KT-176-537

Hutchinson
20th Century Encyclopedia

Hutchinson 20th Century Encyclopedia

Edited by
E.M.Horsley

Hutchinson
London Melbourne Auckland Johannesburg

Century Hutchinson Ltd
Brookmount House
62–65 Chandos Place
London WC2 4NW

Century Hutchinson Group (Australia) Pty Ltd
16–22 Church Street
Hawthorn
Melbourne
Victoria 3122

Century Hutchinson Group (NZ) Ltd
32–34 View Road
PO Box 40–086
Glenfield
Auckland 10

Century Hutchinson Group (SA) Pty Ltd
PO Box 337
Bergvlei 2012
South Africa

Hutchinson's Twentieth Century Encyclopedia
First published 1948
Second revised edition 1951
Third revised edition 1956
Fourth revised edition 1964
(fully revised, re-set, with new illustrations, and re-titled
Hutchinson's New 20th Century Encyclopedia)
Fifth revised edition 1970
Sixth revised edition 1977
(fully revised, newly illustrated, computer-set,
enlarged in new format and re-titled *The New Hutchinson 20th Century Encyclopedia*)
Second impression 1978
Third revised impression 1978
Fourth revised impression 1979
Seventh fully revised edition 1981
Second revised impression 1982
Third revised impression 1984
Fourth revised and updated impression 1986
Fifth revised and updated impression 1987

Illustrations by Oxford Illustrators Ltd and Gordon Cramp Studio

Computer typeset in Times by C. R. Barber & Partners,
Wrotham, Kent
Printed and bound in Great Britain by
Butler & Tanner Ltd, Frome and London

ISBN 0 09 143970 1 (Standard edition)

Editor's Preface

The *Hutchinson 20th Century Encyclopedia* is designed to serve as a single-volume companion to world events, history, arts, and sciences, for home or library use. The aim throughout has been to provide an up-to-date and readable outline of the subject concerned, using clear and non-technical language. It is hoped that the Encyclopedia will be useful in providing background details in such areas as current affairs and major historical events, as well as giving specific facts and dates.

Units are shown both in metric (SI) and imperial forms; some obsolete units have been retained for ease of reference. Lists of abbreviations, titles and forms of address, and a table of weights and measures can be found in an appendix at the end of the volume. Cross-references, indicating where further information can be found on a topic, are shown in SMALL CAPITALS or by the initials (q.v.) after a reference. The entry for each continent is accompanied by a map of physical features; more detailed information about specific countries can be found in the colour atlas section in the centre of the book.

This new impression of the *Hutchinson 20th Century Encyclopedia* takes into account recent political changes around the world, including for example recent changes in leadership in China, and the latest developments in the war between Chad and Libya, as well as noting the deaths of (among others) the sculptor Henry Moore, writer Bernard Malamud, and French aircraft designer Jules Dassault.

Maps

Colour atlas
between pages 666 and 667

Black-and-white maps in text as below

Africa (physical)
Africa (independence)
Antarctica (exploration)
The Arctic (exploration)
Asia (physical)
Auckland
Australia (physical)
Australia (exploration)
Berlin
Continent (geological formation)
Earthquake belts
England and Wales (physical)
Europe (physical)
London (central)
London (boroughs)
Melbourne
Mid-Atlantic Ridge
Moon (physical and Apollo missions)
Moscow
New York
New Zealand (physical)
North America (physical)
Paris
Peking
Quebec
Roman Empire
Scotland (physical)
South America (physical)
Sydney
Tokyo

Appendices following the text

Abbreviations
Customary Forms of Address
Weights and Measures

Note to the Reader

Pronunciation is indicated approximately by the following simple system:

Vowel sounds

a as in rack
ā as in rake
ah as in father
ar as in mare
aw as in raw
e as in wreck
ē as in mete
oi as in boil
oo as in book
o͞o as in boot
ow as in cow
u as in but
ü as in Fr. *dune*
ū as in mute
eh as in Fr. *née*
i as in rick
ī as in mite
o as in rock
ō as in so
ö as in Fr. *jeune*
oh as in Fr. *eau*

Consonant sounds

b, d, f, h, j, k, l, m, n, p, r, t, v, w, z, present no difficulty; c, q, x, are not used in this key.

ch as in chip
dh is soft as in this
g is hard as in get
kh as ch in Scots loch
ks for x
kw as in quick
ň is nasal as in Fr. *bon*
ng as in singer
ngg as in finger
s is hard as in set
th is hard as in think
y is consonantal as in yet
zh as in treasure (trezhur)

Abbreviations follow the standard forms and are included in an appendix, an exception being the adoption of F.W.W. and S.W.W. to indicate the First and Second World Wars. In any article the title word (or words) may be represented by its initial letter (or letters), e.g. in the article AACHEN the letter A. stands for Aachen.

Illustrations have been placed as close as possible to the entry to which they refer. Usually they are on the same page, but occasionally the illustration is on the facing page, or overleaf.

A

The first letter in nearly all the alphabets. The English *a* is derived from the Etruscan *a* through the Lat. alphabet, which is the parent of the West-European alphabets. The Greeks called the first letter *alpha*; the Semites *aleph* or *alph*, which meant 'ox', but more probably because the word began with this letter - a simple mnemonic device - than because the letter was formed as the rough outline of an ox-head, as some scholars have claimed.

AACHEN (ah'khen). German cathedral city and spa in the *Land* of North Rhine-Westphalia, 72km (45m) S.W. of Cologne. It is a thriving industrial centre and one of Germany's principal railway junctions. A. was the Roman Aquisgranum, and from the time of Charlemagne until 1531 the German emperors were crowned there. Charlemagne was b. and buried in A., and he founded the cathedral in 796. The 14th cent. town hall, containing the hall of the emperors, is built on the site of Charlemagne's palace. Leading citizens estab. the annual *Charlemagne prize* (1949) for service to European co-operation: winners incl. Adenauer, Churchill, Heath, Schuman and Spaak. In the S.W.W. Aachen was the first major Ger. town captured by the Allies (20 Oct. 1944). Pop. (1980) 250,000.

AACHEN. Among the treasures of the cathedral is the Shrine of Charlemagne. Completed in 1215, it is a masterpiece of the goldsmith's art, and is decorated with fine reliefs. Here Charlemagne presents a model of the church to the Virgin. *Photo: Marburg*

AALBORG (awl'-). Danish port 32km (20m) inland from the Kattegat, on the S. shore of the Limfjord. One of the oldest towns in Denmark, it has a castle and the fine Budolfi church. Pop. (1970) 100,250.

AALST (ahlst) or **Alost.** Town in E. Flanders, Belgium, on the Dender, with brewing and textile industries. Pop. (1970) 46,750.

AALTONEN (ahl'-), **Wäinö** (1894-1966). Finnish artist. At first a painter, he later turned to sculpture, and was a pioneer in the revival of carving directly from the stone, his favourite medium being granite. His works incl. portrait busts, notably one of Sibelius, and statues for the Finnish Parliament House and the Univ. of Helsinki.

AARDVARK (ahrd'-). Afrikaans name for the ant-bear (*Orycteropus afer*) found in central and southern Africa. A timid, defenceless animal about the size of a pig, it has a long head, pig-like snout, and large asinine ears. It feeds at night on termites, which it licks up with its long, sticky tongue.

AARDWOLF. One of the Carnivora (*Proteles cristatus*), resembling a small striped hyena. It is found in E. and S. Africa, usually in the burrows of the aardvark, and feeds on termites.

AARHUS (awr'hoos). Second city of Denmark, on the E. coast overlooking the Kattegat. It is the cap. of A. co. in Jutland, and a shipping and commercial centre with a univ. Pop. (1970) 187,000.

AARHUS. The 'Old Town', an open-air museum of old buildings gathered together from all over Denmark, and re-erected in part of the botanical gardens. Ancient crafts are carried on, as in the watch-maker's house on the right. *Photo: J. Allan Cash*

AARON (ā'ron). In the Bible, the elder brother of Moses and leader with him of the Israelites in their march from Egypt to the Promised Land of Canaan.

AASEN (aw'sen), **Ivar Andreas** (1813-96). Norwegian philologist, poet and playwright. Through a study of rural dialects he evolved by 1853 a native 'country language', which he called *Landsmaal*, to take the place of literary Dano-Norwegian.

A'BACUS. Method of calculating with a handful of stones on 'a flat surface' (Lat. *abacus*), familiar to the Greeks and Romans, and used by earlier peoples, possibly even in ancient Babylon, and which still survives in the E. in the more sophisticated bead frame form of the Russian *schoty* and the Japanese *soroban*. In the West arithmetic with written Arabic figures, the so-called 'pen-reckoning', replaced 'counter-casting' for some 200 years, but is today being replaced by adding machines and electric calculators, themselves based on the principle of the A. The metal reckoning counters or jettons of the 13th-18th cents. are often very attractive. *See* CAPITAL.

ABACUS. Modern schoolchildren find the fundamentals of arithmetic easier to grasp with the aid of a Roman-type abacus. Behind it is the more familiar bead abacus. *Photo: Courtesy of J. M. Pullan*

ABADA'N. Iranian is. on the E. side of the Shatt-al-Arab. A. is the chief refinery and shipping centre for Iran's oil industry, nationalized 1951. This measure was the beginning of the world-wide movement by oil-producing countries to assume control of profits from their own resources.

ABALONE (abalōn'i). Marine, snail-like animal (family Haliotidae), also known from its shape as the ear shell. It provides a bluish mother-of-pearl much used in ornamental work, and the animal itself is edible. California has several valuable species, and As. are eaten there, as well as in China and Japan.

A'BBAS the Great (*c.* 1557-1628). Shah of Persia from 1586, he defeated the Uzbegs near Herat in 1597 and also the Turks. Bandar-Abbas is named after him. At his death his dominions reached from the Tigris to the Indus.

ABBAS II, Hilmi (1874-1944). Last khedive of Egypt, 1892-1914. On the outbreak of war between Britain and Turkey in 1914, he sided with Turkey and was deposed following the establishment of a British protectorate over Egypt.

ABBASIDS. Dynasty of the Mohammedan empire who reigned as caliphs in Baghdad 750-1258. They were descended from Abbas, Mohammed's uncle, and some of them, e.g. Harun-al-Rashid (786-809) and Mamun (813-33), were outstanding patrons of cultural development. Later their power dwindled, and in 1258 Baghdad was burnt by the Tartars. Thence until 1517 they were caliphs of Egypt.

ABBEVILLE (ahbvēl'). Town in N. France in the Somme dept., 19km (12m) inland from the mouth of the Somme. During the F.W.W. it was an important base for the British armies. Pop. (1973) 25,000.

ABBEY. In the Christian church, a monastery of monks or a nunnery or convent of nuns, all vowed to a life of celibacy and religious seclusion, governed by an abbot or abbess respectively. Sometimes the word is applied to a religious edifice which was once the church of an A., e.g. Westminster A., or to a building or society that has long since been secularized, e.g. Battle Abbey. The first As. as established in Syria or Egypt were mere collections of huts, but in course of time massive and extensive buildings were constructed. St. Benedict's A. at Monte Cassino in Italy - so strongly built that for weeks in 1944 it defied blasting by bomb and shell - set the pattern, and soon every country of Christendom could boast a number of noble As. England, esp. the north, is rich in A. ruins.

ABBEY THEATRE. Playhouse in Dublin associated with the Irish literary revival of the early 1900s that owed its origin to the co-operation of the writers George Russell (A.E.) and W. B. Yeats, with the actors W. G. and Frank Fay. The theatre was opened in 1904, and provided a stage for the works of a number of brilliant dramatists, including Lady Gregory, Yeats, J. M. Synge, Lennox Robinson, Padraic Colum, Conal O'Riordan, St John Ervine, Seumas O'Kelly, and Sean O'Casey. Burned out in 1951, the A. T. was rebuilt 1966.

ABBOTSFORD. Home of Sir Walter Scott (q.v.) from 1811, on the right bank of the Tweed, Borders region. Originally a farmhouse, it was rebuilt 1817-25 as a gothic baronial hall, and is still in the possession of his descendants.

ABD EL-KADER (*c.* 1807-83). Algerian nationalist. Emir of Mascara from 1832, he led a tribal struggle against the French until his surrender in 1847.

ABD EL-KRIM, el-Khettabi (1881-1963). Moroccan Arab chief known as the 'Wolf of the Rif'. With his brother Mohammed, he led the Riff revolt, inflicting disastrous defeat on the Spanish at Anual in 1921, but surrendering to a large French army under Pétain in 1926. Banished to the is. of Réunion, he was released in 1947 and d. in voluntary exile in Cairo.

ABDICATION. Renunciation of an office or dignity, usually the throne, by a ruler or sovereign.

ABDUL-HAMID II (1842-1918). Last sultan of Turkey 1876-1909. In 1908 the Young Turks under Enver Bey forced A.-H. to restore the constitution of 1876, and in 1909 insisted on his deposition. He d. in confinement. For his part in the brutal suppression of the Armenian revolt of 1894 he was known as the Great Assassin.

ABDULLAH, Sheikh Mohammed (1905-82). Kashmiri leader, known as the 'Lion of Kashmir'. He headed the struggle for constitutional government against the Maharajah of Kashmir, and in 1947 became P.M. He agreed to the accession of the state to India to halt tribal infiltration, but was imprisoned from 1953 (with brief intervals) until 1968, when he reaffirmed the right of the people of K. 'to decide the future of the State'. He became P.M. 1975, accepting the sovereignty of India.

ABDULLAH ibn Hussein (1882-1951). King of Jordan. The son of Hussein ibn Ali and brother of Feisal I of Iraq (qq.v.), he worked with Lawrence in the Arab revolt of the F.W.W. From 1921 he was Emir of Transjordan, and assumed the title of King in 1946 when the country - until then a British mandate - became independent. He incorporated Arab Palestine into his kingdom, which then became the Hashemite Kingdom of Jordan, following the 1948-9 Arab-Israeli war. He was assassinated by an Arab fanatic.

ABDUL RAHMAN, Tunku (Prince) (1903-). Malaysian statesman. In 1961-2 he headed the missions to London negotiating the formation of the Fed. of Malaysia, and was the country's first P.M. 1963-70.

Famous Abdications

Sulla, Roman dictator	79 B.C.
Diocletian, Roman emperor	A.D. 305
Edward II of Eng.	1327
Richard II of Eng.	1399
Charles V, Holy Roman emperor	1555
Mary Queen of Scots	1567
Christina of Sweden	1654
Napoleon I	1814 and 1815
Louis Philippe of France	1848
Isabella II of Spain	1870
Abdul Hamid II of Turkey	1909
Manoel II of Portugal	1910
Pu-Yi of China	1912
Nicholas II of Russia	1917
Constantine I of Greece	1917 and 1922
Ferdinand I of Bulgaria	1918
Wilhelm II of Germany	1918
Charles (Karl) of Austria-Hungary	1918
George II of Greece	1923
Edward VIII of United Kingdom	11 Dec. 1936
Carol II of Rumania	1940
Victor Emmanuel III of Italy	1946
Umberto II of Italy	1946
Michael of Rumania	1947
Wilhelmina of the Netherlands	1948
Leopold III of the Belgians	1951
Farouk of Egypt	1952
Constantine II of Greece (deposed)	1973
Zahir Shah of Afghanistan	1973
Shah of Iran (deposed)	1979

ABEL (ā'bel). In Genesis, 2nd son of Adam and Eve. He was a shepherd, and his burnt offerings were more acceptable to the Lord than were the fruits of Cain, his brother. Filled with jealousy, Cain killed A.

Ā'BEL, Sir Frederick Augustus (1827-1902). British scientist. Chemist to the War Dept., he introduced a new method of making gun-cotton, was joint inventor with Dewar of cordite, and invented the Abel close-test instrument for determining the flash point of petroleum.

A'BELARD, Peter (1079-1142). French scholastic philosopher. B. near Nantes, he became canon of Notre Dame in Paris, and master of the cathedral school in 1115. When his seduction of, and secret marriage to, his pupil Héloïse became known, she took the veil and he was castrated by ruffians at the instigation of her uncle, Canon Fulbert, and became a monk. Resuming teaching a year later, he was cited for heresy and became a hermit at Nogent, where he built the oratory of the Paraclete, and later abbot of a monastery in Brittany. His autobiographical *Historia Calamitatum* drew from Héloïse the famous love letters. He d. at Châlon-sur-Saône, on his way to defend himself against a new charge of heresy. Héloïse was buried beside him at the Paraclete in 1164, their remains being taken to Père Lachaise, Paris, in 1817. A. has a great place in medieval thought as a 'conceptualist', for whom 'universals' have only a mental existence.

ABEOKUTA (abē-ōkoo'tah). Agricultural trade centre in Nigeria, West Africa, on the Ogun river, 103km (64m) N. of Lagos. Pop. (1970) 200,000.

ABERBROTHOCK. Another name for ARBROATH.

ABERCROMBY, Sir Ralph (1734-1801). Scots soldier who in 1801 commanded an expedition to the Mediterranean, charged with the liquidation of the French forces left behind by Napoleon in Egypt. He decisively defeated the French at Aboukir Bay, but was mortally wounded in the action.

ABERDĀ'RE. Town in Mid Glamorgan, Wales, formerly producing high-grade coal, and now with electrical and light engineering industries. Pop. (1971) 38,000.

ABERDEEN, George Hamilton Gordon, 4th earl of (1784-1860). British statesman. B. in Edinburgh, he succeeded his grandfather as earl in 1801, and was a prominent diplomat. In 1828 he was Foreign Secretary under Wellington, and again in 1841. Although a Tory, he supported Catholic emancipation and followed Peel in his conversion to Free Trade. In 1852 he became P.M. in a govt of Peelites and Whigs or Liberals, but resigned in 1855 because of the hostile criticism aroused by the miseries and mismanagement of the Crimean War.

ABERDEEN. City, seaport and holiday resort on the E. coast of Scotland, admin. H.Q. of Grampian region. It is Scotland's third largest city, and is rich in historical interest and fine buildings, including the Municipal Buildings (1867); King's College (1494) and Marischal College (founded 1593; housed in one of the largest granite buildings in the world, 1836) which together form Aberdeen University; St Machar Cathedral (1378), and the Auld Brig o'Balgownie (1320). The 2 rivers which flank it, the Dee and the Don, are famous in history and the 2 miles of promenade and the sandy beach attract many holiday visitors. Industries include the manufacture of agricultural machinery, paper and textiles; fishing, shipbuilding, granite-quarrying, and engineering. However, oil discoveries in the North Sea in the 1960-70s transformed A. to the European 'offshore capital,' with an airport and heliport linking the mainland to the rigs, and new sources of employment in the shore-based maintenance and service depots. Pop. (1971) 181,785.

ABERDEEN. The 'Granite City', a focus of the British oil boom of the 1970s, is expanding fast under the impetus of its new prosperity. Office blocks tower over the traditional style buildings. *Photo: Camera Press*

ABERDEENSHIRE. Former co. in E. Scotland, merged in 1975 in Grampian region.

ABERFAN (abervan'). Mining village in Mid Glamorgan, Wales, nr Merthyr Tydfil. An avalanche of coalmine waste overwhelmed a school and houses in 1966: 144 d. incl. 116 children.

ABERRATION. Astronomical term for the apparent displacement of a star resulting from the combined effects of the speed of light, and the speed of Earth as it moves in its orbit round the Sun, about 30km (18.5m) per sec. The *constant of A.* is 20.47 sec. *Chromatic A.* appears as coloured fringes when objects are illuminated and seen through simple lenses.

ABERY'STWYTH. Holiday resort and university town, Dyfed, Wales, at the mouth of the Ystwyth river. The town developed round the fortress rebuilt by Edward I in 1277. The Univ. Coll. of Wales was founded in A. in 1872, and maintains the Welsh Plant Breeding Station. On the outskirts of A. is the National Library of Wales. Tanning is an industry. Pop. (1972) 10,650.

ABIDJA'N. Port and former cap. of the Rep. of Ivory Coast, W. Africa. It trades in coffee, palm oil, cocoa and timber (mahogany); and there is an airport and a rail link with Ougadougou, and a university. Pop. (1984) 2,000,000.

ABILENE (ab'ilēn). Town of Kansas, USA, on the Smoky Hill river. A western railway terminus, A. was a shipping point for cattle in the 1860s, and was a wild city until tamed by Marshal Wild Bill Hickok in 1871. President Eisenhower lived here as a boy and is buried here, and there is an Eisenhower Memorial Museum. Pop. (1970) 6,661.

A'BINGDON. Town in Oxfordshire, England, on the Thames 10km (6m) S. of Oxford. The remains of the 7th cent. abbey incl. Checker Hall, restored as an Elizabethan-type theatre. The 15th cent. bridge was reconstructed in 1929. There are light industries. Pop. (1971) 18,600.

ABOMEY (ahbō'mi). Town and port of Benin. It was once the cap. of the kingdom of Dahomey, which flourished in the 17th-19th cents., and had a mud-built defence-wall 10km (6m) in circumference. Pop. (1970) 45,000.

ABOMINABLE SNOWMAN. Man-like creature, with long arms and a thick-set body covered with reddish-grey hair. Reports of the existence of the A.S. in the Himalayas, where it is locally known as the 'yeti', have been current since 1832, but gained substance from a published photograph of a huge footprint in the snow taken by Eric Shipton of the Everest Reconnaissance Expedition in 1951.

ABORIGINES (abōri'jinēz). Those inhabitants of a country who are believed to have been there from time immemorial (Lat. *ab origine,* from the beginning). The word now more particularly refers to the native peoples of those lands which have become the scene of European settlement, and especially those of Australia. *Australian Aborigines* numbered *c.* 300,000 when British settlers first arrived in 1788: the largest concentration is now in Queensland (24,000) and they total (1973) 116,000, with *c.* 20,000 of mixed blood. They have a rich tradition of legends, songs, rituals, and bark and cave paintings concerned with their 'dreamtime', a long-ago era when men were first on Earth, and when the tribal totem ancestors (the spirit eaglehawk, kangaroo, snake, etc.) wandered abroad. About 40% live tribally in remote desert areas, but are threatened by mineral discoveries on their lands, to which their rights have been officially disputed. The rest live in squalid conditions as casual labour on the town fringes. In recent years there has been a movement for the recognition of A. rights.

ABORIGINES. A fisherman of Arnhem Land in Australia's Northern Territory. Arriving in Australia from Asia 13–30,000 years ago, the Aborigines developed a complex and enduring culture in areas where white settlers were later to find survival difficult. *Photo: Axel Poignant*

ABORTION. In law, the expulsion of the contents of the pregnant womb at any time before full term; in medicine, the expulsion before the foetus is capable of living - before the 6th month. Expulsion after that is called miscarriage or premature labour. Strictly forbidden in times of shortage of manpower, e.g. in France in 1920 after the F.W.W., A. is a recognized method of birth-control in times of over-population, e.g. legalized in Britain 1968 in certain circumstances, but there is risk to the mental and physical health of the mother, with the danger of prematurity or complications in subsequent desired births.

ABOUKIR (abookēr') **BAY, Battle of.** Also known as the Battle of the Nile: Nelson defeated Napoleon's fleet at the Egyptian seaport of A. on 1 Aug. 1798.

ABRAHAM (fl. *c.* 2300 B.C.). Founder of the Jewish nation. B. at Ur, Abram was the son of Terah, and migrated to Haran, N. Mesopotamia, with his father, his wife Sarah, and his nephew Lot. Proceeding to Canaan, he received Jehovah's promise of the land to his descendants, and after sojourning in Egypt during a famine, separated from Lot at Bethel before settling in Hebron. On renaming him Abraham 'father of many nations', Jehovah promised him a legitimate heir, and then tested him by a command to slay the boy Isaac in sacrifice. By his 2nd wife, Keturah, A. had 6 sons. He was buried in Machpelah cave, Hebron. *See* CANAAN.

ABRAHAM, Sir Edward Penley (1913-). British biochemist. Professor of chemical pathology at Oxford from 1964, he succeeded (with his group) in isolating the antibiotic cephalosporin (q.v.), capable of destroying penicillin-resistant bacteria.

ABRAHAM, Plains (or **Heights**) **of.** Plateau near Quebec, Canada, where on 13 Sept. 1759 the French under Montcalm were defeated by Wolfe, whereby Canada was won for the British Empire. It is now the National Battlefield Park.

ABRASIVES. Substances used for cutting and polishing or for removing small amounts of the surface of hard materials. They are divided into *natural* As., e.g. quartz, sandstone, pumice, diamond, corundum, and emery; and *artificial*, e.g. bath brick, rouge, whiting, and carborundum. They are usually referred to Mohs' (q.v.) Scale of Hardness.

ABRUZZI (ahbroots'i). Mountainous area of south central Italy; Gran Sasso d'Italia (2,914 m/9,560 ft) is the highest point of the Apennines.

ABSALOM. In the O.T., the 3rd and favourite son of King David. He headed a revolt against his father, was defeated in battle, and as he fled on a mule, his long hair caught in an overhanging branch. In this predicament he was slain by Joab, David's captain.

A'BSINTH. Strong alcoholic drink containing from 60 to 80 per cent of alcohol, which owes its toxic qualities to the oil of wormwood which gives its characteristic flavour. It attacks the nervous system and causes acute symptoms of narcotic poisoning.

ABSOLUTE ZERO. The lowest temperature which could possibly exist, equivalent to −273.16° C. when molecules would have no energy. Near this temperature the physical properties of materials change substantially, e.g. some metals lose their electrical resistance.

ABSTRACT ART. Abstract works of art may be classified as (1) *semi-abstract* - i.e. those works which are based on nature, though they bear little resemblance to natural forms; and (2) *pure abstract* - i.e. those works which have no relation to nature, but consist of shapes and colours of the artist's own invention. In (1) we may group Cubism, Futurism, Vorticism, and the work of certain artists, such as Henry Moore and Archipenko, who have evolved their own individualistic styles. In (2) we may include Constructivism, Suprematism, and Neo-Plasticism. There are other movements, such as Expressionism, which defy classification. In Expressionist paintings forms are created instinctively, according to the promptings of the artist's emotions, but such works usually consist of lines and shapes, and can therefore be considered as abstract. Surrealist works are also executed in a similar way - they are the expressions of a dream-world - but since their chief interest lies in their subject-matter they cannot, strictly speaking, be classed as A.A. For definitions of the different movements *see* ACTION PAINTING, CUBISM, CONSTRUCTIVISM, FUTURISM, etc.

ABSURD, Theatre of the. *See* ALBEE, E.; BECKETT, S.; IONESCO, E.; and SIMPSON, N. F.

ABU-BEKR (573-634). Mohammed's father-in-law and the first caliph. B. at Mecca and originally named Abd-el-Ka'ba, he was one of the first notable converts to Mohammed's teaching, accompanied the Prophet on his flight to Medina, and took the name Abu-Bekr, 'Father of the Virgin', when Mohammed married his daughter Ayesha (*c.* 618). As Mohammed's successor (632) he proved a vigorous ruler, adding Mesopotamia to the Moslem world.

ABU DHABI (ah'boo dah'bi). Largest of the United Arab Emirates (q.v.), on the Arabian Gulf. The borders are ill defined and there have been disputes with Oman (Buraimi Oasis) and Saudi Arabia (The Liwa). The ruler is Sheikh Zaid. Exploitation of rich oil resources from 1962 has led to rapid expansion. The cap. is Abu Dhabi. Area 67,340 sq.km (26,000 sq.m); pop. (1973) 85,000.

ABU DHABI. Sheikh Zaid, in the foreground, leaves his royal palace followed by his bodyguard, who combine modern efficiency with traditional features of Arab dress. *Photo: John Cowan/Camera Press*

ABUJA (aboo'jah). Fed. cap. terr. of Nigeria, S.E. of Kaduna, in the region of the boundary between the Niger and Plateau states. The decision was made in 1976 to transfer the cap. from Lagos to this healthier, more central area, the transfer to be completed *c.* 1986.

ABYDOS (abī'dos). Ancient city of upper Egypt, W. of the Nile, *c.* 160km (100m) above Asyut. The Great Temple built here by Seti I (*c.* 1300 B.C.), is one of the most imposing Egyptian temples.

ABYSSAL (abis'al) **ZONE.** Deep area of the ocean (q.v.), calm, muddy, dark, not subject to seasonal changes, and with a temperature of approx. 4°C (39°F). Fish and crustaceans may be blind.

ABYSSINIA. Another name for ETHIOPIA.

ACACIA (akā'sha). Genus of trees and shrubs of the family Leguminosae. Most of the 400 species flourish in the tropics of Africa and Australia. *See* WATTLE and MIMOSA.

ACADEMY (Gk *akadēmeia*). Name given to the Platonic school of philosophy, which met in the gardens of Academe, in the N.-W. of Athens. Here among the olive groves Plato and his successors taught their disciples, until in A.D. 529 Justinian closed all the pagan schools.

First of the As., in the modern sense of a recognized society estab. for the promotion of one or more of the arts and sciences, was the Museum of Alexandria, founded by Ptolemy Soter in the 3rd cent. B.C.

The *Académie française* originated as a literary society in 1629, and was granted letters patent by Louis XIII in 1635. Since 1639 its membership has been restricted to 40 at a time, the '40 Immortals'.

The Soviet *A. of Sciences* was originally estab. by Catherine I in 1725 as the Académie Impériale des sciences de Saint-Petersbourg. Responsible for such achievements as the *Sputnik*, the A. formerly admin. many of the country's 3000 scientific establishments, but in 1961 was reorganized to concentrate on the most promising lines of theoretical research. The practical side of scientific research work was entrusted to the newly-created State Committee of the Council of Ministers for the Co-ordination of Scientific Research Work.

In Britain an 'academy' generally means a society dealing with the arts, such as the Royal Academy.

ACADIA, or **ACADIE** (ahkahdē'). Name given to Nova Scotia by the original French settlers in 1604. France renounced her claim to the colony in 1713. Many of its inhabitants migrated to New England and Louisiana: some 4,000 others were expelled in 1755.

ACA'NTHUS. Genus of herbaceous plants, family Acanthaceae, of the Mediterranean region. The A. was frequently used as a motif in classical architecture, the Greeks preferring the species *A. spinosus* and the Romans *A. mollis.* The latter, often grown as an ornamental plant, and also called bear's breech grows some *c.* 1m (3ft). The spineless, hairy leaves are shiny, and the flowers form handsome white or pinkish spikes.

ACAPULCO (ak'apo͞o'lkō). Mexican holiday resort, famed for its beauty and deep-sea fishing, set in an almost land-locked bay 305km (190m) S.W. of Mexico City. Pop. (1970) 234,800.

A'CCAD. Ancient town on the left bank of the Euphrates from which a Semitic people of N. Babylonia took their name - Accadians. It was the chief city of the empire of Sargon I.

ACCELERATION. The rate of increase in the velocity of a moving body, expressed in metres per second squared, m/s^2. The acceleration due to gravity is the A. shown by a body falling freely under the influence of gravity, either in a vacuum or after allowing for the retardation due to air resistance; it varies slightly at different latitudes. Retardation is actually A. in the reverse direction, e.g. a rising rocket is actually being accelerated towards the centre of the earth.

ACCESSARY. An *accessary before the fact* is one who instigates another person to commit a crime which that person then commits. If he is present when the crime is committed, he is not an A. but an *abettor.* An *A. after the fact* is one who assists a person who he knows has committed a crime.

A'CCOLĀDE. Gentle blow on the shoulders with the flat of the sword given by the Sovereign, or a representative, in conferring a knighthood.

ACCOMPLICE. One who is associated with another in the commission of a crime. In law, the word is applied not only to persons who played a minor part in the crime, but also to the principal offenders.

ACCORDION. Portable musical instrument invented by Buschmann in Berlin in 1822. Box-like in form, it comprises a pair of bellows with many folds and a keyboard of up to 50 keys. On these being pressed and the bellows worked, wind is admitted to metal reeds, whose length and thickness determines the notes they emit.

ACCOUNTANCY. The art or practice of an accountant. The accountant today enjoys professional status and is entrusted not only with the control of the book-keeping functions and the preparation of Trading and Profit and Loss Accounts and Balance Sheets, but with numerous other duties in connection with the financial affairs of an organization. The auditing of accounts is the work of professional accountants who may also be required to serve as liquidators of companies, receivers for debenture holders, etc. During the 1970s inflation rendered A. a less exact process, and the CCA (current cost accounting) system was advocated in 1975 by the Sandilands Committee for enforcement in the UK. Accountants, however, maintained that this alone still did not allow for valid comparisons over a period in which the value of money changes and urged its combination with their own CPP (current purchasing power) method of adjustment. A combination of the two was adopted.

In the British Isles there are Inst. of Chartered Accountants for England and Wales, Scotland, and Ireland and other professional organizations; the American Inst. of Accountants dates from 1887.

ACCRA'. Capital and port of Ghana, W. Africa. It is an important commercial and industrial centre with good road, rail, and air communications. The Univ. of Ghana (1961) is at nearby Legon, with its medical school in A. itself. Pop. of the Greater A. region (1970) 851,614. *See* TEMA.

ACCRA. The University of Ghana, where a motif from Ghanaian folk art decorates the wall of the George Padmore library. Construction on stilts over an ornamental pool gives much-needed coolness. *Photo: Camera Press*

ACETALDEHYDE (asetal'-) (CH_3CHO). In chemistry, one of the chief members of the group of organic compounds known as aldehydes. It is a mobile inflammable liquid boiling at 20.8°C (69.6°F).

ACETIC (asē'tik) **ACID** (CH_3COOH). One of the simplest members of a series of organic acids called the fatty acids. In the pure state it is a mobile colourless liquid with an unpleasant pungent odour; it solidifies to an ice-like mass of crystals at 16.7°C, and hence is often called glacial acetic acid. *See* VINEGAR.

Cellulose (derived from wood, etc.) is treated with A.A. to produce a cellulose acetate solution, which is then extruded to form the synthetic textile fibre formerly called acetate rayon and now simply acetate.

ACETONE (CH_3COCH_3). A colourless mobile inflammable liquid used extensively as a solvent. It boils at 56.5°C, is miscible with water in all proportions, and has a pleasant and characteristic odour.

ACE'TYLENE (C_2H_2). A colourless inflammable gas produced by the action of water on calcium carbide. It was discovered by Edmund Davy in 1836 by the action of water on some impure by-products of the preparation of potassium.

The most important modern development in the use of A. is its conversion into artificial rubbers. Since the combustion of A. provides more heat relatively than almost any other fuel known - its calorific power is three times that of coal gas and five times that of hydrogen - the gas is of great value in obtaining an intensely hot flame, e.g. in oxyacetylene welding and cutting.

ACHAEA (akē'a). Ancient name for Greece. The name Achaeans was originally used for the fair-haired invaders from the N. who swept over the whole of Greece some time before 1100 B.C., submerging the ancient Aegean civilization of Mycenae, and who then captured Troy, as told in the *Iliad*.

The Achaean League of 275 B.C. united most of the cities of the northern Peloponnesus, and achieved victory over Sparta, but it was worsted by the Romans in 146 B.C.

ACHAEMENIDS (akimen'ids). Dynasty ruling the Persian Empire 550-330 B.C., and named after Achaemenes, ancestor of Cyrus the Great, founder of the Empire. His successors incl. Cambyses, Darius I, Xerxes I and Darius III, who, as the last Achaemenid ruler, was killed after defeat in battle against Alexander the Great in 330 B.C.

ACHERON (a'keron). In Greek mythology, one of the rivers of the lower world. The name was taken from a river in S. Epirus which flowed through a deep gorge into the Ionian Sea.

A'CHESON, Dean Gooderham (1893-1971). American statesman and lawyer. He was Under-Secretary of State 1945-7, and was closely associated with George C. Marshall in the preparation of the 'Marshall Plan'. He succeeded him as Sec. of State from 1949 till the end of the Truman régime in 1953. He played a leading part in establishing NATO, and is remembered for his comment that Britain had 'lost an empire and not yet found a role.'

ACHILL (ak'il). Largest of the Irish islands, lying off the coast of Mayo. The scenery is wild and mountainous, and on the N. and W. are cliffs reaching 275m (900ft). Area 148 sq.km (57 sq.m).

ACHILLES (akil'ēz). Greek hero, the central figure of Homer's *Iliad*. He was the son of Peleus, king of the Myrmidons in Thessaly. His mother Thetis dipped him into the r. Styx and thereby made him invulnerable except for the heel by which she held him. Bravest and handsomest of all the Greeks, he took part in the Trojan War, and in a mighty combat killed Hector. In the end he was himself slain by Paris, whose poisoned arrow wounded him in the heel.

The *A. tendon* pins the calf muscle to the heelbone, and is one of the largest in the body.

ACID (Lat. *acidus*, acid, sour). In chemistry, a substance which in solution in an ionizing solvent (usually water) gives rise to hydrogen ions. The more obvious properties of As. are their sharp taste, and their ability to turn litmus red, to neutralize alkalis to form well-defined salts, and act as solvents. The first known A. was vinegar. Inorganic As. include boracic, carbonic, hydrochloric, nitric, phosphoric, sulphuric, and sulphuretted hydrogen; and among organic acids are acetic, benzoic, citric, formic, lactic, oxalic, and salicylic. As. combine with bases (alkalis are soluble bases) to form salts. 'Strength' of an acid is measured by its hydrogen-ion concentration, indicated by pH value and expressed on a scale of numbers from 0 = extremely acid, through 7 = neutral, to 14 = extremely alkaline.

ACLINIC (aklin'ik) **LINE.** The magnetic equator, an imaginary line near the equator, where the compass needle has no 'dip' or magnetic inclination.

ACNE (ak'-). A skin eruption due to inflammation of the sebaceous glands that secrete an oily substance called sebum, the natural lubricant of the skin. Sometimes their openings become stopped and they swell; the contents decompose and pimples form.

ACONCA'GUA. An extinct volcano (6,960 m/22,834 ft) in the Andes on the W. border of Argentina. The highest peak in the Americas, it was first climbed in 1897 by Vines and Zurbriggen (FitzGerald Expedition).

A'CONITE. Genus of poisonous plants of the Ranunculaceae family. Of some 60 species, *Aconitum napellus*, or Monkshood, is the common European species; also known as *A. lycoctonum*, wolf's bane. The roots yield aconitine, formerly used for poison arrows.

Ā'CORN. Fruit or seed of the oak tree. It is a nut, based in a shallow cup or cupule. The sea-acorn or acorn-shell (*Balanus*) is a genus of Cirripedia, allied to the barnacles.

ACOUSTICS (akoo'- or akow'-). In general, the experimental and theoretical science of sound; but more specially, that branch of the science that has to do with the phenomena of sound in space, e.g. public buildings, concert halls, cinemas, etc. Acoustical engineering is concerned with the technical control of sound, and the subject also enters into architecture and building, with the necessity for the control of vibration, for sound-proofing and the elimination of noise; it also includes all forms of sound recording and reinforcement, and hearing-aids. See SOUND.

ACQUAVIVA (ahkwah-), **Claudius** (1543-1615). A Neapolitan, he was General of the Jesuits from 1581 and one of their ablest organizers and educators.

ACQUITTAL. In law, the clearing or setting free of a person charged with a crime or accusation. In an English court this follows on a verdict of 'not guilty', but in a Scottish court the verdict may be either 'non-proven' or 'not guilty'. A. by the jury must be confirmed by the judge.

Ā'CRE. City and port of Israel, on a promontory at the northern extremity of the Bay of A. It has played an important part in history, owing to its strategic position. In 1517 it became part of the Turkish empire. Napoleon besieged it in 1799, but was withstood by the Turkish Jezzar Pasha, supported by a British fleet under Sir Sidney Smith. During the F.W.W., General Allenby captured it from the Turks (1918): the Israelis captured it in 1948. A. has lost importance owing to the growth of Haifa, 14km (9m) S. but exports olive oil, corn, and wool. There is a Naval Officers' School. Pop. (1970) 20,000.

Ā'CRE. Traditional English land measure (4,047 sq.m/4,840 sq.yds/0.405 ha). Originally the word meant a field, and it was of a size that a yoke of oxen could plough in a day, but as early as Edward I's reign it was standardized by statute for official use, although local variation in Ireland, Scotland and some English cos. continued.

A'CRIDĪNE ($C_{13}H_9N$). An organic compound which occurs in crude anthracene oil, from which it may be

ACOUSTICS. The anechoic room at the Building Research Station of the Department of the Environment at Watford. Lined with sponge wedges to eliminate echoes, it is for detailed study of sound transmission and general acoustic research. *Photo: Crown copyright*

extracted by dilute acids. It is also obtained synthetically. It gives rise to many dye-stuffs and some valuable drugs.

ACROME'GALY. A disease distinguished by an unsightly enlargement of the prominent parts of the body (Gk. *akra*, high parts), e.g. the hands and feet, and the lips, nose, tongue, and jaws. It is due to an excessive output of growth hormone by the front lobe of the pituitary gland.

ACRONYM. Words formed from the initial letters or syllables of other words, and used as an abbreviation, but also often taking on a life of their own. They first proliferated during the S.W.W., e.g. SHAEF and radar.

ACRO'POLIS. The citadel of an ancient Greek town. Best known is the A. at Athens, famous for the ruins of the beautiful temples built there during the great days of the Athenian empire.

ACROSTIC. A verse or set of verses whose initial letters form a word, phrase, or sentence; the term comes from the Gk for 'at the end of a line or row'.

ACRYLIC (akril'ik) **ACID.** Acid obtained from the aldehyde acrolein derived from glycerol or fats. Glass-like thermoplastic resin is made by polymerizing esters of A. or methacrylic acid, and used for transparent parts, dentures, lenses, etc. Other A. compounds are used for adhesives, artificial fibres such as Acrilan and Orlon, and the resins used as a medium by many modern artists for their brilliant effect.

ACTAEON (aktē'on). Greek mythical hero. The son of Aristaeus and Cadmus' daughter Autonoë, he was a famous hunter. He accidentally spied upon Artemis as she was bathing, and the goddess changed him into a stag, whereupon he was torn to pieces by his own hounds.

ACTINIDES. Those chemical elements with nos. 89-105, all radioactive and man-made above uranium, no. 92. They are grouped because of their chemical similarities,

ACRE. The strong walls guarding the seaward side of the city reflect its troubled history, but, though pitted by shot, still stand firm. *Photo: Courtesy of the Israeli Government Tourist Office*

and also by analogies with the rare-earth elements (lanthanides).

ACTI'NIUM. Rare radioactive element, at. no. 89, at. wt. 227, the first of the actinides, a weak emitter of high-energy alpha-rays. Made in quantity by bombarding radium with neutrons.

ACTION. One of the proceedings whereby a person enforces his civil rights in a court of justice. The best-known proceedings not commenced by action but by petition are bankruptcy and divorce.

ACTION PAINTING. Abstract expressionist style of painting developed in New York in the 1950s. The word was first used by critic Harold Rosenberg, who wrote that the painter's canvas seemed to these artists 'an arena in which to act'. The paint was applied often by violent methods: *see* POLLOCK, JACKSON. Franz Kline and Mark Rothko are also of this school.

A'CTIUM. Ancient name of a promontory in western Greece on the gulf of Arta, where the fleets of Antony and Cleopatra were defeated by Octavian in 31 B.C.

ACT OF CONGRESS. In USA a bill or resolution that has been passed by the Senate and the House of Representatives and has received the President's assent. If he vetoes it, it may become a A. of C. if it is returned to Congress again and passed by a majority of two-thirds in each House.

ACT OF GOD. Legal term meaning some direct, violent, sudden, and irresistible act of nature which could not reasonably have been foreseen, e.g. extraordinary storms, snow, or frost.

ACT OF INDEMNITY. An Act of Parliament passed to relieve some person from the consequences of some action or omission which, at the time the action or omission took place, was illegal, or of which the legality was doubtful.

ACT OF PARLIAMENT. A parliamentary statute; a decree of the sovereign legislature having the force of law. Acts of P. are of two kinds, public and private, but there is no distinction as to their force, only as to their application; i.e. public Acts of P. have a general effect, while private Acts deal with matters of purely local interest.

The body of English statute law comprises all the Acts passed by Parliament, and the existing list opens with the Statute of Merton, passed in 1235. An Act (unless it is stated to be for a definite period and then to come to an end) remains on the statute book until it is repealed.

ACTON, John Emerich Edward Dalberg-Acton, 1st baron A. (1834-1902). British historian. B. at Naples, of old English R.C. stock, he was elected a Liberal M.P. in 1859 and became a friend and admirer of Gladstone. As leader of the Liberal R.Cs. he opposed the promulgation in 1870 of the doctrine of papal infallibility. Appointed prof. of modern history at Cambridge in 1895, he planned and edited the *Cambridge Modern History,* but d. when only the first 2 vols. were completed.

ACTORS STUDIO. Theatre workshop in New York, USA, estab. 1947 by Cheryl Crawford, Elia Kazan and Robert Lewis: there is also a Los Angeles branch. Selected 'life members' here study the 'method' of Stanislavsky (q.v.), etc.

A'CTUARY. An official of a government department, insurance co., or friendly soc., whose task it is to make the calculations concerning human longevity, etc., on which the tables of mortality, sickness, accident, etc., and hence the premiums or charges, are based. Professional bodies are the Inst. of Actuaries (England, 1848), Faculty of Actuaries (Scotland, 1856) and Society of Actuaries (US, 1949, by a merger of 2 earlier bodies).

ACUPUNCTURE (ak'ū-). Method of healing involving the insertion of metal needles into the body (Lat. *acu,* with a needle) at points determined according to a system which in China, where A. originated, requires a decade of study. Electroacupuncture, developed from the 1950s, is widely used in China to produce anaesthesia. In 1980 it was found that A. works partly by stimulating production of the brain's own painkillers: *see* ENKEPHALIN.

ADAM. Four brothers - Robert, John, James, and William - distinguished Scottish architects and interior decorators.

Robert A. (1728-92), was b. at Kirkcaldy, travelled in Italy and Dalmatia, and was appointed Architect to the King in 1762. With the assistance of his brothers, he designed the district of London between Charing Cross and the Thames, which was named after them the Adelphi (from the Gk for brothers). The area was largely rebuilt in 1936. The A. brothers were responsible for a great improvement in architectural taste, and developed a style which was decidedly their own. Robert A. also earned a considerable reputation as a furniture designer.

James A. studied in Rome, and succeeded Robert as Architect to the King in 1768; **William A.** is described as an architect and a banker; and **John A.** succeeded his father as an architect in Edinburgh.

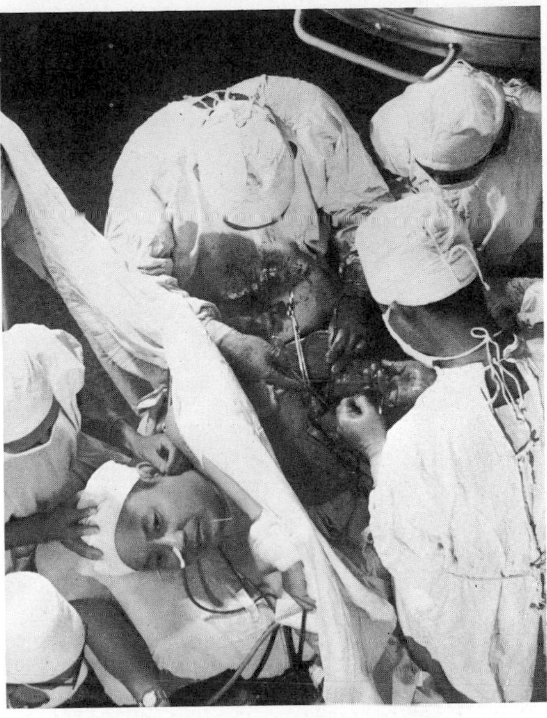

ACUPUNCTURE. Three needles (one in the body, one in the left ear and one in the left forearm) have made this patient unaware of pain, although fully conscious. The operation — at the Peking Medical College — is a major one for removal of a tumour in the oesophagus. *Photo: Camera Press*

ADAM (ahdoṅ'), **Adolphe Charles** (1803-56). French composer of light operas. Some 50 of his works were staged; he is best known for the classic ballet *Giselle.*

ADAM and **EVE.** In the Bible, the first parents of the human race. According to Gen. ii, 7-iii, 24, Jehovah (Yahweh) formed man from the dust, breathed into his nostrils the breath of life, and put him in the Garden of Eden, where the fruit of the Tree of Knowledge of Good and Evil was forbidden him. God formed a woman from a rib of the man while he slept. The woman was tempted by the serpent to eat the forbidden fruit, persuaded A. also to eat, and they were expelled from Eden.

Adam's Peak is a mtn (2,245 m/7,365 ft) in the Kandyan Hills, Sri Lanka. The 'footprint' on the summit is revered by Moslems as that of A., driven from Paradise, and by Buddhists as that of Buddha: it is a place of pilgrimage.

ADAMS, Henry Brooks (1838-1918). American author. A grandson of President John Q. A., his best known works are the studies of the 13th cent. *Mont-Saint-Michel and Chartres* (1904), and of the contrasting complexities of the 20th, *Education of H.A.* (1907).

ADAMS, John (1735-1826). 2nd President of the USA. B. at Quincy, Mass., he was a member of the Continental Congress, 1774-8, and signed the Declaration of Independence. In 1779 he went to France and negotiated the treaties that closed the War of American Independence. In 1785 he became the first American ambassador in London. Returning home, he was Vice-President (1789-97), and President 1797-1801.

ADAM AND EVE. The parents of mankind from an exquisite detail in 'The Virgin and Child with St William of Aquitaine and St John the Baptist', painted by Costa and Maineri for the Oratory of the Conception at Ferrara 1497–1500. *Photo: Courtesy of the National Gallery, London*

ADAMS, John Couch (1819-92). British astronomer. B. in Cornwall, he deduced the existence of the planet Neptune in 1845, and in 1858 became professor of astronomy at Cambridge.

ADAMS, John Quincy (1767-1848). 6th President of the USA. Eldest son of President John Adams, he was b. at Quincy, and became US minister in turn at The Hague, Berlin, St Petersburg, and (1815) London. In 1817 Monroe made him Secretary of State, and 1825-9 he was President.

ADAMS, Léonie (1899-). American poet. B. in N.Y., she became instructor in writing at Columbia Univ. in 1947, and is noted for her romantic, metaphysical lyrics, as in *Those Not Elect* (1925) and *This Measure* (1933).

ADAMS, Samuel (1722-1803). American statesman. B. in Boston, he was a 2nd cousin of President John Adams, and was a leader of the revolutionary party in Massachusetts. He sat in the Continental Congress 1774-81, and signed the Declaration of Independence. In 1776 he anticipated Napoleon in calling the English a nation of shopkeepers.

ADANA (ad'ana). Town in Turkey-in-Asia, on the r. Seyhan. It has cotton, tobacco, and agricultural machinery factories. Pop. (1970) 351,650.

ADDAMS, Jane (1860-1935). American sociologist and feminist. A founder and head of the social settlement of Hull House, Chicago, she was active in the peace movement: co-winner Nobel prize 1931.

ADDER. *See* VIPER.

ADDINGTON, Henry (1757-1844). British Tory statesman, Prime Minister of UK, 1801-4. In 1805 he was created Viscount Sidmouth.

ADDINSELL, Richard (1904-77). British composer. B. in London, he studied at the Royal College of Music and abroad, and wrote music for many theatrical productions and films, e.g. *Dangerous Moonlight*, which includes the 'Warsaw Concerto'.

ADDIS ABABA (Amharic, meaning 'new flower'). Cap. of Ethiopia, and of Shoa prov., founded 1887 by Menelik, then chief of Shoa, at the request of his wife Taitu who found the climate of his existing cap. Entotto, lying farther north, too severe. A. lies at 2,450 m (8,000 ft) a.s.l., but is protected by the surrounding Shoa highlands, and includes hot springs. Eucalyptus woods were planted nearby by Menelik who, when he ascended the throne of Ethiopia in 1889, made A.A. cap. of the whole country. A.A., which is linked by a railway completed 1917 with Djibouti on the coast, was cap. of Italian East Africa 1936-41. Of the four royal palaces in the city, one was presented by Haile Selassie to Ethiopia's first university, inaugurated by him in 1961. It is HQ for UN Economic Commission for Africa, and for OAU. Pop. (1971) 795,900.

ADDISON, Joseph (1672-1719). British essayist and poet, b. in Wilts. In 1699 he was granted a pension to enable him to qualify for the diplomatic service by foreign travel, and in 1704 celebrated Marlborough's victory at Blenheim in his poem 'The Campaign'. In 1706 he became Under-Sec. of State, and in 1708 secretary to the Lord-Lieutenant of Ireland, and an M.P. In 1709 he began to contribute to the *Tatler*, just started by his friend Steele; and in 1711 the two together estab. the *Spectator*, to which A. contributed the 'Coverley Papers'. In 1713 his successful tragedy *Cato* was performed and he contributed to Steele's *Guardian* and in 1714 to the revived *Spectator*. In 1716 he was appointed a commissioner for trade, and in 1717 a Sec. of State, but failing health led to his withdrawal from public life in 1718.

ADDISON, Thomas (1793-1860). Physician. B. nr Newcastle, he became physican to Guy's Hospital, London, in 1837. He was the first to recognize the condition known as *Addison's disease* - a disease of the suprarenal capsules.

ADDITIVE. Chemical substance added to give food longer life (from the traditional salt to modern antibiotics); more attractive colouring or flavour; greater food value (vitamins, etc.); greater convenience in manufacture, etc. Legislation controls the use of As. since many apparently harmless substances may have toxic effects, especially in the long term.

ADELAIDE (1792-1849). Queen of William IV. Daughter of the duke of Saxe-Meiningen, she m. William, then duke of Clarence, in 1818. No children of the marriage survived infancy.

ADELAIDE. Capital of South Australia. Founded in 1836, and named after William IV's queen, it stands on high ground overlooking Holdfast Bay and sheltered on the S. and E. by hills: the highest peak is Mt. Lofty 711 m. (2,334 ft). It is a noteworthy example of town-planning. The residential districts are separated from the commercial by the r. Torrens, dammed to form a lake. The most impressive streets are King William St and North Terrace. A.'s fine buildings include Parliament House (built of marble), Government House, the Anglican

ADDISON. Kneller's portrait for the dining-room of the Kit-Cat Club, to which Congreve, Steele, Vanbrugh and publisher Jacob Tonson belonged. The pictures were less than half-length because the room was low, hence portraits of this size are still called 'kit-cat'. *Photo: National Portrait Gallery*

cathedral of St Peter, the R.C. cathedral, two univs., the State observatory, museum and art gallery. Pop. (1976) 900,379.

ADELAIDE. The city's parkland setting is one of its most attractive features, and Adelaide prides itself on having no slums. This view is taken across the Municipal Golf Course in North Adelaide. *Photo: Courtesy of the South Australian Government*

ADÉLIE LAND. *See* ANTARCTICA.

Ā'DEN. Cap. of the People's Democratic Rep. of Yemen, on a peninsula of barren rock at the S.W. corner of Arabia, commanding the entrance to the Red Sea. It comprises the new admin. centre Madinet al-Sha'ab; the commercial and business quarters of Crater and Tawahi, and the harbour area of Ma'alla. There is an internat. airport. Pop. (1975) 250,000.

A. and its immediate area (121 sq.km/75 sq.m) was annexed by Britain in 1839 and developed as a ship refuelling station after the opening of the Suez Canal. It was a colony 1937-63, and then, after a period of transitional violence between rival nationalist groups and British forces, was combined with the former A. protectorate (290,000 sq.km/112,000 sq.m) to create in 1967 the Southern Yemen People's Rep., later re-named the People's Democratic Rep. of Yemen (q.v.).

ADENAUER (ah'denower), **Konrad** (1876-1967). German statesman. He was Lord Mayor of his native city of Cologne from 1917 until his imprisonment in 1933 by Hitler for opposition to the Nazi régime. After the war he headed the Christian Democratic Union, and was Chancellor of the Federal Republic 1949-63. He strongly supported all measures designed to strengthen the Western bloc in Europe, e.g. his support of Britain's entry into the Common Market.

ADENOIDS. Popular word for the glandular tissue on the back of the upper part of the throat, into which the nose opens. This is apt to overgrow in children as a result of infection, and to cause chronic blocking of the nose and mouth-breathing. The open mouth makes the child's expression look vacant, and the voice has a dull twang. The child is subject to constant colds, is in danger of middle-ear disease and deafness, and often suffers from chronic tonsillitis. The treatment is the removal by surgery of the tonsils and overgrown adenoid tissue.

ADER (ahdār'), **Clement** (1841-1925). French pioneer airman. His first steam-driven machine, the *Éole*, just made the first powered take-off in history (1890), but it could not fly. In 1897, with his *Avion III*, he failed completely, despite his false claims made later.

ADHĒ'SIVE. Substance sticking 2 surfaces together. Natural As. incl. gelatine in its crude industrial form (made from bones, hide fragments and fish offal), and vegetable gums. More recent developments are the synthetic thermoplastic and thermosetting resins, often stronger than the substances they join, replacing nails and screws, etc., and elastomeric (stretching) As. for flexible joins.

ĀDIABA'TIC. The A. expansion or contraction of a gas is one in which a change takes place in the pressure or volume of the gas, although no heat is allowed to enter or leave.

ADIGE (ah'dējeh). Next to the Po, the longest river in Italy, it rises in the lakes of the Resia Pass, traverses the Lombardy Plain, and enters the Adriatic a few miles N. of the Po delta: *c.* 410km/254m long.

ADI GRANTH or **GRANTH SAHIB.** The holy book of Sikhism (q.v.).

ADIRO'NDACKS. Mountainous area in the N.E. of New York State, USA, famous for its scenery and sport facilities: Mt. Marcy 1,629 m/5,345 ft. Lake Placid was the scene of the Winter Olympics 1980.

ADLER (ahd'ler), **Alfred** (1870-1937). Austrian psychologist, founder of the school of Individual Psychology. B. in Vienna, he was a general practitioner and nerve specialist there 1897-1927, serving as an army doctor in F.W.W. He joined the circle of Freudian doctors in Vienna about 1900, but did not accept the more dogmatic Freudian theories of infantile sexuality. After 10 years of collaboration, he parted company with Freud to develop his own distinctive line of thought. His books incl. *Organic Inferiority and Psychic Compensation* (1907) and *Understanding Human Nature* (1927).

ADMINISTRATIVE LAW. The laws made and the judicial decisions arrived at by the Executive under powers delegated to them by the Legislature; such legislative powers have been vastly extended in the 20th cent. in many countries and have been attacked by lawyers. In the US the Administrative Procedure Act (1946) was an attempt to cope with the problem.

In Great Britain the very many new powers delegated to Ministers of the Crown are so wide as frequently to enable the Ministers to make regulations which amend or override Acts of Parliament, and in some cases they further take away from the courts of law the power they have hitherto exercised of confining the legislative activities of the Executive within the limits of the authority delegated to them by Parliament by declaring any regulation that exceeds these limits to be *ultra vires*, and so of no effect.

ADMIRAL. Naval officer of the highest rank: in the RN (in ascending order) rear-admirals, vice-admirals, admirals, and admirals of the fleet; in the USN there are 4 corresponding grades.

ADMIRAL'S CUP. Racing trophy for sailing yachts estab. 1957: teams of 3 yachts for each competing nation take part in 5 races, the most gruelling being the 975km (605m) Fastnet Cup (from Cowes, round the Fastnet Rock off the coast of Cork, Rep. of Ireland, and back to Plymouth). It was first run 1925, and in 1979 ten competitors died in a freak storm. The fifth race was added to this biennial event in 1977.

ADMIRALTY. From the reign of Henry VIII until 1964, the **Board of A.** was the dept of State charged with the provision, control and maintenance of the Royal Navy; its functions - apart from that of management - then passed to the new unified Min. of Defence (q.v.). The 600-year-old office of Lord High Admiral, in commission in the A., then reverted to the Sovereign, to prevent its extinction.

ADŌ'NIS. In classical mythology, a beautiful youth beloved by Aphrodite. While hunting a boar he was gored to death; from his blood sprang the anemone. He was permitted to return each year from the underworld to his mistress for six months. He was worshipped as Adon by the Phoenicians, and earlier still the cult is found in Babylonia and Assyria.

ADOPTION. The legal acquisition of the rights and duties as to the custody and maintenance of a child not one's own legitimate offspring. In antiquity - as in Greece and Rome - emphasis tended to be on the acquisition of an heir, and, as in India, might have religious significance. A. was legalized in England only in 1926, and the modern emphasis is on the welfare of the child and its complete acceptance as if lawfully born to the adopter, e.g. by the Act of 1958 an adopted child inherits on an intestacy as if it were the child of the adopter, and closer restrictions were placed on A. societies. In the US there is a particularly high rate of A., conditions being regulated by the laws of the various states. Stress on care of the child is illustrated by international As., e.g. those of Korean refugee children adopted in the UK through the International Social Service of Great Britain.

Preference is given to young married couples, and all relations with the child's natural parents are severed. Legalized abortion, increased use of contraceptives, and the lessening stigma of being an unmarried mother have combined to decrease the numbers of children available for A. since the S.W.W. and of those 90% are usually illegitimate. In the U.K. the rights of natural parents to prevent A., when the child's welfare might thus be adversely affected, were diminished under the Children Act (1975), and a new legal status of 'custodianship' was created, enabling foster-parents to apply for legal custody after caring for the child for one year. At majority (18) a child is entitled to know its original name.

ADOWA. Alternative form of ADUWA.

ADRĒ'NAL GLANDS. A pair of glands situated on the upper poles of the kidneys and known also as 'suprarenal' glands. They are soft and yellow, and consist of 2 parts. The cortex (outer part) secretes various hormones (steroids) related to sex hormones, controls salt and water metabolism, and other processes. The medulla (inner part) secretes **adrenaline**, whose nature was discovered by Oliver and Schäfer in 1894, and which constricts the blood vessels of the belly, lungs, and skin so that more blood is available for the heart, lungs and voluntary muscles - an emergency preparation for 'fight or flight' causes a large output of adrenalin.

Ā'DRIAN IV. Pope, 1154-9; Nicholas Breakspear, the only Englishman to sit in the papal chair. He was b. at Abbots Langley, became a monk in France, and in 1137 abbot of St Rufus, near Arles. Elected pope at the end of 1154, he secured the execution of Arnold of Brescia, crowned Frederick I Barbarossa as German emperor; refused Henry II's request that Ireland should be granted to the English crown in absolute ownership; and was at the height of a quarrel with the emperor when he d. at Anagni.

ADRIAN, Edgar, 1st baron (1889-1977). British physiologist. He received the Nobel prize for medicine in 1932, for his work with Sherrington in the field of nerve impulses, and was prof. of physiology at Cambridge 1937-51, and Master of Trinity Coll. 1951-65. His books incl. *The Basis of Sensation* (1928) and *The Physical Basis of Perception* (1947). Awarded the O.M. in 1942, he was created a baron in 1955.

ĀDRIANŌ'PLE. Older name of EDIRNE, after the Emperor Hadrian, who rebuilt it *c.* A.D. 125.

ĀDRIA'TIC SEA. Large arm of the Mediterranean Sea, lying N.W. to S.E. between the Italian and the Balkan peninsulas. The western shore is Italian; the eastern Yugoslav and Albanian. The sea is about 805km (500m) long, and its area is 135,250 sq.km (52,220 sq.m).

ADULTERY. Extra-marital act while married. The commission of A. by the respondent is one of the facts considered as demonstrating an 'irretrievable breakdown' of marriage in suits for judicial separation or divorce in Britain. It is almost universally recognized as ground for divorce in USA, and in some states is theoretically punishable by fine or prison.

ADUWA (ad'u-wa). Town in Ethiopia, *c.* 180km (110m) S.S.W. of Massawa at an altitude of 1,910 m (6,270 ft). It was formerly the cap. of Ethiopia, and it was here that the Ethiopians defeated the Italians in 1896. Pop. (1970) 5,750.

ADVENT (Lat. *adventus*, approach, arrival). That season in the Christian calendar which is celebrated as a preparation for the festival of Christmas. It includes the four Sundays before Christmas, beginning with the Sunday which falls nearest (before or after) to St Andrew's Day (30 Nov.).

ADVENTISTS. Those who hold the view that Christ will return to make a second appearance on the earth. Expectation of the Second Coming of Christ is found in N.T. writings generally. Adventist views are held in particular by the Seventh Day Adventists, Christadelphians, Jehovah's Witnesses, and the Four Square Gospel Alliance.

ADVOCATE (Lat. *advocatus*, one summoned to one's aid, esp. in a court of justice). A professional pleader in a court of justice. The English term is barrister or counsel, but A. is retained in Scotland and in other countries, e.g. France, where the Roman law is still retained. The *Lord Advocate* is the principal law-officer of the Crown in Scotland, a political member of the ministry of the day, retiring with the government by whom he was appointed. A *Judge-Advocate* manages the prosecution in courts-martial, the *Judge-Advocate-General* being the chief of the legal department of the respective Service. The term A. has no special significance in the US.

ADVOCATES, Faculty of. Scottish legal body, incorporated in 1532 under James V. Members closely resemble in their powers English barristers.

AEGEAN (ējē'an) **SEA.** Branch of the Mediterranean between Greece and Turkey. The Dardanelles connect it with the Sea of Marmara. The numerous islands in the A. Sea incl. Crete, the Cyclades, the Sporades and the Dodecanese. There is political tension between Greece and Turkey over sea limits claimed by Greece round such islands as Lesbos, Chios, Samos and Kos. By 1980 the possibility of undersea oil reserves in the A.S. had been discounted.

AEGINA (ējī'na). Greek island in the Gulf of A. *c.* 32km (20m) S.W. of Piraeus. In 1811 remarkable sculptures were recovered from a Doric temple in the N.E. (restored by Thorwaldsen) and taken to Munich.

AEGIR (īgir). In Scandinavian mythology, the god of the sea.

AEGIS (ē'jis). In Gk mythology, the shield of Zeus, symbolic of the storm cloud associated with him. In representations of deities it is commonly shown as a protective animal skin.

AELFRIC (*c.* 955-1020). Old-English prose writer. He became a priest and taught at Cernel monastery (now Cerne Abbas) in Dorset, and was abbot of Eynsham from 1005. He is celebrated for his writings in the vernacular, particularly for his two collections of homilies and the *Lives of the Saints.*

AENEAS (ēnē'as). In classical legend, a Trojan prince who became the ancestral hero of the Romans. According to Homer, he was the son of Anchises and the goddess Aphrodite. During the Trojan war he several times owed his life to the intervention of the gods. The legend on which Virgil's *Aeneid* is based describes his escape from Troy and eventual settlement in Latium. The Latins accorded him divine honours, and the house of Julius claimed to be descended from him.

AEOLIAN ISLANDS. Another name for the LIPARI ISLANDS.

AE'OLUS. In Gk mythology, god of the winds, ruler of the Aeolian islands, where he kept the winds imprisoned in a cavern. The *aeolian harp* (popular in the Romantic period) is a wooden sound box, rectangular and fitted with loose gut strings which vibrate in the wind to produce a chordal impression.

AERONAUTICS. The science of aerial locomotion within the earth's atmosphere, including aerial navigation, aerodynamics, aircraft structures, and jet and rocket propulsion. It should not be confused with *Astronautics*, which is the science of travel through space; *Astronavigation* is, however, used in aircraft as in ships and is a part of A. **Aerodynamics** comprises the study of the airflow around bodies moving through it. In subsonic A. (below the speed of sound) aerodynamic forces increase as the square of the speed, and are thus simply calculated, streamlining being necessary. Transonic A. covers the speed range from just below to just above the speed of sound. Ordinary sound waves move at *c.* 1,225 kph (760 mph) at sea level, and air in front of an aircraft moving slower than this is 'warned' by the waves so that it can move aside. But, as the flying speed approaches that of the sound waves, the warning is too late for the air to escape and the aircraft pushes it aside by brute force, creating shock waves which absorb much power and create design problems. On the ground this is heard as 'sonic boom'. Supersonic A. concerns speeds above that of sound and is a much older study than A. itself, since as ballistics (q.v.), the study of the flight of bullets was undertaken soon after the introduction of firearms, and was applied in turn to aeroplanes. Hypersonics is the study of airflows and forces at speeds about 5 times that of sound (mach 5), e.g. for vehicles such as the V2, guided missiles and rockets being launched into space. Superaerodynamics deals with very high speeds in the rarefied air at very high altitudes, i.e. 80-240 km (50-150 m).

AEROPLANE. A heavier than air craft supported in flight by fixed wings (*aerofoils*): it may be unpowered (the glider) or powered, when it is propelled by the reaction from air accelerated rearwards by airscrew(s) (propellers) or jet(s) to overcome the air resistance (*drag*). Drag depends on frontal area (e.g. large, airliner; small, fighter) and shape (*drag coefficient*); it equals *thrust* in straight level flight. Less drag (*streamlining*) means increased speed and lower fuel consumption from given power; less fuel need be carried for a given distance (*range*) and the A.'s weight is reduced.

Aerofoils are so shaped and cambered that air passing above them is speeded up, reducing pressure below atmospheric, while that above is slowed. This produces a vertical force (*lift*) to support the aircraft's weight. (Lift = weight in level flight.) Minimum weight is thus essential to an efficient A., requiring a smaller wing which has less drag. Very strong but light aluminium alloys (with copper, magnesium, etc.) are used, and also for the body (*fuselage*) and where possible for controls and in engines. For supersonic planes special stainless steel and titanium may be used. The thin *skin* (outer) panels, with *ribs* and *stringers* at intervals to prevent buckling, support all flight stresses with no separate structure (semi-monocoque

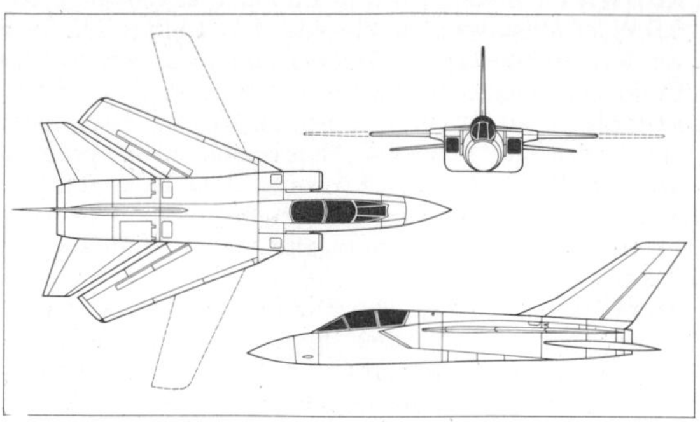

AEROPLANE. The swing-wing Multi Role Combat Aircraft (MRCA) under development for the British, German and Italian air forces, as the backbone of their defence in the 1980s. Able to intercept at high or low altitudes, the Tornado is intended to maintain air superiority over the battlefield, give support to ground or naval forces, and carry out reconnaissance. The diagrams to the right illustrate the full range of the wing sweep, from fully extended at take-off to completely retracted in level flight. *Photo: Courtesy of British Aircraft Corporation*

construction). The *payload* (crew, passengers, bombs, etc.) may be up to one-third all-up weight.

Control. Aerofoils are unstable and a horizontal *tailplane* is installed behind to overcome this, with hinged flaps (*elevators*) to control pitch (*attitude*). Raising the elevator depresses the tail and the aerofoil is inclined (*angle of attack* increased), which further speeds up the airflow above it until lift exceeds weight, when the A. climbs; the steeper attitude increases drag and more power is needed to maintain speed. Descent results from reducing the angle of attack, when speed builds up rapidly (*diving*) if the engine is not throttled back. Descent without power is *gliding*. Turning (changing direction) is effected not by the rudder (hinged to the vertical *tail-fin*), but by banking the A. (rolling) so that the lift force inclines inwards to provide a centripetal component as well as supporting the A.'s weight; to do so it must exceed that for level flight, and the angle of attack is increased by raising the elevators. The A. is banked by applying ailerons (inter-connected hinged flaps at the rear (*trailing edge*) of the wings, working oppositely). In a jet A., such as *Concorde*, which forms a single triangular (delta) wing, the ailerons and elevators are combined (*elevons*). The 'outer' aileron is depressed to increase effectively the camber and therefore the lift, and vice versa. The more aileron applied, the more the A. banks and the quicker it turns, until the wings are nearly vertical. Rudders are fitted only as balance controls, and 'top' rudder (i.e. opposite to the direction of bank) is applied to prevent side-slip inwards when turning, or to fly straight on one engine in a two-engined A.

Flaps are fitted to the rear of wings to increase camber and lift for shorter take-off and landing, and planes have now been developed, e.g. the Harrier jump-jet, which are capable of vertical take-off and landing (VTOL). This is achieved by jet nozzles which swivel downwards to give lift at take-off, and then return to a level position for normal forward flight. To land, the angle of attack of an A. is increased until the airflow over the wing breaks down and lift is lost (*stalling*). The design of an aircraft for sub-sonic flight, e.g. the *c.* 965 kph (600 mph) of the ordinary commercial jetliner operating on short hauls, is less streamlined than that of the supersonic plane. However, even the supersonic plane can use to advantage the out-spread wing position which gives greatest lift and manoeuvrability in take-off and its initial subsonic flight, hence the development of the swing-wing A. This adopts the 'outspread wing' as required, but the wings are subsequently swung back closer to the fuselage to achieve the delta, sweptwing design best adapted to high speed level flight, e.g. the MRCA. On the ground the A. rests on wheels (floats, on water) attached to the *air-frame* by struts; the landing gear (*under-carriage*) is retractable in flight to reduce drag.

These principles apply to all A. types, e.g. biplanes (2 super-imposed wings — now obsolescent), monoplanes, seaplanes, flying boats (obsolete), airliners, freighters, fighters, bombers, trainers, whether propelled by airscrews, driven by piston engines or by gas turbines (jet or turbo-jet) or rocket motors. Helicopters (rotating wing aircraft) and rockets are not As. *See* FLIGHT, JET PROPULSION. Under development, however, is a new kind of aircraft, the 'control configured vehicle' (CCV). Instead of the controls being brought into action by hydraulic lines operated by the pilot through mechanical or electrical linkage, microcomputers have made possible a 'fly-by-wire' system. The pilot instructs the computer which manoeuvre the aircraft must perform, and the computer, which is kept in touch by a series of sensors with the attitude, speed and turning rate of the plane, sends the correct orders to the control devices (ailerons, rudder, throttle, and so on) to enable the manoeuvre to be executed. Such automated high speed response frees the aircraft from some of the restrictions previously imposed by the force of gravity, and, with the addition of one or more vertical fins toward the front and twisting (variable incidence) wings, to turn and move either up or down while still maintaining level flight.

AEROSOL (ā'rōsol). A colloidal system, e.g. mist or fog, in which air is the dispersion medium; and popularly a form of packaging in which gas under pressure, or a liquefied gas with a pressure greater than atmospheric at ordinary temperatures, is used to spray a very fine mist of liquid droplets from a nozzle; it is generally actuated by a press-button device. As. are used for germicides, insecti-cides, fire extinguishers, paints, hair lacquers, perfumes,

AEROPLANE. The radar station in the sky: the Hawker Siddeley Nimrod AEW (airborne early warning) aircraft. The nose radome — the largest of its kind in the world — houses the front radar scanner, and the aircraft carries mission system avionics specially designed and developed by Marconi-Elliott Avionics for the Ministry of Defence. The system is resistant to jamming and incorporates electronic counter-measures to protect it from enemy guided missiles and radar. The Nimrod is equally effective whether seeking out submarines or even small patrol boats at sea, or operating over land where it registers low-flying supersonic aircraft and can direct their interception. *Photo: Courtesy of Hawker Siddeley*

etc. A fear that fluorocarbon propellants used in As. might wear down the ozone (q.v.) layer, protecting Earth against ultra-violet rays from the Sun, led to measures to ban them, but scientists regard the theory as absurd.

AESCHINES (ē'skinēz) (4th cent. B.C.). Orator of ancient Athens, a rival of Demosthenes.

AESCHYLUS (ē'skilus) (*c* 525–456 B.C.). Greek dramatist. B. near Athens, he came of a noble family; fought against the Persians at Marathon (490 B.C.), and wrote nearly 90 plays between 499 and 458 B.C. He twice visited the court of Hiero, king of Syracuse, and d. at Gela in Sicily.

The earliest of his 7 surviving plays is *The Suppliant Women*, performed about 490. There followed *The Persians* (472), *Seven against Thebes* (467) and *Prometheus Bound* (*c.* 460). Then came the trilogy of the *Oresteia* which won the first prize at the festival of Dionysus in 458; the 3 plays - *Agamemnon, Choephori,* and *Eumenides* - deal with the curse on the house of Agamemnon which was eventually resolved by the action and suffering of Orestes.

A. became famous for the majesty of his language, the boldness of his speculation upon problems of religion and human destiny, and the grandeur and simplicity of his plots and characters.

AESCULĀ'PIUS. Lat. form of Asklepios, god of medicine in Gk. mythology. His attribute was a staff with a snake coiled about it, because the snake, since it sloughs its skin, was supposed to renew its youth. Sacred snakes were kept in the sanctuaries of A. at Epidaurus and elsewhere. The customary offering to A. was a cock.

AESOP (ē'-). Fabulist of antiquity. Herodotus says he lived in the reign of Amasis of Egypt (mid-6th cent. B.C.). B. a slave, he may well have been a Negro, and was represented in later art as deformed. He received his freedom and visited Lydia and Greece. No writings by him have survived, and some at least of the fables were current in Egypt many centuries earlier.

AESTHETIC MOVEMENT. Artistic movement of the late 19th cent. in England, the chief doctrine of which was Art for Art's sake. It owed much to Pater and Wilde, and found expression in the *Yellow Book*. It was exemplified by painters such as Whistler, draughtsmen like Aubrey Beardsley, poets such as Lionel Johnson and Ernest Dowson, and among critics by J. A. Symonds.

AETOLIA (ētō'-). District of anc. Greece on the N.W. of the gulf of Corinth. The AETOLIAN LEAGUE was a confederation of the cities of A. which, following the death of Alexander the Great, was the chief rival of the Macedonian power and the Achaean League.

AFARS AND THE ISSAS, Fr. Terr. of the. *See* DJIBOUTI.

AFFINITY (in law). The relationship which exists between a man and his wife's blood relations, or between a woman and her husband's blood relations. It is distinguished from consanguinity or blood relationship. Many relationships by A. prevent marriage, e.g. a man cannot normally marry his step-daughter.

AFFIRMATION (in law). A solemn declaration made instead of taking the oath by a person who has no religious belief or objects to taking an oath on religious grounds.

AFGHAN HOUND. Dog resembling the saluki, though more thickly coated, first introduced to Britain by army officers serving on the N.W. Frontier in the late 19th cent. It has an aloof, aristocratic expression, and in the 1970s became increasingly fashionable.

AFGHANISTAN. Country to the N.W. of Pakistan. It is almost entirely mountainous, the Hindu Kush to the N.E. rising to 7,315 m (24,000 ft). The chief rivers are Amu Darya (Oxus), Kabul, and Helmand. By irrigation of the small areas of level land crops of wheat and other cereals, sugar cane and sugar beet, fruits, tobacco, rice and cotton are grown in the N. and E. The river pastures are grazed by cattle, and fat-tailed sheep and yaks are raised in the mountains. Minerals, for the most part undeveloped, incl. iron, coal, copper, gold and silver, gypsum, asbestos and various gems. Natural gas is piped to Russia, and other exports incl. karakul lamb skins, carpets, fruit and tobacco. Hydro-electric schemes are helping the growth of industry, and there has been a large road-building programme since the 1950s, though there are no railways and few navigable rivers. Air transport has also been developed. The chief passes are the Khyber and Khojak (to Pakistan) and the Salang (to USSR). The frontier with Pakistan (Durand Line 1893) is disputed and A. claims Pakhtoonistan (*see* PATHAN). The cap. is Kabul, other towns incl. Kandahar, Herat and Mazar-i-Sharif.

Area 650,000 sq.km (250,000 sq.m); pop. 15,540,000 whom 90% are Sunni Moslems, and the chief official language is Pushtu. M.U.: afghani.

History. Once part of Aryana, a region of the ancient Persian Empire, A., occupied by many peoples during its early history, first became an independent amirate in 1747. During the 19th cent. Russian influence in the country threatened British India, and in 1838 A. was invaded by a British force, which secured control of the country; but in 1842 the garrison of Kabul was wiped out and the British evacuated A. A second Afghan War followed in 1878, during which General Roberts captured Kabul and, in 1880, marched to Kandahar. A third Afghan War, in

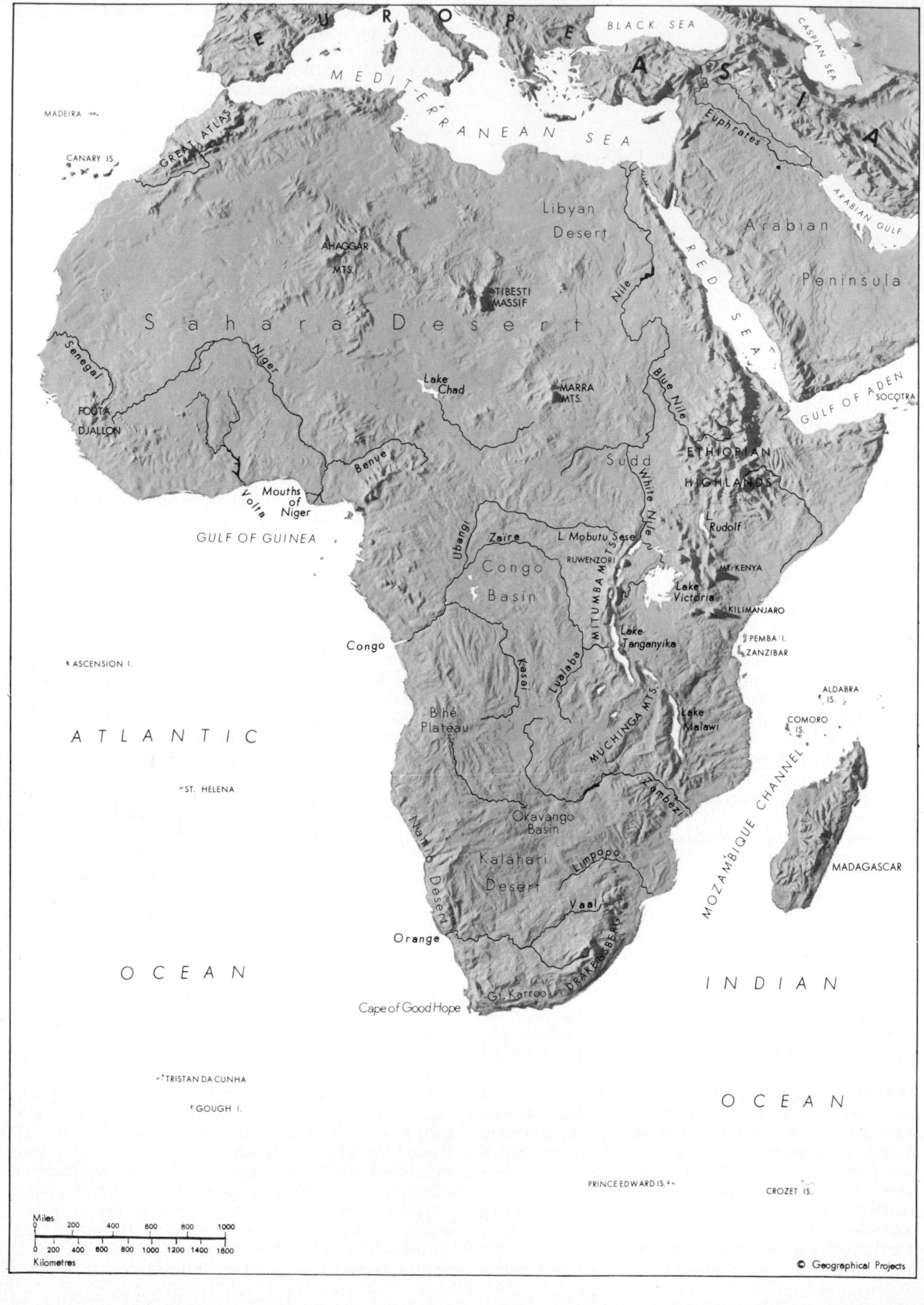

EUROPE
EURASIA
BLACK SEA
CASPIAN SEA
MEDITERRANEAN SEA
MADEIRA
CANARY IS.
GREAT ATLAS
Euphrates
ARABIAN GULF
Libyan Desert
Arabian Peninsula
AHAGGAR MTS.
TIBESTI MASSIF
Nile
RED SEA
Sahara Desert
Senegal
Niger
Lake Chad
MARRA MTS.
Blue Nile
GULF OF ADEN
SOCOTRA
FOUTA DJALLON
Benue
Sudd
White Nile
ETHIOPIAN HIGHLANDS
Volta
Mouths of Niger
L. Rudolf
GULF OF GUINEA
Ubangi
Zaïre
L. Mobutu Sese
RUWENZORI
Congo Basin
MITUMBA MTS.
MT. KENYA
Lake Victoria
KILIMANJARO
Congo
Lake Tanganyika
PEMBA I.
ZANZIBAR
ASCENSION I.
Kasai
Lualaba
ALDABRA IS.
Bihé Plateau
Lake Malawi
COMORO IS.
ATLANTIC
MUCHINGA MTS.
MOZAMBIQUE CHANNEL
ST. HELENA
Zambezi
Okavango Basin
Namib Desert
Kalahari Desert
Limpopo
MADAGASCAR
Vaal
Orange
DRAKENSBERG
OCEAN
INDIAN
Gt. Karroo
Cape of Good Hope
TRISTAN DA CUNHA
GOUGH I.
OCEAN
PRINCE EDWARD IS.
CROZET IS.
Miles
0 200 400 600 800 1000
0 200 400 600 800 1000 1200 1400 1600
Kilometres
© Geographical Projects

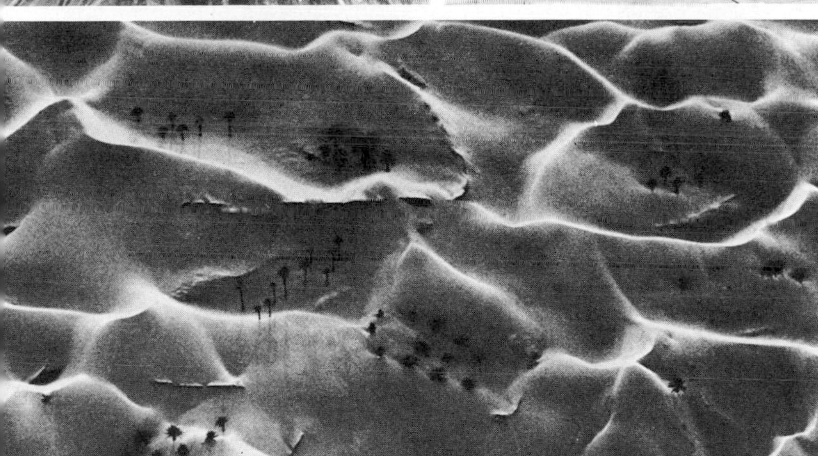

AFRICA. The rich diversity of the continent has astonished the world since ancient times, when the Greeks said 'There is always something new from Africa'. Traditional river life in the tropical forests of central Africa (top left); the *souk* at Marrakesh in Morocco (top right); the crater of the active volcano of Mt Oldony Lengai in the Great Rift Valley (upper centre left); the streamlined modernity of Ibadan University in Nigeria (upper centre right); the shifting sands of the Sahara almost obliterate an oasis (lower centre left); a woman of the Arussi from Ethopia (lower centre right); and Cape Town at night (bottom right). *Photos: Camera Press (Ibadan, Ethiopian woman, river scene, Cape Town), Mireille Vautier (Marrakesh), Popperfoto (volcano, Sahara).*

which the Afghans invaded India, lasted only a few months in 1919. The king Mohammed Zahir Shah, was deposed and assassinated in 1973, and the new republic signed a treaty of friendship with the USSR in 1978. The regime became increasingly Soviet-dominated, which resulted in growing Islamic insurgency. In Dec. 1979–Jan. 1980 there was invasion and occupation by Soviet troops to back up the puppet regime, an action which was condemned by a UN General Assembly resolution. Guerrilla resistance continued. *See* WAKHAN SALIENT.

AFGHANISTAN. A fur tailor at work in Kabul on the coats which are popular, especially among younger people, all over the world. *Photo: Gunter Reitz/Barnaby's Picture Library*

AFGHANS. In Australia the Moslem camel drivers, also known as Ghans, who were brought to work in the outback from 1860 to the 1920s. They actually came from Pakistan. The Ghan (pron. gan) is the train link Adelaide-Alice Springs.

AFRICA. Second largest of the continents of the world; with an area of 30,000,000 sq.km (11,500,000 sq.m), it is smaller than Asia or America, but two-and-a-half times the size of Europe.

Geography and Resources. The proportion of desert to cultivated land is unusually high: the Sahara covers *c.* 8,700,000 sq.km (3,500,000 sq.m), and is expanding. There are few fertile alluvial plains to compensate for the deserts, the continent being composed of a great plateau rising sharply from the sea. The rivers cut their way from the plateau to sea-level by cataracts and are therefore generally not suitable for navigation. The Nile receives no tributaries in its lower reaches, and without artificial irrigation would water only a narrow strip of land: the Zaïre (Congo) and Niger basins are masked by dense tropical forests. The coastline has few good natural harbours, but man-made ports such as Tema are supplying the deficiency. A wide strip of central A., on either side of the equator, experiences a wet tropical climate; the coast lands of W. Africa are hot and damp, while on the E., though drier, it is even hotter. Great tracts between the tropical regions and the deserts of N. and S. Africa are covered by tropical grassland and bush country.

In some minerals A. was formerly considered poor as compared with other continents, e.g. petroleum, but surveys revealed rich reserves in north and west A., and other mineral wealth incl. copper (Zaïre, Zambia), diamonds (Botswana, S. Africa, S.W. Africa, Zaïre), gold (Ghana, S. Africa), manganese (Ghana, S. Africa), phosphates (north Africa), tin (Uganda, Zaïre), uranium (S. Africa, Zaïre). *See* SAHARA.

Large areas of the continent are unsuited to arable agriculture, and in other areas the tse-tse fly prevents stock raising; but chemical and other scientific aids, artificial irrigation, and development of hydro-electric power are increasing A.'s agricultural and industrial production. Important crops include cocoa (Ghana, Nigeria), cotton (Uganda, Egypt), coffee (Kenya), sisal (E. Africa), tobacco (E. Africa); wine is produced in Algeria and S. Africa.

Population. Numbering altogether some 370,000,000, the pop. of A. is composed of Bushmen and Hottentots living in the Kalahari region, S.W. Africa and Botswana; Negritos or Pygmies in Zaïre; Negroes in W. Africa; Hamites in Egypt, the Republic of Sudan, Ethiopia, Somali Rep., N. Africa and parts of the Sahara; various mixed peoples such as the Hamiticized Negroes or Bantus and the Nilotics of the Republic of Sudan; Semites, including the Arabs of N. and E. Africa; recent immigrants of European and Indian origin in E. and S. Africa, Kenya, and other recently developed territories.

AFRICA. The growth of independence.

Territorial Divisions of Africa

Territory	*Area in 1,000 sq. km.*	*Pop. est. in 1,000s*	*Capital*
North Africa:			
Algeria	2,293	22,107	Algiers
Egypt	1,000	49,000	Cairo
Libya	1,780	3,752	Tripoli
Morocco	459	23,117	Rabat
*Western Sahara**	266	100	El Aaiún
Sudan	2,500	22,972	Khartoum
Tunisia	164	7,259	Tunis
East Africa:			
Djibouti	23	297	Djibouti
Ethiopia	1,184	42,266	Addis Ababa
Kenya	583	20,194	Nairobi
Madagascar	594	9,941	Tananarive
Mauritius	2	1,024	Port Louis
Somali Rep.	700	7,595	Mogadishu
Tanzania	943	21,701	Dodoma
Uganda	236	14,689	Kampala
West Africa:			
Benin	113	4,005	Porto Novo
Burkina Faso	274	6,320	Ouagadougou
Cameroon	474	9,737	Yaoundé
Gambia	11	751	Banjul
Ghana	239	13,004	Accra
Guinea, Rep. of	246	5,597	Conakry
Guinea-Bissau	36	858	Bissau
Ivory Coast	322	10,090	Yamoussoukro
Liberia	113	2,232	Monrovia
Mali	1,204	7,721	Bamako
Mauritania	1,031	1,656	Nouakchott
Niger	1,187	6,491	Niamey
Nigeria	924	102,783	Abuja/Lagos
Senegal	198	6,755	Dakar
Sierra Leone	73	3,883	Freetown
Togo	56	3,023	Lomé
Central Africa:			
Burundi	28	4,673	Bujumbura
Central African Rep.	625	2,664	Bangui
Chad	1,284	5,036	N'djamena
Congo	342	1,798	Brazzaville
Gabon	267	988	Libreville
Guinea, Equatorial	28	350	Malabo
Malawi	117	7,056	Lilongwe
Rwanda	26	6,115	Kigali
Zaïre	2,345	30,505	Kinshasa
Zambia	752	6,832	Lusaka
Zimbabwe	391	8,678	Harare
Southern Africa:			
Angola	1,247	7,948	Luanda
Botswana	575	1,068	Gaborone
Lesotho	30	1,512	Maseru
Mozambique	785	13,638	Maputo
*South Africa***	1,180	32,465	Pretoria
S.W. Africa	823	1,090	Windhoek
Swaziland	17	636	Mbabane
	30,097	563,972	

*Under sole control of Morocco from 1979
**See also Bophuthatswana and Transkei

AFRICA, Horn of. The projection constituted by Somalia and adjacent terrs. Because of their common interests, a confederation in this area comprising Ethiopia, Kenya, Somalia, the Sudan and the Rep. of Djibouti, has been proposed.

AFRICAN HISTORY. Possibly the cradle continent of mankind (*see* MAN), Africa also has remains in Egypt of one of the greatest of ancient civilizations. Stimulated into rapid growth *c.* 3,400 B.C. by influence from Mesopotamia, or even some unknown source common to both, Egypt spread her influence northward into Europe via Greece, and deep into Africa itself, e.g. Ethiopia. Here Semitic immigrants from southern Arabia had founded a civilization, which flowered 1-6th cents. A.D. in the kingdom of Aksum (q.v.), and later medieval rulers, tracing a legendary descent from Solomon, were themselves identified in distant Europe with fables of 'Prester John'. In historic times the Sahara has always been a formidable barrier between northern and central Africa, and the struggle for dominance between the lighter races of the north and the Negro south has been concentrated via the Nile Valley and Nubia, where an Egyptianized civilization continued when Egypt has been conquered in turn by Assyria, Persia, Greece and Rome (*see* MEROË). Militant Islam, in its expansion across north Africa (conquest of Egypt A.D. 640), followed the Phoenician settlers of Carthage in invading Europe via Spain, and reinforced the Arab influence exercised since time immemorial down into east and central Africa, where there is an extraordinary tribal and cultural diversity. Written record is scant for this area, apart from references in Arab and European sources, but the memory of the powerful medieval states, such as ancient Ghana, Mali, Songhai, Dahomey, and Ashanti has inspired the establishment of modern African states. Recovery of archaeological material is greatly limited by the destructive climate.

The Phoenicians are said to have rounded the Cape of Good Hope *c.* 600 B.C., but it was not until the 15th cent. (*see* DIAZ and DA GAMA) that European influence began to impinge on Africa by the sea routes from the west, with traders seeking the goods which gave rise to the names Gold Coast and Ivory Coast. Even more important was the trade in 'black ivory'. Slavery was not new to Africa, but the scale of the trade to the New World caused enormous suffering and a drain on Africa's population stock. The mining and agricultural skills the slaves brought to the development of America have tended to be underestimated, e.g. in Brazil, and there is still some light to be thrown on the history of Africa by traditions preserved across the Atlantic.

Further to the south where the Bantu peoples predominate, written record is still sparse, though archaeology begins to fill in some gaps, e.g. the remains of Great Zimbabwe: the Mashona people now have no recollection of the culture their ancestors created. Of such warrior kingdoms as that of the Zulus, we have record only when they clashed with white settlers in comparatively recent times.

The whole of Africa, previously the 'dark continent', was illuminated for the West by the great explorers of the 18-19th cents. (e.g. Mungo Park, Livingstone, Stanley, Burton, Speke), but communication remained difficult and only in the 1970s was a Trans-African Highway (Lagos-Mombasa) practically planned. The harsh climate and endemic diseases made large-scale settlement unattractive to Europeans over huge areas of the continent, West Africa being known as the 'white man's grave'. Exceptions incl. the area of the Rep. of South Africa, settled by the Dutch from the 17th cent. and later by the British, with consequent conflict in the Boer War; Zimbabwe and the highlands of Kenya, settled by the British in the 19-20th cents.; and the north African coast (the French in Algeria in 19-20th cents. and Italians in Libya in 20th cent.). Desire for colonies, for reasons of prestige and hoped-for potential wealth of economic resources, however, meant that the whole of Africa was partitioned among the European states in the 'Scramble for Africa' in the late 19th cent. Belgium, Germany, Italy, Portugal and Spain participated, but the chief protagonists were Britain, on a N.-S. axis, and France E.-W., with the inevitable flashpoint incident at Fashoda in 1898, which almost precipitated a European war. Resistance from the Africans was brave, and often extremely well-organized, but useless against such better-armed opponents, e.g. the Ashanti Wars.

Lack of intensive settlement by Europeans meant that the annexations were comparatively rapid to 'unscramble' in much of Africa after the breakdown of European dominance after the two World Wars: minor campaigns were fought in Africa in the F.W.W., e.g. Tanganyika, and in the S.W.W., the turning-point of the war in the West was the Battle of El Alamein (1942) in N. Egypt. Unfortunate legacies were arbitrary boundaries unrelated to natural African national divisions, and language barriers, where official languages had been English and French, although this aided communication with the outside world. The bitterest conflicts came in Kenya (Mau-Mau), Algeria, and other areas where actual settlement had taken place, and continued underground, as in Mozambique until 1975, Zimbabwe until 1980, and S. Africa. The idea of Pan-Africanism had developed in the 1930s and 1940s, but the idealism which helped to found the new states (*see* MAP) had its counter-balance in the civil war in Nigeria, the Burundi-Rwanda massacres, etc. Parliamentary govt. with one party in power and one or more in official opposition had always been a little alien to the more African concept of a 'tribal consensus', but some of the new regimes proved harshly authoritarian and oppressive. Moreover, the 'old imperialism' which had, within the limitations of its time, been not ignoble in administrators of wider vision, tended to be replaced by a new 'economic imperialism', because most African countries were producers of primary products subject to the vagaries of the commodity markets, and in need of investment and aid from the developed countries of Europe, the USA, USSR and China. In spite of these difficulties substantial progress continued to be made, and the new Africa is an increasingly influential factor in the modern world. *See* OAU.

AFRICAN NEGRO ART. The chief centres of Negro art are in Nigeria, Zaïre, Ghana, the Ivory Coast, and the Rep. of Cameroon. In S. Nigeria the most notable works were produced by the Negro people of Benin and of ancient Ife. The Beni used the *cire-perdue* process - as used in Italy during the Renaissance - in executing their bronze relief work. In Zaïre the Bakuba and Baluba tribes are famous for their wonderful decorative works such as ornamental spoons, bobbins, and head rests. The artists of the Bushango kingdom (15th-16th cents.) produced wood-carvings of singular beauty, and also practised the art of portraiture. The wooden statues of their early kings are most remarkable. Among the most interesting products of Ghana are the brass weights from Ashanti. These are used for measuring gold-dust, and are made in the form of tiny figures which are said to illustrate local legends. The most skilful artists of the Ivory Coast belong to the Baoulé tribe, who are closely related to the Ashanti peoples. Wood-carvings, drinking cups, basketry, statues, and masks are among the artistic products of the Rep. of Cameroon. The masks of the Cross River are particularly famous for their realistic quality.

The Negro art of W. Africa, remarkable for its beauty of form and intense vitality, has had a profound influence on the work of many of the leading European artists, e.g. Picasso, Matisse, Brancusi, Modigliani, and Epstein.

AFRIKAANS. One official language of S. Africa, the other being English. Spoken by the Afrikaners, mainly descendants of the original Dutch colonists, it is a development of the Dutch language, modified by the influence of German, French, and other immigrant and native tongues. Reaching its modern form in the middle of the 18th cent., it did not become a written language until *c.* 1875.

AFRIKA KORPS. Name of the German army in the Western (Libyan) Desert in the S.W.W. They first came into contact with British troops at El Agheila on 24 March 1941, but were driven out of N. Africa by May 1943.

AGA. Title of nobility, probably of Tartar derivation. The Turks applied it to military commanders, and, in general, to men of high station.

AGADIR (-dēr'). Most southern seaport in Morocco, near the mouth of the Sus. When Fez was occupied by the French in July 1911, the *Panther*, a German gunboat, appeared off A., and the Emperor William II of Germany made a claim for territorial concessions. On 1 March 1960, the town was virtually destroyed by an earthquake, about a third of its 30,000 inhabitants being killed. A new town was built on solid rock nearby. Pop. (1970) *c.* 50,000.

AGA KHAN (ah'ga kahn) **IV** (1936-). Spiritual head of the Ismaili Moslem sect. He was the nominated successor of his grandfather, **Aga Khan III** (1877-1957), holder of the office from 1885, and a noted racehorse owner.

AGAME'MNON. Greek hero. The son of Atreus, king of Mycenae he m. Clytemnestra, and became by her the father of three daughters - Iphigenia, Chrysothemis, and Laodice (Electra) - and a son, Orestes. The most powerful of the Greek princes, he was their leader in the Trojan war. When Troy was captured, A. received Cassandra, daughter of King Priam, as his prize, and sailed for home, where he was murdered by Clytemnestra and Aegisthus.

AGAR-AGAR. Organic substance, usually met with as a straw-coloured powder or as pale strips which dissolve in hot water to give a solution which sets to a jelly on cooling. It is obtained from the *Gelidium* species of red algae, and is useful in bacteriology for growing bacteria at blood temperature.

AGA'RICUS or A'GARIC. Genus of fungi of the class Basidiomycetes. It includes the common mushroom (*Agaricus campestris*) and the horse-mushroom (*A. arvensis*): closely allied is the genus Amanita (q.v.) with many poisonous species.

AGATE (ag'ăt). Banded or cloudy kind of silica, used to form ornamental stones and objects of art. A. stones are used to burnish and polish gold deposited on glass and ceramics.

AGRICULTURE. On the left, medieval haymakers at work outside the fortified walls of their town, and, on the right a mammoth modern irrigation system in the San Joaquin Valley, California. The crops include cotton, almonds, figs, walnuts and, as seen here, grapes. *Photo of San Joaquin: Courtesy of Citibank*

AGAVE (agā'vē). Genus of plants of the Amaryllidaceae family. All belong to the New World, and have stiff, spiny leaves, with flowers borne on an upright stalk, *c.* 10m (30ft) high. They were cultivated by the Aztecs of Mexico, and are a source of sisal, and a fermented drink *pulque* (pron. pōōl'kā); introduced to Europe as ornamental plants in 16th cent., they are sometimes called 'century plants', since they flower only after many years and then die. *See* TEQUILA.

AGEING. Process resulting in death. Every living cell is governed in its behaviour by the presence in its nucleus of DNA, a long complex molecule carrying instructions for all the chemical reactions of the cell encoded in a series of chemical groupings along its length. When a cell multiplies by division into 2, the DNA in each new one repeats the same series of genetic instructions. These are in the form of proteins, some of which form part of the cell structure and others are enzymes varying according to cell function, e.g. production of insulin in the pancreas, or waste disposal in the kidney. If during division the DNA is not accurately reproduced, faulty enzymes result, and it has been suggested that it is the accumulation of such errors which causes A. and death.

A'GINCOURT. French village, to the S.E. of Calais, famous for the victory of the English under Henry V over superior French forces on 25 Oct., St Crispin's Day, 1415. Pop. *c.* 300.

AGNEW, Spiro (1918-). American Vice-President. A Republican, he was Gov. of Maryland 1966-9, and as Vice-Pres. to Nixon gained a reputation for homespun forthright speeches. He resigned in 1973, shortly before pleading 'no contest' to a charge of income tax evasion.

AGNI. In Hindu mythology, the god of fire, the protector of men against the powers of darkness, the guardian of their homes.

AGNON, Shmuel Yosef (1888-1970). Israeli novelist. B. in Buczacz, Galicia (now in USSR), setting of his most famous book *A Guest for the Night,* he wrote in Hebrew and shared a Nobel prize 1966.

AGNOSTIC. Word coined by T. H. Huxley in 1869: person believing that in the nature of things we cannot know anything of what lies behind or beyond the world of natural phenomena. It would seem he had in mind the Greek words *Agnosto theo* (To an unknown God) which St Paul found inscribed on an altar in Athens.

An atheist denies the existence of gods or God; an agnostic asserts that God or a First Cause is one of those concepts - others are the Absolute, Infinity, Eternity, Immortality, etc. - which lie beyond the reach of human intelligence.

AGOUTI (agoo'ti). Genus of rodents (*Dasyprocta*), herbivorous, swift-running, and about the size of a rabbit. They are found in the forests of S. America.

AGRA (ah'grah). City of Uttar Pradesh, Republic of India, on the Yamuna, 160km/100m S.E. of Delhi. Baber, the first great Mogul ruler, made it his capital in 1527. His grandson Akbar rebuilt the Red Fort of Salim Shah (1566), and is buried outside the city in the splendid tomb at Sigandra. In the 17th cent. the buildings of Shah Jehan made A. one of the most beautiful cities in the world. The Taj Mahal, completed 1650, and erected as a tomb for the emperor's wife Mumtaz Mahal, took more than 20 years to build. A.'s political importance dwindled from 1658 when Aurangzeb moved the capital back to Delhi. It was taken from the Mahrattas by Lord Lake in 1803. Pop. (1971) 637,785.

AGRA. The lily pools and fountains of the Taj Mahal are useful as well as decorative. Here a gardener fills a goatskin with water as he works to maintain the beauty of this 'Pearl of India'. *Photo: Camera Press*

AGRI'COLA, Gnaeus Julius (A.D. 37-93). Roman general and statesman. B. in Provence, he became consul in A.D. 77, and next year was made Governor of Britain. He advanced the Roman power as far north as the Firth of Forth, defeated the Caledonians at the battle of Mons Graupius (Grampian hills), and built a chain of forts. His fleet sailed round the N. of Scotland, thus proving for the first time that Britain was an island. He was recalled to Rome in A.D. 85. His daughter m. in A.D. 78 the historian Tacitus, who wrote a biography of A.

AGRICULTURE. All the processes of farming in its widest sense. With some peoples A. has still not reached the stage of soil cultivation, e.g. the Australian aborigines and the nomadic pastoralists of Africa, whereas in ancient Egypt there were extensive estates with very varied produce. The settler-farmer was typical of early Greece and Rome, but later huge estates run by slave labour were common. The medieval economy rested on the manorial system which broke down under the enclosure movement: *see* ENCLOSURES. Modern A. first developed principally in Britain: *see* JETHRO TULL, ARTHUR YOUNG. In the US stress was on the individual working his own land, e.g. the Homestead Act (1862) passed by Lincoln, and using every mechanical device for greater productivity and efficiency, so that American practice is greatly influential in the mechanization now overtaking under-developed countries.

From 1900 until the S.W.W. few agricultural chemicals were in use, but these now incl. a wide range of *herbicides*, selective weedkillers of the 'growth regulating' or hormone type; *insecticides* to deal with insect pests in the soil, and on roots and foliage; and *fungicides*, used either in seed dressings or on the growing plant. The persistence of some of these in the soil or crops, with danger to animals and man has led to restriction of their use. The development of fertilizers has been similarly expanded, and in combination with specialized species of wheat, etc. has led to the 'green revolution' in under-developed countries: *see* BORLAUG and BREEDING. The indiscriminate use of these techniques also has its dangers, and may involve exhaustion and erosion in the wake of the expanded population that plenty brings. *See* ORGANIC FARMING.

The Food and Agriculture Organization of the UN (FAO) estab. 1945 has its HQ in Rome.

AGRIGENTO (ahgrējen'toh). Town in Sicily, Italy. The Roman Agrigentum, it was long called Girgenti until renamed Agrigento under the Fascist regime. There are fine remains of Greek temples. Pop. (1970) 55,000.

A'GRIMONY. Species of plants (*Agrimonia eupatoria*) of the family Rosaceae, growing in hedge-banks, dry sunny banks, and fields. The flowers are small and pale yellow, and are borne on a slender spike.

AGRI'PPA, Marcus Vipsanius (63-12 B.C.). Roman general. Commander of the fleet at Actium (q.v.), he m. Augustus' daughter, Julia.

Ā'HAB. King of Israel, *c.* 875-854 B.C. His empire included the suzerainty of Moab, and Judah was his subordinate ally; but his kingdom was weakened by constant wars with Syria. By his marriage with Jezebel, princess of Sidon, A. was led to introduce into Israel the worship of the Phoenician god Baal, thus provoking the hostility of Elijah and the prophets. A. d. in battle against the Syrians at Ramoth Gilead.

AHA'GGAR. Plateau of the central Sahara whose highest point, Tahat, *c.* 3,000 m (9,850 ft), lies between Algiers and the mouth of the Niger. It is the home of the nomadic Tuaregs.

AHASUE'RUS. Latinized Hebrew form of the Persian Khshayarsha (Gk. Xerxes). Name given to several Persian kings in the Bible, notably to the husband of Esther. Traditionally it was also the name of the Wandering Jew.

AHMA'DIYYA. Islamic religious movement founded by Mirza Ghulam Ahmad (1839-1908). His followers reject the doctrine that Mohammed was the last of the prophets and accept Ahmad's claim to be the Mahdi and Promised Messiah. In 1974 the Ahmadis were denounced by their co-religionists as non-Moslems.

AHMAD SHAH (1724-73). First ruler of Afghanistan. Elected king in 1747, he had made himself master of the Punjab by 1751. He defeated the Mahrattas at Panipat in 1761, and then the Sikhs.

AHMEDABA'D or **AHMADABA'D.** City of India, on the Sabarmati, in Gujerat state. It was founded in the reign of Ahmad Shah in 1412, and came under the control of the East India Co. in 1818. It has many edifices of the Hindu, Moslem and Jain faiths. Pop. (1971) 1,588,378.

AHMEDNA'GAR or **AHMADNA'GAR.** City of India in Maharashtra state, 195km (120m) E. of Bombay, on the

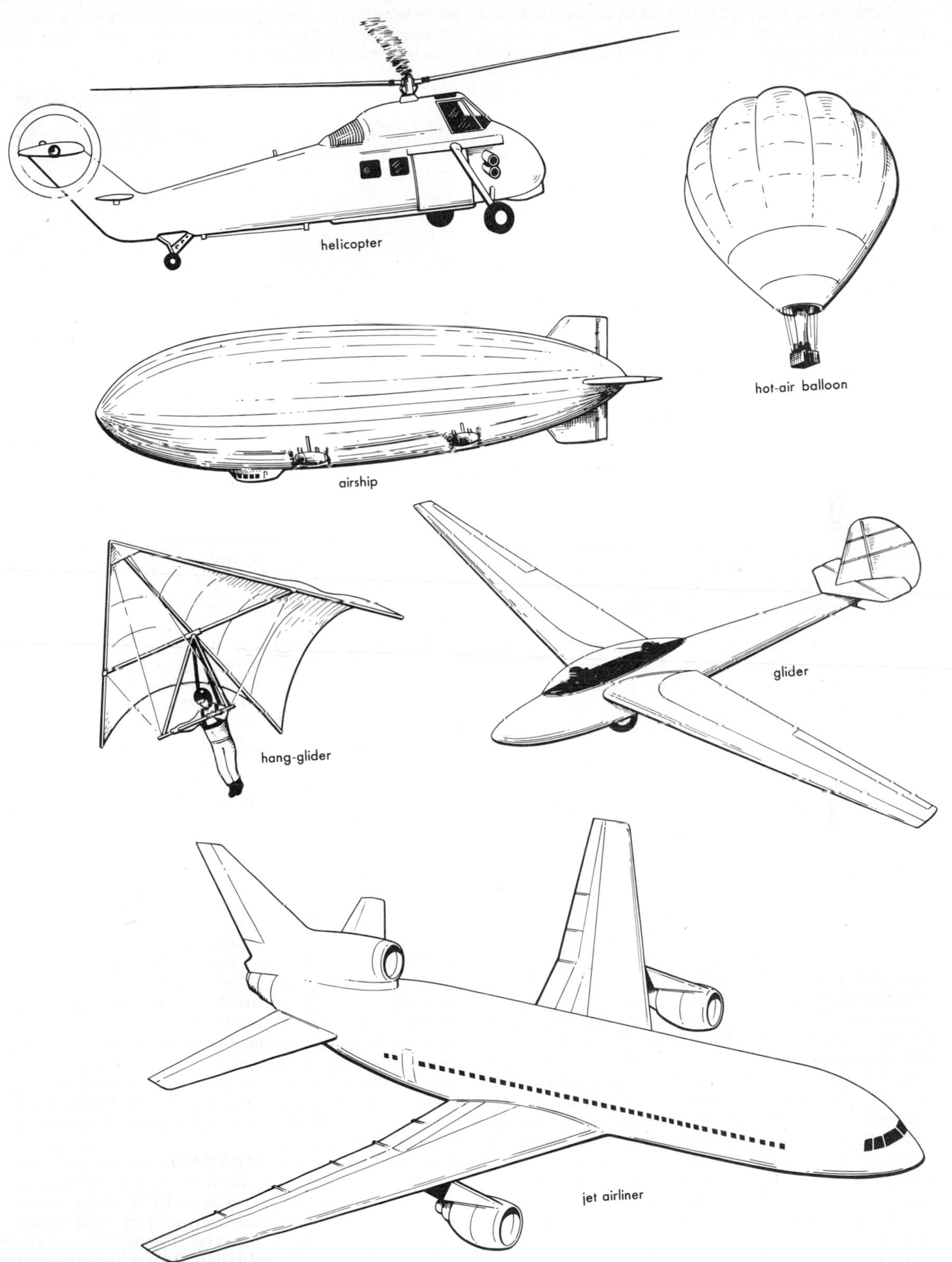

AIRCRAFT. A selection of the different types of aircraft.

left bank of the Sina. It is a centre of cotton trade and manufacture. Pop. (1971) 117,275.

AH'RIMAN. Name given to the evil principle in the Zoroastrian religion (Parseeism). He is the lord of darkness and death, and wages eternal war with Ahura Mazda (Ormuzd).

AHU'RA MA'ZDA or **ORMUZD.** Name given to the supreme good principle in Zoroastrianism. He is the god of life and light, and will finally prevail over his enemy, Ahriman.

AHWA'Z. Cap. of the Arab prov. of Khuzestan, Iran. Pop. (1976) 329,000.

AIDAN, St (d. 651). Monk of Iona; first bishop of Lindisfarne. He christianized Northumbria, settled on Lindisfarne, erected churches and monasteries, and founded a school. He d. at Bamburgh.

AIDS. Disease (*A*quired *I*mmunity *D*eficiency *S*yndrome) which destroys the body's immune system.

AIGUN (ī'goon), **Treaty of.** Signed in 1858 at the port of A. on the Amur river, Heilongjiang prov., China, it ceded the left bank to Russia, but has been repudiated by Communist China.

AIKEN (ā'ken), **Conrad Potter** (1889-1973). American poet and novelist. B. in Georgia, he long lived in Sussex. His first vol., *Earth Triumphant* (1914), was written under the influence of the realist school. He then became associated with the Imagist movement, and all his work shows a lyric facility: *Collected Poems* (1953). Among his novels the most remarkable are *Great Circle* (1933), reflecting events of his own life - when he was a boy his father committed suicide after killing A.'s mother - *Conversation* (1940), and *Ushant* (1962).

AIKEN, Howard (1900-). American mathematician. He began work in 1937 on the first electro-mechanical computer, which incorporated many features retained in modern models, and initiated the concept of 'time-sharing'. He became director of Harvard Computation Laboratory in 1946.

AILSA CRAIG (āl'sa krāg). Rocky islet in the Firth of Clyde, Scotland, about 16km (10m) off the coast of Strathclyde, opposite Girvan.

AINSWORTH, William Harrison (1805-82). British historical novelist. B. at Manchester, the son of a solicitor, he had a great success with his first novel, *Rookwood* (1834), which had Dick Turpin as its hero. He produced in all some 40 novels, of which the best-known are *Jack Sheppard* (1839), *The Tower of London* (1840), *Old St Paul's* (1841), *Windsor Castle* (1843), and *The Lancashire Witches* (1848).

AINTAB. Syrian name of GAZIANTEP.

AINTREE. Racecourse outside Liverpool, Merseyside, where, in addition to flat racing, the Grand National, the premier event of the steeplechase season, was estab. 1839. *See* HORSE-RACING.

AINU (ī'noo). Caucasoid race of hunters and fishermen, fair-skinned, blue-eyed and hairy. Until driven out in the 4th cent. A.D. by the Yamato (ancestors of the modern Japanese), they were the dominant race in Japan, but today only a few thousands survive on Hokkaido, where an Institute of A. Studies at the univ. works to prevent their extinction. Possibly originating in Scandinavia, they have tended to inter-marry with the 'oriental' population, and to decline with the eradication of their culture, which may go back to 7 or 8,000 B.C. Their language may be one of the world's oldest, having few links with any other, and their religion is a complex animalism, one of its features being a communal bear's festival. A blue tattoo of face and lips is practised, especially by the women.

AINU. The women, whose blue-tattooed lips can clearly be seen, also have an attractive costume, and practise varied handicrafts. *Photo: John Hillelson*

AIRCRAFT. Aeronautical vehicle, whether lighter than air (supported by buoyancy) or heavier than air (supported by the dynamic action of air on its surfaces). *See* AEROPLANE, BALLOON, GLIDER, HELICOPTER.

AIRCRAFT CARRIER. A sea-going aerodrome. Although ships were used to carry aircraft in the F.W.W., the first purpose-designed A.C. was the Japan-built *Hosho* (1922). In the S.W.W. the most famous was HMS *Ark Royal* (completed 1938); repeatedly falsely claimed as sunk by the Axis powers, she was eventually torpedoed off Gibraltar, foundering in tow Nov. 1941. After the S.W.W. the cost and vulnerability of such large vessels was considered to outweigh their advantages, and they were built only by the USSR (*Komsomolec* 1979, 40,000 tonnes, 15 fixed-wing aircraft, 20 helicopters) and the USA (*Eisenhower* 1979, 81,600 tonnes, 95 aircraft). By 1980, however, the need to have a means of destroying aircraft beyond the range of a ship's own weapons, espec. on convoy duty, had led to a widespread revival of A.Cs. in the 20-30,000 tonne range (HMS *Invincible* 1980, 19,500 tonnes). They are equipped with combinations of fixed-wing aircraft, helicopters, missile launchers and A.A. guns.

AIREDALE TERRIER. British breed of dog. It originated about 1850 in the Aire and Wharfedale districts of Yorks., as a cross of the otter hound and Irish and Welsh terriers.

AIR FORCE. A nation's fighting aircraft, and the organization to maintain them. The emergence of the aeroplane at first brought only limited recognition of its potential value as a means of waging war; like the balloon, used from the American Civil War, it was considered a way of extending the vision of surface forces. The need for a unified A.F. - foreseen in the UK in 1911 - was realized with the formation of the RAF in 1918 by merging the Royal Naval Air Service and the Royal Flying Corps. During the inter-war period, unity of air control was achieved by Italy (1923), France (1928), Germany (1935, after repudiating the arms limitations of the Versailles treaty), and by the USA in 1947. While the main

AIRCRAFT CARRIER. HMS *Invincible* 1980, played an invaluable role in the retaking of the Falkland Islands in 1982. Carriers of this class, 16,000 tons, are designed to carry 0 Sea Harrier aircraft and 10 Sea King helicopters, are armed with Sea Dart missiles, and have a speed of 28 knots. *Photo: Crown copyright.*

AIR FORCE. A section of the RAF Museum, opened in 1972 at Hendon. In the foreground is the pre Second World War trainer, the Tiger Moth (T-6296); to the right a Gloucester Gladiator (K 8042); and next to that a First World War Sopwith Camel (F 6314). In the background to the left are a Westland Lysander and Vickers Vimy. *Photo: Courtesy of the British Tourist Authority*

specialized groupings formed during the F.W.W. - combat, bombing, reconnaissance, transport, etc. - were adapted and modified in the S.W.W., activity was extended, with self-contained tactical A.Fs. to meet the needs of surface commanders in the main theatres of land operations; and for the attack and defence of shipping over narrow seas.

In 1945-60 the piston engine was superseded by the jet engine which propelled its craft at supersonic speeds; exquisitely precise electronic guidance systems lessened the difference between missile and aircraft; and flights of unlimited duration became a reality by means of air-to-air refuelling. Together with Polaris-armed submarines, the 24 hr.-a-day patrol of the US strategic air command's bombers armed with thermo-nuclear weapons, constitute the West's main ultimate deterrents. It was formerly anticipated that even the pilot might become obsolete, but the continuation of conventional warfare and the evolution of tactical nuclear weapons, has led in the 1960s and 1970s to the development of advanced combat aircraft able to fly supersonically beneath an enemy's radar on strike and reconnaissance missions, e.g. the Phantom FGR2 and Jaguar.

AIR RAID. Aerial attack, usually one involving civilian population. In the F.W.W. 1,316 people were killed in Great Britain, and in the S.W.W. there were 60,584 civilians killed, incl. 29,890 in the London area and 380 in the Coventry raid of 14-15 Nov. 1940. Germany's heaviest casualties were suffered in the triple Allied raid on Dresden 13-14 Feb. 1945, when it is est. 135,000 were killed. In the Far East immediate deaths in the USAF high explosive raid on Tokyo 9-10 March 1945 exceeded those at Hiroshima (q.v.) and totalled 83,793. In the post-S.W.W. hostilities in Korea, non-combatant Laos, and Vietnam the deaths from A.Rs. will never be accurately known.

A comparatively high degree of protection was often possible in the F.W.W. and S.W.W. in large communal shelters or small domestic ones, but the advent of atomic warfare, with the need for very deep, strongly reinforced shelters, self sufficient in food, water, air supply, sanitation, etc. over long periods rendered these obsolete. Development of tactical nuclear weapons, however, and the continuation of conventional warfare, led China to undertake complex systems of tunnels in Peking and other cities, following the border clashes of 1969 with the USSR.

AIRSHIP. Essentially a power-driven balloon. All As. have streamlined envelopes or hulls, which contain the inflation gas, and are either non-rigid, semi-rigid or rigid. Count Ferdinand von Zeppelin (1838-1917) was the pioneer of the rigid type, named after him, and used for bombing raids on Britain in the F.W.W. The destruction by fire of the British R101 in 1930 led to a cessation of building, but after the S.W.W. when large supplies of the non-inflammable gas helium became available there was renewed interest in As. which cause minimum noise pollution, can lift enormous loads, and are economical in fuel. Their comparative silence, and advantage over helicopters that they do not need to be taken to a site by ship, makes them useful in hunting submarines.

AISNE (ān). River of N. France, giving its name to a dept. For the Battles of the Aisne, *see* FIRST and SECOND WORLD WARS.

AIX-EN-PROVENCE (ā'ks-). Town in the dept. of Bouches-du-Rhône, France, 29km (18m) N. of Marseilles. Capital of Provence, it has a fine Gothic cathedral and a university (1409). Pop. (1973) 93,670.

AIX-LA-CHAPELLE. French name of AACHEN.
AIX-LES-BAINS (āks-lā-bań'). Spa in the dept. of Savoie, France, near Lake Bourget, 13km (8m) N. of Chambéry. There are sulphurous hot springs and the climate is healthy. Pop. (1973) 20,720.
AJACCIO (ajas'siō). Cap. of the French island of Corsica. Situated on the W. coast, on the northern shore of the Gulf of A., it has been French since 1768. It was the birthplace of Napoleon. Pop. (1973) 42,300.
AJA'NTA. Village in Maharashtra state, India, famous for its Buddhist cave temples, dating from 200 B.C. to 7th cent. A.D., and discovered in 1817 and first described by J. Ferguson in 1843.
Ā'JAX. Homeric hero. Son of Telamon, king of Salamis, he was second only to Achilles among the Greek heroes in the Trojan War. When Agamemnon awarded the armour of the dead Achilles to Odysseus, A. is said to have died of rage, or to have killed himself.
AJMER (ahjmēr'). Town of Rajasthan state, Rep. of India. Situated in a deep valley in the Aravalli mountains. It has many ancient remains, notably a Jain temple. It was formerly the cap. of the small state of A., which was merged with Rajasthan in 1956. Pop. (1971) 262,480.
AKABA. Alternative transliteration of AQABA.
A'KBAR, Jellaladin Mohammed (1542-1605). Greatest of the Mogul emperors of India. He succeeded his father in 1556, and gradually established his rule throughout the whole of India N. of the Deccan. The firmness and wisdom of his rule won him the title 'Guardian of Mankind'.
À KEMPIS, Thomas. *See* THOMAS À KEMPIS.
AKHETA'TON (modern Tell-el Amarna). New cap. estab. by Ikhnaton (q.v.) - to replace Thebes and its associations with the old religion - when he promulgated his monotheistic cult of Aten, the sun's disc. The name means 'horizon of the sun's disc'.
AK'HNATON. *See* IKHNATON.
Ā'KINS, Zoe (1886-1958). American writer. B. in Missouri, she wrote poems, literary criticism, and plays, of which the best-known is *The Greeks Had a Word for It* (1930).
AKKAIA. *See* ACHAEA.
AKO. Israeli name for ACRE.
AKŌ'LA. Town in Maharashtra state, India, near the Purna r. It is an important centre for the cotton and grain trade. Pop. (1971) 168,454.
AK'RON. City of Ohio, USA, on the Cuyahoga first settled in 1807. Dr B. F. Goodrich estab. a rubber factory there in 1870, and the industry grew immensely with the rising demand for motor car tyres from *c.* 1910. A. has a univ. founded 1870. Pop. met. area (1970) 673,485.
AKSA'KOV, Sergei Timofeyevich (1791-1859). Russian writer. B. at Ufa, in the Urals, he became a civil servant, entered the censorship, and, under the influence of Gogol, wrote autobiographical novels, including *Chronicles of a Russian Family, Years of Childhood,* etc.
AK'SUM or **Axum.** Ancient kingdom which flourished 1st-6th cents. A.D. and covered a large part of modern Ethiopia as well as the Sudan. The ruins of its cap., also called Aksum, lie N.W. of Aduwa, but the site is being developed as a modern city.
ALABAMA (alabah'mă). State of USA, known as the 'cotton state'; it is in the 'Deep South', with an outlet to the Gulf of Mexico. Through this corridor flows the main waterway, the river A. The state comprises the Cumberland Plateau in the N.; the Black Belt, or Canebrake, excellent cotton-growing country, in the centre; and S. of this the coastal plain, or Piny Woods.

AKSUM. The tallest of the obelisks still standing at Aksum. Some 18 m (60 ft) high, it represents a many-storied castle, and like the rest, has an altar at its base. Raised probably in the 1st–3rd cents A.D., these monoliths are thought to be linked with Sun-worship. *Photo: Werner Forman Archive*

A. was settled by the French in the early 18th cent., and passed to Britain in 1763. At the close of the 18th cent. nearly the whole of A. was included in USA, and in 1819 it became a state. It is mainly agricultural. Cotton, sugar, tobacco, rice, and fruits are grown. Some oil is worked. The capital is Montgomery, and Mobile is the only port. The largest town is Birmingham. The state univ. is at Tuscaloosa, and at Tuskegee is an institute founded for Negroes by Booker Washington. Area 133,665 sq.km (51,609 sq.m); pop. (1977) 3,690,000.
ALABAMA. Cruiser (1,040 tonnes) belonging to the Confederate States in the American Civil War. Built at Birkenhead, she was allowed to slip out by the British authorities, and sank many US merchant vessels before being herself sunk by a US man-of-war in 1864. In 1871 a court of arbitration at Geneva decided in favour of the USA, and Britain had to pay damages amounting to $15,500,000.
A'LABASTER. Naturally-occurring form of gypsum which, chemically, is hydrated calcium sulphate, $CaSO_4.2H_2O$. It is a soft material, used for carvings.
ALAIN-FOURNIER (ahlań' foornyeh'). Pseudonym of Henri Fournier (1886-1914), French novelist, who was killed in action on the Meuse in the F.W.W. His reputation rests on *Le Grand Meaulnes* (1913), an autobiographical fantasy of romantic adventure, a search for *The Lost Domain,* as the book was originally titled in English. His life is intimately recorded in his correspondence with his brother-in-law Jacques Rivière.

ALAMAGO'RDO. Town in southern New Mexico, USA. An air force base was estab. here in the S.W.W., and the first atom bomb was exploded 16 July 1945 at Trinity Site to the N.W. There is now a test site for guided missiles. Pop. (1970) 23,000.

ALAMEIN (alamān'). One of the decisive battles of history, fought 23 Oct.-4 Nov. 1942, during the S.W.W., when the British 8th Army, under Montgomery, completely routed the Axis (German and Italian) forces in the Western Desert of North Africa.

A'LAMŌ. Mission-fortress in San Antonio, Texas. It was besieged 23 Feb.-6 March, 1836 by 4,000 Mexicans under Santa Anna (q.v.), and the garrison of *c.* 150 incl. Davy Crockett (q.v.) was massacred.

ALANBROOKE, Alan Francis Brooke, 1st viscount A. (1883-1963). British soldier. Son of Sir Victor Brooke, of co. Fermanagh, he served in the artillery in the F.W.W., and in the S.W.W., as commander of the 2nd Corps 1939-40, did much to aid the extrication of the B.E.F. from Dunkirk. He was C.-in-C. of the Home Forces 1940-1 and while Chief of the Imperial General Staff 1941-6 was largely responsible for the strategy which led to the German defeat. He became a Field-Marshal in 1944, was created a baron 1945 and visct 1946. Sir Arthur Bryant's *The Turn of the Tide* (1957) and *Triumph in the West* (1959) were based on A's. war diaries.

ÅLAND (aw'land) **ISLANDS.** Group of some 300 islands, belonging to Finland, in the Baltic Sea, at the S. extremity of the Gulf of Bothnia. Only 80 are inhabited; the island of A. is the largest and contains a small town, Mariehamn. Area 1,481 sq.km (572 sq.m.); pop. (1971) 20,666.

ALARCON, Pedro Antonio de (1833-91). Spanish journalist and poet, b. at Guadix. Out of his experiences as a soldier in Morocco he produced a *Diario* which was acclaimed as a masterpiece. Among his outstanding works were *El sombrero de tres picos* (The Three-cornered Hat, 1874) and *Cuentos amatorios.*

A'LARIC (*c.* 370-410). King of the Visigoths. In 396 he invaded Greece and retired with much booty to Illyria. In 400 and 408 he invaded Italy, and in 410 captured and sacked Rome, but d. the same year on his way to invade Sicily, and was buried in the r. Busento.

ALA'SKA. Detached state of the USA, at the N.W. extremity of N. America. It was discovered in 1741 by Behring, and a settlement was made in 1744 by Russia, from whom it was bought in 1867 by the USA at a cost of 7,200,000 dollars. Much of A. is mountainous and includes, besides other peaks, Mt McKinley 6,194m (20,320ft), the highest peak in N. America, surrounded by a national park. Reindeer thrive in the Arctic tundra and elsewhere there are extensive forests. Agriculture is rendered difficult by the short summers and the variation of climate from great heat to extreme cold. There are numerous rivers, the largest being the Yukon. The coast is rocky and deeply indented, fringed with many islands; one of these, Little Diomede, is only 3.9 km (2.4m) from Big Diomede (or Ratmanov Is.) in the USSR. The cap. is Juneau, with the eventual prospect of a new cap. to be sited north of Anchorage.

Oil and natural gas, exploited from 1968 especially in the Prudhoe Bay area to the S.E. of Point Barrow, are the most valuable mineral resources. An oil pipeline (1977) runs from Prudhoe Bay to the port of Valdez, and an underground natural gas pipeline is under construction to Chicago and San Francisco. Other minerals incl. coal, copper, iron, gold and tin. There is an important fur trade. Salmon fisheries and canneries, and lumbering are thriving industries. Reindeer provide food for the Eskimoes and hides. The chief railway runs from Seward to Fairbanks, which is linked by motor road (via Canada) with Seattle. Air services are frequent. Near Fairbanks is the Univ. of Alaska. Area 1,500,000 sq.km (586,400 sq.m); pop. (1977) 407,000.

ALASKA. The Trans-Alaska Pipeline runs above ground for half its 1,300 km (800 m) length, as it carries oil south from Prudhoe Bay. The pipe is subject to an enormous temperature range, and to allow for contraction and expansion, the line is built in trapezoidal 'zig-zag' sections. When filled with oil and pumping at full rate, its temperature rises so high that the permafrost could be melted with disastrous environmental results. Consequently 'heat pipes' — the candle-like devices distributed along the pipe — are used, which automatically lower the temperature of the soil as soon as it rises above that of the air. *Photo: Vautier — De Nanxe*

ALASKA HIGHWAY. Road which runs from Fort St John, British Columbia, to Fairbanks, Alaska (2,450 km/1,523 m). It was built in 1942 during the S.W.W., primarily as a defence measure in the event of a Japanese attack on Alaska.

A'LBA. Celtic name for Scotland.

ALBACETE (ahlbahtheh'teh). City in S.E. Spain, cap. of a province of the same name. Once famous for its cutlery and notably for daggers, it is a market town. Pop. (1970) 93,233.

A'LBACORE. Name loosely applied to several sorts of fish found in the Atlantic, in particular to a large tunny and to several species of mackerel.

ALBAN, St (d. A.D. 303). First Christian martyr in England. According to tradition, he was b. at Verulamium, served in the Roman army, became a convert to Christianity after giving shelter to a priest, and on openly professing his belief, was beheaded. In 793 King Offa founded a monastery on the site of A.'s martyrdom, and round this the city of St Albans grew up.

ALBĀ'NIA (Alban. Shqiperia). Republic forming part of the Balkan peninsula. The Dinaric Alps extend over the greater part, with thickly forested slopes which are the haunt of wild boars and wolves. Swift streams descend to the alluvial lowland, which fringes the coast. The lowland soil is fertile, and agriculture is carried on by state farms and collectives. Coal, chrome and nickel are mined, and steel and chemical industries are developing: there is also some oil. The chief towns are Tirana, the cap., Shkodër, Durrës (the chief port), and Vlonë.

After forming part of the East Roman empire, A. was overrun by the Turks in 1468 after the death of the nationalist leader Skanderberg (George Castriota) (1403-68). It remained part of the Turkish empire until 1912, when it became a principality under Prince William of Wied. Civil war followed, in which Italy intervened. A. became a republic in 1925, and in 1928 its president, Ahmed Beg Zogu, was proclaimed as King Zog (1895-1961) and remained on the throne until 1939, when the country was invaded by the Italians. In 1940 the Greeks almost succeeded in expelling the Italians, but were forced to surrender in 1941 to the Germans. These in turn were expelled in 1944, and in 1946 A. became again a republic with a Communist form of govt. Many mosques and churches were closed in 1967 and the govt claimed A. as the world's first atheist state. A. broke off relations with USSR 1961, and cooled to China after the Sino-American detente in the 1970s, pursuing a fiercely independent line. Enver Hoxha (q.v.), who had led the country since 1944, died in 1985, and was succeeded by his deputy Ramiz Alia. Area 28,748 sq.km (11,100 sq.m); pop (1979) 2.9 mill. M.U.: lek.

ALBANIA. Visitors from abroad are left in no doubt of the direction of Albanian sympathies when they arrive to study Marxist-Leninism in practice. Stalin shares pride of place with Enver Hoxha on the front of the coach. *Photo: Malcolm Gilson/Camera Press*

ALBANY. Capital of New York State, one of the oldest towns in USA, on the Hudson, about 225km (140m) N. of New York City. With Schenectady and Troy it forms a met. area: pop. (1970) 710,714. Also a port in Western Australia, which suffered from the initial development of Fremantle, but has grown with the greater exploitation of the surrounding area. The A. Doctor is a cooling breeze from the sea, rising in the afternoon. Pop. (1975) 13,000.

A'LBATROSS. Genus of oceanic birds (*Diomedea*) closely related to the petrels and belonging to the order Procellariiformes. The best-known species is *D. exulans* of the Pacific, which breeds on Tristan da Cunha and other oceanic islands and is the largest sea-bird, having a wingspan of 3m (10ft) or more.

ALBEE, Edward (1928-). American playwright. B. in Washington, D.C., he was adopted as an infant into a N.Y. family with theatrical links, but did not begin writing until he was 30. His plays belong to the drama of the Absurd and incl. *The Zoo Story* (1961), *The American Dream*, and *Who's Afraid of Virginia Woolf?* (1962), and *Little Alice* (1966).

ALBÉNIZ (al-bā-neeth), **Isaac** (1860-1909). Spanish composer and pianist, b. in Catalonia. He composed the suite *Iberia* and other impressive piano pieces, making use of traditional Spanish tunes.

ALBERONI (ahlbehrō'nē), **Giulio** (1664-1752). Spanish-Italian cardinal and statesman. B. in Parma, he became a priest. Philip V made him in 1715 Prime Minister of Spain. In 1717 he became a cardinal. He introduced many reforms, but was forced to flee to Italy in 1719.

ALBERT (1819-61). Prince Consort of the UK. The second son of Ernest, Duke of Saxe-Coburg-Gotha, he was ed. privately and at the Univ. of Bonn, showing great aptitude in natural science and the arts. His union with Queen Victoria, his first cousin, was the cherished plan of their uncle, King Leopold I of Belgium, and the marriage took place in 1840.

Albert planned the Great Exhibition of 1851, and the surplus profits of £186,000 went to purchase the sites of all the South Kensington Museums and Colleges, and the Albert Hall. He d. at Windsor of typhoid, and was buried at Frogmore. Though hard-working and conscientious, he was regarded by the British people with groundless suspicion because of his German connections.

ALBERT I (1875-1934). King of the Belgians. The younger son of Philip, Count of Flanders - the brother of Leopold II - he m. in 1900 the Duchess Elisabeth of Bavaria. He became king in 1909, and in the F.W.W. commanded the Allied army that conquered the Belgian coast in 1918, re-entering Brussels in triumph on 22 Nov. He was killed while mountaineering.

ALBERT (Victor Christian Edward) (1864-92). Duke of Clarence and Avondale and Earl of Athlone. B. at Frogmore Lodge, Windsor, he was the eldest son of Edward, Prince of Wales, afterwards Edward VII, and his consort Alexandra. In 1891 he was betrothed to Princess Victoria Mary of Teck, afterwards Queen Mary, but before the marriage could take place he d. at Sandringham after a short illness.

ALBERT, Lake. *See* MOBUTU SESE SEKO.

ALBERTA. Prov. of Canada, created in 1905 out of part of the North-western Territory. It lies between Saskatchewan and the Rocky Mountains, many of whose highest peaks it includes; and most of it is arable. In the centre and S. is the dry, treeless prairie; towards the N. this merges into a zone of poplar, then mixed forest. The valley of the Peace River is the most northerly farming land in Canada (except Eskimo pastures), and there are good grazing lands in the foothills of the Rockies.

A. is pre-eminently agricultural, producing wheat, barley, and oats on a vast scale. Sugar-beet is grown in the S. More than a million head of cattle are fed on the natural pastures E. of the Rockies.

A. has the most extensive coal resources in Canada, the principal mines being near Edmonton and at Anthracite, Mountain Park, Lethbridge, Canmore, etc. A. is also Canada's leading producer of petroleum and natural gas. An oil pipe line extends from Edmonton to L. Superior. The McMurray district has large deposits of bituminous sand, the Athabasca tar sands, to the S.W. of the lake of that name, which the world energy crisis is rendering economic to exploit. Lumbering is important. There are food manufactures, petroleum refineries, chemical and wood industries.

The cities are Edmonton, the capital; Calgary, Lethbridge, Medicine Hat, Wetaskiwin, Red Deer, and Drumheller. Area 661,187 sq.km; pop. (1972) 1,655,000.

ALBERTA. A wheat farm south of Calgary, owned by one of Canada's flying farmers. Using the most modern equipment enables him to farm a vast area single-handed, hiring help only for a few weeks in harvest time. *Photo: Barnaby's Picture Library*

ALBERT CANAL. Designed as part of Belgium's frontier defences; also links the industrial basin of Liège with the port of Antwerp. Built 1930–9, it was named after King Albert I.

ALBERTUS MAGNUS (Albert the Great) (1193 or 1206–80). Scholastic philosopher. B. in Swabia, he studied at Bologna and Padua, and entered the Dominican order in 1223. He taught at Cologne and lectured from 1245 in Paris University. St Thomas Aquinas was his pupil there, and followed him to Cologne in 1248. In 1254 he became provincial of the Dominicans in Germany, and was made bishop of Ratisbon in 1260. Two years later he resigned and eventually retired to his convent at Cologne. He was a man of vast learning on a variety of subjects - theology and philosophy (especially Aristotle), but also the natural sciences, chemistry, physics, etc. He figures as the *doctor universalis* among the Schoolmen, and as a magician in popular legend. He wrote numerous works and was canonized in 1932.

ALBI (ahlbē'). Chief town in the dept. of Tarn, S. France, on the river Tarn, 72km (45m) N.E. of Toulouse. It was the centre of the Albigensian heresy and has a 13th cent. cathedral. Pop. (1973) 46,615.

ALBIGE'NSES or **CATHARS.** Heretical sect of Christians who flourished in S. France near Albi and Toulouse during the 11th to 13th cent. They adopted the Manichean belief in the duality of good and evil and pictured Jesus as being a rebel against the cruelty of an omnipotent God. They showed a consistently anti-Catholic attitude with distinctive sacraments, especially the *consolamentum,* or baptism of the spirit. In 1209 Pope Innocent III ordered a crusade against the As. Their lands were invaded by armies under Simon de Montfort, and thousands perished before peace was restored by the treaty of Paris (1229).

AL'BINISM. Absence or great deficiency in the body of the dark pigment melanin. As a result the hair is very light or white, the skin is white, and the eyes pink, yellow, or pale blue. It probably occurs sporadically among most races of mankind; it has been observed in most domestic and many wild animals, and also among plants. Poor daylight vision in albinos, formerly only ameliorated by dark glasses, may be overcome even in infants by fitting coloured contact lenses (q.v.).

A'LBION. Ancient name of Britain, mentioned by Pytheas of Massilia (4th cent. B.C.). It is probably of Celtic origin; but the Romans, having in mind the white cliffs of Dover, assumed it to be derived from *albus* (white). The kindred name of Albany was given to the Scottish highlands in the 10th cent.

A'LBOIN (reigned *c.* A.D. 561–73). King of the Lombards, who were at that time settled N. of the Alps. Early in his reign he attacked the Gepidae in Romania, killing their king and taking his dau. Rosamund to wife. About 568 he invaded Italy, conquering the country as far as Rome. He was murdered at the instigation of his wife, whom he had forced to drink from a wine-cup made from her father's skull.

ALBUERA (ahlboo-eh'rah). Spanish village, S.E. of Badajoz, where on 16 May 1811, during the Peninsular War, the French under Soult were defeated by Beresford.

ALBŪ'MIN. A class of proteins which occur in most animal fluids and tissues, and also in the seeds of plants. The most common are: *leucosin,* in the seeds of wheat, rye, and barley; *legumelin,* in the seeds of pea, lentil, soya-bean, etc., *egg-a.,* from the white of hens' eggs; and *serum-a.,* from blood serum.

ALBUQUERQUE (ahlbookār'ke), **Alfonso de** (1453–1515). Viceroy of the Portuguese Indies from 1508. He conquered Goa, Ceylon, Malacca, and Ormuz, and d. at sea on his way home.

ALBUQUERQUE (al'bakerki). Largest city of New Mexico, USA, situated E. of the Rio Grande, in the Pueblo district. It is a holiday resort and industrial centre. Here is the Univ. of New Mexico, founded 1889. Pop. (1970) 243,751.

A'LBURY-WODONGA. Australian twin town: Albury on the New South Wales bank of the river Murray, and Wodonga on the S. and Victorian bank, 320km (200m) from Melbourne and 560km (350m) from Sydney. Close to Hume Weir water resources, it is on the main rail and road link between the two cities, and is planned for development by both states to reduce the pressure of their urban growth. Car components, e.g. automatic gearboxes are made. Pop. of A. (1973) 30,000; and of W. 15,000.

ALCAEUS (alsē'us) (*c.* 611–*c.* 580 B.C.). Greek lyric poet. B. at Mytilene in Lesbos, he was a member of the aristocratic party and went into exile when the popular party triumphed. He wrote odes, and the Alcaic stanza is named after him.

A'LCATRAZ. Small island in San Francisco Bay, Calif., USA. Its fortress was a military prison 1886–1934, and then a famous federal penitentiary until closed in 1963. The dangerous currents meant few successful escapes. American Indian 'nationalists' took over the island in 1970 as a symbol of their lost heritage.

ALCAZAR (ahlkah'thahr). Name of Moorish palaces in Spain. There were 5 in Toledo, of which one, defended by Nationalist troops, held out for 71 days against the Republicans during the Spanish Civil War in 1936.

ALCHEMY. The supposed art of transmuting base metals, such as lead and mercury, into silver and gold. A certain field of A. constituted the chemistry of the Middle Ages. More broadly, however, A. was a system of philosophy which dealt alike with the mystery of life and formation of inanimate substances. A. was a complex and indefinite conglomeration of chemistry, astrology, occultism, and magic, blended with obscure and complex ideas derived from various religious systems and other sources.

ALCHEMY. The alchemist and his assistants at work, as illustrated in a 15th century treatise on alchemy in the British Museum. *Photo: Mansell Collection*

ALCIBIADES (alsibī'adēz) (*c.* 450-404 B.C.). Athenian general and politician. In 422 he became leader of the war party in Athens during the Peloponnesian War, and in 415 he was appointed one of the 3 commanders of the expeditionary force to Sicily. Shortly before its departure the pillars of the god Hermes in the streets of Athens were mutilated, and the sacrilege was attributed to A. who was recalled to stand his trial. He escaped to Sparta, and was condemned to death in his absence. In 411 the Athenians recalled him, and under his leadership they gained a number of victories. But in 407 he was superseded, and retired to the Chersonese. After the fall of Athens in 404 he took refuge in Phrygia, and was there murdered.

ALCMAEONIDAE (alkmē'-o'-nidē). A noble family of anc. Athens; its members include Pericles and Alcibiades.

ALCOCK, Sir John William (1892-1919). British airman. On 14 June 1919, he and Lt Whitten-Brown made the first direct crossing of the Atlantic in an aeroplane, a Vickers-Vimy machine. Both were given the KBE. A. was killed in a flying accident near Rouen.

ALCOFORADO (ahlkohfohrah'doh), **Marianna** (1640-1723). Portuguese nun. The *Letters of a Portuguese Nun* (1699), supposed to have been written by her to a young French nobleman who abandoned her when their relations became known, are no longer accepted as authentic. In 1972 three women writers, the 3 Marias (Maria Isabel Barreno, Maria Teresa Horta, and Maria Velho da Costa) pub. *New Portuguese Letters,* a feminist plea in male-dominated Portugal which led to their trial. They were acquitted after the 1974 coup.

ALCOHOLIC LIQUORS. Alcohol, or, more properly, ethyl alcohol, is the basis of all the common intoxicants. These fall into 3 groups: (1) Wines, ciders, perry, and other drinks in which the alcohol is produced by direct fermentation of their sugars by yeasts; (2) Malt liquors (beers and stouts): the starch of grain is converted into sugar by malting, and the sugar is then fermented into alcohol by the action of yeasts; (3) Spirits, distilled from malted liquors or wines.

Internationally A. strength in beverages is expressed as a percentage of pure A.: table wines 8-15%; port, sherry 15-22%; whisky, rum 70%; vodka 80%. In an average person, a concentration of alcohol in the blood of 0.15% causes mild intoxication, 0.3% causes definite drunkenness and partial loss of consciousness, and 0.6% endangers life.

ALCOHOLS. In chemistry, a group of organic compounds characterized by the presence of one or more OH-groups in the molecule. They may be liquids or solids, according to the size and complexity of the molecule.

The 5 best-known As. form a series in which the carbon and hydrogen atoms increase progressively, i.e. each of the series differs from its predecessors by the presence of an extra CH_2-(methylene) group in the molecule, viz. methyl alcohol or wood spirit (CH_3OH); ethyl A. or spirit of wine (C_2H_5OH), known also as ethanol or simply as A.; propyl A. (C_3H_7OH); butyl A. (C_4H_9OH); and amyl A. ($C_5H_{11}OH$). The lower spirits are liquids miscible with water. The higher members such as amyl A. are oily liquids not miscible with water, and the highest are waxy solids, e.g. cetyl A. ($C_{16}H_{33}OH$) and melissyl A. ($C_{30}H_{61}OH$) which occur in spermaceti and beeswax respectively.

The main uses of A. are: in alcoholic liquors; as a solvent for gums, resins, etc., in the lacquer and varnish industry, and also in the making of dyes; for essential oils in perfumery; and for medical substances in pharmacy. It is also used as a raw material in the manufacture of chloroform, ether, chloral, iodoform, etc. Certain brands of motor spirit contain A., where it is claimed to give increased power to the engine. A. is also used as a fuel.

ALCOTT, Louisa May (1832-88). American writer for girls. B. near Philadelphia, she was the dau. of Amos B. Alcott (1799-1888), a poet and transcendentalist philosopher. Her *Little Women* (1868), the most popular of all American books for girls, had *Good Wives* among its sequels.

A'LCUIN (735-804). English scholar. B. at York, he went to Rome in 780, and in 782 took up his residence at Charlemagne's court in Aachen. From 796 he was abbot of Tours. Though not a profound scholar like Bede, he disseminated the achievements of Anglo-Saxon scholarship, organized education and learning in the Frankish empire, gave a strong impulse to the Carolingian Renaissance, and was a prominent member of Charlemagne's academy.

ALDABRA (ahldah'brah). High limestone is. some 400 km (260 m) N.W. of Madagascar, part of the Brit. Indian Ocean Terr. 1965-76, when it was returned to the admin. of the Seychelles. The island is remarkable for rare animal and plant life, incl. the giant land tortoise.

A'LDEBARAN. Binary star, of which one of the 2 components is the most brilliant star in Taurus constellation.

ALDEHYDES (al'dēhīdz). In chemistry, a group of organic compounds prepared by oxidation of primary alcohols. The name is made up from *al*cohol *dehyd*rogenatum, i.e. alcohol from which hydrogen has been removed. As. are usually liquids and include acetaldehyde, formaldehyde, benzaldehyde, and citral.

ALDER. Genus of trees and shrubs (*Alnus*) of the family Betulaceae, allied to the birch. The common or Black A. (*A. glutinosa*) is found throughout the temperate zone of the northern hemisphere.

ALDERMAN (awl'-, Old Eng. *ealdorman,* older man). Senior member of a borough or county council in England and Wales until 1974, or of a municipal corporation in certain towns in the USA. *See also* LONDON, CITY OF.

ALDERMASTON. Village of Berks., England, site of an atomic weapons research establishment. In 1958 nuclear disarmament campaigners made it the goal of a great Easter protest march from London, and until 1964 marches were made in the reverse direction.

ALDERNEY (awl'-). Third largest of the Channel Islands. The soil is fertile and well suited for grazing the famous A. cattle. The only settlement of importance is St Anne (the capital) with an airport. It suffered severely under the German occupation 1940-5. Pop. (1971) 1,686.

ALDERSHOT (awl'-). English town in Hants, S.W. of London. The military camp and barracks date from 1854, and it is the HQ of the Parachute Regiment. Pop. (1972) 34,540.

ALDHELM (*c.* 640-709). English saint, prelate, and scholar. He was abbot of Malmesbury from 673 and bishop of Sherborne from 705. Of his poems and treatises in Latin, some survive, notably his Riddles in hexameters, but his English verse has perished. He was also a skilled architect.

ALDINGTON, Richard (1892-1962). English writer and poet. B. in Hants, he pub. vols. of Imagist verse, working with Hilda Doolittle (q.v.), to whom he was m. 1913-37. His novels incl. *Death of a Hero* (1929) and *All Men Are Enemies* (1933); his biographical studies of D. H. Lawrence *Portrait of a Genius, but . . .* (1950) and of *Lawrence of Arabia* (1955) were controversial.

ALDISS (awl'dis), **Brian** (1925-). British science fiction writer. One of the best-known exponents of the genre, of which he wrote a history *The Billion Year Spree* (1973), he has pub. many vols. of theoretically sound fantasies, e.g. *Non-Stop* (1958), dealing with a lost space-ship, and *The Moment of Eclipse* (1971).

ALEIXANDRE (ahleksahnd'ra), **Vicente** (1898–1984). Spanish lyric poet. B. in Seville, he suffered from renal tuberculosis and was largely bedridden, so that he remained in Spain as a 'spiritual' rebel under the Franco regime. He was awarded a Nobel prize in 1977.

ALEMBERT (ahloṅbār'), **Jean Le Rond d'** (1717-83). French mathematician and encyclopedist. B. in Paris, he was a foundling, ed. by the Jansenists, and studied law and medicine before devoting himself to mathematics. He was associated with Diderot in planning the great *Dictionnaire Encyclopédique.*

ALENÇON (ahloṅsoṅ). French town, cap. of Orne dept., in a rich agricultural plain, to the S.S.E. of Caen. A. is famed for its lace, now a declining industry. Pop. (1973) 33,400.

ALEPPO. City of N. Syria, situated in the fertile valley of the Kuwaib. A beautiful city, A. was once the trade centre between Europe and Asia, and is still an important market. There is a university. A. dates from *c.* 2,000 B.C. Pop. (1970) 639,360.

ALESSANDRIA (ahlessahn'drēah). City and episcopal see in N. Italy, on the Tanaro, 90km (56m) E.S.E. of Turin. Pop. (1971) 102,000.

ALETSCH (ah'lech). Most extensive glacier in Europe, stretching for 16km (10m) and starting on the southern slope of the Jungfrau in the Bernese Alps.

ALEUTIANS (ale-ōō'shi-anz). Chain of islands in the N. Pacific, stretching from Alaska for 1,900 km (1,200 m) W.S.W. They comprise 14 large and more than a hundred small islands, and many rocks and islets. Politically they are part of Alaska, USA. They are ice-free all the year round, but are often wrapped in fog. The is. are mountainous and volcanic, treeless, but with grass and sedge.

The Aleuts are a branch of the Eskimos. Very few are full-blooded today. Most of them belong to the Greek Orthodox Church. They live by hunting and fishing. Area 17;670 sq.km (6,820 sq.m); pop. *c.* 6,000.

ALEXANDER III. Pope 1159-81. Leader of the papal opposition to the emperor Frederick Barbarossa. Shortly after his election he was compelled to flee to France but in 1178 returned to Rome and received the emperor's homage. He supported Henry II of England in his invasion of Ireland, but humbled him after the murder of Thomas à Becket. He held the 3rd Lateran council in Rome in 1179.

ALEXANDER VI. Pope 1492-1503. The infamous Borgia pope. B. in Spain in 1431, he was speedily advanced in the church by his uncle Pope Calixtus III (1455-8). He secured his own election as pope by bribery, and his papacy became noted for nepotism, immorality, treachery, and ostentatious extravagance. But, himself a man of great gifts, he was a patron of art. When Savonarola in Florence preached against his corrupt practices, A. secured his execution. A. died of poison which he is said to have prepared for his cardinals. He was the father of Cesare and Lucrezia Borgia.

ALEXANDER I (1777-1825). Tsar of Russia. Son of Paul I, he came to the throne in 1801 on his father's assassination, joined the coalition against Napoleon in 1805, and was present at Austerlitz, where his forces were defeated. Defeat at Eylau and Friedland led A. to seek peace, and a treaty was concluded at Tilsit (1807). For a time A. seems to have fallen under the spell of Napoleon's personality, but admiration turned to detestation, and he broke with Napoleon's economic policy and opened his ports to British goods and ships. In 1812 Napoleon invaded Russia, where the determined resistance of the Tsar and his people, the Russian winter and the vastness of the country, proved his undoing. A. led the Russian hosts from Moscow to Paris, and was recognized as the greatest

ALEXANDER. The turning point of the Battle of Issus, when Darius fled from the field in his chariot before the onslaught of Alexander, seen on horseback to the far left. This mosaic, now in the Naples Museum, comes from Pompeii, and probably derives from an almost contemporary Hellenistic painting now lost. *Photo: André Held*

of European potentates. He gave a constitution to Poland, but was also the prime mover in the Holy Alliance which endeavoured to make reaction permanent. His last years were clouded by fear of the liberal movements.

ALEXANDER II (1818-81). Tsar of Russia. Eldest son of Nicholas I, he succeeded him in 1855, when Russia was fighting the Crimean War against Britain, France, and Turkey. The war was concluded in 1856 by the treaty of Paris. In 1863-4 a Polish insurrection was sternly repressed, and in 1877-8 there was war again with Turkey, in which the Russians were successful. Although the serfs were emancipated in 1861, A. became increasingly autocratic and reactionary, and he was assassinated by Nihilists.

ALEXANDER III (1845-94). Tsar of Russia. Son of Alexander II, he succeeded on the assassination of his father in 1881. He m. Dagmar (1847-1928), dau. of Christian IX of Denmark and sister of Queen Alexandra of the UK, in 1866. Essentially a reactionary, he ruled the empire with a firm hand. The Jews were persecuted, and the subject peoples were relentlessly Russified.

ALEXANDER THE GREAT (356-323 B.C.). King of Macedonia and conqueror of the Persian empire. The son of Philip, king of Macedonia, and Olympias, he was ed. by the philosopher Aristotle. He first saw fighting in 340, and at the battle of Chaeronea (338) contributed to the victory by a cavalry charge. When his father was murdered in 336, the Macedonian throne and army passed into his hands. He first secured his northern frontier, suppressed an attempted rising in Greece by his capture of Thebes, and in 334 crossed the Dardanelles for the campaign against the vast Persian empire. A. marched with 20,000 foot and 5,000 horse, and at the r. Granicus near the Dardanelles won his first success. In 333 he routed the Pers. king Darius at Issus, and then set out for Egypt, where he was greeted as Pharaoh, son of the god Ra, and hailed as son of Zeus. He founded Alexandria, the future centre of Hellenistic civilization. Meanwhile, Darius collected half-a-million men, with scythed chariots and elephants, for a final battle, but at Arbela on the Tigris in 331 A. with 47,000 men drove the Persians in headlong retreat.

After the victory he stayed a month in Babylon, then marched to Susa and Persepolis, and in 330 to Ecbatana. Soon after he learned that Darius was dead. In Afghanistan he founded colonies at Herat and Kandahar, and in 328 reached the plains of Sogdiana, where he m. Roxana, dau. of King Oxyartes. India now lay before him, and he pressed on to the Indus. Near the Hydaspes he fought one of his fiercest battles against the rajah Porus. At the r. Hyphasis his men refused to go farther, and reluctantly he turned back down the Indus and along the coast. They reached Susa in 324, where A. took Darius' daughter for his 2nd wife. He d. at Babylon of a malarial fever.

A. left no successor, and his empire broke up into independent kingdoms. But his personality left deep impressions on East and West; peoples of the East all had their traditions of him, whilst medieval romances made him a hero of the type of Arthur and Charlemagne.

ALEXANDER. Name of three kings of Scotland. ALEXANDER I (*c.* 1078-1124), known as 'the Fierce', reigned from 1107. ALEXANDER II (1198-1249), the son of William the Lion, succeeded his father in 1214, and supported the English barons in their struggle with King John after Magna Carta. By the treaty of Newcastle in 1244 A. acknowledged Henry III of England as his liege lord. His son ALEXANDER III (1241-85) reigned from 1249. In 1263 he extended his authority over the Western Isles which had been dependent on Norway, and strengthened the power of the central Scottish government. He d. as the result of a fall from his horse at Kinghorn, leaving as heiress his granddau. Margaret, the Maid of Norway.

ALEXANDER (OBRENOVICH) (1876-1903). King of Serbia from 1889 while still a minor, upon the abdication of his father King Milan. He took power into his own hands in 1893, and in 1900 m. a widow, Mme Draga Mashin. In 1903 A. and his queen were murdered, and Peter Karageorgevich was placed on the throne.

ALEXANDER I (KARAGEORGEVICH) (1888-1934). King of Yugoslavia, 2nd son of Peter Karageorgevich, King of Serbia, he was declared regent for his father in 1912, and in 1921, on his father's death, became king of the state of South Slavs - Yugoslavia - which had come into being in 1918. Rivalries of neighbouring powers and of the Croats, Serbs and Slovenes within the country led A. to estab. a personal dictatorship in 1929. He was assassinated on a state visit to France, and Mussolini's govt was later declared to have instigated the crime.

ALEXANDER, Frederick Matthias (1869-1955). Australian founder and teacher of the psycho-physical method named after him. At one time a professional reciter, he developed throat and voice trouble, and his experiments in curing himself led him to work out the system of mental and bodily control described in his *Use of the Self.*

ALEXANDER, Harold Rupert Leofric George, 1st earl A. of Tunis (1891-1969). British soldier. 3rd s. of the 4th earl of Caledon, he was ed. at Harrow and Sandhurst and commissioned in the Irish Guards. After distinguished service during the F.W.W., he held various staff appointments until 1938 when he commanded the 1st Division taking it to France in 1939. As lieut-general he commanded the 1st Corps, organized the last phases of defence and was the last man to leave Dunkirk. He was then G.O.C.-in-C. Southern Command until he became G.O.C.-in-C. in Burma in March 1942, where he fought a delaying action for 5 months against vastly superior Japanese forces. In Aug. 1942 he went to N. Africa, and in 1943 became deputy to Eisenhower in charge of the Allied forces in Tunisia. When the Axis forces in N. Africa surrendered, A. became deputy C.-in-C. of the Mediterranean Combined Operations and was promoted G.O.C., then Supreme Allied Commander in the Mediterranean and, in 1944, field marshal. Appointed Gov.-Gen. of Canada in 1946, he was created earl A. of Tunis in 1952, and was Min. of Defence 1952-4. In 1959 he was awarded the O.M.

ALEXANDER, Samuel (1859-1938). Australian philosopher, prof. at Manchester 1893-1924, and originator of the theory of Emergent Evolution. According to this, matter is supposed to have emerged from the original space-time matrix, and life to have similarly evolved from matter, which in its turn has given birth to mind; finally God is supposed to emerge from mind. His books incl. *Space, Time and Deity* (1920), and he received the O.M. in 1930.

ALEXANDER NEVSKI (1220-63). Russian hero and saint. Son of the Grand Duke of Novgorod, he was a great warrior and in 1240 defeated the Swedes on the banks of the Neva, thus acquiring the name of Nevski. Two years later he won a victory on Lake Peipus against the Knights of the Teutonic Order.

ALEXANDER SEVĒ'RUS (A.D. 208-35). Roman emperor. B. in Palestine, he succeeded his cousin Heliogabalus in 222. His campaign against the Persians in 232 achieved some success, but in 235 when proceeding to defend Gaul against German invaders he was killed in a mutiny.

ALEXA'NDRA (1844-1925). Queen Consort of Edward VII of the United Kingdom. Eldest dau. of Christian IX of Denmark, she m. Albert Edward, Prince of Wales, in 1863; 3 sons and 3 daus. were born of the marriage. She founded Queen A.'s Imperial Nursing Service in 1902; and in 1912, to mark the 50th anniversary of her coming to England, she instituted A. Rose Day in aid of the hospitals.

ALEXANDRA (1872-1918). Last Tsarina of Russia. Dau. of Louis IV, Grand Duke of Hesse, and Princess Alice, dau. of Queen Victoria. She m. in 1894 Tsar Nicholas II. In 1907 she fell under the spell of Rasputin, a dissolute monk who had been brought to the palace to help cure the young Tsarevitch, who was a victim of haemophilia. Rasputin was murdered in Dec. 1916, and on 15 March 1917 the Tsar was compelled to abdicate. With her husband, their son and daus. A. was sent to Siberia by the Bolsheviks; and on 16 July 1918, in a cellar at Ekaterinburg (Sverdlovsk), the whole royal family were murdered.

ALEXANDRETTA. *See* ISKENDERUN.

ALEXANDRIA. City in the Arab Rep. of Egypt and chief port of Egypt, situated between the Mediterranean and Lake Maryut. It was founded in 331 B.C. by Alexander the Great, and for over 1,000 years was the capital of Egypt and the principal centre of Hellenistic culture. Since the 4th cent. A.D. it has been the seat of a Christian patriarch. In 641 it was captured by the Mohammedan Arabs, and after the opening of the Cape route its trade rapidly declined. Early in the 19th cent. it began to recover its prosperity, and its growth was encouraged by its being the main British naval base in the Mediterranean during both the World Wars: the Egyptian cotton trade passes through the port and there is an oil refinery.

Few relics of antiquity remain. The Pharos, the first lighthouse and one of the Seven Wonders of the ancient world, has long since disappeared. The world-famous Alexandrian Library was finally destroyed by the Arabs in 641. 'Pompey's Pillar' is a column erected, as a landmark from the sea, by Diocletian. Two obelisks that once stood before the Caesareum temple are now in London ('Cleopatra's Needle') and New York respectively. A univ. was founded in 1942. Pop. (1971) 1,900,000.

ALEXANDRIAN SCHOOL. Name given to the writers and scholars of Alexandria who from about 331 B.C. to A.D. 642 made the city the chief centre of culture in the Western World. They include the poets Callimachus, Apollonius Rhodius, and Theocritus; Euclid, father of geometry; Eratosthenes, the geographer; Hipparchus, who developed a system of trigonometry; Ptolemy, who gave his name to the Ptolemaic system of astronomy that endured for over 1,000 years; and Philo, the Jewish philosopher. The Gnostics and Neo-Platonists also flourished in Alexandria.

ALEXANDROVSK. Older name of ZAPOROZHE.

ALEXIUS I COMNENUS (1048-1118). Byzantine emperor 1081-1118. The Latin Crusaders helped him repel Norman and Turkish invasions, and he devoted great skill to buttressing the threatened empire. His dau. **Anna Comnena** (1083-*c.* 1148) wrote the *Alexiad,* descriptive of the Byzantine world.

ALEXANDRIA. Fishermen have for several thousand years drawn in rich catches here, but pollution and the building of the High Dam at Aswan, which retains the nutrient elements which formerly were carried down by the Nile waters, have diminished their hauls. *Photo: Ken Lambert/Camera Press*

ALFA'LFA. Spanish name for a kind of lucerne or medic (*Medicago sativa*) of great importance as a fodder-plant. It is grown in many parts of the Old World, and extensively cultivated in the Canadian prairies.

ALFIERI (ahlfē-ā'rē), **Vittorio,** count (1749-1803). Italian dramatist. B. at Asti in Piedmont, he inherited a large fortune at the age of 14, and travelled abroad 1766-72. In 1775 his tragedy *Cleopatra* was successfully performed. In 1777 he met the Countess of Albany, the separated wife of the 'Young Pretender', in Florence, following her to Rome, Colmar, and Paris. On the outbreak of the Revolution, they fled to Florence, where they resided until A.'s death. His whole output betrays an ardent love for freedom and a glowing hatred of tyranny. The masterpieces among his 28 plays, tragedies most of them, are *Saul* and *Mirra.*

ALFONSO XIII (1886-1941). King of Spain, 1886-1931. The posthumous son of Alfonso XII, he assumed power in 1906, following the regency of his mother, and in the same year m. Princess Ena of Battenburg, granddau. of Queen Victoria. The wedding was marred by one of several attempts at assassination. Popular discontent, aided by economic depression, led to the proclamation of a republic in 1931, and A. settled in Rome, where he d.

ALFRED THE GREAT (*c.* 848-*c.* 900). English king. B. at Wantage, Berks, the youngest son of Ethelwulf, King of the West Saxons, he gained a brilliant victory over the Danes at Ashdown in 871, and succeeded his brother Ethelred after a series of defeats later in the same year. Five years of uneasy peace followed until the Danes attacked once more in 876, and in 878 A. was forced to retire to the stronghold of Athelney, whence he finally emerged to win the victory of Edington, Wilts. By the Peace of Wedmore in 878 the Danish leader Guthrum agreed to withdraw from Wessex and from Mercia W. of Watling Street. A new landing in Kent encouraged a revolt of the East Anglian Danes, which was suppressed (884-6) and after the final foreign invasion under Hasten was defeated (892-6), A. strengthened the navy to prevent fresh incursions.

In the peace that followed, A. extended and consolidated the shire system of local government, and supervised finance, the administration of justice, and the codification of the law. He also revived learning by establishing a school at his court, to which he invited scholars such as Asser of S. Wales and John the Saxon, and encouraged writing in the vernacular. He himself translated Pope Gregory's *Pastoral Care,* Orosius' *Universal History* (to which he made many additions from his own knowledge), Bede's *Ecclesiastical History,* and Boethius' *Consolation of Philosophy,* and fostered the Anglo-Saxon Chronicle. A. was buried at Winchester. *See* ATHELNEY, ISLE OF.

ALFRED THE GREAT. The superbly worked 'Alfred Jewel' was found in 1693 some miles west of the Isle of Athelney. It may have been the head of a bookmark and is of green, red and blue cloisonné enamel work: round the gold rim are the words 'Alfred had me made' (Ælfred mec heht gewyrcan).

ALGAE (al'jē; Lat. seaweeds). Subdivision of plants belonging to the Thallophyta or lower plants distinguished from the more advanced classes by their simplicity of structure, in which there is no distinction of stem, root and leaf; and from the fungi, the other main division of the Thallophyta, by the presence of green colouring-matter (chlorophyll), and in the majority of cases by their aquatic habit. They show great variety of form, the lowest types consisting of only a single cell, while some of the higher seaweeds attain to considerable size and complexity of structure.

They are divisible into 7 groups, largely to be distinguished by their pigmentation, viz. the *Chlorophyta,* green and incl. the Chlorophyceae, the simplest forms, found mostly in fresh water or damp earth and the Charophyceae or stoneworts; *Euglenophyta,* mostly green and freshwater; *Pyrrophyta,* yellow to brown; *Chrysophyta,* yellow-green to yellow-brown, mostly freshwater; *Phaeophyta* or brown seaweeds, ranging from Ectocarpus to the kelps, Laminaria and its allies, the largest of all algae; *Rhodophyta* or red seaweeds, amongst the most specialized A. and mainly marine; and *Cyanophyta,* blue-green of simple cell structure, in which reproduction is never sexual, mostly freshwater or terrestrial. *See* CHLORELLA and SEAWEED. In Britain the Natural Environment Research Council (1965) has a Culture Centre for A. and Protozoa at Cambridge.

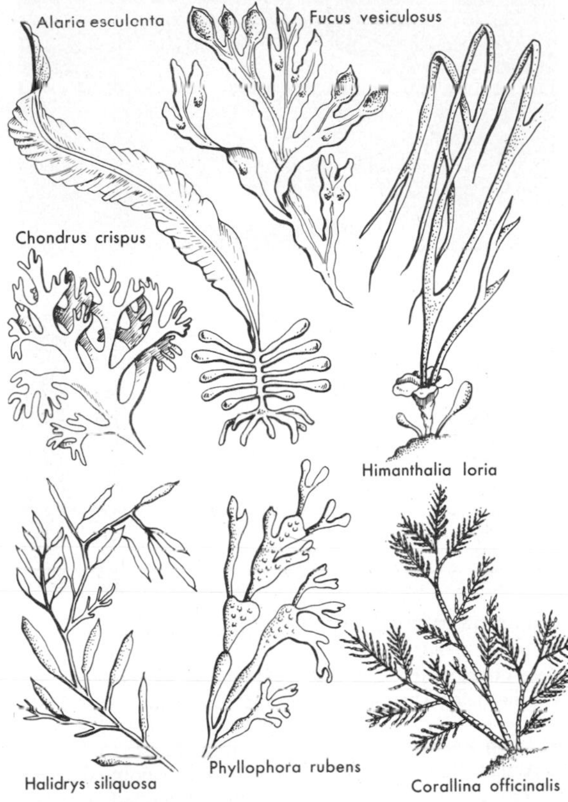

ALGAE. Some of the many varied forms of seaweed.

ALGARVE (ahlgahr'vā). Ancient kingdom in S. Portugal, the modern district of Faro, which began to be wrested from the Moors in the 12th cent. and was united with Portugal as a kingdom in 1253. It incl. the S.W. extremity of Europe, Cape St Vincent, where the British fleet defeated the Spanish in 1797. Today it is a favoured holiday region.

ALGEBRA. That department of mathematics that deals with calculations in which quantities are designated by symbols.

In ancient times it was developed in connection with certain learned professions, such as astronomy, notably in Babylon, Egypt, and India. This knowledge was preserved by the Arabs and later transmitted to Europe. The word is derived from *Al-jebr w'almuqabalah,* the title of one of the works of Mohammed ibn Musa (*c.* A.D. 820). A. received its modern form in the 16th and 17th cents. in Europe. Descartes connected A. with geometry in 1637. Applications of algebra were found in preparing tables for navigation, in the design of gears for clocks, in scientific investigations, in shipbuilding, in military matters, etc. On this foundation of elementary A. mathematicians have built various types of higher mathematics. The function of higher mathematics is to interpret and classify, to investigate what problems can be solved by what methods, and why. *See* BOOLE, GEORGE.

ALGECIRAS (aljesēr'as). Port in Spain, prov. of Cadiz, to the W. of Gibraltar across the Bay of A. Founded by the Moors in 713, A. was taken from them by Alfonso XI of Castile in 1344; virtually destroyed in a fresh attack by the Moors, it was re-founded 1704 by Spanish refugees from Gibraltar when that place was bombarded and captured by the British. Pop. (1970) 81,600.

ALGĒ'RIA. Country of N. Africa. In the north the Atlas area resembles southern Europe in scenery and climate. The coast is rather inhospitable but has a number of ports, incl. Algiers (also the cap.), Oran, Skikda (formerly Philippeville), and Mostaganem. Agriculture is concentrated in the fertile plains and valleys of the north, and the land has been redistributed to peasant co-operatives. Formerly A. was the world's largest exporter of wine, high in alcohol but poor in quality, so that it was used to fortify French wines or even converted to industrial alcohol, but inferior vineyards have been converted to other crops, allowing concentration on quality. Citrus, dates, cereals, and vegetables are grown. Since 1962 there has been industrialization concentrated round Constantine and Annaba in the N.E., and in the N.W. round Arzew: petrochemicals, lorry assembly plants, iron and steel production, sugar refining, paper and textile mills. The changeover from agriculture to industry has been financed by the discoveries of oil and natural gas in the desert areas covering three-quarters of A., and extending south of the mountains which border the coastal strip. The main production centres for oil are Edjélé, Hassi Messaoud and El Gassi; and for gas Djebel Berga and Hassi-R'Mel, and there are pipelines to the coast. Other mineral wealth incl. antimony, coal, iron, copper, lead, marble, mercury, phosphates and zinc. Railways are limited to the coastal area, but a Trans-Sahara highway is under construction.

Area 2,293,190 sq.km (919,590 sq.m); pop. (1980) 20,000,000, of whom 75% are Sunni Moslem Arabs speaking Arabic (the official language) and 25% Berbers, who claim that Berber should also be an official language. French is still widely spoken. M.U.: dinar.

History. A. formed part of the Roman Empire, but was Islamized and subjugated by the Arabs in the 7th cent. A.D. In the 16th cent. it was overrun by the Turks, but the Sultan's rule was often nominal, and in the 18th cent. A. became a pirate state dominated by *deys,* who preyed on Mediterranean shipping. European intervention became inevitable, and in 1816 an Anglo-Dutch force bombarded Algiers. In 1830 a French army landed and seized Algiers; by 1847 the N. had been brought under control, and in 1848 was formed into the depts. of Algiers, Oran, and Constantine. Many French colonists settled in these depts. which in 1881 were made part of Metropolitan France. The mountainous region inland inhabited by the Kabyles, occupied 1850–70, and the Sahara region, subdued 1900–9, remained under military rule.

After the defeat of France in 1940, A. came under the control of the Vichy government until the Allies landed in N. Africa in 1942. Algiers was the HQ of the French Committee of National Liberation from 1943 until it was able to move to a liberated France as the provisional govt. Postwar hopes in France of integrating A. more closely with France were frustrated by opposition in A. from those of both French and non-French origin. An embittered struggle for independence from France continued

1954-62, when referenda in both Algeria and France, held by de Gaulle, resulted in the recognition of A. as an independent republic. Many Moslem Algerians who had fought in the Algerian war of independence on the side of the French (the harkis, pron. ahrki'), afterwards settled in France. Mohamed ben Bella (1916–) was P.M. 1962-5, when he was overthrown and imprisoned by Col. Houari Boumédienne (1925-78) who was pres. and P.M. until his death. He was succeeded as pres. by Col. Benjedid Chadli (q.v.) in 1979. Only one political party, the Nat. Liberation Front (FLN) is permitted. Algeria supports the Sahrawi people's organisation (Polisario) in its resistance to Moroccan occupation of Western Sahara.

ALGERIA. Although modernization has been rapid since independence, the past still lingers in remote areas. On the verge of the desert, a simple wooden plough remains in use. *Photo: Camera Press*

ALGIERS (aljērz'). Cap. of Algeria, N. Africa, situated on the narrow coastal plain between the Atlas mts and the Mediterranean. Founded by the Arabs A.D. 935, A. was taken by the Turks in 1518, and by the French in 1830. The old town is dominated by the Kasbah, the palace and prison of the Turkish rulers. The new town, constructed under French rule, is in European style. Pop. (1980) 2,200,000.

ALGŌ'A BAY. Broad and shallow inlet in South Africa, Cape Province, where Diaz landed after rounding the Cape in 1488.

ALGONQUIN (algong'kwin). Member of Indian tribes living along the upper Ottawa r., and now often referred to as Ottawa Indians.

ALHA'MBRA. Fortified palace at Granada, Spain, built by Moorish kings mainly between 1248 and 1354. It stands on a rocky hill and remains the finest example of Moorish architecture.

ALI (ah'lē) (*c.* 600-61). 4th Caliph. B. at Mecca, he was the son of Abu Talib, uncle to Mohammed, who gave him his dau. Fatima in marriage. On Mohammed's death in 632, A. had a claim to succeed him, but this was not conceded until 656. After a stormy reign, he was assassinated. Around A.'s name has raged the controversy of the Sunnites and the Shiites, the former denying his right to the caliphate and the latter supporting it.

ALHAMBRA. The Court of the Lions. The rich plaster work is decorated in red, green, blue and gold, but the intricate detail never obscures the purity of line of the design or interferes with the ultimate harmony of the structure. *Photo: J. Allan Cash*

ALI (Ali Pasha) (1741-1822). Turkish statesman, known as Arslan (the lion). An Albanian, he was appointed pasha of Janina in 1788, and there he maintained a semi-barbarous court, visited by Byron. He was murdered by the Sultan's order.

ALI, Muhammed (1942–). Name adopted by American boxer Cassius Marcellus Clay on joining the Black Muslim movement. He became world heavyweight champion in 1964, but lost the title in 1967 (for refusing military service). He regained it 1974–Feb. 1978, and Sept. 1978–Oct. 1980.

ALIBI (al'ibī; Lat. elsewhere). In law, a defence to a charge of crime that the person accused was, at the time the crime was committed, at some place other than the scene of the crime and so could not be guilty of it.

ALICANTE (ahlēkan'teh). Leading seaport of Spain on the S.E. coast. Pop. (1970) 184,715.

ALICE SPRINGS. Australian town, on the trans-continental Stuart Highway, in Northern Terr., on Todd r., at 600m (2,000 ft) a.s.l. Terminus of the railway from Adelaide, cap. of S. Australia, it was named after the wife of Sir Charles Todd who directed the construction of the S.-N. transcontinental telegraph line. A.S. is a tourist centre, only town in an area producing livestock and opals, and HQ of the 'flying doctor' service. Pop. (1976) 11,200.

Ā'LIEN. Person owing allegiance to a foreign state. Under the Immigration Act (1971) aliens and Commonwealth citizens were placed under a single system of immigration control. Only those Commonwealth citizens

ALICE SPRINGS. The town lies right in the 'red, dead heart of Australia'. It is a centre for graziers, and increasing numbers of tourists come in by air and along the Stuart Highway. *Photo: Richard Harrington/Camera Press*

in certain complex categories were allowed entry, but the law as to British nationality, as laid down in an act of 1948, was revised under a new law of 1981 which defined three kinds of citizen: *see* under CITIZEN. Citizens of the Republic of Ireland have reciprocal rights, unaffected by the 1981 act, and are not regarded as aliens.

Aliens may hold property as if they are British subjects, but may not accept public office, vote, or own a British ship or aircraft. British women marrying aliens lose their citizenship only if they renounce it formally, and alien women marrying British subjects may apply for registration themselves, but do not acquire citizenship automatically.

In the US all As. are subject on arrival to scrutiny by the Immigration and Naturalization Service and for permanent residence must have an immigrant visa from a US consul located abroad. American women marrying As. only lose their citizenship if they formally renounce it. Certain classes are excluded, e.g. the insane, narcotic drug addicts, and members of 'subversive' organizations.

ALIGARH (ahlēgahr'). City of Uttar Pradesh, India. The Muslim Univ. here, constituted in 1920, was opened to non-Muslims in 1956. Pop. (1971) 254,000.

A'LIMONY. In law, a money allowance which a court may order a husband to pay for the support of his wife or former wife, after separation or divorce; an order may also be made against a wife to pay A. to her husband or former husband in certain circumstances.

ALIPHATIC (alifa'tik) **COMPOUNDS.** Chemical term for a group of organic substances of which the most typical are fats. They also include carbohydrates (starch, sugar, etc.), alcohols, and paraffins.

A'LKALI. In chemistry a base that is soluble in water. As. neutralize acids, turn red litmus to blue, and are soapy to the touch. The word comes from the Arabic *al-qalīy*, 'ashes', since soda and potash were derived from the ashes of plants. The hydroxides of metals are As., those of sodium (caustic soda) and of potassium (caustic potash) being chemically powerful.

ALKALOIDS. Physiologically active and frequently poisonous substances contained in certain plants. The As. or vegetable As. are usually bases, i.e. they form salts with acids and, when soluble, give alkaline solutions. But substances are included in the group rather by custom than by scientific rules. Examples of As. are morphine and cocaine, quinine, strychnine, nicotine, and atropine.

ALKEN, Henry Thomas (1784-1851). British sporting artist. Fox-hunting and steeplechasing were the subjects that most frequently occupied him, but the whole range of field sports was covered in his *National Sports of Great Britain* (1821).

ALKMAAR (ahlkmahr'). Town in N. Holland, to the N.W. of Amsterdam, on the North Holland canal. It is a centre for cheese export. Pop. (1972) 50,725.

AL'LAH (Arabic *al*, the; *ilāh*, God). The name given to the One True God by Moslems.

ALLAHABA'D. Indian city, in the state of Uttar Pradesh, at the junction of the Ganges and Yamuna. A univ. town, it is a centre of culture, commerce, and communication. In the grounds of the fort is one of the surviving pillars bearing edicts of Asoka (d. *c.* 228 B.C.). Remains of a palace built by Akbar are nearby. A. is regarded as a Holy City by Hindus, and is the scene of yearly pilgrimages. Nehru had his home here. Pop. (1971) 514,000.

ALLAN, David (1744-96). Scottish historical painter. He studied in Rome and, after a period in London, he became in 1786 director of the Academy of Arts in Edinburgh. A vein of humour appears in his 'Scotch Wedding', etc.

ALLAN, Sir William (1782-1850). Scottish historical painter, b. at Edinburgh. He spent several years in Russia and neighbouring countries, returned to Edinburgh in 1814, was elected R.A. in 1835, President of the Royal Scottish Academy in 1838, and was knighted in 1842. His paintings include scenes from the Waverley novels.

ALLEGHENY MOUNTAINS. Range more than 800km (500m) long extending from Pennsylvania to Virginia, rising to more than 1,500 m (4,800 ft) and averaging 750m (2,500 ft). In places very beautiful, but wild and difficult, they proved for many years an effective barrier to western migration, the first settlement to the W. being Marietta in 1788.

ALLEGIANCE. The duty of obedience owed by a subject to a Sovereign, who in return gives protection. An *Oath of A.* must be taken by aliens on naturalization, by M.P.s, by certain ministers of the Crown, etc. Aliens becoming US citizens swear A. to the 'Constitution and laws of the USA.'

A'LLEGORY. Figure of speech; the description or illustration of one thing in terms of another, it is equivalent to an extended metaphor or parable, and it makes use of obviously fictitious figures. A well known A. is Bunyan's *Pilgrim's Progress.*

ALLEGRI (ahlleh'grē), **Gregorio** (1582-1652). Italian composer. B. at Rome, he became a priest, and entered the Sistine chapel choir in 1629. His *Miserere* for 9 voices was treasured at the Sistine. Mozart wrote it down from memory at 14, breaking a papal 'monopoly'.

ALLEN, Ethan (1738-89). American hero of the War of Independence. He first led the Green Mountain Boys, an irregular militia, in advancing the independence of Vermont, which came to be known as the Green Mountain state. In the war, he led them in the taking of

Ticonderoga in 1775. He was captured by the British when he took part in an expedition against Montreal, and imprisoned 1775-8.

ALLEN, Hervey (1889-1949). American novelist, best known for his mammoth historical novel *Anthony Adverse* (1933) set in the Napoleonic era. He was a high school teacher at Charleston, S.C.

ALLEN, Woody. Professional name of Allen Stewart Konigsberg (1935-), American comedian, film director and jazz clarinetist. He was writer and actor of the film *Play It Again Sam* (1969/72), and in such films as *Annie Hall* (1977), which won an Oscar and starred Diane Keaton, and *Manhattan* (1979), added the role of director.

ALLEN. Lough or lake in co. Leitrim, Rep. of Ireland, on the upper course of the Shannon. It is 11km (7m) long and 5km (3m) broad.

ALLEN, Bog of. Morasses E. of the Shannon in Rep. of Ireland, comprising about 96,000 ha (240,000 acres) of Offaly, Leix, and Kildare.

ALLENBY, Sir Edmund Henry Hynman, 1st visct A. (1861-1936). British field marshal. In the F.W.W. he was with the BEF in France before taking command in 1917-9 of the British Forces in the Near East. He proceeded to crush the Turks in Palestine, the crowning victory being at Megiddo in Sept. 1918, which was followed almost at once by the capitulation of Turkey.

ALLENDE (ahlyān'dā), **Salvador** (1909-73). Chilean statesman. Elected pres. in 1970, he was the first Marxist to be elected head of state by democratic vote in the Western world. He advocated a peaceful transition to socialism, a 'quiet revolution', and rapidly broke up large estates, and nationalized the banks, factories, and the US-run copper mines. Meanwhile, Communist infiltration throughout the govt (allegedly Moscow-inspired) alienated confidence, and the too-rapid changes undermined the economy. In 1973 he was toppled from power by a revolt of the armed forces and committed suicide.

ALLENDE. Popular support for Allende included many Amerindians, such as those seen carrying placards here. Beneath the portrait of the president is the familiar protest slogan used worldwide: 'We shall overcome'. *Photo: Christian Belpaire/Camera Press*

A'LLERGY. A special sensitiveness of the body which makes it react, with an exaggerated response of the natural defence mechanism, to the introduction of a foreign substance, proteins (organic substances containing nitrogen), etc. The person subject to hayfever in summer is allergic to one or more kinds of pollen. Many asthmatics are allergic to certain kinds of dust; or to micro-organisms in animal fur or feathers. Others come out in nettle-rash, or are violently sick if they eat shellfish or egg. Drugs may be used to reduce sensitivity or produce tolerance, but there is no universal panacea.

ALLIER (ahlyeh'). River in central France, tributary of the Loire; it is 565km (350m) long, and gives its name to a dept. Vichy is the chief town on it.

A'LLIGĀTOR. Genus of reptiles, of which there are 2 species - *A. mississippiensis* in the southern states of USA, and *A. sinensis* of the Chang Jiang in China. The former grows to *c.* 4m (12ft) but the latter is smaller. The genus *Caiman* of Central and South America is closely allied.

As. closely resemble crocodiles in their general habits, swimming well with the assistance of lashing movements of the tail, and feeding on fish and mammals, though seldom attacking man. The eggs are laid in sand. The skin is of value for fancy leather, and A. farms have been established in USA.

ALLIGATOR. Not built for easy turning, these alligators prefer to rest 'in line of battle' ready for rapid retreat to the safety of the river, or to attack any edible target coming within their range on the Amazon. *Photo: Douglas Botting*

ALLINGHAM (al'-), **Margery Louise** (1904-66). British writer of detective fiction, e.g. *Death of a Ghost, Flowers* *for the Judge, The Case of the Late Pig,* and *More Work for the Undertaker.*

A'LLIUM. Genus of plants belonging to the Lily family (Liliaceae). They are usually acrid in their properties, but form bulbs in which sugar is stored. Cultivated species incl. onion, garlic, chives, leek, etc.

ALLOA. *See* CLACKMANNANSHIRE.

ALLO'PATHY. The treatment of disease of one kind by exciting a disease process of another kind or in another part; sometimes incorrectly used as a name for orthodox medicine, in distinction from homoeopathy (q.v.), which means treatment with minute doses of drugs which induce the same ailment.

ALLOY. A blending together of a metal with one or more metallic (or non-metallic) substances. Some As. have been known to mankind for many thousands of years, e.g. bronze. Most are made by liquefying one metal (usually that with the higher melting point) and adding the others, usually in solid form. As. may be several times stronger than any of the metals used in their manufacture, have generally lower melting points than some of their constituents. Duralumin As. were specially developed for strength and resistance to corrosion, copper with a small proportion of beryllium for toughness, and combinations of iron, nickel, titanium, manganese for a wide range of permanent and non-permanent magnets.

ALL SAINTS' DAY. 1 Nov. Also known as All-Hallows or Hallowmas. The festival for all saints and martyrs for whom the Church calendar does not provide a separate day.

ALL SOULS' DAY. Festival in the Catholic Church, held on 2 Nov., following All Saints' Day. It was instituted in 993, and its observation is based on the doctrine of the Communion of Saints and the belief that the faithful on earth are able, by prayers and self-denial, to hasten the deliverance of souls expiating their sins in purgatory.

ALLSPICE. Spice prepared from dried berries of the A. tree or pimento (*Eugenia pimenta*), cultivated chiefly in Jamaica.

ALLSTON, Washington (1779-1843). American artist and writer; he painted chiefly religious subjects.

ALMA. River in Ukraine SSR flowing across the S.W. of the Crimean peninsula; it gives its name to a battle fought on 20 Sept. 1854, when the Russians were defeated by the Franco-British armies.

ALMA ATA (ah'ta). Cap. of Kazakh SSR, USSR, at the foot of the Ala-Tau mts. It is an industrial centre (cotton, food and tobacco processing) with a university and a link in the Turkestan-Siberian railway. Kazakh nationalist riots here in Dec 1986 resulted in some 20 deaths. Population (1983) 1,023,000.

ALMA MATER (mah'ter; Lat., bounteous mother). Title given by the Romans to the goddess Ceres, and now applied to universities and schools, which are considered as the 'foster-mothers' of their pupils.

ALMANSA (ahlmahn'zah). Spanish town in Albacete, about 80km (50m) N.W. of Alicante, where on 25 April 1707 British and allied forces were defeated by the French under the Duke of Berwick. Pop. *c.* 14,500.

ALMA-TADEMA (ah'lma-tah'dema), **Sir Laurence** (1836-1912). Anglo-Dutch painter. B. at Dronrijp, Holland, he settled in England in 1873. Some of his best-known paintings depict scenes from Greek and Roman life. He was knighted in 1899.

ALMEIDA (ahlmā'ēdah), **Francisco de** (*c.* 1450-1510). First viceroy of Portuguese India 1505-8. He was killed in a skirmish with the Hottentots at Table Bay, S. Africa, and was buried where Cape Town now stands.

ALMERÍA (ahlmārē'ah). Spanish city, chief town of a prov. of the same name on the Mediterranean. The prov. is famous for its white grapes and in the Sierra Nevada are rich mineral deposits. Pop. (1970) 114,500.

ALMOND. Fruit of the A. tree (*Prunus amygdalus*), which is closely related to the peach and the apricot. Originally a native of N. Africa and the Near East, it has for a long time been introduced into Europe, and its fruit will ripen in southern England.

ALOE (al'ō). Genus of African plants of the family Liliaceae, distinguished by their long fleshy leaves. From the juice of the leaves of several species is prepared the drug aloes, a powerful cathartic.

ALOST (ah'lōst), or **Aalst.** *See* AALST.

ALOYSIUS (alō-is'i-us), **St** (1568-91). Patron saint of youth. B. Luigi Gonzaga at Castiglione in N. Italy, he joined the Jesuits at Rome, and d. while nursing victims of the plague. He was canonized in 1726.

ALPA'CA. S. American mammal, a domesticated variety of the guanaco (*Llama huanaco*), found in Chile, Peru, and Bolivia, and herded at high elevations in the Andes. Its flesh is eaten, but it is mainly valued for its wool.

ALPHA and Ō'MEGA (A and Ω). The first and last letters of the Greek alphabet; hence the beginning and the ending, or the sum total of anything.

ALPHA (al'fa) **PARTICLE.** Positively charged particle ejected with very great velocity from a nucleus. It is one of the products of the spontaneous disintegration of radioactive substances such as radium and thorium and is identical with the nucleus of a helium atom, i.e. it consists of 2 protons and 2 neutrons.

ALPHABET. A set of conventional symbols (so-called from *alpha* and *beta*, the first letters of the Gk A.), each denoting a given sound or sounds. The many attempts at alphabetic systems discovered by archaeologists in the Palestine-Syria area make it certain that this was the cradle of our A., and the N. Semitic A., in use from the 13th cent. B.C. and consisting of 22 letters, which at first expressed only consonants, developed into all the main modern alphabetic scripts. The chief branches incl. the Aramaic, which produced numerous eastern As., notably the Arabic and Brahmi, parent of *c.* 200 Indian As. and offshoots throughout the Far East; and the Classical As. Of the latter, the Greek A. was adopted from Semitic sources *c.* 9th cent. B.C., and the Etruscan, from which the Latin A. was to be created in the 7th cent., possibly also derived directly from these sources. The Romans changed some of the values of the 21 letters of the early Etruscan A., and also included the 2 last letters of the Greek A., but J, U and W were not added until medieval times. The Cyrillic A., parent of the Russian and other E. European As., is derived from the Greek uncial (capital-type letters of the 4-8th cents. A.D.) script. The Runic As. show peculiarities of Latin and N. Etruscan descent, and the cryptic Ogham script of S. Ireland and Wales (5-6th cents. A.D.) is based on the Runes. Disseminated by the European peoples, the Latin A. has become the script of the greater part of the world, because of its adaptability and easy reproduction.

ALPHEGE (al'fej), **St** (954-1012). Anglo-Saxon churchman, bishop of Winchester from 984, archbishop of

Canterbury from 1006. When the Danes attacked Canterbury he tried to protect the city, was thrown into prison, and, refusing to deliver the treasures of his cathedral, was stoned and beheaded at Greenwich on 19 April, his feast-day.

ALPS. The mountain-chain which forms the northern barrier to Italy and extends in the form of a crescent from the Mediterranean on the W. to the Adriatic on the E. Among the most famous peaks are Mont Blanc 4,810 m (15,781 ft), the Matterhorn 4,505 m (14,782 ft), Monte Rosa or Dufourspitze 4,638 m (15,217 ft), Finsteraarhorn 4,275 m (14,026 ft), and the Eiger 3,975 m (13,000 ft), remarkable for its almost vertical rock wall 2,355 m (7,730 ft), on the north face, first scaled in 1938 by Heinrich Harrer.

Many of the streams and rivers have been harnessed to provide electricity for small iron and textile industries, railways and lighting. 'The Alps' is used by the alpine people to describe the high summer pastures which are of immense importance for agriculture. Cattle are grazed on the lower parts in June, gradually working upwards as summer advances. The economic conditions of the Alpine peoples have been revolutionized in the last two cents., mainly owing to tourist and winter sports traffic. The chief sports resorts and spas incl. St Moritz, Davos, Baden, and Tarasp-Schuls-Vulpera in Switzerland, Garmisch-Partenkirchen in Bavaria and Kitzbühel in Austria. The A. are pierced by many rail and road tunnels.

ALPS, Australian. The highest area of the Eastern Highlands in Victoria and N.S.W. Australia, and which incl. the Snowy Mtns: *see also* MT KOSCIUSKO.

ALPS, Southern. Range of mtns extending along the west central coast throughout the entire length of South Island, New Zealand. They are forested to the W., with scanty scrub to the E. The highest point is Mt Cook 3,764 m (12,349 ft). Scenic features incl. deep gorges, glaciers, lakes and waterfalls. Among the most famous of its lakes are those at the southern end of the range: Manapouri, Te Anau and — the largest — Wakatipu (83 km/52 m long), which lies *c.* 300 m (1,000 ft) a.s.l. and has a depth of 378 m (1,242 ft).

ALSACE-LORRAINE (ahlzahs'-lorān'). Alsace and Lorraine were formerly provs. of N.E. France and form a modern region. Bismarck introduced the term Elsass-Lothringen (Ger. for Alsace-Lorraine) in 1871 for the territory annexed by Germany, i.e. Alsace, and the N.E. part of Lorraine, and comprising the present French depts of Moselle, Bas-Rhin, and Haut-Rhin. The steel industry, based on its coal and iron, which formerly made it prosperous is in decline, but new industries, such as motor vehicles and electronics are being encouraged.

Forming part of Celtic Gaul in Caesar's time, the A.-L. area was invaded by the Alemanni and other Germanic tribes in the 4th cent., remaining part of the German Empire till the 17th cent. In 1648, part of the territory was ceded to France; in 1681, Louis XIV seized Strasbourg. The few remaining districts were seized by the French after the Revolution, but A.-L. was conquered by the Germans 1870-1, and declared 'Imperial Territory' (*Reichsland*). France did not regain possession of A.-L. until 1919. In 1940 the country was again annexed by the Germans until liberated in 1944 by the Allied armies. The German dialect spoken in A.-L. does not have equal rights with French, and there is some autonomist sentiment.

ALSĀ'TIA. The old name for Alsace. In 17th cent. London this name was given to the district of Whitefriars between Fleet St and the Thames. It afforded sanctuary to debtors and other lawless characters, a privilege derived from the convent of Carmelites, estab. there in 1241. In 1697 this privilege was withdrawn.

ALSATIAN. Breed of dog introduced from Germany into Britain after the F.W.W. and known officially from 1977 as the German shepherd. It has a wolf-like appearance, a beautiful coat with many varieties of colouring, and distinctive gait. As war and police dogs, the tractability of the breed has been recognized.

ALTAI (ahltī') **MTS.** Mountain system of W. Siberia and Mongolia. It is divided into 2 parts, the Russian A., which includes the highest peak, Mount Belukha 4,540 m (15,157 ft), and the Mongolian or Great A.

ALTAMIRA (ahltahmē'rah). Cave near the Spanish village of Santillana del Mar in Santander prov. where in 1879 remarkable palaeolithic wall-paintings were discovered.

ALTDORF (ahlt'dorf). Mountain-encircled cap. of the Swiss canton Uri at the head of Lake Lucerne. It is the scene of the legendary exploits of William Tell. Pop. (1970) 7,000.

A'LTDORFER, Albrecht (*c.* 1480-1538). German artist. Probably the first European painter of a finished picture excluding the human figure; his work breaks with the medieval tradition of 'story-telling'. Few of his pictures survive. He was b. at Regensburg, where he worked as an architect.

ALTERNATING CURRENT. Electric current which flows for an interval of time in one direction and then in the opposite direction, i.e. a current which flows in alternately reversed directions through or round a circuit. A.C. power is the usual form in which electric energy is generated in a power station, and A.Cs. may be used for both power and lighting. The value of A.C. over direct current (as from a battery) is that its voltage can be raised or lowered economically by a transformer, high voltage for generation and transmission, and low voltage for utilization and safety, e.g. railways, factories, and domestic appliances.

ALTGELD, John Peter (1847-1902). American political and social reformer. B. in Prussia, he was taken in infancy to USA. During the Civil War he served in the Union Army. He was a judge of the supreme court in Chicago 1886-91, and as Governor of Illinois 1893-7 was champion of the worker against the government-backed power of Big Business.

ALTHING. The parliament of Iceland. Created *c.* 930, the oldest parliamentary assembly in the world.

ALTMARK INCIDENT (1940). The *Altmark*, a German auxiliary cruiser, was intercepted on 15 Feb. 1940, by HM destroyer *Intrepid* off the coast of Norway. She was carrying the captured crews of Allied merchantmen sunk by the German battleship *Admiral Graf Spee* in the S. Atlantic, and took refuge in Jösing fjord. There she was cornered by HMS *Cossack*, under Capt. Vian, and ran aground. Vian's men released 299 British sailors.

A'LUM. A white crystalline powder readily soluble in water. It is a double sulphate of potassium and aluminium. Its chemical formula is K_2SO_4, $Al_2(SO_4)_3$ $24H_2O$, and it is the commonest member of a group of double sulphates called As., all of which have similar formulae, the same

ALTDORFER. Thought to be the earliest European landscape painting — *c.* 1518–20 — 'Landscape with a Footbridge' was acquired by the National Gallery in 1963. The only other purely landscape picture by this artist is in the Alte Pinakothek, Munich. *Photo: Courtesy of the National Gallery, London*

crystalline form, and the same number of molecules of water of crystallization.

ALŪ'MINA (Al_2O_3). Oxide of aluminium which occurs widely distributed over the surface of the earth in clays, slaty rocks, and shales. It is formed by the decomposition of the feldspars in granite. Typically it is a white powder, soluble in most strong acids or caustic alkalis, but not in water, and is used extensively in the manufacture of clay articles such as pipes and of various paints.

ALŪMI'NIUM. The most abundant metal, valuable for its light weight, having at. no. 13, at. wt. 26.98, and chemical symbol Al. Nearly one-twelfth of the substance of the earth's crust is composed of A. compounds, but A. in its pure state was not readily obtained until the middle of the 19th cent., for it oxidizes rapidly, and much energy is needed to separate the metal from chemical combination. Pure A. is a soft white metal. It is one of the lightest of metals, its specific gravity being 2.70, and for this reason is widely used in shipbuilding and aircraft. In the pure state it is a weak metal, but when alloyed with other elements such as copper, silicon, or magnesium, alloys of great strength are obtained. Commercially, A. is obtained from bauxite (q.v.) and requires large supplies of electric power. A. is much used in steel-cored aluminium overhead cables and for canning uranium slugs for reactors. A. is an essential constituent in the Alcomax series of magnetic materials; and as a good conductor of electricity is used in the form of foil in electrical capacitors. A plastic form of A., developed in 1976, which moulds to any shape and extends to several times its original length, has uses in electronics, cars, building construction, etc. In the USA the original name suggested by Sir Humphry Davy ALUMINUM (aloō'-) is retained.

ALVA, or **ALBA, Ferdinand Alvarez de Toledo,** duke of (1508-82). Spanish statesman and general. He commanded the Spanish armies of Charles V and Philip II, and in 1567 was appointed Governor of the Netherlands, where he set up a reign of terror to suppress the revolt against the Spanish tyranny of the Inquisition. In 1573 he retired, and returned to Spain.

ALVARA'DO, Pedro de (*c.* 1485-1541). Spanish conquistador. In 1519 he accompanied Hernando Cortez, and distinguished himself in the conquest of Mexico. In 1523-4, he conquered Guatemala.

ALVAREZ, Luis Walter (1911-). American physicist. Ed. at the Univ. of Chicago, he became prof. of physics at the Univ. of California in 1945, being also Assoc. Director of the Lawrence Radiation Laboratory 1954-9; he headed the research team which in 1959 discovered the Xi-zero atomic particle. He was awarded a Nobel prize in 1968.

ALWAR (ul'war). City in Rajasthan, India, chief town of the district (formerly princely state) of the same name. It has fine palaces, temples and tombs. Pop. (1971) 100,791.

ALWYN, William (1905-). British composer. Prof. of composition at the RAM 1926-55, he is well known as a writer of film music (*Desert Victory, The Way Ahead*).

ALZHEIMER'S DISEASE. *See* DEMENTIA.

AMA'LEKĪTES. Ancient Semitic tribe of S.W. Palestine and the Sinai peninsula. According to Exodus xvii they harried the rear of the Israelites after their crossing of the Red Sea, were defeated by Saul and David, and finally crushed in the reign of Hezekiah.

AMA'LFI. Port of Italy at the foot of Monte Cerrato, on the Gulf of Salerno, 39km (24m) S.E. of Naples. For 7 cents. it was an independent republic. It is an ancient archiepiscopal see, and has a fine Romanesque cathedral. Pop. (1970) 7,000.

AMA'LIA, Anna (1739-1807). Duchess of Saxe-Weimar-Eisenach. As widow of Duke Ernest, from 1758 until her son Karl August succeeded her in 1775, she reigned with admirable prudence and skill, making the court of Weimar a literary centre of Germany. She was a friend of Wieland, Goethe, and Herder.

AMANĪTA. Genus of fungi, closely allied to *Agaricus* (q.v.) and often treated merely as a sub-genus. It is distinguished by having a ring, or *volva*, round the stem, and warty patches on the cap, and by the clear white colour of the gills. Many of the species are brightly coloured and highly poisonous. Fly agaric (*A. muscaria*), with bright red cap and white warty patches, is dangerous, and the Death's Cap (*A. phalloides*) is deadly: both are found in Britain.

AMANUL'LAH KHAN (1892-1960). Emir of Afghanistan, 3rd son of Habibullah Khan. On his father's assassination in 1919 he seized the throne and concluded a treaty with the British, but his policy of westernization led to rebellion in 1928. A. had to flee, abdicated in 1929, and settled in Rome.

AMARI'LLO. Town in the Texas panhandle, USA, centre of the largest cattle-producing area in the world, in the high plains. In the 1970s assembly line procedures were here adapted to cattle, in that the animals are raised, fattened (in feedyards taking up to 100,000 head), slaughtered, and reduced to frozen packages for retail

AMALFI. Set at the mouth of a deep ravine, Amalfi has spectacular cliff scenery. It was Italy's most ancient maritime republic, and its law of the sea, the *Tabula Amalfitana,* was recognized throughout the Mediterranean until the mid-eighteenth century. *Photo: Bernard G. Silberstein/Camera Press*

distribution in a single continuous operation. Pop. (1970) 127,000.

AMA'RNA TABLETS. Collection of clay tablets with cuneiform inscriptions, found in the ruins at Tell-el Amarna (the ancient Akhetaton), about 300km (190m) S. of Cairo on the E. bank of the Nile. The majority of the tablets, which comprise royal archives and letters of 1411-1375 B.C., are in the British Museum. They possibly represent the 'waste-paper basket' of officials who discarded inessential documents when the city was abandoned.

AMARYLLIDACEAE (amarilidā'sē-ē). Family of monocotyledonous flowering plants allied to the Liliaceae, but distinguished by the ovary being inferior. Its European species include the narcissus, daffodil, and snowdrop.

AMA'TERA'SU. In Japanese mythology, the sun-goddess, grandmother of Jimmu Tenno, first ruler of Japan, from whom the emperors claimed to be descended.

AMATI (ahmah'tē). Italian family of violin-makers, fl. in Cremona, *c.* 1550-1692.

A'MATOL. An explosive consisting of ammonium nitrate (A/N) and TNT in almost any proportions.

A'MAZON. South American river. The largest river in the world as regards volume, and the second longest, 6,518 km (4,050 m); its main head-streams, the Marañón and the Ucayali, rise in central Peru and unite to flow eastwards across Brazil for *c.* 4,000 km (2,500 m). The total network is 48,280 km (30,000 m) of navigable waterways, draining 7,000,000 sq.km (2,750,000 sq.m), nearly half the S. American land-mass. The A. reaches the Atlantic on the Equator, its estuary is 80km (50m) wide and discharges a volume of water so immense that 64km (40m) out to sea fresh water remains at the surface. The name A. probably derives from Indian *Amossona* 'destroyer of boats', navigation being hindered by floods, rapids and tidal waves.

AMAZON. Most famous of the tribes of the Amazon basin are the Xingu of the Mato Grosso. Kamaiura and his fellow tribesmen, despite missionary efforts to help preserve their culture, are fighting a losing battle against the settlers whose roads and farms destroy their hunting grounds. *Photo: Mireille Vautier*

A'MAZONS. Legendary nation of female warriors, whom the ancients believed lived in Pontus, near the Black Sea. They were governed by a queen, made warlike excursions into the adjoining lands, and cut off their right breasts so as to use the bow.

AMBALA. Other form of UMBALLA.

AMBASSADOR. Officer of the highest rank in the diplomatic service, who represents the head of one Sovereign State at the court or cap. of another. As personal representatives of the Heads of their States, they enjoy many privileges and powers, which extend also to their families and households.

AMBER. Fossilized gum which exuded from coniferous trees of Middle Tertiary age. A light substance, usually yellow or brown in colour, it is found chiefly on coasts such as the Baltic and in Sicily, having been washed up by the sea. Amber has been used as an ornament since prehistoric times.

AMBERGRIS (-grēs). Fatty substance, resembling wax, found in the stomach and intestines of the sperm whale, and used in perfumery as a fixative. Basically intestinal matter, A. is not the result of disease, but probably the pathological product of an otherwise normal intestine. The name derives from the French *ambre gris* (grey amber).

AMBLER, Eric (1909-). British novelist. B. in London, he makes brilliant use of Balkan/Levant settings in the thrillers *The Mask of Dimitrios* (1939) and *Journey into Fear* (1940).

AMBOI'NA. Small island in the Moluccas, Republic of Indonesia. The town of A., formerly an historic centre of Dutch influence, has shipyards. Pop. (1970) 68,000.

A'MBROSE, St (*c.* 340-397). A Father of the Christian Church. B. at Trèves, in S. Gaul, the son of a Roman prefect, A. became governor of N. Italy. In 374 he was chosen bishop of Milan, although he was not yet a member of the Christian Church. But he was baptized forthwith, and was consecrated as bishop 8 days later, on 7 Dec. (St Ambrose's day). His writings on theological subjects earned him a prominent place among the Latin Fathers of the Church; he also wrote many hymns, and devised the arrangement of church music known as the *Ambrosian Chant.*

AMBRŌ'SIA. In Greek mythology, the food of the gods (from the Gk *ambrotos*, 'immortal'), which was said to confer immortality upon all who ate it.

AMEN. Hebrew word signifying affirmation ('so be it'), commonly used at the close of a prayer or hymn. As used by Jesus Christ in the N.T. it was traditionally translated 'verily'.

AMENHŌ'TEP III. Pharaoh of Egypt, *c.* 1400 B.C. He erected many famous buildings, especially the great monuments at Thebes. His 2 portrait-statues were known to the Greeks as the Colossi of Memnon. *See* IKHNATON.

AMERICA. The western hemisphere of the globe, containing the continents of N. America and S. America, with Cent. America in between. This great land-mass extends from the Arctic to the Antarctic, from beyond 75° N. lat. to past 55° S. lat. The area is *c.* 42,000,000 sq.km (16,000,000 sq.m), and the est. pop. (1970) was some 500,000,000.

The name A. is derived from Amerigo Vespucci, the Florentine navigator who was falsely supposed to have been the first to discover the American mainland in 1497.

AMERICAN CIVIL WAR. *See* UNITED STATES OF AMERICA.

AMERICAN FEDERATION OF LABOR AND CONGRESS OF INDUSTRIAL ORGANIZATIONS (AFL-CIO). Federation of trade unions in the USA. The AFL was founded in 1881, and the CIO in 1935 as a breakaway union opposed to the AFL policy of including only skilled workers, and favouring industrial unionism. A merger reunited them in 1955.

AMERICAN INDEPENDENCE, WAR OF (1775-83). The revolt of the British colonies in N. America, which resulted in the establishment of the USA. The struggle originated in the resentment of the colonists against such measures as the Navigation Acts, which subordinated American to British commercial and industrial interests. When the British government imposed a stamp tax (1765) and later a tea tax on the colonists, they were bitterly opposed, and measures of repression provoked the colonists to arm. The first shots were fired at Lexington (19 April 1775), where troops sent to seize illegal military stores were attacked by the local militia, and the first battle fought at Bunker Hill, near Charlestown (17 June). Soon after, the Continental Congress appointed George Washington to command its ill-armed and undisciplined forces, and on 4 July 1776 it issued the Declaration of Independence.

An American assault on Quebec (Dec. 1775) was bloodily repulsed. Washington occupied Boston and later New York, but after his defeat at Long Island (27 Aug. 1776), had to retire to Pennsylvania, although he won 2 successes at Trenton (26 Dec.) and Princeton (3 Jan. 1777). The British government planned a junction between Sir William Howe, advancing from New York, and General Burgoyne from Canada; Howe was not given precise instructions, however, and Burgoyne was compelled to surrender at Saratoga (17 Oct.). Meanwhile, Howe invaded Pennsylvania, defeated Washington at Brandywine (11 Sept.) and Germantown (4 Oct.), and occupied Philadelphia. During the winter of 1777-8, which he spent at Valley Forge, Washington had great difficulty in keeping his troops together.

In the summer of 1778 France and Spain entered the war as America's allies; a French fleet was sent to American waters, and a small force under Rochambeau went to Washington's assistance. Howe's successor, Clinton, withdrew from Philadelphia to New York, with an indecisive battle at Monmouth (28 June). The British now carried the war into the south, where loyalists were most numerous; Savannah was captured (29 Dec. 1778), followed by Charleston (12 May 1780), and victories were won at Camden (16 Aug. 1780) and Guilford Court House (15 March 1781). Nevertheless, the British attempt to enforce conscription, and certain excesses of the Loyalists, alienated support from them. It had been planned that Cornwallis, having conquered the south, should march north to join Clinton in New York, but the prolonged struggle in S. Carolina delayed him. Entering Virginia, he withdrew to Yorktown, where he was besieged by Washington and Rochambeau and blockaged by a French fleet. His surrender on 19 Oct. 1781 virtually ended the land fighting.

At sea the Americans built up a strong force of privateers, their best-known commander being John Paul Jones. The entry of France and Spain into the war initiated a hard struggle for naval supremacy, which ended with Rodney's victory off Martinique on 12 April 1782. After Yorktown the other southern ports fell, until only New York remained in British hands. Peace negotiations opened in 1782, and on 3 Sept. 1783 the treaty of Paris recognized American independence.

AMERICAN INDEPENDENCE. 'Blessed are the Peace Makers', a political satire published in 1783 after an attack on the peace terms in the House of Commons, which was followed by the fall of the Shelburne ministry. The belligerent powers, Spain and France, lead George III by the neck. Behind the King walks Shelburne, carrying the Preliminary Articles of Peace, and bringing up the rear is America holding a flail, and leading Holland also by the neck. *Photo: British Museum*

AMERICAN INDIANS. *See* INDIANS, AMERICAN.

AMERICAN LEGION. Organization in USA of ex-servicemen of the F.W.W., founded in 1919.

AMERICAN LITERATURE. *See* UNITED STATES OF AMERICA.

AMERICA'S CUP. International yacht-racing trophy, won from the Royal Yacht Squadron in 1851 by the schooner-yacht *America*, owned by J. C. Stephens, in a race round the Isle of Wight. The silver cup was retained by the New York Yacht Club until won by *Australia II* in 1983 after victory in 4 out of the series of 7 races over a course *c.* 39 km (24 m) long, held every 3 yrs internationally at Newport, Rhode Island.

The original J-class sloops were 39.6 m (130 ft) long, but even the modern 12-metre (design formula) yachts which average 19.8 m (65 ft) are too expensive for any but syndicates to finance.

AMERI'CIUM. Man-made transuranic element produced from plutonium. At. no. 95, its isotope of mass 243 has half-life of 480 years. Possible source for radiographic diagnosis because of suitable gamma-emission.

AMERSFOORT (ah'mersfoh'rt). Ancient town of the Netherlands, 19km (12m) E.N.E. of Utrecht. Pop. (1978) 86,850.

Ā'MERY, Leopold Stennett (1873-1955). British Cons. statesman. He was Colonial and Dominions Sec. 1924-9, and Sec. of State for India and Burma 1940-5. His most famous speech was made in May 1940 when he addressed to Neville Chamberlain the words once used by Cromwell - 'In the name of God, go!' His books incl. *India and Freedom* (1942), and *My Political Life* (1953-5). His son **Julian** (1919-) was Cons. Min. for Aviation 1960-4, Housing 1970-2, and FCO 1972-4. He pub. the autobiographical *Approach March* (1973).

A'METHYST. A kind of quartz coloured violet by the presence of small quantities of manganese, and used as a semi-precious stone. As. are found chiefly in Russia, India, the USA, and Brazil.

AMIEL (ahmē-ēl'), **Henri Frédéric** (1821-81). Swiss philosopher and writer. B. at Geneva, he became professor of philosophy at the university there. His fame rests on his *Journal intime*, pub. 1882-4.

AMIENS (ahmē-aṅ'). Ancient city of N.E. France at the confluence of Somme and Avre; capital of Somme dept. It has a magnificent Gothic cathedral with a spire (113m/370ft), and gave its name to the battles of Aug. 1918, when Haig launched his victorious offensive. Pop. (1973) 122,000.

AMIN (ahmēn'), **Idi** (1926-). Ugandan president. A Muslim from N. Uganda, he became C.-in-C. of the armed forces, and led the coup which deposed Obote in 1971, himself becoming president. He expelled Uganda's Asian community in 1972, and imposed a reign of terror which led to his overthrow by Ugandan-Tanzanian forces in 1979. He fled the country.

AMINES (am'inz) and **AMINO COMPOUNDS.** Nitrogenous substances, usually basic, i.e. they will form salts with acids. The parent substance of most is ammonia, NH_3, to which they are related by the substitution of one or more of the hydrogen atoms by the radicals or groups of atoms. The *simple As.* are divided into primary, secondary, or tertiary according to whether 1, 2, or 3 hydrogen atoms of the ammonia molecule are replaced. The *methyl As.* have rather unpleasant ammonia odours and occur in decomposing fish. They are all gases at ordinary temperature. *A. acids* are compounds of which the basic and acidic groups exist in the same molecule. The simplest is glycine. Of the *aromatic A. compounds* the most important is aniline. Other interesting A. compounds are the metal amides and the acid amides.

AMIN. President Idi Amin, surrounded by his bodyguards, talks to reporters concerning the violent death of the Archbishop of Uganda and two cabinet ministers while they were in custody in 1977. *Photo: Popperfoto*

Ā'MIS, Kingsley (1922-). British author. Ed. at Oxford, he lectured in English at Swansea Univ. Coll. 1949-61, and was fellow of Peterhouse, Cambridge, 1961–3. His novels include *Lucky Jim* (1954), *Take a Girl Like You* (1960), and *The Old Devils* (1986), for which he won the Booker Prize.

AMMA'N. Capital and chief industrial centre of Jordan, on the site of the ancient Rabbath-Ammon (Philadelphia). The Univ. of Jordan was estab. here 1962, and A. is the centre of a road network and on the Cairo-Baghdad air route. Pop. (1970) 583,000.

A'MMETER. An instrument which measures electric current. *See* AMPERE.

AMMON. Egyptian deity, identified by the Greeks with Zeus and by the Romans with Jupiter. In art he is represented as a ram, as a man with ram's head, or as a man crowned with feathers.

AMMONIA (NH_3). A colourless, pungent-smelling gas of about two-thirds the density of air, and soluble in water, forming ammonium hydroxide, NH_4OH. The solution is

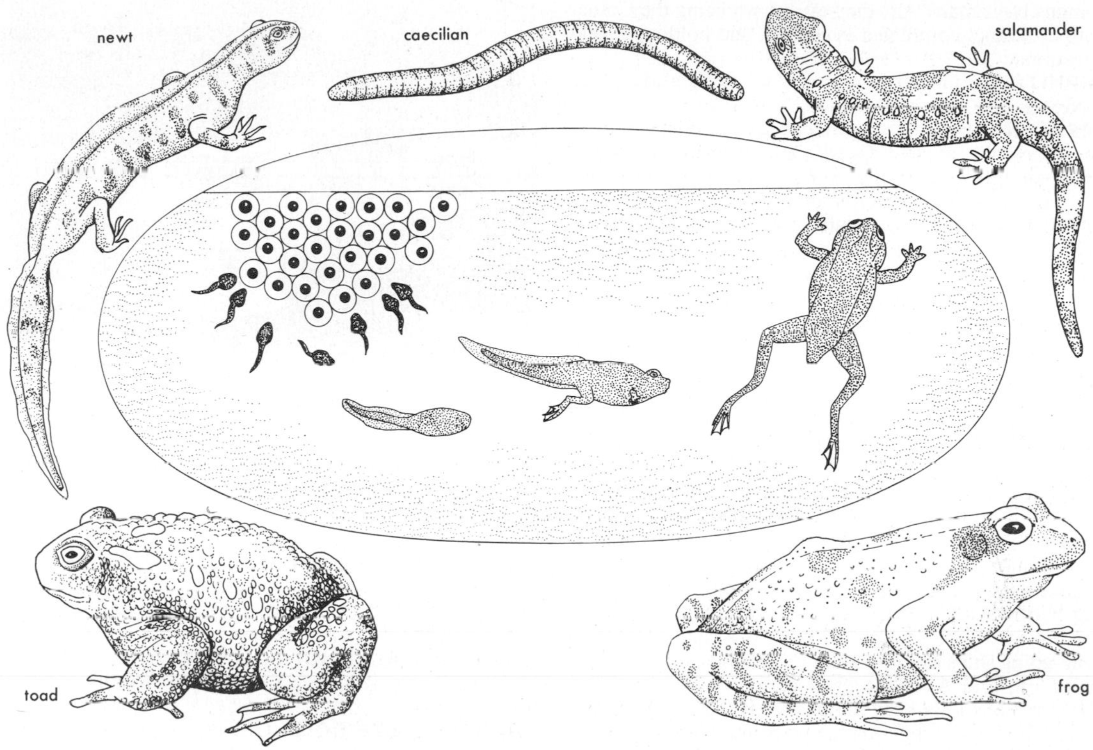

AMPHIBIA. Typical forms of amphibia.

strongly alkaline, and forms crystalline salts on neutralization with acids.

Appreciable amounts of ammonium carbonate are found in the guano deposits of S. America, and in the mineral deposits at Stassfurt. It is also produced synthetically in gas works, being a product of the destructive distillation of coal, and by the Haber and Cyanamide processes.

A'MMONITES. Ancient Semitic people living to the N.W. of the Dead Sea on the edge of the Syrian desert. Worshippers of Moloch, to whom they offered human sacrifices, they were frequently at war with the Israelites.

AMMONITES. Extinct cephalopod molluscs akin to the modern nautilus. The shell is curled in a plane spiral and made up of numerous chambers, only the outermost of which is inhabited by the animal. As. flourished in the Mesozoic times.

AMOEBA (amē'ba). One of the simplest living animals, consisting of a single cell and belonging to the group Protozoa, found in fresh water. The body, which is just visible to the naked eye, consists of colourless protoplasm. The chief organ within the body is the nucleus which largely controls the A.'s activities. The A. feeds by flowing round and enclosing organic debris, etc., which it encounters. It has no eyes or other sense organs, and no sexual reproduction.

AMORITES. Ancient people of Semitic or Indo-European origin, who were among the inhabitants of Canaan at the time of the Israelite invasion.

Ā'MOS. First of the Hebrew O.T. prophets whose utterances were preserved in literary form (*c.* 760 B.C.). A sheep-farmer of Tekoah, he was roused by the increased moral laxity and corruption of Israel under Jeroboam II.

AMOY. *See* XIAMEN.

AMPÈRE (oṅpār'), **André Marie** (1775-1836). Fr. physicist and mathematician, prof. at the Collège de France in Paris. The instrument for measuring current, the *ammeter*, is named after him, as is the *ampere*, the unit of electric current, which would produce a force between parallel conductors (one metre from each other in a vacuum) of 2×10^{-7} newtons per metre length.

AMPHIBIA. Class of vertebrates standing in zoological classification between the fishes and the reptiles. The A. were the first four-legged animals to inhabit the earth, and our knowledge of them goes back to the Carboniferous age. The modern A. are divided into 3 orders: *Apoda* or *Gymnophiona* (the Caecilians, limbless and with very short tail); *Caudata* or *Urodela* (salamanders and newts, with limbs and tail); *Salientia* or *Anura* (frogs and toads, with 4 limbs and no tail).

The A. are cold-blooded vertebrates, with the body covered with skin instead of scales and passing the first part of their life in a larval or tadpole state. The majority spend their adult lives on land, generally near water, and salt water except in great dilution is fatal to them.

AMPHITHEATRE. Large oval or circular building used by the Romans for the exhibition of gladiatorial contests, fights of wild beasts, and other similar spectacles; the arena of an A. is completely surrounded by the seats of the spectators, hence the name (Gk *amphi*, around). The Romans built many As., the best-known being the Colosseum at Rome, completed in A.D. 80, and holding 87,000 spectators.

AMPHITRITE (amfitrī'tē). Greek sea-maiden, daughter of Nereus and wife of Poseidon.

AMPHORA (amf-). Large earthenware vessel in common use among the ancient Greeks and Romans, having a handle on both sides of the neck and a pointed lower end that was thrust into the ground.

AMPULLA. Small vessel with a round body and narrow neck, used for holding oil, perfumes, etc., used by the Greeks and Romans for toilet purposes. At British coronations the oil is contained in an eagle-shaped A.

AMRI'TSAR. City in the Punjab, India, founded 1577. It is the religious centre of the Sikhs and contains the Golden Temple and Guru Nanak Univ. (1969), named after the first Sikh Guru. Pop. (1971) 432,665.

AMSTERDAM. Capital, largest city, commercial and intellectual centre of the Netherlands, on the Amstel where it joins the Ij, an inlet of the Ijsselmeer (remnant of the Zuider Zee). A. became important on the decline of Antwerp in the 16th cent. When vessels became too large to navigate the Zuider Zee the port lost some of its importance, but regained it with the opening of the North Holland Canal to Helder in 1825. In 1876 the 24km (15m) long North Sea Canal to Ijmuiden was opened; this has been repeatedly enlarged and deepened, so that the largest ocean-going ships can now reach A. Various industries are carried on, and A. is the chief diamond market of the world, and has long been famous for its cutting industry. A. has many docks and quays, and is intersected by many canals. Most of the heavy transport is water-borne. Notable buildings are the Royal Palace (1655); the Nieuwe Kerk (1408); the Oude Kerk (14th cent.); the St Antonieswaag, an old weighhouse, used to house the city's archives, and the Rijksmuseum, and the Stedelijk, with the Vincent Van Gogh Museum next to it, opened in 1973. The Rembrandt and Anne Frank Houses are carefully preserved. There are two universities, 1877 and 1905. Pop. (1978) 728,746.

AMU DARYA (ahmoo dah'ryah). River in Soviet Central Asia, rising in the Pamirs and flowing through a wide delta into the Aral Sea. It was anciently known as the Oxus and is 2,540 km (1,490 m) long.

AMU DARYA. *See* ARAL.

AMUNDSEN (ah'moondsen), **Roald** (1872-1928). Norwegian explorer. B. in Borge, he was the first to navigate the N.W. Passage in 1906. In 1910 he set sail in the *Fram* to discover the North Pole, but on hearing that he had been forestalled by Peary, he raced Scott to the South Pole instead (1911). In 1918 he made an unsuccessful attempt to drift across the North Pole in the *Maud*, and in 1925 essayed a flight from Spitzbergen to the Pole by aeroplane. This too failed, but the following year he and Ellsworth joined the Italian General Nobile in his dirigible the *Norge*, which circled the pole twice and landed in Alaska. A. lost his life when searching by plane for Nobile and his airship *Italia*.

AMUR (ahmoor'). River in the Far East of Asia. Formed by the Argun and the Shilka, the A. enters the sea of Okhotsk. At its mouth at Nikolaevsk it is 16km (10m) wide. For much of its course of over 4,345 km (2,700 m) it forms, together with its tributary, the Ussuri (q.v.), the boundary between the RSFSR and China. Under the treaties of Aigun (1858) and Peking (1860) 984,200 sq.km (380,000 sq.m) of territory N. and E. of the 2 rivers were ceded by China to the Tsarist govt, and from 1963 China raised the question of its return.

AMSTERDAM. The Meagre Bridge over the Amstel river, and in the background the high, narrow houses favoured by the careful city burghers who made maximum use of land which sold at a premium in this wealthy port. *Photo: Barnaby's Picture Library*

AMYL (a'mil) **ALCOHOL** ($C_5H_{11}OH$). A clear colourless oily liquid, usually having a characteristic rather choking odour.

ANABO'LIC STE'ROID. One of the synthetic steroid (q.v.) hormones which stimulate constructive chemical processes in living creatures. They are illegally used - the 'bulk bomb' - to give athletes phenomenal size and strength, and are difficult to detect. A single dose, in combination with a high protein diet, is effective in increasing mass over several months, so that As. were at first used chiefly by weight-lifters, javelin throwers, etc. Later, sprinters found that, taken shortly before racing, they improved muscular performance by immediately increasing aggressiveness and competitiveness. In women they tend to produce unwanted tendencies to masculine characteristics.

A'NABRANCH. A stream (Gk *ana*, 'again') which branches from the main river and then re-unites with it. The *Great A.* in Australia leaves the Darling nr. Menindee, and joins the Murray, some distance below the confluence of the Darling and Murray.

ANACO'NDA. World's greatest copper plant in Montana, USA. The city founded as Copperopolis 1883, by the Anaconda Copper Mining Co., was incorporated as A. in 1888. Anaconda is 1,615 m (5,300 ft) a.s.l., and 42km (26m) N.W. of Butte. Pop. (1970) 9,770.

ANACONDA. South American snake, allied to the boa-constrictor; one of the largest snakes, it reaches 9m (30ft) and more.

ANAEMIA (anē'mia). A disease condition in which the patient has too little blood, too few red blood cells or too little haemoglobin. Deficiency in quantity or quality may be due to excessive bleeding, faulty nourishment, or failure to use the food properly. Blood may be destroyed by chemical poisons or infections, and may be impaired by certain diseases of the blood or the lymphatic system. A patient with chronic A. tires quickly on exertion and becomes faint and breathless through lack of oxygen in the tissues. The remedy is proper nutrition and iron.

Pernicious or Addison's A. is a disease due to the failure of the stomach to secrete a certain substance which is necessary to produce blood from the food. It can be rectified by the administration of liver or its extract. Acute A. is also caused by a large whole-body dose of nuclear radiation. *See also* THALASSAEMIA.

ANAESTHESIA (anesthē'sia). Absence of sensation (Gk *an-*, not; *aisthēsis*, sensation). A. of a part of the skin, so that the patient is insensitive to a pin-prick or other stimulus, is a sign of nerve disorder, but the more common meaning of A. is a loss of sensation or consciousness produced by an anaesthetic drug.

The beginning of modern A. was the discovery by Thomas Beddoes in 1776 of nitrous oxide. Sir Humphry Davy, inventor of the miner's lamp, did much of the experimental work and first suggested its application to surgery. Horace Wells, a New England, USA, dentist, had a tooth extracted under nitrous oxide (laughing gas) for the first time in 1844. Ether was successfully used by Dr Crawford Long of Georgia in 1842 for the removal of a tumour of the neck. The credit for the discovery of A. is, however, given to W. T. G. Morton, another dentist, of Boston, Mass., who in 1846 anaesthetized a patient with ether for the removal of a skin tumour at the Massachusetts General Hospital. Prof. James Simpson of Edinburgh used it soon afterwards on women in childbirth, and met great opposition from religious persons. Meanwhile chloroform had been known in France since 1831, and Simpson began to use it in preference to ether. Its use by Queen Victoria at the birth of Prince Leopold in 1853 settled the religious controversy.

Local A. came into use about the beginning of the 20th cent. Cocaine was used as long ago as 1847, but is too poisonous and too likely to lead to addiction to be generally useful. The relatively harmless synthetic substance novocaine, invented about 1905, marked the beginning of the general use of local A. Large areas of the body can be anaesthetized by injecting As. into nerve junctions.

ANALGESICS (-je'siks). Medicines that give freedom from pain, e.g. cocaine and novocaine for local application; opium and its derivatives, antipyrine, aspirin, and certain barbiturate drugs, for internal use. Dangers of increasing dosage and addiction may arise, and in cases of intractable pain, as in some types of cancer or post-operative pain (e.g. thoracic surgery), cryoanalgesia may be used. The relevant sensory nerves are frozen by the application of compressed nitrous oxide, which expands to create intense cold.

ANANDA (fl. 5th cent. B.C.). Favourite disciple of the Buddha. At his plea, a separate order was established for women.

ANARCHISM. A term in political theory derived from the Gk *anarkhos*, 'without ruler'. It does not mean 'without order'; most theories of A. imply an order of a very strict and symmetrical kind, but they maintain that such order can be achieved by co-operation, and they claim that other methods of achieving order, which rely on authority, are both morally reprehensible and politically unstable. A. must not be confused with nihilism, a purely negative and destructive activity directed against society as such: it is essentially a pacifist movement.

The religious type of A., claimed by many anarchists to be exemplified in the early organization of the Christian church, has found expression in modern times in the social philosophy of Tolstoy and Gandhi. The growth of political A. may be traced through William Godwin, Shelley, and P. J. Proudhon to Bakunin (q.v.) who had a strong following in Latin Europe, especially France and Spain, until the suppressive dictatorships of Mussolini and Franco. The theory of A. is best expressed in the works of Kropotkin (q.v.).

From the 1960s there was an outbreak of terrorism popularly identified with A., e.g. the bombing and shooting incidents carried out by the 'Angry Brigade' 1968-71 in Britain.

ANASTA'SIA (1901-1918). Russian Grand Duchess, youngest dau. of Nicholas II (q.v.). She was murdered with her parents, but it has been alleged that A. escaped, and of those who claimed her identity the most famous was Anna Anderson. Alleged by some to be a Pole, Franziska Schanzkowski, she was rescued from a Berlin canal in 1920: the German Federal Supreme Court rejected her claim 1970.

ANATOLIA. Alternative name for TURKEY - in Asia.

ANA'TOMY (Gk, cutting up, dissection). The study of the structure of the parts of the body, as distinguished from physiology, which is the study of their functions.

Herophilus of Chalcedon (fl. *c.* 300 B.C.) and Erasistratus of Chios are regarded as the fathers respectively of anatomy and physiology. In the 2nd cent. A.D. Galen of Pergamum produced an account of A. which was the only source of anatomical knowledge until the period of the Renaissance, in particular until the appearance in 1543 of *On the Working of the Human Body* by the Belgian, Andreas Vesalius (1514-64). In 1628 William Harvey pub. his demonstration of the circulation of the blood. A. was immensely advanced by the invention of the microscope, and the Italian Malpighi (1628-94) and the Hollander Leeuwenhoek (1632-1723) laid the foundations of the study of minute anatomy, or histology. In 1747 B. Albinus (1697-1770), with the help of the artist J. Wandelaar (1691-1759), produced the most beautiful and exact account of the bones and muscles, and in 1757-65 the Swiss Albrecht von Haller (1708-77) gave the most complete and exact description of the organs that had yet appeared. The A. of the nervous system was advanced by the Frenchman Vicq d'Azyr (1748-94), comparative A. by G. Cuvier (1769-1832), whilst in England J. Hunter (1728-93) developed an anatomical museum.

Among the most notable anatomical writers of the early 19th cent. are the London surgeon Sir Ch. Bell (1774-1842), Jonas Quain (1796-1865), and Henry Gray (1825-61). Later in the century came the inventions of staining tissues by dyes for microscopic examination, and the method of mechanically cutting very thin sections of stained tissues. Radiographic A. has been one of the triumphs of the 20th cent. which has also been marked by immense activity in embryological investigation. *See* HUMAN BODY.

ANCESTOR WORSHIP. Religious attitude adopted by many primitive peoples towards the deceased of the tribe or family. Thus the Zulus used to invoke the spirits of the great warriors of their race before engaging in battle. The Greeks deified their early heroes, and the ancient Romans held in reverential honour the *manes* or departed spirits of their forebears. Particularly prevalent in old China, A.W. gives way under Communist teaching.

ANCHORAGE. Port and largest town of Alaska, USA, at the head of Cook Inlet. There is a salmon canning industry, and coal and gold are mined; and A. has an internat. airport. Alaska's new cap., Willow, is to the N. Pop. (1970) 48,000.

ANCHORAGE. Terminus of the Alaska Railroad which runs north to Fairbanks, Anchorage is also served by many airlines, and 90 per cent of the food and goods passing into and out of Alaska passes through this port. *Photo: J. R. Eyerman/Camera Press*

ANCHOVY. A fish (*Engraulis encrasicholus*) of the herring family (Clupeidae). It breeds abundantly in the Mediterranean, and is also found on the Atlantic coast of Europe. It is distinguished by its projecting snout and deep cleft to the mouth, grows to a length of 18-20cm (7-8in), and is dark green, with a broad silvery band on the sides.

ANCIEN RÉGIME (oṅsiaṅ′ rāzhēm′). (Fr., old order of things). The system of government under the French monarchy, which was swept away by the Revolution of 1789.

ANCIENT LIGHTS. In Britain the right of an owner of a building, arising through long use, to receive an uninterrupted flow of light at one or more of the windows of the building. The right may be acquired in various ways, but usually under the Prescription Act, 1832, by the enjoyment of the right for 20 years without interruption.

ANCŌ′NA. Italian town and naval base on the Adriatic Sea, capital of A. province. It has a Romanesque cathedral and a former palace of the popes. Pop. (1971) 110,235.

ANDALŪ′SIA. Region of Spain comprising the provs. of Almería, Cádiz, Córdoba, Granada, Huelva, Jaén, Málaga and Sevilla. It forms an extensive and mostly fertile plain, ringed by mountains, producing copper, manganese, molybdenum, etc., and is watered by the Guadalquivir and many other rivers. It contains the Sierra Nevada. The chief town is Seville, others incl. Málaga, Granada and Córdoba. Autonomy is planned.

A′NDAMANS. Group of islands in the Bay of Bengal, between India and Burma. There are 5 principal islands (forming the Great Andaman), the Little Andaman, and about 204 islets. The A. were formerly used as a penal settlement, abolished 1945, and were occupied by the Japanese 1942-5. Area 6,500 sq.km (2,500 sq.m); pop. (1971) *c.* 100,000. With the Nicobars (q.v.), they form a territory of the Rep. of India. The aboriginal pop. number only a few hundred; they are pygmies, probably the remnants of a race once spread over S.E. Asia.

A′NDERSEN, Hans Christian (1805-75). Danish writer. The son of a shoemaker, he was b. at Odense in Fünen. His first book was pub. when he was only 17, but it was not until 1829 that he attracted notice. In 1835 his novel *The Improvisatore* brought him popularity, and he began to compose the immortal fairy tales which have been translated into all languages. A.'s other works include romances and a genial autobiography.

ANDERSEN. He was backward at school, but in real life realized the theme of his most famous story, 'The Ugly Duckling'. Children and grownups everywhere recognize him as the greatest master of the folk tale. *Photo: Courtesy of the Danish Tourist Board*

ANDERSON, Carl David (1905-). American physicist. B. in New York, he was prof. at the California Institute of Technology 1939-76. Engaged on gamma and cosmic ray research from 1930, he in 1932 discovered the positive electron, or positron, and for this was a 'joint' Nobel prize-winner in 1936.

ANDERSON, Elizabeth Garrett (1836-1917). British pioneer woman doctor, *née* Garrett. She began to study medicine in 1860, and in 1865 was granted a licence to practise by the Society of Apothecaries. She held hospital posts in London, 1866-1903, and m. in 1871 J. G. S. Anderson, shipowner. In 1908 she became mayor of Aldeburgh, the first woman mayor in England.

ANDERSON, Sir John. *See* WAVERLEY.

ANDERSON, John Bayard (1922-). American politician. B. in Rockford, Illinois, he became a Republican Congressman, but in 1980 campaigned for pres. as an Independent with former Democrat Patrick Lucey as vice-pres. running mate. His platform was a blend of conservative and liberal tenets.

ANDERSON, Marian (1902-). American contralto singer. B. in Philadelphia, she made her début in 1924, her voice being of remarkable richness. In 1955 she appeared as Ulrica in Verdi's *The Masked Ball* at the Metropolitan Opera, N.Y., the first Negress to appear there, and achieved outstanding success.

ANDERSON, Maxwell (1888-1959). American dramatist. Son of a Baptist minister, he spent some time in journalism, among other very varied occupations, before making his name in collaboration with Laurence Stallings with *What Price Glory?*, a trenchant war play.

ANDERSON, Sherwood (1876-1941). American short-story writer. B. in Ohio, he became manager of a paint factory but abandoned commerce to join the literary circles of Chicago. He estab. a reputation with *Winesburg, Ohio* (1919), with its relish of small-town life and another short story vol. *The Triumph of the Egg* (1921). He deals with the frustration of instinct in modern industrialized society: his novels incl. *Windy McPherson's Son* (1916) and *Dark Laughter* (1925).

ANDES (an'dēz). The great mountain system or cordillera that forms the western fringe of S. America, extending through some 67° of latitude and the republics of Colombia, Venezuela, Ecuador, Peru, Bolivia, Chile and Argentina. The mts exceed 3,600 m (12,000 ft) for half their length of 6,500 km (4,000 m). Geologically speaking, they are new mountains, having attained their present height by vertical upheaval of the entire strip of the earth's crust as recently as the latter part of the Tertiary era and the Quaternary. But they have been greatly affected by weathering. Rivers have cut profound gorges, and glaciers have produced characteristic valleys. The majority of the individual mountains are volcanic, some are still active volcanoes.

The whole system may be divided into two almost parallel ranges. The southernmost extremity is Cape Horn, but the range extends into the sea and forms islands. Among the highest peaks are Cotopaxi and Chimborazo in Ecuador, Cerro de Pasco and Misti in Peru, Illampu and Illimani in Bolivia, Aconcagua in Argentina (highest mtn in the New World), and Ojos del Salado in Chile.

The A. are rich in minerals, and the extraction of silver and gold has never ceased. The ores which are of present-day world importance are tin, tungsten, and bismuth in Bolivia, and vanadium, copper, and lead in Peru. Difficult communications make mining expensive. Transport was for long chiefly by pack animals, but air transport has greatly reduced difficulties of communications. Three railways cross the A. from Valparaiso to Buenos Aires, Antofagasta to Salta, and Antofagasta via Uyuni to Asuncion. New roads are being built, incl. the Pan-American Highway from Alaska to Cape Horn.

The population is sparse on the whole. The majority are dependent upon agriculture, the nature and products of which vary with the natural environment.

The **Andean Group** - the Latin-American Common Market - was estab. under the treaty of Cartagena (1969) by Bolivia, Chile, Colombia, Ecuador and Peru; Venezuela joined 1973, Mexico assoc. 1972, and Chile withdrew 1976.

A'NDHRA PRADE'SH. State of the Rep. of India, created 1953 from the Telugu-speaking areas of Madras (q.v.), and enlarged 1956 from the former Hyderabad state. Rice and sugar cane are grown, there are textile and paper mills, and Vishakhapatnam has an oil refinery and shipyards. Area 275,280 sq.km (106,285 sq.m); pop. (1971) 43,390,000.

ANDES. Aconcagua, on the border between Argentina and Chile, gives its name to a province of Chile which extends to the Pacific, and also to the river which rises on its southern slopes. *Photo: Mike Andrews*

ANDO'RRA. Small European republic in the eastern Pyrenees between France and Spain, consisting of gorges and narrow valleys surrounded by high mountains. Traditionally it received its independence from Charlemagne, and in 1278 it was placed under the joint suzerainty of the count of Foix in France and the bishop of Urgel in Spain. The former's rights are now vested in the president of the French Republic, but the bishop still retains his prerogatives. Bi-annual dues of 960 francs are paid to France and 460 pesetas to the bishop. There is an elected Council General, and the executive power is wielded by a First Syndic. There are no railways but a road links the French and Spanish frontiers via the cap., Andorra la Vella, pop. c. 8,500. The people speak Catalan and are R.C. Area 465 sq.km (190 sq.m); pop. (1977) 30,700, c. 8,000 citizens, the rest Spanish. M.U.: as France and Spain.

ANDORRA. The enclosing mountains which rise behind the little village of Santa Julia de Loria show the difficult terrain which helped Andorra survive in independence to modern times. *Photo: Dick Huffman/Barnaby's Picture Library*

ANDRÉ (an'drā), **John** (1751-80). British soldier. B. in London, the son of a merchant from Geneva, he served with the British army in America from 1774, and when Arnold offered to betray West Point to the British, Major A. was chosen to negotiate the surrender. Captured by the Americans, he was hanged as a spy. A monument to A. was set up in Westminster Abbey.

ANDREA (ahndrā'ah) **DEL SARTO** (1486-1531). Italian painter, b. at Florence. His name was Andrea d'Agnolo; he was called Del Sarto because he was the son of a tailor. He was apprenticed to a goldsmith, later studied under Giovanni Barile and Piero di Cosimo, but he owed more to his study of Masaccio, Michelangelo, and others. In 1516 he m. Lucrezia del Fede, a beautiful woman who appears in many of his pictures. In 1518 he went to Paris at the invitation of Francis I, and for him painted the 'Charity' now in the Louvre. In 1519 he returned to Florence, and with the money Francis had entrusted to him for the purchase of works of art built a house for himself. In 1525 he painted the 'Madonna del Sacco', a fresco, usually considered his masterpiece. He d. of the plague.

AN'DREW, St (d. *c.* A.D. 70). Apostle. A native of Bethsaida, he was Simon Peter's brother. With Peter, James, and John, who worked with him as fishermen at Capernaum, he formed the inner circle of the 12 disciples. According to tradition he went with John to Ephesus, preached in Scythia, and was crucified at Patras on an X-shaped cross (St Andrew's cross). His feast is held on 30 Nov. He is the patron saint of Scotland.

ANDREWES, Lancelot (1555-1626), C. of E., divine. B. in London, he went to Cambridge, and took holy orders in 1580, becoming bishop successively of Chichester (1605), Ely (1609), and Winchester (1618). He took part in preparing the text of the A.V., and was remarkable for his fine preaching.

ANDREWS, Julie (1935-). British actress and singer. A child star on the British stage, she was the original *My Fair Lady* (1956), and her films incl. *Mary Poppins* (1963) and *The Sound of Music* (1964).

ANDREYEV (andrā'yev), **Leonid Nicolaievich** (1871-1919). Russian author. B. at Orel, he achieved success with a collection of stories in 1901. Later works, obsessed with death and madness, incl. the symbolic drama *Life of Man* (1907), the melodrama *He Who Gets Slapped* (1915); and novels *Red Laugh* (1904), *Seven that were Hanged* (1908), and *S.O.S.* (1919) pub. in Finland, where he had fled from the Revolution.

ANDRIC (andrēch), **Ivo** (1892-1975). Yugoslav novelist. A former member of the nationalist Young Bosnia organization, another member of which shot Francis Ferdinand, he began writing while a political prisoner in Austria. He later became a diplomat and then entered the Yugoslav Parliament. A.'s most outstanding work is the trilogy which incl. *The Bridge on the Drina.* He was awarded a Nobel prize in 1961.

ANDROCLES (and'roklēz) (fl. 1st cent. A.D.). Roman slave. He is said to have fled from a cruel master to a cave in Africa, where he drew a thorn from the foot of a suffering lion. When A. was recaptured and sentenced to fight a lion, he encountered the same animal who repaid his kindness by greeting him as a friend. The emperor Tiberius pardoned A. who was set free, together with the lion.

ANDROMACHE (androm'akē). Heroine of Homer's *Iliad;* the wife of Hector, who was killed in combat with Achilles, and mother of the boy Astyanax, who was flung from the battlements by the conquerors. After the fall of Troy she was awarded to Neoptolemus, Achilles's son.

ANDRO'MEDA. In Gk mythology, a beautiful Ethiopian princess who was chained to a rock and exposed to a sea-monster. Perseus slew the latter and married her. When she d. the gods placed her among the stars.

ANDROPOV (andraw'pof), **Yuri** (1914–84). Soviet statesman. He was involved in suppressing the Hungarian revolt of 1956, and was head of the KGB 1967–May 1982. In 1982 he succeeded Brezhnev as Gen Sec of the Soviet Communist Party, also becoming pres. June 1983.

ANE'MONĒ. Genus of plants of the crowfoot family Ranunculaceae. The wood A. (*A. nemorosa*) or wind-flower is a familiar plant in the shady woods, flowering in spring. *A. pulsatilla*, the Pasque flower, and *A. pratensis* are powerful emetics. *A. hepatica* is common in the Alps. The garden A. (*A. coronaria*) is among the florists' flowers.

ANEROID. *See* BAROMETER.

ANGEL (Gk, messenger). In Christian, Mohammedan, and Jewish belief a class of supernatural beings, intermediate in status between God and man, whose function is to praise and serve the former, and act as the mediators to man. Later Christian belief evolved a celestial hierarchy of 9 orders: the Seraphim, Cherubim, and Thrones, who contemplate God and reflect his glory; Dominations, Virtues, and Powers, who regulate the stars and universe; and Principalities, Archangels, and Angels, who minister to humanity. In R.C. belief each human soul has a Guardian A. to protect and watch over it.

ANGELFISH. Genus of fish (*Squatina*) related to the sharks, found in warmer waters and with wing-like pectoral fins; also small, brightly coloured members of the freshwater Cichlidae found in aquariums.

ANGE'LICA. Genus of umbelliferous plants. *A. sylvestris*, the species found in Britain, is a tall perennial herb, with wedge-shaped leaves and clusters of white, pale violet, or pinkish flowers.

ANGELICO (ahnjel'ēkoh), **Fra** (1387-1455). Italian painter, whose real name was Guido di Pietro. B. in Tuscany, he entered the Dominican order. For 10 years from 1436 he lived in the monastery of S. Marco in Florence where he executed some fine frescoes. In 1446 he moved to Rome at the summons of the Pope. Among his outstanding pictures are 'The Coronation of the Virgin' in the Louvre, and a Christ with 265 saints, in the National Gallery, London. He was a mystic, and his saintly character is revealed in all his works. The name *Angelico* was given him because of the angelic beauty of his nature.

ANGELL (ān'jel), **Sir Norman** (1872-1967). British writer on politics and economics. In 1910 he acquired an international reputation with his book *The Great Illusion*, in which he maintained that any war must prove ruinous to the victors as well as to the vanquished, and in 1933 was awarded a Nobel peace prize.

ANGERS (oṅzhā'). Ancient French town, cap. of Maine-et-Loire dept, on the r. Maine. It has a 12-13th cent. cathedral and castle, and was formerly the cap. of the duchy and prov. of Anjou whose people are called Angevins - a name also applied by the English to the Plantagenet kings. Pop. (1973) 261,435.

ANGINA (anjī'na). Sore throat, an agonizing spasmodic pain. *A. pectoris* is a sudden agonizing pain in the chest, sometimes extending to the left shoulder and down the arm, associated with a terror of immediate death; it is due to spasm of the coronary arteries which supply blood to the heart muscle, or to an aneurysm of the aorta.

A'NGIOSPERMS. One of the 2 great divisions of flowering plants (Phanerogamia). In contrast to the gymnosperms ('naked seeds') - which comprise only the conifers and cycads - the As. have their seeds enclosed in a fruit, and show a generally higher and more advanced organization.

A'NGKOR. Name applied to the ruins in and around the ancient ruined cap. of the Khmers in Cambodia. The remains date mainly from the 10-12th cent. A.D., and comprise temples originally dedicated to the Hindu gods, shrines associated with Hinayana Buddhism, royal palaces, etc. Many are grouped within the great enclosure called Angkor Thom, but the great temple of Angkor Vat (early 12th cent.), one of the most imposing edifices in the world, lies some little distance outside. A. was abandoned in the 15th cent., and the ruins were not adequately described until 1863. Buildings on the site suffered damage during the civil war 1970-5.

ANGKOR. Built in the 12th cent. by Suryavarman II, the great temple of Angkor Vat was devoted to Siva and represents the height of Khmer classical art. *Photo: Mireille Vautier*

ANGLER. A fish (*Lophius piscatorius*) of the order Pediculati, inhabiting the waters of the N. Atlantic, and found off British shores. It has an enormous flattened head and a wide mouth with sharp teeth, and may be 1.5m (5ft) long. Other names for it are sea devil, frog fish, and goose fish.

ANGLESEY, Henry William Paget, 1st marquess of (1768-1854). British cavalry leader during the Napoleonic wars. He led a great charge at Waterloo, in which he lost a leg, and was made a marquess for his conspicuous services. He was twice Lord-Lieutenant of Ireland, and succeeded his father as earl of Uxbridge in 1812.

ANGLESEY. Welsh island, separated from the mainland of Wales by the Menai Straits, which are crossed by the Britannia tubular railway bridge and Telford's suspension bridge, built 1819-26 but since rebuilt. Nature-lovers visit A. for its fauna (especially bird-life) and flora, and antiquarians for its many buildings and relics of historic interest; it is also a popular holiday resort. The ancient granary of Wales, A. now has growing industries, e.g. toy-making, electrical goods, and bromine extraction from the sea. Holyhead is the principal town and port; but Beaumaris was the co. town until the co. of A. was merged in Gwynedd (1974). Area 715 sq.km (276 sq.m); pop. (1971) 59,705.

ANGLICAN COMMUNION, The. Family of churches incl. the Church of England and those holding the same essential doctrines, i.e. the Lambeth Quadrilateral (1888) - Holy Scripture as the basis of all doctrine, the Nicene and Apostles' Creeds, Holy Baptism and Holy Communion, and the historic episcopate.

The Church of England originated during the Roman occupation *c.* 2nd cent., and, after a period of decline, was estab. as part of the Catholic Church by the mission of St Augustine who became first Abp. of Canterbury in 597. At the Reformation the chief change was political, the Sovereign (Henry VIII) replaced the Pope and assumed the right to appoint abps. and bps. The Book of Common Prayer (q.v.), the basis of worship throughout the A.C., dates from Edward VI's reign; the Thirty-Nine Articles, the Church's doctrinal basis, were drawn up under Elizabeth I; and the canons of ecclesiastical discipline are essentially those framed under James I. *See* BIBLE.

The Church was early carried by colonizers and explorers to N. America (where 3 American bps. were consecrated after the War of Independence, whose successors still lead the Episcopal Church in the USA), Australia and New Zealand, and by traders to India. The main missionary effort, however, came in the 19th cent., especially in Africa, and in the 20th cent. work has been extended to S. America.

In England the 2 abps. head the provs. of Canterbury and York (qq.v.), which are subdivided into bishoprics. *See* PARLIAMENT. The Church Assembly (1919) was replaced in 1970 by a General Synod with 3 houses (bps., other clergy, and laity) to regulate Church matters, subject to parliament and the royal assent. A decennial Lambeth Conference (first held 1867) attended by bps. from all parts of the A.C. is presided over in London by the Abp. of Canterbury: it is not legislative but its decisions are often put into practice. The Church Commissioners for England (1948) manage the estates of the Church and endowment of livings.

The 3 main parties, all products of the 19th cent., are: the Evangelical or Low Church, which maintains the Church's Protestant character; the Anglo-Catholic or High Church, which stresses continuity with the pre-Reformation Church (*see* KEBLE, FROUDE, NEWMAN, PUSEY) and is marked by ritualistic practices, the use of confession, maintenance of religious communities of both sexes, etc.; and the Liberal or Modernist, concerned with the reconciliation of the Church with modern thought (*see* J. A. T. ROBINSON, M. STOCKWOOD). In the 20th cent. there have been moves towards reunion with the Methodist and R.C. Churches. The ordination of women has been accepted by some overseas churches, e.g. the American Episcopalian Church in 1976, but the General Synod in Britain, although voting in 1976 that there were no fundamental objections, was reluctant to proceed further.

ANGLING. Fishing with a rod and line, as opposed to the use of nets, and espec. as a 'sport', on which the classic work is Izaak Walton's *Compleat Angler* (1653). The equipment is as light as is consistent with the size and strength of the quarry, the 'game' quality of the species being assessed by its vigour and the length of time, often many hours, during which a fish will fight for its life. Stock may be conserved, or artificially renewed, by A. associations in preserved waters. Freshwater game fish incl. salmon, trout, carp and pike; and saltwater incl. shark, tuna or tunny, marlin and swordfish, which as 'big-game' fish are often caught from specially equipped motor-boats.

Angling has been defended as a sport in that fish were believed to feel no pain, but in 1980 scientists found that the pain-transmitting agent (Substance P), which occurs in mammals, is also present in fish.

ANGLO-SAXONS. The Teutonic invaders who conquered Britain between the 5th and 7th cents. According to Bede they consisted of the Angles, who settled in E. Anglia, Mercia, and Northumbria; the Saxons in Essex, Sussex, and Wessex; and the Jutes, in Kent and S. Hampshire. The Jutes probably came from the Rhineland and not, as was formerly believed, from Jutland. The Angles and Saxons came from Schleswig-Holstein, and may have united before the invasion. There must have been a good deal of inter-marriage with the Romanized Celts, although the latter's language and civilization almost disappeared. After the conquest a number of kingdoms were set up, commonly referred to as the Heptarchy; these were united in the early 9th cent. under the overlordship of Wessex. The English-speaking peoples of Britain, the Commonwealth, and the USA are often referred to today as A.-Ss., but the term is completely unscientific, as the Welsh, Scots, and Irish are mainly of Celtic descent, and by 1971 only 14.4 per cent of Americans were of British stock.

ANGŌ'LA. State in southern Africa, between Zaïre and S.W. Africa, and incl. also the enclave of Cabinda, N. of the Rep. of Zaïre. The coastal area is flat, unproductive and unhealthy, but behind a mountainous edge is a vast fertile plateau. Coffee, maize, sugar, palm kernels and their oil are produced: minerals incl. rich diamond deposits and oil. The cap. is Luanda (formerly São Paulo de Luanda), which is to be replaced by Huambo (formerly Nova Lisbõa): other towns incl. Benguela, Mossamedes and Lobito. Area 1,246,700 sq.km (481,350 sq.m); pop. (1972) 5,800,000. M.U.: kwanza, named after A.'s main river.

Formerly a Portuguese possession, A. became independent in 1975, when there was a civil war. The Marxist faction was victorious, with Soviet and Cuban aid, and the govt. comprises a pres. and (from Nov. 1980) a Nat. People's Assembly. Their opponents continued guerrilla warfare, backed by South Africa, which mounted large-scale border incursions in 1980-1.

ANGORA. Earlier form of Ankara (q.v.), which gave its name to the A. goat (*see* MOHAIR), and hence to other species of long-haired animal, e.g. the A. rabbit, source of A. 'wool', and the A. cat.

ANGOSTURA. *See* CIUDAD BOLIVAR.

ANGOULÊME (aṅgoolām'). French town, cap. of the dept of Charente, on the Charente, with a fine cathedral and a castle and papermills dating from the 16th cent. Pop. (1975) 98,000.

ANGRY PENGUINS. Magazine and literary movement in Australia 1941-6, linked with Adelaide Univ., and specializing in 'advanced' verse. *See* MCAULEY, JAMES.

ANGRY YOUNG MEN. Group of British writers who emerged after the creative hiatus which followed the S.W.W. They included Kingsley Amis, John Wain, John Osborne and Colin Wilson (qq.v.). Also linked to the group were Iris Murdoch and Ken Tynan.

ANGSTRÖM (awng'-), **Anders Jonas** (1814–74). Swedish physicist, noted for his work in spectroscopy and solar physics. The *Angstrom unit* (named after him), and used to express the wavelength of electro-magnetic radiations has been replaced by the SI unit, i.e. the angstrom = 0.1 of a nanometre.

ANGOLA. Among the crops exported is sisal, which also forms the costume of these masked ritual dancers. *Photo: Hubertus Kanus/Barnaby's Picture Library*

ANGUILLA. *See* under LEEWARD ISLANDS.

ANGUS. Former co. on the E. coast of Scotland, merged in 1975 in Tayside region.

ANHUI (ahnhwoo-ē'). Prov. of E China (formerly Anhwei), watered by the Chang Jiang, and producing cereals, etc. in the N and cotton, rice and tea in the S. There are coal mines, and iron and steel works. The cap. is Hefei. Area 139,900 sq.km (54,000 sq.m); pop. (1978) 45,000.

ANHWEI. *See* ANHUI.

A'NILĪNE (Aminobenzene, $C_6H_5NH_2$). The simplest aromatic base known, originally prepared by the dry distillation of indigo, whence its name (Port. *anil*, indigo). When pure it is a colourless oily liquid; it has a characteristic odour, and turns black in contact with air. It occurs in coal tar, and was discovered in 1826. It is highly poisonous.

ANIMALS. One of the two 'kingdoms' of living things, the science of which is zoology, the other being the vegetable kingdom or plants, the science of which is botany.

As. and plants are fundamentally similar in microscopical structure, being composed of a substance, protoplasm, and the tissues in the more elaborately

Phyla of the Animal Kingdom

1.	PORIFERA or PARAZOA	Sponges.
2.	COELENTERATA	Jelly-fish, sea-anemones, corals, sea-pen.
3.	PLATYHELMINTHES	Flat worms, including tapeworms and flukes.
4.	NEMERTINEA	No popular name, but Nemertine worms.
5.	ROTIFERA or ROTATORIA	Wheel-animalcules.
6.	NEMATODA	Round or thread worms.
7	ANNELIDA	Leeches, earthworms, lugworm, sea-mouse
8.	ARTHROPODA	Barnacles, crabs, woodlice, spiders, ticks, scorpions, centipedes, millipedes, insects.
9.	MOLLUSCA	Mussels, oysters, limpets, snails, cuttlefishes, squids, nautilus, ammonites.
10.	POLYZOA	Moss-polyps, sea-mat.
11.	BRACHIOPODA	Lamp-shells.
12.	CHAETOGNATHA	Arrow-worms.
13.	PHORONIDEA or PODAXONIA	No popular name.
14.	ECHINODERMATA	Starfishes, sea-urchins, sea-cucumbers, stone-lilies.
15.	CHORDATA	Sea-squirts, lancelet, vertebrates, including fishes, frogs, reptiles, birds, and mammals with man.

organized examples of the two kingdoms alike consist primarily of minute particles of protoplasm known as cells. But the macroscopical structure of all the familiar As. and plants is so different that there is no difficulty in distinguishing one from the other, and there is also the important physiological difference that As. are capable of living and developing only by the nutritive assimilations of the protoplasmic tissues of other living organisms, plant or A. As. are dependent on plants, and must have succeeded them in the evolution of living things. But these differences, both anatomical and physiological, between the more complex and familiar As. and plants break down in the simplest, most primitive forms of As., the Protozoa, which are so distinct from other As. that they are given the rank of a sub-kingdom, the rest being assigned to the sub-kingdom Metazoa. Owing to the dying out of formerly existing links, the Metazoa can be classified into a number of primary, definable groups, each of which is known as a phylum, meaning a stock or line of descent; and the classification, or taxonomy, of As. is based on the conception that fundamental structural resemblances indicate kinship, not superficial resemblances such as exist between a whale and a shark, and have been acquired as adaptations to a similar mode of life. Today the more obscure problems of classification may be solved by the electronic microscope and computer analysis.

The views of zoologists differ to a certain extent regarding the number of phyla of Metazoa that may be admitted, but the accompanying list is widely adopted, and includes the names of some familiar animals in each phylum.

Some of these phyla, e.g. Chaetognatha and the Phoronidea, are comparatively unimportant, and the chief interest of the Brachiopoda is geological. On the other hand, the Arthropoda, Mollusca, and Chordata contain a vast number of widely different living forms, quite apart from those known only from their fossil remains.

All the more extensive phyla, including the Protozoa, are subdivided into numerous groups of subordinate status, bearing names of Greek or Latin derivation, the principal subdivisions commonly admitted and arranged according to rank, being subphyla, classes, sub-classes, orders, suborders, tribes, families, sub-families, genera, species, and sub-species.

ANIMAL WORSHIP. A common feature of many primitive religions, arising from animism, totemism, belief in the transmigration of souls under animal forms, or from a desire to propitiate the dangerous or encourage the useful animal. Every variety of A. is eligible, although a preference may be shown for particular types, e.g. the widespread cult of the serpent. Among the animals reverenced are the ancient Egyptian bull, cat, jackal, hawk, ibis, and hippopotamus; the Israelite golden calf; the Hindu cow, monkey, and elephant; and the N. American Indian beaver, buffalo, and deer.

ANIMISM (Lat. *anima*, soul). In psychology and physiology, the view of human personality which rejects materialistic mechanism as a valid explanation of man. In religious theory, the primitive conception of a spiritual reality behind the material one: e.g. the native beliefs in the soul as a shadowy duplicate of the body capable of independent activity, both in life and death. Linked with this is the worship of natural objects such as stones and trees, thought to harbour spirits (naturism), fetishism, and ancestor worship.

ANJOU (oṅzhoo'). An old countship and former prov. in the N. of France: cap. Angers. In 1154 the count of A. became King of England as Henry II, but the territory was lost by John in 1204. In 1480 the countship was annexed to the French crown. The depts of Maine-et-Loire and part of Indre-et-Loire, Mayenne, and Sarthe cover the area.

AN'KARA. Cap. of Turkey, standing on the Anatolian plateau of Asia Minor and having Roman and earlier relics. In 1415 it became permanently Turkish. Constantinople (Istanbul) being in Allied occupation 1918-23, after the F.W.W., in 1923 Mustafa Kemal (Atatürk) declared A. the cap. of the Turkish rep., and proceeded to turn the small provincial town into a 20th cent. city. The President's palace, the palace of the Grand National Assembly, and Atatürk's mausoleum are among the chief buildings. There are 3 univs., the technical univ. serving all the Middle East. Pop. (1975) 1,700,000.

ANKH (angk). Ancient Egyptian symbol (derived from the simplest form of sandal), meaning 'eternal life', as in Tut*ankh*amun. It consists of a 'T' shape surmounted by an oval, and is now a world-wide good luck charm.

A'NNABA. Seaport in Algeria (formerly **Bône**), the name meaning 'city of jujube trees'. There are metallurgical

ANIMAL WORSHIP. The desire to combine the wisdom of man with the strength of the bull and the power of flight of the bird, results in the winged man-headed bulls which ornament the doorways of the palace of Ashur-nazir-pal II in the 9th cent. B.C. *Photo: Courtesy of the British Museum*

industries, and iron ore and phosphates are exported. Pop. (1970) 170,000.

ANNAM. Country of S.E. Asia, incorporated in Vietnam (q.v.) in 1946 as Central Vietnam. A flourishing Bronze Age civilization was in existence in the area when Chinese conquerors penetrated it and held it for centuries. Mongolization was not complete and the people remained basically Indonesian. The Chinese named their conquest An-Nam, 'peaceful south'. Their rule ended in 968 when the 1st native dynasty was estab. In 1884 A. became a French protectorate, and the kings were virtually vassals. The Japanese occupied A. during the S.W.W.

ANNA'POLIS. Seaport of the USA, cap. of Maryland, 3km (2m) from Chesapeake Bay on the Severn r. It was founded c. 1648 as Providence, renamed Anne Arundel, and, in 1695, Annapolis. While Congress met here, Nov. 1783-June 1784, it received Washington's resignation of his commission as C.-in-C. (1783) and ratified the peace treaty (1784) of the War of American Independence. The US Naval Academy (1845) is at A.; John Paul Jones is buried in the chapel crypt and there is a museum with relics of US naval history. Pop. (1970) 30,000.

ANNAPUR'NA. Mountain 8,075 m (26,502 ft) in the Himalayas, Nepal. The N. face was climbed by a Fr. expedition (Maurice Herzog) 1950 and the S. by a British 1970.

ANNE (1665-1714). Queen of Great Britain and Ireland. The 2nd daughter of James, duke of York, who became James II, and Anne Hyde, she received a Protestant upbringing, and in 1683 m. Prince George of Denmark. Of their 17 children only one survived infancy, William, duke of Gloucester, who d. at the age of 12. For the greater part of her life A. was a close friend of Sarah Churchill, wife of John Churchill, afterwards duke of Marlborough; the Churchills' influence helped lead her to desert her father for her brother-in-law, William of Orange, during the revolution of 1688, and later to engage in Jacobite intrigues. She succeeded William on the throne in 1702. She aimed at national unity under the Crown, and recent research shows that her replacement of the Tories by a Whig govt. 1703-4 was her own act, not due to Churchillian influence. The outstanding events of her reign were the War of the Spanish Succession (1702-13), Marlborough's victories at Blenheim, Ramillies, Oudenarde, and Malplaquet, and the union of the English and Scottish parliaments in 1707. A. finally broke with the Marlboroughs in 1710, when Mrs Masham succeeded the duchess as her favourite, and supported the Tory government of the same year.

ANNE (1950-). Princess of the UK. She was b. at Clarence House, London, on 15 Aug. 1950, and is the 2nd child of Queen Elizabeth II and the Duke of Edinburgh. She was ed. at Benenden School, Kent, and estab. a reputation as a horsewoman. In 1973 she m. Lieut. Mark Phillips (1949-) of the Queen's Dragoon Guards, equestrian gold medallist 1972 Olympics. Their son, Peter Mark Andrew Phillips (1977-) was the first untitled direct descendant of Elizabeth II. Their home is at Gatcombe Park, Gloucestershire.

ANNEALING (anē'ling). The heating of a glass or metal for a certain period to a predetermined temperature in order to give it greater ductility and strength.

ANNE OF AUSTRIA (1601-66). Queen of France. Daughter of Philip III of Spain, she m. Louis XIII of France in 1615, and on his death in 1643 became regent for her son, Louis XIV. She was much under the influence of Mazarin, to whom she was supposed to be secretly married.

ANNE OF CLEVES (1515-57). 4th wife of Henry VIII of England. Daughter of John, duke of Cleves, she was recommended to Henry by Thomas Cromwell, who desired an alliance with German Protestantism against the emperor. She proved to be so plain and stolid that Henry had the marriage declared null and void, A. receiving a comfortable pension.

ANNE OF DENMARK (1574-1619). Queen consort of Great Britain. Daughter of Frederick II of Denmark and Norway, she m. in 1589 James VI of Scotland, who became James I of Great Britain in 1603. A. was suspected of Catholic leanings, and was notably extravagant.

ANNECY (ahnsē'). Capital of the dept of Haute-Savoie, France, at the northern end of A. Lake. A beautiful town, it has some light industry, incl. precision instruments. Pop. (1975) 53,000.

ANNE'LIDA. Phylum of animals, including the segmented worms. They are distinguished from the Arthropoda by the absence of jointed appendages, and by the presence of a cavity, part of the coelom, surrounding the alimentary canal. There is a distinct head, and the body is divided into a number of similar segments, which are shut off from one another internally by membraneous

ANNE. Princess Anne and Captain Mark Phillips, before leaving as reserves in Britain's Olympic Equestrian Team for the three-day event in Montreal. *Photo: Keystone Press*

partitions. The A. are divided into 3 principal classes, the *Polychaeta* (or many-bristled worms), *Oligochaeta* (or few-bristled worms) - these two together forming the *Chaetopoda* - and the *Hirudinea* (or leeches), which are entirely destitute of bristles.

ANNIGŌ'NI, Pietro (1910-). Italian artist. He is noted for the etherealized Renaissance style of his portraits, e.g. Elizabeth II in 1955: other sitters incl. the Duke of Edinburgh and Princess Margaret.

ANNO DO'MINI (Lat., in the year of our Lord). In the Christian chronological system, dates since the birth of Christ, denoted by the letters A.D. Earlier years are denoted by the letters B.C. (Before Christ). There is no year 0, so A.D. 1 follows immediately after the year 1. B.C. The system is based on the calculations made in A.D. 525 by Dionysius Exiguus, a Scythian monk, but the birth of Christ should more correctly be placed in 3 B.C. or 4 B.C. It became the standard reckoning when adopted by Bede in the 8th cent.

ANNUNCIATION. The tidings brought to Mary by the angel Gabriel concerning the Incarnation (Luke i, 26-38). The Feast of the A. is kept on 25 March, known as Lady Day.

ANOA. *See* BUFFALO.

A'NŌDE. The electrode at which positive current enters a device. It is the positively charged electrode of an electrolytic cell, the electrode on which the primary stream of electrons impinges in a vacuum tube and the negative terminal of a battery.

ANOPHELES. *See* GNAT.

ANOUILH (anōōiy'), **Jean** (1910-). French playwright and film writer. Though b. in Bordeaux, he grew up in Paris and became a law student and advertising agency man before finding his true bent in the theatre. Constantly concerned with the antithesis of innocence and experience, his plays have frequently been staged in English versions *L'invitation au Château* (1947: Ring Round the Moon), *Colombe* (1950), and *Becket, ou l'honneur de Dieu* (1959), concerned with Becket and Henry II.

ANSCHLUSS (ahn'shloos: Ger., joining). Term used for the union of Austria with Germany, accomplished by Hitler on 12 March 1938.

ANSELM, St (1033?-1109). Churchman, b. near Aosta, in Piedmont. Educated at the abbey of Bec in Normandy, which as an abbot (from 1078) he made the greatest centre of scholarship in Europe, he was appointed abp. of Canterbury by William II in 1093, but was later forced into exile. He was recalled by Henry I, with whom he bitterly disagreed on the investiture of the clergy; a final agreement gave the king the right of temporal investiture and the clergy that of spiritual investiture. A. was canonized in 1494. He holds an important place in the development of scholasticism. In his *Proslogion* he developed the ontological proof of theism, which infers God's existence from our capacity to conceive of a perfect Being. His most important work, *Cur deus homo,* deals with the Atonement.

ANSHAN (ahnshahn'). Chinese city and iron and steel centre, in Liaoning prov., 89 km (55 m) S.E. of Shenyang (Mukden). Started here in 1918, expanded by the Japanese, dismantled by the Russians, the iron works were restored by the Communist govt of China: production 6 million tonnes of steel annually. Pop. c. 1,000,000.

ANSON, George, baron (1697-1762). British admiral. B. in Staffs, he entered the navy at the age of 15. In 1740, during the war with Spain, he commanded a squadron of 6 ships with which he attacked Spanish colonies and shipping in S. America. After circumnavigating the globe, he returned to England in 1744 with only a single ship, but bringing back £500,000 of Spanish treasure. In 1747 he routed a French convoy off Cape Finisterre, and was created Baron A. of Soberton. His chaplain's account of his *Voyage Round the World* (1748) is a maritime classic.

ANT. Insect of the family Formicoidae of the order Hymenoptera, to which also belong the wasps and the bees.

About 10,000 different species of As. are known. All are social in habit, and live in nests of various kinds. Each A. society or community consists of a number of sterile wingless females, termed workers, and a smaller number of fertile females and males, which are usually winged. The male is smaller and more slender than the female. At certain times of the year the winged males and females leave the parental nest in large numbers on their nuptial flight. Mating takes place in the air, after which the males soon perish, while the fertilized females (or queens, as they are now called), lose their wings and settle down to colony founding. In some As. the workers are all alike, but in others large-headed 'soldiers' may be distinguished from the small-headed workers.

The most primitive As. are carnivorous and hunt other insects. The tribal As. of the tropics lead a wandering nomadic life. Others are pastoralists, feeding chiefly upon saccharin matter obtained from the extra-floral nectaries of various plants, but more especially on honey dew, discharged by aphids and related insects. The As. induce the aphids to void this substance by stroking them with the antennae; some As. even keep and protect them. Honey As. use certain of their own workers or soldiers as receptacles for storing collected honey dew; when hungry, they stroke these 'repletes' and receive from them regurgitated honey dew. Harvesting As. collect, husk, and store plant seeds in special chambers or granaries. The robber As. (*Formica sanguinea*) raid nests of other As., in particular those of *F. fusca*, and carry off Fusca pupae to their own nests, where they are destined to live as slaves, tending the brood of their captors. The so-called white As. or termites (q.v.) belong to a very different group of insects.

ANT. More than a thousand species of ant are found in Australia, and among those unique to the continent is the bull dog or soldier ant (*Myrmecia gulosa*) which has an extremely powerful sting. Here, one of the workers, who feed the larvae on dead insects brought into the nest, is moving her charges round. *Photo: Courtesy of the Australian Information Service*

ANTANANARIVO. *See* TANANARIVE.

ANTARCTICA. Continent surrounding the South Pole, area *c.* 13,727,000 sq.km (5,300,000 sq.m), and the ice-covered sea surrounding it. In a broad sense the term covers all land and sea S. of about latitude 60° S. There are no permanent inhabitants but research stations are maintained. The continent is a vast faulted plateau of very ancient rocks with flanking Tertiary deposits showing affinity with geological occurrences in New Zealand and S. America. The Vinson Massif in the Ellsworth Mts rises to 5,139 m (16,860 ft) and Mt Erebus, 3,795 m (12,450 ft) on Ross Is. is the most southerly known active volcano. The great ice sheet which covers the continent reaches a thickness of *c.* 650m (2,000 ft). The Ross or Great Ice Barrier is a great shelf of ice formed by several glaciers coalescing in the Ross Sea. The coasts are backed by huge walls of ice. There is thought to be considerable mineral wealth.

A number of islands, all barren and windswept, lie off the continent: these include the S. Shetlands, S. Orkneys, the S. Sandwich islands and Peter 1st Is.

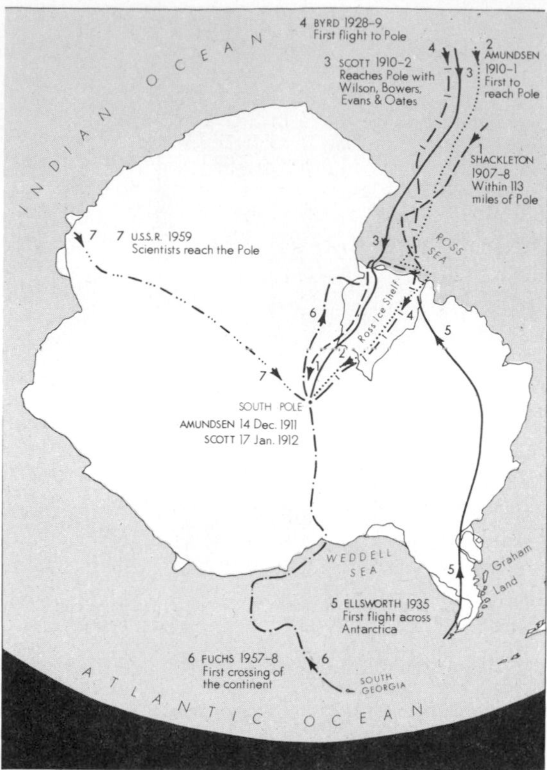

ANTARCTICA. Routes of most famous expeditions.

CLIMATE, VEGETATION. Winter is almost continuous in A., no month being free from frost, and even the summer mean temperature is below freezing-point. Winter temperatures are usually below −18° C/0° F. Southerly winds of great velocity are common. Rain seldom falls. There is very little soil cover. Lichens and mosses encrust the rock faces; there are no trees, and few other plants. Whales, seals, and penguins visit the seas and shore, and many sea birds nest there in summer. The continent once formed part of Gondwanaland, and fossil remains dating back to 230 million years ago have been found which incl. remains of a man-like ape similar to E Africa's Proconsul.

POLITICAL CLAIMS. The international Antarctic Treaty (1959) reserved A. for peaceful purposes of research, and 'froze' existing claims to territorial sovereignty. In 1980 the signatory states (those recognised as conducting substantial research in A., chiefly European powers and the USA) signed a convention on exploitation of resources, notably oil, gas, fish and krill.

Exploration. The first to sail in Antarctic seas was James Cook in 1773-4, and early in the 19th cent. discoveries were made to the south of S. America (E. Bransfield, J. Briscoe, Bellingshausen, and J. Weddell) and Australia (D. d'Urville and C. Wilkes). In 1841-2 James Ross found great land areas in S. Victoria Land and sighted the Great Ice Barrier. The *Challenger* crossed the Antarctic Circle in 1872 and de Gerlache wintered in A. in 1897-9. Scott's initial attempt to reach the S. Pole in 1902-4 (82° 17′ S.) was followed by a number of others, e.g. Shackleton 1908-9; Amundsen succeeded on 16 Dec.

1911, and Scott himself on 18 Jan. 1912. In 1957-8 Vivian Fuchs made the first overland journey across the continent via the Pole.

The first aerial flights were made in 1928 by H. Wilkins over Graham Land, and in 1929 R. E. Byrd flew to to the Pole and back from the Ross Ice Barrier in 19 hours. In 1935 L. Ellsworth flew 2,300 m across unknown territory. The largest expedition ever attempted was that under Byrd in 1946, which consisted of 4,000 men, 13 ships, 29 land-based planes, and 35 seaplanes from tenders.

ANTARCTICA. A group of Adélie penguins in Hope Bay, at the north-east tip of the Antarctic Peninsula. *Photo: N. Leppard/British Antarctic Survey*

ANTARCTIC OCEAN. Popular name for the reaches of the Atlantic, Indian and Pacific Oceans extending S. of the A. Circle (66° 33′ S.). The term is not used by the Internat. Hydrographic Bureau.

ANTEATER. Name given to several mammals that live wholly or mainly on ants, for which diet they are structurally adapted with toothless jaws, extensile tongue, and powerful fore-paws for breaking up the ant-hills. The Great A. or Ant Bear (*Myrmecophaga tridactyla*), is common in Brazil, and stands 30cm (2ft) high. The name is also applied to the aardvark, the echidna, and the pangolins (qq.v.).

A'NTELOPE. Popular name for a number of distinct kinds of hoofed animals of the family Bovidae of the order Artiodactyla. A few medium-sized genera are found in Asia, notably the chiru of Tibet; the saiga of Tartary; several sorts of gazelles that inhabit the deserts of Iran and Arabia spread into India, to which the blackbuck, the four-horned A., and the nilgai are restricted. But most A. are known from Africa where they range from the extreme N. to the Cape Province; some of the duikers do not surpass a cat in height, whereas the eland is as bulky as large cattle. Other important species are the kudu, oryx or gemsbok (q.v.), sable A., gnu or wildebeest (q.v.),hartebeest, water-buck, impala, and springbok (q.v.). There are no true As. in the Americas, although the prongbuck passes under that name in the USA.

ANTHEIL (ahn'tīl), **George** (1900-59). American composer, the son of a Polish political exile. He was at one time a concert pianist, but was best known for his *Ballet Mécanique*, scored for anvils, aeroplane propellers, electric bells, automobile horns, and 16 player pianos.

ANTHĒ'LION. Antisun; a kind of solar halo, sometimes appearing at the same altitude as the Sun, but opposite to it.

ANTHONY (an'toni), **St** (*c.* 250-350). Founder of Christian monasticism. B. in Egypt, he renounced at the age of 20 all his possessions and lived in a tomb, and at 35 sought yet further solitude on a mountain in the desert. In 305 he founded the first cenobitic Order, or community of Christians following a rule of life under a superior. When he was about a hundred, A. went to Alexandria and preached against the Arians. A.'s temptations in the desert were a popular subject in art.

ANTHONY OF PADUA, St (1195-1231). B. at Lisbon, the son of a nobleman, he became an Augustinian monk, but in 1220 joined the Franciscans. He opposed the relaxations introduced into the Order. Like St Francis, he is said to have preached to animals. He d. at Padua and was canonized in 1232.

ANTHOZŌ'A (Gk, flower-animals) or **Actinozoa.** Class of animals of the phylum Coelenterata, including sea-anemones, corals, etc. They are sedentary polyps, and never pass through a medusa stage. The most important divisions are the Alcyonaria, Actiniaria, and Madreporaria.

A'NTHRACENE ($C_{14}H_{10}$). White glistening crystalline hydrocarbon with a faint blue fluorescence when pure. Its melting-point is about 216° C., and its boiling point 351° C. It occurs in the high boiling fractions of coal tar, where it was discovered in 1832 by Laurent and Dumas.

A'NTHRACĪTE (Gk *anthrakos*, coal). A hard, dense glossy variety of coal, containing over 90 per cent of fixed carbon, and a low percentage of ash and of volatilizable matter, which causes it to burn without flame, smoke, or smell. It gives an intense heat, but is slow-burning and slow to catch alight, and is therefore unsuitable for use in open fires. Its characteristic composition is thought to be due to the action of bacteria in disintegrating the coal-forming material when it was laid down in the carboniferous age. Amongst the chief sources of A. coal are S. Wales, Pennsylvania, the Donbas (q.v.), and the Shanxi province of China.

A'NTHRAX. A disease caused by the anthrax bacillus; woolsorters' disease. It is principally a disease of animals, especially cattle and sheep, and is caught by man from infected hides and fleeces. Consequently, most countries have strict laws regulating the importation of these articles. The disease is so deadly to animals and so dangerous to man that to guard against its spread every animal exposed to it must be slaughtered and burnt. The first sign is a boil on the part of the body exposed to contact; after a few days this grows into a large red area with a dark scab surrounded by clear blisters.

A'NTHROPOID APES (from Gk for 'resembling man'). A group of the Primates comprising fossil and extinct species, and also living species (gorilla, chimpanzee, orang-utan, and gibbon, qq.v.), referred to as the family Simiidae, which is associated with the Hominidae (Man) in the section Anthropomorpha.

ANTHROPO'LOGY (Gk *anthropos*, man; *logos*, science). The natural history of Man. The term was first used by Otto Casmann in 1594, but A. did not develop as a science until the general adoption of evolutionary theory in the second half of the 19th cent.

ANTHROPO'METRY. The science that deals with the measurement of the human body, particularly stature, body-weight, cranial capacity, length of limb, etc., in the two sexes and the different living and extinct races of mankind.

ANTHROPOMOR'PHISM. The attribution of human characteristics to beings above or below humanity in the order of the universe. Plants, animals, and even inanimate objects or forces such as stones or the winds are sometimes given human qualities, but A. is generally limited to the conception of gods in human form. Seen in its fullest development in the mythologies of Scandinavia and Greece, it tends in more advanced religions such as Christianity to be reduced to metaphor.

ANTHRŌPO'SOPHY. System of mystical philosophy developed by Rudolf Steiner (q.v.), who claimed to possess a power of intuition giving him access to knowledge not attainable by scientific means.

ANTIBES (oṅtēb'). Town at the W. base of Cap d'A., forming with Juan les Pins at the E. base (developed from 1925), a resort on the Fr. Riviera, dept Alpes Maritimes. Pop. (1973) 48,000.

ANTIBĪO'TIC. A chemical substance produced by living micro-organisms such as moulds and bacteria, which is capable of destroying or preventing the growth of other micro-organisms. Under some conditions a disease-causing organism, originally susceptible, may become resistant to the effect of an A., hence 2 or more As. are often used in combination with other drugs. Since the introduction of the first A., penicillin (q.v.) in the 1940s, they have greatly contributed to the decline of tuberculosis, venereal diseases, pneumonia, etc.

ANTIBODY. Any of the proteins produced in the blood in response to the presence of a bacterium, virus or a transplanted kidney or heart, which attach themselves to the 'invader' or antigen and help destroy it - the immune reaction.

ANTICHRIST. The great opponent of Christ, by whom he is finally to be conquered. Although the term first occurs in Christian writings, the idea of conflict between Light and Darkness is present in Persian, Babylonian, and Jewish literature, and influenced early Christian thought. A. may be a fake Messiah, or be connected with false teaching, or be identified with an individual, e.g. Nero at the time of the persecution, and the Pope and Napoleon in later Christian history.

A'NTICLINE. Geological term for a fold in the earth's crust in which the beds dip on each side of a central axis, thus forming a sort of arch, which, however, is seldom preserved intact. The fold may be undulating or sharply curved. Should one side of an anticlinal fold be compressed until it is nearly vertical, it forms a monocline. A SYNCLINE is the geological term for the converse - the structure produced when beds are folded so that they dip towards a central axis, giving rise to a trough or basin.

ANTI-COM'INTERN PACT (Anti-Communist Pact). Agreement signed between Germany and Japan on 25 Nov. 1936, opposing Communism as a menace to peace and order. The pact received the adhesion of Italy in 1937 and of Hungary, Spain, and Manchukuo in 1939. It became a dead letter in 1945.

ANTI-COSMOS. *See* MOHOLE.

ANTICYCLONE. Area of high atmospheric pressure. As. are caused by descending air, which becomes warm and dry. From a calm centre winds radiate, taking a clockwise direction in the N. hemisphere, and anticlockwise in the S. hemisphere. They are associated with clear weather and are distinguished by the absence of rain and violent winds. In summer they bring hot, sunny days, and in winter fine, frosty spells, though fog and low cloud are not uncommon in winter anticyclonic weather.

ANTIETAM (antē'tam), **Battle of.** Decisive engagement of the American Civil War (sometimes called Battle of Sharpsburg) on 17 Sept. 1862 at A. Creek, off the Potomac r. Gen. McClellan blocked the advance of Lee on Washington.

ANTIGEN. *See* ANTIBODY.

ANTI'GONĒ. In Greek legend, a daughter of Jocasta, by her son Oedipus (q.v.).

ANTI'GONUS (382-301 B.C.). A general of Alexander the Great, after whose death in 323 he made himself master of Asia Minor. He was defeated and slain by Seleucus at the battle of Ipsus.

ANTIGUA (ahntē'gwah) **and Barbuda.** Two of the Leeward Islands. Antigua was discovered by Columbus in 1493, and first settled by Britain in 1632. An assoc. state of the UK from 1967, it became independent with Barbuda within the Commonwealth in 1981. Sea island cotton is exported, and there is a tourist industry. The cap is St John's. Area 442 sq.km (171 sq.m); pop. (1981) 74,000, incl. Barbuda and (uninhabited) Redonda.

ANTIHISTAMINE. *See* HISTAMINE.

ANTI'LLĒS. Name sometimes used to describe the whole group of West Indian Islands, which are divided into Greater A. (Jamaica, Cuba, Puerto Rico, and Haiti-Dominican Rep.), and Lesser A.

ANTIMATTER. In physics, a form of matter in which all the attributes of an ordinary atomic particle, such as electrical charge and spin are reversed. Such antiparticles can be created in particle accelerators, such as those at CERN (q.v.) and America's Fermilab, and are of vital potential importance. For example, nuclear fusion of two ordinary protons would result in a fraction of their mass being converted to energy (about 1%), whereas fusion of a proton and an antiproton would result in the complete destruction of both, with all their mass (100%) being converted into energy.

A'NTIMONY. A metallic element, symbol Sb, at. no. 51, at. wt 121.76. In the ordinary form it is a silver-white metal, brittle, and readily powdered. It occurs chiefly as stibnite, and is used in a number of alloys and as a photo-sensitor, with response in blue and blue-green.

A'NTIOCH (-ok). Ancient capital of the Greek kingdom of Syria, founded 300 B.C. by Seleucus Nicator in memory of his father Antiochus, and for long famed for its splendour and luxury. Under the Romans it was an early centre of Christianity. The site is occupied by the Turkish town of Antakiyah; pop. (1970) 57,600.

ANTĪ'OCHUS (-ok). Name of 13 kings of Syria of the Seleucid dynasty. A. I (b. 324; reigned 281-261 B.C.), son of Seleucus, one of the generals of Alexander the Great, earned the title of A. Soter or Saviour by his defeat of the Gauls in Galatia (278 B.C.). His son A. II (b. 286; reigned 261-246 B.C.), was known as A. Theos, the Divine. During his reign the eastern provinces broke away from the Graeco-Macedonian rule, and set up native princes. A. III the Great (b. *c.* 241; king 223-187 B.C.), grandson of A. II, secured a loose suzerainty over Armenia and Parthia (209), overcame Bactria, received the homage of the

Indian king of the Kabul valley, and returned by way of the Persian Gulf (204 B.C.). He took possession of Palestine, entering Jerusalem in 198 B.C. He crossed into N.W. Greece, but was decisively defeated by the Romans at Thermopylae in 191 and at Magnesia in 190 B.C. He had to abandon his domains in Asia Minor, and perished at the hands of the people of Elymais. A. IV (king 175-164 B.C.), 2nd son of A. III, was known as A. Epiphanes, the Illustrious; he occupied Jerusalem about 170 B.C., seizing much of the Temple treasure, and instituted worship of the Greek type in the Temple. This produced the revolt of the Jewish people under the Maccabees, and A. died before he could suppress it.

A. VII Sidetes (king 138-129 B.C.), the last strong ruler of the dynasty, took Jerusalem in 134 B.C., reducing the Maccabees to subjection, and fought successfully against the Parthians. Under A. XIII Asiaticus (reigned 69-65 B.C.), the last of the dynasty, Syria was converted into a province by Pompey.

ANTI'PODĒS (Gk *anti*, opposite; *podes*, feet). Places exactly opposite one another on the globe. In Britain, Australia and New Zealand are sometimes so called. The Antipodes Islands S.E. of New Zealand are approx. the A. of London.

ANTIRRHINUM (antirīn'um) or **snapdragon.** Genus of plants belonging to the same group as the foxglove and toad flax (Scrophulariaceae). *A. majus*, a native of central and southern Europe, is a familiar garden flower.

ANTI-SEMITISM. *See* JEWS.

ANTISE'PTICS. Substances which kill or hinder the growth of germs. As. began to be evolved almost as soon as Pasteur's discoveries made medical men familiar with the properties of microbes about the middle of the 19th cent. Lord Lister revolutionized surgery by operating in a spray of carbolic acid, but 'antiseptic' has now been almost entirely replaced by 'aseptic' surgery. The number of different As. in use today is very large.

ANTI-VIVISECTION. Movement for the abolition of vivisection, i.e. experiments upon living animals. Vivisection is defended on the grounds that it results, or may result, in discoveries of great importance to medical science. It is attacked on the grounds that it is immoral to inflict pain on helpless creatures, even for the best of motives, that it is unjust that animals should suffer in order that men may benefit, that it is unscientific in that results achieved with animals may not be paralleled with human beings, and that vivisection has not added to man's power over disease. Anti-vivisectionists demand the repeal of legislation permitting experiments on animals by licensed scientific workers.

ANT LION. Larval form of the family of winged insects Myrmeleonidae common in Europe (not Britain) and the US. The common A.L. (*Myrmeleon formicarius*) has at this stage a large head and big toothed mandibles. It snares its prey by making, and lying concealed at the bottom of, a pit of loose sandy soil which sends unwary passing insects slipping down into its waiting jaws.

ANTOFAGA'STA. Port of N. Chile, cap. of a prov. of the same name. Nitrates, etc., from the Atacama desert are exported. There is a univ. (1957). Pop. (1975) 150,000.

ANTONINE'S WALL. Line of fortifications built by the Romans across central Scotland from the Clyde to the Forth in A.D. 142, during the reign of the emperor Antoninus Pius. By 200 it was abandoned in favour of Hadrian's Wall.

ANTONĪ'NUS PĪ'US (A.D. 86-161). Roman emperor. The son of a consul, he was adopted as heir by the emperor Hadrian early in 138, and became emperor a few months later, on Hadrian's death. His long reign was peaceful and prosperous, and he made various legal reforms.

ANTŌNIŌ'NI, Michelangelo (1912-). Italian film director, famous for his subtle analysis of neuroses and personal relationships among the leisured classes of society, e.g. *L'Avventura* (1960), *La Notte* (1961), and *Blow-Up* (1967).

ANTONY, Mark. *See* MARK ANTONY.

ANTRIM. N.E. county of Northern Ireland, separated from Scotland by the 32km (20m) wide North Channel. The coastal districts are hilly, and on the N.W. coast is the remarkable structure of the Giant's Causeway. The boggy lowlands of the interior produce peat. The pop. is mainly Protestant and of Scottish descent. Industries are located in and near Belfast. Area 2,906 sq.km (1,122 sq.m); pop. (1971) 712,700.

A'NTWERP (Antwerpen). City and chief commercial centre of Belgium, one of the principal ports of N.W. Europe; it is situated on the Escaut (Scheldt), 88km (55m) from the North Sea, and its trade passes down the estuary of the Scheldt, which lies in Dutch territory.

It was not until the 15th cent. that A. rose to prosperity; from 1500 to 1560 it was the richest port in N. Europe. After this A. was distracted by religious troubles and the Netherlands revolt against Spain. In 1648 the treaty of Westphalia gave both shores of the Scheldt estuary to the United Provinces, which closed it to Antwerp trade. The treaty of Paris, 1814, opened the estuary to all nations on payment of a small toll to the Dutch, abandoned 1863. During the F.W.W. A. was in German hands from Oct. 1914 to Nov. 1918; during the S.W.W. from May 1940 to Sept. 1944.

Architecturally the city is well laid out. The Gothic cathedral was begun in the 14th cent., but finished only in 1518; also noteworthy are the Bourse (1872), the house of the 16th cent. printer Plantin, and the Museum. Besides the extensive merchant business, A. has a considerable industry in ship-repairing and ship-building, diamond-cutting, oil-refining, petro-chemicals, and textiles in silk, cotton, wool and man-made fibres. Pop. (1971) 673,260.

ANŪ'BIS. Egyptian god of the tomb, usually shown with the head of a jackal. He is often identified with the Greek Hermes.

ANURADHAPU'RA or **Anuradha.** Cap. of N. Central prov., Sri Lanka, with ruins of the cap. of the Sinhalese kings 5th cent. B.C. - 8th cent. A.D., lost until rediscovered in the jungle in the mid 19th cent. It is a Buddhist pilgrimage centre, with a Bo-tree descended from the original.

ANVERS. French form of ANTWERP.

ANYANG (anyahng'). City in Henan prov., China, the cap. of the Shang dynasty (13-12th cents. BC). Rich archaeological remains have been uncovered from the 1930s. Pop. (1970) 225,000.

ANZAC. Acronym (1915) from the initials of the Australia and New Zealand Army Corps, but applied in general to all troops of both countries serving in the F.W.W. and to some extent those in the S.W.W. Most famous of their campaigns was that in Gallipoli: the date of their landing, 25 April 1915, is marked by a public holiday, Anzac Day, in both countries.

ANTWERP. The city's port facilities have been completely modernized since 1956, but there are still magnificent survivals from its past. This elaborately carved staircase is in the home which Rubens had built to his own design, and where he lived from 1610 to 1644. *Photo: Courtesy of the Belgian National Tourist Office*

ANZANI'A. Proposed name of South Africa under black rule.

ANZHERO-SUDENSK (ahnzhe'ro soojensk'). Coal-mining town in W. Siberia, RSFSR, 80km (50m) N. of Kemerovo. Pop. (1977) 105,000.

ANZIO (ahn'tsē-oh). Seaport on the W. coast of Italy, 53km (33m) S.E. of Rome, the site of the Roman town of Antium. The battle of A. beachhead (22 Jan.-23 May 1944), was one of the most bitterly contested operations of the S.W.W.

ANZUS TREATY. Collective security organization estab. 1951 by Australia, New Zealand and the U.S. It was replaced by SEATO (q.v.).

AO'MORI. Port at the head of Mutsu Bay, on the N. coast of Honshu Island, Japan, 40km (25m) N.E. of Hirosaki. The port handles a large local trade. Pop. (1977) 273,000.

AOSTA (ah-os'tah). Italian city, cap. of Valle d'Aosta (French-speaking) autonomous region, 79km (49m) N.W. of Turin. It has extensive Roman remains. Pop. (1971) 35,000.

APACHES (apach'ēs). Group of N. American Indian tribes (Indian 'enemy') related to the Navajo, of whom the surviving members live in reservations in Arizona, the 'A. state', Oklahoma and Mexico. They were considered particularly treacherous by the white settlers, against whom they waged ferocious war. Most famous of their leaders was Geronimo (q.v.). The name A. (pron. apash') has also been given to the Parisian gangster type.

APARTHEID. (apaht'hāt). System of racial segregation practised in the Rep. of South Africa, 'apartness'. Always generally in practice, it was legally formulated in 1948 after the Afrikaners gained control. Pressure of world opinion, the rise of black African states on South Africa's borders, and the need for a larger, skilled labour force internally, has led to its modification, and under Botha (q.v.) the process of rationalisation was being speeded, A. being referred to rather as 'plural democracy'. **Petty A.** refers to racial laws and regulations, such as the prohibition of mixed marriages; **Grand A.** is the long-term plan to create independent homelands on a tribal basis within South Africa. **Neo-apartheid** is the retention of class divisions in the economic field which would mean in effect that the colour power structure remained unaltered. Militant black opposition to the system has grown notably since Soweto (q.v.), for example, the sabotage of Sasolburg (q.v.) in 1980.

APE. Originally a synonym of monkey, and still applied to some species of the latter, such as the Barbary ape of Gibraltar, and the black ape of Celebes; zoologically the term usually signifies the 4 man-like or anthropoid apes (q.v.). Ape City is the popular name for the Yerkes Regional Primate Center, Atlanta, Georgia, USA, where large numbers are kept for physiological and psychological experiment.

APE. A major area of research at Ape City is language. By pushing the buttons on the machine the young chimpanzee can convey the meaning of a vocabulary of words, and develop the rudiments of grammar. *Photo: Courtesy of Yerkes Regional Primate Center*

A'PENNINES. Chain of mountains stretching the length of the Italian peninsula. A continuation of the Maritime Alps, from Genoa it swings across the peninsula to Ancona on the E. coast, and then back to the W. coast and into the 'toe' of Italy. The system is continued over the

Strait of Messina along the N. Sicilian coast, then across the Mediterranean sea in a series of islands to the Atlas mountains of N. Africa. The **Lunar A.** are a mtn. range SE of the Sea of Showers.

APE'RIENT. *See* PURGATIVES.

APHID (ā'fid). Insect of the family Aphididae, also known as the plant louse or greenfly. Colonies live on the leaves and stems of plants, feeding on the sap, and excreting honeydew (*see* ANT). There may be 2,000 million of them in a hectare (2 acres). They also transmit virus disease, and have been regarded as unmitigated pests, but recent research suggests that they remove surplus sugar by making honeydew, which promotes fertility in the soil beneath by raising the rate of nitrogen fixation.

APHRODISIAC (from *Aphrodite* the Greek goddess of love). Anything arousing or increasing sexual desire. Sexual activity can be stimulated in men and animals by drugs affecting the pituitary gland, for clinical and commercial farming purposes, but preparations commonly sold as As. are valueless, e.g. powdered rhinoceros horn in the East, or dangerous, e.g. cantharidin. Psychological tests seem to show that impotence is usually the result of anxiety or other stress. However, there is some evidence that alkaloid substances, e.g. caffeine, cocaine, LSD, morphine and nicotine, affect the brain by increasing any sensual pleasure.

APHRODĪ'TE. Greek goddess of love identified with the Roman Venus, the Syrian Astarte, and the Babylonian Ishtar. According to Homer, A. was the daughter of Zeus and Dione, but Hesiod says she sprang from the foam of the sea. She was the wife of Hephaestus (Vulcan), and the mother of Eros, and received the prize of beauty from Paris. Cyprus, Cythera, Corinth, and Eryx in Sicily were centres of her worship. The Greeks distinguished between A. Urania (goddess of the sky) and A. Pandemos (goddess of all the people, i.e. of marriage and family life), and in the course of time the former became goddess of the higher, purer type of love, while the latter represented sensual lust.

APIA (ah'pē ah). Cap. and port of Western Samoa, on the N. coast of Upolu island, in the West Pacific. It was the home of Robert Louis Stevenson 1889-94. Pop. (1976) 30,000.

Ā'PIS. Sacred bull, worshipped by the anc. Egyptians as a god, chiefly at Memphis.

APO'CALYPSE. Form of religious writing which emerged during the Jewish Hellenistic period. The earliest example is the O.T. book of Daniel; during the 19th cent. many later apocalyptic books were discovered. In the N.T. the book of Revelation is frequently referred to specifically as the A.

All As. share a common purpose of stimulating faith in God in times of distress by graphic portrayal of the future in terms of triumph and deliverance. They also emphasize that the victory of God at the end of the world will be preceded by evil times.

APOCALYPSE. Movement among writers which developed from Surrealism in 1938, and included G. S. Fraser, Henry Treece, J. F. Hendry, Nicholas Moore, and Tom Scott. Largely influenced by the work of Dylan Thomas, it favours Biblical symbolism and thrusts aside the extremes of political theory and the pressures of a mechanized age in an attempt to obtain integrated expression of the self. Apocalyptic writers have also been active in America under the name of the International Workshop.

APOLLINAIRE (ahpollēnār'), **Guillaume.** Abbreviated name of Guillaume Apollinaire de Kostrowitsky (1880-1918), French poet. Of aristocratic Polish descent, although of illegitimate birth, he was b. in Rome and ed. in Monaco, but in 1898 went to Paris. There he was a leader of the *avant garde* in literary and artistic circles. His lyrics (*Alcools* and *Calligrammes*), his novel *Le Poète Assassiné*, and play *Les Mamelles de Tirésias* show him as a representative of the cubist and futurist manner, and his work greatly influenced younger French writers, such as Aragon.

APO'LLO. Greek god, son of Zeus and Leto, and twin brother of Artemis. A. was the leader of the Muses, the god of music, song, and poetry, of agriculture and the pastoral life. He was supposed to have been born on the island of Delos, and he features in a great number of the Greek myths and legends. The chief centres of his cult were Delphi, Delos, and Didyma in Asia Minor. From Delphi his worship spread to Italy, where he was recognized as the god of healing, oracles, and prophecy. Ancient statues show A. as the embodiment of the Greek ideal of male beauty.

The **A. Project** (1961-72) was launched by J. F. Kennedy to land a man on the Moon (q.v.).

APOLLŌ'NIUS OF RHODES (fl. 220-180 B.C.). Greek poet, author of the epic *Argonautica*.

APOLLONIUS OF TY'ANA (fl. A.D. 50). Greek ascetic philosopher of the Neo-Pythagorean school. He travelled in Babylonia and India, where he acquired a wide knowledge of oriental religions and philosophies, and taught at Ephesus. He was credited with many miraculous powers.

APOLLO OF RHODES. *See* COLOSSUS.

APOLOGE'TICS (Gk *apologeisthai*, to speak in defence). Refutation of attacks on the Christian faith. Famous apologists include Justin Martyr, Origen, St Augustine, Thomas Aquinas, Blaise Pascal, and Joseph Butler. The questions raised by modern scientific and historical discoveries have widened the field of A. Principal topics are: the claim that religion is merely a projection of the group mind or a psychological illusion; the denial of the existence of God as a Creative Mind in the light of evolutionary theory; the nature of Revelation; the historical truth of the gospel story; and the basis of Christian ethic, first assailed in modern times by Nietzsche.

A'POPLEXY. *See* CEREBRAL HAEMORRHAGE.

APO'STLE (Gk, envoy). In the N.T., the missionaries sent out by Jesus, esp. the Twelve Disciples. In the earliest days of Christianity the term was extended to include some who had never known Jesus in the flesh, notably St Paul; the *Apostolic Age* in Church history is the period during which the affairs of the infant church were directed by men who either had personal knowledge of Jesus or had received their knowledge and their commission to instruct and preach from members of the Twelve or St Paul.

APOSTLES. Discussion group at the Univ. of Cambridge, founded 1820. Members incl. Tennyson, G. E. Moore, Strachey, Leonard Woolf, Keynes, and Guy Burgess and Anthony Blunt.

APOSTOLIC SUCCESSION. The doctrine in the Christian Church that certain spiritual powers and supernatural grace were received by the first Apostles direct from Christ Himself, and have been handed down in the ceremony of 'laying on of hands' from generation to generation by those who are the only true representatives of the Faith originally entrusted to the Saints.

APO'THECARY. An early name for a person who mixed and dispensed medicines, a pharmacist. The word retains its original meaning in USA and other countries, but in England an A. became a licensed medical practitioner. The Society of Apothecaries (constituted by Royal Charter in 1617) was by Act of Parliament (1815) given the legal right to grant licences to practise medicine in England and Wales.

APPALĀ'CHIANS. Mountain system of eastern N. America, stretching *c.* 2,400 km (1,500 m) from Alabama in the S.W. to Quebec prov. in the N.E., composed of very ancient rocks, much worn down. They consist of 4 zones: the Allegheny and Cumberland plateaus; the great A. valley; the Blue Ridge, containing the highest peak, Mt Mitchell, 2,045 m (6,684 ft); and the Piedmont plateau. The E. edge is marked by a fall line, where Philadelphia, Baltimore, Washington, and other large cities stand. The A. are generally forested; coal is mined in the E. The *A. Trail,* a 3,200 km (2,000 m) scenic foot trail crosses 14 eastern states and runs from Mt Katahdin, Maine, to Springer Mtn, Georgia.

APPALACHIANS. The Blue Ridge mountains, one of the southern ranges of the Appalachians, begin in southern Pennsylvania, but rise to their highest in Virginia. Maby Mill on Blue Ridge Parkway is typical of their still picturesque remoteness. *Photo: Courtesy of U.S. Travel Service*

APPEASEMENT. Name given to the generally conciliatory policy adopted by the British government, particularly under Neville Chamberlain, towards the Nazi-Fascist dictators. It was strongly opposed by Winston Churchill, but the Munich Pact of 1938 was almost universally hailed as its justification. When Czechoslovakia was occupied by the Germans in March 1939, A. was definitely abandoned.

APPENDICITIS (-sī'tis). Inflammation of the vermiform *appendix,* a small blind extension of the bowel about the size of a little finger, leading off the bottom of the caecum or blind gut, which forms the first part of the large bowel and lies low on the right-hand side of the abdomen. The appendix is very liable to inflammation, because it is narrow, can easily become twisted and kinked, and is a blind alley, so that faecal matter is easily trapped in it and decomposes, and the bacteria which swarm in the bowel multiply to a harmful extent. Sometimes a foreign body sets up inflammation. In acute A. the festering contents suddenly break through into the peritoneum, and the infection spreads rapidly through the abdomen. Often the attack comes on suddenly, usually in the night, with a sharp stabbing pain low down in the right side of the belly, making the patient vomit. He has a high temperature and quick pulse and breathing. The belly is very tender and hard. The usual treatment is operation at the earliest moment: the abdomen is cut open and the appendix is removed. The appendix is not necessary to healthy life.

APPERT (ahpār'), **Nicolas** (1750-1841). French pioneer of food preservation by canning; author of *L'art de conserver les substances animales et végétales.*

APPLE. Fruit of *Pyrus malus,* a tree of the family Rosaceae. It has been an important food-plant in Europe from the earliest times, all the cultivated varieties being probably derived from the wild crab-apple. There are several thousand varieties of cultivated As., which may be divided into eating, cooking, and cider apples. They grow best in temperate countries with a cool climate and plenty of rain during the winter. The continent of Europe and N. America (both the USA and Canada) are the main sources of supply, but As. are also produced in Australia, New Zealand, South Africa, and some parts of Asia.

APPLETON, Sir Edward Victor (1892-1965). British physicist. B. in Bradford, Yorks, the son of a millhand, he won scholarships to Cambridge, and from 1920 worked under Rutherford in Cambridge. A.'s researches found the Kennelly-Heaviside (E) layer at 60km and the Appleton (F) layer, with branches, between 3-400 km, with diurnal and seasonal variations affecting radio. A. was prof. of physics at London, 1924-36, and prof. of natural philosophy at Cambridge, 1936-9. Sec. of the Dept of Scientific and Industrial Research 1939-49, he was knighted in 1941. He was closely associated with the initial work in England on the atom bomb. In 1947 he received a Nobel Prize.

APPOMATOX COURT HOUSE. Village in Virginia, USA, 5km (3m) from the modern village of A. and scene of the surrender on 9 April, 1865 of the Confederate Army under General Robert E. Lee to the Federals under General Ulysses S. Grant - the end of the Civil War. In 1954 a National Historical Park was estab. incl. a restored A.C.H.

Ā'PRICOT. Fruit of *Prunus armeniaca,* a tree closely related to the almond, peach, plum, and cherry. A native of the Far East, it has long been cultivated in Armenia, whence it has been introduced into Europe and USA.

APRIL FOOL'S DAY. The first of April, when it is customary in W. Europe to expose somebody to ridicule by causing him to believe some falsehood or to go on a fruitless errand. When he falls into the trap he is known in England as an April Fool; in Scotland as a gowk (cuckoo or fool); and in France as a *poisson d'avril* (April fish).

APSLEY HOUSE. London mansion at Hyde Park Corner, the residence of the dukes of Wellington since the 1st duke acquired it in 1820. In 1947 it was presented to the nation by the 7th duke, and part of it was opened as the Wellington Museum in 1952.

APULEIUS (apūlē'us), **Lucius** (fl. A.D. 160). Roman author and philosopher, who travelled in the eastern parts of the Roman empire, where he became initiated into mystery religions, practised as an advocate at Rome, and retired to N. Africa, giving the rest of his life to literature. In his *Golden Ass* the hero undergoes many romantic adventures. In this work are preserved a number of anc. legends, notably the story of Cupid and Psyche.

APULIA. Region of ITALY.

AQABA (a'kaba), **Gulf of.** Extending for 160km (100m) between the Negev and the Red Sea, its coastline is uninhabited except where at its head the frontiers of Israel, Egypt, Jordan, and Saudi Arabia converge. Here are the 2 ports Eilat or Elath (Israeli) and A. (Jordanian, and the country's only port).

AQUAE SULIS. Roman name of BATH.

AQUARIUM. Institution for the study and display of living aquatic plants and animals. These have been common since Roman times, but the first modern public A. was opened in Regent's Park, London, in 1853. A recent development is the Oceanarium (q.v.).

AQUATINT (a'kwa-). A process of etching in tone. It deals with broad masses in various gradations of tone, and thus differs from the usual type of etching, in which lines are bitten into a metal plate. J. B. le Prince (1734-81) is credited with its invention, and Goya is the most famous exponent of A.

AQUAVIVA (ahkwahvē'vah), **Claudio** (1543-1615). Fifth general of the Society of Jesus. B. at Naples, of noble family, he entered the order in 1567, and became its head in 1581. Under his rule the Society greatly increased in numbers, and the revolt of the Spanish Jesuits was put down. He pub. a treatise on education.

AQUEDUCT (a'kwi-). Artificial channel or conduit for the conveyance of water, commonly an elevated structure of stone, wood, or iron built for conducting water across a valley. Greek As. were marvels of engineering skill, and many of those built by the Romans are still standing, e.g. the A. at Nîmes in S. France, built about A.D. 18. The first modern A. in Britain was that carrying the Bridgewater Canal over the Irwell at Barton, built 1759-72. An outstanding recent A. is the California State Water Project taking water from Lake Oroville in the N., through 2 power plants and across the Tehachapi Mts, more than 177km (110m) to southern California.

AQUĪ'NAS, Thomas (Thomas of Aquino) (*c.* 1226-74). Christian theologian and philosopher, most famous of the Schoolmen of the Middle Ages, and known as *Doctor Angelicus.* Of noble descent, he was b. at the castle of Roccasecca, prov. of Naples, S. Italy, and ed. at Monte Cassino. From 1239 he studied at the univ. of Naples, and in 1244 joined the Dominicans. Under Albertus Magnus he studied at Paris and Cologne. In 1256 he became licentiate in theology at Paris, and soon was remarked for his profound knowledge and dialectical ability. Nine years of teaching, chiefly in Rome (1259-68), were followed by another 4 in Paris. In 1272 he accepted a professorial chair at Naples; he refused the archbishopric, and summoned to the General Council at Lyons by Gregory X, he d. at Fossa Nuova on the way there. In 1323 he was canonized.

A.'s earliest writings were commentaries on the Scriptures, Boethius and Aristotle. In 1259-64 he wrote the *Summa contra gentiles,* showing that reason and faith are complementary and not antagonistic. In 1265 he began to work on the *Summa theologica,* which consists of 3 parts, concerned respectively with the existence and nature of God, the rules of morality, and the life and work of Christ. This last part was not completed. The complete works of A. were pub. in 1787; a modern ed. was launched in 1882 by Leo XIII, who in 1879 directed that A.'s teaching should be the basis of the theology of the Catholic Church.

AQUEDUCT. The Pont du Gard at Nîmes in southern France is a magnificent example dating from *c.* A.D. 18. Water still flows along the top, and the bridge is still used by motor traffic. *Photo: Bernard G. Silberstein/Camera Press*

AQUITAINE. Region of modern France, comprising the depts of Dordogne, Gironde, Landes, Lot-et-Garonne, and Pyrénées-Atlantiques. It coincides roughly with the Roman prov. of Aquitania, and the ancient French prov. of A. It was an English possession 1154-1452.

ARAB EMIRATES, United. State created in 1971 when Britain ended her special relationship with the Trucial Coast sheikhdoms, and comprising Abu Dhabi (q.v.), Ajman, Dubai, Fujairah, Sharjah, Umm el Quwain, and (from 1972) Ras al Khaimah. The largest town of the UAE is Dubai. The pres. is Sheikh Zaid (Abu Dhabi) and the vice-pres. is Sheikh Rashid (Dubai). There are rich oil deposits, espec. in Abu Dhabi. There has been some dissension between the majority who seek greater unity, and those (Dubai and Ras al Khaimah) who fear the greater dominance of Abu Dhabi. Area 83,000 sq.km (32,000 sq.m); pop. (1976) 652,846. M.U.: dirham.

ARABIA. Large peninsula, for the most part desert, in the extreme S.W. of Asia, separated from Africa by the Sinai peninsula, Red Sea, and Gulf of Aden. Arabia proper comprises the independent states of United Arab Emirates, Bahrein, Kuwait, Oman, Qatar, Saudi Arabia, and Yemen (North and South).

A sandy coastal plain of varying width borders the Red Sea, behind which a high mountain chain rises abruptly to *c.* 2,000-2,500m (7-8,000 ft). Behind this range is the extensive plateau of the Nejd, averaging 1,000 m (3,500 ft), with subsidiary ridges imposed on it, and gradually sloping towards the E. coast. The interior (about half of A.'s 3,000,000 sq.km/1,200,000 sq.m) comprises a vast desert area: part of the Hamad (Syrian) desert in the far north; Nafud in northern Saudi Arabia, and Rub' al Khali (Great Sandy Desert) in the south. Rainfall is scanty and day temperatures high. The total pop. is *c.* 12,000,000.

ARAB EMIRATES. The president, Sheikh Zaid of Abu Dhabi, holding a string of 'worry beads', and the vice-president, Sheikh Rashid of Dubai, to the right. *Photo: Courtesy of the Embassy of the United Arab Emirates*

Nomadic Bedouin tribes still roam the interior, rearing camels and sheep, but life in the towns is increasingly sophisticated, e.g. Damman, Dubai, Kuwait and Riyadh.

History. The Arabian civilization was revived by Mohammed during the 7th cent. A.D. from the political chaos which existed, but in the new empire created by militant Islam, A. itself became merely a subordinate state, and its cities were eclipsed by Damascus, Baghdad and Cairo. Nineteenth century colonialism touched only the fringe of A., e.g. Aden (q.v.), and until the 20th cent. the interior was unknown to Europeans. The narratives of the explorers of A. - Gertrude Bell, T. E. Lawrence, H. St John Philby, Freya Stark, and Charles Doughty - are European classics. A new nationalism began actively to emerge at the period of the F.W.W., but only the oil discoveries from 1953 supplied sufficient resources to give the peninsula an important place in the modern world following the S.W.W.

ARABIAN GULF. *See* GULF.

ARABIAN NIGHTS, or **The Thousand and One Nights.** Collection of tales dealing with scenes in Persia. They had been current for many centuries before being introduced to the West by the French orientalist, A. Galland, in 1704. Collections of stories had existed orally since the 10th cent., some being Arabian.

A'RABIC. The main representative of the southern branch of the Semitic languages. Classical Arabic emerged in central Arabia in the 6th cent. A.D. out of the many dialects spoken throughout the peninsula; as the literary language of Islam, with the Koran as its perfect and inimitable ideal, it spread along with the faith of the Prophet to Syria, Palestine, and Mesopotamia; to Egypt, N. Africa, the Sudan, Nigeria, and several more southerly districts; and today, in various distinct dialects, it is the *lingua franca* over a wide area of the Near East and Africa. It has long lost its footholds in Spain (Mozarabic), Sicily, and elsewhere in the Mediterranean, but the Maltese still speak an A. dialect. The A. vocabulary influenced the Persian, Turkish, Hindustani, and Malay languages; it also left traces in Spanish, and other European languages took up terms of astronomy, chemistry, etc., such as *alchemy, alcohol, alkali, alkahest, algebra,* and many more. A. calligraphy was a highly developed art, and ornamental inscriptions play an important part in interior architecture of Islamic countries. The complexity of the script, requiring the printer to use 300 to 1,000 separate characters has been an important factor in maintaining a low level of literacy in Arab countries. Vernacular Arabic differs widely from country to country, the language of Saudi Arabia being considered the purest, and that of Egypt the nearest to a standard version. The media use formal classical Arabic to ensure comprehension throughout the Arab world. There are *c.* 138,000,000 Arabic speakers.

From the 6th cent. and probably earlier Arab poets were skilled, the ode of 30-100 lines with a single rhyme being the favoured form. Arab story-tellers have always been renowned (*see* ARABIAN NIGHTS), but the language barrier hinders appreciation of modern writers in the West. *Al Ahram* (Cairo) is among the world's leading newspapers.

ARABIC NUMERALS. The signs 0 1 2 3 4 5 6 7 8 9 which were in use amongst the Arabs before they were taken over by the peoples of Europe during the Middle Ages in place of the Roman numerals. They appear to have originated in India, and reached Europe by way of Spain.

ARAB-ISRAELI WARS. Series of wars which arose between members of the Arab League (q.v.) and Israel, following the establishment of the Israeli state in Palestine (q.v.). Arab opposition to Zionist aims in Palestine was voiced from 1913, and espec. following the Balfour Declaration (q.v.) of 1917, manifesting itself in anti-Jewish riots during the British mandate in Palestine 1920-48. In 1936 a serious Arab revolt led to a recommendation by a British Royal Commission in 1937 that Palestine be partitioned between the Arabs and the Jews, and a vote in favour was carried in the UN General Assembly in 1947. The Arabs rejected this, and following Britain's surrender of the mandate, hostilities began.

The *First A.-I. War* 1948-9 involved intermittent heavy fighting 14 Oct. 1948-13 Jan./24 Mar. 1949 and resulted in an enlargement on all fronts of the boundaries originally allotted to the new Israeli state by the UN. The *Second A.-I. War* 1956, coincident with the Suez Crisis, 29 Oct.-4 Nov., resulted in the Israeli capture of Sinai and the Gaza strip, but withdrawal after the entry of a UN force. The *Third A.-I. War* 1967, known also as the 'Six Day War' 5-10 June resulted in the Israeli capture of the Golan Heights from Syria; Old Jerusalem and the West Bank from Jordan, and, in the south, the occupation of the Gaza Strip and the Sinai Peninsula as far as the Suez Canal. The *Fourth A.-I. War* 1973, known as the 'October War' 2-22/24 Oct., or sometimes as the 'Yom Kippur War' because Israeli forces were taken by surprise by the Arabs on the 'Day of Atonement', saw the re-crossing of the Suez Canal by well-organized Egyptian forces and initial gains, although some later loss of ground by the Syrians in the North.

The wars resulted in great international tension, in particular from the adoption of the Arab cause by USSR, and of the Israeli by USA, and the misery of the Palestinians led to terrorist outrages by extremist groups, e.g. Black September. By the time of the fourth war, aided by the pressure of oil needs from the Arab countries, world opinion was less sympathetic to the Israeli cause and there was rapprochement between the USA and Egypt.

ARAB-ISRAELI WARS. Having crossed the Suez Canal, Israeli tanks rumble into Egypt on 22 October 1973. Part of the occupied area was within 72 km (45 m) of Cairo. *Photo: Popperfoto*

In 1978 the Camp David Agreements brought Egypt-Israeli peace, but this was denounced by other Arab countries. Israel withdrew from Sinai 1979–82, but no final agreement on Jerusalem and the estab of a Palestinian state on the W Bank was reached.

The *Fifth Arab-Israeli War* resulted from the presence of Palestinian guerrillas in Lebanon, which led to alternate Arab raids on Israel and Israeli retaliatory incursions from 1978. However, on 6 June 1982 Israel launched a full-scale invasion. By 14 June Beirut was encircled, and PLO and Syrian forces were evacuated (mainly to Syria) 21–31 Aug. The president-elect (Bashir Gemayel) of Lebanon was assassinated, and PLO refugees were massacred by Lebanese Christian Phalangist troops. Israeli forces withdrew from Lebanon in 1985.

A'RABISTAN. Former name of the Iranian prov. of Khuzestan, which was revived in the 1980s by the 2 million Sunni Arab inhabitants who demand autonomy. Unrest and sabotage 1979-80 led to a pledge of a degree of autonomy by Ayatollah Khomeini.

ARAB LEAGUE. League formed at Cairo on 22 March 1945, by Egypt, Syria, Iraq, Lebanon, Transjordan (Jordan, 1949), Saudi Arabia, and Yemen. For later members, *see* TABLE OF ARAB COUNTRIES.

Its object was to promote unity among Arab states in particular in opposition to Israel, and most of the members have been involved to varying degrees in the Arab-Israeli Wars (q.v.). In 1976 Palestine, as represented by the Palestine Liberation Organization, was admitted as the 21st member. Because of its negotiations with Israel, Egypt was suspended from membership in 1979, and the HQ were temporarily transferred from Cairo to Tunis.

ARACHNE (arak'-nē). In Greek mythology, a Lydian girl who was so skilful a weaver that she challenged the goddess Athena to a contest. Athena tore A.'s beautiful tapestries to pieces, whereupon A. hanged herself in despair and was transformed into a spider and her weaving became a cobweb. A. in Greek means 'spider'.

ARACHNIDA. A class of animals of the phylum Arthropoda (q.v.), mainly carnivorous, and incl the mites, scorpions and spiders (qq.v.). They have simple eyes and four pairs of legs.

Arab Countries

	Area in 1,000 sq. km.	*Pop. in 1,000s*	*Capital*
Algeria	2,293	22,107	Algiers
Arab Emirates, United	83	1,283	Dubai*
Bahrein	.6	431	Manama
Djibouti	23	297	Djibouti
Egypt	1,000	49,000	Cairo
Iraq	444	15,507	Baghdad
Jordan	98	2,668	Amman
Kuwait	19	1,710	Kuwait
Lebanon	10	2,619	Beirut
Libya	1,780	3,752	Tripoli
Mauritania	1,031	1,656	Nouakchott
Morocco	459	23,117	Rabat
Oman	212	1,228	Muscat
Qatar	11	301	Doha
Saudi Arabia	2,400	11,152	Riyadh
Somalia	700	7,595	Mogadishu
Sudan	2,500	22,972	Khartoum
Syria	186	10,535	Damascus
Tunisia	164	7,259	Tunis
Yemen (North)	195	6,159	San'a
Yemen (South)	160	2,209	Aden
	13,768.6	193,260	

*Largest town, not official capital

ARAD (or'od). Romanian town on the Mures, 160km (100m) N.E. of Belgrade; an important route centre with many industries. Pop. (1971) 139,000.

A'RAFAT, Yassir (1929–). Palestinian politician. Pres. of the Palestine Liberation Organization (PLO) from 1969, he was forced to evacuate Lebanon in 1983, and sought renewed support from Jordan.

ARAFU'RA SEA. Sea between N. Australia and Indonesia, and between the Timor Sea to the W., and Coral Sea to the E.: 1,290 km (800m) long and 560km (350m) wide.

ARAGON (ahrahgoń'), **Louis** (1898–1982). French poet and novelist. Beginning as a Dadaist, he became one of the leaders of Surrealism, pub. vols. of verse and in 1930 joined the Communist party. Taken prisoner in the S.W.W., he escaped to join the underground, experiences reflected in the poetry of *Le Crève-Cœur* (1942) and *Les Yeux d'Elsa* (1944).

A'RAGON. Ancient kingdom of NE Spain, comprising the modern provs. of Huesca, Teruel and Zaragoza, with its cap. at Saragossa. A Roman prov. until taken by the Visigoths, who lost it to the Moors in the 8th cent., it became a kingdom in 1035. United with Castile in 1479, it was in 1978 planned to become an autonomous region.

ARAKA'N. Tapering strip of terr. some 645km (400m) long, on the Bay of Bengal coast and strewn with islands. It is closed in by the Arakan Yoma, a mtn range rising to 3,000 m (1,000 ft). The ancient kingdom of A. was conquered by the Burmese in 1782: Myohaung has ruins of its capital. It was British 1826-1948.

A'RAL SEA. Inland sea or lake, divided between Kazakhstan and Uzbekistan, USSR: 380km (235m) long and 290km (180m) wide, area 62,000 sq.km (24,000 sq.m) decreasing by evaporation. It is fed by the Syr-Darya and Amu Darya.

ARAM, Eugene (1704-59). British murderer. B. in the West Riding, he was a schoolmaster at Knaresborough, and in 1745 was tried and acquitted on a charge of being concerned in the disappearance of a local shoemaker. After achieving some distinction as a philologist, he was arrested at Lynn in Norfolk, following the discovery of a skeleton in a cave at Knaresborough. He was tried at York, confessed to the murder after his conviction, and was hanged. He is the subject of works by Lytton, Hood, etc.

ARAMAIC. A Semitic language in the Near East, the vernacular of Jesus Christ and the Apostles, and probably the one in which the Gospels were first written. The Aramaeans were nomads who set up states in Mesopotamia in the 13th cent. B.C., and flowed over into N. Syria in 12th and 11th cents. B.C. Damascus, Aleppo, and Carchemish were among their chief centres, but all were subjugated by Assyria by the end of the 8th cent. By the end of the 7th cent. Syria and Mesopotamia had become thoroughly Aramaized. A. was the *lingua franca* of the day, and under the Achaemenides it became one of the official languages of the Persian empire. In some isolated villages A. dialects are still spoken by native Christians.

A'RAN. Group of 3 rocky islands (Inishmore, Inishmaan, Inisheer) across the mouth of Galway Bay, Rep. of Ireland, forming a natural breakwater. The inhabitants are Irish-speaking fisherfolk. Area 47 sq.km (18 sq.m); pop. *c.* 2,600.

ARANJUEZ (ahrahn-hweth'). Spanish town on the Tagus, 40km (25m) S.S.E. of Madrid. The palace was for centuries a royal residence. Pop. (1970) 27,300.

ARANY (or'ony), **János** (1817-82). Hungarian writer, b. at Nagyszalonta (now in Romania). His comic epic *The Lost Constitution* (1846) was followed in 1847 by *Toldi*, one of the finest products of the popular national school. In 1860 he settled in Pest as editor of literary reviews. In 1864 appeared his epic masterpiece *The Death of King Buda*. During the last years of his life A. produced the remainder of the *Toldi*-trilogy, and his most personal lyrics.

A'RARAT. Mountain mass in Turkey, near the borders of Armenia S.S.R. and Iran, consisting of Great A., 5,156 m (17,000 ft), and Little A., 3,914 m (12,900 ft). Tradition ascribes to A. the resting-place of the Ark after the deluge.

ARAUCANIAN INDIANS (arōkān'ian). Original inhabitants of central Chile, comprising various tribes. An agricultural and hunting people, they lived in small villages, and were excellent warriors, defeating the Incas and opposing the Spanish forces for 200 years. Some 200,000 still survive living in reserves.

ARAUCĀ'RIA. Genus of coniferous trees allied to the firs, natives of the southern hemisphere, and often attaining a gigantic size. They include the monkey-puzzle tree (*A. imbricata*), the Bunya-Bunya pine (*A. bidwillii*) of Australia, and the Norfolk Island pine (*A. excelsa*).

ARBITRATION. The procedure whereby two nations refer their differences for settlement to a selected person or persons. In the 19th cent. the head of a friendly state or an international commission was usually selected as arbitrator; the 20th cent. has seen 3 attempts to establish permanent machinery for the settlement of disputes - the Hague Court, the League of Nations, and the United Nations.

Proposals for a permanent court were put forward in the 18th cent. by the Abbé de St Pierre and Jeremy Bentham, but the practice of referring disputes to A. did not come into general use until the 19th cent. A well-known example is the dispute between the British and US govts over the *Alabama* during the American Civil War.

The Hague Peace Conference of 1899 led to the setting up of a permanent court of A., and after the F.W.W. the Hague Court was maintained, and a Permanent Court of International Justice also set up to deal with disputes of a legal nature. A number of disputes, mainly frontier problems arising from the peace settlement, were successfully settled between 1920 and 1925. By the Locarno Pact of 1925 France and Germany, and by the Kellogg Pact of 1928 fifty-nine states, agreed to renounce war as an instrument of policy and to refer all differences to A.

Under the Charter drawn up at San Francisco (June 1945), the United Nations pledge themselves to seek a solution to all disputes by negotiation, arbitration, or other peaceful means. If these fail, the parties are to refer the matter to the Security Council. Legal disputes should normally be referred to the International Court of Justice.

ARBOR DAY. Day set apart in USA for the planting of trees along the highways, in parks, etc. It is also observed in S. Australia and New Zealand.

ARBROATH (arbrōth'). Fishing town of Tayside region, Scotland. Created a royal burgh 1186, it was celebrated by Scott as 'Fairport' in *The Antiquary*. In 1320 the Scottish Parliament here asserted their country's independence in a letter to the Pope. Pop. (1971) 22,765.

ARBUTHNOT, John (1667-1735). British physician and author. B. in Kincardineshire, he practised medicine in London, and was physician to Queen Anne 1705-14. He was the friend of Pope, Gay, and Swift, and was the chief author of the satiric *Memoirs of Martinus Scriblerus*. He also developed the national character of John Bull in his *History of John Bull* (1712).

ARBŪ'TUS, or strawberry tree (*Arbutus unedo*). Plant of the family Ericaceae, familiar in cultivated state as an ornamental garden tree. It produces handsome white flowers and bright red fruit.

ARCACHON (ahrkahshoṅ'). Coastal town and fashionable holiday resort in Gironde dept, S.W. France. Pop. (1973) 15,755.

ARCÀ'DIA. Central plateau district of Peloponnesus, S. Greece. In antiquity it was inhabited by shepherds and hunters, whose mode of life has been idealized in literature as idyllic, e.g. by Sidney.

ARC DE TRIOMPHE (ahrk'-de-trēoṅf'). Triumphal arch in the Place de l'étoile, Paris, begun by Napoleon (and completed in 1836) to commemorate his victories of 1805-6. Beneath it rests France's 'Unknown Soldier'.

ARCH, Joseph (1826-1919). British Radical politician and trade unionist. B. at Barford, Warks, the son of an agricultural labourer, he worked in the fields from boyhood. Entirely self-taught, he became a Methodist local preacher, founded the National Agricultural Union (the first of its kind) in 1872, and was Liberal-Labour MP for N.W. Norfolk.

ARCH. A curved structure consisting of several wedge-shaped stones or other hard blocks which are supported by their mutual pressure. The term is also applied to any curved structure which is an A. in form only, but not in function.

ARCHAEAN (arkē'an). In geology, the earliest system of rocks. Underlying rocks of the Cambrian System, they may be composed of igneous, metamorphic, or stratified rocks, and often contain valuable minerals. 'Azoic' and 'Eozoic' are synonymous with A.

ARCHAEBACTERIA (ah'kēbakteria). Single-celled micro-organisms, dating back *c.* 4,000 million years. The molecular sequence of their DNA differs from that of the bacteria, and also from that of plants and animals, so that they seem to represent a third line of evolution. They take in carbon dioxide and hydrogen, and give off methane gas (hence their other name of methanogen). They occur in sewage treatment plants and hot springs, where the temperature is *c.* 70°C (170°F), and the atmosphere is without oxygen.

ARCHAEOLOGY. The study of the material products of the past, providing in the case of prehistoric man, or of peoples who had no written records, our only source of knowledge, but also supplementing our information on the historic and recorded peoples. The oldest man-made implements found are *c.* 1,820,000 yrs old, and the written documents of Egypt and Mesopotamia go back *c.* 5,000 yrs.

Systematic classification began when C. J. Thomsen placed the specimens in the Danish Nat. Museum *c.* 1818 according to 3 periods, which he called the Stone, Bronze, and Iron Ages. Effective recording of excavation and conservation of objects was practised *c.* 1840 by the early marine salvage workers, the brothers Charles and John Deane, and Gen. Sir Charles Pasley, who had meticulous watercolours made of their finds, complete with encrustations. Pioneers on land were Pitt-Rivers and Petrie (qq.v.), *see* also Schliemann, Evans, Rawlinson, Layard, Ventris, Wheeler, Emery, and Leakey.

During the 20th cent. there has been a widening of scope, for example, to medieval and industrial A., and use of scientific 'tools', e.g. carbon-14 dating (*see* CARBON); chemical methods of conservation, as with the Swedish warship *Vasa*; and location of sites by aerial photography and sonar, e.g. Alexander McKee's work on Henry VIII's battleship *Mary Rose* off Portsmouth from 1967.

ARCHAEOPTERYX (arkēop'teriks). The earliest known bird, remarkable for its reptilian features. Two fossil specimens have been dug out of the Jurassic limestone of Bavaria.

ARCHANGEL. Seaport in N. Europe (Russ. Arkhangelsk) in R.S.F.S.R. on the N. Dvina river, at the head of the Gulf of A. It is blocked by ice for some 6 months of the year, but is nevertheless, the chief timber-exporting port of the USSR. Pop. (1977) 391,000.

A. was colonized by Norsemen under Othere in the 10th cent. Chancellor in 1553 built an Eng. factory there. Boris Godunov made it an open port, and it was of prime importance until Peter the Great built St Petersburg. It was a centre for the interventionist armies after the Revolution of 1917, and during the S.W.W. was a receiving station for Anglo-American supplies.

ARCHBISHOP. In the Christian Church, a bishop of superior rank, who has authority over other bishops in his jurisdiction. Very often an A. is also a metropolitan, i.e. the head of an ecclesiastical province. In the Church of England there are two As., both of them metropolitans - the A. of Canterbury ('Primate of All England') and the A. of York ('Primate of England').

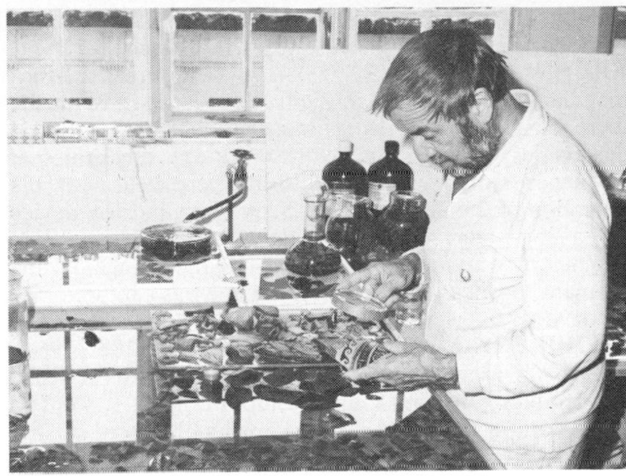

ARCHAEOLOGY. In 1798 Sir William Hamilton, husband of Nelson's Emma, consigned a thousand antique Greek vases — his priceless 'second collection' — to HMS *Colossus* to be carried back from Naples to England. The ship was lost while sheltering off the Scillies, and it was not until 1976 that Roland Morris, seen here examining some of the recovered fragments, located the wreck site and began the difficult task of recovering the invaluable remains of these works of classic art. *Photo: Courtesy of Roland Morris*

ARCHDEACON. Originally an ordained dignitary of the Christian Church charged with the supervision of the deacons attached to a cathedral. Today in the R.C. Church the office is purely titular; in the C. of E. an A. has still many duties of a business character, e.g. the periodic inspection of the churches.

ARCHER, Frederick James (1857–86). British jockey. B. at Cheltenham, he won 2,748 of the 8,084 races in which he rode, incl. 5 Derbys (1877, 1880, 1881, 1885, 1886), 4 Oaks, 6 St Legers, and 5 Two Thousand Guineas. His record of 246 winners in one season was not beaten till 1933 (*see* RICHARDS, GORDON). He shot himself while ill with typhoid fever.

ARCHERFISH. Tropical fish (*Toxotes jaculator*) found off Australia and S.E. Asia: it stuns insects just above the water with a jet of water from its mouth.

ARCHERY. The use of the bow and arrow in war and the chase. Flint arrowheads have been found in very ancient archaeological deposits, and bowmen are depicted in the sculptures of Assyria and Egypt and indeed all the nations of antiquity. Until the introduction of gunpowder in the 14th cent., bands of archers were to be found in every European army. The English archers distinguished themselves in the French wars of the later Middle Ages; and to this day the Queen's bodyguard in Scotland is known as the Royal Company of Archers. The Honourable Artillery Company was originally a body of archers.

Up to the time of Charles II the practice of A. was fostered and encouraged by English rulers. Henry VIII in particular loved the sport, and it was in his reign that Ascham wrote his *Toxophilus.* By the mid-17th cent. A. was no longer important in warfare and interest waned until the 1780s, although in the N. of England shooting for the Scorton Arrow has been carried on, with few breaks, from 1673. Organizations incl. the Fédération Internationale du Tir à l'Arc (1931); the British Grand National A. Soc. (1961); and in the US the National A.

Assocn (1879) and, for actual hunting with the bow, the National Field A. Assocn (1940).

ARCHIMĒ'DĒS (-k-) (*c.* 287-212 B.C.). Greek mathematician. B. at Syracuse in Sicily, he spent most of his life there. Many of his writings have survived, and he made discoveries in geometry, hydrostatics and mechanics of permanent importance. He is also credited with the invention of the *Archimedean Screw,* a cylindrical device for raising water, still in use in the Nile delta. He invented engines of war for the defence of Syracuse against the Romans, but was slain when Syracuse was captured. *See* BUOYANCY.

ARCHIPENKO (ahkhipyen'ko), **Alexander** (1887-1964). Russo-American sculptor and draughtsman, b. at Kiev. He produced his first Cubist sculpture in 1911, went to New York in 1923, and experimented with carved plastic.

ARCHITECTURE. The first of the plastic arts. From earliest times until the mid-19th cent. all permanent building was governed by 3 structural principles: the post and lintel, the wooden truss and the masonry arch. Latterly the steel skeleton and reinforced concrete have revolutionized A., being the first entirely new principles evolved since Roman times, thus liberating it from limitations imposed by the weight of stone and brick at each floor level, allowing great flexibility in design and buildings of immense height. Further developments have entirely removed the need for structural walls and roofs as separate entities, e.g. the geodesic dome of Buckminster Fuller (q.v.). The basic problem of the A. has always been how best to enclose space to fulfil the varied needs of human occupation, and, in so doing, the trends of contemporary life must be considered, and will be reflected in the shape of buildings. The earliest permanent buildings, dating from *c.* 4,000 B.C. in Egypt, reflect the grandeur of the ruling classes and their system of worship. Progressive changes tended to embrace more varied and specialized structures to suit the needs of a greater proportion of the population. In the 19th cent. the acceptance of the division of A. into ecclesiastical (churches, etc.), civil (houses and public buildings), military and naval, illustrates the rigidity which had overtaken the subject, so that the A. had become merely the creator of academic styles. In the 20th cent. men such as Le Corbusier, Gropius, and Mies van der Rohe broke free from these shackles, and contemporary As. widen their scope beyond the individual building or group of buildings to the whole city and its environs, adapting themselves to new synthetic materials and factory-made components, and also to the necessity of making their work capable of change and growth to meet the expansion of a city or the alteration of individual housing requirements as families first increase and then dwindle when children leave home.

Architects throughout the world are linked through the International Union of Architects (1948); important national organizations are the Royal Inst. of British Architects (1835) and the American Inst. of Architects (1857). *See* GOTHIC A. and sections under individual countries.

ARCHIVES. Originally thought of as limited to written and printed documents and papers, A. now not only extend to microfilm and computer tape, but also incl. paintings and photographs (e.g. London's National Portrait Gallery collection), and sound recordings, films and videotapes (of which the BBC has one of the world's largest collections), etc. In England the records of the

ARCHITECTURE. Two of the most influential modern architects, Le Corbusier (left) and Walter Gropius. *Photo: Popperfoto*

courts of law and govt. depts. from the Norman Conquest are housed at the Record Office in London, and (the major number of them) at Kew. Archives are not necessarily factual, e.g. the British National Film Archive and the BBC's collection of television plays. There is also a Nat. Register of Archives (1945).

In the USA the Declaration of Independence, the Constitution of the USA, and the Bill of Rights are exhibited at the National A. Hall, Washington. The National A. and Records Service is responsible for preserving federal records and administration of the presidential libraries.

ARCOSA'NTI. Town under construction to the N of Phoenix, Arizona, USA. The name derives from arcology (architecture concerned with ecology) and cosanti (Italian 'thing before'). Begun in 1970 by Italian-born architect, Paolo Soleri (1917-), it is planned to be self-sufficient, housed under a single glass roof, and with an eventual pop. of 5,000.

ARCOT. Town on the Palar, 105km (65m) S.W. of Madras, India. It is famous for Clive's defence in 1751, when with only 80 Europeans and 150 Sepoys able to carry out their duties he held it for 50 days against 10,000. Pop. (1971) 30,229.

ARCTIC. Regions N of the **Arctic Circle,** an imaginary line which runs round the North Pole at 66°33 N. There is no Arctic continent, but a mass of pack ice surrounding the Pole and floating on the **Arctic Ocean**: area 14,090,000 sq.km (5,440,000 sq.m). This ocean has comparatively low salinity, partly because of the rivers flowing into it from Siberia, and freezes readily. The ice breaks up more readily into floes in summer, with stretches of clear water, and in winter 'packs' together irregularly again. There is a variable fringe area but the NE Passage round the USSR, and the NW Passage round Canada are not easily navigable, although the Soviet Union uses the nuclear-powered ice-breaker *Arktika* to try to maintain all-year-round access to the N Atlantic and Pacific. Some of the pack ice is carried beyond the Arctic Ocean, the main current being a rotary one, which sweeps down the Greenland coast to meet the warm Atlantic drifts, fogs being frequent where the two meet. This is the source of icebergs, such as that which sank the *Titanic*.

The areas of the A. Ocean immediately bordering the major land masses are divided into a number of seas: Beaufort, Chukchi, East Siberian, Laptev, Kara, Barents, Norwegian and Greenland. The average depth is 1330 m (4,362 ft), and artificial islands are used in oil drilling.

Land areas within the A. have a cold winter, in which the Sun disappears below the horizon altogether for a time, and the brief warm summer lasts only up to two months. However, the cold is not so great as in NE Siberia and the Antarctic. Coniferous forest reaches into the area to some extent, but more typical is the tundra marked by stunted vegetation and an outburst of summer alpine flowers. Animals incl. domesticated reindeer, caribou and musk ox; foxes, hares, lemming and wolves; and the polar bear, seal, and walrus. Birds are rare except in summer, when insect life burgeons, espec. hordes of mosquito. The typical people of the A. are the Eskimo of the American/Canadian A. and Greenland, but even the remotest areas now also have transient colonies of oilmen, scientists, and military personnel.

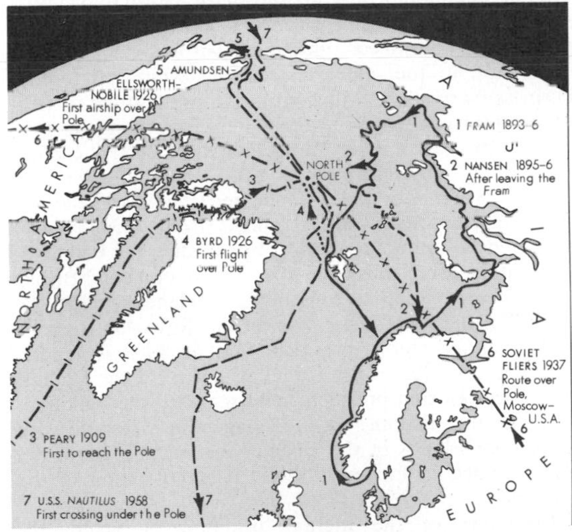

ARCTIC. Routes of famous flights and expeditions.

Exploration. The desire to find trade routes to the E. was the main incentive to early exploration in the N. of America and Asia. First in the long quest for the N.W. Passage was John Cabot in 1497; M. Frobisher in 1576 discovered the Frobisher and Hudson Straits; H. Willoughby and R. Chancellor began the search for the N.E. Passage in 1553. W. Barents (1596) and H. Hudson (1607) tried to cross the Arctic Ocean, Barents discovering Spitsbergen. Franklin discovered the N.W. Passage, but perished in the attempt. The first to sail through it was Amundsen in 1903-5. The N.E. Passage was navigated by A. E. Nordenskjöld in 1878-9. Attention was then turned to the N. Pole which was reached by R. E. Peary on 6 April 1909. R. E. Byrd claimed to have flown over the Pole in a monoplane in 1926, but doubt has been cast on the possibility that he could have covered the distance in the time he took; Nobile accompanied by Amundsen crossed the Pole in an airship in 1926; and C. F. Blair made the first solo flight in 1951. In 1958 the US submarine *Nautilus* crossed the Pole beneath the ice, and in 1977 the Soviet icebreaker *Arktika* made the first surface voyage to the Pole.

Scandinavian Air Lines began the first commercial service on a 'great circle' route over the Pole in 1954, and from 1960 a Russian nuclear-powered ice-breaker has kept open for 150 days a year a 4,000 km (2,500 m) Asia-Europe passage along the N. coast of Siberia. A number of weather stations are maintained.

ARCTIC. Almost more at home in water than on land, the polar bear has broad nearly 'webbed' feet to make it a powerful and rapid swimmer, but does not need a cold climate. Sally, with one of her triplets, is proof of that. *Photo: Zoological Society of London*

ARDEBIL (ahrdebēl'). Iranian town, near the Russian frontier. An important road centre, it also has an airport. A. exports dried fruits, carpets, and rugs. Pop. (1976) 148,000.

ARDÈCHE (ahrdāsh'). River of S.E. France, a tributary of the Rhône. Near Vallon it flows under the Pont d'Arc, a natural bridge. It gives its name to a dept.

ARDENNES. A wooded plateau extending from N. France through S.E. Belgium to N. Luxembourg. It is cut through by the Meuse and other rivers in wooded gorges. Towns incl. Charleville-Mézières and Sedan in the French dept of A., and Malmédy, Dinant and Spa in Belgium.

Early in the F.W.W., the A. was the scene of fierce fighting, while in the S.W.W. the Germans thrust through it in 1940 to separate the British from the French forces. The A. was retaken in 1944, but in Dec. of that year Rundstedt made a last desperate bid to break through once more to Dinant and Liège. This was defeated and the Allied line restored, 31 Jan. 1945. Nearly 77,000 Americans were killed, missing or wounded in this battle.

A'RECA. Genus of palms, native to tropical Asia. The seeds, known as A. nuts, have purgative properties, and *A. catechu* provides the betel-nut chewed with betel leaf.

ARECIBO (aresē'bō). Town in NW Puerto Rico with a large radio telescope. Pop. (1970) 70,000.

AREQUIPA (ahrākē'pa). City of Peru at the base of the volcano El Misti. Founded by Pizarro in 1540, it is the cultural focus of S. Peru, and a busy commercial centre. Pop. (1972) 156,700.

ARES (ā'rēz). Greek god of war, identified by the Romans with Mars. The son of Zeus and Hera, he was worshipped chiefly in Thrace.

ARĒTHŪ'SA. In Greek mythology, a Nereid and nymph of the fountain and spring of A. in the island of Ortygia near Syracuse.

AREZZO (ahret'sō). Italian town in the valley of the Upper Arno, 64km (40m) S.E. of Florence; it has a Gothic cathedral and a citadel. Pop. (1971) 81,500.

ARGALI (ahr'gali) or **arkal.** Wild sheep (*Ovis ammon*) of Central Asia. The ram may stand 120 cm (4 ft) at the shoulder, and has massive spiral horns.

ARGENTEUIL (ahrzhontöy). NW suburb of Paris, France, on the Seine. Pop. (1975) 103,000.

ARGENTINA (ahrjentē'na). Country of South America. It comprizes 22 provs. stretching from within the tropics to the tip of the S. American mainland, and the national terr. of half the island of Tierra del Fuego.

The western part of A. is occupied by the high Andes, increasingly exploited for their mineral wealth of gold, silver, copper, etc., and incl. Aconcagua (q.v.). The long gentle eastward slopes lead down to the rolling plains of central A.; rainfall is sparse, so much is semi-desert, particularly in the Patagonian steppes. Further N. crops can be grown with irrigation, and in the extreme N. (El Gran Chaco) there are forests with extremely valuable timber resources, savannah and swamp. In the E., between the Parana and Colorado rivers, lie the pampas, once covered with the white plumes of the 'pampas grass' now cultivated throughout the world as an ornamental plant. This region is now divided into ranch estates with great herds of cattle (the wildness of the gaucho horsemen who tended them used to be legendary), and farms famous for their wheat and maize. The country is drained N.W. to S.E. by the Uruguay and the Parana, with its tributary the Salado (which enter jointly the estuary of the Plate), the Colorado, the Negro, and lesser streams. The south becomes dank and chill as it runs down towards the Antarctic, and was formerly given over to huge flocks of sheep, but there are new sources of wealth here in oil, and hydro-electric schemes are part of the industrialization overtaking the country. Besides such established industries as meat-packing, there are metallurgical, chemical, textile and other manufactures being developed, notably in Rosario, Cordoba and La Plata. The Federal cap. is Buenos Aires, the centre of the rail and road system, and air services. Area 2,780,000 sq.km (1,073,000 sq.m); pop. (1978) 25,400,000, mostly of Spanish or Italian origin, only *c.* 20,000 Amerindians surviving. The language is Spanish and the religion Roman Catholic (supported by the State). M.U.: peso.

History. The Amerindian people of A. were wandering hunters, who used the bolas, two rounded stones linked by a leather thong, which they swung and threw to bring down such prey as the rhea. They boldly resisted first the Incas, and then, from the 16th cent., the Spaniards, but were finally almost wiped out in the 19th cent. Argentina estab. her independence of Spain 1810–16, under the leadership of Gen. José de San Martín (q.v.), and became a republic. Immigration on a large scale began in the late 19th cent. when settlers from the Latin countries of Europe poured in. Under the federal constitution (basically that of 1853), there is a Senate and House of Deputies, and the pres. is elected through electoral colleges for a 6-yr term. The outstanding figure of 20th cent. politics is Gen. Juan Perón (q.v.), pres. from 1946 until his abandonment of liberalism for a form of dictatorship led to his deposition in 1955. However, a Perónist movement continued, identified with the masses in opposition to the upper classes, the army and foreign business interests, and its continuing strength led in 1973 to the return to power of a new Perónist regime. In 1976 a military junta overthrew the increasingly corrupt Peronist government (*see* PERÓN), and some 15,000 opponents of military rule disappeared (the *desaparecidos*). General Leopoldo Galtieri (pres. from 1981) briefly bolstered his unpopular regime by invading the Falklands (Argentina also claims from Britain S Georgia and British Antarctica). His failure to hold the Falklands precipitated the fall of the junta in 1982, and Gen. Reynaldo Bignone took over as interim president until in 1983 Argentina returned to civilian rule. Raoul Alfonsin (of the Radical party) was elected president, and renewed the Falklands claim against Britain. In 1984 Argentina's dispute with Chile over islands in the Beagle Channel off Tierra del Fuego ended in favour of Chile by intervention of the Vatican.

ARGENTINA. Gauchos on a cattle ranch of the Pampa. Their work is still skilled and sometimes dangerous. *Photo: Mireille Vautier*

Inheritors of the literary tradition of Spain, the Argentinians are noted for a fine journalistic record, and for one author internationally known, Jorge Luis Borges (q.v.). The English writer W. H. Hudson (q.v.) interpreted the Argentinian scene of an earlier period.

A'RGON. Chemically inert gaseous element, at. wt. 39.944, symbol Ar., at. no. 18. Discovered in air by Rayleigh and Ramsay after all oxygen and nitrogen was removed chemically, it is used in electric discharge lamps.

A'RGONAUT, or **paper nautilus.** Genus of dibranchiate cephalopods (*Argonauta*) belonging to the division Octopoda. *A. argo* inhabits the Mediterranean, and was well known to the ancient Greeks.

ARGENTINA. The blind poet, Jorge Luis Borges, is here seen after he received an honorary degree at the University of Oxford. *Photo: Keystone*

ARGONAUTS. In Greek legend the band of heroes who accompanied Jason when he set out in the ship *Argo* to fetch the Golden Fleece. *See* JASON.

ARGONNE (ahrgon'). Wooded plateau in N.E. France, separating Lorraine and Champagne. It was the scene of fierce fighting in the F.W.W.

A'RGOS. Ancient Greek city in the N.E. Peloponnese, near the head of the gulf of Nauplia. In the Homeric age it was one of the chief cities of Greece, and the name Argives was sometimes used instead of Greeks. The modern town is a rly junction. Pop. (1970) 13,200.

A'RGUS. In Greek mythology, a giant with 100 eyes, set by the jealous Hera to watch over Io, the beloved of Zeus, who had been turned into a cow. Hermes charmed A. to sleep with his flute, cut off his head, and Hera transplanted his eyes to the tail of her favourite bird, the peacock.

ARGYLL (argīl'), **Earls and Dukes of.** Line of Scottish peers who trace their descent to the Campbells of Lochow. The earldom dates from 1457. **Archibald,** the 8th earl (1607-61), led the Covenanting party during the Civil Wars, crowned Charles II in 1651, submitted to Cromwell in 1652, and was beheaded after the Restoration. **Archibald,** 9th earl (1629-85), was executed for leading a rebellion in co-operation with Monmouth's rising. **Archibald,** 10th earl (1651-1703), received a dukedom in 1701. John, 2nd duke (1678-1743), became a peer of the UK for helping to promote the Union.

George Douglas, 8th duke (1823-1900), was Secretary for India 1868-74, and opposed Irish home rule. In his writings he attempted to reconcile Christianity with scientific discovery. **John Douglas Sutherland,** 9th duke (1845-1914), m. Princess Louise, dau. of Queen Victoria, in 1871, and was Gov.-Gen. of Canada, 1878-83.

ARGYLLSHIRE. Former co. of Scotland on the W. coast, incl. many of the Western Isles, which was for the most part merged in Strathclyde region in 1975, although a small area to the N.W. incl. Ballachulish, Ardgour and Kingairloch went to Highland region.

ARIA'DNE. In Greek legend, the dau. of Minos, king of Crete. When Theseus came from Athens as one of the victims offered to the Minotaur, she fell in love with him and gave him the ball of thread by means of which he was able to find his way out of the labyrinth.

ARIANE-SPACE. Consortium of banks, electronic and aerospace firms which in 1980 took over from the European Space Agency the production and launching of satellites by Ariane (French form of Ariadne) booster rockets. Geostationary satellites can be placed directly into orbit by this means, and the scheme is in competition with the US Space Shuttle. The launching site is Kourou, French Guiana, nr. the Equator.

ARIANE-SPACE. The three-stage European carrier-rocket Ariane awaiting launch from the island of Kourou. *Photo: Keystone*

Ā'RIANISM. A system of Christian theology, founded about A.D. 310 by Arius (q.v.), and condemned as heretical at the Council of Nicaea in 325. Certain 17th and 18th cent. theologians held Arian views akin to those of modern Unitarianism. In 1979 the heresy again caused concern to the Vatican in the writings of such theologians as Edouard Schillebeeckx of Nijmegen University.

ARICA (arē'ka). Port in N. Chile, just S. of the border with Peru. Much of Bolivia's trade passes through it, and negotiations have been opened to allow her a land corridor to the Pacific at this point. Pop. (1975) 93,000.

ARID ZONES. Infertile areas with a small, infrequent rainfall that rapidly evaporates because of high temperatures, and which form a serious problem in Morocco, Pakistan, Australia, America, etc. The problem

ARICA. Set on a rainless coastline, Arica has a dramatic history. Several times devastated by earthquake, it was razed in 1880 when captured by Chile from Peru. *Photo: Mireille Vautier*

involved is not merely finding new sources of water, although constant research goes on to discover, for example, cheaper methods of distilling sea water, but the conservation of existing sources by avoiding evaporation (e.g. the artificial recharging of natural groundwater reservoirs) and the eradication of salt in irrigation supplies from underground sources or as a surface soil deposit in poorly drained areas.

ARIÈGE (ahrē-āzh'). River in S. France, a tributary of the Garonne. It gives its name to a dept.

ARIOSTO (ahrē-ost'ō), **Ludovico** (1474–1533). Italian poet b. at Reggio. He wrote Latin poems and comedies on classical lines, joined the household of Cardinal Ippolito d'Este in 1503, was frequently engaged in embassies and diplomacy, and pub. the *Orlando Furioso* at Ferrara in 1516. This is a romantic epic, dealing with the wars of Charlemagne against the Saracens, and the love of Orlando (Roland) for Angelica, a princess of Cathay. The perfection of its style and its unflagging narrative interest place A. among the great Italian poets. In 1521 A. became governor of a province in the Apennines, and after 3 years retired to Ferrara, where he d.

ARISTARCHUS OF SAMOS (*c.* 310–264 B.C.). Greek astronomer, famed as being the first to maintain that the earth revolves round the sun.

ARISTĪ'DĒS (*c.* 530–468 B.C.). Athenian statesman. He was one of the 10 Athenian generals at Marathon in 490 B.C., and was elected chief archon. Later he came into conflict with the democratic leader Themistocles, and was exiled *c.* 483 B.C. He returned to fight against the Persians at Salamis in 480 B.C., and next year commanded the Athenians at Plataea. His popular title 'the Just' was probably derived from his just assessment of the contribution to be paid by the Greek states who entered the Delian league against the Persians.

ARISTI'PPUS (*c.* 435–356 B.C.). Greek philosopher, founder of the Cyrenaic or Hedonist school. A pupil of Socrates, he developed the doctrine that pleasure is the only good in life. He lived at the court of Dionysius of Syracuse, and later with his mistress Laïs, the courtesan, at Corinth.

ARISTO'PHANĒS (*c.* 448–380 B.C.). Comic dramatist of ancient Athens. His early comedies are remarkable for the violence of the satire with which he ridiculed the democratic war leaders. In 425 he produced the *Acharnians*, a plea for peace with Sparta. The *Knights* (424) shows the figure of the 'Demos' or 'democracy' beguiled by Cleon. The *Clouds* (423) pours ridicule on the new learning of Socrates. The *Wasps* (422) is a satire on the Athenian love of litigation. The *Peace* (421) was written when negotiations for peace with Sparta were far advanced. In the *Birds* (414), written after the renewed outbreak of the Peloponnesian War, A. tells how two Athenians persuade the birds to build a kingdom in the air known as 'Cloud-cuckoo-land'. In the *Lysistrata* (411) the women, tired of the war, deny conjugal relations to their husbands until they have made peace with Sparta. The *Thesmophoriazusae* (Priestesses of Demeter) (411) satirizes Euripides and the women of Athens. The *Frogs* (405) tells how the god Dionysus was sent to the lower world to bring back Aeschylus to Athens. The *Ecclesiazusae* or *Women in Parliament* (393) describes what happened when the women seized the Athenian parliament. In *Plutus* or *Wealth* (388) the abolition of poverty results in a series of comic episodes. Besides the 11 extant plays A. is known to have written about 40 comedies which are now lost.

A'RISTOTLE (384–322 B.C.). Greek philosopher. B. at Stagira in Thrace, he studied at Athens under Plato, became tutor to Alexander the Great, and in 335 opened a school at Athens. When Alexander d. he was forced to flee to Chalcis, where he d. He is sometimes referred to as 'the Stagirite'.

Of A.'s works some 22 treatises survive, dealing with logic; metaphysics; physics, astronomy, and meteorology; biology; psychology; ethics and politics; and literary criticism.

A. maintained that sense-experience is our only source of knowledge, and that by reasoning we can discover the essences of things, i.e. their distinguishing qualities. The essence of a thing he regards as real, but not as capable of existing apart from it. He conceives of all being as potentiality and actuality, in the physical order represented by matter and form; God alone is all actuality. Change consists in bringing the potentiality of a substance into actuality. All change is caused, the Supreme Cause being God.

A. held that all matter consisted of a single 'prime matter', which was always determined by some form. The simplest kinds of matter were the 4 elements, earth, water, air, and fire, which in varying proportions constituted all the things we know. A. saw nature as always striving to perfect itself, and first classified organisms into species and genera to show how they subserve this purpose.

The principle of life he terms a soul, which he regards as the form of the living creature, not as a substance separable from it. The intellect can discover in sense-impressions the universal, and as the soul thus transcends matter, it must be immortal. In his works on ethics and politics A. suggests that man's happiness consists in living in conformity with nature, according to reason and moderation. He derives his political theory from the recognition that mutual aid is natural to man, and refused to set up any one constitution as universally ideal. Art embodies nature, but in a more perfect fashion, its end being the purifying and ennobling of the affections. The essence of beauty is order and symmetry.

In the Middle Ages A.'s philosophy became the foundation of Islamic philosophy, and was incorporated into Christian theology.

ARISTOTLE. No contemporary portraits of the philosopher survive, but this antique bust from the Vienna Museum expresses the lofty spirit of his thought. *Photo: Kunsthistorischen Museum, Vienna*

ARITHMETIC. The branch of mathematics that deals with all questions into which numbers enter, such as counting, measuring, weighing.

Simple A. existed already in prehistoric times. In China, Egypt, Babylon, and early civilizations generally A. was used for commercial purposes and for records of taxation as well as for astronomy. During the Dark Ages in Europe, knowledge of A. was preserved in India and later among the Arabs. European mathematics revived as conditions became more settled, with the development of trade and overseas exploration. The Arabic numerals replaced Roman numerals and allowed calculations to be made in writing, instead of by the abacus (q.v.) method. With the invention of logarithms in 1614, and of the slide rule in 1620-30, A. reached its modern form. The chief development since then has been the growing use of calculating-machines and ready-reckoners.

The basic operation in A. is counting. Most questions of A. could be answered by counting alone, though with great labour and expenditure of time. The object of formal calculations is to achieve the same result more quickly. The fundamental operations are addition and subtraction, and multiplication and division. Fractions arise naturally in the process of measurement. Decimals are a form of fractions.

Powers, i.e. repeated multiplication of the same number, are represented by an index, e.g. 2^5 = '2 to the 5th' = $2\times2\times2\times2\times2$. Roots are the reverse of powers: If we ask, 'What number multiplied by itself five times gives 32?' the answer is called the 5th root of 32, i.e. 2, since $2\times2\times2\times2\times2 = 32$. *See* also LOGARITHMS.

In the modern teaching of A. stress is laid on understanding the processes involved, espec. the *place-value* system. The decimal numeral system employs ten numerals (0123456789), and each position has a value ten times greater than the position to its right, i.e. the numeral 3 represents the number 3, but moved one place to the left of the first position it equals 3 tens. The Babylonians, however, used a complex base-sixty system; the Mayas base-twenty; and modern computers base-two. This last uses only two numerals (01), and each position has a value twice as great as the position to the right, so that 111 is equal to 7 in the decimal system, and 1111 is equal to 15. *Modular A.* deals with events recurring in regular cycles, and is used in describing the functioning of petrol engines/electrical generators and so on, e.g. in the modulo-twelve system, the answer to a question as to what time it will be in five hours if it is now ten o'clock, can be expressed $10+5=3$.

Ā'RIUS (c. A.D. 256-336). Founder of Arianism, a Christian heresy which denied the complete divinity of Christ. B. in Libya, he became a priest of Alexandria in 311. In 318 he was excommunicated and fled to Palestine, but his heresy spread to such an extent that the emperor Constantine called a council at Nicaea, where Athanasius confuted the Arian doctrines and persuaded the bishops to draw up a creed in which the dogma of the Trinity was categorically affirmed. A. and his adherents were banished, though later he was allowed to return.

ARIZŌ'NA. A south-western state (the 'Grand Canyon' state) of the USA. Its main waterway is the Colorado, which flows through the famous Grand Canyon - one of the most impressive natural features of the world. To the E. of the Colorado is a vast barren area called the Painted Desert which incl. the Petrified Forest (2½ m. years old). In the N.E. lies the Colorado Plateau, another barren region. The Gila desert occupies the S.W. of the state. The deserts of A. are arid, and have the highest temperatures in the USA.

A. is believed to derive its name from the Spanish *arida-zona* (dry belt). The first Spaniard to visit A. was the Franciscan Marcos de Niza in 1539. By 1715 A. was part of New Spain; in 1824 it became part of the United Mexican States. After the Mexican War it passed to USA in 1848, became a territory in 1863, and developed rapidly as a result of the gold-rush in neighbouring California. In 1912 it was admitted as a state of the Union. Irrigation has been carried out on a colossal scale, e.g. the Roosevelt dam on Salt river, and Hoover Dam on the Colorado between A. and Nevada, provide the state with both hydro-electric power and irrigation water. At the end of the 19th cent. rich copper deposits were found in A. and there exist deposits of many other minerals. Phoenix is the capital. Area 295,023 sq.km (113,909 sq.m); pop. (1977) 2,296,000, incl. 100,000 Indians who still own a quarter of the state.

ARKANSAS (ahr'kansaw). South-central state of the USA, called the 'wonder state' because of its remarkable natural features.

The Missippi runs along the eastern boundary; and from the eastern plains the land gradually rises to the Ouachita and Boston mountain ranges, lying S. and N. of the A. river, which runs across the state from W. to E. The climate is warm and healthy. The chief towns are Little Rock, the cap.; Fort Smith, Hot Springs, centre of a Nat. Park, and Pine Bluff.

A. is primarily an agricultural state, producing cotton, rice and fruit, but there is growing industry. Natural gas was discovered in 1888, petroleum in 1901; and there are refineries near El Dorado. Bauxite and diamonds are other mineral products.

The first white man to explore the area was the Spaniard Hernando de Soto in 1541. The first European settlement Arkansas Post was founded by some of the companions of the French explorer La Salle in 1686 who began trading with the local Indians. In 1803 A. formed part of the Louisiana purchase by the USA. There followed a wave of immigration and in 1836 A. was constituted a state of the Union, seceded 1861, readmitted 1868.

Area 137,533 sq.km (53,102 sq.m); pop. (1977) 2,140,000; of whom about 25 per cent were Negroes.

ARKWRIGHT, Sir Richard (1732-92). British inventor and manufacturing pioneer. B. at Preston, Lancs, he experimented in machine-designing with a watchmaker, John Kay of Warrington, and in 1768, with Kay and John Smalley, he set up his celebrated 'spinning-frame' at Preston. He shortly removed to Nottingham to escape the fury of the spinners who feared that their handicraft would be dispensed with. In 1771 he went into partnership with Jedediah Strutt, a Derby man who had improved the stocking-frame, and Samuel Need, and built a water-powered factory at Cromford in Derbyshire. In 1790 he installed steampower in his Nottingham works. His business prospered and he was knighted in 1786.

A'RLEN, Michael (1895-1956). British novelist. B. at Ruschuk, Bulgaria, of Armenian parents, he changed his name from Dikran Kuyumjian when he became a naturalized British subject in 1922. His greatest success was the cynically smart *The Green Hat* (1924), story of a *femme fatale*. He d. in New York.

ARLES (ahrl). Ancient city in Bouches-du-Rhône dept, S.E. France on the left bank of the Rhône, in a great fruit- and vine-growing district. Roman relics include an amphitheatre for 25,000 spectators. The cathedral of St Trophime is the finest Romanesque structure in Provence. Pop. (1975) 50,345.

ARLINGTON. Name of the National Cemetery of the USA, on the banks of the Potomac, in Virginia, facing Washington. The mansion was Robert E. Lee's, and the grounds were first used as a military cemetery in 1864 during the American Civil War. Up to 1975, 165,142 military, naval, and civilian persons from every war in which the USA has been engaged have been buried there, incl. one Unknown Soldier of the F.W.W., one of the S.W.W., and one of the Korean War. Pres. J. F. Kennedy and his brother Robert Kennedy are buried here.

ARMADA. *See* SPANISH ARMADA.

ARMADI'LLO. A mammal of the family Dasypodidae, provided with a protective armour of bony plates, joined in such a way that the body can be rolled up like a hedgehog's. The family ranges from Texas to Patagonia, and contains many species. The largest, the Giant A. (*Priodon gigas*) of Brazil and Surinam is 1m (3ft) long, excl. the tail.

ARMAGH (ahrmah'). Smallest of the 6 cos. of N. Ireland. In the N. it is flat, and there are extensive bogs. The better drained parts are under crops, especially flax. The chief rivers are the Bann and Blackwater, flowing into Lough Neagh, and the Callan tributary of the Blackwater. Chief towns are A., the co. town, Lurgan, Portadown, and Keady. Area, 1,266 sq.km (489 sq.m); pop. (1971) 133,200.

ARMAGNAC (ah'manyak). Former French prov. in S France (cap. Auch), which now survives chiefly as the name of a deep-coloured brandy.

ARMÉNIA. A mountainous region in S.E. Europe and S.W. Asia, divided between USSR, Turkey, and Iran, and situated between the Black Sea, the Little Caucasus, and the plateaux of Iran and Asia Minor. In legend, it is the site of the Garden of Eden, and the Ark, after the Flood, came to rest on the 'Mountains of Ararat', the highest part of the plateau. In the last cents. of the 2nd millenium B.C. the country was occupied by a people called Urartu, Ararat, Vannic, or Khaldian. Their kingdom flourished in the 9th-7th cents. B.C., and was overrun by an Indo-European people from the W. or N., the two peoples amalgamating and representing the ancestors of the modern Armenian. A. owed allegiance in turn to Assyria, Persia, the Romans, the Byzantine Empire (7th cent.), the Seljuks and Mongols, and in the 16th cent. was divided between Persians and Turks, Russia obtaining a portion during the 19th cent.

The *Armenian Question* arose in 1878 when promised reforms never materialized; unrest broke out and there were massacres by Turkish troops in 1895. Again in 1909 and 1915, the Turks massacred altogether more than a million Armenians, and deported others into the N. Syrian desert where they died of starvation; those who could fled to Russia or Persia, and only some 100,000 were left in Turkish Armenia.

After the Russian revolution of 1917, Russian Armenia in 1920 proclaimed itself a republic; it was one of the reps. of the Transcaucasian S.F.S.R. (the others being Georgia and Azerbaijan) from 1922 until it became a constituent republic of the USSR in 1936.

ARMENIAN CHURCH. A. adopted Christianity in the 3rd cent., and about 295 Gregory the Illuminator (*c.* 257-332) was made exarch of the Armenian church, which has developed along national lines. The Seven Sacraments, or Mysteries, are administered, baptism being immediately followed by confirmation. The Catholicos or exarch is the supreme head, and Echmiadzin, near Yerevan, is his traditional seat.

LANGUAGE. The Armenian language constitutes one of the main divisions of Indo-European. Old Armenian, the classic literary language, is still used in the liturgy of the Church. Armenian was not written down until the 5th cent. A.D., when an alphabet of 36 (now 38) letters was evolved. Literature flourished in the 4th-14th cents., revived in the 18th; contemporary Armenian, with modified grammar and enriched with words from other languages, is used by a group of 20th cent. writers.

PEOPLE. There are *c.* 3,600,000 Armenian-speakers in the Soviet Union, and communities continue to exist in India, Iraq, Lebanon, Iran, Syria, Turkey, and the USA.

ARMENIAN S.S.R. Constituent Rep. of the USSR, situated in the S. of Transcaucasia and mainly mountainous and wooded. Livestock are raised in the mountains round Yerevan, the cap., and in the Aras valley cotton, tobacco, fruits are grown with the help of irrigation. There are electrical engineering and machine-tool industries, and rich mineral resources incl. aluminium, copper and zinc, and cement and marble, are increasingly exploited. Area 29,800 sq.km (11,500 sq.m); pop. (1972) 2,606,000.

ARMENTIÈRES (ahrmoñtē-ār'). French manufacturing town in Nord dept, on the Lys, 16km (10m) N.W. of Lille. The song 'Mademoiselle from A.' originated in the F.W.W. when the town was held by the British. Pop. (1975) 27,500.

ARMIDALE. Town on the New England plateau of New South Wales, centre of an agricultural region and seat of the Univ. of New England (1954), originally affiliated to the Univ. of Sydney and first estab. in an old 'squatter' mansion. Pop. (1975) 20,000.

ARMI'NIUS (17 B.C.-A.D. 21). German chieftain, whose annihilation of a Roman army led by Varus in the Teutoburger Wald in A.D. 9 resulted in the Roman withdrawal to the Rhine frontier.

ARMI'NIUS, Jacobus. Latinized form of Jakob Harmensen (1560-1609), the Dutch Protestant divine who founded Arminianism, a school of theology opposed to Calvinism. B. in S. Holland, he was ordained at Amsterdam in 1588, and from 1603 lived as professor of theology at Leyden. A.'s views were developed and systematized after his death by his follower, Episcopius. A. opposed Calvin's doctrine of predestination, and asserted that forgiveness and eternal life are bestowed on all who repent of their sins and unfeignedly believe in Jesus Christ. In England Arminianism was adopted as the theology of Wesleyan Methodism, in opposition to the Calvinist views of the followers of Whitefield.

ARMOUR. Protective covering in warfare. The use of body A. is very ancient and is frequently depicted in Greek and Roman art. In the Middle Ages chain mail was extensively developed, and in the 14-16th cents. came the growth of plate A. which eventually encased the whole body and represented a superb degree of craftsmanship. The invention of gunpowder led, though only by degrees, to the virtual abandonment of A. until in the F.W.W. the helmet reappeared as a defence against shrapnel. The pre-requisites of practical modern A., lightness and flexibility, were not met until the development of the nylon and fibre-glass A. which began to come into use in the S.W.W. and the Korean War. A. is also used on tanks, aircraft, ships, and cars.

ARMSTRONG, Anthony. Pen-name of A. A. Willis (1897-1976). British author of humorous novels and the ingenious thriller play *Ten-Minute Alibi.*

ARMSTRONG, Louis (1900-71). American jazz musician, nicknamed Satchmo. A trumpet-player of virtuoso ability, he was b. in New Orleans, joined Kid Ory's band in 1917, and formed his own 7 yrs later. His reputation is as worldwide as the distribution of his records, and his films incl. *High Society.*

ARMSTRONG, Neil (1930-). American astronaut. B. in Ohio, he took his pilot's licence at 16, and served as a naval aviator in Korea 1949-52 before joining NASA as a test pilot. Selected as an astronaut in 1962, he was the first man to step on the Moon in 1969, when he said: 'That's one small step for a man, one giant leap for mankind.'

ARMY. An organized military force: these were common to all ancient civilizations: Sumeria, Babylonia, Egypt, Assyria, China, India, Persia, Greece, Carthage and - above all - Rome. In Britain the Anglo-Saxon *fyrd*, or local militia, saved the country from being wholly overrun by the Danes, but the first body of standing troops was raised by Canute. After the Norman Conquest military organization was based on the feudal system common to all Europe, whereby vassals supplied their overlords with

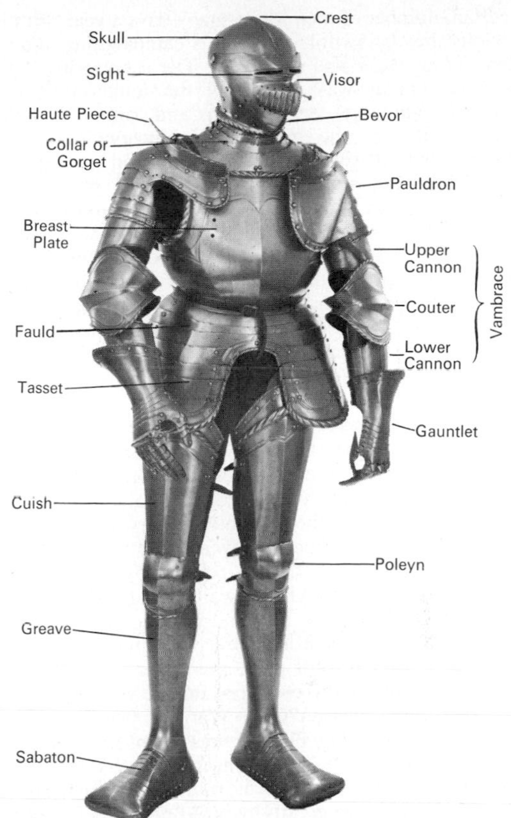

ARMOUR. A medieval suit of armour, made by a master smith is less heavy and more flexible in wear than might be thought. The holes to the left of the illustration on the right breast, show where the lance was held in combat.

ARMSTRONG. One of the founders of classical jazz, Louis was beloved for his personality. *Photo: Popperfoto*

a certain number of men for so many days a year, with its obvious drawbacks for continuous campaigning, though mercenaries were also employed. The superiority of the mounted knight was ended by the longbow (Crécy, Poitiers, Agincourt), and firearms and cannon favoured centralization in the hands of professionals and the development of sustained campaigns and strategy. In Tudor England small standing bodies of troops were employed for external and internal defence, but the defects of raw levies, noble amateurs and mercenaries led to Cromwell's creation of the New Model Army for the larger campaigns of the Civil War. After the Restoration Charles II estab. a small standing army, the beginning of the modern British army, which was expanded under James II and William III. Under George III it failed to subdue the American colonists, showing the superiority of the citizen, or people's army, dramatically illustrated in Europe by the forces of the French Revolution. Conscription was first adopted in Prussia to counter Napoleon's imperial ambitions. The British A. under Wellington which eventually broke Napoleon was one of the best ever put into the field, but it afterwards decreased in numbers and efficiency. Its weaknesses were patent in the Crimean War and, despite reforms by Cardwell and Wolseley, in the South African war. R. B. Haldane (on the advice of Roberts) organized an expeditionary force, and for home defence a territorial force, though these were still inadequate. In the 19th cent. there had been immense development of rapidly produced missile weapons, use of railways (the American Civil War has been called the 'railway war'), etc. The F.W.W. was one of trench warfare in which enormous As. were bogged down, e.g. the British A. expanded from 750,000 to 5½ million men. In the inter-war period As. were greatly reduced until the rise of the Italo-German forces led to reluctant increases: Britain was in many respects less prepared in 1939 than 1914. The As. of the S.W.W. were remarkable for mobility and the enormous distances they covered, notably Allied forces in the Pacific area, and also for close co-ordination of land, sea and air forces.

On the assumption that the nuclear age - especially the perfection of the H-bomb (1952) - meant the virtual end of conventional warfare, the USA (1955) and USSR (1960) announced reductions in their armies, but this theory was disproved by the Vietnam and Arab-Israeli campaigns. Not only were there sophisticated developments in tanks and anti-tank missiles, low-level and very-low-level air defence guided weapons, and mortar locating radar, etc., but tactical nuclear weapons capable of use for strategic purposes without endangering the attacker were evolved. The modern A., however, tends to be smaller than those of the early post-S.W.W. period, and is specialized and professional.

ARNAULD (ahrnoh'). Name of a French family closely associated with the Jansenist movement in the 17th cent. ANTOINE A. (1560-1619) was a Paris advocate, strongly critical of the Jesuits. Many of his 20 children were associated with the abbey of Port Royal, a convent of Cistercian nuns near Versailles, that became the centre of Jansenism: the 2nd daughter, ANGÉLIQUE (1591-1661), became abbess through her father's instrumentality at the age of 8. Later she served as prioress under her sister AGNES (1593-1671), and her niece, LA MÈRE ANGÉLIQUE (1624-84), succeeded to both positions. A.'s youngest child, ANTOINE (1612-94), the 'great Arnauld', was religious director of the nuns at Port Royal. With Pascal, Nicole, and others, he produced not only Jansenist pamphlets, but works on logic, grammar, and geometry. For years he had to live in hiding, and the last 16 years of his life were spent in Brussels. *See* JANSENISM; PORT ROYAL, etc.

ARMY. An 'Honest John' missile being prepared for firing during training by members of the British Army. *Photo: Central Office of Information*

ARNE, Thomas Augustine (1710-78). British composer. B. in London, he composed operas and oratorios, as well as much music for the theatre, but is best remembered for his songs, which include 'Where the bee sucks' and 'Rule, Britannia'.

ARNHEM (arn'hem). Cap. of Gelderland prov. of the Netherlands, on the right bank of the Rhine, to the S.E. of Utrecht. Sir Philip Sidney died there in 1586. Pop. (1973) 129,633. In the S.W.W. it was the scene of a great airborne operation and battle (17-27 Sept. 1944) when 10,095 British troops under Major R. E. Urquhart were dropped in the region of A. with the object of securing a bridgehead over the N. Rhine and facilitating an Allied drive into the heart of Germany. Forces also landed by air at Nijmegen were unable to fight their way along the road to Arnhem, and after a fierce struggle the survivors in that town had to be withdrawn; 7,605 were lost, killed, wounded, or missing.

ARNHEM LAND. Plateau filling the major part of the central peninsula of Australia's Northern Territory. Intersected by forested ravines, it is the largest of the Aboriginal reserves. The only white residents are in mission stations on its rim, such as that at Yirrkala on the coast of the Gove peninsula. Mineral resources, such as the bauxite being mined not far from Yirrkala, threaten the peace of the reserve, where the people still practise hunting, bark and cave painting, etc. in the primeval way.

ARNIM, Ludwig Achim von (1781-1831). German Romantic poet and novelist. B. in Berlin, he wrote short stories, a romance, *Gräfin Dolores* (1810), and plays, but left his finest work, the historical novel *Die Kronenwächter* (1817), unfinished. With Clemens Brentano he collected the Ger. folk-songs in *Des Knaben Wunderhorn* (1805-8). In 1811 he m. Brentano's sister, BETTINA (1785-1859), who as a girl had an intimate friendship with Goethe. In 1835 she pub. her correspondence with the poet, largely spurious.

ARNO. Italian r. 240km (150m) long, rising in the Apennines, and flowing westward to the Mediterranean. Florence and Pisa stand on its banks.

ARNOLD (d. 1155). Italian religious reformer, known as Arnold of Brescia. B. probably at Brescia, he studied in Paris and became an Augustinian monk. Leading a highly ascetic life himself, he strongly condemned the prevailing laxity in the Church, and opposed the temporal power of the papacy. Banished from Italy by Innocent II in 1139, he returned in 1145, and played a part in the short-lived Roman republic. In 1155 he was forced to flee, but was taken, condemned to death, and hanged. His followers were probably merged in the Waldenses.

ARNOLD, Benedict (1741-1801). American soldier, chiefly remembered for an act of treason to the American side in the War of American Independence. A merchant in Newhaven, Conn., he joined the Colonial forces, but in 1780 plotted to betray the strategic post at West Point to the British. Major André was sent by the British to discuss terms with him, but was caught and hanged as a spy. A. escaped to the British, who gave him an army command.

ARNOLD, Sir Edwin (1832-1904). British scholar and poet. After leaving Oxford, he was a schoolmaster and principal of a college at Poona. In 1861 he joined the staff of the *Daily Telegraph.* He is famed for his *Light of Asia* (1879), a rendering of the life and teaching of the Buddha in blank verse. *The Light of the World* (1891) is a less successful attempt to re-tell the life of Christ.

ARNOLD, Malcolm (1921-). British composer. Principal trumpet in the London Philharmonic Orchestra 1941-4 and 1945-8, he has composed symphonies, and film music for *The Bridge on the River Kwai.*

ARNOLD, Matthew (1822-88). British poet. B. at Laleham, he was the son of Dr A., headmaster of Rugby, and after a short period as assistant master at Rugby was one of HM inspectors of schools (1851-86). His first vols. of poetry, *The Strayed Reveller* (1849) and *Empedocles on Etna* (1852), were unsuccessful and anonymous, but 2 further publications under his own name in 1853 and 1855 caused him to be elected professor of poetry at Oxford (1857-67). A classical tragedy, *Merope* (1858) and *New Poems* (1867) followed, and much literary criticism is contained in *Essays in Criticism* (1865 and 1888), and other vols. He also pub. studies in education, *Literature and Dogma* (1873), and a masterly indictment of 19th cent. Philistinism, *Culture and Anarchy* (1869). As a poet and as critic A. held steadfastly to the standard set by classical unity, and demanded 'high seriousness' and 'a criticism of life'.

ARNOLD, Thomas (1795-1842). British schoolmaster. Ordained in the C. of E. in 1818, he was headmaster of Rugby School 1828-42, and his rule there has been graphically described in Thomas Hughes's *Tom Brown's Schooldays.* His emphasis was on training of character, and his influence on public school education was profound.

ARP, Hans or **Jean** (1887-1966). French painter and sculptor. B. at Strasbourg, he was one of the founders of Dadaism in Zurich *c.* 1917, and was later a member of the Surrealist and Abstract-Creation groups. His early painting is fluid, and when he turned to sculpture it was notable for its boneless curves; also remarkable are his *papiers déchirés,* torn paper designs pasted on a white ground.

ARRAN. Large island in the Firth of Clyde, Scotland, in Strathclyde: 32km (20m) by 16km (10m). Area 427 sq.km (165 sq.m); pop. (1971) 4,500.

ARRAS (ahrahs'). French town, cap. of Pas-de-Calais dept, on the Scarpe, N.E. of Paris. Formerly it was famed for its tapestry. Pop. (1975) 50,400.

It gave its name to five battles of the F.W.W., when it was almost destroyed. The fiercest was fought April 1917, with losses on either side in killed, wounded, and missing of 145,000. A. was captured in the German advance on Dunkirk in 1940.

ARRAU (ar'ow), **Claudio** (1903-). Chilean pianist. A concert performer since the age of 5, he excels in Bach and Beethoven.

ARREST. Deprivation of personal liberty with a view to detention. In Britain an A. in civil proceedings now takes place only on a court order, usually for contempt of court. In criminal proceedings an A. may be made on a magistrate's warrant, but a police constable is empowered to arrest without warrant in all cases where he has reasonable ground for thinking a felony has been committed. Under the Vagrancy Act (1824) he could also arrest 'a suspected person loitering with intent to commit an arrestable offence', hence it was known as the 'sus' law and disliked as allegedly used disproportionately against blacks. It was replaced in 1981 by a reformed 'law of attempt'. Private persons may, and are indeed bound to, arrest anyone committing a felony or breach of the peace in their presence. In the US peace officers and private persons have similar rights and duties.

ARRHENIUS (ahrră'nē-oos), **Svante August** (1859-1927). Swedish scientist, the founder of physical chemistry. B. near Uppsala, he became a professor at Stockholm in 1895, and made a special study of electrolysis. He wrote *Worlds in the Making, Destinies of the Stars,* etc., and in 1903 received the Nobel prize for chemistry.

ARROWROOT. Starchy substance derived from the roots and tubers of various plants. The true A. (*Maranta arundinacea*) was used by the Indians of South America as an antidote against the effects of poisoned arrows. The W. Indian island of St Vincent is the main source of supply today.

ARSENIC. Greyish white semi-metallic crystalline element, symbol As, at. wt. 74.91, at. no. 33. It occurs in many ores, and is widely distributed, being present in minute quantities in the soil, the sea, and the human body. The chief source of A. compounds is as a by-product from metallurgical processes. A. is used in insecticides and medicine; as it is a cumulative poison, its presence in food and drugs is very dangerous. The symptoms of A. poisoning are vomiting, diarrhoea, tingling in the limbs and possibly numbness, and collapse.

Arsenious oxide (As_4O_6), or white A., is an important inorganic compound of A. Arsine (AsH_3) has been made as a war gas. Of the organic arsenicals the best known is Salvarsan (q.v.).

ARSON. The wilful setting fire to property, crops, etc., in Britain covered by the Criminal Damage Act (1971).

ART. The creation of something aesthetically satisfying. The *fine* As. incl. painting, sculpture, engraving, and the *useful* As. such activities as weaving, metal work and furniture-making which combine beauty and practical purposes: in modern usage, however, the distinction becomes increasingly blurred.

In the Middle Ages the term was used, chiefly in the plural, to signify a branch of learning which was regarded as an instrument of knowledge; the seven *Liberal Arts* consisted of the *trivium*, i.e. grammar, logic, and rhetoric, and the *quadrivium*, i.e. arithmetic, music, geometry, and astronomy.

ARTAUD (ahrtoh'), **Antonin** (1896-1948). French theatrical director. His play, *The Cenci* (1935), was a failure, but his concept of the 'Theatre of Cruelty', intended to release feelings usually repressed, has become influential in the modern drama. Becoming insane in 1936, he was confined in an asylum.

ART DECO (ahr de'kō). Style originating in the Paris Exposition des arts décoratifs (1925), and continuing through the 1930s: in architecture it is represented by Radio City Music Hall, N.Y. (1932), restored as New York's Entertainment Centre (1979). It had a rather heavy, geometrical simplification of form, intended to be functional and adapted to mass production techniques. By the 1970s A.D. was being favourably re-assessed.

ARTEMIS (ahr'temis). Greek goddess, identified with the Roman Diana. She was the goddess of chastity, the virgin huntress, who presided over childbirth and the young. Ephesus was a chief centre of her cult.

ARTERIOSCLERŌ'SIS. The loss of elasticity of the arteries in later years when they thicken and harden, and which is hastened by unhealthy diet, smoking, alcohol, etc. *Atherosclerosis* is the form of A. in which the innermost layer of the artery is clogged by fatty deposits (thought to form in cases of a high cholesterol diet), which leads to coronary thrombosis, etc.

A'RTERY. One of the vessels which convey blood from the heart. The largest is the aorta, which leads from the left ventricle up over the heart and downwards through the diaphragm into the abdomen. As. are flexible, elastic tubes consisting of 3 layers. The cutting of an A. of any size is a dangerous injury. With middle and old age the As. normally lose their elasticity: *see* ARTERIOSCLEROSIS.

ARTĒ'SIAN WELLS. Artificial borings made through impermeable rock to water-containing beds, when the water rises to the surface by hydrostatic pressure or is pumped up. The name comes from Artois, the French province where they were first adopted in Europe.

ARTHRĪ'TIS. Inflammation of the joints, of which the most widespread form is *rheumatoid A.*, which usually begins in middle age in the small joints of the hands and feet, causing a greater or lesser degree of deformity and painfully restricted movement. Aspirin is still the most commonly used drug. Rheumatoid A. is genetically based, and an autoimmune disease in which the antibodies usually produced for defence of the tissues, attack the joint tissue. It is probably triggered by a virus infection. *See also* CORTISONE and MUSSEL. *Osteoarthritis* tends to affect larger joints, such as the knee and hip. It appears in later life in manual labourers, athletes, dancers, and others whose joints may have been subject to earlier stress or damage. It is now possible to cut out (arthrectomy) badly affected joints replacing them (arthroplasty) with metal alloy or plastic ones, not only in the larger joints, but in the hands, etc.

ARTHRO'PODA. Phylum (Greek 'jointed feet') of invertebrate animals with jointed legs and segmented bodies with a horny or chitinous casing, the latter being shed periodically and replaced as the animal grows. The phylum comprises the Arachnida and king crabs (qq.v.) in one of 2 sub-divisions, and in the other millipedes, centipedes, crustacea and insects (qq.v.). Three-quarters of the some 30 million species are insects.

See also TRILOBITES.

ARTHUR. Legendary early 'king' and hero, probably a Romano-British leader against the pagan Saxon invaders of the 6th cent. The story of the quest for the Holy Grail and the Round Table (which eliminated strife over precedence) for the knights of his court at Camelot (q.v.) was developed in the 12th cent. by Geoffrey of Monmouth. Later writers on the theme of A. incl. the anonymous author of *Sir Gawayn and the Grene Knight* (*c.* 1346), Sir Thomas Malory in *Morte d'Arthur* (1485), Tennyson, *Idylls of the King*, and T. H. White. He was said to have been buried at Glastonbury. **Arthur's seat,** a hill (251m/822ft) of volcanic origin in King's Park, E. of Edinburgh, is linked with the hero only by name.

ARTHUR (1187-1203). English prince, nephew of King John, who is supposed to have had him murdered on 3 April 1203 because he was a possible rival to the English throne. The story of John's order to blind A. is a famous scene in Shakespeare's *King John*.

ARTHUR, Chester Alan (1830-86). 21st President of USA. Son of a Baptist minister, he was b. in Vermont, and became a lawyer and eloquent Republican spokesman. In 1880 he was elected vice-president; and when Garfield was assassinated in the following year, succeeded him as president, holding office until 1885.

ARTHUR'S PASS. Pass in the Southern Alps, NZ, at 926 m (3,038 ft), linking Christchurch by road and rail (through the Otira rock tunnel) with Greymouth on the W. coast.

ARTICHOKE. Two plants of the family Compositae, both familiar as table-vegetables. The true A. (*Cynara scolymus*) is tall, with purplish blue flowers; the bracts of the unopened flower are eaten. The Jerusalem A. (*Helianthus tuberosus*) has edible tubers; it is a native of N. America, and its name is a corruption of the It. *girasole*, sunflower.

ARTIFICIAL INTELLIGENCE. Branch of computer science (AI) which has its own programming languages; is used espec in scientific, medical research, etc, and produces 'models' which show how knowledge is acquired; how humans make deductions and inferences; how emotion and prejudice intervene in decisions; how problems are solved; how creative thought emerges, etc.

ARTIFICIAL RESPIRATION. The process of maintaining breathing in a helpless person, or an unconscious person who has suffered electric shock or is apparently drowned; also in cases of infantile paralysis (anterior poliomyelitis) in which the mechanism of breathing is affected. In cases of electric shock or apparent drowning the first choice is the expired air method (kiss of life), by means of mouth-to-mouth breathing, since it gives greater ventilation than other methods. In paralysis 'iron lungs' are used.

ARTILLERY. One of the 2 main divisions of firearms (q.v.). In general use in Western Europe from the mid-14th cent., A. consisted of very small guns, made of cast iron or bronze, smooth bored; and firing lead, iron or stone balls at low velocities. The barrel, closed at one end (the breech), was filled with a charge of gunpowder, tamped down with a soft 'wad', and the ball placed on top. A tiny 'touch' hole in the breech was filled with powder and lit, forming a 'train' through the barrel to explode the charge. Edward III used guns in his Scottish campaign of 1327, and in the English fleet at the battle of Sluys, 1340. In the 15th cent. attempts were made to eliminate the difficulties involved in obtaining sound metal castings for the bigger guns by fabricating barrels from rods, beaten and welded together lengthwise, and reinforced by iron rings. With the inadequate techniques of the period, this highly unsound method was responsible for many accidents, including the death of James II of Scotland in 1460. With the advent of improved methods, casting prevailed from the 16th cent., but in spite of considerable warfare little progress was made in the next 300 years, except that cannon grew bigger: there had already been a passing fashion in the later 14th cent. for giant cannon, e.g. 'Duille Grete' made in Ghent *c.* 1382, which weighed 15 tonnes and fired a 270kg (600lb) stone ball. The period 1845-85 saw the evolution of the rifled barrel, permitting greater accuracy, and a return to built-up steel construction. Higher velocities and elongated missiles added considerably to penetrating power, diminishing the need for 'big' guns. In the more recent period there have been refinements in construction etc., but even in the S.W.W. the use of A. was still very much 'hit-or-miss'. The modern break-through in the use of electronic devices was dramatically illustrated in the rapid Egyptian advance in the opening phase of the Fourth Arab-Israeli War in 1973. If a target can be seen it can be hit with unerring accuracy, but the consequent heavy casualties among gun crew can be avoided by remote-controlled firing. On board ship also, where A. is referred to as the 'armament', the most modern types of gun turret are unmanned.

ARTILLERY. On exercise in Germany, members of the 5th Regiment Royal Artillery and 3rd Royal Tank Regiment, with an M107 gun. *Photo: Central Office of Information*

AR'TIODA'CTYLA. The 'cloven-hoofed' mammals; more scientifically, those animals distinguished by the structure of their feet, in which the median axis passes between the enlarged, symmetrically-paired 3rd and 4th digits, constituting the main hoof. The 2nd and 5th digits are also commonly represented by a pair of small hoofs, which seldom reach the ground. By the structure of their teeth and stomach the A. are divided into the *Suina* (pig-like animals), comprising the Suidae (pigs and peccaries) and Hippopotamidae (hippopotami); and the *Ruminantia* (ruminant-like animals), including the Tylopoda (camels), the Tragulina (chevrotains), and the Pecora (true ruminants: deer, giraffes, antelopes, goats, sheep, oxen, etc.).

ART NOUVEAU (ahr noovoh'). Decorative style of art (Fr. 'new art') developed in the 1890s and marked by sensuously sinuous line and stylised patterns of flowers and leaves. It was named after a shop in Paris. Exponents incl. Aubrey Beardsley, Sir Alfred Gilbert, C. R. Mackintosh, and René Lalique (qqv). Long under eclipse after 1914, it became a vogue of the 1970s.

ARTOIS (ahrtwah'). Old prov. of N. France, bounded by Flanders and Picardy, and almost corresponding with the modern dept of Pas-de-Calais. Its cap. was Arras.

ARTS COUNCIL OF GREAT BRITAIN. Semi-official organization for the advancement of cultural activities among the people as a whole. It originated in 1940 as a committee of the Pilgrim Trust to encourage the arts in wartime. It was at first known as the Council for the Encouragement of Music and the Arts (CEMA), but in 1945 it was incorporated under its present name. It is assisted by Committees for Scotland and Wales, and specialist panels for music, drama, and the visual arts.

A'RUM. Genus of plants of the family Araceae. The typical species (*A. maculatum*), known as cuckoo-pint or lords-and-ladies, is a common British hedgerow plant. The A. or trumpet lily (*Zantedeschia aethiopica*), a well-known ornamental plant, is a native of Africa.

ARUNACHAL PRADESH. Union Terr. of the Rep. of India in the Himalayas on the borders of China (Tibet) and Burma. Formerly nominally part of Assam, and known as the N.-E. Frontier Agency, it became a Union Terr. in 1972, and was renamed A.P. 'Hills of the Rising Sun'. Its tribal peoples speak 50 different dialects. Boundary disputes led to a Chinese invasion of the area in 1962. The cap. is Shillong. Area 81,426 sq.km (31,438 sq.m); pop. (1971) 444,744.

ARUNDEL, Thomas Howard, 2nd earl of A. (1586-1646). English statesman and patron of the arts. The A. Marbles, part of his collection of Italian sculptures, were given to Oxford university in 1667 by his grandson.

ARUNDEL. Town in Sussex, England, on the r. Arun, 16km (10m) E. of Chichester. Situated in a gap in the S. Downs, it has a magnificent castle (much restored and rebuilt), the seat for centuries of the earls of A. and dukes of Norfolk. The parish church of St Nicolas dates from the 14th cent.; the R.C. church of St Philip Neri was built by the 15th duke in 1873. Pop. (1972) 2,400.

A'RVAL BRETHREN (Lat. *Fratres Arvales,* brothers of the field). Body of priests in ancient Rome who offered annual sacrifices to the *Lares* or divinities of the fields in order to ensure a good harvest. They formed a college of 12 priests, and their chief festival fell in May.

ARYAN (ār'ian or ah'rian). Name given to a broad division of the human race, who are supposed to have inhabited the great stretch of country from Central Asia to Eastern Europe, and to have reached India about 3000 B.C. German theorists conceived of the As. as a white-skinned master race, identifiable with the 'Nordic' or Teutonic race, but there is little or no evidence for such a view. With more reason A. is applied to a division of the Indo-European family of languages, comprising Sanskrit and Iranian, but it ought not to be used as synonymous with Indo-European.

ARYANA. Ancient name of AFGHANISTAN.

ARYA SAMAJ (ah'rya sahmahj'). Hindu religious sect founded by Dayanand Saraswati (1825-88), about 1875. He was a Brahman who renounced idol-worship, and urged a return to the purer principles of the Rig Veda.

ASBESTOS. Any of several related minerals of fibrous structure which offer great heat resistance through their non-inflammability and poor conductivity. Commercial A. is generally made from chrysotile, a kind of serpentine found in Quebec, USSR, and Zimbabwe. It has been used for brake linings, suits for firemen and spacemen, insulation of electric wires in furnaces, and after subjection to heavy neutron bonbardment in reactors and blended with cement, for A. cement sheets and pressure pipes for the building industry. Exposure to A. is a recognized cause of industrial cancer (mesothelioma), espec. in the 'blue' form (from S Africa), rather than the more common 'white', and usage is now subject to stringent regulation. **Asbestosis** is a chronic lung inflammation caused by A. dust.

ASCE'NSION. British island of volcanic origin in the S. Atlantic, 1,126 km (700m) N.W. of St Helena. Area 88 sq.km (34 sq.m). Most of the pop. (1971: 1,231) live in Georgetown, the cap. Discovered on Ascension Day, 1501, by a Portuguese navigator, A. was uninhabited till 1815, when occupied by a British RN garrison: attached to the colony of St Helena in 1922.

ASCENSION DAY. In the Christian calendar, the feast day commemorating Christ's ascension into heaven. Known sometimes as Holy Thursday, it is the 40th day after Easter.

ASCETICISM (aset'isism). The renunciation of the physical pleasures, e.g. in eating and drinking, or the exercise of sexual instincts; and the courting of discomfort, or pain. It ranges from the primitive tabu to the self-denial of the great religions.

ASCHAM (as'kam), **Roger** (*c.* 1515-68). English scholar. Having written a treatise on Henry VIII's favourite sport of archery, he was appointed tutor to the Princess Elizabeth in 1548. He retained favour under Edward VI and Mary (despite his Protestant views), and returned to Elizabeth's service as her secretary after she became queen. His *Scholemaster* (1570) gives still valuable advice on the art of education.

ASCO'RBIC ACID or Vitamin C. A relatively simple organic acid found in fresh fruits and vegetables. It prevents scurvy.

A'SCOT. Village in Berks, 9.5km (6m) S.W. of Windsor. Queen Anne estab. the racecourse on Ascot Heath in 1711, and the Royal A. meeting is still one of the events of the London 'season'. Races incl. the Gold Cup, A. Stakes, Coventry Stakes and King George VI and Queen Elizabeth Stakes.

ASDIC. *See* SONAR.

ASEAN. Association of S.E. Asian Nations (1967) which took over the non-military role of SEATO (q.v.) in 1975.

ASE'PSIS. Freedom from bacteria, particularly in surgery. Modern surgery rests on a meticulously careful technique of A., by which germs are not ever allowed to reach a surgical wound, and are removed from an accidental wound by cutting out damaged tissues and careful cleansing. Similar precautions are used in childbirth and accidents.

ASEXUAL ('without sex'). Biological term applied to those plants and animals which reproduce by division. Unlike sexual reproduction, this does not involve the fusion of two cells, and never needs two parents. Examples are bacteria, amoeba, yeast, strawberry plants, shallots, and apple trees. More recent is the development of the clone (q.v.) method.

ASH. Group of trees of the genus Fraxinus, belonging to the order Oleales. *F. excelsior* is the common species. The timber is of importance. The mountain A. or rowan (*Sorbus aucuparia*) belongs to the Rosaceae.

ASHANTI. Region of Ghana, W. Africa; area 25,100 sq.km (9,700 sq.m); pop. (1970) 1,477,400. Kumasi is the cap. Crops are cocoa and other tropical products. A. art, notably brass figures, gold work, and drums, shows fine craftsmanship.

For more than 200 years forming an independent kingdom, during the 19th cent. the warlike Ashanti people came into conflict with the British on the Gold Coast who sent 4 expeditions against them, and in 1901 formally annexed their country. Otomfuo Sir Osei Agyeman, nephew of the then deposed king, Prempeh I, was made head of the re-established A. confederation in 1935 as Prempeh II, and the Golden Stool, symbol of the A. peoples since the 17th cent., was returned to Kumasi. The Asantahene (King of the A.) still holds durbars - the finest in Africa - in which this stool is ceremonially paraded.

ASHANTI. Bearing the king's stool in procession. An Ashanti king is always 'enstooled' not crowned. *Photo: Werner Forman Archive*

ASHBY-DE-LA-ZOUCH (ash'bi-de-la-zoosh'). Town of Leics, England, 27km (17m) N.W. of Leicester. The 15th cent. castle features in Scott's *Ivanhoe* and Mary Queen of Scots was confined there 1569. Pop. (1971) 8,300.

ASHCROFT, Dame Peggy (1907-). British actress. B. in Croydon (q.v.), she made her first stage appearance with the Birmingham repertory in 1926. Her many parts incl. such Shakespearian roles as Desdemona, Juliet, and

ASIA. Physical features of the great land mass.

Rosalind, and the subtle modernity of Miss Madrigal in *The Chalk Garden*. She was created D.B.E. in 1956.

A'SHDOD. Deepwater port of Israel, on the Mediterranean 32km (20m) S. of Tel-Aviv, which it superseded 1965. It stands on the site of the ancient Philistine stronghold of Askalon. Pop. (1973) 75,000.

ASHES, The. Cricket trophy, theoretically held by the winning team in any series of Test Matches between England and Australia. A humorous obituary notice of 'English cricket', pub. in the *Sporting Times* in 1882, stated that the 'body' would be cremated and the ashes taken to Australia. During the winter of 1882-3, Ivo Bligh, captain of a successful English team visiting Australia, was presented by Melbourne ladies with an urn containing the ashes of the stumps and bails used in the match. The urn is in the keeping of the MCC at Lords.

ASHEVILLE. Town and resort in N. Carolina, USA, on a plateau in the S. Appalachians. Textiles, espec. rayon are made, and traditional hand-weaving is carried on by Biltmore Industries (1901). Thomas Wolfe's home is preserved, and to the S. is the 19th cent. Biltmore mansion, once the home of millionaire George W. Vanderbilt. Nearby are the Great Smoky Mtn nat. park, the Pisgah nat. forest, etc. Pop. (1970) 57,700.

ASHFORD, Daisy (1881-1972). British author of *The Young Visiters* (1919), written when she was nine, and a classic of unconscious humour. The hero of the romance is Mr Salteena: 'I am not quite a gentleman but you would hardly notice it.'

ASHFORD. Town of Kent, England, on the r. Stour, SW of Canterbury. It has locomotive works, now less important, but in 1979 was chosen for expansion as a new commercial and industrial centre for the South-East. Pop. 35,000.

ASHKENÁZIM. Jews of German or E European descent, as opposed to the Sephardim.

ASHKENA'ZY, Vladimir (1937-). Russian pianist. He has a technique rather differing from standard Western practice and in 1962 was joint winner of the Tchaikovsky competition with John Ogdon. He excels in Rachmaninov, Prokofiev and Liszt.

ASHKHABA'D. Cap. of the Turkmen S.S.R. in a region on the fringe of the Kara-Kum desert, but well watered by irrigation canals. Founded in 1881, it produces 'Bukhara' carpets, has a large glass factory, etc., and is the business and cultural centre of the Republic. It is the hottest place in the Soviet Union. Pop. (1977) 302,000.

A'SHMOLE, Elias (1617-92). British antiquary. B. at Lichfield, he became a lawyer, served with the Royal forces during the Civil War, and after the Restoration held posts in the excise and other offices. He wrote books on alchemy, and on antiquarian subjects, amassed a fine library, and a collection of curiosities, both of which he presented to Oxford Univ. His collection was housed in the 'Old Ashmolean' (built 1679-83), and forms the basis of the present Ashmolean Museum, erected in 1897.

ASHMORE AND CARTIER ISLANDS. Territory transferred to the authority of the Commonwealth of Australia by Britain in 1931, and comprising Middle, East and West Is. (the Ashmores) and Cartier Is., in the Indian Ocean *c.* 320km (200m) off the N.W. coast of Australia. They are admin. as part of the Northern Territory and are uninhabited, although W. Ashmore has an automatic weather station.

A'SHRAM. An Indian community, the members of which lead a simple life of discipline and self-denial, and devote themselves to social service, e.g. that of Mahatma Gandhi at Wardha, and the poet Sir Rabindranath Tagore's at Santiniketan.

ASHRIDGE. The former seat of the earls Brownlow near Berkhamsted, Herts, England, which in 1928 was bought and endowed as a college of citizenship on conservative and constitutional lines as a memorial to Bonar Law. After various changes, it was in 1959 converted into a management training centre with the backing of major British industries.

ASHTON, Sir Frederick (1904-). British dancer and choreographer. B. in Ecuador, he joined the Vic-Wells in 1935, he was knighted in 1963 and succeeded De Valois as director of the Royal Ballet (1963-70). Later ballets incl. *Marguerite and Armand* (1963) based on Dumas and *The Dream* (1964) on Shakespeare, and *Rhapsody* (1980). Awarded O.M. 1977.

ASHTON UNDER LYNE. Town in the met. co. of Greater Manchester. There are light industries, coal and cotton. Pop. (1972) 48,760.

ASH WEDNESDAY. The first day of Lent, so called from the use of ashes as a symbol of penance. In the Catholic Church, members of the congregation are marked on the forehead with a cross in ash, obtained by burning the palms from Palm Sunday of the previous year.

ASIA. The largest of the continents, forming the larger eastern part of Eurasia and the main land-mass of the old world. It occupies ⅓ of the total land surface of the globe, stretching from within the Arctic Circle almost to the Equator, the most northerly point being Cape Chelyuskin, 78° N., the most southerly Cape Romania, at the tip of the Malayan peninsula, 1° N. The E. Indian islands extend to 10° S. of the Equator. The continent, which has an area of 44,000,000 sq.km (17,000,000 sq.m), is surrounded by the Arctic, Pacific and Indian Oceans on the N., E., and S., and adjoins Europe along the Urals, and the shores of the Caspian, Black, and Mediterranean Seas. The isthmus of Suez, cut in two by the Suez canal, joins A. to Africa, while Bering Strait in the N.E. separates it from America.

Geography. There are 5 main geographical divisions: (1) The central triangular mountain mass, composed of a number of huge ranges diverging from the Pamir region, and including the Himalayas with the highest mountains in the world. N. of the Himalayas is the great Tibetan plateau, bounded on the N. by the Kunlun Mountains. To the N. of the plateau lie a series of ranges and enclosed basins, most notable of which is the Tarim basin. The Gobi (desert) occupies a vast plateau of central A. (2) The S.W. plateaux and ranges, which form the complicated relief of Afghanistan, Baluchistan, and Iran. (3) The northern lowlands, stretching from the central mountainous mass to the Arctic Ocean, and drained by several huge rivers, e.g. Ob, Yenisei, Lena, which are frozen over for much of their course for some 6 months of the year. Great floods occur in spring when the rivers are full and their mouths still frozen. (4) The eastern margin and the islands, where a large part of the pop. is concentrated. The lowlands are crossed by large rivers, e.g. Menam, Mekong, Xi Jiang, Chang Jiang, and Huang He. Off the E coast of A. lie the islands of Sakhalin, the Kuriles, Japan, Taiwan, etc., while off the S.E. coasts lies the great group of the E. Indian islands, with Sumatra, Java, Borneo, the Philippines, and hundreds of others. Other small groups lie off India and Burma. (5) The southern plateaux and river plains which include the ancient masses of Arabia, the Deccan, and the alluvial plains of the Euphrates and Tigris, Indus, Ganges, and Irrawaddy.

Climate. Climatically, A. experiences great extremes and contrasts, the heart of the continent becoming bitterly cold in winter and greatly heated in summer. It is this fact, with the resulting pressure and wind systems, that is basically responsible for the Asiatic monsoons, which bring heavy rain to all S.E. Asia, China, and Japan, between May and October, with a more or less dry season the other half year. The most southerly latitudes have an equatorial climate, while the far N. is arctic.

Vegetation and Agriculture. The vegetational cover varies with the climate, from tropical rain forest, through temperate grassland, to semi-desert scrub. In the wet tropical parts the main crop is rice, the staple food crop of Asiatic peoples. Where rainfall or temperature is unsuited to rice, millet, maize, wheat, or soya bean takes its place. Cotton, jute, tea, rubber, dates and other fruits, olives, and tobacco are grown and silk is reared where the climate is suitable. Timber is an important product from the coniferous woods of Siberia, the hardwood forests of China, and the tropical zones, where teak is found.

History. Asia has some of the earliest beginnings of culture, e.g. Jericho and Catal Hüyük (Turkey); Indus Valley and China (qq.v.), as well as in the medieval period the destructive nomad empires (Genghiz and Kublai Khan); the great Hindu and Moslem dynasties of India; the exotic civilizations of S.E. Asia; and the isolated flowering of Chinese and Japanese development. The West became dominant in the 19th cent., but led by Japan A. swiftly turned both military and economic weapons against the conquerors in the 20th.

ASIA, Soviet Central. Formerly Russian Turkestan, it consists of the Kazakh, Uzbek, Tadzhik, Turkmen and Kirghiz S.S.Rs. These areas were subdued by Russia as recently as 1866-73, and even under Soviet rule nationalist sentiment persists, leading to shortfalls in agricultural production, etc., and the estab. in 1962 of a Central Asian Bureau to strengthen centralized control by the Party Praesidium in Moscow. These republics are also the home of the majority of Moslems of the USSR.

ASIA MINOR. Historical name for Anatolia.

ASIENTO (ahsē-en'tō; Span., 'contract'). Name given to the treaty of 1713, whereby British traders were permitted by Spain to introduce 144,000 Negro slaves into the Spanish-American colonies in the course of the next 30 years. In 1750 the right was bought out by the Spanish government for £100,000.

ASKHABAD. *See* ASHKHABAD.

ASMARA (asmah'ra). Town in Ethiopa, 64km (40m) S.W. of Massawa on the Red Sea. The cap. of Eritrea, it is an industrial and communications centre, and the Naval School is here. In 1974 it was the focus of unrest which precipitated revolution. Pop. (1973) 200,000.

ASNIÈRES (ahnē-ār'). N.W. suburb of Paris, France, on the left bank of the Seine; a boating centre and pleasure resort. Pop. (1973) 90,000.

ASŌ'KA (reigned 264-228 B.C.). Indian emperor who made Buddhism the state religion. The grandson of Chandragupta, founder of the Maurya dynasty, he reigned over the ancient kingdom of Magadha, became converted to Buddhism, issued edicts enjoining the adoption of the leading tenets of the new faith, and had these carved on pillars (many of which have survived), and on the walls of caves, rocks, etc.

ASP, or **aspic.** Name applied to several species of poisonous snakes. The A. of S. Europe (*Vipera aspis*) is a species of viper closely allied to the adder. The Egyptian horned A. (*Cereastes cornutus*) is supposed to have been the one with which Cleopatra ended her life. The Africa A. (*Naja haje*) is related to the cobras.

ASPA'RAGUS. Genus of plants of the lily family (Liliaceae). *As. officinalis* is cultivated, and the young shoots are eaten as a vegetable.

ASPĀ'SIA (fl. 440 B.C.). Mistress of Pericles, the Athenian statesman; since she was b. in Miletus their marriage was not recognized by Athenian law, but their son, Pericles, was subsequently legitimized. Her salon was a famous meeting-place for the celebrities of Athens.

ASPEN. Winter sports resort in the Rocky Mts., Maryland, USA. The A. Inst. for Humanistic Studies (founded in the 1930s, but now also with an HQ in NY) is influential: Kissinger is a fellow. Pop. (1970) 16,820.

ASPEN. Species (*Populus tremula*) of poplar (q.v.).

ASPEN LODGE. *See* CAMP DAVID.

Territorial Divisions of Asia

Territory	*Area in 1,000 sq. km.*	*Pop. in 1,000s*	*Capital*
Afghanistan	650	15,056	Kabul
Arab Emirates, United	83	1,283	Dubai**
Bahrein	.6	431	Manama
Bangladesh	143	101,408	Dacca
Bhutan	46	1,417	Punakha
Brunei	6	232	Bandar Seri Begawan
Burma	678	36,919	Rangoon
China	9,556	1,037,588	Peking
Taiwan	36	16,500	Taipei
Cyprus	9	665	Nicosia
Hong Kong	1.2	4,700	Victoria
India	3,215	767,681	Delhi
Indonesia	1,915	173,103	Djakarta
Iran	1,648	45,191	Tehran
Iraq	444	15,507	Baghdad
*Israel	89	4,128	Jerusalem
Japan	370	120,731	Tokyo
Jordan	98	2,668	Amman
Kampuchea	181	6,249	Phnôm-penh
Korea, North	121	20,082	Pyongyang
Korea, South	99	42,643	Seoul
Kuwait	19	1,701	Kuwait
Laos	236	3,605	Vientiane
Lebanon	10	2,619	Beirut
Macao	16	280	Macao
Malaysia	332	15,467	Kuala Lumpur
Maldive Islands	.3	182	Malé
Mongolian Rep.	1,560	1,893	Ulan Bator
Nepal	141	16,966	Katmandu
Oman	212	1,228	Muscat
Pakistan	804	99,199	Islamabad
Philippine Rep.	300	56,808	Manila
Qatar	11	301	Doha
Saudi Arabia	2,400	11,152	Riyadh
Singapore	.6	2,556	Singapore
Sri Lanka	66	16,344	Colombo
Syria	186	10,535	Damascus
Thailand	514	51,546	Bangkok
Turkey-in-Asia	757	35,398	Ankara
U.S.S.R. (Asiatic)			
Kazakh S.S.R.	2,717	14,700	Alma-Ata
Kirghiz S.S.R.	198	3,500	Frunze
R.S.F.S.R. in Asia	12,050	34,150	
Tadzhik S.S.R.	143	3,700	Dushanbe
Turkmen S.S.R.	488	2,700	Ashkhabad
Uzbek S.S.R.	448	14,800	Tashkent
Vietnam	336	60,492	Hanoi
Yemen, North	195	6,159	San'a
Yemen, South	160	2,209	Aden
	43,688	2,753,944	

*1967 area **Largest town

A'SPHALT. A mixture of different hydrocarbons forming a kind of semi-solid, brown or black bitumen. Considerable natural deposits occur round the Dead Sea and in the Philippines, Cuba, Venezuela, and in the pitch lake of Trinidad. Bituminous limestone occurs at Neufchâtel. A. is mixed with rock chips to form paving material, and the purer kinds are used for insulating material and for waterproofing masonry.

A'SPHODEL. Genus of plants (*Asphodelus*) belonging to the Liliaceae. *A. albus*, the white A. or king's spear, is found in Italy and Greece, sometimes covering large areas, and providing grazing for sheep. *A. luteus* is the yellow A. These beautiful plants were connected by the Greeks with the dead, and were supposed to grow in the Elysian fields.

ASPIDI'STRA. Small genus of Asiatic Liliaceae. The broad-leaved Japanese A. (*A. lurida*) survives much ill-treatment as an indoor plant, and was popular in Britain in the Victorian parlour.

A'SPIRIN. Name of drug given by the firm of Bayer, Meister & Lucius to a synthetic acetylsalicylic acid which they invented in the early years of the 20th cent., and which soon became immensely popular as a household remedy for headaches and minor pains.

ASPLĒ'NIUM. Genus of ferns of the family Polypodiaceae, and generally known as spleenworts.

ASQUITH, Herbert Henry, 1st earl of Oxford and Asquith (1852-1928). British Liberal statesman. B. in Yorks, he was ed. at the City of London School and Balliol Coll., Oxford, and was called to the Bar in 1876. Elected MP in 1886, he was Home Sec. in Gladstone's 1892-5 govt and in 1905 he became Chancellor of the Exchequer in Campbell-Bannerman's govt; he introduced the first provision for old age pensions, and on the PM's death he succeeded him.

The rejection by the Lords of Lloyd George's budget in 1909 produced a political crisis. In 2 general elections in 1910 the Liberals were returned to power with reduced majorities; the budget was passed, and the Parliament Act (1911) limited the Lords' right to veto legislation. The Home Rule Bill (1912) met with even fiercer opposition, until the outbreak of the F.W.W. temporarily united the nation.

A coalition govt formed in May 1915 lasted till the reverses suffered by the Allies forced A. to resign in Dec. 1916, when he was succeeded by Lloyd George. At the 1918 election A. and his followers were heavily defeated, he himself losing the seat he had held for 32 years. He returned to the House in 1920.

After the collapse of the coalition in 1923 an alliance was formed between the followers of A. and Lloyd George. The Liberals held the balance of power in the next parliament, and it was A.'s support which enabled the Labour Party to take office. Defeated in the 1924 general election, he was raised to the peerage in 1925, and remained leader of the Liberal Party until 1926, when he resigned following dissensions over the general strike.

His eldest son Raymond A. (1878-1916) was killed in action in the F.W.W.; his 2nd son Herbert A. (1881-1947), barrister, poet and novelist, m. Lady Cynthia Charteris (1887-1960), dau. of the 11th earl of Wemyss, who wrote reminiscences and a diary. Most famous of his children were Lady Asquith of Yarnbury (1887-1969) who, as Lady Violet Bonham-Carter (she m. in 1915 Sir Maurice Bonham-Carter, who d. 1960), was an active Liberal, being pres. of the Party Organization 1945-7: *see* GRIMOND. In 1964 she was created a life peeress, taking the title Lady A. Anthony A. (1902-68), director of such films as *Quiet Wedding, The Winslow Boy* and *The Millionairess*; and Elizabeth (1897-1945) who m. Prince Antoine Bibesco and wrote short stories, novels and poems. Both the last-named were his children by his 2nd wife, Margot Tennant (1868-1945), daughter of a Glasgow ironmaster, whom he m. in 1894 and who was a celebrated wit. Her vols. of memoirs offended many by their lack of reticence.

ASQUITH. A man of rare achievement in his peacetime ministry, his motto 'Wait and see' was less appropriate to the demands of war, and he was superseded by Lloyd George.
Photo: Courtesy National Portrait Gallery, London

ASS. A mammal (*Equus asinus*), related to the horse, zebra, and quagga, and with them constituting the family Equidae. The typical form is the African A., which is the source of our domestic breeds. Apart from its familiar 'braying roar', it differs from the horse (*Equus*) chiefly in its smaller size, much larger ears, tufted tail, characteristic fur and markings, narrower hoofs adapted for sure-footed traversing of rocky hillsides. The colour is usually grey.

A'SSAD, Hafez al (1930-). Syrian statesman. A Baathist and Shiah Moslem, he became PM after a bloodless military coup in 1970, and in 1971 was the first pres. of Syria to be elected by popular vote. He estab. close relations with other Arab powers. *See* SHIAH.

ASSA'M. State of the Rep. of India, lying between Bangladesh and Burma, consisting mainly of the valleys of the Surma and Brahmaputra, and surrounded by a fringe of jungle-clad mountains. Half India's tea is grown in A., rice and jute are cultivated and there are timber resources. Oil, first discovered 1888, is refined, and there is coal. By 1980 there was violent native agitation to expel newcomers from other states arriving to settle from 1951. Pending construction of a new cap., the admin. centre is at Shillong. Area 100,730 sq.km (8,706 sq.m); pop. (1980) 19,000,000, incl. 4,000,000 Bengalis and Nepalis.

Part of British India from 1826, A. was made a separate prov. in 1874, and in 1947 was incl. in the Dominion of India, except for most of Silhet district which went to

Pakistan. The Gara, and Khasi and Jaintia tribal hill districts became in 1970 the state of Meghalaya (q.v.). In 1972 the Mizo hill district became the Union Terr. of Mizoram (q.v.). *See also* ARUNACHAL PRADESH.

ASSASSINATION. Treacherous and violent murder, especially of royal or public personages. Some of the famous As. in history are given in the Table.

Famous Assassinations

	B.C.
Sennacherib of Assyria	681
Hipparchus, tyrant of Athens	514
Philip II of Macedon	336
Julius Caesar	44
	A.D.
Caligula, Roman emperor	41
Domitian	96
Thomas à Becket	1170
James I of Scotland	1437
James III of Scotland	1488
William the Silent	1584
Henry III of France	1589
Henry IV of France	1610
Duke of Buckingham	1628
Prince Wallenstein	1634
J.P. Marat	1793
Paul I of Russia	1801
Spencer Perceval	1812
Abraham Lincoln	1865
J.A. Garfield	1881
Alexander II of Russia	1881
Lord F. Cavendish	1882
M.F. Carnot	1894
Humbert I of Italy	1900
W. McKinley	1901
Alexander and Draga of Serbia	1903
Carlos of Portugal	1908
George I of Greece	1913
Archduke Francis Ferdinand	1914
Field Marshal Sir H.H. Wilson	1922
Paul Doumer	1932
Dr. Dollfuss	1934
Alexander of Yugoslavia	1934
Leon Trotsky	1940
Reinhard Heydrich	1942
Lord Moyne	1944
Mahatma Gandhi	1948
Count Bernadotte	1948
Abdullah of Jordan	1951
Liaquat Ali Khan	1951
Feisal II (Iraq)	1958
J.F. Kennedy	1963
H.F. Verwoerd	1966
M. Luther King	1968
R.F. Kennedy	1968
L. Carrero Blanco	1974
Faisal (Saudi Arabia)	1975
Lord Mountbatten	1979
Anwar Sadat	1981
Indira Gandhi	1984

ASSAYING. The determination of the quantity of a given chemical substance present in a given amount of a sample to be tested. Usually it refers to determining the purity of the precious metals. The assay may be carried out by 'wet' methods, when the sample is wholly or partially dissolved in some suitable reagent (often an acid), or by 'dry' or 'fire' methods, in which fusion techniques are used.

ASSENT, Royal. Formal consent given by a British sovereign to the passage of a bill through parliament, after which it becomes an Act of Parliament. The last instance of a royal refusal was the rejection of the Scottish Militia Bill of 1702 by Queen Anne.

ASSISI (ahsē'sē). Town of Umbria, Italy, 19km (12m) S.E. of Perugia. It is the birthplace of St Francis, and the Franciscan monastery, completed in 1253, contains his tomb. The churches of St Francis are adorned with frescoes by Giotto, Cimabue, and others. Pop. (1971) 24,400.

ASSIUT. Alternative transliteration of ASYUT.

ASSĪZ'ES. In Britain, the courts formerly held by judges of the High Court in each co.: they were abolished under the Courts Act (1971).

ASSOCIATED STATE of the United Kingdom. Status proposed in a British Colonial Office White Paper in 1965, as a solution for the problems of the Leeward and Windward Is. It involves full internal self-govt, leaving Britain responsible for external relations and defence, and was first adopted by Antigua in 1966.

ASSOCIATION FOOTBALL. *See* FOOTBALL.

ASSOCIATION OF SOUTH EAST ASIAN NATIONS. Organization (ASEAN) estab. at Bangkok (its HQ) in 1967 to accelerate economic growth, social progress and cultural development in the area. It took over the non-military aspects of the South East Asia Treaty Organization (SEATO), a collective defence system which was phased out after the Vietnam débâcle in 1975.

ASSUAN. Alternative transliteration of ASWAN.

ASSUMPTION. Principal feast of the Blessed Virgin in the R.C. Church, held on 15 Aug., when her translation into heaven is commemorated.

ASSY. Village and sanatorium in Haute-Savoie, France, 994m (3,280 ft) a.s.l., where the church of Notre Dame de Toute Grâce, begun in 1937, consecrated 1950, is adorned by Braque, Chagall, Matisse, Derain, Rouault, and other artists. Pop. (1973) 1,400.

ASSYRIA. Empire of antiquity in the Near East. The land of A. originally consisted of a narrow strip of alluvial soil on each side of the Tigris, starting where the Lower Zab joins the river, and reaching to the foothills beyond Dur-Sharrukin, the old city of Sargon. The area was settled about 3500 B.C., and the empire collapsed in 612 B.C.

Sumerian civilization in Mesopotamia came to an end about 2500 B.C., with the rise to power of Sargon of Akkad; for nearly 200 years A. was subject first to the dynasty of Akkad and then to the Gutians, barbarians from the north. The first Assyrian kings are mentioned during the wars following the decline of the 3rd dynasty of Ur. For many centuries yet, however, A. was under Babylonian and subsequently Egyptian suzerainty. About 1450 B.C. a fresh resurgence of A. began. Under king Ashur-uballit (reigned c. 1380–1340 B.C.) the future greatness of A. as a military power was laid. His work was continued by Adad-nirari I, Shalmaneser I, and Tukulti-enurta I, who conquered Babylonia and assumed the title of king of Sumer and Akkad. During the reign of Nebuchadnezzar I (1150–1110 B.C.), A. was subject to Babylonia, but Tiglath-pileser I threw off the yoke. In the Aramaean invasions, most of the ground gained was lost. From the accession of Adad-nirari II in 911 B.C. A. pursued a triumphant course of expansion and conquest, culminating in the mastery of Elam, Mesopotamia, Syria, Palestine, the Arabian marches, and finally of Egypt. Of this period the O.T. records and many 'documents' such as the Black Obelisk celebrating the conquest of Shalmaneser III in the 9th cent. B.C. survive.

The reign of Ashur-nazir-pal II (885-860 B.C.) was spent in unceasing warfare, in which he is said to have introduced 'frightfulness' as evidenced by many bas-reliefs. Shalmaneser III warred against the Syrian states. At the battle of Qarqar (854 B.C.) the Assyrian advance received a setback, and there followed a period of decline. The final period of Assyrian ascendancy began with the accession of Tiglath-pileser III (746-728 B.C.). Sargon, Sennacherib, Esarhaddon, and Ashurbanipal raised A. to the highest peak of its glory, culminating in the conquest of Egypt by Esarhaddon in 671 B.C. From this time the empire seems to have fallen into decay, and a union of Nabopolassar of Babylonia and Cyaxares of Media led to its destruction. Nineveh was destroyed, and A. became a Median province and subsequently a principality of the Persian empire.

Much of Assyrian religion, law, social structure and artistic achievement was based on, or derived from, neighbouring sources: The Assyrians adopted the cuneiform script invented by the Sumerians, and took over the Sumerian pantheon, although their national god, Ashur (Assur), assumed the chief place in the cult. They adopted in the main the Sumerian structure of society. The famous library of Ashurbanipal excavated at Nineveh witnesses to the thoroughness with which Babylonia culture was being assimilated. *See* BABYLONIA.

ASSYRIA. Relief from the palace at Nimrud, showing Ashur-nazir-pal II engaged in a lion hunt. *Photo: Courtesy of the British Museum*

ASTAIRE, Fred (1899-). American dancer. B. in Omaha, Nebraska, he danced in partnership with his sister Adele A. (1898-1981) 1916 until her mar. with Lord Charles Cavendish, younger son of the Duke of Devonshire, in 1932. Entering films in 1933, he appeared in *Roberta, Top Hat, Follow the Fleet, Easter Parade, Funny Face,* and others which contained many sequences designed by himself. Most famous of his later partners was Ginger Rogers.

ASTA'RTE. Semitic goddess, the Ashtoreth of the Bible. She was the embodiment of the female principle, a great nature goddess watching over fertility, and her rites provided occasion for sexual licence.

ASTATINE. Symbol At, at. no. 85, at. weight 210; halogen-like and highly radioactive. It is artificially made by bombarding bismuth in a cyclotron.

A'STER, or starwort. Genus of plants of the Compositae, belonging to the same division as the daisy. The sea aster (*A. tripolium*) grows wild on sea cliffs in the S.W. of England, but many more species are familiar as cultivated garden flowers. These include the Michaelmas Daisy (*A. tradescanti*). The China aster (*Callistephus hortensis*) belongs to a closely allied genus; it was introduced to Europe from China and Japan in the early 18th cent.

ASTEROIDS. The As., more properly known as Minor Planets, are small bodies circling the Sun between the paths of Mars and Jupiter - though a few, such as Eros, depart from the main swarm and may approach the Earth fairly closely. The largest are Ceres 670km (416m) in diameter; Pallas 450km (280m); Vesta 385km (239m), the brightest and the only one visible to the naked eye; and Juno 240km (149m). They are thought to have condensed from the primordial cloud of gas and dust from which the solar system was formed. Many of the smaller As. are irregular in shape, e.g. Eros is elongated 19×6km (12×4m) and rotates in 5 hr 17 min. A previously unknown A. approached within *c.* 1,200,000 km. (750,000 m.) of Earth in 1976 — close in space distances. They are composed mostly of iron and silicon.

ASTHMA (asth'- or as'ma). Disease distinguished by recurring attacks of breathlessness, caused by a spasm of the diaphragm or breathing tubes, or congestion of the membrane lining the tubes. *Ordinary A.* is essentially a reaction to a foreign protein, e.g. dust, eggs, milk, and the hair or scurf of an animal. As such it belongs to the same group of diseases as hay-fever, nettlerash, and some forms of epilepsy - the so-called allergic diseases. *Cardiac A.* is a distinct condition in which the breathlessness is caused by a form of heart disease.

ASTI (ahs'tē). City of Piedmont, 48km (30m) S.E. of Turin, on the Tanaro. It is the seat of a bishopric and has a Gothic cathedral. The sparkling wine of Asti prov. is famed. Pop. (1971) 68,400.

ASTON, Francis William (1877-1945). British physicist. From 1910 he worked in the Cavendish Laboratory, Cambridge. He pub. his *Isotopes* and received the Nobel Prize for chemistry in 1922. His researches were of the utmost value in the development of atomic theory.

ASTOR, John Jacob (1763-1848). American millionaire. B. near Heidelberg, in Germany, he set up as a fur trader in America, operating from the Great Lakes to the Pacific. He increased his wealth enormously by astute investment, and d. worth $30 million. His eldest son, WILLIAM BACKHOUSE A. (1792-1875), became known as the 'landlord of New York' and made a further fortune by land deals.

ASTOR, William Waldorf, 1st visct (1848-1919). Great-grandson of John Jacob A. (q.v.), he was an American diplomat and writer before becoming a naturalized Briton in 1899. In 1917 he was made a visct. His son, WALDORF ASTOR, 2nd visct (1879-1952), was Cons. MP for Plymouth 1910-9, when he succeeded to the peerage. He was chief proprietor of the *Observer,* Lord Mayor of Plymouth, 1939-44, and was keenly interested in the Turf.

He m. in 1906 Nancy Witcher Langhorne (1879-1964), LADY ASTOR. B. in Virginia, USA, she succeeded her husband as MP for Plymouth (1919-45), and was the 1st woman MP to take her seat in the House of Commons. An opponent of the Drink Trade, she was a famous political hostess, and govt policy was said to be decided before the S.W.W. at her Cliveden (q.v.) house parties.

ASTRAKHAN (ahstrahkhahn'). City in the R.S.F.S.R., on the delta of the Volga, cap. of A. region. Anciently a Tartar cap., it became Russian in 1556. It is the chief port for the Caspian fisheries. Pop. (1977) 466,000.

ASTROLOGY (astrol'oji). So-called art or science of foretelling the future from the positions of the stars (Gk *astron*, star; *legein*, speak). The belief that the fortunes of men and nations are affected for good or evil by the movements of the stars and planets flourished in ancient Babylon. It spread to the Mediterranean world, and was widely held among the Greeks and Romans. During the Middle Ages A. had a powerful vogue, and astrological beliefs are frequently encountered in Elizabethan and Jacobean literature. In spite of the rise of modern science, popular interest in A. has never completely died. The 1st edition of *Old Moore's Almanac* appeared in 1700, and there have been annual editions since. Astrological forecasts are a prominent feature in popular newspapers and journals.

The astrologer 'casts a horoscope' based on the date and hour of his subject's birth, i.e. draws a diagram showing the position at that moment of the sun and moon, the planets, and the 12 signs of the Zodiac. These heavenly bodies are supposed to represent different character traits and influences, and by observing their positions and interrelations the astrologer professes to assess the person's character and to foretell the main outlines of his career.

A'STRON. Large-scale cosmic impact features on the surface of the Earth, Moon, etc., caused by meteorites. The Moon has more than 300,000 craters over 1 km in diameter easily visible; those on Earth are more obscure because they have been more rapidly eroded. It has been suggested that such geographical features as the bulge of W Africa, and the Great Australian Bight, are the remains of As.

ASTRONAUT. US term for man making flights into space. *See* SPACE RESEARCH.

ASTRONOMER ROYAL. Title of the astronomer in charge of the Royal Observatory estab. at Greenwich, England, in 1675. Since 1958 the observatory has been located at Herstmonceux Castle, Sussex, to avoid the obscuring smoke and lights of London.

The A.R. besides his strictly astronomical work has various public duties relating to weather, time, Summer Time, and the broadcast time signal (rhythmic and pips). The A.R. for Scotland is Prof. H. A. Brück.

Astronomers Royal

John Flamsteed	1675	Sir Geo. Biddell Airy	1835
Edmund Halley	1720	Sir W.H.M. Christie	1881
James Bradley	1742	Sir Frank Dyson	1910
Nathaniel Bliss	1762	Sir H. Spencer Jones	1933
Nevil Maskelyne	1765	Sir Richard Woolley	1956
John Pond	1811	Sir Martin Ryle	1972
		F. Graham Scott	1982

ASTRONOMY. The science that deals with the celestial bodies - the Sun; the Moon; the planets and other members of the Solar System; the stars, and the galaxies. It is concerned with the positions and motions of these bodies; with the explanation of their motions; with their distances, sizes, masses, temperatures and physical conditions.

There can be little doubt that A. is the oldest science in the world, since there are observational records from Babylonia, China and Ancient Egypt. The first true astronomers, however, were the Greeks, and the work of men such as Thales, Pythagoras, and Hipparchus will always be remembered. The Greeks knew that the Earth is a sphere, and not flat, as earlier peoples had believed; Eratosthenes of Cyrene even measured the size of the Earth with considerable accuracy. Star-catalogues were drawn up, the most celebrated being that of Hipparchus. Fortunately, the work of the Greek philosophers was summarized by Ptolemy of Alexandria in a great book which has survived in its Arab translation, the *Almagest*. The main defect of Greek A. was that the Earth was still regarded as the centre of the universe - though even this had been doubted by some philosophers, notably Aristarchus of Samos, who maintained that the Earth moves round the Sun.

Ptolemy, the last famous astronomer of the Greek school, died in or about the year A.D. 180, and little progress was made for some cents. When A. revived, it did so by way of the Arabs, who carried out theoretical researches from the 8th and 9th cents., and who also produced good star-catalogues. Unfortunately, true A. was handicapped by a general belief in the pseudo-science of astrology, and this continued to be the case until the end of the Middle Ages.

The dawn of a new era came in 1543, when a Polish canon, Copernicus, pub. a work entitled *De Revolutionibus Orbium Coelestium*, in which he demonstrated that the Sun, not the Earth, is the centre of the planetary system. Copernicus was wrong in many respects - for instance, he still believed that all celestial orbits must be perfectly circular - but he had taken the fundamental step. Tycho Brahe, of Denmark (q.v.), increased the accuracy of observations by means of improved instruments, allied to his own personal skill, and his observations were used by the German mathematician Johann Kepler (q.v.) to prove the validity of the Copernican system. However, there was considerable opposition to the idea of removing the Earth from its proud position in the centre of the universe; the Christian Church was openly hostile, and ironically, Tycho Brahe never accepted the idea that the Earth could move round the Sun. Yet before the end of the 17th cent. the theoretical work of Sir Isaac Newton had placed celestial mechanics upon a really firm footing.

The telescope was invented in or about 1608, by Hans Lippershey in Holland, and was first applied to astronomy by the Italian scientist Galileo (q.v.) in the winter of 1609-10. Immediately Galileo made a series of spectacular discoveries. He found the 4 satellites of Jupiter, which gave strong support to the Copernican theory; he saw the craters of the Moon, the phases of Venus, and the myriad faint stars of the Milky Way. His telescope was feeble by modern standards, and magnified only 30 times, but before long larger telescopes were built, and official observatories were established. Greenwich Observatory, for example, dates from 1675.

Galileo's telescope was a *refractor*; that is to say, it collected its light by means of a glass lens or object-glass. Certain difficulties led Newton, in 1671, to develop the *reflecting telescope*, in which the light is collected by means of a curved mirror. (Newton was not the first to suggest this principle, but he seems to have been the first to construct such an instrument.) *See* TELESCOPE.

Theoretical researches continued, and astronomy made rapid progress in all directions. New planets were discovered - Uranus in 1781, by Herschel, and Neptune in 1846, by Adams and Le Verrier; even more significant was the first measurement of the distance of a star, in 1838, when the German astronomer Bessel established that the star 61 Cygni lies at a distance of about 11 light-years. (A light-year is the distance travelled by light in one year; it is equal to $9,461 \times 10^{12}$ km (5,880,000,000,000 m). Astronomical spectroscopy was developed, first by Fraunhofer in Germany and then by men such as Secchi and Huggins, while Kirchhoff successfully interpreted the spectra of the Sun and stars; and by the 1860s good photographs of the Moon had been obtained, so that by the end of the cent. photographic methods had started to play the leading role in research.

William Herschel (q.v.), probably the greatest observer in the history of A., investigated the shape of the star-system or galaxy during the latter part of the 18th cent., and concluded that the stars are arranged roughly in the form of a double-convex lens. Basically, Herschel was correct, though it is now known that he was wrong in placing the Sun near the centre of the system; in fact, the Sun is well out toward the edge, and lies some 25,000 to 30,000 light-years from the galactic nucleus. Herschel also studied the luminous 'clouds' or nebulae, and made the tentative suggestion that those nebulae capable of resolution into stars might be separate galaxies, far outside the Galaxy in which the Solar System is situated. It was not until 1923 that Hubble (q.v.), using the 254cm (100in) reflector at the Mount Wilson Observatory, was able to prove the correctness of this view. It is now known that the 'starry nebulae' are galaxies in their own right, and that they lie at immense distances. The brightest galaxy visible from Europe, the Great Spiral in Andromeda (faintly visible to the naked eye), is more than 2,000,000 light-years away; the most remote galaxy so far measured lies at about 5,000 million light-years. It was also found that the galaxies tended to form groups, and that each group was apparently receding from each other group at speeds proportional to their distance.

This concept of an expanding and evolving Universe (q.v.) at first rested largely on Hubble's law, relating the distance of objects to the amount their spectra shift towards red — the 'red shift' (*see* DOPPLER). Subsequent evidence derived from objects not to be studied in visible light, but by using other parts of the electromagnetic spectrum, notably the radio and x-ray bands, has provided confirmation. Radioastronomy had estab. its place in probing to — and beyond — the limits attainable by optical astronomy by demonstrating in 1954 that an optically visible distant galaxy was identical with a powerful radio source known as Cygnus A. Later analysis of the comparative number, strength and distance of radio sources suggested that in the distant past these, incl. the quasars (q.v.) discovered in 1964, had been much more powerful and dense in distribution than today. Optical variation in the brilliance of quasars also supports the view that the Universe is not in the state of equilibrium to be expected under a 'steady state' theory, and the discovery in 1965 of microwave background radiation suggested that here was the residue surviving from the tremendous thermal power of the giant explosion or 'big bang' which brought the Universe into existence. *See also* BLACK HOLE, INFRA-RED RADIATION, PULSAR, RADAR ASTRONOMY, etc.

Meanwhile, although the practical limit in size and efficiency of optical telescopes has apparently been reached, the siting of these and other types of telescope, etc., at new observatories in the previously neglected southern hemisphere has opened fresh areas of the sky to search which may be expected to be particularly productive. Australia has been espec. to the fore in these developments. The most remarkable extension of the powers of the astronomer to explore the Universe, however, has lain in the use of rockets, satellites, space stations and space probes. Even the range and accuracy of the conventional telescope may be greatly improved free from the Earth's atmosphere, and only cost has so far prevented the establishment of a large optical telescope permanently in space.

ASTRONOMY. The spiral nebula in Virgo known as the 'sombrero hat' galaxy because of the thick layer of cosmic dust which gives the effect of a hat brim. *Photo: The Hale Observatories*

ASTROPHYSICS. The science that is (a) physical astronomy, the study of the physical conditions in the heavenly bodies; and (b) astronomical physics, a branch of physics in which the behaviour of matter and radiant energy is studied under conditions unattainable on the earth. From this point of view a star or a nebula is a special laboratory in which extremes of temperature and density unknown in terrestrial laboratories are reached, and the effect of these conditions on the familiar elements of chemistry is ascertained. An approach to these extreme conditions is attempted in thermonuclear machines.

ASTŪ'RIAS. An ancient Spanish prov., once a kingdom. The eldest son of a king of Spain is called prince of A. It corresponds to the modern prov. of Oviedo, and autonomy is planned.

ASTŪ'RIAS, Miguel Angel (1899-1974). Guatemalan author and diplomat. He pub. poetry, Guatemalan legends, and novels, such as *The President (1946),* attacking Latin-American dictatorships and 'Yankee imperialism'. Nobel prize 1967.

ASUNCION (ahsoonthēōn'). Cap. of the S. American rep. of Paraguay, on the Paraguay river. Founded in 1537, it is a commercial centre with good docks. There are 2 univs. Pop. (1976) 500,000.

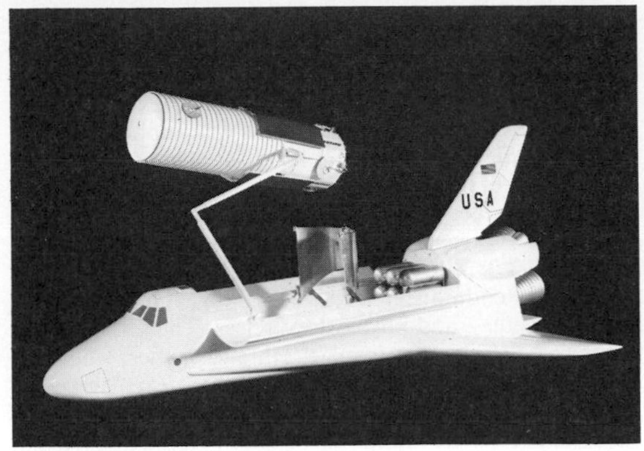

ASTRONOMY. A model of the Large Space Telescope which the world economic crisis has prevented NASA from developing. It is here shown as it would be recaptured by the Space Shuttle for routine maintenance while in orbit. When deployed for operation 520 km (323 m) above the Earth, the telescope would expand to twice its length; the circular cover over the lens (left) would hinge outward; and the solar panels (the dark rectangular features at the top and bottom of the cylinder, to the right) would stretch out like 'wings' to use the Sun's radiation to generate electrical power to operate the telescope. *Photo: Courtesy of Boeing Aerospace Company Ltd.*

ASWAN (ahswahn'). Town of the Arab Rep. of Egypt, in Upper Egypt. It stands near the first or lowest cataract of the Nile, and has famous ruins. Pop. (1971) 60,000. The A. High Dam (1960-70) some 8km (5m) upstream has a storage capacity of 5,500 m.cu metres and maintains the level of the Nile constant throughout the year without flooding.

ASWAN. The High Dam has provided irrigation for more than 400,000 ha (1,000,000 acres), but has also created problems. Stagnant water in the fields has greatly increased the incidence of schistosomiasis. *Photo: Douglas Dickins*

ASYUT (ahsyoot'). City in the Arab Rep. of Egypt in Upper Egypt, near the Nile, 322km (200m) S. of Cairo. An ancient Graeco-Egyptian city, it has many tombs of 11th and 12th dynasty nobles. Asyut Univ. was founded 1957. Pop. (1971) 248,000.

ATACAMA (ahtahkah'mah). Extensive desert in S. America, covering large areas of northern Chile. Inland are mountains, and the coastal area is rainless and barren. Silver and copper mines are worked, and in the N. Chile coastal province of A. are extensive nitrate deposits.

ATAHUALPA (ahtahwahl'pah) (*c.* 1502-33). Last of the Incas of Peru. He was taken prisoner in 1532 when the Spaniards arrived, and agreed to pay a huge ransom, but was accused of plotting against Pizarro and sentenced to be burnt. On his consenting to Christian baptism, the sentence was commuted to strangling.

ATALA'NTA. In Greek mythology, a huntress of Arcadia who declared that a suitor must first compete with her in a foot race; if he lost he must die. Milanion received from Aphrodite three golden apples which he dropped one by one during the race. A. stopped to pick them up and Milanion won.

ATATÜRK (1881-1938). Name assumed by Mustafa Kemal Pasha, Turkish statesman and soldier. B. at Salonika, the son of a customs official, he distinguished himself at a military academy, but was banished in 1904 to Damascus for having joined a revolutionary society. Later he was pardoned and promoted, and was largely responsible for the successful defence of the Dardanelles against the British in 1915. In 1918 he was sent into Anatolia to carry through the demobilization of the Turkish forces in accordance with the armistice terms, but instead estab. a provisional govt opposed to that of Constantinople (under Allied control), and in 1921 led the Turkish armies against the Greeks who had occupied a large part of Asia Minor. He checked the invaders at the 21-day battle of the Sakaria, 23 Aug. to 13 Sept. 1921, for which he was granted the title of Ghazi (the Victorious) by the Assembly, and within a year had finally expelled the Greeks from Turkish soil. War with the British was averted by the statesmanship of K. and Gen. Harrington, and Turkey in Europe passed under K.'s control. On 29 Oct. 1923, Turkey was proclaimed a rep. with K. as 1st president. A one-party dictatorship was set up and a policy of consistent and radical westernization was embarked upon. In 1934 Kemal adopted the surname of Atatürk (Head of the Turks).

ATHABA'SCA. River and lake in Alberta and Saskatchewan, Canada. To the SW of the lake is a huge area of tar sands containing 'heavy' oil, which is difficult but increasingly profitable to extract.

ATHANASIAN CREED. One of the three ancient creeds of the Christian Church consisting in the main of a definition of the doctrine of the Trinity. Although not written for many years after the death of Athanasius, it came to be attributed to him as he was the chief upholder of Trinitarian doctrine.

ATHANĀ'SIUS (*c.* 298-373). Christian bishop of Alexandria and reputed author of the Athanasian creed. Probably b. at Alexandria, he was a disciple of St Anthony the hermit, and became early prominent in the great Arian controversy. Arianism was officially condemned at the council of Nicaea in 325, and in 328 A. was appointed bishop of Alexandria. Banished in 335 by the emperor Constantine because of his intransigence towards the defeated Arians, in 346 he was restored to his see, but suffered three more banishments before his final reinstatement about 366.

Ā'THEISM (Gk, without god). Disbelief in, or denial of, the existence of God or gods. A. takes many forms and expressions. *Dogmatic A.* asserts that there is no God. *Sceptical A.* maintains that the finite mind of man is so constituted as to be incapable of discovering that there is or is not a God. *Critical A.* holds that the evidence for Theism is inadequate. This is akin to *Philosophical A.* which fails to find evidence of a God manifest in the universe. *Speculative A.* comprises the belief of those who, like Kant, find it impossible to demonstrate the existence of God - although, again like Kant, they may believe in the existence of God on other grounds.

There were Atheists in ancient Greece, e.g. Democritus, Leucippus, and their followers of the materialistic schools. In Rome the outstanding A. was Lucretius. The early Christians were called Atheists by the pagans since they denied the familiar gods of the Roman world; and in the centuries of Christian domination the term A. was applied in a similarly opprobrious fashion by the members of one sect and church to those of other sects and churches. Buddhism has been called an atheistic religion since it does not postulate any Supreme Being. The Jains are similarly atheistic; and so are those who adopt the Sankhya system of philosophy in Hinduism. Following the revolution of 1917 Soviet Russia and later Communist states adopted an atheist outlook.

A'THELNEY, Isle of. 'Island' of firm ground, 12m (40ft) above the surrounding marshland, *c.* 7m from Taunton in Somerset, England: the name means 'isle of princes'. In 878 Alfred the Great built a fort here as his guerrilla HQ against the Danes, and the legend of his burning the cakes is set on A.

A'THELSTAN (*c.* 895-939). King of the Mercians and West Saxons. Son of Edward the Elder and grandson of Alfred the Great, he was crowned king in 925 at Kingston-on-Thames. He subdued parts of Cornwall and Wales, and in 937 defeated the Welsh, Scots, and Danes at Brunanburh.

ATHĒ'NA. Greek goddess, identified with the Roman Minerva, and supposed to have been b. from the head of Zeus fully grown and fully armed. She was the maiden goddess of wisdom and of the arts and crafts, and also goddess of war and protectress of the city of Athens, where was her most famous temple - the Parthenon or Maiden's Temple.

ATHENS. Capital city of modern Greece and of ancient Attica. Situated 8km (5m) inland N.E. of its port of Piraeus on the Gulf of Aegina, it is built around the rocky hills of the Acropolis 169m (412ft) and the Areopagus 112m (370ft), and is overlooked from the N.E. by the hill of Lycabettus 277m (909ft). It lies in the S. of the central plain of Attica watered by the mountain streams of Cephissus and Ilissus.

The Acropolis (q.v.) dominates the city. Here stand architectural remains of the great days of ancient Greece, e.g. the Parthenon, the Erechtheum, and the temple of Athena Nikē. Near the site of the ancient Agora or market-place stands the Theseum, and S. of the Acropolis is the theatre of Dionysus. To the S.E. stand the gate of Hadrian and the columns of the temple of Olympian Zeus. Nearby is the marble stadium built about 330 B.C. and restored in 1896.

The site was first inhabited *c.* 3000 B.C. and A. became the capital of a united Attica before 700 B.C. Captured and sacked by the Persians in 480, subsequently under Pericles it was the first city of Greece in power and culture. After the death of Alexander the Great the city fell into comparative decline, but it flourished as an intellectual centre until A.D. 529, when the philosophical schools were shut down by Justinian. In 1458 it was captured by the Turks who held it until 1833; it was chosen as the cap. of modern Greece in 1834. Among the modern buildings are the Royal Palace, and several museums. Pop. Greater A. (including Piraeus) (1971) 2,540,240.

ATHLETICS. The practice of athletic games - i.e. games of skill and endurance, such as hurdling, running, javelin throwing, etc. - and physical exercises. The Greeks were among the first to organize athletic games; the first Olympic games were held about 2,500 years ago. The Romans usually held their games at the festivals of the gods. The Olympic Games (q.v.) were revived in 1896 and the Commonwealth Games are run along similar lines. In Britain, where A. proper is limited to field and track events, the Amateur Athletic Association (1880) is the leading body. In the US, where team games are included, leading associations incl. the Amateur Athletic Union (1888) and - typical of the American interest in inter-collegiate competition - the National Collegiate Athletic Association.

Modern competition in field and track events, with the increasing importance of the 'world record', tends to be less against rivals than a record figure. Computers are used to select ideal potential athletes, e.g. for the sprinter, fast heart beat, thickset build, mental aggressiveness are important factors, and difficult-to-detect drugs are illicitly used to increase endurance, or even in the long-term to increase height and strength. *See* STEROL, TESTOSTERONE. Equipment is also scientifically designed to improve performance, e.g. glass fibre vaulting poles, foam landing pads for jumpers, javelins designed on aerodynamic principles, and springy, non-slip running tracks. The advance by women in breaking records in recent years has surpassed that of men, so that the achievement gap between the sexes narrows. In Channel-swimming (q.v.) the record is held by a woman.

Ā'THOS. A peninsular promontory on the Macedonian coast of Greece. Its peak is a white marble pyramid, 1,935 m (6,670 ft) high. The promontory is occupied by a community of 20 Basilian monasteries inhabited by some 3,000 monks and lay brothers. No female creature is allowed within the peninsula.

ATKINS, Tommy. Popular name for the British soldier. The earliest discoverable use of the name is in a specimen form included in an official handbook circulated by the War Office at the end of the Napoleonic War. A story that T.A. was a British soldier mortally wounded under Wellington in the Netherlands in 1794, and that the Duke chose his name to be used in an army document some 50 years later, seems to have originated in an article by Col. Newnham-Davis in *Printer's Pie.*

ATLA'NTA. Cap. and largest city of Georgia, USA. Founded as Terminus in 1837, and re-named in 1845, it was nearly destroyed in 1864 during the American Civil War. It has 2 universities and a college founded in 1885 for Negro students. Nearby Stone Mountain Memorial 58×93m (190×305ft), the world's largest stone carving, shows Jefferson Davis, Robert E. Lee, and Stonewall Jackson on horseback. Artists were Gutzon Borglum 1923-5, Augustus Lukeman 1925-8, and Walter Hancock

Men's World Athletic Records

High jump 2.41m (7ft 10.75in) Igor Paklin (USSR) 1985
Long jump 8.90m (29ft 2.25in) Robert Beamon (USA) 1968
Triple jump 17.97m (58ft 11.5in) Willie Banks (USA) 1985
Hammer throw 86.66m (284ft 7in) Yuri Sedykh (USSR) 1986
Discus 74.08m (243ft 0.5in) Jurgen Schult (E. Germany) 1986
Javelin 79.86m (262ft) Brian Crouser (USA) 1986
Pole vault 6.01m (19ft 8.75in) Sergei Bubka (USSR) 1986
Hurdling: 110 metres 12.93sec R. Nehemiah (USA), 1981
Walking: 50,000 metres 3hr 41min 39sec R.Gonzalez (Mexico), 1979
Running:
100 metres 9.93sec C. Smith (USA), 1983
200 metres (turn) 19.72sec P. Mennea (Italy), 1979
400 metres 43.86sec L. Evans (USA), 1968
800 metres 1min 41.73sec S. Coe (GB), 1981
1 mile 3 min 46.32 sec Steve Cram (GB), 1985
1,500 metres 3min 29.46 sec Said Aouita (Morocco), 1985
30,000 metres 1hr 29min 18.8sec T.Seko (Japan), 1981
Relay Race: 4 × 100 metres 37.83sec (USA), 1984

1963-70: Hartsfield Internat. Airport has the world's largest air terminal (1980). Pop. met. area (1970) 1,373,629.

ATLANTIC, Battle of the. Name given to the continuous battle fought in the Atlantic Ocean throughout the S.W.W. (1939-45) by the Royal Navy, the Merchant Navy, and Coastal Command aircraft, under the operational control of the Admiralty, against the sea and air power of Germany.

The battle opened on the first night of the War, when on 4 Sept. 1939 the Donaldson liner, *Athenia,* sailing from Glasgow to New York, was torpedoed by a German submarine off the Irish coast. The Germans tried U-boats, surface-raiders, indiscriminate mine-laying, and aircraft, but every enemy method was successfully countered by, e.g., the convoy system and degaussing. Outstanding incidents were the engagements in which the armed merchantmen *Rawalpindi* (23 Nov. 1939) and *Jervis Bay* (5 Nov. 1940) were sunk by German warships, and the destruction of the great German battleship *Bismarck* on 27 May 1941. The total number of U-boats destroyed by the Allies during the whole war was nearly 800. No fewer than 2,200 convoys of 75,000 merchants ships crossed the Atlantic.

ATLANTIC CHARTER. Declaration issued by Winston Churchill and President Roosevelt following meetings on board HMS *Prince of Wales* and the US carrier *Augusta* in Aug. 1941. It stated that Britain and the USA sought no territorial aggrandizement; desired no territorial changes not according with the wishes of the peoples concerned; respected the rights of all peoples to choose their own form of government: wished to see self-government restored to the occupied countries; would further access

ATLANTIC. The operations room at Derby House, Liverpool, where the Battle of the Atlantic was planned throughout the war. In the foreground on the main 'plot' discs of approximately 150 miles radius mark restricted bombing areas for aircraft, where allied submarines are under passage. In the background is the home 'plot' and enemy submarine report board. *Photo: Crown Copyright*

by all states to trade and raw materials; desired international collaboration for the raising of economic standards; hoped to see a peace affording security to all nations and enabling them to cross the seas without hindrance; and proposed the disarmament of the aggressor states as a preliminary to general disarmament.

ATLANTIC CITY. City of USA on the coast of New Jersey, celebrated seaside and pleasure resort. Pop. (1970) 47,859.

ATLANTIC COLLEGE. International educational experiment conceived by Kurt Hahn (q.v.) and Air Marshal Sir Lawrence Darvell. The first A.C. (for boys of 17-18 drawn from N. America and Europe) was opened in 1962 in St Donat's castle (once owned by W. R. Hearst, q.v.), near Cardiff in Wales; there are others at Singapore and Vancouver Is., Canada.

ATLANTIC OCEAN. Sea lying between Europe and Africa to the E. and the Americas to the W., probably named after Atlantis (q.v.). Area of A.O. basin 81,500,000 sq.km (31,500,000 sq.m); incl. Arctic Ocean, Antarctic seas, etc. 106,200,000 sq.km (41,000,000 sq.m). The average depth is 3km (2m); greatest depth the Puerto Rico Trench 9,219 m (27,498 ft). The Mid-Atlantic Ridge, of which the Azores, Ascension, St Helena and Tristan da Cunha form part, divides it from N. to S. Lava welling up from this central area annually widens the distance between S. America and Africa. The N. Atlantic is the saltiest of the main oceans, and its tides are larger.

ATLANTIS. An island continent, which according to Plato once existed in the Atlantic opposite the Straits of Gibraltar, but foundered about 9,600 B.C. as a result of submarine convulsions. The story (as originally told by Egyptian priests to Solon) may refer to the volcanic eruption *c.* 1500 B.C. of Santorini (of which the is. Thera and Therasis 110km (70m) N. of Crete are the remains), causing the collapse of the empire of Minoan Crete by fire and tidal wave.

A'TLAS. In Greek mythology, one of the Titans who revolted against the gods; as a punishment A. was compelled to support the heavens upon his head and

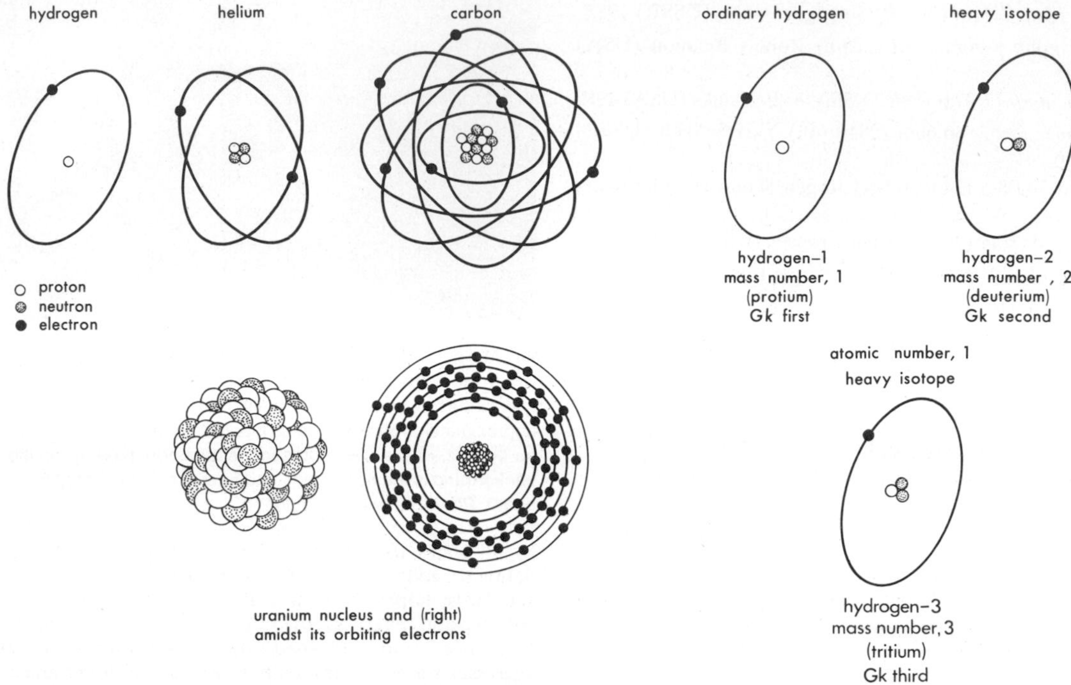

ATOM. The structure of hydrogen, helium and carbon atoms (upper left) in the conventionalised form usually adopted, although for physicists the concepts are much more complex; the clustered nucleus of U-238 (92 protons and 146 neutrons) which has 92 orbiting electrons (lower left); and (right) the three isotopes of hydrogen compared, the heavy isotopes being those used in H-bombs.

shoulders. Growing weary, he asked Perseus to turn him into stone, and he was transformed into Mt Atlas. The use of the word to denote a book of maps was introduced in the 16th cent. by Mercator; such books had a frontispiece showing Atlas supporting the globe.

ATLAS. Mountain system of N.W. Africa, stretching 2,400 km (1,500 m) from the Atlantic coast of Morocco to the Gulf of Gabes, Tunisia, and lying between the Mediterranean on the N. and the Sahara on the S. Geologically the A. mts. compare with the Alps in age, but their structure is much less complex. They are recognized as the continuation of the great Tertiary fold mountain systems of Europe.

ATMOSPHERE. The air which surrounds and forms a permanent covering of the earth's surface. It is a mixture of gases which show no measurable variation near the surface of the earth except for the water vapour. The constitution of dry air from which all water vapour has been removed is as follows (percentage by volume): nitrogen 78.09; oxygen 20.95; argon 0.93; carbon dioxide 0.03. Included in the above are minute quantities of other gases, e.g. neon, helium, krypton, hydrogen, xenon, ozone, and radon, each less than 0.0001.

Atmospheric pressure is normally equivalent at sea-level to 760mm of mercury or 1,013 millibars but varies slightly. It decreases steadily as higher altitudes are reached.

ATOLL. *See* CORAL REEFS.

ATOM (Gk *atomos*, indivisible). Name given to the very small, discrete particles of which all matter is composed. There are 92 kinds of A., occurring naturally in ordinary circumstances, which differ in chemical behaviour and correspond to the 92 elements which cannot be broken up by chemical means to anything simpler. *See* TRANSURANIUM ELEMENTS.

Belief in the existence of As. dates back to the days of the ancient Greek natural philosophers, but it rested on entirely circumstantial evidence, since As. are much too small to be seen even by the microscope; the largest (caesium) is 0.000 000 5 mm in diameter (0.000 01 in). Furthermore, they are in constant motion. Of recent times, however, various methods for detecting the presence of single As. have been devised, all making use of effects which can be produced by the energy of a rapidly-moving A. Rutherford showed that As. of certain radioactive elements shoot out spontaneously the so-called alpha rays, single As. of helium issuing at about 16,000 km (10,000 m) a sec. At this speed an A. has sufficient energy to produce a tiny speck of light when it hits a thin layer of phosphorescent zinc sulphide. Each A. causes a splash of light, and this momentary scintillation can be observed with a microscope. It is then possible to determine its path.

Until near the end of the last century it was believed that every A. was a complete unbreakable entity. Since then the modern theory of atomic structure has been worked out, largely by Rutherford, who by experiments with alpha particles showed that every A. consists of a very minute particle, only one 10,000th as big across as the atom, called the *nucleus*, surrounded by a distribution of particles of negative electricity called *electrons*.

All electrons have identical mass and charge. The different properties of the various chemical elements are due to the different number of electrons in the atom of each element. The simplest element, hydrogen, contains 1 electron; each atom of carbon contains 6; the most complex A. normally found, that of uranium, has 92. The mass of an A. of any kind is several thousand times as great as the mass of the electrons it contains. Moreover, As. in their normal state have no excess of electric charge. Save in hydrogen, each nucleus is composed of 2 kinds of particle, *protons* and *neutrons*. Each proton has a positive electric charge, equal in magnitude but opposite in sign to that of the electron; the neutrons have no charge. Proton and neutron have nearly equal mass, and this is about 1839 times as great as the mass of the electron. Since the proton and electron charges are equal and opposite and the A. as a whole has no charge, the number of protons within the nucleus of any A. must equal the number of electrons outside the nucleus. The number of units of positive charge (protons) in the nucleus is called the *atomic number*.

The problem of the basic structure of the neutrons and protons that make up atomic nuclei will be brought nearer solution when some fundamental (sub-atomic) particles discovered in recent high energy physics research are better understood. They incl. anti-particles (such as the anti-proton and anti-neutron) which are opposite in some properties but identical in others to known charged and neutral particles; hyperons, with masses greater than protons; and mesons, with masses intermediate between electrons and protons. More than 300 kinds of particle are now known, and research has been concentrated on the elucidation of some unifying theory. Experiments by CERN and at the Fermi laboratory in the USA have tended since 1974 to confirm that particles are themselves made up of sub-particles, known as quarks (q.v.), possibly only of 3 or 4 kinds, which are the fundamental building blocks of matter. *See* CHARM, B. RICHTER., FORCES.

Confirmation of the existence of quarks, however, does not complete the solution of the problems of the A., for particles have been shown to change from one form to another, and perhaps most important of all in its implications is that their behaviour is not exactly predictable. There is the likelihood that they will do what physicists have worked out that they should, but no certainty (*see* UNCERTAINTY PRINCIPLE). This is something that Einstein himself was unwilling to accept - that chance rather than exact physical law is at the heart of the Universe. *See* DETERMINISM.

As. which have the same number of protons but differ in their number of neutrons are called *isotopes*; these have identical chemical properties since they have the same number of electrons. Most of the chemical elements consist of mixtures of two or more isotopes; e.g. about 1 atom in 4,000 of natural hydrogen contains 1 neutron in addition to the single proton that forms the nucleus of the ordinary hydrogen A. This kind of hydrogen is called heavy hydrogen or deuterium, and is denoted by the symbol H^2 as opposed to H^1 for the more plentiful isotope. At the other end of the list, natural uranium consists of 3 isotopes, U^{234}, U^{235}, and U^{238}, the last forming over 99 per cent of the mixture.

As. as a whole are held together by the electrical forces of attraction between each negative electron and the positive protons within the nucleus. The latter *repel* one another with relatively enormous forces; a nucleus holds together only because other forces, not of a simple electrical character, attract the protons and neutrons to one another. These additional forces act only so long as the protons and neutrons are virtually in contact with one another. If, therefore, a fragment of a complex nucleus, containing some protons becomes only slightly loosened from the main agglomeration of neutrons and protons, the strong natural repulsion between the protons will cause this fragment to fly apart from the rest of the nucleus with high speed, carrying with it energy that is very much greater than the energy released in chemical reactions between As. - reactions which involve only the weak forces existing between the outer electrons of the As. It is by such fragmentation of atomic nuclei (*nuclear fission*) that 'atomic energy' (more strictly nuclear energy) is released.

Energy is also released by the process of *nuclear fusion*, as in the Sun (q.v.). This involves the building up of more complex nuclei by the combination, or fusion, of simpler ones, and in the case of JET (Joint European Torus experiment — a toroidal experiment being one in which plasma, q.v., is confined within a tube bent into a circle) deuterium (from heavy water) and lithium would be used. Plasma would be held in a strong magnetic field at 50–100 million degrees centigrade, and if a method can be found to maintain the correct temperature and densities for the requisite time, tritium, an isotope of hydrogen produced from the deuterium and lithium would fuse to form heavier elements. The method involves no radioactive waste disposal problems; only a small quantity of commonly available 'fuel' is consumed, so that depletion of natural resources is negligible; and the amount of energy released in such a controlled thermonuclear reaction (CTR) is greater than with nuclear fission.

Some of the most complex natural nuclei, e.g. those of uranium and radium, are radioactive, that is, they spontaneously disintegrate with the emission of a fragment containing 2 neutrons and 2 protons, a so-called alpha particle. If a large number of As. of say U^{238} are considered, about half of them will have disintegrated after about 4,000 million years; for radium the corresponding half-life is *c.* 1,600 years.

ATOM BOMB. Bomb deriving its explosive force from nuclear energy (q.v.). The possibility was explored in Britain from 1940, but work was transferred to USA after America's entry into the S.W.W. As the Manhattan Project, it was under the direction of Oppenheimer at Los Alamos (qq.v.). *See also* BOMB.

ATOMIC ENERGY. *See* NUCLEAR ENERGY.

ATOMIC NUMBER. The number of electrons, or, what is its equivalent, the positive charge on the nucleus, of an atom. The 105 elements are numbered 1 (hydrogen) to 105 (hahnium) in the Periodic Table. *See* CHEMISTRY and INORGANIC CHEMISTRY; also TRANSURANIUM ELEMENTS.

ATOMIC TIME. The time derived from integrating seconds intervals as realized by caesium beam atomic clocks. In 1967 a new definition of the second was adopted in the internat. system of units as the duration of 9 192 631 770 periods of the radiation corresponding to the transition between 2 hyperfine levels of the ground state of the caesium-133 atom. The Internat. A.T. Scale is based on clock data from a number of countries; it is a continuous scale in days, hours, minutes, and seconds from the origin on 1 Jan. 1958, when the A.T. scale was made $0^h0^m0^s$ when Greenwich Mean Time was $0^h0^m0^s$.

ATOMIC WEIGHT. The least weight of a chemical element that is present in a molecular weight of any of its compounds. A.Ws. are relative numbers or ratios, not absolute weights. Formerly the A.W. of hydrogen, the smallest element, was taken as unity but it has been found more convenient to take the A.W. of oxygen as exactly 16, when that of hydrogen is 1.008. The absolute weight (or mass) of a hydrogen atom is 1.6×10^{-24} grams.

ATONALITY. In music, name given to a modern system of harmony, in which there is an absence of key. Towards the end of the 19th cent., the chromaticism of such composers as Wagner had the effect of leading the music farther and farther from the original key. Scriabin's later work showed a distinct tendency towards A., and he was the first to attempt to formulate it into a system by building up his harmonies on certain 'synthetic chords'. The system which is now generally called the atonal system, however, was that worked out by Arnold Schönberg about 1911, and finally perfected by him about 1923. This is more correctly called the 'twelve-tone system'; Schönberg and his followers repudiate the term A. as meaningless. Their system, though totally different from that which underlies diatonic harmony, is by no means arbitrary but is bound by strict rules. The chief exponents of A. are Schönberg, Alban Berg, von Webern, and Křenek.

ATŌ'NEMENT. Literally, a bringing to be 'at one', i.e. reconciliation. In Christian theology, it is the doctrine that Jesus Christ suffered on the Cross as the means of effecting reconciliation and forgiveness between God and man.

ATONEMENT, Day of. Jewish religious fast (Yom Kippur) held on the 10th day of Tishri (Sept.-Oct.), the 7th month of the Jewish year.

ATROPINE (a'tropin). An alkaloid, the active principle of deadly nightshade, or belladonna, named from the Greek *Atropos*, one of the three Fates who cut men's lives short. Usually given as atropine sulphate, it is a mild local anaesthetic.

ATTAR OF ROSES (Pers. *attar*, essence). Perfume derived from the essential oil of roses, obtained by crushing and distilling the petals of the flowers.

ATTENBOROUGH, Sir Richard (1923-). British actor and film producer. Outstanding among his modern, naturalistic roles was Pinkie in *Brighton Rock* (1943); later films incl. *The Guinea Pig, Brothers in Law* and *The Angry Silence* (1959: co-producer). His brother **David A.** (1926-) led zoological expeditions to Indonesia, New Guinea, Madagascar, etc., was director of programmes, television 1969-72, and in 1979 was narrator in the television series *Life on Earth*, on which he also based a book.

ATTERBURY, Francis (1662-1732). C. of E. divine and politician. Taking holy orders in 1687, he was appointed a royal chaplain by William III. Under Queen Anne he received rapid promotion, becoming bishop of Rochester in 1713. His Jacobite sympathies prevented his attaining to the primacy, and in 1722 he was sent to the Tower and subsequently banished. He was a friend of Pope and Swift.

ATTICA. District of ancient Greece, washed on two sides by the Aegean Sea. It is a prefecture of modern Greece with Athens as its cap.

A'TTILA (c. 406-53). King of the Huns, called the 'Scourge of God'. Becoming king in 434 of hordes of Huns roaming the area from the Caspian to the Danube, he embarked on a career of vast conquests ranging from the Rhine to Persia. In 451 he invaded Gaul, but was defeated near Châlons-sur-Marne by the Roman and Visigothic armies under Aëtius and Theodoric. In 452 he led his Huns into Italy and only the personal intervention of Pope Leo I prevented the sacking of Rome. He returned to Pannonia and d. on the night of his marriage with Ildico.

ATT'ILA LINE. The line dividing Greek and Turkish Cyprus, because of a fanciful identification of Turks and Huns.

A'TTIS. A Phrygian god, whose death and resurrection symbolized the end of winter and the arrival of spring. Beloved by the goddess Cybele, he was driven mad by her as a punishment for his infidelity, and castrated himself and bled to death. His worshippers sought identification with the god by castrating themselves.

ATTLEE, Clement Richard, 1st earl (1883-1967). British Labour statesman. B. in Putney, the son of a solicitor, he was ed. at Haileybury and Oxford, and practised at the Bar 1906-9. Social work in E. London and co-operation with the Webbs in Poor Law reform led him to become a Socialist: he joined the Fabian Society and the I.L.P. in 1908. He became sec. to Toynbee Hall in 1910 and lecturer in social science at the London School of Economics in 1913. After distinguished service in the F.W.W. he was mayor of Stepney 1919-20; Labour MP for Limehouse 1922-50 and for W. Walthamstow 1950-5.

In the 1st and 2nd Labour Govts he was Under-Sec. for War (1924), and Chancellor of the Duchy of Lancaster and P.M.G. (1929-31). In 1935 he became Leader of the Opposition. In the wartime Coalition Govt he was Lord Privy Seal (1940-2), Dominions Sec. (1942-3) and Lord Pres. of the Council (1943-5), combining the office of Deputy PM with both these latter posts. In July 1945 he became PM after a Labour landslide in the general election, and introduced a sweeping programme of nationalization and a whole new system of social services. The govt was returned to power with a much reduced majority in 1950 and was defeated in 1951. Following his resignation as PM, he was awarded the O.M. and in 1955 accepted an earldom, on his retirement as Leader of the Opposition. His books incl. *The Labour Party in Perspective* (1937) and *As it Happened* (1954), an autobiography.

ATTORNEY (ater'ni). Person appointed by another to do certain acts in his stead. In Britain the term is largely obsolete, but the head of the English Bar and principal law officer of the Crown is still known as the *A. General*: he is usually prominent in politics. In the US an A. combines the functions of barrister and solicitor: the *A. General*, a member of the cabinet and appointed by the pres., is the chief law officer of the govt and head of the dept of justice.

ATTLEE. After the flamboyance of Churchill, the businesslike cabinets of Attlee were a strong contrast. Quietly undemonstrative, Attlee changed the social structure of Britain.

ATTWELL, Mabel Lucie (1879-1964). British artist, illustrator of many books for children, incl. her own stories and verse. Her apple-faced children are inimitable and have been reproduced on numerous souvenirs. She m. in 1908 Harold Earnshaw who d. in 1937.

AUBE (ōb). River of N.E. France, a tributary of the Seine, giving its name to a dept. It is about 240km (150m) long.

AUBER (ōbār'), **Daniel François Esprit** (1782-1871). French operatic composer. B. at Caen, he studied under Cherubini. Of his about 50 operas, *The Dumb Girl of Portici* (1828) and the comic opera *Fra Diavolo* (1830) are best known.

AUBERGINE (ō'bārzhēn). Plant in the Solanaceae family, often called the eggplant (*Solanum melongena*). The dark purple fruits are eaten as a vegetable. It is a native of Africa and S Asia.

AUBREY (aw'bri), **John** (1626-97). British antiquary. B. in Wilts, he studied law, but became dependent on patrons such as Ashmole and Hobbes. He pub. *Miscellanies* (1696) of folklore and ghost-stories, whilst the material he collected for surveys of Surrey and Wilts appeared posthumously in 1719 and 1862 respectively. His *Brief Lives* (pub. 1898) contain intimate notes on celebrities of his time. A. was the first to claim Stonehenge as a Druid temple.

AUBRIETIA (awbrē'sha). Genus of spring-flowering dwarf perennial plants of the Cruciferae order, trailing in habit and bearing purple flowers. It was named in 1763 by Adanson after Claude Aubriet (*c.* 1665-1742), painter for the French Royal Garden.

AUBUSSON (ōbüsoṅ'). Town in the dept of Creuse, France, famous for its carpets and tapestry, the industry dating from the 15th cent. Pop. (1975) 5,700.

AUCHINLECK (awk'inlek), **Sir Claude John Eyre** (1884-1981). British soldier, known as the 'Auk' because of his reticent dignity. Son of a colonel in the Royal Artillery, he was G.O.C.-in-C. Southern Command in England in 1940, C.-in-C. in India in 1941, and in the Middle East 1941-2. During the summer of 1942 his army was forced back to the Egyptian frontier by Rommel, but there made a magnificent stand. Handing over the command of the 8th Army to Montgomery, he was appointed in 1943 C.-in-C. in India for the second time. In 1946 he was promoted to field marshal, and retired in 1947.

AUCKLAND, George Eden, 1st earl of A. (1784-1849). British statesman. He became Tory MP in 1810, and 1835-41 was Governor-General of India. Auckland in NZ is named after him.

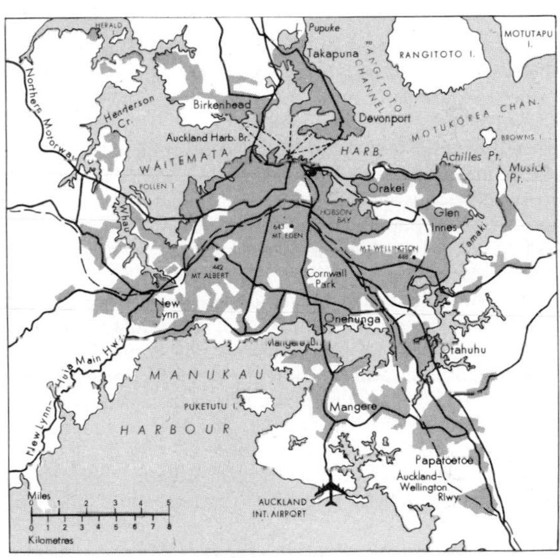

AUCKLAND

AUCKLAND. Largest city of New Zealand. It now fills the isthmus that separates its two harbours (Waitemata and Manukau), and its suburbs spread N. across the Harbour Bridge. There was a small whaling settlement in the 1830s, but A. was officially founded as NZ's cap. in 1840, remaining the cap. until 1865. It is the country's chief port and leading industrial centre — iron and steel, engineering, car assembly, textiles, food-processing, sugar-refining and brewing, and many young Maoris tend to migrate here in search of job opportunites. The univ. was founded in 1882, and there are Anglican and RC cathedrals. The internat. airport at Mangere is the country's chief focus for overseas services. Pop. (1977) 800,000.

AUCKLAND ISLANDS. Six volcanic islands some 480 km (300 m) S. of Invercargill in South Island, NZ.

AUCTION. The sale of property in public, usually to the highest bidder. Auctioneers must take out an annual licence. There are usually conditions of sale by which all

AUCKLAND. Harbour Bridge, which spans Waitemata harbour; top left are the wharves and commercial area of the port. *Photo: Courtesy of the High Commissioner of New Zealand*

bidders are bound. A bid may be withdrawn at any time before the auctioneer brings down the hammer, and the seller is likewise entitled to withdraw any lot before the hammer falls. It is illegal for the seller or anyone on his behalf to make a bid for his own goods unless his right to do so has been reserved and notified before the sale. A reserve price is kept secret, but the amount of an upset price is made public before the sale. An A. where property is first offered at a high price and gradually reduced until a bid is received is known as a *Dutch A.*

AUCTION BRIDGE. Card game played by two pairs of players. A development of bridge, it originated in India among members of the Indian Civil Service, reached England in 1903, and was first played at the Portland Club in 1908. Its chief characteristic is that trumps are decided by preliminary bid or auction. In 1929 it was largely supplanted by Contract Bridge (q.v.).

AUDE (ōd). River of S.E. France, 210km (130m) long, which gives its name to a dept. Carcassonne is the chief town on it.

AUDEN (aw'den), **Wystan Hugh** (1907-73). Anglo-American poet. B. in York and ed. at Oxford, he was with C. Day Lewis and Spender (qq.v.), one of the 'committed' poets of the thirties, and pub. his first vol. in 1930. By the time of *Look Stranger* (1936) much of the earlier obscurity of manner had been discarded, and noteworthy later books are *The Quest* (1941), with some fine sonnets; *Another Time* (1940), excellent conversational verse; *The Age of Anxiety: A Baroque Ecologue* (1947), and *The Shield of Achilles* (1955). Representing a new departure in drama, both in idea and method, were *The Dog Beneath the Skin* (1935), *The Ascent of F6* (1937), and *On the Frontier* (1938), written with Christopher Isherwood (q.v.). In 1939 he became assoc. prof. of English Literature at Ann Arbor Univ., Michigan, and subsequently adopted American citizenship, but in 1956-61 returned to Oxford as prof. of poetry. A. was a poet of great satiric and lyric gifts, although not free from carelessness and cheap effects. By his daring technique, evolved under the influence of Hopkins and Eliot, he cleared the way for younger writers. His effect on modern drama is undeniable.

AUDENARDE. French form of OUDENAARDE.

AUDIOMETER (awd'i-ometer). Electrical instrument for testing the pitch and loudness of sounds that a subject can hear: the various aspects of deafness can be tested and accurately recorded in this way.

AUDITOR. A person whose duty it is to examine accounts. In the UK the Companies Acts 1948 and 1967 require that the accounts of companies to which it applies must be audited annually, that the As. must report to the members stating whether they have obtained all the information required and whether the company's balance sheet exhibits a true view of the company's affairs.

AUDUBON (aw'dūbon), **John James** (1785-1851). American naturalist. B. in Santo Domingo, the son of a French sailor and a Creole woman, he was ed. in Paris and became a trader in Kentucky. In 1827 he pub. the first parts of his *Birds of North America*, with a remarkable series of colour plates. Later he produced a similar work on American quadrupeds. The National A. Soc. (originating 1886) has branches throughout the US and Canada for the study and protection of birds.

AUDUBON. This representation of 'The Wild Turkey Cock' catches not only the detail of its appearance, but the spirit of the bird. *Photo: Courtesy of the New York Historical Society*

AUGIER (ōzhē-ā), **Émile** (1820-9). French dramatist. B. at Valence, he studied law but turned to the stage after the success of his verse-play *La Ciguë* in 1844. His best-known play, *Le Gendre de M. Poirier* (1854), written in prose in collaboration with Jules Sandeau, a realistic delineation of bourgeois society, has become a classic.

AUGSBURG (owgs'boorg). City of W. Germany in Bavaria at the confluence of the Wertach and Lech, 52km (32m) N.W. of Munich. It is named after the Roman emperor Augustus who founded it in 15 B.C. During the Middle Ages its merchants, particularly the families of Fugger and Welser, were world-famous. During the S.W.W. the Messerschmitt and other engineering works were frequently bombed. Pop. (1970) 213,230.

The *Confession of A.* was a statement of the Protestant faith as held by the German Reformers, presented to Charles V at the Diet of A. in 1530. It is the accepted statement of the creed of the Lutheran Church.

AUGURS (aw'gerz). College of Roman priests who interpreted the will of heaven from traditional signs or 'auspices', chief of which were the flight of birds, the entrails of animals sacrificed, and the direction of thunder and lightning. Their advice was sought before the commencement of battle, and on other important occasions. Consuls and other high officials had the right to consult the auspices themselves, and a campaign was said to be conducted 'under the auspices' of the general who had thus consulted the will of the gods.

AUGUSTINE (awgus'tin) (A.D. 354–430). Christian saint, theologian, and a Father of the Church. B. at Tagaste, Numidia, of Roman descent, he studied rhetoric in Carthage where he became the father of a natural son, Adeodatus. He lectured at Tagaste and Carthage and for 10 years was attached to the Manichaean heresy. In 383 he went to Rome, and on moving to Milan came under the influence of Ambrose. After prolonged study of Neo-Platonism A. was converted to Christianity and was baptized by Ambrose together with his son. Resigning his chair in rhetoric, he returned to Africa, his mother St Monica dying at Ostia on the journey, and settled at Tagaste. His son d. at 17. In 391, while visiting Hippo, A. was ordained priest. In 395 he was given the right of succession to the bishopric of Hippo, and in 396 succeeded to the office. He d. at Hippo during its siege by the Vandals.

Many of A.'s books resulted from his share in 3 great controversies: he refuted Manichaeism; attacked and did much to eliminate Donatism (conference of Carthage, 411); and devoted the last 20 years of his life to the Pelagian controversy, in which he maintained the doctrine of original sin and the necessity of divine grace. He estimated the number of his works at 230, and also wrote many sermons, as well as pastoral letters. A.'s most famous productions are his 'Confessions', his spiritual autobiography, and the influential *De Civitate Dei* (City of God) vindicating the Christian Church and Divine Providence in 22 books.

AUGUSTINE, St (d. A.D. 604). First archbishop of Canterbury. Originally prior of the Benedictine monastery of St Andrew, Rome, he was sent to convert England by Pope Gregory I. Landing at Ebbsfleet, Thanet (597), he soon baptized Ethelbert, King of Kent. He was consecrated bishop of the English at Arles (597) and appointed archbishop in 601. In 603 he attempted unsuccessfully to unite the Roman and native Celtic churches at a conference on the Severn. A. was the founder of Christ Church, Canterbury (603), and the abbey of SS. Peter and Paul, now the site of St A.'s Missionary College. His festival is celebrated on 26 May.

AUGUSTINIANS. Name applied to all religious communities which follow the Rule of St Augustine of Hippo. It includes the Canons of St Augustine, Augustinian Friars and Hermits, Premonstratensians, Gilbertines, and Trinitarians.

AUGUSTUS (63 B.C.–A.D. 14). First of the Roman emperors. Caius Julius Caesar Octavianus was the son of a senator who married a niece of Julius Caesar, and he became his great-uncle's adopted son and principal heir. Following Caesar's murder, Octavian (as he was styled) formed with Mark Antony and Lepidus the triumvirate which divided the Roman world between them, and proceeded to eliminate the opposition. Antony's victory in 42 over Brutus and Cassius brought the Republic to an end. Soon after Antony became enamoured of Cleopatra and spent most of his time at Alexandria, while Octavian consolidated his hold on the western part of the Roman dominion. War was declared against Cleopatra, and the naval victory at Actium in 31 left Octavian in unchallenged supremacy, since Lepidus had been forced to retire.

After his return to Rome in 29 B.C., Octavian was created *princeps senatus*, and in 27 he was given the title of Augustus (venerable). He then resigned his extraordinary powers, and received from the Senate in return the proconsular command, which gave him control of the army, and the tribunician power, whereby he could initiate or veto legislation. In his programme of reforms A. received the support of 3 loyal and capable helpers, Agrippa, Maecenas, and his wife, Livia, while Virgil and Horace acted as the poets laureate of the new regime. A firm frontier for the empire was established: on the N., the friendly Batavians held the Rhine delta, and then the line followed the course of the Rhine and Danube; on the E., the Parthians were friendly, and the Euphrates gave the next line; on the S., Africa was protected by the desert, on the W. were Spain and Gaul. The provinces were governed either by imperial legates responsible to the *princeps*, or by proconsuls appointed by the Senate. The army was made a profession, with fixed pay and length of service, and a permanent fleet was established. Finally, Rome itself received an adequate water supply, a fire brigade, a police force, and a large number of public buildings.

The years after 12 B.C. were marked by private and public calamities; the marriage of A.'s daughter Julia to his stepson Tiberius proved disastrous, while a serious revolt occurred in Pannonia in A.D. 6, and in Germany 3 legions under Varus were annihilated in the Teutoburg Forest in A.D. 9. A. d. a broken man, but his work remained secure. He was an enlightened and generous patron of literature and the arts, and the period of his rule lives in history as the Augustan Age. Augustus is often shown wearing the diadem of a Hellenistic king, which he would not have dared to wear in Rome.

AUK (awk). Family of diving birds (Alcidae) allied to the gulls, and generally included with them in the plover order (Charadriiformes). They are marine birds feeding upon fish, and are confined to the northern hemisphere. The largest of the family, the Great Auk (*Pinguinus impennis*), became extinct after 1844. It could not fly, but other As. use their wings for flying short distances, and as oars in the sea. The smallest is the Little A. (*Alle alle*), which is a winter visitor to Britain. Other members of the family are the razorbills, guillemots, and puffins.

AUSTEN. The drawingroom at Chawton in Hampshire. In the foreground is Jane's work-table; her father's Hepplewhite bureau is in the background; and on the wall hangs a portrait of Fanny White, her favourite niece. The portrait of Jane herself (right) is based on a drawing by her sister Cassandra. *Photos: Courtesy of the British Tourist Authority*

AUGUSTUS. In this gem cameo the emperor wears the diadem of a Hellenistic king. The wearing of such a crown would have been abhorrent to Romans, and it is in fact a medieval addition.

AULD (awld) **LANG SYNE** (Scottish for 'old long since' or 'long ago'). Title of a song written by Robert Burns, *c.* 1789, and based on lines attributed to Sir Robert Aytoun; it is sung at the conclusion of social gatherings, and is set to an old Scottish air.

AULD REEKIE ('Old Smoky'). Scottish dialect name formerly applied to Edinburgh, on account of its smokiness and dirty streets.

AUNG SAN (1914-47). Burmese statesman. Imprisoned for his nationalist activities while a student in Rangoon, he escaped in 1940 to Japan, returned to lead the Burma Independence Army, which assisted the Japanese invasion of 1942, and became Defence Minister in the puppet govt set up. Before long, however, he secretly contacted the resistance movement, and from March 1945 openly co-operated with the British in the expulsion of the Japanese. As leader of the Anti-Fascist People's Freedom League he became Vice-President of the Executive Council in Sept. 1946, and was assassinated by political opponents in July 1947.

AU'RANGZEB or **Aurungzebe** (1618-1707). Mogul emperor of Hindustan. 3rd son of Shah Jahan, he made himself master of the court by a palace revolution, and ruled as emperor from 1658. His reign was the most brilliant period of the Mogul dynasty, but A.'s despotic tendencies and Mohammedan fanaticism aroused much opposition. His latter years were spent in war with the princes of Rajputana and Mahrattas.

AURĒ'LIAN (*c.* 214-275). Roman emperor from 270; full name, Lucius Domitius Aurelianus. A successful soldier, he was chosen emperor by his troops on the death of Claudius II. He defeated the Goths and Vandals, defeated and captured Zenobia of Palmyra, and was planning a campaign against Parthia when he was murdered. The *A. Wall,* a fortification surrounding Rome, was built by A. in A.D. 271. It was made of concrete, and substantial ruins exist. The *A. Way* ran from Rome through Pisa and Genoa to Antipolis (Antibes) in Gaul.

AURĒ'LIUS (Antoninus), Marcus. Roman emperor. *See* MARCUS AURELIUS.

AURIC (ohrik'), **Georges** (1899-). French composer. He was one of the musical group known as *Les Six,* who were influenced by Erik Satie. A. composed a comic opera, several ballets, and incidental music.

PACIFIC OCEAN
BORNEO
CELEBES
MOLUCCAS
HALMAHERA
MACASSAR STRAIT
BURU
SERAM
BANDA SEA
NEW GUINEA
SNOW MTS.
BISMARCK ARCHO.
NEW IRELAND
NEW BRITAIN
SOLOMON SEA
JAVA SEA
ARU IS.
TANIMBAR
Fly
BALI
LOMBOK
FLORES
SUMBAWA
SUMBA
TIMOR
ARAFURA SEA
TIMOR SEA
MELVILLE I.
BATHURST I.
TORRES STR.
C. York
Arnhem Land
GULF OF CARPENTARIA
Cape York Pena.
CORAL SEA
Daly
GREAT BARRIER REEF
Kimberley Plateau
Sturt Plain
Barkly Tableland
Fitzroy
Flinders
GREAT DIVIDING RANGE
Great Sandy Desert
Georgina
Fortescue
HAMERSLEY RA.
Ashburton
Diamantina
MACDONNELL RAS
Simpson Desert
Gibson Desert
Lake Eyre Basin
Barcoo
Gascoyne
Finke
PETERMANN RAS.
MUSGRAVE RAS.
Warburton
Warrego
Murchison
Lake Eyre
Coopers Cr.
Great Victoria Desert
L. Torrens
FLINDERS RA.
Nullarbor Plain
Darling
L. Gairdner
Swan
GREAT AUSTRALIAN BIGHT
Lachlan
Murray
Murrumbidgee
SPENCER G.
C. Leeuwin
KANGAROO I.
AUSTR. ALPS
MT. KOSCIUSKO
TASMAN SEA
BASS STRAIT
KING I.
FURNEAUX GROUP
TASMANIA
INDIAN OCEAN
Miles
0 100 200 300 400 500 600
0 100 200 300 400 500 600 700 800 900
Kilometres
© Geographical Projects

AURICULA (awrik'ūla). Species of primrose (*Primula auricula*), well known as a garden flower. It is a native of the Alps, but has been grown in Eng. gardens for 3 centuries.

AURIGNACIAN (awrignā'shan). In archaeology, the name given to an Old Stone Age culture which came between the Mousterian and the Solutrian in the Upper Palaeolithic. It is derived from a cave at Aurignac in the Pyrenees. *See* STONE AGE.

AURIOL (ohriol'), **Vincent** (1884-1966). French Socialist statesman. He acted as pres. of the 2 Constituent Assemblies of 1946 and was first pres. of the 4th Rep. 1947-54.

AUROCHS (aw'roks). The huge wild cattle (*Bos primigenius*) that formerly inhabited central Europe. It probably survived in the Polish forests up to the end of the 16th cent. It was about 2.5m (8ft) high, and black to reddish or grey in colour.

AURO'RA. Roman goddess of the dawn, corresponding to the Greek Eos. Daily before dawn she left her husband Tithonus and rose to heaven in a chariot to announce the coming of daylight.

AURORA. Light in the night sky, known as the *Aurora Borealis* 'northern dawn', a name given by Frenchman Gassendi in 1621, in the northern hemisphere, and *A. Australis* in the southern. Initially it usually forms a luminous arch with its apex towards the magnetic pole, and then forms arcs, bands, rays, curtains and coronas, ranging in colour from smoky black to flaming red. It is emitted chiefly by the atmosphere itself at heights above Earth's surface of *c.* 100km (60m). A fast stream of charged particles originating in the Sun, and consisting mainly of protons and electrons, enters the upper atmosphere and by bombardment of the atmospheric gases causes them to emit visible light. The magnetic field of the Earth causes the concentration into 2 zones.

AUSCULTATION (awskooltā'shon). Listening to sounds inside the body. It is used in the medical examination of the heart, lungs, bowels, arteries, joints, liver, spleen, thyroid gland, and the state of the child within the womb. It was introduced by the French physician Laënnec, who in 1819 invented the stethoscope, originally a trumpet-shaped wooden tube.

AUSGLEICH (ows'glīkh; Ger., settlement, agreement, compromise). Name given to the compromise between Austria and Hungary of 8 Feb. 1867, which established the Austro-Hungarian Dual Monarchy, under Habsburg rule. It endured until the collapse of Austria-Hungary in 1918.

AUSSIE (awz'y). Colloquial name for Australian troops, particularly those of the F.W.W., 1914-18.

AUSTEN (aw'sten), **Jane** (1775-1817). British novelist. B. at Steventon, Hants, where her father was rector, she began writing early, the burlesque *Love and Freindship* (pub. 1922) belonging to 1790. In 1801 the family moved to Bath, and after the death of her father in 1805, to Southampton, finally settling in Chawton, with her brother Edward.

During 1795 to 1798 she worked on 3 novels. The first to be pub. (like its successors, anonymously), was *Sense and Sensibility* (1811: drafted in letter form *c.* 1797). *Pride and Prejudice* (1813) followed, but *Northanger Abbey*, a skit on the contemporary Gothic novel (sold to a London publisher in 1803 and bought back in 1816), did not appear till 1818. The fragmentary *Watsons* and *Lady Susan* (written *c.* 1803-5) remained unfinished.

The success of her pub. works, however, stimulated J.A. to write in rapid succession *Mansfield Park* (1814), *Emma* (1816), *Persuasion* (1818), and the final fragment *Sanditon* (wr. 1817). She d. at Winchester, and is buried in the cathedral. Although she never moved beyond the world of middle-class provincial society, she attains perfection within her range. She shows the utmost delicacy, naturalness, and ironical humour in her character-drawing, and from the outset her style was remarkably mature.

AUSTERLITZ (ow'sterlits). Small town in Czechoslavakia, formerly in Austria, 19km (12m) E. of Brno, where on 2 Dec. 1805 Napoleon defeated Alexander I of Russia and Francis II of Austria. Its Czech name is Slavkov.

AUSTIN (aw'stin), **Alfred** (1835-1913). British poet. He made his name with the satirical poem *The Season* (1861), which was followed by mediocre plays and vols. of poetry; from 1896 he was Poet Laureate.

AUSTIN, Herbert, 1st baron (1866-1941). British pioneer motor-car manufacturer. B. at Little Missenden, he went to Australia and was a works manager in Melbourne. Returning to England, he began manufacturing cars in 1905 at Northfield, Birmingham, notably the 'A. Seven' in 1921.

AUSTIN, John Langshaw (1911-60). British philosopher. Influential in later work on the philosophy of language, A. was a pioneer in the investigation of the way words are used in everyday speech. His lectures *Sense and Sensibilia* and *How to do Things with Words* were posthumously pub. in 1962.

AUSTIN. Cap. of Texas, USA, on the Colorado river. Pop. (1970) 252,000.

AUSTRALASIA. Geographical term covering the Commonwealth of Australia, the Dominion of New Zealand, and the Pacific islands dependent on them.

AUSTRĀ'LIA. Island continent in the southern hemisphere lying between the Pacific and Indian Oceans, with the Timor and Arafura seas to the N. Off the S.E. coast, separated by Bass Strait, is the island of Tasmania, part of the Commonwealth of Australia. The total area is 7,704,441 sq.km (2,974,693 sq.m), more than one-eighth of which lies within the tropics.

GEOGRAPHY. A. may be divided into 5 regions: (1) the narrow E. coastal plain, on which many of the large towns are situated; (2) the Western plateau, mainly semi-desert; (3) the central plains with good cattle and sheep country in the N. relying to a large extent on underground water supplies, and the wheat and cattle lands of the Murray basin in the S.; (4) the eastern highlands, with their mountains rising to 2,229 m (7,316 ft) in Kosciusko; (5) the tropical N.E. coast, protected by the Great Barrier reef, *c.* 2,000 km (1,250 m) long, where sugar and cotton are grown.

The northern part of A. has a true tropical climate, with a monsoonal rainfall in summer (Nov.-April) and continually high temperatures. The S.E. coastal area receives rain all the year round, and has hot summers and warm winters on the coastal plain grading to a cool mountain climate at higher altitudes. The E. mountain slopes are forested, but the W., receiving less rain, form large expanses of open grassland or scrub, which gives way to semi-desert and desert conditions in the heart of the continent. The extreme S.E. and S.W. of A. have a winter rainfall, and a climate and vegetation closely resembling those of the European Mediterranean region. In the whole continent there is only one important river system, the Murray, with its tributaries.

POPULATION. In 1979 the pop. was *c.* 14,331,700 (incl. *c.* 215,000 Aborigines, q.v.). The majority are still of British stock, but one third are immigrants, or children of immigrants, who entered after the S.W.W., and these incl. many from other European countries, e.g. Italy and Yugoslavia. By the 1970s the impact of assisted mass immigration on housing, schools and employment led to a more selective policy, and a re-assessment of A.'s future among her Asian neighbours has led to a repudiation of the 'White A.' policy. Assimilation of the Aborigines or isolation in reserves, the twin methods previously adopted, have also been challenged, and there is a movement for recognition of tribal land rights and independent development.

ECONOMIC DEVELOPMENT. Australia is a world leader in the production of meat, sugar and wool. Huge flocks of sheep are reared in New South Wales, Victoria and Queensland, and in the great plains of E. central Australia, where artesian water is available, cattle are increasingly reared. Today the emphasis is no longer in expanding use of virgin land, but more intensive use of existing holdings. The leading crop is wheat, grown in the Murray basin but Australia is particularly rich in orchard and other fruits, and her wines, espec. those of S. Australia, have a growing world-wide reputation. Fine timber, Karri and jarrah pines, comes from W. Australia.

However, there is lessening dependence on exports of traditional basic commodities as industrialization (shipbuilding, textiles, chemicals, machine tools, aircraft, transport vehicles, etc.) makes A. a leading supplier of finished goods to the Far East. Besides such ventures, as the Snowy River project, which supplies both power and water to Victoria and New South Wales, there were during the 1960s remarkable mineral discoveries, espec. in W. Australia, to hasten industrial progress and self-sufficiency. Minerals incl. gold, silver, uranium, iron, bauxite, lead, zinc, nickel, copper, coal (not of high quality), oil and natural gas. These rapid developments have involved much of A.'s business, industry, and mining concerns being of British or American origin, and there has also been concern that so much of her mineral wealth is exported unprocessed to Japan. M.U.: Australian dollar.

TOWNS AND COMMUNICATIONS. The federal cap. of A. is Canberra. The large industrial and commercial towns are mainly on the coast: Perth, with its port at Fremantle, Adelaide, Melbourne, Sydney and Brisbane. Inland there are mining centres, such as Ballarat, Bendigo and Broken Hill, but it is not until recently that there has been an attempt to relieve pressure on the coastal towns by developing diversified inland centres, e.g. Albury-Wodonga. Standardization of differing state rail gauges proceeds, and in 1970 a trans-continental line linking Perth and Sydney (3,960 km/2,460 m) was opened. Road construction is rapid, especially in Queensland, and the huge distances have necessitated good internal air services.

ADMINISTRATION. The Federal legislature consists of the Sovereign, represented by a Gov.-General, the Senate and the House of Representatives. All states have equal representation in the Senate, but proportional representation is adopted in the elected Lower House. Each state (except Queensland which abolished the upper house in 1922) has a Governor and Parliament of 2 houses. The seat of the Federal Govt was transferred to Canberra, A. Capital Territory, in 1927. The Northern Terr. is admin. by the Federal Govt, with an administrator at Darwin, its cap. For other dependencies, *see* TABLE: Nauru became independent in 1968 and Papua New Guinea in 1975.

History. The main stock of Aborigines (q.v.) were immigrants from southern India, Sri Lanka and S.E. Asia over a period extending from about 30,000 years B.C. to 10,000 B.C. Their intelligent cultural adaptation to a harsh and isolated environment is illustrated by the inability of early European explorers to cope adequately with such conditions. The first European discovery of A. may have long antedated the first recorded sightings. These were in 1606, when the Dutch ship *Duyfken* sighted the W. shore of Cape York, and the Spaniard Luis Vaez de Torres sailed along the coast S. of Cape York, and through Torres Strait. Later voyagers incl. Dutchman Dirk Hartog in 1616 who left an inscribed pewter plate (Australia's most famous early European relic, now in Amsterdam) in W. Australia; Pelsaert, Tasman and Dampier (qq.v.). In April 1770 James Cook made the first sighting of the more hospitable E. coast, and claimed N.S.W. for Britain. By the mid 19th cent. the whole coast was known, the survey work of George Bass (1771-1803) and Flinders (q.v.) being notable.

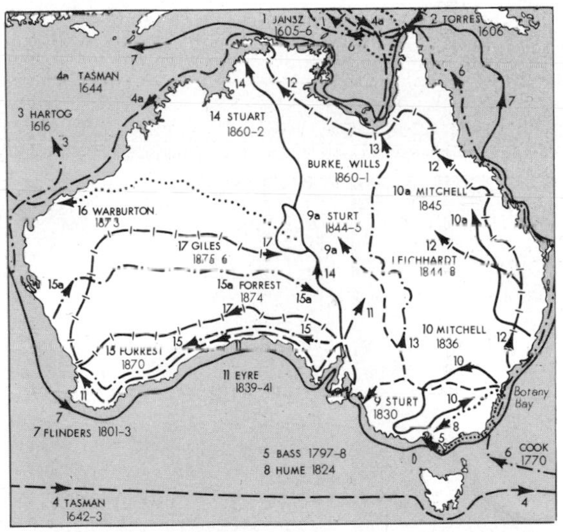

AUSTRALIA. Routes of the first explorers.

Exploration of the interior began with the crossing of the barrier of the Blue Mtns (q.v.) in 1813, and an era of striking discoveries began. Famous names incl. those of Hamilton Hume (1797-1873) and William Hovell (1786-1875) who in 1824 reached Port Phillip Bay and discovered the r. Murray; George Sturt (q.v.), probably the greatest of them all; Sir Thomas Mitchell (1792-1855), Surveyor-General for N.S.W. 1828-55, who opened up the fertile western area of Victoria; Strzelecki, the discoverer of Mt. Kosciuscko; Eyre, Leichhardt, Burke and Wills, and McDouall Stuart (qq.v.). In the 1870s the last gaps were filled in by the famous crossings of Western A., which made the names of Forrest (q.v.), William Giles (1835-97) in 1875-6 and Peter Warburton (1813-89) in 1873.

AUSTRALIA: A koala bear takes a nap in Taronga Park Zoological Gardens in Sydney; cattle ranching in the vast spaces of the Northern Territory (top right); Sydney Harbour Bridge and the Opera House (upper centre left); an old-timer at the gold mines (upper centre right); the radio telescope at Parkes, New South Wales (lower centre left); Captain Cook proclaims New South Wales a British possession (lower centre right); and an Aborigine family in Arnhem Land (bottom left).
Photos: Australian News and Information Service (koala) Axel Poignant (cattle, gold miner, Aborigines), Camera Press (Sydney), CSIRO (radio telescope), Radio Times Hulton Picture Library (Cook).

The gold rushes 1851-61, and sporadically to the early 1890s, contributed to the exploration as well as to the economic and constitutional growth of Australia, as did the pioneer work of the overlanders (q.v.). Following the first settlement in New South Wales at Sydney in 1788, the creation of other separate colonies followed: Tasmania (1825), W. Australia (1829), S. Australia (1836), Victoria (1851), and Queensland (1859). The system of transportation of convicts, never introduced in South Australia and Victoria, ceased within a comparatively short time: in N.S.W. in 1840, Queensland 1849, Tasmania 1853 and W. Australia 1868. Their contribution to the early economic foundation of the country was considerable, and many would not have been convicted under a less harsh and capricious penal system than that operating in Britain at this period. In the 1890s there was a halt in the rapid expansion A. had enjoyed, and a depression developed which gave birth to the Labour Party and the strengthening of unionism, which has proved such a feature of Australian politics ever since; *see also* LIBERAL PARTY. State powers waned following the creation of the Commonwealth in 1901, though more recently showing some revival. In both the World Wars Australia played an important role, notably at Gallipoli in the First (*see* ANZAC) and in the campaigns in Greece and Crete, and at Alamein, as well as the naval battles of Cape Matapan and the Coral Sea in the Second.

After the S.W.W. Australia entered on a fresh period of expansion, new mineral finds again playing a large part in her economic growth, and moved closer to USA in her foreign policy than to Britain. Ties with Britain were further weakened by the latter's entry into the Common Market and in the 1970s A. moved away also from the USA towards a new focal position among her Australasian neighbours. Under the Labour govt. which came to power in 1973 there was a growth of nationalism, e.g. the national honours system adopted in 1975, though the British system was later restored by Fraser. In the constitutional crisis of that year the Senate blocked the budget of the Whitlam govt. following the 'loans scandal' in which ministers were alleged to have tried to raise govt. loans in the Arab money market by unconventional means. For the first time in A.'s history the Gov.-Gen. intervened to dismiss the P.M. After a general election a Liberal-National coalition under Fraser achieved power, and was re-elected 1977 and 1980, but in 1983 Labour achieved victory under Robert Hawke.

THE ARTS. A. painting began in the 18th cent. with the miniatures of John Webber (1752-93), and the drawings and water-colours of Thomas Watling and Thomas Wainewright (1794-1847), both convicts. Conrad Martens, who reached A. in the 1830s, was its first landscape painter; S. T. Gill made sketches of life in the goldfields of Victoria; Louis Buvelot (1814-88), a Swiss, represented the A. scene with an objective eye. Tom Roberts (q.v.), Arthur Streeton (1867-1943), Julian Ashton (1851-1942) are others who became known outside their native country. 20th cent. artists include Sir William Dobell, Russell Drysdale, Sidney Nolan (qq.v.), and the aboriginal Albert Namatjira (1902-59), Phil May (1864-1903) and Will Dyson (1883-1938) were famous cartoonists, and New Zealand born Sir David Low worked for the *Sydney Bulletin* for some years.

Architecture of the colonial period, e.g. Vaucluse House, the Sydney home of William Charles Wentworth still survives, and Queensland has fine old-style homes with screened areas for coolness beneath their floors. Outstanding in the modern period are the Victoria Arts Centre in Melbourne, by Roy Grounds (1905-), who also designed the Academy of Science, Canberra; and the Sydney Opera House, in which the original architect — the Dane, Utzon captured an adventurous Australian spirit.

Music is represented by many fine singers of internat. repute, Dame Nellie Melba, Peter Dawson, Dame Joan Hammond, and Joan Sutherland (qq.v.); the pianist Eileen Joyce, and the composers Arthur Benjamin, Percy Grainger and Malcolm Williamson (qq.v.). In the dance Elaine Fifield (1930-) and Sir Robert Helpmann (q.v.) are famous.

Australian literature begins with the letters, journals, and memoirs of early settlers and explorers. First native poet of note was Charles Harpur (1813-68), and idiom and rhythms typical of the country were developed among others by Henry Kendall (1841-82), Adam Lindsay Gordon, and Andrew Barton (Banjo) Paterson (1864-1941) (qq.v.). More recent poets incl. Christopher Brennan and Judith Wright (qq.v.), Kenneth Sleesor (1901-71), R. D. (Robert David) Fitzgerald (1902-), A. D. (Alec Derwent) Hope (1907-), and James McAuley (1917-76). *See* ANGRY PENGUINS, JINDYWOROBAKS. Among early Australian novelists are Marcus Clarke, Rolfe Boldrewood, and Henry Handel Richardson (qq.v.). Striking a richly harsh vein in contemporary themes are the dramatist Ray Lawler and novelist-playwright Patrick White (qq.v.). The Australian language, familiarly referred to as 'Strine', is developing its own identity as American English has done, and has already progressed to the stage of its own dictionaries, increasingly in use abroad as Australia makes increasing national impact on the worlds of art and entertainment. Such names as Rolf Harris, a serious artist as well as an entertainer, and Barry Humphries, are as well known overseas as at home.

Australian Prime Ministers

Sir Edmund Barton (*Liberal*)	1901	J.A. Lyons (*U.A.P.*)	1932
Alfred Deakin (*Lib.*)	1903	Sir Earle Page (*C.P.*)	1939
John Watson (*Labour*)	1904	R.G. Menzies (*U.A.P.*)	1939
(Sir) G. Reid (*F.T.*)	1904	A.W. Fadden (*C.P.*)	1941
Alfred Deakin (*Lib.*)	1905	John Curtin (*Lab.*)	1941
Andrew Fisher (*Lab.*)	1908	F.M. Forde (*Lab.*)	1945
Alfred Deakin (*Lib.*)	1909	J.B. Chifley (*Lab.*)	1945
Andrew Fisher (*Lab.*)	1910	R.G. Menzies (*Lib.*)	1949
(Sir) J. Cook (*F.T.*)	1913	Harold Holt (*Lib.*)	1966
Andrew Fisher (*Lab.*)	1914	John McEwen (*Lib.*)	1967
W.M. Hughes (*Lab.*)	1915	J.G. Gorton (*Lib.*)	1968
W.M. Hughes (*Nat.*)	1917	William McMahon (*Lib.*)	1971
S.M. Bruce (*Nat.*)	1923	Gough Whitlam (*Lab.*)	1972
J.H. Scullin (*Lab.*)	1929	Malcolm Fraser (*Lib.*)	1975
		Robert Hawke (*Lab.*)	1983

U.A.P.—United Australia Party; *C.P.*—Country Party; *F.T.*—Free Trade.

AUSTRALIA DAY. National commemoration, in Australia, of the foundation of the original British colony in that continent; the date is the anniversary of the arrival

Commonwealth of Australia

States:	Area sq. km.	Pop. 1976	Capital
New South Wales	801,396	4,777,103	Sydney
Victoria	227,620	3,646,981	Melbourne
Queensland	1,736,524	2,037,197	Brisbane
South Australia	984,341	1,244,756	Adelaide
Western Australia	2,527,632	1,144,857	Perth
Tasmania	68,331	402,866	Hobart
Territories:			
Northern Territory	1,356,165	97,090	Darwin
Capital Territory	2,432	197,622	Canberra
	7,704,441	13,548,472	
Dependencies:			
Ashmore and Cartier Is.	1	—	—
A. Antarctic Terr.	5,402,480	—	—
Cocos (Keeling) Is.	14	444	—
Christmas Is.	135	3,255	—
Heard and McDonald Is.	412	—	—
Norfolk Island	34	1,600	—

of Capt. Phillip in Sydney on 26 Jan. 1788. The day is a public holiday.

AUSTRALIAN ANTARCTIC TERRITORY. From 1933, when estab. by a British Order in Council, the islands and terrs. south of 60° S. lat., between 160° E. long. and 45° E. long., excl. of Adèlie Land, and incl. of the Cocos Is. and Christmas Is. (qq.v.). Area 5,402,480 sq.km (2,472,000 sq.m): pop. on the Antarctic continent limited to research personnel.

There are scientific bases at Mawson (1954) in MacRobertson Land, named after the explorer; Davis (1957) on the coast of Princess Elizabeth Land, named in honour of Mawson's second-in-command; Casey (1969) in Wilkes Land named after Lord Casey, and Macquarie Is. (1948).

AUSTRALIAN CAPITAL TERRITORY. An area vested in the Australian Commonwealth since 1911, forming the site of the Federal Capital of Canberra. Its original area was 2,359 sq.km (911 sq.m), to which 73 sq.km (28 sq.m) were added in 1915 at Jervis Bay, on the coast S. of Sydney, to serve as a port. Total area, 2,432 sq.km; pop. (1979) 219,400.

AUSTRIA. Country of Central Europe. It has an area of 83,850 sq.km (32,375 sq.m), and is divided into 9 provs., each with an elected assembly. The head of state is a pres. (popularly elected), and there is an elected National Assembly. Pop. (1977) 7,520,000. The language is German, and about 90 per cent of the people are R.C.

GEOGRAPHY. A. comprises 2 geographical regions: the Alpine zone in the S.W. and the Danube lowlands, incl. the Vienna plain. The Austrian Alps are lower and less impenetrable than the Swiss A., being broken by long, wide valleys. Passes include the Brenner, Arlberg, Semmering, and Schober. Stretching towards the Danube is a broad plain; N. of the river the land rises again towards the Bohemian Forest and Moravian heights in Czechoslovakia. The Vienna plain is a triangular lowland between the Alps and the Carpathians, with fertile alluvial soil.

Much of the formerly extensive Alpine forests has been cleared; above the forest belt lie summer pastures where cattle and goats graze from spring to Sept. Agriculture is general, and A. attracts both summer tourists and winter sports enthusiasts. There is little coal; hydro-electricity is a main source of power. Large iron ore deposits occur in Styria; petroleum and graphite are important. Industries, for the most part state-owned, include metallurgical and engineering works, factories making textiles, chemicals, paper, leather goods, and preparing food products; musical instruments also are made.

TOWNS AND COMMUNICATIONS. Vienna is the cap. and the main route centre. Industrial towns incl. Graz, Wiener-Neustadt, Steyr, Klagenfurt, and Linz. Innsbruck and Salzburg are cultural centres. The Danube is an international route; the head of navigation for large vessels is Linz.

History. A. was inhabited in prehistoric times by Celtic tribes; the country S. of the Danube was conquered by the Romans in 14 B.C., and incorporated in the Roman Empire. After the fall of the empire in the 5th cent. the country now A. was occupied by Vandals, Goths, Huns, Lombards, and Avars. Having conquered the Avars in 791, Charlemagne estab. the East Mark, nucleus of the Austrian empire. In 973 Otto II granted the Mark to the house of Babenberg, who ruled until 1246. Rudolf of Habsburg, who became King of the Romans and Holy Roman Emperor in 1273, seized A. and invested his son as duke in 1282. Until the Empire ceased to exist in 1806 most of the dukes (from 1453 archdukes) of A. were elected Holy Roman Emperor.

A., which in 1526 acquired control of Bohemia, was throughout the 16th cent. a bulwark of resistance against the Turks, who besieged Vienna in vain in 1529. The Thirty Years' War (1618–48) did not touch A., but it weakened its rulers. A 2nd Turkish siege of Vienna was frustrated in 1683, and by 1697 Hungary was liberated from the Turks and incorporated in the Austrian dominion. As a result of their struggle with Louis XIV the Habsburgs in 1713 secured the Spanish Netherlands and Milan. When Charles VI, last male Habsburg in the direct line, d. in 1740, his dau. Maria Theresa became Archduchess of A. and Queen of Hungary, but the Elector of Bavaria was elected emperor as Charles VII. Frederick II of Prussia seized Silesia, and the War of the Austrian Succession (1740–8) followed. Charles VII died in 1745, and Maria Theresa secured the election of her husband as Francis I; but she did not recover Silesia from Frederick.

The Archduke Francis who succeeded in 1792 was also elected Emperor as Francis II; sometimes opposing, sometimes allied with Napoleon, in 1804 he proclaimed himself Emperor of Austria as Francis I, and in 1806 even the name Holy Roman Empire disappeared from history. Under the Treaty of Vienna (1815) Francis failed to recover the Austrian Netherlands (annexed by France in 1797), but received Lombardy and Venetia.

In 1848 the mixed nationalities within the Austrian Empire flared into rebellion, soon crushed. As a result of the Seven Weeks' War of 1866 with Prussia, A. lost Venetia to Italy. In the next year Francis Joseph estab. the Dual Monarchy of Austria-Hungary. The Treaty of Berlin (1878) gave A. the administration of Bosnia-Herçegovina in the Balkans, though they remained nominally Turkish until A. annexed them in 1908. The F.W.W. began with an Austrian attack on Serbia. Austria-Hungary collapsed in

1918, and A. was reduced to Vienna and its immediately surrounding provs. A republic was proclaimed; it had a precarious existence, and internal tensions gave Hitler the opportunity in 1938 of incorporating A. in Germany. A. recovered rapidly economically after the Allied liberation in 1945, although occupied by them until regaining sovereignty under the 1955 peace treaty. Under a Socialist govt. from 1970, Austria has a higher degree of public ownership than any other Western economy.

AUSTRIA. Designed by Fischer von Erlach to rival Versailles, the palace of Schönbrunn at Vienna has associations with Maria Theresa and Napoleon and Marie Louise, whose son was to die there. The main facade, seen from the Neptune Fountain, was completed in 1750. *Photo: Courtesy of the Austrian State Tourist Department*

Provinces of Austria

	Area sq. km.	*Population 1971*	*Capital*
Vienna	415	1,614,340	
Lower Austria	19,170	1,414,160	Wiener Neustadt
Burgenland	3,965	272,120	Eisenstadt
Upper Austria	11,979	1,233,445	Linz
Salzburg	7,153	401,770	Salzburg
Styria	16,385	1,192,100	Graz
Carinthia	9,533	525,730	Klagenfurt
Tirol	12,648	540,770	Innsbruck
Vorarlberg	2,602	271,470	Bregenz
	83,850	7,465,905	

AUSTRIA-HUNGARY. Name given to the 'Dual Monarchy' estab. by Francis Joseph in 1867 between his Empire of Austria and his Kingdom of Hungary. In 1910 it had an area of 261,239 sq.m with a pop. of 51 million. It collapsed in the autumn of 1918. There were only 2 king-emperors: Francis Joseph, 1867-1916, and Charles, 1916-18.

AUSTRIAN SUCCESSION. Name given to a war fought 1740-8 between Austria, supported by England and Holland, and Prussia, France, and Spain. It began when a number of European powers disputed the succession of Maria Theresa, dau. of the Emperor Charles VI, when the latter d. in 1740. Frederick the Great of Prussia seized Silesia from the Austrians. At Dettingen in 1743 an army of British, Austrians, and Hanoverians under the command of George II - the last action in which an English sovereign was personally engaged - was victorious over the French, but at Fontenoy in 1745 an Austro-English army was defeated. British naval superiority was confirmed, and there were gains in America and India. The war was ended by the Treaty of Aix-la-Chapelle in 1748.

AUTISM. (aw'tizm). Condition in young children who fail to develop normally in emotions or intelligence, remaining rigidly withdrawn, although in individual cases some progress has been achieved by psychological and other means. It seems to occur more frequently in families of higher intelligence, but the actual causes are unknown.

AU'TOBĪO'GRAPHY. An account of a man's life, written by himself, and distinguished from the journal or diary by being a connected narrative, and from memoirs by dealing less with contemporary events and personalities. A secondary division of A. is the confession, which is concerned with the inner spiritual life, e.g. the Confessions of St Augustine, Margery Kempe, St Theresa of Avila, Bunyan (*Grace Abounding*), the German physician and pietist Heinrich Jung (Stilling), and Cardinal Newman.

Classical Greek and Roman literature furnishes no notable example of A., nor did the Middle Ages encourage the expression of individual personality; an exception is Abelard's *Historia calamitatum.* With the Renaissance As. began to be written in ever-increasing quantity. Among the best-known of the 16th to 18th cents. are those of Benvenuto Cellini, Lord Herbert of Cherbury, Colley Cibber, Gibbon, Casanova, Alfieri, and Benjamin Franklin. Rousseau's *Confessions* at the close of the 18th cent. set a new vogue by their stress on psychological and emotional development, and influenced Wordsworth's *Prelude,* Byron's *Childe Harold,* De Quincey's *Confessions of an Opium Eater,* and Goethe's *Dichtung und Wahrheit.* Among other 19th cent. autobiographical writers are Leigh Hunt, B. Haydon, Richard Wagner, Berlioz, Rimsky-Korsakov, Bismarck, Béranger, George Sand, the elder Dumas, A. de Musset, A. Daudet, Tolstoy, J. S. Mill, Herbert Spencer, Mark Rutherford, and A. Trollope. In the 20th cent. important political As. and memoirs are those of Hitler (*Mein Kampf*), Lloyd George, W. Churchill, Mahatma Gandhi, Eisenhower, Truman, Johnson, Macmillan and Harold Wilson. Leading figures in arts and literature who have written As. incl. J. Epstein, Salvador Dali, Theodore Dreiser, H. G. Wells, W. B. Yeats, and Malcolm Muggeridge.

AUTO-DA-FÉ (ow'to-dah-fā). Port. for 'act of faith': term for the ceremony, incl. a procession, solemn mass, and sermon, accompanying the sentencing of alleged heretics by the Inquisition. Those found guilty were at once handed over to the secular authorities for punishment, usually burning.

AUTO-IMMUNE DISEASES. Diseases in which the body's immune defence system is turned against itself, e.g. rheumatoid arthritis, Grave's disease, some types of diabetes, and multiple sclerosis.

AUTOLYCUS (awto'likus). In Greek mythology, an accomplished thief and trickster, son of the god Hermes, who gave him the power of invisibility.

AUTOMATION. Term coined by American business consultant John Diebold. It covers the addition of control devices, using electronic sensing and computing techniques which follow the pattern of human nervous and brain functions, to already mechanized physical processes of production and distribution, e.g. steel processing, mining, chemical production, and road, rail and air control. *See* CYBERNETICS.

AUTO'MATON. Mechanical figure imitating human or animal performance, the earliest recorded being a wooden pigeon of 400 BC, and usually of some artistic appeal rather than purely functional. The charm of the A. has been exploited in ballet, e.g. *Coppélia* and *La Boutique Fantasque*. *See* ROBOT.

AUTONOMI'STI. Semi-clandestine amalgam of Marxist student organisations, linked with terrorist groups and such atrocities as the kidnapping and murder of Italian premier Aldo Moro by the Red Brigades in 1978.

AUTONOMIC NERVOUS SYSTEM. The part of the nervous system which controls the involuntary activities of the smooth muscles (of the alimentary canal, blood vessels, etc.), the heart and glands.

AUTO-SUGGESTION. The conscious or unconscious acceptance of an idea as true, without demanding adequate rational proof, but with potential subsequent effect for good or ill on the individual. Coué (q.v.) pioneered A. in healing, and it has been used in modern psychotherapy for conquering nervous habits, ending dependence on tobacco, alcohol, etc.

AUTUN (ōtaṅ'). City in Saône-et-Loire dept, France, on the Arroux. There are metallurgical and textile industries, Roman remains and a 12-15th cent. cathedral, with a portico illustrating the Last Judgment. Pop. (1973) 20,000.

AUVERGNE (ōvār'ny). Ancient prov. of central France and a modern region (depts Allier, Cantal, Haute-Loire and Puy-de-Dôme). Mountainous, it lies in the heart of the Central Plateau, composed chiefly of volcanic rocks in several masses, the Auvergne Mountains.

AUXERRE (ōsār'). Cap. of Yonne dept, France, 170km (106m) S.E. of Paris, on the Yonne. The Gothic cathedral founded in 1215 has fine sculptures and stained glass. Pop. (1973) 40,000.

AVA (ah'vah). Ancient cap. of Burma, on the Irrawaddy; 30 kings reigned here from 1364 to 1783.

A'VALON. In Celtic mythology, the island of the blest or paradise, and in the Arthurian legend the land of heroes, to which the dead king was conveyed. It has been associated with Glastonbury.

AVATAR (avatahr'; Sanskrit, descent). In Hindu mythology, the descent of a deity to earth in a visible form. Most famous are the 10 As. of Vishnu.

Ā'VEBURY, John Lubbock, 1st baron A. (1834-1913). British banker. A partner in the family firm from 1856, he was a Liberal (from 1886 Liberal Unionist) MP 1870-1900, and was largely responsible for the Bank Holidays Act, 1871. He was an original worker in archaeology and physical anthropology.

AVEBURY. Site of Europe's largest stone circle, on which the small village of A. in Wilts, England, has been built. Probably constructed in the neolithic period *c.* 3,500 yrs. ago, it is 412 m (450 yds) in diameter, and the stones have been much depleted by use as building material. It is thought to have had a religious-astronomical purpose, and is linked with nearby Silbury Hill (q.v.).

AVE MARIA (ah'vā' mahrē'ah). Lat. 'hail, Mary'; traditionally, the salutation of the Virgin Mary by the archangel Gabriel (Luke i, 28), when he announced to her that she would be the mother of the Messiah. These words have been set to music by many composers.

AVERNUS. Small circular lake in Italy near Naples and Cumae, which the ancients believed was the entrance to the lower world.

AVERROES (averō'ez) (1126-98). Arabian philosopher; in Arabic, Ibn Roshd. B. at Córdova in Spain, he became judge of Seville and of Córdova, but was accused of heresy and banished (1195). Later he was recalled, and d. at Marrakesh. His philosophical writings, incl. the important commentaries on Aristotle, became known to the West through Latin translations, and exercised a great influence on Christian thinkers. 'Averroism' was taught at Paris and elsewhere by the 'Averroists', who distinguished philosophical truth from revealed religion.

AVICE'NNA (979-1037). Arabian philosopher and physician; in Arabic, Ibn Sina. B. near Bokhara, he made a profound study of the Koran, philosophy, and the science of his day, and won a high reputation as physician. He d. at Hamadan, where he had been vizier. His *Canon Medicinae* was a standard work for centuries. His philosophical writings were influenced by Al-Farabi and by Aristotle and the Neoplatonists, and influenced the Schoolmen of the 13th cent.

AVIEMORE (avimohr'). Winter sports centre in Highland region, Scotland, SE of Inverness among the Cairngorms.

AVIGNON (ahvēnyoṅ'). French city in Provence, cap. of Vaucluse dept, on the Rhône north-west of Marseilles. An important Gallic and Roman city, it has its 14th cent. walls, the famous half-bridge, a 13th cent. cathedral, and the palace built 1334-42 during the residence here of the Popes. A. was papal property 1348-1791. Pop. (1973) 89,000.

Villeneuve-lès-Avignon, virtually a suburb, lies across the Rhône in Gard dept. Pop. (1973) 7,500.

AVILA (ah'vēlah). Spanish town, cap. of prov. of the same name, 90km (56m) N.W. of Madrid. It has remains of the Moorish castle, a Gothic cathedral, and the convent and church of Sta. Teresa of Avila, who was b. here. Pop. (1970) 28,400.

AVOCADO (avokah'dō). Tree of the laurel family (*Persea americana*), first cultivated by S American Indians for its dark green pear-shaped 'fruit', with a flesh of buttery texture, used in salads.

AVOCET (a'voset). Wading-bird (*Recurvirostra avosetta*), belonging to the plover and snipe order (Charadriiformes). It is distinguished by its black and white plumage, long legs, partially webbed feet, and by its upward-curved bill.

AVOGADRO (ahvōgah'drō), **Amedeo,** Conte di Quaregna (1776-1856). Italian physicist. B. at Turin, he became in 1821 prof. of higher physics in the univ. there. In 1811 he pub. a memoir on what has since been known as 'Avogadro's Law' (equal volumes of gases at the same pressure and temperature contain the same number of molecules).

AVON, Anthony Eden, 1st earl of A. (1897-1977). British Cons. statesman. Entering parliament in 1923 as MP for Warwick and Leamington, he became Lord Privy Seal in 1934, and in 1935 Min. for League of Nations Affairs. In 1935 he succeeded Sir Samuel Hoare as For. Sec., but in Feb. 1938 resigned as a protest against Chamberlain's decision to open conversations with Mussolini. He became Dominions Sec. in 1939, and was again For. Sec.

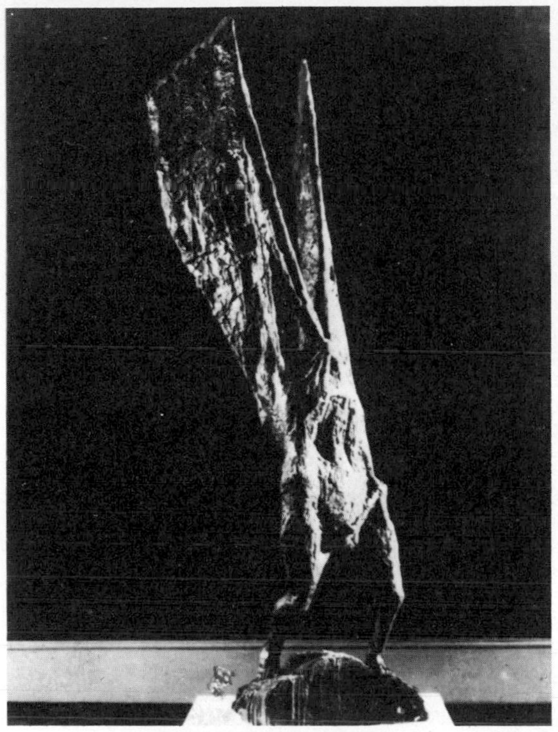

AYRTON. Michael Ayrton with one of his many interpretations of the Icarus myth — a bronze 170 cm (67 in) high. He followed up the same theme in his book *The Testament of Daedalus* (1962). *Photos: Popperfoto and David Farrell*

1940-5, taking part in all the great conferences of the S.W.W. Deputy leader of the Opposition 1945-51, he once more returned to the Foreign Office, also becoming Deputy PM, in 1951. He was created K.G. in 1954 following his diplomatic triumphs in achieving peace in Indo-China at the Geneva Conference and the rapprochement of France and Germany within Western European Union at the London Conference. In 1952 he had m. Clarissa Churchill, niece of Sir Winston Churchill and, on the latter's resignation in April 1955, he succeeded him as PM. He was confirmed in office at the May general election, but resigned shortly after the Suez crisis and received an earldom in 1960.

Ā'VON. Celtic word for 'river', name of several rivers in England and Scotland. The chief are: The Upper, or Warwickshire, A., rising in the Northampton uplands near Naseby, joins the Severn at Tewkesbury; 154km (96m). The Lower, or Bristol, A., 121km (75m) rises in the Cotswolds, and flows into the Bristol Channel at Avonmouth. The East, or Salisbury, A. rises S. of the Marlborough Downs, and flows into the English Channel at Christchurch, length, 104km (65m).

AVON. Co. of S.W. England, created in 1974, and incl. Bristol, the S. part of Gloucestershire, and a large part of Somerset, incl. Bath, Weston-super-Mare, Radstock and Clevedon. Area 1,336 sq.km (516 sq.m); pop. (1978) 921,900.

AWE (aw). Longest 37km (23m) of the Scottish freshwater lochs, in Strathclude, S.E. of Oban. It is drained by the river Awe into Loch Etive. The hydro-electric installations are a tourist attraction.

AXHOLME, ISLE OF. Area of 2,000 ha (5,000 acres) in Humberside, bounded by the Trent, Don, Idle, and Torne rivers, where 'medieval type' open field strip farming is still practised. The largest village, Epworth, is the birthplace of John Wesley.

AXIS. Name given to the union of Nazi Germany and Fascist Italy before and during the S.W.W. The Rome-Berlin Axis was formed in 1936, when Italy was being threatened with 'sanctions' because of her invasion of Abyssinia, and became a full military and political alliance in May 1939. A 10-year alliance between Germany, Italy and Japan (Rome-Berlin-Tokyo A.) was signed in Sept. 1940, and was subsequently joined by Hungary, Bulgaria, Rumania, and the puppet states of Slovakia and Croatia. The A. collapsed with the fall of Mussolini and the surrender of Italy in 1943.

AXMINSTER. Small town in Devon, England, nr Exeter, famous for cut-pile, patterned carpets. Slightly coarser than Wilton, the method permits up to 240 colours. Pop. 4,500.

A'XOLOTL. Usually permanent larval form of *Ambystoma (Siredon) mexicanum,* found in Mexico, which resembles a large, full-grown tadpole (30 cm/1 ft), and reaches sexual maturity in this state. The name is also used for other fully-grown larval salamanders, e.g. *Ambystoma tigrinum.*

AXUM. Alternative transliteration of AKSUM.

AYATOLLAH (īyahto'la). Honorific title 'sign of God' among Shi'ite Moslems in Iran, which is accorded by popular consent to holy men of the faith. *See* KHOMEINI.

AYCKBOURN (ăk'born), **Alan** (1939-). British playwright. As director of the Theatre-in-the Round Library Theatre Co., Scarborough, from 1959, he wrote plays of modernistic technique with an exceptional popular appeal, notably *Absurd Person, Singular* (1973), the trilogy *The Norman Conquests* (1974), and *Just Between Ourselves* (1977).

AYCLIFFE. Town in Durham, England, on the r. Skerne, developed from 1947 as a 'new town'. Pop. (1980) 28,000.

AYE-AYE (ī-ī). A lemur (*Daubentonia* or *Chiromys madagascariensis*) from Madagascar, the sole representative of a special family, distinguished by having its front teeth adapted for gnawing like those of the Rodentia. It is about the size of a cat.

AYER, Sir Alfred Jules (1910-). British philosopher. Wykeham prof. of logic at Oxford from 1959, he estab. his reputation with *Language, Truth and Logic* (1936), an exposition of the theory of 'logical positivism'. Later works incl. *Probability and Evidence* (1972).

AYERS ROCK. Ovate, pinkish monolith in Northern Territory, Australia; 335 m. (1,100 ft.) high and 9 km (6 m) round, named after a premier of South Australia. For the Aboriginals, whose paintings decorate its caves, it has magical significance.

AYERS ROCK. The first European to see the rock was William Giles in 1872. Later it was named after a South Australian premier, Sir Henry Ayers. *Photo: Camera Press*

AYESHA (ah'yesha) (*c.* 611-*c.* 678). Favourite wife of Mohammed, whom she m. when she was 9. Her father, Abu-Bekr, through her influence became Caliph on the Prophet's death in 632.

AYLESBURY (ālz'beri). Admin. HQ of Bucks, England, 63km (39m) N.W. of London in the Vale of A. There are printing, light engineering and dairy industries. Nearby is Waddesdon Manor, a mansion in the French Renaissance style bequeathed to the nation in 1957 by James de Rothschild (q.v.). Pop. (1972) 40,860.

AYMARA (āmerah'). South American Indians of Bolivia and Peru. They were conquered, first by the Incas and then by the Spaniards, but their language survives, and although the majority are now Roman Catholic, their faith incorporates elements of their old beliefs.

AY'OT ST LAWRENCE. Village in Herts, where Shaw's Corner (home of G. B. Shaw) is preserved. Pop. 150.

AYR (ār). Town in Strathclyde region, Scotland, at the mouth of the r. Ayr. The 'Auld Brig' was built in the 15th cent., the 'New Brig' in 1788 (rebuilt 1879). A. has associations with Robert Burns. Pop. (1971) 48,020.

AYRSHIRE. Former co. of S.W. Scotland, with a 113km (70m) coastline on the Firth of Clyde. In 1975 the major part was merged in the region of Strathclyde, the remaining sector, approx. S. of the Water of Girvan and incl. Girvan itself, became part of Dumfries and Galloway.

AYRTON, Michael (1921-75). British artist. Gifted as a painter, sculptor and illustrator, he developed an obsession with the Daedalus myth from 1961, e.g. his bronzes of Icarus, and his fictional autobiography of Daedalus *The Maze Maker* (1967). He himself designed and built a maze with 2 m (6 ft) walls of stone and brick and 1,000 m (3,000 ft) long, in the Catskill Mtns, N.Y. state.

AYTOUN (ā'ten), **Sir Robert** (1570-1638). Scottish poet, one of the first of Scots to write in graceful English. His love poems are his best work. James I knighted him, and gave him employment.

AYTOUN (ā'toon), **William Edmonstoune** (1813-65). Scottish poet, b. in Edinburgh, chiefly remembered for his *Lays of the Scottish Cavaliers* (1848), and for the *Bon Gaultier Ballads* (1855), which he wrote in collaboration with Sir T. Martin.

AYURVEDA (ah'yurvēda). Ancient Hindu system of medicine, the main principles of which are derived from the Vedas. In India there are numerous Ayurvedic hospitals, dispensaries, etc.

AZA'LEA. Group of plants of the order Ericaceae, closely related to Rhododendron, in which genus they are now generally incl. There are several species, natives of Asia and N. America, and from these many cultivated varieties have been derived which make fine ornamental shrubs - particularly the Japanese As. Several species are highly poisonous.

AZERBAIJAN (ahzerbījahn'). Constituent SSR of USSR on the S.W. shore of the Caspian Sea. It is heavily forested and has large mineral deposits, particularly petroleum. Baku, the cap., is one of the chief centres of Soviet oil production. Artificial irrigation is used chiefly for cotton production. Area 86,600 sq.km (33,400 sq.m); pop. (1979) 6,028,000, the majority traditionally Moslem (Shiah) and Turkic-speaking: *see also* AZERBAIJAN, Iranian.

AZERBAIJAN, Iranian. Two provs. of NW Iran, Eastern A. (cap. Tabriz) and Western A. (cap. Rezayeh). Like the people of Soviet A., the people are Moslem (Shiah) ethnic Turks, descendants of the Mongol Khans' followers, whose cap. was also Tabriz. They form over a third of Iran's pop., 5 million in A., and 3 million distributed in the rest of the country where they form a strong middle class (merchants, army officers, teachers).

In 1946, with Soviet backing, they briefly estab. their own republic. Denied autonomy under the Shah, they rose 1979-80 against the supremacy of Ayatollah Khomeini, and were forcibly repressed, although a degree of autonomy was promised.

AZHAR (azahr'), **El.** Moslem mosque and univ. at Cairo. Founded by Jawhar, C.-in-C. of the army of the Fatimid caliph, in 970, it is claimed to be the oldest univ. in the world. It became the centre of Islamic learning, with several subsidiary foundations, and is primarily a school of Koranic teaching.

AZI'LIAN. Name given to an archaeological period following the close of the Old Stone (Palaeolithic) Age, and regarded as one of the cultures of the Mesolithic Age. It was first recognized by Ed. Piette at Mas d'Azil, a village in Ariège, France.

AZINCOURT. French form of AGINCOURT.

AZORES (azorz'). Group of 9 islands in the N. Atlantic, belonging to Portugal, divided into 3 admin. districts. Area 2,388 sq.km (922 sq.m). Of the pop. (1978) 292,200 half live on the is. of San Miguel, on which is the chief tn, Ponta Delgada (pop. 21,350). The islands are volcanic in origin, and have a genial climate. Known to the Carthaginians, they were rediscovered in the 14th cent. and annexed by the Portuguese *c.* 1430. Europe's most westerly land, they were used as an air base in the S.W.W. to protect Allied shipping. The A. gained partial autonomy in 1976, but a separatist movement was supported in the 1980s by Libya and USSR.

AZORES. Mosteiros Village on San Miguel, the main island. The Azores are outlying peaks of the Mid-Atlantic Ridge, and the strata of the rocks offshore show their volcanic origin. *Photo: Dick Huffman/Barnaby's Picture Library*

AZORIN (athorin'). Pseudonym of José Martínez Ruiz (1873-1967), Spanish author. B. in Alicante prov. he studied law, but soon devoted himself to literature. His work was as influential as it is rich and varied in form and incl. vols. of critical essays and short stories, plays and novels, such as the autobiographical *La voluntad* (1902) and *Antonio Azorin* (1903) - the author adopted the name of the eponymous hero of the latter as his pseudonym.

Á'ZOV. Inland sea of the USSR, forming a gulf in the N.E. of the Black Sea.

A'ZTECS. Mexican Indian people who migrated from further N in the 12th cent. AD, and in AD 1325 began reclaiming lake marshland to build their cap., Tenochtitlán, on the site of modern Mexico City (q.v.). Under Montezuma I (reigned from 1440), they created a great empire in central and southern Mexico. Their tribal god was Huitzilopochtli (Humming-bird Wizard), but they also worshipped Quetzalcoatl (q.v.), inherited from the conquered Toltecs, and others. Aztec rule was resented as oppressive, and Montezuma II (reigned from 1502) was able to put up only slight resistance when Cortes landed in 1519. He was killed and Tenochtitlán was subsequently destroyed.

Aztec architecture, jewellery (gold, jade and turquoise), and textiles, were magnificent. Their form of writing combined the hieroglyph and pictograph, and they used a complex calendar, which combined a sacred period of 260 days with the solar year of 365 days. Propitiatory rites were performed at the 'dangerous' period, once in every 52 years, when the beginning of the two coincided, and all temples were rebuilt (useful as a date-mark for archaeologists). Possessed by a degree of religious mania, they practised wholesale human sacrifice, tearing the heart from the living body, and flaying people alive. War captives were obtained for this purpose, but their own people may also have been used. Pictures show that they played a type of 'football', in which legs rather than feet were used to propel a solid rubber ball, and it is not certain whether the losers were sacrificed for having lost, or the winners promoted to the next world for having won.

AZTECS. An Aztec calendar stone, some 4m (12 ft) in diameter. The calendar was based on a sacred period of 260 days in combination with the solar year of 365 days. When the beginning of the two coincided – once in 52 years – great natural disasters were believed to occur. *Photo: Mexican National Tourist Council*

B

Second letter of the alphabet. It corresponds to the Greek *beta* and the Semitic *beth*; and as written in the modern W. European alphabet is derived from the classical Latin.

BĀ'AL. Semitic word meaning 'lord' or 'owner', used as a divine title of their chief male gods by the Phoenicians, Canaanites, etc. Generally deities of fertility, their worship was often orgiastic and of a phallic character, and was strongly denounced by the Hebrew Prophets.

BAALBEK (bahl'bek). City of ancient Syria, in modern Lebanon, 60km (36m) N.E. of Beirut. There are magnificent ruins of Baal temples. The Greeks identified Baal with Helios, the sun, and renamed B. Heliopolis.

BAALBEK. The Temple of Bacchus, built in the second century A.D. is still almost intact. At 1,150 m. (3,000ft.) above sea level, it lies today among orchards of the Bekaa region. *Photo: Courtesy of the Lebanese National Tourist Council*

BĀ'BEL. Hebrew name for Babylon, chiefly associated with the TOWER of B., which, in the Genesis story, was erected in the plain of Shinar by the descendants of Noah. The site has been identified with the temple of E-sagila in Babylon and the mound of Birs Nimrud (Borsippa) near the city.

BABEL, Isaak Emmanuilovich (1894-1939/40). Russian Jewish writer. B. in Odessa, he was an ardent supporter of the Revolution and fought with Budyenny's cavalry in the Polish campaign of 1921-2, an experience which inspired *Konarmiya* (1926: *Red Cavalry*). Best known of his other works is *Odesskie rasskazy* (1924: *Stories from Odessa*), which brilliantly conveys the life of the Odessa Jews.

BAB-EL-MANDEB (bahb-el-mahn'deb). Strait separating Arabia and Africa, and joining the Red Sea and the Gulf of Aden.

BABER (bah'ber) or **Babar** ('Tiger'). Title given to Zahir ud-din Mohammed (1483-1530), first Great Mogul of India. He was the great-grandson of Tamerlane, and at the age of 12 succeeded his father as ruler of Ferghana (Turkestan). In 1526 he defeated the emperor of Delhi at Panipat, captured Delhi and Agra, and estab. a dynasty which endured until 1858.

BABEUF (bahböf'), **François Noël** (1760-97). French revolutionary journalist, a pioneer of practical socialism. In 1794 he founded in Paris a paper, later known as the *Tribune of the People*, in which he demanded the equality of all men and the abolition of property. For conspiring against the Directory he was guillotined.

BÁBÍ FAITH. *See* BAHÁ'Í FAITH.

BABIRUSA (bahbiroo'sa). A wild pig (*B. alfurus*), found in Celebes, characterized by the great development in the male of the upper tusks which grow upwards through the skin of the snout, and curve back towards the forehead.

BABI YAR (bah'bi yahr). Place near Kiev, USSR, where tens of thousands of Jews were killed by the Germans in 1941. Yevgeni Yevtushenko's poem of this title (1961) was a condemnation of anti-semitism in the USSR which led to a rebirth of Jewish consciousness and pressure from 1968 to be allowed to go to Israel.

BABOO'N. A large monkey (*Papio*) found in Africa, S. of the Sahara and in S. Arabia, given the popular name 'dog-faced monkey', because of its elongated muzzle. Well-known species are: the chacma from S. Africa, the small ginger-coloured B. of Guinea, the yellow B. of E. Africa, the olive green Anubis B., ranging from E. Africa to Nigeria, and the Hamadryas or sacred B. from Ethiopia and S. Arabia.

BA'BYLON. Cap. of ancient Babylonia, on the left bank of the Euphrates. The site is in modern Iraq, 88km (55m) S. of Baghdad and 8km (5m) N. of Hilla (pop. 50,000), which is built chiefly of bricks from the ruins of Babylon. B. first rose to importance under Hammurabi, and under Nebuchadrezzar I it was a magnificent city. Stone supports, probably part of the Hanging Gardens built by Nebuchadrezzar II, have been found.

BABYLŌ'NIA. The great alluvial plain of Mesopotamia, watered by the rivers Euphrates and Tigris, now forming the principal portion of Iraq. In the O.T. it is frequently referred to as the plain of Shinar, Babel, and 'the land of the Chaldees'. In history it was the centre of the Babylonian (and later the Assyrian) empire.

The history of B. is bound up with that of the city of Babylon. B. lay at the meeting-point of 2 great avenues of commerce, the one connecting her with the Mediterranean and Egypt, the other with the Black Sea. Her rise to supremacy followed the penetration of the western Semites into Mesopotamia, and their eventual triumph over the Sumerians. They founded the first Amorite dynasty of Babylon in 1950 B.C. Under Hammurabi (1791-1750 B.C.) the first Babylonian empire reached on the S.W. to the borders of Syria. From 1650 B.C. the kings of the first Sea-land dynasty ruled for 368 years. There followed a period of Kassite domination, which lasted for 576 years. The Kassites are generally supposed to have been an Aryan people. The letters from Tell el-Amarna and from the Hittite archives at Boghaz-Keui throw a good light on the history of their later monarchs. The period was terminated in 1174 by an Elamite invasion.

During the next 300 years B. struggled against the advancing power of Assyria. From 732 until 612 B.C. Babylonia was a subject prov. of the Assyrian empire, and her continued resistance was one of the causes of the downfall of Assyria.

The Neo-Babylonian empire was estab. by Nabopolassar, whose son, Nebuchadrezzar II, raised it to a pitch of prosperity and greatness beyond any it had known. Babylonian rule was extended over the whole of Mesopotamia; Egypt became a tributary; Babylon was rebuilt, fortified, and adorned with magnificent buildings; Jerusalem was captured in 586 B.C., and a large part of the population of Judah carried into exile. After Nebuchadrezzar's death there was a swift decline. In 539 B.C. Babylonia became a prov. of the Persian empire.

The civilization of B. was largely derived from the Sumerians. Their cuneiform or wedge-shaped writing was taken over, and the Sumerian language continued to be used for religious purposes. The Sumerian pantheon was also adopted, together with the chief myths, such as those of the Creation and the Deluge, and the epic of Gilgamesh. Babylonian religious ideas and conceptions of the universe passed into Hebrew culture, and into Europe by way of Greece.

BABYLONIAN CAPTIVITY. The period spent by the Jews in Babylon following the capture of Jerusalem by Nebuchadrezzar the Babylonian emperor, in 605, 597 and 586 B.C. Traditionally it lasted 70 years, but Cyrus permitted the exiles to return to Jerusalem in 536 B.C. The term is also applied to the period 1309–77, when the popes were exiled to Avignon.

BACAU (bahk'ow). Town of Romania, 250km (155m) N.N.E. of Bucharest, on the Bistrita. It is an oil centre with refineries. Pop. (1973) 103,500.

BACCARAT (bakarah'). Casino card game, played in two forms, *chemin de fer* and *banque.*

BACCHUS (bak'us). Greek and Roman god of wine, also known in Greece as Dionysus. In Gk legend B. was the son of Zeus and Semele. He toured the cities of Greece, bringing the gift of the vine to those who welcomed him, and overwhelming those who opposed him with madness and intoxication. The worship of B. took the form of wild and licentious revels, called *Bacchanalia.*

BACH (bahkh), **Johann Sebastian** (1685-1750). German composer. B. at Eisenach, in Thuringia, he came of a distinguished musical family. At 15 he became a chorister at Lüneburg, and at 19 organist at Arnstadt. Subsequent appointments incl. positions at the ducal court of Weimar, and finally, in 1723, that of musical director at St Thomas's choir school in Leipzig, where apart from his brief visit to the court of Frederick the Great of Prussia in 1747, he remained until his death. B. m. twice, and had numerous children, many of whom died in infancy. His 2nd wife, Anna Magdalena Wülkens, was a soprano singer; she also acted as his amanuensis, when in later years his sight failed.

B.'s music represents the culmination of the polyphonic style of the 17th and early 18th cents., but it was not until the time of Mendelssohn that it began to be generally appreciated. His influence on later musicians can hardly be overestimated.

His sacred music incl. the 190 church cantatas, the Easter and Christmas oratorios, the 2 great Passions, according to St Matthew and St John, and the Mass in B minor. *Phoebus and Pan* is a secular dramatic cantata. His orchestral music incl. the 6 Brandenburg concertos, and other concertos for clavier and for violin and 4 orchestral suites. B.'s keyboard music, for clavier and for organ, is of equal importance and incl. the collection of 48 preludes and fugues known as *The Well-tempered Clavier,* the Goldberg variations, the Italian concerto, and the French and English suites. Of his organ music the most important examples are the choral preludes. His music also incl. chamber-music and songs, and 2 important works written in his later years illustrate the principles and potentialities of his polyphonic art - the *Musical Offering* and *The Art of Fugue.*

His eldest son, **Wilhelm Friedemann B.** (1710-84), although famous as an organist, improviser, and master of counterpoint, had an unsuccessful career owing to his dissipated habits. J.S.B.'s 3rd and musically most important son, **Karl Philip Emanuel B.** (1714-88), b. at Weimar, studied music under his father, was appointed crown musician to Frederick the Great, then Crown Prince, and became a member of the royal household on the latter's accession in 1740. He wrote over 200 pieces for the clavier, and pub. an important critical textbook on its technique. From 1768 he was Kapellmeister at Hamburg. His church music incl. the oratorio *The Israelites in the Wilderness.* He is important as a pioneer of the new 'harmonic' (as opposed to 'polyphonic') music, and Mozart, Haydn, and Beethoven all owed a considerable debt to him. J.S.B.'s 11th son **Johann Christian B.** (1735-82), b. at Leipzig, became well known in Italy as a composer of operas. In 1762 he was invited to London, where he remained till his death and enjoyed great popularity, both as a composer and performer.

BACILLUS (basil'us). Lat. diminutive of *baculus,* rod; the larger, rod-like forms of bacteria (q.v.).

BACKGA'MMON. Basically a game for 2 players on a board marked with 12 triangles or 'points' of alternate colours along each side, divided into 4 'tables' of 6 points each. The pieces, round and flat like draughtsmen, are set out in a standard pattern, and the players roll 2 dice alternately, moving their pieces round the board according to the numbers thrown. The player begins by bringing all his 15 pieces into his home or 'inner' table, and then removes them from the board, again according to the numbers rolled, the winner being the first to clear his pieces.

Equipment for a similar game was excavated at Ur of the Chaldees (*c.* 2,600 B.C.) and from Tutankhamen's tomb, and it was also played by the Romans. The modern game, then known as 'tables', was introduced to Europe by the returning Crusaders, and was played by Chaucer, Henry VIII and Pepys; from 1750 it became known as B. (Old English 'back game'). In the 1920s it became a casino game, when the rules were amended to allow a group or *chouette* to play against a single opponent, and the American innovation of the doubling cube was introduced (marked 2, 4, 8, 16, 32, 64) - when turned by a player in a potentially winning position it involves doubling of the stakes. In France B. is known as *tric-trac* and the children's game of ludo is a derivative.

BACON, Francis (1561-1626). English statesman and philosopher. Youngest son of Sir Nicholas B., the Elizabethan statesman, he was b. in London, ed. at Cambridge, called to the Bar in 1582, and in 1584 became an MP. Although Lord Burleigh was his uncle, his political ambitions were frustrated and he attached himself to the Earl of Essex. Yet when Essex was disgraced and tried for his life in 1599, B. acted with the prosecuting counsel and in 1601 did much to secure his conviction as a traitor. On

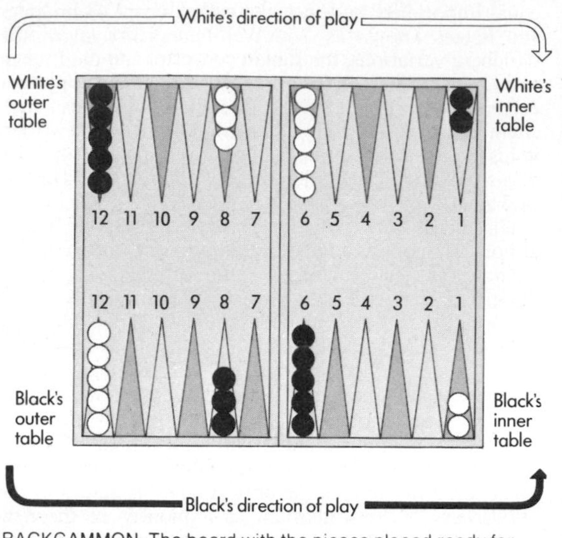

BACKGAMMON. The board with the pieces placed ready for the beginning of play.

the accession of James I, his fortunes improved. He was knighted in 1603, in 1607 became Solicitor-General, and in 1613 Attorney-General. Lord Keeper in 1617, in the next year he was appointed Lord Chancellor and raised to the peerage as Lord Verulam. In 1621 he was created Viscount St Albans; but in the same year he was accused in the House of Lords of taking presents from suitors in cases that he had tried. He offered no defence and was ordered to be fined £40,000, imprisoned indefinitely, and banished from Parliament and the Court. After a few days in the Tower he was allowed to retire to Gorhambury, but never again held office.

B.'s brilliant political career was overshadowed at the last by the misfortunes that his alleged malpractices brought upon him. In literature his fame is far more secure. His famous *Essays or Counsels, Civil and Moral*, a series of short discourses upon truth, death, revenge, friendship, etc., appeared in 1597. In 1605 he pub. *The Advancement of Learning* which gave a general view of his ideas upon scientific method, set out more fully in the *Novum Organum Scientiarum* of 1620. B. sought a means of building a natural science which should not be merely theoretical or philosophical, but the principal means of enlarging man's knowledge and power. Among his other writings are a history of Henry VII, a collection of apophthegms, and the *New Atlantis*, a description of a scientific Utopia. The *Baconian Theory*, originated by the Rev. James Wilmot in 1785, suggests that the works of Shakespeare were written by Bacon.

BACON, Francis (1909-). British artist. B. in Dublin, he was largely self-taught, beginning to paint *c.* 1930 and holding his first one-man show in London in 1949. His work is characterized by lurid colour, and terrifyingly blurred and featureless figures. *Study after Velazquez* (1953) and *Mad Dog* (1952) are in the Tate Gallery, and *Studies of the Human Body* (1947) in the National Gallery of Victoria, Melbourne.

BACON, Roger (*c.* 1214-92). English philosopher and pioneer scientist. B. in Somerset, and ed. at Oxford and Paris, he became a Franciscan friar and until *c.* 1251 was in Paris lecturing on Aristotle. Then he wrote a number of works in Latin, e.g. *On Mirrors, Metaphysical Questions, On the Multiplication of Species*, etc., and in 1266, at the invitation of his friend Pope Clement IV, he began his *Opus Majus*, a compendium of all branches of knowledge. In 1268 he sent this with his *Opus Minus* and other of his writings to the Pope. In 1277 he was condemned by the Church and imprisoned for 'certain novelties', but was released in 1292. One of the most original and bold thinkers of the Middle Ages, B. foresaw the magnifying property of convex lenses, the extensive use of gunpowder, and the possibility of mechanical boats and flying machines.

BACON. Francis Bacon, called by Alexander Pope 'the wisest, brightest, meanest of mankind' had an influence on scientific thought which endures to our own day. *Photo: Courtesy of the National Portrait Gallery.*

BACTERIA (baktēr'ia). Microscopic unicellular organisms. It was formerly assumed that they were the original simplest life form from which all others evolved, but the proteins of bacteria are unlike those of supposedly more 'advanced' organisms. It has therefore been suggested that the bacteria-type may actually be the more advanced form, or even that two different types of cell originated at the period of creation. *See* PROCARYOTE, and also ARCHAEBACTERIA.

Under the microscope bacteria are minute transparent cells without a nucleus. They are now classfied biochemically, but their varying shapes provide a rough classification, e.g. cocci are round or oval, bacilli are cylindrical, and spirochaetae are spiral or undulatory. They reproduce by fission, and since this may occur approximately every 20 minutes, a single bacterium is potentially capable of becoming 16 million in a day. In the laboratory bacteria are grown on culture media, and may mutate, a characteristic which accounts both for the emergence of strains which are resistant to antibiotics, and for the use of bacteria in genetic research. Unlike viruses, bacteria do not necessarily need contact with a live cell to become active.

Bacteria are generally thought of as harmful, and do cause such diseases as anthrax, cholera, diphtheria, enteric fever, pneumonia, scarlet fever, tuberculosis and venereal diseases. However, many other bacteria perform useful functions in the healthy human body, in soil fertility, etc., and are essential in many food and industrial processes, e.g. making butter, cheese, yoghurt and the new synthetic foods, and in curing tobacco, tanning leather, sewage disposal, and (by virtue of the ability of bacteria to attack metal) in cleaning a ship's bottom, de-rusting her tanks, and even extracting minerals from a mine. *See* FRANKENSTEIN LAW.

BĀ'CUP. Town of E. Lancashire, England, 30km (19m) N.E. of Manchester. There are coal mines and slate quarries nearby, but the staple cotton and iron industries have undergone decline. Pop. (1972) 15,100.

BADAJOZ (bahdah-hōs'). Spanish city on the Guadiana. It has the ruins of a Moorish castle; the cathedral dates from the 13th cent. An ancient Roman city, because of its strategic position near the Portuguese frontier it has often been besieged; Wellington stormed it in 1812 with the loss of 59,000 British troops. Pop. (1970) 101,700.

BADEN (bah'den). Former state of S.W. Germany, which had Karlsruhe as its cap. B. was captured from the Romans in 282 by the Alemanni, later it became a margravate, and in 1806 a grand duchy. A state of the German empire 1871-1918, then a rep. and under Hitler a *Gau*, it was divided between the *Länder* of Württemberg-Baden and Baden in 1945, and in 1952 made part of Baden-Württemberg (q.v.).

BADEN. Town of Aargau canton, Switzerland, nr Zurich. The radioactive mineral waters have been visited since Roman times. There are electronic and chemical industries. Pop. (1970) 15,000.

BADEN-BADEN. Health resort of Baden-Württemberg, W. Germany, in the Black Forest. The mineral waters have been known for cents. and in the 19th cent. it became the most fashionable of spas. Pop. (1970) 45,000.

BĀ'DEN-PŌ'WELL, Robert Stephenson Smyth, 1st baron (1857-1941). Soldier, and from 1920 'World Chief Scout'. B. in London, he was ed. at Charterhouse and commissioned in the Hussars in 1876. Worldwide fame came to him for his gallant defence of Mafeking during the S. African War. Invalided home, he was knighted in 1909, and retired in 1910 with the rank of lieut-general. Earlier he had written *Scouting for Boys* (1908), and he now estab. the Boy Scout movement which rapidly spread throughout the World. In 1929 he was created a peer, and in 1937 O.M.

His sister **Agnes Baden-Powell** (1854-1945) helped him found the Girl Guides (1910), and his wife, **Lady (Olave) Baden-Powell** (1889-1977), whom he m. in 1912, was the first and only World Chief Guide 1918-77.

BADEN-WÜRTTEMBERG (bah'den vür'temberg). Land of S.W. Germany formed in 1952 (following a plebiscite) by the merger of the Länder Baden, Württemberg-Baden, and Württemberg-Hohenzollern. The Rhine forms its W. and S. boundaries, and the river valley is devoted to vine and fruit-growing, much of the state is rich agricultural country and forestry is carried on. Textiles, chemicals, iron and steel goods, clocks (espec. in the Black Forest), electrical equipment, etc. are produced. The cap. is Stuttgart. Area 35,750 sq.km (13,805 sq.m); pop. (1978) 9,120,500.

BADER (bah'de), **Sir Douglas** (1910–82) British aviator. He lost both legs in a stunt accident in 1931, but nevertheless became an ace fighter pilot in the S.W.W., scoring 22½ victories in the air. He was knighted in 1976 for his work for the disabled.

BADGER. Mammal of the weasel family, but with larger jaws and molar teeth of a crushing type adapted to a more vegetable diet, and short strong legs with long claws suitable for digging. It has long coarse hair grizzled with black on the upper side, and the underside and legs are black. The face is white with a broad black stripe on each side. The common B. (*Meles meles*) is *c.* 1m (3ft) long. Harmless and of nocturnal habits, it spends the day in deep burrows, called a 'set'. It feeds on insects and roots, but also eggs, mice, and young rabbits.

The so-called sport of *badger-baiting* has been prohibited in Britain since 1850.

BADGER. The badger's set has tunnels that may run long distances in many directions, and when left undisturbed, colonies persist through many generations. *Photo: J.B and S. Bottomley/Ardea*

BAD HOMBURG. *See* HOMBURG.

BA'DMINTON. Game played by 2 or 4 players with rackets and shuttlecocks, usually indoors. The name is derived from B. House, the Gloucestershire seat of the duke of Beaufort, where B. originated in the 1860s. The first rules were drawn up in 1876, and the B. Association was formed in 1895.

BADOGLIO (bahdō'lē-oh), **Pietro** (1871-1956). Italian soldier. A veteran of campaigns against the tribes of Tripoli and Cyrenaica, he in 1935 replaced de Bono as C.-in-C. in Ethiopia, adopting ruthless measures to break patriot resistance, and being created Viceroy of Ethiopia and Duke of Addis Ababa in 1936. Always unfavourable to Fascism, he succeeded Mussolini as PM from July 1943 to June 1944.

BAEDEKER (bād'-), **Karl** (1801-59). German publisher, who started the famous series of travel guides, recording nothing he had not seen himself. In the S.W.W. the German 'B. air raids' were those in which historic buildings in Britain were the targets.

BAEKELAND (bāk'-), **Leo Hendrik** (1863-1944). American chemist. B. in Ghent, he went to USA in 1889, and undertook research on photographic materials, inventing Velox paper. His subsequent researches covered the fields of plastics, electro-chemistry, organic chemistry, synthetic resins, and electrical insulation. He also invented bakelite.

BAER (bār), **Karl Ernst von** (1792-1876). German zoologist. B. in Estonia, he held scientific posts at Königsberg and St Petersburg, and was the founder of comparative embryology.

BAFFIN, William (1584-1622). English navigator and explorer, a Londoner by birth. In 1612 he was chief pilot of an expedition in search of the N.W. passage, and in 1613-4 commanded a whaling fleet near Spitzbergen. In 1615 he became pilot for Robert Bylot on the *Discovery* examining Hudson Strait. In 1616 they discovered Baffin Bay and reached Lat. 77° 45', which for 236 years remained the 'furthest north'. After 1617 B. transferred his services to the E. India Co. and made surveys of the Red Sea and Persian Gulf. In 1622 he was killed in an Anglo-Persian attack on Ormuz.

BAFFIN ISLAND. Island in the Northwest Territories, the largest in the Canadian Arctic. Mtns rise above 2,000 m. (6,000 ft) and there are several large lakes. Area 507,450 sq km (195,930 sq.m.). The northernmost part of the strait separating B.I. from Greenland forms Baffin Bay, the southern end being Davis Strait.

BAGATE'LLE. A game resembling billiards, played on a board with numbered cups instead of pockets. The object is to drive the 9 balls into the cups. In *ordinary B.* each player sends all the balls up in turn. In *French B.* 2 or 4 players, playing alternately, take part.

BAGEHOT (baj'ot), **Walter** (1826-77). British economist. Manager of the London office of his family banking house, he pub. a masterly analysis of the London money market *Lombard Street* (1873). Other books incl. *The English Constitution* (1867), a classic explanation of the political system at the end of the Palmerstonian era, and *Physics and Politics* (1869), applying the laws of natural selection to the development of human communities. He ed. *The Economist* from 1860.

BA'GGARAS. A Beduin tribe whose home is in the Nile Basin, principally in Kordofan, Sudan, W. of the White Nile. They are Moslems, formerly chiefly occupied in cattle-breeding and big-game hunting. Physically they are of a very fine type. The British soldier nicknamed them 'Fuzzy-wuzzies' on account of their mop-like hair fashions.

BAGHDAD (bahgdahd'; Eng. bag'dad). Cap. of Iraq, on the Tigris. B. was founded in the very early days of history; it was a route centre of great importance, a commercial and intellectual centre during the 8th-9th cents. The present city was founded in 762 and enlarged by Harun-al-Rashid. It was overrun in 1258 by the Mongols, who destroyed the irrigation system. In 1639 it was taken by the Turks. During the F.W.W. B. was captured by Gen. Maude in 1917, and in 1921 was made cap. of the new country of Iraq. Pop. (1970) 2,696,000.

Of the old city of 'Arabian Nights' fame not much remains; the modern city is one of metalled roads, railway stations, public buildings, etc. B. Univ. (1958) has colleges in Basra and Mosul. B. is still a great centre of communications.

The **Baghdad Pact** was a treaty made in B. in 1955 between Turkey and Iraq to which Britain, Pakistan, and Iran later adhered. Iraq withdrew from it after the revolution of 1958 and the remaining allies renamed their group the Central Treaty Organization (CENTO) in 1959. The USA signed bilateral agreements of co-operation.

BAFFIN ISLAND. 'Wareham Island, Cumberland Gulf', painted in 1930 by Canadian artist Lawren Harris. This view of one of the offshore islands of Baffin, itself the fifth largest island in the world, captures the stark loneliness and beauty of the Arctic. *Photo: Courtesy of the Canadian Government*

BA'GNOLD, Enid (1889-1981). British author, who m. Sir Roderick Jones of Reuters. Her novel *National Velvet* (1935) achieved great success as a play, and *The Chalk Garden* (1954), staged both in London and N.Y., was a delicate essay in character study.

BAGPIPE. Musical instrument of ancient origin, being known to the Romans and ancient Egyptians and found in different forms in various parts of Europe, as well as in the British Isles. It is developed from the primitive reedpipe, but is distinguished by the presence of a bag for the supply of wind, a chanter or melody pipe and drones, which emit one invariable note and supply a ground-bass. The Scotch B.P. is regarded as the national instrument, and the chanter pipe has a compass of 9 notes. The compass of the Irish bagpipe is wider.

BAGRI'TSKY, Eduard (1895-1934). Pseudonym of the Soviet poet Eduard Dzyubin. One of the Constructivist group, he pub. a vol. of verse, *South-West,* the heroic poem *Lay About Opanas,* and collections of verse called *The Victors* and *The Last Night.*

BAGUIO (bagwi'o). Summer resort on Luzon, Philippine Rep., 200km (125m) N. of Manila, 1,370 m (4,500 ft) a.s.l. Pop. (1970) 45,000.

BAHADUR SHAH II (1775-1862). Last of the Mogul emperors of India. He reigned, though in name only, and under the British, as king of Delhi 1837-57, when he was hailed by the mutineers as an independent emperor at Delhi. After the Mutiny he was deported to Rangoon.

BAHÁ'Í FAITH (bah-hī'). Religion foreshadowed by the teaching of Iranian Mirzá 'Alí Muhammad (1819-50), known as the Bab ('gate'). His claim that Islam was not God's final revelation ended in his being shot by the government at Tabriz. Another of his countrymen, Husayn 'Alí (1817-92), who called himself Bahá'u'lláh ('God's Glory'), claimed to be the prophet the Bab had foretold. His new faith (1863) claims to incorporate the best in all other religions and stresses the oneness of mankind regardless of race, sex, colour, class or creed. The sect still has adherents throughout the world.

BAHAMAS (ba-hah'maz). Group of *c.* 700 islands and *c.* 200 cays in the West Indies, off the S.E. coast of Florida: only 21 is. are inhabited. The chief are New Providence, on which stands Nassau, the cap.; Grand Bahama, Abaco, Eleuthera, Cat, Andros, Exuma, Maguana, Crooked, Long, Great Inagua, and San Salvador (where Columbus made his first landfall in the New World). Cement, petroleum products, crawfish and salt are among exports, but tourism is the chief industry. Land area 13,935 sq.km (5,380 sq.m); pop. (1977) 218,000. M.U.: B. dollar.

The islands were held by the British and Spanish alternately in the 17-18th cents. until they finally became British in 1783. The pirate Edward Teach (Blackbeard) was among many who used the is. as a base. Internal self-govt was granted in 1964; Lynden O. Pindling (1930-) took office as the first black PM in 1967, and led his country to independence as the Commonwealth of the B. in 1973, within the (British) Commonwealth.

BAHAWALPUR (bah-hahwahlpoor'). Town of the Punjab, Pakistan, once cap. of a former state of B. It is on the Sutlej, and has textile factories and rice mills. Pop. (1972) 134,000.

BAHIA (bah-ē'ah). *See* SALVADOR.

BAHIA BLANCA. Industrial town in S. Argentina, on the Naposta, 5km (3m) from its mouth. It has extensive dockyards and is a meat-packing centre. Pop. (1970) 200,000.

BAHRAIN (bahrān'). Group of islands in the Arabian Gulf, 25km (15m) from the mainland of Saudi Arabia, linked by a causeway (opened 1986). Identified with the Sumerian Dilmun of 3000 B.C., they were seized by the Arabs in the 7th cent., were held by Portugal 1521–1602, and then were disputed by various countries until in 1816 the ruling sheikh placed them under British protection. The ruler is Sheikh Isa bin Sulman Al-Khalifa (1933–), under whom B. became independent in 1971.

There are fine quality pearls, dhow-building and fisheries, but oil, discovered in 1932, is the chief product. The cap. is Manama, on the largest island, also called B., which it is intended to link by causeway with the smaller is. of Sitra. The latter has an earth satellite station and is a communications centre for the lower Gulf. Mina Sulman, at the N.E. corner of B. is mainly a re-export port, with an industrial area powered by natural gas, incl. aluminium smelting (Australian ore). Area 600 sq.km (400 sq.m); pop. (1978) 275,550, mainly Moslem Arabs, half Sunni, half Shiite. M.U.: Bahrain dinar.

BAHAMAS. The market on the sea front at Nassau shows the variety of the produce that the island provides. *Photo: J.Allan Cash*

BAIKAL (bī'kahl). Largest freshwater lake in Asia, deepest in the world (up to 1,740 m/5,710 ft), in the R.S.F.S.R. between Irkutsk region and Buriat-Mongol A.S.S.R. Fed by more than 300 rivers, it is drained only by the Lower Angara. It has sturgeon fisheries, and a rich fauna largely unique to it, incl. its own breed of seals, but is threatened by pollution. Area 31,500 sq.km (12,150 sq.m); 630km/390m.

BAIKONOUR (bikohn'or) **COSMODROME.** Official name for the Soviet space launch site at Tyuratam, Kazakh SSR, the nearest centre being the coalmining town of Baikonour.

BAIL. The setting at liberty of a person in the custody of the law on an undertaking, usually backed by some security, given either by him or by someone else, that he will attend at a court at a stated time and place. If he does not attend, the bail is 'estreated', i.e. forfeited.

BAILE ATHA CLIATH (blawklē'). Official Irish name of DUBLIN from 1922.

BAILEY, Sir Donald Coleman (1901–85). British engineer, inventor during the S.W.W. of the Bailey Bridge. Made up of interlocking sections, speedily manhandled, the bridges can be easily transported and erected: the girders are built up from prefabricated panels and all parts are interchangeable.

BAILLIE, Dame Isobel (1895–83). British soprano. B. in Hawick, Scotland, she was celebrated for her work in oratorio, especially Handel's *Messiah*, her voice having a singularly pure quality. DBE 1978.

BAILLY (bahyē'), **Jean Sylvain** (1736-93). French astronomer, who wrote on the satellites of Jupiter and the history of astronomy. Early in the French Revolution he was president of the National Assembly and mayor of Paris, but resigned in 1791, and was guillotined during the Terror.

BAILY, Francis (1774-1844). British astronomer, originally a stockbroker and actuary. In 1836 during an eclipse of the sun he noticed *Baily's beads,* due to the breaking-up of the solar crescent into separate portions of light by prominences on the moon.

BAINBRIDGE (bān'brij), **Beryl** (1933-). British novelist. Born in Liverpool, she was originlly an actress, and her books have the drama and simple economy of a stage play, notably *The Dressmaker* (1973) and *The Bottle Factory Outing* (1974).

BAINBRIDGE, Kenneth Tompkins (1904-). American physicist. B. in Cooperstown, N.Y., he worked at the Cavendish Laboratory, Cambridge, 1933-4. Returning to America, he taught at Harvard, and directed the Alamogordo atom bomb test in 1945. He has also carried out research in radar, and since 1961 has been George Vasmer Leverett prof. of physics at Harvard.

BAIRD, John Logie (1888-1946). British pioneer of television. B. at Helensburgh, Scotland, he studied electrical engineering in Glasgow at what is now the Univ. of Strathclyde, at the same time serving several practical apprenticeships. He was working on television possibly as early as 1912, and took out his first provisional patent in 1923. The first public demonstration was given at Selfridges in 1925, and in the following years he pioneered fibre optics (1926); radar (1926) in advance of Sir Robert Watson-Watt; infra-red television (1926), also for the long-distance detection of objects; video recording on both wax records and magnetic steel discs (1926-7); colour television (1925-8); 3D-colour television (1925-46); transatlantic television (1928), and facsimile television (1944), the forerunner of Ceefax (q.v.). In 1936 his mechanically scanned 240 line system competed with EMI-Marconi's 405 line, and the latter was preferred for the BBC service from 1937, partly because it handled live indoor scenes with smaller, more manoeuvrable cameras. In 1944 Baird demonstrated the world's first all electronic colour and 3D-colour receiver (500 lines).

BAIRNSFATHER, Bruce (1888-1959). British artist, celebrated for his 'Old Bill' cartoons of the F.W.W. In the S.W.W. he was official cartoonist to the US Army in Europe, 1942-4.

BAJA (ba'ha) **CALIFORNIA.** The mountainous peninsula which forms the twin NW states of Lower (Spanish 'baja') California, Mexico. The northern state, Baja California Norte, incl. the busy towns of Mexicali and Tijuana, but the southern, Baja Califonia Sur, is still undeveloped.

BAKER, Sir Benjamin (1840-1907). British civil engineer. B. in Somerset, he was chief assistant to Sir John Fowler in building the Metropolitan and District Railway, London, and with Fowler designed the Forth Bridge (1890) and the original Aswan Dam, Egypt.

BAKER, Dame Janet (1933-). British mezzo-soprano. B. at Yarm-on-Tees, she excels in lieder and oratorio as well as opera, and music of all periods. Her great performances incl. Dido in *The Trojans* and Marguerite in *Faust,* and as soloist in *Dream of Gerontius* and *Song of the Earth.*

BAKER, Richard St Barbe (1889–1982). British forestry expert, founder of the Men of the Trees Society, which in 1932 became world-wide. In 1959 he settled in New Zealand.

BAKER, Sir Samuel White (1821-93). British explorer. B. in London, he founded an agricultural colony in Ceylon, built a railway across the Dobruja, and in 1861 set out to discover the source of the Nile. In 1863 he met Speke and Grant, who had anticipated him, but he pushed on into Central Africa to be the first European to sight the Albert Nyanza and to find that the Nile flowed through it. His wife, Florence von Sass, accompanied him. In 1869-73 he was Gov.-Gen. of the Nile equatorial regions.

BAKEWELL. Market town in Derbyshire, England. Close by are Chatsworth House and Haddon Hall. It has textile industries founded by Arkwright (q.v.). Pop. (1972) 4,000.

BAKKE (bak'a), **Allan** (1940-). American medical student. In 1978 he claimed 'reverse discrimination' when appealing against his exclusion from university, since less well-qualified blacks were to be admitted as part of a special programme for racial minorities. He won his case against quotas before the Supreme Court, although other affirmative action on racial grounds was still endorsed.

BAKST, Leon (1866-1924). Russian artist whose real name was Rosenberg. B. at St Petersburg, he displayed remarkable gifts as a theatrical designer, and from 1900 was scenic artist to the Imperial theatres. In 1909 he painted the scenery for Diaghilev's Russian ballets. The latter part of his life was spent in Paris, and he exercised worldwide influence on the decorative arts of the theatre.

BAKU (bahkoo'). Cap. city of the Azerbaijan S.S.R. (USSR), on the Apsheron peninsula, in the Caspian Sea. It is the principal centre of the Russian oil industry, which began here in the 1870s. Pipelines lead to Batumi on the Black Sea. B. is also chief port on the Caspian. Pop. (1977) 1,435,000.

BAKUNIN (bahkoon'yēn), **Mikhail** (1814-76). Russian anarchist. B. in the Tver prov. of a noble family, he served in the Imperial Guard, but, disgusted with Tsarist methods in Poland, resigned his commission, and travelled abroad. In 1848 he was expelled from France as a revolutionary agitator. For his share in a brief revolt at Dresden in 1849 he was sentenced to death. The sentence was commuted to imprisonment, and he was handed over to the Tsar's government and sent to Siberia (1855). In 1861 he managed to escape to Switzerland, where he became recognized as the leader of the anarchist movement. In 1869 he joined the 'First International', but after stormy conflicts with Marx, was expelled in 1872. He had a large following, particularly in the Latin countries. He wrote books and pamphlets, including *God and the State.*

BALA (bah'lah). Largest natural lake (Llyn Tegid) in Wales. Situated in Gwynedd, N. Wales, it is about 6.4km (4m) long and 1.6km (1m) wide.

BALACLAVA (balaklah'va). Town in Ukraine S.S.R., in the Crimea, 10km (6m) S.E. of Sevastopol, which gives its name to a battle fought on 25 Oct. 1854, during the Crimean War, rendered famous by an ill-timed but gallant charge of the British Light Brigade of cavalry against the Russian entrenched artillery. About 700 all ranks were engaged; only 195 returned.

BALAKIREV (bahlah'kērev), **Mily Alexeievich** (1837-1910). Russian composer, b. at Nijni-Novgorod. At St Petersburg he won fame as a pianist, attached himself to

Glinka, estab. the Free School of Music (1862), which stressed the national element, and was director of the Imperial Chapel 1883-95. He wrote orchestral and pianoforte music and songs, all imbued with the Russian national character and spirit.

BALALAIKA (balalī'ka). Russian musical instrument, not unlike a guitar. It has a triangular sound box and 2, 3 or 4 strings played by plucking with the fingers.

BALANCE OF PAYMENTS. Summary of the financial results of economic relations between one country and the rest of the world over a certain period, usually a year. It consists in effect of 2 lists: on the one side, of the transactions which give rise to a demand for foreign currencies, i.e. to pay for which pounds have to be sold for dollars, francs, etc.; and on the other, of those transactions which are payable in sterling, i.e. foreign currencies have to be sold for pounds.

BALANCHINE (balantschēn'), **Georges** (1904–83). American choreographer. B. in St Petersburg, he left Russia after the revolution, and was ballet master for Diaghilev 1925-9. In 1933 he went to US, became an American citizen, and since 1948 has been artistic director of the N.Y. City Ballet Co. He staged the ballet *Slaughter on Tenth Avenue* for *On Your Toes* (1936): others incl. *The Prodigal Son, Serenade,* and *Ballet Imperial.*

BALANŌGLO'SSUS. Genus of marine wormlike animals which, with a few near allies, forms the class Hemichordata or Enteropneusta, the lowest division of the Chordata. They burrow in sand or mud at the sea bottom, live at moderate depths, and are found in the warm and temperate parts of the world.

BALBŌ'A, Vasco Nuñez de (*c.* 1475-1517). Spanish conquistador and discoverer of the Pacific Ocean. He went to the West Indies and in 1510 joined the expedition which conquered the isthmus of Darien. In 1513 he set out across the mountains, and reached the further shore on 29 Sept. He was made Admiral of the Pacific and Gov. of Panama, but was removed by intrigues at the Spanish court, imprisoned and executed.

BALCHIN, Nigel Marlin (1908-70), British author. During the S.W.W. he was engaged on scientific work for the army with the rank of brigadier, and estab. his reputation as a novelist with *The Small Back Room* (1943), dealing with the psychology of the 'back room boys' of wartime research.

BALCON, Sir Michael (1896-1977). British film producer. His films incl.: *The Lavender Hill Mob, The Cruel Sea,* and *The Long and the Short and the Tall.*

BALDER (bawl'der). In Norse mythology, the son of Odin and Frigga and husband of Nanna, and the best, wisest, and most loved of all the gods. He was killed, at Loki's instigation, by a twig of mistletoe shot by the blind god Hodur.

BALDNESS. Loss of hair from the upper scalp, especially common in older Caucasian men, though its onset and extent is influenced by genetic make-up and the male sex hormones. There is no 'cure' and expedients such as hair implants from elsewhere on the head are expensive and seldom effective. Hair loss in both sexes may occur as a result of various forms of ill-health.

BALDWIN I (1058-1118). Son of the count of Bouillon in the Ardennes, he accompanied his brother Godfrey on the 1st Crusade in 1096 and became King of Jerusalem in 1100. The kingdom he founded endured for nearly a century.

BALDWIN, James (1924-). American author. A Negro, b. in Harlem, N.Y., he has been active in the civil rights movement. He has written plays, e.g. *The Amen Corner* (1955); vols. of essays, e.g. *Notes of a Native Son* (1955) and *The Fire Next Time* (1963); and novels, e.g. *Just Above my Head* (1979).

BALDWIN, Stanley, 1st earl B. of Bewdley (1867-1947). Conservative statesman. B. at Bewdley, Worcs, he was the only son of A. Baldwin, MP, of the iron and steel company known as Baldwin's Ltd. In 1908 he was elected Unionist MP for Bewdley, and in 1916 he became parliamentary private secretary to Bonar Law. He was Financial Secretary to the Treasury 1917-21, and then was appointed to the presidency of the Board of Trade. In 1919 he gave to the Treasury £150,000 of War Loan for cancellation, representing about 20 per cent of his fortune. He took a leading part in the disruption of the Lloyd George Coalition, and became Chancellor of the Exchequer in Bonar Law's Cons. admin. As such he negotiated, on the advice of Montagu Norman, the war debts settlement with the USA. On Bonar Law's retirement in 1923, B. became PM, and later in the year he 'went to the country' in search of a mandate to introduce a measure of Protection, which was necessary to counter the wave of unemployment. The result was adverse, and early in 1924 B. resigned. After the fall of the MacDonald admin., B. became Premier for the 2nd time, holding office until 1929. His premiership was marked by the General Strike of 1926, the Trade Disputes Act of 1927, the grant of widows' and orphans' pensions, and the securing of complete adult suffrage in 1928. In 1931 MacDonald formed in conjunction with B. a Nat. Govt in which B. was Lord President of the Council. In 1935 B. became PM for the 3rd time; he retained the post until 1937, when he made place for Neville Chamberlain, he himself going to the House of Lords as an earl. His handling of the situation that arose from the abdication of Edward VIII was generally applauded, but his attitude towards the dictator powers of Germany and Italy was much criticized.

BÂLE. French form of BASLE.

BALĒA'RICS. Group of islands off the E. coast of Spain; they were conquered by Aragon in the 14th cent. The largest are Majorca (on which is the cap., Palma), Minorca, Iviza, Cabrera, and Formentera. Area 5,014 sq.km (1,935 sq.m); pop. (1970) 558,300.

BALEWA. *See* TAFAWA BALEWA.

BALFE (balf), **Michael William** (1808-70). British composer. B. at Dublin, he was a violinist at Drury Lane, London, when only 16. In 1825 he went to study in Italy, and in 1846 he was appointed conductor at Her Majesty's Theatre. He composed operas of which only *The Bohemian Girl* is now remembered.

BALFOUR, Arthur James, 1st earl of (1848-1930). British Cons. statesman. Son of a Scottish landowner, he was elected a Conservative MP in 1874. In Lord Salisbury's ministry he was Sec. for Ireland (1887) and for his ruthless vigour was called 'Bloody B.' by the nationalists. In 1891, and again in 1895, he became 1st Lord of the Treasury and leader of the Commons, and in 1902 he succeeded Salisbury in the premiership. His cabinet was divided over Chamberlain's Tariff Reform proposals, and at the 1905 elections suffered a crushing defeat. B. retired from the party leadership in 1911. In 1915 he joined the Asquith coalition as 1st Lord of the Admiralty, and he was Foreign Sec. 1916-19; as such he issued the 'B. Declaration' of 1917 in favour of a national home in Palestine for the Jews and signed the Treaty of Versailles. He was Lord Pres. of the Council 1919-22 and 1925-9, and received the O.M. in 1916 and an earldom in 1922. He was also a distinguished philosopher, and wrote *A Defence of Philosophic Doubt* (1879), *Foundations of Belief* and *Theism and Humanism* (Gifford Lectures, 1914).

BALFOUR DECLARATION (1917). Letter written on 2 Nov. 1917 by A. J. Balfour, then British Foreign Sec., to Lord Rothschild, chairman of the British Zionist Federation, stating that 'His Majesty's Govt view with favour the establishment in Palestine of a national home for the Jewish people': this eventually led to the foundation of the modern Jewish State of Israel in 1948.

BALI (bah'lē). Mountainous volcanic island of Indonesia, separated from Java by the mile-wide B. Strait. The climate is equable, the soil fertile, and the vegetation luxuriant. Tropical produce grows to perfection. The Balinese are noted for their fine physique, and the women are often remarkably beautiful. They are Hindus in religion, devoted to the drama and music, and their dances are world-famous. They are skilled craftsmen in gold and silver work, wood-carving, and weaving.

A Hindu culture, brought by settlers from India, was estab. in B. by the 7th cent. A.D. From time to time B. was subject to Javanese princes, but its warlike inhabitants were difficult to control, and in the 17th cent. the kings of B. ruled Lombok and a small part of E. Java. B. remained independent until 1856 when the Dutch occupied it.

B. Strait, between B. and Java, was the scene on 19-20 Feb. 1942 of a naval action between Japanese and US and Dutch forces which served to delay slightly the Japanese invasion of Java.

The cap. is Singaradja, the other important town being Denpasar. Area 5,800 sq.km. (2,240 sq.m); pop. (1970) 1,783,000.

BALI. In traditional costume, two young girls perform a temple dance in Bali, Indonesia. *Photo: Gunter Reitz/Barnaby's Picture Library*

BALIKESIR (bahlikesēr'). Turkish town, cap. of an isl. of the same name, 130km (80m) S.W. of Bursa. It trades in olive oil, and has silver mines near by. Pop. (1970) 85,000.

BA'LIKPA'PAN. Port and petroleum centre in Kalimantan, Indonesia. Pop. (1970) 91,700.

BALKANS (bawl'kanz) (Turkish for mountains). Peninsula in S.E. Europe stretching into the Mediterranean between the Adriatic and Aegean Seas. It is joined to the rest of Europe by an isthmus 1,200 km (750m) wide between Rijeka on the W. and the mouth of the Danube on the Black Sea to the E. It comprises Albania, Bulgaria, Greece, part of Romania, Turkey-in-Europe, and most of Yugoslavia (qq.v.). A byword for political dissension historically, a tendency fostered by the great ethnic diversity resulting from successive waves of invasion, the B. developed comparatively slowly economically until after the S.W.W., largely because of the predominantly mountainous terrain, apart from the plains of the Save-Danube basin in the north. Political differences have remained strong, e.g. the confrontation of Greece and Turkey over Cyprus, and the differing types of Communism prevailing in the rest, but in the later years of the 20th cent. a tendency to regional union emerged both economically and politically, prompted in part by the danger of pro-Soviet coups in individually unstable regimes.

BALKAN WARS (1912-13). Two wars which resulted in the expulsion of Turkey from all but 23,485 sq km (9,068 sq.m.) of Europe. The 1st, in 1912, of Bulgaria, Serbia, Greece, and Montenegro against Turkey, forced the Turks to ask for an armistice, but the peace negotiations, in London, broke down when the Turks, while agreeing to surrender all Turkey-in-Europe W. of Adrianople (Edirne), refused to give up that city. In Feb. 1913 hostilities were resumed, Adrianople fell on 26 March and on 30 May by the Treaty of London Turkey retained in Europe only a small piece of eastern Thrace and the Gallipoli peninsula.

In the 2nd Balkan War, June-July 1913 - among the victors - Bulgaria attacked Greece and Serbia which were joined by Rumania. Bulgaria was defeated, and Turkey secured from that country the cession of Adrianople.

BALKHA'SH. Lake in the Kazakh S.S.R. (USSR). It is 600km (375m) long, receives several rivers, but has no outlet. It is very shallow and is frozen throughout the winter. Area 17,300 sq.km (6,680 sq.m). On its N. shore is the town of B., founded in 1928, pop. 90,000, engaged in refining copper mined nearby.

BALL, John (d. 1381). English agitator, a priest and prominent leader of the Peasants' Revolt of 1381. At Blackheath he preached from the text 'When Adam delved and Eve span, Who was then the gentleman?' When the revolt collapsed he was taken prisoner and executed.

BALLAD (bal'ad). Type of popular poetry. Derived from Late Lat. *ballare*, 'to dance', the B. was primarily intended for singing at the communal ring-dance, the refrains representing the chorus.

Of simple metrical form and dealing with some strongly emotional event, the B. is half-way between the lyric and the epic. The majority of Bs. date from the 15th cent. but were not collected until modern times, the most famous collections being Bishop Percy's *Reliques of Ancient Poetry* (1765), Scott's *Minstrelsy of the Scottish Border* (1802-3), and Prof. F. J. Child's *English and Scottish Popular Ballads* (1857-9). Opinion is divided as to whether the authorship of the Bs. may be attributed to individual poets or to the community. Later Bs. tend to centre round a popular folk-hero, as in the case of the *Gest of Robyn Hode* and in the American cycles concerning

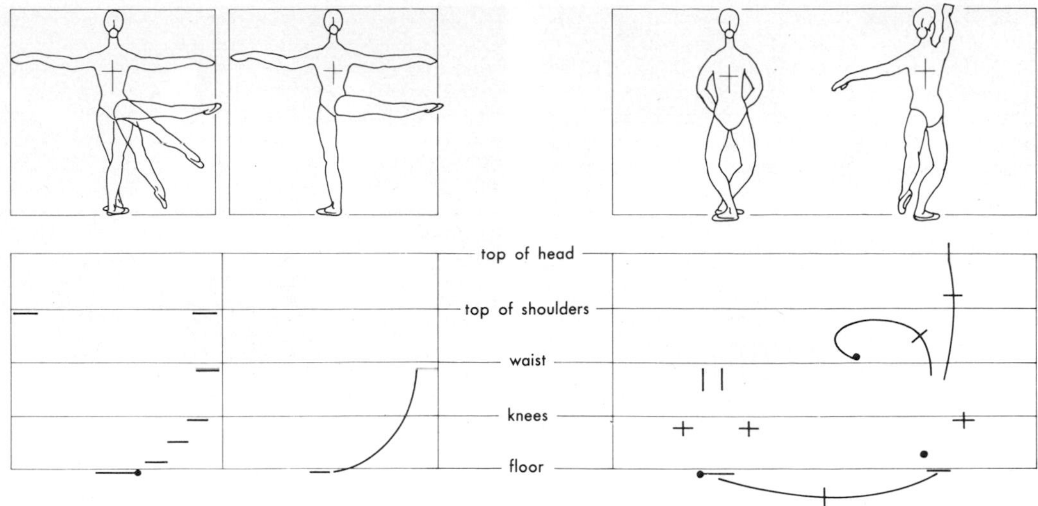

BALLET. Two examples of the Benesh system of notation. On the left, the opening and final stages of a 'grande battement à la seconde' recorded, and, on the right, a forward jump in a 'sissonne ouverte', in which the forward direction is indicated by a dash across the lines of movement.

Jesse James and Yankee Doodle. Other later forms are the 'broadsheets' with a satirical or political motive, and the testamentary 'hanging' Bs. of the condemned criminal. Poets of the Romantic movement both in England and in Germany were largely influenced by the B. revival, e.g., the *Lyrical Ballads* (1798) of Wordsworth and Coleridge. Other writers of modern Bs. include Keats, Southey, Rossetti, S. Dobell, Tennyson, Morris, and Kipling.

In 19th cent. music the refined drawing-room ballad had a vogue, but a more robust tradition survived in the music hall, and folk-song (q.v.) played its part in the growth of pop music (q.v.).

BALLADE (balahd'). Poetic form developed in France in the later Middle Ages from the popular ballad, and generally consisting of 1 or more groups of 3 stanzas of 7 or 8 lines each, followed by a shorter stanza or envoy. The last line of the 1st stanza is repeated as a refrain in each succeeding verse including the envoy. The B. was revived in the 19th cent. by Banville, A. Lang, E. Gosse, and Henley. Also a music form of story-like type, notably used by Chopin.

BALLANCE, John (1839-93). NZ statesman. B. in Ulster, he migrated to NZ, founded and ed. the *Wanganui Herald,* held many cabinet posts, and was PM 1891-3.

BALLANTYNE (bal'antīn), **Robert Michael** (1825-94). British writer of stories for boys. B. in Edinburgh, a nephew of Scott's publishers, James and John B., he went to Canada as a boy and spent 6 years as a trapper in lonely outposts for the Hudson's Bay company. He produced over 100 spirited tales, incl. *The Young Fur Traders, Coral Island,* and *Martin Rattler.*

BALLARAT (bal'arat). Industrial town in Victoria, Australia, founded in the gold rush of 1851. The old mining village and mine workings nearby have been completely reconstructed as a tourist attraction, and there is a Gold Museum. Pop. (1976) 60,700. *See* EUREKA STOCKADE.

BALLET (bal'ā). A theatrical representation combining music and movement in a complex form of dancing. Some such form of entertainment existed in ancient Greece, but the germ of B. as it is known today was brought to France by Catherine de Medici, in the form of a spectacle combining singing, dancing, and declamation.

The first important dramatic B. was mounted in 1581 by Baltasar de Beaujoyeux, and was performed by male courtiers, ladies of the Court forming the *corps de ballet.* In 1661 Louis XIV founded *L'Académie Nationale de Musique et de la Danse,* from which all subsequent B. activities throughout the world can be traced. Long flowing court dress was worn by the dancers. In the 1720s Marie-Anne Camargo, the first ballerina, shortened her skirt to reveal her feet, thus allowing greater movement *à terre* and the development of dancing *en l'air.* In the early 19th cent. a Paris costumier, Maillot, invented tights, thus completing muscular freedom. The first of the great B. masters was J. G. Noverre (1727-1810). Great contemporary dancers were Vestris, Heinel, Dauberval, and Gardel. Carlo Blasis (1803-78) is regarded as the father of classical B.

ROMANTIC BALLET. The great Romantic era of Taglioni, Elssler, Grisi, Grahn, and Cerrito began about 1830, but survives today only in *Giselle* (1841) and *La Sylphide* (1832). The calf-length classical white dress was introduced together with dancing *en pointe.* The technique of the female dancer developed, but the men were reduced to partners.

Russian B. was introduced to the West by Diaghilev (q.v.) who set out for Paris in 1909 at about the same time that Isadora Duncan, a rigid opponent of classical B., was touring the Continent. Associated with him were Michel Fokine, Nijinsky, Pavlova, Massine, Balanchine, Lifar, and Bs. presented by his co. before its break-up on his death in 1929 incl. *Les Sylphides, Schéhérazade, Petrouchka* and *Blue Train.*

BALLET. Eighteenth and twentieth century ballet: To the left, Nicholas Lancret's portrait of Camargo, capturing the grace and fire which owed something to her Spanish descent; and to the right, the Russian ballerina, Natalia Makarova, rehearsing *Giselle* with Anthony Dowell. *Photos: Courtesy of the Trustees of the Wallace Collection and Central Press Photos Ltd.*

In the US Balanchine estab. in 1933 the School of American B., and the de Basil Ballets Russes de Monte Carlo and Massine's Ballet Russe de Monte Carlo also carried on the Diaghilev tradition: since 1948 the N.Y. City Ballet with Maria Tallchief, Nora Kaye, and choreographer Jerome Robbins, under the guiding influence of Balanchine, has developed a genuine American classic style. *See* also GRAHAM, Martha.

In Britain Marie Rambert initiated in 1926 the Ballet Club which developed into the Ballet Rambert, and in 1930 Arnold Haskell and Ninette de Valois formed the Camargo Society, but the modern national co. the Royal Ballet (so named 1957) grew from foundations laid by Ninette de Valois in 1928. British dancers, incl. Margot Fonteyn, Beryl Grey, Alicia Markova, Anton Dolin, Michael Somes, Elaine Fifield, Antoinette Sibley and Anthony Dowell; choreographers incl. Sir Frederick Ashton, Antony Tudor, and Kenneth MacMillan.

In Russia B. continues to flourish, the 2 chief cos. being the Kirov and Bolshoi. Best known ballerinas are Ulanova and Plisetskaya (qq.v.), and among the men Rudolf Nureyev and Alexander Godunov, both now dancing in the West, and husband-and-wife team Vyacheslav Gordeyev and Nadezhda Pavlova, now dancing in the West.

The best-known systems of dance notation are Labanotation, developed by Hungarian Rudolf Laban (d. 1958), and the much simpler Benesh System, using symbols on a horizontal stave, developed by husband and wife Joan and Rudolf Benesh (d. 1975).

BALLISTICS. Study of the motion of projectiles, both while still inside the weapon and after launching. In the case of a gun, the exterior factors include temperature, barometric pressure, and wind strength; and in the case of nuclear missiles extend to the speed at which the Earth turns, etc.

BALLOON. Bag of impermeable fabric which rises from the ground when filled with a gas lighter than air. The first successful human ascent was piloted by Pilâtre de Rozier in Paris in 1783 in a hot-air balloon of the type designed by the Montgolfier brothers. Balloons were first used in war during the French Revolution for observation purposes. Balloons continue in use for sport, and as an economical means of making meteorological, infra-red, gamma ray, ultra-violet and other scientific observations . The first transalantic balloon crossing was made by 3 Americans (Presque Isle, Me to Miserey, France) 11-17 Aug. 1978. *See also* NAZCAR.

BALMO'RAL CASTLE. Royal residence in Scotland on the Dee, 10.5km (6½m) N.E. of Braemar, Grampian region. The castle, built of granite in the Scottish baronial style, is dominated by a square tower and circular turret rising 30m (100ft). It was rebuilt 1853-5 by Prince Albert, who bought the estate in 1852.

BALSAM. In medicine and perfumery, plant oils and resins, e.g. B. of Peru from the tree *Myroxylon pereirae,* and Friar's Balsam (q.v.). Also garden plants of the genus *Impatiens,* usually annuals with red or white flowers.

BALTIC. Large shallow arm of the North Sea, extending N.E. from the narrow Skagerrak and Kattegat, between Sweden and Denmark, to the Gulf of Bothnia between Sweden and Finland. Its coastline is 8,000 km (5,000 m) long, and its area, incl. the Gulfs of Riga, Finland and Bothnia is 422,300 sq.km (163,000 sq.m). Its shore-line is shared by Denmark, Germany, Poland, USSR, Finland, and Sweden. Many large rivers flow into it, including the Oder, Vistula, Niemen, W. Dvina, Narva, and Neva. Tides are hardly perceptible, and weather is often stormy and navigation dangerous. Most ports are closed by ice from Nov. till May. The Kiel canal links the B. and the North Sea, the Göta canal connects the two seas by way of the S. Swedish lakes, and since 1975 it has been linked by the Leningrad-Belomorsk seaway with the White Sea.

BALTIC, Battle of the (1801). Name given to the naval battle fought off Copenhagen on 2 April 1801, in which a British fleet under Sir Hyde Parker, with Nelson as second-in-command, annihilated the Danish navy.

BALTIC PORT. English name of PALDISKI, translation of its German name Baltisch Port.

BALTIC STATES. Collective name sometimes used for Estonia, Latvia, and Lithuania (qq.v.).

BALTIMORE. City and port of USA and largest city in Maryland State, on the W. shore of Chesapeake Bay, at the mouth of the Patapsco, to the N.E. of Washington.

Named after the founder of Maryland, Lord Baltimore (1606-75), the city of B. dates from 1729 and was incorporated in 1797. It is an important commercial, industrial, and educational centre. A road tunnel under B. harbour (opened 1957) relieved a bottle-neck between Washington and N.Y. The homes of Edgar Allen Poe and Babe Ruth are preserved. Pop. met. area (1970) 2,043,667.

BALUCHISTAN (baloochistahn'). Mountainous desert region divided mainly between a prov. of Iran (cap. Zahedan) and of Pakistan (cap. Quetta). Coal, chrome and natural gas are exploited, but the people are chiefly nomadic Moslem (Sunni) tribesmen, with aspirations to independence. In 1980 there were fears that the USSR wished to create a 'United Baluchistan' which would give her a warmwater port (Gwadar, in Pakistani Baluchistan) on the Indian Ocean, and allow her to control the Strait of Hormuz (q.v.). Pop. about 3,000,000, of whom *c.* 1,000,000 are in Iran. There are another 300,000 Baluchis in border areas of Afghanistan.

BALZAC (bahlzahk'), **Honoré de** (1799-1850). French novelist. B. at Tours, the son of the director of the city hospital whose real name was Balssa, he studied law and worked as a notary's clerk in Paris, but turned to literature. His first attempts included tragedies such as *Cromwell* and novels pub. pseudonymously with no great success. A venture in printing and publishing (1825-8) involved him in a lifelong web of debt, but in 1829 he achieved his first success with *Les Chouans* and *Physiologie du mariage.* This was the beginning of the long series of novels the *Comédie humaine,* which according to the complete plan of 1842 was to consist of 143 vols. depicting 19th cent. French life in every conceivable aspect, but of which only some 80 were completed. They incl. studies of human folly and vice such as the miser in *Eugénie Grandet* (1833), the monomaniac of *La recherche de l'absolu* (1834), the weak loving father of *Père Goriot* (1834), the jealous *Cousine Bette* (1846), and the acquisitive *Cousin Pons* (1847); and analyses of professions or ranks such as the commercial traveller of *L'illustre Gaudissart* (1833), the doctor of *Le médicin de la campagne* (1833), the great business man of *La maison de Nucingen* (1838), and the cleric of *Le curé de village* (1839). Apart from the novels stand the collection of Rabelaisian *Contes drôlatiques* (1833).

In 1833, before the death of his patroness, Mme de Berny, who figures in *Le Lys dans la vallée* (1836), B. met the Polish countess Evelina Hanska; he m. her 4 months before his death in Paris. He was buried in Père Lachaise cemetery.

BAMAKŌ'. Cap. of the Rep. of Mali, a port and communications centre on the Niger. Pop. (1972) 170,000.

BAMBERG. City of W. Germany, in Bavaria, on the Regnitz. The cathedral, built by Henry II in 1004, contains sculptures of the 13th cent., and the castle is renowned. Pop. (1970) 73,900.

BAMBOO'. Group of plants *(Bambuseae),* belonging to the family of the grasses (Gramineae), found in tropical and sub-tropical countries, and remarkable for the relatively gigantic size which they attain. The stems are hollow and jointed, and can be used in furniture, house and boat construction, etc. The young shoots are eaten in China; paper is made from the stem.

BA'NABA. *See* OCEAN ISLAND.

BAMBOO. In Cambodia, as throughout the East, bamboo serves a multitude of purposes. Here it is being made into sleeping mats, blinds and partitions. *Photo: Mireille Vautier.*

BANANA (banah'na). Tropical plant (*Musa sapientum* of the family Musaceae) producing a fruit which has been used for human food since before written history. It originated in the moist tropical regions of southern Asia, was carried to Africa by Arab traders, established in the Canary Is. by the Portuguese about 1482, and from there was introduced to the New World. It was scarcely known in Britain prior to 1890, and the first direct shipment of a full cargo of Bs. from Jamaica reached Bristol in 1901.

The B. plant is up to 10m (30ft); it is not a tree, because there is no wood in it. Each plant bears a single bunch of Bs., made up of 6 to 9 'hands' or clusters, each containing from 12 to 18 Bs. or 'fingers'. For export, the fruit is cut green and transported in special refrigerated ships: some is sun-dried. The fruit of the plantain, a larger coarser sub-species is used green, being cooked as a vegetable and forming a staple of the diet in many countries.

BANARAS. Another transliteration of VARANESI.

BANBURY. Town of Oxon, England, on the Cherwell, 32km (20m) N. of Oxford. It is famous for its cake and ale, and also for the B. cross of the nursery rhyme, which was removed in 1602, but replaced by a new one in 1858. Pop. (1972) 30,170.

BANCA. Alternative form of BANKA.

BANCROFT, George (1800-91). American diplomat and historian. A democrat, he was sec. of the navy 1845, when he estab. Annapolis as the US Naval Academy, and as acting sec. of war (May 1846) was instrumental in bringing about the occupation of California, and gave the order to Zachary Taylor to cross the Texas border which started war with Mexico. He wrote a *History of the United States* (1834-76).

BAND. Group of musicians usually specialising in a certain type of instrument or music. **Military bands,** developed in the 18th cent., comprise woodwind, brass and percussion, Kneller Hall (1857) being a world-famous training centre; **brass bands** incl. only brass and percussion, and are particularly typical of the factory and colliery districts of N England; **marching bands** are a variant of the brass band, introduced from USA to Britain, and associated with showmanship, sporting events, a younger membership and a pop repertoire. Other types are the jazz band, dance band and steel band (q.v.).

BANDA (ban'da), **Hastings** (1905-). Malawi statesman. Once a student and practitioner of medicine in Britain, he led his country's independence movement, becoming Prime Minister of Nyasaland in 1963, and first pres. of the new Rep. of Malawi in 1966.

BANDAR. *See* MASULIPATNAM.

BANDAR ABBAS. Iranian port on the Ormuz strait, Persian Gulf; formerly called Gombroon, it was renamed and made prosperous by Shah Abbas I (1587-1629). Its summer pop. is *c.* 10,000; winter, *c.* 15,000.

BANDARANAIKE (bondrahnī'ahkah), **Solomon West Ridgeway Dias** (1899-1959). Sri Lanka statesman. An ardent nationalist he founded in 1951 the Sri Lanka Freedom Party and in 1956 became P.M., pledged to a socialist programme and a neutral foreign policy. He failed to satisfy extremists and was assassinated by a Buddhist monk. In 1940 he had m. **Sirimavo Ratwatte** (1916-) and on his death she entered politics, and was the world's first woman PM 1960-5 and 1970-7. In 1980 judges of the supreme court found that, while in office, she had abused her powers.

BANDAR SERI BEGAWAN. Cap. of Brunei, 15km (9m) from the mouth of the Brunei r. Pop. (1971) 72,500.

BANDAR SHAH. Iranian port on the Caspian Sea, 320km (200m) N.E. of Tehran, and northern terminus of the Trans-Iranian railway. It was a lease-lend supply port for the Russian armies 1941-5.

BA'NDICOOT. Small marsupial mammal of the Peramelidae family, inhabiting Australia, Tasmania, and New Guinea. There are several species, approximately the size of a rabbit and mainly insectivorous. They live in burrows.

BANDUNG. City of Indonesia, a commercial centre. It has technical and medical institutions, an airport and a powerful radio station. Pop. (1971) 1,200,000.

The **Bandung Conference** (1955) was the first held by Afro-Asian nations, who proclaimed their anti-colonialism and neutrality between E. and W.

BANFF. Health and pleasure resort in Alberta, Canada, on the Bow. It is the railway and road centre for the Rocky Mountains national park. Lake Louise is near by. Pop. (1970) 3,000.

BANFFSHIRE. Former county of N.E. Scotland stretching from the Cairngorms to Moray Firth. In 1975 B. was merged in Grampian region, of which Banff (the former co. town) is admin. H.Q. (pop. 3,775).

BANGALISTAN (banga'listan). State advocated by the organisation Amra Bangali (1969) to comprise W Bengal, Tripura, Bengali-speaking areas of Assam, Orissa and Bihar, and possibly Bangladesh.

BANGALORE (bangaloor'). Cap. of the Indian state of Karnataka, formerly the largest British cantonment in S. India. It is an important airport, railway junction, and industrial town. Pop. (1971) 1,648,200.

BANGK'OK. Cap. and chief port of Thailand (Siam) on the Chao Phraya, 40km (25m) from the Gulf of Siam. It has a royal palace, 9 univs., many industries and an important airport. It was estab. as the cap. by Phra Chao Tak in 1769, after the Burmese had burned down the former cap. Avuthia *c.* 65km (40m) to the N. also on the r. Chao Phraya. The temple, Wat Phra Keo, within the palace walls, contains an image in jasper of Buddha: also famous is Wat Arun with a high tower. Pop. (1977) 4,743,000.

BANGLADESH (bangladāsh'). Rep. of the Indian sub-continent: the name means 'Bengal Nation'. Until 1972 it was known as East Pakistan (*see* PAKISTAN), and had been formed on independence in 1947 from the eastern part of the Bengal prov. of British India and the Sylhet district of Assam. Part of the alluvial plain of the Ganges-Brahmaputra river system, annual rainfall 2,540mm/100in., B. is subject to devastating cyclones. The main crops are rice, tea in the hills and jute in the plains, although the market for jute has been affected by the development of artificial fibres. B. has little industry, and her smaller share of Pakistan's development funds, although her jute exports supplied a large part of Pakistan's foreign exchange and she had a larger pop. than West Pakistan, led to agitation for autonomy. Sheikh Mujibar Rahman proclaimed secession in 1971, and following a brief civil war, in which she received Indian aid, E. Pakistan became an independent state in 1972 as Bangladesh ('Bengal Nation'), within the Commonwealth from 1972, and some 10m. refugees returned home across the Indian border. The cap. is Dacca, and the chief port is Chittagong. Sheikh Mujib (q.v.) exercised one-party presidential rule Jan.-Aug. 1975, until his murder. There were subsequently coups and counter-coups, and Gen. Zia ur Rahman (pres 1977-81) was assassinated in 1981. However, a unicameral nat. assembly was restored in 1979. The Pres. is General Ershad. M.U.: taka.

Area 143,000 sq.km (55,000 sq.km); pop (1981) 94,000,000, of whom the majority are Bengali-speaking Moslems. *See* BANGALISTAN.

BANGOR. Cathedral city and seaport, of Gwynedd, N. Wales, seat of the Univ. College of N. Wales. There is an export trade in slate. The cathedral, begun in 1495, was restored in 1866-80. Pop. (1972) 15,760.

BANJERMASIN (bahnyermah'sin). Town and port of Indonesia, in Kilimantan, Borneo. It exports petroleum, rubber, etc. Pop. (1970) 268,700.

BANJO. Musical instrument usually with 4 or more strings. The notes are stopped by the left hand while the strings are plucked by the thumb or fingers of the right, or with a plectrum. It was taken to USA by Negro slaves and Negro minstrels introduced it into England about 1846.

BANJUL (ban'jool). Cap. and chief port of Gambia, W. Africa, on an island at the mouth of the river Gambia. It was known as Bathurst until 1973. Pop. (1971) 54,000.

BANKA. Island of the Rep. of Indonesia off the E. coast of Sumatra. It is one of the world's largest tin producers. Pangkal Pinang is the cap., and Mintok the chief port. Area 12,000 sq.km (4,600 sq.m); pop. (1970) 300,000.

BANKRUPTCY. The process by which the property of a person unable to pay his debts is taken from him and divided rateably among his creditors. Proceedings may be instituted either by the debtor himself (voluntary B.) or by any creditor for a substantial sum (involuntary B.).

BANKS, Sir Joseph (1743-1820). British naturalist and explorer. B. in London, he accompanied Capt. Cook round the world, 1768-71, played a leading part in the development of New S. Wales, was a principal founder of the Botanical Gardens at Kew, introduced fresh food and plants into various parts of the world, and was President of the Royal Society from 1778.

BANKS. Banks are essentially intermediary financing institutions which do not own the larger part of the funds they employ, but owe them in turn to others. A country's

BANGLADESH. A Garo man enjoys smoking a waterpipe. Garo customs are unusual. In marriage it is the woman who makes the proposal, and if the bridegroom accepts her, she lives on probation for a time in his house. *Photo: Mireille Vautier*

monetary supplies are commonly controlled by entrusting the issue of notes to a central bank.

Modern B. originated with the Lombards who disappeared from England at the time of the Reformation, their place being taken by the goldsmiths, who received money for safe custody from their clients, and lent it out again to approved borrowers - the first cheques being their 'notes' or receipts. Firms so specializing developed into private banks. The *Bank of England* was founded with govt backing in 1694, but private banks continued to flourish until the Napoleonic wars: joint-stock B. was legalized in 1826 but such banks were not permitted to operate in London, hitherto the Bank of England's preserve, until 1833. The Bank Charter Act of 1844 practically concentrated the note issue in the Bank of England, but joint-stock banks expanded through the cheque system (reinforced after the S.W.W. by cheque and credit cards qq.v.), the present British 'Big Four' - the result of a long process of amalgamation - being Barclays, Lloyds, Midland, and National Westminster Bank Group. All have subsidiaries at home and abroad. Besides a number of other general bankers, there are also some 'merchant bankers' primarily concerned with commerce. In 1946 the Bank of England, till then a private corporation, was nationalised, but this marked no substantial change of function. The *Bank Rate* (fixed by the Bank of England as a guide to mortgage, HP rates, etc.) was replaced in 1972 by *Minimum Lending Rate* (lowest rate at which the Bank acts as lender of last resort to the money market), which from 1978 was again a 'bank rate' set by the Bank. In Europe there are similar central banks, but in the US it was only in 1914 that a series of independent bank failures led to the estab. of the *Federal Reserve System.* All national banks (those chartered by the Federal controller of the currency) are compulsory members: for State banks (those chartered by individual B. depts) membership is optional. Co-operation between the Federal Reserve System and the US treasury is close, especially since the 1933 crisis in B.: there is no one central bank, but the country is divided into 12 districts each with a Federal Reserve Bank.

Banks obtain payment of the cheques and bills of exchange, etc., drawn upon each other, through a *Bankers' Clearing House.* In the UK each bank has an account at the Bank of England, and the daily balances of amounts due and receivable are made by transfer through these accounts: the London clearing house was estab. 1770 and there are others in the chief provincial cities. There is also a bank giro (q.v.) system enabling payments to be made and received between customers of the various banks, one cheque frequently covering a large number of individual payments, etc. The N.Y. clearing house dates from 1853, and each great city of the US has its own.

The International Bank of Reconstruction and Development was estab. in 1945 and is popularly known as the 'World Bank': its H.Q. are in Washington. It aids international investment for production purposes, supplementing private investment from its own capital in order to improve the balance of world trade and living standards everywhere. The *Economic Development Institute* (estab. 1956) is an offshoot where economic planning can be studied by representatives of member countries, and there is an *International Centre for Settlement of Investment Disputes* (1966) with the pres. of the World Bank as chairman: both are in Washington. Affiliates of the bank are the *Internat. Development Assocn* (IDA: 1960) and *Internat. Finance Corp.* (IFA: 1956) which lend to the public and private sectors in less developed countries on favourable terms. *See* UNITED NATIONS.

BANNISTER, Sir Roger (1929-). British doctor athlete. On 6 May 1954, at Oxford, he became the first man in the history of athletics to run the mile in under 4 min., his time being 3 min. 59.4 sec.

BANNOCKBURN. Town in Central region, Scotland, where on 24 June 1314 Robert Bruce completely defeated an army of English invaders under Edward II. It manufactures woollen goods. Pop. (1973) 4,760.

BA'NTENG. A species (*Bibos banteng*) of wild ox ranging from Indo-China through Burma to Java and Borneo. Its colour varies from pale brown to almost black; its height is about 150cm (5ft).

BANTING, Sir Frederick Grant (1891-1941). Canadian scientist, discoverer with Prof. Macleod, Dr Best, and others, of the insulin treatment for diabetes (1922), for which in 1923 he and Macleod received a Nobel Prize. B. was killed in an aeroplane crash in Newfoundland.

BANTOCK, Sir Granville (1868-1946). British composer. B. in London, he became known as a conductor of musical comedy and modern Eng. music, and was prof. of music at the Univ. of Birmingham 1908-34. He was knighted in 1930. His works incl. the choral symphony *Atalanta in Calydon, Hebridean Symphony,* and a setting of *Omar Khayyám.*

BANKS. An electronic cheque sorter/ reader sorts 700 items per minute into branch and account order and, under control of the central computer, records all the details on magnetic tape. The system originated in the U.S.A. and was first used in Europe by the Westminster Bank. *Photo: Courtesy of the Westminster Bank.*

BANTU (ban'too). A group of related languages, spoken by predominantly Negroid peoples widely spread over the greater part of Africa S. of the Sahara. The word comes from the Zulu (meaning 'people') and illustrates the inflexional use of the prefix which is the main structural peculiarity of B.: *ba-ntu*, people; *mu-ntu*, a man, etc. The origin of the B.-speaking peoples may have been in N. Central Africa. Until 1978 Bantu was the unpopular official designation of the black people of South Africa.

BANTUSTAN. *See* BLACK HOMELAND.

BANVILLE (boṅvēl'), Theodore Faullain de (1823-91). French poet, dramatist, and novelist. B. at Moulins, he made his name among the French Romantic poets with many vols. of verse such as *Les Cariatides* (1841). Of his plays *Gringoire* (1866) is the best-known.

BA'NYAN. A tree (*Ficus benghalensis*) of the family Moraceae. Its roots grow down from its spreading branches, forming supporting pillars which have the appearance of separate trunks.

BAOBAB (bah'obab). Tropical African tree (*Adansonia digitata*) of the family Bombaceae. Its trunk grows 9m (30ft) thick, and it is one of the largest trees known.

BAPTISM (Gk *baptizo*, I dip, submerge). Immersion in or sprinkling with water, particularly as a religious rite of initiation. In antiquity and among primitive people the practice has been widespread; in some of the mystery religions blood took the place of water. B. was universal in the Christian Church from the first days, being administered to adults and by immersion. The B. of infants was not practised until the 2nd cent., but became general in the 6th. B. by sprinkling (christening) when the child is named is now general in the West except for some sects, notably the Baptists (q.v.), where complete immersion of adults is the rule. The Eastern Orthodox Church also practises immersion.

BAOBAB. As ancient as it looks - such trees may live over a thousand years – the baobab in folk-tale was planted upside down, because the trunk and branches look more like roots. One species, *A.Gregorii*, is found only near Kimberley in north-west Australia and is thought to be a relic of Gondwanaland (q.v.). *Photo: Australian Information Service.*

BAPTISTS. A world-wide Christian community, practising baptism by immersion of believers only on profession of faith. They stand in the Protestant and evangelical tradition, seek their authority in the Bible, emphasize the right of the soul to an immediate relation to God, and conceive the Church as a fellowship of the spiritually regenerate.

Bs. originated among the English Separatists who took refuge in Holland in the early 17th cent., the first English B. being Rev. John Smyth, a Cambridge scholar and an ordained minister of the C. of E. The first Baptist Church in America was organized on Rhode Island in 1639 by Roger Williams. In the 19th cent. there was considerable B. development on the continent of Europe. There are flourishing B. communities in the Commonwealth. Of the world total of *c.* 31,000,000, some 26,500,000 are in USA, and 265,000 in UK.

The Baptist Missionary Society, formed in 1792 under the inspiration of William Carey, pioneered in the modern missionary movement. In 1905 the Baptist World Alliance was formed.

BARBĀ'DOS. Most easterly is. of the W. Indies, British since 1627, which became independent within the Commonwealth in 1966. It lies in the Atlantic to the E. of the Windward Is. The soil is fertile, and produces sugar; rum is distilled and tourism is important. Bridgetown is the cap. There is a Senate and an elected House of Assembly dating from 1627. Area 430 sq.km (166 sq.m); pop. (1973) 244,000.

BARBARO'SSA. Name given to the German emperor Frederick I (q.v.), and also to two brothers who were Barbary pirates: Horuk was killed by the Spaniards in 1518, Khair-ed-Din took Tunis in 1534, and d. at Constantinople in 1546. The name means 'red beard'. It was also the code name for the German invasion of Russia in 1941.

BARBARY. Traditional name for N. Africa W. of Egypt and N. of the Sahara, named after the Berbers, its principal inhabitants. *See* CORSAIRS.

BARBARY APE. Species (*Macaca sylvana*) of monkey, native to the mountains of Algeria and Morocco; introduced into Gibraltar, it is the only kind of monkey now found wild in Europe. Yellowish brown, the species has no visible trace of a tail. Legend has it that if the colony dies out, Britain will lose Gibraltar.

BARBASTE'LLE. Species (*Barbastellus barbastella*) of bat found in Britain and neighbouring parts of Europe. Although it is only the size of a mouse, its wings have a span of some 25cm (10in).

BAR'BEL. Genus of freshwater fish (*Barbus*) of the carp family (Cyprinidae), so called because of the soft appendages near the mouth (Lat. *barba*, beard).

BARBE'LLION, W. N. P. Pseudonym of Bruce Frederick Cummings (1889-1919), British biologist and diarist. He held an appointment at the Natural History Museum, London, and was the author of the remarkable *Journal of a Disappointed Man.*

BARBIRO'LLI, Sir John (1899-1970). Brit. conductor. B. in London, of French and Italian stock, he made a name as a cellist, and was permanent conductor to the Hallé Orchestra, Manchester, 1943-58 before becoming principal conductor (1958-68), then conductor laureate for life. He was knighted in 1949. His style had a temperamental brilliance.

BARBIROLLI. Meticulous in preparation as in performance, Barbirolli working on the score of Vaughan Williams' Fifth Symphony in the recording studio. *Photo: Godfrey MacDominic*

BARBITURATE. A salt or ester of barbituric acid, which is derived from malic acid (found in unripe apples and urea). A sedative drug, its various forms are legitimately used in medicine, as a sleeping aid, anaesthetic, and means of controlling epilepsy, but are addictive when prescribed indiscriminately, and in 1979 legal penalties were introduced in the UK for their misuse.

BARBIZON (bahrbāzoṅ). French village on the outskirts of Paris near the forest of Fontainebleau famous for its association with the artists of the 'Barbizon School' who included Millet, Rousseau, Corot, Daubigny, and Courbet.

BARBOUR (bar'ber), **John** (*c.* 1316-95). Scottish poet. He was archdeacon of Aberdeen after 1357, and held small posts at court. His chronicle-poem *The Brus* is almost the first Scottish poem.

BARCELONA (bahrselō'nah). Largest port, chief commercial and industrial centre, and 2nd city of Spain, on the Mediterranean coast 5km (3m) N. of the mouth of the Llobregat. It was founded in the 3rd cent. B.C., and its importance grew until in the 14th cent. it had become one of the leading trading cities of the Mediterranean. As the chief centre of anarchism and Catalonian nationalism it was prominent in the overthrow of the monarchy in 1931, and was the last city of the republic to surrender to Franco in 1939.

The central Plaza de la Cataluña is the largest square in Spain, into which run the Rambla promenades. Besides the 14th cent. cathedral, there is the striking Templo Expiatorio de la Sagrada Familia, designed by Gaudi. The univ. was founded 1450. The Pueblo Espagñol, built 1929 for the World's Fair, has examples of Spanish architecture of all periods and regions, and the 14th cent. shipyards form a Maritime Museum (with a replica of Columbus's *Santa Maria*). A large Picasso collection is housed in palaces of the 13th and 15th cents. There are large modern docks, and industries incl. textiles, engineering, chemicals, etc. Pop. (1970) 1,745,000.

BARDEEN, John (1908-), American physicist. He shared a Nobel prize in 1956 (with W. H. Brattain and W. Shockley) for work on the development of the electronic transistor. In 1972 he became the first prizewinner to receive the award twice in the same subject, when he won it with Leon Cooper and John Schrieffer for their theory of superconductivity. *See* ELECTRICITY.

BAREBONE, Praise God (*c.* 1596-1679). English preacher of the Parliamentary party. A London leather merchant by trade, in 1653 he became a member of the new House of Commons, and in derision the Parliament was nicknamed 'Barebone's Parliament'.

BAREILLY (barālē'). City of India in the state of Uttar Pradesh near the Ramganga. It is an important rly junction and manufacturing centre. Pop. (1971) 326,150.

BĀ'RENBOIM, Daniel (1942-). Israeli pianist and conductor. B. in Buenos Aires, where he made his debut at the piano at 7, he m. in 1967 Brit. violoncellist Jacqueline du Pré (q.v.). He became pianist with the Israeli Philharmonic Orchestra in 1953 and musical director with the Orchestre de Paris in 1975.

BARENTS (bah'rents), **Willem** (1550-97). Dutch explorer, who in 1594-7 made 3 expeditions from Holland in search of a N.E. passage. He d. in course of the last. Barents Sea is named after him.

BARENTS SEA. East section of the Arctic Ocean between Spitsbergen, Novaya Zemlaya and N. Scandinavia. There are rich oil and gas reserves. It is strategically important as the meeting point of the NATO and Warsaw Pact forces.

BARHAM, Richard Harris (1788-1845). British writer and antiquary. He took holy orders and became priest-in-ordinary to the Chapel Royal. He is best known for his verse tales pub. in *The Ingoldsby Legends* under his pseudonym Thomas Ingoldsby.

BARI (bah'rē). Italian port on the Adriatic, 112km (69m) N.W. of Brindisi. The commercial centre of Apulia, it has a univ. (1924), textile and food industries and oil refineries. Pop. (1972) 357,350.

BARING-GOULD, Sabine (1834-1924). British writer, rector of Lew Trenchard in N. Devon from 1881. He was prolific in novels, books of travel, mythology and folklore, and wrote the words of 'Onward, Christian Soldiers'.

BĀ'RIUM. A metallic chemical element, symbol Ba at. no. 56, at wt. 137.36. The name comes from the Greek word for 'heavy', since the presence of B. was first discovered in barytes or heavy spar. It is silver-white in colour, oxidizes very easily, and is a little harder than lead. Being heavy, B. sulphate is added to a meal to reveal abnormalities in the digestive tract during radiography. B. is very important since, with strontium, it forms the emissive surface in every small thermionic valve and cathode-ray tube.

BARK, or **cortex.** The outer rind of the stems of plants, strictly speaking the outer covering of the stems of dicotyledonous plants, especially those of a woody and perennial growth (trees and shrubs). True bark consists of dried-up tissues, and its production is assisted by the formation of a layer of cork outside the growing part of the stem. B. has many economic uses. Some kinds have medicinal qualities, e.g. cinchona (quinine), cascara, and angostura.

BARKER, George (1913-). British poet. His verse has been compared to that of the surrealists, and, though uneven, has great vividness of imagery. His work incl. the long poem *Calamiterror* (1937), *The True Confessions of George Barker* (1950), and *Collected Poems, 1930-50.*

BARKER, Sir Herbert Atkinson (1869-1950). British manipulative surgeon. He achieved thousands of cures by his unorthodox methods, but was subject to bitter attack from the medical profession until late in his life: he was knighted in 1922.

BARKLY TABLELAND. Area of some 100,000 sq.km (40,000 sq.m.) to the S.E. of the Gulf of Carpentaria, Australia, mainly in Northern Territory but partly in Queensland. It is chiefly grassland and open-range cattle are raised on a large scale. The *B. Highway* (c. 650km/400m) links Mt Isa to the Stuart Highway.

BARK PAINTINGS. Paintings on the inner side of strips of tree bark produced by Australian aborigines of Arnhem Land, etc. In red, yellow, white, brown and black pigments, they were often painted with the fingers as the artist lay inside the low bark-roofed shelters.

BARLE'TTA. Italian port on the Adriatic, 55km (34m) N.W. of Bari. There is a Romanesque cathedral, and cement and chemicals are manufactured. Pop. (1972) 80,000.

BARLEY. Genus of cereals (*Hordeum*) belonging to the family Gramineae. The cultivated B. comprises 3 species - six-rowed barley (*H. hexastichon*), four-rowed barley or Scotch Bigg (*H. vulgare*), and two-rowed barley (*H. distichon*).

B. was one of the earliest cereals to be cultivated, and no other cereal can thrive in so wide a range of climate. Polar barley is sown and reaped well within the Arctic circle in Europe. B. is no longer much used in bread-making, but finds a wide use for pig, horse, and cattle foods. Its main importance, however, is in brewing and distilling.

BARNABAS. Christian saint, mentioned in Acts as a 'fellow-labourer' with Paul; he went with Mark on a missionary journey to Cyprus, his birthplace.

BARNACLE. Marine crustacean of the sub-class Cirripedia. The larval form is free-swimming, but after a time it settles down, and fixes itself by its head to a stone, floating wood, etc. The animal then becomes a sedentary creature, enclosed in a shell through the opening of which the cirri protrude. By means of these food is swept into the mouth. The true barnacles (*Lepadidae*) are fixed on long fleshy stalks, and include the common goose barnacle (*Lepas anatifera*) which grows on ships.

BARK PAINTINGS. The traditional designs both abstract and based on animal forms, as with the turtle in the foreground, now have a commercial value. Spears make an adaptable stand. *Photo: Richard Harrington/Camera Press.*

BARNARD (bahrnahrd'), **Christiaan** (1922-), South African cardio-thoracic surgeon. Specialist at Groote Schuur Hospital from 1958, he carried out the first transplant of a human heart there 3 Dec. 1967, when Louis Washkansky received the heart of a woman, but d. 18 days later of pneumonia. He became Hon. Prof. of Surgical Science, Univ. of Cape Town, 1968. *See* HEART.

BARNARDO (barnar'do), **Thomas John** (1845–1905). British philanthropist. Of Irish-Jewish extraction, he was known as 'Dr' Barnardo, though not actually qualified. He opened his first home for destitute children in 1867 in Stepney, London, where the HQ of the Barnardo organisation remains.

BARNAUL (bahrnah-ool'). Admin. centre of Altai Territory, RSFSR (USSR), situated where the r. Barnaulka enters the Ob. Originally a mining town founded 1730, it has cotton mills and food-packing factories. Pop. (1974) 490,000.

BARNES, Ernest William (1874-1953). British modernist churchman. A lecturer in mathematics at Cambridge 1902-15, he was an ardent advocate of the significance in modern religion of scientific thought. In 1924 he became bp of Birmingham and outraged many by his controversial views, as in *The Rise of Christianity* (1947), expressing doubt as to miracles, the virgin birth, and so on.

BARNES, Thomas (1785-1841). British journalist, editor of *The Times* from 1817, developing it into a most powerful organ of informed opinion, the 'Thunderer'.

BARNES, William (1800-86). Dorsetshire poet. B. at Rushay, of farming stock, he was vicar of Whitcombe from 1847 and rector of Winterbourne Came, where he d., from 1862. He pub. vols. of poems in the Dorset dialect.

BARNET. Suburb in the N. of Greater London. In the Battle of B., on 14 April 1471 the Lancastrians under Warwick the Kingmaker were completely defeated by the Yorkists under Edward IV, Warwick himself being killed.

BARNSLEY. Town (admin. H.Q.) in S. Yorkshire, England, N. of Sheffield. On one of Britain's richest coalfields, it has iron and steel, glass, paper, carpet, and clothing industries. Pop. (1971) 75,330.

BARNSTAPLE. Picturesque fishing port of N. Devon, England, once a centre of the woollen trade. Pottery (Barum ware) is made. Pop. (1972) 17,860.

BA'RNUM, Phineas Taylor (1810-91). American showman, who after an adventurous career exhibited 'Tom Thumb', toured USA with Jenny Lind, and in 1871 established the 'Greatest Show on Earth', comprising circus, menagerie, and exhibition of 'freaks', conveyed in 100 railway cars.

BARŌ'DA. *See* VADODARA.

BAROJA (bahrokh'ha), **Pio** (1872-1956). Spanish novelist of Basque extraction and anarchist sentiments. His books incl. a trilogy dealing with the Madrid underworld, *La lucha por la vida* (1904-5), and *Memorias de un hombre de acción*, extending to a score of vols.

BARO'METER. Instrument for measuring atmospheric pressure. In the **mercury barometer** a column of mercury in a glass tube about 0.75 m high (closed at one end and curved upward at the other) is balanced by the pressure of the atmosphere on the open end. Any change in the height of the column reflects a change in pressure. In the **aneroid barometer** a similar result is achieved by changes in the distance between the sides of a shallow cylindrical metal box which is partly exhausted of air.

A rise of 305m (1,000ft) in altitude measured from sea-level corresponds approximately to a change in pressure of 25mm (1in) of mercury, but the relation between height and pressure depends very largely on atmospheric temperature.

A **barograph** creates a permanent record of variations in atmospheric pressure. Usually, a pen, which is governed by the movements of an aneroid barometer, makes a continuous line on a chart placed on the outside of a cylinder which rotates over the period of a day or week. The completed chart is known as a barogram.

BA'RON. Lowest rank in the peerage (q.v.) of the UK, above a baronet and below a viscount. The 1st English barony was created in 1387, but Bs. 'by 'writ' existed earlier. Life peers, created under the Act of 1958, are always of this rank.

BARONET. Hereditary title signifying a rank below that of a baron and above a knight. It was instituted by James I as a means of raising money.

BARONS' WAR. In English history, the civil war between the barons led by Simon de Montfort and Henry III. The former won the battle of Lewes in 1264, but at Evesham in 1265 the position was reversed, Montfort being slain.

BARŌ'QUE. Term used to denote a style of architecture, characterized by bizarre or fantastic ornamentation which prevailed on the Continent during the 17th and 18th cents. The term perhaps derives from the Span. *barrueco*, meaning an irregular-shaped pearl. The most famous exponents of B. were Giovanni Bernini and Francesco Borromini.

BAROSSA VALLEY. Valley in the Mt Lofty Ranges, S. Australia, one of the chief wine-growing areas of the continent.

BAROSSA VALLEY. Named after a Spanish wine-growing locality, the valley produces more than a third of Australia's total wine output and has been under cultivation for vines since 1847. *Photo: Barbara Wace.*

BARO'TSELAND. Former kingdom of W. Zambia. It came under Brit. protection at the request of the ruler, Lewanika (1860-1922) in 1890. Following the estab. of the Rep. of Zambia in 1964, it became the country's Western Province. It is mainly agricultural, with cattle as the chief form of wealth, and the Barotse are of fine physique. The admin. centre is Mongu.

BARRA. Most southerly of the larger Outer Hebrides is., in Western Isles, Scotland, separated from S. Uist by the Sound of B. The is., about 13km (8m) by 6.5km (4m) is barren: Castlebay is a fishing harbour. Area 91 sq.km (35 sq.m); pop. (1971) 1,087.

BARRACUDA (barakoo'dah), **barracouta.** Large carnivorous pike-like fish (*Sphyraena barracuda*) of the family Sphyraenidae, found in the warmer seas of the world. It is esteemed for food.

BARRAGÁN, Luis (1902-). Mexican architect. Noted for his use of basic materials, such as rough wooden beams, cobbles, lava, and adobe, he creates simple houses with walled gardens and makes great use of fountains.

BARRANQUILLA (bahrahnkēl'yah). Chief port, airport and city of Colombia, S. America, near the mouth of the Magdalena. Pop. (1972) 693,900.

BARRAS (bahrrahs'), **Paul François Jean Nicolas,** Count (1755-1829). French revolutionist. B. in Provence, he fought against the English in India, was elected to the National Convention in 1792, and helped to overthrow Robespierre (1794). In 1795 he became a member of the *Directoire.* In 1796 he brought about the marriage of his former mistress, Joséphine de Beauharnais with Napoleon, and assumed dictatorial powers. After Napoleon's *coup d'état* of 19 Nov. 1799, B. fell into disgrace.

BARRAULT (bahroh′), **Jean Louis** (1910-). French actor-director. He was producer-director to the Comédie-Française 1940-6, and was director of the Théâtre de France (formerly Odéon) from 1959 until dismissed 1968 because of statements made during the occupation of the theatre by student rebels. His films incl.: *La Symphonie fantastique, Les Enfants du Paradis* (1944) and *La Ronde* (1950).

BARRE (bahr), **Raymond** (1924-). French statesman. An economist, he was vice-pres. of the European Commission 1967-72, helped organise the Rambouillet Conference, and was Min. of External Trade from Jan. 1976 until he replaced Chirac as P.M. in August.

BARREL ORGAN. Portable musical instrument consisting of a cylinder containing an arrangement of pins and staples which, on the handle being turned, raise keys which open pipe valves, thus admitting air from the wind chest.

BARREN LANDS/GROUNDS. Tundra region in Canada, W of Hudson Bay.

BARRIE, Sir James Matthew (1860-1937). Scottish novelist and playwright. B. in Kirriemuir, Angus, he entered journalism in Nottingham in 1883, and settled in London in 1885. He became known by his studies of Scottish rural life in *Auld Licht Idylls* (1888), and *A Window in Thrums* (1889) which began the vogue of the Kailyard school. His first novel, *The Little Minister*, was dramatized in 1897 and, together with *The Professor's Love Story* (1894), estab. his reputation as a playwright. The most important of his later plays are: *Quality Street* (1901), *The Admirable Crichton* (1902), *What Every Woman Knows* (1908), *Dear Brutus* (1917), and *Mary Rose* (1920). The perennial children's play, *Peter Pan* (1904), was drawn from an idea in the *Little White Bird* (1902). Other works incl. a biography of his mother, *Margaret Ogilvie* (1896). He was made a bart in 1913 and received the O.M. in 1922.

BARRISTER. Lawyer qualified (by study at the Inns of Court) to plead for a client at the bar (a railed division in British courts which separates off the judges and officers of the court). Barristers remain outside the bar until they become King's/Queen's Counsel, when they 'take silk' (wear a 'silk' instead of a 'stuff' gown) and are called 'within the bar'. Barristers usually act for clients only on the instructions of a solicitor, and in the highest courts only a barrister can be heard on behalf of a litigant. In the USA the distinction between barrister and solicitor does not exist, and the functions of both are combined in the courtroom lawyer.

BARROW. A burial mound, usually composed of earth, but sometimes of stones, examples of which are found in many parts of the world. There are 2 main types, long and round.

The *long barrow* is held to be the earlier, dating from the New Stone Age. Sometimes it may be a mere mound, but usually it contained a chamber of wood or stone slabs in which were placed the bodies of the deceased. Such are especially common in the southern counties from Sussex to Dorset. They seem to have been communal burial-places of the long-headed Mediterranean race.

Round barrows were the work of the round-headed or 'beaker' folk of the early Bronze Age. The commonest type is the bell B., consisting of a circular mound, enclosed by a ditch and an outside bank of earth. Many dot the Wiltshire downs. In historic times certain of the Saxon and most of the Danish invaders were barrow-builders.

BARROW. Most northerly town of the USA on Point B. on the N. coast of Alaska. The average winter temperature is 30° below zero, but B. is heated by natural gas. It is the world's largest Eskimo settlement and oil strikes in Prudhoe Bay have brought added prosperity. Pop. (1970) 2,500.

BARROW-IN-FURNESS. Port in Cumbria, England, at the S. end of the Furness peninsula. High quality iron ore, formerly mined locally, founded its prosperity, but in recent years the iron works have closed. The docks have been modernized, and the iron ore traffic has been replaced by the export of scrap metal to the Continent; ships (nuclear subs.) are built. Pop. (1972) 64,340.

BARRY, Sir Charles (1795-1860). British architect, designer of the Houses of Parliament, Westminster (1840-60); he was knighted in 1852.

BARRY, Comtesse du. *See* DU BARRY.

BARRY. Port in S. Glamorgan, Wales, 13km (8m) S.W. of Cardiff. The first docks were built in 1889 for coal export. Between the wars B. and B. island, developed as a resort. Pop. (1972) 41,880.

BARRYMORE. American family of actors, the children of British-born Maurice B. and Georgie Drew, both stage personalities. Lionel B. (1878-1954) first appeared on the stage with his grandmother, Mrs. John Drew, in 1893. After studying art in Paris, he returned to the stage, and from 1909 made numerous films. Ethel B. (1879-1959) played with Irving in London in 1898 and in 1928 opened the Ethel B. Theatre in N.Y.; she also appeared in many films from 1914. John B. (1882-1942), a vitally flamboyant personality, appeared on stage and screen, often with his brother and sister.

BART (bahr), **Jean** (1651-1702). Naval hero of France. B. at Dunkirk, the son of a fisherman, he served in the French navy, and harassed the British fleet in many daring exploits.

BART, Lionel (1930-). British composer, author of the music and lyrics of *Fings Ain't Wot They used T'Be* (1959) and *Oliver!* (1960), based on Dickens's novel.

BARTH (bahrt), **Karl** (1886-1968). Swiss Protestant theologian. B. at Basle, he held chairs of theology in Germany from 1921, and 1935-62 was prof. at Basle. His *Epistle to the Romans* (1919) and *Church Dogmatics* (13 vols. 1932-67) gained him an international reputation.

BARTHOLDI (bahrtol′dē), **Auguste** (1834-1904). French sculptor. He completed the statue of Liberty overlooking New York harbour in 1884.

BARTHOLOMEW. Christian saint and one of the 12 apostles. Legends relate that after the Crucifixion he took Christianity to India, or that he was a missionary in Asia Minor and Armenia, where he suffered martyrdom by being flayed alive. The Catholic Church commemorates him on 24 Aug.

On St Bartholomew's day in 1572 occurred the famous MASSACRE OF ST B., when numbers of the French Huguenots were slaughtered by order of the queen-mother, Catherine de' Medici.

BARTÓK (bor′tōk), **Béla** (1881-1945). Hungarian composer, b. in Transylvania. He was regarded as a child prodigy, studied music at Budapest, and collaborated with Kodály in research into Hungarian folk music, which coloured his later compositions. His large output includes string quartets, violin and piano concertos, orchestral suites, and operas. When Hungary joined Germany in the S.W.W., B. went to America. He d. in New York.

BARTOLOMMEO (bahrtōlommā'ō), **Fra** (1475-1517). Florentine painter, known also as BACCIO DELLA PORTA. He owed much to Leonardo da Vinci. Albertinelli assisted him in painting the fresco of the 'Last Judgment' in Santa Maria Nuova. Deeply moved by Savonarola's death, he entered a Dominican convent, but he soon turned again to painting. His figure of St Mark is regarded as his greatest achievement.

BARTON, Sir Edmund (1849-1920). Australian statesman. B. at Sydney, N.S.W., he was leader of the Federation movement from 1896, and first P.M. of the Commonwealth of A. (1901-3). On his retirement, 1903, he became a High Court Judge.

BART'S. Short for St Bartholomew's Hospital, in Smithfield, one of the great teaching hospitals of London, England. It was founded by Henry VIII at the Reformation.

BARUCH (barook'), Bernard Mannes (1870-1965). American stock market wizard. He was a friend of Churchill and a self-appointed, unpaid adviser to Presidents Wilson, F. D. Roosevelt and Truman. He strongly advocated internat. control of atomic energy.

BASALT. The commonest volcanic rock, usually dark grey, but sometimes green, brown or black. The ground mass may be glassy or finely crystalline, sometimes with large crystals embedded. Successive eruptions have formed the great plateaux of Colorado and the Indian Deccan, and in some places, such as Fingal's Cave and the Giant's Causeway in Antrim, shrinkage during the solidification of the molten lava caused the formation of hexagonal columns.

BASEBALL. The national summer game of the USA, thought by some authorities to have evolved from the English game of rounders, while others claim that it originated in New York, USA in 1839.

It is played with a bat and ball between 2 teams, each of 9 players. The field of play is marked in the form of a diamond.

The side taking first innings bat in regular succession. The opposing side taking the field are: the pitcher, near the centre of the diamond; the catcher, behind the home base; 1st baseman, near the 1st base, which is to the right of the catcher; 2nd and 3rd basemen, near the 2nd and 3rd bases; short stop (in-fielder) about midway between 2nd and 3rd basemen; and outfielders at right, centre and left.

The pitcher may deliver the ball either under or over arm. The batter tries to make a 'fair hit' which means that the ball must fall within the diamond or beyond, but within the 'foul lines'. If his strike is successful the batter tries to make a 'run' which is a complete circuit of the diamond from home base to 1st, 2nd, 3rd bases in regular order and back to home base. This may be in one dash called a 'home run' or by stopping in the circuit at any other base as a safety point.

He is declared out if, (1) he fails to hit the ball after 3 attempts, (2) he strikes the ball in the air and it is caught by a fielder, (3) he is touched by the ball in the hand of one of his opponents while he is between bases, and (4) a fielder standing on one of the bases catches the ball before he reaches the base. A batter may only run for 'fair hits', but he may be put out on a 'foul hit' if the ball is caught before it reaches the ground. The main duty of the infielders is to put out the batsman by touching him with the ball held in the hand, while he is running between the bases, or reaching a base with the ball before the batsman can get there; either method puts the batsman out. The outfielders' duty is to catch or stop long hits and return them to 'basemen'.

The 1st batter is followed by the other members of his team in rotation until 3 members of the batting side are put out: the opposing team then take their turn. This continues until 9 equal innings have been played and the team scoring the most runs wins the game. The game may be controlled by one umpire, but 2 are more usual for important matches.

The ball is formed by yarn wound on a core of cork or rubber and covered with two strips of white horsehide. It weighs 141-155g (5-5½oz) and the diameter is c. 23cm. (9in). The bat is round, and not more than 7cm. (2¾in) in diameter at its thickest part, and c. 1m. (3ft 6in) long.

B. was first played in 1839 at Cooperstown, N.Y., the field being laid out by Abner Doubleday, who organized the game. The 100th anniversary of the game was celebrated at Cooperstown in 1939 with the dedication of the Hall of Fame and National Museum of B. The Select Five, the players whose performances were thought to have stamped them as the greatest players of all, were Ty Cobb (1886-1961), Babe Ruth (q.v.), Christy Mathewson, Honus Wagner, and Walter Johnson, chosen in that order. The Knickerbocker Club, the 1st to be founded, was formed in New York by Alexander J. Cartwright in 1845. The National Association of Baseball Players was formed in 1858 and the 1st professional team was Cincinnati's Red Stockings (1869).

The first serious effort to introduce B. to Britain was made in 1917, when a demonstration match was played at Lord's cricket ground. During the S.W.W. the presence of great numbers of American soldiers in UK led to a considerable increase in the game's popularity.

BASEL. German form of BASLE.

BA'SHKIR. ASSR of the RSFSR, on the W. slopes of the S. Ural Mts. Grains and sunflower seeds are grown; metals worked include iron, copper, gold; petroleum is found; and the forests in the N.E. produce timber. Ufa is the cap. Area 143,600 sq.km (55,400 sq.m); pop. (1972) 3,835,000.

BASHKIRTSEFF (bahshkēr'tsev), **Maria Constantinova** (1860-84). Russian artist and diarist. After studying singing, she turned to painting while at Paris in 1877, and 3 years later began to exhibit at the Salon. She is chiefly known as a writer of letters and of a diary.

BASIC. The 'language' used in computer programming (*B*eginner's *A*ll-purpose *S*ymbolic *I*nstruction *C*ode), designed at Dartmouth, USA. A single error in the special code phrases or even the omission of a semi-colon, results in the machine answering merely 'syntax error'.

BASIC ENGLISH. Named from the initial letters of British - American - Scientific - International - Commercial, B.E. is a simplified form of English, devised as an international auxiliary language. With a vocabulary of 850 words, including only 18 verbs, it expresses more advanced meanings by a combination of these with the 600 nouns or 20 prepositions and adverbs, e.g. 'buy' becomes 'give money for'. The originator was C. K. Ogden, who began his researches in 1926, and was joined by I. A. Richards.

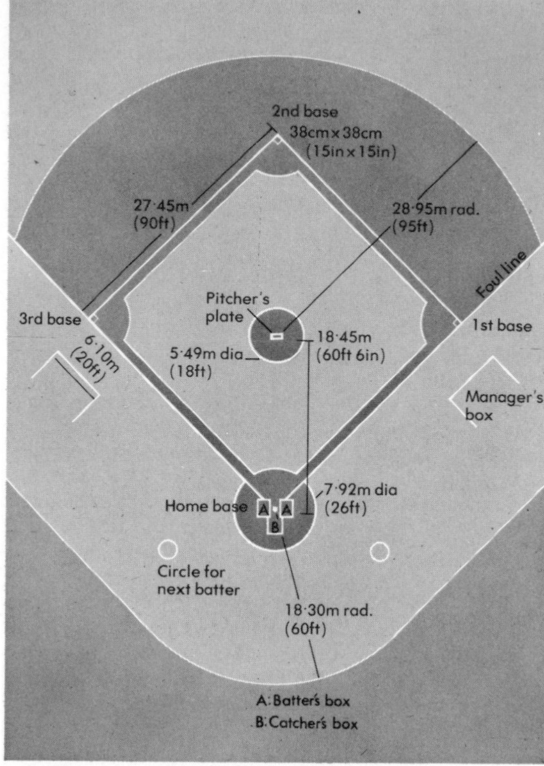

BASEBALL. The 'diamond'.

BA'SIL (*c.* A.D. 330-379). Christian saint, founder of the Basilian monks, and known as THE GREAT. B. at Caesarea, Asia Minor, he studied at Constantinople and Athens, visited the hermit saints of the Egyptian desert, entered a monastery in Asia Minor about 358, and developed a monastic rule based on community life, work, and prayer. These ideas form the basis of monasticism in the Greek Orthodox church, and influenced the foundation of similar monasteries by St Benedict. Elected bishop of Caesarea in 370, B. opposed the heresy of Arianism. He wrote many theological works and composed the 'Liturgy of St Basil', in use in the Orthodox church.

BASIL. A plant (*Ocimum basilicum*) of the family Labiatae. A native of India, it is cultivated in Europe as a potherb and for seasoning.

BASILDON. Village in Essex, England, developed from 1949 as a residential and industrial 'new town' to take London's overspill, and producing chemicals and clothing, and with printing and engineering works. Pop. (1975) 84,000.

BASILICA. Type of Roman public building; a large roofed hall flanked by columns generally having an aisle on each side, used for judicial or other public business. The earliest known B., at Pompeii, dates from the 2nd cent. B.C. The type was adopted by the early Christians for their churches.

BASINGSTOKE. Town in Hants, England, on the Loddon, 72km (45m) W.S.W. of London. Of recent years it has developed industrially. Pop. (1972) 56,330.

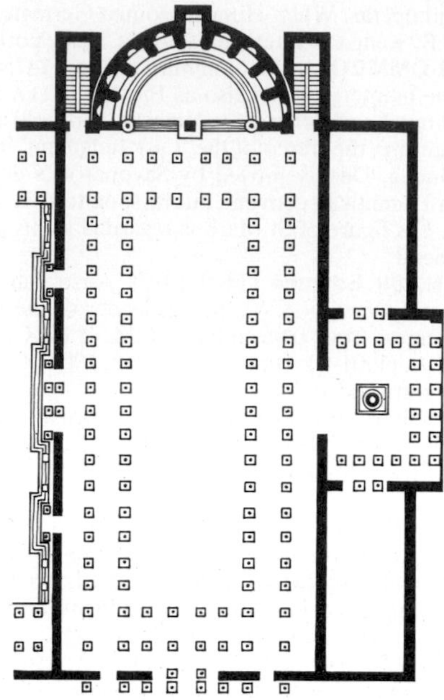

BASILICA. Plan of the Basilica Ulpia at Rome.

BASKERVILLE, John (1706-75). British printer. He began his career as a footman, becoming a writing-master in Birmingham, and from 1750 onwards experimented in casting types. In 1756 he pub. a 4to edition of Virgil, which was followed by 54 books remarkable for their craftsmanship.

BASKETBALL. Indoor game very popular in USA and Canada, invented by Dr J. A. Naismith, of Springfield, Mass., a YMCA instructor in 1891. It is played by 2 teams of 5, substitutes being allowed during play. The object is to throw the ball, similar to a round football, into a basket suspended against a board, 3.05m (10ft) from the ground, at each end of the court. The ball is played by hand only. Most famous of all teams is the Harlem Globetrotters.

BASLE. Conventional English form of the name of the 2nd city of Switzerland (Basel in German, Bâle in French). Situated on the Rhine, on its right-angled bend at the S. end of the middle Rhine plain, it is one of the greatest route centres of Europe, and also a great banking and commercial centre. The Bank for International Settlements was estab. here in 1930. B. manufactures textiles, particularly silks and ribbons, machinery, chemicals, clocks and watches, foodstuffs, etc.

B. was a strong military station under the Romans. In 1501 it joined the Swiss confederation, and later developed as a centre of the Reformation. The 11th cent. cathedral was rebuilt after an earthquake in 1356. The town hall dates from the 16th cent., and the univ. from the 15th. Pop. (1971) 212,000.

BASQUE (bahsk) **REGION.** Spanish autonomous region, estab. in 1980, and comprising the provs. of Álava, Guipúzcoa and Vizcaya: Navarra has the option of joining at a later date.

BASQUES (bahsks). People directly descended from the Stone Age hunters of Altamira, and living in the autonomous Basque region of N Spain and the French

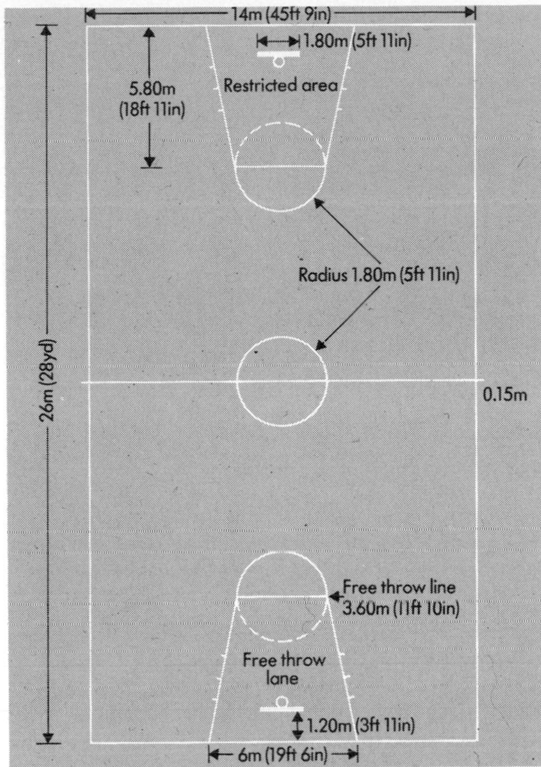

BASKETBALL.

BASLE. The cathedral, built of deep red sandstone, is seen here across the Rhine still surrounded by the houses of the old town. *Photo: Courtesy of the Swiss National Tourist Office.*

dept. of Pyrénées-Atlantiques. They first appeared in history when in 778 they annihilated the rearguard of Charlemagne's army at Roncesvalles (q.v.). In the Civil War 1936-9 the Basques took the Republican side, were vindictively crushed by Franco, and only secured autonomy and the recognition of the Basque language (Euskara - unrelated to French or Spanish) in 1980. From 1968 there had been terrorism by ETA (Euskadi ta Azkatasuna - Basque Nation and Liberty), which claimed responsibility for the assassination of Spanish premier Carrero Blanco in 1974. The French organization is called Enbata (Ocean Wind). The Basque national game is pelota.

BA'SRA. City in Iraq, and its only port situated near the Shatt-al-Arab, 97km (60m) from the Gulf. It is an important railway and air centre; shipping trade is largely with India. Petroleum is worked in the vicinity. The irrigated areas round B. produce the world's finest dates. Pop. (1970) 450,000.

BASS (bas). Various species of fish of the order Percomorphi. The species *Morone labrax* belongs to the family of sea-perches (Serranidae), and is found in shoals off the Mediterranean and Atlantic coasts. *See* GROUPER.

BASSEIN (bahssān'). Port in Burma, on the B. river, 125km (78m) from the sea. Founded in the 13th cent., it was captured by the British in 1852. There are rice mills, and a univ. Pop. (1970) 100,000.

BA'SSET. A French hound for hunting the hare on foot, introduced into Britain in 1866. It is heavy and short-legged, and remarkable for its great powers of scent and for excelling in hound 'music'.

BASSETERRE (bastār'). Cap. and port of St Kitts in the Leeward Is. Pop. (1970) 16,000.

BASSE-TERRE (bahs-tār'). Cap. and port of the French overseas region of Guadeloupe. Pop. (1970) 15,850.

BA'SSET HORN. Obsolete wind musical instrument resembling a clarinet.

BASSOO'N. Woodwind instrument of the oboe family, of which it is the bass. It is descended from the bass pommer which was c. 2m (6ft) in length and perfectly straight, whereas the B. is doubled back on itself. Its tone is rich and deep.

BASS ROCK. Islet in the Firth of Forth, Scotland, c. 107m (350ft) high. It has a lighthouse, and hosts of sea birds.

BASS STRAIT. The channel separating Australia and Tasmania: 290km (180m) long, 129-241km (80-150m) wide. Oil was discovered beneath the sea in the 1960s.

BASTIA (bahstē'ah). Largest town and commercial centre of Corsica, France. Pop. (1970) 51,000.

BASTILLE (bastēl'). Name given to the castle of St Antoine, part of the fortifications of Paris, which was used for centuries as a State prison; it was singled out for the initial attack by the revolutionary mob, which set in train the French Revolution, on 14 July 1789. Only 7 prisoners were found in the B. when it was stormed; the governor and most of the garrison were killed; the B. was razed to the ground.

BASUTOLAND (bahsōō'tōland). *See* LESOTHO.

BAT (Chiroptera). An order of mammals distinguished by having the fore-limbs converted into wings capable of sustained and rapid flight. These wings consist of a thin hairless membrane stretched between the limbs and the body and between 4 of the fingers of the hand, which are greatly lengthened for that purpose, and cleft to the wrist.

The thumb is free and is furnished with a sharp claw to help in climbing. The hind feet have 5 toes provided with sharp hooked claws, which suspend the animal head downwards when resting.

Bats are nocturnal, and those native to temperate countries hibernate in winter. They form the most widely distributed order of mammals, their power of flight taking them all over the world where there are trees, and to oceanic islands which other mammals cannot reach. Bs., like whales and dolphins, use a type of echo-location system.

There are 2 main groups: the large fruit-eaters (*Megachiroptera*), also called Flying Foxes, of Africa, S. Asia and Australia, and the smaller insect-eaters (*Microchiroptera*), of which there are some 600 species, found in all temperate and tropical regions.

BATAAN. Peninsula on Luzon, Philippine Rep., W. of Manila Bay, which was gallantly but in vain defended against the Japanese by American and Filipino troops under MacArthur from 1 Jan. to 9 April 1942.

BATAVIA. Dutch name for DJAKARTA.

BATES, H. E. (Herbert Ernest) (1905-74). British author. B. in Northampton, he was briefly a journalist and clerk, and pub. his first novel *The Two Sisters* (1925). He estab. his reputation as a short-story writer during the S.W.W., under the pen-name 'Flying Officer X', and as the author of the novel *Fair Stood the Wind for France* (1944); *The Purple Plain* (1947) and *The Jacaranda Tree* (1949) dealt with the Burma campaigns. His later series of books about the bucolic Larkin family, beginning with *The Darling Buds of May* (1958), was equally successful.

BATH. City in Avon, England on the right bank of the river Avon, 16km (10m) S.E. of Bristol. A health resort, it claims the only natural hot springs (49°C/120°F) in Britain, usable both for bathing and drinking. The Romans built round the spa the city of Aquae Sulis; the ruins of the great temple and rectangular bathing pool are the finest Roman remains in Britain. During the Middle Ages it became an important walled city; the springs were Crown property, but were administered by the Church. Of medieval B. little remains but the Abbey, a fine perpendicular structure with fan tracery. Early in the 18th cent. B. was transformed by the organizing ability of Beau Nash, the business acumen of Ralph Allen, and the architectural genius of the two John Woods. Guests of high rank thronged the city. The Assembly Rooms (opened in 1771) were the finest suite of 18th cent. entertainment rooms in England until destroyed by German air attack in 1942; reconstructed, they were re-opened 1963. The Grand Pump Room was rebuilt in 1796. Pulteney Bridge is flanked by shops and houses. There is an annual music festival. Spa treatment was ended in 1976, but the establishment of Bath Univ. of Technology in 1966 is symptomatic of the growth of engineering industries. Bath stone, oolitic building stone is quarried nearby. There is a botanic garden in Victoria Park. Pop. (1972) 84,740.

BATH, Order of the. British order of knighthood, believed to have been founded in the reign of Henry IV (1399-1413). Formally instituted 1815, it incl. civilians from 1847 and women from 1970. There are 3 grades: Knights of the Grand Cross (G.C.B.), Knights Commanders (K.C.B.), and Knights Companions (C.B.).

BATHURST (bath'urst). Town of N.S.W., Australia, centre of a mining region. Pop. (1971) 17,170; and town of New Brunswick, Canada, pop. (1971) 19,000. It was also formerly the name of the cap. of the Gambia, now Banjul (q.v.).

BATHURST. Together with Orange (q.v.) Bathurst is being developed as a growth centre for central west New South Wales. The courthouse complex, with its graceful classical design is being carefully preserved. *Photo: Eric Wadsworth/Courtesy of Australian Information Service.*

BATHYSCAPHE and **BATHYSPHERE.** Types of diving apparatus, bell-shaped and spherical respectively, used to investigate animal life and conditions at great depths in the ocean.

BATIK. Javanese technique of applying coloured designs to fabric. The portions which it is desired to protect from the action of a given dye are covered with wax. This is practised throughout Indonesia, and was introduced into Europe by the Dutch.

BATIK. Applying the wax to the cloth preparatory to dyeing, the material being hung on a rack, contrary to European practice when a table is used. *Photo: Mireille Vautier.*

BATON ROUGE (bat'on roozh). Cap. of Louisiana, USA on the Mississippi. A major American deep water port, it is a rail and air centre, has huge oil and sugar refineries. There are two univs. Louisiana State (1860) and Southern (1881). The old Gothic-style State Capitol is an art gallery, and the present capitol building, begun under the admin. of Huey Long (q.v.), is magnificent in bronze and marble. Pop. (1970) 166,000.

BATTEN, Jean (1909-). NZ aviator. B. in New Zealand, she joined the London Aeroplane Club, and obtained her pilot's licence in 1930. She flew solo from England to Australia in 1934 and back in 1935 - the 1st woman to make the return journey, and estab. several world records.

BATTENBERG, Prince Louis Alexander (1854-1921). Admiral of the Fleet. Son of Prince Alexander of Hesse, he became a naturalized British subject in 1858, entered the RN in 1868, m. in 1884, Princess Victoria of Hesse, daughter of Queen Victoria's daughter Alice, and was 1st Sea Lord, 1912-14. In 1917 he renounced his German titles, adopted the surname Mountbatten (q.v.) and was created 1st Marquess of Milford Haven (q.v.).

The 2nd son of Prince Alexander, ALEXANDER JOSEPH (1857-93), became Prince Alexander I of Bulgaria. The 3rd son, Prince HENRY MAURICE (1858-96), m. in 1885 Queen Victoria's youngest daughter, Beatrice (d. 1944), became governor of the Isle of Wight and of Carisbrooke, took part in the Ashanti war, and d. at sea; his daughter, Victoria Eugénie Julia Ena, m. Alfonso XIII of Spain.

BATTERSEA. District of the Inner London bor. of Wandsworth on the S. bank of the Thames, noted for its park (incl. a funfair 1951-74), a classically-styled power station, and B. Dogs' Home (1860) for strays.

BATTLE. Small town in Sussex, England, the name of which is derived from the battle of Hastings, 1066, which was fought in the neighbourhood: the site was acquired for the nation in 1976. B. Abbey, a girls' school, incorporates part of the abbey built by William the Conqueror. Pop. *c.* 5,000.

BATTLE CRUISER. A type of warship with the displacement and armament of a battleship, and the speed and protection of a cruiser. They were considered obsolete after the S.W.W., but the *Kirov* (USSR 1980) is a 28,000 tonne B.C. with formidable anti-aircraft armament.

BATTLESHIP. Type of warship now obsolete, but formerly predominant over all others in armour and fire-power.

BATUMI (bahtōōm'i). Chief town of Adzhar A.S.S.R. Georgia, S.S.R., an important port on the S.E. of the Black Sea. Linked with oilfields of the Baku area by railway and pipelines, it has large oil-cracking plants. Pop. (1972) 106,000.

BAUDELAIRE (bōdlār'), **Charles Pierre** (1821-67). French poet. B. at Paris, he was sent to India (1841-3) by his guardians as a check to his dissipation, but remained so extravagant on his return that his inheritance was placed in the hands of a trustee. He joined the revolutionaries in 1848. His first book of verse, *Les Fleurs du Mal* (1857), caused considerable scandal, and was condemned by the censor as endangering public morals: author and printer were fined, and the most offensive pieces suppressed. In 1949 this sentence was quashed.

B. combined concentrated rhythmic and musical perfection with a morbid romanticism and eroticism which found beauty in decadence and evil. His later works incl. translations of E. A. Poe, whom he greatly admired; *Paradis artificiels, opium et haschisch* (1860), based on his own experience; an appreciation of *Richard Wagner et Tannhäuser à Paris* (1861); and *Petits poèmes en prose* (1868). His excesses impaired his health, and he spent the last 2 years of his life in hospitals at Brussels, where financial difficulties had driven him, and at Paris, where he d. B. prepared the way for Rimbaud, Verlaine, and the Symbolist school.

BAUDOUIN (bōhdoo-aṅ') (1930-). King of Belgium. In 1950 his father, Leopold III (q.v.), relinquished to him his constitutional powers, and B. was known until his succession in July 1951 as *Le Prince Royal.* In 1960 he m. Fabiola de Mora y Aragón (1928-), member of a Spanish noble family and author of fairy tales for children.

BAUHAUS (bow'hows), **Staatliches.** The 'State Building House' was founded in 1919 in an attempt to fuse all the arts and crafts in a unified whole, by the architect Walter Gropius (q.v.) at Weimar. Moved to Dessau under political pressure in 1925, it was closed by the Nazis in 1933. Associated with the B. were Klee, Kandinsky and Ludwig Mies van der Rohe. The tradition never died, and in 1972 the *Bauhaus Archive* was installed in new premises in W. Berlin.

BAUM (bowm), **Lyman Frank** (1856-1919). American author, creator of fantasies for children, such as *The Wonderful Wizard of Oz* (1900).

BAUXITE (boks'īt). The most widely known ore of aluminium, providing the major part of the world's supplies of that metal; it is named from the district of Les Baux, near Arles, in the S. of France, where it was first discovered. Bauxite ($Al_2O_3.2H_2O$) contains aluminium oxide, generally contaminated with compounds of iron, which give it a red colour.

BAVARIA (Ger. **Bayern**). The largest of the *Länder* of W. Germany. It occupies the greater part of the Danube basin, and was formerly predominantly agricultural, wheat, barley, sugar beet, etc. being grown. Since the S.W.W. it has developed into an industrial state: automotive, aero-space, electronics, optics, chemicals, plastics, oil-refining, textiles, glass toys. In the Fichtelgebirge in the N.E. there are large uranium deposits. Towns incl. Munich (cap.), Augsburg, Nuremberg, Ratisbon, Bayreuth. Area 70,550 sq.km (27,230 sq.m); pop. (1978) 10,819,300, of whom 70% are Roman Catholic.

The original Bavarians were Teutonic invaders from Bohemia who occupied the country at the end of the 5th cent. A.D. They were later ruled by dukes who recognized the supremacy of the Emperor. The House of Wittelsbach ruled parts of all of B. from 1181 to 1918; Napoleon made the ruler a king in 1806. In 1871 B. became a state of the German Empire. The last king, Ludwig III (1845-1921), abdicated in 1918, and B. declared itself a rep. Prince Albert (1905-), the present claimant to the throne is also the claimant to the Stuart 'right' to the British throne.

BAX, Sir Arnold Edward Trevor (1883-1953). British composer. His works were often based on Celtic legends, and incl. *The Garden of Fand* (a symphonic poem), *Tintagel* (an orchestral tone poem), and 'Coronation March', his last, played in Westminster Abbey for the Coronation of Queen Elizabeth II. He was Master of the King's Musick from 1943.

BAXTER, George (1804-67). British inventor in 1834 of a special process for printing in oil colours, which he applied successfully in book illustrations.

BAXTER, Richard (1615-91). English churchman. B. in Salop, he took orders in the C. of E. in 1638, became minister at Kidderminster, and during the Civil War he was a chaplain in the parliamentary army. Ill-health caused his retirement to Rouse-Lench, Worcs, where he

BAVARIA. Neuschwanstein Castle, in the Alpine foothills, was created for Ludwig II by Dollmann, Riedel and Hofman to rival the 11th century Wartburg, whose design it closely follows. *Photo: Courtesy of Lufthansa.*

composed that Puritan classic *The Saints' Everlasting Rest* (1650). After the Restoration he lived in London and was a royal chaplain. In 1662 the Act of Uniformity drove him out of the Church. In 1685 he was tried before Judge Jeffreys for alleged sedition, and imprisoned for nearly 18 months.

BAY. Name applied to various species of laurel (*Laurus*) and some other plants. The victor's laurel of the ancients was the sweet bay (*L. nobilis*), a native of S. Europe. Its aromatic evergreen leaves are used in cookery, for flavouring.

BAYARD (bā'ahrd), **Pierre du Terrail** (Chevalier) (1473-1524). French soldier. B. in Dauphiné, he served under Charles VIII, Louis XII, and Francis I, and was killed in action at the crossing of the Sesia in Italy. His heroic exploits in battle and in tournaments, his chivalry and magnanimity, won him the name of 'knight without fear and reproach'.

BAY CITY. Town in Michigan, USA, 160km (100m) N.W. of Detroit, at the mouth of the Saginaw r. on Saginaw Bay. Industries incl. car components, cranes, prefabricated buildings, oil refining, with attendant chemical products, cement, and sugar refining. Pop. (1970) 50,000.

BAYERN. German form of BAVARIA.

BAYEUX (bahyö'). Town in Calvados dept, France, on the Aure, 28km (18m) N.W. of Caen. The fine cathedral is mainly 13th cent. Gothic, and a museum houses the B. Tapestry (q.v.). B. was the first town in W. Europe to be liberated by the Allies, 8 June 1944. Pop. (1973) 12,870.

BAYEUX 'TAPESTRY'. A linen hanging, made about A.D. 1067-70 which gives a vivid pictorial record of the invasion of England by William the Conqueror in 1066. It is 70m (231ft) long, and 50cm (20in) wide, embroidered with woollen threads in blue, green, red, and yellow, and contains 72 separate scenes with descriptive wording in Latin.

BAYLE (bāl), **Pierre** (1647-1706). French critic and controversial writer. Son of a Calvinist pastor, he held chairs of philosophy at Sedan and Rotterdam. Suspected of rationalist views, he was suspended in 1693. Three years later appeared his *Dictionnaire historique et critique*, which had a wide influence, particularly on the French Encyclopedists.

BAYONNE (bahyon'). Town in Pyrénées-Atlantiques dept, France, 5km (3m) from the mouth of the Ardour, nr the Spanish frontier. There are fortifications by Vauban, and the bayonet was invented here. It is a centre of Basque life. There are chemical, metallurgical and leather industries, and the natural gas field at Lacq (1951) is one of the world's largest. Pop. (1975) 120,400.

BAYOU (bī'-oo). Corruption of Fr. *boyau* 'gut': in southern USA an oxbow lake or marshy offshoot of a river. Bs. may be formed, as in the lower Mississippi, by a river flowing in exaggeratedly wide curves in flat country, and then cutting a straight course across them in time of flood, so leaving 'loops' of dead water behind.

BAYREUTH (bī'roit). Town in Bavaria, W. Germany, 68km (42m) N.E. of Nuremberg, famous for its Wagnerian associations. The Wagner Theatre was opened in 1876, and here the Wagner festivals are held, attracting music-lovers from all over the world. Pop. (1971) 60,600.

BAZAINE (bahzān'), **Achille François** (1811-88). Marshal of France. B. at Versailles, he enlisted as a private soldier in 1831 and had a rapid rise. He commanded the French troops in Mexico in 1862-7, and was made a marshal in 1864. In the Franco-Prussian War B. commanded the 3rd Corps of the Army of the Rhine, allowed himself to be cooped up in the fortress of Metz, and capitulated on 27 Oct. 1870, with nearly 180,000 men. For this in 1873 he was court-martialled and sentenced to death; the sentence was at once commuted to 20 years' imprisonment. In 1874 he escaped to Spain.

BEACHY HEAD. Between Seaford and Eastbourne in Sussex, the eastern termination of the S. Downs, and the loftiest headland 162m (531ft) on the S. coast of England. The lighthouse off the shore is 38m (125ft) high. The French name for the promontory is Béveziers.

BEACONSFIELD (bē'konzfēld), **Benjamin Disraeli,** earl of (1804-81). Conservative statesman and novelist. The son of Isaac D., a distinguished Jewish man of letters, he was baptized a Christian at the age of 13. He was ed. at a private school, and after a period in a solicitor's office wrote the novel *Vivian Grey* (1826) and others, and the brilliant pamphlet *Vindication of the English Constitution* (1835). D. entered parliament in 1837 after 4 unsuccessful attempts, and 2 years later he m. Mrs Wyndham Lewis, widow of a parliamentary colleague.

Excluded from Peel's government of 1841-6, D. formed his 'Young England' group to keep a critical eye on Peel's conservatism. Its ideas were expounded in the novels *Coningsby* (1844), *Sybil* (1845), and *Tancred* (1847). When Peel decided in 1846 to repeal the Corn Laws, D. opposed the measure in a series of witty and effective speeches; Peel's govt fell soon after, and D. gradually came to be recognized as the leader of the Conservative Party in the Commons. He gave his own account of these events in his *Life of Lord George Bentinck* (1852).

During the next 20 years the Conservatives formed short-lived minority govts in 1852, in 1858-9, and in 1866-8, with Lord Derby as P.M. and D. as Chancellor of the Exchequer and leader of the Commons. In 1852 D. first proposed discrimination in income tax between earned and unearned income, but without success. The 1858-9 govt legalized the admission of Jews to parliament, and transferred the govt of India from the E. India Co. to the Crown. In 1866 the Conservatives took office after defeating a Liberal Reform Bill, and then attempted to secure the credit of widening the franchise by the Reform Bill of 1867. On Lord Derby's retirement in 1868 D. became P.M., but a few months later he was defeated at a general election. During the 6 years of opposition which followed he pub. another novel, *Lothair* (1870), and estab. a Conservative Central Office, the prototype of modern party organizations.

In 1874 he took office with a majority of 100. Some useful reform measures were carried, such as the Artisans' Dwelling Act, which empowered local authorities to undertake slum-clearance, but the out-standing feature of the government's policy was its Imperialism. It was Disraeli's personal initiative which purchased from the Khedive of Egypt a controlling interest in the Suez Canal, conferred on the Queen the title of Empress of India, and sent the Prince of Wales on the first royal tour of that country. The Bulgarian revolt of 1876 and the subsequent Russo-Turkish War of 1877-8 provoked the most famous of the political duels between Disraeli and Gladstone. The crisis was concluded by the Congress of Berlin (1878), where B. - he had accepted an earldom 2 years before - was principal British delegate, and whence he brought home 'peace with honour'. The government was defeated in 1880, and a year later B. d. after writing *Endymion*. He was the founder and chief inspiration of the modern Conservative Party.

BEACONSFIELD. Benjamin Disraeli, earl of Beaconsfield, prime minister of England 1868, and 1874-1880. *Photo: Camera Press.*

BEACONSFIELD (be'konzfēld). English town in Bucks 37km (23m) W.N.W. of London. Edmund Waller and Burke lived in B., and Benjamin Disraeli, whose seat was Hughenden Manor in the neighbourhood, took his title from it. In 1949 the Manor was opened as a Disraelian Museum. Pop. (1971) 12,000.

BEADLE (bēdl), **George Wells** (1903-). American biologist. B. at Wahoo, Nebraska, he was prof. of biology at the California Inst. of Technology 1946-61, and in 1958 shared a Nobel prize for his work with Edward L. Tatum in biochemical genetics.

BEAGLE. A miniature foxhound used for hunting the hare on foot. Of terrier size, the B. can be of any recognized foxhound colour.

BEAGLE CHANNEL. Channel to the S of Tierra del Fuego, named after the ship of Darwin's voyage. Three islands at its E end are disputed between Argentina and Chile, but what is really at issue is the krill and oil in the sea within the 200 m territorial waters, and the dependent 'sector' of the Antarctic, together with its resources.

BEALE, Dorothea (1831-1906). British pioneer in feminine education. Dau. of a London doctor, she became a teacher at the Queen's Coll. for Ladies, and as headmistress of the Ladies' Coll. at Cheltenham from 1858 was influential in raising the standard of women's education.

BEAM WEAPONS. The 'death ray' weapons of science fiction were under development by the major powers by 1980. Most frequently discussed are: 1. The *high energy laser* (HEL) producing a beam of high accuracy which burns through the surface of its target. The USSR is thought to have an HEL able to put out of action orbiting US reconnaissance spacecraft. 2. The *charged particle beam* (CPB) which uses either electrons or protons, which have been accelerated almost to the speed of light, to slice through its target.

BEAN. Name given to the seeds of various leguminous and other plants, which are rich in nitrogenous or proteid matter, and are grown both for human consumption and as food for cattle and horses. The broad bean (*Vicia faba*) has been cultivated in Europe since prehistoric times. The French bean, kidney bean, or haricot (*Phaseolus vulgaris*) is possibly of S. American origin; the runner bean (*P. multiflorus*) is closely allied to it, but differs in its climbing habit. Among Bs. of warmer countries are the Lima bean (*P. lunatus*) of S. America, the soya of China and Japan (*Glycine soja*), and the winged bean (*Psophocarpus tetragonolobus*) of S.E. Asia, of which the tuberous roots have recently been discovered to contain 20% protein, and which has great potential as a main crop in tropical areas where protein deficiency is common. The tiny Asiatic mung bean (*Phaseolus mung*) forms the bean sprouts of China. Canned baked beans are a variety of *Phaseolus vulgaris* which grows well in the USA: development of a variety suited to the British climate was nearing success in 1980.

BEAR. Large or medium sized, heavily-built mammal, forming the family Ursidae of the order Carnivora, distinguished by their protrusible lips, very short tail, and broad plantigrade feet armed with long, non-retractile claws; the teeth too are characteristic. Bs. are chiefly vegetarian in diet, breed once a year, and usually have 2 cubs in the litter.

The common brown bear *(Ursus arctos)* extends from Europe through Central Asia and is represented by many local races. The colour varies from blackish or reddish brown to grey. These bears hibernate where it is very cold in winter, and eat vegetable food, insects, fish, and small mammals, but sometimes raid farm property, and carry off cattle, pigs, or other livestock. Consequently, and also because of the value of their skins, they have become greatly reduced in numbers. They rarely attack man, except when cornered.

The grizzly B. (*U.a. horribilis*) of N. America is closely related to the European brown bear, which it resembles in size, appearance, and habits. There are several races, chiefly inhabiting the Rocky Mountains; but it has been exterminated in many districts. Stories of its ferocity have probably been exaggerated. The N. American black B. (*Euarctos americanus*) is just under 1m (3ft) high. Other species are the Himalayan Black B. (*Selenarctos tibetanus*), the Malayan B. (*Helarctos malayanus*), the sloth B. (*Melursus ursinus*) of Hindustan and Sri Lanka, and smallest of all, the spectacled B. (*Tremarctos ornatus*) of S. America.

Lastly there is the polar or white B. (*Thalarctos maritimus*) distinguished by its white coat, inability to climb, and hairy soles of the feet - characters that are adaptations to arctic life. Its prey comprises fish, seals, and stranded whales. It will also eat seaweed and, in the summer, lichen and grass. This is one of the largest Bs., a good sized male being *c.* 3m (9ft) long.

A still larger B. was the extinct cave B. (*U. spelaeus*) of prehistoric Europe.

BEAR. The Syrian brown bear, a specimen at Whipsnade. *Photo: Zoological Society of London.*

BEAR BAITING. Brutal sport once popular in Europe; the bear was chained to a stake and baited by dogs. It was abolished in Britain in 1835.

BEAR, Great and **Little.** Two constellations, in Lat. called *Ursa major* and *minor* (q.v.).

BEARDSLEY, Aubrey Vincent (1872-98). British black-and-white artist. A musical phenomenon as a boy, he began to study art at the age of 19 and developed an unconventional style which evoked much criticism. In 1894 he became prominent as illustrator to the *Yellow Book.* He became a R.C. in 1897, and d. at Mentone of consumption.

BEARS AND BULLS. *See* STOCK EXCHANGE.

BEAS (bē'as). One of the 5 rivers which give its name to Punjab, B. is an upper tributary of the Sutlej. The ancient Hyphasis, it marked the limit of the invasion of India by Alexander the Great.

BEAT GENERATION. The beatniks of the 1950s, a word coined by Jack Kerouac (q.v.) whose works were their bible, using a combination of '*beat*itude' and 'sput*nik*'. They rejected the work ethic, wore jeans as a symbolic 'uniform' and used drugs.

BEATIFICATION. *See* CANONIZATION.

BEATITUDES (bē-at'itūdz; Latin *beatitudo*, blessedness, or happiness). The sayings of Jesus reported in Matt. v, 1-12; Lk. vi, 20-38, depicting the spiritual qualities which are to characterize members of the Kingdom of God.

BEATLES. British pop music group formed in 1960. The members who reached fame were all born in Liverpool: George Harrison (1943-), John Winston Lennon (1940-80), James Paul McCartney (1942-) and Richard Starkey, stage-name 'Ringo Starr' (1940-), where they made a reputation in the Cavern Club. Using songs written by Lennon and McCartney they developed a distinctive 'Mersey beat', and the 'Liverpool sound' took the pop world by storm 1963-5. They continued to exert tremendous influence in style of dress, way of life, and lines of thought, e.g. the fashion for mysticism from 1967, beyond their break-up as a group in 1971, when they developed as single performers. Famous numbers incl. 'She Loves You', 'Can't Buy Me Love', 'Yester-day', 'Yellow Submarine', and 'A Hard Day's Night'; and the complex electronic syntheses of 'Sgt Pepper's Lonely Hearts Club Band' took 6 months in the recording studio to produce. Lennon was shot by an unstable fan in NY.

BEATLES. The makers of the modern 'Pop' scene. In the foreground, Ringo; George and Paul decorously on the sofa, and John propping up the wall. *Photo: Bruce McBroom/Camera Press.*

BEATON (bē'ton), **Sir Cecil** (1904-80). British photographer and designer. He produced notable portrait studies and setting for plays and films, e.g. the London and

N.Y. production of *My Fair Lady*; and scenery and costumes for ballets.

BEATON (bē'ton or bā'ton), **David** (1494-1546). Scottish cardinal and statesman. A chief min. of James V, he was made primate of Scotland in 1539. Under Mary Queen of Scots he opposed the alliance with England, persecuted the Reformers, and was assassinated by a band of fanatics at St Andrews.

BEATRIX (bē'atriks) (1936-). Queen of the Netherlands. Eldest daughter of Juliana, she succeeded to the throne on her mother's abdication in 1980. In 1966 she married W German diplomat Claus von Amsberg (1926-), created Prince Claus of the Netherlands, after some initial popular opposition. The heir to the throne is Prince Alexander (1967-).

BEATTY (bē'ti), **David,** 1st earl (1871-1936). British admiral. Entering the navy in 1888, he commanded the cruiser squadron 1912-16, and bore the brunt of the Battle of Jutland. In 1916 he succeeded Jellicoe in command of the Grand Fleet, and in 1918 received the surrender of the German Fleet, being subsequently made Admiral of the Fleet and receiving an earldom and the O.M.

BEAUFORT SCALE. System of recording wind velocity, devised in 1806 by Admiral Sir Francis Beaufort (1774-1857), who became hydrographer to the Royal Navy in 1829. It consists of the numbers 0-17, calm being indicated by 0 and a hurricane by 12: 13-17 indicate degrees of hurricane force. In 1874 it received international recognition.

BEAUFORT SEA. Section of the Arctic Ocean off the N Alaskan coast, named after Sir Francis Beaufort. Oil drilling is allowed only in the winter months because the sea is the breeding and migration route of bowhead whales, the staple diet of local Eskimo.

BEAUHARNAIS (bō ahrnā'), **Alexandre** (1760-94). French viscount, who served in the American War of Independence, joined the popular party in the early days of the Revolution, but was guillotined for lack of zeal. He m. Joséphine Tascher de la Pagerie, afterwards wife and empress of Napoleon I, and had two children: **Hortense** (1783-1837), who m. in 1802 Louis Bonaparte, a younger brother of Napoleon, and became the mother of Napoleon III, and **Eugène** (1781-1824), who was made a prince by Napoleon and viceroy of Italy in 1805. After 1814 he lived in retirement in Bavaria.

BEAUJOLAIS (bōzholeh'). A red wine of the massif central, France, drunk while young. The traditional broaching date was 15 Nov., and the new vintage is still taken to London in a commemorative 'run', as the wine is very popular in England.

BEAULIEU (bew'li). English village in Hants, 10km (6m) N.E. of Lymington. An abbey founded 1204 is the home of Lord Montagu of Beaulieu. Here is the Montagu Motor Museum. Pop. (1974) 1,170.

BEAUMARCHAIS (bōmahrshā'), **Pierre Augustin Caron de** (1732-99). French dramatist. B. in Paris, the son of a watchmaker named Caron, he attracted the notice of Louis XV and was given a court appointment. He m. a wealthy widow, assumed the title of de Beaumarchais, won a fortune by speculation, and on his wife's death made another good match. His great comedies *Le barbier de Seville* (1775) and *Le Mariage de Figaro* (1778, but prohibited until 1784 because of revolutionary tendencies) are best known in England by the operatic versions of Rossini and Mozart. Louis XVI entrusted B. with secret missions, and he was responsible for the shipment of arms to the American colonies during the War of Independence, conducting a private traffic with great profit. Accused of treason in 1792, he fled to poverty in Holland and England. In 1876 he returned to Paris where he died.

BEAUMONT, Francis (1584-1616). English poet and dramatist. B. at Grace Dieu, Leics, the son of a judge and brother to the poet Sir John B. (1583-1627), he studied law and in 1602 pub. a love poem *Salmacis and Hermaphroditus.* From c. 1608 he collaborated with John Fletcher, with whom he lived until the latter's marriage in 1613. The best of their joint works are: *Philaster* (*c.* 1610), *The Maid's Tragedy* (*c.* 1611), and *A King and No King* (*c.* 1611). *The Woman Hater* (*c.* 1606) and *The Knight of the Burning Pestle* (*c.* 1607) are ascribed to B. alone. B. had greater powers of thought and versification than Fletcher, as well as excelling in plot construction. He was buried in Westminster Abbey.

BEAUNE (bōn). French town in the dept of Côte d'Or, 37km (23m) S. by W. of Dijon, a centre of the Burgundy wine trade. Pop. (1975) 17,500.

BEAUTY CULTURE. The art of improving the physical appearance.

The practice of painting the face, of dressing the hair, and of using lotions and perfumes to enhance natural beauty dates back to ancient times. Unguent jars, still fragrant with musk, were found in the 4,000-year-old tomb of King Tutankhamen. Cosmetics, oils for the skin, perfumes, and aromatic baths were known to the Egyptians. Henna, which is still used as a hair dye, was used in the time of Cleopatra to colour the finger and toe nails. The Greeks used perfumes, many of which were imported from Egypt, and also experimented with hair dyes and bleaches. They introduced cosmetics into the Roman Empire, and by the time of Nero it was common for Romans of both sexes to use perfumes, and to indulge in luxurious baths. Kohl was used for painting the eyes, pumice powder for whitening the teeth, and *fucus* as a rouge for the lips and cheeks.

Cosmetics were first used in Britain at the time of the Roman occupation, but they were uncommon until many cents. later. During the 11th and 12th cents. the Crusaders brought all kinds of perfumes and cosmetics from the east. In Elizabethan times powders, rouges, and eye cosmetics were popular; ladies-in-waiting took milk baths; Mary, Queen of Scots, bathed in wine. These practices were suppressed during the Commonwealth, but were revived under Charles II. Smallpox scars and the ravages of other diseases were concealed by means of heavy make-up.

Herbal lotions and packs were later sold to improve the complexion, but it was not until the 20th cent. that make-up became generally accepted by women of all classes. The manufacture of cosmetics has now developed into a major industry, and many women pay regular visits to beauty salons, not only for treatment for their hair (the 1st permanent 'wave', created in 1905 by Charles Nessler, was a painful 9-hr operation), but for massage, skin conditioning, facial treatment and manicure. Since the S.W.W. toilet preparations for men have become increasingly popular, and modern fashions with their revealing lines and emphasis on active leisure clothes have dictated greater attention to the body as well as the face for both sexes. Salons specializing, not merely in getting rid of excess fat, but in developing perfect proportions and fitness by exercises and other means, have multiplied.

BEAUVAIS (bōvā′). French town, cap. of Oise dept, 74km (46m) N.W. of Paris. The cathedral (1247-1558) is one of the noblest in France, and the town is famous for its carpets, rugs, and hand-made tapestries (now made in Paris). Pop. (1975) 56,725.

BEAUVOIR (bohvwahr′), **Simone de** (1908-). French writer, who taught philosophy at the Sorbonne 1931-43. Her books incl. a number of novels illustrating philosophical theories, e.g. *All Men are Mortal* (1947); *The Second Sex* (1949), a sensational attack on the man-made world of values women must inhabit; *Les Mandarins* (1954), a novel of post-war Parisian intellectualism with characters resembling Camus, Koestler and Sartre. Essential to an understanding of her work are the 2 autobiographical vols. *Memoirs of a Dutiful Daughter* and *The Prime of Life.*

BEAVER (bē′ver). Sole representative of the family Castoridae of the order Rodentia; found in Europe, Central Asia, and North America, and distinguished mainly by its broad, flat, scaly tail and webbed hind feet - adaptations to aquatic life.

The European B. (*Castor fiber*) survives in Central Asia and, under strict protection, in small numbers in the Elbe and Rhine, and in Norway and elsewhere in Europe. The American B. (*Castor canadensis*) is widely distributed in N. America. Both species have a coat of thick brown fur impervious to water, grow to just over 1m (3ft) including the tail, attain a weight of 22.5kg (50lb) and live up to 15 years. There are usually 4 young born in the spring in a 'lodge' of logs and mud.

The B. is a valuable fur-bearing animal, and also yields castoreum, secreted by glands at the base of the tail, which is used for perfumes.

BEAVERBROOK, William Maxwell Aitken, 1st baron B. (1879-1964). Canadian newspaper proprietor. B. at Maple, Ontario, he made his fortune by a merger of the principal Canadian cement firms in 1910, when he settled in England and became a Conservative M.P. A close association with Bonar Law and other Conservative leaders gave him a strong influence in the F.W.W., and he received a peerage in 1917 and became Min. of Information in 1918. From 1919 he was in full control of the policy of the *Daily Express,* soon after founding the *Sunday Express* and buying the *Evening Standard.* In 1929-31 he launched a campaign for Empire Free Trade and against Baldwin's leadership of the Conservative Party, while during the 1930s he advocated a policy of 'splendid isolation' in Europe. In the S.W.W. he was Min. of Aircraft Production 1940-1, Min. of Supply 1941-2 and Lord Privy Seal 1943-5. Among his books are *Men and Power* (1956) and *The Decline and Fall of Lloyd George* (1963).

BEBINGTON. English town on the left bank of the Mersey estuary, Merseyside, just S. of Birkenhead. It incl. Port Sunlight (1888, a model estate for Unilever workers), and manufacturing soap, margarine, oils, etc. Pop. (1972) 62,610.

BECCARIA (bekahrē′ah), **Cesare,** marquis of (1738-94). Italian philanthropical writer. B. in Milan, he pub. in 1764 a treatise on *Crimes and Punishments.* His arguments against torture and capital punishment, and in favour of education as a means of preventing crime, had their effect upon penal codes, and his phrase 'the greatest happiness of the greatest number', shortly became the watchword of Bentham, Romilly, and the English Utilitarians.

BEAVER. Branches are painstakingly ferried to dam a stream. In this way the water is kept at the right depth, so that it does not freeze to the bottom and the beavers can still swim under water to their lodges in mid-stream. *Photo: Pat Morris/Ardea.*

BECHUANALAND. *See* BOTSWANA.

BECKET, Thomas (1118-70). English churchman. The son of a rich Norman merchant, he passed from the service of Theobald, Archbishop of Canterbury, to that of Henry II, who created him Chancellor of England in 1155. When he became Archbishop of Canterbury in 1162 he devoted all his energy to resisting royal encroachments on the privileges of the clergy, and as a result Henry's friendship turned to bitter hatred. His opposition to Henry's attempt by the Constitutions of Clarendon (1164) to bring the clergy under the jurisdiction of the royal courts provoked open hostility between them, and B. fled to France. He returned in 1170 when a reconciliation was patched up; but the quarrel soon broke out again, and 4 knights, encouraged by a hasty outburst of the king's, murdered B. in Canterbury Cathedral. He was canonized in 1172, and his shrine remained a popular object of pilgrimage until the Reformation.

BECKETT, Samuel (1906-). Irish dramatist, who settled in Paris as a disciple of Joyce, and published a number of novels and some verse. He made a world reputation with his play *Waiting for Godot* (1952), in which two tramps wait endlessly for 'Godot' and debate equally endlessly. Later plays incl. *Fin de Partie* (End Game: 1957). Nobel prizewinner 1969.

BECKFORD, William (1760-1844). British writer and eccentric. B. at Fonthill, Wilts, he inherited an immense fortune, became a M.P. in 1784, but shortly afterwards was obliged to leave England owing to scandals in his private life. *Vathek,* a fantastic Arabian Nights' tale, was pub. in Paris in 1787. In 1796 B. returned to England, rebuilt Fonthill Abbey, and filled it with fantastic curiosities. This he sold in 1822, and retired to Bath.

BECQUEREL (bekrel'), **Antoine Henri** (1852-1908). French physicist, renowned for his discovery in 1896 of the *Becquerel rays*, the first indications of radio-activity: these were later re-named gamma rays. He shared with the Curies the Nobel Prize for physics in 1903.

BEDDOES, Thomas Lovell (1803-49). British poet and dramatist. A romantic, working under the influence of the Elizabethan dramatists, he started his most famous play, the incoherent *Death's Jest Book*, in 1825, but it was not pub. until 1850, much revised. From Oxford he had gone on to medical studies in Germany, and practised as a physician in Zurich until driven out by political events in 1839. After several suicide attempts, he succeeded in poisoning himself with curare. His lyrics and various dramatic fragments are now highly regarded by connoisseurs.

BEDE (bēd) (*c.* 673-735). English theologian and historian, known as the Venerable Bede. B. at Monkwearmouth, Durham, he entered the local monastery at the age of 7, later transferring to Jarrow, where he became a priest *c.* 703. He devoted his life to writing and teaching, the most famous of his pupils being Egbert, archbishop of York. He wrote many scientific, theological and historical works, the most celebrated being his *Historia Ecclesiastica Gentis Anglorum*, finished in 731. He d. and was buried at Jarrow, but his remains were removed to Durham in the 11th cent.

BEDFORD, John Robert Russell, 13th duke of (1917-). British nobleman. He succeeded his father, a noted naturalist, in the title in 1953. Under his aegis the family seat at Woburn in Bedfordshire was restored and is visited by thousands annually.

BEDFORD. Town in Beds, England, admin. H.Q. of the co., on the Ouse 37km (23m) S.W. of Cambridge. Industries incl. agricultural machinery, diesel engines, bricks, etc. Bunyan began to write *The Pilgrim's Progress* in B. jail; Bunyan Meeting House stands on the site of the barn in which he preached. Pop. (1971) 73,300.

BEDFORDSHIRE (Beds). A S. midland county of England, lying mainly in the Ouse basin, and for the most part lowland, devoted to agriculture. Chief towns are Bedford, admin. H.Q.; Luton (largest town), Dunstable, and Leighton-Linslade. Area 1,235 sq.km (477 sq.m); pop. (1978) 494,700.

BEDLAM. Popular name of Bethlehem hospital, the oldest public lunatic asylum in Europe with the exception of that of Granada in Spain. It was originally founded in Bishopsgate, London, as a priory in 1247, was incorporated by Henry VIII in 1547, and was removed to Moorfields in 1675, in 1815 to Lambeth, and in 1930 to West Wickham, near Croydon.

BEDLINGTON. Breed of terrier dog supposed to have been produced by the Northumberland pitmen of about 100 years ago. It has much in common with the Dandie Dinmont, though in conformation like the greyhound. The colours are blue or liver.

BEDOUIN (bed'ooin) or **Beduin.** Nomadic tribesman (Arabic 'desert-dweller') of Arabia and N Africa, now becoming increasingly settled.

BEE. Four-winged stinging insect of the superfamily Apoidea in the order Hymenoptera. There are over 12,000 species, of which less than a twentieth are social in habit.

The solitary bees incl. species useful in pollinating orchards in spring, and may make their nests in tunnels under the ground, in hollow plant stems, etc. The 'cuckoo'

BEDOUIN. Gradually the Bedouin are becoming urbanized, but in remote areas the traditional way of life survives untouched. The little girls will still adopt the heavy veiling worn by their mothers as soon as they are old enough. *Photo: Fred Peer/Camera Press.*

bees lay their eggs in the nests of the bumblebees, which they closely resemble.

The social bees include the bumblebees, and the hive bee (*Apis mellifera*), which establishes perennial colonies in which membership may rise to about 80,000. These are overwhelmingly infertile females (workers), large fertile males (drones), and the even larger single fertile female (queen). In commercial beekeeping the natural aerial mating of an emergent daughter queen with the most powerful of the drones has been replaced by artificial insemination. Swarming, the exit from the hive of the old queen with her attendants, leaving the new queen in possession, is not allowed to happen. The wax 'comb' (made from a secretion exuded by the workers) of hexagonal cells is used to rear new members of the colony and store honey: to concentrate energy on honey production, partly artificial combs are commercially used. Bees transmit information to each other about honey and pollen sources by a dance, each movement giving rise to sound impulses which are picked up by tiny hairs on the back of the bee's head, and the orientation of the dance also having significance - the 'language of the bees'. Bee and wasp stings may be fatal to those who are particularly allergic, and in 1980 a course of vaccine treatment using concentrated venom was developed.

BEECH. Genus of trees (*Fagus*), of which the common B. (*F. sylvatica*) grows as a forest tree throughout Europe. Its wood rots easily, but is used for making small objects of household use. The nuts or mast are a food for pigs.

BEECHAM, Sir Thomas (1879-1961). English conductor, grandson of Thomas B. (1820-1907), founder of the pharmaceutical firm. As conductor to the B. Orchestra (formed 1908) and the B. Opera Co. (formed 1915; later the British National Opera Co.), he introduced new life into the world of British music, and in 1911 brought the Russian ballet to England. At his death he was still conductor of the Royal Philharmonic Orchestra, which he had founded in 1947. Renowned as an interpreter of Mozart and Haydn he estab. the musical reputation of Delius, of whom he pub. a biography in 1959, by his ceaseless advocacy. He was knighted in 1916, succeeded his father as 2nd bt in the same year, and in 1944 pub. the autobiographical *A Mingled Chime.* His mischievous wit, fiery temper, and personal magnetism rendered him an unforgettable figure.

BEECHER, Lyman (1775-1863). American Presbyterian divine, one of the most influential pulpit orators of his time. He was the father of Harriet Beecher Stowe (q.v.), and of Henry Ward B. (1813-87), Congregational minister, pastor of Plymouth church, Brooklyn, N.Y., from 1847, a leader in the movement for the abolition of slavery, and an eloquent preacher.

BEECHING, Richard, baron (1913–85). British scientist and administrator. A director of I.C.I. 1957–61 and 1965–8, he was chairman of Brit. Railways Board 1963-5, when the *B. Report* (1963) planning concentration on inter-city passenger traffic and a freight system was controversial.

BEERBOHM, Sir Max (1872-1956). British writer, the half-brother of the actor-manager Sir Herbert Beerbohm Tree (1853-1917). B. in London, he contributed to *The Yellow Book,* publishing the essays later ironically as *The Works of Max Beerbohm* (1896), and succeeded Shaw as dramatic critic to the *Saturday Review.* A superb stylist, B. produced one novel *Zuleika Dobson* (1911), parodies - *A Christmas Garland* (1912), and vols. of exquisite caricatures, e.g. *The Poet's Corner* and *Rossetti and his Circle.* From 1910 he lived in Rapallo, Italy, and was knighted in 1939.

BEERSHĒ'BA. Market town and road centre of Israel, cap. of the Negev, 72km (45m) S.W. of Jerusalem. A settlement from the Stone Age, in the 1950s B. developed industrially. Pop. (1971) 81,000.

BEET. Genus of plants (*Beta*) of the order Chenopodiaceae. *B. vulgaris* grows wild on seashores in many parts of the Old World. Several varieties are cultivated for their fleshy taproot, such as the red beet and the mangold-wurzel, or for their leaves, such as the white or spinach-beet. The sugar-beet (q.v.) is the variety with the greatest commercial importance.

BEETHOVEN (bāt'hōven), **Ludwig van** (1770-1827). German composer. Born in Bonn, the son and grandson of musicians, he became deputy organist at the court of the Elector of Cologne at Bonn before he was 12, and later had lessons from Mozart and Haydn, whose influence dominated his early work. From 1801 he was troubled by increasing deafness (total by 1824), but continued composition, and from 1809 had a small allowance from aristocratic patrons. He fell in love, often with his noble pupils, but never married, and the shiftless behaviour of a nephew whose guardian he was caused him great grief. His music which developed increasing complexity and breadth of construction was influential in the development of all forms, but especially the symphony.

His works incl. the *Egmont* overture, the opera *Fidelio,* 5 piano concertos and one for violin, 32 piano sonatas (incl. the *Apassionata*), 16 string quartets, the Mass in D (*Missa Solemnis*), and 9 symphonies, notably the Third ('Eroica', originally intended to be dedicated to Napoleon, with whom Beethoven became disillusioned), the Fifth ('Victory', because the rhythm of the opening corresponds to 'V' in the Morse code and was used in Allied radio broadcasts in the Second World War), Sixth ('Pastoral') and Ninth ('Choral' which incl. the passage chosen as the National Anthem of Europe).

BEETHOVEN. A portrait by Louis Letronne signed by the composer and considered 'very like'. *Photo: Courtesy of the Royal College of Music.*

BEETLE. Common name of insects in the order Coleoptera (Greek sheath-winged), which have leathery fore-wings which fold down in a protective sheath over their membranous hind-wings which are used for flight. They pass through a complete metamorphosis, the young larval forms being very varied, and include some of the largest and smallest of all insects - the South American Hercules beetle (*Dynastes hercules*) reaches 15 cm (6 in) long. They are also the largest single order in the animal kingdom with some 250,000 species. Some are useful, but many are extremely destructive. The more familiar incl. the click beetle, Colorado beetle, cotton boll weevil, death watch beetle, firefly, glow worm, scarab, and woodworm.

BEETON (bē'ton), **Isabella** (1836-65). British housewifery expert. Wife of a publisher, she produced *Beeton's Household Management* (1859), the first really comprehensive work.

BEGIN (bā'gin), **Menachem** (1913-). Israeli statesman. Born in Poland, he became a leader of the extremist Irgun Zvai Leumi organization in Palestine from 1942. He was Prime Minister of Israel 1977–83, as head of the right-wing Likud, and in 1978 shared a Nobel peace prize with Sadat for his share in the Camp David peace agreement. After 1980 he was increasingly criticized for his opposition to a Palestine state, and resigned 1984.

BEGŌ'NIA. Genus of plants of the family Begoniaceae. There are numerous species, natives of the tropics, espec. S. America and India. They have fleshy succulent leaves, and the flowers are often brightly coloured.

BEHAN (bē'an), **Brendan** (1923-64). Irish author and playwright. B. in Dublin, he became an IRA member in 1937. Sentenced to 3yrs Borstal training almost immediately on his arrival in England in 1939 (for carrying explosives), he was deported on release to Dublin. Involved in an Easter Day parade incident there which resulted in the shooting of a policeman, he was sentenced in 1942 to 14yrs imprisonment, but released in 1946. A house-painter by trade, he started writing in 1951, achieving success with the play *The Quare Fellow* (1956), based on his prison experiences. Other works incl. the autobiographical *Borstal Boy* (1958), and the play *The Hostage* (1958). A raconteur of genius, B. had the gift of language, and great warmth of personality.

BEHĀ'VIOURISM. School of psychology originating in USA, of which the leading exponent was John Broadus Watson (1878-1958). Behaviourists maintain that all human activity can ultimately be explained in terms of conditioned reactions or 'reflexes' and habits formed in consequence.

BE'HRENS, Peter (1868-1940). German architect. He pioneered the adaptation of architecture to modern industry, as in the AEG turbine factory in Berlin (1909), and influenced Le Corbusier and Gropius.

BEHRING, Emil von (1854-1917). German bacteriologist, the founder of the science of immunology.

BEHRING (or **Bering**), **Vitus Jonassen** (1680-1741). Danish navigator. In 1728-30 he sailed from Kamchatka northward along the Siberian coast to 67°N., and proved that Asia and America are not connected. In a second expedition 1740-1, during which he d. on B. Island, he sighted Alaska and so discovered America from the east. *Bering Island*, in the S.W. of *B. Sea* (the section of the Pacific between Asia and America to the N. of the Aleutians) and *B. Strait*, which links the Pacific and Arctic Oceans, are named after him.

BEIDERBECKE (bī'debek), **Bix** (**Leon Bismarcke**) (1903-31). American jazz composer, a virtuoso of the piano and cornet.

BEIJING (bājēng'). Pinyin form of Peking.

BEIRA (bā'rah). Port at the mouth of the r. Pungwe, Mozambique. It is an important outlet for Zimbabwe and Malawi, but Zambia now also uses the Tanzam Railway to Dar-es-Salaam. Pop. (1970) 59,200.

BEIRUT (bāroot'). Cap. and port of the Lebanon. Its status as an internat. financial and educational centre was destroyed by the civil war 1975-6: it also had a reputation as the focus of espionage routes. Pop. (1978) 702,000.

BEJAIA (be'jīah). Seaport in Algeria, 193km (120m) E. of Algiers, linked by pipeline with oil wells at Hassi Messaoud. Formerly Bougie, it was renamed B. on independence. Pop. (1974) 104,000.

BELASCO, David (1859-1931). American playwright whose plays incl. *Madame Butterfly* (1900), and *The Girl of the Golden West* (1905), both of which served Puccini as libretti for operas.

BELÉM. Brazilian port, naval base, and air centre. It was founded c. 1615 as Santa Maria de Belém do Grãs Pará, often abbreviated to Pará. Pop. (1975) 771,700.

BELFAST (belfahst'). Capital of N. Ireland, also its chief port and industrial centre. It grew up, where the Lagan enters B. Lough 20km (12m) from the sea, round a castle built in 1177 by John de Courcy. It received its first charter in 1613, and was created a city in 1888, with a Lord Mayor from 1892. Of interest are the Parliament Buildings at Stormont, to the south, St Anne's Protestant Cathedral (1899), the City Hall (1906), Queen's University, and Ulster Museum in the city and Ulster Folk Museum nearby in Co. Down. Industries incl. ships, aircraft, machinery, textiles (linen and synthetics), and tobacco. There is an internat. airport at Aldergrove. From 1968 considerable damage was done by bomb incidents organized by political extremists. Pop. (1971) 360,150.

BELFORT (belfor'). French town, cap. of the territory of B., commanding the important route-way between the Vosges and the Jura mountains. Pop. (1975) 131,400.

BELGAUM (belgawm'). Town of Karnataka, Rep. of India, with textile industries. Pop. (1971) 213,830.

BELGIUM. European state bordering the North Sea, lying between the Netherlands on the N. and France on the S., with Germany and the duchy of Luxembourg on the E. It is mainly low-lying, though in the S.E. the Ardennes, forested and with heavy rainfall, rise in the Botrange to 692m (2,270ft). The coast is backed by sand dunes, sand also occurring in the Campine Heaths in the N., and in parts of the plain, where rye, oats, etc. are grown in soil reclaimed by fertilization and irrigation. In naturally fertile areas sugar beet, wheat, roots and forage crops are grown and cattle are reared, and cattle are also found on the pastures of the Ardennes. The plain is watered by the Scheldt and its many tributaries, and by the Sambre and Meuse.

Before the S.W.W. the French-speaking area of Wallonia in the S. was predominant. Generally anti-clerical and Socialist in outlook, it was rich in the steel and metal-working industries based on the coal of the Mons, Charleroi and Liège area, but these suffered some decline in the face of competition with other fuels - coal production halved 1960-70. Flanders, to the N.W., Flemish-speaking and generally Catholic and Christian Democrat, was before the S.W.W. comparatively less prosperous as the agricultural region, but has since achieved great industrial growth along the North Sea coast, notably petrochemicals round the great port of Antwerp, pharmaceuticals, fertilizers, and plastics. There has been a dramatic increase in the automotive sector, and synthetics have been added to the traditional cotton and woollen textiles and carpets. Poor in natural resources - the loss of the minerals of the Belgian Congo (now Zaïre) was a severe blow - B. has seized the opportunities offered by the country's central position in the Common Market to become a European distribution centre, with modernized road, rail and canal links, and modernized ports at Zeebrugge and Ostend as well as Antwerp. Blankenberghe and Knokke are holiday resorts.

B. is a kingdom (*see* BAUDOUIN) with a Senate and Chamber of Representatives, elected on a basis of proportional representation. The majority are Roman Catholic. French and Flemish are both official languages, but from 1963 the language of admin. and instruction has been decided according to a linguistic frontier: Flemish in Flanders, French in Wallonia, with the Brussels zone bilingual. The cap. is Brussels, and there is a univ. here, as well as in Ghent, Liège and Louvain. Area 30,513 sq.km (11,779 sq. m); pop. (1977) 9,837,400. Of these over 50% are Flemish-speaking, some 30% French-speaking, and 11% bilingual, and there is a small German minority. After continual deadlock over plans for decentralisation, it was agreed in 1980 that directly-elected regional councils should be estab. in 1982 for Flanders and Wallonia, but that the controversial creation of a third autonomous region of Brussels should be temporarily abandoned. M.U.: Belgian franc.

History. Julius Caesar conquered the lands occupied by the Celtic Belgae, and they were incorporated in the Roman Empire in 15 B.C. The Franks overran the area from the 3rd cent. onwards. The peace and order estab. by Charlemagne fostered the growth of such towns as Ghent, Bruges, and Brussels; following the division of his empire in 843 the area was incl. in Lotharingia. By the 11th cent. 7 feudal states had emerged: the counties of Flanders, Hainault, and Namur, the duchies of Brabant, Limburg, and Luxemburg, and the bishopric of Liège, all nominally subject to the French kings or the German emperor, but in practice independent. From the 12th cent. a flourishing economic life developed; Bruges, Ghent and Ypres became centres of the cloth industry, while the artisans of Dinant and Liège exploited the copper and tin of the Meuse valley. During the 15th cent. the states came one by one under the rule of the dukes of Burgundy, and in 1477, by the marriage of Mary, heiress of Charles the Bold, duke of Burgundy, to Maximilian, Archduke of Austria, passed into the Habsburg dominions.

Other dynastic marriages brought all the Low Countries under Spain, and in the 16th cent. the religious and secular tyranny of Philip II led to general revolt in the Netherlands; the independence of the N. as the Dutch Republic was recognized in 1648; the S., reconquered by Spain, remained Spanish until the Treaty of Utrecht, 1713, transferred it to Austria. The Austrian Netherlands was in 1797 annexed by revolutionary France and incorporated in France. The Congress of Vienna reunited the N. and S. Netherlands as one kingdom under William, Prince of Orange-Nassau; but historical differences, and the fact that the language of the wealthy and influential in the S. was (as it remains) French, made the union uneasy. A rising in 1830 of the largely French-speaking part of the people in the S., and continuing disturbances, led in 1839 to the recognition by the Great Powers of the S. Netherlands as the independent and permanently neutral kingdom of Belgium, with Leopold of Saxe-Coburg (widower of Charlotte, dau. of George IV) as king, and a parliamentary constitution. Leopold II (reigned 1865-1909) acquired the Congo, a Belgian colony 1908-60: *see* ZAÏRE.

Although Prussia had been a party to the treaty of 1839 recognizing Belgium's permanent neutrality (Bethmann Hollweg's 'scrap of paper'), Germany invaded Belgium in 1914 and occupied a large part of it until 1918. Again in 1940 B. was overrun by the Germans, to whom Leopold III surrendered. But his govt escaped to London, and inside B. there was a strong resistance movement. After B.'s liberation by the Allies, 1944-5, the king's surrender gave rise to acute controversy, ended only by his abdication in 1951 in favour of his son Baudouin (q.v.). The system of proportional representation has encouraged the formation of coalitions which have frequently collapsed. And, although the country has remained generally stable, the rivalry of France and Wallonia, symbolized by the disputes over language, has led to moves towards regional self-govt in the 1970s.

THE ARTS. The declaration following the revolution of 1830-9, that French was the only official language (it remained so until 1898), actually stimulated interest in the Flemish language (in its written form, the same as Dutch). J. F. Willems (1793-1846) brought out a magazine which revived medieval Flemish works; H. Conscience (1812-83) and J. T. van Ryswyck (1811-49) pub. novels in Flemish; K. L. Ledeganck (1805-47), Prudens van Duyse (1804-59), Jan de Beers (1821-88) wrote poetry. Later writers were Albrecht Rodenbach (1856-80), Pol de Mont (1857-1931), Cyriel Buysse (1859-1932). Writers in French have included Georges Eekhoud (1854-1927), who wrote of Flemish peasant life; Émile Verhaeren and Maurice Maeterlinck (qq.v.).

The noted composer César Franck (1822-90) was of Belgian birth; Eugène Ysayë (1858-1931) was a famous violinist. Belgian painting has its roots in the Flemish Art (q.v.) of medieval and later times; best known modern painter is James Ensor (q.v.).

BELGIUM. The 18th century law courts at Bruges overlook one of the canals which intersect the city. *Photo: Pierre Berger/Barnaby's Picture Library.*

BELGRADE. Cap. of Yugoslavia and of Serbia, one of the federal reps. of Yugoslavia. At the junction of the Save with the Danube, the city is an important inland port and exchange centre. It was formerly defended by walls, and an old citadel still stands on a 60m (200ft) cliff. Except for brief intervals, it was in Turkish hands from 1501 to 1867; in 1878 it became the cap. of newly independent Serbia. In 1976 it was linked by rail with the newly developed port of Bar 476 km (292 m) S.W. on the Adriatic: the line incl. Europe's highest bridge, over the Mala Rijeka r. at 201 m. (660 ft.). Pop. (1971) 741,618.

BELGRÀ'VIA. District of London, laid out in a solid magnificence of squares by Thomas Cubitt 1825-30, and bounded to the N. by Knightsbridge.

BELISARIUS (*c.* 505-65). General under the emperor Justinian (q.v.).

BELITUNG. Island of Indonesia famous for its tin, discovered in 1759 and developed by the Dutch. The cap. is Tanjongpandan.

BELIZE (belēz'). British crown colony on the Caribbean, Central America, adjacent to Guatemala and Mexico. The coastal area is low swampland, with mtns rising to 915m (3,000ft), and many small rivers flow into Honduras Bay. Most of the land is forested, and timber (mahogany, cedar, rosewood, etc.) and chicle is exported. Crops incl. sugar, citrus (espec. grapefruit), and bananas, and cattle are reared. The people are of mixed blood, some Amerindian, some British (woodcutters from Jamaica were the first white settlers in 1638), some Spanish (Spain disputed possession of B. until British control was finally established in

1798), and some Negro (large numbers of slaves were imported during the 18th cent.). The colony attained internal self-govt in 1964, and changed its name from British Honduras to Belize in 1973. Guatemalan claims on B. hindered the granting of full independence, but this was attained in 1981.

The cap. is Belmopan, and the chief seaport is Belize. Area 22,965 sq.km (8,867 sq.m); pop. (1978) 151,600. M.U.: Belize dollar.

BELIZE. A Maya sculpture hidden in a jungle clearing. The god depicted has the same broad head as the modern Amerindian of the area: the average head width is over 85 per cent of the length. *Photo. Mireille Vautier.*

BELL, Alexander Graham (1847–1922). British inventor. B. in Edinburgh, he was ed. at the Univ. of Edinburgh and London, and in 1870 went first to Canada and then to the US where he opened a school for teachers of the deaf in Boston in 1872, and in 1873 became prof. of vocal physiology at the univ. there. In 1876 he patented his invention of the telephone, and later experimented with a type of phonograph and in aeronautics.

BELL, Gertrude Margaret Lowthian (1868-1926). British traveller, who from 1899 spent most of her time in the Near East. She worked in the British intelligence service during the F.W.W. For some years she exercised dominating influence as Oriental Secretary of the High Commissioner of Iraq, and to her Feisal largely owed his throne. Her *Letters* are famous.

BELL. Instrument of hollowed metal struck to produce a musical sound. The oldest inscribed B. is that cast in 698 by Hirokuni Tsukishinenomura for the Myoshinji Temple, Kyoto. The earliest-dated English B. (1296) is at Claughton, Lancs. The largest B. in the world is the Tsar Kolokol (King of bells) in the Kremlin, Moscow; cast in 1734 for Nicholas II, it weighs 220 tonnes and stands on the ground where it fell when being hung. Famous English Bs. are Great Paul in the clock tower of St Paul's, the largest in England; Big Ben (q.v.); Great Peter at York and Great Tom at Oxford. The Peace B. at the UN headquarters in N.Y. was cast in Japan in 1952 from coins given by 64 countries.

BELLADO'NNA. Deadly nightshade (*Atropa belladonna*). The leaves, which contain the alkaloids hyoscyamine, atropine, hyoscine, and belladonnine, are dried and powdered. The plant and all its preparations are highly poisonous, and the cosmetic use of it to enlarge the pupil of the eye (hence the name meaning 'beautiful lady') is dangerous.

BELLARMINE (bel'armin), **Roberto Francesco Romolo** (1542-1621). Italian theologian, cardinal, and controversialist. He taught at the Jesuit College in Rome, and became archbishop of Capua in 1602. *Disputationes de controversersiis fidei christianae* (1581-93) is his chief work. He was canonized in 1930. Saltglaze, stoneware drinking jugs, bearing a bearded face were nicknamed Bs. by the Protestant party in the Netherlands, but the earliest dates to 1550.

BELLAY (belā'), **Joachim du** (1522?-60). French poet and prose-writer, who pub. the great manifesto of the new school of French poetry, the Pléiade: *Défense et illustration de la langue française* (1549).

BELLINGSHAUSEN (bel'ingzhowzen), **Fabian Gottlieb von** (1779-1852). Russian Antarctic explorer, the first to sight the Antarctic continent, though without realizing what it was.

BELLINGSHAUSEN SEA. The section of the S Pacific off the Antarctic coast.

BELLINI (belē'nē). A family of Venetian artists. **Jacopo B.** (*c.* 1400-70) was founder of the Venetian School. Only 5 of his paintings - a 'Crucifixion' and 4 'Madonnas' - have survived. There are, however, 2 books containing his drawings - one in the British Museum, the other in the Louvre. His elder son, **Gentile B.** (*c.* 1429-1507), was a painter of great achievement and versatility. In 1474 he was commissioned to assist in the decoration of the Great Hall of Council in the Ducal Palace, and later he worked in the court of Mohammed II at Constantinople. A portrait of the Sultan is in the National Gallery, London. His other important works incl. paintings of processional groups in the Academy at Venice, the 'Adoration of the Magi' in the National Gallery, London, and 'St Mark Preaching at Alexandria' (1505), in the Brera, Milan. His younger brother, **Giovanni B.** (*c.* 1430-1516), studied under his father. His early works show the influence of the Paduan School, particularly of his brother-in-law, Mantegna. He was one of the first painters to work in oil, and executed altar-pieces.

BELLINI, Vincenzo (1801-35). Italian composer, of the operas *La Sonnambula*, *Norma*, etc.

BELLINZŌ'NA. Cap. of Ticino canton, Switzerland, on the Ticino, 16km (10m) from Lake Maggiore. It is a road and rail centre, with tourist traffic, for the St Gotthard Pass. Pop. (1970) 17,000.

BELLOC, Joseph Hilaire Pierre (1870-1953). Author, the son of a French barrister and an English mother, he became a naturalized British citizen in 1902. In 1911 he founded the *Eye-Witness* with Chesterton's brother, Cecil, with whom he also wrote a political work entitled *The Party System*. With G. K. Chesterton he advocated a return to the Distributist theories of the late Middle Ages, in place of modern capitalism or socialism. His literary versatility is shown by his nonsense verse, by his historical studies, incl. *Danton, Robespierre, James II,* and a *History of England,* by satires such as *Mr. Clutterbuck's Election,* and by *The Path to Rome,* a walker's classic.

BELLOT (belō'), Joseph René (1826-53). French arctic explorer, who discovered Bellot Strait, and lost his life while searching for Franklin.

BELLOW, Saul (1915-). American novelist. B. in Lichine, Quebec, of Russian-Jewish extraction, he moved to Chicago with his family as a boy of nine, and has since made his home there. His books, remarkable both for subtlety and humour, incl. the picaresque *The Adventures of Augie March* (1953); *Herzog* (1964), philosophically speculative; and *Humboldt's Gift* (1975). He was awarded a Nobel prize in 1976.

BELLOW. Acclaiming *Henderson the Rain King* (1959) as his 'most imaginative expedition' the Nobel Committee made their award of a prize for his 'human understanding and subtle analysis of contemporary culture'. *Photo: Popperfoto.*

BELL-RINGING. Change-ringing is a truly British art and was introduced by Fabian Stedman, a Cambridge printer, in the 17th cent. The method he perfected was named after him and is rung at the present day. Change-ringers are organized into Diocesan and County Guilds, the oldest being the 'Ancient Soc. of College Youths' (estab. 1637), responsible for ringing at St Paul's Cathedral, Westminster Abbey, and Southwark Cathedral. On the Continent and in America, the most common form of B.R. is by the Carillon, which comprises a set of 12-70 stationary Bs., operated by a clavier. The keys are wooden levers, operated by hands and feet, and are connected by wires to the clappers of the Bs. In change-ringing, 5 to 12 bells are rung by hand in mathematical permutations, and the 'methods' have picturesque names - Grandsire, Plain Bob, Treble Bob, Stedman (after its 17th cent. originator), etc. The study of bell-ringing is known as campanology (Lat. *campana* 'bell').

BELLS. Nautical term applied to half-hours of watch. A day is divided into 7 watches, 5 of 4 hours each and 2 of 2 hours. Each half-hour of each watch is indicated by the striking of a bell, 'eight bells' being the end of the watch.

BELL'S THEOREM. Hypothesis of Swiss physicist, John S. Bell, that an unknown force, of which space, time and motion are all aspects, continues to link separate parts of the Universe which were once united, and that this force travels faster than the speed of light. Experiments at Berkeley, California, seem to confirm the theory.

BELMÓPAN. Cap. of Belize, in the foothills of the mtns 80km (50m) S.W. of the seaport of Belize (the former cap.), which it replaced in 1973 after the latter was destroyed by a hurricane in 1961. Pop. (1973) 3,000.

BELOFF (be'lof), **Sir Max** (1913-). British historian. In 1974-80 he was principal of the University College at Buckingham, Britain's first independent institution at univ. level. He was knighted in 1980. Life peer 1981.

BELO HORIZONTE (bel'orizon'tā). City of Brazil, cap. of the fast-developing state of Minas Gerais. It is the centre of an area rich in coal and timber, and engineering firms have followed the estab. of steelworks. Cotton textiles are also made. Pop. (1970) 1,126,000.

BELSEN. *See* CONCENTRATION CAMPS.

BELTANE (bel'ten). Celtic name for the 1st day of May, formerly one of the Scottish quarter days. The ancient feasts held on this day were marked by the kindling of B. fires on the hillsides.

BENARES. Another transliteration of VARANESI.

BEN BARKA, Mehdi (1920-65). Moroccan politician. Tutor to King Hassan, he became pres. of the Nat. Consultative Assembly in 1956 on the country's independence from France. Increasingly leftist in his views, he was in 1963 twice sentenced to death in his absence (for alleged involvement in an attempt on the king's life and for supporting Algeria in Algerian-Moroccan border disputes). After being lured to Paris to discuss an anti-colonial film, he was kidnapped and shot by Moroccan agents with the aid of French foreign service men. His body was not found. The case disturbed Franco-Moroccan relations, and led to de Gaulle's reorganisation of the secret service.

BEN BELLA (ben be'la), **Mohamed** (1916-). Algerian leader. Founder in Cairo in 1952 of the National Liberation Front (FLN), he was prime minister of independent Algeria from 1962 until overthrown by Boumedienne in 1965, remaining in custody till 1980.

BENBOW (ben'bō), **John** (1653-1702). English admiral. He ran away to sea as a boy, and from 1689 served in the Royal Navy. He fought at Beachy Head (1690), La Hogue (1692), and d. of wounds received in a great fight with the French off Jamaica. He was a popular hero.

BENCHLEY, Robert (1889-1945). American humorist. B. at Worcester, Mass., he went to N.Y. in 1916 as a journalist and was drama editor to the *New Yorker* 1929-40. His books incl. *Of All Things* (1921) and *Benchley Beside Himself* (1943) and his film skit *How to Sleep* illustrates his superb ability to extract humour from daily living.

BENDA, Julien (1867-1956). French writer. B. in Paris, of Jewish stock, he ed. the *Cahiers de la Quinzine* 1910-4, attacked Bergson's philosophy, and in 1927 pub. a manifesto on the necessity of devotion to the absolute truth which he felt his contemporaries had betrayed *La Trahison des clercs* (The Treason of the Intellectuals, 1927). His last book *La Grande Épreuve des démocraties* (1942) was smuggled to N.Y. from Nazi-occupied Paris.

BE'NDIGŌ. Name under which the British pugilist Wm. Thompson (1811-89) was known. He won his first prize fight in 1832 and fought his last in 1850. Subsequently he was a popular figure and preacher, and B. in Australia is said to be named after him.

BENDIGO. Industrial town in Victoria, Australia, on the flank of the Australian Great Divide, about 120km (75m) N.N.W. of Melbourne. In 1851 alluvial gold was discovered here, and a 'rush' followed, but commercially workable deposits were exhausted by the 1950s. Pop. (1976) 50,200.

BENDS. Caisson disease. Paralytic affliction of divers, arising from too rapid release of nitrogen after solution in the blood under pressure. Immediate treatment is compression and slow decompression in a special chamber.

BENEDICT, St (*c.* A.D. 480-*c.* 547). Founder of Christian monasticism in the West, and of the order of the Benedictine monks. B. of wealthy parents at Nursia, he was sent to be ed. in Rome, but fled from that city and spent 3 years in ascetic solitude. He founded 12 monasteries near Subiaco, and later migrated to Cassino, and founded the monastery of Monte Cassino. Here he wrote out his rule for monastic life, and was visited shortly before his death by the Ostro-gothic king Totila, whom he won to the Christian faith. In 1964 he was proclaimed patron saint of Europe.

BENEDICT XV (1854-1922). Pope from 1914. During the F.W.W. he endeavoured to remain neutral, and his papacy is noted for the renewal of British official relations with the Vatican, suspended since the 17th cent.

BENEDICTINES. Religious order of monks and nuns in the R.C. Church, founded by St Benedict at Subiaco, in Italy, in the 6th cent. St Augustine brought the order to England. At the beginning of the 14th cent. it was at the height of its prosperity, and medieval civilization was largely its creation. At the Reformation there were nearly 300 B. monasteries and nunneries in England, all of which were suppressed. The English novice house survived in France, and in the 19th cent. monks expelled from France removed to England and built abbeys at Downside, Ampleforth, and Woolhampton. The monks from Pierre-qui-vive, who went over in 1882, rebuilt Buckfast Abbey in Devon on the ruins of a Cistercian monastery. Celebrated Benedictine monasteries in the US are at Latrobe, Pennsylvania, and St Meinrad, Indiana.

BENELUX. Name for the BElgium, NEtherlands, LUXembourg customs union, agreed to by the exiled governments of those countries in 1944, and ratified by them after the war. Owing to post-war economic difficulties, it did not come into full effect until 1960.

BENEŠ (ben'esh), **Eduard** (1884-1948). Czech statesman. A devoted pupil and friend of Thomas Masaryk, he followed him into exile in 1915, became sec. of the Czechoslovak national council in Paris, and in 1918 Min. of Foreign Affairs in the Czechoslovak govt recognized by the Allies. He returned with Masaryk to Prague, and was For. Sec., playing a leading part in the Little Entente and League of Nations affairs until 1935, when he was elected Pres. of the rep. on Masaryk's retirement. After the Munich Conference he was compelled to resign through German pressure and left the country. He became leader of the Czechoslovak freedom movement in 1939 and set up a provisional Czechoslovak govt in London. In 1945 he returned to Czechoslovakia, but ill-health and dislike of Communist measures led to his resignation on 7 June 1948.

BENÉT (benā'), **Stephen Vincent** (1898-1943). American writer, whose best-known work is *John Brown's Body* (1928), a poem dealing with the American Civil War.

BENEVE'NTŌ. Town in Campania, Italy, cap. of B. prov., 56km (35m) N.E. of Naples, with many ancient remains. Its 12th cent. cathedral was almost completely destroyed in the fighting in 1943. Pop. (1971) 58,400.

BENGAL (bengawl'). Province of British India, at the head of the Bay of Bengal, in the N.E. of the Indian subcontinent. At independence in 1947, W. Bengal became part of the new state of India, and E. Bengal, after forming the eastern part of Pakistan 1947-72, became the independent state of Bangladesh (q.v.).

WEST BENGAL. State of the Rep. of India. It forms the W. part of the vast alluvial plain created by the Ganges and Brahmaputra, and has an annual rainfall in excess of 250cm (100in). Crops are rice, jute and tea. Coal is mined, and the state is heavily industrialized - iron and steel, cars, rail locomotives, aluminium, fertilizers, and jute products - and overpopulated. Towns incl. Calcutta (cap.), Howrah, and the industrial centre of Durgapur. Area 88,563 sq.km (33,829 sq.m); pop. (1985) 49,800,000

BENGAL. A Darjeeling train in W.Bengal India with a Buddhist monastery in the background. *Photo: Peter Fraenkel.*

BENGALI (bengaw'li). Language of Bangladesh and W Bengal. *See also* BANGALISTAN.

BENGHAZI (bengah'zē). Second city of Libya on the coast of Cyrenaica. It changed hands between Axis and British forces several times 1941-42 in the S.W.W. Oil discoveries in the interior from 1959 have aided growth. Pop. (1977) 282,200.

BENGUELA (bengā'la). Town on the coast of Angola, W. Africa, 32km (20m) S.W. of Lobito Bay. It has an airport and is the W. terminus of B. railway which links it with the central African lines, but the railway was inoperative by 1979 because of attack from anti-Soviet guerrillas. Pop. (1970) 15,400.

BEN GU'RION, David (1886-1973). Israeli statesman. B. in Plonsk, Russian Poland, he settled in Palestine in 1906, but was exiled by the Turks as a Zionist in 1915. In America he became an organizer of the Jewish Legion in which he served under Allenby. He was chairman of the Jewish Agency for Palestine 1935-48, and in 1948 proclaimed the independence of Israel. Leader of the Mapai (Labour) party, he was P.M. and Min. of Defence 1948-53 and 1955-63. He led a breakaway Labour Party (Rafi) 1965-7.

BENIN (benēn'). Country in W. Africa, formerly Dahomey, with a short coastline on the Bight of B. Much of D. is arid, but there are scattered forest areas producing palm kernels and palm oil, the chief exports, and cotton and coffee are grown. The climate is tropical. Porto Novo is the cap.; other towns are Cotonou, the chief port, and Abomey. Area 112,600 sq.km. (43,480 sq.m.); pop. (1973) 2,948,000. M.U.: CFA franc.

The French signed a commercial treaty with the well-organised Negro kingdom of Dahomey in 1851, made it a protectorate in 1863, a colony in 1894. In 1960 it became an independent rep. outside the French Community. A series of military coups followed and Mathieu Kerekou, who seized power in 1972, announced in 1974 the creation of a Marxist-Leninist 'Socialist Society'. In 1975 the name of the country was changed from Dahomey to B., although it has no historical connection with the former Negro kingdom of B.

BENIN. One of the series of bronze plaques from the ancient kingdom of Benin which show the Oba, or ruler, with his attendants. *Photo: Courtesy of the British Museum.*

BENIN (benēn'). City and airport of Nigeria, cap. of Bendel state. Once centre of the kingdom of the Beni, noted for its well-organized but cruel govt (human sacrifice by crucifixion was common), it was a slave-trading port, and made handsome bronzes and ivory carvings. There is a univ. Pop. (1975) 136,000.

BENJAMIN, Arthur (1893-1960). Australian pianist and composer. B. at Brisbane, he taught composition at the R.C.M. from 1926, where Britten was one of his pupils. His works incl. *Jamaican Rumba* inspired by a visit to the W. Indies in 1937; operas such as *A Tale of Two Cities* (1953); and a harmonica concerto for Larry Adler.

BENN, Anthony Wedgwood (1925-). British Labour politician. Elder surviving son of 1st visct Stansgate, a Labour peer, he succeeded his father in 1960, but never used the title or took his seat in the Lords. He attempted renunciation in 1955 and 1960, and in 1963 was the first person to disclaim his title under the Peerage Act, when he re-entered the Commons. He succeeded Cousins as Min. of Technology 1966-70 and was Min. for Industry 1974-5, but mounted a campaign against Labour policy of entry to the Common Market and was transferred to Energy in 1975-9. As the intellectual leader of the Labour left, he supported policies which resulted in the split within the party in 1980-1.

BENN. Tony Benn, here seen with Michael Foot, former leader of the Labour Party, returned to the House of Commons in 1984, after losing his seat at the 1983 General Election. *Photo: Terry Kirk/The Financial Times.*

BENNETT, (Enoch) Arnold (1867-1931). British novelist. B. at Hanley, Staffs, son of a solicitor in whose office he started work, he settled in London in 1893 as a journalist, becoming editor of *Woman* in 1896. His 1st successful novel was *The Grand Babylon Hotel* (1902), but his best books are those set among the 5 towns of the Potteries he knew so well, e.g. *Anna of the Five Towns* (1904), *Sacred and Profane Love* (1905), *The Old Wives' Tale* (1908) - his masterpiece, dealing with the lives of 2 sisters - and the trilogy *Clayhanger, Hilda Lessways* and *These Twain* (1910-15). Of his ventures into drama the more successful were *What the Public Wants* (1909) and *Milestones* (1912: with E. Knoblock): a notable late novel is *Riceyman Steps* (1923).

BENNETT, Richard Rodney (1936-). British composer. Besides jazz and film music (*Far from the Madding Crowd* and *Nicholas and Alexandra*), he has produced symphonies and chamber music, and operas, incl. *Victory* (1970).

BEN NEVIS (nev'is). Highest mountain in the British Isles (1,340m/4,406ft), in the Grampians.

BENŌ'NI. Town in the Transvaal, Rep. of South Africa. Industries incl. gold mining, metallurgy, tyres, electrical goods. Pop. (1970) 160,400.

BENSON, Edward White (1829-96). British churchman, first headmaster of Wellington Coll. 1859-68, and, as Archbishop of Canterbury from 1883, responsible for the 'Lincoln Judgment' on questions of ritual in 1887.

BENTHAM, Jeremy (1748-1832). British philosopher and legal reformer. He rose to fame by the publication in 1776 of his *Fragments on Government.* He declared that the 'utility' of any law is to be measured by the extent to which it promotes the pleasure, good, and happiness of the people concerned, and the essence of his 'Utilitarian' philosophy is found in the pronouncement in his *Principles of Morals and Legislation* (1789), that the object of all legislation should be 'the greatest happiness of the greatest number'. He made suggestions for the reform of the poor law (1798), which formed the basis of the reforms enacted in 1834, and in his *Catechism of Parliamentary Reform* (1817) he proposed annual elections, the secret ballot, and universal manhood suffrage. He was also a pioneer of prison reform. In economics B. was an apostle of *laissez-faire,* and in his *Defence of Usury* (1787) and *Manual of Political Economy* (1798) he contended that his principle of 'utility' was best served by allowing every man to pursue his own interests unhindered by restrictive legislation. He was made a citizen of the French Republic in 1792.

BENTINCK, Lord George (1802-48). British Cons. politician. From 1846 he was the leader of the Protectionists after Peel, the Cons. leader, had repealed the corn laws. He was a great friend of Disraeli, and was well known on the Turf.

BENTINCK, Lord William Cavendish (1774-1839). Son of the 3rd duke of Portland, in 1827 he became Gov.-Gen. of Bengal and in 1828-35 the 1st Gov.-Gen. of India. He took measures against thugs (q.v.), suppressed suttee (q.v.), and to simplify further education, estab. English as the medium of instruction.

BENTLEY, Edmund Clerihew (1875-1956). British author of the classic detective story *Trent's Last Case* (1912) and inventor of the 4-line doggerel verse known as the 'clerihew', as used in *Baseless Biography* (1939).

BENTLEY, Phyllis (1894-1977). British novelist. B. in Halifax, she wrote novels with a Yorkshire industrial background incl. *Inheritance* (1932), and was an expert on the Brontës, e.g. *The Young Brontës* (1960).

BENTLEY, Richard (1662-1742). British classical scholar, famous for his pioneer work in textual criticism and for his controversy (1697-9) with Charles Boyle, in which he demonstrated the spuriousness of the *Letters of Phalaris,* a collection of 148 letters supposed to have been written by the Sicilian tyrant of that name in the 6th cent. B.C. From 1700 he was master of Trinity Coll., Cambridge.

BENUE (bān'wā). River of Nigeria, largest affluent of the Niger. It is navigable for the major part of its length (1,400km/870m).

BENZ (bents), **Karl** (1844-1929). German automobile engineer. B. in Karlsruhe, in 1878 he built his first model engine, and in 1885 produced the world's first petrol-driven motor car.

BENZAL'DĒHYDE (C_6H_5.CHO), or oil of bitter almonds. A clear colourless liquid with the characteristic odour of almonds. It occurs free in certain leaves, such as the cherry, laurel and peach, and in a combined form in certain nuts and kernels. It can be extracted from such natural sources, but the product of commerce is nearly always synthetic, being made from toluene.

BENZEDRINE (ben'zedrēn). Trade name for a stimulant of the central nervous system, a 'pep pill' or amphetamine.

BEN'ZĒNE (C_6H_6). A clear liquid hydrocarbon of characteristic odour, occurring in coal tar. Although useful as a motor fuel, it is more important as a solvent and a starting substance for the synthesis of many important chemicals.

BENZODĪ'AZEPINE. Mood-altering drug, e.g. Librium, Valium.

BENZŌ'IC ACID (C_6H_5COOH). A white crystalline solid, sparingly soluble in water, and used as a permitted food preservative for certain articles. It is obtained chemically by the direct oxidation of benzaldehyde and occurs in certain natural resins, some essential oils, and in the compound state as hippuric acid.

BEN'ZŌIN, or **gum benjamin.** A resin obtained by making incisions in the bark of *Styrax benzoin,* a tree native to the E. Indies. It has a fragrant smell, and is used in the preparation of cosmetics, perfumes, and incense.

BEN ZVI (zvē), **Izhak** (1884-1963). Israeli statesman. B. at Poltava, he was active in the Zionist movement in the Ukraine. In 1907, he went to Palestine and was deported together with Ben Gurion in 1915 and, like him, served in the Jewish Legion under General Allenby. He succeeded Ben Gurion as pres. of Israel 1952-63.

BEOGRAD. Another form of BELGRADE.

BEOWULF (bā'ōwulf). Old English poem (composed *c.* 700), the only complete surviving example of Germanic folk-epic. It is extant in a single MS. copied *c.* 100 in the Cottonian collection of the British Museum. The hero B. delivers the Danish king Hrothgar from the water-demon Grendel, and his monstrous mother, and, returning home, succeeds his cousin Heardred as king of the Geats. After 50 years' prosperity, he is killed in slaying a dragon.

BÉRANGER (behronzheh'), **Pierre Jean de** (1780-1857). French poet, famous for his light satirical *chansons,* treating of love, wine, popular philosophy, and politics. Fined and imprisoned for his republican and Bonapartist views in 1821 and 1825, he was elected to the Constituent Assembly in 1848, but resigned after a few days. *Derniers chansons* and *Ma biographie* appeared in 1857.

BERBERA (ber'bārah). Seaport of Somalia, N.E. Africa, with the only sheltered harbour on the S. side of the Gulf of Aden. British 1884-1960, it exports sheep, cattle products, ghee, frankincense, and myrrh. Pop. 15,000; winter, 30,000.

BERBERS. A people of N. Africa, who since prehistoric times have inhabited Barbary, the Mediterranean coastlands from Egypt to the Atlantic. Their language is Berber, and about one-third of the Algerians and nearly two-thirds of the Moroccans speak it. B. customs are best preserved in the mountain communities, e.g. the Kabyles of Algeria, and the Rifs of the Atlas ranges in Morocco.

BERCHTESGADEN (berkh'tesgah'den). Village in S.E. Bavaria, N. of the Königssee. It has rock-salt mines. Hitler's country residence, the Berghof, stood near by at the base of Obersalzberg, his private retreat at its top. B. was several times bombed by the Allies during the

BERBERS. Magnificent horsemen, they are still used in desert patrol, and here are on parade in Algiers. *Photo: Camera Press.*

S.W.W., and was captured by US troops on 4 May 1945. Pop. (1978) 9,000.

BERDICHEV. Town of the Ukrainian S.S.R., USSR, 48km (30m) S.W. of Zhitomir, scene of bitter German-Russian battles in 1943-44. The town is a railway junction and commercial centre. Pop. (1972) 90,000.

BERDYAEV (berdyah'yef), **Nikolai Alexandrovich** (1874-1948). Russian philosopher. B. in Kiev, he often challenged official viewpoints and although appointed prof. of philosophy in 1919 at the univ. of Moscow, his defence of religion caused his exile in 1922. He based his ideas on Russian Orthodox Christian thought, and a conception of the operation of the spirit of God in history was their focal point. His books incl. *The Meaning of History* (1923) and *The Destiny of Man* (1935).

BERDYA'NSK. Ukrainian port on the Sea of Azov.

BERET (ber'i). Round, flat cap or bonnet, originally worn by the Basques. During the S.W.W. maroon coloured Bs. were worn by the British airborne troops (hence their name 'Red Devils'), black by the tank corps, green by the commando units, and blue by the RAF Regiment.

BEREZNIKI'. Town in the R.S.F.S.R., on the left bank of the Kama r., 145km (90m) N.N.E. of Perm. Formed in 1932 by the amalgamation of several older towns, it has giant chemical works based mainly on local salt and potash deposits. Pop. (1972) 150,000.

BERG, Alban (1885-1935). Austrian composer. B. at Vienna, he studied under Schönberg, and was associated with him as one of the leaders of the atonal school of composition. His most successful work was the opera *Wozzeck*, a grim story of working-class life, first produced in 1925.

BERGAMA. *See* PERGAMUM.

BER'GAMO. City and episcopal see of Lombardy, 48km (30m) N.E. of Milan. There are metal works and a textile industry, specializing in silks. Originating with paintings donated by Count Giacomo Carrara in 1796, the Academia Carrara now contains one of the finest collections in N. Italy. Pop. (1971) 127,300.

BERGAMOT. Tree of the genus citrus (*C. bergamia*); from the rind of its fruit a fragrant orange-scented essence used as a perfume is obtained. The sole source of supply is southern Calabria, but the name comes from the town of Bergamo, in Lombardy.

BER'GEN. Second largest city in Norway, on a deep sound sheltered by islands, about 160km (100m) N. of Stavanger. It is the westernmost port of Norway, with an airport and has a great tourist traffic. Ancient merchants' houses survive from Hanseatic times, and Grieg lived at nearby Troldhaugen. There is a 13th cent cathedral and a univ. (1948). Shipbuilding and engineering are carried on, and fishing is important. Pop. (1971) 212,000.

BERGEN-OP-ZOOM (bergh'en-op-zōm'). Town in N. Brabant province, Netherlands, at the junction of the E. Scheldt and the Zoom, 50km (32m) E. of Flushing. There are anchovy and oyster fisheries, and large pottery works. Pop. (1972) 40,000.

BERGIUS (ber'gē-oos), Friedrich (1884-1949). German research chemist, who received the Nobel Prize for chemistry in 1931. He invented processes for converting coal into oil, and wood into sugar.

BERGMAN (bār'yman), **Ingmar** (1918-). Swedish theatre and film producer. From 1963 to 1966 he was Head of the Royal Dramatic Theatre, Stockholm. His films have an international reputation and incl. *Summer Interlude* (1950), *The Seventh Seal* (1956), and *Cries and Whispers* (1973).

BERGMAN (berg'man), **Ingrid** (1917–82). Swedish actress. B. in Stockholm, where she was trained at the school of the Royal Dramatic Theatre, she was best known for her films, such as *Intermezzo* (1939), *Casablanca* (1942), *Joan of Arc* (1948), *Anastasia* (1957), and *Autumn Sonata* (1978) She m. in 1937 Dr Peter Lindstrom, leaving him for the film producer Roberto Rossellini whom she m. in 1950, and in 1958 m. a Swedish impresario Lars Schmidt.

BERGSON (bergson'), **Henri** (1859-1941). French philosopher. B. in Paris of Anglo-Jewish parentage, he became a naturalized French citizen. He was prof. of Philosophy at the Collège de France (1900-21), and in 1928 was awarded the Nobel Prize for literature. Under the Pétain govt in the S.W.W., he refused exemption from certain anti-Jewish regulations, being unwilling to accept any privileged treatment.

For B. time, change, and development were the essence of reality and he considered that time was not a succession of distinct and separate instants, but a continuous process in which one period merged imperceptibly into the next. His books incl. *Time and Free Will* (1889), *Matter and Memory* (1896), and *Creative Evolution* (1907). In the last-named he expressed his disssatisfaction with the materialist account of evolution popularized by such thinkers as Herbert Spencer, and attempted to prove that all evolution and progress are due to the working of the *élan vital* or life-force.

BERIA, Lavrenti (1899-1953). Soviet politician. B. in Georgia, of peasant parentage, he became head of the Soviet police force and Minister of the Interior. On Stalin's death he, with Malenkov and Molotov, formed a virtual triumvirate, but later he was shot after a secret trial.

BERI-BERI. Endemic polyneuritis, an inflammation of the nerve endings, mostly occurring in the tropics and resulting from deficiency of Vitamin B_1.

BERING ISLAND, SEA, STRAIT. *See* BEHRING, Vitus.

BERIOZŌ'VA, Svetlana (1932-). British ballerina. B. in Lithuania, she was brought up partly in the US and has danced with the Royal Ballet since 1952. Her style has a lyrical dignity and she excels in *The Lady and the Fool, Ondine,* and *Giselle.*

BERKELEY (berk'li), **Busby** (1895-1976). American film director. He was noted for his use in musicals of female dancers to create large-scale pattern effects amidst extravagant sets of fantastic ingenuity, as in *Gold Diggers of 1933.*

BERKELEY (bark'li), **George** (1685-1753). Irish bishop and idealist philosopher. He pub. several of his main philosophical works between 1707, when he became a fellow of Trinity Coll., Dublin, and 1712, when he left Dublin for England. In 1713 he was presented at Court by his friend, Swift, and from 1713 till 1720 he travelled on the Continent. In 1721 he returned to Ireland, became successively dean of Dromore and dean of Derry, and in 1723 inherited a considerable property from Miss Vanhomrigh (Swift's 'Vanessa'). His project to found a college in Bermuda did not materialize, and after spending some years at Rhode Is. he returned to England in 1731. In 1734 he became bishop of Cloyne, where he stayed until his retirement in 1752.

It was as a philosopher and as a critic of the empiricism of Locke that B. became famous. He was unable to accept Locke's theory that our ideas are representations of real objects, and he propounded as an alternative his famous theory of 'Subjective Idealism', according to which all objects exist simply in the mind of the beholder, and 'to be' means simply 'to be perceived'. This theory is contained in his *New Theory of Vision* (1709), *Principles of Human Knowledge* (1710), and *Hylas and Philonous* (1713).

BERKELEY (bah'kli), **Sir Lennox** (1903-). British composer. He excels in composition for the voice, as in 'The Hill of the Graces' (1975), verses from Spenser's *Faerie Queene* set for eight-part unaccompanied chorus; and his operas *Nelson* and *Ruth.* Other works incl. symphonies. He was knighted 1974.

BERKELEY (berk'li). On San Francisco Bay in California, USA it is the seat of the Univ. of California, famous particularly for its atom research. *See* BERKELIUM and table of TRANSURANIUM ELEMENTS. Pop. (1970) 118,000.

BERKELIUM (berkē'li-um). Metallic transuranic element, at no 97, discovered at Berkeley in 1949 by Seaborg and others.

BERKSHIRE (bark-). English co. lying S. of the Thames between Wilts and Surrey. Its northern boundary formerly followed the Thames, but in the re-organization of 1974 it lost a substantial area in the N.W. to Oxfordshire, and extended to the E. beyond the Thames to take in Eton and Slough from Buckinghamshire. In the extreme S. is Inkpen Beacon, at 297m (975ft) one of the highest points of the chalk downs of England. Windsor Forest in the E. and the pinewoods of Bagshot Heath in the S.E. cover a considerable area. It is mainly agricultural, with many pleasant country houses and attractive scenery. Reading is the largest industrial centre: other towns incl. Maidenhead, Newbury and Windsor. Area 1,243 sq.km (480 sq.m); pop. (1978) 672,600.

BE'RLIN, Irving (1888-). Adopted name of Israel Baline, American composer. B. in Russia, he settled in the US in 1893. His international song hits incl. *Alexander's Ragtime Band, Always, What'll I do?, Everybody's Doing It.* Among his stage musicals are *Annie Get Your Gun* and *Call Me Madam.*

BERLIN, Sir Isaiah (1909-). British philosopher. The son of a Jewish refugee from the Russian revolution, he was Chichele prof. of Social and Political Theory, Oxford, 1957-67. His books incl. *Historical Inevitability* (1954) and *Four Essays on Liberty* (1969). O.M. 1971.

BERLIN. City of Germany, on the Spree, cap. of united Germany from 1871 to 1945. First mentioned *c.* 1230, the city grew out of a fishing village, joined the Hanseatic League in the 15th cent., became the permanent seat of the Hohenzollerns, and was cap. of the Brandenburg electorate 1486-1701, of the kingdom of Prussia 1701-1871. From the middle of the 18th cent. it grew rapidly, developing into an important commercial and cultural centre.

After the S.W.W., B. was divided into 4 sectors - British, US, French, and Russian - and until 1948 was under quadripartite govt by the Allies; in that year the Russians withdrew from the combined board and created a separate municipal govt in their sector. The other 3 sectors (W.B.) were made a Land of the Federal Rep. in May 1949, and in Oct. 1949 E.B. was proclaimed cap. of E. Germany *See* BERLIN WALL.

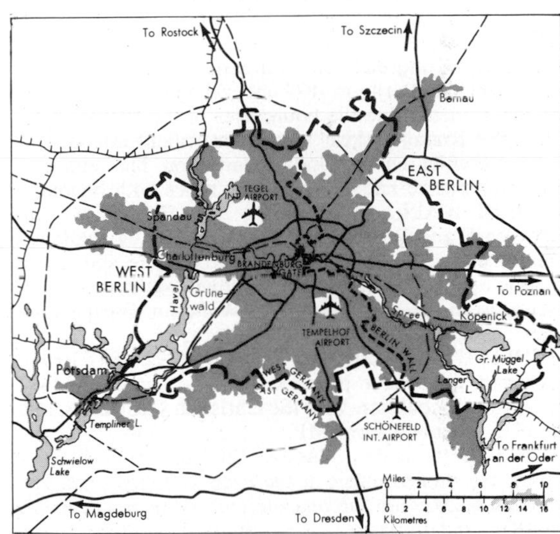

BERLIN

In the S.W.W. air raids and conquest by the Russian army 23 April-2 May 1945 destroyed much of B., but Unter den Linden, the tree-lined avenue once the whole city's focal point has been restored and new projects undertaken on both sides of the wall. In West B. the fashionable shopping area incl. the Kurfürstendamm and Europa-Center; the Alexander-platz complex has a giant hotel and television tower; and the Hansa quarter is a striking residential district. Notable buildings incl. the Kaiser-Wilhelm Gedächtniskirche (rebuilt 1959-61, but with its ruined 19th cent. tower); Reichstag (former parliament building); Schloss Bellevue (Berlin res. of the pres.); Schloss Charlottenburg (housing several museums); Congress Hall; restored 18th cent. State Opera, new Komische Oper, and Philharmonic concert hall; 20th Century Art Gallery and Dahlem picture gallery. The Tiergarten (zoo) has the largest aquarium in Europe. The attractive environs of B. incl. the Grünewald forest and

Wannsee lake. The internat. airport is at Tegel. Industries incl. machine tools, electrical goods, paper and printing. Pop. (1978) E.B. 1,118,142, W.B. 1,926,800.

BERLIN. The Gedächtniskirche and Europa Centre in West Berlin. *Photo: Klaus Lehnartz/Camera Press.*

BERLIN, Congress of. Congress of the European Powers held at Berlin in 1878 under the presidency of Bismarck, to determine the boundaries of the Balkan states after the Russo-Turkish war. Beaconsfield attended as Britain's chief envoy, and declared on his return to England that he had brought back peace with honour.

BERLIN WALL. The dividing line 45 km (28.5 m) between E and W Berlin which, from 13 Aug. 1961 was reinforced by the Russians with barbed wire and armed guards to prevent the escape of unwilling workers of E Berlin to the greater freedom of W Berlin. Escapers are shot on sight.

BERLINGUER (berlingwar'), **Enrico** (1922–84). Italian Communist. Close to power in 1976, he lost ground by a compromise coalition with the Christian Democrats, and in 1979 became a Euro-MP.

BERLIOZ (berlē-ōz'), **Hector** (1803-69). French composer. He studied music at the Paris Conservatoire. His cantata, *La Mort de Sardanapale,* gained the *prix de Rome* in 1830, and he spent 2 years in Italy. In 1833 he m. Henrietta Smithson, an Irish actress playing Shakespearian parts in Paris, but there was a separation in 1842. After some years of poverty and public neglect, B. was invited by Schumann to Germany in 1842, and there conducted his own works with triumphant success. Subsequently he made successful visits to Austria, Russia, and England. In 1854 he m. Marie Recio, a singer.

B. was the founder of modern orchestration. He wrote symphonic works such as *Symphonie fantastique* and *Roméo et Juliette,* built upon a literary or dramatic programme. His dramatic cantatas include *La damnation de Faust* and *L'enfance du Christ,* and his sacred music, a *Te Deum* and a *Requiem* in memory of the French soldiers killed in Algeria. He wrote 3 operas, *Béatrice et Bénédict, Benvenuto Cellini,* and *Les Troyens à Carthage.*

BERLIOZ. Originally an unwilling medical student, Berlioz defied his parents to study music, earning a meagre living by teaching and singing in a theatre chorus. *Photo: Courtesy of the Royal College of Music.*

BERMŪ'DA. Britain's oldest colony comprising some 150 small islands, of which only about 20 are inhabited, in the W. Atlantic 935km (580m) E. of N. Carolina. The entire chain (35km/22m long) is of coral formation, and is connected by bridges and causeways. Tourism, banking, insurance, and internat. business are the mainstay of the local economy, but exports incl Easter lilies and pharmaceuticals. The USA has a naval air base, and there is a NASA tracking station. The cap. and chief port is Hamilton; St George's (former cap) and Freeport are also ports.

B. is named after Juan de Bermudez, a Spaniard who visited the islands in 1515, and was settled by British colonists in 1609. Under the constitution of 1968 there is full self-govt, with a Governor, Senate and elected House of Assembly. The United Bermuda Party was returned to power in 1983 (PM John D. Gibbons); the Progressive Labour Party is in opposition. Area 54 sq.km (21 sq.m); pop. (1980) 55,000. M.U.: Bermuda dollar.

BERMUDA TRIANGLE. The sea area bounded by Bermuda, Florida and Puerto Rico, which gained the nickname Deadly Bermuda Triangle in 1964 when it was suggested that unexplained disappearances of ships and aircraft were exceptionally frequent there: analysis of the data did not eventually confirm the idea.

BERNADETTE (bernahdet') (1844-79). French saint. B. at Lourdes in the French Pyrenees. In Feb. 1858 she had a vision of the Virgin Mary in the grotto of Massabielle, which was later opened to the public by command of Napoleon III. Many sick who were dipped in the water of a spring there were said to be cured. A church built on the rock above the grotto became a shrine of international celebrity. At the age of 20 B. became a nun at Nevers, and nursed the wounded of the Franco-Prussian War. She d. of tuberculosis.

BERNADOTTE, Count Folke (1895-1948). Nephew of the King of Sweden and president of the Swedish Red Cross. In 1945 he conveyed Himmler's offer of capitulation to the British and US govts, and in 1948 was UN mediator in Palestine. He was assassinated by Stern Gang terrorists.

BERNADOTTE (bernahdot'), **Jean-Baptiste Jules** (1764-1844). Marshal in Napoleon's army who in 1818 became Charles XIV of Sweden. Hence, B. is the family name of the present royal house of Sweden.

BERNANOS, Georges (1888-1948). French author. B. in Paris, he achieved fame in 1926 with *Sous Le Soleil de Satan* (The Star of Satan). His strongly Catholic viewpoint emerged equally in his *Journal d'un Curé de Campagne* (1936: The Diary of a Country Priest). After Munich he went into voluntary exile in Brazil, and in the S.W.W. strongly supported de Gaulle, writing his *Lettre aux Anglais* in support of the Allied cause in 1942.

BERNARD, Claude (1813-78). French physiologist. He made many valuable physiological discoveries particularly in connection with the liver, the blood, and the nervous system, and wrote a *Physiologie expérimentale* (1865), which is a standard work.

BERNARD OF CLAIRVAUX (1090-1153). French saint and theologian. He entered the monastery of Cîteaux in 1113, and 2 years later founded and became first abbot of the monastery of Clairvaux, in Champagne. He did much to reinvigorate the Cistercian Order, and many new houses sprang up in France and beyond. In 1146 he preached the 2nd crusade, and induced Louis VII of France and Conrad III of Germany to take the cross. B.'s numerous Latin writings have been often printed and translated, and include letters, sermons, theological treatises, and hymns. He was canonized in 1174.

BERNARD OF MENTHON (923-1008). Christian saint. B. in Savoy, he became archdeacon of Aosta and founded in 962 the St B. hospices on the passes of the Pennine Alps, which bear his name. The St Bernard dogs kept by Augustinian monks in the hospices of the Great St B. have saved many travellers from death from exposure or starvation.

BERNE (bārn). Cap. of the Swiss Confederation, and of B. canton, 69km (43m) S.S.W. of Basle, on the Aar. Its principal features include a minster (begun in 1421), the Town Hall (1406), the Univ. (founded 1834). It makes textiles, chocolate and other foods, and light metal goods; it is the seat of the Universal Postal Union.

The city was founded in 1191, and made a free imperial city by Frederick II in 1218. It joined the Swiss Confederation in 1353, soon taking the lead, and in the 16th cent. championed the Reformed religion. Its name is derived from the bear which forms its coat of arms. The bear-pit in the city has been one of its sights since the 16th cent. Pop. (1971) 162,000.

BERNESE OBERLAND (bārnā'ze ō'berland) or **Bernese Alps.** The mountainous area in the S. of Berne canton which incl. some of the most famous peaks, e.g. the Jungfrau, Eiger, and Finsteraarhorn. Interlaken is the chief town.

BERNHARD (1911-). Prince of the Netherlands. Formerly Prince B. of Lippe-Biesterfeld, he m. Princess Juliana (q.v.) in 1937. When the Germans attacked Holland in 1940, B. led the defence of the royal palace at The Hague. He escaped to England in 1940, and next year became liaison officer for the Netherlands and British forces, playing a part in the organization of the Dutch underground. In 1976 he was censured for his conduct in connection with the purchase of Lockheed aircraft by the Dutch.

BERNHARDT, Sarah. Stage name of the French actress Rosine Bernard (1845-1923). B. in Paris of Jewish parentage, she studied at the Paris Conservatoire, made her début with the Comédie Française in 1862 and came to be recognized as the greatest actress of her day. Her great roles incl. the heroine of Racine's *Phèdre,* Dona Sol in Hugo's *Hernani,* Hamlet (1899) and the duc de Reichstadt in Rostand's *L'Aiglon* (1900). In 1882 she m. a member of her own company, Jacques Damala (or Daria), but they separated the next year. Although she lost her right leg as the result of an accident in 1915, B. continued to act. Her autobiography *Ma Double Vie* appeared in 1907.

BERNINI (bernē'nē), Giovanni Lorenzo (1598-1680). Italian architect, sculptor, and painter; one of the great masters of the baroque style. His most famous piece of sculpture is his 'Apollo and Daphne', while his architectural masterpiece is the colonnade surrounding the piazza outside St Peter's in Rome.

BERNOULLI (bernoolyē'). Swiss family of mathematicians. **Jacques B.** (1654-1705) is remembered for his work relating to 'curves', and for his discovery of *Bernoullian numbers,* a complex series of fractions of considerable value in higher mathematics and the theory of numbers. **Jean B.** (1667-1748), his brother, discovered the exponential calculus. Jean's son, **Daniel B.** (1700-82), was professor of mathematics at St Petersburg, and later held chairs at Basle. When only 24 he invented a clepsydra for recording time at sea, and he made discoveries relating to the inclination of the planets, the tides, etc.

BERNSTEIN, Leonard (1918-). American composer conductor and pianist. B. at Lawrence, Mass., he was ed. at Harvard Univ., and the Curtis Inst. of Music. He has conducted major orchestras throughout the world. His works incl. symphonies - *Jeremiah* (1942), *The Age of Anxiety* (1949); song cycles - *I Hate Music* (1943), *La Bonne Cuisine* (1949); scores for musicals - *Wonderful Town* (1953) and *West Side Story* (1957); and a *Mass* (1971) in memory of J. F. Kennedy.

BERNSTEIN. Noted for his versatility and ability to appeal to the popular as well as to the 'classical' audience, Bernstein is a brilliant executant. He is also well known for his children's concerts. *Photo: Godfrey MacDominic.*

BERRE-L'ÉTANG (behr-lehtaň'). Town on the Étang de Berre, a shallow lake in the Rhône delta, Bouches-du-Rhône dept, France, N.W. of Marseille. It is linked with the Mediterranean by the Martigues canal and Rove tunnel, and is the centre of large oil refining and petro-chemical industries. Pop. (1975) 13,000.

BERRIGAN, Daniel (1921-) and **Philip** (1924-). American R.C. priests. The brothers, opponents of the Vietnam War, broke into the draft records offices at Catonsville to burn the files with napalm, and were sentenced in 1968 to 3 and 6 yrs imprisonment, but went underground. Subsequently Father Philip was tried with others in 1972 for allegedly conspiring to kidnap Henry Kissinger and blow up govt offices in Washington and sentenced to 2 yrs.

BERRY. Family name of Viscount Camrose and Viscount Kemsley. *See* KEMSLEY, Lord.

BERRY (be'ri), **Chuck** (Charles Edward) (1931-). American popularizer of rock-and-roll, and composer of such songs as 'Roll over Beethoven' (1956).

BE'RSERKER. In Scandinavian myth the Bs. were warriors subject in battle to fits of insensate fury, during which they were immune to swords and flame - hence to 'go berserk'.

BERTOLUCCI (bertoloo'chi), **Bernardo** (1940-). Italian film director of *The Spider's Stratagem* (1969), *Last Tango in Paris* (1972) and *La Luna* (1980).

BERTRAND DE BORN (*c.* 1140-*c.* 1215). Provençal troubadour. He was viscount of Hautefort in Périgord, accompanied Richard Cœur de Lion to the Holy Land, and d. a monk.

BERWICK (ber'ik), **James Fitzjames,** duke of (1670-1734). French marshal. Natural son of the duke of York (afterwards James II of England) and Arabella Churchill, sister of the great duke of Marlborough, he was made duke of B. in 1687. After the revolution of 1688 he served under his father in Ireland, joined the French army, fought against William III and Marlborough, and in 1707 defeated the English at Almansa in Spain. He was killed at the siege of Philippsburg.

BERWICKSHIRE (ber'ik-). Former co. of S.E. Scotland, merged in Borders Region 1975, of which it became a district.

BERWICK-UPON-TWEED (be'rik). Seaport and fishing town of England, at the mouth of the Tweed, Northumberland, 5km (3m) S.E. of the Scottish border. Held alternately by the English and Scots for centuries, B. was in 1551 made a neutral town; it was attached to Northumberland in 1885. The Old Bridge (1611-34) over the Tweed, with 15 arches, remains, but was superseded in 1928 by the Royal Tweed Bridge in reinforced ferro-concrete which carries the Great North Road. The Royal Border railway bridge, constructed by Robert Stephenson, was opened in 1850. The town has iron foundries and shipbuilding yards, salmon and other fisheries. Pop. (1972) 11,760.

BERYL (ber'il). Species of precious stone; silicate of beryllium and aluminium. B. usually occurs as green hexagonal crystals sometimes of large size, found chiefly in granites and pegmatites; the dark green crystals are termed emeralds and the light blue-green aquamarines.

BERYLLIUM (glucinum). Light silvery hard metallic element, at. wt 9.013, at. no. 4, symbol Be, sp. gr. 1.84. Its chief uses are as a source of neutrons when bombarded; windows of X-ray tubes, being highly transparent; toughened copper for high-grade gear-wheels and spark-free tools; and, as a neutron reflector, moderator, and uranium sheathing in nuclear reactors.

BERZĒ'LIUS, Jöns Jakob (1779-1848). Swedish chemist. In 1818 he was appointed secretary of the Stockholm Academy of Sciences. His special study was the determination of atomic and molecular weights, and his tables, pub. 1818 and 1826, comprised more than 2,000 chemical substances. He invented the system of chemical symbols now in use, and discovered several elements.

BES. Egyptian god of recreation, music, and dancing, sometimes also associated with childbirth. He was usually represented as a grotesque dwarf wearing a crown of feathers.

BESANÇON (bezoňsoň'). Cap. of Doubs dept, France, 61km (38m) S.W. of Belfort, on the Doubs. The fortress, on a rock 118m (387ft) above the town, was fortified by Vauban. The Roman remains incl. an amphitheatre, aqueduct, and triumphal arch of Marcus Aurelius. B. has also an 11th and 12th cent. cathedral. Watchmaking is the principle industry. B. is a great route centre. Pop. (1975) 124,000.

BESANT (bez'ant), **Annie** (1847-1933). British theosophist. B. in London, *née* Wood, she m. in 1867 the Rev. Frank B., who obtained a separation in 1873. She became closely associated with Charles Bradlaugh (q.v.) and with the Fabian Society. About 1889 she came under the influence of Mme Blavatsky, and henceforth was an enthusiastic theosophist. She went to India, founded the central Hindu college at Benares, and in 1917 was president of the Hindu National Congress. In 1926-7 she visited England and America with J. Krishnamurti, a young protégé in whom she recognized the new Messiah. She wrote many books on theosophical subjects and an autobiography (1893).

BESANT, Sir Walter (1836-1901). British author. He collaborated with James Rice in novels such as *The Golden Butterfly* (1876), and produced an attack on the social evils of the E. End, *All Sorts and Conditions of Men* (1882), and an unfinished *Survey of London* (1902-12). He was a founder of the Soc. of Authors.

BESIER, Rudolf (1878-1942). British playwright, author of the perennially popular *Barretts of Wimpole Street* (1930).

BESSARABIA. Territory of E. Europe. Annexed by Russia in 1812, after the 1917 revolution B. broke away and its union with Romania was agreed to by the Allies in a treaty signed in Paris in 1920. Russia never recognized this cession, and in 1940 reoccupied B. Romania ceded the area to the USSR by the peace treaty in 1947, and it was incorporated partly in Moldavia, partly in Ukraine, S.S.R.s.

BESSEL, Friedrich Wilhelm (1784-1846). German astronomer. Director of the newly-estab. observatory at Königsberg from 1813, he pub. in 1818 a catalogue of more than 3,000 stars and by his systematic research founded modern precision astronomy.

BE'SSEMER, Sir Henry (1813-98). British civil engineer and inventor of the *Bessemer Process* (1856) for converting molten pig-iron into steel.

BEST, Charles Herbert (1899-1978). Canadian physiologist, who was one of the team of Canadian scientists under the leadership of Sir Frederick Banting, whose researches resulted in 1922 in the discovery of insulin as a treatment for diabetes. A Banting-Best Dept of Medical

Research was founded in Toronto, and B. was its director 1941-67.

BETA PARTICLES. Electrons emitted from nuclei of radioactive substances undergoing spontaneous disintegration. Streams of B.P. are called beta rays.

BETELGEUSE (be'teljerz). Star, a red supergiant, in the constellation of Orion. The name is Arabic for 'shoulder of the giant', since that is its position.

BĒ'TEL-NUT. Fruit of the areca palm (*Areca catechu*), used as a masticatory by peoples of the East: chewing it results in blackened teeth and the mouth is stained deep red.

BETHE (bāt'e), **Hans Albrecht** (1906-). German-American physicist. A refugee from Hitler in 1933, he taught first in Britain, then in the USA where he became prof. of theoretical physics at Cornell in 1937. He worked on the first atom bomb, and was in 1967 awarded a Nobel prize, especially for his discoveries concerning energy production in stars.

BE'THLĒHEM. Small town of ancient Palestine 10km (6m) S. of Jerusalem, the reputed birthplace of Jesus Christ, and of King David. It contains the Church of the Nativity, used by Latins, Greeks, and Armenians, beneath the choir of which is the Grotto of the Nativity, much visited as a place of pilgrimage. In the N.W. stands a square-domed building said to mark the site of Rachel's tomb. In 1099 the Crusaders captured B., and Baldwin I was crowned king of Jerusalem there. The modern town of Beit-Lahm, Jordan, on the site, was occupied by Israel in 1967. Pop. (1973) 24,000.

BETHLEHEM. City of Penn., USA, on the Lehigh r., 80km (50m) N.W. of Philadelphia. It is the site of a chief plant of the B. Steel Corporation, one of the largest steel companies in the world. Pop. (1970) 72,700.

BETHMANN HOLLWEG (beht'mahn-holveg), **Theobald von** (1856-1921), German statesman who succeeded Prince Bülow as Imperial Chancellor in 1909. At the outbreak of the F.W.W. he defended Germany's invasion of Belgium and Luxemburg. He was dismissed in 1917.

BÉTHUNE (bātün'). Town in Pas-de-Calais dept, France, 32km (20m) N.N.W. of Arras, on the richest coalfield in France. Machinery, tyres, etc. are manufactured. Pop. (1975) 145,200.

BETJEMAN, Sir John (1906-84). English poet and essayist, originator of a peculiarly English light verse, nostalgic and delighting in Victorian bric-à-brac, Neo-Gothic architecture, and so on. His *Collected Poems* appeared in 1968 and a verse autobiography *Summoned by Bells* in 1960. He was knighted in 1969 and became Poet Laureate in 1972.

BE'TONY. Plant (*Betonica officinalis*) of the family Labiatae, a hedgerow weed in Britain. It has a hairy stem and leaves and dull purple flowers, and was formerly supposed to have curative properties.

BETTERTON, Thomas (*c.* 1635-1710). British actor. A member of the Duke of York's company after the Restoration, he attracted the attention of Charles II, and was particularly famous in such parts as Hamlet and Othello.

BETTI, Ugo (1892-1953). Italian poet and dramatist. In daily life a magistrate, his cleareyed view of things as they are is shot through with poetry. His best-known plays are *The Queen and the Rebels* (1949) and *The Burnt Flower-Bed* (1951).

BETJEMAN. In pensive mood the Poet Laureate waits on inspiration. For his ability to capture the popular mood and his care for the remains of England's past, Sir John Betjeman was regarded with much affection. *Photo: Courtesy of John Murray.*

BETTING. The staking of money, etc., on the result of some future event, generally of a sporting character, e.g. horse-racing, dog-racing, etc. In Britain only credit B. and B. on the course (whether by ready money or on the Tote, q.v., on approved courses on specified days) were formerly legal, but the B. and Gaming Act of 1960 legalized off-course cash B. and the establishment of B. Offices licensed by local authorities. Football 'pools' pay a duty on the stake money, and by the Pool B. Act (1954) a company or person promoting such a business must register with the local authority to whom annual accounts are submitted. The amount of the money prizes is determined by the number of successful forecasts of the results of matches received by the promoter except in fixed odds B.

BETTY, William Henry West (1791-1874). British boy actor, called the 'Young Roscius', after the greatest comic actor of ancient Rome. First appearing in Belfast aged 11, he was enthusiastically received for 6 yrs, especially in Shakespeare. As an adult actor he was not remarkable.

BETWS-Y-COED (betoos'-a-koid). Welsh village and tourist centre on the r. Conway, Gwynedd, in Snowdonia National Park. Pop. (1973) 720.

BEVAN, Aneurin (1897-1960). British Labour politician. B. at Tredegar, Mon., the son of a miner, he entered the pit at 13, later becoming a miner's agent. In 1929 he became M.P. for Ebbw Vale, holding the seat for the rest of his life, and with the establishment of the weekly *Tribune* became prominent in Labour journalism. As Min. of Health 1945-51, he started post-war rehousing and inaugurated the Health Service, and was Min. of Labour Jan.-April

1951, resigning because his opinions increasingly diverged from official Labour policy. As leader of the 'Bevanites' he conducted lively skirmishes, but in Nov. 1956 became 'Shadow' Foreign Sec., having reached a working arrangement with Gaitskell. He was a superb orator. He m. Jennie Lee (1904-), created life peeress 1970.

BEVERIDGE, William Henry, 1st baron (1879-1963). British administrator and economist. In 1908 he joined the Civil Service and acted as Lloyd George's lieutenant in the social legislation of the Liberal govt before the F.W.W. He was at the Board of Trade until 1916, for most of the time as Director of the newly-established Labour Exchanges. Leaving the Civil Service in 1919, he was director of the London School of Economics until 1937, when he was Master of University Coll., Oxford (until 1944). He was chairman of the Committee on Social Insurance and Allied Services (1941), and practically all his recommendations for a unified and greatly improved system of Social Security were at once accepted in principle by the Churchill Govt and embodied in later legislation. His most influential book was *Full Employment in a Free Society* (1944).

BEVERLY HILLS. Residential city adjoining Los Angeles, California, USA, famous as the home of Hollywood stars. Pop. (1970) 33,400.

BEVIN, Ernest (1881-1951). British Labour statesman and Trade Unionist. B. at Winsford, Som., the son of a farm labourer, he worked on a farm as a boy, and was ed. chiefly at evening classes in Bristol. At 29 he became a trade union official, and was largely responsible for the creation of the Transport and General Workers' Union. In 1920, at an official enquiry into dock labour, he won the title of 'Dockers' K.C.'. From 1921 until 1940 he was gen. sec. of the T.G.W.U. In 1940 he was returned as Labour M.P. for Wandsworth, having been already appointed by Churchill Min. of Labour and National Service, and a member of the War Cabinet. He organized the system of choosing boys ('B. boys') of all classes by ballot to work in the mines. He was For. Sec. in the Labour Govt of 1945, resigning owing to ill-health in 1951, when he became Lord Privy Seal.

BEWICK (bū'ik), **Thomas** (1753-1828). British artist. B. nr Newcastle upon Tyne, where at 14 he was apprenticed to an engraver, his wood engravings of animal life are masterly, e.g. *British Birds* (1797-1804).

BEXHILL. Seaside resort to the S.W. of Hastings, E. Sussex, England. The de la Warr Pavilion dates from 1937, and eroded stumps of the ancient forest that once reached to the sea in this part of England can be seen at low tide. Pop. (1971) 33,300.

BEZA (properly **De Bèsze**), **Théodore** (1519-1605). French reformer. He settled at Geneva, where he attached himself to Calvin, and succeeded him in 1564 as head of the reformed church at Geneva, which post he resigned in 1600. He wrote in defence of the burning of Servetus (1554), translated the N.T. into Latin, and presented in 1581 a 5th cent. Graeco-Latin MS. of the Gospels and the Acts, the *Codex Bezae,* to Cambridge univ.

BÉZIERS (behziā'). Town in Hérault dept, S. France, on the Canal du Midi. It is a centre of the wine trade and was once a Roman station. Pop. (1975) 92,530.

BÉZIQUE (behsēk'; Fr. *bésigue).* Card game, supposed to have originated in Spain, and introduced into England in 1861. About 1869 it became very popular in the London clubs. *Rubicon B.* has a code of laws promulgated by the Portland Club in 1887.

BHAGALPUR. Town in Bihar state, India, 193km (120m) E.S.E. of Patna. It has Jain temples, and makes silks. Pop. (1971) 172,700.

BHA'GAVAD-GITA (-gē'tah) (The Song of the Blessed). Religious and philosophical Sanskrit poem forming an episode in the 6th book of the Mahabharata, one of the 2 great Hindu epics. It is the supreme religious work of Hinduism.

BHAMO (bhahmō'). Town in Burma, 48km (30m) S.W. of the nearest point of the Chinese frontier, 480km (300m) N.E. of Mandalay. It stands at the head of navigation of the Irrawaddy r. Pop. *c.* 10,000.

BHARAT. Hindi name of INDIA.

BHARATA NATYAM (ba'rata nat'yam). Type of Indian classical dancing, supposed to have been described by the ancient expert Bharata.

BHATGA'ON. Town in Nepal, 11km (7m) S.E. of Katmandu. It dates from the 9th cent., is a religious centre, and possesses a palace with golden doors. Pop. (1973) 82,250.

BHAVNAGAR. Seaport, railway terminus, and airport of Gujarat, India, in the Kathiawar peninsula on the Gulf of Cambay. It makes and exports textiles, and was cap. of the former Rajput princely state of B. Pop. (1971) 226,000.

BHŌPA'L. Cap. of Madhya Pradesh, India. It stands on the N. slopes of the Vindhya Hills, has an airport, and is developing rapidly as an industrial centre making textiles, chemicals, jewellery, etc. It was cap. of the former princely state of B. The nearby Bhimbetka Caves (*c,* 600 covering an area of 10 sq.km/4 sq.m) were discovered in 1973 to contain the world's largest collection of prehistoric paintings. They incl. tribal battles and dances, and hunts, and date from the Mesolithic period (10,000 yrs ago). Pop. (1971) 392,000.

BHUBANESWAR (boobahnesh'wah). Cap. of Orissa, India. A place of pilgrimage and centre of Siva worship, it has temples of the 6th-12th cents., and was cap. of the Kesaris (Lion) Dynasty of Orissa 474-950. Utkal Univ. (1843) was removed from Cuttack to B. in 1962. Pop. (1971) 105,500.

BHUMIBOL ADULYADEJ (pōō'mipol adōō-leah'desh) (1927-). King of Thailand. Ed. in Bangkok and Switzerland, he succeeded on the assassination of his brother in 1946, formally taking the throne in 1950. In 1973, the king was active, with popular support in overthrowing the military govt of Field-Marshal Kittachorn, and ending a sequence of army-dominated regimes in power from 1932.

BHUTAN (bhootahn'). Independent state in the S. slopes of the Himalayas, between Tibet and Assam. It is very mountainous. The climate is varied, depending on the altitude. The dominant people are of Tibetan origin, and speak a Tibetan dialect. In religion they are normally Buddhist. Maize and rice are grown in the valleys of tributaries of the Brahmaputra. Tasichozong and Punakha are 2 of the chief fortresses of the country. Treaties of 1865 and 1910 with the British govt were replaced in 1949 by one with India, under which B. receives a subsidy and is guided in external relations by the Indian govt. The cap. is Punakha (summer Thimphu). The dynasty was estab. 1907 and King Jigme Singhi Wangchuk (1955-) succeeded in 1972. Area 46,600 sq.km (18,000 sq.m); pop. (1977) 1,100,000. M.U.: ngultrum.

BHUTTO (bōōt'ō), Zulfikar Ali (1928-79). Pakistani statesman. Ed. at Berkeley, Calif. and Oxford, he became a lawyer and in 1967 founder of the Pakistani People's Party. In 1971-3, following the secession of E. Pakistan (Bangladesh), he was pres., and was then P.M. until the military coup of 1977. In 1978 he was sentenced to death for alleged conspiracy to murder a political opponent and, despite international pleas for clemency, was hanged.

BIAFRA, Bight of. *See* BONNY.

BIAFRA (bē-af'rah), **Rep. of.** State proclaimed in 1967 when the predominantly Ibo Eastern Region of Nigeria seceded under Lt-Col. Odumegwu Ojukwu an Oxford-educated Ibo. On the proclamation of B. civil war ensued with the rest of the Federation, but in a bitterly fought campaign Federal forces had confined the Biafrans to a shrinking area of the interior by 1968, and by 1970 B. ceased to exist.

BIALYSTOK (byah'lüstok). City of Poland, cap. of B. region, 170km (105m) N.E. of Warsaw. Dating from 1310, it makes woollen textiles, chemicals, tools, etc. Pop. (1978) 207,000.

BIARRITZ (bē-ahrēts'). French seaside resort and spa on the Bay of Biscay, in Pyrénées-Atlantique dept, S.W. of Bayonne. It was popularized by Queen Victoria and Edward VII. Pop. (1975) 27,000.

BIATHLON (bī-ath'lon). Cross-country race on skis, contestants also shooting at targets with rifles on the way: it is used as a military training exercise.

BIBE'SCO, Princess. *See* ASQUITH.

BIBLE (bībl; Gk *ta biblia*, the books). Collection of books comprising the authoritative documents of the Jewish and Christian religions, and divided into the Old Testament or 'Covenant', the Apocrypha, and the New Testament.

The O.T. contains those books recognized by the Jews and classified by them as: the Law (the Pentateuch or books of Moses; recognized soon after the return from captivity); the Prophets (Joshua, Judges, Samuel, Kings, Isaiah, Jeremiah, Ezekiel and the 12 minor prophets, Hosea to Malachi, recognized by the 3rd cent. B.C.); and the Hagiographa or Sacred Writings (including the remaining books; finally recognized *c.* A.D. 90-100).

The Apocrypha consist for the most part of the books of the Gk Septuagint which were not included in the final Hebrew canon. Included in the Vulgate, and so recognized by Catholics as authoritative, they were excluded by Luther, and segregated by the English translators from Coverdale onwards. Many editions of the A.V. omit them. Texts of other apocryphal works, e.g. *The War between the Children of Light and the Children of Darkness,* were found among the Dead Sea Scrolls (q.v.).

The N.T., containing those books recognized by the Church in the 4th cent. as canonical, is also divided into three parts: history, Matthew to Acts; epistles, Romans to Jude; and prophecy, Revelation.

A copy of the 'lost' *Gospels of St Thomas,* also known as the *logia* or sayings of Jesus, was discovered by peasants in an earthenware jar in 1945 at Nag Hammadi, nr Luxor. A 3rd or 4th cent. translation in Coptic of a Gk original dating from about A.D. 135, it is variously regarded as authentic, or as more probably a later elaboration.

Text. Until the discovery of the Dead Sea Scrolls (q.v.), which revealed the existence of an almost identical text in the 2nd cent. B.C., the earliest dated Hebrew MS of the O.T. belonged to A.D. 916. Of other versions of the O.T. the Gk Septuagint is the chief. The MS material for the Gk text of the N.T. now consists of (1) papyri (2nd and 3rd cents.); (2) MSS. in capital or uncial writing, including the Codex Vaticanus and Codex Sinaiticus of the 4th cent.; (3) MSS. in minuscule writing (9th to 15th cent.). In addition there is the evidence of early translations, notably Jerome's Latin Vulgate (384-91).

English Translations. The 1st complete B. was produced by John Wycliffe (1380-2), from the Latin Vulgate. In 1525 Tyndale printed a version of the N.T., and in 1535 his disciple Coverdale pub. the first complete printed translation on the Continent (in England 1537). A revised version by Coverdale (the Great Bible), commissioned by Thomas Cromwell, was ordered to be placed in all churches in 1539. The Geneva Bible (complete 1560), prepared by the Protestant Marian exiles, was the first to adopt verse divisions and was not superseded until the A.V. of 1611 (subsequently revised: N.T. 1881, O.T. 1885, Apocrypha 1895).

Recent translations incl. the American Revised Standard Version (1946-57; modified for R.Cs. 1966), the New English Bible (1970; also used by R.Cs.), and the New International Version (1973-9), prepared by reformed and evangelical bodies in the USA, with participation by UK, Canada, Australia and NZ.

BIBLE. Although Henry VIII had already broken with the Pope, Coverdale's Bible of 1535, illustrated here, was published on the Continent - probably being printed in Zürich. *Photo: The British and Foreign Bible Society.*

BIBLE SOCIETIES. Societies founded for the promotion of the translation and distribution of the Scriptures. The largest is the British and Foreign B.S., founded in 1804.

BIBLICAL CRITICISM. The subject is generally treated under 3 main headings: (1) *lower or textual C.,* which is directed to the recovery of the original text; (2) *higher* or *documentary C.,* which is concerned with questions of authorship, date, and literary sources; and (3) *historical C.,* which seeks to ascertain the actual historic content of the Bible, aided by archaeological discoveries and the ancient history of neighbouring peoples.

BICARBONATE OF SODA ($NaHCO_3$). A white crystalline compound more properly called sodium hydrogen carbonate. It neutralizes acids and is used in medicine as an antacid. It is also used in baking powders and in effervescing drinks.

Books of the Bible

Old Testament

Genesis	Nehemiah	Hosea
Exodus	Esther	Joel
Leviticus	Job	Amos
Numbers	Psalms	Obadiah
Deuteronomy	Proverbs	Jonah
Joshua	Ecclesiastes	Micah
Judges	Song of Solomon	Nahum
Ruth	Isaiah	Habakkuk
I & II Samuel	Jeremiah	Zephaniah
I & II Kings	Lamentations	Haggai
I & II Chronicles	Ezekiel	Zechariah
Ezra	Daniel	Malachi

Apocrypha

I & II Esdras	Song of the Three Children
Tobit	Story of Susanna
Judith	Bel and the Dragon
Rest of Esther	Prayer of Manasses
Wisdom	I & II Maccabees
Ecclesiasticus (of Jeremiah)	
Baruch, with the Epistle	

New Testament

Matthew	Galatians	Philemon
Mark	Ephesians	Hebrew
Luke	Philippians	James
John	Colossians	I & II Peter
Acts of the Apostles	I & II Thessalonians	I, II & III John
Romans	I & II Timothy	Jude
I & II Corinthians	Titus	Revelation

BICYCLE. *See* CYCLING.

BIDAULT (bēdoh'), **Georges** (1899-). French statesman. Before the S.W.W. he made a reputation as a journalist, fought in the 1940 campaign and also in the resistance movement. As a leader of M.R.P., he held office as PM and For. Min. in a number of unstable administrations of 1944-54. As head of the *Organisation de l'Armée Secrète* from 1962, in succession to Salan, he left the country, but was allowed to return in 1968.

BIDEFORD (bid'iford). Small port of N. Devon, England, on the estuary of the Torridge. It was important in medieval times, and was in the possession of the Grenvilles 11-18th cents., Sir Richard Grenville (q.v.) being active in the colonization of America. Pop. (1971) 11,000.

BIEL. German form of BIENNE.

BIELEFELD (bē'lefeld). Manufacturing town of N. Rhine-Westphalia, Germany, 55km (34m) E. of Münster, at the foot of the Teutoburger Wald. Pop. (1970) 168,600.

BIELOSTOK. Russian form of BIALYSTOK.

BIENNE (byen'). Swiss town and lake in Berne canton, in the Jura mountains, N.W. of Berne. The town stands at the N. end of Lake B., and is the centre of a watchmaking industry. Pop. (1970) 66,000.

BIERCE (bērs), **Ambrose** (**Gwinett**) (1842-1914?). American author. B. in Ohio, he served with the Union army in the Civil War, and spent most of his life as a journalist in San Francisco. He established his reputation as a master of supernatural and psychological horror by his *Tales of Soldiers and Civilians* (1891), and *Can Such Things Be?* (1893). In 1913 he disappeared on a secret mission to Mexico.

BIFFEN, Sir Rowland (1874-1949). British botanist. Prof. of agricultural botany at Cambridge 1908-31, he was the first to use Mendelian principles to improve cereal varieties. He also revolutionized the attitude to plant disease by estab. that resistance is an inherited characteristic.

BI'GAMY. The offence of marrying another person when one's husband or wife is still alive, and the marriage has neither been dissolved nor annulled. It is a good defence to a charge of B. to prove that the husband or wife of the person charged with the crime has been continually absent for the previous 7 years and has not been known to be alive within that time by the accused, or to prove that the accused genuinely believed on reasonable grounds that his or her husband or wife was dead, even though 7 years have not elapsed. Although a person proving any of these defences is not guilty of B., the second marriage will still be invalid. The maximum penalty for B. is 7 years' imprisonment. The position in the USA is similar.

BIG BEN. Bell in the clock tower of the Houses of Parliament, cast at the Whitechapel Bell Foundry in 1858, and popularly known as 'B.B.' after Sir Benjamin Hall, First Commissioner of works at the time. It weighs 13,700 kg (13½ tons).

BIGGIN HILL. Airport in the S.E. London bor. of Bromley. It was the most famous of the R.A.F. stations in the Battle of Britain.

BIGHT (bīt). A coastal indentation, such as the Bight of Bonny and Great Australian Bight.

BIHA'R. State of India, stretching across the Ganges valley from Nepal to Orissa. For the most part it is a flat and fertile plain, and densely populated. Rice, maize, wheat, jute, tobacco, etc., are grown, and some artificial irrigation has been developed. Coal is mined, and B. is India's richest iron-producing area, with iron and steel plants at Jamshedpur. Patna is the cap. Area 174,038 sq.km (67,000 sq.m); pop. (1971) 56,387,000.

BIJAPUR (bējahpoor'). Ancient city of Karnataka, Rep. of India. Cap. of Muslim kingdom of B. 15th-17th cents., it has splendid remains. Pop. (1971) 78,900.

BIKANER (bikanēr'). City in Rajasthan, Rep. of India, once the cap. of the Rajput state of B. It is famous for carpets, and manufactures electrical appliances, etc. Pop. (1971) 188,600.

BIKINI (bēkē'ni). Island and atoll in the Marshall Islands, Pacific. In the atoll in 1946 atom bomb tests were carried out by the USA. *See* BOMB.

BILBAO (bilbah'ō). Cap. of Biscay prov. and an important port of N. Spain, 71km (44m) W. of Santander, on the r. Nervión. There are rich iron deposits near, and much iron is exported to S. Wales. B. also exports wine, lead, olive oil, and has large iron and steel works, chemical, cement and food factories. Pop. (1970) 410,490.

BILBERRY (whortleberry, or blaeberry). Plant (*Vaccinium myrtillus*) of the family Ericaceae closely resembling the cranberry, but distinguished by its bluish berries.

BILE. A brownish fluid secreted by the liver, also called gall. B. is contained in a small pear-shaped bag on the under-surface of the liver called the gall-bladder, and plays an important part in the digestive processes of the intestines.

BILHARZIA. *See* SCHISTOSOMIASIS.

BILLIARDS. Indoor game of skill played with cues and composition balls on a heavy rectangular table covered by green cloth.

There are pockets at each corner and in the middle of each long side of the table, and the surface is marked out with a baulk line, a semicircle known as the 'D', and 4 spots. Three balls are used, a red and two white, and one of the latter has a spot for easy identification. Points are scored by the cannon, i.e. by the cue (player's) ball hitting the other 2 balls successively, or by winning and losing hazards, the former being made by striking the cue ball against one of the object balls, and sending it into a pocket, and the latter by pocketing the cue ball after hitting one of the object balls. Points are awarded for cannons and for going in off, or pocketing, the white and red balls. The amateur game is usually played for 100 up. The player continues until the end of his break, i.e. until he fails to score, when his opponent takes over.

The origin of the game is obscure, but it has been played in England and France for many centuries. The earliest known rules were printed in 1650.

BILLINGHAM. *See* STOCKTON-ON-TEES.

BILLINGSGATE. Originally one of the gates of the city of London giving on to the Thames just below London Bridge. Near by there is a fish-market dating from the 9th cent. The language of the porters was frequently commented upon by 17th cent. writers, until the word has come to mean foul language.

BILLION. In British usage, a million million (1,000,000,000,000); but in USA and France, a thousand million (1,000,000,000), which in Britain is a milliard.

BILLITON. Another form of BELITUNG.

BILL OF EXCHANGE. A form of commercial credit instrument, defined in Britain by the Bills of Exchange Act, 1882, as an unconditional order in writing addressed by one person to another, signed by the person giving it, requiring the person to whom it is addressed to pay on demand or at a fixed or determinable future time a certain sum in money to or to the order of a specified person, or to bearer. A *cheque* is a B. of E. drawn on a bank payable on demand. US practice is governed by the Uniform Negotiable Instruments Law, drafted on the same lines as the British, and accepted by all states by 1927.

BILL OF RIGHTS (1689). The Act embodying the Declaration of Rights drawn up by the House of Commons and presented to William of Orange and his wife before they ascended the throne as William III and Queen Mary in place of James II. It declares the following illegal: the suspension of laws by royal authority without consent of Parliament; the power to dispense with laws; the establishment of special courts of law; levying money by royal prerogative without the consent of Parliament; the raising or keeping of a standing army in time of peace within the kingdom without such consent. The right to petition the King, the freedom of parliamentary elections, freedom of speech in parliamentary debates, and the necessity for frequent parliaments, are also asserted.

The American **Bill of Rights** (1791) comprises the first 10 amendments to the Constitution: 1. freedom of worship, speech, press, assembly and ability to petition the govt; 2. right to bear and keep arms (this has hindered the control of weapons used illicitly in modern times); 3. conditions for billeting soldiers in private homes; 4. regulations for rights of search and seizure; 5. none to be 'deprived of life, liberty or property without due process of law' or compelled in any criminal case to be a witness against himself (the last provision was frequently quoted in the era of McCarthyism); 6. right to speedy trial, witnesses, defence counsel, etc.; 7. right of trial by jury; 8. excessive bail or fines or 'cruel and unusual punishment' not to be inflicted (the last provision has in recent times been used to attempt to prove the death penalty illegal); 9 and 10. safeguard to the states and people all rights not specifically delegated to the central govt.

BILLY THE KID. Nickname of American Wild West 'hero', William H. Bonney (1859–81). A leader in the Lincoln County cattle war in New Mexico, he was sentenced to death for murdering a sheriff, but escaped (killing two guards), and was finally shot trying to escape being retaken.

BILOXI (bilok'si). Port in Mississippi, USA on a peninsula in Mississippi Sound. It was named after a local tribe of Indians, and is now the centre of a large seafood canning industry (shrimps, oysters). Pop. (1970) 48,500.

BIMETALLIC STRIP. Strip made from 2 metals each having a different coefficient of thermal expansion which therefore deflects when subjected to a change in temperature. Used widely for temperature measurement and control.

BIMETALLISM. That monetary system in which gold and silver both circulate together at a ratio fixed by the State, are coined by the Mint on equal terms, and are legal tender to any amount. Advocates of B. have argued that the 'compensatory action of the double standard' makes for a currency more stable than one based only on gold, since the changes in the value of the two metals taken together may be expected to be less than the changes in one of them.

BINARY NUMBER SYSTEM. A system in which numbers are represented by combinations of successive powers of 2, i.e. 1, 2, 4, 8, 16, etc. (cf. decimal system where successive powers of 10 are used). Some examples of binary numbers are:

Decimal notation	*Binary notation*
5	$101 = 1\times2^2 + 0\times2^1 + 1\times2^0$
14	$1110 = 1\times2^3 + 1\times2^2 + 1\times2^1 + 0\times2^0$
43	$101011 = 1\times2^5 + 0\times2^4 + 1\times2^3 + 0\times2^2 + 1\times2^1 + 1\times2^0$

This system is widely used in computers, because electrically 0 can be read as 'off' and 1 as 'on'.

BINARY STAR. A star made up of 2 separate components, moving round their common centre of gravity. In some Bs. (e.g. Gamma Virginis) the components are virtually equal, and widely separated; with others (e.g. Sirius) one component is very much brighter than the companion. The theory that a B. results from the fission of a formerly single star has now been generally rejected. Famous Bs. incl. Mizar, in the Great Bear; Castor, in the Twins; and the brilliant southern star Alpha Centauri. With some Bs. there are more than 2 components, and Castor, for instance, is a complex multiple system.

BINGO. Game played with cards divided into numbered squares. Each player has 1 or more cards and when the 'caller' draws numbered discs from a bag, numbered balls from an automatic machine, etc., he marks off such numbers as appear on his cards. On achieving a full line (horizontal and sometimes also diagonal), the player shouts 'Full House' or 'House', and may win a prize. Long known as a children's game (lotto), and played in the forces as 'housey-housey', it became a gambling craze in the 1960s in Britain, especially among housewives.

BĪNO'CŪLAR. An optical instrument for the viewing of an object with both eyes, e.g. field-glasses and opera-glasses. The first B. telescope was constructed by a Dutchman, J. Lippershey, in 1608, but interest then lapsed until 1823, when the Dutch binocular telescope was re-invented by a Viennese optician, J. Voigtlaender. Later development was largely due to E. Abbé, of Jena, who at the end of the last cent. designed prism Bs. that foreshadowed the instruments of today, in which not only magnification but stereoscopic effect is obtained.

BĪNŌ'MIAL. In algebra, an expression consisting of 2 terms, as a + b, a − b. The BINOMIAL THEOREM discovered by Newton and first pub. in 1676, is a formula whereby any power of a B. quantity may be found without performing the progressive multiplications.

BI'NTŪRONG. Small mammal (*Arctictis binturong*) with a shaggy coat, short muzzle, and tufted ears. The length of the head and body is *c.* 75cm. (30in) and the long prehensile tail measures *c.* 60cm (24in). The B. is black to greyish black, and is a native of S.E. Asia, ranging from Assam to the Philippines. It sleeps in trees during the day and feeds at night on fruit, eggs, and small animals.

BINYON, Laurence (1869–1943). British poet. B. at Lancaster, son of a clergyman, he became keeper of Prints and Drawings at the British Museum (1932–3), and pub. studies of English and Eastern art. His verse vols. incl. *Lyric Poems* (1894) and *London Visions,* but he is best remembered for his fine ode *For the Fallen* (1914).

BIO-BIO (bē'o-bē'o) (Araucanian 'much water'). Longest river of Chile, 370km (230m) from its source in the Andes to its mouth on the Pacific.

BIOCHEMISTRY. Science concerned with the chemistry of living material and processes, sub-divided into the study of fats, proteins, carbohydrates, enzymes, etc. Two principal aspects of this subject are the static, dealing with chemical composition and structure; and the dynamic, dealing with the processes by which food is built up into living matter and then broken down to waste products.

BIOECONOMICS. Theory put forward in 1979 by Chicago economist Gary Becker that the concepts of sociobiology apply also in economics. The competitiveness and self-interest built into human genes are said to make capitalism an effective economic system, whereas the selflessness and collectivism proclaimed as the socialist ideal are contrary to human genetic makeup and so produce an ineffective system.

BIOGENESIS (-jen'esis). Biological term coined in 1870 by T. H. Huxley to express the hypothesis that living matter always arises by the agency of pre-existing living matter. The opposite idea, that of spontaneous generation or abiogenesis, i.e. that living things may arise out of non-living matter, was generally held until comparatively recently, but evidence is inconclusive.

BIO'GRAPHY. The history of a person's life not written by himself. Among ancient biographers are Xenophon, Plutarch, Tacitus, Suetonius, and the authors of the Gospels. Medieval B. was devoted to religious edification and produced chronicles of saints and martyrs; among the Bs. of laymen are Einhard's *Charlemagne* and Asser's *Alfred.*

In England B. really begins with the early Tudor period and such works as Roper's *Sir Thomas More.* More frequently in the 17th cent., B. was established as an art by Johnson's *Lives of the Poets* and Boswell's *Johnson.* The 19th cent. is remarkable for such fine biographers as Southey, Lockhart, Moore, Mrs Gaskell, J. Forster, G. H. Lewes, Morley, and Carlyle, but the general tendency was to irrelevant detail and the suppression of the more 'human' facts. Lytton Strachey's *Eminent Victorians* opened the modern era of frankness, and the new development of the biographical novel was instituted by Maurois with his studies of Byron and Shelley. Orthodox 20th cent. writers include Churchill, John Buchan, David Cecil, Harold Nicolson, Aldous Huxley, Edith Sitwell, Michael Holroyd (Lytton Strachey), Martin Gilbert (Churchill), and Elizabeth Longford (Queen Victoria and Wellington).

The earliest biographical dictionary in the modern sense was that of Pierre Bayle (1696), followed during the 19th cent. by the development of national Bs. on the Continent, and the foundation of the English Dictionary of National B. in 1882 and the Dictionary of American B. in 1928.

BIOKO (bē-ō'kō). Island in the Bight of Bonny, W Africa, part of Equatorial Guinea. Formerly a Spanish possession, as Fernando Poo, it was known 1973–7 as Macías Nguema.

BIOLOGICAL/CHEMICAL WARFARE. The use of living organisms (or infectious material derived from them) to bring about death or disease in man, animals or plants; or the use of gaseous, liquid or solid substances with toxic effects to man, animals or plants. B./C. Warfare was condemned by the Geneva Convention (1925), and the UN has called for all member states to adhere to it. Nevertheless, experimentation does continue in these weapons, otherwise those who refrain would be at the mercy of those who perfect them.

In 1980 the Geneva Conference had the subject under review, and there have been USA-USSR negotiations. Chemical weapons such as NAPALM (q.v.) and defoliants (*see* DIOXIN) were used in Vietnam, and poison gas has allegedly been used in Afghanistan and Laos. Protective equipment for use in the field is cumbersome: masks, rubber gloves, and overgarments of interwoven fibre layers over a black charcoal lining (to trap noxious elements).

BIOLOGICAL SHIELD. Shield round a reactor to protect personnel from the effects of radiation.

BIOLOGY (bī-o'loji). The science of life. The word was first used by the German physician Treviranus in 1802, and was popularized by Lamarck. Strictly speaking, B. includes all the life sciences, e.g. anatomy and physiology, bacteriology, zoology and botany, ecology, genetics, biochemistry and biophysics, animal behaviour, embryology, and plant breeding.

Medical men, such as Hippocrates in the 5th cent. B.C., made the first accurate observations, describing medicinally useful plants and their properties, and Aristotle, in the 4th cent. laid the foundations of a philosophical approach. Attempts at a scientific physiology were bound to fail in the absence of scientific instruments, a tradition of experiment, and a body of organized knowledge with its own terminology. Galen, in the 1st cent. A.D., epitomized what was known of anatomy, but from A.D. 200 to 1200 no scientific advances were made, and only with the Renaissance did free enquiry again come into its own. The 16th cent. saw the production of encyclopaedias of natural history, such as that of Gesner (1516–65), and the beginnings of modern anatomy,

BIRDS. A selection of representative forms.

notably at Padua under Vesalius (1514-64), who was succeeded by Fabricius. William Harvey, a student of the latter, laid the foundation of modern physiology by his work on the circulation of the blood. This was the first time that any basic function of the body had been scientifically explained, or that quantitative considerations were properly applied in B.

In the 17th cent. came the rise of scientific societies, such as Britain's Royal Society, and of scientific journals and museums. The use of alcohol for preserving specimens was a great step forward, but the outlook in B. was transformed by the introduction of the microscope (Malpighi, Grew, Swammerdam, and Leeuwenhoek were pioneers). Meanwhile, in addition to the complex world revealed by the microscope, explorers had been discovering myriads of new plants and animals and by the early 18th cent. it had become urgent to find a means of classification, and Linnaeus introduced a binomial system. Under this, the name was reduced to 2 Latin or Latinized words - the 1st for the genus, or group of similar species, the 2nd for the individual species: later a 3rd or sub-specific name was added to distinguish differing geographical sub-groups.

In modern B. evolution (q.v.) is the guiding principle and this cent. has seen an all-out attack on the central problem - the mechanism of cellular inheritance. The genetic apparatus in the nucleus of a cell determines the character of the other materials there, and so rules its entire activity. The relationship between the genetic material or DNA (deoxyribonucleic acid) and the vital protein materials was long thought to be governed by a 'genetic code' and in 1961 a team of scientists at the Cavendish Laboratory, Cambridge (incl. F. H. C. Crick and S. Brenner), succeeded in breaking it. These advances in cell study (cytology), have been greatly assisted by the development of the electron microscope, which uses a beam of electrons instead of a light beam. *See* also ANATOMY, BIOCHEMISTRY, DARWIN, PASTEUR, MICROSCOPE, etc.

BĪ'OPSY. Removal of tissue from a living body for the purpose of diagnostic examination.

BIO-RHYTHMS. Theory that everyone is governed from birth by 3 cycles or rhythms, which remain unchanged throughout life. The intellectual (33 days) governs reasoning, learning facts and logic; emotional (28 days) governs mood, degree of irritability, etc.; and physical (23 days) governs self-confidence and energy. The day when any of these cycles passes from its positive to its regenerative stage is regarded as 'critical', and when 2 or 3 of them coincide in being critical on the same day, particular care is alleged to be necessary. In Japan and USA commercial cos. have used the theory in an attempt to reduce accident levels.

BĪ'OSPHERE. Region of earth, air and water occupied by living organisms. Man-made modifications have unpredictable consequences, e.g. imbalance of carbon dioxide and oxygen in the atmosphere. Transatlantic jets burn 30 tons of oxygen per flight and produce carbon dioxide, and natural plant sources of oxygen are being reduced by expanding cities, etc.

BIOTECHNOLOGY. The industrial processing of materials by biological agents, such as microorganisms, to create various products and services. For example, a biofuel, such as methane, can be made from biodegradable waste materials, and a food product, such as single cell protein, can be made from methanol (made from methane). A service, such as the more effective displacement of oil from deep wells, may be secured by the use of microbial polysaccharides. *See also* BACTERIA.

BIRCH, John M. (1918-45). American Baptist missionary. B. in Georgia, he served in China, and during the S.W.W. was commissioned in the USAAF to carry out intelligence work behind the lines there. He was killed by Chinese Communists 10 days after the war ended. The ultra-nationalist *J. B. Society* (1958) was named after him.

BIRCH. Tree of the genus *Betula*, including about 25 species, found in the cool temperate parts of the northern hemisphere, of which the white or silver, *Betula alba*, is the best-known. It is of great importance to man, as its timber is quickgrowing and very durable. The bark is used for tanning and dyeing leather, and an oil is obtained from it.

BIRDS. Warm-blooded, vertebrate animals clothed in feathers, and with their fore-limbs transformed into wings. They are oviparous, and feathers and scales originate as epidermal appendages. Except in brain development they are structurally as highly organized as mammals. Their behaviour is largely instinctive. Yet their body temperature is so much higher than that of mammals that they exhibit the emotional side of life in a far greater degree. Physically and mentally they have become highly specialized.

Primarily birds are divided into the *Archaeornithes* (also called Saururae): extinct forms with wellmarked reptilian affinities, represented by a single genus, Archaeopteryx (q.v.) and the *Neornithes* or modern birds, which includes two distinct types. (a) The *Ratitae* are flightless and their breastbone resembles a flat bottomless raft (Lat. *ratis*); they comprise only 5 extant forms, viz. the ostrich, rhea, kiwi, emu, and cassowary. (b) The *Carinatae* comprise the vast majority of living and extinct birds, in which the breastbone is provided with a keel (Lat. *carina*) which amplifies the surface for attachments of the immensely developed muscles of flight. A widely accepted classification of Bs. is given in the Table.

In addition to their use in flight, feathers also give protection and regulate body temperature (ranging from 40° to 43°C). The vocal apparatus is highly specialized, with no 'obstructions' to prevent free passage of the voiced current of air through the open mouth and, though the lungs are relatively small and inelastic, the air supply is reinforced through numerous air sacs, direct prolongations of the lungs. Besides song (used in courtship but continued while the female broods), there are call and alarm notes. Display of plumes and other ornamentations by the male before the female plays the major part in courtship.

Bs. benefit man by eating insect pests (it has been computed that the blue titmouse consumes *c.* 6½ million insects per annum), eliminating rodent pests in the case of birds of prey, and acting as scavengers. Their senses of smell and touch are little developed, but their hearing, despite no external ears, is excellent and even more so their sight - B. migrants are thought to be largely guided by landmarks. The average lifespan is 2 to 6 years. *See* also ARCHAEOPTERYX, DINOSAUR, MIGRATION, ORNITHOLOGY, TERATORN.

BIRDS OF PARADISE. Family of birds (*Paradiseidae*) native to New Guinea and the neighbouring islands. The

Classification of Birds

Passeriformes. Crows, jays, choughs, starlings, birds-of-paradise, orioles, finches, larks, pipits, wagtails, creepers, nuthatches, titmice, goldcrests, shrikes, waxwings, flycatchers, warblers, thrushes, wheatears, wrens, dippers, swallows, lyre-birds.
Apodiformes. Swifts, humming-birds.
Caprimulgiformes. Nightjars.
Trogoniformes. Trogons, quetzals.
Coliiformes. Mouse-birds.
Coraciiformes. Hornbills, hoopoes, kingfishers, rollers, bee-eaters, etc.
Piciformes. Woodpeckers, barbets, toucans, etc.
Cuculiformes. Cuckoos, plantain-eaters.
Psittaciformes. Parrots and cockatoos.
Strigiformes. Owls.
Falconiformes. Vultures, eagles, hawks, falcons.
Ciconiiformes. Herons, storks, ibises, spoonbills, flamingoes.
Anseriformes. Swans, geese, ducks, mergansers, American screamers.
Pelecaniformes. Cormorants, darters, gannets, pelicans, frigate-birds, tropic-birds.
Procellariiformes. Petrels, shearwaters, albatrosses.
Sphenisciformes. Penguins.
Podicipediformes. Grebes.
Gaviiformes. Divers.
Columbiformes. Pigeons, dodo, sand-grouse.
Charadriiformes. Snipe, curlews, godwits, phalaropes, sandpipers, avocets, plovers, pratincoles, coursers, jacanas, gulls, terns, auks, bustards, cranes, trumpeters, etc.
Gruiformes. Rails, crakes, moorhens, coots, etc.
Galliformes. Grouse, pheasants, partridges, domestic fowl, turkeys, peacocks, curassows, etc.
Tinamiformes. Tinamous.
Struthioniformes. Ostriches
Rheiformes. Rheas.
Casuariformes. Cassowaries, emus.
Apterygiformes. Kiwis.

males are noted for the extreme beauty of their plumage; the females are inconspicuously coloured.

BIRKENHEAD, Frederick Edwin Smith, 1st earl of (1872-1930). British Cons. statesman. B. at Birkenhead and ed at Oxford, he was called to the bar in 1899. He was elected Cons. MP for a Liverpool seat in 1906, and fiercely resisted Lloyd George's budget of 1909 and the Parliament Act of 1910-11. When Home Rule for Ireland became a burning topic of debate, 'F.E.' joined with Sir Edward Carson in organizing armed resistance in Ulster, his activities earning him the sobriquet of 'Galloper Smith'. In 1915 he became Solicitor-General, and later in the same year Attorney-General. He was Lord Chancellor 1919-22, and Sec. for India 1924-8, and received an earldom in 1922.

BIRKENHEAD. Seaport and industrial town in Merseyside, England, on the Mersey estuary opposite Liverpool. The first settlement grew up round a Benedictine priory, and B. was still a small village when William Laird estab. a small shipbuilding yard, the forerunner of the huge Cammell Laird yards. In 1929 the first iron vessel in England was laid down at B. Wallasey dock, first of the series, was opened in 1847, and B. now specializes in bulk cargoes. The rail Mersey Tunnel (1886) and road Queensway Tunnel (1934) link B. with Liverpool. Pop. (1972) 137,000.

BIRMINGHAM. Second largest city in the UK in the West Midlands (admin. H.Q.) N.W. of London. Most of the pop. are engaged in metal-based and engineering industries, mainly the production of cars, but incl. machine tools, nuts and bolts, guns and electro-plate. Other industries incl. plastics, food products, chocolate, chemicals, glass, paint and enamels, electrical apparatus, and jewellery. It is a road and rail centre, with an airport at Elmdon to the S., and the industrial canal links are being developed for leisure. The cathedral church of St Philip (1711-19) by Thomas Archer, is one of Britain's few baroque buildings; the 13th cent. St Martin's church was rebuilt 1873; and the R.C. cathedral of St Chad (1839-41) is by Pugin. The old Town Hall (1831) was designed by Hansom (q.v.) and the Central Library (1973) by John Madin. There is a symphony orchestra, an art gallery and museum famed for its Pre-Raphaelites, a Midlands Art Centre (where ordinary people practise arts and crafts), and the repertory theatre, first founded by Sir Barry Jackson (1879-1961) in 1913, was rehoused in 1971. The Bull Ring (1964) is one of Europe's finest shopping centres. There are 2 univs., the Univ. of B. (1900) and the Univ. of Aston in B. (1966), and a School of Music. The Nat. Exhibition Centre (1976) is at Bickenhill to the E. of the city. B. attained city status in 1889. Pop. (1972) 1,006,760.

BIRMINGHAM Built on the site where bulls were baited in former times, the modern shopping centre retains the name. *Photo: Dennis Assinder.*

BIRMINGHAM. Largest city of Alabama, USA, and industrial heart of the South. Although the coal and iron ore in the area, on which its prosperity was first based has been largely worked out, it is still a centre of heavy industry, and besides iron and steel, produces chemicals, building materials, cotton textiles, etc. However, from 1950 it developed also as a business and educational centre and the Medical Center of the Univ. of Alabama is well known. It is a communications centre, well served by rail, road and air. Pop. met. area (1970) 729,984.

BIRO (bērō'), **Lazlo** (1900-). Hungarian inventor. A political refugee to Argentina just before the S.W.W. (where he became a citizen), he patented in 1944 a pen combining capillary action, gravitational attraction and a rapid-drying ink. So popular did it become that all later imitations are known by his name.

BI'ROBIJAN (-jahn). Town in Kharabovsk Terr., R.S.F.S.R., on the Bira r., 160km (100m) W. of Khabarovsk, cap. of the Jewish Autonomous Region 1928-51 (sometimes also called B.) of the R.S.F.S.R. It has sawmills and clothing factories. Pop. (1978) 67,000.

BIRTWHISTLE, Harrison (1934-). British composer. A clarinettist, he has specialized in chamber music, e.g. his chamber opera *Punch and Judy* (1967), and experimented in electronic music. His *Chronometer* is based on clock sounds.

BISCAY, Bay of. Atlantic bay stretching between Point du Raz, France; Cape Ortegal, N. Spain; and Biarritz, S. France. It is roughly triangular in shape, the sides being about 645km (400m) long. At times the Bay is very rough, and it has exceptionally high tides. In French it is the Gulf of Gascony.

BISCUIT. A crisp, flat cake, consisting of flour, sugar, and fat. Other ingredients are used to give variety of flavour - e.g. eggs, milk, coconut, almonds, and spices. Bs. contain only a low percentage of moisture. They are, therefore, a concentrated food. In the USA a B. refers to something resembling a scone, and the British B. is referred to as a cracker or cookie. The name is also applied to pottery before glazing and second firing, and to wares not intended to be glazed, e.g. Wedgwood's jasper.

BISHOP (Gk *episkopos,* an overseer). A clergyman consecrated for the spiritual government or direction of a diocese or see; as such a B. ranks below an archbishop and above priests and deacons.

In N.T. times there was no clear distinction between Bs. and elders, but with the growth in influence and numbers of the Church, the B. became an increasingly important figure. Originally Bs. were chosen by the people, but in time the power of election passed to the other bishops of the province, and next to the cathedral chapter, subject to the veto of the metropolitan, and later of the Pope. Today in some R.C. countries the political authority has secured the right of appointment to bishoprics, but in other countries the Pope nominates the Bs.

Since 1534 the appointment of Bs. of the C. of E. has been vested in the Crown. Theoretically the cathedral chapter make the nomination, but in practice the selection is made by the Prime Minister, usually on the advice of the archbishops. There are 29 dioceses in the province of Canterbury and 14 in the province of York, and there are many suffragan Bs. in the Anglican Church in the Commonwealth.

In the Eastern Orthodox Church a B. is always chosen from the monastic orders, since he must be unmarried. There are also Bs. in certain of the Lutheran churches, the Moravians, and in the Methodist Episcopal Church in the USA.

BISHOP, Sir Henry Rowley (1786-1855). British opera composer, now remembered mainly for his song *Home, Sweet Home.*

BISHOP, William Avery (1894-1956). Canadian air ace. B. at Owen Sound, Ontario, he won the V.C. in 1917, was promoted Air Marshal in 1939 and as Director of the RCAF in the S.W.W. played an important part in the Empire training scheme.

BISKRA (bēs'krah). Oasis, town, and tourist resort in a valley of the Aurès mountains, Algeria, bordering the Sahara. Pop. (1970) 53,200.

BISLEY. English village in Surrey, W.N.W. of Woking. The National Rifle Association moved its ranges here from Wimbledon in 1890. Military and civilian shooting events are regularly held, the most famous being the Queen's Prize.

BI'SMARCK, Otto Eduard Leopold, Prince von (1815-98). German statesman. The son of a Brandenburg landowner, he studied law and was employed for a time in the civil service. He entered the Prussian Landtag in 1847, and during the revolution of 1848-9 upheld the principle of Divine Right. His experiences as Prussian envoy to the Federal Diet (1851-9) inspired his ambition to establish Prussia's hegemony inside Germany, and to eliminate the influence of Austria. After serving as ambassador to St Petersburg and Paris, he was appointed For. Min. in 1862. He secured Austria's support in his war of 1863-4 with Denmark, but in 1866 he went to war with Austria and her allies. Prussia's victory brought about Austria's secession from the German Bund, and the unification of the N. German states in the N. German Confederation under B.'s chancellorship (1867). Napoleon III's alarm at this development enabled B. to manœuvre him in 1870 into the Franco-Prussian War. The proclamation of the German Empire in 1871 and the annexation of Alsace-Lorraine crowned his work. As Imperial Chancellor he sought to secure the peace settlement by forming the Triple Alliance with Austria and Italy (1882). At home he became involved in conflicts with the R.C. Church, and with the Socialist movement, in both of which he was defeated. William II dismissed him in 1890.

BISMUTH. A reddish white metal. It occurs in nature in the native condition (i.e. as the free metal), although ores (i.e. compounds of B.) are also known. It is used chiefly as a medicine and cosmetic. Being heavy, B. subnitrate is used as a shadowing agent in radiography of the digestive tract. B. is also strongly diamagnetic, the electrical resistance varying with magnetic field.

BĪ'SON. Genus of wild cattle, represented by 2 species. The European B. or wisent (*Bison bonasus*) is slightly the larger, standing *c.* 2m (6ft) high and weighing nearly a tonne. Only a few protected herds survive. The American B., or buffalo (*Bison bison*), has a heavier mane, and more sloping hindquarters, but is the same brown colour. Formerly roaming the prairies in vast numbers, it was almost exterminated by the Indians and European settlers, but survives in protected areas. A cross between the latter and domesticated cattle (Hereford and Charolais) has produced a hardy hybrid, the beefalo, with a lean carcass and economical solely grass diet.

BISSAU (bis'ow). Cap. and chief port of Guinea-Bissau. Pop. (1970) 25,500.

BITHYNIA (bithin'ya). District of N.W. Asia which became a Roman province in 74 B.C.

BITOLJ (bito'l). Town in S. Yugoslavia, 32km (20m) N. of the Greek frontier. It was captured from the Turks (under whom it was known as Monastir) by the Serbs in 1912. Pop. (1971) 124,650.

BITTERN. Genus of birds (*Botaurus*) of the heron family (Ardeidae). The typical European species (*B. stellaris*) was formerly abundant in marshy country in Britain and is now found, owing to protection, in the fens and elsewhere. It is a shy, solitary bird, smaller and more stoutly built than the heron, and its yellowish-brown plumage, streaked with black, renders it very inconspicuous. The male has a curious 'booming' cry. The smaller American species (*B. lentiginosus*) and the Little B. (*Ixobrychus minutus*) occasionally visit the British Isles. Australian species incl. the reed-roarer *(Ixobrychus).*

BITTERSWEET. Name of a plant, the woody nightshade. *See* NIGHTSHADE.

BITŪ'MEN. An impure mixture of hydrocarbons, including such deposits as petroleum, asphalt, and natural gas, although sometimes the term is restricted to a soft kind of pitch resembling asphalt. Solid B. may have arisen as a residue left behind by the evaporation of petroleum. If evaporation took place from a pool or lake of petroleum the residue may form a pitch or asphalt lake like the famous asphalt lake of Trinidad. B. was used by the ancients as a mortar, and by the Egyptians for embalming.

BIZE'RTA. Port in Tunisia, 60km (37m) N.W. of Tunis, most northerly town in Africa. Founded by the Phoenicians, it was a French naval base 1882-1963. Metallurgical and oil industries. Pop. (1975) 62,000.

BIZET (bēzeh'), **Georges** (1838-75), French composer. B. near Paris, he studied at the Paris Conservatoire and won the Grand Prix de Rome in 1857. On his return from Italy he became known as a pianist, and began to compose operas, among them *Les Pêchcurs de perles* (1863), *La jolie fille de Perth* (1867), and *Djamileh* (1872), which are still occasionally performed. He also wrote an overture to Sardou's play *Patrie*, and incidental music to Daudet's *L'Arlésienne*. The latter forms the material of two well-known orchestral suites. His operatic masterpiece *Carmen*, on a libretto founded on Prosper Mérimée's story, was produced a few months before his death in 1875.

BJÖRNEBORG. Swedish name of PORI.

BJÖRNSON (byern'son), **Björnstjerne** (1832-1910). Norwegian author. He became a journalist in Oslo, and made his name by the peasant-tale *Synnöve Solbakken* (1857) and the historical dramatic trilogy *Sigurd Slembe* (1862). B. directed the Bergen (1857-9) and Oslo (1865-7) playhouses, and advanced to realism in *The Newly Married Couple* (1865) and *A Bankruptcy* (1875). Later plays are *Leonarda* (1879) and *A Gauntlet* (1883), treating of sexual morality; the political *Paul Lange and Tora Parsberg* (1898), and *Beyond Human Power* (1883). He also wrote *Poems and Songs* (1870), and the novels *Flags are Flying in Town and Port* (1884), and *In God's Way* (1889). In 1903 he received a Nobel Prize.

BLACK, Davidson (1884-1934). Canadian anatomist. In 1927, when professor of anatomy at the Union Medical Coll., Peking, he unearthed the remains of Peking Man (q.v.), a very primitive type.

BLACK, Joseph (1728-99). Scottish physicist and chemist. B. at Bordeaux, of Scottish descent, he qualified as a doctor in Edinburgh. In chemistry he prepared the way for Cavendish, Priestley, and Lavoisier - and in physics, by his work on 'latent heat', he laid the foundation of the work of his pupil, James Watt.

BLACK-AND-TANS. Nickname of a specially raised force of military police employed by the British in 1920-1 to combat the Sinn Feiners in Ireland; the name was derived from the colours of the uniforms.

BLACKBERRY. Fruit of the bramble (*Rubus fruticosus*), a prickly shrub, closely allied to the raspberry. It is native to the northern parts of the Old World, is exceedingly abundant in Britain, and produces pink or white blossoms and edible black, compound fruit. Several of some 500 varieties have been regarded as distinct species, e.g. the dewberry.

BLACKBIRD. British resident bird (*Turdus merula*) belonging to the thrush family (Turdidae). The male has coal-black plumage, set off by the yellow bill and eyelids; the hen is somewhat larger, her plumage is dark brown, and she has a dark beak. The eggs are pale sea-blue, freckled with reddish-brown, and there are 4 or 5 in a clutch. The B.'s song is rich and flute-like.

BLACKBIRDING. The slave trade in South Sea Islanders for plantation labour in Queensland and Fiji c.1860-1900: they were known as Kanakas (Hawaiian 'man').

BLACK BOX. Popular name for the flight (recording behaviour of the plane) and voice (recording conversations of the crew) recorders carried by airliners in case of disaster. They are actually contained in 2 boxes, painted bright red for easy recovery.

BLACKBOY. *See* GRASS-TREE.

BLACKBUCK. An antelope (*Antilope cervicapra*) found in C. and N.W. India. It is related to the gazelles, from which it differs in having the horns spirally twisted. The males are black above and white beneath, whereas the females and young are fawn-coloured above. It is about 76cm ($2\frac{1}{2}$ft) in height.

BLACKBURN. Town in Lancs, England, 32km (20m) N.W. of Manchester. It was preeminently a cotton-weaving town until mechanical and electrical engineering took precedence after the S.W.W. Pop. (1972) 101,170.

BLACKCAP. *See* WARBLER.

BLACKCOCK. *See* GROUSE.

BLACK COUNTRY. Central area of England, about and to the N. of Birmingham, which in 1974 became the new co. of W. Midlands. Heavily industrialized, it gained its name in the 19th cent. from its belching chimneys, but pollution laws have given it a changed aspect.

BLACK DEATH. Modern name (first used in England in the early 19th cent.) for the great epidemic of bubonic plague, which spread from China to devastate Europe in the 14th cent. It completely demoralized society, and it is estimated that one-third to one-half of the population of England succumbed in 1348-9. The disease remained endemic in London for the next 3 cents., the last great outbreak being that of 1665, when c. 100,000 of the 400,000 inhabitants d. *See* PLAGUE.

BLACK EARTH. Name applied to the exceedingly fertile soil which covers a belt of land in Europe and Asia, extending from Bohemia through Hungary, Rumania, S. Russia, and Siberia, as far as Manchuria. It is a kind of loess (q.v.), and was laid down when the great Eurasian inland ice sheet melted at the close of the last ice age.

BLACK ECONOMY. The hidden economy of a country which incl. undeclared earnings from a second job ('moonlighting'), enjoyment of undervalued goods and services (company 'perks'), etc., designed for eluding the taxman.

BLACKETT, Patrick Maynard Stuart, baron (1897-1974). British physicist. He was awarded a Nobel Prize in 1948 for work in cosmic radiation and his perfection of the Wilson 'cloud-chamber'. He was Pres. R.S. 1965-70, was awarded the O.M. in 1967 and became a life peer 1969.

BLACKFOOT. Fierce tribe of Plains Indians, so-called because of their black mocassins; they now live in Saskatchewan.

BLACK POWER. Angela Davis and Martin Luther King reflect contrasting phases of the movement. *Photos: Popperfoto and Keystone Press Agency.*

BLACK FOREST. Mountainous region of coniferous forest, in Baden-Württemberg, W. Germany. Bounded on the W. and S. by the Rhine, which separates it from the Vosges, it has an area of 4,660 sq.km (1,800 sq.m), and rises to 1,493 m (4,905 ft) in the Feldberg.

BLACKHEATH. English common which gives its name to a residential suburb of London partly in Greenwich, partly in Lewisham. Wat Tyler encamped on B. in 1381.

BLACK HILLS. Mountains in Dakota and Wyoming, USA. *See* MOUNT RUSHMORE.

BLACK HOLE. Invisible source of X-ray signals of enormous power, such as exist in large numbers in our own and neighbouring galaxies. They are formed when the thermo-nuclear fires of a giant star burn out, and it shrinks - virtually crushed into annihilation by the momentum of its own gases drawn towards its centre of gravity - until its atoms are so close together that a spoonful weighs millions of tons. Its escape velocity (the speed needed to escape its gravitational pull) becomes so great that it exceeds the speed of light. Anything approaching it is, therefore, sucked in and never seen again, and time is distorted by being stretched out so that a second lasts a billion years. Collapse into a B.H. is thought to be the fate eventually awaiting our own Universe, which would then be reborn in a new cycle of time in superspace, the physical laws we know no longer existing. A giant B.H. may be 100 million miles across. *See* QUASAR.

BLACK HOMELAND. *See* BLACK NATIONAL STATE.

BLACKMAIL (Fr. *mâille,* 'rent' paid in labour or base coin). Legal term for the criminal offence of demanding anything of value with menaces of violence and other injury, or of exposure of some misconduct on the part of the victim (whether actually committed by him or not). It is punishable by 14 years imprisonment.

BLACK MARKET. Illegal trade in food or other rationed goods, such as petrol and clothing, during the S.W.W. and after.

BLACKMORE, Richard Doddridge (1825-1900). British novelist, author of *Lorna Doone* (1869), a romance of Exmoor in the late 17th cent.

BLACK MOUNTAINS. Group of hills in S. Powys, Wales, overlooking the Wye Valley in the N. Waun Fâch is 808m (2,660 ft) high, and a network of beautiful passages and caves, discovered 1966, runs beneath them.

BLACK NATIONAL STATE. Area set aside in the Rep. of S Africa for development to full self-govt by black Africans in accordance with the theory of plural democracy (*See* APARTHEID): before 1980 they were known as Black Homelands or Bantustans. The majority of their populations usually work in white S Africa, and the land may be poor in resources, and form scattered 'blocks'. Those which have so far reached independence are Transkei 1976, Bophuthatswana 1977, Venda 1979, and Ciskei 1981: They are not recognized outside S Africa because of their racial basis, and Transkei does not recognize Ciskei, since it maintains a claim on the area.

BLACKPOOL. Seaside resort in Lancs, England, 45km (28m) N. of Liverpool. Amusement facilities incl. 11km (7m) of promenades, famous for their 'illuminations' of coloured lights, fun fairs, and a tower 152m (500ft) high. Pop. (1972) 150,000.

BLACK POWER. During the 1960s existing civil rights organizations in the USA such as the National Association for Advancement of Colored People and the Southern Christian Leadership Conference were seen to be ineffective in producing major change in Negro status. It was then proposed by Stokely Carmichael that the concept of B.P. be adopted, i.e. the attainment of full citizenship by exploitation of political and economic power, abandonment of non-violence, and a move towards the type of separatism first developed by the Black Muslims. Negro leaders such as Martin Luther King rejected this approach, but nationwide influence was achieved by the Black Panther Party (so named because the panther, though not generally aggressive, will fight to the death under attack) founded in 1966 by Huey Newton and Bobby Seale, which fully adopted it, and put forward as the ultimate aim establishment of a separate Negro state in the USA estab. by a Negro plebiscite under the aegis of the UN. Following a National Black Political Convention in 1972 a Nat. Black Assembly was estab. to exercise pressure on the Democratic and Republican parties. *See* MOSLEMS.

BLACK PRINCE. Name given to Edward (q.v.), Prince of Wales, eldest son of Edward III of England.

BLACK SEA. Inland sea in S.E. Europe (435,000 sq.km/168,000 sq.m), linked to the N.E. with the Sea of Azov, to the S.W. with the Sea of Marmara, and through the Dardanelles with the Mediterranean. There are uranium deposits beneath it.

BLACKSNAKE. Non-poisonous snake (*Zamenis constrictor*), very common in the USA. But in Australia the B. is *Pseudechis porphyriacus*, a highly poisonous species, allied to the cobra.

BLACKSTONE, Sir William (1723-80). British jurist, remembered for his *Commentaries on the Laws of England* (1765-9). Called to the Bar in 1746, he became professor of law at Oxford (1758), and a Justice of the Court of Common Pleas (1770).

BLACKTHORN, or **sloe.** Tree (*Prunus spinosa*) of the family Rosaceae, closely allied to the plum, and producing a cloud of white blossom on black, leafless boughs in early spring.

BLACK THURSDAY. The day of the Wall Street stock market crash, 29 Oct. 1929, followed by the worst depression in American history.

BLACKWATER FEVER. Form of subtertian malaria, characterized by the breakdown of the red blood corpuscles, which stain the urine a reddish brown. It is widespread on the E. and W. coasts of Africa, and in other malarial districts.

BLACKWELL, Elizabeth (1821-1910). First British woman doctor, and first woman to gain medical degree anywhere. Taken to the USA at 11, she became a teacher and qualified as a doctor there in 1849, being admitted to the English medical register in 1859.

BLACK WIDOW. Popular name of a poisonous species of N. American spider (*Lathrodectus mactans*). It is not so deadly as fiction suggests.

BLADDER. Hollow organ in which urine is accumulated. Situated in the pelvis, it is a round bag of muscle lined with mucous membrane. Urine enters the B. through 2 ureters, one leading from each kidney, and leaves it through the urethra; on emptying, the B. collapses in folds.

BLADDERWORT (-wert). Genus of carnivorous aquatic plants (*Utricularia*) of the family Lentibulariaceae, which feeds on small crustacea.

BLAGONRAVOV (blahgonrah'vof), **Anatoly Arkadievich** (1894-1975). Russian specialist in rocketry and instrumentation. He directed the earth satellite programme leading to the launching of Sputnik I and II.

BLAKE, Robert (1599-1657). British admiral. He represented his native Bridgwater in the Short Parliament of 1640, and distinguished himself with the Parliamentary forces in defending Bristol (1643) and Taunton (1644-5). Appointed 'general-at-sea' (1649), he destroyed Prince Rupert's fleet off Cartagena in the next year. In 1652 he won several engagements against the Dutch before being defeated by Tromp off Dungeness, and revenged himself in 1653 by defeating the Dutchman off Portsmouth and the N. Foreland. In 1654 he bombarded Tunis, the stronghold of the Barbary corsairs, and in 1657 captured the Spanish treasure-fleet in Santa Cruz.

BLAKE, William (1757-1827). British poet and artist. B. in Soho, he was apprenticed to an engraver 1771-8, and studied at the Academy under Reynolds. The comparative simplicity of *Songs of Innocence* (1789) and *Songs of Experience* (1794) was lost in the 'prophetic' books portraying through mythological figures the conflict of restrictive morality and anarchical liberty, e.g. *Book of Thel* (1789), *Marriage of Heaven and Hell* (1793), and *Song of Los* (1795), for all of which he engraved illustrations. He kept a print-shop in London (1784-7), and received commissions from booksellers and others, but after the failure of his exhibition in 1809, retired (1810-17), until his final recognition in his last years. Later works include *Milton* (1803-8), the symbolic *Jerusalem* (1804-20), and the fragmentary *Everlasting Gospel*. His most celebrated illustrations are those to Young's *Night Thoughts*, Blair's *Grave*, the *Book of Job*, and Dante.

BLAMEY, Sir Thomas Albert (1884-1951). Australian soldier. B. in NSW, he served at Gallipoli and on the Western Front in the F.W.W., and in the S.W.W. was C.-in-C. Allied Land Forces in the S.W. Pacific 1942-5. He was the first Australian Field Marshal (1950).

BLANC (bloṅ), **Louis** (1811-82). French socialist. In 1839 he founded the *Revue du progrès*, in which he pub. his *Organisation du travail*, advocating the establishment of co-operative workshops and other socialistic schemes. He was a member of the provisional government of 1848, and from its fall lived in England until 1871.

BLANCHARD (bloṅshahr'), **Jean Pierre** (1753-1809). French balloonist, who came to England to make the first balloon flight across the Channel with Dr John Jeffries in 1785. He also made the first balloon flight in the USA in 1793.

BLANK VERSE. The unrhymed iambic pentameter or 10 syllable line of 5 stresses. Originated by the Italian Trissino, *c.* 1515, it was introduced to England by the Earl of Surrey, *c.* 1540, and developed by Marlowe. B. was used with increasing freedom by Shakespeare, Fletcher, Webster, and Middleton. It was remodelled by Milton, who was imitated in the 18th cent. by Thomson, Young, and Cowper, and revived in the early 19th cent. by Wordsworth, Shelley, and Keats, and later by Tennyson, Browning, and Swinburne. Modern exponents include Hardy, T. S. Eliot, and R. Frost.

BLAKE. The prophetic vision of William Blake lent itself to interpretation of the Bible, as in this rendering of the parable of the Wise and Foolish Virgins. *Photo: Courtesy of the Tate Gallery.*

BLANQUI (blonkē'), **Louis Auguste** (1805-81). French revolutionary politician who spent 37 years in prison. He invented the theory of the 'dictatorship of the proletariat', taken over by Marx.

BLANTYRE. Parish in Scotland on the Lanarkshire coalfield, Strathclyde. Here David Livingstone was born. Pop. (1973) 17,000.

BLANTYRE-LIMBE (bla'ntīr-lim'bā). The chief industrial and commercial centre of Malawi, in the Shire highlands, formed by the union of Blantyre, named after Livingstone's birthplace, and Limbe, in 1959. It is linked by rail with Beira, and a first-class road link is planned. There is an airport. The Univ. of Malawi (1965) is in Limbe. Pop. (1977) 228,520.

BLARNEY. Small town with tweed mills in co. Cork, Rep. of Ireland, 11km (7m) N.W. of Cork. High up in the wall of the 15th cent. castle is the *B. Stone,* reputed to give those kissing it wonderfully persuasive speech. Pop. (1971) 1,130.

BLASHFORD-SNELL, John (1936-). British soldier-explorer. From 1963 he organized Adventure Training at Sandhurst, and his most famous expeditions have incl. the first descent and exploration of the Blue Nile (1968); the trans-Americas journey from Alaska to Cape Horn, crossing the Darien Gap (q.v.) for the first time (1971-2); and the first complete navigation of the Zaïre river (1974-5).

BLASIS (blahsē'), **Carlo** (1803-78). Italian *maître de ballet* of French extraction. He had a successful career as a dancer in Paris and in Milan, where he established a famous dancing school (1837).

BLASPHEMY (Gk. *blasphemia,* evil speaking). Written or spoken insult directed against God, Christianity, or the Church, religious beliefs or sacred things, with deliberate intent to outrage belief. B. is still an offence in English law.

BLAST FURNACE. Furnace in which the temperature is raised by the injection of an air blast. It is employed in the extraction of metals from their ores, particularly pig-iron from iron ore. The principle has been known for thousands of years, but the modern B.F. is a heavy engineering development combining a number of special techniques.

BLAUE REITER (blow'e rī'ter). Movement in art which arose in Germany 1911-14, and took its name from a small picture by Kandinsky (q.v.), *Der blaue Reiter* (Blue Rider). It was marked by an aversion to academic rule and a belief in the 'inner necessity' of expression for the artist.

BLAVA'TSKY, Helena Petrovna (1831-91). Russian theosophist. *Née* Hahn, she m. as a girl Nicephore B., a councillor of state, but separated from him after a few months and travelled widely. In Tibet she underwent spiritual training, and later became a Buddhist. The Theosophical Society (*see* THEOSOPHY) was founded while she was in N.Y. in 1875, but its H.Q. have been at Adyar, nr Madras since 1882. Her books incl. *Isis Unveiled* (1877), explaining the mysteries of science and theology, and *The Secret Doctrine* (1888).

BLEACHING. Decolorization of coloured materials. B. processes have been known from antiquity, especially those acting through sunlight. Both natural and modern chemical colouring matters usually possess highly complex molecules, the colour property often being due only to a part of the molecule. B. chemicals usually attack only that small part, giving another substance similar in chemical structure but colourless. The 2 main types of B. agent are the oxidizing (which add oxygen and remove hydrogen, and include the ultra-violet rays in sunshine, hydrogen peroxide, and chlorine), and the redúcing which add hydrogen or remove oxygen, e.g. sulphur dioxide.

BLEAK. Species of freshwater fish (*Alburnus lucidus*), of the carp family (Cyprinidae), found in the rivers of northern and central Europe.

BLEEDING. Loss of blood (haemorrhage) due to injury or disease. Sudden and copious B. may cause death in a few minutes, and even slight B. may endanger life if unchecked for a considerable time. External B. is treated by closing the blood vessels leading to the wound by means of a tourniquet in the case of a limb, or by pads if on the body; internal B. demands hospital treatment. General symptoms of B. are as in shock.

BLENHEIM. German village in Bavaria on the left bank of the Danube, near which Marlborough defeated the French and Bavarians on 13 Aug. 1704. *See* HAWKSMOOR, Nicholas; MARLBOROUGH, duke of, and VANBRUGH, Sir John.

Another **Blenheim** is in the Marlborough area in the NE of South Island, NZ. It is a centre for a sheep-grazing area and on the road/rail communication route between N and S Island.

BLENNY. Family of fishes of world-wide distribution (Bleniidae), distinguished by spiny fins and smooth body, belonging to the order Percomorphi. The Smooth B. or Shanny (*Blennius pholis*) is the most familiar in Britain.

BLÉRIOT, Louis (1872-1936). French aviator. He constructed a monoplane, and in it made the first flight across the English Channel, 25 July 1909.

BLESBOK (*Damaliscus albifrons*). Species of brownish antelope, *c.* 1m (3ft) high, related to the hartebeest (q.v.). Only a few protected herds survive N. of the Orange River in S. Africa.

BLESSINGTON, Marguerite, countess of (1789-1849). Irish writer. She m. as her 2nd husband the earl of B. in 1818, but in later years damaged her reputation by her association with Count D'Orsay. A queen of literary society, she pub. *Conversations with Lord Byron* (1834), travel sketches, and novels. Her husband d. 1829 and, bankrupt by 1849, she fled London for Paris in D'Orsay's wake, and there d.

BLIGH, William (1754-1817). British admiral. He accompanied Capt. Cook in his 2nd voyage (1772-4), and in 1787 commanded HMS *Bounty* on an expedition to the Pacific. On the return voyage the crew mutinied (1789), and cast B. adrift with 18 men in a boat. The mutineers settled in Tahiti and on Pitcairn Is., whilst B. brought his boat 3,618 m to Timor Is., near Java. Appointed Governor of N.S.W. in 1805, his discipline again provoked a mutiny (1808), but on returning to England he was made an admiral in 1811.

BLIGHT. A number of diseases of plants, mainly caused by parasitic plants (e.g. fungi of the family Erysiphaceae, which produce a whitish appearance on leaf and stem surfaces), or insects (e.g. Aphidae or green fly).

BLIGHTY (Hindustani, bilāyati, foreign). Popular name during the F.W.W. among British troops for 'home' or England.

BLIMP. In the F.W.W., British lighter-than-air aircraft were divided into A - rigid, and B - limp (i.e. without rigid internal framework). The barrage balloon is called a B. Low, the cartoonist, adopted the name for his famous character.

BLINDNESS. Absence of sight. Sudden B. is usually due to a general condition, such as hysteria (functional B.), sudden and severe internal bleeding, brain wounds, etc. The main causes of gradual B. are trachoma, onchocerciasis, glaucoma and cataract.

The first institution for the blind was estab. in the 4th cent. A.D., by St Basil at Caesarea in Cappadocia. In 1260 the king St Louis founded an asylum for the blind in Paris, which still exists. Education of the blind was begun by Valentin Haüy, who pub. a book with raised lettering (1784), and founded a school. There are now approx. 10,000,000 blind people in the world incl. 650,000 children, and measures to help them and avoid the incidence of preventible B. are co-ordinated by the World Council for the Welfare of the Blind. The most highly developed system of blind welfare exists in Britain which has in the Royal National Institute for the Blind (founded by Dr T. R. Armitage in 1868) the largest organization of its kind in the world: other large organizations are St Dunstan's (founded by Sir Arthur Pearson in 1915) for the blinded of both World Wars; the National Library (estab. 1882) and the Guide Dogs for the Blind Assocn.

Aids to the blind incl. the use of braille in reading, or of electronic devices now under development which convert print to recognisable mechanical speech; guide dogs; sonic torches which warn of objects in the way more adequately than a white stick, and the eventual possibility (in which experiments have been made) of bypassing the eye and stimulating directly the part of the brain responsible for sight.

BLINDWORM or **slow worm.** Harmless species of lizard (*Anguis fragilis*), common in Europe and Britain. Superficially resembling a snake, it is distinguished by its small mouth and movable eyelids.

BLISS, Sir Arthur (1891-1975). British composer. B. in London, and ed. at Rugby and Pembroke College, Cambridge, he became Master of the Queen's Musick in 1953. His music has a masculine individuality, and his works include *Colour Symphony* (1922), an experimental relation of tone and visual impressions; the ballets *Miracle in the Gorbals* (1944) and *Adam Zero* (1946); the opera *The Olympians* (1949); and dramatic film music, e.g. *Things to Come.*

BLISTER BEETLE. *See* CANTHARIDES.

BLITZKRIEG (Ger., lightning war). Name applied to a swift, shattering campaign, such as those of 1939-41, which resulted in the fall of Poland, France, Yugoslavia, and Greece, and the advance to Moscow.

BLITZSTEIN (blit'stīn), **Marc** (1905-64). American composer. B. in Philadelphia, he appeared as a child prodigy pianist at the age of six. He served with the US Army 8th Air Force 1942-5, for whom he wrote *The Airborne,* a choral symphony. His operas incl. *The Cradle Will Rock* (1937) and *Reuben Reuben* (1953).

BLOCH (blok), **Ernest** (1880-1959). American composer. B. in Geneva, of Jewish parentage, he went to the US in 1916 and became founder-director of the Cleveland Institute of Music (1920-5). He later taught at the San Francisco Conservatoire and the Univ. of Berkeley. His works incl. the lyrical drama *Macbeth* (1910), 5 string quartets, and *Rhapsodie Hébraique* (1951), and he often used themes based on Hebrew liturgical music and folk-song.

BLOCH, Felix (1905–83). American physicist. He was awarded a Nobel Prize jointly with E. M. Purcell in 1952, for work on nuclear-magnetic resonance (NMR). In medical diagnosis it avoids dangerous radiation and painful injections.

BLOCKADE. Obstruction of part of the coast of a belligerent by the ships of its opponents, so as to prevent any ships or aircraft having access to it. Before the F.W.W. such Bs. were maintained by vessels near the coast, but the development of mines and submarines made this impossible and a 'long distance' B. by cruiser 'cordon' was introduced to prevent access to Germany. In the S.W.W. the *Navicert System* made goods or ships which might ultimately reach the enemy, whether by neutral or enemy ports, liable to seizure unless possessing the necessary certificate.

BLOEMFONTEIN (bloom'fontān). Cap. of the Orange Free State, and judicial cap. of the Union of S. Africa. It lies on a plateau 1,392 m (4,568 ft) a.s.l., 320km (200m) N.W. of Durban. Founded in 1846, B. was taken by Lord Roberts in 1900 during the Boer War of 1899-1902. Here is the appellate division of the supreme court of the Union of S. Africa; and the Univ. of the Orange Free State. Last home of the Republican Volksraad, the Town Hall on Pres. Brand Street is used for the Provincial Assembly. Pop. (1970) 180,200.

BLOIS (blwah). Chief town of Loir-et-Cher dept., France, on the Loire, 56km (35m) S.W. of Orléans. It has a château partly dating from the 13th cent. and makes shoes, porcelain, furniture, etc. Pop. (1973) 44,700.

BLOIS. In this château of the Orléans family, Henry duke of Guise was assassinated by the order of Henry III. It is renowned for its spiral staircase tower in Italian Renaissance style. *Photo: Janet March-Penny/Camera Press.*

BLOK, Alexander Alexandrovich (1880-1921). Russian poet. He was influenced by Soloviev and having pub. the mystic *Verses about the Beautiful Lady* (1904), became the foremost Russian symbolist. Later works are the lyrical plays *Puppet Show* (1907) and *The Rose and the Cross* (1913), and the revolutionary poems *The Twelve* and *The Scythians* (1918).

BLONDIN (bloṅ-daṅ'), **Charles.** Name assumed by the French tightrope-walker, Jean François Gravelet (1824-97). He became world-famous when he crossed Niagara Falls on a rope at a height of 160ft in 1859, repeating the feat several times - blindfolded, wheeling a barrow, etc. He later performed in England.

BLOOD. Red liquid circulating in the arteries, veins, and capillaries of the higher animals, and the corresponding fluid in those lesser animals which possess a circulatory system. In man *c.* a 20th part of the body weight, the temperature of B. in health is *c.* 37°C (98.4°F). It consists of a colourless, transparent liquid called plasma, containing microscopic cells of 3 varieties: (1) Red cells, which form nearly one half of the volume of the B. A cu.mm of B. contains *c.* 5,000,000. Their colour, actually a pale yellow, is caused by haemoglobin, which takes oxygen from the air in the lungs, and yields it to the body tissues. (2) White cells of different kinds. A cu.mm of B. contains only *c.* 7,500, but some of them have the power to eat up invading bacteria and so protect the body from disease (phagocytes); others repair injured tissues. (3) Cells called blood platelets, which are manufactured in the bone marrow, and assist in the clotting of B.

Invading disease germs cause the B. to generate 'antibodies', which resist them and give the person immunity to the disease for a time. B. cells constantly wear out and die, and are replaced from the bone marrow. Various chemicals in the B. occur in different people in differing types, e.g. phosphoglucomutase (PGM) has 3 divisions. These differences assist anthropologists in determining tribal relationships, and the police in the detection of crime. *See* B. GROUPS, PLASMAPHERESIS.

BLOOD, Col. Thomas (*c.* 1618-80). Irish adventurer, whose most daring exploit was an attempt to steal the Crown Jewels from the Tower (1671).

BLOOD GROUPS. In 1900 Karl Landsteiner discovered that when the serum of one person's blood was mixed with the red cells of another, agglutination of the red cells would follow. He, therefore, divided human beings into 3 different B.Gs., and 2 years later a 4th was discovered. The serum of group A agglutinates the cells of group B, and vice versa; the cells of group O will not agglutinate in contact with any serum; those of group AB will be agglutinated by serum from an A or B person. B.Gs. are of great importance in B. transfusion and may be of use in cases of disputed paternity. Sometimes another agglutinogen is present in the B., the Rhesus factor. A woman who is Rh negative (lacking it), who becomes pregnant with a child who is Rh positive (possessing it), may in certain circumstances have developed antibodies which will pass into the blood stream of her child and kill it by destroying the red cells.

BLOODHOUND. Ancient breed of dog. Black and tan in colour, it has long, pendulous ears, and distinctive wrinkles on the head. Its phenomenal powers of scent have been employed in tracking and criminal work from very early times.

BLOOD POISONING, or toxaemia. Circulation of a dangerous quantity of poisonous substances in the blood. Such substances may be derived from outside, e.g. carbon monoxide and alcohol, but they are often due to toxins or poisons manufactured by invading microbes, e.g. the poisoning of a system from an abscess in the root of a tooth. When invading microbes penetrate the blood in large numbers and multiply the condition is known as septicaemia.

BLOOD PRESSURE, or tension, is due to the muscular action of the left side of the heart, which forces the blood out of the left ventricle into the arterial system, acting against the elastic muscular coats of the arteries, which tend to contract and to resist the passage of blood. B.P. is also modified by the degree of fluidity of the blood. It varies considerably, gives a valuable indication of the condition of a patient's health, and is measured in terms of the height in millimetres of the column of mercury which the blood will support. Persistent high B.P. shows disease of the arteries. A very high B.P., especially when the arteries are hard, brings with it a danger of apoplectic stroke, the bursting of an artery in the brain. A persistently low B.P. may be included by certain diseases, general ill-health, etc.

BLOOD TESTS. Tests made to provide information of use to the doctor, and also to detect foreign substances such as poisons or alcohol in the blood. B.Ts. in commonest use are cell counts, determination of the time taken to coagulate, and the chemical measurement of the constituents of blood.

BLOOD TRANSFUSION. Injection of blood into the circulation in the treatment of conditions resulting from loss or impairment of blood, such as haemophilia, shock due to injury, poisoning by carbon monoxide, etc. The first human-to-human B.T. was made in 1818. Practically all B.Ts. are now made, not as formerly directly from donor to patient, but with B. stored at refrigerated temperature (treated with sodium citrate to prevent clotting). Unless used within 3 or 4 weeks, the stored blood has its red cells removed, and the remaining liquid is reduced to powder. This dried plasma is kept for emergency use. During the S.W.W. Birmingham Univ. developed a blood plasma substitute, prepared by the large-scale fermentation of sugar. *See* PLASMAPHERESIS.

BLOOM, Claire (1931-). British actress. B. in London, she made her reputation in Shakespearian roles such as Ophelia and Juliet. Her films incl. *Richard III* and *The Brothers Karamazov.*

BLOOMER, Amelia Jenks (1818-94). American dress reformer and supporter of temperance and women's rights. She advocated, *c.* 1849, the wearing of a short skirt with loose trousers gathered at the ankles, hence the name 'bloomers'.

BLOOMSBURY. Parish in W.C. London, England, between Gower Street and High Holborn. It contains London Univ. HQ, the British Museum, and the Royal Academy of Dramatic Art. Between the World Wars it was the home of writers and artists of a particular intellectual type, e.g. Leonard and Virginia Woolf, Lytton Strachey.

BLOW, John (1648-1708). English composer. He was organist at Westminster Abbey, wrote anthems and other church music, and a masque, *Venus and Adonis.*

BLOWFLY. Fly in the family Calliphoridae of the order Diptera, of which the bluebottle is the most familiar.

BLOY (blwah), **Léon-Marie** (1846-1917). French author. He became a clerk in Paris in 1863. Converted to mystic Catholicism *c.* 1870, he achieved a considerable reputation by his literary lampoons, etc., by 1890. Indifferent to politics and philosophy, and believing in the imminence of the Kingdom of Heaven, he taught the need for sharing in Christ's suffering. He wrote biographies, the novels *La Femme pauvre* and *Le Désepéré* and revealing Journals.

BLÜCHER (blükh'er), **Gebhard Leberecht von** (1742-1819). Prussian general field marshal, popular as 'Marshal Forward'. He took an active part in the patriotic movement, and in the War of Liberation defeated the French as C.-in-C. at Leipzig (1813), crossed the Rhine to Paris (1814), and was made prince of Wahlstadt (Silesia). In 1815 he was defeated by Napoleon at Ligny, but shared with Wellington the triumph of Waterloo.

BLUE. A sporting honour at Oxford and Cambridge, awarded to students representing their univ. in some game or form of athletics. It consists of a strip of light or dark B. ribbon, and is said to have originated with the 2nd Oxford and Cambridge boatrace in 1836.

BLUEBEARD. 'Hero' of a popular tale, best known from Charles Perrault's version (*c.* 1697). He murdered 6 wives in turn, who disobeyed his command not to enter a locked room, but was himself slain before he could kill the 7th. In Britanny B. has been identified with Gilles de Rais.

BLUEBELL. Name given in Scotland to the harebell (*Campanula rotundifolia*), and in England to the wild hyacinth (*Endymion nonscriptus*), belonging to the family Liliaceae.

BLUEBIRD. An American bird (*Sialia sialis*) affectionately regarded as the herald of spring. Slightly larger than a robin, it has a similar reddish breast, the upper plumage being sky-blue. The song is sweet.

BLUEBIRD. A male alighting at its nesthole, usually in a hollow tree, with food - often insects caught in the air, worms, larvae, fruit or seeds. *Photo: G.Ronald Austing.*

BLUEBOTTLE. Fly (*Calliphora vomitoria*) in the family Calliphoridae (*see* BLOWFLY). Metallic blue and making a loud hum, it lays its eggs in rotting carcases.

BLUEBUCK. S. African antelope (*Cephalophus monticola*), 33cm/13in high, and blue-grey in colour. It is related to the duikers, and is common in Natal.

BLUECOAT BOYS. *See* CHRIST'S HOSPITAL.

BLUE GRASS. Dense, spreading grass which grows in clumps. The blue-tinged *Poa compressa* provides fine pasture for horses, and Kentucky, where it is abundant, is known as the B.G. state. Another species is totally green.

BLUE MOUNTAINS. Part of the Great Dividing Range, NSW, Australia, blocking Sydney from the interior until the crossing in 1813 by surveyor William Lawson, Gregory Blaxland, and William Wentworth. Ranging 600-1,100 m. (2-3,600 ft), its varied scenery attracts tourists and the *City of B.M.* (1947) comprises the scattered urban development along 130 km (80 m) of the Western Highway, home of many Sydney commuters.

BLUE RIBAND. Term denoting the highest distinction in any particular sphere, derived from the B.R. of the Order of the Garter. The B.R. of the Turf is the Derby. The B.R. of the Atlantic is held by the vessel making the fastest crossing in both E. and W. directions: the *Queen Mary* 1938-52, and the *United States* from 1952.

BLUES. Type of popular jazz or rag-time music that consists of 3 lines of verse, the 2nd of which is a repetition, usually with variations, on the first, giving the singer time to improvise the last line. B. originated among the American Negroes, and the words are melancholy. Composers of B. include J. A. Carpenter, G. Gershwin, Milhaud, D. Ellington and W. C. Handy. Blues are primarily secular, e.g. the classic renderings of Bessie Smith (1894-1937), the religious equivalent being 'gospel' (Mahalia Jackson), but a blending was achieved by blind, Georgia-born Ray Charles after the S.W.W., and from this in the 1960s developed 'soul', the raw, emotionalized joy and pain of daily living, as in the songs of Aretha Franklin (1942-).

BLUE STOCKING. Disparaging term for a learned woman. It originated *c.* 1750 in London with the literary gatherings of Mrs Montagu, which were attended by Benjamin Stillingfleet, who wore unfashionable blue worsted stockings. Most famous of later B.Ss. is Hannah More.

BLUM, Léon (1872-1950). French Jewish statesman. He was converted to Socialism by the Dreyfus affair (1899), and in 1936 he became first Socialist Prime Minister of France. Again Premier for a few weeks in 1938, he was imprisoned in 1942 for his supposed responsibility for the fall of France, but released by the Allies in 1945. He was again Premier for a few weeks in 1946.

BLUNDEN, Edmund (1896-1974). English poet. B. in Kent, he served in France and Belgium in the F.W.W., and published the prose *Undertones of War* (1928). Ed. at Oxford, he was prof. of English at the Univ. of Hong Kong 1953-64, and of poetry at Oxford 1966-68. His poetry is that of a countryman, and shows the influence of Clare.

BLUNT, Anthony (1907–83). British art historian. While a don at Cambridge, he enlisted recruits for the Russian Secret Service, and while himself a member of the British Secret Service 1940-5 passed on information to the Russians. In 1951 he assisted the defection of Burgess and Maclean. Unmasked in 1964, he was given immunity after his confession, and was allowed to continue in his post as adviser to the Queen on art. When the matter became public in 1974 he was stripped of the knighthood granted in 1956.

BLUNT, Wilfred Scawen (1840-1922). British poet and traveller. In 1869 he m. Lady Anne Noel, Byron's granddaughter, with whom he travelled in Arabia, Syria, Persia, and Mesopotamia. Becoming a supporter of Arab aspirations, he sympathized with the Egyptian national movement in 1881-2, visited India twice, and tried to enter Parliament as an advocate of Irish Home Rule. He wrote many anti-imperialist books, and his poems (collected 1914) and prose diaries (1912-20) show vigorous individuality.

BLYTON (blī'ton), **Enid** (1897-1968). British writer for children. She discovered her gift while teaching, and her creations, the little boy Noddy with his gnome-like hat, and the adventures of the 'Famous Five' and 'Secret Seven', secured enduring popularity with children, though they were criticised by educationists.

BOA. Name given to a family (Boidae) of nonpoisonous snakes, natives of both hemispheres, and loosely to other large snakes which kill their prey by constriction, such as the python. Most common is the boa constrictor, which is found in tropical S. and C. America, reaches a length of 3-4m (10-12ft), and feeds on small animals and birds.

BOADICEA. *See* BOUDICCA.

BOAR, Wild. Name given to several members of the pig family. Best known are the Crested W.B. of India (*Sus cristatus*), and the European W.B. (*Sus scrofa*), from which the domesticated breeds derive. The darkish brown or grey coat is made up of coarse bristles overlying underwool. The W.B. is sturdily built, being 1.5m (4½ft) long and 1m (3ft) high, and possesses formidable tusks. Usually neither species is aggressive, roots and berries forming their chief diet.

BOAT RACE. Rowing race between Oxford and Cambridge Univ. crews. First held in 1829 at Henley, it has normally been held since 1845 during the Easter vacation on the Thames from Putney to Mortlake, on a course of 6.8km (4¼m).

BOBCAT. *See* LYNX.

BO'BOLINK. N. American songbird (*Dolichonyx oryzivorus*), so-named from its call.

BOBRUISK'. Town in White Russia S.S.R., USSR; on the Beresina, it is an important railway junction and a timber centre. Pop. (1977) 192,000.

BOCCACCIO (bokkah'chō), **Giovanni** (1313-75). Italian poet. The son of a Florentine merchant, he came to Naples in 1328, where he abandoned trade for literature, and fell in love with the unfaithful 'Fiametta', who inspired his early work. Before returning to Florence in 1341 he had written *Filostrato* and *Teseide* (used by Chaucer in his *Troilus and Criseyde* and *Knight's Tale*), etc. His great work is the *Decameron*, containing 100 stories told by 10 young people seeking refuge in the country from the plague: narrative skill and characterization compensate for their licentiousness, and Shakespeare, Chaucer, Dryden, and Keats were later indebted to them. B. was a friend of Petrarch, and sponsored Leon Pilatus' translation of Homer.

BOCCACCIO. A portrait by Andrea de Castagno from the Convent of Sant'Apollonia in Florence. *Photo: Alinari - Giraudon.*

BOCCHERINI (bōkārē'nē), **Luigi** (1743-1805). Italian composer. Having studied in Rome, he was a great success in Paris in 1768, and held posts as court composer in Prussia and Spain. An outstanding 'cello player, he composed some 350 instrumental works, an opera, oratorios, etc.

BOCHUM (bokh'oom). Town in the Ruhr, between Essen and Dortmund, Land of N. Rhine-Westphalia, W. Germany. It has metallurgical, automotive, and chemical industries and a university. Pop. (1970) 343,800.

BODE (bō'de), **Johann Elert** (1747-1826). German astronomer. He was director of the Berlin observatory, and propounded *Bode's Law*, which states that the proportionate distances of the planets from the Sun out to Uranus are found by adding 4 to each term of the series 0, 3, 6, 12, 24, etc., if the asteroids be included between Mars and Jupiter. The law breaks down for Neptune and Pluto, however.

BODENSEE. German name of LAKE CONSTANCE.

BODH GAYA. Another form of BUDDH GAYA.

BODHIDHARMA (bō'didir'ma) (6th cent.). Indian Buddhist. He entered China from S. India *c.* 520, and was the founder of Zen ('religious meditation', Japanese word derived from Chinese *cha'an*), the school of Mahayana Buddhism in which intuitive meditation, prompted by contemplation of the beautiful, leads to enlightenment. It passed to Japan in the 12th cent., where it is the best-known school.

BODIN (bodań'), **Jean** (1530-96). French political thinker. He became an attorney in Paris, and in 1574 pub. a tract explaining that prevalent high prices were due to the influx of precious metals from the New World. His *De la république* (1576) has been described as originating political economy.

BODLEY, Sir Thomas (1545-1613), English diplomat and scholar. He was employed by Queen Elizabeth on diplomatic missions, but retired in 1597, and began to restore the library at Oxford (originally founded by Humphrey, duke of Gloucester, in the 15th cent.), which was opened in 1602, and is named after him the Bodleian Library. He was knighted in 1604.

BODMIN. Admin. H.Q. of Cornwall, England, 48km (30m) from Plymouth. Pop. (1972) 10,300. *B. Moor* to the N.E. is a granitic area of wild beauty, culminating in Brown Willy 419m (1,375ft).

BODONI (bōdō'nē), **Giambattista** (1740-1813). Italian printer, who managed the printing-press of the duke of Parma and produced books, chiefly editions of the classics, that were magnificent specimens of the craft.

BOEHME (bö'me), **Jakob** (1575-1624). German mystic. He became a shoemaker in Gölitz, and although persecuted as a heretic after the appearance of his mystical *Aurora* (1612) continued to write theosophical treatises, which won followers in Germany, Holland, and England. He claimed divine revelation of the unity of everything and nothing, and found in God's 'eternal nature' a principle to reconcile evil and good.

BOEOTIA (bē-ō'shya). Ancient district of central Greece. The chief city was Thebes. Ten city states formed the *Boeotian League* in the 6th cent., and in the 4th cent. took the leadership of Greece from Sparta. *See* EPAMINONDAS.

BOER (bor; Dutch, farmer). Dutch settler in S. Africa. For BOER WARS *see* SOUTH AFRICA.

BOETHIUS (bō-ēthius), **Anicius Manlius Severinus** (*c.* 480-524). Roman statesman and philosopher. He rose to high rank under the Gothic king Theodoric, but was eventually imprisoned on suspicion of treason, and executed at Pavia. While in prison he wrote his *De Consolatione Philosophiae.*

BŌ'GART, Humphrey (1899-1957). American film actor. B. in New York, son of a wealthy doctor, he achieved fame in 1936 with *The Petrified Forest,* as a gangster. Later were *The Maltese Falcon* (1941), *Casablanca* (1943, with Ingrid Bergman), and *To Have and Have Not* (with Lauren Bacall, who became his 4th wife in 1945), and *The Caine Mutiny* (1954). In the 1970s he became a cult figure as the romantic, tough 'loner'.

BOGHAZKOI (bō'gahzkö'e). Turkish village in Asia Minor, 145km/90m E. of Ankara on the site of Hattusas, the ancient Hittite capital estab. *c.* 1640 B.C. Thousands of tablets discovered by excavations here over a number of years by the German Oriental Society revealed, when their cuneiform writing was deciphered by Bedrich Hrozny (1879-1952), a great deal about the customs, religion, and history of the Hittite people. Pop. (est.) 1,000.

BOGNOR REGIS (rē'jis). English seaside resort in Sussex, 105km (66m) S.W. of London, which owes the Regis in its name to the convalescent visit of George V in 1929. Pop. (1972) 34,000.

BOGORODSK. Name until *c.* 1930 of NOGINSK.

BOGOTÁ (bōgōtah'). Cap. of Colombia, on the edge of the plateau of the E. Cordillera 2,640m (8,660ft) a.s.l. Founded in 1538, it has a cathedral (1563), and the National (1572) and other univs. It is linked by rail with the port of Buenaventura. Industries incl. iron and steel, tobacco, textiles, clothing, and leather. Pop. met. area (1973) 2,855,000.

BOHEMIA. Historic kingdom of Central Europe, consisting of a square block of highland bounded by the Bohemian Forest, the Erzgebirge, the Sudeten Mts., and the Moravian Heights, and drained by the Vltava River, on which Prague stands.

The name B. derives from the Celtic Boii, its earliest-known inhabitants. By the 5th cent. Czechs and other Slav peoples had conquered the country, which became Christian by the end of the 9th cent. The bohemian princes were tributary to the emperor, but the native dynasty became extinct in 1306, and the crown passed to the House of Luxemburg, the 2nd of whom, Charles I (1346-78) was also emperor as Charles IV, and founded Prague Univ. in 1348. Under his son Wenzel (1378-1419) there was a strong reforming movement led by John Huss, whose burning at the stake caused a civil war. In 1457 George of Poděbrad became king, the first native ruler since 1306. He was followed by Vladislav of Poland, whose son Louis was killed at Mohács in 1526; the archduke Ferdinand of Austria was then elected king, and henceforth until 1918 B. was under Habsburg rule. The Hussites supported the reformation, and a revolt in 1618 precipitated the Thirty Years War. The Battle of the White Mountain in 1620 ended Czech freedom. In 1918 B. became a province of the new rep. of Czechoslovakia; it was abolished as an administrative division in 1949.

BOHLEN (bō'len), **Charles 'Chip'** (1904-74). American diplomat. Ed. at Harvard, he entered the foreign service in 1929. Interpreter and adviser to Roosevelt at Tehran and Yalta, and to Truman at Potsdam, he served as ambassador to the USSR 1953-7, and estab. a reputation for realism.

BOHR (bōr), **Niels** (1885-1962). Danish physicist: Nobel prizewinner 1922. After work with Rutherford at Manchester, he became prof. at Copenhagen in 1916 and founded the Institute of Theoretical Physics there, of which he became director, in 1920. He fled from the Nazis in the S.W.W. and took part in work on the atom bomb in the USA. His son, **Aage Bohr** (1922-),also a physicist, shared a Nobel prize in 1975 for work on the theory of the atomic nucleus.

BOIARDO (bōyahrdō), **Matteo Maria,** count (1434-94). Ital. poet, famed for his *Orlando Innamorato* (1486).

BOIL. Inflamed nodule beneath the skin, formed by the infection of the root of a hair by a staphylococcus. Bs. are only likely to occur when general resistance is low, as in those who are fat, overfed, diabetic, or have mild food-poisoning.

BOILEAU (bwalo′), **Nicolas** (1636-1711). French poet and critic. Called to the bar in 1656, he turned to literature on receiving a legacy. After a series of keen contemporary satires, his *Epîtres* (1669-77) led to his joint appointment with Racine as historiographer royal in 1677. Later works include *L'Art poétique* (1674), the mock-heroic *Le Lutrin* (1674-83), and a translation of Longinus *On the Sublime* (1674). The close friend of Racine, Molière, and La Fontaine, he was elected to the Academy in 1684.

BOILING POINT. For any given liquid, the temperature at which the application of heat raises the temperature of the liquid no further, but converts it to vapour. The B.P. of water under normal pressure is 100°C or 212°F. The lower the pressure the lower the B.P. and vice versa.

BOIS-LE-DUC (bwah-le-dük). French form of *'s Hertogenbosch.*

BOKHARA. Another form of BUKHARA.

BOLDREWOOD (bōl′der-), **Rolf** (1826-1915). Pseudonym of the Australian writer Thomas Alexander Browne. B. in London, he was taken to Australia in 1830, where he became a pioneer squatter, etc., and until 1895 was police magistrate in the goldfields. His novels of adventure include *Robbery under Arms* (1888), and *Miner's Right* (1890).

BOLĒ′TUS. Genus of European fungi, resembling mushrooms, and belonging to the Basidiomycetes. *B. edulis* is edible, but some species are poisonous.

BOLEYN (bool′in), **Anne** (*c.* 1507-36). Second queen of Henry VIII. The daughter of Sir Thomas B., she was m. to the king in 1533, and in the same year became the mother of the future Queen Elizabeth. Accused of adultery and incest, she was beheaded.

BOLINGBROKE, Henry St John, visct (1678-1751). British statesman and philosopher. He entered parliament as a Tory in 1701, became Sec. of War (1704-8), and For. Sec. in Harley's ministry in 1710. He was raised to the peerage in 1712, and in 1713 negotiated the Peace of Utrecht. He planned the restoration of the 'Old Pretender', and secured Harley's dismissal in 1714, but his plans were ruined by Anne's death only 5 days later and George I's peaceful succession, and he fled to France in 1715. Allowed to return in 1723, he worked for Walpole's downfall, but after 1739 lost all influence. His political writings, which influenced Disraeli, include *The Patriot King* and *Letters on the Study and Use of History.*

BOLIVAR (bōlē′vahr), **Simón** (1783-1830). S. American soldier-statesmen, known as the Liberator. B. in Venezuela, he joined the patriots working for Venezuelan independence, and was sent to Britain in 1810 as the representative of their govt. Forced to flee to Colombia in 1812, he joined the revolutionists there, and invaded Venezuela in 1813. A bloody civil war followed and in 1814 B. had to withdraw to Colombia, and eventually to the W. Indies, whence he raided the Spanish-American coasts. In 1817 he returned to Venezuela to set up a provisional govt., crossed into Colombia (1819), where he defeated the Spaniards, and returning to Angostura proclaimed the rep. of Colombia, comprising Venezuela, New Granada, and Quito (Ecuador), with himself as president. The independence of Venezuela was finally secured in 1821, and 1822 B. liberated Ecuador. B. was invited to lead the Peruvian struggle in 1823; and final victory having been won by Sucre at Ayacucho in 1824, he turned his attention to framing a constitution. In 1825 the independence of Upper Peru was proclaimed, which adopted the name Bolivia in B.'s honour.

BOLEYN. A portrait of Anne Boleyn by an an unknown artist. *Photo: Courtesy of the National Portrait Gallery.*

BOLIVIA. Land-locked rep. of S. America. The main chains of the Andes run through the W. part, enclosing a great tableland at 3,660m (12,000ft), in which lie Lake Titicaca (only part of which is in Bolivia) and Lake Poopo. This high altiplano is cold, and is the mining region, where tin has taken precedence in importance over the silver of colonial times. Agriculture - wheat and maize - is carried on in the temperate valleys. The people are poor and the area is over-populated, mainly by Sierra Indians. To lessen B.'s dependence on the mining industry, and give land to the Indians the tropical, densely wooded plains of the E. (Santa Cruz dept) are being developed for the cultivation of cotton and sugar, and raising of beef cattle. Oil and natural gas are worked in the S. at Camiri and Sanandita. The chief rivers (Beni, Mamoré and Guaporé), are headstreams of the Amazon. There are rail links from La Paz to the port of Antofagasta in Chile; from Santa Cruz to the Brazilian border (Corumba) and Argentine border (Yacuiba); and one Santa Cruz-Cochabamba is projected. There are 1,000m of the Pan-American Highway in B. and internal air services are useful in the difficult terrain. La Paz is the cap.

BOLIVAR. A portrait of Simon Bolivar by an unknown artist. *Photo: Maxim.*

and seat of govt; Sucre is the legal capital; other towns are Cochabamba, Santa Cruz, Potosi. The pop is mainly R.C. About a third are of Spanish descent, but the Amerindian majority speak Aymara or Quechua, which in 1977 both became official languages. Area 1,098,000 sq.km (424,000 sq.m); pop. (1977) 5,950,000. M.U.: peso boliviano.

History. Before the Spanish Conquest in the 16th cent., B. formed part of the Inca empire. Independence was achieved in 1825, and the country was named in honour of Simon Bolivar, whose lieutenant, Sucre, was the first President. Originally possessing a narrow Pacific coast line, B. lost this in 1883 after its defeat by Chile. B.'s political history is troubled: from 1880 Simon Patino, the 'mining king', was for many years dominant in the state; and there was a disastrous war in the Chaco between B. and Paraguay (1932-5), the boundary line being fixed by arbitration only in 1938. Under President German Busch (1937-9) the oil industry was nationalized, and under Villaroel (1943 to 1946, when he was lynched) important social and economic reforms were initiated. Pres. Hugo Banzer (1971-8) seized power by a military coup, and his attempt to rig the elections on his retirement, to ensure the succession of his chosen candidate, was followed by a general strike in 1980. Lidia Gueiler became interim Pres. pending new elections, but a military coup intervened. Civilian government was resumed in 1982 under Hernan Siles Zuazo; in Aug. 1985 Dr Victor Paz was elected Pres.

BÖLL, Heinrich (1917-). German novelist. B. in Cologne, he served in the infantry in the S.W.W. Both in life and in work he has attacked Germany's political past, and, as a radical Catholic, the materialism of her contemporary society. He estab. his reputation with *Billard um Halbzehn* (1959: Billiards at Half-Past Nine) and following *Gruppenbild mit Dame* (1971: Group Photograph with Lady), was awarded a Nobel prize.

BOLLANDISTS. Body of Belgian Jesuits who edit the *Acta Sanctorum,* the standard collection of saints' lives. They are named after JOHN BOLLAND (1596-1665), who pub. the first 2 vols. in 1643.

BOLL-WEEVIL. Small American beetle (*Anthonomus grandis*) of the family Curculionidae: the female lays eggs in the unripe pods of 'bolls' of the cotton plant, and on these the larva feeds, causing great destruction.

BOLOGNA (bōlō'nyah). City of N. Italy, at the foot of the Apennines on the Reno and Savena, 80km (50m) N. of Florence. The city has 2 leaning towers, a cathedral, a univ. (founded in the 11th cent.), and many industries, principally concerned with foodstuffs. B. was the site of an Etruscan town, later of a Roman colony, became a rep. in the 12th cent., came under Papal rule in 1506, and in 1860 was united with Italy. Pop. (1971) 490,250.

BOLSHEVISM (Russ. *bolshinstvo,* a majority). Doctrines of the extreme Socialist or Communists who effected the Russian Revolution of 1917. The word came into use following a conference of Continental and British Socialists held in London in 1903, at which there was a split between the Russian Social Democratic party led by Lenin, and the moderate delegates. The former being in the majority were called *Bolsheviki,* and their opponents the *Mensheviki* (Russ. *menshinstvo,* a minority). Since 1952 Bolshevik is no longer the official alternative for Communist.

BOLT, Robert (1924-). British playwright. Ed. at Manchester Grammar School, he worked in assurance and as a teacher until the success of his play *Flowering Cherry* (1958). *A Man for all Seasons* (1960), dealing with Sir Thomas More, was filmed in 1967 and (scripted by him) won an Academy Award. His other screenplays incl. *Lawrence of Arabia* (1962), *Dr Zhivago* (1965: Academy Award) and *Lady Caroline Lamb* (1972).

BOLTON. Town in Greater Manchester, England, 18km (11m) N.W. of Manchester; chemicals and textile machinery are made. The Octagon is a modern civic theatre. Pop. (1972) 154,250.

BO'LTZMANN, Ludwig (1844-1906). Austrian physicist and authority on the kinetic theory of gases. B.'s constant **k** (1.375×10^{-16} ergs per degree) is the ratio of the mean total energy of a molecule to its absolute temperature, and the principle of the equi-partition of energy is known as B.'s law.

BOLZANO (boltsah'no). Town in Italy, in Trentino-Alto Adige region (alternate cap. with Trento), on the Isarco at its confluence with the Talvera; formerly in Austria. Pop. (1971) 103,125.

BO'MA. Port in Zaïre, on the estuary of the r. Zaïre 88km (55m) from the Atlantic. The oldest European settlement in Zaïre, it was a slave mart, and cap. of the Belgian Congo until 1927. Pop. (1971) 31,600.

BOMB. An explosive projectile used in warfare. Aerial bombing started in the F.W.W. when the German Air Force carried out 103 raids on Britain, dropping 269 tonnes of bombs. In the S.W.W. nearly twice this tonnage was dropped on London in a single night, and at the peak of the Allied air offensive against Germany more than 10 times this tonnage was regularly dropped in successive

BOMB. The epoch making photo of one of the atom bomb tests carried out at Bikini atoll in the Pacific in 1946. On 25th July a bomb was exploded under water and here the vast atomic cloud towers above the warships which look like toys; the battleship *Arkansas* was sunk by the blast. *Photo: Keystone Press Agency.*

nights, on one target. Raids in which nearly 1,000 heavy bombers participated were frequent and the same town might be subjected to this terrible punishment by day and night.

They were delivered either in 'precision' or 'area' attacks and great advances were made in 'blind' bombing, in which the target is located solely by instruments and is not visible through a bomb-sight. In 1939 B.s were commonly *c.* 115kg (250lb) and 230kg (500lb) but by the end of the conflict the 10-tonner was being produced, though even these paled beside the atom B. This derives its explosive force from nuclear fission as a result of a neutron chain reaction; 3 were exploded during the S.W.W.: 1st a test explosion on 16 July 1945, at Alamogordo, New Mexico, USA; then on 6 Aug. the 1st to be used in actual warfare was dropped over Hiroshima (q.v.) and 3 days later another over Nagasaki. These were 'nominal', i.e. nominally equal in destructive power to 20,000 tonnes of T.N.T. Russia 1st detonated an atom B. in 1949 and Britain in 1952 (in the Monte Bello Islands off Australia). Later developments have incl. the fusion or hydrogen bomb (q.v.), and by the 1960s intercontinental 100-megatonne nuclear warheads could be produced (5,000 times more powerful than those of the S.W.W.) and the USA and USSR between them possessed a stockpile sufficient to destroy all mankind. *See* FALLOUT.

Methods of delivery have also changed since Germany pioneered the V1 flying bomb and V2 rocket bomb, so that in the 1960s it was recognized that the era of bombers with free-falling bombs was over, and that future development would lie with missiles launched from aircraft, land sites or submarines. The danger of such nuclear weapons naturally increases with the number of nations possessing the ability to produce them (France and China became nuclear powers in 1960 and 1964 respectively), and the possibility of 'policing' states to check on their testing of bombs has been complicated by the development of underground testing. It was agreed under the Outer Space Treaty (1966) that nuclear warheads may not be sent into orbit, but this measure has been circumvented by more sophisticated weapons. The Fractional Orbital Bombardment System (FOBS) sends a warhead into a low partial orbit, followed by a rapid descent to Earth. This renders it both less vulnerable to ballistic missile defence systems and cuts the warning time to 3 min. More recent Bs. also tend to produce less fall-out, a 'dirty' B. being one which produces large quantities of radioactive debris from a U-238 casing. Testing grounds incl. Lop Nor (China); Mururoa Atoll in the S. Pacific (France); Nevada Desert, Amchitka Is. in the Aleutians (USA); Semipalatinsk in Central Asia, Novaya Zemlya Is. in the Arctic (USSR).

House of Bonaparte

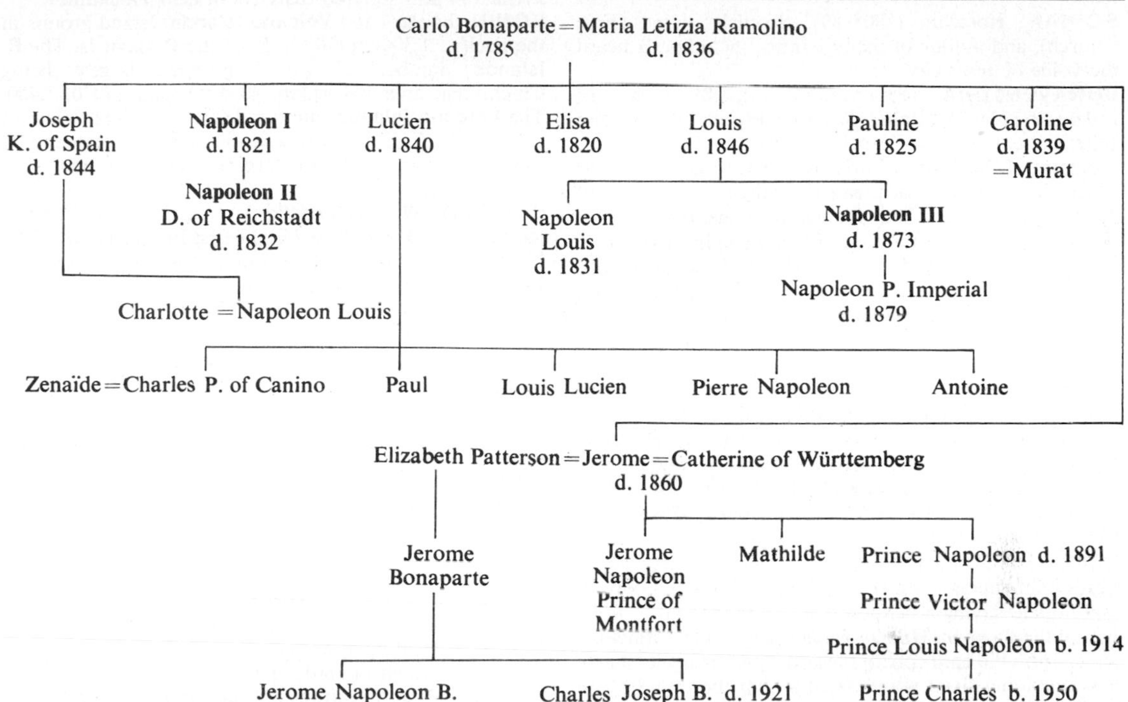

The rapid development of laser guidance systems in the 1970s, however, has meant that precise destruction of small but vital targets can be more effectively achieved with standard 450 kg/1,000 lb high explosive bombs. The laser beam may be directed at the target by the army from the ground, but additional flexibility is gained by coupling ground directed beams with those of guidance carried in high performance aircraft accompanying the bombers, e.g. the Laser Ranging Marler Target System (LRMPS).

BOMBAY (bombā'). Former prov. of Brit. India. Together with a number of interspersed princely states, it was incl. in the Dom. of India in 1947, and the major part became in 1960 the 2 new states of Gujarat and Maharashtra (qq.v.). The cap. was the city of Bombay (q.v.).

BOMBAY. Cap. and chief port of Maharashtra, Rep. of India. B. occupies the former B. Island, joined by reclamation to Salsette Island to the N., with suburbs spreading northwards on Salsette. The great harbour lies to the E. of the city, facing the mainland, here some 11km (7m) away. It is a major financial and industrial city, with a World Trade Centre (1975). Textiles are traditionally dominant (today incl. fashion goods), but hydro-electric power has made engineering and chemical-based industries, espec. pharmaceuticals, increasingly important, and from 1960 there was a revival of the ancient diamond industry. It is India's 'Hollywood', the majority of Hindi films being made here, and a Nat. Centre for the Performing Arts (1969) records music, dance and drama of the past as well as promoting future developments. A twin city, New Bombay, on the mainland, has its own port.

B. was founded in the 13th cent., came under Mogul rule, was occupied by Portugal in 1530, and passed to Britain in 1662 as part of Catherine of Braganza's wedding dowry. Area 603 sq.km (233 sq.m); pop. (1973) 5,969,000.

BOMBAY DUCK. Small fish (*Harpodon nehereus*), found off the B. coast and in other E. waters. Salted and dried, it is eaten with curry, etc.

BŌ'NA FĪ'DE (Lat. in good faith). Legal phrase signifying that a contract is undertaken without intentional misrepresentation.

BŌ'NAPARTE. Corsican family, originally of Italian origin, from whom Napoleon I (q.v.) was descended. Napoleon's father **Carlo B.** (1746-85), was a lawyer of Ajaccio, Corsica, and had a large family by his wife Letizia Ramolino (1750-1836), who joined Napoleon in Paris in 1799, and lived with him in Elba. Among their other children were **Joseph B.** (1768-1844) whom Napoleon made king of Naples in 1806, and of Spain (1808-13), and who fled to the USA on Napoleon's final surrender; **Lucien B.** (1775-1840), whose masterly handling of the Council of Five Hundred on 10 Nov. 1799 helped to secure Napoleon's success; **Louis B.** (1778-1846), whom Napoleon made governor of Paris in 1805 and king of Holland 1806-10; his son Charles Louis Napoleon became emperor of the French as Napoleon III (q.v.); **Caroline B.** (1782-1839), who m. Joachim Murat (q.v.) in 1800; and **Jerome B.** (1784-1860), who became king of Westphalia in 1807, and under Napoleon III was made marshal of France and president of the Senate. A grandson of Jerome by his first wife, Elizabeth Patterson of Baltimore, was Charles Joseph B. (1851-1921), Attorney-General of USA in the Roosevelt cabinet 1906-9. Jerome's son by his 2nd wife, Catherine of Württemberg, Napoleon Joseph Charles (1822-91), known as 'Plon-Plon', held office under Napoleon III, and his grandson

Louis Jerome (b. 1914) is the present Bonaparte 'pretender'.

BO'NAR. Horatius (1808-89). Scottish divine (Free Church), and author of many hymns, including 'I heard the voice of Jesus say'.

BONAVENTURA (bōnahventōō'rah), **St** (John of Fidanza) (1221-74). Italian R.C. theologian, canonized in 1482. He entered the Franciscan order in 1243, became professor of theology at Paris, and in 1256 general of his order. In 1273 he was created cardinal and bishop of Albano, and d. at the 2nd Council of Lyons. His eloquent writings earned him the title of the 'Seraphic Doctor'.

BOND, Edward (1935-). British dramatist. His work has come under attack because of its startling themes. *Saved* (1965) incl. the brutal killing of a baby, symbol of a society producing unwanted children, and *Bingo* (1973) showed Shakespeare committing suicide in retirement. *See* HENZE, H.W.

BONDFIELD, Margaret Grace (1873-1953). British Socialist. From being a shop assistant she became a trade union organizer among women workers. She was a Labour MP (1923-4 and 1926-31), and was the 1st woman to enter the Cabinet - as Min. of Labour, 1929-31.

BÔNE (bohn). *See* ANNABA.

BONE. Hard animal tissue consisting of a network of fibres impregnated with salts of lime. A bone is a portion of B. tissue having a definite size and shape and forming part of the skeleton. Human beings have *c.* 200 distinct Bs. which form the hard core of the body, preserving its shape, and providing fixed points from which the muscles can work, and to which ligaments are anchored.

B. forms early in the unborn child. Plates of B., e.g. those forming the skull, develop from membrane; long Bs. from cartilage or gristle. B. is formed by the cells enlarging and depositing fine granules of phosphate and carbonate of lime in the spaces between them. The original membrane or cartilage disintegrates and is carried away. Experiments have been made in setting broken Bs. with plastic.

BONHAM-CARTER, Lady Violet. *See* ASQUITH OF YARNBURY, **Lady.**

BONHEUR (bonör'), **Rosa** (1822-99). French animal painter, who exhibited at the Paris Salon from 1841. Her best work is 'Horse Fair' (1853).

BONHOEFFER (bon'hohfer), **Dietrich** (1906-45). German Lutheran theologian. Having taken part in the plot against Hitler, he was executed by the Nazis in Flossenburg concentration camp. His *Letters and Papers from Prison* became the textbook of modern 'radical theology', anticipating the possibility of a secular 'religionless' Christianity.

BONIFACE (bon'ifās). Name of 9 popes. The most notable was B. VIII (*c.* 1228-1303). Succeeding to the office in 1294, he exempted the clergy from taxation by the secular government by a bull of 1296. Philip the Fair of France and Henry III of England forced him to give way by excluding the clergy from certain lay privileges. His bull of 1302 asserting the complete temporal and spiritual power of the papacy was equally ineffective.

BONIFACE, St (680-754). 'Apostle of Germany'. Originally named Wynfrith, he was b. in Devon and became a Benedictine monk. After a preliminary missionary journey to Frisia in 716, he was given the task of evangelizing Germany by Pope Gregory II in 718, and was appointed archbishop of Mainz in 746, but returned to Frisia 754 and suffered martyrdom near Dockum.

BONIN (bōnēn') and **Volcano Islands.** Island groups in the Pacific, 1,300km (800m) E. of the Ryukyu Is. The **B. Islands** number 27 (in 3 groups), largest being Chichijima: area 104 sq.km (40sq.m); pop. (1970) 7,400. The **Volcano Islands** number 3, incl. Iwojima, scene of some of the fiercest fighting of the S.W.W.; total area 28 sq.km (11 sq.m). They are Japanese, but were under US control 1952-68.

BONINGTON, Chris(tian) (1934-). British mountaineer. He took part in the first British ascent of the N. face of the Eiger (1962), climbed the central Tower of Paine in Patagonia in 1963, and was the leader of the Everest expedition 1975. *See* KONGUR SHAN.

BONINGTON, Richard Parkes (1801-28). British painter. His family settled in France in 1817 and he rapidly developed a talent for seascapes and landscapes in watercolour. In the last few years of his life he also painted in oils, and excelled in depicting the transitory effects of light. The Wallace Collection has a fine selection of his work. He d. of tuberculosis.

BONITO (bonētō). Popular name of a smaller species of tunny not exceeding 1m (3ft) in length (*Thynnus pelamys*), belonging to the mackerel family (Scombridae), and common in tropical seas.

BONN. Cap. of the W. German Federal Rep. 18km (15m) S.S.E. of Cologne, on the left bank of the Rhine. An important Roman station, it was captured by the French in 1794, annexed by them in 1801, and was allotted to Prussia in 1815. Remarkable features are the cathedral (begun 11th cent.), the univ., the observatory, and Beethoven's birthplace. Industries incl. chemicals, textiles, leather, and ceramics. B. was chosen W. German cap. in 1949. Pop. (1978) 284,000.

BONNARD (bonahr'), **Pierre** (1867-1947). French painter. One of the Nabi group led by Maurice Denis, he made an idea rather than an object his starting point, using colour with a decorative effect in street scenes of Paris, landscapes and interiors with figures.

BONNEVILLE, Lake. Prehistoric lake, of which the Great Salt Lake, Utah, is the surviving remnant; salt flats over 300m (1,000ft) above the present lake level, mark the former boundary and have been used as a track for motor speed records.

BONNY, Bight of. Part of the Gulf of Guinea (formerly the B. of Biafra), between Capes Formosa and Lopez, forming the E. section of Nigeria's continental shelf. The river Niger flows into it. In 1975 it was re-named B. of Bonny, after the port of that name.

BONSAI (bonsī). Dwarf tree cultivation. Formerly limited to Japan, which originated the practice, it has in recent years spread increasingly to the West. Specimens may be several hundred years old.

BOOK. Permanent portable written record. Early substances used in B.-making include leaves, bark, linen, silk, clay, leather, and papyrus. Early in the Christian era (*c.* 100-150), the codex or paged book, as against the roll, began to be adopted. Vellum was generally used for B. production by the beginning of the 4th cent. and its use lasted until the 15th, when it was superseded by paper. *See* MICROFORM.

It is anticipated that by the end of the 1980s, the paper book will have been superseded to some extent by the visual display unit (VDU), a page-size read-out terminal.

BONN. Europe's newest capital has made-to-measure accommodation for the West German government. Members of Parliament have a modern office block (top left); the Upper House (Bundesrat) is in the centre; the Lower House (Bundestag) is at the bottom right. *Photo: Camera Press.*

For quick reference and portability there would be a wrist-size terminal. The 'computer book' would basically consist of a microchip holding information in code (*see* BINARY NUMBER SYSTEM), which would be decoded on the read-out terminal in whatever language the reader preferred.

BOOKBINDING. B. only emerged as a distinct art when printing made less expensive materials than precious metals and wood essential. The principal ornament of leather B., gold tooling, was probably introduced to Europe from the East by the Venetian Aldus Manutius, and adopted in England by Thomas Berthelet, binder to Henry VIII. Famous binders include Nicholas and Clovis Eve (16th cent.), Le Gascon, Samuel Mearne (17th cent.), A. M. Padeloup, N. D. Derome, Roger Paynes (18th cent.), Francis Bedford (19th cent.), and T. J. Cobden-Sanderson, C. Ricketts (20th cent.). Modern cloth binding common to England and America was first introduced by Leighton in 1822, but since the S.W.W. synthetic bindings have been increasingly employed.

BOOKER McCONNELL PRIZE. Prize of £10 000 annually awarded (from 1969) by the conglomerate Booker McConnell to a novel published in the UK. Their activities incl health foods, shipping, engineering and author copyrights (Agatha Christie, Ian Fleming, etc).

BOOKKEEPING. Keeping books of account, i.e., records of commercial transactions, in a systematic and accurate manner (*see* ACCOUNTANCY). The earliest-known work on double entry B. was by Luca Pacioli, pub. in Venice in 1494. The method which he advocated had, however, been practised by the Italian merchants for several hundred years before that date. The first English work on the subject, by the schoolmaster, Hugh Oldcastle, appeared in 1543. Double entry is a system which recognizes the duality inherent in every business transaction, each item being entered in the books twice - as debit and as credit.

BOOK OF THE DEAD. Ancient book of the Egyptians, known to them as the *Book of Coming Forth by Day*, and forming a guide-book for the deceased through Hades to the kingdom of Osiris.

BOOLE, George (1814-64). British mathematician. Self-educated, he in 1847 pub. *The Mathematical Analysis of Logic* which estab. the basis of modern mathematical logic and was prof. at Queen's College, Cork, from 1849. *Boolean Algebra* is used in designing computers.

BOO'MERANG. Hand-thrown wooden missile, usually up to 1m (3ft) long, shaped in a curved angle, which returns if it does not hit its target, developed to perfection by Australian Aborigines. A good return throw is 44m (145ft).

BOONE, Daniel (1734-1820). American frontiersman. He blazed the pioneer Wilderness Road in 1775, from E. Virginia to Kentucky, followed by settlers in the first large-scale westward migration.

BOOTH, Charles (1840-1916). British sociologist and shipowner. He conducted a remarkable investigation into the manner of living of the London poor, recorded in *Life and Labour of the People of London* (1891-1903). B. was also a pioneer in the old-age pensions movement.

BOOTH, John Wilkes (1839-65). American actor, who fired the shot which mortally wounded President Lincoln at Ford's Theatre, Washington, on April 14 1865. B. escaped with a broken leg, and was shot dead in a barn in Virginia on his refusal to surrender.

BOOTH, William (1829-1912). 'General' of the Salvation Army. B. at Nottingham, the son of a builder, he experienced religious conversion at the age of 15. In 1865 he founded in Whitechapel the Christian Mission which in 1878 became the Salvation Army.

His eldest son, **William Bramwell B.** (1856–1929) became chief of staff of the S.A. in 1880 and was General from 1912 until his deposition (1929). **Evangeline B.** (1865-1950), 7th child of General William B., was a prominent S.A. officer, and 1934-9 was General. She became a US citizen.

BOOTHBY, Robert John Graham, baron (1900–86). Scottish politician. Ed. at Eton and Magdalen Coll., Oxon, he became a Unionist MP in 1924 and was P.P.S. to Churchill 1926–9. An ardent advocate of Britain's entry into Europe, a superb speaker and a powerful personality in British politics, he pub. *Recollections of a Rebel* (1978).

BOOTHE, Clare (1903-). American writer. B. in N.Y., she entered journalism, was managing editor of *Vanity Fair* (1933-4), and made a sensational success with her plays, espec. the mordant *The Women* (1936) and *Margin for Error* (1939). A Republican, she was a member of Congress 1943-7, ambassador to Italy 1953-7, and ambassador designate to Brazil in 1959, when she resigned because of a political dispute over her appointment. She married 1935 Henry Robinson Luce (1898-1967), founder of the magazines *Time* (1923) and *Life* (1936).

BORGIA. Sometimes called merely a 'Courtesan', this portrait by Bartolommeo Veneto has also been identified as Lucrezia Borgia. The portrait of her brother is by an unknown artist. *Photos: Stadelschen Kunstinstituts, Frankfurt and Alinari-Giraudon.*

BOOTLE. Town in Merseyside, England, adjoining Liverpool, on the estuary of the Mersey. There are docks, and it is the H.Q. of the National Girobank. Pop. (1972) 73,110.

BOOTLEGGING. In the early days of USA the sale of intoxicating liquor to the Red Indians was prohibited but unscrupulous traders conveyed to them bottles of liquor hidden in the legs of their jack-boots. Thus originated the term B. which came into universal vogue during the period 1920-33 of nation-wide prohibition in the USA.

BOPHUTHATSWANA (bōpootatswah'nah). S. African Black homeland (independent 1977), comprising 6 blocks nr the Botswana border. Minerals incl. platinum, chrome, vanadium, asbestos, manganese, and the cap. is Mmbatho, 16km (10m) N. of Mafikeng (q.v.). Area 40,330 sq km (15,571 sq m); pop. (1978) 2,500,000, of whom over half live in the Rep. of South Africa.

BORAGE (bur'ij). A salad plant (*Borago officinalis*) cultivated in Britain and occasionally found wild. It has small blue flowers and hairy leaves.

BORAH, William Edgar (1865-1940). American Republican politician. B. in Illinois, he was a senator for Idaho from 1906. He is remembered as an arch-isolationist, one of those chiefly responsible for America's repudiation of the League of Nations.

BORAS (-os). Town in Sweden, E. of Gothenburg. Iron is mined, and there are engineering and textile industries. Pop. (1978) 104,150.

BORAX. Hydrated sodium borate, found as soft whitish crystals or incrustations on the shores of hot springs and lakes associated with recent volcanoes. Formerly much of the world's B. came from a salt lake in Tibet, but now it is largely derived from the mineral colemanite. B. is employed in glazing pottery and enamel ware, in calico printing, etc.

BORDEAUX. Major port in France, cap. of Gironde dept on the Garonne, 96km (60m) from the sea. Situated in the fertile plain of Médoc, B. is the centre of the wine trade of the area. Tropical products are imported, and imported oil is refined on a large scale: other industries incl. metallurgy, electronics, chemicals, synthetic rubber, and food preparation. B. was under the English crown for 3 cents. until 1453. In 1870, 1914 and 1940, the French govt was moved here in the face of German invasion. The medieval and 18th cent. areas of the city have been magnificently preserved: the univ. was founded in 1441. Pop. (1975) 591,500.

BORDERS. Region of Scotland, on the eastern border between England and Scotland, created 1975. It incl. the former cos. of Berwick, Peebles, Roxburgh and Selkirk, with a small part of Midlothian, S.E. of the Moorfoot Hills. The admin. H.Q. is Newtown St. Boswells, where Mary Queen of Scots had a home, now a museum. Area 4,662 sq.km (1,800 sq.m); pop. (1971) 99,000.

BORE. A tidal wave which rushes up certain rivers with great violence, forming a wall of water stretching across the stream, sometimes with disastrous results to river craft. It occurs chiefly at spring tide in rivers with a funnel-shaped estuary quickly narrowing upstream so that the wave is steadily concentrated and attains a considerable height, e.g. the Severn B. and the very much larger Bs. on the Amazon and Yangtze-Kiang.

BORGES (bor'khes), **Jorge Luis** (1899–1986). Argentinian poet and author. Grandson of an Englishwoman, and the son of a lawyer, he was encouraged by his father to write, and headed a youthful anti-traditionalist (Ultraiste) movement. Under Perón he was deprived of his post as librarian, but in 1961 became Director of the National Library, Buenos Aires, where he was also prof. of English literature at the univ. His reputation rests chiefly on his short stories, *Ficciones* (1962) being the 1st vol. to appear in translation.

BORGIA (bor'jah), **Cesare** (1476-1507). Italian cardinal and ruler. Illegitimate son of Rodrigo B., who became pope as Alexander VI in 1492, he was made a cardinal by his father at the age of 17, but resigned the honour in exchange for the post of captain-general of the papacy. He led a number of successful campaigns against the Italian city-republics and was suspected of aiming at the establishment of his own kingdom. In 1503 he nearly d. of the poison that killed his father. Faced by a powerful coalition, B. went to Spain and then to Navarre, and was killed at the siege of Viana. Execrated for his crimes and vices, he was yet a patron of the arts and a ruler of unusual ability.

BORGIA, Lucrezia (1480-1519). 5th child of Pope Alexander VI and sister of Cesare B., she was first married at the age of 12 and again at 13. Both marriages were annulled in turn by her father, and at 18 she was married to a Neapolitan noble, who 2 years later was murdered at the instigation of Cesare B. Finally in 1501 she was found a 4th husband in Alfonso of Este, who became duke of Ferrara in 1505. She encouraged authors and artists such as Ariosto and Titian.

BO'RGLUM, Gutzon (1871-1941). American sculptor. Of Danish stock, he was b. in Idaho. He developed a gift for monumental works reminiscent of the achievements of ancient Egypt, e.g. a 6-tonne marble head of Lincoln at Washington and a series of giant heads of Washington, Jefferson, Lincoln and T. Roosevelt carved on Mount Rushmore, S. Dakota.

BORIC ACID (H_3BO_3). Also called boracic acid; an acid formed by the simple combination of hydrogen and oxygen with the non-metallic element boron. It is a weak antiseptic.

BORIS III (1894-1943). Tsar of Bulgaria from 1918, when he succeeded his father, Ferdinand I. From 1934 he was virtual dictator until his sudden and mysterious death following a visit to Hitler. His son Simeon II was Tsar until deposed in 1946.

BORIS GODUNOV' (1552-1605). Tsar of Russia from 1598, when he succeeded Fedor, son of Ivan the Terrible. He was a capable but tyrannical ruler, and he d. during a revolt led by one who professed to be Dmitri, a brother of Fedor and the rightful Tsar, whom B. is supposed to have murdered.

BORLAUG (bor'lowg), **Norman** (1914-). American scientist of Norwegian extraction, 'father of the green revolution'. Sent to Mexico 1944 by the Rockefeller Foundation, he developed high-yielding strains of dwarf wheat invaluable for use with fertilizers and irrigation in countries such as India and Pakistan. He was awarded a Nobel peace prize 1970.

BORMANN, Martin (1900-45). German Nazi politician, b. at Halberstadt. He took part in the abortive Munich Putsch of 1923, and rose to high positions in the National Socialist Party. After Hess's flight to England he became 'party chancellor' in May 1941. He was believed to have escaped the fall of Berlin in May 1945, and was tried in absence and sentenced to death at Nuremberg 1945-6, but a skeleton uncovered by a mechanical excavator in Berlin 1972 was officially recognized as his by forensic experts in 1973.

BORN, Max (1882-1970). Physicist. B. in Germany, he became British in 1939, and was Tait prof. of natural philosophy at Edinburgh 1936-53. In 1954 he was awarded a joint Nobel Prize for his fundamental work in quantum mechanics.

BOR'NEO. Large island in the E. Indies. Politically it comprises Kalimantan (Indonesian), Sarawak and Sabah (*see* MALAYSIA), and Brunei (British protected) (qq.v.). The name B. is a variant of Brunei, first reached by the Portuguese discoverers who gave the name to the whole island. Most of B. is forest-clad and mountainous (Mt Kinabalu, 4,175m/13,680ft, in N.B.), but it has wide alluvial plains and low marshy shores with silted estuaries. The pop. consists of (1) Dayak tribes of the interior, an Indonesian people, animists and formerly head-hunters, who live by the sale of jungle produce, grow rice and maize, and fish; (2) Malays, a later coastal people, Moslems, who plant, fish, and trade; and (3) Chinese who started gold-mining and are now farmers and tradesmen. Area 730,000 sq.km (282,000 sq.m). Pop. (1985) 6,500,000.

BORNHOLM. Danish island in the Baltic Sea, 35km (22m) S.E. of the nearest point of the Swedish coast. Ronne is the cap. Area 587 sq.km (227 sq.m); pop. (1978) 47,340.

BORNU (bornoo'). Negro kingdom of the 9-19th cents. to the W. and S. of Lake Chad. Converted to Islam in the 11th cent., it reached its greatest strength in the 15th-18th cents. From 1901 it was absorbed in the British, French and German colonies in this area, which are now the Reps. of Niger and Cameroon, and the Federation of Nigeria. The largest section of ancient B. falls in the modern state of Bornu in Nigeria, of which the cap. is Maiduguri.

BOROBUDUR. Largest Buddhist monument in Java, 24km (15m) N.W. of Jokjakarta, built between A.D. 750 and 850, and one of the architectural wonders of the world.

BORODI'N, Alexander Porfirievich (1834-87). Russian composer. B. at St Petersburg, the illegitimate son of a Russian prince, he became by profession an expert in medical chemistry, but in his spare time devoted himself to music. His principal work is the opera *Prince Igor;* left unfinished, this was completed by Rimsky-Korsakov and Glazunov. B.'s works include symphonies, songs and chamber music, and are characterized by the use of traditional Russian themes.

BORODINO (borōdē'nō). Russian village, 113km (70m) W. of Moscow, on the road to Smolensk, where on 7 Sept. 1812 Napoleon defeated the Russian army under Kutusov.

BO'RON. A non-metallic element: symbol B.; at. wt. 10.82; atomic number 5. It is a maroon-coloured powder, made by heating a mixture of its oxide with magnesium at a high temperature. Very important in reactor engineering, it absorbs neutrons, transmuting to lithium isotope. Boral (alloy with aluminium) is an excellent shield for neutrons, and B. steel is used for reactor control rods. Arc-made B. carbide is used for steel-cutting tools.

BOROUGH (bur'u). In the UK a former area of local govt. Probably originating in the 8th cent., it was estab. in the form which endured until the local govt reorganization of 1974, by the Munipal Reform Act (1835). Each had councillors directly elected by popular vote (for 3 yrs one-third retiring annually), who elected from among their number the mayor and aldermen (for 6 yrs, half retiring every 3 yrs). They were of 2 types: *Municipal Bs.*, with limited powers, and *County Bs.* The title Borough has been retained as an honorary status. A parliamentary B. is an urban constituency, a unit of political representation.

In the US the name B. largely ceased to be used after the War of Independence: an interesting survival is the administration subdivision of N.Y. City into the 5 Bs. of Manhattan, The Bronx, Brooklyn, Queens and Richmond.

BORROMEO (borōmā'ō), **Carlo** (1538-84). R.C. saint and cardinal. B. at Arona of noble Ital. stock, he was created a cardinal and archbishop of Milan by his uncle Pope Pius IV in 1560. B. wound up the affairs of the Council of Trent, and largely drew up the catechism that contained its findings. He lived the life of an ascetic, and in 1578 founded the community later called the Oblate Fathers of St Charles. He was canonized 1610. His feast day is 4 Nov.

BORROMINI (boromē'ni), **Francesco** (1599-1667). Italian architect, leading practitioner of the baroque style. He worked on St Peter's, Rome under Bernini, and designed St Agnese in Piazza Navona and St Carlo alle Quattro Fontane, Rome.

BORROW, George Henry (1803-81). British author and traveller. B. at E. Dereham, Norfolk, he was articled to a Norwich solicitor, but having studied many languages, including Romany, came to London in 1824 as a translator before taking to the life of a wanderer in 1827. He travelled on foot through England, France, Germany, Russia, Spain, and the East, and acted as agent for the British and Foreign Bible Society for several years. On his marriage in 1840, he settled to writing at Oulton Broad, Norfolk, and produced *Zincali* (1840), an account of the Spanish gipsies, and *The Bible in Spain* (1843). In 1844 he toured the Balkans, and then pub. *Lavengro* (1851), and its sequel, *The Romany Rye* (1857), mingling autobiographical and fictitious material. A later work, *Wild Wales* (1862), was the result of a visit to that country. His knowledge of languages and gipsy lore was wide though unscientific, and he was unrivalled in the creation of the atmosphere of the open road.

BORROWDALE. Famous beauty-spot in the Lake District of England, 8km (5m) S. of Keswick, Cumbria, from Derwentwater to Scafell Pike.

BORSTAL. A reformatory system estab. in Britain under the Prevention of Crimes Act, 1908, for the purpose of retrieving young persons of both sexes who have started on a career of crime, and first put into practice in 1902 at Borstal prison near Rochester in Kent. B. Institutions vary in type and are classified as 'open' (e.g. North Sea Camp, Lincs. and Hollesley Bay Colony, Suffolk) and 'closed' (e.g. Borstal, Kent, and Feltham, Middlesex). From 1963 the minimum age of entry has been 15.

BO'RZOI (Russ. for 'swift'). Russian species of greyhound, first seen in England in 1842, and widely known since 1890. Height for dogs 74cm (29in) upwards at shoulder; long-haired; colour, white with black and tan markings.

BOSCAWEN (boskō'en, -kaw'en), **Edward** (1711-61). English admiral who saw much service against the French in the mid-18th cent. wars. To his men he was known as 'Old Dreadnought'.

BOSCH (bos), **Jerom** (*c.* 1460-1516). Dutch painter named from his birthplace, 's Hertogenbosch. His works, of a bizarre and grotesque style, were greatly admired by Philip II of Spain. His Christian name Jerom is often given its Latinized form Hieronymus.

BOSE, Sir Jagadis Chunder (1858-1937). Indian physicist. B. nr Dacca, he was prof. of physical science at Calcutta 1885-1915, and studied plant-life, especially the growth and minute movements of plants, and their reaction to electrical stimuli. He founded the B. Research Institute, Calcutta.

BOSE, Satyendranath (1894-1974). Indian physicist. With Einstein, he formulated the B.-Einstein law of quantum mechanics, and was prof. of physics at the Univ. of Calcutta 1945-58.

BOSNIA AND HERÇEGOVINA (-hertsego'vena). Federal rep. of Yugoslavia, formed of the 2 provs. of B. and H. Sarajevo is the cap. Wild and mountainous with fertile valleys and forest lands in the E., it produces fruits, tobacco, wheat and other grains, pigs, cattle and sheep. Minerals incl. coal, iron, quicksilver; and there are steelworks and other industrial plants. Area 51,129 sq.km (19,745 sq.m); pop. (1971) 3,717,000, many being Moslem.

Both B. and H. formed part of Roman Illyria; in the 7th cent. they were conquered by the Slavs. B. was an independent kingdom for a short time in the 14th cent. Part of the Turkish empire from 1463, B. and H., still nominally Turkish, were placed under Austrian administration in 1878. Austria annexed the area in 1908, and in 1918 it was made part of the new kingdom of the Serbs, Croats, and Slovenes (renamed Yugoslavia 1931).

BOSPORUS. Strait 27km (17m) long joining the Black Sea with the Sea of Marmara, and forming part of the water division between Europe and Asia. Istanbul stands on its W. side. The *B. Bridge* (1973) links Istanbul and Turkey-in-Asia (1,621m/5,320ft).

BOSSUET (bosü-eh'), **Jacques Bénigne** (1627-1704). French R.C. divine, pulpit orator, and theologian. Appointed to the Chapel Royal in 1662, he won fame by his *Oraisons funèbres*, delivered at the funerals of certain great personages. Then he became tutor to the young Dauphin. Appointed bishop of Meaux in 1681, B. became involved in the Gallican controversy between Louis XIV and the pope and did his best to effect a compromise. His *Exposition de la foi catholique* (1670) and *Histoire des variations des églises protestantes* (1688) are brilliant essays.

BOSTON. Cap. of Massachusetts, USA, at the mouth of the r. Charles where it enters Mass. Bay. B. is a cultural centre, and has been the home of many literary and political figures. The inhabitants, for the main part descendants of the original New England settlers, were long regarded as the aristocrats of the USA, but Irish, Italian, Polish and Czech immigrants have modified the former Puritan basis of the population. There are many fine buildings and historical landmarks, including B. univ., the public library, and the Statehouse on Beacon Hill, overlooking the city. The Boston Symphony Orchestra is world-famous. The Charles is spanned by many bridges, including Harvard, leading to the famous univ. Overlooking the harbour is the J. F. Kennedy library, which also contains the papers of Ernest Hemingway.

BOSPORUS. The slim span of the new Bosporus Bridge links the two continents. The name 'Bosporus' (Gk 'ox-ford') refers to Io, who in her wanderings in the guise of a heifer, was said to have crossed here. *Photo: Courtesy of the Cleveland Bridge & Engineering Company Ltd.*

The industries incl. book publishing and printing, rubber manufacture, shoemaking, confectionery, and machinery.

The site was settled in 1630, and was named after B. in England. The attempt of the British govt to levy a tax on tea led to the 'Boston Tea Party', 1773, when citizens disguised as Red Indians boarded ships carrying tea and threw it into the harbour. Bunker Hill, which gives its name to the 1st battle of the War of American Independence, is now within the city of B. The 'Boston Massacre' was a riot 5 March 1770, also arising from resistance to the payment of duties. Four men were killed by British troops called to the aid of one of their comrades. Pop. met. area (1970) 2,730,228.

BOSTON. Seaport in Lincs, England, on the Witham 6km (4m) from its mouth. St Botolph's is England's largest parish church, and its tower 'Boston stump' is a landmark for seamen. Pop. (1972) 26,230.

BOSTON TERRIER. American breed of dog, but British in origin. It is on terrier lines, but with the short head of the bulldog. The coat is black with a white blaze on the head, white collar and 'socks'.

BOSWELL, James (1740-95). Scottish biographer and man-of-letters. B. at Edinburgh, the son of the judge Alexander B., Lord Auchinleck, he studied law but centred his ambitions on literature and politics. He first met Johnson in 1763 before setting out on the Continental tour during which he met Rousseau, Voltaire, and General Paoli, whom he commemorated in his popular *Account of Corsica* (1768). In 1766 he was admitted as an advocate, and in 1772 renewed his acquaintance with Johnson in London, as became his custom almost every year. Establishing a place in his intimate circle, he became a member of the Literary Club in 1773, and in the same year accompanied Johnson on the journey later recorded in the *Journal of the Tour to the Hebrides* (1785). On his succession to his father's estate in 1782, he made further attempts to enter Parliament, was called to the Eng. bar in 1786, and was Recorder of Carlisle 1788-90. In 1789 he settled in London, and in 1791 produced the greatest of Eng. biographies, the *Life of Johnson.* His long-lost personal papers were acquired for publication by Yale Univ. in 1949, and the *Journals* are of exceptional interest.

BOSWELL. A youthful portrait by George Willison in a costume ill-adapted for the rocky Romantic setting, just as the owl above his head suggests a wisdom at odds with his indiscretions. *Photo: Courtesy of the National Galleries of Scotland.*

BOSWORTH. Last battle of the Wars of the Roses, fought on 22 Aug. 1485 near the village of Market B., 19km (12m) W. of Leicester. Richard III, the Yorkist king, was defeated and slain by Henry of Richmond, who became Henry VII.

BOTANY. The study of plants; this is subdivided into a number of smaller studies, e.g. the distinction of the differences and resemblances of plants is termed taxonomy, their external formation plant morphology, their internal arrangement plant anatomy, their microscopic examination histology, their life history plant physiology, and their distribution over the earth's surface in relation to their surroundings, plant ecology. Palaeobotany concerns the study of fossil plants, while economic B. deals with the utility of plants. Horticulture, agriculture, and forestry are specialized branches of B.

BOTTICELLI. The loveliest of all Botticelli's paintings, the *Primavera*, 'Springtime' in the Uffizi gallery at Florence. It was inspired by a poem of Politian's. *Photo: Mansell Collection*

The most ancient botanical record is carved on the walls of the temple at Karnak, about 1500 B.C. The Greeks in the 5th and 4th cents. B.C. used many plants for medicinal purposes, the first Greek Herbal being drawn up about 350 B.C. by Diocles of Carystus. Botanical information was collected into the works of Theophrastus of Eresus (380-287 B.C.), a pupil of Aristotle, who founded the technical plant nomenclature. Cesalpino in the 16th cent. sketched out a system of classification based on flowers, fruits, and seeds, while Jung (1587-1658) used flowers only as his criterion. John Ray (1627-1705) arranged plants systematically, based on his findings on fruit, leaf, and flower, and described about 18,600 plants. Swedish Carl Linné or Linnaeus (1707-78), who founded systematics, included in his classification all known plants and animals, working them into a rigid framework, and giving each a binomial descriptive label. Banks, Solander, Brown, Bauer, and others travelled throughout the world studying plants, and found that all could be fitted into a systematic classification based on Linnaeus' work. Linnaeus was also the first to recognize and accept the sexual nature of flowers, this work being followed up later by Sprengel, Amici, Robert Brown, and Charles Darwin. Later work revealed the detailed cellular structure of plant tissues, and the exact nature of photosynthesis and the manufacture of plant food. Sachs (1832-97) defined the function of chlorophyll, and the significance of plant stomata. Engelmann (1843-1909) worked on the effect of the spectrum on chlorophyll; the effect of nitrogen on plant life was revealed about the same time, and the study of plant functions has assumed a comprehensive form.

In the period since the S.W.W. much has been achieved towards the clarification of cell function, repair and growth by the hybridization of plant cells (the combination of the nucleus of one cell with the protoplasm of the other), but some problems elude solution. However, the achievement of the first plant-animal hybrid in 1975 (a fusion of red blood cells from a hen with protoplasts derived from yeast cells) was expected to lead to further advances. *See* BREEDING.

BOTANY BAY. Inlet on the E. coast of Australia, 8km (5m) S. of Sydney, N.S.W. Discovered by Capt. Cook in 1770, it was so named by him on account of the variety of plants found on its shores by Joseph Banks, the expedition's botanist. Chosen in 1787 as the site for a penal colony, it proved unsuitable, and the settlement was made where Sydney stands. But the name B.B. continued to be popularly used for any convict settlement in Australia.

BOT-FLIES. Group of dipterous insects, forming the family Oestridae. The larvae are parasitic, internally or externally, on horses, sheep, cattle and deer.

BOTHA (bō'ta), **Louis** (1862-1919). S. African soldier and statesman, b. at Greytown, Natal, of Boer parents. Elected a member of the Volksraad in 1897, he supported the more moderate Joubert against Kruger. On the outbreak of the Boer War he commanded the Boers besieging Ladysmith, and in 1900 succeeded Joubert in command of the Transvaal forces. For 18 months he engaged in guerrilla warfare, but eventually welcomed the conclusion of peace. In 1907 B. became Premier of the Transvaal and in 1910 of the first Union govt. On the outbreak of war in 1914 he rallied S. Africa to the Commonwealth, suppressed the

Boer revolt under de Wet, and conquered German S.W. Africa. At Versailles in 1919 he represented S. Africa.

BOTHA, Pieter Willem (1916-). S. African statesman. As Defence Minister from 1965, he built up the strength of the armed forces, and in 1978 succeeded Vorster in the premiership. In 1979 he warned his own National Party that 'white domination and legally enforced apartheid are a recipe for permanent conflict,' and subequently moved towards modification of the policy.

BOTHWELL, James Hepburn, 4th earl of (*c.* 1536-78). Scottish nobleman, who is alleged to have arranged the explosion which killed Darnley, husband of Mary Queen of Scots, in 1567. Tried and acquitted a few weeks later, he abducted Mary, and (having divorced his wife) married her on 15 May. A revolt ensued, and B. was forced to flee to Norway and thence to Sweden. In 1570 Mary obtained a divorce on the ground that she had been ravished by B. before marriage. Later, B. was confined in a castle in Zeeland, where he d. insane.

BO- (abbr. of *Bohdi* 'wisdom' or 'enlightment') **TREE.** Name given by Indian and Ceylonese Buddhists to the peepul or sacred wild fig (*Ficus religiosa*) under which Buddha (q.v.) was 'enlightened'. The B. planted *c.* 300 B.C. at Anuradhapura (q.v.) is still worshipped by pilgrims.

BOTSWANA (botswah'na). Country in Southern Africa, lying between the Molopo on the S and Zambezi on the N, and S.W. Africa and the Transvaal on the W and E respectively. Cattle are reared and livestock and products exported; field crops are undependable owing to irregular rainfall. In the N the Okovango Swamp (20,800 sq.km/ 8,000 sq.m), into which the Okovango r. empties, is a potential source of irrigation, but at the expense of rich wild life, hippopotami, crocodiles, etc. Southern B. forms part of the Kalahari Desert. Mineral discoveries since the 1960s incl. industrial diamonds, copper, nickel and coal.

The cap. is Gaborone, pop. (1976) 37,300, and the chief tribe, forming 80% of the population, are the Bamangwato, whose cap. is Serowe. M.U.: pula.

The country came within the British sphere of influence in 1885 as Bechuanaland, and in 1966 became a rep. within the Commonwealth, as Botswana. Sir Seretse Khama (q.v.), the first pres., was succeeded in 1980 by Quett Masire, a member of the minority Bangwaketse; as chieftain of the Bamangwato, Sir Seretse was succeeded by his eldest son, Ian. There is a Nat. Assembly, the majority elected by universal suffrage, and an advisory House of Chiefs. Area 575,000 sq.km (222,000 sq.m); pop. (1978) 800,000, the majority being Christian. Both Tswana and English are official languages.

BOTTICELLI (bottĕchel'lē), **Sandro** (1444-1510). Florentine artist, real name Filipepi, but his elder brother's nickname B. 'little barrel' was passed on to him. He studied under Filippo Lippi, and was patronized by the Medici family. His *Primavera* (about 1477) treats a theme from classical mythology in a style which is both graceful and realistic. In 1481-2 he assisted with the decoration of the Sistine chapel in Rome. About 1494 he produced his illustrations of Dante. After the execution in 1498 of Savonarola, B. broke with the Medicis, and his 'Calumny of Apelles' (1498) is said to express his detestation of those who calumniated Savonarola. His pictures became more sombre and religious, though his 'Madonna of the Magnificat' shows all the grace and colour of which B. was capable.

BOTTLEBRUSH. Three genera of trees and shrubs common in Australia, *Melaleuca, Banksia* (named after Sir Joseph Banks, q.v.), and *Callistemon*, with characteristic cylindrical, composite flowerheads, often brightly coloured.

BO'TULISM. A frequently fatal type of food poisoning due to *Clostridium botulinum*, which excretes one of the most powerful toxins known.

BOUCHER (booshch'), **François** (1703-70). French painter. B. in Paris, he became director of the Gobelin tapestry works in 1755, and 10 years later court painter. He is famous for his paintings of maidens, shepherds, cupids, etc.

BOUCHER DE CRÈVECOEUR DE PERTHES (boosheh' de krāvker' de pārt), **Jacques** (1788-1868). French geologist, whose discovery of Palaeolithic hand-axes in 1837 led him to promote the recognition of man's history as ante-dating the popularly accepted limit of 4000 B.C.: He was attacked by traditionalists.

BOUDICCA (boodik'a) (d. A.D. 62). Queen of the Iceni, often referred to by the Lat. form Boadicea (bō-adisēah). Her husband, King Prasutagus, had been a tributary of the Romans, but on his death (A.D. 61), the territory of the Iceni was violently annexed, and B. was scourged and her daughters outraged. B. raised the whole of S.E. England in revolt, and before the main Roman armies could return from campaigning in Wales she burnt London and Colchester. Later the British were annihilated somewhere between London and Chester, and B. poisoned herself.

BOUDIN (boodiṅ'), **Eugène** (1824-98). French painter, a fore-runner of Impressionism noted for his seascapes.

BOUGAINVILLE (boogaṅvēl'), **Louis Antoine de** (1729-1811). French navigator. After service with the French in Canada during the Seven Years War he sailed round the world, 1766-9. Several islands are named after him, and also the climbing plant *Bougainvillea*, a genus of the family Nyctaginaceae, native of S. America, and cultivated for its conspicuous red, purple, or mauve bracts which cover the flowers.

BOUGAINVILLE (boo'ganvil). Is. to the E. of mainland Papua New Guinea, discovered by the French navigator B. in 1768. The copper resources at Panguna are immensely rich, and there was agitation for separate independence till in 1976 B. became a prov. (with substantial autonomy) of Papua New Guinea. The cap. is Kieta. Area 10,620 sq.km (4,100 sq.m); pop. (1975) 90,000.

BOUGHTON (baw'ton), **Rutland** (1878-1960). British composer. B. at Aylesbury, he is best known for his music drama *The Immortal Hour* (1914), with a text based on the work of Fiona Macleod.

BOUGIE (boozhē). *See* BEJAIA.

BOULANGER (booloṅzheh'), **George Ernest Jean Marie** (1837-91). French general. After service in Indo-China and N. Africa, he became Minister of War in 1886. He won immense popularity because of his anti-German speeches, and nearly provoked a war with Germany in 1887. In 1889 he was suspected of aspiring to dictatorial powers by a coup d'état, fled to London, and was tried in his absence for treason. He committed suicide in Brussels on the grave of his mistress.

BOULANGER, Nadia (Juliette) (1887-1979). French music teacher. A pupil of Fauré, and admirer of Stravinsky, she incl. among her pupils at the Conservatoire Américain de Fontainebleau in Paris (from 1921), Leonard Bernstein, Virgil Thomson, Aaron

House of Bourbon and Bourbon-Orleans

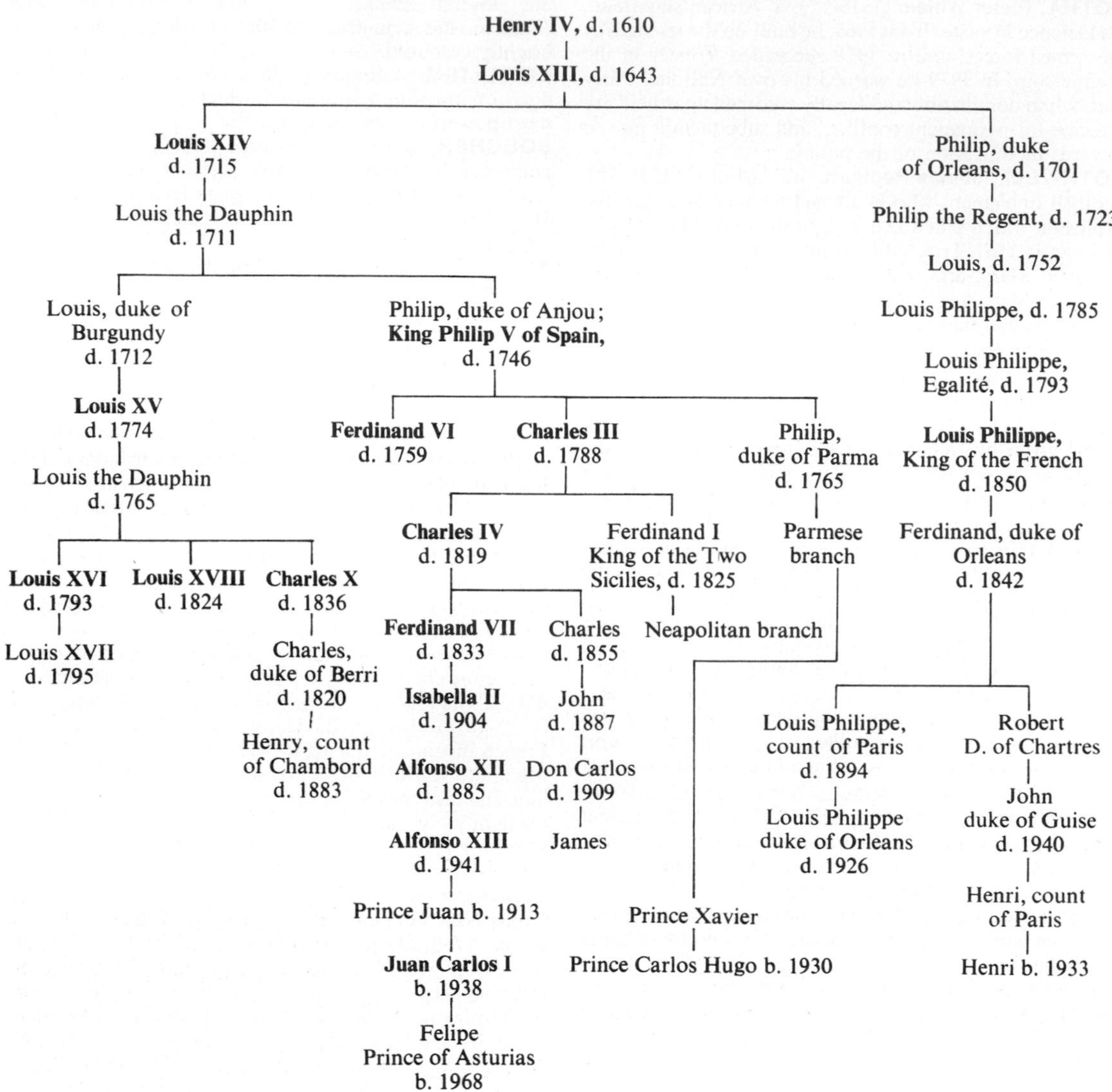

Copland, Roy Harris, Walter Piston and Lennox Berkeley.

BOULES (bōōl). French game (also *boccie*) between 2 players or teams, each of which try to place their boules (Fr. ball), which are 11cm (4⅜in) in diameter, nearer to the target jack than their opponent, and improve the position of their own. Standard length of the pitch is 27.5 metres.

BOULEZ (boo'lāz), **Pierre** (1926–). French composer. He studied with Messiaen, and is a devotee of the abstract in music. His works incl. *Le Visage Nuptial* (1946-50) for 2 solo voices, female choir and orchestra; *Le Marteau sans Maître* (1955) a cantata; and *Poésie pour Pouvoir* (1958) for orchestra and 8-track tape-recorder.

BOULOGNE-SUR-MER (boolōny'-sür-mār). French port and seaside resort on the English Channel, Pas-de-Calais dept. It was a medieval countship, but became part of France in 1477. Napoleon assembled his invading force for England here. In the S.W.W. it was evacuated by the British 23 May 1940 and recaptured by the Canadians 22 Sept. 1944. It is a major fishing port with fish curing and other food industries, oil refining and metallurgical industries. Pop. (1975) 95,500.

BOULT (bōlt), **Sir Adrian** (1889–1983). British conductor. B. at Chester, he studied at Leipzig, and was conductor of the BBC Symphony Orchestra 1930-50 and the London Philharmonic 1950-7. He promoted the work of

Holst and Vaughan Williams, and is a fine interpreter of Elgar. He was knighted in 1937.

BOULTON (bōl'ton), **Matthew** (1728-1809). British engineer. B. at Birmingham, he continued his father's silver-inlaying business, financed James Watt's steam engine, and entered into partnership with him in 1775.

BOUMÉDIENNE (boomehdi-en'), **Houari.** Adopted name of Algerian statesman Mohammed Boukharouba (1925-78). He headed the revolt which brought Ben Bella to power in 1962, then led the military coup which overthrew him, himself becoming president from 1965 till his death.

BOUNTY, Mutiny of the. *See* BLIGH.

BOURBON (boorboṅ'). A royal house of Europe whose members have occupied the thrones of France, Spain, Naples, and ruled several Italian duchies; the name comes from Bourbon l'Archambault, chief town of the feudal lordship of Bourbonnais in central France. Antoine de B. became king of Navarre by marriage in 1554, and his son became king of France in 1589 as Henry IV. The last of the French line was Louis-Philippe, who abdicated in 1848. The present B. Pretender to the French throne is Henry, Count of Paris.

The Spanish Bs. are descended from Philippe, duke of Anjou, younger son of Louis, Dauphin of France (d. 1711); he became Philip V of Spain in 1700. The Spanish king, Alfonso XIII, lost his throne in 1931, but the monarchy was fully restored under his grandson Juan Carlos in 1975.

BOURBON. Name 1649-1815 of RÉUNION.

BOURBON, Charles, duke of (1490-1527). He was made Constable of France for his courage at the battle of Marignano, 1515. Later he served the emperor Charles V, and helped to drive the French from Italy. In 1526 he was made duke of Milan, and in 1527 allowed his troops to sack Rome. He was killed by a shot Cellini claimed to have fired.

BOURGEOIS (boorzhwah'), **Léon Victor Auguste** (1851-1925). French statesman. Entering politics as a Radical, he defeated Gen. Boulanger in 1888, in 1895 was Prime Minister, and later served in many cabinets. He was one of the pioneer advocates of the League of Nations. In 1920 he received the Nobel peace prize.

BOURGEOISIE (boorzhwahzā'). The middle classes. The Fr. word originally meant the freemen of a borough. Hence it came to mean the whole class between the workers and peasants, and the nobility. B. has also acquired a contemptuous sense, as implying commonplace, philistine respectability. By socialists it is applied to the whole propertied class, as distinct from the proletariat.

BOURGES (boorzh). Historic French city, a literary and commercial centre, 200km (125m) S. of Paris. There is a 13th cent. Gothic cathedral, and museums with great art collections. Industries incl. aircraft, engineering, tyres. Pop. (1975) 83,720.

BOURGUIBA (boor'gēbah), **Habib ben Ali** (1903-). Tunisian leader. Ed. at the Univ. of Paris, he became a journalist and was frequently imprisoned by the French for his nationalist aims as leader of the Néo-Destour party. He became PM in 1956, and Pres. (for life from 1974) and PM of the Tunisian Rep. in 1957.

BOURNEMOUTH. Seaside resort in Dorset, England, in the valley of the Bourne stream. Wooded clefts, or 'chines', interrupt the line of cliffs. The town is famous for its high standard of music, and the Russell-Cotes museum has a Victorian/Edwardian collection from all over the world, and a gallery with paintings by Turner, Corot, etc. Pop. (1972) 148,850.

BOUTS, Dierick (*c.* 1400-75). Dutch painter. B. at Haarlem, he settled before 1448 at Louvain, where he executed his finest works such as the 'Last Supper' and the 'Martyrdom of St Erasmus'.

BOUVET (booveh') **ISLAND.** Dependency of Norway since 1930, in the S. Atlantic Ocean. Discovered by the Frenchman Jacques B. in 1738, it was made the subject of a claim by Britain in 1825, but this was waived in Norway's favour in 1928. Area 48 sq.km (19 sq.m); uninhabited.

BOVET (bōbeh'), **Daniel** (1907-). Swiss physiologist. He pioneered research into anti-histamine drugs used in the treatment of nettle rash and hay fever, and was awarded a Nobel prize 1957 for his production of a synthetic form of curare, used as a muscle relaxant in anaesthesia.

BOW BELLS. The bells of St Mary-le-Bow church, Cheapside, London; a person born within their sound is considered to be a true Cockney. The church was nearly destroyed by bombs in 1941. The bells, recast from the old metal, were restored in 1961.

BOWDLER (bowd'ler), **Thomas** (1754-1825). British editor whose prudishly expurgated versions of Shakespeare and other authors gave rise to the verb 'bowdlerize'.

BOWEN (bō'en), **Elizabeth** (1899-1973). British novelist. B. in Dublin, she followed her first vol. of short stories *Encounters* (1923), with *Look at all those Roses* (1941), *Demon Lover* (1945) and others. Her novels incl. *Friends and Relations* (1931), *The Death of the Heart* (1938), *The Heat of the Day* (1949), and *The Little Girls* (1964).

BOWER-BIRD. Family of Australian birds (Ptilonorhynchidae), nearly allied to the birds of paradise; the males construct decorated bowers or playgrounds of sticks, grasses, etc., in which they pay court to the females.

BOWER-BIRD. The Satin Bower-bird *(Ptilonorhynchus violaceus)* found in the coastal districts of eastern Australia. In the breeding season the birds show off by dancing round and through the bowers with a bright shell or feather or flower in their beaks. *Photo: Courtesy of the Australian News and Information Service.*

BOWIE (bow'i), **James 'Jim'** (1796-1836). American folk hero. A colonel in the Texan forces during the Mexican War, he is said to have invented the single-edge, guarded, hunting and throwing knife which is known as a Bowie knife.
BOWLS. Outdoor game played in England at least since the 13th cent. It is played on flat or crown greens with biased bowls of lignum vitae (c. 13cm/5in in diameter), and the object of the game is to draw each bowl as near as possible to the small white jack. The game can be played as singles, pairs, or rinks (4 men a side).
BOX. Genus of shrubs and small trees (*Buxus*) of the family Euphorbiaceae. The common box (*B. sempervirens*) has compact evergreen foliage.
BOXER. Medium-sized dog of continental origin, with a short, smooth coat, and in a wide range of colour.
BOXERS. Name given to bands of fanatical Chinese nationalists who in 1900 at the instigation of the Empress Dowager besieged the foreign legations in Peking, and murdered European Missionaries and thousands of Chinese converts. An international punitive force was dispatched, Peking was captured on 14 Aug. 1900, and China agreed to pay a large indemnity. Mao Tse Tung claimed them as national heroes, but his successors refer to them as 'blind xenophobes'.
BOXING. Fighting with the fists, originally using the bare knuckle and without 'rounds', though later each fall marked the end of a round and a fight of 276 such rounds is on record.

Jack Broughton (1705-89), English champion for many years, is said to have introduced gloves, though only for practice bouts. B. became popular with the nobility or 'Corinthians' (*See* JOHN JACKSON), but only lost its reputation for brutality with the introduction of the Queensberry Rules (drawn up by the 8th Marquess in 1866) which (although modified) are still the basic rules of modern B. Official professional organizations are the B. Board of Control in Britain, Nat. B. Assocn. in the USA, European B. Union, and World B. Council. The professional 'ring' is a roped square 6.10m (20ft) maximum, and 4.3m (14ft) minimum. Champions are classified according to weight: heavyweight, no limit; light heavy-weight 79.378kg (175lb); middleweight 72.574kg (160lb); lightweight 61.235kg (135lb); featherweight 57.153kg (126lb); bantamweight 53.524kg (118lb) and flyweight 50.802kg (112lb). Outstanding heavyweight champions have been John L. Sullivan (bare-knuckle champion) 1882-92, James J. Corbett (1st Marquess of Queensberry champion) 1892-7, Jack Dempsey 1919-26, Joe Louis 1937-49, Floyd Patterson 1956-9 and 1960-2, Muhammad Ali (q.v.) 1964-7, and 1974-Feb. 1978, and Sept. 1978-Oct. 1980.
BOYCOTT, Charles Cunningham (1832-97). Land agent of Lord Erne in co. Mayo, Ireland, who strongly opposed the Irish Land League, with the result that the peasants refused to work for him; thus arose the word 'boycotting'.
BOYD ORR, John, 1st baron (1880-1970). Brit. nutritional expert, and advocate of world federalism. In 1936 he caused a sensation by proving in *Food, Health and Income* that half the nation was undernourished, and was director-general of the F.A.O. 1945-8. In 1949 he was awarded a Nobel peace prize.
BOYER (bwah-yeh'), **Charles** (1899-1977). French actor. Going to Hollywood in 1934, he made a reputation as 'the great lover' in such films as *Mayerling*.

BOXING. The world heavyweight championship at Kuala Lumpur in 1975, in which Muhammad Ali defeated Joe Bugner of the U.K. *Photo: Syndication International Ltd.*

BOYLE, Charles, 4th earl of Orrery (1676-1731). Irish soldier and diplomatist who was worsted in his dispute with Bentley over the authenticity of the *Letters of Phalaris*. The orrery, a contrivance for studying the solar system, is named after him.
BOYLE, Robert (1627-91). Irish natural philosopher, 7th son of the 1st earl of Cork. From 1654 he lived in Oxford. In 1659 he discovered the elasticity of air, and in 1662 enunciated *Boyle's Law:* that the volume of a gas varies inversely with its pressure. He was one of the founders of the Royal Society, and in 1661 pub. *The Sceptical Chemist*. He studied the Bible languages, and by his will founded the B. lectures for the defence of Christianity.
BOYNE. Irish river, 113km (70m) long, flowing past Drogheda into the Irish Sea. It gives its name to the battle fought on 11 July 1690, near Drogheda, in which James II was defeated by William III.
BOY SCOUTS. *See* SCOUTS.
BOZEN. German form of BOLZANO.
BRABANÇONNE (brahboñson'), **La.** National anthem of Belgium, written and composed during the revolution of 1830.
BRABA'NT. District of W. Europe, comprising the Belgian provinces of Brabant and Antwerp and the Dutch province of N. Brabant. During the Middle Ages it was an independent duchy, and after passing to Burgundy, and thence to the Spanish crown, was divided during the Dutch War of Independence. The southern portion was Spanish until 1713, then Austrian until 1815, when the whole area was included in the Netherlands. In 1830 the influential French-speaking part of the pop. in the southern Netherlands rebelled and when Belgium was recognized in 1839, S. Brabant was included in it.
BRACEGIRDLE, Anne (*c.* 1663-1748). English actress who made her first London appearance in 1680 and had a brilliant career on the stage until 1707, esp. in Congreve's plays, and she may have secretly married him.
BRACHIOPODA (braki-o'pōda), or lamp-shells. Group of marine animals, usually treated as a separate, isolated phylum. They have 2 shells placed dorsally and ventrally, and are fixed to stones, corals, etc., by means of a stalk. The shell has something of the appearance of an ancient lamp. Some of the earliest fossils known belong to the B.

BRACKEN. Species of fern (*Pteris aquilina*), abundant in most parts of Europe. It has a perennial root-stock, which throws up large fronds.

BRACKNELL. Town in Berks, England, S.W. of Windsor, developed from 1949 as a 'new town' to take London's overspill. There are furniture, clothing, and engineering industries. Pop. (1975) 40,300.

BRACTON, Henry de (d. 1268). English judge, writer on English law, and chancellor of Exeter cathedral from 1264. He compiled an account of the laws and customs of the English, the first of its kind.

BRADBURY, Ray (1920-). American writer. B. at Waukegan, Illinois, he advanced from pulp magazine stories to science fiction on a serious level, with its basis in developments of existing inventions and mental attitudes: *The Martian Chronicles* (1950) and *Something Wicked This Way Comes* (1962).

BRADFORD. City (1897) in W Yorkshire, England, on the Brad 14 km (9 m) W of Leeds. From the time its first markets were granted in the 13th cent., B. developed first as a great wool manufacturing centre and then as a focus for the world market in wool and cloth, but by 1980 competition from the Third World and 'outward processing' in the Common Market had affected its pre-eminence. There are also heavy engineering, machine tool, electronics, and printing industries. There is a 15th cent. cathedral; the Cartwright Hall (1904) has a gallery and museum; and the univ. (1965) developed from the technical college founded 1882, and incl. a Management Centre. The Central Library incl. a theatre, and there is also a playhouse, and the Alhambra, built as a music hall and restored for ballet, plays and pantomime. The city has received a succession of immigrants, Irish in the 1840s, German merchants (mid 19th cent. - the warehouses of Little Germany are now a tourist attraction), then Poles and Ukrainians, and more recently W Indians and Asians. Pop. (1980) 470,000.

BRADLAUGH (-law), **Charles** (1833-91). British free-thinker and radical politician. He served in the army, was a lawyer's clerk, became well known on the platform and in journalism under the name of Iconoclast, and from 1860 ran the *National Reformer*. In 1880 he was elected Liberal MP for Northampton, but was not allowed to take his seat until 1886 as, being an atheist, he had expressed his un-belief in the efficacy of the oath and claimed to affirm instead.

BRADLEY, Francis Herbert (1846-1924). British philosopher. B. in Brecknock, he became a fellow of Merton Coll., Oxon, in 1870. In *Ethical Studies* (1876) and *Principles of Logic* (1883) he attacked the utilitarianism of J. S. Mill, and in *Appearance and Reality* (1893) and *Truth and Reality* (1914) he outlined his Neo-Hegelian doctrine of the universe as a single ultimate reality. His brother, **Andrew Cecil B.** (1851-1935), became professor of poetry at Oxford (1901-6). His *Shakespearean Tragedy* (1904) is a fine example of the philosophical and psychological approach to the dramatist.

BRADLEY, Omar Nelson (1893-1981). Amer. general. In 1943 he commanded the 2nd US Corps in Tunisia and Sicily, and in 1944 led the US troops in the invasion of France. He was Chief of Staff US Army 1948-9 and chairman of the Joint Chiefs of Staff 1949-53. He was appointed General of the Army in 1950.

BRADMAN, Sir Donald George (1908-). Australian cricketer, and formerly a stockbroker at Adelaide. B. in N.S.W. he played for Australia 1928-48 and was captain 1936-48. He has the highest aggregate score and greatest number of centuries in England v. Australia Test Matches.

BRAEMAR (brām-ahr'). Village in Upper Deeside, Grampian, Scotland. Highland games are held here in August.

BRAGA (brah'gah). Portuguese city 48km (30m) N.N.E. of Oporto. It is the seat of an archbishopric, the archbishop being primate of the Iberian peninsula. Pop. (1970) 41,000.

BRAGANÇA (brahgahn'sah). City in the N.E. corner of Portugal, the seat of a bishopric. It gave its name to the royal house of Portugal, whose members reigned 1640-1853; another branch were emperors of Brazil 1822-89. Pop. (1970) 8,000.

BRAGG, Sir William Henry (1862-1942). British physicist. In 1915 he shared with his son **Sir (William) Lawrence B.** (1890-1971) a Nobel prize for physics for their research work on X-rays and crystal structure.

BRAHÉ (brah'e), **Tycho** (1546-1601). Danish astronomer. In 1576 Frederick II of Denmark gave him the island of Hven in the Sound, together with a pension. Here he erected the observatory of Uraniborg. In 1597 he quarrelled with the authorities, and eventually settled near Prague where Kepler became his assistant.

BRAHMA. In Hinduism, the Supreme Being, or Universal Soul, the Absolute, self-existing and eternal. When referred to in the masculine he is the creator who forms with Vishnu and Siva the 'Trimurti'.

BRAHMANISM. The earliest stage in the development of Hinduism (q.v.). Its sacred scriptures are the Vedas with their accompanying literature of comment and explanation known as Brahmanas, Aranyakas, and Upanishads.

BRAHMAPUTRA (-poot'ra). River in Asia which rises in the Himalayan glaciers as Tsang Po and runs for 1,450 km (900m) through Tibet, to the mountain mass of Namcha Barwa. Turning S., as the Dihang, it enters India near Jido, and flows into the Assam valley near Sadiya. Now known as the B., it flows generally westward until shortly after reaching Bangladesh it turns S. and divides into the B. proper, without much water, and the main stream, the Yamuna, which joins the Padma arm of the Ganges at Goalunda. The r. (2,900 km/1,800 m long) is navigable for 1,285 km/800m from the sea.

BRAHMA SAMÂJ. Indian monotheistic religious movement, founded in 1830 in Calcutta by Ram Mohun Roy who attempted to recover the primitive simple worship of the Vedas and purify Hinduism.

BRAHMS, Johannes (1833-97). German composer. B. at Hamburg, he attracted the attention of the great violinist Joachim in 1853 and was introduced by him to Liszt and Schumann. The latter in particular encouraged him. From 1872 B. made his home in Vienna. Though his music has many romantic qualities, it represents in essence a continuation of the classical tradition from the point to which Beethoven had brought it. As a composer of symphonic music and of songs, he is ranked with the greatest. Among his choral works the German Requiem is best known. He was famed as a pianist and as a performer and conductor of his own works.

BRAILA (brah-ē'lah). Romanian commercial and naval port on the Danube, 170km (106m) from its mouth. It exports grain, is connected with the Romanian oil fields

BRAHMA. A painting in the Kaligat style executed in 1917, but retaining all the traditional features. *Photo: Courtesy of the Victoria and Albert Museum*

BRAHMS. The composer in his study. A life-long bachelor, he remained in furnished rooms even after he became comparatively well-to-do. *Photo: Paul Popper*

and manufactures man-made fibres, iron and steel, machinery, paper, etc. Pop. (1972) 157,840.

BRAILLE (brahy; Eng. brāl), **Louis** (1809-52). French inventor in 1829 of the system of lettering or embossed dots which is named after him. He himself was blinded at the age of 3.

BRAIN. That part of the central nervous system contained within the skull. The B. weighs c. 1.4kg (3lb) and consists of a soft white substance which during life is almost fluid. The greatest part of this is contained in the 2 cerebral hemispheres, which are situated on either side of the middle line of the skull and together form the cerebrum or great B. The cerebellum or small B. lies below the great B. at the back of the head, within the occiput; it also consists of 2 hemispheres. The medulla (marrow), or hind B., is a short conical structure which connects the B. with the spinal cord. The pons (bridge) joins the lower parts of the cerebellar hemispheres. The mid.B. consists of 2 broad strands of nerve tissue which run from the centre of the cerebral hemisphere to the pons, and of the structures lying over these.

The surface of the cerebral hemispheres is wrinkled (convolutions) or furrowed (fissures). These hemispheres are divided into the frontal, temporal, parietal, and occipital lobes, and the frontal lobes are separated from the parietal lobes by the fissure of Rolando, which divides the B. into the effector area in front - the part which is concerned with action, and the receptor area behind - the part which is concerned with receiving stimuli. The outer parts of all the convolutions are made of grey matter which consists of innumerable nerve cells. The remainder of the cerebrum is formed of white matter, made up of nerve fibres. These conduct impulses from the end organs all over the body to the cortex. They cross from one side to the other in the pyramid of the medulla, a fact which explains why each side of the brain governs the opposite side of the body.

The B. is enclosed by 3 membranes, which separate it from the skull. The cerebro-spinal fluid surrounds the whole of the B., spinal cord, and nerves, in a thin layer to form a kind of water-cushion in which the nerve tissues float.

There are 6 layers of B. cells, connected with certain functions. It is not possible to draw an exact map of the cerebral cortex, though many functions have been approximately localised. (In persons suffering from hydrocephalus, for example, in whom the brain may be prevented from growing to full size by the pressure of fluid within the skull, the intelligence may be perfectly normal.) Speech seems usually to be governed by the left hemisphere in the right-handed, and by the right hemisphere in the left-handed. The right hemisphere is specialized to deal with visual-spatial processing. Such specialization for language, etc., occurs later in girls than in boys, and dyslexia and autism are less common in girls. Experiments in psychosurgery have incl. burning an area of the B. thought to trigger aggression (amygdalotomy) in violent (volunteer) convicts in the USA.

In the late 1970s a range of natural chemicals or neurotransmitters was discovered which play a large part in the reaction of the central nervous system to the information passed to it by the human body and its environment. Some are apparently concerned with learning and memory, e.g. dopamine; others control the hormones needed for growth or reproduction; and yet others, such as enkephalin, are produced under stress as natural painkillers.

BRAINE, John (1922-). British novelist. From Bradford grammar school he went on to selling furniture, working in a bookshop and as a laboratory assistant, before making a career as a librarian. His novel *Room at the Top* (1957), which estab. him as an author, created Joe Lampton, a typical modern go-getter.

BRAINS TRUST. Nickname applied to a group of experts who advised President F. D. Roosevelt on his New Deal Policy.

BRAITHWAITE, Eustace Adolph (1912-). Guyanese author. B. in Guyana, he studied physics in England, served in the RAF in the S.W.W., and then taught in London. His teaching experiences prompted *To Sir With Love* (1959), and *Reluctant Neighbours* (1972) deals with black/white relations.

BRAITHWAITE, Richard Bevan (1900-). British philosopher. Originally a physicist and mathematician, he was Knightbridge prof. of moral philosophy at Cambridge 1953-67 and has experimented in the provision of a rational basis for religion and moral choice.

BRAMAH, Ernest. Pseudonym of the British short story writer Ernest Bramah Smith (1868-1948), creator of Kai Lung, a philosophically-minded Chinese, and of Max Carrados, a blind detective.

BRAMA'NTE (LAZZARI), Donato (*c.* 1444-1514). Italian architect and painter, whose real name was Donato d'Agnolo. B. at Urbino, he moved to Rome about 1500 and there under Pope Julius II commenced the rebuilding of St Peter's.

BRAMBLING. A bird (*Fringilla montifringilla*) belonging to the finch family (Fringillidae) which visits Britain in winter, breeding in Asia and N. Europe.

BRANCUSI (brahn'koosh or brahnkoo'zi), **Constantin** (1876-1957). Rumanian sculptor. B. in S. Rumania, he studied at Bucharest before going to Paris in 1904. Important in his work are the abstractions of animal and bird form, such as his bronze 'Bird in Space' (1919). In 1927 this was assessed by the American Customs as a piece of metal not a work of art and therefore dutiable: the claim caused controversy and was over-ruled in 1928. Rodin had an important influence on his work.

BRANDENBURG. Former Prussian and German prov. The area, then inhabited by Slavonic tribes, was conquered in the 12th cent. by Albert the Bear. Frederick of Hohenzollern became margrave in 1415, and an elector of the Holy Roman Empire; the Elector Frederick III achieved the crown of Prussia in 1701. Potsdam was the cap. When Germany was united in 1871, Brandenburg became one of its provs. That part of it E. of the Oder came under Polish administration, in accordance with the Potsdam agreement, in 1945; the remainder became a Land of (E.) Germany, abolished in 1952 when its boundaries were obliterated in the newly created administrative districts of Neubrandenburg, Potsdam, Frankfurt-an-der-Oder, and Kottbus.

BRANDENBURG. Town in (E.) Germany, on the r. Havel, 60km (36m) W. of Berlin. There is a 12th cent. cathedral, and textile, automotive, and aircraft industries. Pop. (1978) 95,000.

BRA'NDES, Georg Morris Cohen (1842-1927). Danish critic. He was belatedly appointed prof. of aesthetics in his native Copenhagen in 1902, but had previously played a major part in the Scandinavian literary awakening, and encouraged Lagerlöf, Björnsen, Ibsen and others.

BRA'NDO, Marlon (1924-). American actor. B. at Omaha, Nebraska, he is the best-known exponent of Method acting. His successes incl. *A Streetcar Named Desire* (both as film and play) and the films *The Wild One* and *Last Tango in Paris.*

BRANDT, Willy (1913-). German statesman. He emigrated to Norway in 1933 as an anti-Nazi and anti-Communist, and was active in the resistance movement, resuming German citizenship 1947. Mayor of W. Berlin from 1957, he became chairman of the Social Democratic Party 1964, Min. of Foreign Affairs under Kiesinger 1966-9, and Fed. Chancellor 1969, re-elected 1972. His *Ostpolitik* resulted 1972-3 in treaties with USSR and Poland, and a 'Basic Treaty' between E. and W. Germany. He was awarded a Nobel peace prize 1971. He resigned 1974 when one of his aides was found to be an E. German spy. In 1979 he became MEP.

BRANDY. A potable spirit obtained by the distillation of the fermented juice of grapes or other fruits. The best and only genuine B. comes from true wine-producing countries. The finished product contains from 40 to 70 per cent ethyl alcohol by volumes.

BRANGWYN, Sir Frank (1867-1956). British artist. Of Welsh extraction, he was b. at Bruges, where his father was working as an ecclesiastical architect. His talent coming to the notice of William Morris, he worked for him as a textile designer, then travelled widely, developing a sense of colour and power of large-scale decorative concepts unusual in British artists and greatly appreciated on the Continent. In 1925 he completed 5 of a series of panels for the Royal Gallery of the House of Lords, but these were rejected after much controversy and now hang in the B. Hall, Swansea. In 1932 he was commissioned to work on panels for Radio City, N.Y. His gifts were varied and he produced furniture, pottery, carpets, schemes for interior decoration and architectural designs, as well as the more expected book illustrations, lithographs and etchings. There is a B. Museum (1936) at Bruges, and at Orange, Vaucluse (1947). He was knighted in 1941.

BRANTÔME (broṅtōm'), **Pierre de Bourdeille,** Seigneur de (*c.* 1540-1614). French historian, who accompanied Mary Stuart to Scotland, served in Malta, Italy, Africa, and Hungary, and in the Huguenot wars. His *Mémoires* give a vivid picture of his time.

BRAQUE (brahk), **Georges** (1882-1963). French artist. B. at Argenteuil, he was associated with Picasso in introducing the Cubist movement in 1908. Eliminating curved lines, he reduced the human figure, landscapes and everyday objects to geometrical shapes. About 1912 he was also the main initiator of *papiers collés* in which oddments of paper, wood, etc., are glued to a canvas and incorporated in the picture.

BRASI'LIA. Cap. of Brazil from 1960, in Goias state, 965km (600m) N.W. of Rio de Janeiro and 915m (3,000 ft) a.s.l. Juscelino Kubitschek de Oliveira, Brazilian pres. 1955-60, pushed through the idea, dating from 1823, of a completely new city bringing life to the interior. It was designed by Lucio Costa in the shape of a bent bow and arrow, and Oscar Niemeyer was chief architect. There is a univ. (1960). Pop. (1975) 763,255.

BRASOV (brahshōv'). Romanian town at the foot of the Transylvanian Alps, an important route centre. producing machine tools, industrial equipment, cement, and woollens, etc. It was called Urasul Stalin (Stalintown) 1948-56. Pop. (1977) 260,550.

BRASS. An alloy of copper and zinc, with not more than 5 or 6 per cent of other metals. The zinc content ranges from 20 to 45 per cent, and the colour of B. varies accordingly from coppery to whitish yellow. Bs. are characterized by the ease with which they may be worked into shape. They are strong and ductile, and resist many forms of corrosion. Usually they are classed into those that can be worked cold (up to 25 per cent zinc) and those which are better worked hot (about 40 per cent zinc).

BRA'SSICA. Genus of plants of the family Cruciferae. The best-known species is the common cabbage (*B. oleracea*) with its varieties broccoli, cauliflower, kale, brussels sprouts, etc.

BRATBY, John (1928-). British artist, popularly regarded as the leader of the 'kitchen-sink' school because of a preoccupation in early work with working-class domestic interiors. He has also pub. books illustrated by himself which have a similar bold energy of style, incl. *Breakdown* (1960).

BRATISLAVA (brahtislah'va). City and chief port of Czechoslovakia, on the Danube, 61km (38m) E. of Vienna. A trans-shipment centre, the town has engineering and chemical industries, oil refineries, shipbuilding yards, and the Slovak univ. founded in 1919. Pop. (1977) 350,000.

BRATTAIN (brat'un), **Walter Houser** (1902-). American physicist. B. in Amoy, China, son of a teacher, he joined 1929-67 the staff of Bell Telephone Laboratories. In 1956 he was awarded a Nobel prize jointly with William Shockley and John Bardeen for their work on the development of the transistor which replaced the comparatively costly and clumsy vacuum tube in electronics.

BRAUCHITSCH (browkh'itsh), **Walther von** (1881-1948). German field marshal. A staff officer in the F.W.W., he replaced in 1938 von Fritsch as C.-in-C. of the army and became a member of Hitler's secret cabinet council. He was dismissed after the failure before Moscow in 1941. Captured in 1945, he d. before being tried.

BRAUN (brown), **Eva** (1910-45). German Nazi. B. at Munich, she became secretary to Hitler's photographer and personal friend, Hoffmann. Her name was associated with Hitler's for years, and she married him in the air-raid shelter of the Chancellory at Berlin on 29th April 1945. They then committed suicide together.

BRAUNAU (brow'now). Town and railway junction in Austria, on the Inn, which here forms the frontier with Bavaria, Germany. Adolf Hitler was b. here, 1889. It has an aluminium plant, tanneries, breweries, etc. Pop. *c.* (1972) 16,500.

BRAZIL. Largest of the S. American countries, occupying the N.E. half of the continent, and having a land frontier with all the S. American states except Ecuador and Chile. It has a 6,600 km (4,100 m) coastline: area 8,512,000 sq.km (3,286,000 sq.m).

Geography. B. is a country of plains and plateaux. There are 3 main plains - those of the Amazon and Paraná-Paraguay rivers and the coastal lowlands some 300km (185m) wide. This last remained the concentrated area of settlement, espec. in the industrial S.E., until the mid-twentieth century. The flat Amazon lowlands in the N. cover some 2,500,000 sq.km (1,000,000 sq.m), and along the N. frontier area run several chains of mtns averaging 1,000-1,500 m (3-5,000 ft), though Mt Roraima (q.v.) rises to 2,630 m (8,625 ft). The whole of the E. and S.E. part of B. is occupied by a great system of scarps and plateaux, with a tipped-up scarp edge along the S.E. coast, reaching over 2,750 m (9,000 ft) behind Rio de Janeiro in Pico da Bandeira. The Amazon is B.'s largest river system but the country also includes a large section of the Rio de la Plata system, and the largest river wholly in B. is the São Francisco, which has a great hydro-electric scheme at Paulo Affonso Falls, and empties into the Atlantic S.W. of Recife. The Equator passes through north B. and the Tropic of Capricorn through the south, so that the Amazon basin has a permanently hot, wet climate and a dense tropical forest. This area has long been a source of natural rubber, Brazil nuts, rosewood and other valuable timber, and is the home of the remaining Amerindian tribes, such as the Xingu, for whom the Villas Boas brothers created the Xingu National Park to save them from extinction. The whole region is being transformed by the *Trans-Amazonian Highway* 1970-3 from João Pessoa and Recife on the Atlantic coast, across the Amazon basin to the south of the river to the Peruvian border. A north/south cross-section links Santarem on the r. Manaus with Cuiabá in Mato Grosso. Huge resources of bauxite, iron and tin lie in the river basin area, and although half the forest cover is being conserved (it is est. that the evergreen trees produce half the world's oxygen), much land has been cleared for cattle-ranching, or cash crops of tomatoes, peppers, jute, rice, etc. However, continuous cultivation rapidly exhausts the thin forest soil, and attention is being turned to the *cerrados* (the savannahs of the S) which could be used for wheat, coffee, eucalyptus, and cattle. In the N the poor prairie country is dominated by cactus.

POPULATION. The Brazilians are mainly of Portuguese descent, although with a considerable admixture of Negro and Amerindian blood. Amerindians, est. at 2,000,000 in 1500 have dwindled to (1970) *c.* 500,000. In the 20th cent. there has been substantial immigration from Europe and Japan. The official language is Portuguese, and the majority of the pop. is Roman Catholic, but there is considerable state/church antagonism. Although elementary education is compulsory, 40% of the pop. are still illiterate: there are 54 univs. Pop. (1980) 120,000,000.

Economic Development. Brazil is still largely agricultural, although undergoing very rapid industrialization with a booming economy in the 1970s, and has the greatest world production of coffee, sugar, soya, and castor oil beans, as well as large crops of oranges, bananas, grapes, cocoa, tobacco, cotton, rice, maize, wheat, cassava (tapioca), potatoes and sweet potatoes. As a livestock producer (cattle, sheep) B. now surpasses Argentina. Lacking oil and coal in large quantities, B. has great hydroelectric resources, and the uranium deposits nr Belo Horizonte for future nuclear power are among the world's largest. A wealth of other minerals include iron, manganese, nickel, chrome, mica, quartz crystal, industrial diamonds, aluminium, gold, beryllium, titanium, thorium, tungsten, and asbestos: Minas Gerais is the chief mining state. Industries incl. textiles, trucks and automobiles, steel, shipbuilding, petrochemicals, paper, etc. The rivers constitute an important means of communication, forming with the canals 35,500 km (22,000 m) of navigable waterway. There is a rail network, principally in the S.E. and along the coast, air services, and a rapidly expanding road system. The cap. is Brasilia; other towns are Rio de

BRAZIL. Modern sophistication in the President's Palace in Brasilia, built in 1960 to a design of Oscar Niemeyer, and Amerindian fishermen in the Mato Grosso. *Photos: Mireille Vautier.*

Janeiro, the former cap., São Paulo, Belo Horizonte, Recife, and Salvador. M.U.: cruzeiro.

ADMINISTRATION. Under the constitution of 1969 B. is a federal rep. with a pres. indirectly elected by an electoral college of members of Congress (Senate and Chamber of Deputies) and members of the state legislatures - there are 21 states, 4 fed. terrs. and 1 fed. dist. - themselves elected by universal suffrage (excl. illiterates).

History. The first European to reach B. in 1500 is reputed to have been a Spaniard, Vicente Yanez Pinzon, and later in the year a Portuguese, Cabral, landed there. B. was claimed by Portugal, and in 1532 coastal settlements were established. From 1632 to 1654 the Dutch had a foothold in the N.E. Rio de Janeiro became the cap. in 1763. When Portugal was invaded by Napoleon, Queen Maria (d. 1816) and her court went to Rio in 1808. Her son, John VI, returned to Lisbon following a rising in Portugal in 1816 leaving behind as regent his son Pedro who in 1822 declared B. independent with himself as emperor. King John, by a treaty of 1825, was made emperor of B., but abdicated immediately in favour of Pedro. War with Buenos Aires from 1825 to 1828 deprived B. of the Banda Oriental prov. (Uruguay from 1828). From 1864 to 1870 B. and the Argentine were at war with Paraguay, which suffered a crushing defeat. The Republic of B. was proclaimed in Nov. 1889 as a result of the abolition of slavery by Pedro II, 1888. B. has a less turbulent later history than other S. American reps., but after the military revolution of 1964 a less democratic regime evolved, and an urban guerrilla movement developed. From 1979 there was a more liberal trend under Pres. João Figueiredo, incl. a partial amnesty for political exiles, investigation of 'missing persons' under the military regime 1964-79, and relaxation of restrictions on the estblishment of new political parties. As part of the trend towards democratisation, General Figueiredo handed over power to Tancredo Neves in 1985, but he died five weeks later, and his Vice Pres. José Sarney became acting President.

BRAZIL NUT. Seed, rich in oil and highly nutritious, of the S. American tree *Bertholletia excelsa*. The nuts are enclosed in a hard outer casing, each fruit containing 10-20 arranged like the segments of an orange. The timber of the tree is also valuable.

BRAZZAVILLE (braht'sahvēl). Cap. of the People's Rep. of Congo, a river port with an airport. Founded by the Italian Count Pierre Savorgnan de Brazza (1852-1905), employed in African expeditions by the French govt, it stands on Pool Malebo (Stanley Pool), opposite Kinshasa, and is linked by railway with Pointe-Noire, at the mouth of the Congo, 622km (240m) to the W.S.W. It has foundries and railway repair shops, builds ships, and makes shoes, soap, furniture, bricks, etc. The Pasteur Institute here dates from 1908, the cathedral from 1892. B. was the African HQ of the Free (later Fighting) French during the S.W.W. Pop. (1972) 250,000.

BREAD. The product obtained by moistening flour, kneading the resulting dough, and baking. Unleavened B. contains no raising agent; leavened B. - the normal product - is usually raised with yeast.

B. consists essentially of flour, yeast, salt and water, with fat, milk powder, eggs and other ingredients added in some cases. Wheaten flour is usually used, but rye flour may be used instead, or in addition, in some countries. White B. is made from flour from which all the outer skins (or bran) have been extracted during milling, but brown and wholemeal incl. part or all of the bran respectively.

BREAD FRUIT. Fruit of a tree (*Artocarpus altilis*) of the fig and mulberry family (Moraceae). When toasted, it is said to taste like bread, and is an important article of food among the people of the South Sea Islands to which it is native.

BREAKSPEAR, Nicholas. The only Englishman to become Pope. *See* ADRIAN IV.

BREAM, Julian (1933-). British virtuoso of the guitar and lute. He revived much Elizabethan lute music, and encouraged composition by contemporaries for both instruments.

BREAM. Name given to 2 quite distinct groups of fishes - the freshwater B. belonging to the carp family (Cyprinidae) and the sea B. (Sparidae) - and various others, which have in common their more or less compressed form. The former Bs. are esteemed by anglers. The latter Bs. are carnivorous fishes, resembling the perch, and are good eating.

BREASTED (bres'ted), **James Henry** (1865-1935). American archaeologist. B. at Rockford, Illinois, he was diverted from entry into the Church to the study of egyptology, intent on linguistic sources, and pub. 5 vols. of *Ancient Records of Egypt* (1906-7). Backed by John D. Rockefeller, jr., he organized the Oriental Institute of Chicago, of which he was director 1919-35, acquired many antiquities for the univ. museum, and pub. the valuable *Development of Religion and Thought in Ancient Egypt* (1912), etc.

BREATHALYSER. Instrument (invented by Borkenstein of Indiana) for checking the amount of alcohol drunk during a given period. Breath samples are taken, e.g. from a suspected drunken driver, in small self-sealing plastic bags, and are bubbled through a diluted solution of potassium dichromate in 50% sulphuric acid. A built-in colorimeter then gives a reading of the degree of colour change in the yellow dichromate to blue, this change being brought about by the presence of alcohol in the air. Since it is known that one part of alcohol is present in air for every 2,100 parts in blood at a temperature of 34°C (the mean breath temperature), the amount of alcohol consumed can thereby be measured.

BRECHT (brekht), **Bertolt** (1898-1955). German poet, playwright and theatre producer. B. of bourgeois family in Augsburg, he became known after the F.W.W. as a dissolute Bohemian out to shock and singing songs to a guitar accompaniment. *Drums in the Night* (1918) is a play with one of his typical returning soldier heroes; *The Threepenny Opera* was an attempt to set Gay to a propagandist tune (*See* KURT WEILL); *Mother Courage* (1939) attacked war and inadvertently made a heroine of 'Mother Courage', actually intended as a symbol of the little people who make war possible; and *Galileo*. A Communist, he went into exile in Scandinavia and the US under the Hitler regime. After the S.W.W. he became an Austrian citizen and eventually settled in E. Berlin to direct his own company, the Berliner Ensemble, founded 1949. His controversial influence has led to varying estimates of his permanent value.

BRECKNOCKSHIRE. Former co. of Wales, bordered on the N.E. by the r. Wye and on the E. and S.E. by the Welsh border: it was merged in Powys in 1974.

BREDA (brādah'). Historic Dutch town in N. Brabant. Charles II made here the Declaration that paved the way for his restoration in 1660. Pop. (1978) 118,220.

BREEDING. The rearing of animals or the cultivation of plants, using the crossing of different varieties to change the characteristics of an existing breed or variety, or produce a new one. Cattle may be bred for increased meat or milk yield, sheep for thicker or finer wool, horses for speed or stamina, bees for better honey, etc. Plants, such as cereals, may be bred for disease resistance, heavier and more rapid cropping, and hardiness to adverse weather or climate. Radiation is among the plant breeder's new tools: *see* RICE. *See also* EUGENICS.

BREEDING. Process in a nuclear reactor in which more fissile material is produced than was used in the operation of the reactor. Thus thorium can be turned into uranium-233, or plutonium-239 from uranium-238, both by the fission of natural uranium-238. The need is to use rare natural fissionable material only to initiate breeding of new fissile material, which can continue the process indefinitely with abundant raw material.

BREIZH (brāzh). Celtic name for Brittany.

BREMEN. City and seaport in B. Land, W. Germany, on the Weser 69km (43m) from the open sea. A Hansa town, and a free imperial city from 1646, it became a member of the N. German Confederation in 1867, and of the German Empire in 1871. There are iron and steel works, oil refineries and chemical industries, and aircraft, ships and cars are made. Pop. (1978) 562,665.

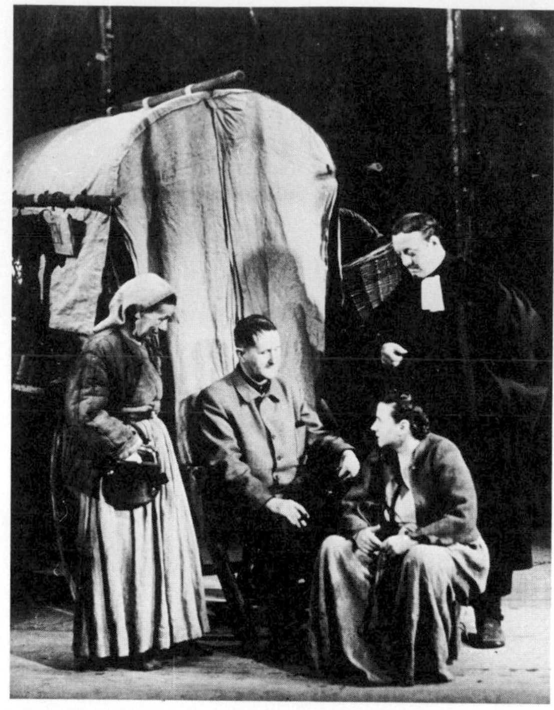

BRECHT. The dramatist (second on the left) takes part in a rehearsal of *Mother Courage* with Helene Weigel (left) who played the title role for many years. *Photo: Popperfoto*

The **Land of B.** consists of the city of B., together with Bremerhaven: area 404sq km. (156sq.m.): pop. (1978) 703,200.

BREMERHAVEN. Port at the mouth of the Weser, Germany, serving as outport for Bremen, 54km (34m) S.S.E. Pop. (1978) 140,500.

BRENNAN, Christopher John (1870-1932). Australian poet. His poems, pub. in Sydney in 1913, clearly reveal the influence of the French symbolists.

BRENNER PASS. Lowest of the Alpine passes, 1,370 m (4,495 ft), it leads from Trentino-Alto Adige, Italy, to Austrian Tirol, and is 19km (12m) long.

BRENTANO (brentah'nō), **Franz** (1838-1916). German-Austrian philosopher. He was noted for his contribution to philosophical psychology, e.g. *Psychology from the Empirical Standpoint* (1874) and *The Origin of Ethical Knowledge* (1889).

BRENTA'NO, Klemens (1778-1842). German poet, novelist, and dramatist. B. at Ehrenbreitstein, the son of an Italian merchant, he became a leader of the Younger Romanticists. His poetry reflects the lyric note of the fold-songs which he and L. A. von Arnim (q.v.) collected (1805-8); his other works include the erotic novel *Godwi* (1802), the mystic religious poems *Romanzen vom Rosenkranz* (1852), and plays. He excelled in lyric narrative and in the popular fairy-story.

BRESCIA (bre'shah). Italian city, the fort of the Brescian Alps, in the Lombardy region, 84km (52m) E. of Milan. It still has medieval walls and 2 cathedrals (12th and 17th cent.), and there are textile and engineering industries. Pop. (1971) 210,432.

BRESLAU. German name of WROCLAW.

BREST. French naval base, commercial port and town on Brest Roads, a great bay at the W. extremity of Brittany 583km (363m) W. of Paris. There are electronic, engineering, and chemical industries. Occupied as a U-boat base by the Germans 1940-4, the town was destroyed by Allied bombing and rebuilt. Pop. (1975) 186,500.

BREST. Town in Byelorussia S.S.R., USSR, on the r. Bug, 238km (210m) S.W. of Minsk: it was in Poland (Brzesc nad Bugiem) 1921-39. The **Treaty of Brest-Litovsk** (an older Russian name of the town) was signed here 3 March 1918 between Russia and the Central Powers. Under it Russia agreed to recognize the independence of the Baltic states, Georgia, the Ukraine and Poland, and pay heavy 'compensation'. Under the Nov. Armistice between the Central Powers and the Allies it was annulled. Pop. (1977) 124,000.

BRÉTIGNY (brātinyē'), **Treaty of.** Treaty made with John II of France in 1360 at the end of the first phase of the Hundred Years' War, under which Edward III of England received Aquitaine and its dependencies in exchange for renunciation of his claim to the French throne.

BRETON (bretoṅ'), **André** (1896-1966). French author. Among the leaders of Dada - *Les Champs magnétiques* (1921), an experiment in automatic writing, was one of the most notable products of the movement - he was also a founder of Surrealism, publishing *Le Manifeste de surréalisme* (1924). Of his other works, *Najda* (1928), the story of his love affair with a medium is the most striking.

BRETON. Celtic vernacular of Brittany, belonging to the Cymric group and closely related to the extinct Cornish tongue. It developed from the speech of British emigrants of the 5th and 6th cents. Although superseded by French in the upper prov., B. has never lost its foothold in Lower Brittany; and in the 19th cent. the Romantic revival led to the collection of popular folk-tales, legends, and ballads, followed by the rise of original national poets such as Jaffrennou and Berthou at the end of the century. Nevertheless, official discrimination against the language continued in education etc. and was a grievance of the Breton Liberation Movement after the S.W.W. *See* BRITTANY.

BRETTON WOODS. Township in New Hampshire, USA, where an International Monetary Conference was held 1-22 July 1944, under presidency of Henry Morgenthau, US Sec. to the Treasury. At the conclusion of the Conference a Draft of a United Nations' Monetary Agreement was published, providing for the creation of an international monetary fund. *See* MONEY.

BREUER (broi'-er), **Josef** (1842-1925). Viennese physician, a discoverer of the form of psychiatric treatment known as Psychoanalysis. He applied it successfully to cases of hysteria, and collaborated with Freud in *Studien über Hysterie* (1895).

BREUER (broi'er), **Marcel** (1902-81). Hungarian-American industrial designer and architect. Assoc. with the Bauhaus, he became famous for his tubular steel chairs. He fled from Germany in 1933, later joining Gropius in America, and was one of the architects of the Whitney Museum of American Art, N.Y. and the UNESCO offices in Paris.

BREUIL (broy), **Henri** (1877-1961). French prehistorian. B. at Mortain, the Abbé B. became prof. of historic ethnography and director of research at the Inst. of Human Palaeontology, Paris, in 1919. He estab. the genuine antiquity of Palaeolithic cave art and stressed the anthropological approach to the early history of man.

BRĒ'VIARY (Lat., a summary or abridgement). The book of the canonical office in use in the R.C. church. It is usually in 4 vols., one for each season.

BREWING. The alcoholic fermentation of an aqueous extract of cereal grains with the addition of hops. The medieval distinction between beer containing hops and ale without hops has now fallen into disuse and in modern terminology beer is strictly a generic term including ale, stout and lager. However, it is usual in Britain to refer to ale as beer and to regard stout and lager as products different from beer. In this usage beer is light coloured and top fermented; stout is dark coloured and top fermented and also contains roasted malt or barley; and lager is light coloured and bottom fermented.

BREWSTER, Sir David (1781-1868). Scottish physicist, famous for his discoveries regarding the diffraction and polarization of light.

BREZHNEV, Leonid Ilyich (1906–82). Russian statesman. Son of a steelworker, he became an engineer and metallurgist. During the S.W.W. he was a political worker with the army and afterwards held party office in his native Ukraine. He was pres. of the USSR 1960-4, succeeded Khrushchev as sec. of the Soviet Communist Party in Oct. 1964, and from 1977 was the first to combine both offices.

The **Brezhnev Doctrine** (1968) designed to justify the invasion of Czechoslovakia, laid down for the USSR as a duty the direct maintenance of 'correct' socialism in countries within the Soviet sphere of influence. In 1979 it was extended, by the invasion of Afghanistan, to the direct establishment of 'correct' socialism in countries not already within its sphere.

BRIAND (brē-oṅ'), **Aristide** (1862-1932). French statesman. B. at Nantes, he became a journalist in Paris. An ardent socialist, he helped Jaurès to found *L'humanité*, and in 1902 was elected to the French Chamber. In 1906, as Minister of Public Instruction and Worship, he carried through the law separating Church and State. Henceforth he was one of the Radical Socialists. B. was several times Prime Minister: 1909-11, when he broke the railway strike of 1910 by mobilizing the strikers for army service; 1913, when he extended the period of military service from 2 to 3 years; 1915-17; 1921-2; 1925-6; and 1929. Subsequently he was often Foreign Minister. In 1925 he concluded the Locarno Pact, and in 1928 the Kellogg Pact; in 1930 he outlined his favourite scheme for the United States of Europe.

BRIANSK (brē-ansk'). Russian town and rly junction in the R.S.F.S.R. on the Desna. It has foundries, sawmills, cement and brickworks, etc. Pop. (1977) 385,000.

BRIDGE. A construction which provides a continuous path or road over water, valleys, ravines, or above other roads. Bs. may be classified into 4 main groups: (1) the arch; (2) the girder; (3) the cantilever; and (4) the suspension B. Examples of these types are: (1) Waterloo B., London, and the Sydney Harbour B., (2) the Rio-Niteroi (1974), Guanabara Bay, Brazil, the world's longest continuous box and plate girder B. (centre span 300m/984ft; length 13,900 metres/8 miles 3,363 ft); (3) the Forth B., which is 1,658 m/5,440 ft long, and has 2 main spans, each consisting of 2 cantilevers, one from each tower; (4) the Verrazano-Narrows B. (1964), the world's longest suspension B., total length 4,174 m (13,700 ft); but the Humber Bridge (1980) has the world's longest main span 1,410 m (4,628 ft). Steel is pre-eminent in the construction of long-span Bs. because of its high strength-to-weight ratio, but reinforced concrete has the advantage of lower maintenance costs. Light alloy may be used in special cases. *See* TUNNEL for B.-TUNNELS.

BRIDGE. The Verrazano Narrows Bridge spans the mouth of New York harbour and was named after the Italian explorer who in 1524 was the first European to sail into the bay. *Photo: Ken Lambert/ Barnaby's Picture Library.*

BRIDGE (Straight Bridge). Card game, probably originating in Greece, which was introduced into Britain about 1880. From the Portland Club, where it was 1st played in 1894, it rapidly spread - to the detriment of whist - but about 1908 was superseded by its offspring, Auction B. *See* AUCTION B.; CONTRACT B.

BRIDGEPORT. City in Conn., USA, the industrial cap. of the state. Situated on the N. shore of Long Island Sound, at the mouth of the Pequonnock river, it developed from an Indian village. Metal goods and tools, electrical appliances, and aircraft are among manufactures. There are several univs., the P.T. Barnum Museum, and, in the nearby town of Stratford, the American Shakespeare Festival Theatre. Pop. (1970) 156,550.

BRIDGES, Robert Seymour (1844-1930). British Poet Laureate. B. at Walmer, he qualified as a doctor in London, but abandoned medicine for literature in 1882. In 1913 he was appointed Poet Laureate and became a founder of the Society for Pure English. He is remembered for his lyrics, and *The Testament of Beauty* (1929), a long philosophical poem which won immediate currency. He was an eager experimenter in metre and was a friend of Hopkins (q.v.), whose poetry he pub. in 1918 when he felt that the time was ripe for such a daring new voice to be heard.

BRIDGET (453-523). A patron saint of Ireland, also known as St Brigit or St Bride. She founded a church and monastery at Kildare, and is said to have been the dau. of a prince of Ulster.

BRIDGETOWN. Cap. of Barbados. Founded on Carlisle Bay in 1628, it has a deep-water harbour (1961). Pop. (1976) 88,000.

BRIDGEWATER, Francis Egerton, 3rd duke of (1736-1803). Pioneer of British inland navigation. With James Brindley as his engineer, he constructed (1762-72) the B. canal from Worsley to Manchester, and thence to the Mersey, a distance of 67.5km (42m).

BRIDGMAN, Percy Williams (1882-1961). American physicist. B. at Cambridge, Mass., he was ed. at Harvard where he was Hollis prof. of mathematics and natural philosophy 1926-50 and Higgins univ. prof. 1950-4. His research in machinery producing high pressure led in 1955 to the creation of synthetic diamonds by General Electric.

BRIDGWATER. Seaport in Somerset, England, on the Parret, 53km (33m) S.W. of Bristol, with plastic and electrical industries. The derelict docks were being developed as a marina in 1980. The Battle of Sedgemoor (1685) site, where Monmouth was defeated, is 8km (5m) to the S.E. Pop. (1973) 26,700.

BRĪ'DIE, James. Pseudonym of Osborne Henry Mavor (1888-1951). Scottish dramatist. B. in Glasgow, where he became prof. of medicine at Anderson Coll., he achieved success in 1931 with *The Anatomist,* dealing with Burke and Hare. Later plays incl. biblical dramas in the modern idiom (*Tobias and the Angel*) and fantasies.

BRIEUX (brē-ö'), **Eugène** (1858-1932). French dramatist, an exponent of the naturalistic problem play attacking social evils. His most powerful plays are *Les trois filles de M. Dupont* (1897); *Les Avariés* (1901; *Damaged Goods*), long banned for its outspoken treatment of syphilis; and *Maternité.*

BRIGGS, Henry (1561-1630). British mathematician. B. near Halifax, and ed. at Cambridge, he was Savilian prof. of geometry at Oxford from 1619. He is best known for his work in constructing the system of logarithms still in popular use.

BRIGHOUSE, Harold (1882-1958). British playwright. B. and bred in Lancs, in his most famous play *Hobson's Choice* (1916) he dealt with a Salford bootmaker's courtship, using the local idiom.

BRIGHT, John (1811-89). Liberal statesman. B. at Rochdale, the son of a Quaker millowner, he became a partner in his father's business. He was among the founders of the Anti-Corn Law League in 1839, and after entering parliament in 1843 led the struggle there for free trade, together with Cobden, which achieved success in 1846. His *laissez-faire* principles also made him a prominent opponent of factory reform. His influence was constantly exerted on behalf of peace, as when he opposed the Crimean War, Palmerston's aggressive policy in China, Disraeli's anti-Russian policy, and the bombardment of Alexandria. During the American Civil War he was outspoken in support of the North, and he was largely instrumental in securing the passage of the reform bill of 1867. He sat in Gladstone's cabinets as President of the Board of Trade 1868-70 and Chancellor of the Duchy of Lancaster 1873-4 and 1880-2, but broke with him over the Irish Home Rule Bill. B. owed much of his influence to his oratorical powers.

BRIGHT, Richard (1789-1858). British physician. He was for many years on the staff of Guy's hospital; 'Bright's Disease', an inflammation of the kidneys, is named after him.

BRIGHTON. Holiday resort on the E. Sussex coast, England, 82km (51m) S. of London, seat of the Univ. of Sussex (1963). Originally a fishing village called Brighthelmstone, it became known as Brighton at the beginning of the 19th cent., when it was already a fashionable health resort. The Prince Regent, afterwards George IV, stayed there and built the Pavilion in oriental style which contains a concert hall, museum, assembly room, etc., and there are still attractive Regency terraces and squares. There are about 9km (5½m) of fine promenades, two piers, a famous aquarium, a racecourse on the Downs, 2 well-known public schools - B. College and Roedean Girls' School, and a polytechnic. Pop. (1972) 163,700.

BRIGHTON. At night, the Pavilion takes on a fairy-tale beauty. During the First World War wounded Indian soldiers were housed here, as it was thought it would make them feel at home. *Photo: Courtesy of the British Tourist Authority.*

BRILL. Flat-fish (*Rhombus laevis*) of the turbot genus, of a sandy brown colour, varied with white spots and darker brown on the upper side. It is abundant off the coast of Britain.

BRILLAT-SAVARIN (brē-yah'-sahvahrañ), **Anthelme** (1755-1826). French gastronomist, the author of *Physiologie du goût*, a witty guide to the pleasures of the table.

BRINDISI (brin'dizi). City and seaport on the Adriatic, in Apulia, 104km (65m) S.E. of Bari. One of the oldest Mediterranean ports, situated at the end of the Appian Way from Rome, it specializes in passenger traffic and is a naval base. There are food processing and petrochemical industries. Pop. (1971) 82,700.

BRINDLEY, James (1716-72). British engineer. B. in Derbyshire, he was employed by the duke of Bridgewater for the construction of the Bridgewater canal, and played a great part in the rapid development of canal construction in Britain.

BRINELL HARDNESS TEST. The hardness of a substance is calculated from the area of indentation made by a 10mm hardened steel or sintered tungsten carbide ball under standard loading conditions in a test machine and is equal to the load (kg) divided by the surface area (mm^2). Johann Auguste B. (1849-1925), inventor of the machine for testing metals and alloys in 1900, was a Swedish engineer.

BRISBANE, Sir Thomas Makdougall (1773-1860). Scottish soldier and astronomer. After serving under Wellington, he was Gov. of N.S.W. 1821-5, and Brisbane in Queensland is named after him.

BRISBANE. Cap. and chief port of Queensland, Australia, on Moreton Bay, near the mouth of B. river, dredged to carry ocean-going ships. It is a rapidly developing commercial and industrial centre, and besides older industries such as brewing, tanning, tobacco and shoe manufacture, there are oil refineries (fed by pipeline from Moonie in S. Queensland) and natural gas is also piped in from elsewhere in the state.

B. is a well-planned city, built on a plain backed by mountains. Sir Thomas B. (q.v.), after whom it is named, took over the site as a penal colony 1824-39, opened to free settlers 1842. It has the Queensland Parliament House, Anglican and R.C. cathedrals, museums, Queensland (1909) and Griffith (1975) Univs and a racecourse to the E. of the city. Pop. (1976) 957, 710.

BRISBANE. Built on both sides of the Brisbane River, the city is one of the largest metropolitan administrative areas in the world. *Photo: Courtesy of the Australian Tourist Commission.*

BRISSOT (brēsō'), **Jacques Pierre** (1754-93). French revolutionary leader. B. at Chartres, he became a member of the Legislative Assembly and the National Convention, but his party of moderate republicans – the Girondins, or Brissotins – fell foul of Robespierre and B. was guillotined.

BRISTOL. English city and seaport in the co. of Avon, 13km (8m) from the mouth of the Avon on the Bristol Channel and admin. HQ of the co. A trading centre since Saxon times, it had a large traffic in wool in the Middle

Ages. It was from here that John Cabot sailed when he discovered Newfoundland, and in the 17-18th cents. trade with the American colonies and the West Indies flourished, B. coming to the fore in the slave trade. B. incl. the docks of Avonmouth and Portishead, and modernization and extension proceeds.

The principal buildings incl. the 12th cent. cathedral, 14th cent. St Mary Redcliffe (linked with Chatterton q.v.), the Council House (1956), and the University (1909). Much of Georgian B. has been destroyed but the Clifton area is preserved. Brunel's *Great Britain* (an essential link between sail and steam) is being restored in dry dock, and a maritime museum is planned. There has been rapid industrial expansion, aided by B. being at the junction of two motorways. Manufactures incl. aircraft engines, microelectronics, shoes, chocolate and cocoa, tobacco, chemicals, and there are nuclear and general engineering, printing paper and packaging, and shipbuilding industries. Wines and spirits are imported. There are also banking, insurance and credit companies. There is an airport at Lulsgate Bottom. Pop. (1972) 421,580.

BRISTOL CHANNEL. Seaward extension of the Severn estuary, 137km (85m) long, width 8km (5m) to 69km (43m) between S. Wales, Lundy Island and N. Devon. It receives the rivers Usk, Wye, Severn, Avon, etc. and has very high tides.

BRITAIN, Ancient. The name B., indicating present-day England, Scotland and Wales, is derived from the Roman name Britannia which is in its turn derived from the ancient Celtic. Before the Celts arrived B. was inhabited for thousands of years by people who had already learnt to tame animals and to grow corn in a primitive fashion; built Stonehenge (perhaps about 1900 B.C.) and buried their chiefs in barrows. About 1000 B.C., Britain was conquered by the Celts, tall, fair-haired people who swept across from the Continent in 2 great waves of migration. First came the Goidelic Celts of whom traces may still be seen in the Gaels of Ireland and the Highlands; there followed the Brythonic Celts or Bretons who were closely allied in blood and culture to the Gauls of France. The early British craftsmen were highly skilled in pottery and metal-work. Tin mines in Cornwall attracted merchant seamen from Carthage.

BRITAIN, Battle of. Air battle over Britain which lasted from 10 July to 31 Oct. 1940: one of the decisive battles of history. It has been divided into 5 phases: (1) 10 July-7 Aug., the preliminary phase; (2) 8-23 Aug., attack on coastal targets; (3) 24 Aug.-6 Sept., attack on Fighter Command airfields; (4) 7-30 Sept., daylight attack on London, chiefly by heavy bombers; and (5) 1-31 Oct., daylight attack on London chiefly by fighter-bombers.

At the outset the Germans had the advantage of airfields almost completely free from attack in the Netherlands, Belgium and France, dominating S.E. England. On 1 Aug. 1940 the Luftwaffe had c. 4,500 aircraft of all kinds, as against c. 3,000 for the R.A.F., but the main battle was between some 600 Hurricanes and Spitfires and the Luftwaffe's 800 Messerschmitt 109s and 1,000 bombers (Dornier 17s, Heinkel 111s and Junkers 88s). Losses Aug.-Sept. were for the RAF: 832 fighters totally destroyed, and for the Luftwaffe 668 fighters and some 700 bombers and other aircraft. The Battle of B. had been intended as a preliminary to the German invasion plan Seeloewe (Sea Lion), which Hitler indefinitely postponed 17 Sept. and abandoned 10 Oct. The battle had been won by the men of Fighter Command under Air Chief Marshal Sir Hugh (later Lord) Dowding (q.v.).

BRITANNICUS, Tiberius Claudius (*c.* 41-55). Roman prince, son of the Emperor Claudius and Messalina, so-called from his father's expedition to Britain. He was poisoned by Nero.

BRITISH ANTARCTIC TERRITORY. Colony created in 1962, and comprising all Brit. terrs. S. of lat. 60°S.: the British sector of the Antarctic continent (Graham Land and areas round the Weddell Sea) approx. 388,500 sq.km (150,000 sq.m); the South Orkneys, 722 sq.km (240 sq.m) and South Shetlands, 337 sq.km (130 sq.m). Scientific personnel are the only population: *c.* 250.

BRITISH BROADCASTING CORPORATION (BBC). *See* BROADCASTING.

BRITISH COLUMBIA. The Pacific coast province of Canada, lying between the Rocky Mts. and the sea; on the N.W. and on the S. it touches the USA. It has 3 great parallel ranges - the Rockies, the Columbia mountain system, and the coast range - interspersed with valleys, lake basins, heavily timbered forests, rolling uplands, and plateaux. Mt. Fairweather on the Alaska border is 4,663 m (15,300 ft). The chief rivers are the Fraser and the Columbia, and there are more than 80 lakes. The coast is deeply indented.

The capital is Victoria, on Vancouver Island; the commercial metropolis is the port and city of Vancouver on the mainland. Other cities are New Westminster, formerly the capital, a freshwater port on the Fraser; Nanaimo, on Vancouver Island, centre of the coal-mining industry; Prince Rupert, centre of the halibut fishery; Nelson, on Kootenay Lake, centre of mining and lumbering; Vernon and Kelowna, both in the Okanagan, in the heart of the fruit-growing area; Trail, headquarters of the Consolidated Mining and Smelting Co.; and Kamloops, at the confluence of the N. and S. Thompson rivers, a ranching and farming centre. The fastest growing prov., B.C. has since the S.W.W. attracted foreign investment, notably from Japan, in the wood, paper and allied industries, and in mining (copper, coal, iron, lead, molybdenum, nickel, zinc, and natural gas and oil).

Vancouver Island was discovered by the Spanish in 1774. The territory was ceded to Britain in 1790, and entered the Canadian Confederation in 1871 as a province. Area 948,599 sq.km (366,255 sq.m); pop. (1971) 2,184,621.

(BRITISH) COMMONWEALTH (OF NATIONS). *See* COMMONWEALTH.

BRITISH COUNCIL. Semi-official organization which was inaugurated in 1935 and granted a royal charter in 1940; has for its chief aims the promotion overseas of a wider knowledge of the UK, excluding political and commercial matters, and the development of cultural relations with other countries.

BRITISH EMPIRE. A British order of chivalry, instituted by George V in 1917. There are military and civil divisions, and the ranks are G.B.E., Knight Grand Cross or Dame Grand Cross; K.B.E., Knight Commander; D.B.E., Dame Commander; C.B.E., Commander; O.B.E., Officer; M.B.E., Member. In 1974 awards for civilian gallantry previously made within the order were replaced by the Queen's Gallantry Medal (Q.G.M.), which ranks after the George Cross and George Medal.

BRITISH COLUMBIA. Kamloops Lake is typical of the spectacular mountain scenery of the province. *Photo: Courtesy of the British Columbian Government.*

BRITISH EXPEDITIONARY FORCE (1939-40). British army that served in France and was evacuated, mainly from Dunkirk, in May-June 1940. It was commanded by Gen. Visct. Gort.

BRITISH HONDURAS. *See* BELIZE.

BRITISH INDIAN OCEAN TERRITORY. British colony in the I.O. estab. in 1965 to provide certain defence facilities for the govts of the UK and USA. It consists of the Chagos Archipelago c.1,900 km (1,200 m.) N.E. of Mauritius, which was admin. until 1965 by Mauritius. The is. of Aldabra (q.v.), Farquhar, and Desroches, some 485 km. (300 m.) N. of Madagascar, originally formed part of the BIOT, but were returned to the admin. of the Seychelles in 1976. The BIOT is directly admin. by officials of the For. and Commonwealth Office.

On Diego Garcia, largest is. of the archipelago, there is an American naval and air base, built as a counter move to the Soviet presence in the Indian Ocean. Copra, salt fish and tortoise shell are exported. Pop. c.500.

Area 186 sq.km. (72 sq.m.) incl. lagoons; pop. (1970) 1,500.

BRITISH ISLES. Group of islands off the N.W. coast of Europe, consisting of Great Britain (England, Wales, and Scotland), Ireland, the Channel Islands, Orkney and Shetlands, Isle of Man, and many others which are included in various counties, e.g. Isle of Wight, Scilly Isles, Lundy Island, and the Inner and Outer Hebrides (qq.v.). The islands are divided from Europe by the North Sea, Strait of Dover, and English Channel, and face the Atlantic to the W.

BRITISH LEGION. Organization to promote the welfare of veterans of war service and their dependants. Estab. under the leadership of Haig in 1921 (royal charter 1925) it became the **Royal B.L.** 1971; it is non-political. The sale on Remembrance Sunday of Flanders poppies made by disabled members raises much of its funds.

BRITISH LIBRARY. Created in 1973, it comprises a reference division (the former library depts of the British Museum, eventually to be housed at a Euston Road site), a lending division (incl. the former Nat. Lending Library for Science and Technology) at Boston Spa, Yorks, and a bibliographic services division (incorporating the Brit. Nat. Bibliography).

BRITISH MUSEUM. Largest and most important museum of the U.K. Founded in 1753 with the purchase of Sir Hans Sloane's library and art collection, and the subsequent acquisition of the Cottonian, Harleian, and other libraries, the B.M. was opened at Montagu House, Bloomsbury, in 1759. Rapid additions led to the construction of the present buildings (designed by Sir Robert Smirke) by 1852, with later extensions in the circular reading room (1857), and the N. wing or Edward VII galleries (1914). In 1881 the Natural History Museum was transferred to S. Kensington.

BRITISH MUSEUM. Although the British Museum remains one of the world's greatest research institutions, the modern presentation of the great collection allows everyone to understand and enjoy its treasures. *Photo: Courtesy of the British Tourist Authority.*

BRITISH VOLUNTEER PROGRAMME. Name by which the various schemes under which volunteers from the UK are sent to work in overseas developing countries have been known since 1966. Voluntary Service Overseas (1958) is the best-known of these organizations, which inspired the American Peace Corps (q.v.).

BRITTAIN, Vera (1894-1970). British writer. B. in Staffs, she was a V.A.D. nurse 1915-19, and pub. a vol. of reminiscences, *Testament of Youth* (1933). Later books were *Testament of Friendship* (1950), a biography of her friend Winifred Holtby (q.v.), and *Testament of Experience* (1957), covering her own later years. In 1925 she m. the political scientist (Sir) George Catlin (1896-1979), and their dau. is the politician Shirley Williams (q.v.).

BRITTAN, Leon (1939-). British Cons. politician. Chief Sec. to Treasury 1981–3, Home Sec. 1983–4, Trade and Industry Sec. 1985. Resigned over Westland affair 1986.

BRITTANY. Region of France from 1973, comprising the N.W. peninsula occupied by the Armorican Massif. Farming is carried on, but the dominant factor is the sea, the Bretons being famed as mariners and fishermen.

B. was the Roman Armorica, which was devastated by the Northmen after the Roman withdrawal. During the Angle and Saxon invasions of Britain, many Celts from that land joined their fellow Celts in B., which thus acquired its name. It became a duchy *c.* 1000, but in 1491 Duchess Anne married the French king Charles VIII, and in 1532 a treaty was signed to mark the union of B. and France, although in theory full political, economic and

BROADCASTING. The radio 'chain' (1) a newsreader (2) the VHF transmitting mast at Wrotham (3) FM transmitters at Sutton Coldfield and (4) the continuity studio, with the panel technical operator in the cubicle in the foreground, and David Hamilton in the studio in the background during a Radio 1 transmission. *Photo: Courtesy of the British Broadcasting Corporation.*

military independence was reserved. However, formal annexation by France ensued in 1547, and in 1790 B. was divided into 5 depts, those of the modern region, plus Loire-Atlantique, and centralized govt was imposed from Paris. Agricultural and industrial development of B. was inhibited, and there was discrimination against the Breton language (close to Welsh and Cornish) which was banned in education in favour of French. After the S.W.W. a regionalist separatist movement grew up, aimed at national independence for B., and in the 1960-70s terrorist outrages occurred. In 1974 both the Liberation Front organizations were banned by the French govt. The historic cap. of B. is Rennes, and Brest is an important port. St Malo is a popular tourist and yachting centre. Area 28,331 sq.km (10,939 sq.m); pop. (1972) 2,515,600.

BRITTEN, Benjamin, baron (1913-76). British composer. B. at Lowestoft, he was ed. at Gresham's School, Holt, and the R.C.M. In America when the S.W.W. broke out, he returned in 1942 and devoted himself to composing at his home in Aldeburgh, Suffolk, where he estab. an annual music festival. He wrote for the individual voice, e.g., Peter Pears and Janet Baker, and is also known for his operas, *Peter Grimes* (1945) based on a tale by Crabbe, the chamber opera *The Rape of Lucretia* (1946), *Billy Budd* (1951), *A Midsummer Night's Dream* (1960) and *Death in Venice* (1973). His oratorio *A War Requiem (1962)* was written for the dedication of Coventry Cathedral. He was awarded the O.M. 1965, and a life peerage in 1976. *See* ALDEBURGH.

BRIXHAM. Old fishing port in Devon, England, which forms with Torquay and Paignton the composite holiday resort of Torbay. William of Orange (William III) landed here in 1688.

BRNO. Industrial town and the 2nd city of Czechoslovakia, at the junction of the Svratka and the Svitava. It has a fortress; the 15th cent. cathedral of St Peter; a 16th cent. Rathaus; and a univ., founded in 1918. The Bren gun was first manufactured here. Pop. (1970) 339,000.

BROAD, Charlie Dunbar (1887-1971). British philosopher. B. in London, he was ed. at Trinity Coll., Cambridge, and was Knightbridge prof. of moral philosophy at the univ. 1933-53. His books incl. *Perception, Physics and Reality* and *Lectures on Psychic Research* (1962), discussing modern scientific evidence for survival after death.

BROAD ARROW. The mark resembling an arrow-head on British govt stores. Of doubtful origin, the B.A. came into general use in the 17th cent. and is still used to mark govt property, such as military supplies, but it has long been abolished on prison dress.

BROADCASTING. The transmission of sound and vision programmes by radio. B. may be organized under complete state control, e.g. Soviet Union; or private enterprise, e.g. the USA, where it is only limited by the issue of licences from the Federal Communications Commission to competing commercial companies; or operate under a compromise system, e.g. Australia (where a govt corporation also sells time to advertisers) and Britain, where there is a television and radio service controlled by the BBC (a centralized body appointed by the State and responsible to Parliament, but with policy and programme content not controlled by the State), and also a

BRONTË. The sisters, Emily, Anne and Charlotte, painted by their brother, Patrick Branwell, c.1835; and the lonely moorland farmhouse 'High Withens', which was the original of 'Wuthering Heights' in Emily's novel. *Photos: Courtesy of the National Portrait Gallery and the British Tourist Authority.*

BRITTEN. The composer rehearses his re-arrangement of John Gay's *The Beggar's Opera* from the original airs. *Photo: Popperfoto.*

commercial Independent Broadcasting Authority (television from 1955, radio from 1973). In Japan, which ranks next to the US in the number of TV sets owned, there is a semi-governmental radio and television B. corporation (NHK) and numerous private TV cos. *See* RADIO and TELEVISION.

BROADMOOR. Place in S.E. Berks, England, the site of a special hospital opened 1863 for persons then described as criminally insane. It was transferred from Home Office to Min. of Health control in 1949.

BROADS, The. A district in Norfolk and Suffolk, England, containing about 12 large freshwater lakes or 'broads' and many small ones. The largest B. is Hickling. The total length of waterway available for light craft is some 320km/200m. The Bs. are famous as a holiday resort. Long thought to be natural, they have recently been found to have been created by the digging out of peat deposits 600 years ago.

BROADSTAIRS. Seaside resort in N.E. Kent, England, on the E. coast of Thanet. Edward Heath was born here. Pop. (1972) 21,050.

BROADWAY. Main street of, and a great theatre and trade centre in, New York City.

BROCH (brokh), **Hermann** (1880-1951). Austrian novelist, best known for *Der Tod des Vergil* (1945: *The Death of Virgil*), a study of the last 18 hours in the poet's life, expressing his own sense of the inadequacy of poetry or any art as a full means of perception of truth. After a period under Nazi arrest he escaped to England and became a US citizen.

BROCKEN. Highest peak of the Harz Mtns (1,142 m/3,746 ft) in E. Germany. On 1 May (Walpurgis night) witches were said to gather here. The *B. Spectre* is a phenomenon of mountainous areas, so named because first scientifically observed at B. in 1780. The greatly enlarged shadow of the observer, accompanied by coloured rings, is cast by a low sun upon a cloud bank.

BROGLIE (brōly'), **Louis,** 7th duc de (1892-). French theoretical physicist. His distinguished ancestors incl. Victor, 2nd duc de B. (1718-1804) who was a Marshal of

France, campaigned in the Seven Years' War, and headed an emigré army in the Revolution. In 1929 the 7th duc was awarded a Nobel Prize, having written much from 1924 on quantum theory and having accounted for certain properties of atomic particles in terms of waves, thus laying the foundations of wave mechanics. His elder brother Maurice, 6th duc de B. (1875-1960) did notable work in the X-ray of crystals.

BROKEN HILL. Mining town in N.S.W., Australia, in a district containing rich deposits of zinc, lead, tin, and silver. Pop. (1976) 28,150. *See also* KABWE.

BROMBERG. German name for BYDGOSZCZ.

BROMFIELD, Louis (1896-1956). American novelist. Some of his books have only the facility of the journalist, a profession he followed for some years, but exceptions are *The Strange Case of Miss Annie Spragg* (1928) and *Mrs. Parkington* (1943) dealing with the golden age of N.Y. society.

BRŌ'MINE. A chemical element, a dark brown-red liquid, very volatile, and with an unpleasant irritating smell - whence the name given to it in 1826 by its discoverer Balard (Gk. *bromos*, a stench). Its symbol is Br; atomic weight 79.92 and atomic number 35. It does not occur free in nature, but its compounds are found in sea water, mineral springs, etc.

Bromides, formed by combining metallic elements with B., are much used in photography, and potassium bromide and sodium bromide are used in medicine as sedatives.

BRONCHITIS. Inflammation of the bronchi. *Acute B.* is the most common acute disease of the lungs. It may be due to sudden exposure to cold, but is more usually caused by extension of a cold in the head. It may develop into *Chronic B.*

BRONTË. Name of three sisters, famous as novelists: CHARLOTTE (1816-55), EMILY JANE (1818-48), and ANNE (1820-49). The daughters of an Irish clergyman, Patrick B. (1777-1861), they were b. at Thornton, near Bradford, whence in 1821 the family moved to Haworth. After their mother's death the sisters and their brother PATRICK BRANWELL (1817-48) were brought up by an aunt. In 1824 the older girls went to a school for clergymen's daughters, but were soon removed; Charlotte later described the school as 'Lowood' in *Jane Eyre.* For some years the sisters earned their living as governesses, and in 1842 Charlotte and Emily entered M. Héger's school at Brussels; Emily returned to Haworth on their aunt's death, but Charlotte, who had conceived a hopeless passion for Héger, did not finally leave Brussels until 1844. Meanwhile Branwell, who shared something of his sisters' genius, had become a drunkard and an opium addict. The sisters now discovered that each was secretly engaged in literary activity, and in 1846 they pub. a joint collection of poems under the pseudonyms of Currer, Ellis, and Acton Bell. Charlotte's first novel, *The Professor,* failed to find a publisher, though Emily's *Wuthering Heights* and Anne's *Agnes Grey* were accepted. *Jane Eyre,* issued in 1847, won a sensational success. During 1848-9 Branwell, Emily, and Anne all d. of consumption. *Shirley,* dealing partly with the Luddite riots, appeared in 1849, and *Villette* in 1853; it derives largely from Charlotte's Brussels experiences. Abandoning her anonymity, she visited London, and made the acquaintance of Thackeray, Harriet Martineau, and her biographer, Mrs Gaskell. In 1854 she m. her father's curate, A. B. Nicholls, but their happy married life was cut short by her death a year later. Emily's only novel, *Wuthering Heights,* a share in which has been claimed for Branwell on insufficient evidence, is a work of strange, wild power unique in English literature. The same power is discernible in her poems, which are greatly superior to those of her sisters. Anne's two novels, *Agnes Grey* and *The Tenant of Wildfell Hall,* are mainly interesting through their author's association with her greater sisters. All four Bs. collaborated as children in stories of the imaginary African Empire of Angria.

BRONX, The. Borough of New York City, USA, N.E. of Harlem river. Largely residential, it has a large Jewish community and features in American literature, e.g. Clifford Odets, who was born there.

BRONZE. Alloy of copper and tin, yellow or brown in colour; one of the first metallic alloys known to man. It is harder than pure copper and more suitable for casting. It contains 4-11 per cent of tin; for bell-metal, bronze containing 15 per cent or more of tin is used. Phosphor B. is hardened by the addition of a small percentage of phosphorus. Silicon B. (for telegraph wires) and aluminium B. are similar alloys of copper with silicon or aluminium, but usually contain no tin.

BRONZE AGE. Period of early history and pre-history when bronze was the chief material used for tools and weapons. It lies between the Stone Age and the Iron Age and may be dated 5000-1200 B.C. in the Near East, and about 2000-500 B.C. in Britain. Mining and metalworking were the first specialized industries, and the invention of the wheel revolutionized transport. Agricultural productivity, and hence the size of the pop. which could be supported, was transformed by the ox-drawn plough.

Recent discoveries in Thailand (q.v.) suggest that the Far East, rather than the Near East, was the cradle of the Bronze Age.

BRONZINO (bronzēnō), **Il** (1503-72). Pseudonym of the Italian artist Agnolo di Cosimo, favourite painter of Cosimo I, duke of Tuscany. His portraits of the Medici circle have a simple elegance and incl. some attactive child studies. He was influenced by Michelangelo.

BROOK, Peter (1925-). British theatrical producer and director. He is known for his work at the Royal Shakespeare Theatre and the Paris-based Le Centre International de Créations Théâtrales. Films he has directed incl. *Lord of the Flies* (1962) and *Meetings with Remarkable Men* (1979).

BROOKE, Sir Basil. *See* BROOKEBOROUGH, VISCT.

BROOKE, Sir James (1803-68). British administrator, known as 'the white rajah'. B. nr Benares, he served in the army of the East India Co. In 1838 he headed a private expedition to Borneo, where he helped to suppress a revolt, and in 1841, the Sultan gave him the title of Rajah of Sarawak. He was suçceeded as Rajah by his nephew, SIR CHARLES JOHNSON B. (1829-1917), who in turn was succeeded by his son, SIR CHARLES VYNER B. (1874-1963), who in 1946 arranged for the transfer of Sarawak to the British Crown.

BROOKE, Rupert Chawner (1887-1915). English poet. B. at Rugby, where he was ed., he travelled abroad after a nervous breakdown in 1911, but in 1913 won a fellowship at King's Coll., Cambridge. Later that year he toured America (*Letters from America,* 1916), NZ and the S. Seas, and in 1914 became an officer in the Royal Naval Division. After fighting at Antwerp, he sailed for the Dardanelles, but died of blood-poisoning on the Greek island of Skyros, where he is buried. The 5 war sonnets pub. immediately after his death made him the symbol of the F.W.W. 'lost generation': 'Grantchester' and 'The Great Lover' are perpetual anthology pieces.

BROOKEBOROUGH, Basil Brooke, visct B. (1888-1973). Statesman of N. Ireland. Entering Parliament as a Unionist in 1929, he was Min. for Agriculture 1933-41, for Commerce 1941-5, and PM of N. Ireland 1943-63. He was a staunch advocate of strong links with Britain.

BROOK FARM. Farm in W. Roxbury, near Boston, Mass., USA, which in 1841-7 was the scene of a liberal communistic experiment led by George Ripley (1802-80), a former Unitarian minister. Financial difficulties and a disastrous fire led to the community's dissolution.

BROOKLANDS. Former motor racing track, near Weybridge, Surrey, England, opened in 1907 as a testing-ground for motor-cars, and closed in 1946. In 1974 it was partly re-opened.

BROOKLYN. Most populous borough of New York City, USA. Occupying the S.W. end of Long Island, on New York Bay and East r., it is connected with Manhattan Island by B. Bridge (1883) and others, and by the Verrazano-Narrows Bridge (1964) to Staten Island. It is an important commercial and industrial centre; its water-front, with many great docks, basins and wharves, extends to 53km/33m; and at Wallabout Bay, East r., is the important Brooklyn US Navy Yard. *See* BRIDGE.

B. is noted for the number and standard of its public buildings; cultural activities are the concern of the Brooklyn Institute, founded in 1823. Of the more than 60 parks, Prospect is the most important. Pop. (1970) 2,602,000.

BROOKS, Van Wyck (1886-1963). American critic. Though b. in New Jersey, B.'s spiritual home was New England, where he settled in Connecticut in 1920. He valued the 'rational intensity of the Puritan ideal' and his study *The Flowering of New England* (1936) was the first of a 5-vol. series covering American literature 1800-1915.

BROUGHAM, Henry Peter, 1st baron B. and Vaux (broom and vawks) (1778-1868). British statesman. B. in Edinburgh, he was a founder of the *Edinburgh Review* to which he contributed from 1802 onwards. From 1811 he was chief adviser of the Princess of Wales (afterwards Queen Caroline), and in 1820 he defeated the attempt of George IV to divorce her. He sat in Parliament 1810-12 and from 1816, and supported the causes of public education and law reform. When the Whigs returned to power in 1830, B. was made Lord Chancellor and created Baron B. and Vaux. His speeches in support of the Reform Bill were a notable effort, but his dictatorial and eccentric ways led to his exclusion from office when the Whigs next assumed power in 1835. After 1837 he took an active part in the business of the House of Lords.

BROUWER (brow'wer), **Adriaen** (*c.* 1605-38). Flemish artist. Influenced by Hals, with whom he may have studied, he developed an animated style of rendering peasant scenes. Avoiding bucolic romanticism, he captured in detail the squalid debauchery, and was himself said to have lived a Bohemian existence.

BROWN, Ford Madox (1821-93). British painter. B. at Calais, he studied in Belgium, and later came to England where he was associated with the Pre-Raphaelites, though he did not actually join the movement. His best-known pictures incl. 'The Last of England' (Birmingham), and 'Christ Washing St Peter's Feet' (Tate Gallery, London), and he had a gift for strong colour.

BROWN, George, baron **George-** (1914-). British Labour politician. Entering Parliament in 1945, he was briefly Min. of Works in 1951 and contested the leadership of the party on the death of Gaitskell. He was Sec. of State and Min. for Economic Affairs 1964-6, and For. Sec. 1966-8. He was created a life peer in 1970.

BROWN, John (1800-59). American anti-slavery leader. B. in Connecticut, he settled as a farmer in Kansas in 1855. In 1856 he was responsible for the 'Pottawatomie massacre' when 5 pro-slavery farmers were killed. In 1858 he formed a plan for a refuge for runaway slaves in the mountains of Virginia. With 18 men, he seized, on the night of 16 Oct. 1859, the govt arsenal at Harper's Ferry in W. Virginia, and resisted all attacks until on 18 Oct. US marines under Col. Lee stormed the place. B. was seriously wounded. He was tried at Charleston and hanged on 2 Dec. In the northern states B. was quickly hailed as a martyr. The words of the song 'John Brown's Body' were written *c.* 1860, probably by Thomas B. Bishop: the tune is of uncertain origin.

BROWN, Lancelot (1716-83). English landscape gardener, known as 'Capability B.', because of his characteristic comment that a garden had 'capabilities'. His work, as at Blenheim, involved the controlled picturesque - curving paths, judicious artificial mounds, and the creation of lakes.

BROWNE, Robert (1550-1633). English Puritan leader, founder of the Brownists. B. near Stamford, he took to preaching in Norwich, and was several times in prison in 1581-2 for attacking Episcopalianism. For a time he retired to Middelburg in Holland, but later made his peace with the Church and became master of Stamford Grammar School. From 1591 he was a rector in Northants.

The community which B. founded in Norwich and Holland continued on Nonconformist lines, developing into modern Congregationalism. In a work pub. in 1582 B. advocated congregationalist doctrine.

BROWNE, Sir Thomas (1605-82). English author and physician. B. in London, he travelled widely on the Continent as a student of medicine before settling at Norwich in 1637. He cultivated a personal mode of expression which still gives value to his main works: *Religio Medici* (1643), a justification of his profession; *Vulgar Errors* (1646), an examination of popular legend and superstition; *Urn Burial* and *The Garden of Cyrus* (1658); and *Christian Morals* (1717). He was knighted in 1671.

BROWNIAN MOVEMENT. When colloidal particles are suspended in a fluid medium they are subjected to impacts from the molecules of the medium and are in continuous random motion. This phenomenon was first observed by Robert Brown in 1827.

BROWNING, Elizabeth Barrett (1806-61). British poet. B. near Durham, *née* Barrett, she fell from her pony in girlhood and injured her spine, and was treated by her father as a confirmed invalid. In 1844 she pub. *Poems* (incl. 'The Cry of the Children'), which led to her friendship and secret marriage with Robert B. in 1846. The *Sonnets from the Portuguese* (1847) were written during their courtship and represent her work at its best. Freed from her father's oppressive influence, B.'s health improved, and during the years in Italy she wrote *Casa*

Guidi Windows (1851), the poetic novel *Aurora Leigh* (1857), and other verse.

BROWNING, Robert (1812-89). Poet. B. in Camberwell, he wrote his first poem *Pauline* (1833) under the influence of Shelley; it was followed by *Paracelsus* (1835) and *Sordello* (1840), which marked the development of his use of psychological analysis and interest in obscure characters of literature and history. In 1837 he achieved moderate success with his play *Strafford*, and in the series of *Bells and Pomegranates* (1841-6), which contained *Pippa Passes* (1841), *Dramatic Lyrics* (1842) and *Dramatic Romances* (1845), he included the dramas *King Victor and King Charles, Return of the Druses* and *Colombe's Birthday*.

In 1846 he met Elizabeth Barrett, whom he m. the same year and took to Italy. Here he wrote *Christmas Eve and Easter Day* (1850); and *Men and Women* (1855), containing some of his finest love-poems and dramatic monologues, which were followed later by *Dramatis Personae* (1864), and *The Ring and the Book* (1868-9), based on an Italian murder story. After his wife's death in 1861 B. had settled in England and now enjoyed an established reputation, although his latest works such as *Red-cotton Night-Cap Country* (1873), *Dramatic Idylls* (1879-80), and *Asolando* (1889), still prompted opposition by their rugged obscurity of style. Although the charge of facile optimism is unfounded, B. is less valued today for his philosophy than for the range of his poetry. The *Pied Piper of Hamelin, Home Thoughts from Abroad, Rabbi ben Ezra*, etc., are constant anthology pieces.

BROWNING. A portrait of Robert Browning by M. Cordigiano, dating from 1858. *Photo: Courtesy of the National Portrait Gallery.*

BROWN SHIRTS. The S.A. (*Sturm-Abteilung*), or Storm Troops, the private army of the German Nazi Party; so called from their uniform.

BRUBECK (broo'bek), **Dave** (David Warren) (1920-). American jazz musician. B. at Concord, California, he studied the piano and worked under Darius Milhaud at Mills Coll., Oakland (1946-9), beginning to record in 1950. He is a jazz 'intellectual' and his quartet (formed 1951) combines improvization with the disciplines of modern classical music.

BRUCE, James (1730-94). Scottish explorer. He was British consul at Algiers (1763-5), and then set out to explore the Roman remains in the Near East. Starting from Alexandria in 1768 he reached the source of the Blue Nile in 1770, and followed the river downstream to Cairo by 1773.

BRUCE, Robert (1274-1329). Scottish hero. He was the grandson of Robert de Bruce (1210-95), who unsuccessfully claimed the Scottish throne in 1290. B. shared in the national rising led by Wallace, and soon after the latter's execution in 1305 he rose again against Edward I, and was crowned king of Scotland in 1306. He defeated Edward II at Bannockburn in 1314, and in 1328 the treaty of Northampton recognized Scottish independence, and B. as king.

BRUCE, Stanley Melbourne, 1st visct. B. of Melbourne (1883-1967). Australian statesman. Called to the Bar in 1906, he practised in England until 1914. After serving in the F.W.W., he returned to Australia, where he was elected to the Commonwealth parliament in 1918 as a member of the National Party, becoming PM and Min. for External Affairs in a National-Country Party coalition (1923-9).

BRUCELLOSIS (broos'elōsis). Undulant fever, named after the Scottish doctor Sir David Bruce (1855-1931), caused by bacteria present in the milk of infected cattle. Vaccination of the animals and pasteurization of the milk has been practised, but eradication is the aim.

BRÜCKE, die. German Expressionist art movement, the 'bridge', which flourished 1905-13. Ernst Ludwig Kirchner was one of its founders and Emil Nolde a member 1906-7. Their work, strongly influenced by Negro art, was marked by pure colours.

BRUCKNER (brook'ner), **Anton** (1824-96). Austrian composer. B. at Ansfelden, son of a country schoolmaster, he was a choirboy at the monastery of St. Florian where he later became apprentice organist. As cathedral organist at Linz 1856-68, he composed in his leisure time and was much influenced by Wagner, and from 1868 was at Vienna, where he became prof. at the Conservatoire in 1871. He wrote numerous choral works, and 9 symphonies, one unfinished.

BRUEGHEL (brö'khel), **Pieter** (*c.* 1525-69). Flemish painter, whose pictures of peasant life are distinguished by vividness of colouring and expression, and by a grotesque and often satirical humour. His son PIETER B. THE YOUNGER (1564-1637), called 'Hell' B., painted chiefly religious subjects; another son JAN B. (1568-1625), known as 'Velvet' B., was a painter of flowers, landscapes, and seascapes, and often collaborated with Rubens.

BRUGES (brüzh). City in Belgium, capital of W. Flanders province, 16km (10m) from the North Sea, with which it is connected by canal, and 93km (58m) N.W. of Brussels. It has its name from the many bridges that cross its many waterways. Among its notable buildings are the

BRUNEL. Isambard Kingdom Brunel's SS *Great Britain* was the first vessel to embody all the constituent parts of a modern ocean-going ship; she was 98 m (322 ft) long, with a maximum width of 15 m (50.5 ft). This drawing of her, as she was when making her maiden trans-Atlantic voyage in 1845 from Liverpool to New York, was specially prepared for exhibition alongside the restored ship in Bristol, by David Ditcher, the figures in period dress being by Joan-Marie Abley. *Photo: Courtesy of the School of Technical Illustration, Bournemouth and Poole College of Art.*

cathedral of St Sauveur, dating from the 7th cent.; the church of Notre Dame, dating from the 8th cent.; the Hôtel de Ville, begun in 1376; and the famous belfry (13th cent.) above the Halles (markets). Medieval B. was the most important place in Flanders, with a thriving woollen industry, but was superseded by Antwerp and Amsterdam, though it is still important for textile and lace manufacturing. The College of Europe (1949) is the oldest centre of European studies. Pop. (1978) 118,300.

BRUGGE. Flemish form of BRUGES.

BRUMMELL, George Bryan (1778-1840). English man of fashion known as 'Beau' B. The friend of the Prince of Wales (later George IV), he was for several years the recognized leader of fashion. Eventually, however, his fortune was exhausted, he quarrelled with the Prince, and in 1816 fled to France.

BRUNEI (brooni'). State in N.W. Borneo, surrounded on the landward side by Sarawak. It came under Brit. protection in 1888, was occupied by the Japanese 1941–5, and in 1984 became independent. Under the amended constitution of 1965 there is a Privy Council, Council of Ministers (elected) and Legislative Council (part nominated, part elected). The Mentri Besar, or chief minister, is appointed by the sultan, Sir Hassanal Bolkiah (1922–), who succeeded on his father's abdication in 1967, and whose dynasty dates from the 15th century. Excellent social services are supported by oil and natural gas revenues; rubber and sago are also exported. The cap.is Bandar Seri Begawan (until 1970 called Brunei Town, pop. (1971) 37,000), on B. river. Area 5,800 sq.km (2,226 sq.m); pop. (1981) 191,770.

BRUNE'L, Sir Marc Isambard (1769-1849). Engineer and inventor. B. in Normandy, he served with the French navy until 1792, when he went to New York. Coming to England in 1799, he did engineering work for the Admiralty, improved the port of Liverpool, and planned a tunnel under the Thames from Wapping to Rotherhithe which was constructed 1825-43. He was knighted in 1841.

His son, **Isambard Kingdom B.** (1806-59), assisted his father in the Thames tunnel project, and in 1833 became engineer to the G.W. Railway, which adopted the 7ft gauge on his advice. In 1838 he designed the *Great Western* which was the first steamship to cross the Atlantic regularly, and sailed from Bristol to New York. His next ship was the *Great Britain* (1845), the first large ship to be constructed of iron and to have a screw propeller; larger still was the *Great Eastern* (1858). Brunel Univ. (1966) at Uxbridge is named after the father and son.

BRUNELLESCHI (broonel-les'kē) or **BRUNELLESCO** (-skō), **Filippo** (1377-1446). Italian architect. The first of the great Renaissance architects, he was a pioneer in the scientific use of perspective. His great work was the completion of the cathedral church of Santa Maria del Fiore in Florence.

BRÜNING, Heinrich (1885-1970). Ger. politician. Elected to the Reichstag in 1924, he led the Catholic Centre Party from 1929, and was Reich Chancellor 1930-2, when political and economic crisis forced his resignation. He then went to the US, but was prof. of political science at Cologne univ. 1951-5.

BRÜNN. German form of BRNO.

BRUNO (broo'nō), **Giordano** (*c.* 1548-1600). Italian philosopher. He became a Dominican in 1563, but his sceptical attitude to Catholic doctrines compelled him to leave Italy *c.* 1577. After visiting Geneva and Paris, he lived in England (1583-5), where he wrote some of his finest works. He then returned to the Continent, and after much wandering was arrested in Venice by the officers of the Inquisition, who took him to Rome in 1593. He was imprisoned, but refused to renounce his heretical religious views and his belief in the Copernican system of astronomy, and was burnt at the stake.

BRUNO, St (*c.* 1030-1101). Founder of the Carthusian order. B. in Cologne, he became a priest, and controlled the cathedral school of Rheims 1057-76. Withdrawing to the mountains near Grenoble, as a result of an ecclesiastical controversy, he founded the monastery at Chartreuse in 1084.

BRUNSWICK. District in the Land of Lower Saxony, (W.) Germany. Once an independent duchy, it became a rep. in 1918.

The city of B., on the Oker, S.E. of Hanover, was one of the chief cities of N. Germany in the Middle Ages, and a member of the Hanseatic League. It was cap. of the duchy of B. from 1671. There is a technical univ. Pop. (1970) 223,275.

BRUSA. Alternative form of BURSA.

BRUSSELS. Capital city of Belgium on the Senne, 43km (27m) S. of Antwerp. Buildings incl. the 13th cent. church of Ste Gudule; the 15th cent. Hôtel de Ville, and the Maison du Roi in the Grande Place; the Royal Palace and the Houses of Parliament dating from the 18th cent.; and the univ. founded 1834. B's. manufactures incl. lace, textiles, silk goods, machinery, chemicals, pottery, clothing, furniture, and *objets d'art.* It has rail and air communications with all the capitals of Europe, and canals connect it with Antwerp and the sea. B. was a Roman settlement, and in the 16th cent. became one of the chief cities of the Low Countries. When these were divided between the Dutch Rep. and Spain, B. remained Spanish, and later became Austrian, then French. It was chosen as cap. of Belgium, recognized by the Powers as independent in 1839. It is the HQ of the Common Market. Pop. (1978) 1,030,000, of whom 80% are French-speaking, although the suburbs are Flemish. For its proposed regional status, *see* BELGIUM.

BRUSSELS, Treaty of. Pact signed in Brussels on 17 March 1948 by the Foreign Ministers of Britain, France, and the Benelux countries (Belgium, Netherlands, Luxemburg), which set up Western Union. The contracting parties pledged themselves to an economic, political, cultural, and military alliance for 50 years. The military side of the alliance was in 1950 merged in the North Atlantic Treaty (q.v.).

Following the London Conference of 1954 the German Federal Rep. and Italy entered Western Union (renamed Western European Union) in 1955.

BRUTUS (broo'tus), **Marcus Junius** (*c.* 78-42 B.C.). Roman leader. He sided with Pompey against Caesar during the civil war, but on Pompey's defeat was pardoned by Caesar and raised to high office. He was, however, persuaded to become one of Caesar's assassins in the belief that the restoration of the rep. would follow. But the bulk of the army adhered to Caesar's lieutenant Antony, and Cassius and B. were defeated at Philippi in 42 B.C., whereupon B. committed suicide.

BRUXELLES. French form of BRUSSELS.

BRYANSK. *See* BRIANSK.

BRYANT, Sir Arthur (1899-). British historian, noted for his studies of Restoration figures such as Pepys and Charles II, and a series covering the Napoleonic Wars of which *The Age of Elegance* (1950) is the most effective. He was knighted in 1954.

BRYANT, William Cullen (1794-1878). American poet. After practising as an attorney, he became a journalist in New York in 1825, and from 1829 was editor-in-chief of the *New York Evening Post.* His verse combines appreciation of nature with Puritan idealism in ethics. His *Thanatopsis* is one of the earliest masterpieces of American poetry.

BRYCE, James, 1st viscount (1838-1922). British statesman. Prof. of civil law at Oxford 1870-93, he entered Parliament as a Liberal in 1880, holding office under Gladstone and Rosebery. An admirer of the US and author of *The American Commonwealth* (1888), he was ambassador to Washington 1907-13, doing much to smooth US-Canadian relations.

BRY'ONY. Two British climbing hedgerow plants. White B. (*Bryonia dioica*) belongs to the gourd family (Cucurbitaceae). Black B. (*Tamus communis*) is of the same family as the yam (Dioscoreaceae).

BRYUSOV (bryoos'of), **Valery** (1873-1924). Russian symbolist poet and critic, who created a sensation by his following of Western as well as Russian classic models.

BRZESC NAD-BUGIEM. Polish name of BREST, Byelorussia.

BRZEZINSKI (brezhin'ski), **Zbigniev** (1928-). American Democrat politician. B. in Warsaw, he taught at Harvard, became a US citizen in 1949, and in 1977 Carter's National Security Adviser. He was the chief deviser of the human rights policy of the pres., and pursued a 'hard line', as opposed to the more moderate stance of Sec. of State Vance, in relation to USSR.

BUBBLE CHAMBER. When an ionizing particle moves through a B.C., a vessel filled with a transparent highly super-heated liquid, it may start violent boiling along its path shown by a string of tiny bubbles. Photographic study of these tracks gives much information about the nature and movement of atomic particles and the interaction of particles and radiations. *See* GLASER, Donald and SPARK CHAMBER.

BUBER (boo'ber), **Martin** (1878-1965). Israeli philosopher. B. in Vienna, he was driven from a professorship in comparative religion at Frankfurt by the Nazis, and taught social philosophy at the Hebrew Univ., Jerusalem, 1937-51. He attempted the re-appraisal of ancient Jewish thought in modern terms.

BUCARAMA'NGA. City in N. central Colombia. It has metallurgical industries and is a tobacco and coffee centre. Pop. (1972) 347,400.

BUCCANEERS (Carib, *boucan,* wooden grid for smoking meat, the use of which was borrowed from the natives of S. Domingo by early French hunters). Name given to the piratical rovers who infested the Spanish American coast in the 17th cent. Though mainly British, some were French, Dutch, and Portuguese; they were united in hatred of Spain and desire to plunder the Spanish Main. Among the most famous Bs. was Henry Morgan (q.v.). The ranks of the Bs. were divided by the outbreak of war between England and France in 1689, and the growth of naval power in the 18th cent. put an end to their activities.

BUCER (boots'er), **Martin** (1491-1551). German Protestant reformer. From 1549 he was regius prof. of divinity at Cambridge. He attempted to reconcile the viewpoints of Luther and Zwingli.

BUCHAN, John, baron Tweedsmuir (1875-1940). Scottish statesman and author. Called to the Bar in 1901, he was Cons. MP for the Scottish Univs. (1927-35), and on his appointment as Gov. Gen. of Canada (1934-40) was raised to the peerage. In addition to biographies of Raleigh, Scott, Cromwell, Julius Caesar, and Augustus, he pub. thrilling adventure stories which won wide popularity and incl. *Prester John* (1910), *The Thirty-Nine Steps* (1915), *Greenmantle* (1916), *Huntingtower* (1922), *The Three Hostages* (1924), and *The House of the Four Winds* (1935); and the autobiographical *Memory Hold the Door* (1940).

BUCHANAN, Sir Colin (1907-). British town planner. In the govt service 1946-63, he developed revolutionary ideas on the handling of traffic in cities. He was Director of the School of Advanced Urban Studies at Bristol 1973-5.

BUCHANAN (bukan'an), **George** (1506-82). Scottish humanist. Forced to flee to France in 1539 owing to some satirical verses on the Franciscans, he returned to Scotland *c.* 1562 as tutor to Queen Mary. He became principal of St Leonard's Coll., St Andrews, in 1566, and wrote *Rerum Scoticarum Historia* (1582).

BUCHANAN (bukan'an), **Jack** (1891-1957). British musical comedy actor. B. at Helensburgh, he played in London and N.Y. in *Charlot's Revue*, etc., and his songs such as 'Good-Night Vienna' epitomized the inter-war period.

BUCHAREST (bookarest'). Cap. of Romania, on the Dombovita. Although open to the plains, except on the W. and S.W., it has a comparatively mild winter. Once a citadel built by Prince Vlad the Impaler to stop the advance of the Ottoman invasion in the 14th cent., it was the cap. of the Princes of Wallachia from 1698, and of Romania from 1861. Little of the old town remains, but there are fine 17-18th cent. churches, the 18th cent. Mogosoaia Palace (now a museum), the univ. (1864), the Palace of the Grand Nat. Assembly, the Fine Arts Museum, Nat. Museum of Antiquities, and the Cismigiu Gardens planned in the 19th cent. There is an international airport at Otopeni, and Baneasa has an internal service. Pop. (1977) 1,948,611.

BUCHENWALD (bookh'envalt). Village N.E. of Weimar, E. Germany, site of a Nazi concentration camp 1937-45.

BUCHMAN (bo͞ok-), **Frank N. D.** (1878-1961). American evangelist. In charge of Christian work at Penn. State Coll. 1909-15, he visited Oxford in 1921 and gathered round him the 'Holy Club', nicknamed the 'Oxford Group' when a number of members, visited S. Africa, noted for its group confessionals. In 1938 he launched in London the anti-Communist campaign for Moral Rearmament (M.R.A.).

BUCK (*née* Sydenstricker), **Pearl S.** (1892-1973). American novelist. Dau. of missionaries to China, she wrote novels of Chinese life, such as *East Wind-West Wind* (1930) and *The Good Earth* (1931), and received a Nobel prize in 1938.

BUCKINGHAM, George Villiers, 1st duke of (1592-1628). English courtier. Introduced to the court of James I in 1614, he soon became his favourite, being made earl of B. in 1617 and a duke in 1623. He failed to arrange the marriage of Prince Charles and the Infanta of Spain (1623), and on returning to England negotiated Charles's alliance with Henrietta Maria, sister to the French king. Following Charles's accession, B. attempted to form a Protestant coalition in Europe and Britain drifted into war with France, but he failed to relieve the Protestants besieged in La Rochelle (1627). His policy was attacked in Parliament, and when about to sail again for La Rochelle he was assassinated at Portsmouth.

BUCKINGHAM. Town in Bucks, England, on the Ouse, 25km (14m) N.W. of Aylesbury. A market town, it has dairy processing and engineering industries, and Univ. College (1974), founded as the basis of an Independent University, free from state finance and control. Its first principal (1974-9) was Sir Max Beloff (1913-). Pop. (1973) 5,300.

BUCKINGHAM PALACE. The London home of the British Sovereign. Originally built in 1705 for the duke of B. it was bought by George III in 1762 and reconstructed by Nash 1825-36. It was permanently occupied by Queen Victoria, and in 1913 a new front was added. It was slightly damaged by bombs during the S.W.W.

BUCKINGHAMSHIRE. S. Midland co. of England. Largely agricultural, the Vale of Aylesbury being very fertile, the co. is also extensively wooded in the N., is crossed by the Chiltern Hills, and is famous for its beeches in the south. The chief rivers are the Thames and the Ouse, and the Grand Union Canal passes through the co. Manufactures incl. furniture, paper, and agricultural machinery. The co. town is Aylesbury: other centres are Buckingham, High Wycombe, Beaconsfield, Marlow and Amersham. In the local govt reorganization of 1974, B. lost its southernmost corner, incl. Eton and Slough, to Berkshire. Area 1,878 sq.km (725 sq.m); pop. (1978) 525,100.

BUCKLEY, William (1780-1856). Australian convict. He escaped from Port Phillip and managed to survive among the Aborigines 1803-35, before giving himself up. Hence the Australian saying 'B.'s chance', meaning an outside chance.

BUCKTHORN. Genus of thorny shrubs (*Rhamnus*) of the family Rhamnaceae, of which 2 species, *R. catharticus* and *R. frangula* (alder B.), are British.

BUCKWHEAT. Plant (*Fagopyrum esculentum*) of the family Polygonaceae, producing a grain of high nutritive value for human and animal consumption, which can be grown on poor soil in a short summer.

BUDAEUS (boodē'-us). Latin form of the name of Guillaume Budé (1467-1540). French scholar. He persuaded Francis I to found the Collège de France, and also the library that formed the nucleus of the Bibliothèque Nationale.

BŪ'DAPEST. City of central Europe, cap. of Hungary. It lies on the Danube, and consists of Buda on the right bank, which includes the former royal palace and coronation church, and Pest on the left, which includes the houses of parliament, palace of justice, govt offices, etc. 8 bridges connect the 2 cities. Pest grew rapidly following the establishment of the Dual Monarchy in 1867 when it was made the cap. of Hungary and became the centre of agriculture and trade; it was united with Buda 1872. Between the wars many new industries incl. textiles and chemicals were estab. at B. There is a univ. (1635) and the technical univ. (1856) was reorganized 1967. In 1944-5 the city saw prolonged fighting between German and Russian armies. Pop. Greater B. (1971) 2,023,000.

BUDDHA and **BUDDHISM** (boo-). Buddhism, one of the great world religions, originated in India, where it later became almost extinct, although influencing the development of Hinduism. However, the number of its adherents there was swelled from 1956 by the mass adoption of B. on the part of the scheduled castes. It exists in 2 main forms: the School of the Elders (Theravada) in southern Asia (Sri Lanka, Thailand and Burma), and the later Mahayana (China, Korea, Japan, and Tibet) in northern Asia.

Buddhism originated with Gautama (*c.* 563-483 B.C.), the son of a king of the Sákyas, a tribe settled near modern Nepal, who was brought up in luxury, but at the age of 29 became aware of human ills and left his wife and home to seek a way of escape from the burdens of existence. After 6 years of extreme austerities he turned to meditation under a tree, the Bodhi tree (tree of Enlightenment) nr Buddh Gaya, and became enlightened - hence his name Buddha (the Enlightened One). Enlightenment consisted of acquiring the four Truths: the fact of pain or ill; that pain has a cause; that pain can be ended; and the Noble Eightfold Way (right views, right intention, right speech, right action, right livelihood, right effort, right mindfulness, and right concentration) whereby pain may be ended. Adoption of the Way leads to a state of peace, *Nirvana*, the extinction of all craving for the things of sense, though not necessarily the annihilation of the individual. After his enlightenment, Buddha removed to Varanesi, where he began his teaching and founded the Sangha, or Order of monks. For the rest of his long life he moved here and there about N. India, but chiefly in the Magadha country (Bihar). He died at Kusinagara in Uttar Pradesh. *See* LUMBINI.

The only complete canon of the Buddhist scriptures is that of the Sinhalese (Sri Lanka) Buddhists, in Pali, but other schools have essentially the same canon in Sanskrit. The scriptures are known as Pitakas or 'baskets', and there are 3 divisions: Vinaya or Discipline, listing offences and rules of life; Sutta (Discourse) or Dhamma (Doctrine), containing an exposition of B. by Buddha and his disciples; and Abhidhamma or Further Doctrine, later discussions of the doctrine by various schools.

In common with other Indian religions, B. holds two fundamental doctrines, that of *karma* or action, the belief that all deeds meet with reward or punishment in this life or in one and another of a long succession of lives; and that of transmigration or rebirth, according to which everyone is reborn in a happy or painful existence, wherein he experiences the fruit of past deeds. In Buddhism there is no belief in a permanent self. The object of the Noble Eightfold Way is to break the chain of *karma* binding the individual to rebirth, by attaining *Nirvana*, when there is final dissociation from the body.

Mahayana, the 'Great Career' form of B., as distinct from the form taught by the School of the Elders, referred to as Hinayana, 'Base Career', arose at about the beginning of the Christian era. In this the individual is exhorted not merely to attain Nirvana for himself, but to train to become a Buddha, and so save countless others. Those adopting this 'Great Career' are called Bodhisattvas, and may be highly revered and even worshipped, much as are the gods of Hinduism. The original B., if not atheistic, at least found no place for God or gods. To this day the real strength of B. lies in its lofty moral teaching, in particular its toleration and feeling of universal brotherhood, and in recent years there has been a growth of laymen's societies with temples of their own.

Most famous of later developments is that of the Ch'an (Sanscrit *dhyāna* 'meditation') Sect, which originated *c.* A.D. 520 with Bodhidharma, a Mahayana monk who went from S. India to teach in China, and proclaimed the importance of intuitive insight in achieving enlightenment. Ch'an emerged as a distinct sect under the 6th patriarch Hui-neng (637-713), and spread in Japan from the 12th cent., under the name Zen, the Japanese form of the word, under which it became familiar to Westerners in the 20th cent. Zen is characterized by anecdotes, to be studied by the aspirant, in which an apparently nonsensical exchange of question and answer between master and pupil results in sudden enlightenment. *See* ZEN.

BUDDHISM The finest examples of Thai art belong to the Sukhodaya school. This 13th century Buddha, with strongly arched brows, aquiline nose and delicately carved lips is typical of the classic period. *Photo: Mireille Vautier.*

BUDDH GAYA (bood'gīa). Indian village 9.5km (6m) S. of Gaya, in Bihar, where Gautama became Buddha while sitting beneath a Bo (Bodhi) tree, of which a supposed descendant is still preserved there.

BUDGERIGAR (bujrigahr'). Small, hardy species of Australian parrakeet (*Melopsittacus undulatus*). Feeding mainly on grass seeds, it breeds freely in captivity, and while normally bright green, yellow, white, blue, and mauve varieties have been produced.

BUDOJOVICE. *See* CESKE BUDEJOVICE.

BUDWEIS. German form of Budejovice: *see* CESKE BUDEJOVICE.

BUENOS AIRES (bwā'nos īr'es). Cap. of the Argentine rep., largest city in the southern hemisphere, on the W. bank of the estuary of the Rio de la Plata, 240km (150m) from the sea. Although founded in 1536, B.A. is almost entirely modern, its development dating from its establishment as the cap. of the Argentine rep. in 1853. It is laid out on the American 'gridiron' plan, and there are many fine thoroughfares: e.g. Avenida de Mayo and Avenida de Julio. In the Plaza de Mayo are the cathedral, presidential palace (known as the 'Pink House'), treasury building, and municipal offices; the Palace of Congress is in the Plaza del Congresso. The city has one of the world's most luxurious shopping precincts. There is also a nat. univ. (estab. 1821) and a great many industrial and manufacturing establishments, incl. meat-packing plants. Hostile Indians caused the first settlers of 1536 to withdraw, but the site was re-occupied in 1586, and in 1776 was

BUDGERIGARS. A poignant contrast to caged specimens, a cloud of wild budgerigars descend on the water hole in the Nullarbor desert of Western Australia. *Photo: Popperfoto.*

made cap. of the viceroyalty of Rio de la Plata. Pop. (1977) 8,435,840.

BUFFALO. City and port of USA, in New York state, at the E. end of Lake Erie, close to the mouth of the r. Niagara. It is a leading commercial, industrial, and transport centre, with many large and small industries. Pop. met. area (1970) 1,336,601.

BUFFALO. Several species of wild cattle, mostly large, distinguished by their horns being flattened at the base and triangular in section. True Bs. are confined to the eastern hemisphere and fall into 2 distinct groups, African and Asiatic.

The typical African B. (*Syncerus caffer*) inhabits open bush country, generally near rivers all over Africa S. of the Sahara. The Cape B. is about 1.6m (5ft) high is black and has horns set close together to form a helmet-like mass on the forehead. Other races inhabit E. Africa. The dwarf C., sometimes called the bush-cow, is just over a metre (3½ft) high. It is red and lives in the Congo forest.

In Asiatic B.s the head is relatively longer and the ears smaller. The common Indian B. or water-B. (*Bubalus bubalis*) is black and up to 1.75m (5½ft high), with long, widely separated horns. They can be domesticated readily, and have been introduced into Australia, Italy, etc. The so-called B. of America is the bison (q.v.).

BUFFET (büfeh'), **Bernard** (1928-). French artist. B. in Paris, he has exhibited annually since 1948, and besides oils and water colours, is known for his lithographs, book illustrations and murals. His rapidly produced canvases are pessimistic, reflecting a feeling of nausea at the unpleasantness of life.

BUFFALO. In the wild, water buffalo inhabit swamp marshland and this domestic herd in Thailand still enjoys a mud wallow. They are kept as draught animals as well as for their rich milk supply. *Photo: Camera Press.*

BUFFON (büfoń'), **Georges Louis Leclerc,** comte de (1707-88). French naturalist. In 1739 he became keeper of the Jardin du Roi, and was elected to the Academy in 1753, when he delivered his *Discours sur le style.* He encouraged the popular study of natural history, and pub. a 'Natural History' in 44 vols. (1749-1804).

BUG. Name loosely applied to various insects, and in the USA to various kinds of beetles (*Coleoptera*), but in England more particularly to the bed-bug and its allies, which form the sub-order Heteroptera of the order Hemiptera.

The bed-bug (*Cimex lectularius*) is a brownish, flattened, wingless insect, with an unpleasant smell, found in old houses, and issuing forth at night to suck the blood of sleepers. The Heteroptera include a number of families. Some are predatory, feeding on other insects; some suck the juice of plants, such as the squash B. (*Anasa tristis*) and the cotton stainer (*Dysdercus suturellus*); other Bs. such as the water-scorpions (Nepidae), water boatmen (Notonectidae), and pond skaters (Hydrometridae), are aquatic; and one genus (*Halobates*) is marine.

BUG (boog). Name of 2 rivers in eastern Europe. The West B. rises E. of Lvov, and flows past Brest to the Vistula 32km (20m) below Warsaw. The South B. rises near Proskurov in the Ukrainian S.S.R. and flows S.E. to enter the Black Sea below Nikolaev.

BUGANDA (boog-). Two provs. (North and South B.) of Uganda, home of the able and ambitious Baganda people, and formerly a kingdom under a 'Kabaka'. Sir Edward Mutesa II (1924-69), popularly known as 'King Freddie', was also the first pres. of independent Uganda from 1962 until his deposition by Milton Obote under the constitution of 1966. He was succeeded as Sabataka (head of the Baganda clans), by his son Ronald Mutebi (1955-), but the boy did not become Kabaka or 'King'. Kampala, the cap. of Uganda, is in Buganda.

BUGLE. Wind instrument, belonging to the brass family. It resembles the trumpet, but has a shorter tube and less expanded bell, and is constructed of copper plate with brass. It has long been in wide use as a military instrument.

BŪ'GLOSS. Name of several plants of the family Boraginaceae, distinguished by their rough bristly leaves and small blue flowers.

BUHL (bool). Process of inlaying various metals, particularly brass and silver, into tortoise-shell or occasionally wood, which was invented by the Frenchman C. A. Boulle (1642-1732).

BUILDING SOCIETY. Institution which attracts investment and from the proceeds makes advances (home loans) on the security of first mortgage on property. They originated in Britain, the earliest being estab. in Birmingham in 1781, and at first were directly concerned in building operations. Most of the capital is provided by way of shares, attractive to small investors because income tax is borne by the B.S.: interest rates for borrowers are cushioned by income tax relief on mortgage payments.

B.Ss. in the British form are found mainly in the old Commonwealth countries. Australia has both permanent (the British type) and terminating (the type in which the B.S. borrows most of its funds from the institutions) societies, as does NZ. The USA has from *c.* 1840 had savings and loans associations with money deposited on both instant withdrawal and term share basis. Practice in Europe varies from virtually no home loan facilities, e.g. Italy, to Austria and Germany, which have *Bausparkassen,* from which regular investors may obtain a mortgage after a few years, and France, where a *credit deferré* (deferred credit) system has operated since 1954, under which investors' funds are pooled, and each year a percentage (only of those investing) are allowed a loan. Generally speaking home ownership is taken less for granted in continental Europe.

BUJUMBURA (bo͞ojumbo͞o'rah). Cap. (formerly called Usumbura) of Burundi, on Lake Tanganyika. The univ. was founded 1960. There is a steamer service to Kigoma in Tanganyika, and an international airport. Pop. (1976) 157,100.

BUKA'VU. Town in Zaïre, formerly called Costermansville, at the southern end of Lake Kivu. It is a trade and communications centre. Pop. (1974) 180,600, incl. many refugees from Burundi and Rwanda.

BUKHARA (bo͝okhah'rah). Ancient city in Central Asia, formerly the capital of the independent emirate of B., annexed to Russia in 1868. It is the cap. of B. region, Uzbek S.S.R., in which it was included in 1924. On a branch of the r. Zarafshan, it is a great Islamic centre, has famous schools and colleges, and makes silk and cotton textiles, leather goods, etc. 'Bukhara carpets' are made in Ashkhabad, but used to be marketed here. There is a medieval citadel, and the Ark, former palace of the emirs, has been meticulously restored. Pop. (1977) 140,000.

BUKHAREST. *See* BUCHAREST.

BUKHOVINA (bo͞okōvē'nah). Region covering *c.* 10,500 sq.km (over 4,000 sq.m) in S.E. Europe. Part of Moldavia during the Turkish régime, it was ceded by Turkey to Austria in 1777, becoming a duchy of the Dual Monarchy, 1867-1918; then it was included in Romania. North B. was ceded to Russia, 1940, and included in Ukraine S.S.R. as the region of Chernovtsy; the cession was confirmed by the peace treaty of 1947. The part of B. remaining in Rumania became the district of Suceava.

BULAWAYO (boolahwah'yō). City of Zimbabwe and former cap. of Matabeleland, at an alt. of 1,355 m (4,450 ft) on the r. Matsheumlope, a trib. of the Zambezi. Founded on the site of the kraal, burned down 1893, of Lobenguela, the Matabele chief, B. has developed with the exploitation of goldmines in the neighbourhood. Notable buildings include Government House, once belonging to Rhodes, who is buried in the Matopo hills above B. It is the centre of the Zimbabwe railway system and has an airport. Pop. (1977) 358,000 (incl. 56,800 Europeans, and 11,600 non-African other races).

BULB. Instrument of vegetative reproduction characteristic of many monocotyledonous plants, e.g. daffodil, snowdrop, onion. It is composed of the fleshy leaf-bases of the previous year's plant, enlarged by the food material they contain for the nourishment of the new plant.

Bs. are grown on a commercial scale in temperate countries, e.g. in parts of E. Anglia (England), and particularly in Holland.

BULGA'NIN, Nikolai (1895-1975). Russian soldier. He helped to organize Moscow's defence in the S.W.W., became a Marshal of the Soviet Union in 1947, and was Min. of Defence 1947-9 and 1953-5. On the fall of Malenkov in 1955 he became 'PM' (Chmn of Council of Ministers 1955-8) until ousted by Krushchev.

BULGARIA. Republic of S.E. Europe between the Danube on the N., Greece and Turkey-in-Europe on the S. The Balkan mountains form the backbone of the country, but in the S. between these and the Rhodope mountains is a stretch of low land drained into the Black Sea by the Maritsa and other rivers.

B. has been divided since 1964 into 28 provinces. Almost wholly agricultural before the S.W.W., B. is now largely industrialized, half her exports consisting of textiles,chemicals (espec. fertilizers), non-ferrous metals, fork-lift trucks and other mechanical goods, and electronic equipment. This development has been speeded from 1970 by the organization of large agricultural-industrial complexes. Crops incl. cereals, sugar beet, tobacco, and rose oil; valuable timber comes from forests covering nearly a third of B.; and minerals incl. iron, manganese, copper, lead, and pyrites, as well as oil discovered in the 1950-60s, which is refined at Pleven and Burgas. The cap. is Sofia; Plovdiv is the agricultural centre, and Burgas and Varna are Black Sea ports. Among new towns is Dimitroygrad, developed from 1947 as a new industrial centre.

Area 110,840 sq.km (42,796 sq.m); pop. (1977) 8,800,000. M.U.: lev.

History. Under the Romans B. formed the prov. of Moesia Inferior. It was later occupied by Slavs who, conquered in the 7th cent. by the Bulgars from Asia, eventually absorbed the invaders though they gave their name to the country. In 865 Khan Boris adopted Eastern Orthodox Christianity (still the national religion), and under his son Simeon (893-927), who assumed the title Tsar, B. became a leading power. In 1014 it was absorbed into the Byzantine empire, and although a 2nd Bulgarian empire was founded after the revolt of 1185, the last independent tsar died *c.* 1393, and B. passed under Ottoman rule until the national revival of the 19th cent. resulted in the creation of an autonomous principality under Turkish suzerainty in 1878, and the declaration of independence by Ferdinand I in 1908. In 1912-13 B. assisted in the defeat of the Turks, but was herself defeated in the 2nd Balkan war in 1913.

In 1915 B. entered the F.W.W. on the side of the Central Powers, and was again defeated; and in 1918 Ferdinand abdicated in favour of his son Boris III, who became virtual dictator from 1934. In 1941 B. became an ally of Germany, and German troops occupied the country, which declared war on Britain and the USA, but never on Russia, though Russia, to compel B. to surrender, declared war against B. in 1943. King Boris d. in 1943 following a visit to Hitler; his son Simeon II lost his throne after a referendum, 1946, and a rep. was proclaimed. Following the 1947 peace treaties, which restored the frontiers of 1919 except that B. retained S. Dubruja ceded by Rumania in 1940, B. adopted a Communist constitution drawn up on the Russian model by Georgi Dimitrov (q.v.). Under a new Constitution adopted in 1971 a council of State, to be elected by the single chamber Nat. Assembly, was introduced, which combines executive and legislative power. Owing her independence to Russian support, B. has always been one of the most loyal satellites of the USSR. *See* THRACE.

Language. Earliest of the Slavonic languages to be reduced to writing (9th cent.), Bulgarian is a member of the southern group, and is written in a modified Cyrillic character. Besides its close link with Serbo-Coat and Russian, it has modern Albanian, Greek and Turkish vocabulary elements.

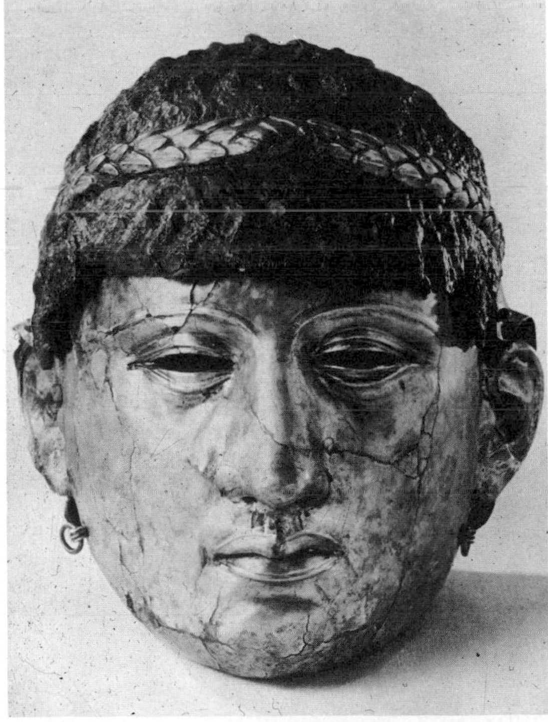

BULGARIA. A helmet mask of the Roman period of Thracian culture. Dating from the 1st century A.D., it comes from Plovdiv. The back is made of iron made to look like hair, a silver band forms the laurel wreath, and the face is of bronze. *Photo: Courtesy of the Bulgarian Government.*

BULL, John. Typical Englishman, especially as represented in cartoons. The name came into popular use after the publication of Dr John Arbuthnot's *History of John Bull* (1712) advocating the Tory policy of peace with France.

BULL, Olav (1883-1933). Norwegian poet. From his first vol., which appeared in 1909, he stood in the front rank of Norway's lyricists.

BULL, Papal. Document or edict issued by the pope; so called from the circular seals (medieval Lat. *bulla*) attached to them. Famous P.Bs. include Leo X's condemnation of Luther in 1520; and Pius IX's proclamation of papal infallibility in 1870.

BULL-BAITING. One-time popular Eng. sport in which a bull was set upon by a pack of vicious dogs. B. was made illegal in 1835.

BULLDOG. British dog of ancient but uncertain origin. Coming into prominence in the days of bull-baiting, it developed the characteristic underjaw which left the nostrils free for breathing whilst the dog retained its grip on the bull's throat. The head is broad and square, with a deeply wrinkled skull, small folded ears, and nose laid back between the eyes.

BULLER, Sir Redvers Henry (1839-1908). British soldier. Joining the army in 1858, he commanded the British armies in S. Africa against the Boers. Defeated at Colenso and Spion Kop, he eventually relieved Ladysmith but was superseded by Lord Roberts.

BULLETIN, The. Weekly Sydney magazine estab. in 1880 which, until the 1920s, was the chief Australian periodical. It did much to foster Australian literature by its criticism, etc.

BULL-FIGHTING. Contests between men and bulls; the national sport of Spain and of Spanish S. America. It was common in Greece and Rome, and was introduced into Spain by the Moors in the 11th cent. B. takes place in an arena, or bull-ring, where a bull is let loose. The animal is at first tormented by men on horseback, called *picadores,* who wound it with lances, and then by the *banderilleros* who plunge darts into its neck. Finally the *matador* with his sword and muleta (a red cloth attached to a stick) enters. Lured by the red cloth, the enraged animal charges at the matador who steps aside, and deals the death blow by plunging his sword between the bull's left shoulder and the shoulder-blade.

BULLFINCH. Species of finch (*Pyrrhula pyrrhula*) of the family Fringillidae, distinguished by its thickset form, silky plumage, and stout parrot-like bill. The male has a pinkish-crimson breast, grey back, and glossy black head, wings and tail. The B. is a common British resident.

BULLHEAD, or **miller's thumb.** Small freshwater fish (*Cottus gobio*), of no food value, with large, broad head, and sharp spines on the gill covers. The marine father lasher, or sting fish (*C. scorpius*), is of the same genus, and is so called because the male guards the eggs, and agitates the water with his tail to ensure them a supply of oxygen.

BULLROARER. Australian aboriginal musical instrument; it consists of a piece of wood of varying size, which is fastened by one of its pointed ends to a cord, by which it is whirled round the head to create a whirring noise. Both among the aborigines and other primitive races the B. is of magical significance.

BULL RUN, Battles of. Two engagements of the American Civil War at a site 48km (30m) S.W. of Washington, D.C. On 21 July 1861 the Northern forces were halted in their advance on the Confederate capital of Richmond, mainly by General Jackson and his brigade, who stood 'like a stone wall'. On 30 August 1862 Confederate forces under Jackson and Lee were again victorious at this site when General Pope was misled into thinking the Confederates were in retreat.

BULL TERRIER. British dog, originating in the 1850s, of which there are 3 recognized varieties, the white, the coloured, and the miniature.

BÜLOW (bü'loh), **Prince Bernhard von** (1849-1929). German statesman. He was Chancellor 1900-09 and, holding that self-interest was the only rule for any state, adopted attitudes to France and Russia which unintentionally precipitated Europe into the opposing power groups of the Entente and Triple Alliance.

BÜLOW (bü'loh), **Hans von** (1830-94). German pianist and conductor. He studied under Wagner and Liszt, and in 1857 m. the latter's dau. Cosima. He was professor of pianoforte at the Stern conservatorium in Berlin (1855-64), and in 1864 obtained a post under Ludwig II of Bavaria, and was the first conductor of *Tristan* and the *Meistersinger*. His wife left him to live with Wagner whom she m. in 1870.

BULWER-LYTTON. *See* LYTTON.

BUMBLE-BEE. Family of social insects (Bombidae) belonging to the super-family Apoidea of the order Hymenoptera. They have broad hairy bodies, which are usually dark brown or black, banded with yellow or orange, and live in small colonies, usually underground. The queen lays her eggs in the hollow nest of moss or grass at the beginning of the season, and the larvae are fed on pollen and honey, and develop into workers. In the summer, males and perfect females are produced, and all die at the end of the season except the fecundated females, which hibernate, to form fresh colonies in the spring. The flight muscles of the B. produce power more efficiently than aero engines, enabling it to fly despite its unaerodynamic shape, and its ability to produce internal central heating enables it to work in cold weather when ordinary bees are confined to the hive.

BUMBLEBEE. These bees are widely distributed throughout the world, except Australia, where they have been introduced to enable some cultivated varieties of clover to be properly pollinated. *Photo: Stephen Dalton/The Natural History Photographic Agency.*

BUNCHE (bunch), **Ralph** (1904-1971). American administrator, specializing in African and colonial affairs. A Negro and grandson of a slave, he was principal director of the UN Dept of Trusteeship 1947-54, and then UN Under-Sec., acting as mediator in Palestine 1948-9 and as special representative in the Congo 1960. In 1950 he was awarded the Nobel peace prize.

BU'NIN, Ivan Alexeyevich (1870-1953). Russian writer. B. in Voronezh, he wrote realistic stories of peasant life: *Derevnya* (1910: *The Village*); and *Gospodin iz San Frantsisko* (1916: *The Gentleman from San Francisco*), dealing with the death of a millionaire on Capri, which won him in 1933 a Nobel prize. Among later books *The Well of Days* (1930) has autobiographical elements and forms part of a longer work. He was also a poet and translated Byron and Longfellow.

BUNKER HILL. Small hill in Charlestown (now part of Boston), Mass., USA, near which on 17 June 1775 the first considerable engagement was fought in the American War of Independence; the colonists were defeated.

BUNSEN (boon'sen), **Robert Wilhelm von** (1811-99). German chemist. He was prof. of chemistry at Heidelberg 1852-98, and is credited with the invention of the B. burner. His name is also given to the carbon-zinc electric cell which he invented in 1841 for use in arc-lamps. About 1859 he discovered 2 new elements, caesium and rubidium.

BUNTING. Group of birds of the family Emberizidae, related to the finches, but of heavier build. The Bs. are best represented in the New World, though a number of species are native to the Old, 5 of which breed in Britain.

BUÑUEL (boon'yōō-el), **Luis** (1900–83). Spanish film director, famous for his controversial and often anticlerical films, e.g., *L'Age d'Or* (1930), and *The Discreet Charm of the Bourgeoisie* (1972).

BUNYAN, John (1628-88). English author. B. nr. Bedford, the son of a tinker, he followed his father's trade, but at 16 was conscripted into the Parliamentary army. Released in 1646, he passed through a period of religious doubt before joining the fellowship of the Baptists in 1653. In 1660 he was committed to Bedford county gaol for preaching, where he remained for 12 years, refusing all offers of release on condition that he would not preach again. Chief of the books written during his confinement was *Grace Abounding* (1666) describing his early spiritual struggles. Set free in 1672, he was elected pastor of the Bedford congregation, but in 1675 was again arrested and imprisoned for 6 months in the gaol on Bedford bridge where he began *The Pilgrim's Progress* (1678). The book achieved instant success, and a second part followed in 1684. Among his many later publications only *The Life and Death of Mr Badman* (1680) and *The Holy War* (1682) retain living interest.

BU'NYIP. Mythical animal of the Australian Aborigines: it is a river creature, rather like a slender, long-necked hippopotamus. The word was adopted by settlers as meaning 'fake' or 'impostor'.

BUOYANCY. The lifting effect of a fluid on a body wholly or partly immersed in it. This was studied by Archimedes in the 3rd cent. B.C. His principle states that the upward thrust or apparent loss of weight of a substance wholly or partly immersed in a fluid is equal to the weight of fluid displaced.

BURBAGE, Richard (*c.* 1567-1619). English actor. He is thought to have been the original Hamlet, Othello and Lear, and built the Globe Theatre *c.* 1599.

BURBOT. *See* COD.

BURKHARDT, Jakob (1818–97). Swiss art historian. Born in Basel, he was professor of history at Basel University 1858–93. His book, *The Civilization of the Renaissance in Italy* (1860), is a pioneering work of cultural analysis.

BURCKHARDT, Johann (1784-1817). Swiss traveller, whose intimate knowledge of Arabic enabled him to travel throughout the Middle East, visiting Mecca disguised as a Moslem pilgrim in 1814.

BURDOCK. A plant (*Arctium lappa*), of the family Compositae, a frequent roadside weed in Britain. It is a bushy herb, with hairy leaves, and ripe fruit enclosed in burs which are provided with strong hooks.

BURGAS (boor'gahs). Black Sea port of Bulgaria, handling a large export trade. There is an oil refinery (1963). Pop. (1976) 144,000.

BURGENLAND (boor'genlahnd). S.E. prov. of Austria, extending from the Danube southwards along the western border of the Hungarian plain.

Extensive forests supply timber. Lignite, antimony, and limestone are worked. Eisenstadt is the cap. Area 3,965 sq.km (1,531 sq.m); pop. (1971) 272,120.

BÜRGER, Gottfried August (1747-94). German poet, b. at Halberstadt. In 1773 he became famous with *Lenore,* and he also wrote many other ballads and lyrics.

BURGESS, Anthony (1917-). British novelist. B. in Manchester, he became a teacher, and in 1959 was invalided home from Borneo, where he was an education officer, because of a suspected brain tumour. With a diagnosis of one year to live he concentrated on writing, e.g. *A Clockwork Orange* (1962) about a London terrorized by teenage gangs, and *Earthly Powers* (1980).

BURGH (bur'o). Unit of Scottish local govt corresponding to the English borough (the town council consisting of provost, magistrates and councillors), and abolished in the local govt reorganization of 1975. The titles B. and Royal B. (formerly giving greater mercantile privilege) remained only as honorary distinctions.

BURGH (boorg), **Hubert de** (d. 1243). Justiciar of England. He rose to high office under Richard I, and in 1215 was appointed chief justiciar. His defeat of the French fleet in the Strait of Dover in 1217 ended French intervention in England. Until his dismissal in 1232, he was Henry III's chief minister.

BURGHLEY (ber'li), **William Cecil,** baron B. (1520-98). English statesman. B. at Bourne, Lincs, and ed. at Cambridge, he became private sec. to the Protector Somerset, and in 1550 one of the king's secretaries. He was deprived of most of his offices under Mary, but on Elizabeth's accession he became one of her most trusted ministers. He was largely responsible for the religious settlement of 1559, and in 1560 persuaded Elizabeth to send an army to Scotland to support the reformers. He also took a prominent part in the events leading up to the execution of Mary Queen of Scots in 1587. In general he was an advocate of caution and moderation, and was at great pains to avoid any breach with Spain before the strength of England was fully prepared. In 1571 he was created Baron Burghley, and in 1572 Lord High Treasurer.

BURGLARY. Formerly the crime of breaking into any dwellinghouse by night, i.e. between 9 p.m. and 6 a.m., with intent to commit a felony: outside these hours the same act was called housebreaking. In 1969, under the Theft Act (1968), the distinction was abolished. B. (maximum sentence 14 years) and aggravated B. (involving the use of firearms, etc., and a maximum of life imprisonment) are limited neither by the type of premises nor time of day. In the USA state law varies, but the crime of B. is not usually limited as it used to be in Britain.

BURGESS. Original and versatile, Anthony Burgess, blends real and surreal, actual and supernatural, in such a book as *Beard's Roman Women* (1977). *Photo: Universal Pictorial Press.*

BURGOS (boor'gōs). Spanish city, 217km (135m) N. of Madrid, cap. of B. prov. and former cap. of the old kingdom of Castile. The Gothic cathedral was built 1221-1567. Pop. (1970) 120,000.

BURGOYNE (bergoin'), **John** (1722-92). British soldier and dramatist. He served in the Seven Years War, and on the outbreak of the American War of Independence was given command of a force intended to invade the colonies from Canada, but was surrounded and surrendered at Saratoga in 1777. He wrote comedies, among them *The Maid of the Oaks* (1775) and *The Heiress* (1786).

BURGUNDY. Ancient kingdom and duchy in the valleys of the Saône and Rhône, France. The Burgundi were a Teutonic tribe and overran the country *c.* 400. From the 9th cent. to the death of the duke Charles the Bold in 1477, it was the nucleus of a powerful principality. On Charles's death the duchy was incorporated into France. The capital of B. was Dijon. The modern region of B. (Bourgogne), comprises the depts of Côte-d'Or, Nièvre, Saône-et-Loire, and Yonne. It is famous for its wines. Area 31,763 sq.km (82,266 sq.m); pop. (1975) 1,570,943.

BURIAT (boor'rē-at). An A.S.S.R. within the R.S.F.S.R. In Central Asia with L. Baikal forming its western boundary, it adopted the Soviet system in 1920. Its name was shortened from Buriat-Mongol in 1958. It is largely steppe, and cattle-breeding is the chief occupation. Ulan-Ude is the cap. Area 351,300 sq.km (135,650 sq.m); pop. (1978) 896,000.

BURKE, Edmund (1729-97). British statesman and author. B. in Dublin and ed. at Trinity Coll., he settled in London in 1750, and achieved literary fame in 1756 by his *Vindication of Natural Society* and *Essay on the Sublime and Beautiful.* He entered Parliament as a Whig in 1765, and took a prominent part, as orator and pamphleteer, in the opposition to George III's attempts to dominate English politics and coerce the Americans, e.g. by his *Thoughts on the Present Discontents* (1770) and *Speech on Conciliation* (1775). He was paymaster of the forces in Rockingham's government of 1782, and in the Fox-North coalition of 1783, and after the collapse of the latter spent the rest of his career in opposition. He then threw himself into the attack on Hastings' misgovernment in India, and was among the managers chosen to conduct his unsuccessful impeachment. As a fanatical opponent of democracy, he denounced the French Revolution in *Reflections on the Revolution in France* (1790), which brought to an end his long friendship with Fox. He defended his conduct in his *Appeal from the New to the Old Whigs* (1791) and *Letter to a Noble Lord* (1796), and attacked the suggestion of peace with France in *Letters on a Regicide Peace* (1795-7). He retired in 1794 with a govt pension to his estate at Beaconsfield, where he died. By modern Conservatives he is regarded as the greatest of their political theorists.

BURKE, Robert O'Hara (1820-61). Australian explorer. B. in Galway, Ireland, he became a police inspector on the goldfields of Victoria. In 1860 he set out for the Gulf of Carpentaria and reached it, but although courageous, he was impetuous, and on the tragic return journey B. and his second-in-command William Wills (1834-61) d. of hunger

BURKE and **HARE.** Murderers. William B. and William H., two Irishmen living in Edinburgh, during 1827-8 murdered at least 15 people and sold their bodies to the anatomists. B. was hanged in 1829 on H.'s evidence. Hare is said to have died a beggar in London in the 1860s.

BURKE'S PEERAGE. Popular name of the annual *Genealogical and Heraldic History of the Peerage, Baronetage, and Knightage of the United Kingdom,* first issued by John Burke (1787-1848) in 1826.

BURKINA FASO. *See* VOLTA, UPPER.

BURMA, Union of. Country of S.E. Asia. A coastal strip running 2,250 km (1,400 m) S.E. from Akyab is cut off from the rest of the country by the Arakan Mtns, except where the delta of the Irrawaddy gives entry into the main plain of B., stretching N. from Rangoon 640km (400m) to Mandalay. To the E. of this plain lies the *Shan State* 155,800 sq.km (60,155 sq.m), a tableland of hilly country, and to the N. of Mandalay is the *Kachin State* 89,042 sq.km (34,379 sq.m), an area of jungle, mtns and patches of cultivation in the river valleys. S. of the Shan State, along the Thai border, are the *Kayah State* 11,730 sq.km (4,529 sq.m) and the *Kawthoolei* (formerly Karen) *State* 30,383 sq.km (11,731 sq.m). To the W. of Mandalay on the Bangladesh-Indian border are the jungle-clad Chin Hills, which form a Special Division for the Chin peoples, 36,019 sq.km (13,907 sq.m). B. proper is centrally admin. but there are separate state govts.

The largest river of B. is the Irrawaddy, its principal tributary the Chindwin. Parallel to the Irrawaddy flow the Sittang, which has its mouth only 80km (50m) to the E., and the Salween, which flows through the E. part of the Shan State. Over half B. is forested, the wetter parts with dense tropical jungle, or a monsoonal forest, in which teak is found; the drier parts have scrub vegetation merging into semi-desert. Rice is the chief crop, and sesame, groundnuts, sugar, cotton, rubber and tobacco are also grown. A wealth of minerals incl. antimony, copper, lead, silver, tin, tungsten, zinc; jade, rubies and sapphires; and oil. Industry is being developed. The cap. is Rangoon; other towns are Mandalay and the port of Moulmein. M.U.: kyat. Area 678,000 sq.km (261,789 sq.m); pop. (1977) 31,510,000. The great majority of the people are Buddhist, and the official language is Burmese, but English is permitted.

History. The Burmese date their era from A.D. 638, when they had arrived from the region where China meets Tibet, and were semi-savage. By 850 they had organized a little state in the centre of the plain at Pagan, and from 1044 until 1287 they maintained a hegemony over most of the area of B. as it now is, and developed a distinctive civilization, one of its chief characteristics being Buddhism, of the original Hinayana type, and the particular ecclesiastical architecture of the pagoda and monastery. In 1287 Kublai Khan's grandson Ye-su Timur occupied B. after destroying the Pagan dynasty. After he withdrew, anarchy supervened. From *c.* 1490 to 1750 the Toungoo dynasty maintained itself, with increasing difficulty; and in 1752 Alaungpaya once more unified the country and founded Rangoon as his cap. In a struggle with Britain, 1824-6, his descendants lost the coastal strip from Chittagong to Cape Negrais. The 2nd Burmese War, 1852, resulted in British annexation of Lower B. (the southern section of the plain, including Rangoon). Thibaw, the last Burmese king, precipitated the 3rd Burmese War, 1885, and the British seized Upper B., 1886. The country was united as a prov. of India until made a separate country with its own constitution in 1937. The Japanese invaded B. in 1941, and occupied the country 1942-5. Negotiations with Britain followed the liberation of B., and on 4 Jan. 1948 B. achieved complete independence outside the British Commonwealth.

In 1962 there was a military coup by General Ne Win, who became Prime Minister, the overthrown Prime Minister, U Nu, continuing to organize revolt from a base in Thailand. From 1970 this was linked with the rebellion of the Karens, insurgent from 1948, who control much of S.E. Burma on the Thai border. There was also continuing revolt in the Shan and Kachin states, supported by the Chinese from 1967. Under the Constitution of 1973 there is a People's Assembly which elects the policy-making Council of State of which U Ne Win became the first chairman, i.e. Pres. of the Rep., in 1974: term renewed for 4 yrs 1978. Civilian rule was restored in 1974, and U Ne Win's Lanzin Party aims at creating a Socialist state in 'the Burmese Way'. Burma is one of the 'non-aligned' countries.

BURNE-JONES, Sir Edward (1833-98). British painter and designer, b. at Birmingham of Welsh ancestry. Under Rossetti's influence he abandoned his intention of taking orders and devoted himself to art. He drew his inspiration from medieval ballads and legends, classical mythology, and the Bible. He received a baronetcy in 1894.

BURNET, Gilbert (1643-1715). British bishop and historian. B. in Edinburgh, he was ordained in the Episcopal Church of Scotland in 1661. He pub. his *History of the Reformation in England* in 1679. His Whig views having brought him into disfavour, he retired to The

BURMA. The Shwe Dagon pagoda in Rangoon is the largest place of Buddhist worship of its kind in the world. Covered with pure gold, it stands on a small hill, and it is itself 118m (368ft) high. It is solid, apart from a relic chamber and worshippers perform their devotions on the great surrounding platform. *Photo: J. Allan Cash.*

Hague on the accession of James II, and became the confidential adviser of Princess Mary and William of Orange. He returned to England with the latter in 1688, and was appointed bp of Salisbury. His best-known work is his *History of His Own Time.*

BURNET, Sir Macfarlane (1899-). Australian virologist. He was awarded the O.M. in 1958 in recognition of his work on such diseases as influenza, polio and cholera, and 1944-65 was director of the Walter and Eliza Hall Inst. for Medical Research and prof. of experimental medicine at Melbourne. *See* MEDAWAR.

BURNE'TT, Frances Eliza Hodgson (1849-1924). Anglo-American writer. B. in Manchester, she lived in the USA from 1865. She wrote many novels and plays, and the famous children's story *Little Lord Fauntleroy* (1886).

BURNEY, Frances (Fanny) (1752-1840). British novelist and diarist. The dau. of Dr Charles B. (1726-1814), historian of music, she belonged to the circle of Dr Johnson, and achieved success with her first novel *Evelina*, pub. anonymously in 1778. She obtained a post at court 1786-91, and in 1793 m. the French émigré General D'Arblay. She pub. 2 further novels, *Cecilia* (1782), and *Camilla* (1796), and her diaries and letters appeared in 1842-6.

BURNHAM, James (1905-). American philosopher. B. at Chicago, he was a Rhodes scholar at Oxford. Prof. of philosophy at N.Y. univ. 1932-54, he argued in *The Managerial Revolution* (1941) that world control is passing from politicians and capitalists to the new class of business executives, the managers.

BURNLEY. Town in Lancs, England, 19km (12m) N.E. of Blackburn. Formerly a leading cotton-manufacturing town, it has suffered some decline with the shrinking of the industry, but is diversifying into new products. Pop. (1972) 74,760.

BURNS, John (1858-1943). British labour leader. B. in Battersea and trained as an engineer, he was sentenced to 6 weeks' imprisonment for his part in the Trafalgar Square demonstration on 'Bloody Sunday' - 13 Nov. 1887 - and in 1889 was a leader of the strike securing the 'dockers' tanner' (wage of 6d. per hr). In 1892 he entered Parliament as an Independent Labour MP and in 1906 was the 1st working man to be a member of the Cabinet (Pres. of the Local Govt Board). In 1914 he was appointed pres. of the Board of Trade, but resigned on the outbreak of war.

BURNS, Robert (1759-96). Scottish poet. B. at Alloway, Ayrshire, the son of a farmer, he became joint tenant, after his father's death in 1784, with his brother in a farm at Mossgiel, where many of his best poems were written. In agriculture he proved less proficient and having in addition been crossed in his love for Jean Armour among others, he decided to emigrate to Jamaica. He was dissuaded by the success of his *Poems, chiefly in the Scottish dialect* (1786), which made him the lion of the Edinburgh season 1786-7. A 2nd enlarged edition in 1787 proved profitable, and in 1788 enabled him at length to marry Jean Armour and settle to farming at Ellisland, near Dumfries. In 1789 he obtained a part-time post as district excise-officer, and when his farm once more failed in 1791, he transferred to a full-time post.

B.'s fame rests equally on his poems and his songs, of which he contributed some 300 to Johnson's *Scots Musical Museum* (1787-1803), and Thomson's *Scottish Airs with Poetry* (1793-1811); sometimes wholly original and at others combining inspiration from several popular versions, they attain lyric perfection. His English verse is negligible; the full vigour of his genius waited on his use of the Scots dialect as in 'Holy Willie's Prayer', 'Tam o' Shanter', and 'Jolly Beggars'.

BURNS. Injuries to the tissues caused by heat, light, or corrosive substances. A 'scald' is a burn caused by hot liquid or vapour; the nature of the injury is the same. Bs. include injuries made by invisible rays, whether these are of lower frequency than visible light (heat, infra-red), or of higher frequency (ultra-violet, X-rays, radium emanations).

Bs. are divided into two classes, superficial and deep, according to whether the skin is partially destroyed, or whether it is wholly destroyed and the muscle beneath it is damaged. All Bs. cause some degree of shock, and this is often more dangerous than the local effect. The treatment of a bad B. or scald is therefore first directed against shock and infection. Local treatment incl. the use of silver nitrate wet soaks to cover the wound; water soluble ointment; temporary grafting from another person before the final grafting from sound areas of the patient's own skin; and the use of anti-biotics to prevent septicaemia.

BURR, Aaron (1756-1836). American politician. B. in New Jersey, he served on Washington's staff during the War of Independence, and in 1800 received the same no. of electoral votes as Jefferson in the presidential election. Through the influence of Alexander Hamilton the House of Representatives voted in favour of Jefferson (Feb. 17,

BURNS. The Alexander Nasmyth portrait painted to illustrate the first Edinburgh edition of his poems. *Photo: Courtesy of the Scottish National Gallery.*

1801), but B. was vice-pres. 1800-4. B. never forgave Hamilton, whom he thought also prevented his becoming Gov. of N.Y. State in 1804, and killed him in a duel that year. As a result he became a social outcast, and had to leave the USA for some years following an attempt to raise an armed force for the invasion of Mexico.

BURRA, Edward (1905-76). British artist. B. in Kensington, his work incl. genre watercolours with a humorous touch, as well as more dramatic works showing the influence of El Greco and Goya. Notable are 'Mexican Church' (1938) and 'Soldiers' (1942), both in the Tate Gallery.

BURROUGHS (bur'ōz), **Edgar Rice** (1875-1950). American novelist. B. at Chicago, he had a varied career, before writing a score of 'Tarzan' books, romantic stories of the adventures of an ape-man, which were widely popular, beginning with *Tarzan of the Apes* (1914). *See* TARZANA.

BURROUGHS, William (1914-). American novelist. Member of a 'big-business' family, he was b. in St Louis, Missouri, ed. at Harvard and has had a variety of jobs as reporter, advertising man, private detective, etc. Well known to devotees of the American 'beat' movement, he estab. his reputation with *The Naked Lunch* (1959) dealing with the world of the drug addict: *The Ticket that Exploded* (1962) is science fiction.

BURSA. City in N.W. Turkey-in-Asia, the cap. of B. il, and cap. of the Ottoman Empire 1326-1423. It is a centre for commerce, and for silk and wool production, with a port at Mudania 26km (16m) N.W. on the Sea of Marmara. It is said that Hannibal suggested its foundation. Pop. (1970) 275,920.

BURT, Sir Cyril Lodowic (1883-1971). British psychologist, a pioneer in intelligence tests and psychological tests for special abilities in schoolchildren. After his death, the evidence on which he based some of his conclusions on the greater influence of heredity rather than environment was questioned.

BURTON, Sir Richard Francis (1821-90). British traveller and orientalist. B. at Torquay, in 1842 he became a subaltern in the Indian army. He made himself master of 35 oriental languages. In 1853 he went on pilgrimage to Mecca; in 1854 he explored the interior of the Somali country, and in 1856 was commissioned by the Foreign Office to explore the sources of the Nile; with J. H. Speke he discovered Lake Tanganyika in 1858. From 1861 he was a British consul - from 1871 at Trieste, where he d. Every country of the many he visited was made the subject of a remarkable book, but he is chiefly remembered for his literal translation of the *Arabian Nights* (1885-8).

BURTON, Robert (1577-1640). English philosopher. B. in Leics, he was ed. at Oxford, and remained there for the rest of his life as a fellow of Christ Church. His fame rests on his *Anatomy of Melancholy* (1621), a remarkable compendium of information on the medical and religious opinions of the time.

BURTON UPON TRENT. Town in Staffs, England, 200km (123m) N.W. of London, noted as a brewing centre, and for its engineering works. Pop. (1972) 50,250.

BURU'NDI. Country of central Africa, to the E. of Lake Tanganyika. The narrow western plain is bordered by the Nile-Congo dividing range at *c.* 2000 m (6,500 ft), which falls away to the central highlands at *c.* 1,525 m (5,000 ft). Export crops are coffee, cotton, and tea; minerals (nickel) are of growing importance; and hides and livestock are exported. There are enormous peat reserves in the basin of the Akanyaru, a tributary of the Nile.

Formerly part of Ruanda-Urundi (q.v.), B. became an independent kingdom in 1962. In 1966 the PM, Michel Micombero (1940-), deposed King Mwami Ntare V, who was killed in the later period of tribal unrest in 1972, and proclaimed himself pres. of the Rep. of B. The majority of the pop. are the small-stature Bantu Hutu, but 15% are the Nilotic Tutsi, a tall people who have exercised a 500-yr dominion over the Hutu. In 1972 exiled Hutu returned and attempted to wipe out the Tutsi, and the latter retaliated by killing many of their Hutu serfs in a double genocide. Many exiled Tutsi from Rwanda (q.v.) are living in B. In 1976 Micombero was himself overthrown by a military coup, and the regime became increasingly dictatorial. The chief towns are the cap., Bujumbura (formerly Usumbura) and Kitega (former royal cap.). Area 27,834 sq.km (10,747 sq.m); pop. (1977) 3,970,000. M.U.: B. franc.

BURY (ber'i). Town in Greater Manchester, England, on the Irwell, 16km (10m) N. of Manchester proper. There are cotton, chemical, and engineering industries. Pop. (1972) 68,580.

BURY ST EDMUNDS. Town in Suffolk, England, on the Lark, 45km (28m) E. of Cambridge. Chief town of the western part of the co., it is a marketing centre with agricultural machinery works and beet sugar factories. It was named after St Edmund (q.v.), and there are remains of the once magnificent Benedictine Abbey founded in 1020. Pop. (1972) 26,420.

BUSHMEN. A Bushman of the Kalahari Gemsbok Park, and the prehistoric Bushman painting, the 'White Lady' of the Brandberg. The method of hunting remains the same. *Photos: Courtesy of SATOUR.*

BUSBY (buz'bi), **Richard** (1606-95). English headmaster of Westminster school from 1640. Among his pupils were Dryden, Locke, Atterbury, and Prior, and he was renowned for his floggings.

BUSH, Alan Dudley (1900-). British composer. As a student under John Ireland, he experimented in 12-note composition, but has subsequently tried to keep his style simple in accordance with the ideas of Marxism, which he adopted when studying philosophy in Berlin. His works incl. the operas *Wat Tyler* (1953) and *Men of Blackmoor* (1956), both much more successful on the Continent than in Britain, and the *Byron Symphony* (1962).

BUSH, George (1924-). American Republican politician. B. in Mass., he was US ambassador to the UN 1970-3, Director of the CIA 1975-6, and in 1981 became vice-president to Reagan.

BUSHBUCK (*Tragelaphus*). African antelopes, with hair tails and only a spiral twist in the horns. The largest c. 1.2m (4ft) high is the mountain or Buxton's B. (*T. buxtoni*) of S. Abyssinia. The common B. (*T. scriptus*), the smallest species (less than 1m/3ft high), is found over most of Africa S. of the Sahara.

BUSHEL. A British imperial dry or liquid measure of 8 gallons (2219.36 cu.in): some US States have different standards according to the goods measured.

BUSHIDO (boo'shidō). Code of honour of the Japanese military caste of *Samurai*, analogous to the English conception of 'chivalry'.

BUSHMEN. A nomadic race of hunters, living in the central parts of S. Africa, particularly the Kalahari Desert. They are thin and of small stature, with dark yellow skins, prominent cheekbones and a low skull. Only about 26,000 survive today. Their language, which is monosyllabic, has the same curious 'clicks' as that of the Hottentots. They have no tribal chiefs, live in holes in the ground or in reed huts, and wear rough skins. Ancient B. paintings found in mountain caves show remarkable artistic talent.

BUSHRANGERS. Australian armed robbers of the 19th cent. The first Bs. were escaped convicts. The last gang was led by the Kelly brothers in 1878-80. They form the subject of many Australian ballads.

BUSONI (boosō'nē), **Ferruccio Benvenuto** (1866-1924). Italian pianist, composer, and musical critic. B. near Florence, he made his first public appearance at the age of 7. In 1891-3 he was at the Conservatoire of Boston, USA, and later lived in Berlin, Bologna, and Zürich. Most of his music was for the piano, but he also composed several operas. As a critic he was influential in suggesting new standards of value.

BUSTAMA'NTE, Sir (William) Alexander (1884-1977). Jamaican statesman, *né* William Alexander Clarke. Of mixed blood, his father being Irish and his mother a mulatto, he was adopted at 15 by a Spanish seaman called Bustamante. As leader of the Labour Party, he was first PM of independent Jamaica 1962-7.

BUSTARD. Family of large running birds (Otidae), with a superficial resemblance to turkeys, inhabiting dry plains in Europe, Asia, and Africa. The great B. (*Otis tarda*) and the little B. (*O. tetrax*) were once familiar in Britain, and attempts are being made by the Great Bustard Trust (1970) to naturalise the former again nr Porton Down. A full-grown male weighs *c.* 18kg. (40 lb). The related Australian B. (*Eupodotis australis*) reaches 1.2 m (4ft) and has a remarkable mating display.

BUTADIENE (būtadī'ēn). An inflammable gas (CH_2:CHCH:CH_2), colourless and liquefying easily, which is derived from petroleum. It also polymerizes readily, and is chiefly used in the manufacture of synthetic rubbers. *See* RUBBER.

BŪ'TĀNE. C_4H_{10} paraffin hydrocarbon b.p. 1°C, density at 0°C=0.60, obtained from petroleum distillation. It is liquefied under pressure in steel cylinders and used as fuel for industrial and domestic purposes, e.g. portable cooking stoves.

BŪTE, John Stuart, 3rd earl of (1713-92). British Tory statesman. He succeeded his father in the title in 1723, and in 1737 was elected a representative peer for Scotland. Upon the accession of George III in 1760, he became the chief instrument in the king's policy for breaking the power of the Whigs and establishing the personal rule of the monarch through Parliament, and in 1762 was appointed Premier. His position as the king's favourite and the supplanter of the popular Pitt made him hated in the country. After the Seven Years War in 1763 he resigned.

BUTE. Scottish island in the Firth of Clyde, separated from the mainland to the N. by the winding channel called the Kyles of B. It is a holiday resort for Glasgow, and the chief town is Rothesay. It is 25km (15½m) long, and has an area of 122 sq.km (47 sq.m). With Arran and the adjacent is. it formed the co. of B., but was merged 1975 in the region of Strathclyde.

BUTLER, Joseph (1692-1752). British theologian. In 1740 he became dean of St Paul's, in 1747 refused the primacy, and in 1750 became bp of Durham. He defined his philosophy in *Fifteen Sermons* (1726) and in his *Analogy of Religion* (1736) refuted Deism, attempting to prove that the element of revealed religion in Christianity is inherently probable even if not capable of logical proof.

BUTLER, Josephine Elizabeth (1828-1906). British social reformer. *Née* Grey, she was b. in Northumberland and m. Dr Butler, later canon of Winchester. She agitated for the admission of women to higher education, helped to secure the Married Women's Property Act, worked for the improvement of the lot of 'fallen' women, and carried on a campaign against the Contagious Diseases Acts of 1864-9, which made women in garrison towns liable to compulsory examination for V.D. The Acts were repealed 1883-6.

BUTLER, Reg (1913-). British sculptor. B. in Herts, he held his 1st one-man show in 1949, and caused a sensation by winning the international Unknown Political Prisoner competition in 1953. He is primarily concerned with the human figure, using distortion to achieve striking effects.

BUTLER, Richard Austen, baron B. of Saffron Walden (1902-82). British Cons. politician, known as 'Rab' from his initials. As Min. of Education in the Coalition 1941-5, he was responsible for the 'Butler' Act of 1944 establishing the lines of post-war educational development, was Chancellor of the Exchequer 1951-5, and Lord Privy Seal 1955-9. A likely candidate for the premiership in 1957, he was given the additional post of Home Sec. under Macmillan, and in 1962 became Depty PM with the new title of First Sec. of State. On the resignation of Macmillan in 1963, he again narrowly missed the premiership, but continued under Douglas-Home as Sec. of State for Foreign Affairs until 1964. He became a life peer and master of Trinity Coll., Cambridge, 1965-78.

BUTLER, Samuel (1612-80). English satirist. The son of a Worcs. farmer, he served in the household of the countess of Kent, and then of Sir Samuel Luke, a colonel in the Parliamentary army. After the Restoration he became secretary to the earl of Carberry. His poem *Hudibras,* pub. in 3 parts in 1663, 1664 and 1678, became immediately popular for its biting satire against the Puritans. His prose *Characters* are also of high merit.

BUTLER, Samuel (1835-1902). British author. B. in Notts, the son of a clergyman, he refused to go into the Church, and became a sheep-farmer in New Zealand (1859-64). He made his name by the satirical *Erewhon* (1872) describing a visit to the imaginary country, Erewhon, i.e. Nowhere reversed. A sequel, *Erewhon Revisited,* was pub. in 1901. *The Fair Haven* (1873) was a satirical examination of the miraculous element in Christianity. *Life and Habit* (1877) and other works were devoted to a criticism of the theory of natural selection. In *The Authoress of the Odyssey* he maintained that the Odyssey was the work of a woman. B.'s fame was greatly increased by the posthumous publication of his *Notebooks* and his largely autobiographical novel, *The Way of All Flesh,* written 1872-85; pub. 1903.

BUTLIN, Sir William 'Billy' (1899-1980). British pioneer of holiday camps. B. in S. Africa, he went in early life to Canada, but later entered the fair business in England. His chain of camps provide 'all-in' holidays with amusements, meals and sleeping chalets at an inclusive price. He was knighted in 1964.

BUTOR (bütor'), **Michel** (1926-). French writer. Ed. at the Univ. of Paris, he is a practitioner of the 'anti-novel' of which Robbe-Grillet (q.v.) is the theoretician. These incl. *Passage de Milan* (1954), *Degrés* (1960) and *L'Emploi du temps* (1963): *Mobile* (1962) is a vol. of essays.

BUTT, Dame Clara (1873-1936). British contralto. B. in Sussex, she had an unusually rich and powerful voice, and Elgar's *Sea Pictures* (1899) was specially written for her. She m. in 1900 the baritone Kennerley Rumford (1870-1957), and in 1917 became D.B.E.

BUTTE (būt). City in Montana, USA 80km (50m) S.W. of the State capital Helena. Here are the copper smelting works of the Anaconda Mining Co., owners also of the copper, silver and other mines in the vicinity. B. was founded in 1864 during a rush for gold, soon exhausted; copper was found some 20 years later. Pop. (1970) 23,368.

BUTTER. A fatty dairy product made from milk by churning the cream. Besides the cow, the goat, sheep, ass, mare, camel, and buffalo have been used for milk production.

BUTTERCUP. Genus (*Ranunculus*) of the family Ranunculaceae, many species having divided leaves which have earned the alternative name of crowfoot, and shining yellow cuplike flowers. Common in Europe and Asia, and naturalized in N. America, are the bulbous B. (*R. bulbosus*), the creeping B. (*R. repens*), and the meadow crowfoot (*R. acris*); native to N. America are the marsh B. of the east (*R. septentrionalis*) and the California B. (*R. californicus*). The florists' B. is *R. asiaticus.*

BUTTERFLY. Name given to those insects which form the series Papilionoidea (or Rhopalocera) of the order Leipidoptera, the remainder of the order consisting of the moths (q.v.). Like moths, Bs. are clothed with microscopic scales, and feed upon nectar and other fluid substances which they imbibe through a tubular proboscis formed by the greatly modified maxillae; but they are distinguished from moths by their clubbed antennae and in the absence of a frenulum from the hind-wings. They are essentially day-flying insects, whereas most moths are nocturnal. Metamorphosis is complete; the caterpillars are very diverse in form, and the pupae or chrysalids are usually without the protection of cocoons. The life of the adult insect is usually only a few weeks, but species which hibernate live until the spring or early summer when they lay their eggs. *See illus.* under LEPIDOPTERA.

The Skippers or Hesperiidae, the most primitive family of Bs., are characterized by all the veins in the fore-wings arising separately from the cell. In the remainder of the Bs. certain of the veins in the fore-wings are coincident and do not arise separately from the cell. The Swallow-tails or Papilionidae are a family of large or very large Bs., mainly tropical.

In the Nymphalidae, the largest family of Bs., with about 6,000 species, the fore-legs are so reduced as to be useless for walking. The subfamily Nymphalinae includes the Peacock, Purple Emperor, Tortoiseshells, Admirals and Fritillaries. The sub-family Satyrinae comprises the Meadow Brown, Grayling, together with the Heaths, Ringlets, and many others.

The family Pieridae includes the Whites, Clouded Yellows, Orange Tips, and their allies. The Garden or Cabbage Whites (*Pieris rapae* and *P. brassicae*) are among the few injurious species. The Lycaenidae are a large family that incl. the Blues, Coppers, and Hairstreaks. They are mostly rather small, often with metallic coloration. The Erycinidae are essentially S. American; the sole British representative is the Duke of Burgundy fritillary (*Nemeobius lucina*).

There occur different seasonal forms among certain Bs., e.g. the European Nymphalid B. *Araschnia levana*, whose spring form is known as *levana* whilst the summer form *prorsa* was considered to belong to a different species. Other Bs., such as the African *Papilio dardanus*, have several distinct forms of female and only one type of male.

Although the caterpillars of most Bs. feed upon flowering plants, those of a few kinds are carnivorous. Modern agricultural practice, the use of sprays and rooting out of hedges, has endangered many species.

BUTTERFLY. A painted lady *(Vanessa cardui)* - a species found almost throughout Africa - just emerged from its pupa. *Photo: Anthony Bannister/NHPA.*

BUXTEHUDE (bookstehōō'de), **Diderik** (1637-1707). Danish composer and organist. Organist at Lübeck, Germany, from 1668, he influenced Bach and Handel. He is best remembered for his cantatas written for performance at his annual concert series of Abendmusiken.

BUXTON. Market town and spa in Derbyshire, England, 58km (36m) N.W. of Derby. It is the highest town of its size in England, just over 300m (1,000 ft) a.s.l. Famous for its healing waters since Roman times, it is a winter resort, and has a restored Edwardian opera house. Pop. (1973) 20,000.

BUZZARD. Name applied to the larger and heavier built hawks, particularly to the subfamily Buteoninae, allied to the eagles. The common B. (*Buteo buteo*) was formerly a common British bird, but is now found in only a few districts. The rough-legged B. (*Archibuteo lagopus*) is an irregular autumn visitor. The honey B. (*Pernis apivorus*) is very scarce as a breeding species. The bird called B. in America is the Turkey B. (*Cartharistes aura*), one of the New World vultures.

BYBLOS (bib'los). Town (modern Jebeil), 32km (20m) N. of Beirut, Lebanon. Known to the Assyrians and Babylonians as Gubla it had a thriving export of cedar and pinewood to Egypt as early as 3000 B.C. In Roman times called B., it boasted an amphitheatre, baths and a temple dedicated to an unknown male god: excavation continues.

BYDGOSZCZ (bid'goshch). Town in Poland, 105km (65m) N.E. of Poznan on the river Brda. It is an important railway and canal junction and was Prussian from 1772 to 1919, when it was restored to Poland. Pop. (1978) 339,000.

BYELORUSSIA (byelōru'shia). SSR of the USSR ('White Russia') bordering on Poland. It is low-lying, and is drained by the W Dvina, Dnieper and its tribs., incl. the Pripet and Beresina. The Pripet Marshes lie in the E; forest covers more than a quarter of its area. The climate is mild and damp. Products incl. potatoes, flax, pigs, cattle, sheep in the agricultural area; chemicals, matches, timber, paper, textiles, lorries, cement, leather are industrial products. Power stations operate on peat from the extensive peat bogs. The rep. suffered severely under German invasion and occupation during the S.W.W. Minsk is the cap. 207,600 sq.km (80,150 sq.m); pop. (1972) 9,100,000.

BYNG (bing), **George,** visct Torrington (1663-1733). British admiral. In 1704 he captured Gibraltar and was knighted by Queen Anne for gallantry in the sea battle of Malaga; in 1708 commanded the fleet which prevented an invasion of England by the Pretender; and in 1718 destroyed the Spanish fleet at Messina. He was created a peer in 1721. John Byng (q.v.) was his fourth son.

BYNG, John (1704-57). British admiral. When in 1756 the island of Minorca was invaded by the French, B. was ordered to sail to the relief of Fort St Philip which was still resisting, but failed in the attempt. After the fort's fall he was court-martialled and condemned to death, and shot at Portsmouth. As Voltaire commented, it was done 'to encourage the others'.

BYNG OF VIMY, Jullian Byng, 1st visct (1862-1935). British general. A son of the 2nd earl of Strafford, he commanded the 3rd Cavalry Division in 1914, the Cavalry Corps in 1915, the IXth Army Corps at the Dardanelles, and the Canadian Army Corps in 1916-17 in France. After his victory at Vimy Ridge he took command of the 3rd Army, and in Nov. 1917 made the brilliant tank attack on Cambrai. He was Gov.-Gen. of Canada 1921-6, and was made a viscount in 1926, and a field marshal in 1932.

BYRD (bird), **Richard Evelyn** (1888-1957). American airman and explorer. B. in Virginia, he served in the navy, but made his reputation by flights to the North (1926) and South (1929) Poles, and by his four land expeditions to the Antarctic 1928-30, 1933-5, 1939-41 and 1946-7. He also led the US Navy's 'Operation Deepfreeze' 1955-7: a mtn range with peaks 5,180 m (17,000 ft) high was discovered in E. Marie Byrd Land.

BYRD, William (1543-1623). English composer, b. probably at Lincoln, where he became organist in 1563. He shared with Tallis the honorary post of organist in Queen Elizabeth's Chapel Royal, and in 1575 he and Tallis were granted a monopoly in the printing and selling of music. B. was the founder of the English school of madrigal writers and also composed music for the virginals, but his church music represents his most important work.

BYRON, George Gordon, 6th baron (1788-1824). British poet. Born in London, he succeeded his great-uncle in the title in 1798. He was ed. at Harrow and Cambridge, and pub. the juvenile poems *Hours of Idleness* in 1807. Their harsh criticism by the *Edinburgh Review* provoked his satire, *English Bards and Scotch Reviewers* (1809). He then undertook the tour of Portugal, Spain, and the Balkans, which he described in the first 2 cantos of *Childe Harold.* Their publication in 1812 made him famous overnight, while the series of Oriental verse romances which followed were even more successful. In 1815 he m. Anne Milbanke, but a year later a separation ensued which caused such a scandal that B. was hounded out of England. He first settled in Switzerland, where he met Shelley, and under his influence wrote *The Prisoner of Chillon* (1816), the 3rd canto of *Childe Harold* (1816), and *Manfred* (1817). The next 3 years he spent in Venice, where in spite of his debauched life he produced much of his finest work, incl. *Beppo* (1818), the 4th canto of *Childe Harold* (1818), and *Mazeppa* (1819), and began work on his masterpiece, *Don Juan* (1819-24). In 1819 he removed to Ravenna, as the lover of Countess Guiccioli, and there dabbled in Italian revolutionary politics, and wrote his rhetorical series of tragedies and the masterly *Vision of Judgment* (1822). He sailed for Greece in 1823, in order to aid the Greek struggle for independence, but d. of fever at Missolonghi in 1824. His writings, his life and his death contributed to make him the patron saint of romanticism and revolutionary liberalism in 19th cent. Europe.

BYRON. A portrait of Lord Byron by Richard Westall, painted in 1813 at the height of the poet's early fame. *Photo: Courtesy of the National Portrait Gallery.*

BYZANTINE (bizan'tīn) **ART.** A style of painting, architecture, etc., which originated in Byzantium (4th-5th cents.) and spread to Italy, throughout the Balkans, and to Russia, where it survived until modern times. It is a mixture of Greek and Oriental elements, and is characterized by the use of rich colours, particularly gold, geometrical designs on a flat surface, distorted figures, and (in architecture) the use of the dome supported on pendentives. Classical examples of B. architecture are St Sophia, Constantinople, and St Mark's, Venice. A modern example is Westminster Cathedral. The first great Italian painters to break away from the formalism of the B. style were Cimabue and Giotto, who painted religious subjects in a naturalistic style.

BYZANTINE EMPIRE. The Eastern Roman Empire, with its capital at Constantinople (Byzantium). The Emperor Constantine removed his capital to Constantinople in A.D. 330, but it was not until 364 that the Empire was finally divided into E. and W. halves. When the W. Empire was overrun by barbarian invaders, the B.E. stood firm, and Justinian I (527-565) temporarily recovered Italy, N. Africa, and parts of Spain. During the 7th cent. Syria, Egypt and N. Africa were lost to the Arabs, who twice besieged Constantinople (673-7, 718), but the Byzantines maintained their hold on Asia Minor. The Iconoclastic controversy of the 8th and 9th cents. brought the emperors into conflict with the papacy, and in 867 the Greek Church broke with the Roman. Under the Macedonian dynasty (867-1056) the B.E. reached the height of its prosperity; the Bulgars proved a formidable danger, but after a long struggle were finally crushed in 1018 by Basil II. After Basil's death the B.E. declined, and in 1071-3 the Seljuk Turks conquered most of Asia Minor. In 1204 the W. crusaders sacked Constantinople and set Baldwin of Flanders on the throne. The Latin Empire was overthrown in 1261, and the B.E. maintained a precarious existence, until in 1453 the Turks captured Constantinople. The B.E. rendered great services to civilization, as the guardian of Greek culture and Roman law during the Dark Ages, as the centre whence Christian civilization penetrated the Balkans and Russia, and as the bulwark of Christendom against Moslems and barbarians.

BYZANTINE LITERATURE. Written mainly in the Gk. *koinē*, a form of Greek accepted as the literary language of the 1st cent. A.D. and increasingly separate from the spoken tongue of the people, it is chiefly concerned with theology, history, and commentaries on the Greek classics. Its chief authors are the theologians St Basil, Gregory of Nyssa, Gregory of Nazianzus, Chrysostom (4th cent. A.D.), and John of Damascus (8th cent.); the historians Zosimus (*c.* 500), Procopius (6th cent.),

Bryennius and his wife Comnena (*c.* 1100), and Georgius Acropolita (1220–82); and the encyclopaedist Suidas (*c.* 975). Drama was non-existent and poetry, save for the hymns of the 6–8th cents., scanty and stilted, but there were many popular saints' lives.

BYZANTIUM. Ancient Greek city on the Bosphorus, founded by the Megarians *c.* 660 B.C. In A.D. 330 the capital of the Roman Empire was transferred there by Constantine the Great, who renamed it Constantinople (q.v.). Its Turkish name Istanbul (q.v.) is commonly used today.

C

Third letter of the alphabet. It corresponds to Heb. *gimel* and Gk *gamma*, both derived from the Semitic word for 'camel'. Originally representing a hard *g*, it was used by the Romans for *k* also.

In the Roman system the numeral C stands for a hundred.

CABA'L. A clique of scheming politicians; applied particularly to Charles II's ministry (1667-73) whose initials made up the word - C(lifford), A(shley), B(uckingham), A(rlington), and L(auderdale).

CABBAGE. A plant (*Brassica oleracea*) of the family Cruciferae, allied to the turnip and wild charlock. It is an important table vegetable, and the numerous cultivated varieties - all probably descended from the wild cabbage or seakale - include kale, Brussels sprouts, common cabbage, savoy, cauliflower, sprouting broccoli, and kohlrabi.

CABBALA. *See* KABBALA.

CĀ'BER, Tossing the (Gaelic *cabar*, a pole). Scottish athletic sport. The C. is a tapering tree-trunk, 6.1m (20ft) long. The tosser rests the C. on his shoulder, holding the thin end which he raises till it is about level with his elbow, runs forward as the C. begins to topple over, and hurls it into the air. A champion may achieve throws of over 12m (40ft).

CABI'NDA or **Kabinda.** Enclave on the African coast between the Congo Rep. and Zaïre, a dependency of Angola (q.v.); and also its cap. of the same name, pop. 22,000. There are oil reserves. Area 7,770 sq.km (3,000 sq.m); pop. (1975) 82,000. It has made claims to separate independence, and rebel activity continues.

CABINET. In Britain the committee of ministers (selected by the PM) holding the most important executive offices, who decide the govt's policy. The C. system originated in the 'C. councils' (C. meaning a small room, and hence implying secrecy), or sub-committees of the Privy Council, which under the Stuarts undertook specialized tasks. Under William III it became customary for the king to select his ministers from the party with a parliamentary majority. When George I ceased to attend C. meetings, the office of PM came into being, to supply a chairman for C. meetings; Walpole is usually considered the first, although the office was not legally recognized until 1905. Cabinet policy is a collective one, and a vote of censure on one minister usually involves the whole C. Meetings are strictly secret, and almost invariably confined to members; minutes are taken by the Sec. of the Cabinet, a high civil servant. In the USA a C. system developed early, the term being used from 1793, though it is not responsible as in Britain for initiating legislation. Members are selected by the Pres. and, again contrary to British practice, may neither be members of either house of Congress nor speak there, being responsible to the Pres. alone.

In Britain the Leader of the Opposition (when a Conservative) appoints certain of his followers to cover foreign affairs, finance, etc., and they are known collectively as the 'Shadow Cabinet'. In the case of the Labour Party the choice of the 'Shadow Cabinet', or Parliamentary Committee, is made by election among members of the Parliamentary Labour Party. The tradition of secrecy for cabinet discussions was breached in books by R. Crossman, B. Castle (qq.v), etc.

CA'BOT, John (*c.* 1450-98). Genoese navigator and discoverer of the N. American mainland. He was naturalized a Venetian, and made many voyages to the Levant. In 1484 he moved to London; and in 1496 C. with his three sons was commissioned by Henry VII to discover lands hitherto unknown. On 2 May 1497, he sailed from Bristol, and after 52 days he landed on Cape Breton Island (which he thought was the N.E. coast of Asia). In 1498 he sailed again and touched Greenland.

His 2nd son, **Sebastian C.** (1474-1557) was cartographer to Henry VIII of England, and then similarly served Ferdinand of Spain. In 1526-30 he explored the Brazilian coast and the river Plate. Returning to England he planned a voyage to China by way of the N.E. passage, encouraged the formation of the Co. of Merchant Adventurers of London in 1551, and in 1553 and 1556 directed the Co.'s expeditions to Russia.

CABOT. A painting of John Cabot by Menescardi Giustino, from the Ducal Palace, Venice. *Photo: Mansell Collection.*

CABRAL (kabrahl'), **Pedro Alvarez** (*c.* 1460-1526). Portuguese explorer. Setting sail from Lisbon March 1500 for the East Indies, he accidentally reached Brazil by taking a course too far west. He claimed the country for

Portugal 25 April, Spain not having followed up Vicente Pinzón's landing there earlier in the year. Sailing on round Africa, he lost 7 of his fleet of 13 ships (Diaz being one of those drowned), and landed in Mozambique, which he was the first to describe accurately. Proceeding to India, he negotiated the first Indo-Portuguese treaties for trade, and returned to Lisbon July 1501.

CABRINI (kahbrē'nē), **Frances** (1850–1917). The first R.C. saint in USA. B. in Lombardy, she founded the Missionary Sisters of the Sacred Heart in America, and estab. many schools and hospitals in the care of her nuns. She was canonized in 1946.

CACHALOT (kash'-) or **sperm-whale** (*Physeter catodon*). The largest of the toothed whales. It has a large blunt snout, with the nostrils opening above at the tip, and an enormous head. The male may attain a length of 18m (60ft); the female is only half that size. The C. favours the warmer oceans and is gregarious; it is much sought by whalers on account of its spermaceti.

CACTOBLASTIS. Genus of moths of the family Pyralidae. The most important species is *C. cactorum*, whose caterpillars feed on the prickly pear (*Opuntia*). For this reason they have been introduced into Australia in order to check the prickly pear menace.

CACTUS. Typical genus of plants of the family Cactaceae, and in common speech applied to the whole family. They are recognized by their woody axis being overlaid with an enlarged fleshy stem, which assumes various forms and is usually covered with spines. The leaves are usually very much reduced, and frequently are absent. The flowers are often large and brightly coloured. The fruit is fleshy and often edible, as in the case of the prickly pear.

The Cactaceae are a New World family, though some species are found in the warmer parts of the Old and others have been introduced from the New to the Old, e.g. in the Mediterranean area, and have become a pest. They grow in the driest and rockiest situations.

CADARACHE (kahdahrahsh'). Location of a French nuclear research centre, N.E. of Aix-en-Provence, Bouches-du-Rhône department.

CADDIS FLY. Common name for all the insects forming the order Trichoptera. They are moth-like in appearance, their wings covered with hairs, and their mouth-parts are of the biting type. They feed on the juices of plants. Their larvae are aquatic.

CADE, Jack (d. 1450). English rebel. A prosperous Kentish landowner, he took the lead when the men of Kent rose in 1450 against the misgovernment of Henry VI. He defeated the royal forces at Sevenoaks and occupied London, whereupon under promise of reforms and pardon the rebels dispersed. But C. was then hunted down and killed near Heathfield, Sussex.

CÁDIZ (Span. kah'dēth). Spanish city and naval base, cap. and seaport of the prov. of C., standing on C. Bay, an inlet of the Atlantic, 103km (64m) S. of Seville. Probably founded by the Phoenicians about 1100 B.C., it was a centre for the tin trade with Cornwall. It was recaptured from the Moors by the king of Castile in 1262, and rose to great importance after the discovery of America in 1492. The English burned it in 1596. Modern development was restricted by its peninsular location until a bridge to the further shore of C. Bay was completed 1969. Pop. (1970) 135,745.

CACTUS. Even in the Galapagos Islands, more than 1100 km (700 m) out in the Pacific, cacti have no difficulty in surviving. In the centre is the candelabra cactus *(Jasminocereus)* and, to the right and left, opuntias. *Photo: Heather Angel.*

CA'DMIUM. Symbol Cd., at. wt. 112.41, at. no. 48. C. is a soft silver-white metal. It is used in standard cells for the accurate determination of electromotive force (e.m.f.) in electroplating; as a constituent of one of the lowest-melting alloys; and in bearing alloys with low coefficients of friction. It is also used as control rods in nuclear reactors on account of its high absorption of neutrons. Its industrial importance has greatly increased in recent years.

CADWA'LADER (d. c. 634). Welsh hero. The son of Cadwallon, King of Gwynedd, N. Wales, he defeated and slew Eadwine of Northumbria in 633. About a year later he was killed in battle.

CAECILIA (sēsi'lia). Typical genus of amphibians of the order Gymnophiona. Small worm-like animals, destitute of limbs, they have a wide distribution in tropical countries.

CAEDMON (kad'mon) (7th cent. A.D.). First English Christian poet. Bede says that he was a cowherd in the monastery of Whitby, when in a dream a stranger ordered him to sing, whereupon on waking he produced a poem on the Creation. Of this Bede appends a Latin translation, but the original Old English poem is preserved in some MSS. C. then became an inmate of the monastery and composed poems on sacred subjects.

CAEN (kaṅ). Cap. of Calvados dept, France, on the r. Orne, linked by canal with the English Channel 14.5km (9m) N.E. The church of St Étienne was founded by William the Conqueror, and the univ. by Henry VI of England in 1432. The town was badly damaged in 5 weeks of heavy fighting in the S.W.W. before its capture by the

British on 9 July 1944. It is a business centre, with ironworks, and electric and electronic industries. Caen building stone is famous. Pop. (1975) 182,700.

CAERLEON (kahrlē'on). Small town in Gwent co., Wales, on the Usk, 5km (3m) N.E. of Newport. It was on the site of the Roman fortress of Isca and there is a Legionary Museum and remains of an amphitheatre. Pop. *c.* 5,000.

CAERNA'RVON (kahr-). Town in Gwynedd, Wales, the admin. HQ of the region. On the S.W. shore of the Menai Strait, it was a Roman station, and is a market town and port. The first Prince of Wales (later Edward II) was born in C. Castle, and in modern times Edward VIII was invested in 1911 and Prince Charles in 1969. The Earl of Snowdon became Constable of the castle in 1963. Pop. (1972) 9,060.

CAERNARVONSHIRE. Former co. in N.W. Wales, merged in Gwynedd in 1974.

CAERPHILLY (kahrfil'li). Market town in Mid Glamorgan, Wales, 11km (7m) N. of Cardiff. The castle was built by Edward I. The town is noted for its mild C. cheese. Pop. (1972 41,480.

CAESAR. Name of one of the most powerful families of ancient Rome. The greatest of the line was Gaius Julius Caesar (q.v.), whose grand-nephew and adopted son Augustus assumed the name of C., and in turn passed it on to his adopted son Tiberius. Henceforth it was borne by the successive emperors, becoming a title of the Roman rulers. The titles Tsar in Russia and Kaiser in Germany are both derived from C.

CAESAR, Gaius Julius (*c.* 102–44 B.C.). Roman statesman, general, and founder of the Empire. Descended from a distinguished patrician family, his sympathies were from the first with the popular or democratic party. He m. Cornelia, daughter of Cinna, and refused to divorce her at Sulla's bidding - whereupon he had to flee to Bithynia.

In 65 B.C. he was elected Aedile and nearly ruined himself with his lavish amusements for the Roman population. In 63 he was elected chief pontiff, although he was a freethinker. Two years later he was appointed governor of Further Spain. Returning to Rome in 60, he formed with Pompey and Crassus the first triumvirate, and was given the two provinces of Cisalpine and Transalpine Gaul. For the next 13 years he was almost continuously engaged in campaigning in Gaul. He defeated the Germans under Ariovistus, and sold thousands of the Belgic tribes into slavery. In 55 C. crossed into Britain, and repeated his visit in the next year. Two years later the Gauls under Vercingetorix rose in revolt and in 51 C. crushed them completely. The series of campaigns thus completed was described by C. himself in his Commentaries.

C.'s governorship expired in 49, and of his two partners Crassus was dead and Pompey was now a rival. He had many enemies in Rome, and Pompey was authorized to lead an army against him. Declaring 'the die is cast', C. crossed the Rubicon from Gaul into Italy, and the Civil War began. In 48 C. followed Pompey to Epirus, defeated him at Pharsalus, and chased him to Egypt, where he was murdered. For the next 9 months C. dallied with Cleopatra, by whom he had a son; then marching into Asia Minor, he defeated King Pharnaces in a lightning campaign which he described in the words *Veni, vidi, vici* (I came, I saw, I conquered). Returning to Italy, he moved from triumph to triumph over the Pompeian party, and in 46 he was firmly established in the seat of power at Rome. He planned to reform the calendar, take a census of the Empire, establish Roman colonies overseas, and improve the law of local govt, but the vigour with which he prosecuted his plans aroused a fear that he was aiming at a personal dictatorship. A band of disgruntled republicans with Brutus and Cassius as their leaders formed a conspiracy to kill him, and on 15 March 44 B.C. - the Ides of March - he was stabbed to death in the Senate House.

CAESAREA. *See* QISARAYA.

CAESAREAN SECTION. The removal of a child from the womb through an incision in the abdominal wall. Julius Caesar is said to have entered the world in this way: hence the name.

CAESIUM (sē'sium). Chemical element. Symbol Cs, at. wt. 132.91, at. no. 55. It is used in the manufacture of photo-electric cells. Highly radioactive C. (Cs-137, half-life 30 years), a waste product from nuclear power-stations, is used for mass radiation and sterilization of foodstuffs, and medically for irradiation of surface tumours. *See* CLOCK.

CAETANO (kah-etah'nō), **Marcello** (1906–80). Portuguese statesman. In 1968 he succeeded Salazar as PM and introduced greater democracy until his curbs on unrest during colonial wars in Angola and Mozambique led to his overthrow by a military coup in 1974, and exile.

CAFETĒ'RIA (Span., a coffee-shop). A help-yourself restaurant; supposed to have originated in New York in the 1880s. The first English use of the word was about 1923.

CAFFEINE (kaf'fē-ïn) ($C_8H_{10}N_4O_2$). The most important member of a group of nitrogenous substances found in tea, coffee, etc., for whose stimulant effect it is partly responsible.

CAGE, John (1912-). American composer. A pupil of Schoenberg, he has re-assessed musical aesthetics, and defines the role of music as 'purposeless play'. All sounds that can be heard are to be available for musical purposes, e.g. electric buzzers and tin cans in 'Imaginary Landscape'. The artist should remain anonymous.

CAGLIARI (kahylyah'rē). City and archiepiscopal see of Sardinia, Italy, cap. of Sardinia and of C. prov., on the Gulf of Ca. The cathedral, completed 1312, was later modernized; the univ. was founded in 1626. Pop. (1978) 242,000.

CAGLIOSTRO (kahlyos'trō), **Alessandro di,** count (1743–95). Italian charlatan, whose real name was Giuseppe Balsamo. B. at Palermo, he travelled widely, married, and set up as a specialist in the occult. In Paris in 1785 he became involved in the affair of the Diamond Necklace (supposed to have been ordered by Queen Marie Antoinette, but in fact by a band of swindlers), and was imprisoned in the Bastille. Later he was arrested by the Inquisition in Rome. A sentence of death for freemasonry was commuted to one of life imprisonment. He d. in the fortress of San Leone. His *Mémoires* are not authentic.

CAGNES-SUR-MER (kany-sür-mar'). Cap. of the dept of Alpes-Maritimes, to the S.W. of Nice, France. The chateau (13–17th cent.) contains mementoes of Renoir. Pop. (1975) 23,000.

CAIN. O.T. character, the first-born son of Adam and Eve. He murdered his brother Abel from motives of jealousy, as Abel's sacrifice was more acceptable to the Lord than his own, and so became the world's first murderer.

CAIN, James Mallahan (1892-1977). American novelist. B. at Annapolis, he entered journalism and was the author of *The Postman Always Rings Twice* (1934), *Double Indemnity*, and *Mildred Pierce* (1941).

ÇA IRA (sah ērah'). Song of the French Revolution, written by a street singer, Ladré, and set to an existing tune by Bécourt, a drummer of the opera.

CAIRN. British breed of terrier dog, the original terrier of the Scottish Highlands. It is shaggy, compact, and short-legged.

CAIRNGORMS. Mountain group in Scotland, N. part of the Grampians, the highest peak being Ben Macdhui (1,309 m/4,296 ft). Aviemore (Britain's first complete holiday and sports centre) was opened in 1966, and 11 km (7m) to the S is the Highland Wild Life Park at Kincraig.

CAIRNS. Seaport of Queensland, Australia, with a fine harbour, concerned largely with the export of sugar. Pop. (1976) 39,305.

CAIRO (kī'rō). Cap. of the Arab Rep. of Egypt, on the E. bank of the Nile 13km (8m) above the apex of the Delta and 160km (100m) from the Mediterranean. El Fustat (Old Cairo) was founded by the Arabs *c.* A.D. 641, Cairo itself *c.* 1000 by the Fatimite ruler Gowhar. The city is 32km (20m) N. of the site of the ancient Egyptian centre of Memphis, and at nearby Gizeh are the Great Pyramids and the Sphinx. The Mosque of 'Amr dates from A.D. 643; the Citadel, built by Saladin in the 12th cent., contains the impressive 19th cent. Mohammed Ali mosque; and the mosque which houses the El Azhar univ. (founded 970) is the heart of traditional Islam, e.g. in its organized opposition to the liberation of women. The modern govt and business quarters reflect the importance of C. as an administrative and commercial centre, and the semi-official newspaper *al Ahram* is an influential voice in the Arab world. At Helwan 24km (15m) to the S. an industrial centre with iron and steel works powered by electricity from the Aswan High Dam is developing. There are 2 secular univs., Cairo Univ. (1908) and Ein Shams (1950). Pop. (1974) 5,715,000.

CAIRO. A view over the Nile from the Cairo tower. *Photo: Ken Lambert/Camera Press.*

CAISSON DISEASE. *See* BENDS.

CAITHNESS (kāth'nes). Co. in the extreme N.E. of Scotland, merged from 1975 in the Highland region. Wick was the admin. H.Q.

CALABAR (kal'abahr). Port and cap. of Cross River state, Nigeria, on the C. river, 64km (40m) from the sea. Rubber, timber, vegetable oils are exported. Pop. (1970) 80,000.

CALA'BRIA. Region occupying the 'toe' of Italy and comprising the provs. of Catanzaro, Cosenza, and Reggio di C. The cap. is Catanzaro; Reggio being developed as the chief industrial centre. Area 15,080 sq.km (5,820 sq.m); pop. (1977) 2,057,900. In Roman times the name C. was given to the 'heel' of Italy.

CALAIS (kahlā'). Seaport in Pas-de-Calais dept., France, 40km (25m) E.S.E. of Dover across the English Channel and 238km (148m) N. by W. of Paris. Taken by Edward III in 1347, it was saved from destruction by the personal surrender of half a dozen of its citizens, the 'Burghers of Calais' immortalized in a monument by Rodin. It was retaken by the French in the reign of Mary I in 1558. The Germans occupied C. in the S.W.W. from May 1940 to 1 Oct. 1944, when it surrendered to the Canadians. It is a fishing as well as a commercial and passenger port, and there are chemical, food, and textile industries. Pop. (1975) 100,450. The *Pas de Calais* is the Strait of Dover.

CALAMINE (kal'amīn). Pink powder (zinc oxide plus ferric oxide) used in soothing lotions and ointments, e.g. in treating eczema.

CALAS (kahlahs'), **Jean** (1698-1762). A French Protestant, who in 1761 was accused of murdering his son to prevent his joining the R.C. Church. In spite of his complete denials, he was found guilty and executed. His widow escaped to Switzerland, and enlisted the aid of Voltaire, who succeeded in getting the trial reviewed and Calas' innocence was proved. A grant was paid to the family by Louis XV.

CALCEOLARIA (kalsēolā'ria), also 'slipper flower' (Lat. *calceolus* 'slipper'). Genus of plants of the family Scrophulariaceae, native to S. America and including shrubby and herbaceous species. The brilliantly coloured flowers, much enlarged in highly cultivated greenhouse specimens, resemble pouches or 2-lipped slippers. Cs. were introduced to Europe *c.* 1830.

CALCITE (-s-). A form of calcium carbonate ($CaCO_3$) and the constituent of chalk, limestone, and marble. There are two distinct crystalline forms, viz. 'nailhead spar', where the crystals are flat and tabular in shape, and 'dog-toothed spar', with sharply pointed pyramidal crystals. Iceland spar, a variety of the first type, possesses the property of double refraction and is used in optical instruments. C. is one of the most abundant mineral constituents of the earth's crust.

CALCIUM. Chemical element, a silvery-white metal, one of the alkaline earth metals. Symbol, Ca; atomic weight 40.07; atomic number 20. It was discovered by Sir Humphry Davy in 1808 and is very widely distributed, mainly in the form of its carbonate $CaCO_3$ which occurs in a fairly pure condition as chalk and limestone. C. is an essential component of bones, teeth, shells and leaves. C. compounds are very important to the chemical industry and include lime (calcium hydroxide $Ca(OH)_2$); plaster of Paris (calcium sulphate $CaSO_4 2H_2 0$); calcium hypochlorite $CaOC1_2$ a bleaching agent; calcium nitrate ($(Ca(NO_3)_2 4H_2 0)$ a nitrogenous fertilizer; calcium carbide CaC_2 which reacts with water to give acetylene (q.v.);

calcium cyanamide ($CaCN_2$), the basis of pharmaceuticals, fertilizers and plastics incl. Melamine; calcium cyanide ($Ca(CN)_2$) used in the extraction of gold and silver and in electro-plating, and others used in baking powders, fillers for paints, etc.

CALCULATING MACHINES. *See* COMPUTER.

CALCULATOR. The hand-held electronic calculating device first commercially launched in 1971. They perform a minimum of arithmetical addition, subtraction, multiplication and division, and the more complex cope with square root, logarithm, sine, cosine; etc., so that they approach the sophistication of a computer (q.v.) and can be programmed, and have a continuous memory to retain data and programmes even when switched off.

CALCULUS. Name given to the methods of calculation which are used to deal with such matters as changing speeds, problems of flight, varying stresses set up in the framework of a bridge, electrical circuits, and in general the study of quantities which are continuously varying.

The INTEGRAL C. deals with the method of summation or adding together of the effects of continuously varying quantities. The DIFFERENTIAL C. deals in a similar way with rates of change. Many of its applications arose from the study of speed. Each of these branches of the C. deals with small quantities which during the process are made smaller and smaller, hence both comprise the INFINITESIMAL C. Differential equations represent complex rates of change and integrals are the empirical solutions. If no known processes are available, the integrations are made graphically or by machine.

The C. originated with Archimedes in the 3rd cent. B.C. in the means he devised for finding the areas of curved figures and for drawing tangents to curves; but his ideas could not germinate until the 17th cent., when Descartes showed how geometrical curves could be described and analysed by means of algebraic formulae. Then Fermat and later Newton and Leibniz immensely advanced the study.

CALCUTTA. City of the Rep. of India, on the Hooghli, the most westerly mouth of the Ganges, some 130km (80m) N. of the Bay of Bengal. It is the cap. of W. Bengal and was the seat of govt of British India 1773-1912.

C. was founded 1686-90 by Job Charnock, head of Hooghli factory of the East India Co., when Hooghli was attacked by Mogul troops. C. was captured by Suraj-ud-Dowlah in 1756, during the Anglo-French wars in India, and it was in a small dungeon in the original Fort William (completed 1702) that he confined 146 British prisoners on 20 June 1756, only 23 surviving the night. This incident became known as the *Black Hole of C.*, and although the story has been disputed it has a foundation in fact. In 1757 C. was re-taken by Clive, who began the new Fort William in the centre of the Maidan or Great Park (completed 1773). Other striking buildings incl. a magnificent Jain temple and the palaces of former Indian princes; and the Law Courts and Government House, survivals of the British Raj. C. has an enormous overseas trade, and is chiefly a great commercial and industrial centre. Industries incl. engineering, shipbuilding, jute and other textiles. Across the river is Howrah, and there is a new port, Haldia, halfway between C. and the sea, to handle bulk cargoes, which is the focus of such additional industrial development as oil refineries, petrochemical plants, and fertilizer factories. Educational institutions incl. the Univ. of Calcutta (1857), oldest of several univs.; the Visva Bharati at Santiniketan, founded by Tagore; the Bose Research Institute; and a fine museum. Pop. (1971) 7,005,000.

CALDECOTT, Randolph (1846-86). British book illustrator, best known for illustrations to Washington Irving and his work for children: *John Gilpin* and *The House that Jack Built.*

CALDER, Alexander (1898-1976). American artist. B. in Philadelphia, Pennsylvania, he studied as an engineer, but in 1923 turned to art and originated 'stabiles' in 1931, and in 1932 'mobiles', with which latter his name is usually associated. One of his most famous large-scale mobiles is 'Point 125' (1957) in the lobby of Kennedy Airport, N.Y.

CALDERON DE LA BARCA, Pedro (1600-81). Spanish dramatist and poet. B. in Madrid, he studied law at Salamanca (1613-19). In 1620 and 1622 he was successful in the poetical contests at Madrid; and while still writing dramas served in the army in Milan and the Netherlands (1625-35). By 1636 his first vol. of plays was pub. and he had been made master of the revels at the court of Philip IV, receiving a knighthood in 1637. In 1640 he assisted in the suppression of the Catalan rebellion. After the death of his mistress he became a Franciscan in 1650, was ordained in 1651, and appointed to a prebend of Toledo in 1653. He resumed playwriting when made honorary chaplain to the king in 1663. Many of these later dramas were *autos sacramentales,* outdoor plays for the festival of the Holy Eucharist. Most famous of his regular plays, of which some 118 survive, are the tragedies *El pintor de su deshonra, El Alcalde de Zalamea, El Médico de su honra* and *El Mayor monstruo los celos*; the historical *El Principe constante*; the dashing intrigue *La Dama duende*; the philosophical *La Vida es sueño*; and the religious *El Purgatorio de San Patricio.* He died in poverty.

CALDWELL, Erskine Preston (1903-). American novelist. B. in Georgia, he worked among the poor whites of the South as a journalist, cotton picker and stage assistant and achieved sensational success with *Tobacco Road* (1932), later dramatized and filmed, telling of a squalid share-cropping family in the back lands of the cotton country, which was banned in many places.

CALDY ISLAND. Island off the coast of Dyfed, Wales, nr Tenby. The small Cistercian monastery is famous for its manufacture of perfume.

CALEDONIAN CANAL. A waterway across the N.W. of Scotland, linking the Atlantic and the North Sea. Of its length of 98km (61m) only a stretch of 37km (23m) is artificial, the rest being composed of lochs Lochy, Oich, and Ness. The C. was built by Thomas Telford, 1803-23.

CALENDAR. A system devised for the distribution of time into periods convenient for the purposes of civil life. The word comes from the Lat. *kalendae* or *calendae,* the first day of each month on which solemn proclamation was made of the appearance of the new moon. All early Cs. except the ancient Egyptian were lunar. The C. in use over a great part of the world today rests on the Roman C. as revised by Julius Caesar and Augustus, but many modifications have been made in the course of time.

Quite early in their history the Romans had a civil year of 355 days; but the seasons depended on the solar year which was about 11 days longer than the lunar, and to bring the 2 years into harmony, additional days were intercalated. In 46 B.C. Caesar introduced the year of 365 days, and an extra day in every 4th year. He took the length of the solar year as 365 days, 6 hours. Actually, however, it is only 365 days, 5 hrs. 48 mins. 46 secs. and through the centuries the discrepancy mounted up until in the 16th cent. it amounted to 10 days. In 1582 Pope Gregory XIII proclaimed his Gregorian or New Style C., with the aim of putting the Julian error right and also to secure uniformity as to the date at which each year should be reckoned as beginning. At first only states in the Roman obedience accepted the new C., but in the 18th cent. Protestant states began to fall into line. Britain adopted it in 1751, by which date the accumulated error amounted to 11 days, so it was enacted that the day following 2 Sept. 1752 should be renumbered 14 Sept. France, which had adopted the Gregorian C. in 1582, abandoned it from 1793 to 1805 in favour of the Revolutionary Calendar. Turkey and Russia did not adopt it until 1917, and the Eastern Orthodox Church in Russia and the Balkans not until 1923.

About 1930 the League of Nations decided that it would be advantageous to change to what is now called the World C., i.e. equal quarters perpetual, with an extra-calendrical day at the end of the year and a similar day in the summer every Leap Year. The proposal is still before the U.N. The 8-day week involved brought objections from orthodox Jewry. *See also* ISLAM.

CA'LGARY. City of Alberta, Canada, on the Bow in the foothills of the Rockies: at 1,048 m (3,440 ft) it is one of the highest Canadian towns. Founded as Fort C. by the N.W. Mounted Police in 1875, it was reached by the C.P.R. in 1885, and with the discovery of oil in 1914 rapidly developed. It is now the oil and financial centre of Alberta and W Canada, and the commercial heart of the city, bounded on the N by the Bow, is known as the 'Golden Crescent'. It has oil-linked industries, fertilizer factories, and agricultural industries, e.g. flour mills, and is also a tourist centre, notably for the annual Calgary Exhibition and Stampede in July. The Univ. of C. became independent of Alberta Univ. 1966. Pop. (1979) 550,000.

CALGARY. Once used for transporting food to cowboy teams on the range, the 'chuck-wagon' now plays a picturesque part in the events of Stampede Week. Here, one races down the track urged on by yelling horsemen. *Photo: Karsh/Camera Press.*

CALHOUN (kalhōōn'), **John Caldwell** (1782-1850). American statesman. B. in S. Carolina, of Scots-Irish descent, he was elected Vice-President in 1824, and again in 1828. Throughout he was a defender of the 'States' Rights' as against the Federal Government and the institution of Negro slavery.

CALI (kahlē'). City in S.W. Colombia, in the Cauca Valley 975m (3,200 ft) a.s.l. Founded 1536, C. has textile, sugar and engineering industries. Pop. (1972) 1,022,200.

CALIBRÄ'TION. Comparison of scale marks with a standard, as in testing the accuracy of measuring instruments.

CA'LICO. A plain woven cotton material; the name derives from Calicut on the Malabar coast, an original source of India Cs.

CALIFORNIA. Pacific state of the USA called the Golden State, originally because of its gold mines, but more recently because of its sunshine. The Sierra Nevada runs along the E. boundary and incl. the Yosemite Nat. Park and Mt Whitney (4,418 m/14,494 ft) highest mtn in the continental USA, excl. Alaska: to the S.E. is Death Valley 86m (282ft) below sea level. Lower and more disconnected than the Sierra are the Coast Ranges. Between the 2 features lies the great valley of C., watered by the Sacramento, the San Joaquin, and tributaries which together drain most of the state. Here, and in reclaimed desert regions such as the Imperial Valley (irrigated from the Colorado) vast quantities of fruit are produced in a year-long growing season. Its fruit and nuts (mainly pistachios and almonds) are more valuable than its vegetables, wheat, rice and cotton, and in 1980 it was the leading agricultural state of the USA. The Mojave and Colorado deserts are in themselves tourist attractions, as are Lake Tahoe, the Sequoia Nat. Park, and the Monterey Peninsula. The art museum founded by Paul Getty (1892-1976), and built in the style of a Roman villa, is at Malibu. California wines are famous.

C. was first settled by the Spaniards in 1769, formed part of Mexico 1822-48, when it was ceded to the USA, and became a state of the union in 1850. The discovery of gold in 1848 led to the gold rush of the 'forty-niners' in the following year, but oil has replaced gold as the leading mineral; asbestos, boron, gypsum, tungsten, etc., are also worked. There are also great reserves of energy (geothermal) in the hot water which lies beneath much of the state. Industries incl. aerospace (aircraft and missiles), oil refining, food products (canned and frozen), electrical and electronic goods, fishing, etc. The chief towns are Los Angeles and San Francisco; Sacramento is the cap. Area 411,013 sq.km (158,693 sq.m); pop. (1970) 19,953,134.

CALIFORNIA, Lower. *See* BAJA CALIFORNIA.

CALIFORNIUM. *See* TRANSURANIUM ELEMENTS.

CALI'GULA, Gaius Caesar (A.D. 12-41). Roman emperor. The son of Germanicus, he ascended the throne in 37 on the death of Tiberius. He revealed a tyrannical character, and is reputed to have become mad. He was assassinated by an officer of his guard.

CALIPH (kā'lif; Arab. *khalifah,* successor). Title adopted by Mohammed's successors as civic and religious heads of the world of Islam. The first C. was Abu Bekr (d. 634). The caliphate was nominally elective, but became hereditary in practice, being held by the Ummayyad dynasty 661-750, and then by the Abbasids. During the 10th cent. the political and military power passed to the leader of the C.'s Turkish bodyguard; about the same time an independent Fatimite caliphate sprang up in Egypt. After the death of the last Abbasid C. (1258) the title was claimed by a number of Moslem chieftains in Egypt, Turkey, and India. The most powerful of these were the Turkish sultans of the Ottoman Empire. In 1924 the last Turkish C. was deposed by Kemal Atatürk.

CALLAGHAN (kal'ahan), **(Leonard) James** (1912–). British Labour politician. The son of a chief petty officer in the RN, in which he himself served during the S.W.W., he entered the Civil Service as a tax officer in 1929. In 1950–1 he was parliamentary and financial sec. to the Admiralty, and as Chancellor of the Exchequer 1964–7, he introduced a corporation and capital gains tax and in 1966, to promote the effective use of manpower, a selective employment tax. Resigning following devaluation in 1967, he was Home Secretary 1967–70, and as Foreign Secretary 1974 dealt with renegotiation of Britain's Common Market membership. In 1976 he succeeded Wilson as PM in a period of increasing economic stress, and in 1977 entered into a pact with the Liberals to maintain his govt. in office. Strikes in the winter of 1978–9 led to his being the first P.M., since Ramsay MacDonald in 1924, to be forced into an election by the will of the Commons, and he was defeated at the polls in May 1979. In 1980 he was under pressure from the Left wing and resigned the leadership.

CALLAGHAN. James Callaghan and the South African Prime Minister, John Vorster, consult on the problem of Rhodesia. *Photo: Jan Kopec/Camera Press.*

CALLAO (kahlyah'ō). Chief commercial and fishing port of Peru, 12km (7m) S.W. of Lima. Founded 1537, it was destroyed by an earthquake in 1746. It is Peru's main naval base, and produces fertilizers, etc. Pop. (1973) 321,700.

CALLAS, Maria. Stage-name of the lyric soprano Maria Calogeropoulos (1923–77), b. in N.Y. of Greek stock. With a voice of fine range and a gift for dramatic expression, she excelled in opera, her roles incl. *Norma, Madame Butterfly, Aïda, Lucia* and *Medea.*

CALLICRATES (kali'kratēz) (5th cent. B.C.). Athenian architect (with Ictinus) of the Parthenon.

CALLIGRAPHY (kali'grafi). The art of beautiful writing, incl. both formal writing with an edged pen and informal writing. Modern letter forms have gradually evolved from originals which were shaped by the tools used to make them – the flat brush and chisel on stone, the stylus on wax and clay, and the reed and quill on papyrus and skin.

The principal formal hands used in early books were written in capital letters or majuscules. In the 4th and 5th cents. A.D. books were written in square capitals derived from classical Roman inscriptions of which the Trajan column is the outstanding example. The rustic capitals of the same period were written more freely, and the uncial capitals, more rounded, were used from the 4th to the 8th cents. During this period the cursive hand was also developing and the interplay of this with the formal hands, coupled with the need for speedier writing, led to the minuscule forms. During the 7th cent. the half-uncial was developed with ascending and descending strokes and was adopted by all countries under Roman rule. The cursive forms developed differently in different countries and in particular in Italy the beautiful italic script was evolved which became the model for italic type faces. The modern calligraphic revival in Britain was largely due to Edward Johnston.

CALLI'MACHUS (*c.* 310–240 B.C.). Greek poet and critic. B. in Cyrene, he taught in Alexandria where he was head of the great library. He is best known for his epigrams.

CALLIOPE (kalī'ōpē). In Greek mythology, the muse of epic poetry.

CALLI'STŌ. In Greek myth a nymph beloved by Zeus (Jupiter), hence one of the moons of Jupiter, distant from the planet c. 1,883,000 km (1,170,000 m), and rather larger than Mercury. The surface has icy patches and dark brown blotches.

CALLOT (kahloh'), **Jacques** (1592–1635). French engraver and painter. He engraved about 1,600 pieces, of which the best known are his 'Miseries of War', his 'Sieges', 'Fairs', 'Temptation of St. Anthony', and 'Conversion of St. Paul'.

CALMETTE (kahlmet'), **Albert** (1863–1933). French bacteriologist. A follower of Pasteur, in 1921 he developed with Camille Guérin (1872–1961) the BCG vaccine effective against tuberculosis.

CALOMEL. Mercurous chloride, Hg_2Cl_2, a white, heavy powder, valuable as a purgative in infections of the bowel.

CALORIE (Lat. *calor,* heat). Unit of quantitative measurement of heat. The original small C. was the amount of heat necessary to raise 1 gram of water through 1°C. But the word is nowadays nearly always used to signify the large C, or kilo-calorie, the amount of heat required to raise 1 litre of water through 1°C – chiefly by dietitians as a measure of the heat-giving properties of foodstuffs. 28 grams (1oz) of protein yields 120, carbohydrate 110, fat 270, and alcohol 200 large calories.

CALPE (kal'pē). Name of GIBRALTAR in antiquity.

CALTANISSE'TTA. Town in Sicily, Italy, 96km (60m) S.E. of Palermo. It is the chief centre of the island's sulphur industry, and has a fine baroque cathedral. Pop. (1971) 64,700.

CA'LVARY (Lat. *calvaria,* a skull). The place of Christ's execution at Jerusalem; also called Golgotha in Aramaic. Two chief sites are suggested. One is that where the Church of the Sepulchre now stands; the other, first suggested by General Gordon, is the skull-like hill beyond the Damascus gate.

The name C. is further applied to a monument commemorating the Crucifixion.

CALVIN, John (1509-64). Swiss reformer and theologian. B. at Noyon, Picardy, he studied theology and then law, and about 1533 adopted reformed opinions and soon came to the front as an evangelical preacher. In 1534 he was obliged to leave Paris and retired to Basle, where he studied Hebrew and wrote his *Institutes of the Christian Religion,* pub. in 1536. In the same year he accepted an invitation to go to Geneva, and assist in the work of reformation. But in 1538 he was expelled because of public resentment at the many and too-drastic changes he introduced. At Strasbourg he m. a widow, and devoted himself to translating the N.T. In 1541 the Genevans invited him back. He accepted and established in the face of strong opposition a theocracy. The black mark on his rule is the burning of Servetus for heresy in 1553. He supported the Huguenots in their struggle in France, and afforded a refuge to English Protestants driven overseas by the Marian persecutions. His theological system is known as Calvinism (q.v.), and his Church government as Presbyterianism (q.v.).

CALVINISM. That interpretation of Christian doctrine that was formulated by John Calvin (q.v.) and became predominant in Scotland, parts of Switzerland and Holland, and has greatly influenced Protestant theology to the present time. Its central doctrine is that of predestination, by which is meant that certain souls (the elect) are predestined by God to salvation (although this does not obviate the need for faith and perseverance), whilst others are doomed to eternal damnation. C. stresses the total depravity of human nature, but insists that salvation is offered through the sacrifice of Christ, made only on behalf of the elect. Faith and repentance are also necessary, but the theory of irresistible grace implies that the operation of Divine grace which makes these possible is predetermined. C. is marked by logic and lucidity, but even those churches originally C. in doctrine rarely accept it in its strict sense nowadays. Nevertheless during the present century there has been a marked revival of Neo-Calvinist thought, largely through the influence of Karl Barth (q.v.).

CALYPSO (kalip'sō). Greek sea-nymph who waylaid the homeward-bound Odysseus for seven years. Also the beguiling witty and scurrilous ballads of local life sung in the W Indies, espec. Trinidad.

CAMAGÜEY. City in Cuba, cap. of C. prov., in the centre of the is. Founded *c.* 1514, it has a 17th cent. cathedral. Pop. (1973) 260,000.

CAMARGO (kahmahrgō'), **Marie-Anne de Cupis de** (1710-70). French dancer. B. in Brussels, she became a ballet star in Paris in 1726. She was the first ballerina to adopt a shortened skirt, and the first to attain the *entrechat à quatre.* She retired in 1751. The Camargo Society, founded in 1930, was named after her.

CAMARGUE (kamahrg'). The marshy area of the Rhône delta, S. of Arles, France: area *c.* 780 sq.km (300 sq.m). It is noted for the bulls and horses bred there, and for the nature reserve rich in bird life which forms the southern part.

CAMBODIA (kambō'dia). *See* KAMPUCHEA.

CAMBORNE-REDRUTH. Town in Cornwall, 16km (10m) S.W. of Truro. World price rises for tin have made the mines here once more economic and there is a School of Metalliferous Mining. Pop. (1972) 43,000.

CAMBRAI (koṅbrā). Chief town of Nord dept., France, on the Escaut (Scheldt). Industries incl. light textiles (cambric is named after the town), confectionery, etc. Pop. (1975) 41,100. The *Peace of C.* or Ladies' Peace (1529) was concluded on behalf of Francis I of France by his mother Louise of Savoy and on behalf of Charles V by his aunt Margaret of Austria.

During the F.W.W. C. was severely damaged while in German hands. It gives its name to 2 battles: (1) Nov.-Dec. 1917, when the 3rd Army under Byng nearly succeeded in recapturing C. in an engagement in which large numbers of tanks were used for the first time; (2) 26 Aug.-5 Oct. 1918, when C. was captured during the final British offensive.

CAMBRIDGE. English city, the admin. HQ of Cambridgeshire on the river Cam (a river sometimes called by its earlier name, Granta), 82km (51m) N. of London. The site was occupied as early as 100 B.C. and a Roman settlement grew up on a slight rise in the low-lying plain, commanding a ford over the river. The most famous colleges back on to the gardens and lawns through which the Cam flows (known as the Backs) and are the chief architectural glory of the city. Other buildings incl. St Benet's church, oldest building in C.; the round church of the Holy Sepulchre; and the Guildhall (1939). Industries incl. scientific instruments, radio and electronics, paper, flour milling, and fertilizers. Pop. (1972) 98,840.

CAMBRIDGE. The 'Bridge of Sighs', St. John's College, bridges the Cam, and students enjoy their moments of leisure on the river. *Photo: Alan Hutchinson Associates/Camera Press.*

CAMBRIDGE. City of Mass., USA, facing Boston on the Charles r. It is a cultural centre, and sprang up round Harvard College (later univ.); there are many other educational institutions, incl. the Massachusetts Inst. of Technology (1861), and the John F. Kennedy School of Govt and Memorial Library. Industries incl. paper and publishing. Pop. (1970) 100,360.

CAMBRIDGESHIRE. Low-lying fen co. of E. England, formed in 1974 by the amalgamation of the former co. of Cambridgeshire and Isle of Ely (*see* ELY, Isle of), and Huntingdonshire and Peterborough (q.v.). It is low-lying, largely fenland, and its chief rivers, the Ouse and Nene are to some extent channelled through artificial courses. The soil is fertile and cereals, vegetables, fruit and dairy foods are produced. There is comparatively little industry. The admin. HQ is Cambridge; other towns are Ely, Huntingdon and Peterborough. Area 3,409 sq.km (1,316 sq.m); pop. (1978) 570,200.

CAMBRIDGE UNIVERSITY. One of the oldest of European univs., founded probably in the 12th cent., though the earliest of the existing colls. was not founded until *c.* 1280-4: *see* Table. The Chancellor is the titular, and the Vice-Chancellor the active, head. The Regent House is the legislative and executive body, with the Senate as the court of appeal. Each coll. has its own corporation, and is largely independent. The head of each coll. (in the case of men's coll. usually called the master), assisted by a council of fellows, manages its affairs.

Cambridge Colleges

Peterhouse	1280-4	Sidney Sussex	1596
Clare	1326	Downing	1800
Pembroke	1347	Girton	1869
Gonville and Caius	1348	Newnham	1871
Trinity Hall	1350	Selwyn	1882
Corpus Christi	1352	Hughes Hall	1885
King's	1441	St. Edmund's House	1896
Queens'	1448	New Hall	1954
St. Catherine's	1473	Churchill	1960
Jesus	1496	Darwin	1964
Christ's	1505	Wolfson College	1965
St. John's	1511	Lucy Cavendish Coll.	1966
Magdalene	1542	Clare Hall	1966
Trinity	1546	Fitzwilliam	1966
Emmanuel	1584	University	1966
		Robinson College	1978

CAMBY'SES (reigned 529-522 B.C.). Emperor of Persia. Succeeding his father Cyrus, he assassinated his brother Smerdis and conquered Egypt in 525. Here he outraged many of the native religious customs, and was said to have become mad. On his way back he d. in Syria by suicide or accident.

CAMDEN, William (1551-1623). English antiquary. B. in London, he pub. his *Britannia* in 1586, and became headmaster of Westminster School in 1593. The C. SOCIETY was founded in 1838.

CAMDEN. Industrial city of New Jersey, USA, on the Delaware, linked with Philadelphia by the Benjamin Franklin suspension bridge (1926). The Walt Whitman House, where the poet lived 1884-92, is a museum. Pop. (1970) 456,300.

CAMDEN TOWN GROUP. British art group (1911-13) based in Camden Town, London, and incl. Sickert, Spencer Gore and Harold Gilman.

CAMEL. A large cud-chewing mammal (*Camelus*) of the order Artiodactyla with a humped back, and differing from typical ruminants by having a three-chambered stomach, tusk-like canines above and below and a similar isolated outer upper incisor, and by the two toes having broad soft soles for walking on the sand, and hoofs resembling nails. With the Llamas they constitute the suborder Tylopoda.

There are 2 species, the Arabian one-humped C. or dromedary (*C. dromedarius*) and the shorter-legged Central Asiatic or Bactrian two-humped C. (*C. bactrianus*). Both have long been domesticated.

The dromedary is adapted to life in the sandy plains of Arabia and N. Africa, and is very hardy and capable of standing great privations. It feeds on desert vegetation and carries a reserve of fatty tissue in the hump, which it can draw on when needed. An extra-large membrane in its nostrils extracts moisture from the air, enabling it to go without drinking for a fortnight.

Cs. vary in colour from dark brown to light cream. From remote times they have been of great value to the tribes which domesticated them, and the wealth of chieftains was assessed by the herds of Cs. they owned. The walking pace of a C. is 5km (3m) an hour, and it can keep this up for 50km (30m) even when carrying 270kg (600lb). A lightly built type of dromedary is capable of twice this speed when not heavily burdened, and camel racing is a favourite sport in such countries as Sudan. In Australia Cs. played a useful part in the development of the interior: *see* AFGHANS.

CAMĒ'LLIA. Genus of oriental evergreen shrubs of the family Theaceae, nearly allied to the tea plant. Numerous species, such as *C. japonica* and *C. reticulata* have been introduced into Europe.

CAMELOT (kam'elot). Legendary capital of King Arthur (q.v.). A possible site is the Iron-Age hill fort of South Cadbury Castle, nr Yeovil in Somerset, where excavations from 1967 have revealed relics dating 3000 B.C. to A.D. 1100, incl. remains of a large 6th cent. settlement.

Because of its combination of idealism and sophistication the name was also given to the 'court' of Pres. J. F. Kennedy.

CAMEO. A precious stone on which a design is carved in relief. Cs. were used by the ancient Greeks and Romans as a means of decorating goblets, vases, etc., and were worn as personal ornaments.

CAMERA. *See* PHOTOGRAPHY.

CAMERON, Charles (*c.* 1740-1812). Scottish architect. He studied architecture in Rome, and in 1779 was summoned to Russia by Catherine the Great. He designed part of the palace and built the cathedral of Tsarskoe Selo (Pushkin).

CAMEROON, Republic of. Country of W. Africa. At the western end of the arc of the Adamawa Mtns, but separate from them, is the country's highest peak Mt Cameroon (4,070 m/13,352 ft), an active volcano on the coast. There is desert in the far N. in the Lake Chad basin, dry savannah plateau in the intermediate area, and in the south there is dense tropical rainforest, a source of rubber and valuable timber, with cocoa, coffee, bananas, and ground-nuts cultivated in clearings. On the coast there is a belt of swamp. Gold and aluminium (smelted at Edéa) are mined. The chief towns are Yaoundé, the cap., and the port of Douala.

History. The Cameroons was a German possession, 1884-1916, when during the F.W.W. it was captured by Allied forces. After that war, it was in 1922 divided and admin. under League of Nations mandate by France and Britain which in 1946 placed their respective areas under UN trusteeship. French Cameroons was in 1960 proclaimed an independent rep. outside the French Community. British Cameroons consisted of 2 detached portions admin. from 1946 as part of Nigeria - the N. within the N. Region, the S. as a separate region. Plebiscites were held in both parts in 1961: the N. chose to remain in Nigeria, the S. chose to join the Federal Rep. of C., which then consisted of East C. (the former French Cameroons), French-speaking, with an area of 431,200 sq.km and pop. 4,500,000, and West C. (the former southern part of Brit. Cameroons), English-speaking, with an area of 42,900 sq.km; pop. 1,200,000. A further plebiscite in 1972 led to C. becoming a United Rep. the same year. President Ahmadou Ahidjo (1924–) held power continuously from 1960–82, and was succeeded by Paul Biya; Ahidjo was exiled the following year. Area 474,000 sq.km (183,580sq.m); population (1985) 9,737,000. M.U.: franc CFA.

CAMOENS (kam'ō-ens) or **CAMOES** (Port. kah-moñ'ēsh), **Luís Vaz de** (1524-80). Portuguese poet. B. at Lisbon or Coimbra, of Galician descent, he studied at Coimbra, and *c.* 1545 went to Lisbon where he is said to have wooed a lady of the court to whom the *Rimas* are addressed. Banished from the cap. on some unknown cause, he served in Africa (1547-9) where he lost an eye fighting at Ceuta. Returning home, he wounded a king's equerry in 1552, and was released on condition of going to India. He arrived in Goa in 1553 and accompanied 2 military expeditions to the Red Sea and Persian Gulf, before being sent to Macao in an official capacity. In 1558 he was shipwrecked while returning to Goa, but the MS. of his epic poem *Os Lusiadas* was saved. In 1567 he left Goa for Mozambique, and by 1570 had reached Lisbon, where in 1572 he pub. the national epic of Portugal, the *Lusiads* (which tells of the voyage of da Gama and incorporates much of Portuguese history). He was granted a small pension in recognition of its success, but d. in poverty of plague. In 1880 his remains were taken to the national pantheon at Belem.

CA'MOMILE. Plant of the daisy (Compositae) family. The most important species *Anthemis nobilis* is a perennial herb common in Europe; the solitary flower-heads have yellow centres surrounded by white florets and when dried make a bitter tonic. It used to be thought that it grew faster the more it was trodden upon.

CAMO'RRA. Secret society in Naples and S. Italy. About 1820, prisoners in the Neapolitan dungeons banded themselves against their gaolers. On their release they maintained their unity, and dominated the life of Naples. They practised smuggling, robbery, and blackmail, and from 1848 went into politics. In 1911 the C. was suppressed.

CAMPAGNA ROMANA (kahmpahn'yah rōmah'nah). Lowland stretch of the Italian peninsula, incl. and surrounding the city of Rome. Lying between the Tyrrhenian Sea and the Sabine Hills to the N.E., the Alban Hills to the S.E., it is drained by the lower course of the Tiber and a number of small streams, most of which dry up in the summer. Prosperous in Roman times, it became virtually derelict later owing to over-grazing, lack of water, and the arrival in the area of the malaria-carrying Anopheles mosquito. Extensive reclamation and drainage in the 19th and 20th cents. restored it to usefulness.

CAMPĀ'NIA. A prov. of ancient Italy, also a considerably more extensive region of modern Italy. It is noted for its climate and scenery. The chief towns are Naples, the cap., and Benevento, Caserta and Salerno, which are developing industrially. Area 13,594 sq.km (5,250 sq.m); pop. (1971) 5,054,825.

CAMPANILE (kahmpahnē'le). Bell-tower erected near, or attached to, churches or town halls in Italy. The leaning tower of Pisa is a famous example; another is the great C. of Florence, 90m (275ft) high.

CAMPANŪLĀ'CEAE (Lat. *campanula*, 'a little bell'). Family of flowering plants, mainly found in the temperate regions of the N hemisphere, e.g. the British harebell (*Campanula rotundifolia*), the garden Canterbury bell (*C. medium*) and the tall bellflower of the N American woodland (*C. americana*).

CAMPBELL, Sir Colin. *See* CLYDE, COLIN CAMPBELL, 1st Baron.

CAMPBELL, Donald Malcolm (1921-66). British car and speedboat enthusiast. His father, Sir Malcolm C. (1885-1949) broke the world's land speed record in 1935 with his *Bluebird* at 301.1 mph and estab. a world water speed record in 1939 at 141.74 mph in a boat of the same name. Donald C. was invalided out of the RAF in the S.W.W. and took up his father's interests: in 1964 he set up the world water speed record of 276.3 mph on Lake Dumbleyung, Australia, with the turbo-jet hydroplane *Bluebird.* He achieved the land speed record of 403.1 mph at Lake Eyre salt flats, Australia, in a car of the same name, 17 July, 1964. He was killed in an attempt to raise his water speed record on Coniston Water, England.

CAMPBELL, Gordon (1886-1953). British vice-admiral. As commander of Q ships (warships masquerading as unarmed merchantmen, so luring German submarines to the surface) he destroyed numerous U-boats in the F.W.W. and won the VC. He wrote *My Mystery Ships* (1928).

CAMPBELL, Mrs Patrick (1865-1940). British actress, *née* Beatrice Stella Tanner. B. in London, she was selected by Pinero to play Paula in *The Second Mrs Tanqueray* (1893); her other roles incl. Rosalind and Eliza Doolittle in *Pygmalion*, specially written for her by Shaw, with whom she conducted an amusing correspondence.

CAMPBELL, Roy (1901-57). S. African poet. B. at Durban, he became a professional jouster and bull-fighter in Spain and Provence. He fought for Franco in the Spanish Civil War, and was with the Commonwealth forces in the S.W.W. He estab. his poetic reputation with the individualistic *The Flaming Terrapin* (1924).

CAMPBELL, Thomas (1777-1844). Scottish poet. Following the successful publication of his *Pleasures of Hope* in 1799, he travelled on the Continent, and there wrote some of his best poems, including 'Hohenlinden' and 'Ye Mariners of England'. In 1803 he settled (govt pension from 1805) in London.

CAMPBELL-BANNERMAN, Sir Henry (1836-1908). British Liberal statesman, b. at Glasgow. He was Liberal MP for Stirling from 1868, Chief Sec. for Ireland in 1884-5, War Min. in 1886 and again in 1892-5, and leader of the Liberals in the House of Commons from 1899. In 1905 he became PM, and led the Liberals to an overwhelming electoral victory in 1906. His period of office was marked by the grant of self-govt to the S. African colonies, the Trades Disputes Act 1906, and the opening of the conflict between Commons and Lords that led to the Parliament Act of 1911. He resigned in 1908 and d. shortly afterwards.

CAMP DAVID. Mountain-top retreat in the Appalachians, Maryland, USA, used as a country home by the Pres. of the USA. Originally named Shangri-la by F. D. Roosevelt, it was re-named Camp D. by Eisenhower (after his grandson), and for a time after the assassination of J. F. Kennedy was referred to as Camp Number Four, for security reasons. It is guarded by the Marines.

It consists of a series of lodges, Aspen Lodge being the presidential residence. *See* CAMP DAVID AGREEMENTS.

CAMP DAVID AGREEMENTS. Two framework peace agreements signed at Camp David in 1978 by Begin and Sadat, under the aegis of Carter. One covered an Egypt-Israel peace treaty (signed 1979), incl. phased withdrawal by Israel from Sinai (partly achieved in 1979). The other covered an overall Middle East settlement, incl. the election by the people of the West Bank and Gaza Strip of a 'self-governing authority'. This was held up by disagreement on the degree of autonomy Israel was prepared to allow the Palestinians, the question of the participation of the P.L.O., and the continuing establishment of Israeli settlements in the West Bank. The Agreements were condemned by most of the Arab states and the General Assembly of the U.N.

CAMPECHE (kampech'e). Port on the Bay of C., Mexico, the cap. of C. state. Timber and fish are exported, and there is a univ. Pop. (1977) 55,000.

CAMPECHE, Bay of. The SW area of the Gulf of Mexico. A blow-out in the vast undersea oilfield off the Yucatan peninsula caused the world's worst oil pollution disaster in 1979.

CAMPERDOWN. Dutch village in N. Holland prov., 13km (8m) NW of Alkmaar, off which on 11 Oct. 1797 the Dutch were defeated by a British fleet under Duncan.

CAMPHOR (kam'for). Volatile, aromatic ketone substance ($C_{10}H_{16}O$) obtained from the C. tree (*Cinnamomum camphora*), a member of the Lauraceae, native to S China, Formosa, and Japan. The C. is distilled from chips of the wood of the root, trunk, and branches which are exposed to the action of steam, and afterwards refined.

CAMPI (kahm'pē). Family of Italian painters practising in Cremona in the 16th cent., the most famous being Giulio C. (*c.* 1502-72).

CAMPINAS (koṅpē'nahs), City of São Paulo state, Brazil, situated on the central plateau; a centre for the coffee-growing areas. There are metallurgical and food industries. Pop. (1975) 472,700.

CAMPION, Edmund (1540-81). English Jesuit and RC martyr. B. in London, he took deacon's orders in the English church, but fled to Douai, where in 1571 he recanted Protestantism. In 1573 he became a Jesuit at Rome, and in 1580 was sent to England as a missionary. He was betrayed as a spy in 1581, committed to the Tower, and hanged, drawn and quartered as a traitor. He was canonized in 1970.

CAMPION, Thomas (1567-1620). English poet and musician. He entered Gray's Inn in 1586 and later qualified as a doctor and practised in London. He pub. Latin *Poemata* (1595); *The Art of English Poesie* (1602); a textbook of music, and 4 *Bookes of Ayres* for which he composed both words and music.

CAMPION. Name given to several plants, belonging to the genera *Lychnis* and *Silene*, of the family Caryophyllaceae, e.g. the garden C. (*L. coronaria*), the wild white and red Cs. (*L. vespertina* and *L. diurna*) and bladder C. (*S. inflata*).

CAMPOBASSO (kahmpōbah'sō). Cap. of Molise region, Italy, *c.* 190km (120m) SE of Rome; it is noted for cutlery. Pop. (1977) 45,000.

CAMPO-FORMIO, Treaty of. Peace settlement concluded 17 Oct. 1797 by Bonaparte with Austria at the Italian village of C-F., which gave France the Austrian Netherlands, the Ionian Is., etc.; Austria was compensated with Dalmatia, Istria and part of Venetia.

CAM RANH (kam ran). Port on C.R. Bay in southern Vietnam, used as an American base in the Vietnam War, and subsequently by the USSR. Pop. 105,000.

CAMUS (kahmü'), **Albert** (1913-60). French writer. Of Breton and Spanish parents, he was b. in Algeria, became a journalist in Metropolitan France and was active in the S.W.W. Resistance, when he edited the clandestine *Combat. L'Étranger* (1942: *The Outsider*) tells of a meaningless killing in the harsh sun of N Africa, and the same sense of the absurdity of the universe was expressed in the essays *Le Mythe de Sisyphe* (1942). Later books are the novel *La Peste* (1948: *The Plague*) and *L'Homme révolté* (1952: *The Rebel*), a study of the inevitable corruption of ideal revolutionary ideas by murder and oppression which marked the end of his association with Sartre. He was awarded a Nobel prize in 1957.

CANAAN (kān'an). Traditionally the area of the Palestinian coast between the Mediterranean and the line of the Dead Sea, in the Bible the 'Promised Land' of Abraham, occupied as early as the 3rd millennium BC by the Canaanites, Semitic-speaking peoples of mixed race who were known to the Greeks of the 1st millennium BC as Phoenicians (*see* PHOENICIA). However, the first known complete Canaanite city was excavated 1965-71 at Arad in the Negev, and in 1976-7 excavations at Tell Mardikh, Syria, revealed the city of Ebla, cap. of a great Canaanite empire incl. Syria, Palestine and part of Mesopotamia c. 2,400 B.C. A vast archive of inscribed tablets incl. refs to placenames such as Gaza and Jerusalem (no excavations at the latter had suggested occupation at so early a date) and to Semitic personal names incl. Abraham, Ishmael, David and Saul. These are not to be identified individually with the characters of the O.T., but illustrate the environment in which such legends might take shape.

CANADA. A federal union of 10 provs. and 2 territories, an independent community within the British Commonwealth of Nations, occupying (except for Alaska, USA), the entire northern half of N America. N and S its territory extends from about the latitude of Rome to well within the Arctic Circle; E and W it stretches across 88° of longitude and embraces 5 Standard Time (hour) zones. It is divided from the USA by the 49th parallel of latitude in the W, the Great Lakes and St Lawrence r. in the centre, and the 45th parallel to the northern hump of Maine in the E., the boundary on the Atlantic being the Saint Crois r. Of 9,975,223 sq.km (3,851,809 sq.m), more than 755,000 sq.km (290,000 sq.m) are freshwater lakes.

Physical Features. In the N and E centre the old Pre-cambrian continent, often called the *Canadian Shield*, has, broadly, the conformation of a great plain, and is profusely dotted with lakes and rock basins. While parts of it support productive forests, it is almost devoid of good agricultural soils; its riches lie in its minerals, furs, and hydro-electric water power. The *Appalachian Region* in Quebec, New Brunswick, and Nova Scotia consists for the most part of rounded hills and shallow valleys; it is productively forested, and contains considerable stretches and numerous pockets of fertile soil. The *St. Lawrence Lowlands*, an area which supports more than half the population, constitutes the southern interior of eastern central Canada. There are no elevated areas except a few intrusions of igneous rock near Montreal. The *Great Plains* or *Prairies* extend from the edge of the Canadian Shield to the Rocky Mts. There are 3 prairie steppes, roughly located in southern Manitoba, Saskatchewan, and

Alberta respectively. Much of the soil is of great depth and very fertile. The *Cordilleran Region,* occupying British Columbia, the Yukon, and a narrow boundary zone of Alberta, consists of 'a sea of mountains' in 3 roughly parallel bands, the Rockies, the Selkirks, and the Coast Ranges. The highest peaks are in Yukon Territory, notably Mount Logan 6,050 m (19,850 ft). British Columbia possesses fertile valleys devoted to fruit growing and dairying.

The chief coastal indentations are on the Atlantic side where the Gulf of St Lawrence and the St Lawrence Seaway give ready access to the heart of the country. The rivers incl. the St Lawrence (q.v.) and Ottawa flowing into the Atlantic; Nelson and Churchill (1,600 km/1,000 m), Saskatchewan (1,939 km/1,205 m) and Albany, flowing into Hudson Bay; Columbia (2,000 km/1,243 m, of which about a third is in C.), and Fraser, flowing into the Pacific, Yukon (2,849 km/1,770 m of which less than half is in C.), flowing into the Bering Sea; and the Mackenzie (4,241 km/2,635 m, from the head of Finlay River, C.'s longest river), Peace, Back, Liard and Coppermine, flowing into the Arctic Ocean.

Canada

Provinces	*Area in sq. km.*	*Population (1976)*	*Capital*
Alberta	661,187	1,838,037	Edmonton
British Columbia	948,599	2,466,608	Victoria
Manitoba	650,088	1,021,506	Winnipeg
New Brunswick	73,437	677,250	Fredericton
Newfoundland	404,517	577,725	St. John's
Nova Scotia	54,558	828,571	Halifax
Ontario	1,068,587	8,264,465	Toronto
Prince Edward Is.	5,657	118,229	Charlottetown
Quebec	1,540,676	6,234,445	Quebec
Saskatchewan	651,901	921,323	Regina
Territories			
Northwest Territories	3,379,689	42,609	Yellowknife
Yukon Territory	536,327	21,836	Whitehorse
	9,975,223	22,992,604	

While climatic conditions are very varied owing to C.'s vast area, the continental type predominates, and only the coastline of British Columbia enjoys a marine climate such as that of Britain and NW Europe. Over most of the central portion the ground is continuously snow-covered from the middle of November until late in March.

History. The first permanent settlements were established by Samuel de Champlain, a French explorer, in what are now Nova Scotia and Quebec province, on the sites of Quebec City and Montreal early in the 17th cent. From the outset the French colonies on the seaboard and along the St Lawrence were bitter rivals of the English colonies to the S. The French régime was doomed to yield ultimately to the growing strength of the New England colonists and the sea-and-land power of Britain. In 1758 Wolfe captured Louisburg, the French stronghold, and a year later the citadel of Quebec. By the Peace of Paris (1763) C. was ceded to Britain. During and immediately after the War of American Independence (1775-83) large numbers of loyalists fled from the Union northward into what is now New Brunswick and Ontario, and, under the name of United Empire Loyalists, played an important part in the creation of these new provinces. In 1791 Canada was divided into (French-speaking) Lower Canada and (English-speaking) Upper Canada. The population was swelled by waves of migration from Great Britain and USA, and by the time of Confederation (1867) there were a million people in Lower Canada and 1½ million in Upper Canada.

Meantime an effort to establish an agricultural colony on the Red River had been made by Lord Selkirk, 1811-12. Winnipeg was founded on the site of a fur-trading post, and a colony was estab. In 1866 two colonies on the Pacific side were united to form British Columbia.

Confederation of Upper and Lower Canada (now Ontario and Quebec), Nova Scotia, and New Brunswick was accomplished by the British North America Act, which came into force on 1 July 1867. Manitoba was created in 1870, and British Columbia joined the union in 1871. The Canadian Pacific Railway was completed in 1885. Prince Edward Island came into federation in 1873. The new provs. of Saskatchewan and Alberta were formed out of the NW Territory in 1905. A change of economic factors for the better about 1895 made it possible to throw open the vast region of fertile soil on the prairies for settlement; and the discovery of gold and other metals, the exploitation of forests for lumber and paper, the development of fisheries and tourist attractions, and heavy investment of capital from other countries in industrial plants, gradually transformed C. from a simple extractive economy to one of the important manufacturing and trading nations of the world. The S.W.W. stimulated further rapid industrialization, and in the post-war period discovery and exploitation of mineral resources was on a vast scale. By the late 1960s there was concern at dependence on raw material exports, and on the USA for two-thirds of C.'s merchandise trade, but C.'s potential, as one of the few industrial nations self-sufficient in energy, was recognized as enormously great. From his coming to power in 1968 Pierre Trudeau promoted a greater Canadian 'nationalism' in all fields.

In 1974 Trudeau, having lost his overall majority in 1973, again achieved an overwhelming majority for his policy of 'vitesse et panache' (speed and style). French-Canadian nationalism, apparent from the 1960s and fostered by the recession of the mid-1970s, led to a referendum in 1980 which resulted in rejection of the demand for independence. However, Trudeau, returned to power after a brief Progressive Conservative govt. 1979-80 under Joe Clark, embarked on constitutional reform. In 1982, following agreement by all the provincial govts except Quebec, the constitution was patriated to Canada, where changes could be made with the consent of the fed govt and 7 provs, comprising at least 70% of the population.

People. The chief racial stocks of C. are British, *c.* 9,624,000; French *c.* 6,180,000; and German *c.* 1,317,000; the aborigines of C. are the Indians, *c.* 300,000 and Eskimoes, *c.* 18,000. The French-speaking Canadians are descendants of the few boatloads of emigrants from Normandy and other provinces of NW France who were settled in New France and Acadia by the French government in the 17th and 18th cents. The British stock is partly descended from the United Empire Loyalists who moved N into C. from the USA during and after the War of American Independence, but in the main is the result of direct immigration. The 'Open Door' policy which began in the 1890s enriched the Canadian racial mosaic with a wide variety of European stocks.

There is no established or State Church.

Government. The Canadian constitution is partly written, partly unwritten. The British North America Act of 1867, and subsequent amendments, define and divide the fields of jurisdiction as between the central government and the 10 provinces. In 1969 the Official Languages Act recognized English and French as the official languages of Canada for all purposes.

The Federal Parliament at Ottawa consists of Queen, Senate, and House of Commons. Queen Elizabeth II of the UK is also Queen of Canada; she is represented in C. by her personal viceroy, the Governor-General, who acts as Chief of State in C. There is a Prime Minister of the Canadian Dominion, and there are Premiers in each prov. govt.

The Senate consists of 104 nominated members, the House of Commons of 264 members who are elected by universal suffrage for 5 years (unless previously dissolved). The leading political parties are the Liberal (John Turner), Progressive Conservative (Brian Mulroney), and New Democratic Party (J. Edward Broadbent), all of a moderate liberal tendency.

Under the Canadian honours system (initiated 1967) no title is conferred, but recipients place the appropriate letters after their name: Companion of the Order of Canada (CC), Officer (OC) Member (CM); and for bravery, Cross of Valour (CV), Star of Courage (SC), Medal of Bravery (MB). The royal anthem is 'God Save the Queen', but from 1980 the nat. anthem is the French-Canadian marching song 'O Canada'. Canada Day (formerly Dominion Day) is 1st July.

Canadian Prime Ministers

Sir John A. Macdonald (*Con.*)	1867
Alexander Mackenzie (*Lib.*)	1873
Sir John A. Macdonald (*Con.*)	1878
Sir John J. Abbott (*Con.*)	1891
Sir John S.D. Thompson (*Con.*)	1892
Sir Mackenzie Bowell (*Con.*)	1894
Sir Charles Tupper (*Con.*)	1896
Sir Wilfrid Laurier (*Lib.*)	1896
Sir Robert L. Borden (*Con.*)	1911
Arthur Meighen (*Con.*)	1920
William Lyon Mackenzie King (*Lib.*)	1921
Arthur Meighen (*Con.*)	1926
William Lyon Mackenzie King (*Lib.*)	1926
Richard Bedford Bennett (*Con.*)	1930
William Lyon Mackenzie King (*Lib.*)	1935
Louis Stephen St. Laurent (*Lib.*)	1948
John G. Diefenbaker (*Con.*)	1957
Lester Bowles Pearson (*Lib.*)	1963
Pierre Elliot Trudeau (*Lib.*)	1968
Joseph Clark (*Prog. Con.*)	1979
Pierre Elliot Trudeau (*Lib.*)	1980
John Turner (*Lib.*)	1984
Brian Mulroney (*Prog. Con.*)	1984

Provincial Governments. The Queen is represented in each prov. by a Lieutenant-Governor, appointed by the Gov.-Gen. in Council. The provincial govt. consists of the Lieutenant-Governor, the Executive Council and a Legislative Assembly (Quebec has, in addition, a Legislative Council). The provs. enjoy sovereign authority in all local matters. Public education comes under the jurisdiction of the provincial govts. and in Quebec there are 2 distinct systems of education - Roman Catholic and Protestant.

Economy. Since the S.W.W. industry has predominated over agriculture, but the latter is still of major importance. Wheat, oats and barley are grown, most especially in Saskatchewan, the granary of C. In stock-raising Alberta is pre-eminent; dairying and also tobacco cultivation are typical of Ontario and Quebec; and fruit farming is carried on in Ontario and British Columbia. Almost half C. is forested, and newsprint is one of C.'s most valuable products. Fur trade with the Indians led to the early exploration of C., but the 'ranching' of mink and fox now surpasses the value of fur trapping. There are rich fisheries - salmon, cod and lobster.

The leading mining provs. are Alberta, Ontario, Quebec, British Columbia and Saskatchewan. Minerals exploited incl. asbestos, copper, gold, iron, lead, molybdenum, nickel, potash, silver, uranium and zinc. The great reserves of oil and natural gas, notably in Alberta, render C., in conjunction with her vast hydro-electric resources and expertise in nuclear power, self-sufficient in energy. Manufacturing industry is largely concentrated in Ontario and Quebec, and incl. iron and steel, aircraft and motor vehicles, machinery, electrical and electronic equipment, pulp and paper, oil refining, chemicals and plastics, fertilizers, flour and animal feed milling, processed food products, textiles, printing and publishing. M.U.: Canadian dollar.

CANADA. A typical country town of the wheat belt, Carstairs in Southern Alberta. As in all prairie towns, the grain elevators dominate the flat landscape. *Photo: Barnaby's Picture Library.*

Communications. In the 1850s the first great period of railway construction began. In 1885 the Canadian Pacific Railway linked the Atlantic and Pacific coasts, and during the F.W.W. the other privately owned systems of the country were consolidated in the state-owned Canadian Nat. Rlwys. In a country with such enormous distances, air travel developed early, and is similarly divided into state-owned Air Canada, and the private enterprise Canadian Pacific Airline. The trans-Canada highway from Halifax, Nova Scotia, to Vancouver, British

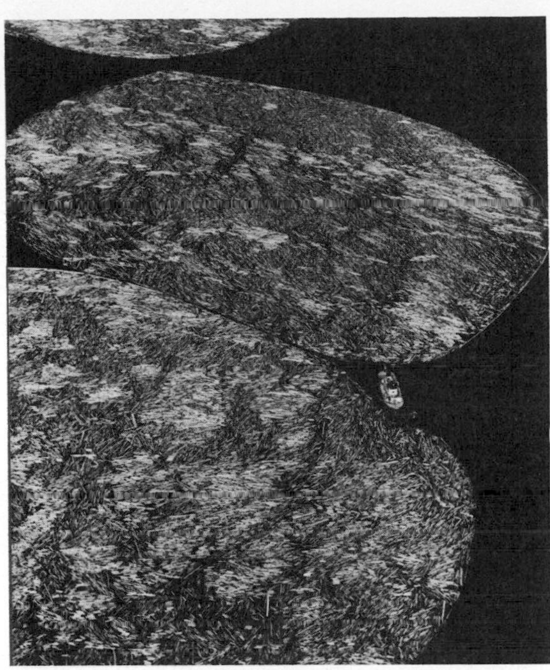

CANADA. Millions of logs from the virgin forests of northern Canada are marshalled inside 'booms' before starting on their journey downstream. Delivered to the pulp mills of the paper industry, they supply the world with newsprint. *Photo: Camera Press.*

Columbia, is an all-weather, continuous motor road, 6,751 km (4,195 m) long.

Besides privately-owned television and radio stations, C. has in the Canadian Broadcasting Corporation a state-owned service remarkable for independence and high quality of its transmissions.

Art. Early painters of note included Cornelius Krieghoff (1812-72), who recorded *habitant* pioneer life; Antoine Plamondon (1804-95), a Quebec portrait painter; and Paul Kane (1810-71), painter of the Plains Indians. A native Canadian style developed with the landscapes of Tom Thomson (1877-1917) and the 'Group of Seven' - J. E. H. MacDonald (1873-1932), Franklin Carmichael (1890-1945), A. J. Casson, Lawren Harris, A. Y. Jackson, Arthur Lismer, and F. H. Varley - who worked as a group 1919-33.

Painters dependent on English or US 19th cent. realism included Horatio Walker (1858-1938), William Brymner (1855-1925), and Homer Watson (1855-1936). Among Impressionist painters were A. Suzor-Côté (1869-1937), Clarence Gagnon (1881-1942) and, most important, J. W. Morrice (1865-1924). Followers of later movements were Emily Carr (1871-1945), Goodridge Roberts (1904-), David Milne (1882-1953), Stanley Cosgrove, P. E. Bordaus (1905-60), Henri Masson, J. P. Riopelle, Alfred Pellan, Jacques de Tonnancour, and Harold Town.

Ecclesiastical wood-carving in the French Norman tradition has been continuous from the early 18th cent. Realist sculptors include Philippe Hébert (1850-1917), Walter Allward, Emmanuel Hahn (1881-1957), Elizabeth Wyn Wood, and Louis Archimbault.

20th cent. architecture has followed international style except in the prov. of Quebec which developed its own traditions.

CANADIAN ART. 'Old House, Parry Sound', a painting by A.J.Casson dated 1932, and a typical example of the work of the legendary and influential Group of Seven. *Photo: Courtesy of the Canadian Government.*

Literature. ENGLISH. Canadian literature in English began early in the 19th cent. in the Maritime Provs. with the humorous tales of T. C. Haliburton (1796-1865); Charles Heavysege (1816-76), a poet of note, belonged to Kingston, Ontario. The later 19th cent. brought the lyrical output of Charles G. D. Roberts (1860-1943), Bliss Carman (1861-1929), Archibald Lampman (1861-99), and Duncan Campbell Scott (1862-1944).

Realism in fiction developed with Frederick P. Grove (1871-1948), Mazo de la Roche (1885-1961), creator of the Jalna series and Hugh MacLennan (1907-). Humour of world-wide appeal emerged in Stephen Leacock (1869-1944), Brian Moore (1921-), author of *The Luck of Ginger Coffey* (1960), and Mordecai Richler (q.v.). Popular outside Canada too, was Lucy Montgomery (1874-1942), whose *Anne of Green Gables* (1908) became a children's classic. Saul Bellow and Marshall McLuhan were both Canadian-born.

Though their merits as poetry are not high, the verses of Robert W. Service (1874-1958), 'Bard of the Yukon', and W. H. Drummond (1854-1907), who affectionately satirized *habitant* life, maintained their popularity. Memories of the F.W.W. lived in the well-known poem 'In Flanders Fields' by John McCrae (1872-1918). In the 'thirties poetry flourished in the work of E. J. Pratt (1883-1964) and the Montreal Group among whom were A. M. Klein, Frank Scott, A. J. Smith, P. K. Page and Patrick Anderson. Later prominent poets included Dorothy Livesay, Ann Marriott, Douglas LePan, Earle Birney (1904-), Roy Daniells, L. A. Mackay, and Jay MacPherson.

FRENCH. F.-X. Garneau's *Histoire du Canada* (1845-8) inspired a school of patriotic verse led by Octave Crémazie (1827-79) and continued by Louis Fréchette (1838-1908). A new movement began after 1900 with such poets as André Lozeau (1878-1924), Paul Morin, Robert

Choquette (1862-1941), Alain Grandbois, St Denys Garneau, Eloi de Grandmont, and Pierre Trottier. Fiction reached a high point with Louis Hémon (1880-1914) whose *Maria Chapdelaine* inspired many genre works. Outstanding later novelists are Germaine Guèvremont, Gabrielle Roy, 'Ringuet' (Philippe Panneton, 1895-), Robert Elie, Roger Lemelin, and Yves Thériault.

Ship Canals and Waterways

	km	*m*
Amsterdam (Netherlands) 1876	26.6	16.5
Baltic-Volga (U.S.S.R.) 1964-	2,430	1,510
Baltic-White Sea (U.S.S.R.) 1933	235	146
Corinth (Greece) 1893	6.4	4
Elbe and Trave (Germany) 1900	66	41
Göta (Sweden) 1832	185	115
Grand Canal (China) 485 B.C. – A.D. 1972	1,050	650
Kiel (W. Germany) 1895	98	61
Manchester (England) 1894	57	35.5
Panama (Panama) 1914	81	50.5
Princess Juliana (Netherlands) 1935	32	20
St. Lawrence (Canada) 1959	3,770	2,342
Saulte Ste. Marie (U.S.A.) 1855	2.6	1.6
Saulte Ste. Marie (Canada) 1895	1.8	1.1
Welland (Canada) 1929	45	28
Suez (Egypt) 1869	166	103

CANAL. A man-made waterway constructed for drainage, irrigation, or navigation.

Irrigation Canals carry water for irrigation from rivers, reservoirs, or wells, and are carefully designed to maintain an even flow of water over the whole length. Irrigation canals fed from the Nile have maintained life in Egypt since the earliest times; the division of the waters of the Upper Indus and its tributaries for the extensive system of irrigation canals in Pakistan and Punjab, India, was for more than 10 years a major cause of dispute between India and Pakistan, settled at last by a treaty in 1960; the flourishing agriculture of the Murray basin, Victoria, Australia, and of the Great Valley of California, USA, are examples of 19th and 20th cent. irrigation canal development.

Navigation and Ship Canals. Constructed at one level between locks, Cs. frequently link with other forms of waterway - natural rivers, modified river channels, and sea links - to form a waterway system. Probably the oldest to be still in use is the Grand Canal waterway in China, which links Tianjin and Hangzhou, and interconnects the Huang He (Yellow River) and Chang Jiang. It was originally built in three stages 485 BC-AD 1283. Large sections silted up in later years, but the entire system was dredged, widened and rebuilt 1958-72 in combination with work on flood protection, irrigation and hydro-electric schemes. *See* TABLE.

The first British C. was the Manchester-Bridgewater C. 1761-76, constructed for the 3rd Duke of Bridgewater to carry coal from his collieries to Manchester. The engineer, Brindley, overcame great difficulties in the route. Today many of Britain's canals form part of an inter-connecting system of waterways some 4,000 km (2,500 m) long. Many which have become disused commercially have been restored for recreation and the use of pleasure craft.

The economy of energy in such a means of goods transport, where speed is not a prime factor, has encouraged a modern revival and Belgium, France, Germany, and the Soviet Union are among countries which have extended and modernized their C. facilities. The Baltic-Volga Waterway begun in the USSR in 1964 will link the northern port of Klaipeda with Kahovka, at the mouth of the Dnieper on the Black Sea, a distance of 2,430 km/1,510 m. A further C. cuts across the N. Crimea, thus shortening the onward voyage of ships from the Dnieper through the Black Sea to the Sea of Azov. *See also* RHINE.

In North America, the great modern example is the St Lawrence and Great Lakes Waterway in which the St Lawrence Seaway 1954-9, extends from Montreal to Lake Ontario (290km/180m) and, with the deepening of the Welland C. and some of the river channels, provides a waterway that enables ocean-going vessels to travel during the ice-free months between the Atlantic and Duluth, Minnesota, USA, at the western end of Lake Superior, some 3,770 km (2,342 m).

CANALE'TTO, Antonio (1697-1768). Venetian painter. He painted many scenes of Venice, his works being remarkable for their handling of perspective and control of colour. He visited England in 1746 and 1753.

CANALETTO. A view along the Grand Canal in Venice, in the Woburn Collection. To the right the 'Palazzo Corner della Ca'Grande', built by Jacopo Sansovino in 1523. The campanile of Santa Maria della Carita, seen in the distance on the left, has been destroyed. *Photo: Courtesy of the British Tourist Authority.*

CANARY. A bird (*Serinus canarius*) belonging to the finch family (Fringillidae). It is nearly allied to the European serin (*S.c. serinus*), which is now regarded as a subspecies only, but in a wild state is confined to Madeira and the Canary Islands. It was first bred in Europe as a cage-bird in Italy, in the 16th cent. As songsters, those known as rollers have the sweetest voice and the most sustained powers.

CANARY ISLANDS. Group of volcanic islands *c.* 100 km (60 m) off the NW coast of Africa. They form a region of Spain, the prov. of Santa Cruz de Tenerife comprising Tenerife, Palma, Gomera and Hierro (cap. Santa Cruz on Tenerife), and the prov. of Las Palmas comprising Gran Canaria, Lanzarote, and Fuerteventura, plus 6 uninhabited islets, (cap. Las Palmas on Gran Canaria). The highest peak in extra-continental Spain is Pico de Teyde (3,713 m/12,182 ft) on Tenerife. Autonomy is planned, but the OAU supports the creation of an independent Guanch Republic (so-called from the indigenous islanders, a branch of the Berbers of N Africa), and restoration of the Guanch language. Area 7,273 sq.km (2,808 sq.m); pop. (1973) 1,170,225.

CANBERRA (kan'bra). Federal cap. of the Commonwealth of Australia, standing in the Australian Capital Territory enclosed within New South Wales, on a tributary of the Murrumbidgee; it was selected as capital in 1908. It contains the Parliament House, first used by the Commonwealth Parliament in 1927, the Australian Nat. Univ. (1946), the C. School of Music (1965), and the Nat. War Memorial. Area (Australian Cap. Terr. incl. the port at Jervis Bay) 2,432 sq.km (939 sq.m); pop. (1976) 215,461.

CANBERRA. A garden city some 320 km (200 m) south west of Sydney, Canberra has its administrative buildings flanking Civic Square. The bronze statue, 'Ethos', is the work of the Australian sculptor Tom Bass and symbolizes,the spirit of the community. *Photo: Courtesy of the Australian News and Information Bureau.*

CANCAN. A stage dance performed by a line of dancers or as a solo. It first appeared about 1830 in Paris and came to symbolize Parisian naughtiness. The music latterly associated with the C. is the *galop* from Offenbach's *Orpheus in the Underworld.* The high kick was a speciality of the C.

CANCER (kan'ser). A group of diseases due to the growth of malignant tumours; a malignant tumour. The chief varieties are *carcinoma,* which grows from skin or mucous membrane, and *sarcoma,* which grows from connective tissue. These 2 categories are subdivided according to the kind of tissue from which the growth takes place.

Such diseases are characterized by the production of C. cells. Recent research suggests that production of such cells is commonplace in the healthy individual and that they become malignant only when the normal control of such unruly cells fails to operate because the body's defence mechanism has been damaged. Cell growth and division goes on constantly, and since each new cell must carry a duplicate of the genetic code (the pattern of a million or so molecules strung together in precise order which regulates its activities), there is great possibility of error. Such a defective or C. cell would normally be destroyed, but when it survives shows its difference from the normal by growing and dividing without restriction (normal cells increase at a rate which exactly matches cell deaths), the increase becoming obvious as a lump, or (as in leukaemia) being distributed throughout the body; by invading other tissues, etc. Damage to the body's defence mechanism may be caused by physical or chemical stimulants, known as carcinogens, such as factory by-products (e.g. asbestos dust, benzpyrene); hormones; parasites; psychological stress (e.g. bereavement); radiation (e.g. X-rays), and viruses. The most usual remedies are surgery; radiation by X-ray, radium or radioactive isotope; and drugs, cystostatic (cell-stopping) agents which prevent cell division. Very many victims of C. can now be helped and many totally cured.

CANDELA OUTERIÑO, Felix (1910-). Mexican architect. Professor at the National School of Architecture, Univ. of Mexico, from 1953, he founded with his brother a firm specializing in the design and construction of reinforced concrete shell structures.

CA'NDIA. Italian name for the Greek island of CRETE, also formerly the name of the largest city, Heraklion (q.v.), founded *c.* 824. It has many Venetian remains.

CANDLE. A source of artificial light consisting of a rod or cylinder made of wax, tallow, or some other solid fatty material, enclosing a wick of cotton or flax. There is a declining demand for household Cs., except for coloured and fancy Cs.

The traditional spermaceti C. flame used as a candle-power standard has been replaced by the *candela,* symbol cd, which is 1/60 of the intensity of one square centimetre of a blackbody radiator at the temperature of solidification of platinum (2046°K).

CANDLEMAS. In the Christian Church, the feast of the Purification of the Blessed Virgin Mary, or the Presentation of the Infant Christ in the Temple, celebrated on 2 Feb.

CANE. Name applied to the reed-like stem of various plants such as the sugar-cane and bamboo, but more particularly to the group of palms called rattans, consisting of the genus *Calamus* and its allies; their slender stems are dried and used for making walking sticks, baskets, and furniture.

CANEA (kahn'ya). Cap. and principal port of Crete, about midway along the N Coast. It was founded in 1252 by the Venetians, and is still surrounded by a wall. Vegetable oils, soap, and leather are exported. Heavy fighting took place round C. during the S.W.W., following the landing of German parachutists in May 1941. Pop. (1971) 40,565.

CANIDAE (kan'idē). Family of mammals belonging to the Carnivora, distinguished by their walking on the toes (digitigrade), having non-retractile claws and an elongated muzzle, and by other anatomical characters. The dogs, wolves, jackals, and foxes are typical members.

CANNABIS. *See* HEMP.

CANNAE (kan'ē). Ancient Italian town in Apulia, where in 216 BC Hannibal defeated the Romans.

CANNES (kahn). Town of the French Riviera in Alpes-Maritimes dept, one of the most fashionable and most popular holiday resorts of the Continent. Until 1834 it was only a little seaport, but then it attracted the patronage of Lord Brougham (who d. here) and other distinguished visitors, and soon a handsome new town (La Bocca) grew up facing the Mediterranean. There is an annual film festival. Pop. (1975) 70,225.

CANNIBALISM. The practice of eating human flesh, also called anthropophagy. The name is derived from the Caribs, a man-eating tribe of S American and W Indian natives, who impressed themselves upon the conquering Spaniards by their savagery.

C. has been practised throughout the ages and in most parts of the world. It has religious and superstitious motives, but modern outbreaks, e.g. in Russia after the Revolution, in the Nazi concentration camps, and in China under Japanese rule, have been caused by overpowering hunger, and food C. is possibly the original form.

CANNING, George (1770–1827). British Tory statesman. The son of a barrister, he was ed. at Eton and Oxford, and in 1793 entered Parliament. His wit and eloquence, best shown in his verse satires and parodies contributed to the *Anti-Jacobin* (1797–8), made him extremely valuable to Pitt, who gave him several appointments. As For. Sec. 1807–10 C. was largely responsible for the seizure of the Danish fleet and British intervention in the Spanish peninsula, but his disapproval of the Walcheren expedition involved him in a duel with Castlereagh and led to his resignation. Except for the presidency of the Board of Control (1816–20) he held no further office until 1822, when on Castlereagh's death he again became For. Sec. He opposed the interventionist policy of the 'Holy Alliance' in Spain, and supported the national movements in Greece and the S American republics. He succeeded Lord Liverpool as PM in 1827, and on the refusal of Wellington, Peel, and other Tories to serve under him formed a coalition with the Whigs. He d. in office a few months later.

His son **Charles John,** earl C. (1812–62), sat in the Lords from 1837 as visct. C. As Gov.-Gen. of India from 1856, he suppressed the Indian Mutiny with an unvindictive firmness which earned him the nickname 'Clemency C.' and became 1st Viceroy of India in 1858, receiving an earldom the next year.

CANNING. The art of preserving foods in hermetically sealed containers by the application of heat. In 1809 the Frenchman Nicolas Appert succeeded in preserving food in glass containers, and in 1810 the Englishman Peter Durand patented tin cans. In 1819 the 1st American C. factory was started in Boston by Underwood, an Englishman. The American Civil War stimulated the development of C. and there was phenomenal expansion following the introduction of scientific methods *c.* 1925.

CANO (kah'nō), **Juan Sebastian del** (d. 1526). Spanish voyager, for whom it is claimed that he was the first circumnavigator. He sailed with Magellan in 1519, and after the latter's death in the Philippines, brought the *Victoria* safe home to Spain.

CANOE (kanōō'). Lightweight boat of shallow draught, pointed at both ends and easily propelled by paddles or sails. Early construction varied from the hollowed tree-trunk of African tribes to the framework covered with bark or skin used by the American Indians, the latter being the basis of modern plastic and fibre-glass versions. Canoeing became a sport in the 19th cent. and the Royal C. Club in Britain was founded 1866. Two types of C. are used, the *kayak* derived from the Eskimo model, which has a keel and in which the canoeist sits, and the Canadian style, which has no keel and in which the canoeist kneels. In addition to straightforward racing, there are slalom courses, with up to 30 'gates' to be negotiated through rapids and round artificial rock formations. Penalty seconds are added to course time for touching suspended gate poles or missing a gate. One to four canoeists are carried.

CANON. In the Catholic Church, a clergyman holding a prebend in a cathedral or collegiate church. He lived within its precinct, and his life was ordered by ecclesiastical rules or canons. About the 11th cent. a distinction was drawn between *regular* or Augustinian canons who observed the rule, and *secular* canons who lived in the world, and were in effect the administrative officers of a cathedral, but in holy orders. Following the Reformation, all Cs. in England became secular Cs.; and the Cs., headed by the dean, are the resident ecclesiastical dignitaries attached to a cathedral and constitute the chapter.

CANON (of scripture). The collection or list of books of the Bible (q.v.) that are accepted by the Christian Church as divinely inspired and authoritative, i.e. the Old and New Testaments. The canon of the OT was drawn up at the assembly of Rabbis held at Jamnia in Palestine between AD 90 and 100; certain excluded books were included in the Apocrypha. The earliest list of NT books is known as the Muratorian Canon (*c.* AD 160–70). Athanasius promulgated *c.* 365 a list which corresponds with that in our Bibles.

CANONICAL HOURS. In the RC Church the daily set periods for the performance of devotion; matins and lauds, prime, terce (9 am), sext (noon), nones (3 pm), evensong or vespers, and compline. In England C.Hs. are also those in which a marriage may legally be performed in a parish church, without a special licence (8 am–6 pm).

CANONIZATION. Procedure in the Roman Catholic Church whereby one (or more) of her members is formally admitted into the Calendar of Saints. Formerly, under a system laid down mainly in the 17th cent., the long process of investigation was seldom completed in under 50 yrs, although in the case of a martyr the final stages were more speedy. In 1969 a simplified procedure was introduced, the gathering of proof of the virtues of the candidate being left to the diocesan bishop of the birthplace, and by 1980, science having made proof of saintly miracles more difficult, stress was shifted to 'extraordinary "favours" or "graces" that can be proved or attested by serious investigation'. The findings are then put before the Congregation for the Causes of Saints, and any objections are put forward by the Promotor Fidei (popularly called the 'devil's advocate'). On papal ratification of a favourable verdict, the stage of beatification is reached (allowing local veneration) and full C. follows after proof of further 'favours'. The ceremony takes place in the Vatican basilica. Many more recent saints come from the

Third World, where expansion of the R.C. Church is most rapid, e.g. the Uganda Martyrs, or non-white racial groups, e.g. the American Mohawk Indian Kateri Tekakwitha (d. 1680), beatified in 1980. In the revised Calendar of Saints (1970) only 58 saints were recognized as of worldwide importance, and some old favourites, such as Christopher and Valentine, were removed as probably non-existent.

CANON LAW. The rules governing the Christian Church, originating in the declarations of Christ and the Apostles, with subsequent ecclesiastical additions. The earliest compilations were in the East, and the C.L. of the Eastern Orthodox Church is comparatively small and easy of access. The condensation of the C.L. of the Western Church achieved in 1917, was again revised in 1983 by John Paul II to incorporate reforms of the Second Vatican Council 1962–5. These incl the reduction of offences carrying automatic excommunication; extension of the provisional for the annulment of marriage; removal of the ban on marriage with non Catholics; extension of the role of women in church services; and a ban on priests taking part in trade union and political party activity.

The Canon Law of the Anglican Communion remained almost unchanged from 1603 until its complete revision in 1969. It is now kept under constant review by the C.L. Commission of the General Synod.

CANO'SSA. Ruined castle 19km (12m) SW of Reggio, Italy. Emperor Henry IV did penance here before pope Gregory VII in 1077 for having opposed him in the question of investitures.

CANOVA (kahnō'vah), **Antonio** (1757-1822). Italian sculptor. B. near Treviso, he traditionally modelled a lion in butter which brought his talent to notice, and his work has a sentimental delicacy which, though it led to the honour of executing the tombs of Clement XIII, Pius VII and Clement XIV, has not served his enduring reputation. 'Cupid and Psyche' in the Louvre and 'The Three Graces' at the Hermitage, Leningrad, are other famous pieces.

CANTAL (koṅtahl'). Range of mountains in central France which gives its name to Cantal dept. It is of volcanic origin. The highest point is the Plomb du Cantal, 1,858 m (6,096 ft).

CANTALOUPE (kan'taloop). Name of several small varieties of the melon (*Cucumis melo*), distinguished by their small and round ribbed fruits.

CANTERBURY. City in Kent, England, on the Stour, some 100km (62m) SE of London. It was the Roman city of Durovernum, and excavation of the areas bombed in German air raids of the S.W.W. has greatly increased our knowledge of this period. The modern name derives from Cantwarabyrig (OE fortress of the men of Kent), and was the capital of the Saxon Kings of Kent. It was King Ethelbert, whose wife Bertha was already a Christian, who welcomed Augustine's mission to England in 597, and C. has since been the metropolis of the Anglican Communion and seat of the Archbishop of Canterbury, Primate of All England. The foundations of the present cathedral were laid by Lanfranc (1070-89), but it has been rebuilt and added to, so that its styles range from Norman to Perpendicular. Throughout medieval times it was a great city, as the 14th cent. surviving West Gate shows, and was a centre of pilgrimage (cf. Chaucer's *Canterbury Tales*) to the shrine of St Thomas à Beckett, who was murdered in the cathedral in 1170. The shrine was destroyed by the commissioners of Henry VIII: close to the site are the tombs of the Black Prince and Henry IV. Christopher Marlowe was born in Canterbury and Somerset Maugham was ed. at King's School (refounded by Henry VIII 1541) on the site of the Benedictine Abbey of St Augustine, of which only fragments remain. The Univ. of Kent was estab. here 1965, and the first college was named after T. S. Eliot. Pop. (1972) 36,300.

CANTERBURY. Part of the stained glass window in St. Thomas' chapel, Canterbury cathedral, believed to represent the saint who was murdered there in 1170. *Photo: Courtesy of the British Tourist Authority.*

CANTERBURY, Archbishops of. The archbishop of C. is the Primate of All England, metropolitan of the Church of England, and first peer of the realm, ranking next to royalty. He crowns the sovereign, has a seat in the House of Lords, and is a member of the Privy Council. He appoints to many livings, and is empowered to confer degrees (Lambeth degrees) in divinity, law and medicine. His seat is Lambeth Palace, London, with a second residence at the Old Palace, Canterbury. The appointment is made by the Prime Minister, formerly by political consultation, but from 1980 on the suggestion of the church group, the Crown Appointments Commission (formed 1977).

The first A. of C. was Augustine, who was despatched from Rome by pope Gregory in AD 597 to convert the Anglo-Saxon Kingdom of Kent. Archbishops appointed this cent. have been: Randal T. Davidson, 1903; C. G. Lang, 1928; Wm. Temple, 1942; G. F. Fisher, 1945; A. M. Ramsey, 1961; D. Coggan, 1974, R. A. K. Runcie, 1980.

CANTERBURY PLAINS. District on the E. coast of South Island, New Zealand, *c.* 10,000 sq.km (4,000 sq.m) in extent, a rich area of grassland between the mountains and the sea. From here comes C. lamb.

CANTERBURY PLAINS. In the foreground the well laid out 'yards' and some of the nine thousand merino sheep run on the picturesque country surrounding Glentanner Station. The white-walled modern homestead nestles behind the plantation in the background. *Photo: Courtesy of the High Commissioner of New Zealand.*

CANTHA'RIDES (blister beetle, or Spanish fly). Family of beetles (Coleoptera) belonging to the section Heteromera. *Cantharis vesicatoria,* the Spanish fly, is the best-known species; it is bright golden-green, and 2cm (.75in) long. The drug C., a dangerous aphrodisiac, is prepared from its dried body.

CA'NTILĒVER. A horizontal beam fixed at one end to a rigid support and free to move at the other end. This type of structure is used widely in building and in C. bridges, where the projecting arms are built inwards from the piers to meet in the centre of the span, and in C. cranes where a straight steel truss rests on a central support.

CANTON. *See* GUANGZHOU.

CANTON. In France, a subdivision of the arrondissement; in Switzerland, a C. is one of the 23 divisions forming the Confederation.

CANTON AND ENDERBURY. Two atolls in the Phoenix group which forms part of the Rep. of Kiribati. They were a UK-USA condominium 1939-80, and there are US aviation, radar and tracking stations.

CANUTE (*c.* 995-1035). King of England, Denmark, and Norway. Son of Sweyn, king of Denmark, he was baptized *c.* 1000, accompanied his father in his invasion of England in 1013, and on the latter's death in 1014 was hailed as king by the army. In 1016 he defeated Edmund Ironside at Assandun in Essex, and then ruled Mercia and Northumbria until on Edmund's death he succeeded to the whole kingdom, and proved himself a just and wise ruler. He invaded Scotland *c.* 1027, and forced King Malcolm to pay homage. In 1018 he succeeded his brother Harold as king of Denmark, and he conquered Norway in 1028. His empire fell to pieces, however, at his death. He was buried at Winchester.

CA'NYON. Anglicized spelling of Span. *cañón,* a deep narrow hollow running through the mountains. There are many Cs. in the western States of the USA and in Mexico, e.g. the Grand C. of the Colorado, the C. in Yellowstone National Park, and the Black C. in Colorado.

CAPACITANCE, ELECTRICAL. The ratio of the electric charge on a body to the resultant change of potential. A capacitor (q.v.) has a C. of one farad when a charge of one coulomb changes its potential by one volt. The farad is an impractically large unit and capacitors normally used in electronic circuits are of the order of millionths of a farad (microfarads) or less.

CAPACITOR. Device for storing electric charge, consisting of conducting plates separated by layers of insulating material (dielectric). They may be flat or rolled up. Multiple air dielectric Cs. are commonly used as adjustable Cs. for tuning radio circuits. (Cs. were formerly called condensers.)

CAPE BRETON. Island forming the N part of the prov. of Nova Scotia, Canada. Bisected by a waterway, it is linked to the mainland across the Strait of Canso by road and rail. C.B. has coal resources and steelworks, and there has been substantial industrial development in the strait area, with docks and oil refineries, newsprint production from local timber, etc. In the N the surface is rugged, rising to 550m (1,800 ft) at North Cape, and the much indented coast has many fine harbours. There are cod fisheries. The climate is mild and very moist. The chief towns are Sydney and Glace Bay.

The first British colony was estab. in 1629, but was driven out by the French. In 1763 C.B. was ceded to Britain and attached to Nova Scotia 1763-84 and from 1820. Area 10,282 sq.km (3,970 sq.m).

CAPE BYRON. The most easterly extremity of Australia, in N.S.W., just south of the border with Queensland.

CAPE CANAVERAL (kanav'eral). Promontory on the Atlantic coast of Florida, USA, 367km (228m) N of Miami. First mentioned in 1513, it was known 1963-73 as Cape Kennedy. The John F. Kennedy Space Center, from which all US orbital and lunar flights have been launched, is here.

CAPE COAST. Port of Ghana, West Africa, 130km (80m) W of Accra, superseded since 1962 by Tema. The town is built on a natural breakwater, adjoining which is the castle, first estab. by the Portuguese in the 16th cent. Pop. (1970) 71,600.

CAPE COD. Peninsula in SE Massachusetts, USA, where in 1620 the Pilgrim Fathers landed at Provincetown.

CAPE COLOURED. Descendants of mixed unions between Europeans and African peoples, living mainly in Cape Province, Rep. of S. Africa.

ČAPEK (chah'pek), **Karel Matěj** (1890-1938). Czech playwright. His great successes were *R.U.R.* (Rossum's Universal Robots) in 1921, in which the mechanical creations of the scientists develop souls and rebel against their masters, and, more bitterly satirical, *The Insect Play* also 1921 (written with his brother Joseph C., 1887-1945) prophetic of totalitarianism.

CAPE HORN. Southernmost point of S America, Horn Island, Tierra del Fuego, Chile. Strong winds make the passage round it dangerous.

CAPE OF GOOD HOPE. South African headland forming a peninsula between Table Bay and False Bay, Cape Town. Discovered by Bartholomew Diaz in 1488, it was named Cape of Storms, but afterwards given its present name by King John II of Portugal.

CAPE PROVINCE (Kaapland). A province – the parent state of the Republic of S. Africa, in the extreme S of the African continent, named after the famous promontory. The Dutch occupied the Cape in 1650, and in 1652 laid out Capetown. The territory, first taken by the British in 1795 after the French Revolutionary armies had occupied the Netherlands, was sold to Britain for £6,000,000 in 1814. The Orange r. was proclaimed the N boundary in 1825. Griqualand W (1880) and the S part of Bechuanaland (1895) were later incorporated; and Walvis Bay, although administered with SW Africa 1922-77, is legally an integral part of Cape Province.

Physically the Cape consists of (a) a high plateau, the veld country, hilly and dotted with isolated kopjes, whose southern limit is the great escarpment which more or less parallels the coast and is called the Drakensberg, Stormberg, etc.; and (b) the area between the escarpment and the sea, comprising the Great Karoo, the SE region about Graaff Reinet, and the Coast Belt.

Rainfall is the dominating climatic factor, although irrigation is extending. Only the SW corner about Capetown has a copious and reliable (winter) rainfall, and here conditions favour the production of fruit and vegetables; the grapes are made into popular wines. The Karoo lends itself to extensive farming, in spite of droughts, since the scrub is nutritious animal food and the soil is fertile. The SE is an area of mixed farming, cattle and maize being the chief products. Kimberley, in Griqualand W, is the centre of great diamond workings; copper, asbestos, and manganese are also important.

The Cape was given self-government in 1872; it joined the Union in 1910. The chief towns are along the coast. Capetown, the cap., is also the legislative cap. of the Rep. of South Africa; Port Elizabeth and East London rank next in size. Other towns are Kimberley, Grahamstown and Stellenbosch. Area 721,000 sq.km (278,400 sq.m) excl. Walvis Bay; pop. (1970) 6,731,820, incl. 1,100,000 white.

CAPER. A shrub (*Capparis spinosa*) of the family Capparidaceae, native to the Mediterranean region. Its buds and unripe fruit are preserved in vinegar and used as a condiment, known as capers.

CAPERCAILZIE (kaperkāl'zi, -kāl'yi). Game bird (*Tetrao urogallus*), the largest member of the grouse family (Tetraonidae). The cock is as large as a hen-turkey, with dark iron-grey, brown and black plumage, glossed with green on the breast.

CAPET (kahpā'), **Hugh** (*c.* 938-96). King of France. He succeeded his father, Hugh the Great, as duke of France in 956, claimed the throne in 987 on the death of Louis V, the last of the Carolingians, and maintained his claim against Charles of Lorraine, Louis's uncle. The dynasty he founded occupied the French throne until the Revolution.

CAPETOWN. City and oldest town of S. Africa, legislative capital of the Republic of South Africa, and the capital of Cape Province. It was founded in 1652 by Johan van Riebeeck, of the Dutch East India Co., and later German and Huguenot refugees joined the small community. C. is a vitally important port and the modern harbour, continually improved, can accommodate vessels of large size. With the expansion of population, new suburbs are developed. The city is well planned, and contains many handsome buildings; they include City Hall, the Houses of Parliament, and the castle, begun in 1666. The university is situated in the grounds of Groote Schuur (great barn), Cecil Rhodes's home, designated by him to be the residence of the Premier. Most industries of C. centre round port activities, but the cultivation of fruit and flowers is also important. Pop. (1970) 825,750 (271,370 white).

CAPE VERDE (verd), **Rep. of.** Archipelago of 10 islands in the Atlantic, 565 km (350 m) W of Cape Verde in Senegal, the most westerly cape in Africa. The cap. is Praia; pop. 6,000. Formerly Portuguese, C.V. became independent in 1975, and eventual union with Guinea-Bissau is planned. C.V. is strategically important because it dominates Western shipping routes. In 1980 the USSR supplied C.V. with the nucleus of a navy. Area 4,033 sq.km (1,557 sq.m); pop. (1976) 360,000, with a large Negro element, incl. many Angolan refugees. A Portuguese dialect is spoken. M.U.: C.V. escudo.

CAPE YORK. The most northerly point (10°41'S) of the Australian mainland, so named by Cook in 1770. The C.Y. Peninsula is c.800 km (500 m) long and c. 640 km (400 m) wide at its junction with the mainland. Its barrenness deterred early Dutch explorers, although the southern part is being developed for cattle (Brahmin type) and in the northern there are large bauxite deposits. There are large aboriginal reservations and some of their best rock paintings are here. *See illus under* CAVE.

CAPILLARY (Lat. *capillus*, a hair). One of the network of innumerable minute blood vessels situated between the small arteries and the small veins. Their size is about 8/1,000 of a millimetre. The term is also applied to any very fine-bore tube or cylindrical space of very small radius. C. pressure is pressure due to C. force, and capillarity deals with the effects of elevation or depression of fluids in fine Cs. the study of which grows much light on surface-tension phenomena, wetting of materials, soils, etc., and separation of gases through porous media.

CA'PITAL. In architecture, a stone placed on the top of a column, pier, or pilaster, and usually wider on the upper surface than the diameter of the supporting shaft. It consists of 3 parts: the top member called the *abacus*, a block which acts as the supporting surface to the superstructure; the middle portion known as the bell or *echinus*; and the lower part called the necking or *astragal*. *See* ORDER.

CAPITALISM. Name given to the economic system in which the principal means of production, distribution, and exchange are in private (individual or corporate) hands. Almost synonymous is 'private enterprise', since reliance is put on the enterprise of private individuals and business companies and firms for the satisfaction of the community's economic wants, and not on government and municipal activities. The 'profit motive' constitutes the prime stimulus to productive exertion, and the 'price mechanism' determines what things shall be made, in what quantities, and under what conditions. The rival system is Socialism or Communism, in which the State is the dominant factor. A 'mixed economy', as in Britain, combines private enterprise and a degree of state monopoly, as in the nationalised industries.

CAPITAL PUNISHMENT. Punishment by death, a form of penalty common to all ages. In England at the end of the 18th cent. more than 200 offences, incl. petty theft, carried the death penalty, though in practice it was imposed only for some 25. From 1810 onwards Sir Samuel Romilly and others conducted a vigorous campaign for the mitigation of the penal laws; several acts were passed at intervals, each reducing the number of crimes liable to so drastic a penalty, until an act of 1861 left only murder, treason, piracy with violence, and the firing of government arsenals and dockyards punishable by death. Disuse abrogated its imposition for the last 2 offences and except for a few exceptions for treason in time of war, all executions in Britain since 1838 have been for murder. Until 1866, they were carried out in public. In 1965 C.P. was in effect abolished.

In the USA the Supreme Court ruled in 1972 that C.P. was a violation of the 8th amendment to the constitution (prohibiting cruel and unusual punishment), but the death penalty was subsequently restored by a number of individual states. A further ruling in 1976 by the Court laid down that it was not 'cruel and unusual' in all circumstances. Execution methods vary from state to state and incl. electrocution, lethal gas, hanging and shooting.

Elsewhere in the world C.P. is still retained by the majority of countries for ordinary crimes and sanctioned by majority public opinion, e.g. in the USSR crimes punishable by death incl. bribe-taking, theft and currency offences. A tendency in more settled states to abolition is countered by an increase in use, often with accompanying additional punishments, where the rule of law is ill-established. All countries tend to invoke it in times of exceptional crisis. France uses the guillotine (q.v.), Spain garrotting, a form of strangulation, and the USSR shooting.

CAPO-DI-MONTE (kah'pō-di-montā). Village, N of Naples, where porcelain known by the same name was first produced under King Charles III of Naples in 1736. Best-known are the figures of tramps, beggars and urchins.

CAPONE (kapōn'), **Alphonse** (1898-1947). American gangster, called Al Capone, b. in Brooklyn, the son of an Italian barber. During the prohibition period C. built up a criminal organization in Chicago city. No charges could be sustained against him until 1931, when he received a 10-year sentence for evading the payment of income tax. He was released in 1939.

CAPORE'TTO. Village on the Isonzo, near to which in 1917 the Italians under Cadorna were defeated by the Austro-Germans under Below. Then in Hungary, it was in Italy from 1918 until trs. to Yugoslavia in 1947.

CAPOTE (kapō'tē), **Truman** (1924-). American novelist. B. in New Orleans, he uses a Southern setting in *The Grass Harp* (1951), etc., and set a trend in 'non-fiction' novels with *In Cold Blood* (1966), reconstructing a Kansas killing.

CAPP, Al. Pseudonym of the American cartoonist Alfred Caplin (1909-79). B. in New Haven, Connecticut, he started his *Li'l Abner* strip in 1934 and the characters of the hill-billy community of Dogpatch, Kentucky, passed into US folklore.

CAPPADOCIA (kapadō'shia). In ancient geography, a mountainous district in the E. of Asia Minor bounded on the S. by the Taurus mts. and on the E by the Euphrates.

CAPRA (kah'prah), **Frank** (1897-). American film director. Sicilian-born, but living in the US from the age of 6, he won Oscars for such films as *Mr Deeds Goes to Town* (1936) and *You Can't Take it With You* (1938), with sentimental, idealistic heroes.

CAPRI (kah'prē). Italian island at the S entrance of the Bay of Naples, 32km (20m) S of Naples. It has two towns, Capri and Anacapri, and is famous for its flowers, beautiful scenery, and ideal climate. Area 13 sq.km (5 sq.m); pop. about 8,000.

CAPRIVI (kahprē'vē), **Georg Leo,** Count von (1831-99). German Imperial Chancellor 1890-4.

CAPSICUM (kap'sikum). Genus of plants in the nightshade family Solanaceae, native to S America. The differing species produce green-to-red fruits which vary from the small ones (used whole to give the hot flavour of chilli, or ground to produce cayenne pepper), to the large pointed or squarish pods of the sweet peppers (mild-flavoured and used as a vegetable).

CAPSULE, space. Vehicle launched by a rocket into space. It may be manned, in which case it contains all the instruments and accessories necessary for survival during launching, flight, re-entry into the atmosphere and recovery, or other projected programme.

CAPUA (kah'poo-ah). Italian town in Caserta province on the Volturno, in a fertile plain N of Naples. There was heavy fighting here in 1943 during the S.W.W., and the Romanesque cathedral was almost destroyed. Pop. (1970) 18,200.

CA'PŪCHIN. A South American monkey (*Cebus*). Sometimes called the Sapajou. Some species have hairy 'cowls' on the forehead, thus giving rise to the popular name from a fancied resemblance to C. monks. They have prehensile tails used for climbing, and go about in troops, feeding on insects and fruit.

CA'PŪCHINS. Order of friars in the RC church, instituted about 1520 by Fr Matteo di Bassi, an Italian monk who wished to return to the literal observance of the rule of St Francis. The brown habit with the pointed hood (Fr *capuche*) which he adopted gave his followers the name. It was recognized by the Holy See in 1619, and has been remarkable for its missionary activity. Despite stress on poverty and austerity, the order has attracted many members of the nobility. *See* FRANCISCANS.

CAPYBĀ'RA The largest of the rodents (*Hydrochoerus hydrochaeris*) and the only representative of the family Caviidae. It has scanty, coarse yellowish hair, and is *c.* 125cm (4ft) long with a large head and a very short tail, and may reach a weight of 45kg (100lb). An expert swimmer, it herds in the forests of South America.

CA'RACAL. A species of lynx (*Lynx caracal*). It lives in bush or desert country in Africa, Arabia, and India, where it was formerly tamed for the purpose of catching game. It is over 90cm (3ft) long, has tufted blackish ears and short fur, fawn above, and white with spots below.

CARACA'LLA, Marcus Aurelius Antoninus (AD 186-217). Roman emperor. He succeeded his father Septimius Severus in 211, ruled with great cruelty and ruinous extravagance, and was assassinated.

CARACAS (karah'kas). Chief city and cap. of Venezuela, on the Andean slopes, 13km (8m) S of its port La Guaira on the Caribbean coast. It has many fine buildings. Founded 1560-67, it has several times suffered severely from earthquakes. Simon Bolivar was b. here. It makes cement, textiles, paper, tobacco, etc., and has an international airport. Pop. of met. area (1979) 3,507,800.

CARA'CTACUS (d. *c.* AD 54). British chieftain, who resisted the Romans, AD 43-51, at the head of the tribes of SE Britain, but was defeated on the southern borders of Wales, and shown in Claudius's triumphal procession; in admiration for his courage Claudius released him, and he d. at Rome.

CA'RADON, Hugh Foot, baron C. (1907-). Brit. Labour politician, son of Isaac Foot (q.v.). As gov. of Cyprus 1957-60, he guided independence negotiations,

CARACAS. Venezuela University forms a city within a city, and the complex of buildings, of which part is seen here, has gates guarded by university police. As in most Latin American countries, the university is independent and self-governing, a privilege jealously guarded, and no state police or soldiers are allowed to enter. This is a necessary precaution in a continent where military coups are frequent. *Photo: Claude Jacoby/Camera Press.*

and was Min. of State for For. Affairs and permanent Brit. rep. at the UN 1964-70.

CA'RAT. Unit of purity in gold. The carat (US karat) is a twenty-fourth part, and chemically pure gold is 24-carat. Jewellery is often composed of 22-carat or 18-carat gold, i.e. a mixture of 22 or 18 parts gold and 2 or 6 parts alloy. The metric C. of 0.200 grams is the unit of weight for diamonds and other precious stones.

CARAVAGGIO (kahrahvahd'jo), **Michelangelo Merisi da** (*c.* 1569-1609). Italian artist. B. at Caravaggio, near Milan, he developed a precocious talent and rapidly estab. a reputation for controversial realism. His life was equally adventurous - he killed a man in a brawl in 1606 and fled from Rome where the Cardinal del Monte had been his patron, working in Naples, Malta and Sicily. His works incl. 'The Supper at Emmaus' (National Gallery), 'The Entombment of Christ (Vatican) and 'The Death of the Virgin' (Louvre).

CA'RAWAY. Genus of plants (*Carum*) of the family Umbelliferae. *C. carvi*, of Europe and Asia, is cultivated for its fruit, known as C. seeds, which are aromatic and pungent, containing a volatile oil, and are used for flavouring and also in medicine.

CA'RBIDES. Compounds of carbon and one other chemical element, the 2nd element being a metal, silicon, or boron. They occupy an important place in chemical technology, particularly calcium C., which, as the generator of acetylene, acts as the starting-point of many basic organic syntheses. In recent years some metallic Cs. have come to hold a place of great importance in engineering technology on account of their extreme hardness and strength. The C. of tungsten and its ore, wolfram, is an essential ingredient of metallic C. tools as well as of ordinary high-speed tools.

CARBOHYDRATES. A group of compounds composed of carbon, hydrogen, and oxygen. On decomposition the Cs. yield water and a residue of carbon. Cs. include sugars - soluble crystalline compounds with a sweet taste; starches - more complex compounds, usually non-crystalline, and insoluble in cold water; and cellulose, which is fibrous and can be woven into textiles. Cs. form the chief foodstuffs of herbivorous animals.

CARBOLIC ACID. Phenol, C_6H_5OH. Extracted from coal tar, pure C.A. consists of colourless crystals, needle-shaped, which readily take up moisture from the atmosphere. The taste is pungent and slightly sweet and the smell strong and characteristic. It is a powerful and penetrating antiseptic, but because of its poisonous properties it is not now much used on human tissues. It is a strong disinfectant.

CARBON. Symbol C, at. wt. 12.011, at. no. 6. One of the most widely distributed non-metallic elements. It occurs free in nature as diamond and graphite (crystalline forms), in carbonaceous rocks such as chalk and limestone, as carbon dioxide in the atmosphere, as hydrocarbons in petroleum, coal and natural gas and as a constituent of all organic substances. *See* ORGANIC CHEMISTRY. In its amorphous form it is familiar as coke, charcoal, soot, etc.

Of the inorganic C. compounds, the most important is *carbon dioxide* (CO_2), a colourless gas with a very slightly acid taste, which is formed wherever C. is burned in an adequate supply of air. *Carbon monoxide* (CO) is formed whenever C. is oxidized in a limited supply of air. It is combustible, does not form an acid solution in water, and is tasteless. It is very poisonous owing to the stable compound it forms with the blood haemoglobin; it is the poisonous constituent of coal gas and motor-car exhaust fumes. *Carbon disulphide* (CS_2), a dense liquid with a sweetish odour, is the sulphur compound corresponding to the oxygen compound C. dioxide. An important group of compounds is known as the *carbon halides*, of which C. tetrachloride (CCl_4) is the best-known. Being non-inflammable it is used in certain fire appliances, but as it reacts with oxygen at high temperatures to produce phosgene ($COCl_2$), a poisonous war gas, the fumes are dangerous.

When added to steel C. forms a wide range of C. steels with useful properties. In pure form it is widely used as a moderator in nuclear reactors; as colloidal graphite (Dag, Aquadag) it is a good lubricant and, when deposited on a surface in a vacuum, obviates photoelectric and secondary emission of electrons. In the form of coal or coke (q.v.) C. is a widespread fuel. The isotope carbon-14 is greatly used as a tracer in biological research, since plants can be grown in an atmosphere containing radioactive C. in carbon dioxide, which passes into chemicals derived from the plant and hence becomes a 'label'. Carbon-14 is also useful for dating, as in archaeology, e.g. on death wood ceases to take up carbon-14 from the air and that already taken up decays at a known rate, allowing the time which has elapsed to be measured.

Carbon fibres - fine, black, silky filaments produced by heat treatment from a special grade of Courtelle and bonded by resin - were developed at the Royal Aircraft Establishment, Farnborough, 1964-5. Light, wear-resistant, cheap to produce, and up to 8 times as strong as high-tensile steel, they are vital in the aerospace, car and electricity industries, manufacture of sports gear, etc.

CARBONARI (kahrbŌnah'rē). A political secret revolutionary society in southern Italy in the first half of the 19th cent. The first members were republican rebels against Murat, the Bonapartist king of Naples, who took refuge in the Abruzzi and called themselves C. ('charcoal burners'). Subsequently the C. rose more than once against the Bourbon king; and though driven underground, played a part in Mazzini's 'Young Italy' movement.

CA'RBONATES. Important group of minerals formed by the combination of carbon dioxide with a basic element. The carbon dioxide dissolved by rain falling through the air, and also liberated by decomposing animals and plants in the soil, forms with water carbonic acid, which unites with various alkaline basic substances to form Cs. Of these, calcium carbonate ($CaCO_3$) is the most important.

CARBORUNDUM. Silicon carbide (SiC). A hard black artificial compound of carbon and silicon, discovered in 1891 by E. G. Acheson. It is harder than corundum but not so hard as diamond.

CARBUNCLE. A mass formed by a cluster of boils, or a garnet cut to resemble it in the shape of a rounded knob.

CARBURATION. Regular combustion, usually in a closed space, of carbon compounds such as petrol, paraffin, or fuel oil; regulated combustion is distinct from much more rapid burning such as explosion or detonation, and the definition applies particularly to combustion in the cylinders of reciprocating petrol engines of the types used in aircraft, road vehicles, or marine vessels. The device by which the liquid fuel is prepared for combustion is termed the *carburetter.*

CARCASSONNE (kahrkahson'). City of SW France, cap. of Aude dept, on the r. Aude, which divides it into the ancient and modern town. Its medieval fortifications (much restored) are the finest in France. Pop. (1973) 46,330.

CARCASSONNE. The fortifications restored by Viollet-le-Duc 1850–80 now look much as they did when unsuccessfully besieged by the Black Prince in 1356. *Photo: Camera Press.*

CARCHEMISH (kahr'k-). Ancient city on the right bank of the upper Euphrates, 80km (50m) NE of Aleppo, once the centre of a New-Hittite empire and in 605 BC the scene of a battle between Nebuchadnezzar and the Egyptians. On its site is the Turkish village of Karkamis; nearby on the Syrian side of the frontier is Jerablus.

CA'RDANO, Girolamo (1501–76). Italian physician, mathematician, philosopher, and astrologer, B. at Pavia, he became professor of medicine there in 1543, and wrote 2 important works on physics and natural science - *De subtilitate rerum* (1551) and *De varietate rerum* (1557).

CÁRDENAS, Lazaro (1895-1970). Mexican general and statesman, in early life a civil servant, he took part in the revolutionary campaigns 1915-29 that followed the fall of President Diaz, was President of the republic 1934-40, and introduced many Socialist measures. He was Min. of National Defence 1943-5.

CARDIFF. Capital of Wales (officially designated 1955), and admin. HQ of S and Mid Glamorgan, at the mouth of the Taff, Rhymney and Ely rivers. The city dates from Roman times, the later town being built round the Norman castle: this, the residence of the earls and marquesses of Bute from the 18th cent., was given to the city in 1947 by the 5th marquess. The modern importance of C. dates from the opening of the docks on the Bristol Channel in 1839, which were greatly extended by the 2nd marquess of Bute (1793-1848). Here a great coal export trade was handled until the 1920s. As this declined iron and steel exports continued to grow, and an import trade in timber, grain and flour, tobacco, meat, and citrus fruit developed. Besides steelworks, there are automotive component, flour milling, paper, cigar and other industries.

In Cathays Park is a group of public buildings incl. the Law Courts, and City Hall, the Nat. Museum of Wales, the Welsh Office (estab. 1964), a major part of the Univ. of Wales (Institute of Science and Technology, Nat. School of Medicine and Univ. Coll. of S Wales), and the Temple of Peace and Health. Llandaff, on the right bank of the Taff, seat of an archbp from the 6th cent. was incl. in C. in 1922; its cathedral, virtually rebuilt in the 19th cent. and restored 1948-57 after air raid damage in the S.W.W., has a giant figure of Christ in Majesty by Epstein. At St Fagan's nr C. is the Welsh Nat. Folk Museum, containing small rebuilt historical buildings from rural Wales in which living crafts are demonstrated. The Royal Mint is at Llantrisant 16km (10m) from C. Pop. (1973) 280,000.

CARDIFF. The City Hall (1906), one of the fine group of civic buildings, including the National Museum of Wales, in Cathays Park. *Photo: Courtesy of the Welsh Office.*

CARDIGANSHIRE. Former co. of Wales facing Cardigan Bay, which was in 1974 merged, together with Pembroke and Carmarthen, in Dyfed. Mainly mountainous, the area rises in the NE to Plynlimmon (752m/2,468 ft), and is drained by the Rheidol, Ystwyth,

Teifi and Towy. The co. town was Cardigan, pop. (1973) 3,800.

CARDINAL. In the RC church, the highest dignitary next to the Pope. Originally a C. was any priest in charge of a major parish; but in 1567 the term was confined to the members of the Sacred College: from 1973 only 120 (below the age of 80) are eligible to elect the Pope. The Cs. assist the Pope in liturgical matters and in the temporal business of the Church, give their advice in all matters of doctrine, canonizations, and convocation of councils, and are responsible for electing the Pope from amongst their number. They are nominated and elected by the Pope and must come to Rome for the ceremony within a year, to receive the red hat which is the badge of office.

CARDUCCI (kahrdooch'ē), **Giosuè** (1835-1907). Italian poet. B. in Tuscany, he was appointed in 1860 professor of Italian literature in Bologna, and won a distinguished place by his lecturing and critical work, and also as a poet. His *Inno a Satana* (Hymn to Satan, 1865) was full of revolutionary feeling, and was followed by several other vols. of verse, in which his nationalist sympathies are apparent. He was awarded the Nobel prize for literature in 1906.

CARDWELL, Edward, visct (1813-86). British Liberal statesman. He entered Parliament as a Peelite in 1842, and 1868-74 was Sec. for War under Gladstone, when he carried out many reforms, including the abolition of the purchase of military commissions and promotions.

CAREW (kăr'i), **Thomas** (1595?-1638?). English poet. B. in Kent, he was in 1628 a gentleman of the privy chamber to Charles I, and was the most brilliant lyricist as well as the most deliberate and finished craftsman of the school of 'Cavalier Poets'.

CAREY, Henry (*c.* 1690-1743). British poet and musician, remembered for the song 'Sally in Our Alley'. 'God Save the King' (both words and music) has also been attributed to him.

CARGO CULT. Religious belief among some natives of Melanesia that the trappings of Western life - the 'cargo' - will be brought to them by ship or aircraft through the agency of some messianic spirit figure. Imitating white usage, they make calls on telephones which they do not realise need to be connected and build 'warehouses' for the expected goods. They also perform various rituals, and may turn on local whites when their expectations are disappointed.

CARIBBE'AN. A sea forming that part of the Atlantic Ocean lying between the N coasts of S and Central American and the West Indies, about 2,740 km (1,700 m) long and 650km (400m)-1,500 km (900m) wide; here the Gulf Stream turns in the direction of Europe.

CARIBBEAN COMMUNITY. Know as Caricom, the C.C. was estab. by the Treaty of Chaguaramas (1973), to secure economic, development, and foreign policy co-operation. The dominant member is Trinidad and Tobago; others are Antigua, Barbados, Belize, Dominica, Grenada, Guyana, Jamaica, Montserrat, St Kitts-Nevis, Anguilla, St Lucia and St Vincent. The left-wing coup in Grenada in 1979 led to the establishment of a 'progressive' regional sub-group by Grenada, St Lucia and Dominica.

CARIBOU. *See* REINDEER.

CARIBS. Name given by Columbus to an aboriginal people of S America and the islands of the W Indies in the Caribbean Sea. They were cannibals, distinguished for their ferocity. In 1796 the English in the W Indies deported most of them to Roatan Island off Honduras. They have since spread extensively in Honduras and Nicaragua. Reddish brown in colour, their features are mongoloid.

CARICATURE. The representation of persons or things by exaggerating characteristic features in such a way as to provoke ridicule or contempt. The word first came into use in England in its Italian form *caricatura* (from It. *caricare*, to exaggerate) *c.* 1680.

C. was not unknown to the Greeks and Romans. Grotesque drawings have been discovered in Pompeii and Herculaneum, and Pliny refers to a grotesque portrait of the poet Hipponax. Humorous drawings were executed by the Carracci and their followers (the Italian 'eclectic' school of the 16th cent.). Pictorial satire was common in England during the Civil War, but true C. begins with Hogarth: later exponents incl. Gillray, Rowlandson, Cruikshank, John and Richard Doyle, Leech, du Maurier, Tenniel, Phil May, Beerbohm, David Low, 'Vicky', 'Giles', Cummings, Osbert Lancaster and Mel Calman (b.1931-) in England, and Jules Feiffer, Herb Block, Bill Mauldin and Saul Steinberg in the USA.

Charles Philipon (1800-62) founded in Paris in 1830 *La Caricature*, probably the first periodical to specialize in C.: notable later was *Punch*, founded 1841.

CARICATURE. Brilliantly caustic in his comments in the Second World War was the Russian cartoonist, Kukrinski. Here, Hitler is being flatteringly painted by Dr Goebbels.

CARINĀ'TAE. One of the two divisions into which the living members of the class Aves (Birds, q.v.) fall, though it is now regarded rather as a rule-of-thumb than a strictly scientific division. It covers the vast majority of the class - all flying birds and the penguins.

CARINTHIA. An independent duchy from 976, and a possession of the Hapsburgs 1276-1918, it is an alpine prov. of Austria, bordering Italy and Yugoslavia in the south. The cap. is Klagenfurt. Area 9,533 sq.km (3,681 sq.m); pop. (1971) 525,730.

CARISBROOKE. Village in the Isle of Wight, SW of Newport, of which it is now a part. Its chief feature is the ruins of the castle in which Charles I was imprisoned (1647-8).

CARL XVI Gustaf (1946-). King of Sweden. He succeeded his grandfather Gustaf VI (q.v.), his father having been killed in an air crash in 1947. Under provisions in the new Swedish constitution which became effective on his grandfather's death, the monarchy was effectively stripped of all power at his accession.

CARLISLE (karlīl'). City in Cumbria, England, on the Eden 13km (8m) S of the Scottish border: it was the co. town of the former co. of Cumberland. It is an important railway centre; textiles, engineering, and biscuit making are the chief industries. The outstanding buildings are the cathedral and the castle, both dating from Norman times, but subsequently much added to. The bishopric dates from 1133. It is admin. HQ of Cumbria. Pop. (1972) 71,440.

CARLISTS. Supporters of the Spanish pretender, Don Maria Isidro Carlos de Bourbon (1788-1855), who claimed the throne on the death of his brother Ferdinand VII in 1833, in opposition to his niece Maria Isabella who had been proclaimed queen. The Carlist revolt continued, espec. in the Basque provs., until 1839, and it was not until 1977 that the Carlist political party was legalised and Carlos Hugo de Bourbon Parma (1930-), who had m. in 1964 Princess Irene of the Netherlands, renounced his claim as pretender and became reconciled with King Juan Carlos. *See* table under BOURBON.

CARLOS I (1863-1908). King of Portugal, of the Braganza-Coburg line, from 1889 until he was assassinated in Lisbon with his elder son Luis. He was succeeded by his younger son Manoel.

CARLOS, Don (1545-68). Spanish prince. Son of Philip II, he was recognized as heir to the thrones of Castile and Aragon, but became a lunatic and had to be placed under restraint following a plot to assassinate his father. His story was made the subject of plays by Schiller, Alfieri, Otway, and others.

CARLOW. Co. of Rep. of Ireland, in the prov. of Leinster. In the S there is a long range of heights, rising to 796m (2,610 ft) in Mt Leinster, but the rest of the co. is a low-lying and undulating plain. The soil, watered by the Barrow and the Slaney, is fertile and dairy farming is important. The co. town is also C. Area 896 sq.km (346 sq.m); pop. (1971) 34,237.

CARLSBAD. German name of KARLOVY VARY.

CARLSON, Chester (1906-68). American inventor. A research worker with Bell Telephone, he was sacked from his post in 1930 during the Depression, and set to work on his own to develop an efficient copying machine. By 1938 he had invented the xerox (q.v.) method.

CARLYLE, Thomas (1795-1881). Scottish author. B. at Ecclefechan in Dumfriesshire, he accepted a mathematical mastership at Annan in 1814, studying meanwhile for the Presbyterian ministry. In 1816 he transferred to Kirkcaldy where he met Edward Irving, and in 1818 to Edinburgh where, having given up thought of the Church, he combined study of the law with miscellaneous literary work. In 1821 he passed through the spiritual crisis described in *Sartor Resartus*, and after a period as a tutor secured the publication in London of his life of Schiller (1825), and a translation of Goethe's *Wilhelm Meister* (1824). He had first met Jane Baillie Welsh (1801-66) in 1821, and after their marriage in 1826 they moved to her farm at isolated Craigenputtock, where *Sartor Resartus* (1836) was written. In 1834 they removed to Cheyne Row, Chelsea, and in 1837 he established his reputation with the *French Revolution*, still unrivalled in vividness of narration. Of the series of lectures he gave (1837-40), the most successful were those *On Heroes, Hero-Worship, and the Heroic in History* (1841). At this period he also wrote *Chartism* (1839), attacking the doctrine of *laissez-faire*; *Past and Present* (1843), a comparison of labour in the 13th and the 19th cents.; and *Latter-Day Pamphlets* (1850), a criticism of popular government. The notable *Letters and Speeches of Cromwell* (1845) was followed by the miniature life of his friend *John Sterling* (1851). C. then began his monumental *History of Frederick the Great* (1858-65), and in the year of its completion was elected rector of Edinburgh university. After the death of his wife in 1866 he devoted most of his time to editing her letters and preparing the *Reminiscences*. The publication of these (in 1883 and 1881 respectively), and of the biography by Froude, caused a public outcry because of the rather unfavourable light thrown on C.'s character.

CARMARTHENSHIRE. Former co. of S Wales, and formerly also the largest Welsh county. It bordered on the Bristol Channel, and was merged in 1974, together with Cardigan and Pembroke in Dyfed. The co. town was Carmarthen, pop. (1973) 12,850.

CARMELITES or **White Friars.** Religious order of mendicants in the RC church. Traditionally they originated in the days of Elijah, who is supposed to have lived on Mt Carmel in Palestine. Historically the first congregation was founded on Carmel by Berthold, a crusader from Calabria, about 1155. According to the rule which the patriarch of Jerusalem drew up for them about 1210, they lived as hermits in separate huts. About 1240 the Saracen conquests compelled them to move from Palestine, and they took root in the west, particularly in France and England, where the order became cenobitical and mendicant. There were many reform movements in the order's history, of which the most important was that initiated by St Teresa. In 1562 she founded in Avila a convent where the rule was stricter than that hitherto observed, and with the co-operation of St John of the Cross and others she established priories and further nunneries, whose members were called the Discalced or bare-footed Cs., to distinguish them from the senior branch of the Calced Cs. The Cs. have devoted themselves largely to missionary work and mystical theology. Their habit consists of a brown tunic with a white overmantle.

CARNAC (kahrnahk'). Village in the dept of Morbihan, France, SE of Lorient. In the neighbourhood there is a fine collection of megalithic remains of the period 2000-1500 BC, incl. various types of tomb and a series of stone alignments. In the largest of the 3 latter (Menec) well over 1,000 stones up to 4m (13ft) high are arranged in 11 rows with a circle at the W end. They were obviously used for processions, possibly linked with rituals for the dead. As with Stonehenge, their arrangement suggests an astronomical use. Pop. (1975) 4,000.

CA'RNAP, Rudolf (1891-1970). American philosopher, the world's foremost exponent of logical empiricism. B. at Wuppertal, Germany, he was a member of the Vienna Circle who adopted Mach (q.v.) as their guide, and in 1935 went to the US, where he was prof. of philosophy at the Univ. of California 1954-62. His books incl. *The Logical Syntax of Language* (1934), and *Meaning and Necessity* (1956).

CARNARVON RANGE. Section of the Great Divide, Queensland, Australia, c. 900 m. (1,000 ft) high. There are many Aboriginal paintings in the sandstone caves along its length of c. 160 km (100m).

CARNATION. Name given to the numerous double-flowered cultivated varieties of the clove-pink (*Dianthus caryophyllus*). They are divided into flake, bizarre, and picotees, according as the petals exhibit one or more colours on their white ground, or have it dispersed in strips, or as a border to the petals.

CARNÉ (kahrneh'), **Marcel** (1909-). French film director. A master of subtle depths of characterization, his films incl. *Quai des brumes* (1938), *Le Jour se lève*, and *Les Enfants du Paradis* (1944).

CARNEGIE (kahrneg'i), **Andrew** (1835-1919). Scottish-American millionaire. B. at Dunfermline, he was taken by his parents to USA in 1848, and at 14 became a telegraph boy in Pittsburg. Subsequently he became a railway employee, rose to be superintendent, and by the introduction of sleeping-cars and successful investments in oil, laid the foundations of a fortune. Next he concerned himself with the development of the Pittsburgh iron and steel industries, and built up a vast 'empire' which he disposed of to the US Steel Trust in 1901. From that time he lived at Skibo castle in Sutherland, and devoted his wealth to philanthropic purposes, notably the provision and equipment of libraries, the endowment of universities, the Carnegie Hero Fund, etc. On his death the C. Trusts continued his benevolent activities. *Carnegie Hall* in New York, opened 1891 as The Music Hall, was renamed in 1898 in recognition of his large contribution to its construction.

CARNEGIE, Dale (1888-1955). American author and teacher. B. in Missouri, he planned a teaching career, but tried journalism and the stage before becoming YMCA instructor on public speaking. An instant success, he achieved world fame with *How to Win Friends and Influence People* (1938).

CARNIOLA. A former crownland and duchy of Austria, most of which was included in Slovenia, part of the kingdom of the Serbs, Croats, and Slovenes (later Yugoslavia) in 1919. The westerly districts of Idrija and Postojna, then allocated to Italy, were transferred to Yugoslavia in 1947.

CARNI'VORA. An order of the mammalia, whose members are flesh eaters - though they are not the only animals which eat flesh and some of them are omnivorous or largely herbivorous. They are classified by variations in the skull and skeleton, the teeth, and various external features. There are 2 sub-orders, the Pinnipedia and the Fissipedia.

The *Fissipedia*, which are terrestrial, semi-arboreal, or amphibious, are sub-divided into 2 tribes, the Arctoidea and the Aeluroidea. The Arctoidea include the families of Ursidae or bears; the Canidae or dogs, wolves and foxes; the Procyonidae containing such dissimilar mammals as the racoon, coatimundi, kinkajou, and cacomistle; the Mustelidae including the otters, skunks and badgers, weasels and polecats; the Ailuropodidae containing the giant panda; the Ailuridae (common panda). The Aeluroidae incl. the Felidae or cats; the Hyaenidae comprising the hyaenas and aard-wolf; the Herpestidae containing the mongooses and suricates; the Cryptoproctidae containing only the fossa; the Viverridae containing the civets, genets, lingsangs, palm civets, binturong.

The 2nd sub-order, the *Pinnipedia*, with the limbs paddle-like in adaptation to a marine habitat, is composed of modified descendants of the terrestrial Arctoid Fissipedia. They fall into 2 main groups. The first contains the Otariidae or sea-lions, and the Odobaenidae or walruses. The 2nd group is composed of the family Phocidae or true seals.

The geographical distribution of the C. is worldwide but for Australia and New Zealand, and our domestic pets include two typical representatives in the dog and the cat.

CARNOT (kahrnō'), **Lazare** (1753-1823). French general. He joined the army as an engineer, and at the Revolution earned the title of 'Organizer of victory', since he not only reformed French fighting methods, but also introduced efficient systems of supplying munitions, clothing, and especially food, to the troops. After the coup d'état of 1797 he went abroad, but returned in 1799 and was made War Minister 1800-1. In 1814 as gov. of Antwerp he put up a brilliantly successful defence. Minister of the Interior during the Hundred Days, he was proscribed at the Restoration and retired to Magdeburg, where he d. His great work on fortification (*De la défense de places fortes*, 1810) became a military textbook.

C.'s elder son, **Nicolas Leonard Sadi C.** (1796-1832), was the founder of thermodynamics. *See* C. CYCLE.

CARNOT, Marie François Sadi (1837-94). French President. Grandson of Lazare Carnot, he entered the government service, was returned to the Assembly for Côte d'Or in 1871, and in 1887 was elected President. He successfully countered the Boulangist movement, and in 1892 the scandals arising out of French financial activities in Panama. He was assassinated by an Italian anarchist at Lyons.

CARNOT CYCLE. For a reversible heat engine a C.C. consists of the following changes, in the order stated, in the physical condition of a gas: (1) isothermal expansion (i.e. without change of temperature), (2) adiabatic expansion (i.e. without change of heat content), (3) isothermal compression and (4) adiabatic compression. The principles derived from a study of this cycle are important in the fundamentals of heat and thermodynamics. The absolute scale of temperature is based on this cycle.

CARNUBA (kahnoo'ba). S American palm (*Copernicia cerifera*) which produces fine quality wax and timber.

CARO (ka'ro), **Anthony** (1924-). British sculptor. Assistant to Henry Moore 1951-3, he shows a bold simplicity of structure in his works, such as 'Fathom', outside the London *Economist* building. Special features are his use of paint, and the absence of a formal base for his sculptures so as to give the impression of immediacy.

CAROB TREE. Small tree of the Mediterranean region (*Ceratonia siliqua*), often called locust tree. The 20cm (8in) pods are used as animal fodder and have been suggested as the 'husks' of the Prodigal Son and the 'locusts' eaten by John the Baptist in the wilderness.

CAROL I (1839-1914). King of Romania. A prince of the house of Hohenzollern-Sigmaringen, he was invited to become Prince of Romania, then under Turkish suzerainty, in 1866. In 1877, in alliance with Russia, he declared war on Turkey, and the treaty of Berlin recognized Romanian independence; in 1881 C. was crowned king.

CAROL II (1893-1953). King of Romania. Son of King Ferdinand, he m. Princess Helen of Greece, who bore him a son, Michael. In 1925 he renounced the succession, and settled in Paris with his mistress, Mme Lupescu. Michael succeeded to the throne in 1927, but in 1930 C. returned to Romania and was proclaimed king. In 1938 he introduced a new constitution under which he became practically absolute. He was forced to abdicate by the pro-German Iron Guard in Sept. 1940, and withdrew to Mexico with Mme Lupescu, whom he m. in 1947.

CAROL. Originally a song associated with a round dance, the term came later to be applied to popular songs (as distinct from hymns) associated with the great annual festivals, such as May Day, the New Year, Easter, and Christmas.

Christmas Cs. were popular as early as the 15th cent. The custom of singing Cs. from house to house, collecting gifts, was associated with 'wassailing'. Many of the best-known Cs., such as 'God rest you merry' and 'Noel', date back at least as far as the 16th cent. Others, such as 'Good King Wenceslas', have modern words but an ancient tune, and yet others are completely modern.

CAROLINA. *See* NORTH C. and SOUTH C.

CAROLINE OF ANSPACH (1683-1737). Queen of George II of Great Britain. The dau. of the Margrave of Brandenburg-Anspach, she m. George, Electoral Prince of Hanover, in 1705, and followed him to England in 1714 when his father became king as George I. As Princess of Wales she held a separate court at Leicester House and was the patron of many of the leading writers and politicians.

CAROLINE OF BRUNSWICK (1768-1821). Queen of George IV of Great Britain. Second dau. of Charles William, duke of Brunswick, and Augusta, sister of George III, she m. her first cousin the Prince of Wales in 1795, but following the birth of the Princess Charlotte a separation was arranged. When her husband ascended the throne in 1820 she was offered an annuity of £50,000 provided she agreed to renounce the title of queen and to continue to live abroad. She returned forthwith to London, where she assumed royal state. In July 1820 the Government brought in a bill to dissolve the royal marriage, but Lord Brougham's splendid defence led to the bill's abandonment. On July 19, 1821, she was prevented by royal order from entering Westminster Abbey for the coronation. She d. on Aug. 7, and her funeral was the occasion of popular riots.

CAROLINES. Scattered archipelago in Micronesia, Pacific Ocean, consisting of more than 500 coral islets; area 1,200 sq.km (463 sq.m). The chief islands are Ponape, Kosrae, and Truk in the eastern group and Yap and Belau in the western. They are well watered and productive. German from 1899, occupied by Japan 1914, and mandated by the League of Nations to that country in 1919, they were fortified, contrary to the terms of the mandate. Under Allied air attack in the S.W.W., they were not conquered. In 1947 they became part of the US Trust Terr. of the Pacific Is. (q.v.). Pop. (1973) 57,100.

CAROLINGIANS. Frankish dynasty descending from Pepin the Short (d. 768) and named after his son Charles the Great (Charlemagne). The last of the Cs. was Louis V who reigned in France 966-87, and was followed by Hugh Capet.

CAROTHERS, Wallace (1896-1937). American chemist. He joined Du Pont, the chemical firm, who sponsored his researches in polymerization. By 1930 he had discovered that some polymers were fibre-forming, and in 1937 perfected nylon.

CARP. A genus of freshwater fishes (*Cyprinus*) of the family Cyprinidae. *C. carpio*, the common species, found in most parts of Europe and Asia, has large scales, a long dorsal fin, and 4 barbels on its mouth. It prefers still waters, and is much esteemed as a food. Also familiar are the goldfish (q.v.) and the Chinese grass C., introduced to British rivers in 1978 for weed control.

CARPACCIO (kahrpah'chō), **Vittorio** (*c.* 1465-1522). Venetian painter. His principal works were painted between 1490 and 1519, and are in Venice.

CARPATHIANS. A mountain chain of Central Europe, forming a great semicircle from the Bohemian massif, girdling the Hungarian Plain, to Orsova (145km (90m) E of Belgrade) on the Danube. The total length is about 1,450 km (900m).

CARPENTĀ'RIA, Gulf of. A great, shallow gulf opening out of the Arafura Sea on the N of Australia, was discovered by Tasman in 1606 and named in 1623 in honour of Pieter Carpentier, Governor-General of the Dutch East Indies. There is an Anglican bishop of C. with his seat on Thursday Is., Queensland.

CARPET. Thick textile fabric, generally made of wool, used for covering floors, stairs, etc. The earliest known Cs. are those excavated at Passypych in SE Siberia by Rudenko and date from *c.* 500 BC, but it was not until the later Middle Ages that Cs. reached Western Europe from Turkey, Cardinal Wolsey being an eager buyer. Persian Cs., which reached a still unrivalled peak of artistry in the 15th and 16th cents., were rare in Britain until the mid-19th cent., reaching America a little later. The subsequent demand led to a revival of organized C.-making in Persia. Other countries with a long tradition of fine carpets are India, Pakistan, and China. Europe copied oriental technique, but developed western designs: France produced beautiful work at the Savonnerie and Beauvais establishments under Louis XIV and XV, and Exeter, Axminster, London and Wilton became famous British centres in the 18th cent., though Kidderminster is the biggest centre today. The 1st C. factory in the USA was estab. at Philadelphia, still a large producing centre, in 1791.

The 3 main types of machine-made Cs. today are the 'Wilton', remarkable for its fine, close texture and lending itself to design effects; the 'Axminster' which economizes in material, each tuft being on the surface with none hidden in the fabric as with 'Wilton'; and the 'tufted' Cs. The last-named are a post-war development, making wide use of the new synthetic fibres: the pile threads are looped through a hessian backing to which they are then anchored by a layer of rubber compound in the form of latex. Tufted Cs., originally inferior in quality and design now rival the traditionally woven Cs., and the latter have adopted the foam rubber and other backings first developed to give resilience, etc. to tufted types.

CARPET. The craft of carpet weaving has been passed on from generation to generation in the East for thousands of years, and children begin work as soon as they can walk. This young girl, from the village of Herannia south of Cairo creates her patterns spontaneously. *Photo: J.P.Charbonnier/Camera Press.*

Cs. and rugs have also often been made in the home as a pastime, cross and tent stitch on canvas being widely used in the 18th and 19th cents.: famous among modern Cs. of this type were those produced by Queen Mary, consort of George V.

CARPET-BAGGER. Name given in US history to the disreputable politicians and office seekers from the North who swarmed into the Southern States following the Civil War of 1861-5 and in co-operation with the local white riffraff (the 'scallawags'), and the Negroes, established governments which were a by-word for oppression and corruption. They were so called because they were supposed to own no property but what they carried in their carpet-bags.

CARPINI (kahrpē'nē), **Johannes de Plano** (*c.* 1182-1252). Franciscan friar and traveller. In 1245 Pope Innocent IV placed him in charge of a fact-finding mission to Mongolia, from which he returned in 1247. His history of the Mongols is a valuable piece of practical research.

CARRACCI (kahrah'chē). Three Italian painters who founded the eclectic school of painting, i.e. those who studied the works of the great masters and chose what they considered to be the chief merits of each and combined those in their own works. **Lodovico C.** (1555-1619), who lived in Bologna, was the initiator of the school. His cousins, **Agostino C.** (1557–1602) and **Annibale C.** (1560-1609), helped him in his work. The school is particularly well represented in Bologna.

CARRAGHEEN (kar'agēn). Species of deep reddish branched seaweed (*Chondrus crispus*), named after C. in Ireland, and found elsewhere in N. Europe. It is exploited commercially in food and medicinal preparations, and as cattle feed.

CARRARA (kahrah'rah). Italian town in the Apennines, 60km (37m) NW of Leghorn, with quarries of the finest white marble in the world. These were worked by the Romans, abandoned in the 5th cent. AD, came into use again with the revival of sculpture and architecture in the 12th cent. C. has a 13th cent. Gothic church. Pop. (1977) 56,000.

CARREL (kahrel'), **Alexis** (1873-1944). French surgeon and biologist, who emigrated to America and in 1906 joined the New York staff of the Rockefeller Institute for Medical Research, winning the Nobel prize in 1912 for his success in the surgery of blood-vessels. Besides a number of medical books he wrote *Man, the Unknown* (1935).

CARRHAE (kar'ē). Ancient town of NW Mesopotamia in modern Turkey, called Haran in the OT (Gen. 12), and scene of a battle in 53 BC in which a Roman army under Crassus was wiped out by the Parthians.

CARRICKFERGUS. Seaport on Belfast Lough, Antrim, N Ireland, NE of Belfast. Pop. (1971) 10,250.

CARRIER, Willis (1876-1950). American engineer. He coined the terms, and invented in 1911 the process of 'air conditioning', as a means of controlling the purity, humidity, temperature and circulation of air indoors.

CARRINGTON, Peter Alexander Rupert Carington, 6th baron (1919–). British Cons. statesman. He led the Opposition in the Lords 1964–70 and 1974–9, was Defence Sec. 1970–4, and as Foreign Sec. 1979–82 settled the Rhodesian question (*see* ZIMBABWE), but resigned following his failure to anticipate the Falklands crisis. He was to become Sec.-Gen. of NATO in June 1984.

CARROLL, Lewis. Pseudonym of Charles Lutwidge Dodgson (1832-98), mathematician and writer of children's books. B. at Daresbury, Cheshire, he became a lecturer on mathematics at Oxford and published under his own name books on mathematics. *Alice's Adventures in Wonderland,* under the pseudonym of L.C., appeared in 1865, and quickly became popular. It grew out of a story told by Dodgson to amuse 3 little girls, including the original 'Alice', the dau. of Dean Liddell, Dean of Christ Church. During his lifetime Dodgson refused to acknowledge any connection with any books not pub. under his own name, but a sequel, *Through the Looking Glass,* followed in 1872. Among later works was the mock-heroic nonsense poem 'The Hunting of the Snark' (1876).

CARROT. Genus of plants (*Daucus*) belonging to the family Umbelliferae. The wild C. (*D. carota*) is a common wayside and meadow weed in Britain, and ranges through Europe and Asia as far as India. Cultivated varieties have long, fleshy tap-roots.

CARSE OF GOWRIE (gow'ri). Fertile plain bordering the Firth of Tay. It is 24km (15m) long, one of Scotland's most productive agricultural areas.

CARSON, Edward Henry, baron (1854-1935). Irish politician and lawyer. As a member of both the English and Irish Bars he made a great name in criminal and civil cases; his part in the Oscar Wilde trial was decisive. In the years before the F.W.W. he was the leader of the Ulstermen in their resolve to resist Irish Home Rule by force of arms if need be. But on the outbreak of war he rallied Ulster to the support of the Government, and took office

33

are ferrets! Where can I have dropped them, I wonder?" Alice guessed in a moment that it was looking for the nosegay and the pair of white kid gloves, and she began hunting for them, but they were now nowhere to be seen — everything seemed to have changed since her swim in the pool, and her walk along the river-bank with its fringe of rushes and forget-me-nots, and the glass table and the little door had vanished.

Soon the rabbit noticed Alice, as she stood looking curiously about her, and at once said in a quick angry tone," why, Mary Ann! what are you doing out here? Go home this moment, and look on my dressing-table for my gloves and nosegay, and fetch them here, as quick as you can run, do you hear?" and Alice was so much frightened that she ran off at once, without

CARROLL. Lewis Carroll was an ardent photographer, and in this portrait by Rejlander, he is caught polishing a lens. To the left is part of the autograph manuscript of *Alice in Wonderland* presented to the British Museum in 1949 by a group of well wishers from the U.S.A. *Photo: Courtesy of the British Museum and the Mansell Collection.*

under both Asquith and Lloyd George (Attorney-General 1915, First Lord of the Admiralty 1916, member of the War Cabinet 1917-18). He was an MP 1892-1921 and a Lord of Appeal in Ordinary, 1921-9.

CARSON, Rachel (1907-64). American naturalist. Aquatic biologist with the US Fish and Wildlife Service 1936-49, when she became its editor-in-chief until 1952, she pub. in 1951 *The Sea Around Us,* and in 1963 *Silent Spring,* attacking indiscriminate use of pesticides.

CARSON CITY. Cap. of Nevada, USA. Smallest of America's cap. cities, it was named after the famous frontiersman Kit Carson (1809-68). Pop. (1970) 15,468.

CARTAGĒ'NA. Spanish industrial city, seaport, and naval base in the prov. of Murcia on the Mediterranean Sea. It was founded about 225 BC by the Carthaginian Hasdrubal, and was then called New Carthage; it continued to flourish under the Romans and the Moors, and was conquered by the Spanish in 1269. It has a 13th cent. cathedral and Roman remains. Pop. (1970) 146,900.

CARTAGENA. City and seaport of Colombia, cap. of the dept of Bolivar. Founded in 1533, it was taken by Drake in 1586. A pipe-line brings petroleum here from the Baranco Dermaja wells. Pop. (1978) 420,000.

CA'RTEL. An amalgamation of industrial businesses that falls short of a trust, in that the firms comprising it retain their identity but pledge themselves to regulate output and to observe a common price list so as to avoid undercutting. The growth of organizations such as EFTA and the EEC increased the danger of the establishment of Cs. and operation of restrictive practices, so that both the Treaty of Rome and Stockholm Convention contain provisions for control.

CARTER, 'Jimmy' (James Earl) (1924-). 39th Pres. of the U.S.A. B. in Georgia, he graduated from the U.S. Naval Academy in 1947, and did advanced study in nuclear physics. In 1953 he left the navy to become a peanut farmer, and then entered politics as a Democrat, serving as gov. of Georgia 1970-4. In 1976 he wrested the presidency from Ford by a narrow margin, becoming the first pres. from the South since 1848. Landmarks of his presidency were the Panama Treaty, the Camp David agreements between Egypt and Israel, restoration of full

Sino-Soviet diplomatic relations, and negotiations over the American embassy hostages in Iran.

The Russian invasion of Afghanistan prompted the **Carter Doctrine** (1980) of the vital US interest in the Gulf region. Any outside attempt to control it would be repelled 'by any means necessary, incl. military force'. Carter was badly defeated by Reagan (q.v.) in 1980.

CARTER. Jimmy Carter and his wife acknowledge applause in his home state of Georgia as he claimed victory in the 1976 presidential election. His daughter, Amy, roused from sleep for the great occasion, is only half awake as she waves. *Photo: Popperfoto.*

CARTHAGE (kahr'thāj). In ancient geography, a rich and powerful Phoenician city in N Africa, on the gulf of Tunis, *c.* 16km (10m) N of modern Tunis.

C. is said to have been founded in 814 BC by Phoenician emigrants from Tyre, led by the princess Dido. It developed an extensive commerce throughout the Mediterranean, and traded with the Tin Islands, which have been located in Cornwall or in SW Spain. After the capture of Tyre by the Babylonians in the 6th cent. BC it became the natural leader of the Phoenician colonies in N Africa and Spain, and there soon began a prolonged struggle with the Greeks which centred mainly in Sicily, the E of which was dominated by Greek colonies, while the W was held by Carthaginian trading stations. About 540 BC the Carthaginians defeated a Greek attempt to land in Corsica, and in 480 a Carthaginian attempt to conquer the whole of Sicily was defeated by the Greeks at Himera. Eventually the Carthaginians came into conflict with Rome, and in the 1st Punic War (264-241 BC) they were defeated at sea and expelled from their strongholds in E Sicily. Under Hamilcar Barca, they next proceeded to build up an empire and army in Spain, whence Hamilcar's son Hannibal launched the 2nd Punic War (218-201 BC); he crossed the Pyrenees and Alps and inflicted crushing defeats upon the Roman armies in Italy before being forced back to Africa and defeated at Zama (202 BC).

In the 3rd Punic War (149-146 BC), C. was finally defeated, and the city itself destroyed by the Romans in 146 BC. About 45 BC Roman colonists were settled in C. by Caesar, and it rose to be the wealthy and important capital of the province of Africa. After its capture by the Vandals in AD 439 it was little more than a pirate stronghold. From 533 it formed part of the Byzantine empire until its final destruction by the Arabs in AD 698.

The population of C. before its destruction by the Romans is said to have numbered over 700,000. The constitution was an aristocratic republic with two chief magistrates elected annually, and a senate of 300 life-members. The religion was Phoenician, including the worship of the goddess Tanit, the great god Baal-Hammon, and the Tyrian Meklarth: human sacrifices were not unknown. The real strength of C. lay in its commerce and its powerful navy; its armies were for the most part mercenaries.

When the French secured the protectorate of Tunisia in 1881, C. became the seat of an RC bishopric (1884) and the Cathedral of St Louis was built upon the supposed site of the camp where Louis IX of France had d. in 1270. Modern C. is a pleasant villa suburb of Tunis.

CARTHUSIANS. Order of monks in the RC Church, founded by St Bruno, who in 1084 estab. their first monastery on the bleak mountain plateau of Chartreuse, near Grenoble in Dauphiné. They lived in unbroken silence, abstained from all meat, took only one meal a day, and supported themselves by their own labours.

The first rule was drawn up by Guigo, the 5th Prior. Between then and 1681 a few important changes were made. The order was introduced into England about 1178, when the first Charterhouse was founded at Witham in Som. They were suppressed at the Reformation, but there is a Charterhouse at Parkminster, Sussex, estab. in 1833.

The famous liqueur called Chartreuse was first made at La Grande Chartreuse after the Revolution to enable the monks to meet the rents which were newly imposed on them for their land. Most of the income is now given to charity.

CARTIER (kahrtyeh'), **Sir Georges Étienne** (1814-73). French-Canadian statesman. He fought against the British in the rebellion of 1837, was elected to the Canadian parliament in 1848, and was joint Premier with Sir John Macdonald 1858-62. He furthered railway development, and brought Quebec into the federation in 1867.

CARTIER, Jacques (1491-1557). French navigator. B. in St Malo, he sailed in 1534 in search of a NW passage, and arrived at Newfoundland. On his 2nd voyage in 1536 he sailed up the St Lawrence and named the Indian village of Hochelaga, Mount Royal (Montreal). In 1541 and 1543 he made further voyages to what was now French Canada.

CARTOON. A preliminary drawing on strong paper used as a design for oil painting, mosaic, and tapestry. When completed the drawing is transferred by tracing or pouncing to the surface on which the finished design, painting, etc., is to be executed. The term is commonly applied to caricatures (q.v.).

CARTWRIGHT, Edmund (1743-1823). Inventor. B. in Notts, he went to Oxford and became a country rector, though he was also a farmer. In 1785 he patented a power-loom. He invented several other machines, but went bankrupt in 1793.

CARUSO (kahroo'sō), **Enrico** (1873-1921). Italian operatic tenor. B. at Naples, he made his first appearance on the stage there at 21. In 1898 he achieved a great success at Milan, in Puccini's *La Bohème.* He subsequently won world-wide fame.

CARVER, George Washington (*c.* 1864-1943). American Negro agricultural chemist. B. in Missouri of slave parents, he worked from 1896 at the Tuskegee Institute,

Alabama. He advocated the diversification of crops in the South, especially the cultivation of the peanut from which he developed some 300 products, and was a pioneer in the field of plastics.

CARY, Joyce (1888-1957). British novelist. B. at Londonderry, he was ed. at Clifton Coll. and studied art before going up to Trinity Coll., Oxford. In 1918 he entered the Colonial Service retiring 2 years later because of ill-health, but Nigeria, where he had served, gave a background to such novels as *Mister Johnson* (1939) concerning a half-educated African clerk. Other books are *Castle Corner* (1938) and *A House of Children* (1941), both with autobiographical elements; *The Horse's Mouth* (1944) telling the story of the outrageous Bohemian artist Gulley Jimson, and *The Captive and the Free* (1959) dealing with faith-healing and written when he was progressively paralysed by muscular atrophy.

CARYATID (karia'tid). Pillar or other support to a building in the form of a woman, the name deriving from the Karyatides, who were the priestesses of the temple of Artemis at Karyai. Similar male columns are called Atlantes (*see* ATLAS) or telamones ('bearers').

CARYATID. The Erectheum, the original temple of the tutelary deities of Athens - Athene, Poseidon and Erectheus - built 421-407 BC and famous for its caryatids. *Photo: J. Allan Cash.*

CASABLA'NCA. Port on the Atlantic coast of Morocco, 320km (200m) SW of Tangier; it was occupied by the French in 1907 and developed by them until Morocco became independent in 1956. It is a great commercial and industrial centre. The Arabic name for C. is **Dar el-Beida.** C. was the scene of the S.W.W. conference between Churchill and Roosevelt in Jan. 1943 which issued the Allied demand for unconditional surrender by Germany, Italy, and Japan. Pop. (1980) 2,175,000.

CASALS (kasals'), **Pablo** (1876-1973). Spanish violoncellist, composer and conductor. B. in Tarragona, he was exiled by Franco in 1936 and lived just over the Spanish border in France. He wrote symphonic, chamber and choral works incl. the Christmas oratorio *The Crib,* which spoke much of his own exile. Noted for his freedom of technique, he was probably the greatest of all cellists.

CASANO'VA DE SEINGALT, Giovanni Jacopo (1725-98). Italian adventurer, author of memoirs largely concerned with his love affairs. B. at Venice, he served in the household of Cardinal Acquaviva, and embarked upon a career of intrigue and adventure which took him into many parts of Europe, especially to Paris, Rome, Berlin, Warsaw, and Madrid. From 1774 he was a police spy in the Venetian service. In 1782 a libel got him into trouble, and after more wanderings he was appointed in 1785 Count Waldstein's librarian at his castle of Dux in Bohemia, where he wrote his *Memoirs* (pub. 1826-38): the unexpurgated text did not appear until 1960-1.

CASCADE RANGE. Volcanic mtns in Washington, USA, 64 km (40 m) NE of Portland, which incl. Mt Lassen (erupted 1914) and Mt St Helens (q.v.). Excl. Alaska and Hawaii, they are the most active in the USA.

CĀ'SĒIN. The coagulate protein of milk, familiar as cheese, where it is mixed with fat and water. It exists in milk, probably as a loose compound with calcium solids, and is obtained commercially by treating separated milk. It has a number of important commercial applications in the manufacture of glues, paints, distempers, artificial silk, and plastics.

CASEMENT, Roger David (1864-1916). Irish nationalist. While in the British consular service he exposed the ruthless exploitation of natives in the Belgian Congo and in Peru, and was knighted in 1911 (degraded 1916). During the F.W.W. he went to Germany in 1914 and attempted to induce Irish prisoners of war to form an Irish brigade to take part in a republican rising. He returned to Ireland in a submarine in 1916 (actually to postpone, not start the Easter rising), was arrested, tried for treason, and hanged. The controversial C. diaries, held by the British govt, were made available in 1959 and show that he was a homosexual. His remains were returned to Ireland by the British govt in 1965 and rest in Glasnevin cemetery, Dublin.

CASE'RTA. Italian town in Campania 33km (21m) NE of Naples, with a palace completed for the Bourbons in 1774 which was made the seat of an air training academy in 1926, and during the S.W.W. was used as Allied HQ in Italy 1943-5. At C. the Germans in Italy surrendered to Field-Marshal Alexander in 1945. Pop. (1971) 61,700.

CASEY, Richard Gardiner, baron (1890-1976). Australian Liberal statesman. A diplomat, noted for his successful liaison between the Australian and British govts. (he occupied a seat in the British war cabinet 1942-3), he was Min. of External Affairs 1951-60, and Gov.-Gen. 1965-9. In 1969 an Antarctic research station was named after him.

CA'SLON, William (1692-1766). British type-founder. Showing Dutch influence, his graceful 'old-face' types were much used until the late 18th cent. and were revived in Britain and the US in the mid-19th cent.

CASPIAN SEA. Inland sea between the Caucasus and Asia: except for the southern coast, which belongs to Iran, it lies in Soviet territory. An under-water ridge divides it into two halves, of which the shallow northern is almost salt-free. There are no tides. Drainage in the N. and the damming of the tributary rivers for hydroelectric power, such as the Volga and Ural, have led to constant shrinkage over the last half century, and the growth of industry along its shores has caused pollution and damaged the Russian and Iranian caviar industries. The chief ports are Astrakhan and Baku. Area *c.* 400,000 sq.km (155,000 sq.m). It is now approximately 28m (90ft) below sea level.

CASSA'NDRA. In Greek legend, the dau. of Priam, king of Troy. She foresaw the doom of Troy, and became the booty of Agamemnon; she was murdered with him by Clytemnestra.

CASSATT (kasat'), **Mary** (1855-1926). American artist. In 1875 she went to Europe and finally settled near Paris. She is best known for her paintings of mothers and children in the Impressionist style.

CASSAVA (kahsah'vah), or **manioc.** The starch-containing roots of plants of the S American genus *Manihot,* which belongs to the family Euphorbiaceae. The bitter C. (*M. utilissima*) yields a meal called Brazilian arrowroot. Tapioca is prepared from it.

CASSAVETES (kasavā'tēz), **John** (1929-). American actor and film director. He appeared in *The Dirty Dozen, Rosemary's Baby,* etc., and directed experimental, apparently improvised films, incl. *Shadows* (1960) and *The Killing of a Chinese Bookie* (1980).

CASSEL. *See* KASSEL.

CASSIA. Bark of a plant (*Cinnamomum cassia*) of the family Lauraceae. It is aromatic, and closely resembles the true cinnamon, for which it is largely used as a substitute.

C. is also a genus of plants of the family Leguminosae, many of which have strong purgative properties and are the source of the laxative senna.

CASSINO. Italian town 80km (50m) NW of Naples, at the foot of Monte C., it was the scene of heavy fighting during S.W.W. in 1944, when most of the town was destroyed. It was rebuilt *c.* 1.5km (1m) to the N. The famous abbey on the summit of Monte C., founded by St Benedict in 529, was destroyed by Allied bombardment in Feb. 1944 since it commanded the entrance to the Liri valley and was in German hands: rebuilding was completed in 1956. Pop. (1971) 24,800.

CA'SSIUS, Gaius (d. 42 BC). Roman soldier, one of the conspirators who slew Julius Caesar. He fought at Carrhae (53), and with the republicans against Caesar at Pharsalus (48), was pardoned and appointed praetor, but became a leader in the conspiracy of 44, and after Caesar's death joined Brutus. Defeated at Philippi (42), he killed himself.

CASSIVELAUNUS (kasēvelow'noos). Chieftain of the Catuvellauni, a tribe of Britons N of the Thames, and leader of the resistance to Caesar in 54 BC.

CA'SSON, Sir Hugh (1910-). British architect. Director of architecture for the Festival of Britain 1948-51, he was knighted in 1952, and became PRA in 1976. His books incl. *Victorian Architecture* (1948).

CASSOWARY (kas'oweri). Genus of flightless ostrich-like birds (*Casuarius*), confined to Australia and the neighbouring islands, and allied to the emu. The C. can run and leap well. The wings are very small, and the plumage is a glossy black.

CASTANETS. Spanish musical instrument of percussion, consisting of a pair of hollow wooden shells, fastened together, bound round the thumb and 2nd finger of the hand. By striking them together a clicking sound is produced. They provide a rhythmical accompaniment to dancing, etc.

CASTE (kahst; Port., *casta,* race). A term generally used to denote the component groups of Indian or more particularly Hindu society. In India the C. system is derived traditionally from the 4 classes of early Hindu society - Brahmans (priests), Kshatriyas (nobles and warriors), Vaisyas (traders and cultivators), and Sudras (servants), which were said to have originated from the head, arms, thighs, and feet respectively of Brahma, the Creator. A

CASSOWARY. In appearance and size, the cassowary is not unlike the emu but is distinguished by the thick bony helmet on the top of its head. It is the chick's father which is here showing such parental concern. *Photo: Popperfoto.*

fifth class, the Untouchables, polluting on account of its origin, its occupations, or its mode of life, remained and still largely remains outside the pale of Hindu society, for although the Indian Constituent Assembly of 1947 abolished 'untouchability', and made discrimination against the Scheduled Castes or Depressed Classes illegal, and attempts have been made to enforce this, strong prejudice continues. The existing Cs. which number probably some 3,000, exclusive of sub-castes, are regarded as having come into being by the interbreeding of these original groups. Recently there has been militancy among Harijan (low caste) youth, e.g. the Dalit (oppressed) Panthers of Maharashtra modelled on the Black Panthers of the USA.

The formation and development of the C. system owes a great deal to taboo, and it rests on a belief in pollution by touch, or even by sight, and in the necessity for purification from such contact. Internally each C. is generally broken up into sub-castes, often endogamous themselves, but often also with limited intermarriage. The 'Bhagavad Gita' lays down the principle that it is the first duty of every Hindu to follow the rules of his C., and a contentment with the C. into which each man is born is inculcated by the doctrine of *karma.* The belief in this doctrine alone makes tolerable the lot of those whose contact is deemed to be polluting to clean Hindus. While C. is opposed to Western ideas, it may be claimed for the C. system that it has preserved a stable Indian society through the ages, given continuity to the exercise of industrial arts and crafts, and has provided a system of social providence and security.

CASTEL GANDOLFO (kahstel′ gahndohl′foh). Italian village 24km (15m) SE of Rome, with a castle, built by pope Urban VIII in the 17th cent., which is used by the Pope as a summer residence. The Vatican estab. an astronomical observatory at C.G. in 1936. Pop. (1971) 4,400.

CASTELLÓN (kahstelyōn′) **DE LA PLANA.** Spanish city, cap. of Castellón prov., which faces the Mediterranean to the E. It is the centre of an orange growing dist. Pop. (1970) 94,000.

CASTELO BRANCO (kahstel′oo brahn′koo), **Camilo** (1825-90). Portuguese novelist. Illegitimate and soon an orphan, he had a dramatic life, and his works have a Balzac-type range, alternating in temper between mysticism and Bohemianism. They incl. *Onde está a felicidade?* (1856: *Where is Happiness?*); *Amor de perdição* (1862: *Love of Perdition*), written during his imprisonment for adultery and showing his obsession with love as a motive force; *Novelas do Minho* (1875), stories of the rural north; and *A brazileira de Prazins* (1882: *The Brazilian girl from Prazins*). Created a visct in 1885, he committed suicide when overtaken by blindness.

CASTIGLIONE (kahstēlyoh′neh), **Baldassare,** count (1478-1529). Italian author and diplomat. B. near Mantua, he served the duke of Milan, and in 1506 was engaged by the duke of Albino on a mission to Henry VII of England. While in Spain in 1524 he was created bishop of Avila. He pub. letters, poems in Lat. and It., and a picture of the perfect Renaissance gentleman *Il Cortegiano* (1528).

CASTILE (kastēl′). Historic kingdom of Spain. It comprised the two great basins separated by the Sierra de Gredos and the Sierra de Guadarrama. The northern basin constitutes the modern region of Old Castile (Castilla la Vieja); area 49,976 sq.km (19,290 sq.m), pop. (1970) 1,542,450. It incl. part of the Cantabrian mts., and reaches to the Bay of Biscay; it is drained by the upper Ebro, the upper Douro, and many tributaries. The southern basin constitutes the modern region of New Castile (Castilla la Nueva); area 72,363 sq.km (27,932 sq.m), pop. (1970) 5,164,026. It is drained by the Tagus system and the Guadiana. The climate is continental and irrigation is essential to agriculture.

The kingdom of C. grew from a small area in the north. In the 11th cent. Old C. was united with Léon; in 1085 the kingdom of Toledo was captured from the Moors and became New C., with Toledo the cap. of the whole. Through the marriage in 1469 of Isabella, heiress of Castile, to Ferdinand, who became king of Aragaon in 1479, C. and Aragon were united Autonomy is planned for both regions. *See* SPAIN.

The Castilian language is the standard form of Spanish. The chief towns are Madrid in New C., and Valladolid, Burgos, and Santander in Old C.

CASTLE, Barbara (1911-). British Labour politician. Née Betts, she m. in 1944 journalist Edward C. (created life peer 1974). She was Min. of Overseas Development 1964-5, Transport 1965-8, and Employment 1968-70. Her White Paper *In Place of Strife* (1969), proposing a compulsory 'conciliation pause' and a ballot of union members before a strike, was abandoned as too controversial. She was Min. of Social Services 1974-6, when she was dropped from the cabinet by Callaghan, an opponent of the White Paper, and her *Diaries* (1980) were critical of him. From 1979 she led the Labour group in the European parliament.

CASTILE. Simancas, a Moorish castle until taken by the Christians in the 9th century, was rebuilt by Alfonso III in the 13th century. It was designated for its present function, as the General Archive of the Realm, by Philip II. *Photo: Courtesy of the Spanish Ministry of Tourist Information.*

CASTLE. A fortified building or stronghold of medieval times. The main parts of a Norman castle were: the keep, a square or oblong tower containing store rooms, dungeons, soldiers' quarters, etc.; the inner bailey or basecourt surrounding the keep; the outer bailey or 2nd courtyard separated from the inner bailey by a wall; the crenellated embattlements through which missiles were discharged against an attacking enemy; round towers known as bastions projecting from the walls; the postern gate used by messengers during a siege; the portcullis, a heavy grating which could be let down to close the main gate; and the drawbridge crossing the ditch or moat surrounding the castle. Sometimes a tower called a barbican was constructed over a gateway as an additional defensive measure.

Excavation of ancient Egyptian fortresses, e.g. that of Buhen in Nubia by W. B. Emery (q.v.), has revealed complex structures which may have influenced the practice of medieval builders.

CASTLE HILL RISING. A revolt among Irish convicts on 4 March 1804 in N.S.W. Australia. Led by William Johnston, who had been transported for taking part in the Irish rebellion in 1798, the men set out for Sydney, but had been betrayed by one of their comrades. They were taken while parleying with the military under a flag of truce, a number being killed.

CASTLEMAINE, Lady (1641-1709). Mistress of Charles II of England. B. Barbara Villiers, she m. in 1659 Roger Palmer (1634-1705) who in 1661 was created earl of C. For 10 years she held first place among the royal mistresses, and in 1670 she was made duchess of Cleveland; 3 of her sons were made dukes: Cleveland, Grafton, and Northumberland.

CASTLEMAINE. Town in Victoria, Australia, c.105 km (65 m) NW of Melbourne, on the Loddon. One of the earliest sites of a gold strike in 1851, it had a pop. rising to 30,000 at that period. It survives as an agricultural marketing centre.

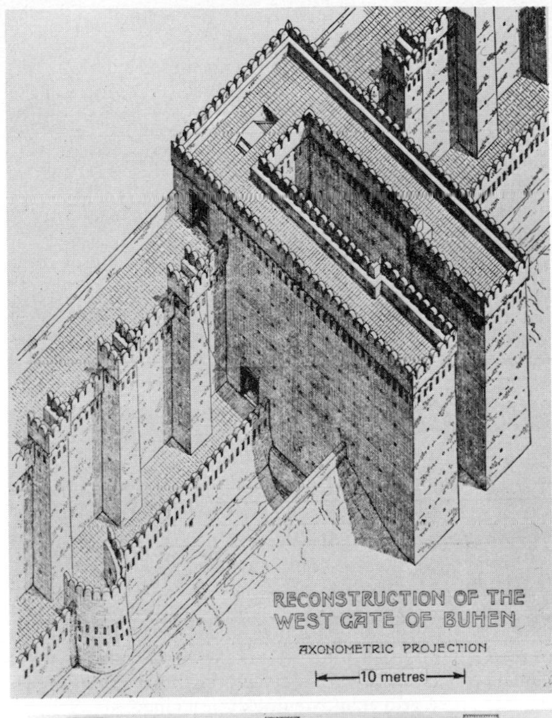

CASTLE. A great chain of forts of which Buhen was the chief, was built by the Twelfth Dynasty pharoahs to safeguard their southern frontier in Nubia. Although Buhen was stormed by the armies of Kush in about 1675 B.C. it was probably only with the aid of treachery. The wonderfully preserved remains on the basis of which Professor W.B. Emery made this reconstruction were submerged beneath the waters of the Nile on completion of the Aswan Dam. Above is the west or main gate and (below) a view along the length of the fortress. *Drawing reproduced by courtesy of W.B.Emery.*

CASTLEREAGH (kahs'elrā), **Robert Stewart,** visct (1769-1822). British Tory statesman. When his father, an Ulster landowner, was made an earl in 1796, he took the courtesy title of visct C. In 1821 he succeeded his father as Marquess of Londonderry. He sat in the Irish House of Commons from 1790, and in 1797 became Chief Secretary in Ireland. He took a leading part in suppressing the rebellion of 1798, and manipulation of the borough-mongers secured the passage in 1800 of the Act of Union. In the Parliament at Westminster he was War Secretary 1805-6 and again in 1807-9. In 1809 he fought a duel with Canning, the For. Sec., as a result of which they both resigned. C. returned to office in 1812 as For. Sec., devoted himself to the overthrow of Napoleon, represented Britain at the peace conferences, and used his influence to secure a just peace for France. Abroad his policy favoured the development of national liberalism, but at home he ruthlessly repressed the Reform movement. Popular opinion held C. responsible for the Peterloo massacre and the repressive legislation. Overwork and the realization of his unpopularity unsettled his mind, and on 12 Aug. 1822 he cut his throat with a penknife. His burial in Westminster Abbey was the scene of great popular rejoicing.

CASTOR and **POLLUX.** In classical mythology, the twin sons of Leda and brothers of Helen and Clytemnestra. They were called the *Dioscuri*, i.e. sons of Zeus, who had loved their mother in the guise of a swan. A temple was dedicated to them at Rome.

CASTŌ'REUM or **Castor.** Substance used in perfumery, consisting of the preputial follicles of the beaver.

CASTOR OIL. Oil obtained from the seeds of the C.O. plant or Palma Christi (*Ricinus communis*). This is a tall shrub of the family Euphorbiaceae, reaching a height of over 2m (6ft), often cultivated as an ornamental garden-plant. The oil is used medicinally as a purgative. The poison ricin is also obtained from the seeds: it causes the rapid collapse of the cardio-vascular system.

CASTRATION. The removal of the testicles or ovaries. It prevents reproduction, and also much modifies the secondary sexual characteristics; e.g. in the male the voice may remain high as in childhood, and growth of hair on the face and body may become weak or cease, owing to the removal of the hormones normally secreted by the testes. In the woman it produces the change of life (menopause).

C. was formerly used to preserve the treble voice of boy singers or, by Moslems, to provide trustworthy harem guards: *see* EUNUCH. Today some Scandinavian countries use C. in the case of persistent male sexual offenders.

Male domestic animals, esp. stallions and bulls, are castrated to prevent undesirable sires from reproducing, to moderate their aggressive and savage disposition, and to make them produce more meat. Cockerels are castrated (capons) to improve their flavour and increase their size.

CASTRO RUZ, Fidel (1927-). Cuban Prime Minister. Of wealthy parentage C. was ed. at Jesuit schools and, after studying law at the Univ. of Havana, he gained a reputation through his work for poor clients. He strongly opposed the Batista dictatorship, and with his brother Raúl took part in an unsuccessful attack on the Army barracks at Santiago de Cuba in 1953. After spending some time in exile in the US and Mexico, C. attempted a secret landing in Cuba in 1956 in which all but 11 of his supporters were killed. He eventually gathered an army of over 5,000 which overthrew Batista in 1959 and he became PM a few months later. His régime is socialist and he was originally a Marxist-Leninist until in 1974 he rejected the Marxian formula 'from each according to his ability and to each according to his need' and decreed that a Cuban should 'receive according to his work'. He became pres. in 1976, and in 1979 also pres. of the Non-Aligned Movement. His brother Raúl was appointed Min. of Armed Forces in 1959.

CASUARINA (kasyoorī'na). Genus of trees, with many Australian and New Guinea species, also found in Africa and Asia. They are gracefully handsome, e.g. the river she-oak *(C. cunninghamiana),* with fronded branches resembling cassowary feathers, hence the name.

CAT. A member of the mammalian family, Felidae, to which belong the lion, tiger, leopard, jaguar, puma, cheetah, etc. But the term is more usually confined to the smaller species, the domestic cat in particular.

Although Cs. have been domesticated since the time of the ancient Egyptians, their characters are so specialized and stable - in contrast with the dog - that only minor variants occur, e.g. the tail-less Manx C., which there is

CASTRO. Seen here on a visit to President Allende in Chile in 1971, Fidel Castro has taken every opportunity to consolidate potential support for the 'revolutionary struggle' in South and Central America and in Africa. *Photo: Diego Goldberg/Camera Press.*

actually no reason to believe originated in the I.O.M. Cs. retaining the ancestral patterning of the coat, or modifications of it, are called 'tabbies', and may be 'striped' - when the pattern hardly varies from that of the European wild C. (*F. silvestris*) - or 'blotched'. Colours range through black, grey (divided into shades known as 'smokes', 'blues', 'chinchillas', and 'silvers'), white, cream, yellow and red (the last predominantly males); combinations of colours are frequent - red and black producing tortoiseshell (predominantly females). All are primarily classified as 'short-haired' or 'long-haired' (also known as Persian, though not known to have originated anywhere in the Middle East): the short-haired 'Abyssinian', 'Siamese', and Manx are separately judged. The National C. Club in Britain was founded in 1887.

Wild Cs., with greyish yellow fur and more distinct dark stripes across the body than those of the tabby, survive in Scotland, and possibly in England.

CAT (Cat-o'-nine-tails). A whip with 9 knotted lashes used in the punishment of criminals. It is now very rarely used, for the Criminal Justice Act of 1948 abolished sentences of whipping except in cases of mutiny, incitement to mutiny, or gross violence to a prison officer. The sentence may be carried out then only after an order of a Visiting Committee or the Home Secretary.

CATACOMBS (kat'akōmz). Subterranean cemeteries. Most of the Christian Cs. belong to the 3rd and 4th cents. The name was first applied to the vaults beneath the basilica of St Sebastian in Rome and afterwards to the network of tunnels there and to similar burial places in Naples, Syracuse, Egypt, etc., where the Christians buried their dead in niches hollowed in the walls. Mass was celebrated at the tombs of martyrs; they became places of pilgrimage; and in times of persecution the Christians would take refuge in the Cs. When Christianity became the State religion, the Christians began to bury their dead in cemeteries above ground.

CATALAN. A Romance language, belonging to the southern Gallo-Roman group, closely related to Provençal, of which it is usually considered a dialect. It is spoken in the NE and E (Mediterranean) provinces of the Spanish mainland, the Balearic Isles, a corner of SE France, Andorra, etc.

CATALAUNIAN FIELDS. Plain near Troyes, France, scene of the defeat of Attila by the Romans and Goths under Aëtius in AD 451. The battle freed Europe from the danger of Asiatic domination.

CA'TALEPSY. In medicine, an abnormal state of complete suspension of the will in which the patient is apparently or actually unconscious and his limbs will remain in the position in which they are placed. He does not respond to stimuli, and the rate of his heart-beat and breathing is slow. A similar condition can be produced by hypnotism, but C. as ordinarily understood occurs spontaneously. It is seen in schizophrenia, hysteria, and sometimes in persons who have no other symptom of mental or nervous disorder. It is essentially an extreme form of resistive stupor, a defence against the environment or reality.

ÇATAL HÜYÜK (chatahl' hoo'yook). Neolithic site (6,000 B.C.) discovered by James Mellaart in 1961 in Anatolia, S.E. of Konya. A true fortified city, it had temples with fine wall paintings, and there were rich finds of jewelry, obsidian, mirrors, etc. With Jericho (q.v.) it demonstrated much earlier development of urban life in the ancient world than previously imagined.

CATALŌ'NIA. Region of NE Spain (Span. Cataluña), comprising the provs. of Barcelona, Gerona, Lérida and Tarragona. Area 31,960 sq.km (12,340 sq.m); pop. (1970) 5,100,000. In the N it is mountainous, but in the S the Castellón mountains are broken through by the lower Ebro, and the basin of its tributaries. The soil is fertile, but the climate in the interior is arid. Hydroelectric power is produced, and C. leads Spain in industrial development, especially in wool and cotton textiles. The cap. is Barcelona.

The region has a long tradition of independence, enjoying autonomy 1932-9, but lost its privileges following its leading part on the Republican side in the Civil War. Autonomy and official use of the Catalan language were restored in 1980. The nat. dance is the *sardana*, a circle dance.

CATA'LPA. Genus of trees found in N America, China, and West Indies, belonging to the Bignoniaceae. The common species, *C. bignoniodes*, has been introduced into Europe. It has large, heart-shaped leaves, and white, yellow and purple streaked bell-shaped flowers.

CATA'LYSIS. Chemical process whereby the speed of a reaction is altered by means of the introduction of another substance into the system, this substance remaining chemically unchanged at the end of the reaction. Such a substance is called a *catalyst*, and in a broad analogy it may be compared with the oil which improves the working of a machine. The most important catalysts are those which increase the speed, i.e. *positive catalysts*, but in some reactions materials which slow down a reaction, i.e. *negative catalysts*, are important.

CATAMARA'N. Type of raft used in S America and the E and W Indies, commonly consisting of a large centre log with 2 smaller ones lashed above it, the crew and cargo being carried between them. Double-hulled yachts designed on the same principle are the fastest craft in sailing.

CATAMARAN. Japan's *Sea Palace* carries 300 passengers on Seto inland sea. *Photo: Courtesy of the Japanese Embassy.*

CATANIA (kahtah'nē-ah). Italian city, chief town of C. province in Sicily. It has Roman remains, including a great amphitheatre. The cathedral is part-Norman. It exports locally produced sulphur, asphalt, and fruits. Pop. (1970) 414,600.

CA'TARACT. Opacity of the lens of the eye. It sometimes occurs in children (lamellar C), although the commonest form is senile C., occurring chiefly in persons over 50. Fluid accumulates between the fibres of the lens and gives place to deposits of albumen; these coalesce into rounded bodies; the lens fibres themselves break down, and areas of the lens become filled with opaque products of degeneration. The condition nearly always affects both eyes, but usually one more than the other. In most cases the treatment is to extract the lens. After the lens is removed the patient can see but cannot alter his focus, so he needs separate reading and distance glasses.

CATARRH. Discharge of fluid from mucous membrane; generally, an excessive secretion of mucous fluid, sometimes mixed with pus, from the nose (rhinitis).

CATASTROPHE THEORY. Mathematical theory developed by Frenchman René Thom, originally as a general theory applied to the development of biological forms in *Stabilité structurelle et morphogénèse* (1972). In this he showed that the growth of an organism proceeds by a series of gradual changes, which are triggered by and in turn trigger 'catastrophic' jumps or large-scale changes. The theory is expressed in 3-dimensional graphs or models which are of 7 types: fold, cusp, swallowtail, butterfly, hyperbolic umbilic, elliptic umbilic, and parabolic umbilic. The theory is thought to be applicable in many practical fields, e.g. optics, civil engineering (as in the collapse of bridges), etc., and tentatively in less exact sciences, such as economics and psychology. For example, in a quarrel between husband and wife, plotted in the form of a cusp (the meeting point between 2 curves), the disagreement develops steadily, resolution being possible at any stage up to a certain point, but once it reaches that point it 'jumps' to a different level of open anger and develops from there.

CATCHMENT AREA. Area from which water is collected by a river valley.

CATECHISM. Instruction, usually in religion, by question and answer. Socrates used this method in his dialogues. A form of C. was used for the catechumens in the early Christian Church. Little books of C. became numerous at the Reformation. Luther pub. simple Cs. for children and unlearned people, and a larger C. for the use of teachers. The most popular RC catechism was that of Peter Canisius (1555); that with the widest circulation now is the 'Explanatory C. of Christian Doctrine'. Among the best-known Protestant Cs. are Calvin's Geneva C. (1537); that composed by Cranmer and Ridley with additions by Overall (1549-1661), incorporated in the Book of Common Prayer; The Presbyterian C. (1647-8); and the Evangelical Free Church C. (1898).

CATECHU (kat'eshoo, -choo). An extract of the leaves and shoots of *Uncaria gambier*, an East Indian acacia. It is rich in tannic acid, which is released slowly, a property which makes it a useful intestinal astringent in diarrhoea.

CATERPILLARS. The larvae of butterflies and moths. They are wormlike in form, and the body consists of 13 segments besides the head. The abdominal segments bear a varying number of pro-legs as well as the 6 true legs on the thoracic segments. The head has strong biting mandibles, silk glands and a spinneret. In many species the body is hairy, and the skin is often provided with scent and other glands. Many Cs. resemble the plant on which they feed, dry twigs, or rolled leaves. Others are highly coloured and rely for their protection on their irritant hairs, disagreeable smell, or on their power to eject a corrosive fluid. Others again take up a peculiar 'terrifying attitude' when attacked.

Cs. emerge from the eggs which have been laid by the female insect on the food plant, and feed greedily, increasing greatly in size and casting their skins several times, until the pupal stage is reached.

CATFISH. Members of the order of Ostariophysi of the bony fishes; so-called because of the long feelers or barbels about the mouth, which give the effect of a cat's whiskers. The group includes several families of which most are wholly freshwater fishes.

In Britain the name C. is commonly given to the wolf-fish (*Anarrhichas lupus*), a sea-fish belonging to blennies, and having nothing to do with the true C.

CATHARS or **Cathari** (medieval Lat., 'the pure'). A sect in medieval Europe usually numbered among the Christian heretics. They started about the 10th cent. in the Balkans where they were called Bogomils, spread to the southern countries of W Europe where they were often identified with the Albigenses, and by the middle of the

CATERPILLAR. The larvae of the birdwing butterfly from Australia resembles a spiny fruit. Threads of silk criss cross the leaf as the caterpillar begins to spin its cocoon. *Photo: G.Pizzet/The Natural History Photographic Agency.*

14th cent. had been destroyed or driven underground by the Inquisition. It seems that they believed that this world is under the domination of Satan, and men and women are the terrestrial embodiment of spirits who were inspired by him to revolt and were driven out of heaven. At death the soul will become again imprisoned in flesh, whether of man or beast, unless it has been united in this life with Christ. If a man has become one of the C., death brings release, the Beatific Vision, and immortality in Christ's presence. Baptism with the spirit - the *consolamentum* - was the central rite, which was held to remedy the disaster of the Fall. The spirit received was the Paraclete, the Comforter, and it was imparted by imposition of hands. Those who received it were included among the Perfect, the ordained priesthood, were implicitly obeyed in everything, and lived lives of the strictest self-denial and chastity, The Believers or *Credentes* could approach God only through the Perfect.

CATHĒ'DRAL (Gk *kathedra*, a seat or throne). Church containing the throne of a bishop or archbishop, which is usually situated on the S. side of the choir. There are Cs. in most of the important cities of Britain, and formerly they were distinguished as monastic and secular Cs., the clergy of the latter not being members of a regular monastic order. The term 'minster' applied to such Cs. as Lincoln and York does not imply that they were at one time monastic churches, but it originated in the name given to the bishop and C. clergy who were often referred to as a *monasterium*. After the dissolution of the monasteries by Henry VIII, most of the monastic churches were refounded and are called Cs. of the New Foundation. Cathedrals of sees founded since 1836 incl. St Albans, Southwark, Truro, Birmingham, and Liverpool. Among the most famous American cathedrals are: St Patrick's and St John the Divine, both in NY, and the Episcopal Cathedral of St Peter and St Paul, Washington, DC. A cathedral is governed by a dean and chapter. *See* COVENTRY.

CATHEDRAL. Notre Dame, built 1163–1240 and situated at the east end of the Ile de la Cité, the oldest part of Paris. *Photo: B.G.Silberstein/Camera Press.*

CATHER (kath'-), **Willa Sibert** (1876-1947). American novelist. Her books deal generally with immigrant life of the Midwest - *O Pioneers* (1913) and *Lucy Gayheart* (1935) - which she knew as a child in Nebraska, but *Sapphira and the Slave Girl* (1940) is set in her native Virginia.

CATHERINE I (1683-1727). Empress of Russia. A Lithuanian peasant girl, Martha Skavronsky m. a Swedish dragoon and eventually became the mistress of Peter the Great. In 1703 she was rechristened as Katarina Alexeievna, and in 1711 the emperor divorced his wife and m. C. She accompanied him in his campaigns, and showed tact and shrewdness. In 1724 she was proclaimed empress, and after Peter's death in 1725 she ruled capably with the help of her ministers. She allied Russia with Austria and Spain in an anti-English bloc.

CATHERINE II, the Great (1729-96). Empress of Russia. Daughter of the prince of Anhalt-Zerbst, she married in 1745 the Russian grand duke Peter, who was an unbalanced weakling, and 6 months after his becoming Tsar in 1762 he was put out of the way. Henceforth C. ruled alone and proved capable and energetic. During her reign Russia extended her boundaries to include territory from Turkey (1774) and Sweden (1790), and profited by the Partitions of Poland.

C.'s private life was notorious throughout Europe, but she did not permit her amours to influence her policy. She admired and aided the Encyclopaedists, and corresponded with Voltaire and D'Alembert.

CATHERINE DE' MEDICI (de meh'dēchē) (1519-89). French queen, wife of Henry II and mother of Francis II, Charles IX, and Henry III. She was a daughter of Lorenzo de' Medici, and m. Henry in 1533. During the reigns of her sons she exercised a powerful political influence. At first she schemed with the Huguenots, but later bitterly opposed them, and the massacre of St Bartholomew (1572) was largely her work. She was a patron of the arts.

CATHERINE DE' MEDICI. Catherine was a true Medici in her love of magnificent architecture, and during her regency much work was carried out on the Palace of the Tuileries. *Photo: Mansell Collection.*

CATHERINE OF ARAGON (1485-1536). First queen of Henry VIII of England. Daughter of Ferdinand and Isabella of Spain, she was betrothed at the age of 2 to Prince Arthur of England and m. him in 1501. He d. in 1502, and C. was then betrothed to his brother Henry, aged 11. When Henry became king in 1509, the marriage took place. C. bore 6 children, but only her daughter Mary lived. Henry desired a male heir, and in 1526 began to seek an annulment of his marriage on the grounds that the union with his brother's widow was invalid in spite of papal dispensation. When the Pope demanded that the case should be referred to him, Henry m. Anne Boleyn and afterwards received the desired decree of nullity from Archbishop Cranmer (1533). The Reformation in England followed. C. went into retirement, and was kept virtually a prisoner until her death.

CATHERINE OF BRAGANZA (1638-1705). Queen of Charles II of England. The daughter of John IV of Portugal, she m. Charles in 1662. Bombay and Tangier formed part of her dowry. Charles was occupied with his mistresses, and she lived in retirement. She had no children, but Charles opposed Shaftesbury's design for a divorce. Her liberty to practise her religion as a Catholic was resented. In 1692 she returned to Lisbon.

CATHERINE OF GENOA (1447-1510). Catholic saint. B. at Genoa of a noble family, she was m. at 16 and in later life devoted herself to the care of the sick, practised an inner life of deep meditation, and left two mystical treatises and a dialogue between the soul and the body. She was canonized in 1737.

CATHERINE OF SIENA (1347-80). Catholic saint and mystic, b. at Siena in Italy. She practised severe mortification while still a child, and at the age of 16 became a Dominican tertiary. She attempted to reconcile the Florentines with the Pope, and persuaded Gregory XI to return to Rome from Avignon in 1376. In 1375 she is said to have received on her body the stigmata, the impression of Christ's wounds. Her *Dialogue* is a remarkable mystical work. She was canonized in 1461.

CATHERINE OF VALOIS (1401-37). Queen of Henry V of England. The 3rd daughter of Charles VI of France, she was m. to Henry in 1420, and bore a son, Henry VI. Henry d. in 1422, and about 1425 she secretly m. Owen Tudor, by whom she had a son, Edmund, who became the father of Henry VII.

CA'THŌDE. The electrode at which positive current leaves a device. It is the negatively charged electrode of an electrolytic cell, the electrode from which the primary stream of electrons is emitted in a vacuum tube, and the positive terminal of a battery.

CATHODE RAYS. Streams of negatively charged particles (electrons) emitted from the cathode of a discharge tube when sufficiently evacuated.

CATHODE RAY TUBE. A special form of vacuum tube in which a beam of electrons is produced and focused on to a fluorescent screen. It is an essential component of television receivers and of oscilloscopes, instruments widely used in electronics for studying waveforms.

CATHOLIC CHURCH (Gk *katholikos*, universal). Term applied to the whole body of the Christian Church (e.g. in the Apostles' Creed). By those Christians who accept the supremacy of the Pope, it is applied exclusively to themselves. Members of other churches, however, add the qualifying term Roman when speaking of them. *See* ROMAN-CATHOLICISM; OLD CATHOLICS.

CATHOLIC EMANCIPATION. Name given to a series of acts passed in Britain between 1780 and 1829 to relieve Catholics from the civil and legal restrictions accumulated from the time of Henry VIII.

CATILINE (kat'ilīn), **(Lucius Sergius Catilina)** (*c.* 108-62 BC). Roman politician. An unscrupulous adventurer, of an impoverished patrician family, he followed a double failure to be elected to the consulship in 64/63 with a plot to seize control of the state. In 4 celebrated orations Cicero (q.v.) laid bare the conspiracy: several of C.'s followers were executed and C. d. in battle at the head of his revolutionary troops.

CĀ'TŌ, Marcus Porcius (234-149 BC). Roman statesman. The son of a farmer, he served in the war against Hannibal, became consul in 195 BC and imposed a Roman peace upon the tribes of Spain. Appointed censor in 184 he used his powers to exclude from the senate all those members who fell short of the ancient Roman standards of dignity and moral uprightness. He was a keen farmer, and his treatise on agriculture is the earliest surviving work in Latin prose. Deeply impressed by the commercial prosperity of Carthage, which he visited in 157, he ended every speech in the senate by declaiming that 'Carthage must be destroyed'.

CATO STREET CONSPIRACY. An unsuccessful plot to murder Castlereagh and his ministers while they were dining with Lord Harrowby on 20 Feb. 1820, to capture the Bank and Mansion House, and to set London on fire, after which it was planned to set up a provisional govt. The conspirators were betrayed, and the 5 leaders were hanged and others sentenced to life transportation. The plot was hatched in Cato St., Edgware Rd, London. *See* THISTLEWOOD.

CATS' CRADLES. Game played by one or more persons with a piece of looped string: world-wide in distribution it has magic connotations in some parts of the world, or may illustrate folktale events.

CATSKILLS. American mountain range, mainly in the state of New York; the highest point is Slide Mt (1,281 m/4,204 ft). They form part of the Appalachian Mtns system.

CATTERICK. Village with an important military camp, nr Richmond, N Yorks, England.

CATTLE. A group of large-sized ruminant Artiodactyla, including the buffaloes, bison, yak, gaur, gayal, and banteng, and the various familiar domesticated breeds. There are 2 main types of domesticated cattle, the European breeds and the zebus or sacred humped cattle of India, which are useful in the tropics for their ability to withstand the heat and diseases to which European breeds succumb. There is also in northern India a domesticated breed called the gayal descended from a wild species termed the gaur or tsain. A smaller related species, the banteng, has been domesticated in Java. The European breeds (*Bos taurus*) are descended from the extinct aurochs (*Bos primigenius*), which, although larger, resembled the White Park Cattle formerly greatly prized in Britain, at Chillingham, Chartley, and elsewhere. *See also* BISON.

CATUL'LUS, Gaius Valerius (*c.* 84-54 BC). Roman lyric poet. B. at Verona, he moved in the best literary and political society of Rome and wrote lyrics describing his unhappy love affair with Clodia, wife of the consul Metellus. He journeyed to Asia Minor on the staff of the Roman governor Memmius, and near Troy visited the tomb of his brother for whom he wrote an epitaph full of sincere feeling. His longer poems include two wedding-songs. Many of his happiest poems are short verses to his friends.

CAUCASUS (kaw'-). Series of mountain ranges which traverse the area between the Black Sea and the Caspian Sea, in USSR. From its westerly extremity, S of the estuary of the Kuban, it runs SE for 1,200 km (750 m), approaching the Caspian shore near the peninsula of Apsheron. The maximum width of the Great C. is about 225 km (140 m). The highest peaks include Elbruz (5,633 m/18,480 ft), Jaikyl, Shkara, and several others.

J. F. Blumenbach *c.* 1800 derived the white race of mankind from this area, hence the use of the word *Caucasian* to denote European types.

CAUCUS (kaw'-). Term originally used in Boston, USA, in the 18th cent. for a meeting of the leaders of a political club or party designed to make arrangements for elections, etc. In England, it was first applied to the organization introduced by Joseph Chamberlain in 1878. Nowadays it means the powerful directive nucleus of a political party.

CAULIFLOWER. Variety of cabbage (*Brassica oleracea*), distinguished by its large flattened head of fleshy, aborted flowers, and by being less hardy than is the broccoli. It is said to have been introduced into England from Cyprus in the 16th cent.

CAVAFY, Constantinos (1863-1933). Greek poet. An Alexandrian, he throws a startlingly up-to-date light on the Greek past, recreating the classical period with zest. In 1923 E. M. Forster translated *Pharos and Pharillon.*

CAVALIER. A term originally applied to horsemen of gentle birth, but referring in particular to the supporters of Charles I in the Civil War. Suckling, Lovelace, etc. are known as 'C. poets'.

CAVALLI (kahvahl'lē), **Francesco** (1602-76). Italian composer, organist at St Mark's, Venice; 27 of his operas survive. C. was the first to make opera a popular entertainment.

CAVAN. Inland co. in that part of the prov. of Ulster that is included in Rep. of Ireland. The r. Erne divides it into a narrow peninsula, some 20m long, between Leitrim and Fermanagh - low-lying country for the most part - and an eastern section of wild and bare hill country. The soil is generally poor, and the climate moist and cold. Agriculture is the chief industry. The chief towns are Cavan, the capital, pop. *c.* 3,000. Kilmore, seat of RC and Protestant bishoprics, Virginia, etc. Area 1,890 sq. km (730 sq. m); pop. (1971) 52,620.

CAVE. A hollow in the earth's crust produced by the action of underground water or by waves on a sea coast. Cs. of the former type commonly occur in limestone, but not in chalk country where the rocks are soluble in water. A *pot-hole* is a vertical hole in rock caused by water descending a crack. C. fauna often show loss of pigmentation or sight, and under isolation specialized species may develop. *See* SPELEOLOGY.

Some of the most famous Cs. are the Mammoth C. in Kentucky, 6.4km (4m) long and 38m (125ft high); the Caverns of Adelsberg (Postumia) near Trieste which extend for many miles; Carlsbad C., the largest in America; the Cheddar Cs., Somerset; Fingal's C., Staffa, Scotland, famous for its range of basalt columns; and Peak Cavern, Derbyshire.

CAVE. Part of a gallery of ancient Aboriginal paintings being admired by Dick Roughsey, himself an Aboriginal artist. Recently discovered nr Laura on Cape York, Queensland, they include the device of painting from an impression of the artist's own hand, which is universal among primitive peoples. *Photo: Barbara Wace*

CAVE, Edward (1691-1754). British printer, founder under the pseudonym 'Sylvanus Urban' of *The Gentleman's Magazine* (1731-1914), the first periodical to be

CAVE. A sophisticated Bodhisattva from Ajanta in India, where caves have often been used as temples. *Photo: Courtesy of the Government of India Tourist Office*

called a 'magazine'. Johnson was an influential contributor 1738-44.

CAVELL (kavl), **Edith Louisa** (1865-1915). British nurse. Dau. of a Norfolk clergyman, she was appointed matron at the new nurses' training institute in Brussels in 1907. In the F.W.W. this became a Red Cross hospital for both sides, and she with Philippe Baucq helped English and French soldiers to escape to the Dutch frontier. On 5 Aug. 1915 she was arrested; and after a court martial she and Baucq were condemned to death. She d. with heroic calmness, her final words being: 'Patriotism is not enough. I must have no hatred or bitterness towards anyone'. Since 1919 her body has rested beside Norwich Cathedral, and there is a statue of her in St Martin's Place, London.

CAVENDISH, Lord Frederick Charles (1836-82). Second son of the 7th duke of Devonshire, he was appointed in 1882 chief secretary to the Lord-Lieutenant of Ireland, and on the evening of his arrival in Dublin was murdered in Phoenix Park with Burke, the Under-Secretary, by members of the society of 'Irish Invincibles'.

CAVENDISH, Henry (1731-1810). British physicist. A grandson of the 2nd duke of Devonshire, he devoted his life to scientific pursuits, living in rigorous seclusion at Clapham Common. He discovered the composition of nitric acid and the composition of water. The C. experiment was a device of his to discover the density of the Earth.

CAVENDISH, Thomas (*c.* 1555-92). English navigator; commander of the third circumnavigation of the world. He sailed in July 1586, touched Brazil, followed down the coast to Patagonia, passed through the Straits of Magellan, and sailed back via the Philippines, Cape of Good Hope, and St Helena, reaching Plymouth after 2 years and 50 days.

CAVE TEMPLES. Examples of rock architecture, of which the finest are found in Western India and the Deccan. *See* AJANTA and ELLORA.

CAVIARE (kavēahr'). Russian delicacy, obtained from the roes of the sturgeon. It is prepared by beating and straining the ovaries until the eggs are free from fats, etc., and then adding salt.

CAVITE (kahvē'teh). Town and port of the Philippine Republic, cap. of C. prov., Luzon, 13km (8m) S of Manila. It was in Japanese hands Dec. 1941 to Feb. 1945 during the S.W.W. After the Philippines attained independence in 1946, the US Seventh Fleet continued to use the naval base. Pop. (1970) 76,000.

CAVOUR (kahvoor'), **Camillo Benso,** count (1810-61). Italian statesman. B. at Turin, he served in the army in early life, and entered politics in 1847 as editor of *Il Risorgimento.* From 1848 he sat in the Piedmontese parliament, and held cabinet posts 1850-2. Becoming Prime Minister in 1852, he sought to secure French and British sympathy for the cause of Italian unity by sending Piedmontese troops to fight in the Crimean War. In 1858 he met Napoleon III secretly at Plombières, and planned with him the war of 1859 against Austria, which resulted in the union of Lombardy with Piedmont. The central Italian states also joined the kingdom of Italy, although Savoy and Nice had to be ceded to France as the price of acquiescence. With C.'s approval Garibaldi overthrew the Neapolitan monarchy, but to prevent him from marching on Rome C. occupied part of the Papal States, which with Naples and Sicily were annexed to Italy.

CA'VY (family Caviidae). Various kinds of short-tailed S American rodents, of which the tame guinea pig (q.v.) is the most familiar example.

CAWNPORE. Another form of KANPUR.

CAXTON, William (*c.* 1422-91). First English printer. B. in Kent, he was apprenticed to a London mercer (1438), and set up his own business in Bruges 1441-70. In 1471 he went to Cologne, where he learned the art of printing, and then set up his own press in Bruges in partnership with Colard Mansion. The first book from his press, and the first book printed in English, was C.'s own version of a French romance, *Recuyell of the Historyes of Troye* (1474). Returning to England in 1476 C. estab. himself in Westminster, where he produced the first book printed in England, *Dictes and Sayenges of the Phylosophers* (1477). Altogether he printed about 100 books, including editions of Chaucer, Gower and Lydgate, and translated many texts from the French or the Lat., in addition to revising others, e.g. Malory's *Morte d'Arthur.*

CAYENNE (kāyen'). Cap., chief port, and international airport of French Guiana, on C. island at the mouth of the r. C. Founded 1634 and destroyed by Indians, it dates actually from 1664; it was used as a penal settlement from 1854 to 1946. Pop. (1974) 30,500.

CAYENNE PEPPER, A condiment derived from the dried fruits of *Capsicum* (q.v.), a genus of plants of the family Solanaceae. It is wholly distinct in its origin from true pepper.

CAYLEY, Arthur (1821-95). British mathematician. Sadlerian prof. at Cambridge from 1863, he was the greatest pure mathematician of the cent. His books incl. *Elliptic Functions* (1876).

CAYLEY, Sir George (1773-1857). British pioneer in aeronautics. In addition to building successful models and full-size gliders from 1804, he laid the foundations of modern aerodynamics 1809-10.

CAYMAN (kīmahn') **ISLANDS.** Three low-lying islands in the W Indies, 290km (180m) WNW of Jamaica. The largest is Grand Cayman (35km/22m long and 6.5-13km/4-8m wide), on which is the cap. George Town; the others are Cayman Brac and Little Cayman. Discovered by Columbus in 1503, they were first settled by military deserters in Cromwellian times, harboured pirates in the 18th cent., and are today attractive to tourists. They are also an international financial centre and 'tax haven'. They were admin. with Jamaica until 1962, when they became a Brit. Crown colony. Green turtle are farmed and there is a valuable strain of seawhip coral used as a source of prostaglandins. Total area, 260 sq.km (100 sq.m); pop. (1981) 18,000, pleasantly racially mixed. M.U.: C.I. dollar.

CEAUSESCU (se-owchesk'oo), **Nicolae** (1918-). Romanian statesman. He became Sec.-General of the Communist Party in 1965, and in 1967 became Pres. of the State Council, the growing importance of Romania's independent foreign policy requiring him to represent the country officially. In 1974 he became first pres. of the republic: re-elected 1980.

CEBU (seboo'). Oldest city, founded 1565 as San Miguel, of the republic of the Philippines, on the island of C. (5,086 sq.km/1,964 sq.m), of which it is the chief port. Pop. (1975) 408,200.

CECIL (si'sil), **Lord David** (1902-). British critic. The younger son of the 4th marquess of Salisbury, he became Goldsmiths' prof. of English literature at Oxford in 1948. His books incl. *The Stricken Deer* (1929), dealing with Cowper, as well as studies of Jane Austen, Scott, and Hardy; and the subtly-penetrating *The Young Melbourne* (1939), with its sequel *Lord M.* (1954).

CECIL, Robert, 1st earl of Salisbury (?1563-1612). Son of Lord Burghley by his 2nd wife, he succeeded him as Sec. of State to Elizabeth, and was afterwards the chief minister of James I, who made him earl of Salisbury in 1605.

CECILIA (sesil'ia). Christian saint, martyred in Rome, in the 2nd or 3rd cent. Her later association with music may derive from the story that she sang hymns while undergoing torture.

CEDAR (sē'der). Genus of coniferous trees (*Cedrus*). The best-known is the C. of Lebanon (*C. libani*), which grows to a great height and age in the mountains of Syria and Asia Minor. Of the famous forests on Mt Lebanon itself, only a few groups of trees remain. Together with the Himalayan C. (*C. deodara*) and the Algerian or Mt Atlas order (*C. atlantica*), it has been introduced into England.

CEEFAX. *See* TELETEXT.

CELANDINE (sel'andīn). Name given to 2 plants belonging to different families, and resembling each other only in their bright yellow flowers. The greater C. (*Chelidonium majus*) belongs to the Papaveraceae, and is common in English hedgerows. The lesser C. (*Ranunculus ficaria*) is a member of the buttercup family, and is a familiar wayside and meadow plant.

CELEBES (selē'biz). Island of the Rep. of Indonesia, also known as Sulawesi, which is one of the Great Sunda Is. (q.v.). It is mountainous and forested, producing copra and nickel. Area, with dependent islands 190,000 sq.km; pop. (1971) 8,500,000.

CELERY (sel'eri). Genus of plants (*Apium*) of the family Umbelliferae. The common species (*A. graveolens*) grows in ditches, salt-marshes, etc., and is coarse and acrid. In cultivation the acrid qualities are removed by blanching.

CELL. A minute portion of living matter; the simplest living organism; the unit of physical life. Bacteria, amoebae, and certain other micro-organisms consist of single cells. Plants and animals are composed entirely of cells of various kinds. The body of a mammal (including that of the human species) originates from an organism consisting of a single cell - an ovum or egg-cell generated by the female and fertilized by fusion with a spermatozoon or seed-cell generated by the male. The fertilized ovum (embryo) is a microscopic body chiefly consisting of protoplasm, or clear jelly, the simplest form of living substance. The protoplasmic part of the cell is called the cytoplasm. It is enclosed in a membranous wall and contains a small spherical body called a nucleus - an essential part of most cells, without which they cannot reproduce. The only cells of the body which have no nucleus are the red blood cells. The nucleus of the embryo contains a denser spot called the nucleolus, but many other kinds of cells do not.

The nucleus of a cell contains genetic material (*see* NUCLEIC ACIDS), and the cytoplasm contains structural and functional units (organelles), such as the minute bodies (mitochondria) incl. enzymes which produce energy.

Cells reproduce by division, a complicated process which starts in the nucleus. The function of the cell is to convert energy from one form into another, e.g. food and oxygen into chemical energy.

Sexual reproduction is performed by the union of two special kinds of cells. When the human ovum is fertilized by fusion with a spermatozoon, the new cell contains the chromosomes from both - 48. The sex of the new individual is determined by the distribution of the special sex chromosomes. The ordinary cells of the female body have two X chromosomes; the cells of the male body have an X and a Y chromosome - two different types. The mature ovum contains one X chromosome and the mature spermatozoon contains either an X or a Y chromosome. If on fertilization two X chromosomes meet, the result is a female; if an X and a Y meet, the result is a male. All men thus inherit from their fathers one Y chromosome which gives their male characteristics: some (perhaps 1 in 300) inherit 2, which give added height, greater emotional instability, inability to bear frustration, and great aggressiveness. These men are often criminally violent, and possession of the Y-factor, immediately detectable under the microscope, has (as in France and Australia 1968) been successfully pleaded in mitigation in murder cases.

Ionization arising from gamma or X-radiation can damage Cs., and in the case of reproduction Cs. this may lead to disruption of the chromosomes and potential degradation of the offspring.

In 1976 the barrier between the plant and animal kingdoms was broken by the achievement in the laboratory (in U.K., U.S.A. and Hungary), of the fusion of a plant and animal cell to form a hybrid, e.g. red blood cell from a hen and a yeast cell, using polyethylene glycol as a fusing agent. There has as yet been no development beyond a single cell.

CELL (Electric). An apparatus in which chemical energy is converted into electrical energy; the popular name is 'battery', but this should be reserved for a collection of cells in one unit. E. Cs. can be divided into: (a) *primary*, which produce electric energy by chemical action and require replenishing after this action is complete; and (b) *secondary*, or accumulators, which are so constituted that the action is reversible, and the original condition can be restored by an electric current. The first battery was made by Volta in 1800. Types of primary cells are the Daniell, Lalande, Leclanché, etc., and the so-called dry cells; secondary cells include Planté, Faure, Edison, etc. Newer types incl. the Mallory (mercury depolarizer), which has a very stable discharge curve and can be made in very small units, e.g. for hearing-aids, and the Venner accumulator, which can be made substantially solid for some purposes.

CELLINI (chellē'nē), **Benvenuto** (1500–71). Italian artist, sculptor, and silversmith; also famous for his autobiography. B. in Florence, he was apprenticed to a goldsmith, and in 1519 went to Rome. C. claims to have killed the Constable de Bourbon during the siege of 1527. Later C. worked for the papal mint, and once was imprisoned on a charge of having embezzled pontifical jewels. In 1546 he began the bronze group of 'Perseus holding the head of Medusa', completed in 1554. He worked for a time in France at the court of Francis I, and finally settled in Florence in 1545, where he d.

CELLULITE (sel'ūlīt). A fatty compound supposedly produced within the body mainly by liver disorder and resulting in lumpy obesity. Medical opinion denies its existence and considers the diets to counteract it, which are recommended by some dieticians, to be potentially harmful in the long-term.

CELLULITIS (selūlī'tis). Inflammation of body tissue, accompanied by swelling, redness and pain.

CELLULOID (sel'ūloid). Transparent or translucent highly inflammable plastic material, now largely replaced by the non-inflammable cellulose acetate. C., chemically, is cellulose nitrate, and is formed by the action of nitric acid on cellulose in the presence of sulphuric acid mixed with camphor.

CELLULOSE. Complex carbohydrate material widely distributed in the plant kingdom, where it is the principal structural material. In various states of combination it is familiar as different kinds of wood; a purer form is cotton, and also paper and linen. It is present in nearly all plants, where it forms the harder parts, the cell walls, the fibres, etc.

CELSIUS (sel'si-us). The degree centigrade (°C) was officially re-named (1948) Celsius to avoid confusion with the angular measure (a hundredth of a grade) known as the centigrade, but remains in use, as in meteorology. *See* CENTIGRADE.

CELTIC (keltik). A group of languages of the Indo-European family. They fall into two well-marked groups: the Goidelic consisting of the Gaelic language, under its 3 forms of Irish, Scottish, and Manx Gaelic, each with several sub-dialects; and the Brythonic, which includes Welsh, Cornish (extinct since *c.* 1800), Breton, and Gallic or Gaulish, the language of Gaul before the introduction of Latin, which seems to have died out in *c.* AD 600. The C. languages had formerly a much wider extension, as is seen by place-names in all parts of the British Isles, France, the N of the Spanish peninsula, Switzerland, S Germany, and N Italy. Native C. speakers grow fewer, but measures to arrest a final decline were undertaken in the mid-20th cent.

CELTIC ART. A style of art which originated in *c.* 500 BC, probably on the Rhine, and spread westwards to Gaul and the British Isles, and southwards to Italy and Asia Minor until it was superseded by Roman influence (2nd–1st cent. BC). It is known conventionally as La Tène art, from a Swiss site where the best examples of the style were found. The chief characteristics are: linear designs - developing at a later state into intricate patterns - and the use of enamel and coral in the decoration of bronze objects.

A Late Celtic period existed only in the British Isles; it corresponds to a period of varying length according to regions in the Christian era, and is characterized by a rich decorative art, especially by enamelled horse-trappings and engraved mirrors.

CELTIC LEAGUE. Nationalist organisation with representatives from Alba (Scotland), Breizh (Brittany), Eire, Kernow (Cornwall), Cymru (Wales) and Ellan Vannin (Isle of Man), which held its first conference in 1975. Its aims incl. a pan-Celtic federation economically and politically independent of Britain and France.

CELTIC LITERATURE. *See* BRETON; CORNISH; IRISH; MANX; SCOTTISH GAELIC; WELSH.

CELTIC SEA. Name coined by oilmen to denote the sea area between Wales, Ireland and SW England being explored for gas and oil in the 1970s. It avoided a narrowly nationalist significance.

CELTS (keltz). The name given, under various forms, by Greek and Roman writers to a people whose first-known territory was an area in the basin of the upper Danube and S Germany. Here they were pioneers of the working of iron, and in the last 6 cents. BC elaborated the La Tène culture. They overran France, Spain, Portugal, N Italy, sacked Rome in 390 BC, the British Isles, and Greece. They appear never to have had a united empire, and their conquests were made by emigrant bands which effected permanent settlements in the lands named, as well as in the part of Asia Minor later known as Galatia from their name. The name C. was given by classical authors to a fair, tall people of N Europe; and it was only gradually that they learned to distinguish the Cs. from the German tribes.

CEMENT (sement'). A bonding agent used to unite particles in one mass or to cause one surface to adhere to another. The term is applied to a variety of materials such as fluxes and pastes, and also bituminous products obtained from tar. In general, however, the name is more applicable to Portland C., a powder obtained from burning together a mixture of lime or chalk, and clay, which is the universal medium for building in brick or stone or for the production of concrete. In 1824 Joseph Aspdin, a Yorkshire bricklayer, discovered and patented the first Portland C., so named because of its resemblance in colour, in the hardened state, to the famous Portland stone.

CENOTAPH (sen'otaf; Gk 'empty tomb'). Sepulchral monument to commemorate a person or persons whose remains are not actually buried at the site. The C. in Whitehall, London, for those who d. in both world wars, was designed by Sir Edwin Lutyens.

CENSOR (sen'-). High official at ancient Rome. Every 5 years 2 censors were elected to hold office for 18 months; besides completing a registration (*census*) of the citizen body, they revised the list of senators.

CENSOR. The psychic function by which, according to Freud and his followers, impulses arising in the subconscious mind are prevented from reaching consciousness if they are for some reason inacceptable, e.g. if they conflict with a moral sentiment, or would cause painful emotion. The rejection of psychic contents on these grounds is repression. *See also* PSYCHOLOGY (*psychoanalysis*).

CENSORSHIP. Supervision by some person or persons in authority of printed matter and other forms of publication with a view to suppressing anything considered immoral, subversive of the govt, or liable to undermine faith. The RC Church exercises a strict censorship, accepted by the faithful in every country, over all reading matter. In England, under the Tudors and Stuarts, the Crown claimed a monopoly of printing presses, and publication could be carried out only under licence until licensing was abolished in 1695. During both world wars, British defence regulations made it an offence to publish anything likely to be useful to the enemy, and censors were appointed to whom newspaper editors and others could submit material before publication, and much advantage was taken of their services; but such submission was not made compulsory. *See* D-NOTICE. Laws relating to obscenity, libel, and defamation act in some respects as a censorship; they differ from one country to another, and much that would not be published in the UK because it would be libellous there can appear with impunity in e.g. the USA or France.

The C. of plays in the UK by the Lord Chamberlain (under the Theatres Act 1843) ended in 1968.

There is no official C. of films in either the UK or the USA, but in both countries films are submitted before public presentation to bodies set up by the film industry: the British Board of Film Censors in the UK, and a body popularly called the Hays Office (after its first president, 1922-45, Will H. Hays) in the USA.

CENSUS. An official enumeration of the inhabitants of a country or state, together with certain other information regarding the age, sex, occupation, etc., of each individual. In most modern states a C. is taken at regular intervals, usually of 5 or 10 years. The first American C. was taken 1790, and for England and Scotland in 1801. A simultaneous C. of all the Common Market countries, Eurocount, took place in 1981. The original purpose of a C. was to assess the no. of men available for military service, but in modern times they are used in an attempt to assess social trends and forecast calls on social services.

CENTAURS (sen'tawrz). In Greek legend, a race of creatures half-man and half-horse. They dwelt in the plains of Thessaly, and (apart from Chiron, the adviser of Hercules) they were noted for their lawless and turbulent character. The earliest representations of Cs. (*c.* 1800-1000 BC) were excavated near Famagusta in 1962, and are two-headed. Some female representations are also known.

CENTIGRADE. The temperature scale in which one degree is taken as 1/100th part of the interval between two fixed points, melting ice (0°C), and steam over boiling water at standard atmospheric pressure (100°C). The C. thermometer was invented by Linnaeus, who illustrated it in the frontispiece of his *Hortus Cliffortianus* (1737): it is also called the Celsius (q.v.) thermometer, the Swedish scientist Anders Celsius (1701-44) having devised in 1742 a similar thermometer divided into 100 degrees, but with zero as the boiling point of water and 100 as freezing point. One degree C. has the same magnitude as one degree of the Kelvin scale, which is based on the thermo-dynamic properties of an ideal gas and is independent of the physical properties of any medium. A temperature expressed on the Kelvin scale is numerically greater by 273.15 deg. than the same temperature on the C. scale.

CENTIPEDES (sen'tipēdz). Name of a class of animals (*Chilopoda*) of the phylum Arthropoda, having a distinct head and a single pair of antennae. They are distinguished from insects by their bodies being composed of numerous segments, all of similar form and bearing appendages, and from millipedes (*Diplopoda*) by the fact that there is only one pair of limbs to each segment. They are mostly nocturnal in their habits, predatory, and carnivorous, feeding on insects and worms, and are equipped with strong jaws provided with poison fangs. The bite of some of the larger species, found in warmer parts of the world, is painful and may be dangerous. Some of the tropical species, such as *Scolopendra gigas*, attain to as much as a foot in length. Several species are British, *Lithobius forficatus* being most common.

CENTRAL. Region of Scotland created in 1975 to incl. the co. of Clackmannan, all of Stirlingshire except a small area in the SW, the SW of Perthshire, and the Bo'ness area of W Lothian. There is a prosperous agriculture and varied industries incl. engineering, electronics, petrochemicals, dyes, textiles, paper, glass, and brewing and distilling. The admin. HQ is Stirling. Area 2,590 sq.km (1,000 sq.m); pop. (1971) 263,000.

CENTRAL AFRICAN REPUBLIC. The country consists mainly of a plateau at 600 m (2,000 ft), and produces cotton, tobacco, coffee, groundnuts, and timber. Although there are important diamond and uranium reserves, industrialisation has only just begun, and it is one of the world's poorest countries. The cap. is Bangui; pop (1971) 302,000. M.U.: CFA franc.

Formerly the French territory of Ubangi-Shari, the country became independent in 1960. Jean Bokassa (1920-) seized power by a coup in 1966, and re-named it in 1976 the Central African Empire, with himself as Emperor Bokassa. His brutal excesses led to his overthrow and exile in 1979. He returned to the country in 1986 to face trial for treason and cannibalism under the present leader Andre Kolingba.

Area 625,000 sq.km (240,000 sq.m); pop. (1974) 2,610,000, split into many Bantu tribal groups, the majority being Christian. French is the official language, but the lingua franca is Sangho.

CENTRAL AMERICA. A geographical division comprising that portion of the American continent which connects Mexico with the Isthmus of Panama. In itself it is also an isthmus, traversed by mountains that form part of the *cordillera.* It comprises 7 states: *see* table below.

The Central American Common Market (ODECA: *Organización de Estados Centro-americanos*) was estab. in 1960 by El Salvador, Guatemala, Honduras and Nicaragua: Costa Rica acceded 1962, Honduras seceded in 1970.

CENTRAL CRIMINAL COURT. Court (usually known as the Old Bailey) which sits to try all treasons, felonies, and misdemeanours committed in the City of London, and the Greater London area. The C.C.C. was established in 1834.

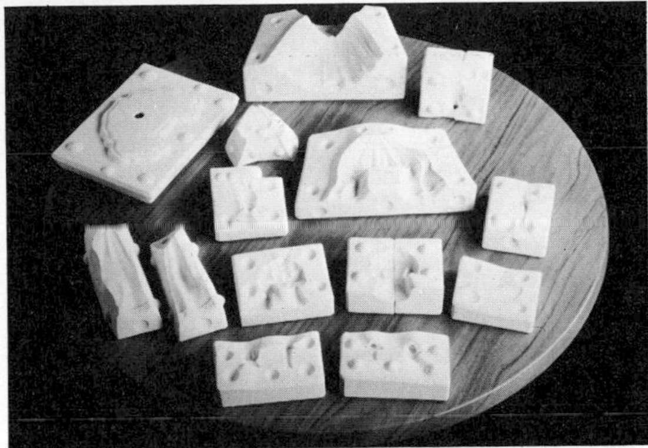

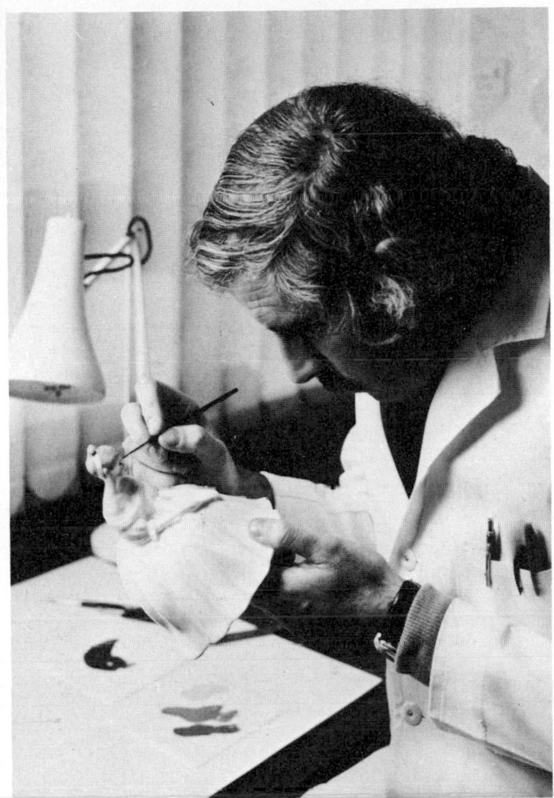

CERAMICS. The making of a Doulton figure. The moulds for the separate pieces involved (top left), the figure partly assembled (lower left), and (right) the delicate task of painting the completed figure. *Photo: Courtesy of Royal Doulton.*

CENTRAL INTELLIGENCE AGENCY. Intelligence organization estab. in 1947 by Pres. Truman on the lines of the British Secret Intelligence Service, and developed from the wartime Office of Strategic Services. Intended solely for use overseas in the 'cold war', it intervened effectively in Iran (under Mossadeq and to restore the Shah in 1953), in S Vietnam, in Zaïre (when it was still the Congo), and against Allende in Chile, but failed in Cuba (*see* PIGS, Bay of). Its involvement in Watergate, when it allegedly undertook illegal domestic espionage, was marginal. During the 1970s there was widespread anti-intelligence agitation in the USA, but the collapse of US influence in Iran, Afghanistan, Nicaragua and N and S Yemen led to a reversal by 1980. *See* BUSH, George.

Countries of Central America

	Area in sq. km.	*Pop. in 1,000s*	*Capital*
Belize	22,965	152	Belmopan
Costa Rica	50,997	2,000	San José
El Salvador	21,393	4,000	San Salvador
Guatemala	108,889	6,800	Guatemala
Honduras	112,088	3,036	Tegucigalpa
Nicaragua	148,000	3,000	Managua
Panama	76,614	1,780	Panama
	540,946	20,768	

CENTRAL MOUNT STUART. Flat-topped mtn 844 m (2,770 ft) high, the approx. central point of Australia. It was originally named in 1860 by explorer J. McDouall Stuart after Sturt (q.v.) - Central Mount Sturt - but later became known by his own name.

CENTRAL PROVINCES AND BERAR. *See* MADHYA PRADESH.

CENTRAL TREATY ORGANIZATION. Defence organization (CENTO) which replaced the Baghdad Pact (q.v.) in 1959. Iran Pakistan and Turkey withdrew in 1979, leaving Britain as the only full member, and it ceased to exist.

CENTRE, The. The central area of Australia which incl. many features increasingly attractive to tourists, e.g. the Musgrave and MacDonnell Ranges, and the area between them in which lie Ayers Rock and Lake Amadeus, as well as the Tanami and Simpson Deserts to the NW and SE respectively, which are all reached from Alice Springs.

CENTRIFUGE (se'ntrifūj). Apparatus for rotating containers at high speeds. One use is for separating substances of different densities. These substances (solid particles, colloids, liquids, gases or mixtures of these) are placed in the containers and the rotation sets up centrifugal forces in the whirling substances acting radially outwards, causing them to separate according to their densities. A common example is the separation of the lighter cream from the

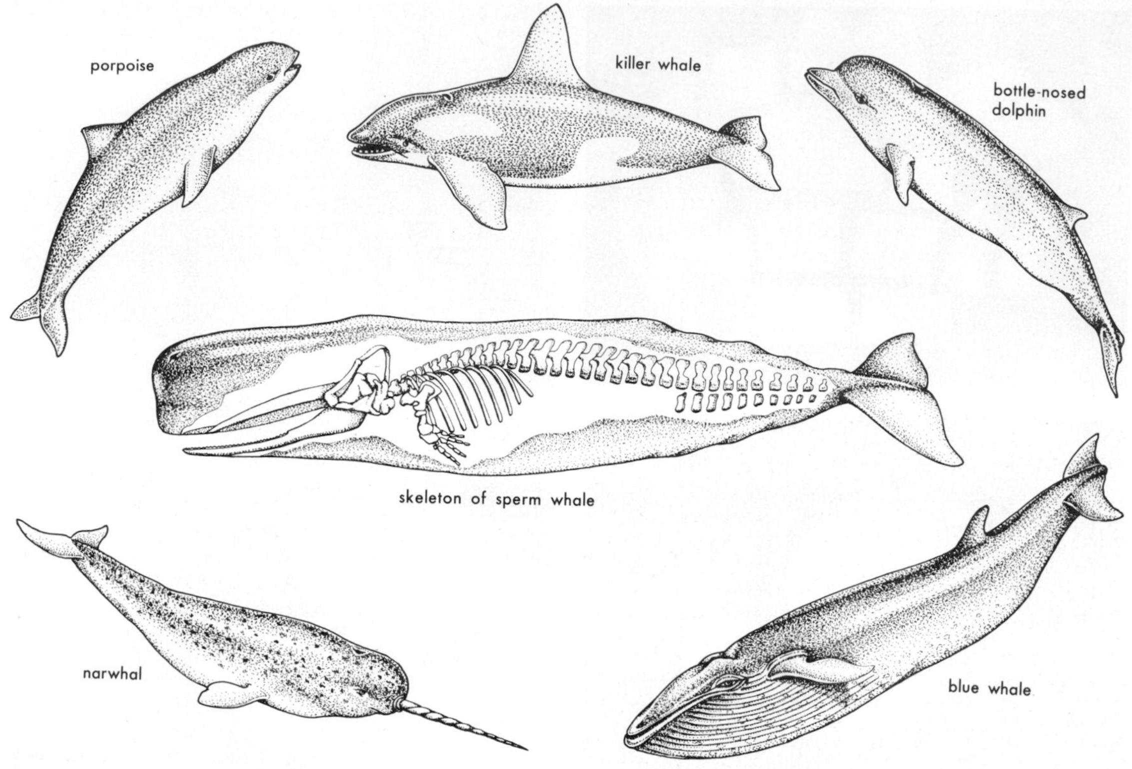

CETACEA. Typical forms of Cetacea.

heavier milk in this way. The ultracentrifuge is a very high-speed C. and is used in colloid- and bio-chemistry. Large Cs. are used for physiological research, e.g. in astronaut training: testing bodily response to many times the normal acceleration due to gravity (g).

CEPHALONIA (sefalō'nia). *See* KEPHALLINÍA.

CEPHALO'PODA (sef-; Gk 'head-footed'). Class of animals of the phylum Mollusca, including the octopus, cuttle-fish, squid, nautilus, etc. They are characterized by the inclusion of the mouth and head in the foot - hence the name - are exclusively marine, and have a very wide range.

CEPHALOSPORIN (sef'alo-). Antibiotic, also known as ceporin, extracted from cephalosporium mould. It was developed at Oxford by E. P. Abraham (q.v.) and others: Dorothy Hodgkin (q.v.) was associated in the early stages. C. is capable of destroying penicillin-resistant bacteria.

CERAMICS (seram'iks). In the widest sense any non-metallic mineral used in articles created from a powder and sintered at high temperatures. C. are divided into heavy clay products (bricks, roof tiles, drainpipes, sanitary ware), refractories or high-temperature materials (linings for furnaces used in steel-making, fuel elements in nuclear reactors), and pottery, which uses china clay, ball clay, china stone and flint. Pottery (q.v.) ranges from the opaque and porous earthenware well adapted to colour, through translucent white bone china (5% calcined bone) to finest porcelain (q.v.).

A super-ceramic, such as silicon carbide, is half the weight of steel, resistant to wear and corrosion, withstands extremes of heat and cold, and is so hard that it cannot be machined but has to be fired to the precise required size and shape. These have great potential in motor and aircraft engine design.

CERBERUS. In classical mythology, the many-headed watchdog at the gates of the underworld.

CEREALS (sē'rē-alz). Grain-bearing plants cultivated for food. The term relates primarily to barley and wheat, but may also be said to cover oats, maize, rye, millet, and rice. Cs. have been of the utmost importance in the history of human society, and different grain-bearing plants are characteristic of different civilizations in various parts of the world. *See* BREEDING.

CEREBRAL HAEMORRHAGE. The breaking of a blood vessel in the brain, or the blocking of one of the arteries of the brain by a blood clot which results in an apoplectic fit or stroke. The cause of the rupture of the blood vessel is usually a combination of high-blood pressure with hardening of the arteries through age or disease, or through chronic poisoning by alcohol or lead.

CERES (sērēs). In Roman mythology, the goddess of agriculture, identified with the Greek Demeter.

CERIUM (sēr'-). The principal chemical element of the group known as the rare earth metals, symbol Ce, at. no. 58. at. wt. 140.13, One of the most common uses of C. is as an alloy for 'flints' for cigarette lighters. Radioactive Ce-140 (half-life 9 months) is a fission product from nuclear power stations and may find a use in giant sources of limited life.

CERN (kern). A European organisation which came into being in 1954 as a cooperative enterprise among European governments. It was originally known as the *Conseil Européen pour la Recherche Nucléaire,* but was subsequently renamed *Organisation Européene pour la R.N.*, although still familiarly known as CERN. At the laboratories at Meyrin, nr Geneva, research is carried out into the fundamental structure of matter by teams of scientists from the 12 member states. In 1965 the original laboratory was doubled in size by extension across the border from Switzerland into France.

In 1980 the construction of a new large electron-positron collider (LEP) was under consideration. From the energy left behind after their collisions, new particles can rematerialise, which would incl. quarks, gluons, and possibly some types whose existence is not yet suspected.

CERN. Aerial view of CERN: in the centre is the 200 m diameter ring of the 28 GeV proton synchotron (PS) or particle accelerator. Beyond it, to the left, is the 300 m diameter ring of the intersecting storage rings (ISR) built for colliding beam physics. In the background, to the right, across the main road, is the second laboratory built from 1971, of which the chief feature is the 2.2 km diameter underground proton synchotron (SPS synchotron à protons souterrain). *Photo: Courtesy of CERN.*

CERNAUTI. Romanian form of CHERNOVTSY.

CERVANTES (servan'tēz; Span. thervahn'thes), Miguel de Cervantes Saavedra (1547-1616). Spanish novelist, playwright, and poet. B. at Alcalá de Henares, he entered the army in Italy and in 1571 was wounded in the battle of Lepanto. In 1575, while on his way back to Spain, he was captured by Barbary pirates and was taken to Algiers, where he became a slave until ransomed in 1580. Returning to Spain he began to support himself by writing. He wrote several plays, and in 1585 his pastoral romance *Galatea* was printed. In 1587 he was employed at Seville in provisioning the Armada. He was more than once imprisoned for failures to make good deficiences in the accounts of moneys he had received as a collector of taxes. He now sank once more into poverty, and little is known of the course of his life till *Don Quixote,* which had previously circulated in manuscript, appeared in 1605 and immediately achieved a great success. Within a few years it had been translated into English and French. In 1613 appeared his *Novelas Exemplares,* a collection of short tales; and in 1614 a burlesque poem, *Viage del Parnaso,* and a spurious 2nd part of *Don Quixote* which prompted C. to bring out his own authentic 2nd part, considered to be superior to the first in construction and in characterization. His last work was *Persiles y Sigismunda.*

ČESKÉ BUDĚJOVICE (ches'ke boo'dyeyovētse). Town in Czechoslovakia, on the r. Vltava, a commercial and industrial centre for southern Bohemia. Pop. (1978) 85,500.

CESSNOCK. Mining town in N.S.W., Australia, NW of Newcastle. Coal has been mined since 1856, and although production was hit by cheap oil, its output recovered following the energy crisis. Pop. (1976) 16,500.

CESTŌ'DA. Class of worms of the phylum Platyhelminthes. They include all those commonly called tapeworms (q.v.).

CETACEA (sitā'sha). A highly specialized order of purely aquatic fish-like mammals, including whales, dolphins, and porpoises. Fossil forms indicate their descent from an extinct group of the carnivora known as the creodonta. They can be readily distinguished from fish by their tail-fins, termed the 'flukes', being horizontal, not vertical. They are grouped in two sub-orders, the *Mystacoceti* or whalebone whales, including the rorqual and also the Greenland whale and the *Odontoceti* or toothed whales, including porpoises, dolphins, narwhal, etc. See WHALES.

CETEWAYO (setiwah'yō) (d. 1884). Ruler of Zululand, S Africa, 1873-83, when he was expelled by his subjects. In 1879 he defeated the British at Isandhlwana, but was defeated himself at Ulundi.

CETINJE (tsetēn'yēh). Town of Montenegro, Yugoslavia, 19km (12m) ESE of Kotor. Founded in 1484 by Ivan the Black, it was cap. of Montenegro until 1918. It has a palace built by Nicholas, the last king of Montenegro. Pop. (1971) 25,000.

CEUTA (sū'ta). Spanish seaport and military base in Morocco, captured in 1580. It is 27km (17m) S of Gibraltar and overlooks the Mediterranean approaches to the Straits of Gibraltar. Pop. (1971) 86,700.

CEVENNES (sehven'). Collective name given to a series of mountain ranges on the S, SE, and E borders of the Central Plateau of France.

CEYLON (sēlon'). *See* SRI LANKA.

CÉZANNE (sehzahn'), **Paul** (1839-1906). French landscape, still-life, and portrait painter, the leader of the Post-Impressionist School. He was b. at Aix-en-Provence, where he studied and was on friendly terms with Émile Zola. In Paris he met Pissarro and other Impressionist painters, with whom at first he was in sympathy; but later he broke away from them and developed a style of painting which showed up their weaknesses. His aim was to give a sense of solidity which Impressionist paintings failed to give. His work has great influence on modern art.

CHÂBLIS (shahblē'). Town in Yonne dept, France; the centre for the production of a white Burgundy wine of the same name. Pop. (1973) 2,000.

CHABRIER (shahbrē-eh'), **Emmanuel** (1841-94). French composer. Abandoning a post in the Ministry of the Interior to devote himself to music, he made his name with *España* (1883), an orchestral rhapsody, and the light opera *Le Roi malgré lui* (1887: 'King Against his Will'). He influenced French composers of the post-1918 era.

CHACMA. *See* BABOON.

CÉZANNE. A self-portrait. *Photo: Courtesy of the National Gallery, London*

CÉZANNE. A landscape, 'Mountains in Provence', which reflects the artist's intense feeling for his native countryside. *Photo: Courtesy of the National Gallery, London*

CHACO (chah'koh). Prov. of Argentina, until 1951 a territory, part of Gran Chaco, a great zone, for the most part level, stretching into Paraguay and Bolivia. The prov., includes many lakes and swamps, and much of it is forested, producing timber and quebracho; the chief crop is cotton. The cap. is Resistencia, in the SE. Area 99,633 sq.km (38,479 sq.m); pop. (1970) 567,000.

The N of Gran Chaco was the scene of the Bolivia-Paraguay war (over boundaries) of 1932-5, settled by arbitration in 1938.

CHAD, Lake. Lake on the NE boundary of Nigeria, first seen by white explorers in 1823. It varies in extent between rainy and dry seasons from 50,000 sq.km (20,000 sq.m) to 20,000 sq.km (7,000 sq.m). The Lake Chad basin is being developed in concert by Cameroon, Chad, Niger and Nigeria.

CHAD (chahd), **Republic of.** Country of central Africa, which takes its name from Lake Chad. The northern area is part of the Sahara, and is subject to terrible drought, but has uranium resources. In the south cotton and groundnuts are grown in the Shari basin, and stockraising is important. The cap. is N'djamena (formerly Fort Lamy). M.U.: CFA franc.

Chad was formerly one of the 4 territories of French Equatorial Africa, but became independent in 1960. Ngarta Tombalbaye (1918–75) was pres. from independence until killed in a military coup. A civil war between the Moslem north and Christian south 1965-80, and then between the victorious Moslem factions, ended in 1981 with defeat for the Libyan-backed Moslem faction. In 1986 large numbers of French troops assisted the Chad army to retake Fada.

Area 1,284,000 sq.km (495,753 sq.m); pop. (1977) 4,200,000. The official language is French.

CHADLI (chad'li), **Benjedid** (1929-). Algerian statesman. An army colonel, he supported Boumédienne in the overthrow of Ben Bella, and succeeded the former in 1979, pursuing less extremist socialist policies.

CHADOR (chud'ar). All-enveloping black mantle (Hindi 'square of cloth') for women, originating in the period of Cyrus the Great and the Achaemenian empire in Persia. Together with the purdah (Persian 'veil') and the idea of female seclusion, it persisted under Alexander the Great and the Byzantine Empire, and was adopted by the Arab conquerors of the Byzantines. Despite its revival by Khomeini in Iran as something fundamentally Islamic, it is not prescribed by the Koran which requests only 'modesty' in dress.

CHADWICK, Sir James (1891-1974). British physicist. He studied at Cambridge under Rutherford, and in 1932 discovered the particle in an atomic nucleus which became known as the neutron, because it has no electric charge. In 1935 he was awarded a Nobel prize, and in 1940 was one of the British scientists reporting on the atom bomb. He was Lyon Jones prof. of physics at Liverpool 1935-48, and Master of Gonville and Caius Coll., Cambridge, 1948-59.

CHAETOGNATHA (kētog'natha) or **arrow-worms.** Class of invertebrate animals of peculiar structure and uncertain position, consisting of *Sagitta* and 7 other genera, comprising 38 species. They usually measure 12-38mm (.5-1.5in), occur in vast numbers on the surface of the sea, and form an important item in the food of fishes.

CHAETOPODA (kētop'oda). Division of annelid worms, distinguished from the Hirudinea by the presence of locomotive organs, in the form of paired bristles, borne on most of the numerous rings or segments into which the body is divided. They include two principal classes. The Polychaeta have many bristles, and include the marine bristle worms. The Oligochaeta, which have fewer bristles, include the earthworms and some freshwater species.

CHĀ'FER. Name given to several beetles of the section Lamellicornia, e.g. the cockchafer (*Melolontha vulgaris*); the summer C. (*Rhizotrogus solstitialis*), another common British species; and the rose C. (*Cetonia aurata*).

CHAFFINCH. A bird (*Fringilla coelebs*), well known as resident in Britain and Europe generally. The male is olive-brown above, with a bright chestnut breast, a bluish-grey cap, and two white bands on the upper part of the wing; the female is duller. The length is 150mm (6in). The C. is a good songster.

CHAGALL (shagal'), **Marc** (1887–1985). Russian artist. B. at Vitebsk, of Jewish parentage, he became a pupil of Bakst and from 1910 to 1914 studied in Paris. In 1922 he returned to France where he has since lived. A precursor of Surrealism, he breaks through the bounds of natural law to a dream world of floating animals and figures, and strange colours and juxtapositions of objects. He has also produced illustrated books - the Bible and La Fontaine's *Fables*.

CHAGOS ARCHIPELAGO. *See* BRITISH INDIAN OCEAN TERRITORY.

CHAILLU (shahyü'), **Paul Belloni du** (1835 1903). American (French-born) traveller. B. in France, in 1855 he began a 4 years' journey of exploration in W Africa. His *Explorations and Adventures in Equatorial Africa* (1861) relates amongst other things his discovery of the gorilla in Gabon.

CHAIN, Sir Ernst Boris (1906-79). British scientist. B. in Berlin, son of a chemist and industrialist, he was driven to Britain by Nazi racial discrimination and worked under F. Gowland Hopkins (q.v.) at Cambridge 1933-5. With Florey (q.v.) he initiated the work on penicillin which led to the discovery of its curative properties, and in 1945 shared the Nobel prize for physiology and medicine with Fleming and Florey.

CHAKA (chah'kah) (c. 1783-1828). Zulu chief who in the early years of the 19th cent. built up by conquest a powerful Zulu realm from the border of Cape Colony to the Zambezi. He was murdered.

CHALDAEA. *See* BABYLONIA.

CHALIAPIN (chahlē-ah'pēn), **Fyodor Ivanovich** (1873-1938). Russian singer. B. at Kazan of peasant parentage, he became a world-famous bass singer, and made his London début in 1913. His greatest role was that of Boris Godunov in Mussorgsky's opera. C. left Russia after the rise of the Soviet régime, and d. in Paris.

CHA'LICE (chal'is). Cup used in celebrating the Eucharist, sometimes of wood or pewter, but often of precious metal.

CHALK. A soft, fine-grained whitish rock composed of carbonate of lime, $CaCO_3$, formerly thought to derive from the remains of microscopic animal organisms or Foraminifera (foraminiferal ooze theory). In 1953, however, it was seen under the electron microscope to be composed chiefly of coccoliths, unicellular lime-secreting algae, and hence to be primarily a vegetable deposit. C. was laid down in the later Cretaceous period and covers a wide area in Europe. In England it stretches in a belt from Wilts continuously across Bucks and Cambs to Lincs and Yorks, and also forms the N and S Downs and the cliffs of SE England. C. is extensively quarried for use in cement, lime, mortar, etc.

Hill figures, formed by the removal of turf to show the underlying chalk, are a feature of the English landscape. Animal figures predominate, such as the 'White Horse' on Bratton Hill, Wiltshire, said to commemorate Alfred the Great's victory over the Danes at Ethandun in 878.

CHALMERS, Thomas (1780-1847). Scottish divine. As minister of Tron Church, Glasgow, from 1815, he became noted for his eloquence and for schemes of social reform. In 1823 he became professor of moral philosophy at St Andrews, and in 1828 of theology at Edinburgh. At the 'Disruption' of the Church of Scotland in 1843, C. withdrew from the church along with a large body of other divines, and became principal of the Free Church college.

CHÂLONS-SUR-MARNE (shaloṅ'-sür-mahrn'). Cap. of the dept of Marne, France, with a fine 13th cent. cathedral. There are food manufactures and a trade in champagne. Pop. (1975) 56,000.

It is traditionally here that Attila was defeated, in his attempt to invade Gaul, at the **Battle of Châlons** (451), by the Roman general Aëtius and the Visigoth Theodoric.

CHALON-SUR-SAÔNE (-sōn'). Town in the dept. of Saône-et-Loire, France, on the r. Saône and the Canal du Centre. There are mechanical and electrical engineering, and chemical industries. Pop. (1975) 70,000.

CHAMBERLAIN, (Arthur) Neville (1869-1940). British Conservative statesman, younger son of Joseph C. and half-brother of Joseph Austen C. B. in Birmingham, of which he was Lord Mayor in 1915, he became Min. of Health in 1923, doing excellent work in slum clearance. After a brief space as Chancellor of the Exchequer he was Minister of Health again 1924-9. In 1931 he was Chancellor of the Exchequer in the National Govt, and in 1937 succeeded Baldwin as PM. In an endeavour to close the old Anglo-Irish feud he agreed to the return to Eire of the ports occupied by the navy, and he made similarly friendly advances towards the dictators, Mussolini in particular. When in 1938 he went to Munich and negotiated with Hitler the settlement of the Czechoslovak question, he was ecstatically received on his return, and claimed that the Munich agreement brought 'Peace With Honour'. Soon, however, he agreed that he had been tricked, and when Britain declared war on Sept. 3, 1939, he summoned the people to fight the 'evil things' that Hitlerism stood for. On May 10, 1940, he resigned, and became Lord President of the Council in the Churchill Cabinet, but d. on Nov. 9, 1940.

CHAMBERLAIN, Joseph (1836-1914). British statesman. B. in London, he entered in 1854 the screw-manufacturing business of his cousin Joseph Nettlefold at Birmingham. By 1874 he had made a sufficient fortune to devote himself entirely to politics; he early adopted radical views, and took an active part in local affairs. Thrice mayor of Birmingham, he carried through many schemes of municipal development. In 1876 he was elected MP for Birmingham as John Bright's colleague, and joined the republican group led by Sir Charles Dilke, the extreme left wing of the Liberal Party. In 1880 he entered Gladstone's Cabinet as Pres. of the Board of Trade. The climax of his radical period was reached with the Unauthorized Programme of 1885, advocating free education, small holdings, graduated taxation, etc. In the next year he broke with Gladstone over Home Rule for Ireland, resigned from the Cabinet, and led the revolt of the Liberal-Unionists. In 1895 C. became Colonial Secretary in Salisbury's Cons. Govt, and as such was responsible for relations with the Boer republics up to the outbreak of war in 1899. In 1903 he advanced proposals for Imperial Preference or 'Tariff Reform' as a general

CHAMBERLAIN. Neville Chamberlain at Heston Airport after his meeting with Hitler in September 1938. He holds the Munich Agreement, by which he claimed to have achieved 'Peace with honour'. *Photo: Popperfoto.*

policy of imperial consolidation, and left the Cabinet in order to leave himself free to propagate his ideas. In 1906 a stroke was followed by the paralysis which kept him out of public life for his remaining years.

C. was one of the most colourful figures of British politics, and his monocle and orchid made him a favourite subject for political cartoonists.

CHAMBERLAIN, Sir (Joseph) Austen (1863-1937). British Conservative statesman. Elder son of Joseph C. he was elected in 1892 as a Liberal-Unionist MP, and after holding several minor posts was Chancellor of the Exchequer 1903-6. During the F.W.W. he was Sec. of State for India 1915-17 and member of the War Cabinet 1918. He was Chancellor of the Exchequer 1919-21 and Lord Privy Seal 1921-2, but, as in 1911 (on Balfour's resignation), failed to secure the leadership of the party in 1922, as many Conservatives resented his share in the Irish settlement. He was For. Sec. in the Baldwin government 1924-9, and negotiated and signed the Locarno Treaty and the Kellogg Pact. After the formation of the Nat. Govt in 1931 he was First Lord of the Admiralty for a few months.

CHAMBERLAIN, Lord. An administrative office in the royal household, responsible for engaging the staff, etc., and for appointing the tradesmen. New plays were submitted to the L.C.'s examiner for a licence before public performance until censorship ended 1968. The office is temporary, and its appointment is in the hands of the Government.

CHAMBERLAIN, Lord Great. The only Officer of State whose position survives from Norman times. His principal duties are to arrange Westminster Hall and the Houses of Parliament at the opening of the Houses by the monarch and to attend the sovereign at the coronation. He is also responsible for the ceremony at the creation of peers and bishops.

CHAMBER MUSIC. That class of music which is suitable for performance in a chamber, as opposed to that intended for the concert hall. As now used the term is applied to music written for a small combination of instruments, played with one instrument to a part. Many such combinations are possible, but of these the string quartet is the most important. A string quartet of G. Allegri (1582-1652) is believed to be the first example of its kind, while among English composers who wrote 'fantasy trios', or 'fancies', were Byrd and Orlando Gibbons. In the 17th and early 18th cents. C.M. generally had the harpsichord as a basis. The C.M. sonata with a figured bass accompaniment was established by the great Italian school of violinists - Vivaldi, Corelli, etc. From the 18th cent. onwards a new type of C.M. was first experimentally worked out by Haydn. In his string quartets each part plays, as it were, on equal terms, the keyboard instrument, as a basis, being eliminated. Haydn also developed the classical sonata form. His quartets influenced those of Mozart, who in turn influenced his master. The last quartets of Beethoven are the personal expression of his own individuality and show many striking departures from the original classical framework. In the 19th cent. C.M. found its way into the concert hall, and this effected a certain coarsening of the texture, and a quasi-orchestral quality, even in the work of Brahms. The early 20th cent. French school of Impressionists, represented by Debussy and Ravel, instituted changes in the classical framework, and during the period which followed various theories such as atonality, polytonality, etc., have found expression in C.M.

Modern composers of C.M. incl. Berg, Webern, Hindemith, Stravinsky, Prokoviev, Shostakovich, Kodály, Bartók, Ireland, Bliss, Tippett, Rubbra, Copland and Roy Harris.

CHAMBERS, Sir (Stanley) Paul (1904-81). British economist. Sec. and Commissioner of the Board of Inland Revenue 1942-7, he devised P.A.Y.E. (q.v.), and 1960-8 was chairman of Imperial Chemical Industries.

CHAMBERS, Sir William (1726-96). British architect. Sailing as supercargo to China at 16, he made drawings of Chinese subjects and his design for the Kew Gardens pagoda shows this influence, which he helped to popularize. His greatest work is Somerset House, London.

CHAMBÉRY (shoṅbārē'). Old capital of Savoy, now cap. of Savoie dept, France. The seat of an archbishopric, it is a railway junction and airport, with a number of industries; also a holiday and health resort. Pop. (1975) 52,300.

CHAMELEON (kamē'lēon). A family of lizards (*Chamaeleontidae*) of peculiar structure and remarkable for their faculty of colour-changing. The headquarters of the family is in Africa, but some species are found outside the limits of that region, including the common C. (*Chamaeleon chamaeleon*) of the Mediterranean countries, and there are also Indian representatives. The tail is long and highly prehensile, assisting the animal when climbing. The tongue is very long, protrusible, and covered with a viscous secretion; it can be shot out with great rapidity to *c.* 200mm (8in) and by means of it the C. captures insects. Cs. are entirely arboreal in their habits, and move very slowly. Their changes of colour are caused by changes in the intensity of light, of temperature, and of emotion, which affect the action of two layers of pigment-containing cells which lie underneath the skin.

CHAMOIS (sham'wah). A species (*Rupicapra rupicapra*) of the so-called goat-antelopes, distinguished by vertical horns 175mm (7in) long and hooked backwards at the tip. It is brown, stands 75cm (2.5ft) and inhabits the mountain ranges of S Europe and Asia Minor. Chamois leather is now also made from the skin of sheep and goats.

CHAMONIX (shahmohnē′). Holiday resort at the foot of Mt Blanc, in the French Alps. Pop. (1973) 8,500.

CHAMPAGNE (shampān′). Ancient prov. of France, of which the cap. was Troyes, famous for its vineyards. The modern region of Champagne-Ardennes comprises the depts of Ardennes, Aube, Marne, and Haute-Marne. Area 25,741 sq.km (9,939 sq.m); pop. (1975) 1,336,832. C. forms the plains E of the Paris basin.

CHAMPAGNE. French wine, produced from specially fine grapes and blended wines, the former grown in a strictly defined area of the Marne region about Reims and Épernay in Champagne. Unlike other wines, fermentation takes place after the bottle has been sealed, this accounting for the effervescence.

CHAMPAIGNE, Philippe de (1602-74). French painter. Of Flemish origin, he settled in Paris at 19, and is famed for portraits, e.g. Richelieu.

CHAMPLAIN (shoṅplaṅ′), **Samuel de** (1567-1635). French pioneer in Canada, soldier, and explorer. He served in the army of Henry IV and with an expedition to the W Indies, and in 1603 began his exploration of Canada. In a third expedition in 1608 he founded and named Quebec, and in 1612 was appointed Lieut.-Governor of French Canada.

CHAMPOLLION (shoṅpolyoṅ′), **Jean François,** le Jeune (1790-1832). French Egyptologist, who in 1822 found the key to the decipherment of the Egyptian hieroglyphics on the Rosetta Stone (now in the British Museum).

CHANCE. The theory of probability. As a science it originated when the Chevalier de Méré consulted Blaise Pascal on methods to reduce his gambling losses. Pascal then worked out in correspondence with another mathematician, Pierre de Fermat, the foundations of the theory of chance which underlie the science of statistics. Among fields in which it is particularly important are life assurance and atomic physics.

CHANCELLOR, Lord High. A high state official who originally acted as royal secretary and keeper of the great seal. Until the 14th cent., the C. was always an ecclesiastic, who also acted as royal chaplain. Under Edward III the C. became head of a permanent court to consider petitions to the king, the Court of Chancery. Today he is a member of the cabinet, and goes out of office with it. In his legal capacity he may preside over the Court of Appeal, and appoints the judges and justices of the peace; he also acts as Speaker of the House of Lords. In order of precedence he comes after the Archbp of Canterbury.

CHANCELLOR OF THE DUCHY OF LANCASTER. An honorary post held by a cabinet minister who has other non-departmental responsibilities. The C. was originally the king's representative controlling his lands and courts within the duchy.

CHANCELLOR OF THE EXCHEQUER. The cabinet minister responsible for the national economy. The office was originally established under Henry III, the C.'s task being that of keeper of the exchequer seal. Since the 19th cent. it has been a cabinet post, regarded as ranking next to that of Prime Minister.

CHANCERY. The court which, until the fusion of the courts in 1875 into the High Court of Justice and the Court of Appeal, administered the rules of equity as distinct from the rules of common law. It dealt with such matters as the administration of the estates of deceased persons, the execution of trusts, foreclosure of mortgages, partnerships, and the estates of minors.

CHANDERNAGO'RE. Indian city, on the Hooghly, in the state of W Bengal. Formerly a French settlement it was ceded to India by treaty in 1952. Pop. (1971) 67,100.

CHANDIGARH. City of the Rep. of India, inaugurated 1953 to replace Lahore (cap. of British Punjab), which went to Pakistan under partition in 1947. Planned by Le Corbusier, in the foothills of the Himalayas north of Ambala, C. became the joint cap. of Hariana and Punjab in 1966. Pop. (1971) 233,000.

CHANDLER, Raymond (1888-1959). American thriller writer. B. in Chicago, he shared with Hammett (q.v.) the invention of tough crime writing and of the 'private eye' hero, such as his own Philip Marlowe. His books incl. *The Big Sleep* (1939), *Farewell, My Lovely* (1940) and *The Lady in the Lake* (1943).

CHANDRAGUPTA MAURYA (called Sandrocottus by the Greeks). Ruled in N India *c.* 321-*c.* 296 BC as king of Magadha.

CHANEL (shanel′), **'Coco' (Gabrielle)** (1883-1970). French fashion designer. She popularised the 'little black dress', the informal cardigan suit, and the perfume Chanel No. 5.

CHANGCHIAKOW. *See* ZHANGJIAKOU.

CHANGCHUN. (chahngchoon′). Industrial city in Jilin prov., China. A rail junction and centre of an agricultural district, it makes machinery and motor vehicles. As Hsingking ('new capital'), it was the cap. of Manchukuo 1932-45. Pop. (1970) 2,000,000.

CHANG JIANG (chahng jē-ahng′). Greatest river (formerly Yangtze Kiang) of China, rising in Tibet and flowing into the Yellow Sea. Length *c.* 5,470 km (3,400 m). In its upper reaches it is known as the Jinsha Jiang.

CHANGSHA (chahngshah′). River port, on the Xiang Jiang, cap. of Hunan prov., China. Pop. (1970) 825,000.

CHANNEL, English. Stretch of water between England and France, leading in the W to the Atlantic Ocean, and in the E via the Strait of Dover to the North Sea: it is known as La Manche 'the sleeve' (from its shape) by the French. It is 450km (280m) long W-E; 27km (17m) wide at its narrowest (Cap Gris Nez-Dover) and 117km (110m) wide at its widest (Ushant-Land's End). In 1979 Bryan Allen (USA) made the first man-powered crossing in a pedal-powered aircraft.

Channel swimming. The first to swim the English Channel was Capt. Webb on 25 Aug. 1875, Dover-Calais 21 hr 45min.; fastest crossing (England to France) Penny Dean (US) in 1978, 7 hr 42 min; and first to swim 'nonstop' in both directions, Argentinian Antonio Abertondo in 1961.

Channel tunnel. A land link was first suggested by a Frenchman, Mathieu, to Napoleon I in 1802. The idea later aroused the interest of Isambard Brunel, and after signature of an Anglo-French convention in 1875, excavations were begun in 1882, but abandoned in 1883 when a House of Commons Committee rejected the idea as a military hazard. In 1972 England and France signed an agreement for the construction of a bored rail tunnel, but, owing to economic problems, the project languished. Anglo-French agreement was again reached on a rail tunnel in 1986.

CHANNEL COUNTRY. Area of SW Queensland, Australia, in which channels such as Cooper's Creek (where Burke and Wills d. in 1861) are cut by intermittent rivers. Summer rains supply rich grass for cattle, and the effect of not infrequent drought is lessened by the 'beef roads', which remove the herds in trains of linked trucks for slaughter, etc.

CHANNEL ISLANDS. Group of islands lying in the English Channel, off the NW coast of France. Since the Norman conquest they have been a possession of the English Crown. They comprise, Jersey, Guernsey, Alderney, Great and Little Sark, Herm, Brechou, Jethou and Lihou. They have a mild climate, productive soil and are famous for cattle and the production of flowers, early potatoes and tomatoes. There is some light industry.

French is an official language, though English is more widely used. English currency is used, in addition to local coinage. The is. have their own laws. Unless specially signified, the C.I. are not bound by Acts of Parliament. They are the only part of the dukedom of Normandy still held by Britain. During the S.W.W. the Germans occupied the is. from June 30, 1940, until May 9, 1945. Area 194 sq.km (75 sq.m); pop. (1971) 126,420.

CHANT. Word used in common speech to denote any vocal melody or song, especially of a slow and solemn character; but applied specifically to a type of melody used in the services of the Christian Church, which is specially adapted for singing the psalms, canticles and other non-metrical portions of the liturgy. The Ambrosian and Gregorian Cs. are forms of plainsong melody.

CHANTILLY (shontēyē'). Town in Oise dept, France, NE of Paris. It has a fine chateau, is the centre of French horseracing, and was the HQ of Joffre 1914-17. Pop. (1973) 10,500.

CHANTREY, Sir Francis Legatt (1781-1841). British sculptor. He made a reputation with his busts and statues of Wellington, Wordsworth, Scott and others, but is most celebrated for his child studies, notably the 'Sleeping Children' (1817) in Lichfield cathedral. The C. Bequest provides for the income from his private fortune to be used by the R.A. for the purchase of works of art for the benefit of the nation: these are housed in the Tate Gallery.

CHAO PHRAYA (chaw-oo prāyah). Chief river of Thailand (formerly Menam), flowing 1,200 km (750 m) into the Gulf of Thailand.

CHAPEL ROYAL. The original C.R. of the English court, existing at least from 1135, was not a building but the royal retinue of priests, singers and musicians. In the 15th and 17th cents. the choirboys contributed to the development of the drama by their presentation of interludes, etc., and musicians attached to the C.R. have incl. Tallis, Byrd and Purcell.

There are C.Rs. at the former royal palaces, St James's Palace, Hampton Court and the Tower of London (St John the Evangelist and St. Peter ad Vincula); there are also private chapels at Buckingham Palace, Windsor Castle (with a royal chapel also in Windsor Great Park), and a royal church at Sandringham.

CHAPLIN, Sir Charles (1889-1977). British film actor-producer. B. in London, he first appeared on stage at 5, but made his world-wide reputation as the down-trodden trampish little character with smudge moustache, bowler hat and cane in silent films, e.g. *The Gold Rush* (1925), *The Circus* (1928), *City Lights* (1931) and *Modern Times* (1938), showing man's predicament in a machine age. In *The Great Dictator* (1940), guying Hitler, he spoke for the first time and in *Monsieur Verdoux* (1947) again abandoned his traditional costume. He was four times married, his fourth wife being Oona, dau. of Eugene O'Neill (q.v.). He was knighted in 1975.

CHAPLIN. Wearing the costume familiar to millions, Chaplin in a bewildered moment in *Modern Times. Photo: Courtesy of the British Film Institute.*

CHAPMAN, George (1559-1634). English poet, who was associated in London with Marlowe, and collaborated with Ben Jonson, but is best known for his fiery translation of Homer 1598-1624, which inspired Keats.

CHAR. Genus of fishes (*Salvelinus*) of the salmon and trout family (Salmonidae). *S. alpinus*, the typical species, is a marine form, but it enters rivers.

CHARADRIIFORMES (karad'ri-for'mēz). Order of birds, including the plover family (Charadriidae) and their allies the snipe and sandpipers.

CHARCOT (shahrkoh'), **Jean-Martin** (1825-93). French neurologist. B. at Paris, he was prof. of pathological anatomy in the Univ. of Paris from 1860. He estab. the neurological clinic at the Salpêtrière, distinguished himself by his researches on the diseases of the nervous system, and initiated the scientific study of hypnotism. He influenced Freud.

CHARDIN (shahrdiń'), **Jean Baptiste Siméon** (1699-1779). French artist. B. in Paris, of a poor family, he is chiefly celebrated for his interiors and still-lifes of kitchen subjects - fruit and pots and pans.

CHARDONNET (shahrdoneh'), **comte Hilaire Bernigaud de** (1839-1924). French chemist. Developing the manufacture of rayon, the first artificial fibre, he founded the synthetic textile industry.

CHARENTE (shahront'). French river, rising in Haute-Vienne dept and flowing past Angoulême and Cognac into the Bay of Biscay below Rochefort. Its wide estuary is much silted up. Length 360km/225m. It gives its name to two depts, Charente and Charente-Maritime (formerly Charente-Inférieure).

CHARGE OF THE LIGHT BRIGADE. *See* BALACLAVA.

CHARING CROSS. District within the city of Westminster, London, lying around Charing Cross (main line) railway station. Its name is derived from one of the stone crosses built by Edward I at the resting-places of the coffin of his queen, Eleanor. The present cross is modern.

CHARLEMAGNE (char'leman), or **Charles the Great** (742-814). King of the Franks and Roman emperor. The son of Pepin the Short, mayor of the palace in Merovingian Neustria, he was crowned by the Pope in 754 along with his father and his younger brother Carloman. When Pepin d. in 768, C. inherited the N part of the Frankish kingdom, and when Carloman d. in 771, C. also took possession of his countries. In 770 he m. the dau. of the king of the Lombards, whom a year later he divorced.

He was engaged in his first Saxon campaign when the Pope's call for help against the Lombards reached him; he crossed the Alps, captured Pavia, and took the title of king of the Lombards. The pacification and Christianizing of the warlike pagan tribes of Saxons occupied the greater part of C.'s reign. The Westphalian leader Widukind did not submit until 785, when he received baptism. From 792 N Saxony was subdued, and in 804 the country was finally pacified. In 777 the emir of Saragossa asked for C.'s help against the emir of Cordova. C. crossed the Pyrenees in 778, and reached the Ebro, but had to turn back from Saragossa. The rearguard action of Roncesvalles in which Roland, warden of the Breton March, and other Frankish nobles were ambushed and killed by Basque hordes, became immortal in the *Chanson de Roland.* In 801 the district between the Pyrenees and the Llobregat was organized as the Spanish March. The independent duchy of Bavaria was incorporated in the kingdom in 788, while the Avars, Turko-Finnish nomads inhabiting Hungary, were subdued in 791-6 and accepted Christianity. The supremacy of the Frankish king in the western world found outward expression in the bestowal of the imperial title: in Rome, during Mass on Christmas Day 800, pope Leo III crowned C. emperor.

C.'s activities were not confined to warfare. Jury-courts were introduced, the laws of the Franks revised, other tribal laws written down. A new coinage was introduced, weights and measures were reformed, and communications were improved. C. also took a lively interest in theology, organized the Church in his dominions, and furthered missionary enterprises and monastic reform. The 'Carolingian Renaissance' of learning began when he persuaded the Northumbrian Alcuin to enter his service in 781. C. gathered a kind of academy around him. He also collected the old heroic lays, began a German grammar, and promoted religious instruction in the vernacular. He died on 28 Jan. 814, at Aachen, where he was buried. Soon a cycle of heroic legends and romances developed round him, and these live on in epics of Ariosto, Boiardo, and Tasso.

The **C. Prize,** estab. by a no. of leading citizens in Aachen in 1949, is awarded annually for services to European understanding and co-operation: winners incl. Churchill, Adenauer, Hallstein, Monnet, Schuman, Spaak and Heath.

CHARLEROI (shahrlrwah'). Belgian industrial town on the Sambre in Hainault prov. The coal industry declined in the 1970s. Pop. (1975) 22,500.

CHARLES I (1600-49). King of Great Britain and Ireland from 1625. B. at Dunfermline, the son of James VI of Scotland, he became heir to the throne on the death of his brother Henry in 1612. He went to Madrid in 1623 to urge his suit to the Infanta of Spain, but without success. In 1625 he became king, and m. Henrietta Maria, dau. of Henry IV of France. Friction with parliament began at once. The parliaments of 1625 and 1626 were dissolved, and that of 1628 refused supplies until C. had accepted the Petition of Right. In 1629 it attacked C.'s illegal taxation and support of the Arminians in the Church, whereupon he dissolved parliament and imprisoned its leaders.

For 11 years he ruled without a parliament, raising money by expedients which alienated the entire nation, while the Star Chamber suppressed opposition by persecuting the Puritans. When C. attempted in 1637 to force a prayer book on the English model on Presbyterian Scotland he found himself confronted with a nation in arms. The Short Parliament, which met in April 1640, refused to grant money until grievances were redressed, and was speedily dissolved. The Scots then advanced into England, and forced their own terms on C. The Long Parliament met on 3 Nov. 1640, and declared extra-parliamentary taxation illegal, abolished the Star Chamber and other prerogative courts, and voted parliament could not be dissolved without its own consent. Laud and other ministers were imprisoned, and Strafford condemned to death. After the failure of his attempt to arrest the parliamentary leaders on 4 Jan 1642, C. withdrew from London, and on 22 Aug. declared war on parliament by raising his standard at Nottingham. His defeat at Naseby in June 1645 ended all hopes of victory; in May 1646 he surrendered at Newark to the Scots, who in Jan. 1647 handed him over to parliament. In June the army seized him, and carried him off to Hampton Court. While the army leaders strove to find a settlement, C. secretly intrigued for a Scottish invasion. In Nov. he escaped to Carisbrooke, but was held there in custody; a Scottish invasion followed in 1648, and was shattered by Cromwell at Preston. In Jan. 1649 the House of Commons set up a high court of justice, which tried C. and condemned him to death. He was beheaded on 30 Jan. before the Banqueting Hall in Whitehall, and was buried in St George's Chapel, Windsor.

CHARLES II (1630-85), King of Great Britain and Ireland from 1660. B. at St James's Palace, the son of Charles I, he lived with his father at Oxford 1642-5, and after the victory of the parliament withdrew to the Continent. Accepting the Covenanters' offer to make him king, he landed in Scotland in 1650, and was crowned at Scone on 1 Jan. 1651. An attempt to invade England was ended on 3 Sept by Cromwell's victory at Worcester. C. escaped, and after many adventures reached the

CHARLES I. The delicate idealisation of the features of the monarch, as shown in Van Dyck's portraits, played its part in the creation of the legend of 'Charles the Martyr'. The small head of the charger was typical of the Flemish horses used at this period. *Photo: Courtesy of the National Gallery, London*

Continent. For 9 years he wandered through France, Germany, Flanders, Spain, and Holland until the opening of negotiations by Monk in 1660 offered new hope. In April C. issued the Declaration of Breda, promising a general amnesty and freedom of conscience. Parliament accepted the Declaration; C. was proclaimed king on 8 May, landed at Dover on the 26th, and entered London 3 days later.

Politically he had 3 aims: 'not to go on his travels again'; to make himself absolute; and to secure toleration, and if possible supremacy, for Catholicism. He hovered in religion between Catholicism and scepticism, but for his subjects he favoured the former as most consistent with absolute monarchy. For the present he entrusted the government to Clarendon, who arranged his marriage in 1662 with Catherine of Braganza, but his tutelage soon became irksome.

The disasters of the Dutch War furnished an excuse in 1667 for banishing him, and he was replaced by the Cabal - Clifford and Arlington, both secret Catholics, and Buckingham, Ashley and Lauderdale, who had links with the Dissenters. In 1670 C. signed the Secret Treaty of Dover, the full details of which were known only to Clifford and Arlington, whereby he promised Louis XIV he would declare himself a Catholic, re-establish Catholicism in England, and support Louis's projected war against the Dutch; in return Louis was to finance C. and in the event of resistance to supply him with troops. War with Holland followed in 1672, and at the same time C. issued the Declaration of Indulgence, suspending all penal laws against Catholics and Dissenters. Parliament forced C. in 1673 to withdraw the Indulgence and accept a Test Act exluding all Catholics from office, and in 1674 to end the war in Holland. This broke up the Cabal, while Ashley (Lord Shaftesbury), who had learned the truth about the treaty, assumed the leadership of the opposition. Danby, the new chief minister, built up a Court Party in the Commons by wholesale bribery, while subsidies from Louis relieved C. from dependence on parliament. In 1678 Oates's announcement of a 'Popish Plot' released a wholesale panic, which Shaftesbury exploited to introduce his Exclusion Bill, excluding James, Duke of York, from the succession as a Papist; instead he hoped to substitute C.'s illegitimate son Monmouth. C. played for time, counting on a Royalist reaction and offering compromises which the opposition rejected. In 1681 his last parliament was summoned at Oxford; the Whigs attended armed, but when Shaftesbury rejected a last compromise, C. dissolved parliament and the Whigs fled in terror.

Henceforward C. ruled without a parliament. For money he relied on subsidies from Louis. When the Whigs plotted a revolt their leaders were executed, while Shaftesbury and Monmouth fled to Holland.

CHARLES II. A portrait by J.M. Wright of the king who, as Rochester wrote, 'never said a foolish thing, nor ever did a wise one'. Charles responded that this was true 'for my words are my own, and my actions are my ministers'. *Photo: Courtesy of the National Portrait Gallery.*

CHARLES (1948-). Prince of the United Kingdom, heir apparent to the British throne, and Prince of Wales. B. at Buckingham Palace on 14 Nov. 1948, he is the first-born child of Queen Elizabeth II and the Duke of Edinburgh. He entered Cheam School, Berks, in 1957 and in 1962 followed in the footsteps of his father to Gordonstoun. In 1958 he was created Prince of Wales (investiture 1969) and studied at Trinity Coll., Cambridge, 1967-70, subsequently serving in the RAF and Royal Navy. In 1980 he acquired a country home, Highgrove, nr Tetbury, Glos. In 1981 he married Lady Diana Spencer (1961-), daughter of the 8th Earl Spencer, and they have two children: William (b. 1982), and Henry (b. 1984).

CHARLES. The Prince and Princess of Wales with Prince William, wearing a smart snow suit for his first real 'royal walkabout', which he tackled with remarkable composure. *Photo: Peter Abbey/Camera Press.*

CHARLES. Name of 7 rulers of the Holy Roman Empire. CHARLES I was Charlemagne (q.v.). CHARLES II, THE BALD (823-77), the younger son of Louis I, the Pious, warred against his eldest brother the Emperor Lothair I, until the treaty of Verdun (843) assigned to C. the W Frankish Kingdom, i.e. modern France and the Spanish March. He was crowned emperor at Rome in 875. CHARLES III, THE FAT (832-88), the youngest son of Louis the German, became king of the W Franks in 885, thus uniting for the last time the whole of Charlemagne's empire. He was deposed in 887. CHARLES IV (1316-78), son of John of Luxemburg, king of Bohemia, was elected king of Germany in 1346, and in 1347 obtained power over all Germany. He founded the first German university, at Prague, in 1348. CHARLES V (1500-58); *see* below. CHARLES VI (1685-1740), the 2nd son of the emperor Leopold I, was put forward as the Austrian claimant to the Spanish dominions (*see* SPANISH SUCCESSION). In 1711 he abandoned Spain on becoming Holy Roman Emperor, and returned to Germany. CHARLES VII (1697-1745) was elector of Bavaria when Charles VI died, and contested the claim of the latter's dau., Maria Theresa, to the imperial crown. In 1742 he himself was crowned emperor.

CHARLES V (1500-58). Holy Roman Emperor. B. at Ghent, the son of Philip, son of the emperor Maximilian, and Joanna of Castile, he was brought up in the Netherlands, which he inherited on his father's death (1506). In 1516 he inherited the possessions of his maternal grandfather Ferdinand V, consisting of Spain, Naples, Sicily, Sardinia, and the Spanish dominions in N Africa and America. When Maximilian d. in 1519, C. came into possession of all the Habsburg dominions, and was elected emperor.

The rivalry of Francis I of France, originating in disputes over possessions in Burgundy and Italy, led to 4 wars, the outstanding events of which were the French king's defeat and capture in the battle of Pavia (1525), and the sacking of Rome - the Pope having become an ally of Francis - by Charles's troops in 1527. The series was concluded in 1544 by the treaty of Crépy-en-Valois in which C. renounced his claims on the duchy of Burgundy, but maintained his other Burgundian possessions and Milan. Francis never ceased to scheme against the emperor, and even allied himself with the Turks, who besieged Vienna in 1529 and again in 1532.

Meanwhile the religious movement started by Luther in 1517 was dividing the empire into two camps, and all Charles's efforts to reach a settlement, culminating in the diet of Augsburg in 1530, were unsuccessful. The Turkish threat obliged C. to conclude a truce with the Lutherans (1532), and not before the French wars had come to an end was he able to crush the Protestant League of Schmalkalden (1546-7). The Protestants then allied themselves with Henry II of France, and allowed him to take Metz, Toul, and Verdun. After years of struggle, the Protestants under Maurice of Saxony forced Charles by the treaty of Passau in 1552 to yield most of the Protestant demands. Disappointed and worn out, C. at last abdicated in favour of his son, Philip II, in the Netherlands (1555) and in Spain (1556), resigned the imperial crown into the hands of his brother Ferdinand, and passed the remainder of his days in the monastery of Yuste in Spain.

CHARLES (Karl) (1887-1922). Emperor of Austria and king of Hungary, the last of the Habsburg emperors. He succeeded his great-uncle, Francis Joseph, in 1916, at the height of the F.W.W., and in 1919 was forced to withdraw to Switzerland, although he refused to abdicate. In 1921 he attempted unsuccessfully to regain the crown of Hungary; and was deported to Madeira, where he d. He m. the Princess Zita of Bourbon-Parma, and their son, the Archduke Otto, maintains the Habsburg claims.

CHARLES. Name of 10 kings of France. Charles I was Charlemagne (q.v.) and for Charles II the Bald, *see* CHARLES, rulers of the Holy Roman Empire.

CHARLES III, THE SIMPLE (879-929), the son of Louis the Stammerer, was crowned at Reims in 893. In 911 he ceded what later became the duchy of Normandy to the Norman chief Rollo. CHARLES IV, THE FAIR (1294-1328), the last of the direct Capetian line, succeeded Philip V in 1322. CHARLES V, THE WISE (1337-80), acted as regent during the captivity of his father John II in England (1356-60), and became king in 1364. He renewed the war with England in 1369, and by 1380 had reconquered nearly all France. CHARLES VI (1368-1422) succeeded his father Charles V in 1380, but until 1388 France was governed by his uncles. In 1392 he went mad; his uncles regained power, and civil war broke out between the dukes of Orleans and Burgundy. Henry V of England invaded France in 1415, conquered Normandy, and in 1420 forced C. to sign the treaty of Troyes, which recognized Henry as his successor. **Charles VII** (1403-61), the son of Charles VI, was excluded from the succession by the treaty of Troyes, but on his father's death he was recognized as king by the S of France. C. remained inactive until 1429 when Joan of Arc raised the siege of Orleans and had him crowned at Reims. C. organized France's first standing army, and by 1453 had expelled the English from all except Calais. **Charles VIII** (1470-98) succeeded his father, Louis XI, in 1483. In 1494 he claimed the Neapolitan crown, invaded Italy, and entered Naples in 1495. Milan, Venice, Spain and the Emperor then formed a coalition against him; C. defeated the allies at Fornovo, but Naples was lost. He d. while preparing a 2nd expedition. **Charles IX** (1550-74), 2nd son of Henry II and Catherine de' Medici, succeeded his brother Francis II in 1560, but remained entirely under his mother's influence for 10 years, during which France was torn by religious wars. In 1570 he fell under the influence of the Huguenot leader Coligny, whereupon Catherine in alarm persuaded him to consent to the massacre of St Bartholomew which led to a new religious war.

Charles X (1757-1836), grandson of Louis XV, and brother of Louis XVI and Louis XVIII, was known before his accession as Count of Artois. At the beginning of the Revolution he fled to England, where he remained until the fall of Napoleon. When he came to the throne in 1824 he attempted to undo the work of the Revolution. In 1830 there was a revolt, and C. again fled to England. He d. at Gorizia.

CHARLES. Name of 15 kings of Sweden. The first 6 were merely local chieftains. CHARLES VII reigned 1161-7. CHARLES VIII, elected king in 1448, was twice expelled by the Danes and twice restored before his death in 1470. CHARLES IX (1550-1611) of Sweden and Poland, in 1595, and king in 1600. This involved him in war with Poland and Denmark. CHARLES X (1622-60) succeeded his cousin Christina in 1654. He waged war with Poland and Denmark, and in 1657 invaded Denmark from the S, leading his army over the frozen sea. CHARLES XI (1655-97), who succeeded in 1660, showed himself a remarkable general, and drastically reformed the administration. CHARLES XIII (1748-1818), who was elected king in 1809, became the 1st king of Sweden and Norway in 1814. CHARLES XV (1826-72) reigned over Sweden and Norway from 1859. For Charles XII and XIV *see* below.

CHARLES XII (1682-1718). King of Sweden. He succeeded his father Charles XI in 1697 and from 1700 was involved continuously in war with Denmark, Poland, and Russia. He won a brilliant succession of victories, until in 1709 while invading Russia he was defeated at Poltava, and forced to take refuge in Turkey until 1714. He was killed in 1718 while besieging Frederiksten.

CHARLES XIV (1763-1844). King of Sweden and Norway, originally Jean Baptiste Jules Bernadotte. B. at Pau, he entered the French army, won rapid promotion during the Revolutionary War, and was created a marshal of France by Napoleon. In 1810 he was elected crown prince of Sweden, under the name of Charles John. He brought Sweden into the alliance against Napoleon in 1813, as a reward for which Sweden received Norway. He succeeded to the throne in 1818, proved a capable ruler, and was the founder of the present dynasty.

CHARLES or **Carlos.** Name of 4 kings of Spain. CHARLES I was Charles V, Holy Roman Emperor (q.v.). CHARLES II (1661-1700) was the last of the Spanish Habsburg kings, 2nd son of Philip IV. He was an invalid and almost an imbecile from birth. On his deathbed he made a will leaving his dominions to Philip of Anjou, grandson of Louis XIV, which led to the War of the Spanish Succession. CHARLES III (1716-88), the son of Philip V, became duke of Parma in 1732, and in 1734 conquered Naples and Sicily. On the death in 1759 of his half-brother Ferdinand VI he became king of Spain, handing over Naples and Sicily to his son Ferdinand. During his reign Spain was twice involved in war with Britain, during the Seven Years War and the War of American Independence. At home C. carried out a programme of reforms and expelled the Jesuits. CHARLES IV (1748-1819) succeeded his father, C. III, in 1788, but left the government wholly in the hands of his wife and her lover Godoy. In 1808 C. abdicated in favour of his son Ferdinand. He became a pensioner of Napoleon, and d. at Rome.

CHARLES ALBERT (1798-1849). King of Sardinia. He showed Liberal sympathies in early life, and after his accession in 1831 introduced certain reforms. On the outbreak of the 1848 revolution he granted a constitution and declared war on Austria. His troops were defeated at Custozza and Novara, and in 1849 he abdicated in favour of his son Victor Emmanuel and retired to a monastery, where he died.

CHARLES AUGUSTUS (1757-1828). Grand Duke of Saxe-Weimar. He succeeded his father in infancy, fought against the French in 1792-4 and 1806, and is remembered as the patron and friend of Goethe.

CHARLES EDWARD STUART (1720-88), 'The Young Pretender'. He was b. at Rome, the son of James, the Old Pretender, and grandson of James II, and created Prince of Wales at birth. In July 1745 he sailed for Scotland, and landed in Inverness-shire with 7 companions. On 19 Aug. he raised his father's standard, and within a week had rallied an army of 2,000 Highlanders. He entered Edinburgh almost without resistance, won an easy victory over General Cope at Prestonpans, invaded England, and by 4 Dec. had reached Derby, where his officers insisted on a retreat. The army returned to Scotland, and won a victory at Falkirk, but was forced to retire to the Highlands before Cumberland's advance. On 16 April at Culloden C.E.'s army was completely routed by Cumberland, and he himself fled. For five months he wandered through the Highlands with a price of £30,000 on his head before escaping to France. He visited England secretly in 1750, and may have made other visits. In later life he degenerated into a friendless drunkard.

CHARLES MARTEL ('the Hammer') (*c.* 688–741). Frankish ruler. An illegitimate son of Pepin of Heristal, he ruled the E of the Frankish kingdom from 717 as mayor of the palace, and the whole kingdom from 731. His victory near Poitiers in 732 ended the Arab invasions of France.

CHARLES THE BOLD (1433-77). Duke of Burgundy. Son of Philip the Good, he inherited Burgundy and the Low Countries from him in 1465 and it was his ambition to create a kingdom stretching from the mouth of the Rhine to the mouth of the Rhône. He formed the League of the Public Weal against Louis XI of France, invaded France in 1471, and laid the country waste as far as Rouen. His ambitions now united against him the Emperor, Lorraine, and the Swiss; he captured Nancy, but was defeated at Granson, and again at Morat (1476). Nancy was lost and while attempting to recapture it he was killed in battle. After his death his possessions in the Netherlands passed, by the marriage of his dau. Mary to Maximilian, to the Habsburgs.

CHARLES'S LAW. This law stated by Jacques Charles (1746-1823), French physicist, in 1787 and independently by Gay-Lussac in 1802 states that the volume of a given mass of gas at constant pressure increases by 1/273 of its

CHARLES EDWARD STUART. The 'Young Pretender' in disguise as a woman during the period of his wanderings in the Highlands after Culloden. *Photo: The Mansell Collection.*

volume at 0°C for each degree C rise of temperature, i.e. the coefficient of expansion of all gases is the same. The law is only approximately true and the coefficient of expansion is generally taken as 0.003663 per deg. C.

CHARLESTON. Main port and city of S Carolina, USA, dating from 1670. Fort Sumter in the sheltered harbour was bombarded by Confederate batteries 12-13 April 1861, thus beginning the Civil War. There are many historic houses and fine gardens. It was here that the Charleston, typical exhibition dance of the 1920s, originated. Pop. (1970) 66,945.

CHARLESTON. Chief city of W virginia, USA, on the Kanawha. It is the centre of a district producing coal and natural gas. Pop. (1970) 71,505.

CHARLOCK or **wild mustard.** A plant (*Sinapis arvensis*) of the family Cruciferae. It is a common annual weed in Britain, reaching a height 60cm (2ft) and with yellow flowers.

CHARLOTTE. City in the S of N Carolina, USA, nr the border with S Carolina. Industries incl. data processing, textiles, chemicals, machinery and food products. It was the gold-mining centre of the country until 1849; the Mint Museum of Arts has paintings, sculpture and ceramics. Pop. (1974) 302,500.

CHARLOTTE AUGUSTA, Princess (1796-1817). Only child of George IV and Caroline of Brunswick, and heir to the throne. She m. in 1816 Prince Leopold of Saxe-Coburg (*see* LEOPOLD, King of the Belgians), but d. in childbed 18 months later.

CHARLOTTE SOPHIA (1744-1818). Queen consort. The dau. of the duke of Mecklenburg-Strelitz, she m. George III in 1761, and bore him 9 sons and 6 daughters.

CHARM. A new property of matter, analogous to an electric charge. A group of sub-atomic particles, known as 'charmed' particles, had been predicted as existing, but it was not until 1976 that a track left by such a particle was identified by Eric Burhop (of Univ. Coll., London) and his team at the Fermi Nat. Accelerator Laboratory, Chicago. A 20-litre stack of photographic emulsion was exposed to a neutrino beam, and one neutrino was shown to enter, split a neutrino in the emulsion to fragments (causing heavy tracks), and then create light tracks of which one decayed into 3 charged tracks - an event only apparently explicable as the production of 'charm'.

CHARON (kā'ron). In Greek legend the ferryman of the souls of the dead over the river Styx. *See* PLUTO.

CHARPENTIER (shahrpoṅtyeh'), **Gustave** (1860-1956). French composer. His great success was *Louise* (1900), an opera dealing with Parisian working-class life.

CHARPENTIER, Marc-Antoine (1634–1704). French composer. His works incl. the opera *Medée*, and a number of masses: interest in him revived in the 1970s.

CHARTERIS, Leslie (1907-). Anglo-American novelist. B. at Singapore, the son of a surgeon, he had a varied career in many exotic occupations which were to give authentic background to some 40 novels of Simon Templar, the 'Saint' - gentleman-adventurer on the wrong side of the law - which have been translated into 16 languages and adapted for films, radio and television. These began with *The Saint Meets the Tiger* (1928). In 1946 he became a US citizen.

CHARTISM. Radical British democratic movement, mainly of the working classes, which flourished c. 1838-50. It derived its name from the 'People's Charter', a programme comprising 6 points: universal manhood suffrage, equal electoral districts, vote by ballot, annual parliaments, abolition of the property qualification for MPs, and payment of MPs.

CHARTRES (shahrtr). Cap. of the dept of Eure-et-Loir, NW France, 96km (59m) SW of Paris, on the Eure. Its cathedral of Notre Dame, completed about 1240, is a masterpiece of Gothic architecture. Pop. (1975) 41,250.

CHARTREUSE (shahrtröz'), **La Grande.** The original home of the Carthusian order of RC monks, estab. by St Bruno c. 1084, in a remote valley 23km (14m) NNE of Grenoble (in modern dept of Isère), France. The present buildings date from the 17th cent. The monks were expelled at the Revolution, returned 1816, were again expelled 1903, but, returning in 1940 as refugees from Italy, were allowed to remain. Since 1607 the monks have distilled a famous liqueur, here and at another house at Tarragona, Spain.

CHARYBDIS (karib'dis). In Greek mythology a monster linked with the whirlpool on one side of the narrow straits of Messina, Sicily, opposite the monster Scylla. Homer tells how the ship of Odysseus contrived to pass unscathed 'between Scylla and Charybdis'.

CHASE, James Hadley. Pen-name of René Raymond (1906–85), who served in the RAF during the S.W.W., and wrote *No Orchids for Miss Blandish* (1939), and other 'tough' novels with a great vogue.

CHASING. Indentation of a design on metal by small chisels and hammers. This method of decoration was familiar in ancient Egypt, Assyria and Greece.

CHA'SŪBLE. The outer garment worn by the priest in the celebration of the Mass. The colour of the C. depends on the feast which is being celebrated.

CHÂTEAU (shah'toh). Term originally applied to a French medieval castle, but now used to describe a country seat or important residence in France. The C. was first used as a domestic building in the late 15th cent.; by the reign of Louis XIII (1610-43) fortifications such as moats, keeps, etc., were no longer used for defensive purposes, but merely as decorative features.

CHATEAUBRIAND (shahtōbrē-oṅ'), **François René**, vicomte de (1768-1848). French author. He visited America in 1791, and returning to France, was exiled by the Revolution (1794-9). In exile he wrote *Atala* and the autobiographical *René*, which formed part of *Le Génie du Christianisme* (1802). He assisted the accession of Louis XVIII, under whom he held diplomatic appointments, and in 1849-50 his *Mémoires d'Outre Tombe* appeared. C. was an important precursor of Romanticism.

CHÂTEAUROUX (shahtohroo'). Cap. of Indre dept, France, on the r. Indre. Dating from the 14th cent., it makes woollen textiles, tobacco products, etc. Pop. (1975) 55,650.

CHÂTEAU-THIERRY (shahtoh'-tyārrē'). Town on the Marne, Aisne dept, France, the scene during the F.W.W. of a US victory in 1918. Pop. (1975) 13,900.

CHATHAM, William Pitt, 1st earl of (1708-78). British statesman and orator. The grandson of Thomas Pitt, governor of Madras, he entered parliament in 1735 as MP for the family pocket borough of Old Sarum, and joined the 'patriots' in opposition to Walpole. After Walpole's fall in 1742 he attacked the policy of his successor, Carteret, during the War of the Austrian Succession, but in 1746 he was given a place in Pelham's Cabinet as Paymaster of the Forces; he refused to use this post, as was customary, to enrich himself, and contented himself with his legal salary. In 1755 he was dismissed from office for attacking the PM, Newcastle, but the disastrous beginning of the Seven Years War led to a popular demand for his recall. He formed a govt in 1756, but in 1757 was forced to form a coalition with Newcastle. His strategy and his choice of military and naval commanders were justified by brilliant success, culminating in the 'year of victories', 1759. By military and financial help to Frederick the Great he kept the French occupied in Europe, while Britain won the command of the sea and expelled the French from Canada and India, while at home he appealed to the patriotism of parliament and the nation by his eloquence and by such measures as the revival of the militia. In 1761 he was forced by George III to resign. He attacked the Peace of Paris in 1763, maintaining that Britain's gains were not proportionate to her efforts, and in 1766 formed an all-party government and accepted the title of earl of Chatham. Ill-health, however, kept him out of public life for 2 years, during which the govt came more and more under the king's control, and in 1768 he resigned. During his last years he championed civil liberties, parliamentary reform and the rights of the American colonies against the king, although he rejected any suggestion of recognizing American independence. While making his last speech in the Lords, opposing the withdrawal of British troops from America, he collapsed (7 April 1778), and on 11 May he d. at Hayes. He was buried in Westminster Abbey.

CHATHAM. English seaport and naval base on the N coast of Kent, on the Medway. The Royal Dockyard dates from 1588. Pop. (1972) 59,000.

CHATHAM ISLANDS. Two is. in the S Pacific, which form a co. of South Island, NZ: Chatham 898 sq.km (347 sq.m) and Pitt 64 sq.km (25 sq.m). Area 963 sq.km (372 sq.m); pop. (1972) 700.

CHATTANOO'GA. City in Tennessee, USA, on the Tennessee r., focus of the TVA area. Pop. met. area (1970) 370,800.

CHATTERJI (chat'erjē), **Bankim Chandra** (1838-94). Indian novelist. B. in Bengal, where he estab. his reputation with his first book *Durges-Nandini* (1864), he became a favourite of the nationalists: *Ananda Math* (1882) contains the Indian national song 'Bande-Mataram'.

CHATTERTON, Thomas (1752-70). British poet. B. in Bristol, he became familiar with ancient documents he found in the church of St Mary Redcliffe, and composed poems which he claimed as the work of Thomas Rowley, an imaginary monk of the 15th cent. Encouraged by his success in imposing on his Bristol acquaintance, he sent specimens to Horace Walpole, but was refused assistance when Walpole was advised by friends that these were forgeries. He then began contributing to periodicals in the style of Junius, and in 1770 went to London. Failing in success, he poisoned himself with arsenic. Although his modern productions show versatility and facility, his pseudo-medieval pieces are the proof of his genius, and greatly influenced the Romantic poets.

CHATTERTON. The rather idealised concept of the poet's suicide, with the torn scraps of his manuscripts beside him, is a Victorian interpretation by Henry Wallis. Yet it captures the pathos of his wasted gifts and life. *Photo: Courtesy of the Tate Gallery.*

CHAUCER (chaw'ser), **Geoffrey** (*c.* 1340-1400). English poet. B. in London, he became a page in the household of Lionel, Duke of Clarence, by 1357, and in 1359 was taken prisoner in the French wars, although ransomed by Edward III in 1360. He m. Philippa Roet, whose sister later became the wife of John of Gaunt, and through her gained the patronage of the latter. C. held various court and official appointments, notably that of controller of customs in the port of London (1374), and was employed on missions abroad. In this way he visited Italy (1372-3), where he may have met Boccaccio and Petrarch, France and Flanders (1377), and Italy again in 1378. His early work is dominated by French influence, either in translation, as in his version of the *Romaunt of the Rose*, or in form, as with *The Boke of the Duchesse* (c. 1369). With his absorption of Italian influence came maturity, and such works as *Troilus and Criseyde* (adapted from Boccaccio), *The House of Fame, The Legend of Good Women*, and the *Knight's Tale* (also from Boccaccio). The last was to be merged in the great work of C.'s final period, the *Canterbury Tales*, which was designed c. 1387, and envisaged a company of pilgrims beguiling their journey by telling stories. The descriptive prologue is a masterpiece of metre and characterization. He also wrote a prose translation of Boethius, and a treatise on the astrolabe for his small son. He is buried in Poets' Corner, Westminster Abbey.

CHAUVINISM (shōv'-). A warlike fervour of patriotism: from Nicholas Chauvin, one of Napoleon I's veterans, and his fanatical admirer. More recently 'male C.', the result of an inveterate conviction of the superiority of the male sex over the female.

CHÁVEZ (chah'vās), **Carlos** (1899-78). Mexican composer. A student of the piano and of the complex rhythms of his country's folk music, he founded the National Symphony Orchestra. His works incl. a number of ballets, 7 symphonies, and concertos for both violin and piano.

CHAYE'FSKY, Sydney (1923–). American playwright known as Paddy C. B. in the Bronx, he estab. his reputation with the television plays *Marty* and *Bachelor Party*, both successfully filmed (1955 and 1957 respectively). His characters have an inarticulate pathos and frustration well adapted to 'Method' acting, and are placed in a detailed urban setting.

CHEAPSIDE. A street running from St Paul's Cathedral to Poultry, in the City of London, England. It was the scene of the 13th cent. 'Cheap', a permanent fair and general market.

CHECK. *See* CHEQUE.

CHEDDAR. Village of Somerset, famous for its gorge, caves, and fine cheeses. In 1962 excavation revealed the site of a Saxon palace.

CHEESE. A compact, concentrated food made usually from whole cows' milk, but also from the milk of goats, ewes, mares, buffaloes, reindeer, etc., and consisting of preserved milk solids. Its popularity is due to its palatability and its satisfactory nutritional quality; cheese such as Cheddar or Cheshire consists of approximately one-third protein, one-third fat, and one-third moisture. Furthermore, the highly nutritious non-bulky solid is easy to handle and is very easily stored.

There are over 500 varieties of cheese, of which the greater number used to be made only in the districts after which they are named. The varieties are divided into 3 main groups: (1) hard pressed, e.g. Cheddar, Cheshire, Cantal, Parmesan, Gruyère, the most important group, economically and nutritionally; (2) semi-hard, e.g. Stilton, Gorgonzola, Wensleydale, Roquefort, Pont l'Evêque, Gouda; (3) soft, e.g. Cambridge, York, Camembert, Coulommier, Brie.

In 1980 France introduced *appellation controlée* status (as with wine) for certain cheeses which have been made for at least a century in precisely defined areas of France by traditional methods, incl. Beaufort, Cantal, Comte, Munster and Roquefort. Others, such as Camembert, Gruyere, Brie, etc., which are also made elsewhere were excluded.

CHEESECLOTH. Originally the fine muslin used to press curds, but in the fashion world from 1967 a cotton hand-woven crepe with a twist yarn, developed in India for export. The surface is permanently crinkled, stretching to fit the body.

CHEETAH (chē'tah). Member of the cat family (Felidae), also known as the hunting-leopard (*Acinonyx jubatus*), used for cents. in India and Persia for hunting game because of its phenomenal speed and comparative tractability. Standing 45cm (1½ft) high, it is yellowish with black spots, and differs from other cats in having claws which are only partially retractile. It is found in open country in Africa and SW Asia, and Zimbabwe has a specially handsome variety, the king C.

CHEEVER, John (1912–82). American writer. B. in Quincy, Mass., he wrote short stories, and novels which incl. *The Wapshot Chronicle* (1937), *Bullet Park* (1969) and *World of Apples* (1973).

CHEFOO. *See* YANTAI.

CHEKA (chā'kah). Secret police operating in the Soviet Union 1918-23. The name is formed from the initials *che* and *ka* of the two Russian words meaning 'extraordinary commission', formed for 'the repression of counter-revolutionary activities and of speculation', and extended to cover such matters as espionage and smuggling. In 1923 the C. was replaced by the Ogpu and ultimately by the MVD (q.v.).

CHEKHOV (chekhof'), **Anton Pavlovich** (1860-1904). Russian writer. B. at Taganrog, he qualified as a doctor in 1884, but devoted himself to writing short stories rather than medical practice. A collection *Particoloured Stories* (1886) consolidated his reputation, and gave him leisure to develop his style: *My Life* (1895), *The Lady with the Dog* (1898) and *In the Ravine* (1900). His first play *Ivanov* (1887) was a failure, as was *The Seagull* (1896) until revived by Stanislavsky in 1898 at the Moscow Arts Theatre, for which C. went on to write *Uncle Vanya* (1899), *The Three Sisters* (1901) and *The Cherry Orchard* (1904). Not influential in Russian literature, he has been widely recognized abroad, espec. in Britain, where there is a tendency to over-solemnify. He relies on the creation of atmosphere and delineation of internal development, rather than external action.

CHEKIANG (chekyang'). *See* ZHEJIANG.

CHELMSFORD. Town of Essex, England, 48km (30m) NE of London. It is the admin. HQ of the co., and a market town with radio, electrical, engineering and agricultural machinery industries. Pop. (1972) 58,330.

CHELONIA (kilō'nia). Order of reptiles, including the tortoises and turtles, and distinguished, among other characteristics, by having their body protected by a bony carapace or shell, into which the head and limbs can be withdrawn.

CHELSEA. Historic area of the Royal Bor. of Kensington and Chelsea, London, immediately N of the Thames, where it is crossed by the Albert and C. bridges. The Royal Hospital (1682) was founded by Charles II for old and disabled soldiers, 'Chelsea Pensioners', and the National Army Museum (1960) covers campaigns 1485-1914. The Physic Garden for botanical research was estab. in the 17th cent.; and the home of Thomas Carlyle in Cheyne Row is a museum. The Chelsea Flower Show is the highpoint of the gardener's year. Ranelagh Gardens (1742-1804) and Cremorne Gardens (1845-77) were celebrated places of entertainment.

CHEKHOV. A delicately languid portrait with the poetic grace that attaches to such a creation as his story 'The Lady with the Dog'. *Photo: Mansell Collection.*

CHELTENHAM. Spa at the foot of the Cotswolds, Glos, England. There are annual festivals of literature and music, and educational institutions incl. C. College (1854). Pop. (1972) 75,560.

CHELYABINSK. Industrial town of the RSFSR, cap. of C. region. It lies E of the Ural Mountains, 240km (150m) SSE of Sverdlovsk. It has ferrous and non-ferrous industries and engineering works, and makes chemicals, motor vehicles, and aircraft. Pop. (1974) 947,000.

CHEMICAL WARFARE. *See* BIOLOGICAL/CHEMICAL WARFARE.

CHEMISORPTION. In chemistry the reaction between a clean solid surface and a foreign substance, such as occurs with a gas in various forms of corrosion. Such interactions are of tremendous importance in many areas of industry.

CHEMISTRY. The science concerned with the composition of matter, and of the changes which take place in it under varying conditions.

The ancient civilizations were familiar with certain chemical processes, e.g. extracting metals from their ores, and making alloys. The alchemists were concerned with endeavouring to turn base metals into gold, and modern chemistry may be said to have evolved from alchemy towards the end of the 17th cent. Robert Boyle (1627-91) defined elements as the simplest substances into which matter could be resolved. The alchemical doctrine of the four elements (earth, air, fire, and water) gradually lost its hold, and the theory that all combustible bodies contained a substance called phlogiston was discredited by the experimental work of Black (1728-99), Lavoisier (1743-94), and Priestley (1733-1804), the last-mentioned discovering the presence of oxygen in the air. Cavendish (1731-1810) discovered the composition of water, and Dalton (1766-1844) put forward the atomic theory, which ascribed a precise relative weight to the 'simple atom' characteristic of each element. Much research then took place leading to the development in modern times of biochemistry, chemotherapy, plastics, etc.

All matter can exist in three states: gas, liquid or solid. It is composed of minute particles termed *molecules* which are constantly moving, and may be further divided into *atoms* (q.v.). Molecules which contain atoms of one kind only are known as *elements*, while those which contain atoms of different kinds are called *compounds*. The separation of compounds into simpler substances is analysis, and the building up of compounds from their components is synthesis. When substances are brought together without changing their molecular structure they are said to be *mixtures*. Chemical compounds are produced by a chemical action which alters the arrangement of the atoms in the molecule. Heat, light, vibration, catalyst, radiation or pressure, as well as moisture (for ionization), may be necessary to produce a chemical change.

To facilitate the expression of chemical composition, symbols are used to denote the elements. The symbol is usually the first letter or letters of the English or Latinized name of the element, e.g. C, carbon; Ca, calcium; Fe, iron (ferrum). These symbols represent one atom of the element; molecules containing more than one atom are denoted by a subscript figure, e.g. water, H_2O. In some substances a group of atoms acts as a single atom, and these are enclosed in brackets in the symbol, e.g. $(NH_2)_2SO_4$, ammonium sulphate. The symbolical representation of a molecule is known as a formula. A figure placed before a formula represents the number of molecules of one substance present in another, e.g. 2 H_2O, two molecules of water. Chemical reactions are expressed by means of equations, viz. $NaCl + H_2SO_4 = NaHSO_4 + HCl$. This equation states the fact that sodium chloride (NaCl) on being treated with sulphuric acid (H_2SO_4) is converted into sodium bisulphate ($NaHSO_4$) and hydrogen chloride (HCl).

Elements are divided into two classes: metals, having lustre, and being conductors of heat and electricity, and non-metals, which usually lack these properties. The Periodic System developed by Newlands (1863) and established by Mendeleyev in 1869, classified elements according to their atomic weights, i.e. the least weight of the element present in a molecular weight of any of its compounds. Those elements which resemble each other in general properties were found to bear a relation to one another by weight, and these were placed in groups or families. Certain anomalies in this system were removed by classifying the elements according to their atomic number. The latter is the equivalent of the charge on the nucleus of the atom.

Organic Chemistry is that branch of C. which deals with carbon compounds. *Inorganic C.* deals with the description, properties, reactions, and preparation of the elements and their compounds, with the exception of carbon

Table of Chemical Elements

Name	Symbol	At. no.	Internat. at. wt.
actinium	Ac	89	227
aluminium (aluminum)	Al	13	26.98
americium	Am	95	(243)
antimony (stibium)	Sb	51	121.76
argon*	Ar	18	39.944
arsenic	As	33	74.91
astatine	At	85	(210)
barium	Ba	56	137.36
berkelium	Bk	97	(249)
beryllium	Be	4	9.013
bismuth	Bi	83	208.99
boron	B	5	10.82
bromine**	Br	35	79.916
cadmium	Cd	48	112.41
caesium (cesium)	Cs	55	132.91
calcium	Ca	20	40.08
californium	Cf	98	(251)
carbon	C	6	12.011
cerium	Ce	58	140.13
chlorine*	Cl	17	35.457
chromium	Cr	24	52.01
cobalt	Co	27	58.94
columbium, *see* niobium			
copper (cuprum)	Cu	29	63.54
curium	Cm	96	(247)
dysprosium	Dy	66	162.51
einsteinium	Es	99	(254)
erbium	Er	68	167.27
europium	Eu	63	152.0
fermium	Fm	100	(253)
fluorine*	F	9	19.00
francium	Fr	87	(223)
gadolinium	Gd	64	157.26
gallium	Ga	31	69.72
germanium	Ge	32	72.60
gold (aurum)	Au	79	197.0
hafnium	Hf	72	178.50
hahnium	Ha	105	(262)
helium*	He	2	4.003
holmium	Ho	67	164.94
hydrogen*	H	1	1.008
indium	In	49	114.82
iodine	I	53	126.91
iridium	Ir	77	192.2
iron (ferrum)	Fe	26	55.85
krypton*	Kr	36	83.80
lanthanum	La	57	138.92
lawrencium	Lr	103	(257)
lead (plumbum)	Pb	82	207.21
lithium	Li	3	6.940
lutetium	Lu	71	174.99
magnesium	Mg	12	24.32
manganese	Mn	25	54.94
mendelevium	Md	101	(256)
mercury (hydrargyrum)**	Hg	80	200.61
molybdenum	Mo	42	95.95
neodymium	Nd	60	144.27
neon*	Ne	10	20.183
neptunium	Np	93	(237)
nickel	Ni	28	58.71
niobium, columbium	Nb	41	92.91
nitrogen*	N	7	14.008
nobelium	No	102	(259)
osmium	Os	76	190.2
oxygen*	O	8	16.000
palladium	Pd	46	106.4
phosphorus	P	15	30.975
platinum	Pt	78	195.09
plutonium	Pu	94	(242)
polonium	Po	84	210
potassium (kalium)	K	19	39.100
praseodymium	Pr	59	140.92
promethium	Pm	61	(147)
protactinium	Pa	91	231
radium	Ra	88	226
radon*	Rn	86	222
rhenium	Re	75	186.22
rhodium	Rh	45	102.91
rubidium	Rb	37	85.48
ruthenium	Ru	44	101.1
rutherfordium	Rf	104	(261)
samarium	Sm	62	150.35
scandium	Sc	21	44.96
selenium	Se	34	78.96
silicon	Si	14	28.09
silver (argentum)	Ag	47	107.873
sodium (natrium)	Na	11	22.991
strontium	Sr	38	87.63
sulphur	S	16	32.066
tantalum	Ta	73	180.95
technetium	Tc	43	(99)
tellurium	Te	52	127.61
terbium	Tb	65	158.93
thallium	Tl	81	204.39
thorium	Th	90	232.05
thulium	Tm	69	168.94
tin (stannum)	Sn	50	118.70
titanium	Ti	22	47.90
tungsten (wolfram)	W	74	183.86
uranium	U	92	238.07
vanadium	V	23	50.95
xenon*	Xe	54	131.30
ytterbium	Yb	70	173.04
yttrium	Y	39	88.91
zinc	Zn	30	65.38
zirconium	Zr	40	91.22

* = gas; ** = liquid; the remainder are solids. Atomic weights are for elements as found in nature, and those in parenthesis in the table are for the most stable isotope of the more recently discovered man-made elements which are represented only by unstable isotopes. They are International atomic weights 1959 based on oxygen 16.000. *See also* Transuranium Elements.

compounds. *Physical C.* treats of the particular changes which materials may undergo in special circumstances. Physical changes are changes of state only, the properties of the material remaining unaltered. This branch studies in particular the movement of molecules, and the effects of temperature and pressure, especially with regard to gases and liquids. *See* ORGANIC CHEMISTRY, INORGANIC CHEMISTRY, etc.

CHEMNITZ. *See* KARL-MARX-STADT.

CHEMULPO. Former name for INCHON.

CHENGCHOW. *See* ZHENGZHOU.

CHENGDE (chungde'). Town (formerly Chengteh) in Hebei prov., China, NE of Peking. It was the summer residence of the Manchu rulers and has an 18th cent. palace and temples. Pop. (1973) 200,000.

CHENGDU (chungdoo'). Ancient city (formerly Chengtu), the cap. of Sichuan prov., China, with well-preserved temples. It is an important rail junction and has railway workshops, textile, electronics and engineering industries. Pop. (1973) 2,000,000.

CHENGTEH. *See* CHENGDE.

CHENGTU. *See* CHENGDU.

CHÉNIER (shehnyeh'), **André de** (1762-94). French poet, b. at Constantinople, son of a French father and a Greek mother. He began to write poetry in imitation of classical models, visited Italy and London, and in 1790 associated himself in Paris with the Feuillant Club, a group of constitutional royalists, and pub. political poems and prose. In 1793 he went into hiding, but continued to write, among other poems, his *Ode à Charlotte Corday*, and his *Ode à Versailles*. Finally he was arrested, and on 25 July 1794, guillotined. While in prison he wrote some of his most famous poems, including the *Jeune Captive* and the political *Iambes*.

CHENOPODIUM (keno-). Genus of plants, known as goose-foot. All-good, or Good King Harry (*C. bonus-Henricus*) is the most familiar species, a common wayside weed in Britain which was formerly cultivated, being used as a substitute for spinach.

CHEPSTOW. Market town in Gwent, Wales, on the Wye. The high tides sometimes 15m (50ft) above low level are the highest in Britain. There is a Norman castle, and the ruins of Tintern Abbey are 6.5km (4m) to the N. Pop. (1972) 6,500.

CHEQUE (chek). A form of bill of exchange, drawn on a bank by a depositor. It need not be on a special form, though this is usual. The essentials of C. are that it should bear the date on which it is payable, name in words and figures a definite sum of money to be paid, to a named person or body or to bearer, and be signed by the drawer. It is then payable presentation at the bank on which it is drawn. If the C. is 'crossed', it is not negotiable and can be paid only through a bank; in the USA a C. (spelled check) cannot be made non-negotiable.

CHEQUE CARD. Card issued from 1968 by savings and clearings banks in Europe (incl. UK), which guarantees payment by the issuing bank when it is presented with a cheque to a bank, shop, etc. It bears the customer's signature and account number, for comparison with those on the cheque, and payment to the vendor by the issuing bank is immediate, no commission being charged. To lessen the dangers of loss and theft, the card is kept separately from the cheque book by the customer. It is less specialised than the CREDIT CARD (q.v.).

CHEQUERS. Country seat of the Prime Minister for the time being of the UK. It is an Elizabethan mansion in the Chiltern hills near Princes Risborough, Bucks, and was given to the nation by Lord Lee of Fareham under the Chequers Estate Act, 1917, which came into effect in Jan. 1921.

CHER (shār). French r. which rises in Creuse dept. and flows into the Loire below Tours. Length 355km (220m). It gives its name to a dept.

CHERBOURG (shārbo͞or'). French port and naval station at the N end of the Cotentin peninsula, in the dept of Manche. There is a nuclear processing plant at Cap la Hague, an institute for nuclear warfare, and shipbuilding yards. Cherbourg was captured by the Allies in June 1944. Pop. (1975) 79,000.

CHERENKOV, Pavel (1904-). Russian physicist. Ed. at Voronezh univ., he discovered in 1934 the *C. Effect*, important in atomic physics: when charged atomic particles pass through water or other media at a speed in excess of that of light itself, a bluish light is emitted. In 1958 C. and his colleagues Ilya Frank and Igor Tamm were awarded a Nobel prize. The C. Effect has also been claimed as the discovery of Fr. scientist Lucien Mallet.

CHERNENKO, Konstantin (1911–85). Soviet statesman. Siberian-born, he specialised in political propaganda, and was a protégé of Brezhnev from 1948. In 1984 he became Gen Sec of the Communist Party. He died in March 1985.

CHERNIGOV (chernēgof'). Town and river port on the Desna in the N of the Ukrainian SSR, it has an 11th cent. cathedral. Lumbering, textiles, chemicals, distilling, and food-canning are among its industries. Pop. (1977) 233,000.

CHERNOVTSY. City of the Ukrainian SSR, on the Prut river. It has a univ. founded 1875. It was in Romania 1918-40. Pop. (1977) 214,000.

CHE'ROKEE. American Indian tribe of Iroquois stock, formerly living in the mtn country of Alabama, the Carolinas, Georgia and Tennessee. They sided with the British against the French, and fought against the rebel colonists in the American War of Independence. One of them, Sequoyah (c.1770-1843), worked out the syllabary used for writing down the Indian languages. They now live mainly in North Carolina and in Oklahoma, where they estab. their cap. at Tahlequah. Nearby is the Cherokee Cultural Center which has a restored Indian village of c.1700.

CHERRY. Sub-genus of trees (*Cerasus*) of the genus *Prunus* distinguished from the plums and apricots by their fruit, a drupe, being spherical and smooth, and not covered with a bloom. They are probably derived from the 2 species, the wild or dwarf C. (*Prunus cerasus*), and the gean (*P. avium*), which grow wild in Britain. The former is the ancestor of the 'sour Cs.' - morello, duke, and Kentish C., and the latter of the 'sweet Cs.' - hearts, mazzards, and bigarreaus. Besides those varieties which are grown for their fruit, others are well-known ornamental trees.

CHERUBINI (keroobē'nē), **Maria Luigi Carlo Zenobio Salvatore** (1760-1842). Italian composer. B. at Florence, his first opera *Quinto Fabio* was produced at Alessandria in 1780. In 1784 he went to London and became composer to the king, but from 1788 Paris became his permanent home. There he produced a number of dramatic works, e.g. *Médée* (1797), the ballet *Anacréon* (1803), and *Les deux Journées*. In 1809 with a Mass in F he began his career as a great church composer. In 1822 he became

CHERNENKO. Defeated in the immediate power struggle after Brezhnev's death, Chernenko succeeded in obtaining the leadership when Andropov died. *Photo: Tass.*

director of the Conservatoire at Paris; in 1835 appeared his treatise *Counterpoint and Fugue*; and in 1836 his Requiem in C minor was written.

CHERVIL. Genus of umbelliferous plants (*Anthriscus*). The garden C. (*A. cerefolium*) has leaves with a sweetish odour, somewhat resembling parsley. It is used as a garnish, and as a pot-herb.

CHERWELL (char′-), **Frederick Alexander Lindemann,** viscount C. (1886-1957). British physicist. Director of the Physical Laboratory of the RAF at Farnborough in the F.W.W., he was personal adviser to Churchill on scientific and statistical matters during the S.W.W. He was prof. of experimental philosophy at Oxford 1919-56.

CHESHIRE, Geoffrey Leonard (1917-). British airman. Commissioned with the RAF on the outbreak of the S.W.W., he won the VC, DSO (with 2 bars) and DFC, and in 1945 was an official observer at the dropping of the atom bomb on Nagasaki: he retired in 1946. A devout Roman Catholic, he founded in 1948 the first C. Foundation Home for the Incurably Sick. He m. in 1959 Susan Ryder (1923-), who estab. a foundation for the sick and disabled of all ages and became a life peeress (as baroness Ryder) in 1978. He was awarded OM in 1981.

CHESHIRE. County in NW England, largely a plain with fertile soil. The chief rivers are the Mersey, Dee, and Weaver.

It was considerably truncated in the local govt reorganization of 1974, losing Birkenhead to the NW, and the northern part of the peninsula on which the town stands, to the new co. of Merseyside, and areas in the NE, incl. Stockport, to Greater Manchester. Still included are the textile centres of Macclesfield and Congleton, and the locomotive works centre and rail junction of Crewe. C. gained Warrington on the further side of the Mersey. There are brine and coal deposits, and the copper workings at Alderley Edge, worked from Roman times until the 1920s, are a tourist attraction because of their geological richness. The admin. HQ is Chester. Area 2,322 sq.km (897 sq.m.); pop. (1978) 919,800.

CHESIL BANK. A shingle bank extending 19km (11m) along the coast of Dorset, England, from Abbotsbury to the Isle of Portland.

CHESS. The board, and the way each piece can move; and (below) the arrangement of the chessmen when the game begins.

CHESS. A game of great antiquity, played by 2 players on a board of 64 squares alternating black and white. Each player has 16 pieces, the one side white and other red or black. These pieces are placed as shown in the accompanying diagram; and (reading from the white square on the player's right) they are: king's rook (or castle), king's knight, king's bishop, king, queen, queen's bishop, queen's knight, queen's rook. In front of these is a line of pawns. The object of the game is to force the king of the opposite side into such a situation that he can neither move nor remain without the danger of being taken by some other piece - this is called being in check. If the king cannot be removed out of check, the game is lost. Each of the pieces can move only in a particular way.

C. was thought to have originated in the 6th cent., but the discovery by Russian archeologists in 1973 of pieces dating to the 2nd cent. AD in the Uzbek Republic, nr the Afghanistan border, places it much earlier. The game is recorded by lettering and numbering the squares. The world championship was estab. in 1866. Recent winners have been Bobby Fischer (1972–5), Anatoli Karpov, who won the title by default when Fischer refused to defend, and Gary Kasparov, who defeated Karpov in a rematch in 1985.

CHESTER. English city and seaport, the admin. HQ of Cheshire, on the Dee 26km (16m) S of Liverpool. Its name derives from the Roman *Castra Devana*, the 'camp on the Dee', and there are many Roman and later remains. The city walls are intact - a unique feature in England. The cathedral dates from the 11th cent. but was restored in 1876. The church of St John the Baptist is one of the finest examples of early Norman architecture. The famous 'Rows' are covered arcades dating from the Middle Ages. From 1070 to the reign of Henry III, C. was the seat of a county palatine. The town hall dates from 1869. Although the silting up of the Dee destroyed C.'s importance as a port, navigation has been greatly improved by dredging. Pop. (1972) 62,320.

CHESTERFIELD, Philip Dormer Stanhope, 4th earl of (1694-1773). English statesman and man of letters. B. in London, he sat in parliament from 1715, and in 1726 succeeded his father as 4th earl. As an opponent of Walpole, he was Lord-Lieutenant of Ireland in 1745 and a Sec. of State in 1746. He moved in the literary circle of Swift, Pope, and Bolingbroke, and is remembered chiefly for his *Letters to his Son* (1774) - his natural son, Philip Stanhope (1732-68).

CHESTERFIELD. Market town of Derbyshire, England, 40km (25m) N of Derby, on the Rother, a coal-mining and industrial centre. All Saints' church is renowned for its crooked spire. Pop. (1972) 69,970.

CHESTERTON, Gilbert Keith (1874-1936). British author. B. in London, he studied art but quickly turned to journalism. His sympathies at this time were with the Socialist attempts to remedy the evils of capitalism, but he later found his own solution in Distributism. In poetry his best work is in satire, in the humorous *Wine, Water, and Song* (1915), and in *The Ballad of the White Horse* (1911). Among his best-known serious prose works are his studies of Browning (1903) and Dickens (1906); and the collections of essays *Twelve Types* (1902), *Heretics* (1905), and *A Short History of England* (1917). The most famous of his novels are the series dealing with the adventures of the naïve priest-detective, who first appeared in *The Innocence of Father Brown* (1911); but others incl. *The Napoleon of Notting Hill* (1904), *The Man who was Thursday* (1908), *The flying Inn* (1914), and *The Man who knew too Much* (1922). In 1922 C. entered the RC Church, and in 1936 his autobiography appeared.

CHESTNUT (ches'nut). Genus of trees (*Castanea*) belonging to the same family as the oak and beech (Fagaceae). The Spanish or Sweet C., *C. sativa,* produces a fruit that is a common article of diet in Europe and USA, and its timber is also valuable. The Horse chestnut or *Aesculus hippocastanum* is quite distinct, belonging to a different family.

CHESTERTON. Chesterton, Belloc and Baring, by H.J. Gunn. *Photo: Courtesy of the National Portrait Gallery.*

CHEVALIER, Maurice (1888-1972). French actor. B. in Paris, he became famous as dancing partner to Mistinguett at the Folies Bergère, and made numerous films incl. *The Innocents of Paris,* which revived his song 'Louise', and *Gigi* (1958).

CHEVENING (chē'vning). Official country residence 1974-80 of the Prince of Wales, nr Sevenoaks, Kent. It was bequeathed to the nation by the 7th Earl of Stanhope (1880-1967) for use by a member of the Royal Family, the PM, or a Cabinet Minister.

CHEVIOTS. Range of hills 56km (35m) long, forming for some 48km (30m) the border between England and Scotland. The highest point is the Cheviot (816m/2,676 ft). For centuries the area was a battleground of English and Scots.

CHEWING GUM. A confectionery mainly composed of chicle (q.v.), sweetened with various flavours. The first patent was taken out in the USA in 1871.

CHIANG KAI-SHEK (chyang kī-shek) (1887-1975). Chinese generalissimo and statesman. B. at Ningpo, he entered the Chinese military academy and in 1907 joined the revolutionary party of Sun Yat-sen. He took part in the Revolution of 1911, and served on Sun Yat-sen's staff at Canton, 1917-20. In 1925 he was made C-in-C of the Kuomintang armies in S China and established a national government at Nanking, of which in 1928 he became President and Generalissimo. From 1931 he was continuously engaged in striving to unite the Chinese against the Japanese menace. In 1936 he was kidnapped by Chang Hsüeh-liang, the 'Young Marshal', but was released after 13 days. Following the 'incident' near Peking on 7 July 1937, C. conducted the war against the Japanese invaders and in the early years suffered many reverses. During the S.W.W., he met Roosevelt and Churchill in 1943, and in 1945 received the surrender of the Japanese in China. But almost at once the former struggle between the Kuomintang and the Chinese Communists was renewed. The Communist victory limited his rule to Taiwan.

Madame Chiang Kai-Shek (Soong Mayling, 1898-), assisted her husband and was prominent in his conferences at Delhi in 1942 and Cairo in 1943.

He was succeeded as pres. by Yen Chia-kan (1905-), but real power rests with his elder son Chiang Ching-kuo (1910-). He was PM 1971-8 and pres from 1978.

CHIB'CHAS. S American Indian people whose civilization in Colombia was overthrown by the Spaniards in 1538. Their rite of powdering their chief with gold dust, after applying an underlay of gum, helped foster the legend of El Dorado.

CHICAGO (shikah'gō). Second city in pop., third in area, of the USA, in Illinois, on the S shore of Lake Michigan: area 583 sq.km (225 sq.m) has a lake frontage of 40km (25m). The Chicago river cuts the city into three 'sides', joined by bridges and tunnels. The site of C. was visited by Jesuit missionaries in 1673, and Fort Dearborn, then a frontier fort, was built here in 1803. The original lay-out of C. was rectangular, but many outer boulevards have been constructed on less rigid lines. As late as 1831 C. was still an insignificant village, but by 1871, when it suffered a disastrous fire, it was a city of more than 300,000 inhabitants. Rapid development began in the 1920s, and C. has become a series of towns rather than a centralized city. During the years of prohibition, 1919-33, the city became notorious for activities of its gangsters. The old business and amusement centre was in the Loop; the newer business district lies to the north of it. C. was the original home of the skyscraper: the first was built here 1887-8, and during the years since many others have been erected, and the Sears Tower (1974) at 443m (1,454 ft) is the world's highest building. In the centre of the city is a plaza with a Picasso sculpture, above which rises the Civic Centre.

There are many fine parks, playgrounds and bathing beaches; cultural institutions incl. the Univ. of C., an art institute and a school of music. It is known as the 'Windy City' because of the icy breezes from the lake, and the liking of its citizens for voluble talk.

C. is the greatest railway centre in the USA; the opening of the St Lawrence Seaway in 1959 brought Atlantic shipping to its docks; it has two major airports and a number of smaller ones. It is the chief world market for grain futures, and food processing is one of its major trades. Its manufactures are on a colossal scale, steel being of outstanding importance. Government is by mayor and common council; the various social and racial groups in the city play an important part in local politics. Pop. met. area (1970) 7,612,300.

CHICANOS (shikan'os). Mexican Americans in the SW of the USA, the word probably deriving from Mexicanos by eliding the first syllable, leaving Xicanos, in which the 'x' has an Aztec pronunciation 'sh'. The 1846-8 War between Mexico and the USA led to problems for Spanish-speaking Mexicans, who became US citizens when the territory was acquired by the USA. Immigration from Mexico to the USA became considerable because of the 1910 Revolution in Mexico, and because of American demand for labour.

CHICAGO. The view over the city from the Sears Tower, the world's highest building. *Photo: Mireille Vautier.*

CHICHEN ITZA (chechān' etsa'). Maya city, Yucatan, Mexico, which flourished 11-13th cent. AD. Excavated by Sylvanus Griswold Morley 1924-40, the remains incl. temples with magnificent sculptures and colour reliefs, an observatory, and a sacred well into which sacrifices, incl. human beings, were cast.

CHICHESTER, Sir Francis (1901-72). British yachtsman. B. in Devon, he became famous as a flier (1931 first E-to-W crossing of Tasman Sea in *Gipsy Moth*), and was knighted (KBE) for his circumnavigation of the world in *Gipsy Moth IV* 1966-7.

CHICHESTER. English city and market town, the admin. HQ of W Sussex, 111km (69m) SW of London, nr C. Harbour. It was an ancient Roman township, and the remains of the Roman palace built c. AD 80 at nearby Fishbourne are unique outside Italy. There is a fine cathedral consecrated 1108, later much rebuilt and restored, and the Chichester Festival Theatre (1962). Pop. (1972) 21,100.

CHICKEN. *See* POULTRY.

CHICKEN POX. Varicella, an acute fever characterized by crops of small blisters and a rash. It is caused by a virus, identical with that which causes shingles (q.v.), the latter representing a re-activation of the C.P. virus. It chiefly attacks children under 10. The virus is often air-borne, in the spray of coughing or speaking, but may also be transmitted on objects such as clothing or toys. The incubation period is 2-3 weeks.

CHICKWEED. A plant (*Stellaria media*) belonging to the pink family Caryophyllaceae. In Britain it is a common garden weed.

CHICLE (chik'l). Juice from the sapodilla tree (*Achras zapota*) of Central America. It is obtained by tapping. Shortly after exposure, the juice hardens into gum. C. is the basis of chewing gum.

CHI'CORY. Plant (*Cichorium intybus*) belonging to the Compositae. It grows wild in Britain, mainly on chalky soils, and has large, usually blue, flowers. Its long tap-root is dried and roasted, to be mixed with coffee.

CHIENGMAI (chi-eng'mī). Town in N Thailand, with a trade in teak and lac, and many handicraft industries. Pop. (1973) 70,000.

CHIFF-CHAFF. A bird (*Phylloscopus collybita*) of the Old World warbler family (Muscicapidae). It is olive-brown above and yellowish-white below, and is a summer migrant in England, being the first to arrive, about the middle of March.

CHIFLEY, Joseph Benedict (1885-1951). Australian Labour statesman. He was Min. of Defence under Scullin 1931-2, and under Curtin was Treasurer 1941-9 and Minister of Post-War Reconstruction 1942-5, when he succeeded him as PM. He united the party in fulfilling a welfare and nationalisation programme 1945-9, initiated the post-S.W.W. immigration programme, and also the Snowy Mtns hydroelectric scheme.

CHIHUAHUA (chēwah'wah). Mexican city, cap. of C. state, 1,285 km (800m) NW of Mexico City. It was founded 1707 and is the centre of a mining district. Pop. (1978) 387,000.

CHIHUAHUA. Breed of dog, developed in Mexico where they may have been introduced from Malta or N. Africa by the Spaniards. The C. is the smallest existing dog. Smooth and short-coated, prick-eared, skull large in comparison to body, in colour varied, it may weigh as little as .9kg (2lb).

CHIHUAHUA. Champion Rozavel Hasta la Vista. These little dogs were probably taken to Malta from North Africa by the Carthaginians c. 700 BC, and only received their name from the Mexican state when travellers from the USA took them home. *Photo: Thomas Fall Ltd.*

CHILBLAIN. A painful inflammation of the skin of the feet or hands, due to damp cold. The parts turn red, swell, itch violently, and are very tender. In a bad case the skin cracks, blisters, or ulcerates, or may even become gangrenous.

CHILDBIRTH. The expulsion of a child from its mother's body; labour. Normally a child grows within the womb (uterus) for 40 weeks from the date of conception; but birth may take place at any earlier time, and may be delayed by several weeks after the normal term. A child born before the end of the 7th month usually requires medical assistance to survive. The birth of a dead child is called a stillbirth. Normal labour is spontaneous childbirth without assistance or complications.

CHILDE (chīld), **V. Gordon** (1892-1957). Australian archaeologist, director of the London Institute of Archaeology 1946-57. He discovered the pre-historic village of Skara Brae in the Orkneys, and in 1939 pub. *The Dawn of European Civilisation.*

CHILDERS (chil'derz), **Robert Erskine** (1870-1922). Irish Sinn Fein politician and writer. Before turning to Irish politics, he was a clerk in the House of Commons in London and author of the 'German spy' novel, *The Riddle of the Sands* (1903). In 1921 he was elected to the Irish Parliament as a supporter of De Valera, and as a Republican took up arms against the Irish Free State in 1922. Shortly afterwards he was captured, court-martialled and shot by the Irish Free State govt of William T. Cosgrave (q.v.). His son, **Erskine C.** (1905-74), although a Protestant, succeeded De Valera as Pres. of Ireland in 1973-4.

CHI'LE. S American republic occupying the W or Pacific slope of the Andes, S of Peru. It is 4,000 km (2,500 m) long, average width 160km (100m). The country may be divided into 3 main areas: the chain of the Andes in the E, which extends through most of the length of C; the central valley or tableland, and the coastal chain of mountains. The climate varies a great deal in different parts; the N receives no rain and is desert, the S is cold, wet, and heavily forested; the centre has a Mediterranean climate, and is the heart of C. This central area, which includes the largest cities - Santiago (the cap.), Valparaiso, and Concepción - is covered by farms and vineyards.

The principal rivers flow from E to W; they are short and of little importance for transport. The lakes are chiefly in the S. The chief ports from N to S are Arica, Iquique, Antofagasta, Coquimbo, Valparaiso, Talcahuano (port of Concepción), Puerto Montt, and Punta Arenas. There are 25 provs.

C. is the principal mining country in S America. Sodium nitrate is found in Tarapacá and the Atacama desert; and in this region about 70 per cent of the world's iodine (an element which exists in nitrate deposits) is produced. Copper is mined in the mountainous region in the N and is exported from Antofagasta and Tocopilla. Iron, coal, and many other minerals are worked.

The first European to see what is now Chile was Magellan who discovered and sailed through Magellan Strait in 1520. A Spanish expedition under Pedro de Valdivia founded Santiago in 1541. In 1810 there was a rising against Spain and a rep. was proclaimed; Spanish rule ended in 1818. The discovery of nitrates and guano in the borderlands to the N led to disputes from 1866 onwards with Bolivia and Peru over frontiers which in 1879 came to war, ended in 1883 by a treaty under which C. gained Tacna (returned to Peru in 1929) and Arica provs. from Peru, Antofagasta prov. from Bolivia.

The socialist regime of Allende (q.v.) was overthrown by a revolt of the armed forces in 1973, unrest having been fanned by rampant inflation and general economic chaos (*see also* CENTRAL INTELLIGENCE AGENCY). The leader of the revolt, Gen. Augusto Pinochet (Ugarte) (1915-), became Supreme Head of State in 1974, and all legislative and executive powers were assumed by the junta. After the coup there were *c.* 600 'missing persons' (*desaparecidos*), but by 1980 there was some liberalisation, and by the application of Friedmanite policies inflation was being reduced and growth stimulated. Under the constitution approved by referendum in 1980, Pinochet was to remain pres. until at least 1989, and possibly until free elections in 1997. There is a dispute with Argentina concerning islands in the Beagle Channel (q.v.).

Area 741,765 sq.km (286,400 sq.m); pop. (1977) 10,660,000, mainly Spanish-speaking descendants of the Spanish conquerors and Amerindian women. M.U.: peso.

CHILLON (she-yoń'). A fortress on an island rock at the E end of Lake Geneva, Switzerland, made famous by a poem of Byron. It dates from the 8th cent.

CHILOPODA (kilo'poda). An important sub-division of the Arthropoda (q.v.) comprising the centipedes (q.v.).

CHILTERN HUNDREDS. The stewardship of the C.H. is a nominal 'office of profit under the Crown' which may be accepted by a MP who wishes to resign his seat. Another is the stewardship of Northstead in Yorks.

CHILTERNS. Range of chalk hills extending for some 72km (45m) in a curve from a point N of Reading to the Suffolk border. The highest point is Haddington Hill near Wendover 261m (857ft).

CHIMAERA (ki-mē'rah). Genus of fishes, typical of the order Holocephali of the class Selachia. They resemble the sharks and rays in having a cartilaginous skeleton, and in laying large, single eggs, enclosed in a horny case. The Arctic C. or rabbit fish (*C. monstrosa*) is sometimes taken in British waters.

CHIMPANZEE (*Anthropopithecus troglodytes*). An anthropoid ape, which, apart from the gorilla, is the most man-like in structure. Like the gorilla it lives in the forests of West and Central Africa, but it is easily distinguished by its smaller size, larger ears, and unswollen nostrils. Its arms are somewhat shorter, reaching to the knees in the erect posture, and the hands and feet are narrower. An adult male is about 1.35m (4½ft) in the upright position and the female is some 15cm (6in) shorter. Cs. feed mainly on fruit.

Study of the chromosomes of Cs. and man indicated in 1980 that 99% of their genes are the same. They also share man's aggressive behaviour (being capable of cannibalism, infanticide and mass murder); can combine to hunt, and are primitive tool users. Some success has been achieved in teaching Cs. to 'talk' with the aid of machines (*see* APE) or sign language, but it is doubtful whether the constructive element in language has been attained.

CHIMU (chē'moo). Pre-Inca civilisation which flourished in Peru A.D. 1200–c.1470. The Chimu people built enormous adobe brick mounds or *huacas* (pron. wak'az) as the base of temples and palaces, produced fine work in gold, boldly realistic portrait pottery and savage fanged images in clay, and possibly a system of 'writing' or recording by painting beans in particular patterns. Their agricultural system depended on remarkable irrigations schemes with aqueducts carrying water many miles, defaulting peasants seem to have been ritually mutilated. Their greatest monument is the maze-like city of Chan Chan 36 sq.km. (14 sq.m.) on the coast nr. Trujillo. It consists of 9 complexes, probably built by successive kings and forming their eventual tombs, where they were buried with much human sacrifice. The C. were conquered by the Incas who ensured victory by cutting their aqueducts.

CHINA. Country of E Asia (*see also* ZHONGHUA), one of the largest in the world, and the most populous. The territory of the Chinese Republic is organized for political purposes in 6 regions, among which the 22 provs., 5 autonomous regions and 3 municipalities are divided. Taiwan, seat of the Nationalist govt, is counted as part of E region.

Physical. China proper consists of 3 great river systems - the Huang He, or Yellow river, in the N; the Chang Jiang (Yangtze-Kiang) in central China; and the Xi Jiang (Si-Kiang) in the S. Their basins are separated by mountain ranges. In the far N, beyond the Huang He, is the

CHIMU. A bottle in the form of a musician and high on the neck, a monkey. Such animals were always used to ornament Chimu pottery. *Photo: Mireille Vautier*

Mongolian plateau, merging into the loess-covered plateau of NW China. The S part of the country is occupied by a rugged plateau, much dissected. In the W is the Sichuan or Red basin, surrounded by mountains, except for the gorge where the Chang Jiang breaks through the plain of central China. Beyond Sichuan, to the W, rises the lofty plateau of Xizang (Tibet). Covering such a huge area, and with such varying surface conditions, C. has a very diverse climate, with January temperatures below −18°C (0°F) in the NE and as high as 18°C (65°F) in Hainan. Rainfall is very heavy in the S, being over 2,000 mm (80in) at Beihai in Guangxi Zhuang (Kwangsi-Chuang).

Economic. Originally much of C. was forested, and felling of trees over large areas caused severe erosion, now being remedied by re-afforestation; teak and tung oil are valuable products. The great majority of the people work in agricultural communes, but may have small private holdings. The ox and buffalo are the traditional draught animals of the S, and the mule and horse in the N, but there has been large-scale mechanization (some 25 million tractors), although manual labour is still overwhelmingly important. The use of animal and human manure is complemented by modern fertilizers, and there has been improvement of crop varieties and widespread extension of irrigation. In the S rice and sugar are the main crops, giving way in the N to wheat and soya beans, and N again to millet. Cotton is grown in the Huang He and Chang Jiang basins, tea in the centre and S, and groundnuts, maize and potatoes are also important. Sheep are grazed in the N and NW, cattle are increasingly raised, and poultry are widely kept, but the pig is the major domestic animal, est. at 300 million, with its valuable by-products such as bristles.

Industrialization, stimulated by the Japanese partial occupation, was intensified under the Communist regime, a series of 5-year plans having been put into operation since 1952. In more recent years, espec. following the withdrawal of Soviet aid, there has been concentration on dispersed, small-scale, industrial development, resistant to destruction in the event of war, and utilizing to advantage abundant manpower. Industries incl. cotton, wool and silk

Divisions of China

Provinces	Area in sq. km.	Pop. (1979) in 1,000s	Capital
N. Region			
Hebei	202,700	50,000	Shijiazhuang
Beijing*	17,800	8,000	—
Tianjin*	4,800	7,000	—
Nei Monggol**	450,000	8,500	Hohhot
Shanxi	157,100	23,000	Taiyuan
N.E. Region			
Heilongjiang	710,000	32,000	Harbin
Jilin	290,000	24,000	Changchun
Liaoning	230,000	36,000	Shenyang
E. Region			
Anhui	139,900	45,000	Hefei
Fujian	123,100	24,000	Fuzhou
Jiangsu	102,200	57,000	Nanjing
Shanghai*	5,800	10,000	—
Jiangxi	164,800	28,000	Nanchang
Shandong	153,300	70,000	Jinan
Taiwan§	36,000	16,500	Taipei
Zhejiang	101,800	36,000	Hangzhou
Central – S. Region			
Guangdong	231,400	53,500	Guangzhou
Guangxi Zhuang**	220,400	33,000	Nanning
Henan	167,000	70,000	Zhengzhou
Hubei	187,500	42,000	Wuhan
Hunan	210,500	50,000	Changsha
S.W. Region			
Guizhou	174,000	25,000	Guiyang
Sichuan	569,000	90,000	Chengdu
Xizang**	1,221,600	1,700	Lhasa
Yunnan	436,200	30,000	Kunming
N.W. Region			
Gansu	530,000	19,000	Lanzhou
Ningxia Hui**	170,000	3,000	Yinchuan
Qinghai	721,000	3,500	Xining
Shaanxi	195,800	27,000	Zian
Xinjiang Uygur**	1,646,800	11,000	Urumqi
	9,569,700	933,700	

*municipality **autonomous region
§seat of the Nationalist govt.

textiles, iron and steel (notably at Anshan, Baotou (Paotow) and Wuhan), machine tools and motor vehicles, fertilizers, flour and rice milling, cement and paper. Minerals incl. coal and iron reserves widely spread throughout the country, as well as antimony, bauxite, copper, manganese, tin, and tungsten, C. being the world's largest producer of the last-named. Oil reserves are also well distributed on the mainland and offshore, and since 1973 C. has been an exporter. There are good communications, road (mainly unmetalled), rail and air, and the ancient canal system has been improved and extended. The chief ports are Guangzhou (Canton), Shanghai, Luda (Ta-lien), Tianjin (Tientsin), and Qingdao (Tsingtao); other major cities are the cap. Beijing (Peking), and Nanjing (Nanking), Shenyang, Wuhan, Chongqing (Chungking), Harbin, Xian (Sian) and Chengdu (Chengtu). M.U.: yuan.

As part of the Cultural Revolution the educational system was reorganised to avoid creating an intellectual elite. The student body was diluted with soldiers and agricultural and industrial workers, and study had to be combined with manual labour. Disastrously falling standards led to a reversal of the policy from 1975. By 1978 special schools had been estab. for able pupils, advanced study was encouraged, and in the drive for modernisation many students were being sent to Western universities.

Government. Under the constitution of 1982 there is a president (maximum two 5-yr terms), and in 1983 Li Xiannian (b. 1905–) was elected. A Nat. People's Congress, is also elected for 5 years, and chooses the Prime Minister (Zhao Zi-yang, q.v.), who recommends his own ministers for appointment to the State Council. Zhao Ziyang is also General Secretary of the Communist Party, in which Deng Xiaoping (q.v.) also remains influential. Since 1980 both the Prime Minister and the newly instituted elected people's govts (replacing party-run revolutionary committees) in the 29 provs, autonomous regions and special municipalities, have been freer from Party control.

History. Chinese civilization is the oldest in existence. The social system which endured until this cent. was stabilized fully 3,500 years ago. The so-called Sage Kings (2800-2205 BC) were all associated with civilizing developments - agriculture, medicine, river conservancy, etc. There followed the Hsia dynasty (2205-1557 BC) of which little is known. Then came the Shang dynasty, whose artistic genius is illustrated in the still existing bronze vases; it was replaced about 1050 by the Chou dynasty, followed in 221 BC by the shortest and most remarkable of the dynasties, the Ch'in, comprising the reign of Shih Huang Ti, who curbed the feudal nobility and introduced a widespread system of orderly government; he also built the Great Wall to keep out the northern barbarians. The next dynasty was the Han (206 BC-AD 220) under which the keeping of historical records was systematized and the idea of the unity of China was so firmly implanted that, though that unity has often been broken, it always reasserted itself. After a period of division between N and S came the T'angs (618-906), the most brilliant centuries in China's history. After another period of disruption the Sungs ruled (960-1279) in an age of culture and refinement. The Mongols reigned from 1279-1368, when they were expelled by the 1st of the Mings (1368-1644); during their rule, in the 16th cent., Europeans began to arrive in China.

The Portuguese reached Canton in 1517, and were followed by Spanish, Dutch, French, British and Americans. During the 19th cent. it seemed likely that C. would be partitioned amongst the Powers, all trade being conducted through Treaty Ports in their control, and the system not being ended until new agreements were made 1943-7. The last Chinese effort under the Empire to throw off western influence was the Boxer Rising of 1900, suppressed by European troops.

The last of the dynasties was the Manchu (1644-1912) which gave several great rulers to C., up to the empress dowager Tz'e Hsi who d. in 1908. Three years later revolution broke out, and in 1912 the infant emperor (*see* PU

CHINA. A glazed pottery model of the square pagoda so characteristic of Chinese architecture for some 2000 years (upper left); a quaint example of a Scottish motif in a plate now in the Royal Museum of Scotland (lower left); 'acrobatic' workers on China's first electrified rail line (top right); wool convoys on their way to the textile mills (centre right); and the bronze 'celestial' horse excavated in 1969 in Gansu, the finest representation of the new breed of tall Western or 'flying' horses introduced to China in the 1st century AD. *Photos: Courtesy of Anglo-Chinese Educational Institute, Royal Museum of Scotland, and Society for Anglo-Chinese Understanding.*

YI, HENRY) was deposed. The principal maker of the revolution was Sun Yat-sen, who became President of the Republic. He d. in 1925, and for years afterwards C. was distracted by civil war conducted by rival war lords. Then the country was divided between the nationalist Kuomintang under Chiang Kai-shek and the Communists, who received Russian support. In 1931 the Japanese began their penetration of Manchuria, and in 1937 the so-called 'China Incident' outside Peking marked the beginning of open war which continued until 1945 when C., as one of the Allied Powers, received the surrender of the Japanese. The Civil War was then resumed, and in 1949, following their elimination of Nationalist resistance on the mainland, the Communists inaugurated the People's Republic of China. The Nationalists retired to Taiwan (q.v.).

Dissension developed in the Communist Party from 1957 when Mao Tse-tung (q.v.) attempted to achieve 'pure' Communist aims at home and abroad. He failed and moderate policies prevailed 1959-62 when Liu Shao Chi replaced him as chairman of the rep., but he struggled to regain power and launched 1964 the Great Proletarian Cultural Revolution, adopted as Party policy 1966 and put into force by the youthful Red Guards and adult Revolutionary Rebels. Widespread disturbances ensued 1967-8, and industry and education were disrupted.

Relations with Britain and Russia deteriorated sharply, but improved with the former in 1970 when the disorder in the country ceased. Lin Piao (q.v.), an opponent of rapprochement with the West and espec. the USA, fell into disgrace from 1970. The post of Head of State was abolished in 1970, but Mao Tse-tung retained the Communist Party chairmanship, with Chou En-lai as Prime Minister. In 1972 the end of the 'cold war' maintained with USA since the establishment of Communism was consolidated by Nixon's visit to Peking, but even 1980 saw no significant improvement in Sino-Soviet relations.

After the successive deaths of Mao and Chou in 1976, middle-of-the-road Hua Guofeng (formerly Hua Kuofeng) ousted the radical devotees of Mao's tenet of perpetual revolution and concentrated on the 'Four Modernisations' - agriculture, industry, science and technology, and defence. Relaxation in freedom of expression, e.g. 'Democracy Wall' (*see* PEKING), was limited. An infusion of capitalist enterprise followed the return of many overseas Chinese, and in 1980 the replacement of Hua Guofeng by Zhao Ziyang, the protégé of Deng Xiaoping (qq.v.), marked a transition to even greater stress on economic pragmatism.

Area 9,569,700 sq.km (3,694,000 sq.m); pop. (1980) 975,000,000, incl. 17 million on Taiwan. By AD 2000, at the present birthrate, it will be over 2,000,000,000, so that couples with 1 child are now rewarded and those with more than 2 lose 'workpoints' (on which communal income is assessed). The Chinese vary widely in physical type. *See* CHINESE LANGUAGE. They traditionally practise Confucianism, Buddhism and Taoism, often in combination. None is fully consistent with Communism, but by 1980 such attacks as those on Confucianism in 1974 had ceased and attitudes even to the Moslem and Christian minorities became benevolent.

CHINA CLAY. *See* KAOLIN.

CHINA SEA. Area of the Pacific Ocean bordered by China, Vietnam, Borneo, the Philippines and Japan: north of Taiwan it is known as the *East C.S.* and to the south as the *South C.S.* Various groups of small is. and shoals in the centre, W and E of the South C.S., e.g. the Paracels 500 km (300m) E of Vietnam have been disputed by China and other powers because they lie in oil bearing areas.

CHINCHIL'LA (family, Chinchillidae). Name given to several species of South American rodents allied to porcupines. They have long hind legs, longish ears, and a bushy tail; vary in size from a large squirrel to a small rabbit, are very active, and live in groups in burrows and rock crevices in the Andes of Bolivia and Chile. The common C. (*Chinchilla laniger*) is famous for its beautiful, soft, silvery-grey fur.

CHINDITS. Name given to the 3rd Indian Division (Long Range Penetration Group) under the command of Brigadier Wingate (q.v.) in the S.W.W. The name derived from the mythical Chinthay - half lion, half eagle - at the entrance of Burmese pagodas to scare evil spirits.

CHINESE ARCHITECTURE. Since early times Chinese buildings have been constructed chiefly of timber, and consequently they do not usually last long. There are few buildings which date back earlier than the Ming dynasty (1368-1644), but there are records, such as the Ying Tsao Fa Shih (Method of Architecture), pub. in AD 1103, which describe and illustrate early Chinese buildings. These records reveal that C.A. has remained very much the same in style throughout the ages. Chinese buildings usually face S, a convention which can be traced back to the 'Hall of Brightness', a famous building of the Chou dynasty (*c.* 1050-221 BC). One of the most characteristic features of C.A. is the curved roof, believed to have been imported with Buddhism from India.

The Chinese are also famous for their walls. The Great Wall of China was built, *c.* 228-210 BC, by the Emperor Ch'in Shih Huang Ti along the northern frontier as a defence against the hostile nomadic tribes of the north. The fine city walls of Peking (of which some sections have been demolished in modernisation of the city) date to the Ming dynasty, as also do some of the buildings in or near Peking, notably the Altar of Heaven, the ancestral temple of the Ming tombs, and the Five Pagoda Temple. The pagoda with its tiled roofs one above the other is typically Chinese.

Modern C.A. has tended to be functionally western in construction, with some traditional features.

CHINESE ART. During China's Stone Age painted pottery and jade objects were made, but there was not a Chinese culture until the acquisition of bronze. During the Shang period, which lasted till *c.* 1050 BC, beautiful bronze vessels were produced, and motifs, such as the dragon, the elephant, and the ogre's mask, were already in use. Under the Chou dynasty a feudal system emerged, together with important developments in the field of art. Buildings were often decorated with mural paintings, and this art is said to have won the praise of Confucius. The brush had been used for painting on pottery, and lacquer workers used brushes as early as 2 or 3 cents. BC. The use of finer brushes resulted in the invention by Mêng T'ien of the writing brush, *c.* 200 BC, and the development of calligraphy, which the Chinese have long regarded as the greatest of the fine arts.

The Han period (206 BC-AD 220) was very important in art. Silk weavings appeared, glaze was used to brighten pottery, great architectural schemes were carried out, relief sculpture, portrait and other painting developed.

The first of the great painters whose name we know - Ku K'ai Chih - worked *c.* AD 3500-400 in S China. Some of his illustrations on the inscribed scroll entitled *The Admonitions of the Instructress to the Court Ladies* are in the British Museum.

During the T'ang period (618-906) the art of painting reached its zenith, and porcelain was perfected. This was a period of great expansion, and China began to take an interest in her neighbours, both oriental and occidental. The shapes of vessels show the influence of Persian designs. The Sung period (960-1279) is famous for its many beautiful landscape paintings, and its many animal, flower, and bird paintings which were executed with great delicacy and charm. An Imperial Academy of Painting was founded by the emperor Hui Tsung, who was himself a talented painter of birds. Then with the Mings (1386-1644) there was an outburst of patriotism which was reflected by artists and craftsmen in bold masses, free flowing line, and brilliant colour. Chinese architecture, pottery, and painting of the period display all these qualities. There was a flourishing trade in porcelain, and typical of the time are the large wine jars of sturdy design, tall and imposing vases with heavily outlined floral designs. Enamelling on metal was perfected.

The Ming dynasty was overthrown by invaders from Manchuria who proved to be excellent rulers. The Manchus fostered the arts and encouraged learning. Closer contact was made with western civilization. The two great liberal rulers of the period were K'ang Hsi, whose reign began in 1662, and Ch'ien Lung, who reigned from 1736 till almost the end of the 18th cent. Under K'ang Hsi porcelain became the most typical medium of expression. K'ang Hsi wares were chiefly the blue and white (called 'Nanking' in England), and the enamelled porcelains. During the 18th cent. there was a growing fad for intricacy of design. Although some fine pieces were produced during the reign of Ch'ien Lung, C.A. began to deteriorate, and it has never since recovered.

CHINESE LANGUAGE. Chinese is generally believed to belong to the Sinitic or Indo-Chinese family related to Tibetan, Burmese, Thai, etc. Its chief characteristics are the possession of significant tones whereby the pitch or inflection of the voice entirely alters the meaning of a syllable, and monosyllabism. In course of time the spoken language has been affected by many innovations, but syllables which have become identical to the ear have remained distinguished to the eye. Thus the spoken language is distinguished from the written, and it was not until our own day that the spoken language has been given written form. The dialects of Chinese are many, and are so profoundly different as to constitute almost separate languages.

The classical written language has remained the same since about the 10th cent. AD, while the spoken language moved further and further towards its modern form. Thus a good written style can be attained only after many years of study. After the establishment of the Republic, this was recognized as a hindrance to democratic development and Common Speech (Putonghua), based on the Peking dialect (Mandarin), was cultivated as a nat. spoken and written language. To speed reading and writing the characters, formerly vertical and read right to left, were from 1956 placed horizontally and read left to right, and *c.* 1,000 simplified characters were gradually introduced. A 25-letter Roman alphabet (excl. 'v'), introduced in primary schools 1957, is intended to help with pronunciation. Transliteration into the Roman alphabet presents difficulties, but the official system is Pinyin (q.v.).

CHINESE LITERATURE. POETRY. Written in the ancient literary language understood throughout China, C. poems, often only 4 lines long, consist of rhymed lines of a fixed number of syllables, ornamented by parallel phrasing and tonal pattern. The oldest poems are contained in the *Book of Songs* (800-600 BC). Among the most famous C. poets are the nature poet T'ao Ch'ien (AD 372-427), the master of technique Li Po (701-62), the autobiographical Po Chüi (772-846), and the wide-ranging Su Tung-p'o (1036-1101); and among the moderns using the colloquial language under European influence and experimenting in free verse are Hsu Chih-mo (1895-1931), and Pien Chih-lin (1910-).

PROSE. Typical C. history is less literary than an editing of assembled documents with moral comment, but the essay has long been cultivated under strict rules of form and style. Among the most famous essays is that of Han Yü (AD 768-824) *Upon the Original Way*, recalling the nation to Confucianism. Until the 16th cent. the short story was confined to the anecdote, startling by its strangeness, related in the literary language, e.g. those of the poetic Tuan Ch'eng-shih (d. AD 863), but after that time the more novelistic type in the colloquial tongue developed by its side. The C. novel has evolved entirely from the street storyteller's art, and has consequently always existed in the vulgar tongue. The early romances *Three Kingdoms, All Men are Brothers,* and *Golden Lotus* are anonymous, the earliest known author being Wu Che'ng-en (*c.* 1505-80); the most realistic of the great novelists is Ts'ao Chan (d. 1763).

20th cent. C. novels have largely adopted European form, and have been particularly influenced by Russia, as have the realistic stories of Lu Hsün (q.v.). In typical C. drama, the stage presentation far surpasses the text in importance (the dialogue was not even preserved in early plays), but the present cent. has seen experiments in the European manner.

CHINGHAI. *See* QINGHAI.

CH'IN SHIH HUANG TI (chin shē hoo-ahng tē) (*d.* 210 BC). Emperor of China. Coming to the throne of the state of Ch'in in 246 BC, he re-united the country as an empire by 228 BC. He was the builder of the Great Wall, and his tomb complex, guarded by 10,000 individualised, life-size pottery warriors was being excavated in 1980. His 'burning of the books' in 213 BC was intended to destroy all ties with the past and destroy the status of the feudal princes, but he had so over-extended his power that the dynasty ended with the death of his feeble successor in 207 BC, and the empire collapsed. (Pinyin form: Qin S.H.T.)

CHIOGGIA (kēoh'jah). City and port in NE Italy, S of Venice, built on C. island at the S end of the Venice lagoon and connected by bridge with the mainland. Pop. (1971) 47,800.

CHIOS (kē'os). Greek island (Khíos) in the Aegean Sea, off the coast of Turkey. Cap. Chios, pop. (1971) 24,000. Area 831 sq.km (321 sq.m).

CHIP. In electronics the minute square of semiconductor material, made of silicon or gallium arsenide (qq.v.), or using Josephson junction components (q.v.), which is essential to the integrated circuits of computers, etc.

CHIPMUNK (*Tamias*). A kind of ground-squirrel found in N America and E Asia. Of small size and ornamented with white stripes, they are sometimes called striped gophers, and are distinguished from ordinary squirrels by having cheek-pouches. They inhabit woods, living in burrows or hollow logs.

CHIPPENDALE, Thomas (c. 1718-79). English cabinet-maker. The son of a joiner of Otley, Yorks, he went to London at the age of 20, and from 1753 had his workshop in St Martin's Lane. His book *The Gentleman and Cabinet Maker's Director* (1754) was a landmark in furniture design, and illustrates his favourite styles - Louis XV, Chinese and Gothic. He worked mainly in dark mahogany.

CHIRAC (shirahk'), **Jaques** (1932-). French statesman. A member of Pompidou's personal staff, who nicknamed him 'my bulldozer', he held varied ministerial posts before being chosen by Giscard d'Estaing as Prime Minister in 1974. He opposed Britain's renegotiation of entry into the Common Market. Following his resignation in 1976, he reorganised the Gaullist party as the Rassemblement pour la républiqųe, offering a political challenge to Giscard d'Estaing. In 1977 he became mayor of Paris, and was a presidential candidate 1981.

CHIRICO (kē'rēkō), **Giorgio de** (1888-1978). Italian artist. B. in Greece, of Italian parents, he was associated with the Dadaists and Surrealists.

CHIRON (kī'ron). In Greek mythology, the wise centaur, son of Cronos and a sea nymph, and tutor of Jason, Achilles, and other heroes.

CHIROPODY (kīrop'odi). The care and treatment of the hands and feet. The first centre to deal with common foot disorders was the Pedic Clinic (1913), which later became the London Foot Hospital; and the Soc. of Chiropodists was estab. 1945.

CHIROPRACTIC (kīroprak'tik). The manipulation of the joints. There is a British Chiropractors Assocn (1925) in London, and the profession is legally recognized in Canada, NZ, Switzerland and USA, and was incl. in 1972 in the US Medicare programme.

CHIROPTERA (kīrop'terah). An order of mammals comprising the bats (q.v.), which are readily distinguished by the conversion of the fore-limbs into wings for the purpose of flight.

CHITA. Russian town in eastern Siberia, on the C. river. It is on the Trans-Siberian railway, and has engineering works, coal mines, etc. Pop. (1977) 294,000.

CHITTAGO'NG. Town and port in Bangladesh, 16km (10m) from the mouth of the Karnaphuli r., on the Bay of Bengal. Industries incl. steel, engineering, chemicals and textiles. Pop. (1974) 416,733.

CHIVALRY (shiv'alri). Originally the knightly class of the feudal Middle Ages; subsequently the word came to mean the code of gallantry and honour that the knights were supposed to observe. The Court of C. endured from Edward III's reign to 1737.

CHĪVE. A plant (*Allium schoenoprasum*) that sometimes grows wild in Britain, and is cultivated as a vegetable.

CHKALOV (chkah'lof). Name 1938-57 of ORENBURG.

CHLADNI (khlahd'nē), **Ernest Florens Friedrich** (1756-1827). German physicist, a pioneer in the field of acoustics.

CHLORACNE (klorak'nē). Cutaneous eruption caused by contact with chlorinated organic chemicals which may cause disfigurement. It also indicates the presence of a chemical which may be dangerous to human beings in other ways and to the environment.

CHLORAL (klor-) (CCl_3-CHO) or **Trichloracetaldehyde.** An oily colourless liquid with a characteristic pungent smeli. It is very soluble in water, and its compound chloral hydrate is a powerful hypnotic.

CHLORATES. In chemistry, the salts of chloric acid, the common ones being those of sodium, potassium, and barium.

CHLORELLA (klore'la). A single-celled, freshwater green alga, 3-10 microns in diam., obtaining its growth energy from light. C. is capable of increasing its weight four-fold in a 12 hr period, and, already an essential tool for the study of photosynthesis in the laboratory, it may prove even more valuable as a staple foodstuff, particularly for space travellers. Although unpalatable, its nutritive content is high, consisting of 50% protein, 20% fat, 20% carbohydrate and 10% phosphate, calcium and other inorganic substances.

CHLORIDES (klor'īds). Salts of hydrochloric acid commonly formed by its action on various metals or by the direct combination of metal and chlorine.

CHLORINE (klor'ēn). A chemical element, a greenish-yellow gas with an irritating, suffocating smell. Symbol Cl; atomic number 17; atomic weight, 35.457. It rapidly attacks the membranes of the nose, throat, and lungs, producing bronchitis or pneumonia, and during the F.W.W. it was used as a weapon. It is never found uncombined in nature, but is widely distributed in combination with the alkali metals. Common or rock salt is sodium chloride. C. was discovered in 1774 by Scheele, but Sir H. Davy in 1810 first proved it to be an element. C. is an important bleaching agent and is used universally as a germicide for drinking water. It is also an oxidizing agent and finds many applications in organic chemistry.

CHLOROFORM. Trichloromethane, $CHCl_3$, with 1 or 2 per cent of alcohol to prevent it from decomposing on exposure to light. It is a clear, colourless liquid with a characteristic pungent, sweet, rather sickly smell and taste. It had been known to chemists long before David Waldie, chemist to the Apothecaries' Company of Liverpool, suggested to Professor James Young Simpson of Edinburgh in 1847 that it might be used as a general anaesthetic.

CHLOROMYCETIN (klō'rōmīsetin). Antibiotic which attacks viruses as well as bacteria, used in treatment of scrub-typhus, typhus and psittacosis.

CHLO'ROPHYLL (klo'rofil). The green colouring matter found in plants, being formed in the parts exposed to light. By its means, plants absorb and decompose carbon dioxide in order to produce oxygen and to form new organic substances. *See* PHOTOSYNTHESIS.

CHOCOLATE. *See* COCOA.

CHODOWIECKI (kohdohvyets'kē), **Daniel Nicolas** (1726-1801). German painter and engraver. B. at Danzig of Polish descent, he is particularly famous for his engravings of scenes from the Seven Years War and the life of Christ, and for a picture of 'Jean Calas and his family'.

CHOIR (kwīr). A trained body of singers, esp. as taking part in religious services, either leading the congregation or singing alone. The use of a C. in worship was taken over by the Christian Church from the Jews. In the Anglican Church, the C. consists, traditionally of boys and men only, singing in 4 parts, but women and girls increasingly take part.

CHOISEUL (shwahzöl′), **Étienne François,** duke of (1719-85). French statesman. Originally a protégé of Mme de Pompadour, he became Minister for Foreign Affairs in 1758 and held this and other offices until 1770. He banished the Jesuits, and was a supporter of the *Philosophes.*

CHOLERA. Asiatic cholera, an acute epidemic disease, most common in India, due to a specific microorganism (vibrio, spirillum) and characterized by violent diarrhoea, cramps, and a high death rate; this, however, has been reduced to about one per cent by Leonard Roger's treatment with copious injections of saline fluid.

CHOLESTEROL (koles′terol). Fatty alcohol occurring in bile and nervous tissue, and forming gall stones and causing arterio-sclerosis. Konrad Bloch (Harvard) and Feodor Lynen (Munich) received a Nobel prize 1964 for their research on C.

CHOMSKY, Noam (1928-). American linguist. His *Syntactic Structures* (1957) maintains that language supplies evidence for the rationalist theory of innate ideas; he is opposed to centralized political power.

CHONGQING (chawngcheng). City (formerly Chungking) in Sichuan prov., China. A former treaty port, opened to foreign trade in 1891, it stands at the confluence of the Chang Jiang and the Jialing Jiang. For more than 4,000 years it has been an important commercial and route centre in one of the most remote and economically backward regions of China, and it remains a focal point of road, river and rail transport. Industries incl. iron and steel, chemicals, synthetic rubber, textiles, etc., and there is a university. When both Peking and Nanjing were in Japanese hands, it was the cap. of China 1938-46. Pop. (1980) 4,000,000.

CHOPIN (shopań′), **Frédéric François** (1810-49). Polish composer. B. near Warsaw, the son of a French father and a Polish mother, he made his first public appearance as a pianist at the age of 9, and from 1831 made his home in Paris. Here he became well known in the fashionable salons, though he rarely performed in public. In 1836 Liszt introduced him to Mme Dudevant (George Sand, q.v.), with whom he had a liaison from 1839 which lasted for 7 years. At Majorca, George Sand nursed him - he was consumptive - and for a time he regained his health. He d. on 17 Oct. 1849 and was interred in Père Lachaise cemetery in Paris.

As a performer C. revolutionized the technique of pianoforte-playing. He excelled in the performance of his own works, and was at his best in the intimate atmosphere of a salon. As a composer, he made little attempt to handle the larger forms, but in his pieces for piano solo he is without a rival. These stand alone for their lyrical and poetic quality; in them Slavonic passion and melancholy are combined with French grace and refinement. Besides sonatas, his works incl. collections of waltzes, preludes, études, nocturnes, ballades, impromptus, fantasias, polonaises, and mazurkas.

CHORDATA (kordā′ta). The highest phylum of the animal kingdom, consisting of the Vertebrata, together with certain primitive forms lacking a true backbone, but agreeing in other characters, e.g. the sea squirts, lancelet, and Balanoglossus.

CHOPIN. A daguerrotype of the composer. *Photo: Mansell Collection.*

CHOU EN-LAI (chō-enlī) (1898-1976). Chinese statesman (Pinyin: Zhou Enlai). B. in S China, he studied Communist organization in Europe and became head of the political dept of Whampoa Military Academy. Purged by Chiang Kai-shek in 1927, he went 'underground', and then was Communist representative to the National Govt at Nanking and Chungking 1937-46. He became premier in 1949, and was also For. Min. 1949-58. Always a moderating influence, he restored orderly progress after the Great Leap Forward and the Cultural Revolution, and although opposed to Soviet 'revisionism' averted outright border confrontation by negotiation with Kosygin in Peking in 1969, and in 1972 modified Chinese hostility to USA by receiving Nixon.

CHOUGH (chuf). Genus of birds (*Pyrrhocorax*) belonging to the crow family (Corvidae). The common C. (*Pyrrhocorax pyrrhocorax*) is black with red feet and bill.

CHOW CHOW. Chinese breed of dog, popular in Britain as a pet. Its name is pidgin-English for 'food', and in China the C. is killed for human consumption. Its coat should be of one colour, and its chief peculiarity is its black tongue.

CHRÉTIEN DE TROYES (krehtē-ań′ de trwah). Medieval French poet, b. in Champagne, about the middle of the 12th cent. His epics include *Le Chevalier de la Charrette*; *Perceval,* written for Philip, count of Flanders; *Erec*; *Yvain,* and other Arthurian romances.

CHRIST. *See* JESUS CHRIST.

CHRISTCHURCH (krīst′-). English town in Dorset, adjoining Bournemouth at the junction of the Stour and the Avon, with a fine Norman and Early English priory church. Pop. (1972) 31,000.

CHRISTCHURCH. City of South Island, New Zealand, on the Avon, 11km (7m) from its mouth. Principal city of the Canterbury plains, it has an Anglican cathedral, designed by Sir Gilbert Scott, and an RC cathedral; and is the seat of the Univ. of Canterbury. Industries incl. fertilizers and chemicals, canning and meat-processing, rail workshops, and shoes. The Avon estuary is obstructed by a bar, and C. uses as its port a bay in the sheltered Lyttelton Harbour on the N. shore of the Banks Peninsula, which forms a denuded volcanic mass. Land has been reclaimed for service facilities, and rail and road tunnels (1867 and 1964 respectively) link C. with Lyttelton. Pop. (1975) 326,400.

CHRISTCHURCH. A striking example of modern architecture, the Ferrier Fountain and restaurant complex at Canterbury, Christchurch. *Photo: Courtesy of the High Commissioner for New Zealand.*

CHRISTENING. (kris'ning). The Christian ceremony of baptism of infants, including giving a name.

CHRISTIAN. A professor of the religion founded by Jesus Christ. In Acts xi, 26, it is stated that the first to be called Christians were the disciples in Antioch.

CHRISTIAN. Name of 8 kings of Denmark and Norway. CHRISTIAN I (1426–81) was the first of the dynasty; in 1450 he established the union of Denmark and Norway which lasted until 1814. Under CHRISTIAN III, who reigned 1535–59, the Reformation was introduced. CHRISTIAN IV reigned 1588–1648, sided with the Protestants in the Thirty Years War, and founded Christiania (now Oslo, capital of Norway).

CHRISTIAN VIII was king of Denmark 1839–48. CHRISTIAN IX (1818–1906) was king of Denmark from 1863. His daughter Alexandra m. Edward VII of the UK and another m. Tsar Alexander III; his second son, George, became king of Greece. In 1864 he lost Schleswig-Holstein following a war with Austria and Prussia.

CHRISTIAN X (1870–1947) succeeded his father Frederick VIII as king of Denmark and Iceland in 1912. He m. Alexandrine, Duchess of Mecklenburg-Schwerin; and because of his democratic ways was highly popular. During the S.W.W. he was a semi-prisoner of the Germans in Copenhagen.

CHRISTIANIA. *See* OSLO.

CHRISTIANITY. One of the great world religions; regarded as having been founded by Jesus of Nazareth in the first third of the first Christian century. Like Buddhism and Islam it is a universal religion, claiming to be the true religion which ought to be believed by all men. It has, therefore, always been a missionary religion, and in the late 20th cent. is expanding most rapidly in Africa and S America.

C. includes a vast number of sects which represent different versions of the faith. The 3 main sections are: the Roman Catholic Church; the Eastern Orthodox Church; and the Evangelical communions which have since the Réformation repudiated the authority of the Pope. The schism between Eastern and Western churches was finally effected in 1054. The Reformation in the 16th cent. gave rise to 2 large groups of reformed churches - those which followed Luther and those which regarded Calvin as their teacher. The Protestant movement has since given birth to a very large number of smaller sects, but in the 20th cent., beginning with the Edinburgh Conference (1910) there has been a current towards reunion among the Protestant sects and to some extent from 1949 with the RC Church - the Ecumenical Movement (Gk *oikoumenē* the whole inhabited world). The World Council of Churches (1948) incl. Anglican and other Protestant denominations, Orthodox and Old Catholics, and receives increasing co-operation from the RC Church. Its financial support for liberation movements with terrorist associations has been controversial. The HQ are in Geneva. *See* CHURCH HISTORY.

C. is grounded on the Bible, the NT in particular; in addition most Christians profess belief in the statements of the 3 creeds - the Apostles', the Nicene, and the Athanasian. Belief in God the Father, Who is all-good, all-wise and all-powerful, is the fundamental concept, combined with the doctrine of the Trinity, i.e. of the union of the three Persons of the Father, Son, and Holy Ghost in one Godhead. Only the comparatively few Unitarians reject the dogma of the divinity of Christ. Most Christians profess belief in the Incarnation and the Resurrection of Christ, although there are many Modernists of whom this can hardly be said. The universal belief of Christians is that Christ is the Redeemer, but there is no universal agreement as to the nature of the Atonement. Belief in a historical Fall in the Garden of Eden has declined since the propagation of the theory of Evolution in the last century.

There are about 1,024 million Christians, of whom 585 million are returned as Roman Catholics. Rather more than 320 million are Protestants, and the rest are Eastern Orthodox, Copts, etc.

In the 1970s there was a revival of interest in C. among young people which was divorced from the estab. churches, e.g. the rock operas *Godspell* and *Jesus Christ Superstar*; the Jesus Freaks; and the Children of God, originating in the USA (HQ Los Angeles). *See also* LIBERATION THEOLOGY and PENTECOSTAL MOVEMENT.

CHRISTIAN SCIENCE. The religion, or interpretation of the Christian religion, discovered and founded by Mary Baker Eddy (q.v.). It is regarded by Christian Scientists themselves as the restatement of primitive Christianity with its full gospel of salvation from all evil, including sickness and disease as well as sin. Christian Scientists believe that since God is good and is Spirit, matter and evil are not truly real; and the application of this belief constitutes C.S. practice. According to its adherents, C.S. healing is brought about by the operation of Truth in human conscience and not by mental suggestion, psycho-therapy, etc. In those who are properly attuned to the Divine Spirit there can be no place for evil, sin, and disease.

CHRISTIANITY. The new approach to Christian doctrine in the 1970s symbolised in the popular appeal of the rock musical Jesus Christ Superstar. Here Jesus preaches. *Photo: Donald Cooper.*

There is no ordained priesthood, but there are public practitioners of C.S. healing who are officially authorized and listed by the Church of Christ, Scientist, that was estab. by Mrs Eddy in 1879. The Mother Church - the First Church of Christ, Scientist - is situated in Boston, Mass., USA, and it has branches in most parts of the world. The textbook of C.S. is Mrs. Eddy's *Science and Health with Key to the Scriptures,* first pub. in 1875. Among the Christian Science publications is the *C.S. Monitor,* an international daily newspaper.

CHRISTIANS OF ST THOMAS. Sect of Indian Christians on the Malabar coast; named after the apostle who is supposed to have carried his mission to India, although they were estab in the 5th cent. by Nestorians from Persia. They now form part of the Syrian Church with their own patriarch.

CHRISTIE, Dame Agatha (1890-1976). British novelist, *née* Miller. B. in Torquay, her first ambition was to be a concert singer, but in 1914 she m. Col Archibald Christie and served during the war as a nurse. Skilfully constructed and with strong characterization, her crime novels began with *The Mysterious Affair at Styles* (1920), introducing Hercule Poirot, the Belgian detective, and she subsequently created one of the few convincing woman detectives in the elderly spinster Miss Marple. She often broke 'purist' rules, as in *The Murder of Roger Ackroyd* (1926) in which the narrator is the murderer, and in *Ten Little Niggers* (1939), in which all the suspects are killed. Her plays incl. *The Mousetrap* (1952, and still running at her death), and a number of her books were filmed, e.g. *Murder on the Orient Express* (1975). After her divorce in 1928, she m. in 1930 Sir Max Mallowan (1904-78), the archaeologist, and a number of her books, e.g. *Death on the Nile* (1937), have an archaeological setting. She was created DBE in 1971.

CHRISTIE'S. Popular name for the firm of Christie, Manson, and Woods, Ltd, the principal art dealers in London, estab. 1766.

CHRISTINA (kris'tēna) (1626-89). Queen of Sweden. She succeeded her father Gustavus Adolphus in 1632, and until she was 18 the country was ruled by the great chancellor Oxenstjerna. In 1644 she assumed the royal power, and proved in many ways a wise and enlightened ruler. But she was extravagant and capricious, and refused

CHRISTIE. Among the detective novelists who formed the 'classical' school of the twenties and thirties, the name of Agatha Christie remains pre-eminent. *Photo: Angus McBean.*

to marry and thus secure the succession, as her ministers repeatedly advised her to do. At length she nominated her cousin Charles Gustavus as her successor, and then embarked upon a career of dissipation. In 1654 she abdicated and removed to Innsbruck, where she was received into the RC Church, and then maintained a court in Rome. Twice she returned to Sweden with a view to recovering the throne, but d. in Rome as a pensioner of the Pope.

CHRISTMAS. The mass of Christ; the day on which the birth of Christ is commemorated, constituting a feast of the Christian Church. The actual day of the Nativity has never been decided, and as late as the 5th cent. AD the feast was variously held on 25 Dec., 6 Jan., and 25 March; 25 Dec. the winter solstice was a highly significant date in pagan mythology - the Mithraists, for instance, kept it as the birthday of the 'Unconquered Sun' - and its increasing acceptance in the Western Church from the 4th cent. onwards owed much to the desire to facilitate the conversion of the pagans to Christianity. In Britain, 25 Dec. has been kept as a festival since long before the introduction of Christianity.

In the RC Church, the Church of England, and most of the Protestant denominations, Christmas Day is celebrated with religious services; and in most Christian countries it is kept as a public holiday. Many of the popular usages have a heathen origin. The yule log was taken from the pagan Norse festival. The holly, ivy, and mistletoe used to decorate churches and homes are symbols of fertility with their winter berries. Fir trees used to adorn the Roman Saturnalia, but the spread of their use as

Christmas trees is said to date from their introduction to England from Germany by Prince Albert. Christmas puddings and cakes date from the Middle Ages. Carols were originally secular songs, until the Franciscans succeeded in giving them a religious application. Santa Claus is a corruption of San Nicolaas, patron saint of children, whose feast is properly 6 Dec. The first Christmas card was designed in 1843, by J. C. Horsley, RA; the custom of sending them was estab. by 1870 in England, and spread to the USA a few years later.

CHRISTMAS. (i) Island in the Indian Ocean, 360km (250m) S of Java. Uninhabited when discovered on Christmas Day 1643 by Capt. Wm. Mynors, it was annexed by Britain in 1888; there are phosphate deposits. Japan occupied C. island 1942-5; it was transferred to Australia 1958. Area 135 sqkm (52 sq.m); pop. (1971) 3,000. (ii) HQ of the Line Islands, lying about 2°N, 157°W, area 360 sq.km (140 sq.m); pop. (1970) 370. Discovered on Christmas Eve 1777, by Capt. Cook, and annexed by Britain in 1888, it is the largest coral atoll in the Pacific. Copra is exported. Hydrogen bomb experiments were carried out here in 1957.

CHRISTOFF, Boris (1919-). Bulgarian bass singer. B. nr Sofia, he gained a scholarship to study singing in Rome, and in 1946 made his début in opera. His roles incl. Boris Godunov, Ivan the Terrible and Mephistopheles.

CHRISTOPHE (krēstof'), **Henri** (1767-1820). Negro slave in the West Indies who was one of the leaders of the revolt against the French in 1790, and in 1812 was crowned king of Haiti. In spite of his capable rule he alienated support by his cruelty; when he was deserted by his troops he shot himself.

CHRISTOPHER. Patron saint of ferrymen and travellers. Traditionally he was a Christian martyr in Syria in the 3rd cent., and the best-known legend concerning him describes his carrying the Christ child over the stream; despite his great strength he found the burden increasingly heavy, whereupon he was told that this was no wonder as Christ was bearing the sins of all the world. *See* CANONIZATION.

CHRIST'S HOSPITAL. English public school for boys, generally known as the Blue Coat school from the blue gown which forms part of the boys' dress. Founded in 1552, it was removed from Newgate Street, London, to Horsham, Sussex, in 1902. At Hertford there is a girls' school on the same foundation. Coleridge and Lamb (qq.v.) were C.H. boys.

CHRŌMATO'GRAPHY. A method of analysing substances by spatial separation. It may be carried out either: (1) by passing solutions of different substances up a column of an absorbent when they will be separated according to their affinity for the absorbent; or (2) by putting drops of a mixture of components in solution on filter paper when the different components will be separated by differential diffusion through the paper (paper C.); or (3) by evaporating the liquid to be analyzed into an inert gas which is allowed to flow into a partition column containing a substance, such as a high-boiling-point liquid, in which the materials of the sample have different partition coefficients, and are separated because they travel at different speeds (gas C.). These methods are extremely sensitive and enable very small quantities of substances to be detected and analyzed.

CHROMIUM. Chemical element, symbol Cr, at. no. 24. at. wt. 52.01. A bluish-white metal capable of taking a high polish, and with a high melting-point, it is much used decoratively and (alloyed with nickel) for electrical heating wires. Resistant to abrasion and corrosion, it is used to harden steel, and is a constituent of stainless steel and many useful alloys. It is used extensively in C. plating and as a catalyst. Its most important compounds are sodium and potassium chromates and dichromates (for tanning leather) and potassium and ammonium chrome alums. It occurs chiefly as chrome iron ore: USSR, Zimbabwe and Brazil are important sources.

CHROMOSOMES. *See* GENETICS.

CHROMOSPHERE (krō'mosfēr). The upper portion of the Sun's atmosphere, consisting mainly of hydrogen and ionized calcium. It may be observed through the spectroscope and visually when the Sun is totally eclipsed.

CHRONOMETER. An instrument for measuring equal intervals of time with the greatest accuracy, espec. one used for determining position in navigation.

CHRYSANTHEMUM (krisan'thēmum). Genus of plants of the family Compositae, containing nearly 300 species, most of which have been developed by cultivation. The Chinese and Japanese varieties are derived by hybridization from *C. indicum* and *C. morifolium.* In the Far East the common C. has been cultivated for more than 2,000 years, and it is the national emblem of Japan. The first C. was introduced into England in 1789, but *C. leucanthemum* and *C. segetum,* the ox-ėye daisy and the corn marigold respectively, are common weeds in Britain. Cs. may be grown from seed, but are more usually reproduced by cutting or division.

CHRYSOLITE. *See* OLIVINE.

CHUB. A freshwater fish (*Leuciscus cephalus*) belonging to the carp family (Cyprinidae). It has a plump, thick body and heavy head, and is dark bluish or greenish on the back, with silvery sides.

CHUBB CRATER. Crater discovered in 1950 by a prospector, F. W. Chubb, in northern Quebec, 96km (60m) from Hudson Strait, Canada. Made by a meteor, in prehistoric times, it is 411m (1,350 ft) deep with a rim of 168m (550ft) above the local land level. In the centre is a lake 224m (800ft) deep.

CHUKCHI (chook'chi) **SEA.** Part of the Arctic Ocean to the N of Bering Strait between Asia and N America. The Chukchi people are semi-nomadic hunters of NE Siberia, who are fiercely independent: Soviet rule was only fully estab. in the 1930s.

CHUKO'VSKY, Kornei Ivanovitch (1882-1969). Russian critic and poet. The leading authority on Nekrasov, he was also an expert on the Russian language, e.g. *Zhivoi kak zhizn* (1963: *Alife as Life*), and beloved as 'Grandpa' K.C. for his nonsense poems which owe much to the English nursery rhymes and nonsense verse he admired.

CHUNGKING. *See* CHONGQING.

CHURCH. Frederick Edwin (1826-1900). American landscape artist of the Hudson River School. Noted for its effects of light and colour, his work was rediscovered after the S.W.W. 'Icebergs' was found in a boys' remand home in Manchester, England, in 1979, after being lost for a hundred years.

CHURCH ARMY. Religious organization within the Church of England founded in 1882 by Wilson Carlile (1847-1942), a business man converted after the failure of his textile-firm, who took orders in 1880. Originally intended for evangelical and social work in the Westminster slums, it developed along Salvation Army lines, and has done much work among ex-prisoners and for the soldiers of both world wars.

CHURCH HISTORY. The Christian C. is traditionally said to have originated on the first Whitsun Day, but was only finally separated from the parent Jewish C. by the declaration of SS Barnabas and Paul that the distinctive rites of Judaism were not necessary for entry into the Christian C.

For the first 2 cents. the C. was not much more than a spasmodically persecuted minority, but in the 3rd cent. more determined efforts to extirpate it were made under Severus, Decius, and Diocletian. Toleration was obtained by the victory of Constantine at Milvian Bridge (312), and Christianity became the estab. religion of the Roman Empire. Security and increasing wealth brought some deterioration, and the outbreak of heresies such as Montanism and Gnosticism, to which the C. opposed a developed creed, a canon of estab. scriptures, and her threefold ministry with its succession from the Apostles. Questions of discipline also threatened disruption within the C.; and to settle these Constantine called the Council of Arles (314), which was followed by the Councils of Nicaea (325), Constantinople (381), Ephesus (431), and Chalcedon (451). A settled doctrine of Christian belief evolved, but failed to prevent the schism of the churches of the East.

During the Dark Ages the Church, esp. as represented by the Celtic and Benedictine monks, preserved the best features of the Graeco-Roman civilization and taught the northern barbarians, e.g. SS Colomba and Augustine in England. The C fostered agriculture and education, and assisted the growth of the feudal system of which it formed the apex, as recognized by Charlemagne (800) in seeking coronation by the Pope.

The Middle Ages, despite an underlying unity symbolized by the theology of St Thomas Aquinas, saw much controversy between secular and spiritual jurisdiction, e.g. Emperor Henry IV and Pope Gregory VII, Henry II of England and Becket. Moreover, increasing worldliness (against which the foundation of the Dominicans and Franciscans was a protest) and other ecclesiastical abuses, led to dissatisfaction in the 14th cent. and the appearance of the reformers Wycliffe and Huss.

In N Europe the Renaissance brought a re-examination of Christian truth by More, Colet, and Erasmus; and with the advent of Luther, Calvin, and Zwingli came the Reformation, an attempt to return to primitive Christianity. In England Henry VIII and Elizabeth found a middle way between Romanism and Puritanism in the C. of England. During the 18th cent. Christianity was brought to the test of reason; the Scriptures were then examined on the same basis as secular literature, and the shock to orthodox belief was confirmed by the evolutionary theories of the 19th cent.

Meanwhile in England the Church of England suffered the loss of large numbers of Nonconformists, who estab. the denominations known today as the Free churches. In the 18th cent. arose the Methodist movement, and in the 19th cent. the Oxford movement led by Newman, Keble and Pusey, which eventually developed into present-day Anglo-Catholicism. Of the Presbyterian churches founded in the Reformation period the most important is the Church of Scotland. *See* CHRISTIANITY.

CHURCHILL, Charles (1731-64). British satiric poet. Once a clergyman in the C of E, he wrote coarse and highly personal satires dealing to a large extent with political issues.

CHURCHILL, Lord Randolph Henry Spencer (1849-95). British Cons. statesman. B. at Blenheim, son of the 7th duke of Marlborough, he entered parliament in 1874 as a Cons. MP. After 1880 he formed the '4th party' with Drummond Wolff, Gorst, and Arthur Balfour, and in 1885 his policy of Tory democracy was widely accepted by the party. In 1886 he became Chancellor of the Exchequer, but resigned within 6 months because he did not agree with the demands made on the Treasury by the War Office and the Admiralty. He was a founder and the first member of the Primrose League, and was prominent on the Turf. He m. in 1874 Jenny Jerome, dau. of a wealthy New Yorker, and had 2 sons, the elder of whom was Winston C.

CHURCHILL, Winston (1871-1947). American novelist. B. at St Louis, he wrote successful novels incl. *Richard Carvel* (1899), *Coniston* (1906), and *The Uncharted Way* (1941).

CHURCHILL. A striking VE day portrait taken in his study in 1945. *Photo: Popperfoto.*

CHURCHILL, Sir Winston Leonard Spencer (1874-1965). British statesman. A descendent of the great duke of Marlborough, he was b. at Blenheim Palace on 30 Nov. 1874, being the elder son of Lord Randolph C. (q.v.) and his wife, Jenny Jerome. Ed. at Harrow, he was commissioned in the 4th Hussars in 1895 and saw active service in a series of minor campaigns. During the Boer

War he was the *Morning Post's* war correspondent and made a dramatic escape from imprisonment in Pretoria. In 1900 he was elected Cons. MP for Oldham, but he disagreed with Chamberlain's tariff reform policy, and joined the Liberals. In 1908 Asquith made him Pres. of the Board of Trade, in which capacity he introduced legislation for the establishment of Labour Exchanges. In 1910 he became Home Sec. and was present at the notorious incident in the East End of London known as the siege of Sydney Street, when he authorized the use of troops against some armed gangsters. Then in 1911 Asquith appointed him First Lord of the Admiralty with the instruction to put the fleet into a state of instant readiness for war. C. ordered naval mobilization on the eve of war without waiting for Cabinet authority, and early in the war sent the Naval Brigade to Antwerp. He was then involved in acute controversy over the Dardanelles operation which he sponsored, and when the first Coalition govt was formed in 1915 he was excluded. Until the autumn of 1916 he served in the trenches in France as lieut.-col. of the 6th Royal Scots Fusiliers, but then resumed his parliamentary duties and was Min. of Munitions under Lloyd George in 1917, when he had much to do with the development of the tank. After the Armistice he was Sec. for War, 1918-21, and then as Colonial Sec. played a leading part in the establishment of the Irish Free State. During these post-war years he was active in support of the anti-Bolshevik (white) generals in Russia.

From 1922-4 C. was out of parliament, left the Liberals in 1923, and in 1924 was returned for Epping as a Constitutionalist. Baldwin made him Chancellor of the Exchequer, and he brought about Britain's return to the Gold Standard and was prominent in the defeat of the General Strike of 1926. In 1929-39 he was out of office as he disagreed with the Conservatives on India, re-armament, and Chamberlain's policy of appeasement.

On the first day of the S.W.W. he went back to his old post at the Admiralty, and there he remained until 10 May 1940, when he was called to the Premiership as head of an all-party admin. On 13 May he presented himself to the House of Commons with the historic 'blood and tears, toil and sweat' speech. One of the decisive decisions of the war was his broadcast announcement of the evening of 22 June 1941, that Britain allied herself with the Soviet Union. He effected the closest personal contact with President Roosevelt, and in Aug. 1941 concluded with him the Atlantic Charter. On 20 Dec. 1941 he addressed a joint session of the American Congress. He travelled to Washington, Casablanca, Cairo, Moscow, and Teheran, meeting the other great leaders of the Allied war effort; and at Christmas 1944 he made a dramatic flight to Athens to avert civil war in Greece. In Feb. 1945 he met Stalin and Roosevelt in the Crimea, and agreed on the final plans for victory. On 8 May he announced the unconditional surrender of Germany.

Then on 23 May the Coalition was dissolved, and C. formed a 'caretaker' govt drawn mainly from the Cons. Defeated in the gen. election in July, he resigned office to become Leader of the Opposition until the gen. election of Oct. 1951 brought his return to power as PM. He received the OM in 1946, and was created KG in 1953. On 5 April 1955 he resigned.

Also a great writer, C. won the Nobel prize for literature in 1953. His first books were accounts of the campaigns in which he had participated. His life of his father was pub. in 1906, and his *World Crisis,* (4 vols., 1923-9) is a history of the F.W.W. In 1933-8 appeared his life of the Great Duke of Marlborough later followed by vols. of speeches, and Memoirs of the S.W.W. He was also a capable artist. He was buried at Bladon, nr Blenheim Palace, and his home from 1922, Chartwell in Kent, was opened as a museum.

C. m. in 1908 Clementine Hozier (1885-1977), created GBE in 1946 and in 1965 a life peeress as Lady Spencer-Churchill. Their children are: Diana (1909-63), who m. Duncan-Sandys (q.v.) in 1935 (m. diss. 1960); Randolph (1911-68), Cons. MP 1940-5, well known as a journalist and author of studies of Eden (1959) and Derby (1960); Sarah (1914-82), an actress, who m. Vic Oliver the musician and comedian in 1936 (m. diss. 1945), then Anthony Beauchamp, photographer, in 1949 (d. 1957) and in 1962 Lord Audley (d. 1963); and Mary (1922-) who m. in 1947 Christopher Soames (q.v.).

CHURCHILL. Sir Winston Churchill's home at Chartwell in Kent, now preserved for the nation. *Photo: Courtesy of the British Tourist Authority*

CHURCH OF ENGLAND. *See* ANGLICAN COMMUNION.
CHURCH OF SCOTLAND. *See* SCOTLAND, CH. OF.
CHU TEH (1886-1976). Chinese marshal (Pinyin: Zhu De). Son of a wealthy landlord, he studied Communism in Germany 1922-5, and led the Chinese Red Army with Mao Tse-tung on the legendary long march to Shaanxi 1934-5, in the Japanese War and the civil war of 1946-9. From 1975, as chairman of the Standing Committee of the National People's Congress, he functioned as 'head of state'.
CHUVASH (choovahsh'). An Autonomous Soviet Socialist Republic of the RSFSR. It lies W of the Volga, 560km (350m) E of Moscow. The cap. is Cheboksary, pop. (1977) 292,000. Lumbering and grain-growing are important and there are phosphate and limestone deposits, and electrical and engineering industries. Area 18,300 sq.km (7,100 sq.m); pop. (1978) 1,288,000.
CIANO (chēah'noh), **Galeazzo** (1903-44). Italian Fascist politician. Son-in-law of Mussolini, he was For. Min. 1936-43, when his loyalty became suspect. He voted against Mussolini at the meeting of the Grand Council on

25 July which overthrew the dictator, and was tried for treason and shot by the Fascists.

CICADA (sikā'da). A family of insects (Cicadidae) of the sub-order Homoptera of the order Hemiptera, nearly allied to the frog-hoppers. The adult insects live on trees, whose juices they suck, and are remarkable for the chirping noise made by the males.

CICERO (sis-), **Marcus Tullius** (106–43 BC). Roman orator, writer, and statesman. B. at Arpinum, he became an advocate in Rome, spent 3 years in Greece studying oratory, and after Sulla's death distinguished himself in Rome on the side of the popular party. In 63 BC he was appointed consul; later in the year he saved the Republic when it was threatened by Catiline's conspiracy. When the 1st Triumvirate of Caesar, Crassus, and Pompey was formed in 59, C. was exiled, and devoted himself to literature. On the outbreak of the Civil War in 49 he followed Pompey to Greece, but in 48 returned to Italy where he was well treated by Caesar. After the latter's assassination in 44 BC he took the lead in the Senate in an attempt to restore the republican form of govt, and in 14 great speeches he supported Octavian (the future Augustus) and denounced Mark Antony. These speeches are known as the Philippics after the denunciations of King Philip of Macedon by Demosthenes in the 4th cent. BC. In the autumn of 43, however, Antony and Octavian came to terms and C. was killed while trying to escape to the East.

As a statesman, C. attempted unsuccessfully to carry out a moderate policy. His influence on the future of literature was immense. His speeches were soon recorded as models of Latin prose, and his philosophical essays are full of common sense and practical sympathies. His letters are of interest.

CICERO. His informal letters, with their references to his wives - both of whom he divorced - and to his beloved daughter, Tullia, who died while still a young woman, make him a very real person for us. *Photo: Mansell Collection.*

CID (Span., thēdh), **Rodrigo Diaz de Bivar** (*c.* 1040–99). Spanish national hero, was b. in Castile of a noble family, fought against the king at Navarre, and won his nickname *el Campeador* (the Champion) by killing the Navarrese champion in single combat. Eventually he became a soldier of fortune, and d. while defending Valencia against the Moors. 'The Cid' (the Lord) was a name given to him by the Moors, and he soon became a hero of romance.

CIDER (sīder). A fermented drink made from the juice of the apple. As a beverage it has been known for more than 2,000 years, and for many centuries it has been a popular drink in France and England, which are now its main centres of production. The French output is by far the greater, Normandy and Brittany being chiefly concerned. In a good year *c.* 30 million gallons are produced in Britain. The West of England from Hereford to Devon has long been famous for its C. Most of the apple crop is sold to factories estab. in the region and also in Kent and Norfolk. In the USA the term usually refers to unfermented apple juice.

CIERVA (thē-ervah), **Juan de la** (1895–1936). Spanish engineer. In trying to produce an aircraft which would not stall and could fly slowly, he invented the autogyro, the forerunner of the helicopter, but differing from it in having unpowered rotors which revolved freely.

CIGAR (sigahr'). Originally a sheath of palm leaves filled with tobacco, smoked by the Indians of Central and N America. The modern C. is a compact roll of tobacco leaves. C.-smoking was introduced into Spain soon after the discovery of America, and then spread all over Europe. The first C. factory was opened in Hamburg in 1788, and about that time the taste for C.-smoking became well marked in England. The first Cs. were made by hand - as still are the more expensive Cs., incl. most of those made in Cuba - but in USA from about the 1850s various machine methods were employed. From about 1890 C.-smoking was gradually supplanted in popularity in England by cigarette-smoking. The 'little cigar' has been in some demand of recent years.

CIGARETTE. Literally, a little cigar. The first Cs. were the *papelitos* smoked in S America about 1750. The habit spread to Spain, and then throughout the world, and is today the most general form of tobacco-smoking. In some countries, through the tax on tobacco, smokers contribute a large part of the national revenue. Following the estab. of a direct link between C. smoking and lung cancer in the 1960s, there was concentration by manufacturers on filtering harmful substances. Production of Cs. using a cellulose tobacco substitute 1977–80 failed ignominiously.

CIGARETTE CARDS. Cards incl. in packets of cigarettes, and bearing printed views, drawings, portraits, etc. They originated in the USA in the 1870s.

CIMABUE (chēmahboo'-eh), **Giovanni** (1240–*c.* 1302). Italian painter; the master of Giotto, and styled the 'father of Italian painting'. Among the best-known works attributed to him are a 'Madonna and Child' in the Uffizi, Florence, and other paintings of the same subject in the Louvre, Paris, and the National Gallery, London. C. was one of the first artists to paint from a living model.

CIMAROSA (chēmahroh'zah), **Domenico** (1749–1801). Italian composer of operas extremely popular in their day, of which the best is *Il Matrimonio Segreto* (1792: The Secret Marriage).

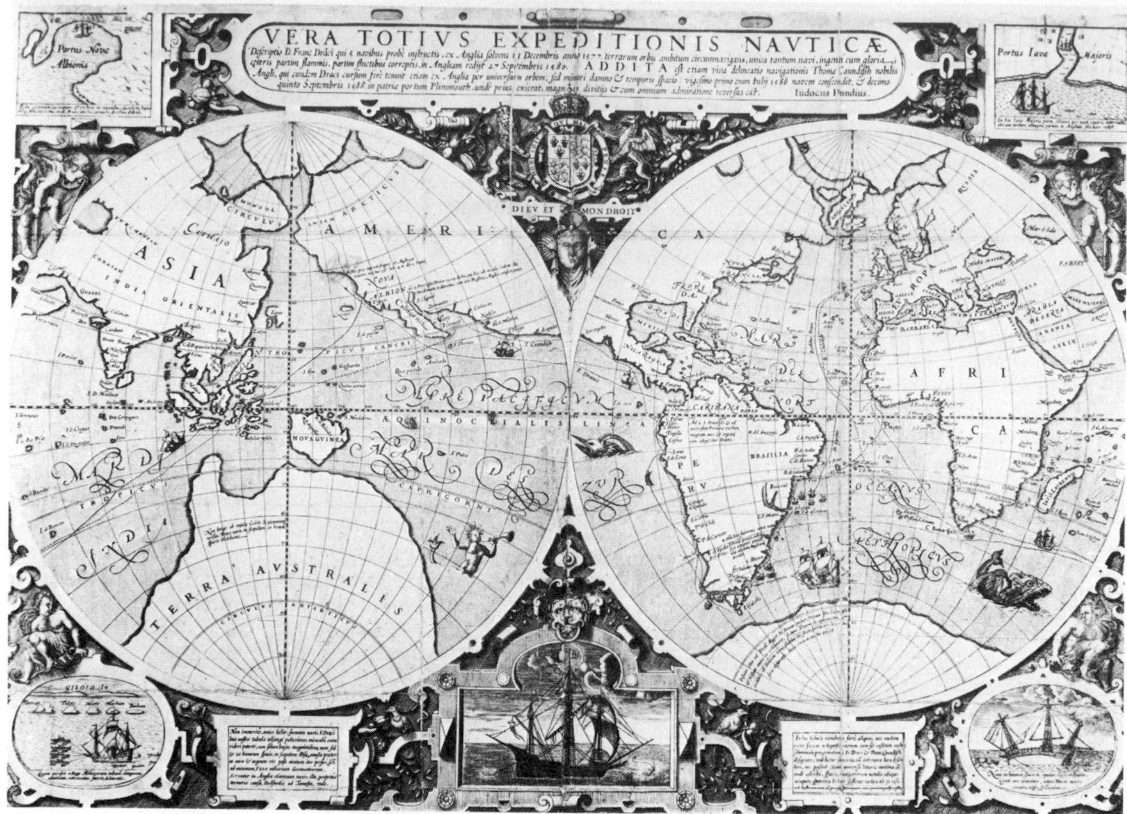

CIRCUMNAVIGATION. The route of Drake's voyage round the world in 1577–80, and that of Thomas Cavendish in 1586–8, in maps prepared by Jodocus Hondius c.1590. *Photo: The Mansell Collection.*

CINCHONA (sinkō'na). Genus of shrubs and trees belonging to the family Rubiaceae and growing wild in the Amazonian forests. From the bark of some species is produced quinine (q.v.), and C. culture has been introduced into India, Sri Lanka, the Philippines, and Indonesia, with marked success.

CINCINNATI (sinsina'ti). American city in Ohio on the Ohio r. Founded in 1788, it became a city in 1819, and during the middle years of the 19th cent. grew rapidly as it attracted large numbers of European immigrants, particularly Germans. It has one of the finest railway stations in the USA and is well served by air. The symphony orchestra of the municipal univ. (oldest mun. univ. in the USA) is famous; there is also a RC univ. Among the chief industries are machine-tool, clothing, and furniture making, and meat-packing. Pop. met. area (1972) 1,412,000.

CINCINNATUS, Lucius Quinctius. Early Roman general, famous for his frugal simplicity. Appointed dictator in 458 BC he defeated the Aequi in a brief campaign, then resumed life as a yeoman farmer.

CINNABAR (sin'abar). Mercuric sulphide, HgS, the only important ore of mercury. It is found in Spain (Almaden), USA (California), Peru, Yugoslavia, etc. The mineral itself is used as a pigment, commonly known as vermilion.

CINNAMON (si'namon). Bark of a tree (*Cinnamomum zeylanicum*) which is a member of the family Lauraceae and is grown in Sri Lanka, Java, Brazil, W Indies, etc. Oil of C. is obtained from the inner bark, and is used as a flavouring and in medicine.

CINQUEFOIL (singk'foil). Genus of plants (*Potentilla*) belonging to the rose family (Rosaceae). The typical species *(P. reptans)*, is a creeping perennial, widely distributed throughout the British Isles, growing in pastures and meadows and on banks.

CINQUE (sink) **PORTS** (Fr. *cinq*, five). An association of ports in S England, originally Sandwich, Dover, Hythe, Romney, and Hastings, to which were added later Rye and Winchelsea, and a number of other places. Founded probably in Roman times, they rose to importance after the Norman conquest, and until the end of the 15th cent. were bound to supply the ships and men necessary against invasion. The office of Lord Warden survives as an honorary distinction (Churchill 1941-65, Menzies 1965-78, the Queen Mother from 1979). The official residence is Walmer Castle.

CIRCADIAN (serkăd'ian) **RHYTHM.** The human metabolic rhythm which in most people coincides with the twenty-four hour day, but which may be slightly longer or shorter, so that it gradually shifts out of phase, and the person concerned feels out of sorts. *See* BIORHYTHMS, CLOCK, JETLAG.

CIRCASSIA (serkas'ia). Former name of an area of the N Caucasus, now part of the RSFSR. The Circassians or Cherkesses differ from other tribes of the area in origin and their women were formerly highly prized by Turkish merchants for the harems of the East.

CIRCUITS. In England and Wales the periodic travels by High Court and Circuit Judges to try civil and criminal cases at centres (graded as 1st, 2nd or 3rd-tier) on 6 circuits (Midland and Oxford, N Eastern, Northern, S Eastern, Wales and Chester, and Western). In the USA the Court of Appeals sits in 10 judicial circuits - hence circuit courts - and Washington DC.

CIRCUMCISION. Surgical operation, practised from early times and usually accompanied by ritual, consisting of the removal of a small part of the foreskin. Performed for sanitary reasons in infancy, it is sometimes necessitated on medical grounds. All Jewish and Moslem boys must be circumcised as a religious rite, and the custom prevails among Arabs, Australian aboriginals, Kaffirs, and Papuans.

CIRCUMCISION, Feast of. Anglican and RC religious festival, celebrated annually on 1 Jan. in commemoration of Christ's circumcision.

CIRCU'MFERENCE. In geometry, the curved line that encloses a plane figure, e.g. a circle, an ellipse. Its length varies according to the nature of the curve, and may be ascertained by the appropriate formula. Thus the C. of a circle is $2\pi r$, where r is the radius and $\pi = 3.1415927\ldots$ or roughly $^{22}/_{7}$.

CIRCUMNAVIGATION. The first ship to sail round the world was the *Victoria*, one of the Spanish squadron of 5 vessels that sailed from Seville in Aug. 1519 under F. de Magellan (q.v.). Four vessels were lost on the way, but the *Victoria* arrived back in Spain in Sept. 1522. Magellan himself did not complete the voyage, as he d. in the Philippines in 1521 (*see* CANO). The first English circumnavigator was Drake in 1577–80.

CIRENCESTER (sis'iter). Market town in Gloucestershire, 24km (15m) SE of Gloucester, with engineering industries. Pop. (1972) 14,500.

CISALPINE (sis-) **GAUL.** The southern region of the Roman prov. of Gallia, i.e. N Italy; the northern, Transalpine Gaul, comprised modern Belgium, France, Netherlands and Switzerland. The **Cisalpine Republic** was the creation of Napoleon in N Italy in 1797, and known as the Italian Rep. 1802–4 and the Kingdom of Italy 1804–15.

CISTERCIANS (sister'sh-). A monastic order of the RC Church, estab. at Cîteaux in 1098 by Robert de Champagne, abbot of Molesme. Its purpose was to restore in its full rigour the rule of St Benedict, and the Cs., living mainly by agricultural labour, were responsible for much of the advance in farming methods in the Middle Ages.

CITHARA (sith'ara), **cithern,** or **cittern.** Ancient musical instrument, resembling a lute but with a flat back. It was strung with wire and plucked with a plectrum or (after the 16th cent.) with the fingers. It is now obsolete, but the bandurria and laud, still popular in Spain, are instruments of the same type.

CITIZEN. A national of a state. In Britain citizenship, as defined in the Nationality Act of 1948, was outdated by subsequent changes in the Commonwealth. Under the British Nationality Bill (1981), only a British citizen has a right of abode in the UK, i.e. basically anyone born in the UK to a parent who is a British citizen, or who is lawfully settled in the UK. Other categories are: Citizen of British Dependent Territories, e.g. Hong Kong; and British Overseas Citizen, i.e. the remainder of existing 'citizens of the UK and Colonies'. No changes were proposed for Irish citizens. *See* ALIEN.

CITIZENS' BAND. Short-range radio communication (27 MHz AM) facility used by members of the public in USA and many Continental countries - espec. when on the road - to chat or call for assistance in emergency. Legalisation of a form of C.B. called Open Channel was legalised (27 MHz/930 MHz FM) in the UK in 1981.

CITRIC ACID. An organic acid widely distributed in the plant kingdom, especially in citrus fruits. It is a white crystalline powder with an acid taste. At one time it was prepared from concentrated lemon juice, but now the main source is the fermentation of sugar with certain moulds. It is widely used in effervescent saline drinks, calico-printing, etc. Its chemical formula is $C_6H_8O_7$.

CITRUS. Genus of trees and shrubs, belonging to the family Rutaceae, and found in the warmer parts of the world, particularly Asia. They are evergreen and aromatic, and several species (orange, lemon, lime, citron, grapefruit, etc.) are cultivated for fruit.

CITY. Generally speaking, a large and important town. In the ancient world Cs. were states in themselves. In the early Middle Ages, Cs. were usually those towns which were episcopal sees, and to this day the English cathedral towns are called Cs. In present-day Britain the term is chiefly of historical and ceremonial importance. In the USSR ten hero cities were created for their role in the S.W.W. incl. Minsk, Moscow and Volgograd (Stalingrad).

CITY, The. *See* LONDON.

CIUDAD BOLÍVAR (thē-oodadh' bohlē'vahr). City of Venezuela on the Orinoco, 400km (250m) from its mouth, and linked with Soledad across the river by the Angostura bridge (1967) - first to span the Orinoco. It was called Angostura 1824–49. Gold is mined in the vicinity. Pop. (1972) 110,000.

CIUDAD GUAYANA. City of Venezuela formed by the union of Puerto Ordaz and San Felix, an iron and steel centre. It is on the S bank of the Orinoco, at its junction with the Caroni, and has been opened to ocean-going ships by dredging. Pop. (1972) 150,000.

CIUDAD JUAREZ. City of Mexico, in the valley of the Rio Grande, close to the American border. Pop. (1973) 490,000.

CIUDAD REAL (re-ahl'). City of central Spain, capital of C.R. prov., 170km (105m) S of Madrid. Its chief feature is its huge Gothic cathedral. Pop. (1970) 38,000.

CIUDAD TRUJILLO. Trujillo City: name 1936–61 of Santo Domingo (q.v.).

CIVET (siv'et) or **civet cat** (*Viverra*). Mammals of the family Viverridae, related to the cats (Felidae), but distinguished principally by their longer head and jaws, numerous dog-like teeth, and by having a perfume gland in the inguinal region. There are many different kinds inhabiting tropical Asia and Africa. A few species are of commercial value on account of their perfume.

CIVIL AVIATION. Passenger and freight service organization, and aircraft development.

The International C.A. Organization (1947) has its HQ in Montreal, and is a UN agency. In the UK there are about 170 airports, those for London (Heathrow and Gatwick) and Prestwick and Edinburgh being managed by the British Airports Authority (1965), and the British Airways Board supervises British Airways, formerly British

CIVIL AVIATION. British Airways Concorde 206 (foreground) lands after its historic inaugural flight, London – Kennedy Airport, New York, on 22 Nov. 1977. Its supersonic cruising speed of 2,300 km/h (1,450 mph) cuts transatlantic flying time from seven to three hours. *Photo: Courtesy of British Aerospace.*

European Airways (BEA) and British Overseas Airways Corporation (BOAC); there are also independent companies.

Close co-operation is maintained with authorities in other countries, incl. the Federal Aviation Agency, which is responsible for development of aircraft, air navigation, traffic control and communications in the USA: the Civil Aeronautics Board is the American authority prescribing safety regulations and investigating accidents. There are no state airlines in the USA, although many of the private airlines are large. The world's largest airline is the govt-owned Aeroflot (USSR).

With increasing traffic, control of air space is a major problem, and in 1963 Eurocontrol was estab. by Belgium, Britain, France, W Germany, Luxembourg, and the Netherlands to supervise both military and civil movement in the air space over member countries. There is also a tendency to co-ordinate services and pool services and other facilities between national airlines, e.g. the estab. of Air Union by France (Air France), W. Germany (Lufthansa), Italy (Alitalia) and Belgium (Sabena) in 1963.

CIVIL DEFENCE. Organization of the civil population to mitigate the effects of enemy attack. In Britain the Min. of Home Security was constituted 1939 to direct Air Raid Precautions in the S.W.W., the country being divided into 12 regions, each under a commissioner to act on behalf of the central govt in the event of cut communications. Associated with the 'air-raid wardens' were ambulance and rescue parties, gas officers, breakdown gangs, etc., and a Nat. Fire Service, based on existing local services, and *c.* 5,000,000 citizens were enrolled as firewatchers and firefighters. The C.D. Corps and Auxiliary Fire Service were disbanded in 1968. In 1980 it was proposed to create a renamed structure of 'Home Defence' in which the voluntary services, local authorities and the Territorial Army would co-operate.

In the USA the Office of Civil Defense (1961) of the Dept of Defense has a Staff College and 3 warning centres. Public shelter from fall-out is available for 160,000,000 and special attention is given to incorporating shelter in all new constructions.

China has a remarkably comprehensive C.D. system, networks of tunnels in the cities enabling the population to escape 'fallout' and reach the countryside, although not protecting against actual blast.

CIVIL DISOBEDIENCE. Movement in India led by Gandhi (q.v.) and aimed at peaceful withdrawal of Brit. power.

CIVIL ENGINEERING. That department of engineering that is concerned with such works as construction of roads, bridges, aqueducts, water-works, tunnels, canals, irrigation works, harbours, etc. The professional organization in Britain is the Institution of Civil Engineers, which was founded in 1818 and is the oldest engineering institution in the world.

CIVIL LIST. The annual sum provided to meet the expenses of the British Sovereign; the consort of a Sovereign; children of a Sovereign (except the Prince of Wales, who is provided for from the revenues of the Duchy of Cornwall); and widows of those children. The basic amounts are charged on the Consolidated Fund, and until the reign of Elizabeth II, when inflation necessitated a more flexible procedure, were traditionally fixed at the beginning of each reign. Under the C.L. Act (1975) such sums were to be supplemented as needed by means of a grant in aid through the normal parliamentary supply estimate procedure. Payments to other individual members of the Royal Family have been covered since 1976 by a contribution from the Queen. Three-quarters of the C.L. is spent on wages for the Royal Household. *See also* PRIVY PURSE.

There is no equivalent of the C.L. in the USA. A President receives, by Act of Congress, a salary of $200,000 a year taxable plus $50,000 (also taxable) for defraying expenses connected with his official duties, and may spend up to $100,000 (not taxable) a year on travel and official entertaining expenses; ex-presidents receive a life pension of $60,000 plus free office space and post facilities, and up to $90,000 for office staff, and their widows a life pension of $20,000 a year. The Vice-Pres. has a salary of $75,000 and $10,000 expenses, all taxable.

CIVIL LIST PENSIONS. Pensions originally paid out of the sovereign's Civil List, but granted separately since the accession of Queen Victoria. They are paid to persons in need, who have just claims on the royal beneficence, who have rendered personal service to the Crown, or who have rendered service to the public by their discoveries in science and attainments in literature and art, etc. The recipients are nominated by the Prime Minister, and the List is approved by Parliament.

CIVIL SERVICE. The body of civilian staffs working in the different departments of state of a country. In England, civil servants were originally in the personal service of the sovereign. They were recruited by patronage, and many of them did little except nominal duties. The great increase in public expenditure during the Napoleonic Wars led to a move in Parliament for reform of the C.S., but it was not until 1854 that two civil servants, Charles Trevelyan and Stafford Northcote, issued a report as a result of which recruitment of competitive examination, carried out under the C.S. Commission (1855), came into force. Some appointments still went by patronage, but by *c.* 1900 competitive entry was the rule, even those recruited from time to time (e.g. during the world wars) on a temporary basis having to pass some form of examination.

The 2 main divisions of the British C.S. are the Home and Diplomatic services, the latter created 1965 by amalgamation of the Foreign, Commonwealth and Trade Commission Services. All are paid out of funds voted annually for the purpose by Parliament.

In 1981 the C.S. Dept created in 1968 was abolished and responsibilities for manpower and remuneration were transferred to the Treasury. The Prime Minister (as Min. for the Civil Service) remained responsible for the Management and Personnel Office (MPO). The present emphasis is on the professional specialist, and the C.S. College (Sunningdale Park, Ascot) was estab. in 1970 to develop training. Members of the British C.S. may not take an active part in politics, and do not change with the government. Their permanence gives those in the upper echelons an advantage over ministers who are a comparatively brief time in office, and in the 1970s and 1980s it was alleged that ministerial policies in conflict with C.S. views tended to be blocked from being put into practice.

In the USA, until 1883 all C.S. posts were given as rewards for political services, and changed hands with a change of the party in power; the Pendleton Act 1883, estab. competitive examinations and permanency for certain posts, and that system has been steadily extended. The govt agency concerned is the C.S. Commission.

CIVIL WAR. In English history, the name usually applied to the struggle in the middle years of the 17th cent. between the king and his Royalist supporters on the one hand, and the Parliamentarians (also called Roundheads) on the other. It falls into two parts. The first C.W. began on 22 Aug. 1642, when Charles I raised his standard at Nottingham, and was ended on 5 May 1646, when he surrendered to the Scottish army. The most important battles were Edgehill (23 Oct. 1642) which was indecisive, Marston Moor (2 July 1644) and Naseby (14 June 1645) both of which were great Parliamentary victories won largely by Cromwell. The second C.W. was the Royalist and Presbyterian rising of March to Aug. 1648, which was soon crushed by Cromwell and his New Model Army.

Extensions of the C.W. were Cromwell's invasion of Ireland, 1649-50, and the campaign in which he defeated the Royalists under Prince Charles (Charles II) at Dunbar, 1650, and Worcester, 1651.

For the American Civil War, *see* UNITED STATES OF AMERICA. *See also* SPAIN.

CIVITAVECCHIA (chē'vētah-vek'kē-ah). Ancient port on the W coast of Italy 64km (40m) NW of Rome. Pop. (1971) 42,300.

CLACKMA'NNANSHIRE. Former co. - the smallest - in Scotland, bordering the Firth of Forth, which was in 1975 merged in Central Region. The co. town was Alloa.

CLACTON-ON-SEA. Seaside resort, Essex, England, 19km (12m) SE of Colchester. The 16th cent. St Osyth's priory (16th cent.) is nearby. Pop. (1972) 38,500.

CLADI'STICS. Method of determining patterns of relationships used in biological classification, from Gk. 'branch'.

CLAIR (klār), **René.** Pseudonym of the French film producer René-Lucien Chomette (1898-1981). Originally a poet, novelist, and journalist, he produced the first sound film of artistic value *Sous les Toits de Paris* (1930).

CLAM. Various bivalve molluscs of the class Lamellibranchia, valuable as food. In England it usually refers to the gaper, *Mya truncata*, but in Scotland to the scallop. The hard C. *Venus mercenaria* of N America has a shell used formerly as money (wampum) by the Amerindians. The giant C. of East Indian waters may weigh, with the shell, 225 kg (500lb).

CLAM. The giant clam *(Tridacna gigas)*, showing its mantle folds. If the two valves close on the foot of a diver, he may not be able to free himself. In the foreground, to the left, are fan worms, which are also filter feeders. *Photo: Heather Angel.*

CLAN. A patriarchal division of human society usually restricted to the clans of Scotland and Ireland, but similar institutions exist among many other peoples. In theory, all members of the C. are of common origin, tracing their descent from one ancestor from whom in general the name is derived, e.g. the clan MacGregor (son of Gregor) believed themselves to be descendants of Griogar, a son of King Alpin of Scotland, and the Irish O'Donnells were the grandsons of Donnell, i.e. Donald.

In Scottish history the Cs. played a prominent part until after the Jacobite rebellion of 1745, when their distinctive dress was prohibited and a determined attempt was made to break the allegiance of the clansmen to their chiefs. In modern times the chieftainship of some Cs. is still maintained as a title.

CLARE (*c.* 1194-1253), **St.** Christian saint. B. at Assisi, she became at 18 a follower of St Francis, who founded for her the convent of San Damiano. Here were gathered the first members of the Order of *Poor Clares.* Canonized in 1255, she was in 1958 proclaimed by Pius XII the patron saint of television, since in 1252 she saw from her convent sickbed the services celebrating Christmas in the Basilica of St Francis at Assisi.

CLARE, John (1793-1864). Poet. B. near Peterborough, the son of a farm labourer, he passed most of his days in poverty. His *Poems of Rural Life* (1820), and *The Village Minstrel* (1821) were followed in 1827 by *The Shepherd's Calendar.* He was given an annuity from the duke of Exeter and other patrons, but had to turn to work on the land and spent his last years in Northampton asylum.

CLARE. Co. in Rep. of Ireland, in the prov. of Munster, bounded on the W by the Atlantic, with a wild and dangerous coastline. Inland C. is an undulating plain, with fringing mountains on the E, W, and NW, the chief range being the Slieve Bernagh mts in the SE rising to over 518m (1,700 ft). The principal rivers are the Shannon and its tributary, the Fergus. There are more than 100 lakes in the co., Lough Derg is on the eastern border. The co. town is Ennis. At Ardnachusha, 5km (3m) N of Limerick, is the chief power station of the Shannon hydroelectric installations. The co. is said to be named after Thomas de Clare, an Anglo-Norman settler to whom this area was granted in 1276. Area 3,188 sq.km (1,231 sq.m); pop. (1971) 75,000.

CLARENCE. English ducal title, which has been conferred on a number of princes. The last was Albert Victor (1864-92), eldest son of Edward VII. *See* JACK THE RIPPER.

CLARENDON, Edward Hyde, 1st earl of (1609-74). Statesman and historian. He sat in the Short Parliament of 1640 and in the Long Parliament, where he attacked Charles I's unconstitutional actions, and supported the impeachment of Strafford. In 1641, however, he broke with the revolutionary party, and became one of the royal advisers. When war began he followed Charles to Oxford, and was knighted and made Chancellor of the Exchequer. On the king's defeat in 1646 he withdrew to Jersey, but in 1651 became chief adviser to the exiled Charles II. At the Restoration he was created earl of C., while his influence was further increased by the marriage of his daughter Anne to James, duke of York. The 'Clarendon Code' was designed to secure the supremacy of the C of E, but his moderation earned the hatred of the extremists, and finally he lost the support of Charles by his openly expressed disapproval of his private life. The disasters of 1667, when the Dutch sailed up the Medway, brought about his downfall. His last years were passed in exile in France. He d. at Rouen, and was buried in Westminster Abbey. C.'s claim to literary fame rests on his *History of the Rebellion* (1702-4).

CLARENDON, George William Frederick Villiers, 4th earl of (1800-70). British Liberal diplomat. He was Lord-Lieutenant of Ireland 1847-52, and in 1853 became For. Sec. His diplomatic skill was shown at the Congress of Paris, 1855. He was again For. Sec. in 1865-6 and 1868-70, and an outstanding achievement was the settlement of the *Alabama* dispute with the USA.

CLARENDON, Constitutions of. A code of laws accepted by the royal council at C., near Salisbury, in 1164, and intended to regulate the relations between Church and State. Becket refused to accept the Constitutions, and his ensuing quarrel with Henry II led to his murder.

CLARET. Since the 17th cent. the English term for the light red wines of Bordeaux.

CLARINET. A single-reed woodwind instrument, invented in its present form by Joseph Christian Denner (1655-1707). It has a mouthpiece containing the reed, a cylindrical tube, and a bell-mouthpiece. The tube is pierced by 18 holes, of which 9 are closed by the fingers and 9 by keys. Its tone is full, mellow, and sweet.

CLARK, Joe (Joseph) Charles (1939-). Canadian Progressive Conservative statesman. B. in Alberta, he was party leader 1976–83, and in May 1979 defeated Trudeau at the polls to become the youngest P.M. in Canada's history. Following the rejection of his govt.'s budget, he was himself defeated in a second election in Feb. 1980.

CLARK, Kenneth, baron (1903-). Brit. art expert. As director of the National Gallery (1934-45) he did much to humanize relations with the public and through television he has stimulated lay interest in art, e.g. the series *Civilisation* (1969). His books incl. *Leonardo da Vinci* (1939), *The Nude* (1955), and the autobiography *Another Part of the Wood* (1974).

CLARK, Mark Wayne (1896–1984). American soldier. B. in New York, he fought in France in the F.W.W. and between the wars held various military appointments in USA. In 1942, during the S.W.W., he became Chief of Staff for ground forces, led a successful secret mission by submarine to get information in N Africa preparatory to the Allied invasion, and commanded the 5th Army in the invasion of Italy and the capture of Rome. He succeeded Ridgway as C.-in-C. of the UN armies in Korea 1952-3. He was created hon. KBE 1944.

CLARKE, Arthur Charles (1917-). British scientist. He is best known for his work on space exploration - he originated the plan for the modern system of communications satellites in 1945 - and collaborated with the astronauts in their book *First on the Moon* (1970), and for his science fiction, e.g. *2001: A Space Odyssey* (1968). He has also carried out underwater exploration on the coast of Sri Lanka, where he lives, and on the Great Barrier Reef. *See* ELEVATOR.

CLARKE, Jeremiah (c.1659-1707). English composer. Organist at St. Paul's, he composed 'The Prince of Denmark's March', a harpsichord piece, which was arranged by Sir Henry Wood as a 'Trumpet Voluntary' and wrongly attributed to Purcell. Clarke shot himself when disappointed in love.

CLARKE, Marcus Andrew Hislop (1846-81). Australian writer. B. in London, he went to Australia when he was 18, and worked as a journalist in Victoria. He wrote *For the Term of his Natural Life* (1874), a powerful novel dealing with life in the early Australian prison settlements.

CLARKSON, Thomas (1760-1846). British philanthropist. From 1785 he devoted himself to a campaign against African slavery. He was one of the founders of the Anti-Slavery Society in 1823 and was largely responsible for the abolition of slavery in the British colonies in 1833.

CLASSICISM. In literature, music, and art, the opposite to Romanticism (q.v.). It may be said to denote that style which emphasizes the qualities considered as characteristic of Greek and Roman art, i.e. reason, objectivity, restraint, definiteness, strictness and simplicity of form - as opposed to those Romantic qualities supposed to be derived from Gothic art and literature.

CLAUDEL (klohdel'), **Paul** (1868-1955). French author. Entering the diplomatic service in 1892, he was ambassador to Tokyo, Washington and Brussels. A fervent Catholic, he was influenced by the Symbolists and achieved an effect of mystic allegory in such plays as *L'Annonce faite à Marie* (1912) and *Le Soulier de satin* (1929), set in 16th cent. Spain. His verse incl. *Cinq Grandes Odes* (1910).

CLAUDE LORRAIN (klohd lorān') (1600-82). Properly Claude Gellée, a landscape painter of the French school, b. in Lorraine. In 1627 he estab. himself in Rome, where he executed several pictures for pope Urban VIII. He was

CLAUDE LORRAIN. This landscape, known as 'The marriage of Isaac and Rebekah' does not follow the text of Genesis XXIV.61, and is sometimes called 'The Mill'. The subject is less important than the serene composition of trees, sky and water. *Photo: Courtesy of the National Gallery, London.*

the first great artist to devote himself entirely to landscapes, of which he painted about 400, and had an unequalled ability to render light and the atmosphere of a place at a particular time of day. His *Liber Veritatis* contains some 200 drawings after his finished works, useful for dating.

CLAUDIAN (klaw'dian), or CLAUDIUS CLAUDIANUS (d. 408?). Last of the great Latin poets. He was b. probably in Alexandria, and fl. at the end of the 4th cent. AD. He wrote official panegyrics, and may have been a Christian.

CLAUDIUS (klaw'di-us) (10 BC-AD 54). Roman emperor. A nephew of Tiberius, he was made emperor by the soldiers in AD 41, though he was much more inclined to scholarly pursuits. For many years he was under the thumb of his 3rd wife Messalina, notorious for her debaucheries and intrigues, whom ultimately he had executed. He d. of poison. During his reign the Empire was considerably extended.

CLAUSEWITZ (klow'sewitz), **Karl von** (1780-1831). Prussian soldier and writer on war, b. near Magdeburg. Outstanding among his writings is *Vom Kriege* (Eng. ed. 'On War', 1873) which gave a new philosophical foundation to the science of war, and put forward a conception of strategy which was dominant at least to the time of the F.W.W.

CLAUSIUS (klow'zē-oos), **Rudolf Julius Emanuel** (1822-88). German physicist, one of the founders of the science of thermodynamics. In 1850 he enunciated its second law; Heat cannot of itself pass from a colder to a hotter body.

CLAVERHOUSE (klā'ver-), **John Graham of,** visct Dundee (*c.* 1649-89). Scottish soldier. Employed in the suppression of the Covenanters, he was routed at Drumclog in 1679, but 3 weeks later won the battle of Bothwell Bridge, in which the rebellion was crushed. Until 1688 he was engaged in the work of persecution, and as 'Bloody Clavers' he became an almost diabolical figure among the peasantry. In 1688 he took up arms in support of James II and defeated Mackay in the pass of Killiecrankie, but was mortally wounded.

CLAVICHORD. Stringed keyboard instrument, popular in the Middle Ages and in 18th cent. Germany. Notes are sounded by a metal blade striking the string. It was a forerunner of the pianoforte.

CLAY, Cassius. *See* ALI, MUHAMMAD.

CLAUDIUS. One of the most intriguing of the Roman emperors, Claudius wrote historical works and an autobiography none of which survives, although Robert Graves supplied his own version of the latter. This statue of the deified Claudius is from the Lateran Museum, Rome. *Photo: The Mansell Collection.*

CLAY, Frederic (1838-89). British composer. B. in Paris, he wrote light operas and the cantata *Lalla Rookh* (1877), after Moore, which incl. 'I'll Sing Thee Songs of Araby'.

CLAY, Henry (1777-1852). American statesman and orator. B. in Virginia, he was one of the founders of the Republican Party and thrice stood unsuccessfully for the presidency. He was chiefly responsible for the Missouri compromise of 1821 and for the compromise of 1850 that endeavoured to reconcile the interests of the slavery and antislavery parties in the USA.

CLAY, Lucius DuBignon (1897-1978). American general. C-in-C of the US occupation forces in Germany 1947-9, he broke the Berlin blockade of 1948 (a 'siege' by the Russians lasting 327 days) with the 'airlift', a term he brought into general use.

CLAY. A mud which has undergone a greater or lesser degree of consolidation. It may be white, grey, red, yellow, bluish, or black, and consists essentially of hydrated silicate of alumina, together with sand, lime, iron, oxides, magnesium, potassium, soda and organic substances. When mixed with water it is rendered plastic. The more important clays are adobe, alluvial, building, brick, cement, china, ferruginous, fusible, refractory, vitrifiable, fireclays, etc. Clays have an immense variety of uses, some of which, e.g. pottery and bricks, date back to prehistoric times. According to international classification, in mechanical analysis of soil C. has a grain size less than 0.002mm.

CLAYTON, Philip Thomas Byard (1885-1972). C of E clergyman. B. in Queensland, he was an army chaplain in France and Flanders during the F.W.W. He opened the rest centre Talbot House (named after Gilbert Talbot, son of a former bp of Winchester killed in action) in Poperinghe in Dec. 1915, and in 1920 refounded it in London as Toc H (a signaller's abbrev.). He was vicar of All Hallows, Barking-by-the-Tower, London (1922-63), which he made the Guild Church of Toc H.

CLEETHORPES. Seaside resort in Humberside, England, on the Humber estuary, nr Grimsby. Pop. (1972) 36,480.

CLELAND, John (1709-89). British author. Consul at Smyrna and one-time employee of the E. India Co. at Bombay, he wrote *Fanny Hill - Memoirs of a Woman of Pleasure* (1748-9) to extract himself from the grip of his London creditors. Called before the Privy Council, he escaped with a pension to prevent his falling into more mischief.

CLEMATIS. Genus of plants of the family Ranunculaceae. They are mostly climbing plants, and have a wide distribution. *C. vitalba* (traveller's joy or old man's beard) is the only British species. Many beautiful species are also grown in gardens, e.g. *C. flammula* (sweet virgin's bower), with small, white, very fragrant flowers, and *C. viticella,* whose bell-like, purple or pink flowers hang downwards.

CLEMENCEAU (klemoṅsoh'), **Georges** (1841-1929). French statesman. B. in La Vendée, he was mayor of Montmartre, Paris, in the war of 1870, and in 1871 was elected a member of the National Assembly at Bordeaux. He was elected a deputy in 1876, and soon earned the nickname of 'The Tiger' on account of his ferocious attacks on politicians whom he disliked. At this time he was an extreme radical. In 1893 he lost his seat and spent the next 10 years in journalism. He was prominent in defence of Dreyfus. In 1902 he was elected senator for the Var, and henceforth was one of the most powerful politicians. He was PM 1906-9; and in 1917, in the darkest hour of the F.W.W., he was again called to the premiership. His appointment of Foch as generalissimo was a stroke of the first importance. Victory won, he presided over the Peace Conference in Paris, but failed to secure for France the Rhine as a frontier. In 1920 he resigned, and withdrew his candidature for the presidency of the Rep. for lack of support. C. founded and edited a succession of political papers, wrote novels and works of philosophy. *The Grandeur and Misery of Victory* (1930) was his final testament. In 1922 he toured USA, pleading unavailingly for American co-operation in the new European order.

CLEMENS, Samuel Langhorne. *See* TWAIN, MARK.

CLEMENTI (klehmen'tē), **Muzio** (1752-1832). Italian pianist and composer. He conducted the Italian opera in London in 1777, and settled there in 1782 as a teacher and then as proprietor of a successful pianoforte and music business. He was the founder of the new technique of piano-playing, and his *Gradus ad Parnassum* (1817) is still in use.

CLEMENT OF ROME (fl. *c.* AD 96). Saint and Father of the Church. According to tradition he was the 3rd or 4th bp of Rome, and a disciple of St Peter. He wrote a letter addressed to the church at Corinth (First Epistle of Clement), and many other writings have been attributed to him.

CLEMENCEAU. By forming his 'victory cabinet' in 1917, Clemenceau had restored French morale. Our portrait shows him after the victory in 1919, when an attempt on his life was made by Cottin, as resentment grew over his concentration of negotiations in his own hands. *Photo: The Mansell Collection.*

CLEOPATRA. By descent, Cleopatra was Macedonian not Egyptian, and the line of forehead and nose in this relief suggests it may have elements of a genuine portrait. *Photo: Werner Forman Archive.*

CLEMENTS, Sir John (1910-). Brit. actor-producer. He founded the Intimate Theatre (1935) at Palmers Green, and excels in Shaw and Restoration Comedy. He m. in 1946 the actress, Kay Hammond.

CLEON (klē'on) (d. 422 BC). An Athenian demagogue and military leader in the Peloponnesian War. After the death of Pericles, to whom he was opposed, he won power as representative of the commercial classes and leader of the party advocating a vigorous war policy. He was killed fighting the Spartans at Amphipolis.

CLEOPATRA (*c.* 68-30 BC). Queen of Egypt, famous for her beauty. Upon the death of her father in 51 BC she ascended the throne in Alexandria together with her younger brother Ptolemy XIII, whom she was expected to marry according to the tradition of the Pharaohs. In 49 BC Julius Caesar arrived in Egypt and she became his mistress, bore him a son, Caesarion, and returned with him to Rome. After Caesar's murder she returned to Alexandria and resumed her position as queen of Egypt. In 41 BC she met Mark Antony in Cilicia, who, after having m. Octavia, sister of Octavian, in 40, returned to the E to live in sumptuous magnificence with C., who bore him 3 sons. In 32 BC open war broke out between Antony and Octavian (the future Augustus). In the crucial battle of Actium (31 BC), fought at sea off the W coast of Greece, C. took to flight with her 60 Egyptian ships, whereupon Antony abandoned the struggle and followed her to Egypt. Next year they were besieged in Alexandria. Antony committed suicide, and C. killed herself by applying an asp to her bosom.

CLEOPATRA'S NEEDLE. Name given to each of 2 ancient Egyptian granite obelisks erected at Heliopolis 15th cent. BC by Thothmes III, and removed to Alexandria by Augustus *c.* 14 BC - so, much older than Cleopatra's reign. One of the pair was taken to London in 1878 and erected on the Victoria Embankment; it is 21m (68½ft) high. The other was given by the Khedive to USA, and erected in Central Park, NY, in 1881.

CLERK MAXWELL (klark-), **James** (1831-79). British physicist. B. in Edinburgh, he was prof. of natural philosophy at Aberdeen 1856-60, and then of physics and astronomy at London. In 1871 he became prof. of experimental physics at Cambridge. C.M.'s short life was rich in contributions of the first order to every branch of physical science, particularly on gases, optics and colour sensation, electricity and magnetism. His theoretical work in the last sphere prepared the way for wireless telegraphy and telephony. His principal works incl. *Perception of Colour, Colour Blindness* (1860), *Theory of Heat* (1871), *Electricity and Magnetism* (1873), *Matter and Motion* (1876).

CLERMONT-FERRAND (klermoṅ'-feroṅ'). French industrial city, capital of Puy-de-Dôme dept. Its rubber industry is the largest in France; motor-car tyres are manufactured. Other products incl. chemicals, preserves, foodstuffs, and clothing, and C.-F. is an important agricultural market. The Gothic cathedral is 13th cent. At a council at C. Urban II ordered the First Crusade in 1095. Pop. (1975) 153,379.

CLEVELAND, Stephen Grover (1837-1908). President of the USA; notable as the first Democratic pres. elected after the Civil War, and as the only pres. to hold office for 2 terms (1885-9 and 1893-7) which were not consecutive. He attempted to check corruption in public life, and in 1895 settled the Venezuela dispute with Britain.

CLEVELAND. Largest city of Ohio, USA, standing on Lake Erie at the mouth of the r. Cuyahoga, where the iron ore from the Lake Superior region is brought to meet the coal from the mines in Ohio and Pennsylvania. Its chief industries centre round the many great iron and steel works; petroleum refining is also important. C. is a railway centre and has an airport. Pop. met. area (1970) 2,043,797.

CLEVELAND. Co. in NE England created in 1974 from areas on both banks of the r. Tees, formerly incl. in Durham and the N Riding of Yorks. It is the terminal for the southern gas fields of the North Sea and for gas piped down from Scotland, and there is a chemical industry based on gas and local potash deposits. It incl. Stockton on Tees, Hartlepool, and Middlesbrough (the admin. HQ). Area 583 sq.km (225 sq.m); pop. (1978) 568,200.

CLÈVES. French form of KLEVE.

CLICK-BEETLE or **SKIP-JACK.** Name given to the members of the family Elaterideae of beetles (Coleoptera), which can be recognized by their long, narrow, rather flattened bodies, short legs, and the lengthening of the hinder end of the thorax backwards into 2 sharp spines. They can get on to their feet again from lying on their backs, by jumping into the air and turning over, making loud clicks in the process. The larvae are known as wireworms.

CLIMATE. The primary factors which determine the variations of C. over the surface of the earth are (a) the effect of latitude and the tilt of the earth's axis to the plane of the orbit about the sun (66½°); (b) the difference between land and sea; and (c) contours of the ground.

The amount of heat received from the sun varies in different latitudes and at different times of the year. In the equatorial region the mean daily temperature of the air near the ground has no large seasonal variation. In the polar regions the temperature in the long winter, when there is no incoming solar radiation, falls far below the summer value.

The temperature of the sea, and of the air above it, varies very little in the course of day or night, while the surface of the land is rapidly cooled by radiation to a clear sky. In the same way, the annual change of temperature is relatively small over the sea, and great over the land. Thus the land is colder than the sea in winter, and warmer than the sea in summer. The winds which blow from the sea are warm in winter and cool in summer, while winds from the central parts of continents are hot in summer, and cold in winter.

On average, air temperature falls off with height at a rate of 1 deg C (1.8 deg F) per 90m (300ft). Thus places situated at an elevation above mean sea-level will usually have lower temperatures than places at a lower level. Even in equatorial regions, high mountains are snow-covered during the whole year. Rainfall is produced by the ascent of air. When an air current blows against a range of mountains, so that it is forced to ascend over the high ground, it gives rainfall, of amount depending on the height of the ground and the dampness of the air.

The complexity of the distribution of land and sea, and the consequent complexity of the general circulation of the atmosphere, makes the distribution of the climate extremely complicated. Centred on the equator is a belt of tropical rain-forest which may be either constantly wet or monsoonal, i.e. seasonal with wet and dry seasons in each year. Bordering each side of this belt is a belt of savannah, with lighter rainfall, and less dense vegetation. After this usually comes a transition through steppe (semi-arid) to desert (arid), with a further transition through steppe to Mediterranean climate with dry summer, followed by the moist temperate climate of middle latitudes. Next comes a zone of cold climate with moist winter, but where the desert extends into middle latitudes the zones of Mediterranean and moist temperate climates are missing, and the transition is from desert to a cold climate with moist winter. In the extreme E of Asia a cold climate with dry winters extends from about 70° N to 35° N. The polar caps have tundra and ice-cap climates, with little or no precipitation.

CLĪNO'METER. A hand surveying instrument for measuring angles of slope.

CLIVE, Robert, baron (1725-74). Soldier and statesman, founder of the British Empire in India. B. at Market Drayton, in 1743 he became a writer in the East India Company's service in Madras and was given an ensign's commission. In 1751, during a dispute over the succession to the Carnatic in which the French took the side of one claimant and the British of the other, C. marched from Madras with 500 men, seized Arcot, the cap. of the Carnatic, defended it for 7 weeks against 10,000 French and Indian troops, and then sallied out and relieved the British besieged in Trichinopoli. In 1753 C. returned to England a national hero.

In 1755 he went back to India as a lieutenant-colonel and governor of Fort St David. In the next yr the Nawab of Bengal, Suraj-ud-Dowlah, seized Calcutta, and shut up 146 British prisoners in the 'black hole' where all but 23 perished (20 June 1756). In Feb. 1757 C., with 1,900 men, defeated the Nawab's army of 34,000 men outside Calcutta, and forced him to make peace. In Europe the Seven Years War had begun; and C., discovering that Suraj-ud-Dowlah intended to assist the French, set out from Chandernagore with 3,200 men, and on 23 June completely defeated the Nawab's army at Plassey. By this victory Bengal practically fell to the East India Company.

In 1760 ill-health forced C. to return to England. In 1762 he was created Baron C. of Plassey. He returned to India in 1765 as Governor of Bengal and C-in-C, and executed many great and necessary reforms. But he made many enemies, and on his return to England for the last time, in 1766, he was fiercely attacked and threatened with impeachment. In 1772-3 a parliamentary enquiry was held and he was virtually acquitted, but the charges preyed on his mind. In a fit of depression he committed suicide.

CLIVEDEN (cleev'den). Estate in Bucks, England, on the Thames 5km (3m) NW of Maidenhead. Acquired in 1893 by Lord Astor, whose wife used it for politically influential house-parties, it was presented to the Nat. Trust in 1942 by the 2nd Visct, who remained as tenant. In the grounds are the Canadian Red Cross War Memorial Hospital, and the cottage let to Stephen Ward which became notorious as the setting for events connected with the Profumo Affair 1961-3.

CLOCK. Any device that can be used for measuring the passage of time, though customarily a timepiece consisting of a train of wheels driven by a spring or weight controlled by a balance wheel or pendulum. The purpose of a C. is to perform the subdivision of the day into smaller time intervals. In ancient Egypt the time during the day was measured by a shadow-clock, a primitive form of sundial, and at night the water-clock was used. Up to the late 16th cent. the only C. available for use at sea was the sand-clock, of which the most familiar form is the hour-glass. The Royal Navy kept time by half-hour sand-glasses until 1820. During the Middle Ages various types of sundials were widely used, and portable sundials were in use from the 16th to the 18th cent. Watches were invented in the 16th cent. - the first were made in Nuremberg shortly after 1500 - but it was not until the 19th cent. that they became cheap enough to be available to the ordinary man or woman.

The first known public C. was set up at Milan in 1353; the first in England was the Salisbury cathedral C. of 1386. The time-keeping of both Cs. and watches was revolutionized in the 17th cent. by the application of pendulums to Cs. and of balance-springs to watches.

The marine chronometer is a precision timepiece of special design and of the finest workmanship, used at sea for giving Greenwich mean time. Electric timepieces were made possible by the discovery early in the last century of the magnetic effects of electric currents. One of the earliest and most satisfactory methods of electrical control of a C. was invented by Matthaeus Hipp in 1842. In the modern mains electric C., the place of the pendulum or spring-controlled balance-wheel is taken by a small multipolar synchronous motor which counts up the alternations of the mains electric supply, and then by a suitable train of wheels records the time by means of hands on a dial.

The quartz crystal C. (made possible by the piezo-electric property of certain crystals) has even greater precision, with a short-term accuracy of about one-thousandth of a second per day. More recently still it has been shown that resonance associated with some atoms, e.g. caesium, comes within the range of estab. microwave techniques and with the use of electronic circuits a link can be maintained with the atomic resonance to control the frequency of a quartz crystal oscillator. This system is called an atomic clock and provides a time scale with a stability better than one millionth of a second per day.

Biological. As early as the 18th cent. endogenous circadian cycles had been discovered, and by 1950 the existence of the circadian C. (*see* CIRCADIAN RHYTHM) was widely recognized, espec. when 'jet-lag' was the consequence of the internal and external Cs. being at variance. Except in organisms without a discrete nucleus, such as bacteria and the majority of algae, such Cs. are common to all animals, and also to many plants, fungi and unicellular organisms. Some Cs. may control several activities, but in higher organisms, there appears to be a series of Cs. of graded importance. For example, although body temperature and activity cycles in human beings are normally 'set' to 24 hours, the 2 cycles may vary independently, showing that two C. mechanisms are here concerned, and yet other Cs. control other functions. Research into the exact nature of these Cs. is being directed into enzyme systems and membrane activity.

CLOISTER. A convent or monastery, and more particularly a covered walk within these, often opening onto a courtyard.

CLOISTERS, The. Branch of the Metropolitan Museum of Art in Fort Tryon Park, upper Manhattan. Lovingly re-assembled are parts of a number of medieval buildings transported to America from Europe, and priceless medieval tapestries, pictures, books, etc. are among the exhibits.

CLONE (klōn). The asexual reproduction of a genetic carbon copy of an animal or plant, from the Gk for 'twig'. With animals such as mice this has been done, and in the future it may become possible for the nucleus of an unfertilized human egg cell to be replaced by the nucleus of a cell from the person to be cloned. The egg, being in this way provided with the full set of chromosomes which normally follows only on fertilization, would then divide and develop in the usual way. The result would be a more perfect copy of the man or woman concerned than if they had an 'identical twin', and it has been suggested that such Cs. might be kept in deepfreeze to provide the original person with organ transplants in case of disease or accident. Since the number of Cs. would be unlimited, there would also be the prospect of producing as many copies of outstanding athletes or intellectual giants as society required. With plants test-tube culture of an almost invisible segment of flowering tissue produces true Cs. Orchids have been grown by this means for many years, and by 1980 it was in commercial use for improving such products as palm oil. Palms grown by this means have a consistent high yield, and uniform growth to facilitate mechanical harvesting.

CLOSED SHOP. Name given to a company or firm, public corporation or other body which requires its employees to be members of the appropriate trade union. With the growth of trade union power, enforcement of the C.S. has been widely extended, e.g. in the motor industry, and in the UK the Trade Unions and Labour Relations Act (1976) provided for its universal legal enforcement. In 1980 the Cons. govt. Employment Act modified the C.S. legislation (*see* TRADE UNION), but insufficiently, as regards exemption, to avoid the question being brought before the European Court of Human Rights in 1981. In the USA the C.S. was made illegal by the Taft-Hartley Act (1947), passed by Congress over Truman's veto.

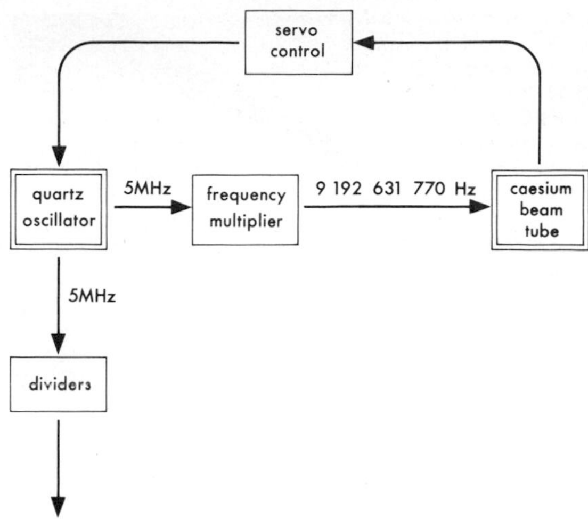

CLOCK. In a caesium beam atomic clock, the 5MHz output from the quartz oscillator is multiplied up to produce a radiofrequency very near to that at which energy transitions take place in the caesium atom. When this frequency is injected into the caesium beam tube transitions are induced. If this frequency is not exactly the same as the caesium frequency an error signal is developed which corrects the quartz oscillator frequency. Thus by servo control the output signal of the quartz oscillator is kept at a frequency which is directly related to the caesium frequency. This stable and accurate output from the quartz oscillator is used to drive a clock which gives microsecond accuracy.

CLOUD. A sky(left) frequently seen after the passage of an intense subsidiary depression moving on the border of a primary cyclone. Above are bands of cirrostratus, merging into cirro-cumulus, moving and radiating from the south. Below are small cumulus and fracto-cumulus (ie. torn cumulus) from WNW. The view is to the south-west. And (right) a heat thunderstorm after a fine hot day. Vigorous convection is evident within the cloud mass, with a recently- formed anvil canopy spreading out from the cloud- top. *Photos. Courtesy of the Meteorological Office.*

CLOTH. *See* TEXTILES.

CLOTHES MOTHS. Moths of the family Tineidae. The larvae feed on clothes, upholstery, etc., and often do considerable damage. The lesser C.M. (*Tinea pellionella*) has yellow larvae.

CLOUD. Water vapour condensed into minute water particles which float in masses in the atmosphere. Like fogs or mists, from which they are distinguished by the height at which they occur above the ground, they are formed by the cooling of air charged with water vapour which condenses generally on tiny dust particles.

Clouds are usually classified according to the height at which they occur. *Cirrus* and *cirro-stratus* clouds are met with at 10,000 m (30,000 ft). The former, sometimes called mare's-tails, consist of minute specks of ice and appear as feathery white wisps, while cirro-stratus clouds stretch across the sky as a thin white sheet. Three types of cloud are found at 3-7,500 m (10-24,000 ft): cirro-cumulus, alto-cumulus, and alto-stratus. *Cirro-cumulus* Cs. occur in small or large rounded tufts, sometimes arranged in the familiar pattern called 'mackerel sky'. *Alto-cumulus* clouds are similar but larger white clouds, also arranged in lines. *Alto-stratus* clouds are like heavy cirro-stratus clouds and may stretch across the sky as a grey sheet.

The lower clouds, occurring at heights of up to 2,000 m (7,000 ft), may be of 2 types, the strato-cumulus or the nimbus. The *strato-cumulus* Cs. are the dull grey clouds which give rise to a so-called 'leaden' sky which, however, may not yield rain. *Nimbus* Cs. are dark grey, shapeless, rain-clouds. Two types of C., the *cumulus* and *cumulo-nimbus*, are placed in a special category because they are produced by diurnal ascending currents which take moisture into the cooler regions of the atmosphere. Cumulus Cs. have a flat base generally at 1,500 m (4,500 ft) where condensation begins, while the upper part is dome-shaped and extends to about 2,000 m (6,000 ft). Cumulo-nimbus Cs. have their base at much the same level, but extend much higher, often up to over 6,000 m (20,000 ft). Short heavy showers and sometimes thunder may accompany them. *Stratus* clouds, met with below 1,000 m (3,500 ft), have the appearance of sheets parallel to the horizon. They are, practically speaking, high fogs.

CLOUD CHAMBER. Apparatus devised by C. T. R. Wilson of Cambridge for tracking ionized particles. It consists of a vessel filled with air or gas, saturated with water vapour. When suddenly expanded this cools and a cloud of tiny droplets forms on the nuclei, dust or ions present. If single fast-moving ionizing particles are allowed to traverse a dust-free chamber just before expansion a trail of droplets will appear where the ionizing particles collide with the air or gas molecules, showing as visible tracks. Much information about interactions between particles and radiations has been obtained from photographs of these tracks. This system has been developed in recent years by the use of liquid hydrogen or helium instead of air or gas. *See* BUBBLE CHAMBER.

CLOUD CHAMBER. Following its sudden cooling, these tiny condensation trails were formed in the wake of a neutral hyperon particle. *Photo: Courtesy of the Imperial College of Science and Technology.*

CLOUET (kloo-eh'), **Jean** (*c.* 1486-1541). French artist, court painter to Francis I, known as Janet. He portrayed Francis and the members of his court with great skill. His son François (b. before 1522, d. 1572), also known as Janet, succeeded his father as court painter to Francis, holding the same office under Henry II and Charles IX. Both produced oils, chalk drawings and miniatures of exquisite life.

CLOUGH (kluf), **Arthur Hugh** (1819–61). British poet. B. at Liverpool, the son of a rich cotton merchant, he was at Rugby under Dr Arnold, and at Oxford came under the influence of Newman. Eventually he became an unbeliever in religion, and many of his lyrics are marked by a melancholy scepticism. One of his best-known poems is the pastoral 'Tober-na-Vuolich' (1848). *Amours de Voyage* (1849) is a novel in verse. His lyric 'Say not the struggle nought availeth' was made famous in the S.W.W. through a Churchillian quotation. He d. at Florence. His sister **Anne Jemima C.** (1820–92) was the first principal of Newnham Coll., Cambridge.

CLOVE'LLY. Village of N Devon, England, famous for its steep cobbled main street which descends 122m (400ft) down the side of a beautifully wooded cliff. Pop. (1974) 450.

CLOVER. A genus of leguminous plants (*Trifolium*), of which there are a great number of species, found mostly in the temperate regions; 20 are British. Herbaceous plants, they have trifoliate leaves and roundish heads or a spike of small flowers. Many are cultivated as fodder plants. The most important is the Red C. (*T. pratense*). White or Dutch C. (*T. repens*) is common in pastures.

CLOVES. The unopened flower-buds of the clove tree *Eugenia aromatica*, a member of the order Myrtaceae. Their aromatic quality is shared to a large degree by the leaves, bark and fruit of the tree, which is a native of the Moluccas. Cs. are used for flavouring in cookery and confectionery. Oil of Cs., which has tonic and carminative qualities, is employed in medicine.

CLOVIS (465–511). King of the Franks. One of the Merovingians, he succeeded his father Childeric in 481 as king of the Salian Franks, defeated the Gallo-Romans near Soissons, and also the Alemanni near Cologne in 496, embraced Christianity and subsequently proved a powerful defender of orthodoxy against the Arian Visigoths, whom he defeated at Poitiers (507). He made Paris his capital.

CLUB. An association of persons for social intercourse, indulgence in sport or hobbies, discussion of matters of common interest, etc. There were Cs. of a sort in the ancient world, but the London Cs. of today developed from the taverns and coffee-houses of the 17th and 18th cents. The oldest is White's, evolved from a chocolate-house of the same name in 1693. Other famous London clubs incl. Boodles, 1762; Brooks's, 1764; the Portland (cards), 1816; The Athenaeum, 1824; the Garrick (dramatic and literary), 1831; the Carlton (Conservative), 1832; the Reform (Liberal), 1836; the Savage (literary and art), 1857; the Press Club, 1882; the Royal Automobile, 1897. Best-known of the women's clubs is the University Women's (1887).

The clubland of London is in the St James's and Pall Mall area, but there are clubs in all British cities and many towns. The Working Men's Club and Institute Union (1862) comprises more than 3,000 Cs. with approx. 2 million members.

Club life in the USA is common in pursuit of a particular interest, notably sports and country Cs., and such bodies as the Antique Automobile Club of America (1935). The Yale Club of New York and the Harvard Club of New York, drawing membership in the main from the universities from which they take their names, are more like a London C. than many so-called Cs. in America. The most prominent type of C. in the USA, however, is the women's club, with regular lunches followed by lectures and debates; this form of C. was well estab. all over the country when the Federation of Women's Clubs was formed in 1889.

CLUB MOSS. A class of flowerless plants (Lycopodiales) belonging to the Pteridophyta and allied to the ferns and horsetails. They have a wide distribution, but were far more numerous in Palaeozoic times, the Lepidodendroids of the coal measures being large trees. The living species are all of small size. The common C.M. or stag's horn moss (*Lycopodium clavatum*) is found on upland heaths.

CLUB-ROOT. Disease affecting cabbages, turnips, and allied plants. It is caused by one of the organisms known as Mycetozoa or slime-moulds - *Plasmodiophora brassicae*; this attacks the root of the plant, which sends out knotty outgrowths, and the whole plant decays.

CLUJ (kloozh). City in Transylvania, Romania, on the Somes, a communications centre for Romania and the Hungarian plain. There is a 14th cent. cathedral, and Romanian (1872) and Hungarian (1945) univs., and industries incl. machine tools, furniture and knitwear. Pop. (1971) 205,450.

CLUNIES-ROSS. Family which estab. a benevolently paternal rule in the Cocos Is. (q.v.). John C.-R. settled on Home Is. in 1827: the family's rule ended in 1978 with the purchase of the Cocos by the Australian govt.

CLUNY (klünē'). Town in Saône-et-Loire dept, France, on the Grosne r. Here from 910 to 1790 was a celebrated abbey, foundation house of the Cluniac order, originally a reformed branch of the Benedictines; some remains of the abbey exist. C., once famous for lace, has an important cattle market. Pop. (1975) 3,800.

CLUTHA (kloo'tha). Longest river in South Island, NZ, 338 km (210 m) long. It rises in the Southern Alps, has hydroelectric installations (Roxburgh), and flows out on the E coast.

CLWYD (kloo'id). Co. of Wales, formed in 1974 by the merging of most of Denbigh (except its border on the Conway) with Flint (qq.v.), together with a small NE corner of Merioneth. The admin. HQ is Mold. Area 2,424 sq.km (6,278 sq.m); pop. (1973) 371,000.

CLYDE, Colin Campbell, 1st baron C. (1792–1863). British soldier. B. at Glasgow, he entered the army in 1808, and served in the Peninsular War, in China 1842–6, the Sikh War of 1848–9, and during the Crimean War commanded the Highland Brigade at Balaclava. During the Indian Mutiny he was C-in-C, raised the siege of Lucknow, and captured Cawnpore. He was created Baron C. in 1858 and promoted to field marshal in 1862.

CLYDE. Scottish river, one of the chief commercial waterways of the world. It rises in Strathclyde in the Lowther hills, runs through Clydesdale, and after 170km (106m) enters the Firth of Clyde, a broad tidal inlet nearly 64km (40m) wide at its southern end. Between Glasgow and Greenock some of the world's greatest shipbuilding firms were established, but declined after the S.W.W. Among the chief towns on the C. are Lanark, Hamilton, Bothwell, Glasgow, Port Glasgow, and Greenock. Ayr is on the Firth in which are the islands of Bute and Arran

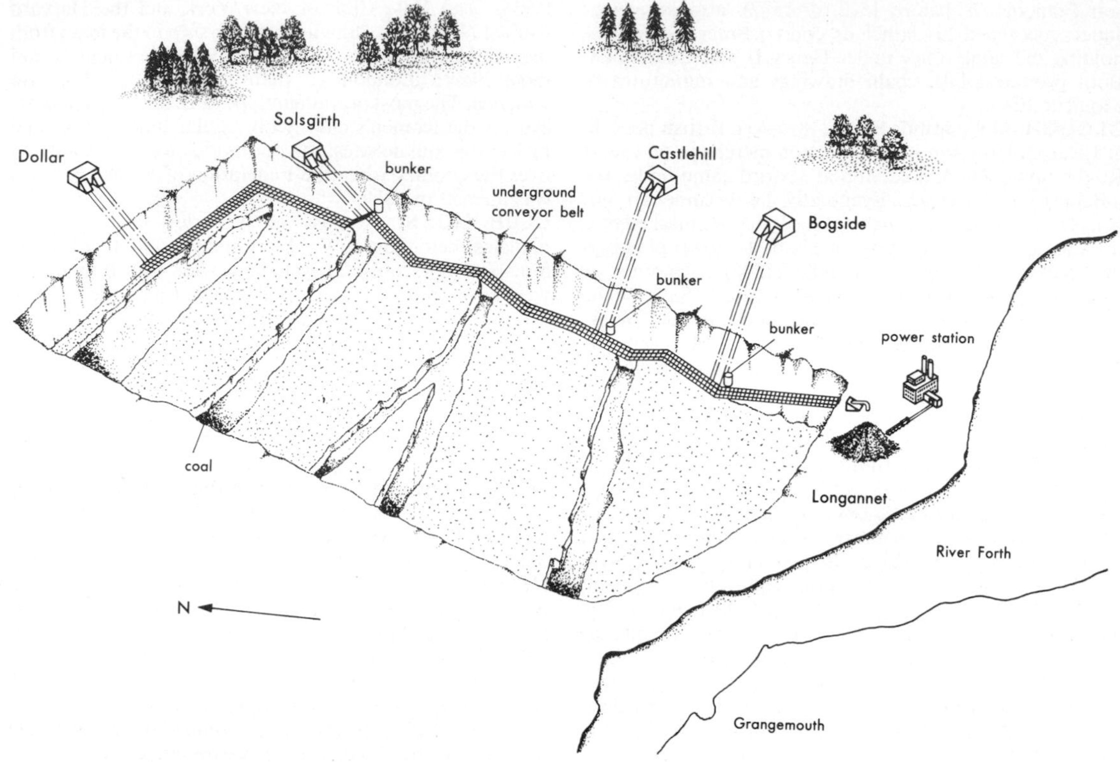

COAL. The surface of a modern mine looks no different from a new factory, and here at Longannet in Scotland the new drift mines, sloping up to the surface from shallow seams, were designed to blend into the landscape. They supply Longannet power station which generates enough power to supply Edinburgh and Glasgow. Self-advancing, power-operated steel roof supports provide a working area along which chain hauled power loaders operate, cutting the coal and automatically loading it onto the face conveyors. These in turn feed (via bunkers) the world's longest conveyor-belt system 9 km (5½m), a central computer controlling the flow for mix of qualities on its way to the power station. *Courtesy of the National Coal Board*

and a number of smaller islands. The C. is connected to the Firth of Forth by the Forth and Clyde canal, 56km (35m).

CLYDEBANK. Town on the Clyde, Strathclyde, Scotland, 10km (6m) NW of Glasgow. At the John Brown yard the famous liners, the Atlantic 'queens' of the 1930s were built. Pop. (1971) 48,170.

CLYTEMNESTRA (klītemnest'ra). In Greek legend, daughter of Tyndareus and Leda, and wife of Agamemnon. Their children were Orestes, Electra, and Iphigenia. During her husband's absence at the Trojan war, C. was seduced by Aegisthus, and on his return murdered him with the connivance of her lover. C. and Aegisthus were eventually slain by Orestes.

CNOSSUS. Alternative form of KNOSSOS.

COACHING. Conveyance by a coach - a horse-drawn passenger carriage on 4 wheels, sprung and roofed in. Famous coaches still in use are those of the Lord Mayor of London (1757) and the state coach built in 1761 for George III. Stage coaches made their appearance in the middle of the 17th cent.; the first mail coach ran in 1784. Between about that time and 1840, when railways became the vogue, was the golden age of C. The main roads were kept in good repair by turnpike trusts, and large numbers of inns - many of which still exist - arose to cater for man and beast. The influence of coach design may be seen in the normal railway carriage.

COAL. Mineral substance of fossil origin, the result of the transformation of organic matter: the main types are anthracite (bright and with more than 90 per cent carbon), bituminous C. (bright and dull patches) and lignite (woody, grading into peat) and brown C. (no woody structure but only 70 per cent carbon). Fields are widely distributed in the temperate N hemisphere, the greatest reserves being in Europe, W Siberia and USA: the York, Derby and Notts is Britain's chief reserve, extending N of Selby. In the southern, Australia is important.

C. has probably been worked in England since Roman times and in the 2nd half of the 18th cent. became the basis of Britain's rise to industrial power. There was increasing use 1950-70 of cheap natural gas and oil as fuel and for the production of electricity, but the energy crisis of the 1970s led to an expansion of the exploitation of coal resources throughout the world. Under the C. Industry Nationalization Act (1946) Britain's mines are admin. by the Nat. Coal Board.

Extraction is now almost entirely mechanical, whether below ground or by the 'open-cast' method, when the soil is stripped from near-surface deposits and afterwards replaced. However, where seams are thick, near the surface, and of the bituminous type which shrinks when heated (allowing air to enter) underground gasification is used, and in the USA this is now the preferred method.

In the 1980s coal will be increasingly important as a source of synfuel (synthetic petrol). In the Fischer-Tropsch process (used in Germany in the S.W.W. and today in S Africa) the coal is gasified and then catalysts are used to reconstitute it into diesel and jet fuel. In the degradation process (under development in USA for high-octane motor fuel), a liquid fuel is directly produced by adding hydrogen or removing carbon from the coal.

COAL TAR. The black oily material resulting from the destructive distillation of coal in the gas-works. After distillation a number of fractions are obtained, viz. light oil, middle oil, heavy oil, and anthracene oil; the residue is called pitch. On further fractionation a large number of substances - some 200 have been isolated - used as dyes, in medicines, etc., are obtained.

COASTAL COMMAND. Combined British naval and RAF system of defence organized during the S.W.W. (1939-45). It was divided into groups which worked in close co-operation with Naval Command, both services being directed from an Area Combined Headquarters. In addition to the groups which operated in England, N Ireland, Scotland, and Wales, there was a separate group in Iceland and a station at Gibraltar.

COASTGUARD. Organization to prevent smuggling, assist distressed vessels, watch for oil slicks, etc. In Britain the C. was originally formed to prevent smuggling after the Napoleonic Wars, and is now admin. by the Dept of Trade. The US Coast Guard (1915) has wider duties incl. enforcement of law and order on the high seas and navigable waters; prevention of smuggling; maintenance of lighthouses, buoys and bells; carrying out of an ice patrol for ships crossing the N Atlantic, etc. It had its beginnings in the revenue cutter service estab. by Washington in 1790.

The **Coastwatchers** of Australia (1919), a volunteer civilian organisation, were originally formed to maintain a defensive watch on the home coast, but in the S.W.W. won distinction in an active role from 1942 in New Guinea and the Pacific Islands against the Japanese.

COATBRIDGE. Town in Strathclyde, Scotland, 13km (8m) E of Glasgow. Coal and iron are mined nearby, and there is an iron and steel industry. Pop. (1973) 52,800.

COATES, Eric (1886-1957). British composer. B. in Notts, he was a viola player, but from 1918 devoted himself to composing, e.g. *The London Suite,* which incl. the 'Knightsbridge March'; 'The Dam Busters March'; the songs 'Bird Songs at Eventide' and 'The Green Hills of Somerset'; and 'Sleepy Lagoon'.

COATI (ko-ah'ti) A mammal (*Nasua*) of the order Carnivora, family Procyonidae, related to the racoon. It has a long tail and a long, flexible, pig-like snout, and its paws are furnished with long claws for climbing and digging. It is found in the forests of S and Central America.

COBALT. Metallic element, closely resembling nickel in appearance, symbol Co, at. no. 27, at. wt. 58.94. It occurs in a number of ores, though not in great quantities, and is used as a pigment and in alloys: because it maintains its hardness at great heat, it is used to cement carbides in tools in the high-speed machining of metals. The chief sources of supply are Zaïre and Zambia. Radioactive cobalt-60 (half-life 5.3 years) is produced by neutron radiation in heavy-water reactors, and is used in large sources for gamma-rays in cancer therapy, substituting for the much more costly radium. The C. 'bomb' contains C.-60 and is used in routine radio-therapy in hospitals.

COBBETT, William (1763-1835). English politician and journalist. B. at Farnham in Surrey, the son of a farmer, he enlisted in the army in 1784 and saw service in Canada. Having obtained his discharge, he lived in USA as a teacher of English, and became known as a vigorous pamphleteer, at this time on the Tory side. In 1800 he returned to England, and in 1802 launched his *Political Register,* a weekly journal. Gradually C.'s views changed to out-and-out Radicalism, largely because of his increasing knowledge of the sufferings of the farm labourers whose champion he constituted himself. In 1809 he was imprisoned for having criticized the flogging of English troops by German mercenaries, and in the post-war years he became the protagonist of the working-class movement. From 1817 to 1819 he was in America, and on his return wrote the *Rural Rides* for his newspaper, which were collected in book form in 1830. He was a strong advocate of parliamentary reform, and sat in the Reformed parliament from 1832.

COBDEN, Richard (1804-65). British Liberal statesman. B. in Sussex, the son of a farmer, he became a calico manufacturer at Manchester. With other business men he founded in 1838 the Anti-Corn Law League and began his lifelong association with John Bright. In 1841 he was elected Liberal MP for Stockport, and until 1845 devoted himself to the repeal of the Corn Laws. A typical early Victorian radical, he believed in the abolition of class and religious privileges, a minimum of govt interference, and the securing of international peace by disarmament and arbitration. He opposed trade unionism and most of the factory legislation of his time, because he regarded them as opposed to liberty of contract. His opposition to the Crimean War made him unpopular, but in 1859 Palmerston offered him a seat in the Cabinet, which he refused. C. was largely responsible for the commercial treaty with France in 1860.

COBDEN-SANDERSON, Thomas James (1840-1922). British bookbinder and painter. Influenced by William Morris and Burne-Jones, he opened his own workshop in Maiden Lane, Strand, in 1884, and soon established a reputation as a bookbinder with faultless technique and admirable taste. Later he founded the Doves Press (1900-16).

COBH (cōve). Irish seaport and market town on Great Island, in the estuary of the Lee, co. Cork, Rep. of Ireland. Pop. (1971) 6,700.

COBLENZ. *See* KOBLENZ.

COBRA. Venomous snakes of the genera *Naja* and *Sepedon,* characterized by the fact that their necks are dilatable into a broad hood. They have cylindrical bodies with long tails and smooth scales. The Indian C., or Cobra da Capello (*Naja naja tripudians*), attains 2m (7ft), and is black to pale brown, with generally a spectacle-shaped marking on the upper surface of the neck. Its bite is deadly. The king C. or hamadryad (*N. hannah bungarus*) may be 4m (14ft), and is one of the fiercest and most aggressive of snakes. It is yellowish brown or olive, with black cross-bands, and feeds on other snakes. African Cs. include the Egyptian or hooded C. (*N. haje*) and the black-necked C. (*N. nigricollis*).

COBURG (koh'boorg). Town in Bavaria, W Germany, on the Itz, 80km (50m) SE of Gotha. Formerly the cap. of the duchy of C., it was part of Saxe-Coburg-Gotha 1826-1918, and a residence of its dukes. Pop. (1978) 47,500.

COCA. A S American shrub (*Erythroxylon coca*) belonging to the Erythroxylaceae, whose dried leaves are the source of cocaine. It is cultivated in Bolivia.

COCAINE. The chief alkaloid found in the leaves of the coca tree. It is used in medicine to produce local anaesthesia, etc. It is a dangerous drug, increasing the heart rate and blood pressure, and in chronic use creates a pychosis resembling delirium tremens as well as psychological dependence.

COCHABA'MBA. City in Bolivia, SE of La Paz. At 2,550m (8,370 ft), it has a refinery linked by pipeline with the Camiri oilfields. Pop. (1970) 149,900.

COCHIN. Indian town and seaport, also fishing port and naval training base, in Kerala state, on the Malabar coast. It exports coir, copra, tea, spices; makes ropes, clothing, and there are oil refineries, etc.; and has an airport and railway terminus. Vasco da Gama established a Portuguese factory at C. in 1502, and in 1530 St Francis Xavier made it a missionary centre. The Dutch held C. 1663-1795 when it was taken by the English. Pop. (1971) 438,420.

COCHIN. Formerly princely state lying W of the Anamalai hills in S India. It was part of Travancore-Cochin from 1949 until merged in Kerala in 1956.

COCHIN-CHINA. Former French colony in Indo-China, from 1949 part of Vietnam (q.v.).

COCHINEAL (coch' inēl). Red dye obtained from the bodies of *Dactylopius coccus*, one of the scale-insects (Coccidae) belonging to the sub-order Homoptera of the order Hemiptera. It is a native of S America, and feeds on various species of cactus.

COCHRAN, Sir Charles Blake ('C.B.') (1872-1951). British impresario, who promoted everything from wrestling and roller-skating to the introduction to London of the Diaghilev Ballet. C.'s 'young ladies' incl. many musical comedy stars of later years. He was knighted in 1948.

COCKATOO'. Group of birds in the parrot family, Psittacidae, confined to Australia, New Guinea and the Malay Archipelago. Most familiar is the Australian sulphur-crested C. (*Kakatoe galerita*) which is white with a characteristic high erectile crest of yellow feathers.

COCKCHAFER. A number of beetles in the family Scarabeidae. The common C. (*Melolontha vulgaris*) is reddish-brown and 25 mm (1 in) long. The larvae feed on the roots of crops, and the adults - known as maybugs because of the season when they emerge from the soil - attack the leaves of trees.

COCKCROFT, Sir John Douglas (1897-67). British physicist. B. at Todmorden, Yorks, he held an engineering appointment with Metropolitan-Vickers, and took up research work under Rutherford at the Cavendish Laboratory, Cambridge. He succeeded (with E. T. S. Walton) in splitting the nucleus of the atom for the first time in 1932, and in 1951 they were jointly awarded a Nobel prize. Succeeding Appleton as Jacksonian prof. of natural philosophy, Cambridge (1939-46), he was engaged in the S.W.W. on scientific work for the govt, latterly in connection with the atom bomb. He was director at Harwell 1946-58, and in 1960 became 1st Master of Churchill Coll., Cambridge. Knighted in 1948, he was awarded the OM in 1957.

COCKATOO. The sulphur-crested cockatoo is one of the handsomest of the group, and one of the most intelligent, excelling as a 'talker' and mimic of various noises. *Photo: Courtesy of the Australian Information Service.*

COCKERELL, Sir Christopher (1910-). British engineer, inventor of the hovercraft (q.v.). From a first interest in radio, he switched to electronics, working with the Marconi Co. 1935-50. In 1953 he began work on the hovercraft, carrying out his early experiments on Oulton Broad, Norfolk, and was knighted in 1969.

COCK-FIGHTING. The pitting of game-cocks against one another to make sport for onlookers and gamblers - a diversion now, in most countries, illegal because of its cruelty. It was extremely popular in feudal England. A royal cockpit was built in Whitehall by Henry VIII, and royal patronage continued in the next century. During the Cromwellian period it was banned, but at the Restoration it received a new lease of life until it was banned in 1849. C. continues surreptitiously in advanced countries, and is still legal in many others. Fighting cocks are 1-2 yrs when matched and steel spurs are attached to their legs.

COCKLE. Family of bivalve molluscs (Cardiidae), recognized by their prominently ribbed, heart-shaped shell. The common C. (*Cardium edule*) is found in large numbers on the British coasts, and is gathered for food (after boiling to destroy typhoid bacilli).

COCKNEY. A native of the city of London. According to tradition he must be born within sound of Bow bells (q.v.) in Cheapside. The term C. is also applied to the racy dialect of the Londoner, of which a striking feature is the C. rhyming slang.

COCKROACH. A sub-order of insects (Blattaria), commonly but wrongly called 'black beetles'; they belong to the order Dictyoptera and have nothing to do with the true beetles. In Britain only 2 small species, of the genus *Ectobia,* which do not enter human habitations, are truly native, but several species have been introduced with imported food, etc., and are great pests, e.g. common C. (*Blatta orientalis*) which is common in old houses, and nocturnal and omnivorous in its habits. It leaves a disgusting smell, caused by its saliva, on whatever it touches.

The co-called German C. (*Blattella germanica*) and the American C. (*Periplaneta americana*) are found in bakeries, warehouses, etc.

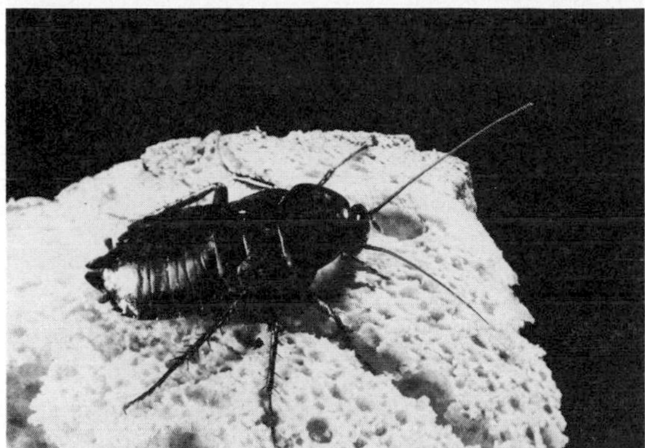

COCKROACH. Damaging and soiling far more food than it actually eats, the oriental, or common cockroach, is very much at home in poorly cleaned restaurants in Europe. *Photo: Heather Angel.*

COCOA and **CHOCOLATE.** Food products both made from the cacao (or cocoa) bean, fruit of a tropical tree (*Theobroma cacao*) growing chiefly in W Africa (Ghana, Nigeria), parts of S America, the West Indies, Java, and Sri Lanka. Cacao is believed to be indigenous to the forests of the Amazon and Orinoco, and the use of the beans was introduced into Europe following the conquest of Mexico by Cortez in the 16th cent. A 'cocoa-house' was opened in London in 1657; others followed and became centres for the fashionable and the wits. In Mexico *chocolatl* (its native name) was mixed with hot spices, whisked to a froth and drunk cold. Cocoa powder was a later development.

The cacao tree when fully grown is some 6m (20ft) high. It begins bearing fruit about the 5th year; this matures rapidly as a pod, 12.5-22.5 cm (5-9 in) long, containing 20 to 40 seeds (beans), embedded in juicy white pulp. The trees bear all the year round and there are 2, sometimes 3, harvests. Preparation consists chiefly in roasting, winnowing, and grinding the nib (the edible portion of the bean). If drinking cocoa is required, a proportion of the cocoa butter is removed by hydraulic pressure and the cocoa which remains is reduced by further grinding and sieving to a fine powder. Chocolate, on the other hand, contains all the original butter.

COCONUT. Fruit of the palm (*Cocos nucifera*), native to India and SE Asia. The trees grow 18-24 m (60-80 ft), mature in 5-7 years, and bear up to 100 nuts a year until 70-80 years old. The kernel of the mature nut contains 70 per cent of oil and when dried this 'copra' is sold for use in making margarine and nut butter. The sap of the tree is fermented to produce a potent spirit, "arrack', or may be boiled down to yield sugar, as in India. The leaves are woven into mats, baskets and sails, and the fibrous husk of the nut is used for mats, cordage and ropes. Indonesia, the Philippines, Malaysia, and Sri Lanka are among the chief exporters.

COCONUT. Copra cutters at work on Rotuma in the Fiji Islands. The smoothcoated fibrous husk on the whole nuts (in the foreground) is removed together with the shell by a few dexterous cuts of their incredibly sharp knives. *Photo: Rob Wright/Camera Press.*

COCOS. Group of 27 small coral islands in the Indian Ocean some 1,770 km (1,720 m) NW of Perth, Australia. Discovered by William Keeling 1609, they were uninhabited till 1826, were annexed by Britain 1857, and transferred to Australia as the Terr. of C. (Keeling) Islands 1955. In 1978 the Australian govt. purchased them from John Clunies-Ross (q.v.). West Island has an airport. Area 14 sq.km (5.5 sq.m); pop. (1973) 625.

COCTEAU (koktoh'), **Jean** (1891-1963). French writer of multifarious talents. Young in an era which worshipped youth, he produced Dadaist verse, a miscellany-novel *Le Potomak* (1919), ballets such as *Le Bœuf sur le toit*, or *The Nothing doing Bar* (1920), plays, e.g. *Orphée* (1926), and a mature novel of bourgeois French life, *Les Enfants terribles* (1929), which he made into a fine film in 1950.

COD. The typical fish of the family Gadidae. The common species (*Gadus morhua*) is found in the Atlantic and Baltic, and when freshly taken is brown to grey along the sides, with the belly shining white. The most important cod-fisheries are on the Newfoundland banks, Iceland, and the North Sea. The majority of the catch is salted and dried. Formerly one of the cheapest fish, over-fishing, etc., has made it one of the more expensive. For 'Cod Wars', *see* ICELAND.

CODEX. An ancient book, with pages stitched together and bound, somewhat after the modern fashion; during the 2nd cent. AD codices began to replace the earlier rolls.

COD LIVER OIL. Oil obtained by subjecting fresh cod livers to pressure at a temperature of about 85°C. When prepared by modern methods, it is nearly tasteless and odourless and is highly nutritious. It is also a valuable source of the vitamins A and D.

CODY, Samuel Franklin (1862-1913). Anglo-American aviation pioneer. B. in Texas, U.S.A., he took British nationality in 1909. He spent his early days with a cowboy stage and circus act, and made successful man-lifting kites. He made the first powered flight on 16 Oct. 1908 at Farnborough, England, in a machine of his own design. He was killed in a flying accident.

CODY, William Frederick (1846-1917). American scout and showman known as Buffalo Bill from a contract he made with the Kansas Pacific Railway to supply buffalo meat to its labourers in 1867: he killed 4,280 buffalo in 18 months. He saw service against the Red Indians and from 1883 organized a 'Wild West' show with which he toured USA and Europe.

CO-EDUCATION. The teaching of boys and girls together, on equal terms and in the same classes. With the rise of modern national systems, economy dictated the adoption of C., as in 17th cent. Scotland and after the Education Act of 1870 in England. Yet it has never been universally approved, either in England, on the Continent, or in many parts of the emergent world, and segregation is still often practised, particularly at the adolescent stage, and in the old-established schools. In 1954 the USSR returned to her earlier co-educational system, partly abolished in 1944. In the US 90 per cent of schools and colleges are co-educational, and an overwhelming majority of teachers are women. In Islamic practice C. is frowned on beyond the infant stage.

COELACANTH (sē'lakanth). Archaic fish, formerly believed extinct. In 1938 a skin, in 1952 a complete fish, and subsequently other specimens, were obtained near Madagascar. It is directly related to the ancestors from whom human beings descend.

COELENTERATA (sēlenterā'ta). One of the phyla or primary divisions of the animal kingdom, distinguished from all the higher animals, or Coelomata, by having a single body cavity, which has only one opening, the mouth, through which food is taken into the body, and the waste products subsequently rejected. They thus correspond to the gastrula stage of the developing embryo of higher animals, and rank next in order above the Protozoa and sponges.

With one or two exceptions the C. are a marine group, and exhibit two main forms of organization: the free-swimming Medusa or jelly-fish form, and the fixed polyp. A special feature is the possession of special stinging cells, or nematocysts, by means of which they are able to paralyse their prey. Many C., e.g. the corals, build up skeletons for themselves from carbonate of lime.

The C. are divided into the 3 great classes of Hydrozoa, Scyphozoa, and Anthozoa (qq.v.).

COFFEE. The seeds or berries of cultivated forms of *Coffea arabica, C. liberica* and allied species - natives of Africa and probably Arabia. Naturally *c.* 5m (17ft), the shrub is pruned to *c.* 2m (7ft) in cultivation, is in full bearing in 5-6 years and lasts for 30 years. Susceptibility to frost and disease, and the length of time before a tree begins to bear, results in periodic scarcity, as in the late 1970s. C. is a tropical crop and does best on frost-free hillsides with moderate rainfall. The largest producer is Brazil; others are Colombia, Ivory Coast, Angola, Uganda, Zaïre, Guyana, Mexico, El Salvador, Guatemala and Indonesia. Chicory (q.v.) is often mixed with C. to give it a distinctive bitter flavour and rich colour. The species *C. robusta*, grown espec. in Angola, is that used in most 'instant' coffee.

In Arabia C. drinking dates from about the 14th cent., but did not become common in Europe until 300 years later. In the 17th cent. C. houses were opened in London, but C. was largely superseded by tea until it regained ground in the 20th: in USA and on the Continent C. has always been more popular.

COFFEE. Ripe coffee berries of the species used to make most 'instant' coffee. *Photo: Camera Press.*

COGNAC (koṅyahk'). Town in Charente dept, France, 40km (25m) W of Angoulême. Situated in a vine-growing district, C. has given its name to a world-famous brandy. Pop. (1975) 22,600.

COIMBATORE (kō-imbator'). City in Tamil Nadu, India, on the Noyel r. There are textile industries and the Indian Air Force Admin. College. Pop. (1971) 393,100.

COIMBRA (koh-ēm'brah). City in Portugal on the Mondego r., 32km (20m) from the sea. There is a 12th cent. Romanesque cathedral incorporating part of an older mosque, and the univ., founded in Lisbon 1290 and transferred to C. 1537, is celebrated. C. was cap. of Portugal 1139-1385. Pop. (1970) 46,320.

COINS. *See* NUMISMATICS.

COKE, Edward (1552-1634). Lord Chief Justice of England. B. in Norfolk, he was called to the Bar in 1578, and in 1592 became Speaker of the House of Commons and Solicitor-Gen. In 1594 he was appointed Attorney-Gen., and as such conducted the prosecution at the trials of Essex, Raleigh, and the Gunpowder Plot conspirators. In 1606 he became Chief Justice of the Common Pleas, and began his struggle, as champion of the common law, against James I.'s attempts to exalt the royal prerogative.

An attempt to silence him by promoting him to the dignity of Lord Chief Justice proved unsuccessful, and from 1620 he was a leader of the parliamentary opposition. Under Charles I he drew up the Petition of Right, and led the attack on Buckingham. His *Institutes* are a legal classic, and he ranks as the supreme common lawyer.

COKE, Thomas William, earl of Leicester of Holkham (1752-1842). British agriculturist, known as C. of Norfolk. He succeeded to his estates at Holkham in 1776, and devoted himself to agricultural improvements, and especially to improving the breed of sheep. He was MP for Norfolk for most of his life as a Whig, and was raised to the peerage in 1837.

COKE. A clean, light fuel produced by the carbonization of certain types or blends of coal. When this coal is strongly heated in airtight ovens, in order to release all volatile constituents, the brittle, silver-grey C. is left. It comprises 90 per cent carbon together with very small quantities of water, hydrogen, oxygen, etc., and makes a most useful industrial and domestic fuel. An inferior grade of C. is produced as a by-product in the manufacture of coal-gas.

COLA (kō'la). Genus of tropical trees in the family Sterculiaceae, bearing nuts with a high caffeine content, which are chewed locally in W Africa as the social equivalent of coffee-drinking. In the West they are used in combination with coca leaves to flavour soft drinks.

COLBERT (kolbār'), **Jean-Baptiste** (1619-83). French statesman. B. at Reims, he entered the service of Mazarin, and after his death became Chief Minister to Louis XIV. In 1661 he set to work to reform the Treasury, and in 1665 was appointed Controller-General. The national debt was largely repaid, and the system of tax collection was drastically reformed. Industry was brought under state control, and a high standard of workmanship was insisted on. Shipbuilding was encouraged by bounties, companies were established to trade with India and America, and colonies were founded in Louisiana, Guiana, and Madagascar. Above all, C. tried to make France a naval power equal to England or Holland. He favoured a peaceful foreign policy, but in his later years was supplanted in Louis's favour by Louvois, with a policy of conquests.

COLCHESTER (kōl'chester). English town and river port on the Colne, Essex, 80km (50m) NE of London. In an agricultural area, it is a market centre with clothing manufacture and engineering and printing works. The Univ. of Essex (1962) is at Wivenhoe to the SE.

C. goes back to the time of Cymbeline (*c.* AD 10-43). Made a colony of Roman ex-soldiers in AD 50, it became one of the most prosperous towns in Roman Britain despite its burning by Boudicca (Boadicea) in 61. Most of the Roman walls remain as well as ruins of the Norman castle, St Botolph's priory, etc. Holly Tree Mansion (1718) is a museum of 18-19th cent. social life. Pop. (1974) 80,000.

COLD, common. A minor disease caused by a variety of viruses, and which is a major cause of industrial absenteeism. Symptoms: headache, chill, nasal discharge, sore throat and occasionally cough. Reseach at the Common Colds Research Unit at Salisbury indicates that the virulence of a cold depends on psychological factors and either reduction or increase of social or work activity as a result of stress in the previous 6 months. There is no immediate hope of an effective cure since the viruses transform themselves so rapidly.

COLD HARBOR, Battle of. Engagement nr Richmond, Virginia, 1-12 June 1864, during the American Civil War in which the Confederate Army under Lee repulsed Union attacks under Grant.

COLDITZ (kold'its). Town in E Germany on the Mulde, in the middle of the triangle formed by Leipzig, Dresden and Chemnitz. The moated castle on a cliff above the town, built by Augustus the Strong, King of Poland and Elector of Saxony 1694-1733, was a high-security POW camp (Oflag IVC) in the S.W.W. Many daring escapes were made, e.g. by Capt. Patrick Reid and 3 others in Oct. 1942. All C. prisoners had already escaped from other camps.

COLDITZ. The castle, supposedly escape-proof, which was turned into a special prisoner-of-war camp by the Germans early in the Second World War. *Photo: Courtesy of the B.B.C.*

COLE'NSO, John William (1814-83). Anglican cleric. Bishop of Natal from 1853, he incurred furious attack from traditionalists by his *Pentateuch and Book of Joshua critically examined* (1862). Deposed in 1863 by the bishop of Capetown, he was reinstated on appeal to the Privy Council. He was later under attack for championing the Zulus against the white settlers.

COLEOPTERA. *See* BEETLE.

COLERIDGE, Samuel Taylor (1772-1834). British poet, critic, and philosopher. B. 21 Oct. 1772 in Ottery St Mary, Devon, he was a contemporary of Charles Lamb at Christ's Hospital, and while at Cambridge was driven by debt to enlist for a time in the Dragoons. In 1795, as part of a plan to found a communist colony in America with Robert Southey and others, he m. Sarah Fricker, from whom he afterwards separated. On the failure of this project, he turned to lecturing, and in 1796 pub. both the unsuccessful periodical *The Watchman* and his first vol. of *Poems.* In 1795 he had met Wordsworth, and now collaborated with him in the *Lyrical Ballads* (1798), in which the 'Ancient Mariner' appeared. 'Kubla Khan' and 'Christabel' were also written at this time. In 1798 he also visited Germany, becoming interested in German literature and philosophy, and 1800-4 he settled at Keswick, near Wordsworth, with whom he later quarrelled, and finally became enslaved by opium. He lectured in London during the next dozen years, and pub. another unsuccessful periodical, *The Friend,* in 1809. From 1816 he resided largely in the care of the physician

James Gillman at Highgate, where his remarkable conversational powers attracted many young disciples.

His poetry is largely fragmentary, but unequalled in magic and music; and in criticism, the best of which is found in the *Biographia Literaria* (1817), lectures on Shakespeare, and *Table Talk*, he was the first to bring philosophical and psychological methods into the consideration of poetry. As a philosopher, he is less important as a creative thinker than as introducing idealistic German philosophy to England.

COLERIDGE. The portrait by W. Allston, painted in 1814.
Photo: Courtesy of the National Portrait Gallery.

COLERIDGE-TAYLOR, Samuel (1875-1912). Brit. composer. B. in London, he was the son of a West African Negro doctor and an English mother. While still a student at the Royal College of Music he had a symphony performed at St James's Hall in 1896. His choral work *Hiawatha* (1898-1900), a setting in 3 parts of Longfellow's poem, won immediate popularity. He was a student and champion of trad. Negro music.

COLET, John (1467?-1519). English humanist. B. in London, he set out on a tour of the Continent in 1493 and in Italy fell under the influence of Savonarola. On his return in 1496 he was ordained, and began lecturing at Oxford on the Pauline epistles. His interpretation represented a reaction against the scholastic tradition, and Erasmus was strongly influenced by him. In 1505 C. became dean of St. Paul's and about 1508 refounded St Paul's school. C. is the founder of modern biblical exegesis.

COLETTE (kolet'), **Sidonie-Gabrielle** (1873-1954). French writer. She was b. in the Burgundian countryside, whence she derived a great love of animals and natural scenery. At twenty she m. her 'Svengali', Henri Gauthier-Villars, a journalist known as 'Willy', who signed with his own name her 4 'Claudine' novels loosely based on her early life, which took Paris by storm. A period in music-hall as strip-tease artist and mime followed their divorce, but she continued to write, her later books incl. *Chéri* (1920) and *La Fin de Chéri* (1926), dealing with a love affair between a young man and an older woman, and *Gigi* (1944). Her 2nd husband was the journalist Henri de Jouvenel (m. diss. 1925) and her 3rd Maurice Goudeket.

COLIGNY (kolēnyē'), **Gaspard de** (1519-72). French admiral and soldier, and prominent Huguenot. About 1557 he joined the Protestant party, and in 1569 achieved an advantageous peace. He became a favourite of the young king Charles IX, but on the eve of the massacre of St Bartholomew's Day was killed by a servant of the duc de Guise.

COLĪ'TIS. Inflammation of the walls of the colon. Sulphonamides are among the drugs used in its treatment.

COLLAGE (kolahzh). Dada technique originated by Max Ernst, and named from the French for 'gluing' or 'pasting'. Disparate items such as fragments of newsprint or photographs are stuck alongside one another, and linked by brush or pencil to create a new artistic whole.

COLLECTIVE FARMS. System of farming developed in the Soviet Union. A C.F. is formed by a group of peasant farmers, who pool their land, horses, and agricultural implements, each household retaining as private property a plot of land and domestic animals for its own requirements. The profits of the farm are divided among its members in proportion to work done. The system has developed gradually since 1917, and became general after 1930. State farms also exist which are owned and run by the State, and employ their workers for wages. The State supplies the C.F.s with stock and equipment, and loans agricultural machinery as required. The system obtains in other Communist countries, and was adopted (1953) as an objective in China, but by 1954 had been considerably modified in Yugoslavia. Israel also has a large number of C.Fs.

COLLECTIVE SECURITY. The principle laid down in the covenant of the League of Nations, that all nations collectively should guarantee the security of each individual nation. When put to the test in Manchuria in 1931, in Abyssinia in 1935, in Spain in 1936, and in China in 1937, the principle was not enforced.

COLLECTIVE UNCONSCIOUS. The shared pool of memories inherited from ancestors which Carl Jung (q.v.) suggested co-existed with individual unconscious recollections, and which might be active both for evil in precipitating mental disturbance or for good in prompting achievements in the arts, etc.

COLLEGE OF ARMS. *See* HERALDS' COLLEGE.

COLLIE. British sheepdog. There are 3 main varieties, rough, smooth, and bearded; and two lesser, the Welsh and Border working Cs. Commonly known as the 'Scotch C.' the rough has been bred for centuries in the Highlands for herding. Of medium size, its long, narrow head and muzzle, and its strikingly handsome coat and colouring, are its chief features. The smooth variety differs in coat and colour. But the bearded C. resembles the Old English sheepdog.

COLLIER, Jeremy (1650-1726). Anglican divine. On the Revolution of 1688 he was one of the Non-jurors, refusing the oath of allegiance to William III, and was several times imprisoned. In 1696 he was outlawed for having granted absolution on the scaffold to 2 men who had tried to assassinate William. In 1698 appeared his *Short View of* *the Immorality and Profaneness of the English Stage,* aimed at Congreve and Vanbrugh, and temporarily effective. In 1713 he was consecrated a bishop of the Non-jurors.

COLL'IMATOR. An optical device for producing parallel light. A small point source or an illuminated slit is placed at the focus of a convex lens, from which the rays emerge parallel.

COLLINGWOOD, Cuthbert Collingwood, baron (1750-1810). British admiral. Entering the navy at the age of 11, he formed a close friendship with Nelson while serving in the W Indies. He distinguished himself on the 'glorious 1st June' and at St Vincent, was promoted to Rear-Admiral in 1799, and was with the Channel fleet blockading Brest 1803-5, until Villeneuve's return from the W Indies, when he blockaded him in Cadiz. Here he was joined by Nelson as his commander-in-chief, and after Nelson's death he took command at Trafalgar. He was buried beside Nelson in St Paul's.

COLLINS, Michael (1890-1922). Irish Sinn Féin leader. B. in Co. Cork, he became an active member of the Irish Republican Brotherhood, and in 1916 fought in the Easter Rebellion. In 1918 he was elected a Sinn Féin member to the Dáil, and became a minister in the Republican Provisional Govt, and in 1921 he and Arthur Griffith were mainly responsible for the treaty which established the Irish Free State. In spite of the opposition of De Valera and the Republicans, he persuaded the Dáil to accept the treaty, and in 1922 became Min. for Finance in the Prov. Govt. During the ensuing civil war C. took command of the Free State forces, and crushed the opposition in Dublin and the large towns within a few weeks. When Griffith d. on 12 Aug., C. became head of the State and the army, but he was ambushed near Cork by fellow Irishmen 10 days later and killed.

COLLINS, William (1721-59). British poet. B. at Chichester, he was ed. at Winchester and Magdalen Coll., Oxford. His *Persian Eclogues* (1742) were followed in 1746 by the great series of endlessly imitated 'Odes', the best-known being 'To Evening'. After 1750 he became insane.

COLLINS, William Wilkie (1824-89). British novelist. Although called to the Bar, he turned instead to literature, and in 1860 contributed *The Woman in White* (a crime novel remarkable for its fat villain, Count Fosco) to Dickens' periodical *Household Words.* Best-known of his later books was *The Moonstone* (1868), with Sergeant Cuff, one of the first detectives in English literature. Still highly dramatic, his stories suffer for modern readers from repetition and very involved narrative technique.

COLLODI (kolō'di), **Carlo.** Pseudonym of Italian writer Carlo Lorenzini (1826-90), adopted from the birthplace of his mother. B. himself at Firenze, he was a journalist, and in 1881-3 wrote *The Adventure of Pinocchio* the children's story of a wooden puppet who became a human boy.

CO'LLOIDS. Non-crystalline substances of high molecular weight such as glue, egg-white, soaps, and starch which exhibit special properties in solution. A colloidal solution that retains the liquid form is known as a *sol,* but many Cs. can retain the colloidal state when in liquid form as a jelly or *gel.* The study of Cs. has thrown much light on the study of vital processes and has proved valuable in such industries as rubber and artificial silk.

COLMAN, Ronald (1891-1958). British actor. B. at Richmond, Surrey, he went to the US in 1920 where his charm, good looks and speaking voice soon brought success in romantic Hollywood roles - *Beau Geste, The Prisoner of Zenda, Lost Horizon,* and *A Double Life* (1948), for which he received an Oscar.

COLMAR. Cap. of Haut-Rhin dept, France, between the Rhine and the Vosges mts. It is an industrial centre. The church of St Martin is 13-14th cent., and the former Dominican monastery, now the Unterlinden Museum, contains a famed Grünewald alterpiece. Pop. (1975) 62,400.

COLOGNE (kolōn'). German port, and industrial and commercial city (Köln), in N Rhine-Westphalia, W Germany, on the left bank of the Rhine, 35km (22m) from Düsseldorf. It can be reached by ocean-going vessels and has developed into a great trans-shipment centre, and is also the HQ of Lufthansa, the state air line. Some 48km to the N is the Ruhr coalfield, and many of C.'s industries are based on Ruhr coal. They incl. motor vehicles, railway wagons, chemicals, and machine tools.

Founded by the Romans *c.* 38 BC and made a colony in AD 50 under the name Colonia Claudia Arae Agrippinensis (hence the name Cologne), it became an important Frankish city and during the Middle Ages was ruled by its arch-bishops. It was a free imperial city from 1288 until the Napoleonic age. In 1815 it passed to Prussia. The great Gothic cathedral was begun in the 13th cent. but its towers were not built until the 19th cent. (completed 1880). C. univ. (1388-1797) was refounded 1919. C. suffered severely from aerial bombardment during the S.W.W.; some 85 per cent of the city was wrecked and its three Rhine bridges were destroyed. Pop. (1978) 976,760.

COLOMBES (kolońb'). Cap. of Hauts-de-Seine dept, France, on the Seine. Tyres, electronic equipment, and chemicals are manufactures. Pop. (1975) 83,500.

COLOMBEY-les-Deux-Églises (kolombā'-lā-döz-āglēz'). Village (the name means C. with the two churches) in Haute-Marne, France. Gen. de Gaulle lived and was buried here. Pop. (1975) 420.

COLO'MBIA. S. American republic, in the NW corner of the continent, with coasts on the Pacific Ocean and Caribbean Sea. It is traversed by the Andes from N to S. In the E there are vast llanos and forested plains watered by tributaries of the Amazon and Orinoco. The Magdalena is an entirely Colombian river nearly 1,600 km (1,000 m) in length. Though C. is a tropical country its climate and temperature vary greatly according to the altitude.

The largest town is Bogotá, the cap.: others are Medellín and Cali, and the ports Barranquilla and Cartagena on the Caribbean, and Buenaventura on the Pacific. Half the pop., the majority of whom are of mixed Spanish-Amerindian descent, are city dwellers. The settled area is mainly at an altitude of 1,500-3,000 m (4-9,000 ft).

C. is the most important emerald-producing country in the world, and also ranks high as a producer of platinum; gold, silver, uranium are worked, and C. has many other minerals, including coal and iron. Petroleum is an important export, and some 25% is refined in C., chiefly at Barrancabermeja. Coffee and bananas are the chief crops grown for export; cotton, rice, tobacco, sugar are other important crops. Air transport has greatly simplified communications. An interoceanic seaway linking the Caribbean and Pacific via the Choco Valley, and formed

COLOGNE. A miracle of survival. The magnificent cathedral, its roof shattered, but its structure intact, stands triumphant amidst the surrounding devastation in March 1945. *Photo: Archiv Benno Wundshammer.*

by damming the Atrato and San Juan rivers, has been projected.

Illiteracy has been reduced to under 30%. The predominant religion is RC, and the language Spanish. Under the constitution of 1957 there is a pres. and congress (House of Representatives and Senate) directly elected for 4 yrs. Women received the vote in 1954.

Conflict between the Liberal and Conservative parties was ended in 1957 by the formation of a National Front sharing power, which successfully fought off the challenge of the Nat. Popular Alliance in the elections of 1970, 1974 and 1978.

Area 1,139,000 sq.km (456,500 sq.m); pop. (1978) 26,500,000. M.U.: peso.

COLOMBO. Cap. and principal seaport of Sri Lanka, on the W coast nr the mouth of the Kelani. The chief govt offices are here. The Univ. of Sri Lanka (1942), formerly in C., is now at Peradeniya, nr Kandy.

C. was mentioned as Kalambu in *c.* 1340, but the Portuguese renamed it in honour of Columbus. The Dutch seized it in 1656 and it was surrendered to Britain in 1796. Pop. (1977) 562,200.

COLOMBO PLAN. Commonwealth plan for co-operative economic development in S and SE Asia which came into operation in 1951. The plan covers large-scale irrigation and hydro-electric schemes, technical training, an Asian nuclear centre at Manila, etc., and is not limited to Commonwealth members. A Staff College for Technician Education was estab. at Singapore in 1974.

COLÓN. City of Panama at the Caribbean end of the Panama Canal. Founded in 1850, and named Aspinwall in 1852, it was renamed C. in 1890 in honour of Columbus (Span. Colon). Once notorious for yellow fever, it has been transformed into a healthy and prosperous town. Pop. (1975) 1,400,000.

COLÓN, Archipiélago de. Official name of the Galápagos Islands.

COLOPHON (kol'ofon). Originally an inscription on the last page of a book giving the writer or printer's name, place and year of publication, etc. In modern practice it is a decorative device on the title page or spine of a book, the 'trade-mark' of the individual publisher.

COLORADO (kolorah'dō). One of the mountain states of the USA, west of the Mississippi basin in the Rocky Mountains. The eastern half is mainly rolling plains, but the west is mountainous with numerous peaks of more than 4,250 m (14,000 ft). The largest river is the Colorado, and this and other rivers travel in deep, narrow canyons. Tourist attractions incl. the Rocky Mtn Nat. Park, the cliff dwellings of the Mesa Verde Nat. Park, Pikes Peak, and 'ghost' mining towns.

First settled by the Spanish, C. later attracted fur traders, and Denver, the cap., was founded in the gold rush which followed the discoveries of 1858. Other towns incl. Colorado Springs, Aurora, Pueblo, and Lakewood. C. became a state in 1876. Sheep and cattle are raised, and there are meat, and dairy product industries. Crops incl. sugar beet, cereals and orchard fruits. Mineral wealth is great and varied, incl. gold, molybdenum (Climax has one of the world's largest reserves), tin, uranium, vanadium, and petroleum, incl. unexploited rich shale deposits. There are metallurgical, engineering, aerospace, and other industries. Area 270,240 sq.km (104,247 sq.m); pop. (1970) 2,207,259.

COLORADO. The Great Sand Dunes National Monument, near Alamosa. Cradled in the spectacular Sangre de Cristo(Blood of Christ) Mountains, are 150 sq.km (60 sq.m) of sparkling white sand, rising to 180m (600ft) in wind-sculptured dunes. *Photo: Courtesy of the United States Travel Service.*

COLORADO. River of N America, rising in the Rocky Mtns, and flowing 2,300 km (1,450 m) to the Gulf of California through C. state, Utah and Arizona, and northern Mexico. The many dams along its course to provide power and irrigation water, e.g. Hoover and Glen Canyon, have been destructive of wildlife and scenery, and very little water even reaches the sea. To the W. of the river in SE California is the **Colorado Desert,** an arid area of 5,000 sq.km. (2,000 sq.m).

COLORADO BEETLE. A beetle (*Leptinotarsa decemlineata*) of the family Chrysomelidae. A native of the USA, it first appeared in England in 1933, and was at once dealt with as a menace to agriculture. It is a small, oval beetle, dark in colour with longitudinal yellowish stripes, and club-shaped antennae. The six-legged grub is orange-yellow. Both larvae and perfect insects feed on the leaves of the potato, etc., and the damage done extends to the tubers.

COLORADO SPRINGS. Health resort in Colorado, USA, 120km (75m) SSE of Denver. At an alt. of *c.* 1,800 m (6,000 ft) and surrounded by magnificent scenery, it is also a local trade centre. Pop. (1970) 135,000.

COLOSSEUM (kolosē'um). The largest amphitheatre in ancient Rome. Begun by the emperor Vespasian to replace the amphitheatre destroyed by fire in the reign of Nero, and completed by Titus in AD 80, it was 187m (615ft) long and 49m (160ft) high, and seated *c.* 50,000 people. Its ruins are amongst the most notable antiquities of Rome. Early Christians were martyred here by lions and gladiators.

COLOSSUS OF RHODES. Bronze statue of Apollo erected at the entrance to the harbour at Rhodes 292–280 BC. Said to have been about 30m (100ft) high, it was counted as one of the seven Wonders of the World, but in 224 BC fell as a result of an earthquake.

COLOUR. A quality of the visual sensation. It is not known what is going on in the mind of an observer when he sees a colour, but it is possible to analyse the quality of the light coming from a coloured object. Light consists of electro-magnetic radiations of various wavelengths or frequencies of vibration, and if a beam of light is refracted through a prism it can be spread out into a spectrum, each part of the spectrum corresponding to a particular wavelength. At the long-wave end of the spectrum there are the red radiations; at the short-wave end the violet colours; and in between are the orange, yellow, yellow-green, green, blue-green, and blue hues. Purples are a mixture of radiations from the two ends of the spectrum. When the surface of an object is illuminated by white light, some parts of the spectrum are absorbed, depending on the molecular structure of the material of the surface and of the dyes or pigments which may have been applied to it. Thus a red surface will absorb the light from the blue end of the spectrum, but have a high reflection for light at the long-wave end. Colours vary in brightness or luminosity, in hue, and in saturation - i.e. in the extent to which they are admixed with white.

COLOUR BLINDNESS. An incurable defect of vision which reduces the ability to discriminate one colour from another. In the most common types confusion among the red-yellow-green range of colours is very prevalent - e.g. many colour-blind observers are unable to distinguish red from yellow or yellow from green. The cause of congenital C.B. is not known, although it probably arises from some defect in the retinal receptors. Toxic conditions caused by excessive smoking, lead poisoning, etc., can lead to C.B. Statistics show that from 2 to 6 per cent of males suffer from the defect, but among women the number of cases is under 1 per cent.

COLOURS, Military. Flags or standards carried by regiments, so called because of the various combinations of colours employed to distinguish one regiment from another. Each battalion carries the Sovereign's colour - i.e. a Union Jack on a blue ground - and the regimental colour which bears the title, crest, and motto of the regiment with the names of battle honours. Rifle regiments do not carry colours.

COLT, Samuel (1814–62). American inventor of the revolver named after him (1835). At Hartford, Conn., his birthplace, he built up an immense arms-manufacturing business.

COLUGO. Two species of mammal constituting the order Dermoptera, also known as flying lemurs, though not related to the lemurs. About the size of a small cat, they are chiefly vegetarian, and are active at night rather than during the day. They do not actually fly, but use a membrane extending forelimb-hindleg-tip of tail to glide from branch to branch. They are found from the Philippines to Malaysia.

COLUM, Padraic (1881–1972). Irish writer. He was associated with the foundation of the Abbey Theatre, Dublin, where his best-known plays *Land* (1905), *Fiddler's House,* and *Thomas Muskerry,* were performed. His *Collected Poems* (1932) show a homely lyric gift.

COLUMBA (521–97). Latin form of Colum or Columcille ('C. of the cell'). Irish saint and apostle of Scotland. B. in co. Donegal of royal descent, he founded monasteries and churches in Ireland. In 563 he sailed with 12 companions to Iona, and built there the monastery famous in the history of the conversion of Britain. He crowned king Aidan. In 1958 his cell, with the broad slab of rock on which he slept, was discovered.

COLUMBAN (543–615). Irish saint. B. in Leinster, he studied at Bangor, and *c.* 585 went to the Vosges with 12 other monks and founded the monastery of Luxeuil. Later he preached to the barbarians in Switzerland, then went to Italy, where he built the abbey of Bobbio in the Apennines.

COLUMBIA. River in western N America, famous for salmon. It rises in B.C., Canada, and flows through Washington state, USA, to the Pacific below Astoria. It is harnessed for irrigation and power by the Grand Coulee and other great dams.

COLUMBIA. US city, cap. of S Carolina, on the Congaree river. A distributing centre and seat of S Carolina university, it makes textiles, fertilizers, hosiery, etc. Pop. (1970) 113,540.

COLUMBIA, District of. Seat of the federal govt. of the USA. It is conterminous with the capital, Washington (q.v.).

COLUMBIFORMES. Order of birds including the various forms known as pigeons and doves (family Columbidae) together with the extinct dodo and solitaire (family Raphidae). The sand-grouse (Pteroclidae) are often added as a 3rd family.

COLUMBINE (kol'umbīn). A plant (*Aquilegia vulgaris*) belonging to the Ranunculaceae. It is a perennial herb, with deeply divided leaves, and purple flowers with spurred petals. It grows wild in woods and is a familiar garden plant.

COLU'MBIUM. *See* NIOBIUM.

COLU'MBUS, Christopher (1451–1506). Discoverer of America. B. at Genoa, he went to sea at an early age, and in 1478 settled in Portugal. Having come to the conclusion that Asia could be reached by sailing westward, he sought

COMET. Halley's comet was first recorded by the Chinese in 240B.C. and filled Englishmen with dread when it made its appearance in 1066, as depicted in this scene from the Bayeux Tapestry. When they rushed to tell King Harold he saw it as an ill omen, and his defeat at the Battle of Hastings ensued. On the right, a photograph taken in 1910 at the Helwan Observatory, Egypt. *Photos: The Mansell Collection and Courtesy of the Royal Astronomical Society.*

for many years for a patron to finance such a voyage. After many delays he won the support of the king of Spain, and on 3 Aug. 1492 sailed from Palos with 3 small ships. On 12 Oct. land was sighted (probably Watling Island), and within a few weeks Cuba and Haiti were also discovered. On his return to Spain in March 1493, C. was loaded with honours. During his 2nd voyage (1493-6) he discovered Guadalupe, Montserrat, Antigua, Porto Rico and Jamaica. In 1498 he discovered Trinidad, and sighted the mainland of S America for the first time. He now became involved in quarrels among the colonists sent to Haiti, and in 1500 the governor sent him back to Spain in chains. Released and compensated by the king, he made his last voyage in 1502-4, during which he explored the coast of Honduras and Nicaragua in the hope of finding a strait leading to India. He d. in poverty in Valladolid, and lies buried in Seville cathedral. In many states of the USA *Columbus Day* (12 October) is a public holiday. In 1968 the site of the wreck of his flagship, *Santa Maria*, sunk off Hispaniola 25 Dec. 1492, was located.

COLUMBUS. Capital city of Ohio, USA, on the rivers Scioto and Olentangy. It is near a coalfield and natural gas resources, and industries incl. cars, planes, missiles, electrical goods, mining machinery, refrigerators, and telephones. There are 3 Univs. and a symphony orchestra. Pop. of the met. area (1970) 1,017,850.

COLUMN. In architecture, a structure, round or polygonal in plan, erected vertically as a support for some part of a building. Cretan paintings reveal the existence of wooden Cs. in Aegean architecture, about 1500 BC. The Hittites, Assyrians, and Egyptians also used wooden Cs., and in modern times they are a great feature in the monumental architecture of China and Japan. In classic architecture there are 3 principal types of Cs., viz. *Doric* which is a tapering shaft with a simple capital consisting of an echinus and abacus, and no base; the *Ionic* which is more slender than the Doric, its most distinctive feature being the capital which has 2 large volutes in the front and 2 at the back; and the *Corinthian* which is similar to the Ionic, but has a capital ornamented with conventional acanthus leaves. *See* ORDER.

COLUMBUS. An engraving of the portrait by Piombo, of which the original is in the Uffizi, Florence. *Photo: The Mansell Collection.*

COLWYN BAY. Seaside town, Clwyd, N Wales, known as the 'garden resort of Wales'. The Welsh Mountain Zoo is the only one of its kind in Eruope. Pop. (1972) 25,470.

COMA (kō'ma). In medicine, a state of complete unconsciousness from which the subject cannot be roused even by powerful stimuli; and in optics one of the geometrical aberrations of a lens, whereby skew rays from a point object make a comet-shaped spot on the image plane instead of meeting at a point, hence the name.

COMBINATION ACTS. Laws passed in Britain in 1799 and 1800 making trade unionism illegal. Their introduction was the result of the anti-Jacobin panic following the French Revolution, and the fear that the unions would become centres of political agitation. The unions continued to exist, but claimed to be friendly societies or went underground, until the acts were repealed in 1824, largely due to Francis Place.

COMBINED OPERATIONS. *See* COMMANDOS.

COMECON. The Council for Mutual Economic Co-operation was estab. 1949 by USSR in opposition to the Marshall Plan (q.v.), and is known in Russian as Sovet Ekonomischeskoi Vzaimopomoshchi (SEV). Founder members were USSR, Bulgaria, Czechoslovakia, Hungary, Poland and Romania; later Albania 1949-61, E Germany 1950, Mongolia 1962, and Vietnam 1978. A number of other countries either have 'observer status' or co-operate in some measure.

Industrial production increased but COMECON lagged behind the scientific-technical developments of the West, and its share of world trade declined. In the 1950s there was a demand for specialization of production in the East, and better trade between COMECON and the West, especially with the development of the European Common Market. Khrushchev in 1962 proposed to achieve this by a supranational organization, but this was opposed by Hungary, Poland, Romania and China. Czechoslovakia, which attempted independent relations with the West, was invaded in 1968. From 1973, however, Romania made separate agreements with the EEC, reaching a comprehensive trade pact in 1980. This breaking of the ranks is discouraged by the USSR which, by making large-scale deals with the West herself, tends to control the spread of Western-derived science and technology in the East, which remains a captive market for Russian exports of cars, etc.

COMÉDIE FRANÇAISE (komehdē' fronsāz'). The French national theatre in Paris, formally estab. in 1680 by Louis XIV. Rules laid down by Napoleon in 1812 are still in force. It receives a govt subsidy, and from Molière's time has been associated with the leading French dramatists and players. Its base is the Salle Richelieu on the right bank, and the Théatre de l'Odéon, on the left bank, is a testing-ground for avant-garde ideas.

COMET (Gk *kome*, hair). A member of the Solar System, composed of relatively small particles surrounded by an envelope of tenuous gas. Some Cs. move round the sun in short periods, but the only periodical C. visible to the naked eye is Halley's, which has a period of 76 years and is due to return in the year 1986. Strictly speaking, all Cs. are periodical, but the 'great Cs.' have periods amounting to thousands or even millions of years, so that they cannot be predicted. Large Cs. have long tails, but the small, short-period Cs. are often tail-less. The last really brilliant C. was Halley's in 1910. It has been suggested that the Tunguska 'event'; which levelled Siberian forests NW of Lake Baikal in 1908, may have been caused by collision of a C. nucleus with Earth. Cs. have also been suggested as causing Ice Ages (their dust particles cooling Earth's upper atmosphere), or even carrying the basic building blocks of life to our own and other planets.

COMINES (komēn'), **Philippe de** (*c.* 1445-1509). French statesman and historian. He was a minister of Charles the Bold, duke of Burgundy, but from 1472 was in the service of Louis XI of France. In 1489-91 he wrote his *Mémoires* (pub. 1524), one of the most valuable historical documents of the age.

COMINFORM. *See* INTERNATIONAL.

COMINTERN. Abbreviation of Communist International. *See* INTERNATIONAL.

COMMANDOS. British troops of Combined Operations Command who raided enemy-occupied territory in the S.W.W. The name was suggested by Lt-Col D. W. Clarke who, after Dunkirk, prepared a scheme for 'amphibious guerrilla warfare'. Among the most important C. raids were those on the Lofoten Islands (3-4 Mar. 1941), Vaagsö, Norway (27 Dec. 1941), St Nazaire (28 Mar. 1942), and Dieppe (19 Aug. 1942). In 1940 Cs. were sent to the Middle East. One of their most daring exploits was the raid in Nov. 1941 on Rommel's HQ in the desert. Cs. were later active in other theatres of war, e.g. in French North Africa, Sicily, and Italy, and went into action on D-Day, taking part in some of the hardest fighting in Normandy. In Nov. 1944 Cs. took part in the capture of the island of Walcheren at the mouth of the Scheldt, and later distinguished themselves in the crossing of the Rhine. Cs. also fought in Burma. At the end of the war the army Cs. were disbanded, but the organization was carried on by the Royal Marines. The term C. originated in S Africa, where it was used for Boer military reprisal raids against African tribesmen, and later, in the S African War, against the British.

COMMANDO. A scene during the commando raid on Vaagsö Island in 1941, during the Second World War. *Photo: Popperfoto.*

COMMISSIONERS FOR OATHS. In England persons appointed by the Lord Chancellor with power to administer the oath or take an affidavit. They are usually practising solicitors.

COMMITTAL PROCEEDINGS. In the UK a hearing before local magistrates of evidence as to whether there is a case to answer before a higher court. From 1967 the proceedings were unreported unless a defendant, or one of them, wished the restriction lifted. The system came under debate following the Jeremy Thorpe case in 1978.

CO'MMŌDUS, Lucius Aelius Aurelius (AD 161-92). Roman emperor from 180. Son of Marcus Aurelius, he proved an ignoble tyrant and was strangled by members of his household.

COMMON LAW. That part of the English law not embodied in legislation. In contrast with legislation, C.L. consists of rules of law embodied in judicial decisions. It is also described as 'unwritten law' as opposed to the 'written law' of legislation. English C.L. became the basis of law in the USA.

With the growth of law reports grew the doctrine of 'judicial precedent', i.e., that, in deciding cases, the courts must have regard to the principles of law laid down in earlier reported decisions which relate to the same point, or to a similar point, in the particular case before them. This rule does not prevent the courts from making reasonable extensions of such principles to suit variant facts, or from laying down a new principle if the case before them is unconnected with any existing principle. Hence, the C.L. (sometimes also called 'case law' or 'judge-made law') is an important agency in keeping the law in harmony with the needs of the community, where no legislation is applicable, or where, if there is, its exact meaning has to be interpreted by the courts.

A narrower meaning of C.L. is that it comprises the law embodied in decisions of the C.L. Courts, as opposed to that contained in 'Equity', i.e. the decisions of the Court of Chancery.

COMMON MARKET. Another name for European Economic Community. *See under* EUROPEAN UNION; ANDES; CARIBBEAN COMMUNITY, etc.

COMMON PRAYER, Book of. The service book of the C of E, based very largely on the Roman Breviary. The first Book of Common Prayer in English was that known as the First Prayer Book of Edward VI, pub. in 1549. The Second Prayer Book of Edward VI appeared in 1552, but was withdrawn in 1553 on Mary's accession. In 1559 the Revised Prayer Book was issued, closely resembling that of 1549. This was suppressed by parliament in 1645, but its use was restored in 1660 and a number of revisions were made. This Book of C.P. is still officially recognized, but (as permitted by acts of 1968 and 1974) the *Church's Alternative Service Book* (1980) contains modern language services authorized by the General Synod.

COMMONS. Unenclosed wastes and pastures used in common by the inhabitants of a parish or district or the community at large. It is a popular misconception that a C. belongs to 'the public' and that therefore anyone may use it as he pleases. Cs. originated in the manorial system. In every manor there was a large area of unenclosed and uncultivated land over which the freeholders and copyholders had the right to take or use what the soil naturally produced.

COMMONS, House of. *See* PARLIAMENT.

COMMONWEALTH, The. On 15 May 1917 Jan Christian Smuts, then S. African Min. of Defence, and in London as representative of his country in the Imperial War Cabinet of the F.W.W., suggested that 'British commonwealth of nations' was the right title for the British Empire. The name was recognized in the Statute of Westminster (1931), but after the S.W.W. a growing sense of independent nationhood led to the simplification of the title to THE COMMONWEALTH.

The C. is now a free association of sovereign independent states, the full 'members of the C.', together with a number of dependent terrs., such as colonies and protectorates, which rank as 'C. countries'.

In the case of C. countries which have reached self-governing maturity but are too small to bear the full responsibilities of 'members of the C.' there may be special status, for example, as an Associated State of the UK (q.v.) or 'special member', *see* NAURU.

There were 3 impulses behind the growth of the British Empire. The 1st, the impulse to seek freedom of religious practice, was the main element in the creation of the original colonies in N America. The 2nd, the search for trade, had some part in N America (notably through the Hudson's Bay Company) and was the overriding influence in the Far East and in many parts of Africa. The 3rd, which came into play in the 19th cent., was the urge felt by the Christian community in Britain to carry the gospel to the heathen; it resulted in the exploration and opening up of the interior of the 'dark continent' of Africa.

HISTORY. England, Wales, Ireland, and Scotland, the 4 countries of the British Isles, came under one sovereign with the accession of James VI of Scotland as James I of England in 1603; and it was in the reign of this monarch that, in 1607, the 1st successful English colony was founded overseas, in N America at Jamestown, Virginia. British settlement spread up and down the E coast of that continent until in 1664, when the British secured New Amsterdam (New York) from the Dutch, there was a continuous fringe of colonies from the present S Carolina in the S to what is now New Hampshire in the N. These colonies, and others formed later, had democratic institutions and a good deal of freedom, and it was the attempt of George III and his unwise minister Lord North to coerce their inhabitants into paying taxes to the home government that roused the colonists to resistance which came to a head in the War of American Independence, 1775-83, and led to the creation of a new independent state, the United States of America, from the 13 English colonies then lost.

But before this happened, the British had set up colonies and trading posts in other parts of the world, and conquered territories from other European empire builders. Settlements were made in Gambia and on the Gold Coast (1618) in Bermuda (1609) and others of the W Indian islands; Jamaica was taken from Spain in 1655; Acadia (Nova Scotia) was secured from France by the Treaty of Utrecht, 1713, which recognized Newfoundland and Hudson Bay (as well as Gibraltar in Europe) as British. New France (Quebec), Cape Breton Island, and Prince Edward Island became British as a result of the Seven Years War, 1756-63.

In the Far East, the East India Company, chartered 1600, set up factories, as their trading posts were called, on the W coast of India at Surat, 1612; on the E coast at Madras, 1639; and on the Hooghli, one of the mouths of the Ganges, 1640. Bombay came to the British Crown in 1662, and was granted to the E India Company for £10 a year. A struggle in the following century between the French and English E India Companies ended in 1763 in the triumph of the English. The Company, subsequently involved in more than one war with Indian Princes, steadily increased its possessions and the territories over which it held treaty rights up to the eve of the Indian Mutiny, 1857. That rising was put down, but it resulted in the taking over of the govt of British India by the Crown, 1858; Queen Victoria was proclaimed Empress of India on 1 Jan. 1877. Ceylon had also been annexed to the E

The Commonwealth

	Area in 1,000 sq. km.	*Pop. in 1,000s*	*Capital*
In Africa			
*Botswana	575	1,001	Gaborone
British Indian Ocean Terr.	.2	2	Victoria
*Gambia	11	700	Banjul
*Ghana	239	13,367	Accra
*Kenya	583	18,580	Nairobi
*Lesotho	30	1,438	Maseru
*Malawi	117	6,612	Zomba
*Mauritius	2	1,002	Port Louis
*Nigeria	924	85,219	Lagos
St. Helena	.1	5	Jamestown
*Seychelles	.3	65	Victoria
*Sierra Leone	73	3,705	Freetown
*Swaziland	17	632	Mbabane
*Tanzania	943	20,524	Dodoma
*Uganda	236	13,819	Kampala
*Zambia	752	6,346	Lusaka
*Zimbabwe	391	8,077	Salisbury
In the Americas			
Anguilla	.09	7	The Valley
*Antigua	.4	80	St. John's
*Bahamas	14	223	Nassau
*Barbados	.4	251	Bridgetown
*Belize	23	154	Belmopan
Bermuda	.05	55	Hamilton
Brit. Virgin Is.	.2	10	Road Town
*Canada	9,976	24,882	Ottawa
Cayman Islands	.3	14	Georgetown
*Dominica	.7	74	Roseau
Falkland Is.	12	2	Stanley
*Grenada	.3	111	St. George's
*Guyana	210	833	Georgetown
*Jamaica	12	2,347	Kingston
Montserrat	.1	113	Plymouth
*St. Christopher-Nevis	.4	44	Basseterre Charlestown
*St. Lucia	.6	119	Castries
*St. Vincent and the Grenadines	.2	134	Kingstown
*Trinidad and Tobago	.5	1,149	Port-of-Spain
Turks and Caicos Is.	.4	7	Grand Turk
In the Antarctic			
Australian Antarctic Terr.	5,403	—	

	Area in 1,000 sq. km.	*Pop. in 1,000s*	*Capital*
Brit. Antarctic Terr.	390	—	—
Falkland Island Dependencies	1.6	—	—
(N.Z.) Ross Dependency	453	—	—
In Asia			
*Bangladesh	143	96,535	Dacca
*Brunei	6	209	Bandar Seri Begawan
*Cyprus	9	653	Nicosia
Hong Kong	1.2		Victoria
*India	3,215	730,572	Delhi
*Malaysia, Rep. of	332	14,995	Kuala Lumpur
*Maldives	.3	168	Malé
*Singapore	.6	2,501	Singapore
*Sri Lanka	66	15,300	Colombo
In Australasia and the Pacific			
*Australia	7,704	15,265	Canberra
Norfolk Island	.03	2	—
*Fiji	18	676	Suva
*Kiribati	.7	60	Tarawa
**Nauru	.02	8	—
*New Zealand	269	3,203	Wellington
Cook Islands	.2	18	—
Niue Island	.3	4	—
Tokelau Islands	.01	2	—
*Papua New Guinea	475	3,259	Port Moresby
Pitcairn	.005	.1	—
*Solomon Islands	30	254	Honiara
*Tonga	.7	104	Nuku'alofa
**Tuvalu	.02	8	Funafuti
*Vanuatu	15	127	Vila
*Western Samoa	3	160	Apia
In Europe			
*United Kingdom			
England	131	56,009	London
Wales	21	2,768	Cardiff
Scotland	79	5,226	Edinburgh
N. Ireland	14	1,536	Belfast
Isle of Man	.5	60	Douglas
Channel Islands	.2	131	—
Gibraltar	.006	29	Gibraltar
*Malta	.3	308	Valletta
	33,932	2,846,447	

*Independent members of the Commonwealth
**Special members

India Co. in 1796, and Burma, after a series of Anglo-Burmese Wars from 1824, became a prov. of British India in 1886.

Constitutional development in Canada started with an act of 1791 which set up Lower Canada (Quebec), mainly French-speaking, and Upper Canada (Ontario), mainly English-speaking. In the American War of 1812, the USA assumed, erroneously as was soon apparent, that Canada would gladly join the Union; but there was nevertheless enough discontent there to lead in 1837 to rebellion in both Canadas. After the suppression of these risings, Lord Durham was sent out to advise on the affairs of British N America; his report, published in 1839, became the basis for the future structure of the Empire. In accordance with its recommendations, the 2 Canadas were united in 1840 and given a representative legislative council: the beginning of colonial self-government. With the British N America Act, 1867, the self-governing dominion of Canada came into existence; to the original union of Ontario, Quebec, New Brunswick, and Nova Scotia were later added further territories until the federal govt of Canada controlled all the N part of the continent except Alaska.

Far away in the Antipodes, colonization began with the need to find a place for penal settlement after the loss of the original American colonies. The first shipload of convicts was landed in Australia in 1788 on the site of the future city of Sydney; New South Wales was opened to free settlers in 1819; and in 1853 transportation of convicts was abolished. Before the end of the century 5 Australian colonies - NSW, W Australia, S Australia, Victoria, Queensland - and the island colony of Tasmania had each achieved responsible govt; an act of the Imperial Parliament at Westminster created from them the federal commonwealth of Australia, an independent dominion, 1901. New Zealand, annexed in 1840, was at first a dependency of NSW; made a separate colony in 1853, it was created a dominion 1907.

The Cape of Good Hope in S Africa was occupied by 2 English captains in 1620; but neither the home govt nor the E India Company was interested. The Dutch occupied it in 1650, and Cape Town remained a port of call for their E India Company until 1795 when, French revolutionary armies having occupied the Dutch Republic, the British seized it to keep it from the French, and under the Treaty of Paris, 1814, bought it from the new kingdom of the Netherlands for £6,000,000. British settlement began in 1824 on the coast of Natal, proclaimed a British colony in 1843.

Resentment over the abolition of slavery (1833) in all British possessions led a body of Boers (Dutch for farmers) from the Cape to make the great trek north-eastwards, 1836, and found Transvaal and Orange Free State. Conflict between the British govt, which claimed sovereignty over those areas (since the settlers were legally British subjects), and the Boers culminated, after the discovery of gold in the Boer territories, in the S African War of 1899-1902, which brought Transvaal and Orange Free State definitely under British sovereignty. Given self-govt in 1907, they were in 1910, with Cape Colony (self-governing 1872) and Natal (self-governing 1893), formed into the Union of S Africa, 4th dominion of the Empire.

The British S Africa Company, chartered 1889, extended British influence over S Rhodesia (a colony in 1923) and N Rhodesia (a protectorate in 1924); with Nyasaland, taken under British protection in 1891, the Rhodesias were in 1953 formed into a federation (1953-63) with representative govt. Uganda was made a British protectorate in 1894, to put an end to inter-tribal wars. Kenya, formerly a protectorate, became a colony in 1920, certain districts on the coast forming part of the Sultan of Zanzibar's dominions remaining a protectorate.

In W Africa, British control was extended from time to time in Gambia and the Gold Coast. Sierra Leone colony started in 1788 with the cession of a strip of land to provide a home for liberated slaves; a protectorate was established over the hinterland in 1896. British influence in Nigeria began through the activities of the National Africa Company (the Royal Niger Company from 1886) which bought Lagos from an African chief in 1861 and steadily extended its hold over the Niger Valley until it surrendered its charter in 1899; in 1900 the two protectorates of N and S Nigeria were proclaimed.

The F.W.W. ousted Germany from the African continent, and in 1921-2, under League of Nations mandate, Tanganyika was transferred to British administration, SW Africa to South Africa; Cameroons and Togoland, in W Africa, were divided between Britain and France.

The establishment of the greater part of Ireland as the Irish Free State, with dominion status, came in 1922. A new constitution adopted by the Free State in 1937 dropped the name and declared Ireland (Eire) to be a 'sovereign independent state'; 12 years later S Ireland became a republic outside the Commonwealth, though remaining in a special relationship with Britain.

British India was given independence in 1947 as the 2 dominions of India (predominantly Hindu in religion) and Pakistan (predominantly Moslem). A startling constitutional development came in 1950 with India's decision to become a republic but, with the full consent of the other members, to remain within the Commonwealth. This made it simple for other members of the C. to adopt a similar status on becoming independent, since it entails recognition of the Queen as Head of the Commonwealth, but not as ruler of the individual state. The progress to independent statehood throughout the C. may be judged from the following list of members:

United Kingdom, Canada (1867), Australia (1901), New Zealand (1907), India (1947), Sri Lanka (Ceylon, 1948), Ghana (Gold Coast, 1957), Malaysia (Malaya, 1957-63), Nigeria (1960), Cyprus (1961), Sierra Leone (1961), Tanzania (Tanganyika and Zanzibar, 1961-3), Jamaica (1962), Trinidad and Tobago (1962), Uganda (1962), Kenya (1963), Malawi (Nyasaland, 1964), Malta (1964), Zambia (N Rhodesia, 1964), Gambia (1965), Singapore (1965), Guyana (Brit. Guiana, 1966), Botswana (Bechuanaland, 1966), Lesotho (Basutoland, 1966), Barbados (1966), Mauritius (1968), Swaziland (1968), Nauru (1968), Tonga (1970), W Samoa (1970), Fiji (1970), Bangladesh (E Pakistan, 1972), Bahamas (1973), Grenada (1974), Papua New Guinea (1975), Seychelles (1976), Solomon Islands (1978), Tuvalu (1978), Dominica (1978), St. Lucia (1979), Kiribati (Gilbert Islands, 1979), St. Vincent and the Grenadines (1979), Zimbabwe (1980), Vanuatu (1980), Antigua and Barbuda (1981), Belize (1981), Maldives (1982), St Christopher-Nevis (1983), Brunei (1984).

The emergence of C. members inhabited by pops. of non-British blood brought about changes of attitude within the group. When the Union of S Africa adopted a rep. form of govt in 1961, it decided not to seek re-admission to the C., because of differences with other members (incl. Britain) over apartheid. A similar crisis occurred when Rhodesia made a unilateral declaration of independence in 1965, rather than accept the principle of the granting of independence on terms 'acceptable to the people of Rhodesia as a whole'. The ultimate solution in 1980 was the return of Rhodesia to its legal status as

COMMONWEALTH. The London conference in 1977. From left to right: front row – Malawi (H. Kamuzu Banda), India (M.R. Desai), Australia (M. Fraser), Jamaica (M. Manley), Cyprus (Abp. Makarios), H.M. the Queen, United Kingdom (J. Callaghan), Zambia (K.D. Kaunda), Bangladesh (Z. Rahman), New Zealand (R.D. Muldoon), Nigeria (S. Yar'Adua); middle row – Papua New Guinea (M. Soarce), Sierra Leone (S.P. Stevens), Mauritius (Sir Seewoosagur Rangoolam), Barbados (J.M. Adams), Grenada (E.M. Gairy), Tanzania (A. Jumbe), Ghana (F.W. Akuffo), Bahamas (L.O. Pindling), Tonga (HRH Prince Fatafehi Tu'ipelehake); back row – W. Samoa (T. Efi), Malaysia (D. Hussein bin Onn), Fiji (Sir Kamisese Mara), Lesotho (L. Jonathan), Kenya (D.T. arap Moi), Singapore (Lee Kuan Yew), Sri Lanka (F.R.D. Bandaranaike), Guyana (F.R. Wills), Swaziland (M. Dlamini), Trinidad and Tobago (J. Donaldson), Gambia (Sir Dawda Jawara), Botswana (Sir Seretse Khama), Canada (P. Trudeau). *Photo: Central Press.*

'Southern Rhodesia' before official independence as Zimbabwe. The urge to national independence has also led to breakaway movements within members of the C., as with Biafra in Nigeria in 1967, Bangladesh from Pakistan in 1971-2 (which led to Pakistan's leaving the C. in 1971), unrest in Canada from the 1960s on the Quebec question, dissension among is. in the Caribbean and Pacific, and in 1975 within the UK itself when devolution was being discussed for Scotland and Wales.

Special members of the C. are those of very small size which enjoy the functional benefits of membership, but have no representation at meetings of heads of govermnents: Nauru, Tuvalu, and St Vincent and the Grenadines.

Consultation at top level on major topics takes place at *Commonwealth Conferences* especially convened, but there was no permanent organization until at the 1965 conference it was suggested, mainly by the Afro-Asian members, that one should be estab. on the lines of the United Nations. The Secretaries-General have been Canadian diplomat Arnold Smith 1965–75, and 'Sonny' Ramphal (q.v.) from 1975. The Secretariat HQ is at Marlborough House, Pall Mall, London. The Commonwealth Office, formerly the only day-to-day link with the C. countries, was merged with the foreign Office in 1968.

Bodies dealing with C. affairs incl. the *Royal Commonwealth Society* (1868), *Commonwealth Institute* (q.v.), *Commonwealth Development Corporation* (q.v.), and *Commonwealth Foundation* (1965) estab. to assist contacts between professional people and organizations in the C. countries. *See* COMMONWEALTH DAY.

COMMONWEALTH. The Secretary General Shridath Ramphal straddles three of the five continents which enrich the Commonwealth. A Guyanese of Indian origin, he met his English wife in Britain. *Photo: Courtesy of the Central Office of Information.*

COMMONWEALTH CONFERENCE. Popular name for a meeting between the Prime Ministers (or Defence, Finance, Foreign or other Mins.) of the sovereign independent members of the Commonwealth. Colonial Cs. had been instituted in 1887, also meeting in 1894, 1897 and 1902. The 1907 Conference resolved that Imperial Cs. be held every 4 years, and these met regularly till 1937 (the most notable being in 1926 which defined the relationship of the self-governing members of the Commonwealth). From 1937 the tendency was towards the present more informal discussions now known as C.Cs., but although these are purely consultative, the implementation of policies being decided by individual govts, results may be far-reaching.

Notable recent C.Cs. have been Singapore (1971) the first outside the UK; Sydney (1978) the first regional meeting; and Lusaka (1979) the first regular session in Africa.

COMMONWEALTH DAY. Celebrated on the official birthday of Elizabeth II, it was called Empire Day till 1958 and celebrated on 24 May (Qu. Victoria's birthday) till 1966.

COMMONWEALTH DEVELOPMENT CORPORATION. An organization founded as the Colonial D.C. in 1948 to aid the development of dependent Commonwealth territories; the change of name and extension of its activities to include those now independent were announced in 1962. It works in close co-operation with the govts concerned.

COMMONWEALTH INSTITUTE. The major centre in the UK for information about the Commonwealth and its dependent territories, founded in 1887. The permanent galleries are in Kensington High St.

COMMUNE OF PARIS. The revolutionary govts set up in Paris in 1789-94 and 1871. The former, a purely municipal govt set up after the storming of the Bastille, played a prominent part in the French Revolution until the fall of Robespierre. The latter, a provisional govt of Socialist and left-wing Republicans, was elected in March 1871 after an attempt by the right-wing National Assembly at Versailles to disarm the Paris National Guard, and held power until May, when the Versailles troops captured Paris and massacred at least 20,000 people. It is famous as the first socialist govt in history.

COMMUNISM. The revolutionary socialist movement basing its theory and practice on the teachings of Marx (q.v.). The first organization of those sharing this outlook was the Communist League, for which Marx and Engels wrote the *Communist Manifesto* (1848), setting out the general theory of C. According to this, human society has passed through successive stages - primitive society, slavery, feudalism and capitalism; that each phase was at first progressive, but later became a drag upon human progress and had to be superseded by a higher phase, through the taking of power by a new class which represented the new social system. Capitalism, progressive in its early stages, appears as a barrier to progress in its monopoly stage, so that in order for mankind to advance the working class must take power, end the capitalist system of production for private profit, and build a socialist society based on common ownership of the means of production and a planned economy.

The Social Democratic parties formed in Europe in the second half of last century professed to be Marxist, but their outlook gradually became 'reformist' - aiming at reforms of capitalist society rather than at the radical social change envisaged by Marx. The Russian Social Democratic Labour Party, however, led by Lenin, remained Marxist, and led the Russian workers in the November 1917 revolution, and in the subsequent building up in the Soviet Union of a socialist society on Marxist principles. It changed its name to 'Communist Party' to emphasize its difference from Social Democratic parties elsewhere. Revolutionary socialist parties and groups united to form Communist Parties in other countries (in Britain in 1920), and China, at first under Russian tutelage, swiftly emerged after the S.W.W. as a rival to the Soviet Union in world leadership. Both took strong measures to maintain or establish their own types of 'orthodox' C. in countries on their borders (USSR in Hungary and Czechoslovakia, qq.v.) and China in Korea and Vietnam (qq.v.), and in more remote areas (USSR in the Arab world and Cuba, and China in Albania); and both of them in the newly-emergent African countries.

During the late 1960s and the 1970s two issues were dominant *Firstly*, whether the state requires to be maintained as 'the dictatorship of the proletariat' once revolution on the economic front has been achieved (so that classes may also be abolished beyond revival on the political, ideological, cultural and traditional fronts), or whether it may then become the state of the entire people: Engels, Lenin, Khrushchev, and Liu Shao-chi held the latter view, and Stalin and Mao Tse-tung the former. *See* CHINA, HISTORY. *Secondly*, the Brezhnev Doctrine (*see* BREZHNEV).

In 1976 the Euro-Communists (French, Italian, Romanian, Spanish and Yugoslav) repudiated any attempt to restore Soviet dominance and the rule of any internat. organisation such as the Comintern or Cominform. Typical of more recent thought also was the abandonment by the Japanese Communist Party of the concept of the 'dictatorship of the proletariat' (suggestive of violent revolution), and of the term Marxist-Leninism (the names of historic individuals being inappropriate), which was replaced by 'scientific socialism'.

In the USA under the Internal Security Act of 1950 (known as the MacCarran Act: *see* MACCARRAN, PATRICK) all Communist organizations were required to register with the Attorney General and members might not hold a US passport. However, in 1964 the Supreme Court reversed the conviction of the Communist Party for failure to register in 1962, and ruled that passport provision unconstitutional.

COMMUNITY SERVICE. Scheme introduced in Britain by the Criminal Justice Act (1972), under which minor criminals are sentenced to spare time work in the service of the community (aiding children, the elderly or the handicapped), instead of prison. The offender must give his consent, be 17 or over, and have committed no violence.

CO'MMUTĀTOR. A device in an electric motor or generator whereby electric contact is made to the armature or rotor. It usually consists of a cylindrical insulator mounted on the armature shaft with metal contacts mounted on the insulator and connected to the armature coils through carbon or metal brushes. In a dc motor or generator the brushes and contacts are so arranged that the armature current is reversed at the appropriate time.

COMO (koh'moh). Italian city in Lombardy, on Lake C. at the foot of the Alps. The r. Adda flows through the lake from N to S, and the shores are famous for their beauty. C. has a marble cathedral (1396-1732), and is a tourist resort. Pop. (1971) 95,600.

CO'MORIN. The cape that is the most southerly point of India, in Tamil Nadu. Here meet the Indian Ocean, Bay of Bengal and Arabian Sea.

COMORO (komoro') **ISLANDS.** Archipelago of small is. in the Mozambique Channel NW of Madagascar. The main is. are Grand Comore, Anjouan, Mayotte, and Moheli. Cap. Moroni. Copra and vanilla are produced. Formerly a French Overseas Territory, the C.I. became in

1978 the Fed. and Islamic Rep. of the Comoros, except for Mayotte which remained united with France by its own wish. Area 2,170 sq.km (838 sq.m); pop. (1973) 300,000. M.U.: CFA franc.

COMPANIES. Cs. may be either public (to which the general public is invited to subscribe) or private (the great majority), at least 7 members being required for the former and 2 for the latter. In the majority of Cs. in Britain the liability of the members is limited liability to the amount of their subscription, under an act of 1855 promoted by Judge Lord Bramwell, by which British law came into line with Continental practice, which had already been largely adopted in the US. This limitation of liability is essential to commercial expansion when large capital sums must be raised by the contributions of many individuals. The affairs of Cs. are managed by directors, a public company having at least 2, and their accounts must be audited. *See* AUDITOR. The American equivalent of the company is the 'corporation', which has developed along similar lines although its activities are complicated on occasion by state law, i.e. a corporation of one state may not be allowed to operate in another.

The development of multinational Cs., world-wide in their operations, enabled them to avoid tax laws, affect currency stability, and be independent of elected govts. It has been est. that by 1985 some 400 Cs. may control 80% of all industrial capital assets. A counter-factor was the wide-spread demand for worker participation, common in Europe, where a supervisory board represents share-holders, workers and (where necessary) the public interest, and can appoint and dismiss the board of manage-ment. This two-tier structure may become mandatory throughout the Common Market.

COMPANIONS OF HONOUR. British Order of Chivalry, founded by George V in 1917. It is of one class only, and carries no title, but Companions append C.H. to their names. The number is limited to 65 and the award is made to both men and women.

COMPASS. An instrument for finding direction. The most commonly used is a magnetic C. consisting of a thin piece of magnetic material with the north-seeking pole indicated, free to rotate on a pivot perpendicular to its length and mounted on a C. card on which the points of the C. are marked. When the C. is properly adjusted and used the north-seeking pole will point to the magnetic N from which true N can be found from tables of magnetic corrections.

Cs. not dependent on the magnet are gyrocompasses dependent on the gyroscope and radiocompasses, depending on the use of radio.

COMPIÈGNE (koṅpē-ān'). Town with an airport in Oise dept, France, on the Oise near its confluence with the Aisne. It has an enormous château, built by Louis XV. Nearby is the forest of C. in a clearing of which the armistices of 1918 and 1940 were signed. Pop. (1975) 40,720.

COMPLEX. In psychology, a group of ideas and feelings which have become repressed because they are distasteful to the person in whose mind they arose; but which are still active in the depths of the person's unconscious mind, and which continue to affect his life and actions, even though he is no longer fully aware of their existence. Typical examples of a C. are the Oedipus C. and the Inferiority C.

COMPOSITAE. Family of Dicotyledonous flowering plants, characterized by having the flowers crowded into composite heads. It is the largest family of flowering plants, and the most highly advanced.

COMPOSITE. In industry a purpose-designed engineer-ing material created by combining single materials with complementary properties into a composite form. Most Cs. have a structure in which one component consists of discrete elements such as fibres (e.g. asbestos, glass or carbon steel in continuous or short lengths, or 'whiskers', specially grown crystals a few mm long, such as silicon car-bide) dispersed in a continuous matrix, e.g. plastics, concrete, steel.

COMPTON-BURNETT, Dame Ivy (1892-1969). English novelist. She relied on dialogue to show reactions of small groups of characters dominated by the tyranny of family relationships. Set at the turn of the century, they incl. *Pastors and Masters* (1925), *More Women than Men* (1933), *Mother and Son* (1955) and *The Mighty and Their Fall* (1961). DBE 1967.

COMPUTER. A device for performing accurate calcula-tions at extremely high speeds; usually utilizing electronic circuits and components. There are 3 types of electronic computer. An *analogue C.* in which information is repre-sented by smooth variations of some physical quality – thus the speedometer in a car uses 'analogue representa-tion'. Their main use is for the simulation of continuous processes. An everyday, non-electronic, analogue C. is a slide rule. A *digital C.* in which information is represented by groups of digits formed from binary numbers which use only two symbols 'O' and 'I' to represent quantities. These can equate to the 'on/off' state of circuits or other two state devices. When Cs. are referred to without qualifica-tion, digital Cs. are usually meant. A *hybrid C.* uses both digital and analogue elements. Their main use is as control devices in process control and manufacturing systems.

A digital computer system currently consists of *hard-ware* and *software*. The *hardware* is the electronic and electro-mechanical equipment in a computer system and performs 5 principal functions: data storage; arithmetic and logical processing; data transfer; data input and output; and programmed control. The *software* is the group of programs that make the computer system operate generally and specifically perform numerous applications. A *program* is a written list of coded data presented in a form upon which the C. can act.

The concepts behind the modern C. were devised by Charles Babbage (1792-1871) *c.* 1835, using mechanical devices. Theoretical papers were pub. in 1936 by Dr A. M. Turing in the UK and by C. Shannon in the USA. The first electronic computer was 'Colossus', developed in 1943 in Britain during the SWW by Thomas Flowers, head of the switching group at the Post Office research station. It was used at Bletchley Park to break the codes of the German High Command, and the achievement remained secret until 1977. *See* ULTRA.

By the 1980s computers had dramatically increased memory capacity and speed, but were also much smaller. *See* MICROCOMPUTER and CALCULATOR. In 1983 the British *transputer* had one piece of silicon smaller than a finger-nail combining various functions formerly requiring separate chips (q.v.), and operated at 5 million instruc-tions per second (MIPS).

Computers can already write their own programs, more complex than a human being could devise, and sometimes making it difficult to understand the reasoning behind C. results used in making key decisions. However, a '5th generation' of computers is under research in which molecules (q.v.) would be used to store information and act as transistors. Complementary to human brain processes, they would select from a range of facts, make inferences, learn from mistakes, and so generate new information. Calculations of ten billion per second are envisaged.

Information stored on computers raises problems of confidentiality, e.g. in the case of medical records, and also of security, e.g. the US embassy computers in Tehran in 1979. Special minicomputers have now been devised for US embassies so that sensitive data can be erased in moments.

COMPUTER. A bronze computer, the earliest known, made *c.* 30 BC and recovered from an ancient Greek shipwreck off the Mediterranen island of Antikythera in 1953. *Photo: Courtesy of Derek Price.*

COMPUTER. This 32-bit microprocessor is the equivalent, on a single piece of silicon, of the central processing unit of a small main- frame computer, operating at 1 million MIPS. It is used for multi-user business systems, in which several people use the computer at one time, and for the most advanced personal computers. *Photo: National Semiconductor.*

COMTE (koṅt), **Auguste** (1798-1857). French philosopher, founder of Positivism or the Religion of Humanity. B. at Montpellier, he studied at the Paris École Polytechnique, being expelled for leading a student revolt in 1816, and began teaching mathematics in Paris. In 1818 he became secretary to Saint-Simon and was much influenced by him. He began lecturing on the 'Positive Philosophy' in 1826, but was almost immediately attacked by a nervous disorder and once tried to commit suicide in the Seine. On his recovery he resumed his lectures and mathematical teaching. His first great work, the *Cours de Philosophie Positive,* was pub. in 6 vols., 1830-42. In 1848 he founded the Positivist Society, out of which grew the Positivist Church, which secured members not only in France but in Brazil and England. His second work of importance was the *Système de Politique Positive* (4 vols., 1851-4). For many years C. was in correspondence with J. S. Mill, who was the means of securing financial assistance from English sympathizers to enable him to carry on his work. C. d. of cancer and was buried in Père La Chaise cemetery in Paris. *See* POSITIVISM.

CONAKRY (kō'nakri). Cap. and chief port of Rep. of Guinea on the is. of Tombo, linked with the mainland by a causeway and by rail with Kankan 480km (300m) NE. Bauxite and iron ore are mined nearby. Pop. (1972) 525,700.

CONCENTRATION CAMPS. Prison camps used by the Nazis for the detention, and later for the mass extermination, of the Jews and political opponents. In 1939 some 40,000 Germans were est. to be in C.Cs. and over 200,000 had previously passed through them. During the S.W.W. the numbers of inmates were swollen by many millions of Jews and political suspects from occupied Europe, and when Germany was overrun the Allies found 80,000 prisoners at Buchenwald, 30,000 at Belsen, 32,000 at Dachau, 16,000 at Mauthausen and 16,000 at Ebensee - all near to starvation and many diseased. At the Polish camps conditions were even worse: at Oswiecim the total number sent to the gas-chambers exceeded 4 million and medical experiments were carried out on living persons, and at Maidanek *c.* 1½ million people were exterminated, cremated, and their ashes used as fertilizers. Many camp officials and others responsible were executed by the Allies as war criminals. *See* EICHMANN.

CONCEPCIÓN (konthepthē-on'). City of Chile, capital of the province of C., near the mouth of the Bió-Bió in a rich agricultural district. Nearby are a coalfield and a large steel plant. Pop. (1975) 180,000.

CONCERTINA (konsertē'na). A wind musical instrument with free reeds consisting of 2 keyboards connected by expansible and folding bellows. It is played by compressing and expanding the bellows while at the same time pressing the knobs on the keyboard. By these means air is admitted to the reeds, which are set in vibration. The

CONCRETE. The new building (left) of the Independent Broadcasting Authority at Crawley Court, near Winchester. Elegant cruciform units of exposed aggregate precast white concrete produce a bold cloistered effect among beautiful, mature trees. To the right, part of a mural by Philippa Threlfall at the new Greenwich District Hospital. A concrete 'tapestry' of coloured pebbles and ceramic pieces embedded in precast concrete slabs, it depicts the maritime history of Greenwich from mariners to modern dockers. *Photos: Courtesy of the Cement and Concrete Association.*

English C., or melodion, was invented by Wheatstone (q.v.) in 1829.

CONCERTO (konchār'tō). Composition, usually in 3 movements, for solo instrument or instruments and orchestra. Corelli and Torelli were early composers in the form, and Mozart wrote some 50 Cs. for various instruments. Modern C. composers incl. Schoenberg, Berg and Bartók, who have developed it along new lines.

CONCLAVE. Literally, a room locked with a key. Usually the word refers to the papal C. which is held in Rome immediately following the funeral of a pope. Wooden cells are erected inside the Vatican Palace near the Sistine Chapel, one for each cardinal, who is accompanied by his secretary and a servant, and all are sworn to secrecy on the deliberations. This section of the palace is then locked and no communication with the outside world is allowed until a new pope is elected, the result of each ballot being announced by a smoke signal - black for an indecisive vote and white when the choice is made.

CONCORD. Town in Mass., USA, on the C. river, 32km (20m) NW of Boston. Site of the first battle of the War of American Independence, 19 April 1775, it also has associations with Emerson, Thoreau. Hawthorne, Louisa Alcott and her father. Pop. (1970) 16,150.

CONCORDANCE. Book containing an alphabetical list of the words in some important work with references to the places in which they occur. The first C. was one prepared to the Vulgate by a Dominican in the 13th cent. The most famous C. is A. Cruden's (1737), of which many editions have appeared. There are also Cs. to Shakespeare, Milton, etc.

CONCO'RDAT. An agreement between the Pope as head of the RC Church and the temporal ruler of a state, concerning matters which are of mutual concern, e.g. the appointment of the clergy, education, taxation, etc. The C. effected between Napoleon and Pius VII in 1801 lasted in France until 1905. Mussolini's C. with the Holy See endured 1929-78: *see* ITALY.

CONCRETE. A building material composed of cement, sand, and crushed stone or gravel, mixed in varying proportions so that when dry there results a solid stone-like substance of very great durability.

C. was used by the Romans before 500 BC, and many examples of Roman work nearly 2,000 years old still exist. In medieval times it was used for the foundations, etc., of Westminster Abbey, Salisbury and York Cathedrals, etc. C. of the type known today was not used until the middle of the last century, following the discovery of Portland cement by Aspdin in 1824.

The life of C. is almost unlimited, and it is not affected by extremes of weather conditions, but durability may be affected by chemical additives to achieve faster setting. Additional strength is imparted by the use of steel reinforcement in the form of rods. Owing to its fireproofing qualities C. is frequently used as a coating for steel structural bars.

Pre-cast C. units such as paving slabs, lamp posts, drainpipes, walling blocks, etc., are now common, but the more recent development of larger units not only speeds the construction time of tunnels, blocks of flats and offices, etc., but minimizes interruptions due to bad weather. C. can be applied to other substances by means of a cement coating, and coloured C. is decoratively effective.

CONDÉ (kondeh'). A noble French family, related to the house of Bourbon. The founder of the family, Louis de Bourbon (1530-69), was an uncle of Henry IV of France, and was prominent as a Huguenot leader in the Wars of Religion. Louis II, called the Great C. (1621-86), won brilliant victories during the Thirty Years War at Rocroi (1643) and Lens (1648), rebelled in 1651 and entered the Spanish service, was pardoned in 1660, and commanded Louis XIV's armies against the Spaniards and the Dutch.

CONDER, Charles (1868-1909). English artist who painted in water-colour and oil, and executed a number of lithographs including the 'Balzac' (1899) and the 'Carnival' sets (1905).

CONDITIONED REFLEX. A response to an associated stimulus, e.g. a dog secretes saliva not only at the sight of food but in answer to a bell rung at mealtimes. It is considered to occur without conscious learning as a result of nerve processes in the brain. *See* BEHAVIOURISM and PAVLOV. Contrasted with the C.R. is a *simple* or *unconditioned* reflex - an action occurring automatically or intensively in immediate response to a stimulus, without involving the higher brain centres.

CONDOMINIUM. The joint rule of a territory by two or more states, e.g. Canton and Enderbury Islands, in the Phoenix Group (under the joint control of Britain and the USA for 50 years from 1939).

CONDOR. One of the largest of all flying birds (*Vultur gryphus*), one of the American vultures (*Cathartidae*), with up to a 3m (10ft) wing span. The plumage is black, except for a white frill at the base of the neck which (like the head) is bare and bright red. Ranging from Ecuador to Patagonia, the C. hunts by sight and is carnivorous. Another species (*Gymnogyps californianus*) frequents the mountains of Lower California to Arizona, but is so nearly extinct that a special breeding programme has been undertaken.

CONDOR. A sacred bird for the Indians, it is reverenced in this dance of the condor at the Inti-Raymi, or festival of the sun-god. This is celebrated at Cuzco on 24th June, as in the days of the Incas. *Photo: Vautier-Decool.*

CONDORCET (koṅdorsā'), **Marie Jean Antoine Nicolas Caritat,** marquis de (1743-94). French philosopher and statesman. His essay on the theory of probabilities (1785), contributed to the *Encyclopédie,* won him a high reputation as a mathematician. He welcomed the Revolution in 1789, was elected to the Legislative Assembly of 1791-2, and his plan for state education (1792) formed the basis of the scheme adopted. One of the Girondins, he opposed the execution of Louis XVI, and was outlawed. Whilst in hiding, he wrote *Esquisse d'un tableau historique des progrès de l'esprit humain.* Arrested at length, he was found dead in his cell, probably having taken poison.

CONEY (kōn'i) **ISLAND.** Pleasure resort on a peninsula in the SW of Long Island, New York City, USA, part of Brooklyn. It has a famous board-walk 3km (2m) long.

CONFECTIONERY. A term of wide application covering food preparations having sugar as the principal ingredient and comprising 2 main classes, (*a*) sweetmeats and (*b*) cakes and pastries.

Prior to the 19th cent., sweet manufacture was carried out by apothecaries, who produced sweetmeats to mask the taste of their drugs, and by the chefs attached to the courts of kings and nobles. The manufacture of sugar-coated nuts, etc., known as dragées, is said to have been introduced by a Roman, Julius Dragatus, about 177 BC. Bon-bons were first made in France in the 13th cent., pastilles in the 15th, and fondants in the 17th cent. The great present-day volume of manufacture is due to the introduction of automatic and semi-automatic machines about the middle of the 19th cent.

CONFEDERATION OF BRITISH INDUSTRY. Organization estab. in 1965, combining the former Federation of British Industries (founded 1916), British Employers' Confederation, and National Association of British Manufacturers. The unified body voices general policy on economic, fiscal, commercial, labour, social and technical questions, and increased efficiency.

CONFESSION. The C. of sins originated with the Jews, and both John the Baptist's converts and the early Church practised public C. The Lateran Council of 1215 made auricular confession (the accusation by the penitent of himself of his sins to a priest who in Catholic doctrine is divinely invested with authority to give him absolution) obligatory once a year. Auricular C. is practised in Roman Catholic, Orthodox and most Oriental Churches and since the early 19th cent. has been revived in Anglican and Lutheran Churches.

The R.C. penitent in modern times has always confessed alone to the priest in a confessional box, but from 1977 such individual C. might be preceded by group discussion, or the C. itself might be made openly by members of the group. *See* PENANCE.

CONFIRMATION. Rite by which a previously baptized person is admitted to full membership of the Christian Church. It consists in the laying on of hands by a bishop, in order that the confirmed person may receive the gift of the Holy Spirit. Among Anglicans, the rite is deferred until the child is able to learn a catechism containing the fundamentals of Christian doctrine, and an unconfirmed person is not usually allowed to receive Holy Communion.

CONFUCIANISM. The body of beliefs and practices that are based on the Chinese classics and are supported by the authority of Confucius, although he himself maintained that he was a transmitter rather than a creator. For some 2,500 years C. has been the religion of the great masses of Chinese.

The scriptures of C. are the 5 Chinese classics or canonical books, viz. the Shu King, or book of historical documents; the Shih King, or ancient poems; the Li Ki, or book of rites and ancient ceremonies and institutions; the Yi King, or book of changes; and the Annals of Lu, otherwise known as Spring and Autumn. Only the last may be attributed with any confidence to Confucius's authorship, but the material in the other books may owe something to his editing.

From these scriptures the Chinese in countless generations have derived their ideas of cosmology, political government, social organization, and individual conduct. The origin of things is seen in the union of Yin and Yang, the negative and positive principles. Human relationships follow the patriarchal pattern; until 1912 the emperor was regarded as the father of his people, appointed by heaven to rule. The Superior Man was the ideal human, filial piety was the virtue of virtues, and in general human relationships were to be regulated by the Golden Rule. Accompanying this lofty morality is a kind of ancestor worship. Under the emperor, sacrifices were offered to heaven and earth, the heavenly bodies, the imperial ancestors, various nature gods, and Confucius himself. These were abolished at the Revolution in 1912, but ancestor worship (better expressed as reverence and remembrance) remained a regular practice in the home.

Under Communism C. continued, Lin Piao (q.v.) being associated with the cult, but Mao Tse-tung undertook an anti-Confucius campaign 1974-6, which was not pursued by the succeeding regime.

CONFUCIUS (*c.* 550-478 BC). Latinized form of K'ung Fu-tzu (K'ung the master), the Chinese sage whose name is given to Confucianism (q.v.). He was b. in Lu, a small state in what is now the province of Shandong, and his early years were spent in povery. At 15 his mind was 'set on learning'. At 19 he m., and about this time he was a minor official. Very early he began his career as a teacher, and gradually attracted a number of disciples on whose voluntary contributions he made a meagre living. In 517 there was an uprising in Lu, and C. spent the next year or two in the adjoining state of Ch'i, where the ruler treated him with marked respect. On his return he held aloof from public life until he was nearly 50, when he accepted the governorship of a small town and distinguished himself in the suppression of crime and in the promotion of morality. Then for 14 years he wandered from state to state accompanied by a handful of disciples. At last he returned to Lu and devoted himself to the revision of the ancient Chinese scriptures, some parts of which have been attributed, though on slight evidence, to his pen. At his death he was buried with great pomp, and his grave outside Qufu has remained ever since a centre of devout pilgrimage.

CONGER. *See* EELS.

CONGO. *See* ZAÏRE.

CONGO, People's Rep. of the. Country of central Africa, lying on the Equator. It has a narrow Atlantic coastline, where Pointe Noire is the chief port, and inland has the Zaïre and its tributary, the Oubangui, as its SE boundary and water highway. Sugar is grown, and though agriculture is generally undeveloped, products incl. cotton, coffee, palm oil, cocoa, peanuts, etc., and timber is exported. Mineral resources incl. potash, lead, zinc, and offshore oil, and there are textile, cement, plastic and other industries. Hydro-electric potential is very great. The cap. is Brazzaville. MU.: CFA franc.

Formerly the French colony of Middle Congo, it achieved independence in 1960. There are still close links with France (French is still the official language), but relations are also maintained with USSR and Cuba. In 1979, following sporadic fighting and military interventions throughout the period from independence, Col. Denis Sassou-Ngouesesso became pres., and under a new constitution a National People's Assembly was elected. Ngouesesso was unanimously re-elected leader in 1984.

Area 342,000 sq.km (132,000 sq.m); pop. (1977) 1,440,000, of whom half are Christian, mainly R.C.

CONGO, Republic of. *See* ZAÏRE.

CONGREGATIONALISM. The form of church govt adopted by those Protestant Christians known as Congregationalists, in which each congregation manages its own affairs. The first Congregationalists were the Brownists, named after Robert Browne, who in 1580 defined the congregational principle. In the next cent. they were known as Independents, e.g. Cromwell and many of his Ironsides, and in 1662 hundreds of their ministers were driven from their churches and estab. separate congregations. The Congregational Church in Eng. and Wales and the Presbyterian Church in England joined in 1972 to form the United Reformed Church. The latter, like its counterpart the Congregational Union of Scotland, has no control over individual churches but is simply consultative. Similar unions have been carried out in Canada (United Church of Canada, 1925) and USA (United Church of Christ, 1957).

CONGRESS. National legislature of USA, consisting of a House of Representatives (435 members, apportioned to the States of the Union on the basis of population, and elected for 2-year terms) and the Senate (100 senators, 2 for each State, elected for 6 years, one third elected every 2 years). Both representatives and senators are elected by direct popular vote. C. meets at Washington in the Capitol. Members of both houses receive a salary of $42,500.

CONGRESS OF INDUSTRIAL ORGANIZATIONS. *See* AMERICAN FEDERATION OF LABOR AND CONGRESS OF INDUSTRIAL ORGANIZATIONS.

CONGRESS PARTY. The Indian National Congress, founded by the Englishman A. O. Hume in 1885, was a moderate body until the F.W.W. when, under Gandhi's leadership, it began a campaign of non-violent non-co-operation. Declared illegal 1932-4, under Nehru's guidance, it was recognized as the paramount power in India at the granting of independence in 1947, and won the elections of 1952, 1957, 1962, 1967 and 1971. In 1977 it was defeated for the first time and Mrs Gandhi lost the leadership she had held since 1966. Heading a splinter group, known by her initial as Congress (I), she achieved an overwhelming victory, engineered by her son Sanjay, in the elections of 1980, and reduced the main C. party in turn to a splinter group.

CONGREVE (kon'grēv), **William** (1670-1729). English dramatist and poet. B. nr Leeds, he was a friend of Swift at Trinity Coll., Dublin, and in 1691 began studying law in London. He won immediate success with his first comedy *The Old Bachelor* (1693), which was followed by *The Double Dealer* (1694), *Love for Love* (1695) and the tragedy *The Mourning Bride* (1697). In 1698 he pub. a reply to Jeremy Collier's (q.v.) attack on the contemporary stage, and 2 years later his masterpiece, *The Way of the World*, appeared, but was at the time a failure.

Among the friends of his later years were the actress Mrs Bracegirdle, and Henrietta, duchess of Marlborough, to whom he left his fortune. C. is the most brilliant of the Restoration comic dramatists, and achieves perfection of construction and style.

CONIC SECTIONS. The curves obtained when a cone is intersected by a plane; they were first discovered by the ancient Greeks and have been of great importance in mathematics. If the intersecting plane cuts both extensions of the cone it yields a hyperbola, if it is parallel to the side of the C. it produces a parabola; other intersecting planes produce circles and ellipses.

CONIFERAE (kōnif'erē) or **CONIFERALES.** Division of plants, forming the largest and most important order of the Gymnosperms, and contained in about 46 genera, and about 500 species. They are trees and shrubs, often of a characteristic pyramidal form, and the leaves are linear 'needles', or small and scale-like, usually evergreen. The reproductive elements are borne in male and female cones, and the pollen is distributed by the wind. They usually grow in forests, and are specially characteristic of the colder and temperate parts of the world, particularly the N hemisphere.

The C. are divided into 5 families: the Araucariaceae, including the monkey-puzzle tree and the kauri pine; Podocarpaceae, including half-a-dozen genera of trees, shrubs, or small undershrubs; the Pinaceae, including the spruce, pine, fir, larch, and cedar; the Cupressaceae, including the juniper, cypress, arbor vitae, umbrella-pine, and the gigantic *Sequoia*; and the Taxaceae, which includes the yew.

CONJUNCTIVĪ'TIS. Inflammation of the conjunctiva or membrane which covers the front of the eye.

CONNACHT. Province of Rep. of Ireland, consisting of the cos. of Mayo, Galway, Roscommon, Sligo, and Leitrim. Mainly lowland, it is agricultural and stock-raising country with very poor land in the W. The chief rivers are the Shannon, Moy, and Suck, and there are a number of lakes. The chief towns are Galway, Roscommon, Castlebar, Sligo, and Carrick-on-Shannon. The Gaelic language has maintained itself better in C. than in the other provinces, and the C. dialect has been adopted as the standard of the national language. Area 17,122 sq.km (6,611 sq.m); pop. (1971) 390,900.

CONNECTICUT (konet'ikut). One of the New England States of the USA, bounded by the States of New York, Massachusetts, and Rhode Is., and Long Is. Sound. Most of it is plain, but there are highlands in the NW. The chief rivers are the Connecticut, the Thames, the Naugatuck, and the Housatonic. The chief towns are Hartford (the cap.), New Haven, Bridgeport, Waterbury, and Stamford. Although retaining a picturesque countryside, and producing poultry, dairy products, tobacco, and fruits and vegetables, C. is also highly industrialized. Among its complex products are silverware and cutlery, watches and clocks, typewriters, helicopters and jet engines, nuclear submarines, and ball bearings. Most famous of its institutions is Yale University at New Haven. The American Shakespeare Festival is held at Stratford, and Mystic Seaport, at the E end of Long Island Sound, is a re-creation of a 19th cent. village, with a collection of more than 150 old ships, some having been refitted and refloated.

Settled in 1635 by Puritan colonists from Massachusetts, C. in 1639 adopted the famous Fundamental Orders, foreshadowing in many respects the United States constitution. It was one of the original 13 states of the American union. Area 12,973 sq.km (5,009 sq.m); pop. (1970) 3,032,217.

CONNELL, James (d. 1929). Irish socialist writer, remembered as the author of *The Red Flag*.

CONNEMARA (konemah'rah). The western division of co. Galway, Rep. of Ireland, much visited by tourists for its wild scenery.

CONNECTICUT. Mystic Seaport is a recreated 19th century village, with a chapel, school and blacksmith's forge, and alongside the quays, famous sailing ships including the wooden whaler, *Charles W. Morgan* and the square-rigged *Joseph Conrad. Photo: Courtesy of the U.S. Travel Service.*

CO'NNOLLY, Cyril (1903-74). English writer. As founder-editor of the literary magazine *Horizon* (1930-50), he exercised considerable critical influence. His books incl. *The Rock Pool* (1935), a novel of artists on the Riviera and *The Unquiet Grave* (1945), a vol. of essays under the pseudonym 'Palinurus'.

CONQUISTADOR (konkistador'). Spanish word for 'conqueror', applied to such explorers and adventurers in the Americas as Cortes and Pizarro.

CONRAD. Name of several kings of the Germans. **Conrad I** (d. 918) succeeded Louis the Child, the last of the Ger. Carolingians, in 911, and during his reign the realm was harassed by Magyar invaders. **Conrad II** (d. 1039) reigned from 1024 and ceded the march Sleswick to Canute. **Conrad III** (1093-1152), the 1st king of the Hohenstaufen dynasty, was crowned at Aachen in 1138, and throughout his reign a fierce struggle between his followers, the Ghibellines, and the Guelphs, the followers of Henry the Proud, duke of Saxony and Bavaria, and his son Henry the Lion, continued. C. took part in the 2nd crusade. **Conrad IV** (1228-54), son of the emperor Frederick II, was elected king in 1237, and had to defend his right of succession against Henry Raspe of Thuringia and William of Holland. His son **Conradin** (1252-68), the last of the Hohenstaufen, was defeated and captured by Charles of Anjou at Tagliacozzo in 1268, and beheaded in Naples.

CONRAD, Joseph (1857-1924). British novelist. Of Polish parentage, he was b. Teodor Jozef Konrad Korzeniowski in the Ukraine, and was taken to Warsaw in 1861 by his father. He joined the French merchant marine in 1874, and transferred to the British service in 1878, when he first landed at Lowestoft with no knowledge of English. In 1886 he gained his master mariner's certificate and became a naturalized British subject, but retired from the sea in 1894 to write. His first novel, *Almayer's Folly*, appeared in 1895 and was followed by - among others - *An Outcast of the Islands* (1896), *The Nigger of the 'Narcissus'* (1897), *Lord Jim* (1900) and *Nostromo* (1904). Showing increasing power and mastery of technique, he not only brought home to English readers the mysteries of sea life and exotic foreign settings, but plumbed the

CONQUISTADOR. The Amerindians of Mexico had seen nothing like the ships, artillery and horses which Cortés brought with him, and at first assumed that only a descendant of the Sun-god could possess such things. *Photo: The Mansell Collection*

psychological isolation of the 'outsider'. C.'s earlier period closes with the autobiographical *Mirror of the Sea* (1906). Among later books were *Under Western Eyes* (1911), with a tsarist Russian background, *The Secret Agent* (1907), and *Chance* (1914), his first popular success.

CONSANGUINITY. Relationship by blood, whether lineal, i.e. by direct descent, or collateral, i.e. by virtue of a common ancestor. The degree of C. is of importance in laws relating to the inheritance of property and also in relation to marriage, which is forbidden between parties closely related by blood.

CONSCIENTIOUS OBJECTORS. A term originally denoting parents who objected to compulsory vaccination, later applied to persons refusing compulsory service, usually in the army, on moral, religious or political grounds.

CONSCRIPTION. The system under which all able-bodied male citizens are legally liable to serve with the armed forces. It originated in France in 1792, during the Revolutionary War, and in the 19th cent. it became the established practice in almost all European states. C. was unknown in Britain before the F.W.W., although a campaign in its favour was carried on by Lord Roberts for some years. During F.W.W. it was introduced for single men between 18 and 41 in March 1916 and for married men 2 months later, but was abolished after the war. It was introduced for the first time in peace in April 1939, when all men aged 20 became liable to 6 months' military training. The National Service Act, passed in Sept. 1939, made all men between 18 and 41 liable to military service, and in 1941 women also became liable to be called up for the women's services as an alternative to industrial service. Men reaching the age of 18 continued to be called up until 1960.

In the USA conscription (the 'draft') was introduced during the Civil War - by the Confederates 1862 and by the Union side 1863. In the F.W.W. a Selective Service Act was passed in 1917, and again in 1940 in anticipation of America's entry into the S.W.W. It remained in force, except for 15 months 1947-8, until abolished by Nixon following the withdrawal from Vietnam. In 1980 Carter restored registration for a possible military draft for men at 18, but his proposal that it be extended to women was rejected by Congress.

CONSENT, Age of. The age at which consent may legally be given to sexual intercourse by a girl or boy. In the UK it is sixteen.

CONSERVATION. Concept that the Earth, together with its atmosphere, animal and plant life, and mineral and agricultural resources, form an interdependent whole which is in danger of irreversible depletion and eventual destruction unless positive measures are taken to conserve a balance. Action by govts has been supplemented by private agencies, e.g. the World Wildlife Fund.

CONSERVATIVE PARTY. One of the 2 historic British parties, the name replacing 'Tory' in general use from 1830 onwards. Traditionally the party of landed interests, opposed to the *laissez-faire* of the Liberal manufacturers, it supported, to some extent, the struggle of the working-class against the harshness of conditions arising from the Industrial Revolution. The split of 1846 over Peel's corn-law policy led to 20 years out of office, or in office without power, until Disraeli 'educated' his party into accepting parliamentary and social change, extended the franchise to the artisan (winning considerable working-class support), launched imperial expansion, and estab. an alliance with industry and finance. The Home Rule issue of 1886 drove Radical Imperialists and old-fashioned Whigs into alliance with the Conservatives, so that the party had nearly 20 years of office, but Joseph Chamberlain's proposals for Imperial Preference and the general fear that Protection meant higher prices led to a Liberal landslide in 1906. The C.P. fought a rearguard action against the sweeping reforms which followed and only the outbreak of the F.W.W. averted a major crisis.

During 1915-45, except briefly in 1924 and 1929-31, the Conservatives were continually in office, whether alone or as part of a coalition, the main factor in maintaining this ascendance being the break-up of the traditional 2-party system by the rise of Labour. At the elections following the end of the S.W.W. Labour swept to power, but the C.P. formulated a new policy in their Industrial Charter of 1947, visualizing an economic and social system in which employers and employed, private enterprise and the State, work to mutual advantage. Antagonism to further nationalization reduced the Labour majority in the 1950 election, and in 1951 returned the Conservatives to power with a small majority. This was slightly increased in the general elections of 1955 and 1959 - despite such setbacks as Suez - because of maintained prosperity. Narrowly defeated in 1964 under Home (q.v.), the C.P. chose in 1965 its first elected leader, Edward Heath (q.v.) and was again defeated 1966, but in 1970 achieved a small majority. However, the C. govt's imposition of wage controls led to confrontation with the unions and, when Heath sought a mandate Feb. 1974, a narrow defeat, repeated in a further election in Oct. 1974. In 1975 Margaret Thatcher replaced Heath, and won a majority of 43 over all other parties in the election of May 1979, raised to 143 in the landslide of June 1983, though on a reduced vote. In the European Parliament it forms the majority of the European Democratic Group.

CONSTABLE, John (1776-1837). English landscape painter. B. at E Bergholt, Suffolk, the son of a miller, he first worked in his father's mills, but in 1795 was sent to study art in London, where he copied Reynolds, painted religious pictures and studied Ruysdael. In 1799 he entered the RA schools and from 1802 exhibited every year in the RA. His marriage to Mary Bicknell in 1816 followed a long period of waiting, due to her relatives' stubborn opposition. He was elected ARA in 1819, and his picture 'The Haywain' created a sensation when exhibited in the Paris Salon in 1821. From 1830 to 1833 he was mainly occupied with the famous series of mezzotints engraved by David Lucas. His pictures are remarkable for the way in which they evoke a sense of warmth or coolness, according to the kind of weather he is depicting. Among the most famous are 'Flatford Mill' (1825), 'Stratford Mill' (1820), 'The Leaping Horse' (1825), 'The Cornfield' (1826), 'Dedham Vale', and 'Salisbury Cathedral' (1831). In 1978 it was recognized that a number of his other famous works had been produced by other members of the family, incl. his son Lionel.

CONSTABLE. A self-portrait of John Constable in pencil and watercolour. *Photo: Courtesy of the National Portrait Gallery.*

CONSTABLE. The artist's best-loved picture, and one which helped to change the course of European art. *Photo: Courtesy of the National Gallery, London.*

CONSTANCE. Town in Baden-Württemberg, Germany, on the section of the Rhine joining Lake C. and the Untersee. Suburbs stretch across the frontier into Switzerland. C. has clothing, machinery, and chemical factories and printing works. The council of C., 1414-17, ended the Great Schism, 1378-1417, with rival popes at Rome and Avignon. Pop. (1978) 65,000.

CONSTANCE, Lake (Ger. Bodensee). Lake lying between Germany, Austria, and Switzerland; the Rhine flows through it. Area 540 sq.km (200 sq.m).

CONSTA'NTA. Chief seaport of Romania on the Black Sea, cap. of C. region. The exporting centre for the Romanian oilfields, to which it is connected by pipeline, it has refineries, shipbuilding yards, and food factories. Pop. (1977) 260,330.

CONSTANTAN. A high-resistance alloy of approximately 40 per cent Ni and 60 per cent Cu with a very low temperature coefficient. It is used as a resistance wire in items of physical apparatus.

CONSTANT DE REBECQUE, Henri Benjamin (1767-1830). French writer and politician. B. at Lausanne, he travelled widely, began a liaison with Mme de Staël in 1796, and in 1803 went into exile because of his liberal views. Returning to Paris on the fall of Napoleon in 1814, he advocated a constitutional monarchy, and after Waterloo he withdrew to London, where he pub. the autobiographical novel *Adolphe.* He went back to Paris in 1816, and for the rest of his life defended constitutional liberalism. His most ambitious work is *De la Religion* (1825-31).

CONSTANTINE II (1940-). King of the Hellenes. In 1964 he succeeded his father Paul I (q.v.) and later that year m. Princess Anne-Marie of Denmark: his heir is Crown Prince Paul (1967-). He went into exile 1967; formally deposed 1973.

CONSTANTINE THE GREAT (*c.* AD 274-337). First Christian emperor of Rome, and founder of Constantinople. B. at Naissus (Nish, Yugoslavia), he was the son of Constantius. He was already well known as a soldier when his father d. at York in 306 and he was acclaimed by the troops there as joint-emperor in his father's place. His authority over Britain and Gaul was at first recognized by the other emperors, but a few years later Maxentius, the joint-emperor at Rome (whose sister C. had married), mobilized his armies to invade Gaul. C. won a crushing victory outside Rome at the Milvian Bridge (312). It was during this campaign that he was said to have seen a vision of the cross of Christ superimposed upon the sun, accompanied by the words, 'In this sign conquer'. By the Edict of Milan (313) he formally recognized Christianity as one of the religions legally permitted within the Roman Empire, and in 314 summoned the bishops of the western world to the Council of Arles. Since 312 C. had been sole emperor of the West, and by defeating Licinius, the emperor in the East, C. became sole ruler of the Roman world (324).

He now set to work to consolidate and reorganize his empire. He increased the autocratic power of the emperor, issued legislation which tied the farmers and workpeople to their crafts in a sort of caste system, and enlisted the support of the Christian Church. He summoned, and presided over, the first general council of the Church at Nicaea (q.v.) in 325.

C. moved his capital to Byzantium on the Bosphorus in 330 and renamed it Constantinople. In 337 he set out to defend the Euphrates frontier against the Persians, but d. at Nicomedia in Asia Minor.

CONSTANTINE THE GREAT. A gold medallion minted at Siscia AD 326–327. The emperor's biographer, Eusebius, interpreted his upward gaze as an attitude of prayer. *Photo: Courtesy of the British Museum.*

CONSTANTINE. City of Algeria, 320km (200m) E of Algiers. An ancient town, it was captured by the French in 1837. Carpets and leather goods are made. Pop. (1974) 350,200.

CONSTANTINO'PLE. The former capital of the Eastern Roman and Turkish Empires, now called by its Turkish name, Istanbul (q.v.). It was founded by Constantine the Great by the enlargement of the Greek city of Byzantium in 328, and became the seat of the imperial government in 330. Its elaborate fortifications enabled it to resist a succession of sieges, but it was captured by crusaders in 1204, and was the seat of a Latin kingdom until in 1261 the Greeks recaptured it. An attack by the Turks in 1422 proved unsuccessful, but after a gallant defence lasting nearly a year another Turkish army took the city by storm on 29 May 1453.

CONSTELLATION. A group of stars. Many received their names in antiquity from some mythological figure with which they were associated. *See* ZODIAC. In 1930 the International Astronomical Union standardized the boundaries of 88 Cs., the chief being: NORTHERN: Andromeda, Aquila, Auriga, Boötes, Cassiopeia, Cepheus, Corona Borealis, Cygnus, Draco, Hercules, Lyra, Ophiuchus, Pegasus, Perseus, Sagitta, Ursa Major, Ursa Minor. *Zodiacal:* Aquarius, Aries, Cancer, Capricornus, Gemini, Leo, Libra, Pisces, Sagittarius, Scorpius, Taurus, Virgo. SOUTHERN: Canis Major, Centaurus, Cetus, Corona Austrina, Corvus, Crater, Crux Australis, Eridanus, Hydra, Lepus, Lupus, Orion.

CONSTITUTION. The fundamental laws of a state, laying down the system of government, and defining the relations of the legislative, executive and judiciary to each other and to the citizens. The British C. is unique, in that it does not exist in the form of a single document; it consists rather of an accumulation of customs and precedents, which have arisen in the course of national development, together with a number of laws defining certain of its aspects. Among the most important of the latter are Magna Carta (1215), the Petition of Right (1628), and the Habeas Corpus Act (1679), limiting the royal powers of taxation and of imprisonment; the Bill of Rights (1689) and the Act of Settlement (1701), establishing parliamentary supremacy and the independence of the judiciary; and the Parliament Acts (1911 and 1949), limiting the powers of the Lords. The Triennial Act (1694), the Septennial Act (1716), and the Parliament Act (1911) limited the duration of parliament, while the Reform Acts of 1832, 1867, 1884, 1918, and 1928 extended the electorate. Relations between states of the Commonwealth are regulated by the Statute of Westminster (1931). By the Republic of Ireland Act (1948), S Ireland ceased to be a member of the Commonwealth, but neither the Irish Rep. nor the UK regards the other as a foreign state. The adoption of Republican status by India (1950) and others does not affect their membership and they accept the Queen as Head of the Commonwealth. In certain countries of the 'Old Commonwealth', such as Canada, the Queen, as Queen of Canada, is personally represented by a Governor-General, appointed on the recommendation of the country concerned. Constitutional crises in this connection are rare, but occurred in 1975 when the Australian Gov.-Gen. dismissed the PM after deadlock had been reached between the 2 Houses of Parliament, and the PM refused to call a general election.

The British C. is that of a parliamentary monarchy, sovereignty being vested in the Queen, Lords, and Commons. The legislature consists of the House of Lords and the elected House of Commons. Considerable numbers of Life Peers, espec. since 1958, have modified the hereditary basis of the Lords, but the natural bias of the House towards conservative-type legislation led to friction with the Wilson govt in 1968 and 1975, and with that of Callaghan in 1976, and a strengthening demand for its abolition. Nevertheless, creation of Labour peers continued. *See* PARLIAMENT. All legislation requires the royal assent (q.v.). The Queen, as the head of the executive, appoints her ministers, but since the revolution of 1688 it has become customary for her to choose them from the party commanding a majority in the Commons, on the advice of the leader of the party. The judges are

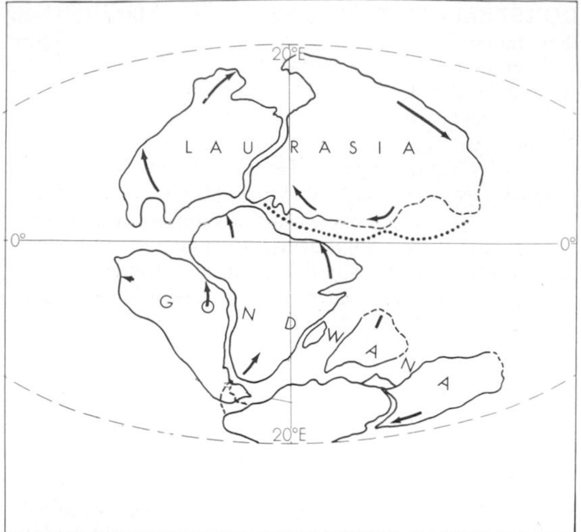

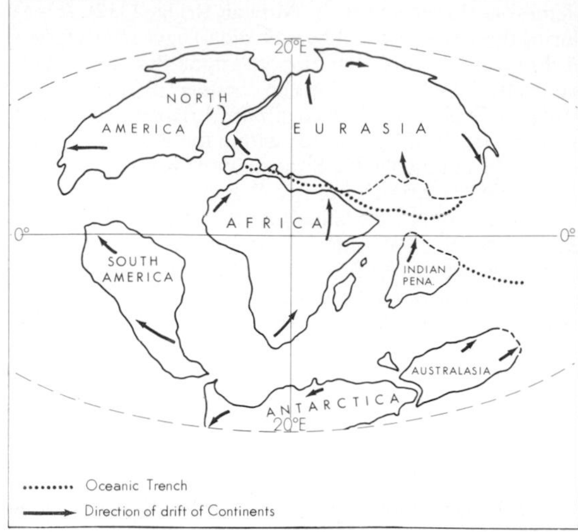

CONTINENT. The continents as they were at the end of the Triassic period 195,000,000 years ago (left) and the position (right) they had reached at the end of the Cretaceous period 65,000,000 years ago.

appointed by the Crown for life, and can be removed only on a petition from both Houses.

The C. of the USA, adopted in 1787, is the oldest written C. in existence. Subsequently modifications incl. the Bill of Rights, 1791 - this contained 12 amendments of which 10 were adopted, among them the '5th amendment' including the provision none should be compelled 'to be a witness against himself' which has frequently been quoted by those accused as Communists - the abolition of slavery 1865, equal rights for white and coloured 1870, and limitation of presidential terms to two, which came into effect in 1951 and was inspired by F. D. Roosevelt's unique achievement in being elected for a 4th term. The majority of judges are elected by popular vote, but *see* SUPREME COURT. *See* UNITED STATES.

Since the French Revolution almost all states have adopted written Cs. The present C. of the Soviet Union was adopted in 1936; it, too, is written. The proliferation of legislation during the 1970s in Britain, often carried on the basis of a small majority in the Commons and by govts. elected by an overall minority of votes, led to demands for the introduction of a written constitution as an additional safeguard for the liberty of the individual.

CONSTRUCTIVISM. Art movement which arose in the 1930s out of cubism (q.v.), having as its aim the creation of works - sculpture, painting, etc. - which exist in their own right and are unrelated to natural forms. Among the chief exponents of the movement are N. Gabo, B. Nicholson, B. Hepworth, and Mondrian (qq.v.).

CONSUL. The chief magistrate of ancient Rome following the expulsion of the last king in 510 BC. The Cs. were two annually elected magistrates, both of equal power; they jointly held full civil power at Rome, and the chief military command in the field. After the establishment of the Roman Empire the office became purely honorary. *See* FOREIGN RELATIONS.

CONSUMER PROTECTION. In early days the purchaser or 'consumer' of goods and services could be largely safeguarded by his own common sense, by test before purchase, and by being able to confront the seller personally in case of dissatisfaction. Today the technical complexities of products and their purchase from outlets which are only remotely connected with the original producer, tend to baffle the consumer, who is also under pressure from massive advertising which ranges from the merely optimistic to the deliberately deceptive. An early organization attempting C.P. was the British Standards Institution (1901) which lays down specifications of quality, performance and safety: goods reaching these standards may carry a certification, known from its shape as the 'kitemark'. Legal protection was given by the Trade Descriptions Act (1968), rendering it a criminal offence to describe goods or provisions falsely. In the USA there is special provision by both federal and state govts for C.P., and in 1962 Pres. Kennedy set out the 4 basic rights of the consumer as the right to safety, to be informed, to choose,

CONSTITUTION. The Australian constitutional crisis bubbles over into the Royal Jubilee visit in 1977. A lively demonstration against Sir John Kerr, the Governor-General, demands his resignation and Southern Cross flags are waved in support of a republic. *Photo: Penny Tweedie/Camera Press.*

and to be heard. There are many private consumer associations, and among the most influential of crusaders for greater protection is Ralph Nader (q.v.). A more positive approach to C.P. in the UK was the creation in 1974 of a govt dept of Prices and C.P. by subdivision of the Dept of Trade and Industry.

CONTACT LENSES. Lenses placed under the eyelids in contact with the eye, separated in most cases only by a film of tears. They may be used as a substitute for spectacles in the correction of refractive defects or, in special circumstances, as protective shells, or to correct cosmetic defects, or refractive errors which cannot be coped with by the normal spectacle lens. The earliest use of C.L. in the late 19th cent. was protective, or in the correction of corneal malformation, for it was not until the 1930s that simplification of fitting technique by taking eye impressions made their general use possible. The most recent development has been the 'soft' plastic lens which avoids the often severe discomfort suffered by prolonged use of earlier types, and enables the C.L. to be worn night and day for lengthy periods without removal.

CONTINENT. A major division of the land surface of the Earth. There are usually said to be seven: Africa, N America (incl. Central America), S America, Antarctica, Asia, Europe, and Oceania. Each C. is continued under the sea in a *continental shelf,* which varies in width according to the nature of the coastline. The shelf reaches a depth of about 200m (600ft), then drops more sharply, by the *continental slope,* to the ocean deeps. Only approx. five-sixteenths of the Earth's surface, the *continental area,* is above sea level. In 1915 Alfred Wegener (q.v.) advanced the theory, now generally accepted, that the way in which the shores of Europe/Africa and N/S America fit together indicates that the Cs. reached their present position by *continental drift,* this movement having followed the break-up of 2 super-continents, Laurasia in the N and Gondwanaland in the S, which themselves had once formed a single land mass, Pangaea. The Cs. 'float' on the rocks of the mantle of the Earth, proof of their movement coming from study of the movement of ancient rocks, etc., by Blackett, Runcorn, and others. For example, the folding of the Himalayas is the result of the comparatively recent drifting together of India and Asia. Africa is growing closer to Europe, so that the Algerian coast will eventually lock into the Riviera, and, in reverse, South America and Africa grow further apart by a few centimetres every year because of the thrust of lava rising from the Mid-Atlantic Rift. It is possible that Earth was originally smaller than today, so that the continents once covered the whole globe, and that there was a later expansion.

CONTINENTAL CONGRESS. In American history the several legislative bodies existing from 1774 to 1789, when the Constitution was adopted. The second C.C. convened May 1775 was that responsible for drawing up the Declaration of Independence.

CONTINENTAL SYSTEM. Napoleon's attempted economic blockade of Britain 1806–12.

CONTRACEPTION. *See* FAMILY PLANNING.

CONTRACT. An agreement between two or more parties which will be enforced by law. Every agreement is not a C., which always consists of an offer and an acceptance of that offer. In English law a C. must either be made under seal (i.e. in a deed) or there must be consideration to support it, i.e. there must be some benefit to one party to the C. or some detriment to the other.

A C., even though it is made in the proper form and the parties to it have the necessary capacity, may be unenforceable because it is made under a mistake, misrepresentation, duress, or undue influence.

Cs. which are illegal are void. Among illegal Cs. are those to commit a crime or civil wrong, to trade with the enemy, immoral Cs., and Cs. in restraint of trade, i.e. Cs. by which a servant binds himself not to compete with his master after his service is over. Cs. by way of gaming and wagering are void.

CONTRACT BRIDGE. Probably the most popular card game, played all over the world since 1930. It originated in 1925 in a bridge game on a steamer *en route* from Los Angeles to Havannah, and was introduced to New York clubs by H. S. Vanderbilt, one of the players. Subsequently the most famous expert was Ely Culbertson (q.v.).

C.B. is a development of Auction B. and like it is based on whist. It is played by 2 pairs of players as partners, and its distinctive feature is that trumps are settled by a preliminary process of bidding. The partner of the caller is 'dummy', and his hand is laid face upwards on the table. Scoring is above the line for honours and below the line for tricks; only the tricks actually contracted for and won count towards the game. Each trick over six contracted for and won counts 30 if spades or hearts, and 20 if diamonds or clubs, are trumps; in no trumps, 40 is counted for the first trick and 30 thereafter. A game is won when a pair scores 100 points below the line, and the pair which first wins 2 games wins the rubber (500 points if 3 games have been played, 700 if only 2). Extra points are awarded for over tricks, small slam, grand slam, etc., and penalties are imposed for under tricks. Once the bidding has been completed, play is very much as in 'auction' or whist, although in the various highly complicated systems there are numerous 'conventions'.

CONVOCATION. In the Church of England, the synods of the clergy of the provinces of Canterbury and York. The General Synod estab. 1970 took over the functions and authority of the Cs. of Canterbury and York which continued to exist only in a restricted form.

CONVO'LVŪLUS, or **bindweed.** Genus of plants, typical of the family Convolvulaceae. They are characterized by their twining stems, and by having their petals united into a tube. The common bindweed (*C. arvensis*), a trailing plant with handsome white or pink-and-white-streaked flowers, is a frequent weed in Britain.

CONVOY SYSTEM. The grouping of ships to sail together under naval escort in wartime. In the F.W.W. Royal Navy escort vessels were at first used only to accompany troopships, but the C.S. was adopted for merchant shipping when the unrestricted German submarine campaign opened in 1917. In the S.W.W. it was widely used by the Allies, and was generally successful, although there were heavy losses.

CONWY. Welsh port on the river C., Gwynedd, known until 1972 by the anglicized form *Conway.* Still surrounded by walls, C. has picturesque ruins of a castle rebuilt by Edward I in 1284. Pop. (1972) 12,160.

COOBER PEDY (ko͞o'ber pē'di). Town (Aboriginal 'white man in a hole') in the Great Central Desert, Australia. Opals were discovered in 1915, and are mined amid a moonscape of diggings in temperatures up to 60°C (140°F).

COOCH BEHAR. District of W. Bengal, India. Once a princely state it was merged in W. Bengal in 1950.

COOK, James (1728-79). British explorer. B. at Marton, Yorks., he joined the RN in 1755, and in 1768 was given command of an expedition to the S Pacific to witness the transit of Venus. He sailed in the *Endeavour* with Joseph Banks and other scientists, reaching Tahiti in April 1769. The transit was observed in June, after which C. sailed round New Zealand and charted the coasts. He then went on to make a detailed survey of the E coast of Australia, naming New South Wales, Botany Bay, etc., and arriving back in England on 12 June 1771.

Now a commander, C. set out in 1772 with the *Resolution* and *Adventure* to search for the southern continent. The location of Easter Island was determined, and the Marquesas and Tonga Islands plotted. Among other discoveries were New Caledonia and Norfolk Island, and New Zealand was revisited. C. returned on 25 July 1775, having sailed 60,000 m in 3 years.

The object of his 3rd and last voyage with the *Resolution* and *Discovery*, on which he set out 25 June 1776, was the discovery of the NW Passage from the Pacific end. On the way to New Zealand, he discovered several of the Cook or Hervey Islands and rediscovered the Hawaiian or Sandwich Islands. The ships sighted the American coast in lat. 45° N, and sailed N, making a continuous survey as far as the Bering Strait, when the way was blocked by ice. C. then surveyed the opposite coast of the strait (Siberia), and returned to Hawaii early in 1779. In Kealakekua Bay, one of the *Discovery*'s boats was stolen by the islanders, and C. was clubbed from behind on 14 Feb. in a scuffle on the beach when trying to recover it, and was buried at sea.

C. made enormous additions to geographical knowledge, was responsible for Britain's acquisition of the Australasian territories, and his accounts of his discoveries are classics.

COOK, Peter (1937-). British writer-comedian. Ed. at Cambridge Univ., he was in revue, *Beyond the Fringe* 1959-64, opened London's first satirical nightclub *The Establishment* (1960) with Dudley Moore (1935-), his partner in comic dialogues, who is also a jazz musician. Cook also owns a major share in the satirical magazine *Private Eye*.

COOK, Thomas (1808-92). Pioneer British travel agent, founder of Thos. C. & Son. B. in Derbyshire of poor parents, he started work at 10, and at 20 became a Baptist travelling missionary and temperance worker. He organized his first excursion in 1841 for a temperance meeting at Loughborough, and his first tour to Switzerland in 1863. Tours of America (1866), the Middle East (1868), and round the world (1872) followed. Travellers' cheques, known as 'circular notes', were introduced in the early 1870s. In 1884 C. was given charge of transport of Gordon's Sudan expedition.

COOK, Mt. See ALPS, Southern.

COOKE, Alistair (1908-). American journalist. B. in England, he was ed. at Cambridge, Yale and Harvard, and estab. a reputation for humorously penetrating interpretation of American affairs for British audiences, e.g. his television narrative *America* (1972–3). He was *Guardian* correspondent 1948–72. Hon KBE 1973.

COOKHAM-ON-THAMES. Village in Berkshire, England. The artist Stanley Spencer (q.v.) lived here for many years and a memorial gallery of his work was opened in 1962.

COOK. A portrait of Captain James Cook by Dance, presented to the National Maritime Museum, Greenwich, by the executors of Sir Joseph Banks. *Photo: RTHPL.*

COOK ISLANDS. Group of 6 large and a number of smaller islands 2,600 km (1,600 m) NE of Auckland, N.Z. Rarotonga, site of an internat. airport and of Avarua, the seat of govt, is the chief island. Niue, geographically part of the group, is separately administered. The C.I. were discovered by Capt. Cook 1773, annexed by Britain 1888, transferred to NZ 1901 and became a self-governing overseas terr. in 1964. Area 230 sq.km (90 sq.m); pop. (1976) 18,100.

COOK STRAIT. Strait dividing North and South Island, NZ, on which Wellington stands. A submarine cable transfers electricity from South to North Island.

COOL'ABAH. Aboriginal name for the Australian tree, *Eucalyptus microtheca*, found near inland rivers and hence also known as the flooded box. It is referred to as being by the camp site in 'Waltzing Matilda'.

COOLIDGE, John Calvin (1872-1933). 30th President of the USA. B. in Vermont, the son of a farmer and storekeeper, he became a lawyer and was Governor of Massachusetts in 1919, when he won fame by the vigour with which he crushed the Boston police strike. A republican, he became Vice-President in 1921 and President, on the death of Harding, in 1923. He was re-elected in 1924, and his period of office was marked by great economic prosperity.

COOPER, Alfred Duff. *See* NORWICH, LORD.

COOPER, Gary (1901-62). American actor. B. in Montana, he epitomized the lean, true-hearted Yankee, slow of speech but capable of besting the 'badmen' in *A Bengal Lancer, Mr. Deeds Goes to Town, Sergeant York* (Academy award 1941), and *For Whom the Bell Tolls.*

COOPER, Henry (1934-). Brit. heavyweight boxer. Noted for his left - Henry's hammer - he held the British and Empire titles 1959-71, and the European 1964 and 1968-71. In 1967 he became the first to win 3 Lonsdale belts outright.

COOPER, James Fenimore (1789-1851). American writer. B. in New Jersey of Quaker stock, he sailed before the mast to Europe and in 1808 became a midshipman. In 1811 he made a happy marriage, and spent most of the rest of his life on the family estate of Cooperstown. He wrote some 30 novels, first becoming popular with *The Spy* (1821). Most notable were the volumes of *Leather Stocking* stories (so called because they were linked by the figure of Hawk-eye or Leather Stocking) comprising *The Pioneers* (1823), *The Last of the Mohicans* (1826), *The Prairie* (1827), *The Pathfinder* and *The Deerslayer* (1841), all exciting stories of settlers and Redskins in the middle 18th century.

COOPER, Samuel (1609-72). English artist. He was probably b. in London, and his works - the finest of all miniatures - incl. portraits of Milton, Cromwell, and members of Charles II's court. Pepys commissioned him to paint his wife.

CO-OPERATION. The banding together of bodies of persons for mutual assistance in trade, manufacture, the supply of credit, or other services. In Britain the predominant type of C. is the Consumers' Co-operative Society, a retail trading concern whose shops sell at current market prices, but return the bulk of their profits (less any sums placed to reserve) to their members as 'dividends' on the sums spent there. Control is in the hands of a management committee elected by the members. Societies of this type in Britain have nearly 13,000,000 members, and in Scandinavia the rate is also high - in Denmark they cover approx. 45 per cent of the population. Usually the local societies are federated nationally in co-operative wholesale societies, which carry on wholesale trade and factory production. The original principles of consumers' C. were laid down in 1844 by the Rochdale Pioneers, under the influence of Robert Owen (q.v.). Producers' Co-operative societies, formed on a basis of co-partnership among the employees, exist on a large scale in France, Italy, and the Soviet Union, but are of little importance in Britain. Agricultural Co-operative Societies have been formed in Britain for the collective purchase of seeds, fertilizers, etc., while societies for co-operative marketing of agricultural produce are prominent in the US, Ireland, Denmark, the British Commonwealth, and many other countries. Often both functions are discharged by a single society. Agricultural Credit Societies are strong in the peasant countries of Europe and Asia, including parts of India. The US also has a Co-operative Farm Credit System.

CO-OPERATIVE COMMONWEALTH FEDERATION (CCF). *See* NEW DEMOCRATIC PARTY.

CO-OPERATIVE PARTY. Founded in Britain in 1918 by the C. movement, to maintain its principles in parliamentary and local govt, it contests seats by agreement with the Labour Party.

CO-OPERATIVE WHOLESALE SOCIETY (C.W.S.). The largest co-operative organization in the world, this British concern is owned and controlled by the numerous co-operative retail societies, who are also its customers. Founded in 1863, it acts as wholesaler, manufacturer, banker, etc., and owns factories, farms and estates, in addition to offices and warehouses, etc.

COOPER'S CREEK. *See* CHANNEL COUNTRY.

COORG (koorg). District of the state of Karnataka, India. Formerly the princely state of C., it was merged in Karnataka in 1956.

COOT. Genus of birds (*Fulica*), belonging to the rail family (Rallidae) and closely resembling the moorhens in habits and appearance. The European species (*F. atra*) is common in Britain. Its plumage is sooty black, and there is a large, bare white patch on the forehead (hence 'bald as a coot').

COOTE, Sir Eyre (1726-83). Irish soldier. B. near Limerick, he took part in Clive's occupation of Calcutta and the battle of Plassey. In 1759 he was transferred to the Carnatic, where his victory in 1760 at Wandiwash, followed by the capture of Pondicherry, ended French hopes of supremacy. He returned to India as C-in-C in 1779, and several times defeated Hyder Ali, sultan of Mysore.

COPE. Ecclesiastical vestment. It is a semi-circular cape, without sleeves, worn by priests of the Western Church in processions and on certain other formal occasions, but not when officiating at Mass.

COPENHAGEN. Capital of Denmark, on the islands of Zealand and Amager. The harbour occupies the channel between the two islands and forms the headquarters of most of the Danish shipping lines. The centre of the city is the Kongens Nytorv, an irregular open space adjacent to the harbour, on which focus the main thoroughfares of the city. To the NE are the citadel and the royal palace at Amalienborg. Buildings round the square include the Charlottenburg palace (1672-83), occupied 1754 by the Academy of Arts, the Kunstudstilling (1883), Thotts Palais (c. 1685), the Royal Theatre, Foreign Office, etc. The cathedral church was rebuilt early in the 19th cent. The new town hall dates from 1901. The Christiansborg, in the Slottsholm, an island formed by an arm of the harbour, is used for meetings of parliament. The univ. was founded in 1479.

C. was a fishing village until 1167, when the castle was built on the site of the present Christiansborg palace by the bishop of Roskilde. A settlement grew up, and it became the Danish cap. in 1443. On 9 April 1940 C. was occupied by the Germans, remaining in their hands until 5 May 1945. Pop. (1978) 1,268,428.

COPENHAGEN, Battle of. Naval victory won on 2 April 1801 by a British fleet under Sir Hyde Parker and Nelson over the Danish fleet. Here it was that Nelson put his telescope to his blind eye and refused to see Parker's signal for withdrawal.

COPE'PODA. Sub-class of Crustacea, incl. a great variety of forms, nearly all microscopic, abundant in the sea and fresh water.

COPERNICUS, Nicolaus (1473-1543). Polish astronomer. B. at Thorn on the Vistula, then under the Polish king, he studied at Cracow and in Italy, and lectured on astronomy at Rome. On his return to Pomerania in 1505 he became physician to his uncle, the bishop of Ermland, and was made canon at Frauenburg, although he did not take holy orders. Living there until his death, he interspersed astronomical work with the duties of various civil offices. For 30 years he worked on the hypothesis that the motion of the Earth was responsible for the apparent

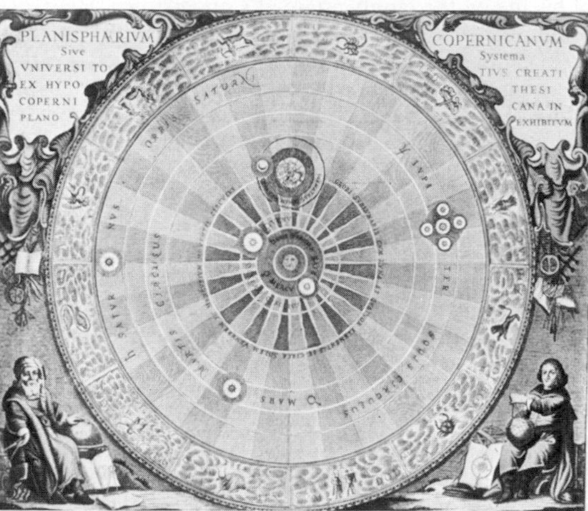

COPERNICUS. A representation of the planetary system which bears the astronomer's name. The signs of the zodiac surrounding the diagram show how closely astronomy and astrology were then linked. *Photos: The Mansell Collection*

COPENHAGEN. At the entrance to the harbour stands Edvard Eriksen's famous statue of Hans Christian Andersen's 'Little Mermaid'. *Photo: Courtesy of the Danish Tourist Board.*

movements of the heavenly bodies, but his great work *De revolutionibus orbium coelestium* was not pub. until the year of his death. In this work he proved that the Sun is the centre of our system, and he thus became a prime founder of modern astronomy.

CŌ'PLAND, Aaron (1900-). American composer. B. in NY, he studied in France with Nadia Boulanger, and in 1940 became instructor in composition at the Berkshire Music Center - from 1945 assistant director. C.'s early works, such as the piano concerto of 1926, were in the jazz idiom then popular in America, but he gradually developed a gentler style with a regional flavour drawn from American folk music. Later works incl. the ballets *Billy the Kid* (1939) - which contains a variant of the cowboy song 'Bury Me Not on the Lone Prairie' - *Rodeo* (1942) and *Appalachian Spring* (1944), based on a poem by Hart Crane; and *Inscape for Orchestra* (1967).

COPLEY, John Singleton (1737-1815). American artist. B. at Boston, Mass., of Anglo-Irish parents, he became the leading portraitist of the colonial period. From 1774 he lived mainly in England, where he also painted historical scenes incl. 'The Death of Chatham', which gained him his RA.

COPPER. A chemical element, one of the earliest metals used by man. Chemical symbol Cu; at. no. 29; at. wt. 63.54. It is salmon pink, very malleable and ductile, and used principally on account of its toughness, softness, and pliability, high thermal and electrical conductivity, and resistance to corrosion. When alloyed with tin it forms bronze, a relatively hard metal, the discovery of which opened a new age in human pre-history.

COPLAND. The American composer is also a skilled conductor, and often - as here - conducts his own compositions. *Photo: Godfrey MacDominic.*

Until about a century ago, Spain and Cornwall were the chief producers, but these are now of minor importance compared with the USA (which produces about a quarter of the world's output), Chile, Canada, Zambia, and the Shaba region of Zaïre. C. is usually commercially extracted from C. pyrites. Large deposits containing C. sulphide occur in the Lake Superior district in N America, and in Spain. Other ores from which C. is extracted include malachite, crysocolla, and atacamite.

COPRA. Dried kernel of the coconut (q.v.).

COPTIC. The latest phase of the old Egyptian language, and still the ritual language of the Coptic Church. It is written in the Greek alphabet with the addition of 8 characters derived from the demotic. Of the several dialects, that of Upper Egypt, known as Sahidic, became the literary medium. The literature is wholly religious.

COPTS. The descendants of the ancient Egyptians who had accepted Christianity in the 1st cent. and refused to adopt Islam after the Arab conquest. Prior to the Arab conquest a majority of Christian Egyptians had adopted Monophysite views, and when this doctrine was condemned by the Council of Chalcedon in 451 they became schismatic and were persecuted by the orthodox party, to which they were opposed on nationalistic as well as religious grounds. They therefore readily accepted Arab rule, but were later subjected to persecution by their new masters. They now form a small minority (*c.* 3,000,000) of the population, mainly town-dwellers, and are distinguishable in dress and customs, but hardly in physical features, from their Moslem fellow-countrymen. They rarely marry outside their own sect. The head of the Coptic Church is the Patriarch of Alexandria. The revival of militant Islam has led to some renewed agitation against them.

COPYRIGHT. Generally speaking, the law of C. applies to literary, musical or artistic works, including plays, recordings, films, and radio and television broadcasts. It prevents the reproduction of the work, either whole or in part, without the consent of the author, but is essentially a safeguard, not for the basic idea or theme, but for the individual interpretation by the author, composer, or artist through which it takes on concrete form. For example, the basic plots of 2 novels might be identical without infringing the law of C., but should details in the descriptions and development of characters make it clear that one author had copied from the other, then C. would be infringed. Translations of literary works are also protected.

Under the Universal C. Convention (1952) each contracting country offers authors of other signatories the same protection it gives its own: it came into force USA 1955, UK 1957 and USSR 1973, when the last-named also estab. a C. Agency as the sole body to deal with foreign publishers, and made it illegal for an author to do so on his own behalf. Revision of the Convention of Berne (1886, mainly European) at Stockholm 1967 introduced a controversial protocol allowing countries regarded by the UN as 'developing' to modify C. conditions extensively: Britain did not sign the protocol. Under English law, C. subsists for 50 years from end of year of author's death, or from date of publication, where posthumous. Duration of C. in the USA used to be for 28 years from date of publication, with a right to renewal for another 28, but under an act effective 1978 this was amended to the life of the author plus 50 years.

In the 1980s there were increasingly complex problems of C. which constituted a threat to the production of new original material in literature, music, television programmes, etc. The invention of ever-cheaper copying devices meant that a single advance copy of a book produced in Europe or the USA could be copied and distributed on a vast scale at a much lower price in Asia, even before the book was formally published in its country of origin. Similarly, a pop music disc, or a television film, could be pirated and sold, the almost indistinguishable copies even making their way back, or originating in, the countries where C. is legally enforceable because their illicit sources were difficult to trace. This meant that the original producers of the book, music or film found it increasingly difficult to recoup sufficient profit to enable them to continue to operate, and authors and composers lost royalties. The existence of copies and recorders in homes, offices and schools also meant that innumerable individuals were infringing copyright by making copies of textbook material, sheet music, etc., often without any realisation that their actions were illegal. In 1981 a precedent was set in the UK by legal action on behalf of the C. owners against multiple copying of sheet music in schools for class use, and a judgment obtained against such infringement.

An anomaly in the law of C. has been that although fees are paid on performance of a piece of music or play, a book may be borrowed from a library repeatedly without benefit to the author. A solution has been sought in the creation of a Public Lending Right (PLR). Introduced in Australia in 1974, it involved payment, to authors resident in the country and with books in a minimum of 50 libraries there, of 50 cents per copy annually, plus 25 per cent of this amount to the publisher. A form of PLR was enacted

1979 in the UK, though not immediately put into operation as the details of the scheme had yet to be agreed.

CORAL. Name given to the hard skeletons of various marine organisms, belonging to the phylum Coelenterata. Most of them are members of the class Anthozoa, but a few are placed in the Hydrozoa. The skeleton is composed of carbonate of lime extracted from the surrounding waters. In the simplest solitary Cs., such as the Devonshire cup coral (*Caryophyllia smithii*), the skeleton takes the form of a cup, into which the polyp can contract itself. The majority of Cs., however, form large colonies, and it is from the accumulated skeletons of these polyps that C. reefs are built up. The red C. of the Mediterranean (*Corallium rubrum*) has been valued from very ancient times as an ornament.

CORALLI, Jean (1779-1854). French dancer and choreographer. B. in Paris of Italian descent, he made his début as a dancer in Paris in 1802. He chorographed *Giselle* (1841) and *La Péri* (1843), both for Grisi; *Le Diable Boiteux* for Fanny Elssler, and many other famous ballets.

CORAL REEFS are built up from the accumulated skeletons of marine organisms, including certain algae as well as Cs. These flourish in the warmer seas and at moderate depths. C. reefs take the 3 distinct forms of fringing reefs, barrier reefs, and atolls. *Fringing reefs* are so called because they built up on the shores of continents or islands; the living Cs. mainly occupy the outer edges of the reef. *Barrier reefs* are separated from the shore by a salt-water lagoon, which may be as much as 30 km (20 m) wide; there are usually navigable passes through the barrier into the lagoon. The Great Barrier Reef, to the NE of Australia, is *c.* 1,600 km (1,000 m). *Atolls* resemble a ring surrounding a lagoon, and do not enclose an island; they are usually formed by the gradual subsidence of an extinct volcano, the C. growing on the raised rim.

CORAL SEA. Part of the Pacific Ocean lying between NE Australia, New Guinea, the Solomon Islands, New Hebrides, and New Caledonia. It contains numerous coral islands and reefs. The BATTLE OF THE C.S. was fought 4-8 May 1942 and ended with the victory of American naval and air forces over a Japanese fleet. The first Allied success in the Pacific, it saved Australia from invasion.

CORAL TREE. Name given to several tropical species of the *Erythrina* genus, family Papilionaceae, with bright red or orange flowers, and producing a particularly lightweight wood.

CŌ'RAM, Thomas (1668-1751). British philanthropist. B. in Lyme Regis, he became a farmer and shipwright in Massachusetts, returned to England in 1703 and founded the Foundling Hospital in London in 1741. He nearly became bankrupt through his many philanthropic schemes and also promoted the settlement of Georgia and Nova Scotia.

COR ANGLAIS (kōr-angglā') or **English horn.** Musical instrument; it is not a horn, but a member of the oboe family, and its English origin is doubtful. A metal tube, bent backwards to the mouth of the player, contains the reed. The C.A. was introduced into the orchestra in the time of Wagner, has an expressive tone, and is used in slow melodic passages.

CORBIÈRE (korbē-ār'), **Tristan** (1845-75). French poet. The merits of his *Les Amours jaunes* (1873) went unrecognized until Verlaine called attention to it in 1884. Many of his poems, such as *La Rhapsodie Foraine,* deal with life in his native Brittany.

CORBY. Town in Northants, England, formerly a major steel-making centre, but after the closures of 1980 retaining only a tube-milling plant. Pop. (1980) 55,000.

CORDAY (kordā'), **Charlotte** (1768-93). Frenchwoman who assassinated Marat. She belonged to the Girondist party and went to Paris in 1793 resolved to rid the country of one or other of the Jacobin leaders, Robespierre or Marat. Having secured admission to the latter's apartment, she stabbed him to the heart with a bread-knife as he was sitting in his bath. She was guillotined 4 days later.

CÓRDOBA. City in Argentina, on the Rio Primero, here harnessed for power. Founded in 1573, it has a univ. founded 1613, a military aviation college, an observatory, and a cathedral. Pop. (1970) 798,700.

CÓRDOBA. Spanish city, cap. of C. prov., on the Guadalquivir. It has many Moorish remains. Its glory is the mosque, now a cathedral, founded by Abder-Rahman I in 785; it is 180×130m (590×425ft) and except for St Peter's, Rome, is the largest Christian church in the world. C. was founded probably by the Carthaginians, and from 711 until 1236 was held by the Moors. Pop. (1970) 253,650.

CORE'LLI, Arcangelo (1653-1713). Italian composer and violinist. B. in Milan, he studied in Bologna and in *c.* 1685 settled in Rome, under the patronage of Cardinal Pietro Ottoboni, where he pub. his first violin sonatas. He was one of the first great violinists and his music, marked by graceful melody, incl. a set of concerti grossi and 5 sets of chamber sonatas.

CORE'LLI, Marie. Pseudonym of the British novelist Mary Mackay (1855-1924). Trained for a musical career, she turned instead to writing and from the appearance of *The Romance of Two Worlds* (1886) was highly popular, though literary critics were far from kind.

CORFE (korf) **CASTLE.** Village in the Isle of Purbeck, Dorset, built round the ruins of a Norman castle destroyed in the Civil War. Pop. (1974) 1,400.

CORFU (korfōō'). Most northerly, second largest of the Ionian islands (Gk Kérkyra), off the coast of Epirus in the Ionian Sea. The chief town, also C. (Kérkyra) (pop. (1971) 28,630), is a port and seat of an RC archbishopric. C. was colonized by Corinthians *c.* 700 BC. Venice held it 1386-1797, Britain from 1815-64. Area 1,072 sq.km (414 sq.m); pop. (1971) 92,750.

CORI'NNA. Greek lyric poetess of 6th cent. BC, said to have instructed Pindar. Only fragments of her poetry survive.

CO'RINTH. Ancient city of Greece (Gk Korinthía), on the isthmus connecting the Peloponnesus with the mainland. The isthmus is rocky, and is now cut by the 6.5km (4m) C. canal, opened in 1893. C. was already a place of some importance in the 9th cent. BC. At the end of the 6th cent. BC it joined the Peloponnesian League, and it took a prominent part in the Persian and the Peloponnesian wars. In 146 BC it was conquered by the Romans. St Paul visited it, and addressed two epistles to the churches there. After many changes of ownership it became part of independent Greece in 1822. The most outstanding of C.'s ancient monuments is the ruined temple of Apollo (6th cent. BC). Pop. (1971) 20,800.

CORIŌ'LIS EFFECT. Named after its discoverer, French mathematician Gaspard C. (1792-1843), it results from the deflective force of the Earth's W-to-E rotation. Winds and ocean currents are deflected to the right in the N and to the left in the S hemisphere. It has to be allowed for in launching guided missiles, but has negligible effect on the clockwise or anti-clockwise direction of water running out of a bath.

CORK. The light cellular outer layers of the bark of the stems and roots of almost all trees and shrubs, which is impermeable by water. In particular, the word is used for the corky outer layers of the bark of the cork-oak (*Quercus suber*), a native of S Europe and N Africa, which is cultivated in Spain and Portugal and provides the cork of commerce. Manufactured C. is C. ground up and then formed into sheets with a binder: it is much used for engine gaskets and isolation of vibration, as well as for heat insulation.

CORK. Co. of Rep. of Ireland, in Munster prov., with a coastline on the Atlantic Ocean. The co. is occupied by a series of ridges and vales, running from NE to SW. Across its centre run the Nagles and Boggeragh mts, which separate the two main drainage systems, the Blackwater and the Lee. There are many smaller rivers, such as the Bandon, Ilen, etc. C. is an agricultural co., but there is some mining of copper, manganese, etc., marble-quarrying, and river and sea fishing. The co. town is Cork. Other towns are Cobh, Bantry, Youghal, Fermoy, and Mallow. Area 7,459 sq.km (2,880 sq.m); pop. (1971) 352,473.

CORK. City, episcopal see, and seaport of co. Cork, at the head of the long inlet of Cork harbour, on the Lee. It is the 2nd port of the Rep. of Ireland. The lower section of the harbour can berth liners, and the town has distilleries, shipyards, iron-foundries, etc. There is a Protestant cathedral dedicated to St Finbarr, an RC cathedral of St Mary and St Finbarr. University College (1845) became in 1968 the University of Cork. The city hall was opened in 1937.

St Finbarr's 7th cent. monastery was the original foundation of C. It was eventually settled by Danes, who were dispossessed by the English in 1172. Pop. (1971) 128,235.

CORMORANT. Genus of birds (*Phalacrocorax*) included with the gannets in the Pelicaniformes. They are divers, with long necks and strong, solid beaks. Of the 30 species, 2 are British. The common C., *P. carbo*, is a familiar sea-bird, and is black glossed with bronze. The shag or green C. (*P. aristotelis*) is rather smaller and has a greenish gloss on its plumage. Cs. feed on fish, and are proverbially voracious.

CORNCRAKE. *See* RAIL.

CORNEILLE (kornāy'), **Pierre** (1606-84). French dramatist. B. at Rouen, he had his first play *Mélite* performed in 1629. It was followed by others of skilful construction, which were approved by Richelieu, and gained him an appointment as one of the 5 poets engaged to mould the cardinal's ideas for the stage, (1634). But C. proved intractable and was soon dismissed.

His first important play, the tragedy *Médée* (1635), was followed in 1636 by *Le Cid*, which achieved sensational success with the public, although it was fiercely attacked by Academicians under the influence of Richelieu. After 3 years' retirement, C. returned to the cardinal's favour and a pension with *Horace* (1639), which like all his later plays was based on Aristotle's unities. Continuing his success with *Cinna* (1640), *Polyeucte*, the comedy *Le Menteur*, and *Rodogune*, he was elected to the Academy in 1647. He then encountered a run of failures, and retiring from the stage in 1652 devoted himself to translation and criticism, notably his *Discours du poème dramatique*. He returned with *Oedipe* (1659), approved by Louis XIV, and *La Toison d'or* (1661). His last great play was *Sertorius* (1662), although he continued to write until 1674. His tragedies glorify the strength of will governed by reason, and although unequal in style and construction, established the French classical drama of the next two centuries.

His younger brother **Thomas Corneille** (1625-1709), wrote some 40 plays, of which the most famous are *Ariane* (1672), and *Comte d'Essex* (1678).

CORMORANT. Fishing with cormorants on Nagara River in Japan. The flares attract the fish to the surface and the cormorants dive to seize them. Lines round the neck of the birds draw them back to the boats, and prevent their swallowing the fish before their masters can retrieve them. *Photo: Courtesy of the Japan Information Centre.*

CORNET. Musical instrument. Originally the name of a family of woodwind instruments; it now refers to the *cornet à pistons*, which is without fixed notes, notes of different pitch being obtained by over-blowing and by means of 3 pistons. It is often used as a substitute for the trumpet in brass bands.

CORNFLOUR. The purified starch content of maize (Indian corn) used in milk puddings, etc.

CORNFLOWER. A plant (*Centaurea cyanus*) belonging to the Compositae. It is distinguished from the knapweeds by its deep azure blue flowers, and was formerly a common weed in cornfields in Britain.

CORNFORTH, Sir John (1917-). Australian chemist. B. in Sydney, Australia, and completely deaf since boyhood, he settled in England in 1941. In 1975 he shared a Nobel prize with Vladimir Prelog for work utilizing radioisotopes as 'markers' to find out how enzymes help the formation of chemicals which are mirror images of one another: this research has potential value in fighting disease. He was knighted 1977.

CORNICHE (kornēsh'). La Grande (Great) C. (Italian 'mountain ledge'), a road with superb alpine and coastal scenery, was built between Nice and Menton by Napoleon: it rises to 520m (1,700 ft). La Moyenne (Middle) and Petite (Little) C., are supplementary parallel roads, the latter being nearest the coast.

CORNISH. An extinct branch of the Brythonic group of the Celtic languages, spoken in Cornwall till the beginning of the 19th cent. Written C. first appears in 10th cent. glosses and similar documents. C. verse is first represented by a (dramatic?) fragment of the 14th cent. and a slightly later poem on the Passion of Our Lord. There are a number of religious plays of the 15th and 16th cents.

which draw on Lat. and Eng. sources. Later C. literature is scanty, and consists of an occasional folk-tale or poem and other scraps of verse and prose. However, attempts at the revival of C. are being made as a result of the Cornish nationalist movement.

CORN LAWS. Laws to regulate the export or import of cereals, in order to maintain an adequate supply for the consumers and a fair price for the producers. For centuries they formed an integral part of the Mercantile System in England, and it was not until after the Napoleonic wars that they aroused any strong opposition. They were modified in 1828, again in 1842, and practically repealed by Peel in 1846, as being an unwarranted tax on food.

CORNWALL. County occupying the extreme SW of England and including the Scilly Is. It is surrounded by the Atlantic Ocean and the English Channel, except in the E where it adjoins Devon. C. is renowned for its fine coastal scenery culminating in Land's End, and for its moorland stretches. Bodmin Moor rises to 419m (1,375 ft) in Brown Willy; everywhere the co. is rugged and hilly. The main rivers are the Tamar, Fowey, Fal, and Camel. Creeks along the coast have given shelter to fishing fleets for centuries. The climate is mild and sunny, particularly in the south round Falmouth and Penzance (Cornish Riviera). Agriculture is general, and there are specialized 'pockets' for early vegetables. The Scilly Is. are famous for spring flowers. Among the rocks of C. there is considerable mineral wealth, the best-known deposits being those of tin. Exploited from the Bronze Age, they were for many years superseded by Malayan discoveries until renewed workings in the 1960s. Tungsten, lead, zinc, and silver are also mined. Kaolin occurs near St Austell. The Cornish have been fishermen for many centuries. Tourism is important.

The admin. HQ is Truro; other centres are Bodmin and Launceston, the picturesque fishing villages and ports are all tourist resorts - Bude, Falmouth, Looe, Newquay, Padstow, Penzance, and St Ives. Area 3,546 sq.km (1,369 sq.m); pop. (1978) 416,700.

Cornish separatism in recent years was illus. by the revival in 1974 of the Stannary or Tinners' Parliament, comprising 6 members from each of the 4 Stannary towns (Lostwithiel, Launceston, Helston and Truro): they must be Cornish and with mining connections. Chartered in the 11th cent., it ceased to meet in 1752, but its powers had never been rescinded at Westminster. *See* St Piran. The flag of the saint, used by the separatist movement, consists of a white 'St George's cross' on a black ground.

CORNWALLIS, Charles, 1st marquess (1738-1805). British soldier, eldest son of the 1st earl C., he had a distinguished career in the army until 1781, when he and the force under his command were forced to surrender at Yorktown, thus virtually ending the War of American Independence. Subsequently he was twice Governor-General of India, and Viceroy of Ireland, and was made a marquess in 1793.

COROMANDEL. The east coast of Tamil Nadu, India. Also the **C. Peninsula** of North Island, NZ, to the E. of Auckland.

CORONATION. The ceremony of investing a king with the emblems of royalty, as a symbol of his inauguration in office. The British C. ceremony combines the Hebrew rite of anointing with customs of Germanic origin, e.g. the actual crowning and the presentation of the king to his subjects to receive homage. Its main features are the

CORNWALL. Polruan, with Fowey in the background. In medieval times a boom, between the ruined foot on the headland and its twin on the further shore, prevented unwanted ships from sailing in. *Photo: Courtesy of the British Tourist Authority.*

presentation to the people; the administration of the oath; the presentation of the Bible; the anointing of the sovereign with holy oil on hands, breast, and head; the presentation of the spurs and the sword of state, the emblems of knighthood; the presentation of the armills, robe royal, the orb, the ring, the sceptre with the cross, and the rod with the dove; the coronation with St Edward's Crown; the benediction; the enthroning; and the homage of the princes of the blood and the peerage. A queen consort is anointed on the head, presented with a ring, crowned, and finally presented with the sceptre and the ivory rod. Since the C. of Harold in 1066 English sovereigns have been crowned in Westminster Abbey.

CORONEL. Port of Chile, off which on 1 Nov. 1914 a German squadron under Admiral von Spee defeated a technically inferior squadron under Rear-Ad. Cradock, who went down with his ship.

CORONER. In England an officer appointed by a county council to inquire into the deaths of persons who have died suddenly by acts of violence, under suspicious circumstances, or, formerly, in prison at the hands of the hangman. They may also inquire into instances of treasure trove. The office may date back to the days of King Alfred.

A C. is appointed for life, and must be a barrister, solicitor, or medical practitioner with at least 5 years' professional service. Some county councils insist on the double medical and legal qualification.

At an inquest, a C. is assisted by a jury of not less than 7 or more than 11 persons. Evidence is on oath, and medical and other witnesses may be summoned. If the jury return a verdict of murder or manslaughter, the C. can commit the accused for trial.

In Scotland similar duties are performed by the procurator-fiscal. In the USA coroners are usually elected by the qualified voters of the co.

CORONET. A small crown worn by a peer at the Coronation and the state opening of parliament. A duke's

C. consists of a golden circlet, above which are 8 strawberry leaves; a marquess's has 4 strawberry leaves with 4 points surmounted by pearls between them, an earl's 8 strawberry leaves with 8 tall points surmounted by pearls between them, a viscount's 16 small pearls, and a baron's 6 large pearls.

COROT (koroh'), **Jean Baptiste Camille** (1796–1875). French landscape painter. B. in Paris, he was at first employed in a linen-draper business there, but from the age of 26 devoted himself to painting, and became famous as one of the painters of the 'Barbizon school'. Though he exhibited regularly at the Paris Salon from 1827, his pictures did not begin to attract attention until he was about 60. He was one of the most poetical of landscape painters; much of his best work was executed in the early hours of the morning or at twilight.

CORPORATIVE STATE. A state in which the members are organized and represented not on a local basis as citizens, but as producers working in a particular trade, industry, or profession. The conception first appeared in modern politics in the theories of the Syndicalist movement of the early 20th cent., which proposed that all industries should be taken over and run by the trade unions, a federation of whom should replace the state. Similar views were put forward in Britain by the Guild Socialists. Certain features of Syndicalist theory were adopted and given a right-wing tendency by the Fascist régime in Italy, under which employers' and workers' organizations were represented in the National Council of Corporations, but this was completely dominated by the Fascist Party and had no real powers. Catholic social theory, as expounded in recent papal encyclicals, also favours the C.S. as a means of eliminating class conflict. Corporative institutions were set up by the Franco and Salazar régimes in Spain and Portugal, under the influence of Fascist and Catholic theories. In Spain representatives of the national syndicates were included in the *Cortes*, and in Portugal a Corporative Chamber existed alongside the National Assembly.

CORPUS CHRISTI (Lat., Body of Christ). A feast celebrated in the R.C. and Greek churches, and to some extent in the Anglican Church, on the Thursday after Trinity Sunday. It was instituted in the 13th cent. through the devotion of St Juliana, prioress of Mount Cornillon, near Liège, in honour of the Real Presence of Christ in the Eucharist.

CORREGGIO (kohr-rej'oh), **Antonio Allegri da** (*c.* 1494–1534). Italian painter, named after his birthplace near Modena. The son of a prosperous merchant, he came under the influence of Mantegna, Leonardo da Vinci, and Raphael, but developed a style of his own which is remarkable for its fine sense of colouring and its treatment of light and shade. His best-known works incl. 'Adoration of the Shepherds' or 'Night' in the Dresden Gallery, 'The Marriage of St Catherine' in the Louvre, and 'Mercury instructing Cupid before Venus' and 'Ecce Homo' in the National Gallery, London.

CORREGIDO'R. Fortified island at the mouth of Manila Bay, Luzon, Philippine Rep. It became famous for its heroic defence in the S.W.W. by survivors of the Bataan campaign under Gen. Wainwright from 9 April until resistance ceased on 6 May 1942. US parachute troops recaptured it 15 Feb. 1945.

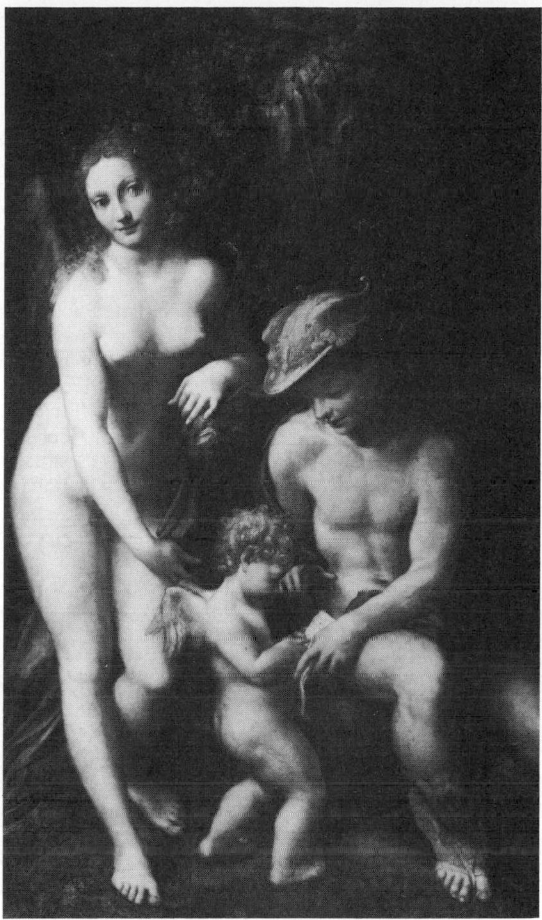

CORREGGIO. 'Mercury instructing Cupid before Venus'. *Photo: Courtesy of the National Gallery, London.*

CORRÈZE (korrāz'). River of central France flowing 89km (55m) from the Plateau des Millevaches, past Tulle, cap. of C. dept. (to which it gives its name), to join the Vézère. It is harnessed for power at Bar, 9.5km (6m) NW of Tulle.

CORRIENTES (korrē-en'tes). City of Argentina, cap. of C. prov., on the Paraná: an important river port in a stock-raising district. Pop. (1970) 136,000.

CORRO'BOREE. Dance of the Australian aborigines. Some Cs. record events in history; others have a religious significance, connected with fertility and rejuvenation, or are just theatrical entertainment.

CORSAIRS (kor'sārz). Moorish pirates who from the 16th cent. onward plundered shipping in the Mediterranean and Atlantic. Although many punitive expeditions were sent against them, they were not suppressed until France occupied Algiers in 1830. Some Englishmen of good birth joined the Barbary pirates or C., e.g. the half-brother of Sir Edmund Verney (q.v.), Sir Francis Verney.

CORSE. French name of CORSICA.

CORSICA. Island in the Mediterranean off the W coast of Italy, and immediately N of Sardinia. It forms a region of France, and is composed of a granitic plateau. The only part with a coastal plain is in the east. C. has a very favourable climate. Much of the land is covered by the characteristic maquis vegetation, herbs, evergreens, and bushes, but parts have fine chestnut forests and pine woods. Sheep are kept on the highland pastures, while on the coastlands wheat, vines, tobacco, olives, and fruits are grown. Fishing is important, marble is quarried; there is little industry.

The Corsican is renowned for his pride and dignity, his hospitality towards visitors, and formerly was famed for the relentless nature of the vendetta, or blood feud. The chief town and port is Ajaccio; other towns are Bastia, Bonifacio, Calvi, and Corte.

The first civilized inhabitants of C. were the Phocaeans of Ionia, who founded Alalia about 560 BC. They were succeeded in turn by the Etruscans, the Carthaginians, the Romans, the Vandals, and the Arabs. In the 14th cent. C. fell to the Genoese, and in the second half of the 18th cent. Paoli led an independence movement. Genoa sold her rights to France in 1768 and French rule was eventually established. In the S.W.W. C. was occupied by the Italians 1942-3. From 1962 French refugees from Algeria, espec. vine growers, were settled in C. and their prosperity helped to fan nationalist feeling, which demands an independent C. The island is the main base of the Foreign Legion. Area 8,722 sq.km (3,367 sq.m); pop. (1980) 270,000, of whom 130,000 are native Corsicans.

CORT, Henry (1740-1800). British ironmaster. He invented the puddling process and developed the rolling mill in the manufacture of wrought iron, which were of vast importance early in the Industrial Revolution.

CORTES (kortehs'), **Hernando** (1485-1547). Spanish soldier. He went to the W Indies as a young man, and in 1518 was given command of an expedition to Mexico. Landing with only 600 men, he was at first received as a god by the emperor, but was finally expelled from Mexico City by a revolt. With the aid of native allies he recaptured the city in 1521, and conquered the whole country. After ruling as governor for some years he returned to Spain, where he d., neglected by the court.

CORTISONE (Compound E.). Substance discovered by T. Reichstein of Basle, Switzerland, and put to practical clinical use for rheumatoid arthritis by P. S. Hench and E. C. Kendall in the USA (all 3 shared a Nobel prize in 1950). A product of the adrenal gland, it was first synthesized from a constituent of ox-bile, and is now produced commercially from a Mexican yam and from a by-product of the sisal plant.

CORTŌ'NA. Town in Italy, 22km (14m) SE of Arezzo, one of Europe's oldest cities. It is encircled by walls built by the Etruscans and has a medieval castle, and an 11th cent. cathedral. Pop. (1970) 30,000.

CORU'NDUM. Native aluminium oxide (Al_2O_3), occurring in cleavable masses or in pyramidal crystals. It includes the ruby and sapphire, and is next on the scale of hardness to diamond. It occurs as crystals distributed through granites, cyanites, and schists in many parts of the world.

CORUNNA (kohroon'yah). Town, cap. of C. prov., in the extreme NW of Spain. Its activities are for the most part based on the fisheries, but it has tobacco and match factories, sugar refineries, linen and cotton mills, etc. Nearby in 1809 was fought the battle in which Sir John Moore was killed. Pop. (1970) 189,655.

CORVETTE (korvet'). Term, now obsolete, for a class of vessels in the Royal Navy, which guarded convoys, etc., during the S.W.W. The term was a revival from the days of sail.

CORVIDAE. Family of birds including the crow, magpie, chough, and jay (qq.v.).

CORVO, Baron. *See* ROLFE, F. R.

CORYPHAENA (korefē'na). Genus of ocean fishes of the mackerel family, known to sailors as dorados or 'dolphins'. *C. hippurus*, the best-known species, is brilliant blue with golden reflections and deep blue spots. They grow to *c.* 2m (6ft).

COS. Fertile Greek island (Gk Kos), one of the Dodecanese, in the Aegean Sea. It gives its name to the Cos lettuce. Area 287 sq.km (111 sq.m); pop. (1970) 19,000.

COSE'NZA. Italian town of Calabria at the junction of the Crati and the Busento, cap. of C. prov., an archiepiscopal see, and the burial place of Alaric. Pop. (1973) 103,000.

COSGRAVE, William Thomas (1880-1965). Irish statesman. B. in Dublin, he took part in the Easter Rebellion of 1916, and sat in the Sinn Féin cabinet of 1919-21. Head of the Free State govt. from 1922 until his defeat by De Valera in 1932, he led the Fine Gael opposition 1933-44. His eldest son **Liam Cosgrave** (1920-) was leader of Fine Gael 1965-77, and in 1973-77 was PM of a Fine Gael-Labour coalition. Improved relations developed between the Irish and British govts under his premiership.

COSMETICS. *See* BEAUTY CULTURE.

COSMIC RADIATION. The so-called cosmic rays are not true rays, but high-speed particles (atomic nuclei) moving at tremendous velocities. The cosmic-ray primaries are relatively heavy, since the nuclei appear to have atomic weights as high as that of tin, and may well be dangerous to living matter; fortunately, the Earth's atmosphere provides an effective screen, and the primaries are broken up, so that only their fragments reach the ground. The origin of C.R. is still rather uncertain. The Sun is one source, but most of the cosmic rays come from beyond the Solar System. They were first studied by Millikan (q.v.) in 1925. Their energy far exceeds that of particles from a laboratory accelerator, and they present a marginal hazard to manned space flights.

Most C. rays of comparatively low energy seem to be of galactic origin. To attempt to locate the extra-galactic sources of high energy C. Rs., large-size detectors have been built in the USA, USSR, Australia and the UK, where the water-Cerenkov detectors at Haverah Park, nr Leeds have an area of 12 sq. km (4.5 sq.m). The rotating disc of infalling matter round black holes has been suggested as one possible source.

COSMONAUT (kos'monawt). Russian term for man making flights into space. *See* SPACE RESEARCH.

COSSACKS. A section of the Russian population, of mixed descent, which originally held land in return for military service. Before 1917 C. households had a larger allotment of land than that of the ordinary peasant, and in return all the men were bound to serve in the army for 20 years. This special position made them bitterly opposed to the Soviet regime, and their resistance was brutally suppressed. In the S.W.W. some fought for the Germans. Their chief pursuits are agriculture and the breeding of sheep and cattle. Their fine horsemanship is proverbial.

COSTA RICA (rē'kah). Country of Central America, the name means 'rich coast', lying between the Caribbean and Pacific. Most of C.R. is an elevated tableland, crossed by three mountain ranges which incl. many volcanic peaks. The chief river is the San Juan. Coffee and bananas are export products, and industrialisation is limited. The chief towns are the cap., San José, Alajuela, Cartago, and Liberia; and the ports of Limón (Caribbean) and Puntarenas (Pacific).

Discovered by Colombus, C.R. was inhabited by Guaymi Indians (now *c.* 1,000), who were conquered by the Spaniards by 1563. The modern pop. is almost entirely of Spanish blood. Independence from Spain was achieved in 1821. There were boundary disputes with C.R.'s neighbours in the late 19th and early 20th cents., but C.R. has had no army since the civil war in 1948-9. Govt. is by a popularly elected pres. and single-chamber Legislative assembly, both elected for 4 years. Long politically stable, C.R. developed economic difficulties by the 1980s. The language is Spanish, but English is taught in all secondary schools. Area 50,997 sq.km (19,690 sq.m); pop. (1978) 2,700,000, the official religion being R.C. M.U.: colón.

COSTA RICA. To fetch top prices bananas must be kept unblemished, and in these plantations the fruit is grown in plastic bags to protect it from insect pests. *Photo: Mireille Vautier.*

COSTER, Charles de (1827-79). Belgian writer. B. at Munich, he was one of a group of young writers who set out to produce a distinctively Flemish literature instead of using French. In *La Légende de Thyl Uylenspiegel* (1867) he achieved a true masterpiece.

COSTER, Laurens Janszoon (1370-1440). Dutch printer, b. at Haarlem. According to some authorities, he invented movable type, but after his death an apprentice ran off to Mainz with the blocks and, taking Gutenberg into his confidence, began a printing business with him.

COST OF LIVING. This phrase came into common use during the F.W.W., when it was desired to measure the rise in prices of goods in general consumption, partly as a guide to necessary increases in wages. In Britain the first C.O.L. index was introduced in 1914 and based on the expenditure of a working-class family of man, wife and 3 children; the standard is 100. This, officially known from 1947 as the *Index of Retail Prices,* has been revised from time to time, as a result of inflation and a general rise in prices. Supplementary to it in reaching estimates of C. of L. is the *Consumer Price Index,* calculated from 1938 on the expenditure of all consumers. A *Tax and Price Index* (TPI) was introduced Aug. 1979 to illustrate the offsetting of inflation provided by cuts in taxation.

As a means of controlling inflation there has been advocacy of comprehensive *indexation,* the linking of all forms of income (wages, investment, etc.), contractual debts and tax scales, to the retail price index. Brazil and many European countries have used varying indexation systems with varying success; it would seem that it is effective in slowing inflation in certain circumstances, e.g. when one particular section of society is exerting pressures which are accelerating inflation. Index-linked savings schemes were introduced in the UK in 1975.

In the US a Consumer Price Index, based on the expenditure of families in the iron, steel and related industries, was introduced in 1890. The modern index is based on the expenditure of the urban wage-earner and clerical-worker families in 46 large, medium and small cities, the standard being 100.

COSTUME. *See* DRESS.

COSWAY, Richard (1742-1821). British artist. Elected RA in 1771, he was the most accomplished of the 18th cent. miniaturists and painted the chief members of the Prince Regent's court.

COT DEATH. Death of a young baby during sleep when it has apparently been in good health, also known as Sudden Infant Death Syndrome (SIDS). Possible causes incl. poor heart rhythm and irregular breathing.

COTMAN, John Sell (1782-1842). British landscape painter. B. at Norwich, he went to London to study *c.* 1798, returning to Norwich in 1807 as a drawing master. In 1834 Turner helped him to an appointment at King's Coll., London. He achieved a balanced harmony of forms in subdued tones, and was fond of depicting ships and bridges. His sons, Miles Edmund (1810-58) and Joseph John (1814-78) were also landscape painters.

COTONEASTER (kōtōnē-as'ter). Genus of trees and shrubs belonging to the Rosaceae and closely allied to the hawthorn and medlar. Its leaves are simple and entire, and woolly beneath, and the conspicuous but small and unpalatable fruits persist through the winter.

COTONOU (kot'onoo). Chief port of Benin, on the Gulf of Benin. It is a road and rail centre, and has an airport. Palm products and timber are exported. Pop. (1976) 178,000.

COTOPA'XI. Formerly the world's highest active volcano (q.v.) situated to the S of Quito in Ecuador. It is 5,897 m (19,347 ft) high, and was climbed first in 1872. Its name is Quechua for 'shining peak'. *See* VOLCANO.

COTSWOLDS (kots'wōldz). Range of hills in Avon-Glos., England, some 80km (50m) long, between Bristol and Chipping Camden. They rise to 330m (1,083 ft), but average *c.* 200m (600ft).

COTTON, Sir Robert Bruce (1571-1631). English antiquary. At his home in Westminster he built up a fine collection of MSS. and coins, many of which had come from the despoiled monasteries. His son, Sir Thomas C., added to the library, and in 1700 it was bestowed on the nation by Sir John Cotton. Its contents are in the British Museum.

COTTON. Commercial cotton mainly processed by industry consists of the fibres surrounding the seeds in the ripened fruit or boll. Most frequently cultivated is *Gossypium herbaceum,* believed to be of eastern origin, but introduced to America in the 18th cent. However, the longest fibres come from Sea Island Cotton (*Gossypium barbadense*), considered to be a native of the New World and now grown in the West Indies, which is so named from its early cultivation on the islands that fringe Georgia and South Carolina. Many cultivated cottons are hybrids.

The C. shrub grows 1.5m (5ft) and needs 200 days free from frost coupled with moderate rainfall or irrigation. Bright sunshine and rich soil are important for the ripening of the bolls. Among the chief producers are USA (Texas, Mississippi, California, and Arkansas), USSR, China, Egypt, India and Brazil.

The C. industry in Britain grew up in Lancashire and remains there. Its varied products range from apparel fabrics and household and surgical textiles to industrial fabrics and Service equipment. In recent years increasing competition, both from cheap imports produced by the developing countries and from man-made fibres, has stimulated new developments in machinery, and in new processes and finishes, as well as combination of C. with synthetics. The Shirley Institute has a world-wide reputation for fundamental and applied research in C., silk, and man-made fibres.

A by-product of C. cultivation is cotton seed, from which can be extracted a reddish oil containing glycerides of palmitic, oleic, stearic and linoleic acids. Refined, it turns yellow and is used in the manufacture of edible products such as cooking fats, margarine and salad oils. Other derivatives are soaps, tars, paints, chemicals, etc. C. cake is used as cattle food and as a fertilizer, since it contains nitrogen, phosphates and potash. Cotton seed flour blended with wheat flour is used by bakers and confectioners and the hard covering of the kernel is used for making insulating materials and fertilizers. Gossypel, used as a male contraceptive, is derived from cotton.

COTTON. Each shrub produces some 20 flowers (left). The petals fall after only 3 days, leaving small green pods with 30-40 seeds in each, and every seed has soft downy hairs like those of dandelion clocks. After two months the swollen pods open (right), revealing the cotton. *Photo: Courtesy of the Cotton Board, Manchester.*

COTTONWOOD. Name given to several species of N. American poplar, espec. *Populus angulata,* which has been widely planted in Australia in recent years. And also to a tree of the family Malvaceae, *Hibiscus tiliaceus,* native to Australia and the S.W. Pacific, which flourishes in salt coastal marshlands.

COUCH GRASS. A plant (*Agropyron repens*), one of the commonest of the grasses (Gramineae). It is closely allied to wheat, but is generally regarded as an undesirable weed.

COUÉ (koo-eh'), **Emile** (1857-1926). French psychological healer, famous for his slogan, 'Every day, and in every way, I am becoming better and better'. 'Couéism' reached the height of its popularity in the 1920s.

COULOMB (koolon'), **Charles Auguste de** (1736-1806). French scientist, inventor of the torsion balance for measuring the force of electric and magnetic attraction. The name *coulomb* was given to the practical unit of quantity of electricity - the quantity conveyed by a current of one ampere in a second.

COUNCIL. In English local govt a popularly elected local assembly charged with the good govt of the area within its boundaries. Under the Local Govt. Act of 1972, they were simplified in structure and reduced in number, and their powers were re-allocated. They now comprise three types: County Cs., District Cs., and Parish Cs. (qq.v.).

COUNCIL FOR MUTUAL ECONOMIC ASSISTANCE. *See* COMECON.

COUNCIL OF EUROPE. Body constituted in 1949 to secure 'a greater measure of unity between the European countries'. The first session of the Consultative Assembly opened at Strasbourg in August 1949, the members then being Great Britain, France, Italy, Belgium, the Netherlands, Sweden, Denmark, Norway, the Repub. of Ireland, Luxembourg, Greece, and Turkey; Iceland, W Germany, Austria, Cyprus, Switzerland, Malta, Portugal, Spain and Liechtenstein joined subsequently. The Assembly operates through 12 general committees; a standing committee preserves its existence between sessions. Its seat is Strasbourg, France.

COUNTER-ESPIONAGE. *See* SECRET SERVICE.

COUNTERFEITING. The production of fraudulent imitations, particularly of money. The problem is increased today by the rapidity with which large sums, produced by modern printing and photographic techniques, can be distributed over great distances.

COUNTERPOINT. In music, the combination of melodies to form an artistic and satisfying musical texture. Derived from the Lat. *punctus contra punctum,* 'note against note', it originated in Plainsong where 2 vocal lines, independent but sung simultaneously, produced a certain texture. The greatest period for C. was the 16th century.

COUNTERTENOR. The highest naturally produced male voice, sometimes called 'male alto'. It was favoured by Elizabethan composers, and Purcell himself sang in this range. It was revived in Britain by Alfred Deller (1912-79), and has a strange unearthly quality.

COUNTRY AND WESTERN. Style of popular music deriving from Anglo-American folk song, and sometimes called 'hillbilly'. Since 1925 its HQ has been Nashville, Tennessee. In the 1940s and 1950s it developed as a minority cult, and in the 1970s had become a nationwide interest. The songs have a traditional guitar accompaniment, usually avoid political protests and may be cheerful, e.g. 'You are my Sunshine' by Governor Davis of Tennessee, but more frequently tell stories of unhappy love. Well-known singers have incl. Hank Williams, Jerry Bradley, Elvis Presley, Charlie Pride, Johnny Cash, Gene Autry and Merle Haggard.

COUNTRY DANCING. *See* FOLK DANCING.

COUNTRY PARTY. *See* NATIONAL COUNTRY PARTY.

COUNTRYSIDE COMMISSION. Created for England and Wales under the Countryside Act (1968), it replaced the Nat. Parks Commission, and had by 1980 created over 160 Country Parks. Here, as in all other activities, such as its Demonstration Farms Project, it aims at conservation, improvement, and the reconciliation of working activity with public recreational use. There is a separate commission for Scotland.

COUNTY. In Britain, an administrative unit, nowadays synonymous with 'shire', although historically the two had different origins. Many of the English cos. can be traced back to Saxon times, but a number have proved either too large or too small for modern administrative purposes, and others have cut across the lines of new development. Under the Local Govt Act of 1972, which came into effect in 1974, the existing English admin. Cs. were replaced by 45 new county areas of local govt (6 being metropolitan Cs. on the plan of Greater London, already reorganized under the London Govt Act of 1963), and the 13 Welsh Cs. were reduced by amalgamation to eight. Under the Local Govt (Scotland) Act of 1973 the 33 Cs. of Scotland were amalgamated in 1975 in 9 new regions and 3 island areas. N Ireland has 6 geographical Cs., but under the Local Govt Act of 1973 admin. is through 26 district councils (single-tier authorities) each based on a main town or centre. The Rep. of Ireland has 26 geographical and 27 admin. Cs.

COUNTY COUNCIL. Under the Local Govt Act of 1972, which created a new county structure for England and Wales, the powers and functions of C.Cs. were considerably modified. The C.Cs. consist of a chairman and councillors only, the former distinction between councillors and specially privileged aldermen (q.v.) having been abolished under the act. Councillors are elected for 4 years, the franchise being the same as for parliamentary elections, and elect the chairman from among their own number. The revised responsibilities of C.Cs. are defined as including broad planning policy; highways; education, personal social services and libraries; police, fire and traffic control; and refuse disposal. Certain exceptions occur in some of these responsibilities in metropolitan areas, where district councils are responsible.

COUNTY COURT. An English court of law created by the County Courts Act, 1846. It exists to try civil cases, and actions on contract and most actions on tort may be brought before it if the claim does not exceed £2000. C.Cs. are presided over by one or more Circuit Judges. An appeal on a point of law lies to the Court of Appeal. *See* COURTS, Small Claims.

COUPERIN (kooprañ'), **François** (1668-1733). French composer, called *le Grand,* as being the most famous of a distinguished musical family. B. in Paris, he held various court appointments and wrote exquisite pieces for the harpsichord.

COURBET (koorbeh'), **Gustave** (1819-77). French landscape and genre painter. From 1841 he was associated with the Barbizon school, and his paintings created a sensation at the Salon of 1850, because of their Impressionistic technique. Manet was influenced by him. In 1871 C. became a member of the Paris Commune and was sentenced to 6 months' imprisonment and a fine. His last years were spent at Vevey in Switzerland.

COURRÈGES, André (1923-). French dress designer. Originally with Balenciaga, he founded his own firm in 1961, and in 1964 invented the 'mini-skirt'.

COURSING. The chasing of hares by greyhounds, not by scent but by sight, as a 'sport', and as a test of the greyhound's speed, etc. It is one of the most ancient of field sports. Since the 1880s it has been practised on enclosed or park courses. The governing body in Great Britain is the National Coursing Club, formed in 1858.

The C. season lasts September-March: the Altcar or Waterloo meeting, which decides the championship, is held in Feb. The Waterloo Cup race is known as the Courser's Derby.

COURTAULD, Samuel (1793-1881). British industrialist. He founded the firm of Courtaulds in 1816 at Bocking, Essex, which at first specialized in silk and crepe manufacture, but from 1904 developed the production of viscose rayon. His great nephew, **Samuel C.** (1876-1947), was chairman of the firm from 1921, and in 1931 transferred his house and art collection to the Univ. of London as the C. Institute. The firm has more recently developed other man-made fibres.

COURT-MARTIAL. A court convened for the trial of persons subject to service discipline. British Cs.-M. are governed by the code of the service concerned - Naval Discipline, Army, or Air Force Acts - and in 1951 an appeal court was estab. for all 3 services by the Cs.-M. (Appeals) Act. The procedure prescribed for the US services is similar, being originally based on British practice.

COURTNEIDGE (kawrt'nēj), **Dame Cicely** (1893-1980). British actress. B. in Sydney, she estab. herself on stage and screen as a comedienne with a gift for rousing songs, e.g. 'Vitality'. She m. comedian Jack Hulbert (1892-1978).

COURT OF SESSION. The supreme Civil Court in Scotland, estab. 1532. Cases come in the first place before one of the 8 Lords Ordinary, and from their decisions an appeal lies to the Inner House which sits in 2 divisions called the First and Second Division. From the decisions of the Inner House an appeal lies to the House of Lords.

COURT OF THE LORD LYON. Scottish heraldic body composed of 1 King of Arms, 3 Heralds, and 3 Pursuivants. It embodies the High Seanachie of Scotland's Celtic kings.

COURTRAI. Belgian industrial town on the Lys, in W Flanders (Flemish Kortrijk). It is connected by canal to the coast, and by river and canal to Antwerp and Brussels. It has a large textile industry, esp. damask, linens, and lace. Here in 1302 was fought a battle in which the Flemings of Ghent and Bruges defeated an army of French knights. Pop. (1978) 77,200.

COURTS, Law. *See* LAW COURTS.

COURTS, Small Claims. In most cities in the USA there are S.C.Cs. where small claims are settled at evening session, both parties appearing without legal representation and putting their case to a lawyer who acts as 'judge'. There is the minimum of formality and all those concerned sit round a table. Influenced by this American precedent, similar courts, but outside the judicial system, were estab. in the UK in Manchester and Westminster, presided over by solicitors acting in their spare time. They depend on goodwill by both complainant and defendant, since both must agree to abide by his decision. S.C. procedures were subsequently also introduced in the County Courts.

COUSIN (koozan'), **Victor** (1792-1867). French philosopher. B. at Paris, he became a lecturer at the Sorbonne when 23, and did much to introduce German philosophical ideas into France. In 1840 he was Minister of Public Instruction and reorganized the system of elementary education.

COUSTEAU (koostoh'), **Jacques-Yves** (1910-). French naval officer. Celebrated for his oceanographic researches in command of the *Calypso* from 1951, he shared in the invention of the Aqualung in 1943 and was the first to use television under water. *The Silent World* (1953) and other books recount his adventures, and he pioneered in underwater archaeology.

COUTTS (koots), **Thomas** (1735-1822). British banker. He estab. with his brother the firm of Coutts & Co. (one of London's oldest banking houses, first originating in 1692 in the Strand, which it has never left), becoming sole head on the latter's death in 1778. Since the reign of George III an account has been maintained there by every succeeding sovereign and other customers incl. Chatham, William Pitt, Fox, Wellington, Reynolds, and Boswell.

COVENANTERS. The Presbyterian adherents of the National Covenant in 17th cent. Scotland. The National Covenant was occasioned by Charles I's attempt in 1637 to introduce a liturgy on the English model into Scotland. The Presbyterians revived the covenant drawn up by John Craig in 1581, swearing to uphold Presbyterianism, and added an appendix condemning recent innovations. This document was signed at Greyfriars' church, Edinburgh, on 28 Feb. 1638 and a general assembly abolished episcopacy. In 1643 the Cs. signed with the English parliament the *Solemn League and Covenant*, whereby they promised military aid in return for the establishment of Presbyterianism in England, and a Scottish army entered England and fought at Marston Moor.

At the Restoration Charles II revived episcopacy in Scotland, and ministers who resisted the change were evicted. Conventicles began to be held, and those who attended them were savagely persecuted. Rebellions followed in 1666, 1679, and 1685, and led to the intensification of persecution, but Presbyterianism was restored as the national religion of Scotland after the revolution of 1688.

COVENT GARDEN. London square (named from the Convent Garden once on the site) laid out by Inigo Jones in 1631. In 1831 the present fruit, vegetable and flower market buildings were erected, and when the market was removed to Nine Elms, Wandsworth, in 1973, they were adapted for shops and leisure use. It is also the site of the Royal Opera House.

COVENTRY (kov'entri). City in West Midlands, England on the r. Sherbourne, 29km (18m) SE of Birmingham. It originated with the foundation of a priory in 1043 by Leofric, earl of Mercia, whose wife was Lady Godiva (q.v.). Until about 1700 C. was a centre of woollen and cloth manufacture, but its modern industrial wealth began with the manufacture of bicycles in 1870. Today it produces cars, electronic equipment, machine tools on a very large scale, agricultural machinery, etc.

C., sometimes called the 'City of Three Steeples', was one of the most heavily bombed cities in Britain in the S.W.W. The cathedral, built 1373-95 on the site of an earlier building, was destroyed in the raid of 14 Nov. 1940, but the steeple survived to be incorporated in the plan of the new cathedral designed by Sir Basil Spence. Christ Church was also destroyed in the S.W.W., although the 14th cent. spire remains, and the 17th cent. Trinity Church, with the 3rd of the spires, was only slightly damaged. St Mary's Hall, built 1394-1414 as a guild centre, and two gates of the old city walls (1356) also survive. Recent buildings incl. the Belgrade Theatre (1958), the Art Gallery and Museum, and Lanchester Polytechnic. Pop. (1973) 336,500.

COVERDALE, Miles (1488-1569). Translator of the Bible into English. B. in Yorks, he became a Catholic priest, but turned to Protestantism and in 1528 went abroad to avoid persecution. His translation of the Bible appeared in 1535, and was dedicated to Henry VIII - the first complete translation of the Bible to be printed in English. His translations of the psalms is that retained in the Book of Common Prayer. In 1539 he ed. the Great Bible which was ordered to be placed in churches. After some years in Germany, he returned to England in 1548, and in 1551 was made bishop of Exeter. Under Mary he again left the country, but in the early part of Elizabeth's reign he held the living of St. Magnus near London Bridge.

COWARD, Sir Noël (1899-1973). Brit. man-of-the-theatre. He first appeared on the stage in 1910, and estab. himself as a dramatist with *The Young Idea* (1923), going on to consolidate his reputation in the '20s and '30s with the sharp sophistication of *The Vortex* (1924); the brilliant comedy *Hay Fever* (1925); the revue *This Year of Grace* (1928); the operetta *Bitter Sweet* (1929); *Private Lives* (1930), which gave a great role to Gertrude Lawrence; and the sentimental *Cavalcade* (1931). Besides stage appearances in his own plays, etc., he acted in the film *In Which We Serve* (1942), which he also scripted, and wrote scripts for films of his later plays, *Blithe Spirit* (1941), a venture in spiritualism, and *This Happy Breed* (1942); and for the subtle *Brief Encounter* (1945).

COWES (kowz). Seaport and resort on the N coast of the Isle of Wight, on the Medina estuary, opposite Southampton Water. It is the HQ of the Royal Yacht Squadron which holds the annual Cowes Regatta, and has maritime industries. In East C. is Osborne House (q.v.), used as a museum. Pop. (1972) 17,000.

COWLEY, Abraham (1618-67). British poet. Joining King Charles at Oxford in 1644, he fled to France after Marston Moor, and was employed in Royalist intrigues. He returned to England in 1655, and although arrested was released on bail, and in 1656 pub. his collected works, including the epic *Davideis*, 'The Mistress', 'Pindarique Odes', and 'Miscellanies'. Highly valued in his own day, his fondness for 'conceits' now makes him unreadable except in his lighter pieces and unstudied essays.

COWPER (koo'per), **William** (1731-1800). British poet. B. in Herts, he was called to the Bar in 1754, but suffered from intense melancholic depression, which in 1763 was aggravated to madness. While in a St Albans asylum he underwent a great religious experience, and on his recovery in 1765 settled in Huntingdon with Mr and Mrs Unwin. On the death of the former, C. and Mrs Unwin removed to Olney, where he was subjected to the evangelical influence of the converted slave-trader, the Rev. John Newton, with whom he collaborated in the *Olney Hymns* (1779). In 1773 C. suffered another attack of madness which prevented his marriage with Mrs Unwin, but on the removal of the influence of Newton in 1779, C. turned to secular poetry, and in 1782 pub. *Table Talk*. This was followed in 1785 by *The Task* and *John Gilpin*, but in 1787

COWARD. The works of Noël Coward suffered an eclipse in the atmosphere of the 1950s and 1960s, but their suave wit came into its own again before his death with many revivals. *Photo: Keystone Press Agency*

and 1794 he again suffered from insanity. Many of C.'s best minor poems belong to these later years, and in 1794 he received a state pension. The outstanding qualities of his poetry, delicate observation and kindly humour, are also present in his letters.

COWRY. A family of marine gasteropod molluscs (Cypraeidae), belonging to the Streptoneura. They are distinguished by the peculiar form of the shell, in which the last wall conceals the others, and the outer lip of the elongated border is bent in towards the inner. Cs. are shallow-water dwellers, and are found in many parts of the world, particularly in the Indian and Pacific Oceans. C. shells are often beautifully coloured and polished. They have been used as ornaments and charms, and were worn by women to produce fertility. They have also been used as money in the S Seas.

COWSLIP. A plant (*Primula veris*) belonging to the Primulaceae, being placed in the same genus as the primrose. It is common in English meadows, and in some parts the flowers are made into C. wine. The oxlip (*P. elatior*) is closely allied to it.

COX, David (1783-1859). British artist. B. nr Birmingham, the son of a blacksmith, he studied under John Varley and made a living as a drawing master. His water-colour landscapes have attractive cloud effects, and his renderings of scenes in N Wales are excellent.

COYŌ'TE. Name for several races of small wolf (*Canis latrans*) inhabiting N America from southern Canada to Mexico, and representing the jackals of the New World. They live in burrows, and are a great nuisance to poultry farmers, but their food consists chiefly of hares, mice, and wild birds.

COYPU (koi'poo). S American water rodent (*Myocaster coypus*) of the porcupine group, *c.* 50cm (2ft) long, excl. its scaly rat-like tail, and weighing *c.* 9kg (20lb). It has webbed hind feet, a blunt-muzzled head on a short, thick neck, and its strong front teeth are orange-yellow. Introduced into East Anglia in the 1930s for its fur (nutria), the C. escaped, bred, and did such damage to growing crops and waterways that it was officially recognized as a pest in 1960.

COYPU. Although harmless in the Argentine the coypu developed in Britain where it had no enemies to check its numbers - a dangerous liking for root crops and young corn. It also undermines marsh roadways and the banks of waterways. *Photo: Crown Copyright*

COZENS (kuz'enz), **Alexander** (*c.* 1717-86). British artist. B. in Russia, he was rumoured to be a natural son of Peter the Great, but was probably the son of Richard C., employed by the Tsar as a shipbuilder. Coming to England in 1742, he taught at Eton and George III's sons were his pupils. He is famous for his water-colour landscapes done in brown, grey or black washes, and sometimes used blots as the inspiration of a study to be finished with brush or pen. His son, **John Robert C.** (*c.* 1752-97) was also a water-colourist, influencing Girtin and Turner, but became mentally unstable.

CRAB. Name given to the crustacea of the sub-order Brachyura, and to many of the Anomura (hermit crabs, etc.) of the order Decapodoa. The true Cs. (Brachyura) are characterized by having the abdomen small, and tucked under the cephalothorax, which is covered with a broad carapace. They have 10 legs, of which the first pair are modified as claws, or nippers, and the remaining 4 pairs are used for swimming and walking. They are active, intelligent crustaceans, mainly carnivorous in their diet, and acting as scavengers. Most of them have a characteristic sidelong mode of progression. The young pass through a metamorphosis, the zoëa and megalopa stages, before the familiar adult form is reached; and growth, both in these larval free-swimming forms and the adult, is effected by periodic casting of the outer shell.

Cs. vary greatly in habit and type. Common between tide-marks in Britain and Europe is the shore or green C. (*Carcinus maenas*); species of commercial value incl. the British and European edible C. (*Cancer pagurus*) and the blue C. (*Callinectes sapidus*) of the American Atlantic coast; freshwater Cs. incl. the S European river C. (*Thelphusa fluviatilis*); and the hermit Cs. have a soft, spirally twisted abdomen and rely on the empty shells of gasteropod molluscs such as the whelk and periwinkle to afford them protection. Some tropical hermit Cs. live most of their lives a considerable distance from the sea, and the robber C. *(Birgus latro)* a member of the family that has developed armour on the upper surface of the abdomen - climbs palm trees for the nuts. The Australian sidewalker (*Holthusiana transversa*), living in the desert, can tolerate loss of half its body water without inconvenience.

CRAB APPLE. The wild form (*Malus sylvestris*) from which the cultivated apple has been derived; it differs chiefly in the smaller size and bitter flavour of the fruit, used in C.A. jelly. The tree is common in woods and hedgerows in southern Britain and varies from a mere bush to 10m (30ft) in height.

CRABBE, George (1754-1832). British poet. B. in Suffolk, he was apprenticed to an apothecary and practised medicine until he went to London in 1780 and was assisted by Burke in furthering his literary career. In 1781 he took orders and pub. his first poem *The Library*, which was followed by *The Village* (1783), *The Parish Register* (1807), *The Borough* (1810), *Tales* (1812), and *Tales of the Hall* (1819). In 1782 C. became chaplain to the duke of Rutland, and in 1814 settled as vicar of Trowbridge. Reacting against the romantic idealized conception of country life, he dealt realistically with the agricultural poor. *See* BRITTEN, B.

CRACOW. Alternative form of KRAKOW.

CRAIG, Edward Gordon (1872-1966). British theatrical producer, actor, dramatist and writer. The son of Ellen Terry, he went on the stage at 6, and joined Irving's company in 1889. His first stage production, Purcell's *Dido and Aeneas* (1900), introduced new effects in staging and lighting.

CRAIGAVON (krăgav'on). Town in Armagh, Northern Ireland, created from 1965 by the merging of Lurgan and Portadown, and intended to become the second city of Northern Ireland. It was named after the first P.M. of Northern Ireland. Pop. (1971) 73,100.

CRAIK, Dinah Maria (1826-87). British novelist. B. at Stoke-on-Trent, the dau. of Thomas Mulock, an eccentric Irishman, she pub. *John Halifax, Gentleman* in 1857, still an English classic. In 1864 she m. G. L. Craik, partner in Macmillan's the publishers.

CRAIOVA (krahyoh'vah). Romanian town near the r. Jiu. It is an important commercial and manufacturing centre. Pop. (1971) 179,360.

CRAKE. *See* RAIL.

CRANACH (krah'nakh), **Lucas** (1472-1553). German artist. B. at Kronach in Bavaria, he settled at Wittenberg in 1504 to work for the elector of Saxony. He was a close friend of Luther, whose portrait he painted several times, and his work is highly finished and gaily inventive in the use of classical themes. He produced numerous woodcuts and copperplates. His 2nd son **Lucas C. the Younger** (1515-86) had a similar style, and succeeded his father as director of the C. workshop.

CRANBERRY. A plant (*Vaccinium oxycoccus*) allied to the bilberry, and belonging to the heaths (Ericaceae). It is a small evergreen, growing in marshy places, and bearing small, acid, edible crimson berries.

CRANE, Hart (1899-1932). American poet. B. in Ohio, he had little education and at 15 was working in his father's sweet factory. His long heroic poem *The Bridge* (1930) lives only in parts. He drowned after jumping overboard from the steamer bringing him back to the USA after a visit to Mexico.

CRANE, Stephen (1871-1900). American writer. B. in NJ, he became a journalist, and won fame in 1895 with *Red Badge of Courage*, dealing vividly with the American Civil War.

CRANE, Walter (1845-1915). British artist. While apprenticed to W. J. Linton, the wood engraver, he came under pre-Raphaelite influence. He excelled as a book illustrator for children and adults, his finest work being for an edition of Spenser's *Faerie Queene* (1894-6).

CRANE. A family of birds (*Gruidae*), distinguished by long legs and neck, powerful wings. They are marsh- and plain-haunting birds, feeding on plants as well as insects, small animals, etc., fly well and are usually migratory. They are found in all parts of the world except S America. The common C. (*Grus grus*) is an occasional visitor to Britain, and is still common in many parts of Europe, and winters in Africa and India. It stands over a metre (4ft) high and the plumage of the adult bird is grey, varied with black and white, and a red patch of bare skin on the head and neck.

CRANE. The brolga (*Grus rubicunda*) is the only Australian crane. Its call is trumpet-like. *Photo: Douglas Baglin/NHPA*

CRANE. Machine for raising, lowering, or placing in position, heavy bodies. The jib C. revolves, and an arm which juts from the base carries the load. The overhead travelling C., which is chiefly used in workshops, is mounted on rails laid on girders.

CRANE-FLY or **daddy-long-legs.** Family of insects (Tipulidae), belonging to the Diptera. They have long, slender, and very fragile legs. The larvae of the typical genus (*Tipula*) are known as 'leather-jackets' and live underground, doing damage to the roots of plants, esp. grasses.

CRANE'S BILL. Plants of the genus *Geranium*, which contains about 300 species and is typical of the family Geraniaceae. They are so called because of the long, beak-like process which is attached to the seed-vessels. When ripe, this splits into spiral, coiling processes which jerk the seeds out, thus assisting in their distribution. The genus incl. 14 British species, including herb-robert (*G. robertianum*) and bloody C. (*G. sanguineum*).

CRANKO, John (1927-73). British choreographer. B. in S Africa, he joined Sadler's Wells in 1946, and excelled in the creation of comedy characters, as in the *Tritsch-Tratsch Polka* (1946) and *Pineapple Poll* (1951). His revue *Cranks* (1952) was a sensational success.

CRANMER, Thomas (1489-1556). English churchman. B. in Notts, he went to Cambridge and was ordained a Catholic priest in 1523. In 1529 he suggested that the question of Henry VIII's marriage to Catherine of Aragon should be referred to the universities of Europe, and Henry received him into his favour. In 1530 and 1531 he was sent on foreign embassies, and in 1532 m. a German Lutheran. In 1533 he was appointed Archbishop of Canterbury, declared the King's marriage to Catherine of Aragon null and void, and crowned Anne Boleyn queen.

Having by now adopted Protestant views, he encouraged the translation of the Bible, ordering a copy to be placed in every church, and issued an English litany, the basis of that now in use. Under Edward VI he was responsible for the issue of the Prayer Books of 1549 and 1552, and took a large part in their compilation. On Edward's death he supported the movement to place Lady Jane Grey on the throne, and in 1553 was condemned to death for treason. Taken to Oxford, he was tried for heresy, found guilty, excommunicated, and degraded. He signed 6 recantations of his heresies, but when Mary refused to spare his life he repudiated them and was burnt at the stake.

CRAPS. American game with 2 dice, originating in the 19th cent. and now also a British casino game. A player throwing 7 or 11 wins, and loses with 2, 3 and 12.

CRASHAW, Richard (1613-49). English religious poet of the metaphysical school. B. in London, he pub. a book of Latin sacred epigrams in 1634. Developing Catholic leanings, he fled to France, and in Paris joined the RC Church, and his *Steps to the Temple* appeared in 1646. In 1649 he became sub-canon of the Holy House at Loretto and d. there of fever or possibly of poison.

CRASSUS, Marcus Licinius (*c.* 108-53 BC). Roman general, statesman, and financier. He crushed the rising of gladiators and slaves under Spartacus in 71, and in 70 became consul with Pompey. In 60 he joined with Caesar and Pompey in the first Triumvirate and in 55 obtained a command in the East. Invading Mesopotamia, he was defeated by the Parthians, captured, and put to death.

CRATER LAKE. *See* CHUBB CRATER.

CRAWFORD, Joan (1908-77). American actress. B. in Texas, she was originally a dancer, but made her name from 1925 in such strongly dramatic films as *Mildred Pierce* and *Whatever Happened to Baby Jane?*

CRAWFORD, Osbert Guy Stanhope (1886-1957). British archaeologist. He introduced aerial survey as means of finding and interpreting remains, an idea conceived in the F.W.W., and was founder-editor of *Antiquity* from 1927.

CRAWLEY. Town in W Sussex, England, NE of Horsham, Chartered by King John in 1202, it was developed as a 'new town' from 1946. Industries incl. plastics, engineering and printing. Pop. (1975) 70,700.

CRAYFISH. Name given to freshwater crustaceans of the family Astacidae, which closely resemble the lobsters, and like them belong to the division Macrura of the order Decapoda. *Astacus pallipes* is common in rivers and streams in England and Ireland, living in burrows in the mud, and emerging chiefly at night. This, and a number of other species are edible, and are increasingly farmed. The initial stocking is comparatively costly, but feeding is not usually necessary; the warmer the water the more rapid the growth.

The name C. or CRAWFISH is also given by fishermen to a marine Crustacean, the spiny or rock lobster (*Palinurus vulgaris*), which belongs to quite a different family of the Macrura. It is abundant on the S and W coasts of Britain; in France it is much valued for the table, and is known as *langouste*.

CREATIONISM. Creation science (unrecognized by scientists as having any scientific basis) claims that the world was suddenly created by a supernatural force, or Creator, about 6000 yrs ago. Human beings are said to remain as when they were created, and to be unconnected with the great apes.

CRÉCY-EN-PONTHIEU (krehsē'-oṅ-poṅtyö'). A village in Somme dept., France, 18km (11m) NNE of Abbeville, where in 1346 Philip VI of France was defeated by Edward III. Pop. (1973) 1,400.

CREDIT CARD. Card issued by a bank or organization which enables the holder to obtain goods or services on credit (usually to a specified limit), or, in the case of a bank card, also to obtain money more easily from branches of his bank at which he has no account without special arrangement.

The pioneer of C.Cs. was Diners Club in 1950 in the USA. An alternative is the cheque card (q.v.).

CREED, Frederick George (1871-1957). Canadian inventor. B. in Nova Scotia, he came to Britain in 1897 and perfected the teleprinter, or C. telegraphy system, first used in Fleet Street in 1912 and now used in newspaper offices all over the world.

CREEDS (Lat. *credo*, I believe). Name given to the verbal confessions of faith expressing the accepted doctrines of the Christian Church. The oldest is the APOSTLES' CREED, which, though not the work of the apostles, was probably first formulated in the 2nd cent. The full version of the Apostles' Creed, as now given, first appeared about 750. The use of Cs. as a mode of combating heresy was established by the appearance of the NICENE CREED, introduced by the Council of Nicaea in 325, when the Arian heresy was widespread. The Nicene C., as used today, is substantially the same as the version adopted at the Church Council at Constantinople in 381.

The so-called ATHANASIAN CREED is much later in origin than the time of Athanasius (d. 373) although it represents his views in a detailed exposition of the doctrines of the Trinity and the Incarnation. Some authorities suppose it to have been composed in the 8th or

9th cent. but others place it as early as the 4th or 5th cent. The only Creed recognized by the Eastern Orthodox Church is the Nicene.

CREEVEY, Thomas (1768-1838). British politician and diarist. B. at Liverpool, the son of a slave-trader, he entered parliament as a follower of Fox, m. a rich widow, and in 1830 became Treasurer of the Ordnance. His lively letters and journals give information on early 19th cent. society and politics.

CREMATION. The method of disposing of the dead by burning. The custom was universal among Indo-European peoples, e.g. Greeks, Romans, Teutons, etc., but was discontinued among Christians on account of the belief in the bodily resurrection of the dead.

C. was revived in Italy about 1870, and shortly afterwards introduced into England. The C. Society was formed in 1874, but it was not until 1885 that C. was legalized and the first crematorium in England was opened at Woking. In the UK an application for C. must be accompanied by 2 medical certificates. C. is usually carried out by means of gas-fired furnaces. Ashes are scattered in Gardens of Remembrance or deposited in urns at the crematorium or in private graves.

CREMŌ'NA. Italian city, capital of C. prov. in Lombardy, on the Po, 72km (45m) SE of Milan. It has a 12th cent. cathedral, and was a famous violin-making centre. Pop. (1971) 79,100.

CREOLE (krē'ōl). In the West Indies and Spanish America, people of European descent b. in the New World; in Louisiana and other states on the Gulf of Mexico, either someone of French or Spanish descent, or (popularly) someone of mixed European and African descent. The French *patois* spoken in Louisiana is also known by this name.

CREOSOTE (krē'-osōt). A constituent of coal-tar and wood-tar used as a preservative and disinfectant.

CRESCENT. Term applied to the curved shape of the moon during its first quarter when its points or horns are seen at the left (in the N hemisphere). Also applied to any object, symbol, etc., resembling the C. moon. Often associated with Islam, it was first used by the Turks on their standards after the capture of Constantinople in 1453, and appears on the flags of many Moslem countries The *Red Crescent* is the Moslem equivalent of the Red Cross.

CRESS. Name given to several plants, mostly belonging to the Cruciferae, and characterized by a pungent taste, but especially to the common garden C. (*Lepidium sativum*). This is cultivated in Europe, N Africa, and parts of Asia, the young plants being grown along with white mustard to be eaten while in the seed-leaf stage as 'mustard and cress'.

CRETE (krēt). Large island in the Mediterranean belonging to Greece, lying SE of the Greek mainland. Its backbone is a limestone ridge, rising into 4 main mountain groups; snow covers the highest peaks for most of the year. The valleys and lower slopes are very fertile, and produce the usual Mediterranean fruits, etc.

The chief towns are Canea, the capital, on the northern coast; Heraklion (formerly Candia), seat of the abp. of C. and formerly the capital; Rethymnon; and Hierapetra. Most of the people belong to the Eastern Orthodox Church.

Archaeologists have unearthed many traces of early civilization in C. beginning somewhere about 3000 BC, before which time there are traces of a Neolithic population. Between about 1900 and 1400 BC was the flowering time of the Minoan culture, named after the legendary king Minos of Knossos (q.v.). About 1000 BC it was overthrown by Dorian invaders from Greece. Subsequent changes in ownership have been many. From 1669 to 1898 C. was under Turkish rule, and in 1913 it was allowed to join Greece.

During the S.W.W. an Allied force of Greek, British, and NZ troops under General Freyberg made a desperate stand against German airborne troops, 19 May-1 June 1941. The survivors withdrew to Egypt. Area 8,378 sq.km (3,235 sq.m); pop. (1971) 456,640.

CRETE. The queen's *megaron*, or hall, in the royal palace at Knossos, with its attractive dolphin fresco. Adjoining are a small bedroom, and a lavatory with what appears to have been a flush mechanism. *Photo: Peter Clayton*

CREUSE (krōz). River in central France flowing 255km (158m) generally N from the Plateau des Millevaches to the Vienne r. It traverses Creuse dept., to which it gives its name.

CREUSOT (krōzō'), **Le.** Industrial and coal-mining centre in Saône-et-Loire dept., France. It has foundries, locomotive shops, armaments factories, etc. Pop. (1975) 34,100.

CREWE. English industrial town in Cheshire, which owes its growth to its position as a railway junction. At C. are the chief construction workshops of British Rail. Pop. (1972) 51,200.

CRICHTON (krīt'on), **James** (*c.* 1560-82). Scottish scholar. Commonly called 'the Admirable C.' because of his extraordinary gifts as a poet, scholar, and linguist, he was also an athlete and swordsman. According to one account he was killed at Mantua in a street brawl.

The killer is said to have been C.'s pupil, Vincenzo di Gonzaga, son of the Duke of Mantua, whose enmity had been aroused by his master's popularity.

CRICK, Francis (1916-). British molecular biologist. During the S.W.W. he worked on the development of radar, but from 1949 did research into DNA (deoxyribonucleic acid) at the Cavendish Laboratory, Cambridge. For his discoveries as to its molecular structure (the means whereby characteristics are transmitted from one generation to another), he was awarded a Nobel prize (with Maurice Wilkins of Harvard and John D. Watson of London) in 1962. In 1977 he became research prof. at the Kieckhefer Center for Molecular Biology at La Jolla, California.

CRICKET. Name applied to insects of the family Gryllidae, which are allied to the grasshoppers and like them belong to the order Orthoptera or Saltatoria. They have long, slender antennae, and the males make a chirping note by rubbing together their wing-cases, which are provided with special stridulating organs, the purpose being to attract the females. The latter have a long ovipositor, and the males, also, are provided with special organs for transferring the sperm to the female. They are typically subterranean insects, but the most familiar, the house C. (*Gryllus domesticus*), 12mm (½ in) is common in old houses and bakehouses in the Old and New Worlds. The field C. (*G. campestris*) is larger and darker, and lives in burrows in the ground; the American *G. assimilis* closely resembles it.

CRICKET. England's national summer game, played in the open air with bat and ball. Its origin is obscure, but some form of bat and ball game has been played since the 13th cent. In 1711 Kent played All England, and in 1735 a match was played between teams chosen by the Prince of Wales and the Earl of Middlesex. The Hambledon Club at Broad-Halfpenny Down in Hampshire was the first to be formed, in 1750. The Marylebone Cricket Club (MCC) was established in Thomas Lord's ground in Dorset Square in 1787, and in 1814 it moved to St John's Wood. Since then it has been the controlling authority, and its ground the acknowledged HQ of the game.

The rules of the game have been changed from time to time. At first the wicket consisted of only 2 stumps, first without, then with a single bail. The third stump was introduced in the middle of the 18th cent. The first rules of the game were drawn up in 1774. Only underhand bowling was allowed at first, but over-arm bowling was introduced in 1865. The game is played between 2 sides of 11 men each. Wickets are pitched at 20m (22yds) apart. A batsman stands at each wicket and the object of the game is to score more runs than do the opponents. The bowler bowls to the batsman a stipulated number of balls (usually 6), after which another bowler bowls from the other wicket. A run is normally scored by the batsman after striking the ball, exchanging ends with his partner, or by hitting the ball to the boundary line for an automatic 4 runs. A batsman is usually got out by being (1) bowled; (2) caught; (3) run out; (4) stumped; (5) l.b.w. - when the ball hits his leg which is placed before the wicket. Games comprise either one or two innings per team.

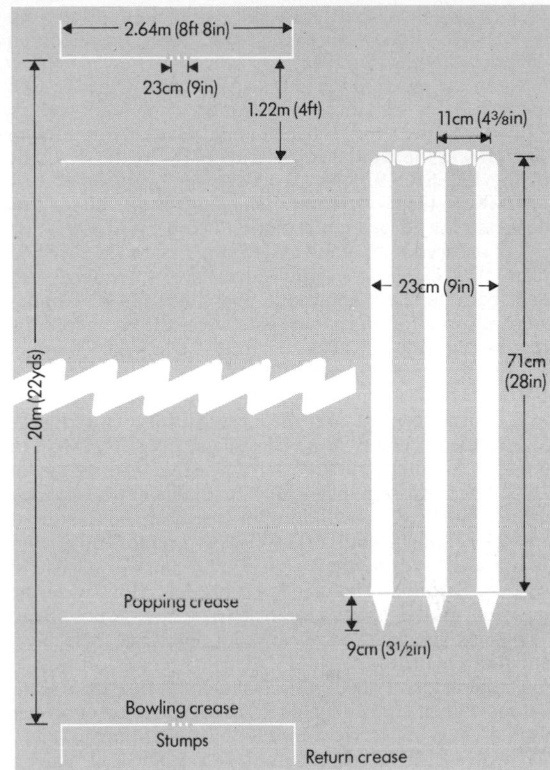

CRICKET. The pitch and wickets; the jagged line indicates that the full length of the pitch is not proportionately shown.

Every year series of Test Matches are played among member countries of the Commonwealth, where the game has its greatest popularity: Australia, India, NZ, Pakistan, UK, and W Indies. *See* ASHES. In Britain there is a County Championship Table (1850), and a County Knock-Out Competition for the Gillette Cup. The Eton v Harrow (1805, in which Lord Byron played) and Oxford v Cambridge (1827) matches are social occasions.

Famous grounds, besides Lord's, incl. Kennington Oval, Old Trafford (Manchester), the Melbourne Ground and Sydney Oval (Australia); and the Wanderers' Ground (Johannesburg). Great cricketers have incl. W. G. Grace, Sir Jack Hobbs, W. R. Hammond, and Sir Len Hutton; the Australian Sir Don Bradman; the Indian K. S. Ranjitsinhji; the South African A. D. Nourse; and the West Indians Sir Leary Constantine, Sir Frank Worrell and Sir Gary Sobers.

Test matches take several days, but otherwise the majority of matches last one day. The Cricket Memorial Gallery at Lord's is a museum. From 1977 Australian businessman Kerry Packer (1937-) staged controversial fast-moving World Series C. matches between 'star' teams, often by floodlight.

CRIMEA. Peninsula on the N shore of the Black Sea, forming a region of Ukraine SSR. Most of its surface is steppe, but the Kerch peninsula on the E is rich in iron ore and petroleum is worked. The southern coastal strip has a Mediterranean climate and a fertile soil, making it a favourite health resort. The cap. is Simferopol. Sevastopol is a great port and naval base. Smaller places are Yevpatoria, Feodosia, Kerch, and Yalta, scene of an Allied conference in 1945.

At an early period the C. was colonized by the Greeks; overrun later by successive invaders, it was Turkish 1475-1774, then independent until seized by Russia in 1783. It was the republic of Taurida 1917-20, the C. ASSR of the RSFSR 1920-44. The Germans occupied it July 1942-May 1944; its Tatar inhabitants were afterwards deported for alleged collaboration (exonerated 1967) and it was reduced to the rank of a region, first of the RSFSR, from 1954 of Ukraine. The Tatars have since tended to drift back to their homeland, and some 16,000 families were allowed to return, but some were still being forcibly returned to exile in Uzbekistan in 1979. Area 60,500 sq.km (23,500 sq.m); pop. 2½m.

CRIMEAN WAR (1854-6). The war arose nominally from a disagreement over the custody of the Holy Places at Jerusalem, actually from British and French mistrust of Russia's ambitions in the Balkans. Hostilities began in 1853 with a Russian invasion of the Balkans (whence they were compelled to withdraw by Austrian intervention) and the sinking of the Turkish fleet at Sinope. Britain and France declared war on Russia in 1854, and were joined in 1855 by Sardinia. The main military operations were the invasion of the Crimea, the siege of Sevastopol (Sept. 1854-Sept. 1855), and the battles of the Alma, Balaclava, and Inkerman, fought in 1854. The French lost 62,500 men, the British 19,600 - 15,700 of them by disease, a scandalous state of affairs that led to the organization of proper military nursing services by Florence Nightingale (q.v.).

CRIMINAL APPEAL, Court of. In England and Wales a court constituted under the Criminal Appeal Act of 1907 (amended 1908) and consisting of the Lord Chief Justice as president, and all the judges of the Queen's Bench Division. A similar court was estab. for Scotland in 1926.

CRIMINAL INJURIES COMPENSATION BOARD. In Britain the board estab. in 1964 to admin. the govt. scheme for compensation of victims of crimes of violence.

CRIMINAL INVESTIGATION DEPARTMENT (New Scotland Yard). Detective branch of the London Metropolitan Police, estab. in 1878, and comprising a force of *c.* 4,000 men and women, which is recruited entirely from the uniformed police and controlled by an Assistant Commissioner.

Some 1,000 are stationed at New Scotland Yard, where are housed: the *Central Office*, which deals with international offences and serious crimes in London and the provinces, and controls the Flying Squad; the *Criminal Intelligence Department*, which studies criminals and their methods; the *Fingerprint Department*, which contains *c.* 2,000,000 prints of convicted persons; the *Criminal Record Office*, which has information on all known criminals, and pub. the 'Police Gazette' and a pawn list daily; the *Scientific Laboratory*, which also serves police forces in the Home Counties; the *Stolen Car Squad*; and the *Special Branch*, which deals with offences against the State. The remaining 3,000 detectives are stationed locally in the Metropolitan Police District. *See* SCOTLAND YARD.

Developed outside London in the later 19th cent., such depts now exist in all UK forces. In practice they had been autonomous, but in 1979 new admin., arrangements were introduced so that all police officers, incl. CID, came under the uniformed chief superintentendent of the division, so putting into practice the former theoretical position. Also originating in London (1954), but extended across the country from 1965, are Regional Crime Squads. These comprise detectives drawn from the various local forces of region to deal with major crime, and are kept in touch by a London-based national co-ordinator.

CRIMINAL LAW. It is distinguished from Civil Law, which redresses the private wrong of the individual, by being the attempt of the State to preserve public order, at first by limitation of private vengeance, and later exclusively by state-inflicted punishment.

In England before the Norman Conquest, machinery for the enforcement of C.L. was rudimentary, and rested on the organization of the local territorial unit, e.g. the hundred. The principal court was the shire court, at which the freemen of the county were represented, and in which the law was declared from oral tradition. The main tendency of Saxon times was to extend money penalties for all offences, except for those that were *botless*, for example, murder, arson, rape.

After the Conquest the Saxon conception of the king's peace, at first limited to the vicinity of the king's person, was extended to include the whole kingdom, and offences against this, together with the crimes that were *botless*, form the basis of modern English C.L. Under Henry II more modern procedure was introduced into C.L. by the institution of a formal 'presentation' of persons suspected of felonies, i.e. homicide, treason, arson, before a grand jury, and their ultimate trial before one of the king's justices. Lesser offences or misdemeanours were for a time dealt with by the county courts, and later by the Justices of the Peace. The distinction between felonies and misdemeanours was afterwards lost, when, owing to the extreme penalties inflicted for the former, new crimes created by statute were commonly placed in the latter class.

Early law does not differentiate sharply between offences which are committed intentionally and those which cannot be attributed in law to the doer, but today the first test of criminal liability is guilty intention. This may be affected by the accused being a minor, e.g. it is presumed that no child under 14 may have guilty intention; by insanity; irresistible impulse (admitted as a defence in some states of America, although not in England); drunkenness (generally no excuse to a criminal charge, and sometimes an aggravation); necessity (apparently no defence in English C.L.); duress or threat of it.

During the last cent., however, a great many minor offences have been created by legislation which may be crimes of absolute liability, i.e. offences committed independent of any question of intention, e.g. selling adulterated food; or impose vicarious liability on certain persons, e.g. a publican is liable if his servant permits any unlawful game on licensed premises. By 1980 there were also suggestions that a number of offences should be removed from the C.L. which may be prejudicial to the smooth running of society, but are not criminal, e.g. some traffic offences, and to rename them 'contraventions'.

After the S.W.W. the growth of crime led to overcrowding of prisons, particularly by the inadequate and by the professional criminal in organized crime, who used violence. The Criminal Justice Act (1972) made provision in Britain for non-custodial penalties for the former, and for the latter introduced life imprisonment as the maximum penalty for the use of firearms; reparation for personal injury or loss of/damage to property of the victim; and criminal bankruptcy proceedings to recover the proceeds of crime.

In the USA each of the States has its own individual body of C.L., but these have a common origin in English practice.

CRIMINOLOGY. The study of crime in its various forms; of its causation and prevention; of the types of individuals who commit crimes; and of the methods used in studying these problems. C. as an independent branch of scientific study dates from the first half of the 19th cent., but criminological research remained a comparatively little-developed field in Britain until the continued increase of crime in the years following the S.W.W. prompted the endowment of an Institute of C. at Cambridge Univ. in 1959 by the Isaac Wolfson Foundation.

CRINOI'DĒA. Class of Echinoderms mainly known as feather-stars and sea-lilies. They are distinguished from the other living members of the phylum by being fixed by a stalk for at least part of their existence. The majority are known only as fossils.

CRIPPEN, Henry Hawley (1861-1910). American murderer. He killed his wife, variety artist Belle Elmore, and tried to burn the remains, but finally buried them in the cellar of his house in Hilldrop Crescent, Islington, London. Trying to escape to the USA, with his mistress Ethel le Neve (dressed as a boy), he was arrested on board ship following a radio message to the captain. He was the first criminal captured 'by radio', and was executed at Pentonville.

CRIPPS, Sir (Richard) Stafford (1889-1952). British Labour statesman. The youngest son of the 1st baron Parmoor and Theresa Potter, sister of Beatrice Webb, he was called to the Bar in 1913. Knighted in 1930, he was Solicitor-General in the MacDonald govt and was elected a Labour MP in 1931. During the 1930s he became, as leader of the Socialist League, which he helped to found, an outstanding figure in the left wing of the Labour Party but was expelled from the latter in 1939 for supporting the proposal for a 'Popular Front' of all opposed to the Chamberlain appeasement policy, and was not readmitted until 1945. In 1940 he was appointed British ambassador to Moscow and did much to improve Anglo-Soviet relations during a difficult period. From 1942 to 1945 he was Min. of Aircraft Production, and in the Attlee govt made great efforts to curb inflation while Chancellor of the Exchequer 1947-50.

CRISIS, Arc of. Term coined 1980 by US Nat. Security Adviser Brzezinski to describe the crescent area (Indian sub-continent - Turkey - Arabia - Horn of Africa) where US/Soviet influence clashes most immediately.

CRIVE'LLI, Carlo (*c.* 1430-*c.* 1493). Italian artist. B. in Venice, probably the son of a painter, he fled from his native city after a sentence for rape. His numerous paintings of sacred subjects are sharply defined and often incl. swags of realistic fruit.

CROATIA (krō-ā'shia). Federal republic of Yugoslavia. It has a long coastline on the Adriatic with the r. Drava forming its eastern boundary. Although the majority of the pop. is engaged in agriculture, coal, iron, and other minerals are mined, and there are various industries. The people are mainly Serbs and Croats (nearly 90 per cent), and about 75 per cent are RC, most of the remainder being Greek Orthodox. Zagreb is the cap., other towns are Rijeka, Split, Dubrovnik, Zadar.

CRIVELLI. Detail head of the Virgin, from the Demidoff altarpiece. *Photo: Courtesy of the National Gallery, London*

C. was in Roman times part of Pannonia, but in the 7th cent. was settled by Carpathian Croats. From 1102 it was for 800 years an autonomous kingdom under the Hungarian Crown. An Austrian crownland 1849, a Hungarian crownland 1868, it was included in the kingdom of the Serbs, Croats, and Slovenes (called Yugoslavia from 1931) in 1918. In the 1970s C. became the chief hotbed for violent nationalist separatism in Yugoslavia, and there were demands for complete autonomy. Area 56,470 sq.km (21,824 sq.m); pop. (1971) 4,423,000.

CROCE (krō'cheh), **Benedetto** (1866-1952). Italian philosopher. B. in the Abruzzi, he studied at Rome Univ. and continued as a private scholar in Naples. He was Min. of Public Instruction 1920-1, but the gradual hardening of his opposition to Fascism prevented his holding further office until he was briefly Min. without portfolio in Badoglio's cabinet in 1944. He was, however, allowed to pub. his journal *La Critica*, which he founded in 1903, and continued from 1945 as *Quaderni della Critica*.

C. like Hegel held that ideas do not *represent* reality but *are* reality; but unlike his master he rejected every kind of transcendence.

CROCKETT, Davy (1786-1836). American folk-hero. Tennessee-born, he was a Congressman (Democrat) 1827-31 and 1833-5. A series of books, of which he may have been part-author, made him into a mythical hero of the frontier, but their Whig associations cost him his office. He d. defending the Alamo during the war for Texan independence.

CROCKFORD, John. Managing clerk to Edward Cox, Sergeant-at-Law, who pub. in Britain in 1858 the first edition of *Crockford's Clerical Directory*, and who preferred to use his clerk's name because of his own official position. The anonymous prefaces have estab. an influential tradition.

CROCKFORD, William (1775–1844). British gambler. Son of a fishmonger, he founded in 1827 C.'s Club in St James's Street, which became the fashionable place for London society to gamble. Closed 1970, it re-opened with the original décor restored in 1972.

CROCODILE. Name given to reptiles of the order Crocodilia, and esp. to that section which includes the genera *Crocodylus* and *Osteolaemus*, distinguished from the alligators and caimans by their short, triangular or rounded snout, and a notch in the upper jaw into which the 4th tooth in the lower jaw fits. There are about a dozen known species, found in the tropical regions of Africa, Asia, Australasia, and Central America. The largest is the salt-water or estuarine C. (*Crocodylus porosus*), which ranges from the eastern shores of India, through the Malay Region, to N and E Australia, New Guinea, and the Fiji Is. Lengths of 6m (20ft) are not uncommon. The Nile C. (*C. niloticus*) ranges from the Upper Nile to the Cape, incl. Madagascar.

The members of the order Crocodilia are distinguished by their more or less ponderous, lizard-like form, short legs and amphibious habits.

Cs. are generally sluggish when on land, but can move with considerable speed when alarmed. They are largely nocturnal, and wholly carnivorous, and will not hesitate to attack man. All the Crocodilia are oviparous; their eggs are relatively small and are covered with a hard, white shell. Wholesale shooting for the fancy leather goods trade threatens their survival.

CROCODILE. Shooting for the sake of their valuable skins is making such monster specimens rare, and will soon threaten the existence of the species. *Photo: Courtesy of the South African Information Service*

CROCUS. Genus of plants of the family Iridaceae, natives of the N parts of the Old World, esp. S Europe and Asia Minor. During the dry season of the year they remain underground in the form of a 'corm', and produce fresh shoots and flowers in spring or autumn. At the end of the season of growth fresh corms are produced. Several species are cultivated as garden plants, the familiar mauve, white and orange forms being varieties of *C. vernus, C. versicolor,* and *C. aureus.* To the same genus belongs the saffron (*C. sativus*). The so-called autumn C. or meadow saffron (*Colchicum*) is not a true C., but belongs to the Liliaceae.

CROESUS (krē'sus) (d. *c.* 546 BC). Last king of Lydia. He secured dominion over the Greek cities of Asia Minor, and welcomed at his court their wise men, among them Solon, the Athenian lawgiver, who warned him that no man could be called happy till his life had ended happily. Later C. was overthrown by Cyrus the Persian and condemned to be burnt to death. When on the pyre, he called three times the name of Solon; and Cyrus, having learnt the reason, was moved to spare his life. *See* NUMISMATICS.

CROFTS, Freeman Wills (1879–1957). Irish writer. B. in Dublin, he was a railway engineer until 1929, but pub. the first of many detective novels, *The Cask,* in 1919. He was precisely detailed in his settings and his detective, Inspector French, was a member of the British regular force.

CROKER, Richard (1841–1922). American politician, known as 'Boss C.' B. in Co. Cork, he was taken to New York in infancy and there became 'Boss' of Tammany Hall, the notorious political organization of the Democratic Party (1886–1902). Accused of every crime from corruption to murder, he was only once in prison, and lived from 1900 in retirement in England.

CROMAGNON (kroman'yoñ). Name given to a race of prehistoric man, the first skeletons of whom were found in 1868 in the C. cave near Les Eyzies, in the Dordogne region of France. They are supposed to have been rather larger in build than modern man, and to have been possessed of considerable artistic gifts.

CRO'MARTY. *See* ROSS AND CROMARTY.

CROME, John (1768–1821). British artist, known as Old Crome. B. at Norwich, the son of a journeyman weaver, he was apprenticed to a housepainter. In his spare time he drew from nature, his work showing Dutch influence, and in 1803 founded the Norwich Society. Chiefly using oils, he also produced water-colours and etchings, and is important in the development of English landscape art. His most important pictures incl. 'Mousehold Heath' (National Gallery), 'The Poringland Oak', and 'Carrow Abbey'.

CROMER, Evelyn Baring, 1st earl of (1841–1917). British statesman. A member of the banking family of Baring, he was appointed British commissioner of the Egyptian public debt office in 1877, and then financial member of the Viceroy of India's council in 1880. He returned to Egypt in 1883 as British agent and consul-general, and until his resignation in 1907 remained the real ruler of the country.

CROMER. Seaside resort, fishing port and touring centre for Norfolk, England, 39km (24m) N of Norwich. Pop. (1972) 5,550.

CROMLECH (krom'lek). A prehistoric burial chamber, consisting of 2 or more upright stone slabs, on top of which a flat stone is placed as a roof. A well-known example is Kit's Coty House, near Aylesford, Kent.

CROMPTON, Richmal. Pseudonym of the British author R. C. Lamburn (1890–1969). B. in Lancs, and originally a teacher, she is best known for her scape-grace schoolboy creation 'William'.

CROMPTON, Samuel (1753–1827). British inventor. B. in Lancs, he invented in 1779 the 'spinning mule', an improved version of Hargreaves' spinning-jenny. His contribution to the supremacy of British manufactures was inadequately rewarded, and he d. in comparative poverty.

CROMWELL, Oliver (1599-1658). English soldier and statesman. B. at Huntingdon, the son of a small landowner, he was ed. at the local grammar school and at Cambridge. He represented Huntingdon in the parliament of 1628-9, and Cambridge in the Short Parliament of 1640, and the Long Parliament. Active in the events leading to the Civil War, he raised a troop of horse with which he did good work at Edgehill. After this experience he worked with the Eastern Association, raising more cavalry forces. These were chiefly responsible for the victory at Marston Moor in 1644, being called 'Ironsides' by Prince Rupert. By 1645, C. was the only member of either House allowed to retain his commission. The New Model Army was now raised, and under Fairfax and C. inflicted a decisive defeat on the royalists at Naseby.

Throughout 1646-8 C. worked to secure a constitutional settlement with the king acceptable to all parties. The 2nd Civil War of 1648, during which C. defeated a Scottish invasion at Preston, ended all hopes of a compromise; the army purged parliament of its Presbyterian right wing, a special commission, of which C. was a member, tried the king and condemned him to death, the monarchy and House of Lords were abolished, and a republic was set up. The democratic party or Levellers wished to go further, but in 1649 C. suppressed them and executed their leaders. During 1649-50 he crushed the resistance of the Irish clans and their royalist allies by terrorist methods. He then turned on the Scots, who had acknowledged Charles II, defeated them at Dunbar on 3 Sept. 1650, and a year later ended their attempt to invade England at Worcester.

In 1653 C. forcibly expelled the 'Rump' parliament, whose corruption was discrediting the republic, and summoned a convention known as 'Barebone's Parliament', which was soon dissolved as too radical. Under a constitution drawn up by the army leaders, the Instrument of Government, C. assumed the title of Protector, with almost royal powers. A parliament which met in 1654-5 proved refractory; it was dissolved, and a period of military dictatorship followed. C.'s last parliament, that of 1657-8, offered him the crown, which only fear of the army's republicanism restrained him from accepting. His greatest achievement as a ruler was the broad, though not complete, system of religious toleration he established. His foreign policy restored English prestige, but its whole basis, of an alliance with France against Spain, was anachronistic. He d. at Whitehall on 3 Sept. 1658; his body was buried in Westminster Abbey, whence it was removed in 1661.

His eldest surviving son **Richard Cromwell** (1626-1712) succeeded him as Protector, but resigned in May 1659. After the Restoration he lived in exile until 1680, and subsequently in retirement in England. C.'s 4th son **Henry Cromwell** (1628-74) served in the Irish campaign and ruled Ireland 1655-9 with considerable success.

CROMWELL, Thomas, earl of Essex (*c.* 1485-1540). English statesman. B. at Putney, he entered Wolsey's service in 1514, and after his fall transferred to that of Henry VIII. He soon won his new master's favour, and from 1534 acted as royal secretary and the real director of government policy. Aiming at the establishment of an absolute monarchy unchecked by Church or parliament, he had Henry proclaimed head of the Church, suppressed the monasteries, ruthlessly crushed all opposition, and favoured Protestantism, which upheld the divine right of

CROMWELL. Oliver Cromwell after Samuel Cooper. *Photo: National Portrait Gallery*

kings against the divine right of the Pope. The failure of Henry's marriage to Anne of Cleves, which C. arranged in 1539 to cement an alliance with the German Protestant princes against France and the Empire, brought about his downfall. In 1540, shortly after being created earl of Essex, he was accused of treason, attainted, and beheaded.

CRŌ'NIN, Archibald Joseph (1896-1981). British novelist. B. in Scotland, he practised as a doctor, and then in 1930 settled to creative writing. *Hatter's Castle* (1931), the story of a tradesman's lust for power, was immediately successful: later books incl. *The Citadel* (1937), exposing the methods of certain 'society doctors'. He was also creator of 'Dr Finlay's Casebook', celebrated television series.

CRONJE (krōn'ye), **Piet Arnoldus** (*c.* 1840-1911). Boer general in the South African War of 1899-1902. In 1899 he besieged Mafeking and defeated Gatacre at Magersfontein, but early in 1900 he was surrounded by Kitchener's force near Paardeberg, and forced to surrender with 4,000 men.

CRONKITE (kronk'īt), **Walter** (1916-). American broadcast journalist. Television correspondent with CBS 1950-81, he made US political history in some of his interviews, e.g. that with Gerald Ford in 1980 when Ford was considering acceptance of the Reagan vice-presidential candidacy.

CROOKES, Sir William (1832-1919). British scientist. B. in London, he was from 1856 engaged on scientific research. Among his many chemical and physical discoveries were the metal thallium (1861), the radiometer (1875), and C.'s high vacuum tube used in X-ray techniques. He was an authority on town sewage disposal, and interested in other problems, including dyeing and printing, artificial manures, and spiritualism (q.v.). Elected FRS in 1863, he was awarded the OM in 1910.

CROQUET (krō'ke). Open-air game played with mallets and balls on a level grass lawn not less than 27m (90ft) long by 18m (60ft) wide. Two or more players try to drive the balls through a series of hoops set to a pattern on the ground, leading to the winning peg. During the game a player may have his ball advanced by his partner or retarded by his opponent. These conflicts are the chief interest of the game. C. was played in France (16th-17th cent.), and was popular in England during the 1850s, before being superseded by lawn tennis (*c.* 1875); but from the 1950s a revival began. The tactical skills involved have invited comparison with chess, and membership of the Croquet Association (1897) at the Hurlingham Club, London, was rapidly increasing in the 1980s.

CROSBY, Harry Lillis (1904-77). American singer, known as 'Bing' C. B. at Tacoma, Washington, he started singing with dance bands in 1925 and achieved world success with such songs as *Pennies from Heaven, Blue Skies, White Christmas, The Bells of St Mary's* - which were featured in films with the same titles. He also made a series of 'road' film comedies with Dorothy Lamour and Bob Hope, the last being *Road to Hong Kong.*

CROSS (Lat. *crux*). Stake used in ancient times as an instrument of punishment; particularly, the C. on which Christ was crucified. It was commonly used by the Carthaginians, and the Romans employed it as a means of executing malefactors of the lowest class. The simplest form of cross (*crux simplex*) is an upright stake, without the transverse bar, on which criminals were bound or nailed. The form of C. best known in the West is the Latin cross, or *crux immissa,* which has a transverse bar fixed towards the top of the upright stake. The *crux commissa* or C. of St Anthony has the transverse bar at the top of the stake. St Andrew's C., or *crux decussata,* is formed of 2 diagonal beams, and the C. of St George or Greek C. of equal upright and horizontal beams, intersecting at the centre.

The C. is the recognized symbol of the Christian faith, but long before the Christian era it was used as a religious emblem or for ornamental purposes. Traditionally, St Helena, Constantine's mother, discovered the C. on which Christ was crucified when she made a pilgrimage to Jerusalem in 326.

The ankh (q.v.) or *crux ansata* (Lat. cross with a handle or loop at the top) is used in Egyptian inscriptions, etc., as a symbol of life.

CROSSBILL. Genus of birds (*Loxia*) of the finch family, distinguished by the crossed tips of the bill. This peculiar formation enables the C. to lever up the scales of pine cones and scoop out the seeds with its tongue.

CROSSMAN, Richard (1907-74). British Labour politician. A 'Bevanite' (*see* ANEURIN BEVAN), he consistently opposed the Labour Party's official defence policy, and in 1960 left the shadow cabinet following a disagreement on this with Gaitskell, returning in 1963. He was Min. of Housing and Local Govt 1964-6, Min. of Health and Social Security 1968-70, and editor of the *New Statesman* 1970-72. His posthumously pub. memoirs created a furore because of their revelation of confidential Cabinet discussion.

CROSSWORD. Short for a crossword puzzle, consisting of a diagram divided with squares, some of which are cancelled, but the remainder are numbered and have to be filled in with the letters of words of which numbered clues ('down' and 'across') are given at the side. The modern vogue dates from 1923, when Cs. became very popular in USA and soon after in Britain.

CROUP. In children, a cough and attacks of severe breathlessness caused by inflammation of the larynx and trachea.

CROW. Bird of the genus *Corvus* which also incl. the raven, rook and jackdaw, in the family Corvidae. The carrion C. (*C. corone*), resident in Britain, is wholly black, without the patch of bare white skin at the base of the bill which marks the rook - it is also less gregarious and more carnivorous. It is highly intelligent and sometimes destructive. The hooded or grey C. (*C. cornix*) takes its place in Ireland and parts of Scotland. The American C. (*C. brachyrhynchos*) is rather smaller.

CROWFOOT. Name applied to plants of the genus *Ranunculus.* Of this genus, some members are terrestrial, and have yellow flowers, while others are aquatic, and have white flowers, with only a touch of yellow at the base of the petals. In the former are included the buttercup, lesser celandine, and spearwort.

CROWLEY, Aleister (1875-1947). British would-be magician, *né* Edward Alexander C. Self-styled the 'Great Beast' and the 'wickedest man alive', he estab. in 1920 the Abbey of Thélème (named after the lay community devoted to pleasure imagined by Rabelais in his *Gargantua*) at Cefalu in Sicily, as a shrine of drugs, sex and magic. A posing publicity-seeker, he was somewhat unbalanced.

CROWN. An official head-dress worn by a king or queen. The modern C. originated with the diadem, an embroidered fillet worn by eastern rulers, for which a golden band was later substituted. A laurel C. was granted by the Greeks to a victor in the games, and by the Romans to a triumphant general. Cs. came into use among the Byzantine emperors and the barbarian kings after the fall of the Western Empire. Perhaps the oldest in Europe is the Iron C. of Lombardy, made in 591. The C. of Charlemagne, preserved at Vienna, consists of 8 gold plates.

Before the Conquest kings of England certainly wore Cs., and from the Conquest to the Commonwealth each king had two Cs. The old regalia was broken up under the Commonwealth, and a new set had to be made after the Restoration. *See* REGALIA.

CROWN AGENTS for Overseas Governments and Administrations. The officially appointed business and financial agents in the UK for many govts (inside and outside the Commonwealth) and public authorities, incl. the UN. It originated as the C.A. for the Colonies (1833), and in 1970-4 made some ill-judged investments which led to financial rescue by the govt. and its conversion to a public corporation in 1976.

CROWN COLONIES. British colonies which are under the direct legislative control of the Crown, and do not possess their own systems of fully responsible or representative government. They are administered either by a Crown-appointed governor or by elected or nominated legislative and executive councils with an official majority. Usually the Crown retains rights of veto and of direct legislation by orders in Council.

CROWN COURTS. On the abolition of quarter sessions and assizes in England and Wales by the Courts Act (1971), C.Cs. were estab. which may sit at any number of different centres. They are presided over by a High Court judge, for more serious cases, and by Circuit judges or Recorders for lesser ones. Appeals against conviction or sentence at magistrates' courts may be heard in C.Cs.

CROWN JEWELS. *See* REGALIA.

CROWN PROCEEDINGS ACT. An Act of Parliament passed in 1947 providing that, as from 1 Jan. 1948, the Crown (i.e. Government departments, etc.) may be sued like a private person.

CROYDON. Bor. of Greater London from 1965. Lanfranc's palace (11th cent.), residence of the Archbishops of Canterbury until *c.* 1750, survives in part. The Peggy Ashcroft (q.v.) Theatre was opened 1962. Opened 1920, C. airport was once one of the world's busiest: closed 1959. Office development to relieve congestion in central London has led to rapid growth. Pop. (1972) 334,000.

CRUCIFERAE (kroosi'ferē). Family of dicotyledonous flowering plants, so called because of the cross-like arrangement of their four petals. They are annuals or biennials, and comprise about 220 genera and 1,000-2,000 species.

CRUCIFIX (kroo'sifiks). A cross, or a representation of a cross, with the image of Christ on it.

CRUDEN (krōō'den), **Alexander** (1701-70). Scottish scholar who became a bookseller in London, and was the author of *The Complete Concordance of the Holy Scriptures,* first pub. in 1737. For much of his life he was mentally unbalanced.

CRUELTY, Theatre of. *See* ARTAUD, Antonin.

CRUFT, Charles (1852-1938). British dog expert. He organized his first dog show in 1886, and hence-forward annual shows were held in Islington - Cruft's being the premier event of the dog year in Britain.

CRUIKSHANK (krook'-), **George** (1792-1878). British caricaturist, painter and illustrator. B. in London, he owed much to Gillray for his mastery of technique. His best-known illustrations include those for Dickens's *Oliver Twist,* and *Sketches by Boz*; *The Ingoldsby Legends*; Ainsworth's *Tower of London,* and works by Fielding, Smollett, and Sterne. He was an ardent teetotaller, and his oil-painting, 'The Worship of Bacchus', now in the National Gallery, illustrates the evils of drink.

CRUISER. Medium-sized warship, less heavily armoured than a battleship, and designed for high speed and long 'cruising' range. They may be specialized for anti-aircraft, submarine or guided missile work, and the USA has a number that are nuclear-powered. The Soviet *Ochakov,* launched in 1976, is only 8,000 tonnes, but has 2 quadruple surface-to-surface missile launchers and 4 twin surface-to-air missile launchers.

CRUSADES. The wars undertaken 1096-1291 to recover the Holy Land from the Moslems. The term was also applied to wars undertaken, with the blessing of the Church, against the Spanish Moors, the Baltic pagans, heretics, and excommunicated princes. The motives combining to produce them included religious zeal, the territorial ambitions of feudal princes, and the desire of the Italian cities to secure trading bases. The 1st CRUSADE 1095-9 was occasioned by the conquest of Asia Minor and the capture of Jerusalem by the Seljuk Turks; it resulted in the recovery of Jerusalem and the establishment of a chain of Latin kingdoms along the Syrian coast. The 2nd CRUSADE 1147-9, led by Louis VII of France and the Emperor Conrad III, was a complete failure. The 3rd CRUSADE 1189-92, led by Philip Augustus of France and Richard I of England, failed to recapture Jerusalem, which had fallen to Saladin in 1187. The 4th CRUSADE 1202-4, originally intended for Egypt, was diverted against Constantinople by the intrigues of Venice; the city was sacked, and its empire divided among the crusaders. The 5th CRUSADE 1218-21, again directed towards Egypt, captured Damietta only to lose it again. The 6th CRUSADE 1228-9 was led by the Emperor Frederick II, himself under excommunication at the time, who recovered Jerusalem from the Sultan of Egypt by negotiation. The city was finally lost in 1244. The 7th CRUSADE 1249-54 and the 8th CRUSADE 1270-2 were both led by Louis IX of France, with whom in the latter was associated Edward I of England. Acre, the last Christian fortress in Syria, was lost in 1291.

CRUSADES. Built c. 1131 by Fulc V (1090–1142), count of Anjou and from 1131 king of Jerusalem, Le Krak des Chevaliers, some 150 km (93 m) N of Damascus, is an outstanding Crusader castle. It illustrates the principle of mutual defence of all the parts of a stronghold which western engineers learnt from the Byzantines. *Photo: Aerofilms Ltd.*

CRUSTACEA (krustā'shia). Class of animals in the phylum Arthropoda, comprising the crabs, lobsters, crayfish, prawns, and shrimps, besides a very large number of less familiar forms. The name is derived from the Lat., *crusta,* a shell or crust, as the stiff outer skin of chitin is further strengthened by lime salts, and forms a covering of shelly plates. C. are mostly aquatic and often develop by metamorphosis. The class is divided into sub-classes: e.g. Branchiopoda, including certain shrimps and water-fleas; Ostracoda, minute forms with the body completely enclosed in a bivalved shell; Copepoda, minute forms with a simple unpaired eye and paddle-like two-branched feet; Cirripedia, the barnacles and acorn shells; and Malacostraca, comprising all the larger and better-known examples of the class, with the body divided into two regions, and the appendages sharply distinguished.

In point of size the C. have, probably, a greater range than any other of the major divisions of the animal kingdom, varying from less than one hundredth of an inch (0.25mm) to over 3m (11ft).

Most of the C. live in sea water and are found all over the world. There are a few terrestrial species, but most of these breed in water. The most familiar of the terrestrial C. are the woodlice, whose whole life is spent on the land.

Some varieties such as crabs, lobsters, etc., serve as human food, but the importance of the Cs. lies in the part they play in the 'food-chains' in the sea.

CRYOGENICS (krī-ōjen'iks). The science of very low temperatures (approaching the absolute zero) and its applications. C. includes the production of these low temperatures, the liquefaction of gases such as nitrogen, helium, hydrogen, etc. Most substances have peculiar properties at these low temperatures which in recent years have been exploited. These include the disappearance of electrical resistance (superconductivity) and the application of this phenomenon to the production of very intense magnetic fields, masers such as that used in connection with Telstar, and high-speed switching devices for computers.

CRYONICS (krī-oniks). Freezing at the moment of clinical death to arrest 'cellular death' and so enable eventual resuscitation. The process was described by Prof. Robert Ettinger of Detroit in 1964, and the first 'candidate' - James H. Bedford, a lung cancer patient of 74 - was frozen in 1967. Treatment incl. draining the body of blood and its placing for indefinite preservation in a thermos-type container filled with liquid nitrogen at −196°C.

CRYONICS. 'Forever Flasks' in store in San Francisco in 1976. Each flask accommodates the bodies of two people frozen at the temperature of liquid nitrogen. *Photo: Michael Abrahams*

CRYPTOGRAPHY (kripto'grafi). The analysis and deciphering of codes intended to ensure the secrecy of messages en route between their sender and the intended recipient. The Enigma coding machine used by the Germans in the S.W.W., which was decoded by the Allies (*see* ULTRA) is the most famous example. Codes extend beyond military use, for example, uncrackable commercial codes are essential to banks encoding electronic fund transfer messages, business firms sending computer-conveyed memos between headquarters, and in the growing field of electronic mail. The latest development is **public-key C.** which uses an asymmetrical coding system, for which the codebooks are publishable, and which involves the use of a property of prime numbers discovered by Euler (q.v.). Putting the message into code (encrypting) is simple, but deciphering requires the inverse reading-key to be known.

CRYSTAL. Nearly all known substances, organic and inorganic, natural or artificial are crystalline; that is, they possess directional properties and their ultimate structure is a highly symmetrical arrangement of electrically-bonded atoms or molecules. A crystalline substance often grows with the characteristic shape of a geometrical solid called a crystal, which is bounded by plane surfaces termed 'faces'. Each geometrical figure or form, many of which may be combined in one crystal, consists of 2 or more faces, e.g., dome, prism, pyramid, etc. A mineral can often be identified by the shape of its crystals and the system of crystallization determined. A single crystal can vary in size from a sub-microscopic particle to a huge mass some hundred feet in length.

CRYSTALLO'GRAPHY. The scientific study of crystals, a type of solid body which shows a pattern of atoms extended in all directions. Scientific interest in crystals has greatly increased in recent years owing to the discovery of yet more remarkable properties possessed by them. Thus in 1912 it was found that the shape and size of the unit cell of a crystal can be discovered by X-rays and also the exact nature of the cell contents, thus opening up an entirely new way of 'seeing' atoms and how they cling together to form crystalline solids. This means of determining the atomic patterns in a crystal is known as X-ray diffraction. By this method it has been found that many substances have unit cells or boxes which are exact cubes, e.g. ordinary table salt (sodium chloride). The unit boxes into which a crystal structure can be divided are not always cubic; many have boxes whose edges are all of different lengths and not all at right-angles to one another.

The interest of chemists now lies in a detailed study of the complex groupings which occur in living matter. It has been shown that even protein molecules of living matter can form crystals, and such compounds may now be studied by X-ray C. Another field of application of X-ray analysis lies in the study of metals and alloys. C. is also of use to the geologist, since X-ray analysis of crystals can tell how atoms are arranged in the rocks and soils. Many materials were not even suspected of being crystals until they were examined by X-ray crystallography.

CRYSTAL PALACE. Building of glass and iron designed by Paxton, originally erected in Hyde Park, London, England, to house the Great Exhibition of 1851, and rebuilt in a modified form at Sydenham Hill 1854, where it burnt down in 1936. The site was used for a Nat. Sports Centre (1964).

CS gas. Gas affecting breathing and making the eyes water, $C_6H_4ClCH{:}C(CN)_2$, used in war or during riots for crowd control, and so-called from the initials of its American inventors, *C*arson and *S*taughton.

CTESIPHON (tes'ifon). Ruined city of the Sassanians 19km (12m) SE of Baghdad. A palace of the 4th cent. still has its throne-room standing, spanned by a single vault of unreinforced brickwork some 24m (80ft) across.

CŪ'BA. Largest of the islands of the West Indies; it lies across the entrance to the Gulf of Mexico; and is an independent republic. C. is long and narrow, and is mountainous at either end. For the rest there are large areas of well-watered, fertile plain, on which tropical agriculture flourishes. The staple products are tobacco and sugar: and C. is the largest producer of sugar in the world after the USSR. Tobacco is chiefly grown in the Vuelta-Abajo district in the W. Coffee, cocoa, pineapples, bananas, etc., are also exported. There is much valuable wood in the

Carlisle: Kendal is a prosperous centre of light industry. Area 6,808 sq.km (2,628 sq.m); pop. (1978) 472,400.

CUMIN (kum'in). Spice, the seed-like fruit of the plant *Cuminum cyminium*, with a bitter flavour.

CUMMING, Sir Mansfield (1859-1923). British naval officer. The first head of the British S.I.S., he steered M16 through the F.W.W. The head of the service has always since been known by the initial letter of Cumming's surname - 'C'. The tradition that C. should be a sailor was only broken in 1939 when Amiral Hugh Sinclair retired and was succeeded by Col. Stewart Menzies, who held the post though the S.W.W.

CUMMINGS, Bruce F., *See* W.N.P. BARBELLION.

CUMMINGS, Edward Estlin (1894-1962). American artist-poet. B. in Mass. and ed. at Harvard, he wrote much verse, characterized by a peculiar use of punctuation and typographical devices, and the French prison camp novel *The Enormous Room* (1922).

CUNEIFORM (kūnē'iform). An ancient system of writing formed of combinations of wedge-shaped strokes, usually impressed on clay. It was probably invented by the Sumerians, and was in use in Mesopotamia as early as the middle of the 4th millennium BC. It was adopted and modified by the Assyrians, Babylonians, Elamites, Hittites, Persians, and many other peoples of different races and languages. In the 5th cent. BC it fell into disuse, but sporadically reappeared in later cents. BC. The decipherment of the C. scripts was due to the efforts of G. F. Grotefend (1802) and H. C. Rawlinson (1846).

CUNNINGHAM, Allan (1784-1842). Scottish man of letters. B. in Dumfriesshire, he was apprenticed to a stonemason, and became clerk of works in Chantrey's studio in London. His best-known poem is 'A Wet Sheet and a Flowing Sea'.

CUNNINGHAM, Andrew Browne, 1st visct C. of Hyndhope (1883-1963). British admiral. From the training ship *Britannia*, he entered the RN in 1898, served in the F.W.W. and as C-in-C in the Mediterranean 1939-42 maintained British control. He was Naval C-in-C of the Expeditionary Force to N Africa in 1942 and Feb.-Oct. 1943 was C-in-C Allied Naval Forces in the Mediterranean and Admiral of the Fleet, receiving in Sept. the surrender of the Italian fleet. He succeeded Dudley-Pound as First Sea Lord and Chief of Naval Staff 1943-6, when he was created a visct and awarded the OM. His autobiography *A Sailor's Odyssey* (1951) records his story as the greatest fighting sailor since Nelson.

CUNNINGHAM, Sir John (1885-1962). British admiral. In 1940 he assisted in the evacuation of Norway, taking the Norwegian King to England in his flagship, and as 4th Sea Lord in charge of supplies and transport 1941-3 prepared the way for the N African invasion in 1942. He was C-in-C Mediterranean 1943-6, 1st Sea Lord 1946-8 and became Admiral of the Fleet in 1948.

CUNNINGHAME GRAHAM, Robert Bontine (1852-1936). Scottish writer and politician. Of Scottish and Spanish descent, he travelled widely in C and S America, Spain and Morocco. He was a Liberal MP 1886-92, became president of the Scottish Labour Party in 1888, and in later life was associated with the Scottish Nationalist movement. His writings deal with Morocco, e.g. *Mogreb-el-Acksa* (1898), or Latin America, e.g. *A Vanished Arcadia* (1901). For using the word 'damn' in the House of Commons he was once suspended.

CUPAR (koo'pahr). Town in Fife region, Scotland, on the left bank of the Eden. Pop. (1971) 6,850.

CŪ'PID. Roman name for the Greek god Eros (q.v.).

CŪ'PRĪTE. Red oxide of copper, Cu_2O, occurring crystalline in cubes or octahedra or massive. It resembles haematite in its reddish colour, but is much softer. In Arizona it is an important source of copper.

CŪPRO-NICKEL. Copper alloy (75 per cent copper and 25 per cent nickel) substituted in the UK in 1946 for the 'silver' (50 per cent silver, 40 per cent copper, 5 per cent nickel and 5 per cent zinc) previously used in currency. The change was prompted by the rising cost of silver, obtained chiefly from the US and paid for in dollars.

CURAÇAO (kūrasō'). Island in the West Indies, one of the Netherlands Antilles (q.v.). Area 338 sq.km (210 sq.m); pop. (1975) 155,000.

Willemstad, the cap. has a fine harbour. There is some agriculture, but the principal industry, dating from 1918, is the refining of petroleum from Venezuela. C., discovered in 1499, colonized by Spain 1527, annexed by the Dutch West India Company 1634, gave its name from 1924 to the group of islands renamed Netherlands Antilles in 1948.

CURAÇAO. Liqueur, originally the produce of the island of C. in the Netherlands W Indies, but now made in other countries, notably Latvia. Both dry and sweet C. is produced and marketed, the alcohol content varying between 36 and 40 per cent.

CURARE (kūrah'ri). S American native poison obtained from the bark of the tree *Strychnos toxifera* by macerating in water: used on arrow tips it paralyses the victim. An alkaloid derivative, curarine, is used as a muscle relaxant in surgical operations.

CURATE (kū'ret). Literally, a priest who has the cure of souls in a parish, and so used on the Continent. In England, however, it is generally applied to an unbeneficed clergyman who acts as assistant to a parish priest, more exactly an 'assistant C'.

CURIA ROMANA. The judicial and administrative bodies through which the Pope carries on the government of the RC Church. It includes certain tribunals; the chancellery which issues papal bulls, and various offices including that of the Cardinal Secretary of State; and the Congregations, or councils of cardinals, each with a particular department of work.

CURIE (kūrē'), **Marie** (1867-1934). Polish scientist. B. in Warsaw (née Sklodovska), she went to study in Paris in 1891, where she m. the scientist **Pierre Curie** (1859-1906), in 1895. Impressed by the publication of Becquerel's experiments, Marie decided to investigate the nature of uranium rays; and in 1898 she reported the possible existence of some new powerful radioactive element in pitchblende ores. Her husband abandoned his own researches to assist her, and in the same year the existence of polonium and radium was announced, the pure elements being isolated in 1902. Both scientists refused to take out a patent on their discovery, and were jointly awarded the Davy Medal (1903) and the Nobel Prize for physics (1903; with Becquerel). In 1904 Pierre was appointed to a chair in physics at Sorbonne, and on his death in a street accident was succeeded by his wife. She wrote a *Treatise on Radioactivity* in 1910, and was awarded the Nobel Prize for chemistry in 1911. She d. a victim of the radiations among which she had worked in her laboratory, as seen below.

CURIE. Madame Curie in her Paris laboratory. The simplicity of the apparatus she used is in striking contrast to that of today. *Photo: The Mansell Collection*

CURIE. Unit of radioactivity equal to that emitted by one gramme of radium, named after Marie C.

CURITIBA (kōōrētē'ba). Brazilian city, cap. of Paraná state on the C. river. It has a univ. (1912) and makes paper, furniture, textiles, chemicals, etc. It dates from 1654. Coffee, timber and maté are exported. Pop. (1970) 600,000.

CURIUM. Element at. no. 96, at. wt. 247, radioactive transuranic metal produced from americium and named after the Curies.

CURLEW (ker'lū). Genus of wading birds (*Numenius*) of the snipe family Charadriidae, distinguished by their long curved bills. The typical European C. or whaup (*N. arquata*) breeds on upland moors, and is *c.* 50cm (2ft) long with brownish, mottled plumage. A more northern species is the smaller whimbrel (*N. phaeopus*), which also has a shorter bill. Closely allied is the American whimbrel (*N. hudsonicus*). The stone-C. or thick-knee (*Oedicnemus crepitans*) belongs to the Oedicnemidae, a family intermediate between plovers and bustards.

CURLING. Game played on ice with stones; sometimes described as 'bowls on ice'. One of the most distinctive national games of Scotland, where it probably originated, it has spread to many countries. It can also be played on artificial (cement or tarmacadam) ponds. Two tees are erected c.35m (38yd) apart. There are 2 teams of 4 players. The object of the game is to deliver the stones near the tee, those nearest scoring. Each player has 2 stones, of equal size, fitted with a handle. The usual weight of the stone, which is shaped like a small flat cheese, is c.16-20kg (36-42lb). In Canada the weight is greater (about 27kg (60lb)) and iron replaces stone. The stone is slid on one of its flat surfaces and it may be curled in one direction or another according to the twist given as it leaves the hand. The match is played for an agreed number of heads or shots, or by time.

CURRAGH (kur'a), **The.** Plain in Co. Kildare, Rep. of Ireland, H.Q. of Irish racing and site of the national stud. The **Curragh 'Mutiny'** was the demand in March 1914 by Gen. Hubert Gough and his officers, stationed at the army camp there, that they should not be asked to take part in forcing Protestant Ulster to participate in Home Rule. They were subsequently allowed to return to duty, and after the F.W.W. the solution of partition was adopted.

CURRANT. Variety of grape first cultivated near Corinth (hence the name), with a small round seedless berry. Dried, these are used extensively in cakes and are grown on a large scale in Greece and California. Because of the similarity of the fruit, the same name is given to several species of shrubs in the genus *Ribes* (family Grossulariaceae). The red C. (*Ribes rubrum*) is a native of S Europe, Asia and N America, occasionally growing wild in Britain. The white C. is a cultivated, less acid variety, but the black C. (*R. nigrum*) is the most favoured for cooking. The flowering C. (*R. sanguineum*) is a native of N America.

CURRENCY. *See* MONEY.

CURRENT. A body of water flowing in a particular direction. Oceanic Cs. are of two kinds, viz. drifts which are broad and move slowly, and streams which are narrow and move swiftly. Of stream currents the best-known are the Gulf Stream and the Kuroshio or Japan C.

CURTIN, John (1885-1945). Australian Labour statesman. B. in Victoria, he rose to prominence as a trade-union leader and journalist, entered the House of Representatives in 1928, and was elected leader of the Labour Party in 1935. Becoming Prime Minister in 1941, he organized the mobilization of Australia's resources to meet the danger of Japanese invasion, and was confirmed in office in 1943.

CURVE. In geometry, the locus of a point moving according to specified conditions. The best-known of all Cs. is the circle, which is the locus of all points equidistant from a given point (the centre). Other common geometrical Cs. are the ellipse, parabola, and hyperbola; these curves are produced when a cone is cut by a plane at different angles. Many Cs. have been invented for the solution of special problems in geometry and mechanics, e.g. the cissoid and the cycloid.

CURWEN (ker'wen), **John** (1816-80). British musician. A Nonconformist minister, he retired in 1864 to propagate the tonic sol-fa system of music notation which he adapted from that originated by Sarah Ann Glover (1785-1867).

CURZON LINE. The Polish-Russian frontier proposed by the territorial commission of the Versailles conference in 1919, based on the eastward limit of areas with a predominantly Polish population. It acquired its name after Lord Curzon (q.v.) suggested in 1920 that the Poles, who had invaded Russia, should retire to this line pending a Russo-Polish peace conference. The frontier established in 1945 in general follows the C.L.

CURZON OF KEDLESTON, George Nathaniel Curzon, 1st marquess (1859-1925). British Cons. statesman. Son of a clergyman, he entered Parliament in 1886 and acquired an expert knowledge of Asian affairs by foreign travel 1887-94. Created baron C. in the Irish peerage on his appointment as Viceroy of India in 1899, he was the inaugurator of the North West Frontier prov. and of various reforms, but resigned in 1905 following a controversy with Kitchener. In 1911 he accepted an earldom and in 1921 a marquessate. He was For. Sec. 1919-22 and 1922-4, but on Bonar Law's resignation in 1923 he was bitterly disappointed when passed over for the premiership in favour of Baldwin. He was the lover of Elinor Glyn.

CUSTARD APPLE. Name give to several tropical fruits, produced by trees and shrubs belonging to the genus *Anona, of the family Anonceae. A. reticulata.* the common C.A., or 'bullock's heart', bears a large dark-brown fruit, containing a sweet reddish-yellow pulp. It is a native of the W Indies.

CUSTER, George Armstrong (1839–76). American Civil War general. He subsequently campaigned against the Sioux from 1874, and was killed with his troops, by the forces of Sitting Bull, in the Battle of Little Big Horn, Montana: 'Custer's last stand', 25 June 1876.

CUSTER. Frederic Remington's interpretation of 'Custer's last Charge' in the battle of the Little Big Horn. *Photo: The Mansell Collection*

CUSTOMS AND EXCISE. C. duties are taxes levied on certain imports, e.g. tobacco, wines and spirits, perfumery and jewellery; E. duties are levied on certain goods produced (e.g. beer) and incl. VAT; or on licences to carry on certain trades (sale of wines and spirits, etc.) or other activities (theatrical entertainments, betting, etc.) within a country. In the UK both come under the Board of C. and E., which also admin. VAT generally, although there are independent tax tribunals for appeal against the decisions of the commissioners; in the USA Excise duties are classed as Internal Revenue and C. are controlled by the C. Bureau.

CUTHBERT (d. 687). Christian saint. He was a shepherd of Northumbria till after a vision he entered the monastery of Melrose, travelled as a missionary far and wide, and because of his miracles was known as the 'wonderworker of Britain'. He became prior of Lindisfarne, but retired in 676 to Farne Island. In 684 he became bishop of Hexham and later of Lindisfarne. His body was removed to Durham in 995.

CUTTACK (kut-tak'). Indian city and minor port in Orissa state, of which it was the cap. until 1950. It is on the Mahanadi river delta. The old fort (Kataka) from which the town takes its name is in ruins. Pop. (1971) 194,800.

CUTTLE-FISH. Name applied to various ten-armed molluscs of the class Cephalopoda, chiefly those belonging to the family Sepiidae, which are distinguished by their internal calcareous shell (cuttle-bone). The common European C.F. (*Sepia officinalis*) is 150–250mm (6–10in) long and swims actively by means of the fins into which the sides of its oval, flattened body are expanded, and also jerks itself backwards by emitting a jet of water from its siphon. It varies from dark brown to grey, and is capable of rapid changes of hue. The large head is provided with conspicuous eyes, and 10 arms provided with suckers. Two of these are very much elongated, and with them the animal seizes its prey. The C.F. is provided with an 'ink-bag', from which a black fluid can be discharged into the water, whereby the animal can cover its retreat when alarmed; from this sepia, the well-known dark-brown pigment, is obtained.

CUTTY SARK. Most famous of the tea clippers which used to compete in the 19th cent. to bring their cargoes home first from China to Britain. The name meaning 'short chemise', comes from that of the witch in Robert Burns's poem 'Tam O'Shanter'. Built 1869, she was permanently preserved in dry dock at Greenwich in 1957. The biennial C.S. International Tall Ships Race also commemorates her.

CUVIER (küvyā'), **Georges,** baron (1769–1832). French comparative anatomist. In 1798 appeared his *Tableau élémentaire de l'histoire naturelle des animaux,* in which his scheme of classification is outlined. He was prof. of natural history in the Collège de France from 1799, and at the Jardin des Plantes from 1802; and at the Restoration in 1815 he was elected Chancellor of the University of Paris. C. was the first to relate the structure of fossil animals to that of their living allies. His great work, *Le Règne animal,* embodies a systematic survey of the animal kingdom.

CUXHAVEN (kooks'hahfen). German seaport on the S side of the Elbe estuary, at its entrance into the North Sea. It acts as an outport for Hamburg. Pop. (1970) 43,500.

CUYP (koip), **Albert** (1620–91). Dutch artist. The son of Jacob Gerritsz C. (1594–1652), a landscape and portrait painter, he himself painted views of rivers remarkable for their purity of colour and simplicity of design, people on horseback, seascapes, etc. His 'Riders with the Boy and Herdsman' is in the National Gallery, and 'Piper with Cows' in the Louvre.

CUZCO (kooz'koh). City of S Peru, cap. of C. dept, in the Andes, over 3,350 m (11,000 ft) a.s.l. some 560km (350m) SE of Lima. It was the ancient cap. of the Inca empire, and has many Inca remains as well as a fine Renaissance cathedral and other relics of the early Spanish conquerors. Founded in the 11th cent. by the first of the Incas, it was captured by Pizarro in 1533. The univ. was founded in 1598. In the 1970s and 1980s the Inca irrigation canals and terracing nearby were being restored to increase cultivation. Pop. (1972) 105,400.

CWMBRAN (koombrahn'). Admin. HQ of Gwent, Wales, NW of Newport, on the Afon Lywel, a tributary of Usk. It was estab. 1949, the name meaning 'Vale of the Crow', to provide a focus for new industrial growth in a depressed area, producing car components, nylon, biscuits, etc. Pop. (1975) 43,000.

CYANIDES (sī'anīdz). In chemistry, salts of prussic or hydrocyanic acid, produced when this is neutralized by alkalis. The principal are potassium, sodium, calcium, mercuric, gold, and cupric.

CYBELE (sib'elē). In the pantheon of W Asia, the Great Mother Goddess, whose worship, originally of Phrygian origin, was introduced among the Greeks and Romans. The Greeks identified her with Rhea. The Corybantes celebrated her worship with wild orgiastic dances, and in Rome the Galli, the priests of her cult, castrated themselves in her honour. Attis (q.v.) was beloved by her.

CYBERNETICS (sīberne'tiks). Name, derived from the Gk. 'steersman', for the science concerned with how systems organize, regulate and reproduce themselves, and also how they evolve and learn. It was founded and named

CUZCO. In the ruins of Sacsay Huaman at Cuzco the 'sacred fire' of the festival of the Sun-god (Inti Raymi) is kindled with the aid of a mirror. The ceremony has continued to take place each year in June since the beginning of the Inca era. *Photo: Mireille Vautier.*

by Norbert Wiener (1894-1964), an American mathematician. In the laboratory inanimate objects are created that behave like living systems. The uses of C. range from the creation of electronic artificial limbs to the creation of the fully automated factory where decision-making machines operate even at managerial level.

CYCADS (si'kadz). An order of plants (Cycadales) belonging to the Gymnosperms. Some have a superficial resemblance to palms, others to ferns. There are 9 genera and about 80 species, natives of tropical and sub-tropical countries. The stems of many species yield an edible starchy substance resembling sago.

CYCLADES (sik'ladēz). Group of about 200 Greek islands (Gk. Kiklådhes) in the Aegean Sea, lying between Greece and Turkey. They include Andros, Melos, Paros, Naxos and Siros on which is the cap. Hermoupolis. Area 2,579 sq.km (996 sq.m); pop. (1971) 121,000.

CYCLAMATES (sīk'lamāts). Derivatives of cyclohexysulphamic acid formerly used as cheap artificial sweeteners, because 30 times as sweet as sugar, without after-taste, and free of calories. They were banned in UK and USA from 1970, because of harmful side effects.

CYCLAMEN (sik'lamen). Genus of perennial plants of the Primulaceae, with heart-shaped leaves and the lobes of the corolla twisted and bent back. The flowers are usually white or pink, and several species are cultivated.

CYCLING. Riding a bicycle for sport, pleasure or transport. The bicycle derived from the hobby-horse which consisted of 2 wheels connected by a wooden beam carrying a saddle. The rider propelled himself by thrusting his feet against the ground. By the 1860s it had assumed a practical form; being driven from the front wheel by pedals and cranks. Structural improvements, including wire wheels, metal frames, and solid rubber tyres followed in the 1870s and 1880s, and an increase in the diameter of the front wheel to gain extra speed, gave rise to the graceful 'penny-farthing'. Further developments led to the chain drive 'safety' bicycle, equipped with pneumatic tyres (J. B. Dunlop, 1888), which exists virtually unchanged to the present day. Slight variants are the small-wheel Moulton bicycle, and folding machines for carriage in a car boot.

Cycle racing is on oval artificial tracks: or on the road, e.g. the French Tour de France (q.v.) or the British Milk Race; or across country (cyclo-cross).

CYCLONE (sī'klōn). Area of low atmospheric pressure. Cs. are formed by the mixture of cold, dry polar air with warm, moist equatorial air. These masses of air meet in temperate latitudes; the warm air rises over the cold, resulting in rain. Winds blow in towards the centre in an anticlockwise direction in the N hemisphere, clockwise in the S hemisphere; the systems are characterized by variable weather, and are common over the British Isles. They bring rain or snow, winds up to gale force, low cloud, and sometimes fog. Tropical Cs. are a great danger to shipping. The tornado is a rapidly moving cyclone.

CYCLOPES (sī'klōpēz). In Gk mythology, a race of one-eyed giants, inhabiting Sicily. As described by Homer, they were savages, subsisting on their flocks of sheep and goats, but of cannibalistic propensities.

The name C. was also given to a legendary race of builders, supposed to have come from Thrace or Lycia, and to be responsible for the so-called Cyclopean walls, a feature of the prehistoric architecture of Mycenae and other places in Greece and Italy.

CYMBAL (sim'bel). Musical instrument of percussion, consisting of a pair of round metal plates, fastened to the hand with a leather strap, and struck together to produce a loud clashing sound.

CYMRU (koom'ri). Celtic name for Wales.

CYNEWULF (kin'ewoolf) (fl. 750). Anglo-Saxon poet. He is thought to have been a Northumbrian monk, and is the undoubted author of 'Juliana' and part of the 'Christ' in the Exeter Book, and of the 'Fates of the Apostles' and 'Elene' in the Vercelli Book, in all of which he inserted his name in form of runic acrostics.

CYNIC (sin'ik). Originally the name of a school of ancient Greek philosophy, founded at Athens *c.* 400 BC by Antisthenes, a disciple of Socrates. He advocated a stern and simple morality, and a complete disregard of pleasure and comfort. His followers led by Diogenes (fl. 340 BC) not only showed a contemptuous disregard for pleasure, but despised all human affection as a source of weakness. Their 'snarling contempt' for ordinary men earned them the name of C., which in Gk means 'dog-like'.

CYPRESS (sī'pres). Genus of coniferous trees (*Cypressus*) of the family Cupressaceae. There are 20 species, which are evergreen trees and shrubs, found mainly in the warm temperate regions of the N hemisphere. They have minute scale-like leaves and small globular cones, made up of peltate woody scales, and exude an aromatic resin.

CYPRIAN (si'prian) (*c.* 210-258). Christian saint and martyr, one of the earliest Christian writers and bishop of Carthage about 249. His most famous work is a treatise on the unity of the Church.

CYPRUS (sī'prus). Large island (Gk. Kypros, Turkish Kibris) in the E Mediterranean, *c.* 64km (40m) S of Turkey in Asia. Between the Kyrenia range to the NE and the Troodos mts to the SE lies the broad and fertile plain of the Messaoria, in which is the cap. Nicosia. The small streams dry up in summer, but lack of water is being remedied by extensive irrigation work, and afforestation is being carried out. Minerals incl. copper and iron pyrites and there are some manufactures. Citrus fruit and grapes are also exported, and Cyprus sherry is famous. The chief port is Famagusta; other towns are Kyrenia, Larnaca and

Limassol. The majority of the pop. are members of the Greek Orthodox Church, but 18% are Moslems of the Turkish minority. Besides Greek and Turkish, English is widely spoken. Area 9,251 sq.km (3,572 sq.m); pop. (1975) 639,000; some 200,000 Greek Cypriots displaced from the N by the Turkish invasion are still living in the S. M.U.: Cyprus pound.

From the 15th cent BC C. was colonized by a succession of peoples from the mainland. In the 8th cent. it was within the Assyrian empire, then the Babylonian, Egyptian, and Persian. As part of Ptolemaic Egypt, it was seized by Rome in 58 BC. The Lusignan family ruled it from 1191 until Venice captured it in 1489, and from 1571 it belonged to the Turks until in 1878 they surrendered its administration to Britain, by whom it was annexed 1914 and made a colony in 1925. A movement for enosis (pron. en'ōsis, union with Greece) developed among Greek Cypriots from 1930, the Turks responding by asking for partition. In 1960 C. became an independent republic (admitted to the Commonwealth 1961), after negotiations among the 3 interested govts, with Abp Makarios (q.v.) as first pres. Britain retained 3 military bases on the S coast: Akrotiri, Episkopi and Dhekelia. Gen. George Grivas (1898-1974) continued terrorist attacks against the Makarios govt in a renewed attempt to achieve enosis, and after his death Makarios was overthrown in 1974 by a Greek-supported military coup. Turkey thereupon invaded C., occupying a third of the island N of the 'Attila Line' passing through, and including, Nicosia (part) and Famagusta. The UN peacekeeping force in C. from 1964 tried to minimize hostilities. In 1975 a Turkish Cypriot Federated state was proclaimed in the north, but Greek Cypriots (under President Spyros Kyprianou from 1977) opposed a bi-regional federation, and in 1983 the north (under President Rauf Denktash from 1976) was unilaterally proclaimed a republic.

CYPRUS. St. Hilarion castle in the Kyrenia Mountains, which were the scene of much bloodshed in the guerrilla warfare which preceded independence. *Photo: J. Allan Cash*

CYRANO DE BERGERAC (sērah'noh-de-berzherahk'), **Savinien de** (1619-55). French writer. B. in Paris, he joined a corps of guards at 19, and performed heroic feats which made him famous. He wrote plays and is the hero of a well-known play by Rostand (q.v.).

CYRENAICA (sīrenā'ika). Area of E Libya, N Africa. The Greeks estab. colonies here in the 7th cent. BC which passed under the rule of Ptolemys in 322 BC, and in 174 BC became a Roman province. It was conquered by the Arabs in the 7th cent., by Turkey in the 16th and by Italy in 1912, when it was developed as a colony which became a prov. of the new kingdom of Libya from 1951 until it was split into a number of smaller divisions under the constitutional reorganization of 1963. Modern cities, rapidly growing following discoveries of oil, incl. Benghazi, Derna and Tobruk, and there are magnificent ruins at Cyrene, Apollonia, etc.

CYRENAICS (sīrenā'iks). A school of ancient Greek philosophy founded *c.* 400 BC by Aristippus of Cyrene. He regarded pleasure as the only absolutely worth-while thing in life, but taught that self-control and intelligence were necessary to choose the best pleasures.

CYRIL (sir'il) **OF ALEXANDRIA** (376-444). Christian prelate and saint. B. at Alexandria he was made archbp in 412. He persecuted Jews and heathens, and his conjectured part in the death of Hypatia, the girl philosopher, aroused indignation. His violence arose out of hatred of heresy, but he himself was charged with unorthodoxy.

CYRIL and **METHODIUS.** Christian saints, apostles of the Slavs in the 9th cent. They were brothers, b. in Thessalonica, and were sent in 863 as missionaries to Moravia. They translated the scriptures and liturgy into Slavonic, and are said to have invented the **Cyrillic alphabet,** a variation of the Greek alphabet, with some additional signs, which is still in use among the Serbs, Bulgars, and Russians.

CYRUS (sī'rus) (d. 529 BC). The founder of the Persian empire. He became king of the Persians while they were still a small tribe of hardy warriors subordinate to the king of Media. In 550 BC he overthrew his suzerain Astyages of Media, and in 546 captured Croesus, king of Lydia, and became master of the whole of Asia Minor, including the Greek cities on the coast. Finally in 539 he captured Babylon and added Babylonia and Syria to his empire. As part of his policy of toleration he allowed the exiled Jews to return to Jerusalem. He d. fighting in Afghanistan.

CYSTIC FIBROSIS (sis'tik fibrō'sis). Genetic disorder which involves a thickening of the mucus throughout the body with resulting blockage, e.g. obstruction of the pancreatic duct so that the enzymes necessary for digestion are not produced.

CYSTITIS (sistī'tis). Inflammation of the bladder caused by bacterial infection. It is more common in women, and results in frequent and painful urination.

CZAR. *See* TSAR.

CZECHOSLOVAKIA (chekōslōvah'kē-a). Federal republic of central Europe.

C. may be divided into two main areas separated by the valley of the Morava. To the W lies a densely populated area with good communications; to the E a district that is sparsely populated and comparatively backward. The continental character of the climate increases towards the E.

Agriculture is highly developed. In the low-lying regions sugar-beet, wheat, maize, and barley are grown, in the higher parts potatoes, oats, and rye. Hops for the production of beer and for export are cultivated. Fruit is grown in many districts, and there are numerous vineyards.

Many of the important industries obtain their raw materials from agricultural products, e.g. the sugar and beer-brewing industries, the numerous factories for the production of preserved fruit, cheese, smoked meat. C. is rich in minerals, there are important coalfields at Most, Chomutoc, Kladno, Ostrava, and elsewhere; iron, silver, copper, lead, uranium, and rock-salt are mined. Parts of C. are among the most densely wooded regions of Europe, and the timber industry is important. Manufactures incl. machine tools, cars, glass, imitation jewellery, toys and woodware.

The capital is Prague; other large towns are Brno, Bratislava, Ostrava, and Plzen. The languages are Czech, a member of the western branch of the Slavonic languages, and Slovak, a closely related tongue. The majority are RC. Area 127,895 sq.km (49,381 sq.m); pop. (1978) 15,030,000, of whom a third are Slovak. M.U.: koruna.

Government. Under the Federalization Law (1969) there is a pres. and a bicameral federal assembly: directly elected Chamber of the People (2 to 1 Czech majority) and Chamber of Nations (150 deputies: half chosen by each of the Czech and Slovak Nat. Councils), with safeguards to prevent domination by either nationality.

CZECHOSLOVAKIA. Hradčany Castle, originally the fortified palace of the Bohemian kings, now houses the presidential residence and government headquarters. On the west bank of the river Vltava, it encloses the cathedral of St Vitus, founded by King Wenceslas in the 10th century. *Photo: Camera Press*

History. C. came into existence as an independent republic in 1918, after the break-up of the Austro-Hungarian empire at the end of the F.W.W. It consisted originally of the Bohemian crownlands (Bohemia, Moravia, and part of Silesia) and Slovakia, the area of Hungary inhabited by Slavonic peoples; to which was added as a trust part of Ruthenia when the Allies and Associated Powers recognized the new republic under the treaty of St Germain-en-Laye. (For the earlier history of the regions concerned, see those headings.) Besides the related Czech and Slovak peoples, the country included substantial minorities of German origin long settled in the N, of Hungarian (or Magyar) origin in the S. But despite the problems of welding into a nation such a mixed group of people, until the troubled 1930s C., under the presidency of Thomas Masaryk (q.v.), made considerable political and economic progress.

The rise of Hitler to power in Germany produced a revival of opposition among the German-speaking part of the pop., and irredentism revived among the Magyar-speakers; in addition, the Slovakian clerical party demanded autonomy for Slovakia. These difficulties led on to crisis in 1938 and the Munich agreement (q.v.) between Britain, France, Germany, and Italy, made without consultation with or the consent of C., which detached from C. the Sudetenland and gave it to Germany. Six months later Hitler occupied all C. A government-in-exile under Beneš was estab. in London until the liberation in 1945 by Russian and US troops. The same year saw some 2,000,000 Sudeten Germans expelled and Czech Ruthenia transferred to Ukraine SSR. Elections in 1946 gave the Left a slight majority and by 1948 the Communists were in full control (*see* MASARYK, JAN). The historic provs. were subsequently abolished, the country being divided into 10 regions plus Prague and Bratislava. A slight liberalization of the economy initiated 1965 became in 1968, under the leadership of Alexander Dubcek (1921-) the First Sec. of the Communist Party, a 'Socialist Democratic Revolution'. Its programme, incl. restoration of freedom of assembly, speech and movement, and restriction of the secret police, was regarded with suspicion by the USSR, and in Aug. 1968 Soviet, Bulgarian, E German, Hungarian and Polish troops invaded C. to restore the orthodox line. This was intended to secure that the concept of 'socialism with a human face' should be wholly eradicated. Nevertheless, C. went ahead with the adoption of a federal structure with equal status for Czechs and Slovaks, and attempted to retain some shadow of freedom of action.

In Czech literature, although it is the oldest of the Slavonic literatures, the only internationally known names are those of Thomas Masaryk, Karel Capek, and Jaroslav Hašek (qq.v.). The greatest modern playwright, Vaclav Havel is a leader of the Charter '77 human rights movement, estab. in 1977 to protest against the non-observance of human rights in C.

Czech composers incl. Smetana, Dvořák, Janáček and Weinberger (qq.v.).

CZESTOCHOWA (chestokhoh'vah). Industrial town in Poland, 193km (120m) SW of Warsaw, making iron goods, chemicals, paper, cement, etc. It is a railway junction. The Shrine of the 'Black Madonna' at Jasna Gora is Poland's holiest place, and Pope John Paul II spent several days there in 1979. The madonna is credited with raising the siege of C. monastery by the Swedes in 1655. Pop. (1978) 227,000.

D

Fourth letter of the alphabet, answering to the Semitic *daleth* and the Greek *delta.*

In the Latin numeral system D stands for 500. In English money d. was the sign for a penny (Lat. *denarius),* until decimalisation of the currency.

DAB. Species of flatfish (*Limanda limanda*) belonging to the plaice family (Pleuronectidae). Light brown or grey, with dull brown spots, it is commonly about 25cm (10in) long.

DABCHICK or **little grebe.** Freshwater bird (*Podiceps ruficollis*) belonging to the Podicipedidae. *See* GREBES.

DACCA (dak'ah). Capital of Bangladesh, 240km (150m) NE of Calcutta, on the Burhi Ganga. It makes jute goods, chemicals, muslin, etc. Chittagong and Chalna are its ports, and there is a major airport. The univ. was founded in 1921. Pop. (1974) 1,310,976.

DACE. A freshwater fish (*Leuciscus leuciscus*) of the carp family (Cyprinidae). Common in England, it is silvery, and reaches a length of about 30 cm (12in).

DACHAU (dakh'ow). *See* CONCENTRATION CAMPS.

DACHSHUND (daks') Small hound of German origin, (Ger., badger-dog), intended for use in badger digging, whence its name. Black-and-tan or self-coloured tan, it is long in body and short-legged.

DACOI'T. Indian term for an armed robber, member of a gang numbering 5 and over: also used in Burma. Dacoity remained troublesome after India's independence. Up to the 1970s more than 5,000 had been arrested.

DACRE, Hugh Trevor-Roper, baron D. (1914-). British historian. Regius prof. of history at Oxford 1957-80, he made his name with *The Last Days of Hitler* (1947), written after he had been sent to Berlin to probe the facts. He was created a life peer 1979.

DADAISM. Irrational literary and artistic movement developed between 1915 and 1922, born of reaction and disillusion during the F.W.W. D. appeared almost simultaneously in New York, with Marcel Duchamp's exhibition of 'ready-made' sculptures; and in Zürich, the Romanian poet Tzara with German writers Ball and Hillsenbeck founded the 'Cabaret Voltaire' in 1916, where works by Jean Arp, Max Ernst, Klee, Modigliani and Picasso were exhibited. D. was a preparatory phase in the development of Surrealism (q.v.).

DADD, Richard (1817-1886). British artist. In 1844 he brutally murdered his father and was confined as a criminal lunatic, but continued to paint haunting pictures. His figures have a mad intensity, and the distorted detail and vivid colour appealed to the taste of the 1970s, e.g. 'The Fairy Feller's Master-Stroke'.

DADDY-LONG-LEGS. *See* CRANE FLY.

DAEDALUS (dē'dalus). In Greek mythology, an Athenian craftsman who constructed for King Minos the labyrinth in which the Minotaur was imprisoned, and fled from Crete with his son Icarus by means of wings made from feathers and fastened with wax. Icarus flew too near the Sun, so that the wax melted and he drowned in the Aegean. *See* AYRTON, MICHAEL.

Project Daedalus is the plan by the British Interplanetary Society for unmanned star probe.

DA'FFODIL. Name given to several species of plants of the genus *Narcissus,* distinguished by their bell-shaped corollas. The common D. of N Europe (*N. pseudonarcissus*) has large yellow flowers, and grows from a large bulb. There are numerous cultivated forms.

DAGHESTAN (dahgestahn'). An ASSR of the RSFSR, at the E extremity of the Caucasus, bordering the Caspian Sea. It is mountainous, dissected by deep valleys and inhabited by numerous distinct peoples, each with its own language. Makhach-Kala, the cap., is a useful port on the Caspian, with petroleum refineries. D. was annexed from Persia in 1723, made an autonomous republic in 1921. Area 50,300 sq.km (14,700 sq.m); (1978) 1,600,000.

DAGLISH, Eric Fitch (1892-1966). British artist and author. B. in London, he wrote a number of natural-history books, and illustrated both these and such classics as Izaac Walton, Thoreau, Gilbert White, and W. H. Hudson with exquisite wood engravings.

DAGUERRE (dahgār'), **Louis Jacques Mandé** (1789-1851). French painter and pioneer of photography. He worked from 1829 with J. N. Niepce (d. 1833) who, like himself, had discovered the possibility of using sunlight to obtain permanent pictures. D. perfected the process, which was pub. in 1839 and is known as daguerreotype.

DAHLIA (dā'lia). Genus of plants of the family Compositae, named after Andrew Dahl, a Swedish botanist. There are 20 species of the genus, which is a native of Mexico, but was introduced to England in 1789. There are many cultivated forms.

DAHRENDORF, Ralf (1929–). German sociologist. Director of the London School of Economics 1974–84, his works incl. Life Chances (1980), which sees the aim of society as the improvement of the range of opportunities open to the individual, and of the 'ligatures' which tie him to family, community, country, etc. Hon. KBE 1982.

DAHOMEY (dahō'mi). *See* BENIN.

DÁIL ÉIRANN (doil-ār'an). The lower house of the legislature of Eire. It consists of 148 members elected by adult suffrage on a basis of proportional representation.

DAIMLER (dīm'ler), **Gottlieb** (1834-1900). German motor-car pioneer. B. in Württemberg, he had engineering experience at the Whitworth works, Manchester, before joining in 1872 N. A. Otto of Cologne in the production of new-type gas engines. In 1886 he produced his first 'motor vehicle', and a motor-bicycle. He was one of the true pioneers of the high-speed 4-stroke petrol engine.

DAIREN (dīren'). *See* LÜDA.

DAIRYING. The business of producing and handling milk and milk products. Liquid whole milk is the nearest approach which is known to a perfect food. In England and Wales, over 70 per cent of the milk produced is consumed in its liquid form, consequently D. is dominated by the needs of the home liquid milk market, whereas countries such as New Zealand rely on easily transportable milk products such as butter, cheese, condensed and dried milk. It is now usual for dairy farms to concentrate on the production of milk and for factories to take over the handling, processing, and distribution of milk as well as the manufacture of dairy products. In Britain the Milk Marketing Board (1933), to which all producers must sell their milk, forms a connecting link between farms and factories. Research is carried out at the National Institute for Research in Dairying at Reading, the Hannah Dairy Research Institute in Scotland, etc. *See* MILK.

DAIRYING. The pale gold abundance of butter coming from the giant churns of the Morrinsville Co-op Dairy at Waikato in Auckland province, New Zealand. *Photo: Courtesy of the High Commissioner for New Zealand.*

DAISY. Genus of plants (*Bellis*) of the family Compositae. The best-known species is the common D. (*B. perennis*), a British wild flower. A single white or pink flower-head rises from a rosette of spoon-shaped leaves. There are many cultivated varieties.

DA'KAR. Chief port and cap. of Senegal, W Africa, on Cape Verde peninsula. Founded in 1862, it has an artificial harbour, extensive docks, and an airport. It is an industrial centre, and there is a univ. (1957). It was formerly the seat of govt of French W Africa, and in July 1940 an unsuccessful naval action was undertaken by British and Free French forces to seize D. as an Allied base. Pop. (1976) 789,000.

DAKHLA (dahkh'lah). Coastal town in Western Sahara, formerly (as Villa Cisneros) cap. of the Spanish prov. of Rio de Oro. Pop. (1970) 2,600.

DAKOTA. *See* NORTH DAKOTA; SOUTH DAKOTA.

DALADIER (dahlahdyeh'), **Édouard** (1884-1970). French statesman. Originally a teacher, he entered the Chamber as a Radical in 1919, and was PM Jan.-Oct. 1933 and Jan.-Feb. 1934. Once more Premier April 1938-March 1940, he was largely responsible both for the Munich Agreement and France's declaration of war on Germany, was arrested on the fall of France, and was a prisoner in Germany 1943-5. He was re-elected to the Chamber 1946-58.

DALAI LAMA (dahlī' lah'mah), 14th Incarnation (1935-). Spiritual and temporal head of the Tibetan State until 1959. Enthroned in 1940, he temporarily fled 1950-1 when the Chinese overran Tibet, and in March 1959 made a dramatic escape from Lhasa to India, following a local uprising against Chinese rule. He then settled at Dharmsala, in the Punjab. His people continued to demand his return and the Chinese made unavailing overtures to him in 1980. *See* LAMAISM.

DALCROZE (dahlcrōz'), **Émile-Jaques.** *See* JAQUES-DALCROZE, ÉMILE.

DALE, Sir Henry Hallett (1875-1968). Brit. scientist. B. in London, he was director of the National Institute for Medical Research 1928-42 and in 1936 shared the Nobel prize for medicine with Otto Loewi of Graz for work on the chemical transmission of nervous effects. In 1942-6 he was prof. of chemistry at the Royal Institution, and was awarded the OM 1944.

D'ALEMBERT. *See* ALEMBERT.

DALGARNO, George (1626-87). Scottish schoolmaster and inventor of the first deaf-and-dumb alphabet (1680).

DALHOUSIE (dalhow'zi), **James Andrew Broun Ramsay,** 1st marquess and 10th earl of D. (1812-60). British administrator. He worked with Gladstone at the Board of Trade, succeeding him as pres. from 1845 until his appointment as Gov.-Gen. of India in 1847. For his successful handling of the 2nd Sikh War he received a marquessate, annexed the Punjab (1849) and, following the Burmese War, Lower Burma (1853). He also reformed the Army and Civil Service, and furthered social and economic progress before retiring in 1856.

DALI (dah'lē), **Salvador** (1904-). Spanish artist. B. near Barcelona, he came under the influence of the Italian Futurists, but in 1929 joined the Surrealists. A student of Freud, he claimed that his work could be appreciated only by the unconscious, and shocked the public into startled recognition of his gifts. His later work shows a reversion to classicism. He collaborated with L. Bunuel in surrealist films, and has designed ballet costumes and scenery. *Secret Life of S.D.* and *Diary of a Genius* (1966) are autobiographical.

DALLAS. City in Texas, USA. Founded as a trading post in 1844, it developed as the focus of a cotton area, and then as a mineral and oil-producing centre, with banking and insurance operations. After the S.W.W. growth increased rapidly with aviation, aerospace, electronic and machinery industries, clothing, food processing, printing and publishing. It is a road, rail and air centre, the D.-Fort Worth Regional Airport (1973) being the world's largest. There are many colleges and univs. in the area, and D. has a symphony orchestra, opera, ballet and theatre centre. The Texas State Fair is held annually. It was in D. that J. F. Kennedy was assassinated. Pop. of D.-Fort Worth metro. area (1971) 2,544,900.

DALMATIA (dalmā'shia). Region of Croatia, Yugoslavia. The cap. is Split. It lies along the E shore of the Adriatic and incl. a number of islands. The interior is mountainous. Important products are wine, olives, and fish. Notable towns in addition to the cap. are Zadar, Sibenik, and Dubrovnik. D. became Austrian in 1815, and by the treaty of Rapallo, 1920, went to the kingdom of the Serbs, Croats, and Slovenes (Yugoslavia from 1931), except for the town of Zadar (Zara), and the island of Lastovo (Lagosta) with neighbouring islets, given to Italy until transferred to Yugoslavia in 1947. D. was made a region of Croatia in 1949.

DALMATIAN. Breed of dog, familiar as the 'spotted' or 'plum pudding' dog. Medium-sized and smooth-coated, white with characteristic liver or black spots, it is classified as a pointer.

DALMA'TIC. The outer liturgical vestment of the deacon in the RC Church; a mantle worn at Mass and in solemn processions.

DALNY. Russian form of DAIREN.

DALTON, Hugh, baron (1887-1962). British economist and Labour politician. Chancellor of the Exchequer in 1945, he resigned in 1947 following an indiscreet disclosure to a Lobby correspondent before a Budget speech. His name is associated with the 2½% Irredeemable Treasury Stock known as 'Daltons', introduced in 1946 and bought by many savers, but rapidly depreciating in value. In 1960 he was created a life peer.

DALTON, John (1776-1844). British scientist. B. in Cumberland, he taught at New College, Manchester 1793-9, his first important work *Meteorological Observations and Essays* appearing in 1793. He is remembered for his tentative formulation of the atomic theory of chemical composition in 'Absorption of Gases' (1805), with a list of atomic weights, and elaborated in his *New System of Chemical Philosophy* (1808).

DALY, Augustin (1838-99). American theatrical manager. Of Irish descent, he was at first a drama critic and playwright, then in 1879 built Daly's theatre in New York and another Daly's in London (1893-1939). His company was a great training ground for the American stage.

DALZIEL (dal'zēl). British family of wood-engravers. George D. (1815-1902), Edward D. (1817-1905), John D. (1822-60), and Thomas Bolton D. (1823-1906), were all sons of Alexander D. of Wooler, Northumberland. George went to London in 1835 and was joined in due course by his brothers. They produced a large number of illustrations for the classics and magazines.

DAM. Engineering structure built to hold up water so as to prevent floods, provide water for irrigation and storage, and produce hydro-electric power. The world's largest dams (in 1,000 cubic metres/yards vol.) are the Tarbela, Pakistan 142,300 (186,000) and Fort Peck, Missouri 96,400,000 (126,000). Such major Ds. are usually earth or rockfill, sometimes incl. concrete sections.

DAMAN or **Damão.** Port on the W coast of India, some 160km (100m) N of Bombay. A Portuguese settlement (area 386 sq.km/149 sq.m) from the 16th cent., it was annexed by India in 1961 and incorporated in the Union Terr. of Goa, Daman and Diu (q.v.).

DAMA'RALAND. Central region of SW Africa, lying about Windhoek. It is inhabited by the Hereros (q.v.).

DAMA'SCUS. City of western Asia, the capital of Syria, said to be the oldest still inhabited city of the world. It stands on the Barada, SE of Beirut, on the edge of a highly fertile area, and has road, rail and air links.

D. was an ancient city even in OT times. The Assyrians destroyed it in *c.* 733 BC. In 332 BC it fell to one of the generals of Alexander the Great; in 63 BC it became Roman. In AD 635 it was taken by the Arabs, and has since been captured many times, by Egyptians, Mongolians, Turks, etc. During the F.W.W. it was taken by the British, 1918, and in 1920 became cap. of French-mandated Syria.

The 'street which is called straight' is associated with St Paul who was converted while on the road to D., and the tomb of Saladin is here. The most notable of the old buildings is the Great Mosque, completed as a Christian church in the 5th cent. AD. The fortress dates from 1219. A Syrian univ. was founded in 1924. From ancient times, D. has been a trading centre and was once famous for its swords. Pop. (1971) 850,000.

DA'MASK. In textiles: linen, cotton, silk, etc., fabrics that possess a figured pattern. The name derives from the city of Damascus.

DAME. Legal title of the wife (or widow) of a knight or baronet, also of Dames of the Order of the British Empire. *See* CUSTOMARY FORMS OF ADDRESS.

DAMIEN (dahmyań'), **Father** (1840-89). Belgian missionary; his original name was Joseph de Veuster. He entered the order of the Fathers of the Sacred Heart at Louvain, went to Hawaii, and from 1873 was resident priest in the leper settlement at Molokai; he became himself infected.

DAMIE'TTA. River-port of Egypt on the E branch of the Nile delta, 16km (10m) from its mouth. Pop. (1970) 100,000.

DAMOCLES (dam'ōklēz) (fl. 4th cent. BC). A courtier to the elder Dionysius, ruler of Syracuse. Having extolled the happiness of his sovereign, D. was invited by him to a great feast, and in the midst of his enjoyment beheld above his head a sword suspended by a single hair. He recognized this as a symbol of the insecurity of the great.

DAMŌ'DAR. Indian river flowing 560km (350m) from Chota Nagpur plateau in Bihar through Bihar and W Bengal states to join the Hooghli 40km (25m) SW of Calcutta. The D. Valley is a great centre of heavy industry with a hydroelectric project, combined with irrigation works.

DAMPIER (dam'pēr), **William** (1652-1715). English explorer. B. in Somerset, he went to sea in 1668, led a life of buccaneering adventure, circumnavigated the globe, and pub. his *New Voyage Round the World* in 1697. In 1699 he was sent by the government on a voyage to Australia and New Guinea, and again circled the world. He accomplished a 3rd circumnavigation 1703-7, and on his final voyage 1708-11 rescued Alexander Selkirk, the original of Robinson Crusoe, from Juan Fernandez.

Named after him are: *Dampier,* a newly-developed port on the remote N coast of Western Australia, where salt from sea water is exported to Japan's soda industry; *D. Archipelago* in the Indian Ocean, NW of the coast of Western Australia, of which Enderby Is. is the largest (area 54 sq.km/21 sq.m); and *Mt Dampier,* a peak of the Southern Alps in S Island, NZ (3,440 m/11,287ft).

DAMSON. Variety of the plum (Prunus insititia) distinguished by its small, oval fruit, which in colour ranges from yellow, through dark purple or blue to black.

DANA (dā'na), **Richard Henry** (1815-82). American author. Son of Richard Henry D., poet and essayist, he went to sea and worked his passage round Cape Horn to California and back, publishing in 1840 an account in *Two Years before the Mast.*

DANAE (dan'ā-ē). In Gk mythology, dau. of Acrisius, king of Argos, who shut her up in a brazen tower because of a prophecy that her son would kill his grandfather. Zeus became enamoured of her and descended in a shower of gold, and by him she became the mother of Perseus.

DA NANG (dah nang). Port and second city (formerly Tourane) of S Vietnam, 80km (50m) SE of Hué. Following the reunion of N and S Vietnam, the major part of the pop. was dispersed in 1976 to rural areas. Used as an American base in the Vietmam War, it was subsequently used by the USSR. Pop. (1973) 500,000.

DANBY, Thomas Osborne, earl of (1631-1712). British Tory statesman. Entering parliament in 1665, he acted 1673-8 as Charles II's chief minister, and in 1674 was created earl of D. He endeavoured to strengthen the Crown, although his foreign policy was hostile to France. In 1678 he was impeached, and sent to the Tower until 1684. In 1688 he signed the invitation to William of Orange which led to the Revolution, was again chief minister 1690-5, and in 1694 was created duke of Leeds.

DANCE. Rhythmic movement of the body, usually performed in time to music by one, two or more people. Its primary purpose is not for exercise, but may be religious, magical, martial, social or artistic - the last 2 being characteristic of contemporary 'advanced' societies.

Dances have always tended to rise upward through the social scale, i.e. the medieval court dances derived from peasant country dances. One form of D. tends to typify a whole period, e.g. the galliard the 16th cent., the minuet the 18th, the waltz the 19th and the quickstep the 20th. In this cent. new dances have tended to reach Britain from the Americas, the pioneers in popularizing them being Vernon and Irene Castle and the Astaires. The 9 Ds. of the modern World Championships in ballroom dancing are the standard 4 (waltz, foxtrot, tango and quick-step) the Latin-American styles (samba, rumba, cha-cha-cha, and paso doble), and the Viennese waltz: a British development since the '30s, which has spread to some extent abroad, is 'formation' dancing in which each team (usually 8 couples) performs a series of ballroom steps in strict co-ordination. Popular dance crazes, also American imports, have been the jitterbug in the '40s, jive in the '50s and the twist in the '60s. There is also today a great interest in Old Time (lancers, polka, two-step) and sequence D. In general, however, popular D. in the West moved away from any prescribed sequence of movements and physical contact between participants, the dancers performing as individuals with no distinction between the male and female role. By the late 1970s there were signs of a reversal of the trend, and nostalgic revivals of jive, etc., but the breakthrough came with disco dancing (*see* DISCOTHEQUE). Dances were developed requiring skilled athletic performance, espec. by the male dancer, e.g. the Grapevine, Hustles, and New Yorker. A key figure was John Travolta in his films *Grease* and *Saturday Night Fever* (both 1978). By 1980 a further degree of skill was demanded by putting the participants on wheels in 'roller disco', which also demanded young-style clothing, brilliant and glittering.. The post-war world has also produced a great cross-fertilisation from dances of different cultures. Troupes have visited the West, not only from Russia and E. Europe, but from Afro-Asia e.g. India (notably Kathakali from Kerala state), Indonesia, Japan, South Korea (Little Angels), Nigeria and Senegal. The result in the 1970s was Jazz Dance, pioneered in the U.S.A. by Matt Mattox, which includes elements of ballet, modern dance, tap, Indian classical, Latin American and Afro-American, and may be summed up as 'free-style dance'. *See also* BALLET.

DANCE. Shiva as Lord of the Dance, a bronze in the Chola style from Tamil Nadu, dating from the 11th century A.D. *Photo: Courtesy of the Victoria and Albert Museum.*

DANDELION (dan'delī-on). Perennial British wild flower *(Taraxacum officinale)* belonging to the Compositae. The stout root-stalk rises from a rosette of leaves, deeply indented like a lion's tooth, hence the name (from Fr. *dent de lion).* The flower-heads are bright yellow. The fruit is surmounted by the hairs of the calyx which constitutes the familiar D. 'puff'. The milky juice of the D. has laxative properties, and the young leaves are sometimes eaten in salads. In the Russian species *T. kok-saghyz* the juice forms an industrially usable latex, relied upon espec. during the S.W.W. as a source of rubber.

DANDIE DINMONT. Breed of terrier dog, which originated in the Scottish border country, and was made famous through the character Dandie Dinmont (and his terriers) in Scott's *Guy Mannering.*

DA'NDOLO. Celebrated Venetian family which produced 4 doges, of whom the most outstanding was Enrico D. (c. 1120-1205) who became doge in 1193. He greatly increased the dominions of the Venetian republic and accompanied the crusading army which took Constantinople (1203).

DANIEL, Glyn (1914–81). British archaeologist. A pioneer in the development of the subject, he became Disney prof. of archaeology, Cambridge, in 1974. His books incl. *The Origins and Growth of Archaeology* (1967), and *Megaliths in History* (1973).

DANIEL, Samuel (1562-1619). English sonneteer and playwright. Master of the revels at court from 1603, he wrote masques, e.g. *Hymen's Triumph* (1615).

DA'NIKEN, Erich von (1935-). Swiss writer. B. in Schaffhausen, he devoted himself from 1955 to travel and investigation of the possibility of visits to Earth by beings from outer space in earlier times. In *Chariots of the Gods* he advanced the theory that the gigantic geometric lines laid out at the ancient Peruvian city of Nazca in the Andes could have served as an 'airfield' for such visitors.

DANINOS (dahnēnoh'), **Pierre** (1913-). French author. Originally a journalist, he was liaison agent with the British Army at Dunkirk in 1940, and created in *Les Carnets du Major Thompson* (1954) a humorous-type Englishman who caught the French imagination.

DANISH LANGUAGE, LITERATURE, ART. *See under* DENMARK.

DANKWORTH, John (1927-). British jazz musician. Influential in the development of British jazz after the S.W.W., he formed a large orchestra in 1953 and in 1960 m. singer Cleo Laine. His film scores incl. *Saturday Night and Sunday Morning*, and *The Servant*.

D'ANNUNZIO (dahnoon'tsyō), **Gabriele** (1863-1938). Italian writer. His 1st vol. of poetry, *Primo Vere* (1879), was followed by further collections of verse, short stories, novels, and plays, such as *La Gioconda* (1898) for Duse; *Francesca da Rimini* (1902), etc. After serving in the F.W.W., he led an expedition in 1919 to capture Fiume, which he held until 1921. He prepared the way for Fascism by his mystic nationalism, and was created Prince of Montenevoso in 1924.

DANTE ALIGHIERI (ahlēgi-ā'ri) (1265-1321). Italian poet. B. in Florence, he first met Beatrice in 1274 and conceived a love for her which survived her marriage to another and her death in 1290, as he described in *Vita Nuova (c.* 1295). In 1289 D. fought in the battle of Campaldino, won by Florence against Arezzo, and from 1295 took an active part in Florentine politics. In 1300 he was one of the 6 Priors of the Republic, and since he favoured the moderate White Guelphs rather than the Black, was convicted in his absence of misapplication of public moneys in 1302 when the latter became predominant. He spent the remainder of his life in exile, in central and N. Italy. His works include the prose philosophical treatise *Convivio* (1306-8); *Monarchia* (1310-13), expounding his political theories; *De vulgari eloquentia* (1304-6), an original Latin work on Italian, its dialects, and kindred languages; *Canzoniere*, containing his scattered lyrics; and the *Divina Commedia (c.* 1300-21) an imaginary journey through Hell, Purgatory, and Paradise, under the guidance of Reason and Faith, represented by Virgil and Beatrice respectively. It is the greatest poem of the Middle Ages.

DANTON (doṅtoṅ), **Georges Jacques** (1759-94). French revolutionary. B. at Arcis-sur-Aube, he practised law, and during the early years of the Revolution he was one of the most influential men in Paris. He organized the rising of 10 Aug. 1792 which overthrew the monarchy, roused the country to expel the Prussian invaders, and procured the formation in April 1793 of the revolutionary tribunal and the Committee of Public Safety, of which until July he was the real leader. Thereafter he sank into the background. When he attempted to recover power, he was arrested and guillotined.

DA'NŪBE. Second longest of European rivers. It rises on the E slopes of the Black Forest, and flows 2,820 km/1,750 m across Europe to enter the Black Sea in Rumania by a swampy delta. The head of river navigation is Ulm, in Baden-Württemberg; Braila, Rumania, is the limit for ocean-going ships. Large towns on the D. include Linz, Vienna, Bratislava, Budapest, Belgrade, Ruse, Braila, and Galati. The D. is connected with the Main by canal, and thus with the Rhine system.

DANUBE. The quiet of the marshes in the delta of the great river in Rumania, where it reaches the Black Sea. *Photo: Mireille Vautier*

DANZIG. German form of GDANSK.

DA'PHNĒ. Genus of shrubs, natives of the N hemisphere of the Old World, and included in the Thymeleaceae. Best known of the 40 species is the British spurge laurel (*D. laureola*). The leaves are evergreen, the flowers green, and the berries black and poisonous.

D'ARBLAY, Madame. *See* BURNEY, FANNY.

DARDANELLES. Turkish strait that joins the Sea of Marmara with the Aegean Sea; its shores are formed by the Gallipoli (q.v.) peninsula on the NW and the mainland of Turkey-in-Asia on the SE. It is 75km (47m) long and 5-6km (3-4m) wide.

DAR EL-BEIDA. *See* CASABLANCA.

DAR ES SALAAM (dahr-es-salahm') (Arab. 'haven of peace'). Seaport in Tanzania, on mainland Tanganyika, and until its replacement by Dodoma the cap. of Tanzania. It is the Indian Ocean terminus of the TanZam Railway, and a line also runs to the lake port of Kigoma; a road links it with Ndola in the Zambian copperbelt, and oil is carried to Zambia by pipeline from D.'s refineries; there is also an internat. airport. Univ. College (1963) became the Univ. of D. in 1970, and there is a Technical College. Pop. (1978) 870,000.

DARFUR (dar'foor). Prov. in the W of the Republic of Sudan, a vast rolling plain producing gum arabic; there is also stock raising. The cap is El Fasher (pop. 30,000). D. was an independent sultanate until conquered by Egypt in 1874. Area 357,806 sq.km (138,150 sq.m); pop. *c.* 1½ million.

DARIEN (dār'ien). Former name for the Panama isthmus as a whole, and still the name of an eastern prov. of Panama. The *Gulf of D.*, part of the Caribbean, lies between Panama and Colombia. The *D. Gap* was the complex of swamp, jungle and ravines, which long prevented the linking of the N American and S American sections of the Pan-American Highway, stretching about 300km/200m, between Canitas, Panama and Chigorodo, Colombia. At the Columbian end is the Great Atrato Swamp, 60km/35m across, and of unplumbed depth (over 300m/1,000ft). The Brit. Trans-Americas Expedition (led by John Blashford-Snell) made the first motorized crossing in 1972.

The *D. Expedition* was a Scottish attempt to colonize the isthmus 1698-9, which failed disastrously owing to the climate and Span. hostility.

DARÍO (dahrē-oh'), **Rubén.** Pseudonym of the Nicaraguan poet, Félix Rubén Sarmiento (1867-1916). After holding various diplomatic appointments, he came to Madrid in 1892. He estab. the Modernist movement by his *Azure* (1888), a collection of prose and verse, and *Profane Prose* (1896). Greatest of the later works is *Songs of Life and Hope* (1905).

DARĪ'US, the Great, king of Persia, 521–485 BC. A member of a younger branch of the royal family of the Achaemenidae, he won the throne from the usurper Gaumata, reorganized the govt, and in 512 marched against the Scythians and subjugated Thrace and Macedonia. An expedition in 492 to crush a rebellion in Greece failed, and the army sent into Attica (490 BC) was defeated at Marathon. D. had an account of his reign inscribed on the mountain at Behistun, Persia.

DARJEELING (dahrjē'ling). Town and health resort in W Bengal, India, 2,150 m (7,000 ft) a.s.l. on the S slopes of the Himalayas, and connected by rail with Calcutta, 595km (370m) to the S. It is the centre of a tea-producing district. Pop. (1971) 40,700.

DARKHA'N. Industrial town in Outer Mongolia, nr the Soviet border. Cement and bricks are made, and to the S is Erdenet, site of the legendary Copper Mountain, now being exploited with Soviet aid for both copper and molybdenum. Pop. (1975) 47,000.

DARLAN (dahrloń'), **Jean François** (1881-1942). French admiral and politician. He entered the navy in 1899, and in 1939 was appointed admiral and C-in-C. He commanded the French navy 1939-40, took part in the evacuation of Dunkirk, and entered the Pétain Cabinet as Naval Minister. In 1941 he was appointed Vice-Premier, and became strongly anti-British and pro-German, but in 1942 he was dropped from the Cabinet by Laval. He was recognized as Chief of State by the Americans when they landed in French N Africa, and was assassinated by a young Frenchman.

DARLING, Grace (1815-42). British heroine. She was the dau. of a lighthouse keeper on the Farne Islands. On 7 Sept. 1838 the *Forfarshire* was wrecked, and at considerable danger Grace and her father rowed to the wreck and 9 lives were saved. She was awarded a medal for her bravery.

DARLING. Australian river, a tributary of the Murray, which it joins at Wentworth; 3,075 km (1,910 m). D. is also the name of a mountain range in W Australia, and of Downs in SE Queensland. The name comes from Sir Ralph Darling (1775-1858), governor of NSW 1825-31.

DARLINGTON. Town in Durham, England, on the Skerne, near its junction with the Tees. It has coal and ironstone mines, and makes iron and steel goods, knitting wool, etc. The world's first passenger railway was opened between D. and Stockton 27 September 1825. Pop. (1972) 85,890.

DARMSTADT. Town in the Land of Hessen, W Germany, 29km (18m) S of Frankfurt-am-Main. It has a ducal palace and a technical university. Its industries include iron founding and the manufacture of chemicals. Pop. (1978) 138,600.

DARNLEY, Henry Stewart or **Stuart,** lord (1545-67). Second husband of Mary, Queen of Scots. He was b. in England the son of the earl of Lennox and Lady Margaret Douglas, through whom he inherited a claim to the English throne. In 1565 he m. Mary, who was his first cousin. By the advice of her secretary, David Rizzio, Mary refused D. the crown matrimonial; in revenge D. led a band of nobles who murdered Rizzio in Mary's presence. Within a few days Mary and D. were reconciled,and a son, later James I and VI, was b. in June, but soon D. alienated all parties and a plot was formed against him by Bothwell. While he was lying ill at Kirk o'Field, a lonely house at Edinburgh, it was blown up on 10 Feb. 1567, D.'s body being found strangled in a neighbouring garden. Mary's share in the plot remains a subject of controversy.

DARROW, Clarence Seward (1857-1938). American lawyer. B. in Ohio, he appeared on behalf of labour organizations in many famous cases, notably the trial of Eugene Debs in 1895, and was counsel for the defence in the Loeb and Leopold murder trial of 1924, and the Dayton 'monkey' trial of 1925.

DART, Raymond (1893–1984). Australian anthropologist. His discovery of the fossil remains of the 'southern African ape' *Australopithecus africanus* in 1924, nr Taungs in Botswana, was a landmark in the study of early man. However, by 1975, it had been estab. that this was not a direct ancestor of modern man, but represented a branch that had died out.

DARTFORD. English market town in Kent, 27km (17m) ESE of London. Manufactures cement, chemicals and paper. The D. Tunnel (1963) runs under the Thames to Purfleet, Essex. Pop. (1972) 45,250.

DARTMOOR. Plateau of SW Devon, over 1,000 sq.km (400 sq.m) in extent, of which half is some 300m (1,000 ft) a.s.l. The moor is noted for its wild aspect, and rugged blocks of granite, or 'tors', crown its higher points, the highest being Yes Tor 618m (2,028 ft) and High Willhays 621m (2,039 ft). The chief rivers of Devon have their sources on D. There are numerous prehistoric relics. Most of D. is a National Park. Near Hemerdon there are tungsten reserves.

D. Prison, opened in 1809 originally to house French prisoners-of-war, is at Princetown in the centre of the moor, 11km (7m) E of Tavistock.

DARTMOUTH. English seaport at the mouth of the Dart, 43km (27m) E of Plymouth, on the Devon coast, a noted centre for yachting, with an excellent harbour. The Britannia Royal Naval Coll. dates from 1905. Pop. (1972) 5,480.

DARTMOUTH. Port in Nova Scotia, Canada, on the NE of Halifax harbour, and virtually part of the capital city itself. It has engineering industries. Pop. (1971) 64,770.

DARTS. Game possibly derived from target practice with broken arrow-hafts, in the days when archery was a compulsory military exercise for all able-bodied men. The shortening of the dart and segmentation of the board date from the 17th cent. During the 1970s the game became popular in the USA, and *c.* 7,000,000 players take part in the World Cup.

DARWIN, Charles Robert (1809-82). British scientist; discoverer of the principle of natural selection. B. at Shrewsbury, the grandson of Erasmus D. (q.v.), he studied medicine at Edinburgh and theology at Cambridge. As naturalist on the surveying voyage in the southern hemisphere of HMS *Beagle* 1831-6, he made the observations leading to his theory of modification of species. Having m. in 1839 his cousin Emma Wedgwood, he settled in Down, Kent, for the rest of his life. By 1844 he had enlarged his notes to a sketch of his conclusions, and in 1858 A. R.

Wallace (q.v.) sent a memoir to D. embodying the same theory. In 1859 D. pub. *On the Origin of Species by Means of Natural Selection* which placed the whole world of living things in an intelligible pattern, a genealogical tree, but aroused bitter controversy because it did not agree with the literal sense of the Book of Genesis. D. himself played little part in the debates, but his *Descent of Man* (1871) added fuel to the theological discussion in which T. H. Huxley and Haeckel (qq.v.) took leading parts. D. then devoted himself chiefly to botanical subjects till his death. He was buried in Westminster Abbey. Down House is maintained as a museum by the Royal College of Surgeons.

DARWIN. Charles Darwin in 1854 a few years before the publication of his great work. Conventionally respectable in dress and appearance, he was to cause uproar as much among laymen as scientists. *Photo: Radio Times Hulton Picture Library*

DARWIN, Erasmus (1731-1802). British poet, physician and naturalist. Grandfather of Charles D., he wrote *The Botanic Garden* (1792), which incl. a versification of the Linnaean system 'The Loves of the Plants', and *Zoonomia* (1794-6), which anticipated some aspects of evolutionary theory, but tending to Lamarck's interpretation.

DARWIN. Cap. and port in Northern Territory, Australia, in NW Arnhem Land. It serves the uranium mining site at Rum Jungle to the S, and commercial fruit and vegetable growing is being developed in the area. The N terminus of the rail line from Birdum, D. also has an airport and is a telecommunications centre. Founded in 1872, and named after Charles D., it was destroyed in 1974 by a cyclone, but rebuilt on the same site. It is a centre for tourists, espec. for wildlife safaris. Pop. (1973) 40,000.

DASHT-EKAVIR DESERT. Great Salt Desert SE of Tehran, Iran, where US planes landed in 1980 in the abortive mission to rescue the American Embassy hostages.

DARWIN. An aerial view of the port and man-made harbour in Northern Territory, Australia. *Photo: Courtesy of the Australian Information Service*

DASSAULT (dahsoh'), **Marcel** (1892–1986). French aircraft designer and manufacturer. Active in the F.W.W., he refused to collaborate with the Nazis in the S.W.W., and was imprisoned in Buchenwald. After the war he produced the Mystère and Mirage jets.

DASYURUS (dasi-ū'rus). Genus of marsupial cats. Nocturnal animals found in Australia and New Guinea, they are usually brown, spotted with white, and have a long fairly bushy tail, and feet adapted for climbing and running.

DATE. Genus of palms (*Phoenix*), of which *P. dactylifera*, a native of N Africa, SW Asia, and parts of India, is the most important. It is 9-18m (30-60ft) high. The fruit are produced by the female tree in bunches, weighing 9-11kg (20-25lb) and with 180-200 fruit. Ds. are an important source of food in the Near and Middle East, being exceedingly rich in sugar, and when dried are exported. Their juice is made into a kind of wine. The tree also supplies timber, and materials for baskets, rope, animal feed, etc.

DAUDET (dohdeh'), **Alphonse** (1840-97). French novelist. He became a journalist in Paris. Among his works, which show a Dickensian realism, are the sketches *Lettres de mon moulin* (1866); *Tartarin de Tarascon* (1872) with its 2 sequels; *Fromont jeune et Risler aîné* (1874); the play *L'Arlésienne* (1872), for which Bizet composed the music; and *Souvenirs d'un homme de lettres* (1889).

Alphonse D.'s son, **Léon D.** (1867-1942), also became a journalist, and founded in 1899, after the Dreyfus case, the militant royalist periodical *Action Française*. He wrote novels and philosophical treatises, and frank *Souvenirs* (1914). During the S.W.W. he was a collaborator.

DAUGAVPILS. Town in Latvia SSR, on the Daugava (W Dvina). A fortress of the Livonian Knights, 1278, it became the cap. of Polish Livonia. There is a timber industry. Pop. (1975) 110,000.

DAUMIER (dohmyeh'), **Honoré** (1808-79). French artist. B. at Marseilles, he was taken to Paris as a child and entered a lithographer's studio. He became famous for his cartoons for *La Caricature, Charivari* and other periodicals, once being imprisoned for an attack on Louis Philippe. His output was enormous and incl. 4,000 lithographs, but his popular success hindered appreciation of his work as a painter, e.g. his realistic 'Les Bohémiens de Paris', 'Christ Mocked' and illustrations of incidents from Cervantes.

DAUMIER. The artist's characteristic bold brushwork depicts 'Don Quixote and Sancho Panza'. *Photo: Courtesy of the National Gallery, London*

DAUPHIN (dohfan'). Title of the eldest sons of the kings of France from 1349 to 1830. It was originally attached to the rulers of the provinces of Vienne and Auvergne, known as the Dauphiné.

DAUPHINÉ (dohfēneh'). Old prov. of France, comprising the depts of Isère, Drôme, and Hautes-Alpes. After the collapse of Rome it belonged to Burgundy, then was under Frankish domination; afterwards part of Arles, it was sold by its ruler to France in 1349. The cap. was Grenoble.

DÁVAO. Town in the Philippine Republic, cap. of D. prov., at the mouth of D. river on the island of Mindanao. It is the centre of a fertile district and is a busy port. Pop. (1975) 482,300.

DA'VENANT, Sir William (1606-68). English poet and dramatist. B. at Oxford, he was rumoured to be a son of Shakespeare. In 1638 he became poet laureate, and during the Civil Wars was imprisoned by Parliament. His *Siege of Rhodes* (1656) is considered the first English opera.

DAVENTRY (dān'tri). Town in Northants, England, 19km (12m) W of Northampton. Because of its central position, it became in 1925 the site of the BBC high-power radio transmitter. Originally specializing in footwear, it received London and Birmingham overspill from the 1950s, and developed varied light industries. Pop. (1973) 13,400.

DAVID (*c.* 1060-970 BC). Second king of Israel. Youngest son of Jesse of Bethlehem, while still a shepherd boy he was anointed by Samuel to succeed Saul. He played the harp before Saul to banish his melancholy, and later slew the Philistine giant, Goliath, with a sling and stone. Saul's son, Jonathan, became his friend, but Saul, jealous of his prowess, schemed to murder him. D. married Michal, Saul's dau., but following further attempts on his life went into exile until Saul and Jonathan fell in battle with the Philistines at Gilboa. D. was anointed king at Hebron, took Jerusalem, made it his capital, and housed the Ark there. Absalom, his favourite son, led a rebellion but was defeated and slain. D. sent Uriah to his death in order that he might marry his widow. He probably wrote a few of the psalms, was a skilled harpist, and was celebrated as a secular poet.

DAVID (or **Dewi**) (fl. 5th-6th cent.). Patron saint of Wales, traditionally the son of a prince of Cardiganshire and uncle of King Arthur. He founded a monastery at Menevia, and presided over a synod at Brefi and condemned the Pelagian heresy. It is said that D. was responsible for the adoption of the leek as the national emblem of Wales.

DAVID I (1084-1153). King of Scotland. The youngest son of Malcolm Ceanmhor and St Margaret, he was brought up in the English court of Henry I, m. in 1113 Matilda, widow of the earl of Northampton, and in 1124 became king. He invaded England in 1138 in support of Queen Matilda, dau. of Henry I, but was defeated at Northallerton in the 'Battle of the Standard', and again in 1141.

DAVID II (1324-71). King of Scotland. Son of Robert the Bruce, he was m. at the age of 4 to Joanna, dau. of Edward II of England, and in 1329 succeeded to the throne. After the defeat of the Scots by Edward III at Halidon Hill, D. and Joanna were sent to France for safety. They returned in 1341 and in 1346 D. invaded England and was captured at the battle of Neville's Cross and imprisoned for 11 years. On Joanna's death in 1362 D. m. Margaret Logie, but divorced her in 1370.

DAVID (dahvēd'), **Félicien César** (1810-76). French composer. He travelled in Palestine, and became famous with the performance of his symphonic fantasy *Desert* (1844). He was one of the first Western composers to introduce oriental scales and melodies into his music.

DAVID, Gerard (*c.* 1450-1523). Flemish painter. The last great artist of the Bruges school, he is famous chiefly for his altar-pieces.

DAVID (dahvēd'), **Jacques Louis** (1748-1825). French painter. He studied under Boucher, won the Prix de Rome in 1774, and during the Revolution he was an ardent supporter of the republicans; he was elected to the Convention and a member of the Committee of Public Safety, and narrowly escaped the guillotine. His most famous paintings are 'The Sabine Women' and 'Mme Récamier'. He became court painter to Napoleon, but was banished by the Bourbons and settled in Brussels.

DAVIDSON, John (1857-1909). Scottish poet. B. in Renfrewshire, he developed an interest in science as assistant to the public analyst at Greenock, spent some years as a schoolmaster, and in 1889 went to London. At first mildly successful with *Fleet Street Eclogues* (1893) he declined into poverty and drowned himself. The modern, realistic idiom of such a poem as 'Thirty bob a week' influenced Eliot.

DAVIES, Sir Henry Walford (1869-1941). English composer. B. in Salop of Welsh parentage, he was knighted in 1922, and was organist at St George's Chapel, Windsor 1927-32. From 1934 he was Master of the King's Musick, and he was influential in the musical education of Britain through his attractive radio talks. His compositions incl. the cantata *Everyman* (1904), the 'Solemn Melody' for organ and strings, chamber music and part songs.

DAVIES, Peter Maxwell (1934-). British composer and conductor. He composed much music for chamber ensembles, and has a particular interest in the work of the

16th cent. composer John Taverner, whose life is the basis of his opera *Taverner* (1972).

DAVIES, William Henry (1871-1940). British poet. B. in Mon. he went to America, where he lived the life of a 'hobo', and lost his right foot 'riding the rods'. Returning to England he raised the money to pub. his first vol. of poems, *Soul's Destroyer* (1906), as a wandering pedlar. G. B. Shaw recognized its merit and assured his success. D. pub. further vols. of simple direct verse and the prose *Autobiography of a Super-Tramp* (1908).

DA VINCI. *See* LEONARDO DA VINCI.

DAVIS, Angela (1944-). American Communist activist. B. in Alabama of a middle-class Negro family, she was ed. at Brandeis Univ., Mass. and in Europe. At the Univ. of California, she studied under Marcuse, becoming asst. prof. of philosophy in 1969 but being dismissed 1970 because of her politics. Later in 1970 she was arrested as allegedly having supplied guns which were used in the murder of a judge, seized as a hostage in an attempt to secure the release of 3 Negro convicts (known as the Soledad brothers from the name of their prison), but was acquitted in 1972. One of them - George Jackson - was shot in mysterious circumstances in 1971 in San Quentin, where he had been transferred. *See* BLACK POWER.

DAVIS, Bette (1908-). American actress. B. in Mass., she entered films in 1930, estab. a reputation with *Of Human Bondage* as a forceful dramatic actress. Later films incl. *Dangerous* (1935) and *Jezebel* (1938), both winning her Academy Awards, *Private Lives of Elizabeth and Essex*, and *Whatever happened to Baby Jane* (1963).

DAVIS, Sir Colin (1927-). British conductor. Musical director at Sadler's Wells 1961-5, and chief conductor BBC Symphony Orchestra 1967-71, musical director of the Royal Opera 1981–6. He was knighted in 1980.

DAVIS. Sir Colin Davis, relaxing at home, in contrast to his more characteristic role of sustained activity as a professional conductor. *Photo: Clive Barda*

DAVIS, Dwight Filley (1879-1945). American tennis player, donor in 1900 of the *Davis Cup* - more properly, the Dwight Davis International Bowl.

DAVIS, Jefferson (1808-89). American statesman. B. in Kentucky, he served in the US army before becoming a cotton planter in Mississippi. He sat in the Senate 1847-51, and was Secretary of War 1853-7. He returned to the Senate in 1857 as a leader of the Southern Democrats, and a defender of slavery; in 1860 he issued a declaration in favour of secession, and early in 1861 he was elected president of the Confederate States. During the Civil War he ably directed the home front, but his strategy was less successful. He left Richmond on its fall in 1865, and shortly after was captured in Georgia, and spent 2 years in prison.

DAVIS, Joe (1901-78). British billiards and snooker player. He was world snooker champion 1927-46, and virtually the creator of the sophisticated modern game.

DAVIS, John (c. 1550-1605). English navigator and explorer. B. near Dartmouth, he sailed in search of a NW passage in 1585, and in 1587 sailed to Baffin Bay through the straits named after him. In 1588 he fought against the Armada. He was killed by Japanese pirates in the straits of Malacca.

DAVISSON, Clinton (1881-1958). American scientist. B. in Illinois, he worked under O. W. Richardson at Princeton before joining the Bell Telephone organization in 1917, and proved de Broglie's theory that electrons - and therefore all matter - have wave structure: G. P. Thompson carried through the same research independently and in 1937 the 2 men shared a Nobel prize.

DAVITT, Michael (1846-1906). Irish revolutionary. B. in co. Mayo, he began work in a factory at the age of 10, joined the Fenians in 1865, and was sentenced in 1870 to 15 years' imprisonment for treason-felony. After his release in 1877 he and Parnell founded the Land League in 1879. Imprisoned several times for his share in the land agitation, he was a MP 1895-9.

DAVOS (dahvohs'). Town at 1,559 m (5,115 ft) a.s.l. in an Alpine valley in Grisons canton, Switzerland, famous as a health resort and as a winter-sports centre. Pop. (1970) 11,500.

DAVY, Sir Humphry (1778-1829). British chemist. Initially an apprentice surgeon, he also studied metaphysics, ethics and mathematics, before devoting himself to chemistry. While laboratory superintendent at the Bristol Pneumatic Institute he discovered the respiratory effects of 'laughing gas' (nitrous oxide) in 1799, and as a result was invited to the Royal Institution, London, where he became prof. of chemistry in 1802. He soon estab. a fine reputation for his lecturing and research, and at govt. request gave a course of lectures on agricultural chemistry (1803), later pub., which remained the standard work for nearly 50 years. During his classic 'Bakerian' lectures (1806-10) on electro-chemistry, he demonstrated his discovery of the metals sodium, potassium, calcium, magnesium, strontium and barium, by electrolysis. During a continental tour in 1813, with his assistant Faraday (q.v.), he investigated the electricity of torpedo-fish, burnt diamonds in oxygen to prove that they were made of carbon, and examined volcanic activity. On returning to England he investigated fire damp in coal mines and constructed the safety lamp, used from 1816. He was elected pres. of the Royal Society in 1820. Throughout his life he wrote poetry for relaxation.

DAVY JONES. Sailor's name, generally occurring in the phrase 'gone to D.J.'s locker' applied to those drowned at sea, and taken as the name of a sea-spirit or devil.

DAWES (dawz), **Charles Gates** (1865-1951). American statesman. In 1923 he was appointed by the Allied Reparations Commission president of the committee which produced the 'Dawes Plan' - aiming at securing that Germany should pay as much as possible as war debts. It was superseded by the Young Plan in 1929. D. was elected vice-president of the USA in 1924, received the Nobel peace prize in 1925, and was ambassador to Britain 1929-32.

DAWSON, Peter (1882-1961). Australian baritone, noted for marching songs, ballads, etc.

DAWSON. Canadian 'ghost town', cap. until 1953 of the Yukon Territory, at the junction of the Yukon and Klondike rivers, founded 1896 at the time of the Klondike gold rush when its pop. was 25,000; pop. (1971) 500.

DAWSON CREEK. Town in British Columbia, SE terminus of the Alaska Highway. Pop. (1976) 10,500.

DAY, Sir Robin (1923-). British broadcasting journalist. A barrister, he pioneered the probing political interview, notably when he questioned Macmillan on the composition of his cabinet in 1958. Knighted 1981.

DAYAKS (dī'aks) or **Dyaks.** Tribal people of Borneo. They are taller and less dark-skinned than the Malays, and are skilled in many arts and crafts. For hunting purposes they use the blowpipe. The custom of head-hunting has tended to die out.

DAYAN (dahyahn'), **Moshe** (1915–81). Israeli general. He was Chief of Army Staff 1953–8, and, as Minister of Defence 1967–74, was said to be responsible for the victory in the Six Day War, but was criticised for the conduct of the October War. He resigned as Foreign Minister (1977–9) when Begin failed to negotiate with the Palestinians.

DAY LEWIS, Cecil (1904-72). British poet. B. at Ballintubber, Ireland, he was ed. at Oxford and then became a schoolmaster, teaching at Cheltenham Coll. 1930-5. With Auden and Spender he was one of the influential Leftist poets of the 1930s, and first showed an individual quality in *From Feathers to Iron* (1931). In maturity he developed a gift for tangy, accomplished lyrics, and sustained narrative power, e.g. 'The Loss of the Nabara' in *Overtures to Death* (1938). Prof. of poetry at Oxford 1951-6, he pub. critical works, translations of the *Georgics* and *Aeneid,* and detective novels under the pseudonym Nicholas Blake. In 1968 he succeeded Masefield as Poet Laureate.

DAYTON. City of Ohio, USA, producing precision machinery, household appliances, electrical equipment, etc. It has an aeronautical research centre and an RC university. It was the birthplace of Orville Wright (q.v.). Pop. met. area (1970) 842,147.

DAYTON. Small town in Tennessee, USA, notorious as the scene of the trial (1925) of John T. Scopes, a science teacher at the high school, accused of teaching, contrary to a law of the State, that 'man is descended from the lower animals'. Scopes was fined $100, but this was waived on a technical point. Pop. (1970) 4,360.

DAYTONA BEACH. Popular US seaside resort and motor-racing centre on the Atlantic coast of Florida. Pop. (1970) 45,327.

DAZAI, Osamu. Pseudonym of Shuji Tsushima (1909-48), Japanese author. His work reflects the drunkenness and drug addiction of his life, and his ultimately successful penchant for suicide. The title of his novel *The Setting Sun* (1947) has become in Japanese synonymous with the dead of the S.W.W.

D-DAY. Name given to the day - 6 June 1944 - when the Allied invasion of Europe took place during the S.W.W. It was originally fixed for 5 June, but owing to unfavourable weather the invasion was postponed for 24 hrs. *See* S.W.W. In military jargon D-Day was any day for which an operation was planned, but in ordinary usage it has acquired this specialized sense.

D.D.T. (Dichloro-Diphenyl-Trichloroethane). Powerful insecticide, in the form of a white powder, discovered in 1940 by the Swiss firm J. R. Geigy. Effective against flies, mosquitoes, sand flies, lice, fleas, etc., it is valuable in the control of diseases such as malaria, typhus, yellow fever and plague which they spread. Unfortunately, there is evidence that these pests develop resistant strains in response. DDT also persists in the aquatic and terrestrial environment, and was banned or restricted in use by most industrialized nations 1970-1. Developing countries oppose restriction as entailing dear food and re-establishment of malaria and other diseases. *See* MÜLLER, P.

DEACON. Third and last order of the Christian min. It dates from Apostolic times, and originally the Ds. were entrusted with the care of the material needs of the Christian community. Subsequently it became the preliminary stage to the priesthood, and in the C of E a candidate for holy orders is ordained D., proceeding to obtain priest's orders after a year. In the Presbyterian and Free Churches a D. is a layman chosen to assist the min. Deaconesses existed in the early Church, but as known today are a modern institution, having been revived in the C of E in 1862 and legally recognized in 1968. They may not admin. the Sacraments, but may conduct public worship and preach.

DEAD SEA. Large lake partly in Israel partly in Jordan; it is 74×13km (46×8m), and lies 394m (1,292 ft) below sea-level. The chief river entering it is the Jordan; it has no outlet to the sea, and the water is very salt. Since both Israel and Jordan are using the waters of the Jordan river, the D.S. is now dried up in the centre and divided into two halves, but in 1980 Israel announced a plan to link it by canal with the Mediterranean. The Dead Sea Rift is part of the fault between the African and Arab plates.

DEAD SEA SCROLLS. Collection of ancient scrolls (some intact in their jars) and fragments of scrolls found 1947-56 in caves on the W side of the Jordan 12km (7m) S of Jericho and 2km (1m) from the N end of the Dead Sea. The most valuable date from *c.* 150 BC to AD 68, when the monastic community which owned them was destroyed by the Romans because of its support for a revolt against their rule from AD 66. They incl. scripts of OT books a thousand years earlier than those previously known. *See* QUMRAN.

DEAFNESS. Absence or deficiency of the sense of hearing. It may be inborn and due to abnormality of development, but is usually caused by injury or disease of the inner ear. After the habit of speech has been fully formed, the ability to speak will be retained, and some relief may be given by electrical hearing aids (q.v.), but deafness in young children necessarily implies mutism as well unless special training is given. Experiments are in progress with implants using micro-electronics technology.

The Deaf and Dumb Alphabet is a finger alphabet rather tedious in use; much more rapid is American Sign Language (A.S.L.), a language with manually produced signs, of which some are iconic but the majority symbolic; the grammar differs from that of spoken English.

DEAKIN, Alfred (1856-1919). Australian Liberal statesman. He was attorney-general in the first Federal Cabinet of 1901, and P.M. 1903-4, 1905-8, and 1909-10.

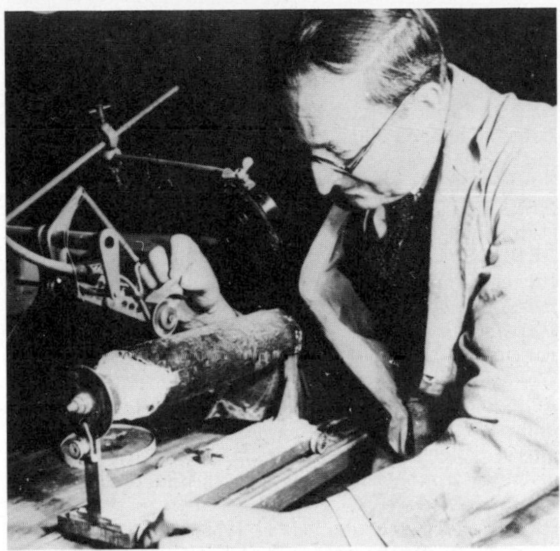

DEAD SEA SCROLLS. Among the leather scrolls from Qumran, were two of bronze, of which only metallic salts remained. Professor H. Wright Baker (above) of the Manchester College of Science and Technology solved the problem by bonding the salts together and cutting the scrolls into strips with a tiny circular saw. They record the location of the treasures of the temple at Jerusalem. A transcription from one segment of a scroll is seen below. *Photo: Courtesy of Prof. H. Wright Baker*

In his second administration, legislation on defence, protection and the provision of pensions was wide-reaching and long-lasting. His posthumous *The Federal Story* (1944) described the negotiations which estab. the Commonwealth and the drafting of its constitution.

DEAL. English port and resort on the E. coast of Kent, one of the Cinque ports. Julius Caesar is said to have landed there in 55 BC. The castle was built by Henry VIII and houses the town museum. Pop. (1972) 26,120.

DEAN. In the C of E, the head of the chapter of a cathedral or collegiate church. A rural D. is a clergyman who is invested with jurisdiction or precedence over a division of an archdeaconry. There are also Ds. in the colleges of Oxford and Cambridge, being fellows charged with the maintenance of discipline; and in medical schools, univs., etc.

DEAN, Basil (1888-1978). British man of the theatre. In the S.W.W. he was founder and director-general of ENSA, providing entertainment for the forces.

DEAN, Forest of. Wooded area in W Gloucestershire, England, much of it Crown property. Iron and coal are mined.

DEAKIN. Alfred Deakin was a leading figure in the negotiations to establish the Australian Commonwealth, and in drafting the constitution. *Photo: Courtesy of the Australian Information Service*

DEAN, James (1931-55). American actor, *né* James Byron. Killed in a road accident when only his first film, *East of Eden*, had been shown, he posthumously became the focus of a cult with *Rebel Without a Cause* and *Giant*, as the 'first American teenager'.

DEARBORN. Motor manufacturing city in Michigan, USA, 16km (10m) SW of Detroit. Settled in 1795, it was the birthplace and home of Henry Ford (q.v.) who built here the first Ford works. D. also makes aircraft parts, steel, bricks. Pop. (1970) 184,000, incl. D. Heights.

DEATH. The permanent ending of all life processes in an animal or plant. The exact moment of its occurrence is sometimes uncertain, and modern resuscitation techniques render definition difficult, the one sure sign being putrefaction. The development of transplant surgery, however, led in 1968 to an agreed definition of D. by a conference at the World Health Organization HQ in Geneva: a potential donor is considered dead when his brain has totally and irreversibly ceased to work, i.e. there is no brain-body connection, muscular activity, blood pressure, or ability to breathe unaided by machine.

DEATH VALLEY. Depression 225km (140m) long and 6-26km (4-16m) wide, in SE California, USA. At 85m (280ft) below sea level, it is the lowest point in N America. Bordering mtns rise to 3,000 m (10,000ft) average rainfall is 35mm (1.4in) annually, and it is one of the world's hottest regions.

DEATH WATCH. Species of beetle (*Xestobium rufovillosum*) of the family Anobiidae. It bores in old furniture, etc., and the male, in order to attract the female, produces a ticking sound by striking its head upon a wooden surface; this is taken by the superstitious as a warning of approaching death.

DEAUVILLE (dohvēl'). Holiday resort of Normandy in Calvados dept, France, on the Eng. Channel and at the mouth of the Touques, opposite Trouville. Pop. (1975) 5,200.

DE BŌ'NŌ, Edward (1933-). British doctor. Lecturer at the Dept. of Investigative Medicine, Cambridge Univ., from 1976, he is chiefly famous for his concept of *The Use of Lateral Thinking* (1967).

DEBRAY, Régis (1941-). French Marxist theorist. In 1967 he was sentenced to 30 yrs imprisonment in Bolivia for his association with Che Guevara, but released after 3 years. His writings on Latin-American politics incl. *Strategy for Revolution* (1970).

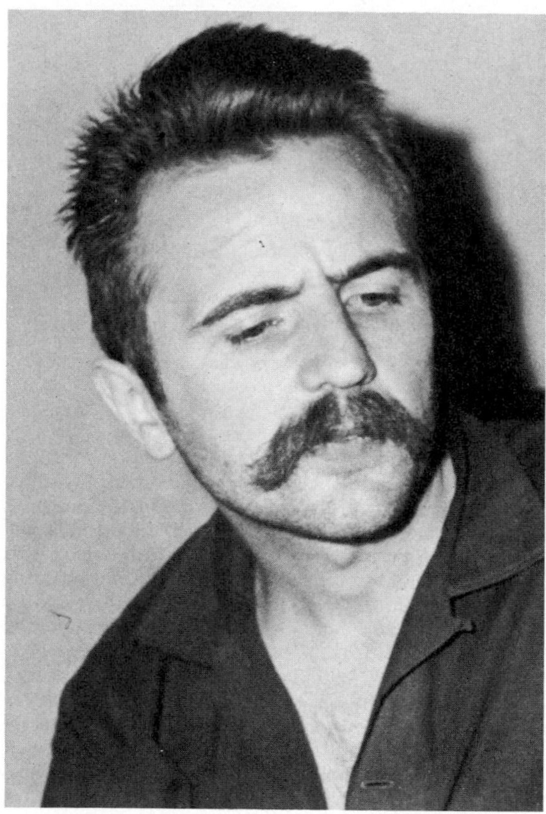

DEBRAY. One of the influential theorists of the new revolutionary movements of Latin-America, Régis Debray. *Photo: Mireille Vautier*

DEBRECEN (de'bretsen). Hungarian town, 193km (120m) E of Budapest. It is a commercial centre, and has a univ. founded 1912. Pop. (1978) 196,000.

DEBRETT, John (1753-1822). London publisher who in 1802 pub. a *Peerage* followed by a *Baronetage* in 1808, still called by his name.

DE BROGLIE (de brōly'), **Maurice,** 6th duc (1875-1960). French scientist, noted for his work on atomic physics and X-rays. He was succeeded in the title by his brother **Louis Victor de B.,** 7th duc (1892-), well known for his research in nuclear physics and the relations between wave and corpuscular theories. The latter was awarded a Nobel prize in 1929, and became prof. of physics at Paris in 1932.

DEBS, Eugene Victor (1855-1926). American Socialist. B. in Indiana, he organized the American Railway Union in 1893, and was Socialist candidate for the presidency in every election from 1900 to 1920, except that of 1916. He opposed US intervention in the F.W.W., and was imprisoned 1918-21.

DEBUSSY (debüsē'), **Claude Achille** (1862-1918). French composer. B. at St Germain-en-Laye, he studied at Paris, and won the Grand Prix de Rome with his cantata *L'enfant prodigue* (1884). After studying in Rome and Russia, he returned to Paris and won fame with his *L'après-midi d'un faune* (1894). His opera *Pelléas et Mélisande* was first performed in 1902. He also wrote orchestral music and numerous piano pieces, chamber music, ballets, songs, etc. For his rejection of classical diatonic harmony he may be called the first of the modern composers.

DEBYE (debī'), **Peter** (1884-1966). Dutch-American physicist. In 1940 he went to the US where he was prof. of chemistry at Cornell univ. 1940-52. A pioneer of X-ray powder photography, and famed for his work on polar molecules, dipole moments and molecular structure, he was awarded a Nobel prize in 1936.

DE'CALOGUE. The 10 commandments delivered by Jehovah to Moses, and stated in Ex. xx, 1-17, and Deut. v, 6-21. The D. is recognized as the basis of morality by both Jews and Christians.

DECA'PODA. An important order of crustaceans of the division Malacostraca. The name is derived from the limitation of the feet to 10. They are divided into Natantia (prawns and shrimps) and Reptantia (lobsters, crayfish, hermit-crabs, crabs).

DECATUR (dekā'tur), **Stephen** (1779-1820). American naval hero. Of French ancestry, he was b. in Maryland and greatly distinguished himself in the war with Tripoli (1801-5), when he succeeded in burning the *Philadelphia*, which the enemy had captured. During the war with England he surrendered only after a desperate resistance in 1814, and in 1815 was active against the Algerian pirates. He was killed in a duel. He is famed for his toast which incl. the phrase 'our country, right or wrong'.

DECATUR. City in central Illinois, USA, on Lake D., with engineering, food processing, and plastics industries. It was founded in 1829 and named after Stephen D. Pop. (1970) 90,400.

DE'CCAN. Triangular tableland in the peninsula of India, stretching between the Vindhya Hills in the N and the Western and Eastern Ghats.

DECIBEL (des'ibel). A logarithmic unit, symbol dB, used to express ratios of power, voltage current or sound intensity. It is expressed as 10 times the logarithm to the base 10 of the power ratio, that is $10 \log_{10} p_1/p_2$ where p_1 and p_2 are the powers being compared. The unit is the tenth of a bel, and 3 dB is equivalent to roughly doubling the power.

Sound intensity which is proportional to the square of the sound pressure is often quoted in Ds. with reference to a standard intensity, which is usually taken to be a pressure of 0.002 dyn/cm^2. Hence a sound intensity corresponding to this pressure would, by definition, be 0 dB. *See* NOISE.

DECIMAL FRACTIONS (Lat. *decem*, ten). The system of fractions expressed by the use of the decimal point, which are in fact all those fractions where the denominator is 10, 100, 1,000 or any higher power of 10. Thus 3/10, 51/100, 23/1,000 are D.Fs. and are normally expressed as 0.3, 0.51, 0.023. The regular use of the decimal point appears to have been introduced about 1585, but the occasional use of D.Fs. can be traced as early as the 12th cent.

DECIMAL SYSTEM. A system of weights and measures, or coinage based on one standard unit (e.g. the metre, the dollar), which is divided into or multiplied by multiples of 10. Since the USA and France set the example in the late 18th cent., many leading countries of the world have adopted the D.S. for their coinage. Canada early adopted D. coinage, but it was not until after the S.W.W. that many other Commonwealth countries did so, e.g. India 1957, Australia 1966, NZ 1967 and UK 1971. The D.S. system of weights and measures was first suggested by James Watt and first adopted by France during the Revolution. It is almost universally used throughout the world, espec. by scientists and technologists, and was adopted in the UK from 1975. *See* METRIC and DUODECIMAL SYSTEMS.

DECIUS (dē'shius), **Gaius Messius Quintus Traianus** (AD 201-51). Roman emperor. He fought a number of campaigns against the Goths, but was finally beaten and killed by them near Abritum. He ruthlessly persecuted the Christians.

DECLARATION OF INDEPENDENCE. The statement issued by the American Continental Congress on 4 July 1776, renouncing all allegiance to the British Crown, and ending the political connection with Britain. Following a resolution moved on 7 June, 'that these United Colonies are, and of right ought to be, free and independent States', a committee incl. Jefferson and Franklin was set up to draft a declaration; most of the work was done by Jefferson.

The resolution was adopted by the representatives of 12 colonies, New York abstaining, on 2 July, and the Declaration on 4 July; the latter date has ever since been celebrated as the 'birthday' of the USA. The representatives of New York announced their adhesion on 15 July, and the Declaration was afterwards signed by the members of Congress on 2 August.

DECLARATION OF RIGHTS. The statement issued by the Convention Parliament in Feb. 1689, laying down the conditions on which the crown was to be offered to William and Mary. Its clauses were later incorporated in the Bill of Rights (q.v.).

DECORATED. Name given in architecture to the 2nd period of English Gothic, covering the latter part of the 13th cent. and the 14th cent. Its chief characteristics are highly ornate window tracery, the window itself being divided into several lights by vertical bars called mullions; sharp spires ornamented with crockets and pinnacles; complex church vaulting; and slender arcade piers. Exeter cathedral is a notable example.

DEE, John (1527-1608). English alchemist and mathematician. B. in London, he lived for many years on the Continent, and claimed to have transmuted metals into gold. He long enjoyed the favour of Elizabeth I, and was employed as a secret diplomatic agent. He d. in poverty. His reputation has been restored among modern students of extra-sensory perception.

DECLARATION OF INDEPENDENCE. The committee who were appointed to draft the document - John Adams, Roger Sherman, Robert Livingston, Jefferson and Franklin - are seen at the table in 'The Signing of the Declaration of Independence' by John Trumbull. *Photo: Mary Evans Picture Library*

DEED. A legal document serving to pass an interest in property or to bind a person to perform or abstain from some action. Ds. are of two kinds: indentures and Ds. poll. Indentures are those which bind two parties in mutual obligations; Ds. poll concern one party only, as where a person changes his name.

DEEP FREEZING. Method of preserving food by rapid freezing, and storage at −18°C (0°F). Rapid freezing avoids structural change destructive of palatability, e.g. the shrinkage and distortion of cells by formation of enlarged ice crystals in the extra-cellular spaces. Some 'quick frozen' foods require pre-thawing before use, and cooking must then be prompt. Commercial freezing is usually by blast, circulation of air at −40°C (−40°F); contact, in which a refrigerant is circulated through hollow shelves; immersion, e.g. fruit in a solution of sugar and glycerol; or cryogenic, e.g. by liquid nitrogen spray. Accelerated freeze-drying (AFD) involves rapid freezing followed by heat drying in a vacuum, e.g. prawns for later rehydration. The product does not have to be stored in frozen condition.

DEER. Family of ruminant hoofed mammals (Cervidae) akin to antelopes and cattle but distinguished by the presence of antlers in almost all species. In the typical D. the antlers are usually branched and with rough surfaces and are carried only by the male, but they occur in both sexes in the reindeer (*Rangifer tarandus*).

Most species of D. are forest-dwellers, and the family is distributed throughout Europe, Asia, and America; it is absent from Australia, and in Africa occurs only in Morocco, where the Red D. (*Cervus elaphus*) is found. This is the typical wild D. of Europe, including Great Britain, increasingly being 'farmed'.

DEERHOUND. Breed of dog traced as far back as the 14th cent., and formerly used for stag-hunting; similar to the greyhound, but of larger size.

DE FALLA, Manuel. *See* FALLA, MANUEL DE.

DEFAMATION. *See* LIBEL, SLANDER.

DEFENCE, Ministry of. British government dept. created in 1964, which absorbed the existing Ministry of D. (estab. after the S.W.W., in which the PM had been Min. of D. 1940-6, to assist co-ordination), and the 3 other depts. previously responsible: the Admiralty, Air Ministry, and War Office. It is headed by the Sec. of State for D., under whom is the Min. of State for Defence; individual Service Ministers were replaced 1967 by Under-Secs. for the Royal Navy, Army, and RAF. This centralization was influenced by the example of the USA, where the army, navy, and air force were unified by the National Security Act, 1947, under the **Dept of Defense,** presided over by a Sec. of Defense with a seat in the President's Cabinet; each of the 3 services has a civilian sec. at its head, not of cabinet rank. The defence commands of both countries interlock with those of Europe in the North Atlantic Treaty Organisation. In Britain the Imperial Defence College was replaced in 1971 by a Royal College of Defence Studies, with a curriculum slanted towards Europe rather than the 'Empire'.

DEFENDER OF THE FAITH (Lat. *Fidei Defensor*). One of the titles of the English sovereign, conferred on Henry VIII in 1521 by Pope Leo X in recognition of the king's treatise against Luther. It appears on British coins in the shortened form *Fid. Def.*

DEFLATION. *See* INFLATION.

DEFOE (defō'), **Daniel** (*c.* 1660-1731). English novelist and journalist. B. in Cripplegate, the son of a butcher, James Foe. He was ed. for the Nonconformist min., but became a hosier. He took part in Monmouth's rebellion, and joined William of Orange in 1688. After his business had failed, he held a Civil Service post (1695-9). He wrote numerous pamphlets, and first achieved fame with the satire *The True-Born Englishman* (1701), followed in 1702 by the ironic *The Shortest Way with Dissenters,* for which he was fined, imprisoned, and pilloried. In Newgate he wrote his 'Hymn to the Pillory' and started a paper, *The Review* (1704-13). Released in 1704 he travelled in Scotland (1706-7), working to promote the Union, and pub. in 1709 *A History of the Union.* During the next 10 years he was almost constantly employed as a political controversialist etc. His version of the contemporary short story 'Apparition of Mrs Veal' (1706) had revealed a gift for realistic narrative, and *Robinson Crusoe,* based on the story of Alexander Selkirk, appeared in 1719. It was followed among others by the pirate story *Captain Singleton* (1720); *A Journal of the Plague Year* and picaresque novels *Moll Flanders* and *Colonel Jack* in 1722, and *Roxana* (1724).

His last years were given to more 'solid' work, beginning in 1724 with *A Tour through the Whole Island of Great Britain.*

DEGAS (degah'), **Hilaire Germain Edgard** (1834-1917). French impressionist painter. B. in Paris, the son of a French father and a Creole mother from New Orleans, he abandoned law in order to study at the *École des Beaux-Arts,* where he came under the influence of Ingres. He worked in Italy for 5 years, and in 1870, during the Franco-Prussian War, he served in the National Guard. He avoided the Paris Salon, and became one of the chief exponents of the French impressionist technique, working almost exclusively in pastel, and devoting himself to studies of ballet, horses and jockeys, and representations of contemporary life. He was also a sculptor. He became blind, and d. in Paris.

DEGAS. Ballet was a favourite subject with Degas, and one of his most famous works is 'Danseuse au bouquet saluant'. *Photo: Popperfoto*

DE GAULLE, Charles (1890-1970). French statesman. B. at Lille, he graduated from Saint-Cyr in 1911 and in 1916 was severely wounded and captured by the Germans. In his *The Army of the Future* (1934) he attacked French dependence on an 'impregnable' Maginot Line, and in 1940 refused to accept Pétain's truce with the Germans, becoming leader of the Free French in England. In 1944 he entered Paris in triumph and was briefly head of the provisional govt before resigning in protest at the defects of the new constitution of the Fourth Republic in 1946. In 1947 he founded the Rassemblement du Peuple Français (RPF) a non-party constitutional reform movement, and when bankruptcy and civil war loomed in 1958 D.G. was called by Coty to form a govt. As Premier he promulgated a constitution subordinating the legislature to the presidency and in 1959 took office as President. Economic recovery and eventual solution of colonial problems followed, but in pursuit of his Grand Design he opposed 'Anglo-Saxon' influence in Europe. Re-elected pres. in 1965, he quelled student-worker unrest which endangered the economy in 1968, and the Gaullist party, reorganized as *Union des democrats pour la Cinquième République,* won an overwhelming majority in the elections of the same year. In 1969 he resigned after the defeat of the govt in a referendum on constitutional reform. His *Mémoires* cover the war and his years of political power. *See also* COLOMBEY-les-Deux-Églises.

DEGAUSSING (dēgōs'ing). The neutralization of the magnetic field of a body by encircling it with a conductor through which a current is maintained. Ships were degaussed in the S.W.W. to avoid detonating magnetic mines.

DEGREE. The 360th part of the circumference of a circle; it is symbolized by the sign ° after a figure, e.g. 32°. It is subdivided into 60 minutes (1° = 60′). A degree of latitude is the length along a meridian such that the difference between its N and S ends is 1°. A degree of longitude is the length between 2 meridians making an angle of 1° at the centre of the earth. *Temperature* is also measured in Ds. but in this case the D. is divided decimally, not into minutes and seconds.

DE HAVILLAND, Sir Geoffrey (1882-1965). British aircraft designer. Founder in 1920 of the De H. Aircraft Co., he had already designed planes for the F.W.W. Later were the *Moth,* the *Mosquito* fighter-bomber of the S.W.W.,

DE GAULLE. Broadcasting from London in 1941, when as leader of the Free French Forces, he kept alive the spirit of resistance of his countrymen. *Photo: United Press International*

and the post-war *Comet* - the world's first jet-driven air liner. He was knighted in 1944 and received the OM in 1962.

DEHRA DUN (deh'rah doon). Town of India in Uttar Pradesh, capital of D.D. district. It has a military academy, a college, and a Sikh temple built in 1699. Pop. (1971) 199,445.

DEHYDRATION. Process whereby food is reduced to powder form by removing its water content. Research, begun in 1937, was carried on at the Cambridge Low Temperature Research Station and elsewhere and was stimulated by the need to save shipping space during the S.W.W. D. was applied to milk, butter, eggs, meat, fish, and vegetables, but there was loss of flavour until the process was perfected in the 1960s. In accelerated freeze drying (AFD) food is quick-frozen to preserve the flavour, before being dehydrated in vacuo. *See* DEEP FREEZING.

DEISM (dē'izm). Literally, belief in one Supreme Being; but especially a movement of religious thought in England in the 17th-18th cents., characterized by belief in the 'religion of nature' as opposed to the revealed religion of Christianity. The father of English D. was Lord Herbert of Cherbury (1583-1648), and the chief writers were John Toland (1670-1722), Anthony Collins (1676-1729), Matthew Tindal (1657-1733), Thomas Woolston (1670-1733), Thomas Chubb (1679-1747). Later, D. came to mean a belief in a personal deity who is distinct from the world and not very intimately interested in its concerns. *See* THEISM.

DEKKER, Thomas (*c.* 1572-*c.* 1632). English dramatist and pamphleteer. B. in London, he wrote realistic plays incl. *The Shoemaker's Holiday* (1600), *Old Fortunatus* (1600); *The Honest Whore* and *Roaring Girl* (both with Middleton); *Sir Thomas Wyat* (with Webster), *Virgin Martyr* (with Massinger), and *The Witch of Edmonton* (with Ford and Rowley).

DELACROIX (delahkrwah'), **Ferdinand Victor Eugène** (1798-1863). French artist. Possibly the son of Talleyrand, whom he resembled, he was b. near Paris. Outstanding in his early romantically heroic style is 'Liberty Leading the People' (1831), and a visit to Morocco in 1832 (as a member of a French military mission) and to Spain introduced a colourfully exotic element to his work. He excelled in religious and historical subjects, animal studies, illustrations of Shakespeare, Dante and Byron, and painted superb portraits of Paganini and Chopin. Leader of the romantic movement, he encountered great opposition to his daring use of colour and freedom of approach. His lithographs and murals are notable. As striking in his personality as in his work he kept a remarkable *Journal*.

DELAFIELD, E. M. Pseudonym of British writer Edmée Elizabeth Monica de la Pasture (1890-1943). Author of a number of psychologically competent novels, she is best remembered for her amusing *Diary of a Provincial Lady* (1931), skilfully exploiting the foibles of middle-class existence.

DE LA MARE, Walter (1873-1956). English poet. Of Huguenot descent, he was born in Kent, and wrote superlative verse for children, such as *Songs of Childhood* (1902), which appeared under the pseudonym Walter Ramal. Later vols. of poetry incl. *The Listeners* (1912) and *Collected Poems* (1942). He was also a gifted anthologist, as in *Come Hither* (1923) and *Behold this Dreamer* (1939), and wrote attractive prose, e.g. *The Memoirs of a Midget* (1921). He received the OM in 1953. He had a gift for the weirdly mysterious.

DELANE (delān'), **John Thaddeus** (1817-79). British journalist. As editor of *The Times* (1841-77), he first gave it international standing.

DE LA RAMÉE, Louise. *See* OUIDA.

DELAROCHE (delarosh'), **Hippolyte,** called **Paul** (1797-1856). French artist. B. in Paris, he first exhibited in the Salon of 1822, and with his friends Géricault and Delacroix was in the forefront of the revolt against the classicism of David and his followers. D.'s historical paintings were very popular.

DE LA ROCHE (-rosh), **Mazo** (1885-1961). Canadian novelist, author of the 'Whiteoaks' series, a family chronicle of 3 generations on an estate in Ontario, ruled by an autocratic old lady.

DELAUNAY (delōneh'), **Robert** (1855-1941). French painter. B. in Paris, he made fruitful experiments in the constructive use of colour in non-representational works and in subject pictures of runners, etc. His 'Windows' (1912) is believed to be the first Cubist painting in colour.

DELAWARE. Atlantic maritime state of the USA. It is divided into 2 physical areas, one hilly and wooded, and the other gently undulating. The state is generally agricultural. The chief towns are Wilmington, Dover (cap.), and Newark. D. is named after Lord de la Warr, Governor of Virginia 1610-18. The first settlers were Dutch and Swedes about 1638, but in 1664 the area was captured by the British. D. was made a separate colony in 1702, organized as a state in 1776; it was one of the original 13 states of the USA. Area 5,328 sq.km (2,057 sq.m); pop. (1970) 548,104.

DE LA WARR, Thomas West, baron (1577-1618). American colonial governor. Appointed Gov. of Virginia in 1609, he arrived in 1610 just in time to prevent the desertion of the Jamestown colonists and by 1611 had reorganized the settlement. Both the river and state of D. are named after him.

DELCASSÉ (delkahseh'), **Théophile** (1852-1923). French statesman. He became Foreign Min. in 1898, but had to resign in 1905 because of German hostility: and again 1914-15. To a large extent he was responsible for the *Entente Cordiale* with Britain.

DELFT. Town in the Netherlands in the prov. of S Holland, 14km (9m) NW of Rotterdam, famous for its china. William the Silent (q.v.) was murdered at D., 1584. Pop. (1972) 87,000.

DELHI (de'li). Union territory of the Rep. of India from 1956. The chief town is Delhi, capital of the Republic. Grains, sugar cane, fruits, and vegetables are the chief crops. Area 1,484 sq.km (573 sq.m); pop. (1971) 4,044,000.

DELHI. Capital of the Republic of India. *Old D.* on the Jumna is an ancient city that was reconstructed by the emperor Shah Jehan in the 17th cent. and remained the capital of the Mogul Empire until the establishment of British rule in 1857. It is surrounded by a wall with 7 gates, and its chief features are the Red Fort, formerly the imperial palace (1638-48), and the Great Mosque (1644-58).

New D., on the Jumna 8km (5m) SW, was designed to house government departments when the capital of British India was moved in 1912 from Calcutta to D. Constructed to plans by Sir Edwin Lutyens and Sir Herbert Baker, it was inaugurated in 1931. There is an international airport 16km (10m) to the SW. *Old D.* is a centre of skilled craftsmanship (ivory carving, gold and silver embroidery, jewellery, etc.). New D. has chemical, engineering and textile industries. The Univ. of Delhi was founded in 1922. Pop. of Old and New D. (1971) 3,630,000.

DELHI. The working day begins in Delhi: the early risers cycle along the Raj Path Highway. *Photo: Camera Press*

DĒ'LIUS, Frederick (1862-1934). British composer. B. at Bradford, son of a German-born wool merchant, he spent an abortive period in the trade and tried orange-growing in Florida, before going to study music in Leipzig in 1887. Encouraged by Grieg, he settled in Paris to work in 1888, and in 1903 m. the artist Jelka Rosen, the couple making their home at Grez-sur-Loing, where - after being blind and paralyzed from 1925 - he d. His works incl. choral works (*Appalachia, Sea Drift, A Mass of Life, A Song of the High Hills*); the opera *A Village Romeo and Juliet* (1906) and music for the very popular play *Hassan* (1923); orchestral works such as *Brigg Fair* and *In a Summer Garden*; chamber music and songs. A shifting texture of harmonies, his music depends greatly on skilled interpretation, and his reputation owes much to the untiring advocacy of Sir Thomas Beecham (q.v.).

DELL, Ethel M. (1881-1939). British romance writer. B. in Streatham, she was sensationally successful with her emotional stories, in which the heroes were usually ugly:

DELIUS. The blind composer listening to his 'Mass of Life' at the Queen's Hall. Portrait by Ernest Proctor. *Photo: RTHPL*

Way of an Eagle (1912), *The Keeper of the Door* (1915), and *Storm Drift* (1930).

DELLER, Alfred. *See* COUNTER-TENOR.

DĒ'LOS. Greek island, smallest in the Cyclades group, in the Aegean. The great temple of Apollo (4th cent. BC) is still standing.

DELPHI (delfī). City of ancient Greece, situated in a rocky valley to the north of the gulf of Corinth, on the S slopes of Mt Parnassus, site of a famous oracle. Here in the temple of Apollo was the *Omphalos* or conical stone supposed to stand at the centre of the earth; the oracle was interpreted by priests from the inspired utterances of the Pythian priestess. A European Cultural Centre was built nearby 1966-7.

DELPHI. Partly hewn from the hillside the stadium to the NW of the temple is well-preserved. It is narrower than modern stadia, and the runners in foot-races turned a post at the far end. *Photo: Courtesy of Prof. Harold A. Harris*

DELPHI'NIUM or **larkspur.** Genus of plants belonging to the Ranunculaceae. There are some 150 species, incl.

rocket larkspur (*D. ajacis*), and great flowered larkspur (*D. grandiflorum*).

DEL SARTO, Andrea (1486-1531). Florentine artist whose work is a rather 'sweeter' blend of the style of Leonardo and Michelangelo.

DELTA. A triangular tract of land at a river's mouth, formed by deposited silt or sediment. Familiar examples of large Ds. are those of the Mississippi, Ganges and Brahmaputra, Rhône, Po, Danube, and Nile; the shape of the last-named is like the Greek letter Δ, and thus gave rise to the name.

The *Grand Delta* is the area of southern France from Marseille to Lyon, and incl. the Provence-Côte d'Azur and Rhône-Alpes regions. The Fos-sur-Mer harbour NW of Marseille and the projected Rhône-Rhine canal link would enable cargo to be transported by barge direct to the North Sea at Rotterdam, and there are plans for a link with Eastern Europe via the Danube. In combination with the Suez Canal a short route to the East would be opened, and the Delta would be the focal point of a network of pipelines, canals and motorways serving all Europe.

DEMENTIA. Mental deterioration accompanied by emotional disturbance. It may be caused by faulty blood supply to the brain, but 80% of those over 55 who die from dementia suffer from **Alzheimer's disease** (loss of brain cells, tangling and distortion of those remaining, and biochemical imbalance). In 1983 evidence was found that it was linked with enzyme deficiency in the area of the brain controlling memory and learning ability.

DEMERĀ'RA. River in Guyana, 174km (180m) which gives its name to one of the country's counties. Demerara county is the chief growing area for sugar-cane in the country, and D. sugar is named after it.

DEMĒ'TER. Greek goddess of agriculture (equivalent to the Roman Ceres) dau. of Kronos and Rhea. By Zeus she became the mother of Persephone.

DE MILLE (demil'), **Cecil B. (Blount)** (1881-1959). American film director. B. in Mass., he entered films with Jesse L. Lasky in 1913 (with whom he later estab. Paramount), and was one of the founders of Hollywood's long supremacy. He specialized in biblical-type epics, e.g. *The Sign of the Cross* and *The Ten Commandments.*

DEMIRE'L, Suleyman (1924-). Turkish statesman. Leader from 1964 of the Justice Party (J.P.), he was Prime Minister 1965-71, 1975-77, and 1979-80. He favoured links with the West, full membership of the EEC and foreign investment in Turkish industry.

DEMO'CRACY. As defined by Abraham Lincoln, 'Government of the people, by the people, for the people'. A distinction may be made between direct D., where the whole people meet for the making of laws or the direction of executive officers, and indirect D., where the people entrust such power to elected representatives. The most famous example of direct D. is that of Athens in the 5th cent. BC. Direct D. today is represented mainly by the use of the referendum, as in the U.K., Switzerland and certain states of the USA. In the modern world D. has developed from the American and French Revolutions. Representative parliamentary government has existed in England since the 13th cent., but the working classes were excluded almost entirely from the franchise until 1867, and women were admitted and property qualifications abolished only in 1918.

Recent controversy has centred on the 'western' conception of D., as accepted in Britain, France and the USA, and the 'eastern', as in the USSR and Communist Asia and E Europe. The former emphasizes the control of the govt by the electorate and freedom of speech and the Press. The latter envisages economic control by the govt for the benefit of the community, both political and economic power resting in the Communist Party under a single-party system.

DEMOCRATIC PARTY. One of the two great parties of the USA. Founded by Jefferson in 1792 to defend the rights of the individual states against the centralizing policy of the Federalists, it tends to be the party of the 'small man', as opposed to the Republicans, the party of 'big business', but the divisions between the two are not clear-cut. Its stronghold is the Southern states, or 'solid south'. The D.P. held power almost continuously 1800-60, and later returned Cleveland, Wilson, F. D. Roosevelt, Truman, Kennedy, Johnson, and Carter. In the 20th cent. it has become associated with more liberal policies than the Republican.

DEMO'CRITUS (*c.* 460-361 BC). Greek philosopher and speculative scientist. B. in Thrace, he travelled widely in the E in search of knowledge. His most important contribution to philosophy is the atomic theory of the universe.

DEMO'STHENES (*c.* 384-322 BC). Athenian orator and statesman. From 351 BC he led the party which advocated resistance to the growing power of Philip of Macedon and in his 'Philippics' incited the Athenians to war. This policy resulted in the defeat of Chaeronea in 338, and the establishment of Macedonian supremacy. After the death of Alexander he organized a revolt, and when it failed took poison to avoid capture by the Macedonians.

DĒMO'TIC WRITING. A cursive script derived from Egyptian hieratic, itself a cursive form of hieroglyphic. D. documents are known from the 6th cent. BC to about AD 470. It was written horizontally, from right to left.

DEMPSEY, 'Jack' (William Harrison) (1895-). American boxer, known from his birthplace in Colorado as the Manassa Mauler. In 1919 he defeated Jess Willard to become world heavyweight champion till he lost to Gene Tunney in 1926. He first estab. boxing as a 'respectable' sport.

DENBIGHSHIRE (den'bishēr). Former co. of Wales, largely merged in 1974, together with Flint and part of Merioneth in Clwyd, although a small area along the W border was incl. in Gwynedd. The co. town was Denbigh in the Clwyd valley. Pop. (1973) 8,000.

DENDROCHRONOLOGY. Study of annual tree growth rings in relation to archaeology and climatology, founded by American astronomer A.E. Douglass in 1935. The use of radiocarbon in tree rings to calculate solar activity originated in the 1960s.

DENGUE (deng'i). Viral fever transmitted by mosquitoes and accompanied by joint pains, a rash and glandular swelling. A more virulent form, D. haemorrhagic fever, thought to be caused by a second infection on top of the first, also causes internal bleeding.

DENG XIAOPING (dung shē-owping) (1904-). Chinese statesman (formerly Teng Hsiao-ping), *né* Kan Tse-Kao, he adopted the name X. 'Little Peace' in 1925. Dimissed during the Cultural Revolution as a 'capitalist roader', he was acting P.M. following Chou En-lai's heart attack in 1974. Again disgraced in 1976, he was rehabilitated in 1977, and as Vice-Premier 1977-80 was in charge of the 'Four Modernisations' of agriculture, industry, science and technology. He remained vice-chairman of the party, and helped to oust Hua Guofeng in favour of Zhao Ziyang (qq.v.).

DEN HAAG. Dutch form of THE HAGUE.

DEN HELDER (dān hel'der). Fishing port and naval base in N Holland prov., Netherlands, 65km (40m) N of Amsterdam, on the entrance to the N Holland Canal from the North Sea. Pop. (1974) 61,200.

DE'NIER. System of measuring fine yarns, both natural and man-made, derived from the old French silk industry. The D. was an old French silver coin. Thus 9,000 metres of 15 D. nylon, commonly used in nylon stockings, weighs 15g and in this case the thickness of thread would be .00425mm (.0017in).

DENIKIN (dene'kin), **Anton Ivanovich** (1872-1946). Russian general. He distinguished himself in the Russo-Japanese and the F.W.Ws. After the outbreak of the Revolution he organized a volunteer army of 60,000 'Whites', but in 1919 was routed and escaped abroad. He wrote a history of the Revolution and the Civil War.

DENIS, St (Dionysius). First bishop of Paris and one of the patron saints of France. He was martyred by the Romans about AD 275.

DENMARK. Kingdom of NW Europe, occupying the N two-thirds of the Jutland peninsula and the islands lying between the peninsula and Sweden. It is a low-lying, flat country, the highest point being Yding Skovhöj (173m/567ft) in E Jutland. The W part is sandy, terminating in a sand-dune coast, behind which lies a succession of lagoons. The E coast is broken by long inlets, on which are most of D.'s towns. The largest is. are Zealand, Fünen, Lolland, Falster and Langeland, separated by narrow channels, and Bornholm 128km (80m) to the E.

A highly advanced co-operative system among the intensely cultivated smallholdings results in a very efficient agricultural industry producing meat, espec. bacon, dairy produce and eggs for export. There is also a fishing industry. In the postwar period, however, D. has become industrialized and exports highly specialized manufactured goods, particularly to other European countries, e.g. semi-finished products to the Swedish car and aircraft industries. Tobacco, textiles, clothing, paper and chemicals are among other industries, and some 3 million mink pelts are produced annually.

Copenhagen, the cap. has rail and ferry links across the Sound with Sweden, and a bridge-tunnel was under construction 1973-85 to Malmö, as well as a new underwater rail link Helsingör/Helsingborg. Other towns are Odense on Fünen, and the ports of Aarhus, Aalborg and Esbjerg on the coasts of Jutland. There are ferry services across the Skagerrak and Kattegat to Norway and Sweden, and D. is served by the Scandinavian Airlines System.

Area 43,039 sq.km (16,619 sq.m); pop. (1978) 5,096,960. M.U.: krone.

Government. D. is a constitutional monarchy. The House of Oldenburg ruled from the election of Christian I in 1448 as king of D. and Norway up to 1863 when the crown passed to the House of Schleswig-Holstein-Sonderburg-Gluckstein in the person of Christian IX. Margrethe II (1940-   ) succeeded 1972, D.'s first reigning queen for 500 years.

Three-quarters of the single-chamber Folketing are elected by proportional representation, the remaining quarter being distributed among parties with insufficient votes to gain any elective seats. The Faeroes and Greenland (qq.v.) both send 2 representatives, but autonomy was achieved by Greenland in 1979. There is a comprehensive social security system. The educational system is good, with univs. at Copenhagen, Aarhus and Odense, and folk high schools for adults.

History. The original home of the Danes was S Sweden, whence they migrated in 5th and 6th cents. Ruled by local chieftains, they terrified Europe by their piratical raids in the 8th-10th cents. until Harald Bluetooth (*c.* 940-85) unified D. and estab. Christianity. Canute (1014-35) founded an empire embracing D., England, and Norway, which fell to pieces at his death. After a cent. of confusion D. again dominated the Baltic under Valdemar I, Canute VI, and Valdemar II (1157-1241). Domestic conflict then produced anarchy, until Valdemar IV (1340-75) restored order. D., Norway, and Sweden were united under one sovereign in 1397. Sweden broke away in 1449 and after a long struggle had its independence recognized in 1523. Christian I (1448-81) secured the duchies of Schleswig and Holstein, fiefs of the Holy Roman Empire, in 1460; they were held by his descendants until 1863. Christian II (1513-23) was deposed in favour of his uncle Frederick whose son Christian III (1534-59) in 1536 made Lutheranism the established religion. Attempts to regain Sweden led to disastrous wars with that country, 1563-70, 1643-5, 1657-60; equally disastrous was Christian V's intervention, 1625-9, on the Protestant side of the Thirty Years War.

Frederick III (1648-70) made himself absolute in 1665, and ruled through a burgher bureaucracy. Serfdom was abolished in 1788. D.'s adherence in 1780 to the Armed Neutrality against Britain resulted in the naval defeat of Copenhagen (1801), and in 1807 the British bombarded Copenhagen and seized the Danish fleet to save it from Napoleon. This incident drove D. into the arms of France, and the Allies at the Congress of Vienna took Norway from D. and gave it to Sweden, 1815. A liberal movement then arose, which in 1848-9 compelled Frederick VII (1848-63) to grant a democratic constitution. In 1848-50 the Germans in Schleswig-Holstein revolted with Prussian support, and in 1864 Prussia seized the provinces after a short war. N Schleswig was recovered after a plebiscite in 1920. D. was occupied by Germany 1940-5, but a strong resistance movement was maintained. D. entered the Common Market in 1973 together with Britain. The elections of 1973 demonstrated disillusion with the long-estab. political parties. The Social Democrats formed a further minority govt., but the new Progress Party emerged as the strongest minority group. Their leader Mogens Glistrup claimed to have become a millionaire by tax avoidance, and promised to abolish income tax and most of the civil service. In 1979 he was convicted for tax evasion, though pending appeal at the time of the general election of that year in which his share of the vote fell. Yet another minority Social Democrat govt. was formed.

Language. Danish, like the other languages of Scandinavia, belongs to the Germanic language group; it evolved from old Norse, becoming a separate language in the 11th and 12th cents. It was recorded on parchment in runic script towards the end of the 13th cent. and in the

14th began to be written in Latin script. By the beginning of the 16th cent. the characteristic accent with its glottal stop had become established. The literary language developed from the Jutland dialect during the 18th cent.

Literature and the arts. Writers of world fame emerged in the 19th cent.: Hans Andersen, the philosopher Soren Kierkegaard, and the critic Georg Brandes (1842-1927), who played a major part in the Scandinavian literary awakening, encouraging Ibsen and others. The novelists Henrik Pontoppidan (1857-1943), Karl Gjellerup (1857-1919), and Johannes Jensen (1873-1950) were all Nobel prize-winners, but did not achieve an enduring reputation outside Scandinavia. *See also* KIERKEGAARD.

The composer-organist Diderik Buxtehude (1637-1707) is increasingly recognized internationally, and Bartel Thorwaldsen (1770-1844) became well-known as a sculptor, but the most famous Danish statue is the 'Little Mermaid' at Copenhagen by E. Eriksen (1877-1959).

DENMARK. One of the most precious prehistoric treasures of Denmark is the Trundholm 'Sun-car', a votive offering recovered from a peat-bog in 1902. Made probably in the 13th century in bronze and gold, it is much earlier than any other example of the *cire-perdue* process to survive in Scandinavia. *Photo: Courtesy of the National Museum, Copenhagen*

DENSITY. The D. of a substance is its mass per unit volume and in the metric system is usually measured in kilograms per cubic metre. The specific gravity of a substance is the ratio of the D. of the substance to that of water which is taken to be unity at 4°C. As the D. of water varies with temperature it is more convenient for precision work to deal with Ds. than with specific gravities.

DENTISTRY. The care and treatment of the teeth and their supporting tissues. The bacteria which start the process of dental decay are normal, non-pathogenic members of a large and varied group of micro-organisms present in the mouth. They are strains of oral streptococci, but it is only in the presence of sucrose (from refined sugar) in the mouth that they become damaging to the teeth. Fluoride (q.v.) in the water supply is one attempted solution, but in 1979 a vaccine was developed from a modified form of the bacterium *Streptococcus mutans.* Orthodontics deals with the straightening of the teeth, and periodontology with care of the supporting tissue.

The earliest dental school was opened at Baltimore in 1839; in Britain the predecessors of the modern Univ. Coll. Hospital Dental School and Royal Dental Hospital and School, both within the Univ. of London, were estab. 1859 and 1860. There is an International Dental Federation (1900).

DENVER. City in Colorado, USA, on the South Platte river, nr the foothills of the Rocky Mountains. It was founded in 1858, with the discovery of gold, becoming a mining camp supply centre, and the US mint is sited here. Coal is also mined nearby, and D. became a big industrial centre with rubber, mining machinery, canning and meat packing brewing, and many other varied manufactures. In the 1970s the development of oil and gas finds in the Rocky Mtns. overthrust belt made it a rival oil capital to Houston, and it is also important as a communications and distribution centre for the western USA. There is a univ., a mining School, and many medical institutions. Pop. met. area (1978) 1,574,000.

DE'ODAR. Species of cedar (*Cedrus deodara*), native to the Himalayas, Afghanistan, and N Baluchistan. It forms forests at high elevations, and is a valuable timber-tree.

DEPI'LATORY. An instrument or substance used to eradicate growing hair. For ringworm of the scalp in children, X-rays or thallium acetate are generally employed, but the only sure method of removing facial hair for cosmetic reasons is the destruction of each hair root separately with an electrolytic needle or an electro-cautery.

DE QUINCEY (de kwin'si), **Thomas** (1785-1859). British author. B. in Manchester, he ran away from school there to wander and study in Wales. He then went to London where he lived in extreme poverty, but with the constant companionship of the young orphan Anne, of whom he writes in the *Confessions.* In 1803 he was reconciled to his guardians and was sent to Oxford, entering the Middle Temple in 1808. In 1809 he settled with the Wordsworths and Coleridge in the Lake District, and in 1816 m. Margaret Simpson. His addiction to opium had begun while he was at college, and in 1820 he removed to London where he pub. his *Confessions of an English Opium-eater* in 1821 in the *London Magazine.* He devoted the rest of his life to miscellaneous writing; most notable are his essays. In 1828 he moved to Edinburgh, where he died.

DERAIN (derañ'), **André** (1880-1954). French post-impressionist artist. He originally estab. himself as one of the leaders of the Fauve movement with a number of landscapes and studies of the Paris suburbs in 1905, and went on to produce work of astonishing diversity. His gift for fantasy emerged in his scenery and costumes for Diaghileff's ballet *La Boutique Fantasque.*

DERBY (dar'bi), **Edward Geoffrey Smith Stanley,** 14th earl of (1799-1869). British statesman. Son of the 13th earl, he entered parliament in 1820 as a Whig. In 1830 he became Sec. for Ireland, and in 1833 Sec. for the Colonies, introducing the bill for the abolition of slavery. He broke with the Whigs in 1834 and joined the Tories, the split in the Tory Party over Peel's free-trade policy giving him the leadership for 20 years, with Disraeli as his lieutenant in the Commons. He succeeded to the earldom in 1851. He was thrice PM: in 1852, in 1858-9, and 1866-8.

DERBY, Edward George Villiers Stanley, 17th earl of (1865-1948). British Cons. statesman. He became an MP in 1892 and succeeded to the earldom in 1908. In 1915 he was appointed director-general of recruiting, and was responsible for the system known as the Derby Scheme. In the Lloyd George coalition of 1916-18 he was Sec. for War, and held the same post in 1922-4. In 1918-20 he was ambassador to France. He was well known on the Turf. He was succeeded by his grandson **Edward John Stanley,** 18th earl of D. (1918-).

DERBY. City in Derbyshire, England, on the Derwent 23km (14m) W of Nottingham. It is a great industrial centre manufacturing locomotives and wagons, Rolls-Royce cars and aero-engines, Crown Derby china, electrical, mining and engineering equipment, chemicals, paper, etc. There is a theatre - the Playhouse - and local museums have a fine Derby porcelain collection and the Rolls-Royce collection of aero engines. Created a City 1977. Pop. (1974) 218,000.

DERBY. The most important horse-race in England, run for the D. stakes (estab. by the 12th earl of D. in 1780) on the 2nd day of the Epsom summer meeting. The distance is 2.4km (1½m): record time 2 min. 33.8 sec. by Mahmoud 1936. The American equivalent is the Kentucky D. (1875), run at Churchill Downs, Louisville over 2km (1½m).

Recent Derby Winners

Year	*Horse*	*Owner*
1972	*Roberto*	John Galbreath
1973	*Morston*	A.M. Budgett
1974	*Snow Knight*	Mrs Sharon Phillips
1975	*Grundy*	Carlo Vittadini
1976	*Empery*	Nelson Bunker Hunt
1977	*The Minstrel*	R. Sangster
1978	*Shirley Heights*	Earl of Halifax
1979	*Troy*	Sobell/Weinstock
1980	*Henbit*	Mrs Arpad Plesch
1981	*Shergar*	Aga Khan
1982	*Golden Fleece*	Robert Sangster
1983	*Teenoso*	E. Moller
1984	*Secreto*	L. Miglitti
1985	*Slip Anchor*	Lord Howard de Walden
1986	*Shahrastani*	Aga Khan

DERBYSHIRE. Co. in the English midlands, lying to the S of Yorkshire. The NW incl. the S end of the Pennines, with the Peak district (q.v.). To the S and E the land is lower and flatter, and yields heavy cereal crops, etc. There is dairy farming and sheep are grazed on the limestone hills. The closure of pits in the E and shut down of engineering factories made this a depressed area, which began to be redeveloped from 1973 when it was flanked by the M1 motorway network. Besides coal, iron and large reserves of fluorspar are present. The chief rivers are the Derwent, Dove, Rother and Trent. Matlock is the admin. HQ: other towns are Derby, Buxton, Chesterfield, Glossop and Ilkeston. Area 2,630 sq.km (1,015 sq.m); pop. (1978) 896,200.

DERMATĪ'TIS. Inflammation of the skin. It may occur in nearly any skin disease, but the best-known varieties, because of their legal implications, are those caused in persons engaged in occupations bringing them into contact with irritating substances such as dyes, paints, solvents or even flour, or in persons wearing clothing, such as woollen garments or fur coats, to which their skin is sensitive.

DERBYSHIRE. Chatsworth House, Bakewell, the chief seat of the Duke of Devonshire, with a remarkable collection of paintings and other treasures. *Photo: Camera Press*

DERRY. *See* LONDONDERRY.

DERVISH. In Iran and Turkey, a religious mendicant, and throughout the rest of Islam a member of a Moslem religious brotherhood, not necessarily mendicant in character. The Arabic equivalent is *fakir.* There are various orders of Ds., each with its 'rule', and a special ritual. The 'howling Ds.' gash themselves with knives and claim miraculous healing powers.

DESAI (desī'), **Morarji** (1896-). Indian statesman. An early follower of Mahatma Gandhi, he was Prime Minister, as leader of the Janata Party 1977-9, after toppling Indira Gandhi. Party in-fighting led to his resignation of both the premiership and party leadership.

DESALINATION. The removal of salt, espec. from seawater, to produce fresh water for irrigation, etc. Distillation has usually been the method adopted, but in the 1970s a cheaper process, using certain polymer materials which filter the molecules of salt from the water by reverse osmosis, was developed.

DESCARTES (dākahrt'), **René** (1596-1650). French philosopher. B. near Tours, he served in the army of Prince Maurice of Nassau, and in 1619, while travelling on the Continent, he experienced an illumination which determined him to apply the certain methods of mathematics to metaphysics and science. He settled in Holland in 1628, where he was likely to be free from interference by the ecclesiastical authorities. In 1649 he visited the court of Queen Christina of Sweden, and d. at Stockholm.

D.'s philosophic and scientific works were elaborated by application of the method of doubt, which eliminated everything except certain clear and distinct ideas, e.g. his own existence, which could not be denied because the very act of denial asserted his own existence (*Cogito ergo sum,*

'I think, therefore I am'); everything has a cause; nothing can result from nothing; and matter is extended substance. He aimed at showing that the entire material universe can be completely explained in terms of mathematical physics, on the basis of the fewest possible ultimates - his 'clear ideas' of extended substance and its ultimate properties, divisibility, and mobility. But although all matter is in motion, matter does not move of its own accord - the initial impulse comes from God; and he also postulated two quite distinct substances - spatial substance or matter, and thinking substance or mind. This dualism preserved him from serious controversy with the Church.

D. is regarded as the discoverer of analytical geometry and the founder of the science of optics. His works include *Discourse on Method* (1637), *Meditations on the First Philosophy* (1641), and *Principles of Philosophy* (1644), and numerous books on physiology, optics, geometry, etc.

DESCHAMPS (dāshoṅ'), **Eustache** (*c.* 1346-*c.* 1406). French poet. B. in Champagne, he was the author of more than 1,000 ballades, etc., and the *Miroir de Mariage,* an attack on women.

DESERT. Area without sufficient vegetation to support human life, and scientifically incl. the ice areas of the polar regions, although generally thought of as restricted to the Earth's warmer zones. *See* GOBI, GREAT SANDY, KALAHARI, SAHARA DS., etc.

Ds., which constitute almost a third of the Earth's surface, may have existed from time immemorial, or be created by changes in climate, over-grazing, destruction of timber shelter belts, and the overpopulation which leads to exhaustion of the soil by too intensive cultivation without restoration of fertility.

DESERT RATS. Popular name for the British 8th Army, originating from the shoulder-flash worn by the 7th Armoured Division showing a jerboa, or desert rat, a rodent noted for its prodigious leaps.

DE SICA (sē'ka), **Vittorio** (1901-74). Italian director and actor. B. in Sora, Caserta, he achieved international fame in 1946 with *Bicycle Thieves,* a film of subtle realism. Later were *Umberto D* (1952) and *The Garden of the Finzi-Continis* (1972).

DESIGN CENTRE, THE. Estab. in the Haymarket, London, in 1956 by the Council of Industrial Design (an official body set up in 1944 to improve standards in British products), the centre displays goods such as building fittings, furniture, cutlery, etc., and includes in a Design Index selected examples of good design. Since 1957 D. Awards have been given annually for 20 outstanding specimens. Scottish D.C. in Glasgow is run on similar lines.

DES MOINES (de moin). Cap. and largest town in Iowa, USA, on the D.M. river, a tributary of the Mississippi. It is an important road, railway, and air centre with many manufactures. Pop. (1970) 286,100.

DESMOULINS (dāmoolan'), **Camille** (1760-94). French revolutionary, who summoned the mob to arms on 12 July 1789, so precipitating the revolt that culminated in the storming of the Bastille. A prominent Jacobin, he was elected to the National Convention in 1792, and his *Histoire des Brissotins* was largely responsible for the overthrow of the Girondins. But shortly after he went to the guillotine.

DESSALINES (desahlēn'), **Jean Jacques** (1758-1806). Negro emperor of Haiti. B. in Guinea, he was taken to Haiti as a slave, where he led the revolt against the French

DESERT. Here at Ica in Peru, the desertification process now operating in half the countries of the world, is reversed. Irrigated fields rise green amidst the desert. *Photo: Victor Englebert/ Susan Griggs Agency*

in 1791, and became emperor in 1804. He proclaimed himself emperor, as Jean-Jacques I, but was killed when trying to suppress a revolt.

DESSAU (des'ow). Town of Halle district, E Germany, on the Mulde, 115km (70m) SW of Berlin, the former cap. of Anhalt duchy and state. It manufactures chemicals, machinery, chocolate, etc., and was the seat of the great Junkers aeroplane works. Pop. (1978) 101,100.

DESTROYER. Small, fast warship, originally introduced as a 'torpedo boat D.' In the F.W.W. they were developed for anti-submarine work, serving in this capacity with convoys, etc., in the S.W.W. Modern guided-missile Ds. are of c.3,700-5,650 tonnes, and in 1977 the last of the Royal Navy's conventional Ds., the 2,600-tonne *Cavalier* was preserved at Southampton as a museum. *See* WARSHIP.

DETECTIVE FICTION. Novels of crime, in which a prominent part is played by an amateur or professional sleuth. The first great detective of fiction was E. A. Poe's Dupin in *The Murders in the Rue Morgue* (1841). The earliest English example was the Sergeant Cuff of Wilkie Collins (q.v.), but the real vogue of D.F. began with Sherlock Holmes (see CONAN DOYLE). Later writers incl. Agatha Christie, Dorothy Sayers, F. W. Crofts, G. K. Chesterton (qq.v.), and Maurice Leblanc, whose Arsène Lupin was both criminal and detective. One striking departure was in books by Dennis Wheatley in which the reader was presented with data and clues to solve the problem himself. Successor to the more formal detective is the 'private eye' and adventurer-investigator of Charteris, Hammett, Chandler and others. Yet another variant of the basic D. theme is the story in which much of the interest arises from the psychological springs of character and motive, as with Georges Simenon (q.v.), and more recently Ruth Rendell (1930-).

DÉTENTE (dātahnt'). French word meaning 'a relaxation of tension', and used in politics espec. in referring to improved relations between the USA and USSR and those allied with them. Western diplomats usually accept an agreed reduction of arms as indicating acceptance of the existing balance of power, but this is contrary to the essential assumption of Eastern diplomats that the spread and consolidation of Communism is historically inevitable. From their viewpoint D. is merely a matter of bargaining to avoid direct armed confrontation with the USA and its immediate allies, and the costly necessity of an expanded nuclear arms programme to meet and overcome such a challenge.

DETENTION CENTRE. In Britain an establishment for the short-term detention of young offenders (14–21). In 1980 those at New Hall (Wakefield, Yorks) and Send (Woking, Surrey) were selected to give 'short, sharp shock' treatment to those sentenced to 3 months by the courts.

DETE'RGENT. In the broadest sense any cleansing agent including soap is a D., but the term is generally limited to a special class of surface-active agents. The common Ds. are made from fats or hydrocarbons and sulphuric acid, and their long-chain molecules have a type of structure similar to that of soap molecules - a salt group at one end attached to a long hydrocarbon 'tail'. The mechanism of removing dirt, which is generally attached to materials by oil or grease, is that the hydrocarbon 'tails' (soluble in oil or grease) penetrate the oil or grease drops, while the 'heads' (soluble in water but insoluble in grease) remain in the water, and being salts become ionized. Consequently the oil drops become negatively charged and tend to repel one another; thus they remain in suspension and are washed away with the dirt. They have the advantage over soap in that they do not produce scum by forming insoluble salts with the calcium and magnesium ions present in hard water.

Ds. were first developed from coal tar in Germany during the F.W.W., and synthetic organic Ds. came into ever-increasing use after the S.W.W. Domestic powder Ds. for use in hot water have alkyl benzene as their main base, but also incl. bleaches and fluorescers for the whiter-than-white look, perborates to free stain-removing oxygen, and nitrilo-tri-acetic acid (used as a substitute for phosphates which cause eutrophication, (q.v.), but which itself causes cancer in laboratory animals) and silicates to soften the water. Liquid Ds. for washing dishes are based on ethylene oxide. Cold water Ds., consisting of a mixture of various alcohols. plus an ingredient for breaking down the surface tension of the water, so enabling the liquid to penetrate fibres and remove the dirt, have been produced. They would be used in far smaller quantity, and use no energy for water heating, but manufacturers claim that cold water is not so effective against stains. Problems of pollution are caused by Ds. when surface-active materials escape the normal processing of sewage and cause troublesome foam in rivers.

DETERMINISM. Theory which maintains that everything which happens, incl. all human thoughts and actions, is completely determined or caused by past conditions. It is the opposite of Free Will, and involves the denial of moral choice and responsibility; the causes which determine men's actions are not limited to their external circumstances, but incl. also their own past mental states and their motives. In antiquity the theory of D. was held by the Stoics. In Christian theology the Calvinist doctrine of Predestination is deterministic. Psychoanalysis provided support for D., but quantum theory and the 'uncertainty principle' lends support to the other side of the argument.

DETROIT. City of Mich., USA, situated on D. river. It was founded in 1701 and is the oldest city of any size W of the original colonies of the coast. In 1805 it was completely destroyed by fire, but was soon rebuilt and is today a great industrial centre with the HQ of Ford, Chrysler and General Motors. A recent major development is the waterfront Renaissance Center complex. Once a famous centre for jazz, D. became in the 1960s and 1970s noted for the rock and soul of Diana Ross, Stevie Wonder, Aretha Franklin and Alice Cooper. The fine reputation of its symphony orchestra was estab. by Antal Dorati. Pop. met. area (1970) 4,161,660.

DETSKOE SELO. *See* PUSHKIN.

DETTINGEN. Bavarian village where on 27 June 1743, in the War of the Austrian Succession, an army of British, Hanoverians, and Austrians under George II defeated the French under Noailles. It was the last battle in which a British sovereign took part.

DEUTERIUM (dūtēr'ium). Heavy isotope of hydrogen, mass number 2, discovered in 1932 by Urey. Combined with oxygen it produces heavy water.

DEUTERON (dū'-). Nucleus of the deuterium atom, or the ion of deuterium. It is of mass 2 and carries a unit positive charge.

DE VALERA (de valā'ra), **Éamon** (1882–1975). Irish statesman. B. in New York, the son of a Spanish father and an Ir. mother, he was sent to Ireland as a child, and became a teacher of mathematics. He was sentenced to death for his part in the Easter Rebellion, but the sentence was commuted to penal servitude for life, and in 1917 he was released under an amnesty. In the same year he was elected MP for E Clare, and president of Sinn Féin. In May 1918 he was re-arrested and imprisoned in Lincoln gaol, but in 1919 escaped to the USA. Elected Pres. of the Irish Rep., he returned to Ireland in 1920, and directed the struggle against the British govt from a hiding-place in Dublin. He authorized the negotiations of 1921, but refused to accept the treaty which ensued. Civil war followed, and in 1923 De V. was arrested by the Free State govt, and spent a year in prison. In 1926 he formed a new party, *Fianna Fáil* ('soldiers of destiny'), which in 1932 secured a majority. De V. became PM and For. Min., and at once abolished the oath of allegiance and suspended payment of the annuities due under the Land Purchase Acts. In 1938 he negotiated an agreement with Britain, under which all outstanding points were settled. Throughout the S.W.W. he maintained a strict neutrality. He resigned after his defeat at the 1948 elections, but was again PM 1951–4 and 1957–9, and was pres. of the republic 1959–73.

DE VALOIS (de vahl'wah), **Dame Ninette** (1898–). Stage-name of the British dancer and choreographer Edris Stannus. B. in co. Wicklow, of Huguenot ancestry, she was a member of Diaghilev's Russian ballet, but from 1931 devoted herself (as director) to the development of the Vic-Wells Ballet, later the Royal Ballet, being created DBE in 1951 and retiring in 1963. She was also founder of the Royal Ballet School, and created such ballets as *Job, Checkmate,* and *The Rake's Progress.*

DEVALUATION. In a financial crisis, when a country is badly in deficit in its balance of payments, the lowering of the value of its currency in the international market. The goods it produces are initially made cheaper abroad, so that the economy is stimulated, but in the longer term imports of food, raw materials and manufactured goods become dearer. Hence prices at home rise, wages lose their value, and, since govts fear to curb their own spending because this causes unemployment, chronic inflation sets in with further Ds., espec. when commodities such as oil are rising in price because of increased world demand. *Revaluation* is the opposite process. Ds. upset the balance of the world's money markets and allow speculators to operate, so that in an attempt to promote greater stability, many countries have allowed the value of their currencies to 'float', i.e. to fluctuate in value.

DE'VENTER. Town in Overijssel prov., the Netherlands, on the Ijssel, 45km (28m) S of the Ijssel Meer. It is an agricultural and transport centre. Pop. (1978) 64,600.

DEVLOPMENT AID, Official. The aid (ODA) usually given by the rich, industrial 'developed' countries to 'less-developed countries' (ldcs). Aid may take the form of money, goods, technical assistance, etc. The donors act for idealistic reasons, for commercial reasons (to estab. a future lucrative pattern of trade), or for geo-political reasons (to obtain base facilities in the recipient country).

DEVIL. In Christian theology, the supreme spirit of Evil, or an evil spirit generally. The D. or Satan is mentioned only in the later books of the OT, written after the Exile, but the later Jewish doctrine is that found in the NT. Jesus recognized as a reality the kingdom of evil, of which Satan or Beelzebub was the prince. The conception of the D. thus passed into the early Church; and theology till at least the time of St Anselm represented the Atonement as primarily the deliverance, through Christ's death, of mankind from the bondage of the D. In the Middle Ages the D. in popular superstition assumed the attributes of the horned fertility gods of paganism, and was regarded as the god of the witches. The belief in a personal D. continued at the Reformation; Luther regarded himself as the object of a personal Satanic persecution. With the development of liberal Protestant theology in the 19th cent. came a strong tendency to deny the existence of a positive spirit of evil, and to explain the D. as merely a personification. But the traditional conception was never abandoned by the RC Church, and such theologians as C. S. Lewis maintain the assumption of the existence of a power of positive evil.

DEVIL FISH. Name given to several marine animals, on account of their formidable and ugly appearance. These include the octopus, the angler-fish (*Lophius piscatorius*), and the largest rays.

DEVIL'S COACH-HORSE. A beetle (*Ocypus olens*) of the Staphylinidae. It is a common British species, black, very pugnacious, and feeding mainly on carrion. When alarmed it turns up the tip of its abdomen, and emits an evil-smelling fluid.

DEVIL'S ISLAND. Island of French Guiana, 43km (27m) NW of Cayenne. It was a convict settlement, noted for its terrible conditions, until 1950: Dreyfus was imprisoned here 1895–9.

DEVIL'S MARBLES. Area of granite boulders, S. of Tennant Creek, off the Stuart Highway in Northern Territory, Australia.

DEVIL'S MARBLES. About 1450 million years old and up to some 3 m (10 ft) in diameter, this strange rock formation plays its part in Aborigine legend. *Photo: Courtesy of the Australian Information Service*

DEVIZES (dēvī'zez). Historic town in Wilts, England. There are ancient British earthworks and shattered remains of the splendid Norman castle stormed by Cromwell in 1645. Pop. (1972) 10,150.

DEVOLUTION. The delegation of authority and duties, espec. in the later 20th cent. the movement to decentralize governmental power, as in the case of the UK where a bill for the setting up of Scottish and Welsh assemblies was introduced in 1976. *See* SCOTLAND AND WALES. The word was first widely used in this sense in connection with the Irish question, Redmond claiming in 1898 that the Liberals wished to diminish 'Home Rule' into 'some scheme of devolution or federalism'.

DEVOLUTION, War of (1667–8). War waged by Louis XIV to gain Spanish territory in the Netherlands, of which ownership had allegedly 'devolved' on his wife Maria Theresa. It was ended by the Treaty of Aix-la-Chapelle. Turenne conducted a remarkable series of sieges.

DEVON. Co. in the SW of England, lying between Cornwall and Somerset, with a wild and rocky coast on N and S. The NE is occupied by the mass of Exmoor, and towards the S is the granite area of Dartmoor (q.v.). Elsewhere, the co. is lower, and much of it is covered with rich red soil. There is a high percentage of pastureland, and in favoured areas of the S coast specialized crops are grown. Devon cider is famous. Sheep are grazed on Exmoor and the drier parts of Dartmoor. The chief rivers are the Taw and Torridge, Axe, Otter, Exe, Teign, Dart, and the Tamar. Kaolin is worked in the S. Plymouth and Dartmouth have shipbuilding yards, and Honiton is known for its lace. The tourist industry is of great importance: leading resorts incl. Sidmouth, Exmouth, Teignmouth, Paignton, and Torquay in the S, and Lynton, Ilfracombe, Barnstaple, and Bideford in the N. Exeter is the co. town.

Plymouth-Devonport forms the great naval centre. Area 6,525 sq.km (2,519 sq.m); pop. (1978) 948,000.

DEVON. The coastline abounds in beautiful inlets, such as Hope Cove, with its lobster fishermen. *Photo: Courtesy of the British Tourist Authority*

DEVONSHIRE, William Cavendish, 7th duke of (1808-91). British nobleman. He was largely responsible for the development of Eastbourne as an early example of town planning. His son **Spencer Compton Cavendish,** 8th duke of D. (1833-1908), was known from his father's accession to the title in 1858 as the marquess of Hartington. As a Liberal MP, he held many cabinet posts until 1885, when he broke with Gladstone over the Irish Home Rule Bill, and became leader of the Liberal Unionists. He was Lord President of the Council 1895-1903, when, as a free trader, he resigned from Balfour's Cabinet.

DEW (dū). Moisture which collects on the ground during clear, calm nights, particularly after a warm day. As temperature falls during the night the air and the water vapour it contains become chilled. Condensation takes place on the cooled surfaces of grass, leaves, etc. When the moisture begins to form, the surrounding air is said to have reached its dew-point. If the temperature falls below freezing point during the night, the dew will freeze, or if the temperature is low, and the dew-point is below freezing point, the water vapour condenses directly into ice; in both cases hoar frost is formed.

DEWAR (dū'ar), **Sir James** (1842-1923). Scottish chemist and physicist; Fullerian prof. of chemistry at the Royal Institution, London, from 1877. He invented cordite jointly with Abel (q.v.); and while working on the liquefaction of gases and low temperatures evolved the vacuum flask.

DE WET (de vet), **Christian** (1854-1922). Boer general and politician. B. in the Orange Free State, he served in the Boer Wars of 1880 and 1899; in 1907 became Min. of Agriculture in the Orange River Colony; and when the F.W.W. broke out in 1914 he headed a rising that was soon suppressed by Botha.

DEWEY, John (1859-1952). American philosopher. B. in Vermont, from 1904 he was prof. of philosophy at Columbia univ. D. early recognized that the exigencies of a modern democratic and industrial society demand new educ. technique. He expounded his ideas in numerous writings, esp. in *School and Society* (1899), and founded a progressive school in Chicago. A pragmatist thinker, influenced by William James, D. maintained that there is only the reality of experience, and made 'inquiry' the essence of logic. D.'s influence on American thought and educ. has been profound. His writings incl. *Experimental Logic* (1916), *Reconstruction in Philosophy* (1920), *Quest for Certainty* (1929), *Problems of Men* (1946), etc.

DEWEY, Melvil (1851-1931). American librarian. He devised in 1876 the D. decimal system of classification for books, now very widely used in libraries.

DEWEY, Thomas Edmund (1902-71). American Republican politician. B. in Michigan, he became a noted New York lawyer and was US Attorney 1933-4. In 1935 he was appointed to conduct a special campaign against organized crime in New York, and was Gov. of the state 1942-54. He failed to defeat Roosevelt in the presidential elections of 1944, and Truman in 1948.

DE WINT, Peter (1784-1849). English landscape artist. B. in Staffs, of Dutch descent, he was a notable watercolourist.

DHAULAGIRI (dow'lagiri). Mtn in the Himalayas, Nepal, W of Annapurna: 8,172 m (26,810 ft).

DHOFAR (dōfahr'). Mountainous western prov. of Oman. It is on the border with S Yemen, and the latter supported guerrilla activity here in the 1970s; Britain and Iran supported the government military operations. The cap. is Salalah (pop. 40,000), which has a port at Raysut.

DHŌLE. Wild dog of India, reddish-brown in colour, larger than the jackal, but, like it, hunting in packs.

DĪABĒ'TES. Disease (*diabetes mellitus*) in which a deficiency in the islets of the pancreas prevents the body reducing sugars properly. Adult D. (frequently inherited) can often be controlled by diet, though dosage with insulin (q.v.) may also be needed; juvenile D., which is possibly viral and may eventually be treated by vaccine, needs daily injections of insulin. Unless treated, D. causes incapacity, weakens resistance to infection, and ends in death in a coma.

DIAGHILEV (dēah'gilef), **Sergei Pavlovich** (1872-1929). Russian impresario. B. in the prov. of Novgorod, he studied law at St Petersburg, and in 1908 went to Paris and produced *Boris Godunov* with Chaliapin in the title role. In 1909 he founded the Ballet Russe, with its HQ in Monte Carlo, which he was to direct for 20 years. Its artists incl. Pavlova and Nijinsky, and Falla, Ravel and Stravinsky provided scores, so that first Paris, and then in 1911 London, were taken by storm.

DIALECTICAL MATERIALISM. The philosophy developed by Marx and Engels. From Hegel they derived the conception that all material and mental phenomena constitute a single system, developing through the tension between opposites, which resolves itself in a transition to a higher form of organization. But reversing Hegel's view, D.M. teaches that matter preceded mind, that in the course of evolution it gave rise to life, and subsequently to mind, and that the mental always remains a function of matter. D.M. assumes that things do not always remain the same, but possess latent potentialities which emerge as conditions change. What things are and how they behave depends on the relationships in which they are found, and only in relation to surrounding phenomena can they be understood. Institutions change their nature as social and political developments transform conditions. As one social order, by developing its internal contradictions, is compelled to change into a higher order, the new society will evoke new qualities in man, and transform law, politics, economics, morals, and art.

DĪA'LYSIS. The separation of colloids and substances in solution by diffusion through a semipermeable membrane. The process is made use of in the artificial kidney machine for dialysing accumulated impurities, normally removed by healthy kidneys, out of the blood.

DIAMOND. A precious gem stone, the hardest natural substance known (10 on Mohs' scale). Composed of carbon, it crystallizes in the cubic system, other common crystals being octahedra and dodecahedra. The high refractive index of 2.42 and the high dispersion or 'fire' accounts for the displays of colours seen in cut Ds. Rough Ds. are dull or greasy before being cut, and only some 20 per cent are suitable as gems. There are 4 chief varieties: well-crystallized transparent stones, colourless or only slightly tinted, valued as gems; *bort,* poorly crystallized or inferior Ds.; *balas,* an industrial variety, extremely hard and tough; and *carbonado,* or industrial D., also called black D. or carbon, which is opaque, black or grey, and very tough. *See* CARAT.

Ds. were known before 3000 BC; and until their discovery in Brazil in 1725 India was the principal source of supply. Modern sources are Angola, Ghana, Guyana, Sierra Leone, S Africa, SW Africa, Tanzania, and Yakutia; Brazil and Zaïre are noted for industrial Ds. They may be found as alluvial Ds., on or close to the earth's surface in river beds or dried watercourses, or on the sea bottom (off W Africa); or else in 'pipes' composed of blue ground or kimberlite, where the original matrix has penetrated the earth's crust. In the latter case the blue ground is extracted, then washed until completely disintegrated, and the residue made to flow over vibrating, sloping tables where a layer of petroleum grease arrests the Ds. This involves wastage and X-ray sorting is increasingly used. Natural Ds. may be exhausted by 2000 unless new deposits are found: *See* GEM.

Famous rough Ds. incl. the Cullinan (3,025.75 carats, S Africa 1905); Excelsior (995.2 carats, S Africa 1893) and Star of Sierra Leone (968.9 carats, Yengema 1972). Ds. are cut by the use of D. dust. The 2 most frequent forms of cutting gem Ds. are the 'brilliant' (for thicker stones) and the 'rose' for shallower ones. By 1980 India was on the way to replacing Antwep and Tel Aviv as the world's major cutting and polishing centre.

DĪA'NA. Roman goddess identified with the Gk Artemis. The dau. of Jove and twin-sister of Apollo, she was the goddess of hunting and of the moon.

DIANE (dē-ahn'). The EEC computer network, operational from 1980.

DIARRHOEA (dī-arē'-a). Excessive action of the bowels so that the motions are fluid or semi-fluid. It is usually due to irritation by a poisonous substance taken with the food or generated by microbes in the food itself (food poisoning), or by a disease organism, as in dysentery or cholera.

DIARY (dī'-ari). A daily record of personal events. The earliest D. extant in English is that of Edward VI, but full development of the form came in the 17th cent. with Pepys, Evelyn, and George Fox. The following cent. provides Swift's *Journal to Stella,* Boswell's *Journal of a Tour to the Hebrides* and the Ds. of John Wesley, Fanny Burney, and the country parson James Woodforde. Very detailed diaries were often kept in the 19th and early 20th cents., e.g. those of C. Greville, T. Creevey, Queen Victoria, Gladstone, Francis Kilvert, W. N. P. Barbellion, K. Mansfield, Sir Harold Nicolson, and Lady Cynthia Asquith. Foreign diarists include Emerson, Saint-Simon, Jules and Edmond Goncourt, Henri Amiel, Marie Bashkirtseff, Gide, etc. A more modern development of the D. is the fictitious form, e.g. George and Weedon Grossmith's *D. of a Nobody,* E. M. Delafield's *D. of a Provincial Lady,* and A. Loos's *Gentlemen Prefer Blondes.*

DIAMOND. The Cullinan diamond, found in 1905, the world's largest, before cutting. *Photo: Courtesy of the Diamond Corporation*

DĪAS'PORA. A dispersal, espec. of the Jews after the fall of Jerusalem in AD 70.

DĪ'ATHERMY. The generation of heat in body tissues by the passage of high-frequency electric currents through the body between two electrodes placed on the body. In diathermic surgery one electrode is very much reduced for cutting purposes and the other correspondingly enlarged and placed at a distance on the body. The high-frequency current produces at the tip of the cutting electrode sufficient heat to cut tissues, or to coagulate and kill tissue cells, with less bleeding than in normal surgical methods.

DĪ'ATOMS. Class of microscopic algae, found in all parts of the world. They consist of single cells, known as *frustrules*; the cell-wall is made up of 2 similar valves, which are usually impregnated with silica, and which fit together like the lid and body of a pill-box. Diatomaceous earths (diatomite) are made up of the valves of fossil Ds., and are used in the manufacture of dynamite and in the rubber and plastic industries.

DIAZ (dē'ahs), **Bartolomeu** (fl. 1481-1500). Portuguese explorer. He extended Port. explorations down the W coast of Africa, discovered the Cape of Good Hope (1488) and a route round the S extremity of Africa. He served under Vasco da Gama in 1497, and d. during an expedition led by Cabral, off the Cape of Good Hope.

DIAZ (dē'ahth), **José de la Cruz Porfirio** (1830-1915). Mexican President 1877-80 and 1884-1911. He gave Mexico its longest period of stable govt but was at length driven from power and fled to Europe.

DICKENS, Charles (1812-70). British novelist. B. on 7 Feb. 1812, in Portsea, the son of a clerk, he received little systematic education, although a short period spent working in a blacking factory in S. London, while his father was imprisoned for debt in the Marshalsea during 1824, was followed by 3 years in a private school. In 1827 he became a lawyer's clerk, and then after 4 years as a reporter in Doctors' Commons, became parliamentary reporter for the *Morning Chronicle,* to which he contributed the *Sketches by Boz.* In 1836 he m. Katherine Hogarth, three days after the publication of the first number of the *Pickwick Papers.* Originally intended merely as an accompaniment to a series of sporting illustrations, the adventures of Pickwick outgrew their setting and established D.'s position as a writer. He followed up this success with *Oliver Twist* (1838), the first of his 'reforming' novels; *Nicholas Nickleby* (1839); *Barnaby Rudge* (1840), set in the period of the Gordon riots; and *The Old Curiosity Shop* (1841). In 1842 he visited the USA, where his attacks on the pirating of English books by American publishers chilled his welcome; his experiences are reflected in *American Notes* and *Martin Chuzzlewit* (1843). In 1843 he pub. the first of his Christmas books, *A Christmas Carol,* followed in 1844 by *The Chimes,* written in Genoa during his first long sojourn abroad, and in 1845 by the even more successful *Cricket on the Hearth.* A venture as editor of the Liberal newspaper, *The Daily News,* in 1846 was short-lived, and *Dombey and Son* (1848) was largely written abroad. *David Copperfield,* his most popular novel, appeared in 1849, and contains many autobiographical incidents and characters.

Reverting to journalism, D. inaugurated the weekly magazine *Household Words* in 1850, reorganizing it in 1859 as *All the Year Round*; many of his later stories were pub. serially in these periodicals. His married life had long been unsatisfactory, and in 1856 he agreed with his wife on a separation: his sister-in-law remained with him to care for his children, while D. himself formed an association with the actress Ellen Ternan. In 1858 he began making public readings from his novels, which proved such a success that he was invited to make a 2nd tour of America in 1867. Among his later books are *Bleak House* (1853), which mirrors his legal experience; *Hard Times* (1854); *Little Dorrit* (1857), in which he evoked his memories of the Marshalsea prison; *A Tale of Two Cities* (1859), indebted to Carlyle's *French Revolution*; *Great Expectations* (1861); and *Our Mutual Friend* (1864). He d. at Gadshill, his home near Rochester, on 9 June 1870. *Edwin Drood,* left incomplete, was a mystery story influenced by the style of his friend, Wilkie Collins.

Dickens's life was written by John Forster (1872-4), who also edited his letters. He had 7 sons and 3 daughters. The 6th son was **Sir Henry Dickens** (1849-1933), an eminent barrister.

DICKENS, Monica Enid (1915-). British novelist. A great-granddau. of Charles D., she became a hospital nurse and wrote *One Pair of Hands, Happy Prisoner,* and *Flowers on the Grass.*

DICKINSON, Emily (1830-86). American poetess. B. in Mass., she had an unhappy love affair while visiting Philadelphia in 1854, and from 1862 lived in complete seclusion at Amherst. There she wrote a large number of short poems of an increasingly mystical character. During her lifetime very few of her poems were pub., but numerous vols. have since appeared, including *Bolts of Melody* (1947). D.'s poetry has been described as among the most remarkable ever written by a woman.

DICKENS. In his 'readings' Charles Dickens acted the parts of his characters to such effect that he electrified his audience and exhausted himself. *Photo: Popperfoto*

DICK-READ, Grantly (1890-1959). British gynaecologist. In private practice in London 1923-48, he developed the theory of natural childbirth, i.e. that by the elimination of fear and tension childbirth pain could be minimized and anaesthetics rendered unnecessary.

DICOTYLEDONS (dīkotilē'donz). In botany, class of Angiosperms, containing the great majority of flowering plants. They are characterized by the presence of 2 seed-leaves or cotyledons in the embryo, which is usually surrounded by an endosperm.

DICTATOR. Originally a Roman magistrate invested with extraordinary powers for 6 months in order to cope with a grave emergency, but in modern usage an absolute ruler possessing extra-constitutional powers. A king overriding the constitution and assuming extraordinary powers may constitute himself a D. Although dictatorships were common in Latin America during the 19th cent., the only European example during this period is the rule of Napoleon III. The crises following the F.W.W. produced many dictatorships in Europe; these included the régimes of Atatürk, Mussolini, Hitler, Pilsudski, Primo de Rivera, Franco, and Salazar.

Dictatorships also occur in Communist regimes, e.g. Stalin, and in the Third World after the S.W.W. there were many with both right-wing and left-wing characteristics.

DICTATORSHIP OF THE PROLETARIAT. Marxist term for a revolutionary dictatorship estab. after a socialist revolution, during the period of transition from capitalism to complete communism.

DICTIONARY. Book containing the words of a language, with their meanings - either definitions or equivalents in another language - usually arranged alphabetically. The term is also applied to books containing specialized information on some particular subject and to lexicons of the special terms of some particular art or science.

The earliest Ds. in England were written for the purpose of explaining Latin words in English. Dr Johnson's D. (1755) was the first standard English D.; it long held foremost place in English lexicography, as did that of Noah Webster (1828), in USA. The Oxford *New English Dictionary* appeared in 10 vols., 1884-1928, and a revision began in 1958.

DIDEROT (dēderoh'), **Denis** (1713-84). French man of letters, b. in Langres. His first notable publication, *Les Pensées philosophiques* (1746), was burnt by order of the *parlement*. His *Lettre sur les Aveugles* (1749) was also condemned, and the author was imprisoned for several months. In 1749 he was commissioned to edit a vast Encyclopedia, and obtained the collaboration of Voltaire, D'Alembert, Rousseau, Montesquieu, etc. They aimed not merely to impart information but to mould opinion, and although the *Encyclopédie* was often in danger of being suppressed, D.'s indomitable spirit had carried it through by 1772.

DIDEROT. A portrait of the encyclopedist by L.M. van Loo, now in the Louvre. *Photo: The Mansell Collection*

DIDJERIDU (di'jeridoo'). Hollow section of bamboo c. 1.5 m (4ft) long, blown to produce rhythmic, booming notes by Australian Aborigines.

DĪ'DO. Phoenician goddess, legendary founder of Carthage. Virgil makes her fall in love with Aeneas.

DIEFENBAKER (dēf'enbaker), **John George** (1895-1979). Canadian Progressive Conservative statesman. B. in Ontario, he became known as the 'prairie lawyer' because of his brilliance as a defence counsel. Becoming leader of his party in 1956, he became Prime Minister in 1957, and going to the country to get an absolute majority, achieved the greatest landslide in Canadian history. In 1963 he was defeated after criticism of the proposed manufacture of nuclear weapons in Canada, and lost the leadership in 1967, following his repudiation of a 'two nations' policy for Canada. A 'radical' Tory, he was also a strong supporter of Commonwealth unity, and attacked Soviet imperialism.

DIEGO GARCIA. Island in the Chagos Archipelago, named after its Portuguese discoverer in 1532. *See* BRITISH INDIAN OCEAN TERRITORY.

DĪELE'CTRIC. A D., which is always an insulating material, is a substance capable of supporting electric stress. The D. constant of a substance may be measured by the ratio of the capacity of a capacitor with the medium as D. to that of a similar capacitor when the D. is replaced by a vacuum. Common examples of good insulators are ceramics, glass and paraffin wax.

DIELS (dēls), **Otto** (1876-1954). German chemist. He was prof. of chemistry at the Berlin univ. inst. 1906-15, and at Kiel univ. 1916-45. In 1950 he and his former assistant, Kurt Alder, were jointly awarded the Nobel prize for chemistry for their research into carbon synthesis.

DIEMEN (dē'men), **Anthony van** (1593-1645). Dutch admiral, b. at Kuilenberg. In 1636 he was appointed Governor-General of Dutch settlements in the E Indies, and wrested Ceylon and Malacca from the Portuguese. In 1636 and 1642 he supervised expeditions to Australia, on the 2nd of which Abel Tasman discovered land which he named Van Diemen's Land, now Tasmania.

DIEN BIEN PHU (dyen byen fōō'). Town of N Vietnam, nr the Laotian border, 320km (200m) from Hanoi. General de Castries and some 10,000 troops were besieged in the Fr. Union fortress 13 March-7 May 1954 by the Communist Vietminh. Its fall led to the partition of Vietnam and indirectly to the end of the Fourth Republic in France.

DIEPPE (dē-ep'). Seaport at the mouth of the Arques, Seine-Maritime dept, N France. From 1066-87 and 1135-1204 D. was in English hands. It has a good harbour, with sea services to Newhaven and elsewhere; fishing is carried on, and there are shipbuilding and pharmaceutical industries. There is an airport. Pop. (1975) 35,000.

During the S.W.W. the first Allied combined-operations raid was carried out on D. on 19 Aug. 1942; a force of 7,000, most of them Canadians, was put ashore and remained there for 9 hours. There were some 3,500 casualties.

DIESEL (dēzl) **ENGINE.** A type of internal combustion engine which burns heavy oil. Air, which is mixed with the oil, is compressed and thereby heated to the ignition temperature of the oil. The principle was invented in England by Herbert Akroyd Stuart (1864-1937) in 1890, and developed by Rudolf Diesel (1858-1913) in Germany.

D., or compression ignition engines, are used for road, rail and marine transport.

DIET. A meeting or convention of the princes and other dignitaries of the Holy Roman (German) Empire.

DIETETICS. The science and practical application of the principles of diet or nutrition. Therapeutic D. is very important in the treatment of certain illnesses, e.g. diabetes, being used sometimes alone, and often in conjunction with drugs.

DIETRICH (dēt'rikh), **Marlene.** Stage-name of the German-American actress Magdalene von Losch (1904-). B. in Berlin, she won fame by her appearance with Emil Jannings in *The Blue Angel,* and went to Hollywood, becoming a US citizen in 1937. Her husky, sultry singing voice added to her appeal.

DIFFERENTIAL CALCULUS. *See* CALCULUS.

DIFFERENTIAL GEOMETRY. An offspring of coordinate geometry and the differential calculus; it deals with the problems of curves and curvature, leads beyond the concepts of Euclidean geometry to those of Riemannian geometry, named after B. Riemann (1826-66), whose work on this subject is of inestimable value; joins hands with hyperspatial geometry; and ultimately touches upon Einstein's theory of relativity.

DIFFRA'CTION. The interference phenomena observed at the edges of opaque objects, or discontinuities between different media in the path of a wave train. The phenomena give rise to slight spreading of light into light and dark bands at the shadow of a straight edge. The D. grating is a device for separating a wave train such as a beam of incident light into its component frequencies (white light results in a spectrum). The regular spacing of atoms in crystals are used to diffract X-rays, and in this way the structure of many substances has been elucidated, including recently that of proteins. Sound waves can also be diffracted by a suitable array of solid objects.

DIFFUSION. Term used in physical chemistry to describe at least 3 similar processes: the spontaneous mixing of gases or liquids (classed together as *fluids* in scientific usage) when brought into contact without mechanical mixing or stirring; the spontaneous passage of fluids through membranes; and the spontaneous passage of dissolved materials both through the material in which they are dissolved and also through membranes.

One important application of the D. principle is for the separation of isotopes, particularly those of uranium. When uranium hexafluoride is forced through a porous plate the ratio of the 235 and 238 isotopes is changed slightly. With sufficient number of passages, the separation is nearly complete. There are large plants both in UK and USA for obtaining enriched fuel for fast reactors and the fissile uranium-235, originally required for the first atom bombs. Another application is the D. pump, used extensively in vacuum work, in which the gas to be evacuated diffuses into a chamber where it is carried away by the vapour of a suitable medium, usually oil or mercury.

DIGGERS or **TRUE LEVELLERS.** A 17th cent. socialist sect who became prominent in April 1649, when, headed by Gerrard Winstanley, they set up communal colonies near Cobham, Surrey, and elsewhere. They were broken up by mobs and, being pacifists, made no resistance. Their ideas considerably influenced the early Quakers.

DIGITAL COMPUTER. *See* COMPUTER.

DIGITĀ'LIS. Genus of plants of the family Scrophulariaceae, incl. the foxgloves. The leaves are the source of the drug D., used in the treatment of heart trouble.

DIJON (dēzhoṅ'). Capital of Côte d'Or dept, France, and once capital of Burgundy. It is 265km (165m) SE of Paris, has a large wine trade, produces famous mustard, and has metallurgical and chemical industries, etc. The univ. dates from 1722. Pop. (1975) 156,790.

DILKE (dilk), **Sir Charles Wentworth** (1843-1911). British Liberal politician. B. in London, he became an MP in 1868, and expressed republican, radical, and strong imperialist views. In 1885 his political career was ended by his involvement in a divorce case. In *Greater Britain* (1868) he advocated a union of the British Empire and the USA.

DILL. A plant (*Anethum graveolens*) belonging to the family Umbelliferae and resembling fennel. It is a native of S Europe and Africa. Oil of D. and D. water, prepared from the seeds, are used medicinally.

DILL, Sir John (1881-1944). British soldier-diplomat. An Ulsterman, he became CIGS in 1940 at the time of the evacuation from Dunkirk, and in 1941 was promoted field marshal and sent by Churchill on a special mission to Washington. Roosevelt had full confidence in him, and he attended the conferences at Casablanca, Quebec, Cairo and Tehran as senior British representative on the Combined Chiefs of Staff.

DIMBLEBY, Richard (1913-65). British broadcaster and provincial-newspaper owner. He joined the BBC in 1936 and estab. himself as the foremost commentator on royal and state events, and current affairs (*Panorama*), on radio and television.

DIMETHYL SULPHOXIDE (dīmē'thīl sulfok'sīd). By-product (DMSO) of the processing of wood to paper, used as an antifreeze and industrial solvent. Because of its ability to penetrate the skin, it has also been claimed as a 'wonder-drug' in the treament of cystitis, rheumatoid arthritis, etc., but harmful side-effects have been claimed.

DIMITROV, Georgi (1882-1949). Bulgarian Communist. He was elected a deputy in 1913, and from 1919 was a member of the executive of the Comintern. In 1933 he was arrested in Berlin and charged with others with having set fire to the Reichstag. So forceful was his defence that the court was obliged to acquit him, and he went to the USSR, where he was general secretary of the Comintern until its dissolution in 1943. He returned to Bulgaria in 1945 and in 1946 became PM. He d. in Russia.

DINAN (dēnoṅ'). Town in Côtes-du-Nord dept, N France, on the Rance, with textile industries. Pop. (1975) 32,600.

DINANT (dēnoṅ'). Ancient town in Namur prov., Belgium, on the Meuse, a tourist centre for the Ardennes. It was almost destroyed by the Germans in August 1914. Pop. *c.* 6,500.

DINGAAN (d. 1840). Zulu king. Obtaining the throne in 1828 by murdering his predecessor, he was noted for his cruelty. In warfare with the Boer immigrants into Natal he was defeated on 16 Dec. 1838 - 'Dingaan's Day'. Escaping to Swaziland, he was murdered there.

DINGLE. The most westerly town in Ireland, situated on an inlet of D. Bay, co. Kerry, Ireland. It was a Celtic fort, and is now a fishing and market town. Pop. (1970) 1,500.

DINGO. The Australian wild dog (*Canis dingo*), descended from a domesticated breed introduced by the aborigines from Asia. It is the size of a small wolf, with yellowish fur.

DINGO. The only carnivorous mammal native to Australia before white settlers arrived. It is a danger to sheep. *Photo: Courtesy of the Australian News and Information Service*

DINOSAUR (dī'nosawr). One of a group of extinct creatures of the Mesozoic age, ranging up to *c.* 20m (70ft) long and a weight of about 35 tonnes. The name means 'terrible lizard', and it was assumed in the 1820s when giant skeletons were first identifiably discovered, that Ds. had been reptiles and their small brains indicated limited intelligence. However, from *c.* 1970 small Ds., with large brains, stereo vision, and 'hands' adapted for grasping were discovered. These were undoubtedly warm-blooded, and it seems likely that all Ds. were, so that they should be placed in a class of their own, being neither mammals nor lizards. The reason for their extinction is elusive, but they possibly disappeared following climatic changes attending the final break-up of the continents. An alternative theory has it that a line of their descendants survives, birds having evolved from little, fast-moving Ds.

DIOCLETIAN (dīoklē'shian), **Gaius Valerius** (AD 245-313). Roman emperor. B. in Dalmatia, he was proclaimed emperor in 284, and estab. a fourfold division of the Empire with two joint and two subordinate emperors. Under him there was a severe persecution of the Christians (303). In 305 he abdicated in favour of Galerius, and retired to his books and gardens at Salona, on the Dalmatian coast.

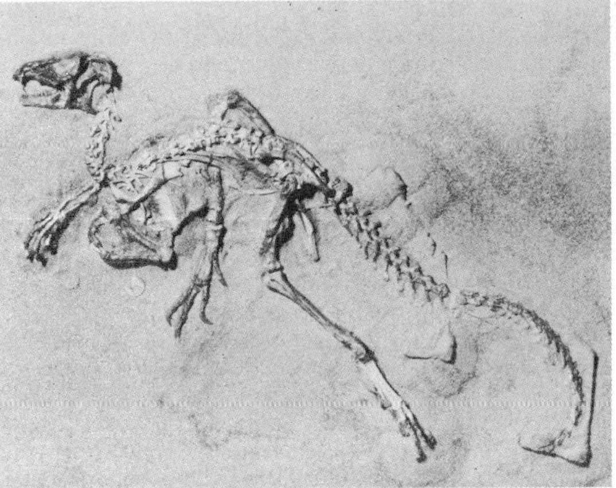

DINOSAUR. The first-ever reconstruction of a Triassic ornithischian. Some 200 million years old, this mini-dinosaur *(Heterodontosaurus tucki)* from South Africa was only 90 cm (3ft) from head to tail, and was a fast-moving bipedal herbivore. *Photo: Courtesy of Nature*

DĪ'ŌDE. An electronic device containing only 2 electrodes, an anode and a cathode, with marked unidirectional characteristics.

DIOGENES (dī-o'jenēz) (*c.* 412-323 BC). Ascetic Greek philosopher of the Cynic school, b. at Sinope. The story for his having lived in a tub like a dog arose only from Seneca having said that was where a man so crabbed ought to have lived. He was captured by pirates and sold as a slave to a Corinthian named Xeniades, of whose 2 sons he was appointed tutor. He spent the rest of his life in Corinth and won a great reputation for cynical wisdom.

DIOMEDE (dī'ōmēd). Two is. off the tip of the Seward peninsula, Alaska. Little D. (6.2 sq.km / 2.4 sq.m) belongs to the USA, and is only 3.9 km (2.4m) from Big D. (29.3 sq.km/11.3 sq.m) owned by USSR. They were first sighted by Vitus Bering 1728.

DION CASSIUS (dī'on kash'ius) (**Cocceianus**) (*c.* AD 150-235). Roman historian. He wrote in Greek a Roman History, in 80 books (of which 26 survive), covering the period from the foundation of the city to AD 229, giving the only surviving account of Claudius's invasion of Britain.

DIONNE QUINTUPLETS. Five girls, b. at Callander, Ontario, in 1934, the daughters of Oliva and Elzire Dionne. They were greatly under weight at birth, and their survival was largely due to the doctor in attendance, Allan Dafoe. Only 3 of the sisters still survive.

DĪONY'SIA. Festivals of Dionysus (Bacchus) celebrated in ancient Greece, esp. in Athens. The most important were the lesser D. in December, chiefly a rural festival, and the greater D., at the end of March, when new plays were performed.

DĪONY'SIUS. Name of 2 tyrants of the ancient Greek city of Syracuse in Sicily. **D. the Elder** (*c.* 432-367 BC) seized power in 405. His first 2 wars with Carthage further extended the power of Syracuse, but in a 3rd (383-378) he was defeated. He was succeeded by his son, **D. the Younger.** Driven out of Syracuse by Dion in 356, he was tyrant again in 353, but in 343 returned to Corinth.

DIONYSUS. *See* BACCHUS.

DIOPHANTUS (dī-ōfan'tus). Greek mathematician who lived at Alexandria *c.* AD 250 and wrote *Arithmetica*, a treatise on the theory of numbers, which is the first known work on problems in algebra.

DIO'PTRE. An optical unit in which the power of a lens is expressed as the reciprocal of its focal length in metres. The usual convention is that convergent lenses are positive and divergent lenses negative.

DIOR (dē-or'), **Christian** (1905-57). French fashion designer. He estab. his own Paris salon in 1947, and made an immediate hit with the 'New Look' (very feminine after the stark wartime fashions) and a series of styles named after the letters of the alphabet Y, X, H, and A.

DIOXIN (dī-ok'sin). One of the most toxic chemicals known (tetrachlorodibenzodioxin), produced as an impurity during the manufacture of Agent Orange, a defoliant used in the Vietnam War, and of the weedkiller 245-T, used in ordinary farming and gardening. Developed in the USA, both have been linked with chloracne, cancer, miscarriages, and deformed births. *See* SEVESO.

DIPHTHERIA (difthēr'ia). An infectious disease in which a false membrane forms on a mucous surface, usually in the throat, and death may result either from asphyxiation or from general collapse. The death rate has been much reduced by the discovery of an efficient antitoxin and a means of immunization and testing of susceptibility (Schick's method).

DIPLO'DŌCUS. Genus of herbivorous dinosaurs, belonging to the division Sauropoda, whose fossil remains were found in the Upper Jurassic rocks of western USA. They were of enormous size.

DIPLOMATIC SERVICE. *See* FOREIGN RELATIONS.

DIPLO'PODA. Class of Arthropods, commonly known as millipedes (q.v.).

DIPNOI (dip'nō-ī) (double breathers). An order of fishes, characterized, among other things, by having the swim bladder modified as a lung, so that when the rivers which they inhabit dry up in the hot season they are able to live buried in the mud. The living representatives of the group are hence called lung fishes or mud fishes.

DIPPER or **water ouzel.** Name of a bird (*Cinclus cinclus*), the type of a small family (Cinclidae) of the order Passeriformes. They are allied to the wrens and thrushes, but are distinguished from all other members of the order by their aquatic habits.

DIPSOMANIA. A morbid craving for alcohol, usually appearing at intervals. It is considered to be a symptom of an underlying mental disturbance or chemical imbalance.

DI'PTERA. Order of insects, characterized by the presence of a single pair of wings, and having the mouthparts modified for sucking. It comprises the two-winged flies.

DIRAC (derak'), **Paul Adrien Maurice** (1902–84). British physicist. Lucasian prof. of mathematics at Cambridge 1932-69, he has done important work in the field of quantum mechanics, and was awarded the Nobel prize in physics in 1933. OM 1973.

DISCALCULUS. *See* DYSLEXIA.

DISCOTHEQUE (disk'ōtek). Club for dancing to pop music on records. The most famous, Studio 54 (1977-80) in Manhattan, N.Y., gained notoriety when its owner, Steven Rubell, operated a policy of selective admission. *See* DANCE.

'DISCOVERY'. The vessel in which Captain Scott, commanding the National Antarctic Expedition in 1900-4, sailed to the Antarctic and back. In 1980 she was in St Katherine's Dock, London, being prepared for a new life as a Maritime Trust museum of exploration.

DISCUS. Circular disc used in ancient times at gymnastic contests, esp. at the Olympic Games, and also in modern Olympic and other athletic games.

DISINFECTANT. An agent which kills or prevents the growth of germs. Since the introduction of carbolic acid (phenol) by Lister (q.v.) in the 1870s, many different types of D. have been developed for special purposes, e.g. treatment of cuts and burns; cleansing of clothes, bedding, food processing equipment, and medical and surgical instruments. *See* ANTISEPTICS.

DISNEY, Walt (Walter Elias) (1901-66). American filmmaker. B. in Chicago, he estab. his own studio in Hollywood in 1923, and his first Mickey Mouse cartoon (*Plane Crazy*) appeared in 1928: among other notable creations was the surly Donald Duck. He developed the 'Silly Symphony', a new type of cartoon based on a musical element conceived in close association with the visual image, of which *Fantasia* (1940) was the culmination. His first feature-length cartoon was *Snow White and the Seven Dwarfs* (1938), followed by *Pinocchio* (1940), *Dumbo* (1940) and others. From 1953, when *The Living Desert* was shown, D. also made some remarkable nature-study films as well as features with human casts e.g. *The Swiss Family Robinson* (1960).

DISPLACED PERSONS. Citizens of occupied countries brought into Germany as slave labour during the S.W.W. The Allies found *c.* 7½ million, and when IRO funds ran out in 1952 the remaining 100,000 became the responsibility of the country (chiefly W Germany) in which they were living. The United Nations High Commissioner for Refugees, appointed principally to cope with Arab refugees (1951) after the establishment of Israel, helped with the remaining D.P. and later refugees, e.g. 200,000 Hungarians. The Germans who fled before the advancing Russians, and the Germans and German-speakers expelled from Poland, Czechoslovakia, and Polish-occupied E Germany, are sometimes loosely referred to as D.P.: they numbered *c.* 9 million. The 1960-80s saw renewed problems of D.P. in Africa, Asia and the Americas.

DISRAELI. *See* BEACONSFIELD, EARL OF.

D'ISRAELI (dizrā'li), **Isaac** (1766-1848). British scholar. Son of a Spanish Jew, who had emigrated to England from Venice, he was the father of Lord Beaconsfield (q.v.) and author of *Curiosities of Literature* (1791-3 and 1823).

DISSENTERS. Those who dissent from the Established Church in England or in Scotland. Usually the term refers to those legally styled Protestant Ds., viz. Baptists, Presbyterians, and Independents (now known as Congregationalists).

DISSIDENTS. Those intellectually dissenting from the official party line in Communist countries, espec. the Soviet Union following the advent of Khrushchev, and increasingly from 1968. They comprise those who are convinced Communists, but who advocate a more democratic and humanitarian approach; those whose main emphasis is on religious regeneration (Moslem and Christian); and those who aim at the restoration of national independence to non-Russian peoples within the USSR (e.g. Armenians, Lithuanians, Ukrainians, and

Tartars), or are Jews wishing to emigrate. Their views are expressed through the Samisdat (q.v.), and by publication abroad. They are dealt with by means of prison, labour camps and mental institutions, or in lesser cases by being deprived of their jobs. The most famous names are those of Sakharov and Solzhenitsyn.

DISTEMPER. A disease common in young dogs, characterized by catarrh, cough, and general weakness. It is caused by a virus, and is very contagious, but is controlled by inoculation.

DISTRICT COUNCIL. In Britain, under the Local Govt Act (1972), 300 new D.Cs. (incl. 37 in Wales) were created to replace the former county borough, borough, and urban and rural district councils. These incl. 34 metropolitan D.Cs. to operate within the metropolitan counties. The D.Cs. are headed by an annually-elected chairman, or in cases where the place has honorary borough or city status, mayor or lord mayor. Councillors are elected for 4 years, and one-third retire at a time, district elections being held in 3 out of 4 years, county council elections taking place in the fourth. Their responsibilities cover housing, local planning and development, roads (excl. trunk and classified), bus services, environmental health (e.g. refuse collection, clean air, food safety and hygiene, and enforcement of the Offices, Shops and Rlwy Premises Act), rating, museums and art galleries, parks and playing fields, swimming baths, cemeteries, etc. In the case of met. D.Cs. education, personal social services and libraries are also included.

DISTRICT OF COLUMBIA. *See* WASHINGTON.

DIU (dē'-oo). Island (11km/7m long) and town, off the Kathiawar pen., NW India, part of the Union Terr. of Goa, Daman and Diu (q.v.).

DIVER, or loon. A family of birds (Gaviidae) of the order Gaviiformes. They are confined to the N hemisphere, and usually breed in fresh water, but at other seasons of the year are mainly marine in their habits. On land the birds are scarcely able to stand, but their flight is powerful and in the water they swim and dive readily.

DĪVERTI'CŪLĪTIS. Inflammation of outward protruding 'pockets' or hernias in the large intestine, which frequently seem to form as a result of modern 'civilized' diet which lacks bulk and causes constipation, etc.

DIVINATION. Art of ascertaining future events or eliciting other hidden knowledge by supernatural or irrational means. There are 2 main types of D. The first depends on the interpretation of the mechanical operations of chance or natural law, and includes the casting of lots and ordeals by water, fire, single combat, etc.; consultation of texts obtained by a random opening of such books as the Bible, etc.; omens drawn from the behaviour of birds and animals; examination of the entrails of sacrificed animals; and the observation of the stars in astrology. On the borderline of the subjective forms of D. are fortune-telling by cards and palmistry; manipulation of a Bible and key or the reaction of a suspended ring; and the use of the divining rod in finding water, metals, etc. To the 2nd or almost entirely subjective class, which uses external aids only to a minor extent, belong clairvoyance by crystal gazing, etc.; oracular trance-speaking and automatic writing; necromancy, or the raising of the spirits of the dead; and dreams, often specially induced.

D. played a large part in the ancient civilizations of the Egyptians, Greeks, and Romans, and is still active throughout the world at every stage of culture.

DIVINE RIGHT OF KINGS. The political doctrine that monarchy is divinely ordained, hereditary right is indefeasible, kings are accountable to God alone for their actions, and rebellion against the lawful sovereign is thus a sin against God. The doctrine became prominent in 16th cent. Europe as a weapon against the claims of the Papacy, and in 17th cent. England was maintained by the supporters of the Stuarts in opposition to the democratic theories of the Puritans and Whigs.

DIVINE RIGHT OF KINGS. The concept of the divine right of kings allegorized. Charles I enthroned has the deity blessing his regime: 'Kings reign by my authority'. *Photo: Mary Evans Picture Library*

DIVING. The sport of entering the water, either from a springboard (3 m/c.9 ft.) above the water, or from a highboard (10 m/c.30 ft.) above the water. Various differing starts are adopted, and twists and somersaults performed in mid-air.

DIVING APPARATUS. Diving bells, using the principal of an inverted jam jar were in use in construction work in the 18th cent., but the first really practical individual diving suit was developed in Britain by the brothers John and Charles Deane in 1828. Such suits had to be heavily weighted and supplied with air by pipeline from a surface pump. Freedom of movement for the diver came with the invention of the aqualung in 1943 (*see* COUSTEAU), but at great depths a diver might still have to spend 12 hours in ascending and descending to avoid being affected by the bends (q.v.). During the 1970s the technique of saturation diving was developed by which divers live in a special chamber on the seafloor for 3 weeks at a time, breathing a mixture of 4 oxygen and 96% helium: readjustment to surface conditions takes 4 days. *See also* SUBMARINE.

DIVORCE. The legal dissolution of a lawful marriage. In England, divorce could be secured only by the passing of a private Act of Parliament until the Matrimonial Causes Act, 1857, set up the Divorce Court and enacted that a wife could be divorced for adultery, a husband for adultery plus cruelty or desertion. Under the *Divorce Act* (1969) the sole ground for D. from 1971 is the irretrievable breakdown of the marriage.

In the USA divorce laws differ from state to state. Everywhere adultery is a ground, in NY until 1967 the only ground; other grounds are cruelty, desertion, alcoholism, drug addiction and insanity. Minimum periods of residence before a D. is granted are from 6 weeks, and the Supreme Court ruled in 1949 that quick divorces instituted by one side without notification to the partner may be challenged. The so-called *Enoch Arden Laws* prescribe the number of years which must elapse before remarriage in instances where one partner disappears and is not known to be dead: they are named after the sailor of Tennyson's poem who returned after many years to find his wife remarried. In the USSR, under laws introduced in the 1960s, D. is easy and cheap.

Alimony (q.v.) for a wife after D. is decreasing in importance, but she is likely to benefit by a more equitable division of property. Custody and maintenance of children is tending to become a joint responsibility. In the USA unmarried couples cohabiting are increasingly negotiating 'pre-cohabitatation agreements' which make an advance settlement of division of property, assets, etc., in anticipation of a break-up, the woman sometimes stipulating for subsequent financial payments based on the number of years the arrangement lasts.

The Roman Catholic Church does not permit divorce among its members, but in certain circumstances may adopt an elastic attitude to 'annulment'. Among Moslems a wife cannot divorce her husband, but he may divorce her by repeating the formula 'I divorce you' three times: property settlements, etc., by careful parents make this a right not too frequently exercised.

DIXIE. Word of uncertain origin, denoting the southern states of the USA.

DIYARBAKIR. (dēyah'baki-a). Town in Asiatic Turkey on the Tigris, with a trade in copper, wool and mohair, and manufacturing textiles and leather goods. Pop. (1975) 170,000.

DJAKARTA. *See* JAKARTA.

DJERBA (jer'ba). Island, linked to the mainland by a causeway in Roman times, off S Tunisia. Rendered fertile by springs, it has been identified with the island of the lotus-eaters. Area 513 sq.km (198 sq.m); pop. (1970) 70,000.

DJIBOUTI (jiboo'ti). Rep. of E Africa (formerly French Somaliland 1892-1967 and Fr. Terr. of the Afars and the Issas, 1967-77). On the coast of the Gulf of Aden, it incl. the Gonda Mtns inland, which rise to 1,676 m (5,500 ft.). The climate is hot and dry. The nomadic tribes herd cattle, and there are fisheries. The cap. is the port of Djibouti (pop. 70,000) on the Gulf of Aden, founded 1888, and linked by rail with Addis Ababa. Area 23,000 sq.km (8,500 sq.m); pop. (1973) 200,000. The great majority are Moslems. M.U.: D. franc.

D.N.A. *See* NUCLEIC ACID.

DNEPRODZERZHINSK. Town in the Ukraine SSR, Russia, on the Dnieper, 48km (30m) NW of Dnepropetrovsk. There are chemical works, etc. Pop. (1977) 257,000.

DNEPROPETROVSK. Town in Ukraine SSR, Russia. On the right bank of the Dnieper, it is the centre of an important industrial region, linked with the Dnieper Dam, 60km (37m) downstream. D., founded in 1786, was originally named Ekaterinoslav (Catherine's glory) after Catherine the Great. Pop. (1977) 995,000.

DNIEPER (dnē'per). Russian river, rising in the Smolensk region and flowing S past Kiev, Dnepropetrovsk, and Zaporozhe, to enter the Black Sea E of Odessa. Total length 2,250 km (1,400 m).

D-NOTICE SYSTEM. British voluntary method of self-censorship set up in 1922 and admin. by the Defence (4 Whitehall officials), Press and Broadcasting (11 members between them) Committee. In matters of national security, guidance is given in the form of D-notices, and in cases of doubt material is referred back for clearance.

DOBELL, Sir William (1899-1970). Australian portraitist and genre painter. B. in New S Wales, he worked as an architect until, in 1929, he won a travelling scholarship, and went to study art in England and in Holland. He returned to Australia in 1939, and during the S.W.W. became an official war artist. His best-known portraits incl. 'Joshua Smith', 'Margaret Olley', and 'Helena Rubinstein'. He was knighted in 1966.

DŌ'BERMANN. Medium-sized, smooth-coated terrier, often with erect or cropped ears, and a close docked tail. It is noted for its aggressiveness as a guard dog, a trait acquired from its pinscher strain. It is named after Ludwig Dobermann, a 19th cent. German dog breeder.

DOBRUJA (dōbroo'jah). District in the Balkans between the Danube, on the N and W, and the Black Sea on the E. It is low-lying, partly marshland, partly fertile steppe land. Constanta is the chief town. D. was divided between Romania and Bulgaria in 1878; in 1913 after the 2nd Balkan War Bulgaria ceded its part to Romania, but received it back in 1940, a cession confirmed by the peace treaty of 1947.

DOCK. Name applied to a number of plants of the genus *Rumex*, belonging to the Polygonaceae. They are perennial herbs, natives of the temperate parts of the world, with lance-shaped leaves and small, greenish-coloured flowers. There are several British species and some 30 N American.

DOCKS. Accommodation at ports for commercial and naval vessels. In the 20th cent. the tendency has been away from an elaborate, inelastic system of 'wet' Ds. (for loading and unloading) and 'dry' or 'graving' Ds. (for ship overhaul), towards simple linear quayage which can accommodate ships of ever-increasing size and the flexible 'floating' D. for repairs. The latter are constructed of steel pontoons filled with water, so that the floor of the D. sinks below the ship to be worked on, whereupon the water is pumped out and the D. rises, lifting the ship with it. It has also been found increasingly necessary to provide specialized quayage as cargo ships themselves become more specialized, e.g. bulk cargo carriers of grain and sugar; carriers of cargoes requiring special handling, such as timber or refrigerated products (bananas, meat, dairy produce); container traffic; and oil tankers. Dock facilities have often moved downstream on rivers and away from city centres, e.g. the closure of many London docks combined with extensive new development at Tilbury, in order to gain greater space and manoeuvrability, and achieve the quick turn-round essential for profitable management.

DODDER. A genus of parasitic plants (*Cuscuta*), belonging to the bindweed family (Convolvulaceae). There are about 100 species, of wide distribution. The plant is without leaves or root; but has a slender stem which twines round that of some other plant, from which it draws its nourishment, penetrating its cells by means of suckers.

DODDS, Sir Charles (1899-1973). British biochemist. Courtauld prof. of biochemistry at London 1927-65, and pres. of the Royal Coll. of Physicians 1962, he was largely responsible for the discovery of stilboestrol, the powerful synthetic hormone used in treating prostate conditions and also for fattening cattle.

DŌDECANĒ'SE (Gk '12 islands'). Group of islands of the Aegean Sea belonging to Greece. The inhabitants - mostly Greeks - are noted as sponge-fishers. Under Turkish domination from the 16th cent., the D. were occupied by Italy in 1912, and in 1947 were ceded to Greece. With Rhodes (q.v.) they were formed into a nome called D., area 2,683 sq.km (1,036 sq.m); pop. (1971) 54,000.

DODGSON (dods'on), C. L. *See* Carroll, Lewis.

DŌ'DŌ. Bird (*Raphus cucullatus*) which formerly inhabited the island of Mauritius, but became extinct at the end of the 17th cent. It belonged to the pigeon order (Columbiformes), but is the type of a distinct family, Dididae. It was larger than a turkey, with a bulky body and very short wings and tail which rendered it incapable of flight.

DODGE CITY. City in SW Kansas, USA, on the Arkansas. On the Santa Fé Trail, it was a noted frontier cattle town in the days of the Wild West. Pop. (1970) 14,000.

DODŌ'MA. Cap. of Tanzania from 1975, when it replaced Dar-es-Salaam. It is approx. in the centre of Tanganyika 1,132 m (3,713 ft) a.s.l., and a hub of communications, linked by rail with Dar-es-Salaam and Kigoma on Lake Tanganyika, and by road with Kenya to the N, and Zambia and Malawi to the S. Pop. (1973) 20,000.

DOG. Member (*Canis familiaris*) of the family Canidae in the order Carnivora, which also incl. the jackals, wolves and foxes. Domestic Ds. have been in existence since prehistoric times, but it is hotly debated whether they derive by selective breeding from the wolf. Wild Ds. are found in Africa, America, Asia and Australia.

There are some 400 different breeds of D. throughout the world, the Kennel Club (1873) grouping those eligible for registration (150 breeds) into sporting breeds (hound, gundog, and terrier) and non-sporting (utility, working, and toy); the American Kennel Club (1884) adopts the classification sporting Ds., hounds, working Ds., terriers, toys, and non-sporting Ds. The premier event of the D. year is Crufts Show, Olympia, London: *see* Cruft, Charles.

DOGE (dōj). The chief magistrate in the ancient constitutions of Venice and Genoa. The first D. of Venice was appointed in AD 697 with absolute power (modified in 1297), and from his accession dates Venice's prominence in history. The last Venetian D., Lodovico Manin, retired in 1797.

DOGE. Leonardo Loredan, doge of Venice 1501-21, who ruled the great city-state at the turning point of its history. A portrait by Giovanni Bellini. *Photo: Courtesy of the National Gallery, London*

DOGFISH. Name given to a number of fishes of the order Pleurotremata. They are essentially members of the various families of sharks, differing only in their smaller size. The piked D. or spur D. (*Squalus acanthias*) is viviparous, and is the most abundant species of the British coasts.

DOGGER BANK. Shoal in the North Sea, about 115km (70m) off the coast of Yorkshire. In places the water is only 11m (36ft) deep, but the general depth is 18-36m (60-120ft); it is a well-known fishing ground. An indecisive naval action was fought near the D.B. in 1915 during the F.W.W.

DOGGETT, Thomas (d. 1721). British actor, b. in Dublin, whose memory has been preserved by the prize of 'D.'s Coat and Badge', given to the winner of a sculling race on 1 Aug., open to Thames watermen in the year following their apprenticeship.

DOGS, Isle of. District of E London, England, part of the Greater London bor. of Tower Hamlets.

DOMESTIC ANIMALS. The musk ox and (of ancient British lineage) the multi-horned Manx Loghtan sheep, exploited for wool; the silver fox and mink farmed for fur; poultry for eggs and meat; carp, kept captive for food since Roman times; red deer, now commercially culled, and the Tamworth pig, bred since the Iron Age, for meat.

DŌ'HA. Cap. and chief port of Qatar. Formerly a pirate stronghold, it has a deep-water harbour and internat. airport. Govt. House was completed 1969. Pop. (1983) 190,000.

DOLERITE (dol'erīt). A dark, heavy, coarsely crystalline rock, resembling basalt, but generally found as a dyke or sill intruded into other rocks and not as a volcanic lava.

DOLGELLAU (dolgeth'li). Tourist centre and market town in Gwynedd N Wales, at the foot of Cader Idris. Pop. (1971) 2,400.

DOLLAR. A monetary unit containing 100 cents (from the Ger. *thaler*) adopted as the standard unit in the USA in 1785; Australia, Canada, Hong Kong, and a number of other countries have also adopted the name for their standard unit.

Eurodollar. Following the S.W.W. a large American dollar reserve accumulated in Europe and London became the centre of this Eurodollar market. **Asian dollar.** Large reserves of US dollars also accumulated in Asia and Singapore became from 1968 the centre of the Asian dollar market, working in co-operation with London.

Following the depreciation of the D. after the Vietnam War expenditure and the oil crisis of 1973, the European monetary system became anchored on the German mark, and in Asia the Japanese yen became important as a trading currency.

DOLLFUSS, Engelbert (1892-1934). Austrian statesman. A Christian Socialist, he was appointed Chancellor in 1932, and in 1933 suppressed parliament and ruled by decree. Negotiations for an alliance with the Austrian Nazis broke down. On 12 Feb. 1934 he crushed the Social Democrats by force, and in May Austria was declared a corporative state. The Nazis attempted a coup d'état on 25 July; the Chancellery was seized and D. murdered. He was known as the 'pocket chancellor' because of his diminutive stature.

DOLMEN. Type of prehistoric monument, taking the form of a chamber built of large stone slabs, which are roofed over by a flat stone which they support. Ds. are grave chambers of the Neolithic period, found in Europe and Africa, and occasionally in Asia as far as Japan. In Wales they are known as cromlechs.

DOLPHIN (dol'fin). Genus of cetaceans, of which the typical member is the true, or common, D. (*Delphinus delphis*), found in all temperate and tropical seas. Dark grey to black on the upper part the D. is whitish beneath, reaches over 2m (*c.* 7ft) and has about 100 teeth in its 152mm (6in) 'beak'. Of high intelligence (they are popular performers in oceanariums), Ds. have been the subject of much research in recent years. They are thought once to have gone about on land (their flippers have the bone structure of a 5-toed limb and there are vestiges of hind limbs), and to have been covered with hair. They emit sounds (some audible to humans) which they use for echo-ranging or sonar, so that they can detect objects otherwise invisible in clouded water, and reach speeds in the water of up to 56kph (35mph) through specialized modifications of the skin, etc., which are not yet fully understood. In the US the Ds. are often known as porpoises. The name D. is also given to the beautiful game fish *Coryphaena hippurus*, which may be up to 1.5m (5ft).

DOLPHIN. The first baby dolphin born in captivity in Australia, at Tweed Heads, near Brisbane. Dolphins suckle their young for a year. *Photo: Camera Press*

DOMAGK (dō'mahk), **Gerhard** (1895-1964). German biochemist. He was awarded a Nobel prize in 1939 for his work on the sulpha drugs, effective in protecting from and curing streptococcal infection.

DOMESDAY BOOK. Record of the survey of England carried out in 1086 by officials of William the Conqueror. Its purpose was to provide the necessary information for the levying of the land-tax and other dues, and to ascertain the value of the crown lands. It also enabled the king to discover the wealth and power of his barons, and who were their vassals. Northumberland and Durham were omitted, and also London, Winchester, and certain other towns. The D.B. is preserved in 2 vols. at the Public Record Office, London. The name is derived from the belief that its judgment was as final as that of Doomsday.

DOMESTIC ANIMALS. Animals tamed, or otherwise brought under man's control for exploitation in respect of their labour; use of their feathers, hides or skins; consumption of their eggs, milk, or meat, etc. Almost co-existent with the emergence of man himself, the use of D.A. has only since the S.W.W. developed to factory farming and the inclusion of an increasing number of formerly wild species, with increasing stress on scientific breeding for desired characteristics.

DOMESTIC SERVICE. The oldest form of employment for women, it was generally ill-paid and little-esteemed, and the mobilization of women in the S.W.W. combined with later widened opportunities in other fields to shrink available labour. The National Institute of Houseworkers (1946) helped to raise prestige in Britain by issuing diplomas, etc., but a recent development both in the US and Britain is the rise of the *au pair* girl. Generally from the Continent and studying the English language, she lives as family and receives pocket-money for her services, but increased labour-saving devices are the more usual answer to household problems.

DOMINGO, Placido (1941-). Spanish tenor. B. in Madrid, of a celebrated musical family, he emigrated with them to Mexico as a boy. Self-taught, and also a skilled pianist, he excels in romantic parts, and is a superb *Otello*.

DOMINIC, St (1170-1221). Founder of the RC order of preaching friars, called Dominicans. B. in Old Castile, he was sent by pope Innocent III on a mission to the Provençal Albigenses, and remained preaching among them 1205-15. In 1208 the pope substituted the Albigensian crusade to suppress the heretics by force, and this was supported by D. From D.'s mission grew the Dominican order, and in 1215 it was given premises at Toulouse. Pope Honorius III, in 1218, permitted D. to constitute his 'holy preaching' as an order, and by the time of his death it was estab. all over W Europe. D. was canonized in 1234.

DOMINICA (domine'ka). Island in the West Indies, most northerly of the Windward Is., about 47km (29m) long and containing the highest land in the group. It produces timber, limes, oranges, bananas, cocoa, and rum. The chief town is Roseau, on the W coast; Portsmouth, the only other town, has a good harbour. D. was discovered and named by Columbus, 1493, became British in the 19th cent., and in 1978 became independent within the Commonwealth as the Commonwealth of Dominica. The last remaining Caribs (*c.* 500) have a reserve here. Area 750 sq.km (290 sq.m); pop. (1976) 78,000. M.U.: The East Caribbean dollar, pound sterling and French franc are all legal tender.

DOMINICAN REPUBLIC. Republic occupying the eastern two-thirds of the island of Hispaniola, W Indies; formerly a Spanish colony, it is the oldest settlement of European founding in America. The land is mountainous, rising in the central range to *c.* 3,050 m (10,300 ft), and the most densely settled part is the long E-W valley between the central and N ranges. The lower lands produce sugar, bananas, rice, tobacco, coffee, and cocoa; the soils of the S parts are poorer and arid. Minerals incl. bauxite, platinum and silver. The pop. is partly of Spanish descent, but mainly comprises people of mixed European, Indian, and African origin. The language is Spanish, and the state religion RC. The cap. is Santo Domingo on the S coast. Area 48,430 sq.km (18,700 sq.m); pop. (1978) 4,700,000. M.U.: peso.

Columbus discovered the island in 1492, and it was named Hispaniola ('little Spain'). After centuries of Spanish rule it became independent in 1821, and in 1844 the D.R. seceded from Haiti. It was occupied 1916-24 by the USA. Under the regime of Trujillo (q.v.) stability was achieved at the cost of democracy, but after his assassination fighting broke out between rival factions and US troops landed in 1965. Free elections were held in 1966, and from 1970 land reform was carried out. In 1978 Silvestre Guzmán Fernandez was elected pres., the first peaceful transfer of power to an opposition leader in the country's history.

DOMINICANS. The order of friars founded by St Dominic; they are also known as Friars Preachers, Black Friars, or Jacobins. The first house was estab. at Toulouse in 1215; in 1216 the order received papal recognition, and their rule was drawn up in 1220-1. They soon spread all over Europe, the first house in England being estab. at

Oxford in 1221. The English Ds. were suppressed in 1559, but were restored to a corporate existence in 1622. Today the order is worldwide.

DOMINIONS. *See* COMMONWEALTH.

DOMITIAN (dōmi'shian) (Titus Flavius Domitianus; AD 51-96). Roman emperor. B. at Rome, he became emperor in 81. His reign was troubled by barbarian attacks on the Danube frontier, and in 88 the armies of the Rhine rose in revolt, but were quickly suppressed. From this time D. began a reign of terror, and was eventually assassinated.

DON. Russian river, rising in the Moscow region of the RSFSR, and entering the N-E extremity of the Sea of Azov: length 1,900 km (1,200 m). In its lower reaches the D. is 1.5km (1m) wide, and for about 4 months of the year it is closed by ice. The upper course is linked with the Volga by a canal.

DONATE'LLO, or Donato di Niccolo di Betto Bardi (1386-1466). Italian sculptor. With Brunelleschi he revived the classical style, and exercised a profound influence on the masters of the Italian Renaissance. After he had completed his studies in Rome he returned to his native Florence, where he executed many famous sculptures. Among his important works are: the 'David' at Florence; the equestrian statue of Gattamelata at Padua; the 'St John' in Siena cathedral, etc.

DONBAS. One of the most important industrial regions in the Soviet Union. It incl. Donetsk and Voroshilovgrad regions in E Ukraine and the W part of Rostov region in the RSFSR. It is bounded by the Don and its trib. the Donets. About 40 per cent of the coal mined in the USSR comes from the D., which has also extensive deposits of salt, mercury, lead, and other minerals.

DO'NCASTER. Town in S Yorks, England, on the Don. There are coal mines, engineering works and synthetic textiles are made. Famous races at the D. course are the St Leger (1776) in September and the Lincolnshire Handicap in March. It was originally a Roman station, and Conisbrough, a ruined Norman castle to the SW, features in Scott's *Ivanhoe* as Athelstan's stronghold. Pop. (1972) 85,000.

DONEGAL (don'ēgawl). Co. in Ulster, Rep. of Ireland, washed by the Atlantic on the N, W, and SW. Most of it is mountainous, being geologically a continuation of the Highlands of Scotland. Agriculture is limited to the W. Sheep and cattle are kept. There is little industrial development, but tweed and linen are made. Deep-sea fishing is carried on. The r. Erne hydro-electric project (1952) involved the building of large power stations at Ballyshannon. The co. town is Lifford. The market town and port of D. is at the head of D. Bay in the SW. Area 4,830 sq.km (1,865 sq.m); pop. (1971) 108,345.

DONE'TS. River of the USSR rising in Kursk region and flowing 1,080 km (670m) to join the Don 100km (60m) E of Rostov. In the bend formed by the Don and the D. lies one of the richest coalfields in Europe. *See* DONBAS.

DONE'TSK. City in the Ukrainian SSR, cap. of D. region, 600km (380m) SE of Kiev. In the Donbas, D. is a rail centre and has an airport. It has blast furnaces, rolling mills, and other works engaged in heavy industry. It developed from 1872 when a Welshman, John Hughes, estab. a metallurgical factory, and the town was first called Yuzovka after him; renamed Stalino 1924, and Donetsk in 1961. Pop. (1977) 984,000.

DO'NGOLA. Region of the Northern prov. of the Rep. of the Sudan, lying on both banks of the Nile. Its chief town is New D., 72km (45m) above the 3rd cataract, which was founded *c.* 1812 to replace Old D., 120km (75m) up river, destroyed by the Mamelukes. The latter was cap. of the Christian kingdom of D. 6th-15th cents.

DÖNITZ (dön'its), **Karl** (1891-1980). Ger. admiral. As C-in-C of the German navy, he devised the 'wolf pack' technique used in submarine attacks on Allied convoys in the S.W.W., with the resultant loss of 15 m. tonnes of Allied shipping. Succeeding Hitler as Head of State, he capitulated in 1945, was sentenced to 10 yrs imprisonment at Nuremberg in 1946, and was released 1956.

DONIZETTI (donēdzet'tē), **Gaetano** (1797-1848). Italian composer. B. in Lombardy, he composed 64 operas, of which the best known are *Lucrezia Borgia* (1833), *Lucia di Lammermoor* (1835), *La Fille du Régiment* and *La Favorita* (1840), and *Don Pasquale* (1843). They show the influence of Rossini and Bellini, and their chief feature is their unfailing flow of brilliant and expressive melodies.

DON JUAN (hwahn). Character of Spanish legend, Don Juan Tenorio, supposed to have lived in the 14th cent., and notorious for his debauchery. Tirso de Molina, Molière, Mozart, Byron and G. B. Shaw have utilised the legend.

DONKEY. Popular name for Ass (q.v.).

DONNE (dun), **John** (1571-1631). British poet. He was brought up in the RC faith, and matriculated early at Oxford to avoid taking the oath of supremacy. Before entering Lincoln's Inn as a law student in 1592 he travelled on the Continent. During his 4 years at the law courts he was notorious for his wit and reckless living. In 1596 he sailed as a volunteer with Essex and Raleigh, and on his return became private secretary to Egerton, Keeper of the Seal. This appointment was ended by his marriage to Ann More, niece of Egerton's wife, and they endured many years of poverty. The more passionate and tender of his love poems were probably written to her. In 1615 D. took orders in the C of E. His wife d. 2 years later; and from 1621 to his death he was Dean of St Paul's. His sermons placed him among the greatest orators of his century, and his passionate poems of love and hate, violent, tender, or abusive, give him a unique position among English poets. His verse was not pub. in collected form until after his death.

DONNYBROOK. Locality, formerly a village, in co. Dublin, Rep. of Ireland, famous for riotous fairs which were stopped in 1855. It is now part of Dublin city.

DONOGHUE (don'ohū), **Stephen** ('Steve') (1884-1945). British jockey. Between 1915 and 1925 he rode 6 Derby winners, thus beating Fred Archer's record of 5 Derby victories, and 1921-3 achieved the 'hat-trick' by winning 3 successive Derbys.

DOOLITTLE, Hilda (1886-1961). American poetess. She went to Europe in 1911, and was associated with Ezra Pound and the British writer, Richard Aldington (q.v., to whom she was m. 1913-37), in founding the Imagist school of poets, whose members advocated the presentation of a clear-cut visual image in poetry, and the writing of short, concentrated poems in free rhythms.

DOOMSDAY BOOK. *See* DOMESDAY BOOK.

DOONE. Family of freebooters who lived on Exmoor, according to legend, until they were exterminated in the 17th cent. They feature in Blackmore's novel *Lorna Doone* (1869). The D. Valley is near Lynton.

DONNE. A miniature by Isaac Oliver dated 1616, and possibly the original from which the engraver Merian took the likeness included in the title-page of the 1640 edition of Donne's sermons. *Photo: Collection of H.M. the Queen*

DOPPLER, Christian Johann (1803-53). Austrian physicist. He became prof. of experimental physics at Vienna, and formulated 'D.'s Principle', which states that in the same way as the pitch of a sound alters if the body from which it proceeds is moving relatively to a fixed observer, so the light from a moving star varies in colour.

D.O.R.A. Short for the Defence of the Realm Act, passed in Nov. 1914, which conferred extraordinary powers on the Govt with a view to the proper prosecution of the war.

DORCHESTER. Town in Dorset, England, on the r. Frome N of Weymouth. Roman remains incl. a theatre, encampments and walls. Thomas Hardy was born nearby, and D. is the Casterbridge of the novels. It is the admin. HQ of the co. Pop. (1972) 13,950.

DORDOGNE (-dōn'). River of France rising in Puy-de-Dôme dept and flowing 490km (300m) to join the Garonne 23km (14m) N of Bordeaux. It gives its name to a dept and is harnessed for power. The caves of the wooded valleys of its tributary, the Vezère, offered a home to primitive man, and famous sites incl. Cromagnon, Moustier, and Lascaux with its cave paintings.

DORDRECHT (-rekht). River port on an island in the Maas, S Holland, Netherlands, 19km (12m) SE of Rotterdam. It is an inland port with shipbuilding yards and makes heavy machinery, plastics, etc. Pop. (1978) 104,300.

DORÉ (dohreh'), **Gustave** (1832-83). French artist. B. at Strasbourg, he was a skilled lithographer at 11, and was also active as a painter, etcher, and sculptor. His lasting reputation rests on his illustrations for Rabelais (1854), Dante, Cervantes, the Bible, Milton and Poe, which range from the sardonically humorous to the dark and harrowing.

DŌ'RIANS. Race of ancient Greece. They entered Greece from the N and conquered most of the Peloponnese from the Achaeans; this invasion appears to have been completed before 1000 BC. Their chief cities were Sparta, Argos, and Corinth.

DORIC ORDER. *See* ORDER.

DORMOUSE. Small group of rodents, akin to rats and mice, which comprise the family Muscardinidae. They can be distinguished by their hairy tails. They are arboreal and nocturnal and in cold latitudes hibernate in winter. The Common D. (*Muscardinus avellanarius*) is reddish fawn in colour.

DORMOUSE. The European edible dormouse, *Glis vulgaris*, is grey with black markings and about twice the size of the common dormouse. *Photo: Michael Lyster/The Zoological Society of London*

DORNEYWOOD. Country house nr Burnham Beeches, Bucks, England. Presented to the nation by Lord Courtauld-Thomson (1865-1954), as an official residence for a minister of the Crown, it is used by the For. Secretary. Admin. by the National Trust, it is open to the public.

DORNIER (-ych), **Claude** (1884-1969). German aircraft designer. B. in Bavaria, he founded the D. Metallbau works at Friedrichshafen, Lake Constance, in 1922. He invented the seaplane and during the S.W.W. supplied the Luftwaffe with the 'flying pencil' bomber.

DORPAT. German name of TARTU.

D'ORSAY (dorsā), **Alfred Guillaume Gabriel**, count (1801-52). French dandy. After serving in the French army, he accompanied the earl and countess of Blessington on a tour of Italy. For 20 years he resided with Lady Blessington in London at Gore House, where he became known for his taste and accomplishments. In 1849 he returned to Paris, and shortly before his death was appointed director of fine arts.

DORSET, Earl of. *See* SACKVILLE.

DORSET. Co. of SW England on the English Channel, between Hants and Devon. The centre is occupied by the chalky Dorset Heights, rising to over 275m (900ft) in the E. Elsewhere the co. is lowlying. Sheep and cattle are kept, and marble and building stones quarried. The eastern coastal area has oil deposits. The co. town is Dorchester. Along the S coast are many holiday resorts, incl. Lyme Regis and Weymouth. Other towns include Poole, Shaftesbury, and Sherborne. The co. contains the village and ruins of Corfe Castle and fine religious buildings, incl. Wimborne Minster. D. is the centre of Thomas Hardy's Wessex. In 1974, D. acquired the SW corner of Hants, incl. Bournemouth and Christchurch. Area 2,688 sq.km (1,038 sq.m); pop. (1978) 586,500.

DORSET. The county has countless hidden villages along its byeways, with original names. This church and its attendant thatched cottages are at Piddletrenthide. *Photo: Courtesy of the British Tourist Authority.*

DORT. Another name for DORDRECHT.

DORTMUND (dort'moond). Industrial centre in the Ruhr, W. Germany, 58km (36m) NE of Düsseldorf; it is the S terminus of the D.-Ems canal with large docks and has an airport. D. owes its importance to the Westphalian coalfield, of which it is the largest mining town. D. was bombed repeatedly during the S.W.W. Pop. (1978) 617,600.

DŌ'RY or **John Dory.** A sea-fish (*Zeus faber*), the type of the family Zeidae and the order Zeomorphae; found in the Mediterranean and Atlantic. There are 9-10 spines on the dorsal fin, and bony plates on the abdomen and back. In colour D. is olive brown or dull grey, with a conspicuous blotch on each side of the body. It is an excellent food fish and grows to *c.* 50cm (20in).

DOS PASSOS (dus-pas'sus), **John** (1896-1970). American author. B. in Chicago, he made a reputation with the war novels *One Man's Initiation* (1919), and *Three Soldiers* (1921). His acknowledged masterpiece is the *USA* trilogy (1930-6), which attains a panoramic view of American existence by placing fictitious characters against the real setting of newspaper headlines, and contemporary events.

DOSTOIEVSKY (dostōyef'skē), **Fyodor Mihailovich** (1821-81). Russian novelist. B. in Moscow, the son of a physician, he was for a short time an army officer. His first novel, *Poor Folk,* appeared in 1846. In 1849 D. was arrested as a Socialist revolutionary, and after being reprieved from death at the last moment was sent to the penal settlement at Omsk for 4 years, where the terrible conditions increased his epileptic tendency. Finally pardoned in 1859, he pub. the humorous *Village of Stepanchikovo*; *The House of the Dead* (1861), recalling his prison experiences; and *The Insulted and the Injured* (1862). Meanwhile he had launched 2 unsuccessful liberal periodicals in the second of which his *Letters from the Underworld* appeared. Compelled to work by pressure of debt he quickly produced *Crime and Punishment* (1866), an analysis of a murderer's reactions, and *The Gambler* (1867), and then fled abroad from his creditors. He then wrote *The Idiot* (1868-9), in which the hero is an epileptic like himself; *The Eternal Husband* (1870); and *The Possessed* (1871-2).

Returning to Russia in 1871 he again entered journalism and issued the personal miscellany *Journal of an Author* in which he discussed contemporary problems. In 1875 he pub. *A Raw Youth,* but the great work of his last years is *The Brothers Karamazov* (1880).

Remarkable for their profound psychological insight D.'s novels have greatly influenced Russian writers, and since the beginning of the 20th cent. have been increasingly admired and imitated abroad.

DOSTOIEVSKY. A portrait of the writer by V.G. Perov. *Photo: Popperfoto*

DOTTEREL. Bird (*Eudromias morinellus*) of the plover family (Charadriidae). About the shape and size of the golden plover, it is mostly plain brown in colour, with white eyebrows and breast-band. In Britain it is a summer migrant, frequenting moors.

DOUAI (doo-ā'). French industrial town on the r. Scarpe, Nord dept. It has coal-mines, iron foundries, breweries, etc. In the English RC college, founded there in 1568, removed to England 1903, the D. Bible was prepared. Pop. (1975) 47,570.

DOUBS (doo). French river rising in the Jura mtns and flowing 430km (265m) to join the Saône at Verdun-sur-le-Doubs. It gives its name to a dept.

DOUGHBOY (dō'-). Nickname for USA soldiers in the two world wars. One derivation is from the large buttons on the uniforms of the soldiers of the American Civil War, which were so called. In the 17th cent. a D. was a dumpling.

DOUGHTY (dow'ti), **Charles Montagu** (1843-1926). British poet and prose-writer. B. in Suffolk, he travelled in Arabia, 1876-8, and recorded his experiences in antique prose in *Travels in Arabia Deserta* (1888). In 1906 appeared his epic *Dawn in Britain*, a chronicle of legendary British history.

DOUGLAS (dug'las), **Lord Alfred (Bruce)** (1870-1945). British poet. The 3rd son of the 8th marquess of Queensbury, he became closely associated in London with Oscar Wilde. This friendship led to Wilde's action for libel against D.'s father, and ultimately resulted in Wilde's own imprisonment.

DOUGLAS, Gavin (or **Gawain**) (1475-1522). Scottish poet. A son of the earl of Angus, he became bishop of Dunkeld in 1515, and was very active in Scottish politics. He wrote 2 allegories, *The Palace of Honour* and *King Hart*, but his best work is his translation of Virgil's *Aeneid*, the first Eng. version of one of the great classical poets.

DOUGLAS, Norman (1868-1952). English writer. His travel books, such as *Siren Land* (1911) and *Old Calabria* (1915), are witty and sensually appreciative, as is his famous novel *South Wind* (1917). *Looking Back* and *Late Harvest* are autobiographical.

DOUGLAS OF KIRTLESIDE, William Sholto Douglas, 1st Baron (1893-1969). British air marshal. During the S.W.W. he was AO C-in-C of Fighter Command 1940-2, Middle East Command 1943-4, and Coastal Command 1944-5. In 1946-7 he was Military Gov. of the British Zone of Germany, and in 1949-64 was chairman of BEA.

DOUGLAS. Cap. of the Isle of Man, on the E coast of the island. It is a holiday resort, and terminus of the shipping routes from and to Fleetwood and Liverpool. Pop. (1971) 20,400.

DOUKHOBORS (dōō') or **Dukhobortzi.** Russian religious sect, also known as 'Christians of the Universal Brotherhood', some of their teachings resembling those of the Quakers. They were long persecuted, mainly for refusing military service - Tolstoy organized a relief fund for them - but in 1898 were permitted to emigrate and settled in Canada where they number *c.* 13,000, mainly in British Columbia and Saskatchewan. Refusing to send their children to school (where militarism might be taught) the extremist group, 'The Sons of Freedom', staged demonstrations and terrorism in the 1960s leading to the imprisonment of *c.* 100 members of the sect.

DOULTON (dol'ton), **Sir Henry** (1820-97). British ceramist. He developed special wares for the chemical, electrical and building industries and in 1846 estab. the world's first stoneware drainpipe factory. From 1870 he created at Lambeth and Burslem a reputation for art pottery and domestic tablewares.

DOUMER (doomār'), **Paul** (1857-1932). French statesman. He was elected pres. of the Chamber in 1905, in 1927 became pres. of the Senate, and in 1931 Pres. of the Rep. He was assassinated by Gorgulov, a mad White Russian émigré.

DOURO (doo'rō). River rising in N central Spain and flowing through N Portugal to the Atlantic at Oporto. There are hydro-electric installations. It is 800km (500m) long. At the river mouth navigation is hindered by sand bars.

DOUW (dow) or **DOW, Gerard** (1613-75). Dutch painter. B. at Leyden, he studied under Rembrandt. He was fond of painting half-length figures in window alcoves, and is famous for exactitude in detail.

DOVE. *See* PIGEON.

DOVER. One of the Cinque Ports, a market town and seaport on the SE coast of Kent, and the nearest point of Britain to the Continent, being only 34km (21m) from Calais. D.'s modern development has been chiefly due to the cross-Channel traffic, which includes train-ferry and other passenger and goods services. D., the terminus of Watling Street, was the Roman Portus Dubris. The beacon, or pharos, on the cliffs, built *c.* AD 50 is reputed to be one of the oldest buildings in Britain. The Lord Warden of the Cinque Ports is Constable of Dover Castle. Pop. (1972) 34,000.

DOVER, Strait of. Strip of water separating England from France, and connecting the English Channel with the North Sea. It is about 35km (22m) long and 34km (21m) wide at the narrowest part. With increasing traffic, collisions and shipwrecks became so frequent that traffic-routeing schemes were enforced in 1972.

DOWDING, Hugh Caswall Tremenheere, 1st baron (1882-1970). British air chief marshal. A member of the RFC (later RAF) in 1914, he was chief of Fighter Command at the outbreak of war in 1939, a post he held through the Battle of Britain. He retired in 1942 and was created a baron in 1943. He wrote works on spiritualism.

DOWELL, Anthony (1943-). British ballet dancer. Noted for the classical perfection of his style, he became senior principal with the Royal Ballet in 1967. He excels in *Enigma Variations, Sleeping Beauty* and *Four Schumann Pieces.*

DOWLAND, John (1563-1626). English composer. He failed to estab. himself at Elizabeth's court - he was an RC convert - but later reverted to Protestantism and from 1612 was patronized by the Stuarts. He is remembered for his songs to lute accompaniment.

DOWN. Co. in the SE of N Ireland, facing the Irish Sea on the E, and adjoining Armagh on the W, Antrim on the N. In the S are the Mourne mts., in the E Strangford sea lough. The co. town is Downpatrick. Area 2,465 sq.km (952 sq.m); pop. (1971) 310,620.

DOWNING STREET. Street in Westminster, England, leading from Whitehall to St James's Park, named after Sir George Downing (d. 1684), a diplomat under Cromwell and Charles II: No. 10 is the official residence of the Prime Minister. No. 11 is the residence of the Chancellor of the Exchequer, and No. 12 the office of the Government Whips.

DOWNS, North and **South.** Two lines of chalk hills in SE England. They form two scarps which face each other across the Weald of Kent and Sussex, and are much used for sheep pasture. The N Downs run from Salisbury Plain across Hampshire, Surrey, and Kent to the cliffs of S Foreland. The S Downs run across Sussex to Beachy Head.

DOWNS, The. Roadstead off E Kent, England, between Deal and the Goodwin Sands. Several 17th cent. naval battles took place here, incl. a defeat of Spain by the Dutch in 1639.

DOWN'S SYNDROME. Chromosomal abnormality (the presence of an additional chromosome in all their cells) which causes a child to have the rather flattened face and fold of skin at the inner edge of the eye which gave the condition its old name of 'mongolism'. With early treatment and training the accompanying mental retardation may be reduced, and the children are often sweet-natured.

DOWSING. The ascertaining of the presence of water or minerals with a forked twig, pendulum, etc. Unconscious muscular action by the dowser moves the twig, usually held with one fork in each hand, possibly in response to a local change in the pattern of electrical forces. The ability has been known since at least the 16th cent., and though not widely recognised by science diviners are commercially in demand.

DOWSON, Ernest (1867-1900). British poet. Perhaps the best of the 'decadent' poets of the 1890s, he suffered from tuberculosis, and in later life was very poor. His lyric 'Cynara' has a famous refrain: 'I have been faithful to thee, Cynara! in my fashion'.

DOYLE, Sir Arthur Conan (1859-1930). British writer. B. in Edinburgh, he qualified as a doctor, and practised at Southsea, 1882-90. Later he travelled in the Arctic and on the W coast of Africa, and during the Boer War was senior physician of a field hospital in S Africa. He wrote *The Great Boer War* (1900), and was knighted in 1902.

The first of D.'s books, *A Study in Scarlet*, appeared in 1887 and introduced to the public the famous private detective, Sherlock Holmes, and his ingenuous companion, Dr Watson. Other books featuring the same characters followed, incl. *The Sign of Four* (1889), *The Hound of the Baskervilles* (1902), and *The Valley of Fear* (1915), as well as several vols. of short stories. D. also wrote historical novels (*Micah Clarke*, 1889, and *The White Company*, 1891) and scientific romances (*The Lost World*, 1912). In his later years he became a spiritualist.

DOYLE, Richard (1824-83). British caricaturist. He illustrated many books, and was the designer of the original cover for *Punch*.

D'OYLY CARTE, Richard (1844-1901). British producer of the Gilbert and Sullivan operas at the Savoy Theatre, London, which he built.

DRABBLE, Margaret (1939-). British novelist. Dau. of a judge, she was ed. at a Quaker school at York and Newnham Coll., Cambridge, and in 1960 m. actor Clive Swift. Her books deal with the convolutions and frustrations of suburban life, and its moments of illumination. They incl. *The Millstone* (1966), filmed as *The Touch of Love*, and *The Middle Ground* (1980).

DRĀ'CO or **flying dragon.** Genus of small lizards, inhabiting the E Indies, Malaya, etc., of which *D. volans* is the type. They are arboreal in their habits. The ribs are prolonged and support a parachute of skin, by means of which the animal is able to glide from bough to bough.

DRACO (7th cent. BC). Athenian statesman, the first to codify the laws of the Athenian city-state. These were notorious for their severity; hence Draconian, meaning particularly harsh.

DOYLE. A corner of the famous room at 221B Baker Street where Sherlock Holmes and Dr Watson discussed the great detective's cases. *Photo: Courtesy of Whitbread.*

DRACULA (drak'ūlah). In the novel by Bram Stoker (q.v.), the caped count who, as a vampire, drank the blood of beautiful women. The original nucleus of the character was a 15th cent. prince of Rumania, Vlad V, known as 'the impaler' because he slowly impaled the Turkish invaders of his country, 20,000 at a time, and was no less cruel to his own people. The name D. derives from his father, who was known as Vlad Drakul (the Devil), and Castle D., N of Bucharest in the Carpathians, is a tourist attraction. His vampirism is a later addition. *See* ROMANIA.

DRAFT. *See* CONSCRIPTION.

DRAGON. Name popularly given to various kinds of lizard. These incl. the flying D. *(see* DRACO); the members of the family Agamidae, found in Australia, which are often spined, prickled or frilled in bizarre fashion; and the Indonesian komodo *(Varanus komodensis),* at over 3 m (10 ft) the largest living lizard, although an extinct Australian species was twice the length.

DRAGON. The Australian frill-neck *(Chlamydosaurus kingii),* just under a metre (2.5 ft) long. It disconcerts its enemies with its wide erectile frill, supported on umbrella-like spokes. *Photo Courtesy of the Australian Information Service.*

DRAGON-FLIES. Insects found throughout the world which form the order Odonata. Mostly large and brilliant coloured, Ds. have narrow, elongated bodies, prominent, protruding eyes and minute, bristlelike antennae. The mouthparts are modified for seizing and chewing, and have strong teeth. Their 2 pairs of approximately equal, membranous, glassy wings have a net-like venation.

The nearly 5,000 species of Ds. are classified into 2 main groups or sub-orders: the Anisoptera incl. the larger and stouter members, the Zygoptera the smaller and weaker kinds. They are often known as damsel-flies.

DRAGOON (dragoon'). Name derived from the 'dragon' or short musket used by the French in the 16th cent., and applied to a mounted soldier who carried this or some other infantry weapon. The name has been retained by certain regiments, though it no longer has its original meaning.

DRAKE, Sir Francis (*c.* 1545-96). English sea-captain. B. near Tavistock, he was apprenticed to the master of a coasting vessel, who left him the ship at his death. He accompanied Sir John Hawkins (q.v.) in 1567, and then after 2 voyages of reconnaissance he set out in 1572 to plunder the Spanish Main. He returned to England in 1573 with considerable booty. After serving in Ireland as a volunteer, he suggested to the Queen an expedition to the Pacific, and in Dec. 1577 he sailed in the *Pelican* with 4 other ships and 166 men. In Aug. 1578 the fleet passed through the Straits of Magellan in 16 days and was then blown S to Cape Horn. The remaining ships became separated and returned to England, leaving the *Pelican,* now renamed the *Golden Hind,* alone in the Pacific. D. sailed N along the coast of Chile and Peru, plundering Spanish ships as far N as California, and then, in July 1579, SW across the Pacific. He rounded the Cape in June 1580, and reached England in Sept. Thus the second voyage round the world, and the first made by an Englishman, was completed in a little under 3 years. When the Spanish ambassador demanded D.'s punishment, the Queen knighted him on the deck of the *Golden Hind* at Deptford.

In 1582 D. was chosen mayor of Plymouth, and in 1584-5 he represented Bosinney in parliament. In a raid on Cadiz in 1587 he burnt 10,000 tons of shipping, 'singed the King of Spain's beard', and delayed the Armada for a year. He was stationed off Ushant in 1588 to intercept the Armada, but was driven back to England by unfavourable winds. During the fight in the Channel he served as a vice-admiral in the *Revenge.* D. sailed on his last expedition to the W. Indies with Hawkins in 1595, and in Jan. 1596 d. on his ship off Nombre de Dios.

In 1579 D. anchored the *Golden Hind* off the California coast, and a Nat. Park at San Francisco marks the approx. site.

DRAKENSBERG (drah'kens-). Mountain range in S Africa, on the boundary of Lesotho and Orange Free State with Natal; highest point is Mont aux Sources, 3,482 m (10,822 ft), near which is Natal National Park.

DRAMA. A story interpreted to an audience by actors, in which such elements as dancing, music, singing, etc., are only subsidiary. The earliest known D. is probably the ancient Egyptian *The Triumph of Horus,* inscribed in verse *c.* 88 BC on the outer wall of the Temple of Edfu, but thought to be based on a prototype written *c.* 2700 BC.

ORIENTAL D. is characterized by fixed conventions and an avoidance of all semblance of reality. This is true in Japan of both the aristocratic *No* plays developed in the 14-16th cents. and of the popular *Kabuki* which originated in the 17th cent., and also applies to the less literate Chinese theatre and to Indian drama.

GREEK D. arose from the lyrical dithyramb chanted by a chorus in praise of Dionysus when, according to tradition, Thespis added a single actor. D. rapidly developed with the inauguration of the Athenian festivals: Aeschylus, Sophocles, and Euripides perfected tragedy, and comedy reached its greatest heights under Aristophanes and Menander.

All that survives of ROMAN D., e.g. the comedies of Terence, the farces of Plautus, and the tragedies of Seneca, is directly based on the Greek tradition.

MEDIEVAL. Something of the classical tradition was probably carried on into the Dark Ages by wandering entertainers. But in about the 10th cent. Church ritual began to assume dramatic form, and thence developed the mystery cycles and miracle plays. Essentially amateur productions, they were popular all over Europe in the 12-16th cents.

RENAISSANCE. The rediscovery of classical D. brought a new beginning in the Italian courts at the end of the 15th cent., and at the same time the *commedia dell' arte,* depending on the actors' improvisation, was evolved among the people. This cleavage did not exist in Spain, where Lope de Vega and Calderón de la Barca were the outstanding dramatists.

In England, too, there was no rigid class demarcation. Early experiments in the morality, interlude, comedy, and tragedy, were followed by the work of the young univ. men, Lyly, Greene, Peele, Kyd, and Marlowe, which prepared the way for Shakespeare.

17TH CENT. In England tragedy declined, although erratic strength still appears in Webster, Massinger, Middleton, and Ford. New vitality in comedy came with the comedy of humours of Jonson, which, combining with the witty comedy of Beaumont and Fletcher, produced the early plays of Shirley, and the later Restoration works of Etherege, Wycherley, and Congreve. The playhouses became the resort of the courtier, so that although the comedy of manners flourished, there was no place for great tragedy, despite the efforts of Dryden, Otway, and Lee.

In France the intellectual interests of the age found expression after the middle of the cent. in the work of Corneille, Racine, and Molière.

18TH CENT. In this period less vital examples of the older types of tragedy and comedy were written by Sheridan, Goldsmith, Marivaux and Voltaire, but a new sentimental genre was exploited by Cumberland and Kelly in England; and by Diderot, Beaumarchais, Goldoni, and Lessing abroad. This sentimentalism was coloured by romantic aspirations in Schiller and Kotzebue.

19TH CENT. The most popular form was the melodrama, which left nothing behind of literary value. In France Victor Hugo gave full expression to romanticism, but otherwise it was the period of the sentimental problem drama represented by S. Knowles, B. Lytton, and Boucicault in England; and Hebbel, Augier, and Dumas fils on the Continent. The latent vitality of the latter was exploited by Ibsen and Strindberg, who secured the triumph of realism - a development paralleled less forcefully by Robertson, Pinero, and H. A. Jones in England;

and by Sardou, Hervieu, Lavedan, Becque, Brieux, Sudermann, Hauptmann, and Wedekind in Europe.

20TH CENT. In Russia, the native realistic tradition combined with the inspiration of Ibsen to produce the Moscow Arts Theatre and Chekhov, and elsewhere the plays of Oscar Wilde, Shaw, Bridie and Pirandello also reflected a preoccupation with the individual in society. The cynical mood prevalent after the F.W.W. gave rise to the comedies of Coward and later Rattigan in England, and to the general trend elsewhere towards satire, experiment and fantasy shown in the work of Cocteau, Mayakovsky, and O'Neill, and in the early plays of Capek, Brecht, Toller and Elmer Rice. With the advent of the Depression and the rise of Fascism, the latter writers became committed to action, and the 'thirties saw some of Brecht's best work, and the rise of the American playwrights, Odets, A. MacLeish and Irwin Shaw. The dramatists produced by the S.W.W. incl. Camus, Sartre, Anouilh and Salacrou. The nihilistic mood of the 'fifties was reflected by the 'Theatre of the Absurd' in work by Ionesco, Simpson, Beckett, and Albee; this was accompanied by the more realistic drama of Osborne, Wesker, Pinter and John Arden in England, Brendan Behan in Ireland, Genet, Dürrenmatt and Ugo Betti on the Continent, and Miller, Jack Gelber and Tennessee Williams in America.

The re-association, begun by Claudel, of the poet and the playhouse in the 20th cent. led to the rise of the Irish Abbey Theatre, with plays by J. M. Synge and W. B. Yeats, and to the poetic drama of Lorca in Spain, and of T. S. Eliot, Spender, Auden and Isherwood, MacLeish and Fry, in England and America. The logical culmination of this trend was in the pure-sound plays of Dylan Thomas.

In the 1960s the British director Peter Brook (1925-) revived from the Continent the ideas of Artaud's Theatre of Cruelty with Weiss's *Marat/Sade*, and besides more traditional plays, such as those of Robert Bolt, there was the more experimental output of Tom Stoppard, Peter Schaffer and Joe Orton, and - in America - Neil Simon. By the 1970s, however, the outstanding figure in the British theatre was Alan Ayckbourn, whose 'black' comedies have intellectual and emotional maturity - you need to have been 'kicked in the stomach by life', as the author says, to appreciate them.

DRAUGHTS, or **checkers.** A game played by 2 players on a square checkered board of 64 squares. Each player has a set of 12 men which at the start of the game occupy alternate squares of the first 3 rows on 2 opposite sides of the board. A man may be moved forwards diagonally left or right to a contiguous and unoccupied square. When a man reaches the opponent's back line he becomes a king, and as a distinguishing sign another man of the same colour is placed on top of him. A king may move backwards as well as forwards. When there is a hostile piece on a contiguous square, and there is an empty square on the further side, the man or king may be moved to the empty square and the hostile piece removed from the board. If after making such a capturing move there is another hostile piece contiguous and with an empty square beyond it, such piece, being *en prise,* must be captured also. The object of the game is to leave the opponent without a move, either by capturing all his pieces or by blocking them so that they cannot move.

DRAMA. Four of today's dramatists: Edward Albee (top left), Alan Ayckbourn (top right), Harold Pinter (lower left) and Tom Stoppard. *Photos: Courtesy of Jonathan Cape Ltd., Margaret Ramsay Ltd., The Observer, and Angela Clements.*

DRAVI'DIAN. Name applied to a group of non-Indo-Aryan peoples, of the Deccan and northern Sri Lanka. They generally are of darker skin and shorter stature than the Aryan types of the N, and developed their own style of temple architecture. The D. languages include Tamil, Telugu, Malayalam, and Canarese.

DRAYTON, Michael (1563-1631). English poet. B. in Warwickshire, he came to London in 1590, where he pub. a vol. of poems, *The Harmony of the Church* (1591), which was destroyed by order of the Archbishop of Canterbury. His greatest poetical work was the topographical survey of England, *Polyolbion* (1613-22), in 30 books. D. was buried in Westminster Abbey.

DREAM. Fantasy experienced during sleep. Until the 18th cent. Ds. were closely studied, especially as indications of future events, a whole code arising for their interpretation, but then came to be regarded as an unimportant reaction to physical stimuli. In 1900 Freud revived the importance of Ds., concluding that they were an expression of unconscious wish-fulfilment, nightmares being failed Ds. induced by intense fear of 'repressed' impulses. Periods of rapid eye movement (swivelling from side to side) and twitches of the extremities coincide with Ds. which occupy about a fifth of sleeping time. Research has shown that Ds. are vital to rest, and that to interrupt or stop them completely - as with sleeping tablets - causes confusion, restlessness and tiredness. Ds. perform an important function for the brain in co-ordinating and sorting new information gathered during the working day, rather like the 'clearing the banks' time for a computer.

Ds. are not rapidly fleeting (as was once claimed), but occupy the same period of time as they appear to do to the dreamer. This is ascertainable by measurement of mental and physical activity during sleep, the sleeper reacting in the same way to D. stimuli as to real stimuli when awake.

DREISER, Theodore (1871-1945). American novelist, noted for his large-scale realism. B. in Indiana, he pub. in 1910 *Sister Carrie*, which was suppressed as immoral, and only became known with *Jennie Gerhardt* (1911). Later were the companion studies of big business *The Financier* (1912) and *The Titan* (1914), and his masterly study of an unscrupulous climber who ends as a murderer, *An American Tragedy* (1925), based on a real-life crime. In his later years he became a Communist. His brother, **Paul Dreiser** (1857–1911), wrote popular songs such as 'On the Banks of the Wabash'.

DRESDEN. City of (E) Germany, cap. of D. district, formerly cap. of Saxony. It is on the Elbe, to the S of Berlin, and is first mentioned in 1206 as a place fortified by the margraves of Meissen. D. became one of the most beautiful Ger. cities under the elector Augustus II the Strong (1694-1733), who made it a centre of art and culture, and erected the Zwinger and other rococo buildings. Count Brühl built a famous palace and the Brühl terrace. The museums contain well-known works of art. There is a conservatory of music and a technical coll. Manufactures incl. chemicals, machinery, glassware, musical instruments, and luxury goods. The manufacture of D. china, started at D. in 1709, was transferred to Meissen in 1710. Napoleon won a famous battle at D. 1813. D. was devastatingly bombed by the Allies on the night 13-14 Feb. 1945 15.5 sq.km (6 sq.m) of the inner town being destroyed, and *c.* 135,000 killed. The Russians took the city on 8 May. Pop. (1978) 512,500.

DRESS. The various garments which cover the human form. In ancient times D. usually remained unmodified for cents. Greek D. was extremely simple; from the 7th to the 1st cent. BC the main D. for both men and women was the tunic, called the *chiton*, which consisted of a rectangular woollen cloth fastened on each shoulder by a pin. The male garment of the Romans was the *toga*, which was usually white.

MIDDLE AGES. During the Middle Ages costumes did not change much in style for cents., but differed widely from place to place. There was also a wide difference between the costumes of different classes. The typical head-gear was the hood. Women wore a veil or fold of mantle, but this was abandoned in the 15th cent. for various kinds of caps, some with horns, some with butterfly-wings of gauze. Fashion, in the modern sense, was evident in the 15th cent., the two main centres being Venice and Paris.

16TH CENT. In the 16th cent. all points became blunted. As an instance, in the previous cent. shoes were excessively pointed - men's shoes became so long that the points were curled up and attached to the knees - but in the 16th cent. they seemed for a time excessively wide. In the first part of the cent. women's clothes were bell-shaped and kept in position by petticoats. Later the ruff developed, and men wore the doublet, the legs being exposed and covered with tight-fitting hose.

17TH CENT. The main outlines of Elizabethan costume were retained during the reign of James I, but with the accession of Charles I costumes became more elegant. Women were not so tightly waisted. The short puffed breeches of the men extended downwards to the knee and were adorned with rosettes of ribbon, as were also the shoes. Puritans wore the same styles in general outline, but the materials were plainer. Cavaliers and Roundheads wore the same kind of wide-brimmed, high-crowned hat, but the Roundheads abandoned the plume. French modes were introduced at the restoration of Charles II, and the male costume became more elaborate than that under Charles I. Men began to wear flowing wigs in imitation of Louis XIV. During the rest of the cent. the costume of both sexes gradually stiffened, and the male D. began to consist of the 3 garments which, with various modifications, have remained the typical male attire ever since.

18TH CENT. Women's clothes lost some of their stiffness. Men's coats were richly embroidered, and the waistcoat assumed something of its present form. In the 1770s the head-dress of both men and women became very high - women's hair was sometimes dressed to the height of a metre and was crowned with ships, windmills, and various other ornaments. Towards the end of the cent. men adopted the plain cloth of the English country gentleman, and wore a high-crowned hat.

19TH CENT. Trousers were worn by all classes, and men's clothes became more sombre in tone, until about 1850 black clothes were introduced for evening and formal wear. The top hat was by this time universal. Women's clothes were more varied than men's. The crinoline was introduced in the '40s, but was later replaced by the bustle. In the middle '90s the chief eccentricity was the leg-o'-mutton sleeve. Men's clothes developed a new informality with the introduction of the 'suit' and of the bowler hat and 'gent's boater'.

20TH CENT. During the Edwardian epoch men became more formal, and the frock coat was revived. Women had narrow waists, and wore much lace. The 'hobble' skirt, worn with a large hat, was introduced about 1910. By 1925 a new type of female D. appeared - the narrow straight garment extending down to the knees, and having the waist round the hips. Plus-fours were worn by men, and the Homburg or Trilby was introduced. In the '30s skirts grew longer, and after the S.W.W. austerity came the even longer skirts and femininity of the 1948 'New Look'. In the 1950s came the return to modified 'Edwardian' for men (so-called 'Teddy Boys'), and (for women) to the straight line and dropped waist of the '20s in the Dior H-look and A-line of 1954-5. Late in the 1950s the waist disappeared altogether with the advent of the 'Sack', and in the early 1960s of a modified and better-cut version of this - the 'Shift', and the hem-line rose to just below the knee. The development of man-made fabrics, and of the ready-to-wear industry catering largely for a teenage market, led in the mid-1960s to the 'swinging' era of London's Carnaby Street in Soho, and mini-skirts (*see* COURRÈGES) high above the knee. The best-known fashion designer later in the period was British - Mary Quant - but by the 1970s fashion had become more individualized. Both men and women 'did their own thing', and there were many designers, Italian, Japanese, and other nationalities, each with their own following. There was also a reaction, espec. among the young, against synthetics, and in favour of natural, cotton, wool and silk. Hand-crafted clothes of earlier periods became greatly sought after, and styles were eagerly re-copied. By the 1980s dress had to a great extent become unisex in that more than a third of British

DRESS. The development of women's dress in fashion plates of the 19th century: the Empire style in 1807, the crinoline in 1830, and the bustle in 1887. *Photos: Courtesy of the Victoria and Albert Museum.*

couples were found to share jeans, socks, scarves and boots.

DREYFUS, Alfred (1859-1935). French soldier. B. in Mulhouse of a Jewish family, he held a post in the War Ministry when in 1894 he was accused of betraying military secrets to Germany, court-martialled, and sent to Devil's Island. In 1896 it was discovered that the real criminal was a Maj. Esterhazy; the High Command nevertheless attempted to suppress the facts, and used forged documents to strengthen their case. After a violent controversy, during which Clemenceau and Zola were prominent among D.'s champions, a re-trial in 1899 found him guilty with extenuating circumstances and he received a pardon. In 1906 the Court of Appeal declared him innocent, and he was reinstated in his military rank.

DRILL. A large baboon (*Mandrillus leucophaeus*) of W Africa, characterized by a very short tail and a long prehensile great toe. Its face is black with no colouring as in the mandrill. It is mainly arboreal.

DRINKWATER, John (1882-1937). British poet. B. in Leytonstone, Essex, he was an insurance clerk for 12 years, before becoming associated as manager and producer with the Birmingham Repertory Co. His first vol. of verse appeared in 1906, and he contributed accomplished lyrics to *Georgian Poetry.* His outstanding revival of the chronicle play *Abraham Lincoln* (1918) won great success, and was followed by *Mary Stuart* (1921), *Oliver Cromwell* (1921), *Robert E. Lee* and *Robert Burns* (1925).

DROGHEDA (drokh'eda). Seaport (bor.) near the mouth of the Boyne, co. Louth, Rep. of Ireland. The town was stormed by Cromwell in 1649, and in 1690 it surrendered to William III after the battle of the Boyne. Pop. (1971) 19,745.

DRÔME. French river rising in Dauphiné Pre-Alps and flowing WNW for 101km (63m) to join the Rhône below Livron. It gives its name to D. dept.

DRO'MEDARY. The Arabian one-humped camel (*Camelus dromedarius*). All Ds. are now domesticated and are suited to life in the sandy deserts of Arabia and N Africa. The hump contains fatty tissue on which the D. subsists when food is scarce.

DROMEDARY. A herd in the Moroccan Sahara. The animals are hardy and longlived, not reaching maturity till their teens, and often attaining their half century. *Photo: Mireille Vautier.*

DROPSY. An accumulation of lymph in body cavities or tissues. If in the abdomen, it is called ascites; if local, oedema. General D. is usually a sign of disease of the heart, kidneys, or lungs. Tapping or a drug which will dilate the blood-vessels sometimes gives relief.

DRO'SERA. *See* INSECTIVOROUS PLANTS.

DROSOPHILA (drōsof'ila). Genus of flies, belonging to the family Muscidae and the order Diptera. The best-known species is the fruit-fly, *D. melanogaster.* Because of the rapidity with which it can be bred, and its well-marked variations, it is most suitable for the study of the laws of heredity.

DROUGHT. Period of prolonged dry weather. The area of the world subject to serious Ds. is increasing because of destruction of forests, etc.

DROUGHT. A dam in north-east Queensland illustrates the effects of one of the continent's great droughts. *Photo: Camera Press.*

DROWNING. *See* ARTIFICIAL RESPIRATION.

DRUGS, Misuse of. The taking of dangerous substances, some of which have medicinal value, for non-medicinal purposes: a problem since the earliest times, it is in the 20th cent. increasingly so. In the UK the Misuse of D. Act (1971) divided them into 3 categories according to their degree of harmfulness: (a) heroin, morphine, opium and other narcotics; hallucinogens (commercially developed after the S.W.W.) such as mescalin and LSD; injectable amphetamines, e.g. methedrine. (b) narcotics such as codeine and cannabis (*see* HEMP), stimulants of the amphetamine type, e.g. Benzedrine, Dexedrine and Drinamyl (purple hearts), and (from 1979) barbiturates. (c) less dangerous drugs of the amphetamine type. Hospitalization is the most effective form of treatment, since psychological factors are almost always involved.

Most countries strictly control production and distribution by legislation. In the USA the Justice Dept. has its Bureau of Narcotics and Dangerous Drugs and, since 1972, a special Office of Drug Abuse Law Enforcement; and Scotland Yard has a Dangerous Drugs Squad dealing with the problem. Internationally, a new Narcotics Control Board was estab. in 1965, and in 1971 a UN convention was approved on psychotropic substances (those affecting the central nervous system) to control hallucinogens, stimulants and tranquillizers. Burma is one important source of smuggled narcotics, the point where Burma, Laos and Thailand meet being known as the 'golden triangle'. Others are Mexico (espec. for USA), and China (via Hong Kong) and increasingly the Middle East for the West generally. New drugs, such as Angel's Dust (phencycladine) in the 1970s, which besides producing a feeling of weightlessness and of dying, gives an Alice-in Wonderland sense of diminished body size, continue to appear. After a temporary decline in the 1970s drug misuse, espec. of heroin, was rapidly increasing in the West in the 1980s.

DRU'IDISM. Ancient religion of the Celtic peoples of pre-Christian Britain and Gaul. The word is generally connected with a root meaning 'oak', this tree being regarded as sacred. Druids taught the immortality of the soul and a reincarnation doctrine, and were also expert in astronomy; their chief religious rite consisted in the cutting off of a mistletoe bough from the sacred oak with a golden knife. They are supposed to have offered human sacrifices.

D. was stamped out in Gaul after the Roman conquest. In Britain their stronghold was Anglesey, where they were extirpated by Agricola. They also existed in Scotland and Ireland until the coming of the Christian missionaries. What are often termed Druidic monuments - cromlechs, stone circles, etc. - are of Neolithic origin, though they may later have been used for religious purposes by the Druids.

DRUM. Musical instrument of percussion. It consists of a piece of skin, parchment, plastic or nylon, which is struck with a stick or with the hands and thus set in vibration, and which is stretched over one or both ends of a wooden or metal frame acting as a resonator. Ds. were adopted into military bands from the Turks during the 18th cent.

DRUMMOND, William, called 'of Hawthornden' (1585-1649). Scottish poet. B. at Hawthornden, near Edinburgh, he became laird there in 1610. He was the first notable Scottish poet to adopt southern English as his mode of expression.

DRURY LANE THEATRE (Theatre Royal, Drury Lane). London playhouse. The first theatre bearing this name opened in 1663 on the site of earlier playhouses; the present building dates from 1812.

DRUSES (droo'zēz). A religious sect of Syria and the Lebanon, founded in the 11th cent. AD. They are monotheists, and their scriptures are drawn from the Christian gospels, the Pentateuch, the Koran, and the Sufi allegories.

DRYAD (drī'ad). In Greek mythology, a wood nymph; each tree was supposed to be personified in its own D. or nymph. They were sometimes called hamadryads.

DRY CLEANING. Method of cleaning textiles based on the use of volatile solvents, discovered by accident in 1849 when a French tailor, John Baptiste Jolly-Bellin, noted the cleansing effect on a portion of a tablecloth on which turpentine had spread from an overturned lamp; introduced into Britain in 1886. Various non-inflammable solvents are now used.

DRYDEN, John (1631-1700). British poet. B. at Aldwinkle, Northants, he came to London in 1657, and although in 1659 he pub. *Heroic Stanzas,* in memory of Oliver Cromwell, he hastened to celebrate the Restoration with *Astraea Redux* (1660). In 1663 he m. Lady Elizabeth Howard, and was already embarked on his career as a dramatist. He produced more than a score of plays, including the comedy *Marriage à la mode* (1672); *Tyrannic Love* (1669) and *The Conquest of Granada* (1669-70), which represent the culmination of 'Heroic Tragedy'; and *All for Love* (1678). Much excellent criticism is contained in the prefaces to D.'s plays and in his *Essay of Dramatic Poesy* (1668). D.'s work as a satirist and didactic poet begins with *Absalom and Achitophel* (1681), which was followed by *The Medal* (1682); *MacFlecknoe; Religio Laici,* a justification of Protestantism; and *The Hind and the Panther* (1687), a defence of Roman Catholicism, to which he was converted after the accession of James II. At the Revolution of 1688 D. as an RC was deprived of the laureateship to which he had been appointed in 1668, and having also lost his pension supported himself by writing for the stage, and by translations, notably that of Virgil (1697). Among his many other works are *Annus Mirabilis* (1667); his odes on 'St Cecilia's

Day' (1687), and to the 'Memory of Mrs Anne Killigrew' (1686); and *Fables* (1699), verse paraphrases of stories from Chaucer, Boccaccio, and Ovid. D. was buried in Chaucer's grave in Westminster Abbey.

He was the greatest literary figure of his age; a master of all verse forms, he particularly excelled in the heroic couplet, and created modern English prose style.

DRY-POINT. A method of drawing on a metal plate with a sharp point; 'dry' indicates that no acid is used in its production. The incision made on the plate makes a furrow which turns up a rough edge or fringe of metal called the 'burr'. When the plate is inked for printing, the burr collects the ink and gives an effect of great richness and a soft velvety quality to the dark portions. Dürer made a few D.-Ps., and it was much used by Rembrandt in his later work, and in more recent times by J. M. Whistler, A. Legros, W. Strang, Muirhead Bone, F. Dodd, and H. Rushbury.

DRY ROT. The infection of timber in damp conditions by fungi, such as *Merulius lachrymans*, which forms a thread-like surface whitish at first, later reddening where it forms reproductive spores. Dry rot also spreads fungoid 'tentacles' though the fabric of the timber, rendering it brittle. The spores are rapidly spread though a building.

DRYSDALE, Sir George Russell (1912-69). Australian artist. B. in Sussex, England, he went to Australia as a child. He studied art in Melbourne, London and Paris, and became known particularly for his drawings and paintings of the Australian Outback. He was awarded the Wynne Prize in 1947 and in 1962 became a member of the Commonwealth Art Advisory Board. He was created knight bachelor 1969.

DRYSDALE. The artist with some of his works, penetrating in their sombre realism. *Photo: Axel Poignant.*

DUBAI (dūbī'). Second largest of the United Arab Emirates (q.v.). It is an entrepot centre and Port Rashid, constructed 1964-72 and named after D.'s ruler, Sheikh Rashid (1915-), is the greatest man-made harbour in the area. The cap. is D. (pop. 60,000), which has an airport. Smuggled goods are important, e.g. gold to India and Pakistan. There is also growing industrial development, and D. is the financial cap. of the UAE. Pop. (1976) 207,000.

DU BARRY, Marie Jeanne Bécu, comtesse (1743-93), Mistress of Louis XV of France. The dau. of a dressmaker, she m. Comte Guillaume du B., and in 1769 was presented at court. She is said to have been strikingly handsome, not without wit, and frank to the point of vulgarity. She exercised great influence on Louis. On the latter's death in 1774 she was banished to a convent, but later went to live at Luciennes. At the Revolution she fled to London, but returned to Paris in 1793, when she was arrested and guillotined.

DUBCEK (dōōb'chek), **Alexander** (1921-). Czechoslovak statesman. A Slovak, he lived in the Soviet Union 1925-38, and during the S.W.W. was a resistance leader in the Tatra mtns. In 1968-9 he was First Sec. of the Czechoslovak Communist Party and launched a liberalization campaign. He was arrested by invading Soviet troops but later released and given minor govt. posts.

DUBLIN. Cap. and co. bor. of Rep. of Ireland, at the mouth of the Liffey, on the coast of co. D., facing the Irish Sea: the official Gaelic name is BAILE ATHA CLIATH, pron. bah'la aw klē'ah. The greatest port of the republic, D. draws its exports from the whole state, and is the largest collecting and distributing centre. In D. is one of the world's largest breweries (Guinness); other industries incl. textiles, biscuits, pharmaceuticals, electrical goods, machine tools, etc., and there are shipyards, flour-mills, railway yards, and engineering shops. The city is a great route focus, roads, railways, and canals converging there, and has a handsome airport 10km (6m) to the N. The river channel has been artificially deepened and miles of granite quays built.

The present city was founded in 840 by the Danes who were finally defeated in 1014 at Clontarf, a N suburb of the city. From 1171, when Henry II landed in Ireland, D. was the centre of English rule until 1922; D. castle dates from 1200. The 18th cent. saw the architectural development of D. as it increased in importance. A good deal of damage was done to prominent buildings (e.g. the Custom House) in the rising of 1916 and in 1922. There are 2 cathedrals, both Protestant: St Patrick's founded in 1190, Christ Church in 1038, rebuilt in 1172. There are 2 univs., Univ. of Dublin (Trinity College, 1592), and University College (formerly part of the Nat. University, which became an independent university in 1979). Other interesting buildings are the City Hall (1779), the Four Courts (1796), the Art Galleries and Museum, the General Post Office, the RC pro-Cathedral of St Mary (1816), the Bank of Ireland, Leinster House in which the Dáil Eireann sits, and the Abbey and Gate theatres. Pop. (1971) 567,900.

DUBLIN. Co. of the Rep. of Ireland, facing the Irish Sea. It is level and low-lying, though in the S it rises to 753m (2,473 ft) in Kippure, part of the Wicklow mts. The only river of importance is the Liffey, which enters D. bay. Agriculture is chiefly directed towards supplying the needs of Dublin city. Dun Laoghaire is the only other large town. Area 922 sq.km (356 sq.m); pop. (1971) 852,220, incl. D. city.

DUBNA (dōōb'nah). Town in RSFSR, 40km (25m) W of Tula. It is a metal-working centre, and nuclear research is also carried on. The Germans held it for a short time in 1941 during their attempt to capture Moscow. Pop. (1977) 45,000.

DUBROVNIK. Yugoslav port on the Adriatic Sea. It was a Roman station, and after centuries as an independent rep. was under Austrian rule, 1814-1919. Pop. (1972) 30,000. *See* RAGUSA.

DUBUFFET (dübüfa'), **Jean** (1901–85). French exponent of *art brut* 'raw art'. Using unusual materials, such as coal or steel wool, he preached in the 1940s the value of the naively primitive, the productions of children and lunatics, and drew inspiration from graffiti.

DUCCIO DI BUONINSEGNA (doo'choh dē bwonēnsen'yah) (*c.* 1255-1319). Italian painter, the earliest of the Sienese school. His greatest work is his altar-piece for Siena cathedral (1308-11). His 'Virgin and Child with Four Angels', one wing of a diptych, is in the National Gallery.

DUCE (doo'cheh). Ital. for 'Leader'. The title was bestowed on Mussolini by his followers, and was later adopted as his official title.

DUCHAMP (düshaṁ'), **Marcel** (1887-1968). French artist. He achieved fame with his *Nude Descending a Staircase* exhibited at the Armoury Show in NY 1913, which used schematized human forms. With Picabia he founded the Dadaist movement, and was associated with the Surrealists.

DUCK. Bird of the family Anatidae found mainly in the northern hemisphere. The family is a large one, and comprises several sub-families such as the geese (Anserinae), swans (Cygninae), mergansers (Merginae), surface-feeding Ds. (Anatinae), and diving Ds. (Nyrocinae).

The Anatinae are distinguished by the flattened bill, moderately long and covered with a soft skin except for the nail at the tip, and provided with lamellae through which the birds are able to strain their food from the water and mud. The front toes are webbed, and the small hind toe is free. They are mostly freshwater species, feeding on worms, insects, etc., as well as vegetable matter. The typical species is the wild D. or mallard (*Anas platyrhynchos*).

The diving Ds. (Nyrocinae), have the feet set farther back, and the hind toe lobed. The nail of the beak is usually prominent, and many of them are marine in their habits. The most familiar species is the tufted D. (*Nyroca fuligula*).

DUCKBILL. *See* PLATYPUS.

DUCTLESS GLANDS. Certain glands, including the pituitary, thyroid, parathyroid, adrenal, and sex, in the human body which have no ducts or canals for carrying away their products. Known as internal secretions, the latter pass directly into the blood stream. Another name for D.Gs. is endocrine glands.

DUDI'NTSEV, Vladimir Dmitriyevitch (1918-). Russian writer. B. near Kharkov, he studied law in Moscow. In 1956 he pub. the controversial novel *Not by Bread Alone*, a product of the de-Stalinization era, which permitted criticism of injustice and the bureaucratic attitude in the individual, although not of the Communist system in general.

DUDLEY. Town, NW of Birmingham, W Midlands, England. Industries incl. light engineering and clothing Pop. (1972) 185,920.

DUFY (düfē'), **Raoul** (1877-1953). French painter and designer. He was noted for his calligraphic style, varied use of colour, and for his pictures of sport and recreation.

DŪ'GONG. A mammal (*Dugong dugong*) of the order Sirenia, or sea-cows, found in the Indian seas. It is sometimes c. 2.5m (8ft) long, and has a tapering body with a notched tail and 2 fore-flippers. Leather, ivory, and oil are obtained from it, and its flesh is edible.

DUGONG. Slow-moving and harmless, the dugong is herbivorous and becoming rare. It is sometimes suggested as the original of the mermaid legend, but a close-up view is disillusioning. *Photo: Associated Press.*

DUISBURG (do͞o'-is boorg). Industrial city of the Ruhr, Germany, at the confluence of the Rhine and the Ruhr. It is the largest inland port in W Germany, with important coal-mines, iron and steel, chemical, shipbuilding and engineering industries. The N suburb of Hamborn was incorporated in 1929, and until 1935 it was called D.-Hamborn. During the S.W.W., D. was heavily bombed from 1940 until its capture by US troops after severe fighting 30 March 1945. Pop. (1978) 572,000.

DUKAS (dükahs'), **Paul** (1865-1935). French composer. B. in Paris, he was prof. of composition at the Paris Conservatoire, and composed the opera *Ariane et Barbebleue*, the ballet *Le Péri*, and the very popular orchestral scherzo *L'Apprenti Sorcier* (The Sorcerer's Apprentice).

DUKE (Lat. *dux*, a general). Highest title in the English peerage. It was unknown in England until 1337, when Edward III created his son Edward D. of Cornwall. The oldest Scottish duchy is Hamilton, 1643.

DUKERIES, The. District of NW Nottinghamshire, forming a woodland recreation area, part of Sherwood Forest. It comprises the parks of four former ducal estates.

DULCIMER (dul'simer). Musical instrument, consisting of a shallow box strung with wire strings which are struck with small wooden hammers.

DU'LLES, John Foster (1888-1959). American statesman. B. in Washington the s. of a Presbyterian minister, he was ed. at Princeton, the Sorbonne and George Washington univ., before being admitted to the Bar. At 19 he attended the Hague Peace Conference of 1907, and took part in the 1919 Paris Peace Conference. He was senior US adviser at the UN founding conference in 1945 and was prominent in the drafting of the Japanese Peace Treaty in 1951. D. became Sec. of State in 1952 and criticized Britain's actions during the Suez crisis in 1956. Suffering from cancer, he resigned office and d. in 1959.

His brother, **Allen D.** (1893-1969), a lawyer, was director of the Central Intelligence Agency 1953-61.

DULUTH (dulooth′). US port on Lake Superior by the mouth of the St Louis river, Minnesota. It manufactures steel, flour, timber, and dairy produce. Pop. (1970) 100,580.

DULWICH. Suburb of London, England, part of the inner London bor. of Southwark. It contains D. college (founded 1619 by Edward Alleyn, the Elizabethan actor), the Horniman Museum (1901) with a fine ethnological collection, D. Picture Gallery (1814, rebuilt 1953 after S.W.W. bombing), D. Park and D. Village, still pleasantly rural.

DUMAS (dūmah′), **Alexandre** (1802-70). French novelist and dramatist, called D. the Elder. B. at Villers-Cotterets, he was the son of a French general, and through his paternal grandmother inherited a strain of Negro blood. When he was 20 he went to Paris, and in 1829 had a resounding success with his play *Henri III et sa Cour.* Another great success was *Antony* (1831), and altogether he wrote more than 20 plays. The famous historical novels began to appear in 1836, and in a vast output D. was assisted by collaborators, incl. Auguste Maquet. It was with Maquet's help that he wrote *Les Trois Mousquetaires* (*The Three Musketeers,* 1844) and its sequels; also in 1844 he pub. the *Comte de Monte-Cristo.* Another series centres round Henri IV, and a 3rd deals with the French Revolution, e.g. *Le Collier de la Reine* (*The Queen's Necklace*). Best known of the many other novels are *La Tulipe Noire* (*The Black Tulip*) and *Les frères Corses* (*The Corsican Brothers*). In 1832 appeared *Impressions de Voyage,* the first of a series of entertaining travel books. *Mes Mémoires* gives the story of his life to 1832. His natural son Alexandre D. the Younger (q.v.) was also a writer.

DUMAS, Alexandre (1824-95). French dramatist and novelist known as D. the Younger, to distinguish him from his father, Alexandre Dumas the Elder (q.v.). His novels and miscellaneous writings have been eclipsed by his plays, of which the first, *La Dame aux Camélias* (1852), had an outstanding success as the first important comedy of manners of the 19th cent. in France: the novel had appeared 1848.

DU MAURIER (dü mō′ryā′), **Dame Daphne** (1907-). British novelist. The dau. of actor-manager Sir Gerald D.M. (1873-1934) and grand-dau. of George D.M. (q.v.), she m. in 1932 Sir Frederick Browning (1896-1965), who was deputy commander of the 1st Airborne Army at Arnhem in 1944. She estab. her reputation with *Jamaica Inn* (1936), a story of wreckers in Cornwall, the co. she made her home. Later books incl. *Rebecca* (1938), *Frenchman's Creek* (1941), and *My Cousin Rachel* - all filmed - and studies of her father and grandfather. She was created DBE in 1969.

DU MAURIER, George Louis Palmella Busson (1834-96). British author and artist. B. in Paris, the son of a French refugee who became an English subject during the Revolution, he settled in London in 1860 and secured a place on the staff of *Punch.* Besides illustrating books and periodicals, he wrote novels: *Peter Ibbetson* (1891) and *Trilby* (1894) - story of a natural singer able to perform only under the hypnosis of Svengali, her tutor.

DUMBA′RTON. Town in the region of Strathclyde, Scotland. On the Clyde estuary at the mouth of the Leven, it has whisky distilling, engineering, boiler and tube making industries. The hovercraft was first developed here. Pop. (1971) 25,240.

DUMAS. The creator of the Three Musketeers, the prince of romantic storytellers, Alexandre Dumas. *Photo: Popperfoto.*

DUMBARTON OAKS. An 18th cent. mansion near Washington, DC, USA, scene of a conference held 21 Aug.-29 Sept. 1944, between Britain, the USA, and the USSR for preliminary discussions of the structure and aims of a new international league to enforce peace. After the Russians (who were not then at war with Japan) had left, a Chinese delegation arrived. The conference ended on 7 Oct., agreement having been reached for a draft programme for a conference held at San Francisco 25 April-25 June 1945, at which the United Nations was founded.

DUMFRIES (dumfrēs′) **and Galloway.** Region of Scotland, created in 1975 from the cos. of Dumfriesshire, Kirkcudbright, Wigtown and S Ayrshire, incl. Girvan. Over half is mountainous moorland, incl. Glen Trool Nat. Park, and most of the pop. is concentrated in the coastal plain and r. valleys, where there is some industry, and agriculture and forestry are carried on. The climate is the mildest in Scotland. The admin. HQ is Dumfries, which has knitwear, plastics and other industries; pop. (1973) 29,300, and Stranraer provides the shortest sea route to Ireland. Area 6,475 sq.km (2,500 sq.m); pop. (1979) 142,427.

DUMFRIESSHIRE. Former co. of S Scotland, merged in 1975 in the region of Dumfries and Galloway.

DUMOURIEZ (dümooryeh′), **Charles François du Périer** (1739-1823). French general. In 1792 he was appointed Foreign Minister, supported the declaration of war against Austria, and after the fall of the monarchy was given command of the army defending Paris; he won the battle of Jemappes, but was defeated at Neerwinden in 1793, and after intriguing with the Royalists he had to flee for his life. From 1804 he lived in England.

DUNANT (dünoṅ'), **Jean Henri** (1828-1910). Swiss philanthropist; the originator of the Red Cross. B. at Geneva, he became a physician and witnessed the battle of Solferino (1859). He helped to tend the wounded, and described their distress in *Un Souvenir de Solférino* (1862) wherein he proposed the establishment of an international body for the aid of the wounded - an idea that was realized in the Geneva Convention of 1864.

DUNBAR, William (*c.* 1460-*c.* 1520). Scottish poet. Said to have become a Franciscan and to have travelled in France, he returned to Scotland about 1500, and appears to have become prominent in the court of James IV. D. is generally accounted the greatest Scottish poet before Burns.

DUNBAR. Port and resort in Lothian region, Scotland. Cromwell won a victory over the Scots here in 1650. Pop. (1971) 4,000.

DUNBARTONSHIRE. Former co. of Scotland, bordering the N bank of the Clyde estuary, on which stand Dumbarton (the former co. town), Clydebank and Helensburgh. It was merged in 1975 in the region of Strathclyde.

DUNCAN, Isadora (1878-1927). American dancer. B. in San Francisco, she created a sensation by her lightly clad interpretations of Greek dances, reconstructed from vase paintings and other art relics. *My Life* (1928) is her autobiography.

DUNCAN-SANDYS, Duncan Edwin Sandys, baron (1908-). British Cons. politician. He held numerous ministerial posts, incl. Min. of Defence 1957-9, and of Aviation 1959-60, and as Sec. of State for Commonwealth Relations 1960-4, negotiated the agreement of 1963 on the Malaysian Federation. He was m. 1935-60 to Diana, dau. of Sir Winston Churchill, and was created a life peer 1974.

DUNDALK (dundawk'). Co. town and seaport in Louth, Rep. of Ireland at the mouth of the Castletown r. in D. Bay. Cattle and meat are exported, and there are clothing and engineering industries, and products also incl. shoes, electrical goods and tobacco Pop. (1971) 21,700.

DUNDA'S, Henry, 1st visct Melville (1742-1811). British Tory statesman. In 1791 he became Home Secretary, and carried through the prosecution of the English and Scottish reformers. After holding other high Cabinet posts, he was impeached in 1806 for corruption, and although acquitted on the main charge held no further office.

DUNDEE (dundē'). City and seaport of Scotland in Tayside, on the N side of the Firth of Tay. It is the chief centre of the British jute industry; other industries incl. shipbuilding, engineering, and watches and clocks; linen weaving and textile dyeing; canning of fruit and preserves such as marmalade, and confectionery. Fishing is carried on and D. is an important shipping and rail centre, which is sharing in the benefits of Scotland's oil discoveries. There is a univ. (1967: derived from Queen's Coll., founded 1881), an inst. of art and technology, and other notable buildings incl. the Albert Institute (1867) and Caird Hall. It is the admin. HQ of Tayside. Pop. (1971) 182,930.

DUNDEE, Visct. *See* CLAVERHOUSE.

DUNĒ'DIN. Port on Otago harbour, South Island, New Zealand, also a road, rail and air centre. There are engineering and textile industries, and Otago univ. was estab. 1869. The city itself was founded 1848 by members of the Free Church of Scotland. Pop. (1975) 120,900.

DUNFERMLINE (dumferm'lin). Industrial town nr the Firth of Forth in Fife region, Scotland, and incl. the naval base of Rosyth. Many Scottish kings, incl. Robert the Bruce, are buried in D. Abbey. Industries, incl. engineering, shipbuilding and textiles. Pop. (1971) 51,750.

DUNGENESS (dunjenes'). Accumulation of shingle and sand which has been built up (and still forms) by deposition and sea currents on the S coast of Kent, England. It has a lighthouse, bird sanctuary (1932) and a nuclear power station (1959).

DUNHAM, Katherine (1910-). American Negro dancer. B. in Chicago, she studied ethnology and dance at the univ. there and in 1938 went to the W Indies to study Negro dancing. In 1940 she began presenting her own dances, which portray ritualized emotion, and in 1945 she founded her own school and dance company.

DUNKIRK. Seaport of N France (Fr. Dunkerque) in Nord dept, on the Strait of Dover, to the N of Paris. Its harbour, greatly enlarged in 1975, is one of the most important in France, and canals link the town with the industrial centres of Nord and Pas-de-Calais and other regions of France, and with Belgium. Industries incl. oil refining, shipbuilding, and fishing; and textiles, machinery, and soap are manufactured. The town grew up round the church of St Éloi, founded in the 7th cent. During the F.W.W. the front was for most of the time close to D.; during the S.W.W. D. was the scene of one of the most momentous events in British history - the evacuation of the bulk of the BEF and a large number of French troops, 337,131 in all. The port was reopened to shipping in 1946, and Dunkirk gives its name to the 50-year Anglo-French treaty of 1947. Pop. (1975) 83,760.

DUNKIRK. Under a storm of shells and bombs the little ships came across the Channel to the rescue. The troops waited in orderly files for their embarkation.

DUN LAOGHAIRE (doon lā'reh). Port of Dublin, Rep. of Ireland, 10km (6m) SE of Dublin, known as Kingstown 1821-1922. It has sea services with Holyhead and Liverpool. Pop. (1971) 53,200.

DU'NLIN. A species of sandpiper (*Calidris alpina*) belonging to the snipe family (Charadriidae). Very common as a shore bird on all coasts of the the British Isles, it is about the size of a lark, and in summer is chestnut above, with a black patch on the breast.

DUNLOP, John Boyd (1840-1921). Scottish inventor. B. in Ayrshire, he practised as a veterinary surgeon in Belfast. To help his child win a tricycle race, he bound on rubber hose to the wheels and inflated it (1887). Later he took out a patent for pneumatic rubber tyres and was one of the founders of the D. Co. formed to market them.

DUNMOW (dun'mō). GREAT D. is an English market town on the Chelmer, Essex, on the site of a Roman station. LITTLE D., 3km (2m) away, is the scene of the annual D. Flitch trial. The ceremony, first held in 1244, consists of the presentation of a flitch of bacon to any married couple who 'will swear that they have not quarrelled nor repented of their marriage within a year and a day after its celebration'. Pop. Gt D. (1974) 4,000.

DUNNE, John William (1875-1949). British philosopher. In *An Experiment with Time* (1927) he developed *Serialism*, a theory framed to afford a rational explanation of phenomena ascribed to telepathy or clairvoyance. D.'s other important works incl. *The Serial Universe* (1934), *The New Immortality* (1938), and *Nothing Dies* (1940).

DUNS SCOTUS, John (*c.* 1265-*c.* 1308). Medieval scholastic philosopher, known as *doctor subtilis*. B. in Scotland, he became a Franciscan monk and was ordained in 1291. He studied and lectured at Oxford and Paris, and was later transferred to Cologne, where he d. D.S. wrote commentaries on the Bible and Aristotle, and is generally regarded as the leader of the Franciscan school which criticized the Aristotelianism of the Dominican, St Thomas Aquinas.

DUNSTABLE (dun'stabl). English town in SW Beds, 48km (30m) NW London. Whipsnade zoo is near. Printing, engineering, etc., are carried on. Pop. (1972) 32,000.

DUNSTABLE, John (?-1453). English composer. Little is known of his life, though he may have had some connection with St Albans Cathedral, and seems to have travelled widely on the Continent, achieving a reputation also as mathematician and astrologer. He had remarkable gifts of melodic invention.

DUNSTAN, St (*c.* 924-88). English prelate and statesman. B. near Glastonbury, the son of a West Saxon noble, he became a monk, and *c.* 945 was appointed abbot of Glastonbury. There he rebuilt the church and made the abbey a famous centre of education. Under Edred and Edgar he was chief minister, and in 959 he became bishop of London and in 961 archbishop of Canterbury.

DUODECIMAL SYSTEM. System of arithmetic notation using 12 as a base, superior to the decimal system in that 12 has a high divisibility (2, 3, 4, 6) and the gross (12 dozen) also has numerous divisors. D. societies exist for its promotion in the UK and US.

DUPARC (düpahrk') (**Marie Eugène**) **Henri** (**Fouques**) (1848-1933). French composer. B. in Paris, he studied under César Franck, and later helped to found the National Musical Society. His songs, though only 15 in number, are of great importance for their high intrinsic quality and their place in the history of French song-writing.

DU PRÉ (düprā'). Jacqueline (1945-). British cellist. One of the finest executants, she m. Daniel Barenboim (q.v.) in 1967, and worked with him in concerts as a duo and in a conductor-solist relationship until her career, except as a teacher, was ended by multiple sclerosis.

DURALUMIN. An aluminium base alloy containing copper, manganese, magnesium, silicon, and iron. Developed by a German engineer, Wilm, before the F.W.W., it possesses the remarkable property of 'age hardening', and is exclusively used in the rolled or forged condition.

DURAS (dürah'), **Marguerite** (1914-). French writer. Ed. at the Sorbonne, she graduated in law, and her works incl. short stories (*Des Journées entières dans les Arbres*), plays (*La Musica*), filmscripts (*Hiroshima Mon Amour*), and novels such as *Le Vice-Consul* (1966), evoking an existentialist world from the actual setting of Calcutta.

DURAZZO. Italian form of DÜRRES.

DURBAN. Principal port of Natal, S. Africa, and second port of the rep. Founded in 1824 as Port Natal, it was renamed in 1835 after General Sir Benjamin d'Urban (1777-1849), lieut.-governor of the eastern district of Cape Colony 1834-7. D.'s exports consist of coal, maize, wool, etc., whilst heavy machinery and mining equipment for the Rand is imported. It is also an important holiday resort. Natal univ. (1949) is divided between Durban and Pietermaritzburg. Pop. (1970) 874,000, incl. 244,000 whites.

DÜRER. A self-portrait painted in 1498 and now in the Prado. The artist notes his age at the time he carried out the work in the inscription under the window, and adds his characteristic initials. *Photo: The Mansell Collection.*

DÜRER, Albrecht (1471-1528). German engraver and painter. B. at Nuremberg, in 1486 he was apprenticed to Michael Wohlgemuth, a distinguished artist, and at the age of 13 he drew a portrait of himself from the mirror, the first self-portrait in the history of European art. After some years of travel, D. m. in 1494 Agnes Fey, whose portrait he drew many times. In 1494-5 he visited Venice. After his return to Nuremberg he executed a number of copperplates, and also his famous series of woodcuts of the 'Apocalypse'. His first important painting, 'The Adoration of the Magi', is dated 1504. In 1505 he went to

Venice again, where he painted 'The Feast of the Rosary' and 'The Martyrdom of St Bartholomew'. In 1512 he first became associated with the Emperor Maximilian I, for whom he did a great deal of work. In 1520 he travelled to the Netherlands, and became court painter to Charles V. He was a friend of Luther, and was greatly influenced by the Reformation. D.'s drawings and engravings are among the finest in the world.

DURGA (door'gah). Hindu goddess; one of the many names for Siva's wife.

DURHAM (dur'am), **John George Lambton,** 1st earl of (1792-1840). British statesman. He inherited a large estate while still a child, served in the army, became an MP in 1813, and in 1816 m. Lord Grey's dau. In 1828 he was created baron D. and in 1830 became Lord Privy Seal and drew up the Reform Bill. Ambassador to Russia in 1832, he became an earl in 1833; and in 1837 went to Canada as Gov.-Gen., to deal with the situation created by the rebellions. His arbitrary methods were disowned by the govt and he at once resigned. In 1839 he laid before parliament his *Report on the Affairs of British N. America,* which marks a turning-point in the history of the Empire; it advocated that the government of the colony should be entrusted to the colonists themselves, and that Upper and Lower Canada should be united as a first step towards a federation of the N American colonies.

DURHAM. Lord Durham by T. Phillips. *Photo: Courtesy of the National Portrait Gallery.*

DURHAM. Co. of NE England, facing the North Sea. To the W the land rises to the crest of the Pennines (q.v.), sheep being pastured on the hills, and to the E slopes down to a fertile coastal plain. D. lies on one of England's richest coalfields, Horden, Blackhall and Easington being further developed with grants from EEC, and Dawdon being one of Europe's most technically advanced pits. However, in the local govt re-organization of 1974, D. lost major industrial areas in the NE (the S bank of the Tyne estuary, with Gateshead, S Shields and Jarrow, and Sunderland on the Wear) to the new co. of Tyne and Wear, and in the SE (W Hartlepool and Stockton on Tees, on Tees Bay and the r. Tees) to the new co. of Cleveland. It retained Darlington, and in the SW gained a section of the former N Riding of Yorks. incl. Barnard Castle. The admin. HQ is Durham. Area 2,436 sq.km (6,309 sq.m); pop. (1978) 603,800.

DURHAM. City in co. D. (of which it is admin. HQ), England, on the Wear. D. was founded in 995 when a church was built on an eminence almost surrounded by the river; the Norman cathedral was built on the same site, and with later additions is one of England's finest ecclesiastical edifices. The remains of Bede, who d. at Jarrow, were transferred to D. Cathedral in 1370. On the same hill stands the castle, built by William I in 1072; the univ. was founded 1832, and reconstituted in 1963. Pop. (1972) 27,550.

DURHAM. The cathedral has one of the most beautiful sites in England. It was here that the monks of Lindisfarne brought the body of St Cuthbert in fear of Viking raids. *Photo: A.G.Hutchinson/Camera Press.*

DURKHEIM (dürkem'), **Émile** (1858-1917). French philosopher. Prof. of sociology at Paris from 1892, he maintained that human progress is mechanically determined, and stressed the importance of precision and scientific method in all social investigations.

DURRA (doo'ra) or **dourra.** Genus of grasses (*Sorghum*), also known as Indian millet, grown as cereals in parts of Asia, Africa, etc. *S. vulgare,* is the chief cereal of many parts of Africa.

DU'RRELL, Lawrence George (1912–). English poet and novelist. B. in India, he was for a time in the Foreign Service, and has lived mostly in the E Mediterranean countries about which he writes. His verse incl. *A Private*

Country (1943), *Cities, Plains and People* (1946), and *On Seeming to Presume* (1948); and his tetralogy *Justine, Balthazar, Mountolive* and *Clea* (1957-60) made him one of England's leading novelists: on the Continent his reputation stands even higher. His brother, **Gerald Malcolm D.** (1925-) is a zoologist and writer and runs the Jersey Zoological Park.

DÜ'RRENMATT, Friedrich (1921-). Swiss dramatist. The son of a Protestant pastor, he writes in German, and takes crime and violence as the mainstay of his grotesquely farcical tragedies. These incl. *The Visit* in which a millionairess corrupts a village by bribing the people to avenge her grudge against a girlhood lover, and *The Physicists* (1962), dealing with 3 normal nuclear physicists who take refuge from mad reality in a Swiss asylum.

DURRES (doo'rās). Chief port of Albania, cap. of D. district, chief commercial and communications centre of the country with flour mills, soap and cigarette factories, distilleries and an electronics plant. It is 32km (20m) W of Tirana. Pop. (1970) 53,000.

DUSE (doo'se), **Eleonora** (1859-1924). Italian actress. B. in Lombardy, she began acting at the age of 4, and when 14 played Juliet in Verona. In 1879 her success in Zola's *Thérèse Raquin* led to her engagement as leading lady in Cesare Rossi's company. She estab. a reputation as one of the greatest actresses of all time. Her association with D'Annunzio began in 1897, and is recorded in his novel *Il Fuoco* (*The Flame of Life*). He wrote *La Gioconda* for her.

DUSHANBE (dooshan'bā). Cap. of Tadzhik SSR, USSR, c. 160km (100m) N of the Afghan frontier and 320km (200m) S of Tashkent. An important road, rail and air centre, D. has cotton mills, tanneries, meat-packing factories, printing works, etc., and is the seat of Tadzhik state univ. Developed as Stalinabad from 1929 on the site of the ancient village of D., it reverted to its old name in 1961. Pop. (1972) 400,000.

DÜ'SSELDORF. Industrial city of W Germany on the right bank of the Rhine, 26 km (16 m) NW of Cologne, cap. of N Rhine-Westphalia. It is a great river port, and the commercial and financial centre of the Ruhr area, with large exhibition facilities. There are food processing, brewing, agricultural machiney, textile and chemical industries. It is also a university city. Pop. (1978) 607,500.

DUSTBOWL. Name given to a large area in the USA covering western Kansas, and parts ('pan-handles') of Oklahoma and Texas which lie just to the S. It is swept by winds from N to S. The native grasses which formerly covered it and held down the soil were removed to make way for wheat-farming, and during the drought years of 1934-7 hundreds of tons of loose topsoil were blown away into the Gulf of Mexico. Many of the farmers abandoned their worthless farms and migrated westward (as described in Steinbeck's novel *Grapes of Wrath*). By planting trees as windbreaks and re-introducing suitable grasses, etc., much of the area has been rehabilitated.

DUTCH ART, LANGUAGE, LITERATURE. *See* under NETHERLANDS.

DUTCH EAST INDIES. *See* INDONESIA.

DUTCH GUIANA. *See* SURINAM.

DUVAL (düvahl'), **Claude** (1643-70). English highwayman. B. in Normandy, he came to England at the Restoration as a valet, but turned highwayman, and his gallantry was as famous as his robberies. He was hanged at Tyburn.

DUVALIER (düvahlyeh'), **Jean Claude** (1951-). Haitian statesman. His father François Duvalier (1907-71), known as 'Papa Doc', became pres. of Haiti in 1957 and ruled till his death with the aid of a private army of Tontons Macoute 'bogeymen'. Under Jean Claude, who succeeded his father in the presidency, and is known as 'Baby Doc', were replaced, as presidential bodyguard, by the less aggressive Les Léopards, trained by American veterans, and the modernization of Haiti by agricultural and industrial development was speeded. In 1973 he held the first elections since 1961, and in 1979 allowed the formation of other political parties. Censorship remained strict.

DUVE (düv), **Christian de** (1917-). French scientist, working with Albert Claude and George Emil Palade (with whom he shared a Nobel medicine prize in 1974), on the structural and functional organization of the cell, he collaborated in the creation of a new discipline - cell biology.

DUVIVIER (düvivyeh'), **Julien** (1896-). French film director, of such French classics as *Poil de Carotte, Un Carnet de Bal, La Fin du Jour* (1938).

DVINSK. Russian name of DAUGAVPILS.

DVOŘÁK (dvor'zhahk), **Antonin** (1841-1904). Czech composer. B. near Prague, the son of a butcher, he early showed a talent for music, and in 1857 went to Prague. There he entered an organ school and supported himself by playing the viola in cafés, etc. In 1862 he joined the orchestra of the Prague National Theatre, later gained an appointment as a church organist, and also taught. A patriotic hymn for chorus and orchestra gained him popularity in 1872, and in 1875 an annual allowance from the Austrian govt gave him financial independence. His series of Slavonic dances (1877) were a further success, and his *Stabat Mater* was performed by the London Musical Society in 1883. In 1892-5 he was director of the National Conservatory in New York. His interest in Negro music is evident in the *New World Symphony* (1893) and such works as the *American Quartet.* In 1895 he returned to Prague, where he later became head of the Conservatoire. D. wrote 9 operas, incl. *The Water Nymph* (*Rusalka*); large-scale choral works, the *Carnival* and other overtures, violin and 'cello concertos, chamber music, piano pieces, songs, etc.

DYE. Substance which, applied in solution to fabrics, imparts a colour resistant to washing. Direct Ds. combine with the material of the fabric, yielding a coloured compound; indirect Ds. require the presence of another substance (a mordant), with which the fabric must first be treated, and which will cause precipitation of the coloured compound in the fibres; vat Ds. are usually colourless soluble substances which on oxidation by exposure to air yield an insoluble coloured compound.

Naturally occurring Ds. incl. indigo, madder (alizarin), logwood and cochineal, but industrial Ds. are usually synthetic, and are classified according to the substances from which they are produced, or the characteristic chemical groupings in the molecules, e.g. the azo-dyestuffs, acridine, anthracene and aniline. Colour can now be diagnosed by photo-electric instruments which measure the red, blue and green contents: the recipe for producing it can then be calculated exactly by a computer.

DYFED (duv'ed). Co. of Wales formed in 1974 by the merging of Cardigan, Carmarthen and Pembroke (qq.v.).

DVOŘÁK. Always open to new influences, the composer delighted in the variety of his works, and his prolific output. *Photo: Courtesy of the Royal College of Music.*

The admin. HQ is Carmarthen. Area 5,767 sq.km (2,227 sq.m); pop. (1978) 323,000.

DYLAN (di'lahn), **Bob** (1941-). American singer. He exercised an enormous influence on pop music in the 1960s with songs typical of the social chaos of modern USA, e.g. 'The Times They Are A-Changin' and 'A Hard Rain's A-Gonna Fall'. His album 'Slow Train Coming' (1979) marked his conversion to Christianity.

DYNAMICS. The branch of mechanics that deals with the mathematical and physical study of the behaviour of bodies under the action of forces which produce changes of motion in them.

DYNAMITE. A high explosive consisting of a mixture of nitroglycerine and kieselguhr; it was first devised by Alfred Nobel (q.v.).

DYNAMO (dī'namo), also called generator. A machine for transforming mechanical energy into electrical energy. Present-day Ds. work on the principles described by Faraday in 1830, that an electromotive force (e.m.f.) is developed in a conductor when it is passed through a magnetic field. A simple form of D. consists of a powerful field magnet, between the poles of which a suitable conductor, usually in the form of a coil (armature), is rotated. The mechanical energy of rotation is thus converted into an electric current in the armature.

DYNE (dīn). Symbol dyn. In physics, the absolute unit of force in the centimetre-gramme-second (c.g.s.) system; it is defined as the force which produces an acceleration of one centimetre per second per second in a mass of one gram. In SI units 1 dyne = 10^{-5} newton. *See* NEWTON.

DYSENTERY (dis'enteri'). Infective ulceration of the large bowel, causing copious passage of blood and mucus (the 'bloody flux'). It may be due to *Entamoeba histolytica* (amoebic dysentery); a dysentery bacillus, especially *B. dysenteriae Shiga*; or a variety of intestinal worms.

DYSLEXIA (dislek'sia). A malfunction in the brain's synthesis and interpretation of sensory information (Gk bad, pertaining to words), popularly 'word blindness'. It results in poor ability to read and write, though the child may otherwise excel, e.g. in mathematics. A similar disability with figures is called discalculus.

DYSPEPSIA (dispeps'ia). Disturbance of digestion. Of the numerous possible causes the chief are a faulty diet, excessive drinking or smoking, nervous disorder, general lack of tone with sagging of the stomach (visceroptosis), chronic inflammation of the stomach lining (gastritis), and cancer of the stomach.

DYSPROSIUM (disprō'zium). One of the yttrium group of rare earths (symbol Dy, at. no. 66, at. wt. 162.51) discovered in 1886 by Lecoq de Boisbaudran. One of the lanthanide group, it is used in nuclear reactors and laser material.

DZERZHINSK (djerzhinsk'). Town in central RSFSR, USSR, on the Oka r., 32km (20m) W of Gorki. There are engineering, chemical and timber industries. Pop. (1977) 248,000.

DZHAMBU'L. Town in Kazakhstan, USSR, in a fruit-growing area. Industries incl. fruit canning and sugar refining, and phosphate fertilizers. Pop. (1977) 240,000.

DZUNGARIAN (dzōōngah'rēahn) **GATES.** Ancient route in central Asia on the border of Kazakh SSR (USSR) and Xinjiang Uygur region (China), 470km (290m) NW of Urümqi. Long abandoned, since the Mongol hordes passed through on their way to Europe, it has potential as a road/rail route.

E

The second vowel and fifth and most often used letter of our alphabet. In Lloyd's Register of Shipping it formerly represented a 2nd-class rating.

EAGLE. Name given to a number of genera of large birds of prey of the family Falconidae. The typical genus *Aquila* includes the golden E. (*A. chrysaëtos*). It has a 2m (6ft) wing-span and is dark brown; in Britain it is now confined to the highlands of Scotland. The larger spotted E. (*A. clanga*), of Central Europe and Asia, is a very rare visitor to Britain.

The sea Es. (*Haliaëtus*) incl. the white-tailed sea E. (*H. albicilla*) which is now only an irregular visitor to Britain; mainly a carrion-feeder, it breeds on sea cliffs. The American white-headed sea E. or bald E. (*H. leucocephalus*) is the symbol of the USA; rendered infertile through the ingestion of agricultural chemicals, it is rapidly becoming extinct.

The E. was anciently regarded as sacred to Zeus, and the bearer of his thunderbolts. It was the standard of the Roman legions, and hence was adopted as an imperial symbol by the Russian, German, and Austrian empires, and also by Napoleon.

EAGLE. Neither Benjamin Franklin nor Audubon, whose dramatic rendering of the bird is seen above, thought the bald eagle a suitable national symbol for the USA. It will allow itself to be chased by the much smaller kingbird, and often scavenges its prey.

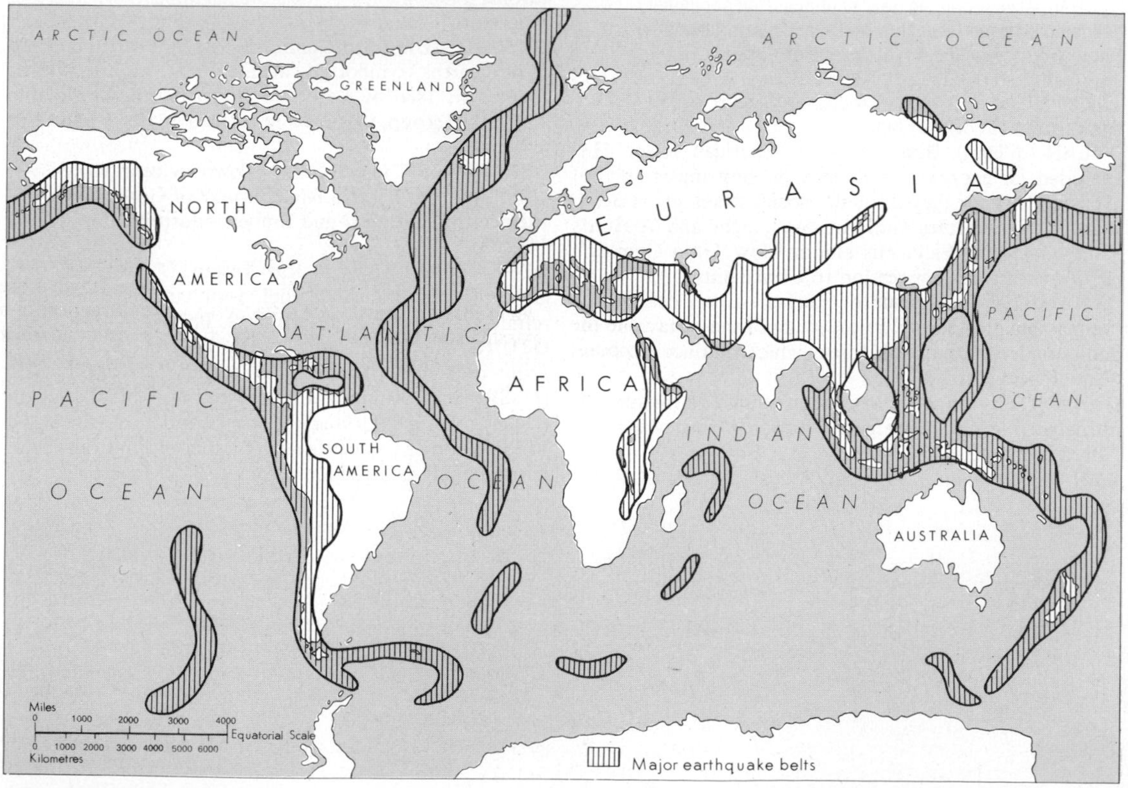

ARCTIC OCEAN
GREENLAND
ARCTIC OCEAN
NORTH AMERICA
EURASIA
ATLANTIC OCEAN
PACIFIC OCEAN
AFRICA
PACIFIC OCEAN
SOUTH AMERICA
INDIAN OCEAN
AUSTRALIA
Miles 0 1000 2000 3000 4000
0 1000 2000 3000 4000 5000 6000 Kilometres
Equatorial Scale
Major earthquake belts

EARTHQUAKE. The world's major earthquake belts.

EALING. Residential district, bor. of Greater London, England. The first British sound-film studio was built here in 1931, and 'E. comedies' became a noted genre in British film-making. The Questors, an amateur drama co. founded 1925, has a world-wide reputation: the present theatre dates from 1964. Pop. (1973) 300,000.

EARTH. Most of Africa and portions of Europe and Asia can be seen in this photograph taken from the Apollo 11 spacecraft. Astronauts Neil Armstrong, Edward Aldrin and Michael Collins were 170,000 km from Earth when this shot was obtained. *Photo: Courtesy of USIS.*

EANES (ā-ah'nesh), **Antonio dos Santos Ramalho** (1935-). Portuguese statesman. A close friend of Spinola, he helped plan the 1974 coup, and as Army Chief of Staff put down the left-wing revolt of Nov. 1975. In 1976 he became president; re-elected 1980.

EAR. The organ of hearing. The external ear (pinna) is a funnel to collect sound. From it a short tunnel leads to the middle ear (tympanum), a small cavity in the temporal bone from which the Eustachian tube runs to the back of the nose, connecting it with the outside air. The tough membrane of the ear-drum completely separates the middle from the outer ear; it vibrates when struck by sound waves, and nerves convey the impressions to the brain.

EARHART, Amelia (1898-1937). American airwoman. B. in Kansas, she was the first woman to fly the Atlantic - in 1928, as a passenger from Newfoundland to Burry Port, Wales; also the first woman to fly the Atlantic alone, in 1932 from Harbour Grace to Londonderry, in 15hrs 18min. While making a Pacific flight in July 1937 she disappeared without trace. She was the wife of G. P. Putnam, American publisher.

EARL. In the British peerage, the third title in order of rank, coming between marquess and viscount; it is the oldest of British titles, being of Scandinavian origin. The premier earldom is Arundel, now united with the dukedom of Norfolk. An earl's wife is a countess.

EARL MARSHAL. In England, the 8th of the great Officers of State; the office has been hereditary since 1672 in the family of Howard, the dukes of Norfolk. The E.M. is head of the College of Arms, and arranges State processions and ceremonies.

EARLY ENGLISH. In architecture, name given by Thomas Rickman (1776-1841) to the first of the 3 periods of English Gothic. It covers the period from about 1189 to about 1280, and is characterized by lancet-windows without mullions, often grouped in threes, fives, or sevens; the pointed arch; pillars of stone centres surrounded by shafts of black Purbeck marble; dog-tooth ornament, etc. Salisbury cathedral is almost entirely Early English.

EARTH. The planet on which we live: it is the third planet outward from the Sun, lying with its satellite, the Moon, between Venus and Mars. Its path round the Sun, i.e. that of its revolution, is an ellipse of which one focus is formed by the Sun. The mean distance of E. from the Sun is *c.* 149.5 million km (93 million miles). The plane of its orbit is called the ecliptic, and it is inclined to Earth's equatorial plane at an angle of 23½°; it is this inclination that is responsible for the phenomena of the seasons. The E., moving at an average speed of 30km (18.5m) a second, makes a complete circuit in the solar year, which measures 365 days 5hr 48min 46sec. It has also a daily movement, rotating about its own axis in 23hr 56min 4.1sec, which is responsible for day and night. By using atomic clocks it has been possible to prove that E.'s rate of rotation is slowing down.

The E. is an oblate spheroid or, taking into account an 18 metre rise at the N Pole and a 26 metre depression at the S Pole, 'pear-shaped'. The equatorial diameter is 12,756 km (7,926.5 m) and the polar diameter 12,713 km (7,900 m); its equatorial circumference is 40,076 km (24,902 m) and its polar circumference 40,009 km (24,860 m). The land surface is *c.* 150 million sq. km (57.5 million sq. m) and the sea floor covers *c.* 361 million sq. km (139.4 million sq. m), or over 70%. The greatest known height is Mount Everest (q.v.), and the greatest oceanic depth is 11,034 m (36,198 ft) in the Mariana Trench off Guam in the Pacific.

The origin of E. is disputed, one theory being that it may have been formed from a swarm of meteorites which arose when matter, drawn from the Sun by the attraction of a passing star, condensed. It is thought to consist of an inner core *c.* 1,300 km (800 m) from the centre, which is possibly solid iron and nickel; an outer core *c.* 2,250 km (1,400 m) thick, which is possibly molten iron and nickel; and a mantle of solid rock *c.* 2,900 km (1,800 m) thick, separated from the outer crust by the Mohorovicić Discontinuity which modifies the speed of earthquake waves. This outer crust varies in thickness, being 5-8km/3-5m thick beneath certain points in the oceans, and *c.* 32km/20m thick beneath the continents. It is not, as formerly thought, in one piece, but composed of about half a dozen 'plates' on top of which the continents (q.v.) slowly drift. Judged by analysis of radioactive materials within it, it was formed about 2,800 million years ago, E. itself having originated *c.* 4,500 million years ago. Fresh material from within E.'s mantle is still attaching itself to the crustal plates, as from the Mid-Atlantic Rift.

EARTHQUAKE. A shaking or convulsion of the Earth's surface, the scientific study of which is called seismology. Most Es. are due to sudden earth movements, generally along faults (fractures or breaks) in the strata - these

ATMOSPHERE

Earth

EARTH. The structure of the Earth: the atmosphere above its surface (left) and the levels of the sea (right).

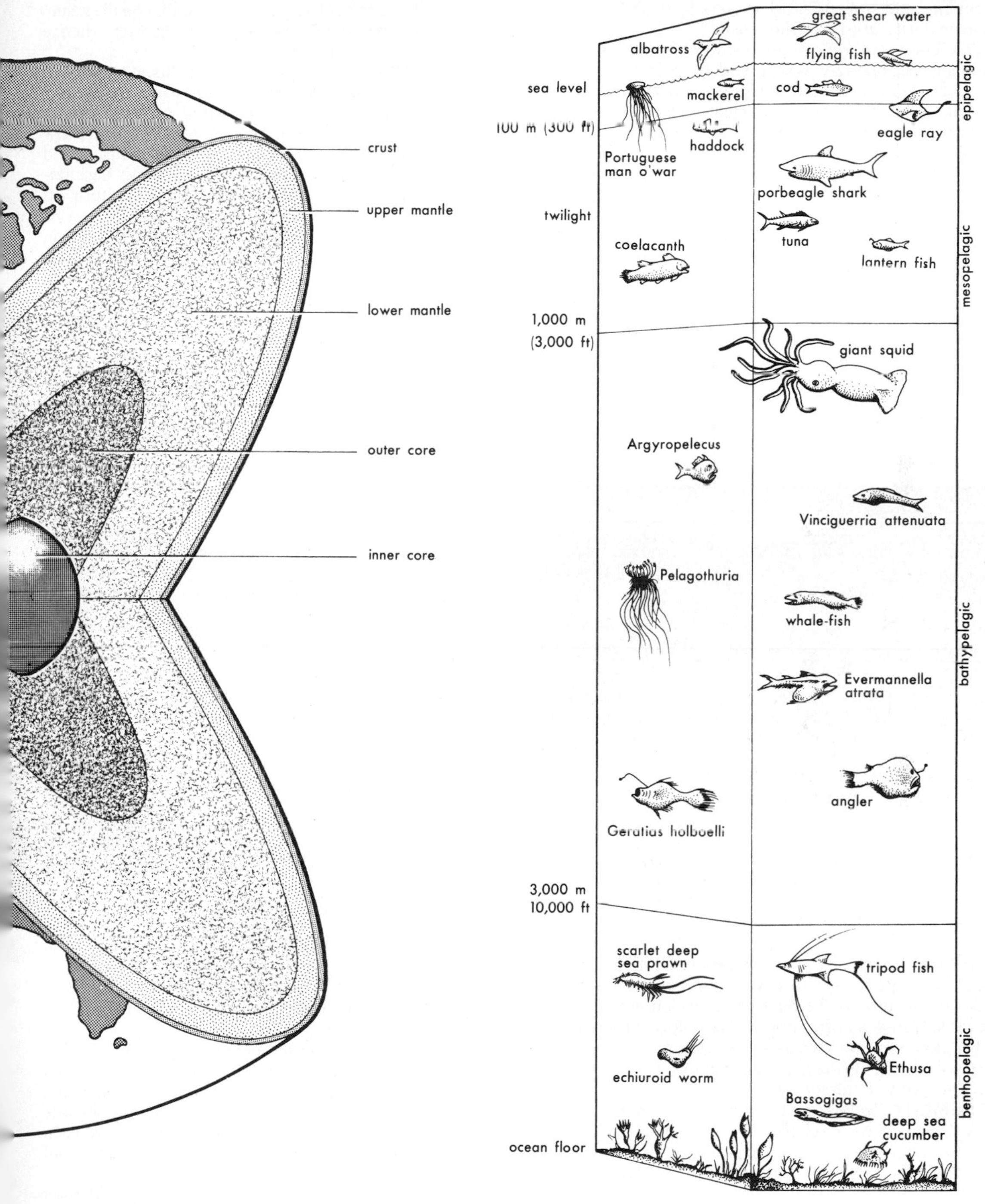
crust
upper mantle
lower mantle
outer core
inner core
OCEAN
zones
sea level
100 m (300 ft)
twilight
1,000 m
(3,000 ft)
3,000 m
10,000 ft
ocean floor
albatross
great shear water
flying fish
mackerel
cod
eagle ray
haddock
Portuguese man o'war
porbeagle shark
coelacanth
tuna
lantern fish
giant squid
Argyropelecus
Vinciguerria attenuata
Pelagothuria
whale-fish
Evermannella atrata
angler
Geratias holboelli
scarlet deep sea prawn
tripod fish
echiuroid worm
Ethusa
Bassogigas
deep sea cucumber
epipelagic
mesopelagic
bathypelagic
benthopelagic

tectonic Es. are the greatest and most widespread in their effects. Es. of one kind or another are constantly occurring, and severe Es. occur every fortnight or so. The great majority are in marine areas.

Prediction is to some extent possible by measurement of underground pressure waves, and there is the eventual prospect of prevention in pressure zones within reach of drilling technology. Rock slippage might be slowed at 'movement' points, or promoted at 'stoppage' points by the extraction or injection of huge quantities of water underground, which serves as a lubricant. This would ease overall pressure. *See* RICHTER, C.F.

EARTHWORMS. Name given to those members of the Oligochaeta which are mainly terrestrial in their habits. Es. are hermaphrodite, and deposit their eggs in cocoons. They live by burrowing in the soil, feeding on the organic matter it contains. They play a most important role in the formation of humus, by irrigating the soil, and levelling it by transferring earth from the deeper levels to the surface as castings. The common British Es. belong to the genera *Lumbricus* and *Allolobophora.* These are comparatively small, but some tropical forms reach over a metre (3ft) and *Megascolides australis*, of Queensland, over 3m (11ft).

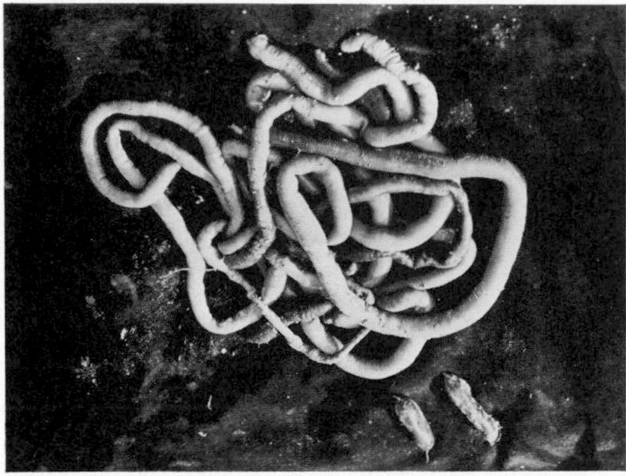

EARTHWORM. The giant earthworm *(Megascolides australis)* is unique to the wet river slopes of Southern Gippsland, Victoria, Australia. It may reach 3.6 m (12 ft). Several are seen here, with two eggs below the writhing heap. *Photo: Courtesy of the Australian Information Service.*

EARWIG. Insects, forming the family Forficulidae and order Dermaptera. The fore-wings are short and leathery, and serve to protect the hind-wings, which are large and are folded fan-wise when at rest. The family is represented in Britain by several species. It feeds at night on the tender parts of plants, flowers, etc., and also on other insects, dead or living. It rarely flies.

EASEMENT. In law, a class of rights which a person or persons may have over the land of another. The commonest example is a right of way; others are rights to bring water over another's land, and to prevent building so as to exclude light from existing windows.

EAST. Point of the compass indicating that part of the horizon where the Sun rises, i.e. when facing N, E. is to the right. The E. has held an important place in various religions; ancient pagan temples had their altars at the E. end, a practice bound up with sun-cult and sacrifices made facing the rising sun. In the 2nd cent. it became customary for Christians to worship facing the E., and also to bury the dead with their feet towards the E., so that on the resurrection-morn they would be facing the quarter whence Christ was to come in glory.

EAST AFRICA. For countries within this area, see the Africa table. The *East African Community* (1967) superseded earlier organizations for shared services among Kenya, Tanzania and Uganda - communications, coordination of commerce and industry and industry and finance, etc. It was dissolved 1977, following Uganda-Tanzania tension from 1971, but Obote's return to Uganda led to reconciliation in 1981.

EAST ANGLIA. District of E England, formerly a Saxon kingdom, roughly corresponding to Norfolk and Suffolk. Once almost isolated by fens and woods, E.A. remains a specialized region. The Univ. of E.A. was founded at Norwich in 1962, and the Sainsbury Centre for the Visual Arts (1978) has a collection of primitive art and sculpture.

EASTBOURNE. English seaside resort in Sussex, 103km (64m) SSE of London. The old town lies about a mile inland; the modern town extends along the coast for 5km (3m), with a pier and fine marine parades; its development, as a model of town planning, was largely due to the 7th duke of Devonshire. At E. the South Downs terminate in Beachy Head (q.v.). Pop. (1973) 71,850.

EASTER. Feast of the Christian Church, commemorating the Resurrection of Christ. Its English name is derived from Eostre, a goddess of Spring honoured by the pagan Anglo-Saxons during April. The festival grew out of the early Christians' observance of the Jewish Passover, and from very early times there has been considerable variation in the date of the annual celebration. By an Act of Parliament passed in 1752 Easter Day is the first Sunday after the full moon which happens upon or next after March 21, and if the full moon happens upon a Sunday then Easter Day is the Sunday following. Yet the full moon referred to is not the real moon, but a hypothetical one, and tables are given in the Book of Common Prayer for determining Easter in any given year. Easter may fall on one of 35 days from 22 March to 25 April, and several attempts have been made (e.g. in 1928) to avoid the inconvenience of a movable feast by establishing a fixed Easter. So far, however, ecclesiastical influence has told against it.

E. has been from ancient times the most important feast in the Christian year. Many popular customs, which probably go back to pagan times, are also associated with it throughout Europe, e.g. the giving of E. eggs. Eggs are a symbol of life and fertility, and the breaking of the chicken through the shell was taken as symbolical of Christ's resurrection.

EASTER. Island, *c.* 166 sq.km (64 sq.m), in the S Pacific Ocean, about 5,960 km (2,300 m) W of Chile, to which country it belongs. It was discovered on Easter Sunday, 1722, and is famous for its huge carved statues and stone houses, the work of neolithic peoples who may have been of South American origin. Pop. (1970) 1,000, nearly all Polynesians.

EASTERN ORTHODOX CHURCH. The Christian Church of many nations inhabiting the eastern part of Europe and the N and W of Asia, including Greeks, Russians, Romanians, Serbians, Bulgarians, Georgians, and Albanians; in the last 200 years it has spread into China, Korea, Japan, and Alaska, as well as among the

EASTER ISLAND. The giant figures, raised on stepped ceremonial platforms of beautifully carved and fitted stone masonry, look out to sea. *Photo: Mireille Vautier.*

tribes of Siberia and central Asia. Today it is a federation of self-governing Churches, some of which were founded by the Apostles and their disciples, which conduct services in their own language, and follow their own customs and traditions, but are in full communion with one another. The senior church of Eastern Christendom is that of Constantinople, whose chief bishop bears the title of oecumenical patriarch, and has primacy of honour.

The Church's teaching is based on the Bible; and the Nicene-Constantinopolitan Creed (325-81) is the only confession of faith used. The centre of Eastern worship is the Eucharist, celebrated with little change since the 6th cent. The ritual is elaborate, and accompanied by singing in which both men and women take part, but no instrumental music is used. Besides the seven sacraments the prayer book contains many other services for daily life. There is an impressive marriage service during which the bride and groom are crowned. There are many monasteries, the most famous being Mt Athos in Greece, which has flourished since the 10th cent. During the last century contacts between Eastern and Anglican Christians have become more frequent, and several societies have been started for its promotion, e.g. the Fellowship of St Alban and St Sergius.

EAST INDIA COMPANY. An English commercial company that was chartered by Queen Elizabeth I in 1600 and given the monopoly of trade between England and the E. In the 18th cent. it became in effect the ruler of a large part of India, and a form of dual control by the Company and a committee responsible to Parliament in London was introduced by Pitt's India Act, 1784; following the Indian Mutiny in 1857, the Crown took complete control of the govt of British India, and the India Act of 1858 abolished the Company.

EAST KILBRIDE. Old village in Strathclyde, Scotland, 11km (6m) SE of Glasgow, for which it was developed as a 'new town' from 1947 to take overspill. There are varied light industries and some engineering, incl. jet engines. Pop. (1975) 70,000.

EAST LONDON. Port and resort on the SE coast of Cape Province, S Africa. It has a good harbour, is the terminus of a railway from the interior, and is a leading wool-exporting port. Pop. (1970) 136,780.

EAST LOTHIAN. South-eastern co. of Scotland, merged with West Lothian and Midlothian in 1975 in the new region of Lothian. Haddington was the co. town.

EAST RIVER. Tidal strait (26km/16m long) between Manhattan and the Bronx, and Long Island. It links Long Island Sound with NY Bay, and is also connected via the Harlem r. with the Hudson. There are both commercial and naval docks, and most famous of many bridges is the Brooklyn.

EAST SIBERIAN SEA. Part of the Arctic Ocean, off the N coast of USSR, between the New Siberian Is. and Chukchi Sea.

EASTWOOD, Clint (1930-). American film actor. As the 'man with no name' caught up in gang warfare in *A Fistful of Dollars,* he started the vogue for 'spaghetti westerns'.

EAU DE COLOGNE (ō de kolōn'). A refreshing perfume whose invention is ascribed to Giovanni Maria Farina (1685-1766) who moved from Italy to Cologne in 1709, and there manufactured the perfume.

EBBW (e'boo) **VALE.** Industrial town in Gwent, Wales. Iron and steelmaking ended in the 1970s, but tin-plate manufacture continues. Aneurin Bevan (q.v.) was MP for E.V. 1929-60. Pop. (1972) 25,710.

E'BONITE. A dark brown, horny substance produced by the prolonged heating of rubber with approx. half its weight of sulphur. It is mainly used as an electrical insulator.

E'BONY. Hardwood, obtained from trees of the genus *Diospyros* of the family Ebenaceae found in the tropics. It is very heavy, hard and black; takes a fine polish; and is used in cabinet-making, inlaying, and also for piano-keys, knife-handles, etc.

EBO'RACUM. Roman name for YORK. The archbp of York subscribes himself 'Ebor'.

E'BRŌ. River in NE Spain, which rises in the Cantabrian Mts. and flows SE, some 800km (500m) SE to the Mediterranean, 130km (80m) SW of Barcelona. Saragossa is on its course, and ocean-going ships can penetrate as far as Tortosa, 35km (22m) from its mouth. It is a major source of hydro-electric power.

During the Spanish Civil War the Nationalist forces were held up by the Republicans along the Ebro July-Nov. 1938, before their final offensives which ended the war in March 1939.

ECCLES, Sir John Carew (1903-). Australian physiologist. A student of Sir Charles Sherrington (q.v.) he worked at Oxford until 1937, and was prof. of physiology at the Australian Nat. Univ., Canberra, from 1951-66, when he undertook research in Chicago for the American Medical Assocn. For his research on conduction in the central nervous system he was elected FRS in 1941, and in 1963 shared the Nobel prize (with Hodgkin, q.v., and Huxley) for physiology and medicine.

ECCLES (ekelz). Town in Greater Manchester, England, 8km (5m) W of Manchester, on the Irwell and Manchester Ship Canal. Industries incl. cotton textiles, machinery, and pharmaceuticals, and Manchester's airport is here. Eccles cakes are rounded pastries with a fruit mixture filling. Pop. (1974) 37,400.

ECHEGARAY (āchāgahrah'-i), **José** (1832-1916). Spanish dramatist. B. at Madrid, he became an engineer and professor of mathematics, and later was a cabinet minister, but is chiefly remembered as a playwright. He wrote some 60 dramas, the best of them being *O locura o santidad* (1877) and *El gran galeoto* (1881), and received the Nobel prize in 1904.

ECHIDNA (ekid'na) or **spiny ant-eater.** Name given to a family comprising 2 genera of mammals, in the order Monotremata, found in Australia and New Guinea. They slightly resemble the hedgehog, are terrestrial in their habits, and subsist entirely upon ants, which they dig out by their powerful claws and lick up by their prehensile tongue. When attacked Es. roll themselves into a ball, or try to hide by burrowing in the sand.

ECHIDNA. The echidna *(Tachyglossus aculeatus)* uses its long, sticky tongue to lick up ants and termites. At certain times of the year, it sometimes invades Australian towns and cities, and flourishes in an urban environment. *Photo: Courtesy of the Australian Information Service.*

ECHINODERMA or **echinoderms** (eki'no-). One of the great phyla of the animal kingdon, divided into 5 main classes typified by the sea urchins (Echinoid), the starfish (Asteroid), the brittle star (Ophiuroid), the feather-star or sea-lily (Crinoid), and the sea-cucumber (Holothuroid). They are exclusively marine animals, and most of them have a body covered with knobs or spines (echinoderma - Gk for 'prickle-skinned') and small stalked out-growths which normally keep them fixed to the sea bottom.

ECKHART (*c.* 1260-1327). German mystic, called Meister E. B. near Gotha, he became a Dominican, was provincial of the order for Saxony 1304-11, taught in Paris, Strasbourg, and Cologne, where in 1326 he was accused of heresy; in 1329 a number of his doctrines were condemned.

ECLIPSE (ĕklips'). Es. are of 2 kinds: solar and lunar. A solar E. occurs when the Moon passes in front of the Sun, and conceals it either totally or partially; during a total E. the Sun's outer atmosphere (the corona) is visible to the naked eye. The next British total E. will take place in 1999. A lunar E. occurs when the Moon passes into the shadow of the Earth; direct sunlight is then cut off from the Moon's surface, and the Moon becomes dim until emerging from the shadow. Lunar Es. may be either total or partial.

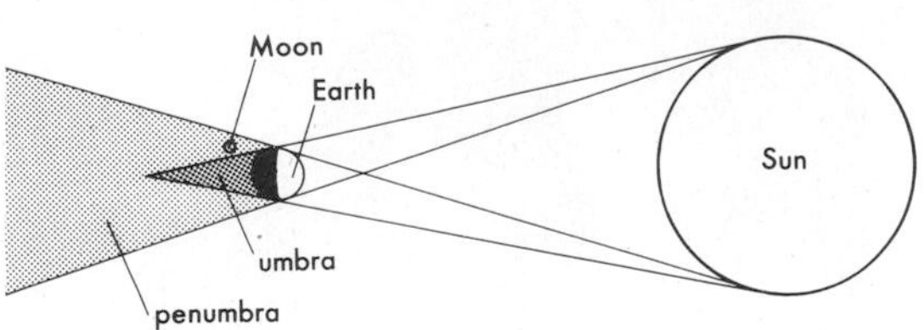

ECLIPSE. In an eclipse of the Moon, the Earth moves between the Sun and the Moon, obscuring its satellite at the apex of the umbra, or region of total darkness. The penumbra is the area in partial darkness surrounding the umbra.

ECLIPSE. A total eclipse in 1976 brings midnight darkness to Melbourne at half-past four in the afternoon. Animals in the zoo panicked, and even human observers found the experience eery. *Photo: Fred Adler/Camera Press.*

ĒCO'LOGY. The study of living organisms as they exist in their natural habitats. The term was first introduced by the German biologist, Ernst Haeckel, in 1866, but it did not come into general use until the present cent. The field of E. embraces all living organisms, and therefore the human race; but in the latter case it merges with sociology, etc. An **ecosystem** is the live interaction between a 'community' of plants and animals and its environment.

ECONOME'TRICS. In economics, the use of mathematical and statistical approaches to its problems.

ECONOMICS. The scientific study (formerly known as 'political economy') of the production, distribution and exchange of 'wealth' - anything and everything conducive to material welfare. Notable economists incl. Adam Smith, Ricardo, Malthus, J. S. Mill, Marx, W. S. Jevons, J. M. Keynes, F. von Hayek, Wassily Leontief, and Milton Friedman (qq.v.). The chief point in dispute in modern times is the respective spheres of state and private enterprise.

In the W the private enterprise system has often been considerably modified, e.g. the nationalization measures of Britain's Labour govts. In the E the Stalinist command economy has also been modified. Poland, Romania, E Germany and the Soviet Union have adopted a system allowing enterprises some freedom to make decisions within the plan's framework and award workers bonuses from profits. In Hungary enterprises are free to vary their prices and dispose of their own profits within wider limits, and in Yugoslavia ownership is vested in the workers' collectives, but market considerations largely govern the economy.

The respective spheres of state and private enterprise, long a theoretically contested area in the West, became an urgently practical problem in the period of world inflation and recession which developed in the mid-1970s. The concept of monetarism (q.v.) was hotly discussed, and the 'science' of econometrics (the mathematical treatment of E.) first estab. by Ragnar Frisch (q.v.) in the 1930s, was developed both in the Communist and non-Communist world: see KANTOROVICH, Leonid.

ECUADOR (ek'wador). A republic of S America, situated on the W coast, across the equator (from which it derives its name), and bounded by Colombia and Peru.

E. falls into 4 zones: (1) The Andean region or Sierra, formed by the Eastern and the Western Cordillera (the highest mountain is Chimborazo, 6,266 m/20,561 ft), with the inter-Andean valleys; this district supplies the principal agricultural produce for home consumption, wheat, maize, potatoes, etc. (2) The tropical coastal region, producing coffee, cocoa, sugar and bananas for export. (3) The Oriente, stretching E from the Andes to the Amazon basin, has valuable unexploited timber in its great forests. There are also oil resources here, and discoveries of oil and natural gas nr the Peruvian border may make E. a major oil producing state. (4) The Archipelago of Colon (Galapagos Is., q.v.). The chief river is the Guayas. Quito is the cap.; Guayaquil, linked by road and rail with Quito, is the chief port and largest town; others are Portoviejo, Ambato and Cuenca.

Still predominantly agricultural, E. had a growing industrial output in the 1960s and 1970s, incl. textiles, electrical goods, pharmaceuticals and cement. Shrimps and fish products are exported, espec. to the USA. Besides oil there is coal, copper, iron, lead and sulphur. Area (govt est.) 301,150 sq.km (116,270 sq.m); in 1942 E. ceded half her Amazonian terrs., occupied by Peru in 1941, but there was renewed fighting in the oil-rich area in 1981. Pop. (1977) 7,560,000, of whom the majority are either Amerindian or of mixed descent; the whites are mainly of Spanish descent, and the official language is Spanish, with Quechua as the chief Amerindian language. The prevailing religion is Roman Catholicism. M.U.: sucre.

HISTORY. E. was conquered by the Incas shortly before the arrival of the Spaniards in the 16th cent. After an abortive revolt in 1809, E. became in 1822 part of Bolivar's rep. of Colombia, seceding peacefully to become an independent republic in 1830. There have been many revolutions, and the constitution of 1967 was designed to prevent recurrence of rule by a military junta. In 1972, however, José Maria Velasco Ibarra (1893-1979), who had been pres. 1944-7, 1952-6, 1960-1, and 1968-72, was deposed and a military dictatorship was established. Under a new constitution (1979) a single-chamber congress was elected, with Jaime Roldós Aguilera as president. The current president, Leon Fébres Cordero, was elected in May 1984.

ECUADOR. The country having been named after the Equator on which it stands, emphasises its place at the centre of things by this monument 24 km (15 m) north of Quito. *Photo: Richard Harrington/Camera Press.*

ECZEMA (ek'zema). An inflammatory skin affection marked by itching, the formation of vesicles, and the exudation of fluid. It may sometimes be allergic in origin, and is often complicated by infection due to scratching.

Ē'DAM. Town in the Netherlands on the river Ij, N Holland prov., famous for its round red cheeses. Pop. (1972) 14,200.

EDDA. Name given to 2 collections of early Icelandic literature, which together constitute our chief source for the old Scandinavian mythology. The term strictly applies to the *Younger* or *Prose E.*, compiled by Snorri Sturluson, a priest, about 1230. The *Elder* or *Poetic E.* is the name given to a collection of poems, discovered by Brynjólfr Sveinsson, about 1643, and written by unknown Norwegian poets of the 9th to 12th cents.

EDDINGTON, Sir Arthur Stanley (1882-1944). British astronomer. Prof. of astronomy at Cambridge from 1913, and director of the univ. observatory from 1914, he did work of the highest importance on the motions and equilibrium of stars, their luminosity and atomic structure, and became a leading exponent of Einstein's relativity theory. In his *Expanding Universe* (1933) he expressed the theory that in the spherical universe the outer galaxies or spiral nebulae are receding from one another. He anticipated the modern recognition of similarities between modern physics and Eastern mysticism by saying 'the stuff of the world is mind-stuff'. He was knighted in 1930 and received the OM in 1938.

EDDY, Mary Baker (1821-1910). American founder of the Christian Science movement. *Née* Baker, she was b. in New Hampshire, and was brought up as a Congregationalist. Her faith in Divine healing was confirmed by her recovery from injuries caused by a fall in 1866, and a pamphlet *Science of Man* (1869) was followed by *Science and Health* (1875), which she constantly revised until her death. In 1876 she founded the Christian Science Association, and among her disciples was A. G. Eddy, whom she m. as her 3rd husband in 1877. In 1879 the Church of Christ, Scientist, was estab., and although living in retirement after 1892 Mrs E. continued to direct the activities of the movement until her death.

EDDYSTONE. Lighthouse (1882) in the English Channel, 23km (14m) S of Plymouth, the fourth on this exposed site.

EDELWEISS (eh'delvīs). Alpine plant (*Leontopodium alpinum*) belonging to the family Compositae. It has white flower-heads and grows at great heights.

EDEN, Sir Anthony. *See* LORD AVON.

EDEN. The 'garden' in which, according to the book of Genesis, Adam and Eve were placed after their creation, and from which they were expelled for disobedience. It is usually assumed that it was in Mesopotamia, and that two of its rivers were the Euphrates and the Tigris.

EDENTA'TA. An order of mammals, comprising the families of sloths, ant-eaters, armadillos, pangolins, and ant-bears. They are practically confined to South and Central America.

EDGAR (944-75). King of all England from 959. Called the Peaceful, he was the younger son of King Edmund, and strove successfully to unite English and Danes as fellow subjects.

EDGAR (*c.* 1050-*c.* 1130). English prince, known as 'the Atheling', meaning 'of royal blood'. Grandson of Edmund II, he was supplanted as heir to Edward the Confessor by William the Conqueror. He led two rebellions against William in 1068 and 1069, but made his peace with him in 1074.

EDGEHILL. Ridge in S Warwicks, England, where the first battle of the Civil War took place in 1642, between Royalists under Charles I and Parliamentarians under the Earl of Essex. The result was indecisive.

EDGEWORTH, Maria (1767-1849). Irish novelist. B. in Oxfordshire, she was the dau. of the writer, inventor and educationist, Richard Lovell E. (1744-1817). Her first novel, *Castle Rackrent* (1800), dealt with Anglo-Irish country society, and was followed by the similar *The Absentee* (1812) and *Ormond* (1817), and the English *Belinda* (1801).

EDINBURGH. City and capital of Scotland in the region of Lothian (of which it is the admin. HQ), nr the S shores of the Firth of Forth. The site during Roman times was occupied by British or Welsh tribes, and *c.* 617 was taken by Edwin of Northumbria, from whom the town took its name. The early settlement grew up round a castle on Castle Rock, whilst about a mile to the E another burgh, called Canongate, grew up round the abbey of Holyrood, founded in 1128 by David I. It remained separate from E. until 1856. Robert Bruce made E. a burgh in 1329, and estab. its port at Leith. In 1544 the town was destroyed by the English. After the union with England in 1707, E. lost its political importance, but remained culturally pre-eminent, and under the devolution proposals of 1976 would have once again become the political capital. Edinburgh Univ., with a famous medical school, dates from 1583 and Heriot-Watt Univ. (1885: univ. status 1966) is a technical institution.

E. castle contains St Margaret's chapel, the oldest building in Edinburgh. The palace of Holyrood House was built in the 15th and 16th cents. The Parliament House, begun in 1632, is now the seat of the high courts. The episcopal cathedral of St Mary, opened in 1879, and St Giles parish church (mostly 15th cent.) are the principal churches. The two most renowned thoroughfares are Princes Street and the Royal Mile. The part known as New Town was started in 1767.

E. is not a great industrial city, but printing and publishing, banking and insurance are carried on and there are chemical manufactures, distilling and brewing, and some shipbuilding. It attracts many tourists, espec. to the annual E. festival of music and the arts. The port of Leith was incorporated in 1920. Pop. (1972) 449,630.

EDINBURGH. Edinburgh castle rises over the city, which by its beauty and its cultural life has earned the title 'Athens of the North'. *Photo: Ken Lambert/Camera Press.*

EDIRNE (edĕr'ne). Town in Turkey, on the Maritza, about 225km (140m) NW of Istanbul. It was formerly known as Adrianople (q.v.). Pop. (1975) 54,000.

EDISON, Thomas Alva (1847-1931). American inventor. B. in Ohio, of Dutch-Scottish parentage, he became first a newsboy and then a telegraph operator. His first invention was an automatic repeater for telegraphic messages, and was followed by over 1,000 others, including various telegraphic devices; the carbon transmitter (of assistance in the production of the Bell telephone); the phonograph; the incandescent lamp; a new type of storage battery; and the kinetiescopic camera, an early form of cinematography. He anticipated the Fleming diode thermionic valve.

EDMONTON. Locality, once a town, part of the Greater London bor. of Enfield. Keats lived at E., Charles Lamb lived and d. here: the Bell inn is referred to in Cowper's *John Gilpin*.

EDISON In his physics laboratory at West Orange, New Jersey, the great inventor holds one of his 'Edison Effect' lamps. By his discovery of this 'effect' in 1880 he revealed one of the fundamental principles on which modern electronics rests. *Photo: Courtesy of US Dept. of the Interior.*

EDMONTON. Capital of Alberta Province, Canada, on the N Saskatchewan river. It is the centre for a mining and petroleum-bearing area to the N and also for an agricultural and dairying region. Petroleum pipelines link E. with Superior, Wisconsin, USA, and with Vancouver, BC. Pop. (1978) 478,000.

EDMUND (*c.* 840-70). King of East Anglia from 855. In 870 he was defeated and captured by the Danes at Hoxne, and martyred on refusing to renounce Christianity. He was canonized and his shrine at Bury St Edmunds became a place of pilgrimage.

EDMUND IRONSIDE (*c.* 989-1016). King of England. The son of Ethelred the Unready, he led the resistance to Canute's invasion in 1015, and on Ethelred's death in 1016 was chosen as king by the citizens of London, while the Witan elected Canute. E. was defeated by Canute at Assandun (Ashington), Essex, and they divided the kingdom between them.

Ē'DOM. The southern district of Palestine, which stretched from the Dead Sea to the Gulf of Aqaba. The original settlers are supposed to have been descendants of Esau.

EDUCATION. In its widest sense, E. begins at birth and continues so long as the mind is capable of receiving impressions. The most primitive human groups have always prepared the young for the sort of life they have to live: had they not done so the group would soon have vanished; and some sort of instruction of the young is common among other mammals and birds. In the more restricted sense of imparting knowledge dependent on literacy, E. has become almost world wide.

Formal E. in the present-day sense is of European origin, though China can boast of an allied form of instruction dating from an imperial decree of 165 BC which set up open competitive examinations for the recruitment of members of the Civil Service. The earliest known European educational systems are those of ancient Greece - in Sparta, devoted particularly to development of military virtues, in Athens to the good of the rep. in a wider sense, but both, as in China, accorded only to the privileged few.

Rome took over much of the Greek notion of E., as of so many other aspects of civilized life, and spread it over western Europe. With the barbarian invasions and the extinction of the Roman Empire, E. vanished from Europe, though monks preserved both learning and the Latin tongue. Charlemagne's monastic schools which taught the 'seven liberal arts' - grammar, logic, rhetoric, arithmetic, geometry, music, and astronomy - produced the 'Schoolmen' and the Scholastic Movement, which in the 11th to 13th cents. led to the foundation of the universities of Paris, Bologna, Padua, Oxford, Cambridge. The capture of Constantinople by the Turks in 1453 sent into exile across Europe the Christian scholars who had congregated there, and revived European interest in learning.

Until the 19th cent. in England no attempts were made to spread literacy downwards. The Factory Act of 1802 required owners of the newly rising factories to have children taught reading, writing, and arithmetic during the first four years of their apprenticeship: the clause was not everywhere observed, but it embodied a new principle. The British and Foreign Schools Society (1808) and the National Society for Promoting the E. of the Poor in the Principles of the Established Church (1811) set up schools in which the 'three Rs' as well as religious knowledge were taught. In 1862 govt grants became available for the first time for schools attended by children up to 12. The Elementary E. Act of 1870 (Forster's Act) estab. district school boards all over the country whose duty was to provide accommodation for the elementary E. of all children not otherwise receiving E. Once the principle of elementary E. for all was accepted, the idea of higher E. for everyone capable of benefiting from it gradually asserted itself.

By the mid 20th cent. E. was free and compulsory in most countries of the world from about 6 to 16, except where the terrain was exceptionally difficult or resources were insufficient to support the burden. Nevertheless, inadequate teaching meant that literacy was by no means universal even in countries with long-established E. systems, and attempts to promote it in the Arab world and in China by the use of the Latin alphabet encountered opposition. Besides the vested interest in the existing scripts of those already expert, there were advantages inherent in them, e.g. the non-phonetic script can be understood throughout China, whereas the spoken dialects are not mutually intelligible.

Increasing stress on science and technology, espec. in secondary and higher education, had also led to an impoverishment of E. as regards the 'liberal arts', very markedly so in USSR and USA, though less so in the UK, so that by the 1970s there was a degree of teacher and student revolt. The new tendency was towards socio-political subjects, the achievements in certain areas of science and technology having prompted disillusion, and the earlier traditional studies being associated with what was considered an outworn system. Previously accepted lines of educational organization were also broken down, e.g. the British scheme for 'comprehensive' schools and the advocacy in both Britain and USA of specially favourable treatment for the 'under-privileged'. A parallel movement in China, prompted by similar egalitarian principles, was the advocacy of political acceptability rather than intellectual achievement as the criterion of selection for higher education. This was reversed under the successors of Mao Tse-tung.

In the UK the **Dept of Education and Science** (1964), is responsible for civil science and universities throughout Great Britain, but primary and secondary E. in Wales is the responsibility of the Welsh Education Office. There is a Scottish Education Dept, under the Sec. of State for Scotland. The 1986 Education Act increased the powers and the numbers of school governing bodies as part of a move towards greater parental involvement in schools. In the USA, E. is in the main the responsibility of the states, but the **Dept of Health, Education and Welfare** (1953), includes a Commissioner of Education responsible for federal aspects.

EDWARD I (1239-1307). King of England. The son of Henry III, he commanded the royal forces in the Barons' War of 1264-7, and was on a crusade when he succeeded to the throne in 1272. He estab. English rule over all Wales for the first time in 1282-4, and attempted to extend it to Scotland, at first by securing a recognition of his overlordship from the Scottish king, and later by direct conquest. The Scots maintained a fierce resistance under the leadership of Wallace and Bruce, and the struggle was still undecided when he d. At home his reign is notable for the emergence of Parliament in roughly its modern form with the Model Parliament of 1295.

EDWARD II (1284-1327). King of England. B. at Caernarvon, he was created the first prince of Wales in 1301, and succeeded his father Edward I in 1307. He soon showed himself incompetent and frivolous, falling entirely under the influence of favourites, and his reign was occupied by struggles with the discontented barons. His invasion of Scotland in 1314, undertaken to suppress Bruce's revolt, resulted in the defeat of Bannockburn. E. was deposed in 1327 by his wife Isabella and her lover Mortimer, and murdered in Berkeley castle.

EDWARD III (1312-77). King of England. B. at Windsor, he succeeded his father, Edward II, in 1327, and assumed charge of the government in 1330. He began his reign by attempting to force his suzerainty on Scotland, winning a victory at Halidon Hill (1333). In 1337 he began the 100 Years War by claiming the French throne in right of his mother. During the first stage of the war E. defeated the French at Crécy (1346), won naval victories at Sluys (1340) and Winchelsea (1350), and captured Calais (1347), while his son, the Black Prince, defeated and captured the French king at Poitiers (1356). The war ended temporarily in 1360 with the treaty of Brétigny, by which E. surrendered his claim to the throne in return for Calais, Aquitaine, and Gascony. After its renewal in 1369 the French recaptured all the English dominions in France but Calais, Bordeaux, and Bayonne.

EDWARD IV (1442-83). King of England. He was the son of Richard, duke of York, and before his accession was known as earl of March. After his father's death E. occupied London in 1461, and was proclaimed king in place of Henry VI by a council of peers. His position was secured by the defeat of the Lancastrians at Towton (1461) and by the capture of Henry. He quarrelled, however, with Warwick, his strongest supporter, who in 1470-1 temporarily restored Henry, until E. recovered the throne by his victories at Barnet and Tewkesbury.

EDWARD V (1470-83). King of England. He succeeded his father, Edward IV, in 1483, but was deposed 3 months later in favour of his uncle Richard, duke of Gloucester. He is generally believed to have been murdered with his brother in the Tower of London by Richard's orders.

EDWARD VI (1537-53). King of England. The son of Henry VIII and Jane Seymour, he became king in 1547. The government was entrusted to his uncle the duke of Somerset, and after his fall in 1549 to the earl of Warwick, later created duke of Northumberland. While still a child, E. became a strong Protestant, and strongly supported the policy of advancing the Reformation adopted by both Somerset and Northumberland. He d. of consumption.

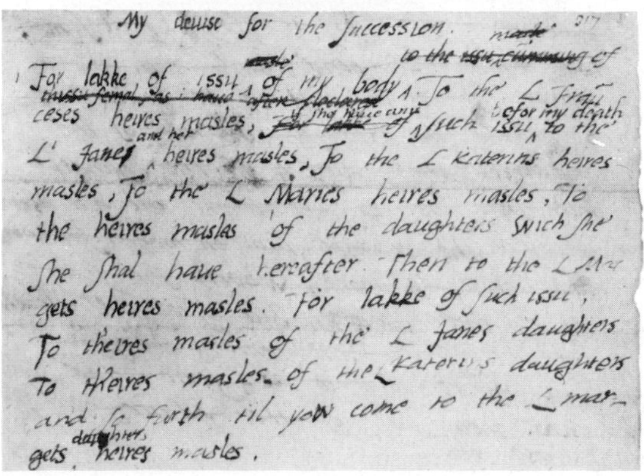

My deuise for the Succession.

For lakke of issu of my body, To the L Fraunceses heires masles, of such issu befor my death to the L' Janes and her heires masles, To the L Katerins heires masles, To the L Maries heires masles, To the heires masles of the daughters wich she shal haue hereafter. Then to the L Margets heires masles. For lakke of such issu, To theires masles of the L Janes daughters To theires masles of the L Katerins daughters and so forth til yow come to the L Margets daughters heires masles.

EDWARD VI. An extract from the young king's will, written in his own boyish hand, and giving 'My devise for the succession'. The vital alteration seen here from 'the L. Janes heires masles' to 'the L. Jane and her heirs masles', is said to have been made by the Duke of Northumberland to ensure his own continuance in power. *Reproduced by courtesy of the Master and Benchers of the Inner Temple.*

EDWARD VII (1841-1910). King of Great Britain and Ireland. B. at Buckingham Palace, the eldest son of Queen Victoria and Prince Albert, he received a careful education. In 1860 he made the first tour of Canada and the USA ever undertaken by a British prince. After his father's death in 1861 he undertook many public duties, although the Queen refused to allow him to take any part in political life. Nevertheless, he took a close interest in politics, and was on friendly terms with Gladstone, Chamberlain, and other party leaders. In 1863 he m. Princess Alexandra of Denmark, by whom he had 6 children. He toured India in 1875-6, played an active part in the life of society, and was a keen sportsman. He succeeded to the throne in 1901, and was crowned in 1902. His influence contributed to the *Entente Cordiale* of 1904 with France, and Anglo-Russian agreement of 1907.

EDWARD VIII (1894-1972). King of Great Britain and Ireland. Eldest son of George V, he was created Prince of Wales in 1910, received a naval training at Dartmouth and studied in Paris and at Magdalen College, Oxford. He saw active service in the F.W.W., and subsequently travelled widely both within and outside the Commonwealth. Succeeding to the throne on January 20, 1936, he showed great concern for the problems of the Glasgow slums and the distressed areas of S Wales. In Nov. a constitutional crisis arose when he wished to marry Mrs Wallis Warfield

EDWARD VII. A portrait of the king, who won affection and respect in his comparatively short reign, by Luke Fildes. *Photo: Courtesy of the National Portrait Gallery.*

EDWARD VIII. A portrait by James Gunn, which captures the charm and sincerity by which Edward established his popularity as Prince of Wales. *Photo: Courtesy of the National Portrait Gallery.*

(Simpson), an American, since it was felt that as she had been divorced she would be unacceptable as Queen. On Dec. 11, E. abdicated and left for France where the couple were m. 3 June 1937, at the Château de Candé, Tours. He received the title of duke of Windsor and was Gov. of the Bahamas 1940-5, subsequently settling in France. His autobiography *A King's Story* appeared in 1951.

EDWARD, called the **Black Prince** (1330-76). Prince of Wales. The eldest son of Edward III, he served at Crécy, and in 1356 defeated and captured the French king at Poitiers. He ruled Aquitaine as his father's representative 1362-71, and in 1367 invaded Castile and restored to the throne the deposed king, Pedro the Cruel. After attempting unsuccessfully to suppress a revolt in Aquitaine he was obliged by ill-health to return to England in 1371, and thereafter took little part in public life. The name 'The Black Prince', said to be derived from his black armour, was probably a later invention.

EDWARD the Confessor (d. 1066). King of England. The son of Ethelred II, he lived in Normandy until shortly before his accession in 1042. The government remained in the hands of Earl Godwin, and, after his death, of his son Harold, while E. devoted himself to religious exercises. E. was buried in Westminster Abbey, which he had rebuilt.

EDWARD the Elder (d. 924). King of England. The son of King Alfred, he succeeded him in 901. He crushed Danish risings and extended his kingdom to the Humber.

EDWARD the Martyr (*c.* 963-78). King of England. On the death of his father, King Edgar, in 975, his stepmother Aelfthryth attempted to secure the crown for her son Ethelred, but through Dunstan's influence E. was crowned king. In 978 E. was murdered, probably at Aelfthryth's instigation.

EDWARD, Lake. Lake in Uganda, at *c.* 900m (3,000 ft) in the Albertine rift valley. In 1973-9 it was known as Lake Idi Amin Dada, after Pres. Amin of Uganda.

EDWARDS, Sir George (1908-). British aircraft designer. Chairman and managing director of the British Aircraft Corporation 1963-75, he was associated with the design of civil and military aircraft, e.g. *Viking, Viscount, Valiant V-bomber, VC-10* and *Concorde.* He was awarded the OM in 1971.

EDWARDS, Jonathan (1703-58). American divine. B. in Connecticut, he became in 1727 pastor at Northampton, Mass. Here he developed Calvinistic views of predestination and initiated the religious revival known as the 'Great Awakening'.

For 200 yrs regarded as an anachronism, he has in the 20th cent. been recognized as a brilliantly original thinker. His important works are *The Freedom of the Will* (defending Determinism), *Nature of the True Virtue,* and *Religious Affections* (defending the emotive basis of religious experience).

EDWIN (*c.* 585-633). King of Northumbria from 617. He fortified Edinburgh, named after him, and was killed in battle with Penda of Mercia.

EEL. Fish of the order Apodes, characterized by a serpent-like body, small gill openings, and reduced fins. The common E. of European and African rivers (*Anguilla anguilla*) reaches 1.6m (5ft) and *c.* 6kg (12-15lb). On becoming mature some 6 yrs later, and assuming a silver breeding livery instead of their earlier yellowish colouring, these Es. were then thought to make their way back to the Sargasso Sea (from which they originally came as larvae) to spawn. It is now suggested, however, that these Es. cannot muster strength for the return journey and consequently never breed and that they are actually of the same species as the American common E. (*Anguilla rostrata*), although the latter may reach 4 times their weight because of more favourable conditions. The eggs of American Es. laid at the northern limits of the spawning grounds would be held in the Sargasso Sea for a year before being carried by the Gulf Stream to Europe, Africa and the Mediterranean; those laid at the southern limits would be carried much more rapidly to the richer feeding grounds of the American coasts by the Antilles and Florida ocean currents, with resultant differences in development.

The morays or painted Es. are represented by some 100 species in tropical and temperate seas; they are often brilliantly coloured and very fierce. The conger Es. are all marine and are distinguished from freshwater species by the total absence of scales, and are common on British coasts.

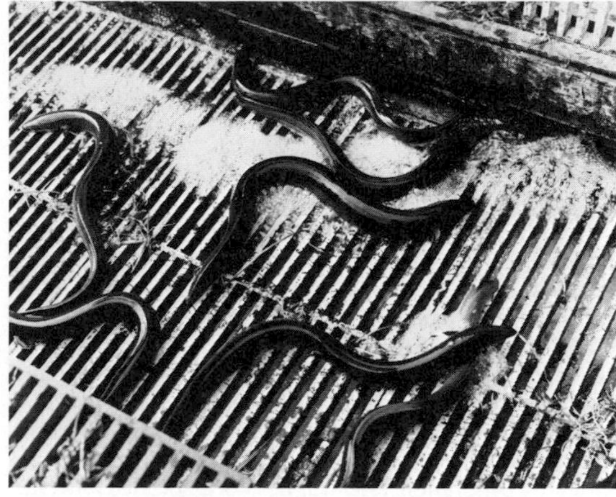

EEL. Mature common eels *(Anguilla anguilla)*, caught on an eel trap built into the river, on their downward migration to the sea. *Photo: Heather Angel.*

EEL GRASS or **glass wrack.** A genus of plants (*Zostera*) belonging to the family Zosteraceae. *Z. marina* is the typical species. They are remarkable among flowering plants in being adapted for a marine life, being completely submerged at high tide.

EGBERT (d. 839). King of the W Saxons. The son of Ealhmund, an under-king of Kent, he succeeded to the W Saxon throne in 802, and by 829 he had united England for the first time under one king.

EGG. In animals, the ovum, or female reproductive cell. It corresponds to the sperm cell or spermatozoon of the male, and when fecundated by this develops by division into further cells, into the embryo.

EGMONT, Lamoral, count of (1522-68). Flemish patriot. B. in Hainault, he defeated the French at St Quentin in 1557 and Gravelines in 1558, and became stadtholder of Flanders and Artois. From 1561 he helped to lead the movement against Spanish misrule, but in 1567 the duke of Alva was sent to crush the resistance, and E. was beheaded.

EGMONT, Mount. Symmetrical extinct volcano in the SW of North Island, NZ, 2,517 m (8,260 ft) high.

Ē'GRET. Genus of birds (*Egretta*) in which both sexes develop a long train of loose-webbed feathers during the breeding season. These snowy-white plumes were formerly so much in demand for hat ornaments that Es. were almost exterminated until the wearing of them was prohibited by law. The great white heron (*E. alba*) which grows to a length of 1m (3ft) and the little E. (*E. garzetta*), 0.6m (2ft), are found in Asia, Africa, S Europe and Australia and rarely visit Britain.

EGYPT (ĕ'jipt). Country of NE Africa, lying between the Mediterranean in the N and the Republic of Sudan in the S. Egypt consists in the main of a low plateau through which the Nile flows towards the N, depositing alluvium which forms a narrow strip of fertile land on both banks, bounded on the E by the Eastern (Arabian) and on the W by the Western (Libyan) Desert. Before reaching the Mediterranean the Nile forms a triangular delta with a width of 240km (150m) at the seaward end. Since most of E. is almost rainless, extension of the irrigated area has been secured through conservation of the Nile flood waters by construction of the Aswan High Dam, with Lake Nasser behind it, which also increases electricity production. In addition a 'second' Nile or New Valley is being created, using this electricity to draw on the underground reservoirs linking the oases of the Western Desert, which run from El Alamein to the Sudanese border (Siwa, Bahariya, Farafra, Dakhla, Kharga). The electricity is also used to power new industries, e.g. aluminium and fertilizer plants. Eventually there is a plan to reclaim the Sinai desert by pumping surplus Nile water through culverts beneath the Suez Canal.

E. is still basically agricultural. Cotton and rice are major exports, and wheat, barley, citrus fruit, sugar and vegetables are also grown. The chief tree is the date palm. Asses, camels, sheep and buffalo are reared. Under Nasser large landowners were eliminated, holdings being limited to an area cultivable by individual *fellahin* or peasants. However, industrialization was greatly accelerated under Nasser, and a programme of nationalization of banks, manufacturing and trading concerns undertaken. Sugar, flour, soap, pottery and glass, and cement are produced. Oil has been discovered in the NE, and further exploration is being undertaken; there are also deposits of coal, cobalt, copper, iron, manganese, nickel, phosphate, and various building stones. Tourism is very important.

The cap. is Cairo at the head of the Nile Delta, where the major towns of Alexandria (the chief port), Mansura, Tanta, Mahalla el Kubra and Damietta are concentrated; on the Nile above Cairo are Faiyum, Asyut, and Aswan; Port Said, Ismailia and Suez, in the canal zone, were evacuated in the course of the Arab-Israeli wars, but in the 1970s were reconstructed and enlarged.

Under the revised constitution of 1980 there is a pres. (indefinitely re-electable), an elected Nat. Assembly and Consultative Council, and the Sharia (*see* ISLAM) is the principal source of legislation. The political system was redefined as 'socialist democratic', and other parties beside the ruling Nat. Democratic Party, are allowed. For local govt. the 2 districts of Upper and Lower E. are subdivided into governorates.

Area 1,000,000 sq.km (386,198 sq.m); pop. (1976) 39,000,000, about one-fifth in the Cairo area. The majority are of Hamito-Semitic origin, with minorities of desert Bedouin and Nubians in the far south. The great majority are Sunni Moslems, but there are *c.* 2,000,000 Coptic Christians. The official language is Arabic. M.U.: Egyptian pound.

EGYPT. The city of Aswan, where dhows still traverse the Nile rapids. The building of the High Dam at this point on the river has enabled the country to leap into the industrial era. *Photo: Bunte/Camera Press.*

History. ANCIENT. The Egyptian state was founded *c.* 3200 BC by the semi-legendary Menes, who united Lower E., in the delta, to his own kingdom of Upper E. in the Nile valley. Following the Archaic Period of the 1st and 2nd Dynasties (32nd-29th cents.), the 'Old Kingdom' reached the height of its power under the 4th Dynasty kings, who built the great pyramids at Gizeh (*c.* 26th cent. BC), and then gradually sank into anarchy. Unity was recovered under the 11th and 12th Dynasties (the 'Middle Kingdom', *c.* 22nd-18th cents. BC); there followed another period of anarchy, resulting in the conquest of E. by the Semitic Hyksos. Their expulsion in 1580 BC marks the beginning of the 'New Kingdom'. Under the 18th Dynasty (1580-1370) a succession of able kings, notably Thothmes III (reigned 1484-1451), founded an empire in Palestine and Syria extending to the Euphrates. The golden age of Amenhotep III probably continued under Ikhnaton (q.v.) - although it is thought by some historians that his neglect of imperial defence for religious reforms led to the loss of most of E.'s possessions in Asia - and also under the 19th Dynasty (Ramses II and Ramses III). However, during the 20th Dynasty there was undoubtedly a decline in Egyptian strength, and power within the country passed from the pharaohs to the priests of Ammon. Under the Late New Kingdom (1090-663 BC) E. was often divided between 2 or more dynasties; the nobles became virtually independent, and in the 7th cent. the Assyrians established their suzerainty over E. Psammetichus I (633-609) and his successors restored to E. its independence and unity, and attempted to restore the empire. This national revival ended when Cambyses in 525 brought E. under Persian rule, which survived, except for a period of independence *c.* 405-340, until Alexander conquered E. in 332. When his empire was divided E. went to Ptolemy, whose descendants ruled until Cleopatra's death in 30 BC.

EGYPT. The temple of Edfu, just north of Aswan, has beautifully decorated panels. Inscribed in the sandstone is the world's earliest play (see DRAMA). *Photo: Camera Press.*

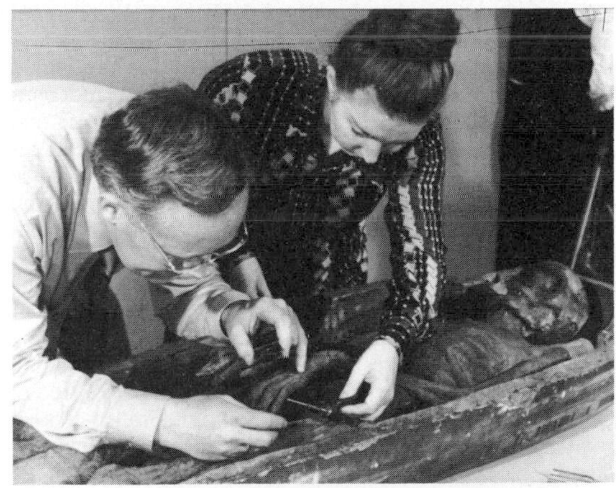

EGYPT. The mummy of Asru, a singer in the great temple at Karnak, being examined at Manchester University. Police finger-printing equipment was used (as here) to aid in the study of the hands of this delicately-boned woman who died 2,600 years ago. *Photo: Keystone.*

RELIGION. The prehistoric Egyptian religion turned on the worship of totemic animals believed to be the ancestors of the clan. Totems later developed into gods, represented with the heads of the animals sacred to them, e.g. the hawk was sacred to Ra and Horus, the ibis to Thoth, the jackal to Anubis. The cult of Osiris, who was murdered, was mourned by his sister and wife Isis, and rose again, was a fertility ritual similar to those of Tammuz and Dionysus; by a natural development Osiris became a god of the underworld. Under the 18th Dynasty a local deity of Thebes, Ammon, came to be regarded as supreme, a reflection of recovered national unity. Ikhnaton attempted, without success, to establish the monotheistic cult of Aton, the solar disc, as the one national god. Immortality, conferred by the magical rite of mummification, was originally the sole prerogative of the king, but was extended under the New Kingdom to all who could afford it.

MEDIEVAL AND MODERN. After its conquest by Augustus in 30 BC Egypt passed under the rule of Roman, and later of Byzantine, governors, and after the Arab conquest of 641 under that of representatives of the Caliphs. Christianity succeeded paganism as the national religion, and was succeeded in turn by Islam. After the 9th cent. Egypt passed to a series of native dynasties, and in the 13th cent. to the Mamelukes, or military aristocracy. The Turks conquered Egypt in 1517, but after 2 cents. of rule by Turkish pashas the Mamelukes regained control.

Contact with Europe began with Napoleon's invasion and the French occupation of 1798-1801. A period of anarchy followed, until in 1805 an Albanian officer, Mehemet Ali, was appointed pasha; the title was later made hereditary in his family. Under his successors large sums of British and French capital were invested in Egypt, while the opening of the Suez Canal in 1869 made the country of great strategic importance. Discontent with foreign domination led to a nationalist revolt in 1881-2, put down by British forces. Henceforward the govt. was mainly in the hands of British civilian agents who directed their efforts particularly to the improvement of E.'s finances. On the outbreak of the F.W.W. in 1914, nominal Turkish suzerainty was abolished and E. was declared a British protectorate. Post-war agitation by the nationalist Wafd party led the way to establishment of an independent kingdom in 1922 under Fuad I., Britain retaining responsibility for the military protection of E. In 1936 all British troops were withdrawn except from the Suez Canal zone. Following a military coup in 1952 the monarchy was abolished in 1953, King Farouk going into exile, and Gen. Neguib declared E. a republic with himself as president; Neguib was displaced in 1954 by his prime minister, Lt-Col. Nasser. By an agreement reached that year the last British units left the canal zone on 13 June 1956; on 26 July Pres. Nasser nationalized the canal. Border clashes between Egyptian and Israeli patrols led in Oct. to an Israeli invasion of E., and joint Franco-British military intervention to protect the canal. Nasser immediately blocked it, and although after the UN ended hostilities 3 weeks later, it was temporarily cleared, it was again closed 1967-75 after further hostilities: *see* ARAB-ISRAELI WARS. Nasser was succeeded in 1970 by Anwar Sadat (q.v.), whose conduct of the October War of 1973 restored Egyptian morale. Cementation of peace with Israel by the Camp David Agreements (q.v.) resulted in the recovery of Sinai, but failed to solve the Palestinian problem. Egypt had been known from 1958 as the United Arab Republic, but the union with Syria (on which the change had been based) collapsed in 1961, so that the style of Arab Rep. of Egypt was adopted in 1971. On the assassination of Sadat in 1981, Hosni Mubarak (q.v.) became president, and was faced by growing fundamentalist Islam. *See* also SUDAN.

For the monuments of Egyptian history, *see* ABYDOS (Great Temple), AKHETATON/TELL EL AMARNA, ALEXANDRIA, CLEOPATRA'S NEEDLE, HATSHEPSUT, MEMPHIS (SAKKARA), THEBES (LUXOR and KARNAK), NUBIA, PHILAE, PYRAMID, SAKKARA, SPHINX, VALLEY OF THE KINGS).

EGYPTO'LOGY. The study of ancient Egypt. Interest in the subject was first stimulated by Napoleon's expedition of 1798, during which the Rosetta Stone was discovered. As this contained the same inscription in Gk as well as the hieroglyphic and demotic scripts, it afforded the clue to the decipherment of the Egyptian inscriptions. Excavation continued throughout the 19th cent., and gradually assumed a more scientific character, largely as a result of the work of Sir Flinders Petrie from 1880 onwards, and the formation of the Egyptian Exploration Fund in 1892. The most sensational discovery so far made was Tutankhamen's tomb in 1922, the only royal tomb with all its treasures intact. Special branches of E. developed in more recent years are the study of prehistoric Egypt, and the search for papyri, preserved by the dryness of the climate; besides ancient Egyptian writings, many lost Gk and early Christian works have been recovered. *See* EMERY, W.B.

EHRENBURG, Ilya Grigorievich (1891-1967). Russian writer. B. in Kiev, he spent many years in France before returning permanently to Russia in 1940. Apart from his brilliance as a war correspondent during both world wars, he is noted for *The Adventures of Julio Jurenito* (1930), a satire on the post-war decay of European civilization, *The Fall of Paris* (1942), and the controversial *The Thaw* (1954), which depicted artistic circles in the USSR, and contributed to the temporary slackening of literary restraint in the 1950s. He was awarded the Order of Lenin in 1944. He pub. 5 vols. of autobiography 1961-4.

EHRLICH (ehr'likh), **Paul** (1854-1915). German bacteriologist. B. in Silesia, he became director of the Royal Institute for Experimental Therapy at Frankfurt in 1906. He discovered the arsenical compounds used in the treatment of syphilis before the discovery of antibiotics, and made great advances possible in chemotherapy. With Mechnikov he shared the Nobel price for physiology in 1908.

EICHENDORFF (ī'khendorf), **Joseph,** Freiherr von (1788-1857). German poet and novelist. B. in Upper Silesia, he held various judicial posts, wrote romantic stories, but is chiefly remembered as one of the greatest lyricists in the German tongue.

EICHMANN (īkh'man), **Karl Adolf** (1906-62). Austrian Nazi war criminal. As an SS official he was responsible for immense atrocities against the Jews, and fled at the fall of Germany. In 1960 he was abducted from Argentina by Israeli agents, tried in Israel during 1961 for the extermination of 6 million Jews, and executed.

EIDER (ī'der). Large marine duck, *Somateria mollissima,* highly valued for its soft down, used in stuffing quilts and cushions. It breeds in northern latitudes, from the Farne Islands to Spitzbergen, and in Iceland and Norway it is bred for its down.

EIFFEL (ī'fel) **TOWER.** Iron tower in the Champ de Mars, Paris, built 1887-9 to the design of the French engineer Gustave Alexandre Eiffel (1832-1923) for the Exhibition of 1889: 320m (1,050 ft).

EIGER. *See* ALPS.

EIGHTH ROUTE ARMY. The Chinese 'Red Army' formed in 1927 when the Communists broke away from the Kuomintang and estab. a Soviet government in Kiangsi, in SE China. When the Japanese invaded China in 1937 it was recognized as a section of the national forces under the name 8th R.A.

EIJKMAN (īk'man), **Christiaan** (1858-1930). Dutch bacteriologist. He isolated vitamin B_1, present in unmilled rice, as a cure for beri-beri, and was a pioneer in the recognition of vitamins as essential to health. He received a Nobel prize 1929.

EILAT. *See* ELAT.

EINDHOVEN. Town in N Brabant prov., the Netherlands, on the Dommel. It is a manufacturing centre, chiefly of electric light bulbs and equipment. Pop. (1978) 192,160.

EINSTEIN (īn'stīn), **Albert** (1879-1955). German-Swiss physicist, framer of the theories of Relativity (q.v.). B. at Ulm, in Württemberg, of Jewish stock, he lived with his parents in Munich and then in Italy. After teaching at the polytechnic school at Zürich he became a Swiss citizen and was appointed an inspector of patents at Berne. In his spare time he took his degree of Ph.D at Zürich, and some of his papers on physics were of so high a quality that in 1909 he was given a chair of theoretical physics at the university. After holding a similar post at Prague (1911), he returned to teach at Zürich (1912), and in 1913 took up a specially created post as director of the Kaiser Wilhelm Institute for Physics, Berlin. In 1905 he had pub. his first theory - the so-called special theory of Relativity - and in 1915 he issued his general theory. His latest conception of the basic laws governing the universe was outlined in his unified field theory made public in 1953; and of the 'Relativistic Theory of the Non-symmetric Field', completed 1955, E. wrote that this simplified the derivations as well as the form of the field equations and the whole theory becomes thereby more transparent, without changing its content. He received the Nobel prize for physics in 1921. He was deprived of his post at Berlin in 1933 and became professor of mathematics and a permanent member of the Institute for Advanced Study at Princeton, NJ, USA, and during the S.W.W. worked for the US Navy Ordnance Bureau. Besides his treatises on Relativity, he wrote *My Philosophy* (1933), *The World as I See It* (1935), and (with Leopold Infeld) *The Evolution of Physics* (1938).

EINSTEINIUM. *See* TRANSURANIUM ELEMENTS.

EINTHOVEN (īnt'hōven), **William** (1860-1927). Dutch physiologist. He invented the electrocardiograph, basically that used in modern medicine, and invaluable in detecting disease of the coronary arteries, etc.

EIRE (ār'e). Irish name for Ireland (q.v.). It was used 1937-49 for the part of the island called the Irish Free State 1922-37.

EISENACH (ī'senakh). Town on the r. Hörsel, Erfurt district, E Germany. Wartburg Castle, where Martin Luther made the first translation of the Bible into German, stands on a ridge above the town. J. S. Bach was born here, and there is a museum of musical instruments. E. is the tourist gateway to the Thuringian Forest. Manufactures incl. pottery, vehicles and machinery. Pop. (1973) 51,000.

EISENHOWER (ī'zenhower), **Dwight David** (1890-1969). 34th President of the USA; Supreme Commander of all the Allied armies in the west during the S.W.W. B. at Denison, Texas, he graduated at West Point Military Academy in 1915, but saw no active service during the F.W.W. In 1935 he served in the Philippines at Manila under MacArthur, and from 1940 held high staff appointments at Washington. In June 1942 he was sent to England as US Commander in the European theatre. In Nov. 1942 he became C-in-C of the American and British forces on the occasion of the invasion of N Africa, and in July 1943 he took command of the Allied invasion of Sicily. It was E. who announced the unconditional surrender of Italy on 8 Sept 1943. In Dec. he was appointed Supreme Commander of the Allied invasion of Europe, and from Oct. 1944 he was in command of all the Allied armies in the west. After the war 'Ike', as he was familiarly styled by his men, was given an official reception in Washington; in Sept. 1945 he was appointed Military Governor of the US zone of Germany, and in Nov. Chief of Staff of the American Army. In Dec. 1950 he became Supreme Allied Commander, Europe, resigning in 1952 when, as a Republican, he was elected President. Re-elected in 1956 (the first Republican since 1900 to hold the Presidency twice in succession), in 1957 he introd. his 'Eisenhower Doctrine', a policy of giving aid, in consultation with the UN, to any Middle Eastern countries requesting it, especially against international Communist aggression.

EINSTEIN. In a broadcast following the development of the H-bomb, Einstein declared that the only way out of the impasse that man had created was the establishment of 'a supra-national judicial and executive body', and effective world government. *Photo: Popperfoto*

EISENHOWER, Mt. Rocky Mtn peak in Alberta, Canada, incl. in Banff Nat. Park, 2,862 m (9,390 ft).

EISENSTEIN (ī'senstīn), **Sergei Mikhailovich** (1898-1948). Soviet film director. A pioneer in the use of editing techniques, notably montage (as a means of propaganda) in *The Battleship Potemkin* (1925), he was also noted for his costume dramas (with his own designs), and won the Order of Lenin in 1938 with *Alexander Nevsky*, the first part of a planned but uncompleted trilogy. The second part, *Ivan the Terrible* (1944), was banned in Russia. He is also famous for his beautiful sense of composition.

EISTEDDFOD (īstedh'vod) (Welsh, 'sitting'). Traditional Welsh gathering for the encouragement of the bardic arts of music, poetry, literature, etc. The E. traditionally dates from pre-Christian times, but it was discontinued from the late 17th until the beginning of the 19th cent., since when it has been held annually. The meetings last 3-4 days.

EISENHOWER. Together during the presidential campaign of 1952, Eisenhower and the vice-presidential candidate, Richard Nixon (far left). Nixon had been under attack for acceptance of financial backing from private sources. *Photo: Popperfoto.*

Musical and literary contests take place, prizes, medals, and bardic degrees being awarded. The culminating ceremony is that of the 'chairing' of the bard.

EKATERINBURG. Pre-revolutionary name of SVERDLOVSK.

EKATERINODAR. Pre-revolutionary name of KRASNODAR.

EKATERINOSLAV. Pre-revolutionary name of DNEPROPETROVSK.

EL AAIÚN (el īyoon'). Cap. (also La'youn) of Western Sahara, nr. the Atlantic coast. Pop. (1970) 24,050.

Ē'LAND. S African antelope (*Taurotragus oryx*). Pale fawn in colour, it is *c.* 2m (6ft) high, and both sexes have spiral horns *c.* 45cm (18in) long.

ELASTICITY. The property possessed by a body of automatically recovering its original shape when deforming forces are removed. There are several types of E. According to Hooke's law for an elastic solid, the stress set up within the body is proportional to the strain to which it is subjected. Stress is measured as a force per unit area and strain as the change in length per unit length. The ratio of stress to strain is called the modulus of E., and the value of the stress at which the material ceases to obey Hooke's law is called the elastic limit.

ELAT (ālaht'). Port at the head of the Gulf of Aqaba, Israel's only outlet to the Red Sea. Founded 1948, on the site of the Biblical Elath, it is linked by road with Beersheba. There are copper mines and granite quarries nearby, and a major geophysical observatory (1968) is 16 km (10 m) to the N. Pop. (1971) 16,000.

ELBA. Rugged island in the Mediterranean Sea, 10km (6m) off the W coast of Italy. Iron ore is exported from Portoferraio, the capital, to the Italian mainland, and there is fishing. E. was the place of exile of Napoleon 1814-15. Area 223 sq.km (86 sq.m); pop. (1971) 29,000.

ELBE. One of the principal rivers of Germany, rising on the S slopes of the Riesengebirge in Czechoslovakia, and flowing NW across the German plain to the North Sea. It is 1,166 km (725m) long.

ELBERFELD. *See* WUPPERTAL.

ELBING. German form of ELBLAG.

ELBLAG. Polish port 11km (7m) from the mouth of the r. E. which debouches into the Zalew Wislany (Frisches Haff). It has shipyards, engineering works, car and tractor factories, etc. Pop. (1978) 93,000.

ELBRUZ. Highest mt. in Europe, 5,642 m (18,510 ft) in the Caucasus, Georgia SSR.

ELBURZ. Volcanic mt. range in NW Iran, close to the S shore of the Caspian, rising in Mt Demavend to 5,770 m (18,934 ft).

ELDER. In the Presbyterian Church the Es. or ruling Es. are laymen who assist the minister (or teaching E.) in the government of the church.

ELDER. Genus of small trees or shrubs (*Sambucus*) of the family Caprifoliaceae. The common *S. nigra*, found in Europe, N Africa, and W Asia, has a smooth bark, pinnate leaves, and in early summer bears heavy heads of small, sweet-scented, white flowers, which are succeeded by clusters of small, black berries. The most handsome species, the scarlet-berried *S. racemosa*, is found in parts of Europe, Asia and N America.

ELDON, John Scott, 1st earl of E. (1751-1838). British Lord Chancellor. B. at Newcastle, he became an MP in 1782, and was Lord Chancellor in 1801-6 and 1807-27, during which period the rules governing the use of the injunction and precedent in Equity finally became fixed.

EL DORADO (dorah'dō). The fabled city of gold believed by 16th cent. Spaniards to exist somewhere in the Americas. *See* CHIBCHAS.

ELEANOR (el'anor) **OF AQUITAINE** (*c.* 1122-1204). Queen of Henry II of England. The dau. of the duke of Aquitaine, she m. Louis VII of France in 1137, but the marriage was annulled on grounds of consanguinity in 1151, and she shortly after m. Henry of Anjou, who in 1154 became king of England as Henry II.

ELEANOR OF CASTILE (d. 1290). Queen of Edward I of England. The dau. of Ferdinand III of Castile, she m. Prince Edward in 1254, and accompanied him on his crusade in 1270. She d. at Harby, Notts.

ELECTORAL COLLEGE. The indirect system whereby voters in the USA elect their president and vice-president. The people theoretically vote, not for the presidential candidate, but for a list of electors nominated by one of the two parties. The whole electoral college vote of the state then goes to the winning party (and candidate). Each state has as many electors as it has senators and representatives in congress, so that the E.C. numbers 538, and a majority of 270 electoral votes is needed to win.

The system can lead to a presidential candidate being elected with a minority of the popular vote behind him, and it has been proposed, for example, by Carter in 1977, to substitute a direct popular vote. A constitutional amendment to this effect failed in 1979, partly because Black and Jewish groups argued that this would deprive them of their politically influential bloc vote in key states.

ELECTORS. The seven German princes who elected the emperor from the 13th cent. until the dissolution of the Holy Roman Empire in 1806. These were commonly the archbishops of Mainz, Cologne, and Trier, the king of Bohemia, the duke of Saxony, the margrave of Brandenburg, and the palatine of the Rhine.

ELECTRIC FISH. Name given to certain fish that have electricity-producing powers. The best-known example is the S American *Electrophorus electricus,* in which the lateral tail muscles are modified to form electric organs;

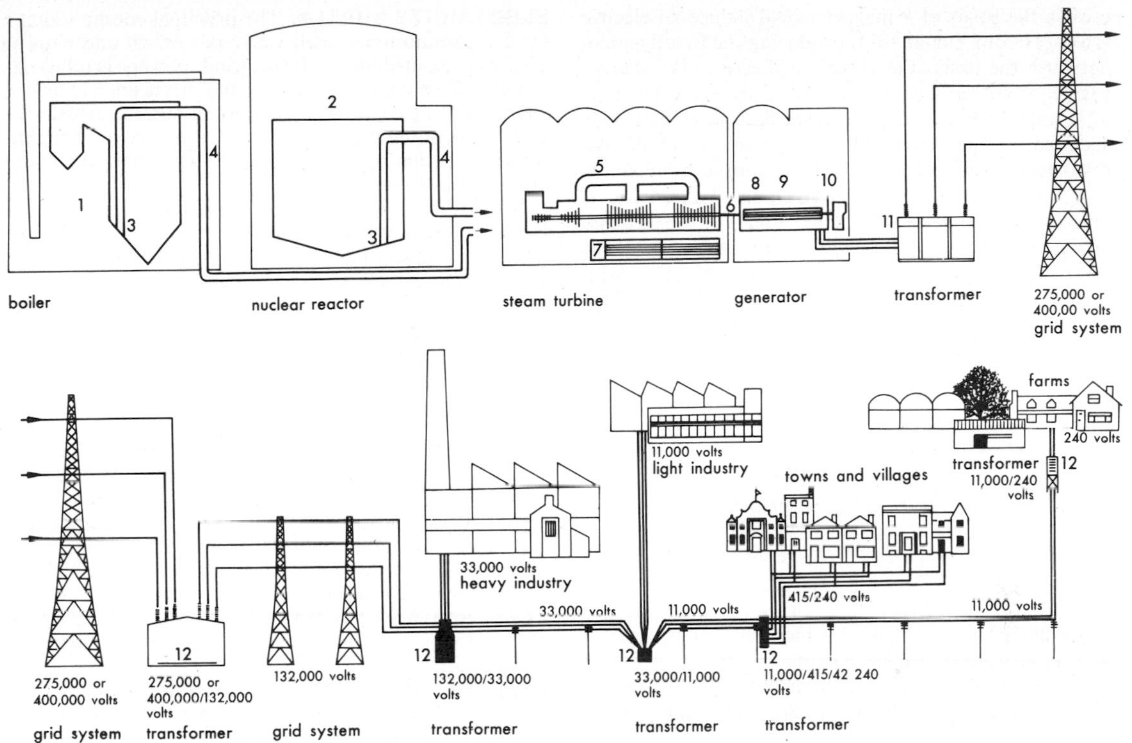

ELECTRICITY SUPPLY. Coal or oil is burned in the boiler (1) of a power station, or carbon dioxide is heated in the reactor (2) of a nuclear power station and the heat boils water circulating at high pressure in the boiler tubes (3) to create high-pressure steam (4). The steam is taken by pipes to the turbine (5) where it is used to drive the shaft (6) at high speed. From the turbine, the steam enters the condenser (7) and passes over tubes containing cooling water. It is thus condensed back into water and creates a vacuum which helps improve the flow of steam through the turbine. The water is returned to the boiler under pressure by a series of pumps. The generator consists of a rotor (8) and a stator (9). The rotor (an electro-magnet made of a number of windings mounted on a shaft) is coupled to the turbine shaft so that it is turned at high speed and generates electricity in more windings that make up the stator. A small generator (10), driven from the end of the rotor shaft, produces the current required to energise the rotor. In the largest modern generators electricity may be generated at about 25,000 volts but for efficient transmission over long distances the voltage is increased by transformers (11), to 132,000, 275,000 or 400,000 volts. The voltage is reduced again by other transformers (12) for distribution to consumers at suitable voltages – 33,000 volts for heavy industries, 11,000 volts for light industries and 240 volts for homes and farms.

current passing from tail to head is strong enough to stun another animal.

ELECTRICITY. The fundamental constituent of matter. A general term used for all phenomena caused by electric charge whether static or in motion. The fact that amber has the power, after being rubbed, of attracting light objects, such as bits of straw and feather, is said to have been known to Thales of Miletus (600 BC) and to Pliny (AD 70). In his studies on these attractions, William Gilbert (1544–1603), Queen Elizabeth I's physician, found that many substances possess this power, and he called it electric after the Greek word meaning amber. The attracting power may be transferred by contact from one body to another by conductors, such as metals. On the other hand, paraffin wax, hard rubber and dry glass do not transmit the power, and are called insulators. It was not until the early 1700s that 2 types of E. were recognized, and that unlike kinds attract each other and like kinds repel. The charge on glass rubbed with silk came to be known as positive E., and the charge on amber rubbed with wool as negative E. These two charges were found to annul one another when brought together. In 1800, Volta found that a series of little cells containing brine, in which were dipped plates of zinc and copper, gave an electric current, which later in the same year was shown to evolve hydrogen and oxygen when passed through water (known as electrolysis). Humphry Davy, in 1807, decomposed soda and potash, both thought to be elements, and separated the metals sodium and potassium; a discovery which led the way to electroplating (q.v.). Other properties of electric currents discovered were the heating effect, now used in lighting and warming our homes, and the deflection of a magnetic needle, described by Oersted in 1820 and elaborated by Ampère in 1825. This work made possible the electric telegraph. For Michael Faraday the fact that an electric current passing through a wire caused a magnet to move suggested that moving a wire or coil of wire rapidly between the poles of a magnet would induce an electric current. He did this in 1831, producing the first dynamo, afterwards the basis of electrical engineering. The characteristics of currents were crystallized by G. S. Ohm (*c.* 1827) who showed that the current passing along a wire was equal to the electromotive force (e.m.f., or driving press.) across the wire multiplied by a constant, which was the conductivity of the wire. The unit of resistance is named after Ohm, e.m.f. is named after Volta (volt), and current after Ampère (amp). The work of the late 1800s indicated the wide interconnections of E. (with magnetism, heat and light), and the discovery by J. Clerk Maxwell (*c.* 1855) of a single electro-magnetic theory explaining both electric waves and light. The universal importance of E. was decisively proved, by the connection between atoms and E. The structure of the atom itself, hitherto thought to be the ultimate particle of matter, was found to be composed of a positively charged central core, the nucleus, about which negatively charged electrons rotate in various orbits. E. generated on a commercial scale was available from the early 1880s and used for electric motors driving all kinds of machinery; for lighting, by carbon arc, but later by incandescent filaments, first of carbon and then of tungsten, enclosed in glass bulbs partially filled with inert gas under vacuum. Light is also produced by passing E. through a gas or metal vapour, or a fluorescent lamp. Other practical applications include telephone, radio, television, X-ray machines, etc.

ELECTRICITY. Controversial as major producers of electric power in the future are the fast breeder reactors. This is the reactor hall of the prototype installation at Dounreay in Scotland. *Photo Courtesy of UKAEA.*

ELECTRICITY SUPPLY. The principal energy sources for E. generation are coal, water power, oil and natural gas, with contributions from wind power, geothermal power, tidal power (see RANCE), and increasingly, nuclear energy. E. is generated as alternating current, usually in large turbo-alternators, because of the ease of changing the voltage (that is, 'pressure') for transmission and distribution. *See* RANCE.

Britain has one of the world's largest inter-connected E.S. systems, comprising large power stations feeding into a national grid: highest voltage 400,000. Coal, made uneconomic by cheap oil in the 1960s, was again in demand after the 1970s oil crisis. Nuclear fuel provides the cheapest form of electricity generation in Britain. Elsewhere there are co-ordinated systems through transmission links, involving for example power pools of groups of undertakings in the USA, and inter-country connections on the continent of Europe. Among specialized power units which convert energy directly to electrical energy without the intervention of any moving mechanisms, the most promising are thermionic converters. These may use conventional fuels such as propane gas, as in portable military power packs, or, when refuelling is to be avoided, expensive radioactive fuels, as in unmanned navigational aids, and spacecraft.

ELECTROCA'RDIOGRAM. A recording on a chart of the electrical impulses from the heart, used to diagnose heart conditions, e.g. heart attacks.

ELECTROCUTION. Popular name for a method of execution in use in many of the states of the USA. The criminal is strapped in a special electric chair and an electric shock at 1,800-2,000 v. administered.

ELE'CTRŌDE. A conductor by means of which a current passes into or out of a substance, e.g. the electrodes of an electrolytic cell, an electric furnace, a discharge-tube, or a radio valve. The term is also applied to conducting elements separated by an insulating material as in a capacitor. *See also* ANODE and CATHODE.

ELECTRODYNAMICS. The study of the motion and interaction of electrically charged matter, and how the electromagnetic fields created by these motions behave, particularly electromagnetic waves, e.g. light and radio waves. *Quantum Electrodynamics* (QED) combines quantum theory and relativity mathematically to make possible detailed calculations of subatomic processes involving charged particles, e.g. electrons and protons.

ELECTRO-ENCEPHALO'GRAPHY. In E.-E. electrodes are fixed to the scalp and by means of electronic apparatus the electrical discharges of the brain can be studied. It is used in studying and diagnosing conditions in the brain, such as epilepsy and tumours.

ELECTRO'LYSIS. The production of chemical changes by ionic migration and discharge. Certain compounds, principally acids, bases, and salts, are decomposed by the passage of an electric current. Its most important application is in electro-plating (q.v.).

ELE'CTROLYTE. A conducting medium or solution in which the electric current flows by virtue of chemical changes or decomposition and the consequent movement and discharge of ions in accordance with Faraday's laws of electrolysis (q.v.). The term E. is frequently used to denote a substance which, when dissolved in a specified solvent, produces a conducting medium. The term 'ionogen' has been suggested as an alternative to the term E. when used with this meaning.

ELECTROMAGNETIC INDUCTION. The production of an electromotive force in a circuit by a change of magnetic flux through the circuit. The e.m.f. so produced is known as an induced e.m.f., and any current that may result therefrom as an induced current. If the change of magnetic flux is due to a variation in the current flowing in the same circuit the phenomenon is known as self-induction; if due to a change of current flowing in another circuit, as mutual induction.

ELECTROMAGNETIC WAVES. The 'waves' which occur in the natural process by which electric and magnetic effects are propagated. Electromagnetic waves are known as radio-waves, heat rays, infra-red rays, light, ultra-violet rays, X-rays, etc., depending on their frequencies.

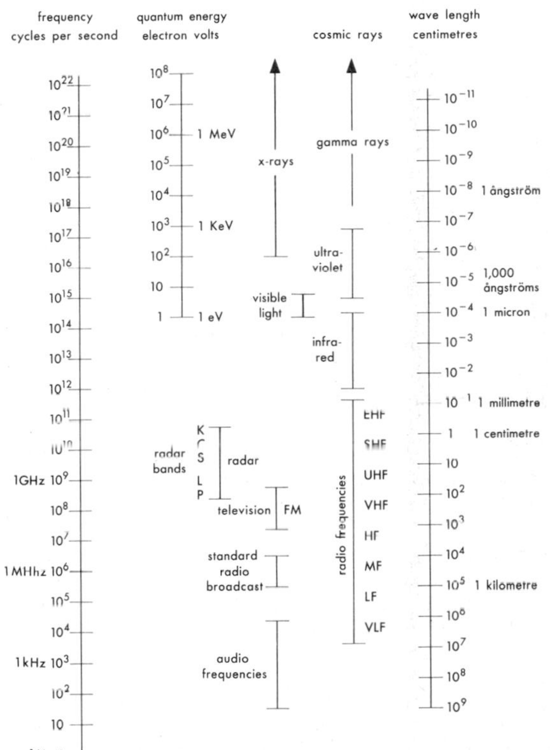

ELECTROMAGNETIC WAVES. Frequency spectrum of radiation from the sub-audible long waves (bottom), to the short wave cosmic rays (top). Courtesy of Penguin Books from *A Dictionary of Electronics* by S. Handel

ELECTROMOTIVE FORCE. That force (e.m.f.) which tends to cause a movement of electricity in a circuit. The electrical condition for generating electromagnetic energy by the transfer of electricity in a certain direction. It is measured by the amount of energy generated by the transfer of unit quantity of positive electricity in that direction. This direction is called the direction of e.m.f.

The e.m.f. in a circuit is the excess of the sum of the e.m.fs. of its constituent parts in one direction over the sum of those in the other direction. Symbol E. Practical unit: volt.

ELECTRON. Stable negatively charged elementary particle which is a common constituent of all atoms. The positron, of equal mass, is the electron's positively charged counter-part. The number of electrons orbiting the atomic nucleus corresponds to the atomic number of the element.

ELECTRON GUN. A structure comprising a cathode and one or more electrodes for producing an electron beam. It is an essential part of many electronic devices such as cathode-ray tubes (television tubes), electron microscopes, etc.

ELECTRONIC FUNDS TRANSFER. The transfer of funds from one bank account, etc., to another by electronic means. For example, a bank customer inserts a plastic card in a point of sale computer terminal in a supermarket, and telephone lines are used to make an automatic debit from his bank account to settle the bill.

ELECTRONICS. Adjusting the transmitter (radar type LAR-2) of the long-range air route surveillance in use at major modern airports: the illustration above shows the antenna. *Photo: Courtesy of Signaal.*

ELECTRONICS. The branch of science which deals with the emission of electrons from conductors, with the subsequent motion of these electrons, and with the construction of electronic devices. From 1940 E. developed at an enormous rate due to the war-time need for radar (q.v.), and this impetus was maintained after the S.W.W. both for military and civil purposes. In the defence field E. forms an integral part of control and guidance systems for ballistic missiles, and methods for their detection, i.e. the Distant Early Warning system. Research into space requires the most advanced electronic techniques, for the control of artificial satellites from take-off to landing. In the civilian field E. played an integral part in the development of computers (q.v.). With the increasing complexity of electronic equipment there was an urgent need to save weight (in spacecraft) and bulk (in computers, etc.) which led to miniaturization. This followed the invention of the transistor (q.v.) and by the mid-1970s the use of standard 'blocks' of electronics was usual.

ELECTRONICS. The complex type of music synthesizer (q.v.) used by exponents such as Walter Carlos. It can easily create series of intervals ranging from less than quarter-tone scales, to whole-tone scales and beyond. *Photo: Courtesy of CBS Records.*

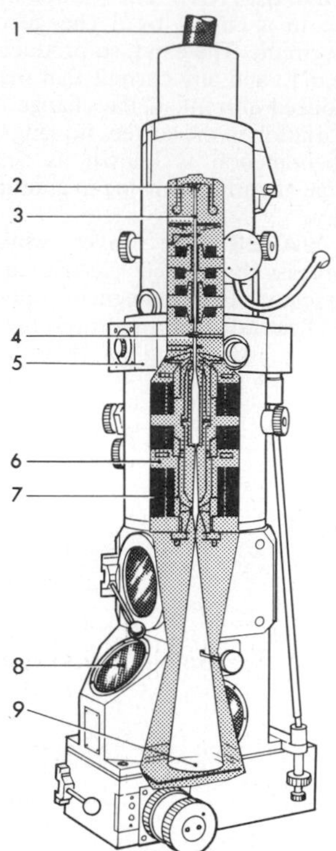

ELECTRON MICROSCOPE

ELECTRON MICROSCOPE. An instrument similar to an optical microscope but using a beam of electrons instead of a beam of light, and electron instead of optical lenses. An electron lens is an electromagnetic or magnetic arrangement to control and focus the beam. Electrons are not visible to the naked eye, so instead of an eyepiece there is a fluorescent screen or a photographic plate on which the electrons are made to form an image. Since the wavelength associated with electrons is very much shorter than that of light much greater magnifications and resolutions are possible. Using a high resolution E.M. (HREM) a 7 million times magnification can be made. The development of the E.M. has made possible the observation of very minute organisms, viruses, and even molecules.

ELECTRON VOLT. A convenient unit for energy in atomic physics. It is the energy acquired by a particle carrying unit electronic charge when it falls through a potential difference of 1 volt, and is approximately equal to $1.602\ 19 \times 10^{-19}$ J.

ELECTRO-PLATING. The electro-deposition of metals upon metallic surfaces for decorative and/or protective purposes. A current is passed through a bath containing a solution of a salt of the plating metal, the object to be plated being the cathode; the anode is either an inert substance or the plating metal. Among the metals most commonly used for plating are zinc, nickel, chromium, cadmium, copper, silver, and gold. E. is used in the preparation of printers' blocks, 'master' gramophone records, and in many other processes.

In electro-polishing the object to be polished is made the anode in an electrolytic solution and by carefully controlling the conditions the high spots on the surface are dissolved away leaving a high-quality stain-free surface. This technique is useful in polishing irregular stainless steel articles, etc. In electro-refining the impure metal is made the anode with a thin sheet of pure metal as the cathode in an electrolytic bath. When a current is passed pure metal deposits on the cathode, leaving the impurities either as an insoluble sludge or in solution. *See also* ION-PLATING.

ELECTROSTATICS. That branch of electricity which deals with the behaviour of stationary electric charges.

ELEMENTS. *See* CHEMISTRY, INORGANIC CHEMISTRY and individual elements.

ELEPHANT. Name given to the 2 surviving species of the Proboscidea, the Asiatic (*Elephas maximus*) and African (*Loxodonta africanus*) Es. The E. reaches 3m (10ft), has a thick, grey, wrinkled skin, a large head, and a long trunk used to obtain food and water. The upper incisors or tusks, which grow to a considerable length, are a source of ivory. The African E. has very large ears and a convex forehead, and the Indian species has smaller ears and a flattened forehead. Es. are herbivorous, and live in herds. With a reputation for intelligence, the E. is quickly tamed, and in India, Burma and Thailand is widely used for transport. The period of gestation is about 19-22 months (the longest amongst mammals) and the life span is probably about 60-70 yrs. Es. do not breed readily in captivity, and this, together with the (now illegal) slaughter of African Es. for ivory, is leading to their extinction. Having the lowest mammalian metabolic rate, which slows down their process of forgetting, Es. are rightly credited with long memories.

ELEPHANT. A cloud of egrets surround the members of this herd of elephants, waiting to feed on the ticks which infest the animals' skin. It is an attention that the great beasts welcome. *Photo: M. Myers/Camera Press.*

ELEPHANTA. Island in Bombay harbour, some 8km (5m) from Bombay. The Temple Caves (6th cent. AD), cut out of the living rock, have sculptures of many Hindu deities incl. Siva.

ELEPHANTĪ'ASIS. In the human body, a gross local enlargement and deformity, especially of a leg, the scrotum, a labium of the vulva, or a breast. The commonest is the tropical variety due to infestation by the parasite filaria; the enlargement is due to chronic blocking of the lymph channels and consequent overgrowth of the skin and tissues.

ELEUSIS (elū'sis). Town in Attica, Greece, NW of Athens, on E. bay with shipyards, iron and steel and cement works. There are substantial remains of the temple of Demeter, in which the **Eleusinian Mysteries** were celebrated. In honour of Demeter, Persephone and Dionysus (qq.v.), they reached a climax in visions seen by the participants in the darkened temple, possibly connected with the underworld. It is thought that the visions may have been induced by fungi containing LSD. Pop. (1971) 2,500.

ELEVATOR. Mechanical device for raising or lowering goods or people on a conveyor belt, or within a shaft inside or outside a building, etc. In 1979 a 'space elevator' was advocated by Arthur C. Clarke (q.v.) as eventually the most economical method of carrying people or freight into high orbit. A cable (37,000 km/23,000,m long) would be attached to a point on Earth's equator, the other end being fastened to a satellite in geostationary orbit, and an E. would then travel up and down at speeds of about 8,000 kph (5,000 mph).

EL FERROL DEL CAUDILLO. *See* FERROL.

ELGAR, Sir Edward (1857-1934). British composer. B. in Broadheath, Worcs., the son of an RC church organist and music-seller, E. had little formal musical education and he gained his first experience in conducting when appointed bandmaster of the staff of a lunatic asylum in 1879. He gained fame as a composer with his *Enigma* variations in 1899, and although his most celebrated work, the magnificent oratorio setting of Newman's *The Dream of Gerontius,* was a failure when performed in Birmingham the following year, it was a great success at Düsseldorf in 1902. Many of his earlier and hitherto unknown works were then performed and are now well known, incl. the popular *Pomp and Circumstance* marches. He was knighted in 1904, and became Master of the King's Musick in 1924. Among his later works are several oratorios, 2 symphonies, chamber music, songs and the tone-poem *Falstaff.*

E'LGIN. Town in Grampian region, Scotland, on the Lossie 8km (5m) S of its port of Lossiemouth on the S shore of the Moray Firth. There are sawmills and whisky distilleries. Pop. (1974) 17,050.

ELGIN MARBLES. Collection of ancient Greek sculptures mainly from the Parthenon at Athens, assembled by the 7th earl of Elgin. Sent to England in 1812, bought for the nation in 1816 for £35,000, they are now in the British Museum.

ELGIN MARBLES. A panel from the Parthenon frieze showing horsemen in the procession of the great Panathenaic festival held every four years at Athens. *Photo: Courtesy of the British Museum.*

ELIJAH (ēlī'jah). Hebrew prophet during the reigns of Ahab and Ahaziah (*c.* mid-9th cent. BC). A native of Gilead and representative of Jehovah, he defeated the prophets of Baal, and was said to have been borne up to heaven in a fiery chariot in a whirlwind.

ELIOT, George. Pseudonym of the British writer Mary Ann Evans (1819-80). B. at Chilvers Coton, Warwicks, she received a strictly evangelical upbringing, but on moving to Coventry with her father in 1841 was converted to free thinking. In 1844 she undertook a translation of Strauss's *Leben Jesu,* and in 1850 began contributing to the *Westminster Review,* of which she became assistant editor under John Chapman 1851-3. At this period she made the acquaintance of Carlyle, Harriet Martineau, Herbert Spencer, and George Henry Lewes. Lewes was married but separated from his wife, and in 1854 E. entered upon a union with him which she regarded as a true marriage and which continued until his death. With Lewes' encouragement she pub. 'Amos Barton', the first of the *Scenes of Clerical Life,* in 1857 under the name of George Eliot. These were successful, and in the following years she won fame with *Adam Bede,* which like its successors, *Mill on the Floss* (1860) and *Silas Marner* (1861), was set in her native county. Less happy were *Romola* (1863), dealing with 15th cent. Italy, and *Felix Holt, the Radical* (1866), which entered the political field. Her next novel, *Middlemarch* (1872), returned to a Warwicks background and is now recognized as E.'s finest work and one of the greatest novels of the cent. Her final work, *Daniel*

Deronda (1876), an impassioned plea against anti-semitism, tends to lose itself in obscurity. She also wrote some poetry. In 1880 she m. her old friend John Cross (1840-1924).

ELIOT, Sir John (1592-1632). English statesman. B. in Cornwall, he became an MP in 1614, a vice-admiral, through Buckingham's patronage, in 1619, and in 1626 was sent to the Tower for demanding Buckingham's impeachment. In 1628 he was primarily responsible for the Petition of Right, and with other parliamentary leaders was imprisoned in the Tower in 1629, where, refusing to submit, he died.

ELIOT, Thomas Stearns (1888-1965). American-born poet and critic; a British subject from 1927. B. at St Louis, Missouri, he was ed. at Harvard, Paris, and Oxford. He settled in London in 1915 and was for a time a bank clerk, later lecturing and entering publishing. In 1917 E.'s first book of verse, *Prufrock and other Observations*, caused a sensation by its daringly experimental verse form and rhythms. His reputation was estab. by the desolate modernity of *The Waste Land* (1922). *The Hollow Men* (1925) renewed the same note, but *Ash Wednesday* (1930) revealed the change in religious attitude which led him to become an Anglo-Catholic. Among his other works are *Four Quartets* (1944), a religious sequence in which he seeks the eternal reality, and the poetic dramas *Murder in the Cathedral* (1935), *The Cocktail Party* (1949), *The Confidential Clerk* (1953), and *The Elder Statesman* (1958). His perceptive critical works incl. *The Sacred Wood* (1920) and *Notes toward the Definition of Culture* (1949), and as editor of *The Criterion* 1922-39, he exercised a moulding influence on the thought of his generation. In 1948 he received the OM and a Nobel prize: Medal of Freedom 1964.

ELIOT. The most classic, and possibly the most enduring poet of the thirties, T.S.Eliot. *Photo: Angus McBean.*

ĖLISABETHVILLE. *See* LUBUMBASHI.

ELĪ'SHA. Hebrew prophet, the successor of Elijah in the mid-9th cent., BC.

ELIZABETH I (1533-1603). Queen of England. The dau. of Henry VIII and Anne Boleyn, she was b. at Greenwich on 7 Sept. 1533. In Mary's reign her Protestant sympathies brought her under suspicion, and she lived in retirement at Hatfield until in Nov. 1558 she became queen. Her first task was to bring about a religious settlement sufficiently broad to exclude any extremists.

Many unsuccessful attempts were made by Parliament to persuade E. to marry or settle the succession. Courtship she found a useful diplomatic weapon, and she sought emotional relief in flirtation with a succession of favourites, among them Leicester, Raleigh, and Essex.

The arrival in England in 1568 of Mary, Queen of Scots, and her imprisonment by E. caused a political crisis and a rebellion of the feudal nobility of the N followed in 1569. Friction between English and Spanish seamen hastened the breach with Spain. When the Dutch rebelled against Spanish tyranny E. secretly encouraged them; Philip II retaliated by aiding Catholic conspiracies against her. This undeclared war continued for many years, until the landing of an English army in the Netherlands in 1585, and Mary's execution in 1587, brought it into the open. Philip's Armada, in 1588, met with total disaster.

The war with Spain continued with varying fortunes to the end of the reign, while events at home foreshadowed the conflicts of the 17th cent. Among the Puritans discontent was developing with E.'s religious settlement; and several were imprisoned or executed. Parliament showed a new independence, and in 1601 forced E. to retreat on the monopolies question. Yet her prestige remained unabated, as was shown by the failure of Essex's rebellion in 1601.

ELIZABETH II (1926-). Queen of the UK. The elder dau. of King George VI, Princess Elizabeth Alexandra Mary was b. at 17 Bruton Street, London, W1, the home of her maternal grandparents, on 21 April 1926. She was ed. privately, and although she became heiress presumptive to the throne on King George's accession did not undertake any official duties until she was 16. During the S.W.W. she served in the ATS, and by an amendment to the Regency Act she became a State Counsellor on her 18th birthday, acting in this capacity during the King's visit to Italy in 1944. She m. her third cousin, the Duke of Edinburgh (*see* PHILIP), in Westminster Abbey on 20 Nov. 1947, and they have 4 children, Prince Charles Philip Arthur George, b. 14 Nov. 1948, Princess Anne Elizabeth Alice Louise, b. 15 Aug. 1950, Prince Andrew Albert Christian Edward, b. 19 Feb. 1960, and Prince Edward Antony Richard Louis, b. 10 March 1964. On the death of George VI in 1952 she succeeded to the throne while in Kenya with her husband at the beginning of a projected tour of Ceylon, Australia and NZ. Since the Coronation in 1953 they have made numerous goodwill tours - in the Commonwealth, the USA, etc. - and in 1977 celebrated a Silver Jubilee.

ELIZABETH (1900-). Consort of George VI. Born the Lady Elizabeth Angela Marguerite Bowes-Lyon, she is the 3rd dau. of the 14th Earl of Strathmore and Kinghorne (d. 1944), through whom she is descended from King Robert Bruce. Ed. privately, she spent most of her early life at her birthplace or at her father's Scottish seat,

ELIZABETH I. A pen-and-ink drawing on vellum by Isaac Oliver. The Queen is traditionally said to be in the dress in which she gave thanks for the defeat of the Armada. *Photo. Courtesy of H.M. the Queen.*

Glamis Castle, Angus. On 26 April 1923, she m. Albert duke of York and their 2 children, Queen Elizabeth II and Princess Margaret [Rose], were b. in 1926 and 1930 respectively. When her husband ascended the throne as King George VI in 1936 she became Queen Consort, and was crowned with him in 1937. She adopted the style Queen Mother after his death.

ELIZABETH (1709-62). Empress of Russia. Dau. of Peter the Great, she carried through a palace revolution in 1741 and supplanted her cousin, the infant Ivan VI, on the throne. She possessed much of her father's energy and statesmanship, continued his policy of westernization, and allied herself with Austria against Prussia.

ELIZABETH. City in New Jersey, USA, the first English settlement in NJ, 1664. It has motorcar and tool factories, oil refineries, chemical works, etc. and sewing machines are made. Pop. (1970) 112,650.

ELIZAVETPOL. Former name of KIROVABAD.

ELK. Largest deer (*Alces alces*) inhabiting N Europe, Asia, Scandinavia, and America, where it is known as the moose. It is brown in colour, stands *c.* 2m (6ft) at the shoulders, has very large palmate antlers, a fleshy muzzle, short neck, and long legs; and feeds on leaves and shoots.

ELLESMERE. Second largest is. of the Canadian Arctic archipelago, Northwest Terrs. It is for the most part glacier-covered. Area 212,687 sq.km (82,119 sq.m).

ELIZABETH II. Her Majesty the Queen has two birthdays, the real one and the official one, usually fixed for a day in June. This official birthday portrait was taken in the '1844 Room' in Buckingham Palace. *Photo: Constantine/Camera Press.*

ELLESMERE PORT. Town in Cheshire, England, on the r. Mersey and the Manchester Ship Canal, an oil port with large refineries. Because of its cross-section of other industries it is used as an 'indicator' of boom and recession. Pop. (1972) 62,850.

ELLICE ISLANDS. *See* TUVALU.

ELLINGTON, Edward Kennedy (1899-1974). American musician, known as 'Duke' E. because of his impeccable clothes. B. in Washington of part Negro origin, he became pianist in NY's Cotton Club in 1927 before forming his own band. He also became one of the world's finest jazz composers, e.g. *Mood Indigo, Sophisticated Lady, In My Solitude,* and *Black and Tan Fantasy.*

ELLIPSE (eli'ps). In geometry, a closed curve which is the locus of a point which moves so that the sum of its distances from 2 fixed points, the foci, is constant. The diameter passing through the foci is the major axis, and the diameter bisecting this at right angles is the minor axis.

ELLIS, Henry Havelock (1859-1939). British writer. He is chiefly famous as the author of many works on the psychology of sex, incl. *Studies in the Psychology of Sex* (7 vols., 1898-1928), but he was also a literary critic and essayist of note.

ELLIS ISLAND. Island off the shore of New Jersey, USA, where steerage class immigrants were processed on arrival in New York, often being cheated and abused, so that it was called Island of Tears. No longer used, it was declared a Nat. Historic Site in 1965 by Johnson. Sam Goldwyn, Irving Berlin, and Elia Kazan were among the *c.* 16 million who entered the USA through Ellis Island.

ELLO'RA. Archaeological site in the N-W Deccan, Maharashtra State, India, with 35 cave temples - Buddhist, Hindu and Jain - varying in date from the late 6th cent. to the 9th cent. They incl. some of the greatest of India's architectural treasures: Visvakarma (a hall *c.* 26m (86ft) long with a huge image of the Buddha), Tin Thal (a 3-storeyed Buddhist monastery cave), the Rameswara cave (with beautiful sculptures) and Siva's Paradise, the great temple of Kailasa.

ELLORA. Goddesses in stone, in the porch of the Rameswara cave temple. *Photo: Courtesy of the Government of India Tourist Office.*

ELM. A common genus (*Ulmus*) of trees of the Ulmaceae family, distributed throughout the temperate latitudes of the N hemisphere, and in mountainous parts of the tropics. The common European E. (*U. procera*) is distributed widely throughout Europe, N Africa and Asia Minor and reaches 46m/150ft; its small, purplish-brown flowers are borne in tufts and appear before the leaves. Other species are the Scotch or wych E. (*U. glabra*) found in N Britain, where it is indigenous, and the N American white E. (*U. americana*) and red or slippery E. (*U. fulva*). The fungus disease *Ceratocystis ulmi*, known as Dutch E. disease, because of a severe outbreak in that country 1924, has reduced the numbers of E. trees in Europe and N America. It is carried by a beetle from tree to tree, and although individual trees may be saved by chemical injection, the process is expensive.

ELM. The underside of elm bark showing the galleries made by elm bark beetles and their larvae. In the process of transmitting Dutch elm disease, they create an abstract pattern an artist might envy. *Photo: Heather Angel.*

EL OBEID (elobā'-id). Cap. of Kordofan prov., Sudan. Linked by rail with Khartoum, it is a market for cattle, gum arabic and durra. Pop. (1975) 91,000.

EL PASO (pah'soh). City in Texas, USA, on the Rio Grande, at the base of the Franklin Mts., where it meets the Mexican border. Centre of an agricultural and cattle raising area., it has industries based on local iron and copper mines, oil refineries, and electronic, food processing and packing, and leather industries. Pop. (1973) 337,800; its twin city on the Mexican side, Juarez, has a pop. of 837,000.

EL SALVADOR. *See* SALVADOR, EL.

ELSINORE. Another form of HELSINGÖR.

ELTON, Charles (1900-). British ecologist. A pioneer of the study of animal and plant life in their natural settings, and of animal behaviour as part of a complex whole, he pub. *Animal Ecology and Evolution* (1930), *The Pattern of Animal Communities* (1966), etc. He was director of the Bureau of Animal Population at Oxford 1932-67.

ÉLUARD (ehlü-ard'), **Paul.** Pseudonym of the French poet Eugène Grindel (1895-1952). B. in Paris of working-class parents, he expressed the suffering poverty of the people in his verse, and was a leader of the Surrealists. He fought in the F.W.W. which inspired his *Poèmes pour la Paix* (1918), and was a member of the Resistance in the S.W.W. His other vols. incl. *Chanson complète, Au Rendezvous Allemand* and *Un Leçon de morale.*

ELY. City in Cambs, England, on the Ouse 24km (15m) NE of Cambridge. It was the chief town of the former admin. co. of the **Isle of Ely,** so-called because the area was once cut off from the surrounding countryside by the fens. Hereward the Wake (q.v.) had his stronghold here. The 11th cent. cathedral is one of the largest in England. At the annual feast of St Ethelreda (Audrey), founder of a religious community at E. in the 7th cent., shoddy or 'tawdry' souvenirs were sold. There are sugar beet factories. Pop. (1972) 10,460.

ELYOT, Sir Thomas (*c.* 1490-1546). English diplomat and scholar. In 1523 he was made clerk to the Privy Council by Wolsey, and in 1531 pub. *The Governour*, the first treatise on education in English.

ÉLYSÉE (ālēzā'), **Palace of the.** Building in Paris erected in 1718 for Louis d'Auvergne, count of Evreux. It was later the home of Mme de Pompadour, Napoleon I and Napoleon III, and in 1870 became the official residence of the presidents of France.

ELYSIUM (ili'zium), or the **Elysian Fields.** In classical mythology, a paradise (sometimes called the Islands of the Blessed) for those who found favour with the gods; it was situated near the r. Oceanus.

ELYTIS (elī'tis), **Odysseus.** Pseudonym of Odysseus Alepoudelis (1911-), Greek poet. B. in Crete, he celebrates the importance of man's fight to shape his own existence in freedom. His major work *To Axion Esti* ('Worthy it is . . .') pub. in 1959, is a lyric cycle, parts of which have been set to music by Theodorakis. Awarded Nobel prize 1979.

ELZEVIR (el'zevēr). Dutch printing house of the 17th cent., founded by **Louis E.** (1540-1617), b. at Louvain. Obliged to leave Belgium in 1580 on account of his Protestant and political views, he settled at Leyden as a bookseller and printer. Of his 7 sons, 5 went into the printing business. Among the firm's publications were editions of Latin, Greek, and Hebrew works, French and Italian classics, etc.

EMBA. River (612km/380m), in the Kazakh SSR, Russia, draining into the N part of the Caspian Sea. It flows through country rich in petroleum.

EMBROIDERY. The art of decoration by means of a needle and thread. Ancient Egypt, Greece, Phrygia, Babylon, and China were renowned for their E. There are many references to such work in the Bible. The earliest Anglo-Saxon work extant is the stole and maniple found in the tomb of St Cuthbert at Durham (AD 905). E. has been used for the adornment of costumes, gloves, book covers, curtains, ecclesiastical vestments, etc. In Britain, early in the 20th cent., E. on canvas and linen for household purposes, together with appliqué, was popular, usually in conventional designs. After the S.W.W., however, there was a revival in creative E. as a craft by designers in many countries.

EMBRYO'LOGY. The study of the changes undergone by living matter in the early life-history or ontogeny of a new individual, during the period in which it acquires the adult form of its species. Recent years have seen the use of frozen embryo transplants in commercial use, e.g. in building up a prize dairy herd quickly at low cost. Some 20 transplants at a time may be removed from one prize cow and re-implanted in inferior foster mothers.

EMDEN. Port of W Germany at the mouth of the r. Ems. Connected with the Ruhr by the Dortmund-Ems canal, E. became an importer of Scandinavian iron ore and timber, exporting Ruhr coal. Oil is refined. Pop. (1978) 65,000.

E'MERALD. A precious stone, a bright, grass-green variety of beryl. It is transparent or translucent, and the finest come from Muzo, in Colombia: other sources are Zambia and Brazil. *See* RUBY.

EMERGENCE, or **Emergent Evolution.** Philosophical theory, propounded in the 20th cent. by C. Lloyd Morgan, S. Alexander, and C. D. Broad, who maintain that life 'emerges' or 'grows naturally' out of matter, and mind emerges out of life.

E'MERSON, Ralph Waldo (1803-82). American poet and essayist. B. at Boston, Mass., and ed. at Harvard, he became a Unitarian minister at Boston. In 1832 he resigned and went abroad, meeting Carlyle, who had a deep and lasting influence on his thought. On his return to America in 1833 he settled at Concord, where he led the Transcendentalists. He made a second visit to England in 1847, and incorporated his impressions in *English Traits* (1856). This had been preceded by two vols. of *Essays* (1841, 1844), and *Representative Men* (1850). Later works incl. *The Conduct of Life* (1860), *Society and Solitude* (1870), and *Letters and Social Aims* (1876). His verse (1847 and 1864) is remarkable for its quality of thought, and as a prose-writer E. possessed a brilliant and clear style.

EMERY, Walter Bryan (1903-71). British archaeologist. In 1929-34 he excavated in Nubia the tumuli at Ballana and Qustol, rich royal tombs of the mysterious X-group people (3-6th cents. AD), and surveyed the whole country 1963-4 before its flooding as a result of the building of the Aswan High Dam. He d. while excavating the site of the tomb and temple of Imhotep at Sakkara.

E'MERY. A variety of corundum (q.v.), greyish-black and opaque, and containing a quantity of haematite and magnetite. Its hardness is second only to the diamond's, and it is much used as an abrasive.

ÉMINENCE GRISE (ehmēnoṅs' grēz; Fr., 'grey eminence'). Name given to the Capuchin friar François Leclerc du Tremblay (1577-1638), who from 1612 was the intimate friend and adviser of Richelieu. Always he worked behind the scenes, and since his time the term *éminence grise* has been applied to other manipulators of power without immediate responsibility. He was also known as Père Joseph.

EMMENTAL (e'mentahl). District in the valley of the Emme r., Berne, Switzerland, where a hard rennet cheese has been made since the mid 15th cent.

EMMET, Robert (1778-1803). Irish patriot. In 1803 he led an unsuccessful revolt in Dublin, was captured, tried, and hanged. His youth and courage have made him the best-loved of Ireland's heroes.

EMPE'DOCLĒS (*c.* 490-430 BC). Greek philosopher and scientist. He lived at Acragas (Agrigentum) in Sicily, and is famous for his analysis of the universe into the 4 elements - fire, air, earth, and water - which through the action of love and discord are eternally constructed, destroyed, and constructed anew. According to tradition, he commited suicide by throwing himself into the crater of Mt Etna.

EMPHYSEMA (emfizē'mah). Lung disease, so-named (meaning 'blown-up lungs') by René Laennec in 1819. The air spaces of the lungs are over-filled with air, the latter having lost much of their recoil force, which enables air to be expelled. Tobacco smoking appears to be a prime cause.

EMPI'RICISM (-isizm). Philosophical theory which maintains that all human knowledge is based ultimately on sense experience (Gk *empeiria*, experience or experiment). It is the opposite of intuitionalism.

EMPLOYERS' ASSOCIATIONS. Employers' organizations formed for purposes of collective action. In the UK there were formerly 3 main organizations, which in 1965 combined as the Confederation of British Industry (q.v.); one of the largest in the USA is the National Assoc. of Manufacturers.

EMINENCE GRISE. Père Joseph, the Capuchin friar who was the friend and confidant of Richelieu. *Photo: Mary Evans Picture Library.*

EMPLOYMENT EXCHANGES. Agencies for bringing together employers requiring labour and workers seeking employment. In the UK these may be organized by the State or a local authority (where they are known as Employment Offices or Job Centres), or as a business venture; a similar system operates in the USA.

EMPSON, Sir William (1906–84). English poet. B. in Yorks, he was prof. of English literature at Tokyo, Peking and 1953-71 at Sheffield. His verse, *Collected Poems* (1955), is obscure and he pub. unusual critical studies, e.g. *Seven Types of Ambiguity* (1930) and *The Structure of Complex Words* (1951). He was knighted in 1979.

EMU (ē'mū). Bird of the Dromaeidae family of the *Ratitae* type. With the exception of the ostrich, the largest of living birds, it is found only in Australia and stands about 2m. (6ft) high. The E. has small rudimentary wings, short feathers on the head and neck, and a curious bag or pouch in the windpipe of the female that enables it to emit the characteristic loud booming note. In appearance it is dull and dowdy.

ENA'MEL. A vitrified substance used as a coating for pottery and porcelain; when transparent it is known as a 'glaze'. Also a vitreous substance of various colours used for decorative purposes on a metallic or porcelain surface.

EMU. An emu father with his chicks, whom he cares for over a period of 18 months from their hatching. His wives meantime enjoy a carefree life. *Photo: Popperfoto.*

In *cloisonné* the various sections of the design are separated by thin metal wires or strips soldered to the metal base.

The art of enamelling dates back to ancient times, and is believed to be of Western Asiatic origin. The Egyptians, Greeks, and Romans enamelled their jewellery, and enamel-work dating from between the 6th and the 9th cents. has been found in the British Isles. Byzantium was famed for enamels from about the 9th to the 11th cents., the finest known work of this period being the famous altar-piece at St Mark's, Venice, which was brought from Constantinople. These were emulated in Europe, and some magnificent work was produced in Saxony, Brunswick, and in the Rhine valley. German enamellers were later employed in France, and during the 13th and 14th cents. the art was introduced into Italy. The chief centres of enamelling during the 15th and 16th cents. were the cities of Lorraine and Limoges. Enamelling was not introduced into China until about the 13th cent.

ENCAUSTIC PAINTING. A process of painting, commonly used in ancient times by the Egyptians, Greeks, and Romans, in which a medium consisting chiefly of wax was employed.

ENCLOSURES. The conversion of common lands into private property, or the substitution of enclosed fields for the open-field system. This process, which has been almost entirely limited to England, began in the 14th cent. and became widespread in the 15th and 16th, the enclosed fields often being used for sheep-rearing. The distress thus caused led to serious rebellions in 1536, 1569, and 1607, while the numerous government measures against depopulation introduced during 1489-1640 were sabotaged by the land-owning JPs. A new wave of E. during 1760-1820 reduced the yeomanry to agricultural labourers, or drove them off the land. A reaction came after 1860, and in 1876 E. of commons was limited by statutes.

ENCYCLICAL (ensī'klikal). Ecclesiastical term, denoting a letter addressed by the Pope to all the bishops of the RC Church.

ENCYCLOPEDIA (ensīklōpē'dia). An alphabetical work of reference covering either the entire field of human knowledge or one specific subject. The earliest extant E. is the *Historia Naturalis* of Pliny the Elder (AD 23-79). The first alphabetical E. in English was the *Lexicon Technicum* (1704), compiled by John Harris. In 1728 Ephraim Chambers pub. his *Cyclopaedia,* which co-ordinated the scattered articles by a system of cross-references, and was translated into French (1743-5). This translation formed the basis of the *Encyclopédie* ed. by Diderot and d'Alembert, pub. 1751-72. By this time the system of engaging a body of expert compilers and editors was estab., and in 1768-71 the *Encyclopaedia Britannica* first made its appearance.

Famous foreign Es. incl. the Chinese E. (printed 1726); the German *Conversations-Lexikon* of Brockhaus; and the French *Grand Dictionnaire Universel du XIX*^{e} *Siècle* of Pierre Larousse (1865-76).

ENCYCLOPÉDIE,
OU
DICTIONNAIRE RAISONNÉ
DES SCIENCES,
DES ARTS ET DES MÉTIERS,
PAR UNE SOCIETÉ DE GENS DE LETTRES.

Mis en ordre & publié par M. DIDEROT, de l'Académie Royale des Sciences & des Belles-Lettres de Prusse; & quant à la PARTIE MATHÉMATIQUE, par M. D'ALEMBERT, de l'Académie Royale des Sciences de Paris, de celle de Prusse, & de la Société Royale de Londres.

Tantùm series juncturaque pollet,
Tantùm de medio sumptis accedit honoris! HORAT.

TOME PREMIER.

A PARIS,

Chez BRIASSON, *rue Saint Jacques, à la Science.*
DAVID l'aîné, *rue Saint Jacques, à la Plume d'or.*
LE BRETON, Imprimeur ordinaire du Roy, *rue de la Harpe.*
DURAND, *rue Saint Jacques, à Saint Landry, & au Griffon.*

M. DCC. LI.
AVEC APPROBATION ET PRIVILEGE DU ROY.

ENCYCLOPEDIA. The title-page of Diderot's *Encyclopédie,* a landmark in the making of modern encyclopedias. *Photo: The Mansell Collection.*

ENDERS, John Franklin (1897-). American virologist. With Weller and Robbins, he discovered the ability of the polio virus to grow in cultures of different tissues, which led to the perfection of an effective vaccine: they were awarded a Nobel prize in 1954. He also succeeded in isolating the measles virus.

ENDIVE (en'div). Annual plant (*Cichorium endivia*) of the Compositae family, related to chicory (q.v.) and grown for use in salads and cooking.

ENDOCRINE GLANDS. *See* DUCTLESS GLANDS.

ENERGY. There are many forms of E. - the ability to do work - mechanical, electrical, chemical, thermal, nuclear, etc. According to the special relativity theory, E. and mass are equivalent, being related by Einstein's equation $E = mc^2$ where E is energy, m is the equivalent mass and c is the velocity of light. The interchangeability of mass and energy is illustrated by the fact that when 2 particles collide they can disappear in a burst of energy, and that an X-ray (beam of energy) may be used to produce thousands of particles.

The chief direct sources of E. have been oil, coal, wood and gas, and indirectly, electricity produced by the use of such fuels or derived from water power or nuclear fission. Increasing costs and the prospect of exhaustion of coal, oil and gas resources, led in the 1970s to consideration of alternative sources. These included solar power, which provides completely 'clean' energy; wind power, tidal power, which like geothermal power, is geographically limited in application; utilization of organic waste, such as chicken manure; photosynthetic power, produced by the use of simple, fast-reproducing plants as fuel; nuclear power, by fusion rather than fission.

ENFIELD. NE bor. of Greater London. Industries incl. engineering - the Royal Small Arms factory having been famous for its production of the E. rifle - textiles, furniture and cement. Little remains of Edward VI's palace, but the royal hunting ground of E. Chase partly survives in the 'green belt'. The Lea Valley has been developed from the 1970s as the cap.'s first regional park. Pop. (1973) 266,000.

ENGELS, Friedrich (1820-95). German socialist. B. at Barmen, he was sent in 1842 to work in the family cotton-factory at Manchester by his father, and there he estab. contact with the Chartists, and collected material for his *Condition of the Working Class in England* (1845). In 1844 began his lifelong friendship with Marx, in collaboration with whom he worked out the materialist interpretation of history and in 1847-8 wrote the *Communist Manifesto.* Returning to Germany during the 1848-9 revolution, E. worked with Marx on the *Neue Rheinische Zeitung,* and fought on the Barricades in Baden. After its defeat he returned to Manchester, and for the rest of his life largely supported Marx and his family. The lessons of 1848 he summed up in his *Peasants' War in Germany* (1850) and *Revolution and Counter-Revolution in Germany* (1851).

ENGINEERING. The design, construction and maintenance of works, machinery, and installations for civil or military purposes, e.g. roads, railways, bridges, harbour installations, engines, ships, aircraft and airports, spacecraft and space stations, generation, transmission and use of electrical power, and a very wide range of applications of science to civilization. To practise E. professionally a university or college training in addition to practical experience is required, but technician engineers usually receive their training through apprenticeships or similar training schemes. The main divisions of E. are aeronautical, chemical, civil, electrical, gas, marine, mechanical, mining, metallurgical, municipal, production, radio and structural E.

ENGLAND. A country of Europe, part of the United Kingdom of Great Britain and Northern Ireland. It occupies the largest part of the island of Great Britain, bounded on the N by Scotland, on the W by Wales; its E coast is washed by the North Sea, its S coast by the

English Channel, and its W coast by the Atlantic Ocean and the Irish Sea. Area 130,763 sq.km (50,487 sq.m); pop. (1978) 46,349,000.

Physical. The main physical features are, in the extreme N, the Cheviot Hills, and, southward, the Cumbrian Mountains and the Pennines which reach as far south as Derbyshire. The Welsh borderlands include Radnor Forest and the Black Mountains. In Devon and Cornwall, Dartmoor, Exmoor, and Bodmin Moor are other stretches of high land. The Cotswold Hills extend from Bristol into Lincolnshire; to the SE, and separated by a broad vale, is a parallel line of hills, consisting of the Marlborough Downs, Chiltern Hills, and East Anglian Heights. Between London and the S coast the N and S Downs enclose the Weald. At their W end they are joined to Marlborough Downs by the extensive, low, chalk plateau of Salisbury Plain. Smaller groups of hills occur particularly in the W. Midlands, Dorset, and Somerset, and NE Yorkshire. The principal lowlands are the Vale of York, East Anglia, the Midlands, the London Basin, the Cheshire Plain, and Hampshire.

The whole of England is well watered, and the many good estuaries have encouraged the growth of great ports (London on the Thames, Bristol on the Avon, Liverpool on the Mersey, Hull on the Humber, Newcastle on the Tyne). Of the rivers the most important is the Thames which flows from the Cotswolds to the N Sea, passing through Oxford, Windsor, and London. The Severn rises in Wales and reaches the Bristol Channel below Gloucester. Other important rivers are the Trent and the Great Ouse, both flowing into the N Sea, and the Mersey. A network of canals linking the ports with centres of industry, constructed in the 18th and 19th cents., lost importance with the growth of modern road and rail transport, but is being increasingly used for recreation and amenity. In the Cumbrian Mountains Windermere and other lakes are famed for their beauty. E. includes several smaller islands, among them the Isle of Wight and the Scilly Isles. (*See also* ISLE OF MAN.)

CLIMATE. The climate is temperate (mean coldest temperature about 5°C, warmest 15°C), and for most of the year the country lies within the influence of the south-westerly variable winds which are cool and generally rain-bearing, though their impact changes unpredictably. Considerable seasonal and regional variations occur, and there are three climatic areas: (1) the west, with warm summers, mild winters, and abundant rainfall; (2) the south-east, with warm summers, cold winters, and less rain; (3) the north-east, with cool summers and cold winters. Throughout its length the W coast is warmer than the E.

VEGETATION. E. was once a land of forests, with grasslands and bogs where the soil did not favour the growth of trees. Through the centuries the woodlands have been cleared until today they cover only a small percentage of their former area. The N mountains lie within the sub-arctic belt of coniferous forests, while Sherwood, Dean, and the New Forests are deciduous. The oak and the beech are the most common native species, but Forestry Commission plantations naturally tend to the more rapidly exploited conifers.

Economic life. England is primarily industrial, relying on imports to fill many of her needs, and since the S.W.W. has encountered recurrent difficulties in achieving a 'balance of payments' by an expansion of exports. Her industrial power was first built on the reserves of coal in the N and Midlands, the iron and steel industries which grew up nearby, and their dependent railway engineering works, shipbuilding yards, etc. These are all still of importance, as are the cottons of Lancs and the woollens of Yorks, but the emphasis has shifted to the newer and more diversified industries. These incl. the manufacture of cars and commercial vehicles; all types of aircraft; hovercraft; electronic, nuclear power and telecommunications equipment; mining, agriculture and textile machinery; scientific instruments; pharmaceuticals, fertilizers and other chemical products, espec. those from petroleum; all kinds of man-made fibres; paper, leather and plastic goods; pottery and glass - for industrial and domestic use; film and television programmes; sound recordings and fashion goods. Exports of these are supplemented by 'invisible earnings' from world-wide banking and insurance interests and overseas investments. Tourism is also important.

By the 1980s the continuing oil crisis and competition from the Third World had enforced further streamlining of major industries, notably in motor vehicle plants and steel. Under the Thatcher govt. there was a drive to return nationalised industry to the private sector, and to revitalize declining areas, as well as redress the general imbalance between the more prosperous Midlands and South East, and the depressed North East, by the introduction of enterprise zones (q.v.). The coal industry made more viable by modernisation, closure of uneconomic pits, and discoveries such as the new field N of Selby, was assured of a role in view of the energy shortage. Other minerals incl. salt, gypsum, Cornish tin and China clay, Yorkshire potash and Derbyshire fluorspar, but above all the oil and natural gas of the North Sea, and more recently the Channel coast, as in Dorset. The cap. is London, and other important towns are Birmingham, Bradford, Bristol, Canterbury, Coventry, Leeds, Leicester, Liverpool, Manchester, Newcastle, Norwich, Oxford, Plymouth, Portsmouth, Sheffield, Southampton, Stoke-on-Trent, Winchester and York.

The agricultural industry is increasingly mechanized, requiring fewer workers, and intensive. The chief crops are cereals (wheat, barley, oats and rye), vegetables (potatoes, beans, peas, cabbages, turnips), and sugar beet. Breeding cattle are exported and excellent meat, butter, cheese and milk produced on high quality grazing. Sheep are important both for meat and wool, and pigs for fresh meat and a bacon industry. Eggs and chicken, espec. on the controversial broiler-house system, are produced. Fruit - apples, pears, plums, cherries and strawberries - is grown in the southern half of the country; and tomatoes, salad crops, and flowers are grown under glass or in the open in favourable areas. Fishing from the great east coast ports of Hull, Grimsby, Yarmouth and Lowestoft was badly affected by decline in herring catches, loss of the Iceland fisheries and dumping by foreign trawlers, but in 1980 the industry was receiving aid to adapt to new conditions. Fish farming is being increasingly developed, and Whitstable oysters and Cornish lobsters are luxury exports.

Communications. The road and rail systems are closely co-ordinated. British Rail (London, Midland, Western, Southern, Eastern and North-Eastern regions) provides fast passenger links between the principal towns, and freight-liner trains for goods, and the road system is being modernized with a series of fast motorways. Internal

GRAMPIAN MTS
MULL
FIRTH OF TAY
SCOTLAND
FIRTH OF FORTH
Clyde
SOUTHERN UPLANDS
Tweed
FIRTH OF CLYDE
ARRAN
CHEVIOT HILLS
NORTH SEA
NORTH CHANNEL
Tyne
SOLWAY FIRTH
Eden
Lake District
PENNINES
Tees
CLEVELAND HILLS
SCAFELL PIKE
Swale
Yorkshire Moors
I. OF MAN
IRELAND
Vale of York
Yorkshire Wolds
Flamborough Hd.
IRISH SEA
Ouse
Aire
Ribble
Spurn Head
Humber
Mersey
LINCOLN EDGE
Lincoln Wolds
ANGLESEY
HOLY I.
Dee
Witham
SNOWDON
THE WASH
Trent
Severn
Nene
The Fens
EAST ANGLIAN HEIGHTS
Yare
The Broads
CARDIGAN BAY
WALES
CAMBRIAN MTS
Ouse
ST. GEORGE'S CHANNEL
Teifi
Avon
Wye
COTSWOLDS
Stour
The Naze
Ure
Thames
CHILTERNS
Gower
Severn
Avon
Kennet
Thames
SHEPPEY
NORTH DOWNS
BRISTOL CHANNEL
MENDIPS
Salisbury Plain
Exmoor
The Weald
STRAIT OF DOVER
SOUTH DOWNS
Arun
Beachy Hd.
Dartmoor
I. OF WIGHT
Bodmin Moor
Exe
Portland Bill
ENGLISH CHANNEL
Miles
0 10 20 30 40 50 60 70 80
0 10 20 30 40 50 60 70 80 90 100 110 120
Kilometres
FRANCE
Land's End
© Geographical Projects

ENGLAND. A silver dish from the Mildenhall treasure, dated to the 4th century A.D.; the bathing pool at Bath, one of the finest British remains of the Roman period (top right); the Pilgrims' Gate at Canterbury (centre left); the poet, Geoffrey Chaucer; a model of a typical Elizabethan playhouse designed and made by Dr Richard Southern, with C. Walter Hodges (centre right); and St. George's Hall, Liverpool, a splendid example of 19th century classicism. *Photos: Courtesy of the British Tourist Authority, British Museum, British Tourist Authority, National Portrait Gallery, British Council and RTHPL*

and external air services are good, and there has been general modernization of seaports, besides such developments as the Milford Haven oil terminal and the bulk handling facilities at Immingham (q.v.).

Population. The English people are descended in the main from Anglo-Saxon and Danish stock, but with a British or Celtic strain surviving in the SW and on the Welsh border. Through the cents. there has been an intermixture of Norman, French, Flemish, German and Jewish elements, and many have Scottish, Irish or Welsh blood in their veins. Before, during and after the S.W.W. there was a substantial influx of Continental refugees - Jewish, German, Polish, Lithuanian, Hungarian, Czech, etc. - and of people from the Irish Republic. Labour shortage in the 1950s and 1960s, and other special conditions, led to the arrival of the Italian and Spanish workers, and such increasing numbers from the West Indies, India, Pakistan and other Commonwealth countries that legislation was introduced to stem the flow. The table gives the administrative cos.

Religion. The Church of England (*see* ANGLICAN COMMUNION) is the estab. church, but there are substantial other Protestant and Roman Catholic denominations, as well as Jewish, Hindu, Moslem and other communities.

ENGLEHEART, George (1752-1829). English miniature painter. B. at Kew, he studied under Joshua Reynolds and in 40 years painted nearly 5,000 miniatures incl. copies of many of Reynolds' portraits.

ENGLISH ART. Painting. English medieval art incl. some fine illuminated MSS, and although some of the surviving wall paintings have been deliberately damaged on religious grounds or been incompetently restored, there have been discoveries in recent years which show that an excellent tradition was established. In Tudor times painting became for the first time mainly secular, and the first well-known artist is Holbein, who came from Germany to paint the court of Henry VIII. Among his followers was the miniaturist Nicholas Hilliard, who estab. a tradition of English excellence in this field which was continued by Samuel Cooper, Richard Cosway and George Engleheart. The Flemish Van Dyck, employed as a court painter by Charles I from 1632, greatly influenced English portrait painters, as in turn did Sir Peter Lely and Godfrey Kneller.

William Hogarth was the first great English artist, Thomas Rowlandson following in the same tradition. More sedate are the famous painters of the 18th cent. conversation piece, the German-born Johann Zoffany and Arthur Devis. A truly indigenous form is the sporting picture, George Stubbs being the great 18th cent. master, although the Sartorius and Alken families also produced fine work, as did Sir Edwin Landseer in the next cent. and Sir Alfred Munnings in the 20th. George Morland's pictures of rural life have a similar vigorous realism.

Among the native portrait painters Sir Joshua Reynolds, Thomas Gainsborough - also a superb landscape artist - and Sir Thomas Lawrence hold high place in the late 18th and early 19th cents. Rather apart was the genius of the visionary William Blake, the water-colourist Samuel Palmer, who came under his influence, and the errant genius of John Martin. Among painters specializing in landscape in the same period were Richard Wilson, Paul Sandby, Alexander Cozens, J. R. Cozens, John Crome, Thomas Girtin, J. S. Cotman, David Cox, Peter

Counties of England

	Area in sq. km.	*Pop. in 1978*	*Admin. H.Q.*
Avon§	1,340	921,900	Bristol
Bedfordshire	1,234	494,700	Bedford
Berkshire	1,243	672,600	Reading
Buckinghamshire	1,878	525,100	Aylesbury
Cambridgeshire	3,409	570,200	Cambridge
Cheshire	2,322	919,800	Chester
Cleveland§	583	568,200	Middlesbrough
Cornwall	3,546	416,700	Truro
Cumbria§	6,808	472,400	Carlisle
Derbyshire	2,630	896,200	Matlock
Devon	6,525	948,000	Exeter
Dorset	2,688	586,500	Dorchester
Durham	2,436	603,800	Durham
Essex	3,674	1,435,600	Chelmsford
Gloucestershire	3,117	495,300	Gloucester
Hampshire	3,772	1,453,400	Winchester
Hereford and Worcester§	3,925	610,100	Worcester
Herefordshire	1,634	947,100	Hertford
Humberside§	3,512	844,900	Kingston upon Hull
Isle of Wight	381	114,300	Newport
Kent	3,730	1,449,000	Maidstone
Lancashire	3,005	1,369,600	Preston
Leicestershire	2,553	833,300	Leicester
Lincolnshire	5,885	530,100	Lincoln
London, Greater**	1,580	6,918,000	
Manchester, Greater*§	1,284	2,663,500	
Merseyside*§	648	1,545,500	Liverpool
Midlands, West*§	958	2,711,600	Birmingham
Norfolk	5,515	679,800	Norwich
Northamptonshire	2,367	516,400	Northampton
Northumberland	5,034	289,200	Newcastle upon Tyne
Nottinghamshire	2,108	973,700	Nottingham
Oxfordshire	2,612	540,600	Oxford
Shropshire	3,490	365,900	Shrewsbury
Somerset	3,458	411,100	Taunton
Staffordshire	2,660	997,000	Stafford
Suffolk	3,807	592,700	Ipswich
Surrey	1,655	995,400	Kingston upon Thames
Sussex, East	1,795	652,500	Lewes
Sussex, West	2,017	633,600	Chichester
Tyne and Wear*§	567	1,165,100	Newcastle
Warwickshire	1,980	469,500	Warwick
Wiltshire	3,481	516,200	Trowbridge
Yorkshire, North	8,316	661,300	Northallerton
Yorkshire, South*	1,562	1,304,100	Barnsley
Yorkshire, West*	2,039	2,067,900	Wakefield
	130,763	46,349,400	

*metropolitan counties
**metropolitan type
§new counties

de Wint and - the giants in genius and influence - J. W. M. Turner and John Constable.

In Victorian times the subject picture was popular and there was a pleasant domestic school which incl. J. C. Horsley. An outstanding group were the Pre-Raphaelites - Millais, Holman Hunt and Rossetti, but these and G. F. Watts, Ford Madox Brown, Lord Leighton and Sir Edward Burne-Jones have suffered in reputation in the 20th cent., although interest in them revived in the 1970s.

J. M. Whistler, the American who introduced the doctrine of Art for Art's Sake and settled in Chelsea, had as his disciple W. R. Sickert, who also admired Degas and with Wilson Steer introduced Impressionism to England. Sickert headed the Camden Town group which incl. Spencer Gore and Harold Gilman. Among artists of the 20th cent. are Duncan Grant, Sir Frank Brangwyn, Sir William Nicholson, Augustus John, Paul Nash, Ben Nicholson, Christopher Wood, Graham Sutherland, Ivon Hitchens, Stanley Spencer, John Bratby, Francis Bacon and Victor Pasmore.

In more recent years there has been a tendency to individualism divorced from schools and particular genres, of which the multi-figure townscapes of Lowry and the brightly attractive colour of the work of David Hockney are disparate examples.

ENGLISH ART. 'The Fighting Temeraire' one of the masterpieces of England's most original artist, J.M.W. Turner. *Photo: Courtesy of the National Gallery, London.*

Sculpture. In addition to some early Celtic work, there are some fine medieval ecclesiastical sculptures, e.g. Wells Cathedral and the Henry VII chapel in Westminster Abbey. Foreign artists such as Roubillac were extremely popular in the 18th cent. but John Flaxman is the first outstanding English name. Well known in the 19th cent. were Sir Francis Chantrey, Alfred Stevens, and Lord Leighton, and Sir George Frampton at the turn of the cent. The 20th cent. has seen a remarkable flowering with the work of Epstein, Eric Gill, Frank Dobson, Henry Moore, Barbara Hepworth, Michael Ayrton, and Reg Butler.

Architecture. The main styles in English architecture are: Saxon, Norman, Early English (of which Westminster Abbey is an example), Decorated, Perpendicular (15th cent.), Tudor (a name chiefly applied to domestic buildings of the period, *c.* 1485-1558), Jacobean, Stuart (incl. the Renaissance and Queen Anne styles), Georgian, and the Gothic revival of the 19th cent. Notable architects incl. Wren, Inigo Jones, Vanbrugh, Hawksmoor, Sir Charles Barry, Sir Edwin Lutyens, Sir Hugh Casson, Sir Basil Spence, Sir Frederick Gibberd, and Sir Denys Lasdun.

Universality of materials - steel, glass - has merged the English tradition with the international trend to austere skyscrapers, but recent years have seen such strikingly imaginative works as Coventry Cathedral by Sir Basil Spence, with the integrally designed tapestry by Graham Sutherland, Liverpool Cathedral by Sir Frederick Gibberd, incorporating in the lantern glass panels designed by John Piper, and Sir Denys Lasdun's National Theatre on the South Bank.

ENGLISH CHANNEL. *See* CHANNEL.

ENGLISH CIVIL WAR. *See* CIVIL WAR.

ENGLISH HISTORY. PREHISTORIC AND ROMAN BRITAIN. From *c.* 2500 Britain was inhabited by people who came from the E and S; they practised agriculture and left as their monument the long barrows in S England. Another group, called 'beaker folk', introduced bronze-working *c.* 1800 BC; they constructed Stonehenge and other great religious structures. Several waves of Celtic invaders followed from *c.* 1000 BC; the use of iron was introduced *c.* 450 BC. The Celts traded with Europe and their tribal organization was developing into a system of kingdoms when Julius Caesar made his visits in 55 and 54 BC. The Roman conquest began in AD 43 and by AD 80 had reached the Scottish Lowlands. After a brief period of resistance Roman culture was accepted, the upper classes becoming completely Romanized. Christianity was introduced from Ireland in the 4th cent.

ANGLO-SAXON ENGLAND (407-1066). An obscure 200 years followed the withdrawal of the Romans in 407, during which the Germanic Angles and Saxons overran all England except Cornwall, Wales, and Cumberland; how far the Celts survived is uncertain. Roman partial military re-occupations possibly occurred 417-*c.* 427 and *c.* 450. In the 6th cent. Christianity was introduced among the pagan invaders by missionaries from Rome. England was divided into several kingdoms, the chief being Northumbria, Mercia, Kent, and Wessex, whose kings battled for supremacy until in 829 they all accepted Egbert of Wessex as overlord. His successors were confronted with the Danish raiders, and although Alfred expelled the Danes from Wessex in 878 he had to cede to them the N and E of England. During the 10th cent. this was reconquered and a real national unity achieved, but Danish raids began again in 991, and during 1016-42 England was ruled by Danish kings. Norman influence, predominant under Edward the Confessor, led toward the Norman conquest of 1066.

EARLY MIDDLE AGES (1066-1307). As England advanced towards unity, the Anglo-Saxons had developed from a tribal society to a system somewhat akin to the feudalism introduced by the Norman kings. The contrast between the law and order they had established, and the disorder of Stephen's reign, made a return to a strong monarchy generally acceptable; nevertheless, when John attempted to claim more than was his due by feudal standards, barons, Church, and towns united against him to assert their privileges in Magna Carta (1215). This alliance was renewed against Henry III, in a struggle whence emerged the House of Commons, an assembly of knights and burgesses, side by side with the older baronial assembly, or House of Lords. The combination of king, lords, and commons began with Edward I's Model Parliament of 1295. Edward completed the conquest of Wales begun by the Normans, and attempted unsuccessfully to conquer Scotland. In Ireland Henry II had estab. a lasting colony in 1171.

ENGLISH HISTORY. An Anglo-Saxon king consults with his witan, an early equivalent of a 'privy council', in this drawing in an 11th century manuscript in the British Museum. On the right, an execution is in progress.

LATER MIDDLE AGES (1307-1485). Dynastic, trade and other interests led to the 100 Years War with France (1338-1453). The financial problems created by this war enabled parliament to secure control of taxation, and of the king's choice of ministers by the weapon of impeachment. The later 14th cent. was filled with unrest. The Black Death (1348-9) created a serious labour shortage, and attempts to deal with it led to bitter class struggles, culminating in the Peasants' Revolt, 1381. In spite of the failure of the rising, serfdom steadily declined during the 15th cent. Popular anticlericalism found expression in the Lollard movement, which anticipated the Reformation. When Richard II moved towards absolutism, parliament replaced him by Henry IV, who was obliged to grant it unprecedented powers. Henry V's attempt to conciliate the nobility by renewing the French war ended in his son's reign in disaster, and led directly to the Wars of the Roses (1455-85). Order, restored by Edward IV, was maintained after a change of dynasty by Henry VII, who broke the political power of the feudal nobility.

TUDOR ENGLAND (1485-1603). Henry VIII followed this up by bringing the Church under royal control, repudiating the papal power, dissolving the monasteries, and confiscating their wealth. In this policy he received the enthusiastic support of parliament and the landowners, who benefited by the confiscated lands. Under Edward VI the English Church adopted Protestant doctrines; after a Catholic reaction under Mary I, Elizabeth I adopted a compromise whereby the Church's doctrines became Protestant and its ritual semi-Catholic. These changes coincided with, and encouraged, a movement whereby many of the free peasantry who had arisen after the disappearance of serfdom were evicted to make room for sheep-farms. Modern capitalism began with the development of the woollen industry and of trade with Russia, Turkey, and later with India. Trade rivalries combined with political reasons to involve England under Elizabeth I in war with Spain, whence the country emerged as a major naval power.

The accession in 1603 of James VI of Scotland as James I of England united the crowns of the two countries. *See* UNITED KINGDOM; also COMMONWEALTH; IRELAND; SCOTLAND; WALES.

THE ENGLISH REVOLUTION (1603-89). Under James I the uneasy co-operation between king and parliament, which had continued through the Tudor period, ended. The gentry and merchants, enriched by Church lands, enclosures, foreign trade, and industry, took advantage of the Crown's financial needs, produced by the inflation which followed the import of American silver, to seize control of the state machine. The issues were complicated by the struggle between the State Church and the Puritans, who became identified with the parliamentary opposition. During the revolution of 1640-60 England passed through civil war to republicanism, and thence to military dictatorship. The Restoration of 1660 restored to the monarchy the show rather than the substance of power. Charles II worked with considerable success to reverse the work of the revolution, but James II's attempts to carry this process further provoked a new revolution in 1688-9, which placed political power in the hands of the Whig landowners and merchants. Ireland, which had been finally conquered by the Tudors, rose for her independence in 1641 and 1689, only to be reduced to the status of a colony. Meanwhile the foundations of the Empire were laid in N America and India, a process which involved England in three wars with the Dutch. The accession of James I had brought England and Scotland under one king. Among the results of the revolution of 1688 was the union of their parliaments in 1707.

THE 18TH CENTURY (1689-1815). Another result of 1688 was the second 100 Years War with France, the successor of Holland as England's commercial and colonial rival. In this series of seven wars British sea-power proved decisive, and the French were ousted from N America and India. At home the supremacy of parliament found expression in the establishment of cabinet government under Walpole (1721-42). The power of the Whig landowning and merchant oligarchy, supreme since 1714, was challenged by George III, and for 70 years (1760-1830) the Tories were almost continuously in office. Those years were troubled by the successful revolt of the American colonies (1775-83) and the French Revolution (1789-99), which stimulated the growth of the democratic movement in England. In Ireland a powerful movement arose for complete independence, which Pitt countered by carrying through a parliamentary union with Britain (1800). At home agriculture was revolutionized by a new wave of enclosures, whereby the small farmer was driven off the land or reduced to being a landless labourer. At the same time mechanical progress and the rise of the factory system converted England from an agricultural to an industrial country without a serious rival. Two new classes emerged from the change, the industrialists and the exploited industrial workers, bitterly hostile to one another yet united in a demand for parliamentary reform.

THE 19TH CENTURY (1815-1900). The alliance of the industrialists with the Whigs produced a new party, the Liberals, who in 1832 carried a Reform Bill transferring political power from the aristocracy to the middle classes. For the next 40 years Liberalism, with its ideology of free trade and *laissez-faire,* was triumphant. The working classes, excluded from the franchise, created their own organizations in the trade unions and the Chartist movement, although the latter disappeared during the years of mid-Victorian peace and prosperity (1850-75). After 1875

Britain's industrial monopoly found rivals in Germany and the USA, and she was obliged to seek new markets and sources of raw materials. The Conservatives made themselves the mouthpiece of the new imperialism, and launched Britain on a career of expansion in Egypt, S Africa, and elsewhere. The outstanding feature of the history of the Empire in the 19th cent. was the development of Canada, New Zealand, Australia, and later of S Africa, into self-governing dominions. The economic crisis of the later 19th cent., which encouraged imperial development, also induced the working classes, largely enfranchised in 1867 and 1885, to revive the militant trade unionism and political movement of Chartist days. From an alliance of trade unions and small socialist bodies emerged the Labour Party in 1900.

ENGLISH HISTORY. The old House of Commons with Sir Robert Walpole - the first Prime Minister - and Arthur Onslow, the Speaker. An engraving by A. Fogg after Hogarth.

THE 20TH CENTURY. After 1900 Britain's commercial and colonial rivalry with Germany led to her abandonment of her traditional isolationist policy, and to her entry into the system of alliances dividing Europe and into a feverish armaments race. At home a Liberal government attempted to satisfy with social reforms a working class demanding a higher standard of living. In 1914 a general strike and a civil war in Ireland seemed imminent, and the F.W.W. created a host of new problems. During the post-war years Ireland won her independence, unrest swept India, and a wave of mass strikes culminated in the general strike of 1926. After a few years of comparative prosperity an unprecedented economic crisis devastated most of the world during 1929-31; among its results was the coming to power of the British National Government in 1931. The years that followed were dominated by the approach of the S.W.W. of 1939-45. Like the F.W.W. this was followed by a general movement towards the Left throughout Europe, one feature of which was the return in 1945 for the first time of a Labour government with an overall majority, whose programme included nationalization (q.v.) and a generally planned economy. The Conservatives returned to power 1951, Eden taking over from Churchill in 1955 until superseded, following Suez, by Macmillan in 1957. The latter's ill-health led to his replacement by Sir Alec Douglas-Home in 1963, and Labour, under Harold Wilson, narrowly returned to power in 1964. The Conservatives, under Edward Heath, were again defeated in 1966, but returned to power 1970-4, before being twice defeated (Feb. and Oct. 1974) by Labour. The Labour majority was small, and dissatisfaction with both major parties was shown by a substantial Liberal vote and strong nationalist votes in Wales and Scotland, so that devolution for these 2 countries became a live issue. Heath had taken E. into Europe in 1973, a decision confirmed 1975 by a referendum under Wilson. Unemployment, inflation and the Northern Ireland question continued to dominate the situation, and following labour unrest in the winter of 1978–9, a Cons. govt. was returned to office, and was re-elected in 1983. Monetarist measures to control inflation then brought an expected increase in unemployment, but with some signs towards the end of 1980 of their becoming effective. Increasing bankruptcies, however, caused worries of long-term damage to the economy. In a major constitutional reform new Select Committees (q.v.) were introduced to strengthen Parliament's control of the executive. A split between Labour right and left led in 1981 to the formation of a 'third' Social Democratic Party.

ENGLISH LANGUAGE. In its origin E. belongs to the western division of the Germanic languages. Towards the end of the 7th cent. 4 main dialects can be distinguished, the Jutish of Kent, the Saxon of the south, the S Anglian or Mercian of the Midlands, and the N Anglian or Northumbrian north of the Humber, which collectively form Anglo-Saxon or O.E. This tongue retained much of the complex Germanic grammar, and was inflectional.

King Alfred's active interest in literature made the W Saxon dialect the prevailing literary language until the early part of the 10th cent.

The Norman Conquest did not at first greatly affect English, and it is possible that interaction with the related speech of the Danes settled in the country played the greater part in the dropping of many inflections, and the creation of a much simpler language than O.E. by the end of the 12th cent.; but it had no standard form, and documents of the M.E. period (*c.* 1200-1400) are written in a variety of dialects. Thanks in particular to the influence of Chaucer, the dialect of London came to be accepted as a literary standard, an early indication of this being that Gower (*c.* 1330-1408), though of Kentish origin, wrote in the London, not the Kentish, dialect. This tendency was confirmed by the setting up in London in 1477 of the first printing press; Caxton, like Gower from Kent, used the London dialect in his publications in English. By *c.* 1650 printers had generally adopted a fixed orthography. But adoption of a standard form of written English did not abolish spoken dialects and local variations of pronunciation in different parts of E., many of which survive into the second half of the 20th cent. despite the widespread levelling influence of broadcasting. From the 1960s a

Waller, and Denham. Drama is represented by Dryden; Otway and Lee in tragedy; Etherege, Wycherley, Congreve, Vanbrugh, and Farquhar in comedy.

With the 18th cent. opened the Augustan Age in England. Pope perfected the poetic technique of Dryden; while in prose Steele and Addison evolved the form of the polite essay, Swift achieved supremacy in satire, and Defoe exploited his gifts as the genius of journalism. This cent. also saw the development of the novel through the long-drawn intricacies of Richardson to the robust narrative of Fielding and Smollett, the sentiment of Sterne, and the Gothic 'terror' of Horace Walpole. The standards established by the 'Augustans' were maintained by Johnson and the members of his circle - Goldsmith, Burke, Reynolds, Sheridan, etc. - but the 'romantic' element present in the work of the poets Thomson, Gray, Young, and Collins was soon to overturn them. The forgeries of Chatterton, Macpherson's *Ossian*, and the work of the Wartons are significant of the new attitude.

The poetry of Cowper, Blake, and Crabbe no longer fits into the old categories, and the *Lyrical Ballads* (1798) of Wordsworth and Coleridge forms the manifesto of the new age. Byron, Shelley, and Keats form a second generation of Romantic poets. In fiction Scott took over the Gothic tradition from Mrs Radcliffe, to create the historical novel, and the quiet genius of Jane Austen estab. the novel of the comedy of manners. Criticism attained new heights in Coleridge, Lamb, Hazlitt, and De Quincey.

During the 19th cent. the novel was further developed by Dickens, Thackeray, the Brontës, George Eliot, Trollope, and the lesser Disraeli, Reade, Kingsley, Bulwer Lytton, etc. The principal poets of the reign of Victoria are Tennyson, Browning, Arnold, the members of Rossetti's circle, Morris and Swinburne, and the solitary Fitzgerald. Among the other great prose writers of the era are Macaulay, Newman, Mill, Carlyle, Ruskin, and Pater. To the transition period at the end of the cent. belong the poetry and novels of Meredith and Hardy; the work of Butler and Gissing; and the plays of Pinero, Jones, and the Irishman Oscar Wilde.

The Victorian tradition in poetry was continued in the new cent. by Bridges; his contemporary Hopkins was a notable experimenter in verse forms. Kipling, Newbolt, Belloc, Davies, Hodgson, De la Mare, Housman, Chesterton, Masefield, Noyes, and Drinkwater were other poets of the opening cent. Best-remembered poets of the F.W.W. are Sassoon, Brooke, Owen, and Graves. Poets of the succeeding years incl. Dame Edith Sitwell, T. S. Eliot, Auden, Day Lewis, MacNeice and Spender. Unusual elements entered the novel with Henry James, Conrad, Kipling, and George Moore. New middle-class realism was in the novels of Wells, Bennett, E. M. Forster, and Galsworthy. Maugham, Hugh Walpole, James Joyce, D. H. Lawrence, Aldous Huxley, Priestley, Virginia Woolf, Christopher Isherwood, Evelyn Waugh, Graham Greene, and Ivy Compton Burnett are later writers of fiction. Writers for the English stage incl. another outstanding Irishman, Bernard Shaw, as well as Galsworthy, Maugham, Priestley, Barrie, Lonsdale, Coward, Graham Greene, Bridie, Rattigan, Emlyn Williams, and the writers of poetic drama, e.g. T. S. Eliot, Fry, Auden, Isherwood, and Dylan Thomas. The '50s and '60s produced what has been called the 'kitchen sink' school of dramatists - e.g. Osborne and Wesker - and the English 'Theatre of the Absurd' in the plays of N. F. Simpson; other leading playwrights were Harold Pinter, John Arden, Tom Stoppard, Peter Schaffer, Joe Orton and Robert Bolt. Outstandingly successful in the 1970s were the 'black comedies' of Alan Ayckbourn. Post-S.W.W. poets included Thom Gunn, Roy Fuller, Philip Larkin, and Sir John Betjeman; and novelists of the same period were William Golding, Iris Murdoch, Angus Wilson, Muriel Spark, Lawrence Durrell, John Braine, Kingsley Amis, C. P. Snow, Pamela Hansford Johnson, John Wain, Anthony Powell, Alan Sillitoe, Anthony Burgess, and John Fowles. Among prose writers of the cent. are W. H. Hudson, Lytton Strachey, T. E. Lawrence, Osbert Sitwell, Winston Churchill, G. M. Trevelyan, Arnold Toynbee, George Orwell, and Bertrand Russell. For other literatures in English, *see under* AUSTRALIA, CANADA, IRELAND, NEW ZEALAND, SCOTLAND, SOUTH AFRICA, UNITED STATES OF AMERICA, WALES.

ENGLISH LITERATURE. John Keats, a portrait by Joseph Severn. *Photo: Courtesy of the National Portrait Gallery.*

ENGLISH-SPEAKING UNION. Society for promoting the fellowship of the English-speaking peoples of the world, founded in 1918 by Sir Evelyn Wrench.

ENGRAVING. The art of incising marks of any kind upon any hard substance, esp. on blocks of metal or wood for purposes of reproduction. There are three main types of print-making: (1) relief prints made by means of woodcutting and wood engraving; (2) intaglio prints made by means of engraving and etching upon metal; and (3) surface prints made by means of lithography. *See* AQUATINT; DRY-POINT; ETCHING; MEZZOTINT.

ENGLISH LITERATURE. George Eliot as a young woman, a portrait by F. D'A. Durade. *Photo: Courtesy of the National Portrait Gallery.*

ENGRAVING. An engraving by Bewick after R. Johnson, illustrating a scene from Goldsmith's 'Deserted Village'. *Photo: Mary Evans Picture Library.*

ENHANCED RADIATION WARFARE. *See* NEUTRON BOMB.

ENIWETOK (eniwē'tok). Atoll in the Marshall Islands taken from the Japanese by the USA in 1944, and used from 1947 for 43 atomic tests. The islanders, re-settled at Ujelang, insisted on returning home in 1980 though radiation danger persisted. Nuclear debris and contaminated soil had been removed to the islet of Runit by the USA and restoration work carried out. Pop. (1980) 453.

ENKEPHALIN (enkef'alin). Brain pain-killer, produced by the brain itself, which acts in a similar way to morphine.

E'NNIS. Co. town of Clare co., Rep. of Ireland, on the Fergus, 32km (20m) NW of Limerick. There are distilleries, flour mills, and furniture is made. Pop. (1971) 6,000.

ENNISKI'LLEN. Co. town of Fermanagh co., N. Ireland, between Upper and Lower Lough Erne. There is some light industry, and it has been designated for further industrial growth. Pop. (1972) 7,000.

ENNIUS (en'i-us), **Quintus** (239–169 BC). Early Roman poet. B. near Tarentum in S Italy, he wrote tragedies based on Greek models. His epic poem, the *Annales,* deals with Roman history and earned him the name of 'father of Roman poetry'.

ENOSIS. *See* CYPRUS.

ENSCHEDE (ens'khedā). Textile manufacturing centre in Overijssel prov., the Netherlands. Pop. (1978) 141,200.

ENSOR, James, baron (1860–1949). Belgian artist. B. at Ostend, he became noted particularly for his dissonant use of colour and his 'decadent' and satiric pictures, whose skeletons and masked figures represented his view of humanity and its falsity. One of his best-known paintings is 'Entrance of Christ into Brussels' (1888).

ENTAIL. The settlement of land on a successive line of persons, usually the 'heirs of the body' of the settlor. 'Estates tail' are (1) general or (2) special. The former descend to the eldest child, regardless of sex, the latter to the eldest male child or the eldest female child or according to some other specific arrangement. Such settlements are increasingly rare in modern times, and the power to make them has often been destroyed by legislation, cf. restrictions in certain states of the US.

ENTE'BBE. Town in Uganda, on the NW shore of L Victoria, 20km (19m) SW of Kampala. It lies 1,177 m (3,863 ft) a.s.l., and has technical schools, a botanical garden, and a first-class international airport. Founded 1893, it was the admin. centre of Uganda 1894–1962. Pop. (1970) 13,500.

The *E. Incident* involved the hi-jacking of a French aircraft by a Palestinian liberation group 27 June 1976. It was taken to E., whence the Israeli hostages were rescued 3-4 July by Israeli aircraft.

ENTENTE CORDIALE (aṅtaṅt' kordē-ahl'). The 'friendly understanding' estab. between Britain and France in 1904, when France recognized Britain's 'special interests' in Egypt, while Britain professed herself disinterested in Morocco.

ENTE'RIC. A general name for infective fevers of the intestine, especially typhoid and paratyphoid.

ENTERPRISE ZONE. In the UK (1980) a special zone in which there is total exemption from rates on industrial and commercial property, from development land tax, and from certain other restrictions. They were introduced to counter industrial recession and decline.

ENTOMO'LOGY. *See* INSECT.
ENUGU (enōō'gōō). Town in Nigeria, cap. of East Central state. It is a coalmining centre, with steel and cement works, and is linked by rail with Port Harcourt. Pop. (1975) 187,000.
ENVER PASHA (1881-1922). Turkish statesman and soldier. He led the military revolt in 1908 which resulted in the Young Turk revolution, and was killed fighting the Bolsheviks in Turkestan.
ENZYME (en'zīm). A biological catalyst which converts one chemical to another very swiftly, without itself being destroyed. Enzymes in the body digest food, and from ancient times substances incl. Es have been used to make cheese (rennet) and alcohol (yeast). Bacteria now produce Es. for industrial purposes (detergents, high-fructose sweeteners, etc), the pure extracted Es. being repeatedly re-used after being bonded with glass, etc. Enzymes are also used medically to correct faulty metabolism in the body. Totally synthetic Es. are being researched.
EOLITHS (ē'-oliths). The simplest and most primitive form of specially shaped stone implements, dating from the Tertiary period. Their recognition as artifacts was largely due to Benjamin Harrison in 1899 and Reid Moir more recently in E Anglia.
Ē'OS. Greek goddess of the dawn, better known by the Roman name of Aurora.
EOTVOS (öt'vösh), **Roland von,** baron (1848-1919). Hungarian scientist. B. at Budapest, he investigated problems of gravitation, and constructed the double-armed torsion balance for determining variations of gravity.
EPAMINONDAS (ēpaminon'das) (*c.* 420-362 BC). Theban general and statesman, who won a decisive victory over the Spartans at Leuctra in 371, and fell in the moment of victory at Mantinea.
ÉPERNAY (ehpernā'). Town in Marne dept, France, centre of the champagne industry. Pop. (1975) 26,500.
EPHEDRINE (ef'edrin). A member of a group of drugs, called sympathomimetic amines, which incl. adrenalin and benzedrine. It occurs in the *Ephedra* genus of shrubs, found in warm temperate zones.
EPHESUS (ef'esus). Ancient city of Asia Minor, a centre of the Ionian Greeks, with a famous temple of Artemis (Diana). St Paul visited the city and addressed one of his epistles to the Christians there. E. was destroyed by the Goths in AD 262.
EPIC. A narrative poem dealing at length with some great action such as the Babylonian *Gilgamesh,* Homer's *Iliad* and *Odyssey,* the Indian *Rāmāyana* and the *Mahābhārata,* and the Anglo-Saxon *Beowulf.* The primary or authentic epics were chanted at great feasts, and their main theme is always the deeds of heroes. The literary or secondary epic is written in imitation of the older epics, and is intended for reading. Virgil's *Aeneid* is the greatest Latin epic poem, and later examples are Milton's *Paradise Lost,* Tasso's *Jerusalem Delivered,* and Hardy's *Dynasts.*
EPICTĒ'TUS (fl. *c.* AD 90). Greek Stoic philosopher. B. at Hierapolis in Phrygia, he lived for many years in Rome as a slave, but eventually secured his freedom, attended the lectures of a Stoic, and became a Stoic philosopher himself. He taught that men are in the hands of an all-wise providence, and that they should endeavour to do their duty in the position to which they are called.
EPICŪRĒ'ANISM. System of philosophy named after Epicurus (341-270 BC), a Greek philosopher who taught in Athens from 306 BC. E. held human happiness to be the highest good, and his scheme of morality has been summed up in 4 canons: the pleasure which produces no pain is to be embraced; the pain which produces no pleasure is to be avoided; the pleasure is to be avoided which prevents a greater pleasure or produces a greater pain; and the pain is to be endured which averts a greater pain or secures a greater pleasure. His 'pleasure' was not sensual gratification, but the rational satisfaction of a healthy mind in a healthy body. The most distinguished Roman Epicurean was Lucretius.
EPIDAU'RUS. Ancient Greek city on the E coast of Argolis. Originally famous for the temple of the god of healing, Aesculapius, E. is now noted for its beautiful and well-preserved amphitheatre where the Nat. Theatre holds an annual festival.
EPIGRAM. A short poem, originally an inscription of a votive or funerary character, but later a short, witty, and pithy saying. The chief Latin epigrammatists were Catullus and Martial; in English literature the E. has been employed by Ben Jonson, Herrick, Pope, Swift, Prior, Landor, and Yeats.
EPI'GRAPHY (Gk *epigráphein,* 'to write on'). The art of writing with a sharp instrument on hard, durable materials, and also the scientific study of that art. Epigraphical writings are called inscriptions.
E'PILEPSY. A chronic disorder marked by attacks of loss or alteration of consciousness, usually with convulsions, corresponding to a sudden release of psychic pressure. The cause may be hereditary defect, injury, or disease. Anti-convulsant drugs, e.g. Valium, control E. so that the patient may lead a normal life.
ÉPINAL (ehpēnahl'). Capital of Vosges dept, France, on the Moselle. A cotton textile centre, it dates from the 10th cent. Pop. (1975) 40,000.
EPIPHANY (ēpi'fani). A feast of the Christian Church, held on Jan. 6 in commemoration of the manifestation of Christ to the world.
EPĪ'RUS (Gk 'mainland'). Country of ancient Greece; the N part is in modern Albania; the remainder, in NW Greece, is divided into four nomes, Arta, Thesprotia, Yanina, Preveza.
EPI'SCOPACY. That system of Church govt in which administrative and spiritual power over a district (diocese) is held by a bishop. The Roman Catholic, Eastern Orthodox, Anglican and Protestant and Methodist Episcopal (US) churches are episcopalian; E. also exists in some branches of the Lutheran Church, esp. in Scandinavia.
EPISTLE (epi'sl). In modern usage a word applied to letters of antiquity, or with a suggestion of pomposity and literary style. The best-known Es. are those contained in the NT, and those of Horace, Boileau, Voltaire, Ben Jonson, Dryden, and Pope.
EPPING FOREST. Forest in Essex, N of London, England. Once a royal hunting ground, it has been controlled from 1882 by the Corpn of the City of London. Area *c.* 25 sq.km (10 sq.m).
E'PSOM. Town in Surrey, England, SW of London. Epsom salts were obtained from its mineral springs from 1618 and it became a spa. Epsom racecourse lies to the S, and the site of Henry VIII's palace of Nonsuch (excavated 1959) to the NE. Pop. (1972) of E. and Ewell, 72,170.

EPSOM SALTS. Hydrated magnesium sulphate, $MgSO_4.7H_2O$, known as a saline purgative. The name is derived from a bitter saline spring at Epsom, Surrey, which contains the salt in solution, but the E.S. of commerce come from Germany and USA.

EPSTEIN (ep'stīn), **Sir Jacob** (1880-1959). British sculptor. B. in New York of Russo-Polish parents, in 1904 he came to England, where most of his major work was done. In 1907-8 his series of figures for the British Medical Assoc.'s building in the Strand, London, provoked a storm of criticism, as did the tomb of Oscar Wilde in Paris (1909). These were followed by, amongst others, the 'Rima' memorial to W. H. Hudson in Hyde Park, 1925; 'Genesis', 1931; 'Ecce Homo', 1933; 'Adam', 1939; 'Lucifer', 1945; the aluminium 'Christ in Majesty' for Llandaff Cathedral, 1957; and 'St Michael and the Devil' for Coventry Cathedral, 1959. All his great sculptures were carved in stone or marble as expressions of human emotions, and their lack of the purely aesthetic conventions of form and elegance almost invariably aroused furious protest. E. became equally well known for his portrait busts, e.g. of Vaughan Williams, Einstein and Blake, whose vitality and insight earned him his reputation as a romantic sculptor. Knighted in 1954.

EPSTEIN. The sculptor seen with his statue 'Lazarus' just before the award of a knighthood in 1954 crowned a career fraught with controversy. *Photo: Popperfoto.*

EQUĀ'TOR. The *terrestrial equator* is the great circle whose plane is perpendicular to the earth's axis, i.e. to the line joining the poles. Its length is 40,076 km (24,901.8 m), divided into 360° of longitude. The *celestial equator* or Equinoctial is the circle in which the plane of the terrestrial equator intersects the celestial sphere.

EQUATORIAL GUINEA. *See* GUINEA, Equatorial.

EQUESTRIANISM (ekwest'-). Skill in horsemanship, espec. in the events for which the International Equestrian Federation is the governing body. It comprises: (1) dressage or *haute école* (high school), in which the horse is guided through various difficult exercises with minimum use of reins or hands; (2) cross-country, in which a difficult tract of country is covered at speed; and (3) show-jumping (q.v.). It is an Olympic sport, World Championships are held and the Royal International Horse Show, Wembley, is a major annual event.

EQUINOXES (ēkwinoksēz; Lat., 'equal nights'). The two points at which the sun during its apparent annual course among the stars crosses the celestial equator; when the sun is in either equinox the day and night are of equal length, 12 hours each, all over the earth.

EQUITIES. Stocks and shares (qq.v.) which differ from debentures and preference shares in not paying interest at fixed rates.

EQUITY (ek'witi). In law, a term denoting the mitigation of the ordinary rules of law where the application of these would operate harshly in a particular case; sometimes it is regarded as an attempt to achieve 'natural justice'. So understood, E. appears as an element in practically all mature legal systems, and in a number of modern codes the judge is instructed to apply to the decision of particular cases both the rules of strict law and the principles of E.

In England E. originated in decisions of the Lord Chancellor's court, the Court of Chancery, on matters that were remitted to it because there was no remedy available in the Common Law courts, or the remedy there was inadequate. Gradually it assumed the appearance of a distinct system of legal rules, as precise and limited in their operation as the rules of Common Law, and developed by the same method as the Common Law, i.e. by the doctrine of judicial precedent. Thus, in the 19th cent., there existed two great systems of English law - Common Law and E. - side by side, and applied in separate law courts, until the Judicature Acts, 1873-5, established a single High Court of Justice, in which each judge was given full powers to apply both Common Law and E. to the decision of any case before him. Equitable principles exist side by side with principles of Common Law in many branches of the law, and particularly in the law of contracts, of real and personal property, and of torts (or civil wrongs). One of the greatest contributions made by E. to English law is the institution of the trust.

ERASMUS, Desiderius (?1466-1536). Dutch scholar and humanist. B. at Rotterdam, the illegitimate son of Rogerius Gerardus (whose story is told in Charles Reade's novel, *The Cloister and the Hearth*), he himself adopted the Latin-Greek name which means 'beloved'. As a youth he was a monk in an Augustinian monastery near Gouda, but in 1495, after becoming a priest, he went to study at Paris, and in 1499 paid the first of a number of visits to England. Here he met Linacre, More, and Colet, and for a time he was Lady Margaret professor of Divinity and of Greek at Cambridge. His pioneer edition of the Greek NT was pub. in 1516, and an edition of St Jerome and the *Colloquia*, a series of dialogues on contemporary topics, in 1519. In 1521 he went to Basle, where he edited the

Christian Fathers. More than 3,000 of his letters have survived.

The *Erasmus Prize* (1958) is awarded annually to outstanding contributors to internat. understanding, usually in social or cultural fields, e.g. Martin Buber, Sir Herbert Read, Robert Schuman, Jan Tinbergen.

ERASTIANISM. The theory that the Church should be subordinated to the State. The name is derived from Thomas Erastus (1524-83), a German-Swiss theologian, who maintained in his writings that the Church should not have the power of excluding persons as a punishment for sin.

ERATO'STHENĒS (fl. 235 BC). Greek geographer and mathematician. His map of the ancient world was the first to contain lines of latitude and longitude; he calculated the earth's circumference with an error of less than 200 m.

ERBIUM. Metallic element; symbol Er, atomic number 68, at. wt. 167.27. It is one of the rare earths, and was discovered in 1843 by Mosander.

E'REBUS. In Greek myth, the god of darkness and also the intermediary region between the upper world and Hades.

EREBUS, Mount. The world's southernmost active volcano (3,794 m/12,520 ft), Ross Island, Antarctica. It contains a lake of molten lava which scientists are investigating in the belief that it can provide a 'window' onto the magma beneath the Earth's crust which fuels volcanoes.

ERFURT (er'foort). City in (E) Germany, on the Gera, cap. of E. district, in a rich agricultural area. The cathedral (12-15th cent.) has fine stained glass, and the Augustinian monastery where Luther spent some years as a monk is now an orphanage. Manufactures incl. textiles, typewriters and electrical goods. Pop. (1971) 198,265.

ERG. In physics, the unit of energy in the c.g.s. system. It is the energy expended when a force of 1 dyne is exerted through a distance of 1cm. It is exactly equal to 10^{-7}J.

ERGONŌ'MICS. The study of the relationship between a man and his work. The main objective is to optimize the performance of a skill in the sense of mechanical efficiency, physiological compatibility (i.e. reducing muscular stress) and psychological effectiveness (i.e. reducing fatigue, coding displayed data to suit perceptual characteristics, taking account of peculiarities of memory). Some emphasis is laid upon dynamic systems, for example, in designing optimum instrument layout in vehicle control, but the science also deals with static optimization of work benches, furniture, and the whole environment.

ERGO'STEROL. The substance which, under the action of the ultra-violet rays in sunlight, gives rise to vitamin D - the vitamin which affects bone-formation and deficiency of which produces rickets. The sterol occurs in ergot (hence the name), in yeast, and in other fungi. The principal source of commercial E. is yeast.

E'RGOT. A parasitic fungus, *Claviceps purpurea*, which attacks the rye plant. It forms large grains usually black in colour from which E. alkaloids (used in childbirth) are extracted. Infected bread causes ergotism, with gangrene or convulsions. *See* LSD.

ERHARD, Ludwig (1897-1977). German statesman. He succeeded Adenauer as Chancellor of the Federal Rep. (1963-6). The 'economic miracle' of W Germany's recovery after the S.W.W. is largely attributed to E.'s policy of 'social free enterprise' (*Marktwirtschaft*).

ERICA (erī'ka). In botany, the heaths; the typical genus of the family Ericaceae. There are about 500 species, distributed through Africa and Europe.

ERICACEAE (erikā'sē-ē). Family of dicotyledonous flowering plants. They are herbs, small shrubs, or small trees, but mostly have woody, creeping stems and are often evergreen. Widely distributed in the cool and temperate parts of the world, they incl. the heaths and the rhododendron.

ERICSSON (er'ikson), **Leif.** Norse explorer who traditionally sailed W from Greenland *c.* AD 1000 to find a country first sighted by one of his predecessors in 986. Landing with 35 companions in N America, he called it 'Vinland', because he discovered grape vines growing, and spent a winter there. The story was confirmed in 1963 when a Norwegian expedition, led by Helge Ingstad, discovered remains of a Viking settlement (dated *c.* 1000) near the fishing village of L'Anse-aux-Meadows at the northern tip of Newfoundland.

ERIC THE RED (fl. 982-1000). The alleged discoverer of Greenland. According to a 13th cent. saga he was the son of a Norwegian chieftain, was banished from Iceland *c.* 982 for homicide, sailed westward, and discovered a land which he called Greenland.

ERIDU (ā'ridoo). Ancient city of Mesopotamia *c.* 5000 BC, according to tradition the cradle of Sumerian civilization. On its site is the Iraqi village of Tell Abu Shahrain.

ERIE (ē'ri). City on the Pennsylvania bank of Lake E., USA, with heavy industries and a trade in iron, grain, and freshwater fish. Pop. (1970) 186,650.

ERIE, Lake. Fourth largest of the 'Great Lakes' of N America connected to L. Ontario by the Niagara river, on which are the famous falls, by-passed by the Welland Canal. It is 400km (250m) long.

ERIGENA (erē'jena), **Johannes Scotus** (*c.* 815-77). Medieval philosopher. He was probably an Irishman and according to tradition travelled in Greece and Italy before Charles the Bald invited him to France (before 847), where he became head of the court school. He is said to have visited Oxford, to have taught at Malmesbury, and to have been stabbed to death by his pupils. As a thinker he tried to combine Christianity with Neo-Platonism.

ERIN (ē'rin). Poetic name for Ireland derived from the dative case Érinn of the Gaelic name Ériu, possibly derived from Sanskrit 'western'.

ERITREA (ārētrā'-a). Country with a coastline of over 1,000 km (670m) on the Red Sea. The interior is mountainous, but the valleys and intermediate plains are cultivated with the aid of irrigation. The cap. is Asmara. E. is Moslem rather than Christian by tradition. Under Egyptian, Ethiopian and Turkish rule in earlier times, E. was an Italian colony from 1889 until taken under British military admin. 1941-52. Following a UN decision, it was then federated with Ethiopia, but after an autonomous period 1952-62 was harshly subordinated as an Ethiopian prov., so that the Eritrean Liberation Front (ELF) demanded complete independence. The 1974 Ethiopian revolution originated in E., but the new regime was similarly opposed to E.'s independence (Assab and Massawa are Ethiopia's outlets to the sea), and armed resistance continued, backed by the Arab world. Eritrean successes in 1980 led towards peace moves. Area 118,500 sq.km (45,745 sq.m); pop. (1971) 1,527,000.

ERIVAN. Alternative transliteration of YEREVAN.

ER'LANGEN. Industrial town, 16km (10m) N of Nuremberg, Bavaria, W Germany, at the confluence of the Regnitz and Schwabach. Textiles and electrical goods are made, and there is a univ. (1743). Pop. (1978) 100,600.

ERMINE (er'min). Name given to the stoat when in its white winter coat. In northern latitudes the coat becomes completely white, except for a black tip to the tail, but in warmer regions the back may remain brownish. The fur is used commercially.

ERNIE. Electronic Random Number Indicator Equipment. Machine designed and produced by the Post Office Research Station to select and print out a long series of random 9-figure numbers to indicate the prize-winners in premium-bond draws.

ERNST, Max (1891–1976). German Surrealist painter. B. in Brühl, nr Cologne, he studied philosophy at the Univ. of Bonn and first exhibited in Berlin in 1916. He was an active Dadaist and in 1922 went to Paris where he helped found the Surrealist movement in 1924.

Ē'ROS (Cupid, Amor). In the Hellenic and Roman pantheon, the god of love. Originally a god of fertility and son of Chaos, he is later described as the son of Aphrodite, and is represented as a youth blindfolded, armed with arrows and winged.

EROS. Asteroid. Elongated, 19 × 6 km (12 × 4 m), it rotates in 5 hr 17 min: mean distance from Earth 217,000,000 m.

ERSE (ers). An early Scottish form of 'Irish', the word was applied in the 18th cent. English literary world to the Gaelic language of Scotland, and occasionally to the Irish Gaelic as well.

ERSKINE, Thomas, 1st baron (1750-1823). British Lord Chancellor. B. in Edinburgh and called to the Bar in 1778, he appeared for the defence in a number of trials of parliamentary reformers for sedition, and when the Whigs returned to power in 1806 he became Lord Chancellor and a baron. Among his most famous speeches were those in defence of Lord George Gordon, Thomas Paine, and Queen Caroline.

ERYSIPELAS (erisip'elas). An acute disease of the skin due to infection by a streptococcus. Starting at some point where the skin is broken or injured, the infection spreads, producing a swollen red patch with small blisters, and general fever.

ERZGEBIRGE (ārz'gebērge). Mountain range - the 'ore mountains' - on the German-Czech frontier, where the rare metals uranium, cobalt, bismuth, arsenic and antimony are mined. Some 145km (90m) long, its highest summit is Mt Klinovec (Keilberg) in Czechoslovakia (1,244 m/4,080 ft).

ERZURUM (ār'zeroom). Turkish town on the Armenian plateau, a commercial centre at the meeting-place of routes from Europe and Asia. It was captured from the Turks by the Russians in the Caucasus Campaign of 1916. Pop. (1970) 134,700.

ESAU (ē'saw; Heb. 'hairy'). OT character; the son of Isaac and Rebekah, and the elder twin brother of Jacob, who tricked Isaac into giving him the blessing intended for E. by donning goatskins. Earlier E. had sold his birthright to Jacob for a 'mess of red pottage'. He was the ancestor of the Edomites. Typically he was a nomadic hunter, compared with Jacob the less barbaric pastoralist.

ESBJERG (ez'byerg). Port of Denmark on the W coast of Jutland, and W termination of the rail and ferry service across Denmark and Sweden to Stockholm. Pop. (1970) 68,100.

ESCALATOR. A mechanism consisting of a continuous series of steps (or trolleys), which travel in ascending or descending direction. Es. are driven by a motor generally housed in the upper landing. This motor drives the gears and the sprockets, which in turn operate the driving chains which carry the steps and also the wheels which drive the hand rail. The first E. was exhibited in Paris in 1900. Es. normally move at a minimum speed of about 3km (2m) per hour. Travelators are similar devices operating on a level surface to speed passengers through airports, etc.

ESCAPE VELOCITY. The V. which would have to be imparted to a body in order for it to escape from the planet of origin, without the application of further power. In the case of Earth, E.V. is 11.3km (7m) per sec; the Moon 2.5km (1.5m); Mars 5km (3.1m); and Jupiter 60km (37m).

ESCAUT. French form of SCHELDT.

ESCHER (e'sher), **Maurits Cornelis** (1902-72). Dutch graphic artist. His drawings, often based on mathematical principles of symmetry or pattern, usually originate in paradox, illusion, or double-meaning. Especially notable are such lithographs as 'Relativity' (1953) and 'Ascending and Descending' (1960).

ESCORIA'L, El. Group of buildings 42km (26m) N of Madrid, commissioned by Philip II. It incl. a palace, with works by El Greco, Titian, and Velasquez; church with a library and a royal mausoleum.

ESENIN (yesay'nin), **Sergey** (1895-1925). Soviet poet. B. in Konstantinovo (renamed Esenino in his honour), of peasant stock, he went to Petrograd in 1915, attached himself to the Symbolists, greeted the Revolution, revived peasant traditions and folklore, and initiated the Imaginist group of poets (1919). Disillusioned by the political development, he went abroad, m. the American dancer, Isadora Duncan, and afterwards a granddau. of Leo Tolstoy, became the head of the Moscow bohemians and committed suicide.

E'SKILSTUNA (-toonah). Manufacturing town W of Stockholm, Sweden, with iron foundries, steel and armament works. Pop. (1978) 91,600.

ESKIMO. People inhabiting the Arctic coasts of N America, the eastern islands of the Canadian Arctic, and the ice-free coasts of Greenland. With the Aleuts, they are decended from Bering Sea mongoloids, they are generally long-headed, of medium height, flat-faced, with prominent cheekbones, sallow complexion, dark eyes, and lank black hair. They refer to themselves as Inuit ('the people'), and were first called E. ('eaters of raw meat') by the N American Indians. Traditionally, they construct their homes from stones, peat, bones, driftwood and skins - snow igloos being used only for temporary camps in winter travel - and rely on oil from blubber for light and heat and on their reindeer herds for all other wants. In practice this picture is increasingly modified as western civilization extends in the Arctic. The skill which the Es. show in the construction of their *kayaks* (skin-covered canoes) and in their remarkable small-scale carvings is easily adapted to the modern situation, and they are first-class mechanics. In 1975 the E. of the Canadian Arctic (*c.* 14,500) demanded the creation of an autonomous state, Nunavat 'Our Land', to comprise part of the mainland of the Northwest Terrs., and many Arctic Is., incl. Baffin Is.

The area claimed is rich in minerals inc. iron, gold, lead, zinc and copper, and the sea has oil and natural gas. Area 2,400,000 sq.km (930,000 sq.m).

The E. language possesses dialects, but has no striking divergencies. The conditions of their life make rather for individualism than distinctive tribal organization. The E. has belief in a soul, in survival after death, in taboos, charms and amulets and formerly in the medicine man or *angakok*, but Christianity has been adopted by many. They number (1974) *c.* 73,000.

ESKIMO. Fur-trapping still provides a living for many Eskimos. These white fox skins are the result of many visits to Kalaut's traps. *Photo: Camera Press.*

ESKIMO DOG. Semi-domesticated dog kept by Eskimos in Alaska for drawing sledges. They are strong and fierce, and are known as huskies.

ESKISEHIR (eskē'shehēr). City in Turkey, 200km (125m) W. of Ankara, exports meerschaum, chromium, and magnesite; makes cotton goods, tiles; assembles aircraft. Pop. (1970) 216,330.

ESPA'RTO. A grass (*Stipa tenacissima*), native to S Spain and N Africa, now widely grown in dry, sandy situations throughout the world. The plant is just over a metre (3ft) high, producing greyish-green leaves, which are used for paper-making, ropes, baskets, mats, cables, etc.

ESPEHAN. *See* ISFAHAN.

ESPERA'NTO. International language invented by Dr L. L. Zamenhof of Warsaw (1859-1917), who pub. the first book on it in 1887. It consists of natural roots and develops on natural lines, and has a literature of original and translated works.

ESPIONAGE. *See* SECRET SERVICE.

ESPRONCEDA (espronthā'dah), **José de** (1808-42). Spanish poet. Originally one of the Queen's guards, he lost his commission because of his political activity, and was involved in the risings of 1835 and 1836. His lyric poetry and life style both owed much to Byron.

ESQUIMALT (eskwī'malt). Canadian naval station, at S of Vancouver Island, B.C. Pop. (1971) 4,000.

ESQUIVEL (eskivel'), **Adolfo** (1932-). Argentinian sculptor and architect. As leader of the Servicio de Paz y Justicia, a Catholic-Protestant human rights organization, he was awarded a Nobel peace prize in 1980.

ESSAY. Literary form, dealing in a discursive meditative way with some particular subject; a personal note is more or less marked. The E. first became a recognized genre and name with the first edition of Montaigne's essays in 1580. Bacon's essays (1597) are among the most famous in English. Abraham Cowley, whose Es. appeared in 1668, was the first English essayist to bring ease and freedom to the genre, but it was with the development of periodical literature in the 18th cent. that the E. became a widely used form. The great names are Addison and Steele, with their *Tatler* and *Spectator* papers, and later Johnson and Goldsmith. A new era was inaugurated by Lamb's *Essays of Elia* (1820); to the same period belong Leigh Hunt, Hazlitt, Sainte Beuve and De Quincey and the Americans Emerson and Thoreau; Hazlitt may be regarded as the originator of the modern critical E., and his successors incl. Arnold and Gosse. Macaulay, whose Es. began to appear shortly after those of Lamb, presents a strong contrast in his vigorous but less personal tone. There was a considerable revival of the form during the closing years of the 19th and beginning of the 20th cent., in the work of R. L. Stevenson, Anatole France, Gautier, Sir Max Beerbohm, and later of Chesterton and Belloc. The literary journalistic tradition of the E. was continued by E. V. Lucas, Robert Lynd, the American James Thurber, Sir Desmond MacCarthy, etc., and the critical essay by George Orwell, Cyril Connolly, F. R. Leavis, T. S. Eliot, etc. The E. was generally adopted in 19th cent. Europe as a vehicle for literary criticism, but the 'true' E. is usually regarded as being particularly English in spirit. However, its leisured approach made it a less-used form by the mid 20th cent., although its spirit survived in the radio 'Es.' of Alistair Cooke. More in tune with the modern mood is the acerbity and penetrating humour of short 'articles' on similar disparate subjects by writers such as Bernard Levin.

ESSEN. City in North Rhine-Westphalia, W Germany. Admin. centre of the Ruhr, it has textile, chemical, electrical and other industries. The Krupp steel and armament works, repeatedly bombed in the S.W.W., have been converted to other industrial use. Pop. (1978) 664,500.

ESSENES (esēnz'). A body of pre-Christian Jewish ascetics in Palestine who regulated their life according to rules resembling those of later monasticism, and practised community of goods. It has been claimed that both St John the Baptist and Christ himself may possibly have lived for a time among the E., perhaps at Qumran (q.v.), and sayings of Jesus seem to reflect both the influence of Essene teaching and antipathy to certain aspects.

ESSEQUIBO (esekē'bō). Principal river of Guyana. Navigable for 80km (50m), it rises in the Acari mts. on the Brazilian border and flows N 960km (600m). It has many rapids, but is navigable by larger ships for 80km (50m) to Bartica. Bauxite and timber are brought down to the coast.

ESSEX, Robert Devereux, 2nd earl of (1566-1601). English soldier and statesman. Eldest son of the 1st earl, he saw service in the Netherlands in 1585-6 and distinguished himself by his courage at the battle of Zutphen. From 1587 he became a favourite with Elizabeth, who created him Master of the Horse and a KG. In 1599 he led an army against Tyrone in Ulster, but was outgeneralled, made an unauthorized truce with Tyrone, and returned without permission to England. He was forbidden to return to court, and Elizabeth's refusal to renew the monopoly of sweet wines he had enjoyed goaded him to madness. At the head of a body of supporters, he marched into the City, but was promptly arrested, tried for treason, and beheaded on Tower Green.

ESSEX. Robert Devereux, 2nd earl of Essex, the tempestuous favourite of Elizabeth I. *Photo: Courtesy of the National Portrait Gallery.*

ESSEX, Robert Devereux, 3rd earl of (1591-1646). English soldier. Eldest son of the 2nd earl, he commanded the Parliamentary army at the drawn battle of Edgehill in 1642. Following a disastrous campaign in Cornwall, he resigned his command in 1645.

ESSEX. Co. of SE England, bounded on the S by the Thames estuary, and on the E by the North Sea. It is for the most part predominantly low-lying but undulating, the only high land is in the NW. The N two-thirds of E. belong geologically to E Anglia: the soil is composed of the same highly fertile glacial clays which yield heavy crops of cereals, sugar beet, fruits, and vegetables. The southern part is composed of heavier clays, and was originally densely forested. Parts of the forest remain, e.g. Epping Forest, but most have been cleared, and dairying is an important industry. In the SW the co. borders on Greater London. The admin. HQ is Chelmsford; other towns incl. Colchester; the ports Harwich and Tilbury; and the seaside resorts Southend and Clacton. Maplin Sands, a shallow-water area at Foulness off the E coast nr Southend was considered as the site of a third airport for London, and the Port of London authority still advocates the establishment there of a deep-sea container and oil port. Area 3,674 sq.km (1,419 sq.m); pop. (1978) 1,435,600.

ESTATE. In law, the interest which a person has in any property. *Real E.* is an interest in any freehold land; *personal E.* the interest in any other kind of property.

ESTER. An organic compound formed by the reaction between an alcohol and an acid, with the elimination of water. Es. correspond to inorganic salts. They are important in explosives, plastics, photographic films, and rayon; vegetable and animal fats and oils, soaps, paints and varnishes; flavourings and perfume.

ESTHER. Chief character in the OT book of E., which relates that as consort of the Persian king Ahasuerus, she prevented the extermination of her people by the vizier Haman - a deliverance celebrated at the Jewish festival of Purim.

ESTŌ'NIA (Estonian Soviet Socialist Republic). A constituent republic of the USSR, occupying the peninsula between the Gulf of Finland and the Baltic Sea, and bordering Latvia to the S. It is a low-lying extension of the Russian plain, but much marshland has been drained. Cereals, and potatoes are grown, and there is dairy-farming and a lumber industry. Shale deposits provide oil and natural gas, and superphosphate fertilizers are produced. The capital is Tallinn, a port on the Gulf of Finland; Paldiski and Parnu are other ports; the largest town inland is Tartu, which has a university.

E. was Russian from 1721 until, following the Revolution of 1917, it won independence in 1920 after a struggle. In 1939 E. was occupied by Russia, and in 1940 became a SSR of the USSR. The Germans overran E. in 1941, were ejected in 1944. The Estonian language is akin to Finnish. In the 1970s there were anti-Russian demonstrations; protests at the suppression of the Estonian language, and against the introduction of large numbers of Russians. Area 45,100 sq.km (17,400 sq.m); pop. (1978) 1,500,000, of whom a third are Russian.

ESTORI'L. Select seaside resort 21km (13m) W of Lisbon, Portugal, a haven of exiled royalty until the end of the Salazar regime. Pop. *c.* 5,000.

ESZTERGOM (es'ter-). Hungarian city on the Danube, NW of Budapest, birthplace of St Stephen, and former ecclesiastical cap. of Hungary, with a fine cathedral. There are hot springs. Pop. (1978) 27,250.

ÉTAPLES (ehtah'pl). Fishing port and seaside resort on the Canche estuary, Pas de Calais dept., France. During the F.W.W. it was an important British base and hospital centre. Pop. (1973) 9,150.

ETCHING. A print or impression on paper, taken from a metal (usually copper) plate, in which the picture has been 'etched' or bitten-in by means of some corrosive acid or chemical. The method was invented in Germany about 1500, the earliest dated print being of 1513. Whereas in the earlier method of engraving (q.v.) on metal the picture is cut into the metal surface by means of a sharp instrument called a burin or graver, used with a pushing action, in etching it is drawn on the plate by means of a sharp delicate metal point, which allows much greater freedom of action. Among the earliest etchers were Dürer, van

Dyck, Hollar, and Rembrandt. Since then great interest has been shown in it by many artists, e.g. Whistler, W. Strang, D. Y. Cameron, F. Brangwyn, W. Sickert, Muirhead Bone, etc.

E'THĀNE. A colourless, odourless gas, formula C_2H_6, b.p. 88°C, the second member of the series of paraffin hydrocarbons of the general formula C_nH_{2n+2}. Its chief importance is as a fuel in the form of natural gas.

ETHELBERT (*c.* 552-616). King of Kent, England. He succeeded his father, Eormenric, in 560, and gradually extended his authority over Middlesex, Essex, E Anglia, and Mercia. He m. the Frankish princess, Bertha, who was a Christian, and favourably received St Augustine in 597. In due course he was baptized.

ETHELRED I (d. 871). King of Wessex, England, elder brother of Alfred the Great. He succeeded his brother Ethelbert in 866, and his reign was spent in war with the Danish invaders. A defeat at Reading was followed by a victory at Ashdown.

ETHELRED II (968-1016). King of England; called the Unready, i.e. redeless, lacking in foresight. The son of King Edgar, he became king in 978 after the murder of his half-brother, Edward the Martyr. He tried to buy off the Danish raiders by paying Danegeld, and in 1002 ordered the massacre of the Danish settlers - so provoking an invasion by Sweyn of Denmark. War with Sweyn and Sweyn's son, Canute, occupied the rest of E.'s reign.

ETHER or **ETHYL ether** $(C_2H_5)_2O$. Colourless, volatile, inflammable liquid, b.p. 35°C, slightly soluble in water, miscible with alcohol. It is prepared by treatment of ethyl alcohol with excess concentrated sulphuric acid at 140°C. It is used as an anaesthetic by vapour inhalation and as an external cleansing agent before surgical operations. It is also used as a solvent in the preparation of explosives and collodion and in the extraction of oils, fats, waxes, resins, and alkaloids.

The term E. is also applied to a series of organic compounds of the general formula R-O-R′, where R and R′ are different radicals.

ETHEREGE (eth'erej) or **ETHEREDGE, Sir George** (*c.* 1635-*c.* 1691). British dramatist. His first play, *Love in a Tub*, was produced in 1664, and was a great success. *She Would If She Could*, a lively but immoral piece, followed in 1667, and his best comedy, *The Man of Mode*, in 1676. E. is the founder of the comedy of intrigue.

ETHICAL MOVEMENT. Movement designed to establish, maintain, and further the moral or ethical factor as the real substance and fundamental part of religion. It had its rise in USA in 1876, when Felix Adler founded an Ethical Society in New York. In 1888 the first English E. Society was founded by Dr Stanton Coit, the successor of M. D. Conway, at the Chapel in South Place, Finsbury, that became the South Place Ethical Society.

ETHICS. The branch of philosophy that is concerned with moral judgments of right and wrong, good and bad. So far as Europe is concerned, it may be said to have originated as a systematic intellectual study with Socrates in the 5th cent. BC, but considerably earlier there was intense ethical speculation in India and China. Plato's *Republic* is an exposition of the nature of justice or righteousness, and ethical theory was advanced by Aristotle's *Nicomachean Ethics* and kindred writings. The Cyrenaics, Epicureans, and Stoics advanced theories that have been many times revived. The 'Christian ethic' is mainly a combination of NT moral teaching with ideas drawn from Plato and Aristotle. Hobbes, Shaftesbury, Hutcheson, Hume, and Bishop Butler are notable 17-18th cent. British ethical philosophers. One of the greatest individual contributors to ethical theory was Kant, with his 'categorical imperative'. The utilitarian ethic was ably expounded by Bentham, J. S. Mill, Sidgwick, and Herbert Spencer; they were opposed by such thinkers as F. H. Bradley and T. H. Green, who linked ethics with metaphysics, and emphasized the place of the individual in organized society. Ethicists of the 20th cent. incl. G. E. Moore, C. D. Broad, John Dewey, Nicolai Hartmann (qq.v.), and Stephen Toulmin (1922-), whose *Place of Reason in Ethics* (1950) first put forward the viewpoint of modern linguistic analysis.

ETHIŌ'PIA. Name originally given by the ancient Greeks to the whole of N Africa, later restricted to much of what is today the Rep. of Sudan and the W part of Ethiopia.

Modern E. consists of elevated plateaux and mtn ranges, with the Danakil Desert to the NE and the Ogaden Desert to the SE, and Eritrea gives the country a coastline on the Red Sea. Ethiopia is watered by the headstreams of tributaries of the Nile, e.g. the Takazze, the Abbai (which drains L. Tana, one of several large lakes), and the Blue Nile. Coffee, said to have first been 'discovered' at Kaffa in the SW, is the main export: other crops are wheat, barley and maize, and sheep, cattle, and goats are raised. Minerals incl. gold, potash, copper and oil, but there has been little exploitation: resources of hydro-electric power for future industrialization are great. A road network has been estab. with overseas aid, and the cap., Addis Ababa, has a rail link with Djibouti on the Gulf of Aden, and Asmara, the Eritrean cap., with the port of Massawa on the Red Sea. Other towns incl. Dire Dawa, Dessie, Harar, Jimma and Gondar.

The dominant Amhara and related peoples of mixed Hamitic and Semitic origin live in the central and northern highlands, and are Coptic Christians. Eritrea is half Moslem and half Christian, and in the S and E Moslem Gallas of Hamitic origin predominate and form more than half the country's total pop., Harar being the chief Moslem centre. There are also pagan minorities, and the Falashas, to the N of Lake Tana, form a Jewish minority. The official language is Amharic, but English is widely taught. Area 1,184,000 sq.km (395,000 sq.m); pop. (1980) 30,200,000. M.U.: birr.

HISTORY. Long subject to Egypt, E. became independent about the 11th cent. BC. Christianity was introduced from Egypt *c.* AD 330 and was adopted as the national religion, but the Arab conquests of the 7th cent. isolated E. from the rest of Christendom. Diplomatic relations were estab. *c.* 1500 by the Portuguese, and contact with Europe was renewed when the explorer Bruce arrived in 1769. From 1850 Ethiopian history turned on the attempt to establish the authority of the central government over the local chieftains. National unity was attained under Menelek (reigned 1889-1913). Italian penetration from Eritrea resulted in war in 1895-6, ending with the Ethiopian victory of Adowa. Menelek's successors were Lej Yasu, deposed in 1916, and the empress Zauditu; with her was associated Ras Tafari, who succeeded as Haile Selassie in 1930. E. was conquered by the Italians in 1935-6, but in 1941 Haile Selassie returned from exile and with the aid of British forces expelled the Italians. He was deposed in a bloodstained military coup in 1974 and a

ETHIOPIA. Water is one of the country's most desperately needed commodities. Here Kirihu tribeswomen are filling *gerbers* - water-tight animal skins - which take on a ghastly resemblance to their former living state. *Photo: Sarah Errington/Camera Press.*

unitary socialist one-party state established. From 1962 a campaign (with Soviet aid) has been waged against guerrillas in Eritrea (q.v.), and 1977-8 against invaders from Somalia trying to obtain the return to them of the Ogaden (q.v.). The chairman of the provisional military admin. from 1977, Lt.-Col. Mengistu Haile Maraim, is becoming less Marxist and more pragmatic.

LANGUAGE AND LITERATURE. The various languages of Ethiopia constitute today the chief representatives of the S branch of the Semitic family. The chief literary and the ecclesiastical language is Ge'ez; Amharic is the principal colloquial language of the highlands; other languages spoken include Tigrina, round Aksum, and Tigré in Eritrea, both dialects of Ge'ez. Ethiopian literature can be traced from the 5th cent. but there is little original material.

ETHNO'LOGY. That branch of anthropology that is concerned with the characteristics and distribution over the globe of the races of mankind; also of their cultural conditions and achievements.

ĒTHO'LOGY. The comparative study of animal behaviour, founded by K. Lorenz and K. von Frisch.

ETHYL ALCOHOL. Colourless liquid C_2H_5OH with a pleasant odour, b.p. 78.5°C, density 0.789 g/ml miscible with water or ether, and burning in air with a pale blue flame. The vapour forms an explosive mixture with air and may be used in high-compression internal combustion engines.

It is made by fermentation of many carbohydrates, by absorption of ethylene and subsequent reaction with water, or by the reduction of acetaldehyde in the presence of a catalyst. It is rapidly absorbed in the human body from the stomach and upper intestine and affects nearly every tissue, particularly the central nervous system. Tests have shown that the feeling of elation, etc., usually associated with drinking alcoholic liquors is due to the loss of inhibitions or removal of the restraining influences of the higher cerebral centres. It also results in dilation of the blood vessels, particularly of the skin where a flushing is commonly observed. This loss of heat from the skin actually produces a physical cooling inside the body, despite the feeling of warmth experienced.

The digestive system is also affected and alcohol is absorbed unchanged from the gastro-intestinal tract into the circulation and intoxication depends on its degree of concentration. It can be detected and measured in the blood (legal limit for British motorists 80 mg in 100 millilitres) and in the breath.

E'TNA. Volcano on the E coast of Sicily, 3,323 m (10,902 ft) - the highest European volcano. There have been many violent eruptions.

ETON. English town in Berks on the N bank of the Thames, opposite Windsor. Pop. (1973) 5,000.

E. College, one of the largest and most famous of England's public schools, was founded in 1440 by Henry VI. The present constitution dates from 1871, and the governing body consists of a Provost appointed by the Crown and 10 fellows. The boys number over a thousand; seventy Collegers (the King's Scholars) live in the College, the remainder, Scholars and Oppidans, in houses held by the masters. King George III's birthday is celebrated each year on 4 June. Famous old Etonians include Chatham, Wellington, Gladstone, Lord Avon, Macmillan, and Lord Home.

ETRU'SCANS. Ancient people of northern Italy. Their chief settlements were the twelve cities of Etruria, including Volaterrae, Tarquinii, Clusium, Caere, and Vetulonia, each of which seems to have been independent. The height of their power was reached about 500 BC. In 474 BC they were defeated by the Carthaginians in a naval battle off Cumae, and about 400 BC their northern conquests were lost by the irruption of the Celts into N Italy. Thereafter the E. entered into a period of decline, and they gradually succumbed to the rising power of Rome.

Some knowledge of their art, religion, and language has been obtained from excavated tombs. The principal medium is sculpture, but pottery, bronze-ware, and mural painting are also noteworthy. Etruscan religion seems to have been derived from Asia Minor, and shows many signs of Greek influence. The language, despite a large number of inscriptions, mainly funerary, and a certain number of words derived by the Romans from Etruscan, is still very imperfectly known.

ETTY, William (1787-1849). British artist. B. at York, he served 7 years' apprenticeship to a Hull printer, before becoming a student of Sir Thomas Lawrence in 1807, and first gained success at the Academy with 'Telemachus rescuing Antiope' in 1811. In his work E. aimed to paint great moral truth and regarded his numerous nude paintings as a dedication to 'God's most glorious work'.

ETYMO'LOGY. The branch of linguistic science which deals with the ultimate origin and history of individual words. It has 2 chief aspects: *phonetic,* dealing with the changes in sounds, and *semantic,* with the changes in meaning.

EUBOEA (ūbē'-a). Largest of the Greek islands. It lies off the E coast of Greece, in the Aegean Sea, and is about 177km (110m) long. It is mountainous, Mt Delphi reaching 1,743 m (5,718 ft). The chief town is Chalcis, connected by a bridge to the mainland. Area 3,755 sq.km (1,480 sq.m).

EUCALYPTUS (ūkalip'tus). Genus of trees of the Myrtaceae family, practically confined, in the natural state, to Australia and Tasmania, where they are commonly known as gum trees. About 90 per cent of Australian timber belongs to the E. group, which comprises about

400 species. EUCALYPTUS OIL, used in medicine, is obtained from the leaves of certain species by aqueous distillation. Methanol obtained from its wood is a potential petrol substitute.

EUCARYOTE (ū'kari-ōt). One of the two classes of living cell, that in which there is a defined nucleus, as in most living things, incl. man. *See* PROCARYOTE, BACTERIA.

EUCHARIST (ū'karist). The most solemn and universally observed of the Christian sacraments. The word comes from the Greek for 'thanksgiving', and refers to the statement in the Gospel narrative that Christ gave thanks over the bread and the cup. Other names for it are the Lord's Supper, Holy Communion, and (amongst Catholics) the Mass. Members of the C of E are required to participate in the E. at least 3 times a year, Easter to be one.

EUCLID (u'klid) (fl. 300 BC). Greek mathematician, who lived at Alexandria and wrote the *Stoicheia* (Elements) in 13 books, of which 9 deal with plane and solid geometry, and 4 with arithmetic. His main work lay in the systematic arrangement of previous discoveries, and the geometrical books remained a standard textbook for over 2,000 years and were still in regular use in English schools in the present cent.

EUGÈNE (ūjēn') **of Savoy,** Prince (1663–1736). Austrian general. The son of Prince Eugène Maurice of Savoy-Carignano, he was b. in Paris. When Louis XIV refused him a commission he entered the Austrian army, and served against the Turks at the defence of Vienna in 1683, and against the French on the Rhine and in Italy 10 years later. In 1697 he expelled the Turks from Hungary by his triumph at Zenta. In the War of the Spanish Succession he shared with Marlborough in his great victories, and won many successes as an independent commander in Italy. He vainly protested against the dismissal of Marlborough, and suffered several defeats before the peace settlement at Rastatt in 1714. He again defeated the Turks in 1716–18, and fought a last campaign against the French in 1734–5.

EUGENICS (ūjen'iks). Term derived from the Greek for 'well born', coined by Sir Francis Galton (q.v.) for the science that he defined as the study of agencies under social control which may improve or impair the racial qualities of future generations either physically or mentally.

EUGÉNIE (öjehnē') (1826–1920). Empress of the French. Dau. of a grandee of Spain, the count of Montijo, she m. in 1853 Louis Napoleon, soon after he became French emperor as Napoleon III. After Sedan she fled to England, and settled with him at Chislehurst. Later she lived at Farnborough, where she built a mausoleum in which she, her husband and her son, who was killed in the Zulu War, were buried.

EULER (oi'ler), **Leonhard** (1707–83). Swiss mathematician. B. at Basle, he became professor of physics at St Petersburg in 1730. Summoned to Berlin in 1741 by Frederick the Great, he spent 25 years there and then returned to Russia. He worked not only in pure mathematics, but also in astronomy, optics, etc.

EUMEN'IDĒS. In Greek mythology the Furies or spirits of vengeance, usually represented as winged women with snake-like hair. They were sometimes known as *Erīnyes* (Furies) and sometimes by the propitiatory name of E. (Kindly ones).

EUNUCH (ū'nuk; Gk *eunoukhos*, one in charge of a bed). In Eastern countries originally a bed-chamber attendant (generally a castrated male person) employed in a harem or zenana. Es. often filled high offices of state in China, India, Persia, etc. The *castrati* of Italy were famous throughout the cents. for the beauty of their voices, but on the accession of pope Leo XIII in 1878 the practice of castrating boys for this purpose ceased.

EUPHRATES (ūfrā'tēz). River, rising in E Turkey, which flows through Syria and Iraq to link with the Tigris above Basra to form the Shatt-el-Arab, at the head of the Persian/Arabian Gulf: 3,600 km (2,235 m). The ancient cities of Babylon, Eridu and Ur were along its course.

EURASIAN (ūrā'shan). In India and the E Indies a term formerly used to denote a person born of a European and an Asiatic, and his or her progeny; it was almost exclusively derogatory and often insulting.

EURATOM (European Atomic Energy Community). *See under* EUROPEAN UNION. The Joint Research Centre is at Ispra, Italy.

EURE (ör). French river rising in Orne dept and flowing SE, then N, to the Seine. Chartres is on its banks; length 115 km (70 m).

EUREKA STOCKADE. Incident at Ballarat, Australia, when c. 150 goldminers or 'diggers', with many justifiable grievances, rebelled against authority. They took refuge behind a wooden stockade, which was taken in a few minutes by the military on 3 Dec. 1854. Some thirty diggers were killed, and a few soldiers were killed or wounded, but the majority of the rebels were taken prisoner. Among those who escaped was Peter Lalor, their leader. Of the thirteen tried for treason, all were acquitted and the E.S. is regarded as marking the emergence of Australian democracy.

EURHYTHMICS (ūrith'miks). Practice of co-ordinated bodily movement as a help to musical development. It was founded by the Swiss musician Jaques-Dalcroze (q.v.), prof. of harmony at Geneva. He devised a series of 'gesture' songs, designed to be sung simultaneously with certain bodily actions.

EURI'PIDES (c. 484–407 BC). Ancient Greek dramatist. The youngest of the 3 great tragedians of ancient Athens, he lived in retirement (apart from his normal terms of service with the Athenian conscript army) and wrote over 80 plays, of which 19 have survived. These show marked innovations in dramatic technique and in the treatment of dramatic themes, and E. was bitterly criticized for his 'impiety' and religious unorthodoxy, and for the sympathy he showed to slaves, beggars, and to women characters like Medea. All the plays are marked by realistic character drawing and, whereas earlier playwrights had presented ideal heroes, E. shows ordinary men amd women as they really were. Towards the end of his life he went into voluntary exile at the court of Macedonia.

His surviving plays are: *Rhesus, Cyclops* (a satiric drama), *Alcestis* (438), *Medea* (431), *Hippolytus* (428), *Hecuba* (*c.* 426), *Children of Heracles* (*c.* 425), *Suppliant Women* (*c.* 424), *Madness of Heracles* (*c.* 423), *Andromache* (*c.* 420), *Ion* (*c.* 418), *Trojan Women* (415), *Electra* (*c.* 413), *Iphigenia in Tauris* (*c.* 413), *Helen* (412), *Phoenissae* (*c.* 410), *Orestes* (408), *Iphigenia in Aulis* (405), and *Bacchae* (405). There are verse translations of a number of these by Gilbert Murray.

EURŌ'PA. In Greek myth the dau. of the King of Tyre, whom Zeus carried off on his back, having assumed the form of a bull. She personifies the European continent.

EUROPA. Moon of Jupiter, diameter 2,900 km (1,800 m) and distant from the planet 676,000 km (420,000 m). It is covered by ice and criss-crossed by thousands of thin cracks 50,000 km (30,000 m) long.

EUROPA NOSTRA (Our Europe). International federation estab. in 1963 by the representatives of 18 organizations (e.g. Italia Nostra, National Trust, Irish Georgian Soc., Vieilles Maisons Françaises) in 11 European countries for the preservation of historic sites, buildings and monuments.

EUROPE. Continent forming the western extremity of the Euroasiatic land mass; the Ural Mountains are usually considered to mark its eastern limit, the frontier between the USSR and Turkey and Iran its south-eastern. At one time the Caucasus Mountains were considered to mark the limit of Europe in this area, but the extension of European Russia into former Asiatic territories has pushed the line farther to the S. On all other sides E. meets the sea; it narrows towards the west. E. which forms about 1/14 of the world's land surface, has a length of 3,850 km/2,400 m from the North Cape to Cape Matapan, in S Greece, and a breadth from Cape St Vincent to the Urals of 5,050 km/3,150 m. The surface of E. is divided into 3 main areas: (1) the North European Plain, which includes S England and contains many great cities, such as London, Paris, Berlin, and Moscow, besides fertile agricultural lands; (2) the Central European Highlands, consisting of the Sierra Nevada, Pyrenees, Alps, Apennines, Carpathians and Balkans; and (3) the Scandinavian highland, including the N of the British Isles.

The main rivers flow into northern or inland seas. The Volga, the Don, the Dnieper, the Northern Dvina, and the Western Dvina rise on the Valdaian plateau, to the NW of Moscow, and the Danube, the Rhine, the Rhône, the Po, and the Adige flow from the Alps. E. has many lakes, notably Geneva, Constance, Lucerne, Neuchâtel, Maggiore, Garda, and Como in the Alps; Vänern, Vättern, Mälar, Mjosa, and Randsfjord in the peninsula formed by Norway and Sweden; Ladoga, Onega, Peipus, and Ilmen in N Russia; Saïma and innumerable others in Finland. The largest islands are Spitsbergen, Iceland, Britain, Ireland, Sardinia, Corsica, Sicily, Novaya Zemlya, and Crete.

GEOLOGY. The oldest rocks found in Europe, those of the Archaean and Palaeozoic periods, cover most of the northern part of the continent including the N and W of Gt Britain, and are also found in Brittany, Central France, and Spain. The more recent rocks of the Mesozoic and Cainozoic periods form a continuous belt in the central plain from the North Sea into Russia. Fossils found in the Canadian Arctic suggest that 45,000,000 years ago Europe and N America may have been linked by a land bridge represented today by the is. of the Canadian Arctic, Greenland, Iceland and Spitsbergen.

CLIMATE. Most of E. lies within the N temperate zone, but parts of Norway, Sweden, and Russia are N of the Arctic Circle. The British Isles and the western coastal areas of continental countries are washed by the Gulf Stream. There are four main climatic regions in E.: (1) southern in the Mediterranean region, characterized by an absence of rainfall in summer; (2) western, near the Atlantic and eastward to the Oder, with warm summers and cold winters, and rainfall evenly distributed throughout the year; (3) eastern or continental, with extremes of heat in summer and cold in winter; and (4) the sub-Arctic climate of the northern regions.

POPULATION. E. is remarkable for the high average density of its population. Several countries of the W support an average of over 600 persons per sq.km. On the N European Plain the highest densities are towards the W. There is a zone of high density along the S edge of the plain, from the Ukraine to NE France, caused by the high quality of the soils and the occurrence of the major coalfields. Anthropologically 3 main racial types are found, though most Europeans show physically a blending of types. The 'Alpine' people, broad-headed and rather stocky, are found in Central E., especially the highlands. The 'Slavs' of Eastern E. are similar to the 'Alpine'. The 'Nordic' type of NW Europe have long heads, blond colouring, and blue eyes. The 'Mediterranean' type are long-headed with dark hair and eyes. A racial admixture from the Third World followed the S.W.W., e.g. from India, Pakistan and W Indies in UK; Indonesia in the Netherlands; and N Africa in France.

LANGUAGES. Most European languages belong to the Aryan group. Celtic is still spoken to some extent in Wales, the Isle of Man, the Scottish Highlands, Ireland, and Brittany. The main divisions of the Teutonic group of languages are High and Low German; English; Dutch and Flemish; Scandinavian in Iceland, Denmark, Norway, and Sweden. Slav languages are spoken by Russians, Poles, Lithuanians, Letts, Wends, Czechs, etc., while French, Spanish, Portuguese, Italian, and Rumanian are Romanic languages. The few non-Aryan tongues include Magyar, Basque, and Turkish.

VEGETATION. S of the Alps the trees are mainly evergreens. Rice, maize, millet, and wheat are among the cereals cultivated in this region, and olives, grapes, oranges, lemons, figs, and chestnuts thrive. Central E. is particularly rich in cereals and also produces large quantities of fruit. Most of its forests are deciduous, oak, beech, ash, etc. In the N the chief trees are pines, larches, firs, birches, and willows.

MINERALS. Coal is found in Great Britain, Germany, France, Belgium, Czechoslovakia, Poland, and Russia; Great Britain, Germany, France, Belgium, Sweden, Austria, Czechoslovakia, Russia, and Spain have deposits of iron ore. Copper, lead, zinc, gold, platinum, silver, quicksilver, salt, sulphur, and graphite are all obtained in E. There are large oilfields in the Caucasus and W Ukraine and both oil and natural gas offshore beneath the North Sea.

Industrialization began in the W where the aptitude of the people, presence of minerals that could be worked with comparative ease, and accessibility to overseas territories offering both raw materials and markets all helped the process; but after the F.W.W. industrial development spread eastwards, and was accelerated after the S.W.W. especially in Ukraine and other countries of the USSR or under Russian influence.

RELIGION. The majority are Christian (45% Roman Catholic and 25% Protestant or Orthodox), the rest incl. Moslems in the Balkans and Caucasia, and in Britain; Jews; and - espec. in Communist countries - an increasing proportion of atheists.

Countries of Europe

	Area in sq. km.	*Pop. in 1,000s*	*Capital*
Albania	28,748	2,620	Tirana
Andorra	465	31	Andorra la Vella
Austria	83,850	7,520	Vienna
Belgium	30,513	9,837	Brussels
Bulgaria	110,840	8,800	Sofia
Czechoslovakia	127,895	15,030	Prague
Denmark	43,039	5,097	Copenhagen
Faeroes	1,339	42	
Finland	337,050	4,747	Helsinki
France	551,553	53,200	Paris
Germany, E	108,180	16,758	East Berlin
Germany, W	248,600	61,666	Bonn
Greece	131,944	9,170	Athens
Hungary	93,000	10,671	Budapest
Iceland	103,000	220	Reykjavik
Irish Republic	68,892	3,220	Dublin
Italy	301,195	56,600	Rome
Liechtenstein	160	25	Vaduz
Luxembourg	2,586	360	Luxembourg
Malta	316	309	Valletta
Monaco	1.5	25	Monaco Ville
Netherlands	34,000	13,898	The Hague
Norway	324,219	4,051	Oslo
Svalbard	62,000	3	Long Year City
Poland	312,000	34,850	Warsaw
Portugal	91,920	9,730	Lisbon
Romania	237,500	21,650	Bucharest
San Marino	58	20	San Marino
Spain	503,556	36,350	Madrid
Sweden	449,700	8,260	Stockholm
Switzerland	41,288	6,300	Bern/Berne
Turkey-in-Europe	23,300	4,800	Ankara
United Kingdom	245,700	55,794	London
Gibraltar	6.5	29	Gibraltar
U.S.S.R. in Europe			
Armenia	29,800	3,031	Yerevan
Azerbaijan	86,600	6,028	Baku
Byelorussia	207,600	9,559	Minsk
Estonia	45,100	1,466	Tallinn
Georgia	69,700	5,016	Tbilisi
Latvia	63,700	2,521	Riga
Lithuania	65,200	3,339	Vilnius
Moldavia	33,700	3,948	Kishinev
R.S.F.S.R.	5,025,000	103,402	Moscow
Ukraine	603,700	49,757	Kiev
Vatican	.4	1	Vatican City
Yugoslavia	255,800	21,560	Belgrade
	11,188,801	668,660	

ORGANIZATION. As yet the European Community (*see* EUROPEAN UNION) is militarily inferior to both USA and USSR, and financially and industrially inferior to the USA, but in trade it is the largest world importer of industrial and agricultural products, and of commodities from the developing countries. In 1979 its annual gross national product surpassed that of the USA for the first time, and parts of Europe were beginning to enjoy an even higher standard of living.

EUROPEAN HISTORY. Ancient. Throughout the many thousands of years of the Palaeolithic Age the inhabitants of E. lived by hunting or fishing; then came the Neolithic Age, during which agriculture and the domestication of animals began. The working of bronze may have developed independently of the Near East civilisations, and was practised in Crete *c.* 3000 BC, and in Britain and Germany after 1750 BC.

Greece was overrun *c.* 1500 BC by Greek-speaking barbarians, who founded the Mycenaean civilization, and *c.* 1100 BC subdued the Cretan Minoan civilization. Iron-smelting, introduced into Greece from Armenia *c.* 1000 BC, reached N and W Europe *c.* 750–500 BC. New invaders overran Greece *c.* 1100 BC and destroyed the Mycenaean civilization. In the city-states they established, monarchy gave place to the rule of a landed aristocracy, which with the growth of a merchant class yielded in turn to democracy. During the 6th–4th cents. BC the distinctively Greek culture arose, which the conquests of Alexander (334–323) spread over the Near East.

By the 3rd cent. BC the city-republic of Rome had become mistress of the Italian peninsula. The Carthaginian wars added Sicily and Spain to its empire, and in 146 BC Greece became a Roman province. Meanwhile the Celtic peoples of C Europe had spread over what is now France, Britain, Ireland and N Italy, and penetrated Spain. Rome subdued the Celts of Italy and Spain in the 2nd cent. BC, France in the 1st, and Britain in the 1st cent. AD. Under Augustus the Rhine and the Danube became the Empire's northern frontiers. Rome's conquests made possible not only the maintenance of order, the circulation of trade, and the diffusion of Graeco-Roman culture, but the dissemination of Christianity, the toleration of which Constantine ordered in 312. But the expansion of the Empire ended in the 2nd cent. AD, and economic and administrative defects, added to the successive invasions by the barbarians on the northern frontiers, led to its disintegration.

Medieval. During the 4th–6th cents. W Europe was overrun by Anglo-Saxons, Franks, Goths, and Lombards, although the traditions of Roman culture and administration were kept alive by the Church. In E Europe the Empire survived, with its capital at Constantinople, whence Christianity reached the Balkans and Russia; the rival claims of the Pope and the Byzantine Patriarch led to a cleavage which became permanent in 1054. During the 7th–8th cents. Christendom was threatened by the Arabs, who conquered Spain.

Charlemagne united France, W Germany and N Italy, and in 800 received the title of emperor from the Pope. With the dissolution of his empire France and Germany came into existence as separate states. A period of confusion followed, accentuated by the Viking raids, during which the feudal system arose. As revived in 962 by Otto I the Empire was confined to Germany and N Italy; he adopted for it the title Holy Roman Empire, used, long after the reality had become shadowy, until 1806. The claim to authority over secular princes put forward by Gregory VII (1073–85) and his successors provoked a conflict between empire and papacy which lasted for nearly 200 years and discredited both. Papal influence was strengthened by the Crusades (1096–1272), but the

EUROPE. The herdsman takes his reindeer across a lake in Finland (top left); looking out to Continental Europe from Beachy Head in Sussex (top right); the headquarters of the European Economic Community in Brussels, Belgium (centre left); Lichtenstein Castle, near Stuttgart, Germany (centre right); the château at Chambord, France (bottom left); the monastery of Las Huelcas at Burgos in Spain (bottom right); and (on the facing page) the Ponte Vecchio, bridging the Arno in Florence, Italy, and Rab in Yugoslavia. *Photos: Courtesy of the British, Spanish, Italian and Yugoslav national tourist offices, B. and C. Alexander, Camera Press, Chemical Bank and Mansell Collection.*

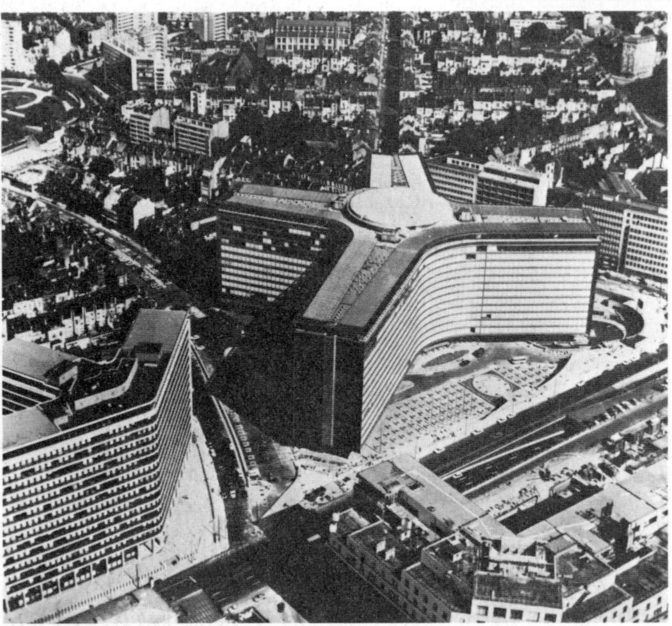

GREENLAND
DENMARK STR.
ICELAND
ATLANTIC
OCEAN
FAEROE IS.
SHETLAND IS.
ORKNEY IS.
BRITISH ISLES
IRELAND
NORWEGIAN SEA
NORTH SEA
NOVAYA ZEMLYA
BARENTS SEA
KOLGUEV I.
WHITE SEA
Scandinavia
GULF OF BOTHNIA
L. Vänern
G. OF FINLAND
BALTIC SEA
GOTLAND
L. Onega
L. Ladoga
L. Chudskoye
N. Dvina
VALDAI UPLANDS
Western Dvina
URAL MOUNTAINS
Siberian
Ob
Plain
Ural
ENGLISH CHANNEL
North European Plain
Vistula
Elbe
Oder
Rhine
Danube
Loire
BAY OF BISCAY
CENTRAL RUSSIAN UPLANDS
Don
Volga
Dnieper
CARPATHIANS
Plain of Hungary
ALPS
SEA OF AZOV
Crimea
CASPIAN SEA
CAUCASUS
BLACK SEA
BOSPHORUS
Iberian
Peninsula
Tagus
PYRENEES
Ebro
Rhône
CORSICA
ADRIATIC SEA
APENNINES
BALEARIC IS.
SARDINIA
STR. OF GIBRALTAR
MEDITERRANEAN SEA
AEGEAN SEA
Asia Minor
ASIA
Tigris
Euphrates
SICILY
MALTA
RHODES
CRETE
CYPRUS
Suez Canal
Dead Sea
Arabian Peninsula
RED SEA
Nile
AFRICA
Miles
0 250 500 750 1000 1250 1500
0 250 500 750 1000 1250 1500 1750 2000 2250
Kilometres
© Geographical Projects

transfer of the papacy to Avignon (1309-71) and the Great Schism (1378-1417) weakened its prestige.

Town life and trade, which had declined under the barbarians, revived after Charlemagne's day. The revival began in the Italian cities, notably Venice, Genoa, Florence, and Milan, which traded with the Near East, and thence with C Asia and China. From the 12th cent. these cities, like the German and Flemish cities, estab. themselves as self-governing republics, and in the 14th-15th cents. fostered the culture of the 'Renaissance'.

From the conflict of monarchy with feudal nobility centralized nation-states emerged in W Europe in the 14th-15th cents.; a feature common to most of the new states was the existence of parliamentary assemblies, representing both landowners and cities. In E Europe the political situation was unsettled by the Turkish conquest of the Balkans, culminating in the capture of Constantinople in 1453.

Modern. Throughout the 16th-17th cents. European politics turned on the rivalry of France and the Habsburgs, who held Spain and its empire, Austria, the Netherlands and the imperial crown, while after 1517 they were further complicated by the Protestant Reformation. Protestantism took 2 main forms: the more conservative Lutheranism, which was adopted by many German princes, and in Scandinavia; and the radical and democratic Calvinism, which gained many adherents in the Netherlands, Scotland, and France. The Catholic Church attempted to meet the challenge with the Counter-Reformation.

The struggle against Spain of the Netherlands and England in the later 16th cent. ended in the establishment of the United Provinces (or Dutch Rep.), 1648, and the emergence of the United Provinces and England as maritime powers. France was torn by religious wars (1562-98), until Henry IV introduced toleration and consolidated the absolute monarchy. Inside Germany the attempt of the Habsburgs to restore the power of Church and Empire led to the Thirty Years War (1618-48), as a result of which France succeeded Spain as the dominant power of Europe.

During the 17th cent. the supremacy of parliament was estab. in England; elsewhere, parliamentary institutions gave way to absolute monarchy, which found its supreme expression in Louis XIV of France (1643-1715). Until 1688 he successfully pursued an aggressive foreign policy but thereafter his ambitions united Europe against him. In N Europe Sweden, after a cent. of glory, ceased to be a great power with the death of Charles XII (1697-1718), while 2 new powers arose: Russia, regenerated by Peter the Great (1682-1725), and Prussia. The rivalries of Prussia and Austria, and of Britain and France in India and Canada, produced the War of the Austrian Succession (1740-8), and the Seven Years War (1756-63); when they ended Prussia was estab. as a European power, and France had lost its colonial empire to Britain.

The spirit of revolt against absolute monarchy was voiced by the *philosophes*, whose humanitarian doctrines prepared the way for the French Revolution (1789-95). The opposition of the Austrian and Prussian monarchies provoked the wars of 1792-1815, during which the French armies spread revolutionary ideas throughout Europe. The dictatorship of the Jacobins (1792-4) saved France in 1792, but the Terror (1793-4) so terrified the bourgeoisie that they accepted the military despotism of Napoleon (1799-1814). His aggressions aroused throughout Europe a popular resistance which brought about his overthrow.

For 30 years the Holy Alliance attempted to hold back the popular movements which had arisen from the French and Industrial Revolutions, Liberalism, nationalism, and Socialism. In spite of the failure of the 1848 revolutions, by 1871 Germany and Italy were unified, and France was a republic.

With the Greek War of Independence (1821-9) the decadence of Turkey became evident. A struggle for the domination of the Balkans followed, in which Russia was matched at first against Britain and France, and later against Austria and Germany. The Balkan question, Franco-German hostility, and colonial rivalries divided Europe into 2 armed camps - the Triple Alliance (1882) of Germany, Austria and Italy, and the Franco-Russian Alliance (1891), with which Britain was linked by the Entente Cordiale, 1904, and an agreement with Russia, 1907. The last of a succession of international crises plunged Europe into the F.W.W. of 1914-18.

Russia became a Communist republic in 1917 and after the war Germany and Austria became democratic republics, Italy and Hungary Fascist dictatorships. The Austrian and Turkish empires disappeared, new states - e.g. Poland, Czechoslovakia, Yugoslavia - arising from the ruins. A new stage opened with Hitler's coming to power in 1933. Germany and Italy embarked on a policy of aggression in Spain, Austria, Czechoslovakia, and Albania, while Britain and France wavered between appeasement and resistance until the S.W.W. broke out in 1939. During 1939-41 Germany overran much of Europe, incl. most of European Russia. Germany's attack on Russia in June 1941, coupled with Japan's attack on the USA later that year, brought both Russia and the USA into the war and eventually turned the tide. Completely defeated, Germany and Austria were occupied by the Allied powers.

Russia emerged from the war as the greatest European power, with the small countries of E Europe as satellites under Russian domination. Treaties of peace were concluded by the Allies in 1947 with Hungary, Italy, Finland, Rumania, and Bulgaria, in 1955 with Austria. The British, US, and French zones of (W) Germany were recognized by those occupying powers in 1949 as the Federal German Republic; the Russian zone of (E) Germany was proclaimed a separate democratic republic later the same year. Russian hostility to western Europe drew the countries of that part of the continent together and into close alliance with the USA through the North Atlantic Treaty, but the closing of the gap between standards of life E and W of the Iron Curtain, reinforced by doctrinal differences between the Soviet Union and China, led to a relaxation of the Cold War. Tension was renewed in 1956 over Hungary and 1968 over Czechoslovakia, but the needs of Comecon (q.v.) for Western goods and technology, and the EEC desire for increased trade sustained a stable relationship into the mid-1970s, which incl. closer links also between the USA and USSR. Nevertheless, the arms race between the Warsaw Treaty countries and Nato did not cease, and the return of the USA to a degree of isolation after her disastrous involvement in Vietnam corresponded with the extension of Soviet influence via rapid naval expansion. The détente of the Helsinki Conference (1975) was contradicted by Soviet acquisition of Indian Ocean bases, and her intervention in Africa, and S and

Central America (via Cuba); in SE Asia (via Vietnam); and directly in Afghanistan. These moves outflanked European, US and Chinese defence positions, and the situation was further destabilised in 1980 by unrest within the Soviet bloc (in Poland), and by the growing E-W rivalry for the oil of the Gulf States.

EUROPEAN DEMOCRATIC GROUP. Group in the European Parliament, in 1980 comprising 60 members of the British Conservative Party, plus 3 Danes and 1 Ulster Unionist. The name was adopted by the British because the word 'Conservative' has in Europe an extremist connotation. Their chairman, appointed 1979 by Margaret Thatcher and elected 1980, is James Scott-Hopkins (1921-). The group works in informal alliance with the Christian Democrats and Liberals.

EUROPEAN MONETARY SYSTEM. On 1 Jan. 1979 a European Monetary System (EMS) was estab. (excl. UK, which expressed an intention of later accession), based on the ecu (European Currency Unit), which is a weighted average of all the currencies in the system. Members aid each other's currencies when they vary in value by 2.25% from a fixed point.

EUROPEAN UNION. Since the break-up of the Roman Empire, which had united southern and western Europe, incl. Britain, within the fence of Roman peace, the idea of a united Europe has been many times revived. Military re-unions, such as those imposed by Charlemagne, Napoleon, and Hitler did not last, but peaceful achievement of the aim was advocated by Grotius (17th cent.), Kant (18th cent.), and Briand, Robert Schuman, Adenauer and de Gasperi (qq.v.) in the 20th cent. A start was made towards the end of the S.W.W. in the economic field through Benelux (q.v.). After the war came the European Recovery Programme (*see* MARSHALL, GEORGE C.) estab. as the Organization for European Economic Co-operation (OEEC) 1948, and renamed Organization for Economic Co-operation and Development (q.v.) in 1961. Also in 1948 the Brussels Treaty (q.v.) was signed, from which came Western European Union and the Council of Europe (q.v.).

The EUROPEAN COMMUNITY consists of the European Coal and Steel Community (1952), European Economic Community (EEC, popularly called the Common Market, 1957), and the European Atomic Energy Community (Euratom, 1957). These 3 share from 1967 the following institutions; **The Commission** (HQ Brussels) of 13 members pledged to independence of national interests, who initiate community action (president Gaston Thorn 1981–4; Jacques Delors 1985-); **The Council of Ministers** (HQ Brussels) which makes decisions on the Commission's proposals and, originally comprising the Foreign Ministers of member countries, was intended to direct and control the other subsidiary councils (Agriculture, Energy, Finance, etc.), that have now become largely autonomous; **European Parliament** (secretariat Luxembourg), directly elected from 1979, which must be consulted on major issues and can dismiss the Commission by an adverse vote (*see also* PARLIAMENT); and **European Court of Justice** (HQ Luxembourg, to safeguard interpretation of the Rome treaties, q.v.). The original members (the 'Six') were Belgium, France, W Germany, Italy, Luxembourg, and the Netherlands; British applications for membership (by a Cons. govt 1961 and Labour 1967) were blocked by France. However, a parallel trading group, the European Free Trade Assocn. (EFTA) had been estab. in 1959 by Austria, Britain, Denmark, Norway, Portugal, Sweden and Switzerland, who came to be known from their geographical relationship to the Common Market countries as the 'Outer Seven'. Linked with Britain in her final successful application for Common Market membership from 1973 were Denmark, Norway (who withdrew after a referendum 1972) and the Irish Republic. Following the advent of a Labour govt. in Britain in 1974, her membership was confirmed by a referendum. Following their introduction of democratic regimes, Greece (from 1981) and Spain and Portugal (on 1 January 1986) were admitted to membership, and trading links outside the market, e.g. under the Lomé Convention (q.v.) with developing countries of Africa, the Caribbean and Pacific, have been widely extended. Agreements with EFTA later joined by Liechtenstein, created an industrial-free-trade system of 18 countries: total pop. over 300 million.

See also EUROPEAN MONETARY SYSTEM.

EUROPEAN UNION. The signature of the Rome Treaties on 25 March 1957 in Palazzo dei Conservatori on the Capitoline Hill, which established the European Economic Community and Euratom. *Photo: Courtesy of the Information Service of the European Communities.*

EURŌ'PIUM. An extremely rare chemical element. Symbol Eu; atomic number 63; atomic weight 152. One of the lanthanide series of metals, it is used in lasers and in colour television.

EUSĒ'BIUS (*c.* 260-*c.* 340). Bishop of Caesarea from *c.* 313. Prominent in the Council of Nicaea, he wrote an Ecclesiastical History down to AD 324.

EUSTACHIO (ā-oostah'kē-ō), **Bartolommeo** (d. 1574). Italian anatomist, the discoverer of the Eustachian tube, leading from the middle ear to the pharynx, and of the Eustachian valve in the right auricles of the heart. He was physician to the popes.

EUTHANASIA (yūthanā'zia). Literally, from the Gk. 'to die well', but popularly the painless killing of a patient suffering from painful and incurable illness, espec. the old. Bills for voluntary E. failed to pass Parliament in the UK in 1969 and 1976, it being argued that modern drugs control pain, and that such a measure would bring to bear intolerable pressures on the patient and destroy trust between doctor and patient.

EVEREST. Everest seen from Nepal, a banner of cloud blowing from the peak, and New Zealander Sir Edmund Hillary (right) and Sherpa Tensing during their ascent in 1953. *Photos: Popperfoto and the Royal Geographical Society.*

EUTROPHICATION (yōō'trofik-). The over-enrichment of lake waters, primarily by phosphates from detergents in municipal sewage, until their use was discontinued. These encouraged the growth of plant life to the extent of eliminating oxygen, making the water uninhabitable for fish and other animal life.

EVANGELICALISM. In the Protestant Church the movement closely adhering to the Bible authority, relying on faith as the only means of salvation, stressing the need for personal commitment to Christ (the 'born-again' experience) and to spread the gospel. It includes Fundamentalism, preachers such as Billy Graham, and was given impetus in the USA in the 1970s by Pres. Carter, himself a 'born-again' Southern Baptist, and Bob Dylan. Although in a sense all protestants are evangelical, in the Anglican Communion the term refers rather to Low Church Anglicans.

EVANGELIST (Gk *euangelos* 'bringing good news'). Term used in the NT for one who is charged with a travelling mission to spread the gospel among the heathen. With reference to one of the authors of the four Gospels, it does not occur until the 3rd cent.

EVANS, Sir Arthur John (1851-1941). British archaeologist. B. in Herts, he was the son of Sir John E. (1823-1908), an authority on the Neolithic and Bronze Age periods in Europe. His excavation of Knossos (q.v.) on Crete resulted in the discovery of the pre-Phoenician Minoan script and in proving the existence of the Minoan civilization of which all trace had disappeared except in legend. Notable among his pub. works are *Scripta Minoa* (1909) and 4 vols. on the *Palace of Minos.*

EVANS, Dame Edith (1888-1976). British actress. B. in London, she was best known for her playing of Lady Bracknell in *The Importance of Being Earnest* (1939). A very versatile actress, she appeared in Shakespeare, Restoration Comedy, Shaw, etc.

EVANSVILLE. City on the Ohio r., Indiana, USA, nr the border with Illinois. Industries incl. refrigerating and air-conditioning equipment, pharmaceuticals, plastics, and aluminium. The boyhood home of Abraham Lincoln was in Spencer co. nearby. Pop. met. area (1970) 287,600.

EVE. *See* ADAM.

EVELYN, John (1620-1706). English diarist and author. B. in Surrey, he enlisted for 3 years in the Royalist army (1624), but withdrew on finding his estate exposed to the enemy and lived mostly abroad until 1652. He declined all office under the Commonwealth, but after the Restoration enjoyed great favour, received court appointments, and was one of the founders of the Royal Society. He was the friend of Pepys, and like him remained in London during the Plague and the Great Fire. Of his more than 30 books the most important is his diary, first pub. in 1818, which covers the period 1640-1706.

EVEREST, Mount. The highest mtn in the world, in the Himalayan range on the China-Nepal frontier (8,847 m/29,028 ft - formerly 29,002 ft, but the range is rising). Its English name derives from Sir George Everest (1790-1866), Surveyor-General of India, but the Nepalese name is Sagarmatha 'Head of the Earth' and in Tibetan it is Chomo Lungma, 'Mother of the Snows'. Of the many early attempts on E. the most famous was that of 1924 when George Mallory and A. C. Irvine disappeared when only 245m (800ft) from the summit, using the North Col (col = a pass between peaks) route. It has never been estab. whether they reached the top. The mtn was first ascertainably climbed in 1953 by New Zealander Edmund Hillary and the Sherpa Tensing, members of the British expedition led by Lord Hunt, using the South Col route pioneered by Eric Shipton in 1951. The even more dangerous SW face was first conquered by Dougal Haston and Doug Scott in the British expedition led by Chris Bonington in 1975.

EVERSHED, John (1864-1956). British astronomer. B. in Surrey, he devoted himself to solar observations, surveying solar prominences in particular detail, and in 1909 discovered the radial movement of gases in sunspots ('E. effect'). He also gave his name to a spectroheliograph, the 'E. spectroscope'.

EVESHAM (ēvz'-). Town in Hereford and Worcester, England, on the Avon SE of Worcester, in the fertile Vale of E. In the battle of E., 4 Aug. 1265, Edward, Prince of Wales, defeated Simon de Montfort, who was killed. Pop. (1972) 14,150.

EVOLUTION. Most usually, the organic E. of living creatures. Some conception of an evolutionary process may be traced in antiquity in writers such as Lucretius (1st cent. BC), but serious speculation was not renewed until the 18th cent. by Erasmus Darwin, grandfather of Charles Darwin, and Lord Monboddo. J. B. Lamarck in 1809 advanced a general theory of E., but the main contribution to the rise of evolutionary doctrine before Charles Darwin's *The Origin of Species* (1859) was the work of the geologist Lyell (q.v.). The evidence for continuous E. of living matter is provided by fossils, by vestigial organs or limbs in living species which are found to be fully functioning in other animals of similar construction, by geographical distribution and geology. Darwin assigned the major role in E. to natural selection, which resulted in the survival of the fittest, but the method by which E. takes place is still uncertain. Later followers of Lamarck maintain that an organism is moulded by its environment, to which it in turn endeavours to adapt itself, the consequent alterations in structure being transmitted to later generations - the concept of 'inheritance of acquired characters'. This theory became discredited and it was thought that the vital factors in E. are the random changes in the hereditary constitution of an organism, upon which the environment may exert an encouraging or discouraging influence. For example, in areas where the atmospheric pollution of the 19th cent. industrial revolution turned the tree trunks black, moths which were previously only known in light-coloured forms developed black forms, thus assisting their survival by making them less visible to predators - a phenomenon known as 'industrial melanism'. However, in the 1970s the case for Lamarck's theory of the 'inheritance of acquired characters' was further explored by writers such as Arthur Koestler, and the controversy revived.

ÉVREUX (ehvrö'). Chief town of Eure dept., Normandy, France, on the Iton. It has an 11th cent. cathedral and a bishop's palace. Rubber and pharmaceutical goods are made. Pop. (1975) 50,400.

EVZONES (ev'zōnz). Riflemen of the Greek army, characterized mainly by their picturesque dress with its spreading skirt.

EXCAVATOR. Machine designed for soil stripping, earth moving, ore extraction, etc., and usually of the track-mounted 'crawler' or more easily manœuvred and adaptable rubber-tyred type. Modern multi-storey concrete buildings which need very deep foundations have led to their increasing use on building sites.

EXCISE. *See* CUSTOMS AND EXCISE.

EXCOMMUNICATION. The temporary or permanent exclusion of an offender from the rights and privileges of membership of a religious community. In the Middle Ages the popes claimed the right to excommunicate recalcitrant sovereigns, and the emperors Henry IV, Frederick I and Frederick II; and John, Henry VIII, and Queen Elizabeth I of England were among those excommunicated.

EXE'CUTOR. The person appointed by Will to carry out the testamentary instructions of the deceased. An E. can be appointed only by a Will or a Codicil to a Will, and he may refuse to act. The duties of an E. are to bury the deceased and to prove the Will and obtain a grant of probate thereof. He must then pay the deceased's debts from the estate, collect any monies due, and distribute the estate according to the testamentary directions.

EXETER. City in Devon, England, on the Exe, 15km (9m) from its mouth: it is the admin. HQ of the co. A market centre, it manufactures agricultural machinery. The cathedral was built 1280-1369, and restored in the 1870s; the guildhall is Elizabethan, and there is a Maritime Museum. The univ. was founded in 1955. Pop. (1972) 94,180.

EXHIBITION. Term used to denote a collection of works of art, industrial products, etc., displayed to the public at a museum, art gallery, etc. A national E. had been held in Paris as early as 1798, but the first great international E. was that held in London in 1851 under the patronage of the Prince Consort (*see* CRYSTAL PALACE). Notable later Es. were the one held in Paris in 1889, for which the Eiffel Tower was erected; the British Empire E. at Wembley, 1924-5; the Festival of Britain, 1951 - for which the Royal Festival Hall on the South Bank of the Thames was built; Expo '70 in Osaka, Japan; and Expo '74 in Spokane, Washington. Few recent exhibitions have rivalled the success, financial and cultural, of the early examples. Britain has a Nat. E. Centre (1976) at Bickenhill, near Birmingham.

EXISTENTIALISM. Philosophical system propounded about 1943 by the French philosopher J. P. Sartre. Its main tenet is that in all important matters 'Existence precedes Essence', or in simpler language 'Facts come before Ideas'. In the evolution of man the facts of human nature come first and it is these facts which determine man's qualities, his purpose, and his 'essence'. Therefore E. is a philosophy which insists on facing the facts of man's nature. Historically speaking, E. is derived partly from the German philosopher Heidegger's cynical and subjective attitude to humanity, and partly from Kierkegaard's conception of man as an isolated and lonely individual dependent solely on God. Sartre himself ignores the religious element in Kierkegaard and is an example of an atheist Existentialist, but it is possible to be a Christian Existentialist, e.g. Jaspers.

E'XMOOR. Moorland in Devon and Somerset, England, nr the Bristol Channel, which (together with the coast from Minehead to Combe Martin) became a Nat. Park 1954. Much is over 300m (1,000 ft); highest point Dunkery Beacon 520m (1,707 ft). The Doone Valley is identified with either Lank Combe or Hoccombe.

EXMOOR. Boulder-strewn streams and lonely heights in Exmoor National Park. *Photo: Courtesy of the British Tourist Authority.*

EXMOUTH. Port and resort in S Devon, England, at the mouth of the Exe, SW of Exeter. There is some fine architecture dating from the 18th cent. Pop. (1972) 26,120.

EXOBIOLOGY. The study of life-forms such as may be found elsewhere in the Universe than on Earth.

EXORCISM. The expulsion of so-called 'evil spirits' by magical or religious rites. The R.C. Church has a special rite for those considered 'possessed', but the advent of psychological medicine has made it comparatively little used. Today the chief practitioners are the charismatics of the Pentecostal Movement (q.v.), by whom it is sometimes referred to as 'deliverance'.

EXPANDING UNIVERSE. In astronomy, a theory framed to account for phenomena exhibited by the extra-galactic nebulae (q.v.), viz. their even distribution through space, and the fact that the spectral lines in the light which they emit are displaced towards the long wave (red) end of the spectrum, of which the only known cause can be motion away from us. This even distribution in space and 'red-shift' was thought to indicate an expansion of the universe, whereby every galaxy is receding from all the others, but *see* ASTRONOMY.

EXPLOSIVES. Materials capable of a sudden release of energy and rapid formation of a large volume of gas, leading when compressed to the development of a high-pressure wave (blast). Combustion, explosion, and detonation differ essentially only in rate of reaction, and many explosives are capable under suitable conditions of undergoing relatively slow combustion. The explosive violence of atomic and hydrogen bombs arises from the tremendous amount of energy released by the conversion of mass into energy, according to Einstein's mass-energy equivalence, $E = mc^2$, where c is the velocity of light. It has been calculated that if it were possible to convert one pound of matter completely into energy it would be equivalent to eleven thousand million kilowatt hours of energy.

EXPRESSIONISM. Term applied to a style of painting, sculpture, or literary composition which is concerned with the inner world of feeling rather than the outer world of fact. An expressionist painting does not imitate nature but distorts natural appearance in order to convey what the artist feels about some subject; or it may consist purely of colours and forms which are entirely unrelated to nature, but express the mood of an artist. Some of Van Gogh's paintings may be described as 'expressionist'. Picasso in his picture of 'Guernica' expresses all the horror of war by means of distorted forms. Matisse's works are (in his own words) expressions of 'balance, of purity and serenity, devoid of any troubling subject matter'. The most important painters associated with the movement were Klee, Marc, Kandinsky, and Chagall.

EXTROVERT and **INTROVERT.** Two psychological types first defined by the Swiss psychologist C. G. Jung about 1916. The E. is the practical person whose energies are directed outwards towards the objective world; the soldier and the engineer are typical Es. The I., on the other hand, is the dreamer whose main energies are turned inwards in contemplation of his own imaginations and fancies; typical Is. include the poet and the musician.

EYCK (īk), **Van.** Family of early Flemish artists. **Hubert van E.** (*c.* 1370-1426) was probably b. at Maas Eyck or Alden Eyck on the Maas. Little of his work has survived. His 'Adoration of the Lamb', an altarpiece originally painted for Jodocus Vijdts who presented it to the cathedral of St Bavon in Ghent, was finished after Hubert's death by his brother **Jan van E.** (*c.* 1390-1441), who like Hubert was court painter to Philip the Good, duke of Burgundy. He is chiefly famous for his portraits, painted with great care and exact likeness; his 'The Marriage of Giovanni Arnolfini' (1434) and 'Man in a Red Turban' are in the National Gallery.

EYE. The organ of sight. It is a roughly spherical structure contained in a bony socket and having considerable freedom of rotatory movement. It is kept moist by the secretion of the lacrimal glands. Light enters it through the circular opening of the iris, passes through the lens, where it is focused, and strikes on the delicate inner membrane, the retina; thence the impulse is transmitted to the brain by the optic nerve. Minute electrodes are used by neurophysiologists to record from single nerve cells in the brain how it is linked with the eye, and experimental work in enabling robots on a production line 'to see' are throwing fresh light on the processes involved.

EYEBRIGHT. Common wild flower of the genus *Euphrasia*, Scrophulariaceae family, found in fields throughout Britain. It is 50-150mm (2-6in) high, bearing whitish flowers streaked with purple. The name indicates its former use as an eye-medicine.

EYRE (ār), **Edward John** (1815-1901). British colonial governor. B. in Yorks, he emigrated to Australia and made journeys into the interior, described in his *Expeditions into Central Australia* (1845), and in 1864 became gov. of Jamaica. In 1865 he suppressed a Negro rising with harshness, was suspended and not reinstated.

EYRE. Lake in S Australia, discovered by E. J. Eyre in 1840, area *c.* 7,770 sq.km (3,000 sq.m). In dry seasons it is a salt marsh, in wet a lake; it was full in 1950 for the first time since its discovery.

EYRE PENINSULA. Peninsula in S Australia, Australia, between the Great Australian Bight and Spencer's Gulf: Port Lincoln is at the S extremity. Iron is mined in the NE in the Middleback Range.

EYSENCK (ī'senk), **Hans Jurgen** (1916-). British psychologist. Ed. at the Univ. of London, he became prof. of psychology there in 1955. He has controversial views, preferring the treatment of symptoms to Freudian psychoanalyis, and stressing the role of heredity rather than environment in intelligence. In 1980 he developed an intelligence test, based on the measurement of brain waves, claimed to be independent of the subject's class, racial or cultural background.

EZEKIEL (ezē'ki-el) (b. *c.* 622 BC). Prophet of the OT. A priest of Jerusalem and member of the family of Zadok, he was carried into captivity with King Jehoiachin by Nebuchadnezzar in 597 BC. While in Babylonia he preached the downfall of Jerusalem as retribution for the sins of Israel.

EZRA. Scribe of the clan of Zadok, who by permission of Artaxerxes led *c.* 1,500 Jews from Babylonia back to Jerusalem (458 BC) where he instituted 'reforms', including the eradication of intermarriage, and re-establishment of the Mosaic Law, as told in the OT book named after him.

F

The sixth letter of the alphabet. Its capital form has changed little from what we see in the earlier Semitic alphabets.

FABER, Frederick William (1814-63). British hymn writer. A clergyman of the C of E, he became an RC priest in 1845, and superior of the Oratory of St Philip Neri (Brompton Oratory) in 1849. He wrote 'Hark, Hark, my Soul'.

FABERGÉ (fahbārjeh'), **Peter Carl** (1846-1920). Russian goldsmith. Of Huguenot descent, he was b. at St Petersburg, and his workshops there and in Moscow were celebrated for the exquisite delicacy of their products, especially the use of gold in different shades. Among F.'s masterpieces was the series of imperial Easter eggs, the first of which was commissioned by Alexander III for the Tsarina in 1884. He d. in exile.

FĀ'BIAN SOCIETY. Socialist propagandist and research organization, founded in 1884. Its name is derived from Fabius Cunctator (q.v.), and refers to the evolutionary methods by which it hopes to attain socialism by a succession of gradual reforms. In its early days it was dominated by Bernard Shaw and Sidney Webb: it still plays its part and in 1963 Harold Wilson first outlined in a F.S. meeting his plans for changing the machinery of British govt.

FĀ'BIUS. Name of an ancient Roman family, of whom the best known is **Quintus F. Maximus,** known as *Cunctator* (Delayer). As commander against Hannibal 217-214 BC, he continually harassed his armies without ever risking a set battle.

FABLE. A story, either in verse or prose, in which the animal kingdom, and even inanimate objects, are endowed with the mentality and speech of human beings in order to point a moral. The best-known Fs. include those of Aesop (5th cent. BC), Phaedrus and Avianus, La Fontaine, Gay, Lessing, etc.

FABRE (fahbr), **Jean Henri** (1823-1915). French entomologist, called the 'Insects' Homer' because of his remarkably vivid and intimate descriptions of wasps, bees, and other insects. B. in Aveyron, he became a schoolmaster but retired in 1871 to Sérignan. He pub. *Souvenirs entomologiques.*

FABRI'CIUS, Geronimo (1537-1619). Italian anatomist. He was prof. of surgery and anatomy at Padua from 1562, and did pioneer work that won him the title of the father of embryology.

FACTORY ACTS. Acts of parliament concerned with conditions of work, hours of labour, safety, and sanitary provisions in factories and workshops. The first was the Health and Morals of Apprentices Act 1802, and this was followed in 1819 by the Cotton Mills Act, which forbade the labour of children under 9 and reduced the hours of labour of those under 16 to 72 per week. Ashley's Act of 1845 forbade night work to women, and in 1847 Ashley (later the 7th earl of Shaftesbury) was responsible for passing the 10-hours bill. The first factory inspectors were appointed in 1833. Legislation was subsequently extended and consolidated, and by an act of 1963 offices, shops, and railway premises, in which conditions had often been unsatisfactory, were covered.

FACTORY ACTS. In the Saab-Scania factory near Stockholm, where trucks and car engines are assembled, there is an island of potted plants enclosing a tea-garden style café right alongside the 'assembly line'. In effect, the 'line' has been abolished, and workers decide themselves whether they want to assemble a whole engine or divide the work among them. *Photo: Courtesy of Saab-Scania.*

FADDEN, Sir Arthur 'Artie' (1895-1973). Australian statesman. B. in Queensland, he led the Country Party 1941-58, and was PM Aug.-Oct. 1941.

FAENZA (fah-en'tsah). City on the r. Lamone in Ravenna prov., Emilia-Romagna, Italy. It has many medieval remains, incl. the 15th cent. walls, and has been famous since the 13th cent. for 'faience pottery'. Pop. (1971) 52,000.

FAEROES (fār'ōz). Group of 21 islands (18 inhabited), which form an outlying part of Denmark, but have since 1948 exercised home rule. They lie in the N Atlantic between the Shetlands and Iceland, and the name means 'Sheep Islands'. The largest are Stromo, Ostero, Vaago, Sudero, and Sando, and the cap. is Thorshavn on Stromo. Sheep are reared, and cod and other fish, and crafted goods are exported. The F. were first settled by the Norsemen in the 9th cent. Area 1,399 sq.km (540 sq.m); pop. (1977) 42,000.

FAHRENHEIT (-hīt), **Gabriel Daniel** (1686-1736). German physicist, inventor of the Fahrenheit thermometric scale, in which freezing point of pot. chlor. was 0°, the freezing point of water was 32° and boiling point 212°.

FAINTING. A sudden and temporary suspension of consciousness and movement, due to failure of the supply of blood, and consequently of oxygen, to the brain. The cause is generally a fall in blood pressure due to shock, heart disease, fatigue, privation, or - in air pilots - to the action of centrifugal force in drawing blood away from the head.

FAIRBANKS, Douglas (1883-1939). American actor. B. at Denver, Colorado, he starred from 1915 in films such as *The Three Musketeers, The Thief of Baghdad* and *Don Q*, and was the most famous of the silent screen's swashbuckling heroes. He and Mary Pickford, whom he m. in 1920, were idolized as 'the world's sweethearts'. His son by a previous marriage, **Douglas F.** (1909-), achieved similar screen renown in *Catherine the Great* and *The Prisoner of Zenda*. He was created an hon. KBE in 1949 for his distinguished efforts in the Allied cause.

FAIRBANKS. Town in Alaska, USA, on the Chena Slough, a trib. of the r. Tanana, terminus of the Alaska Railroad and of the Pan-American Highway. It is a centre for goldmining and the fur trade and has sawmills. The University of Alaska is at College, 5km (3m) NW. Pop. met. area (1970) 42,000.

FAIRFAX OF CAMERON, Thomas Fairfax, 3rd baron (1612-71). English soldier, C-in-C of the parliamentary army in the Civil War. With Cromwell he formed the New Model Army, defeated Charles I at Naseby, and suppressed the risings of 1648.

FAISAL, Ibn Abdul Aziz (1905-75). King of Saudi Arabia. The younger brother of King Saud, on whose accession in 1953 he was declared Crown Prince, he was PM 1953-60 and from 1962. In 1964 he emerged victorious from a lengthy conflict with his brother, the reactionary King Saud, and was proclaimed king. Remarkable for his balanced statesmanship, he assisted the steady modernization of his country. He was assassinated (shot) by his nephew.

FAIZABAD (fīzahbahd'). Town in Uttar Pradesh, India, at the head of navigation of the r. Gogra, with sugar refineries and an agricultural trade. Pop. (1971) 109,765.

FAKIR. In Oriental countries, a religious beggar, usually a member of a sect, order, or special caste. Originally a Moslem term for mendicants akin to dervishes, it is widely used in India for ascetics who practise varieties of self-torture.

FALAISE. French town 32km (20m) SSE of Caen, in Calvados dept, Normandy. It is a market centre, and manufactures cotton and leather goods. The castle was that of the first dukes of Normandy, and William the Conqueror was b. at F. Pop. (1975) 7,100.

FALANGE ESPAÑOLA (fahlahn'khe espahnyō'-lah) (Spanish phalanx). Spanish Fascist Party, founded by José Antonio de Rivera, son of Primo de Rivera. It was closely modelled in programme and organization on the Italian Fascists, and on the Nazis. In 1937, when Franco assumed its leadership, it was declared the only legal party, and altered its name to Traditionalist Spanish Phalanx.

FALCON. Bird of the genus *Falco* in the family Falconidae. Of world-wide distribution, the Fs. are birds of prey with short, hooked beaks and sharp claws, remarkable for their keen sight and swiftness of flight. Notable are the wide-ranging peregrine (*F. peregrinus*), persecuted almost to extinction in Britain, of which there are American and Australian varieties, and which is blue-grey with dark markings on the back and a white breast; the Scandinavian gyrfalcon (*F. gyrfalco*); the Greenland F. (*F. candicans*) almost white and lightest of the true Fs.; the 'saker' and the much smaller 'lanner', both Mediterranean species; the hobby (*F. subbuteo*); the merlin (q.v.); and the kestrel (q.v.) - all the last 3 breeding in Britain. *See* FALCONRY.

FALCON. The peregrine ranges wide, even to Australia, and is here seen with its prey. The kill is quick in those great talons. *Photo: Courtesy of the Australian Information Service.*

FALCONRY. The use of specially trained falcons and hawks to capture birds or small mammals, practised from ancient times in the Near East, and introduced from the Continent to Britain in Saxon times. The Normans, the Tudors and Stuarts were all fond of F., but it fell into desuetude after the Civil War.

FALKENDER, Marcia Falkender, baroness (1932-). British politician. Secretary to Harold Wilson from 1956, she was an influential member of the so-called 'kitchen cabinet' during the 1964-70 Labour ministry of which she pub. a controversial account, *Inside No 10* (1972), and was created a life peer 1974. She was m. 1955-60 to G. Williams.

FALKIRK (fawl'-). Town in Central Region, Scotland, overlooking the fertile Carse of F. A centre of light-casting on the central coalfield, F. has brewing, distilling, tanning and chemical industries. Pop. (1971) 37,500.

FALKLAND (fawk'-), **Lucius Cary,** 2nd viscount (*c.* 1610-43). English royalist. Before the Civil War he earned a high reputation as a patron of literature and scholarship. Elected to the Long Parliament, he showed himself a zealous opponent of absolute monarchy, but the proposal to abolish episcopacy alienated him, and he went over to the king. Plunged into despair by his failure to secure a compromise peace, he flung away his life at the battle of Newbury.

FALKLAND ISLANDS. British Crown Colony in the S Atlantic *c.* 480km (300m) E of the southern part of S America. After the recovery of the Falklands in 1982, the Governor, Rex Hunt, returned as Civil Commissioner.

There are 2 main islands, E Falkland (on which is the cap. Port Stanley), and W Falkland, and a number of islets. Resources incl sheep, alginates from the seaweed beds, and offshore oil. Area 12,173 sq.km (4,700 sq.m); pop (1982) 1800. Admin with the Falklands, but separate dependencies of the UK, are South Georgia (q.v.) and the S Sandwich Is, 775 km (470 m) SE of the former; area 337 sq.km (130 sq.m), uninhabited. *See* also BRITISH ANTARCTIC TERRITORY.

The F.I. were discovered by Englishman John Davis in 1592, and later named after Lord Falkland (q.v.). W Falkland was settled by Britain in 1765. Spain bought out a French settlement in 1766, and ejected the British 1770-1, which almost caused an Anglo-Spanish war. The F.I. were at periods unpopulated, but British sovereignty was never ceded, and from 1833, when a few Argentines were expelled, British settlement was continuous. Argentina asserts its succession to the Spanish claim to the 'Islas Malvinas', but the population has opposed cession. An Argentine invasion and occupation 2 Apr-14 June 1982, was ended by a British expeditionary force.

In the BATTLE OF THE FALKLAND ISLANDS, a British naval victory of the F.W.W. fought off E Falkland on 8 Dec., 1914, a British force under Vice-Admiral Sturdee destroyed almost the entire German squadron commanded by Admiral von Spee that had just been successful in the battle of Coronel (q.v.).

FALLA (fahl'yah), **Manuel de** (1876-1946). Spanish composer. B. at Cadiz, he lived in France where he was influenced by the impressionists, esp. Debussy and Ravel. His first work of importance, the opera *La Vida Breve* (1905), was followed by the ballets *El Amor Brujo* and *The Three-Cornered Hat* (1919); *Nights in the Gardens of Spain*, songs, pieces for the piano and the guitar. The folk-idiom is an integral part of his compositions.

FALLŌ'PIUS, Gabriello (1523-62). Italian anatomist. He taught at Ferrara, Pisa, and Padua, and made a particular study of the generative organs; the Fallopian tubes are named after him.

FALL-OUT. Radiation scattered in the debris of a nuclear explosion. In war-time attack the first danger, provided that the blast and fire hazards have been survived, is gamma radiation. In tests, however, the deposit of F. on the ground is delayed, and the chief peril is from radioactive components, e.g. strontium, which either enter the body and cause cancer, or burn on contact with the skin.

Radiation is measured in rads, and is cumulative in effect. Comparative safety lies below 100 rads, though long-term genetic or carcinogenic changes are probable up to 300; deaths begin at 450 and there is a 50 per cent chance of death occurring over a period of days or weeks.

FALL RIVER. City in Mass, USA, a port at the mouth of the Taunton r. and built over the little Fall r. which gave it its name. Cotton, rubber and paper are the chief industries. Pop. (1970) 96,900.

FALMOUTH. Port on the S coast of Cornwall, England, on the estuary of the Fal. There are ship repairing and marine engineering industries, and the port has potential for container traffic. Piran Round, the nearby open-air theatre has performances of Cornish miracle plays. Pop. (1972) 17,450.

FAMAGUSTA (fahmahgoos'tah). Seaport on the E coast of Cyprus, the chief port of the island, with a trade in citrus fruit, etc. To the N the site of Enkomi-Alasia has yielded undeciphered inscriptions of *c.* 1200 BC, and models of two-headed centaurs (q.v.). Pop. (1975) 39,400.

FAMILY PLANNING. The spacing of the birth of children to safeguard the health of the mother and the balance of family life. The prevention of conception is opposed on religious grounds in that it is immoral to frustrate the natural purpose of the sexual relationship, but is often advocated by medical men to prevent the transmission of hereditary disease and by economists to mitigate poverty, especially in eastern countries such as India, which are undergoing a population 'explosion'. Birth control by contraception has only become a generally adopted practice, most commonly using some chemical or mechanical means, in the last few generations. In the 1960s an oral contraceptive taken by the woman to induce an extension of the 'safe period' was developed but, though initially popular, side effects and possible drawbacks in long-term use later led to a decline. There was also increasing use of vasectomy for men. Abortion, one of the earliest and crudest forms of F.P., lost some of its dangers and difficulties when the vacuum aspiration method was developed in the 1970s for use in the earliest stages of pregnancy. However, F.P. is least practised in any form by those whose circumstances most encourage large families of children for whom they are unable to provide adequately, e.g. those pressured by poverty and high child mortality to insure against destitution in old age, etc., by having many children. In the later 1970s injections (the hormone progesteron) to prevent pregnancy for 3 months or more were being experimentally used. *See also* ABORTION and STERILIZATION.

FANCY, The. Formerly the popular name for pugilists and for those who frequented the prize-ring.

FANTIN-LATOUR (fońtań'-lahtōōr'), **Henri** (1836-1904). French artist. B. at Grenoble, he excelled in lightly delicate still-lifes and flower paintings, genre pictures and portraiture. 'Homage to Delacroix' is a portrait group of Baudelaire, Champfleury, Legros, Whistler, and himself.

FARADAY, Michael (1791-1867). British chemist and natural philosopher. B. in London, the son of a blacksmith, he became a laboratory assistant to Sir Humphry Davy at the Royal Institution in 1813, and in 1827 succeeded him as professor of chemistry there. As early as 1812 he began researches into the problems of electricity, and in that year made his first electric battery. In 1821 he began experimenting on electro-magnetism, and ten years later discovered the induction of electric currents and made the first dynamo. Many more epoch-making discoveries in all fields of electricity followed; and in 1845 he began a second great period of research in which he discovered what he announced as the magnetization of light. He delivered highly popular lectures at the Royal Institution, and pub. many treatises on scientific subjects. In 1835 he was given a government pension, and in 1858 a house at Hampton Court, where he d. Deeply religious, he was a member of the Sandemanian sect. F.'s *laws of electrolysis* are (1) the chemical effect resulting from electrolysis is directly proportional to the quantity of electricity which has passed through the electrolyte; and (2) the quantity of each substance chemically changed, or liberated, at an electrode by the passage of a definite quantity of electricity is directly proportionate to the equivalent weight (q.v.) of the substance. F.'s *law of induced e.m.f.*, associated with him but not enunciated by him, is: the induced e.m.f. round any circuit is proportional to the rate of change of magnetic flux (q.v.) through the circuit. A *farad* is the practical unit of electrostatic capacitance and it is equivalent to 9×10^{11} E.S. units. It is the capacitance of a capacitor in which a charge of 1 coulomb produces a change of potential difference of 1 volt between its terminals.

FARADAY. A portrait of the great chemist by Thomas Phillips painted in 1842. *Photo: Courtesy of the National Portrait Gallery.*

FAR EAST. Geographical term for all that part of Asia lying E. of the Indian sub-continent. *See also* SOVIET FAR EAST.

FAREHAM (fār'am). Town in Hants, England, 10 km. (6 m.) N.W. of Portsmouth. Bricks, ceramics, rope, etc. are made and there are engineering and boatbuilding as well as varied light industries. Pop. (1973) 25,000.

FARGO, William George (1818-81). American pioneer expressman. In 1844 he estab. with Henry Wells (1805-78) and Daniel Dunning the first express company to carry freight west of Buffalo. Its success led to his appointment as sec. of the newly estab. American Express Co. in 1850, of which he was pres. 1868-81. He also estab. Wells Fargo & Co. (1851) carrying goods express between N.Y. and San Francisco via Panama.

Fargo, a town on the Red r., in North Dakota, is named after him. Pop. (1970) 53,365.

FARMAN (fahrmoṅ'), **Henry** (1874-1958). Anglo-French air pioneer. Making his first flying experiments in 1907, he designed and flew his classic biplane in 1909. With his brother Maurice he founded an aircraft works at Billancourt, important as a source of machines for the French army, and other countries, incl. England, which also made use of F.'s inventions, e.g. air-screw reduction gears, in the S.W.W. He became a naturalized Frenchman in 1937.

FARNABY, Giles (*c.* 1550-1650). English composer. He is thought to have been b. in Cornwall and studied at Oxford. He composed pieces for the virginal, and for voices (madrigals).

FARNBOROUGH. Town in Hants, England, N. of Aldershot. The mansion of Farnborough Hill was occupied by the Empress Eugénie, and she, her husband and her son, are buried in a mausoleum at the R.C. church she built. Experimental work is carried out at the Royal Aircraft Establishment. Pop. (1972) 41,680.

FARNE. Group of small rocky is. off the coast of Northumberland, England. A chapel stands on the site of the hermitage of St. Cuthbert (q.v.), and there are 2 lighthouses, that on Longstone being the scene of the rescue by Grace Darling (q.v.). It is a bird sanctuary and a breeding ground for grey seal.

FARNESE (fahrneh'se). Name of a famous Italian family who held the duchy of Parma 1545-1731.

FARNHAM. Town in Surrey, England on the Wey. The parish church was once part of Waverley Abbey (1128), the first Cistercian house in England: Scott named his first novel after the abbey. At Moor Park, Swift (q.v.) met Stella. Pop. (1972) 31,850.

FAROE ISLANDS, FAROES. *See* FAEROES.

FAROUK (fahrōōk') (1920-65). King of Egypt. The son of Fuad (q.v.), he succeeded him in 1936. In 1952 he was compelled to abdicate, his own son Fuad being temporarily proclaimed in his stead.

FARQUHAR (far'kar), **George** (1677-1707). Irish dramatist. B. in Londonderry, he became an actor in Dublin, but in 1698 went to London, where in 1699 his first play *Love and a Bottle* was produced. *The Constant Couple* (1700), was followed by a sequel *Sir Harry Wildair* (1701). The best of his later plays are *The Recruiting Officer* (1706), and *The Beaux' Stratagem* (1707).

FA'RRAGUT, David Glasgow (1801-70). American seaman. B. nr. Knoxville, Tennessee, son of a Spanish emigrant, he took New Orleans in 1862, after destroying the Confederate fleet, and in 1864 effectively put an end to blockade-running at Mobile, besides other dashingly heroic exploits. The ranks of vice-admiral (1864) and admiral (1866) were specially created for him by Congress.

FARRELL, J(ames) G(ordon) (1935-79). British historical novelist. B. in Liverpool, he is best remembered for *Troubles* (1970), dealing with Ireland, and *The Siege of Krishnapur* (1973).

FARRELL, James T(homas) (1904-79). American novelist. B. in Chicago, he worked as a clerk, filling station assistant, and reporter. In his trilogy *Studs Lonigan* (1932-5) he described a youth growing up in the district of the city in which he lived during the depression.

FARS. Prov. of Iran, comprising fertile valleys among mtn ranges running NW to SE. The cap. is Shiraz, and there are imposing ruins of Cyrus the Great's city of Parargardae and of Persepolis (q.v.).

FARTHING. Formerly the smallest English coin, a quarter of a penny. It was introduced, originally as a silver coin, in Edward I's reign. The copper F. became general in Charles II's time, and the bronze in 1860. It became obsolete Jan. 1, 1961.

FASCES (fa'sēz). In ancient Rome, bundles of rods carried in procession by the lictors in front of the chief magistrates, as a symbol of their power over the lives and liberties of the people. An axe was included in the bundle. The F. were adopted by the Fascists as their badge.

FASCHING (fash'ing). Period preceding Lent in R.C. German-speaking towns, Cologne, Munich and Vienna, devoted to masquerades, formal balls and street parades: the word is from the German 'to pour from a barrel'.

FASCISM (fash'ism). The totalitarian nationalist movement founded in Italy by Mussolini; also similar movements elsewhere. Its units were originally called *fasci di combattimento, fascio* meaning a bundle or group; later it adopted as its emblem the *fasces* (q.v.). Between the 2 world wars F. movements arose in many other countries.

F. was essentially a product of the economic and political crisis of the inter-war years. It protected the existing social order by its forcible suppression of the working-class movement, and by providing scapegoats for popular anger in the Jew or the foreigner or the Negro: it also provided the machinery for the economic and psychological mobilization of the nation for war. In its propaganda it made great use of revolutionary phrases. Its ideology denied all rights to the individual in his relations with the State, personified in the infallible 'leader' *(Duce, Fuehrer)*. Science, art, and education were brought under state control. Women were driven from economic and public life.

In Italy F. arose in 1919. In Oct. 1922 Mussolini was invited to take power by the king, and the Fascist regime ended with his fall in July 1943. In the 1970s the neo-Fascist Movimento Sociale Italiano grew in strength especially in less developed areas of the country.

Outside Italy and Nazi Germany, Fascist or semi-Fascist régimes included the dictatorships of Horthy in Hungary, Pilsudski in Poland, Dollfuss in Austria, Franco in Spain, Salazar in Portugal, Pétain in France, and Perón in Argentina. The Fascist movements in Belgium, Holland, and Norway all assisted in the conquest of their countries by the Nazis. Sir Oswald Mosley's British Union of Fascists gained considerable notoriety 1932-9 and was revived as the Union Movement after the S.W.W., and in 1962 the National Socialist Movement was founded by Colin Jordan, having strong links with the U.S. Nazi Party (founded 1958) and led by George Lincoln Rockwell (assassinated 1967). *See also* NATIONAL FRONT. Japanese F., which held power 1932-45, combined European ideas with emperor-worship, Shintoism, and feudal ideology.

FAT. The principal component of the adipose tissue in animal bodies. In chemistry the name is applied to the glyceryl esters of certain fatty acids.

FATES. In Greek and Roman mythology, the spirits who determined the destiny of each newborn child, and in particular the length of its life. They are pictured as three old women spinning, their names being Clotho, Lachesis, and Atropos.

FATHERS OF THE CHURCH. Name applied to certain teachers and writers of the early Christian Church, particularly eminent for their learning and orthodoxy, experience, and sanctity of life, who lived from the end of the 1st to the end of the 7th cent., a period of 600 years divided by the Council of Nicaea (325) into the Ante-Nicene and Post-Nicene Fathers. The most important of the Ante-Nicene Fs. are the Apostolic Fathers - Clement of Rome, Ignatius of Antioch, Polycarp of Smyrna, and 'Barnabas' - Justin Martyr, Tatian, Irenaeus, Clement, Origen, Tertullian, Cyprian, and Gregory Thaumaturgus. Of the Post-Nicene Fs. the most memorable are Cyril of Alexandria, Athanasius, John Chrysostom, Eusebius of Caesarea, Cyril of Jerusalem, Basil the Great, Ambrose of Milan, Hilary of Poitiers, Augustine, pope Leo I, Boethius, Jerome, Gregory of Tours, pope Gregory the Great, and Bede.

FATHOM. Traditional unit of measurement, originally the distance between the finger tips with the arms outstretched, used until metrication in marine soundings and equal to 6 ft (1.829 m). In mining and handling timber signified a measurement 6 ft square (1.829 m.square).

FATIMITES. Name given to a Moslem dynasty which was founded by Obaidallah, who claimed to be a descendant of Fatima, Mohammed's daughter, and her husband, Ali, in N. Africa in A.D. 909. In 969 Egypt was conquered and the dynasty continued until overthrown by Saladin in 1171. The Fatimites were Shiites.

FATTY ACIDS. Group of organic compounds, the higher members of which are found combined with glycerol in fats. They include formic acid, acetic acid, butyric acid, palmitic acid, and stearic acid.

FAULKNER, Brian, baron (1921-77). N. Ireland Unionist statesman. He was the last P.M. of N. Ireland 1971-2 before the Stormont Parliament was prorogued.

FAULKNER, William (1897-1962). American novelist. Son of a declined aristocratic family, he was b. in Mississippi, and after service in the R.C.A.F. and R.A.F. during the F.W.W. wrote prolifically but without publishing anything of importance, until his first novel of a war veteran, *Soldier's Pay* (1926). However, he did not strike his true vein until he returned to Oxford, the town in which he had spent his youth and on which he was to model Jefferson in the co. of Yoknapatawpha, the setting of his major novels. These began with *Sartoris* (1929); *The Sound and the Fury* (1929), dealing with a Southern family in decline and sometimes rated as his finest work; *As I Lay Dying* (1930); *Light in August* (1932), a study of segregation which concerned him deeply; *The Unvanquished* (1938), stories of the Civil War; and *The Hamlet* (1940), *The Town* (1957) and *The Mansion* (1959), a trilogy covering the rise of the materialist Snopes family. His experimental and turgid style - sentences sometimes running over a page - hindered popular recognition and a book such as *Sanctuary* (1931) was deliberately conceived as a horrific moneyspinner. Also notable are *Intruder in the Dust* (1948), *Requiem for a Nun* (1953, dramatized 1955), and *The Reivers* (1962). In 1949 he was awarded a Nobel prize.

FAURE (fohreh'), **Gabriel Urbain** (1845-1924). French composer. A pupil of Saint-Saëns, he became prof. of composition at the Conservatoire in 1896, and was director 1905-20. He is remembered for his songs, chamber music, and a *Requiem* (1887).

FAUST (fowst). Legendary magician. The historical F. appears to have been a wandering mountebank, who appeared in Germany during the opening decade of the 16th cent. But earlier figures such as Simon Magus and Theophilus contributed to the F. legend. In 1587 appeared the first of a series of Faust books. Marlowe's tragedy of *Dr Faustus* was acted in 1594. In the 18th cent. the story was a subject for pantomime in England and puppet plays in Germany. In Germany the serious possibilities of the theme were first pointed out by Lessing; Goethe made F. a symbol of Man's striving after the infinite. Later Lunarcharski, Dorothy Sayers, and Paul Valéry took up the theme. F. has also inspired musical works by Schumann, Berlioz, Gounod, Boito, and Busoni.

FAUVISM. Art movement originating in Paris with the founding of the Salon d'automne in 1903, by Matisse and his friends. Their chief source of inspiration was the work of Van Gogh. Others who participated in the movement were Roualt, Derain, Bonnard, and Vlaminck. In 1905 the art critic L. Vauxcelles called the gallery in which they exhibited 'une cage aux fauves' (cage of wild beasts).

FAWCETT, Percy Harrison (1867-1925). British explorer. After several expeditions to delineate frontiers in S America during the rubber boom, he set off in 1925, with his eldest son John and a friend, into the Mato Grosso to find the 'cradle of Brazilian civilization'. Their fate is unknown although Colonel F.'s younger son Brian F., who edited an account of his father's expeditions in *Exploration Fawcett* (1953), tried to follow up the trail.

FAWKES (fawks), **Guy** (1570-1606). English conspirator. B. at York, he was converted to Catholicism as a youth, served in the Spanish army in 1593, and in 1604 joined in the Gunpowder Plot to blow up the King and the members of both houses of Parliament. He was arrested in the cellar underneath the House on Nov. 4 1605, tortured and executed.

FAWKES. The only known contemporary portrait of the conspirator. *Photo: Courtesy of Sotheby Parke Bernet & Co.*

FAX. Abbreviation for 'fast facsimile machine', used to transmit documents in facsimile. The original document is scanned horizontally, the lengths of black and white along each line being measured and given a compact digital code. The standard transmission is then at the rate of 4,800 'bits' of information per second.

FAYUM (fīyoom'). Prov. of Upper Egypt, SW of Cairo. Numerous very realistic mummy portraits of the 1st-4th cents. A.D. have been found here: they probably reflect Greek influence, since the area was largely settled by Greeks.

FÉCAMP (fehko'ń). A seaport and resort of N France, NNE of Havre in the dept of Seine Maritime. The main industries are shipbuilding and fishing. Pop. (1975) 20,000.

FECHNER (fekh'ner), **Gustav Theodor** (1801-87). German psychologist. He became prof. of physics at Leipzig in 1834, but in 1839 through failing eyesight turned to the study of psychophysics, i.e. the relationship of physiology and psychology. He devised a method (Fechner's Law) for the exact measurement of sensation.

FEDERAL BUREAU OF INVESTIGATION (F.B.I.). Agency of the Dept of Justice in the USA which investigates those violations of federal law not specifically assigned to other agencies, being particularly concerned with internal security. Field divisions are maintained in over 59 major cities, and there are *c.* 160,000,000 finger print cards on its files. Its special agents, known as G-men from the dept's code letter, are 23-36 on entry, with special qualifications in law, accounting or auditing. The dept built up a unique position in the earlier years of the directorship of J. Edgar Hoover 1924-72, but during the S.W.W., when the F.B.I. shared espionage duties with the armed forces, Hoover ignored a report on the planned Japanese attack on Pearl Harbor. In 1964 the F.B.I. was criticised by the Warren Commission for failing to warn the Secret Service that Oswald was a potential threat to Pres. Kennedy, and in 1973 L. Patrick Gray, the acting director, resigned when it was revealed that he had destroyed relevant material in the Watergate investigation. Clarence M. Kelley was director 1973-8, and William Webster from 1978.

FEDERALISM. A system of govt under which two or more separate states unite under a common central govt, while retaining a considerable degree of local autonomy. A federation should be distinguished from a confederation, a looser union of states for mutual assistance. Switzerland, the Soviet Union, the USA, Canada, Australia and Malaysia, are all examples of federal government, and many supporters of the Common Market see it as the forerunner of a federal Europe.

FEDERATION OF BRITISH INDUSTRIES. *See* CONFEDERATION OF BRITISH INDUSTRY.

FEININGER (fī'-), **Lyonel** (1871-1956). American artist. B. in New York, the son of German immigrants, he worked for a time at the Bauhaus, and helped to found the Bauhaus in Chicago. Fond of the sea and ships, he portrayed them with romantic sensitivity in dreamlike translucence and purity of line.

FEISAL I (fī'sal) (1885-1933). King of Iraq. Descended from Mohammed, he was elected king of Iraq in 1921. His grandson **Feisal II** (1935-58) succeeded his father, King Ghazi, in 1939, and following the regency of his uncle Abdul Illah was king of Iraq 1953-8. He was assassinated with his uncle when an army revolt estab. a rep.

FELDSPARS, FELSPARS, Important mineral group in rock formation, particularly of igneous rocks. They range through a great number of minerals, containing aluminium silicate and varying proportions of silicates of sodium, potassium, calcium, and barium; are white, grey, or pink in colour; and crystallize in the monoclinic or triclinic system.

FELIDAE (fēl'idē). Family of carnivores, which includes the lion, tiger, leopard, European wild cat, domesticated cat, etc.

FELIXSTOWE. Popular English holiday resort on the coast of Suffolk between the Orwell and Deben estuaries. The docks are increasingly important, and are being developed to rival Harwich. Pop. (1973) 19,500.

FELLI'NI, Federico (1920-). Italian film director. With strongly subjective poetic imagery, he has directed *I Vitelloni* (1953), *La Strada* (1954), *La Dolce Vita* (1960), *8½* (1963) - i.e. he had by this time made 8½ films, and *Casanova* (1975).

FELONY. *See* CRIMINAL LAW.

FENCING. Art of sword play. The foil used in the most popular modern form of the sport is derived from the Italian *floretta*, a light practice sword used in rehearsing for duels: the point is covered by a plastic button. As a sport it developed from the late 18th cent., masks being introduced 1780 to protect the eyes and protective jackets being worn. Hits, registered electronically in competition, are made to the trunk with the point alone (5 hits in 6 min for men, and 4 in 5 for women). Fencing with the heavier epée, derives from duelling proper, in the later more formal period when 'first blood' rather than death would satisfy honour, so that hits to any part of the body or equipment are possible. In sabre F., the body above the waist is the target, and the weapon has 2 cutting edges, cuts as well as thrusts being counted. Both epée and sabre are for men only.

FÉNÉLON, François de Salignac de la Mothe (1651-1715). French writer and ecclesiastic. A son of the comte de Fénélon, he entered the priesthood in 1675 and in 1679 was made spiritual director to a sisterhood of ex-Huguenot proselytes, for whom he wrote his *Traité de l'Education des Filles* (1687). His *Démonstration de l'Existence de Dieu* was intended to bring the philosophy of Descartes into line with Catholic thought. In 1689 he was appointed tutor to the duke of Burgundy, grandson of Louis XIV, and wrote for him his *Fables, Dialogues des Morts, Télémaque,* and *Plans de Gouvernement. Télémaque* (1699) with its picture of an ideal commonwealth had the effect of a political manifesto, and Louis banished F. to Cambrai, where in 1695 he had been consecrated archbishop.

F.'s mystical *Maximes des Saints* (1697) led to a quarrel with the Jansenists, rupture with Bossuet, and condemnation by pope Innocent XII.

FĒ'NIANS. Irish-American revolutionary secret society, founded in 1858 and named after the ancient legendary warrior band of the Fianna. It aimed at the establishment of an Irish republic. An attempt to invade Canada from the USA in 1866 and a rising in Ireland in 1867 failed completely, but the society continued down to the Irish civil war of 1922.

FENNEC. Species of fox (*Fennecus zerda*) found in the Sahara desert. Its coat is mainly pale fawn, and it has large ears.

FENNEL. Genus of plants (*Foeniculum*) of the Umbelliferae. The common F. is a perennial, reaching *c.* 1m (3ft) in height, and bearing large umbels of fragrant yellow flowers. It grows wild in S Britain, and is used in cookery and sauces and as a garnish.

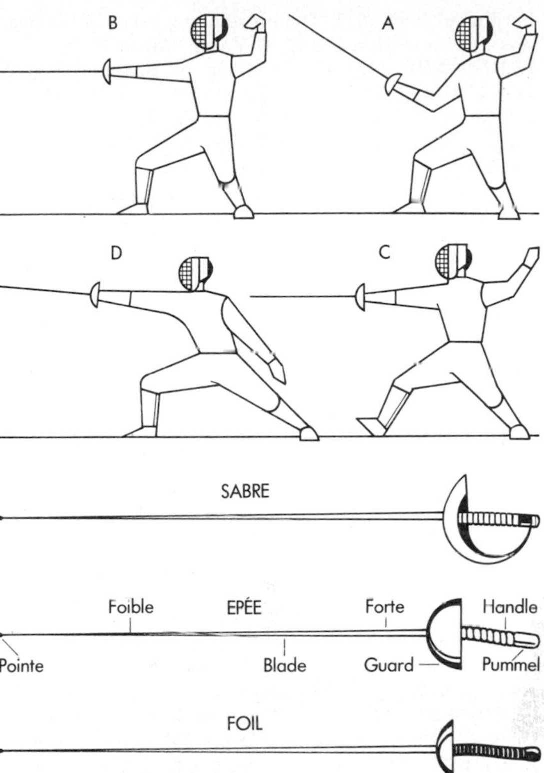

FENCING. The lunge: the on-guard position (A); the arm extended, both establishing attack and giving protection (B); the beginning of the lunge as the rear arm is lowered (C); and the completion of the lunge (D). Below, the weapons – sabre, epée and foil.

FENS. Level, low-lying tracts of land in E England, W and S of the Wash, *c.* 115km (70m) N-S and *c.* 55km (35m) E-W. They fall within the counties of Lincs, Cambs, and Norfolk, consisting of a huge area once a bay of the North Sea, but now crossed by numerous drainage canals and forming some of the most productive agricultural land in Britain. The first drainage attempts were made by the Romans, but later attempts were unsuccessful until in 1634 the 4th earl of Bedford brought over the Dutch water-engineer Vermuyden who introduced Dutch methods. Burwell Fen and Wicken Fen, NE of Cambridge, have been preserved undrained as plant and animal reserves.

FERBER, Edna (1887-1968). American author. B. in Michigan, she was originally a reporter for the *Chicago Tribune*. Her novel *Show Boat* (1926) was adapted as an operetta by Jerome Kern and Oscar Hammerstein II, and her plays, in which she collaborated with G. S. Kaufmann, incl. *Dinner at Eight* (1932) and *Stage Door* (1936).

FERDINAND. Name of 3 Holy Roman emperors. **Ferdinand I** (1503-64) succeeded his brother Charles V as emperor in 1556. **Ferdinand II** (1578-1637), king of Bohemia and Hungary, succeeded his uncle Matthias as emperor in 1619, and by his fanatical Catholicism provoked the Bohemian revolt, which led to the 30 Years War. **Ferdinand III** (1608-57) succeeded his father

Ferdinand II in 1637. The outstanding event of his reign was the conclusion of the 30 Years War in 1648.

FERDINAND (1861-1948). King of Bulgaria. Son of Prince Augustus of Saxe-Coburg-Gotha, he was elected prince of Bulgaria in 1887, and in 1908 proclaimed Bulgaria's independence of Turkey and assumed the title of Tsar. In 1915 he entered the F.W.W. as Germany's ally, and in 1918 abdicated and retired to Coburg.

FERDINAND I, called the Great (d. 1065). King of Castile. He united all NW Spain under his rule or that of his brothers, and began the reconquest of Spain from the Moors.

FERDINAND V of Castile, and **II** of Aragon (1452-1516). First king of all Spain. In 1469 he m. his cousin Isabella, who in 1474 succeeded to the throne of Castile. When in 1479 F. inherited the throne of Aragon the 2 great Spanish kingdoms were brought under a single government for the first time. The outstanding events of his reign included the introduction of the Inquisition in 1480, the expulsion of the Jews and the surrender of the Moors at Granada in 1492, Columbus' discovery of America, and the conquest of Naples in 1500-3.

FERDINAND (1865-1927). King of Romania. He succeeded his uncle Charles I in 1914, and in 1916 declared war on Austria. The Allied victory was followed by the acquisition of Transylvania and Bukovina from Austria-Hungary and Bessarabia from Russia, and in 1922 F. was crowned king of All Romanians.

FERGHANA (fergah'na). Town in Uzbek SSR, in the fertile F. valley, capital of the important cotton- and fruit-growing F. region; nearby are petroleum fields. Pop. (1972) 111,000.

FERGUSON, Harry (1884-1960). British engineer. B. in Co. Down, a farmer's son, he pioneered the development of the tractor, joining forces with Henry Ford in 1938 to manufacture in America. He also experimented in automobile and aircraft development.

FERMANAGH (fermah'nah). Co. in the southern part of N Ireland. The centre is occupied by a broad trough of lowland, in which lie Upper and Lower Loughs Erne. The highest point is Cuilcagh 667m (2,188 ft), and the main river is the Erne. The chief occupation is agriculture, and livestock are raised. The co. town is Enniskillen; smaller towns include Lisnaskea and Irvinestown. Area 1,701 sq.km (657 sq.m); pop. (1971) 50,255.

FERMAT (fermah'), **Pierre de** (1601-65). French mathematician. His method of calculating probability developed from his work with Pascal on the properties of numbers, and he is regarded as a founder of modern theory. His *Last Theorem,* though he himself may have discovered a complete proof, has never been demonstrated by anyone else. *See* CHANCE.

FE'RMI, Enrico (1901-54). American physicist. B. in Rome, he was prof. of theoretical physics there 1926-38, when he settled in the US. The same year he was awarded a Nobel prize for having proved the existence of new radioactive elements produced by bombardment with neutrons and his discovery of nuclear reactions produced by slow neutrons. He was prof. at Columbia Univ., NY, 1939-42 and from 1946 at Chicago. The US Atomic Energy Commission made a special award to him in 1954 for outstanding work in nuclear physics, and these annual awards have subsequently been known as F. Awards.

FERMOY'. Town on the r. Blackwater, co. Cork, Rep. of Ireland; once an important garrison town, it is a salmon fishing centre. Pop. *c.* 3,500.

FERNANDEZ (fernahn'deth), **Juan** (fl. 1570). Spanish navigator. As a pilot on the Pacific coast of S America, he discovered in 1563 the islands off the coast of Chile that now bear his name; on one of these Alexander Selkirk, the original Robinson Crusoe, lived. In 1576 he may have sighted Easter Island, as well as Australia and New Zealand.

FERNANDO POO. *See* EQUATORIAL GUINEA.

FERNS. Name used loosely to cover all groups of the Pteridophyta, the best-known of which are the Equisetaceae (Horse Tail), Lycopodiaceae (Club Moss), and Selaginellaceae (Selaginella) families, and the Filicales, the true fern group.

The true Fs. are a group of non-flowering plants represented by about 150 living genera and a number of fossil forms; they are perennial herbs, with usually a low-growing rootstock, while the leaves, known as fronds, vary widely in size and shape.

Fs. are classified into 8 main families. By far the most common in Britain is the Polypodiaceae, in which are included the polypody (*Polypodium*), shield fern and male fern (*Aspidium*), hart's tongue (*Scolopendrium*), maiden hair (*Adiantum*), and bracken (*Pteris*).

FERNS. Tree ferns in the New Zealand 'bush'. *Photo: Heather Angel.*

FERRAR, Nicolas (1592-1637). Founder of the Anglican monastic community at Little Gidding, Hunts, in 1625, which devoted itself to religious offices and the preparation of harmonies of the Scriptures, and was broken up by the Puritans in 1647.

FERRARA. City and archbishopric in Emilia-Romagna region, N Italy, on a branch of the Po delta, 52km/32m W of the Adriatic Sea. It has a Gothic palace and a cathedral, consecrated 1135. The free univ. was founded in 1391. There are chemical industries and textile manufactures. Pop. (1971) 153,165.

FERRET. Small mammal (*Mustela putorius*) of the Mustelidae family, a domesticated albino polecat. It is about 35cm (14in) long, with yellowish-white fur, and pink eyes. It is used to hunt rabbits, rats, etc.

FERRIER, Kathleen (1912-53). British contralto singer. B. in Lancs, and originally a student of the piano, she made a brilliant reputation in oratorio and opera. Notable appearances were in *The Rape of Lucretia* (1946) and *Das Lied von der Erde* (1947).

FERRIER, Susan Edmundstone (1782-1854). Scottish novelist. B. in Edinburgh, she became a close friend of Sir W. Scott. Her first novel, *Marriage* (1818), was followed by *Inheritance* (1824), and *Destiny* (1831), all of which give a lively picture of Scottish manners and society.

FERRO-ALLOYS. Alloys of iron with a high proportion of manganese, silicon, chromium, molybdenum, etc. They are used in the manufacture of alloy steels.

FERRŌ'L. City, port, and naval station on an inlet on the NW coast of Spain. It possesses a good sheltered harbour, whose narrow entrance is strongly guarded by forts, and there are shipbuilding and ship repairing industries, etc. It was the birthplace of Franco. Pop. (1970) 87,735.

FERTILITY DRUGS. Drugs developed in Sweden in the mid-1950s, the best-known being gonadotrophin. Made from hormone extracts (FSH and LH) taken from the human pituitary gland, it stimulates ovulation in women. Multiple births are a risk, and in 1974 the first sextuplets to survive were born to Susan Rosenkowitz of S Africa.

FERTILIZERS. Substances containing the twenty-odd chemical elements necessary for healthy plant growth, and which are used to compensate the deficiencies of poor soil or of soil depleted by repeated cropping. They may be (a) *Organic*, e.g. farmyard manure, composts, bonemeal, blood and fishmeal, which have been in immemorial use. (b) *Inorganic*, in the form of compounds, mainly of nitrogen, phosphate and potash, which have come into use on a tremendously increased scale since the S.W.W. The compounds are most frequently administered in solid form, but 'non-pressure' liquid Fs. are frequently used in market gardening and 'pressure' liquids, such as anhydrous ammonia (containing 82 per cent nitrogen), are being increasingly used on larger farms and by contractors. The cost of Fs., greatly increased by rises in the prices of fuels needed to make them, and also the fact that externally applied Fs. tend to be in excess of plant requirements and leach away to affect lakes and rivers (*see* EUTROPHICATION), have turned attention to the modification of crop plants themselves. Plants of the pea family, incl. the bean, clover and lupin, live in symbiosis with bacteria, *Rhizobia*, located in root nodules, which fix nitrogen from the atmosphere. Research is now directed to producing a similar relationship between such bacteria and crops such as wheat.

FESCUE (fes'kū). Widely distributed genus (*Festuca*) of grasses. Two species are common in Britain: meadow F., up to 1.5m (5ft) high, and sheep's F., which is up to *c.* .5m (2ft) high.

FETISHISM. Belief in the supernormal power of some object, inanimate or otherwise, which is known as a fetish. Any object that can pass into the possession of an individual can become a fetish to him, but it may be communally owned. F. in some form is common to most civilizations, and in Africa has religio-magical significance.

FEUDALISM (fūd'-) (Lat. *feudum*, a fief). The system which arose during the 4th-10th cents., whereby land was held in return for service. Under it all land, in theory, belonged ultimately to the king, who might hold his kingdom from another king, and grant the use of the land and the right to exact services, and often to administer justice and levy taxes, to a tenant-in-chief, who in turn might grant portions of it to vassals, and so on. The most important of a vassal's obligations was that of military service. The economic basis of F. was the manor, cultivated by serfs bound to the soil, who held portions of the manor fields in return for labour services. The system declined from the 13th cent. onward, owing partly to the development of a money economy, partly to the many peasants' revolts of 1350-1550. In England serfdom became extinct in the 16th cent. and feudal dues paid by landowners to the Crown were abolished in 1660.

FEVER. Disorder due to raising of the body temperature above normal. It is generally the reaction of the organism to the presence in the blood stream of a foreign substance, usually a protein. This is most often produced by invading micro-organisms.

FEZ. Former cap. of Morocco (808-1062, 1296-1548 and 1662-1912), in a valley N of the Great Atlas Mts., 160km (100m) E of Rabat. It is a religious centre, the Kairwan Islamic Univ. dating from 859: a second univ. was founded 1961. Textiles are manufactured and the fez is traditionally said to have originated here. Pop. (1971) 1,071,500.

FEZ. The Kairwan Mosque, decorated according to Islamic custom with geometric design and the graceful script of the Koran, but avoiding representation of living things. *Photo: Mireille Vautier.*

FEZZA'N. Former desert prov. of Libya, with many oases, split into smaller divisions in 1963.

FIANNA fáil (fē-an'a foil) (Soldiers of Destiny). Irish republican party, founded by De Valera in 1926. It aims at the establishment of a united and completely independent all-Ireland republic.

FIBONACCI (fibonah'chē), **Leonardo** (fl. 13th cent.). Italian mathematician. He pub. his *Liber abaci* in Pisa in 1202, which led to the introduction of Arabic notation into Europe. From 1960 interest developed in his discovery of the *F. Numbers*, in their simplest form a series in which each number is the sum of its two predecessors (i.e., 1, 1, 2, 3, 5, 8, 13). They have unusual characteristics with possible applications in botany, psychology, astronomy, etc., for example, a more exact correspondence than Bode's Law to the distances between the planets and the Sun.

FIBRE OPTICS. The transmission of light by reflection down the inside of bundles of very fine optically insulated glass or plastic fibres. An undistorted image can be sent from one end to the other, enabling otherwise inaccessible parts of a machine or the human body to be inspected. The light may also be used, by modulating the signal at high frequency, to transmit data, e.g. telephone conversations, and television programmes.

FIBRES, man-made. The original stimulus to the development of extruded F. was the search for an alternative to carbon filaments in electric lighting, and Sir Joseph W. Swan patented an artificial silk in 1883, but the pioneer of commercial textiles was Count Hilaire de Chardonnet (1839-1924). Artificial silk, called rayon from 1926, began a social revolution in textiles, Courtaulds being the pioneers of the viscose process (patented by C. F. Cross and E. J. Bevan 1892). The revolution was completed by the introduction of the first fully synthetic fibre in 1938, nylon (q.v.) developed by DuPont. Today the 4 main fibre types are nylon; the acrylics used in knitwear (also developed by DuPont, e.g. Orlon 1944); the polyesters (e.g. Terylene, discovered by J. R. Whinfield and J. Dickson of the Calico Printers Association 1940 and developed by ICI); and the spandex or elastomeric F. (e.g. Lycra, DuPont 1959) which replace traditional rubber yarns. The variants are as endless as their uses in clothes, carpets, industry, etc., but espec. notable are the foambacks or laminates, and texturized types (e.g. Crimplene 1959). A world-wide industry has resulted, since air-conditioning renders climate immaterial, and both raw materials and finished product are easily transported. *See* KNITTING.

FIBROSĪ'TIS. Inflammation and overgrowth of fibrous tissue, especially of the sheaths of muscles; fibrositis is also known as muscular rheumatism.

FICHTE (fikh'te), **Johann Gottlieb** (1762-1814). German philosopher. B. in Silesia and ed. at Jena and Leipzig, he was an admirer of Kant and in 1792 pub. a *Critique of Religious Revelation* a critical study on Kantian lines. While professor at Jena (1793-9), F. wrote a number of important works on the theory of knowledge. In 1799 he was accused of atheism, and was forced to resign his post. He moved to Berlin, where he lectured and devoted himself to public affairs. At the same time he delivered his *Addresses to the German People* on the foundations of true prosperity; his *Staatslehre* (Theory of Politics) describes a Utopian state founded on rational principles, but with a tendency towards dictatorship.

FICHTELGEBIRGE (fikh'telgebērge). Chain of mtns in Bavaria, W Germany, on the Czechoslovak border. The highest peak is the Schneeberg 1,051 m (3,448 ft). There are granite quarries, uranium mining, china and glass industries, and forestry is carried on.

FIDEI DEFENSOR (fid'ē-ī dēfen'sōr). (Lat., 'defender of the faith'). The title conferred by pope Leo X upon Henry VIII of England in recognition of a treatise that the latter had written against Martin Luther. The title has ever since been included in the style of English sovereigns.

FIELDFARE. A bird (*Turdus pilaris*) of the thrush family (Turdidae), a winter migrant in Britain, breeding in Scandinavia, N Russia, and Siberia. It has a pale-grey lower back, with black tail.

FIELDING, Henry (1707-54). English novelist. B. in Somerset, he was a contemporary of the elder Pitt and H. Fox at Eton. In 1725 he attempted to abduct an heiress at Lyme Regis, and after some years of life as a man-about-town began writing for the stage, his chief successes in this medium being the burlesque *Author's Farce* (1730), and *Tom Thumb* (1730), and his adaptations from Molière. His first novel was *Joseph Andrews* (1742), a parody of Richardson's *Pamela*; it was followed by the ironic *Jonathan Wild the Great* (1743), and in 1749 by his masterpiece *Tom Jones*, 'a comic *epic in prose*'. F. had been called to the Bar in 1740, and in 1748 was appointed JP for Middlesex and Westminster. Here he was eminently successful, and his concern for social evils, especially prison conditions, emerges in his last novel *Amelia* (1751). In 1754 F. sailed to Portugal to improve his health, writing on the way *A Journal of a Voyage to Lisbon*, and d. and was buried at Lisbon two months after his arrival.

FIELD-MARSHAL. Title given to the highest ranking officer in the British Army, introduced from Germany by George II in 1736.

FIELD MOUSE. *See* MOUSE.

FIELD OF THE CLOTH OF GOLD. Name given to the meeting between Henry VIII and Francis I of France in June 1520, between Guînes and Ardres, near Calais. The magnificence of the dresses was the origin of the name.

FIELDS, Dame Gracie. Stage-name of British comedienne and singer Grace Stansfield (1898-1979). B. in Rochdale, she was originally a mill-girl, but achieved fame in the musical *Mr Tower of London* (1918). Her film successes from 1931 incl. *Sally in our Alley, Sing as We Go*, and *Keep Smiling*.

FIELD STUDIES. The study of ecology, geography, geology, history, archaeology, and allied subjects, in their natural environment. The Council for the Promotion of F.S. was estab. in Britain in 1943, and Flatford Mill, Suffolk, was the first research centre estab.

FIESOLE (fē-ā'sōlā). Italian town 6km (4m) NE of Florence, with many Etruscan and Roman relics. The Romanesque cathedral was completed 1028. Pop. (1971) 13,000.

FIFE, Alexander William George Duff, duke of (1849-1912). Son-in-law of Edward VII. He succeeded his father as 6th earl in 1879, and was created a duke in 1889 on his marriage to Princess Louise Victoria Alexandra Dagmar (1867-1931), later Princess Royal, eldest dau. of Edward VII. They had two daughters: Alexandra, duchess of F. in her own right (1891-1959), m. in 1913 Prince Arthur of Connaught (1883-1938); and Maud (1893-1945) m. Lord Carnegie, later 11th earl of Southesk.

FIFE (fīf). Region of E Scotland (formerly the co. of F.), facing the North Sea and the Firth of Forth; the only high land is in the NW, the Lomond Hills. The chief rivers are the Eden and Leven. Agriculture is important, but coal-mining has declined, superseded by new industries incl. electronics, chemicals, and marine and light engineering.

Early man possibly settled first in this area of Scotland, e.g. Tentsmuir. The ancient palace of the Stuarts was at Falkland and 8 Scottish kings are buried at Dunfermline; St Andrews (q.v.) is another historic centre. The admin. HQ is Glenrothes. Area 1,295 sq.km (500 sq.m); pop. (1979) 332,933.

FIFE. A kind of small flute. Originally from Switzerland, it was known as the Swiss pipe and has long been used by British Army bands.

FIFTEEN, The. Name given to the Jacobite rebellion of 1715, which was led by the 'Old Pretender' (James Edward Stuart) and the earl of Mar, with the object of placing the former on the throne. Mar was checked at Sheriffmuir, and the revolt collapsed.

FIFTH COLUMN. A group within a country secretly aiding an enemy attacking from without. The term originated in 1936, during the Spanish Civil War, when General Mola boasted that the Franco supporters were attacking Madrid with 4 columns, and that they had a 'fifth column' inside the city. This technique was employed by the Nazis in the S.W.W.

FIG. Fruit of *Ficus carica,* the cultivated F. tree, and of a number of other species. The tree is grown particularly in Mediterranean lands, and in California, parts of Australia, S Africa, etc. The fruit is exported fresh or dried; besides its use as a food, it is used in the preparation of laxatives.

FIJI. Independent state which consists of about 322 mainly volcanic islands in the Melanesian archipelago, Pacific Ocean. About 106 is. are inhabited; the largest are Viti Levu (10,386 sq.km/4,010 sq.m), and Vanua Levu (5,535 sq.km/2,137 sq.m). Jungle and forests, providing valuable timber, occupy generally the SE sides of the islands. The drier parts are under grass. Bananas, coconuts, sugar cane, rice, fruit, and vegetables are grown. Fishing is carried on. There is considerable industrial development, e.g. sugar and rice mills; copra, biscuit, and soap factories; and gold is mined. The cap. is the city of Suva, on Viti Levu. Tourism is important, and the internat. airport at Nadi is a staging point for Pacific services.

The group was discovered by Tasman in 1643, visited by Cook in 1773, and ceded to Britain in 1874. The native peoples are of Negroid stock with a Polynesian admixture, but from *c.* 1880 Indians were introduced to work the sugar plantations and now outnumber them. There has been little intermarriage and there is racial tension: the Indians are industrially and commercially predominant and the Fijians own 80% of the land communally. F. attained Dominion status 1970, as an independent member of the Commonwealth, and there is a Gov.-Gen., Senate and House of Representatives elected on 3 communal rolls (Fijian, Indian, and other races). The Fijians are chiefly Methodists and the Indians Hindu. Area 18,272 sq.km (7,055 sq.m); pop. (1976) 588,000; 293,000 Indians, 260,000 Fijians, and Chinese and European minorities. M.U.: Fiji dollar.

FILLMORE, Millard (1800-74). 13th President of the USA. B. in New York, he was elected Vice-President in 1848, and succeeded on the death of Zachary Taylor; he was President 1850-3. A Whig, he advocated reconciliation of North and South, and compromise on the slavery issue, and since he pleased neither side failed to gain renomination.

FILM. Roll of specially coated thin transparent material on which a series of photographs can be recorded, and, by the eye's persistence of vision, 'moving pictures' projected from it on to a screen. The first moving pictures were shown in the 1890s: Edison persuaded James J. Corbett (1866-1933), American world boxing champion (1892-7), to act a boxing match for a film. Lumière in France; R. W. Paul in England; Latham in the USA and others were making moving pictures of a few minutes' duration of actual events (e.g. the Derby, shown in London, on the evening of the race, 1896), and of simple scenes such as a train coming into a station.

In 1902 Georges Méliès of France made a fantastic story film, *A Trip to the Moon,* which ran in London for 9 months; and in 1903 Edwin S. Porter directed for Edison *The Great Train Robbery,* a story in a contemporary setting: it cost about £100, was shown all over the world, and earned more than £20,000.

For a number of years, films even of 'indoor' happenings were 'shot' out of doors by daylight - and its admirable climate was the basis of Hollywood's outstanding success as a centre of film production, though the first film studio was Edison's at Fort Lee, NJ, USA. In England, the pioneer company of Cricks and Martin set up a studio at Mitcham (where a romantic domestic drama, *For Baby's Sake,* was made in 1908).

D. W. Griffith, the great American director, revolutionized film technique and made it in essentials what it is today. He introduced, e.g., the close-up, the flash-back, the fade-out and the fade-in. His first 'epic' was *The Birth of a Nation* (1915), and his second, *Intolerance,* with magnificent and spectacular scenes in the Babylonian section that have never been surpassed, followed in 1916.

At first, the players' names were considered of no importance, though one who appeared nameless in *The Great Train Robbery,* G. M. Anderson, afterwards became famous as 'Bronco Billy' in a series of cowboy films - the first 'Westerns'. The first 'movie' performer to become a name was Mary Pickford - cinemagoers found this young actress so attractive that they insisted on knowing who she was; and in the Hollywood of the 'twenties - helped to pre-eminence by the F.W.W. which virtually stopped film production in Europe - many stars were created: Rudolph Valentino, Douglas Fairbanks Sr, Lillian Gish, Gloria Swanson, Richard Barthelmess, and Greta Garbo outstanding among dramatic actors; Charles Chaplin, Harry Langdon, Buster Keaton, Harold Lloyd among comedians.

Concern for artistry began with Griffith; but developed in Europe, particularly Russia and Germany, whose directors exploited the film's artistic possibilities, during both the silent and the sound era. It is important to remember that silent films were never silent; there was always a musical background, integral to the film, whether played by the solo pianist in the suburban cinema, or the 100-piece orchestra in the big city theatre. The arrival of talking films (*The Jazz Singer,* 1928) proved a setback only to those artists with limited vision who exploited the mere novelty value of sound. Other directors, actors and actresses survived the transition and achieved a wider perspective by the marriage of sight and sound. Among the directors who succeeded were Jean Renoir in France, Lang and Murnau in Germany, Hitchcock in Britain and America, and Pudovkin and Eisenstein in Russia. After the S.W.W. Japanese films were first seen in the Western

FILM. Still unmatched for its huge scientific devices and mass crowd scenes, Fritz Lang's *Metropolis* (1926) dealt with a city of the future (left), in which the workers lived underground and were the slaves of their machines and of the small administrative class living above ground. Australia produced in 1905-6 one of the world's earliest full-length features, *The Kelly Gang,* and later fine films include Peter Weir's *'Picnic at Hanging Rock* (1976), from which a still is seen right. *Photos: Courtesy of the National Film Archive, G.T.O. films and Transit films.*

world (although the industry dates back to the silent days), and India produced some films of merit. Among post-war directors are Woody Allen, Antonioni, Bergman, Bertolucci, Buñuel, Cassavetes, Godard, Kazan, Kubrik, Lean, Preminger, (qq.v.), etc.

The introduction of sound banished silent stars with unsuitable voices, and changed the style of acting to an intimate, realism: stage stars making the transition incl. Edith Evans, Alec Guinness, Laurence Olivier, and Ralph Richardson. Great names of the golden Hollywood era incl. Clark Gable, the Marx Brothers, Marilyn Monroe, Judy Garland, and Elizabeth Taylor.

Apart from story films, the industry produced news films; 'documentaries', depicting factual life, of which the pioneers were the American Robert Flaherty (*Nanook of the North,* 1920, *Man of Aran,* 1932-4, etc.) and the Scottish John Grierson (e.g. *Drifters,* 1929, *Night Mail,* 1936); cartoon films, which achieved their first success with Patrick Sullivan's Felix the Cat (1917), later surpassed in popularity by Walt Disney's Mickey Mouse.

Interest in the history and development of film technique led to the formation in Britain of the British Film Institute (1933) with which is linked the National Film Theatre (1951) where borrowed films as well as the Institute's treasures are shown to members; the Film Library of the Museum of Art in NYC caters for a similar public. Storage needs special conditions and early films are transferred to modern safety stock. Colour films from the 1950s made on a single negative rather than 3 (one for each primary) change colour with time, and by the 1980s some film-makers were reverting to black-and-white for permanence.

After the S.W.W. increasing competition from television led the industry either to make films for the new medium, or to concentrate on the wide-screen spectaculars dealing with historical and biblical themes, e.g. *Cleopatra* (1963). Also exploited were areas of sexuality still considered unsuitable for family television viewing, e.g. *Last Tango in Paris* (1973). The Chinese 'western' or kung-fu film, in which the hero deals with multitudinous enemies by various violent means was also popular. The chief star was e.g. Bruce Lee (1941-1973), an American-born Chinese, as in *Enter the Dragon.* More recently science fiction, such as *Star Wars* (1977) and *Close Encounters of the Third Kind* (1977), with its expensive special effects has attracted large audiences. Censorship of sex and violence remained a controversial topic.

FINCH. Name applied to birds of the family Fringillidae of the order Passeriformes. They have a short, stout, conical bill, and are mainly seed-eaters, e.g. chaffinch, goldfinch, canary, etc. Allied to them are the buntings (Emberizidae) and weaver Fs. (Ploceidae).

FINE GAEL (fin'i gāl') (United Ireland). Irish political party, founded and led by W. J. Cosgrave 1933-44, by his son 1965-77, and by Garret FitzGerald (1926-) from 1977. Since the introduction of the republic by Costello, the basic conservatism of F.G. has weakened.

FINGAL'S CAVE. Cave on the is. of Staffa, Inner Hebrides, Scotland. Lined with natural basalt columns it is 60m (200ft) long and 20m (65ft) high. Fingal, based on Irish hero Finn mac Cumhaill, was the leading character in Macpherson's Ossianic forgeries. Visited by Mendelssohn in 1829, the cave was the inspiration of his *Hebrides* overture, otherwise known as F.C.

FINGERPRINTS. A system of identification by means of the ridges on the skin of a person's finger tips. No two F.Ps. are exactly alike, and they remain constant in pattern throughout life. The classification was originated and practised in India and adopted by the police in England in 1901. Latent Fs. up to 10 yrs old will fluoresce under laser illumination. *See also* VOICEPRINT.

FINISTÈRE (finistār'). Dept of Brittany, France.

FINISTERRE (finistār'), **Cape.** Promontory in the extreme NW of Spain.

FINLAND. A republic of N Europe lying N of latitude 60°, one-third being N of the Arctic Circle. The Åland Islands, in the Gulf of Bothnia, are a Finnish dept.

The many lakes form the principal means of communication, by water in summer; by ice in winter. Winters in F. are long and severe, and most of the harbours are ice-bound for at least 5 months. Over two-thirds of the land area is forested, the northern part having a tundra scrub vegetation.

The Saimaa Canal, linking the Saimaa lake area of Finland and the Gulf of Finland, but with half its length in the USSR, was modernized 1968.

Although Finnish is now spoken by over 90%, Swedish is still recognized as an official language; Lapp is spoken by *c.* 2,000 in the far north. The majority of Finns are Lutheran, but the Gk Orthodox Church is also recognized. There are univs. at Helsinki, Jyvaskyla, Oulu, Tampere and Turku (2).

Timber, pulp and paper are still important, but textile, electronic, chemical, metal and engineering industries have developed, and copper and iron are mined. Finnish architecture, furniture, ceramics and glass are renowned. Agriculture - cereals and dairy products - is confined to the better land of the south. The chief towns are Helsinki, the cap. and main port, Turku (former cap.) and Tampere, the largest industrial centre. The pres. is elected for 6 years, and appoints a Council of State, and there is a single legislative Chamber. The govt is usually a coalition slightly left of centre.

Area 337,050 sq.km (130,125 sq.m), incl. 31,575 sq.km (12,200 sq.m) inland water; pop. (1972) 4,634,000. M.U.: Finnish mark.

FINLAND. The Finlandia Hall concert and congress centre designed by Alvar Aalto in Helsinki. *Photo: Courtesy of the Finnish Tourist Board.*

History. The Finns are of Asiatic origin and migrated to present-day F. in the 7th and 8th cents., finding there a people from whom the Lapps of today are probably descended. Sweden conquered and attempted to Christianize the Finns in the 12th cent., but it was some 150 years before they abandoned paganism. F. was part of the kingdom of Sweden for 600 years, but had a fair amount of self-govt. From early in the 18th cent. Russia and Sweden disputed possession of F. which in 1809 became a grand duchy of Russia with almost complete autonomy except in foreign affairs. A national movement secured the recognition of Finnish as the official language in 1863 (before that it had been Swedish). Later Russia attempted to reduce Finnish liberties, and after the Russian Revolution F. proclaimed itself an independent republic in 1917. In 1939 Russia attacked and defeated F. which in 1940 ceded territory NW of Leningrad to Russia. In 1941 F. joined Germany in attacking Russia and advanced to its old frontier. The Russian offensive in 1944 regained the disputed land and led to an armistice by which, besides the cessions made in 1940, F. ceded the Petsamo area on the Arctic coast, giving the RSFSR a frontier with Norway (cessions confirmed by the peace treaty between F. and the Allies, 1947).

LANGUAGE AND LITERATURE. Finnish, like Estonian, to which it is closely related, belongs to the Finno-Ugrian family of languages. Some fragments in Finnish have come down from the 12th cent.; the first book was an ABC published in 1544. A complete Bible in Finnish was issued at Stockholm in 1642. But the predominance of the Swedes and Swedish in F. inhibited the growth of a Finnish literature until the 19th cent. when it was launched with the publication in 1835 of Lönnrot's verse epic *Kalevala* (q.v.). The novelist Emil Sillanpää (1888-1964) was awarded a Nobel prize 1939.

Finland has also given to the world the architect Alvar Aalto (1898-1976), designer of the Finlandia concert hall Helsinki; the sculptor Wäinö Aaltonen (q.v.), and the composer Sibelius (q.v.).

FINLAND, Gulf of. An eastern arm of the Baltic Sea, with USSR on the S and Finland on the N.

FINLANDISATION. Political shorthand term for the reduction of a state to docile co-operation by the pressure of an overwhelmingly powerful neighbour, as with Finland and the USSR.

FINN MAC CUMHAILL (fin makool'). Hero of Gaelic folklore. He is believed to be identical with the general who organized a regular army for Ireland at the bidding of Cormac mac Airt (fl. *c.* AD 250), and his braves are sharply individualized. *See* FINGAL'S CAVE.

FINSEN, Niels Ryberg (1860-1904). Danish physician. He was the first to develop light treatment scientifically, using artificial light, particularly the carbon arc. He received a Nobel prize in 1903.

FIORD (fyord), or **fjord.** Name given to narrow sea inlets in Norway, enclosed by high cliffs, and now to similar formations elsewhere. **Fiordland** is the deeply indented SW coast of South Island, NZ: one of the most magnificent inlets is Milford Sound.

FIR. A term widely applied to trees of the order Coniferales, but correctly referring only to members of the genus *Abies* and a few other species. The F. is distinguished from the pine by bearing its needle-like leaves singly, trees of the genus *Pinus* bearing theirs in groups. The Fs. are pyramidal and evergreen, retaining their leaves for 6-9 years, but shedding a number every year, so that the tree is never without foliage. Common European Fs. include the silver F. (*Abies alba*), spruce F. or Christmas tree (*Picea abies*), and Douglas F. (*Pseudotsuga menziesii*). N. America has 10 native species.

FIRBANK, Ronald (1886-1926). English novelist. Set in the Edwardian decadent period, his work appeals to a small band of enthusiasts, but his malicious humour palls in large quantities. It incl. *Caprice* (1916), *Valmouth* (1918), set in an imaginary West Country, and the posthumous *Concerning the Eccentricities of Cardinal Pirelli* (1926).

FIRDOUSI (*c.* AD 940-1020). Persian poet, famous for the epic poem *Shahnama*, the Book of Kings, which relates the history of Persia in 60,000 verses.

FIREARMS. Weapons from which missiles are discharged by the combustion of an explosive. They are generally divided into 2 main sections: artillery (q.v.), (ordnance or cannon) which have a bore greater than 1in, and small arms (q.v.), with a bore of less than 1in. Although gunpowder was known 60 years previously, the invention of guns dates from 1300-25, and is attrib. to Berthold Schwartz, a German monk. *See also* PISTOL, MACHINE GUN.

FIRECLAY. A clay that is resistant to very high temperatures, and is therefore suitable for lining furnaces. Its refractory characteristics are due to its chemical composition, which contains a high percentage of silica and alumina and a low percentage of oxides of sodium, potassium, iron, calcium, etc. Fs. underlie the coal seams in the British Isles.

FIREDAMP. Gas which occurs in coal-mines and is explosive when mixed with air in certain proportions. It consists chiefly of methane (marsh gas) but always contains small quantities of other gases, e.g. nitrogen, carbon dioxide, hydrogen, and sometimes ethane and carbon monoxide.

FIREFLY. Popular name of certain beetles in the families Lampyridae and Elateridae. The genus *Pyrophorus*, in the latter family, contains many species which are usually found in western tropical countries. The main luminous organs are situated on the prothorax, and the light is linked with the sexual activities of the insects. *See* GLOW-WORM.

FIRENZE. Italian form of FLORENCE.

FIRE PROTECTION. Fire constitutes a considerable cause of loss of life and one of the greatest causes of damage to property, and protection has always depended on a combination of public service and private enterprise. In Britain Acts of 1707 and 1774 required every parish to provide engines, hoses and ladders, but insurance cos. estab. their own more efficient brigades for the benefit of buildings bearing their own fire marks. The latter amalgamated in the 19th cent. to form the basis of the present-day service which is run by the local authorities who cooperate closely: experimentation in new methods, etc., is carried out at the Fire Research Station at Boreham Wood, in Herts. Similar services operate in other countries. Since early detection enhances the chance of success, a valuable method of protection for industrial and commercial buildings is by automatic sprinkler system: heat opens the sprinkler heads on a network of water pipes and immediately sprays the seat of the fire. In certain circumstances water is less effective and may be dangerous, e.g. for oil and petrol storage tanks foam systems are used, and, for plant containing inflammable vapours, carbon dioxide. Fire-resistant materials are also increasingly used in building construction. Forest Fs. and oilwell Fs. are among the most spectacular disasters, the latter often being tackled by international specialists.

FIREWORKS. Pyrotechny, the art of firework-making. A firework consists of a container or 'case', usually cylindrical in shape and of rolled paper, enclosing a mixture capable of burning independently of the oxygen of the air, since it includes an ingredient holding a supply of oxygen which it readily gives up to the other burnable ingredients.

FIRST AID. Action taken immediately after an accident in order to save the life of a victim, prevent further damage, or facilitate later treatment. A practicable technique is taught by the Red Cross Society and the Order of St John of Jerusalem.

FIRST WORLD WAR. The war of 1914-18, fought between the Allied Powers (the British Empire, France, Russia, Italy, the USA, Japan, Belgium, Serbia, Montenegro, Greece, Romania, Portugal) and the Central European Powers (Germany, Austria-Hungary, Turkey, and Bulgaria).

Three main conflicts went to produce the war. The first arose from the French desire to recover Alsace-Lorraine, and the struggle of French and German industrialists to control the iron of Lorraine and the coal of the Ruhr. The second was caused by the desire of Russia to dominate the Balkans as an outlet to the Mediterranean, and of Germany to do the same as a step to economic control of the Near East. The third lay in the colonial ambitions of the Powers, who had partitioned Africa and divided China into spheres of influence, and especially in the ambitions

FIRE PROTECTION. After a series of mild winters, America experienced a colder one in 1976-7 than had ever previously been recorded. The unusual hazards that the ice offered to firefighters can be seen here as a fireman tries to adjust a hose. *Photo: Popperfoto.*

FIREWORKS. In China and Japan they have an even greater fondness for fireworks than Westerners. This display is at Sasebo City, Kyushu. *Photo: Courtesy of Japan Information Centre.*

of Germany, which had been left behind in the scramble. The Powers were divided into 2 rival alliances: the Triple Alliance of Germany, Austria, and Italy, formed in 1882, and the Triple Entente of Britain, France, and Russia, formed 1895-1907. The final crisis was caused by the murder of the heir to the Austrian throne at Sarajevo on 28 June 1914. Austria made this an excuse to declare war on Serbia on 28 July. When Russia mobilized, Germany declared war on Russia and France, and invaded Belgium, whereupon on 4 August Britain declared war on Germany.

In spite of the resistance of the Belgian fortresses, the Germans advanced rapidly through Belgium, forcing back the French Army and the BEF, which had been positioned at Mons. On 6 Sept., when the Germans were a few miles from Paris, the Allied counter-attack opened on the Marne, and drove the Germans back to the Aisne. The Belgian Army, driven into Antwerp, evacuated it on 9 Oct. with British assistance, and retreated down the coast to join the Allies. By 19 Oct. the opposing lines had been extended to the sea at Nieuport, and the struggle had settled down into trench warfare. German attempts to break through at Arras and Ypres failed to change the situation.

An immediate offensive was launched by the Russians into E Prussia, forcing the Germans to withdraw troops from the W, until stopped by Hindenburg's victory at Tannenberg (26-30 Aug.). The Russians also overran Galicia.

The German fleet early withdrew to its bases, and confined itself mainly to submarine raids and minelaying. Australia, New Zealand, or Japanese forces soon occupied German Pacific possessions - Japan had declared war on 22 Aug. The German Pacific squadron escaped to the Atlantic and defeated a British squadron off Coronel on 1 Nov, but was itself destroyed on 8 Dec. off the Falkland Isles. By Sept. 1916 the German colonies in Africa were in Allied hands.

Throughout 1915 both sides made attempts to break through on the western front, with little result. These offensives incl. those made by the Allies at Neuve Chapelle (March), Vimy Ridge (May), and Loos (Sept.), and by the Germans at Ypres (April), during which poison gas was first used. In Dec. Sir Douglas Haig replaced Sir John French as British C-in-C. On the eastern front German offensives by Mackensen in the S and Hindenburg in the N regained all that had been lost, and expelled the Russians from Poland.

Turkey, which entered the war on 1 Nov. 1914, launched an offensive in the Caucasus, and in 1915 unsuccessfully attacked the Suez Canal from Palestine. A British force invaded Mesopotamia, occupied Kut, and threatened Baghdad. A naval attack on the Dardanelles in Feb.-March, intended to open communication with Russia through the Black Sea, was followed by landings on the Gallipoli peninsula in April. Although further ground was gained in Aug., Gallipoli had to be evacuated in Jan. 1916.

Italy, hoping to secure control of the Adriatic, declared war on Austria in May 1915, while Greece, Bulgaria, and Rumania were still hesitating. The German victories in the E and the Gallipoli failure persuaded Bulgaria to join the German and Austrian attack on Serbia. The Serbian armies retreated to the Adriatic, and at Salonika finally joined the Allied forces, which had landed at the invitation of the pro-British Greek PM Venizelos.

The Germans opened 1916 on the western front with an attack in Feb. on the Verdun salient which continued till June, and 'bled France white', but failed to break through. The Allies replied with their offensive on the Somme, during which tanks were first used, and between July and Nov. carried their line forward 7m. A further French offensive at Verdun in Oct.-Dec. recovered some lost ground. During June-Aug. the Russians' successful advance in S Galicia encouraged the Romanians to declare war and invade Transylvania. The Germans hit back from Transylvania and Bulgaria, and in Dec. occupied Bucharest.

In Mesopotamia a British force defended Kut against the Turks from Dec. 1915 to April 1916, when it had to surrender. The Arabs of the Hejaz rebelled against Turkish rule in 1916, and the revolt, aided by T. E. Lawrence, rapidly spread as far N as Damascus; nevertheless, the Turks made another unsuccessful attack on the Suez Canal in August.

In Feb. 1915 the Germans announced they would use submarines to sink merchant-ships found in British waters, to which Britain replied by seizing all cargoes destined for Germany. The sinking of the *Lusitania* with many Americans on board aroused deep indignation in the USA, and American protests forced Germany to abandon the submarine campaign in April 1916. On 30 May the High Sea Fleet put to sea, and the following day a general fleet action was fought off Jutland. Although the British losses were the heavier, the battered German fleet remained in port for the rest of the war. Renewed submarine warfare in Feb. 1917 resulted in the USA entering the war in April.

In March 1917 anti-war feeling led to the overthrow of the Russian monarchy. The attempts of the new Liberal government to continue the war destroyed its popularity, and on 7 Nov. the Bolsheviks took power with a programme of immediate peace. Fighting ceased on the eastern front in Dec., and in March 1918 peace was signed at Brest Litovsk. The example of the Russian Revolution did much to strengthen the anti-war movement in Germany.

Early in 1917 the Germans withdrew N of the Somme to their new defences, the Hindenburg Line. The Allied offensive of April captured Vimy Ridge, but French losses were so heavy that widespread mutinies resulted. In June the British captured Messines Ridge and straightened out the Ypres salient, but an advance from Ypres towards the coast (Passchendaele offensive) in July-Nov. failed. The French during Aug.-Oct. recovered considerable ground before Verdun, and took the Chemin des Dames.

The war on the Italian front went on the whole in favour of the Italians, until in Oct. 1917 the Germans and Austrians attacked at Caporetto. The Italian line collapsed, and was pushed back beyond the Piave with very heavy losses. British and French troops were sent to the Italian front, and an Allied Council was set up to secure a unified strategy.

In Mesopotamia Gen. Maude captured Kut in Feb. 1917 and Baghdad in March. An advance from Egypt into Palestine, halted at Gaza in April, was resumed under Gen. Allenby in Oct., and captured Jerusalem in Dec.

The German submarine campaign reached its height in April 1917, when 196 British ships were lost, but the convoy system then put into operation caused losses to diminish steadily. The submarine was also combated by

FIRST WORLD WAR. The war leaders at Downing Street in 1918: left to right, Marshal Foch, Georges Clemenceau, Lloyd George, Vittorio Orlando and Baron Sonino. And (right) one of the maze of trenches on the western front in France and Flanders. In winter the men might be up to their armpits in water in the low-lying sections. *Photos: Central Press and Imperial War Museum.*

extensive mine-laying, while the naval raids on Zeebrugge and Ostend in April-May 1918 blocked 2 dangerous bases.

On the western front the Germans began what was intended to be the final offensive on 21 March 1918; by June the Allies had lost all they had gained since 1915, and the Germans had again reached the Marne. They had nowhere succeeded, however, in breaking the Allied line, and the Allies were now being reinforced by US troops, who first saw fire in June. The danger forced the Allies to appoint a supreme commander, Gen. Foch, in April.

Greece had declared war in June 1917, when the Allies deposed the pro-German Constantine. In Sept. 1918 the Allies attacked Bulgaria, which quickly made peace, and in Oct. they expelled the Austrians from Serbia. An Austrian offensive on the Piave in June failed, and in Oct. the last Allied offensive on the Italian front began. On 3 Nov. Austria signed an armistice. In Palestine Allenby captured almost the entire Turkish army at Megiddo in Sept.; Syria was overrun, and Damascus and Aleppo surrendered. The Turkish army on the Tigris also surrendered, and Constantinople itself was threatened. Turkey signed an armistice on 30 Oct.

To a German offensive at Rheims on 15 July Foch replied on 18 July by an attack on the Marne, which by 3 Aug. had reached Soissons. On 8 Aug. a British attack at Amiens drove the Germans back 7m. At the beginning of Sept. they were back behind the Hindenburg Line, which by the end of the month the British had broken. The Americans went into action as an independent army on the French right. During Oct. the Belgian coastline was occupied, the British reached the Scheldt, the French advanced over the Aisne, and the Americans down the Meuse.

Inside Germany revolutionary feeling was growing, and when on 29 Oct. the fleet at Kiel was ordered to prepare for sea, mutiny followed. Within a few days the revolution spread to all the main cities. Negotiations for an armistice began on 6 Nov.; the Kaiser abdicated on 9 Nov., and on 11 Nov. the armistice was signed in the forest of Compiègne. Peace with Germany was signed at Versailles on 28 June 1919, and with Austria, Bulgaria, and Hungary respectively at St Germain (10 Sept.), Neuilly (27 Nov.), and Trianon (4 June 1920). A final settlement with Turkey was not reached until the Treaty of Lausanne was signed in 1923.

The Versailles Treaty was not signed by China, and on Wilson's submitting it to the US senate it was rejected as insufficiently safeguarding American sovereignty in the League of Nations: instead a joint congressional resolution declaring peace with Germany and Austria was signed 2 July 1921 by Pres. Harding, and ratified by the senate 18 Oct. Strictly speaking, the USA was an 'associated' rather than an 'allied' power.

FISCHER (fi'sher), **Emil** (1852-1919). German chemist. Working with Julius Tufel, he produced synthetic sugars and from these the various enzymes. He was a pioneer biochemist and received a Nobel prize in 1902.

FISCHER, Hans (1881-1945). German chemist. Prof. at the Technische Hochschule at Munich, he received the Nobel prize in chemistry in 1930 for his discovery of the red colouring matter in blood.

FISCHER-DIESKAU (fisher-dē'skow), **Dietrich** (1925-). German singer. A baritone, he is a member of the Berlin and Vienna Operas, and has sung in concerts and festivals all over Europe. He is particularly famous for his interpretation of Schubertian songs.

FISH. Name applied to 3 classes of aquatic vertebrate animals. The body is adapted for freedom of movement in water. In most families the skeleton is composed of bone, but in the lamprey, shark and skate families it is of cartilage. The fins vary in number. Those in front are termed the pectoral fins, and those beneath the abdomen the ventral fins; behind these appears the anal fin, and on the median line of the back the dorsal fin. The fins are composed of thin bones lightly covered with skin. Fishes are usually covered with scales of varying size and thickness, whose number remains constant throughout life. Along the side of most Fs. appears the 'lateral line' which is the chief sense organ; the number of scales appearing on this line is used as a means of identification of species.

Fs. breathe by means of gills, i.e. layers of tissue supported on bony arches, situated in the head. Water enters through the mouth and passes over the gills where the oxygen is absorbed by the blood vessels. The water then goes out through the gill slits at the sides of the head. Many Fs. have an air bladder; in the base of the lungfishes this serves as a lung, but in other fishes it alters the specific gravity of the fish in accordance with the surrounding water.

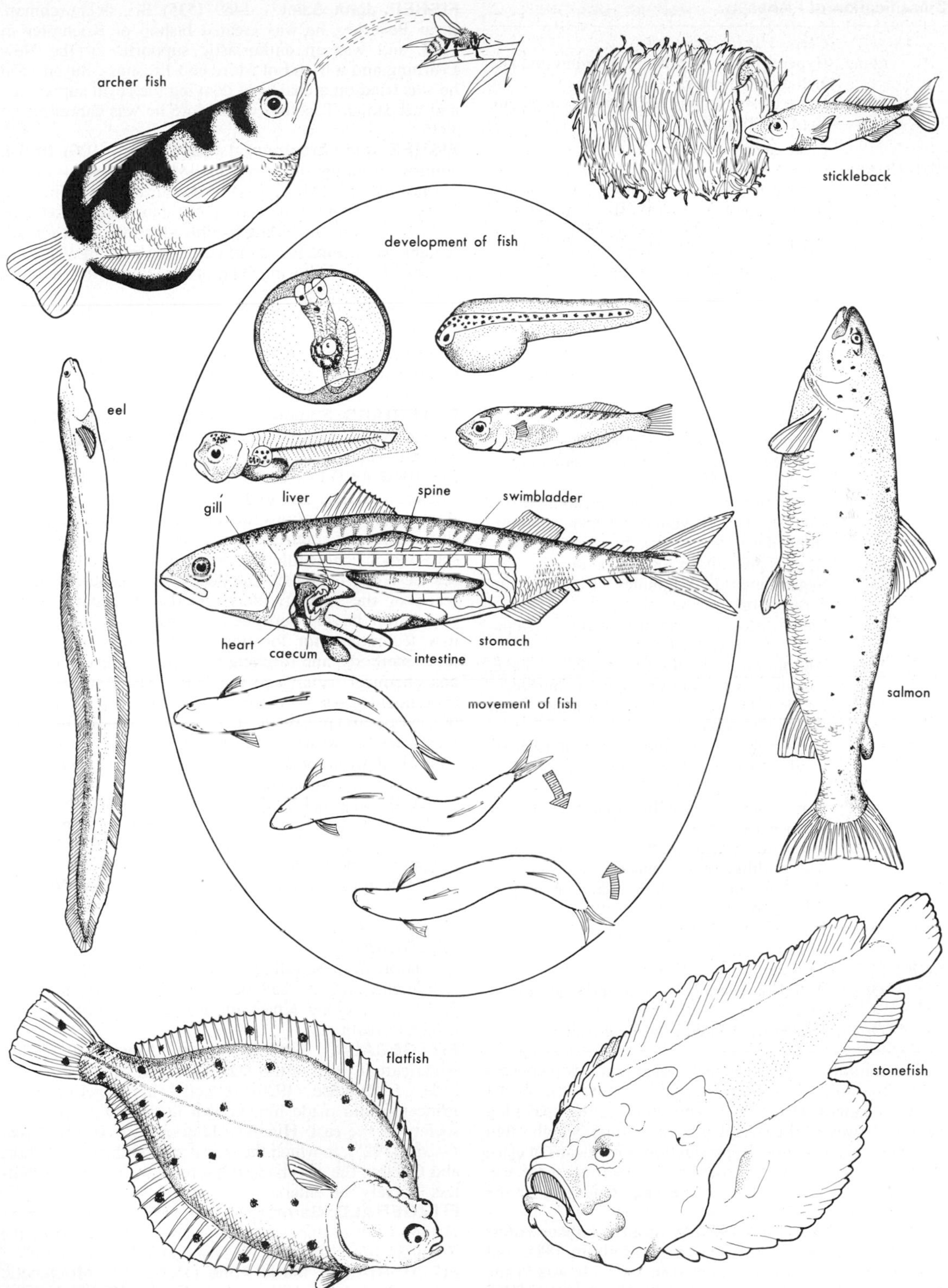

FISH. Representative species and a diagram of the typical features.

Classification of Fishes

Class Marsipobranchii

Order, Hyperoartia; family: Petromysonidae; including lampreys.

Order, Hyperotreta; family: Myxinidae, including hag-fish, borer.

Class Selachii

SUB-CLASS, Euselachii

Order, Pleurotremata; 7 families, including the sharks, dog-fish, monk-fish or angel-fish.

Order, Hypotremata; 5 families including the rays, torpedo, skate, devil-fish.

SUB-CLASS, Holocephali; family Chimaeridae; chimaera, rabbit-fish.

Class Pisces

SUB-CLASS, Palaeopterygii

Order, Chondrostei; family Acipenseridae; sturgeon.

SUB-CLASS, Neopterygii

Order, Isospondyli; 9 families, including the herring, sprat, shad, pilchard, sardine, anchovy, salmon, trout, char, grayling.

Order, Haplomi; family Esocidae; pike.

Order, Ostariophysi ; 2 families including carp, goldfish, barbel, gudgeon, tench, minnow, chub, dace, roach, bream.

Order, Apodes; 6 families including eels, conger.

Order, Synentognathi; 3 families including skipper, gar-fish, flying-fish

Order, Solenichthyes; 2 families including snipe-fish, pipe-fish, sea-horse.

Order, Anacanthini; 3 families including hake, cod, haddock, whiting, pollack, burbot.

Order, Zeomorphi; 2 families including John Dory, boar-fish.

Order, Percomorphi; 31 families including bass, perch, horse mackerel, bream, red mullet, wrasse, sand eels, weevers, mackerel, tunny, sword-fish, goby, dragonet, cat-fish, sticklebacks.

Order, Heterosomata; 3 families including turbot, brill, halibut, dabs, plaice, soles.

Order, Plectognathi; 3 families including trigger-fish, globe-fish or puffer, sun-fish.

Order, Pediculati; family: Lophiidae; angler, fishing-frog.

SUB-CLASS, Crossopterygii

Order, Actinistia; family; Coelacanthidae; coelacanth.

Order, Dipneusti; 2 families of lung-fishes

The coloration of Fs. is usually such that it will conceal the animal in its surroundings, and in many varieties the colour changes with the background. At the spawning season, however, they display their colours, which often become much brighter. Reproduction is by means of eggs, which are frequently very small and numerous: some, e.g. guppies, are live-bearers and the eggs hatch inside the body.

FISHER, Andrew (1862-1928). Australian Labour statesman. B. in Scotland, he went to Australia in 1885, and entered the Australian parliament in 1901. He was Prime Minister in 1908, 1910-13, and 1914-15, and then High Commissioner in London until 1921.

FISHER, John, Saint (*c.* 1469-1535). British churchman. B. at Beverley, he was created bishop of Rochester in 1504, and was an enthusiastic supporter of the New Learning and a friend of More and Erasmus. But in 1535 he was tried on a charge of denying the royal supremacy and beheaded. Together with More he was canonized in 1935.

FISHER, John Arbuthnot, 1st baron (1841-1920). British admiral. Joining the navy in 1854, he served in the Crimean War, held various commands and was First Sea Lord 1904-10, when he carried out many radical reforms and innovations, including the introduction of the Dreadnought battleship. He returned to the post in 1914, but resigned in the following year, disagreeing with Churchill over Dardanelles policy.

FISHER of Lambeth, Geoffrey, baron (1887-1972). British churchman. Headmaster of Repton 1914-32, and bp of London from 1939, he succeeded Temple as abp of Canterbury 1945-61. He was the first holder of his office to visit the Pope for 600 yrs.

FISHGUARD. Seaport on an inlet on the S side of F. Bay, Dyfed, Wales. There is a ferry connection to Rosslare in the Rep. of Ireland. Pop. (1971) 5,000.

FISHING AND FISHERIES. The increasing demand for fish as food has led to the development of improved marketing organizations for the catches, and of powerful ships with special refrigerating equipment, or fish-factory ships which enable filleting, processing, etc., to be done at sea, designed to exploit the deep-water resources out of reach of the smaller, older-type boats. Japan, with a population largely dependent on sea-food, has evolved new techniques for locating shoals (e.g. sonorific and radar methods) and catching them (e.g. electrical charges and chemical baits); and the North Sea countries have experimented less successfully with the artificial breeding of fish eggs and release of small fry into the sea. The future seems to lie with intensive breeding and farming in controlled areas for high quality fish, management being by underwater workers.

Over-fishing had by the later 20th cent. led to serious depletion of stocks, e.g. off British coasts by continental trawlers using methods designed to take all fish, even immature specimens, and in the case of Iceland competition for the remaining catch led to 'Cod Wars'. A partial solution was the extension of fishing limits.

FISSION, Nuclear. *See* NUCLEAR ENERGY.

FITZGERALD, Edward (1809-83). British poet and translator. B. in Suffolk, he lived a life of quiet study and retirement, and in 1859 pub. his poetic version of the *Rubaiyat of Omar Khayyam,* less a translation than an original creation.

FITZGERALD, Francis Scott Key (1896-1940). American novelist of the Jazz Age, b. in Minnesota. *This Side of Paradise* (1920) reflected his experiences at Princeton and made him known in the bright post-war society of the east. His most famous book is *The Great Gatsby* (1925), in which the narrator resembles his author, and Gatsby, the self-made millionaire, is lost in the soulless 'Society' he enters.

FITZGERALD, Garret (1926-). Irish stateman. Leader of Fine Gael in opposition from 1977, he was PM of the Republic June 1981–Jan 1982, and Dec 1982–Mar 1987.

FITZHERBERT, Maria Anne (1756-1837). Morganatic wife of the Prince of Wales, later George IV. She became Mrs F. by her 2nd marriage in 1778, and after her husband's death in 1781 entered London society. She secretly m. the Prince of Wales in 1785, and finally parted from him in 1803. Henceforward she lived in retirement in Brighton.

FITZROY, Robert (1805-65). British vice-admiral and meteorologist. B. in Suffolk, he entered the navy in 1819, and in 1828 succeeded to the command of HMS *Beagle*, then engaged on a survey of the Patagonian coast, and in 1831 was accompanied by Charles Darwin on a 5 years' survey. In 1843-5 he was Gov. of New Zealand.

FIVES. A game of handball played by 2 or 4 players in a court enclosed on 3 or 4 sides: the ball is struck by the hand. It dates from the 14th cent., and was probably derived from the French *jeu de paume*. The name F. may refer to the 5 fingers, or that there were originally 5 players, who had to make 5 points to win. In Britain the game is practically confined to public schools and colleges, and there are 3 main forms, viz. Eton F., Rugby F., and Winchester F.

FIVE-YEAR PLAN. An overall economic plan for an extended period with specific targets. From 1928 the basis of economic planning in the USSR, aimed particularly at developing heavy and light industry in a primarily agricultural country, the idea has since been adopted by other Communist countries, and also in the West, to increase agricultural as well as industrial production - not always successfully.

FLAG. Plant of the *Iris* genus, which grows in damp places and in marshes in Britain and throughout Europe. It has a thick rootstock, from which rise stiff, blade-like monocotyledonous leaves, and stems *c.* 60cm (2ft) high. The flowers are large, and usually yellow. Cultivated varieties include the purple Garden F.

FLAG. The British National F., the so-called 'Union Jack', unites the crosses of St George, St Andrew, and St Patrick, representing England, Scotland, and Ireland; the Merchant F. places the National F. in the canton of a red F.; similarly placed on a large St George's Cross it becomes the distinguishing F. of the Royal Navy. The Stars and Stripes, 'Old Glory', is the F. of the United States; the 50 stars represent the 50 States now in the Union, the 13 stripes the 13 original States. The F. of Russia places the crossed hammer and sickle, representing the workers of town and country, on the red F., the emblem of revolution. The Fs. of the Scandinavian countries bear crosses; the Danish 'Dannebrog' (strength of Denmark) is the oldest national F., used for 700 years. The Red Cross originated in Switzerland, and its emblem is the Swiss F. with its colours reversed. Moslem states often incorporate in their Fs. the crescent emblem of Islam and the colour green, also assoc. with their faith.

The countries of the 'old Commonwealth' incl. the 'Union Jack' as part of their national F. in the case of Australia and N.Z., the stars representing the Southern Cross; Canada omitted it on the introduction of the new maple leaf design, and S. Africa, though now outside the Commonwealth, continues to incl. it as symbolic of the British element in the population.

A flag is flown upside-down as a signal of distress; is dipped as a salute; and when flown a little below the mast-head is a sign of mourning. The 'Blue Peter', blue with a white centre, announces that a vessel is about to sail; a F. half red and half white that a pilot is on board. Many public bodies, as well as shipping lines and yacht clubs, have their own distinguishing Fs.

The British Royal Standard combines the emblems of England, Scotland, and Ireland; the United States Presidential Standard displays the American Eagle, surrounded by 50 stars.

FLAGELLANTS (flajel'ants). Religious fanatics who either allow others to scourge them as a means of discipline and penance, or who scourge themselves. Such flagellation is known in many religions from ancient times, and there were notable outbreaks of this type of extremist devotion in Christian Europe in the 11th-16th cents.: it is still practised to a minor extent in some RC countries.

FLAGELLATA (flagelā'ta). Order of microscopic animals in the sub-kingdom Protozoa. The name is derived from the presence in each individual of one or more flagella - whip-like processes - usually at the front end of the body, which by actively lashing the water drive the protozoan forwards.

FLAGSTAD, Kirsten (1895-1962). Norwegian soprano singer. She was without rival in Wagnerian opera.

FLA'HERTY, Robert (1884-1951). American film director. B. in Michigan, he exerted great influence by his pioneer documentary of Eskimo life *Nanook of the North* (1920): later were *Man of Aran* and *Elephant Boy*.

FLAMBOYANT. In architecture, term applied to late Gothic style of French architecture, contemporary with the Perpendicular style in England. It is characterized by flame-like decorative work in windows, balustrades, and other projecting features.

FLAMEN (flā'men). The sacrificial priest in ancient Rome. The office was held for life, but was terminated by the death of the F.'s wife (who assisted him at ceremonies) or some breach of demeanour. At first there were 3 Fs., but another 12 were later added.

FLAMI'NGO. A bird (*Phoenicopterus*) of the order Ciconiiformes. All members of the family (Phoenicopteridae) have very long legs and down-bent bills, specially adapted for sifting mud, from which they obtain their food of worms and molluscs, etc. They are able to swim and to fly, but usually confine themselves to wading. They live in large colonies, the nest being built of mud in shallow water, and are found in great numbers in the Camargue, in S America, etc.

The common F. (*P. roseus*) is white tinted with pink; the wings, as in all species, are bright red bordered with black.

FLAMI'NIUS, Gaius (d. 217 BC). Roman statesman and general. He had constructed the Flaminian Way northward from Rome to Rimini 220 BC., and was killed at the battle of Lake Trasimene against Hannibal.

FLAMSTEED, John (1646-1719). First Astronomer Royal of England. B. near Derby, he was appointed astronomer to Charles II in 1675, and began systematic observations at Greenwich in the following year. From 1684 he was rector of Burstow in Surrey.

FLANAGAN, Bud. Stage-name of the British comedian Robert Winthrop (1896-1968). Leader of the 'Crazy Gang' (1931-62), he also played in variety all over the world, and with his partner Chesney Allen popularized such songs as 'Underneath the Arches'.

FLANDERS. A region of the Low Countries which in the 8th and 9th cents. extended from Calais to the Scheldt, and is now covered by the Belgian provinces of E and W Flanders, the French dept of Nord, and part of the Dutch prov. of Zeeland.

Fierce battles were fought here in the F.W.W., *see* REMEMBRANCE SUNDAY (q.v.). In the S.W.W. the *Battle of F.* began with the German breakthrough of 10 May 1940 and ended with Dunkirk.

FLASH POINT. The temperature at which a liquid when heated under standard conditions gives off sufficient vapour to ignite on the application of a small flame. F.P. tests are carried out with the Pensky-Martens instrument. The Fire Point of the material itself is obtained by continuing the test and noting the temperature at which ignition occurs. For safe storage (fuel oil, etc) the Flash and Fire Points must be high enough to reduce fire risks to a minimum, and such that no appreciable quantity of oils are driven off during exposure to the weather.

FLAUBERT (flohbār'), **Gustave** (1821-80). French novelist. B. at Rouen, he entered Paris literary circles in 1840, but in 1846 retired to his native place, where he remained for the rest of his life. His masterpiece *Madame Bovary* appeared in 1857 and aroused much controversy by its psychological portrayal of the wife of a country doctor, driven to suicide by a series of unhappy love affairs. *Salammbô* (1862) earned him the Legion of Honour in 1866, and was followed by *L'Éducation sentimentale* (1869), and *La Tentation de Saint Antoine* (1874). F. estab. himself as the master of the short story by his *Trois Contes: Un Cœur simple, Hérodias,* and *Le Legende de Saint-Julien l'Hospitalier* (pub. 1877).

FLAX. A plant of the Linaceae family which yields valuable commercial products. The common F. or linseed plant (*Linum usitatissimum*) is of almost world-wide distribution. It has a stem 125cm (50in) high, bearing small leaves and bright blue flowers. Apart from the fibres yielded by the stem, the seeds produce linseed oil and their residue forms cattle food. The long fibres are used in the manufacture of linen, the shorter fibres are made into twine, and the shortest of all used in paper manufacture. The chief producing areas are in Russia, Belgium, Holland, the Baltic countries, and Northern Ireland.

FLAX. The flax harvest at Courtrai in Belgium. *Photo: Courtesy of the Belgian National Tourist Office.*

FLAX, New Zealand. Unrelated to either flax or hemp, *Phormium tenax* belongs to the Liliaceae, and is commercially grown for the fibre in its sword-shaped leaves which may be 2 m (6 ft) long.

FLAXMAN, John (1755-1826). British sculptor. B. at York, he studied at the RA and for 12 years was employed by Wedgwood as a designer. He became an RA in 1800, and in 1810 he was appointed first prof. of sculpture at the academy. His best-known works incl. the monument to Reynolds in St Paul's, and the statues of Burns and Kemble in Westminster Abbey.

FLEABANE. Plants of the genus *Erigeron,* Compositae family, resembling a dwarf michaelmas daisy.

FLEAS (*Siphonaptera* or *Aphaniptera*). Group of wingless insects, with mouth-parts adapted for sucking the blood of their host. The most important varieties are *Pulex irritans*, which lives on man, and the rat F. (*Xenopsylla cheopis*) which transmits plague.

FLECKER, James Elroy (1884-1915). British poet. B. at Lewisham, he entered the consular service, and went to Constantinople in 1910 and in 1911 to Smyrna. In 1913 ill-health obliged him to visit Switzerland, where he d. of consumption. He pub. several vols. of verse, incl. *The Bridge of Fire* (1907), *The Golden Journey to Samarkand* (1913) and *The Old Ships* (1915). He also wrote the dramas *Don Juan* and *Hassan,* the latter being performed in 1923 with incidental music by Delius.

FLEET STREET. Street in London, England, running from Temple Bar eastwards to Ludgate Circus, named after the River F. With adjoining streets it contains the offices and printing works of many leading British newspapers.

FLEETWOOD. Port and seaside resort in Lancs, England, at the mouth of the Wyre. The fishing industry has declined, but the port also handles timber, petroleum and chemicals. Pop. (1972) 29,530.

FLEMING, Sir Alexander (1881-1955). British bacteriologist. B. in Ayrshire, he studied medicine in London, and was prof. of bacteriology at London univ. 1928-48. His first notable discovery was lysozyme (1922), followed in 1928 by penicillin (q.v.), an antibiotic which saved many lives in the S.W.W. In 1945 he shared the Nobel prize with E. B. Chain and Sir Howard Florey, who had developed penicillin for practical use, and was knighted in 1944.

FLEMING, Ian (1908-64). British author. Son of an army officer, he was ed. at Eton, Sandhurst, and Munich and Geneva univs. After a number of years with Reuters, he worked successively with banking and stockbroking firms, and in the S.W.W. was personal asst. to the Director of Naval Intelligence. From 1953 he became famous as the author of suspense novels featuring the ruthless, laconic 'James Bond', Secret Service agent, No. 007 - the prefixed '00' meaning licensed to kill.

FLEMING, Sir John Ambrose (1849-1945). British electrical physicist and engineer. B. at Lancaster, he was prof. of electrical engineering at Univ. College, London, 1885-1926, and invented the thermionic valve (1904).

FLEMISH. A branch of the West Germanic, or more especially the German division of the Germanic languages (q.v.), spoken in the northern half of Belgium and in the Nord dept of France. In opposition to the introduction of French as the official language in the F. provinces of Belgium after 1830 there arose a strong Flemish movement, led by scholars like J. F. Willems (1793-1846) and writers such as H. Conscience (1812-83), and although equality of French and F. was not achieved until 1898, it brought about a cultural and political revival of F. The F.

FLIGHT. The cross-Channel flight by Bleriot in 1909 which established flying as a practical proposition. Madame Bleriot crossed by torpedo-boat to join her husband as he landed: the Bleriot monoplane is in the air above them. On the right: Orville Wright pilots the Wright biplane making the first powered, sustained and controlled flight at Kittlhawk, N. Carolina, on 17 Dec. 1903: he covered 36.5 m (120 ft). On foot, in the corner of the picture, is Wilbur Wright. In the centre illustration: the Hawker P-1127 strike aircraft, first of the vertical take-off type to be designed for operational service in 1961. And, in the bottom illustration, the USAF rocket aircraft X-15 at the moment of its release from the 'mother' plane on 27 June 1962. Piloted by Robert M. White, it reached 6,605 kph (4,105mph). *Photos: Illustrated London News, Bristol Siddeley and USIS.*

movement was promoted for political reasons by the Germans in both world wars, and in the 1970s and 1980s threatened Belgian unity.

The great figures of F. literature are the poet Guido Gezelle, and the novelists Cyriel Buysse, Stijn Streuvels, and Felix Timmermanns.

FLEMISH ART. The style of painting developed in Flanders (Belgium) from the 14th cent. and distinguished by colourful realism, keen observation, and masterful technique. Hubert and Jan van Eyck made Bruges the first centre of F.A.; other schools arose in Tournai, Ghent, and Louvain. The great names of that period were Roger van der Weyden, Dierick Bouts, Hugo van der Goes, Hans Memlinc, and Gheerardt David. In the 16th cent. Italian influences made themselves felt, and the centre shifted to Antwerp, where Quinten Matsys worked. Whilst Jerome Bosch painted creatures of his own wild imagination, the pictures of P. Brueghel are faithful reflections of F. life. The Italian influence was strong in Mabuse, Jan Massys, and others. Peter Paul Rubens and his school created a new powerful style, which was continued by van Dyck, Jordaens, etc. Brouwer and Teniers kept up the earlier tradition.

FLENSBURG. Port on the E. coast of Schleswig-Holstein, W Germany, with shipyards and breweries. Pop. (1978) 96,000.

FLETCHER, John (1579-1625). English dramatist. B. at Rye, Sussex, he was left an orphan of restricted means when his father d. in disgrace with Queen Elizabeth. Of the 50 plays once attributed to his partnership with Beaumont (q.v.), only 7 are now generally recognized: the remainder are divided between F. and collaborators such as Massinger. Among those credited to F. alone are the pastoral drama *The Faithful Shepherdess* (1610), the

FLEMISH ART. A quaint interpretation of 'The Fall of Icarus' by Brueghel. *Photo: Mansell Collection.*

tragedy *Bonduca* (*c.* 1614), and *Rule a Wife and Have a Wife* (*c.* 1624).

FLEUR-DE-LIS (flör de lē; Fr. flower of the lily). A heraldic device which represents a lily, borne on coats of arms since the 12th cent., and adopted by the Bourbons of France.

FLIGHT, History of. The aeroplane is a development of the model glider, first flown by Sir George Cayley (1773-1857) in 1804, but not until the invention of the petrol engine did powered flight become feasible with the building of the Wright brothers' biplane in 1903-08. In Europe, inspired by the Wrights, France led in aeroplane design (Voisin brothers) and Louis Blériot brought aviation much publicity by crossing the Channel in 1909, as did the Reims meeting of that year. The first powered flight in England was by S.F. Cody in 1908. In 1912 Sopwith and Bristol both built small biplanes and the first big twin-engined aeroplane was the Handley Page bomber in 1917.

The stimulus of the F.W.W. and rapid development of the petrol engine led to increased power and speeds rose to 320 kph (200mph). Streamlining then became imperative: non-essential excrescences were retracted into the body and wings and exposed parts were shaped to reduce drag, and eventually the biplane was replaced by the internally braced monoplane structure, e.g. the Hawker Hurricane and Supermarine Spitfire fighters and Avro Lancaster and Boeing Flying Fortress bombers of the S.W.W. The German jet, the first turbo-jet to fly, the Heinkel 178, flew in 1939.

On 15 May, 1941, the first British jet aircraft, the Gloster E. 28/39, flew from Cranwell, Lincs, powered by a turbo-jet i.c. engine invented by Sir Frank Whittle. The rapid development of this new power-plant led to enormous increases in power and speed until air-compressibility effects were felt near the speed of sound. Twin-jet Meteor fighters were in use at the end of the war and the jet has since ousted the piston engine on nearly all military types and for civil use also, either as a turbo-prop or pure jet, since by flying high over 15,500 m (50,000 ft) these engines are more economical as well as more powerful.

To exceed sonic speed, mere retraction of excrescences was insufficient, and wings were swept back, engines buried in wings and tail units, and even bodies eliminated in all-wing, delta designs. Supersonic airliner projects were the Anglo-French Concorde (*see illus.* CIVIL AVIATION) and the Soviet Tu-144.

For speed, combined with flexibility in operation of flights below 800kph (500mph), V/STOL (vertical and/or short take-off) aircraft provided a solution, e.g. tilt-wing machines which rotate the entire wing to the vertical position in landing and take-off, and use the propellers as helicopter rotors to provide lift. The Hawker P-1127 is also capable of supersonic level flight. Development of swing wing or variable geometry aircraft, capable of much higher speed, encountered setbacks in both Europe and the USA in the 1960s, but by 1974 problems had been solved. The Tornado Multi Role Combat Aircraft (MRCA), produced by the British Aircraft Corporation in partnership with Germany and Italy (1974), can intercept at high or low altitudes, maintain air superiority over the battle-field, cut off enemy supplies, support ground or naval forces, and carry out reconnaissance. *See* AEROPLANE, BALLOON, HELICOPTER, HOVERCRAFT, GLIDING, JET PROPULSION.

FLINDERS, Matthew (1774-1814). British navigator. B. in Lincs, he joined the navy in 1789, and explored the Australian coasts, 1795-9 and 1801-3.

Named after him are *F. Island,* NE of Tasmania, Australia, in Bass Strait, area 2,080 sq.km (800 sq.m); the *F. Range* in S Australia, which reaches 1,165m (3,822 ft) in St Mary Peak and has copper, lead and uranium; and *F. River* in Queensland, Australia, which rises in the Great Dividing Range and flows NW to the Gulf of Carpentaria 840km (520m).

FLINT, Sir William Russell (1880-1970). Scottish artist. B. in Edinburgh, he was pres. of the Royal Soc. of Painters in Water Colours 1936-56; he was knighted in 1947.

FLINT. City of Michigan, USA, on the F. river. Manufacture of motor-cars is the chief industry. Pop. (1970) 193,320. Also, a small town of Clwyd, Wales, on the r. Dee, Pop. (1973) 15,000.

FLINT. A compact, hard, brittle rock, brown, black, or grey in colour, found in nodules in chalk deposits. It consists of fine-grained silica, compressed into a homogeneous mass. When broken, the nodule has a shell-like fracture. Owing to their hardness, F. splinters are used for abrasive purposes, and when ground into powder for pottery manufacture.

Flint implements made by chipping one F. against another were widely used by Palaeolithic and Neolithic Man. The earliest F. implements, belonging to the Palaeolithic Age, are simple, while those of the Neolithic Age are more expertly cut, and are often ground or polished. Such are found in many parts of Britain. In historic times they were used for making fire, by striking a F. against steel, which produces a spark, and for discharging guns. Cigarette-lighter Fs. are made from cerium alloy.

FLINTSHIRE. Formerly the smallest of the Welsh cos., it was merged in 1974, with Denbigh and a small part of Merioneth, to form the new co. of Clwyd: the co. town of Mold became the admin. HQ of the new region. It occupied a rectangular area bordering the Dee estuary and the Irish Sea, incl. Rhyl, Flint and Hawarden, and a small detached area to the SE.

FLODDEN. Site 5km (3m) SE of Coldstream, Northumberland, England, of the battle fought on Sept. 9, 1513, between the Scots under James IV and the English under the earl of Surrey, in which James and the flower of his nobility were slain.

FLINT. Fine flint stone abounds in Denmark, and the Stone Age lasted longer there than elsewhere, so that a skill in flint work was developed which was greater than anywhere else in Europe. Small daggers, such as that illustrated, are beautifully chiselled. *Photo: Courtesy of the Danish Tourist Board*

FLOOD. The disaster which, according to Genesis, obliterated the human race except for a chosen few. *See* NOAH. Excavations at Ur by Woolley (q.v.) revealed (2.5m/8ft) of water-laid clay, suggesting a local deluge prior to 4000 BC over an area *c.* 645km (400m) by 160km (100m) which may have been the origin of the story.

FLORA. Roman goddess of flowers, youth, and of spring. Festivals were held in her honour.

FLORENCE. City in central Italy, cap. of Tuscany region, on the Arno 88km (55m) from its mouth. There are engineering industries.

The Roman town of Florentia was built *c.* 187 BC on a former Etruscan site. It was besieged by the Goths, AD 405, visited by Charlemagne 786. In 1052, with the rest of Tuscany, F. passed to the countess Matilda of Tuscany. It was the scene of many later conflicts between the popes and the emperors, and was governed by nobles. 'Arti' or trade guilds began to grow up, until the feudal lords and the emperors were overcome, and in 1250 F. was proclaimed a republic. Ten years of Guelph supremacy made F. one of Italy's chief cities, but thereafter the struggle between papal supporters (Guelphs) and those of the emperors (Ghibellines) continued. From 1434 the city's history was bound up with the Medici family. In 1532 she lost her independence, and became capital of the duchy of Tuscany.

F. is famed for its art treasures; the Pitti Palace, the Uffizi Gallery, the cathedral of Santa Maria del Fiore, 1420-34, and many other fine buildings. It was heavily damaged in the S.W.W., and in 1966 by the worst floods for 700 years, but has been carefully restored. In 1973 the European Univ. Institute was opened in the Villa Tolomei. Pop. (1971) 461,800.

FLOREY, Howard Walter, baron (1898-1968). British pathologist. B. in Australia, he was prof. of pathology at Oxford 1935-62. He began work on penicillin in 1938, and in 1945 won with Sir Alexander Fleming (q.v.) the Nobel prize for medicine. He was awarded a life peerage and OM 1965.

FLORIANÓPOLIS. Port on Santa Caterina Is., Brazil, which is linked to the mainland by suspension bridge. Pop. (1974) 142,000.

FLORIDA. The most southern state of USA; mainly a large peninsula jutting into the Atlantic which it separates from the Gulf of Mexico. For the most part rolling countryside, suitable for agriculture, it has many lakes in the central region, incl. Okeechobee 1,800 sq.km (700 sq.m); in the S a great expanse of standing water, the Everglades, is being drained for agriculture, but over 5,000 sq.km (2,000 sq.m) are preserved as a National Park. Miami is the largest city; other towns are Tallahassee (the capital), Jacksonville and Tampa. Oranges, grapefruit, water-melon and vegetables are produced in great quantity; fish and shellfish are important; growing industries incl. food processing; chemicals and paper; and minerals incl. phosphate and rare earth metals. The John F. Kennedy Space Center is at Cape Canaveral. There are famous tourist resorts at Miami Beach and Palm Beach, and it is a popular retirement haven as the 'Sunshine State'. Ruled by Spain 1513-1763, it was ceded to Britain 1763-83, and then purchased from Spain by USA in 1819, becoming the 27th state in 1845. Area 151,700 sq.km (58,560 sq.m); pop. (1970) 6,789,443. In the 1970s and 1980s many refugees from Cuba and Haiti settled in the state.

FLORIDA KEYS. Series of small coral is. which curve over 160km (100m) SW from the end of the F. panhandle. Sponges, fish and tourism espec. on the largest, Key Largo, and on Key West, are the chief source of income.

FLORIN. Coin, common to many European lands, first minted in Florence in 1252. The obverse bore the image of a lily, which led to the coin being called *fiorino* (from *fiore*, flower). This F. was a gold coin. The British silver F. of 2s. was first struck 1849, and continued in use after decimalization as the equivalent of 10p.

FLORIO, Giovanni (*c.* 1553-1625). English translator. B. in London, the son of Italian refugees, he taught French and Italian at Oxford, but is best known for his translation of Montaigne (1603).

FLOTOW (floh'toh), **Friedrich, Freiherr von** (1812-83). German composer. Of his 18 operas only *Martha* (1847) is remembered.

FLOTSAM AND JETSAM. F.: goods found floating on the sea after a shipwreck. J.: goods deliberately sunk in the sea to lighten a vessel which is wrecked. Under British law F. and J. belong to the Crown, unless the true owner is known or a franchise has been granted to such goods.

FLOUNDER A species (*Platichthys flesus*) of salt- and freshwater flat-fish, whose skin varies in colour from black to grey, the underside being white. Both eyes are on the same side of the body. It is related to the dab and plaice and is used as a food.

FLOWER. The blossom of a plant. The F. is a characteristic of the Phanerogams (flowering plants), its function being the production of reproductive organs and the formation of seed. The essential parts of the F. are the androecium, which includes the anthers (containing the pollen) or male nucleus, and the filaments on which they are borne; and the gynaecium, which consists of the ovary (containing ovules) or female nuclei and the style, culminating in the stigma.

FLUIDS, Supercritical. Fluids brought by a combination of heat and pressure to the point when, as a near vapour, they combine the properties of gases and fluids. Used as solvents in chemical processes, such as the extraction of lubricating oil from refinery residues or the decaffeination of coffee, they avoid the energy-expensive need for phase changes - from liquid to gas and back again - which are required in conventional distillation processes.

FLUKE. Parasitic flat worm (*Fasciola hepatica*), belonging to the order Trematoda, that causes rot and dropsy of the liver, in sheep, cattle, horses, dogs, and man. Only the adult encysted stage of its life history is passed within the body, after ingestion by the host. The cyst

FLYING FISH and FOX. On the left, the flying fish *(Exocetus spilopterus)* of tropic waters, and on the right the flying fox, which raids the orchards of Queensland and New South Wales during the 'flying fox moon' - note the big claw, used in climbing, protruding from the folded wing on the right. *Photos: Popperfoto and Australian Information Service.*

dissolves in the stomach and the young fluke passes to the liver.

FLUORE'SCENCE. The process of emission of electromagnetic radiation resulting from the absorption of certain types of energy, in which case it is a luminescence lasting a minute fraction of a second after the exciting energy is removed. F. is also used to mean the radiation emitted as well as the emission process, and in X-ray F. it is the characteristic X-rays emitted when X-rays of a higher frequency are absorbed. This is used in analysis. F. is made use of in strip and other lighting, and was developed rapidly during the S.W.W. because of its greater efficiency of illumination, compared with the incandescent lamp. Other important applications are in fluorescent screens for television, cathode-ray tubes, etc.

FLU'ORĪDES. Salts of hydrofluoric acid. F. occur naturally in all water to a differing extent. Pilot experiments in Great Britain, America and elsewhere have indicated that a concentration of fluoride of 1 part per million in water retards the decay of teeth in children by more than 50 per cent. If the natural concentration of F. is less than 1 part per million, the recommended policy of the Min. of Health in Britain is to add sufficient sodium fluoride to the water to bring it up to this amount, but implementation is entirely up to each local authority.

FLU'ORINE. Chemical element, symbol F., at no. 9, at. wt. 19, which was discovered by Scheele in 1771 and isolated by Moissan in 1886. It occurs naturally as the minerals fluorspar (CaF_2) and cryolite (Na_3AlFe_6) and is a member of the halogen family. At ordinary temperatures it is a pale yellow, highly poisonous and reactive gas and it unites directly with nearly all the elements. Hydrogen fluoride is used in etching glass, and the Freons, which all contain fluorine, are widely used as refrigerants and propellants. Combined with uranium as UF_6 it is used in the separation of uranium isotopes.

FLUOROCARBON. More correctly chlorofluorocarbon, an inert compound of carbon and fluoride used as a lubricant, in the manufacture of plastics and synthetic resins, and as a propellent in aerosols. There was concern from 1974 that F. molecules from aerosols were floating into the stratosphere where their chlorine atoms were liberated by ultra-violet rays. The chlorine would then react with ozone to form oxygen which lacks the ability of ozone to filter out harmful solar radiation, with the consequent danger of climatic changes and increase in skin cancer. There was research to modify Fs. or substitute hydrocarbon propellents.

FLUORSPAR or **fluorite.** A cubic mineral (CaF_2), usually violet-tinted. The Blue-john from Derbyshire is a fibrous variety used as an ornamental stone. Colourless F. is used in the manufacture of microscope lenses, for the glaze on pottery, and in the Bessemer process of steel manufacture.

FLUSHING. Port (Dutch Vlissingen) on Walcheren Island, Zeeland, Netherlands, commanding the entrance to the navigable Scheldt estuary, one of the principal sea entries to the continent of Europe. It is a fishing port, and industries incl. shipbuilding and petrochemicals; there is a ferry service to Harwich. De Ruyter was b. at F. and is commemorated in the Jacobskerk. Pop. (1978) 44,000.

FLUTE. Genus of musical instruments, including the piccolo, the concert F., the bass or alto F., etc. They are cylindrical in shape, with a narrowed end, containing the aperture, across which the player blows. The air vibrations produce the note, which can be altered by placing fingers over lateral holes. Certain keys can be depressed to extend the range of the F. to three octaves.

FLUX, MAGNETIC. *See* MAGNETIC FLUX.

FLY. Name given to the winged stage of many insects, such as dragon-fly, butterfly, caddis-fly, etc.: by zoologists it is used to mean a two-winged insect of the order Diptera. Flies form one of the largest orders of insects, and number about 90,000 described species, of which more than 5,200 inhabit the British Isles. They normally possess a single pair of membraneous wings. Hind-wings are represented by a pair of knob-like organs borne on slender stalks. These are the halteres or balancers: they function in maintaining equilibrium during flight. The mouth-parts project from the head in the form of a proboscis. In most Fs. they are used for sucking in fluid substances, but in blood-sucking Fs. they are modified in order to pierce the skin of their victims.

Fs. undergo complete metamorphosis; their larvae are always without true legs, and the pupae are only rarely enclosed in cocoons. They are generally sombrely coloured, but some species are banded with yellow or white, others are metallic green or blue, while some are densely hairy. The sexes are usually very closely alike.

Fs. are usually classified into three sub-orders, viz. Nematocera, including the crane-flies, mosquitoes, midges, and gall-flies; Brachycera, including the horse-flies and robber-flies; and Cyclorhapha, including the house-fly, blow-fly, flesh-fly, etc.

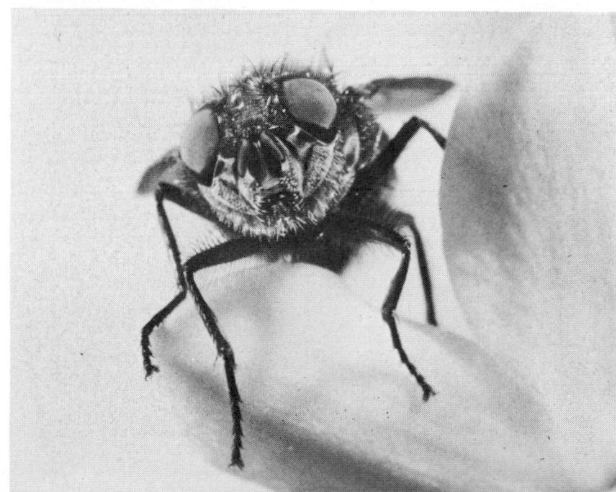

FLY. An adult blowfly *(Calliphora)* encountered head-on. *Photo: Heather Angel.*

FLY. River in Papua New Guinea, which rises in the Victor Emanuel mtns and flows 1,300 km (800m) SE to the Gulf of Papua. Navigable for 800km (500m), it drains a vast area long noted as unhealthy for Europeans.

FLYING FISH. Fish of tropical seas in the family Exocoetidae. They do not in fact 'fly', but have enlarged pectoral fins which enable them to glide through the air after making an initial upward thrust from the water.

FLYING FOX or **fox-bat.** Giant fruit-eating bat of the genus *Pteropus,* of which various species occur in Tropical Asia and Australia. They may reach 1.5 m (5 ft), are nocturnal, and do much damage in orchard areas.

FLYING LEMUR. Small insectivorous mammal, Colugo (q.v.), or Galeopithecus.

FLYNN, Errol (1909-59). Australian actor. B. in Tasmania, he tackled every kind of job before his good looks and gaily reckless personality attracted the film scouts. His films incl. *Captain Blood* (1935) and *The Master of Ballantrae* (1953). In his autobiographics hc was characteristically frank.

FLYNN, John (1880-1951). Australian missionary. Inspired by the use of aircraft to transport the wounded of the F.W.W., he instituted in 1928 the 'flying doctor' service, which can be summoned to the outback by radios in individual homesteads.

FOCH (fosh), **Ferdinand** (1851-1929). Marshal of France. B. at Tarbes, he was commissioned in 1873, and was appointed to the general staff. He was largely responsible for the victory of the Marne, and commanded on the NW front Oct. 1914-Sept. 1916. He was appointed chief of general staff in 1917, entrusted with the co-ordination of the Allied armies in March 1918, and created generalissimo in April. He launched the Allied advance in July which ended the war.

FOG or **MIST.** Cloud which collects at the surface of the earth, composed of water vapour which has condensed on particles of dust in the atmosphere. Cloud and fog are both caused by the air temperature falling below dew point (*see* DEW). The thickness of F. is dependent on the number of water particles it contains. Usually, F. is formed by the meeting of 2 currents of air, one cooler than the other, or by warm air flowing over a cold surface. Sea Fs. commonly occur where warm and cold currents meet, and the air above them mixes. F. frequently forms on calm nights over the land, as the land surface cools more rapidly than the air immediately above it. Officially, F. refers to a condition when visibility is reduced to 1 kilometre (1,100 yards) or less, and mist or haze to that giving a visibility of 1-2 kilometres. A mist is produced by condensed water particles, and a haze by smoke or dust. Industrial areas uncontrolled by pollution laws have a continual haze of smoke over them, and if the temperature falls suddenly, a dense yellow F. forms. To enable small bomber forces to take off in the S.W.W. from 1942 heat from petrol jets was used to clear F., the method being known as FIDO (Fog Intensive Dispersal Of), but it is too expensive for normal use. Subsequent research concentrated on navigation by electronic means, and by 1975 it was possible for aircraft to land and take off 'blind'. *See* SMOG.

FOGGIA (fod'jah). City and episcopal see of Apulia region, S Italy. The cathedral, dating from c. 1170, was rebuilt after an earthquake in 1731. Natural gas is found nearby. Pop. (1971) 142,145.

FÖHN. Warm, unpleasantly desiccating wind which occurs in the valleys of the European Alps. A similar effect occurs elsewhere, e.g. in both North and South Island, NZ, when the NW wind, having left its rain on the W of the mtns blows down the E side, espec. onto the Canterbury Plains.

FOKINE (fokēn′), **Michel** (1880-1942). Russian choreographer. B. in St Petersburg, he became chief choreographer to the Russian Ballet, and by his work with Diaghilev revitalized the art of ballet. His creations incl. the 'Dying Swan' for Pavlova; *Les Sylphides, Le Spectre de la Rose, Petrouchka, Carnaval*; and for the Ballet Theatre of NY *Paganini* and *Barbe Bleu*. He d. in NY.
FOLIES-BERGÈRE (folē′ berzhār′). Music-hall in Paris named after its original proprietor and famous for its lavish productions.
FOLK DANCE. A dance peculiar to a particular people, nation, or country. European F.Ds. are derived from the dances accompanying the native customs and ceremonies of pre-Christian times. Distinctive national characteristics are particularly noticeable in those countries which have had to struggle for national independence. F.D. has tended to die out in industrialized countries; its preservation in England was largely the work of Cecil J. Sharp.
FOLKESTONE (fōk′ston). English port and holiday resort on the SE coast of Kent, 10km (6m) SW of Dover. There is a regular sea service between F. and Boulogne. Pop. (1972) 45,490.
FOLKLORE. The oral traditions and culture of the people. The term F. was coined in 1846 by W. J. Thoms (1803-85), but the founder of the scientific study of the subject was Jacob Grimm (1785-1863). The approach to F. has varied greatly: M. Müller (1823-1900) interpreted it as evidence of nature myths; J. G. Frazer (1854-1941) was the exponent of the comparative study of primitive and popular F. as mutually explanatory; Sir Laurence Gomme (1853-1916) adopted the historical method; Bronislaw Malinowski (1884-1942) and Alfred Radcliffe-Brown (1881-1955) examined the material as an integral element in a living culture; and among those who have specialized in the F. of a single country, Christina Hole (1896-) is outstanding for her work in British F.
FOLK SONG. Body of traditional song forming the spontaneous musical expression of a people. Many F.Ss. originated as a rhythmic accompaniment to manual work. Pure F.S. is melodic not harmonic, and the modes used are distinctive of the country from which it comes. The interest in ballad poetry in the later 18th cent. led to the discovery of a rich body of F.S. in Britain and on the Continent. In addition to Negro F.S., the cosmopolitan background of the USA has brought forth a wealth of material derived from European and S American sources. A great revival of interest, starting in the 1950s, was led by Alan Lomax, John Jacob Niles, Theo Bikel, Pete Seeger, Woody Guthrie and Bob Dylan, and dealt with contemporary topics, e.g. atomic warfare and racial prejudice.
FOLSOM. Settlement in New Mexico, USA, where in 1926 a flint projectile point was found embedded among the bones of an extinct type of bison, so proving that man had existed in America in the Pleistocene period.
FONDA, Henry (1905–82). American actor-director, born in Omaha, Nebraska. His films incl. *Grapes of Wrath* (1940), *My Darling Clementine* (1946), *12 Angry Men* (1957, also director), and *On Golden Pond* (1982:special Oscar). His dau. **Jane F.** (1937-) is also an actress, winning an academy award for her performance in *Klute* (1971) and *Coming Home* (1979), and is active in left-wing politics.

FONTAINEBLEAU (fontānblō). French town to the SE of Paris, in Seine-et-Marne dept. It lies in one of the most beautiful forests of France, for long a favourite haunt of landscape painters. The town is renowned for its royal palace, founded in the 10th cent. Mme de Montespan lived there in the reign of Louis XIV and Mme du Barry in that of Louis XV. Napoleon signed his abdication there in 1814. Pop. (1975) 19,600.
FONTANA (fontah′nah), **Domenico** (1543-1607). Italian architect. He was employed by pope Sixtus V, and his principal works include the Vatican library, the completion of the dome and lantern of St Peter's, and the royal palace at Naples.
FONTANNE, Lynn. *See* ALFRED LUNT.
FONTENOY (foṅtnwah′). Village in Hainaut prov., Belgium SE of Tournai, where Marshal Saxe and the French defeated the British, Dutch, and Hanoverians under the Duke of Cumberland in 1745. Pop. (1970) 600.
FONTEYN, Dame Margot (1919-). British dancer. Née Margaret Hookham, she made her début with the Sadler's Wells Ballet in *The Haunted Ballroom* in 1934 and first appeared as Giselle in 1937, eventually becoming prima ballerina of the Royal Ballet. Technically impeccable and with unique beauty of line, she is supreme among the world's classical dancers. She was created DBE in 1956, and since 1954 has been pres. of the Royal Academy of Dancing. In 1955 she m. Roberto E. Arias, Panamanian ambassador to the UK 1955-8 and 1960-2: a one-time political colleague shot and severely wounded him 1964.

FONTEYN. One of the greatest partnerships in the history of ballet - Margot Fonteyn and Rudolf Nureyev in *Giselle. Photo: Popperfoto.*

FOOCHOW. *See* FUZHOU.
FOOD. The general term for what is eaten by man and other creatures to sustain life. It is used in the formation and repair of body tissues, and for the production of heat

and energy. Certain necessary chemical elements and complex groupings must be provided from which the body can make all it needs. These are the essential constituents: *proteins* for body building and repair, found in meat, fish, eggs, and some vegetables; *fats* to provide energy, e.g. butter, lard, and suet; *carbohydrates* also provide energy and are found in bread, potatoes, sugar, and cereals, which form the bulk of the diet; *vitamins* (q.v.) required only in small quantities to assist the body to make full use of its F.; *minerals,* also needed in small quantities, incl. salt; calcium (bone building) from milk; and iron (blood formation) from meats and green vegetables. The energy value of F. is expressed in calories.

FOOD POISONING. Acute illness caused by poisonous food, or by micro-organisms contained in food, or their products. Some fish and mushrooms are naturally poisonous. Lead or arsenic are sometimes introduced into food during manufacture. Preservatives have caused illness. Milk, oysters, etc., may carry typhoid fever. Uncooked meat may carry harmful organisms. Pork may carry the round-worm Trichinella, and rye the parasitic fungus ergot. The most dangerous food poison is the bacillus which causes botulism (q.v.).

FOOT, Isaac (1880-1960). British liberal politician. A staunch Nonconformist, an ardent collector of Cromwelliana, and an effective fighter against privilege, he held office (Min. of Mines 1931-2) only briefly. Of his sons **Sir Dingle F.** (1905-78), once a Liberal, was Solicitor-General in the Labour govt 1964-7; and **Michael F.** (1913-) is a leading member of the parliamentary group associated with the left-wing weekly *Tribune.* He was Sec. of State for Employment 1974-6, became Lord Pres. of the Council and Leader of the House 1976-9, and succeeded Callaghan as leader of the Labour Party 1980-3. *See also* CARADON, LORD.

FOOT AND MOUTH DISEASE. A highly contagious eruptive fever caused by a virus that attacks cattle and other animals, causing the milk yield of cows to deteriorate, and animals with young to abort. Control is by destruction of affected animals, or, on the Continent, inoculation.

FOOTBALL (American). The first formal game was played between Princeton Univ. and Rutgers Univ., in 1869. The field, popularly known as the 'gridiron', is 109.72m (360ft) long by 48.80m (160ft), marked in lines at intervals of 4.57m (5yds), with goal-lines 9.15m (30ft) from each end. The goals and ball are those used for English Rugby. The 2 teams, each of 11 men, consist of 7 linemen or forwards (a 'centre', 2 'guards', 2 'tackles', 2 'ends'), a quarterback, 2 half-backs and a full-back. Each team's objective is to score the most points.

A touch-down scores 6 points and allows the scoring team to try for an extra point. This they can do when the ball is put into play again on the '2yd line', by getting the ball over the line again by running or passing or by kicking a goal. A field goal (3 points) is scored by either a drop kick or place kick. A touch-down behind their own line by the defending team is called a 'safety' and scores 2 points to the other side. Padded clothing and helmets are worn and substitutes are allowed for injured players. Forward passing is allowed. Only the man with the ball may be tackled and his team-mates may run with him to block opponents from tackling. The side 'in possession' must make at least 10yds in every 4 attempts or the ball goes to the opponents. The game is divided into four 15-minute periods. Four officials are required to handle a college game. There are 3 sets of rules - collegiate, professional, and high school; they are very complicated and change from year to year.

FOOTBALL (Association). 'Soccer' has developed from robust, rural football of the past. In 1863 the Football Association was formed to co-ordinate existing rules. It is popular in every country in the world with the exception of the USA.

The game is played between 2 teams each of 11 players, on a field 90-120m (100-130yds) long and 45-90m (50-100yds) wide with a spherical, inflated leather ball, circumference 0.71-0.68m (27-28in) and weight 396-453 grams (14-16 oz). The object of the game is to propel the ball with the feet or head through the opponents' goal, an area 7.32m (8yds) wide and 2.44m (8ft) high. A team is broadly divided into defence, a goal-keeper, 2 full-backs, and 3 half-backs; and attack, 5 forwards. The 5 backs now generally each mark an opposing forward. The field has a half-way line, marked with a centre circle, 2 penalty areas, and 2 goal areas. Corner kicks are taken from a 1m (1yd) segment, when the ball goes behind the goal-line off a defender; a ball kicked over the touch-lines is thrown in by one of the opposing side. The goal-keeper only is allowed to touch the ball with his hands, then only in his own penalty area and he must clear the ball after 4 paces. For major offences committed within defenders' penalty area, a penalty kick may be awarded by the referee to the attacking team. This is taken 11m (12yds) from the goal centre, with the goal-keeper only within the area. The game is started from the centre spot. It is played for 2 periods of 45 minutes each, the teams change ends at half-time. The game is controlled by a referee; 2 linesmen indicate when the ball is kicked into touch.

The Football Association Cup competition was inaugurated in 1872. The Football League was founded in 1888. The Fédération Internationale de Football Association (1904) organized in 1930 the first of the quadrennial competitions for the 'World Cup' or Jules Rimet trophy: winners 1930 Uruguay; 1934, 1938 Italy; 1950 Uruguay; 1954, 1974 W Germany; 1958, 1962, 1970 Brazil; 1966 England; 1978 Argentina: by their 3rd victory 1970 Brazil won the cup outright. The European Cup (1958) is contested annually.

FOOTBALL (Australian). Australia has its own code of football. It is played with 18 men a side, 2 reserves being allowed for each team. Each side is placed in 5 lines of 3 men each. Three men follow the ball all the time. The 2 goal-posts, at each end, are 6m high and 6.4m apart. On either side are 2 smaller posts. The football is oval, and weighs a little more than a Rugby ball. A goal (6 points) is scored when the ball is kicked between the goalposts, if it is not touched on the way. If the ball passes between a goal-post and one of the smaller posts, or hits a post, the score is a 'behind', or one point. There are no scrums, line-outs, or off-side rules. A player must get rid of the ball as soon as he starts to run, by kicking, punching or bouncing it every 10m. No tackling is allowed as in Rugby.

The Code originated on the Australian goldfields in the '50s of last century.

FOOTBALL (Rugby). 'Rugger' originated at Rugby school in 1823. The game takes place between 2 teams of 15 players a side, on a playing field not to exceed 100m by 69m with areas behind each goal terminated by a dead-ball line. The goal is 5.6m wide and the cross-bar 3.0m from

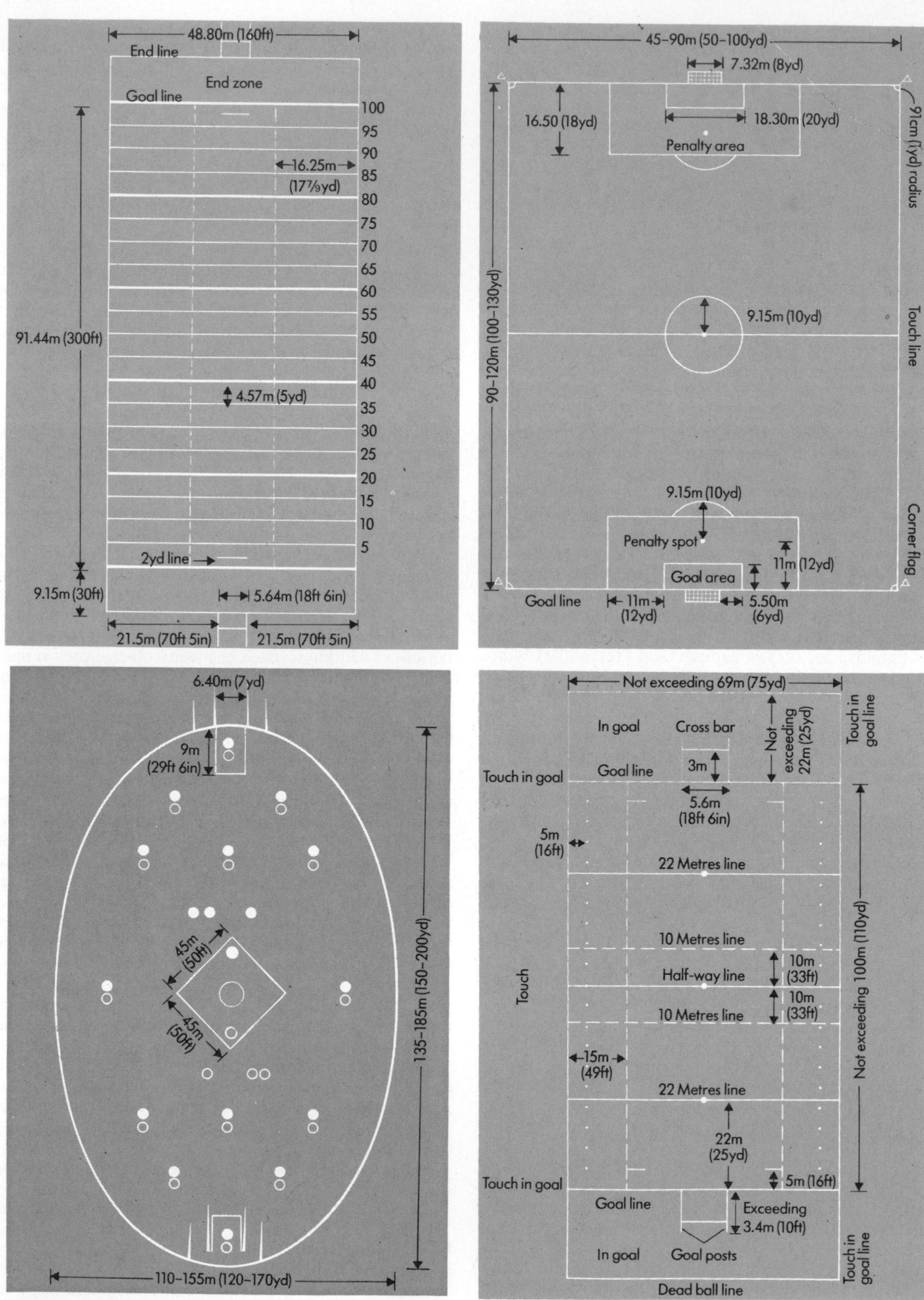

FOOTBALL. American football (upper left), Association football (upper right), Australian football (lower left) and Rugby.

FOOTBALL. Probably the world's most coveted trophy, the World Cup. *Photo: Camera Press.*

the ground, with goal-posts extending beyond this height. The object is to score goals or tries with an oval leather ball. A try is made by touching down the ball by hand over the opposing side's goal-line. A try is converted into a goal if a member of the scoring team kicks the ball through the goal-posts at any height above the cross-bar. The kick may be taken from any point on a line parallel to the touch-lines, passing through the point where the try was scored. Scoring is based on points, 4 for a try, 6 for a try converted into a goal, 3 for a drop goal, and 3 for a penalty or free kick.

The scrummage, a feature of Rugger, is used to re-start the game after certain infringements of the laws. The 15 players on each side usually comprise 8 forwards, 2 half-backs, 4 three-quarter backs and 1 full-back. In all matches a referee and 2 touch-judges must be appointed or mutually agreed upon.

The Rugby Union, governing amateur Rugby, was formed in 1871. The Rugby League was founded in 1895 and plays under Northern Union rules. In this game there are only 13 players a side.

FORAMINI'FERA. Single-celled marine animals of the Protozoa enclosed by a thin shell.

FORCE. In mechanics F. is that which tends to change the state of rest or uniform motion of a body in a straight line and is measured by the product of its mass (m) and its acceleration (a). F = ma. *See* NEWTON, ISAAC.

FORCES, Natural. At subatomic level there are only 4 fundamental interactions underlying the workings of the Universe, and physicists have tried to reduce these to a single unified force. They are 1) electromagnetism, 2) gravity, 3) the strong nuclear force, the most powerful in nature, since it binds the atomic nucleus together against the intense disruptive electric repulsion of its constituent charged protons, and 4) the weak nuclear force, which operates in some forms of radioactive decay within the atomic nucleus. In 1979 Nobel prizewinners Steven Weinberg, Sheldon Glashow (both USA) and Abdus Salam (Pakistan) demonstrated the underlying unity of 1 and 4. They have also postulated that if protons within the atomic nucleus, which were formerly thought to be immutable could be shown to decay into lighter subatomic fragments, then this would establish a relationship between 1, 4 and 3. In 1979 an artificial pool was being excavated in a salt mine near Cleveland, USA, ready to be filled with purified water in order that, in this controlled environment, a detector system might be able to trace any wakes of light left by particles leaving such disinegrating protons. If such disintegration is detected it will end the present belief in the permanence of matter.

FORD, Ford Madox (1873-1939). English writer, *né* Ford Madox Hueffer - he changed his name in 1919 - he was a grandson of Ford Madox Brown (q.v.). He was founder-editor of the *English Review* (1908), to which Hardy, D. H. Lawrence, and Conrad contributed. His verse is forgotten, but his novels incl. the historical trilogy *The Fifth Queen, Privy Seal* and the *Fifth Queen Crowned* (1906-8), dealing with Catherine Howard, and the war tetralogy *Parade's End* (*Some Do Not, No More Parades, A Man Could Stand Up* and *Last Post,* 1924-8), with its hero Christopher Tietjens.

FORD, Gerald R(udolph) (1913-). 38th President of the USA. He was b. in Omaha, Nebraska, as Leslie King, but following the divorce of his parents when he was two years old, he took the name of his stepfather, eminent in the Republican Party. An exceptional footballer at college, he turned down offers to become professional, and after working his way through Michigan Univ., went on the Yale Law School. After service in the navy in the S.W.W., he resumed law practice, was elected to the House of Representatives as a Republican in 1948, and became in 1964 House minority leader. On Spiro Agnew's resignation in 1973, he was nominated to the vice-presidency by Nixon in 1973, and in 1974 succeeded Nixon himself in the presidency, the first president to serve without being chosen in a national election. His decisions to pardon his predecessor and to amnesty Vietnam draft dodgers, were controversial. He was narrowly defeated by Carter in 1976.

FORD, Henry (1863-1947). American motor-car manufacturer. B. in Michigan, he built his first car in 1893 and 10 yrs later founded the F. Motor Co. His model T (1908-27) was the first to be constructed by purely mass-production methods, and 15,000,000 of these historic cars were made. A pacifist, he visited Europe 1915-16 in an attempt to end the war, and in 1936 he founded with his son **Edsel B. Ford** (1893-1943) the philanthropic Ford Foundation. *See* DEARBORN.

FORD, John (1586-1640). English poet and dramatist. B. in Devon, he was noted for an imaginative and dramatic study of incest between brother and sister in *'Tis Pity She's a Whore* (1633). The best of his other pieces are *The*

FORD. Gerald Ford, the first American president ever to serve without being chosen by the American people in a national election, either as president or vice-president. *Photo: USIS.*

FOREIGN LEGION. On parade before the monument to their dead at Sidi bel-Abbès in Algeria, their famous headquarters until 1962. *Photo: Fleet Street News.*

Broken Heart (1633) and the chronicle play *Perkin Warbeck* (1634).

FORD, John (1895-1973). Irish-American film director. Active since the silent days, he was one of the original creators of the 'western'; *Stagecoach* being a masterpiece of the genre. His other films incl. *The Informer, Grapes of Wrath. Two Rode Together,* and he was co-director of the first cinerama story film *How the West was Won.*

FOREIGN LEGION (*Légion Étrangère*). Popular name of the French *régiments étrangers,* formed in 1835. Enlisted men are of any nationality (about half are now French), but practically all the officers are French. Aubagne, nr Marseilles is its reception HQ; its main base is on Corsica.

FOREIGN RELATIONS. Formal relations between one sovereign state and another. In the UK foreign affairs were dealt with, together with home affairs, by the King's principal secretary in medieval times, an office split into two under Henry VIII. While there were two principal secs. of state - for the Northern and Southern Depts - Irish and colonial affairs and relations with the Mediterranean countries, were the responsibility of the latter, and the rest of Europe of the former. In 1782, however, the Southern Dept. became the Home Office and the Northern Dept the Foreign Office, and colonial affairs demonstrated their increased importance by becoming the responsibility of separate depts - Colonial Office 1854, India Office 1858, Dominions Office 1925, Commonwealth Office 1947. However, by 1968, so many members of the Commonwealth had graduated to independent nationhood that the Foreign Office was re-named the Foreign and Commonwealth Office, the staffs being merged in the new HM Diplomatic Service. *See also* CIVIL SERVICE.

In the USA, F.R. are the concern of the State Dept (1789). Thomas Jefferson, then Min. to France, was appointed Sec. of State by Washington in 1789 and took office in 1790. The Sec. of State is charged, under the direction of the President, 'with the duties appertaining to correspondence with the public ministers and the consuls of the United States, and with representatives of foreign powers accredited to the United States, and to negotiations of whatever character relating to the foreign affairs of the United States'.

Most other countries of the world have a Min. of Foreign Affairs who is a member of the cabinet (or equivalent body).

Up to the 18th cent. there was no specialized diplomatic body in any European country. After 1818 diplomatic agents were divided into: ambassadors, papal legates, and nuncios; envoys extraordinary and ministers plenipotentiary and other ministers accredited to the head of state; ministers resident; *chargés d'affaires* who may deputize for an ambassador or minister, or be themselves the representative accredited to a minor country. Heads of diplomatic missions are assisted by counsellors, secretaries, and attachés (military, labour, cultural, press, etc.). After the S.W.W. there was a great increase, partly owing to newly-created states, in the number of countries represented by diplomats of ambassadorial rank, rather than by a minister, envoy or *chargé d'affaires.* Consuls are state agents with commercial and political responsibilities in foreign towns, but are not travel agents.

Instantaneous communications systems have in recent years lessened the importance of the career diplomat as the 'man on the spot'. One less happy development in both E and W was the use of the professionally trained spy in the diplomatic ranks.

FORELAND, North and **South.** Headlands on the Kent coast, England. N.F., with one lighthouse, lies 4 km (2.5m) E of Margate; S.F., with two, lies 4.8km (3m) NE of Dover.

FOREST, Lee de (1873–1961). American inventor. B. in Iowa, and ed. at Yale and Chicago univs., he perfected the audion tube and contributed to the development of radio, radar, and television.

FORESTER, Cecil Scott (1899–1966). British author. His dual reputation rests on the varied excellence of such books as *Payment Deferred* (1926), a subtle crime novel; *Brown on Resolution* (1938), a study of patriotism; *The African Queen* (1938); and *The Earthly Paradise* (1940), dealing with Columbus: and on his series of the Napoleonic era covering the career - from midshipman to admiral - of the redoubtable Horatio Hornblower.

FOREST HILLS. Residential district on Long Island, New York City, USA, noted for tournaments at its West Side Tennis Club.

FORESTRY. The science of forest management. In the past 3 cents. forest areas throughout the world have been drastically reduced, with consequent soil erosion and adverse modification of the climate, as in the Sahel region, and potential danger to the atmosphere we breathe, as with the increasing destruction of the Amazonian forest. Too often the practice of F. has in effect reduced the total yield of a natural forest, having been confined to the planting of a single species, such as one of the rapid-growing conifers providing 'softwood' for paper pulp and construction timber, for which world demand is greatest. In Britain there has been much criticism of the neglect of native, more slow-growing 'hardwoods', to the detriment of the landscape and elimination of the varied wildlife which does not survive in the new plantations. The best modern F. practice aims at multi-purpose cropping, preserving the forest as an ecological entity, and allowing the preservation of varied plant species, animal life, and human crafts dependent on them. A tropical forest may thus yield medicinal plants, oils (cedar, juniper, cinnamon, sandalwood), spices, gums, resins (pines, and others used in inks, lacquers, linoleum, etc.), tanning and dyeing materials, forage for animals, beverages, insect and rodent poisons, green manure, rubber, and animal products (feathers, hides, honey, ivory and musk).

FORFARSHIRE. Name from 16th cent. until 1928 of ANGUS, absorbed in Tayside in 1975.

FORGERY. The falsification of any written document or object, such as a painting or archaeological item.

FORGET-ME-NOT or **scorpion grass.** Common wild flower belonging to the Boraginaceae family (genus *Myosotis*) found in Europe, N America, N Asia, and Australia. Most species have blue flowers.

FORLI (forlē'). City and market centre in Emilia-Romagna region, Italy, S of Ravenna. It has a cathedral, old churches, and a citadel. Felt, majolica, paper are made. Pop. (1971) 105,000.

FORMALDEHYDE. A gas, H_2CO at ordinary temperatures, condensing at -21°C. It has a powerful penetrating smell and burning taste. In aqueous solution it is used as a biological preservative, and is an important base material for chemicals used in the construction industry.

FORMBY, George (1904–61). English comedian. Following the death in 1921 of his father George F. sen., one of music-hall's famed comedians, he appeared under a pseudonym for 18 months, until he had proved his worth. On stage and screen he estab. a reputation as the not-so-gormless Lancashire lad, and sang such songs as 'Mr Wu' and 'Cleaning Windows', accompanying himself on the ukelele.

FORMENTOR, Cape. Northern extremity of Majorca in the Balearic Is., noted for its majestic cliffs and a favoured holiday location.

FORMIC ACID (CH_2O_2). One of the fatty acids, a colourless, slightly fuming liquid that melts at 8°C and boils at 101°C. Specific gravity 1.22. It occurs in stinging ants, nettles, sweat, and pine needles.

FORMŌ'SA. *See* TAIWAN.

FORREST, John, 1st baron (1847–1918). Australian explorer. B. in Western Australia, he is best-known for his dual crossing of the state W to E in 1870, when he went along the southern coast route of Eyre and in 1874 when he crossed much further N, exploring the Musgrave Ranges. He was the first premier of the state in 1890–1901.

FORRESTAL, James Vincent (1892–1949). American Democratic statesman. As sec. of the Navy from 1944, he visited the war zones, accompanying the assault troops at Iwo Jima. He was the first Sec. of the Dept of National Defense (1947–9), a post created to unify the 3 services at the end of the S.W.W.

FORSSMANN, Werner (1904–79). W German heart specialist. In 1929 he originated by experiment on himself the technique of cardiac catheterization, passing a thin tube from an arm artery up into the heart itself and then having X-ray photographs taken. In 1956 he was awarded a joint Nobel prize with A. F. Cournand and D. W. Richards of America.

FORSTER, Edward Morgan (1879–1970). British author. B. in London and ed. at King's Coll. Cambridge, he pub. his first novel *Where Angels Fear to Tread* in 1905. He undermines the superficial situations of his plots with unexpected insights in *The Longest Journey* (1907), *A Room with a View* (1908), and *Howard's End* (1910). *A Passage to India* (1924), his most famous book, explores the relationship between English and Indians through the incident of a possibly non-existent assault on a stolid Englishwoman by the charming Dr Aziz. Forster was concerned with the interplay of personality and the contrast between the conventional and the instinctive. His critical work incl. *Aspects of the Novel* (1927). Awarded OM 1969.

FORSTER, William Edward (1818–86). British reformer. He was a Bradford woollen manufacturer, who entered parliament in 1861 as a Liberal. In Gladstone's government of 1868–74 he was Vice-President of the Council, and secured the passing of the Education Act (1870) and the Ballot Act (1872). He was Chief Secretary for Ireland, 1880–2.

FORSYTH (forsīth'), **Frederick** (1938–). British novelist. Ed. at Tonbridge, he was a Reuters correspondent, and BBC radio and television reporter before making his name with *The Day of the Jackal* (1970), dealing with an attempted assassination of de Gaulle; later novels were *The Odessa File* (1972), *The Dogs of War* (1974), and *The Devil's Alternative* (1979).

FORSYTHIA (forsī'thia). Flowering shrub, allied to the olive (Oleaceae family); the bright yellow flowers appear in spring before the leaves.

FORTALEZA (fortahlā'zah). Port in NE Brazil, with textile, flour-milling and sugar-refining industries. Pop. (1975) 1,110,000.

FORT DE FRANCE (for de froṅs). Cap., chief commercial centre, and port of the French West Indian island of Martinique. Pop. (1974) 99,000.

FORTH. River in SE Scotland, with its headstreams rising on the NE slopes of Ben Lomond, which flows *c.* 72km (45m) to Kincardine where the *Firth of Forth* begins; the Firth is *c.* 80km (50m) long and *c.* 26km (16m) wide where it joins the North Sea. At Queensferry nr Edinburgh are the Forth rail (1890) and road (1964) bridges. The *Forth and Clyde Canal* (1768-90) across the lowlands of Scotland links the Firth with the r. Clyde, Grangemouth to Bowling (53km/33m). A rich coalfield was located beneath the Firth of F. in 1976.

FORT KNOX. US army post and gold depository in Kentucky, established 1917 as a training camp.

FORT LAMY. *See* N'DJAMENA.

FORT SUMTER. Fort in Charleston harbour, S Carolina, 6.5km (4m) SE of Charleston, where the first shots of the Civil War were fired on 12 April 1861, after its commander had refused the call to surrender made by the Confederate General Beauregard.

FORTŪ'NA. In Roman mythology, the goddess of chance and good fortune.

FORT WAYNE. City at the confluence of the St Joseph, St Mary's and Maumee rivers, Indiana, USA. It was originally a French settlement, *c.* 1680, but a fort was built on the site against the Indians in 1794 by Gen. Anthony Wayne (1745-96), hero of a surprise attack on a British force at Stony Point, NY, in 1779, which earned him the nickname 'Mad Anthony'. It was not till 1815 that a safe permanent civilian settlement was estab. The chief industries are electrical equipment, incl. radio and television, and agricultural machinery. Pop. met. area (1974) 377,900.

FORT WORTH. City of Texas, USA; it is one of the great grain, petroleum, and railway centres of the southern USA. Pop. (1970) 757,105.

FORTY-FIVE, The. Name given to the Jacobite rebellion of 1745, led by Prince Charles Edward. With his army of Highlanders 'Prince Charlie' occupied Edinburgh and advanced into England as far as Derby, but then turned back. The rising was crushed by the duke of Cumberland at Culloden in 1746.

FOSSIL (Lat., *fossilis,* dug up). Organic remains which have been preserved in rocks; the majority are of marine origin or lived in swamps, lakes, etc. Fs. may be formed by refrigeration, e.g. the N Siberian mammoths; the preservation merely of the skeleton; carbonization, e.g. wood and leaves converted into coal; the formation of a mould or cast round the organism; petrification, etc. Fs. provide evidence of the condition of the Earth at successive epochs, and of the life-history of the world.

FOS-SUR-MER. *See* MARSEILLE.

FOSTER, Stephen Collins (1826-64). American songwriter, author of 'The Old Folks at Home', 'My Old Kentucky Home', etc.

FOUCAULT (fookoh'), **Jean Bernard Léon** (1819-68). French physicist. He produced in 1851 the pendulum named after him, which demonstrates the rotation of the Earth on its axis, and was the inventor of the gyroscope.

FOUCHÉ (foosheh'), **Joseph,** duke of Otranto (1759-1820). French statesman. B. near Nantes, he was elected to the National Convention, and organized the conspiracy which overthrew Robespierre. Napoleon employed him as Police Minister.

FOU-LIANG. *see* JINGDEZHEN.

FOUNTAINS ABBEY. Cistercian abbey situated 13km (8m) N of Harrogate, in N Yorks, England. It was founded *c.* 1132, and suppressed in 1540. The ruins, set in beautiful park, meadows and woodland, have been beautifully preserved.

FOUR FREEDOMS. President Roosevelt in his address to Congress on Jan. 6, 1941, defined the 'four essential human freedoms' as freedom of speech and expression, freedom of every person to worship God in his own way, freedom from want, and freedom from fear.

FOURIER (fooryeh'), **François Charles Marie** (1772-1837). French Socialist. B. at Besançon, he spent most of his life as a clerk, and d. at Paris. In his *Le nouveau monde industriel* (1829-30), he advocated that society should be organized in units of *c.* 1,800 people living and working in co-operation.

FOURTEEN POINTS. The terms proposed by President Wilson of the USA in his address to Congress on 8 Jan., 1918, as a basis for the settlement of the F.W.W. that was shortly about to reach its climax. They included: open diplomacy; freedom of the seas; removal of economic barriers; international disarmament; adjustment of colonial claims; German evacuation of Russian, Belgian, French, and Balkan territories; the restoration of Alsace-Lorraine to France; autonomy for the Austro-Hungarian peoples and those under Turkish rule; an independent Poland; and a general association of nations. Many of the 'points' were embodied in the peace treaties following the war.

FOURTH (of July). Independence Day in USA; the anniversary of the day in 1776 when the Declaration of Independence was adopted by the Continental Congress.

FOURTH ESTATE. Name applied to the Press. The first to do so was Burke. The **Fourth Republic** was the French regime of 3 June 1944 to 4 Oct. 1958.

FOVEAUX (fov'ō) **Strait.** Strait between the extreme S of South Island, NZ, and Stewart Island. Fishing is carried on and there is a considerable oyster catch.

FOWEY (foi). English port and holiday resort in Cornwall nr the mouth of the Fowey estuary. It is an outlet for the Cornish clay mining industry. Pop. (1971) 2,500.

FOWLER, Henry Watson (1858-1933) and **Francis George** (1870-1918). British scholars, authors of a number of English dictionaries: *Modern English Usage* (1926), the work of the elder brother, rev. by Sir Ernest Gowers (1880-1966) in 1965, provides a widely accepted standard.

FOWLES, John (1926-). English author. Ed. at Bedford School and New Coll., Oxford, he has pub. complex and strange novels, such as *The Collector* (1963), which was filmed; *The Aristos* (1965), and *The French Lieutenant's Woman* (1969).

FOX, Charles James (1749-1806). English Whig statesman. The son of the 1st baron Holland, he entered parliament in 1769 as a supporter of the court, but in 1774 went over to the opposition. In 1782 he became Sec. of State in Rockingham's govt, but resigned when Shelburne succeeded Rockingham. He allied with North in 1783 to overthrow Shelburne, and formed a coalition ministry. When the Lords threw out F.'s bill to reform the govt of India, George III dismissed the ministry, and in their place installed Pitt.

F. now became leader of the opposition, although co-operating with Pitt in the impeachment of Hastings, etc. He welcomed the French Revolution, but the 'Old Whigs' deserted to the govt in 1792, leaving F. and a small group of 'New Whigs' to oppose Pitt's war of intervention and his persecution of the reformers. On Pitt's death in 1806 a ministry was formed with F. as For. Sec., which at F.'s insistence abolished the slave trade. He opened peace negotiations with France, but d. before their completion, and was buried in Westminster Abbey.

FOX, George (1624-91). Founder of the Society of Friends. B. in Leics, he was apprenticed to a shoemaker, but in 1647 became a travelling preacher. In 1650 he was imprisoned for blasphemy at Derby, where the name of 'Quakers' was first applied to him and his followers, and altogether spent 6 years in prison. He later went on missionary journeys to the W Indies, America, Germany, and Holland. His *Journal* appeared in 1694.

FOX. A dog-like carnivorous mammal; fem. vixen. *Vulpes vulpes*, the common European red fox, is reddish-brown, changing to white underneath, with a white-tipped tail. In Britain it is hunted as a sport. Silver or black F. is farmed for its pelt.

FOXE, John (1516-87). English Protestant propagandist. B. at Boston, he became a canon of Salisbury in 1563. His *Book of Martyrs* (1563), by its lurid descriptions of the Marian persecutions, helped to make hatred of popery a force in English life.

FOXGLOVE. Genus of flowering plants (*Digitalis*) of the family Scrophulariaceae found in Europe, W Asia, and the Canaries; they bear showy spikes of bell-like flowers, up to 1.5m (5ft) high. The wild species produce purple to reddish flowers.

FOXHOUND. Small hound specially trained for fox-hunting. It is a combination of the old southern hound, with its keen nose, and the speedy greyhound, and has been bred in England for over 300 years.

FOX-HUNTING. As a recognized sport, this dates from the last half of the 17th cent. In the 18th cent. it was practised by noblemen and country squires, but at the beginning of the 19th cent. it developed into a national pastime. Among the most famous 'hunts' are the Quorn, Pytchley, Belvoir, and Cottesmore. There is a recognized F.-H. season from the first Monday in November until the following April. F.-H. was introduced to the US by early settlers from England, and continues in the south and middle-eastern regions.

FOX-TERRIER. A small, smooth- or rough-haired dog, originally used to run with the hounds but now kept mainly as a house dog.

FOX-TROT. Modern ballroom dance of transatlantic origin that made its appearance just prior to the F.W.W. Its name derives from the alternately rapid and slow movements of the fox.

FOYLE. Sea-lough on the N coast of Ireland, traversed by the frontier of N Ireland and the Irish Republic.

FRACTIONATION. *See* PLANT.

FRACTIONS. In mathematics a fraction is a number which indicates one or more equal parts of a whole. The usual way of denoting this is to place below a horizontal line the number of equal parts into which the unit is divided, and above the line the number of these parts actually comprising the fraction, thus $\frac{3}{4}$. Such fractions are called *vulgar Fs.* A *proper F.* is one in which the numerator is less than the denominator; an *improper F.* is one in which the numerator is greater than the denominator, e.g. $\frac{3}{2}$. An improper F. can therefore be expressed as a mixed number, e.g. $1\frac{1}{2}$.

A *decimal F.* is one in which the F. is expressed by figures written to the right of the units figure after a dot or point (the decimal point). The digits on the right of the decimal point indicate the numerators of vulgar Fs. whose denominators are 10, 100 . . .

FRA DIAVOLO (frah dyah'-). Name by which the Italian brigand Michele Pezza (1771-1806) was known. A renegade monk, he led a gang in the mountains of Calabria for many years, but was eventually executed at Naples. He has no link with Auber's opera.

FRAGONARD (frahgonahr'), **Jean Honoré** (1732-1806). French artist. He studied under Boucher in Paris, and is famous chiefly for his light-hearted *rococo* paintings of love in romantic settings.

FRAMPTON, Sir George James (1860-1928). British sculptor. His most famous works are 'Peter Pan' in Kensington Gdns. and the Nurse Cavell memorial nr St Martin's, London.

FRANC. French coin, so named from *Francorum Rex* (king of the Franks) that was inscribed thereon about 1360 when it was a gold coin. It is divided into 100 centimes. The franc CFA is the monetary unit of the French Community in Africa; CFP in the Pacific. The M.U. of Belgium, Luxembourg, and Switzerland is also called a franc.

FRANCE (froṅs), **Anatole.** Pseudonym of the French writer Jacques Anatole Thibault (1844-1924). B. in Paris, he pub. a critical study of Alfred de Vigny (1868), which was followed by several vols. of poetry and short stories. His earliest novel was *Le Crime de Sylvestre Bonnard* (1881): later books include *Thaïs* (1890), *Crainquebille* (1905), the satiric *L'île des Pingouins* (1908), and *La révolte des Anges* (1914), and the autobiographical series beginning with *Le Livre de mon Ami* (1885). He was elected to the French Academy in 1896, and in 1921 was awarded a Nobel prize for literature.

FRANCE. Republic of western Europe, bordering on Spain in the SW, Italy, Switzerland, and Germany in the E, Belgium and Luxembourg in the NE, and facing the Mediterranean, Atlantic Ocean, and English Channel on the S, W, and N respectively. Area (incl. Corsica) 551,553 sq.km (212,960 sq.m); pop. (1978) 53,200,000. For other terrs. associated with France, both past and present, *see* FRENCH COMMUNITY.

PHYSICAL FEATURES. F. may be roughly divided into 2 parts: to the N. of a line from Bordeaux to Rheims, with a bay in the SW to include the basin of Aquitaine, are lowlands, while to the S are highlands. The core of the mountainous area is the *massif central.* Westward, the mountains of Auvergne merge into the plateau of the Limousin and the hills of Quercy. To the E the Auvergne merge into the Cevennes. The Pyrenees, forming a natural boundary between France and Spain, stretch from the Mediterranean to the Atlantic. The Alps, with their foot-hills and subsidiary ranges, cover most of F's. surface to the E of the Rhône. The highlands of the S are cut through by the valleys of the Rhône and the Aude. N of the Rhône, the Jura mts. curve round to the Rhine at Basle. W of the Rhine are the Vosges, merging into the Langres plateau in the N. The Ardennes farther N abut on the low-lying country stretching to the North Sea.

With the exception of Sète, there is no natural harbour between the Spanish frontier on the Mediterranean and the Rhône estuary. Farther E only Marseille and Toulon are of importance. The principal port of SW France is

Regions and Departments of France

	Area in sq. km.	Population (1975)
Alsace		
Bas-Rhin *Strasbourg;* Haut-Rhin *Colmar*	8,324	1,517,330
Aquitaine		
Dordogne *Périgueux;* Gironde *Bordeaux;* Landes *Mont-de-Marsan;* Lot-et-Garonne *Agen;* Pyrénées-Atlantiques *Pau*	42,411	2,550,340
Auvergne		
Allier *Moulins;* Cantal *Aurillac;* Haute-Loire *Le Puy;* Puy-de-Dôme *Clermont-Ferrand*	26,178	1,330,479
Bourgogne		
Côte-d'Or *Dijon;* Nièvre *Nevers;* Saône-et-Loire *Mâcon;* Yonne *Auxerre*	31,763	1,570,943
Bretagne		
Côtes-du-Nord *St. Brieuc;* Finistère *Quimper;* Ille-et-Vilaine *Rennes;* Morbihan *Vannes*	28,331	22,595,431
Centre		
Cher *Bourges;* Eure-et-Loir *Chartres;* Indre *Châteauroux;* Indre-et-Loire *Tours;* Loir-et-Cher *Blois;* Loiret *Orléans*	39,542	2,1252,500
Champagne-Ardennes		
Ardennes *Charleville-Mézières;* Aube *Troyes;* Marne *Châlons-sur-Marne;* Haute-Marne *Chaumont*	25,741	1,336,832
Corsica		
Haute Corse *Bastia;* Corse du Sud *Ajaccio*	8,772	289,842
Franche-Comté		
Doubs *Besançon;* Jura *Lons-le-Saunier;* Haute Saône *Vesoul;* Terre de Belfort *Belfort*	16,298	1,060,317
Île de France		
Essonne *Évry;* Val-de-Marne *Créteil;* Val d'Oise *Cergy-Pontoise;* Ville de Paris, Seine-et-Marne *Melun;* Hauts-de-Seine *Nanterre;* Seine-Saint-Denis *Bobigny;* Yvelines *Versailles*	12,022	9,878,524
Languedoc-Roussillon		
Aude *Carcassonne;* Gard *Nîmes;* Hérault *Montpellier;* Lozère *Mende;* Pyrénées-Orientales *Perpignan*	27,771	1,789,474
Limousin		
Corrèze *Tulle;* Creuse Guéret; Haute-Vienne *Limoges*	17,049	738,726
Lorraine		
Meurthe-et-Moselle *Nancy;* Meuse *Bar-le-Duc;* Moselle *Metz;* Vosges *Épinal*	23,677	2,330,821
Midi-Pyrénées		
Ariège *Foix;* Aveyron *Rodez;* Haute-Garonne *Toulouse;* Gers *Auch;* Lot *Cahors;* Hautes-Pyrénées *Tarbes;* Tarn *Albi;* Tarn-et-Garonne *Montauban*	45,603	2,268,245
Nord—Pas-de-Calais		
Nord *Lille;* Pas-de-Calais *Arras*	12,526	3,913,773
Basse-Normandie		
Calvados *Caen;* Manche *St. Lô;* Orne *Alençon*	18,249	1,306,152
Haute-Normandie		
Eure *Evreux;* Seine-Maritime *Rouen*	12,379	1,595,695
Pays de la Loire		
Loire Atlantique *Nantes;* Maine-et-Loire *Angers;* Mayenne *Laval;* Sarthe *Le Mans;* Vendée *La Roche-sur-Yon*	32,671	2,767,163
Picardie		
Aisne *Laon;* Oise *Beauvais;* Somme *Amiens*	19,592	1,678,644
Poitou-Charentes		
Charente *Angoulême;* Charente-Maritime *La Rochelle;* Deux-Sèvres *Niort;* Vienne *Poitiers*	26,302	1,528,118
Provence-Côte d'Azur		
Alpes-de-Haute-Provence *Digne;* Hautes-Alpes *Gap;* Alpes-Maritimes *Nice;* Bouches-du-Rhône *Marseille;* Var *Draguignan* Vaucluse *Avignon*	31,778	3,675,730
Rhône-Alpes		
Ain *Bourg-en-Bresse;* Ardèche *Privas;* Drôme *Valence;* Isère *Grenoble;* Loire *St. Étienne;* Rhône *Lyon;* Savoie *Chambéry;* Haute-Savoie *Annecy*	44,624	4,780,723
	551,553	52,655,802

[Capitals of depts. italicized.]

FRANCESCA. The ideal city was a concept that fascinated Renaissance Man. Piero della Francesca was no exception and his balanced, classical constructions are harmoniously attractive. *Photo: Mansell Collection.*

Bordeaux on the Garonne, 96km (60m) from the sea. The shores of Brittany afford some good natural harbours, including Lorient and Brest. From Normandy, where Cherbourg is of great importance, to the Belgian frontier, most of the harbours are either in estuaries or are man-made. Of the 4 river systems, the Rhône rises in the Swiss Alps; and the Garonne, although the r. Garonne itself rises in the Pyrenees, draws much of its waters from the massif central, whence the Loire and Seine systems also rise.

AGRICULTURE. About one-third of the crops raised in F. are cereals, of which wheat is the most important, followed by oats, barley, and rye. Sugar beet is grown in the NW. Among the other crops are flax, hemp, forage crops, hops, tobacco, colza, potatoes, fruits, of which the grape is most important: some 12,000 sq.km (4,500 sq.m) are under the vine and F. has the reputation of producing the world's finest wines. The principal wine-producing areas are the S with Hérault dept as a centre; the Bordeaux district; Touraine and Anjou; the Rhône valley; Burgundy; Champagne; Alsace; and the Charentes (brandy). Silk is produced in 15 depts. Market-gardening and the growing of early vegetables are widespread. The richest pastoral areas are Normandy, Perche, and Flanders. Forestry and fishing are important. F. is self-sufficing in foodstuffs.

INDUSTRY. Minerals incl. coal in the NE, the richest seams being in the Nancy and Longwy-Briey areas; iron and bauxite; oil from the Parentis field in the Landes; natural gas in the Lacq area in the Pyrenean foothills; and uranium near Autun, Clermont-Ferrand, Limoges and Nantes. Industry was formerly concentrated almost entirely in the NE Paris and Rhône valley areas, but is now being developed at regional centres. Declining coal and gas reserves, and the limitations of hydroelectric resources have led to concentration from 1969 on nuclear power. The chief manufactures are motor vehicles, radio and television sets, chemicals, textiles and processed foods. France is now primarily an industrial country with a strong agriculture, her economic expansion having been achieved under a series of five-year 'Monnet plans' from 1945, so-called after the director of the planning office, Jean Monnet (q.v.).

GOVERNMENT. Under the constitution of 1958, as amended 1962, the 5th Republic has a pres. directly elected by universal suffrage, a National Assembly and a Senate which incl. overseas representatives. The 96 depts are organized into 22 regions which, together with the overseas regions of Martinique, Réunion, and French Guiana, have regional councils. These consist of the Nat. Assembly and Senate members for the region plus representatives of the appropriate departmental *conseils généraux*, and of the economic and social advisory councils which are nominated by local professional, business and trade union organizations.

FRANCE. The essence of rural France, an idyllic scene on 'La route des lacs' in the Landes. *Photo: Courtesy of the French Government Tourist Office*

POPULATION. With a basis of 'Alpine' and 'Mediterranean', the French show representatives of every European physical type. The majority of the pop. is Roman Catholic. Immigration, Moslems from Algeria and Portuguese, was halted in 1974.

The largest towns are Paris, the cap., Lyon, Marseille, Lille, Bordeaux, Toulouse, Nantes, Nice, Rouen, Toulon, Strasbourg, Grenoble, St Etienne, and Lens. M.U.: franc. *See* FRENCH COMMUNITY, HISTORY, LANGUAGE, LITERATURE, etc.

FRANCESCA (frañhches'kah), **Piero della** (*c.* 1418–92). Italian artist. A member of the Umbrian school, he was one of the earliest painters in oils. His masterpiece is the series of frescoes of the Legend of the True Cross in the church of San Francesco, Arezzo. Described as the greatest geometrician of his day, he has since been called the first Cubist because of the geometrical construction of his work.

FRANCHE-COMTÉ (fronsh-kontā'). Region of France, comprising the depts of Jura, Doubs, Haute-Saône and Belfort. The traditional caps. of the 'countship' were Dôle and Besançon: it was a bone of contention among France, Burgundy, Austria and Spain from the 9th cent. until it finally passed to France as a prov. under the Treaty of Nijmwegen in 1678. In the mountainous Jura farming and forestry are carried on, with industries such as engineering and plastics elsewhere.

FRANCIS II (1768-1835). Holy Roman Emperor. He succeeded his father, Leopold II, in 1792. During his reign Austria was 5 times involved in war with France, in 1792-7, 1798-1801, 1805, 1809, and 1813-14. He assumed the title of emperor of Austria in 1804, and abandoned that of Holy Roman Emperor in 1806.

FRANCIS I (1494-1547). King of France. He succeeded his cousin Louis XII, and from 1519 European politics turned on the rivalry between him and Charles V, which led to war in 1521-9, 1536-8, and 1542-4. In 1525 F. was defeated and captured at Pavia, and released only on signing a humiliating treaty. At home F. developed absolute monarchy.

FRANCIS I. Unstable and vacillating as a ruler, he is remembered for the brilliance of the artists and writers of his court. *Photo: Courtesy of the Trustees of the Wallace Collection.*

FRANCIS II (1544-60). King of France. He m. Mary, Queen of Scots, in 1558, and succeeded his father, Henry II, in 1559. He was completely under the influence of his mother, Catherine de' Medici.

FRANCISCANS, Friars Minor, or **Grey Friars.** RC order of friars founded in 1209 by Francis of Assisi (q.v.). Sub-divisions were the strict Observants, the Conventuals, who were allowed to own property corporately, and the Capuchins. The F. were noted for their preaching and ministrations amongst the poor, and included such scholars as Roger Bacon. There was also a Second Order of nuns known as Poor Clares after St Clare (q.v.). The Third Order, or Tertiaries, consisted of lay men and women who adopted a modified form of the Franciscan régime, without abandoning business and family life.

FRANCIS FERDINAND (1863-1914). Archduke of Austria. He became heir to his uncle, the Emperor Francis Joseph, in 1889. While visiting Sarajevo on June 28, 1914, he and his wife were assassinated by Serb nationalists; Austria used the episode as an excuse for attacking Serbia, precipitating the F.W.W.

FRANCIS JOSEPH (1830-1916). Emperor of Austria-Hungary. He succeeded his uncle, Ferdinand I, on his abdication in 1848, and after the suppression of the 1848 revolution set out to estab. an absolute monarchy. But he was defeated in the Italian War of 1859 and the Prussian War of 1866, and had to grant Austria a parliamentary constitution in 1861 and Hungary equality with Austria in 1867. His only son committed suicide in 1889, and the empress was assassinated in 1897.

FRANCIS OF ASSISI (asē'sē) (1182-1226). Italian R. Catholic saint. The son of a wealthy merchant, his life was changed by two dreams during an illness following spells of military service when he was in his early twenties. He resolved to follow literally the behests of the NT and to live a life of poverty and service while preaching a simple form of the Christian gospel. F. attracted many followers, and in 1209 founded an Order of friars.

Many stories are told of his ability to charm wild animals and to influence men in all walks of life. In 1219 he went to Egypt to convert the Sultan, and lived for a month in his camp. Returning to Italy, he resigned his leadership of the friars, and in 1224 he suffered a mystical experience during which he is said to have received the *stigmata* or 5 wounds of Christ. He d. at Assisi, and was canonized in 1228.

FRANCIS OF SALES (1567-1622). French R. Catholic saint. B. in Savoy, he became bishop of Geneva in 1602, and in 1610 he founded the Order of the Visitation, a congregation of nuns.

FRANCIUM. Element. Symbol Fr, at. no. 87, at. wt. 223. Discovered by Mlle Perey in 1939, it is a radioactive metal. *See* TABLE OF TRANSURANIUM ELEMENTS.

FRANCK (fronk), **César Auguste** (1822-90). Belgian composer. B. at Liége, he became a teacher and in 1858 organist at the church of St. Clotilde, Paris. There he remained until his death. Much of his music is religious in character and subject. Best known are the Symphonic Variations for piano and orchestra, the violin sonata, and the oratorios *Redemption,* and *Les Béatitudes,* a choral masterpiece.

FRANCO BAHAMONDE, Francisco (1892-1975). Spanish dictator. B. in Galicia, he entered the army in 1910, served in Morocco, and was appointed Chief of Staff in 1935 and Gov. of the Canary Islands in 1936. Dismissed from this post by the Popular Front govt, he plotted an uprising with German and Italian assistance, and on the outbreak of civil war organized the invasion of Spain by Moorish troops and foreign legionaries. After the death of General Sanjurjo, he took command of the insurgents (Nationalists), proclaiming himself *Caudillo* (leader) of Spain, and the defeat of the Republic with the surrender of

FRANCIS OF ASSISI. A portrait of the saint which is said to date from 1225.

Madrid in 1939 brought all Spain under his govt. On the outbreak of the S.W.W., in spite of Spain's official attitude of 'Strictest neutrality', his pro-axis sympathies led him to send aid, later withdrawn, to the German side. At home, he curbed the growing power of the *Falange*, and in 1942 reinstated the *Cortes*, which in 1947 passed an act by which F. became head of state for life. In later years F. trimmed his regime in a slightly more liberal direction, and by 1973 had relinquished the premiership. In 1969 he nominated as his successor and future king of Spain, Juan Carlos (q.v.).

FRANCO-GERMAN ENTENTE. Rapprochement between France and Germany, initiated by de Gaulle's personal mission to W Germany in 1962, followed by the Franco-German Treaty of Friendship and Co-operation (1963).

FRANCO-PRUSSIAN WAR, 1870-1. *See* FRENCH HISTORY.

FRANGIPANI (franzhipah'ni). Tropical tree of the *Plumeria* genus, Apocynaceae family. All the species have beautiful, strongly scented flowers, espec. the red jasmine (*P. rubra*), from which perfume is made. The dessert F. or *frangipane*, concocted from cream, sugar and almonds, is unconnected, being named after its inventor a 16th cent. Italian marquis of Frangipani.

FRANK, Anne (1929-45). German diarist. B. at Frankfurt-am-Main, she fled to Holland with her family in 1933 to escape Nazi anti-Semitism. Under the occupation they remained in a sealed-off room in Amsterdam 1942-4, when betrayal resulted in Anne's death in Belsen concentration camp: the house is preserved as a museum. Her diary during her period in hiding was pub. in 1947.

FRANKEL, Benjamin (1906-73). British composer, Originally a watchmaker's assistant, he studied the piano in Germany, and continued his studies in London while playing jazz as a violinist in night-clubs. He wrote numerous film scores, and chamber music of an individual, serious quality.

FRANKENSTEIN LAW. In the USA the ruling by the Supreme Court (1980) that new forms of life created in the laboratory may be patented.

FRANKFURT-AM-MAIN. City in Hesse, W. Germany, 72km (45m) NE of Mannheim. A free city until 1886, when it was incorporated in Prussia, F. is a very important commercial and banking centre, univ. city, and inland port. There are electrical and machine industries, and an annual internat. Book Fair is held. It was the HQ of the US zone of occupation in the S.W.W. and of the Anglo-US zone 1947-9. Pop. (1972) 667,450.

FRANKFURT-AN-DER-ODER. City in E Germany 80km (50m) SE of Berlin, cap. of F. district. Industries incl. chemicals, engineering, paper, leather, etc. It is linked by the Oder and its canals to the Vistula and Elbe. Pop. (1972) 58,500.

FRANKINCENSE. A resinous product obtained from trees of the *Boswellia* genus, Burseraceae family, natives of Africa, India, and Arabia, and used in incense.

FRANKLIN, Benjamin (1706-90). American statesman, scientist, and writer. B. in Boston of poor parents, he ran a printing business in Philadelphia so successfully that by 1749 he could retire and devote himself to science. His proof that lightning is a form of electricity, his discovery of the distinction between negative and positive electricity, and his invention of the lightning-conductor, made him internationally famous. He was elected to the Pennsylvania Assembly, and in 1754 put forward the first plan for a federation of the American colonies. As agent for Pennsylvania in London 1764-75, he used his influence to procure the repeal of the Stamp Act. Returning to America, he helped to draw up the Declaration of Independence, and as ambassador to France, 1776-85, negotiated an alliance with France and the peace settlement with Britain. He was president of Pennsylvania 1785-8, and took part in the drafting of the US constitution. During his later years he wrote an autobiography.

FRANKLIN, Sir John (1786-1847). British explorer. B. in Lincs, he fought at Copenhagen and Trafalgar, took part in expeditions to Australia, the Arctic, and N Canada, and in 1845 commanded an expedition in search of the NW Passage on which he perished. His fate remained a mystery until 1859, when records were discovered by a search party.

FRANKLIN. A district of Northwest Territories, Canada; area 1,422,550 sq.km (549,253 sq.m).

FRANKS. A Germanic people from whom France derived its name. They overran Belgium and N France in the 4th-5th cents.; their king, Clovis, accepted Christianity and founded the French monarchy. His successors extended their rule over all France and W Germany. In France the Fs. and Gallo-Romans became fused in the 9th cent. into a single people speaking a modified form of Latin.

FRANZ FERDINAND. *See* FRANCIS FERDINAND.

FRANZ JOSEF LAND. Archipelago of *c.* 85 islands in the Arctic Ocean, E of Spitsbergen and NW of Novaya Zemlya, USSR. There are scientific stations. Area 20,720 sq.km (8,000 sq.m).

FRANZ JOSEPH. *See* FRANCIS JOSEPH.

FRASER, Malcolm (1930-). Australian statesman, nicknamed the 'Prefect' because of a supposed disregard of subordinates. Ed. at Oxford, he became a millionaire sheep farmer, and in March 1975 replaced Snedden as leader of the Liberal Party. In Nov., following the Whitlam govt's loan and other economic difficulties, he blocked finance bills in the Senate, became PM of a 'caretaker govt, and won the Dec. election. Re- elected 1977 and 1980, he was defeated 1983.

FRASER, Peter (1884-1950). New Zealand Labour statesman. B. in Scotland, he joined the ILP in 1908. In 1910 he went to NZ and soon became prominent in the Labour movement there. He held various cabinet posts 1935-40, and was PM of the Dominion 1940-9.

FRASER. Canadian river, in British Columbia. It rises in the Yellowhead Pass of the Rockies and flows NW, then S, then W to the Strait of Georgia. It is 1,370 km (850m) long and famous for salmon.

FRATERNITIES. Student societies peculiar to US univs. and colls. Usually named with Gk letters, they are nominally secret, with badge, pass-words, motto and initiation rites, some of a degrading nature. They have a central governing body and a 'chapter' at each coll. Although mainly residential, some Fs. are purely honorary, membership being on the basis of scholastic distinction, e.g. Phi Beta Kappa, earliest of the Fs. founded at William and Mary Coll., Va., in 1776. Sororities are the feminine equivalent.

FRAUD. In law, to establish F., three things are essential: (1) The statement must be factually untrue and made with the intent that it should be acted upon; (2) the person making the statement knows it is untrue or remains deliberately careless whether it is true or not; (3) the party to whom the statement is made acts upon it to his detriment. A contract based on F. may be avoided by the injured party in addition to his having an action for damages.

FRAUNHOFER (frown'hōfer), **Joseph von** (1787-1826). German physicist. B. in Bavaria, he was apprenticed to a glass cutter, and in 1807 founded an optical institute. The dark lines in the solar spectrum (F. lines), that revealed the chemical composition of the Sun's atmosphere, were first accurately mapped by him.

FRAY BENTOS (frah'-ē bān'tos). River port in Uruguay, famous for its meat-packing industry, and particularly for corned beef. It is linked by bridge over the Uruguay r. with Puerto Unzue in Argentina (1976). Pop. (1975) 20,000.

FRAZER, Sir James George (1854-1941). Scottish anthropologist. B. at Glasgow, he was ed. at the univ. and at Cambridge, and in 1890 won acclaim with *The Golden Bough*. This study of primitive religion and sociology on a comparative basis was a pioneer work, still valuable although F.'s attitude was romantic rather than scientific.

FREDERICK I (*c.* 1123-90). Holy Roman Emperor, known as **Barbarossa** (red-beard). Originally duke of Swabia, he was elected emperor in 1152, and was engaged in a struggle with the papacy 1159-77, which ended in his submission; the Lombard cities, headed by Milan, took advantage of this to establish their independence of imperial control. F. joined the 3rd Crusade, and was drowned in Asia Minor.

FREDERICK II (1194-1250). Holy Roman Emperor, called 'the Wonder of the World'. Son of Henry VI, he was elected emperor in 1212. He led a crusade in 1228-9 which recovered Jerusalem by treaty without fighting. At the same time he quarrelled with the Pope, and a feud began which lasted at intervals till the end of his reign. F., who was a complete sceptic in religion, was perhaps the most cultured man of his age.

FREDERICK III (1831-88). King of Prussia and German Emperor. The son of William I, he m. Princess Victoria, eldest dau. of Queen Victoria, in 1858. In outlook he was a liberal, and frequently opposed Bismarck's policy. He became emperor in 1888, but d. of cancer 3 months later.

FREDERICK I (1657-1713). King of Prussia. He became elector of Brandenburg in 1688, and assumed the title of king of Prussia in 1701.

FREDERICK II, called **the Great** (1712-86). King of Prussia. He received a Spartan education from his father, Frederick William I, and in 1730 was threatened with death for attempting to run away. Soon after his accession in 1740 he attacked Austria, and by the peace of 1745 secured Silesia. The struggle was renewed in 1756-63, and in spite of assistance from Britain F. had a hard task to hold his own against the Austrians and their Russian allies; the skill with which he did so proved him to be one of the great soldiers of history. At home he encouraged industry and agriculture, reformed the judicial system, fostered education, and established religious toleration.

FREDERICK WILLIAM. Name of 4 kings of Prussia. **Frederick William I** (1688-1740), who succeeded in 1713, largely founded the Prussian army. **Frederick William II** (1744-97), king from 1786, waged war on the French Revolution. **Frederick William III** (1770-1840), who succeeded him in 1797, warred with France in 1806 and 1813-15. He permitted the abolition of serfdom and other reforms, but in his later years persecuted the Liberals. **Frederick William IV** (1795-1861), king from 1840, was a firm believer in the divine right of kings; the Prussian revolution of 1848 occurred during his reign.

FREDERICK WILLIAM (1620-88). Elector of Brandenburg, called 'the Great Elector'. He succeeded to Brandenburg-Prussia in 1640, and by successful wars with Sweden and Poland made it the second state in Germany.

FREDERICK WILLIAM (1882-1951). Last Crown Prince of Germany, eldest son of Wilhelm II. During the F.W.W. he commanded a group of armies on the western front. In 1918 'Little Willie', as he was called in England, retired into private life.

FREDERICTON. Canadian city, cap. of New Brunswick prov., on the r. St John. The University of New Brunswick, founded 1785, is at F., which is a lumbering and mining centre. Pop. (1976) 44,245.

FREDRIKSSTAD. Norwegian port at the mouth of the r. Glommen, dating from 1570, a centre of the timber trade with shipyards. Pop. (1978) 28,570.

FREE CHURCHES. Those Protestant denominations in England and Wales, that, unlike the C of E, are not established by the State. The chief are the Methodist Church, Baptist Union, and United Reformed Church (Congregational and Presbyterian). Since 1940 they have joined for common action in the Free Church Federal Council.

FREE CHURCH OF SCOTLAND. Name given to the body of Scottish Presbyterians who seceded from the Established Church of Scotland in 1843. In 1900 all but a small section that retains the old name combined with the United Presbyterian Church to form the United Free Church, which reunited with the Church of Scotland in 1929.

FREEDOM (of a city, etc.). In England the right of participating in the privileges of a city or borough. Persons possessing such are known as freemen. Birth, apprenticeship, and marriage are qualifications and a borough may admit distinguished persons as honorary freemen. Today the privileges are almost entirely honorary.

FREEDOM, Presidential Medal of. Highest civilian honour conferred in the USA in peacetime. Instituted by Kennedy in 1963, it is awarded to those 'who contribute significantly to the quality of American life' and a list of recipients is pub. each Independence Day. It replaced the Medal of Freedom, instituted 1945, which had been conferred on no regular basis; only 24 awards had been made.

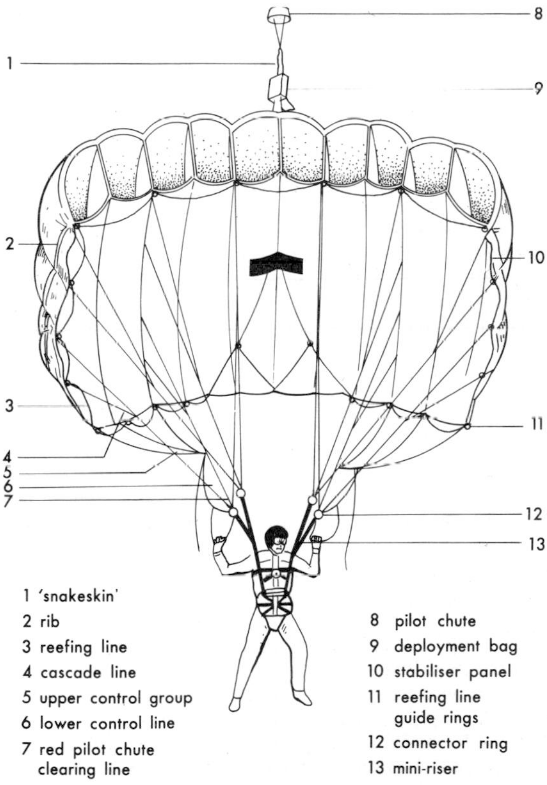

FREEFALLING. The ram-air square parachute, developed in the late 1960s, enables the jumper to travel into the wind and hover over his mark so that he lands with greatly increased accuracy. Above, is the Strato-Star design.

FREEFALLING. Sport also known as skydiving, which entails falling from an aircraft and then, by a correct positioning of the body, gliding down from anything up to 3,650 m (12,000 ft) until the level at which a parachute must be opened - 600m (2,000 ft).

FREEFALLING. A sport of daring rather than strength, it has been widely taken up by women. These two intrepid parachutists were photographed by Dave Waterman, falling at the same speed himself - about 190 kph (120 mph). *Photo: Camera Press.*

FREE FRENCH. Movement formed by Gen. de Gaulle in England in June 1940, consisting of French soldiers who continued to fight against the Axis after the Franco-German armistice. They took the name Fighting France in 1942 and served in many campaigns, among them Gen. Leclerc's advance from Chad to Tripolitania 1942, the Syrian campaigns 1941, the campaigns in the Western Desert, the Italian campaign, the liberation of France, and the invasion of Germany. Their emblem was the Cross of Lorraine (with 2 'bars'), which was used by Joan of Arc.

FREEHOLD. An estate in land which is for an indefinite period and is therefore contrasted with a leasehold, which is always for a fixed term of years. In practical effect, a F. is absolute ownership.

FREEMASONRY. Linked national organizations open to men over 21, united by the possession of a common code of morals and beliefs, and of certain traditional 'secrets'. Apart from requiring a belief in the 'Great Architect of the Universe' and acceptance of its moral code, English F. maintains strict impartiality in politics and religion. F. is descended from an operative guild of masons which existed in the 14th cent., and by the 16th was admitting men unconnected with the building trade. The name 'freemason' may mean a full member of the guild, or one working in free-stone, i.e. a mason of the highest class. Modern F. originated with the formation of the first Grand Lodge, or governing body, in 1717, and during the 18th cent. spread from Britain to America, the colonies, and Europe. In France and other European countries, F. assumed a political and anti-clerical character; it has been condemned by the papacy, and in certain countries was suppressed by the State. Both in Britain and the USA the freemasons maintain hospitals and institutions for their sick or aged members, and schools for their orphans.

FREESIA. Genus of plants of the Iridaceae family. It grows from a corm and produces funnel-shaped flowers in a wide range of colours.

FREETHOUGHT. The intellectual movement which arose in Europe following the Reformation, chiefly in critical opposition to the dogmatic statement of the Christian faith. In Britain it was represented by the Deists in the 17th and 18th cents., who were followed by Carlile, Holyoake, Bradlaugh, Lord Morley, J. B. Bury, Bertrand Russell, and many others. Its propagating organizations are the Rationalist Press Association and the Secular Society.

FREETOWN. Capital of Sierra Leone, W Africa. A commercial port and also a naval station, it has an excellent harbour, and there is an internat. airport at Lungi. Pop. (1975) 274,000.

FREE TRADE. International trade free from all tariffs except those levied for revenue purposes only. The case for F.T., first put forward in the 17th cent., received its classic statement in Adam Smith's *Wealth of Nations* (1776). The movement towards F.T. began with Pitt's commercial treaty with France in 1786, and triumphed with the repeal of the Corn Laws (1846). Britain's superiority to all rivals as a manufacturing country in the Victorian age made F.T. to her advantage, but when that superiority was lost the demand for Protection was raised, notably by Joseph Chamberlain. The Ottawa Agreements (q.v.) of 1932 marked the end of F.T. until in 1948 an international treaty, the *General Agreement on Tariffs and Trade* (GATT), came into operation. A drastic series of resultant international tariff reductions was agreed in the Kennedy Round Conference 1964-7, and the Tokyo Round (1973-9) made substantial special concessions to less developed countries. *See also* EUROPEAN UNION.

FREE WILL. The metaphysical doctrine that men are endowed with a Will as an independent faculty that enables them to choose between different courses of action. The theological dogma of F.W. states that man was so created by God that he may choose between good and evil. The opposite view is determinism (q.v.), necessitarianism, or predestination.

FREEZING. The change from a liquid to a solid state, as when water becomes ice. For a given substance, F. occurs at a definite temperature, known as the *freezing point,* that is invariable under similar conditions of pressure, and the temperature remains at this point until all the liquid is frozen. The amount of heat per unit mass that has to be removed to freeze a substance is a constant for each particular substance and is known as the latent heat of fusion. Water expands just before freezing point is reached. Ice is lighter than water, therefore: and if pressure is applied the freezing point will be lowered, as expansion is retarded. The presence of dissolved substances in the liquid also lowers the freezing point, the amount of lowering being proportional to the molecular concentration of the solution: 2 practical applications of this principle are seen in anti-freeze mixtures for car radiators and the use of salt to melt icy roads.

FREGE (frā'ge), **Gottlob** (1848-1925). German philosopher. The founder of modern mathematical logic, he pub. in 1884 *The Foundations of Arithmetic* which was to influence Wittgenstein. His work, neglected for a time, has attracted renewed attention in recent years in Britain and the US.

FREIBURG-IM-BREISGAU (frī'boorg-im-brīsgow). City in Baden-Württemberg, Germany. It is the seat of an archbishopric and a univ., and manufactures tobacco, paper, etc. Pop. (1972) 171,450.

FREMANTLE. Chief port of W Australia, at the mouth of the Swan r., SW of Perth. It has boat-building yards, sawmills, iron foundries, etc., and exports wheat and timber. Pop. (1973) 25,700.

FRENCH, Sir John. *See* YPRES, EARL OF.

FRENCH ANTARCTICA. Territory, in full French Southern and Antarctic Territories, created 1955 and consisting of Adélie Land, on the antarctic continent (136° to 142°E long.), and the Kerguelen and Crozet archipelagos and Saint Paul and Nouvelle Amsterdam islands in the southern seas. It is admin. from Paris, but Port-aux-Français on Kerguelen is the chief centre, with several research stations. There are also research stations on Amsterdam and in Adélie Land; and a meteorological station on Possession Is. in the Crozet archipelago: Saint Paul is uninhabited. Total area 10,100 sq.km (3,900 sq.m); pop. *c.* 200.

FRENCH ART. Prior to the 15th cent. the artistic genius of the French was best expressed in architecture and sculpture. The miniatures of Jean Fouquet and the Limbourgs' *Très riches heures* stand out in the 15th cent. The 16th cent. artists were influenced by the Italians, but the miniature tradition was kept up by the Clouets and Corneille de Lyons. A great sculptor of the age was Jean Goujon. The most famous names of the 17th cent. include Poussin, Claude Lorrain, Philippe de Champaigne, Blanchard, and Bourdon.

In the 18th cent. F.A. became dominant throughout Europe. The great masters were Watteau, Chardin, Fragonard, Lancret, Boucher, and the sculptor Houdon. The neo-Classical school was founded by David. He was followed by Ingres. Delacroix was the leader of the Romantic movement. Géricault excelled as a history and animal painter.

The 19th cent. produced 2 famous schools of painting – the *Barbizon* and the *Impressionist.* The landscape painters of the Barbizon school incl. Millet, Corot, Daubigny, and Theodore Rousseau; the most famous Impressionists were Monet, Manet, Pissarro, Sisley, Degas, and Renoir. More subjective painters were Toulouse-Lautrec and Van Gogh, and it was the latter, with Cézanne and Gauguin, whose fresh approach to the technique of painting prepared the way for many 20th cent. developments. In the 1850s the graphic artists Daumier and Guys did their best work; and other outstanding artists were Courbet, the Douanier Rousseau, Bonnard, the *Pointillist* Seurat, and the sculptor Rodin.

The 20th cent. saw Paris as the home of 2 schools of painting in particular: Fauvism, showing the influence of Gauguin with his emphasis on pure colour, e.g. Matisse, Derain, Vlaminck, Dufy, and Friesz; and Cubism, deriving from Cézanne, and with exponents as diverse as Matisse and Derain, Picasso, Braque, and Juan Gris. Other notable artists are Chagall, the Dadaist Duchamp, the Surrealist Max Ernst, Rouault, Soutine, Utrillo, Modigliani, and Maillol the sculptor.

FRENCH COMMUNITY. Title taken by France and those overseas territories which adhered to it in the referendum held in 1958 on the proposed new constitution of the 5th Republic.

FRENCH GUIANA (gē-ah'nah). French overseas region (from 1976) in the N of S America, adjoining Surinam. Only a very small area is cultivated, but the forests are rich in timber, gold is mined, and there is commercial shrimp

FRENCH ART. A self-portrait by the leader of the French romantic school - Eugène Delacroix. *Photo: Mansell Collection.*

fishing. The cap. is Cayenne. Off the coast is Devil's Island (q.v.). Area 91,000 sq.km (34,740 sq.m); pop. (1977) 57,600.

FRENCH HISTORY. Before its conquest by Caesar (57-51 BC), France, then called Gaul, was occupied by independent tribes, mostly Celtic. During the 5 cents. of Roman rule they accepted Roman civilization and the Latin language. As the empire declined in the 5th cent. Germanic tribes overran the country, until a Frankish chief, Clovis (481-511), brought the other tribes under his rule and accepted Christianity. Under his successors, the Merovingians, the country sank into anarchy, until unity was restored by Pepin (741-68), founder of the Carolingian dynasty. Charlemagne (768-814) made France the centre of a great empire, but under his incompetent successors the great nobles became semi-independent, and the Norsemen invaded France and settled in Normandy. The first kings of the house of Capet, which assumed the crown in 987, ruled only the district round Paris, and were surrounded by vassals stronger than themselves. During the 11th-13th cents. the royal power was gradually extended, with the support of the Church and the townspeople, but progress was later retarded by the 100 Years War (1337-1453). The restoration of the royal power was finally achieved by 1500, through the policies of Louis XI (1461-83) and the annexation of Burgundy and Brittany to the crown.

Charles VIII's Italian wars initiated a struggle with Spain for supremacy in W Europe which lasted 2 cents. (1503-1697). Protestantism made considerable progress in France, and was adopted by a party of the nobles for political reasons; the result was a succession of civil wars, fought under religious slogans (1592-98). Henry IV (1589-1610) restored peace, established religious toleration, and made the monarchy absolute. His work was continued by the great ministers Richelieu and Mazarin, who by their intervention in the 30 Years War secured Alsace and made France the leading power in Europe. Louis XIV (1643-1715) embarked on an aggressive policy which united Europe against him; in his reign began the conflict with Britain which lost France her colonies in Canada and India. Misgovernment and unsuccessful wars aroused increasing discontent and resulted in the French Revolution (q.v.).

The revolution abolished feudalism and absolute monarchy, but failed to establish democracy. Foreign attempts at intervention led to wars (1792-1802, 1803-15), which gave Napoleon his opportunity to set up his military dictatorship. After Waterloo the Bourbon monarchy was restored. Charles X's attempt in 1830 to substitute absolute for limited monarchy provoked a revolution which placed his cousin, Louis Philippe, on the throne; he in turn was overthrown in 1848, and the 2nd Republic set up. Its president, Louis Napoleon, Napoleon I's nephew, restored the empire in 1852, with the title of Napoleon III. His ambitious foreign policy ended in defeat in the Franco-Prussian War (1870-1) and the foundation of the 3rd Republic.

The new republic had an uneasy career, and on several occasions conflict between the clerical and militarist right and the Radical and Socialist left threatened civil war. Meanwhile a new colonial empire was being built up in Africa and Indo-China. After 1900 politics were largely dominated by the approach of the F.W.W. The war left France exhausted, and desperately seeking security in a system of E European alliances. An unsuccessful Fascist coup in 1934 prepared the way for the victory in 1936 of a Radical-Socialist-Communist alliance, which introduced many social reforms; this broke down in 1938, and it was an alliance of the Radicals with the right which declared war on Germany in 1939. The German invasion of 1940 allowed the extreme right to set up a puppet dictatorship under Pétain, but resistance was maintained by the Free French under de Gaulle and the *maquis* until the liberation of 1944. The republic was re-established by a national govt., from which de Gaulle broke away to form a right-wing opposition in 1946-7, and the Communists were ejected in 1947. Open warfare with the Communists in Indo-China (q.v.) ended after 7½ years in the Geneva agreement of 1954, but a series of unstable govts paved the way for the return to power of de Gaulle in 1958 and the inauguration of the 5th Republic. In 1962 independence was granted to Algeria (q.v.). The Gaullists achieved only a bare majority in the 1967 elections, but in reaction to student unrest and mass strikes, achieved in 1968 the largest majority in Fr. republican history. Yet continuing unrest led to a referendum 1969 on an increased degree of regional govt and reform of the senate, and on the rejection of his proposals de Gaulle himself resigned and was succeeded by Georges Pompidou (q.v.). The rapid economic growth of the de Gaulle era continued, but Communist agitation aimed at the removal of the govt from presidential control continued, and in 1974 Giscard d'Estaing (q.v.) only narrowly defeated the candidate of the Left, François Mitterand, in the presidential elections. In 1981 Mitterand (q.v.) achieved a Socialist victory.

FRENCH INDIA. Former French possessions in India consisted of Pondichéry, Chandernagore, Karikal, Mahé, and Yanaon (Yanam). By 1954 they had been transferred to India.

FRENCH LITERATURE. Two varied aspects of French literary genius exemplified by Baudelaire and Colette. *Photos: Mansell Collection and Camera Press.*

FRENCH HISTORY. A detail from the picture by J.L. David of the army taking the oath of allegiance after Napoleon's distribution of the eagle standards. *Photo: Mansell Collection.*

FRENCH LANGUAGE. One of the Romance languages, F. is a development of the Vulgar Latin used for ordinary intercourse in Roman Gaul. Dialects spoken N of the Loire formed the *langue d'oïl* and to the S the *langue d'oc*, and by 813, when an assembly of bishops at Tours decided to abandon Latin in their preaching, the tongue spoken in N Gaul differed sufficiently from Latin for the existence of a F.L. to be affirmed. Modern F. was evolved from Francien, the dialect of the Île de France, which gained supremacy over other northern rivals in the 13th cent. Although the medium of a rich and varied literature, it remained a vulgar tongue until in 1539 the Decree of Villers-Cotterêts enforced F. as the vehicle of administration and justice.

From the beginning of the 17th cent. the F.L. became fixed: the F. Academy (founded in 1635) became its guardian, and Richelet's *Dictionnaire* (1680) stabilized its form and meaning. Developed by the *salons* and by the classical writers, F. became the polite language of Europe. The democratization of France at the Revolution assisted the gradual disappearance of the *patois*, and prepared the way for the rejuvenation of the romantic period. After the S.W.W. the F.L. experienced an incursion of foreign terms, espec. Anglo-American, and in 1976 the use of *franglais* (frahṅglā′) in broadcasting, etc., where a French equivalent was possible was made illegal. French is also spoken in Belgium, Luxembourg, Switzerland, and countries, such as Canada, which either have existing or former colonial links with France. In 1980 it is spoken by *c.* 90 million.

FRENCH LITERATURE. The Middle Ages. The *Chanson de Roland* (*c.* 1080) is the greatest of the early *chansons de geste* which were superseded by the Arthurian romances (seen at their finest in the work of Chrétien de Troyes in the 12th cent.), and by the classical themes of Alexander, Troy, and Thebes. Other aspects of F. medieval L. are represented by the charming *Aucassin et Nicolette*, the allegorical *Roman de la Rose* of Guillaume de Lorris (*c.* 1230) and Jean de Meung (*c.* 1275), and the satiric *Roman de Renart*, the historians Villehardouin, Joinville, Froissart, and Comines, and the first great F. poet, François Villon.

Renaissance to the 18th cent. Greatest poet of the Renaissance is Ronsard, leader of the Pléiade, set between Marot who opens the 16th cent. and Régnier at its close. In prose the period produced the broad genius of Rabelais and the essayist Montaigne. In the 17th cent. came the triumph of form with the great classical dramatists Corneille, Racine, and Molière, and the graceful brilliance of La Fontaine, and the poet-critic Boileau. Masters of prose in the same period include the philosophers Pascal and Descartes; the preacher Bossuet; the critics La Bruyère, Fénelon and Malebranche; and La Rochefoucauld, Cardinal de Retz, Mme de Sévigné, and Le Sage.

The 18th cent. was the era of prose, with Montesquieu, Voltaire, Rousseau; the scientist Buffon; the encyclopaedist Diderot; Vauvenargues; the novelists Prévost and Marivaux; and the memoir writer Saint-Simon, whose observations greatly illuminated the age.

The 19th and 20th cents. Poetry was reborn with the 'Romantics' Lamartine, Hugo, Vigny, Musset, Leconte de Lisle, and Gautier; novelists of the same school were George Sand, Stendhal and Dumas père, while criticism is represented by Sainte-Beuve, and history by Thierry, Michelet, and Taine. The realist novelist Balzac was followed by the school of Naturalism, whose representatives were Flaubert, Zola, the Goncourt brothers, Alphonse Daudet, Maupassant, and Huysmans. 19th cent. dramatists incl. Hugo, Musset, Dumas fils, and Mirbeau. Symbolism, a movement of experiment and revolt against classical verse and the materialist attitude, with the philosopher Bergson as one of its main exponents, found its first expression in the work of Gérard de Nerval, who was later followed by Baudelaire, Verlaine, Mallarmé, Rimbaud, Corbière, and the prose writer Villiers de l'Isle Adam; later writers in the same tradition were Henri de Régnier and Laforgue.

In the late 19th and early 20th cents. drama and poetry revived with Valéry, Claudel, and Paul Fort, who advocated 'pure poetry'; other writers were the novelists Gide and Proust, and the critics Thibaudet (1874-1936) and later St John Perse, also a well known poet. The Surrealist movement, which developed from 'pure poetry' through the work of Éluard and Apollinaire, influenced writers as diverse as Giraudoux, Louis Aragon, and Cocteau. The inevitable literary reaction against the Symbolists incl. Charles Péguy, Rostand, Mme de Noailles, and Romain Rolland. 20th cent. novelists in the Naturalist tradition were Henri Barbusse, Jules Romains, Julian Green, François Mauriac, Francis Carco, and Georges Duhamel. Other prose writers are Maurois, Malraux, Montherlant, Anatole France, Saint-Exupéry, Alain-Fournier, Pierre Hamp, and J. R. Bloch, while the theatre flourished with plays by J. J. Bernard, Anouilh, Beckett, and Ionesco. The S.W.W. had a profound effect on French writing, and distinguished post-war writers incl. the Existentialist Sartre, and Camus, 'Vercors', Simone de Beauvoir, Alain Robbe-Grillet, Romain Gary, Nathalie Sarraute and Marguerite Duras.

FRENCH POLYNESIA. The French island possessions in the S Pacific, comprising the Society, Marquesas, Tubuai, Tuamotu and Gambier Islands: the cap. is Papeete, on Tahiti, in the Society Islands. Tourism is important, and products incl. copra, coffee, vanilla and mother-of-pearl. Area 4,000 sq.km (1,550 sq.m); pop. (1973) 120,000.

FRENCH REVOLUTION. The revolution of 1789-99 which abolished feudalism and absolute monarchy in France. It began with the meeting in 1789 of the States General, later called the National Assembly. An attempt at counter-revolution was frustrated by the storming of the Bastille. The Assembly abolished feudal privileges and drew up a constitution which in 1791 was accepted by Louis XVI. Threats of foreign intervention led to war with Austria and Prussia in 1792. The monarchy was overthrown, the National Convention declared France a republic, and Louis was executed for treason. The democratic party, or Jacobins, estab. the dictatorship of the Committee of Public Safety, headed by Robespierre, and crushed opposition through the Revolutionary Tribunal. In 1794 the right overthrew Robespierre, and set up the Directory, which maintained a middle course between royalism and Jacobinism until Napoleon seized power in 1799.

FRENCH REVOLUTION. The 'Demolition of the Bastille', by Hubert Robert. The contractors made an excellent profit by selling the stones made up as souvenirs. *Photo: Giraudon.*

FRENCH SOMALILAND. *See* DJIBOUTI.

FRENCH SUDAN. *See* MALI.

FRENCH WEST AFRICA. Former grouping of French colonies (Senegal, Guinea, Ivory Coast, Burkina Faso, Benin (Dahomey), Sudan, Mauritania, Niger) administered by a governor-general from Dakar. It broke up following the birth of the Fifth Republic in 1958.

FRENEAU (frenō'), **Philip Morin** (1752-1832). American poet. Earliest outstanding poet of American birth, he was b. in NY. His *A Political Litany* (1775) was a mock prayer for deliverance from British tyranny, and he was twice captured by the British in voyages to and from the W Indies, where some of his best poems were written.

FREQUENCY. The rate of repetition of a cycle; the reciprocal of the period. The unit of F. is the hertz (Hz), a term which in the UK has only recently superseded the use of cycles per sec (symbol c/s). Audio F. is F. within the range audible to the normal human ear; ultrasonic F. is above the audio F. range, and radio F. is any F. at which electromagnetic radiation is used for telecommunications. Radio Fs. are given in kilohertz kHz (thousands of cycles per second), megahertz MHz (millions of cycles per second), or kilomegahertz kMHz (thousands of millions of cycles per second). The standard F. for a.c. generation is 50 Hz (cycles per second). *See* ELECTROMAGNETIC WAVES.

FRERE (frēr), **John** (1740-1807). British archaeologist. High Sheriff of Suffolk and MP for Norwich, he discovered at Hoxne, Suffolk, deposits of palaeolithic tools in 1790. His deduction that these must, from their situation, ante-date the conventional biblical time-scale was very much ahead of his era.

FRESCO (fres'kō). Term applied to a process of painting on plaster walls before the plaster is dry; also applied to the picture or design produced in this way. Some of the earliest frescoes are on the walls of the palace of Knossos in Crete.

FREUD (froid), **Sigmund** (1856-1939). Originator of psychoanalysis (q.v.). He was b. of Jewish parents in Freiberg, Moravia, and from 1860 lived at Vienna until, following the Nazi occupation in 1938, he migrated to London. He was influenced by Charcot and the researches into hysteria by the Viennese physician, Josef Breuer. With the latter he collaborated in the development of the cathartic method, which employed a hypnotic technique, but he soon abandoned hypnotism and developed the method of free association; this still remains the basic procedure in psychoanalysis. F.'s many books include *The Interpretation of Dreams* (1900), *The Psychopathology of Everyday Life* (1901), *Totem and Taboo* (1913), *The Ego and the Id* (1923), *The Future of an Illusion* (1927), and *Civilization and its Discontents* (1930).

FREYBERG (frī'), **Bernard Cyril,** baron (1889-1963). New Zealand soldier. B. in London, he was ed. at Wellington Coll., NZ, and served in the F.W.W., becoming the youngest brigadier-general in the British Army; he won the VC and DSO with 2 bars, and his courage became legendary. During the S.W.W. he commanded the NZ expeditionary force, and Allied forces in Crete in 1941, and later fought in the Western Desert and in Italy, receiving a third bar to his DSO. He was Gov.-Gen. of NZ 1946-52.

FRIAR (Lat. *frater,* Fr. *frère*). Name given to monks of all orders, but originally the title of members of the mendicant orders, the chief of which were the Franciscans or Minors (Grey Friars), the Dominicans or Preachers (Black Fs.), the Carmelites (White Fs.), and Austin Friars (Augustinians).

FRIAR'S BALSAM. A compound tincture of benzoin. It is used (1) in boiling water as an inhalant, (2) internally, a few drops swallowed often on a lump of sugar against coughs and colds, and (3) externally to cover abrasions.

FRIBOURG (frēboor'). City in Switzerland, on the r. Sarine, cap. of the canton of the same name. It is noted for its food products, and the cheese of the Gruyère district of the canton is famous. The univ. was founded in 1889. Pop. (1971) 39,500.

FRICTION. F. is the force which prevents one body sliding over another, and it occurs in solids, liquids, and gases. The coefficient of F. between 2 solid surfaces is equal to the force required to move one surface over the other, divided by the total force pressing the 2 surfaces together. F. is greatly reduced by the use of lubricants such as oil, grease, and graphite, and air bearings are now used to minimize the F. in high-speed rotational machinery. In other instances F. is deliberately increased by making the surfaces rough, e.g. brake linings, driving belts, soles of shoes, and tyres. F. is also important in problems of fluid flow.

FRIEDMAN (frēd'-), **Milton** (1912-). American economist. Prof. of Economics at the Univ. of Chicago from 1948, he maintains that a country's economy - and hence inflation - can be controlled through its money supply. Govts lack the 'political will' to do so because of the unpopularity of the recession and unemployment consequent on cuts in govt spending and increased taxes. He received a Nobel prize in 1976. *See* MONETARISM.

FRIEDRICHSHAFEN (frē'drikshahfen). Town on Lake Constance, Baden-Württemberg, W Germany. Cars are manufactured and - formerly - Zeppelins. Pop. (1978) 52,500.

FRIENDLY SOCIETY. The F.S. movement arose mainly as an attempt to meet the needs caused by loss of income through sickness. In Great Britain the movement was the successor in this field of the great medieval guilds, but the period of its greatest expansion was in the late 18th and early 19th cents., following the passing 1797 of the first legislation providing for the registration of F.Ss. There are now some 6,500 registered Ss. and their funds total *c.* £385,000,000: among the largest are the National Deposit, Odd Fellows, Foresters, and Hearts of Oak. In the US similar 'fraternal insurance' bodies incl. the Modern Woodmen of America (1883) and the Fraternal Order of Eagles (1898).

FRIENDS, Society of. *See* QUAKERS.

FRIESE-GREENE (frēz-), **William** (1855-1921). British photographer and early experimenter in cinematography. Although his patent of 1890 was upheld in US in 1910, the first functional moving-picture camera is generally credited to the French physiologist Marey in 1888.

FRIESLAND (frēz'-). Province of the Netherlands, bordering the Ijssel Meer. Parts are below sea-level; reclamation of the former Zuyder Zee is adding to its agricultural area. The Frisian breed of cattle is famous. Leeuwarden is the cap. and largest town. Area 3,340 sq.km (1,290 sq.m); pop. (1978) 572,850.

FRIGATE. Originally a small swift undecked sailing vessel, used in the Mediterranean. The name was first applied to a type of warship in the 18th cent., and in modern times Fs. are the most numerous type of larger surface vessel in the British Royal Navy. They are essentially general purpose anti-aircraft, anti-submarine escort vessels of up to 3,000 tonnes carrying various combinations of anti-aircraft and other guns; guided weapons; depth charge mortars; and homing torpedo tubes, and a helicopter also with homing torpedoes.

FRIGATE. The *Amazon,* 2,500 tonnes, first British warship designed to operate entirely on gas turbines. Her operations room is largely automated and the gun turret requires no crew when firing. *Photo: Courtesy of Vosper Thorneycroft.*

FRINGILLIDAE (frinjil'idē). Family of birds in the order Passeriformes. They are small, hard-billed birds, living in the northern hemisphere, and include the finches, linnets, sparrows, etc.

FRISCH (frish), **Karl von** (1886–1982). German zoologist, founder with Konrad Lorenz of ethology. Specializing in bees, he discovered how they communicate as to sources of nectar, etc. by 'dances': *The Dance Language and Orientation of Bees* (1967). He shared a Nobel prize in 1973 with Lorenz and N. Tinbergen (qq.v.).

FRISCH, Max (1911–). Swiss writer. Ed. at Zürich univ. and technical high school, he was first a foreign correspondent and then an architect until 1955, when he had just estab. a reputation with his satirical novel *Stiller* (1954: *I'm not Stiller*). Among his works are the plays *Nun singen sie wieder* (1945), and *Andorra* (1961), and the novel *Homo Faber* (1957).

FRISCH, Ragnar (1895-1973). Norwegian economist. Prof. at Oslo from 1931, he was the virtual inventor of econometrics, and in 1969 shared a Nobel prize with J. Tinbergen.

FRISIANS (fri'zians). Chain of low-lying islands 5-32km (3-20m) off the NW coasts of the Netherlands and the NW coast of Germany, with a northerly extension off the W coast of Denmark. They are divided among Germany, the Netherlands, and Denmark.

FRISIANS. A Germanic people who in Roman times occupied the coast of Holland, and may have taken part in the Anglo-Saxon invasions of Britain. Their language was closely akin to Anglo-Saxon, with which it formed the Anglo-Frisian branch of the West Germanic languages. It is almost extinct in the Ger. districts of E Friesland, has attained some literary importance in the N Frisian Is. and Schleswig, and developed a considerable literature in the W Frisian dialect of the Dutch prov. of Friesland.

FRITH, William Powell (1818-1905). British artist. He was especially noted for his large-scale works with numerous accurately observed figures, e.g. 'Ramsgate Sands', bought by Queen Victoria; and 'Derby Day' in the Tate Gallery.

FRITILLARY. Name of several butterflies in the family Nymphalidae. All the Fs. are orange in colour with black markings, but vary in size, the silver-washed F. (*Argynnis paphia*) being the largest. The Fs. are common in British woodlands.

FRIULI-VENEZIA GIULIA (frē'oolē venet'sēah). Autonomous region of Italy, bordered on the E by Yugoslavia. Formed in 1947 from the provs. of Udine and Gorizia, to which Trieste was added after its cession to Italy in 1954, it was granted autonomy in 1963. The name Friuli, derived from Forum Juli, a Roman settlement in the area, was long used for the greater part of the two provs. forming the region.

The Slav minority numbers *c.* 100,000, and in Friuli there is a movement for complete independence. Area 7,844 sq.km (3,030 sq.m); pop. (1971) 1,209,810.

FRŌ'BISHER, Sir Martin (*c.* 1535-94). English navigator. B. in Yorks, he made his first voyage to Guinea in 1554. In 1576 he set out in search of the NW Passage; and visited Labrador, and Frobisher Bay, in Baffin Land. A 2nd and 3rd expedition sailed in 1577 and 1578. F. served as vice-admiral in Drake's W Indian expedition of 1585, and in 1588 was knighted for his share in the defeat of the Armada. He was mortally wounded in 1594 while attempting to relieve Brest.

FROEBEL (frö'bel), **Friedrich August Wilhelm** (1782-1852). German educationist. B. in Thuringia, he came into contact with Pestalozzi, and evolved a new system of education utilizing instructive play, described in *Education of Man* (1826), etc. In 1836 the first kindergarten was founded, in Blankenburg.

FROG. Amphibian of the family Ranidae with a world-wide distribution, especially abundant in tropical and sub-tropical areas and generally sharing with the toad (q.v.) a lengthy larval period, when the eggs hatch into fish-like 'tadpoles', which gradually lose their gill slits and tail and develop lungs and legs. The common English Grass F. (*Rana temporaria*) is typical of its genus; the body is yellowish-brown, short and stout; the eyes large and prominent; and the fore-limbs short, with only 4 fingers, whereas the hind-legs are long and powerful with 5 webbed toes enabling it to jump and swim rapidly. It hibernates in winter, lives in damp places, migrating to water to spawn in the spring, and captures its prey (slugs, insects, etc.) by shooting out the tip of its tongue which carries a viscid secretion. Other species of interest are the edible F. (*R. esculenta*), of England and Europe, of which only the legs are eaten; the bull-frog of eastern N America (*R. catesbyana*), 175mm (7in) long (excl. of the legs) and with a croak that carries for miles; the flying Fs. of the Malayan area (*Rhacophorus*) which have completely webbed fore- and hind-feet which serve as 'parachutes', and the giant Fs. (*Telmatobius culeus*) of Lake Titicaca which reach *c.* 50cm (20in), and are edible.

FROG. The European tree frog (*Hyla arborea*) photographed through glass to show suction-cup pads on the feet. *Photo: Heather Angel.*

FROGBIT. Small water plant (*Hydrocharis*) with submerged roots, floating leaves, and small green and white flowers. It is common in England.

FROG-HOPPERS. Family of small brown insects (*Ceropidae*) in the division Exopterygota, which leap a considerable distance when touched, and live by sucking the juice from plants. The larvae, known as *froth-flies*, are pale green, and surround themselves with a mass of froth.
FROGMOUTH. Nocturnal bird, rather resembling an owl, of which the commonest species, *Podargus strigoides*, is found throughout Australia, incl. Tasmania. Well-camouflaged, it sits and awaits its prey.

FROGMOUTH. The tawny frogmouth, so-called from the yellow-coloured cavity which appears when it opens its mouth to take its prey. *Photo: Australian Information Service.*

FROISSART (frwahsahr'), **Jean** (1338-1410). French chronicler. B. at Valenciennes, he became secretary to Queen Philippa, wife of Edward III of England. He travelled in Scotland and Brittany, accompanied the Black Prince to Aquitaine, and in 1368 was in Milan in the company of Chaucer and Petrarch. Later he entered the Church, and d. canon at Chimay. His *Chronique de France, d'Angleterre, d'Écosse, d'Espagne*, etc., records often at first hand the events of the years 1326-1400.
FRONDE. The French civil wars of 1648-53. They fall into 2 stages: the attempt of the Paris *parlement* in 1648-9 to limit the powers of the monarchy, and the revolt of the great nobles, headed by Condé, against the rule of Mazarin in 1650-3.
FRONTENAC ET PALLUAU (froñtnahk'e pahlüoh'), **Louis de Buade,** comte de (1620-98). Governor of French Canada. He began his military career in 1635, and was appointed Governor of Canada in 1672. Although efficient he quarrelled with the local bishop and his followers and was recalled in 1682. A disastrous war with the Iroquois followed, and F. was reinstated in 1689.
FROST, Robert Lee (1874-1963). American poet. B. in San Francisco, he had no formal ed. until 11, and 1900-12 farmed unsuccessfully in New Hampshire, combining this with teaching and writing poetry. In 1912 he sailed to England where he pub. *A Boy's Will* (1913), and with this and *North of Boston* (1914), estab. his reputation. Returning to the US and to farming in 1915, he won Pulitzer poetry prizes with *New Hampshire* (1923), *Collected Poems* (1930), *A Further Range* (1936), and *A Witness Tree* (1942). He wrote with an American individuality, and a simplicity that masked a penetrating vision.
FROST. Condition of the weather when the temperature of the air is below freezing 0°C (32°F). Water in the atmosphere then freezes and crystallizes on exposed objects. As cold air is heavier than warm, *Ground Fs.* are the more common type. *Hoar F.* is formed by the condensation of water particles in the same way as dew collects.
FROSTBITE. Change produced in tissues by the action of cold, most common in the feet, hands, nose, and ears. The blood supply being cut off, the affected part starts to die (gangrene; necrosis). The treatment is massage with snow or cold water.
FROUDE (frood), **James Anthony** (1818-94). British historian. B. in Devon he was at first strongly influenced by the Oxford Movement, but subsequently became sceptical and was affected by the teaching of Carlyle. His *History of England from the Fall of Wolsey to the Defeat of the Spanish Armada* (1856-70) revealed his gift for dramatic realization of historic events. As Carlyle's literary executor he pub. his *Reminiscences* (1881) and the *Letters and Memorials of Jane Welsh Carlyle* (1883). He was prof. of modern history at Oxford 1892-4. His brother, **Richard Hurrell F.** (1803-36), collaborated with Newman in the Oxford Movement.
FRUCTOSE or **fruit sugar** ($C_6H_{12}O_6$). A sugar occurring with glucose in honey and cane sugar, and in grape juice, etc. It is somewhat sweeter than cane sugar, from which it is prepared on a large scale.
FRUIT FLY. A small yellow fly (*Drosophila melanogaster*) which breeds in fermenting fruit juices. Because of its rapid reproduction and simple structure - it has 8 chromosomes - it has been of great use to geneticists in the study of heredity.
FRUNZE (froon'ze). Capital (formerly Pishpek) of Kirgiz SSR, USSR, and F. region, situated in the fertile Chu valley. Its industries include the making of textiles, metal goods, and leather, and food preserving. A univ. was estab. in 1951. Pop. (1977) 511,000.
FRY, Christopher (1907-). British dramatist. Originally a teacher, he was a leader of the revival of verse drama after the S.W.W., notably *The Lady's Not for Burning* (1948), *Venus Observed* (1950), and *A Sleep of Prisoners* (1951).
FRY, Elizabeth (1780-1845). British philanthropist. B. at Norwich, *née* Gurney, she joined the Society of Friends in 1798, and in 1800 m. **Joseph F.**, a London merchant. In 1810 she became a minister in the society. She first visited Newgate prison in 1813, and formed an association for the improvement of female prisoners in 1817. In 1818 she inspected the prisons of northern England and Scotland with her brother, **Joseph Gurney,** and their report pub. 1819 had great influence both at home and abroad. She subsequently travelled widely on the Continent.
FRY, Roger Elliott (1866-1934). British painter and art critic. B. in London, he was chiefly responsible for introducing the French post-impressionist painters to England.

His own paintings show a fine sense of design and mastery of technique.

FUAD I (foo'ahd) (1868-1936). King of Egypt. The son of the Khedive Ismail, he succeeded his elder brother, Hussein Kiamil, as sultan of Egypt in 1917, and when Egypt was declared independent in 1922 he assumed the title of king. **FUAD II** (1952-), grandson of Fuad I, was king of Egypt 1952-3 between the abdication of his father Farouk (q.v.) and the establishment of the republic.

FUCHS, Klaus. *See under* SECRET SERVICE.

FUCHS (fookhs), **Sir Vivian** (1908-). British explorer. Before the S.W.W. he accompanied several Cambridge expeditions as geologist, exploring in Greenland and Africa as well as Antarctica, and in 1957-8 led the Commonwealth Trans-Antarctic Expedition and was knighted on his return. *See* ANTARCTICA.

FUCHSIA (fū'shia). Genus of exotic plants of the Onagraceae family, composed of a number of small shrubs native to S America but frequently cultivated in Britain. The genus was named in 1703 after Leonhard Fuchs, German botanist (1501-66). The red, purple, or pink flowers hang downwards, and are bell-shaped.

FUEHRER (fü'rer), **Der.** German for 'the leader'; the name given to Adolf Hitler (q.v.) by his followers.

FUEL. Any source of heat or energy embracing the entire range of all combustibles and including anything which burns, i.e. nuclear Fs.

FUJIAN (foojēahn'). Prov. of SE China (formerly Fukien), bordering Taiwan Strait, opposite Taiwan. It is largely mountainous: crops incl. tobacco, sugar cane, rice and timber, and specially aromatic teas. In 1980 it was designated a pace-setting prov. for modernisation. The cap. is Fuzhou. Area 123,100 sq.km (47,516 sq.m); pop. (1979) 24,000,000.

FUJIYAMA (fooji-yah'mah). Volcano on Honshu is., Japan, 97km (60m) SW of Tokyo. Extinct since 1707, it rises 3,778 m (12,390 ft), features often in Japanese art, and has a weather station on the summit.

FUKIEN *See* FUJIAN.

FUKUOKA. Japanese industrial town and port on the NW coast of Kyushu island. Pop. (1977) 981,000.

FUKUSHIMA (fookooshē'ma). City in N Honshu, Japan. There is a silk industry. Pop. (1977) 251,000.

FUKUYAMA (fookooyah'ma). Port in Honshu, at the mouth of the Ashida r., with cotton, rubber and other industries. Pop. (1977) 337,000.

FULBRIGHT, William (1905-). American politician. A Rhodes Scholar, he was responsible for the *F. Act* (1946) which enabled thousands of Americans to study overseas and overseas students to enter the US. Chairman of the Foreign Relations Committee 1959-74, he is a strong internationalist and supporter of the UN.

FULLER, Richard Buckminster (1895–1983). American architect, born in Milton, Mass. He invented the geodesic dome (light polygonal framework covered with plastic, metal sheeting, etc) in 1947. Works incl the St Louis climatron and New Delhi airport.

FULLER, Roy (1912-). British poet and novelist. A London solicitor, he pub. his first *Poems* (1939), and in 1968 became prof. of poetry at Oxford. Later vols. incl. *Epitaphs and Occasions* (1951), *Brutus's Orchard* (1957) and *Collected Poems* (1962); and the novel *My Child, My Sister* (1965).

FULLER, Thomas (1608-61). English author. Rector at Broadwindsor, Dorset, from 1634, he served as a chaplain to the Royalist army, and at the Restoration became the king's chaplain. He is known for his *Worthies of England* (1662).

FULMAR (fool'-). Name given to several species of petrels of the family Procellariidae, which are similar in size and colour to the common gull. The F. (*Fulmarus glacialis*) is found in the N Atlantic and visits land only to deposit its single egg. The giant Pacific F. (*Macronectes gigantea*) has a wingspan of over 2m (7ft).

FU'LMINATES. The salts of fulminic acid (C:NOH), the chief being silver and mercury. They detonate, i.e. are exploded by a blow.

FULTON, Robert (1765-1815). American engineer and inventor. B. in Pennsylvania, he went to England in 1787 where he devoted himself to engineering in connection with inland navigation. In 1797 he moved to Paris where he produced a submarine, the *Nautilus*. After experimenting in steam navigation on the Seine in 1803, he returned to America and the first steam vessel of note, the *Clermont*, appeared on the Hudson in 1807, sailing between New York and Albany. The first steam warship was the *Fulton* of 38 tonnes, made in 1814-15.

FŪ'MITORY. Genus (*Fumaria*) of the plant family Fumariaceae, native to Europe and Asia. The common F. grows abundantly as a weed in Britain, and produces red or white flowers.

FUNCHAL (foonshahl'). Portuguese name for the island of Madeira, and also the name of the island cap. on the E coast, which has a harbour accommodating ocean-going ships, and is a popular holiday and health resort. There is a wine trade. Pop. (1973) 55,000.

FUNCTIONALISM. Term applied to a style of architecture and furniture characterized by a tendency to exclude everything that serves no practical purpose. It was a reaction against the 19th cent. practice of imitating earlier styles, and its finest achievements are in the realm of industrial building. Its leading exponents were the German Bauhaus school, and the Dutch group de Stijl; the most prominent architects in the field were Le Corbusier and Walter Gropius (qq.v.).

FUNDAMENTALISM. Name given to a religious movement which arose in USA just after the F.W.W. and was characterized by insistence on complete belief in the literal inspiration of the Bible and such doctrines as the Virgin Birth, the physical resurrection of Christ, the Atonement, and the Bible miracles which were regarded as fundamental to the Christian faith. In 1925 F. was publicized by the 'Dayton Trial'. *See* DAYTON. There is a similar modern movement in Islamic countries.

FU'NDY, Bay of. Atlantic inlet between New Brunswick and Nova Scotia, where the tides rapidly rise and fall up to 18m (60ft): its dangers are increased in summer by fog.

FÜNEN. German form of FYN.

FÜNFKIRCHEN (five churches). German name of PÉCS.

FUNGI (fun'jī). In botany, class of plants forming with the algae the Thallophyta. Unlike the algae they have no chlorophyll, and hence must get their food from organic substances. They are either parasites, living on living plants or animals, or saprophytes living on dead matter. F. include bacteria, the slime fungi, moulds, mildew, rusts and smuts, mushrooms, toadstools, puff-balls, etc. F. reproduce by means of spores. Some fungi are edible, but many are highly poisonous.

FUNGI. The penny bun bolete or cêpe *Boletus aestivalis*, growing up amongst sweet chestnut leaves. This forms the staple of many packet soups being adaptable to processing. *Photo: Heather Angel.*

FUR. Animal skin bearing handsome hair worn for warmth: also, in the case of rarer species, regarded as a luxury, e.g. in ancient China, Greece and Rome, and as a status symbol in medieval Europe and, especially for women, in modern times. The modern F. trade originated with the exploitation of N America from the late 17th cent. by the Hudson's Bay Co., etc.: the principal distributing centres are London, New York, and Leningrad. Mink (q.v.) is hard-wearing and long-lasting and has long been the most popular of the high-priced Fs., and lends itself to ranch breeding - more humane than trapping - but chinchilla and Russian sable are even more valuable. In the 1960s there was a trend in fashion towards longer-haired and colourful Fs. with deleterious effect on wildlife, e.g. the leopard, but in the 1970s legislation offered some protection. Artificial F. fabrics formerly offered little competition, but since the S.W.W. there has been increasingly successful use of synthetic fibres such as nylon.

FŪ'RIES. In Greek mythology, the Erinyes or Eumenides, the daughters of Earth or of Night, represented as winged maidens, with serpents twined in their hair. They punished such crimes as filial disobedience, murder, and inhospitality.

FURLONG. Traditional measure of length - 220yds (201m) or 40 rods, poles, or perches: 8 Fs. made one statute mile. Originally it was the length of the furrow in the common field characteristic of medieval husbandry.

FURNESS. Peninsula, formerly a N detached portion of Lancs, separated from the main part by Morecambe Bay. In 1974 it was incl. in the new co. of Cumbria. Barrow is a ship-building and industrial centre.

FURNITURE. Term that includes everything movable that is needed in buildings for human habitation and work. It includes those forms of F. which are used for (1) rest, e.g. chairs, couches, and beds; (2) work, e.g. desks and tables; (3) storage, e.g. chests and cupboards; and (4) decoration, e.g. picture frames. F. is made of a variety of materials incl. wood, metal, stone, glass, plastic, and textiles.

FURNITURE BEETLE. *See* WOODWORM.

FURNITURE. A superb mahogany bookcase by Chippendale in the Gothic style c.1755. *Photo: Courtesy of the Lady Lever Collection.*

FÜRTH (fürt). Town in Bavaria, W Germany, adjoining Nuremberg, it has electrical, chemical, textile and toy industries. Pop. (1978) 105,000.

FURTWÄNGLER (foort'vengler), **Wilhelm** (1886-1954). German conductor. He succeeded Nikisch at Leipzig, and with the Berlin Philharmonic Orchestra. His interpretations of Tchaikovsky and the German romantics, especially Wagner, were regarded as classically definitive. A denazification tribunal cleared him of the charge of having favoured the Hitler régime.

FUSELI (fūz'eli), **Henry Johann Heinrich** (1741-1825). Swiss-born British artist whose work, influenced by Blake, had a fanciful macabre quality which later endeared him to the Surrealists.

FUSEL OIL ($C_5H_{12}O$), also called potato spirit. A liquid with a characteristic unpleasant smell, obtained as a by-product when distilling the product of any alcoholic fermentation, and used in paints, varnishes, essential oils, and plastics.

FUSHUN (foo-shoon). Great coal-mining centre in Liaoning prov., China, 40km (25m) E of Shenyang. It has aluminium, steel, and chemical works. Pop. (1979) 1,100,000.

FUSION, Nuclear. *See* ATOM.

FUTURISM. Literary and artistic movement which burst on Paris in 1909 with a general manifesto by F. P. Marinetti, Italian poet and mountebank, extolling 'a new beauty . . . a roaring motor-car, which runs like a machine gun, is more beautiful than the Winged Victory of Samothrace . . . we wish to glorify war'. Together he and Carrà, Boccioni and Russolo issued further manifestos praising the dynamism of modern life. These artists differed from Cubists in fragmenting their forms with penetrating shafts of light, which, together with their use of colour, infused a feeling of dynamic motion into their work. F. flourished until the advent of the F.W.W.

FUZHOU (foojaw-oo'). Port and cap. (formerly Foochow) of Fujian prov., SE China. It is an important industrial city, and joint foreign and Chinese manufacturing ventures are planned. Mazu (Matsu) Is., occupied by the Nationalists is offshore. Pop. (1979) 990,000.

FYFE, David Maxwell. *See* LORD, KILMUIR.

FYFFE, Will (1885-1947). Scots comedian. He began acting with his father's stock company but by 1921 had achieved great success on the halls, with his vividly portrayed character sketches. His greatest hit was the song 'I Belong to Glasgow'.

FYLINGDALES. (fī'lingdālz). Site in the N Yorkshire Moors Nat. Park, England, of an early-warning radar station, linked with similar stations in Greenland and Alaska, to give a 4-min. warning of nuclear attack.

FYN (fin). Island forming part of Denmark; it lies between the mainland and Zealand. The cap. is Odense. Area 2,976 sq.km (1,149 sq.m).

FYLINGDALES. Erected in 1961, the glass fibre domes of the early warning radar station measure 44 m (145 ft) across. *Photo: Courtesy of the British Tourist Authority.*

FYN. Egeskov in southern Fyn is one of the most beautiful manor-houses in Denmark. Built c.1550 on oak piles rammed into the lake bed, it has walls that rise directly from the surface of the moat. *Photo: Courtesy of the Danish Tourist Board.*

G

The 7th letter of our alphabet. It was formed by the Romans by adding a 'tail' to the letter C which represented the K sound.

GABÈS (gah'bes). Town and port on the Gulf of G., Tunisia, N Africa, 113km (70m) SW of Sfax, standing on the site of the Roman town of Tacapae. Fertilizers and dates are exported. Pop. (1970) 80,000.

GABLE, Clark (1901-60). American actor. A star for more than 30 years in 90 films; he was celebrated for his romantic nonchalance and tough-with-women roles, e.g. as Rhett Butler in *Gone with the Wind.* He was nicknamed the 'King' of Hollywood, and the third of his five wives was actress Carole Lombard, killed in an air crash in 1942.

GABO, Naum (1890-1977). Russian sculptor. One of the leading exponents of Constructivism, he left Russia in 1923 and settled first in London, in USA from 1946. In his sculpture he made use of modern synthetic materials.

GABON (gahbōōn'). Republic on the Atlantic coast of Africa, S of Cameroon. Formerly a French territory, it remained within the French Community on attaining independence in 1960. It has a broad coastal plain, rising to a hilly interior; the equator passes through it. Cocoa, coffee and timber are produced and minerals incl. manganese, uranium, oil and natural gas, and gold. The cap. and chief port is Libreville. Under Pres. Omar Bongo (1935-) from 1967 (re-elected 1973, 1979) there has been social and economic development. Area 266,700 sq.km (103,000 sq.m); pop. (1974) 950,000, of whom a quarter are Fang. The official language is French; M.U. CFA franc.

GABOR (gah'bor), **Dennis** (1900-79). Hungarian-British physicist. In 1958 he invented a type of colour TV tube of greatly reduced depth, and in 1971 was awarded a Nobel prize for his invention of the holographic method of 3-dimensional photography in 1947.

GABORONE (gahborōn'ā). Cap. of Botswana from 1964, mainly an admin. centre, it is near the Transvaal border. Pop. (1977) 34,000.

GABRIEL. An archangel who is mentioned in the book of Daniel, and in the NT announces the birth of John the Baptist to Zacharias and of Christ to the Virgin Mary.

GADDI (gah'dē). Name of three Florentine religious painters, viz. **Gaddo G.** (*c.* 1260-1333), and his son **Taddeo G.** (1300-66) and grandson **Agnoli G.** (*c.* 1333-96).

GADIDAE (gad'idē). Family of fish found in the northern hemisphere, incl. haddock, cod, and turbot.

GAELIC (gā'lik). One of the two main branches of the Celtic languages (q.v.), comprising Irish Gaelic, Scottish Gaelic, and Manx (qq.v.).

GA'FSA. Oasis town in central Tunisia, centre of the phosphate mining area. In Jan. 1980 it was attacked by allegedly Libyan-trained insurgents trying to overthrow the regime. Pop. (1980) 30,000.

GAGA'RIN, Yuri (1934-68). Russian cosmonaut. B. in Smolensk Region, son of a collective farmer, he qualified as a foundryman. He became a pilot 1957 and completed the first manned space flight 12 April 1961, orbiting Earth at *c.* 30,000 kph. He d. on a routine training flight. In 1973 an asteroid in the constellation Leo was named after him.

GAIA (gā'a) or **Ge.** Greek goddess of the Earth sprung from primordial Chaos, she herself produced Uranus (q.v.), by whom she was the mother of the Cyclopes and Titans (qq.v.), etc. *See* LIFE.

GAINSBOROUGH, Thomas (1727-88). British artist. B. at Sudbury, Suffolk, he began to paint while still at school, and in 1741 went to London where he learnt etching and studied at the Academy of Arts, but remained largely self-taught. In 1759 he settled at Bath, becoming famous as a painter of high society - his portraits of Sir Charles Holte, Garrick, and the 'Blue Boy' belong to this period. In 1768 he became one of the original members of the Royal Academy, and in 1774 went to London where his sitters incl. the royal family, Mrs Siddons, Dr Johnson, Burke, and Sheridan. His portraits are noted for their clear tones, graceful lines and a naturalistic approach, generally free from classical influence. In landscape, which he preferred to the portraiture which earned his living, he followed the Dutch as one of the first English artists to substitute real scenery for imaginary Italian.

GAINSBOROUGH. Town on the r. Trent, Lincs, England, 24km (15m) NW of Lincoln. An agricultural marketing centre; it has flour mills, makes agricultural machinery, etc. Pop. (1974) 18,000.

GAITSKELL (gāt'skel), **Hugh Todd Naylor** (1906-63). British Labour statesman. Ed. at Oxford, he became head of the dept of Political Economy at Univ. Coll., London, in 1938. In 1945 he was elected MP for S Leeds, and was Min. of Fuel and Power 1947-50, when he succeeded Cripps, first as Min. of Economic Affairs and then as Chancellor of the Exchequer until Oct. 1951. When the 'Bevanite' controversy arose within the Labour Party, he took the official line, and had a resounding victory over Bevan when elected party leader in 1955. His attempt in 1959 to modify party policy on nationalization and the split in 1960 between advocates of unilateral disarmament and the official multilateralist line threatened his position, but he was re-elected in 1960 and at his death had achieved undisputed authority.

GALAPAGOS ISLANDS. Group of 13 large and many smaller is. in the Pacific Ocean 1,120 km (695m) W of Ecuador, to whom they belong: their Spanish name is Archipiélago de Colón. The cap. is San Cristobal, on the is. of the same name. The unique fauna, studied by Darwin, incl. giant tortoises (*galapagos*), and the is. are a nature reserve. Area 7,800 sq.km (3,000 sq.m); pop. (1974) 4,000.

GALATEA (galatē'a). In Greek mythology, a sea nymph who loved Acis, and when he was killed by Polyphemus transformed his blood into the river Acis. Pygmalion made a statue (later named G.) which was brought to life by Aphrodite.

GALATI (galats'). Port in Romania, on the Danube below its confluence with the Seret. There are ship-building, iron and steel, textile, food processing, perfume and cosmetic industries. Pop. (1977) 244,000.

GALAPAGOS. The giant tortoise *(Testudo elephantopus)* which is now carefully preserved on the islands. *Photo: Mireille Vautier.*

GALĀ'TIA. Ancient prov. of Asia Minor, occupying part of the inland plateau. It was occupied by the Gauls in the 3rd cent. BC, and in 25 BC became a Roman province.

GALAXY. A star system such as that in which our Solar System lies, and which contains about 100,000 million stars. There are two main types: the spiral, which are flattened and comparatively rapidly rotating disc-shaped systems - of which our galaxy is one - and the elliptical, which are cigar-shaped and rotate only slowly, and are thought to have been formed by interaction between originally spiral galaxies by a kind of tidal action.

Some 90% of the mass of any galaxy is spread in the form of small dark objects across a halo, which surrounds the bright stars that form the remaining 10%, and the halo may spread twenty times as far across space as the brightly visible section. Our own galaxy is about 100,000 light years across. All the galaxies, except those such as Andromeda which are part of our own 'Local Group', are receding from us at tremendous speeds.

GALAZ. German form of GALATI.

GALBRAITH, John Kenneth (1908-). Canadian political economist. Prof. at Harvard 1949-75, he wrote *The Affluent Society* (1958) and *Economics and the Public Purpose* (1974), the latter introducing 'the convenient social virtue,' e.g. the praise given by men to women in the role of housewives.

GALEN (gā'len) (*c.* 130-*c.* 200). Greek physician B. at Pergamum, Mysia, Asia Minor, he was accounted second only to Hippocrates among the physicians of antiquity. He was skilled in anatomy and physiology. Some 80 of his 500 treatises have survived.

GALICIA (galish'ia). Former kingdom and modern region of NW Spain, comprising the provs. of La Coruña, Lugo, Orense and Pontevedra. Autonomy was attained in 1981. The language is close to Portuguese. Galicians have a reputation for caution, and Franco came from this area. Galicia was also the name of a prov. of central Europe, formerly a part of Austria, part of Poland after the F.W.W., divided 1945 between Poland and Russia. It occupied the northern slopes of the Carpathians, stretching southwards to the frontiers of Czechoslovakia and Romania.

GALILEE (gal'ilē). A Roman prov. of Palestine, bounded by Samaria on the S, Phoenicia on the W, Coele Syria on the N, the r. Jordan on the E. The SEA OF GALILEE, or Lake Tiberias, lies in the Jordan valley 105km (65m) N of the Dead Sea, and is frequently mentioned in the Gospels.

GALILEO (galēlā'ō) **Galilei** (1564-1642). Italian scientist. B. at Pisa, he studied at the univ. there, and was prof. of mathematics. An opponent's demonstration - by dropping 2 stones of unequal weight from the top of the Leaning Tower - confirmed his view that all falling bodies, great or small, descend with equal velocity, making him unpopular with the orthodox scientists, and he resigned his chair in 1591. From 1592 to 1610 he was prof. of mathematics at Padua. He improved the recently invented telescope, and with it was the first man to see satellites of Jupiter. His astronomical observations led him to accept the Copernican system, which he advocated in his *Dialogues on the two chief systems of the Universe*, pub. in 1632. The book was banned, and G. was summoned to Rome by the Inquisition, and eventually made to recant his views.

GALL (gahl), **Franz Joseph.** *See* PHRENOLOGY.

GALLAS. Race of Hamitic people inhabiting a large area of E Africa in Ethiopia and Kenya.

GALLE (gahl'leh), **Johann Gottfried** (1812-1910). German astronomer, who in 1846 discovered the planet Neptune.

GALL FLY. Small hymenopterous insects of the family Cynipidae. They are similar in appearance to wasps and lay their eggs in leaves, twigs, or roots of plants causing galls, i.e. swellings of various kinds.

GA'LLICO, Paul William (1897-1976). American author. Of Italo-Austrian parentage, G. was b. in New York. Originally a leading American sports columnist, he began writing fiction in 1936, and his books incl. *The Snow Goose* (1941), illustrated by Sir Peter Scott.

GALLIFO'RMĒS. The order of birds that includes the game birds.

GALLI'POLI. City and port in European Turkey, on the W shore of the Dardanelles, giving its name to the peninsula on which it stands. In the F.W.W. an unsuccessful campaign was undertaken, from Feb. 1915 to Jan. 1916, first naval and then military with British Empire and French troops under Sir Ian Hamilton, to force these narrows and thus open up communication with Russia.

GALLIUM. Chemical element. Symbol Ga; at. wt. 69.72; at. no. 31. A grey metal liquid at near room temperatures, it is very scarce and was discovered in 1875 by Lecoq de Boisbaudran. **Gallium arsenide** is being used in the new generation of microelectronic 'superchips', since electrons travel a thousand times faster through it than they do through silicon.

GÄLLIVARE (galēvah're). Iron-mining centre in Swedish Lapland, 65km (40m) N of the Arctic Circle. Pop. (1972) 27,500.

GALILEO. The story that, after his recantation, he rose from his knees, stamped on the Earth and said, 'Yet it does move!' is apocryphal, but typical of his impetuosity. *Photo: Popperfoto.*

GALLON. Imperial liquid and dry measure. Its capacity is 4 quarts or 8 pints or 277.274 cu.in, and 2 gallons make a peck. It equals 4.546 litres.

GALLOWAY (gal'ō-). Ancient division of SW Scotland, famous for horses and cattle, and incl. Wigtown and Kirkcudbright. *See* DUMFRIES AND G.

GALLS. On plants, vegetative growths caused by the presence of insects of the Cynipidae (gall fly, q.v.) family, which lay their eggs on the plant. An irritation is set up, and a swelling arises. The grubs live within the swelling. Among the commonest Gs. are bedeguar (on roses) and oak apples.

GALLSTONE. Biliary calculus; a hard, insoluble, pebble-like accretion formed in the human gall-bladder or bile duct by the precipitation of salts, chiefly cholesterol, from relatively stagnant bile. The size varies from a grain of sand to a walnut.

GALLUP, George Horace (1901-). American journalist and statistician, founder in 1935 of the American Institute of Public Opinion and deviser of the *G. Polls,* in which public opinion is gauged by questioning a number of representative individuals.

GALSWORTHY (gawlz'-), **John** (1867-1933). British novelist and dramatist. B. at Kingston, Surrey, he achieved success with *The Man of Property* (1906), the first instalment of *The Forsyte Saga* (1922), which included *In Chancery* and *To Let.* Soames Forsyte is the embodiment of the Victorian feeling for property, and the wife whom he also 'owns' - Irene - was based on G.'s wife.

GALLIPOLI. Men of the Royal Naval Division and Australian troops sharing a trench. One man is using a periscope (left) and another a 'sniperscope'. *Photo: Courtesy of the Imperial War Museum.*

Later additions to the series are *A Modern Comedy* (1929), which contained *The White Monkey, The Silver Spoon,* and *Swan Song,* and the short stories *On Forsyte Change* (1930). Among G.'s novels outside the Forsyte group are *The Country House* (1907), *Fraternity* (1909), *The Patrician* (1911), and *The Dark Flower* (1913). In 1906 G. also estab. himself as a dramatist with *The Silver Box*: later plays include *Strife* (1909), *Justice* (1910), *The Skin Game* (1920), *Loyalties* (1922), and *Old English* (1924). In all his work G. was deeply concerned with social conditions, and tackled problems such as the conflicts between employers and workmen, landed gentry and the manufacturers, and the prison system. OM 1929.

GALT, John (1779-1839). Scottish novelist. B. in Ayrshire, he moved to London in 1804 and 1826-9 was in Canada. He is best known for the *Annals of the Parish* (1821) in which he portrays the life of a Lowlands village, using the local dialect. He founded the Canadian town of Guelph, and Galt, on the Grand r. in Ontario, was named after him.

GALTON, Sir Francis (1822-1911). British anthropologist. B. at Birmingham, he studied medicine, explored in Africa, made pioneer researches in meteorology, and then, under the influence of his cousin Charles Darwin, studied heredity. He wrote *Hereditary Genius* (1869), *Natural Inheritance* (1889), etc., and endowed a chair of Eugenics, a study he founded, at London.

GALVANI (gahlvah'nē), **Luigi** (1737-98). Italian scientist. B. at Bologna, where he taught anatomy, he discovered galvanic or voltaic electricity in 1762, when investigating the contractions produced in the muscles of dead frogs by contact with charged metal.

GALVANIZING. Process for rendering iron rust-proof, by plunging it into molten zinc (the dipping method), or by electro-deposition, in which zinc is electro-plated from aqueous solution.

GALVANOMETER. Instrument for indicating small electric current by means of its magnetic effect.

GALVESTON. City and port in Texas, USA, at the entrance to G. Bay. It exports cotton, petroleum, wheat, timber; and has chemical works, petroleum refineries, etc. It is subject to hurricanes, one in 1900 killing 8,000 people. Pop. (1970) 61,810.

GALWAY, James (1939–) British flautist B. in Belfast, he was a member of the Berlin Philharmonic Orchestra 1969-75, before becoming a virtuoso, with works written for him by Rodney Bennett and Thea Musgrave.

GALWAY (gawl'wā). County of Rep. of Ireland on the W coast, in Connacht. The E part is low-lying. In the S are the Slieve Aughty mts. W of Lough Corrib is Connemara, a wild area of moors, hills, lakes, and bogs. In the S is G. Bay with the Aran islands. The Shannon is the principal river. G. is the county town; other towns include Ballinasloe, Tuam, Clifden, and Loughrea, near which deposits of lead, zinc and copper were found 1959. Area 5,939 sq.km (2,293 sq.m); pop. (1971) 149,220.

GALWAY. Co. town and fishing port of G. co., Rep. of Ireland, on G. Bay, at the mouth of the Corrib. G. Univ. was estab. 1968. Pop. (1971) 26,896.

GAMA (gah'mah), **Vasco da** (*c.* 1460-1524). Portuguese navigator. B. at Sines, he was chosen by Emanuel I to command an expedition sent in 1497 to discover the Cape route to India. The land he touched on Christmas Day, 1497, he named Natal. Crossing the Indian Ocean, he arrived at Calicut in May 1498, and arrived back in Portugal in Sept. 1499. In 1502 he founded a Portuguese colony at Mozambique and sacked Calicut in revenge for the murder of some Portuguese seamen. After 20 years of retirement, he was despatched to India again as Portuguese viceroy in 1524, but d. 2 months after his arrival in Goa.

GAMBETTA, Léon Michel (1838-82). French statesman. After Sedan he was one of the founders of the French Republic and organized a fierce resistance against the German invaders. In 1881-2 he was Prime Minister for a few weeks.

GA'MBIA, The. Country of W Africa comprising the is. of Banjul (area 76 sq.km/29 sq.m), on which is the cap., also Banjul (formerly Bathurst), and a strip up to 32km (20m) wide extending inland 320km (200m) on both sides of the r. Gambia. The river is bordered by swamps from which the land rises to bush country. Groundnuts are the chief export: there is no known mineral wealth.

British traders estab. a settlement in the area in 1618, and G. became a Crown Colony 1888, and independent within the Commonwealth 1965, adopting republican status 1970. Area 11,000 sq.km (4,000 sq.m); pop. (1978) 568,000, of whom the largest tribe are the Mandingo. They are chiefly Moslem. M.U.: dalasi. A confederal Senegambia was proclaimed in 1982: *See* SENEGAL.

GAMBIA. River in W Africa, which rises in the Fouta Djallon plateau, Guinea, and flows 1,000 km (620m) through Senegal and Gambia to enter the Atlantic at Banjul. It is navigable for ocean-going ships for *c.* 300km.

GAMBLING. The playing of games of pure chance into which skill does not enter, e.g. roulette and all games in which dice (or other mechanical means) are used to decide the chance; or wagering on some fortuitous event. In the UK the Betting and Gaming Act (1960) relaxed previous prohibitions and in 1966 licence duties on gaming were introduced; in the USA gambling is regulated by individual states.

GAME LAWS. In Britain the laws relating to game preservation and the punishment of poachers and trespassers 'in pursuit of game'. The Game Act, 1831, defines game as hares, pheasants, partridges, grouse, heath or moor game, black game, and bustards.

GAMELIN (gahmlañ'), **Maurice Gustave** (1872-1958) French general. French C-in-C and Generalissimo of the Allied armies in France in 1939, he was replaced by Weygand on the enemy breakthrough at Sedan in 1940, and tried as a scapegoat before the Riom 'War Guilt' court in 1942. He refused to defend himself, and was deported to Germany until released by the Allies in 1945.

GAMMA RADIATION. Very high-frequency electromagnetic radiation emitted by the nuclei of radioactive substances during decay, similar in nature to X-rays. *See* diagram under entry ELECTROMAGNETIC WAVES.

GANDHI, Indira (1917–84). Indian stateswoman. The dau. of Nehru (q.v.), she studied at Oxford and was imprisoned during the struggle for independence. In 1942 she m. Feroze Gandhi (d. 1960), not related to the Mahatma, and acted as hostess for her father from 1947. In 1966 she succeeded Shastri as PM and leader of the Congress Parliamentary Party. In 1975 her election to the Lok Sabha was declared invalid and she declared a state of emergency. During this time her son Sanjay (1946-80) entered politics, and his social and economic programme, incl. a ruthless family planning policy, aroused much opposition. She was consequently defeated in 1977, but re-elected in 1980. She was assassinated in 1984, reportedly by Sikh extremists, and succeeded by her eldest son Rajiv Gandhi.

GANDHI, Mohandas Karamchand (1869-1948). Indian social and political leader, called Mahatma (Great Soul) G. Born in Porbandar state, he studied law in London, and in 1893 went to S Africa, where he stayed for some years successfully leading the Indian community in their passive resistance to discriminatory legislation. In 1915 he returned to India to struggle for Indian home rule, by the method of 'non-violent non-co-operation' (*satyagraha*, defence of and by truth). During a series of campaigns of non-co-operation 1920–44, in the course of which he was imprisoned several times, he estab. an influence over the British authorities, and over the Congress (nationalist) Party, which he was to retain all his life although never himself taking office; in the negotiations which eventually resulted in the attainment of independence in 1947 he played an active part behind the scenes. He undertook several 'fasts unto death' on behalf of the 'Untouchables', and during the last weeks of 1947 undertook fasts to end the rioting and anti-Moslem violence which followed Partition. He was assassinated by a Hindu nationalist on 30 Jan. 1948.

GANESA (ganā'sa). One of the principal Hindu gods, represented as elephant-headed, and worshipped as a remover of obstacles.

GANGES. Great river of India and Bangladesh, the most sacred river of the Hindus. It rises in the Himalayas and flows 2,506 km (1,557 m) to reach the Bay of Bengal through a wide delta, the main stream flowing through Bangladesh as the Padma and the Meghna. At Allahabad it receives its chief tributary, the Yamuna.

GA'NGRĒNE. Local death of tissues, due to destruction of tissue through injury, burning, freezing, etc.; poisoning; or failure of the blood supply, as where a bandage is too tight or the vessels are abnormally contracted, or where a vessel is blocked with a blood clot (thrombosis). The affected parts are painful and sensitive and feel cold, and their skin turns brownish or violet. The mass may become infected (wet G). Amputation may be necessary.

GANNET or **solan goose.** Sea-bird (*Sula bassana*) in the family Sulidae. When full-grown it is white with black-tipped wings, but the young are speckled. It breeds on cliffs, the nest being roughly made of grass and seaweed. Only one white egg is laid.

GANSU (gahnsoo'). Prov. of NW China (formerly Kansu). It is mountainous in the S and W, has an extreme climate, and is subject to earthquakes. The ancient caravan 'Silk Road' to central Asia through G. is now a motor road, and there is a rail route into Xinjiang. Cereals and fruit are grown; minerals incl. coal and a major oilfield, and the hydroelectric station (1974) on the Yellow r. is one of China's largest. The cap. is Lanzhou. Area 530,000. sq.km (204,633 sq.m); pop. (1979) 19,000,000.

GANYMEDE (ga'nimēd). In Greek myth a youth so beautiful he was chosen as cupbearer to Zeus (Jupiter), hence one of planet Jupiter's moons is named after him. About the same size as Callisto, it has the same icy surface, patches and brown blotches.

GARBO, Greta. Assumed name of the Swedish actress Greta Lovisa Gustafsson (1905-). She was trained at the Royal Theatre dramatic school, Stockholm, made her first film *The Story of Gosta Berling* in 1924, and then went to the USA, where she played in *The Torrent* (1926), becoming one of Hollywood's first 'stars'. Her later films incl. *Anna Christie* (1930), her first 'talkie', *Mata Hari* (1931), *Queen Christina* (1933), *Anna Karenina* (1935), *Camille* (1936), and *Ninotchka* (1939). A great personality rather than a great actress, she has become a legend.

GA'RCHING. Location NE of Munich, W Germany, of a nuclear research centre.

GARCIA LORCA (gahrthē'-ah lork'ah), **Federico** (1899-1936). Spanish poet. B. in Granada, he had a special affinity with the gipsies of the region, and his *Romancero gitano* (1928, *Gipsy Ballad-book*) has all the spirit of Andalusian songs. In 1929-30 L. visited New York, and his experiences are reflected in *Poeta en Nuevo York*. Returning to Spain, he founded a touring theatrical company and himself wrote plays such as *Bodas de sangre* (*Blood Wedding*) and *La Casa de Bernarda Alba* (*The House of Bernarda Alba*). His finest poem is his *Lament* for the bullfighter Mejías. He was shot by the Falangists.

GARD (gahr). French river, 133km (83m) long, a tributary of the Rhône, which it joins above Beaucaire. It gives its name to G. dept.

GARDA, Lake. Largest lake in Italy, in Lombardy and Veneto: area 370 sq.km (143 sq.m).

GARDEN CITY. Town built in a rural area and designed to combine town and country advantages, with its own industries, controlled developments, private and public gardens, cultural centre, etc. The idea was proposed by the Englishman Ebenezer Howard, who in 1899 formed the G.C. Association, and the first G.C. was Letchworth near Hitchin. A second, Welwyn, 35km (22m) from London, was started in 1919. The New Towns Act, 1946, provided machinery for developing new towns on some of the principles advocated by Howard (e.g. Stevenage, begun in 1947), and there have been various similar schemes in Europe and in the US, but on the whole these have not kept the economic structure, or the industrial self-sufficiency or the permanent rural belt which formed an integral part of Howard's original idea.

GARDEN OF THE GODS. Site NW of Colorado Springs, Colorado, USA, where natural sandstone 'sculptures' are a tourist attraction.

GARDINER, Stephen (*c.* 1493-1555). English churchman and statesman. After being secretary to Wolsey, he entered the king's service, became bishop of Winchester in 1531, and on Mary's accession was created Lord Chancellor. He played a prominent part in the attempted restoration of Catholicism.

GARDNER, Erle Stanley (1889-1970). American author. B. in Mass., he was in 1911 admitted to the California Bar, and in 1932 wrote his first crime story featuring the lawyer-detective Perry Mason, hero of film and television versions of later cases.

GARDNER, Dame Helen (1908-). British scholar. She ed. the poetry and prose of Donne, and the *New Oxford Book of English Verse* (1972), was Merton Prof. of English Literature at Oxford 1966-75, and was created DBE 1967.

GARDNER, John (1917-). British composer. Prof. at the RAM from 1956, he has produced a symphony (1947), the opera *The Moon and Sixpence* (1957), based on the Maugham novel; and other works incl. film music.

GARFIELD, James Abram (1831-81). 20th President of the USA. B. in a log cabin in Ohio, he entered politics as a Republican and served with distinction in the Civil War on the side of the North. He was inaugurated President in 1881, but a few months later was shot in a Washington station by a madman.

GARGOYLE. Spout projecting from the roof-gutter of a building with the purpose of directing water away from the wall. The term is usually applied to the ornamental forms found in Gothic architecture; these were carved in stone and took the shape of fantastic animals, angels, or human heads.

GARIBALDI (gahrēbahl'dē), **Giuseppe** (1807-82). Italian patriot. B. in Nice, he became a sailor, and in 1834 joined Mazzini's Young Italy society. Condemned to death for treason, he escaped to S America where he lived the life of a soldier of fortune. He returned to Italy during the 1848 revolution, served with the Sardinian army against the Austrians, and commanded the army of the Roman republic in its defence of the city against the French. He subsequently lived in exile until 1854, when he settled on Caprera. He again fought against the Austrians in the war of 1859; and in 1860, at the head of his 1,000 Redshirts, conquered Sicily and Naples for the new kingdom of Italy. He led 2 unsuccessful expeditions to liberate Rome from papal rule in 1862 and 1867, served in the Austrian War of 1866, and fought for the French in the Franco-Prussian War.

GARLAND, Judy (1922-69). American singer and actress, *née* Frances Gumm. B. in Grand Rapids, she leapt to stardom in the film *The Wizard of Oz* (1939), featuring the song 'Over the Rainbow'. She had great warmth of personality. Her dau. Liza Minnelli (1946-) also a singer and actress, won an academy award for *Cabaret* (1972).

GARLIC. Perennial plant of the Liliaceae family, the bulb of which has a strong odour and flavour. The edible G. is *Allium sativum*.

GARNET. A group of minerals used as gems and abrasives. They are usually pale pink to deep red, and are of common occurrence in gneiss and schist, crystallized limestones, etc.

GARO'NNE. River rising in the Spanish Pyrenees, then flowing NW through France to the Gironde estuary. Toulouse and Bordeaux are the chief towns on it. It gives its names to the depts of Haute-Garonne, Tarn-et-Garonne, and Lot-et-Garonne.

GARRICK, David (1717–79). British actor. B. in Hereford, he was ed. at Lichfield grammar school and also briefly under Johnson, of whose circle in London he was to become a member, and both set out for the capital together in 1737. He made his début in 1741, and his Richard III and Lear brought him fame, so that he was engaged for Drury Lane. In 1747 he became joint-patentee of the theatre with his own co. The expressiveness and naturalness of his acting, and his gift of mimicry, broke startlingly with the traditional chanting delivery and he excelled in a variety of parts incl. Hamlet, Benedick, Archer in *The Beaux' Stratagem* and Abel Drugger in *The Alchemist.* He himself wrote plays, e.g. *The Clandestine Marriage* (1766, with Colman), and made numerous adaptations. He retired from the stage in 1766, but continued as a manager.

GARRICK. David Garrick as Richard III. William Hogarth has chosen to depict the moment when the King wakes from a nightmare before the fatal Battle of Bosworth. *Photo: Popperfoto.*

GARTER, Order of the. The senior British order of knighthood, founded by Edward III *c.* 1347. Its distinctive badge is a garter of dark blue velvet, with the motto of the order, *Honi soit qui mal y pense,* in gold letters, worn below the left knee. Membership is limited to 25 knights, and to members of the royal family and foreign royalties; appointments are made by the sovereign without ministerial recommendation. St George's Chapel, Windsor, is the chapel of the order. *See* BLUE RIBAND.

GARVEY, Marcus (1887–1940). Jamaican Negro leader. Founder of the Universal Negro Improvement Assocn (1911), he campaigned to colonize Africa with black Americans, the 'Back to Africa' movement. This also influenced peasants in S America.

GARVEY. The founder of the 'Back to Africa' movement in a New York parade. The gorgeous uniform was of his own devising. *Photo: Popperfoto.*

GARY. City in Indiana, USA, at the southern end of Lake Michigan. It contains the largest steel and cement works in the world, those of the United States Steel Corporation, and was named after E. H. Gary (1846-1927) its chairman. Pop. (1970) 175,415.

GAS. Word first used by J. B. van Helmont (1577-1644) for what may be defined as a form of matter that has neither volume nor shape, and such that when a given quantity of it is introduced into a vessel, it will fill the vessel completely. Gs. behave according to certain fundamental laws relating pressure, volume, and temperature. *See* BOYLE, R. and CHARLES'S LAW. Examples of gases are the elements hydrogen, helium, nitrogen, neon, etc., and among compounds, carbon monoxide, carbon dioxide, and nitrous oxide.

Natural gas is the gaseous form of the complex mixture of hydrocarbons called petroleum; crude oil is the liquid form, and bitumen the solid form, which is found at the surface when the lighter hydrocarbons have escaped to the atmosphere. Natural G. and oil are retained below the surface only if there is an adequate impervious capping layer laid down over the top of the accumulation, which is usually found in association with coal reserves. The capping is usually shale.

When oil deposits first began to be exploited the G. was regarded as a waste product, but since the S.W.W. has been increasingly utilized as fuel, and large deposits have been discovered, notably under the North Sea, in Siberia, in the Netherlands, North Africa, and Australia. Natural G. is usually 90% methane, but may also contain varying proportions of ethane, propane, and butane - used in the petrochemical industry - helium, hydrogen, sulphur, etc., all industrially utilizable.

For 150 years the traditional gas-making process was by coal carbonization, but from *c.* 1960 the process was increasingly based on oil, and then from 1965 increasingly on natural gas.

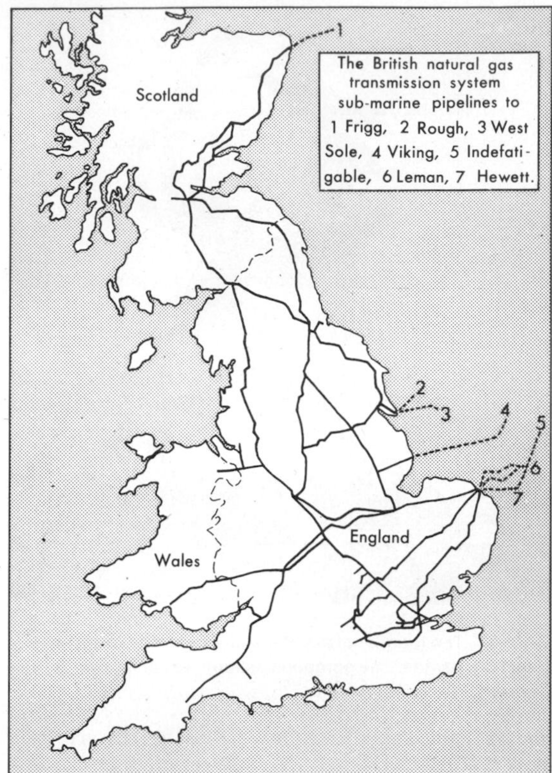

GAS. The British Gas high pressure transmission system for the distribution of natural gas from the fields in the North Sea. *Courtesy of the British Gas Corporation*

GASCONY. Ancient province of SW France. Henry II of England gained possession of it through his marriage to Eleanor of Aquitaine in 1152, and it was often in English hands until 1451. It was united with the royal domain in 1607 under Henry IV.

GAS ENGINES. Type of internal combustion engine, in which G. (coal, producer, natural, or gas from a blast furnace) is used as the fuel. The first practical G.E. was built in 1860 by Lenoir, and the type was subsequently developed by Otto.

GASKELL, Elizabeth Cleghorn (1810-65). British novelist. B. at Chelsea, *née* Stevenson, she was brought up by an aunt in Knutsford, Cheshire, the Cranford of her later writings. She m. William G., a Unitarian minister. Her first novel, *Mary Barton* (1848), depicts the problems of life among Manchester factory-hands. Her masterpiece was *Cranford* (1853), a delicate study of village life. Later books include *Ruth* (1853), *North and South* (1855), *Sylvia's Lovers* (1863-4), and the unfinished *Wives and Daughters* (1866). She was a friend of Charlotte Brontë, and her life of her is a standard work.

GA'SOHOL. Motor fuel, 90% petrol, plus 10% alcohol, usually distilled from maize, wheat, potatoes or sugar cane. It was used in early cars before cheap petrol, and was revived in the energy shortage.

GASOLENE. A mixture of hydrocarbons derived from petroleum, whose main use is as a fuel for internal combustion engines. It is colourless and highly volatile. In USA petrol is called gasoline.

GASPÉ PENINSULA (gahspā'). Mountainous peninsula in SE Quebec, Canada, S of the St Lawrence. Fishing and lumbering are carried on. Area 29,500 sq.km (11,390 sq.m).

GASPERI (gahspā'rē), **Alcide de** (1881-1954). Italian statesman. Imprisoned by the Fascists 1926-8, he was released to work in the Vatican Library. A founder of the Christian Democrat party, he was PM 1945-53, and worked for European unification.

GASTERO'PODA. Class of molluscs, including snails, whelks, etc. They have a well-developed head and a rough tongue, and move by means of muscular contractions of the ventral surface or 'foot'. Except in the very simplest forms, the body is asymmetrical.

GASTRĪTIS. Inflammation of the lining of the stomach. It may be caused by corrosive poisons (e.g. lysol, caustic soda, strong acids), too high a concentration of alcohol, or infection.

GASTRŌENTERĪ'TIS. Inflammation of the stomach and intestines leading to vomiting and diarrhoea, usually caused by contaminated food.

GAS WARFARE. The offensive use of G. to produce a toxic, irritant, or lethal effect on the human body. The idea of G.W. developed with industrial chemistry, so that by 1899 at The Hague Conference the use of toxic substances for war was foreseen by the Great Powers, who (with the exception of the US) pledged abstinence from their employment. However, in 1915 during the F.W.W., the Germans launched a cylinder attack with chlorine against the Allies, who subsequently retaliated in kind. G. shells and mustard G. were also used, accounting for many casualties - immediate and long-term. Chlorine is an example of a lung irritant and mustard G. of a vesicant; other types incl. adamsite, a sneeze gas, and chloropicrin, a tear gas. Most insidious and difficult to detect are nerve Gs., found on German airfields after the S.W.W.; these attack the central nervous system through any moist surface of the body, esp. the eyes. In the S.W.W. there was no G.W. - largely because of more effective countermeasures, e.g. respirators to filter out the noxious substances. In the Vietnam War the USA used tear gas, but in 1975 ratified the Geneva Protocol of 1925 banning the first use of asphyxiating, poisonous and other gases in war.

Forms of tear G. are also used as a last resort in civil disturbances (N Ireland 1969), or against armed criminals, to avoid greater casualties by other means: a common type is the irritant CS gas (ortho-chlorobenzylidenemalononitrile).

GATESHEAD. Port in Tyne and Wear, England, on the Tyne opposite Newcastle. It is an engineering centre with chemical, glass and shipbuilding industries and rail workshops. Pop. (1972) 93,490.

GA'TWICK. Location in Surrey, England, 43km (27m) S of London, site of G. Airport, London, constructed 1956-8.

GAUCHO (gow'chō). South American tribe, part Indian part Spanish, inhabiting the Argentine and Uraguayan pampas. They are nomadic, fine horsemen, and expert in the use of the lasso and bolas.

GAUDI (gowdē'), **Antonio** (1852-1926). Spanish architect. Noted for his flamboyantly individual style, influenced by Moorish and medieval buildings, he is most famous for his incomplete Church of the Holy Family in Barcelona, begun in 1883, on which he was still working when he died.

GAUDIER-BRZESKA (gōdyā'-bresh'ka), **Henri** (1891-1915). French sculptor. He studied art at Bristol, Nuremberg and Munich, and became a member of the English Vorticist movement. His sculptures incl. 'The Dancer' and 'The Embracers'.

GAUGE (gāj). A scientific measuring instrument, e.g. wire-G., pressure-G. The term is also applied to the width of a railway or tramway track.

GAUGUIN (gōgań'), **Paul** (1848-1903). French artist. B. in Paris, he joined a banking firm, but threw up his career in 1881 in order to paint. After a visit to Martinique in 1887, he went to Pont Aven in Brittany, becoming the leading artist in the movement known as *Synthesism.* In 1891 he left Paris for Tahiti, where he remained from 1895 until his death, finding inspiration in the simple life and tropical colouring of the islands. A friend of Van Gogh, he disliked theories and rules of painting, and his pictures are Expressionist compositions characterized by his use of pure, unmixed colours. Among his most famous paintings is 'Le Christe Jaune'.

GAULS. The Celtic-speaking peoples who inhabited France and Belgium in Roman times. They were divided into several tribes, but united by a common religion controlled by the Druid priesthood. Certain tribes invaded Italy *c.* 400 BC, sacked Rome, and settled between the Alps and the Apennines; this district, known as Cisalpine Gaul, was conquered by Rome *c.* 225 BC. The Romans conquered S Gaul between the Mediterranean and the Cevennes *c.* 125 BC, and the remaining Gs. up to the Rhine were conquered by Caesar 58-51 BC.

GAUR (gowr). Indian wild ox (*Bibos gaurus*). It is dark grey with white legs, measures nearly 2m (6ft) high, and has a ridge between the horns.

GAUSS (gows), **Karl Friedrich** (1777-1855). German mathematician and physicist. B. in Brunswick, he became professor of astronomy at Göttingen in 1807. His *Disquisitiones Arithmeticae* (1801) became a standard work on the theory of numbers. The unit of magnetic-field strength is known as a *gauss*, and the method devised to counter the German magnetic mine in 1939 was named *degaussing.*

GAUTIER (gōtyā'), **Théophile** (1811-72). French writer. Influenced by the Romantics, his poetry expresses his passion for beauty, and is distinguished by an instinct for descriptive language and imagery. He was a gifted prose writer also, his best-known novel being *Mlle de Maupin* (1835); soon after this he turned to journalism, writing short stories, dramatic and literary criticism and travel sketches.

GAY, John (1685-1732). British poet. B. at Barnstaple, he was the friend of Pope and Arbuthnot, and produced in his *Trivia* (1716) an excellent verse picture of 18th cent. London. His *The Beggar's Opera* (1728), 'a Newgate pastoral' telling of the love of Polly for highwayman Capt. Macheath, has held the stage ever since and inspired Brecht (q.v.): it was the first opera in English (as opposed to Italian) and used English folk tunes. Its satiric political touches led to the banning of *Polly,* a sequel.

GAYA (gī'ah). Ancient Indian city, in Bihar state, which is famous for its association with Buddhism and includes Buddh Gaya (q.v.) with a temple dating back to 543 BC. Pop. (1971) 180,000.

GAY-LUSSAC (gā-lüsahk'), **Joseph Louis** (1778-1850). French physicist and chemist. B. near Limoges, he became professor of physics at Paris in 1808. In 1804 he made balloon ascents to study the weather. He investigated the physical properties of gases and discovered new methods of producing sulphuric and oxalic acids.

GAZA (gah'zah). Town near the coast of SW Palestine, once chief of the 5 Philistine cities and scene of 3 battles in the F.W.W. Pop. 38,000. It was captured by Egypt on the proclamation of Israel 1948, and became cap. of the coastal *Gaza Strip* where 200,000 Arab refugees remained. Israel invaded the strip 1956, and reoccupied it after withdrawal of UN troops 1967. It was retained in the October war of 1973. Area 260 sq.km (100 sq.m); pop. (1972) 365,000.

GAZIANTEP (gahzēahntep'). Turkish town, 185km (115m) NE of Adana, with textile and tanning industries. Pop. (1970) 225,900.

GDANSK. Polish port (Ger. Danzig), cap. of G. voivodship, on the r. Mottla, S of its mouth on the Gulf of G. Founded 1343, G. became a member of the Hanseatic League in 1361. A free city under Polish protection from 1455 until occupied by Prussia 1793, it again became a free city under League of Nations protection in 1919. The remains of a blockhouse on the Westerplatte commemorate G.'s resistance to the Germans 1-7 Sept. 1939: it remained in German occupation 1939-45, but its churches and fine merchant houses were later carefully restored. Shipyard strikes in 1980 enforced democratic concessions from the Communist authorities. Pop. (1978) 444,000.

GDYNIA (gdin'ia). Polish port on the Gulf of Gdansk, founded in 1920 to provide newly constituted Poland with an outlet to the sea. Pop. (1978) 230,000.

GE (jē). *See* GAIA.

GECKO LIZARD. Small soft-skinned lizard in the family Geckonidae. They are common in warm climates, and have a large head, and short, stout body. Gecko is derived from the clicking sound which the animal makes.

GEELONG (gēlong'). Port and city on an inlet of Port Phillip Bay, Victoria, Australia. It exports wool and wheat, and manufactures textiles, glass, fertilizers, etc. Prince Charles was a student at the C of E Grammar School, the 'Eton of Australia', in 1966. Pop. (1976) 122,000.

GEIGER (gī'ger) **COUNTER.** Geiger-Müller, Geiger-Klemperer, Rutherford-Geiger counters are devices often referred to under the generic name G.C. (derived from the name of **Hans G.** (1882-1945), one-time student of Rutherford and prof. of physics at Kiel who was active in their development). They are used for detecting and/or counting nuclear radiations and particles. The principle on which the G.C. operates is the detection of the momentary current which passes between electrodes in a suitable gas when a nuclear particle or a radiation pulse causes ionization in the gas. The electrodes are connected to electronic devices which enable the intensity of radiation or the number of particles passing to be measured.

GEISHA (gā'sha). Female entertainer (music, singing, dancing, etc.), in Japanese teahouses and private parties. Gs. survive mainly as a tourist attraction.

GELATINE (jel'atēn). A protein prepared by boiling hide and bone, which melts when heated and sets when cold. Industrially, it is used in glues and photographic emulsions, and in cookery to make jellies, etc.

GEISHA. Geisha girls selling flowers at the entrance to a Shinto shrine on a festival day in Osaka. *Photo: Mireille Vautier.*

GELBER, Jack (1932-). American playwright. Ed. at the univ. of Illinois, he was unknown until his very frank study of drug addiction *The Connection* was produced 'off-Broadway' in 1959.

GE'LDERLAND. Prov. of the Netherlands lying between the Ijssel Meer on the NW and the German frontier on the SE. It is drained by the Ijssel, the Waal, and the Maas, and is a cattle-rearing area with flax, wheat, sugar beet, and tobacco as important crops. The scrubland in the NW, called the Valuwe, is a favourite holiday district. The cap. is Arnhem; other towns are Nijmegen, Apeldoorn, and Zutphen. Area 5,000 sq.km (1,930 sq.m); pop. (1978) 1,668,250.

GELL-MANN, Murray (1929-). American Physicist. R. A. Millikan prof. of theoretical physics at the California Inst. of Technology from 1967, he was awarded a Nobel prize 1969 for his work on elementary particles and their interaction. He formulated in 1964 the theory of the 'quark' as the fundamental constituent of all matter and smallest particle in the universe.

GELSENKIRCHEN (gel'zenkĕr'khen). City in the Ruhr, W Germany, 10km (6m) NE of Essen, still with iron and steel works, but with growing oil (from coal), chemical, glass and metallurgical industries. Pop. (1978) 313,450.

GEM. A mineral, precious by virtue of its composition, hardness, and rarity, cut and polished for ornamental use, or engraved. Of 120 minerals known to have been used as gemstones, only about 25 are in common use in jewellery; of these the diamond, emerald, ruby and sapphire are classified as precious, and the topaz, amethyst, opal, aquamarine, etc., as semi-precious. Among synthetic precious stones to have been produced successfully, are rubies and sapphires, emeralds, and diamonds (first made by G.E.C. in USA in 1955). Pearls are not technically Gs.

GEMAYEL, Amin 1943– . Lebanese statesman. He became president in Sept 1982 immediately following the assassination of his younger brother (Bashir Gemayel) who had been president-elect.

GEMSBOK. *See* ORYX.

GENE (jēn). The unit of inherited material situated on the chromosome within the cell nucleus. It has a constant effect on the development of the individual bearing it, other conditions being constant. Gs. are indivisible, duplicate themselves, and are highly stable, though occasionally they mutate. In 1976 an American team under Har Gobind Khorana artifically constructed the first complete G. to function naturally when implanted in a bacterial cell.

GĒNEA'LOGY. The study and tracing of family pedigrees. Formerly of limited aristocratic interest, G. is increasingly popular both in Britain and the USA. The Soc. of Genealogists in London (estab. 1911) with its library, thousands of family papers, marriage index (6,000,000 names of persons married before 1837), collection of parish register copies, etc., undertakes and assists research.

GENÉE (zhenā'), **Adeline.** Stage-name of the British dancer Dame Adeline Genée-Isitt (1878-1970). B. in Denmark, she went to London at 19 where she danced many years and was pres. of the Royal Academy of Dancing 1920-54, being created DBE 1950. The *Adeline G. Theatre* (1967) at E Grinstead, Sussex, commemorates her work.

GENERAL. An official of superior rank having wide authority. Usually in military sense - a G. officer commanding a body of troops larger than a regiment, or more than one arm of the service. In the British and US armies the ranks are Maj.-G., Lt.-G. and G. Supreme commanders in Britain are field marshals, and in the US Gs. of the army.

GENERAL ASSEMBLY. *See* SCOTLAND, CHURCH OF.

GENETIC EFFECT of radiation. Changes in the reproductive cells of living matter due to the absorption of ionizing radiations.

GENE'TICS. The scientific study of heredity, variation, development, and evolution. It accounts for the resemblances and differences to be found among organisms of related descent. Normal cells contain paired chromosomes, which separate during the formation of the germ cell, ultimately containing only one set. When male and female germ cells fuse, the chromosomes pair themselves off independently, and since they may be up to 100 in number the possible combinations are enormous (as enunciated by J. G. Mendel 1866), and account for the many differences in appearance among offspring in the same family; and between offspring and parents.

In 1962 the Nobel medicine and physiology prize was awarded to Francis Crick (molecular biologist at the Cavendish Laboratory, Cambridge), Maurice Wilkins (of King's Coll., London) and John D. Watson (of Harvard). Their researches on DNA (deoxyribonucleic acid, a biological structure which makes transmission of characteristics possible) help to explain why species and individuals differ.

Genetic engineering. The natural course of heredity is interfered with by any breeding programme, but true G.E. is restricted to deliberate manipulation of genetic material in the cell nucleus. This is achieved by (a) mutagenic agents, such as radiation or various chemicals or (b) introduction of new DNA carrying information, ordinarily by means of an infecting virus.

Transplantation of genes is used to increase our knowledge of cell function and reproduction, and also to achieve practical ends, e.g. plants grown for food may be given the ability to fix nitrogen, and so reduce the need for expensive fertilisers, or simple bacteria may be enabled to produce rare drugs. However, there is a risk that in

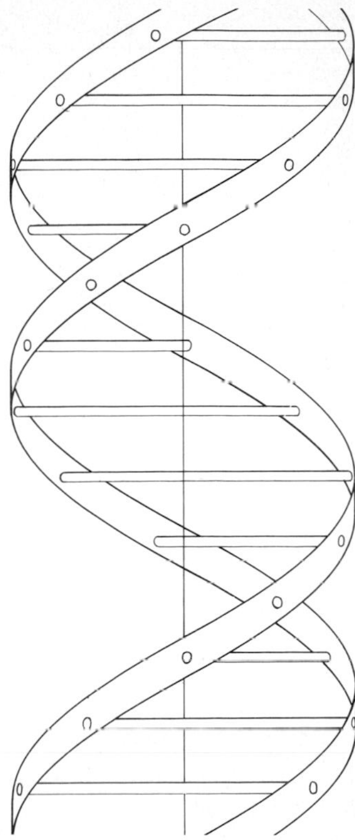

GENETICS. A simplified diagram of the 'double helix' structure of DNA, as postulated by Watson and Crick. A photograph of the original model they constructed accompanies the entry on nucleic acids. Gene replication starts with the separation of the two identical chains.

NORMAL MALE KARYOTYPE

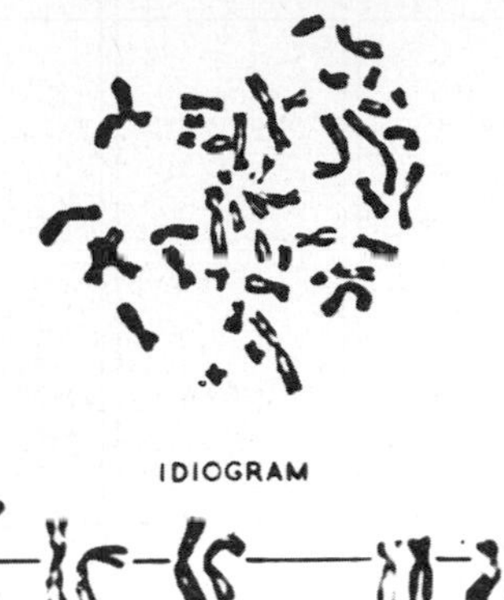

IDIOGRAM

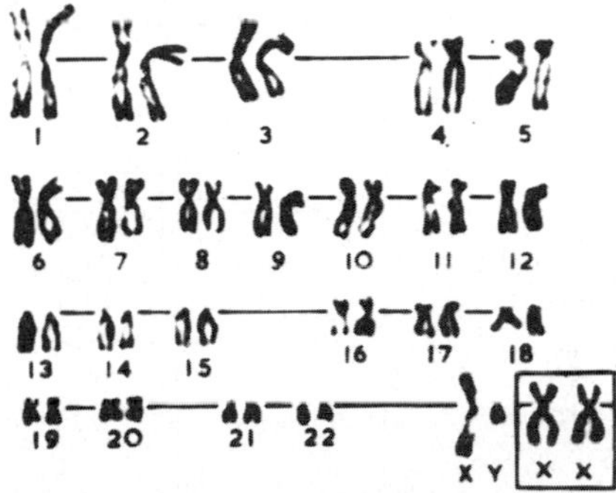

GENETICS. The number and shape of the chromosomes, formed by the linking together of the DNA molecules of a cell, are characteristic of a species. Above are the human chromosomes (male) in a very thinly spread-out skin cell grown in tissue culture. Below, they have been arranged in order of size. The last pair are the sex chromosomes, the male Y being very small, and the inset shows a slightly enlarged XX pair from a female cell. *Photo: Dr D. Hughes, Chester Beatty Research Institute.*

transplanting genes between different types of bacteria *(Escherichia coli,* which lives in the human intestine, is often used) unique pathogenic bacteria might be produced which on escape from the laboratory, might start an uncontrollable epidemic. One solution, apart from strict safety precautions, is to render the bacteria genetically unable to exist outside the laboratory.

GENEVA (jenē'va). Swiss city, cap. of G. canton, on the shore of Lake G. It is a natural route focus, and is a cultural and commercial centre. Industries incl. the manufacture of watches, scientific and optical instruments, foodstuffs, jewellery, musical boxes, etc. The site on which G. now stands was the chief settlement of the Allobroges; Caesar built an entrenched camp here. In the Middle Ages G. was controlled by the prince-bishops of G. and the rulers of Savoy. Under Calvin it became a centre of the Reformation 1536-64; the Academy, founded by him in 1559, became a univ. in 1892. G. was annexed by France in 1798; when freed in 1814 it entered the Swiss Confederation in 1815. In 1864 the International Red Cross Society was estab. at G. It was the H.Q. of the League of Nations whose properties at G. passed in 1946 into the possession of the U.N. Pop. urban area (1971) 318,500.

GENEVA, Lake. Largest of the central European lakes. The northern shores are in Switzerland, and most of the southern are in France. It is c.72 km (45 m) long; area 580 sq km (225 sq m). In French it is Lac Léman (in classical times Lacus Lemannus).

GENEVA CONVENTION. An international agreement regulating the treatment of the wounded in war was reached at a conference held in 1864, and later extended to cover the treatment of the sick and prisoners and the protection of civilians in war-time. The rules were revised at conventions held in 1906, 1929, and 1949.

GENF. German form of GENEVA (Fr. Genève).

GENGHIS (jen'gis) **Khan** (1162-1227). Mongol conqueror. Temujin, as he was originally called, was the son of a local chieftain. After a long struggle he estab. his supremacy over all the Mongol tribes by 1206, when he assumed the title of Chingis or 'perfect warrior'. He began the conquest of N. China in 1213, overran the empire of the shah of Khiva 1219-25, and invaded N. India, while his lieutenants advanced as far as the Crimea. At his death he ruled from the Yellow Sea to the Black Sea. His alleged remains are preserved at Ejin Horo, Inner Mongolia, and in 1980 the spring ceremonies celebrating his achievement were revived by the Chinese govt., but he is disapproved of by the Soviet regime of Outer Mongolia. *See also* GOLDEN HORDE.

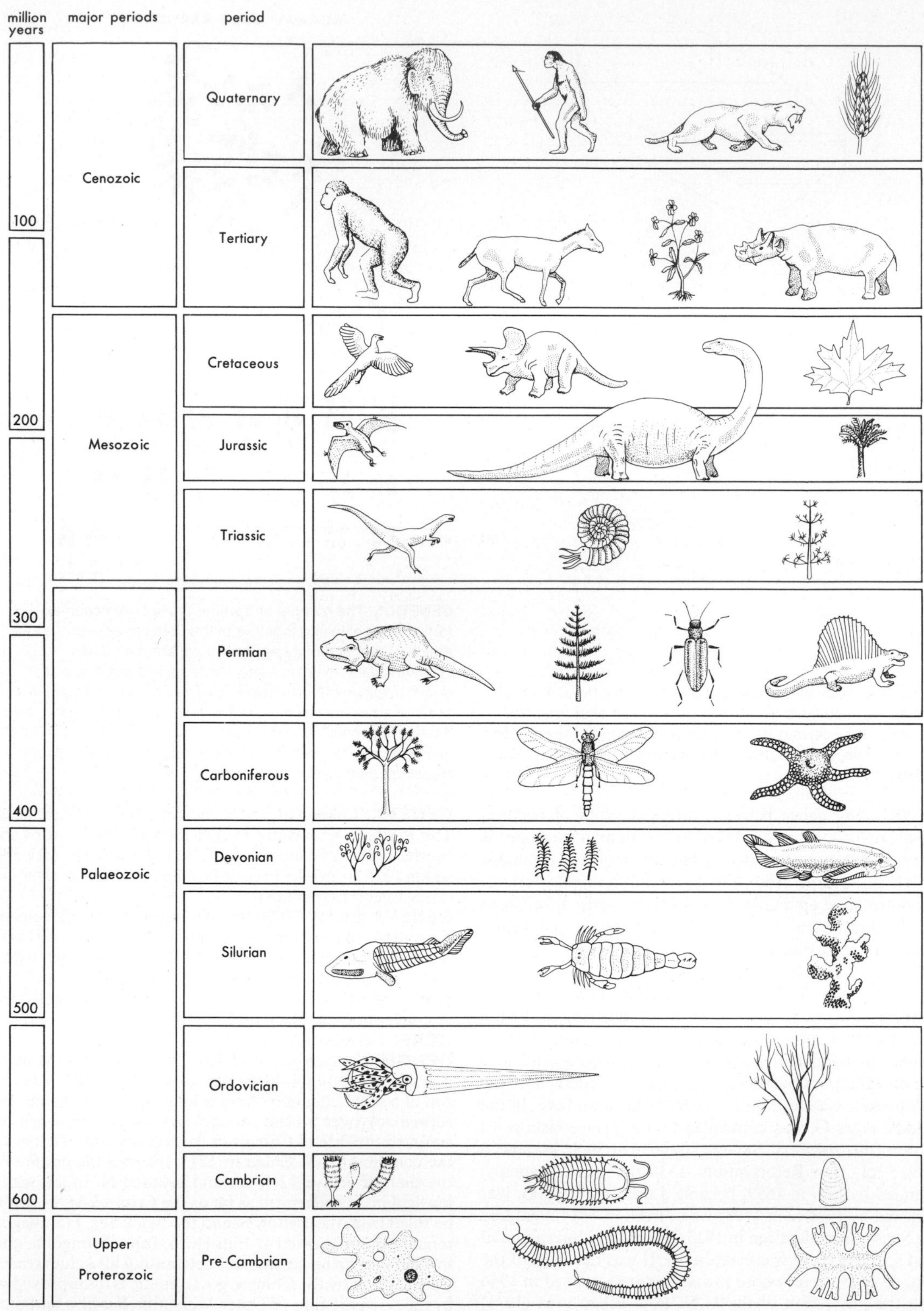

GEOLOGY. The story of the Earth in the increasing complexity of its life-forms.

GENNESARET, Lake of. Another name for the SEA OF GALILEE.

GENOA (jen'ō-ah). City in N. Italy (Italian *Genova)* cap. of the region of Ligura, on the Gulf of G. It is the country's chief port, and a new port area has been developed at Voltri on the W. outskirts, with a rail link to the interior by a tunnel under the Apennines. There are shipbuilding, oil refining, chemical, engineering, and textile industries. Pop. (1971) 812,500.

GENOVA. Italian form of GENOA.

GENRE (zhahr). French word meaning 'kind', and originally used in conjunction with an adjective to describe certain 'kinds' of painting, e.g. *genre du paysage* (landscapes) or *genre historique* (historical paintings). But *genre* is now usually applied to a special kind of painting, one in which some scene of everyday life is depicted. The most famous G. pictures were painted by Flemish artists such as Pieter Brueghel and Adriaen Brouwer, and by Dutch artists such as Teniers and Frans Hals. Of the English G. painters the best-known incl. Hogarth, George Morland, William Mulready, and Sir David Wilkie.

GENTIAN (jen'shan). Alpine plant belonging to the Genus *Gentiana* of the Gentianaceae family. They grow abundantly in mountainous regions, esp. on the Swiss Alps; the flowers may be a brilliant blue, or white or yellow.

GENTILI (jentē'lē), **Alberico** (1552-1608). Italian jurist. He practised law in Italy, but having adopted protestantism was compelled to flee to England, where he lectured on Roman Law in Oxford. His *De Jure Belli libri tres* (1598) constitutes the real foundation of international law.

GENTLEMEN-AT-ARMS, Honourable Corps of. Estab. in 1509, the Corps is, next to the Yeomen of the Guard, the oldest in the British Army: it was reconstituted in 1862. It consists of army officers of distinction under a captain, a peer, whose appointment is political. Theoretically the first bodyguard of the Sovereign, its functions are ceremonial.

GENUS (jē'nus). A number of species in the animal or plant world, when recognized to be related, are grouped together into a genus; in the Linnean nomenclature each species is given 2 names, the former of which is that of the genus; e.g. the domestic dog is known biologically as *Canis familiaris.* Genera are grouped into families, and these into orders.

GEOGRAPHY. The study of the distribution and interrelation of phenomena connected with the Earth's surface.

GEOLOGICAL SURVEY. Great Britain was the 1st country to institute an official G.S. The 1st map, of part of Devon, was completed in 1834. The one inch to one mile survey of England was completed in 1883. A larger-scale survey of England, Wales and Scotland is in continuous progress.

GEOLOGY. The study of the Earth, its origin, structure and history, incl. the remains of extinct life.

GEOMETRY. That branch of mathematics which is concerned with the investigation of the properties of space. It probably originated in Egypt, in the land measurements made necessary by the periodic inundations of the Nile. Early geometers were Thales, Pythagoras, and Euclid (285 BC); the theorems of the last two still find a place in education. Analytical methods were introduced and developed by Descartes in the 17th cent. The subject is usually divided into pure G., which embraces roughly the plane and solid geometry covered by Euclid's 'elements'; and analytical or co-ordinate G. in which problems are solved by algebraical methods. Two-dimensional G. treats of figures on plane or spherical surfaces; and solid G. of three-dimensional figures. Of recent years, non-Euclidean geometries have been devised by the mathematician Riemann and others.

GEOPHYSICS. Branch of geology using physics to study Earth's surface, interior and atmosphere.

GEORGE I (1660-1727). King of Great Britain. The son of the elector of Hanover, whom he succeeded in 1698, and a great-grandson of James I. He succeeded to the throne in 1714, but spent most of his reign in Hanover. He m. Sophia of Zell in 1682.

GEORGE II (1683-1760). King of Great Britain. He succeeded his father, George I, in 1727. Although he had little political ability, he distinguished himself as a soldier; his victory at Dettingen in 1743 was the last battle at which a British king commanded. He m. Caroline of Anspach in 1705.

GEORGE III (1738-1820). King of Great Britain. He succeeded his grandfather George II in 1760. Although he set himself to recover royal influence, his alleged domination of parliament by corrupt 'King's friends' was a Whig invention, now discredited. Obdurate - in support of his ministers - towards the American colonies, he also opposed Catholic emancipation and other reforms. Possibly a sufferer from porphyria, he underwent repeated attacks of lunacy, permanent from 1811. He m. in 1761 Princess Charlotte of Mecklenburg-Strelitz.

GEORGE IV (1762-1830). King of Great Britain. He received a strict upbringing from his father, George III, and early reacted into a life of debauchery. He secretly m. an RC widow, Mrs Fitzherbert, in 1785, but in 1795 he also m. Princess Caroline of Brunswick in return for a settlement of his debts. He acted as regent during his father's madness 1811-20, and succeeded him as king. On his accession in 1820 he attempted to divorce Caroline, but the project was dropped for fear of revolution.

GEORGE V (1865-1936). King of Great Britain. The 2nd son of Edward VII, he served in the navy until 1892, when on his elder brother's death he became heir to the throne. In 1893 he m. Princess May of Teck (Queen Mary) and had 5 sons and a dau. He succeeded his father in 1910 and was crowned in 1911. During the F.W.W. he paid several visits to the front, and concerned himself actively with war policy. During all the great crises of his reign, notably in 1910, 1914, and 1931, he played the part of a wise but unobtrusive counsellor.

GEORGE VI (1895-1952). King of Great Britain. The 2nd son of George V, he served in the navy in the F.W.W. (being present at the battle of Jutland) and then in the RAF; subsequently studying at Cambridge. Created duke of York in 1920, he m. in 1923 the Lady Elizabeth Bowes-Lyon, and 2 dau. were born, Elizabeth (q.v.) in 1926 and Margaret (Rose) (q.v.) in 1930. On Edward VIII's abdication in 1936 he succeeded to the throne, and was crowned in 1937. With his consort he visited France (1938), Canada and USA (1939), and S Africa (1947). During the S.W.W. he visited the Normandy and Italian battlefields. He was endeared to his people by an exemplary family life, a strong sense of duty, and the personal courage to overcome a speech impediment and endure ill-health.

GEORGE IV. A portrait by Thomas Lawrence. *Photo: Courtesy of the National Portrait Gallery.*

GEORGE VI. Called unexpectedly to the throne after the abdication of his popular brother, he won the affection of his people by his devotion to duty. *Photo: Popperfoto.*

GEORGE. Name of 2 kings of Greece. **George I** (1845-1913), 2nd son of Christian IX of Denmark, became king of Greece in 1863. He was assassinated at Salonika in 1913. **George II** (1890-1947) became king on the expulsion of his father king Constantine in 1922, but in 1923 was himself overthrown. He was restored by a military coup d'état in 1935, and soon abolished the constitution and set up a dictatorship under Metaxas (q.v.). He went into exile 1941-6.

GEORGE, St. Patron saint of England. He is said to have been martyred at Lydda in Palestine, probably under Diocletian, but the other elements of his legend are of doubtful historicity. The story of St G. and the Dragon, evidently derived from the Perseus legend, first appears in the 6th cent. The cultus of St G. was introduced into western Europe by the Crusaders, and his feast day is 23 April.

GEORGE (geh-ohr'ge), **Stefan** (1868-1933). German poet. His early poetry was influenced by the French Symbolists but his conception of himself as the seer and leader of a small band regenerating the German spirit first appears in *Der Teppich des Lebens* (1899). *Der Siebente Ring* (1907, *(The Seventh Ring)* contains some of his finest verse and deifies the young man whom he sees as a substitute for Christ. *Das Neue Reich* (1928) shows his realization that the F.W.W. had failed to exert the purifying effect he had hoped for. He rejected Nazi overtures, and went to Switzerland, where he died.

GEORGE CROSS. The supreme civilian award in Britain for acts of the greatest courage in circumstances of extreme danger, instituted in 1940. It consists of a silver cross with a medallion in the centre bearing a design of St George and the Dragon, and is worn on the left breast before all other medals except the VC. The GC was conferred on the island of Malta in 1942. The **George Medal,** also instituted in 1940, is a civilian award for acts of great courage. The medal is silver and circular, bearing on one side a crowned effigy of the sovereign, and on the reverse St George and the Dragon. It is worn on the left breast.

GEORGETOWN. Seaport and cap. of Guyana, near the mouth of the Demerara. Founded 1781, and named by the British, it was held 1784-1812 by the Dutch who re-named it Stabroek; it was ceded to Britain in 1814. Pop. (1975) 182,000.

The *Declaration of G.* (1972), issued at a conference of non-aligned countries, called for the emergence of a multipolar system to replace the 2 world power blocs, the Mediterranean and Indian Ocean to be neutral.

GEORGE TOWN. Chief port of the Federation of Malaysia, cap. also of Penang state, on the island of Penang. Its chief exports are rice, sugar, pepper, tin. Pop. (1970) 270,000.

GEORGIA. The most southern of the 13 original states of the USA. It produces groundnuts, cotton, tobacco, pulpwood, and fruits, e.g. peaches. Industries incl. cotton textiles, clothing, paper, food products, and chemicals. In the SE is the Okefenokee swampland (1,700 sq.km/660 sq.m), a nature reserve for alligators, bears, birdlife, etc. The cap. is Atlanta; Savanna and Brunswick are ports. Named after George II, G. was founded 1733. Area 152,500 sq.km (58,880 sq.m); pop. (1970) 4,589,575.

GEORGIA SSR of the USSR, bordering Turkey and including Abkhaz ASSR, Adzhar ASSR and S Ossetian autonomous region. An area of mountain and plateau, it produces cereals, tea, mulberries (as food for silkworms), tobacco, fruit, etc. Manganese is the chief mineral resource; steel, cement, and fertilizers are among its manufactures. The cap. is Tbilisi. The Georgian language does not belong to the Indo-European language family; it has been preserved by the inhabitants of G. for more than 2,000 years. Stalin was a Georgian. Area 69,700 sq.km (26,900 sq.m); pop. (1979) 5,016,000

GEOSTATIONARY ORBIT. Path, about 274,000 km (170,000 m) in circumference, and 36,000 km (22,300 m) above the equator, used for communications satellites because, travelling within it, a satellite appears to hover fixed above the same place on Earth.

GEOTHERMAL ENERGY. Subterranean energy source, either (1) *hot water*, pumped to the surface and turned into steam or run through a heat exchanger; or (2) *dry steam*, which is directed through turbines to produce electricity.

GERANIUM (jerā'nium) or **crane's bill.** Genus of plants of the Geraniaceae family. Many of the Gs. common in Britain are not members of the genus G., but of *Pelargonium*. *See* CRANE'S BILL.

GERBIL (jer'bil). Small, long-tailed burrowing rodent (family Cricetidae), found in Asia and Africa. Its keen sense of smell has been used in detecting bombs at airports, etc.

GÉRICAULT (zhārikō'), **Jean Louis André Théodore** (1791-1824). French artist. An enthusiastic horseman - he d. as a result of a riding accident - he excelled in pictures introducing horses, e.g. 'The Riderless Horse Race' and 'The Derby at Epsom' - painted on a visit to England. His dramatic 'Raft of the Medusa', recording an incident in which shipwrecked seamen were deliberately set adrift, had political repercussions.

GERMAN, Sir Edward. Name used by British composer Edward German Jones (1862-1936). He studied at the RAM and became a renowned theatrical conductor. His chief works are the operettas *Tom Jones* and *Merrie England*, and the incidental music to Shakespeare's *Henry VIII*. Besides these he wrote much instrumental, orchestral, and vocal music.

GERMAN. A branch of the Germanic group of the Indo-European languages, and more especially of its West Germanic division. The *High G.* of the S and the centre differs from the *Low G.* of the N chiefly in its having been affected by the second or High German sound-shift which changed Germanic *b d g* to *p t k*; and, according to position, *p* to *pf* or *ff*, *t* to *z* (*ts*) or *zz* (*ss*), and *k* to *ch* or *hh*. *See* GERMANIC LANGUAGES.

GERMAN ART. Characterized always by intensity of feeling which finds expression in the mystic and in a realism pushed to the grotesque, G.A. also has a tradition of skilled craftsmanship. In the 13th cent. G.A. first emerged in the sculptures of Bamberg and Naumberg cathedrals, the wood carvings of Veit Stoss, sometimes claimed as Polish (Wit Swosz), and the bronzes of Peter Vischer. The earliest paintings resembled the miniatures of illuminated MSS, but with the series of panels of the life of Christ *c.* 1350 by the Master of Hohenfurth (Czech Vissy Brod), and the altar *c.* 1380 for the monastery of Trebon by the Master of Wittingau (Czech Trebon), a high level was reached. To the 15th cent. belong the charming Stefan Lochner, the realists Hans Multscher (*c.* 1400-57) and Konrad Witz (*c.* 1400-*c.* 1446), and the painter-sculptor Michael Pacher (*c.* 1435-98). Incarnation of the Renaissance in Germany was Albrecht Dürer: other 16th cent. masters incl. Hans Baldung Grien (*c.* 1484-1545), Lucas Cranach, Albrecht Altdorfer, Grünewald, and Hans Holbein. The only notable name in the 17th cent. is that of Adam Elsheimer (1578-1610): in the 18th Chodowiecki's work is of historical value. Among the Romantics are the almost 'expressionist' portrait painter Philipp Otto Runge (1777-1810) and the landscapist Caspar David Friedrich (1774-1840). Max Liebermann (1847-1935) was the first to feel the influence of such foreign developments as Impressionism. At the turn of the cent. came Jugendstil (corresponding to French Art Nouveau), and then parallel with Fauvism the movement known as Die Brücke (The Bridge) which incl. Emil Nolde. Also important were the Blaue Reiter (Blue Rider) group - *see* KANDINSKY - and in architecture and the arts generally the Bauhaus (q.v.) was influential abroad. Later artists incl. Max Ernst and Käthe Kollwitz (1867-1945).

GERMAN ART. The 'Mocking of Christ' (1503) in the Alte Pinakothek, Munich by 'Grünewald'.

GERMAN HISTORY. The W Germanic tribes, originating in Scandinavia, early overran the region between the Rhine, Elbe, and Danube, where they were confined by the Roman power. In the 4th-5th cents. the Franks occupied Belgium and France, and there founded a kingdom which by Charlemagne's day had extended its authority over Germany. Under the Frankish kings the Germans accepted Christianity. After Charlemagne's death Germany was separated from France under its own kings while the local officials or dukes became virtually independent until the central power was restored by the Saxon dynasty (919-1002). Otto I, who in 962 revived the title of emperor, began the colonization of the Slav lands E of the Elbe. This period of progress was ended by the feud between emperors and popes (1075-1250), which enabled the princes to recover their independence. A temporary revival of imperial power took place under Maximilian I (1493-1519), but he and his successor, Charles V (1519-56), were mainly concerned with dynastic interests outside Germany which brought them into conflict with France. The reformation increased Germany's disunity, and led to the Thirty Years War (1618-48). The war not only reduced the Empire to a mere name, but destroyed Germany's economic and cultural life.

The rise of Brandenburg-Prussia as a military power began in the 17th cent., and reached its height under Frederick II (1740-86). Germany's regeneration was due, however, to Napoleon, who united W Germany in the Confederation of the Rhine (1806) and introduced the ideas and reforms of the French Revolution: his reforms were subsequently imitated in Prussia. The Empire was abolished in 1806, and after 1815 Germany became a loose federation. In spite of persecution, the ideas of democracy and national unity spread, and inspired the unsuccessful revolutions of 1848. The growth of industry from 1850 also made national unity an economic necessity. Under Bismarck's leadership Prussia united Germany in 1871, after victorious wars with Austria and France. In the years following industry expanded greatly; the beginnings of a colonial empire and a fleet were made, and at home a powerful Socialist movement arose. Political, industrial, and colonial rivalries with Britain, France, and Russia all combined to produce the F.W.W.

In 1918 a revolution overthrew the monarchy, and the Socialists seized power, and estab. the democratic Weimar republic. The economic crisis of 1929-33 brought Germany near to revolution, until in 1933 the reaction manœuvred the Nazis into power. At home they solved the unemployment problem by a vast rearmament programme, abolished the democratic constitution, and ruthlessly destroyed all opposition; abroad the policy of aggression led to eventual defeat in the S.W.W. Germany was then divided, within her 1937 frontiers, into British, American, French, and Russian occupation zones until 1952.

Subsequent G.H. is overshadowed by the partition into the rival German Democratic Republic under a Communist régime and German Federal Republic under a Christian Democrat coalition, tension being periodically heightened by the anomalous position of Berlin (q.v.). *See* GERMANY.

GERMANIC LANGUAGES. A branch of the Indo-European family. They are divided into: (1) *East* Germanic, consisting of Gothic, now extinct; (2) *North* Germanic or Scandinavian (Icelandic, Norwegian, Danish, Swedish); (3) *West* Germanic, divided into German, Dutch, Friesian, and English, the 2 last being somewhat more closely related between themselves. The chief feature which marks off the G.L. as a distinct group is the change in consonants collectively known as the first Germanic sound-shift, and popularly referred to as *Grimm's Law*, whereby the Indo-European voiced aspirates became voiced spirants, later in certain cases voiced stops;

GERMAN HISTORY. The German delegates sign the document of surrender on 4 May 1945, as Field Marshal Montgomery stands by. *Photo: Imperial War Museum.*

p, t, and *k* changed to the corresponding unvoiced fricatives, and *b, d, g* to *p, t, k* respectively. There are certain exceptions to each of these rules, caused by the varying accent in Indo-European. Whereas in I.-E. the accent might fall on any syllable of the word, the G.L. stabilized it on the first syllable, the only exception being adverbial prefixes.

GERMANICUS CAESAR (15 BC-AD 19). Roman general. The son of Nero Claudius Drusus, stepson of Augustus, he m. the latter's grand-dau., Agrippina. He made an early reputation as a soldier, but on the death of Augustus, refused his troops' suggestion that he claim the empire. Nevertheless, his continuing military success in Germany aroused the jealousy of Tiberius, who sent him to the east. He d. nr Antioch, possibly poisoned at the order of Tiberius. He was the father of the emperor Gaius and of Nero's mother, Agrippina.

GERMĀ'NIUM. Chemical element, symbol Ge; at. no. 32; at. wt. 72.6, which was discovered in 1886. A grey-white, brittle, crystalline metal, it is in the silicon group, and its chemical and physical properties lie between those of silicon and tin. G. is widely used in the manufacture of transistors and rectifiers.

GERMAN LITERATURE. The fragmentary alliterative poem the *Hildebrandslied* (*c.* 800), the most substantial relic of the *Old High German* period, bears no comparison with the Old English literature of the same era, but in the *Middle High German* period there was a great flowering in the vernacular which had been forced into subservience to Latin since the early attempts at encouragement by Charlemagne. The court epics of Hartmann von Aue, Gottfried von Strassburg and Wolfram von Eschenbach in the early 13th cent. were modelled on the French in style and material, but the folk-epic *Nibelungenlied* revived the spirit of the old heroic Germanic sagas. Adopted - in the more limited meaning - from France and Provence, the *Minnesang* reached its height in the lyric poetry of Walther von der Vogelweide.

Modern German literature begins in the 16th cent. with the standard of language set by Luther's Bible and then also came the climax of popular drama in the *Fastnachtsspiel* as handled by Hans Sachs. In the later 16th and early 17th cents. French influence was renewed and English influence, notably by troupes of players, was introduced: Martin Opitz's *Buch von der deutschen Poeterey* (1624),

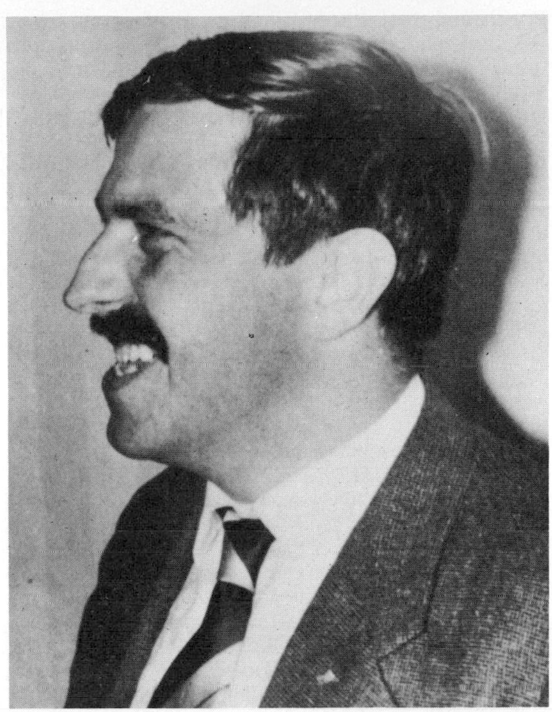

GERMAN LITERATURE. Two of Germany's most successful recent novelists, Heinrich Böll and Günter Grass. *Photos: Courtesy of Secker and Warburg and Sophie Baker.*

in which he advocates the imitation of foreign models, epitomizes the German Renaissance which was followed by the Thirty Years War vividly described in Grimmelshausen's *Simplicissimus.*

In the 18th cent. French Classicism predominated, extolled by Gottsched but opposed by Bodmer and Breitinger, whose writings prompted the Germanic *Messias* of Klopstock. Both Lessing and Herder were admirers of Shakespeare, and Herder's enthusiasm inaugurated the *Sturm und Drang* phase which emphasized individual inspiration, and his collection of folk songs was symptomatic of the feeling which inspired Bürger's modern ballad *Lenore.* Greatest representatives of the Classical period at the end of the cent. were Goethe and Schiller, but their ideals were combated by the new Romantic school which based its theories on the work of the brothers Schlegel, and Tieck, and which incl. Novalis, Arnim, Brentano, Eichendorff, Chamisso, Uhland, and Hoffmann.

With Kleist and Grillparzer in the early 19th cent. stress on the poetic in drama ends, and with Hebbel the psychological aspect becomes the more important. Notable *c.* 1830 was the 'Young German' movement led by Heine, Gutzkow, and Laube, which the authorities tried to suppress. Other excellent writers of the cent. incl. Jeremias Gotthelf, story-teller of peasant life; the psychological novelist Friedrich Spielhagen; the masters of the *Novelle,* Gottfried Keller and Theodor Storm, also both fine poets; and Wilhelm Raabe and Theodor Fontane, novelists of realism. Naturalistic drama found its chief exponents in Hauptmann and Sudermann. Influential in literature, as in politics and economics, were Marx and Nietzsche.

Outstanding in the early years of the 20th cent. were the lyric poets Richard Dehmel, Stefan George, and Rainer Maria Rilke; von Hofmannsthal both poet and dramatist, and the novelists Thomas and Heinrich Mann, Ludwig Renn, E. M. Remarque, and Hermann Hesse. Just before the F.W.W. Expressionism emerged in the poetry of Georg Trakl, dominated the novels of Franz Kafka and the plays of Ernst Toller, Franz Werfel, Georg Kaiser and Karl Sternheim, and was later to influence Bertold Brecht. Under National Socialism many major writers left the country, others were silenced or ignored: to the period after the S.W.W. belong the Swiss dramatists Max Frisch and Friedrich Dürrenmatt, the novelists Heinrich Böll and Heimito von Doderer, and the poets Paul Celan and Günter Grass.

GERMAN MEASLES. Rubella; an acute infectious fever, usually of children, having an incubation period of 10-15 days. The first signs are slight fever, catarrh, and a general rash, paler than that of measles. The patient is usually well in 10 days, but in the case of a pregnant woman her unborn child may be affected, and vaccination is advisable for women at risk.

GERMAN OCEAN. Ger. name for the North Sea.

GERMANY. Country of central Europe. Before the S.W.W. a single state, it was divided after Germany's defeat into 4 occupation zones (British, French, United States, and USSR), and subsequently into 2 separate states, East and West Germany. By the Potsdam Agreement (1945) those parts of the country lying E of the Oder-western Neisse rivers were placed (i) under Russian admin.: the northern part of former E Prussia; (ii) under Polish administration: the southern part of former E

Prussia and the territory lying between the pre-war and post-war frontiers of E Germany. This involved a loss of a third of G.'s former area, more than 117,000 sq.km (45,000 sq.m), and the *Vertreibung* or expulsion of *c.* 15,000,000 Germans from their former homes in the E territories. A treaty normalizing W German-Polish relations (1970) recognized the existing boundary on the Oder and western Neisse. *See also* BERLIN. Pressure for reunion of the 2 German states, and for restoration of the former frontier and the 'lost' territories, sometimes incl. the Sudetenland (q.v.), has been a factor in post-war European politics.

EAST GERMANY (**German Democratic Republic**), formerly the Russian zone of occupation, was estab. 7 Oct. 1949, becoming a sovereign state in 1954, but was recognized only by the Communist powers until in 1973 a Basic Treaty governing relations between E and W Germany was ratified by both states, which were then admitted to the UN.

The N German plain ends in lagoons along the Baltic coast, and is crossed by the river Elbe and its tributaries, and part of the Oder system. Collective farms produce wheat, rye and barley, and cattle and pigs are reared. The climate is less mild than that of W Germany, with short summers and cold winters. In the south the land rises to the Erzgebirge, source of antimony, arsenic, bismuth, cobalt and uranium and the Thuringian Forest in the SW. East Germany also has large reserves of lignite, but the division of the country cut off many other former sources of raw material, and there was initially economic decline and emigration to the W on a large scale. However, from 1963 factory managers were given greater freedom within an overall plan, and greater emphasis was placed on petrochemicals, electronics and precision engineering (needing comparatively little raw materials), and large funds were devoted to scientific research. East Germany then took her place by the 1970s as a world industrial power. However, by the 1980s E Germany was suffering like the West from world recession, and emigration to W Germany was rendered virtually impossible by an electronically guarded frontier. Her most notable leaders have been Ulbricht and Honecker (qq.v.).

Under the constitution of 1968 there is a single party, popularly elected people's chamber (*Volkskammer*), which nominates the members of the Council of State (supreme legislative and executive organ) and Council of Ministers. The Communist Party retains all real power. East Germany was divided 1945-52 into *Länder* (Brandenburg, Mecklenburg, Saxony, Saxony-Anhalt, Thuringia) based on the old duchies, but these were then abolished to obliterate old associations, and the country reorganized into 14 districts (*Bezirke*) each named after its chief town. The cap. is East Berlin.

Area 108,180 sq.km (41,768 sq.m); pop. (1978) 16,757,857, about half being Protestant, less than 10% RC and the remainder having no religious affiliation. M.U.: GDR mark.

WEST GERMANY (**Federal Republic of Germany**) was formed 21 Sept. 1949, by the union of the British French and USA zones (excl. at that time the Saarland, q.v.), achieving full sovereignty and recognition by the Western powers in 1955.

The marshy coast on the North Sea gives way to the N German plain which incl. sandy wastes such as Lüneberg Heath. The mountainous central area pivots on the Fichtelgebirge in N Bavaria; to the NW are the Harz Mtns (partly in E Germany); to the SW the Franconian and Swabian Juras, and the Black Forest; and the Taunus Mts. to the W. In SE the Bavarian Alps culminate in the Zugspitze (2,963 m/9,719 ft). The chief rivers are the Rhine, with its tributaries, and the Ems, Weser and Danube.

GERMANY. Some of the most beautiful scenery in Germany is in the *Land* of Bavaria, with its mountains, forests and lakes. *Photo: J. Allan Cash.*

The chief crops are wheat, barley, and rye; potatoes and sugar beet; and the vines of the Rhine, Main and Moselle valleys which produce famous wines, and reflect the mildness of the climate as compared with E Germany. Cattle, horses, sheep and pigs are reared. The former great iron and steel works of the Ruhr and Saar, originally based on native coal and iron ore, have declined since the S.W.W. and been replaced by a far more extensively varied industry. By the 1970s West Germany had become easily the chief industrial power of W Europe, although chiefly in the conventional range of industries: cars, chemicals, electricals, engineering, and textiles. Some 4 million Gastarbeiter 'guest workers' from Italy, Spain, Turkey, etc., assisted in this economic expansion, but unemployment later in the decade led to the repatriation of more than a million.

There is an excellent rail network; a road system with fine *Autobahnen* or motorways; and internal and external air services centred in Cologne. The main rivers are navigable and the canals incl. Rhine-Herne, Dortmund-Ems, Mittelland, Kiel and Ludwig - the last linking the Rhine and Danube. Tourism is important, espec. in the Black Forest. The chief towns are Berlin (West), Hamburg, Munich, Cologne, Essen, Frankfurt-am-Main, Dortmund and Düsseldorf. The cap. is Bonn.

The newly-created W German state achieved rapprochement with France under Adenauer (q.v.), and under Erhard (q.v.) achieved an 'economic miracle' which in practice made it also politically the dominant power of Western Europe. Under Brandt and Schmidt there was a greater degree of co-operation with Eastern Europe (*Ostpolitik*), which came in question as Russian expansionism increased. At home the unions became less docile in recession, seeking a greater degree of social change.

There is a parliament of 2 houses: the *Bundestag*, or federal diet, elected by universal suffrage for 4 years, and the *Bundesrat*, or federal council, consisting of the members of the govts of the Länder or states. The pres. is elected for 5 years, with a maximum of 2 terms, by the federal assembly which consists of the *Bundestag* and an equal number of popularly elected representatives from the *Länder*. The govt is headed by the federal chancellor, chosen by the *Bundestag*, who usually leads a coalition, the liberal Free Democratic Party (FDP) collaborating in turn with the Christian Democratic Union (CDU) and Social Democratic Party (SPD). An SPD-FDP coalition, successively under Brandt and Schmidt (qq.v.), came into power in 1969. In 1982, after a 'constructive vote of no confidence', Schmidt was replaced by Helmut Kohl (q.v.). Heading a CDU/CSU (Christian Social Union)/FDP coalition, he was confirmed in office by the 1983 election.

Area 248,590 sq.km (95,984 sq.m); pop. (1981) 61,666,000, of whom slightly over half are Protestant and the rest RC. M.U.: deutsche mark (DM).

GERMISTON. Industrial town in the Transvaal, Rep. of S Africa. It is in the Witwatersrand gold-mining area, and there are gold refineries, chemical and steel plants, and textile mills. Pop. (1970) 132,500.

GERONA (khārōn'ah). Cap. of Gerona prov., Catalonia, Spain, 86km (55m) NE of Barcelona: textiles and chemicals are made. The E coastline of the prov. on the Mediterranean, the Costa Brava, is a tourist area. Pop. (1970) 50,350.

GERONIMO (jeron'imo) (1829-1909). Apache Indian chief. Captured in 1886, following a hard-fought campaign against General George Crook, he escaped. He later surrendered, conditionally on his warriors being returned to their homes in Florida. They were instead imprisoned, and later settled elsewhere.

GERRY (ger'i), **Elbridge** (1744-1814). American politician. Gov. of Massachusetts, in 1812 he had his men redraw the map of the state's senatorial districts to gain congressional election, the shape resembling a salamander: hence 'gerrymandering' to denote politic revision of electoral boundaries.

GERS (zhār). Fr. river, 178km (110m) long, rising in the Lannemezan Plateau and flowing N to join the Garonne 8km (5m) above Agen.

GE'RSHWIN, George (1898-1937). American jazz musician. B. in Brooklyn of Jewish parents, he composed popular jazz songs, notable for their instinctive rhythm and melody. He also wrote more serious music, in which he incorporated the essentials of jazz, e.g. the tone poem *An American in Paris*, *Rhapsody in Blue* (1924), and the opera *Porgy and Bess* (1935).

GESTAPO. An abbreviated form of *Geheime Staatspolizei*, the Nazi secret political police, formed in 1933. It was one of the organizations accused at the Nuremberg war-guilt trials (q.v.) in 1946, and was condemned.

GETHSEMANE (geth-sem'an-ē). Site on the Mount of Olives, just E of Jerusalem, of the garden in which, according to tradition, Judas betrayed Jesus. When Jerusalem was divided in 1948 between Israel and Jordan, G. fell within Jordanian territory.

GETTY, John Paul (1892-1976). American millionaire, pres. of the G. Oil Co. from 1947, and founder of the J. Paul Getty Museum, California, noted for its 18th cent. French furniture and tapestries and an art collection ranging the 15-17th cents.

Divisions of Germany

	Area in sq. km.	*Pop. in 1978*	*Capital*
Democratic Republic of (Eastern) Germany			East Berlin
Bezirke			
Berlin, East	400	1,118,142	
Dresden	6,740	1,821,694	Dresden
Erfurt	7,350	1,238,040	Erfurt
Frankfurt-on-Oder	7,185	693,901	Frankfurt
Gera	4,005	737,178	Gera
Halle	8,770	1,855,633	Halle
Karl-Marx-Stadt	6,010	1,953,158	Karl-Marx-Stadt
Cottbus	8,260	877,370	Cottbus
Leipzig	4,970	1,429,526	Leipzig
Magdeburg	11,525	1,279,323	Magdeburg
Neubrandenburg	10,790	624,477	Neubrandenburg
Potsdam	12,570	1,116,151	Potsdam
Rostock	7,075	875,897	Rostock
Schwerin	8,670	589,246	Schwerin
Suhl	3,860	548,121	Suhl
	108,180	16,757,857	
Federal Republic of (Western) Germany			Bonn
Länder			
Baden-Württemberg	35,750	9,120,500	Stuttgart
Bavaria	70,550	10,819,300	Munich
Bremen	404	703,200	Bremen
Hamburg	756	1,680,300	Hamburg
Hessen	21,125	5,540,600	Wiesbaden
Lower Saxony	47,475	7,224,200	Hanover
North-Rhine-Westphalia	34,150	17,030,300	Düsseldorf
Rhineland-Palatinate	19,400	3,639,300	Mainz
Saarland	2,695	1,081,100	Saarbrücken
Schleswig-Holstein	15,785	2,587,200	Kiel
Berlin, West	500	1,926,800	
	248,590	61,352,700	

GETTYSBURG (get'iz-). Borough of south Pa., USA, where in 1863 the battle of G. was fought. It was a Northern victory, and marked the turning-point of the American Civil War. The site is a national cemetery at the dedication of which Lincoln delivered his famous G. address 19 Nov. 1863. Pop. (1970) 7,275.

GEYSER (gā'ser). A natural spring which, at more or less regular intervals, explosively discharges into the air a column of steam and hot water. One of the best-known Gs. is Old Faithful, in Yellowstone National Park, Wyoming, USA; Gs. occur also in New Zealand and Iceland.

GEZIRA (gezē'rah), El. Plain in the Rep. of Sudan, above the confluence of the White and Blue Niles at Khartoum. Cotton, sorghum, wheat and groundnuts are grown by irrigation.

GHADAMÈS (gadah'mez). Oasis in W Libya, close to the Tunisian/Algerian frontier, and hence a route centre. Pop. (1970) 7,000.

GHA'NA. Country in W Africa. The coastal plains are rendered productive by irrigation, and inland the country rises to tropical forested upland. Here cocoa (G. is the world's largest producer), coffee, rubber, oil palms, cashews, and fruits are cultivated. In the savannah to the north groundnuts, maize, rice, millet, yams and tobacco are produced. Minerals incl. bauxite, industrial diamonds, gold, and manganese. The Volta river, dammed at Akosombo to provide power, runs N-S through eastern G., and Lake Volta supports large fisheries. The chief cities are Accra, the cap.; the ports of Sekondi-Takoradi and Tema; and Kumasi and Tamale, which are all industrial centres.

Ghana was created in 1956 by the union, after a plebiscite, of the British colony of the Gold Coast and the part of Togoland under British trusteeship. It achieved independence in 1957 and became a rep. within the Commonwealth in 1960. The name derives from the ancient Sudanese empire of G. (fl. 4th-10th cent. AD), whose cap. was Timbuktoo. One of its nine regions consists of the former kingdom of Ashanti (q.v.).

The flamboyant rule of the first pres., Nkrumah (q.v.), ended in a military coup in 1966, and a return to civilian rule ended similarly in the case of Kofi Busia 1969-72, and of Ignatius Acheompong 1972-8, the last-named being shot for corruption. Under the constitution of 1979, there is a pres. directly elected for a 4-yr term, a council of state, and a parliament expressly forbidden to introduce a one-party regime. Flt Lt Jerry Rawlings, who had achieved power by a coup in 1979, then handed over to a civil govt, took over by a second coup in 1981 when Pres. Limann proved incompetent.

Area 238,537 sq.km (92,100 sq.m); pop. (1973) 8,546,000, the majority Sudanese Negroes, and mainly fetishist in belief. M.U.: cedi.

GHATS (gawts), **Eastern and Western.** Twin mtn ranges in S India, which bound the central plateau to the E and to the W (where they run closely parallel to the coast), and converge towards Cape Comorin. They average 1,000 m (3,000 ft), but rise to almost 3,000 m (9,000 ft) in a few peaks to E and W. The name is actually a European misnomer, the Indian word *ghat* meaning pass not mtn; the bathing G. are steps leading down to a river, as at Varanesi.

GHENT. Cap. of E Flanders (Fr. Gand), Belgium, at the junction of the rivers Scheldt and Lys. G. is connected with the Scheldt estuary at Terneuzen by ship canal. There are textile, chemical and metallurgical industries. The cathedral of St Bavon (12-14th cents.) has paintings by van Eyck and Rubens, and there is a univ. (1816). Pop. (1978) 241,170.

GHETTO. The quarter of a town set aside by law for Jewish residence, and enclosed by gates and walls. The G., the origins of which go back to the Middle Ages, was first enforced by papal bull in Italy in 1555. It was largely swept away at the time of the French Revolution, save in Eastern Europe, but was revived by the Germans 1940-5. Also used generally for any minority slum quarter in a city.

GHIBERTI (gēber'tē), **Lorenzo** (1378-1455). Italian sculptor. A goldsmith by training, he created in the bronze doors for the baptistry of Florence - his native city - one of the most beautiful works of the Italian Renaissance. He also wrote *Commentarii* on art history.

GHIRLANDAIO (gērlahndah'yō), **Domenico.** Name by which the Florentine painter Domenico Bigordi (c. 1449-94) is known. He painted chiefly frescoes in his native city of Florence.

GHANA. Cocoa is one of the country's most important crops. The pods contain 20-40 seeds or 'beans'. *Photo: Courtesy of Cadbury Bros.*

GIANT'S CAUSEWAY. Stretch of columnal basalt on the N coast of Antrim, N Ireland, forming a headland jutting out to sea. It was formed by an outflow of lava in Tertiary times which has solidified in polygonal columns.

GIBBERD, Sir Frederick (1908–84). British architect and town planner. His works incl. the the RC Cathedral, Liverpool, and the Central London mosque at Regent's Park. Knighted 1967.

GIBBON, Edward (1737-94). British historian. B. at Putney, he was withdrawn from Oxford owing to his conversion to Roman Catholicism in 1753. Sent to Lausanne by his father, he was reconverted in 1754, met Voltaire in 1757, and fell in love with the future Mme Necker, from whom parental disapproval parted him. Setting out on a tour of Europe in 1763, he conceived the idea of *The History of the Decline and Fall of the Roman Empire,* while in Rome in 1764. The first vol. appeared in 1776, and was immediately successful, although he was compelled to reply to attacks on his account of the early development of Christianity by a *Vindication* (1779). The work was completed in 1788. From 1783 he had lived in Lausanne, but returned to England and d. in London.

GIBBON, Lewis Grassic. Pseudonym of Anglo-Scottish novelist James Leslie Mitchell (1901-35). His great work was the trilogy *A Scots Quair* (*Sunset Song, Cloud Howe* and *Grey Granite,* 1932-4), set against the background of the countryside and towns of eastern Scotland where he was born and bred. Written in a unique prose style, and reflecting the author's left-wing ideas, it won high praise. Under his real name he wrote *Spartacus* (1933), which deals with the great Roman slave rebellion of 73-71 BC.

GIBBON. Genus of apes (*Hylobates*). The body is hairy except for the buttocks, which distinguishes them from other families of apes. They have long limbs, no tail, and are arboreal in habit, but when on the ground walk upright. They are found from Assam, through the Malay peninsula to Borneo.

GIBBONS, Grinling (1648-1721). Woodcarver and sculptor, his origin - English or Dutch - is disputed. On the recommendation of Evelyn, he worked for Charles II and from 1714 was master carver to George I. For Sir Christopher Wren he did work on St Paul's cathedral choir, and country houses such as Petworth have fine examples of his carvings of flowers, birds, and foliage executed in great detail and with exquisite delicacy.

GIBBONS, Orlando (1583-1625). English composer. B. at Cambridge, he was the most distinguished of a family of musicians, and was appointed organist at Westminster Abbey in 1623. His finest works are his madrigals and motets.

GIBBONS, Stella Dorothea (1902-). British novelist. B. in London, she became a journalist, and is best known for her *Cold Comfort Farm* (1932), a satire on the regional novel.

GIBRALTAR (jibrawl'tar), **City of.** Naval and air base, and fortress occupying a rocky promontory near the extreme S of Spain. The town is on the NW side, and the harbour is enclosed by moles.

Captured by Sir George Rooke in 1704, G. was ceded to Britain under the Treaty of Utrecht (1713); Spanish attempts to retake it incl. the siege of 1779-83 and Franco imposed a blockade (1969) not lifted till 1980. A referendum in 1967 resulted in an overwhelming majority in G. for continued assocn. with Britain. In 1969 G. ceased to be a Crown Colony, becoming known as the *City of G.* Under the new constitution there is a Gov. and an elected House of Assembly of 15 members. There is an underground communications centre, invaluable to NATO, which monitors Soviet shipping in the strait. Area 6.5 sq.km (2½ sq.m); pop. (1971) 28,700. *See* BARBARY APE.

GIBRALTAR. The harbour, and on the fortress wall, two of the apes which, according to legend, ensure by their presence that the 'Rock' remains British. *Photo: Camera Press.*

GIBRALTAR, Strait of. The strait between N Africa and Spain which forms the western entrance to the Mediterranean Sea from the Atlantic. It varies in width from 15km (9m) to 37km (23m) and is 56km (35m) long. In 1980 Spain and Morocco were discussing the construction of a bridge or tunnel across the strait.

GIBSON, Charles Dana (1867-1944). American illustrator. B. in Mass., he became famous for his portrayal of an idealized type of American young woman, known as the 'Gibson Girl'.

GIBSON DESERT. Central Australian desert between the Great Sandy and Victoria deserts. Area 220,000 sq.km (85,000 sq.m).

GIDE (zhēd), **André** (1869-1951). French author. B. in Paris, of a Calvinist family, he pub. his first book *Les Cahiers d'André Walter*, a complex psychological confession, in 1891. In later books, *L'Immoraliste* (1902), *La Porte étroite* (1909), *La Symphonie pastorale* (1919), the autobiographical *Si le grain ne meurt* (1926), and his one real novel, *Les Faux-Monnayeurs* (1926, *The Coiners*), he develops the themes of self-fulfilment and renunciation, the two extremes between which he himself swung. In 1947 he was awarded the Nobel Prize for Literature. The Journal (1939–50), describes his thoughts and experiences until the age of eighty, and is possibly his greatest work.

GIDEONS INTERNATIONAL, The. A Christian business and professional men's association with *c.* 20,000 members in more than 50 countries, which aims at winning the lost for Christ, founded in 1899, at Jamesville, Wisconsin. It is most celebrated for its scripture programme, which incl. the placing of Bibles in hotel and motel rooms: total distribution since 1908 *c.* 7,000,000 Bibles and 45,000,000 NTs. The International HQ is at Nashville, Tennessee and the name derives from the might of the minority illus. by the Biblical story of Gideon.

GIELGUD (gēl'good), **Sir John** (1904-). British actor-producer. A great-nephew of Ellen Terry (q.v.), he made his début at the Old Vic in 1921, attracted notice as Romeo in 1924, and created his most famous role as Hamlet in 1929. He has since produced and appeared in numerous plays incl. many by Chekhov and Shakespeare. His film roles incl. Clarence in *Richard III* (1955) and the Earl of Warwick in *St Joan* (1957). His elder brother **Val G.** (1900-81) was Head of BBC Sound Drama 1929-63, and wrote plays and novels.

GIESSEN (gē'sen). Manufacturing town on the Lahn, Hesse, W Germany, with a famous univ. (1605). Pop. (1978) 79,000.

GIGLI (jel'yi), **Beniamino** (1890–1957). Italian tenor. From his operatic début in 1914, he was specially successful in roles from Puccini, Gounod, and Massenet. His sensuous lyrical voice was unforced and perfect throughout its range.

GIJON (hēhōn'). Port on the Bay of Biscay, Oviedo prov., N Spain. There are iron and steel industries, chemical plants and oil refineries. Pop. (1970) 187,600.

GILBERT, Sir Alfred (1854-1934). British sculptor and goldsmith, b. in London, best known for his 'Eros' (memorial fountain to the 7th earl of Shaftesbury) in Piccadilly Circus, London.

GILBERT, Cass (1859-1934). American architect. B. in Ohio, he was famous for his 'skyscrapers', incl. the Woolworth Building, New York.

GILBERT, Sir Humphrey (*c.* 1539-83). English navigator. B. at Dartmouth, the half-brother of Sir Walter Raleigh, he sailed from Plymouth for Newfoundland in 1583, and landed at the site of St John's, taking possession in the queen's name - whence Newfoundland claims to be the oldest British colony. His ship foundered on the return voyage.

GILBERT, Sir William Schwenk (1836-1911). British humorist and dramatist. B. in London, he was called to the Bar in 1863, but in 1869 pub. a collection of his humorous verse and drawings, *Bab Ballads* - 'Bab' being his own early nickname - which was followed by a second vol. in 1873. His collaboration with Arthur Sullivan (q.v.) in their great series of comic operas dates from 1871. The popularity of these was due as much to G.'s witty lyrics and plots as to Sullivan's music, but personal relations between the 2 men were often cool. He was knighted in 1907.

GILBERT. Sir William Schwenk Gilbert, a portrait by Frank Holl. *Photo: Courtesy of the National Portrait Gallery.*

GILBERT AND ELLICE ISLANDS. Former British colony (a protectorate 1892-1915), which comprised the present states of Tuvalu and Kiribati (qq.v.).

GILES (jīlz), **Carl Ronald** (1916-). British cartoonist for the *Daily* and *Sunday Express* from 1943, especially noted for his 'typical' British family complete from realistic infants-in-arms to a redoubtable grandma.

GILGAMESH. Hero of Sumerian, Hittite, Akkadian and Assyrian legend. The 12 verse 'books' of the *Epic of G.* were recorded in a standard version on a dozen cuneiform tablets by Ashurbanipal's scholars in the 7th cent. BC and the epic itself is older than the *Iliad* by at least 1,500 years. One-third mortal and two-thirds divine, G. is Lord of Uruk, and his friend Enkidu (half beast, half man) dies for him: the incident of the Flood was later drawn upon by OT writers.

GI'LGIT. District in the mtns of NW Kashmir: Nanga Parbat 8,125 m (26,660 ft) is the highest peak.

GILL, Eric (1882-1940). British sculptor and engraver. He studied lettering at the Central School under Edward Johnston, and began his career carving inscriptions for tombstones. Interested in lettering and book production, he devised the famous types Perpetua (1925) and Gill Sans (1927), i.e. 'sans serif', without serifs. His sculptures incl. those on Broadcasting House, London (1933).

GILLETTE (jilet'), **King Camp** (1855-1932). American inventor of the G. safety-razor.

GILLRAY, James (1757-1815). English caricaturist. His 1,500 cartoons, full of broad humour and keen satire (1779-1811), were aimed at the French, George III, politicians, and social follies of his day. He died after 4 years' insanity.

GILPIN, William (1724-1804). British artist. Vicar of Boldre from 1777 and a keen educationist, he is remembered as the inventor of the 'picturesque', establishing precise rules for the production of this effect in his essays.

GIN (jin). A potable spirit, prepared by distilling a mash containing maize, malt, and rye, and flavouring it with juniper, etc. In Holland it is called geneva, a corruption of the French *genièvre*, juniper.

GINGER (jin'jer). Spice derived from the underground stem of *Zingiber officinale*, a reed-like perennial plant, native to SE Asia.

GINGER ALE and **BEER.** Sweetened, carbonated, and non-excisable beverages, aerated by fermentation or artificial means. They include ginger rhizome flavouring, sugar, syrup, harmless acid and colouring. The only difference between them is the employment of bitters in the preparation of G.B.

GI'NGKO. Tree (*Gingko biloba*), also known from the resemblance of its leaves to those of the maidenhair fern - though much enlarged - as the maidenhair tree. A 'living fossil', unchanged since prehistoric times, now only cultivated in Japan and China. First planted in England in the 18th cent., it does well in towns, e.g. Cardiff and New York. In 200 years it may reach *c.* 30m (100ft), and the fruits have edible kernels, although the pulp is poisonous.

GINNER, Charles (1878-1952). British painter. B. at Cannes, he settled in London in 1910, and was one of the London Group from 1914. He was noted for the treatment of buildings in his landscapes.

GINSENG (jin'seng). Plant (*Panax schinseng*) used in medicine in China for 3,000 yrs, and the subject of much present-day controversy. It is claimed to lessen fatigue, stimulate effort, and promote resistance to disease and stress, hence lengthening life. Russian astronauts have used it on space flights.

GIOLITTI (jōlit'i), **Giovanni** (1842-1928). Italian statesman. B. at Mondovi, he was PM in 1892-3, 1903-5, 1906-9, 1911-14, and 1920-1. He opposed Italian intervention in the F.W.W. A Liberal, he pursued a policy of broad coalitions, which was ineffective in the face of the rise of Fascism.

GIONO (jō'nō), **Jean** (1895-1970). French novelist, whose books are chiefly set in Provence. *Que ma joie demeure* (1935: *Joy of Man's Desiring*) is an attack on life in towns and a plea for a return to country life. In 1956 he pub. a defence of Gaston Dominici, who allegedly murdered an English family on holiday, maintaining that the old farmer exemplified the misunderstandings between town and country people.

GIORGIONE (jorjō'ne) (1478-1511). Name by which the Venetian artist, Giorgio of Castelfranco, is known. He was a leader of the High Renaissance, and influenced Titian and others. His masterpiece is the 'Madonna and Child Enthroned with Two Saints', an altar-piece for the church of Castelfranco.

GIOTTO (jot'tō) **DI BONDŌ'NE** (1266/76-1337). Italian painter, sculptor, and architect. B. at Vespignano, N of Florence, he infused new life into Italian art, painting in a naturalistic style and depicting sacred personages as real people. He is chiefly famous for his frescoes in churches at Assisi, Padua, and Florence. In 1334 he was appointed master of the cathedral at Florence and official architect of the city. He collaborated with Andrea Pisano in decorating the cathedral façade with statues, and designed the Campanile, which was completed after his death. *See* ITALIAN ART.

GIRAFFE (jiraf'). Tallest mammal, in the family Giraffidae. It measures over 5.5m (15ft), the neck accounting for nearly half this amount. The G. has 2 small skin-covered horns on the head and a long tufted tail. The skin has a mottled appearance and is reddish brown and cream. Gs. are now found only in Africa, S of the Sahara Desert.

GIRAFFE. Superbly marked specimens among the acacia trees of the Serengeti Park, Tanzania. *Photo: Heather Angel.*

GIRA'LDUS CAMBRE'NSIS (Gerald the Welshman) (c. 1146-1220). Welsh bishop and historian. B. in Pembrokeshire, he was elected bishop of St David's in 1198. One of the foremost Latinists of his age, he wrote a history of the conquest of Ireland by Henry II and *Itinerarium Cambrense.*

GIRAUDOUX (zhērohdōō'), **Jean** (1882-1944). French diplomat, author of light-weight novels, e.g. *Simon le pathétique* (1918), an autobiographical window on adolescence, and plays incl. the humorous renderings of Greek legends *Amphitryon 38* (1929) and *La guerre de Troie n'aura pas lieu* (1935).

GIRGENTI. Another form of AGRIGENTO.

GIRL GUIDES. A youth organization for girls estab. in 1910 by Lord Baden-Powell and his sister, Agnes Baden-Powell. As reorganized 1967 it has 3 branches: Brownie G. (7-11), Guides (10-16), and Ranger G. (14-20) with adult leaders known as Guiders. The World Assocn of G.G. and Girl Scouts (the name by which they are known in USA) ensures international co-operation. World membership is over 6½million.

GIRO (jī'rō). System of making payments by direct transfer between one bank or post office account and another. Originating in Austria in 1883, the idea was introduced in the UK in 1968, the beginning of the present Nat. Girobank run by the Post Office (HQ Bootle). The name derives from Gk *guros* 'circle', since the money goes round and round.

GIRONDE (zhērońd'). Navigable French estuary off the Bay of Biscay, formed by the mouths of the Garonne and Dordogne rivers. It is 80km (50m) long and 3-10 km (2-6 m) wide. It gives its name to the largest dept of France.

GIRON'DINS. The right-wing republican party in the French Revolution, so called because a number of their leaders came from the Gironde. They were driven from power by the Jacobins in 1793.

GIRTIN, Thomas (1775-1802). English painter. The poetic spirit and technical innovations of this friend and contemporary of Turner revolutionized landscape painting in water-colour, and were part of the romantic attitude of the early 19th cent.

GISBORNE. Town and port on the E coast of North Island, NZ, exporting dairy products, wool and meat. Pop. (1976) 31,790.

GISCARD D'ESTAING (zhēskahr' destań'), **Valéry** (1926-). French Independent Republican statesman. Son of a wealthy inspector of finance, he is descended from Louis XV, and by his intellectuality and financial wizardry earned the nickname 'Computer on stilts'. He was Min. of Finance 1962-6, being dropped by de Gaulle at the beginning of his second presidency, and serving again in this post during the presidency of Pompidou from 1969. He succeeded him as pres. in 1974, after a campaign for 'change without risk', only narrowly defeating Mitterand, who in turn defeated him in 1981.

GISCARD D'ESTAING. The future president (left), then Minister of Finance, together with President Pompidou, and Peyrefitte, Minister of Information. *Photo: Popperfoto.*

GISSING, George Robert (1857-1903). British author. B. in Yorks, he taught for many years in London and the USA, leading a life of near destitution. His first novel, *Workers in the Dawn,* appeared in 1880 but it was not until *Demos* (1886), which dealt with socialist ideas, that G. became at all widely read. Among his later books are *New Grub Street* (1891), the autobiographical *Private Papers of Henry Ryecroft* (1903), and a study of Dickens. His books depict, with a realism and sincerity born of experience, the degrading effects on men and women of the struggle against circumstances and poverty.

GIULINI (jūlē'ni), **Carlo Maria** (1914-). Italian conductor. Principal conductor at La Scala, Milan, 1953-5, he is the outstanding conductor today of Italian grand opera, e.g. Verdi's *Don Carlos* at Covent Garden in 1958. He is also a fine interpreter of modern composers, as well as of Brahms, Haydn and Mozart.

GLACE (glas) **BAY.** Port on Cape Breton Island, Nova Scotia, Canada, centre of a coal-mining area. Pop. (1971) 22,500.

GLĀ'CIER. A compacted mass of ice which originates in mountains in the snowfields above the snowline, where the annual snowfall exceeds the annual melting and drainage. It moves slowly down a valley or depression, and is constantly replenished from its source. The scenery produced by the passing of Gs. is characteristic. When a G. moves over an uneven surface crevasses are formed in it; if it reaches the sea it breaks up to form icebergs.

GLADIĀ'TORS. Professional fighters, recruited mainly from slaves, criminals, and prisoners of war, who fought to the death for the entertainment of the ancient Romans. The custom, which originated in the practice of slaughtering slaves on a chieftain's grave, was introduced into Rome from Etruria in 264 BC, and survived until the 5th cent. AD.

GLADIŌ'LUS. Genus of plants of the Iridaceae (Iris) family. The tall leafy stems arise from corms and bear a spike of brightly coloured, irregular flowers. The perianth is funnel-shaped, and in the cultivated varieties may be any shade but blue.

GLADSTONE, William Ewart (1809-98). British Liberal statesman. B. in Liverpool, the son of a rich merchant, he was ed. at Eton and Oxford, and entered parliament as a Tory in 1833. In Peel's govt he was Pres. of the Board of Trade 1843-5, and Colonial Sec. 1845-6. He left the Tory Party with the Peelite group in 1846, and after 1859 identified himself with the Liberals. He was Chancellor of the Exchequer in Aberdeen's govt 1852-5, and in Palmerston and Russell's govts 1859-66. Becoming PM in 1868-74, he carried through a series of important reforms, incl. the disestablishment of the Church of Ireland, the Irish Land Act, the abolition of the purchase of army commissions and of religious tests in the universities, and the introduction of elementary education and of vote by ballot.

During Disraeli's govt of 1874-80 G. strongly resisted his imperialist and pro-Turkish policy, and by his Midlothian campaign of 1879 helped to overthrow him. G.'s second govt of 1880-5 was confronted with difficult problems in Ireland, Egypt and S Africa, and lost prestige through its failure to relieve Gen. Gordon. Returning to office in 1886, G. introduced his Home Rule Bill, which was defeated by the secession of the Liberal Unionists, and he thereupon resigned. After 6 years' opposition he formed his last govt in 1892; his second Home Rule Bill was rejected by the Lords, and in 1894 he resigned. He is buried in Westminster Abbey.

GLAMIS (glahmz). Village in Tayside, Scotland. Nearby G. Castle is the seat of the earl of Strathmore, where Princess Margaret was born. It is haunted by the legend of the 'monster of G'.

GLAMO'RGAN. Three cos. of S Wales - Mid, South and West Glamorgan - created in 1974 from the former co. of Glamorganshire. All are on the Bristol Channel, and the admin. HQ of Mid and South G. is Cardiff; the HQ of West G. is Swansea. **Mid G.,** which also takes in a small area of the former co. of Monmouthshire to the E, contains the important coalmining towns of Aberdare, Merthyr Tydfil, and Rhondda in the valleys of the mtns in the northern part of the co. Area 1,019 sq.km (394 sq.m); pop. (1978) 537,900. In **South G.,** there is mixed farming in the fertile Vale of G., and towns incl. Cardiff, Penarth and Barry. Area 416 sq.km (161 sq.m); pop. (1978) 385,600. **West G.** incl. Swansea, with tin-plating and copper industries; Margam, with large steel rolling mills; Port Talbot and Neath. Area 815 sq.km (315 sq.m); pop. (1978) 366,900.

GLASER, Donald A. (1926-). American physicist. B. in Cleveland, he was ed. at the Case Inst. of Technology and in 1960 became prof. at the Univ. of California. In 1960 he was awarded a Nobel prize for his invention of the 'bubble chamber' (q.v.) for observing high-energy nuclear phenomena. By using a pressurized liquid medium instead of a gas, it overcomes drawbacks inherent in the earlier 'cloud chamber'.

GLASGOW (glahs'gō). City in Strathclyde, Scotland, on the r. Clyde, the country's leading commercial centre. The river channel has been blasted and dredged to accommodate large vessels, and shipbuilding is one of the most important industries. The great transatlantic passenger liners, of which the *Queen Elizabeth II* is the last, were built here. Other industries incl. iron and steel, engineering, chemicals, leather, textiles, clothing, tobacco and distilling. The cathedral of St Mungo (patron saint and founder of the city in the 6th cent.) was built in the 12-13th cents. The Cross Steeple is all that remains of the old Tolbooth (*c.* 1628). The Univ. of G. (1450) is housed in buildings designed by Sir Gilbert Scott, and the Univ. of Strathclyde was founded 1963. Also notable are the Royal Exchange and Stock Exchange, the Kelvingrove Art Gallery, which has a fine impressionist collection, and the Mitchell Library. The Gorbals district, once notorious for the vitality of its slum life, has been subject to clearance. Prestwick internat. airport is 55km (28m) to the SW. G. is the admin. HQ of Strathclyde. Pop. (1973) 835,650.

GLASS. An inorganic substance in a condition which is continuous with its liquid state, but which, as the result of having been cooled from a fused condition, has become for all practical purposes rigid. As such, it is transparent or translucent and may become to some extent opaque. It is a mixture of silicates of lime, soda, and potash, to which are added metallic oxides, for colouring and opacity, and borates, phosphates, etc., for special purposes.

There are three main divisions of manufactured glass. Blown G. contains silica, potash, and lead oxide, which are mixed with broken G. (cullet) in crucibles, heated therein till viscous, when the G. is blown or drawn into tube. Plate G., which required grinding and polishing, has since 1959 been replaced by float G., produced by allowing the molten G. to flow out of the furnace into a chamber 45m long containing molten tin, where it is 'fire-polished' by heating from above and cooled, solidifying at a much higher temperature than the tin. Optical G., homogeneous and transparent, is cooled slowly in crucibles, reheated, and then subjected to prolonged cooling.

Modern advances have led to safety G., laminated G., ultra-violet ray G., heat-treated G., and G. fibres. These fibres were first manufactured as a heat-insulating material, later for vibration control. They have recently been developed as yarn for electric motor and domestic appliances, dress materials, etc. Glass reinforced plastic (GRP) consists of a thermo-setting resin reinforced with G. fibres, these filaments having high tensile strength, good electrical, chemical and weathering properties. It is used for boat hulls, motor bodies, aircraft components, non-corroding equipment for chemical plants, and in buildings. *See also* METALLIC GLASS.

The decorative use of G. is very ancient, blown G. reaching perfection in 18th dynasty Egypt, the Chinese excelling in imitation of rare stones, and the Graeco-Roman era being represented by the Portland vase. High points in later glassware are the Byzantine G. mosaics, medieval European stained G., the delicate filigree of 15th cent. Venice, and English table glass of the 18th cent. Engraved G. by individual artists (e.g. Laurence Whistler, and the products of the Steuben works in the US) is today often used for presentation pieces, the methods being diamond-point engraving (developed in 16th cent. Italy) and copper-wheel engraving (originating in Bohemia): the commercial processes are sand-blasting and acid etching.

GLASS. Glass fibre is one of the principal constituents in the modern composite materials which are increasingly used today. Here continuous filament glass fibre is being fed to the chopped strand mat plant. *Photo: Courtesy of Turner & Newall.*

GLASTONBURY. Market town in Somerset, England. Nearby are 2 excavated lake villages thought to have been occupied for *c.* 150 years before the Romans came to Britain.

The first church on the site was traditionally founded in the 1st cent. by Joseph of Arimathea: the ruins of the great Benedictine abbey built in the 10th-11th cents. by Dunstan (q.v.) and his followers were excavated in 1963 and the site of the grave of King Arthur and Queen Guinevere was thought to have been identified. Pop. (1971) 6,500.

GLAUBER'S SALT. Crystallized form of hydrated sodium sulphate, first described by J. R. Glauber (1604-68), German chemist. It is used as an aperient.

GLENCOE (glenkō′). Glen in Highland region, Scotland, where members of the Macdonald clan were massacred in 1692, John Campbell, earl of Breadalbane, being the chief instigator. It is now a winter sports area.

GLENDOWER, Owen (*c.* 1359-*c.* 1415). Welsh hero. He headed a revolt against the English in N Wales, and defeated Henry IV in three campaigns, 1400-2. But from 1405 the struggle went against him and Wales was reconquered by 1413.

GLENEAGLES. Glen in Tayside, Scotland. The **G. Principle** was formulated 1977 at the G. Hotel, famous as a golfing venue. Agreed by the heads of Commonwealth govts., it states that 'every practical step *(*should be taken*)* to discourage contact or competition by their nationals' with S. Africa, in disapproval of apartheid.

GLENROTHES (glenrōdh′ez). Town in Fife, Scotland, 10km (6m) N of Kirkcaldy, developed as a 'new town' from 1948, and admin. H.Q. of Fife. Pop. (1975) 32,000.

GLIDING. The art of using air currents to fly heavier-than-air craft without engines. Technically speaking G. involves the gradual loss of altitude; gliders designed for soaring flight (utilizing air rising up a cliff face or hill, warm air rising as a 'thermal' above sun-heated ground, etc.) are known as sail-planes. Pioneers incl. Cayley, Lilienthal, Octave Chanute (1832-1910), and the Wright brothers, the last-named perfecting G. technique in 1902. The British G. Assoc. dates from 1929. Launching may be by rubber catapault from a hilltop; by a winch which raises the glider like a kite; or by aircraft tow. In the S.W.W. towed troop-carrying gliders were used by the Germans in Crete and the Allies at Arnhem. In 'hang G.', perfected by US engineer Rogallo in the 1970s, the aeronaut is strapped into a carrier, attached to a sail wing of nylon stretched on an aluminium frame shaped like a paper dart, and launches himself from a height.

GLINKA, Michael (1803-57). Russian composer. B. near Smolensk, he broke away from the prevailing Italian influence, and turned to Russian folk-music as the inspiration of *A Life for the Tsar* (1836). His later works incl. another opera *Russlan and Ludmilla* (1842), and the orchestral *Kamarinskaya.*

GLIWICE (glēvē′tse). Town in Poland, formerly in German Silesia, with coal-mining, iron, steel, and electrical industries. Pop. (1978) 200,000.

GLOBE THEATRE. Octagonal theatre open to the sky, built by Burbage, Shakespeare, and others in 1599 on the Bankside, Southwark, and burnt down in 1613. A replica on the same site was planned in 1976.

GLOBIGERINA (glōbijerī′na). Genus of Foraminifera which are preserved in chalk. The conical spiral shells accumulate at the bottom of deep seas, forming 'G. ooze'.

GLOMMA (glō′ma). Largest r. in Norway; 570km (350m) long, it flows into the Skaggerak at Frederiksstad.

GLOUCESTER (glos′ter), **Richard Alexander Walter George,** duke of (1944-). Prince of the UK. Second son of Prince Henry, duke of G. (1900-74), third son of George V, he succeeded his father owing to the death of his elder brother Prince William (1941-72) in an air crash. Known as an architect, under the name 'Richard Gloucester', and as a photographer, he m. in 1972 Birgitte von Deurs, dau. of a Danish lawyer.

GLOUCESTER. City and port in Glos, England, on the Severn, with aircraft, agricultural machinery works, etc. It is the admin HQ of Glos. The cathedral was founded 1022 as the church of a Benedictine Abbey. At nearby Cranham, in the Cotswolds, is Prinknash Abbey (1928: rebuilt 1939-72) famous for its pottery. Pop. (1974) 90,550.

GLOUCESTERSHIRE. English co. in the western Midlands. The Cotswolds cross it SW to NE, Cleve Cloud reaching 326m (1,070 ft), and to the N and W of them is the fertile Vale of Gloucester, drained by the Severn and its tributaries. Coal is mined in the Forest of Dean. The admin. HQ is Gloucester: other towns incl. Stroud, Cheltenham, Tewkesbury and Cirencester. In the local govt reorganization 1974, G. lost a section in the SW to Avon (q.v.). Area 3,117 sq.km (1,203 sq.m); pop. (1978) 495,300.

GLOVE-BOX. A form of protection used when working with certain radioactive materials. Gloves fixed to ports in the walls of a box allow manipulation of work within the box. Contamination through inhalation of fine air-borne particles of poisonous alpha-active or other materials is prevented by maintaining a slight vacuum inside the box, so that any air flow is inwards.

GLOUCESTER. With a Norman nucleus, the cathedral has additions in every style of Gothic. The cloisters have some of the earliest and loveliest fan tracery in England. *Photo: Michael Charity.*

GLOW-WORM. The wingless female of various luminous beetles in the family Lampyridae. The luminous organs are situated under the abdomen, and the light has a sexual significance. The species are distributed throughout Europe and Siberia. *See* FIREFLY.

GLŌZEL'. Village in Allier dept, France, nr Vichy. An archaeological find in 1924 was attacked as a hoax because of the disparate age of the objects: bones with drawings of animals 10,000 BC, axes 4-2,000 BC, inscribed clay tablets 700 BC-AD 100, and a glass kiln, possibly medieval. Thermoluminescent analysis 1975-6 suggested the objects were genuine.

GLUBB, Sir John Bagot (1897-). British soldier, known until the general abolition of the title in 1952 as G. Pasha. As OC the Arab Legion 1939-56 he was its creator in its modern form. He was dismissed in 1956 as a result of anti-British sentiment in Jordan, and created KCB.

GLUCK (glook), **Christoph Willibald** (1714-87). German composer. B. at Weidenwang, nr Neumarkt, Bavaria, he studied music at Prague, Vienna, and Milan, came to London in 1745 to compose operas for the Haymarket, but returned to Vienna in 1746. He was knighted by the Pope, and in 1756 settled at Vienna as Kapellmeister to Maria Theresa. In 1762 his *Orfeo ed Euridice* revolutionized the whole 18th cent. conception of opera. G. threw overboard the traditional operatic conventions and restrictions and gave free scope to dramatic effects of a serene and classic beauty. *Orfeo* was followed by *Alceste* (1767) and *Paris ed Elena* (1769). *Iphigénie en Aulide* (1774), produced in Paris, gave rise to furious controversies in which G. had the support of Marie Antoinette, whilst his Italian rival Piccini was patronized by Mme Du Barry. With *Armide* (1777) and *Iphigénie en Tauride* (1779) G. won a complete victory over Piccini. He d. at Vienna.

GLUCOSE ($C_6H_{12}O_6$). Form of sugar, also known as grape-sugar or dextrose. It is present in the blood, and in honey and fruit juices. In more complex formations it occurs as cellulose, starch, and glycogen, and it is usually prepared by hydrolysis from cane sugar or starch. Generally a yellowish syrup, it may be purified to a white crystalline powder.

GLUE. *See* ADHESIVE.

GLYCERINE (glis'erin), **GLYCEROL** ($CH_2OH.CHOH.CH_2OH$). Colourless, viscous, odourless, sweetish liquid b.p. 290 °C, m.p. 18 °C, miscible with water and alcohol, insoluble in ether. Obtained from vegetable and animal oils and fats (by treatment with acid, alkali, superheated steam or an enzyme, or by fermentation of glucose), it is used in the manufacture of high explosives, in antifreeze solutions, to maintain moist conditions in fruits and tobacco, in cosmetics, etc.

GLYCINE (glī'sēn). The simplest amino acid, a sweet, colourless crystalline compound. It is stored in the liver of animals and burnt by the muscles to produce energy. Detection of its characteristic radio signal is a means of checking by radio telescope that animal life of the same chemical type as our own exists in space. *See* AMINES.

GLYCOL (glī'kol) ($CH_2OH.CH_2OH$). Colourless, odourless, viscous liquid with a sweetish taste; b.p. 197 °C; m.p. −17 °C; miscible with water and alcohol; density 1.115 g/ml. It is used in antifreeze solutions, in the preparation of ethers and esters, especially for explosives, and as a solvent; a substitute for glycerol.

GLYN (glin), **Elinor** (1865-1943). British writer. Her novel of an exotic love-affair, *Three Weeks* (1907), scandalized Edwardian society, as did her passion for tiger skins, and the beauty of her white skin and red hair: her admirers incl. Lord Curzon.

GLYNDEBOURNE (glīnd-). An English estate nr Lewes, Sussex, with opera house estab. by J. Christie (1882-1962) for staging new and old operatic works at an annual summer festival.

GNAT. Family of flies (Culicidae) in the order Diptera, also known as mosquitoes. The eggs are laid in water, where they hatch into worm-like larvae, which after passing through a pupal stage emerge as perfect insects. Well-known species are the Common G. (*Culex pipiens*), abundant in England: the carrier of malaria (*Anopheles maculipennis*); and the banded mosquito (*Aedes aegypti*) which transmits yellow fever. Only the female is capable of drawing blood, since the male possesses no piercing mandibles.

GNEISS (nīs). Metamorphic rock, often found in association with schists and granites. It has a foliated structure, consisting of an alternation of micaceous and granular bands. Garnets commonly occur in G.

GNOSTICISM (nost'isizm). Name applied to a religious movement contemporary with the rise of Christianity, that is sometimes regarded as a series of Christian heresies, but is better represented as an attempt to form a synthesis of Christian theology, Greek philosophy, and elements derived from the ancient mystery cults of the Mediterranean world. The Gnostics maintained that they possessed an esoteric knowledge of the inner meaning of religion, the *gnosis*, by means of which they were able to attain to illumination and immortality. They conceived the world as a series of emanations or aeons proceeding from the highest of several gods, and they recognized a clear distinction between spirit and essentially evil matter. The Albigenses and other heretics were probably inheritors of Gnostic ideas, as were the Sufis, or mystics of Islam.

GNU (noo). A large, white-tailed S African antelope (*Connochaetes gnou*). Also a larger brindled gnu (*C. taurinus*) of central and E Africa.

GŌ. Game first played in China 3,000 yrs ago, and now the national game of Japan. The board, squared off by 19 horizontal and 19 vertical lines, begins empty and gradually fills up with black and white flattish, rounded stones, as the players win territory by surrounding areas of the board with 'men' and capturing the enemy armies by surrounding them. A handicapping system enables expert and amateur to play against each other. It is far more complex and subtle than chess, the mathematical possibilities being 10 to the 720.

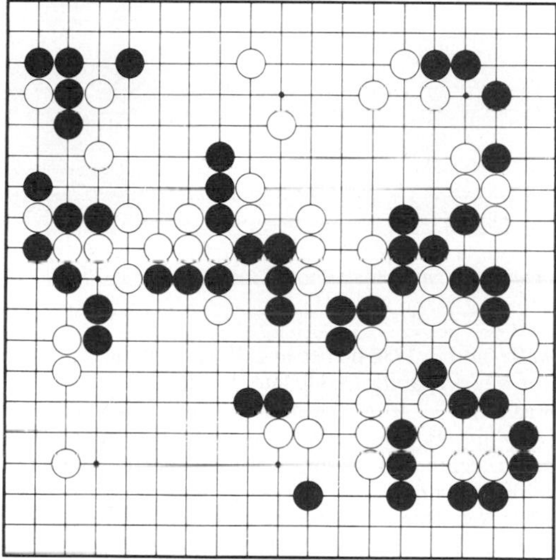

GO. A go board showing a typical tactical manoeuvre.

GOA (gō'ah). Former Portuguese prov. in India, it included besides Goa proper, on the Malabar coast, the settlements of Diu and Damao. Although it had been Portuguese since 1505, from 1950 India demanded its transfer to her, and forcibly seized G. (1961), incorporating it in the Rep. of India (1962): G. rejected by referendum a merger with Maharashtra (1967) and remains a Union Territory. The cap. is Panjim. Area 3,693 sq.km (1,431 sq.m); pop. (1971) 858,000.

GOAT. Genus of ruminants (*Capra*), similar in appearance to the sheep. It is probably Persian in origin, but various species are now found in all parts of the world. Gs. are frequently kept for milk, but the angora and cashmere Gs. produce mohair. There are many species of G.; the English type (*Capra hircus*) is usually brown, sometimes with white patches, has short hair and tapering horns. Gs. are usually bearded and the males have an unpleasant smell. The Rocky Mountain G. of America and the ibex are wild varieties.

GOBELIN (goblań'). Name of a French tapestry manufactory, originally founded as a dyeworks in Paris by Gilles and Jean G. about 1450. The firm began to produce tapestries in the 16th cent., and in 1662 the establishment was purchased by Colbert for Louis XIV. With the support of the State it still continues to make tapestries.

GŌ'BI. Desert in Asia lying partly in the Mongolian People's Republic, partly in Inner Mongolia region, China. It is 800km (500m) N-S and 1,600 km (1,000 m) E-W. The sandy, waterless part occurs in the SW, while the rest is a succession of stony plains and ranges of hills. In some parts sheep and cattle are reared, and where water is available for irrigation crops are grown by the nomadic Mongol and Kalmuck inhabitants. In the desert, relics of prehistoric cultures have been discovered.

GOBINEAU (gōbēnō'), **Joseph Arthur,** comte de (1816-82). French diplomat and writer. His most influential work was his *Essai sur l'inégalité des races humaines* (1855), where he maintained the doctrine of the innate superiority of the white or 'Aryan' race. This quasi-scientific thesis fitted well with the rising nationalist spirit in Germany.

GOD. In its most highly evolved form, the concept of a supreme being, a unique personal creative entity, assumed to be completely good. In the 19th and early 20th cents., with the prevalence of the belief in science and that the only valid statements were those verifiable by the senses, support for the idea of G. waned, but by the 1980s was reviving, as being provable by reason, among philosophers. *See also* FETISHISM, MONOTHEISM and POLYTHEISM; DEISM, THEISM, and PANTHEISM; RELIGION and THEOLOGY.

GO'DALMING. Town in Surrey, England, on the r. Wey. Charterhouse School (1611) was removed here from London in 1872. Pop. (1972) 19,200.

GODARD (gohdahr'), **Jean-Luc** (1930-). French film director. With films such as *À Bout de Souffle* (1959) *Masculin-Féminin,* etc., he pioneered a sharply casual approach to cutting and visual juxtapositions, suggestive of journalism.

GŌDAVA'RI. Sacred r. flowing from W Ghats, India, to the Bay of Bengal: 1,450 km (900m).

GÖDEL (ger'del), **Kurt** (1906-78). American mathematician. B. in Austria-Hungary, he gave his name to a concept of a rotating universe which would make time travel possible.

GODFREY DE BOUILLON (*c.* 1060-1100). Crusader. The 2nd son of Count Eustace II of Boulogne, with his brothers Baldwin and Eustace he led in 1096 a force of 40,000 Germans to take part in the 1st Crusade. After Jerusalem was taken in 1099, he was elected its ruler, but refused the title of king.

GŌDĪ'VA, Lady. Wife of Leofric, earl of Mercia, who founded a Benedictine monastery at Coventry during the 11th cent., where she was buried. According to legend, the earl promised to remit a heavy tax imposed upon the people of the town if his wife rode naked through the streets at noonday. This she did, but by arrangement the people remained indoors; with the exception of 'Peeping Tom', who bored a hole in his shutters, and was struck blind.

GOD SAVE THE KING/QUEEN. The British national anthem. The origin of both tune and words is obscure; the former resembles a composition by John Bull (1563-1628) and a number of other 16th cent. works. The words can also be traced in various forms back to the 16th cent. The song assumed substantially its present form during the 1745 rebellion, when it was used as an anti-Jacobite Party

GOGH. A self-portrait, and one of Van Gogh's most famous works 'A Cornfield with Cypresses'. *Photos: Courtesy of the Courtauld Institute and the National Gallery, London.*

song. The tune has been used for patriotic songs in the USA ('My country, 'tis of thee') and Germany.

GODWIN (d. 1053). Earl of Wessex from 1020. Secured succession to throne in 1042 of Edward the Confessor, to whom he m. his dau. Edith, and whose chief minister he became. King Harold was his son.

GODWIN, William (1756-1836). British philosopher and novelist. At first a Nonconformist minister, he later became an atheist and a philosopher, achieving fame in 1793 through his *Enquiry concerning Political Justice,* which advocated an anarchic society based on a faith in man's essential rationality. He subsequently pub. *Caleb Williams* (1794), a story written in illustration of his theories, and many other works. His first wife, the feminist Mary Wollstonecraft (1759-97), whose *Vindication of the Rights of Women* (1792) demanded equal educational opportunities for men and women, d. in giving birth to a dau., later Mary Shelley.

GOEBBELS, Paul Josef (1897-1945). German Nazi leader. B. in the Rhineland, he became a journalist, joined the Nazi Party in its early days, and was given control of its propaganda in 1929. On becoming Minister of Propaganda in 1933, he brought all cultural and educational activities completely under Nazi control, and built up sympathetic movements abroad to carry on the 'war of nerves' against Hitler's intended victims. On the capture of Berlin by the Allies he poisoned himself.

GOERING, Hermann Wilhelm (1893-1946). German Nazi leader. B. in Bavaria, he served in the F.W.W. as an ace flyer. He joined the Nazi Party in 1922, and organized and commanded the SA (Storm Troops). Appointed PM of Prussia and Min. of the Interior in 1933, he arranged the Reichstag fire, and directed the reign of terror which followed. As Commissioner for Aviation he built up the Luftwaffe, and in 1936 he became director of the four-year plan for war preparations. He later lost favour with Hitler, and was expelled from the Nazi Party in 1945. He was tried at Nuremberg as a war criminal in 1945-6 and condemned to death, but poisoned himself shortly before the execution was due.

GOES (gōōs), **Hugo van der** (*c.* 1440-82). Flemish artist. B. probably in Ter Goes, he spent his later years in a monastery subject to fits of insanity. His works, e.g. the Portinari altar-piece now in the Uffizi and the 'Death of the Virgin' at Bruges, have great emotional impact.

GOETHE (gö'te), **Johann Wolfgang von** (1749-1832). German poet and man-of-letters, statesman and natural philosopher. B. in Frankfurt-am-Main, he first discovered his poetic vocation while studying law at Leipzig; to this period belong the *Laune des Verliebten, Die Mitschuldigen* and the book of lyrics *Annette.* After meeting Herder at Strasbourg (1770-1) he shook off the influence of French rococo and became the leader of the 'Storm and Stress' movement, writing the dramas *Götz von Berlichingen, Faust* (not completed until 60 years later), *Clavigo, Stella*; and the novel *Die Leiden des Jungen Werthers* (1774). In 1775 G. moved to Weimar, entering the service of the Duke Karl August, and his administrative duties there helped him to discipline his genius. A visit to Italy (1786-8) inspired *Römische Elegien* (1795), which was followed by the classical dramas *Iphigenie* (1787) and *Tasso* (1790), and by the novel Wilhelm Meister (1794). The first part of *Faust* was pub. in 1808, but the second did not appear until 1831. Among G.'s later works were the poetic *West-Östlicher Divan* (1819), the novel *Die Wahlverwandschaften* (1809), and the autobiographical *Dichtung und Wahrheit* (1811-33).

GOETHE. A portrait of J.W.Goethe by Schwerdgeburth, sketched two months before his death.

GŌ'GARTY, Oliver St John (1878-1957). Irish writer. An ear, nose, and throat specialist with a large Dublin practice, G. was a member of the literary circle which incl. Yeats, George Moore, and Joyce, and figures in *Ulysses* as Buck Mulligan. A wit and a poet, he wrote several books incl. the autobiographical *As I was going down Sackville Street* (1937). He took an active interest in Irish politics, being a senator of the Irish Free State 1922-36.

GOGH (khokh), **Vincent Van** (1853-90). Dutch painter. B. at Zundert, he tried various vocations, working for a time as a schoolmaster in England, before he took up painting. He studied under Van Mauve at The Hague. In 1886 he went to Paris where he became a friend of Gauguin, and the two painters worked together for a short time in Arles, Provence. One of the leaders of the Post-Impressionist painters, he executed still-lifes, portraits, and landscapes, some of the best-known being 'A Cornfield with Cypresses' 'The Yellow Chair', and 'Sunflowers', all of which are in the Tate Gallery. He spent the last years of his life in asylums, and committed suicide. Our illus. shows him in 1889 bandaged and convalescent after a violent scene with Gauguin - with whom he had been living - in which he cut off a piece of his own ear.

GŌ'GOL, Nicolai Vasilyevich (1809-52). Russian writer. B. nr Poltava, he tried several careers before entering the St Petersburg Civil Service. His first collection of stories, *Evenings on a Farm near Dikanka* (1831-2), had an immediate success, and his second, *Mirgorod,* was warmly praised by Pushkin. Later were *Arabesques* (1835), one of the world's great short stories, 'The Cloak', and his great comedy *The Inspector General* (1836), an attack on bureaucracy. From 1835 he had been a restless traveller in Europe, and it was in Rome that he completed the earlier part of his masterpiece, the picaresque novel *Dead Souls* (1842), depicting Russian provincial society.

GOITRE. Name applied to a swelling on the front of the neck caused by an enlargement of the thyroid gland. Simple G., or Derbyshire Neck, occurs in certain hilly regions and arises from lack of iodine in the water. In Exophthalmic G., also known as Graves's disease, the enlargement of the thyroid gland is accompanied by protrusion of the eyeballs, palpitation, etc.

GŌLA'N HEIGHTS. Plateau on the Syrian border with Israel, commanding the Israeli settlements below, and hence bitterly fought over in the Arab-Israeli Wars.

GOLD. A heavy, valuable, yellow metallic element, with symbol Au, atomic number 79, and atomic weight 197.0. G. has long been valued for its durability, malleability, and ductility, and because it may be easily recognized. It is unaffected by temperature changes and is highly resistant to acids. The major producers are S Africa, the Soviet Union, Canada, USA, and Australia. For manufacture, G. is alloyed with another strengthening metal, fineness being measured by the parts of pure G. in 24. *See* CARAT.

The *gold standard* was the monetary system under which G. coins such as the British sovereign were the monetary unit and worth their face value: bank notes were freely convertible to gold coin. This system, widely estab. at the beginning of the 20th cent., was broken by the F.W.W., and attempts to revive it were undermined by the Great Depression. After the S.W.W. the par values of the currency units of the Internat. Monetary Fund (which incl. nearly all members of the UN not in the immediate Soviet Communist bloc) were fixed in terms of G. and the US dollar. Consequently, they were also related to the price at which the USA dealt in G. with central banks and official monetary authorities, a price kept artificially low to encourage stability. The G. crisis of 1968 began the breakdown of this framework, and in 1976 the official G. price was abolished: floating exchange rates, within varying limits, which had already operated in practice since 1971 were now made legal. The attempt by the USA and IMF to substitute a dollar exchange standard by selling off their stocks of gold failed, owing to lack of world confidence in the dollar, and G. was increasingly used as an inflation hedge. Gold pieces used by investors for this purpose incl. the sovereign, Krugerrand, Canadian Gold Maple Leaf (1979), Mexican Centenario (1980), and the US ½ and 1 oz medallions (1980) bearing portraits of American artists, the first being Marian Anderson and Grant Wood.

Paper G. refers to the Special Drawing Rights (SDRs) created by the Internat. Monetary Fund to increase world liquidity and aid trade. They were formerly defined in G., but in 1974 were redefined in terms of a 'basket' of the 16 currencies of countries doing 1% or more of the world's trade.

GOLD COAST. Name given by Europeans, on account of the alluvial gold washed down by the rivers, to part of the W coast of Africa, from Cape Three Points to the mouth of the Volta r. Portuguese and French navigators visited this coast in the 14th cent., and in 1618 the British set up a trading settlement which developed into the colony of the Gold Coast 72,000 sq.km (24,000 sq.m); with its Ashanti and Northern Territories dependencies plus British Togoland it became Ghana (q.v.) in 1957.

GOLD COAST. Resort, 64km (40m) SE of Brisbane, Queensland, Australia. Pop. (1976) 106,000.

GOLDCREST. The smallest British bird (*Regulus regulus*), it is sometimes called the golden-crested wren, but has no link with the wrens. Olive green, with a bright yellow streak across the crown, it builds usually in conifers.

GOLDEN CALF. Image made by Aaron in response to the request of the Israelites for a god, when they despaired of Moses' return from Mt Sinai.

GOLDEN EAGLE. Bird of prey (*Aquila chrysaetos*) found in mountainous and forested districts of the northern hemisphere. It is persecuted by farmers, who fear for their lambs, but lives mainly on rabbits, hares, grouse, etc.

GOLDEN EAGLE. Two to three young are born, but the nesting sites of these magnificent birds have to be strictly protected from egg collectors. *Photo: Popperfoto.*

GOLDEN FLEECE. In Greek legend, the F. of the ram Chrysomallus, which hung on an oak tree at Colchis guarded by a dragon, and was taken by Jason and the Argonauts. It is also the name of an order of knighthood formerly awarded in Spain and in Austria, which was instituted by Philip the Good, duke of Burgundy, in 1429, and freshly inaugurated in Vienna in 1713 by Charles VI.

GOLDEN GATE, California, USA. Strait linking San Francisco Bay and the Pacific, spanned by a bridge which was completed in 1937. Longest span 1280 m (4,200ft).

GOLDEN HORDE. The invading Mongol-Tatar army which first terrorised Europe from *c.* 1237 under the leadership of Batu, a grandson of Genghis Khan. Tamerlane (q.v.) broke their power in 1395.

GOLDEN ROD. Popular name for the tall, leafy perennials of the *Solidago* genus of the Compositae. Each stem bears a head consisting of a great number of small yellow flowers.

GOLDFINCH. Songbird (*Carduelis carduelis*) commonly found in Europe and N Africa, and in many other parts of the world. It is brilliantly coloured - black, white, and red about the head, and gold and black wings. Most Gs. leave Britain in the autumn.

GOLDFISH. Fish of the carp family (*Carassius auratus*) found in eastern Asia. Greenish brown in its natural state, it has for cents. been bred by the Chinese, taking on highly coloured and freakishly shaped forms. In Japan G. breeding developed rapidly among low-class warriors dismissed by their feudal lords on the Emperor's restoration in 1868, and keeping them became an almost universal Japanese hobby: today enormous quantities are shipped abroad.

GOLDING, William (1911-). English poet and novelist, whose books have a deep moral significance, e.g. *Lord of the Flies* (1954) in which savagery takes over among a group of English schoolboys on a Pacific island and *Rites of Passage* (1980) based on a true 19th cent. story of ship's parson. Nobel prize 1983.

GOLDŌ'NI, Carlo (1707-93). Italian dramatist. B. at Venice, he wrote popular comedies for the Sant'Angelo theatre, incl. *Don Giovanni Tenorio* (1736), *La bottega di caffè, La locandiera, La casa nova,* etc. In 1761 G. moved to Paris, where he directed the Italian theatre, gave It. lessons at the court, and d. in extreme poverty.

GOLDSMITH, Oliver (1728-74). British author. B. in Ireland, the son of a clergyman, he was ed. at Trinity Coll., Dublin and went to Edinburgh to study medicine in 1752. After 18 months he proceeded to Leyden, but left without a degree and wandered through France, Switzerland, and Italy. Returning to England in 1756 he became an usher, before settling to hackwork from which he never escaped, e.g. his *History of England,* and *Animated Nature.* His earliest work of literary importance was *The Citizen of the World* (1762), a series of letters by an imaginary Chinese traveller. In 1761 he met Johnson, and became a member of his 'club'. In 1764 he estab. his reputation with his poem *The Traveller,* and followed it with his collected essays in 1765, and his novel, *The Vicar of Wakefield* (1766), sold according to Johnson's account to save him from imprisonment for debt. A further poem, *The Deserted Village* (1770), was followed by his dramatic masterpiece, *She Stoops to Conquer* (1773), which far exceeds the earlier comedy, *The Good-Natur'd Man* (1768).

GOLDWATER, Barry (1909-). American Republican politician. Senator for his native Arizona 1953-64 and from 1969. He opposes govt intervention in economic life. As presidential candidate in 1964, he was badly defeated by Johnson.

GOLDWYN, Samuel (1882-1974). American film producer. B. in Warsaw, he emigrated to the USA in 1896 and became a pioneer film-maker. He was famed for his 'goldwynisms', e.g. 'Anyone who visits a psychiatrist should have his head examined.'

GOLF. A game consisting of hitting a ball from a starting tee into a standard-sized hole (10.8cm/4.25in diam. and at least 10cm/4in deep) by means of various clubs; 18 (on smaller courses 9) such holes played constitute a round. In 'medalplay' the competitive object is to take fewer strokes than an opponent, but in match-play the result depends on the winner of individual holes. The ball weighs not more than 46 grams/1.62 oz and is no smaller than 41mm/1.62in diam. The clubs, 14 in a full set, are of 2 types. The woods, driver, brassie, spoon and No. 4 wood, now with steel shafts, are the most powerful and are used for initial tee drives and long 'fairway' play. The irons, with steel heads and shafts, are numbered 1 to 9 according to the shape of the blade. No. 1 is set upright and is most powerful; No. 9 is set back the farthest. High-numbered irons are used for gaining height rather than distance. The putter is reserved for shots when the ball is on the green - the small area surrounding each hole. After raising the ball for play from each tee it may not again be touched by hand but must be played as it lies.

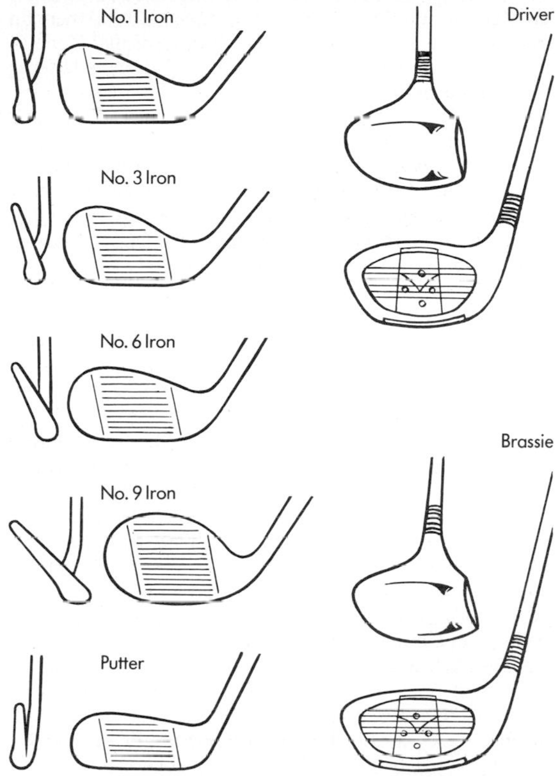

GOLF. A selection of the most frequently used clubs.

Holes vary from 100-450m (100-500yds), the majority being nearer 275m (300yds). They consist of a platform tee, a main fairway, where grass is cut short and which is bounded by rough grass, and the green. Sand bunkers are laid at vulnerable points, often ringing the green. A course now measures about 5,500 m (6,000 yds) for which leading players return scores of under 70. For average players, handicaps are employed as a method of matching unequal opponents.

Originally an ancient game of Scotland, G. has spread during the last century to all parts of the world. The Royal and Ancient Club at St Andrews was founded in 1754. Major events are the British and US Open and Amateur championships; Masters Tournament; Ryder Cup, and biennial Internat. Walker Cup. Former champions incl. Henry Cotton (GB) and Bobby Jones (USA); modern players incl. Tony Jacklin (GB), Gary Player (S Africa), and J. W. Nicklaus and L. Trevino (both USA).

GŌL'ĪATH. The giant champion of the Philistines, who, according to I Sam., xvii, was slain with a stone from a sling by David in single combat before the opposing armies of Israelites and Philistines.

GOLLANCZ, Sir Victor (1893-1967). British left-wing writer and publisher. Founder in 1936 of the influential Left Book Club.

GŌNADOTRŌ'PHIN. *See* FERTILITY DRUGS.

GO'NCHAROV, Ivan Alexandrovitch (1812-91). Russian novelist. B. at Simbirsk, he became a civil servant. His first novel, *A Common Story* (1847), was followed in 1858 by his humorous masterpiece, *Oblomov*, which summarized the indolent and impotent determinism of Russian landed gentry.

GONCOURT (goṅkoor'), **de**, the brothers **Edmond** (1822-96) and **Jules** (1830-70). French writers. They collaborated in producing a compendium, *L'Art du XVIIIe Siècle* (1859-75), and various historical studies which like their *Journal* (1887-96), obtained their effect by cumulative detail. Their joint novels include *Renée Mauperin, Germinie Lacerteux*, and *Madame Gervaisais* (1869). Edmond continued to write after his brother's death, e.g. *Chérie* (1884).

Edmond de G. founded the *Académie Goncourt*, opened in 1903, which awards an annual prize to the author of the best novel of the year.

GO'NDAR. Town in Ethiopia *c.* 2,300 m (7,500 ft) a.s.l. and 40km (25m) N of Lake Tana. Pop. (1974) 43,000.

GONDWA'NALAND. The Mesozoic southern continent which later split apart to form South America, Africa, Australia and Antarctica. *See* WEGENER.

GONORRHOEA (gonorē'a). Infection by the gonococcus, the commonest form of venereal disease. It is usually transmitted by sexual intercourse, but sometimes, especially in children, by contact with an infected person. A copious opaque discharge from the infected part appears in a few days and infection of the eyes must be guarded against. G. became increasingly resistant to penicillin and streptomycin, but in 1963 a new antibiotic actinospectacin effected cures by a single injection.

GOOD FRIDAY (probably a corruption of God's Friday). In the Christian Church, the Friday before Easter, which is kept in memory of the Crucifixion.

GOODMAN, Benny (1909-). American clarinetist, the 'king of swing'. B. in Chicago, he has had his own band since 1934, and has made celebrated recordings, e.g. 'Blue Skies' and 'King Porter Stomp'. Bartók's *Rhapsody* for clarinet and violin was written for him.

GOODWIN SANDS. Group of shoals about 10km (6m) off the E coast of Kent, England, 13-16km (8-10m) from N-S. The sands are exposed at low tide, but despite lightships and buoys, ships frequently go aground. According to legend, the sands represent the submerged island of Lomea, which in the 11th cent. belong to earl Godwin.

GOODWOOD. Racecourse, NE of Chichester, W Sussex, England. There was a motor-racing track 1948-66.

GOODYEAR, Charles (1800-60). American inventor, who developed vulcanized rubber in 1839.

GOONHI'LLY. Post Office satellite tracking station in Cornwall, England. It is equipped with a communications satellite transmitter-receiver in permanent contact with most parts of the world.

GOOSE. Name given to birds forming the genus *Anser*. Both sexes are similar in appearance; they have short, webbed feet, placed nearer the front of the body than in other members of the order Anatidae, and the beak is slightly hooked. They feed entirely on grass and plants, 'grey' geese being very destructive to young crops. The commonest variety is the grey-lag G. (*Anser anser*) which is the ancestor of the tame goose. This is the only variety which nests in Gt Britain. The genus also includes the bean G. (*A. fabalis*), the pink-footed G. (*A. brachyrhynchus*), and the white-fronted G. (*A. albifrons*), all of which breed in the Old World, and visit Britain in winter. The G. builds a nest of grass and twigs on the ground, and from 5 to 9 eggs are laid, white or cream-coloured.

GOOSEBERRY. Edible fruit of (*Ribes grossularia*), a low-growing bush allied to the currant bushes. The bush is straggling in its growth, bearing straight sharp spines singly or in groups, and rounded, lobed leaves. The flowers are green, and hang on short stalks. The fruits are generally globular, green, and hairy, but there are reddish and whitish varieties.

GOPHER (gō'fer). Burrowing rodents (family Geomyidae) of N and Central America, remarkable for their cheek pouches, and harmful to crops.

GORBACHEV, Mikhail Sergeyevich (1931–) Soviet Politician. A former machine operator, he became the Soviet Leader (Gen. Sec. of Soviet Communist Party) in Mar. 1985.

GO'RDIAN KNOT. In Gk mythology, the knot tied by King Gordius of Phrygia, which could only be unravelled by the future conqueror of Asia. Alexander cut it with his sword in 334 BC.

GORDIMER, Nadine (1923–). S African writer. Her first novel appeared in 1953, *The Lying Days*, and has been followed by a number of others incl. *The Conservationist* (1974), and vols. of short stories (*A Soldier's Embrace*, 1980). She gives a delicately observant picture of S African life.

GORDON, Adam Lindsay (1833-70). Australian poet. B. in the Azores, he was sent to Australia in 1853, and lived a varied life as mounted policeman, sheep farmer, politician, etc. *Sea Spray and Smoke Drift*, a collection of some of his best poems, was pub. in 1867, followed in 1870 by *Bush Ballads and Galloping Rhymes*. He committed suicide.

GORDON, Charles George (1833-85). British general. B. at Woolwich, he joined the Royal Engineers in 1852, and served in the Crimean War, and in the Chinese War of 1860. In the latter he suppressed the Taiping rebellion and became known as 'Chinese G.'. In 1874 he went to Egypt, and 1877-9 was governor of the Sudan. He spent the next few years in India, China, Ireland, Mauritius, the Cape, and Palestine. He was sent back to the Sudan in 1884 to rescue English garrisons which were at the mercy of native rebels under the Mahdi, but was himself besieged by the Mahdi's army in Khartoum. A relief expedition under Wolseley arrived on 28 Jan. 1885, to find that Khartoum, after a siege of 10 months, had been captured, and G. killed, 2 days before.

GORDON, Lord George (1751-93). Protestant fanatic, who organized the Protestant protest against the Catholic Relief Act of 1778, which led to the disgraceful 'Gordon Riots'. G. was tried for treason, but acquitted. G. and the 'No Popery' riots figure in Dickens' *Barnaby Rudge*.

GORDON, Richard O. (1921–). British author. After qualifying and practising as a doctor, he pub. a series of light-hearted novels on the career of a young medical aspirant beginning with *Doctor in the House* (1952).

GORDONSTOUN. Public school nr Elgin, Grampian, Scotland, founded by Kurt Hahn (q.v.) in 1935, which emphasizes a spartan outdoor life and achievement of objectives, e.g. in mountain-climbing and sailing. Prince Philip and Prince Charles were both ed. there. The estate was formerly the seat of the Gordon Cumming family, Sir William Gordon Cumming, 4th bt, being the centre of the baccarat scandal of 1890 when he was accused of cheating in a game which included the Prince of Wales (Edward VII), who gave evidence in the subsequent court case.

GORGAS, William Crawford (1854-1920). American military doctor, who cleared the Panama Canal Zone of malaria and yellow fever, and discovered that the latter is transmitted by the mosquito.

GO'RGON. In Greek mythology, Stheno, Euryale, and Medusa, the 3 daus. of Phorcys and Ceto, who were possessed of wings, claws, enormous teeth, and snakes in place of hair. So terrible was the face of Medusa (the only one who was mortal) that the sight of it, even after her death at the hands of Perseus, turned the gazer to stone.

GORGONZŌ'LA. Town in Lombardy, Italy 20km (12m) NE of Milan, famous for its cheeses. Pop. (1971) 9,100.

GORI'. Town in Georgia, USSR. It has a large Stalin museum, and the only outdoor statue monument left standing after his denunciation by Khrushchev in 1956. The little wooden house where Stalin, son of a cobbler, was born stands nearby. Pop. (1977) 50,000.

GORILLA. Largest of the anthropoid apes (*Gorilla gorilla*) found in the dense forests of W Africa. The mountain species (*G. berengei*) is slightly larger and heavier.

The G. stands *c.* 2m (5.5ft), the female being slightly smaller, and the body is covered with blackish hair, silvered on the back in the male in a 'saddlemark'. Almost entirely vegetarian, they travel in search of food in family parties of a senior male, several females, some younger males, and a number of little ones. They construct stoutly built nests in trees for overnight use. The 'breast-beating' movement once thought to indicate rage, only indicates nervous excitement and they will not attack except in self-defence. They are dwindling in numbers, being shot for food by some tribespeople, or by poachers seeking the young ones for zoos, but protective measures are having some effect.

GORIZIA (gōrēt'sē-ah). Town in Friuli-Venezia-Giulia region, N Italy, on the Isonzo, SE of Udine. During the F.W.W. a number of battles were fought round it. Pop. (1971) 42,100.

GORKY, Arshile (1904-48). American artist. B. in Armenia, he went to the USA in 1920 and was an initiator of Abstract Impressionism, his work having a broodingly introspective quality.

GORKY, Maxim. Pseudonym of the Russian writer Alexei Peshkov (1868-1936). B. at Nijni-Novgorod, now renamed G. in his honour, he is unique in playing an equally important part in his country before and after the Revolution, which he strongly supported, enduring exile 1906-13 for his revolutionary principles. Intimate contact with men and life during his restless wanderings in search of work in SE Russia gave G. a strong sense of reality, coupled with a romantic dream of a different world and a better life. This duality pervades such a play as *Na dne* (1902: *The Lower Depths*). Despite the terrible pressure of events, G. never lost his faith in the human race, e.g. *Chelovek* (1903: *Man*), a prose poem; *Mat* (1907: *Mother*), a novel celebrating the potential power of the industrial proletariat; the recollections *Detstvo* (1913: *My Childhood*), and *Yegor Bulychov* (1932), a play forming part of an unfinished trilogy. He suffered from tuberculosis and stayed in S Italy in 1922-8, but then returned to a hero's welcome.

GORILLA. The most famous gorilla in the world, Guy of London's Zoo, as gentle as he was strong. *Photo: Harry Miller/Camera Press.*

GORKY. Town in the RSFSR, cap. of G. region, situated at the junction of the Oka and Volga. An ancient city with a kremlin or castle, it was, as Nijni-Novgorod, long famous for its great annual fair. It remains a great trade centre, making also cars, locomotives, aircraft, etc. It has a univ. Its name was changed in 1932 in honour of Maxim Gorky who was b. there. Pop. (1977) 1,319,000.

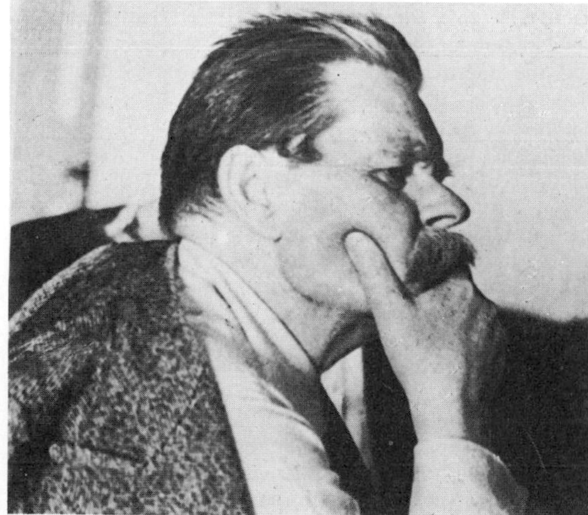

GORKY. One of the few ardently Communist writers to be admired both in the Soviet Union and the West. *Photo: Novosti Press Agency.*

GÖRLITZ. Manufacturing town in E Germany, 89km (55m) E of Dresden. Pop. (1978) 87,500.

GORLOVKA. Industrial town on the Donbas coalfield, in the Ukrainian SSR. Pop. (1977) 342,000.

GORSE, furze, or **whin.** Genus of plants (*Ulex*) of the Leguminosae family, consisting of thorny shrubs with spine-shaped leaves densely clustered along the stems, and bright yellow flowers. The gorse bush (*U. europaeus*) is an evergreen, and grows on heaths and sandy areas throughout western Europe, and abundantly in Britain.

GORT, John Vereker, 1st visct G. (1886-1946). British soldier. He succeeded his father as 6th visct G. in the peerage of Ireland in 1902, won the VC in the F.W.W., and as CIGS from 1937 commanded the BEF 1939-40, conducting a fighting retreat to the Channel and Dunkirk.

GORTON, Sir John Grey (1911-). Australian Liberal statesman. He was Min. for Education and Science 1966-8, and then PM on the death of Holt (q.v.) until he resigned in 1971.

GOSCHEN (gō'shen), **George Joachim,** 1st visct (1831-1907). British Liberal politician. He held several cabinet posts under Gladstone 1868-74, but broke with him in 1886 over Irish Home Rule. In Salisbury's Unionist govt of 1886-92 he was Chancellor of the Exchequer after Lord Randolph Churchill's resignation, and 1895-1900 was 1st Lord of the Admiralty.

GOSHAWK. Bird (*Accipiter gentilis*) used in falconry; similar in appearance to the peregrine falcon, but with short wings and short legs.

GOSPEL. Word used in the NT generally to signify the message of salvation; later it was applied to the 4 written Gs. of Matthew, Mark, Luke, and John. Although the first 3 give approximately the same account or synopsis (thus giving rise to the name Synoptic Gs.), their differences from John have raised many problems, discussed in a vast literature.

The so-called 5th G., or G. of St Thomas, is a 2nd cent. collection of 114 sayings of Jesus found in a Coptic translation in one of 13 papyrus codices, discovered in Upper Egypt in 1945, which were apparently the library of a Gnostic community. Strongly influenced by Gnostic teaching, it is nevertheless interesting for comparison with the canonical Gs.: there is no reason to believe that it was written by St Thomas, the name being used merely to give authority.

GOSPORT. *See* PORTSMOUTH.

GOSSE (gos), **Sir Edmund William** (1849-1928). English author. Son of a marine biologist, who was a member of the Plymouth Brethren, G.'s childhood was shadowed by the narrow tenets of the sect in Victorian times, and in his one great original book *Father and Son* (published anonymously in 1907) he describes the conflict between the generations, even where affection exists. G. worked as a librarian, first at the British Museum, and from 1904-19 in the House of Lords, and was knighted in 1925. He was influential as a critic and an authority on French and Scandinavian literature.

GÖTEBORG. Swedish port at the mouth of the Göta and at the W end of the Göta canal. Pop. (1978) 440,000.

GOTHA (gō'tah). Town in E Germany, at the N edge of the Thuringian forest, 24km (15m) SW of Erfurt. It was a former cap. of the duchy of Saxe-Coburg-Gotha, and has a castle and 2 observatories; it makes pottery, soap, aircraft, etc. The *Almanach de G.*, an annual survey of the royalty, aristocracy and diplomatic ranks of Europe, was pub. here

1763-1944. A successor, *Le Petit Gotha,* has been pub. in Paris from 1968. Pop. (1978) 58,000.

GOTHENBURG. German form of GÖTEBORG.

GOTHIC ARCHITECTURE. The various styles of architecture which are grouped under the heading of Gothic have certain features in common, viz. the vertical lines - tall pillars, spires, etc. - which take the place of the horizontal lines of previous styles, the pointed arch, rib vaulting, and the flying buttress. G.A. originated in Normandy and Burgundy in the 12th cent., and prevailed in W Europe until the 16th cent. when classic architecture was revived. The term Gothic was at first used disparagingly of medieval art by Renaissance architects.

In France, G.A. may be divided into 4 periods, viz. (a) early Gothic, 1130-90, when ogival vaults were introduced; (b) lancet Gothic, 1190-1240, when pointed arches were tall and narrow; (c) radiating Gothic, 1240-1350, which takes its name from the series of chapels which radiate from the cathedral apse; and (d) late Gothic or the Flamboyant style, 1350-1520. Examples of the different periods are (a) Notre Dame, Paris (begun 1160); (b) Chartres (begun 1194); Bourges (begun 1209); Rheims (begun 1211); and Amiens (begun 1221); (c) Sainte Chapelle, Paris (1226-30); and (d) St Gervais, Paris.

In Italy Gothic had a classical basis. A notable example of Italian Gothic is Milan cathedral.

The Gothic style in Germany appeared, until the end of the 13th cent., to have been imported from France, e.g. Cologne Cathedral, the largest in N Europe, was built after the model of Amiens (q.v.).

In England the Gothic style is divided into Early English (1200-75), Decorated (1300-75), and Perpendicular (1400-1575), qq.v. A *G. Revival,* imitating the medieval style, took place in the late 18th and the 19th cent., e.g. the House of Commons.

GOTHIC NOVEL. Genre establ. by Horace Walpole with *The Castle of Otranto* (1765), and characterized by mystery, violence and horror: *see also* MRS RADCLIFFE. It was revived in the 1970s, sometimes with literary quality, e.g. Gordon Honeycombe's *Dragon under the Hill.*

GOTHS. An E Germanic people who settled on the shores of the Black Sea, about the 2nd cent. AD. One branch, the Ostrogoths, was conquered by the Huns *c.* 370, while another, the Visigoths, migrated to Thrace. The latter raided Greece and Italy under Alaric (395-410), sacked Rome, and set up a kingdom in S France. Expelled thence by the Franks, they estab. a Spanish kingdom which lasted until the Moorish conquest of 711. The Ostrogoths regained their independence in 454, and under Theodoric conquered Italy in 488-93; they disappeared as a nation after Justinian reconquered Italy in 535-55.

GO'TLAND. Swedish island in the Baltic Sea. Its cap. is Visby. Area 3,160 sq.km (1,220 sq.m).

GOTTFRIED VON STRASSBURG (fl. *c.* 1210). German poet, author of *Tristan und Isolde.* Hardly anything is known about his life, but he may have been a member of one of the patrician families of Strasbourg. His unfinished *Tristan* epic, which shows a formal refinement and splendour of diction unprecedented in Ger. epic poetry, is a free version of that of the Anglo-Norman Thomas (*c.* 1170).

GÖTTINGEN. W German univ. town in Lower Saxony on the Leine, 42km (26m) NE of Kassel. The univ. was founded in 1734 by George II of England, elector of Hanover, and became a famous seat of learning. The main

GOTHIC ARCHITECTURE. Winchester cathedral (1475) is a fine example of Perpendicualar Gothic architecture. The lines of vertical tracery give an effect of lacework in stone. *Photo: A.W.Kerr.*

industry is printing and publishing; scientific instruments and chemicals are made. Pop. (1978) 121,000.

GOUDA (gow'da). Dutch town in S Holland prov., 19km (12m) NE of Rotterdam; it is famous for its round flat cheeses. Pop. (1978) 58,200.

GOUGH (gof), **Sir Hubert** (1870-1963). British general. As commander of the 5th Army (1916-18), he was blamed for the German break-through on the Somme and superseded, but it was subsequently admitted that the number of his troops was far from sufficient to hold such a length of front: he was created GCB in 1937.

GOULBURN. Australian town, in NSW, 220km (137m) SW of Sydney. A railway junction, it is an agricultural centre and manufactures incl. bricks and tiles, pottery and footwear. Pop. (1971) 21,750.

GOULD, Jay (1836-92). American financier. B. in New York, he set up as a stockbroker in 1859, and in 1868 was elected president of the Erie rly. In 1872 he was compelled to resign following the discovery that he had issued large amounts of fraudulent stock. Some years earlier his speculations in gold had caused a financial panic on 'Black Friday', 24 Sept. 1869. Subsequently he developed a large railway system in the SW states.

GOUNOD (goonoh'), **Charles François** (1818-93). French composer. B. in Paris, he studied at the Conservatoire and in Rome. His first opera, *Sapho,* was produced in Paris in 1851, and was followed by an operatic version of Molière's *Le Médecin malgré lui, Faust* (1859), *Philémon et Baucis* (1860), and *Roméo et Juliette* (1867).

He also wrote sacred songs, masses, and an oratorio, *The Redemption.*

GOURD (gōrd). Name applied to various members of the plant family Cucurbitaceae, including the melon, pumpkin, etc. In a narrower sense, the name applies only to the genus *Lagenaria*, of which the bottle G. (*L. vulgaris*) is best known.

GOUT. Disease due to excess of uric acid in the blood, and almost entirely confined to men. The tendency to it may be inherited. It usually appears between 30 and 50. Attacks are brought on especially by sweet wines, beer, and meat. A typical attack comes suddenly in the night with inflammation of a big toe joint and fever. The disease may become chronic and shorten life by affecting the kidneys. Commonly there is a generalized inflammation of the joints. Treatment aims at removing, more recently at preventing, the deposits of urate of soda in the system by diet and drugs.

GOW, Niel (1727-1807). Scottish violinist. B. near Dunkeld, he was famed as a player and composer of reels; nearly 100 tunes are attributed to him. His 4 sons were also musicians, and 1784-1822 the family pub. the Gow collection of Scottish airs.

GOWER, John (*c.* 1330-1408). British poet. B. in Kent, he was a friend of Chaucer and wrote in English a long poem, *Confessio Amantis*, and other poems in French and Latin. He was buried in Southwark cathedral.

GOWER PENINSULA. Peninsula in W Glamorgan, Wales, W of Swansea. Its scenic beauty attracts tourists.

GOWO'N, Yakubu (1934-). Nigerian statesman. Ed. at Sandhurst, he became Chief of Staff and in the military coup of 1966 became Head of State. After the Biafran civil war 1967-70, he re-united the country with his policy of 'no victor, no vanquished'. In 1975 he was overthrown while on a visit to Kampala.

GOYA Y LUCIENTES (gō'yah ē loothē-en'tes), **Francisco José de** (1746-1828). Spanish painter and etcher. B. in Aragon, of humble parentage, he lived a wild and dissolute life in Madrid, and for a time joined a troupe of bull-fighters, thus obtaining a knowledge of the bull-ring that he employed in some of his finest etchings. After studying art in Italy he returned to Spain, was employed on a number of paintings for the royal tapestry manufactory, and in 1786 became court painter to Charles IV. He is famous for his portraits of 4 successive kings of Spain and of many other great personages, and for his etchings, 'The Disasters of War', depicting the horrors of the French invasion of Spain, 1808-14.

GPU. *See* M.V.D.

GRAAF, Regnier de (1641-73). Dutch physician at Delft, who wrote a treatise in 1663 on the pancreatic secretions, and in 1672 discovered the follicles of the female ovary that are named after him.

GRACCHUS, Tiberius (163-133 BC) and **Gaius** (153-121 BC). Roman agrarian reformers. Tiberius, when elected tribune in 133, attempted to end the process whereby the small farmers were being ruined by the competition of large estates cultivated by slave labour. He introduced an agrarian law for the resumption by the state of public lands in private hands and their redistribution in small lots, but was murdered by a mob of landowners. His brother Gaius, elected tribune in 123 and 122, revived the agrarian law, and introduced a sweeping programme of social and political reforms. Outlawed by the Senate, he committed suicide.

GRACE, William Gilbert (1848-1915). British cricketer and physician. B. at Downend, Glos, he began playing in first-class matches at 15, and helped to estab. cricket as the national game. In 1871 he scored 2,739 runs in the season, and by 1900, when his career as a first-class cricketer ended, he had scored over 54,000 runs. *See* CRICKET.

GRACES. Three goddesses of ancient Greece, who were the personifications of light, joy, and fertility, and the inspirers of the arts, the sciences, and all graceful activities. Their names were Aglaia, Euphrosyne, and Thalia.

GRAFTON, Augustus Henry, 3rd duke of (1735-1811). British statesman. Grandson of the first duke, who was the son of Charles II and Barbara Villiers, duchess of Cleveland, he became 1st Lord of the Treasury in 1766 and acting Prime Minister 1767-70.

GRAFTON. Town of NSW, Australia, on the r. Clarence, 72km (45m) from its mouth; it is an important dairying and sugar centre, with bacon factories, tanneries, etc. Pop. (1977) 17,300.

GRAHAM, Billy (1918-). American evangelist. Of Scottish-Irish parents, he was brought up in N Carolina, and at 17 was converted at a revival. He has crusaded, holding emotional mass meetings, throughout the US and in Britain.

GRAHAM, Martha (1894-). American choreographer and dancer. B. in Pittsburgh, she became a Broadway cult in the 'twenties because of her break with tradition and her repertoire incl. *Appalachian Spring* (score by Aaron Copland) and *Clytemnestra* (1958), one of a number of classical theme dances.

GRAHAME (grā'-am), **Kenneth** (1859-1932). British author. B. at Edinburgh, son of an advocate, he worked at the Bank of England 1878-1908. The early vols. of sketches of childhood, *The Golden Age* (1895) and *Dream Days* (1898), were followed by his masterpiece *The Wind in the Willows* (1908), an animal fantasy originally created for his little son. It has been successfully staged in A. A. Milne's dramatization: *Toad of Toad Hall.*

GRAHAM LAND. Peninsula of the Antarctic continent, formerly a dependency of the Falkland Islands and from 1962 part of the British Antarctic Territory (q.v.). Discovered by John Biscoe in 1832, it was thought to be an archipelago until 1934; it is mountainous and covered with ice and snow.

GRAHAMSTOWN. Town in Cape Prov., S Africa, 137km (85m) WSW of East London. It has 2 bishops, Anglican and Roman Catholic, and is the seat of Rhodes University (1951; founded 1904 as Rhodes Univ. College). Pop. (1970) 40,000.

GRAIL, Holy. The dish or cup used by Christ at the Last Supper, which, together with the spear with which He was wounded at the Crucifixion, appears as an object of quest by King Arthur's knights in certain stories incorporated in the Arthurian legend. According to one story, the Blood of Christ was collected in it by Joseph of Arimathea at the Crucifixion, and he brought it to Britain.

GRAINGER, Percy Aldridge (1882-1961). Australo-American composer. B. in Melbourne, he was a sensitive and technically brilliant concert pianist. His interest in folk music led to his making many popular settings, e.g. *Molly on the Shore* and *Shepherd's Hey.* His brief 'Country gardens' is perennially popular.

GRAIL. The Antioch chalice is in silver and parcel gilt and dates to c. AD400, but the plain inner wooden cup is much older and is believed by some to be the true Holy Grail used at the Last Supper. *Photo: Courtesy of the Metropolitan Museum of Art, New York.*

GRAM/GRAMME. In the metric system the unit of mass, i.e. the thousandth part of the standard kilogram mass.

GRAMPIAN. Region of Scotland, created in 1975 to incl. the cos. of Aberdeenshire and Kincardine; most of Banff and Moray, excl. the area incl. in the Highland region. The admin. HQ is Aberdeen. Area 8,702 sq.km (3,360 sq.m); pop. (1979) 463,130.

The **G. Mtns,** which separate the Highlands from the Lowlands of Scotland, stretch across N Strathclyde, the S Highland region (which incl. Ben Nevis), northern Tayside, and the S border of Grampian region itself.

GRAMPIANS. In Victoria, Australia, the Western end of Australia's eastern highlands: Mt William reaches 1,167 m (3,829 ft).

GRAMPUS. *See* KILLER-WHALE.

GRAMSCI (grahm'shi), **Antonio** (1891-1937). Sard Marxist theorist. Brought up in rural Sardinia, he studied at Turin, and graduated from socialism to Marxism. He preached the need for a stable alliance between the workers of N Italy and the masses of the S, and a practical approach to local problems. He was a founder of the Italian Communist party.

GRANADA (granah'da). City in Spain, cap. of the prov. of G. in Andalusia, on the r. Genil *c.* 670m (2,200 ft) a.s.l. in the Sierra Nevada. Founded by the Moors in the 8th cent., it became the cap. of an independent kingdom in 1236 which, until its surrender to the Spaniards in 1492, was the last Moorish bulwark in Spain. Many Moorish buildings remain, among them the Alhambra (q.v.). The cathedral, built 1529-1703, contains the tomb of Ferdinand and Isabella, first sovereigns of a united Spain. There is also a univ. (1531). Pop. (1970) 190,450.

GRANADA. City in Nicaragua, linked by rail with Managua. On the NW side of Lake Nicaragua, it has shipyards, and manufactures incl. sugar, soap, clothing and furniture. Pop. (1977) 40,200.

GRANA'DOS, Enrique (1867-1916). Spanish composer. A brilliant pianist, he was inspired by the work of Goya to write his important piano work *Goyescas* (1911), converted to an opera in 1916. He d. when the liner in which he travelled back from its performance in NY was torpedoed by a German submarine.

GRANBY, John Manners, marquess of (1721-70). British soldier. His head appears on many inn-signs in England as a result of his popularity as a commander of the British forces fighting on the Continent in the Seven Years War.

GRAN CHACO. *See* CHACO.

GRAND BANKS. In the N Atlantic the continental shelf off SE Newfoundland, where the comparatively shallow waters form one of the world's great fishing grounds, espec. cod.

GRAND CANAL. *See* CANAL, and VENICE.

GRAND CANYON. Great, many-coloured gorge through which flows the Colorado r., in Arizona, USA. It is 6-29km (4-18m) in width, reaches depths of more than 1.5km (1m), and is 350km (217m) long; made a national park 1919.

GRAND CANYON. The entrance to Labyrinth Canyon, part of the great complex along the Colorado River, which is now filled by Lake Powell. *Photo: Tad Nichols.*

GRAND DESIGN. Plan attributed by Sully to Henry IV of France, and rendered abortive by his assassination, for a great Protestant Union against the Holy Roman Empire; the term is also applied to Pres. de Gaulle's vision of France's place in a united Europe.

GRAND FALLS. Town of Newfoundland, Canada, site of large paper and pulp mills. Pop. (1976) 8,800.

GRAND GUIGNOL (grañ gēnyol'). Type of horror play produced at the G.G. theatre in Montmartre, Paris, itself named from the character Guignol, in the traditional bloodthirsty plots of the French marionette theatre in the late 18th cent.

GRAND NATIONAL. A steeplechase (1839) run at Aintree during the Liverpool Spring meeting in March or April over 7km 220m (4m 856yd) with 30 formidable jumps and casualties are not infrequent.

GRAND RAPIDS. City in Michigan, USA, on the Grand r., noted for furniture; makes also motor bodies, plumbing fixtures, electrical goods, paints, etc. Pop. (1970) 197,650.

GRANITE (gra'nit). An acidic igneous rock, of plutonic origin, occurring in intrusions in many parts of the British Isles. The rock is coarse-grained, the characteristic minerals being quartz, feldspars, particularly orthoclase, and mica. It often comprises the core of a range of mountains, the surrounding rocks having been metamorphosed by the heat of the intrusion. Granitic areas produce a very characteristic scenery type, e.g. in the Grampians and Scottish Highlands, the Lake District, Dartmoor, Bodmin Moor in Cornwall, the Mourne mountains, etc. *See* FELDSPAR.

GRANT, Cary. Stage-name of American actor Archibald Leach (1904–86). B. in Bristol, England, he went to the US in 1921, becoming a citizen in 1942. He estab. himself as the most skilled of light-comedy actors, e.g. *Notorious* (1946 with Bergman), *Arsenic and Old Lace* (1944).

GRANT, Duncan (1885–1978). Scottish painter. A member of the 'Bloomsbury' group which incl. Roger Fry and Virginia Woolf, he showed in later works, e.g. 'Snow Scene' (1921), the influence of the Post-impressionists, esp. Cézanne.

GRANT, Ulysses Simpson (1822–85). American general and 18th President of the USA. The son of an Ohio farmer, he had an unsuccessful career in the army 1839–54 and in business, and on the outbreak of the Civil War received a commission on the Mississippi front. He took command there in 1862, and by his capture of Vicksburg in 1863 brought the whole Mississippi under Northern control. Appointed commander-in-chief in 1864, he slowly wore down Lee's resistance, and in 1865 received his surrender at Appomattox. He was elected Pres. in 1868 and 1872, and carried through a liberal reconstruction policy in the S, although he failed in his attempts to suppress political corruption.

GRANTHAM (grant'am). Market town on the r. Witham, in SE Lincs, England. Dating from Saxon times, it has always been the market centre for the surrounding agricultural area. Margaret Thatcher was born here. Pop. (1972) 28,100.

GRANVILLE-BARKER, Harley (1877–1946). British theatre director and dramatist. During 1904–18 he produced, with J. E. Vedrenne, plays of Shaw, and introduced works of Galsworthy, Housman, and Masefield with simple provocative productions and new scenic and lighting principles. His own plays incl. *The Voysey Inheritance* (1905), *The Madras House* (1907) and *Waste* (1909).

GRAPE. *See* VINE.

GRAPEFRUIT. Common name for the large yellow fruit of *Citrus paradisi,* grown chiefly in Florida, California, S Africa, and the W Indies.

GRA'PHĪTE, plumbago or **black lead.** Crystalline form of carbon. Iron-grey to black, with a metallic lustre, it splits up easily into flakes, each flake breaking into smaller flakes - the property which is responsible for its wide use as a lubricant. G. occurs in veins in gneiss, crystalline limestone, and metamorphic rocks. When used as a moderator in nuclear reactors, G. has to be of particularly high purity.

GRASMERE (gras'mēr). English lake and village in the Lake District, Cumbria. Wordsworth lived at Dove Cottage (now a Wordsworth Museum) 1799–1808, De Quincey later making his home in the same house, and both S. T. Coleridge and Wordsworth are buried in the churchyard of St Oswald's.

GRASS (grahs), **Günter** (1927–). German sculptor and writer. B. in Danzig, he studied at the art academies of Düsseldorf and Berlin, worked as a writer and sculptor, first in Paris and later in Berlin, and in 1958 won the coveted 'Group 47' prize. The grotesque humour of his novel *Die Blechtrommel* (*The Tin Drum*: 1963) is again shown in many of his poems. G. has also written plays, incl. *Onkel, Onkel* (1958).

GRASS. Crop of specially balanced mixed grasses (q.v.) used for winter fodder as *hay,* when it is cut and dried naturally in the open; as *silage* packed in a silo (airtight cylindrical structure) without being dried, and is then fermented by anaerobic lactic acid bacteria, molasses sometimes being added; or, increasingly, *artificially dried.*

GRASSE (grahs). Town in Alpes-Maritimes dept, S France, 13km (8m) NW of Cannes. Around the town, orange blossom and roses are grown for the production of perfumes. Pop. (1976) 31,000.

GRASSES. Plants belonging to the Gramineae family; the most important and one of the largest of the families of monocotyledonous plants. They are distributed throughout the world, and include all the cereals, the grasses of meadows and pastures, and other plants of economic importance, including sugar cane, the bamboo, the reed, etc. The leaves of G. are long and narrow, with parallel veins, the lower part enclosing the stem in a sheath. The stem is mainly hollow, and the flowers are borne in one or more spikelets, terminating the stem. The fruit is single seeded, and is known as caryopsis. It contains a small embryo set at the base of a hard, albuminous endosperm. When the flower is ready for pollination, the large stamens break through to the outside of the spike and shed their pollen outside. *See* GRASS.

GRASSHOPPERS. Insects of the order Orthoptera, usually with strongly developed hind legs which enable them to leap. The short-horned Gs. (Acridiidae) incl. the locust (q.v.), and all members of the family feed voraciously on vegetation. The femur of each hind leg in the male usually has a row of protruding joints which produce the characteristic chirping when rubbed against the hard wing veins. Eggs are laid in a small hole in the ground, and the unwinged larvae become adult after about 6 moults. There are several sober-coloured, small and harmless species in Britain. The long-horned Gs. (Tettigoniidae) have a similar life-history, but differ from the Acridiidae in having long antennae, etc., and in producing their chirping by the friction of the wing covers over one another. The large green G. (*Phasgonura viridissima*), 38mm (1½in) long, is a British species of this family, which also comprises the N American katydids (Phanopterinae), notable stridulators.

GRASS SNAKE. Harmless reptile (*Natrix natrix*), commonly found in wet districts of Britain. Attaining 1-2m (3-6ft), it is olive-brown or grey with black spots above and mottled white below, with a yellow and black collar. It feeds on frogs or fish, one meal often sufficing 1-2 months, and the soft oval eggs are laid in July/August.

GRASS-TREE. Genus (*Xanthorrhoea*) of resinous Australian plants in the family Xanthorrhoeaceae.

GRASS-TREE. In the half-light the plants look like a group of spear-carrying warriors. *Photo: Camera Press.*

GRATTAN, Henry (1746-1820). Irish statesman. B. in Dublin, he entered the Irish parliament in 1775. As leader of the opposition he secured the abolition of all claims by the British parliament to legislate for Ireland in 1782. Although he strongly opposed the Act of Union, he sat in the British parliament from 1805.

's GRAVENHAGE. Formal Dutch name of THE HAGUE.

GRAVES, Robert Ranke (1895–1985). English poet and author. B. in London, he was the son of the Irish writer Alfred Perceval G. (1846-1931) whose songs and poetry contributed largely to the Celtic revival. He was severely wounded on the Somme in the F.W.W. and his frank autobiography *Goodbye to All That* (1929) is one of the outstanding war books. In 1927 he joined Laura Riding (q.v.) in directing the Seizin Press and collaborated with her in several books. His first book of verse was *Over the Brazier* (1916) and other vols. followed incl. *Collected Poems* (1959). Particularly striking are his novels of Imperial Rome, *I Claudius* and *Claudius the God* (1934) and *They Hanged My Saintly Billy* (1957), a defence of William Palmer, a forger and supposed poisoner of 14 people, hanged in 1856. He is an avid student of myth and has published notable volumes of literary criticism: he was prof. of poetry at Oxford 1961-6.

GRĀVESE'ND. Town on the Thames, Kent, England, opposite Tilbury, with which there is a ferry service. It is the Thames Pilot Station. Pop. (1973) 53,500.

GRAVES. Robert Graves at work in his study at Deya in Mallorca. *Photo: Popperfoto.*

GRAVITĀ'TION. Fundamental property of space: *see* NEWTON, RELATIVITY. **Gravitational waves,** according to Einstein's general theory of relativity, should be produced when massive bodies are violently disturbed. However, gravity is such a comparatively weak force that their existence was not even indirectly confirmed until 1979. Tests with a radio telescope then showed that the two stars of a binary pulsar were losing energy (in the form of gravity waves), and consequently drifting spirally towards each other.

GRAY, Thomas (1716-71). English poet. B. in London, he formed at Eton a close friendship with Horace Walpole, with whom in 1739 he started on a tour of France and Italy, vividly described in his letters. In 1741 he returned to London, where he lived for a year, making occasional visits to his mother and sister at Stoke Poges; to this period belong the 'Ode on a Distant Prospect of Eton College' and the 'Hymn to Adversity'. In 1748 his first poems appeared anonymously in Dodsley's *Miscellany,* and in 1750 he wrote the 'Elegy written in a Country Churchyard' at Stoke Poges. A vol. of *Poems* was pub. by Dodsley in 1752, and in 1757 Walpole issued G.'s Pindaric Odes, 'The Bard' and 'The Progress of Poesy' from his private press.

GRAYLING. Freshwater fish (*Thymallus thymallus*) of the family Thymallidae. It is found locally in England and has been introduced into Scotland. It exhibits a coloration shading from purple to pink, and may be distinguished by its long dorsal fin.

GRAZ (grahts). Capital of Styria prov., Austria, on the Mur at the foot of the Styrian Alps. It has a 15th cent. cathedral and a univ. founded 1573. Pop. (1971) 248,500.

GRAZIANI (grahtsē-ah'nē), **Rodolfo** (1882-1955). Italian general. With experience in colonial warfare in Libya, Cyrenaica, and Abyssinia, G. became G-in-C of Italian forces in N Africa in the S.W.W., but was soundly beaten by Wavell (1940), and subsequently superseded. Later, as Defence Min. in the new Mussolini govt he failed to reorganize a Republican Fascist army, was captured by the Allies (1945), tried by an Italian military court, and finally released in 1950.

GREAT AUSTRALIAN BIGHT. The broad bay in S Australia between Cape Pasley and the Eyre Peninsula. *See* ASTRON.

GREEK ARCHITECTURE. A reconstruction of the Acropolis of Athens. In the centre the Propylaea or great entranceway; to the left the statue of Athena Promachus (the Champion), with the Erechtheum behind it, and, on the far right, the Parthenon. *Photo: Mansell Collection.*

GREAT BARRIER REEF. A collection of coral reefs and islands stretching *c.* 2,000 km (1,250 m) at a distance of 15-45km (10-30m) from the E coast of Queensland, Australia, and forming an immense natural breakwater.

GREAT BARRIER REEF. A collection of variously formed corals and shells from the reef. *Photo: Australian Information Service.*

GREAT BRITAIN. Name used for England, Scotland, and Wales, and the adjacent islands, that came into official use in 1603, when the English and Scottish crowns were united in the person of James VI of Scotland, I of England. With Northern Ireland it forms the United Kingdom.

GREAT CIRCLE. A plane cutting through a sphere, and passing through the centre point of the sphere, cuts the surface along a G.C. Thus, on the Earth, all meridians of longitude are half G.Cs.; of the parallels of latitude, only the Equator is a G.C. The shortest route between 2 points on the Earth's surface is along a G.C.

GREAT DANE. Large, usually fawn, hunting dog, of which fine specimens were imported from Britain by the Romans: there is no ascertainable connection with Denmark. The average height is *c.* 75cm (30in).

GREAT GRIMSBY. *See* GRIMSBY.

GREAT LAKE. Australia's largest freshwater lake, on the central plateau of Tasmania 1,025 m (3,380ft) a.s.l.; area 114 sq km (44 sq m). It is used for hydroelectric power and is a tourist attraction.

GREAT LAKES. Series of 5 freshwater lakes along the US-Canadian border, comprising Lakes Superior, Michigan, Huron, Erie, and Ontario. All are connected and inter-connected by rivers and canals. The lakes, lying in a plain, are invisible from a few miles' distance; they are drained by the St Lawrence.

In Africa the **Great Lakes** are the group in the east-central area, which incl. Lakes Malawi, Tanganyika and Victoria. In 1976 Burundi, Rwanda and Zaïre estab. an Economic Community of the G.L., with its H.Q. at Gisenye in Rwanda.

GREAT RIFT VALLEY. Geological feature whose eastern arm stretches from the Sea of Galilee on the Israel-Jordan frontier (historically Palestine), through the Red Sea to near Kilimanjaro in E Africa, and the western from Lake Albert to the mouth of the Zambezi. Total length about 8,000 km (5,000 m).

GREEK ART. A gold death mask found at Mycenae by Schliemann, who believed it to be that of Agamemnon, but it probably antedates Homer's hero by four centuries. To the right, Theseus slaying the Minotaur, one of the Attic red-figure *craters,* used for mixing wine and water before the cups were filled. *Photos: Peter Clayton.*

GREAT SANDY DESERT. Desert area in northern Western Australia. Area 415,000 sq.km (160,000 sq.m).

GREAT WALL OF CHINA. System of frontier defences in N China consolidated to a continuous wall *c.* 725km (450m) under the Ch'in dynasty in 214 BC. It consists of a brick-faced wall of earth and stone *c.* 8m (25ft) high and interspersed with square watch towers, eventually extended to *c.* 2,250 km (1,400 m) and intended to prevent incursions by Turkish and Mongol tribesmen. Under the Communist regime it has been carefully restored.

GREAT YARMOUTH. *See* YARMOUTH.

GREBES. Aquatic birds of the family Podicipedidae. The legs are placed far back on the body, causing the birds to stand upright like penguins. There are 5 European species, the best-known being the Little G. or Dabchick (*Podiceps fluviatilis*).

GRECO (gre'kō), **El.** Name given to the Spanish immigrant artist Doménico Theotocopuli (1541-1614) because of his birth in Crete. Some time before 1570 he travelled to Venice, where he studied under Titian, and while visiting Rome was influenced by the works of Michelangelo. In 1575 he first went to Spain, where he found the spiritual atmosphere suited his deeply religious temperament, and settled in Toledo. His works have a fanatic intensity, an almost lurid sense of colour, and exaggeratedly elongated forms, e.g. 'The Burial of Count Orgaz' and 'The Agony in the Garden'.

GREAT WALL OF CHINA. The square watch towers built at intervals along its winding length served as signal fire stations. *Photo: Courtesy of the Society for Anglo-Chinese Understanding.*

GREECE. Country of Europe in the southern Balkans. It is mainly composed of the complicated series of mountain ridges and enclosed valleys forming the Pindus mountains. The coastline is very broken, and is lined with scores of islands. Although winters are cold in the N, southern G. has a typical mediterranean climate. Only about a third of the land is cultivable - being extended by irrigation - but almost half the pop. live by agriculture. Tobacco, cotton, vegetables, olives and fruits, espec. currants, are grown for export, and other crops incl. cereals and sugar beet. Industries incl. wine and other food products, textiles, cigarettes, and chemicals. Minerals incl. bauxite, iron, nickel, magnesite, sulphur, marble and oil. The cap. is Athens, other important towns being Thessaloniki, Patras, Heraklion, Larisa, Volos, Kavala, Yannina, Canea, and Corinth. Under the 1952 constitution, as revised 1974, G. is a rep., the pres. being elected by a unicameral parliament.

Area 131,944 sq.km (50,944 sq.m); pop. (1977) 9,170,000, of whom the great majority belong to the Eastern (Greek) Orthodox Church. M.U.: drachma. *See* GREEK ART, HISTORY, etc.

GREEK ARCHITECTURE. The architecture of Greece stands foremost among the arts of the world as the most perfect. It is divided into 3 styles, viz. Doric, Ionic, and Corinthian. Of these the Doric is the oldest; it is said to have evolved from a former timber prototype. The finest example of a Doric temple is the Parthenon at Athens (447-438 BC). The origin of the Ionic is uncertain. The earliest building in which the Ionic capital appears is the temple of Diana at Ephesus (530 BC). The famous gateway to the Acropolis at Athens (known as the Propylaea) has internal columns of the Ionic order. The most perfect example is the Erechtheum at Athens. The Corinthian order belongs to a later period of Greek art. The most important example of the order is the temple of Jupiter (Zeus) Olympus at Athens (174 BC), completed under Roman influence in AD 129. The Mausoleum at Halicarnassus (353 BC) was one of the Seven Wonders of the World. In modern times Constantinos Doxiadis (1913-75), planner of Islamabad, had a worldwide reputation as an architect. *See* ORDERS.

GREEK ART. The sculpture, painting, vases, gems, etc., produced in Greek cities during the first millennium BC. Chronologically G.A. can be divided into Archaic (to 530 BC), Classical (530-320 BC), and Hellenistic (320 BC-AD 1).

By *Archaic* G.A. is meant the period beginning with the geometric style (900-700 BC) in which decoration consists of geometric elements - circles, triangles, etc. - followed by a transition to more naturalistic decoration showing the influence of Oriental, Egyptian, and Cyprian art, and ending with the red-figure style of vase painting (530 BC).

The *Classical* period may be subdivided into (a) Post-Persian, a name given to the art of the first half of the 5th cent. BC when archaic conventions were abandoned for three-dimensional composition; (b) Periclean art which is sunnier and freer than previous styles - e.g. heavy ornate drapery gives way to more decorative flowing folds; (c) the period of the Sophists when Periclean 'beauty with extravagance' is dissolved into the two extremes of emotional realism and luxuriant artificiality; and (d) the mid-4th cent., the period of the great sculptors Praxiteles, Skopas, and Lysippos, and the great painters Pausius, Nikias, and Apelles.

The *Hellenistic* period saw an increase in the variety of types of sculpture, painting, etc. Works produced during the period include the Tanagra terracottas, the Victory from Samothrace, the altar of Zeus (Pergamum), etc.

GREEK HISTORY: Ancient. The first Greek civilization, that known as Mycenaean (fl. *c.* 1600-1200 BC), owed much to the Minoan civilization of Crete, and may have been produced by the inter-marriage of Greek-speaking invaders with the original inhabitants. From the 14th cent. BC a new wave of invasions began. The Achaeans overran Greece and Crete, destroying the Minoan and Mycenaean civilizations, and penetrated Asia Minor; to this period belongs the siege of Troy (*c.* 1180). The latest of the invaders were the Dorians (*c.* 1100), who settled in the Peloponnese and founded Sparta. An obscure period followed (1100-800) during which the great city-states arose. The mountainous geography of Greece prevented the cities from attaining any national unity, and compelled them to take to the sea. During the years 750-550 the Greeks not only became great traders, but founded colonies around the coasts of the Mediterranean and the Black Sea, in Asia Minor, Sicily, S Italy, S France, Spain, and N Africa. The main centres of Greek culture in the 6th cent. were the wealthy Ionian ports of Asia Minor, where Greek philosophy, science, and lyric poetry originated.

Most of the Greek cities passed from monarchy to the rule of a landowning or merchant oligarchy, and thence to democracy; in many states a 'tyranny', or rule of a popular dictator, formed an intermediate stage between oligarchy and democracy. Thus Athens passed through the democratic reforms of Solon (594), the enlightened 'tyranny' of Peisistratus (560-527), and the establishment of democracy by Cleisthenes (*c.* 507). Sparta remained unique, a state in which a ruling race, organized on military lines, tyrannized over the original population.

After 545 the Ionian cities fell under the suzerainty of the Persian empire. Aid given them by Athens in an unsuccessful revolt in 499-494 provoked Darius of Persia to invade Greece in 490, only to be defeated by the Athenians at Marathon and forced to withdraw. Another invasion by Xerxes, after being delayed by the heroic defence of Thermopylae by 300 Spartans, was defeated on sea at Salamis in 480, and on land at Plataea in 479. The Ionian cities were liberated, and formed a naval alliance with Athens, the Confederacy of Delos. Pericles, the real ruler of Athens 461-429, attempted to convert this into an Athenian empire, and in addition to form a land empire in Greece. Mistrust of his ambitions led to the Peloponnesian War (431-404), which destroyed Athens' political power. In 5th cent. Athens, Greek tragedy, comedy, sculpture, and architecture reached their height, and Socrates and Plato founded moral philosophy.

After the Peloponnesian War, Sparta became the leading Greek power, until she in turn was overthrown by Thebes (378-371). The constant wars between the cities gave Philip II of Macedon (358-336) his opportunity gradually to establish his supremacy over Greece. His son Alexander overthrew the decadent Persian empire, conquered Syria and Egypt, and invaded the Punjab. After his death in 323 his empire was divided among his generals, but his conquest had nevertheless spread Greek culture all over the Near East.

During the 3rd cent. BC the cities attempted to maintain their independence against Macedon, Egypt, and Rome by forming federations, e.g. the Achaean and Aetolian Leagues. Roman intervention began in 212, and ended in the annexation of Greece in 146 BC. Under Roman rule Greece remained important mainly as a cultural centre, until Justinian closed the univ. of Athens in AD 529.

Medieval and Modern. Medieval Greek history begins with Constantine's grant of toleration to Christianity in 313, and the transference of the capital of the Roman Empire to Constantinople in 330. In 1453 the Turks captured Constantinople, and by 1460 they had conquered all Greece.

Except for the years 1686–1715, when the Morea was occupied by the Venetians, Greece remained Turkish until the outbreak of the War of Independence in 1821. British, French, and Russian intervention in 1827, which brought about the destruction of the Turkish fleet at Navarino, led to the establishment of Greek independence in 1829. Prince Otto of Bavaria was placed on thc throne in 1832; his despotic rule provoked a revolution in 1843, which set up parliamentary government, and another in 1862, when he was deposed and replaced by Prince George of Denmark. Relations with Turkey were embittered by the Greeks' desire to recover Macedonia, Crete, and other Turkish territories with Greek populations; a war in 1897 ended in disaster, but the Balkan Wars (q.v.) of 1912–13 won for Greece most of the disputed areas.

In a period of internal conflict from 1914, two monarchs were deposed, and there was a republic 1923–35, when a military coup restored George II (q.v.), who estab. in the following year a dictatorship under Metaxas.

An Italian invasion in 1940 was successfully resisted, but a German *blitzkrieg* in 1941 overwhelmed the Greeks, despite British assistance. On the German withdrawal in 1944, British troops occupied the country and assisted the royalists against the left-wing groups in the civil war which had broken out. A plebiscite in 1946 led to the return of George II, succeeded on his death in 1947 by his brother Paul. In April 1967 there was a bloodless military coup, King Constantine (q.v.) fleeing the country in Dec., after failing in a counter-coup. A rep. was estab. after a referendum in 1973, with Col. George Papadopoulos as pres., but the regime of 'the colonels' became increasingly oppressive, the composer Theodorakis (q.v.) being among those imprisoned. Following the Cyprus (q.v.) crisis in 1974, the military dictatorship collapsed. Lt.-Gen. Phaedon Ghizikis, who had succeeded Papadopoulos as pres. by another coup late in 1973, recalled Karamanlis (q.v.). Free elections were held and a referendum overwhelmingly rejected restoration of the monarchy. In 1980 Karamanlis became pres., and was succeeded as P.M. by George Rallis (also New Democratic Party), and then, in 1981, by the Socialist leader Andreas Papandreou. Greece joined the Common Market in 1981. The current Prime Minister, elected in June 1985, is Christos Sartzetakis, the electorate showing continuing support for socialist policies.

GREEK LANGUAGE. A member of the Indo-European family of languages. Of the ancient G. dialects, the Attic form of Ionic had won the supremacy over the other dialects (Aeolic, Arcadian, Doric) by the 4th cent. BC and a common tongue, based on Attic, spread to the colonies, to Mesopotamia, Syria, Egypt, etc. Modern G. uses the ancient G. alphabet, but the language has undergone decisive changes in phonetics and grammar. Under the Turkish occupation, G. was essentially the language of the common people and, although in free Greece purists aimed at a return to the classical standard, the 'popular' language of everyday speech dominated poetry and fiction, and in 1976 was adopted in schools.

GREEK LITERATURE. Ancient. The three greatest names of early G.L. are those of Homer (fl. *c.* 950 BC), author of the epic *Iliad* and *Odyssey; Hesiod (fl. 800* BC), whose *Works and Days* deals with agricultural life; and the lyric poet Pindar (b. 522 BC). Prose came to perfection with the historians Herodotus (b. 485 BC) and Thucydides (460–400 BC). The 5th cent. also saw the development of the Athenian drama through the works of the tragic dramatists Aeschylus (b. 524 BC), Sophocles (b. 495 BC), and Euripides (480–406 BC), and the comic genius of Aristophanes (*c.* 445–385 BC). After the fall of Athens came a period of prose with the historian Xenophon (434–353 BC), the idealist philosopher Plato (b. 427 BC), the orators Isocrates (436–338 BC) and Demosthenes (*c.* 383–322 BC), and the scientific teacher Aristotle (b. 384 BC).

After 323 BC Athens lost her political importance, but was still a university town with teachers such as Epicurus (341–270 BC), Zeno, and Theophrastus, and the comic dramatist Menander (342–291 BC). Meanwhile Alexandria was becoming the centre of Greek culture: the court of Philadelphus was graced by scientists such as Euclid, and the poets Callimachus, Apollonius, and Theocritus. During the 2nd cent. BC Rome became the new centre for G.L., and Polybius, the historian, spent most of his life there; in the 1st cent. BC Rome also sheltered the poets Archias, Antipater of Sidon, Philodemus the Epicurean, and Meleager of Gadara, who compiled the first *Greek Anthology.* In the 1st cent. AD Latin writers overshadow the Greek, but there are still the geographer Strabo (63 BC–AD 21), the critic Dionysius of Halicarnassus (fl. 10 BC), the Jewish writers Philo Judaeus and Josephus, the NT writers, and the biographer Plutarch (AD 45–125). A revival came in the 2nd cent. with Lucian (AD 125–95). To the 3rd cent. belong the historians Cassius Dio and Herodian, the Christian fathers Clement and Origen, and the neo-Platonists. For Medieval G.L., *see* BYZANTINE LITERATURE.

Modern. After the fall of Constantinople, the Byzantine tradition was perpetuated in the classical Gk writing of e.g. the 15th cent. chronicles of Cyprus, various historical works in the 16th and 17th cents., and educational and theological works in the 18th cent. The 17th and 18th cents. saw much controversy over the various merits of the Gk vernacular ('demotic'), the classical language ('katharevousa'), and the language of the Church, as a literary medium. Adamantios Korais (1748–1833), the first great modern, produced a compromise language, and was followed by the prose and drama writer, and poet, Alexandros Rhangavis ('Rangabe') (1810–92), and many others. The 10th cent. epic of *Digenis Akritas* is usually considered to mark the beginnings of modern Gk vernacular literature, and the demotic was kept alive in the flourishing Cretan lit. of the 16th and 17th cents., in numerous popular songs, and in the Klephtic ballads of the 18th cent. With independence in the 19th cent. the popular movement became prominent with the Ionian poet Dionysios Solomos (1798–1857), Andreas Kalvos (1796–1869), and others, and later with Iannis Psichari (1854–1929), short-story writer and dramatist, and the prose writer Alexandros Papadiamandis (1851–1911), who influenced many younger writers, e.g. Konstantinos Hatzopoulos (1868–1921), poet and essayist. After the 1920s, the novel began to emerge with Stratis Myrivilis (1892–1969) and Nikos Kazantzakis (1885–1957), author of *Zorba the Greek* (1946) and also a poet. *See also* the Nobel poets George SEFERIS and Odysseus ELYTIS.

GREEN, Thomas Hill (1836–82). British philosopher. B. in Yorks, he was prof. of Moral Philosophy at Oxford from 1878. He gave a new direction to 19th cent. philosophical thought by showing the limitations of

Spencer and Mill, and advocated the study of Kant and Hegel. His chief works are *Prolegomena to Ethics* (1883) and *Principles of Political Obligation* (1895).

GREENAWAY, Kate (1846-1901). British artist and illustrator. B. in London, she became famous for her drawings of children, which are full of charm and humour. In 1877 she first exhibited at the RA, and began her collaboration with the colour printer Edmund Evans, with whom she produced a number of books, incl. the popular *Mother Goose*.

GREENE, Graham (1904-). English author. B. at Berkhamsted, son of a headmaster, he was ed. at Oxon. He was then on the staff of *The Times* 1926-30, literary editor of the *Spectator* 1940-1, and during the S.W.W. served in the Foreign Office. Intensely concerned with religious issues - he is an RC convert - he creates characters dominated by the conflict of right and wrong. His novels incl. *Brighton Rock* (1938) depicting race-gang warfare, *The Power and the Glory* (1940), *The Heart of the Matter* (1948), *Our Man in Havana* (1958) and *A Burnt-Out Case* (1961), set in a leper colony in Africa. Rather less effective, but still thought-provoking, are his plays, e.g. *The Living Room* (1953) and *The Potting Shed* (1957). *Lord Rochester's Monkey (1974)* is a biography of the poet. His brother **Sir Hugh Carleton G.** (1910-) was director-gen. of the BBC 1960-8.

GREENFINCH. Bird (*Carduelis chloris*), also known as the green linnet, common in Europe and N Africa. The male is green with a yellow breast and the female a drab greenish-brown.

GREENLAND. The world's largest island. It lies between the North Atlantic and the Arctic Oceans. The whole of the interior is covered by a vast ice-sheet. The Greenlanders are of mixed Eskimo, Danish and other European stocks. The language is Greenlandic. Area 2,140,000 sq.km (826,000 sq.m); pop. (1978) 50,000.

G. was discovered *c.* 982 by Eric the Red who founded colonies on the W coast. Christianity was introduced *c.* 1000. In 1261 the colonies accepted the sovereignty of Norway; but early in the 15th cent. all communication with Europe ceased, and when G. was re-discovered in the 16th the colonies had died out. G. became a Danish colony in the 18th cent., and following a referendum (1979) achieved autonomy that year. The island has importance in civil aviation and strategically, and defence responsibilities are shared with America. There are deposits of lead and cryolite, and offshore oil is being explored. Fishing and fish processing industries are important. The cap. is Godthaab on the W coast.

GREENLAND SEA. Area of the Arctic Ocean between Spitsbergen and Greenland, and N of the Norwegian Sea.

GREEN MONKEY DISEASE. *See* Marburg Disease.

GREEN MOUNTAIN BOYS. Irregulars who fought to keep Vermont free from New York interference, and in the War of Am. Independence captured Ticonderoga. Their leader was Ethan Allen (1738-89), who was later captured by the British. Vermont is popularly called the G.M. state.

GREENOCK. Scottish seaport and industrial centre in Strathclyde. Industries incl. shipbuilding, engineering, and sugar refining. Pop. (1971) 69,170.

GREENSHANK. Greyish bird (*Tringa nebularia*) of the sandpiper group. The name is derived from its long olive-green legs, which distinguish it from the redshank. It breeds in Scotland and N Europe.

GREENLAND. An iceberg stranded offshore. The soaring architecture of this opening along its side, where melting ice falls in a fine gold curtain in the sun's rays resembles that of a cathedral. *Photo: Courtesy of the Danish Tourist Authority.*

GREENWICH (grin'ij). Inner bor. of Greater London, England. The Blackwall tunnel connects G. to the N bank of the Thames.

Charles II built *G. Hospital* to designs by Inigo Jones on the site of an earlier palace, where Henry VIII, Mary, and Elizabeth I were born, and Edward VI died. A hospital for superannuated seamen 1705-1869, it became the Royal Naval College 1873. The *Cutty Sark*, most celebrated of the great tea clippers, is preserved as a museum of sail. The Royal Observatory (founded here in 1675), source of British Standard Time, has been moved to Herstmonceux (q.v.), but the G. meridian (0°) remains unchanged. Part of the buildings have been taken over by the National Maritime Museum, and named Flamsteed House after the first Astronomer Royal. Pop. (1973) 215,000.

GREENWOOD, Walter (1903-74). British novelist and playwright. B. at Salford, he had repeated experience of unemployment to give authenticity to his novel *Love on the Dole* (1933), later dramatized and filmed.

GREGG, Sir Norman (1892-1966). Australian ophthalmic surgeon. He discovered in 1941 that German measles in a pregnant woman could cause physical defects in her child. Knighted 1953.

GREGORY. Name of 16 popes. **Gregory I** or St Gregory the Great (*c.* 540-604), a Roman patrician, was elected pope in 590. He asserted the supremacy of Rome over the other patriarchates of the Church, and within Italy assumed an almost imperial position, making peace and war and negotiating with kings as an equal. In

596 he sent St Augustine's mission to England. **St Gregory VII** or HILDEBRAND (*c.* 1023-85) acted as chief minister to several popes before his election in 1073. His claim to a power superior to that of kings, including the right to depose them, and his denial that laymen could make appointments to ecclesiastical offices, involved him in conflicts with many rulers, while his attempts to suppress simony and enforce clerical celibacy raised him enemies within the Church. In 1077 he forced the emperor Henry IV to wait in the snow at Canossa for 4 days, dressed as a penitent, before receiving pardon. G., driven from Rome, d. in exile. **Gregory XIII** (1502-85), who was elected in 1572, introduced in 1582 the reformed calendar known as the Gregorian.

GREGORY, Isabella Augusta, Lady (1852-1932). Irish playwright, *née* Persse, associated with W. B. Yeats in the creation of the Abbey Theatre (1904). B. in co. Galway, she m. in 1881 Sir William G. She wrote many plays, incl. the comedies *Spreading the News* and *Rising of the Moon,* and the tragic *Gaol Gate* and *Grania.* Her *Journals 1916-30* were pub. 1946.

GREGORY OF TOURS, St (538-94). French bishop and historian. B. at Clermont-Ferrand, he was elected bishop of Tours in 573. His *History of the Franks* is of value.

GRENĀ'DA. One of the Windward Is., an assoc. state of the UK 1967–74 and independent within the Commonwealth, incl the island of **Carriacou** (34 sq.km/13 sq.m, with a pop of 8,200) from 1974. Products incl. cocoa, bananas, spices, and coconuts. The cap. is St George's (pop. 8,600). Premier Eric Gairy's autocratic regime was overthrown in 1979 by Maurice Bishop, of the left-wing New Jewel Movement, but in Oct 1983, Bishop's overthrow by a military council, he and 3 other ministers being murdered, led to US military intervention. Elections in 1984 resulted in a victory for a centrist coalition headed by Herbert Blaize. Area 344 sq.km (133 sq.m); pop. (1975) 111,000.

GRENADINES (gren'adēnz). Chain of small islands in the Caribbean. Those to the N which incl. Mustique (q.v.) form part of St Vincent and the Grenadines (q.v.), and those to the S (incl. Carriacou) form part of Grenada (q.v.).

GRENFELL, Julian Henry Francis (1888-1915). British soldier-poet. Eldest son of Lord Desborough, he d. of wounds in the F.W.W., and is remembered for his poem 'Into Battle'.

GRENOBLE (grenōbl'). Cap. of Isère dept, on the Isère, 97km (60m) SE of Lyon, SE France. There is a fine 12-13th cent. cathedral, and a univ. (1339). It was the birthplace of Stendhal, commemorated by a museum, and the Beaux-Arts gallery has a good modern collection. A major industrial centre, G. has electrical engineering, electronics, cement, textile and glove-making industries. The Franco-German Paul Langevin-Max von Laue Inst. (1967) carries out nuclear research, etc. Pop. met. area (1975) 389,000.

GRENVILLE, George (1712-70). British Whig statesman. He entered parliament in 1741, and was PM and Chancellor of the Exchequer 1763-5. His govt is notable for the prosecution of Wilkes in 1763, and the Stamp Act of 1765, which precipitated the American War of Independence.

GRENVILLE, Sir Richard (*c.* 1541-91). English naval hero. B. of an old Cornish family, he commanded the fleet sent by his cousin, Sir Walter Raleigh, to colonize Virginia in 1585, and organized the defence of W England in 1586-8. In 1591 he sailed to the Azores as 2nd-in-command to Lord Thomas Howard to intercept a Spanish treasure-fleet. Cut off by the Spaniards from the main force, G. commanded the *Revenge* (500 tons) in a fight against 15 Spanish ships for 15 hours. When most of his crew were dead and he was fatally wounded, he ordered the master-gunner to blow up the ship. The crew surrendered, however, and G. was taken aboard the Spanish flagship, where he d.

GRENVILLE. A portrait by an unknown artist of Sir Richard Grenville, whose greatest exploit was commemorated in Tennyson's ballad 'The Revenge'. *Photo: Courtesy of the National Portrait Gallery.*

GRENVILLE, William Wyndham, baron (1759-1834). British Whig statesman. The son of George Grenville (q.v.), he was raised to the peerage in 1790, and in 1806-7 headed the 'All the Talents' coalition.

GRESHAM, Sir Thomas (*c.* 1519-79). English economist. B. in London, the son of Sir Richard G., Lord Mayor in 1537, he was admitted to the Mercers' Co. in 1543, and in 1566-8 paid for the building of the first Royal Exchange. He bequeathed money and his house to found G. College, and his name has been given to *Gresham's Law,* which asserts that bad money tends to drive out good money from circulation.

GRETNA GREEN. Scottish village in Dumfries and Galloway, just over the border from England, which became famous as a centre for runaway marriages after 1754, when an act of 1753 forbidding clandestine marriages in England became effective. In 1856 a law was passed requiring 3 weeks' previous residence in Scotland, and the wedding traffic almost ceased.

GREUZE (gröz), **Jean Baptiste** (1725-1805). French painter. B. at Tournus, he gained sudden success with 'A Father Explaining the Bible to his Children' in the Salon of 1755. Mainly a genre painter, he also produced a number of portraits and his best-known works incl. 'Innocence' and 'The Broken Pitcher'.

GREVILLE, Charles Cavendish Fulke (1794-1865). British diarist. He was Clerk of the Council in Ordinary 1821-59, an office which brought him into close contact with all the noted personalities of the court and of both political parties. This gives the *Greville Memoirs 1817-60* unrivalled interest.

GREY, Beryl (1927-). British ballerina. Making her début with the Sadler's Wells Co. in 1941, she was their prima ballerina 1942-57, then danced internationally, and was artistic director, London Festival Ballet 1968-79. Tall for a ballet dancer, and with impeccable technique, she excelled in dramatic character parts, e.g. the Black Queen in *Checkmate,* and the dual role in *Swan Lake.*

GREY, Charles, 2nd earl (1764-1845). British Whig statesman. He entered parliament in 1786 and in 1806 became 1st Lord of the Admiralty in the 'all the Talents' ministry, succeeding Fox as For. Sec. soon afterwards. He was PM 1830-4, and in 1832 carried the great Reform Bill.

His son **Henry,** 3rd earl G. (1802-94) served under him as Under-Sec. for the Colonies 1830-3, resigning because the Cabinet would not back the immediate emancipation of slaves, was Sec.-at-War 1835-9, and Colonial Sec. 1846-52. He was unique among statesmen of the period in maintaining that the colonies should be governed for their own benefit, not that of the mother country, and in his policy of granting self-govt wherever possible. Yet he advocated convict transportation, and was in opposition to Gladstone's Home Rule policy.

GREY, Sir George (1812-98). British colonial governor. B. at Lisbon, he became Gov. of S Australia in 1841, and of New Zealand in 1845. He succeeded in restoring prosperity to both colonies, and won the gratitude of the Maoris by his care for them. Sent to Cape Colony as Governor in 1853, he quelled a Kaffir rising. Returning to New Zealand as Gov. in 1861, he was PM there 1877-9.

GREY, Lady Jane (1537-54). Queen of England. B. in Leics, the dau. of Henry G., duke of Suffolk, and a great-grand-dau. of Henry VII, she was m. in 1553 to Lord Guildford Dudley, son of the duke of Northumberland, and shortly after Northumberland persuaded Edward VI to make a will bequeathing the crown to her, setting aside the claims of his sisters Mary and Elizabeth. When Edward d. on 6 July Jane reluctantly accepted the crown and was proclaimed queen 4 days later. Mary, however, received universal support and G. was executed on Tower Green.

GREY, Zane (1875-1939). American author of 'Westerns', e.g. *Riders of the Purple Sage* (1912). B. in Ohio, he was a dentist.

GREYHOUND. Ancient breed of dog, with a long narrow muzzle, slight build, and long legs, renowned for its swiftness. As its sense of smell is defective, it hunts by sight. The English G. has smooth sandy or slate-grey hair, and weighs 25kg (60lb). Other varieties incl. the delicate Italian G., Borzoi, and Afghan hound. *See* COURSING and WHIPPET.

GREY. Remarkable for her learning even in an age of scholars, Lady Jane Grey was a master of Latin and Greek and knew also some Hebrew, Chaldee and Arabic. *Photo: Courtesy of the National Portrait Gallery.*

GREYHOUND RACING. A sport held on circular enclosed tracks where Gs. pursue a mechanically propelled hare. It attained popularity in England and USA after the F.W.W.

GREY OF FALLODON, Edward Grey, 1st visct (1862-1933). British Liberal statesman. For. Sec. in Campbell Bannerman's govt in 1905, he followed up Lord Lansdowne's entente with France and concluded an entente with Russia in 1907. Despite worsening relations with Germany after Agadir in 1911 he tried to secure a settlement, and in 1914 commented: 'The lamps are going out all over Europe; we shall not see them lit again in our lifetime.' Eye trouble forced his retirement in 1916, when he accepted a peerage.

GRIEG (grēg), **Edvard Hagerup** (1843-1907). Norwegian composer. B. at Bergen, he studied at Leipzig Conservatoire and in Copenhagen, and settled as a teacher and conductor at Christiana in 1867. He won success with his incidental music for *Peer Gynt* (1876). His works, often inspired by the folk tunes of his country, include a piano concerto, the Holberg Suite for strings, songs, etc.

GRIERSON, John (1898-1972). Brit. film producer. B. in Perthshire, he was a sociologist who pioneered the documentary film in Britain. Used as a social force, it is 'the creative treatment of actuality'. He directed *Drifters* (1929) and produced (1930-5) *Industrial Britain, Song of Ceylon, Night Mail,* etc. During the S.W.W. he created the National Film Board of Canada.

GRIFFIN. Mythical monster, the supposed guardian of hidden treasure, with the body, tail and hind legs of a lion, and the head, forelegs and wings of an eagle. It is often found in heraldry, e.g. the armorial crest of the City of London, and 2 Gs. on the Thames Embankment guard its W boundary.

GRIFFITH, David Wark (1875-1948). American film director. Son of a Kentucky colonel, he was an actor then a director, making many hundreds of 'one reelers' (12 min) 1908-13, in which he introduced the now current techniques of the flash-back, cross-cut, close-up and longshot, completely breaking with theatrical tradition. His masterpiece *Birth of a Nation* (1915) estab. the film as a work of art and entertainment, and was followed by the mammoth *Intolerance* (1916), and *Broken Blossoms* (1919). In decline, from the advent of 'talkies', he d. in poverty.

GRILLPARZER (gril'pahrtser), **Franz** (1791-1872). Austrian poet and dramatist. B. in Vienna, he followed his sensational tragedy *Die Ahnfrau* (1817) with the classical *Sappho* (1818) and the trilogy *Das goldene Vliess* (1821). His historical tragedies *König Ottokars Glück und Ende* and *Ein treuer Diener seines Herrn* (1826) both involved him with the censor. Two of his greatest dramas followed, *Des Meeres und der Liebe Wellen* (1831), returning to the Hellenic world, and *Der Traum, ein Leben* (1834). The bitter cycle of poems *Tristia ex Ponto* (1835) followed an unhappy love-affair. G. is Austria's finest dramatic poet.

GRIMA'LDI, Joseph (1779-1837). British clown. B. in London, the son of an Italian actor, he appeared on the stage when 2 years old, and since his day the clown has been called 'Joey'. His best part was in *Mother Goose* at Covent Garden in 1806.

GRIMM, Jacob Ludwig Carl (1785-1863) and **Wilhelm Carl** (1786-1859). German philologists and folklorists. Brothers, they collaborated in the world-famous *Fairy Tales,* ed. medieval texts, and collected the historical legends *Deutsche Sagen* (1816-18). Jacob's chief work was his *Deutsche Grammatik,* which gave the first historical treatment of the Germanic languages (q.v.).

GRI'MMELSHAUSEN (-howzen), **Hans Jacob Christoffel von** (*c.* 1625-76). German author of the great realistic picaresque novel *Der Abenteuerliche Simplicissimus* (*The Adventurous Simplicissimus*: 1669), whose hero shares his own experiences as a soldier in the Thirty Years War.

GRI'MOND, Joseph (1913-). British Liberal politician. As leader of the party 1956-67, he aimed at making it 'a new Radical Party to take the place of the Socialist Party as an alternative to Conservatism'.

GRIMSBY. Port in Humberside, England, at the mouth of the Humber, 24km (15m) SE of Hull. Long Britain's premier fishing port, with fleets sailing to the Arctic Ocean and Mediterranean, it declined in the 1970s, espec. when Icelandic waters were closed to its ships. There are also shipbuilding and food preserving industries. Some 8km (5m) to the NW, further up the Humber, is **Immingham.** Originally a dock built by the railway co. in 1912 for ships too large to enter G., it developed rapidly and, following construction in 1968 of the largest bulk handling terminal in Europe, became Britain's premier port in terms of tonnage handled. Pop. (1974) 95,150.

GRISONS (grēzoń') (Ger. **Graubünden**). Largest of the cantons of Switzerland. The inner valleys are Europe's highest, and the r. Rhine has its main sources in the canton. It also incl. the fashionable tourist resorts of Davos, and, in the Upper Engadine, St Moritz. The cap, is Chur. Romansh (q.v.) is still widely spoken. Area 7,110 sq.km (2,746 sq.m); pop. (1970) 162,100. It entered the Swiss Confederation in 1803.

GRIVAS (grē'vahs), **George.** *See* CYPRUS.

GRO'DNO. Industrial and market town in White Russia, cap. of G. region on the Niemen, east of the Polish frontier. Once part of Lithuania, it was a meeting place of the diet after the union of Poland and Lithuania in 1569. The 1793 partition of Poland gave it to Russia; it was ceded to Poland 1923, ceded back to Russia 1945. Pop. (1977) 168,500.

GROMYKO (gromē'ko), **Andrei** (1909-). Russian diplomat. As UN representative 1946-58 he was celebrated for the frequency with which he said 'niet' (he exercised the Soviet veto 26 times), and his appointment as Foreign Minister in 1957 was seen as a return to Stalinist traditions. He became President of the Supreme Soviet in 1985.

GRŌ'NINGEN. Cap. of a NE prov. of the Netherlands of the same name, a market centre, with a univ. (1614), and textile and sugar refining industries. Pop. (1978) 160,500. There are large natural gas deposits in the prov., parts of which are reclaimed land below sea level.

GRŌ'PIUS, Walter Adolf (1883-1969). German-American architect. Founder-director of the *Bauhaus* Weimar (1919-28), he exerted great influence through his concepts of team architecture, and the application of artistic standards to industrial production. Later he left Germany, and 1937-52 was prof. of architecture at Harvard where he designed the Harvard Graduate Centre (1949-50).

GRŌS'BEAK. Name given to several thick-billed birds. The pine G. (*Pinicola enucleator*), also known as the pine-finch, breeds in Arctic forests; its plumage is similar to the crossbill's.

GROSSMITH, George (1847-1912). British actor. From journalism he turned to the stage, and in 1877 began his long association with the Gilbert and Sullivan operas, in which he created a number of parts. He collaborated with his brother **Weedon G.** (1853-1919) in the comic *Diary of a Nobody* (1894). The latter was also an artist, and actor-manager.

GROTEFEND (grōt'efent), **George Frederick** (1775-1853). German scholar. A student of the classical rather than the oriental languages, he nevertheless ingeniously solved the riddle of the cuneiform script as used in ancient Persia: decipherment of Babylonian cuneiform followed on the basis of his work.

GROTIUS (grō'shius), **Hugo** (1583-1645). Dutch jurist and statesman. B. at Delft, he became a lawyer, and later received political preferments. In 1618 he was arrested as a republican and sentenced to imprisonment for life: his wife contrived his escape in 1620, and he settled in France, where he composed the *De Jure Belli et Pacis* (1625), a classic of international law, and 1634-45 was Swedish ambassador in Paris.

GROTIUS. A portrait of Hugo Grotius, founder of international law, by A. Moro. *Photo: Mansell Collection.*

GROUND-NUT. Name given to the fruit of a number of plants, but especially to that of the annual *Arachis hypogaea* in the family Leguminosae (which is also known as the pea-nut, earth-nut or monkey-nut), because the pods - borne on stalks after the death of the flower - bury themselves in the earth to ripen. A native of S America, though now widely grown in all tropical countries, the plant is *c.* 50cm (1½ft) high, and the nuts are a valuable source of vegetable oil.

GROUPER. Name given to a number of species of sea bass (Serranidae) found in warm waters off the Atlantic coast of America. The spotted giant G. (*Promicrops itaiara*) is 2-2.5cm (6-8ft) long, may weigh over 300kg (700lb) and is sluggish in movement. Formerly primarily game fish, they are now commercially exploited as food.

GROUSE. Game birds of the family Tetraonidae common in N America and northern Europe. Among the most familiar are the red G. (*Lagopus scoticus*), a native of Britain; the ptarmigans (q.v.); the ruffed G. (*Bonasia umbellus*), common in N American woods; and the capercailzie (*Tetrao urogallus*) and the blackcock (*T. tetrix*), both known in Britain. G. are shot over dogs or by driving in Britain 12 Aug.-10 Dec.

GROUND-NUT. Pyramids of ground-nuts stored at Kaduna in northern Nigeria. *Photo: Popperfoto.*

GROZNY. Russian industrial town, cap. of Chechen-Ingush ASSR on the r. Assa. It is about 145km (90m) W of the Caspian Sea, and is the centre of an important oil field; pipelines link it to Mahachkala on the Caspian and Tuapse on the Black Sea. Pop. (1977) 387,000.

GRUNDY, Mrs. The personification of British respectability. She is first mentioned in Thomas Morton's play *Speed the Plough* (1798), when though she does not actually appear she is constantly appealed to as one who knows the proprieties.

GRÜNEWALD (grün'evalt). German artist identified in 1938 as Mathis Gothardt Neithardt (*c.* 1460-1528). Little is known of his life, but his work shows extremes of emotion with terrible religious intensity. Last and most important of the Gothic painters in Germany, he achieved his masterpiece in the expressive Isenheim altar-piece now in the Colmar Museum.

GRUYÈRE (grū-yār'). District in Fribourg canton, Switzerland, famous for its cheese.

GUADALAJARA (gwah'dalakhah'ra). Mexican city, capital of the state of Jalisco; 485km (300m) NW of Mexico City. Pop. (1970) 1,196,200.

GUADALCANAL (gwah'-). Largest is. of the Brit. Solomon Is., SW Pacific. Invaded by the Japanese in Jan. 1942, it was retaken by US forces Aug. 1942-Feb. 1943 after bitter fighting. Honiara, cap. of the prot., grew from the military base the Americans left behind. Area 4,000 sq.km (2,500 sq.m); pop. (1976) 31,700.

GUADELOUPE (gwahd-loop'). French West Indian overseas region in the Lesser Antilles, consisting of the islands of Guadeloupe proper and Grande-Terre, separated by the narrow Rivière Salée channel. The cap. is Basse-Terre on G. proper. Area 1,702 sq.km (657 sq.m); pop. (1974) 325,000.

GUAM (gwahm). American island in the W Pacific, the largest of the Mariana group. Agaña is the cap., Piti the port of entry. A naval station and radio centre, G. was ceded to USA by Spain in 1898, and occupied by Japan 1941-4. Area 535 sq.km (206 sq.m); pop. (1975) 105,400.

GUANCH (goo-ahnsh') **REPUBLIC.** *See* CANARIES.

GUANGDONG (goo-ahngdawng'). Prov. of S China (formerly Kwangtung), which incl. the Leizhou peninsula to the S and the is. of Hainan. Drained by the Xi Jiang system, it produces rice, sweet potatoes, tobacco, fruit, sugar and silk. Minerals incl. tungsten, iron and oil. Coastal fisheries centre on Guangzhou, the cap., which stands on the estuary of the Xi Jiang: Hong Kong and Macao are situated at the mouth of the delta. Area 231,400 sq.km (89,320 sq.m); pop. (1979) 53,500,000.

GUANGXI ZHUANG (goo-ahngsi jawoo-ahng'). Autonomous region of S China, bordering Vietnam, which incl. the upper part of the basin of the Xi Jiang. Products incl. rice, sugar, and fruit. The Zhuang people are akin to the Thai and form China's largest ethnic minority. Area 220,400 sq.km (85,074 sq.m); pop. (1979) 33,000,000.

GUANGZHOU (goo-ahngzhaw-oo'). Cap. (formerly Canton) of Guangdong prov., China, and chief commercial centre of S China, NW of Hong Kong. It was the first Chinese port opened to foreign trade, the Portuguese visiting it in 1516, and was a treaty port from 1842 until its occupation by the Japanese in 1938. Guangzhou stands at the apex of the Xi Jiang delta, with its deepwater port at Huang-pu. Industries incl. textiles, chemicals, cement, paper, sugar refining, and shipbuilding, and natural gas is found nearby. There is a rail link with Peking and one is planned with Liuzhou. It was the birthplace of Sun Yat-sen, whose home is preserved, and who founded Sun Yat-sen Univ. (1924). Pop. (1977) 5,000,000.

GUARANA (gwahrahnah'). Woody climbing plant (*Paullinia cupana*) of the Amazonian jungle from which a drug containing caffeine is made, known as Zoom in USA.

GUARANI (gwahrani'). South American Indian people who were assimilated with their Spanish conquerors to form the modern mestizo pop. of Paraguay, and who are also found in S Brazil and Bolivia.

GUARDI (gwahr'dē), **Francesco** (1712-93). Italian artist. He was once regarded merely as a follower of Canaletto, but his brilliant evocations of his native Venice, using an almost impressionist technique, are now highly valued.

GUARESCHI (gwahres'ki), **Giovanni** (1909-68). Italian author. B. at Parma, he studied law, but after the S.W.W. became editor of the magazine *Candido*. In this his short stories of the friendly feud between parish priest Don Camillo and the Communist mayor, originally written in haste as space-fillers, first appeared.

GUARNIERI (gwahrnyā'rē). Celebrated family of violin-makers at Cremona, of whom Giuseppe Antonio G. (1687-1745) produced the finest models.

GUATEMALA (gwahtāmah'la). Country of Central America, adjoining Mexico, Belize, Honduras, and Salvador. It is divided into the Great plain of Petén to the N, the Pacific and Caribbean lowlands, and the central region of volcanic mtns and high valleys. The chief crops are coffee, bananas, cotton and sugar; minerals incl. lead, nickel, zinc and oil. Industries incl. textiles chemicals and food processing. The cap. and chief commercial centre is G. City, which is 1,488 m (4,880 ft) a.s.l. on a wide plateau traversed by the Rio de las Vacas. Other towns incl. Quetzaltenango, Matzatenango and the Atlantic ports of Santo Tomas and Puerto Barrios.

The rep. was estab. in 1839, after being part of the Central American federation. Its boundaries were not fixed until 1936, and claims made on Belize prevented the granting of independence to the latter until in 1981 G. agreed to be satisfied with free access to the sea through Belize, and unrestricted navigation rights in coastal waters. The constitution of 1965 provides for a pres., elected for 4 yrs, a council of state, and unicameral congress. However, the military regime is oppressively right-wing, the leader of the opposition having been murdered in 1979, and the USA has pressed for human rights. Mineral wealth ensures a buoyant economy.

Area 108,889 sq.km (42,042 sq.m); pop. (1978) 6,800,000, of whom half are pure Amerindian, the rest, mixed Indian and Spanish (*ladinos*) providing the ruling class; over 35% are illiterate. The official language is Spanish, the religion RC. M.U.: quetzal.

GUATEMALA CITY. Cap. of Guatemala in the Sierra Madre, founded 1776 to replace the old cap. of Antigua, destroyed in an earthquake. It is the country's industrial and commercial centre, and has fine govt. buildings. Pop. (1973) 717,000.

GUAYAQUIL (gwī-ahkē'). City and chief port of Ecuador nr the mouth of the Guayas. Pop. (1974) 823,200.

GUDERIAN (goodār'ē-ahn), **Heinz** (1888-1954). German general. He created the Panzer or 'armoured' divisions of the German army which formed the ground spearhead of Hitler's *blitz-krieg* strategy, and achieved the break-through at Sedan in 1940 and the advance to Moscow in 1941.

GUDGEON (guj'en). Freshwater cyprinid fish (*Gobio gobio*) found in Europe and N Asia on the gravel bottoms of streams. Olive-brown, spotted with black and attaining *c.* 200cm (8in), it has a distinctive barbel at each side of the mouth.

GUELDER ROSE or **gelder rose.** Flowering shrub (*Viburnum opulus*) of the Caprifoliaceae (honeysuckle) family. The wild variety bears its flowers in a head, followed by a cluster of blackish-red berries. The flowers of the garden shrub are enlarged and grouped into a heavy globular head.

GUELDERS. *See* GELDERLAND.

GUELPH (gwelf). Town in Ontario, Canada, 70km (43m) SW of Toronto. It is an agricultural centre, distributing fruit, grain, and livestock, and industries incl. food processing, electrical goods, and pharmaceuticals. Pop. (1971) 60,000.

GUELPHS AND GHIBELLINES (gib-). Names of rival parties, originally in 12th cent. Germany, and later in medieval Italy. They were the partisans of the rival German houses of Welf, dukes of Bavaria and later of Saxony, and of the lords of Hohenstaufen and Waiblingen, who struggled for the imperial crown after the death of Henry VI in 1197, until the Hohenstaufen died out in 1268. In Italy, the papalists were known as Guelphs and the imperialists as Ghibellines.

GUERNICA (gernē'ka). Spanish town, in Biscay prov. Under its famous oak the Castilian kings formerly swore to respect the rights of the Basques. G. was destroyed in 1937 by German bombers fighting for Franco, an event which inspired a famous painting by Picasso. Re-building was completed in 1946. Pop. (1970) 7,800.

GUERNSEY (gern'zi). One of the Channel Islands, second in area to Jersey. The island specializes in the cultivation of grapes and tomatoes under glass, and also produces flowers and vegetables, as well as its own breed of cattle. G., which has belonged to the English Crown since 1066, was occupied by German forces 1940-5. St Peter Port is the cap. and chief harbour: there is an airport at La Villiaze. Area 65 sq.km (25sq.m); pop. (1971) 51,500.

GUEVARA (gevah'rah), **Ernesto 'Che'** (1928-67). Argentine revolutionary. B. in the Argentine, he was trained as a doctor, but in 1953 left the country because of his opposition to Peron. In effecting the Cuban revolution of 1959, he was second only to Castro and his brother, but in 1965 moved on to fight against white mercenaries in the Congo, and then to Bolivia, where he was killed in an unsuccessful attempt to lead a peasant rising. His revolutionary technique using minimum resources has been influential, but his orthodox Marxism has been obscured by romanticizing disciples.

GUEVARA. Che Guevara and his guerrilla techniques have been a potent influence on similar movements worldwide. *Photo: Keystone.*

GUIANA (gē-ah'nah). *See* FRENCH G., GUYANA, *and* SURINAM.

GUIDO. *See* RENI.

GUIENNE (gē-en'). Old prov. of SW France that formed with Gascony the duchy of Acquitaine. Its cap. was Bordeaux. It became English in 1154 and passed to France in 1451.

GUILDFORD (gil'ford). Historic town, admin. HQ of Surrey, England, on the river Wey, where it cuts through the N Downs, to the E of the Hog's Back, 47km (29m) SW of London. It has 16th and 17th cent. buildings, ruins of a Norman castle, and a modern cathedral (1936-61), below which is the Univ. of Surrey (1966), specializing in technology. Yvonne Arnaud (1895-1958), the sophisticated comedy actress, was b. in G. and a theatre (1964) is named after her. There is a cattle market and industries include flour-milling, plastics and engineering. Pop. (1974) 122,600.

GUILDFORD. The well-preserved keep of the Norman castle. *Photo: Courtesy of Dr Gordon Copley.*

GUILDS, or **gilds.** Medieval associations, particularly of craftsmen or merchants, formed for mutual aid and protection and the pursuit of a common purpose, religious or economic. Gs. fulfilling charitable or religious functions, such as the maintenance of schools, roads, or bridges, the assistance of members in misfortune, or the provision of masses for the souls of dead members, flourished in England from the 9th cent. down to 1547, when they were suppressed.

The earliest form of economic G., the *G. Merchant,* arose in the 11th-12th cents.; this was an organization of the traders of a town, who had been granted by charter a practical monopoly of its trade. As the merchants often strove to exclude craftsmen from the G., and to monopolize control of local government, the *Craft Gs.* came into existence in the 12th-13th cents. These, which included journeymen and apprentices as well as employers, regulated prices, wages, working conditions and apprenticeship, prevented unfair practices, and maintained high standards of craftmanship; they also fulfilled many social, religious and charitable functions. By the 14th cent. they had taken control of local government, ousting the G. Merchant.

After the 16th cent. the position of the Gs. was undermined by the growth of the domestic system, which removed industry into the country, where G. regulations had no force, and of the factory system.

GUILLEMOT (gil'emot). Diving sea-fowl of the auk family, which breeds in large numbers on the rocky N Atlantic coasts. The common G. (*Uria aalge*) has a sharp bill and short tail, and sooty-brown and white plumage. Gs. build no nest, but lay one large, almost conical, egg on the rock.

GUILLOTINE (gilotēn'). A beheading instrument, in use from the Middle Ages. Introduced in France during the Revolution, it was named after the physician Joseph Ignace Guillotin (1738-1814), who recommended its adoption as humane and improved the design: it was first used 25 April 1792. It is still used in France and other countries.

GUINEA (gin'i). English gold coin, not minted since 1817, when it was superseded by the gold sovereign. The term continued in use - signifying 21*s* *(£1.05)* - for professional fees and for limited commercial purposes.

GUINEA. Country of W. Africa. Tropical on the coast, it has a cooler climate in the interior plateaux and uplands. Products incl. coffee, rice, palm kernels, and pineapples; and minerals incl. great bauxite deposits at Boke, diamonds and iron ore. The cap. is Conakry. Formerly a French colony, G. became in 1958 the independent Rep. of G., and from 1979 the People's Revolutionary Rep. of Guinea. On the death in 1984 of the President Sékou Touré, who had held power since 1961, the 2nd Republic of Guinea was proclaimed, with Lansana Conté as President (and PM since 12.84). The official languge is French. Area 245,860 sq.km. (95,000 sq.m); pop. (1977) 5,143,000. M.U.: sily.

GUINEA, Equatorial. Country of Central Africa. It comprises: (1) the mainland Rio Muni, plus the small is. of Corisco, Elobey Grande and Elobey Chico, and (2) Bioko Is. (formerly Macias Nguema/Fernando Poo) together with Pigalu Is. (formerly Annobon). The cap. is Malabo (formerly Santa Isabel). Cocoa, coffee, bananas and high grade timber are the chief products. These provs. were formerly the 2 overseas provs. of Spanish Guinea, which achieved independence as Equatorial G. in 1968. The official language is Spanish, but pidgin English is widely spoken. Under the constitution of 1973 G. is a rep. with a pres. and assembly, both elected for 5 yrs, but the first pres., Francisco Macias Nguema, was appointed for life. He was deposed and executed in 1979, and succeeded by Teodoro Obiang Nguema. Total area 28,100 sq.km (10,852 sq.m); pop. (1978) 325,000. M.U.: ekpwele.

GUINEA-BISSAU (gin'i bis'ow). Country of W. Africa, which incl the Bijagós Archipelago. Discovered by the Portuguese in the 15th cent., it was known as Portuguese G. until it obtained independence in 1974 as the Rep. of G.-B. It is thickly forested. Rice, coconuts and groundnuts are grown and minerals incl. bauxite. In 1974 Medina de Boe in the E. interior was named as the provisional cap.; other towns are Bissau, port and cap. until 1974, and Bolama, also a port and former cap. Area 36,125 sq.km (14,000 sq.m); pop. (1974) 600,000, of whom one-third are Moslem. M.U.: peso. *See* CAPE VERDE.

GUINEA COAST. Geographical name for the coast of W. Africa from Gambia to Cape Lopez.

GUINEA-FOWL. Gallinaceous bird (*Numida*), of the family Numididae. The plumage is slate-grey with white spots, and the head is crowned with a bony crest or tuft of feathers. The commonest variety is the African *N. meleagris*, introduced to poultry farms.

GUINEA PIG. Small vegetarian rodent in the family Caviidae. The domestic species is probably derived from the Peruvian cavy (*Cavia cutleri*), and may be black, white, or brown. They breed readily and are extensively used in laboratory experiments.

GUINNESS (gin'es), **Sir Alec** (1914-). British actor. A Londoner, he joined the Old Vic in 1936, played Hamlet in modern dress in 1938 and gave another unorthodox portrayal in 1951. He is celebrated for the humorous versatility of his characterizations, e.g. *Kind Hearts and Coronets* (a film in which he played a number of related characters); and his subtlety, as in the film *The Bridge on the River Kwai* (1957), and his interpretation on stage of Lawrence of Arabia in *Ross* (1960). He was knighted in 1959, and received a 'lifetime achievement' Oscar in 1980.

GUISE (gü-ez'). French noble family, prominent in the period of religious wars in the 16th cent. **Francis** (1519-63), the second duke, commanded against the Huguenots, and was assassinated by a fanatic. His son, **Henry** (1550-88), 3rd duke, was largely responsible for the massacre of St Bartholomew. He, too, was assassinated.

GUITAR (gitahr'). Musical instrument, flat-backed and waisted, and with 6 strings plucked by the fingers, a later development of the lute (q.v.). Traditionally the instrument of Italy and Spain, Gs. reached their peak of popularity from the 17th to mid-19th cent., and then lost favour to the piano until revived for concert purposes by Andrés Segovia, and more recently Julian Bream, who encouraged contemporary composition for the instrument. The G. also achieved popularity among American mountain folk musicians from 1890, and in the early 1930s electrically amplified models became a feature of jazz and dance bands. After the S.W.W. the solid-bodied electric G. became the dominant instrument of 'pop' music, espec. with groups such as the Beatles, and the sophistication of the electronic effects achieved with it was remarkable.

GUIYANG (goo-ēyahng'). Cap. and industrial centre (formerly Kweiyang) of the SW Chinese prov. of Guizhou. Pop. (1973) 670,000.

GUIZHOU (goo-ējawoo'). Prov. of S China (formerly Kweichow), to the NW of Guangxi prov., drained by the Wu Jiang in the N and the Beipan Jiang in the S. Crops incl. rice, maize and wheat, but its chief wealth lies in its mercury, bauxite, manganese, gold and silver. The cap. is Guiyang. Area 174,000 sq.km (67,164 sq.m); pop. (1979) 25,000,000.

GUIZOT (gēzō'), **François Pierre Guillaume** (1787-1874). French statesman and historian. B. at Nîmes, he was a Protestant, and 1812-30 was prof. of modern history at the Sorbonne. He wrote on the history of civilization, and became PM in 1847. His resistance to all reforms led up to the Revolution of 1848.

GUJARAT (goojraht'). State of the rep. of India, formed in 1960 on a linguistic basis (the majority of the inhabitants speaking Gujarati) from the northern part of former Bombay state. The cap. is Gandhinagar. Area 187,091 sq.km (72,154 sq.m); pop. (1971) 26,697,000.

GULF. Name given to any large sea inlet. The G. States are (1) the states of USA bordering on the G. of Mexico (Alabama, Florida, Louisiana, Mississippi, and Texas); and (2) the oil-rich countries sharing the coastline of the Arabian/Persian G., which runs NW between Iran and Arabia (i.e. Iran, Iraq, Kuwait, Qatar, Saudi-Arabia, and United Arab Emirates), and which is 800 km (500 m) long, average width 240 km (150 m).

GULF STREAM. The most pronounced element in the circulation of the upper waters of the North Atlantic, and the most widely known of the permanent ocean currents. The name is often applied to the whole of the surface-current which issues from the Gulf of Mexico through the Strait of Florida, flows northwards off the E coast of the USA, and crosses the Atlantic in several branches, one of which skirts the British Isles to enter Norwegian waters and so on to the Arctic Ocean, but should properly be restricted to that part of the current between Cape Hatteras, USA, and the Grand Banks of Newfoundland. The average width of the stream is 200km/125m, and the annual mean temperature of the surface-water in its central part is about 25°C (78°F). The continuation of the G.S. in the G.S. Drift is a prime cause of the mild winter climate of NW Europe. *See* CURRENT.

GULF WAR. *See* IRAN and IRAQ.

GULL. Seabird of the Laridae family. A typical G. of the genus *Larus* is the black-headed G. (*L. ridibundus*), common in Britain, which is grey and white with (in summer) dark brown head and red beak; it breeds in large colonies on marshland, making a nest of dead rushes, averaging 3 eggs. Allied are the larger laughing G. of America, and the great black-headed G. (*L. ichthyaëtus*) of Asia. Other notable Gs. are the herring G. (*L. argentatus*), often known in the US as the harbour G., which has white and pearl-grey adult plumage and yellow beak; and the oceanic great black-backed G. (*L. marinus*), found in the Atlantic and over 75cm (2½ft) long.

GULL. The herring gull is familiar on the beach, but comparatively few see their nests, high in sheltered spots in the cliffs. *Photo: Heather Angel.*

GUM ARABIC. Exudation from a low thorn bush *Acacia senegal* used in jellies, sweets and soft drinks. There is no synthetic substitute, and 90% of the world's supplies come from the Sudan.

GUMS. The soft tissues surrounding the bases of the teeth. They are liable to inflammation or to infection by microbes from food deposits and tartar, or by Vincent's angina. Pyorrhoea is a general infection of the margins extending down the walls of the teeth. Gumboil is a local infection of one gum.

GUMS. Complex hydrocarbons formed by many plants and trees, particularly by those from dry regions. Tasteless odourless substances, insoluble in alcohol and ether but generally soluble in water, Gs. are used for adhesives, sizing fabrics, in confectionery, medicine and calico printing.

They form 5 main groups: plant and tree exudates; marine plant extracts; seed extracts; fruit and vegetable extracts; and processed gums.

GUN. *See* ARTILLERY, MACHINE G., PISTOL, SMALL ARMS.

GUNMETAL. An alloy of copper and tin, usually in the proportions of about 90 and 10 per cent respectively, with small quantities of zinc or lead. A tough metal, it is used in castings, etc.

GUNPOWDER. Oldest known explosive, a mixture of sulphur, saltpetre, and charcoal. Though no longer used as a propellant, it is in wide use for blasting and fireworks.

GUNPOWDER PLOT. The Catholic conspiracy to blow up James I and his parliament on 5 November 1605. It was discovered through an anonymous letter sent to Lord Monteagle, and Guy Fawkes was found in the cellar beneath the House, ready to fire a store of combustibles. Several of the conspirators were slain, and Guy Fawkes and 7 others were executed. The searching of the vaults of parliament before the opening of each new session, however, was not instituted until the 'Popish Plot' of 1678.

GURDJIEFF (gerd'yef), **George Ivanovitch** (1877-1949). Russian philosopher. His Zen-like search for spiritual truth greatly influenced the modern human-potential movement. He grew up on the Russo-Turkish border, and travelled widely, perfecting his theory that human beings are not aware of their full capabilities, but have to be awakened to a higher level of consciousness by various means, e.g. by a demanding type of dancing.

GURKHAS (goor'kahz). The ruling Hindu caste in Nepal. In the military sense soldiers recruited since 1815 from Nepal for service in British India and overseas in both World Wars. The Brigade of G. still serves with the British Army (HQ Hong Kong) and its bravery is legendary.

GURNARD. Genus of coastal fish (*Trigla*) in the family Triglidae, which creep along the sea bottom by means of 3 finger-like appendages detached from the pectoral fins. They are both tropic and temperate zone fish, half a dozen species being found in British waters, where they are trawled for food.

GUSH EMUNIM (goosh emoo'nim). Israeli group (Bloc of the Faithful), founded 1973, who believe that the W Bank, Gaza Strip and Golan Heights form an permanent part of Israel by divine intention, and pursue an active policy of settlement. This Yeretz Yisrael extends in their more extreme claims to the Euphrates.

GUSTAF V (1858-1950). King of Sweden. Son of Oscar II, he m. Princess Victoria (1862-1930), dau. of the Grand Duke of Baden, in 1881, thus uniting the reigning Bernadotte dynasty with the former royal house of Vasa. He succeeded his father in 1907. His son **Gustaf VI** (1882-1973) was an archaeologist and expert on Chinese art. His first wife was Princess Margaret of Connaught (1882-1920), and in 1923 he m. Lady Louise Mountbatten (1889-1965), sister of Earl Mountbatten of Burma. He was succeeded by his grandson Carl XVI Gustaf (q.v.).

GUSTAVUS ADOLPHUS (1594-1632). King of Sweden. Son of Charles IX, whom he succeeded in 1611, he waged successful wars with Denmark, Russia, and Poland, and in the Thirty Years War became a champion of the Protestant cause. Landing in Germany in 1630, he defeated Wallenstein at Lützen on 6 Nov. 1632, but was killed in the battle. He was known as the 'Lion of the North'.

GUSTAVUS VASA (1496-1560). Son of a nobleman, he led the Swedish movement of independence against the Danes, and in 1523 was elected king of Sweden. Under him Lutheranism was established as the State religion.

GUTENBERG (goot'en-), **Johann** (*c.* 1400-68). German printer, considered the inventor of printing from metal movable types. B. at Mainz, he lived at Strasbourg, and about 1448 was in Mainz where, with Johann Fust as a partner, he carried on a printing business. The partnership was dissolved through monetary difficulties, but G. set up another printing press. He is believed to have printed the Mazarin and the Bamberg Bibles. *See* COSTER, LAURENS JANSZOON.

GUTHRIE, Sir Tyrone (1900-71). British man-of-the theatre. Administrator of the Old Vic and Sadler's Wells 1939-45, he helped found the Shakespeare Festival at Stratford, Ontario, 1953, and was noted for such experiments as *Hamlet* in modern dress in 1936. The T.G. theatre Minneapolis is named after him.

GUTTA-PERCHA. The coagulated juice of various tropical trees belonging to the Sapotaceae family. G.P. is similar to rubber, but is thermoplastic and when stretched will not spring back to its original shape. Its chief use is in insulating cables.

GUYANA (gē-ah'nah). Country of S America between Surinam and Venezuela. Most of the crops (sugar, rice, coconuts, coffee and fruits) are grown in the low coastal region; gold, diamonds, and bauxite are worked in an intermediate area; and the hinterland is mountain and savannah. The chief rivers - Demerara, Essequibo, and Berbice - give their names to the 3 counties into which G. is divided; chief towns are Georgetown, the cap., New Amsterdam, Springlands, and Bartica. First settled about 1620 by the Dutch West Indian Co., G. was captured by the British 1796 (formally ceded 1814), and in 1966 British Guiana became independent as Guyana. In 1970 G. was proclaimed a 'co-operative republic' within the Commonwealth. Area 210,000 sq.km (83,000 sq.m); pop. (1977) 800,000: 50% are East Indians brought in to run the sugar estates after abolition of slavery; some 30% Negroes concentrated in the towns; 5% Amerindians of the interior: and the rest Portuguese and of mixed blood. Under the constitution of 1980, there is an executive president, and a unilateral National Assembly elected by proportional representation (single list system). Party divisions tend to be racial. Forbes Burnham (1923–85), the long-serving President who was also PM 1966–80, was succeeded as President after his death by Desmond Hoyte. The ruling party is the predominantly black People's National Congress, with Ptolemy Reid as Prime Minister. The opposition People's Progressive Party (PPP), headed by Cheddi Jagan (q.v.) is chiefly Indian.

Venezuela maintains a claim to the major part of the great W co. of Essequibo, and Surinam to the New River Triangle in the SE of the E co. of Berbice.

GUYANA. President Burnham (right) examines a highyielding strain of wheat. The country aims at self-sufficiency in food production. *Photo: Courtesy of the Guyana Information Service.*

GUYS (gēs), **Constantin** (1805-92). French artist. He was with Byron at Missolonghi and during the Crimean War sent sketches to the *Illustrated London News.* His delicately realistic drawings of Parisian life, ranging from high society to the street corner, were not fully appreciated until the mid-20th cent.

GWALIOR (gwah'lior). Indian city in Madhya Pradesh, 346km (215m) NE of Bhopal. It contains Jain and Hindu monuments and was formerly in the princely state of G. Pop. (1971) 406,755.

GWENT. Co. of Wales, created in 1974 from the former co. of Monmouth, with minor border adjustments. The admin. HQ is Cwmbran. Area 1,377 sq.km (532 sq.m); pop. (1978) 438,000.

GWYN, Nell (Eleanor) (1651-87). English actress. As a girl she was an orange-seller at Drury Lane Theatre, but became an actress in 1665. Her dramatic gifts tended to low comedy, and Dryden was particularly appreciative of her talent, and wrote her suitable parts. She became the mistress of Charles II in 1669, and had 2 sons by him, the elder of whom was created duke of St. Albans in 1684. The relationship continued until Charles's death, and almost his last wish, made to the duke of York, was 'Let not poor Nellie starve'. She outlived Charles by 2 years only, and was buried at St Martin-in-the-Fields, London. She was largely instrumental in the establishment of the Royal Hospital for old soldiers at Chelsea.

GWYNEDD (gwin'eth). Co. of Wales, created in 1974 from the former cos. of Anglesey, Caernarvon, Merioneth (the major part), and small areas on the W border of Denbigh; admin. HQ is Caernarvon. Area 3,865 sq.km (1,492 sq.m); pop. (1978) 226,400.

GYMNASTICS. Performance of physical exercises to promote health, so named from Gk *gymnos*, 'naked', all ancient Greek athletics having been performed stripped and the *gymnasia* being schools for training competitors for public games. In the 19th cent. the cult was first revived since ancient times in Germany as an aid to

GWYN. A portrait of Nell Gwyn by Sir Peter Lely preserved at Raby Castle. *Photo: Mansell Collection.*

military strength, and was also taken up by educationists incl. Froebel and Pestalozzi, becoming a recognized part of the school curriculum in the present century. International competition is governed by the rules of the *Fédération Internationale de Gymnastique* (1923). Artistic merit is highly rated in modern competition, and the Russian Olga Korbut (Olympic Games 1972) popularized the new image of the sport. *See* PHYSIOTHERAPY.

GYMNOSPERMS. Plants whose seeds are not borne within a fruit. They form one of the major divisions of the flowering plants, the other being the Angiosperms, in which the ovules are enclosed in an ovary which ripens to form the fruit. Pollen is carried directly on to the gymnospermous ovule on the scale of the cone; after pollination the cone scales close until the seed is ripe. There are 3 orders: Coniferales (the pines), Cycadales, and Gnetales.

GYPSIES. A wandering folk, scattered over most parts of the world, whose name is a corruption of 'Egyptian'. The name they apply to themselves is Rom, which may be derived from Romanoi, the name assumed by the inhabitants of the Byzantine Empire in which the Gs. are believed to have originated. In the 14th cent. they crossed the Bosporus into Europe and settled in the Balkan peninsula. During the next cent. they spread over Germany, Italy, and France, and they arrived in England about 1500. A long period of persecution followed, including accusations of cannibalism and child-stealing. They are assoc. with music, various crafts, incl. fortune-telling, but their traditional skills with horses have given way to car-breaking and scrap metal dealing. Attempts have been made to encourage them to settle, and to provide those still nomadic with official camp sites and educational facilities.

The G. language, known as Romany, has relations with the Indo-Aryan group, and some of its words correspond with words in Hindustani. All the countries through which the Gs. have passed have added to their word-stock, Greek and Slavonic being the chief.

GYPSUM (jip'sum). Mineral of common occurrence, composed of hydrated calcium sulphate, $CaSO_4.2H_2O$. It has a number of commercial uses. A fine-grained G., called alabaster, is used for ornamental work, and burnt G. is known as plaster of Paris, since it was obtained for a long time from the G. quarries of the Montmartre district.

GYROSCOPE (jīr'o-). In its simplest form, a mechanical instrument consisting of a heavy wheel mounted on an axis which is fixed in a ring, which ring in turn is capable of rotation about another axis, fixed in another ring capable of rotation about a third axis. The whole is arranged so that the 3 axes of rotation in any position pass through the wheel's centre of gravity. The wheel is thus capable of rotation about 3 mutually perpendicular axes, and its axis may take up any direction. The G. is used as a stabilizing device. If the axis of the spinning wheel is displaced a restoring movement is developed which returns it to its initial direction. Important practical applications of the G. are seen in the gyro-compass, the gyropilot for automatic steering, gyro-directed torpedoes.

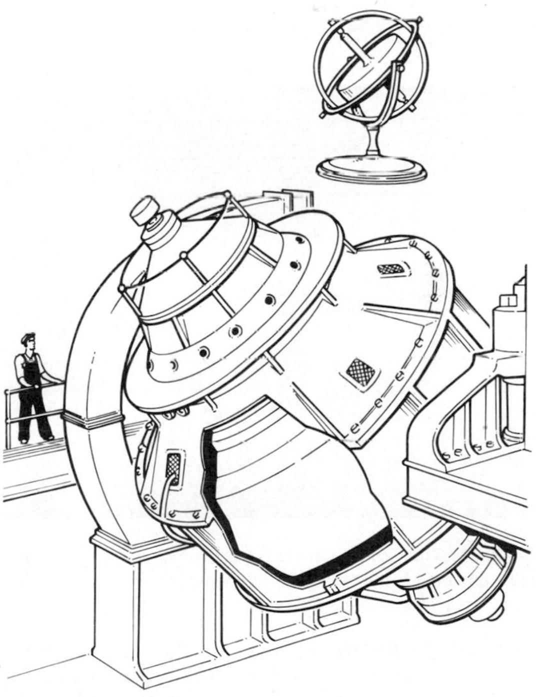

GYROSCOPE. The familiar model (top), and a huge gyroscopic ship's stabiliser.

H

Eighth letter of the Roman alphabet, representing an aspirate in all modern alphabets derived from the Latin except in those languages, especially the Romance languages, where the aspirate is lost. The 'dropping of initial h', often regarded as a corruption in modern dialects, is a phenomenon traceable at least as far back as Tudor times.

HAAKON (haw'kon) **VII** (1872-1957). King of Norway. B. Prince Charles, the 2nd son of Frederick VIII of Denmark, he m. in 1896 Princess Maud (1869-1938), youngest dau. of Edward VII of the UK. He was elected king of Norway in 1905 on the separation of that country from Sweden, and at his coronation in 1906 he took the name of H. When the Germans invaded Norway in 1940 he refused to surrender; and, when armed resistance in Norway was no longer possible, carried on the struggle from Britain until his triumphant return in 1945.

HAARLEM (hahr'lem). Town in the Netherlands, in N Holland prov., 20km (12m) W of Amsterdam. At Velsen to the N a road-rail tunnel runs under the North Sea Canal and is an important link between N and S Holland. H., a famous centre for bulbs, has also textile factories and printing works. The Frans Hals Museum is at H. Pop. (1978) 161,300.

HAARLEM. The Groote Kerk or Great Church, dedicated to St. Bavo, and built in the 15th and 16th centuries. *Photo: Courtesy of the Royal Netherlands Embassy.*

HABEAS CORPUS (hā'bēas kōr'pus) (Lat. 'have the body'). In England a writ directed to a person who has custody of a prisoner, ordering him to produce the prisoner before the court issuing the writ, and to explain why the prisoner is detained in custody. Traditional rights were enforced, mainly due to Lord Shaftesbury, under the H.C. Act (1679); the Scottish equivalent is the Wrongous Imprisonment Act (1701). The main principles were adopted in the US constitution.

HABER (hah'ber), **Fritz** (1868-1934). German chemist. His fixation of atmospheric nitrogen by producing synthetic ammonia opened the way for the synthetic fertilizer industry. In the F.W.W. he worked on poison gas, so that protests were made against his Nobel prize in 1918. He also devised gas masks.

HABSBURG or **Hapsburg.** European royal family, to which the former imperial house of Austria-Hungary belongs. The name comes from the family castle in Switzerland. The Hs. held the title of Holy Roman Emperor 1273-91, 1298-1308, 1438-1740, and 1745-1806. They ruled Austria from 1278, and in 1806 adopted the title of emperor of Austria, which they held until 1918. The archduke Otto, son of the last emperor, Charles, is the present H. pretender and became a Euro-M.P. in 1979.

HADDINGTON. Town in Lothian, Scotland, on the r. Tyne, 16km (10m) SW of Dunbar. It is the birthplace of John Knox and an agricultural centre. Pop. (1971) 6,000.

HADDINGTONSHIRE. Name until 1921 of EAST LOTHIAN.

HADDOCK. Important food fish (*Melanogrammus aeglefinus*), one of the Gadidae family of marine carnivorous fish, found off the N Atlantic coasts. H. may be eaten fresh, but split and smoked H., especially from Finnan, near Aberdeen, is a delicacy.

HĀ'DĒS. In Greek mythology the underworld where the spirits of the departed went after death, usually depicted as a cavern or pit underneath the earth. It was presided over by Pluto, and its entrance was guarded by the three-headed dog Cerberus.

HADHRAMAUT (hahdrahmawt'). District of the People's Democratic Rep. of Yemen (South Yemen), which was formerly ruled by Arab chiefs in protective relations with Britain. A plateau region at 1,400 m. (4,500 ft), it long remained unknown to westerners and attracted such travellers as H. St John Philby and Dame Freya Stark. Cereals and dates are grown by settled farmers and there are nomadic Bedouin.

HĀ'DRIAN (AD 76-138). Roman emperor. B. in Spain, he was adopted by his kinsman, the emperor Trajan, whom he succeeded in 117. He abandoned Trajan's conquests in Mesopotamia, and adopted a defensive policy which included the building of H.'s Wall in Britain.

HADRIAN'S WALL. Roman fortification built in AD 122-6 to mark the northern boundary of Britain, and abandoned c. 383. The wall runs from Wallsend on the Tyne to Bowness on the Solway, then on to Maryport (*c.* 185km/115m) and possibly farther south.

HAECKEL (ha'kel), **Ernst Heinrich** (1834-1919). German scientist and philosopher. B. at Potsdam, he became in 1865 prof. of zoology at Jena, and for more than 50 years laboured to propagate his recapitulation theory of evolution.

HAEMATITE or **HEMATITE** (hem'atīt). Ferric oxide, Fe_2O_3, a valuable iron ore, containing 70 per cent of iron and a low proportion of phosphorus.

HAEMOGLOBIN (hēmoglō'bin). The colouring matter of the red blood cells, which makes the blood red. As it carries oxygen to all the cells of the body, it is necessary to life.

HADRIAN. The Canopus pool of the Emperor's Villa at Rome, built AD 118-138. The building in the background, now a museum, was built to house Hadrian's house servants and guards. *Photo: Stephanie Dinkins/Camera Press.*

HAEMOPHILIA (hēmofil'ia). A tendency to uncontrollable bleeding through deficiency in the blood of the normal clotting substances. It is hereditary, occurs only in males, and is transmitted through the mother. A degree of control by drugs is possible, but the pain of bleeding into the joints, consequent crippling, etc., has not been eliminated. Tests can ascertain the sex of a child before birth, and affected males be aborted.

HAEMORRHAGE (hem'orij). Loss of blood from the circulation. It is 'manifest' when the blood can be seen, as when it flows from a wound, and 'occult' when the blood is lost internally, as from an ulcer or cancer of the stomach or an internal injury. The condition produced by severe haemorrhage is shock, by slow haemorrhage anaemia.

HAEMORRHOIDS (hem'oroids). *See* PILES.

HAFI'Z (*c.* 1300-88). Persian poet. B. in Shiraz, he became prof. in a Dervish college there. His fame rests on his *Diwan*, a collection of short odes, some extolling the pleasures of life, others satirizing his fellow Dervishes.

HAFNIUM. Metallic element; symbol Hf, atomic number 72, atomic weight 178.6. It was discovered by the Danish chemists D. Coster and G. von Hevesy. It occurs in zircon, and its properties and compounds resemble closely those of zirconium. It is highly absorbent of neutrons, and is used for control rods in nuclear reactors.

HAGANA'H (Heb. 'Defence'). Zionist military organization in Palestine. It originated under Turkish rule to protect Jewish settlements, and many of its members served in the British forces in both wars. After the S.W.W. it condemned terrorism, opposing the British authorities only passively. It formed the basis of the Israeli army.

HAGEN (hah'gen). Industrial centre of the Ruhr, W Germany, with iron and steel works, textile mills, etc. Pop. (1978) 224,345.

HAGENBECK (hah'gen-), **Carl** (1844-1913). German zoo proprietor. He founded in 1907 H.'s Zoo, nr. his native Hamburg, and was a pioneer in the display of animals in comparative freedom, against a natural setting.

HAG-FISH. One of the Cyclostomata (*Myxine glutinosa*), found in temperate seas and common off the E coast of Scotland. It is eel-shaped and has toothed jaws, and bores into the body of a fish on which it feeds.

HAGGADAH (hagah'da). The part of the Talmudic literature not given to religious law (the *Halacha*), but devoted to stories of heroes, folklore, etc.

HAGGAI (hag'ī). Minor OT prophet (520 BC) devoted to promoting the rebuilding of the Temple.

HA'GGARD, Sir Henry Rider (1856-1925). British novelist. B. in Norfolk, he held colonial service posts in Natal and the Transvaal 1875-9, then returned to England to read for the Bar. He turned his S African experience to good use in his romantic adventure tales *King Solomon's Mines* (1885), *She* (1887), etc.

HAGGIS. Popular Scottish dish, of ancient origin, consisting of a sheep's or calf's heart, liver, and lungs, etc., minced up with onion, oatmeal, suet, spice, pepper and salt, and boiled in the animal's stomach.

HAGUE (hāg), **The.** Seat of Govt of the Netherlands (Dutch 's-Gravenhage or Den Haag), and cap. of S Holland prov. 4km (2.5m) from the North Sea, and linked by canal and railway with Rotterdam and Amsterdam. The H. is reputed to be the richest of Dutch cities, and has many fine buildings. The H. is the seat of the UN International Court of Justice. Pop. (1978) 465,000.

Virtually incorporated in The Hague is the formerly fashionable seaside resort of **Scheveningen** (pron. skhe'veninge), patronized by Wilhelm II, Hirohito and Churchill. In the 1970s it was refurbished incl. the *fin de siècle* Kurhaus, now a nat. monument.

HAGUE. The Sovereign rides in the Golden Coach to the Knight's Hall for the State Opening of Parliament. *Photo: Thuring.*

HAHN, Kurt (1886-1974). German educationist. Founder and headmaster (1920-33) of Salem School in Germany, after his expulsion from Germany by Hitler he founded Gordonstoun (q.v.) and was headmaster 1934-53. He returned to Salem 1953, and was co-founder of the Atlantic College project (q.v.) in 1960. He was also assoc.

with the Outward Bound schools, whose mountain rescue teams, etc., incorporate his educational theories.

HAHN, Otto (1879-1968). W German physical chemist. B. at Frankfurt-am-Main, he worked with Rutherford and Ramsay, becoming director of the Kaiser-Wilhelm Inst. for Chemistry in 1928. With Strassmann (1938) he discovered nuclear fission of uranium when bombarded with neutrons, which led to the A-bomb, first used in 1945, when he received the Nobel prize for chemistry.

HAIFA (hī'fa). Principal port of Israel, on the S shore of the Bay of Acre, at the foot of Mt Carmel. It has a fine harbour, technical inst. and univ. college, and there are oil refining, chemical and cement industries. Pop. (1978) 228,000.

HAIG, Alexander Meigs (1924-). American general. Aide to Kissinger on the Nat. Security Council, he succeeded Haldeman in 1973-4 at the height of Watergate as Nixon's White House Chief of Staff, and was NATO commander 1974-9. In 1981-2 he was Sec. of State to Reagan.

HAIG, Douglas, 1st earl (1861-1928). British soldier. B. at Edinburgh, he served in the Omdurman and S African campaigns, and in the F.W.W. commanded the 1st Army Corps 1914-15, and the 1st Army in 1915 until he succeeded French as C-in-C the same year. His Somme offensive in the summer of 1916 made considerable advances only at heavy cost, and his Passchendaele offensive (July-Nov. 1917) achieved little at huge loss. He then loyally supprted Foch in his appointment as supreme commander and in his victorious 1918 offensive, and it was his foresight which persuaded Foch to extend his attack N, so breaking the Hindenburg Line. Created field marshal in 1917, and awarded the OM, an earldom, and £100,000 in 1919, he retired in 1921 and devoted himself to ex-service interests as first pres. of the British Legion. He has been stringently criticized, however, for the appalling losses on the Somme and at Passchendaele by modern historians.

HAILE SELASSIE (hī'lē sela'sē) (1891-1975). Emperor of Ethiopia. Appointed heir to the empress Zauditu in 1916, he became emperor on her death in 1930. He pleaded unavailingly to the League of Nations against Italian conquest of his country 1935-6, and lived in England until his restoration in 1941. In 1974 he was deposed by a military coup and d. in captivity.

HAILSHAM of St Marylebone, Quintin Hogg, baron (1907-). Brit. lawyer and Cons. politician. Grandson of Quintin Hogg (1845-1903), the merchant philanthropist who founded in 1882 the institution which developed into the Regent Street Polytechnic, he succeeded his father in 1950 as 2nd visct Hailsham. He renounced the title in 1963 to re-enter the Commons, but took a life peerage in 1970 on his appointment as Lord Chancellor (1970-4). He was the first Min. for Science and Technology 1959-64, and is remembered for his rallying of the party conference at Brighton in 1957 by ringing a handbell. He was again Lord Chancellor from 1979.

HAILSHAM. Market town of E Sussex, England in the Cuckmere Valley, 11km (7m) N of Eastbourne. Michelham Priory is 13th cent. Pop. (1972) 23,000.

HAINAN (hīnahn'). Large island off the Leizhou peninsula, China, in the prov. of Guangdong. The N is low-lying, the centre and S are mountainous. The rainfall is high and the valleys and coastal areas are productive, the principal crop being rice. The farmers are principally Chinese settlers, but aboriginal tribes survive in the mountains which have valuable timber resources. The chief town and port is Haikou. Area 34,000 sq.km (13,000 sq.m).

HAINAUT (hānō'). Province of SW Belgium, adjoining France. It is low-lying, drained by the Scheldt and Sambre, and crossed by several canals. There are important coalfields and much iron and steel is produced. Mons is the capital; Charleroi, Tournai, and Soignies are industrial centres. Area 3,720 sq.km (1,436 sq.m); pop. (1978) 1,318,000.

HAIPHONG (hīfong'). Chief port of N Vietnam, on an arm of the Thaibinh r. delta, near the Gulf of Tonkin, 96km (60m) ESE of Hanoi. It has shipyards and cement and textile factories, and is also a naval station. Pop. (1976) 1,443,500.

HAIR. A fine structure proceeding from the skin and consisting of a root which is embedded in the follicle, a cavity in the second layer (true skin); and a shaft composed of horny material. A H. grows from the root, and consists of 3 layers: the cuticle (outer), cortex (middle), and core (inner). The colouring matter is in the 2 outer layers. The Hs. of different species of animals differ and are distinguishable under the microscope. Most diseases of H. are due to faulty nourishment or pests, e.g. ringworm.

The care and arrangement of the H. has been of social importance from the most ancient times, cf. the elaborate hairstyles of ancient Egypt and Assyria, and among the most primitive tribes. The H. may indicate age-group (the Victorian girl was adult once her hair was 'up'), marital status (African tribes), political allegiance (Roundheads and Cavaliers), rank (the styles, up to 60cm (2ft) high, developed among the 18th cent. aristocracy of France, and imported to England, mourning (the shaven heads of ancient Greeks and Hebrews), disgrace (women collaborators in the S.W.W. were often shaven by their compatriots), religious vocation (the tonsure of the RC and E Orthodox Churches), or social attitudes (the long hair of the 'drop-out' of the 1960s as opposed to the 'short-back-and-sides' of the conventionally conforming). The modern western styles for women, increasingly adopted throughout the world, tend to daytime simplicity, with avoidance of any 'crimping' in the permanent waving (often replaced by special methods of cutting), and more elaborate evening creations made feasible by 'lacquers' or sprays, and often supplemented by nylon or real hair 'switches', etc. Besides semi-permanent and permanent 'rinses', there are hair dyes of every colour - blue, pink, orange, and green often being used by punk rockers in the 1970s-80s - and, for complete transformation, full wigs.

HAIRSTREAKS. Group of butterflies (q.v.), belonging to the Blues (Lycaenidae), and represented in both temperate and tropical regions. Most of them are brownish in their adult form, and they are nearly all tailed.

HAITI (hā'ti). Republic in the western part of the West Indian island of Hispaniola. Ceded to France by Spain in 1697, it gained independence in 1804 under Dessalines (q.v.), who was followed by a colourful series of 'monarchs', until H. became a republic in 1859: H. embraced the whole island 1821-44 (*see* DOMINICAN REPUBLIC). H. was occupied by the USA 1915-34.

H. is mountainous, but well-wooded with fertile plains. Hurricanes are frequent. The economy is agricultural, the chief crops being coffee, sugar, sisal, cotton, cocoa, rice and maize. There are bauxite, copper and other varied minerals. Industries incl. textiles, soap, cement, pharmaceuticals and plastics. The cap. is Port au Prince.

Under the revised constitution of 1964, there is a pres. and single-chamber legislature. François Duvalier (q.v.) ("Papa Doc") came to power in 1957, and was succeeded in 1971 by his son Jean-Claude Duvalier ("Baby Doc"), who moderated the activities of, but continued to use, the notorious private army, the National Security Volunteers (VSN), created by his father in 1958. Both regimes were accused of major violations of human rights and of rule by terror. "Baby Doc" hurriedly fled the country in Feb. 1986, and was replaced by a government headed by Gen. Henry Namphy. The official language is French – spoken by the mulatto bourgeoisie – but the 90% Negro majority speak the Créole dialect. There is acute racial tension between the two groups and political plots are frequent. Area 27,740 sq.km (10,710 sq.m); pop. (1978) 5,500,000. M.U.: gourde.

HAITI. A voodoo ceremony, the bitten lips and clenched fists of the girl dancer showing the tension reached as the participants strive to reach the semi-conscious state in which the gods speak to them. *Photo: Guido Mangold/Camera Press.*

HAKE. Important food fish (*Merluccius vulgaris*) of the Gadidae family, found in N European and N American waters. Its silvery, elongated body attains *c.* 1m (3ft).

HAKLUYT (hak'loot), **Richard** (*c.* 1553-1616). English geographer. B. in London, he entered the Church and became archdeacon of Westminster in 1603. H. lectured on cartography at Oxford, became geographical adviser to the E India Co., and was an original member of the Virginia Co. His chief work is his great compilation, *The Principal Navigations, Voyages and Discoveries of the English Nation* (1589-1600), in which he was assisted by Raleigh.

The *Hakluyt Society* (founded in 1846) pub. original accounts of journeys and geog. records.

HAKODATE (hahkōdah'teh). Japanese city on the S coast of Hokkaido island. It has an excellent harbour. Pop. (1977) 311,000.

HALDANE, Richard Burdon, visct. (1856-1928). British Liberal statesman. As Sec. for War 1905-12, he sponsored the army reforms which estab. an expeditionary force, backed by a territorial army, and under the unified control of an imperial general staff. He was Lord Chancellor 1912-15 and in the Labour govt of 1924. His writings on German philosophy led to popular accusations of his being pro-German.

HALE, Nathan (1755-76). American patriot. Hanged by the British as a spy in the War of Independence, he is remembered for his final words: 'I regret that I have but one life to give for my country'.

HALE, Sarah Josepha Buell (1788-1879). American poetess, author of 'Mary had a Little Lamb' (1830).

HALÉVY, Ludovic (1834-1908). French author and librettist. He collaborated with Hector Crémieux in the libretto for Offenbach's *Orpheus in the Underworld*; and with Henri Meilhac in those for the same composer's *La Belle Hélène* and *La Vie Parisienne*, and for Bizet's *Carmen*. His best novel is *L'Abbé Constantin* (1882).

HALF-LIFE. The time in which the strength of a radioactive source decays to half its original value. It may vary from millionths of a second to thousands of millions of years.

HALF-TONE. A device used in printing by which the intensity of a printed colour can be varied from full strength to the lightest shades, although only one colour of ink and one of paper is used.

The picture to be reproduced is photographed through a screen ruled with a rectangular mesh of fine lines, which breaks up the tones of the original into dots which vary in size according to the intensity of the tone. In the darker shades the dots are large and run together, in the lighter shades they are small and separate.

In the same way, colour pictures are broken down into a pattern of dots, the original being photographed through a number of colour filters. These are then printed in sequence, yellow, magenta (blue-red), cyan (blue-green) and black, which combine to give the full colour range.

HALIBUT. Valuable food fish (*Hippoglossus hippoglossus*) of the family Pleuronectidae. Largest of the flat fish, it may reach over 2m (6ft) and weigh 90-135kg (2-300lb), and is very dark mottled brown or green above and pure white beneath. It prefers the colder seas from the English Channel to the Arctic.

HALICARNA'SSUS. Ancient city of Asia Minor. The tomb of Mausolus, built *c.* 350 BC by widowed Queen Artemisia, was one of the 7 wonders of the world. Herodotus was born here.

HALIFAX, Charles Montagu, earl of (1661-1715). English financier. Appointed Commissioner of the Treasury in 1692, he raised money for the French war by instituting the National Debt, and in 1694 carried out William Paterson's plan for a national bank (the Bank of England), and became Chancellor of the Exchequer. In 1695 he reformed the currency and issued the first 'Exchequer Bills', and in 1696 inaugurated the Consolidated Fund, used to pay interest on foreign loans. He was created a baron in 1700, and at the accession of George I became again 1st Lord of the Treasury and was made an earl.

HALIFAX, Edward Frederick Lindley Wood, 1st earl of H. (1881-1959). British Cons. statesman. Son of the 2nd visct H., he succeeded Reading as Viceroy of India (1926-31) and did much to further independence. As For. Sec. 1938-40 he was assoc. with 'appeasement', and when in line to succeed Neville Chamberlain as premier tacitly stood aside in favour of Churchill. He received an earldom in 1944 for services to the Allied cause while ambassador to the USA 1941-6, and the OM in 1946.

HALIFAX, George Savile, 1st marquess of (1633-95). English statesman. He entered parliament in 1660, and was raised to the peerage by Charles II. He strove to steer a middle course between extremists, and became known as 'the trimmer'. He played a prominent part in the revolution of 1688.

HALIFAX. Capital city of Nova Scotia, and Canada's chief winter port. Founded in 1749, it has a fine harbour and is a naval station with dock and shipyards. Industries include lumber, foundries, and sugar refineries. It is the terminus of the 2 great transcontinental railways. Pop. met. area (1976) 117,880.

HALIFAX. Town in W Yorks, England, on the Hebble. The leading industry is woollen textiles. Notable are the parish church in Perpendicular Gothic, and the 18th cent. Piece Hall, once a cloth market and adapted 1979 for more varied use. Pop. (1972) 90,320.

HALITŌ'SIS. Offensive breath. It may be due to dirty teeth, disease of the mouth, throat, nose, or lungs, or disturbance of the digestion.

HALL, Sir Peter Reginald Frederick (1930-). British theatre director. One of the liveliest minds of the British stage, he was in 1960-8 director of the Royal Shakespeare Theatre at Stratford and developed the Royal Shakespeare Co. as director from 1968 until appointed director of the Nat. Theatre in 1973, in succession to Olivier. His striking productions incl. *Waiting for Godot* (1955), *The Wars of the Roses* (1963), and *The Homecoming* (stage 1967 and film 1973).

HALLAM, Henry (1777-1859). British historian. He was called to the Bar, but a private fortune enabled him to devote himself to historical study from 1812 and his *Constitutional History of England* (1827) estab. his reputation. His eldest son, the poet Arthur Henry H. (1811-33), was commemorated by Tennyson in the elegiac *In Memoriam*.

HALLÉ Town in E Germany, cap. of H. district, on the Saale, 32km (20m) NW of Leipzig. Varied industries incl. the production of salt from brine springs, and lignite is mined. The univ. was founded 1964. Pop. (1978) 231,480.

HALLEY, Edmund (1656-1742). English astronomer. B. in London, he became friendly with Sir Isaac Newton, whose *Principia* he financed. He is remembered as having observed H.'s Comet in 1682 and for accurately predicting (in 1704) that it would reappear in 1759. He was Astronomer Royal from 1720.

HALLMARK. Instituted in 1300 for the prevention of fraud, Hs. are in the UK the official marks stamped on gold, silver and (from 1973) platinum wares. Tests are carried out by authorised Assay Offices at Goldsmiths' Hall, London, Birmingham, Sheffield and Edinburgh, which each have their distinguishing mark, to which is added a maker's mark, date letter and mark guaranteeing the standard. In 1975 an internat. H., accepted as alternative to individual nat. Hs. by participating countries, was introduced, comprising a responsibility mark (name or symbol of the article's sponsor); fineness mark, incorporated in the common control mark, and an assay office mark. Standards of quality are expressed in parts per thousand of pure (fine) gold, silver or platinum in a thousand parts of alloy. *See also* CARAT.

HALLOWE'EN. The evening of 31 Oct., immediately preceding Hallowmas or All Saints' Day, the Christian festival kept in honour of all the saints. Many of the customs associated with the festival date back to pre-Christian days.

	Standard of Fineness	*Fineness Mark*
Gold	750 parts per thousand	750
	585 " " "	585
	375 " " "	375
Silver	925 " " "	925
	830 " " "	830
	800 " " "	800
Platinum	950 " " "	950

HALLMARK. The standards of fineness in the international system, and (above) the symbols for gold, silver and platinum.

HALLSTATT (hahl'shtaht). Village in Upper Austria, 48km (30m) SW of Salzburg. The salt workings date from prehistoric times, and there have been distinctive archaeological finds, notably in a cemetery of more than 3,000 graves discovered in 1846, of a transitional Celtic civilization - between the Bronze and Iron Ages - known as the H. culture, 9th-5th cent. B.C.

HALS (hahls), **Frans** (1580/81-1666). Dutch portrait and genre painter. B. at Antwerp, he was carefree and irresponsible, and some of his best-known pictures are of tavern scenes. Though some would place him next to Rembrandt for his skill as a portrait painter, others have criticized him for his lack of insight in delineating character. In his ability to seize and set down a passing mood he anticipated the French Impressionists. His principal works are at Haarlem, but his famous 'Laughing Cavalier' is in the Wallace Collection, London.

HALSEY, William Frederick (1882-1959). American admiral. Entering the navy in 1905, he was appointed to command of the Third Fleet in the S Pacific in 1942 and compelled the Japanese to withdraw 1943-4. On his flagship, the *Missouri*, the Japanese signed the surrender document ending the S.W.W.

HAMBLEDON. English village in SE Hants, famous in the history of cricket. In its prime the original H. cricket club was strong enough to beat any other team in England; its last important match was at Lord's in 1793, and it was disbanded in 1796. It played on Broadhalfpenny Down until *c.* 1782 then on Windmill Down. A H. cricket club continued to exist after the disbandment of the famous one.

HAMBURG. W. German city and major European port, cap. of H. Land, with which it is contiguous, on the right bank of the Elbe estuary at the head of tidal navigation, 120km (75m) from the N Sea. Industries incl. shipbuilding, engineering, and food processing.

H. was an archbishopric from 834. From its alliance with Lübeck in 1241 the Hanseatic League arose. In 1510 the emperor Maximilian I created it a free imperial city, and in 1871 it became a state of the German Empire. During the S.W.W. it was the target of concentrated air attacks. There is a univ. (1919) and the H. Schauspielhaus is one of the rep.'s leading theatres.

The *hamburger* (chopped beef and seasoning fried as a flattened round) is said to have been invented by the medieval Tartar invaders of the Baltic area. Sailors from H. took the idea home, but although naturalized in the 19th cent. in the USA by German immigrants, the H. dropped out of use in Germany until reintroduced in the 1960s via England.

The LAND OF HAMBURG consists of the city and surrounding districts. Area 756 sq.km (292 sq.m); pop. (1978) 1,680,340.

HAMBURG. On the 'Reeperbahn', the 'Grosse Freiheit' and other streets and alleys of the amusement district of St Pauli, are the city's dance halls, casinos, bars and clubs. *Photo: Courtesy of Lufthansa.*

HAMELN (hah'meln). Town on the Weser, W Germany, 40km (25m) SW of Hanover. Buildings of interest include the Rattenfängerhaus (rat-catcher's house) and the minster. The town is famous for the Pied Piper legend. Pop. (1978) 64,000.

HAMERSLEY RANGE. Range of hills above the H. Plateau, in Western Australia, c. 275 km (170 m) long and remarkable for its coloured rocks and picturesque river (Ashburton and Fortescue) gorges. There are rich iron reserves.

HAMI'LCAR BARCA (*c.* 270-228 BC). Carthaginian general, father of Hannibal. From 247 to 241 he harassed the Romans in Italy, and then led an expedition to Spain where he d. in battle.

HAMILTON, Alexander (1757-1804). American statesman. B. in the W Indies, he served during the War of Independence as captain and from 1777 to 1781 was Washington's secretary and aide-de-camp. After the war he practised as a lawyer. He was a member of the Constitutional Convention of 1787, and in the *Federalist* influenced public opinion in favour of the ratification of the constitution. H. was Sec. of the Treasury, 1789-95, and proved an able controller of the national finances. He led the Federal Party, and incurred the bitter hatred of Aaron Burr when he cast the deciding vote against Burr and in favour of Jefferson for the presidency in 1801. Eventually he fought a duel with Burr, was wounded, and died the next day.

HAMILTON, Lady (Emma) (*c.* 1765-1815). British courtesan. *Née* Amy Lyon the dau. of a Cheshire blacksmith, she obtained employment in London, and in 1782 became the mistress of Charles Greville, and in 1786 of his uncle Sir William Hamilton (1730-1803), the British envoy at Naples. She at once became a leading figure in the society of Naples, and Hamilton married her in 1791. After Nelson's return from the Nile in 1798 she became well known as his mistress and her dau. by him, Horatia, was b. in 1801. After the death of Hamilton and Nelson, Lady H. was imprisoned for debt, but later escaped to Calais where she d. in poor circumstances.

HAMILTON, Iain Ellis (1922-). Scottish composer. Glasgow-born, he worked as an aircraft engineer 1939-46, and studied at the RAM 1947-51. Intensely emotional and harmonically rich, his works incl. the striking viola and 'cello sonatas, a ballet (*Clerk Saunders*), the *Pharsalia* cantata, and symphonies. His opera *The Royal Hunt of the Sun* (1977) renounced melody for inventive chordal formations.

HAMILTON, Sir Ian (1853-1947). Scottish soldier. He was chief-of-staff and deputy to Lord Kitchener, C-in-C, in the S African War. In 1914 he was C-in-C of the Home Defence Army and in 1915 he directed the land operations in Gallipoli. He had become a full general in 1914.

HAMILTON, James Hamilton, 1st duke of (1606-49). Scottish royalist. He acted as Charles I's adviser on Scottish affairs and in 1639 commanded an army against the Covenanters. Subsequently he took part in the negotiations between Charles and the Scots. During the 2nd Civil War he led the Scottish invasion of England, but was captured at Preston and executed.

HAMILTON, Sir William Rowan. *See* QUATERNIONS.

HAMILTON. Town in Strathclyde, Scotland, nr the Clyde, 16km (10m) SE of Glasgow. Industries incl. textiles, engineering, etc. Pop. (1971) 46,375.

HAMILTON. City and port in Ontario, Canada, at the western extremity of Lake Ontario, to which it is linked by the Burlington Canal (1830), and 65km (40m) W of Niagara Falls, with a large hydro-electric plant. More than half Canada's steel is produced here, so that it is nicknamed Steel City, and there are heavy machinery, electrical, chemical, and textile industries. McMaster Univ. has an outstanding medical centre, and there is a Philharmonic Orchestra and Art Gallery. Pop. met. area (1976) 529,370.

HAMILTON. Town on the Waikato river, near the W coast of North Island, New Zealand. Waikato Univ. was estab. here 1964. It is an increasingly important industrial centre. Pop. met. area (1976) 154,600.
HAMILTON. Cap. of Bermuda, on Bermuda Island. Pop. (1970) 3,000.
HAMITE (ham'īt). Member of an African group of peoples (so-called from their traditional descent from Ham, the son of Noah), incl. the ancient Egyptians, and the modern Berbers of N Africa and Tuareg of the Sudan. The Hamitic languages are related to the Semitic. *See* LANGUAGES.
HAMM. Town on the r. Lippe, North Rhine-Westphalia, W. Germany. There are coal mines, chemical and engineering industries, and large rail marshalling yards, frequently bombed in the S.W.W. Pop. (1971) 71,500.
HAMMARSKJOLD (ha'mershold), **Dag** (1905-61). 'World civil servant.' Son of a Swedish PM, he was Sec.-Gen. of UN 1953-8. He dealt with the Suez Crisis (1956) in which he opposed Britain, and his attempts to solve the problem of the Congo (now Zaïre), where he was killed in a plane crash, were attacked by the Soviet Union.
HAMMERFEST. Town on Kvalö island off the NW coast of Norway; the northernmost town of Europe. Fishing is carried on, and there are canning industries. Pop. (1973) 5,200.
HAMMERHEAD. Several species of shark in the genus *Sphyrna*, characterized by a hammer-shaped head, and found in tropical seas. The eyes are at the ends of the double-headed 'hammer'.
HAMMERSTEIN, Oscar. *See* RODGERS, RICHARD.
HAMMETT, Dashiell (1894-1961). American crime-novelist, a pioneer of the tough-guy school, who had himself been a 'private eye'. His best books were *The Maltese Falcon* (1930) and *The Thin Man* (1932).
HAMMOND, Dame Joan (1912-). Australian soprano. She studied both violin and singing in Sydney, and was a fine athlete and golfer. A concert artist, she also sang in oratorio and opera, e.g. *Madame Butterfly, Tosca* and *Martha*.
HAMMURABI (hamoōrah'be). King of Babylon (reigned *c.* 1792-50 BC) of the 1st or Amorite dynasty. He expelled the Elamites and united the country, but is best remembered for his legal code, a consolidation of material already traditional, which survives in several copies: the punishments are bloodthirsty.
HAMPDEN, John (*c.* 1594-1643). English statesman. The son of a wealthy landowner, he was b. at Great Hampden, Bucks, sat in the parliaments of 1621, 1625, and 1626, and became conspicuous when in 1627 he was imprisoned for refusing to pay a forced loan. His refusal in 1636 to pay Ship Money made him a national figure. In the Short and Long parliaments he proved himself a skilful debater and parliamentary strategist. Charles's attempt to arrest him and four other leading MPs made war inevitable. He raised his own regiment on the outbreak of hostilities, and on 18 June 1643 was mortally wounded at the skirmish of Chalgrove Field.
HAMPSHIRE. Co. of southern England lying W of Sussex on the English Channel. It is crossed by the downs, on which sheep are reared, and on lower ground wheat, hay, fodder crops, and fruit are grown and cattle pastured. The chief rivers are the Test, Itchen, and Avon. The admin. HQ is Winchester and other important towns are the port of Southampton, and the naval ports of Portsmouth and Gosport. There are large oil refineries at Fawley. The New Forest is in the SW of the co. In the local govt reorganization of 1974, H. lost a small area to the SW incl. Bournemouth and Christchurch to Dorset. Area 3,772 sq.km (1,456 sq.m); pop. (1978) 1,453,400.
HAMPSTEAD. Locality in the bor. of Camden, Greater London. Famous for its picturesque village atmosphere, it is fashionable and expensive, and reaches 135m (443ft) a.s.l. in parts. **H. Heath** is a noted open-air resort; **H. Garden Suburb** originated 1907.
HAMPTON COURT PALACE. Palace erected in H.C. Park, on the N bank of the Thames, in the Greater London bor. of Richmond-upon-Thames, England, by Cardinal Wolsey in the early 16th cent. In 1526 he presented it to Henry VIII, who added the chapel and the Great Hall. The later additions made by Wren for William III included the Fountain Court, and the E and S fronts.

HAMPTON COURT PALACE. A remarkable cloud formation, cumulonimbus capillatus or 'hairy' cumulonimbus, above the Renaissance front designed by Sir Christopher Wren. *Photo: G.Nicholson/Meteorological Office.*

HAMSTER. The H. (*Cricetus frumentarius*) of Europe and N Asia is the typical member of the cricetine group of rodents. The thickset body is about 30cm (1ft) long incl. the tail, and the fur usually golden-brown above and darker below. It excavates cleanly kept and complex chambered burrows which may be up to 2m (6ft) deep in winter, when it hibernates. It is prolific.
HAMSUN (hahm'soon), **Knut** (1859-1952). Norwegian novelist. The son of a farmer, he suffered from poverty, twice emigrating to the US, and his novel *Sult* (1890: *Hunger*) had a terrible truth which at once made him famous. Of his later books *Growth of the Soil* (1917), after which he received a Nobel prize, in 1920, was the best. His ideas were in sympathy with Nazism in some respects and in 1946 he was fined for collaboration.
HANCOCK, John (1737-93). American politician. He was the first to sign the Declaration of Independence, and his name is often used as the equivalent of 'a signature'. He was later gov. of Massachusetts.
HANCOCK, Tony (1924-68). British radio and television comedian. In 'Hancock's Half Hour', etc., he was the little man whose romantic ideas and schemes were always at odds with everyday life.

HANDBALL. Ball game current in three versions: English fives (q.v.), indoor fourwall, and field handball (a German outdoor version). The rules have elements of ice hockey, basketball and volleyball: there are 7 members to a team and possession of the ball is limited to 3 secs. and 3 steps.

HA'NDEL, George Frederick (1685-1759). German-born composer, who became a British subject in 1726. B. at Halle, he abandoned the study of law at the univ. in 1703, to become a violinist at Keiser's Opera House in Hamburg, where his first opera *Almira* was performed in 1705. Visits to Italy (1706-10) inspired a number of operas and oratorios, and in 1711 his opera *Rinaldo* was performed in London. Appointed Kapellmeister to the elector of Hanover in 1709, he took French leave in 1712 to settle in England, and was for a time in disgrace when the elector succeeded as George I in 1714. However, he wrote for him in 1715 the 'Water Music' and from 1720 directed the opera at the King's Theatre, Haymarket. The rivalry of the fashionable Italian composer Bononcini, and Gay's ridicule in *The Beggar's Opera* (1728), led him to abandon Italianate opera for English oratorio. *Saul* and *Israel in Egypt* (both 1739) were unsuccessful, but his masterpiece *Messiah* was acclaimed on its first performance in Dublin in 1742 and maintains unrivalled popularity. His great contribution is to choral music, later oratorios incl. *Samson* (1744), *Belshazzar* (1745), *Judas Maccabaeus* (1747) and *Jephtha* (1752). From 1751 he became totally blind, and throughout his career suffered financial difficulty.

HANDLEY, Tommy (1896-1949). British comedian. B. in Liverpool, he became famous for his immensely popular radio programme 'ITMA' (It's That Man Again) with its catch-phrases, e.g. 'After you, Claud', and such characters as 'Mrs Mop' and 'Mona Lot'; it ran from 1939 till his death.

HANGCHOW'. *See* HANGZHOU.

HANGING. Suspension by the neck usually with a noose. The base of the tongue is forced into the back of the throat and blocks the air passages; the large blood-vessels supplying the brain are shut off and the vagus nerve and carotid arteries are compressed, causing the heart to stop. Unconsciousness and death therefore follow very quickly. In judicial hanging the condemned person is allowed to drop c. 2m (6ft) so that the powerful jerk of the tightened rope breaks his neck.

HANGZHOU (hahngjow'). Cap. and port (formerly Hangchow) of Zhejiang prov., China, at the mouth of the Fuchun Jiang, and southern terminus of the Grand Canal. Under the Sung Dynasty it was the cap. of China (1127-1278), and today has 2 univs. founded in 1927 and 1959. There are jute, chemical, tea and silk industries. Pop. (1970) 1,100,000.

HANKOW. *See* WUHAN.

HANLEY. *See* STOKE-ON-TRENT.

HANNIBAL (247-182 BC). Carthaginian general, the son of Hamilcar Barca (q.v.). Chosen as general by the army in 221 he besieged Saguntum (in Spain) in 219, whereupon the Romans declared war on Carthage. H. then fought a brilliant campaign in Italy, culminating in his victory at Cannae (216). However, he failed to capture Rome, and after spending some years in S Italy was recalled to Carthage in 203 to meet a Roman invasion which culminated in H.'s defeat at Zama (202). He then became head of the Carthaginian government, but was exiled in

HANDEL. A portrait by Thomas Hudson, 1756. *Photo: National Portrait Gallery.*

196 at the wish of the Romans, fleeing to the court of Antiochus in Asia Minor. He poisoned himself in Bithynia to avoid extradition to Rome.

HANOI (hanō'i). Cap. of Vietnam, on the Red r., c. 130km (80m) from the Gulf of Tonkin, a trade and communications centre, with an airport. Captured by the French in 1873, it was the cap. of French Indochina 1902-40, and was finally evacuated in 1954. Industries incl. textiles, paper, engineering. Hanoi Univ. was founded 1918, and a polytechnic univ. (1965). Pop. (1976) 1,443,500.

HA'NŌVER. W. German city, at the junction of the Leine and Ihme, capital of the Land of Lower Saxony. It is an important river and canal port with a noted institute of technology and many industries, incl. the making of machinery, vehicles, electrical equipment, rubber, textiles, chocolate, biscuits, tobacco; and petroleum refining. The seat of a Lutheran bp., it is first mentioned in 1163, was chartered 1241, passed to Brunswick 1369, joined the Hanseatic League 1386. Pop. (1978) 542,200.

From 1692 H. was the cap. of the former electorate (after 1815, kingdom) of H. George Louis, elector of H., great-grandson of James I, became king of the UK in 1714, and the ruler of the 2 countries was the same person until Victoria's accession in 1837 when H., where a woman could not hold the throne, passed to her uncle Ernest Augustus, duke of Cumberland. His son, George V of H., was forced by Bismarck to abdicate in 1866, H. becoming a prov. of Prussia. In 1946 H. was merged with Brunswick and Oldenburg to form the Land of Lower Saxony.

HANSARD. Name given to the official report of the proceedings of the British parliament. Luke H. commenced printing the *House of Commons Journal* in 1774, but the first 'official' reports were pub. from 1803 by Cobbett, who during his imprisonment of 1810-12 sold the business to his printer, Thomas Curson H., son of Luke H. The publication of the debates remained in the hands of the family until 1889, and is now the responsibility of the Stationery Office. The name H. was officially adopted 1943.

HANSEATIC (hansēat'ik) **LEAGUE.** A medieval confederation of N German trading cities. The earliest association had its headquarters at Wisby; it included over 30 cities, but was gradually supplanted by that headed by Lübeck. Hamburg and Lübeck estab. their own trading-stations in London in 1266 and 1267 respectively, which coalesced in 1282 with that of Cologne to form the so-called Steelyard. There were 3 other such stations: Bruges, Bergen, and Novgorod. At its height in the later 14th cent. the H.L. included over 70 towns, among them Lübeck, Hamburg, Cologne, Breslau, and Cracow. The basis of its power was its monopoly of the Baltic trade and its relations with Flanders and England.

The decline of the H.L. from the 15th cent. onwards was due to the movement of trade routes, and to the development of national states. The last general assembly (1669) marks the end of the League.

HANSEATIC LEAGUE. A reconstruction of the famous 'Cog of Bremen', excavated from the river Weser in 1962. This new type of merchant vessel developed c.1200 and played a major role in the rise of the Hanseatic League. *Photo: Courtesy of the Focke Museum, Bremen.*

HANSOM, Joseph Aloysius (1803-82). British architect. His works incl. the town hall of Birmingham (1831), but he is remembered as the introducer of the H. cab in 1834.

HANUMAN (ha'noomahn). The monkey god and king of Hindustan. He assisted Rama to recover his wife Sita, abducted by Ravana of Lanka (modern Sri Lanka).

HANWAY, Jonas (1712-86). British traveller - he wrote of his experiences in Persia - and advocate of prison reform. He is believed to have been the first Englishman to carry an umbrella.

HANYANG. *See* WUHAN.

HAPSBURG. *See* HABSBURG.

HARA-KIRI (harahkir'i). Form of suicide by disembowelment still sometimes practised in Japan, usually to avoid capture or other ignominy. It dates back to the Middle Ages and was widely practised by the Japanese forces during the S.W.W. It is more correctly called *seppuku*.

HARA'PPA. Archaeological site in Pakistan with remains of the Indus Valley Civilization (q.v.). Of the series of great mounds, the most important is the Citadel - the ramparts still risng 15m (50ft) above the level of the plain - which Sir Mortimer Wheeler identified in 1946.

HARAR (hahrahr'). Chief town of H. prov. in E Ethiopia. An ancient walled city, H. is the Moslem centre of Ethiopia. Pop. (1974) 53,560.

HARARE (hahrah'rā). Cap. (formerly Salisbury) of Zimbabwe, on the Mashonaland plateau *c.* 1,525 m (5,000 ft) a.s.l. It is the centre of a rich farming area (tobacco and maize), with tobacco, metallurgical, food processing and other industries, and is a hub of communications and commerce, with an internat. airport. Pop. (1980) 654,000.

HARBIN. Cap of Heilongjiang prov., China, on the Sungari. A railway and river centre, it makes machinery, linen, etc. Its growth began with the opening of the Chinese Eastern Railway in 1897. Pop. (1977) 2,100,000.

HARCOURT, Sir William Vernon (1827-1904). British Lib. statesman. Under Gladstone he was Home Sec. 1880-5, and Chancellor of the Exchequer 1886 and 1892-5. He was disappointed in his hopes to succeed him as PM. He is remembered for his remark in 1892: 'We are all Socialists now.'

HARDICANUTE (hahr'dikanūt') (*c.* 1019-42). King of England. The son of Canute, he ascended the throne in 1040 and was a harsh ruler.

HARDIE, James Keir (1856-1915). British socialist. B. in Lanarks, he worked in the mines as a boy, and in 1886 became Sec. of the Scottish Miners' Federation. In 1888 he was the 1st Labour candidate to stand for Parliament and was a chief founder of the ILP in 1893. A pacifist, he desperately opposed the Boer War, and the flame of his idealism in his work for socialism and the unemployed made his name a legend: he was MP for West Ham 1892-5 and for Merthyr Tydfil from 1900.

HARDING, Warren Gamaliel (1865-1923). 29th President of the USA. B. in Ohio, he entered the US Senate in 1914 as a Republican, and opposed the Peace Treaty of 1919. In 1920 he was elected President of the USA. He concluded the peace treaties of 1921 with Germany, Austria, and Hungary, and in the same year called the Washington Conference. After the conference there were charges of corruption among members of his Cabinet.

HARDING OF PETHERTON, John, 1st baron (1896-). British field marshal. Chief-of-staff to Alexander in Italy in the S.W.W., he was C-in-C BAOR 1951-2, and CIGS 1952-5. As Gov. of Cyprus 1955-7, during part of the period of terrorism and political agitation prior to independence (1960) he was responsible for the controversial deportation of Makarios (q.v.) from Cyprus in 1955, and for the reorganization of the security forces to combat the Eoka terrorists.

HARDWAR (hurdwahr'). Indian town in Uttar Pradesh, on the right bank of the Ganges, one of the holy places of the Hindu religion and a pilgrimage centre. The

Kumbhmela festival, held every twelfth year in honour of Siva, is the most important and attracts some million pilgrims. The name means door of Hari (or Vishnu). Pop. (1971) 70,000.

HARDY, Thomas (1840-1928). British poet and novelist. B. nr Dorchester in the heart of the 'Wessex' which was to form the background of his novels, he was trained as an architect. His first success was *Far From the Madding Crowd* (1874), followed among others by *The Return of the Native* (1878), *The Mayor of Casterbridge* (1886) and *The Woodlanders* (1887) - all remarkable for the background contrast of richly humorous rustic characters, and the brooding intensity of human loves and hates played out before the onrush of the harshly indifferent force that H. believed governs the world. *Tess of the D'Urbervilles* (1891) - subtitled 'A Pure Woman' - outraged public opinion by portraying as its heroine a woman who had been seduced, and the even greater outcry which followed *Jude the Obscure* (1895) helped to reinforce H.'s decision to confine himself to verse. Beginning with *Wessex Poems* (1898), he pub. several vols. of lyrics and a gigantic blank-verse panorama of the Napoleonic wars, *The Dynasts* (1904-8). In 1910 he was awarded the OM.

HARDY. Thomas Hardy valued his poetry more than his novels, but it is still primarily as a novelist that he is remembered. *Photo: Keystone.*

HARDY, Sir Thomas Masterman (1769-1839). British sailor. He entered the navy in 1781, and at Trafalgar was Nelson's flag-captain in the *Victory*, attending him during his dying moments. He was promoted rear-admiral in 1825, and became 1st Sea Lord in 1830.

HARE. Lagomorph of the family Leporidae, incl. the species not classified as rabbits. The common H. (*Lepus europaeus*) is found in England, and southern and central Europe and the smaller blue or mountain H. (*L. timidus*) in Scotland and Scandinavia. The H. is found in most parts of the world and those of the very north, the polar (*L. arcticus*) and Greenland (*L. groenlandicus*) Hs., turn white in winter. *See* COURSING.

HAREBELL. Wild flower (*Campanula rotundifolia*), sometimes called the bluebell of Scotland. It bears a group of blue bell-shaped flowers on a stem, with heart-shaped leaves at the base, and is found in the N of the northern hemisphere, the Rockies, and Sierra Nevada.

HARE-LIP. A deformity of the face consisting of a cleft in the upper lip and jaw. The cause is failure of union between the right and left sections of the jaw. The cleft may extend back into the palate. Surgery and re-education can often prove a remedy.

HAREWOOD (har'wood), **George Henry Hubert Lascelles,** 7th earl of H. (1923-). The elder son of the 6th earl and HRH Princess Mary, the Princess Royal, he served in the Grenadier Guards in the S.W.W. and was a POW 1944-5. A patron of music, he ed. the magazine *Opera* 1950-3 and was in 1961-5 artistic director of the Edinburgh Festival. His brother, **Gerald David Lascelles** (1924-), is an ardent supporter of jazz.

HARFLEUR (ahrflör'). Port on the N side of the Seine estuary, Seine-Maritime dept, France. During the Middle Ages it was leading port of NW France. Pop. (1976) 11,000.

HARGEISA (hahrgās'a). Second-largest town of the Somali Rep., connected by air service to Aden and Asmara and by highway to Berbera and Addis Ababa. Pop. (1976) 60,000.

HARGRAVES, Edmund Hammond (1815-91). British discoverer of the Australian goldfields. B. in Hants, he found gold in the Blue Hills of NSW in 1851, was made temporary Commissioner of Crown Lands and given a govt award of £10,000.

HARGREAVES, James (d. 1778). British inventor. B. nr Blackburn, he became a weaver, and in 1760 was co-inventor of a carding machine. About 1764 he invented his 'spinning-jenny', which enabled a number of threads to be spun simultaneously by one person.

HA'RIJAN. Hindi 'children of god', name coined by Mahatma Gandhi for the untouchables: see CASTE.

HARLECH (hahr'lekh). Town in Gwynedd, Wales. The castle, built by Edward I, was captured 1468 by the Yorkists from the Lancastrians in the Wars of the Roses: the song 'March of the Men of H.' originated in this siege. Pop. (1971) 1,200.

HARLEM (hahr'lem). District of Manhattan, New York City, with a large Black population.

HARLEY, Robert, 1st earl of Oxford (1661-1724). British Tory statesman. He was Speaker of the Commons from 1701 to 1705 and entered the govt in 1704 as Sec. of State. In 1708 the Whigs procured his dismissal, but in 1710 he returned to power as Chancellor of the Exchequer, and became subsequently a peer, received the Garter, and occupied the office of Lord Treasurer. In 1714, however, he was dismissed. After the accession of George I he was accused of treason, and imprisoned until 1717.

HARLOW, Jean (1911-37). American film actress, née Harlean Carpentier. Discovered by Ben Lyon, she was the first 'platinum blonde', a toughly frank sex symbol of the Thirties, in *Hell's Angels* (1930) and *Saratoga* (1937).

HARLOW. Town in Essex, England, N of Epping, developed as a 'new town' from 1947. Pop. (1973) 81,000.

HARMONICA. Name given to a variety of musical instruments of varying periods, incl. sets of musical glasses (graded in size or containing varying quantities of water) played with wetted fingers or small hammers - both Mozart and Beethoven composed for these; and the mouth organ. The latter, said to have been invented by Wheatstone (q.v.) in 1829, consists of a narrow box containing a metal plate in which there are a number of slots, each having a small metal reed affixed - the size of the reed is varied according to the note to be produced. Easily mastered by the amateur, it can by a few be used at the level of a concert instrument, e.g. Larry Adler.

HARMONIUM. Musical instrument: a pipeless, reed-vibrated organ, worked by air compression with a 5-octave keyboard and an air chamber filled by the action of foot-worked pedals.

HARMONY. The art of combining musical sounds into chords, and the moving from one chord to another. It is distinguished from counterpoint (q.v.), the combination of harmonic textures. H. first took the form of added parts moving parallel to a plainsong. New chord forms appeared in the 16th cent., when the shortcomings of the ecclesiastical modes became more and more apparent, resulting in the evolution of modern major and minor scales. J. S. Bach advanced consonance and dissonance, while chromatic notes began to appear. The practical advancement of H., by Beethoven, Wagner, Stravinsky, etc., had frequently aroused the hostility of academic critics, as it long did in the case of the atonality, abandonment of a fixed key note, and double and treble tonality of Bartók and Holst. Our universal diatonic scale was nearly attained by Pythagoras and perfected by Zarlino.

HARMSWORTH, Alfred. *See* LORD NORTHCLIFFE.

HARNESS RACING. Sport popular in the US and Canada, originating in the 18th cent., in which standardbred horses (rather sturdier than thoroughbreds) pull two-wheeled sulkies on which the driver sits. They compete in trotting (in which the diagonally opposite legs move forward simultaneously) and pacing (in which the 2 right legs, then the 2 left legs, are alternately moved forward) races and the winner may be decided by the best 2 out of 3 heats. The most famous race (trotting) is the Hambletonian at Goshen, NY, named after the mid-19th cent. horse Hambletonian, from which 90 per cent of modern standardbreds are said to descend in the male line. Attempts to popularize H.R. in Britain have failed, but it flourishes in Australia, France, Italy and Sweden.

HAROLD I (d. 1040). King of England, known as 'Harefoot'. The illegitimate son of Canute, he claimed the throne on his father's death in 1035, and in 1037 was elected king.

HAROLD II (*c.* 1022-66). King of England. The son of Earl Godwin, he was early appointed earl of E. Anglia. He succeeded his father in 1053 in the earldom of Wessex and became the most powerful man in England. Soon after 1063 William of Normandy tricked him into swearing to support his claim to the English throne. In Jan. 1066 H. was elected king by the Witan; William began to prepare an invasion. With the assistance of Tostig, H.'s brother, the king of Norway, Harald Hardrada, invaded Northumbria; H. marched north, and routed the invaders at Stamford Bridge on 25 Sept. Three days later William landed at Pevensey; H. took up his position at Battle. The battle of Hastings (14 Oct. 1066) ended with the death of H.

HARP. Musical instrument, the largest to be plucked by hand. It consists of 46 strings, stretched between an upright triangular frame, and is provided with several pedals at the base. These are used to alter the pitch of the instrument.

HARPER'S FERRY. Town in W Va., USA, at the confluence of the Shenandoah and Potomac rivers, scene of several battles in the Civil War. John Brown raided the arsenal here in 1859.

HARPIES. In classical mythology originally feminine wind-spirits. In later legend they became rapacious monsters who retained their human heads but possessed the bodies of vultures.

HARPSICHORD. Keyboard musical instrument popular in the 16-18th cents., until its supersession by the piano. The strings were plucked by quills, not struck by hammers.

HARPSICHORD. Made by Giovanni Baffor of Venice, this beautiful instrument is painted with grotesques and a cartouche of Orpheus and the Muses. *Photo: Courtesy of the Victoria and Albert Museum.*

HARRIER. Genus (*Circus*) of birds of prey in the family Accipitridae. They are found throughout the world, and 3 species occur in Britain: the moorland hen H. (*C. cyaneus*), Montagu's H. (*C. pygargus*), and the marsh H. (*C. aeruginosus*).

HARRIER. A dog hunting the hare by scent. It resembles a foxhound, though smaller and slower.

HARRIMAN (William) Averell (1891-). American administrator. Originally a Republican he became a Democrat in 1927, and was apt. by Roosevelt State Director of the National Recovery Administration in 1933. During the S.W.W. he was active in the admin. of Lease-Lend (q.v.) and was present at the Atlantic Charter (q.v.) meetings in 1941. Ambassador to the USSR 1943-6 and to Great Britain for a few months in 1946, he headed the European division of ECA 1948-50 (MSA 1951-3), and was Gov. of New York 1955-8. He was Ass Sec. of State for Far Eastern Affairs 1961-3, Under-Sec. for Political Affairs 1963-4, and ambassador-at-large 1961 and 1965-9.

HARRIS, Sir Arthur Travers (1892–1984). British Marshal of the RAF. He was C-in-C of Bomber Command 1942–5, becoming known as 'Bomber H.'.

HARRIS, Frank (1856-1931). Irish journalist. B. in Galway, he was active both in New York and London and wrote ephemeral fiction. He is best remembered for his highly coloured biographies of Wilde and Shaw, and his sensational autobiography, *My Life* (1926), banned in the UK and US.

HARRIS, Joel Chandler (1848-1908). American writer. B. in Georgia, he first pub. his 'Uncle Remus' stories in the Atlanta *Constitution*, which he edited 1890-1905; these tales were written in Negro dialect and gained world-wide popularity. His autobiography, *On the Plantation*, appeared in 1892.

HARRIS, Paul P. (1878-1947). American lawyer, founder of Rotary. B. in Wisconsin, he became a lawyer in Chicago in 1896, where he founded the first Rotary Club in 1905, and the International Association in 1912.

HARRIS, Roy (1898-1979). American composer. B. in Oklahoma, son of a farmer and an English-born mother, he served in the F.W.W., was then a truck-driver until 1921, when he studied music at the Univ. of California. Notable among his symphonies are the Third, Fifth and Sixth ('Lincoln'), and among other works his cantata *Abraham Lincoln walks at Midnight* and the orchestral piece *When Johnny Comes Marching Home*.

HARRIS. Southern part of Lewis-with-Harris Island, in the Outer Hebrides, Western Isles, Scotland. It is a barren stretch cultivated by crofters; sheep are reared on the rough upland pastures. Harris Tweed is made from the hand-woven wool of the black face or Cheviot sheep. Tarbert is the chief town. Area 456 sq.km (176 sq.m).

HARRISBURG. Cap. of Pennsylvania, USA, on the Susquehanna r., with food processing and machine industries. In 1979 a reactor breakdown at the nearby Three Mile Is. plant focused agitation against nuclear development. Pop. met area (1970) 411,000.

HARRISON, Benjamin (1833-1901). 23rd President of the USA. He defeated Cleveland in 1888, being pres. as a Republican 1889-93, when he was succeeded by Cleveland. In 1889 he called the first Pan-American Conference.

HARRISON, Rex Carey (1908-). British actor. Lancashire-born, he had his first big success in *French Without Tears* (1936), and subsequently often appeared in London and New York, notably as Prof. Higgins in the musical *My Fair Lady* (1956). His films incl. *Blithe Spirit* (1944), and Caesar in *Cleopatra* (1962).

HARRISON, William (1773-1841). 9th Pres. of the USA. B. in Virginia, he entered the army, became gov. of the newly formed Indiana Territory, and was elected Pres. in 1840, but d. a month after taking office. His grandson, **Benjamin H.** (1833-1901), a Republican, served as 23rd Pres. of the USA from 1889 to 1893.

HARRISSON, Tom (1911-76). British anthropologist. After working among Borneo headhunters, he decided to apply the same study techniques among Bolton cotton mill operators, and set up with Charles Madge in 1937 Mass Observation, earliest of the organizations for the analysis of public opinions and attitudes.

HARROGATE. Town and spa in N Yorks, England, 23km (14m) N of Leeds, a tourist resort and holiday centre. Pop. (1972) 64,280.

HARROW. Bor. of Greater London, England. The parish church was founded by Lanfranc in the 11th cent. H. school was founded by John Lyon in 1571, and opened in 1611; it became a leading public school during the 18th cent.; among its former scholars are Byron, Sheridan, Peel, Palmerston, and Sir Winston Churchill. Pop. (1973) 204,660.

HART, Basil Henry Liddell. *See* LIDDELL-HART.

HART, Dame Judith (1924-). British Labour politician and sociologist. She became MP for Lanark 1959, was Min. of Social Security 1967-8, Paymaster-General with Cabinet rank 1968-9, her assignment incl. decentralization of govt, and Min. of Overseas Development 1967-70, and 1974-5 returning as Min. of State, Overseas Development 1977-79.

HARTE, Francis Bret (1839-1902). American author. B. in Albany, NY, he became a gold-miner in California at the age of 18. While secretary of the California Mint (1864-70) he founded the *Overland Monthly* (1868), in which he pub. short stories of the pioneer West, e.g. 'The Luck of Roaring Camp', and poems, e.g. the 'Heathen Chinee'. In 1878 he entered the consular service, and after his retirement in 1885 settled in England, where he d.

HARTEBEEST. Name given to various species of African antelope, particularly the Caama (*Alcelaphus buselaphus*). It is a brownish-red, and *c.* 120cm (4ft) high.

HARTEBEEST. A statuesque group of Coke's hartebeest (*Alcelaphus buselaphus Cokei*) in East Africa. *Photo: Heather Angel.*

HARTFORD. Capital of Connecticut, USA, on Connecticut r. It is a centre of the insurance business and of various manufactures, e.g. aircraft engines, typewriters and tools. Pop. met. area (1970) 657,104.

HARTLEPOOL (hart'li-). Seaport in Cleveland, England. The old town of H., dating from 640, is on the N side of H. bay, on a promontory. West H., to the SW, grew up with the development of the Durham coalfield. Industries incl. shipbuilding, engineering, paper manufacture, brewing and fishing. Pop. (1973) 99,360.

HARTLEY, L(eslie) P(oles) (1895-1972). English novelist. Son of a wealthy solicitor, he was ed. at Harrow and Balliol Coll., Oxford. After publishing a vol. of short stories, *Night Fears* (1924) and a novella, *Simonetta Perkins* (1925), he gave up serious creative writing until his trilogy of the growing up and intertwined lives of a brother and sister, *The Shrimp and the Anemone* (1944), *The Sixth Heaven* (1946), and *Eustace and Hilda* (1947). Of his later books, *The Go-Between* (1953) successfully filmed, is the most famous, and all show the influence of Jane Austen and Henry James.

HARTMANN, Karl Robert Eduard von (1842-1906). German philosopher. His *Philosophy of the Unconscious* (1869) derived its pessimistic idealism from Hegel and Schopenhauer; and in it he maintains that the unconscious, composed of will and reason, is the absolute of existence.

HARTZ MTNS. Range running N to S in Tasmania, with 2 remarkable peaks: H. Mt. 1,254 m (4,113 ft) and Adamson's Peak 1,224 m (4,017 ft). Part of it forms a national park.

HARUN AL-RASHID (ha-roon'ahl-rah'shēd) (763-809). Caliph of Baghdad. B. near Tehran, he succeeded his brother in 786, and was a lavish patron of music, poetry, and letters.

HARVARD. Senior univ. and oldest educational institution in the USA, founded in 1636 at New Towne (later Cambridge), Mass., and named after John Harvard (1607-38), who bequeathed half his estate (valued at £799 17s. 2d.) and his library to it. Women were first admitted in 1969.

HARVEST-BUG or **harvest-mite.** Scarlet or rusty brown mites belonging to the Trombiculidae family of the Acarina order of the Arachnida. Common in summer and autumn, they are parasitic, and their bites are intensely irritating to humans.

HARVESTMEN. An order (Opiliones) of the Arachnida; found in late summer and early autumn, they may be distinguished from true spiders by the absence of a waist or constriction in the oval body. They are carnivorous, and are found from the Arctic to the tropics; the long-legged H. (*Phalangium*) is often found in Britain.

HARVEY, William (1578-1657). English physician who discovered the circulation of blood. In 1609 he became physician to St. Bartholomew's hospital in London, and in 1615 lecturer at the College of Physicians. His theory of circulation was pub. in 1628. He was physician to James I and Charles I, and was in attendance on the latter at the battle of Edgehill.

HA'RWELL. Main research establishment of the United Kingdom Atomic Energy Authority, close to the village of H. in Berkshire, after which it is often called. It has many reactors, chemical and metallurgical laboratories, workshops and the reactor school.

HARWICH (ha'rij). English seaport on the Essex coast, occupying a peninsula at the E end of the Stour and Orwell estuary. Ferry services run to ports in the Netherlands, Belgium, and Denmark. Pop. (1971) 15,000.

HARYA'NA. State in the NW of the Rep. of India, created in 1966 from the Hindi-speaking areas of the state of Punjab. Cotton, oil seeds and sugar are grown and manufactures incl. wool and cotton textiles, scientific instruments, agricultural machinery and glass. Area 44,056 sq.km (17,010 sq.m); pop. (1971) 10,037,000. The cap. is Chandigarh.

HARZ (hahrts) **MTNS.** Range in Lower Saxony, W Germany, of which the highest point is the granite massif of the Brocken (q.v.).

HA'SDRUBAL (d. 207 BC). Carthaginian general, the brother of Hannibal (q.v.). He remained in command in Spain in 218 when Hannibal invaded Italy, and, after fighting there against the Scipios until 208, marched to Hannibal's relief. He was defeated and killed on the Metaurus.

HAŠEK (ha'sek), **Jaroslav** (1883-1923). Czech writer. B. in Prague, he became a bank clerk, and in 1909 the facetious editor of the entirely serious journal *The Animal World.* In 1915 he was called up, deserted to the Russians at the battle of Chorupan, later fighting in the Czech legion and eventually joining the Bolsheviks. His comic masterpiece is the unfinished *The Good Soldier Schweik,* based on his earlier experiences, which was condemned by authority as detrimental to discipline.

HASHISH. *See* HEMP.

HASLEMERE (hāz'elmēr). Town in Surrey, England, location of the Dolmetsch family music workshops, re-creating instruments of the 16-18th cents. They have held an annual music of festival since 1925. Pop. (1973) 14,000.

HA'SSALL, John (1868-1948). British 'king of poster artists', his most famous being the 'So bracing' poster of Skegness.

HASSA'N II (1930-). King of Morocco, 17th monarch of the Alouite dynasty. He personally suppressed the Rif revolt of 1958-9 and succeeded to the throne on the death of his father Mohammed V in 1961. He introduced his country's first constitution in 1962. He has survived several dramatic assassination attempts. From 1976 he undertook the occupation of Western Sahara (q.v.).

HASTINGS, Warren (1732-1818). British administrator. B. in Oxon, he went to India in 1750 as a clerk in the E India Co.'s service. His services during the war in Bengal attracted Clive's attention, and in 1761 he was promoted to the council at Calcutta. After leave in England 1764-9 he received an appointment at Madras, and in 1772 was appointed Gov. of Bengal; this title was exchanged in 1774 for that of Gov.-Gen. of India. His aggressive war against the Rohillas, and the hanging of a Brahman who had accused H. of forgery, aroused a strong opposition against him. When in 1780 the Indian empire was threatened by the French and their ally Hyder Ali of Mysore, H. saved the situation by prompt action. He resigned and returned to England in 1785. He was impeached in 1788 for corruption and cruelty, but acquitted in 1795.

HASTINGS. Holiday resort and Cinque Port, E Sussex, England. Ruins of the Norman castle survive on the West Cliff, and 3m to the W the almost intact wreck of a Dutch East Indiaman, the *Amsterdam* (1749), embedded in the shore, forms a major archaeological site. St Leonards, adjoining H. to the W and now part of it, developed as a fashionable resort in the 19th cent. The town is scheduled for major redevelopment. The *Battle of H.* on 14 Oct. 1066 in which William the Conqueror defeated Harold, took place at Senlac, 10km (6m) inland; the site is marked by Battle Abbey. Pop. (1974) 74,500.

HATFIELD. Town in Herts, England, 8km (5m) E of St Albans. The 12th cent. palace of the bishops of Ely was seized by Henry VIII, and Edward VI and Elizabeth I lived there before their accession. James I exchanged it for Theobalds with Robert Cecil, earl of Salisbury, who replaced the palace by the existing magnificent Jacobean H. House (1611). There are engineering industries, and a polytechnic. Pop. (1973) 45,500.

HA'THAWAY, Anne (1556-1623). Englishwoman, dau. of a yeoman farmer, who m. Shakespeare in 1582. Her cottage at Shottery is a showplace.

HA'THOR. Sky goddess worshipped in ancient Egypt. On her head she usually wears a cow's horns with the solar disc.

HASTINGS. The *Amsterdam*, a Dutch East Indiaman with a rich cargo, was wrecked here in 1748, and still lies embedded in the shore. It is hoped eventually to raise and restore her. *Photo: Courtesy of Peter Marsden.*

HATSHEP'SUT (fl. 1500 BC). Queen of Egypt, of the 18th Dynasty, *c.* 1489–*c.* 1469 BC. Half sister and queen of Thothmes II, she m. after his death her young half-brother Thothmes III. She arrogated power to herself, ruling as a man, and when she d. or was forced to abdicate, Thothmes III defaced her monuments. The ruins of her magnificent temple at Deir el-Bahri survive.
HA'TTERAS. US cape on the Atlantic coast, N Carolina, site of many shipwrecks. H. Inlet is a noted fishing ground.
HATTERSLEY, Roy (1932–). Labour politician. On the right wing, he was Prices Secretary 1976–9, and in 1983 became deputy leader of the party. His books incl. *Politics Apart* (1982).
HAUGHEY (haw'hē), **Charles** (1925-). Irish statesman. Of Ulster descent, he was dismissed in 1970 from Jack Lynch's cabinet for alleged complicity in an IRA gun-running scheme, but was subsequently acquitted. He succeeded Lynch as PM (and leader of Fianna Fail) 1979–81, and Mar–Nov 1982.
HAUSAS (how'saz). Moslem Negro people of W Africa, chiefly inhabiting N Nigeria. The H. language is accepted as a *lingua franca* over much of W Africa; it is assigned to the Hamitic family.
HAUSSMANN (ōsmahn'), **Georges Eugène,** baron (1809-91). French administrator, chiefly famous for his re-planning of Paris. He became a prefect of the Seine in 1853, and widened streets, laid out boulevards and parks, and improved the water supply.
HAVA'NA. Capital, commercial centre, and chief port of Cuba, situated on the N coast of the island, occupying a peninsula W of the excellent harbour. Ancient buildings incl. the palace of the Spanish governors, and the stronghold of La Fuerza (1583). H. was founded on the S coast in 1515, transferred to present site 1519. The Univ. of H. was founded in 1728. In 1898 the blowing up of the US battleship *Maine* in the harbour precipitated the Spanish-American war. Chief manufactures are cigars and tobacco. Pop. (1970) 1,755,360.
HA'VELOCK, Sir Henry (1795-1857). British soldier. He saw service in Burma 1824-6 and in the Afghan War of 1839. On the outbreak of the Indian Mutiny in 1857 he was engaged in Persia, but returning to India he retook Cawnpore and relieved Lucknow, but d. of dysentery soon after.
HAVRE (ahvr), **Le.** French port on the N bank of the Seine estuary in the dept of Seine-Maritime. It was held by the Germans 1940–44. Pop. (1975) 264 000.
HAWAII (hawī-i). 50th state of the USA. It consists of a chain of islands in the N Pacific of which the chief are H., Maui, Oahu, Kauai, Molokai, Lanai, Niihau, and Kahoolawa. They are volcanic, and H. itself contains Mauna Kea (4,201 m/13,784 ft), one of the world's highest island mountains, and Mauna Loa (4,170 m/13,680 ft), the world's largest active crater. Lake Waiau on Mauna Kea is the highest lake in the USA (3,968 m/13,020 ft), and Ka Lae (South Cape) on H. is the southernmost point of the USA. In Oahu are the cap., Honolulu, and the naval base Pearl Harbor, the Japanese attack on which, 7 Dec. 1941, brought the USA into the S.W.W. The climate is tropical and the flora rich and varied. The chief products are sugar, pineapples, coffee, bananas and flowers. The chief industry is tourism, but fishing, handicrafts, etc., are carried on. *See* INFRA-RED ASTRONOMY.

Capt. Cook landed in the islands (which he named Sandwich Islands) in 1778, but navigators from Europe are thought to have visited them in the 16th cent. The original population, estimated at 300,000 in 1778, was Polynesian; the number of people with aboriginal blood was about 105,000 in 1960, including those (the majority) of only partly Hawaiian ancestry. After 1852 immigration was encouraged, and the population is now heterogeneous, European and Japanese blood predominating. H. was a kingdom until 1893, became a rep. 1894, which ceded itself to the USA in 1898 and was admitted to the Union in 1959. Area 16,705 sq.km (6,450 sq.m); pop. (1970) 769,900.

The **Hawaiian guitar,** also known as the ukelele ('jumping flea'), was introduced to the is. by the Portuguese in 1877, and thence became popular in Europe and the USA in jazz bands. The strings are distinctively tuned, and are not 'stopped' by the fingers but by a metal bar or 'steel' which goes across them all. Sliding this up and down gives the characteristic 'singing' tone of the instrument.
HAWARDEN (har'den). Town in Clwyd, N Wales, on a tributary of the Dee, 10km (6m) SW of Chester. For many years H. Castle (1752) was the home of W. E. Gladstone, and he founded St Deiniol's theological library in H. Pop. *c.* 8,500.
HAW-HAW, Lord. *See* JOYCE, WILLIAM.
HAWICK. Town in Borders, Scotland, on the r. Teviot, 16km (10m) SW of Jedburgh. It makes woollens. Pop. (1973) 16,500.

HAWAII. As the wave crashes and breaks behind him a surfer cuts a diagonal path just beneath the roller's crest, as it starts its final run onto the shores of the island. *Photo: LeRoy Grannis/Camera Press.*

HAWK. Name of various birds of prey in the family Falconidae, excluding eagles and vultures. They have an untoothed bill and short wings.

HAWKE. As Prime Minister Bob Hawke reached consensus with unions and employers on a strategy to lift the country from recession. *Photo: Australian Information Service.*

HAWKE, Bob (Robert) (1929–). Australian self-styled democratic socialist. He was pres. of the Australian Council of Trade Unions 1970–80, and became Prime Minister in 1983.

HAWKE, Edward, 1st baron (1705-81). British admiral. In 1759 he destroyed in Quiberon Bay the French fleet which had been intended to cover an invasion of Britain. He was 1st Lord of the Admiralty 1766-71, and in 1776 was created a baron.

HAWKE BAY. Bay on the E coast of North Island, NZ, between the Mahia Peninsula and Cape Kidnappers, on which Napier stands. The coastal area is noted for sheep.

HAWKER, Robert Stephen (1803-75). British poet. B. in Devon, he became vicar of Morwenstow, Cornwall, in 1834, and introduced the harvest festival now generally adopted. His *Cornish Ballads* (1869) contains the 'Song of the Western Men'.

HAWKES, Jacquetta (1910-). British author. Dau. of Sir F. G. Hopkins (q.v.), she m. in 1933 Prof. Christopher H., with whom she collaborated in *Prehistoric Britain* (1944), and is a keen anthropologist and archaeologist. Following the dissolution of this marriage, she became the wife of J. B. Priestley (q.v.) in 1953, with whom she has also collaborated.

HAWKESBURY. River in NSW, known in its upper reaches as the Wollondilly, Warragamba and Nepean. After a course of some 480 km (300 m) it reaches the sea N. of Sydney, for which it is a major source of water supply.

HAWKING, Stephen (1942-) British physicist. Prof. of gravitational physics at Cambridge from 1977, he is confined to a wheelchair by amyotrophic lateral sclerosis, which also affects his speech. He has made such discoveries as that the strong gravitational field around a black hole can radiate particles of matter. Commenting on Einstein's remark: 'God does not play dice with the Universe,' he said: 'God not only plays dice, he throws them where they can't be seen.'

HAWKINS, Sir Anthony Hope. *See* HOPE, A.

HAWKINS, Sir John (1532-95). English navigator. B. in Plymouth, he made 2 successful voyages to the Guinea coast, but a 3rd in 1567, in which he was accompanied by his cousin Francis Drake, ended in the almost complete destruction of his fleet. In 1573 he became treasurer (later comptroller) of the navy, and in 1588 was knighted for his services against the Armada. He d. while on an expedition to the W Indies.

HAWKINS, Sir Richard (*c.* 1562-1622). English navigator. The son of Sir John H., he sailed to the W Indies with his uncle, William H., in 1582, and in 1588 was given a command against the Armada. In 1593 he set out on an expedition against Spanish possessions, was captured in 1594, and not released until 1602. In 1603 he was knighted, and in 1604 became MP for Plymouth and vice-admiral of Devon.

HAWK-MOTH. Family of moths (Sphingidae) incl. some 1,000 species distributed throughout the world, but mainly tropical. The death's head H. (*Acherontia atropos*) is the largest of British moths. Some S American Hs. closely resemble humming birds and the humming bird H. (*Macroglossa stellatarum*) is found in southern England.

HAWKSMOOR, Nicholas (1661-1736). English architect. He entered Wren's office at 18, and assisted him at the City churches, Greenwich Hospital and St Paul's. Later he was joint architect with Vanbrugh of Castle Howard and Blenheim. The dramatic originality of his work was long undervalued, e.g. the west towers of Westminster Abbey long attributed to Wren.

HAWORTH. Small town in W Yorks, England, 6km (4m) S of Keighley, of which it forms part. The parsonage that was the home of the Brontës is preserved as a museum.

HAWTHORN. Common name for shrubs and trees of the *Crataegus* genus, of the Rosaceae family. The Common H., may or whitethorn (*C. oxyacantha*), a thorny shrub or small tree 3-4m (10-12ft) in height, bears clusters of white or pink flowers followed by groups of red berries. It is indigenous to Britain and much of Europe, N Africa and

W Asia, and has been naturalized in N America and Australia.

HAWTHORNE, Nathaniel (1804-64). American author. B. at Salem, Mass., he was strongly impressed in boyhood with the Puritan tradition of the area. His early attempts at writing stories and sketches were financially unrewarding, but he won immediate success with *The Scarlet Letter* (1850), a story of the retribution overtaking the parents of an illegitimate child, written while working as a customs official (surveyor of the Port of Salem 1846-9). Later were *The House of the Seven Gables* (1851), *The Blithedale Romance* (1852) and such vols. of tales for children as the classic legends of *Tanglewood Tales* (1853).

HAY, Will (1888-1949). British comedian, celebrated as the incompetent schoolmaster of St Michael's on music-hall and screen: he was also a notable amateur astronomer.

HAYDEN, William (1933-). Australian Labor politician. B. in Brisbane, he became leader of the Australian Labor Party and of the opposition in 1977.

HAYDN (hīdn), **Franz Joseph** (1732-1809). Austrian composer. B. in Lower Austria, he was Kapellmeister 1761-90 to Prince Esterházy at Eisenstadt and Esterház, where he had ample opportunity to develop his native originality. He visited London in 1791-2 and again 1794-5, and to these visits we owe the 'Surprise', 'Military', 'Clock', 'Drum-roll', 'London', and 'Oxford' symphonies. For the Eng. public also were written the still popular oratorios *The Creation* and *The Seasons*.

H. established the regular symphonic form and the composition of the orchestra which were to be used by Mozart and Beethoven. He was the first great master of the quartet. He wrote operas, church music, pieces for various instruments, and songs, and composed the 'Emperor's Hymn', subsequently adopted as the Ger. national anthem.

HAYDON, Benjamin Robert (1786-1846). British artist. B. at Plymouth, he settled in London and became celebrated for his gigantic canvases, attempts at 'high art', incl. 'Christ's Entry into Jerusalem' (1820, now in Philadelphia). He is now better appreciated in genre pictures, e.g. 'The Mock Election' and 'Chairing the Member'; and for his lively autobiography and journals. Perpetually harassed financially, he shot himself.

HAYEK (hī-ek), **Friedrich August von** (1899-). Austrian economist. B. in Vienna, he taught at the LSE 1931-50, becoming a British subject in 1938, and was prof. of social and moral science at the Univ. of Chicago 1950-62. His *The Road to Serfdom* (1944) was a critical study of socialistic trends in Britain. Nobel prize 1974.

HAYES, Rutherford Birchard (1822-93). 19th President of the USA. B. in Ohio, he was a major-general in the Civil War and prominent Republican politician. During his presidency (1877-81), the army of occupation was withdrawn from the southern states and the Civil Service reformed.

HAY-FEVER. An acute watery catarrh produced by pollen, etc., in the specially sensitive. As in asthma, nettle-rash and other allergic diseases, large quantities of fluid are released from the blood at the place where the foreign protein (in this case the pollen) enters. Remedies are detection and avoidance of the offending pollen, antiseptic sprays, zinc ionization, ephedrine, and desensitization by vaccine.

HAZARDOUS SUBSTANCES. Waste substances, for the most part generated by industry, which represent a hazard to the environment, e.g. acidic resins, arsenic residues, residual hardening salts, lead, mercury, non-ferrous sludges, organic solvents and pesticides. Their economic disposal or recycling is the subject of intense research.

HAZEL. Popular name for shrubs or trees of the *Corylus* genus, Betulaceae family, also called filbert (the official US name) and cobnut. The nuts are enclosed by a husk.

HAZLITT, William (1778-1830). British writer. B. at Maidstone, son of a Unitarian minister, he himself thought of entering the ministry and dabbled in portrait painting, but ultimately settled to writing in which he had been encouraged by Coleridge. Going to London in 1812 he worked for the daily press and magazines, incl. the *Edinburgh Review*, writing from the liberal viewpoint. He was a superb controversialist, with a unique, clear, hard-hitting prose style which served him equally well in his critical essays: *Characters of Shakespeare's Plays* (1817-18), *Lectures on the English Poets* (1818-19), *English Comic Writers* (1819) and *Dramatic Literature of the Age of Elizabeth* (1820). Other notable works are his *Table Talk* (1821-2); *The Spirit of the Age* (1825), perceptive appreciations of his contemporaries; and the curious *Liber Amoris* (1823) record of his infatuation with the dau. of a tailor with whom he lodged. The latter affair was sandwiched between his 2 marriages: 1st to a friend of Mary Lamb in 1808 (divorce 1822) and 2nd to a widow in 1824, who left him on the return from their honeymoon trip to Italy. His invective, scathing irony and gift for epigram were symptomatic of a temperament which, though sincere, was ill-fated to cope with ordinary people and ordinary life.

HEADACHE. Pain in the head arising from sometimes minor (temporary eye strain) to major (brain tumour) causes, and marked by dilation of the cerebral blood vessels, and irritation of the brain linings (meninges) and of the nerves, etc. *See* MIGRAINE.

HEALEY, Denis (1917-). British Labour politician. He entered Parliament in 1952, and while Min. of Defence 1964-70 was in charge of the reduction of Brit. forces under the policy of concentration on Europe and withdrawal E of Suez. As Chancellor of the Exchequer 1947-9, he attempted to control inflation and in his 1976 budget made reduction in personal income tax dependent on union agreement to minimum wage increases. On the resignation of Callaghan in 1980, he became deputy leader of the party under Foot.

HEARD and McDONALD ISLANDS. Group of is. in the southern Indian Ocean. *c.* 4,000 km (2,500 m) SW of Fremantle, discovered 1833, annexed by Britain 1910 and transferred to Australia 1947. Heard Is. (42km by 19km/26m by 12m) is glacier-covered, although the volcanic mtn Big Ben (2,743 m/9,000 ft) is still active: there is a weather station (1947). Shag Is. is 8km (5m) to the N and the craggy McDonalds are 42km (26m) to the W.

HEARST, William Randolph (1863-1951). American newspaper proprietor, celebrated for his introduction of banner headlines, lavish illustration, and the sensational approach known as 'yellow journalism'. A campaigner in numerous controversies, and a strong isolationist, he was the original of *Citizen Kane* (*see* WELLES, ORSON). He collected art treasures, antiques, and castles - one of which, San Simeon (Hearst Castle) in California, is a state museum. His grand-dau. **Patty H.** (1955-) was kidnapped in 1974 by the Symbionese Liberation Army, and having joined her captors in a bank raid, was imprisoned 1975–79.

HEART. The muscular organ which supplies blood to all parts of the body. Hollow and pear-shaped, it contains two pairs of chambers divided by a vertical muscular wall. The upper pair, the auricles, are smaller and communicate through valves with the lower and larger pair, the ventricles. When the heart beats its muscle contracts strongly (systole) and the following actions occur. The auricles feed blood to the ventricles, which contract an instant later, and the left ventricle pumps blood into the aorta - the main artery through which the whole of the body except the lungs is supplied. The heart muscle itself is supplied with blood through the coronary arteries, leading from the aorta. Valves prevent the blood from returning after the impulse. At the same time the right ventricle pumps used blood to the lungs through the pulmonary artery to be aerated. After the heart's contraction it dilates (diastole) and refills, used blood from the veins entering the right auricle and aerated blood from the lungs entering the left auricle. The timing of the heart's beat is regulated by its own local nervous system. Heart disease is due chiefly to disease or overwork of its muscle, defects of its valves, or disorder of its nervous system.

The first transplant of a human H. was carried out 3rd Dec. 1967 at Groote Schuur Hospital, Cape Town, by Christiaan N. Barnard (q.v.).

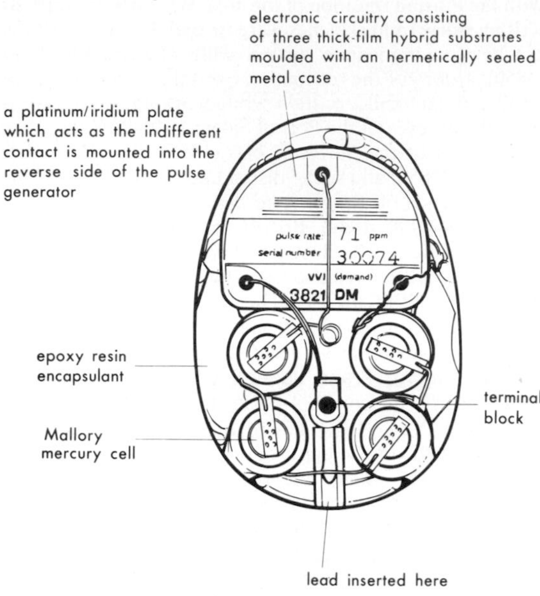

HEART. A heart pacemaker, or 'demand pulse generator', which is powered by 4 Mallory mercury cells, and produces a normal pulse of 71 per minute. It is 74 mm long, 53 mm wide and 23 mm thick, and weighs 150 grams. *Courtesy of Devices Ltd.*

HEARTBURN. Irritation of the gullet by excessively acid stomach contents. The acid may be the hydrochloric acid which is a normal part of the digestive fluid, but present in excess. This is often associated with duodenal ulcer, and the pain is worst when the stomach is empty, and is relieved by eating. The acid may, on the other hand, be one of the organic acids produced by fermentation when the hydrochloric acid is deficient, e.g. lactic, acetic, and butyric acids. This is common in pregnancy.

HEAT. A form of energy which by its addition to or abstraction from a body causes a rise or fall in its temperature. It always tends to flow from a region of higher temperature to one of lower temperature. The effect of heat on a substance may be simply to raise its temperature, to cause it to expand, to melt it if it is a solid, to vaporize it if it is liquid, or to increase its pressure if it is a gas.

The quantity of heat is measured by the extent to which it will raise the temperature of a standard substance.

The name *specific heat* is given to the ratio between the heat required to raise the temperature of a given mass of a substance through a given range of temperature, to the heat required to raise the temperature of an equal mass of water through the same range. The *mechanical equivalent of heat* is the ratio of the amount of work done to the quantity of heat produced.

There are three ways by which heat may be transferred from one place to another, viz. (a) *convection* - transmission through a fluid or a gas by currents, as when the air in a room is warmed by a fire or radiator, or the water is heated in a domestic hot-water system; (b) *conduction* - when the heat passes from one part of a medium to neighbouring parts with no visible motion of the medium accompanying the transfer of heat, as when the whole length of a metal rod is heated when one end is held in a fire; (c) *radiation.* Radiant heat is of the same nature as light. It can pass through a vacuum, travels at the same speed as light, can be reflected and refracted, and does not affect the medium through which it passes.

HEATH, Edward Richard George (1916-). British Cons. politician. In the admin. Civil Service 1946-7, he entered parliament in 1950, was Min. of Labour 1959-60, and as Lord Privy Seal 1960-3 conducted abortive negotiations for Common Market membership. He was at the Board of Trade 1963-4, and succeeded Home as Cons. leader in 1965 - the first elected leader of his party. Defeated in the general election of 1966, he achieved a surprise victory in 1970, but his confrontation with the striking miners as part of his campaign to control inflation led to his defeat in Feb. 1974 and again, by a larger margin in Oct. 1974. He was replaced in the party leadership by Margaret Thatcher in 1975. In 1971 he captained the winning Admiral's Cup Team in his yacht *Morning Cloud.*

HEATH and **HEATHER.** Popular names for plants of the Ericaceae family. The most common in Britain, known in Scotland as ling, is *Calluna vulgaris.* It is up to 1m. (3ft) high, with white, red or purple flowers, and small leaves on a shrubby stem.

HEATHROW (hēth'rō). Location in the Greater London bor. of Hounslow, England, site of Heathrow Airport, London, opened 1946.

HEAT STROKE. Condition caused in human beings when the body temperature rises above 40°C (104°F). The brain swells, resulting in confusion of thought; the body becomes dehydrated, blood circulation slows, and organs, such as the kidneys, fail to function. Coma ensues and ends in cardiac arrest. Treatment is by suspension on a mesh bed across a water bath, with a spray of warm water to keep skin temperature at 32°C and relieve dehydration.

HEAVEN. In the theology of Christianity and most of the other world religions, the place of the blessed in the next world. Many attempts have been made, particularly by Christian and Moslem writers, to describe its joys, but modern theologians usually prefer to describe it as a place or state in which the soul sees God as He really is - enjoys the Beatific vision.

HEAVISIDE, Oliver (1850-1925). British physicist. His theoretical studies of electricity pub. in *Electrical Papers* (1892) had considerable influence on long-distance telephony. In 1902 he predicted the existence of an ionized layer of air in the upper atmosphere which was verified by Kennelly (q.v.) and was later known as the Kennelly-H. or H. layer but is now called the E layer. Deflection from it makes possible the transmission of radio signals round the world, which would otherwise be lost in outer space, and its presence is connected with the phenomenon of radio fading. *See* IONOSPHERE.

HEAVY METAL POISONING. Some heavy metals, such as zinc and copper, are essential to living cells. Others, such as plutonium and cadmium, to which workers in industry may be exposed, are highly toxic. Treatment is difficult because it is not yet possible to produce a drug which can distinguish, when removing them from the body cells, between those which are vital and those which are poisonous.

HEAVY WATER. Deuterium oxide (D_2O), i.e. water containing deuterium (q.v.) instead of hydrogen (mol. wt. 20 against 18 for ordinary water). Its chemical properties are identical with those of ordinary water, its physical properties differ slightly, density at 25°C, 1.1056; m.p. 3.8°C; b.p. 101.42°C; temperature of maximum density 11.6°C. It occurs in ordinary water in the ratio of about one part by weight of deuterium to 5,000 parts by weight of ordinary hydrogen and can be concentrated by electrolysis, the ordinary water being more readily decomposed by this means than the H.W.

HĒ'BĒ. In Greek mythology, the goddess of youth, dau. of Zeus and Hera, and handmaiden of the gods.

HEBEI (hubā'). Prov. of NE China (formerly Hopei), mountainous in the N and W. Wheat, cotton, fruit and oilseeds are grown, and coal, iron, gold, copper and salt are mined. There are textile and iron and steel industries. Hebei incl. the special municipalities of Tianjin and Peking; the cap. is Shijiazhuang. The port of Qinhuangdao was modernised with Japanese aid in 1980. Area 202,700 sq.km (79,053 sq.m); pop. (1979) 42,000,000.

HEBREW. The language of the OT; a branch of the Semitic languages, and closely related to Aramaic. By the 1st cent. AD it had become the language of the schools, being supplanted by Aramaic as the language of the people. The majority of the roots are tri-consonantal, and the modifications of the sense are effected by changing the vowels, or adding prefixes or affixes. The script, written from right to left, originally represented only the consonants; in the 7th and 8th cents. systems of vocalization by means of adding points and strokes were devised.

During the 18th and 19th cents. an improved Hebrew, based on classical models, was evolved and adapted to a mod. literature of Jewry.

HE'BRIDĒS. Group of over 500 islands off the W coast of Scotland. They are divided into the *Inner H.*, including Skye, Mull, Jura, and Islay, and the *Outer H.* (separated from Inner H. by the Little Minch) incl. Lewis-with-Harris and N and S Uist. Fewer than 100 of the H. are inhabited. The principal industries are cattle and sheep raising, distilling, and the production of Harris Tweed. Measures to stem depopulation incl. a fisheries scheme for Lewis-with-Harris, and the estab. of the main site for testing British guided missiles at Geirnish on S Uist. The H. were settled by Scandinavians in the 6th-9th cents., and passed under Norwegian rule from *c.* 890 till 1266. The *Outer H.* form the islands area of Western Isles: area 2,900 sq.km (1,120 sq.m); pop. (1971) 31,000. The *Inner H.* are divided between the Highland and Strathclyde regions: area 4,400 sq.km (1,700 sq.m).

HĒ'BRON. City (Arabic El Khalil) on the W Bank of Jordan, 32km (20m) SW of Jerusalem, occupied by Israel 1967. The traditional sites of the tombs of Abraham, Isaac, Jacob and their wives are within the mosque. Pop. (1980) 54,000, incl. 4,000 Jews.

HEB-SED. Festival celebrated by the kings of ancient Egypt, apparently commemorating Menes' union of Upper and Lower Egypt.

HE'CATĒ. Greek goddess of witchcraft and magic, sometimes identified with Artemis and the moon.

HE'CTARE. Unit of area in the metric system (Gk *hekaton* 100) equalling 100 ares or 10,000 sq. metres or 2.471 acres. Trafalgar Square was laid out as one H., the only square in London conforming to metric.

HECTOR. Legendary Trojan prince, the son of Priam, who during the siege of Troy was the foremost warrior on the Trojan side until he was killed by Achilles.

HE'CŪBA. Legendary Trojan queen, the wife of Priam and mother of Hector and Paris. After the fall of Troy she was carried off by the Greeks.

HEDGEHOG. Mammal (*Erinaceus europaeus*) common in Europe, western Asia, Africa, and India. The body, incl. the tail, is 30cm (1ft) long. It is speckled-brown in colour, has a pig-like snout, and is covered with sharp spines. When alarmed it can roll the body into a ball.

HEDGE SPARROW. European bird (*Prunella modularis*) similar in size and colouring to the sparrow, but with slate-grey head and breast, and more slender bill. It nests in bushes and hedges.

HĒ'DONISM (Gk. *hēdonē*, pleasure). The ethical theory that pleasure or happiness is, or should be, the chief end of life. Hedonist sects in Greece were the Cyrenaics, who held that the sentient pleasure of the moment is man's only good, and the Epicureans, who advocated the pursuit of pleasure under the direction of reason. Modern hedonistic philosophies, such as those of Bentham and Mill, regard the happiness of society as the aim, and not that of the single individual.

HEFEI (hawfā'). Cap. (formerly Hofei) of Anhui prov. in SE China. Pop. (1970) 630,000.

HEGEL (heh'gel), **Georg Wilhelm Friedrich** (1770-1831). German philosopher. B. at Stuttgart, he lectured at Jena and Nuremberg, and was prof. of philosophy at Heidelberg 1817-18, and at Berlin 1818-31. His writings incl. *The Phenomenology of Spirit, Logic, Encyclopaedia of the Philosophical Sciences* (1817), and *Philosophy of*

HEDGEHOG. Its spines not yet fully developed, this young hedgehog is only a week old. *Photo: Heather Angel.*

Right. His German disciples split into 'Right Hegelians', who like H. himself championed religion, the Prussian State and the existing order, and 'Left Hegelians', among them Marx, who used H.'s dialectic to show the inevitability of radical change and criticized both religion and society.

H. conceived of consciousness and the external object as forming a unity, in which neither factor can exist independently. Mind and nature are two abstractions of one indivisible whole. Thus the world is the unfolding and expression of one all-embracing absolute idea, an organism constantly developing by its own internal necessity so as to become the gradual embodiment of reason. The laws of thinking are in principle the laws of reality, e.g. logic must reflect the contradictions within nature, whereby everything not only is something, but is striving to become something else. The whole of history is realization of the Absolute through phases of culture, each of which is embodied in a great nation. Each system by its own development brings about its opposite (antithesis), and finally a higher synthesis unifies and embodies both.

HĒGE'MONY. First used of the dominant leadership exercised over the other Greek city states by Athens, etc., it was adopted later in reference to Prussia in Germany, and by China in propaganda against Vietnam in SE Asia, and the USA and USSR throughout the world.

HE'GIRA or **HEJIRA** (Arabic, 'flight'). Name given to the Mohammedan era. The word denotes the escape of Mohammed from Mecca to Medina on 16 July, AD 622, the date when the era begins. The Mohammedan year is indicated by the letters AH *anno hegirae* (Latin, in the year of the H.).

HEIDEGGER (hī'deger), **Martin** (1889-1976). German philosopher. A student of Husserl, he pub. his influential *Sein und Zeit* (*Being and Time*) in 1927, but his arguments tend to be illogical. Often regarded as the chief exponent of existentialism, he denied ever having been an existentialist.

HEIDELBERG (hīd'el-). W German town on the S bank of the Neckar, 19km (12m) SE of Mannheim. H. univ., the oldest in Germany, was estab. in 1386. The town is overlooked by its ruined castle, built in the 13th-17th cents., 100m (330ft) above the river. Pop. (1978) 129,200.

Also a village near Melbourne, Australia, which gave its name - the **Heidelberg School** - to a group of artists working in teaching camps in the neighbourhood. They incl. Roberts, Streeton and Conder, and used an impressionistic technique. Flourishing 1888-90, the school has its most famous exhibition in 1889, the '9 by 5', from the size of the cigar-box lids used.

HEIFETZ (hī'fets), Jascha (1901-). Violinist. B. at Vilna, he first performed at the age of 5, and before he was 17 had played in most European capitals, and in America, where he settled.

HEILBRONN (hīl-). W. German town on the r. Neckar, Baden-Württemberg. Pop. (1978) 111,700.

HEILONGJIANG (hāloongjē-ahng'). Most northerly Chinese prov. (formerly Heilungkiang), with the H. river (Black Dragon r.) on its N border. Crops incl. wheat, soya beans, sugar beet and flax; gold and coal are mined, and China's largest oilfield is nr. Anda NW of the cap. Harbin. Area 710,000 sq.km (274,060 sq.m); pop. (1979) 32,000,000.

HEILUNGKIANG. *See* HEILONGJIANG.

HEINE (hī'ne), **Heinrich** (1797-1856). German poet. B. at Düsseldorf, of Jewish parents, he pub. his first book of poems in 1821. His *Reisebilder,* which announced his revolutionary sympathies, appeared in 1826, and the *Buch der Lieder* in 1827. After 1831 he lived mainly in Paris, as a correspondent for German papers, but the publication of his writings was forbidden on political grounds in 1835. Later poems include the satire *Atta Troll* (1847), and *Romanzero* (1851). From 1848 he was confined to his bed by spinal paralysis. Much of his prose is topical journalism, but displays his characteristic gifts of fancy, irony, and satirical humour.

HEINKEL (hīn'kel), **Ernst** (1888-1958). German aircraft designer. He founded his firm in 1922, and built the first jet aircraft 1939 (developed independently of the Whittle jet of 1941). During the S.W.W. he was Germany's biggest producer of warplanes.

HEISENBERG (hī'sen-), **Werner Carl** (1901-76). German physicist. The originator of quantum mechanics, and of the principle of indeterminacy (i.e. that there is an ultimate limit on physical measurement or observation in scientific experiment because the very act of measurement changes the behaviour of objects under scrutiny) in physics, he was awarded a Nobel prize in 1932. His attempt to formulate a single natural law accounting for the existence of all known and to-be-discovered atomic particles failed.

HEJAZ (hejahz'). Part of Saudi Arabia, lying along the shores of the Red Sea. It consists of a coastal plain rising sharply to a line of mountains parallel to the coast, and in the E a desert plateau. Where water is available for irrigation wheat, barley, fruit, and date palms flourish. The chief towns are the holy cities of Mecca (the cap.) and Medina, and the port of Jidda. The desert areas are inhabited by wandering Bedouin. H. was under Turkish rule from 1517 until 1916, when Hussein revolted and made himself king of H. He was forced to abdicate in 1924 by Ibn Saud, sultan of Nejd, who in 1925 proclaimed himself king of H., and in 1932 changed the name of his united dominions to the kingdom of Saudi Arabia. Area *c.* 390,000 sq.km (150,000 sq.m); pop. *c.* 2,000,000.

HEL or **HELA.** Norse goddess of the underworld.

HELEN. In Greek mythology the dau. of Zeus and Leda, and the most beautiful of women. She m. Menelaus, king of Sparta, but during his absence eloped with Paris, prince of Troy, whereupon the Greek princes sent their expedition against Troy to recover her. After the Trojan war H. returned to Sparta with Menelaus.

HELENA, St. (*c.* 247-327). Mother of the emperor Constantine the Great, and according to legend the discoverer at Jerusalem of the True Cross of Christ.

HELICOPTER. An aircraft with one or more power-driven horizontal rotors that enable it to take off and land vertically, to move in any direction or to remain stationary in the air. Hs. are used in passenger service; life-saving in floods, earthquakes, and sea and mountain rescue; and in firefighting, agriculture, etc. In war they carry men and equipment in difficult terrain, and make aerial reconnaissance and attacks. Naval carriers are being increasingly built, Hs. with depth charges and homing torpedoes being guided to submarine or surface targets beyond the carrier's attack range. The H. may also use dunking sonar to find targets beyond the carrier's own radar horizon. As many as 30 Hs. may be used on larger carriers, in combination with V/STOL aircraft.

HELICOPTER. A miniature helicopter, the Westland Wisp, which acts as a 'spy-in-the-sky'. Less easy to shoot down than a full-size aircraft and much less expensive, it is ideal for reconnaissance behind enemy lines. *Photo: Associated Press.*

HELIGOLAND. Small island in the North Sea off the mouth of the Elbe. It was taken from the Danes in 1807 by the British, who ceded it to Germany in 1890. The Germans strongly fortified it, and used it as a naval base in both world wars. The fortifications were destroyed in 1947. Area 0.6 sq.km (150 acres); pop. *c.* 3,000.

HELIO'PŌLIS. Chief centre of the worship of the sun-god Ra in ancient Egypt, near the modern village of Matariah, *c.* 10km (6m) NE of Cairo; it appears in the Bible as On.

HĒ'LIOS. The Greek sun-god, who was thought to make his daily journey across the sky in a chariot.

HĒ'LIOTROPE. Genus of plants of the Boraginaceae family (*Heliotropium*), a few of which are found in Europe. The forked spikes of blue, lilac, or white flowers, and also the leaves, alter their position constantly so as to face the sun. The garden H. (*H. arborescens*) was introduced into Europe from Peru.

HĒ'LIUM (Gk. *helios*, the sun). Symbol He, at. wt. 4.003, at. no. 2. Evidence of its existence in the Sun was first obtained by Janssen in 1868 from a line in the solar spectrum and Ramsay isolated it in 1895. H. is a colourless, odourless, inert, non-inflammable and very light gas. It is present in natural gases issuing from the earth in Kansas and other parts of N America, in radioactive minerals and in small quantities in the atmosphere, and is obtained by compression and fractionation of the natural gas. When ionized, by losing its two electrons in a high electric field, H. becomes identified with the alpha-particles ejected by many natural and man-made isotopes. Because of its short de-ionization time it is used in thyratrons. H.-oxygen atmospheres are used in high-pressure breathing work, as required by divers. H. being less soluble than nitrogen in blood it does not give rise to the 'bends'. Liquid H. is very important in cryogenics (q.v.). It is of value in nuclear work on account of its very low cross-section for absorbing neutrons, and because it is a good heat-transfer medium, and in airships because of its non-inflammability.

HELL. In the Bible, the word is used to translate Hebrew and Greek words all meaning the place of departed spirits, the abode of the dead. In popular speech, however, H. is the place in which unrepentant sinners suffer the eternal torments of the damned. Vivid descriptions of the physical and spiritual pains of H. have been frequently given by theologians, but during the last century the tendency, save among Roman Catholics, has been to regard H. as a legendary conception, or at least as a state rather than a place. The idea of H. is also contained in Islam and most of the other great religions.

HE'LLEBORE. Plants of the genus *Helleborus*, Ranunculaceae family. The green H., or bear's-foot, flowers in early spring, and has pale yellowish-green flowers. Stinking H. produces a flower stem up to a foot tall, with drooping pale green flowers.

HE'LLEBORINE. Name applied to several British wild flowers, principally of the *Epipactis* genus of the Orchidaceae. Broad H. bears greenish-purple flowers. Marsh H. grows in moist places, producing pink or white flowers.

HELLENES (hel'ēnz). The name by which the ancient Greeks knew themselves, and which is still used by the modern Greeks. Their country is called Hellas.

HELLESPONT. The ancient name for the Dardanelles (q.v.).

HELLMAN, Lillian (1907–84). American playwright. B. in New Orleans, she worked as a journalist in New York before achieving fame as a dramatist. Her plays, which are largely concerned with contemporary political and social issues, incl. *The Children's Hour* (1934), *The Little Foxes*

HELL. Medieval concepts of Hell were often crudely physical. Among the deadly sins, anger was punished by dismemberment in *Le grant kalendrier et compost des Bergiers,* printed by Nicolas Le Rouge, at Troyes, in 1496.

(1939), *Watch on the Rhine* (1941), and *Toys in the Attic* (1960).

HELMHOLTZ, Hermann Ludwig Ferdinand von (1821-94). German scientist. B. at Potsdam, he became prof. of physics at Berlin. In 1847 he pub. an epoch-making treatise on the conservation of energy. He investigated the mechanics of vision, wrote a *Manual of Physiological Optics* (1856-66), invented the ophthalmoscope, and in his *Doctrine of the Sensations of Tone* (1862) gave a complete study of sound.

HE'LMONT, Jean Baptiste van (1577-1644). Belgian scientist. B. in Brussels, he studied at Louvain, and practised medicine at Vilvorde, near Brussels. He was the first to realize that gases exist apart from the atmosphere, and claimed to have invented the word 'gas'. He was a pioneer experimental biologist, and his carefully controlled 5-year experiment on tree growth was a model of sound scientific method.

HĒ'LOTS. The class of slaves in ancient Sparta, who probably represented the aboriginal inhabitants. Their cruel treatment by the Spartans became proverbial.

HELPMANN, Sir Robert (1909-). Australian dancer, choreographer and actor. B. in Adelaide, he was the leading male dancer with the Sadler's Wells Ballet 1933-50, successfully partnering Margot Fonteyn (q.v.) in the war years. He was noted for his gift for mime and for his dramatic sense, also apparent in his choreographic work, e.g. *Miracle in the Gorbals* (1944). Knighted 1968.

HE'LSINGBORG. Port on the SW coast of Sweden, facing Helsingör across the Sound. Industries incl. copper-smelting, rubber and chemical manufacture, and sugar refining. Pop. (1978) 101,000.

HELSINGFORS. Swedish name of HELSINKI.

HE'LSINGÖR. Port on the NE coast of Denmark, linked by a ferry with Helsingborg across the Sound, here only 5km (3m) wide. It has shipyards. Shakespeare made it the scene of *Hamlet.* Pop. (1975) 55,700.

HELSINGÖR. Kronborg Castle some 45 km (28 m) north of Copenhagen, built by Frederik II 1574–85, the setting for Shakespeare's *Hamlet. Photo: Courtesy of the Danish Tourist Board.*

HE'LSINKI. Capital city and port on the S coast of Finland. Its natural harbour has to be kept open by ice-breakers in winter. There are many fine modern buildings, among them the parliament house. Older buildings incl. the cathedral and the univ. Pop. met. area (1977) 825,400.

At the *H. Conference* (1975) on European security agreement was reached among 35 countries (incl. the Soviet bloc and the USA) on questions of security, economics, science, technology, environment and co-operation in humanitarian fields. The practical outcome was not marked.

HELVE'LLYN. Peak of the English Lake District 950m (3,118 ft) between Thirlmere and Ullswater.

HELVETIA (helvēsh'a). Region, corresponding to W Switzerland, occupied by the Celtic Helvetii in the 1st cent. BC-5th cent. AD. In 58 BC Caesar repulsed their invasion of southern Gaul at Bibracte (nr Autun) and H. became subject to Rome.

HELVETIUS (elvehsē-us'), **Claude Adrien** (1715-71). French philosopher. B. in Paris, he became a farmer-general of taxes in 1738. In *De l'Esprit* (1758) he maintained that self-interest, however disguised, is the mainspring of all human action, and that since conceptions of good and evil vary according to period and locality there is no absolute good or evil.

HEMANS (hem'anz), **Felicia Dorothea** (1793-1835). British poetess, *née* Browne. B. in Liverpool, she pub. many vols. of sentimental verse which attained great popularity. Her best-known poem is 'Casabianca'.

HEMEL HEMPSTEAD (hem'el hemp'sted). Market town in Herts, England, 40km (25m) NW of London, developed from 1946 as a 'new town'. Paper, electrical goods and office equipment are made. Pop. (1975) 73,500.

HEMINGWAY, Ernest (1898-1961). American novelist. B. in Illinois, the son of a doctor, he became a newspaper correspondent in Kansas City. Wounded while serving as a volunteer ambulance man in Italy during the F.W.W., he used these experiences for his war book *Farewell to Arms* (1929). He was much influenced by Gertrude Stein (q.v.) who introduced him to bull-fighting, the theme of his first novel *Fiesta* (1926: US *The Sun Also Rises*) and of *Death in the Afternoon* (1932). *For Whom the Bell Tolls* (1940), has a Spanish Civil War setting, and he served as a correspondent both in this conflict and in the S.W.W. His passion for big-game hunting emerges in short stories, such as 'The Snows of Kilimanjaro' and 'The Short Happy Life of Francis Macomber', and *The Old Man and the Sea* (1952), telling of the duel between a Cuban fisherman and an enormous fish. In 1954 he was awarded a Nobel prize for his 'forceful mastery, which has created a new style in the contemporary art of narration'. His simple, curt sentences attracted imitation. He shot himself.

HĒMI'PTERA (or **Rhynchota**). Order of insects with mouth-parts adapted for feeding by puncture and suction. There are 2 sub-orders, the Homoptera (q.v.) and the Heteroptera (including the bedbug, cotton stainer and chinch bug).

HEMLOCK. Genus of plants (*Conium*) of the Umbelliferae, the only important species being common H. (*C. maculatum*), found in Britain and Europe, and naturalized in the Americas. Reaching 90-150cm (3-5ft), it bears umbels of small white flowers, and the whole plant, but especially the root and fruit, is poisonous, causing paralysis of the nervous system. The ancient Greeks used it as a mode of capital punishment (*see* SOCRATES).

HEMP. Annual plant (*Cannabis sativa*) of the Urticaceae family cultivated in most temperate countries for its fibres, produced in the outer layer of the stem (1-4.5m/3-15ft high), and used in ropes, twines and, occasionally, in a type of linen or lace. Russia is the largest producer, Italy has the finest quality, and it is important in N India and the USA. Dried leaves or resin form a hallucinogen which may be smoked, made into a drink, or eaten. Use of the drug results in loss of inhibitions, uncontrolled giggling and talking, distortion of perception of space and time, and impairment of judgment and memory. Long-term effects have yet to be fully studied, but it soon creates great psychological dependence. H. is also known as bhang (India), dagga (S Africa), hashish (Arabia), kif (N Africa), and pot or marijuana (in W hemisphere).

The name H. is extended to similar types of fibre, e.g. sisal H. or henequen (obtained from the leaves of *Agave rigida* and other species native to Yucatan and cultivated in many tropical countries) and manila H. (from a plant native to the Philippines and Moluccas).

HENAN (hunahn'). Prov. of N China (formerly Honan). It is chiefly agricultural and wheat, maize, sesame and cotton are grown on the river plains of the Huang Ho. The cap. is Zhengzhou. Area 167,000 sq.km (64,462 sq.m.); pop. (1979) 70,000,000.

HENBANE. Wild plant (*Hyoscyamus niger*) common on waste ground in Britain, central and S Europe, and W Asia. A branching plant, 30-120cm (1-4ft) high, it has hairy leaves and a nauseous smell. The yellow flowers are bell-shaped. It is sometimes grown for medicinal purposes, but its use is dangerous.

HEMP. The source of infinite controversy: a fine specimen of Indian hemp *(Cannabis sativa). Photo: Heather Angel.*

HENDERSON, Arthur (1863-1935). British Lab. statesman. B. in Glasgow, he worked 20 yrs as an iron-moulder in Newcastle, entered parliament in 1903 and did much for Lab.'s political organization. He was Home Sec. in the first Lab. govt in 1924, and was For. Sec. 1929-31, when he accorded the Soviet govt full recognition. For his constant endeavour to secure international limitation of arms he was awarded a Nobel peace prize in 1934.

HENDON. Residential district in the bor. of Barnet, Greater London. Its airport (1910-57) was important in the early days of flying. The Met. Police Detective Training and Motor Driving Schools are here, and the R.A.F. Museum (1972) incl. the Battle of Britain Museum (1980).

HENIE (hen'i), **Sonja** (1913-69). Norwegian skater. Norwegian champion at 11, she won 10 world championships and 3 Olympic titles, turning professional in 1936 and making numerous films.

HENLEY-ON-THAMES. English town in Oxon, 10km (6m) NE of Reading. It stands at the foot of the Chilterns on the left bank of the Thames, which is crossed by a fine stone bridge. It is famous for its annual regatta, held first in 1839, and taking place usually in July. Pop. (1972) 11,780.

HENNA. Small shrub (*Lawsonia inermis*) found in Iran, India, Egypt and N Africa. The leaves and young twigs are ground to powder, mixed with hot water to a paste and applied to the fingernails and hair of women, and beards of

HENRY VIII. Probably commissioned by Henry himself, this portrait group shows the King with his family. Princess Mary enters left; Prince Edward and Queen Jane Seymour (who actually died at the birth of her son) are with the King centre; and Princess Elizabeth enters right. *Photo: By gracious permission of H.M. the Queen.*

HENLEY-ON-THAMES. Henley regatta, still one of the major events of the London season after more than 100 years. *Photo: Courtesy of the British Tourist Authority.*

men, giving an orange-red hue. The colour may then be changed to black by applying a preparation of indigo.

HENRIETTA MARIA (1609-69). Queen of England. The daughter of Henry IV of France, she m. Charles I in 1625. As she used her influence to encourage him to make himself absolute, she became highly unpopular, and had to go into exile 1644-60. She returned to England at the Restoration, but retired in 1665 to France.

HENRY I (1068-1135). King of England. The youngest son of William I, he succeeded his brother William II in 1100, and won the support of the Saxons by granting them a charter and marrying a Saxon princess. He was an able administrator, who built up a professional bureaucracy and estab. the system of sending out itinerant justices.

HENRY II (1133-89). King of England. The son of Matilda, daughter of Henry I, and of Geoffrey of Anjou, he inherited Normandy and Anjou, and acquired Poitou, Guienne, and Gascony by marriage. He succeeded Stephen as king in 1154, and successfully restored order and curbed the power of the barons. His attempt to bring the Church courts under royal control led to a long struggle with Becket, after whose murder it had to be abandoned. During his reign the English conquest of Ireland began.

HENRY III (1207-72). King of England. He succeeded his father John in 1216, and assumed royal power in 1227. His subservience to the papacy and generosity to foreign favourites provoked many protests from the barons, who in 1264 rebelled under de Montfort's leadership, defeated H. at Lewes, and held him a prisoner. After the royalist victory at Evesham in 1265 H. was restored to the throne.

HENRY IV (1367-1413). King of England. The son of John of Gaunt, he took an active part in politics under Richard II, and was banished in 1398. He returned in 1399, headed a revolt, and was accepted as king by parliament. His reign was troubled by baronial rebellions and Glendower's rising in Wales, and in order to win support he had to conciliate the Church by a law for the burning of heretics, and to make many concessions to parliament.

HENRY V (1387-1422). King of England. The son of Henry IV, he devoted his life after 1400 to war and statecraft, and succeeded to the throne in 1413. He invaded Normandy in 1415, captured Harfleur, and defeated the French at Agincourt. In 1417-19 he overran Normandy and captured Rouen, and in 1420 he was recognized as his heir by the French king.

HENRY VI (1421-71). King of England. He succeeded his father Henry V in infancy, and came of age in 1442. He identified himself completely with the party opposed to the continuation of the French war, and after his marriage in 1445 was dominated by his wife, Margaret of Anjou. The unpopularity of the government, especially after the loss of the English conquests in France, encouraged the duke of York to claim the crown, and although York was killed in 1460 his son Edward proclaimed himself king in 1461. H. was captured in 1465, and although temporarily restored to the throne in 1470 was again imprisoned in 1471 and soon murdered.

HENRY VII (1457-1509). King of England. The son of Edmund Tudor, earl of Richmond, he was descended through his mother Margaret Beaufort from John of Gaunt. He spent his early life in Brittany, until in 1485 he landed in England, raised a rebellion, and defeated and killed Richard III at Bosworth. He was recognized as king by parliament, although Yorkist rebellions continued until 1497, and by means of the Star Chamber restored order after the Wars of the Roses. By the confiscation of rebels' property, heavy fines, and forced loans he accumulated a large fortune, which rendered him practically independent of parliament.

HENRY VIII (1491-1547). King of England. He succeeded his father Henry VII in 1509, and m. Catherine of Aragon, the widow of his brother Arthur. During the period 1511-29 he pursued an active foreign policy, largely under the guidance of Wolsey. In 1529, as Wolsey had failed to persuade the Pope to grant H. a divorce, he was disgraced. With parliament's approval H. renounced the papal supremacy, proclaimed himself Head of the Church, and dissolved the monasteries; in this policy his chief assistant was Thomas Cromwell. H. nevertheless remained orthodox in theology, and while executing as traitors RCs who denied the royal supremacy he also burned Protestants for heresy. Catherine was divorced in 1533, and H. m. Anne Boleyn, who in 1536 was beheaded for adultery. H.'s 3rd wife, Jane Seymour, d. in 1537. Anne of Cleves he m. in 1540 in pursuance of Cromwell's policy of allying with the German Protestants, but rapidly abandoned this policy, divorced Anne, and beheaded Cromwell. His 5th wife, Catherine Howard, was beheaded in 1542, and the following year he m. Catherine Parr, who survived him.

HENRY. Name of 4 kings of France. HENRY I (1008-60), who succeeded in 1031, spent much of his reign in a struggle with William the Conqueror, duke of Normandy. HENRY II (1519-59), who succeeded his father Francis I in 1547, captured Metz and Verdun from the emperor, and Calais from the English. He was killed in a tournament. HENRY III (1551-89), who succeeded his brother Charles IX in 1574, became involved in a struggle both with the Huguenots, headed by Henry of Navarre, and the Catholic League, headed by the duke of Guise. Expelled from Paris by the League in 1588, H. allied with the Huguenots, but was assassinated by a monk while besieging Paris. HENRY IV (1533-1610), the son of Antoine de Bourbon and Jeanne, queen of Navarre, was brought up as a Protestant, and from 1576 led the Huguenots in the wars of religion. Having succeeded Henry III in 1589, he settled the religious question by himself accepting Catholicism, while granting toleration to Protestants. He restored peace and strong government to France, and brought back prosperity by measures for the promotion of industry and agriculture and the improvement of communications. He was assassinated in 1610 by an RC fanatic.

HENRY. Name of 7 Holy Roman Emperors. HENRY I, called THE FOWLER (*c.* 876-936), became duke of Saxony in 912, and German king in 919. HENRY III (1017-56), who succeeded in 1093, raised the Empire to the height of its power, and extended its authority over Poland, Bohemia and Hungary. HENRY IV (1050-1106), who succeeded in 1056, was involved from 1075 in a struggle with the papacy under Gregory VII. HENRY V (1081-1125), son of Henry IV, continued the struggle with the Church until a settlement on the investitures question was reached in 1122. HENRY VI (1165-97) inherited Sicily by marriage in 1189, and the Empire from his father Frederick I in 1190. As part of his plan for making the Empire universal he captured and imprisoned Richard I of England, and compelled him to do homage. HENRY VII (*c.* 1269-1313), originally count of Luxembourg, was elected emperor in 1308, and attempted unsuccessfully to revive the imperial supremacy in Italy.

HENRY, Joseph (1797-1878). American scientist. B. at Albany, NY, he became prof. of natural philosophy at Princeton 1832-46, and secretary of the Smithsonian Institution in 1846. He invented the first electromagnetic motor in 1829, and a telegraphic apparatus; he also discovered the principle of electromagnetic induction, simultaneously with Faraday, and the phenomenon of self-induction. He later estab. a nation-wide meteorological service, investigated the properties of sound-waves in fog, and perfected a system of fog signals. His name is given to the unit of electrical induction.

HENRY, O. Pseudonym of the American short-story writer William Sydney Porter (1862-1910). B. in N Carolina, he worked in Texas as a bank clerk and a journalist, and was imprisoned for 3 years on a charge of embezzlement. After his release he lived in New York, devoting himself entirely to the short story, and pub. several collections, beginning with *Cabbages and Kings* (1904) and *The Four Million* (1906). His stories, which deal mainly with New York or southern and western life, are marked by a brilliant colloquial style, skilled construction with 'twist' endings, and a deep sense of pity.

HENRY, Patrick (1736-99). American statesman. He is remembered as an orator, espec. his speeches against the Stamp Act 1765 telling George III 'If this be treason, make the most of it!' and supporting the arming of the Virginia militia 1775 'Give me liberty or give me death!' He was governor of the state 1776-9 and 1784-6.

HENRY, William (1774-1836). British chemist. In 1803 he formulated *Henry's law*: when a gas is dissolved in a liquid at a given temperature, its weight is in direct proportion to the gas pressure.

HENRYSON, Robert (*c.* 1430-*c.* 1505). Scottish poet. His works incl. lively versions of Aesop and the *Testament of Cresseid*, a continuation of Chaucer.

HENRY THE NAVIGATOR (1394-1460). Portuguese prince. The son of John I, he devoted himself largely to the promotion of exploration and colonization. Under his patronage Portuguese seamen explored and colonized Madeira and the Azores, and sailed down the African coast almost to Sierra Leone.

HENZE (hen'tse), **Hans Werner** (1926-). German composer. Well known for his operas *Boulevard Solitude* (1952: based on *Manon Lescaut*) and *King Stag* (1956), and more recently *The Bassarids* (1974: based on the *Bacchae* of Euripides), and the radically left-wing *We Come to the River* (1976) with libretto by Edward Bond, as well as for his ballet *Ondine* (1958), he shows in his music the influence of Schoenberg, and he often uses a modified 12-note technique (dodecaphony).

HENZE. One of the most impressive composers of modern opera, Hans Werner Henze. *Photo: Christian Steiner.*

HEPATĪ'TIS, viral. Infection of the liver causing inflammation and jaundice, the result of contaminated water or food, blood transfusion from a carrier, etc. It is a prostrating disease, recalcitrant to all drugs, and increasingly widespread. By 1980 a vaccine had been developed.

HEPBURN, Katherine (1909-). American actress. B. in Connecticut, her gangly grace and husky voice brought stardom in such films as *Morning Glory* (1933), *Guess Who's Coming to Dinner* (1967) and *The Lion in Winter* (1968), for all of which she received academy awards.

HEPHAESTUS (hifēst'us). Greek god of fire and metal craftsmanship, identified with the Roman Vulcan. The son of Zeus and Hera, he was lame and was m. to Aphrodite.

HEPPLEWHITE, George (d. 1786). British craftsman. In his furniture workshop at St. Giles, Cripplegate, in London, he developed a simple elegant style, especially in his chairs, often with shield- or heart-shaped backs. He worked mainly in mahogany or satinwood, and his characteristic decorations of feathers, shells, or wheat-ears were inlaid or painted, rather than carved.

HEPTARCHY (hept'arki). Term coined by 16th cent. historians to denote the 7 Saxon kingdoms supposed to exist prior to AD 800: Northumbria, Mercia, E Anglia, Essex, Kent, Sussex, and Wessex.

HEPWORTH, Dame Barbara (1903-75). British sculptor. B. at Wakefield, she studied at Leeds School of Art and the Royal College of Art, and from 1939 lived at St Ives, Cornwall, where her studio is a museum. She worked in concrete, bronze, wood and aluminium, but her favourite medium was stone. She m. 1st sculptor John Skeaping, and 2nd Ben Nicholson (q.v.); both marriages were dissolved.

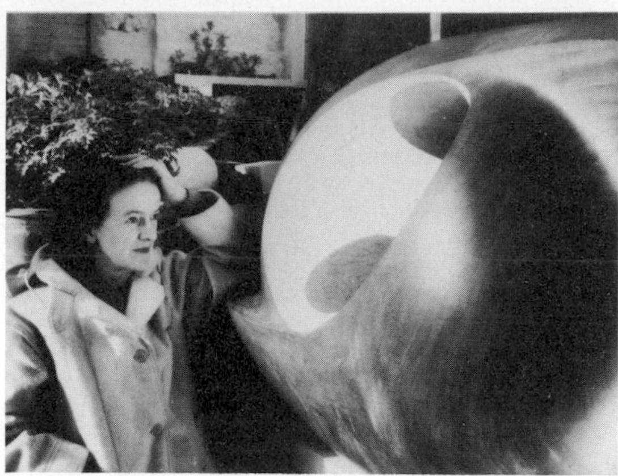

HEPWORTH. The sculptor, Barbara Hepworth, with a favourite among her works, a pierced oval in stone titled 'Delos', a reference to its being the birthplace of Apollo. *Courtesy of Barbara Hepworth.*

HĒ'RA. Greek goddess. The sister and consort of Zeus, she was the mother of Hephaestus, Hebe, and Ares. The protectress of women and marriage, she was identified with the Roman Juno.

HERACLĪ'TUS (c. 540-475 BC). Greek philosopher. B. at Ephesus, he maintained in his chief work, *On Nature*, that the ultimate principle is fire, and that everything is in a state of eternal flux, producing a notably coherent system.

HERAKLION. Largest city of Crete, formerly known as Candia (q.v.). Pop. (1971) 77,500.

HERALDS' COLLEGE or **College of Arms.** English heraldic body formed in 1484 by Richard III incorporating the heralds attached to the Royal Household; re-incorporated by Royal Charter of Philip and Mary in 1555. There are 3 Kings of Arms, 6 Heralds, and 4 Pursuivants, who specialize in genealogical and heraldic work. The College establishes the right to bear Arms, and the Kings of Arms grant Arms by letters patent. In Ireland the office of Ulster King of Arms was transferred in 1943 to the College of Arms in London and placed with that of Norroy King of Arms, who now has jurisdiction in Northern Ireland as well as in the north of England.

HERAT (heraht'). Cap. of H. province, Afghanistan, on the N banks of the Hari Rud. A principal road junction, it was a great city in ancient and medieval times. Pop. (1980) 160,000.

HÉRAULT (ārō'). River in S France, 160km (100m) long, rising in the Cevennes and flowing into the Gulf of Lyons near Agde. It gives its name to a dept.

HERB. A plant which does not possess a permanent woody stem, the parts above ground dying every winter. Also a plant with a sweet, bitter, aromatic, or pungent taste, used in cookery, medicine, or perfumery.

HERBERT, George (1593-1633). English poet. He became in 1619 orator to Cambridge university, and in 1625 a prebendary in Hunts, where his friends incl. Donne, Walton, and Bacon. After ordination in 1630 he became vicar of Bemerton, Wilts, and d. of consumption. His vol. of religious poems, *The Temple*, appeared in 1633. His brother, **Lord Edward H. of Cherbury** (1583-1648), was also a poet and religious philosopher and in his *De veritate* (1624) propounded a theory of natural religion, which makes him the founder of English Deism.

HERBERT, Wally (Walter) (1934-). British surveyor-explorer. His first surface crossing by dog sledge of the Arctic Ocean 1968-9, from Alaska to Spitzbergen, was the longest sustained sledging journey 6,000 km (3,800 m) in polar exploration.

HERBERT OF LEA, Sidney Herbert, 1st baron (1810-61). British statesman. He was Sec. for War in Aberdeen's Liberal-Peelite coalition of 1852-5, and during the Crimean War was responsible for sending Florence Nightingale to the front. After the war he supported army reforms and became a peer in 1861.

HERB ROBERT. Common wild flower of the Geraniaceae family (genus *Geranium*), found throughout Europe, central Asia, and N America. About 30cm (12in), it bears hairy leaves and small purplish flowers, and has a reddish hairy stem. When rubbed, the leaves have an unpleasant smell.

HERCEGOVINA, HERZEGOVINA. *See* BOSNIA-HERCEGOVINA.

HERCŪLĀ'NĒUM. Ancient city of Italy between Naples and Pompeii. H. was overwhelmed during the eruption of Vesuvius (AD 79), which also destroyed Pompeii. It was excavated from the 18th cent. onward.

HERCULES (Gk Heracles). Greek hero, the son of Zeus and Alcmene, famed for his strength. While serving Eurystheus, king of Argos, he performed the celebrated 12 Labours which included the cleansing of the Augean stables. The *Pillars of H.* are the great rocks guarding the entrance to the Mediterranean - Gibraltar and Ceuta.

HERDER, Johann Gottfried von (1744-1803). German poet, critic, and philosopher. B. in E Prussia, he studied at Königsberg where he was influenced by Kant, became pastor at Riga, met Goethe in Strasbourg (1770), and in 1776 was called to Weimar as court preacher. H.'s critical writings indicate his intuitive rather than reasoning trend of thought. He gave considerable impulse to the Storm and Stress movement in Ger. literature. He collected folk songs of all nations (1778) and in the *Ideen zur Philosophie der Geschichte der Menschheit* (1784-91) he outlined the stages of cultural development of mankind.

HEREFORD (her'e-). Town in Hereford and Worcester, England, on the Wye 39km (24m) NW of Gloucester. The present cathedral was begun in 1079. Pop. (1972) 47,150.

HEREFORD and Worcester. Co. of England created in 1974 from the combined former cos. of Herefordshire and Worcestershire (q.v.). The W half, formerly Herefordshire, lies on the Welsh border, and is broken hilly country drained by the Wye and its tributaries. Pears and apples and vegetables are grown and Hereford cattle are famous. The Malvern Hills are in the E, running along the former border with Worcestershire. The admin. HQ is Worcester. Area 3,925 sq.km (1,515 sq.m); pop. (1978) 610,100.

HEREROS (her'ārōz). A nomadic Bantu-speaking people living in SW Africa.

HERESY. A doctrine or system of thought opposed to orthodox belief, especially in religion, e.g. those held by the Gnostics, Arians, Pelagians, Montanists, Albigenses, Waldenses, Lollards, Anabaptists, Unitarians, Quakers, etc.

HEREWARD (her'e-), called **the Wake** (fl. 1070). English patriot. A small Lincs. landowner, he led a rebellion against Norman rule in 1070. William the Conqueror captured his stronghold in the Isle of Ely in 1071. H. escaped with a few companions, and his fate is obscure. *See* CHARLES KINGSLEY.

HERMAPHRODĪ'TUS. In Gk. mythology, the son of Hermes and Aphrodite. He was beloved by a nymph whose prayer to the gods for perpetual union with him was answered in that she and H. became one body, but possessed of the characteristics of both sexes. Hence the modern 'hermaphrodite'.

The true hermaphrodite has both ovaries and sperm-producing organs; pseudo-hermaphrodites have the internal organs of one sex, but appear externally to be of the opposite sex. The true sex of the latter only becomes apparent at adolescence when the normal hormonic activity appropriate to the internal organs begins to function. In some simpler animal species, hermaphroditism is the norm, e.g. the snail and oyster, and it is the standard form in flowering plants.

HE'RMĒS. In Gk mythology, the son of Zeus and Maia and messenger of the gods, usually appearing with winged sandals and bearing a staff around which serpents are coiled. Identified with Mercury and Thoth, he was the god of thieves, travellers and merchants.

HERMES TRISMEGISTUS. Supposed author of the *Hermetica* (2-3rd cents. AD) inculcating a cosmic religion, in which the Sun is regarded as the visible manifestation of God. In the Renaissance they were thought to be by an Egyptian priest contemporary with Moses, and it is possible they do contain some Egyptian material. Copernicus studied them closely.

HERMIT. Religious votary living in seclusion, often practising extremes of mortification, e.g. Simeon Stylites. Modern Hs., e.g. the Anglican community at Bede House, Kent, have bungalow 'cells'.

HERMIT CRAB. Genus of crustaceans (Paguridea). The abdominal segments are not encased as in true crabs, but the H.C. lives in the shell of a gastropod. They are found on the coasts of Europe, America, and the West Indies, usually in close association with sea-anemones and sponges.

HE'RMON (Arab. Jebel esh-Sheikh). Snow-topped mtn 2,814 m (9,232 ft), the highest in Syria. It is the traditional scene of the transfiguration of Jesus.

HERNE BAY. Seaside resort in Kent, England, on the Thames estuary. Reculver, 5km (3m) to the E was the site of a Roman station. Pop. (1972) 25,870.

HERNIA. Protrusion of a part of the bowel through a weak spot in the abdominal wall, usually in the groin or navel. The appearance is that of a rounded, soft tumour.

HERO and LEANDER. In ancient Gk story, H. was the priestess of Aphrodite at Sestos on the Hellespont. She was loved by Leander, who visited her nightly by swimming across the strait from Abydos on the opposite shore. One stormy night he was drowned; and H. cast herself into the sea out of grief.

HERO of Alexandria. A Greek mathematician and writer, probably of the 2nd cent. AD, who invented an automatic fountain, and perhaps a kind of stationary steam-engine.

HE'ROD (74-4 BC). King of the Jews; known as HEROD THE GREAT. The son of Antipater, he was declared king of Judaea by the Romans in 40 BC, and with Antony's assistance estab. his government in Jerusalem in 37 BC. He rebuilt the Temple at Jerusalem, but his Hellenizing tendencies made him suspect to orthodox Jewry. His last years were akin to a reign of terror, and St Matthew alleges that he ordered the slaughter of all the infants in Bethlehem to ensure the death of Christ, whom he visualized as a rival. His son **Herod Antipas** was tetrarch of Galilee and Peraea, 4 BC-AD 39. He m. Herodias, the divorced wife of his half-brother Herod Philip, and ordered the execution of John the Baptist. Christ was brought before him on Pontius Pilate's discovery that He was a Galilean and hence of Herod's jurisdiction. In AD 38 H.A. went to Rome to solicit the title of king, but Caligula was prejudiced against him, and he was banished. The rock citadel of Masada, built by Herod 37-31 BC, was excavated 1963-4: there were important finds of ancient texts; mosaic floors and decorated walls of the royal palace; reservoirs, etc.

HEROD AGRIPPA I (d. AD 44). Jewish ruler of Palestine under the Romans. A grandson of Herod the Great, Caligula made him a tetrarch in Palestine, and Claudius gave him the title of king. He put St James to death and imprisoned St Peter. His son **Herod Agrippa II** (d. AD 100) as king of Chalcis assisted Titus in his siege of Jerusalem, and on the fall of the city in AD 70 went to Rome, where he d. St Paul defended himself before him in AD 60.

HERO'DOTUS (*c.* 484-*c.* 424 BC). Greek historian and prose writer, who travelled widely, recording in his history observations of habits and creeds of many races. After 4 years in Athens, he settled in S Italy in 443 at Thurii, apparently staying there the rest of his life. His history, written lucidly and with charm, deals with the Greek-Persian struggle which culminated in the defeat of the Persian invasion attempts in 490 and 480 BC. The majority of the work is devoted to an early perspective history of the states involved. H. was the first historian to apply a critical sense.

HEROIN (her'ō-in). Diamorphine hydrochloride, an alkaloid obtained from morphine. A white crystalline powder, it depresses the nerve centres controlling breathing and is valuable as a sedative in conditions producing a cough, but the danger of addiction has led to its being widely banned for medical use.

HERON. Large bird in the family Ardeidae, which also includes bitterns, egrets, night-herons, and boatbills. The Common H. (*Ardea cinerea*) nests in Europe and Asia in large colonies at the tops of trees. The bird has a long neck and long legs. The plumage is chiefly grey, but there are black patches on the sides and a black crest. The legs are olive-green, and the beak yellow, except during the breeding season when it is pink. It is a wading bird, but is rarely seen to swim or walk. It feeds on fish, frogs, rats, etc.

HERPES (her'pēz). A variety of viruses which cause cold sores, chicken pox (q.v.), glandular fever, shingles, etc. Cold sores, which occur espec. on the lips are caused by *Herpes simplex*; a second type of this same virus produces sores on the genitals. The viruses remain in the body and are triggered to activity by sunburn, stress, etc. In 1980 the drug acyclovir (ACV) was developed to combat the second type, but it has side-effects. In shingles (*Herpes zoster*), red spots and small blisters appear on the skin over a set of nerve endings, accompanied by neuralgic pain and irritation, sometimes over the ribs like a girdle.

HERON. A pied heron from one of the great rookeries near the mouth of the East Alligator River in Australia's Northern Territory. *Photo: Australian Information Service.*

HERRERA (errā'ra), **Francisco** (1576-1656). Spanish artist, surnamed **El Viejo** (the Old). B. in Seville, he is remarkable for his realism, and skilled use of light and shade. His son Francisco H. (1622-85), called **El Mozo** (the Young), also b. in Seville, was remarkable for his still-lifes.

HERRICK, Robert (1591-1674). English poet. B. in Cheapside, London, he was a friend of Ben Jonson. In 1629 he became vicar of Dean Prior, near Totnes. He pub. *Hesperides* (1648), a collection of sacred and pastoral poetry unrivalled in lyric quality.

HERRING. One of the most important food fish (*Clupea harengus*), the leading member of the Clupeidae. A salt-water fish, it swims close to the surface and may be 25-45cm (10-18in) long. A silvered greenish-blue, it has only one dorsal fin and one short ventral. Young Hs. *c.* 5cm (2in) long, largely compose the delicacy known as 'whitebait'.

The H. is found in large quantities off the shores of Britain, Scandinavia, the E coast of N America, the White Sea, and in the Sea of Japan, but not in the Mediterranean. Shoals have recently diminished, partly due to over-fishing, pollution, etc., but there have been dramatic fluctuations in catches at least from the medieval period.

HERRIOT (ārē-ō'), **Édouard** (1872-1957). French Radical statesman. An opponent of Poincaré, especially his advocacy of French occupation of the Ruhr, he was briefly PM in 1924-5, 1926, and 1932. As Pres. of the Chamber in 1940 he opposed the policies of the Vichy govt, was arrested and later taken to Germany until released in 1945 by the Russians.

HERRIOT, James. Pseudonym of James Alfred Wight (1916-), British author. A practising veterinary surgeon in Thirsk, Yorks from 1940, he began writing of his experiences only at the age of fifty, e.g. *If Only They Could Talk* (1970) and *All Creatures Great and Small* (1972).

HERSCHEL, Sir William (1738-1822). British astronomer. B. at Hanover, he went to England in 1757, earning his living as a musician, whilst instructing himself in mathematics and astronomy. In 1781 he discovered Uranus, and later several of its satellites. During his appointment as astronomer to George III from 1782 he discovered the motion of the double stars round one another, and recorded it in his *Motion of the Solar System in Space* (1783). He constructed a 4ft telescope, of 40ft focal length, at Slough, in 1789, and discovered infra-red solar rays in 1800. His son **Sir John Frederick William H.** (1792-1871) was also an astronomer and estab. an observatory near Capetown in 1834, where he discovered thousands of close double stars, clusters and nebulae, reported in 1847. His inventions incl. astronomical instruments, sensitized photographic paper, and the use of sodium hyposulphite for fixing it.

HERSTMONCEUX (hurstmonsoo′). Village in E Sussex, England, 11km (7m) N of Eastbourne. The castle was first built by Sir Roger de Fiennes, a hero of Agincourt, in 1446. Greatly restored it has been since 1958 the home of the Royal Greenwich Observatory.

HERSTMONCEUX. Side by side with the 15th century castle since 1958 have been the new buildings of the Royal Greenwich Observatory. *Photo: Courtesy of the British Tourist Authority.*

HERTFORD (harf′). Admin. HQ of Herts, England, on the Lea; 3km (2m) to the SE is Haileybury College, and there are brewing and brick industries. Pop. (1972) 21,060.

HERTFORDSHIRE. County of SE England, lying N of Greater London. Across the co. from SW to NE run the Chiltern Hills. H. is drained by the Colne, Lea, and Stort, and is predominantly an agricultural county. On the chalk uplands sheep are grazed, while elsewhere the principal crops are wheat, oats, roots, beans, and potatoes. In the SW fruit is grown; other specialized products include flowers, early vegetables, and watercress. Dairy cattle are pastured by the Stort and Colne. The admin HQ is Hertford; other towns include St Albans, Watford, Bishop's Stortford, Letchworth, and Hemel Hempstead. Area 1,634 sq.km (632 sq.m); pop. (1973) 941,000.

'sHERTOGENBOSCH (s-her′tōgenbosh) (Fr., *Bois-le-Duc*). Capital of N Brabant, Netherlands, 45km (28m) SSE of Utrecht. There are shipbuilding, tobacco, and electrical industries. Pop. (1978) 86,775.

HERTZ (her′ts), **Heinrich** (1857-94). German physicist. Continuing the work of Clerk Maxwell (q.v.) in electromagnetic (*Hertzian*) waves, he prepared the way for radio communication, and showed that their behaviour resembled that of light and heat waves. The unit of frequency, the *hertz*, is also named after him.

HERTZOG (her′tsōg), **James Barry Munnik** (1866–1942). South African statesman. Founder of the Nationalist Party in 1913, he opposed S African participation in the F.W.W. In 1924 he beame PM, forming a coalition in 1924 with Smuts (q.v.). He resigned Sept. 1939 when his motion against participation in the S.W.W. was rejected.

HERZL (hertsl), **Theodor** (1860-1904). Founder of the Zionist movement. B. at Budapest, he became a successful playwright and journalist, but the Dreyfus case convinced him that the only solution to the problem of the Jews was their resettlement in a state of their own in Palestine. His *Jewish State* (1896) launched political Zionism.

HESELTINE, Michael 1933– . British Cons politician. Secretary of State for the Environment 1979–83, he succeeded John Nott as Min. for Defence in Jan. 1983. He resigned dramatically in 1986 over the Westland affair.

HE′SIOD (*c.* 700 BC). One of the earliest of the poets of ancient Greece. He is supposed to have lived a little later than Homer, and according to his own account he was b. in Boeotia. He is the author of *Works and Days*, a poem that tells of the country life, and the *Theogony*, an account of the origin of the world and of the gods.

HESPE′RIDĒS. In Gk mythology, the maidens who, far away in the west, guard the tree that produces golden apples.

HESS, Dame Myra (1890-1965). British pianist. She is remembered for her morale-boosting National Gallery concerts in the S.W.W., her transcription of the Bach chorale 'Jesu, joy of man's desiring', and her interpretations of Beethoven.

HESS, Victor (1883-1964). American physicist. B. in Austria, he was prof. at Fordham Univ., NY, from 1938. In 1936 he was awarded half a Nobel prize for his discovery of cosmic rays.

HESS, Walter Richard Rudolf (1894-). German Nazi leader. Imprisoned with Hitler 1923-5, he became his private sec., taking down *Mein Kampf* from his dictation. In 1932 he was appointed deputy to the Fuehrer, and in 1939 was nominated as Hitler's successor after Goering. He was head of the *Ausland* organization responsible for fifth-column activities abroad. On 10 May 1941 he landed by air in Britain with compromise peace proposals, and was held a prisoner-of-war till 1945, when he was tried at Nuremberg and was sentenced to life imprisonment.

HESSE, Hermann (1877-1962). German-born writer who became a Swiss citizen in 1923. A conscientious objector in the F.W.W. and a pacifist opponent of Hitler, he pub. short stories, poetry and novels, e.g. *Peter Camenzind* (1904) and *Unterm Rad* (1906). Later works, such as *Das Glasperlenspiel* (1943), tend towards the occult. He received a Nobel prize in 1946.

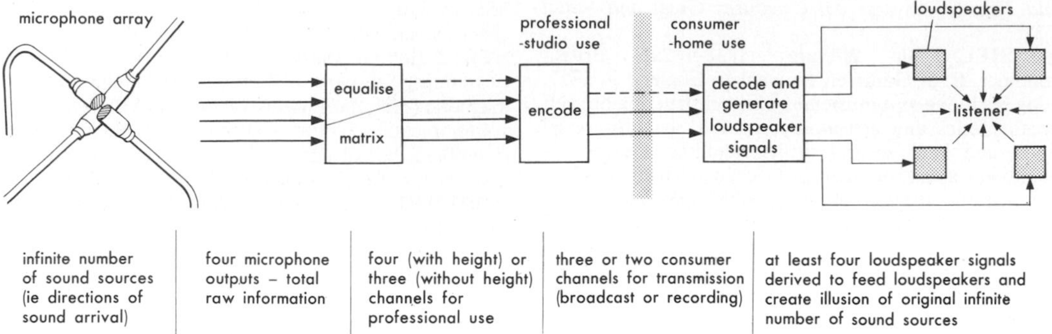

HI-FI. The tetrahedral microphone array developed for Ambisonics, and the stages through which the sound passes before reaching the listener.

HE'SSEN. State (Land) of W Germany, estab. in 1946. The cap. is Wiesbaden. About a quarter of the working pop. is engaged in agriculture, chief products being wheat, rye, oats, and potatoes, with dairying important; chemicals, motor-cars, and machines are made, and there are electrical engineering works. Area 21,125 sq.km (8,156 sq.m); pop. (1978) 5,540,600.

The Land of Hessen occupies generally the area of 2 former territories: (1) **Hesse,** a state divided into 2 separate parts by a strip of Prussian territory, the S portion consisting chiefly of the valleys of the Rhine and Main, the N being dominated by the Vogelsberg 774m (2,539 ft). Darmstadt, the cap., Giessen, Mainz, and Worms were among its towns. (2) **Hesse-Nassau,** a prov. of Prussia, a hilly region with rich timber, metal, and vine resources. Kassel, Fulda, Frankfurt, and Wiesbaden were the main towns.

HE'STIA. In Gk mythology, the goddess of the hearth. She was a daughter of Cronos (Saturn) and Rhea, and the Romans identified her with Vesta.

HEWISH, Antony (1924-). British radio-astronomer. Professor at Cambridge from 1971, he was awarded a Nobel physics prize, with Sir Martin Ryle, in 1974. In 1967-8 he discovered pulsars (q.v.), suspecting at first from the regularity of the stars' radio pulses that they might be signals from an alien civilization, but further research showed them to be natural.

HEXACHLOROPHENE (heksaklor'ofēn). Bactericide, used in minute quantities in soaps and surgical disinfectants. Trichlorophenol is used in its preparation, and without precise temperature control, TCDD (tetrachlorodibenzo-p-dioxin) may form as a by-product. The latter is highly toxic with varied long-term effects, and in 1976 at Seveso, Italy, a large area was accidentally contaminated by a factory explosion.

HEYDRICH (hīd'rikh), **Reinhard** (1904-42). German Nazi terrorist. Whilst deputy 'protector' of Bohemia and Moravia from 1941, he was ambushed and killed by 3 members of the Czech forces in Britain, who had landed by parachute. Reprisals followed incl. several hundred executions and the massacre of Lidice.

HEYERDAHL (hī'-), **Thor** (1914-). Norwegian ethnologist. He achieved world fame with the Kon-Tiki Expedition of 1947. With 5 companions he built a balsawood raft and sailed from Peru to the Pacific Is. along the Humboldt Current, proving it feasible that the Polynesians could have been migrants from S America. In 1969-70 he used reed boats of papyrus stem, like those of ancient Egypt, to demonstrate that they could have been used to cross the Atlantic, thus explaining the introduction of a sun-orientated pyramid (q.v.) culture.

HEYWOOD, Thomas (*c.* 1570-*c.* 1650). English dramatist. B. in Lincs, he became an actor in London, and wrote or adapted over 220 plays. The best was his masterly domestic tragedy, *A Woman kilde with kindnesse* (1607).

HEZEKIAH (hezekī'ah). King of Judah 719-699 BC: son of Ahaz, and father of Manasseh. Against the advice of Isaiah he rebelled against Assyrian suzerainty in alliance with Egypt, but was defeated by Sennacherib. He carried out religious reforms.

HIAWATHA (hīawaw'tha). North American Indian teacher and Onondaga chieftain of the 15th or 16th cents. who welded the Six Nations of the Iroquois (q.v.) into the league of the Long House. Longfellow's epic *Hiawatha* (1855) was based on the data collected by Henry R. Schoolcraft (1793-1864).

HIBI'SCUS. Genus of the Malvaceae (mallow) family, ranging from large herbaceous plants to trees. Favourite ornamental plants because of their brilliantly coloured (red through to white) bell-shaped flowers, they incl. the rose of Sharon (*H. Syriacus*) and the rose of China (*H. rosa-sinensis*). Some tropical species are also useful, e.g. *H. esculentus,* of which the edible fruit is known in the W Indies as the gobbo; *H. tiliaceus,* which supplies timber and fibrous bark to S Sea islanders; and *H. sabdariffa,* cultivated in the W Indies and elsewhere for its fruit.

HICCUP, or **hiccough.** Sharp noise caused by a sudden spasm of or irritation to the diaphragm with closing of the windpipe, commonly due to digestive disorder, etc. The remedy for ordinary H. is to cause a feeling of suffocation by breathing into a paper bag.

HICKEY, William (1749–1830?). British writer. Ed. at Westminster School, he was intended to follow his father as an attorney in England but dissipation led to his being packed off first to the East Indies and then to Jamaica, before he finally made good at the Indian Bar. His *Memoirs*, written in retirement, give one of the raciest accounts of the age.

HICKOK, James Butler 'Wild Bill' (1837–76). American frontiersman. In the Civil War he was a sharpshooter and scout for the Union army, and then served as marshal in Kansas, killing many desperadoes. A legendary figure, he was shot from behind in Deadwood, S Dakota.

HICKORY. Common genus (*Carya*) of trees native to N America. It provides a valuable timber, and all species bear nuts, although some are inedible. The pecan (*C. illinoensis*) is widely cultivated in the S, and the shagbark (*C. ovata*) in the N.

HIEROGLYPHIC (hī-eroglif'ik). One of the most important ancient systems of writing, originating in Egypt. It was in existence about the middle of the 4th millennium BC, and did not develop into a proper 'alphabet'. On the whole, picture-signs, triliteral, biliteral, and uniliteral signs and determinatives were combined into a complicated script, and this was maintained during 3,500 years. The latest H. inscriptions belong to the 3rd cent. AD. The direction of writing is normally from right to left, the signs facing the beginning of the line. The 'Rosetta Stone' of 197 BC, carved in H., Demotic, and Greek, furnished the key to decipherment, which was mainly due to J. F. Champollion in 1822.

HĪ-FĪ. The 'high fidelity' reproduction of the complete audio range of the original signal of sounds (music, speech, etc.) via radio, record player, or cassette tape-player. Two or four speakers give a stereophonic effect. In an advanced system such as the British Ambisonics, an array of 4 microphones is arranged in the form of a tetrahedron or triangular pyramid, so that they point when recording - left-back-down, left-front-up, right-front-down, and right-back-up. Each picks up only sound directly striking one of the 4 plane faces of the pyramid they form, and after processing according to phase, frequency and amplitude characteristics, the sound is broadcast or directly received from the disc or cassette through a minimum of 4 speakers to achieve an effect of the natural concert hall environment with the sound coming from all directions.

HIGH COMMISSIONER. The representative of one independent Commonwealth country in the cap. of another. Equal in rank to ambassadors (q.v.), they have the same duties and powers.

HIGH COUNTRY. NZ name for the generally mountainous land above the 750-1,000 m (2,500-3,000 ft) level, most of which is in South Island. The lakes, fed by melting snow, are used for hydro-electric power, and it is a paradise for the skier, mountaineer and tourist.

HIGHLAND. Region of Scotland - almost half the country - created 1975 and comprising the former cos. of Caithness and Sutherland; Ross and Cromarty and Inverness (excl. the is. of the Outer Hebrides now incl. in Western Isles); Nairn; a small part of Moray and part of N Argyll.

The **Highlands,** a broken plateau of ancient rocks cover almost all Scotland N of the boundary Helensburgh to Stonehaven, extending S of the H. region itself. There are many mtn peaks (*see* BEN NEVIS), and in the valleys lie many lochs. There is fishing and shooting, and winter sports, as at Aviemore in the Spey Valley, where there is also a wild life park, with the bears and wolves once native here. The traditional **Highland Games** incl. such events as tossing the caber (a tree trunk), dancing and bagpipe playing. The H. people and language have always differed from the Lowland: *see* SCOTTISH GAELIC.

Depopulation, the crofters finding the farming of impoverished land uneconomic, is only partly met by tourism. The Highlands and Islands Development Board also promotes more general schemes. The Moray Firth area is being developed as a linear city from Tain to Inverness, cheap hydro-electric power serving such industries as aluminium smelting, petro-chemicals, etc., and further prosperity may be expected from Scotland's offshore oil. Area of H. region 25,149 sq.km (9,710 sq.m); pop. (1979) 189,858. The admin. HQ is Banff.

HIGHSMITH, Patricia (1921–). American crime novelist. Her first book *Strangers on a Train* (1950) was filmed by Hitchcock, and she excels in the contrast of the bad and the good-but-corruptible. Notable is her series dealing with the amoral Tom Ripley.

HIGHWAY. In British law, any road over which an inalienable right of way has been estab., as by 21 years' uninterrupted use. In American usage, any one of the national trunk roads, controlled and partly sponsored by the Federal Govt. After the Roman exodus English roads were sadly neglected until the 16th cent. when parishes were made responsible in their localities, and in the 18th and 19th cents. when turnpike trusts maintained Hs. outside towns, and charged tolls. Development was delayed because of competition from water and rail transport, but from 1888, when County Councils took over, using the methods of Telford and McAdam, communications improved, particularly between towns. The Central Govt assumed entire responsibility for trunk roads in 1946. In America early European settlement was along the seaboard, and the sea provided the means of communication. With migration inland, development in 18th and 19th cents. was similar to that in England. The first real impetus to improved Hs. came with the bicycle and was strengthened by the increasing use of motor-cars. They were built by the State Govts rather than the towns (1891–1913), but intracontinental Hs. were undertaken under the Federal Aid bills of 1916–21. Recognition of the need for rapid, efficient Hs. in Europe came between the wars - the *autostrada* in Italy and the *autobahnen* in Germany; but belatedly in Britain, with the *motorways,* constructed after the S.W.W. Famous trans-continental Hs. incl. the *Pan-American* (mainly constructed 1923-60) which links the USA from the Texas border with Central and S America, running through Mexico City to Panama City, then down the W side of S America to Valparaiso, Chile, where it crosses the Andes and goes to Buenos Aires, Argentina: *see* DARIEN. The *Asian Highway* (1964–73) has 2 routes, Iran-S Vietnam and Iran-Singapore. Others in various stages of construction incl. the *Trans-African* Lagos-Mombasa, the *Trans-Sahara,* and the *East European* Vienna - branching to Moscow and Istanbul. Highways in Australia are often historically interesting as following the routes of early explorers and bearing their names, e.g. Eyre (Port Augusta-Kalgoorlie), Hume (Melbourne-Sydney), and Stuart (q.v.).

HIGHWAY. A key feature of the Midland motorway system is Spaghetti Junction, the multi-level intersection at Gravelly Hill, North Birmingham, completed in 1971. *Photo: Courtesy of the City of Birmingham.*

HIGHWAYMEN. Term applied to thieves on horseback who robbed travellers on the highway, those who did so on foot being known as footpads. With the development of regular coach services in the 17th and 18th cents. their activities became notorious, and the Bow Street Runners were organized to suppress them. Favourite haunts were Hounslow and Bagshot heaths, and Epping Forest, and they continued to flourish well into the 19th cent. Among the best-known H. were Jonathan Wild, Claude Duval (1643-70), John Nevison (1639-84), the original hero of the 'ride to York', Dick Turpin (1706-39), and his partner Tom King, and Jerry Abershaw (*c.* 1773-95).

HIGH WYCOMBE (wi'kom). Market town in SW Bucks, England, in a valley in the Chilterns, famous for its furniture. Disraeli's home, Hughenden Manor, is 2m to the N. Pop. (1972) 60,510.

HIJACKING. *See* PIRACY.

HILDEBRAND. *See* GREGORY VII.

HILDESHEIM (hil'des-hīm). Town of Lower Saxony, W Germany, at the foot of the Harz mts. A bishopric from the 9th cent., H. became a free city of the Holy Roman Empire in the 13th cent. It was under Prussia 1866-1945. Pop. (1972) 99,500.

HILL, Sir Rowland (1795-1879). British reformer. In a pamphlet 'Post Office Reform' he proposed the introduction of the penny pre-paid post (letters had previously been paid for by the recipient on a rate varied according to distance) initiated in Jan. 1840. He was sec. to the Post Office 1854-64.

HILLARY, Sir Edmund (1919-). New Zealand mountaineer and apiarist. B. in Auckland, he was one of the reconnaissance party to Everest in 1951, and in 1953, together with the Sherpa Tensing, conquered the summit. As leader of the NZ section at Scott Base of the Commonwealth Transantarctic Expedition 1957-8, he was the first man to reach the South Pole overland since Scott (q.v.) on 3 Jan. 1958: on the way he was laying depots for Fuchs's (q.v.) completion of the crossing of the continent.

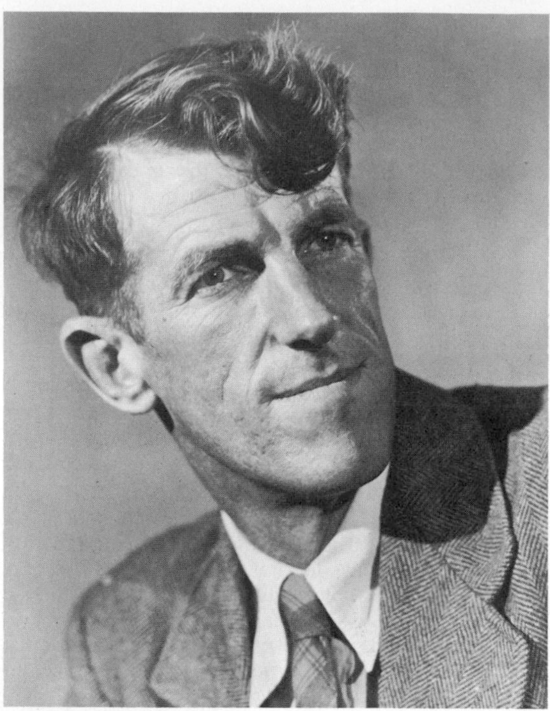

HILLARY. Sir Edmund Hillary, the conqueror of Everest. *Photo: Baron/Camera Press.*

HILLER, Dame Wendy (1912-). British actress. An excellent character actress, she has played successfully parts as varied as Sally Hardcastle in *Love on the Dole* (1935), Catherine Sloper in *The Heiress* (1947), and Eliza in the film of *Pygmalion* (1938).

HILLIARD, Nicholas (*c.* 1547-1619). The earliest English miniaturist, and the first great painter of the English school. B. in Exeter, he became miniaturist and goldsmith to Queen Elizabeth.

HILTON, James (1900-54). British novelist. Lancashire-born, he was to settle in Hollywood as one of its most successful script writers, e.g. *Mrs Miniver.* His books incl. *Lost Horizon* (1933), envisaging Shangri-la, a remote district of Tibet where time stands still; *Mr Chips* (1934), a portrait of an old schoolmaster; and *Random Harvest* (1941).

HILVERSUM. Town in N Holland prov. of the Netherlands, 27km (17m) SE of Amsterdam. Besides being a summer resort, H. is the chief centre of Dutch broadcasting. Pop. (1978) 94,300.

HIMACHAL PRADESH (himah'chel predăsh'). State of the Rep. of India, between Punjab and Tibet. Created as a union territory in 1948, it attained full statehood in 1971. Certain hill areas were transferred from the Punjab to H.P. in 1966. The cap. is Simla. The state is agricultural (maize, wheat, fruit), with coniferous forests supplying timber. Area 55,658 sq.km (21,520 sq.m); pop. (1971) 3,460,000.

HIMALĀ'YA (abode of snow). System of mountain ranges of central Asia, lying along the S edge of the Tibetan plateau in an E-W arc convex to the S. In the most northerly range, average alt. 6,000 m (20,000 ft), a number of peaks exceed 7,500 m (25,000 ft), incl. Everest and Kanchenjunga (qq.v.). The local pron. is himah'lia.

HIMMLER, Heinrich (1900-45). German Nazi leader. B. at Munich, he joined the Nazi Party in its early days, and became leader of the SS in 1929, and chief of the Bavarian police in 1933. His promotion in 1936 to the command of all German police forces, including the Gestapo, made him one of the most powerful men in Germany, and during the S.W.W. he replaced Goering as Hitler's second-in-command. In April 1945 he made a proposal to the Allies that Germany should surrender to Britain and the USA but not to Russia, which was rejected. He was captured in May, and committed suicide.

HINCKLEY. English market town in Leicestershire, 19km (12m) SW of Leicester. It manufactures boots, shoes, and hosiery. Pop. (1972) 48,960.

HINDEMITH (-mit), **Paul** (1895-1963). German composer. A fine viola player, he led the Frankfurt Opera Orchestra at 20, and taught composition at the Berlin Hochschule for music 1927-33, when the modernity of his work, e.g. the *Philharmonic Concerto,* led to a Nazi ban. In 1939 he went to the US, where he taught at Yale, and in 1952 became prof. of musical theory at Zürich. His works incl. many for chamber ensemble and orchestra, and the operas *Cardillac* (1926, revised 1952) and *Mathis der Maler* (1938).

HINDENBURG, Paul Ludwig Hans von Beneckendorf und von (1847-1934). German soldier and statesman. B. at Posen of a Prussian junker family, he was commissioned in 1866, served in the Austro-Prussian and Franco-German wars, and retired in 1911. Given the command in E Prussia in Aug. 1914, he received the credit for the defeat of the Russians at Tannenberg, and was promoted to supreme commander and made a field marshal. Henceforward he and Ludendorff practically directed Germany's policy until the end of the war. He was elected Pres. of the German rep. in 1925, and re-elected in 1932. He invited Hitler to assume the Chancellorship in Jan. 1933, and his last public act was to congratulate him on the 'blood-bath' of June 1934. He d. on his Prussian estate, and was buried at Tannenberg.

HINDENBURG. Name given 1915-45 to ZABRZE in honour of General H.

HINDI. An Indian language, comprising an Eastern and a Western variety, ultimately derivable from Sanskrit, but descended from different Prakrit dialects. From Western H. Hindustani (q.v.) was derived; it is the official language of the Rep. of India.

HINDUISM. The religion of the Hindus; but the term includes the religious beliefs and also the system of caste and other social customs which have been inherited through the ages. Brahma, the Supreme Spirit, always existing and eternal, the original cause and the final home of everything that is, is envisaged as existing in and working through a triad of gods (the Trimurti), known as Brahma the creator, Vishnu the preserver, and Siva the destroyer and also the generator of new life. Vishnu and Siva are the principal objects of popular adoration, and the Vaishnavas and Saivas are the chief religious sects. Vishnu is considered to have been incarnated in a number of *avataras,* one of whom, Krishna, is perhaps the most popular deity. In addition to these principal gods, there is a vast host of minor divinities, demons, ghosts, and spirits, etc., who are popularly worshipped. But educated Hindus regard these and the Trimurti as expressions of the one great, all-comprehending Supreme Spirit.

The basic theological beliefs are the transmigration of souls, and karma (q.v.). The practice of H. is a complex of rites and cremonies performed within the framework of the caste system under the supervision of the Brahman priests and teachers. Temple worship is almost universally performed, and there are many festivals. Benares is the principal of the holy cities, and the Ganges is the holiest river. In India and the rest of Asia there are over 475 million Hindus.

HINDUISM. Vishnu and his consort Lakshmi riding on Garuda, in an 18th century Kulu-style painting. *Photo: Courtesy of the Victoria and Albert Museum.*

HINDU KUSH (hin'doo koosh). Range of mountains in central Asia running WSW from the Pamir region to the Koh-i-Baba, a distance of about 800km (500m). The highest summit is Tirich Mir, 7,690 m (25,230 ft), in Pakistan.

HINDUSTANI. An Indian language, called by Indians Urdu. Originally the language of the bazaars of Delhi, and a local variety of Western Hindi, it was adopted by the troops of the Mogul Empire, and rapidly became a *lingua franca* throughout India.

HINKLER, Herbert John Louis (1892-1933). Australian pilot who in 1928 made the first solo flight from England to Australia. He was killed while making another attempt to fly to Australia.

HIPPARCHUS (hipahr'kus) (*c.* 555-514 BC). Greek tyrant. Son of Pisistratus (q.v.), he was assoc. with his elder brother Hippias as ruler of Athens 527-14. His affection being spurned by Harmodius, he insulted the latter's sister, and was assassinated by Harmodius and Aristogiton.

HIPPA'RCHUS (fl. 160-145 BC). Gk astronomer, a native of Nicaea in Bithynia. He invented trigonometry, calculated the lengths of the solar year and the lunar month, discovered the precession of the equinoxes, made a catalogue of 800 fixed stars, and advanced Eratosthenes's method of determining the situation of places on the Earth's surface by lines of latitude and longitude.

HIPPO'CRATĒS (*c.* 460-*c.* 357 BC). Gk physician commonly styled the Father of Medicine, B. in the island of Cos, he practised and taught medicine in his native place, travelled in the mainland of Greece, and d. in Thessaly. He was the author of a number of medical works, and set a high standard of professional ethics. For more than 2,000 years the Hippocratic Oath has epitomised the medical ethic.

HIPPO'LYTUS. In Gk mythology, son of Theseus. He was accused by his step-mother Phaedra of dishonourable advances, and Theseus placed a curse on him. By the agency of the god Poseidon he was killed while riding in his chariot near the sea. Later he was proved innocent and restored to life.

HIPPOPO'TAMUS (Gk, river-horse). Large mammal of the family Hippopotamidae. The common H. (*H. amphibius*) is found in Central Africa. It is over 4m (13ft) long, 1.2m (4ft) high, weighs between 3 and 4 tonnes, and has a slate-grey skin. The pygmy H. (*H. liberiensis*) inhabits W Africa. Hs. are good swimmers, but leave the water at night to graze.

HIPPOPOTAMUS. Hippos are vegetarians but these great jaws are capable of severing a man's arm. *Photo: Zoological Society of London.*

HIRE PURCHASE. The system of retail trading whereby the purchaser contracts to make partial payments at fixed intervals over a certain period, and the way in which most durable consumer goods are paid for. Increasing rapidly after the F.W.W., the H.P. debt outstanding in USA rose from $3,000 million in 1929 to $100,000 million in 1975, at annual interest rates of 15-18 per cent. The amount owing in Britain in 1975 was over £2,000 million, and the Consumer Credit Act (1974) introduced new protection for the consumer. H.P. is still expanding and covers an increasingly wide range of goods and services.

HIROHITO (hērōhē'tō) (1901-). Emperor of Japan. In 1921 he was the first Japanese crown prince to visit Europe, and in 1926 succeeded his father Yoshihito. After the defeat of Japan in 1945 he formally rejected belief in the divinity of the emperor and Japanese racial superiority, and accepted the 1946 constitution greatly curtailing his powers. The Imperial Palace, destroyed by fire in air raids 1945, was rebuilt within the same spacious wooded compound in 1969. Distinguished as a botanist and zoologist, H. has pub. several books.

HIROSHI'GE, Ando (1797-1858). Japanese artist. B. in Tokyo, he produced paintings, but was best known for his colour prints, his landscapes influencing the Impressionists, e.g. Whistler.

HIROSHIMA (hērō'shima). City and port on the S coast of Honshu, Japan; during the S.W.W. H. was utterly devastated on 6 Aug. 1945 by the first atom bomb to be used in wartime. Over 10 sq.km (4 sq.m) was obliterated, with very heavy damage outside that area. Casualties totalled 136,989 out of a pop. of 343,000: 78,150 were found dead, others died later. The Peace Memorial Park has hauntingly tragic sculptures and a museum of atomic relics. Pop. (1977) 844,000.

HIROSHIMA. The rest of the city has been reconstructed since the atom bomb, but beneath the memorial in the Peace Park can be seen the skeleton of the famous dome which was directly beneath the blast. *Photo: Popperfoto.*

HISPA'NIC. In the USA anyone within the country who is Spanish-speaking, either native-born or immigrant from Mexico, Cuba, Puerto Rico, etc.

HISPANIŌ'LA. W Indian is., first landing place in the New World of Columbus, 6 Dec. 1492. It is divided into Haiti and the Dominican Rep. (qq.v.).

HISPANO-SUIZA. Motor-car designed by a Swiss engineer Marc Birkigt (1878-1947), who emigrated to Barcelona where he founded a factory which produced cars *c.* 1900-38, which were popular among the cognoscenti, incl. Alphonso XIII of Spain, after whom the 1911 sports model was named. During the F.W.W. a Paris factory produced the famous light-alloy aero-engine used by the 'stork' squadron of the French air force, whose emblem, a flying stork, became the mascot of later cars, which incorporated improvements based on war-time experience and incl. the '37.2' and 9 litre V12, still of legendary fame for their handling, elegance and speed.

HISS, Alger (1904-). American politician. B. in Baltimore, he was one of the bright young men recruited under Roosevelt's New Deal. He denied before a federal grand jury having in 1938 passed secret State Dept papers to Whittaker Chambers (an editor of *Time* and a self-confessed Communist). An inconclusive trial for perjury in 1949 was followed by his conviction in 1950: he was released from prison in 1954. His actual guilt is still hotly disputed. Richard Nixon first made his name on the House of Rep. Un-American Activities Committee by pressing the case against Hiss. *See* NIXON, RICHARD.

HISTAMINE (hist'amēn). A substance (an amine) which dilates blood vessels, stimulates gastric secretions, and so on, and is formed at the site of an injury or in allergic reactions such as hay fever and travel sickness. Drugs used to neutralise such effects are antihistamines.

HISTORY. The written record of the development of human societies. The earliest surviving historical records are the inscriptions denoting the achievements of Egyptian and Babylonian kings. As a literary form H. begins with Herodotus (*c.* 484-425 BC), who first passed beyond the limits of a purely national outlook. Thucydides (*c.* 471-401 BC) brought to H. not only literary gifts but the interests of a scientific investigator and political philosopher. Later Greek H. degenerated into rhetoric, nor was Roman H. free from this vice; Sallust (86-35 BC) preserved the scientific spirit of Thucydides, but Livy (59-17 BC) and Tacitus (*c.* AD 54-118), in spite of their great powers, tended to subordinate truth to patriotic or party considerations. Medieval H. suffered from its domination by a ready-made religious philosophy imposed by the Church. English chroniclers of this period are Bede (673-735), William of Malmesbury (d. 1143), and Matthew Paris (d. 1259). France produced great chroniclers of contemporary events in Froissart (1337-1401) and Comines (1447-1511).

The Renaissance revivified H. both by restoring classical models and by creating the science of textual criticism. A product of the new secular spirit is Machiavelli's *History of Florence* (1520-3). The Reformation, especially in Germany, furthered the cause of scientific H. by sending controversialists back to the original documents, while in England the constitutional controversies of the 17th cent. performed a similar service. The 18th cent. 'enlightenment' finally disposed of the attempt to explain H. in theological terms, but it made little progress in the search for an alternative philosophy, although it produced one masterpiece in Gibbon's *Decline and Fall of the Roman Empire* (1776-88). The most remarkable attempt to formulate a philosophy of H., that of Vico (1668-1744), remained almost unknown until the 19th cent. Romanticism left its mark on H. in the tendency to exalt the contribution of the individual 'hero', and in the introduction of a more colourful and dramatic style and treatment, variously illustrated in the works of Michelet, Carlyle, and Macaulay.

During the last cent. H. has been revolutionized. The deciphering of the Egyptian and Babylonian inscriptions opened up a new world. The researches of archaeologists have enabled us to trace the development of prehistoric man, and have revealed forgotten civilizations such as that of Crete. The anthropological studies of primitive society and religion, headed by Frazer's *Golden Bough*, have laid bare the bases of later forms of social organization and belief. The changes brought about by the Industrial Revolution, and the accompanying rise of political economy to the status of a science, forced the historian to turn his attention to economic questions. Marx's attempt to find in economic development the most important, though by no means the only, determining factor in social change, an argument partly paralleled in Buckle's *History of Civilization* (1857), has influenced all serious historians since. A comparative study of civilizations is offered in A. J. Toynbee's *Study of History (1934-54)*, and on a smaller scale by J. M. Roberts' *History of the World* (1976).

HITACHI. City in Honshu, Japan, with electrical industries. Pop. (1973) 182,000.

HITCHCOCK, Sir Alfred (1899-1980). British-American film director. He was a master of suspense and film technique, and his films incl. *Thirty-nine Steps* (1935), *Rebecca* (1940), *Rope* (1948), *Strangers on a Train* (1951), *Rear Window* (1954), *Vertigo* (1958), *Psycho* (1960), *The Birds* (1963), and *Family Plot* (1976). Naturalised US citizen 1955, he was knighted 1980.

HITCHIN. Market town in Herts, 48km (30m) NW of London. The cultivation and distillation of lavender, introduced from Naples in the 16th cent., still continues. Pop. (1972) 29,110.

HITLER, Adolf (1889-1945). German dictator. B. at Braunau-am-Inn, in Austria, the son of a customs official, he spent his early years in poverty in Vienna and Munich. After serving as a volunteer in the German army during the F.W.W., he was employed as a spy by the military authorities in Munich, and in 1919 joined in this capacity the German Workers' Party, founded by Anton Drexler. By 1921 he had assumed its leadership, renamed it the National Socialist German Workers' Party, provided it with a programme, and rallied a following. Having led an unsuccessful rising at Munich in 1923, he was sentenced to 9 months' imprisonment, during which he wrote his political testament, *Mein Kampf (My Struggle)*. The party achieved national importance only in 1930, when the big industrialists began to support it; by 1932, although Hindenburg defeated H. in the presidential elections, it formed the largest group in the Reichstag. As the result of an intrigue directed by von Papen, H. became Chancellor in a Nazi-Nationalist coalition on 30 Jan. 1933.

The opposition were rapidly suppressed, the Nationalists removed from the govt, and the Nazis declared the only legal party. In 1934 H. succeeded Hindenburg as Head of the State, with the title of Fuehrer. Meanwhile, the drive to war began; Germany left the League of Nations, conscription was reintroduced, and in 1936 the Rhineland was occupied. H. and Mussolini, who were already co-operating in Spain, formed an alliance in 1937. The new year saw the annexation of Austria, and the cession of Sudetenland under the Munich agreement. The rest of Czechoslovakia was annexed in March 1939. The non-aggression pact with Russia in Aug. was followed in Sept. by the invasion of Poland and the declaration of war by Britain and France. (*See* SECOND WORLD WAR.) H. narrowly escaped death in 1944 from a bomb explosion prepared by high-ranking officers. On 29 April 1945, when Berlin was largely in Russian hands, he m. Eva Braun in the Reichschancellery, and on the following day committed suicide with her, both bodies afterwards being destroyed by burning. *See* FASCISM, JEWS, NAZISM.

HITTITES (hit'īts). A group of peoples who inhabited Asia Minor and N Syria from the 3rd to the 1st millennium BC. The original Hs., a people of Armenoid type, inhabited a number of city-states in E Asia Minor, one of which, Hatti, gained supremacy over the others. An Indo-European people invaded the country *c.* 2000 BC, made themselves the ruling class, and intermarried with the original inhabitants. Hatti, then known as Hattushash, became the capital of a strong kingdom, which overthrew the Babylonian empire. After a period of eclipse the H. New Empire became a great power (*c.* 1400-1200 BC) which successfully waged war with Egypt, until it was overthrown by the so-called Sea Peoples. Small H. states then arose in N Syria, the most important of which was

HITLER. An unexpected 'holiday snap' of the dictator with his mistress Eva Braun. *Photo: Keystone.*

Carchemish; these were conquered by the Assyrians in the 8th cent. BC, Carchemish in 717.

The Hs. used a cuneiform script, modelled on the Babylonian for ordinary purposes, and a 'hieroglyphic' script for monumental inscriptions. The H. royal archives were discovered at Hattushash in 1906-7, and deciphered in 1915 by Hrozný.

HOATZIN (hō-at'sin). Tropical S American bird (*Opisthocomus hoatzin*), the only representative of its family and resembling a small pheasant in size and appearance: adults are olive with white markings above and red-brown below. The young are hatched naked, and have well-developed claws on the 'thumb and index fingers' of the wing, so that they can crawl reptilian-fashion about the tree - a reminder of their ancestry.

HOBART. Capital of Tasmania, Australia, situated on the estuary of the river Derwent, on the S coast. Founded in 1804, the city was called after Lord H., who was Secretary of State for the Colonies at the time. It has a fine harbour, and the University of Tasmania (1890). Pop. (1976) 162,000.

HOB'BEMA, Meindert (1638-1709). Dutch landscape painter. B. at Amsterdam, he came under the influence of Ruysdael, and his pictures show the peace and charm of the Dutch countryside. Most of his best works, incl. his masterpiece, 'Avenue at Middelharnis' (National Gallery) are in English galleries.

HOBBES, Thomas (1588-1679). English political philosopher. B. near Malmesbury, he was ed. at Oxford, and as a strong royalist withdrew to Paris in 1640, and was tutor to the exiled Prince Charles 1646-8. His most important work was his *Leviathan* (1651), an exposition of the totalitarian state.

HOBART. The Sydney-Hobart yacht race first held 1945-6 is the classic of Australian yachting, and there are always yachts on the Derwent River. Mount Wellington is in the background. *Photo: Australian Information Service.*

HO'BŌKEN. City and port of New Jersey, USA, on the Hudson, adjoining Jersey City. H., incorporated 1849, is on the site of a Dutch farm destroyed by Indians in 1643. Pop. (1970) 45,380.

HOCHHUTH (hohkh'hoot), **Rolf** (1933-). Swiss dramatist. Municipal playwright at Basle from 1953, he is best-known for the controversial *Soldiers* (1968), with its implication that Churchill was involved in a plot to assassinate Sikorski (q.v.).

HO CHI MINH (1892-1969). N Vietnamese politician. B. in N Vietnam, he was trained in Moscow, headed the Communist Vietminh from 1941, and, having campaigned against the French 1946-54, became Pres. and PM of the Democratic Rep. at the armistice. Aided by the Communist bloc, he did much to develop industrial potential, and although he relinquished the premiership in 1955, he was re-elected Pres. in 1960.

HO CHI MINH CITY. Soviet-made armoured personnel carriers trundling past a podium topped by a portrait of the late Ho Chi Minh in the recently 'liberated' Ho Chi Minh City, formerly Saigon. *Photo: Camera Press.*

The *Ho Chi Minh Trails* were the N Vietnamese troop and supply routes to the interior of S Vietnam through Laos.

HO CHI MINH CITY. Chief port and commercial centre of southern Vietnam, on the Saigon r. 43 km (27 m) from the sea. Industries incl. shipbuilding, textiles, rice, sugar, soap, and rubber, chiefly concentrated in the mainly Chinese twin city of Cholon. There is a univ. As Saigon, it was the cap. of the Rep. of Vietnam (S Vietnam) from 1954 to 1976, when it was renamed Ho Chi-minh City. Pop. (1976) 3,460,500.

HOCKEY. A game using hooked sticks, not unlike the modern ones, was played by the ancient Greeks, and under the names of 'hurley' and 'shinty' a primitive form of the game was played in Ireland and Scotland. Modern H. dates from 1886 when the Men's H. Association rules were drafted.

It is played between 2 teams, each of not more than 11 players. The ground is 91.50m (100yd) long and 54.90m (60yd) wide. Goals 2.13m (7ft) high and 3.65m (4yd) wide, are placed within a striking circle of 14.64m (16yd) radius, from which all shots at goal must be made. The white ball weighs c. 155 grams/5½ oz, circumference c. 228mm/9in, and the stick must not exceed 50mm/2in diameter. The game is started by a 'bully-off' in which the centre-forwards strike the ground and the other's stick 3 times before playing the ball. The ball may be stopped with the hand, but not held, picked up, thrown or kicked, except by the goalkeeper in his own striking circle. If the ball is sent into touch, it is returned to play by a 'push in'. The game is divided into two 35 min. periods; it is controlled by two umpires, one for each half of the field. The women's game is governed by the All England Women's Hockey Association founded in 1895.

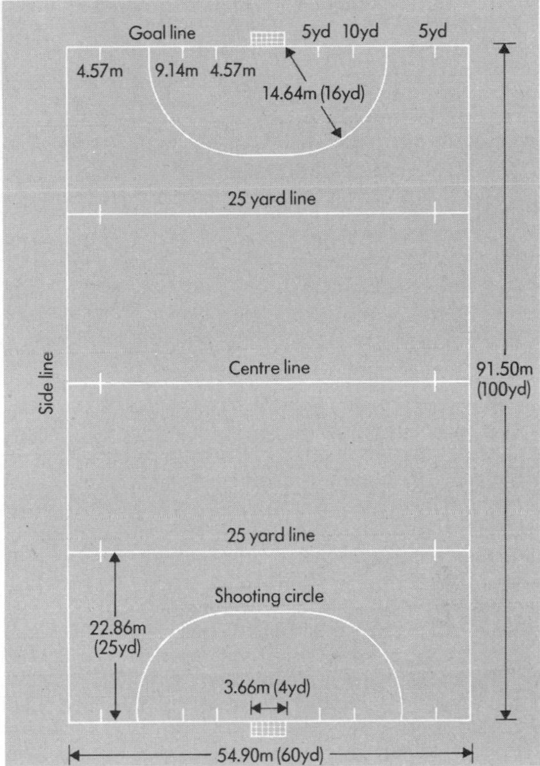

HOCKEY

HOCKNEY, David (1937-). British artist. Trained at Bradford School of Art and the Royal College of Art, he made his first reputation in the Young Contemporaries Show of 1961. His work is colourful, inventive and innocently joyous, as in his representations of water.

HODGKIN, Sir Alan Lloyd (1914-). British physiologist. Both H. and A. F. Huxley, former students of Lord Adrian (q.v.), were engaged in research on the mechanism of conduction in peripheral nerves 1946-60, and in 1963 with Sir John Eccles (q.v.) shared the Nobel prize for physiology and medicine. He was pres. of the Royal Society 1970-5. OM 1973.

HODGKIN, Dorothy Crowfoot (1910-). British chemist. She was awarded a Nobel prize 1964 for work on the determination by X-ray studies of the structure of important biochemical compounds, e.g. vitamin B12, a liver extract used in combating pernicious anaemia, and penicillin. In 1965 she was awarded the OM.

HODGKIN, Thomas (1798-1856). British physician. He first analysed **Hodgkin's Disease,** a cancerous enlargement of the lymphatic glands.

HOFEI. *See* HEFEI.

HOFFA, James Riddle (1913-75). American trade unionist. Pres. of the powerful Internat. Brotherhood of Teamsters, he was jailed 1964-71 for trying to bribe a Federal Court Jury after charges of corruption, and in 1975 disappeared, believed disposed of in a paper-shredder by the Mafia.

HOFFMANN, Ernst Theodor Amadeus (1776-1822). German composer and writer. A lawyer in Berlin, he enjoyed great success with his opera *Undine* (1816) and his *Fantastic Tales* inspired Offenbach's *Tales of H.*

HOGARTH, William (1697-1764). British artist and engraver. B. in London, he was apprenticed to an engraver, and from 1720 studied painting with Sir James Thornhill whose daughter he clandestinely married in 1729. His *A Harlot's Progress* (1731), a series of 6 pictures, engraved in 1732, estab. his fame and was followed by *A Rake's Progress* (1735); his masterpiece *Marriage à la Mode* (1745); *Industry and Idleness* (1749) and *The Four Stages of Cruelty* (1751). His penetrating satire of the follies and vices of his age, command of group composition and skill in genre painting are uniquely English in tone. In portraiture he has a sympathetic directness that did not appeal to the fashionable world of his time.

HOGG, James (1770-1835). Scottish poet, known as the 'Ettrick Shepherd'. B. in Ettrick Forest, Selkirkshire, he worked as a shepherd at Yarrow (1790-9), and until 30 was illiterate. His *Scottish Pastorals* (1801) are now forgotten, but his novel *Confessions of a Justified Sinner* (1824) is a masterly portrayal of personified evil.

HOGG, Quintin. *See* HAILSHAM, LORD.

HOGGAR. Another form of AHAGGAR.

HOGMANAY (hog'manā). Scottish name for the last day of the year and also for the oatmeal cakes given to the children as they go from house to house singing carols.

HOGWEED, giant. Plant (*Heracleum mantegazzianum*), of which the sap makes the skin more sensitive to ultraviolet light, and if cut *in sunshine* brings the gardener out in a very nasty rash.

HOHENLINDEN (hō-enlinden), **Battle of.** In the French Revolutionary Wars, a defeat of the Austrians by the French 3 Dec. 1800 which, in conjunction with Marengo (q.v.), led the Austrians to make peace: Treaty of Lunéville 1801.

HOHENSTAUFEN (hō'enstowfen). Name of a German princely family, members of which held the title of Holy Roman Emperor 1138-1208 and 1214-54. The most notable of the H. emperors were Frederick I, Henry VI, and Frederick II (qq.v.).

HOHENZOLLERN (hō'entsollern). Name of a German family, originating in Württemberg, the main branch of which held the titles of elector of Brandenburg from 1415, king of Prussia from 1701, and German Emperor from 1871. The last emperor, William II, was dethroned in 1918. Another branch of the family were kings of Romania 1881-1947.

HOHHOT (hawhot'). Cap. (formerly Huhehot) of Inner Mongolia (Nei Monggol) autonomous region, China. Centre of a farming district, it has textile industries and a univ. (1957). Pop. (1973) 341,000.

HOKKAIDO (hokī'dō). Most northerly of the 4 main islands of Japan, separated from Honshu on the S by Tsugaru Strait and from Sakhalin on the N by Soya Strait. Snow-covered for 6 months of the year, H. was little developed until the Meiji Restoration of 1868 when disbanded Samurai were settled. Natural resources incl. coal, mercury, manganese, oil and natural gas, timber and rich fisheries. Intensive exploitation followed the S.W.W. incl. heavy and chemical industrial plants, development of electric power, and dairy farming. The cap. is Sapporo. An artificial harbour has been constructed at Tomakomai, and an undersea rail tunnel is planned to link Hakodate with Aomori (Honshu). Area 78,508 sq.km (30,265 sq.m); pop. (1970) 5,171,000 incl. 16,000 Ainus (q.v.).

HOKUSAI (hō'kōōsahi) (1760-1849). Japanese artist. B. at Yedo, he was originally a student of engraving. Very prolific, he produced vital interpretations of everyday Japanese life in prints, water-colours and book illustrations, and was equally at home with a picture on a grain of rice or more than life-size figures.

HOKUSAI. The artist's most famous painting, 'The Wave', the little boats dwarfed beneath its grasping fronds. *Photo: Courtesy of the Japanese Information Service.*

HOLBEIN (hol'bīn), **Hans, the Younger** (1497-1543). German painter. B. at Augsburg, he was the son and pupil of **Hans H., the Elder** (*c.* 1460-1524), who was also b. at Augsburg, and whose masterpiece is the altar-piece of St Sebastian (1515) in the Munich Pinakothek. In 1515 H. went to Basle, where he became friendly with Erasmus, and in 1517 to Lucerne, where he painted the façades of houses. He was working in Basle again 1519-26, and to this period belong the wood engravings for the *Dance of Death.* He also executed title pages for Luther's translation of the NT and More's *Utopia,* and did a number of woodcuts of OT subjects. One of his most famous works is the 'Meyer Madonna', a fine altar-piece at Darmstadt. In 1527 he came to England, and in 1536 became court painter to Henry VIII. He d. of the plague.

HOLDEN, Edith (1871-1920). British artist-naturalist. Dau. of a Birmingham manufacturer, she made most of her observations near her native city, and her journal, illus. with her own watercolours, was pub. in 1977 as *The Country Diary of an Edwardian Lady.* In 1911 she m. a sculptor 7 years her junior, and was drowned nr Kew Gardens, having overbalanced in a Thames backwater while reaching for a botanical specimen.

HOLFORD, William, baron (1907-75). British architect. B. in Johannesburg, he was the most influential architect-planner of his generation, and was prof. of Town Planning at Univ. Coll., London, 1948-70. He was responsible for much redevelopment after the S.W.W., incl. St Paul's Cathedral Precinct.

HOLIDAY, Billie (1915–59). American jazz singer, known as 'Lady Day'. She made her debut in Harlem clubs, and achieved an emotionally charged delivery born of her own unhappy personal life. Addicted to drugs, she d. of their effects. She pub. her autobiography *Lady Sings the Blues*.

HOLINSHED, Ralph (*c.* 1520-*c.* 1580). English chronicler. B. probably in Cheshire, he went to London as assistant to a printer, and pub. in 1578 2 vols. of the *Chronicles of England, Scotland and Ireland,* which were largely used by Shakespeare.

HOLLAND, Henry Richard Vassall Fox, 3rd baron H. (1773-1840). British Whig statesman. The son of the 2nd Lord Holland, he became Lord Privy Seal in 1806-7. His seat at Holland House was for many years the centre of Whig political and literary society.

HOLLAND, North and **South.** Two provs. of the Netherlands. N.H. occupies the peninsula jutting northwards between the North Sea and the Ijsselmeer. Most of it is below sea-level, protected from the sea by a series of sand dunes and artificial dykes. The cap. is Haarlem; other towns are Amsterdam, the largest and most important, Hilversum, Den Helder, and the cheese centres Alkmaar and Edam. Area 2,656 sq.km (1,025 sq.m); pop. (1978) 2,999,500.

S.H., to the S of N.H., is also low-lying. The Hague is its cap.; other important towns are Rotterdam, Leyden, Gouda, and Delft. Dairy cattle are reared and dairy products are important; there are petroleum refineries at Rotterdam, distilleries at Schiedam. Area 2,867 sq.km (1,107 sq.m); pop. (1978) 3,053,000.

Because the provs. of N and S H. have always been the wealthiest part of the Netherlands (q.v.), the name HOLLAND is frequently used for the whole country - even by Dutchmen.

HOLLAND, Parts of. Former separate administrative co. of SE Lincolnshire, England.

HOLLAR, Wenceslaus (1607-77). Bohemian engraver. B. at Prague, he went to England in 1637, and was appointed drawing master to the Prince of Wales. He made numerous plates of views of London and of various other cities which he visited.

HOLLY. Trees and bushes of the *Ilex* genus of the Aquifoliaceae family. The evergreen European H. (*I. aquifolium*) may grow 20m (60ft) high and has a smooth grey bark and highly polished leaves, wavy and spined at the edges. The small whitish flowers, borne in May, are followed by scarlet berries. Branches of both the British and American species are used for Christmas decoration.

HOLLYHOCK. Garden perennial, *Althaea rosea*, of the Malvaceae family. Originally a native of Asia, the H. was introduced into Britain some 3 cents. ago. The flower spikes are *c.* 3m (10ft) high.

HOLLYWOOD. Suburb of Los Angeles, California, USA, from 1911 the centre of the US film industry. The film stars' homes are chiefly situated at Beverly Hills nearby.

HOLMES, Oliver Wendell (1809-94). American writer. B. at Cambridge, Mass., he became prof. of anatomy at Dartmouth (1838-40) and at Harvard (1847-82). In 1857 he founded with Lowell the *Atlantic Monthly*, in which were pub. the essays and verse collected in 1858 as *The Autocrat of the Breakfast-Table*, a record of the imaginary conversation of boarding-house guests. This was followed by *The Professor at the Breakfast-Table* and the novel *Elsie Venner* (1861).

HO'LMIUM (Lat. *Holmia* for Stockholm). Symbol Ho, at. no. 67, at. wt. 164.94. Discovered by Cleve in 1897, H. is one of the rare earth metals and occurs in various minerals such as gadolinite.

HOLOCAUST. Wholesale destruction, from the Greek word meaning the burning of a sacrificed animal in its entirety. It is espec. applied today to the annihilation of about 6 million Jews under the Hitler regime 1933-45 at the concentration camps of Auschwitz, Belsen, Buchenwald, Dachau and Maidanek.

HOLO'GRAPHY. The technique of reconstructing a 3-dimensional image from the reflected waves of a source of single frequency: it operates equally well in sound and light. It is thought that bats owe their ability to weave through wire obstructions etc. to a system of bio-holography. *See* GABOR, D. *and* LASER.

HOLST, Gustav Theodore (1874-1934). British composer. B. at Cheltenham, of Swedish descent, he studied at the RCM under Stanford, became a trombonist, and was a teacher in London and Reading. He composed operas (*Sāvitri, At the Boar's Head*, etc.), ballets, choral works ('Hymns from the Rig Veda', 'The Hymn of Jesus', etc.), orchestral suites (among which is 'The Planets'), songs, etc.

HOLT, Harold Edward (1908-67). Australian statesman. B. in Sydney, son of a teacher, he was Min. of Labour 1940-1 and 1949-58, and Federal Treasurer 1958-66, when he succeeded Menzies as PM. He was drowned in a swimming accident.

HOLTBY, Winifred (1898-1935). British novelist. An ardent advocate of women's freedom and racial toleration, she is best known for her novel *South Riding* (1936), set in her native Yorkshire. *See also* VERA BRITTAIN.

HOLYHEAD (hol'ihed). Seaport on the N coast of H. Island, off Anglesey, Wales. H. Island is linked by road and railway bridges with Anglesey, and there are regular sailings between H. and Dublin. Pop. (1971) 11,000.

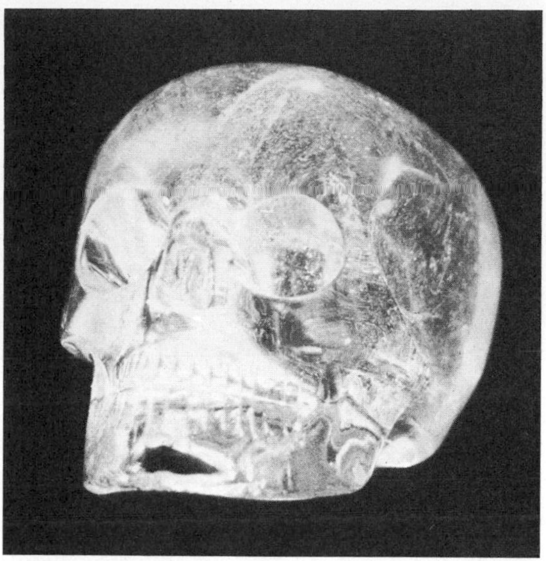

HOLOGRAPHY. A crystal Aztec skull, used in priestly ceremonies, reconstructed by holography. *Photo: Theo Bergström.*

HOLY ISLAND. English island 3km (2m) off Northumberland, to which it is connected by a causeway. St Aidan founded a monastery there in 635.

HOLYHEAD ISLAND is sometimes called Holy Island.

HOLY LAND. *See* PALESTINE.

HOLY LOCH. Western inlet of the Firth of Clyde, W Scotland, with a US nuclear submarine base.

HOLYOAKE, Sir Keith Jacka (1904–83). New Zealand National Party statesman. He succeeded Sir Sidney Holland as PM for 2 months in 1957. Favouring a property-owning democracy, he was returned to power in 1960, 1963, 1966, 1969, retiring 1972.

HOLY OFFICE. The Inquisition (q.v.).

HOLY ORDERS. The estate or condition of Christian priests, conferred by the laying on of hands of a bishop. In the C of E there are three orders - bishop, priest, and deacon; but in the RC Church H.O. include, in addition, sub-deacons, acolytes, exorcists, readers, and door-keepers.

HOLY ROMAN EMPIRE. Name applied to the empire of Charlemagne and his successors, and to the German Empire 962-1806, both being regarded as a revival of the Roman Empire. *See* GERMAN HISTORY; CHARLEMAGNE; HABSBURGS; etc.

HOLYROOD HOUSE. Royal residence in Edinburgh, Scotland. The palace was built (1498-1503) on the site of a 12th cent. abbey by James IV. It has associations with Mary Queen of Scots and Charles Edward, the Young Pretender.

HOLY SHROUD. *See* TURIN.

HOMBURG. Town and spa at the foot of the Taunus mts., W Germany; has given its name to a soft felt hat, made fashionable at H. by Edward VII. Pop. (est.) 25,000.

HOME (hūm) **of the Hirsel, Alec Douglas-H.,** baron (1903-). British Cons. politician. He was Sec. of State for Commonwealth Relations 1955-60, and Foreign Affairs 1960-3. Chosen to succeed Macmillan as PM in

HOLYOAKE. Keith Jacka Holyoake, one of New Zealand's longest serving statesmen. *Photo: Courtesy of the High Commissioner for New Zealand.*

HOME GUARD. Members of the real 'Dad's Army', cleaning their sten guns beneath Big Ben, and as smart as any professional soldier. *Photo: Popperfoto.*

1963, he renounced his peerages, but failed to win the general election of 1964 and resigned as Cons. leader in 1965. He was Sec. for Foreign and Cw. Afairs 1970-4, when he received a life peerage. His younger brother **William Douglas-Home** (1912-) is a playwright, e.g. *The Chiltern Hundreds* and *The Reluctant Peer.*

HOME, Daniel Dunglas (1833-86). British spiritualist medium: related to the earls of H. Evidence of his levitation was attested to in US; and in England, by Lord Lindsay, Lord Adare and Sir William Crookes. He held *séances* before sovereigns of France, Prussia and Holland (1857-8), and while in Italy became a Roman Catholic, but in 1864 was expelled from Rome as a sorcerer.

HOME COUNTIES. Name given to the counties in close proximity to London, viz. Herts, Essex, Kent, Surrey, and formerly Middlesex.

HOME GUARD. Unpaid force formed in Britain in May 1940 to repel the expected German invasion, and known until July 1940 as the Local Defence Volunteers. It consisted of men of 17-65 who had not been called up, formed part of the armed forces of the Crown, and was subject to military law. Over 2,000,000 strong in 1944, it was disbanded 31 Dec. 1945, but revived in 1951, then placed on a reserve basis in 1955, and ceased activities in 1957.

HOME OFFICE. Govt Dept estab. in 1782; it deals with all the internal affairs of England and Wales except those specifically assigned to other Depts. The Home Secretary, the head of the Dept, holds cabinet rank, and is the channel of communication between the sovereign and his subjects. There is a separate Sec. of State for Scotland, and, since 1964, for Wales. The Home Sec. has certain duties in respect of N Ireland, the Channel Islands, and the Isle of Man.

HŌ'MER. Legendary Greek epic poet, the traditional author of the *Iliad* and the *Odyssey.* According to tradition he was a blind wandering minstrel; seven cities claimed to be his birthplace, while he has been given dates ranging 11th to 7th cent. BC.

The *Iliad* tells of an incident of the siege of Troy, the wrath of Achilles and the death of Hector; the *Odyssey* of the wanderings of Odysseus after the siege and his return to Ithaca. Both formed part of a cycle of epics on the siege of Troy, the remainder of which has been lost. The capture of Troy *c.* 1200 BC was an episode in the Achaean invasions of Asia Minor. Songs glorifying princely houses, combining historical elements with myth and folklore, arose at the courts of Achaean chieftains, and assumed artistic form at the hands of professional bards in the Ionian trading cities. In the course of transmission they were greatly modified, e.g. only slight traces of human sacrifice remain. Peisistratus, tyrant of Athens, is said to have first collected the complete texts from reciters at the Panathenaian festival *c.* 550 BC and committed them to writing. Early quotations show many variations from the received texts, which may have been produced by Alexandrian editors 3rd-2nd cents. BC.

Modern Homeric criticism began in 1795 with Wolf's *Prolegomena,* which attempted to prove that the *Iliad* was derived from earlier ballads. The origin of the poems remains a subject of controversy; in its later stages the controversy has been much affected by excavations at Troy, Mycenae, and in Crete.

HOMER, Winslow (1836-1910). American artist. B. in Boston, he estab. his reputation as a realist genre painter with 'Prisoners from the Front' (1866). He is celebrated for his farm and sea scenes, and for water-colours (influenced by English practice) of free brilliance, as in his West Indian studies.

HOME RULE. The slogan of the Irish nationalist movement 1870-1914; it stood for the repeal of the Act of Union, and the establishment of an Irish parliament within the framework of the British Empire. The slogan was popularized after 1870 by Isaac Butt and Parnell, his successor in the nationalist leadership. Gladstone's H.R. bills of 1886 and 1893 were both defeated; Asquith's H.R. bill became law in 1914, but was suspended during the F.W.W. After 1918 the demand for an independent Irish republic replaced that for H.R.

HOMOEOPATHY (homi-o'pathi). A system of medicine, introduced by the German physician Samuel Hahnemann (1755-1843), based on the treatment of morbid conditions by what would induce such diseases in healthy bodies, and on the administration of simple drugs in small quantities only. It is opposed to allopathy (q.v.).

HOMO'PTERA. Sub-order of insects in the order Hemiptera (q.v.), generally distinguished from the Heteroptera by the uniform consistency of the front wings. It includes the cicadas, aphides, and scale insects.

HOMOSEXUALITY. Homosexuals are definite males or females in whom a hormonal imbalance leads them to be attracted less to the opposite sex than their own. A more extreme sex reversal occurs in trans-sexuals who think and feel emotionally like members of the opposite sex, and may prefer the clothing of that sex. Studies of identical and non-identical twins suggest that it is of genetic origin.

HŌMS. City, cap. of H. district, in Syria, nr the Orontes. Silk, cereals and fruit are produced in the area, and industries incl. silk textiles, oil refining, and jewellery. Zenobia, Queen of Palmyra, was defeated at H. by Aurelian in 272. Pop. (1970) 215,525.

HŌNA'N. *See* HENAN.

HONDECOETER (hon'dekooter), **Melchior** (1636-95). Dutch artist. B. at Utrecht, he became famous for his paintings of birds.

HONDO. Another name for HONSHU.

HONDŪ'RAS. Country of Central America. H. is mountainous, the highest range being the Montañas de Selaque, rising to over 2,000 m (7,000 ft). Almost half H. is forest, providing mahogany, etc., and rich minerals, not yet fully exploited, incl. gold, silver, lead, and zinc. Bananas, coffee, cotton, maize, tobacco, sugar and fruit are grown on the coastal plains. Road and rail links are limited, air transport being much used. The cap. is Tegucigalpa.

H. was discovered by Columbus in 1502, and first settled by Spaniards in 1523. Freedom from Spain was gained in 1821, and H. left the Fed. of Central America to become an independent state in 1838. Gen. Oswaldo López Arellano seized power in 1963, and led H. in the 'football War' of 1969 when H. was defeated by Salvador. The President since 1982, Roberto Suazo Cordova, was in 1986 struggling (with US assistance) to hold power against the armed forces. Area 112,088 sq.km (43,227 sq.m); pop. (1974) 4.24 million (including some 50,000 refugees from El Salvador and Nicaragua). M.U.: lempira/peso.

HONDURAS, British. *See* BELIZE.

HO'NECKER, Erich (1912-). East German politician. B. in the Saar, the son of a miner, he specialised in security in the 1950s, and became a politburo member in 1958. In 1971 he took over from Ulbricht (q.v.) as First Sec. of the East Ger. Socialist Unity Party, and after Ulbricht's death became the country's leading political figure.

HONEGGER, Arthur (1892-1955). Swiss composer. B. at Le Havre, he was ed. at Zürich and Paris, and in the 1920s joined the group of French composers known as *Les Six*. Later his work became more deeply expressive, and is very varied in form, e.g. opera (*Antigone*), ballet (*Skating Rink*), oratorio (*Le roi David*), programme music ('Pacific 231' inspired by a railway engine), and the *Symphonie liturgique*.

HONEY (hu'ni). A sweet sticky liquid manufactured in the hive by bees from nectar collected from flowers. It is stored in the honeycombs as a food for the bees' future use, but as more H. is produced than is needed, the surplus may be removed for human use. H. consists of various sugars, particularly laevulose and dextrose, with enzymes and various other constituents such as colouring matter, acids, pollen grains, etc.

HONEY-EATER, or **honey-sucker.** Name given to Australasian birds in the family Meliphagidae. They possess long tongues by means of which they can collect nectar from flowers.

HONEYSUCKLE. Popular name for plants of the *Lonicera* genus of the Caprifoliaceae family. The common British H., or Woodbine (*L. periclymenum*), is a climbing plant with sweet-scented flowers, purple and yellow-tinted outside and creamy-white inside. The N American trumpet H. (*L. sempervirens*) is very handsome and incl. scarlet and yellow varieties.

HONFLEUR (oṅflör'). Seaport on the N coast of France, on the S shore of the Seine estuary opposite Le Havre, in Calvados dept. Much of its trade is carried on with England. Pop. (1973) 9,200.

HONG KONG (Cantonese, 'fragrant harbour'). British Crown colony on the SE coast of Kwantung prov., China. The colony incl. Hong Kong Is., Stonecutters' Is., the territory of Kowloon, and the New Territories. H.K. Is. was ceded to Britain in 1841, Kowloon peninsula was added in 1860, and in 1898 Britain obtained a 99 year lease of the New Territories, incl. the remainder of the Kowloon Peninsula. Under a treaty between Britain and China signed December 1984, H.K. will become a "Special Administrative Region" of China in 1997. The harbour is excellent, and H.K. is one of the world's greatest ports, a large proportion of the exports and imports of S China being transhipped here. An underground railway (1980) links H.K. Island and Kowloon. Textiles, clothing and shipbuilding are traditional industries, with modern diversification into plastics, electronics, etc. The H.K. stock market has 4 exchanges. The cap. is Victoria. Govt is by a Governor, Eecutive and Legislative Councils. H.K. was occupied by the Japanese 1941–5. Area 1,243 sq.km (403.8 sq.m); pop. (1980) 6,000,000.

HONITON. Market town in Devon, England, on the Otter, 25km (16m) NE of Exeter, famous for its handmade 'pillow' lace. Pop. (1972) 5,600.

HONOLULU (honōloo'loo). Capital city and port of Hawaii, USA, on the S coast of Oahu. Noted for its beauty and tropical vegetation, it is a holiday resort, with some industry: 11km (7m) SW is Pearl Harbor with naval and military installations. Waikiki Beach and the extinct

HONG KONG. A general view of the city, the magnificent harbour and Kowloon, taken from the peak. Shrouded in mist are the distant hills of Communist China. *Photo: Hong Kong Government Office.*

volcano Diamond Head are tourist attractions. In Hawaiian H. means 'sheltered bay'. Pop. (1970) 325,000.

HONOURS LIST. In the UK the military and civil awards approved by the Sovereign at the New Year, on her official birthday (celebrated on some selected date in June), and also on other special occasions. *See also* AUSTRALIA, CANADA, etc.

HO'NSHU (Mainland). Principal is. of Japan. It lies betwen Hokkaido on the N and Kyushu on the S. A chain of volcanic mts. extends the length of the is., which is subject to frequent earthquakes. Tokyo and Yokohama stand on a triangular plain. On the Inland Sea in the S are the ports of Osaka, Kobe, Kure, and Hiroshima. Honshu is linked by bridges and tunnels with the islands of Hokkaido, Kyushu and Shikoku. Area 230,448 sq.km (88,839 sq.m), incl. 382 smaller islands; pop. (1970) 76,758,000.

HO'NTHORST, Gerard van (1590-1656). Dutch artist, especially noted for his portraits.

HOOCH (hōkh), **Pieter de** (1629-after 1683). Dutch painter. B. in Rotterdam, he came under the influence of Jacob Le Duck, Kick, and Vermeer. He is famous for courtyard and garden scenes and interiors.

HOOD, Samuel, 1st visct (1724-1816). British admiral. B. in Dorset, he distinguished himself at Dominica in 1782, being created a baron, and was created visct. after his brilliant handling of the Mediterranean command 1793-4. He was a masterly tactician.

HOOD, Thomas (1799-1845). British poet. B. in London, he entered journalism, and edited periodicals, e.g. *Hood's Magazine* (1843). Although best known by his comic verse, e.g. 'Miss Kilmansegg', he also wrote such universally known serious poems as 'Song of the Shirt' and 'Bridge of Sighs'.

HOOGHLI. Indian r. and town, in West Bengal. The r. is the western stream of the Ganges delta. The town is on the site of a factory set up by the E India Co. in 1640 which was moved to Calcutta, 40km (25m) downstream, 1686-90. Pop. (1971) *c.* 100,000.

HOOKE, Robert (1635-1703). British experimental physicist, elected to the Royal Society in 1663, becoming also its curator for the rest of his life. His inventions incl. a double-barrelled air-pump, the spirit-level, marine barometer, and sea gauge.

HOOKER, Richard (1554-1600). English theologian. B. nr Exeter, in 1585 he became Master of the Temple and in 1591 rector of Boscombe, near Salisbury, where he commenced *The Laws of Ecclesiastical Polity,* a defence of the episcopalian system of the C-of-E. He became rector of Bishopsbourne, near Canterbury, in 1595, and d. there.

HOOK OF HOLLAND. Small peninsula and village in S Holland, Netherlands, important as the terminus for a sea service with England (Harwich, Parkeston Quay); in Dutch, Hoek van Holland, meaning corner of Holland.

HOOPER, John (*c.* 1495-1555). English Protestant reformer and martyr. B. in Somerset, he adopted Zwinglian views, he was appointed in 1550 bishop of Gloucester, and in 1555 was burnt for heresy.

HOOPOE (hōō'pōō). Bird (*Upupa epops*) in the order Coraciiformes. About the size of a missel thrush, it has a long thin bill and a bright buff-coloured crest which expands into a fan shape as the bird alights. The wings are banded with black and white and the rest of the plumage is black, white, and buff.

HOOVER, Herbert Clark (1874-1964). 31st President of the USA. As a mining engineer he travelled widely before the F.W.W., during which he organized relief work in occupied Europe; a talented administrator, he was subsequently associated with numerous international relief organizations, and became Food Administrator for the US 1917-19. Sec. of Commerce 1921-8, he then defeated the Democratic candidate for the Presidency, 'Al' Smith, but lost public confidence after the stock-market crash of 1929, when he opposed direct govt aid for the unemployed in the depression that followed, and in 1933 was succeeded by Roosevelt.

The **H. Dam** (1928-36) on the Colorado r. is the highest concrete dam in the USA (221m/726ft high and 378m/1,244 ft long), Lake Mead reservoir being 185km/115m long. Named after H., it was renamed Boulder Dam when he became unpopular in 1933, but the name was restored by Truman in 1947.

HOOVER, John Edgar (1895-1972). American lawyer. As director of the FBI (q.v.) from 1924, he reorganized it, and after his men gunned down the gangster John Dillinger 'public enemy No. 1' in 1934, obtained greatly extended powers. He tracked down the atom spies after the S.W.W., but was subsequently criticized for 'hysterical anti-Communism'. He had the confidence of 8 presidents.

HOOVER, William Henry (1849-1932). American manufacturer. Threatened in his business as a leather manufacturer for carriages and waggons by the advent of the car, he concentrated on developing a primitive existing cleaner into an effective tool for the housewife, the H. Vacuum cleaner, which became a generic name for the type. *See* VACUUM.

HOPE, Anthony. Pseudonym of British novelist Sir Anthony Hope Hawkins (1863-1933). B. in London, he is best known for his romance *The Prisoner of Zenda* (1894), set in the imaginary Balkan state of Ruritania, and its sequel *Rupert of Hentzau* (1898). His *Dolly Dialogues* (1894) are a social satire.

HOPE, Bob. Stage-name of comedian Leslie Townes H. (1904-), b. in Britain but taken to the US in 1907. The most expert exponent of the deadpan wise-crack, he has made numerous films, incl. the celebrated 'Road' series with Dorothy Lamour and Bing Crosby.

HOPEI. *See* HEBEI.

HOPKINS, Sir Frederick Gowland (1861-1947). British biochemist. Prof. at Cambridge from 1914 and Sir William Dunn prof. 1921-43, he revolutionized the conception of the sources of muscular energy and oxidation of tissues, and did fundamental research on vitamins. In 1929 he was awarded the Nobel prize for medicine, and in 1935 the OM. His dau. is Jacquetta Hawkes (q.v.).

HOPKINS, Gerard Manley (1844-89). British poet. B. at Stratford, Essex, he was converted in 1866 to the Church of Rome, and in 1868 began training as a Jesuit. He preached and ministered as a priest in Ireland and England and subsequently taught. He d. of typhoid. His poetry is profoundly religious and records his struggle to gain faith and peace, but also shows great freshness of feeling and delight in nature. A complete edition was issued by Robert Bridges in 1918. His employment of 'sprung rhythm', allied to the Old and Middle English alliterative verse, has greatly influenced later 20th cent. poetry. His *Journals and Papers* were published in 1959, and three volumes of letters 1955-6.

HOPKINS. A portrait of Gerard Manley Hopkins, painted in 1859 by A.E. Hopkins. *Photo: Courtesy of the National Portrait Gallery.*

HOPKINS, Harry L. (1890-1946). American statesman. B. in Iowa, he became in 1935 head of W.P.A. (Works Progress Administration). After a period as Sec. of Commerce 1938-40 he was appointed supervisor of the Lend-Lease programme in 1941, and undertook wartime missions to Britain and Russia.

HOPPNER, John (1758-1810). British artist. B. in London, he was ed. at the RA by George III, and specialized in portraits, notably of the royal princesses, William Pitt, Lord Grenville, Rodney and Nelson. He became portrait painter to the Prince of Wales in 1789 and RA in 1795. Lawrence was a rival.

HOPS. Female cone-heads of the hop plant, *Humulus lupulus*, Moraceae family. The plant has a perennial rootstock, climbs by a twining stem, and produces green leaves and small flowers. H. grow in rich soil throughout Europe and N America, and are picked and dried in oast houses. In designated areas in Europe no male hops may be grown, since seedless H. (produced by the unpollinated female plant) contain a greater proportion of alpha acid which gives beer its bitter taste. They are used as a tonic and as a flavouring in beer.

HOPS. Inveterate climbers, hops here make graceful use of a wire supporting a telegraph pole. *Photo: Heather Angel.*

HORACE (ho'ras) (**Quintus Horatius Flaccus**) (65-8 BC). Roman poet. B. at Venusia, S Italy, the son of a freedman, he fought with the republicans at Philippi, lost his estate, and was reduced to poverty. Virgil introduced him *c.* 38 to Maecenas, who gave him a small estate and procured him the friendship and patronage of Augustus. His Satires, pub. 35-30 BC, survey the follies of contemporary society. His lyrical poems, the Epodes and the 4 books of Odes (*c.* 24-15 BC), written in a variety of metres, deal with both personal and political themes. In later life H. wrote his Epistles, a series of verse letters, and the critical treatise in verse *De Arte Poetica.* His works are distinguished by their style, their wit, and their good sense.

HORDER, Thomas Jeeves, 1st baron (1871-1955). British physician. He attended Edward VII, Edward VIII, George VI, and Elizabeth II, and was a determined opponent of the Health Service as lowering professional standards.

HORE-BELISHA (hawr-bele̅'sha), **Leslie,** baron (1895–1957). British politician. A National Lib., he was Min. of Transport 1934–7, introducing 'B. beacons' to mark pedestrian crossings, and as War Min. from 1937, until removal by Chamberlain in 1940 on grounds of temperament, introduced peace-time conscription in 1939. He was created a peer in 1954.

HOREHOUND. Genus of plants (*Marrubium*) of the Labiatae family. The common H. (*M. vulgare*), found in Europe, N Africa and W Asia and naturalized in N America, has a thick hairy stem and clusters of dirty-white flowers: it has medicinal uses.

HORIZON. The distance to which one can see across the surface of the sea or a level plain, i.e. *c.* 5km (3m) at 1.5m (5ft) above sea level, and *c.* 65km (40m) at 300m (1,000 ft).

HO'RMONES. Products of the endocrine glands. The chief are those of the thyroid, parathyroid, pituitary, suprarenal, pancreas, ovaries, and testicles. They have been called 'blood messengers'. Their purpose is to bring about changes in the functions of various organs according to the body's requirements. Their combined action and interaction are delicately balanced and closely bound up with those of the nervous system. Generally speaking, the pituitary gland, in the skull, is the 'leader of the orchestra'; the thyroid secretion determines the rate at which the organism shall live; the suprarenal secretion prepares the organism for 'fight or flight'; and the sexual secretions govern the reproductive functions. Most hormones are complex chemical substances, and many diseases due to deficiency of one or other of them can be relieved with hormone preparations. **Plant Hs.** are organic compounds produced by plants which are necessary for growth.

HO'RMUZ. Small is. (41 sq.km/16 sq.m), in the **Strait of H.** belonging to Iran. Oil tanker traffic leaving the Gulf for Japan and the West has to pass through this outlet.

HORN, Philip de Montmorency, count of (1518–68). Flemish statesman. He held high offices under Charles V and Philip II, and from 1563 he was one of the leaders of the opposition to the rule of Cardinal Granvella and to the introduction of the Inquisition. In 1567 he was arrested together with Egmont, and both were beheaded in Brussels.

HORN. A family of musical instruments. They originated from animal horns, and are divided into the modern French H., hunting H., and natural H. They are circular in shape, and generally *c.* 3.3m (11ft) long, with a narrow mouthpiece widening to a bell. The natural H. is now replaced by the more varied valve or French H.

HORN, Cape. Most southerly point of the American continent, in the Chilean part of the archipelago of Tierra del Fuego. It was named in 1616 by its Dutch discoverer Willem Schouten (1580–1625) after his birthplace (Hoorn).

HORNBEAM. Genus of trees (*Carpinus*) of the Betulaceae division of the Amentaceae (catkin) family. The common H. (*C. betulus*) is found in woods and hedges throughout the temperate parts of Europe and Asia, and is planted in Britain. It is a small tree with a twisted stem and smooth grey bark. The leaves are oval and hairy on the undersurface. The flowers are borne in catkins, and the fruits are small nuts borne in groups.

HORNBILL. Birds of the family of Bucerotidae, found in Africa, India and Malaya, and so called from the powerful bill surmounted by a bony growth or casque. The H. nests in holes in trees where the female is voluntarily immured, herself assisting in the plastering over of most of the entrance, and fed by her mate throughout incubation.

HORNBLENDE. Mineral of the Amphibole group. It is greenish black, with a glassy, translucent appearance, and is found in the Scottish Highlands, the Alps, N America, etc.

HORNET. *See* WASP.

HORNIMAN, Annie Elizabeth Fredericka (1860–1937). British repertory-theatre pioneer. The dau. of Frederick John H. (1835–1906) founder in 1897 of the H. Museum at Forest Hill, London, she subsidized the Abbey Theatre, Dublin, and founded the Manchester repertory (1907–21). Her brother, **Roy H.** (1872–1909), was an actor and author of *Israel Rank* (1907), in which the hero gains a coronet by poisoning relatives standing between himself and a title (filmed as *Kind Hearts and Coronets*).

HORNUNG, Ernest William (1866–1921). British novelist, creator of Raffles, the gentleman-burglar, and his assistant Bunny in *The Amateur Cracksman* (1899). The idea originated with Conan Doyle, H.'s brother-in-law, who suggested counterparts of Holmes and Watson on the wrong side of the law.

HO'ROSCŌPE. The relative position of the stars and planets at the moment of birth, used by astrologists to forecast the future of the subject. *See* ASTROLOGY. To cope with increased demand in the 20th cent. the casting of Hs. has been computerized.

HO'ROWITZ (-vits), **Vladimir** (1904–). American pianist. B. in Kiev, he made his début in the US in 1928 with the NY Philharmonic Orchestra. He is a masterful technician. In 1933 he m. Wanda, dau. of Toscanini.

HORROCKS, Sir Brian Gwynne (1895–). British general. He served in the F.W.W., and in the S.W.W. under Montgomery at Alamein and with the British Liberation Army in Europe. His TV programmes on military history, etc., were popular.

HORSE. Ungulate mammal (*Equus caballus*) of the family Equidae. The evolution of the H. has been traced from the Eocene age; it is thought to have originated in Asia or Africa, and it was early domesticated as a beast of burden. The teeth became adapted to cropping close grass, and the feet to swift running. The horse now stands on one toe (the hoof), the other toes having been reduced to small digits or splints. The Equidae also includes the zebra, ass, and quagga. The wild horse (*Equus przewalskii*) is now found only in Mongolia. Domesticated breeds are divided into 3 groups - riding, carriage, and carthorses. Riding Hs. incl. the thoroughbred and hunter, which are derived from the Arab H. Carriage Hs. incl. the Hackney, Cleveland Bay, and Coachhorses; the Shire H., Clydesdale, and Suffolk Punch are incl. in the category of carthorses. *See* PONY.

The young male H. is called a colt, and the female a filly; the adult male is called a stallion and the female a mare. There is a large vocabulary covering the coloration, peculiarities of shape, and measurement of Hs. The unit of height, termed a hand, is 10cm (4in). London's first annual International H. Show was held in 1907, but the American National H. Show, held annually in NY, dates from 1883.

HORSE, Master of the. In England an official responsible for the royal stables, and head of one of the departments of the royal household.

HORSE CHESTNUT. Tree common throughout Britain and the temperate regions. The generic name is *Aesculus.* The common H.C. (*A. hippocastanum*) is a fast-growing

HORSE. One of the magnificent sculptures of the imperial war horses of ancient Persia which once decorated Persepolis in Iran. *Photo: Mireille Vautier.*

tree reaching a height of *c.* 20m (60ft). The scented, white or pink flowers are borne in May and June in spikes. The fruits, known to schoolboys as 'conkers', are hard, brown and shiny, and are borne in green spiky cases. *See* CHESTNUT.

HORSE-FLY or **forest fly.** Insect (*Hippobosca Equina*) of the family Tabanidae. Yellowish-brown, it feeds by sucking blood from the flanks of horses.

HORSE GUARDS. Name given to a building in Whitehall, London, England, erected in 1753 by Vardy from a design by Kent, on the site of the Tilt Yard of Whitehall palace. This spot has been occupied by the Household Cavalry or 'Horse Guards' since the Royal Horse Guards were formed in 1661.

HORSE RACING. Sometimes called the national sport of England, where it had its origin in organized form, it has been popular there since at least the 12th cent. and was greatly encouraged by the Stuarts, James I instituting H.R. on Newmarket Heath, where it developed further under Charles I and Charles II, and Queen Anne having Ascot racecourse laid out in 1711. All English thoroughbreds, and through them most of the world's best horses, descend in direct male line from 3 Arabian Hs. introduced in the 18th cent., the Byerly Turk, Darley Arabian, and Godolphin Arabian. Among the chief flat races are the Derby (1780) St Leger (1776), 2,000 Guineas (1809) - these 3 constituting the Triple Crown - Oaks (1779), 1,000 Guineas (1814) - both for fillies only - and Ascot Gold Cup (1807), Eclipse Stakes (1886), and King George VI and Queen Elizabeth Stakes (1951). The Jockey Club (1751) is the governing body and the season is March-Nov. Steeplechasing was not regularized as a sport until the 19th cent., the most important event being the Grand National (q.v.) at Aintree (1839): Liverpool then became the chief seat of steeplechasing, for which the season is August Bank Holiday to Whitsun, and the governing body is the National Hunt Committee. Certain rules governing H.R. generally were laid down by Parliament in 1740, and incl. the basis of the present weight-for-age scale: mechanical starting gates, almost universal elsewhere, were first used for all British classic races in 1967. Bookmaking is subject to legal provisions (*see* BETTING) and the law does not recognize betting debts unless incurred with the Totalizator (q.v.). The chief courses are Epsom, Newmarket, Ascot, Goodwood, Doncaster, Sandown Park, York, and Aintree.

H.R. has spread all over the world, to France (where the most important race is the Prix de l'Arc de Triomphe, Longchamp), Australia, S America, and the USA, where it was introduced by Col. Richard Nicolls, commander of the English forces invading New Amsterdam (New York) in 1664, who laid out a 2-mile course very near the present one at Belmont Park. Now a year-round institution, race meetings may last 50-60 days, and the races are over shorter distances than in Britain. There is no centralized governing body. The scale of American H.R. dwarfs that of other countries, betting on the Totalizator (the only legal method) is on an immense scale, and prize money is high. Classic races incl. the Kentucky Derby (1875), Churchill Downs, Louisville; Preakness Stakes (1773), Pimlico, Baltimore; and Belmont Stakes (1867), Belmont Park, NY - the American Triple Crown. *See also* HARNESS RACING. In Australia the sport is followed with enormous enthusiasm, and the Australian Jockey Club dates from 1842. The most famous race is the Melbourne Cup (1861) at Flemington race course in November: the day is a public holiday in the state of Victoria.

HORSERADISH. Plant (*Armoracia rusticana*) armoracia) of the Cruciferae family, native to SE Europe and naturalized in Britain and America. The thick, cream-coloured and tapering root is used in pharmacy and cookery (a piquant condiment with beef).

HORSETAIL. Genus of plants (*Equisetum*) which, with certain fossil forms, constitutes the family Equisetaceae. The common H. (*E. arvense*) is a frequent weed in Britain and N America. The giant H. (*E. telemateia*) has sterile stems up to 3m (10ft) high and occurs both in the Old World and on the N American Pacific seaboard.

HORSE TRIALS. Competitive sport, also known as 'eventing', which provides an all-round test of a horse in a 3-day event. The first is given to dressage (testing a horse's response to control); the second to speed and endurance across country; and the third to a modified showjumping contest. It is the favourite sport of Elizabeth II, and the only one in which she mixes so closely with the public. *See* BADMINTON.

HORSHAM. English town and market centre on the r. Arun, in W Sussex, 26km (16m) SE of Guildford. Christ's Hospital is *c.* 3km (2m) SW. Pop. (1974) 89,630.

HORSLEY, John Calcott (1817-1903). English artist. B. in London, he was a skilled painter of attractive domestic scenes, but his frescoes for the Houses of Parliament are less happy. He is credited with designing the first Christmas card.

HORST-WESSEL-LIED. Song introduced by the Nazis as a second German national anthem. The text was written by Horst Wessel (1907-30), a Nazi 'martyr', to a traditional tune.

HORTHY DE NAGYBANYA (hortē de nodybahn'yo), **Nicolas** (1868-1957). Hungarian statesman. Leader of the counter-revolutionary 'White' govt., he became regent in 1920, on the overthrow of the Communist Bela Kun régime by Romanian intervention. He pursued a moderate policy, trying (although allied to Hitler) to retain independence of action: in 1944 his country was taken over by the Nazis and he was deported to Germany.

HORTICULTURE. The art of growing flowers, fruit, and vegetables. Courses in H. usually include outdoor gardening, poultry farming, and hothouse care. In Britain the Royal Horticultural Soc. (1804) holds shows at Westminster, and has gardens at Wisley, in Surrey. In the USA there is no general organization like the RHS, but many local societies based upon geography and particular crops, e.g. American Rose Society and Mass. Fruit Growers Association, as there are also in Britain.

HORTICULTURE. One of the world's loveliest harvests, Easter lilies being gathered in Bermuda, whence they are exported by air, especially to the United States. *Photo: Bermuda News Bureau.*

HŌ'RUS. Hawk-headed Egyptian god, the son of Isis and Osiris. The Greeks called him Harpocrates.

HOSPITAL. Institution for the care of the sick and injured. In ancient times temples of deities such as Aesculapius (q.v.) offered facilities for treatment, and the Church had by the 4th cent. founded Hs. for lepers, cripples, the blind, and sick poor. The oldest surviving H. in Europe is the Hôtel Dieu, Paris; in Britain the most ancient are St Bartholomew's (1132) and St Thomas's (1200); and in N America the H. of Jesus of Nazareth, Mexico (1524). Medical knowledge advanced during the Renaissance, and Hs. increasingly became secularized following the Reformation. In the 19th cent. real progress was made in H. design, administration and staffing, cf. Florence Nightingale, and in the 20th there has been a dominant trend to specialization.

In Britain Hs. have formed part of the National Health Service since 1948 and give free treatment, but there are a number of private nursing homes and clinics. In the USA the Hs. may be public (federal or state) or private (voluntary, i.e. non-profitmaking, and proprietary, i.e. profitmaking). From 1966 the over-65s have come under the state Medicare H. insurance scheme, extended 1973 to needy younger people with long-term disablement. Most other Americans belong to voluntary H. insurance schemes, e.g. the non-profitmaking Blue Cross (1929) and the Blue Shield (1917).

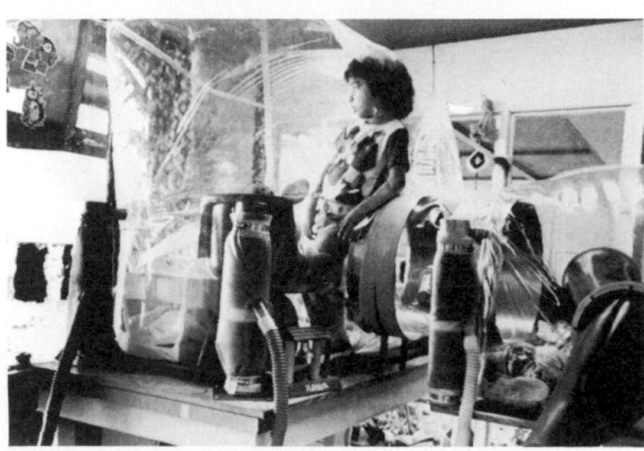

HOSPITAL. Plastic isolation bubbles are used, as here, to protect a child with severe combined immune deficiency, who would die if exposed to the world of germs, but also to protect nursing staff and the outside world against patients with infections such as Marburg disease. *Photo: Popperfoto.*

HOSTAGE. Person taken prisoner as a means of exerting pressure on a third party, usually with threats of death or injury. Most significant internationally have been the *c.* 50 staff of the US embassy taken by the Iranians in 1979. An internat. convention against such acts was being prepared by the UN in 1980.

HOTEL. A house providing for the lodging and refreshment of travellers. European Hs. tend to be smaller (up to 500 rooms), and have more personal service, whereas the American (up to 3,000 rooms) rely much more on mechanization. In the absence of an international rating system, guides are pub. on a national basis, and incl. RAC and AA (Britain), Michelin (France), Warter (Germany), and AAA tour book (USA). *See* MOTEL.

HO'TTENTOTS. S African people inhabiting the SW corner of the continent when Europeans first settled there. They were a pastoral race, composed of Bushmen and Bantu, who have now largely mixed with Dutch and other blood; the Namaqua tribe approximates nearest to the original H. The language bears a resemblance to Bushman, and has mainly monosyllabic roots with explosive consonants which produce peculiar clicking sounds.

HOUDINI (hoodē'nē), **Harry** (1874-1926). American escapologist and conjuror. B. in Wisconsin, he attained fame by his escapes from ropes and handcuffs. He also reproduced some of the phenomena of spiritualist séances by purely mechanical means.

HOUDON (oodoṅ'), **Jean Antoine** (1741-1828). French sculptor. The breathing realism of his portrait busts of Voltaire, Rousseau, Napoleon, etc., is unsurpassed.

HOUNSFIELD, Sir Godfrey (1919-). Brit. scientist. He was a pioneer in the development of tomography (q.v.).

HOUNSLOW. English garrison town and borough of Greater London, England. Situated at the junction of the Bath and Exeter roads, it was an important coaching station, and H. Heath was a resort of highwaymen. Pop. (1972) 206,460.

HOUPHOUËT-BOIGNY (oofwā'-bwahnyē'), **Felix** (1905-). Ivory Coast statesman. He held posts in French ministries, and became pres. of the rep. on independence in 1960: re-elected for a fifth term 1980.

HOUSE FLY. Insect (*Musca domestica*) belonging to the order Diptera. It breeds in stables, garbage dumps, etc., and is most abundant in summer. The female lays about 150 eggs at a time, and may produce 1,000 in a lifetime. It has a dark grey, hairy body, with compound eyes, and feeds through a proboscis. The H. is responsible for carrying a number of diseases, notably typhoid fever.

HOUSEHOLD, Royal. *See* ROYAL HOUSEHOLD.

HOUSEMAID'S KNEE. Inflammation and enlargement of the prepatellar bursa, a small fluid cushion beneath the skin in front of the kneecap.

HOUSING. It is only in the last 100 years that H. has become a matter of state concern, legislation in Britain beginning with measures passed in 1851 and first consolidated in the H. of the Working Classes Act (1890). Private enterprise still provides a proportion of British H., but flats and houses to rent - intended for lower-income groups - are built on a large scale by local authorities under the direction of the Sec. of State for Environment. Local authorities also have wide powers to ensure that all existing houses are well maintained, to clear and redevelop unhealthy or congested areas, to abate overcrowding, and to assist private owners and landlords to improve and convert their property.

Whether operating on a free-enterprise or Communist basis, all modern states have found some degree of state provision or subsidy essential, as in the US through the Housing and Home Finance Agency, with special consideration for 'senior citizens', etc. Nevertheless, growth of population tends always to outstrip any provision made, especially at the income level where it is most needed, and increasing attention is being given to replacing traditional methods by mass-production factory techniques which can make features such as central heating, well-designed plumbing units, etc., available at a fraction of normal cost, and reduce work on site to a minimum.

HOUSMAN, Alfred Edward (1859-1936). B. in Worcestershire, he was ed. at Oxford, and wrote most of the poems of *A Shropshire Lad* (1896) while working as a clerk in HM Patents Office from 1882. Apparently simple, these poems bear the mark of his brilliant classical scholarship and he became prof. of Latin at Univ. Coll., London, in 1892 and held a similar post at Cambridge from 1911. He greatly influenced the 'Georgian' school. His brother, **Laurence H.** (1865-1959), wrote the anonymous novel *An Englishwoman's Love Letters* (1900) and plays, e.g. *Victoria Regina.*

HOUSTON (hyoo'ston). City and port of SE Texas, USA, connected to the Gulf of Mexico by a canal 94km (58.5m) long. H. is a major petroleum centre, with large refineries, and natural gas and sulphur are also exploited. Chemicals, petrochemicals, plastics, synthetic rubber, electronic instruments, etc., are produced, and H. is an agricultural centre, espec. for rice. The Univ. of H. dates from 1934.

H. was founded 1836 and named after Gen. Sam Houston (1793-1863) who won Texan independence from Mexico. It is often known as Space City from the Lyndon B. Johnson Space Center nearby. Pop. met. area (1970) 1,958,491.

HOVE. Sedate seaside resort in E Sussex, England, adjoining Brighton. Pop. (1974) 90,000.

HOVELL, William Hilton. *See* HUME, H.

HOVERCRAFT. Amphibious air-cushion vehicle riding on a cushion of air, free of all contact with the surface beneath. Although H. need a smooth terrain when operating overland, it need not be metalled, and snow and ice present no difficulties, but they are at present best adapted to use on lakes, sheltered coastal waters, river estuaries and swamps. A first experimental passenger ferry service, between Rhyl and Wallasey, was operated in the summer of 1962. The H. owing to its lack of dependence on harbours is specially useful in under-developed countries. They are officially called Air Cushion Vehicles (ACVs). *See* COCKERELL.

HOVERCRAFT. A Mountbatten class hovercraft, *Princess Margaret*, on the cross-Channel service between Dover, Ramsgate, Boulogne and Calais. *Photo: Courtesy of the British Hovercraft Corporation.*

HOWARD, Catherine (d. 1542). Queen of England, the daughter of Lord Edmund H., she was m. to Henry VIII in 1540. In 1541 Cranmer accused her to Henry of unchastity before marriage. In 1542 her adultery was also discovered, and she was beheaded.

HOWARD, Sir Ebenezer (1850-1928). British housing reformer, founder in 1899 of the Garden City Association. He was knighted in 1927.

HOWARD, John (1726-90). British philanthropist. On his appointment as high sheriff for Bedford county in 1773, he undertook a tour of English prisons which led to 2 acts of Parliament in 1774, making gaolers salaried officers and setting standards of cleanliness. After touring Europe in 1775 he pub. his *State of the Prisons in England and Wales, with an account of some Foreign Prisons* (1777). He d. of typhus fever while visiting Russian military hospitals at Kherson in the Crimea. The *Howard League for Penal Reform* (1866) exists to continue his work.

HOWARD, Leslie. Stage-name of British actor Leslie Stainer (1893-1943). He starred in the films *The Petrified Forest, The Scarlet Pimpernel, Pygmalion,* and *Gone with the Wind,* and he was also a talented director and producer. His plane was shot down on his return from a lecture tour in Spain and Portugal, and it has been suggested that the Germans imagined that Churchill was on board.

HOWARD, Trevor Wallace (1916-). British actor. B. at Margate, he was ed. at Clifton Coll., and served with the 1st Airborne Division in the S.W.W. His style of acting ranges from the reckless bravura of *The Devil's General* (1953) to the quiet impact of the film *Brief Encounter* (1945).

HOWARD OF EFFINGHAM, Charles, 2nd baron and 1st earl of Nottingham (1536-1624). English admiral. The son of the 1st baron and a cousin of Queen Elizabeth, he served as ambassador to France 1559, and as Lord High Admiral 1585-1618 commanded the fleet which defeated the Armada. In 1596 he co-operated in the expedition against Cadiz.

HOWE, Elias. *See* SEWING MACHINE.

HOWE, Sir Geoffrey (1926–). British Cons. politician. As Solicitor-General under Heath 1970–2, he drafted the Industrial Relations and European Communities Acts, was Min for Trade 1972–4, and as Chancellor ofthe Exchequer 1979–83 put into practice the monetarist policy of Margaret Thatcher to defeat inflation. In June 1983, he became Foreign Minister.

HOWE. The Conservative Secretary for Foreign Affairs, Sir Geoffrey Howe. *Photo: Courtesy of the C.C.O.*

HOWE (how), **Julia Ward** (1819-1910). American poet and philanthropist. B. in New York City, she m. Samuel Gridley H. in 1843, and ed. with him an anti-slavery newspaper. In 1862 she pub. the 'Battle Hymn of the Republic', sung to the tune of 'John Brown's Body'. Later she advocated women's suffrage and prison reform.

HOWE, Richard, earl (1726-99). British admiral. The son of the 2nd viscount H., he saw service in the War of the Austrian Succession and the 7 Years War, and was promoted to vice-admiral in 1775. In 1776 he was given command of the N American station, and in 1782 he relieved Gibraltar. He was 1st Lord of the Admiralty 1783-8, and in 1788 was created an earl. On the outbreak of the French Revolutionary War he took command in the Channel, and in 1794 won the victory of the 'Glorious 1st of June'.

HOWE, William, 5th visct. (1729-1814). British general. Younger brother of Earl Howe (q.v.), he fought at Bunker Hill. As C-in-C of the British forces in America, he captured New York, defeated Washington at Brandywine Creek and Germantown in 1777, and then settled in Philadelphia while the Americans regrouped at Valley Forge. He resigned 1778 because of lack of support from the home govt.

HOW'ITZER. A piece of ordnance in use since the 16th cent. for steep angle descent in sieges, and much developed in the F.W.W. for demolishing the fortresses of the trench system. The multi-national NATO FH70 field H. is mobile, with its own engine, and fires under computer control three 43 kg (95lb) shells at 32 km (20 m) range in 15 sec. *See* FIREARMS.

HOW'RAH. City of W Bengal, India, on the right bank of the Hooghli, opposite Calcutta. The cap. of H. dist., it has jute and cotton factories, rice, flour and saw mills, chemical factories, engineering works, etc. H suspension bridge, opened in 1943, spans the r. Pop. (1971) 590,400.

HOXHA (haw'ja), **Enver** (1908–85). Albanian statesman. Once a schoolmaster, he founded the Albanian Communist Party in 1941, and headed the liberation movement of 1939–44. He was PM 1944–54, combining this with For. Affairs 1946–53, and from 1954 was First Sec. of the Albanian Workers (Communist) Party. In policy he was fiercely independent both of Chinese and Soviet Communism.

HOYLE, Sir Fred (1915-). British astronomer. Prof. of astronomy at the Royal Institution from 1969, his radio talks and such science fiction as *The Black Cloud* (1957) and *Ossian's Ride* (1959) have estab. his popular reputation, and he is noted for his contribution to cosmological theory (continuous creation) and such books as *Nuclei and Quasars* (1966).

The 'steady state' theory, developed by H., supposes that the universe has always looked the same as it does today. The thinning out arising from expansion is compensated by the continuous creation of matter in the spaces between the stars. *See also* ASTRONOMY.

HUA GUOFENG (hoo-ah goo-awfung'). Chinese statesman (formerly Hua Kuo-feng). On the death of Zhou Enlai in 1976, he succeeded him as PM, being chosen as a compromise candidate in preference to the pragmatic Deng Xiaoping, Zhou's expected successor. In 1976 he also became chairman of the Communist Party Central Committee on Mao Tse-tung's death. However, Deng's renewed influence led to his resignation as PM in 1980, and his retention of the chairmanship with reduced powers only until 1981.

HUA KUO-FENG. *See* HUA GUOFENG.

HUAMBO (hoo-am'bō). Town in central Angola, W Africa, founded in 1912, and known as Nova Lisboa 1928-73 when it was designated by the Portuguese as the future cap. It is an agricultural centre, with rlwy repair shops, and an airport. Pop. (1973) 18,000.

HUANG HE (hoo-ahng'hö). River of China (formerly Hwang-ho), which gained the name (meaning Yellow River) from the yellow loess carried down by its waters. It rises in the A'nyêmaqên Shan, in the western prov. of Qinghai, and flows 4,410 km (2,740 m) in a tortuous course to reach the Yellow Sea in the Bo Hai (formerly Gulf of Chihli). The chief tributaries are the western Wei Hei and eastern Fen Hei, and the main cities standing on it

HUA GUOFENG. His conservative party orthodoxy had to give way in 1980 to the more pragmatic ideas of Deng Xiaoping. *Photo: Hsinhua Press Agency.*

are Lanzhou, Kaifeng, and Jinan. The river has several times changes its lower course and mouth, and disastrous floods earned it the name 'China's sorrow', but since the S.W.W. hydro-electric and flood control schemes have been carried out.

HUASCAR (ōō-ah'skahr) (d. 1533). King of the Incas. He was overthrown by his half brother Atahualpa, with whom he shared the throne 1525-32, and was murdered.

HUASCARAN (ōō-ahskahrahn'). Extinct volcano in the Andes, highest mountain in Peru 6,768 m (22,205 ft).

HUBBLE, Edwin Powell (1889-1953). American astronomer. His researches with the Mount Polamar telescope confirmed the theory, enunciated by de Sitter *c.* 1917, that the universe is expanding. He postulated that the outward velocity of a receding stellar system is proportional to its distance - H.'s law. *See* ASTRONOMY.

HUBBLE'S CONSTANT. Number used by astronomers to calculate the distance and speed of motion of remote objects in space. Thought until 1979 to be 30 miles per second per million parsecs, it was then suggested that it should be 60 miles per second per million parsecs. This would mean the Universe is about 9,000 million years old instead of 15-18 billion (15-15,000 million) years.

HUBEI (hoobā'). Prov. of central China (formerly Hupei), through which flow the Chang Jiang and its tributary the Han Shui. In the W the land is high, the Chang breaking through from Sichuan in gorges, but elsewhere the prov. is low-lying fertile land, and there are many lakes. In summer rice and cotton are grown, and in winter cereals, beans, and vegetables. The cap. is Wuhan. Area 187,500 sq.km (72,375 sq.m); pop. (1979) 42,000,000.

HUDDERSFIELD. Industrial town in W Yorks, on the Colne, and linked by canal with Manchester and other N of England centres. An Anglo-Saxon village, it was a thriving centre of woollen manufacture by the end of the 18th cent., and in modern times has diversified to dyestuffs, chemicals, electrical and mechanical engineering. Pop. (1972) 130,200.

HUDSON, Henry (d. 1611). English explorer. Under the auspices of the Muscovy Company in 1607 and 1608 he made unsuccessful attempts to reach China by way of the NE passage along the N of Asia. In 1609 he was commissioned by the Dutch East India Co., and in Sept. reached New York Bay and sailed 240km (150m) up the river which now bears his name. In 1610 he sailed from London in the *Discovery* and entered what is now the Hudson Strait. The ship was icebound for the winter in the present Hudson Bay. Next spring some of the crew mutinied, and H. and 8 others were turned adrift.

HUDSON, William Henry (1841-1922). Anglo-American author. B. at Florencio near Buenos Aires, of American parents, he was inspired by recollections of early days in Argentina to write his romances *The Purple Land* (1885) and *Green Mansions* (1904), with its bird-like heroine 'Rima', and his autobiographical *Far Away and Long Ago* (1918). His middle and later years were spent in England, and in 1900 he became British by naturalization. He wrote several books on birds, and was a sympathetic interpreter of the English countryside, e.g. *Nature in Down-Land* (1900) and *A Shepherd's Life* (1910). His birthplace has been preserved as a museum since 1956.

HUDSON. River of the USA at whose mouth New York City stands. It rises in the Adirondacks, and flows almost due S for *c.* 485km (300m) to the Atlantic. Discovered in 1524, it was explored in 1609 by Henry Hudson (q.v.), in whose honour it was named.

HUDSON. A festival gathering of old sailing ships on the Hudson River, New York. *Photo: Mireille Vautier.*

HUDSON BAY. Extensive inland sea of NE Canada, connected to the Atlantic by Hudson Strait, and to the Arctic by Foxe Channel. Its area is *c.* 1,233,000 sq.km (476,000 sq.m); length N-S 1,368 km (850m), width 965km (600m).

HUDSON'S BAY COMPANY. A chartered company founded by Prince Rupert in 1670 to trade in furs with the Red Indians. In 1783 the rival North-West Fur Company was formed, but in 1851 this became amalgamated with the H.B.C. which lost its monopoly in 1859. It is still Canada's biggest fur co., but today sales of general merchandise, in towns through large modern dept stores, oil and natural-gas interests, etc., are more important.

HUÉ (hoo-ā). Town in S Vietnam, formerly cap. of Annam (Central Vietnam), 13km (8m) from the China Sea. The Citadel, within which is the Imperial City enclosing the palace of the former emperor, lies to the W of the Old City on the N bank of the Huong (Perfume) River; the New City, incl. the univ., is on the S bank. H. was once an architecturally beautiful cultural and religious centre, but large areas were devastated, with many casualties, during the *Battle of H.* 31 Jan.-24 Feb. 1968 when US and S Vietnamese forces retook the city after Viet Cong occupation by infiltration. There is an airport. Pop. (1973) 156,500.

HUELVA (wel'vah). Seaport in Andalusia, SW Spain, nr the mouth of the Odiel, cap. of H. prov. Columbus began and ended his voyage to America at nearby Palos de la Frontera. Pop. (1970) 96,700.

HUESCA (wes'kah). Cap. of H. prov. in Aragon, N Spain, with a fine 13th cent. cathedral and the former palace of the kings of Aragon. Pop. (1970) 24,400.

HUGGINS, Sir William (1824-1910). British astronomer. He built a private observatory at Tulse Hill, London, in 1856, where he embarked on research in spectrum analysis that marked the beginning of astrophysics: he was also a pioneer in photographic astronomy. Knighted in 1897, he was awarded the OM in 1902.

HUGHES, Howard (1905-76). American tycoon. Inheriting wealth from his father, who had patented an indispensable oil-drilling bit, he created a legendary financial empire. A skilled pilot, he manufactured and designed aircraft, and made the classic film *Hell's Angels* about airmen of the F.W.W.: later successes incl. *Scarface* and *The Outlaw.* From his middle years he was a hypochondriac recluse.

HUGHES, Richard Arthur Warren (1900-1976). British author, chiefly known for his study of childhood, *High Wind in Jamaica* (1929), and the trilogy *The Human Predicament* (1961-73).

HUGHES, Ted (1930-). British poet, B. in W Yorks, he m. in 1956 the American poet Sylvia Plath (1932-63), and has pub. numerous vols. incl. *The Hawk in the Rain* (1957) and *Remains of Elmet* (1979).

HUGHES, Thomas (1822-96). British author. Called to the Bar in 1848, he became a county court judge in 1882. He joined the Christian Socialists, and became principal of the Working Men's College in London. He is chiefly remembered for his boys' book, *Tom Brown's School Days* (1857), a story of Rugby under Arnold. It had a successor, *Tom Brown at Oxford* (1861).

HUGHES, William Morris (1864-1952). Australian statesman. B. in London, he emigrated to Australia in 1884, and in 1915 succeeded Fisher as PM, proving a vigorous war leader. Originally Labor, he headed a National cabinet. He represented Australia at Versailles, and resigned in 1923, but held many other cabinet posts 1934-41.

HUGO (ügō'), **Victor Marie** (1802-85). French poet, novelist, and dramatist. B. at Besançon, the son of one of Napoleon's generals, he pub. *Odes et Poésies diverses* in 1822, and estab. himself as the leader of French Romanticism with the verse play *Hernani* (1830). Later plays include *Lucrèce Borgia* (1833), in which the courtesan

HUGHES. William Morris Hughes, seen here with P.G. Stewart, was one of the most controversial of Australia's statesmen. Small of stature, he was affectionately nicknamed the 'Little Digger' when he visited England during the First World War. *Photo: Australian News and Information Service.*

Juliette Drouet, who was his mistress for 50 years, appeared, and *Ruy Blas* (1838). Of his 25 vols. of verse *Odes et Ballades, Les Chants du Crépuscule* (1835), and *Les Rayons et les Ombres* (1840), may be mentioned. In 1841 he was elected to the academy, became a peer in 1845, but was banished in 1851 for opposing Louis Napoleon's coup d'état, and settled in Guernsey, where he wrote the vols. of verse *Les Contemplations* (1856) and *La Légende des Siècles.* His great series of novels began with *Notre Dame de Paris* (1831), and included *Les Misérables* (1862), *Les Travailleurs de la Mer* (1866), *L'Homme qui rit* and *Quatre-Vingt-Treize* (1874). On the fall of the empire in 1870 H. returned to France, later becoming a senator. He d. in Paris and was buried in the Panthéon.

HUGUENOTS (hū'genots). Name applied to the French Protestants in the 16th cent.; probably a corruption of Ger. *eidgenossen,* 'confederates'. Mainly Calvinist, they were severely persecuted under Francis I and Henry II, but the massacre of St Bartholomew in 1572 and the 30 years of religious wars which followed failed to exterminate them. In 1598 the former Huguenot, Henry IV, granted a measure of toleration by the Edict of Nantes, and although they lost military power after the revolt at La Rochelle 1627-9, the Hs. were still tolerated by Richelieu and Mazarin. In 1685 Louis XIV revoked the Edict of Nantes and attempted their forcible conversion, with the result that 400,000 left France, and many settled in England.

HUHEHOT. *See* HOHHOT.

HULL, Cordell (1871-1955). American statesman. B. in Tennessee, he was a member of Congress 1907-33, and, as Roosevelt's Sec. of State 1933-44, was identified with the 'good neighbour' policy, and opposed German and Japanese aggression. In his last months of office he paved the way for an international security system and was called 'father' of the UN. He was awarded the Nobel peace prize in 1945.

HULL. City and port, more properly **Kingston upon Hull,** in Humberside (of which it is admin. HQ), England. Given its name by Edward I, it stands on the N bank of the Humber estuary, where the r. Hull flows into it, *c.* 35 km (22 m) from the North Sea, and is linked with the S bank by the nearby Humber Bridge (1980). It was once Europe's biggest fishing port, but surviving near and medium water boats are now at Grimsby, nearer the sea, though fish processing (fishmeal and fish fingers) is carried on with continental imports and there are ferry links with Rotterdam and Zeebrugge. Industries incl. vegetable oils, flour milling, electricals, textiles, paint, chemicals, pharmaceuticals, caravans and aircraft. Notable buildings incl. Holy Trinity Church (13th cent.), guildhall, Ferens Art Gallery (1927), and the univ. (1954). Pop. (1947) 281,560.

HULME (hüm), **Thomas Edward** (1881-1917). British philosopher, critic and poet. He was killed on active service in the F.W.W., but his *Speculations* (1924) influenced T. S. Eliot, and his few poems originated the Imagist movement.

HULME-BEAMAN (hūm-bē'man), Sydney George (1887-1932). British author. B. in Tottenham, London, he wrote a series of plays, performed in the puppet theatre he made and operated himself with beautiful hand-carved puppets, which were set in 'Toytown', and incl. such characters as Larry the Lamb, Ernest the Policeman and His Worship the Mayor.

HUM, Environmental. A disturbing sound of frequency about 40 Hz, which is heard by individuals sensitive to this range, but is inaudible to the rest of the population. It may be caused by industrial noise pollution, or have a more exotic origin, such as the jet stream, a fast-flowing high altitude (about 15,000 metres) mass of air.

HUMAN BODY. The physical vehicle of human consciousness. It develops for nine months in the womb from the single cell of the fertilized ovum, through all the stages of human evolution, and reaches maturity between 18 and 24 years of age.

Structure. The bony framework (*skeleton*) consists of 200 bones, over half of which are in the hands and feet. The skull is mounted on the spinal column, a slightly undulant chain of 24 vertebrae. The ribs, 12 on each side, are articulated (jointed) to the spinal column behind, and the upper 7 meet the breast-bone (sternum) in front. The lower end of the spine rests on the triangular sacrum, to which are attached the two hip-bones (ilia), which are fused in front (symphysis pubis). Below the sacrum is the tail-bone (coccyx). These last 4 bones constitute the pelvis. The shoulder blades (scapulae) are held in place behind the upper ribs by muscles, and connected in front to the breast-bone by the two collar-bones (clavicles). Each carries a cup (glenoid cavity) into which fits the upper end of the arm-bone (humerus). This articulates below with the two forearm-bones, the radius and the ulna. The radius is articulated at the wrist to the bones of the hand. The upper end of each thigh-bone (femur) fits into a depression in the hip-bone; its lower end is articulated at the knee to both the leg-bones (tibia and fibula), which are articulated at the angle to the bones of the foot.

Bones are held together by joints (articulations). Some, but not all, of these allow movement of one bone on the other. At a moving joint the end of each bone is formed of tough, smooth cartilage, lubricated by synovial fluid. Points of special stress are reinforced by bands of fibrous tissue (ligaments).

Muscles (flesh) are bundles of fibres which have the power of contracting and relaxing. They perform all the movements of the body, whether of bones or of organs. Muscles under voluntary control are attached to bones (skeletal or voluntary muscles). Those not under voluntary control (involuntary muscles) are found in internal organs and the walls of blood vessels. Muscle bundles are wrapped in thin, tough layers of connective tissue (fascia); these are usually prolonged at the ends into strong, white cords (tendons, sinews) or sheets (aponeuroses), which connect the muscles to bones and organs and through which the muscles do their work. Membranes of connective tissue also wrap the organs and line the interior cavities of the body, and secrete lubricating fluid (serum). Blood vessels, branching into multitudes of very fine tubes (capillaries), supply all parts of the muscles and organs with blood, which carries the oxygen and food necessary to their life. The food passes out of the blood to the cells in a clear fluid (lymph); this returns with waste matter through a system of lymphatic vessels to the large veins below the collar-bones (subclavian), and thence to the heart. A finely branching system of nerves regulates the function of the muscles and organs, and makes their needs known to the controlling centres.

The skull contains the brain, which with the spinal cord comprises the *central nervous system.* This governs the voluntary processes of the body. The spinal cord runs down within the vertebrae of the spinal column for c.43cm (17in), after which a fine terminal filament continues through the rest of the spine. The central nervous system is composed of nerve cells, the bodies of which form the grey matter and the fibres the white. The cell bodies are disposed over the surface of the brain and the interior of the spinal cord; the fibres run together into nerve trunks, which extend all over the body. The inner spaces of the brain and the cord contain cerebro-spinal fluid. On the sides of the spinal column are situated about 22 pairs of nerve junctions (sympathetic ganglia): these, with certain other nerves, make up the *autonomic nervous system,* which governs the involuntary processes of the body. These processes are further regulated by the hormones secreted by the endocrine glands.

The upper part of the trunk, enclosed by the ribs (thorax), contains the *lungs* and the *heart* lying between them. The thorax has a stout muscular floor, the diaphragm, which with the rib muscles expands and contracts the lungs in the act of breathing. The part of the trunk below the diaphragm, the abdomen, contains the *digestive organs* (stomach and intestines), the liver, spleen and pancreas, the urinary organs (kidneys, ureters and bladder), and, in the woman, the *reproductive organs* (ovaries, uterus, and vagina). In the man the prostate gland and seminal vesicles only of the reproductive system are situated in the abdomen, the testicles being housed in the scrotum, which, with the penis, is suspended in front of

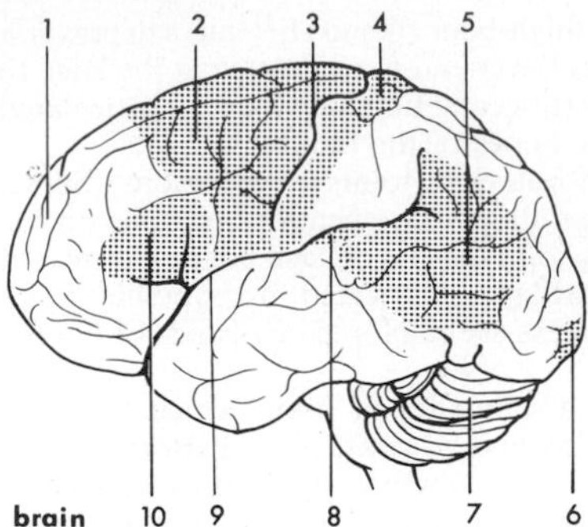

brain

1 association areas (unshaded), as yet not completely understood, but concerned with the analysis of incoming information and formulation of action accordingly
2 motor area, controlling (with 6) movement of the limbs
3 fissure of Rolando, or central fissure
4 somatosensory area, concerned with bodily sensations
5 posterior (Wernicke's) speech area, concerned with understanding of language
6 visual area
7 cerebellum, controlling muscle co-ordination
8 cerebellum, auditory area
9 fissure of Sylvius
10 anterior (Broca's) speech area, concerned with production of speech

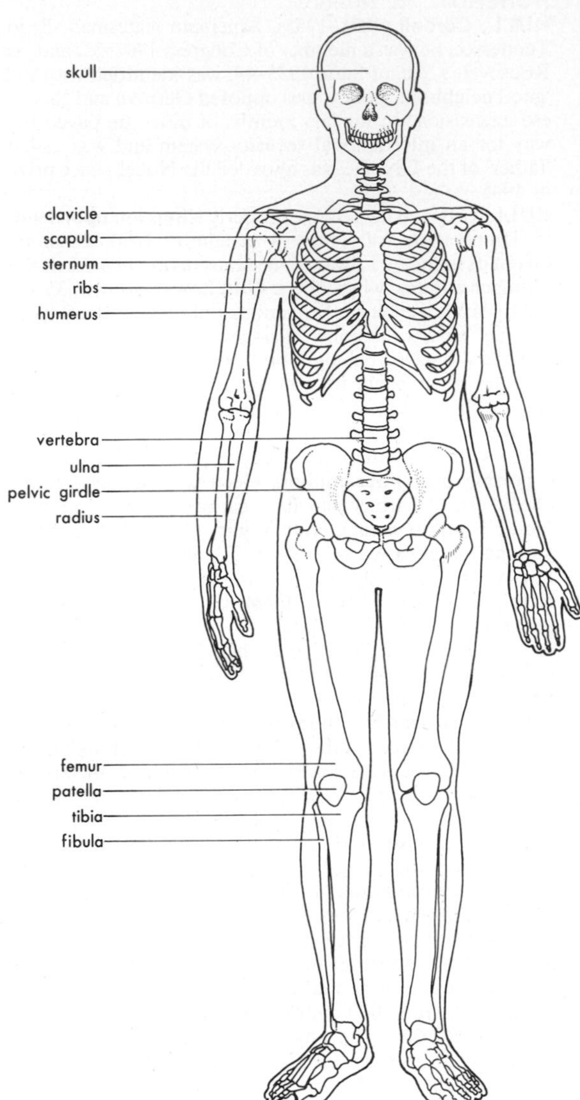

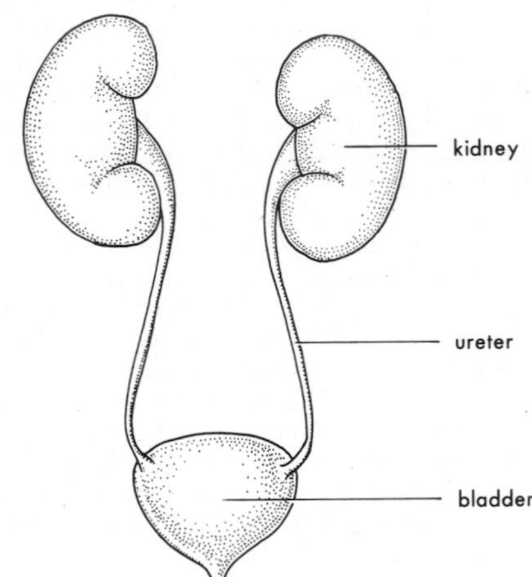

foetal development

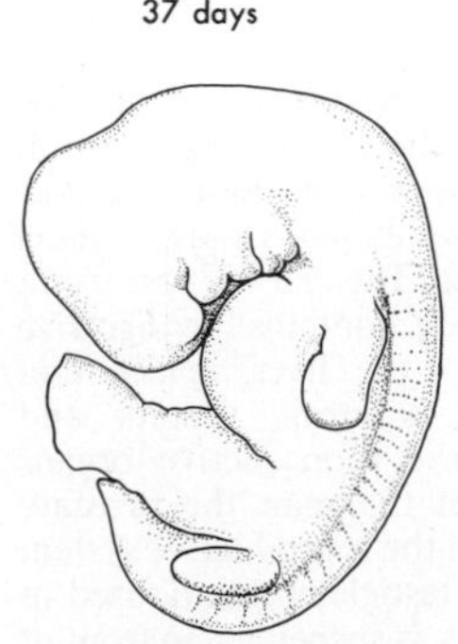

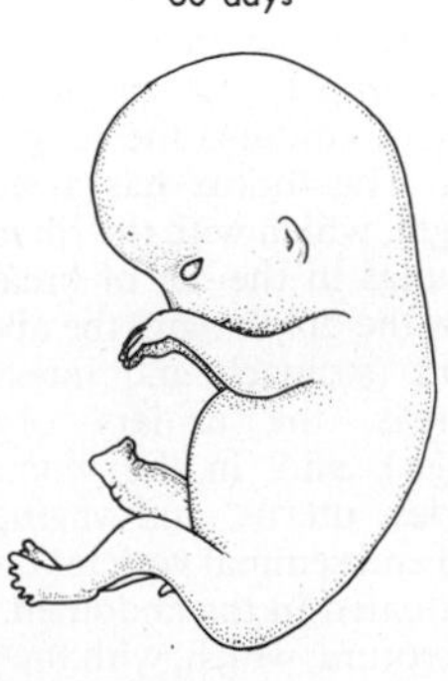

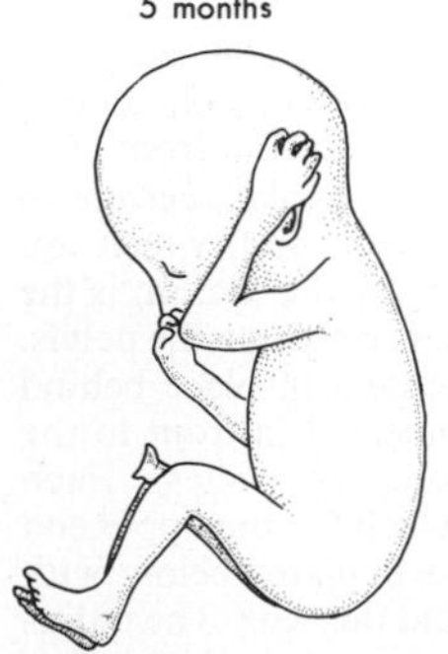

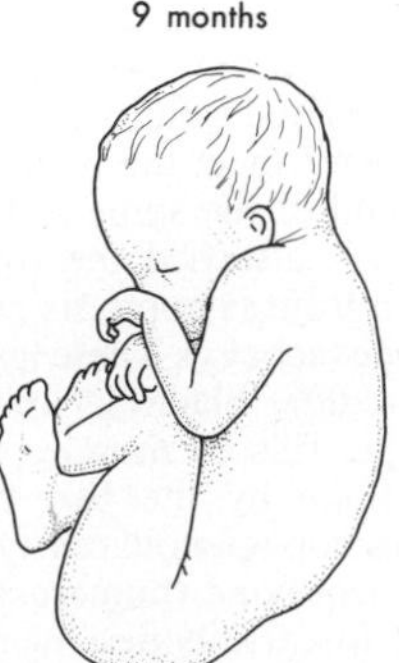

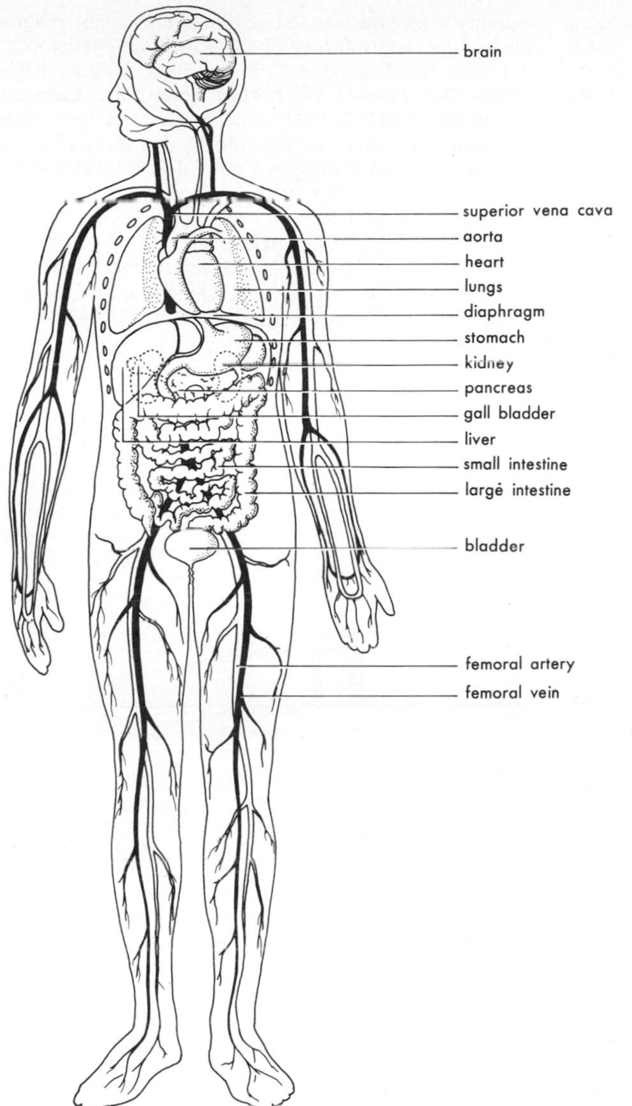

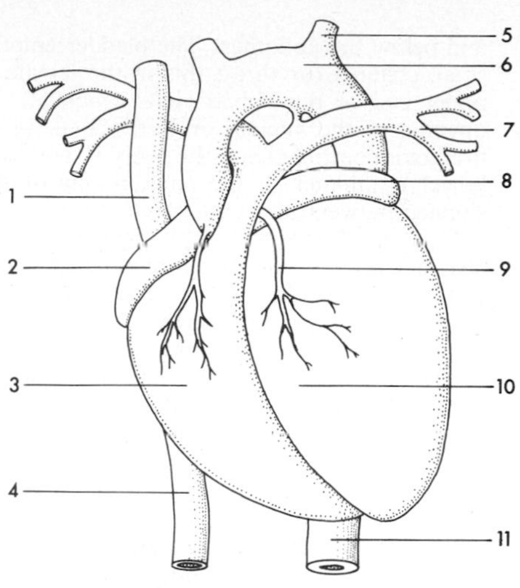

heart

1 superior vena cava
2 right atrium
3 right ventricle
4 inferior vena cava
5 artery to head
6 aorta
7 pulmonary artery
8 left atrium
9 coronary artery
10 left ventricle
11 aorta

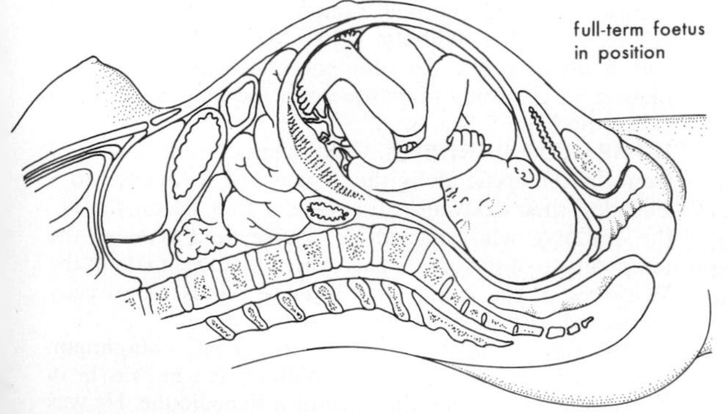

full-term foetus
in position

Aspects of the Human Body

and below the abdomen. The bladder empties through a small channel (urethra); this in the female opens in the upper end of the vulval cleft, which also contains the opening of the vagina, or birth canal. In the male the urethra is continued into the penis. In both sexes the lower bowel terminates in the anus, a ring of strong muscle situated between the buttocks.

Cavities of the body opening on to the surface are coated with *mucous membrane*, which secretes a lubricating fluid (mucus). The exterior surface of the body is coated with *skin*. Within the skin grow the sebaceous glands, which secrete sebum, an oily fluid which makes the skin soft and pliable, and the sweat glands, which secrete water and various salts. From the skin grow hair, chiefly on the head, in the armpits, and around the sexual organs; and nails shielding the tips of the fingers and toes; both these structures are modifications of skin tissue. The skin also contains nerves of touch, pain, heat and cold.

Respiration and Circulation. Like an engine, the body derives energy from the combination of carbon, supplied in the food, with oxygen supplied in the air it breathes. The left side of the heart pumps blood through a system of arteries to all parts of the body, through which it circulates in a network of fine capillary vessels. These lead into veins, by which the blood returns to the right side of the heart, which pumps it to the lungs. Here it passes through minute vessels in which it comes into contact with air drawn through a network of tubes (bronchi) into a multitude of small air cells. The blood gives up carbon dioxide, receives oxygen, and returns to the left side of the heart to be sent again round the body. The beat of the heart is controlled by involuntary nerves; the expansion and contraction of the lungs are partly controlled by the will and partly involuntary.

Digestion. Food is mixed with saliva in the mouth by chewing and is swallowed. It enters the stomach, where it is gently churned for some time and mixed with acid gastric juice. It then passes into the small intestine. In the first part of this, the duodenum, it is more finely divided by the juice of the pancreas and of the duodenal glands and mixed with bile from the liver, which splits up the fat. The jejunum and ileum continue the work of digestion and absorb most of the nutritive substances from the food. The large bowel (colon) completes the process and ejects the useless residue.

The Urinary System. The body, to be healthy, must contain water and various salts in the right proportions. The blood is therefore filtered in the two kidneys, which remove such water and salts as are not needed. These, with a yellow pigment derived from bile, are the urine, which passes down through two fine tubes (ureters) into the bladder, a reservoir, from which the urine is emptied at intervals (micturition) through the urethra.

Heat Regulation. Heat is constantly generated by the combustion of food in the muscles and glands, and dissipated through the skin by conduction to the clothing and evaporation of sweat, through the lungs in the expired air, and in the other excreted substances. The body works best at a temperature of *c.* 38°C/100°F (37°C/98.4°F in the mouth), maintained by a nerve centre in the brain, which regulates the activity of the skin and lungs. *See* parts of body, SEX AND REPRODUCTION, etc.

HUMAN RIGHTS, Universal Declaration of. Proclamation by the UN General Assembly in 1948 which incl. assertion of the rights to life, liberty, education and equality before the law; to freedom of movement, religion, association, and information; and to a nationality.

Under the European Convention of Human Rights (1950) the Council of Europe estab. the **European Commission of H.R.** (HQ Strasbourg), which investigates complaints by states or individuals, and its findings are examined by the European Court of H.R. (1959) whose compulsory jurisdiction has been recognised by a number of states incl. the UK.

HUMBERSIDE. Co. of England, created 1974 from areas of the former E Riding of Yorks and the N of Lincs, and enclosing the Humber estuary. The admin. HQ is Hull. Area 3,512 sq.km (1,356 sq.m); pop. (1978) 844,900.

HUMBERSIDE. Some 8 km (5 m) west of Kingston upon Hull, the Humber Bridge was completed in 1980, when its main span 1,410m (4,626ft) became the longest of any single-span suspension bridge in the world. *Photo: Courtesy of the Humber Bridge Board.*

HUMBERT I (1844-1900). King of Italy. Son of Victor Emmanuel II, he saw service during the war of National Liberation and became king on his father's death in 1878. He was assassinated by an anarchist. For Humbert II *see* UMBERTO II.

HUMBOLDT (hoom'bolt), **Friedrich Heinrich Alexander,** baron von (1769-1859). German scientist. B. in Berlin, he explored the regions of the Orinoco and the Amazon, 1800-4, and on his return devoted 21 years to writing an account of his journeys. His greatest work, *Cosmos* (1845-62), is an account of the physical sciences. His elder brother, **Wilhelm** (1767-1835), held diplomatic and political posts. An eminent philologist, he was a pioneer in the study of Basque and the languages of the Orient and the S Sea Is.

HUMBOLDT CURRENT. Cold ocean current flowing N from the Antarctic along the W coast of S America to S Ecuador, then westwards. It is named after Baron von H., the explorer who charted its course, and reduces the temperature of the coasts past which it flows, making the W slopes of the Andes arid because winds are already chilled when they cross the coast.

HUME (hūm), **Basil** (1923-). British RC churchman. Son of a heart consultant, Sir William H., he was b. in Newcastle upon Tyne, and became a Benedictine. He was abbot of Ampleforth in Yorks 1963-76, to which Ampleforth Coll. (a public school) is attached, and in 1976

HUNGARY. The Hungarian Houses of Parliament in Budapest, built by Aimery Steindel in 1893–1902 on Rudolph Quay. And (right) Béla Bartók, most famous of the country's composers, who exerted a strong influence on the development of modern music.
Photo: Mireille Vautier and Popperfoto.

succeeded Heenan as Abp. of Westminster, the first monk to hold the office.

HUME, David (1711-76). Scottish philosopher and historian. B. at Edinburgh, he studied in France and in 1739 pub. his treatise on *Human Nature*, followed in 1741 by *Essays Moral and Political.* In 1751 appeared his *Inquiry into the Principles of Morals*, an exposition of the Utilitarian philosophy. In 1752 he became librarian to the Faculty of Advocates in Edinburgh. His *History of England* reaches from the Roman period to 1761. His essays criticized belief in miracles and other Christian dogmas.

HUME, Fergus (1859-1932). British writer. Ed. in New Zealand, he returned to his native England in 1888: his *Mystery of a Hansom Cab* (1887) was one of the first popular detective stories.

HUME, Hamilton (1797-1873). Australian explorer. B. in the country, he headed an expedition from Sydney in 1824 in company with William Hilton Hovell (1786-1875), which discovered the Murray r., and reached Port Phillip. The Melbourne-Sydney **H. Highway** is named after him.

HUME, Joseph (1777-1855). British Radical politician. B. at Montrose, he went out to India as an army surgeon in 1797, made a fortune, and on his return bought a seat in parliament. In 1818 he secured election as a Philosophic Radical and supported many progressive measures. His son **Allan Octavian H.** (1829-1912) was largely responsible for the establishment of the Indian National Congress in 1885.

HŪMI'DITY. Absolute H. is the quantity of water vapour in a given volume of the atmosphere, but the more useful quantity is the relative H. which is the ratio of the amount of water vapour in the atmosphere to the saturation value at the same temperature. At the dew-point the relative H. is 100 per cent. Measurements of relative H. are generally made with a wet and dry bulb thermometer (technical name psychrometer). *See* HYGROMETER.

HUMMING BIRD. Name given to many birds forming the family Trochilidae and found in America. They derive their name from the sound produced by the rapid vibration of their wings, and are the only birds able to fly backwards. They are brilliantly coloured, and have a long tongue with which they obtain nectar from flowers and capture insects.

HUMPERDINCK (hoom'perdinck), **Engelbert** (1854-1921). German composer. B. at Siegburg, he studied music in Munich and in Italy and assisted Rich. Wagner at Bayreuth. Fame came to him with his musical fairy operas, *Hansel and Gretel* (1893), *Königskinder*, etc.

HUNAN (hoonahn'). Prov. of central China lying S of the Chang Jiang, Most of it is broken mountainous country watered by the Xiang Jiang and the Yuan Jiang, both of which flow into Dongting lake, a natural overflow reservoir of the Chang Jiang. The cap. is Changsha; other towns incl. Xiangtan and Hengyang. Rice, tea, tobacco and cotton are grown, and it is rich in non-ferrous minerals espec. antimony and mercury. Area 210,500 sq.km (81,253 sq.m); pop. (1979) 50,000,000.

HUNDRED YEARS WAR. Name given to the struggle between England and France that was carried on from 1337 to 1453. It began with the claim of Edward III, through his mother, to the crown of France, and at the outset the English were victorious at the naval battle of Sluys in 1340 and on land at Crécy in 1346 and Poitiers in 1356. After 1369 the tide turned in favour of the French, and when Edward III d. in 1377 only Calais, Bordeaux, and Bayonne were in English hands. A state of half-war continued for many years until Henry V invaded France in 1415 and won a victory at Agincourt. After his death his brother Bedford was generally successful until Joan of Arc raised the siege of Orléans in 1429. Even after her capture and death the French continued their successful counter-offensive, and in 1453 only Calais was left in English hands.

HUNGARIAN or **Magyar.** One of the few languages spoken in Europe that are not of Indo-European stock; with Finnish and Estonian it belongs to the Finno-Ugrian family. Its vocabulary is basically Finno-Ugrian, although many words are importations from Iranian, Slavonic, Turkish, and modern European languages.

HUNGARY. Republic of central Europe, bordering on Romania in the E and Austria in the W. H. consists for the most part of the plains of the middle Danube; the river forms the NW boundary with Czechoslovakia, then turns S and, through Budapest, the cap., flows right across the country in a southerly direction. The Great Hungarian Plain, watered by the r. Tisza and its tributaries, lies E of the Danube. Once almost exclusively vast pastures, it is now for the most part under cultivation. For part of its course the Drava forms the southern boundary with Yugoslavia. N of Lake Balaton, the largest of the central European lakes, in the SW of the country, stretches the mountainous Bákony forest, between which and the Danube lies the Little Hungarian Plain. There is a large timber industry.

Agriculture is still important; main crops incl. wheat, maize, rye, barley, potatoes, and sugar beet. Wine comes from N of Lake Balaton and from the NE hills (Tokay). Horses, cattle, sheep, and pigs are reared. Fishing is important in the Danube and Tisza and Lake Balaton. Minerals incl. oil and natural gas, coal, iron, and bauxite; the chemical, machine and electric power industries are being rapidly expanded and textiles, cement, sugar, etc., are produced. The chief univs. are at Budapest, Debrecen, Szeged, and Pécs.

Area 93,000 sq.km (35,920 sq.m); pop. (1978) 10,671,000, of whom more than 90% are Magyar-speaking. M.U.: forint.

History. Originally inhabited by Celtic and Slavonic tribes, H. was partly occupied by the Romans and after their withdrawal was overrun by Germanic tribes, by the Huns, and by the Avars. The Hungarian state was founded in the 9th cent. by the Magyars, a federation of Finno-Ugrian tribes under a chieftain named Árpád. St Stephen (997-1038) adopted the title of king, and estab. Latin Christianity. After the house of Árpád died out in 1301, H. came under the rule of foreign princes. The Turks were held at bay by John Hunyadi and his son, Matthias Corvinus (1458-90), but in 1526 the Turks annihilated the Hungarian army at Mohács, King Louis II being accidentally drowned as he fled, and secured the centre and S of the country. The Habsburgs estab. themselves in the N and W, while semi-independent princes under Turkish suzerainty ruled Transylvania, which had been part of Hungary since its conquest by St Stephen in 1000 (it became part of Rumania in 1920). Habsburg attempts to suppress Protestantism and the privileges of the nobles led in the 17th cent. to several revolts, ruthlessly put down. By 1697 the Habsburgs had driven out the Turks and secured the whole of H., confirmed by the peace of Karlowitz, 1699. A peasant rising under Rakoczi led to the granting of a constitution in 1711 by Charles III of H. (VI of Austria).

After 1815 a national renaissance began, under the leadership of Kossuth. The revolution of 1848-9 proclaimed a republic and abolished serfdom, but with the help of Russia Austria suppressed the revolt. Francis Joseph in 1867 gave H. autonomy within the Dual Monarchy (*see* AUSTRIA; AUSTRIA-HUNGARY). In 1918, in the last days of the F.W.W., H. was proclaimed a republic, and for a few weeks in 1919 was ruled by a Bolshevik govt under Bela Kun, who, following a coup d'état, escaped to Russia. A popularly elected assembly in 1920 chose Admiral Horthy (q.v.) as regent for an unnamed king; he remained in power until 1944. After 1933 H. fell more and more under German influence and, having joined Hitler in the invasion of Russia in 1941, was overrun by the Red Army 1944-5. Horthy fled, and a provisional govt distributed land to the peasants, later reclaimed for collectivisation. An elected assembly inaugurated a rep. in 1946; it soon fell under Russian Communist domination, although only 70 Communists had been returned out of a total of 409. A popular rising in 1956 was harshly suppressed by Russian forces. Slightly more widely-based elections were held 1967 and far-reaching economic reforms were launched 1968, and by 1980 the 'new economic mechanism' had elements of a free market economy.

Literature. After the H. state was estab. in 895, and Christianity adopted in *c.* 100, Latin chronicles and devotional works dominated the lit. until *c.* 1500. The political upheavals which followed the battle of Mohács (1526), inspired the 16th, 17th, and early 18th cent. chronicle songs and folk poetry which helped preserve the national identity. To the 19th cent. renaissance belong the epic poet Mihály Vörösmarty (1800-55); the patriotic revolutionary Sándor Petöfi (1823-49), famous for his lyrics, the two poets János Arany (1817-82) and his son László (1844-98), and the novelist Mór Jokai (1825-1904). Later poets incl. Mihály Babits (1883-1941) and the lyricist Endre Ady (1877-1919), and Zsigmond Móricz (1879-1942) wrote novels of peasant life. Popular in the West was Ferenc Molnár (1878-1952), with his novel *Paul Street Boys* (1907), and *Liliom* (1909), study of a circus barker, adapted as the musical *Carousel.*

The Arts. Besides music (*see* BARTÓK and KODÁLY) H. excels in crafts such as glass, pottery and metalwork, in which there is a modern revival.

HUNS. Name applied to a number of nomad Mongol peoples who first appeared in history in the 2nd cent. BC as raiding across the Great Wall into China. They entered Europe *c.* AD 372, settled in Hungary, and imposed their supremacy on the Ostrogoths and other Germanic peoples. Under the leadership of Attila they attacked the Eastern Empire, invaded Gaul, and threatened Rome, but after his death in 453 their power was broken by a revolt of their subject peoples. The White Hs. or Ephthalites, a kindred people, raided Persia and N India in the 5th-6th cents.

HUNT, James Henry Leigh (1784-1859). British poet and essayist. B. at Southgate, Middx, he began to edit *The Examiner* in 1808 and in 1813 was sentenced to 2 years' imprisonment for an attack on the Prince Regent, which made him widely acclaimed in radical circles. His narrative poem *The Story of Rimini,* written in prison, appeared in 1816. In 1822 he visited Byron and Shelley in Italy, and in 1828 H. pub. *Lord Byron and some of his Contemporaries.* Hampered by sickness and poverty, he was granted a civil-list pension in 1847. He did much to widen the public taste for early English and Italian poetry; but his own best work is largely in narrative verse.

HUNT, John, baron (1910-). British mountaineer. An army officer, he served in India and in the S.W.W., and led the British expedition which first climbed Mt Everest in 1953.

HUNT, William Holman (1827-1910). British artist. B. in Cheapside, London, he first exhibited at the RA in 1846, and in 1848 helped to found the Pre-Raphaelite Brotherhood. In 1854 H. travelled to Syria and Palestine to paint realistic pictures of Biblical subjects. His most famous work, 'The Light of the World' (1854), is in Keble Coll., Oxford, a replica of it (1904) in St Paul's.

HUNTER, John (1728-93). British surgeon and physiologist. B. in Lanarkshire, he became house-surgeon at St George's hospital, London, in 1756, collaborated with his brother William in the anatomical school; and from 1768 was surgeon. He experimented extensively on animals, collected a large number of specimens and preparations (Hunterian Collections), now in the Royal College of Surgeons, and greatly furthered the art of surgery.

His brother **William H.** (1718-83), anatomist and obstetrician, became prof. of anatomy in the Royal Academy in 1768, and pres. of the Medical Society in 1781. His collections are now in the Hunterian museum of Glasgow univ.

HUNTER. River in NSW, Australia, which rises in the Mt. Royal Range and flows into the Pacific nr. Newcastle, after a course of c. 465 km (290 m). It is liable to flooding, but there is dairying and market gardening, and Hunter Valley wines are famous.

HUNTINGDON. Town in Cambridgeshire, on the Ouse, 26km (16m) NW of Cambridge. It is a market town with a number of light industries. A bridge (1332) connects H. with Godmanchester on the S bank of the river, and the 2 towns were united in 1961. Pepys and Cromwell attended the grammar school founded in 1565 in a 12th cent. building, formerly part of the medieval hospital; it was opened in 1962 as a museum of Cromwelliana. Pop. (1972) 18,000.

HUNTINGDONSHIRE and Peterborough. Former English co., formed in 1965 from the co. of H. and the Soke of Peterborough (q.v.), and merged in a much enlarged Cambridgeshire in 1974.

HUNTSVILLE. Town in NE Alabama, USA. It is an aerospace research centre. Pop. (1973) 138,000.

HUNYADI (hoon'yodi), **János Corvinus** (1387-1456). Hungarian statesman and general. B. in Transylvania, reputedly the natural son of the emperor Sigismund, he campaigned successfully against the Turks. He had just driven them from before Belgrade when he d. of the plague.

HUPEI. *See* HUBEI.

HU'RONS. French nickname (*hure*, head of pig, etc.) for the Wyandot, nomadic Red Indian tribes related to the Iroquois, and living near Lakes Huron, Erie and Ontario in the 16-17th cents. They were almost wiped out by the Iroquois, but some still survive in Quebec and Oklahoma. *Lake Huron,* second largest of the Great Lakes (q.v.), has an area of *c.* 59,600 sq.km (23,000 sq.m) - 36,000 sq.km (14,000 sq.m) in Canada.

HURRICANE. A violent revolving storm. The name is derived from a Carib word *huracan,* and applied originally only to the W Indies, but is now used in many countries, though in the E Indies and the China Seas similar storms are known as typhoons. Hs. are accompanied by a fall in pressure, have a revolving speed of 16-24kmph (10-15mph), and blow at over 120km (75m). On the Beaufort scale it is force 12; the severer stages of H. are force 13 (134-149km/83-92m), 14 (150-166km/-93-103m), 15 (167-184km/104-114m), 16 (185-201km/-115-125m) and 17 (202-219km/126-136m). In weather reports Hs. were formerly given female Christian names, but in 1979 the first male name - Bob - was introduced.

HURSTMONCEUX. *See* HERSTMONCEUX.

HUSKY. Eskimo sledge dog *c.* 70 cm (2 ft) high, with pricked ears, thick fur and a bushy tail.

HUSS, John (*c.* 1373-1415). Bohemian reformer. B. in S Bohemia, he was ed. at Prague univ. of which he became rector in 1402. He attacked ecclesiastical abuses and was excommunicated. His preaching attracted popular support, and in 1411 Prague was laid under a papal interdict. In 1413 he was summoned to appear before the Council of Constance. There he defended Wycliffe and rejected the Pope's authority, and was burnt at the stake on 6 July 1415.

His followers were known as *Hussites,* and from a body of religious reformers they developed into a nationalist party opposed to German and papal influence in Bohemia. War began in 1419, and the Bohemians were for some years successful under the leadership of Žižka. Subsequently the movement split; and Roman Catholicism was re-established in 1620. The traditions of one section, the Taborites, are carried on by the Moravian Church.

HUSSEIN Ibn Ali (hoosān') (*c.* 1854-1931). King of the Hejaz. B. in Mecca, he was appointed Sherif of Mecca in 1908. After negotiations with the British he headed an Arab revolt in 1916, and with the aid of T. E. Lawrence raised an army against the Turks. He assumed the title of king of the Hejaz in 1916, but in 1924 was driven out by the Wahabis under Ibn Saud. He d. in Transjordan. His great-grandson **Hussein I** (1935-), grandson of Abdullah (q.v.), succeeded his father Talal as king of Jordan in 1952 on the latter's declared incapacity. In the Arab-Israeli Wars (q.v.), he had by 1967 lost all his kingdom W of the Jordan, but subsequently achieved tolerable relations with Israel and attempted to control Palestinian guerrillas, not being very active in the war of 1973. At Rabat (1974) H. conceded West Bank sovereignty to the Palestine Liberation Organization. In the Iran-Iraq conflict of 1980 he supported Iraq. His heir, according to Arab custom, is Prince Hassan, his younger brother.

HUSSERL (hoos'-), **Edmund Gustav Albrecht** (1859-1938). Austrian philosopher. Prof. at Freiburg from 1916, he was the founder of phenomenology which gave birth to *gestalt* psychology and influenced Heidegger.

HUSTON, John (1906-). American film director. Son of the actor Walter H. (1884-1950), he has a powerful technique at its best in *The Maltese Falcon* (1941), *The African Queen* (1951), and *Moby Dick* (1956).

HUTTON, Barbara. *See* WOOLWORTH.

HUTTON, James (1726-97). Scottish geologist, the 'founder of geology'. In 1785 he developed the Huttonian theory of the igneous origin of many rocks.

HUTTON, Sir Leonard (1916-). British cricketer. B. in Yorks, he captained England in 23 Test matches and was the first professional to captain England (1952-6).

HUXLEY, Aldous (1894-1963). British author, grandson of Thomas H. and brother of Julian H. (qq.v.). From Eton and Balliol, where his education had been hampered by a disease of the eyes that permanently affected his sight, he went on to literary journalism, a Sitwellian book of verse *The Burning Wheel* (1916) and a witty first novel *Crome Yellow* (1921). Satiric disillusion continued throughout *Antic Hay* (1923), *Those Barren Leaves* (1925) and *Point Counter Point* (1928) with its impression of D. H. Lawrence, whose letters he edited. The fantasy *Brave New World* (1932) reproduced the unlikable human race by mass production in the laboratory, and H.'s sensitivity to the foul and disgusting in life led him to a retreat symbolized by his emigration to California in 1938 and a devotion to mysticism which ended in his experiments with mescalin recorded in *The Doors of Perception* (1954). His other works incl. *Grey Eminence* (1941), a study of Richelieu's adviser Père Joseph, and piquant short stories, e.g. 'The Gioconda Smile' which was successfully staged and filmed.

HUXLEY, Sir Andrew (1917-). British physiologist, the half-brother of Sir Julian and Aldous H. He was Jodrell prof. 1960-9 and from 1969 Royal Soc. Research prof. at University College, London, and in 1963 was awarded a Nobel prize for medicine (with Hodgkin and Eccles) for work on nerve impulses. He was knighted in 1974.

HUXLEY, Thomas Henry (1825-95). British scientist, humanist, and agnostic thinker. Following the publication of *The Origin of Species* in 1859, he won fame as 'Darwin's bulldog', and for many years was the most prominent and popular champion of Evolution. He wrote *Man's Place in Nature* (1863), and textbooks on physiology, and innumerable papers. In 1869 he coined the word 'agnostic' to express his own religious attitude; and his later books, e.g. *Lay Sermons* (1870), *Science and Culture* (1881), and *Evolution and Ethics* were expositions of scientific humanism. His grandson, **Sir Julian Huxley** (1887-1975) was a biologist, popularly remembered as one of the original members of the BBC radio Brains Trust. *See also* Aldous and Sir Andrew HUXLEY.

HU YAOBANG (hoo yowbahng') (1915–). Chinese statesman, chairman Chinese Communist Party 1981–87.

HUYGENS (hē'genz), **Christiaan** (1629-95). Dutch physicist. B. at The Hague, he developed several of Galileo's ideas, propounded the wave theory of light, and discovered polarization. In 1660 he visited England and was made an FRS.

HUYSMANS (üismoṅs'), **Joris Karl** (1848-1907). French novelist. B. in Paris of Dutch ancestry, he spent 30 years as a civil servant. *Marthe* (1876), the story of a courtesan, was followed by other realistic novels.

HWA'NG-HŌ. *See* HUANG HE.

HYACINTH (hī'asinth). Popular spring flower belonging to the family Liliaceae, grown from a bulb, and producing large cylindrical heads of pink, blue, or white sweetly scented flowers. Cultivation has reached its highest development in Holland, particularly around Haarlem. The original plant, *Hyacinthus orientalis,* resembles the bluebell or wild H.

The water H. (*Eichhornia crassipes*), of the family Pontederiaceae, grows in tropical and subtropical regions, and becomes a pest in rivers, since it can double in number every 8-10 days. However, its ability to grow in sewage-polluted water and purify it, and to absorb minerals rapidly, give it a future in environmental control. It can also provide silage or meal for animal feed, fertilizer, soil conditioner, and a means of producing methane gas when harvested.

HYDASPES. Classical name of r. JHELUM.

HYDE, Douglas (1860-1949). Irish scholar and statesman, known in Gaelic as 'the lovely little branch'. Founder-pres. of the Gaelic League 1893-1915, he was Pres. of Eire 1938-45. His works incl. *Love Songs of Connacht* (1894).

HYDE PARK. One of the largest open spaces in London, England. It occupies *c.* 146 ha. (350 acres) in Westminster. It adjoins Kensington Gardens, and incl. the Serpentine, a boating lake with a 'lido' for swimming. Here was held in 1851 the Great Exhibition. Rotten Row is a famous riding track. The name is a corruption of *route du roi.*

HYDERABAD. Capital city of the Indian state of Andhra Pradesh on the Musi, a tributary of the Kistna. Most famous of its buildings is the Jama Masjid mosque. Pop. (1971) 1,798,910.

H. was formerly cap. of the princely state of H. which occupied the greater part of the Deccan, and was by far the largest of the Indian princely states. In 1956 H. was divided between Bombay state (included in that part of it in 1960 created Maharashtra), Mysore, and Andhra.

HYDERABAD. City of Pakistan. H. was the capital of Sind until 1843, when Sind was conquered by the British. Still a military headquarters, it has many industries and a medical school. Pop. (1972) 550,000.

HYDER ALI (hī'der ah'lē) (*c.* 1722-82). Indian Moslem warrior. In command of the army in Mysore from 1749, he became the actual ruler of the state 1759 and rivalled British power in the area until his triple defeat by Sir Eyre Coote in 1781 during the Anglo-French wars. He was the father of Tippoo (q.v.).

HYDRA (hī'dra). Genus of freshwater animals, simplest of the order Hydrozoa. The body is a double-layered tube (with 6-10 hollow tentacles round the mouth) 1.25cm (0.5in) extended but capable of contracting to a small knob. Multiplication is by the formation of buds, by division into 2 or more pieces, and by sexual reproduction (there are no organs except those of reproduction). Usually fixed to waterweed, the H. feeds on minute animals which are caught and paralyzed by the stinging cells on the tentacles.

HYDRANGEA (hidrān'jya). Flowering shrub (*Hydrangea macrophylla*) of the Saxifragaceae family and native to Japan, so named from the Gk for water vessel, after its cup-like seed capsules. Also called hortensia, it normally produces round heads of pink flowers, but these may be blue if certain chemicals, e.g. alum or iron, are in the soil.

HYDRAULICS (hīdraw'liks). The science that deals with the dynamics of liquids (hydrodynamics) especially as applied to engineering.

HYDROCEPHALUS (hīdrosef'alus). Excess of fluid within the skull; 'water on the brain'. In infants it may be congenital and was once commonly due to tubercular inflammation of the brain membranes (meninges), or to blocking by local inflammation of the channel between the ventricles of the brain and the spinal column. The head is much enlarged, and the condition may be fatal; but sometimes can resolve spontaneously or be treated by surgical inclusion of a valve.

HYDROCHLORIC (hīdrōklōrik) **ACID** (HCl aq.). A chemical reagent, known also as muriatic acid or spirits of salts, consisting of gaseous hydrogen chloride in water. H.A. is used extensively in industry in reactions with metals, e.g. the recovery of zinc from galvanized scrap iron and the production of chlorides and chlorine. Highly corrosive, it will attack most metals and dissolve metallic oxides. Oxidizing agents react with it to form chlorine, the salts of H.A. being known as chlorides.

HYDROCYANIC (hīdrosī-a-'nik) **ACID.** Also known as prussic acid, H.A. is a solution of hydrocyanic gas (HCN) in water and is a colourless, highly poisonous, volatile liquid with a characteristic smell of bitter almonds. Hydrogen cyanide is made by the reaction of sodium cyanide with dilute sulphuric acid and is used for fumigation. It forms a series of salts called cyanides, sodium cyanide being used in the cyanide process for extracting gold and silver from ores.

HYDRODYNAMICS. Science of fluids in motion. The theory of H. is concerned almost entirely with perfect fluids, such as water, alcohol, and ether, and indeed most liquids which are not classed as viscous fluids (i.e. fluids in which change of form takes place gradually, as is the case with pitch). The perfect, or inviscid, fluid, cannot sustain any tangential stress.

HYDRO-ELECTRIC POWER. Electricity generated by water power. The first large H.E. installation was completed at Niagara in 1892. The world's largest hydro-electric generating plants today have a capacity of over 10,000 megawatts, e.g. Itaipu (Brazil/Paraguay) 12,600 MW.

HYDROFOIL. Boat or ship rising at speed on struts fitted with horizontal foils, which (with speed) lift the hull out of the water so that only the foils and propeller are left under water. *See* JETFOIL.

HYDROGEN (hī'drojen) (Gk *hydro*, water, and *genes*, forming). Symbol H; at. wt. 1.008; at. no. 1. Colourless, odourless and tasteless, it is the lightest known gas. It does not support combustion but burns in air to form water, and when mixed with air or oxygen forms an explosive mixture. H. was first recognized as a substance by Cavendish in 1766 who called it 'inflammable air'.

H. occurs chiefly in combination with oxygen as water, with carbon as hydrocarbons, and in most organic substances, particularly those used for foods and fuels, and in many minerals. It is manufactured by many processes among which are the action of steam on heated carbon, the electrolysis of water, the reaction of acids on certain metals. The isotope deuterium, at. wt. 2.0147, was announced by Urey in 1932, and tritium, at. wt. 3.0170, in 1934.

The many commercial uses of H. incl. the production of high-temperature flames for welding, cutting, and melting metals; the fixation of atmospheric nitrogen by the Haber ammonia process; the hydrogenation of fats and oils, e.g. in the preparation of margarine; the production of methyl alcohol by catalytic reaction with carbon monoxide; the filling of balloons; as a component in rocket fuel, and, in its liquid form, for cooling.

When an atom of H. is ionized by losing an electron it becomes a proton. H. is the fuel of the stars, releasing energy turning to helium in their interiors. When H. is subjected to a pressure of half a million atmospheres (i.e. pressures 500,000 times greater than Earth's atmosphere at sea-level), it becomes a solid metal.

HYDROGEN BOMB. Large-scale explosion resulting from the thermo-nuclear release of energy when hydrogen nuclei are condensed to helium nuclei. This is the continuing reaction in the Sun and other stars, but on Earth may result from the triggering of tritium (hydrogen isotope of atomic weight 3.0170) by an ordinary atom bomb. The first H.B. was exploded at Eniwetok Atoll by the US in 1952.

HYDROGRAPHY. The study of the waters of the earth's surface - the sea, lakes, and rivers. It includes their physical properties and boundaries, the conformation of the sea floor, particularly the arrangement of deeps, shoals, sandbanks, etc., the measuring of currents, tides, and all movements within the water, effects of surface winds, and the mapping and charting of hydrographical features.

HYDROLYSIS (hīdro'lisis). The term applied to a chemical reaction in which decomposition into simpler forms is effected by the action of water or its ions. H. occurs in the case of certain inorganic salts in solution; in nearly all non-metallic chlorides, in esters, and in other organic substances. It plays an important part in the utilization of food materials by the body.

HYDRO'METER. Instrument used to measure the density of liquids compared with that of water, usually expressed in grammes per cu. cm. The H., based on the theory that any body floating in a liquid equals in weight the volume of the displaced liquid, consists of a thin glass tube ending in a sphere which leads into a smaller sphere, the latter being loaded so that the H. floats upright, sinking deeper into lighter liquids than heavier. The density of the liquid is inversely proportional to the volume immersed.

HYDROPHOBIA (hīdrofō'bia). *See* RABIES.

HY'DROPHONE. An underwater microphone and ancillary equipment which converts water-borne sound waves into electrical signals, originally developed to detect enemy submarines.

HY'DROPLANE. Specially constructed motor boats which skim over the surface of the water when driven at high speed.

HYDROPŌ'NICS. The cultivation of plants without soil, using specially prepared solutions of mineral salts. J. von Sachs in 1860 and W. Knop in 1865 developed a system of plant culture in water whereby the relation of mineral salts to plant growth could be determined, but it was not until about 1936 that large crops were grown by H. methods, at first in California, but since in many other parts of the world.

HYDROSTATICS. The science which deals with the mechanical problems of fluids in equilibrium, i.e. in a static condition. An important practical application concerns the problems connected with floating bodies, as in shipbuilding. Another is concerned with the design of dams.

HYDRO'XĪDE. The term applied to a compound containing one or more hydroxyl (OH) groups, generally combined with a metal. The most important Hs. are caustic soda, caustic potash, and slaked lime.

HYDROZŌ'A. Class of mainly marine animals in the phylum Coelenterata (q.v.).

HYENA (hī-ēna). Genus of quadrupeds, of which there are 3 living species, the striped H. (*Hyaena hyaena*) found in India and northern Africa; the allied brown H. (*H. brunnea*) found on the S African coasts; and the spotted

HYDROPONICS. Commercially grown tomatoes. The nutrient film trough has been opened up to show the strong root development. *Photo: Courtesy of ICI.*

H. (*H. crocuta*) common S of the Sahara. Remarkably strong, both in its bone-cracking jaws and muscular power, the H. has always had value as a scavenger, though it will also attack live cattle and sometimes human beings.

HYÈRES (ē-ār′). French town in the dept of Var. It has a mild climate, and is a popular winter health resort, with some industry: e.g. olive-oil presses, export of violets, strawberries, vegetables. Pop. (1976) 40,000.

HYGIEIA (hēj-ē′ya). In Gk mythology, the goddess of health, the dau. of Aesculapius.

HYGIENE (hījēn). The science of health, whose aim is the preservation of health, the prevention of disease, and the prolongation of life by proper attention to physical laws. It is chiefly concerned with such external conditions as the purity of air and water, sunlight, the cleanliness of body and dwellingplace, dietary rules, conditions of labour and recreation, etc.

HYGROMETER (hīgrom′-). Instrument for measuring the absolute or relative humidity (q.v.) of the atmosphere. The relative humidity is usually measured by means of a special type of H. consisting of 2 identical mercury thermometers, the bulb of one being dry and that of the other kept moist by a covering of muslin dipping into a reservoir of water. The evaporation from the wet bulb cools that thermometer relatively to the dry one, and tables are supplied giving values of the relative humidity at the temperature of the dry bulb for various values of the difference of temperature between the 2 thermometers.

HYKSOS (hik′sōz) ('Shepherd kings' or 'princes of the desert'). A Semitic people which overran Egypt in the 18th cent. BC and established their own dynasty, which lasted till 1580 BC.

HYMEN (hī′men). In Greek mythology, the son of Apollo and one of the Muses, he was the god of marriage and in art is represented as a youth carrying a bridal torch.

HYMENO′PTERA. Order of insects, including ants, bees, etc., with a waist, and the saw-flies without a waist. They have 4 membraneous wings. The female possesses an ovipositor or a sting, and the mouth-parts of both sexes are suited to biting or sucking. They go through a complete metamorphosis.

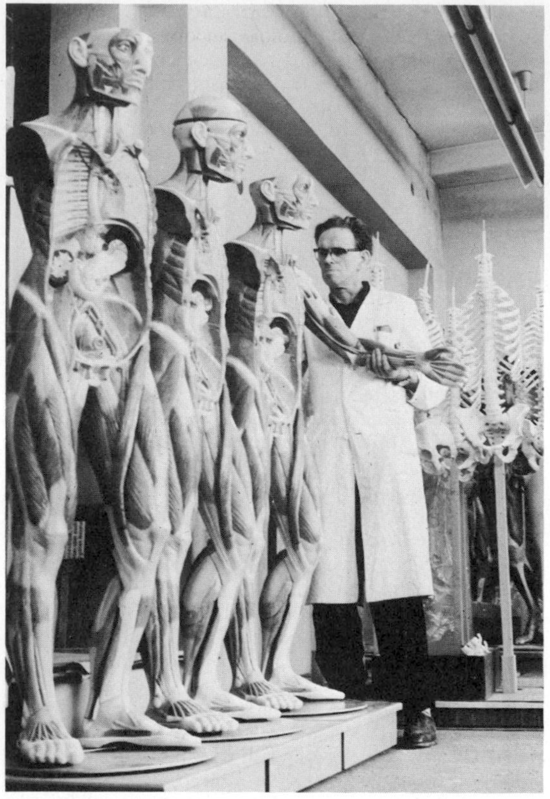

HYGIENE. The German Hygiene Museum, founded in Dresden in 1912, is world-famous for its export of anatomical and biological teaching materials. Models of men are seen here in the final stage of assembly. *Photo: Camera Press.*

HYMNS. Any compositions celebrating a deity which are intended to be sung or chanted. Christian hymnology originates with the OT psalms, those in the NT following closely in the same tradition. St Ambrose is thought to have introduced congregational singing and the full development of church music. In the 6th cent. pope Gregory the Great instituted the more severe mode of the Gregorian chant. Greatest of the medieval hymn-writers was the 12th cent. Adam of St Victor.

The earliest English hymn is the 7th cent. fragment by Caedmon, but in general hymn-writing in the vernacular waited on the Reformation. Among 17th cent. writers are Herbert, Baxter, Ken, and Bunyan. In 1737 the first modern hymn book was pub. by John and Charles Wesley; other writers are Toplady, Newton, the poet Cowper, Watts, and the Taylor sisters. To counterbalance the Nonconformist predominance of the 18th cent. the 19th produced Heber, Newman, Keble, Lyte, and many others. Anglican worship was long limited to *Hymns Ancient and Modern* (1861), notable for translations of ancient hymns, often by J. M. Neale. Most famous of the Scottish writers was Horatius Bonar. Richest of the Continental countries was Germany, with writers such as Luther and Gerhardt. The popular H. was developed in America by the evangelists Dwight Moody (1837-99) and Ira Sankey (1840-1908), and in Britain by the Salvation

Army. It was not until the second half of the 20th cent., however, that a new hymnology, incorporating 'classical' as well as 'pop' elements, and drawing on fresh sources of inspiration in Africa, etc., began to be a feature of all churches.

HYPATIA (hīpā'shia) (AD 370–415). Greek woman philosopher, b. at Alexandria. She studied Neo-Platonism at Athens, and succeeded her father Theon as prof. of philosophy at Alexandria. St Cyril, bishop of Alexandria, becoming jealous of her influence, denounced her as a pagan enchantress, and inspired a mob of monks to murder her.

HYPERACTIVITY. Condition of excessive activity in children, combined with inability to concentrate and difficulty in learning. Modification of the diet may help, and in the majority of cases there is improvement at puberty. The cause is not known.

HYPHASIS. Classical name of the r. BEAS.

HYPNO'TICS. Substances which produce a state like natural sleep. They depress the brain centres governing consciousness and mental activity. Taken in excess they suspend sensation and the power of movement, or even the action of the lungs and heart. The best-known are the alcohols, chlorals, and barbiturates.

HY'PNOTISM. The production of a state in which consciousness and will are suspended but other functions are not impaired. The patient is then extremely susceptible to suggestion and will carry out orders at once or long after he has been awakened, and may be made insensible to pain. The H. Act 1952 controlled exploitation of H. as entertainment.

HYPODERMIC (hīpo-) **SYRINGE.** An instrument used for injecting fluids beneath the skin. It consists of a small graduated tube of glass, metal or plastic, with a close-fitting piston and a nozzle on to which a hollow needle can be fitted.

HYPO'TENUSE. The side of a right-angled triangle opposite the right angle. *See also* PYTHAGORAS.

HYPŌTHE'RMIA. Use of cooling anaesthesia - also known as hibernation - to lower the temperature of the body for heart surgery and to tide over a dangerous phase of illness. The body's metabolism slows down at low temperatures, and less strain is imposed upon the vital organs, particularly the brain and the heart. A less extreme degree of H., a lowering of body temperature below 35.5°C (95°F), tends to occur among the elderly in poorly heated homes, causing death directly or by giving rise to broncho-pneumonia, etc.

HYPSOMETER (hipsom'-). A double steam vessel for testing the accuracy of a thermometer at the boiling point of water. It was originally used for determining heights by changes in the b.p. with changes in pressure - hence the name from the Gk *hypsos*, height.

HYRAX (hī'raks). Order of mammals (Hyracoidea) found in Africa and Syria. They are about the size of a rabbit, with a plump body, short legs, and brownish fur. There are 4 toes on the front limbs, and 3 on the hind, each of which has a hoof. They are good climbers, and live among rocks and in desert places.

HYSSOP (his'op). Herb (*Hyssopus officinalis*) of the Labiatae family, once grown for its medical properties. It produces small blue flowers and narrow, pointed, aromatic leaves.

HYSTERE'CTOMY. Surgical removal of the womb, usually for fibroid or malignant tumours.

HYSTĒ'RIA. A nervous disorder in which the patient simulates various kinds of disabilities in order to avoid responsibility or an unpleasant situation. In contrast with the deceptions of the malingerer, those of the hysteric are involuntary and for the most part unrealized. The commonest symptoms include paralysis of one or more limbs, deafness, blindness, dumbness, recurrent cough, vomiting, and general illness. The object of the hysterical reaction is to enable the hysteric to be dependent on others without loss of self-regard. The patient is commonly extremely selfish, self-centred and emotionally insincere and immature.

HYTHE (hīdh). English seaside resort, one of the Cinque Ports on the S coast of Kent, 8km (5m) W of Folkestone. Pop. (1972) 12,000.

I

Ninth letter of the Roman alphabet, deriving, as regards its form, from the sign for one of the several breaths of the Semitic languages. Its vocalic value was first given it by the Greeks.

IASI (yash'ē). Romanian city, 16km (10m) W of the Prut. There are machine, chemical and textile industries, and a univ. (1860). Pop. (1977) 270,000.

IBADAN (ebah'dahn). Cap. of Oyo state, Nigeria, a major economic and cultural centre. There are plastics and motor vehicle industries, but *c.* 18 km (11 m) of its ancient protective walls still stand. Pop. (1977) 1,500,000.

IBAÑEZ (ēvahn'yeth), **Vincente Blasco** (1867-1928). Spanish novelist and politician. B. at Valencia, he played an active part in revolutionary politics. His novels incl. *Blood and Sand* (1913), and *The Four Horsemen of the Apocalypse* (1918).

IBĒ'RIA. Name given by ancient Greek navigators to the Spanish peninsula, derived from the r. Iberus (Ebro). Anthropologists have given the name Iberians to a pre-Celtish Neolithic race, traces of whom are found in the Span. peninsula, S France, the Canary Is., Corsica, and part of N Africa.

I'BEX. Wild goats (*Capra ibex*), native to the snowy regions of the Alps. The name has also been applied to the Asiatic ibex (*C. sibirica*).

I'BIS. Genus of wading birds related to the storks and herons, but having a long curved beak. Various species occur in the warmer regions of the world, including the scarlet I. of America and the glossy I. found in all 5 continents. The sacred I. of ancient Egypt (*Threskiornis aethiopica*) is still found in the Nile basin.

IBIZA (ivi'tha). One of the Balearic Is., a popular tourist resort. The cap. and port, also called I. has a cathedral. Pop. *c.* 17,000. Area 596 sq.km (230 sq.m); pop. *c.* 45,000.

IBN SAUD (sowd) (1880-1953). King of Saudi Arabia. His father was the son of the sultan of Nejd, at whose capital, Riyadh, I.S. was born. In 1891 a rival tribe seized Riyadh, and I.S. went into exile with his father, who resigned his claim to the throne in his favour. In 1902 I.S. recaptured Riyadh and recovered the kingdom, and by 1921 he had brought all C. Arabia under his rule. In 1924 he invaded the Hejaz, of which he was proclaimed king in 1926. Nejd and the Hejaz were united in 1932 in the kingdom of Saudi Arabia.

IBSEN, Henrik Johan (1828-1906). Norwegian poet-dramatist. B. at Skien, he failed entry to Christiania univ. in 1850, and became dramatic adviser to theatres at Bergen and Christiania, for which he wrote a number of plays. The satirical *Love's Comedy* (1862) aroused opposition, and he spent the years 1864-91 mainly abroad in Italy or Germany. The great verse dramas *Brand* (1866) and *Peer Gynt* (1867) were the first fruits of his exile.

The political satire *The League of Youth* (1869) began the series of realistic dramas which revolutionized the European theatre. There followed the *Pillars of Society; A Doll's House; Ghosts,* which aroused furious opposition; I.'s rejoinder, *An Enemy of the People* (1882); the satiric tragi-comedy *The Wild Duck* (1884); *Rosmersholm* (1886); *The Lady from the Sea* (1888); and *Hedda Gabler* (1890). In 1891 I. returned to Norway, recognized at length as her greatest living writer. His last plays were *The Master Builder* (1892), which recaptures the poetic spirit of his earlier work; *Little Eyolf* (1894); *John Gabriel Borkman* (1896); and *When We Dead Awaken* (1899), a final statement of his philosophy.

I'CARUS. Asteroid *c.* 1.5km (1m) diameter, discovered 1949 and named after the son of Daedalus (q.v.), whose orbital plane intersects with that of Earth. Its orbital period is 409 days and it passes through the plane twice a year. Unlike planets, asteroids are subject to severe orbital perturbations, and collision is theoretically possible.

ICE. The solid formed by water when it freezes. It is colourless, crystalline, and shapes hexagonally. The freezing point, adopted as a thermometric standard, is 0° for the Centigrade and Réaumur scales, and 32° for the Fahrenheit. I. expands in the act of freezing, becoming less dense than water (0.9175 at 0°C). The absorption of heat on melting, and its expulsion on freezing, are expressed as the latent heat of fusion of I.

ICE AGE. Period of glaciation occurring in the earlier part of the Pleistocene period in geology, immediately preceding historic times. Northern Europe and America underwent glacial conditions similar to the polar regions. The American mountains show signs of former glacial activity, and the ice sheet spread over N Europe, reaching Ireland and the Atlantic, leaving its remains as far south as Switzerland. There were formerly thought to have been only 3 or 4 such periods, but recent research has shown about 20 major incidences. For example, ocean-bed cores record the absence or presence in their various layers of such cold-loving small marine animals as radiolaria, which indicate a fall in ocean temperature at regular intervals. The occurrence of I.As. is governed by a combination of factors (the Milankovitch hypothesis): (1) the Earth's change of 'attitude' in relation to the Sun, i.e. the way it tilts in a 42,000 year cycle and at the same time 'wobbles' on its axis in a 23,000 year cycle, making the time of its closest approach to the Sun come at different seasons; and (2) the 100,000 year cycle of eccentricity in its orbit round the Sun, i.e. its change from an elliptical to a near-circular orbit, the severest period of an I.A. coinciding with the approach to circularity. According to calculations, the ice reached a minimum in the present cycle 6,000 years ago and will reach maximum in another 60,000 years.

ICEBERG. A floating mass or hill of ice, rising sometimes to 100m (300ft) a.s.l. Polar glaciers which reach the coast become extended into a broad foot; as this enters the sea, masses break off and drift towards temperate latitudes, becoming a menace to shipping. The sinking of the *Titanic* in 1912 was caused by collision with an iceberg.

ICE-CREAM. Ideally made of cream, eggs, and sugar whipped together and frozen, with various flavourings of syrup and fruit, I.-C. is commercially made from various milk products and sugar, with artificial additives to give colour and flavour, improve its keeping qualities and ease of serving. Traditionally a trade in the hands of Italian immigrants, it became a mechanized industry first in the

USA and then in the 1920s in Britain. A new-type 'hard' I.-C. was used, adapted for storage and transport, but technical developments from the 1950s made possible the mass distribution of a 'soft' I.-C. resembling the original type in appearance.

ICE HOCKEY. Game played on ice between 2 teams, each of 6 players. Derived from ordinary H., the game was first played on ice in Canada in 1867, and is the national sport.

The skating space or rink is 61m long and 30m wide, divided into 3 zones by 2 blue lines. The goals (1.22m high by 1.83m wide) stand at either end of the rink on lines which are 4m from the ends of the rink. All players wear protective clothing. The 6 players are: Goal Keeper, Right Defence, Left Defence, Centre, Right Wing and Left Wing, and 8 reserves are allowed to each team. The puck is a rubber disc, 7.62cm (3in) in diameter and 2.54cm (1in) in depth. It must not be passed forward from one zone to the other between 2 players of the same side, and must precede the attacking players into the attacking zone. The puck must be kept continually in motion. Rough tackling is prohibited. The game is increasingly popular in Britain.

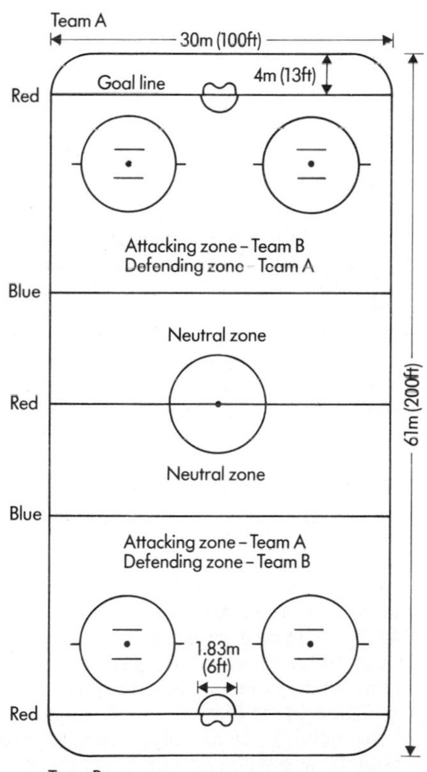

ICE HOCKEY

ICELAND. Island forming an independent rep. in the N Atlantic just S of the Arctic Circle and 370km (230m) SE of Greenland. It is mainly a volcanic plateau *c.* 760m (2,500ft) high, rising to 2,120m (6,952 ft) in the glacier Vatnajökull. The most famous volcano is Hekla, thought in the Middle Ages to be the gateway to Hell. Eruptions on and near I. continue, e.g. the new island of Surtsey thrown up in 1963. There are also many geysers, and underground hot water is used to heat many island homes, offices and shops.

The climate is mild and wet. The pop. is almost all Icelandic. Reykjavik, the cap., is the only large town. There is an aluminium plant, and I.'s hydro-electric and geothermal power are being used for heavy industry. Fishing is the chief occupation, cod and herring being the principal exports. There are regular air services within I. and abroad.

Norse voyagers had probably visited I. before 874, when a few hundred settlers arrived. In 930 the first general assembly or Althing founded the republic of I. In 1000 the people adopted Christianity, and in *c.* 1263 submitted to the authority of the king of Norway. Norway, and with it I., came under Danish rule in 1381. I. remained attached to Denmark after Norway became independent in 1814; it received its own legislature (Althing) in 1871, home rule in 1903, and in 1918 was recognized by Denmark as independent (except for foreign affairs), but linked with Denmark by having the same king. After the German invasion of Denmark in 1940, a small British force was sent to help in the defence of I., which in 1941 proclaimed itself an independent rep., a status confirmed by an act of the Althing in 1944. Keflavik is used as a NATO base. Traditionally, other nations incl. Britain, had been used to fish in I.'s rich waters, and extension of I.'s fishing limits led to disputes, known as 'Cod Wars' 1952-6, 1971-3, and 1975-6. Area 103,000 sq.km (39,758 sq.m); pop. (1977) 220,000. M.U.: krona.

ICELAND. The fishing village of Vestmannaeyjar on Heimsey Island dwarfed by the volcanic eruption of Helgafell which lights up the sky. *Photo: Astor Magnusson/Camera Press*

ICELANDIC. The I. language is the most archaic of the Scandinavian group, and has retained many primitive forms. Early I. literature is mainly anonymous, and seems to have arisen in the Norse colonies in the British Isles. It consists largely in the 2 Eddas (q.v.), and in numerous narratives in prose and verse called *sagas*, among which the *Saga of Burnt Nial* is the best. Ari Thorgilsson (1067-1148) composed a history of the kings of Norway; the *Landnámabók*, narrating the early settlement of Iceland, was the work of a number of writers. Snorri Sturlason wrote the later, or prose, Edda, based partly on Ari. After a period of translation and adaptation of medieval romances, there followed, from 1300, a long eclipse of I. literature, which was ended by hymn-writers of the Reformation. A renaissance took place in the 19th cent., especially in the fields of lyric poetry and the novel, and in the 20th Halldor Laxness (1902-), whose books deal with Icelandic life in the manner of the sagas, was awarded a Nobel prize in 1955.

ICELAND MOSS. Lichen (*Cetraria islandica*) - not a moss - which is common in I., and in other mountainous areas of the northern hemisphere. A lightish brown and up to 10cm (4in) high, it can be processed as a foodstuff.

ICELAND SPAR. Form of calcite (q.v.) originally found in Iceland. The crystals cleave into perfect rhombohedra; in its purest form, which is not uncommon, I.S. is quite transparent, and is used in optical instruments.

ICENI (īsā'nī). British tribe in E England, who revolted against the Romans: *see* BOUDICCA.

ICHANG *See* YICHANG.

ICHNEUMON FLY. Name given to parasitic flies in the family Ichneumonidae. There are several thousand species in Europe, N America and other regions. The eggs are laid in the eggs, larvae or pupae of insects usually in the order Lepidoptera.

ĪCON. Representations in the Greek or Orthodox Eastern Church of Christ, of an angel or a saint, in painting, low relief or mosaic. A *riza*, or gold and silver covering which leaves only the face and hands visible, and often adorned with jewels presented by the faithful in thanksgiving, is often added as a protection. One of the most famous Is. is the Virgin of Kazan (q.v.).

ĪCŌ'NIUM. *See* KONYA.

ĪCO'NOCLASTS (Gk image-breakers). Name applied in the 8th and 9th cents. to the Christian party in Byzantium, who refused to tolerate the use of images in churches. In 843 the Is. were finally defeated. The same name was applied to those opposing the use of images, etc., at the Reformation.

Ī'DAHŌ. A NW state of the USA. Much of I. is mountainous arid land, drained by waterways on which many rapids and waterfalls prevent navigation. The chief river is the Snake, which runs through spectacular Hells Canyon: on the plains of its upper reaches the Atomic Energy Commission has its National Reactor Testing Station. About one third of I. is forested, so that lumbering is important. On fertile areas potatoes, sugar beet, barley, wheat and apples are grown, and I. is famous for its sheep and wool. Minerals incl. rich silver resources, as well as antimony, lead, zinc and mercury. Industries are increasingly important and incl. paper, food processing and phosphates. Tourist attractions incl. the Craters of the Moon Nat. Monument. The chief towns are Boise, the cap., Pocatello and Idaho Falls. I. was admitted to the Union in 1890. Area 216,412 sq.km (83,557 sq.m); pop. (1970) 713,008.

ĪDE'NTIKIT. *See* PHOTOFIT.

IDES (īdz). In the calendar of ancient Rome, the 15th day in March, May, July, and October, and the 13th day in all the other months. The word originally indicated the day of the full moon. Julius Caesar was assassinated on the I. or 15th of March, 44 BC.

IDI AMIN DADA, Lake. *See* EDWARD, Lake.

IF (ēf). Small French is. in the Mediterranean about 3km (2m) off Marseilles, with a castle, Château d'If, built *c.* 1529. This was used as a state prison, and is the scene of the imprisonment of Dantès in Dumas' *Count of Monte Cristo.*

I'FNI. Territory in NW Africa held by Spain 1860-1969, when it was transferred to Morocco. The pop. are nomadic Berbers, and camels, goats, and sheep are raised. The chief town is Sidi Ifni, pop. 20,000. Area 1,920 sq.km (740 sq.m).

IGLS (ēgls). Winter sports resort in the Austrian Tirol, nr Innsbruck.

IGNATIUS (ignā'shius) (1st-2nd cent. AD). Early Christian Father. Traditionally he was a disciple of St John the Apostle and the successor of St Peter as bishop of Antioch. He was thrown to the wild beasts at Rome *c.* AD 115-17. Seven Epistles attributed to him are generally regarded as genuine.

I'GNIS FA'TŪUS. Name applied to the pale flame sometimes seen over marshy land and caused by the spontaneous combustion of methane formed by rotting vegetation. It is also known as will-o'-the-wisp.

IGUANA. Lizard of the family Iguanidae, which incl. *c.* 700 species and is chiefly confined to the Americas. The common I. (*Iguana iguana*) of Central and S America may reach 2m (6ft) and is a favourite food of the Indians.

IGUA'NODON. Amphibious reptile belonging to the herbivorous dinosaurs (q.v.), whose remains are found in strata of the Lower Cretaceous age. The I. varied in length from 5 to 10m (16-32ft), and when standing upright was 4m (13ft) tall. It walked on its hind legs, balancing its body by its long tail.

IJSSELMEER (ē'selmāer). Lake in the Netherlands, the remains after land reclamation of the former Zuider Zee, which was cut off from the North Sea in 1932 by the closing of a dyke *c.* 35km (22m) from N Holland via the former is. of Wieringen to Friesland. By 1944 the water of the lake had become fresh. Area 1,217 sq.km (470 sq.m).

IKEBA'NA. The Japanese art of flower arrangement. It dates from the 7th cent. when arrangements of flowers were placed as offerings in Buddhist temples, a practice learned from China. In the 15th cent. I. became a favourite pastime of the nobility. Oldest of modern Japanese I. schools is Ikenobo at Kyoto (7th cent.), and there is an I. International.

IKHNA'TON. Pharaoh of Egypt of the 18th dynasty, son of Amenhotep III (q.v.), with whom he may have ruled jointly for a time. One of his wives was Nefertiti, by whom he had 6 daus. and who is frequently represented with him. Two of his daus. were m. to his successors Smenkhare and Tutankaton (later Tutankhamen, q.v.), but though he developed (rather than originated) the cult of Aten or Aton, changing his name from Amenhotep to I., it is unlikely that he neglected imperial affairs.

IGUANA. An iguana from the Galapagos *(Conolophus subcristatus)* sheds his skin. *Photo: Mireille Vautier*

ÎLE-DE-FRANCE (ēl-de-froṅs). District and former prov. of France, bounded by the Marne, Seine, and Oise, with Paris as its centre, from which the early kings spread their authority over the country.

ILFRACOMBE (-koom). Picturesque resort and touring centre on the N coast of Devon, England. Pop. (1971) 9,000.

ILKESTON. Town in Derbyshire, with coalmines and making knitted goods. Pop. (1972) 34,100.

ILKLEY. Inland resort and spa in W Yorks, on the r. Wharfe, once a Roman military station. *I. Moor,* lies to the S. Pop. (1972) 22,000.

ILLE (ēl). French r. 45km (28m) long, which rises in Lake Boulet and enters the Vilaine at Rennes. It gives its name to the dept. of Ille-et-Vilaine.

ILLEGITIMACY. Birth outside a legal marriage, such children still suffering certain disadvantages. In the UK the mother has custody and may obtain payment towards the child's maintenance and education from the father, on application to the courts. A child may be legitimated by the subsequent marriage of the parents, and recent acts have given rights of inheritance when parents die intestate, etc., but an illegitimate child may not inherit a title.

ILLINOIS (illinoi'). North-central state of the USA, forming part of the great central prairie. The chief rivers are the Mississippi, Illinois, Ohio, and Rock. The soil is fertile and crops incl. maize and soya beans. The raising of pigs and cattle, and dairying are important. The chief minerals are coal and oil. It is a major manufacturing state, industries incl. machine tools, farm machinery, processing of food, incl. meat-packing and distilling, electric and electronic goods, chemicals, iron and steel, and transport equipment. The cap. is Springfield, other towns incl. Chicago, second largest city of the USA, Peoria, Rockford and Decatur. The first Europeans to reach I. were French missionaries in the 17th cent. I. became part of the French province of Louisiana, 1712, but in 1763 was ceded to Britain. In 1783 it passed to the USA, and was admitted to the Union in 1818. Area 146,075 sq.km (56,400 sq.m); pop. (1970) 11,113,976.

IKHNATON. A stele on which Ikhnaton and Nefertiti make their offerings to the Aton, the disc of the Sun, while the god reaches down through his rays to bless them. Behind the queen one of the little princesses holds the same sign of life that the Sun-god also displays. *Photo: Werner Forman Archive*

ILLY'RIA. Name anciently given to the region lying along the E coast of the Adriatic from the Corinthian Gulf northwards. It was conquered by Philip of Macedon, and became a Roman province in AD 9. Several Roman emperors came from Illyria.

ILMENITE (ilmenīt). Ore of iron, composed of the oxides of iron and titanium, $FeO. TiO_2$, with some magnesia. The mineral is black, with a metallic lustre, and closely resembles haematite.

IMAGISTS. Name given to a school of poets which flourished in England and America from 1909 to 1917. It originated with T.E. Hulme and incl F.S. Flint, Richard Aldington and T.S. Eliot in England, and Ezra Pound, 'H.D.' (Hilda Doolittle) and Amy Lowell in America. It inculcated precision of language and the use of clear, hard images.

IMĀ'GO. The sexually mature stage of an insect.

IMAM (imahm'). Arabic word denoting: (1) one of the 4 successors of Mohammed or one of the 4 leaders of the orthodox sects; (2) one of the great leaders of Shi'ites; or (3) one who leads the prayers in a mosque.

IMBROS. Island in the Aegean (Turkish **Imroz**). Occupied by the Greeks in the F.W.W., it became Turkish under the Treaty of Lausanne (1923). Area 280 sq.km (108 sq.m); pop. 6,000.

IMHOTEP (fl. *c.* 2800 BC). Egyptian physician. Adviser to King Zoser (3rd dynasty), he is thought to have designed the step-pyramid at Sakkara, and was later worshipped as son of the god Ptah, being identified by the Greeks with Aesculapius (q.v.). His tomb, later a centre of healing, is believed to lie somewhere in the N Sakkara necropolis.

IMMACULATE CONCEPTION. A dogma of the RC Church which states that the Virgin Mary was by a special act of grace preserved free from original sin from the very moment of her conception. This article of the Catholic faith was for cents. the subject of heated controversy, but became a dogma in 1854.

IMMIGRATION and **EMIGRATION.** The movement of people into a foreign country in which they intend to settle. Notable immigrants into Britain incl. the Flemish weavers, and wool-traders of the 16th cent.; the French Protestants persecuted after the Edict of Nantes in 1685; refugees from eastern Europe in the 2nd half of the 19th cent.; from Nazi Germany between 1933 and 1939, and from many European countries during and after the S.W.W. Immigration from the New Commonwealth after the S.W.W., espec. the W Indies, India and Pakistan, raised problems of housing and education. The govt est. was that there would be *c.* 2,500,000 coloured immigrants and their descendants in the UK by 1985. Commonwealth Immigration Acts were passed in 1962 and 1968, and replaced by a single system of control under the Immigration Act of 1971. According to the 1971 census nearly 3,000,000 of the 53,000,000 pop. were born outside the UK, of whom 1,290,000 were from the Commonwealth. Some 20,000,000 people emigrated from the UK to countries outside Europe 1815-1939, and after the S.W.W. annual emigration rose to *c.* 300,000 annually in the 1960s. The concern over the 'brain drain' of doctors, engineers, scientists and technologists, espec. to N America, was reversed in the 1970s when qualified people migrated to the UK from the 'Third World' where their services were most needed. The USA has received immigrants on a larger scale than any other country, *c.* 46,000,000 during 1820-1977.

In NW Europe there were 9-10,000,000 unskilled migrant workers supporting its industrial expansion by 1975, and from 1967 a similar situation developed in E Europe, though on a smaller scale, with an influx of workers known as 'foreign friends'. In the recession of the late 1970s and early 1980s there were repatratriation measures in W Germany, etc.

IMMINGHAM. *See* GRIMSBY.

IMMŪ'NITY. Resistance to poison or, more usually, to infection. Natural immunity is in the inborn power to resist micro-organisms or their toxins; but I. can be acquired by an attack of the disease, e.g. a person rarely contracts smallpox or typhoid fever twice; by repeated exposure to small doses of infection, e.g. the resistance of the normal person to tuberculosis; or by treatment (artificial I.), e.g. vaccination against smallpox, inoculation against typhoid. Artificial I. is either active, when the resistance is developed in the body as a reaction to the organism or its toxins; or passive, as when a quantity of serum from an immune person or animal is injected into the body. *See* ANTIBODY, AUTO-IMMUNE DISEASES, and INTERFERON.

IMPEACHMENT. A judicial procedure whereby ministers and high officers of state are brought to trial before the House of Lords for serious offences, the Commons acting as prosecutors. Before the rise of the cabinet system, I. provided a means whereby parliament could control the king's ministers. The first example occurred in 1376. Later Is. were those of Bacon (1621), Strafford (1641), and Warren Hastings (1788). Under the US constitution persons may be impeached by the House of Representatives and tried by the Senate; the best-known example is the trial of Pres. Andrew Johnson in 1868. *See* NIXON, Richard.

IMPERIAL COLLEGE OF SCIENCE AND TECHNOLOGY. Institution estab. at S Kensington, London, in 1907, for advanced scientific training and research, applied especially to industry. It is part of the Univ. of London.

IMPERIALISM. In its original sense, the system of government by an emperor, or a policy of colonial expansion, I. is often used to denote any policy of political, military or economic expansion carried out at the expense of weaker peoples. The heyday of British I. was between *c.* 1880 and 1900, but since the S.W.W. the increasing demand for self-determination has led to independence in most of the colonial countries, and as regards Britain a furtherance of the Commonwealth at the expense of the Empire. From the growing consciousness of her new-found strength in the 1890s, the USA began to look outward. After the Spanish American War, the Philippines, Puerto Rico and Guam were obtained, the Hawaiian is. annexed, and the Panama Canal zone acquired in 1903. The Philippines became a repub. in 1946, Puerto Rico a Commonwealth in 1952, and Hawaii the 50th state of the Union in 1959. Communist countries have developed their own variants of I., and the Soviet Union is the chief remaining imperialist country, e.g. the Baltic states (Estonia, Latvia and Lithuania), the southern areas of the USSR, e.g. the Caucasus (*see* SHAMYL), and in the Far East (*see* SINKIANG-UIGHUR).

IMPERIAL WAR MUSEUM. National museum founded in 1917, as a memorial to the men and women of the Empire in the F.W.W. Its scope has since been extended to incl. records of all operations fought by British forces since 1914. Its present building (formerly the Royal Bethlehem, or Bedlam, Hospital) in Lambeth Rd, London, was opened 1936.

IMPETĪ'GO. A minor skin disease of children. Pimples appear, usually on the face, and start to exude pus; they break, run together, and dry into yellow crusts, which eventually fall off and leave no scar unless scratched. The cause is infection by a streptococcus, sometimes introduced by louse bites, and later a staphylococcus. It is highly contagious.

I'MPHAL. Indian city, cap. of Manipur state, 225km (140m) ESE of Shillong. It is a communications and trade centre. In 1944, when the Japanese invaded Assam, it was besieged from March to June, but held out with the help of supplies dropped by air. Pop. (1971) 100,600.

IMPRESSIONISM. Movement in painting which originated in France in the 1860s, its chief exponents being Manet, Monet, Degas, Renoir, and Pissarro (qq.v.). They sought to capture a fleeting aspect of some scene, guided not by their memory or knowledge of the object, but painting it as though seen for the first time. In nature, they argued, colour is an illusion created by the play of light upon an object, and there are no outlines. Colours are modified by atmosphere and the inclination of the sunlight at different times of day, and even shadows are not entirely colourless. The Impressionists did not mix their pigments but dabbed them side by side on the canvas in the pure state. Their technique was influenced by the work of Constable and Turner, and also by contemporary spectroscopic discoveries.

The starting-point of the movement was the *Salon des Refusés*, an exhibition in 1863 of work rejected by the official Salon, followed by their own exhibitions 1874-86. Their work aroused fierce opposition; the term I. was first used abusively to describe Monet's painting 'Impression, Sunrise'. Among their followers were the American Whistler (q.v.), who introduced the term into England, and the Englishmen Sickert and Wilson Steer (qq.v.).

IMROZ. Turkish form of IMBROS.

INCANDE'SCENCE. The emission of light from a substance in consequence of its high temperature. The colour of the emitted light from liquids or solids depends on their temperature, and for solids generally the higher the temperature the whiter the light. Gases may become incandescent through ionization as in the glowing vacuum discharge tube. The oxides of cerium and thorium are highly incandescent and for this reason are used in gas mantles. The light from a filament lamp is due to the I. of the filament, rendered white-hot when a current is passing through it.

INCARNATION (Lat. *caro*, flesh). In Christian theology, the doctrine that the Second Person of the Trinity assumed human form and human nature as Jesus Christ. I. is also a feature of many other religions, e.g. Hinduism.

INCAS (ing'kahs). Name ordinarily given to the population of Peru before the coming of the Spaniards, but rightly restricted to the ruling caste; the ruler himself was known as the Inca. They probably entered Peru from the SE *c.* 1100, and estab. the only empire of the old world type ever to have existed in the Americas - the first emperor being Manco Capac *c.* AD 1200 - with its cap. at Cuzco. From the mid. 15th cent. a period of expansion began, extending Inca rule over a range of 4,000 km (2,500 m) from Quito in Ecuador beyond Santiago to S Chile. The intricate state organization was a theocratic socialism headed by the godlike emperor, descendant of the Sun. Crafts, agriculture and the army were run with ruthless efficiency, and although writing was unknown, numerical records were kept by knotted cords (quipu) stored at Cuzco. The wheel and the horse were unknown, but excellent roads were maintained for foot soldiers and couriers, and temples and fortresses were built of stone blocks, fitted skilfully together without mortar. Medicine and advanced surgery were practised, and they mummified their dead. The last of the emperors was Atahualpa (q.v.), executed by Pizarro. The descendants of the I. are the modern Quechua (q.v.).

INCAS. Inti-Rayni, the festival of the Sun-god at Cuzco, held in June as in the time of the ancient Incas: the descendant of the Inca rulers is borne along on this throne. *Photo: Mireille Vautier*

INCENDIARY BOMB. Usually dropped by aircraft, I.Bs. containing inflammable matter were used in the F.W.W., and in the S.W.W. were a major weapon in attacks on cities. To hinder firefighters, delayed-action high-explosive Bs. were usually dropped with them.

INCEST. Sexual intercourse between persons so related that marriage between them is barred by law. I. is biologically undesirable because hereditary weaknesses are emphasized by inbreeding, and sociologically because it affects the emotional stability of the family unit.

INCH. In *place-names* in Scotland and Ireland, an islet or land by a river. As a measure of *length*, it is a twelfth of a foot (2.540 cm).

INCHON. Port and summer resort on the W coast of S Korea, 32km (20m) WSW of Seoul. Its ice-free harbour was opened to foreign trade in 1883. It has steel mills and textile and match factories, etc. Pop. (1970) 525,000.

INCOME TAX. Direct tax levied on annual income which, so far as the tax is concerned, may incl. the value of receipts other than in cash. In the UK, the rate of tax and allowances vary from time to time; they are set out yearly in the annual Finance Act which implements the recommendations agreed to by the House of Commons in the Budget presented to it by the Chancellor of the Exchequer. William Pitt introduced an I.T. 1799-1801 to finance the wars with revolutionary France; it was re-imposed 1803-16 for the same purpose, and was so hated that all records were destroyed when it came to an end. Peel reintroduced the tax in 1842 and it has been levied ever since, becoming a more and more important part of govt finance. At its lowest, 1874-6, it was 2d in the £; at its highest, 1941-6, the standard rate was 10s in the £. *See* PAYE.

In the USA every citizen or resident with a gross income of $3,300 or more must file a report for federal income-tax consideration unless he or she was 65 before the end of the tax year, when a return has to be made only if the gross income is $4,300 or more. Rate of tax, which is reckoned on a percentage basis, and allowances, are fixed by Congress from year to year. A state I.T. also is levied in almost all states, the amount of tax and allowances varying from state to state; and in many instances there is a city I.T. varying from city to city.

Most countries levy I.T., generally considered as bearing less heavily on the poor than indirect taxes: *see* TAXATION. However, in Communist states in which the salaries of most workers are fixed by the state, I.T. becomes illogical. From 1960 the USSR gradually began abolition, factory and office workers becoming exempt, and higher grades - to reduce differentials - having their salaries reduced by the amount of tax they would otherwise have paid.

I'NCŪBUS. A male spirit who in the popular belief of the Middle Ages cohabited with women in their sleep. Witches and demons were supposed to result from such intercourse.

INCŪNA'BŪLA. Bibliographical term signifying the books printed during the 15th century.

INDEMNITY. An undertaking to compensate another for damage, loss, trouble, or expenses, or the money paid by way of such compensation. An *Act of I.* is one passed with the object of relieving persons from certain penalties to which they have become liable, or to legalize transactions which infringe the law.

INDEPENDENCE. Residential and industrial city in Missouri, USA, lying E of Kansas City. Pres. Harry S. Truman spent his boyhood at I., later making it his home and the Harry S. Truman Federal Library was estab. in 1957. Industries incl. making of steel and Portland cement, petroleum refining, flour milling. Mormons are the largest religious group. Pop. (1970) 111,650.

INDEPENDENCE DAY. The day (4 July) on which the Declaration of Independence of 1776 is commemorated in the USA. It is a public holiday.

INDEPENDENT LABOUR PARTY. Soc. party, founded at Bradford in 1893. In 1900 it joined with trade unions and Fabians in founding the Labour Representation Committee, the nucleus of the Lab. Party. Many members left the I.L.P. to join the Com. Party in 1921, and in 1932 all connections with the Lab. Party were severed. After the S.W.W. it consistently dwindled. James Maxton (1885-1946) was its chairman 1926-46: *see* also Keir HARDIE.

INDEX. In finance, usually the selection of 30 leading industrial ordinary shares used by the *Financial Times* as an indicator of the general movement of the Stock Exchange market; the US equivalent is the Dow Jones Index. For **Indexation,** *see* COST OF LIVING and SAVING.

INDEX LIBRORUM PROHIBITORUM. The list of books formerly officially forbidden to members of the RC Church. The process of condemning books and bringing the Index up to date was in the hands of a congregation of cardinals, consultors, and examiners from the 16th cent. until 1966.

INDIA. Geographical and historical name for the great S Asian peninsula or sub-continent lying between the Himalayas and the Indian Ocean. It incl. the reps. of Bangladesh, India (incl. Sikkim), Pakistan, and the small states of Bhutan and Nepal. Total area 4,196,000 sq.km (1,620,000 sq.m); pop. (1973) 636,000,000.

Physical. The peninsula is in the form of a large triangle based on the Himalaya mountains, the Arabian Sea lying on the W coast, and the Bay of Bengal on the E. It has common land frontiers with Iran, Afghanistan, China (Tibet), and Burma. There are 3 main geographical divisions: (1) the Himalayas, a vast crescent-shaped range including the highest mountains in the world. (2) the river plains, extending across the widest part of the country and comprising the systems of the Indus, the Ganges, and the Brahmaputra. This region is the most populous. (3) The Deccan or southern tableland, which forms the greater part of the peninsula proper. The northern side of the tableland is formed by the Vindhya mts. The other sides of the triangular plateau are formed by the E and W Ghats.

Climate. In the N the peninsula has a continental climate, with considerable variations of temperature between winter and summer, when the thermometer at Jacobadad in Pakistan may reach 53°C (127°F) in the shade. In the S the climate is more equable, though the winter temperature at Bombay (well within the tropics) has been as low as 11°C (52°F). Rainfall varies greatly, but is constantly heavy in Bengal and in upper Assam (up to 10m/400in annually); while the monsoon brings heavy seasonal rain to the alluvial plains south of the mountains. Farther south there is an arid region, with waterless deserts. The weather system of the peninsula falls into 2 parts. N of the Vindhyas there is copious rainfall during the SW monsoon; to the south the rains are more moderate, but the monsoon continues some weeks longer. The cold months in the peninsula are Jan. and Feb.; March, April, and May are hot. In June, July, Aug., Sept., and Oct. comes the SE monsoon, which is reversed during the remaining 2 months.

INDIA. Women play an increasing part in guiding India's destiny. Thousands sit listening to opposition leaders speak at New Delhi in an election campaign. *Photo: Rex Features*

Peoples. Descendants of the earliest known inhabitants, a Negrito or Negroid people, are still found in scattered tribes in S India; the Andamanese also belong to this group. Southern India is mainly inhabited by Dravidians, and the Aryo-Dravidian (Hindustani) type is

INDIA. Indira Gandhi, Prime Minister 1966–77 and 1980–4. Her rule stressed social reform but was marred by religious conflict. *Photo: High Commissioner for India.*

found in the Ganges valley. People of Indo-Aryan stock occur in Kashmir and neighbouring regions, and Scytho-Dravidian and Mongolo-Dravidian peoples inhabit regions east of the Indus and Bengal respectively. In the NW Turco-Iranian types prevail, and Mongolians have penetrated into the NE.

History. The earliest Indian civilization was that of the Indus valley (*c.* 2500–*c.* 1600 BC); this may have been built up by the Dravidians, the ancestors of the main people of the S. From *c.* 1500 BC waves of Aryans entered I. from the NW, and gradually overran the N and the Deccan, intermarrying with the Dravidians. From their religious beliefs developed the system of Brahmanism; this was periodically modified by reforming movements, the most important of which, Buddhism and Jainism, arose *c.* 500 BC. The sub-continent, except the far S, was first unified under the Mauryan emperors (321–184 BC), one of whom, Asoka (264–*c.* 227), who was a Buddhist, ranks among the most enlightened rulers in history. The N was not again united until the period of the Gupta dynasty (*c.* AD 300–500), 'the golden age of Hinduism'; its rule was ended by the raids of the White Huns, which plunged I. into anarchy.

During the 11th and 12th cents. raids on I. were made by Moslem adventurers, Turkish, Arab, and Afghan, and in 1206 the first Moslem dynasty was set up at Delhi. The next 3 cents. witnessed the establishment of Moslem rule throughout the N and the Deccan, although the S maintained its independence under the Hindu Vijayanagar dynasty (14th–16th cents.). The most brilliant period of Moslem India began with the founding of the Mogul empire by Babur in 1527, and its consolidation by his grandson Akbar (1556–1605). After 1707 the Mogul empire (which lasted nominally until 1858) fell into decline, and a period of anarchy ensued.

INDIA. The transformation of India's industry to the modern era. This base plate for the pressure tubes of a heavy water nuclear reactor is under construction at Larsen and Toubro's Bombay factory. *Photo: The Times*

Portuguese, Dutch, French, and English traders had been establishing trading bases on the coast since the 16th cent. During the Seven Years War (1756–63) the E India Co., eliminating their French rivals, made themselves masters of Bengal and the Carnatic, and within a cent. direct or indirect British rule was established all over I. After the mutiny of 1857–8 the rule of the E India Co. was abolished, and I. passed under the British crown. National feeling found a rallying-point in the National Congress (founded 1885), and from 1906 onward periodic waves of nationalist agitation - after the F.W.W. under the leadership of Gandhi - swept the country. These were met by concessions in the direction of self-govt, culminating in 1947 in the division of British I. into the dominions of India (predominantly Hindu) and Pakistan (predominantly Moslem). *See* INDIA OF THE PRINCES.

INDIA, UNION OF. Rep. in Asia: Hindi *Bharat*, from Bharata, a legendary king. Covering the greater part of the India sub-continent, it incl. the most fertile areas, in particular the Ganges valley. Agriculture, long handicapped by the social, religious and economic system and the small-size holdings, has achieved a rising standard of technology since independence, with extended irrigation, although failure of the monsoon is still a near disaster. Rice, wheat and cereals are grown, and industrial crops incl. cotton, jute, tea, oil seeds, and cane sugar. Industry has been modernized and expanded, and alongside the

Tata iron and steel works at Jamshedpur on the Bihar coalfield, there are new industrial complexes such as Hindustan Steel, with plants at Rourkela, Bhilai and Durgapur, which is also I.'s largest supplier of nitrogenous fertilizers. Machinery and machine tools, petroleum products, textiles, etc., are produced, and hydro-electric installations have been built and extended, espec. in the Deccan. Cut and polished diamonds, the rough gems being imported, top India's exports. In science and technology there have been rapid advances, India being the first non-aligned country to detonate a nuclear device in 1974, and the second developing country after China to join the space club in 1980 by putting a satellite in orbit. Progress is still hindered by too rapid population growth despite official sterilisation and birth control schemes.

On coming into existence in 1947, as the Dom. of India, the Union consisted of the former Brit. Provs.: the United Provs. (Uttar Pradesh), Bihar, Bombay, Central Provs., Orissa, Madras, most of Assam, W Bengal and E Punjab; by 1950 all the princely states within this area (*see* INDIA OF THE PRINCES, also KASHMIR) had been absorbed by the Union. In 1950 I. became a rep. within the Brit. Commonwealth. Internal developments have since incl. reorganization of some states on linguistic and other grounds, fluctuating violence in communal disturbances between Hindu and Moslem, and the emergence in the late 1960s of regional agitation, as in Assam and Maharashtra, against immigrants from other states. Relations with Pakistan have continued to be complicated by such issues as Kashmir and Kutch (q.v.), and there was open war between the two countries 3-17 Dec. 1971 over the secession of E Pakistan, now Bangladesh (q.v.), a peace treaty being signed 1972. There has also been border tension with Communist China, a supporter of the Pakistan viewpoint. The Congress Party had maintained political supremacy under the successive premierships of Nehru, Shastri and Indira Gandhi (qq.v.), but in 1975 opposition leaders combined to call for a civil disobedience campaign to force Mrs Gandhi's resignation. A state of emergency was proclaimed, many opposition leaders were arrested, and press censorship was introduced. The opposition Janata (People's) Front defeated the Congress Party in the 1977 elections and Morarji Desai became prime minister. In 1979 he was superseded by India's first coalition (under Charan Singh) since independence, but party in-fighting and growing chaos in the country led to Indira Gandhi's re-election in 1980. She was assassinated, allegedly by Sikh extremists, in June 1984, and succeeded by her son Rajiv Gandhi, confirmed as leader in the elections of December 1984.

See also INDIAN ART and INDIAN LITERATURE. In modern times India has made her particular mark in the art of the film. e.g. Satyajit Ray (q.v.), and in music, e.g. Ravi Shankar (q.v.).

A pres., elected for 5 years by an electoral college, is head of state; there is a cabinet under a PM - a post first held by Nehru (q.v.); parliament consists of the House of the People, Lok Sabha, directly elected, on a basis of adult suffrage, for 6 years, and the indissoluble Council of States, Rajya Sabha, indirectly elected, one-third of whose members retire every 2 years. Delhi is the cap.; other large cities are Calcutta, Bombay and Madras. Area 3,208,274 sq.km (1,175,410 sq.m); pop. (1981) 683,880,000, incl. 100,000,000 Moslems. M.U.: rupee.

The Union of India

States	*Area in sq. km*	*Pop in 1,000s*	*Capital*
Andra Pradesh	275,281	53,403	Hyderabad
Assam	101,730	19,902	Shillong
Bihar	174,038	69,823	Patna
Gujarat	187,091	33,960	Gandhinagar
Haryana	44,056	12,850	Chandigarh
Himachal Pradesh	55,658	4,237	Simla
*Jammu and Kashmir	138,236	5,981	Srinagar
Karnataka	191,757	37,043	Bangalore
Kerala	38,855	25,403	Trivandrum
Madhya Pradesh	443,452	52,131	Bhopal
Maharashtra	307,762	62,693	Bombay
Manipur	22,346	1,433	Imphal
Meghalaya	22,445	1,327	Shillong
Mizoram	21,230	487	Shillong
Nagaland	16,488	773	Kohima
Orissa	155,825	26,272	Bhubaneswar
Punjab	50,376	16,669	Chandigarh
Rajasthan	342,274	34,102	Jaipur
Sikkim	7,298	315	Gangtok
Tamil Nadu	130,357	48,297	Madras
Tripura	10,453	2,060	Agartala
Uttar Pradesh	294,366	110,858	Lucknow
West Bengal	88,563	54,485	Calcutta
Union Territories			
Andaman and Nicobar Is.	8,120	188	Port Blair
Arunachal Pradesh	81,426	628	Shillong
Chandigarh	26	450	—
Dadra and Nagar Haveli	489	103	Silvassa
Delhi	1,484	6,196	—
Goa, Daman and Diu	3,693	1,082	Panjim
Lakshadweep	28	40	Kavaratti Is.
Pondicherry	469	604	Pondicherry City
	3,215,672	683,810	

**Area occupied by India; another 84,000 sq. km. of Kashmir are occupied by Pakistan.*

INDIA'NA. E north-central state of the USA. The surface is undulating prairie, except in the S along the r. Ohio where there is a range of hills. The chief rivers are the Wabash and its tributaries. The soil is fertile, and agriculture is an important industry. The chief crops are maize, winter wheat, rye, and oats. Tobacco also is cultivated. Mineral products incl. coal, limestone, natural gas, and petroleum; steel, agricultural machinery, motorcars, refrigerators and other domestic appliances are manufactured. The chief towns are Indianapolis, the cap., Fort Wayne, Gary, South Bend, Evansville, and Hammond. In the early 18th cent. French traders reached I., and the first settlements were established in 1731-5. It was admitted to the Union in 1816. Area 93,994 sq.km (36,291 sq.m); pop. (1970) 5,193,669.

INDIANA'POLIS. Capital and largest city of Indiana, USA. There is a large grain trade, and industries include meat packing and chemical and motor-vehicle manufacture. I. is a centre of communications. Pop. met. area (1970) 1,099,628.

INDIAN ART. The history of Indian art may be traced back to the ancient Indus valley civilization of *c.* 3000 BC, which seems to have had a definite influence on the Brahmanical art of later periods. The Maurya period (3rd cent. BC) has its most notable example in the palace of Asoka, and was characterized by sculptured gateways and reliefs. The Kusana and Andhra periods (1st-4th cents. AD) led to the mature and voluptuous art of the Gupta period, which spread widely over SE Asia. Mathura, Sarnath, Ajanta, and Aurangabad were centres of Buddhist sculpture, and remarkable examples of Brahmanical art were also produced. The same tradition led in the 6th and 7th cents. to the painting of frescoes, usually depicting incidents in the legends of the Buddhist, Hindu, and Jain religions. The 7th cent. saw the highest peak of I.A.; the magnificent rock sculpture of the descent of the Ganges at Mamallapuram bears witness to the virility of this period. Medieval art gradually lost the simplicity and force of the classical period, and while continuing on the same general lines tended to become more and more elaborate. Sculpture was generally of a religious character, but the Gujarat school also excelled in decorating dwelling houses. A brilliant school of miniature paintings arose in 16th cent. Rajputana. The Moguls introduced a school of painting based on Persian forms; Indian artists absorbed and expanded this art with great technical virtuosity.

After a period of decline I.A. has enjoyed a renaissance in modern times, e.g. the work of Abanindranath Tagore (q.v.) Amrita Sher-Gil, Jamini Roy, and Sailoz Mookherjee. For recent discoveries in prehistoric art, *see* BHOPAL.

INDIAN CORN. *See* MAIZE.

INDIAN LANGUAGES. Languages spoken in India total 220, falling into 5 main groups. Much the most important is the Indo-European or Aryan, languages belonging to which are spoken by over 506,000,000 people. This group includes Hindi (q.v.), Pushtu, Pali, Urdu, etc., and is ultimately derived from the ancient Sanskrit. Its range includes the whole of N India. Dravidian languages come next, with about 152,000,000 speakers, mainly in the south, where they include the 4 literary languages. Dravidian tongues are also used in the hills of central India, and an isolated pocket exists in Baluchistan. The Tibeto-Chinese group includes no fewer than 145 languages, some of which are spoken in Assam and on the slopes of the Himalayas. English is also widely spoken.

INDIAN LITERATURE. For the literature of ancient India *see* SANSKRIT; VEDA; PALI; PRAKRIT. The great no. of Indian languages and the wealth of the literary output in India through medieval to modern times makes any brief survey impossible. Among recent developments the emergence in the last cent. of Bengali as an important literary tongue is remarkable, cf. the work of philologist Ram Mohan Roy, founder of Brahma Samaj (q.v.), who paved the way for such writers as novelist Bankim Chandra Chatterji (q.v.) and Romesh Chunder Dutt (1848-1909). A token of the reputation of Bengali among literatures of the modern world was the award to Rabindranath Tagore of a Nobel prize in 1913: notable among later writers are the poets Buddhadeva Bose and Amiya Chakravarty. Hindi has been developed rather as a political weapon than a literary medium during the struggle for independence and its aftermath, but especially important as literary languages are Urdu (the novelist

INDIAN ART. Radha and Krishna, a gouache on paper by one of the Pahari School, from the Punjab Hills in northern India c.1800. *Photo: Courtesy of the Victoria and Albert Museum*

Prem Chand and the poet and thinker Muhammed Iqbal, and Gujarati (the poet Nanalal Devi and the writings of Gandhi). The long association with Britain has estab. English as almost a native tongue for many Indians, and writers in English - though wholly Indian in the character of their work - incl. the novelist Dhan Gopal Mukerji, the poet Sarojini Naidu (1879-1949), Sri Aurobindo (1872-1950), and Dom Moraes, and Nehru. Tagore wrote little creatively in English, but translated many of his own works. Among overseas writers of Indian descent, the most famous is V. S. Naipaul (q.v.).

INDIAN MUTINY. The revolt against the British in India of the Bengal army in 1857-8. The movement was confined to the N, from Bengal to the Punjab, and C India; it drew its main support from the army and the recently dethroned princes, but in certain areas it developed into a peasant rising or a general revolt. Outstanding episodes were the seizure of Delhi by the rebels and its siege and recapture by the British, and the defence of Lucknow by a British garrison. The I.M. led to the substitution in 1858 of direct administration by the Crown for the rule of the E India Co.

INDIAN OCEAN. Ocean lying between Africa and Australia, with India to the N. In the S it merges into the Antarctic seas, the arbitrary boundary being a line from Cape Agulhas to S Tasmania. In the 1970s increasing activity by the British, US and Soviet navies made is. bases of vital importance. *See* BRITISH I.O. TERRITORY, SOCOTRA, etc. Area 73,500,000 sq.km (28,350,500 sq.m); greatest depth, Java Trench, 7,725 m (25,344 ft); average depth 3,872 m (12,704 ft).

INDIANS, American. The aboriginal peoples of the Americas, called Indians because Columbus believed he had found, not the New World, but a new route to India. The A.I. entered N America from Asia via the land-bridge, Beringia, which existed in early times. The migration possibly began as early as *c.* 60,000 BC, and was predominantly Mongoloid. The A.I. incl. some of the shortest as well as (in Patagonia) some of the tallest races, and have great cultural diversity.

In Canada there are today *c.* 300,000, incl. the Eskimo, and the largest group are the Six Nations (Iroquois); and in the USA there are *c.* 1,000,000, and the largest reservation is that of the Navajo. Modern movements for Indian rights incl. the Nat. Indian Brotherhood (Canada) and American Indian Movement (AIM: USA).

Latin America has comparatively few surviving pure Indians, the majority being mestizo of Indian-Spanish descent, e.g. half the 12 million in Peru and Bolivia, but there is increasing stress on their Indian inheritance in language and culture. The handful of tribes previously beyond white contact are being eliminated, espec. in the clearing of the Amazon Basin for cultivation and settlement.

See APACHE, ARAUCANIAN, AYMARA, AZTEC, CARIB, CHIMU, ESKIMO, GUARANI, INCA, IROQUOIS, JIVARO, MAYA, MOHICAN, NAVAJO, PUEBLO, QUECHUA, SIOUX, TOLTEC.

INDIA OF THE PRINCES (Indian states). Name formerly applied to the 562 native states ruled by Indian princes. Occupying an area of 715,964 sq.m (45 per cent of the total area of pre-partition India) and with a population of over 93 million they were inextricably mixed up with the former British provs. Most of the states were Hindu, and their rulers mainly Rajputs (q.v.). When India was overwhelmed by the Moslems, the Rajput states in the deserts of the NW, the outer Himalayas, and the central highlands, were saved by their isolation and by the fine fighting qualities of their inhabitants. As the Mogul empire disintegrated other states were set up by soldiers of fortune, e.g. Baroda, Hyderabad, Gwalior, Indore, Bhopal, Patiala, Bahawalpur, and Kolhapur: Mysore, Travancore, and Cochin were also non-Rajput states. At partition of British India in 1947 the princes were given independence by the British govt, but were advised to adhere to either India or Pakistan. Between 1947 and 1950 all except Kashmir (q.v.) were incorporated in the one or the other country.

INDIGENOUS (indij'enus). A people, etc., original and native to a country. Human migration and conquest has been so extensive, and is so lost to memory, that indigenity is impossible to establish, but today refers usually to peoples whose territory has been colonised by whites in more recent times. A World Council of Indigenous Peoples is based in Canada, and the first conference of Latin American I. Peoples was held in Cuzco in 1980.

INDIGESTION. *See* DYSPEPSIA.

I'NDIGO. Deep violet-blue dye originally obtained from plants of the *Indigofera* genus of the Leguminosae, but now replaced by the synthetic product.

INDIUM. Soft, silvery, malleable, rare metallic element; symbol In, at. wt. 114.82, at. no. 49. Discovered in 1863 by Reich and Richter, it was named I. after its indigo-blue spectrum. It occurs in minute traces in zinc ores, etc., and is obtained by eletrolysis from solutions of complex salts. Due to its large neutron capture cross-section, I. is used to monitor the neutron emission from reactors. Other uses incl. the manufacture of junctions in semi-conductor devices, and corrosion-resistant coatings for aircraft sleeve bearings.

INDO-ARYAN LANGUAGES. One of the 2 branches of the Aryan group of the Indo-European family, the other being the Iranian (q.v.). Aryan tribes entered India *c.* 2000-1500 BC, and from the latter date comes the earliest specimen of I.-A., the *Rig-Veda.* Its language, called Vedic, is distinguished from Sanskrit, the later classical language which represents a codification of the language in use on the watershed between the Indus and the Ganges; Sanskrit has remained in use for sacred and literary purposes. Buddhism and Jainism were important in the development of local forms, or Prakrits, which are the direct ancestors of the modern Aryan vernaculars of N India. They fall into 2 major groups - the languages of the centre: W Hindi (whence Hindustani or Urdu), E Hindi, Punjabi, Gujarati, and Rajasthani, while Sinhalese, spoken by the majority in Sri Lanka, is a descendant of the now extinct Pali; and those of the outer band: Kashmiri, Lahnda, Sindhi, Marathi, Bihari, Bengali, and Assamese.

INDO-CHINA, French. Former collective name for a group of Asian countries that became independent after the S.W.W. *See* KAMPUCHEA, LAOS, VIETNAM.

INDO-EUROPEAN (Indo-Germanic). Name of one of the world's largest families of languages, to which English and the majority of modern European languages belong. The common I.-E. language must have begun to split into branches as early as 2000 BC. What we know of its phonology, syntax, morphology, and vocabulary is a reconstruction, based on a comparison of the features of those languages now existing, or which have died out in historical times.

In classifying the I.-E. languages, use is made of the broad cleavage resulting from the different treatment of the palatal stops, which in one group, called the *centum* languages (from the Lat. for 100), have become simple velars, and in the other, the *satem* group (from the Zend form of the same word), have become fricatives. In the main, the former group is found W of a line from the SE corner of the Baltic Sea to the head of the Adriatic, but including Greek; the latter E of that line.

INDONĒ'SIA, Republic of. Asian state composed of the E Indian islands of Sumatra, Java, Madura, the Lesser Sundas (Nusa Tenggaru), the Moluccas (Maluku), Celebes (Sulawesi), and *c.* 3,000 smaller islands, together with Kalimantan (S part of Borneo), Irian Jaya (W part of New Guinea, incorporated 1963) and E Timor (incorporated 1976). The economy is chiefly agricultural, the main crops being rice, sugar, tea, coffee, cassava, sweet potatoes and soya beans. Plantation-grown rubber, copra, coconut oil, kapok and pepper are valuable exports, as is teak from the forests. The chief mineral is oil, but tin, coal, nickel, bauxite, etc. are mined. Other industries incl. textiles, plastics, paper, matches, and chemicals. The cap. is Jakarta Raya (Djakarta); other towns incl. Surabaya, Bandung, Semarang, Malang and Surakarta.

Before the S.W.W. the rep. formed the Netherlands Indies, occupied 1942-5 by the Japanese who actively promoted the movement for independence from the Dutch. At the end of the fighting, the rep. of I., incl. all the Netherlands Indies except western New Guinea, was proclaimed, and was recognized by the Dutch in 1949; a union set up between the two countries at the same time was abrogated by I. in 1956. Under the leadership of Pres. Sukarno (q.v.), the rep. laid claim to Netherlands New Guinea which in 1962 was ceded to the UN, in 1963 to Indonesia, but the 'confrontation' of Malaysia over Sabah and Sarawak 1963-6 ended in *détente*. This was a consequence of a revision of policy by Gen. Suharto (q.v.) who took power 1966 and banned the Communist Party. He became pres. 1968 (re-elected for a third term in 1978), and encouraged investment and development, and commerce. Tribal revolt against the govt. in Irian Jaya in favour of independence, following its incorporation by I., has led to border friction with Papua New Guinea, which has been accused of supporting the rebels.

Area 1,925,000 sq.km (741,000 sq.m); pop. (1978) 141,600,000 the majority being Moslem, with *c.* 6,000,000 Christians. Javanese form nearly half the pop., the largest minority being the Sundanese, over 10%. The official language, Bahasa Indonesia, is almost identical with Malay, and a common spelling was introduced in 1972. M.U.: Rupiah.

INDONESIA. A sculpture from a temple on Bali, in which the enthusiasm of the dancers and their audience still lives in stone. *Photo: Mireille Vautier*

INDO'RE. Indian city in Madhya Pradesh, on the Malwa plain, N of the Vindhya hills. It is the seat of several colleges, and has a fine palace, residence of the maharaja when I. was cap. of the former princely state of I. Pop. (1971) 572,622.

INDRA. Hindu deity of the early Vedic era. He was the god of the firmament and thus the god of all-pervading power, and is depicted as a man on a white elephant. In one of his 4 arms he carried a thunderbolt.

INDRE (añdr). French r. rising in the Auvergne mountains and flowing for 170km (115m) generally NW to join the Loire below Tours. It gives its name to the depts. of Indre and Indre-et-Loire.

INDU'CTANCE. Either that property of an element, or circuit, which when carrying a current is characterized by the formation of a magnetic field and the storage of magnetic energy; or the magnitude of the capability of an element or a circuit to store magnetic energy when carrying a current.

INDU'CTOR. An element possessing the characteristic of inductance.

INDULGENCES (Lat. *indulgere*, to grant). According to the RC Church the total or partial remission of temporal punishment for sins which remain to be expiated after penitence and confession has secured exemption from eternal punishment. The doctrine of I. began as the commutation of the Church penances for sin, such as fasting, for suitable works of charity or money gifts to the Church, and became a great source of church revenue. The system was grossly abused, and the height of degradation was reached when abp Albert of Mainz and Magdeburg sold Is. through the agency of the Dominican Tetzel. This trade in Is. roused Luther in 1517 to draw up his 95 'Theses' and initiate the Reformation. The Council of Trent in 1563 recommended moderate retention of Is., and they continue, notably in 'Holy Years'.

I'NDUS. River of Asia which rises in Tibet in glaciers on the N slopes of Kailas range in the Himalayas, flows NW across Kashmir, then turns SW to flow through Pakistan to the Arabian Sea which it enters through a delta, 200km (125m) wide, below Hyderabad. It is *c.* 2,900 km (1,800 m) long, and with its 5 tributaries forms a river system with twice the annual flow of the Nile. The lower I. has an extensive irrigation system dependent on the Lloyd barrage (1932), but the system for the upper I. area was cut in two by the partition of Punjab in 1947. A treaty of 1960 allotted India the use of the 3 eastern rivers (Ravi, Beas and Sutlej) and Pakistan the 3 western (Indus, Jhelum, and Chenab). *See* INDUS VALLEY CIVILIZATION.

INDUSTRIAL RELATIONS. The interaction of 'workers' and 'management' in industry: ideally complete co-operation to achieve maximum quality output combined with maximum job satisfaction, wage rates and security. In communist systems, wherein the workers are theoretically the management, this should be achieved, but production problems and worker dissatisfaction still arise.

In the West the situation is often one of embittered conflict, as illustrated by the fate of the I.R. Act (1971) in Britain (*see* TRADE UNIONS). In W Germany worker participation (*Mitbestimmung*) was introduced by law in 1952, giving the 'works council' of a firm a right of veto in hirings, redundancies, etc., and making at least one-third of the 'supervisory board' workers' representatives, the rest being 'shareholders' - in Germany often banks. In Britain employers were inclined to favour introduction of a similar system (provided that there were secret ballots and that non-union workers, espec. middle management were included), but the major trade unions preferred an extension of the subjects covered by collective bargaining. The majority recommendation of the Bullock Report (1977) that union-nominated worker-directors be introduced was controversial. *Co-ownership*, as often advocated in Britain, means that the co. is entirely owned by the employees with any profits not ploughed back being distributed as a bonus to the workers.

INDUSTRIAL REVOLUTION. The sudden acceleration of technical development which occurred in Europe from the late 18th cent., and which transferred the balance of political power from the landowner to the industrial capitalist, and created an organized industrial working class. The great achievement of the first phase (to 1830) was the invention of the steam engine in Britain, originally developed for draining mines (*see* NEWCOMEN), but rapidly put to use in factories and in the railways (*see* WATT, ARKWRIGHT, and Samuel CROMPTON). In the second phase, from 1830 to the early 20th cent., the I.R. enlarged its scope from Europe to the world, with some initial exploitation of 'colonial' possessions by European powers as a preliminary to their independent development, and the internal combustion engine and electricity were developed. Then in 1911 Rutherford split the atom at Manchester and the prospect of nuclear power opened, and electronic devices were developed which made possible automation (q.v.), with the eventual prospect of even managerial decision-making being in the hands of 'machines'. *See* CYBERNETICS.

INDUS VALLEY CIVILIZATION. The prehistoric culture of the NW Indian sub-continent. From the 1920s the cities of Harappa (Punjab) and Mohenjo Daro (Sind) in Pakistan were excavated, both being excellent examples of town planning and sanitation. *See* WHEELER, Sir Mortimer. Both belong to the 3rd millenium BC. Among the discoveries were figurines of deities, and numerous seals with animal engravings and inscriptions in a still undeciphered script. It was a wealthy economy in which agriculture, cattle raising, spinning and weaving, and trade flourished. By 1980 many further sites had been found, some dating back to the 7th and 8th millenia BC, so rivalling in age the civilisation of Sumeria. In the same general area there are also Stone Age sites dating back *c.* 50,000 years. The manufacture of flints can be seen by the size of the workings to have been carried on as a 'factory system' which presupposes an unexpectedly complex trading and distribution network.

INDY (aṅdē'), **Vincent d'** (1851-1931). French composer. B. in Paris, he studied under César Franck, and was one of the founders of the *Schola Cantorum,* in which the ideals of Franck were embodied. His works incl. operas (*Fervaal*), symphonies, tone poems (*Istar*), chamber music, etc.

INFANT. *See* MINOR.

INFANTE and **INFANTA** (Lat. *infans,* an infant). Title given in Spain and Portugal to the sons (other than the heir-apparent) and daughters respectively of the sovereign. The heir-apparent in Spain bears the title of Prince of Asturias. The title of I. was also given to other members of the royal family.

INFANTICIDE. In modern states the killing of children is a criminal offence, but it was a recognized practice until recent times as the simplest method of population control in India and China, and among ancient peoples incl. the Greeks. Girls were the most frequent victims, but in communities where bride-prices were high they might be regarded as the greater asset and boys were disposed of.

INFANTILE PARALYSIS. *See* POLIOMYELITIS.

INFANT MORTALITY. The number of infants dying under one year of age. Improved nutrition and medical care have considerably lowered figures throughout the world, e.g. in the 18th cent. in the UK 50 per cent died, compared with under 2 per cent in 1971.

INFECTION. Invasion of the body by micro-organisms. These may be viruses (q.v.) or bacteria (q.v.) incl. cocci and bacilli. Among other diseases, viruses cause smallpox, chickenpox, shingles, measles, mumps, German measles, infantile paralysis, influenza, colds, and sleeping sickness; cocci cause diseases with short incubation periods and acute fever, e.g. scarlet fever, meningitis, and gonorrhoea; bacilli cause diseases with long incubation periods and course, e.g. diphtheria, whooping cough, and typhus. Both cocci and bacilli tend to be carried by immune persons. The effects of I. are due to the body's reaction to the poisons (toxins) produced by the organisms (*see* IMMUNITY). I. may be contracted from a sufferer from the disease; or from a carrier who may be immune or developing the disease himself or convalescent; or from contaminated objects, such as food, drink, bedclothes, or books; or from discharges, such as spray expelled in coughing or sneezing (common cold), or spittle (tuberculosis), or faeces (typhoid). Some infections are carried by insects (malaria by the mosquito, typhus by the louse), or on the feet of flies (food poisoning). Some may be introduced through a breach in the skin, e.g. gonorrhoea and lockjaw (tetanus). Contagion is infection by direct contact.

INFERIORITY COMPLEX. Term used in psychoanalysis for a complex pattern of richly emotional ideas connected with what the patient rightly or wrongly believes to be his inferiority. In order to compensate for his inferiority he often tends to assume an opposite character.

INFLAMMATION. The reaction of tissues to injury. This may be caused by violence, a foreign body, poison, or invasion by harmful bacteria. The signs are heat, swelling, redness, pain, and loss of function. These result from the pouring of white blood cells and lymph into the affected region, with the object of combating the injurious agent and repairing the damage. Collections of dead white cells form the thick, yellowish fluid called pus. When the body's local defences win the fight the inflammation resolves. When they lose it, the I. spreads and may endanger life.

INFLATION and **DEFLATION.** Traditionally, an excess of demand due to an expansion of the money supply, 'too much money chasing too few goods': deflation is the reverse situation. It may arise internally owing to fiscal policy, the govt spending more than its income from taxation; or monetary policy, as when banks lend too easily. Such I. does not occur when the currency remains convertible at par into gold or a convertible foreign currency, but 'convertibility' does not prevent price rise inflation, which may result from worker demand for higher wages, manufacturer demand for higher profits, and lack of consumer resistance. Workers and management tend to make larger demands in anticipation of continued I., and thus make their expectation self-fulfilling. Govts attempt to control I. by strict fiscal policy, monitoring monetary policy, and wage and price 'freezes' - despite the risk of unemployment - but I. may still race ahead because of external factors. In Elizabethan times I. was caused by the influx into Europe of gold and silver from Spanish colonies in the New World, as happened again world-wide in the 19th cent. following gold discoveries in Australia and California. In the 1970s world prices of essential raw materials, such as oil, for which there is increasing competition have risen, causing extreme inflation. Moderate I. is traditionally associated with an expanding economy, higher prices stimulating production and reducing employment, but in the 1970s the term *stagflation* was coined to denote a situation in which, although prices continued to rise, production remained stagnant and unemployment persisted. Contributory factors in such a situation are the lack of confidence which prevents manufacturers from investing in new plant, and the redundancies caused by automation when this new plant is introduced. *Hyperinflation* is I. at over 20 per cent, when it may become so effectively self-feeding that it is no longer controllable by normal economic means, as in Germany after the F.W.W. and parts of modern S America.

INFLUENZA. Acute infectious respiratory disease caused by various types of virus, with an incubation period of 2-5 days. It is marked by catarrh, fever, shivering and aching, and the onset is sharp, the whole attack being clear-cut, as distinct from the heavy cold often miscalled influenza. A malignant type may become pandemic, as with 'Spanish flu' which killed *c.* 20 millions in 1918, and this virus (virtually identical with that which gives rise to swine I.) re-emerged in man in the USA to prompt Pres. Ford's proposal for mass vaccination in 1976. The World I. Centre, financed by WHO is at Mill Hill, N London.

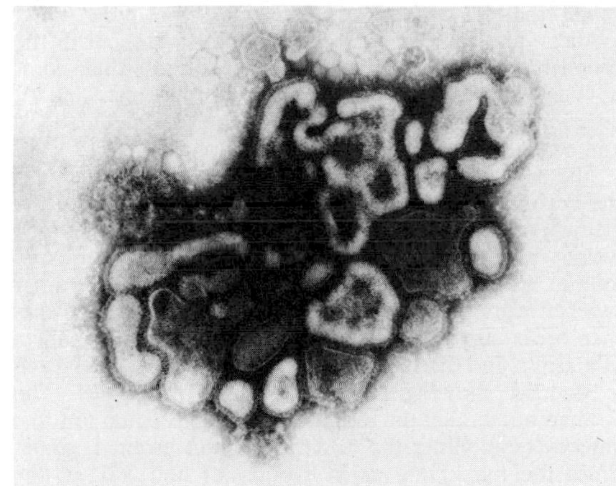

INFLUENZA. A virus, magnified under an electron microscope over 132,000 times, of the strain current in the USA in 1976. *Photo:Popperfoto*

INFRA-RED RADIATION. Invisible electro-magnetic radiation of wavelength between about 0.75-1,000 microns (1 micron is a millionth of a metre), i.e. between the limit of the red end of the visible spectrum and the shortest microwaves. All bodies above the absolute zero of temperature absorb and radiate I-R.R. Absoption spectra are made use of in chemical analysis, particularly for organic compounds, and objects which radiate I-R.R. can be photographed or made visible in the dark, or through mist or fog, on specially sensitized emulsions. This is important for military purposes. I-R.R. is also used in medical photography and treatment, in industry, astronomy and criminology. The strong absorption of many substances for I-R.R. is a useful method of applying heat, as in baking and toasting.

In *infra-red astronomy* I.R. is used in measuring the diameters of remote bodies in the Solar System beyond the accurate reach of optical telescopes. The amount of I.R. radiation from a planet, asteroid, etc., indicates its reflecting power which, in combination with its apparent brightness, is used to gauge its size.

INFRA-RED ASTRONOMY. The 3.8 m (150 in) main mirror for the UK's infra-red telescope on the extinct volcano of Mauna Kea in Hawaii. Grinding and polishing take two years, but at a wavelength of c.10 micrometres the grinding does not need to be so accurate as for an optical telescope. This mirror is half of a failed optical mirror, which it took two months to cut in half with a diamond band saw. *Photo: Courtesy of Grubb Parsons*

INGRES (añgr), **Jean Auguste Dominique** (1780-1867). French painter. After studying under David (1797-8) he worked in Rome (1806-20) and Florence (1820-4), executing some of his finest portraits. In 1826 he became prof. of the fine arts at the Academy in Paris, and in 1832 director of the French Academy in Rome, returning to Paris in 1841. His draughtsmanship, whether in his highly finished portraits or his female nudes, e.g. 'Odalisque' (1814) and 'La Source' (1856), is superb.

INHOMOGENEITY. Name given by astronomers to a very large dense area of the Universe believed to exist ten thousand million light years from Earth. Its gravity appears to be pulling Earth and the rest of the Galaxy towards it, and this would account for the steady movement of Earth which has been detected in relation to the microwave background of X-ray radiation caused by energy left over after the formation of matter in the Universe.

INITIATIVE and **REFERENDUM.** Devices whereby the voters may play a direct part in making laws. In the case of the *Initiative* a proposed law is drawn up and signed by petitioners, and submitted to the legislature. A *Referendum* may be taken on a law that has been passed by the legislature but which will not become operative until the people have expressed their will concerning it. If the R. gives an affirmative vote, then the law is confirmed and comes into force. Switzerland was the pioneer in these devices, but both have been introduced into a number of the states and cities of USA, and a referendum on membership of the Common Market was held in Britain in 1975. It is argued that Rs. undermine parliamentary authority, but they do allow the elector to participate directly in govt.

Another device is the *Recall*, whereby the voters are given the opportunity of demanding the dismissal from office of officials.

INK. The various kinds of ink include: (1) *writing inks*, the essential ingredients of which are hot-water extract of galls or some other vegetable material furnishing gallic acid, tannic acid, and other essentially phenolic compounds; (2) *copying and stamp-pad inks*, consisting of concentrated solutions of basic dyes in a hygroscopic medium; (3) *marking inks*, solutions of silver or copper compounds, with the possible addition of aniline; (4) *printing inks*, consisting of a resin/oil complex dissolved in a thin petroleum distillate, or finely balanced resin solutions in petroleum distillate.

INKERMAN. A battle of the Crimean War, fought on 5 Nov. 1854, during which an attack by the Russians on I. ridge, occupied by the British army besieging Sebastopol, was repulsed.

INLAND SEA. Sea (Jap. *Seto Naikai*), 390km (240m) long, almost enclosed by the Japanese is. of Honshu, Kyushu and Shikoku. Very beautiful, it has *c.* 300 small islands.

INNOCENT III (1161-1216). Pope. B. at Anagni, he was elected pope in 1198. He was successful in asserting the power of the papacy over secular princes, and played a decisive role in the struggles over the imperial succession. His greatest triumph was over King John, whom he compelled to accept Langton as archbishop of Canterbury, and to hold England as the Pope's vassal. I. promoted the 4th Crusade, and crusades against the pagan Livonians and Letts, and the Albigensian heretics.

INNOCENTS' DAY or **Childermas.** Festival of the Catholic Church, celebrated on 28 Dec. in memory of the children who were slaughtered by Herod following upon the birth of Jesus Christ.

INNS and **INNKEEPERS.** An I. may be defined as a house whose owner is according to law prepared to provide shelter and refreshment to all travellers able and willing to pay a reasonable price for the accommodation offered. An innkeeper is bound in law to receive and to provide this accommodation for every guest, so far as he is able, unless the guest be drunk, disorderly, or suffering from infectious disease. Is. differ from hotels in the US only in being picturesque buildings set in attractive surroundings.

INNSBRUCK (-brook). Town on the r. Inn, cap. of Tirol, Austria. I. is a tourist centre, and important as a route junction, esp. as the junction for the Brenner Pass. I. is the seat of a univ. founded 1677. Ancient monuments incl. a 16th cent. Franciscan church. Pop. (1971) 115,200.

INNS OF COURT. Voluntary societies which have the power to call law students to the English Bar. There are now 4, viz. Lincoln's Inn, Gray's Inn, Inner Temple, and Middle Temple; each pursues its separate existence, though joint lectures are given, and a common examination board has been formed. Each is under the administration of a body of Benchers.

INOCULATION. The injection into the body of dead organisms, toxins, antitoxins, etc., with the object of producing immunity by provoking a mild attack of the disease.

INORGANIC CHEMISTRY. Science dealing with the preparation and properties of the elements and their compounds, except those carbon compounds considered in Organic Chemistry (q.v.). Many groups of analogous compounds exist, the oldest known being acids, bases, and salts. Acids usually have a sour taste, change blue vegetable colours (e.g. litmus) red, and react with alkalis to form salts. Alkalis restore the colours of indicators changed by acids, with which they react to form salts. All acids contain hydrogen. Acids containing oxygen are called oxy-acids; those of the same element may contain different amounts of oxygen, the name then ending in -ous and -ic when less or more oxygen is present; the names of the corresponding salts end in -ite and -ate. Salts are formed by the replacement of the acidic hydrogen by a metal or radical. Oxides are classified into: (i) acidic oxides, forming acids with water; (ii) basic oxides, forming bases (containing the hydroxyl group OH) with water; (iii) neutral oxides; and (iv) peroxides (containing more oxygen than the normal oxide). Acidic and basic oxides combine to form salts, whilst in the reaction between acids and bases water is formed as well. An acid containing in the molecule one, two, or three atoms of replaceable hydrogen is called mono-, di-, or tri-basic, respectively. If only part of the hydrogen is replaced, an acid salt is formed. A basic salt is usually a compound of a normal salt (in which all the acidic hydrogen is replaced) with excess of base. Other groups are the compounds of metals with halogens (fluorine, chlorine, bromine, and iodine), called halides (fluorides, chlorides, bromides, and iodides), and with sulphur (sulphides). It is usual in the chemistry of non-metallic elements to discuss their compounds with hydrogen, oxygen, and halogens; and in describing the metals to deal with their oxides, halides, and oxysalts (carbonates, nitrates, sulphates, etc.).

The basis of the modern description of the elements is the Periodic Table, accompanying this entry. In this, the elements are arranged in the order of increasing atomic weight with one or two inversions (e.g. tellurium and iodine), or more correctly in the order of atomic number (nuclear charge). The continuous sequence of elements then breaks up into 7 periods and 8 groups, the members of a group and the sub-groups (a) and (b) into which each is divided showing related chemical properties. The Roman numeral at the top of each group is equal to some valency (sometimes the minimum, as in group I, sometimes the maximum, as in groups VI and VII, of the elements it contains). *See also* table accompanying CHEMISTRY.

The sequence of atomic numbers shows that there are now no 'missing' elements, nos. 43, 61, 85, 87, etc., all highly radioactive, having been made. The last period contains similar elements, and since preceding periods contain 2, 8, 8, 18, 18, and 32 elements, it would be expected that the last should be a very long period and 13 elements beyond uranium have been prepared artificially (plutonium, neptunium, americium, curium, berkelium, californium, einsteinium, fermium, mendelevium, nobelium, lawrencium, rutherfordium and hahnium). Research continues, as in the unsuccessful attempt at Berkeley in 1968 to find traces of no. 110 - thought to be relatively stable - in platinum ore.

The modern quantum theory of the atom (unlike the old Rutherford-Bohr theory) is able to give a satisfactory explanation of the numbers 2, 8, 18, and 32, of elements in the periods, and the structures of the shells of electrons in practically all atoms are known from the spectroscopic data; the explanation of the appearance of the 15 rare

Periodic System of the Chemical Elements

← *metals* → | *non-metals* | *transition elements* | *increasingly electropositive* ↓ | *increasingly electronegative* →

	IA	IIA	IIIA	IVA	VA	VIA	VIIA	VIII	VIII	VIII	IB	IIB	IIIB	IVB	VB	VIB	VIIB	O
	H 1																	He 2
	Li 3	Be 4											B 5	C 6	N 7	O 8	F 9	Ne 10
	Na 11	Mg 12											Al 13	Si 14	P 15	S 16	Cl 17	Ar 18
	K 19	Ca 20	Sc 21	Ti 22	V 23	Cr 24	Mn 25	Fe 26	Co 27	Ni 28	Cu 29	Zn 30	Ga 31	Ge 32	As 33	Se 34	Br 35	Kr 36
	Rb 37	Sr 38	Y 39	Zr 40	Nb 41	Mo 42	Tc 43	Ru 44	Rh 45	Pd 46	Ag 47	Cd 48	In 49	Sn 50	Sb 51	Te 52	I 53	Xe 54
	Cs 55	Ba 56	La 57	Hf 72	Ta 73	W 74	Re 75	Os 76	Ir 77	Pt 78	Au 79	Hg 80	Tl 81	Pb 82	Bi 83	Po 84	At 85	Rn 86
	Fr 87	Ra 88	Ac 89	Th 90	Pa 91	U 92												
Rare Earths (Lanthanides)			La 57	Ce 58	Pr 59	Nd 60	Pm 61	Sm 62	Eu 63	Gd 64	Tb 65	Dy 66	Ho 67	Er 68	Tm 69	Yb 70	Lu 71	
Transuranics (Actinides)			Ac 89	Th 90	Pa 91	U 92	Np 93	Pu 94	Am 95	Cm 96	Bk 97	Cf 98	Es 99	Fm 100	Md 101	No 102	Lr 103	Rf 104 Ha 105

earth elements in period 6 is due to the filling up of an incomplete inner shell by successive additions of electrons as the atomic number increases in steps, whilst the outer valency shell, on which the chemical properties depend, remains unaltered. Elements, the atoms of which have incomplete inner shells, are called transitional elements in the wider sense: they include, besides the rare earths proper, and the group VIII metals, the elements from scandium to zinc, from yttrium to cadmium, and from hafnium to mercury, inclusive.

INQUEST. Inquiry held by a coroner (q.v.).

INQUISITION. An ecclesiastical tribunal in the RC Church, charged with the suppression of heresy. Its existence is usually dated from the Synod of Toulouse in 1229. The *Medieval I.* operated mainly in France and Italy, and to a lesser extent in the Empire and Spain; it never gained a footing in England. The Reformation led to a great revival in its activity in Italy and Spain. The I. or Holy Office (re-named Sacred Congregation for the Doctrine of the Faith 1965) still deals with ecclesiastical discipline, its jurisdiction confined to the Vatican City.

The *Spanish I.* was reorganized in 1480 under royal, not papal, control. Its jurisdiction was extended in the 16th cent. to the Spanish colonies in America. Executions continued until 1781. Napoleon suppressed it in 1808, but it was restored by Ferdinand VII in 1814, only to be abolished again in 1834.

Trials by the I. were conducted in secret, and torture was used to force the prisoner to admit his guilt. Those who confessed were condemned to flogging, fines, or penances; the obstinate to imprisonment or to death by burning.

INSANITY. Social inadequacy due to mental disorder. The word as used popularly has much the same meaning as the legal term mental disease, formerly lunacy. This means a condition which renders the patient so dangerous to himself or others or both, or so helpless, that he should be placed under care. Many mentally diseased or disordered persons are not socially inadequate. In medicine the corresponding term is psychosis.

INSECT. Small invertebrate animal whose body is divided into head, thorax, and abdomen. The head bears a pair of feelers or antennae, and attached to the thorax are 3 pairs of legs and usually 2 pairs of wings. Is. are placed in the class Insecta of the phylum Arthropoda, and their scientific study forms that branch of zoology termed Entomology. About 1,000,000 species are known, and several thousand new ones are discovered every year. Is. vary in size very considerably from 0.02 of a cm (0.007in) to 35cm (13.5in) in length.

The skeleton is almost entirely external and is composed of chitin. It remains membranous at the joints, but elsewhere is hard and gives attachment to the muscles and other internal organs.

The head is its feeding and sensory centre. It bears the antennae, eyes, and mouth-parts. By means of the *antennae,* the I. detects odours and experiences the sense of touch. The *eyes* comprise *compound eyes* and simple eyes or *ocelli.* The compound eyes are formed of a large number of individual facets or lenses. There are about 4,000 lenses to each compound eye in the house-fly. The mouth-parts include a *labrum* or upper lip; a pair of principal jaws or *mandibles,* used for seizing and crushing the food; a pair of accessory jaws or *maxillae*; and a *labium,* or lower lip. The mouth-parts are modified in Is. which feed upon a fluid diet.

The *thorax* is the locomotory centre, and is made up of 3 segments - the *pro-, meso-,* and *metathorax.* Each bears a pair of legs and, in flying insects, the 2nd and 3rd of these segments also bears a pair of wings. Legs vary greatly in form according to use.

Wings are outgrowths of the integument of the meso- and metathorax. A wing is composed of an upper and a lower membrane, and between these 2 layers it is strengthened by a framework of chitinous tubes known as *veins.*

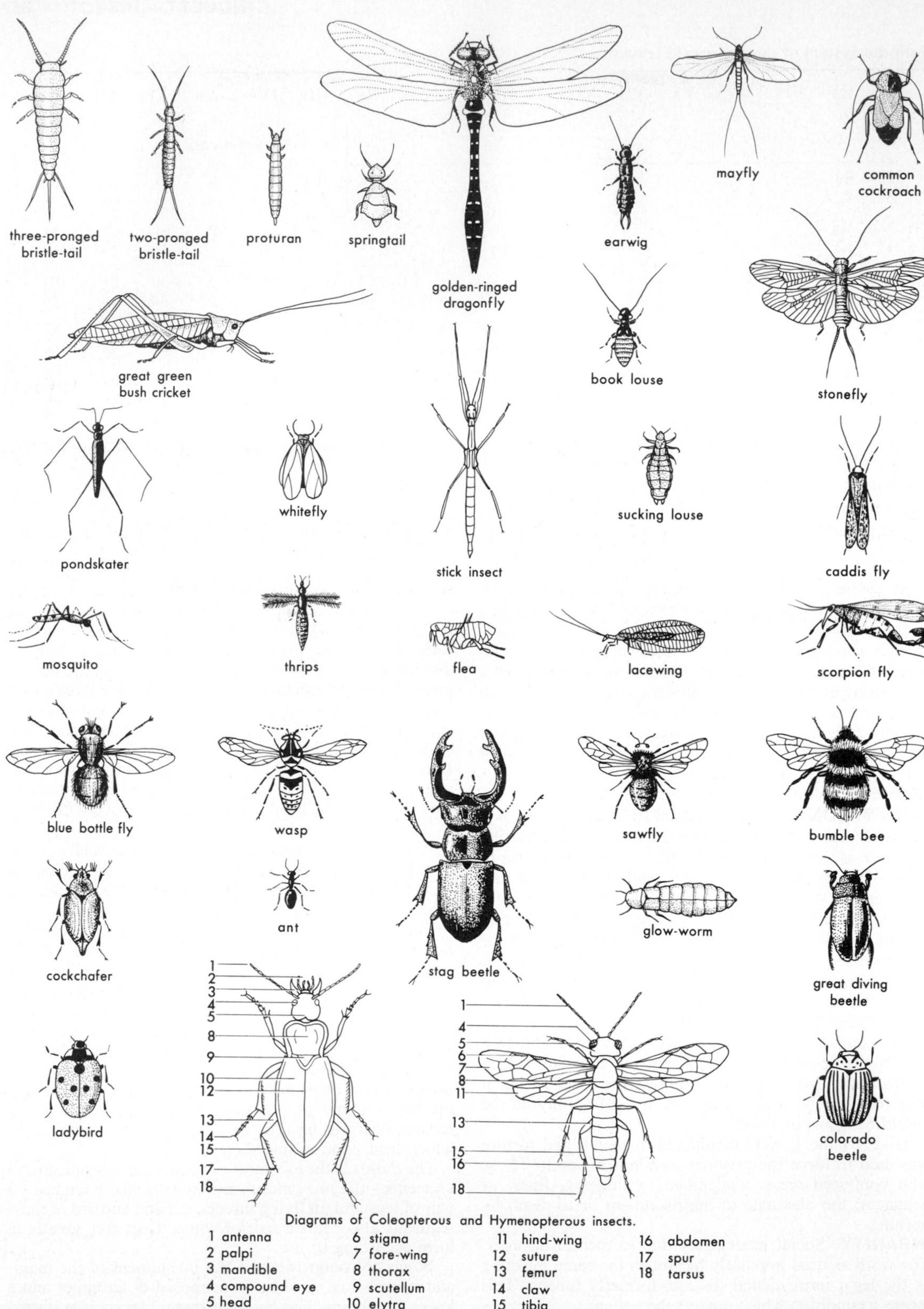

INSECT. A selection of varied insect forms, and diagrams of the typical Coleopterous (left) and Hymenopterous (right) forms.

INSECTIVOROUS PLANTS. The Venus fly-trap (*Dionaea*), which is mainly found in North Carolina. The rose-tinted digestive glands attract the fly to step inside (left), and when the sensitive hairs, hinged at their bases, are touched the trap closes. *Photos: Popperfoto*

The venation or arrangement of this framework is of great importance in the classification of insects. The hind-body or abdomen is the metabolic and reproductive centre: it is here that digestion, excretion, and the sexual functions take place. Usually the abdomen consists of 10 segments. In the female there is very commonly an egg-laying instrument or *ovipositor*, and many insects have a pair of tail feelers or *cerci*. Most insects breathe by means of fine air-tubes called *tracheae* which open to the exterior by a pair of breathing pores or *spiracles*.

Growth and metamorphosis. When ready to issue from the egg the young I. forces its way through the *chorion*, or egg-shell, and growth takes place in cycles that are interrupted by successive moults. After moulting the new cuticle is soft and pliable and able to adapt itself to increase in size and change of form. Moulting is caused by a hormone discharged into the blood. The growth changes constitute metamorphosis.

Most of the lower orders of Is. pass through a direct or incomplete metamorphosis. The young closely resemble the parents and are known as nymphs. The transformation to adult stage is gradual and feeding goes on throughout life.

The higher groups of Is. undergo indirect or complete metamorphosis. They issue from the eggs at an earlier stage of growth than nymphs and are termed *larvae*. The life of the I. is interrupted by a resting *pupal* stage when no food is taken. During this stage the larval organs and tissues are transformed into those of the *imago* or adult. Before pupating the I. protects itself by selecting a suitable hiding place, or making a cocoon of some material which will merge in with its surroundings. When an I. is about to emerge from the pupa it undergoes its final moult, which consists in shedding the pupal cuticle. When in the adult stage the I. no longer grows or moults.

Reproduction is by diverse means. In most Is. mating occurs once only, and death soon follows. Many Is. are pests which may be controlled by chemical pesticides (which may also kill useful Is.), importation of natural predators (which may themselves become pests), or more recently use of artificially reared sterile Is., either the males only or in 'population flushing' both sexes, so sharply reducing succeeding generations.

The classification of Is. (*see* accompanying Table) is largely based upon characters of the mouth-parts, wings and metamorphosis.

INSECTIVORA. Order of mammals incl. hedgehogs, moles and shrews, which is comparatively primitive and mainly insect-eating.

INSECTIVOROUS PLANTS. Plants which attract and trap small insects, and digest them. Unique for their ability to use animal protein as a source of nitrogen, they are common to marshy ground where there is a shortage of nitrogen. The sundews (*Drosera*) are of world-wide occurrence, and the largest species, *D. gigantea*, found in Australia, can reach a height of 1m (3ft). The butterwort (*Pinguicula*) found in Britain, has a rosette of pale green leaves, each with turned-up edges, and a greasy surface covered with tiny points to trap insects. Bladderworts (*Utricularia*) q.v. are floating plants growing in quiet waters or muddy soils, and trap insects by small green bladders among the leaves. The Venus' fly trap (*Dionaea*)

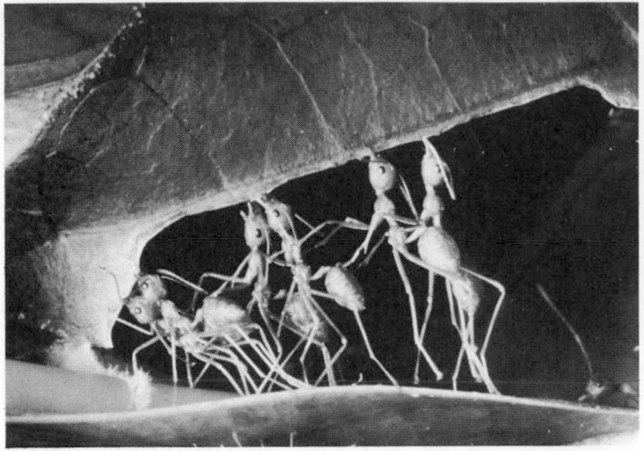

INSECT. An ant colony functions almost as a single intelligent being. Immediately a slit is made in the nest, these worker weaving ants *(Oecophylla smaragdina)* combine to pull the edges together. They then prod their larvae (held in their jaws) to make them produce silk, and pass them to and fro as living shuttles to bind the leaf edges and close the breach. *Photo: M.W.F. Tweedie/NHPA*

Classification of Insects

	Class—INSECTA
	Sub-class **Apterygota**
Thysanura	Three-pronged bristle-tails
Diplura	Two-pronged bristle-tails
Protura	Proturans
Collembola	Springtails
	Sub-class **Pterygota**
	Division 1. **Exopterygota**
Orthoptera	Grasshoppers, locusts, crickets, etc.
Dictyoptera	Cockroaches, praying mantids
Phasmida	Stick and leaf insects
Grylloblattodea	Few primitive, secondarily wingless forms
Plecoptera	Stone-flies
Isoptera	Termites or white ants
Embioptera	Web-spinners
Dermaptera	Earwigs
Ephemeroptera	May-flies
Odonata	Dragon-flies
Psocoptera	Psocids or book-lice
Anoplura	Sucking or true-lice and bird-lice
Thysanoptera	Thrips
Hemiptera	Plant-bugs, cicadas, leaf-hoppers, aphids, etc.
	Division 2. **Endopterygota**
Neuroptera	Lace-wings, alder-flies, etc.
Mecoptera	Scorpion flies
Trichoptera	Caddis-flies
Lepidoptera	Butterflies and moths
Coleoptera	Beetles
Strepsiptera	Stylops
Hymenoptera	Saw-flies, ants, bees, wasps, ichneumon flies, etc.
Diptera	Two-winged or true flies
Aphaniptera	Fleas

is common in S America, and pitcher plants (*Nepenthes*) are native to the wet tropics of the Old World.

INSEMINATION, Artificial. The artificial introduction of semen to the reproductive tract of the female to effect fertilization. Largely used as a means of improving cattle herds through outstanding sires, it has also been used in the case of human beings. Semen may sometimes be obtained from the husband - A.I.H(usband). - or from a stranger who usually remains unknown except to the doctor involved - A.I.D(onor). In the UK, Under the existing law in 1980, an AID child is illegitimate, and if the husband has consented this is immaterial. An extension of A.I. was the birth in 1978 in the UK of Louise Brown, following the external fertilisation of an egg from her mother and sperm from her father, the fertilised egg then being reimplanted in the mother's womb. The logical sequel is the growth of an egg to maturity in the laboratory. *See also* CLONE and GENETICS.

INSTALMENT CREDIT. *See* HIRE PURCHASE.

I'NSŪLIN. The hormone secreted by the islets of Langerhans in the pancreas. It is necessary for the utilization of sugar by the body and its deficiency causes diabetes. McLeod, Banting, and Best discovered its existence in 1921, and how to extract it from the pancreas of animals to treat the disease. By 1980 linkage of synthetic insulin genes to bacterial genes had been achieved, and commercial production of I. by bacteria on a commercial scale was planned.

INSURANCE. By a contract of I. the insured party is guaranteed a specific indemnity in return for valuable consideration, otherwise known as the premium, which is scientifically calculated on the basis of experience in proportion to the risk involved. As practised by I. companies, mutual associations and societies, I. can be classified under the headings: fire, marine, accident and life - the last division being distinguished by the term 'assurance'. An assurance policy guarantees the payment of a definite sum upon the occurrence of a specific event which is accepted as being inevitable, e.g. death, where I. is strictly the provision effected by prudent men against a fortuitous and 'unexpected' contingency.

The practice of I. is strictly governed by various correlated common-law principles, of which indemnity is the most important. This ensures that an insured person shall not be more than fully indemnified, thus preventing anyone profiting, as a result of his loss or misfortune, from the I. fund of which the I. co., is the trustee. It is also affected by various statutes. *See* LLOYDS, SOCIAL SECURITY.

INTAGLIO (intal'yō). Term applied to an engraving which is cut into some material. It is applied more specifically to a gem which has a pattern cut into one surface. In printing, the term is applied to a process in which ink is laid in incisions and hollows on the plate, as in etching, photogravure, etc.

INTEGRATED CIRCUIT. Electronic circuit produced as a single unit on a silicon 'chip' from 1959, superseding the printed circuit (q.v.).

INTELLIGENCE. Ability to cope mentally with the problems life presents. Its distribution follows a tapered curve, the subnormal and highly gifted both being few in number, and both heredity and environment play their part in its determination. It has traditionally been estimated that in a random group of 64 parents, 4 will be very intelligent, with an I.Q. (intelligence quotient) of *c.*

140 and work in the higher professions; 16 will be intelligent (I.Q. *c.* 120) and work in the lower professions; 24 will be average (I.Q. *c.* 100) and be in clerical or other skilled work; 16 will be dull (I.Q. *c.* 85) and semi-skilled; and 4 will be very dull (I.Q. *c.* 70) and in unskilled labour. However, in the next generation the factor of 'regression' would mean that the very intelligent would tend to have less intelligent children and the dull to have more intelligent ones. Achievement in education, career and general happiness would also be modified by factors of character, such as courage and persistence. However, by the mid-1970s the stereotype of the I.Q. had given way to a wider assessment of overall mental activity, such as the British one based on 300 pointers. Factors such as race and heredity were given far less importance, and education and environment far more, I. being no longer regarded as a comparatively fixed endowment, but capable of expansion even beyond the age limits of conventional education. *See* H. J. EYSENCK AND INTELLIGENCE TEST.

INTELLIGENCE AGENCY, Central. *See* CENTRAL INTELLIGENCE AGENCY.

INTELLIGENCE, Military and Political. *See under* SECRET SERVICE.

INTELLIGENCE TEST. The first I.T. was devised by Binet (q.v.) in 1905. The intelligence quotient (IQ) is calculated according to the formula: $IQ = MA/CA \times 100$ in which MA is 'mental age' (the age at which an average child is able to perform given tasks) and CA is 'chronological age', hence the average person would have an IQ of 100. *See also* MENTAL TEST.

INTEREST. Payment for the use of borrowed money or capital. It is calculated at so much per cent (UK £100; US $100; etc.) per annum. The money lent is called the principal, and principal and interest equal the amount. *Simple Interest* is charged on the principal alone. *Compound I.* is charged on the amount of principal and interest as and when it falls due.

INTERFĒ'RON. Natural anti-viral substance, a protein manufactured in cells infected by any virus as part of the body's defences. If applied to cells that are not infected, it renders them resistant to all animal viruses, not merely the virus originally putting the mechanism into operation. Cells treated with I. can be penetrated by viruses in the normal way, but their replication is prevented. Alick Isaacs and Jean Lindenmann discovered I. in 1957 at the Nat. Inst. for Medical Research, London.

INTERIOR DECORATION. The decoration of the inside of a building. Among early names associated with I.D. in England are those of Inigo Jones and Grinling Gibbons, but the first architects to design a building as an integrated whole were the Adam brothers, e.g. Syon House, Middlesex. Craftsmen who have given their names to different styles of furniture design include Chippendale, Hepplewhite and Sheraton. In Victorian times William Morris became famous for his designs of carpets, wallpaper, furniture, etc. Associated with him were the Pre-Raphaelites: Burne-Jones, D. G. Rossetti, and others. In more recent times the trend has been to a less ornate and more functional style, fostered by the interaction of architects and designers working in teams, whether to remodel existing interiors, e.g. Misha Black and Hugh Casson, in British post offices, or in new buildings, e.g. Gio Ponti's Pirelli building (Milan), Oscar Niemeyer's capital city of Brasilia; and the many works of Le Corbusier (France), Eero Saarinen, and Skidmore Owings and Merrill (USA).

INTERLAKEN (in'terlahken). Chief town of the Bernese Oberland, on the Aar between lakes Brienz and Thun, Switzerland. The site was first occupied in 1130 by a monastery, suppressed in 1528. Pop. (1970) 4,700.

INTERNAL COMBUSTION ENGINE. An engine in which energy supplied by a burning fuel is directly transformed into mechanical energy by the controlled burning of the fuel in an enclosed cylinder behind a piston. The term is usually applied to the petrol engine.

INTERNATIONAL, The. Name given to a number of international bodies set up by Socialist and labour organizations to co-ordinate their policies. The 1st International (International Working Men's Association) was formed in London in 1864, under the virtual leadership of Karl Marx (q.v.). The 2nd (Socialist) International, founded in 1889, was a loose federation of national Socialist parties, which lasted until 1939.

The 3rd (Communist) International, generally known as the Comintern, was founded at Moscow in 1919. Like the 1st I. it had a common programme and a strongly centralized leadership, and after the triumph of Hitler in 1933 it advocated a 'popular front' of Communists, Socialists, and Liberals against Fascism. In 1943 it was dissolved. The 4th International, founded in 1936, consists of a number of groups supporting the policy of Trotsky (q.v.).

The Cominform (Communist Information Bureau) 1947–56, estab. by Andrei Zhdanov, was less concerned with world revolution than establishing the Soviet party line. The revolutionary aspect is now covered by the Internat. Dept of the Party's Central Committee, headed by Boris Ponomarev (1905–) from 1954. Training in guerrilla warfare, sabotage and terrorism is given at the Lenin Institute for overt overseas Communists and at the Patrice Lumumba Friendship Univ. for nationalist 'freedom fighters'.

INTERNATIONAL ATOMIC ENERGY AGENCY. Estab. 1957, it has its HQ in Vienna, and is responsible for research centres in Austria and Monaco, and the Internat. Centre for Theoretical Physics (1964) in Trieste. It advises and assists member states in the development and application of nuclear power and guards against its misuse.

INTERNATIONAL BANK for Reconstruction and Development. *See* BANKING.

INTERNATIONAL BRIGADE. The international volunteer force which fought on the republican side in the Spanish Civil War of 1936–9.

INTERNATIONAL CIVIL AVIATION ORGANIZATION. Estab. in 1947 (provisionally 1945) and related to the UN, it encourages safety measures, and uniform regulations in the operation of air services; simplified procedures for customs, immigration and public health; and more safety efficient techniques and equipment.

INTERNATIONAL COURT OF JUSTICE. International court at The Hague, the main judicial organ of the UN. Its statute follows closely that of the *Permanent C. of J.*, set up in 1921, which was associated with the League of Nations.

INTERNATIONAL DATE LINE. A modification of the 180th meridian which marks the difference in time between E and W. The date is put forward a day when crossing the Line going W, and back a day when going E.

INTERNATIONALE. International Communist anthem with words by Eugène Pottier (1871) and music by Pierre

Degeyter (*c.* 1891): it was the nat. anthem of the USSR 1917-19 Dec. 1943.

INTERNATIONAL LABOUR ORGANIZATION. An organization, with HQ at Geneva, which formulates standards for labour and social conditions, to be ratified by member-states. An independent body, first estab. in 1919, it was assoc. with the League of Nations, and in 1945 became affiliated to the UN. Owing to the increasing politicization of the I.L.O., the USA withdrew from membership 1975-80.

INTERNATIONAL LAW. That body of law or collection of rules regarded by civilized states as binding in their relations with each other. The chief framers of modern I.L. were classical jurists, e.g. Hugo Grotius (q.v.), who believed in the uncodified and continually evolving 'law of nature' of reasonable man as a member of society. Its most fundamental rules, covering not only political matters and the conduct of war but broad questions of human welfare, are elucidated in treaties and pacts between countries. The weakness of I.L. is that no body has yet proved strong enough to impose its rulings, although the L. of N. (q.v.) made several attempts and the UN (q.v.) has succeeded to some extent.

Space research has further enlarged the scope of I.L. On the analogy of the high seas outside territorial and economic limits being regarded as the common property of all states, it has been accepted practice since the F.W.W. that each state has absolute sovereignty over air space (the upward limit being undefined in view of the newness of the problem), but that air space over unclaimed territory and the open sea is free for all. Outer space is being customarily treated as free for all, subject only to its use by rockets and satellites of one state having no harmful effect on any other state over which they pass - or which pass under them. Other planets - should these prove available for appropriation - would preferably be internationally controlled. Britain, USSR, and USA signed a treaty 1967 banning nuclear weapons from outer space and in 1968 reached agreement on the rescue and return of astronauts, etc. *See* SEA, LAW OF THE.

INTERNATIONAL SETTLEMENTS, Bank for. Although originated in 1930 to handle the reparation transactions arising from the Young Plan, the bank lost this business with Germany's default, but continued to operate by providing a foreign exchange reserve for central banks and by supplying funds to aid weakened currencies. In addition since the S.W.W., it has been financial agent for the Marshall Plan, OEEC, etc. Its HQ are in Basle.

INTERNATIONAL TRADE UNIONISM. The first internat. body was the *I. Fed. of Trade Unions* (1913), estab. with the beginning of companies with world-wide operations, able to switch their activities to countries where unionism is weak. The modern organizations are the *Internat. Confederation of Free Trade Unions* (ICFTU 1949), which incl. the AF of L/CIO and TUC; *World Fed. of Trade Unions* (WFTU 1945), Communist-dominated; and *World Confederation of Labour* (WCL 1920), mainly Roman Catholic.

INTERPLANETARY MATTER. Material distributed in space, between the planets. It was formerly thought that space must be entirely empty, but this view is now known to be wrong; the material in the Solar System is very thinly spread, but it is still very appreciable. Studies of the interplanetary material have been carried out with the aid of lunar and planetary probes, but information is incomplete.

INTERPOL. Abbreviation of *International Criminal Police Commission,* founded following the Second International Judicial Police Conference (1923) with its HQ in Vienna, but reconstituted after the S.W.W. with its HQ in Paris: it has an international criminal register, fingerprint file and methods index.

INTESTINES. The bowels; the digestive tract. The small intestine (6m/20ft in man), consists of the duodenum, jejunum, and ileum; the large intestine 150cm (5ft) of the caecum, colon, and rectum. Both Is. are muscular tubes comprising an inner lining which secretes alkaline digestive juice, a submucous coat containing fine blood vessels and nerves, a muscular coat with an inner layer of circular and an outer of longitudinal fibres, and a serous coat covering all. The muscle contracts in a series of waves (peristalsis) so as to pass the contents slowly along. The whole tract is supported by a strong band or sling of connective tissue (peritoneum) carrying the blood and lymph vessels and nerves (mesentery, omentum); this keeps the organs in place and isolates infection by pouring out lymph and sealing off the affected region.

INTOXICATION. Affection by a poison (toxin); in popular language usually by alcohol, but scientifically also by poisonous substances, including those generated within the body, e.g. in an abscess under a tooth, or in an inflamed appendix.

INVALIDES, Hôtel des (ōtel′ dāzaṅvahlēd′). Large building in Paris, S of the Seine. It was founded in 1670 as a home for disabled soldiers. The church Dôme des Invalides contains the tomb of Napoleon I. The military gov. of Paris has his HQ at the I.

INVERCARGILL. City at the extreme S of South Island, New Zealand. I. is situated on a deep inlet, and is the centre of a great grazing area. It has sawmills, meat-packing plants, and a smelter at nearby Bluff to process alumina from Queensland. Pop. (1975) 54,000.

INVERNE′SS. Town in Highland region, Scotland, in a sheltered site at the mouth of the Ness. It is a tourist centre, and sheep and wool are gathered from throughout the Highlands for the annual market. Besides tweed manufacture, there are tanning, engineering and distilling industries. It was formerly the co. town of Inverness-shire. Pop. (1973) 35,800.

INVERNESS-SHIRE. Largest of the former Scottish cos., it was merged in Highland region 1975.

INVESTMENT TRUST. *See* SAVING and TRUST.

INYŌKE′RN. Village in the Mojave desert, California, USA, 72km (45m) NNW of Mojave. Founded 1944, it is the site of a US Naval Ordnance test station at which research is carried out in rocket flight and propulsion.

ĪO. In Greek myth a princess loved by Zeus, who transformed her to a heifer to hide her from his jealous wife, Hera.

IO. The moon nearest to Jupiter (422,000 km/260,000 m), diameter 3,658 km (2,273 m). It has at least 8 active volcanoes, each erupting more fiercely than Vesuvius at its most violent, and has a mottled yellow-orange surface, possibly from salts and sulphurs left by evaporated surface water.

IOÁNNINA (yawan′ina). Town in Greece on Lake I., about 80 km (50 m) from the sea. It was conquered by the Turks in the 15th cent., and Ali Pasha, the 'Lion of

INVALIDES. Established by Louis XIV, the Hôtel des Invalides was mainly executed by Jules Hardouin-Mansart. Napoleon was buried beneath the dome of its church in 1840. *Photo: J. Allan Cash*

Ioannina', held it 1788-1822. In 1913 the town reverted to Greece. Pop. (1971) 40,130.

IODINE (ī'odin). A non-metallic element (Gk *iodes,* violet) discovered by Courtois in 1811: symbol I, at. wt. 126.91, at. no. 53. It is a violet-black lustrous solid volatilizing at ordinary temperatures to a bluish-violet gas with an irritating odour, and forming a characteristic blue colour with starch. Not found in the free state, it occurs in saltpetre and as iodides in sea-water from which it is taken up by seaweeds and sponges and may be extracted from their ashes. Most of the world's supplies were formerly extracted from Chile saltpetre deposits but the current process, using finely divided silver on brines from salt wells, has greatly increased production and lowered cost. It is used in photography, externally in medicine (tincture of I. is an alcoholic solution) as an antiseptic, and also internally; and in chemicals and dyes. It collects in the thyroid gland; lack of it producing goitre, and excess myxoedema. Iodine-131 (a radio-active isotope) is widely used in medical diagnosis, research and treatment.

IŌ'DOFORM (CHI_3). An antiseptic which crystallizes into yellow hexagonal plates. It is soluble in ether, alcohol, and chloroform, but not in water.

Ī'ON. An atom or group of atoms which carries a positive or negative electric charge. When neutral atoms or molecules lose valence electrons, positive Is. are formed, when they gain valence electrons, negative Is. are formed. In general salts such as chlorides, sulphates, nitrates, etc., dissolve in water to form both positive and negative Is. in equal quantities, the metal I. being the positive one. Gaseous Is. may be produced by the action of radiation or charged particles. *See* ION-PLATING.

IŌ'NA. Small island of the Inner Hebrides, Scotland, in Highland region. In 563 St Columba founded a monastery which became a great centre of Celtic Christianity; it was destroyed in 807 by Norse pirates. A new Benedictine monastery, founded in 1203, later fell into ruin. Restoration began shortly after it was presented to the Church of Scotland by the duke of Argyll in 1899, and, from the establishment of the I. Community in 1938, was completed by them. Pop. (1971) 150.

IONESCO (ēones'kō), **Eugène** (1912-). French playwright. B. in Rumania, and for a time prof. of literature at Bucharest, he settled in Paris in 1938. Barely staged and allegorical in content, his plays incl. *Les Chaises* (*The Chairs:* 1952), in which a senile married couple converse, and *Rhinocéros* (*The Rhinoceros:* 1959), an attack on totalitarianism, in which every character except one turns into a rhinoceros.

IŌ'NIA. District on the W coast of Asia Minor, inhabited in classical times by Greeks of the Ionian branch. It incl. a number of cities, e.g. Ephesus, Miletus, and later Smyrna, which were subject in turn to Lydia, Persia, Macedonia, and Rome (133 BC).

IŌ'NIAN ISLANDS. island group off the W coast of Greece: British protectorate from 1815 until ceded to Greece 1864. They comprise Corfu (Kerkira), Zanta (Zákinthos), Ithaca (Itháki), Cepahallonia (Kefallinía), Levkás, Cythera and Paxos. Area 332 sq.km (860 sq.m).

IONIAN SEA. That part of the Mediterranean that lies between Italy and Greece, to the S of the Adriatic and containing the Ionian islands.

IONIANS. A Hellenic people who came from beyond the Black Sea and crossed the Balkans *c.* 1980 BC. They then probably invaded Asia Minor before being driven back, possibly by the Hittites. They then spread over mainland Greece, and were later ousted from there to a large extent by the Achaeans.

IONĪZĀ'TION CHAMBER. Device for measuring the amount of ionizing radiation. The radiation ionizes gas in the chamber and the ions are collected and measured as an electric charge.

Ī'ONĪZING RADIATION. Radiation which knocks electrons from atoms during its passage, thereby leaving ions in its path. Electrons and alpha-particles are much more ionizing than neutrons or gamma-radiation (q.v.).

IŌ'NOSPHERE. The ionized layer of the Earth's outer atmosphere, in which free electrons are normally present in sufficient quantities to modify the propagation of radio waves traversing it. There are 3 regions, approx. spherical and concentric, lying 50-640km (30-400m) from the Earth's surface. Knowledge of the I. is important for radio communication and space travel. The lower regions (*see* KENNELLY-HEAVISIDE LAYER) are investigated by sending out radio waves and receiving them back at different places, after they have been reflected and refracted between the I. and earth. The upper boundaries of the I. are investigated with radio sounding from above, by satellites. A great deal of information is being collected in this way concerning daily and seasonal variations. The I. is assumed to be produced by absorption of Sun's ultra-violet radiation.

ION-PLATING. Method of applying corrosion-resistant metal coatings used in the aerospace industry, etc. It has the advantage over electroplating (which uses cyanide in the liquid solution in which the article to be plated is placed), that it is non-polluting, and can be applied to substances such as plastic. The article to be coated is placed in argon gas together with a quantity of the coating metal. The latter is heated, vaporises and becomes ionised as it diffuses through the gas, and forms a metal coating.

I O U. Short for 'I owe you'. A written acknowledgment of debt, signed by the debtor.

I'ŌWA. North central state of the USA. A prairie tableland, it is drained by tributaries of the bordering Mississippi and Missouri, and has great climatic extremes. Varied industries now surpass in value its traditional stockraising (espec. pigs and cattle) and agriculture (maize, soya beans, lucerne, etc.). Minerals incl. cement and coal. First visited by Frenchmen in 1673, I. was admitted to the Union in 1846. The chief cities are Des Moines, the capital, Sioux City, Davenport, Cedar Rapids, and Waterloo. Area 145,790 sq.km (56,290 sq.m); pop. (1970) 2,825,041.

IPECACUANHA (ipikakū-a'na). A small shrubby plant (*Psychotria ipecacuanha*) found in Brazil and Colombia. The root is used as an emetic.

IPHIGENIA (ifijēnī'a). In Gk mythology, the dau. of Agamemnon and Clytemnestra.

IPSWICH. Town and river port of Suffolk, on the Orwell, 26km (16m) NE of Colchester. Increasing trade with Europe has rapidly expanded the port facilities, and there are engineering, agricultural machinery, electrical and fertilizer industries. Christchurch Museum has works by local artists, incl. Constable, Gainsborough and Steer. The PO research estab. is at nearby Martlesham. It is admin. HQ of Suffolk. Pop. (1974) 122,670.

IQUIQUE (ēkē'kā). City and seaport of Chile, cap. of the prov. of Tarapaca. It exports nitrate of soda, from the desert region. Pop. (1972) 63,600.

IQUITOS (ēkē'tōs). Peruvian river port on the upper Amazon, cap. of Loreto dept. The town is a general clearing house for most of eastern Peru. Ecuador claims I. Pop. (1972) 540,560.

IRAN (irahn'). Country in S W Asia, formerly known as Persia (q.v.), which lies between the Caspian Sea to the north, and the Persian Gulf to the south. The central area is occupied by a plateau crossed by mtn ranges, and only about a tenth of I. is fertile; crops incl. wheat, rice, cotton, sugar-beet, tobacco, and tea. Climatic conditions are variable, a general dryness being combined with extremes of heat and cold. The herds of mtn sheep supply wool for the traditionally famous carpets, but I's greatest strength comes from the oil wells of the S, first developed by British enterprise. *See* ABADAN. Oil revenues were used by the Shah to industrialize the country in anticipation of the eventual exhaustion of oil resources, e.g. textiles, glass, pharmaceuticals, fertilizers, cars, steel, etc. Other minerals, not yet fully exploited, incl. iron, copper, lead, zinc and chromite. There is a road and rail network, and an internat. airport at Tehran. The chief towns are Tehran, the cap., Isfahan, Meshed, Tabriz, Rezayeh, Abadan and Ahwaz.

Under the constitution of 1979 supreme authority is given to the Wali Faqih (Theological Ruler) - Ayatollah Khomeini - or failing such another recognised spiritual leader, a Council of Guardians. The country's religion is Shi'ite Islam. The unicameral parliament (majlis) is directly elected as is the pres. (for 4 or 5 years, re-eligible once only). The economy is to be largely state-controlled.

Area 1,648,000 sq. km (636,000sq.m); pop. (1977) 34,000,000, the majority Shi'ite Moslem (*c.* 1,000,000 Sunni). M.U.: rial. The chief language is Farsi: *see* IRANIAN.

History. Persia was overrun from *c.* 1600 B.C. by Aryan (from which the name Iran derives) tribes, incl. the Persians and the Medes. Cyrus II, who seized the Median throne in 550, formed an empire incl. Babylonia, Syria, and Asia Minor, to which Egypt, Thrace, and Macedonia were later added. During 334-328 it was conquered by Alexander, then passed to Seleucus and his descendants, until overrun in the 3rd cent. B.C. by the Parthians. The Parthian dynasty was overthrown in A.D. 226 by Ardashir, founder of the Sassanid dynasty. During 633-41 Persia was conquered for Islam by the Arabs, and then in 1037-55 came under the Seljuk Turks. Their empire broke up in the 12th cent., and was conquered during the 13th cent. by the Mongols. After 1334 P. was again divided until its conquest by Tamerlane in 1380s. A period of anarchy in the later 15th cent. was ended by the accession of the Safavi dynasty, who ruled 1499-1736, but were deposed by the great warrior Nadir Shah (1736-47), after whose death a confused period followed until the accession of the Qajar dynasty (1794-1925). During the 18th cent. Persia was threatened by Russian expansion, culminating in the loss of Georgia in 1801 and a large part of Armenia in 1828. Persian claims on Herat, Afghanistan, led to war with Britain in 1856-7. Revolutions in 1905 and 1909 resulted in the establishment of a parliamentary régime. During the F.W.W. the country was occupied by British and Russian forces. An officer, Riza Khan, seized power in 1921, and was proclaimed shah in 1925. His Axist sympathies led to the Allied occupation of Iran 1941-6, and he abdicated in 1941 in favour of his son (*see* PAHLAVI DYNASTY). The Shah embarked on a 'white revolution' of social and economic reform, celebrating its culmination by his coronation as Shahanshah (King of Kings) in 1967. His pro-Western modernisation programme alienated both leftist and fundamentalist Moslem opposition, and in 1979 he went into exile. The exiled religious leader Ayatollah Khomeini (q.v.) returned and became the supreme power in the new Islamic Rep. of I. There was unrest among the country's minorities *see* AZERBAIJAN, BALUCHISTAN, KHUZESTAN and KURDISTAN. Relations with the USA, formerly supporters of the Shah, were strained by the taking of the US embassy staff in Tehran hostage in 1979, and in 1980 the Ayatollah's encouragement to Iraqi Shi'ites to revolt against their govt. led to an invasion of Iran by Iraq. In 1984 the pro-Soviet Toudeh party leaders were largely eliminated. By 1986 the continuing war with Iraq was taking up over 33% of the national budget in defence expenditure.

IRANIAN. The main language of Iran, Persian or Farsi, is one of the Indo-European group. Old Persian was highly inflected, resembling Sanscrit, but the modern language is as lacking in grammatical forms as English. Written in Arabic script, it incorporates a high proportion of Arabic words. *See also* PERSIAN.

IRAQ (ērahk'). Republic in the Middle East. Flowing across the country are the 2 great rivers Tigris and Euphrates. Rising on either side of the river-plain is plateau country. A great part of I. has a hot desert climate with a scanty rainfall. Natural vegetation of I. is greatly restricted, and cultivation is dependent in the main on artificial irrigation. The plain of I. is potentially highly fertile,

IRELAND. Two of the most influential authors of the 20th century, James Joyce (left), the great experimenter in prose, both in form and language, and the lyric poet W.B. Yeats. *Photos: Camera Press*

much of its surface receiving a new covering of alluvium with each year's floods. In winter, wheat and barley are the main crops, while in summer rice, cotton, and maize are grown, and I. produces most of the world's dates. Sheep, goats, horses, donkeys, and camels are reared. There is a large construction industry and further industrial development is being encouraged by Soviet aid. There are rich oilfields, espec. at Kirkuk (1927). The cap. is Baghdad; chief ports are Basra and, below it nr the Kuwaiti border, Um Qasr, used for freight and as a naval base by the Soviet Union. Area 444,000 sq.km (172,000 sq.m); pop. (1977) 12,200,000, two-thirds Shi'ite and one-third Sunni Moslems. The chief language is Arabic. M.U.: Iraqi dinar.

History. Formerly a Turkish prov., I. became a British mandate after the F.W.W. In 1921 the Emir Faisal was elected king and in 1924 adopted a parliamentary constitution. The mandate ended in 1932, and Faisal was succeeded by his son Ghazi (reigned 1933-9) and grandson Faisal II (assassinated 1958). A rep. was declared which from 1963 came under the control of the Baath Party (Socialist Party of the Arab Renaissance). Unrest among the Kurds (*see* KURDISTAN), backed by Iran, led to a treaty in 1975 which ceded a small area of territory and sovereignty over half the Shatt al Arab to the Shah in return for an end to support for the Kurdish rebels. However, this treaty was abrogated in 1980 by Pres. Saddam Hussein (1936-), who invaded Iran, intent on toppling the Khomeini regime which had been inciting the Shi'ite majority in Iraq to overthrow the Hussein govt. led by the Sunni majority. By 1986 all 250,000 students were conscripted, losses continued to mount, and the government was losing favour with the population.

IRAQ. The Ishtar Gate leads into the Processional Way in ancient Babylon, and is built of bricks so modelled that they form bas-relief figures of bulls and dragons. The surfaces of these were then overlaid with thick coloured enamels.

IRELAND, John (1879-1962). British composer. B. at Bowden, Cheshire, he studied under Stanford at the RCM, returning as prof. of composition (1923-39), when his pupils incl. Britten, Searle and Arnell. Strongly self-critical, he destroyed much early work, but is revealed at his best in the mystic orchestral prelude *The Forgotten Rite* (1915) and piano solo *Sarnia* (1941), both inspired by his love for the Channel Islands where he lived for many years. Himself a brilliant pianist, he also wrote a fine Piano Concerto (1930) and other piano music (incl. London Pieces, 1919, and his Trio No. 3, 1938), as well as chamber music in which the piano takes the leading role. Notable, too, are his choral setting of John Addington Symonds' 'These Things Shall Be' (1937), and song settings, e.g. Masefield's 'Sea Fever'.

IRELAND. One of the British Isles, lying to the west of Great Britain, from which it is separated by the Irish Sea. It is divided into 4 provs.: Ulster, Leinster, Munster, and Connacht; 2 states, Northern Ireland and Rep. of Ireland (*see* table, and under those heads).

The centre of Ireland is a lowland, *c.* 60-120m (200-400ft), but hills are present especially round the coasts, although there are few peaks above 1,000m (3,000ft) high, the highest being Carrantuohill (the inverted reaping hook), 1,041m (3,414ft), in Macgillicuddy's Reeks, co. Kerry. The entire western coastline is an intricate alternation of bays and estuaries. Several of the rivers flow in sluggish courses through the central lowland, and then cut through fiord-like valleys to the sea. The Shannon in particular falls 30m (100ft) in its last 26km (16m) above Limerick and is harnessed for power: *see* SHANNON.

The lowland bogs, which cover parts of central Ireland, are intermingled with fertile limestone country where dairy farming is the chief occupation. The bogs are an important source of fuel, in the form of peat, I. being poorly supplied with coal.

The climate is mild, moist, and changeable. The annual rainfall on the lowlands varies from 76cm (30in) in the E to 203cm (80in) in some W districts, but much higher falls are recorded in the mountains, hence the name 'the emerald isle'.

History. In prehistoric times I. underwent a number of invasions from Europe, the most important of which was that of the Gaels in the 3rd cent. BC. Gaelic I. was divided into kingdoms, nominally subject to an *Ardri* or High King; the chiefs were elected under the tribal or Brehon law, and were usually at war with one another. Christianity was introduced by St Patrick in *c.* AD 432, and during the 5th-6th cents. I. became the home of a high civilization, sending out missionaries to Britain and Europe. From *c.* 800 the Danes began to raid I., and later to colonize, founding Dublin and other coast towns, until they were decisively defeated by Brian Boru at Clontarf in 1014.

Anglo-Norman adventurers invaded I. in 1167, but by the end of the Middle Ages English rule was still confined to the Pale, the territory around Dublin. The Tudors adopted a policy of conquest, confiscation of Irish land, and plantation by English settlers, and further imposed the Reformation and English Law on I. The most important of the plantations was that of Ulster, carried out under James I in 1610. The Irish in 1641 took advantage of the opening struggle in England between king and parliament to begin a revolt which was crushed in 1649 by Cromwell, the estates of all 'rebels' being confiscated. Another revolt in 1689-91 was also defeated, and the RC majority held down by penal laws. The subordination of the Irish parliament to that of England, and of Irish economic interests to English, led to the rise of a Protestant patriot party, which in 1782 forced the British government to remove many commercial restrictions and grant the Irish parliament its independence. This did not satisfy the mass of the people, who in 1798, influenced by French revolutionary ideas, rose in rebellion, but were again defeated; and in 1800 Pitt induced the Irish parliament to vote itself out of existence by the Act of Union, effective 1 Jan. 1801, under which Ireland was given parliamentary representation at Westminster.

The national movement was revived by O'Connell (q.v.), who secured Catholic emancipation in 1829, and raised the demand for repeal of the union. The Young Ireland and Fenian movements, which organized revolts in 1848 and 1867 respectively, adopted a completely separatist policy. The agitation of the Fenians, and later of the Land League (founded 1879), combined with the parliamentary tactics of Parnell (q.v.), drove Gladstone in turn to disestablish the Irish Church, carry 2 Land Acts safeguarding tenants' rights, and introduce 2 unsuccessful Home Rule Bills. Conservative governments sought to conciliate the peasantry by enabling them to buy their holdings. A new Home Rule Bill in 1912 nearly led to civil war between armed nationalist and N Irish Unionist volunteers. Its outbreak was postponed by the F.W.W., but a rebellion took place in Dublin at Easter 1916, and during 1919-21 the Irish Republican Army waged war on the British govt. This was ended by the treaty of 1921, which divided I. into the Irish Free State and N Ireland.

IRELAND, Republic of. A sovereign independent state, occupying the larger part of Ireland.

The country came into existence in 1922 as the Irish Free State, with dominion status in the British Commonwealth. A govt formed by Cosgrave (q.v.) met with a good deal of violent opposition from Irish republicans. De Valera (q.v.) came to office in 1932, and in 1937 introduced a new constitution in which the description Free State was dropped and Eire (Ireland) was declared a sovereign independent state under a president. But the British govt, with the agreement of the other Commonwealth govts, continued to regard Eire as a member of the Commonwealth. Eire was neutral during the S.W.W. When an Irish govt led by J. A. Costello (q.v.) passed legislation which took it, as the Republic of Ireland, outside the Commonwealth in 1949, the British govt passed legislation maintaining for Irish citizens in the UK most of the advantages of British subjects, and a free trade area was estab. with the UK 1966. There is an increasing drift from the land, and growing industrial development by British, US and Continental firms. The chief industries are food processing, brewing and distilling; engineering, vehicle assembly and tyres; mining and electronics, chemicals and tobacco. Tourism is important. The cap. is Dublin, other towns incl. Cork, Limerick, Dun Laoghaire, and Waterford.

There is a pres., normally elected by direct vote for 7 years; a House of Representatives (Dáil Éirann) and Senate (Seanad Éireann), the former elected on a system of proportional representation. The P.M. is known as the Taoiseach; and the chief parties are Fianna Fail and Fine Gael (qq.v.), the former in power 1932–48, 1951–4, 1957–73, 1977–81, and Feb–Dec 1982. Garret Fitzgerald of Fine Gael, PM in coalition with Labour from Dec 1982, promised a review of the constitution to remove obstacles

World Atlas

Legend

Railways	
Canals	
Oil Pipe Lines	
Intermittent Lakes	
Antarctic Base Station	Showa
International Boundaries	
Capital of Country	**Madrid**
Heights in Metres	MT. BLANC 4007
Marsh	
Shipping Routes (in Nautical Miles)	SYDNEY 650

These maps must not be regarded as representing offical recognition of boundaries in dispute or awaiting definition by treaty

63 Fleet Street, London EC4

Contents

THE WORLD

on a Modified Galls Projection

SCALE at 30° Latitude 1:148,500,000

SCALE OF KILOMETRES FOR EACH DEGREE OF LATITUDE

EQUATOR 0 1600 3200 4800 EQUATOR 30° 60° 0 1600 3200 4800 KILOMETRES

APPROXIMATE MILEAGE EQUIVALENTS

KILOMETRES	STATUTE MILES
800	500
1600	1000
3200	2000
4800	3000

ARCTIC OCEAN

NORTH AMERICA

CANADA

UNITED STATES

GREENLAND (DENMARK)

CENTRAL AMERICA

WEST INDIES

SOUTH AMERICA

BRAZIL

ARGENTINA

EUROPE

UNION OF SOVIET SOCIALIST REPUBLICS

ASIA

PEOPLE'S REPUBLIC OF CHINA

INDIA

EAST INDIES

INDONESIA

AFRICA

SAHARA

ATLANTIC OCEAN

PACIFIC OCEAN

INDIAN OCEAN

AUSTRALIA

OCEANIA

POLYNESIA

MELANESIA

MICRONESIA

NEW ZEALAND

GREATER ANTARCTICA

LESSER ANTARCTICA

ANTARCTICA

TROPIC OF CANCER

EQUATOR

TROPIC OF CAPRICORN

ARCTIC CIRCLE

ANTARCTIC CIRCLE

INTERNATIONAL DATE LINE

MONDAY SUNDAY

3
TRADE COMMUNITIES
E.E.C.
E.F.T.A.
0 Kilometres 800
0 Miles 500
SCALE
Kilometres
0 200 400 600
0 100 200 300 400
Miles
© GEOGRAPHIA
ICELAND
Reykjavik
Akureyri
Thorshöfn
Seydisfjördur
Höfn
Vestmannaeyjar
VATNA JÖKULL 2120
Grimsey
Bordeyri
Norwegian Sea
ARCTIC CIRCLE
(DENMARK) FAEROE ISLANDS
Strömö
Thorshavn
Syderø
(U.K.) SHETLAND ISLANDS
ORKNEY ISLANDS
Rockall (U.K.)
HEBRIDES
St.Kilda
Lewis
Cape Wrath
UNITED KINGDOM OF GREAT BRITAIN & NORTHERN IRELAND
BRITISH ISLES
REPUBLIC OF IRELAND
SCOTLAND
ENGLAND
WALES
Glasgow
Edinburgh
Aberdeen
Dundee
Inverness
Wick
Newcastle
Sunderland
Leeds
Hull
Manchester
Liverpool
Birmingham
London
Bristol
Southampton
Plymouth
Dover
Norwich
Harwich
Belfast
Londonderry
Dublin
Cork
Limerick
Waterford
Galway
Sligo
Cobh
English Channel
Channel Is.
ATLANTIC OCEAN
Bay of Biscay
CAPE FINISTERRE
NORTH SEA
DENMARK
Copenhagen
Esbjerg
Århus
Ålborg
Skagerrak
Kattegat
NORWAY
Oslo
Bergen
Stavanger
Kristiansand
Trondheim
Narvik
Tromsø
Bodø
Mo i Rana
Namsos
Ålesund
Kristiansund
Andalsnes
Dombås
JOTUNHEIMEN
Haugesund
Drammen
Halden
LOFOTEN
VESTERÅLEN
SWEDEN
Stockholm
Göthenburg
Malmö
Uppsala
Örebro
Norrköping
Kiruna
Gällivare
Luleå
Umeå
Sundsvall
Östersund
Gävle
Kalmar
Gotland
Öland
Bornholm
FINLAND
Helsinki
Turku
Tampere
Oulu
Kemi
Vaasa
Jakobstad
Lahti
Pori
Joensuu
Kuopio
LAPLAND
Gulf of Bothnia
Gulf of Finland
BALTIC SEA
NETHERLANDS
Amsterdam
The Hague
Rotterdam
BELGIUM
Brussels
Antwerp
Ostend
LUX.
GERMAN FED. REPUBLIC
Bonn
Hamburg
Bremen
Hanover
Essen
Cologne
Frankfurt
Stuttgart
Munich
Kiel
GERMAN DEM. REPUBLIC
Berlin
Rostock
Leipzig
Dresden
POLAND
Warsaw
Gdansk
Szczecin
Poznan
Łódź
Wrocław
Katowice
Kraków
Lublin
Białystok
Bydgoszcz
CZECHOSLOVAKIA
Prague
Brno
Bratislava
Ostrava
Plzen
Košice
AUSTRIA
Vienna
Salzburg
Graz
Linz
HUNGARY
Budapest
Szeged
SWITZ.
Bern
Zurich
Basle
Geneva
LIECH.
FRANCE
Paris
Lyon
Marseille
Bordeaux
Toulouse
Nantes
Rennes
Le Havre
Rouen
Reims
Lille
Calais
Cherbourg
Brest
Strasbourg
Nancy
Dijon
Orleans
Tours
Le Mans
La Rochelle
Limoges
Clermont Ferrand
St.Etienne
Nimes
Grenoble
Nice
Toulon
Perpignan
Biarritz
MONACO
MT BLANC 4807
CORSICA
Ajaccio
Bastia
SPAIN
Madrid
Barcelona
Valencia
Seville
Cordoba
Granada
Malaga
Bilbao
San Sebastian
Santander
Oviedo
La Coruña
Vigo
Burgos
Valladolid
Zaragoza
Tarragona
Toledo
Badajoz
Murcia
Cartagena
Alicante
Almeria
Cadiz
ANDORRA
PYRENEES
BALEARIC ISLANDS (SPAIN)
Majorca
Minorca
Ibiza
Palma
Formentera
PORTUGAL
Lisbon
Oporto
Coimbra
Faro
Cape St. Vincent
Gibraltar (U.K.)
Ceuta (SPAIN)
Tangier
MOROCCO
Rabat
Casablanca
Fès
Oujda
MOYEN ATLAS
ALGERIA
Algiers
Oran
Bejaia
Skikda
Annaba
Constantine
ATLAS SAHARIEN
Melilla (SPAIN)
TUNISIA
Tunis
Bizerte
Sousse
Sfax
GREENWICH West 0 East
ITALY
Rome
Milan
Turin
Genoa
Venice
Verona
Bologna
Florence
Perugia
Naples
Bari
Brindisi
Taranto
Pescara
Foggia
Catanzaro
Reggio
Messina
Palermo
Catania
Syracuse
Trieste
SAN MARINO
APENNINES
VESUVIUS 1277
ETNA 3340
SICILY
SARDINIA
Cagliari
Sassari
Alghero
MALTA
Valletta
Ligurian Sea
Tyrrhenian Sea
Adriatic Sea
Ionian Sea
MEDITERRANEAN SEA
YUGOSLAVIA
Belgrade
Zagreb
Ljubljana
Rijeka
Split
Sarajevo
Dubrovnik
Skopje
Niš
ALBANIA
Tirane
GREECE
Athens
Thessaloniki
Larisa
Patras
Kalamata
Corfu
CRETE
Iraklion
Rhodes
SPORADHES
Aegean Sea
BULGARIA
Sofia
Plovdiv
Varna
Burgas
Ruse
ROMANIA
Bucharest
Timişoara
Arad
Oradea
Braşov
Ploieşti
Galaţi
Iaşi
Constanta
CARPATHIANS
TURKEY
Ankara
Istanbul
Izmir
Bursa
Edirne
Izmit
Zonguldak
Samsun
Sinop
Trabzon
Erzurum
Sivas
Malatya
Adana
Mersin
Antalya
Afyon
Konya
Iskenderun
ANATOLIA
TOROS DAGLARI
MT. ARARAT (BUYUK AGRI) 5165
Lake Van
DARDANELLES
Sea of Marmara
BOSPORUS
CYPRUS
Nicosia
Famagusta
LEBANON
Beirut
SYRIA
Aleppo
Homs
IRAQ
Baghdad
Mosul
Kirkuk
Basra
IRAN
Tehran
Tabriz
Rasht
Qazvin
Hamadan
Dezful
Lake Urmia
BLACK SEA
Sea of Azov
CRIMEA
CASPIAN SEA
Aral Sea
U.S.S.R.
RUSSIAN S.F.S. REPUBLIC
Moscow
Leningrad
Gorki
Kazan
Kuybyshev
Saratov
Volgograd
Astrakhan
Ufa
Orenburg
Magnitogorsk
Orsk
Ural'sk
Vol'sk
Saransk
Penza
Ryazan
Tula
Kaluga
Orel
Kursk
Voronezh
Bryansk
Smolensk
Kalinin
Yaroslavl'
Ivanovo
Vladimir
Rybinsk
Vologda
Novgorod
Pskov
Vyborg
Petrozavodsk
Arkhangelsk
Murmansk
Kandalaksha
Kirovsk
Kem
Onega
Obozerskiy
Vytegra
Kamenka
Pechenga
Kola Peninsula
Kanin Peninsula
White Sea
Lake Ladoga
Lake Onega
Rybinsk Reservoir
Tambov
Michurinsk
Rostov-na-Donu
Krasnodar
Stavropol
Armavir
Novorossiysk
Tuapse
Sochi
Elista
Kizlyar
Makhachkala
Groznyy
CAUCASUS
ELBRUS 5633
ESTONIAN S.S.R.
Tallinn
Tartu
LATVIAN S.S.R.
Riga
Daugavpils
Liepaja
LITHUANIAN S.S.R.
Vilnius
Kaunas
Kaliningrad
R.S.F.S.R.
WHITE RUSSIAN S.S.R.
Minsk
Vitebsk
Mogilev
Gomel
Brest
Pinsk
UKRANIAN S.S.R.
Kiev
Kharkov
Dnepropetrovsk
Donetsk
Voroshilovgrad
Zhitomir
Lvov
Berdichev
Vinnitsa
Chernovtsy
Kovel
Chernigov
Sumy
Poltava
Odessa
Nikolayev
Kherson
Taganrog
Simferopol
Sevastopol
Yalta
MOLDAVIAN S.S.R.
Kishinev
GEORGIAN S.S.R.
Tbilisi
Batumi
Poti
Sukhumi
ARMENIAN S.S.R.
Yerevan
AZERBAIJAN S.S.R.
Baku
Kirovabad
KAZAKH S.S.R.
Gur'yev
Kulsary
Shevchenko
USTURT PLATEAU
Krasnovodsk
Volga
Don
Dnieper
Dniester
Danube
Vistula
Oder
Rhine
Seine
Loire
Rhône
Garonne
Ebro
Tagus
Douro
Guadiana
Guadalquivir
Po
Drava
Sava
Bug
Pripyat
Desna
Khoper
Ural
Emba
Kuma
Aras
Tigris
Euphrates
Dvina
AFRICA
Irish Sea
Donegal Bay
Mizen Head
Lands End
Scilly Isles
Frisian Is.
Sognefjorden
Vestfjorden
Storsjön
Vänern
Vättern
Hiiumaa
Saaremaa
Lake Chudskoye
Hango
Ahvenanmaa
Cape Kanin Nos
Porsangen
Varangerfjord
Vardø
Kirkenes
Kemijärvi
Tornio
Sörøya
Inari
Cape Passero
Fishguard
Holyhead
Cardiff
Carlisle
Ayr
Stoke
Isle of Man
Ben Nevis 1343
NORTH
CZ.
E.
N.
U.K.
LUX.
B.
NETH.
DEN.
PORT.
SPAIN
FRANCE
ITALY
SWITZ.
AUSTRIA
HUN.
YUGOSLAVIA
BULG.
GREECE
TURKEY
NORWAY
SWEDEN
FINLAND
ICELAND
IRELAND
UNITED KINGDOM
GERMANY
POLAND
ROMANIA
U.S.S.R.
Berlin
Warsaw
Moscow
Paris
London
Madrid
Rome
BLACK SEA
CASPIAN SEA
MEDITERRANEAN SEA
NORTH SEA
BALTIC SEA
ATLANTIC OCEAN
ARCTIC CIRCLE
AFRICA
60
50
40
30
20
10
0
60
50
40
30
20
10

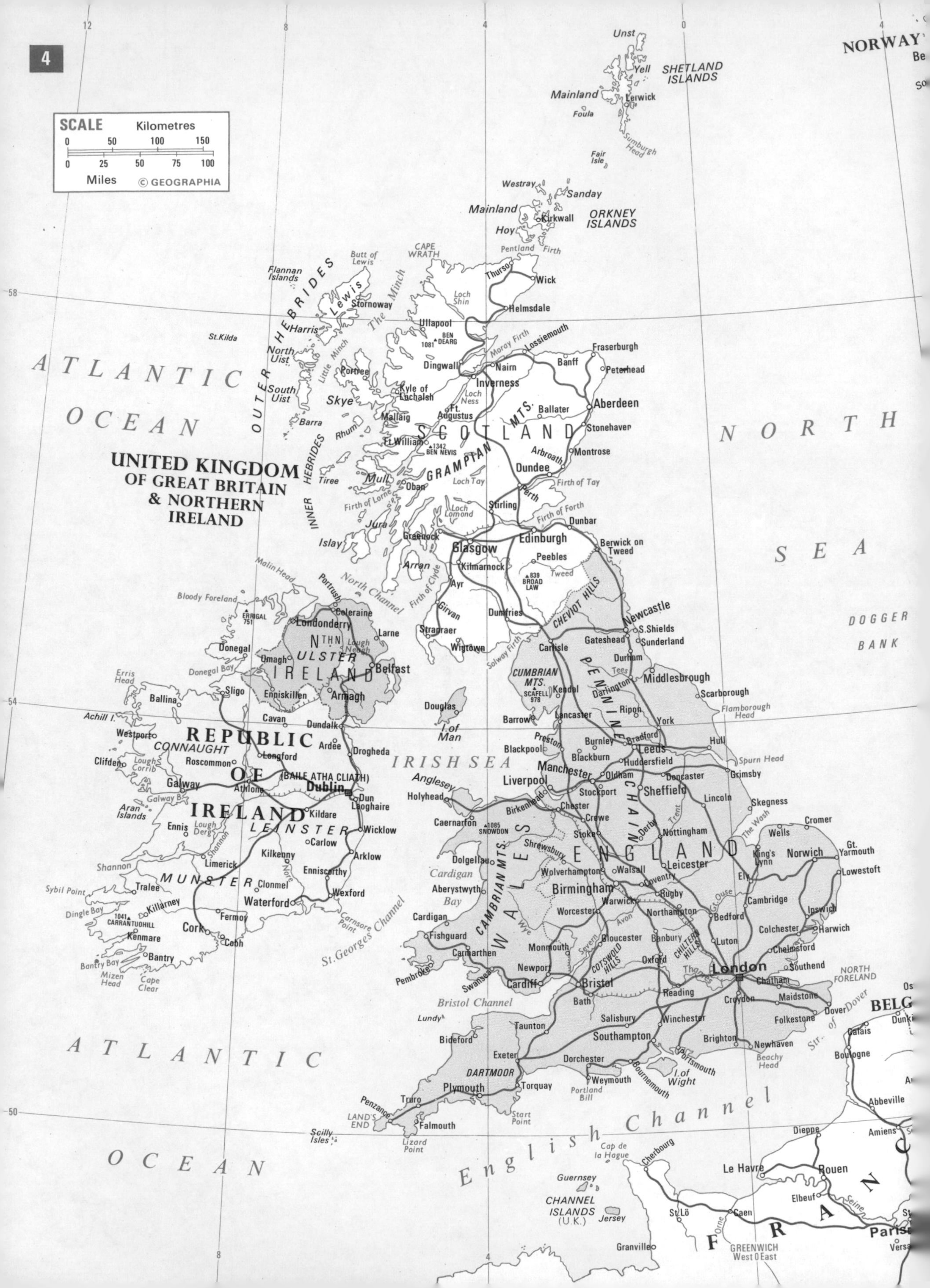

4

UNITED KINGDOM OF GREAT BRITAIN & NORTHERN IRELAND

SCALE Kilometres 0 50 100 150
0 25 50 75 100 Miles
© GEOGRAPHIA

12 8 4 0 4

58 54 50

ATLANTIC OCEAN

NORTH SEA

IRISH SEA

English Channel

NORWAY

Unst
Yell
SHETLAND ISLANDS
Mainland
Lerwick
Foula
Sumburgh Head
Fair Isle
Westray
Sanday
Mainland
Kirkwall
ORKNEY ISLANDS
Hoy
Pentland Firth
Thurso
Wick
CAPE WRATH
Butt of Lewis
Flannan Islands
OUTER HEBRIDES
Lewis
Stornoway
The Minch
Loch Shin
Helmsdale
Harris
Ullapool
BEN DEARG 1081
St. Kilda
North Uist
Little Minch
Moray Firth
Lossiemouth
Fraserburgh
Banff
Peterhead
Dingwall
Nairn
Inverness
Portree
South Uist
Kyle of Lochalsh
Loch Ness
Skye
Ft. Augustus
Ballater
Aberdeen
Mallaig
Barra
Stonehaven
Rhum
SCOTLAND
Ft. William
1342 BEN NEVIS
GRAMPIAN MTS.
Arbroath
Montrose
INNER HEBRIDES
Dundee
Tiree
Mull
Oban
Loch Tay
Firth of Tay
Perth
Firth of Lorne
Loch Lomond
Stirling
Firth of Forth
Dunbar
Jura
Greenock
Edinburgh
Islay
Glasgow
Berwick on Tweed
Peebles
Arran
Kilmarnock
839 BROAD LAW
Tweed
Malin Head
Portrush
North Channel
Firth of Clyde
Ayr
CHEVIOT HILLS
Bloody Foreland
Coleraine
Girvan
Dumfries
Newcastle
ERRIGAL 751
Londonderry
Larne
Stranraer
S. Shields
Gateshead
Sunderland
Donegal
NTHN. IRELAND
Lough Neagh
ULSTER
Wigtown
Carlisle
Solway Firth
Omagh
Belfast
Durham
Donegal Bay
Tees
Erris Head
CUMBRIAN MTS.
Middlesbrough
Sligo
Enniskillen
Armagh
Darlington
Ballina
SCAFELL 978
Kendal
PENNINE CHAIN
Scarborough
Douglas
Ripon
Flamborough Head
Achill I.
Cavan
Dundalk
I. of Man
Barrow
Lancaster
York
Westport
REPUBLIC OF IRELAND
CONNAUGHT
Ardee
Preston
Burnley
Bradford
Hull
Drogheda
Blackpool
Leeds
Clifden
Lough Corrib
Roscommon
Longford
Blackburn
Huddersfield
Spurn Head
(BAILE ATHA CLIATH)
Manchester
Oldham
Doncaster
Grimsby
Anglesey
Liverpool
Galway
Athlone
Dublin
Stockport
Sheffield
Galway B.
Dun Laoghaire
Holyhead
Birkenhead
Lincoln
Aran Islands
Chester
Skegness
Kildare
Crewe
The Wash
Cromer
Ennis
Lough Derg
LEINSTER
Wicklow
Caernarfon
1085 SNOWDON
Trent
Derby
Nottingham
Shannon
Carlow
Stoke
Wells
Gt. Yarmouth
Kilkenny
Shrewsbury
ENGLAND
King's Lynn
Norwich
Shannon
Limerick
Arklow
Dolgellau
Nore
CAMBRIAN MTS.
Wolverhampton
Walsall
Leicester
Lowestoft
MUNSTER
Enniscorthy
Cardigan Bay
Clonmel
Coventry
Ely
Sybil Point
Tralee
Aberystwyth
Birmingham
Rugby
Killarney
Waterford
Wexford
Warwick
Ouse
Cambridge
Dingle Bay
1041 CARRANTUOHILL
Fermoy
Worcester
Avon
Northampton
Bedford
Ipswich
Cardigan
WALES
Wye
Carnsore Point
St. Georges Channel
Kenmare
Cork
Cobh
Fishguard
Severn
Gloucester
Banbury
Luton
Colchester
Harwich
CHILTERN HILLS
Carmarthen
Monmouth
COTSWOLD HILLS
Chelmsford
Bantry
Bantry Bay
Oxford
Thames
London
Southend
Newport
Swansea
Cardiff
Bristol
Chatham
NORTH FORELAND
Pembroke
Mizen Head
Cape Clear
Reading
Bath
Maidstone
Croydon
Bristol Channel
Dover
Str. of Dover
BELG.
Lundy
Salisbury
Winchester
Folkestone
Calais
Taunton
Bideford
Southampton
Brighton
Newhaven
Boulogne
Exeter
Dorchester
Beachy Head
DARTMOOR
Portsmouth
Weymouth
Bournemouth
I. of Wight
Torquay
Plymouth
Portland Bill
Truro
Penzance
Start Point
Abbeville
LAND'S END
Falmouth
Lizard Point
Scilly Isles
Dieppe
Amiens
Cap de la Hague
Cherbourg
Le Havre
Rouen
Guernsey
Elbeuf
Seine
CHANNEL ISLANDS (U.K.)
Jersey
St. Lô
Caen
Orne
FRANCE
Paris
Granville
GREENWICH West 0 East

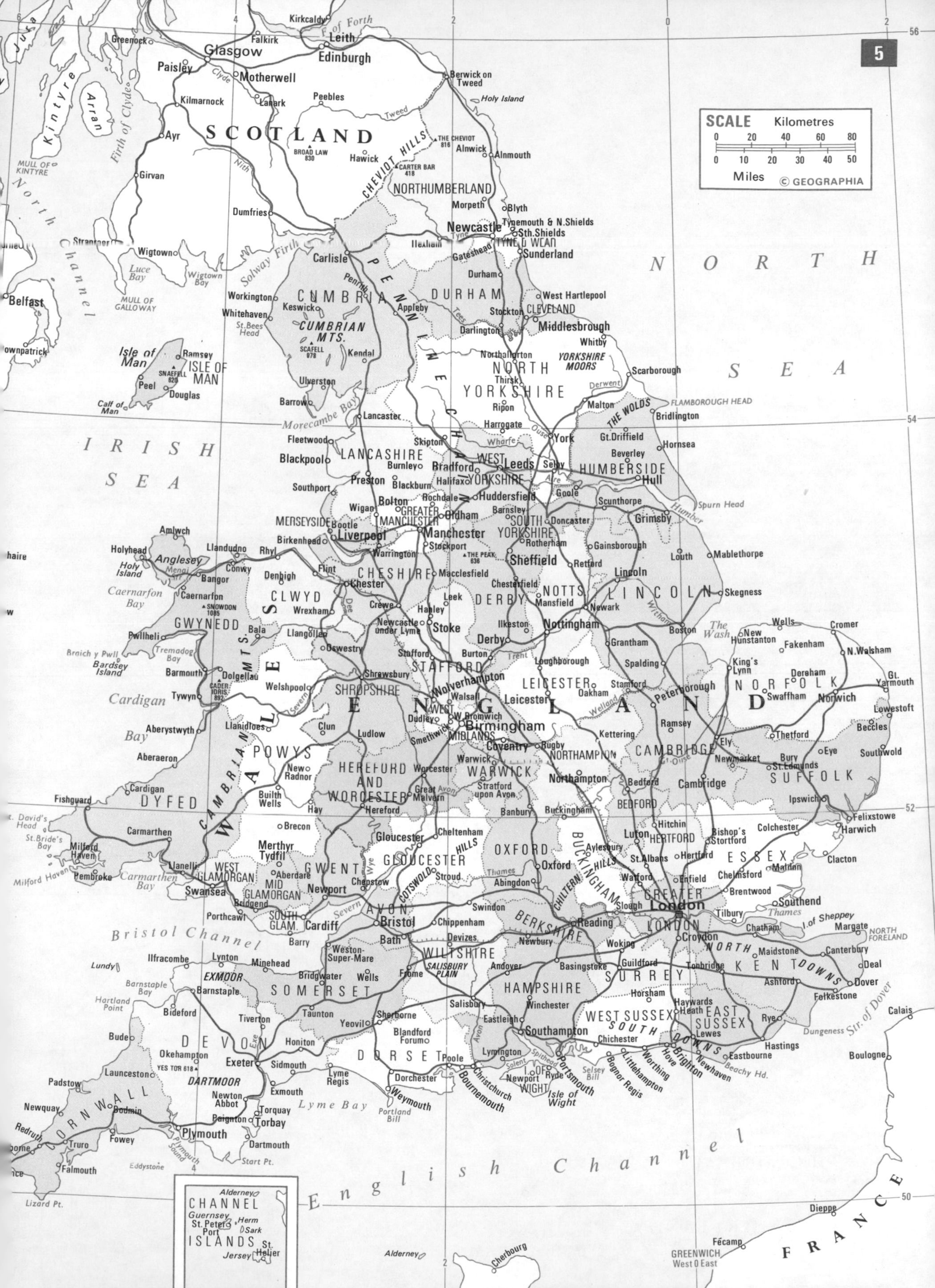
5
SCALE Kilometres
0 20 40 60 80
0 10 20 30 40 50
Miles
© GEOGRAPHIA
SCOTLAND
Glasgow
Edinburgh
Leith
Kirkcaldy
Firth of Forth
Falkirk
Greenock
Paisley
Motherwell
Clyde
Lanark
Kilmarnock
Peebles
Tweed
Berwick on Tweed
Holy Island
Ayr
Arran
Kintyre
Jura
Firth of Clyde
BROAD LAW 830
Hawick
CHEVIOT HILLS
THE CHEVIOT 816
CARTER BAR 418
Alnwick
Alnmouth
MULL OF KINTYRE
Girvan
Nith
NORTHUMBERLAND
Morpeth
Blyth
Dumfries
Tynemouth & N.Shields
Newcastle
Sth.Shields
TYNE & WEAR
Hexham
Tyne
Stranraer
Wigtown
Solway Firth
Carlisle
Gateshead
Sunderland
North Channel
Luce Bay
Wigtown Bay
MULL OF GALLOWAY
Belfast
Workington
CUMBRIA
PENNINE CHAIN
Penrith
DURHAM
Durham
West Hartlepool
Keswick
Appleby
Whitehaven
St.Bees Head
CUMBRIAN MTS.
SCAFELL 978
Tees
Stockton
CLEVELAND
Darlington
Middlesbrough
Whitby
Downpatrick
Isle of Man
Ramsey
SNAEFELL 620
ISLE OF MAN
Peel
Douglas
Calf of Man
Kendal
Northallerton
NORTH YORKSHIRE
YORKSHIRE MOORS
Thirsk
Scarborough
Ulverston
Barrow
Ripon
Derwent
Malton
FLAMBOROUGH HEAD
THE WOLDS
Bridlington
Morecambe Bay
Lancaster
Harrogate
Wharfe
Ouse
York
Gt.Driffield
NORTH SEA
IRISH SEA
Fleetwood
Skipton
Hornsea
Beverley
Blackpool
LANCASHIRE
WEST YORKSHIRE
Leeds
Bradford
Burnley
Selby
HUMBERSIDE
Preston
Blackburn
Halifax
Aire
Hull
Southport
Rochdale
Huddersfield
Goole
Spurn Head
Humber
Wigan
Bolton
Scunthorpe
Grimsby
GREATER MANCHESTER
Oldham
Barnsley
SOUTH YORKSHIRE
Doncaster
MERSEYSIDE
Bootle
Liverpool
Manchester
Amlwch
Birkenhead
Stockport
Rotherham
Gainsborough
Holyhead
Llandudno
Rhyl
Warrington
THE PEAK 636
Anglesey
Holy Island
Menai Str.
Conwy
Flint
CHESHIRE
Macclesfield
Sheffield
Retford
Louth
Mablethorpe
Bangor
Denbigh
Chester
Chesterfield
Lincoln
Caernarfon Bay
Caernarfon
CLWYD
NOTTS
LINCOLN
Skegness
SNOWDON 1085
Wrexham
Crewe
Leek
DERBY
Mansfield
Newark
GWYNEDD
Dee
Hanley
Witham
Pwllheli
Bala
Llangollen
Newcastle under Lyme
Stoke
Ilkeston
Nottingham
Boston
Wells
Cromer
The Wash
New Hunstanton
Fakenham
Tremadog Bay
Oswestry
Derby
Grantham
N.Walsham
Braich y Pwll
Bardsey Island
Stafford
Burton
Trent
Loughborough
Spalding
King's Lynn
Dereham
Barmouth
Dolgellau
CAMBRIAN MTS.
STAFFORD
Shrewsbury
Wolverhampton
LEICESTER
Stamford
NORFOLK
Gt. Yarmouth
CADER IDRIS 892
Welshpool
SHROPSHIRE
Walsall
Leicester
Oakham
Peterborough
Swaffham
Norwich
Cardigan Bay
Tywyn
Severn
WALES
ENGLAND
WEST MIDLANDS
W.Bromwich
Welland
Lowestoft
Dudley
Birmingham
Beccles
Llanidloes
Clun
Smethwick
Kettering
Ramsey
Aberystwyth
Ludlow
Coventry
Rugby
Thetford
Ely
POWYS
Warwick
NORTHAMPTON
CAMBRIDGE
Gt. Ouse
Eye
Southwold
Aberaeron
New Radnor
HEREFORD AND WORCESTER
Worcester
WARWICK
Newmarket
Bury St.Edmunds
SUFFOLK
Northampton
Bedford
Cambridge
Fishguard
Cardigan
Builth Wells
Great Malvern
Avon
Stratford upon Avon
DYFED
Hay
Hereford
Banbury
BEDFORD
Ipswich
Buckingham
Felixstowe
St. David's Head
Harwich
Carmarthen
Brecon
Cheltenham
Hitchin
Bishop's Stortford
Colchester
St.Bride's Bay
Gloucester
Luton
HERTFORD
HILLS
OXFORD
BUCKINGHAM
Aylesbury
Milford Haven
Merthyr Tydfil
GLOUCESTER
Hertford
ESSEX
Clacton
St.Albans
Maldon
Llanelli
WEST GLAMORGAN
Aberdare
GWENT
Wye
Oxford
Chelmsford
Pembroke
Carmarthen Bay
MID GLAMORGAN
COTSWOLD HILLS
Stroud
Thames
Watford
Enfield
Swansea
Chepstow
Abingdon
CHILTERN HILLS
GREATER LONDON
Brentwood
Newport
Bridgend
Southend
Porthcawl
Severn
AVON
Swindon
Slough
London
SOUTH GLAM.
Cardiff
Bristol
Chippenham
BERKSHIRE
Reading
Tilbury
I. of Sheppey
Bristol Channel
Barry
Bath
Devizes
Newbury
Croydon
Chatham
Margate
NORTH FORELAND
Weston-Super-Mare
WILTSHIRE
Woking
NORTH DOWNS
Maidstone
Canterbury
Ilfracombe
Lynton
Minehead
Lundy
Bridgwater
Wells
Frome
SALISBURY PLAIN
Andover
Basingstoke
Guildford
Tonbridge
KENT
Deal
EXMOOR
SOMERSET
HAMPSHIRE
SURREY
Ashford
Dover
Barnstaple Bay
Barnstaple
Horsham
Folkestone
Hartland Point
Bideford
Taunton
Salisbury
Winchester
Haywards Heath
EAST SUSSEX
Str. of Dover
Calais
Tiverton
Sherborne
WEST SUSSEX
Rye
Yeovil
Eastleigh
Bude
DEVON
Exe
Blandford Forum
Southampton
SOUTH DOWNS
Lewes
Dungeness
Honiton
Chichester
Okehampton
DORSET
Poole
Lymington
Solent
Spithead
Portsmouth
Hove
Brighton
Hastings
YES TOR 618
Exeter
Sidmouth
Worthing
Eastbourne
Boulogne
Launceston
Lyme Regis
Dorchester
Christchurch
Bournemouth
I. OF WIGHT
Newport
Ryde
Selsey Bill
Bognor Regis
Littlehampton
Newhaven
Beachy Hd.
DARTMOOR
Padstow
Exmouth
Weymouth
Isle of Wight
Newton Abbot
Torquay
Lyme Bay
Portland Bill
Newquay
CORNWALL
Bodmin
Paignton
Torbay
Redruth
Plymouth
Truro
Fowey
Plymouth Sound
Dartmouth
Start Pt.
Falmouth
Eddystone
English Channel
Lizard Pt.
CHANNEL ISLANDS
Alderney
Guernsey
Herm
Sark
St. Peter Port
Jersey
St. Helier
Dieppe
FRANCE
Fécamp
Cherbourg
GREENWICH
West 0 East
56
54
52
50
6
4
2
0
2

SCALE Kilometres
0 20 40 60
0 10 20 30 40
Miles © GEOGRAPHIA
Fair Isle
North Ronaldsay
Westray
Sanday
ORKNEY ISLANDS
Rousay
Eday
Stronsay
Mainland
Shapinsay
Stromness
Kirkwall
Scapa Flow
Hoy
South Ronaldsay
Pentland Firth
Dunnet Head
Dunnet Bay
DUNCANSBY HEAD
John O'Groats Ho.
Thurso
Wick
Ness Head
Lybster
705 MORVEN
Ord of Caithness
Helmsdale
Brora
Golspie
Dornoch
Dornoch Firth
Tarbat Ness
Tain
Rona
Sula Sgeir
Sule Skerry
Stack Skerry
SHETLAND ISLANDS
Herma Ness
Point of Fethaland
Yell Sound
Yell
St. Magnus Bay
Papa Stour
Walls
Lerwick
Foula
Mousa
Sumburgh Hd
SAME SCALE AS THE MAIN MAP
CAPE WRATH
Kyle of Durness
L. Eriboll
Kyle of Tongue
Strathy Pt.
Durness
Tongue
Naver
BEN HOPE 927
L. Naver
L. Laxford
Scourie
Eddrachillis Bay
Point of Stoer
Lochinver
Enard Bay
BEN MORE 998
Loch Shin
Rimsdale
Helmsdale
Brora
Lairg
Oykel
Bonar Bridge
Carron
Ullapool
L. Broom
Gruinard Bay
Loch Ewe
Gairloch
Loch Gairloch
Loch Maree
B. DEARG 1081
B. WYVIS 1046
Cromarty
Cromarty Firth
Moray Firth
L. Torridon
L. Fannich
Dingwall
Fortrose
Torridon
HIGHLAND
Beauly Firth
Beauly
CALEDONIAN CANAL
Inverness
Nairn
Forres
Elgin
Lossiemouth
Buckie
Cullen
Banff
Macduff
Troup Head
Kinnairds Head
Fraserburgh
Rattray Head
Peterhead
BUCHAN NESS
Cruden Bay
Fochabers
Keith
Rothes
Deveron
Turriff
Huntly
Dufftown
Ythan
Ellon
STRATH SPEY
Grantown
GRAMPIAN
Inverurie
Tomintoul
Alford
Aberdeen
Nigg Bay
Don
Dee
Aboyne
Ballater
Balmoral
Braemar
Banchory
Stonehaven
B. MACDUI 1311
CAIRN TOUL 1293
LOCHNAGAR 1154
North Esk
Inverbervie
Laurencekirk
STRATHMORE
Brechin
Montrose
South Esk
Forfar
Arbroath
Carnoustie
Bell Rock
SIDLAW HILLS
Dundee
Broughty Ferry
Tayport
St. Andrews
Fife Ness
Anstruther
Isle of May
Elie
Firth of Forth
Bass Rock
North Berwick
Dunbar
ST. ABBS HEAD
Eyemouth
Berwick on Tweed
Tweedmouth
Holy Island
FARNE ISLANDS
BUTT OF LEWIS
FLANNAN ISLANDS
OUTER HEBRIDES
WESTERN ISLES
LEWIS
L. Roag
Stornoway
Broad Bay
Eye Pen.
L. Erisort
Scarp
West L. Tarbert
HARRIS
SHIANT ISLANDS
Seaforth
East L. Tarbert
Sound of Harris
Pabbay
The Minch
Little Minch
MONACH ISLANDS
North Uist
Benbecula
South Uist
620 BEN MHOR
L. Boisdale
Eriskay
Barra
Vatersay
Sandray
Mingulay
Barra Head
Snizort
THE STORR 719
Portree
Raasay
Inner Sound
Applecross
L. Bracadale
SKYE
CUILLIN HILLS
Stromeferry
Kyle of Lochalsh
MAM SODHAIL 1178
Farrar
Affric
B. ATTOW 1032
Loch Ness
GLEN MOR
Fort Augustus
MONADHLIATH MTS.
Findhorn
Spey
Kingussie
L. Hourn
Sound of Sleat
Cuillin Sound
Canna
Rhum
GLEN GARRY
Loch Nevis
L. Quoich
Mallaig
Loch Arkaig
L. Lochy
Arisaig
Loch Morar
Eigg
Muck
Sound of Arisaig
CALEDONIAN CANAL
Spean
Fort William
L. Eil
L. Shiel
BEN NEVIS 1342
B. ALDER 1148
L. Laggan
L. Ericht
GRAMPIAN MOUNTAINS
GLEN GARRY
Blair Atholl
TAYSIDE
Pitlochry
Rannoch
Tummel
L. Rannoch
Ardnamurchan Point
L. Sunart
L. Leven
Res.
GLEN COE
Loch Linnhe
Coll
Tobermory
SCOTLAND
Sound of Mull
Ballachulish
RANNOCH MOOR
B. LAWERS 1214
Aberfeldy
Tay
Dunkeld
Blairgowrie
Tiree
Mull
B. MORE 966
Ulva
Staffa
L. Scridain
Iona
Skerryvore Lighthouse
Loch Etive
B. CRUACHAN 1124
Killin
L. Tay
Almond
Oban
Awe
Orchy
B. MORE 1174
L. Earn
Crieff
Perth
Comrie
Earn
Firth of Tay
Cupar
Eden
FIFE
Firth of Lorn
Loch Awe
THE TROSSACHS
L. Katrine
Callander
OCHIL HILLS
Kinross
Leven
Inveraray
Loch Fyne
B. LOMOND 974
Dunblane
Teith
Forth
Scarba
Loch Long
Loch Lomond
Stirling
Alloa
Cowdenbeath
Kirkcaldy
Colonsay
Oronsay
Lochgilphead
Helensburgh
CENTRAL
Dunfermline
Inverkeithing
Jura
Sound of Jura
Ardrishaig
Grangemouth
Linlithgow
Leith
Haddington
Dunoon
Dumbarton
Falkirk
Edinburgh
Musselburgh
Tarbert
Greenock
Renfrew
Coatbridge
Airdrie
LOTHIAN
LAMMERMUIR HILLS
Bowmore
Islay
Rothesay
Bute
Largs
Paisley
Glasgow
Motherwell
PENTLAND HILLS
MOORFOOT HILLS
Duns
STRATHCLYDE
Hamilton
Lauder
Rhinns Point
Gigha
Dalry
Carstairs
Laggan Bay
Port Ellen
Mull of Oa
KINTYRE
Kilbrannan Sd.
Ardrossan
Irvine
Lanark
Peebles
Tweed
Galashiels
Coldstream
Brodick
Arran
Kilmarnock
BORDERS
Kelso
Wooler
Troon
Biggar
Clyde
North Channel
Prestwick
BROAD LAW 839
Selkirk
Teviot
Jedburgh
THE CHEVIOT 816
Inishtrahull
Ayr
Campbeltown
Cumnock
Leadhills
HART FELL 808
Hawick
CHEVIOT HILLS
Alnmouth
Alnwick
Coquet I.
MALIN HEAD
Glengad Head
Firth of Clyde
Maybole
Sanquhar
Moffat
CARTER BAR 418
Aln
Rothbury
Coquet
L. Swilly
Carndonagh
GIANTS CAUSEWAY
Rathlin Island
Sanda
Mull of Kintyre
Ailsa Craig
CAIRNSMORE 796
Nith
Thornhill
Rede
Esk
NORTHUMBERLAND
SL. SNAGHT 615
Moville
Portrush
Ballycastle
Fair Head
Girvan
L. Doon
Annan
Langholm
Morpeth
Blyth
Buncrana
Inch
L. Foyle
Coleraine
ANTRIM MTS.
Cushendall
Stinchar
MERRICK 843
RHINNS OF KELLS
DUMFRIES AND GALLOWAY
Lockerbie
Liddel
N. Tyne
Bellingham
Ramelton
Limavady
Ballymoney
Bush
TROSTAN 554
Garron Point
Ballantrae
L. Ryan
New Galloway
Dee
Dumfries
Gretna Green
Newcastle upon Tyne
Londonderry
Foyle
Kilrea
Glenarm
Newton Stewart
Cree
Castle Douglas
Annan
Longtown
Haltwhistle
S. Tyne
Hexham
Tyne
Gateshead
Letterkenny
LONDONDERRY
Ballymena
Stranraer
Wigtown
Kirkcudbright
Carlisle
ENGLAND
Lifford
Strabane
SPERRIN MTS.
Maghera
Bann
Larne
Portpatrick
Wigtown Bay
Solway Firth
Eden
Alston
Durham
Castlederg
Newtown-stewart
Magherafelt
ANTRIM
I. Magee
Luce Bay
Wigton
CROSS FELL 893
DURHAM
Antrim
Carrickfergus
Belfast L.
Whithorn
CUMBRIA
Bishop Auckland
NORTHERN IRELAND
Bangor
Maryport
Derwent
Tees
Omagh
TYRONE
Cookstown
Belfast
Donaghadee
Burrow Head
SKIDDAW 931
Penrith
Barnard Castle
Darlington
Fintona
Dungannon
Neagh
Lurgan
Lisburn
Newtownards
MULL OF GALLOWAY
Workington
Keswick
Bassenthwaite
Appleby
Strangford L.
WEST 5 OF GREENWICH
St. Bees Head
Whitehaven
Ullswater
7
5
3
1
59
57
55
60

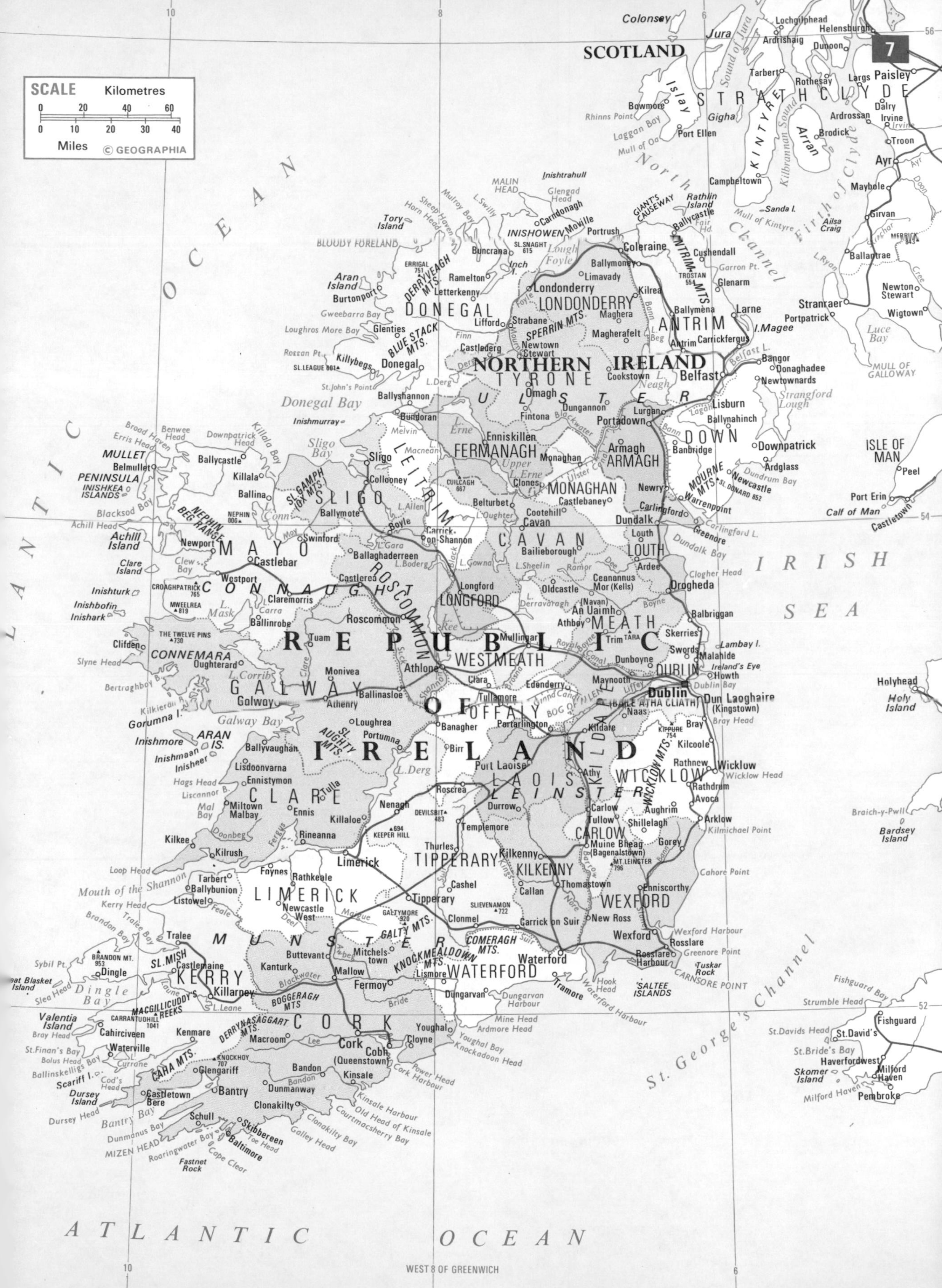

7
SCALE
Kilometres
0 20 40 60
0 10 20 30 40
Miles
© GEOGRAPHIA
SCOTLAND
Colonsay
Jura
Sound of Jura
Lochgilphead
Ardrishaig
Helensburgh
Dunoon
Tarbert
Rothesay
Largs
Paisley
STRATHCLYDE
Islay
Bowmore
Rhinns Point
Laggan Bay
Mull of Oa
Port Ellen
Gigha
KINTYRE
Kilbrannan Sound
Arran
Brodick
Ardrossan
Dalry
Irvine
Troon
Ayr
Doon
Firth of Clyde
Campbeltown
Maybole
North Channel
Sanda I.
Mull of Kintyre
Ailsa Craig
Girvan
MERRICK 843
Ballantrae
Newton Stewart
Stranraer
Wigtown
Portpatrick
Luce Bay
MULL OF GALLOWAY
ATLANTIC OCEAN
Inishtrahull
MALIN HEAD
Glengad Head
Tory Island
Sheep Haven
Horn Head
Mulroy Bay
L. Swilly
Carndonagh
INISHOWEN
Moville
SL. SNAGHT 615
Lough Foyle
Portrush
GIANT'S CAUSEWAY
Rathlin Island
Ballycastle
Fair Hd.
BLOODY FORELAND
Buncrana
Inch I.
Coleraine
Ballymoney
Limavady
ANTRIM MTS.
Cushendall
Garron Pt.
TROSTAN 554
Glenarm
ERRIGAL 751
DERRYVEAGH MTS.
Ramelton
Letterkenny
Aran Island
Burtonport
Londonderry
LONDONDERRY
Kilrea
Ballymena
Larne
I. Magee
Gweebarra Bay
DONEGAL
Lifford
Strabane
SPERRIN MTS.
Maghera
ANTRIM
Carrickfergus
Loughros More Bay
Glenties
BLUE STACK MTS.
Finn
Magherafelt
Antrim
Belfast L.
Bangor
Donaghadee
Newtownards
Rossan Pt.
Killybegs
SL. LEAGUE 601
Donegal
Castlederg
Newtown Stewart
NORTHERN IRELAND
TYRONE
Cookstown
L. Neagh
Belfast
St. John's Point
L. Derg
Omagh
ULSTER
Dungannon
Lisburn
Strangford Lough
Donegal Bay
Ballyshannon
Fintona
Portadown
Lurgan
Ballynahinch
Inishmurray
Bundoran
L. Erne
Blackwater
Bann
DOWN
Downpatrick
ISLE OF MAN
Broad Haven
Benwee Head
Erris Head
Downpatrick Head
Killala Bay
Sligo Bay
Melvin
Enniskillen
FERMANAGH
Armagh
ARMAGH
Banbridge
Peel
MULLET PENINSULA
Belmullet
Ballycastle
Killala
Sligo
Macnean
LEITRIM
Monaghan
Upper L. Erne
Ulster Canal
MOURNE MTS.
Newcastle
Dundrum Bay
Ardglass
INISHKEA ISLANDS
Ballina
SL. GAMPH (OX MTS.)
Collooney
CUILCAGH 667
Clones
MONAGHAN
Newry
SL. DONARD 852
Warrenpoint
SLIGO
Castlebaney
Carlingford
Port Erin
Calf of Man
Castletown
Blacksod Bay
NEPHIN BEG RANGE
NEPHIN 806
Conn
Ballymote
L. Allen
Belturbet
L. Oughter
Cootehill
Cavan
Dundalk
Greenore
Carlingford L.
Achill Head
Achill Island
Newport
MAYO
Moy
Swinford
Boyle
Carrick-on-Shannon
L. Gara
CAVAN
Bailieborough
Louth
LOUTH
Dundalk Bay
IRISH SEA
Clare Island
Clew Bay
Castlebar
Ballaghaderreen
L. Boderg
L. Gownal
L. Sheelin
L. Ramor
Ardee
Westport
CROAGHPATRICK 765
CONNAUGHT
Castlerea
ROSCOMMON
Longford
Ceanannus Mor (Kells)
Clogher Head
Drogheda
Inishturk
Claremorris
LONGFORD
Oldcastle
L. Derravaragh
(Navan) An Uaimh
Boyne
Inishbofin
Inishark
MWEELREA 819
L. Mask
Carra
Ballinrobe
Roscommon
L. Ree
Athboy
MEATH
Balbriggan
THE TWELVE PINS 730
REPUBLIC OF IRELAND
Tuam
Mullingar
Trim
TARA
Skerries
Clifden
CONNEMARA
Oughterard
Suck
Royal Canal
Swords
Lambay I.
Malahide
Slyne Head
Monivea
Athlone
WESTMEATH
Dunboyne
DUBLIN
Ireland's Eye
Howth
L. Corrib
Shannon
Clara
Maynooth
Dublin
Dublin Bay
Holyhead
Bertraghboy B.
GALWAY
Ballinasloe
Tullamore
Edenderry
Grand Canal
Liffey
(BAILE ATHA CLIATH)
Dun Laoghaire (Kingstown)
Holy Island
Kilkieran B.
Galway
Athenry
OFFALY
BOG OF ALLEN
Naas
Gorumna I.
Galway Bay
Loughrea
SL. AUGHTY MTS.
Portumna
Banagher
Portarlington
Kildare
KILDARE
KIPPURE 754
Bray
Bray Head
Inishmore
ARAN IS.
Ballyvaughan
Birr
Kilcoole
Inishmaan
Inisheer
Lisdoonvarna
L. Derg
Port Laoise
LAOIS
Athy
WICKLOW MTS.
Rathnew
Wicklow
WICKLOW
Wicklow Head
Hags Head
Ennistymon
Tulla
Roscrea
LEINSTER
Rathdrum
Avoca
Liscannor B.
CLARE
Durrow
Carlow
Aughrim
Mal Bay
Miltown Malbay
Ennis
Killaloe
Nenagh
DEVILSBIT 483
Tullow
Shillelagh
Arklow
Kilmichael Point
Braich-y-Pwll
Doonbeg
Fergus
Rineanna
694 KEEPER HILL
Templemore
CARLOW
Bardsey Island
Kilkee
Kilrush
Thurles
Muine Bheag (Bagenalstown)
Gorey
Limerick
TIPPERARY
Kilkenny
MT. LEINSTER 796
Loop Head
Foynes
Rathkeale
KILKENNY
Barrow
Slaney
Cahore Point
Mouth of the Shannon
Tarbert
Ballybunion
LIMERICK
Cashel
Callan
Thomastown
Enniscorthy
Listowel
Newcastle West
Tipperary
Nore
WEXFORD
Kerry Head
Feale
Deel
Maigue
GALTYMORE 920
SLIEVENAMON 722
Clonmel
Carrick on Suir
New Ross
Brandon Bay
Tralee Bay
GALTY MTS.
Wexford Harbour
Tralee
MUNSTER
Suir
Wexford
Rosslare
BRANDON MT. 953
Sybil Pt.
SL. MISH
Castlemaine
Buttevant
Awbeg
Mitchelstown
COMERAGH MTS.
KNOCKMEALDOWN MTS.
Waterford
Rosslare Harbour
Greenore Point
Tuskar Rock
Dingle
KERRY
Kanturk
Blackwater
Mallow
Lismore
WATERFORD
CARNSORE POINT
Great Blasket Island
Slea Head
Dingle Bay
Laune
Killarney
L. Leane
Fermoy
Bride
Dungarvan
Dungarvan Harbour
Tramore
Hook Head
Waterford Harbour
SALTEE ISLANDS
St. George's Channel
Fishguard Bay
Strumble Head
MACGILLICUDDY'S REEKS
BOGGERAGH MTS
Valentia Island
CARRANTUOHILL 1041
CORK
Mine Head
Fishguard
Bray Head
Cahirciveen
Kenmare
DERRYNASAGGART MTS.
Macroom
Youghal
Ardmore Head
St. Davids Head
St. David's
St. Finan's Bay
Waterville
Lee
Cork
Cloyne
Youghal Bay
Knockadoon Head
St. Bride's Bay
Bolus Head
Currane
CAHA MTS.
KNOCKHOY 707
Cobh (Queenstown)
Haverfordwest
Ballinskelligs Bay
Glengariff
Bandon
Power Head
Cork Harbour
Skomer Island
Milford Haven
Scariff I.
Cod's Head
Dunmanway
Kinsale
Dursey Island
Castletown Bere
Bantry
Milford Haven
Pembroke
Clonakilty
Kinsale Harbour
Dursey Head
Bantry Bay
Old Head of Kinsale
Schull
Skibbereen
Clonakilty Bay
Courtmacsherry Bay
Dunmanus Bay
Galley Head
MIZEN HEAD
Roaringwater Bay
Toe Head
Baltimore
Cape Clear
Fastnet Rock
ATLANTIC OCEAN
WEST 8 OF GREENWICH
10
8
6
56
54
52

8
Iceland
SAME SCALE AS THE MAIN MAP
WEST 16 OF GREENWICH
Greenland Sea
ARCTIC CIRCLE
Grimsey
ICELAND
Hesteyri
Isafjördur
DRANGA JÖKULL
GLAMA 920
Hólmavík
Húna Flói
Skaga Fjörd
Eyja Fd.
Axar Fd.
Siglufjördur
Húsavík
Thorshöfn
Bakka Flói
Vopna Fjord
Vopnafjördur
Akureyri
Bordeyri
Breida Fjord
Ólafsvík
Snoksdalur
Bru
Seydisfjördur
SNAEFELLS JÖKULL
LANG JÖKULL
HOFS JÖKULL
1460 TROLLADYNGJA
ARNARFELLS JÖKULL
SNAEFELL 1833
VATNA JÖKULL
ORAEFA JÖKULL 2120
Djúpivogur
Faxa Flói
Akranes
Reykjavík
Thingvalla Vatn
Höfn
Keflavík
HEKLA 1492
Oddi
Fagurhólsmýri
Reykja Nes
Eyrarbakki
Vík
Langholt
Vestmannaeyjar
Surtsey
ATLANTIC OCEAN
SCALE
Kilometres
0 50 100 150 200 250
0 50 100 150
Miles
© GEOGRAPHIA
Barents Sea
NORWEGIAN SEA
NORTH SEA
Skagerrak
Kattegat
Gulf of Bothnia
BALTIC SEA
Gulf of Finland
Gulf of Riga
NORWAY
SWEDEN
FINLAND
LAPLAND
DENMARK
ESTONIAN S.S.R.
LATVIAN S.S.R.
LITHUANIAN S.S.R.
U.S.S.R.
R.S.F.S.R.
POLAND
G.D.R.
EAST 16 OF GREENWICH
(North Cape) NORDKAPP
Nordkinn Halvoya
Magerøya
Hammerfest
Söröya
Vardö
Varanger Halvoya
Vadsö
Kirkenes
Pechenga
Rybachi Poluostrov
Tana
Alta
Ringvassöy
Kvalöy
Tromsö
Senja
Andöy
VESTERÅLEN
Langöy
Harstad
Hinnöy
Svolvaer
LOFOTEN
Narvik
Vestfjorden
FROSTISEN 1745
Torneträsk
Karesuando
Kiruna
2117 KEBNEKAISE
SAREKTJAKKO 2090
1913 SULITJELMA
Bodö
Saltfjord
Saltdal
Gällivare
Porjus
Muonio
Kolari
Sodankylä
Inari
Ivalo
Murmansk
Kola
Monchegorsk
Lake Imandra
Kandalaksha
Kuolayarvi
Kemijärvi
Rovaniemi
Tärendö
SVARTISEN 1599
Mo i Rana
Jokkmokk
Övertorneå
Haparanda
Tornio
Kestenga
Kuusamo
Kalevala
Mosjöen
Tjötta
Vega
Arjeplog
Arvidsjaur
Boden
Luleå
Piteå
Älvsby
Tärna
Sorsele
Brönnöysund
BÖRGEFJELLET
Vikna
Foldafjorden
Storuman
Ii
Oulu
Suomussalmi
Raahe
Kalajoki
Kajaani
Namsos
Grong
Vilhelmina
Lycksele
Skellefteå
Hällnäs
Ylivieska
Nurmes
Iisalmi
Lieksa
Pielinen
Frøya
Hitra
Smöla
Kristiansund
Trondheim
Steinkjer
Levanger
Hoting
Strömsund
Kallsjön
Vännäs
Umeå
Kokkola
Jakobstad
Happäjarvi
Molde
TROLL-HEIMEN
Stören
Östersund
Storsjön
Örnsköldsvik
Sollefteå
Vaasa
Seinäjoki
Kuopio
Ålesund
Åndalsnes
SNÖHETTA 2288
Röros
Bräcke
Ange
Härnösand
Sundsvall
Kaskö (Kaskinen)
Jyväskylä
Varkaus
Savonlinna
Dombås
Alvdal
Hede
Kristinestad (Kristiinankaupunki)
Parkano
Florö
Nordfjorden
JOSTEDALSBREEN
GALDHÖPIGGEN 2469
2470 GLITTERTIND
JOTUNHEIMEN
Femund
Sveg
Hudiksvall
Mikkeli
Tampere
Särna
Ljusdal
Pori
Heinola
Lahti
Sognefjorden
Fagernes
Lillehammer
Hamar
Älvdalen
Bollnäs
Söderhamn
Rauma
Toijala
Kouvola
Bergen
Voss
Gjövik
Elverum
Mora
Siljan
Uusikaupunki
Hyvinkää
Kotka
Vyborg
Björnefjorden
Odda
HARDANGER VIDDA
Hönefoss
Falun
Gävle
Turku
Salo
Helsinki
Borlänge
Östhammar
Mariehamn
Porkkala
Haugesund
Oslo
Kongsvinger
Ludvika
Avesta
Uppsala
AHVENANMAA (FINLAND)
Hango (Hanko)
Tallinn
Kunda
Narva
Leningrad
Drammen
Sand
TELEMARK
Ski
Moss
Arvika
Västerås
Mälaren
Haapsalu
Tapa
Rakvere
Gdov
Horten
Fredrikstad
Karlstad
Örebro
Eskilstuna
Stockholm
Hiiumaa
Lake Chudskoye
Boknafjorden
Stavanger
Skien
Larvik
Halden
Kristine-hamn
Hjalmaren
Södertälje
Kragerö
Oslofjorden
Vänern
Nyköping
Pärnu
Tartu
Egersund
Grimstad
Arendal
Mellerud
Motala
Gotska Sandön
Viljandi
Flekkefjord
Kristiansand
Mandal
Vänersborg
Skövde
Norrköping
Saaremaa
Valga
Trollhättan
Mjölby
Linköping
Vättern
Fårö
Alnazi
Grenen
Skagen
Gothenburg
Borås
Jönköping
Västervik
Visby
Gotland
Mazirbe
Cesis
Madona
Hjørring
Frederikshavn
Nässjö
Oskarshamn
Ventspils
Kuldiga
Tukums
Riga
Gauja
Thisted
Ålborg
Læsø
Bolmen
Emån
Lemvig
Viborg
Anholt
Växjö
Borgholm
Aizpute
Jelgava
Krustpils
Rezekne
Holstebro
Randers
Halmstad
Asnen
Kalmar
Öland
Liepaja
Herning
Silkeborg
Århus
Helsingborg
Kristianstad
Karlskrona
Karlshamn
Šiauliai
Panevežis
Fredericia
Copenhagen
Lund
Hanö Bay
Klaipeda
Esbjerg
Ribe
Odense
Fyn
Sjaelland
Store Baelt
Malmö
Ystad
Kursky Zaliv
Taurage
Ukmerge
Glubokoye
Tønder
Åbenrå
Naestved
Mon
Rönne
Bornholm
Bornholmsgattet
Sovetsk
Neman
Kaunas
NORTH FRISIAN ISLANDS
Flensburg
Lolland
Nykøbing
Kaliningrad
Vilnius
Heligoland
Schleswig
Kiel
Kieler Bay
Sassnitz
Rugen
Gulf of Gdańsk
Stupsk
Gdańsk
Kapsukas
Cuxhaven
KIEL CANAL
Lübecker Bay
Swinoujscie
Koszalin
Tczew
Elbląg
Chernyakhovsk
Ełk
Lida
FRISIAN ISLANDS
Lübeck
Rostock
Kołobrzeg
Grodno
Hamburg

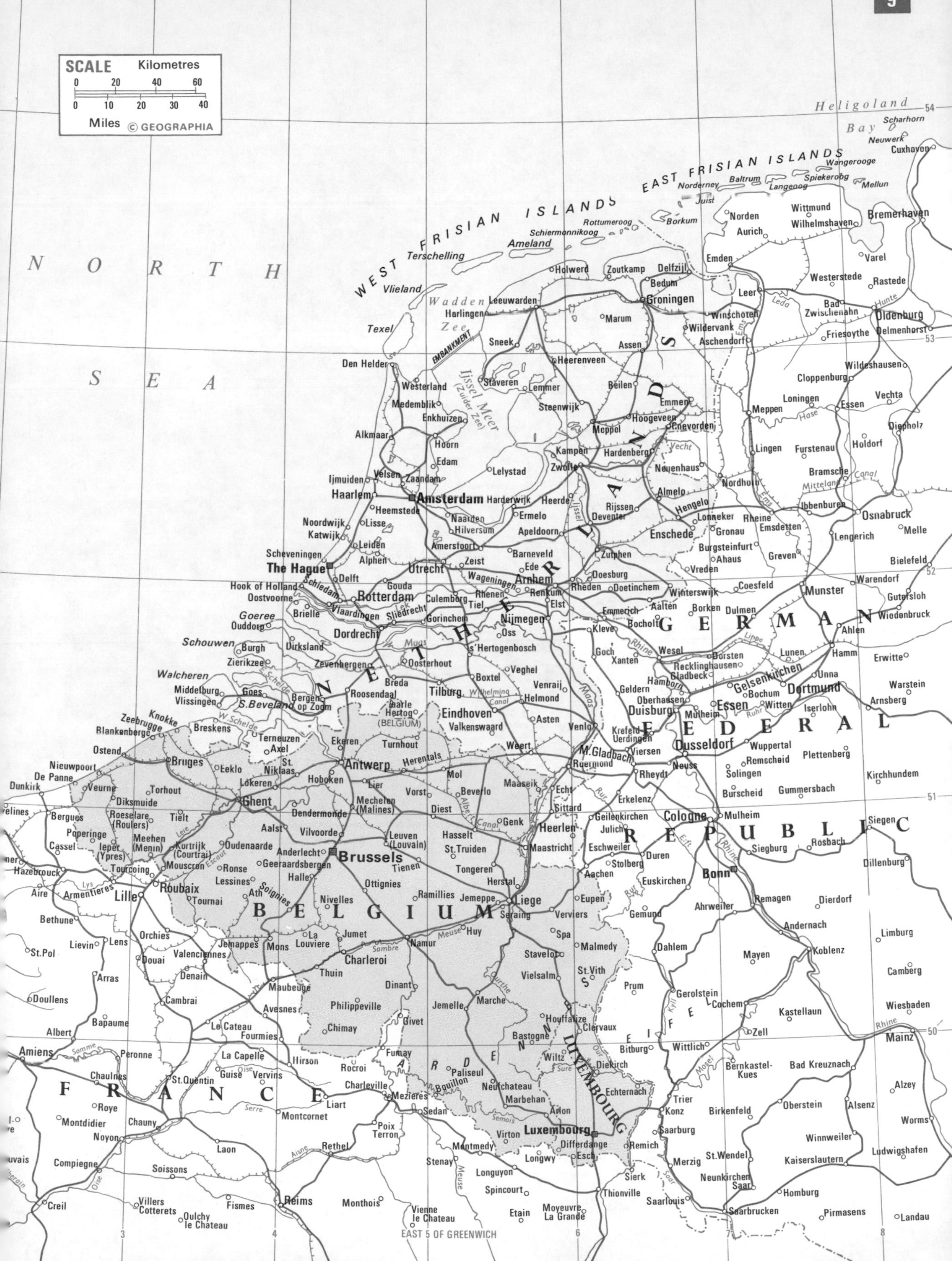
SCALE Kilometres
0 20 40 60
0 10 20 30 40
Miles © GEOGRAPHIA
NORTH SEA
Heligoland Bay
Scharhorn
Neuwerk
Cuxhaven
EAST FRISIAN ISLANDS
Wangerooge
Spiekeroog
Mellun
Norderney
Baltrum
Langeoog
Juist
Borkum
WEST FRISIAN ISLANDS
Rottumeroog
Schiermonnikoog
Ameland
Terschelling
Vlieland
Texel
Wadden Zee
EMBANKMENT
Ijssel Meer (Zuider Zee)
Norden
Aurich
Wittmund
Wilhelmshaven
Bremerhaven
Emden
Varel
Westerstede
Rastede
Leer
Leda
Hunte
Bad Zwischenahn
Oldenburg
Delmenhorst
Friesoythe
Holwerd
Zoutkamp
Delfzijl
Bedum
Groningen
Leeuwarden
Harlingen
Marum
Winschoten
Wildervank
Ems
Aschendorf
Sneek
Assen
Heerenveen
Den Helder
Westerland
Staveren
Lemmer
Beilen
Medemblik
Enkhuizen
Steenwijk
Emmen
Meppen
Loningen
Essen
Vechta
Wildeshausen
Cloppenburg
Diepholz
Hase
Hoogeveen
Coevorden
Meppel
Alkmaar
Hoorn
Edam
Kampen
Hardenberg
Vecht
Zwolle
Neuenhaus
Lingen
Fürstenau
Holdorf
Bramsche
Mittelland Canal
Lelystad
Ijmuiden
Velsen
Zaandam
Haarlem
Amsterdam
Harderwijk
Heerde
Nordhorn
Almelo
Hengelo
Ibbenburen
Osnabruck
Melle
Heemstede
Naarden
Hilversum
Ermelo
Rijssen
Deventer
Ijssel
Lonneker
Rheine
Emsdetten
Noordwijk
Katwijk
Lisse
Leiden
Apeldoorn
Enschede
Gronau
Lengerich
Scheveningen
The Hague
Alphen
Amersfoort
Barneveld
Zutphen
Burgsteinfurt
Ahaus
Greven
Bielefeld
Utrecht
Zeist
Ede
Vreden
Delft
Gouda
Wageningen
Arnhem
Doesburg
Hook of Holland
Schiedam
Oostvoorne
Rotterdam
Culemborg
Rhenen
Renkum
Rheden
Doetinchem
Winterswijk
Coesfeld
Munster
Warendorf
Gutersloh
Vlaardingen
Brielle
Lek
Tiel
Elst
Aalten
Borken
Dulmen
Wiedenbruck
Goeree
Ouddorp
Sliedrecht
Gorinchem
Nijmegen
Emmerich
Bocholt
GERMAN FEDERAL REPUBLIC
Dordrecht
Oss
Kleve
Ahlen
Schouwen
Burgh
Dirksland
Maas
's Hertogenbosch
Rhine
Wesel
Lippe
Hamm
Zierikzee
Zevenbergen
Oosterhout
Goch
Xanten
Dorsten
Lunen
Erwitte
Walcheren
Breda
Boxtel
Veghel
Recklinghausen
Gladbeck
Unna
Middelburg
Goes
Venraij
Hamborn
Gelsenkirchen
Warstein
Vlissingen
S.Beveland
Bergen op Zoom
Roosendaal
Tilburg
Wilhelmina Canal
Helmond
Geldern
Oberhausen
Bochum
Dortmund
Arnsberg
NETHERLANDS
Schelde
Baarle Hertog (BELGIUM)
Eindhoven
Duisburg
Essen
Witten
Iserlohn
W. Schelde
Asten
Mulheim
Ruhr
Knokke
Zeebrugge
Blankenberge
Breskens
Terneuzen
Valkenswaard
Venlo
Krefeld Uerdingen
Axel
Ekeren
Turnhout
Dusseldorf
Wuppertal
Ostend
St. Niklaas
Weert
M.Gladbach
Viersen
Remscheid
Plettenberg
Nieuwpoort
Bruges
Eeklo
Antwerp
Herentals
Roermond
Neuss
De Panne
Lokeren
Hoboken
Mol
Maaseik
Rheydt
Solingen
Kirchhundem
Dunkirk
Veurne
Torhout
Lier
Vorst
Beverlo
Echt
Diksmuide
Ghent
Mechelen (Malines)
Diest
Albert Canal
Rur
Erkelenz
Burscheid
Gummersbach
Bergues
Roeselare (Roulers)
Tielt
Dendermonde
Sittard
Geilenkirchen
Cologne
Mulheim
Siegen
Poperinge
Aalst
Vilvoorde
Hasselt
Genk
Heerlen
Julich
REPUBLIC
Cassel
Ieper (Ypres)
Meenen (Menin)
Kortrijk (Courtrai)
Oudenaarde
Lys
Leie
Anderlecht
Leuven (Louvain)
St.Truiden
Maastricht
Eschweiler
Erft
Siegburg
Rosbach
Brussels
Escaut
Ronse
Geeraardsbergen
Tongeren
Stolberg
Duren
Dillenburg
Hazebrouck
Tourcoing
Mouscron
Lessines
Halle
Tienen
Aachen
Euskirchen
Bonn
Aire
Armentieres
Lille
Roubaix
Ath
Soignies
Ottignies
Herstal
Tournai
Nivelles
Ramillies
Jemeppe
Liege
Eupen
Remagen
Dierdorf
Bethune
BELGIUM
Seraing
Verviers
Gemund
Ahrweiler
Lievin
Lens
Orchies
La Louviere
Jumet
Meuse
Huy
Spa
Andernach
Limburg
St.Pol
Valenciennes
Jemappes
Mons
Namur
Sambre
Malmedy
Dahlem
Koblenz
Douai
Charleroi
Stavelot
Mayen
Arras
Denain
Thuin
Vielsalm
St.Vith
Camberg
Maubeuge
Dinant
Prum
Gerolstein
Doullens
Cambrai
Philippeville
Jemelle
Marche
Ourthe
Kyll
EIFEL
Cochem
Kastellaun
Wiesbaden
Avesnes
Givet
Houffalize
Clervaux
Bapaume
Le Cateau
Chimay
Bastogne
Zell
Albert
Fourmies
Mainz
Amiens
Somme
Peronne
La Capelle
Hirson
Fumay
ARDENNES
Wiltz
Bitburg
Wittlich
Our
Diekirch
Sure
Mosel
Bernkastel-Kues
Bad Kreuznach
Chaulnes
St.Quentin
Guise
Oise
Vervins
Rocroi
Paliseul
Bouillon
LUXEMBOURG
FRANCE
Charleville
Mezieres
Neufchateau
Echternach
Trier
Alzey
Roye
Serre
Liart
Sedan
Marbehan
Arlon
Konz
Birkenfeld
Oberstein
Alsenz
Montdidier
Chauny
Montcornet
Poix Terron
Semois
Luxembourg
Saarburg
Worms
Noyon
Virton
Differdange
Esch
Remich
Winnweiler
Ludwigshafen
Laon
Aisne
Rethel
Montmedy
Longwy
Merzig
St.Wendel
Kaiserslautern
Compiegne
Stenay
Soissons
Longuyon
Sierk
Saar
Neunkirchen
Spincourt
Homburg
Thionville
Creil
Villers Cotterets
Fismes
Reims
Monthois
Vienne le Chateau
Etain
Moyeuvre La Grande
Saarlouis
Saarbrucken
Pirmasens
Oulchy le Chateau
Landau
EAST 5 OF GREENWICH
2
3
4
5
6
7
8
54
53
52
51
50

10
ENGLAND
Bideford
Exeter
Torquay
Plymouth
Falmouth
Penzance
LAND'S END
SCILLY ISLES
Lizard Pt.
Start Pt.
Southampton
Weymouth
Bournemouth
Isle of Wight
Portsmouth
Brighton
Beachy Hd.
Dover
Str. of Dover
English Channel
C. de la Hague
Guernsey
CHANNEL ISLANDS
(U.K.)
Jersey
Ushant
Pte. de St. Mathieu
Pte. de Penmarch
I. de Groix
Belle Ile
I. de Noirmoutier
I. d'Yeu
I. de Re
I. d'Oleron
Bay of Biscay
FRANCE
Brest
Morlaix
Guingamp
St.Brieuc
St.Malo
Dinan
Loudeac
Douarnenez
Quimper
Quimperle
Concarneau
Lorient
Vannes
Sarzeau
St.Nazaire
Redon
Rennes
Fougeres
Avranches
Granville
Coutances
St.Lo
Vire
Flers
Cherbourg
Bayeux
Caen
Le Havre
Seine Bay
Fecamp
Dieppe
Eu
Yvetot
Rouen
Elbeuf
Evreux
Argentan
Alencon
Mayenne
Laval
Le Mans
Angers
Nantes
Saumur
Chinon
Tours
Thouars
La Roche -s-Yon
Les Sables d'Olonne
Lucon
La Rochelle
Rochefort
Niort
Poitiers
Chatellerault
Civray
Marennes
Royan
Cognac
Pons
Angouleme
St.Junien
St.Yrieix
Limoges
Perigueux
Pauillac
MEDOC
Bordeaux
Libourne
Bergerac
Arcachon
E. de Cazaux
E.de Biscarosse
La Teste de Buch
LES LANDES
La Reole
Tonneins
Nerac
Agen
Morcenx
Mont de Marsan
Condom
Dax
Aire-sur-l'Adour
Biarritz
Bayonne
Orthez
Pau
Tarbes
Lourdes
Toulouse
Montauban
Castelnaudary
Pamiers
St.Girons
Foix
Carcassonne
Limoux
Narbonne
Beziers
Sete
Perpignan
Port Bou
C. Creus
Gulf of Lions
Montpellier
Nimes
Avignon
Arles
Ales
Marseille
La Ciotat
Toulon
I'd'Hyeres
Aix-en-Provence
Draguignan
Grasse
Cannes
Nice
MONACO
Monte Carlo
San Remo
Imperia
Digne
Gap
Embrun
Briancon
Carpentras
Montelimar
Valence
Romans
Grenoble
Chambery
Aix-les-Bains
Annecy
Geneva
Lake Geneva
Lyon
Vienne
Givors
St.Etienne
Le Puy
M. MEZENC 1754
Mende
Millau
Rodez
Castres
Lavaur
Figeac
Cahors
Souillac
Aurillac
St. Flour
Brive
Tulle
Ussel
M. DORE 1886
AUVERGNE
Clermont Ferrand
Vichy
Roanne
Villefranche
Macon
Bourg en Bresse
Chalon-sur-Saone
Le Creusot
Moulins
Montlucon
Gueret
Chateauroux
Argenton
Nevers
Bourges
Romorantin
Blois
Orleans
Gien
Montargis
Pithiviers
Chartres
Versailles
St. Denis
Paris
Meaux
Melun
Provins
Sens
Auxerre
Avallon
Troyes
Arcis-sur Aube
Chatillon sur-Seine
Beaune
Dijon
Dole
Gray
Besancon
Vesoul
Langres
Chaumont
Bar-le-Duc
St. Mihiel
Toul
Nancy
Metz
Verdun
Chalons-sur-Marne
Epernay
Reims
Soissons
Chateau Thierry
Laon
St.Quentin
Noyon
Montdidier
Beauvais
Amiens
Abbeville
St. Valery
Etaples
Boulogne
Calais
Dunkirk
St.Omer
Lille
Roubaix
Lens
Arras
Cambrai
Valenciennes
Maubeuge
Charleville
Sedan
Thionville
Sarreguemines
Epinal
Colmar
Mulhouse
Belfort
Strasbourg
VOSGES
JURA MTS.
CEVENNES
Ostend
Roeselare
Ghent
BELGIUM
Brussels
Antwerp
Mechelen
Namur
Dinant
ARDENNES
Liege
Maastricht
Verviers
Malmedy
LUX.
Luxembourg
Arlon
Aachen
Cologne
Dusseldorf
Mulheim
Bonn
EIFEL
Prum
Trier
Koblenz
Neuwied
HUNSRUCK MTS.
Siegen
Giessen
Wiesbaden
Mainz
Frankfurt
Offenbach
Darmstadt
Mannheim
Ludwigshafen
Kaiserslautern
Saarbrucken
Heidelberg
Heilbronn
Karlsruhe
Stuttgart
Schwabisch Gmund
Tubingen
Ulm
Kehl
BLACK FOREST
Freiburg
Schaffhausen
Konstanz
Lake Constance
Tuttlingen
SWABIAN JURA
GERMAN FEDERAL REPUBLIC
G.D.R.
THURINGIAN FOREST
Gotha
Erfurt
Jena
Zwickau
Saalfeld
Coburg
Fulda
Schweinfurt
Bayreuth
Cheb
Wurzburg
Furth
Nuremberg
Ansbach
Regensburg
Ingolstadt
Landshut
Augsburg
Munich
Rosenheim
Kempten
Garmisch
Kitzbuhel
ALLGAUER ALPS
BAVARIAN ALPS
AUSTRIA
Innsbruck
BRENNER PASS
LIECH.
SWITZERLAND
Basle
Zurich
Zug
Lucerne
Bern
Neuchatel
Lake Neuchatel
Lausanne
Chur
Davos
St.Moritz
BERNESE ALPS
4158 JUNGFRAU
ST.GOTTHARD PASS
RHAETIAN ALPS
LEPONTINE ALPS
Brig
PENNINE ALPS
M. ROSA 4638
MATTERHORN 4483
M.BLANC 4810
GRAIAN ALPS
M.CENIS PASS
Aosta
COTTIAN ALPS
M.VISO 3841
MARITIME ALPS
ALPS
ITALY
Lugano
Lake Como
Lake Maggiore
Lake Orta
Como
BERGAMASQUE ALPS
L.Iseo
Lake Garda
Bergamo
Brescia
Riva
Trento
Bolzano
Bressanone
DOLOMITES
Vicenza
Padua
Verona
Mantua
Cremona
Milan
Novara
Pavia
Piacenza
Turin
Asti
Alessandria
Savigliano
Cuneo
Savona
Genoa
Gulf of Genoa
Parma
Reggio
Modena
Ferrara
Bologna
Imola
APENNINE MTS.
Massa
La Spezia
Lucca
Pistoia
Florence
Pisa
Livorno
Siena
Grosseto
Piombino
Elba
Capraia
Orbetello
Giglio
Ligurian Sea
RIVIERA
C. Corse
Bastia
Calvi
Ponte Leccia
Corte
M.CINTO 2710
Aleria
CORSICA
(FRANCE)
Ajaccio
Solenzara
Sartene
Porto Vecchio
MEDITERRANEAN SEA
SPAIN
C. de Penas
Gijon
Oviedo
Ribadesella
Santander
CANTABRIAN MTS.
Riano
Reinosa
Leon
Bilbao
San Sebastian
Irun
Vitoria
Pamplona
Tafalla
Logrono
Calahorra
Tudela
Tarazona
Soria
Zamora
Valladolid
Jaca
PYRENEES
P. DU MIDI D'OSSAU 2885
M. PERDIDO 3355
MALADETTA 3406
P. DE MONTCALM 3080
ANDORRA
Puigcerda
Llivia
Monzon
Manresa
Gerona
Figueras
San Feliu
Palamos
Lloret de Mar
COSTA BRAVA
Loire
Seine
Rhone
Garonne
Dordogne
Rhine
Danube
Meuse
Moselle
Saone
SCALE
Kilometres
0 50 100 150
0 25 50 75 100
Miles
© GEOGRAPHIA

11
FRANCE
SPAIN
PORTUGAL
MOROCCO
ALGERIA
ATLANTIC OCEAN
MEDITERRANEAN SEA
BALEARIC ISLANDS
Gulf of Lions
Gulf of Valencia
Gulf of Cadiz
Gulf of Almeria
Str. of Gibraltar
CANTABRIAN MTS.
PYRENEES
SIERRA DE GUADARRAMA
SIERRA DE GREDOS
SIERRA DE GATA
TOLEDO MTS.
SIERRA DE GUADALUPE
SIERRA MORENA
SIERRA NEVADA
SIERRA DE ALCARAZ
SIERRA DEL MONCAYO
SIERRA DE GUARA
SIERRA CABRERA
SIERRAS DE ARACENA
SERRA DA ESTRELA
COSTA BRAVA
COSTA BLANCA
COSTA DE SOL
CAPE FINISTERRE
CAPE ST. VINCENT
Cape Trafalgar
Cape Carvoeiro
Cape Tortosa
C. de la Nao
C. de Palos
C. de Gata
C. Tres Forcas
C. Formentor
CAPE CREUS
Madrid
Lisbon
Barcelona
Valencia
Seville
Oporto
Zaragoza
Bilbao
Malaga
Cordoba
Granada
Murcia
Alicante
Cartagena
Valladolid
Salamanca
Burgos
Santander
San Sebastian
La Coruna
Santiago
Vigo
Gijon
Oviedo
Leon
Toledo
Badajoz
Caceres
Huelva
Cadiz
Almeria
Albacete
Cuenca
Teruel
Tarragona
Lerida
Gerona
Pamplona
Logrono
Vitoria
Huesca
Palma
Majorca
Minorca
Ibiza
Formentera
Mahon
Ciudadela
Cabrera
ANDORRA
Toulouse
Montpellier
Marseille
Bayonne
Biarritz
Perpignan
Algiers
Oran
Tangier
Ceuta (SPAIN)
Melilla (SPAIN)
GIBRALTAR (U.K.)
La Linea
Algeciras
Tarifa
Coimbra
Braga
Setubal
Faro
Lagos
Sagres
Evora
Beja
Santarem
Abrantes
Guarda
Viseu
Aveiro
Braganca
Chaves
Vila Real
MULHACEN 3483
M. PERDIDO 3355
MALADETTA 3404
P. DU MIDI D'OSSAU 2885
LA SAGRA 2381
Ebro
Duero
Douro
Tagus
Guadiana
Guadalquivir
Jucar
Segura
Minho
GREENWICH West of East
SCALE
Kilometres
0 50 100 150
0 25 50 75 100
Miles
© GEOGRAPHIA
42
38

12
SCALE
Kilometres
0 50 100 150
0 25 50 75 100
Miles
© GEOGRAPHIA
EAST 16 OF GREENWICH
BALTIC SEA
DENMARK
SWEDEN
NETHERLANDS
BELGIUM
LUX
FRANCE
SWITZERLAND
LIECHTENSTEIN
AUSTRIA
HUNGARY
ROMANIA
CZECHOSLOVAKIA
POLAND
GERMAN DEMOCRATIC REPUBLIC
GERMAN FEDERAL REPUBLIC
LITHUANIAN S.S.R.
WHITE RUSSIAN S.S.R.
U.S.S.R.
R.S.F.S.R. (PART OF)
UKRAINIAN S.S.R.
Bornholm
Rugen
BOHEMIA
MORAVIA
CARPATHIAN MOUNTAINS
EAST BESKIDS
WEST BESKIDS
ERZ GEBIRGE
BOHMER WALD
SCHWARZ WALD
THURINGER WALD
BAVARIAN ALPS
HOHE TAUERN
ARDENNES
EIFEL
HUNSRUCK
VOSGES
Copenhagen
Berlin
Warsaw
Prague
Vienna
Budapest
Brussels
Amsterdam
Luxembourg
Bern

13
HUNGARY
ROMANIA
YUGOSLAVIA
BULGARIA
ALBANIA
GREECE
TURKEY
U.S.S.R.
MOLDAVIAN S.S.R.
ALY
BLACK SEA
ADRIATIC SEA
Ionian Sea
MEDITERRANEAN SEA
AEGEAN SEA
Sea of Marmara
Sea of Crete
CARPATHIAN MOUNTAINS
TRANSYLVANIAN ALPS
BALKAN MOUNTAINS
RHODOPE MTS.
PINDUS MTS.
OTHRIS MTS.
BIHORULUI MTS
KOPAONIK MTS.
NTH. ALBANIAN ALPS
DINARIC ALPS
DALMATIA
CYCLADES
DODECANESE
NTHN. SPORADES
STHN. SPORADES
IONIAN IS.
CRETE
Budapest
Ujpest
Vac
Esztergom
Gyor
Egor
Papa
Székesfehérvar
Veszprém
Keszthely
Lake Balaton
Lake Neusiedler
Nagykanizsa
Kaposvár
Pécs
Mohács
Baja
Szeged
Kecskemét
Nagykörös
Cegléd
Szolnok
Karcag
Debrecen
Hajduböszörmény
Nyiregyhaza
Mezötúr
Szarvas
Szentes
Orosháza
Hódmezö-vásárhely
Békés
Békéscsaba
Csongrád
Kiskunfélegyháza
Kiskunhalas
Dunaföldvár
Paks
Subotica
Senta
Sombor
Kikinda
Timisoara
Arad
Oradea
Satu-Mare
Baia-Mare
Sighet
Carei
Valea-lui-Mihai
Marghita
Zalău
Dej
Cluj
Huedin
Beiuş
Abrud
Aiud
Alba Iulia
Brad
Deva
Orăstie
Lugoj
Făget
Caransebeş
Resita
Anina
Feregova
Bela Crkva
Vršac
Pančevo
Belgrade
Zemun
Novi Sad
Vinkovci
Osijek
Slavonski Brod
Požega
Pakrac
Slatina
Virovitica
Barcs
Ruma
Mitrovica
Sabac
Loznica
Valjevo
Smederevo
Požarevac
Petrovac
Palanka
Svilajnac
Negotin
Kragujevac
Paracin
Zaječar
Čačak
Titovo Užice
Visegrad
Priboj
Nova Varoš
Ivanjica
Trstenik
Kruševac
Knjaževac
Prokuplje
Niš
Pirot
Kuršumlija
Leskovac
Kosovska Mitrovica
Priština
Vranje
Peć
Prizren
Dakovica
Tetovo
Kumanovo
Skopje
Titov Veles
Štip
Debar
Krusevo
Prilep
Strumica
Bitolj
Ohrid
Sarajevo
Zenica
Tuzla
Doboj
Maglaj
Jajce
Travnik
Bugojno
Livno
Banja Luka
Modrica
Konjic
Mostar
Makarska
Metković
Dubrovnik
Trebinje
Nikšić
Bijelo Polje
Sjenica
Titograd
Cetinje
Kotor
Budva
Bar
Ulcinj
Shkodër
Lesh
Krujë
Durrës
Tiranë
Elbasan
Berat
Vlonë
Korce
Tepelenë
Gjinokaster
Sarandë
Delvinë
Corfu
Brindisi
Taranto
Lecce
Otranto
Sibiu
Mediaş
Sighisoara
Făgăraş
Brasov
Reghin
Târgul Mures
Gheorgheni
Bistriţa
Năsăud
Vatra Dornei
Câmpulung
Dorohoi
Botoşani
Harlau
Târgu Neamţ
Iasi
Vaslui
Bacău
Târgu Ocna
Barlad
Tecuci
Focşani
Galati
Brăila
Râmnicu-Sărat
Buzău
Făurei
Ploesti
Campina
Târgoviste
Piteşti
Râmnicu Vâlcea
Petroşani
Craiova
Filiasi
Turnu Severin
Orşova
Calafat
Vidin
Caracal
Slatina
Rosiorii de Vede
Turnu Măgurele
Giurgiu
Bucharest
Urziceni
Olteniţa
Feteşti
Cernavoda
Medgidia
Constanţa
Mangalia
Hârsova
Babadag
Tulcea
Ismail
Kiliya
Bolgrad
Kagul
Komrat
Leovo
Husi
Bendery
Tiraspol
Kishinev
Dubossary
Rybnitsa
Beltsy
Ruse
Tutrakan
Silistra
Dobrich
Balchik
Varna
Shumen
Razgrad
Popovo
Svishtov
Nikopol
Pleven
Lovech
Sevlievo
Trnovo
Oryakhovo
Lom
Mikhailovgrad
Berkovitsa
Vratsa
Teteven
Sofia
Karlovo
Kotel
Sliven
Aitos
Burgas
Stara Zagora
Nova Zagora
Yambol
Elkhovo
Akhtopol
Radomir
Samokov
Kyustendil
Stanke Dimitrov
Pazardzhik
Plovdiv
Chirpan
Khaskovo
Bansko
Melnik
Petrich
Smolyan
Momchilgrad
Edirne
Kirklareli
Midye
Iğneada
Lüleburgaz
Uzunköprü
Dhidhimótikhon
Silivri
Catalca
Istanbul
Uskudar
Tekirdağ
Sarköy
Gelibolu
Çanakkale
Bandirma
Bursa
Gönen
Edremit
Ayvacik
Ayvalik
Balikesir
Bergama
Kirkağaç
Akhisar
Simav
Candarli
Manisa
Menemen
Foça
Izmir
Turgutlu
Alaşehir
Ödemiş
Torbali
Tire
Aydin
Nazilli
Söke
Bozdoğan
Milas
Muğla
Marmaris
Çeşme
Serrai
Drama
Xánthi
Komotini
Kavalla
Alexandroupolis
Enez
Kilkís
Langadhás
Thessaloníki
Edhessa
Flórina
Kastoria
Kozáni
Siátista
Katerini
Leskovic
Kónitsa
Métsovon
Ioánnina
Kalabáka
Trikkala
Lárisa
Vólos
Kardhitsa
Fársala
Árta
Lamia
Agrínion
Mesolongion
Atalándi
Chalcis
Thebes
Marathón
Patrai
Aiyion
Mégara
Athens
Piraeus
Lávrion
Corinth
Argos
Navplion
Tripolis
Pirgos
Olympia
Killíni
Kiparissia
Filiatrá
Messíni
Pilos
Kalamai
Methóni
Sparta
Yithion
Monemvasía
Argostólion
Cephalonia
Ithaca
Levkás
Zante
Paxoi
Thásos
Samothráki
Imroz
Limnos
Bozcaada
Skiathos
Skopelos
Skíros
Iliodhrómia
Euboea
Lesvos
Mithimna
Mitilini
Psará
Khíos
Sámos
Ikaría
Andros
Tinos
Míkonos
Kéa
Siros
Kithnos
Sérifos
Sífnos
Páros
Náxos
Ios
Amorgós
Mílos
Thíra
Anáfi
Astipalaia
Patmos
Leros
Kalimnos
Kos
Nisiros
Tilos
Rhodes
Karpathos
Kasos
Aiyina
Idhra
Kíthira
Andikíthira
Khania
Rethimnon
Iraklion
Sitia
Kastélli
C. Spátha
C. Sidheros
C. Matapan
Mesara Bay
Merabellou Bay
M. ATHOS 2033
M. OLYMPUS 2918
M. ZIRIA 2375
MT. NEGOIU 2548
PIETROSUL 2102
DURMITOR 2528
SHIPKA PASS
IRON GATE
DARDANELLES
BOSPORUS
DANUBE DELTA
Danube
Drava
Sava
Tisa
Mures
Somes
Siret
Prut
Dniester
Morava
Vardar
Struma
Maritsa
Tundzha
Ibar
Drina
Bosna
Olt
Arges
Ialomita
Drin
Aliakmon
Akheloos
Gediz
Menderes
Koros
Timis
Jiu
Corabia
Veliki Backi Canal
Mali Canal
Raba
Lake Ohridsko
L. Prespa
L. Shkodër
B. of Drinit
Str. of Otranto
G. of Saros
G. of Thessaloniki
G. of Toronaios
Singitikos G.
G. of Amvrakia
G. of Patrai
G. of Corinth
G. of Kiparissia
G. of Argolis
G. of Messini
G. of Lakonia
G. of Kerme
G. of Taranto
20
24
28
38
42
46
SCALE
Kilometres
0 50 100 150
0 25 50 75 100
Miles
© GEOGRAPHIA
EAST 20 OF GREENWICH

14
GERMAN FED. REP.
AUSTRIA
HUNGARY
SWITZERLAND
LIECHTENSTEIN
FRANCE
YUGOSLAVIA
CORSICA
(FRANCE)
SARDINIA
(ITALY)
SICILY
MALTA
TUNISIA
ALGERIA
MONACO
SAN MARINO
VATICAN
(TUNISIA)
Galite I.
Pantelleria
(ITALY)
Linosa
(ITALY)
Lampione.
(ITALY)
Lampedusa
(ITALY)
JURA MTS.
THE ALPS
PENNINE ALPS
LEPONTINE ALPS
RHAETIAN ALPS
BERGAMASQUE ALPS
ALLGAUER ALPS
BAVARIAN ALPS
NIEDERE TAUERN
CARNIC ALPS
DOLOMITES
GRAIAN ALPS
COTTIAN ALPS
MARITIME ALPS
APENNINES
ABRUZZI MOUNTAINS
DINARIC ALPS
DALMATIA
Ligurian Sea
Tyrrhenian Sea
ADRIATIC SEA
MEDITERRANEAN SEA
Ionian Sea
Gulf of Genoa
Gulf of Venice
Gulf of Gaeta
B. of Naples
G. of Salerno
G. of Policastro
G. of Gioia
G. of Squillace
Gulf of Taranto
G. of Manfredonia
G. of Asinara
G. of Tunis
G. of Hammamet
Str. of Bonifacio
Str. of Messina
Str. of Otranto
Lake Constance
L. Neuchatel
Lake Geneva
Lake Balaton
Lake Neusiedler
L. Como
Lake Orta
Lake Maggiore
L. Garda
Lake Trasimeno
Lake Bolsena
Valli di Comacchio
L. Shkoder
Rhine
Rhône
Inn
Enns
Mur
Drau
Drava
Sava
Danube
Raba
Kupa
Una
Bosna
Drina
Po
Ticino
Adda
Dora Baltea
Adige
Piave
Reno
Arno
Tiber
Tronto
Sangro
Volturno
Medjerda
Mellegue
JUNGFRAU 4158
ST. GOTTHARD PASS
BRENNER PASS
ORTLES 3903
M. BLANC 4810
MATTERHORN 4483
M. ROSA 4638
M. CENIS PASS
M. CINTO 2710
M. GENNARGENTU 1834
VESUVIUS 1277
M. DEL PAPA 2005
M. ETNA 3340
DURMITOR 2528
Stromboli 925
Belfort
Mulhouse
Schaffhausen
Konstanz
Kempten
Garmisch
Salzburg
Bischofshofen
Kitzbuhel
Innsbruck
Landeck
Basle
Zurich
Zug
Lucerne
Neuchatel
Bern
Chur
Davos
Lausanne
Brig
St. Moritz
Lugano
Sondrio
Edolo
Merano
Bolzano
Bressanone
Lienz
Spittal
Villach
Klagenfurt
Graz
Bruck
Murzzuschlag
Wiener Neustadt
Sopron
Gyor
Esztergom
Ujpest
Budapest
Szekesfehervar
Szombathely
Kecskemet
Paks
Kaposvar
Nagykanizsa
Pecs
Baja
Subotica
Sombor
Radkersburg
Maribor
Celje
Kranj
Varazdin
Koprivnica
Krizevci
Ljubljana
Zagreb
Virovitica
Osijek
Vinkovci
Sisak
Pakrac
Slavonski Brod
Kocevje
Karlovac
Ogulin
Susak
Rijeka
Krk
Cres
Losinj
Pag
Gospic
Bihac
Prijedor
Doboj
Jajce
Travnik
Zenica
Zvornik
Sarajevo
Konjic
Mostar
Metkovic
Niksic
Kotor
Cetinje
Budva
Bar
Titograd
Dubrovnik
Mljet
Korcula
Vis
Hvar
Brač
Split
Makarska
Sibenik
Knin
Zadar
Dugi Otok
Gorizia
Trieste
Piran
Rovinj
Pula
Udine
Gemona
Belluno
Trento
Riva
Bassano
Vittorio Veneto
Treviso
Vicenza
Venice
Padua
Chioggia
Adria
Rovigo
Ferrara
Verona
Mantua
Brescia
Bergamo
Como
Milan
Lodi
Cremona
Piacenza
Pavia
Novara
Vercelli
Biella
Aosta
Turin
Brianςon
Asti
Alessandria
Bra
Savigliano
Cuneo
Savona
Genoa
San Remo
Imperia
Menton
Monte Carlo
Nice
Cannes
La Spezia
Massa
Lucca
Pistoia
Pisa
Livorno
Parma
Reggio
Modena
Bologna
Imola
Faenza
Forli
Ravenna
Cesena
Rimini
Pesaro
Urbino
Vergato
Florence
Arezzo
Siena
Senigallia
Ancona
Macerata
Perugia
Foligno
Spoleto
Terni
Ascoli Piceno
Teramo
Orvieto
Grosseto
Piombino
Capraia
Elba
Monte Cristo
Giglio
Orbetello
Viterbo
Civitavecchia
Rieti
L'Aquila
Pescara
Chieti
Ortona
Vasto
Termoli
TREMITI ISLANDS
Avezzano
Rome
Ostia
Anzio
Latina
Frosinone
Cassino
Terracina
Gaeta
PONTINE ISLANDS
Ischia
Capri
Capua
Caserta
Naples
Castellammare
Salerno
Eboli
Avellino
Benevento
Campobasso
Lucera
Foggia
Vieste
Barletta
Canosa
Corato
Bari
Melfi
Altamura
Gioia
Potenza
Matera
Brindisi
Taranto
Manduria
Lecce
Otranto
Gallipoli
C.S. Maria di Leuca
C. Gjuhez
Vallo della Lucania
Lauria
Rossano
Corigliano
Cosenza
Crotone
C. Colonne
Nicastro
Catanzaro
Vibo Valentia
Palmi
Cittanova
Reggio di Calabria
C. Spartivento
LIPARI ISLANDS
Lipari
Ustica
Messina
Barcellona
Palermo
Cefalu
C.S. Vito
Trapani
EGADI ISLANDS
Alcamo
Termini
Marsala
Castelvetrano
Sciacca
Agrigento
Gangi
Nicosia
Enna
Adrano
Acireale
Catania
Caltanissetta
Canicatti
Caltagirone
Licata
Vittoria
Ragusa
Syracuse
Noto
C. Passero
Gozo
Valletta
Rabat
C. Corse
Calvi
Bastia
Ponte Leccia
Corte
Ajaccio
Solenzara
Porto Vecchio
Bonifacio
Asinara
Porto Torres
Sassari
Tempio
Olbia
Alghero
Ozieri
Bosa
Nurri
C. Comino
Oristano
Arbatax
Iglesias
Portoscuso
S. Pietro
S. Antioco
Cagliari
C. Carbonara
C. Spartivento
C. de Fer
Annaba
El Kala
C. Blanc
Bizerte
Mateur
CARTHAGE
Tunis
C. Bon
Kelibia
Tabarka
Guelma
Souk Ahras
Nebeur
Ez Kef
Hammamet
Sousse
Moknine
Kairouan
Mahdia
Tebessa
El Djem
C. Kabudia
Feriana
SCALE Kilometres
0 50 100 150
0 25 50 75 100
Miles
© GEOGRAPHIA
EAST 12 OF GREENWICH
8
16
46
42
38

15
EUROPE
ASIA
AFRICA
UNION OF SOVIET SOCIALIST REPUBLICS
RUSSIAN SOVIET FEDERATIVE SOCIALIST REPUBLIC
SIBERIA
PEOPLE'S REPUBLIC OF CHINA
MONGOLIAN PEOPLE'S REPUBLIC
INDIA
PACIFIC OCEAN
INDIAN OCEAN
ARCTIC OCEAN
ATLANTIC OCEAN
ARCTIC CIRCLE
TROPIC OF CANCER
EQUATOR
EAST 80 OF GREENWICH
UNITED KINGDOM
IRELAND
ICELAND
NORWAY
SWEDEN
FINLAND
PORTUGAL
SPAIN
FRANCE
ITALY
SWITZ.
AUSTRIA
GERMANY
POLAND
CZECHOSL.
HUNGARY
ROMANIA
YUGOSLAVIA
BULGARIA
GREECE
ALB.
TURKEY
CYPRUS
SYRIA
ISRAEL
JORDAN
IRAQ
IRAN
KUWAIT
SAUDI ARABIA
QATAR
UN. ARAB EMIRATES
OMAN
YEMEN
P.D.R. OF YEMEN
AFGHANISTAN
PAKISTAN
NEPAL
BH.
BANGLADESH
BURMA
THAILAND
LAOS
CAMBODIA
VIETNAM
MALAYSIA
MALAYA
SINGAPORE
BRUNEI
SARAWAK
SABAH
INDONESIA
PHILIPPINES
NORTH KOREA
SOUTH KOREA
JAPAN
TAIWAN
HONG KONG
MACAU
SRI LANKA
MALDIVES
UKRAINIAN S.S.R.
WHITE RUSSIAN S.S.R.
LITH. S.S.R.
LATVIAN S.S.R.
EST. S.S.R.
KAZAKH S.S.R.
UZBEK S.S.R.
TURKMEN S.S.R.
KIRGIZ S.S.R.
TADZHIK S.S.R.
MANCHURIA
INNER MONGOLIA
SINKIANG UIGHUR
TIBET
ALGERIA
TUNISIA
LIBYA
EGYPT
NIGER
CHAD
SUDAN
ETHIOPIA
SOMALI DEM. REPUBLIC
UGANDA
KENYA
TANZANIA
ZAIRE
ZAMBIA
MOZAMBIQUE
SAHARA
AUSTRALIA
UNITED STATES TRUST TERRITORY
CAROLINE ISLANDS
PALAU ISLANDS
MARIANA ISLANDS
Guam
Yap
Ogasawara Jima
Minami Tori Shima
RYUKYU ISLANDS
KURILSKIE OST.
COMMANDER ISLANDS
ALEUTIAN IS.
NEW SIBERIAN IS.
LACCADIVE ISLANDS
ANDAMAN ISLANDS
NICOBAR ISLANDS
AMIRANTE ISLANDS
SEYCHELLES
KURIA MURIA ISLANDS
SUNDA ISLANDS
Mergui Archipelago
Svalbard
Franz Josef Land
Novaya Zemlya
North Land
Taimyr Pen.
C. Chelyuskin
Kamchatka Pen.
Sakhalin
Hokkaido
Honshu
Shikoku
Kyushu
Luzon
Samar
Mindanao
Palawan
Hainan
Sumatra
Java
Kalimantan (Borneo)
Sulawesi (Celebes)
Halmahera
Seram
Timor
Sumba
Sumbawa
Flores
Irian Jaya
Nias
Socotra
Barents Sea
Kara Sea
Laptev Sea
East Siberian Sea
Bering Sea
Sea of Okhotsk
Sea of Japan
Yellow Sea
South China Sea
Sulu Sea
Celebes Sea
Banda Sea
Arafura Sea
Timor Sea
Java Sea
Flores Sea
Str. of Makasar
G. of Siam
Bay of Bengal
Arabian Sea
Gulf of Aden
G. of Oman
Arabian Gulf
Red Sea
Caspian Sea
Aral Sea
Black Sea
Mediterranean Sea
Adriatic Sea
Baltic Sea
North Sea
L. Ladoga
L. Onega
L. Baikal
L. Balkhash
Ob
Yenisei
Lena
Kolyma
Indigirka
Aldan
Amur
Irtysh
Volga
Don
Dnieper
Syr Darya
Amu Darya
Tigris
Euphrates
Nile
Blue Nile
White Nile
Indus
Ganges
Brahmaputra
Irrawaddy
Mekong
Yangtze
Hwang
Selenga
URAL MOUNTAINS
ALTAI MTS.
GOBI DESERT
KUNLUN SHAN
HIMALAYAS
TSA DAM
Lisbon
Madrid
Gibraltar
Paris
London
Glasgow
Oslo
Stockholm
Helsinki
Berlin
Warsaw
Vienna
Budapest
Belgrade
Bucharest
Sofia
Rome
Athens
Istanbul
Izmir
Ankara
Algiers
Tunis
Tripoli
Alexandria
Cairo
Wadi Halfa
Khartoum
Pt. Sudan
Asmera
Addis Ababa
Djibouti
Berbera
Mogadiscio
Nairobi
Leningrad
Moscow
Kalinin
Tula
Gorki
Kirov
Kazan
Kuybyshev
Ufa
Magnitogorsk
Chelyabinsk
Sverdlovsk
Kiev
Kharkov
Odessa
Rostov
Volgograd
Astrakhan
Krasnodar
Tbilisi
Batumi
Baku
Murmansk
Arkhangelsk
Salekhard
Petropavlovsk
Omsk
Semipalatinsk
Ayaguz
Kzyl Orda
Alma Ata
Tashkent
Samarkand
Dushanbe
Tomsk
Novosibirsk
Novokuznetsk
Krasnoyarsk
Irkutsk
Ulan Ude
Chita
Mogocha
Blagoveshchensk
Khabarovsk
Ussuriysk
Vladivostok
Nikolaevsk
Aleksandrovsk
Okhotsk
Ayano
Aldan
Yakutsk
Vitim
Verkhoyansk
Bulkur
Khatanga
Dudinka
Turukhansk
Jerusalem
Damascus
Aleppo
Mosul
Baghdad
Basra
Tabriz
Tehran
Esfahan
Shiraz
Bandar Abbas
Mashhad
Herat
Kabul
Kandahar
Quetta
Kalat
Peshawar
Lahore
Amritsar
Karachi
Hyderabad
Medina
Mecca
Riyadh
Sana
Aden
Muscat
Delhi
Agra
Lucknow
Ahmedabad
Indore
Daman
Bombay
Nagpur
Pune
Goa
Bangalore
Mysore
Madurai
Madras
Pondicherry
Jaffna
Colombo
Galle
Calcutta
Cuttack
Visakhapatnam
Kashgar
Kuldja
Urumchi
Bulun Tokhoi
Lhasa
Paan
Mandalay
Rangoon
Moulmein
Chiang Mai
Bangkok
Songkhla
Penang
Kuala Lumpur
Padang
Jakarta
Surabaya
Banjarmasin
Makasar
Davao
Manila
Laoag
Hanoi
Vinh
Binh Dinh
Ho Chi Minh City
Kunming
Chungking
Ningsia
Lanchow
Ulan Bator
Hailar
Nenkiang
Tsitsihar
Harbin
Changchun
Shenyang
Chengte
Peking
Tientsin
Tsingtao
Luta
Pyongyang
Seoul
Pusan
Kitakyushu
Kobe
Osaka
Yokohama
Tokyo
Sendai
Hakodate
Nanking
Wusih
Shanghai
Hangchow
Yungkia
Wuhan
Wuchang
Changsha
Kweilin
Kwangchow
Amoy
Darwin
SCALE
Kilometres
0
500
1000
1500
0
250
500
750
1000
Miles
© GEOGRAPHIA

16
ARCTIC OCEAN
NORTH POLE
UNION OF SOVIET SOCIALIST REPUBLICS
RUSSIAN SOVIET FEDERATIVE SOCIALIST REPUBLIC
SIBERIA
URAL MOUNTAINS
ARCTIC CIRCLE
KAZAKH S.S.R.
UZBEK S.S.R.
TURKMEN S.S.R.
UKRAINIAN S.S.R.
YAKUT A.S.S.R.
KOMI A.S.S.R.
BURYAT A.S.S.R.
MONGOLIAN PEOPLE'S REPUBLIC
PEOPLE'S REPUBLIC OF CHINA
MANCHURIA
SINKIANG UIGHUR
TAKLA MAKAN
GOBI DESERT
ALTAI
KUNLUN SHAN
CHANG TANG
TIBET
HIMALAYA
NORTH KOREA
SOUTH KOREA
JAPAN
AFGHANISTAN
IRAN
IRAQ
TURKEY
SYRIA
KUWAIT
SAUDI ARABIA
PAKISTAN
NORWAY
SWEDEN
FINLAND
POLAND
DENMARK
UNITED KINGDOM
ALASKA (U.S.A.)
SVALBARD (Spitsbergen) (NORWAY)
Bear I. (NORWAY)
(DENMARK) The Faeroes
ZEM. FRANTSA IOSIFA (Franz Josef Land) (U.S.S.R.)
(U.S.S.R.) SEVERNAYA ZEMLYA (North Land)
(U.S.S.R.) NOVOSIBIRSKIYE OSTROVA (New Siberian Islands)
O. Vrangelya (Wrangel I.) (U.S.S.R.)
KURILSKIYE OSTROVA (U.S.S.R.)
Novaya Zemlya
Norwegian Sea
Greenland Sea
Barents Sea
Kara Sea
Laptev Sea
East Siberian Sea
Chukchi Sea
Bering Str.
Sea of Okhotsk
Sea of Japan
Yellow Sea
Black Sea
Sea of Azov
Caspian Sea
Aral Sea
L. Balkhash
L. Baikal
Baltic Sea
G. of Bothnia
White Sea
G. of Ob
Taimyr Pen.
Yamal Pen.
Chukotski Pen.
Kamchatka Peninsula
Sakhalin
Hokkaido
Honshu
Shikoku
CHUKOTSKIY KHREBET
KORYAKSKIY KHREBET
SREDINNY KHREBET
VERKHOYANSKIY KHREBET
KHREBET DZHUGDZHUR
KHREBET SIKHOTE ALIN
YABLONOVIY KHREBET
VILYUYSKIY GORY
Ob
Yenisei
Lena
Amur
Volga
Don
Dnieper
Ural
Irtysh
Ishim
Angara
Aldan
Kolyma
Indigirka
Vilyuy
Olenek
Pechora
Syr Darya
Indus
Tigris
Euphrates
Yangtze
Hwang
Moscow
Leningrad
Kiev
Minsk
Riga
Tallinn
Vilnius
Kishinev
Tbilisi
Yerevan
Baku
Tashkent
Alma Ata
Frunze
Dushanbe
Ashkhabad
Gorki
Kuybyshev
Sverdlovsk
Chelyabinsk
Novosibirsk
Omsk
Krasnoyarsk
Irkutsk
Khabarovsk
Vladivostok
Karaganda
Volgograd
Kharkov
Odessa
Murmansk
Arkhangelsk
Magadan
Yakutsk
Petropavlovsk Kamchatskiy
Ulan Bator
Peking
Tientsin
Pyongyang
Seoul
Tokyo
Kabul
Tehran
Baghdad
Stockholm
Helsinki
Oslo
Copenhagen
Warsaw
Key to U.S.S.R. Administrative Areas
SOVIET SOCIALIST REPUBLICS
ARMENIAN 1
AZERBAIJAN 2
BELORUSSIAN 3
ESTONIAN 4
GEORGIAN 5
KAZAKH 6
KIRGIZ 7
LATVIAN 8
LITHUANIAN 9
MOLDAVIAN 10
TADZHIK 11
TURKMEN 12
UKRAINIAN 13
UZBEK 14
AUTONOMOUS S. S REPUBLICS
ABKHAZ 1
ADZHAR 2
BASHKIR 3
BURYAT 4
CHECHENO-INGUSH 5
CHUVASH 6
DAGESTAN 7
KARELIAN 11
KOMI 12
MARI 13
MORDOVIAN 14
NAKHICHEVAN 15
NTH. OSETIAN 16
TATAR 17
SCALE
Kilometres
0 250 500 750 1000
0 200 400 600
Miles
© GEOGRAPHIA

17
TURKEY
ANATOLIA
TAURUS MTS.
CANIK (PONTINE) MTS.
GREECE
Athens
Ankara
Bursa
Izmir
Konya
Kayseri
Sivas
Malatya
Adana
Mersin
Iskenderun
Antakya
Erzurum
Erzincan
Yerevan
Leninakan
Nakhichevan
MT. ARARAT 5165
ARMENIAN S.S.R.
AZERBAIJAN S.S.R.
Baku
Tbilisi
CASPIAN SEA
TURKMEN S.S.R.
KARA KUM
Krasnovodsk
Ashkhabad
Mary
Bukhara
Samarkand
Chardzhou
Karshi
Termez
Dushanbe
TADZHIK S.S.R.
KIRGIZ S.S.R.
Leninabad
AFGHANISTAN
HINDU KUSH
Kabul
Herat
Kandahar
Ghazni
Jalalabad
KHYBER PASS
Mazar-i-Sharif
Farah
Girishk
PAKISTAN
Quetta
Karachi
Hyderabad
Sukkur
Shikarpur
SULAIMAN RANGE
KIRTHAR RANGE
SIAHAN RANGE
CHAGAI HILLS
BALUCHISTAN
MAKRAN
INDUS DELTA
RANN OF KUTCH
G. of Kutch
IRAN
Tehran
ELBURZ MOUNTAINS
DASHT-I-KAVIR
DASHT-I-LUT
ZAGROS MOUNTAINS
Mashhad
Tabriz
Isfahan
Esfahan
Shiraz
Kerman
Yazd
Qom
Kashan
Hamadan
Rasht
Abadan
Ahwaz
Bandar Abbas
Zahedan
Bam
Neyriz
Bushehr
Kazerun
Str. of Hormuz
Gulf of Oman
IRAQ
Baghdad
Basra
Mosul
Kirkuk
Karbala
An Najaf
An Nasiriya
As Samawah
Euphrates
Tigris
SYRIA
Damascus
Aleppo
Homs
Hama
Latakia
LEBANON
Beirut
Tripoli
Tyre
Haifa
CYPRUS
Nicosia
Crete
Rhodes
DODECANESE
Aegean Sea
MEDITERRANEAN SEA
ISRAEL
Tel Aviv-Yafo
Jerusalem
JORDAN
Amman
SYRIAN DESERT
KUWAIT
Al Kuwayt
SAUDI ARABIA
Riyadh
MECCA
Medina
Jiddah
At Ta'if
AN NAFUD
JABAL SHAMMAR
AD DAHNA
NAFUD AD DAHI
JABAL AT TUWAIQ
HEJAZ
ASIR
HASA
AR RIMAL
RUB AL KHALI
Al Manamah
BAHRAIN
QATAR
Doha
UNITED ARAB EMIRATES
Abu Dhabi
Dubai
Arabian Gulf
OMAN
Muscat
Masira
KURIA MURIA ISLANDS
ARABIAN SEA
YEMEN
San'a
Al Hudaydah
Al Mukha
P.D.R. OF YEMEN
HADHRAMAUT
Aden
Mukalla
Gulf of Aden
Socotra (P.D.R.YEMEN)
Abd al Kuri
Perim I.
RED SEA
FARASAN ISLANDS
DAHLAK ARCHIPELAGO
EGYPT
Cairo
Alexandria
Port Said
Suez
Aswan
Luxor
Asyut
Qena
SINAI
MT SINAI 2285
G. of Suez
G. of Aqaba
ARABIAN DESERT
WESTERN DESERT
QATTARA DEPRESSION
Lake Nasser
TROPIC OF CANCER
AFRICA
LIBYAN DESERT
Tobruk
SUDAN
Khartoum
Omdurman
Khartoum North
Port Sudan
Wadi Halfa
Atbara
Kassala
El Obeid
NUBIAN DESERT
Nile
Blue Nile
White Nile
ETHIOPIA
ERITREA
Lake Tana
EAST 40 OF GREENWICH
SCALE
Kilometres
0 100 300 500
0 100 200 300
Miles
© GEOGRAPHIA

U.S.S.R.
SINKIANG UIGHUR
PEOPLE'S REPUBLIC OF CHINA
TIBET
AFGHANISTAN
IRAN
PAKISTAN
INDIA
NEPAL
BHUTAN
BANGLADESH
BURMA
THAILAND
LAOS
SRI LANKA
JAMMU AND KASHMIR
HIMACHAL PRADESH
PUNJAB
HARYANA
UTTAR PRADESH
RAJASTHAN
GUJARAT
MADHYA PRADESH
BIHAR
WEST BENGAL
SIKKIM
ASSAM
ARUNACHAL PRADESH
MEGHALAYA
NAGALAND
MANIPUR
MIZORAM
TRIPURA
ORISSA
MAHARASHTRA
GOA
KARNATAKA
ANDHRA PRADESH
TAMIL NADU
KERALA
BALUCHISTAN
MAKRAN
REGISTAN
DASHT-E-LUT
DASHT-I-MARGO
HINDU KUSH
KARAKORAM
KUNLUN SHAN
KOKO SHILI
CHANG TANG
TANGLHA RANGE
NYENCHENTANGLHA RANGE
KAILAS RANGE
HIMALAYA
SULAIMAN RA.
SATPURA RA.
THAR OR INDIAN DESERT
WESTERN GHATS
EASTERN GHATS
MALABAR COAST
COROMANDEL COAST
ARAKAN YOMA
CHIN HILLS
PATKAI HILLS
TENASSERIM
MIN SHAN
TSAIDAM
ARABIAN SEA
Bay of Bengal
G. of Siam
G. of Kutch
G. of Camboy
G. of Martaban
G. of Mannar
Palk Str.
INDUS DELTA
GANGES DELTA
IRRAWADDY DELTA
SUNDARBANS
RANN OF KUTCH
LACCADIVE ISLANDS (INDIA)
ANDAMAN ISLANDS (INDIA)
NICOBAR
Nine Degree Channel
Ten Degree Channel
Mergui Archipelago
Isthmus of Kra
Malay Peninsula
TROPIC OF CANCER
Ras al Hadd
GODWIN AUSTEN 8611
MUZTAGH 7236
NANGA PARBAT 8126
KHYBER PASS 2109
KARAKORAM PASS
LANAK PASS 5466
LUNGNAK PASS 5490
THAGCHAB GANGRI 6396
KAMET 7761
NANDA DEVI 7822
DHAULAGIRI 8221
8853 MT. EVEREST
KANCHENJUNGA 8598
PIDURUTALAGALA 2524
Indus
Ganges
Brahmaputra
Yamuna
Chambal
Son
Narmada
Tapti
Godavari
Krishna
Mahanadi
Cauvery
Irrawaddy
Chindwin
Salween
Mekong
Yangtze
Helmand
Kabul
Delhi
Islamabad
Kabul
Katmandu
Thimbu
Dhaka
Rangoon
Bangkok
Colombo
Karachi
Hyderabad
Quetta
Lahore
Rawalpindi
Peshawar
Multan
Bombay
Calcutta
Madras
Bangalore
Ahmadabad
Kanpur
Lucknow
Mandalay
Lhasa
Chengtu
Kunming
Herat
Kandahar
Jaffna
Kandy
Trincomalee
SCALE
Kilometres 0 100 300 500
Miles 0 100 200 300
© GEOGRAPHIA

19
MONGOLIAN PEOPLE'S REPUBLIC
PEOPLE'S REPUBLIC OF CHINA
INNER MONGOLIA
MANCHURIA
SINKIANG-UIGHUR
TSINGHAI
TIBET
SZECHWAN
YUNNAN
KWEICHOW
KWANGSI CHUANG
KWANGTUNG
HUNAN
KIANGSI
FUKIEN
CHEKIANG
KIANGSU
ANHWEI
HUPEI
HONAN
SHANTUNG
SHANSI
SHENSI
KANSU
HOPEI
NINGSIA-HUI
LIAONING
KIRIN
HEILUNGKIANG
NORTH KOREA
SOUTH KOREA
JAPAN
INDIA
NEPAL
SIKKIM
BHUTAN
BANGLA-DESH
BURMA
LAOS
THAILAND
VIETNAM
TAIWAN
REPUBLIC OF THE PHILIPPINES
JAMMU & KASHMIR
U.S.S.R.
GOBI DESERT
TAKLA MAKAN (DESERT)
ALTAI MOUNTAINS
TIEN SHAN
KUNLUN SHAN
HIMALAYA MOUNTAINS
KARAKORAM RANGE
TANGLHA RANGE
NYENCHENTANGLHA RANGE
NAN SHAN
ALA SHAN
GREAT KHINGAN MTS
KHREBET SIKHOTE ALIN
EASTERN GHATS
ARAKAN YOMA
NAGA HILLS
DZUNGARIAN BASIN
TURFAN DEPRESSION
TSAIDAM
GREAT WALL
Peking
Shanghai
Ulan Bator
Pyongyang
Seoul
Delhi
Katmandu
Thimbu
Dhaka
Rangoon
Hanoi
Vientiane
Taipei
Victoria
HONG KONG (U.K.)
MACAU (PORT.)
Sea of Japan
Yellow Sea
EAST CHINA SEA
SOUTH CHINA SEA
PACIFIC OCEAN
Bay of Bengal
Gulf of Tonkin
RYUKYU ISLANDS (JAPAN)
PARACEL ISLANDS
TROPIC OF CANCER
EAST 110 OF GREENWICH
SCALE
Kilometres
0 200 400 600
Miles
0 100 200 300 400
© GEOGRAPHIA

SCALE Kilometres
Miles
© GEOGRAPHIA
U.S.S.R.
MONGOLIAN PEOPLE'S REPUBLIC
GOBI DESERT
INNER MONGOLIA
MANCHURIA
PEOPLE'S REPUBLIC OF CHINA
NORTH KOREA
SOUTH KOREA
JAPAN
Sea of Japan
Yellow Sea
EAST CHINA SEA
TAIWAN
PACIFIC OCEAN
BURMA
LAOS
THAILAND
VIETNAM
DEM. CAMBODIA
SOUTH CHINA SEA
REPUBLIC OF THE PHILIPPINES
UNITED STATES TRUST TERRITORY
MALAYSIA
INDONESIA
INDIAN OCEAN
Peking
Tokyo
Seoul
Pyongyang
Shanghai
Hanoi
Bangkok
Rangoon
Vientiane
Phnom Penh
Manila
Kuala Lumpur
Singapore
Jakarta
Taipei
Ho Chi Minh City (SAIGON)
Kowloon
HONG KONG
TROPIC OF CANCER
EQUATOR
EAST 110 OF GREENWICH

EUROPE
ATLANTIC OCEAN
Bay of Biscay
Paris
WEST GERMANY
Vienna
AUS.
FRANCE
Rostov
U. S. S. R.
Caspian Sea
Odessa
ROMANIA
Bucharest
Black Sea
Genoa
ITALY
YUGOSLAVIA
Belgrade
BULGARIA
Batumi
Baku
Krasnovodsk
AZORES (PORTUGAL)
Sao Miguel
Marseille
PORTUGAL
Madrid
SPAIN
Barcelona
Rome
Naples
Istanbul
Ankara
TURKEY
Lisbon
GREECE
Izmir
Bandar Shah
Tehran
Gibraltar (U.K.)
MEDITERRANEAN SEA
Athens
Mosul
MADEIRA ISLANDS (PORTUGAL)
Funchal
Tangier
Ceuta (SPAIN)
Algiers
Annaba
Bizerte
Tunis
Aleppo
SYRIA
IRAN
Rabat
Casablanca
MOROCCO
Fès
Oran
Constantine
TUNISIA
MALTA
Baghdad
CANARY ISLANDS (SPAIN)
Marrakech
ATLAS MOUNTAINS
Sfax
Damascus
IRAQ
Agadir
Tripoli
ASIA
Sta. Cruz de Tenerife
Las Palmas
Béchar
Ouargla
Touggourt
Al Khums
Misratah
Al Bayda
Darnah
Benghazi
Tubruq
Bardiyah
Barrani
Matrûh
Alexandria
Port Said
ISRAEL
JORDAN
Bandar Shahpur
KUWAIT
Persian Gulf
Smara
Ghudamis
TRIPOLITANIA
CYRENAICA
El Alamein
Cairo
Suez
G. of Suez
El Aaiun
ALGERIA
Adrar
TADEMAIT PLATEAU
Reggane
Ain Salah
Al Uqaylah
Al Jaghbub
Siwa
El Faiyûm
El Minya
Asyût
WESTERN DESERT
EGYPT
LIBYA
FEZZAN
Marzūq
LIBYAN DESERT
QATAR
Dakhla
MAURITANIA
IGIDI DESERT
Ghat
AL KUFRA OASIS
Qena
SAUDI ARABIA
Riyadh
Medina
TROPIC OF CANCER
Nouadhibou
SAHARA
HOGGAR MASSIF
El Khârga
Aswân
RED SEA
Tamanrasset
Wadi Halfa
Lake Nasser
Mecca
EL DJOUF
PLATEAU DU DJADO
NUBIAN DESERT
J. ODDA 2260
ADRAR DES IFORAS
TIBESTI MASSIF
EMI KOUSSI 3415
Port Sudan
Suakin
MALI
TÉNÉRÉ
Karima
Merowe
Haiya
P.D.R. OF YEMEN
SENEGAL
Tombouctou
AIR MASSIF
Largeau
ENNEDI PLATEAU
Gao
NIGER
Ed Damer
ERITREA
Mesewa
San'a
YEMEN
Omdurman
Kassala
Khartoum
Asmera
Bissau
Niamey
CHAD
Wad Medani
Adwa
Aden
Gulf of Aden
Abd al Kuri
Bamako
BURKINA FASO
Ouagadougou
Zinder
El Fasher
SUDAN
Asab
GUINEA
Kankan
Sokoto
Kaura Namoda
Nguru
Hadejia
Ndjamena
Lake Chad
El Obeid
Sennar
Singa
Gonder
DJIBOUTI
Djibouti
Bobo Dioulasso
Kaduna
Kano
J. GIMBALA 3088
ETHIOPIAN HIGHLANDS
Berbera
Freetown
AFRICA
Chari
Nyala
Malakal
Debre Markos
Dire Dawa
Hargeisa
Pendembu
IVORY COAST
Bouaké
Tamale
GHANA
TOGO
BENIN
Parakou
NIGERIA
Jos
Sarh
Bahr Aouk
Blue Nile
Addis Ababa
Harer
Monrovia
LIBERIA
Kumasi
Ibadan
Benue
ETHIOPIA
SOMALI DEM. REPUBLIC
Abidjan
Accra
Lomé
Porto Novo
Lagos
CAMEROON
White Nile
Wau
Akobo
CHILLALO 3657
Shibeli
C. Palmas
Takoradi
Sekondi
Port Harcourt
CENTRAL AFRICAN REPUBLIC
L. Abaya
Negele
Bight of Benin
Douala
Bangui
Bangassou
Bomu
Mongalla
Juba
Dolo
(EQUAT. GUINEA)
Yaounde
Bondo
Uele
Lake Turkana
Bight of Bonny
Businga
Isiro
Tigieglo
Gulf of Guinea
SÃO TOMÉ & PRINCIPE
São Tomé
EQUAT. GUINEA
Zaire
I. Mobutu Sese Seko
UGANDA
Soroti
MT. ELGON 4321
KENYA
Mogadiscio
EQUATOR
Kisangani
RUWENZORI 5120
Kampala
Libreville
C. Lopez
GABON
Ubangui
Mbandaka
Stanley Falls
Lake Idi Amin Dada
Kisumu
KENYA 5200
Entebbe
Nairobi
Chisimaio
Pagalu (EQUAT GUINEA)
Port Gentil
CONGO
Lake Ndombe
Kindu
Bukavu
RWANDA
Kigali
Lake Victoria
Mwanza
UHURU PEAK (KILIMANJARO) 5895
Brazzaville
ZAIRE
BURUNDI
Bujumbura
Arusha
Moshi
Mombasa
Pointe Noire
CABINDA (ANGOLA)
Kinshasa
Ilebo
Sankuru
Lusambo
Kongolo
Kigoma
Tabora
Tanga
Pemba
ZANZIBAR
Ascension (U.K.)
SOUTH ATLANTIC OCEAN
Boma
Matadi
Kwango
Kananga
Kasai
Kabalo
Kalemie
TANZANIA
Dodoma
Dar es Salaam
Lake Tanganyika
Luanda
Dondo
Malange
Bukama
Lake Mweru
Mbeya
RUNGWE 3177
Rufiji
Lindi
ALDABRA ISLANDS
(SEYCHELLES)
COSMOLEDO ISLANDS
Assumption Island
Cuanza
Kolwezi
Tenke
Chtimbe
Cape Delgado
Cap d'Ambre
Lobito
Benguela
ANGOLA
Lubumbashi
MUCHINGA MTS.
MALAWI
Lake Malawi
Pemba
COMOROS ISLANDS
Antsiranana
Huambo
Kabwe
Salima
Lilongwe
Malema
Mahajanga
St. Helena (U.K.)
Namibe
Pt. Albina
Lubango
ZAMBIA
Zomba
Mozambique
Nampula
Mozambique Channel
DEM. REPUBLIC OF MADAGASCAR
Andreba
Cunene
Cuando
Zambezi
Lusaka
Zawi
Livingstone
Harare
MOZAMBIQUE
Quelimane
Antananarivo
Toamasina
Okavango
ETOSHA PAN
Grootfontein
VICTORIA FALLS
ZIMBABWE
Chinde
Antsirabe
Okavango Basin
Masvingo
Beira
Fianarantsoa
Mananjary
NAMIBIA
BOTSWANA
Bulawayo
MADAGASCAR
Manakara
TROPIC OF CAPRICORN
Swakopmund
Windhoek
KALAHARI DESERT
Limpopo
Walvis Bay
NAMIB DESERT
Gaborone
Serowe
Soekmekaar
Toliara
Inhambane
Mariental
Mafikeng
Pretoria
TRANSVAAL
Maputo
Faradofay
Johannesburg
Mbabane
Delagoa Bay
SWAZILAND
C. Ste. Marie
Lüderitz
Keetmanshoop
REPUBLIC OF SOUTH AFRICA
DRAKENSBERG
Gollel
Kimberley
O.F.S.
Maseru
Pietermaritzburg
Port Nolloth
Orange
Bloemfontein
LESOTHO
Durban
Bitterfontein
Calvinia
Port Shepstone
CAPE OF GOOD HOPE
Maclear
Cape Town
GT. KAROO
East London
Port Alfred
Knysna
Pt. Elizabeth
Worcester
Cape Agulhas
Mosselbaai
INDIAN OCEAN
SCALE
Kilometres
0 200 600 1000
0 250 500 700
Miles
© GEOGRAPHIA
EAST 20 OF GREENWICH

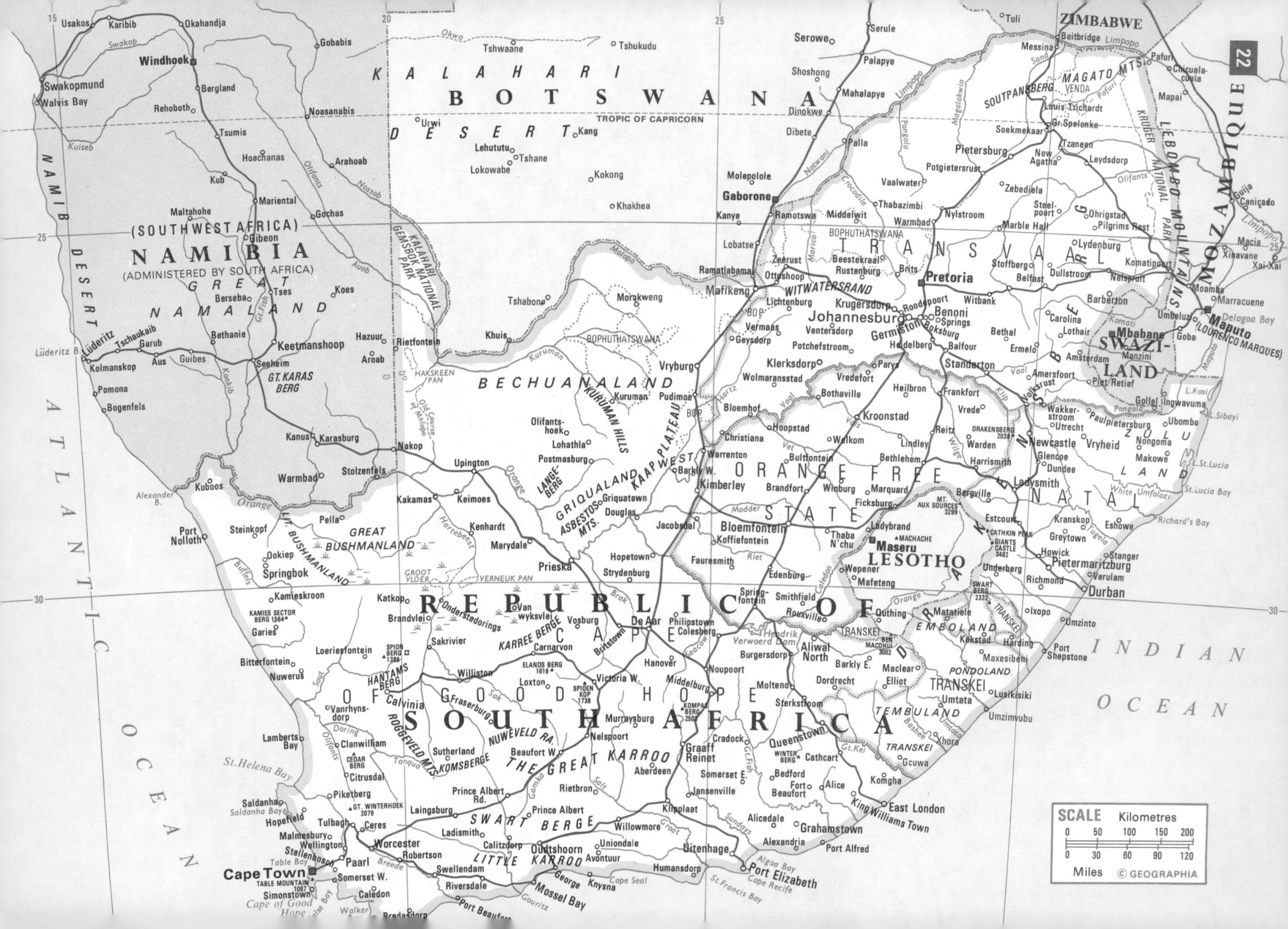

22
BOTSWANA
KALAHARI DESERT
TROPIC OF CAPRICORN
NAMIBIA
(SOUTHWEST AFRICA)
(ADMINISTERED BY SOUTH AFRICA)
GREAT NAMALAND
NAMIB DESERT
ZIMBABWE
MOZAMBIQUE
SWAZI-LAND
LESOTHO
REPUBLIC OF SOUTH AFRICA
TRANSVAAL
ORANGE FREE STATE
NATAL
CAPE OF GOOD HOPE
ZULU LAND
TRANSKEI
BECHUANALAND
GRIQUALAND WEST
KAAP PLATEAU
KURUMAN HILLS
ASBESTOS MTS.
GREAT BUSHMANLAND
LIT. BUSHMANLAND
THE GREAT KARROO
LITTLE KARROO
SWART BERGE
NUWEVELD RA.
ROGGEVELD MTS.
KOMSBERGE
KARREE BERGE
HANTAMS BERG
LEBOMBO MOUNTAINS
KRUGER NATIONAL PARK
KALAHARI GEMSBOK NATIONAL PARK
MAGATO MTS
SOUTPANSBERG
DRAKENSBERG
WITWATERSRAND
BOPHUTHATSWANA
VENDA
EMBOLAND
PONDOLAND
TEMBULAND
GT. KARAS BERG
ATLANTIC OCEAN
INDIAN OCEAN
Windhoek
Swakopmund
Walvis Bay
Usakos
Karibib
Okahandja
Gobabis
Rehoboth
Tsumis
Mariental
Gibeon
Keetmanshoop
Lüderitz
Aus
Karasburg
Gaborone
Serowe
Mafikeng
Vryburg
Kimberley
Bloemfontein
Johannesburg
Pretoria
Pietersburg
Maseru
Mbabane
Maputo (LOURENÇO MARQUES)
Durban
Pietermaritzburg
Ladysmith
Newcastle
East London
King Williams Town
Port Elizabeth
Grahamstown
Uitenhage
Mossel Bay
George
Knysna
Oudtshoorn
Cape Town
TABLE MOUNTAIN 1087
Paarl
Stellenbosch
Worcester
Springbok
Port Nolloth
Upington
Prieska
De Aar
Colesberg
Graaff Reinet
Beaufort W.
Calvinia
Aliwal North
Queenstown
Umtata
Kroonstad
Welkom
Klerksdorp
Potchefstroom
Vereeniging
Benoni
Germiston
Springs
Witbank
Rustenburg
SCALE
Kilometres
0 50 100 150 200
0 30 60 90 120
Miles
© GEOGRAPHIA

UNITED STATES
MEXICO
CANADA
ONTARIO
QUEBEC
WEST INDIES
GREATER ANTILLES
CUBA
HISPANIOLA
PACIFIC OCEAN
ATLANTIC OCEAN
CARIBBEAN SEA
Gulf of Mexico
Gulf of California
Bay of Campeche
Straits of Florida
Yucatan Channel
TROPIC OF CANCER
WEST 110 OF GREENWICH
WASHINGTON
OREGON
CALIFORNIA
NEVADA
IDAHO
MONTANA
WYOMING
UTAH
COLORADO
ARIZONA
NEW MEXICO
N. DAKOTA
S. DAKOTA
NEBRASKA
KANSAS
OKLAHOMA
TEXAS
MINNESOTA
IOWA
MISSOURI
ARKANSAS
LOUISIANA
WISCONSIN
ILLINOIS
MICHIGAN
INDIANA
OHIO
KENTUCKY
TENNESSEE
MISSISSIPPI
ALABAMA
GEORGIA
FLORIDA
S.CAROLINA
N. CAROLINA
VIRGINIA
W.VIR.
PENN.
N.Y.
MAINE
NEW BRUNSWICK
NOVA SCOTIA
BAHAMAS
JAMAICA
HAITI
DOMINICAN REP.
PUERTO RICO
BELIZE
GUATEMALA
HONDURAS
EL SALVADOR
NICARAGUA
ROCKY MTS.
COAST RANGE
SIERRA NEVADA
CASCADE RA.
APPALACHIAN MTS.
WESTERN SIERRA MADRE
EASTERN SIERRA MADRE
SOUTHERN SIERRA MADRE
LOWER CALIFORNIA
YUCATÁN
Washington
Ottawa
Mexico City
New York
Chicago
Los Angeles
San Francisco
Seattle
Philadelphia
Montreal
Toronto
Havana
SCALE
Kilometres
0 200 400 600
0 100 200 300 400
Miles
© GEOGRAPHIA
23

CANADA
U.S.A.
ALASKA
(U.S.A.)
GREENLAND
(DENMARK)
ICELAND
Reykjavik
NORTHWEST TERRITORIES
Mackenzie
Keewatin
Franklin
YUKON
BRITISH COLUMBIA
ALBERTA
SASKATCHEWAN
MANITOBA
ONTARIO
QUEBEC
NEWFOUNDLAND
LABRADOR
NEW BRUNSWICK
NOVA SCOTIA
PR. EDWARD IS.
QUEEN ELIZABETH ISLANDS
SVERDRUP ISLANDS
PARRY ISLANDS
VICTORIA ISLAND
BAFFIN ISLAND
ELLESMERE I.
Devon I.
Banks Island
Melville I.
Prince Patrick Island
Southampton Island
Vancouver Island
QUEEN CHARLOTTE ISLANDS
ALEXANDER ARCHIPELAGO
ARCTIC OCEAN
Beaufort Sea
Baffin Bay
Davis Strait
Hudson Strait
Hudson Bay
James Bay
Ungava Bay
Foxe Basin
Denmark Str.
Bering Strait
Gulf of Alaska
PACIFIC OCEAN
ATLANTIC OCEAN
G. of St. Lawrence
ARCTIC CIRCLE
BROOKS RANGE
ALASKA RANGE
CHUGACH MTS.
MACKENZIE MTS.
ROCKY MOUNTAINS
COAST MTS.
CASSIAR MTS.
CARIBOO MTS.
SELKIRK MTS.
Great Bear Lake
Great Slave Lake
Lake Athabasca
Lake Winnipeg
Lake Superior
L. Huron
L. Ontario
L. Erie
Anchorage
Fairbanks
Nome
Dawson
Whitehorse
Yellowknife
Fort Smith
Edmonton
Calgary
Vancouver
Victoria
Prince Rupert
Saskatoon
Regina
Winnipeg
Churchill
Thunder Bay
Toronto
Ottawa
Montreal
Quebec
Halifax
St. Johns
Seattle
Portland
Spokane
Minneapolis
St. Paul
Milwaukee
Boston
Buffalo
MONTANA
N. DAKOTA
S. DAKOTA
MINNESOTA
WISCONSIN
MICHIGAN
IDAHO
WYOMING
WASHINGTON
OREGON
MAINE
NEW YORK
SCALE
Kilometres
0 200 400 600
0 100 200 300 400
Miles
© GEOGRAPHIA

NORTH AMERICA
CANADA
UNITED STATES
MEXICO
CENTRAL AMERICA
SOUTH AMERICA
GREENLAND (DENMARK)
ICELAND
Reykjavik
U.S.S.R.
Uelen
Bering Str.
Chukchi Sea
ARCTIC OCEAN
Nome
Seward Pen.
Norton Sd.
Pt. Hope
Pt. Barrow
BROOKS RANGE
ALASKA (U.S.A.)
Yukon
Prudhoe Bay
Beaufort Sea
Fort Yukon
Circle
Fairbanks
Anchorage
MT. MCKINLEY 6196
Seward
Cordova
Gulf of Alaska
Aklavik
Dawson
Carmacks
Whitehorse
Skagway
Juneau
Sitka
ALEXANDER ARCHIPELAGO
Prince of Wales I.
Ketchikan
Prince Rupert
QUEEN CHARLOTTE ISLANDS
Qn. Charlotte Sound
Vancouver I.
Victoria
Vancouver
MACKENZIE MTS
Mackenzie
Fort Norman
Great Bear Lake
Fort Simpson
Liard
Fort Resolution
Gt. Slave Lake
Fort Vermilion
Peace River
CHURCHILL PEAK 3202
Prince George
Edmonton
MT. ROBSON 3957
Red Deer
Calgary
Kamloops
Medicine Hat
Saskatoon
Regina
Moose Jaw
Brandon
Winnipeg
Lake Winnipeg
Lake Athabasca
Reindeer Lake
Lynn Lake
Churchill
Port Nelson
York Factory
Nelson
Sioux Lookout
Albany
Moosonee
Cochrane
Thunder Bay
Coppermine
Garry Lake
ARCTIC CIRCLE
QUEEN ELIZABETH ISLANDS
Borden I.
Prince Patrick I.
SVERDRUP ISLANDS
ELLESMERE ISLAND
PARRY ISLANDS
Melville I.
Bathurst I.
NORTH MAGNETIC POLE
Devon I.
M'Clure Strait
Melville Sd.
Barrow Str.
Banks I.
Prince of Wales I.
VICTORIA ISLAND
Amundsen G.
C. Bathurst
Boothia Pen.
G. of Boothia
BAFFIN ISLAND
Baffin Bay
Davis Strait
Foxe Basin
Cumberland Sd.
Wager Bay
Southampton I.
Coats I.
Mansel I.
Hudson Str.
Resolution I.
C. Chidley
Ungava B.
Hudson Bay
BELCHER ISLANDS
James Bay
Ft. George
Eastmain
Hayes Pen.
Thule Air Base
Kavdlorssuaq
Jakobshavn
Disko
Godthab
Julianehab
CAPE FAREWELL
KING CHRISTIAN X LAND
KING CHRISTIAN IX LAND
KING FREDERICK VI COAST
Angmagssalik
Denmark Str.
Scoresby Sd.
Nain
Schefferville
LABRADOR
Battle Harbour
Str. of Belle I.
Botwood
NEWFOUNDLAND
St. John's
C. Race
Mingan
Sept Iles
Anticosti I.
G. of St. Lawrence
Prince Edward I.
Cape Breton I.
Sydney
St. Pierre & Miquelon (FRANCE)
Saint John
Halifax
NOVA SCOTIA
C. Sable
Quebec
Trois Rivieres
Montreal
Ottawa
Sault Sainte Marie
L. Superior
L. Nipigon
L. of the Woods
Duluth
L. Huron
L. Michigan
L. Ontario
L. Erie
Toronto
Hamilton
Buffalo
Portland
Albany
Boston
New Haven
New York
Newark
Philadelphia
Baltimore
Washington
Norfolk
Richmond
CAPE HATTERAS
Bermuda (U.K.)
Seattle
Tacoma
Spokane
Portland
Columbia
Eugene
CASCADE RA
CAPE MENDOCINO
Boise
Snake
Butte
Great Falls
Yellowstone
Laurel
Bismarck
Fargo
Minneapolis
St. Paul
Milwaukee
Sioux City
Omaha
Des Moines
Chicago
Detroit
Toledo
Cleveland
Pittsburgh
Indianapolis
Cincinnati
Louisville
Ohio
Sacramento
Reno
Carlin
Gt. Salt Lake
Salt Lake City
N. Platte
Cheyenne
Kearney
Denver
Pueblo
San Francisco
Oakland
Fresno
SIERRA NEVADA
MT. WHITNEY 4420
Colorado
COLORADO PLATEAU
Los Angeles
Long Beach
San Diego
Santa Fe
Phoenix
Yuma
Kansas City
St. Louis
Wichita
Arkansas
Oklahoma City
Canadian
Little Rock
Red
LLANO ESTACADO
Ft. Worth
Dallas
Memphis
Mississippi
Nashville
APPALACHIAN MOUNTAINS
Charlotte
Wilmington
Atlanta
Charleston
Savannah
Birmingham
Montgomery
Jackson
Mobile
Baton Rouge
New Orleans
Jacksonville
Houston
San Antonio
Galveston
FLORIDA
Cape Canaveral
Tampa
Miami
Key West
BAHAMAS
Nassau
TROPIC OF CANCER
Guadalupe I. (MEXICO)
Ciudad Juárez
El Paso
Rio Grande
Chihuahua
LOWER CALIFORNIA
Gulf of California
WESTERN SIERRA MADRE
Brownsville
Saltillo
Torreón
Monterrey
Gulf of Mexico
C.S. Lucas
Mazatlán
San Luis Potosí
Tampico
León
Guadalajara
Santiago
Pachuca
Mérida
C. Catoche
Yucatan Channel
B. of Campeche
REVILLA GIGEDO ISLANDS (MEXICO)
Manzanillo
Mexico
POPOCATEPETL 5452
Puebla
Veracruz
YUCATÁN
Isthmus of Tehuantepec
Acapulco
Salina Cruz
G. of Tehuantepec
GUATEMALA
Guatemala
Belmopan
Belize
BELIZE
Trujillo
HONDURAS
Tegucigalpa
San Salvador
EL SALVADOR
NICARAGUA
León
Managua
L. Nicaragua
San José
COSTA RICA
PANAMA CANAL
PANAMA
Panamá
G. of Panamá
Havana
Matanzas
CUBA
Camaguey
Santiago de Cuba
Grand Cayman (U.K.)
JAMAICA
Kingston
HAITI
Port-au-Prince
DOMINICAN REPUBLIC
Santo Domingo
HISPANIOLA
PUERTO RICO
San Juan
GREATER ANTILLES
WEST INDIES
Caribbean Sea
Guajira Pen.
G. of Venezuela
Maracaibo
Caracas
Barranquilla
Cartagena
Medellín
Bogotá
ATLANTIC OCEAN
PACIFIC OCEAN
SCALE
Kilometres
0 250 500 750 1000
0 200 400 600
Miles
© GEOGRAPHIA
LONGITUDE WEST OF GREENWICH
70 160 140 120 100 80 60 40 20
110 100 90 80 70
60 50 40 30 20 10

26
SCALE Kilometres
0 200 600 1000
0 200 400 600
Miles
© GEOGRAPHIA
CARIBBEAN SEA
ATLANTIC OCEAN
PACIFIC OCEAN
BRAZIL
COLOMBIA
VENEZUELA
ECUADOR
PERU
BOLIVIA
PARAGUAY
URUGUAY
CHILE
GUYANA
SURINAM
FRENCH GUIANA
CENTRAL AMERICA
SELVAS
CATINGAS
PLATEAU OF MATO GROSSO
GRAN CHACO
PAMPAS
PATAGONIA
ANDES
EQUATOR
TROPIC OF CAPRICORN
WEST 60 OF GREENWICH
Rio de Janeiro
São Paulo
Buenos Aires
Montevideo
Santiago
Lima
Bogotá
Caracas
La Paz
Asunción
Quito
Brasília
FALKLAND ISLANDS (U.K.)
South Georgia (U.K.)
CAPE HORN
Drake Strait

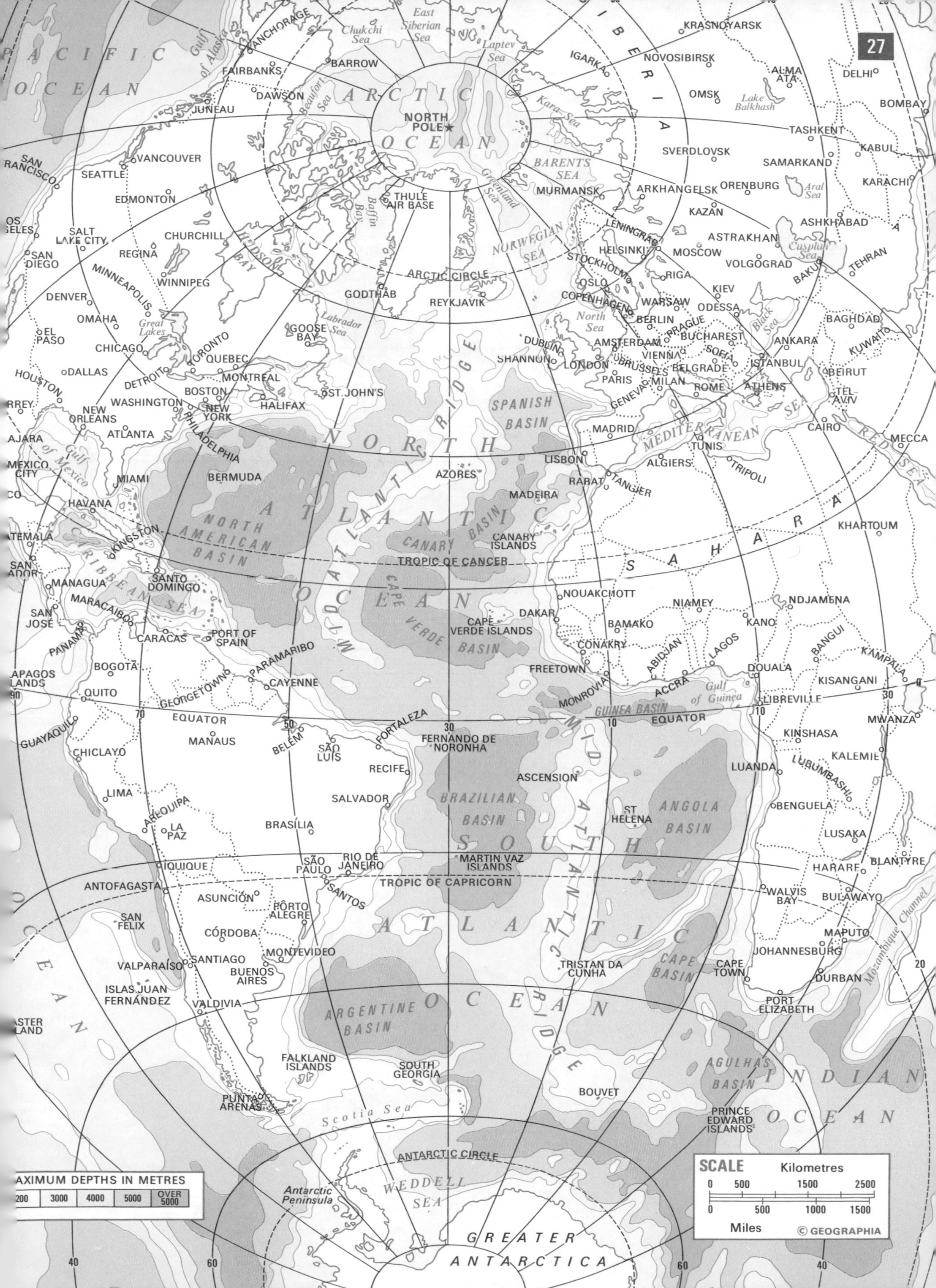
PACIFIC OCEAN
ARCTIC OCEAN
NORTH POLE
SIBERIA
NORTH ATLANTIC OCEAN
SOUTH ATLANTIC OCEAN
INDIAN OCEAN
SAHARA
GREATER ANTARCTICA
MID ATLANTIC RIDGE
ARCTIC CIRCLE
TROPIC OF CANCER
EQUATOR
TROPIC OF CAPRICORN
ANTARCTIC CIRCLE
SPANISH BASIN
NORTH AMERICAN BASIN
CANARY BASIN
CAPE VERDE BASIN
GUINEA BASIN
BRAZILIAN BASIN
ANGOLA BASIN
CAPE BASIN
ARGENTINE BASIN
AGULHAS BASIN
WEDDELL SEA
Scotia Sea
MEDITERRANEAN SEA
CARIBBEAN SEA
RED SEA
NORWEGIAN SEA
BARENTS SEA
HUDSON BAY
Gulf of Mexico
Gulf of Alaska
Gulf of Guinea
Mozambique Channel
Labrador Sea
North Sea
Black Sea
Caspian Sea
Aral Sea
Lake Balkhash
Great Lakes
Baffin Bay
Greenland Sea
Kara Sea
Laptev Sea
East Siberian Sea
Chukchi Sea
Beaufort Sea
Antarctic Peninsula
ANCHORAGE
BARROW
FAIRBANKS
DAWSON
JUNEAU
VANCOUVER
SEATTLE
SAN FRANCISCO
EDMONTON
SALT LAKE CITY
SAN DIEGO
REGINA
CHURCHILL
WINNIPEG
MINNEAPOLIS
DENVER
OMAHA
EL PASO
CHICAGO
TORONTO
QUEBEC
MONTREAL
DETROIT
DALLAS
HOUSTON
BOSTON
NEW YORK
WASHINGTON
PHILADELPHIA
NEW ORLEANS
ATLANTA
MIAMI
HAVANA
MEXICO CITY
KINGSTON
SANTO DOMINGO
MANAGUA
MARACAIBO
SAN JOSÉ
PANAMA
CARACAS
PORT OF SPAIN
BOGOTÁ
PARAMARIBO
GEORGETOWN
CAYENNE
QUITO
GUAYAQUIL
CHICLAYO
MANAUS
BELÉM
SÃO LUÍS
FORTALEZA
RECIFE
SALVADOR
BRASÍLIA
LIMA
AREQUIPA
LA PAZ
IQUIQUE
ANTOFAGASTA
SÃO PAULO
RIO DE JANEIRO
SANTOS
ASUNCIÓN
PÔRTO ALEGRE
SAN FELIX
CÓRDOBA
SANTIAGO
VALPARAÍSO
MONTEVIDEO
BUENOS AIRES
ISLAS JUAN FERNÁNDEZ
VALDIVIA
FALKLAND ISLANDS
SOUTH GEORGIA
PUNTA ARENAS
BERMUDA
THULE AIR BASE
GODTHÅB
REYKJAVIK
GOOSE BAY
ST. JOHN'S
HALIFAX
AZORES
MADEIRA
CANARY ISLANDS
CAPE VERDE ISLANDS
FERNANDO DE NORONHA
ASCENSION
ST HELENA
MARTIN VAZ ISLANDS
TRISTAN DA CUNHA
BOUVET
PRINCE EDWARD ISLANDS
KRASNOYARSK
NOVOSIBIRSK
IGARKA
OMSK
ALMA ATA
DELHI
BOMBAY
TASHKENT
KABUL
SVERDLOVSK
SAMARKAND
KARACHI
MURMANSK
ARKHANGELSK
ORENBURG
KAZAN
ASHKHABAD
LENINGRAD
HELSINKI
MOSCOW
ASTRAKHAN
VOLGOGRAD
BAKU
TEHRAN
STOCKHOLM
OSLO
RIGA
COPENHAGEN
KIEV
WARSAW
ODESSA
BERLIN
PRAGUE
BUCHAREST
DUBLIN
SHANNON
AMSTERDAM
LONDON
BRUSSELS
VIENNA
SOFIA
PARIS
GENEVA
MILAN
BELGRADE
ROME
ISTANBUL
ANKARA
ATHENS
BAGHDAD
KUWAIT
BEIRUT
TEL AVIV
CAIRO
MECCA
MADRID
LISBON
RABAT
TANGIER
ALGIERS
TUNIS
TRIPOLI
KHARTOUM
NOUAKCHOTT
DAKAR
BAMAKO
NIAMEY
KANO
NDJAMENA
CONAKRY
FREETOWN
MONROVIA
ABIDJAN
ACCRA
LAGOS
BANGUI
DOUALA
KAMPALA
KISANGANI
LIBREVILLE
MWANZA
KINSHASA
KALEMIE
LUANDA
LUBUMBASHI
BENGUELA
LUSAKA
BLANTYRE
HARARE
WALVIS BAY
BULAWAYO
MAPUTO
JOHANNESBURG
CAPE TOWN
DURBAN
PORT ELIZABETH
EASTER ISLAND
MAXIMUM DEPTHS IN METRES
200
3000
4000
5000
OVER 5000
SCALE
Kilometres
0 500 1500 2500
0 500 1000 1500
Miles
© GEOGRAPHIA

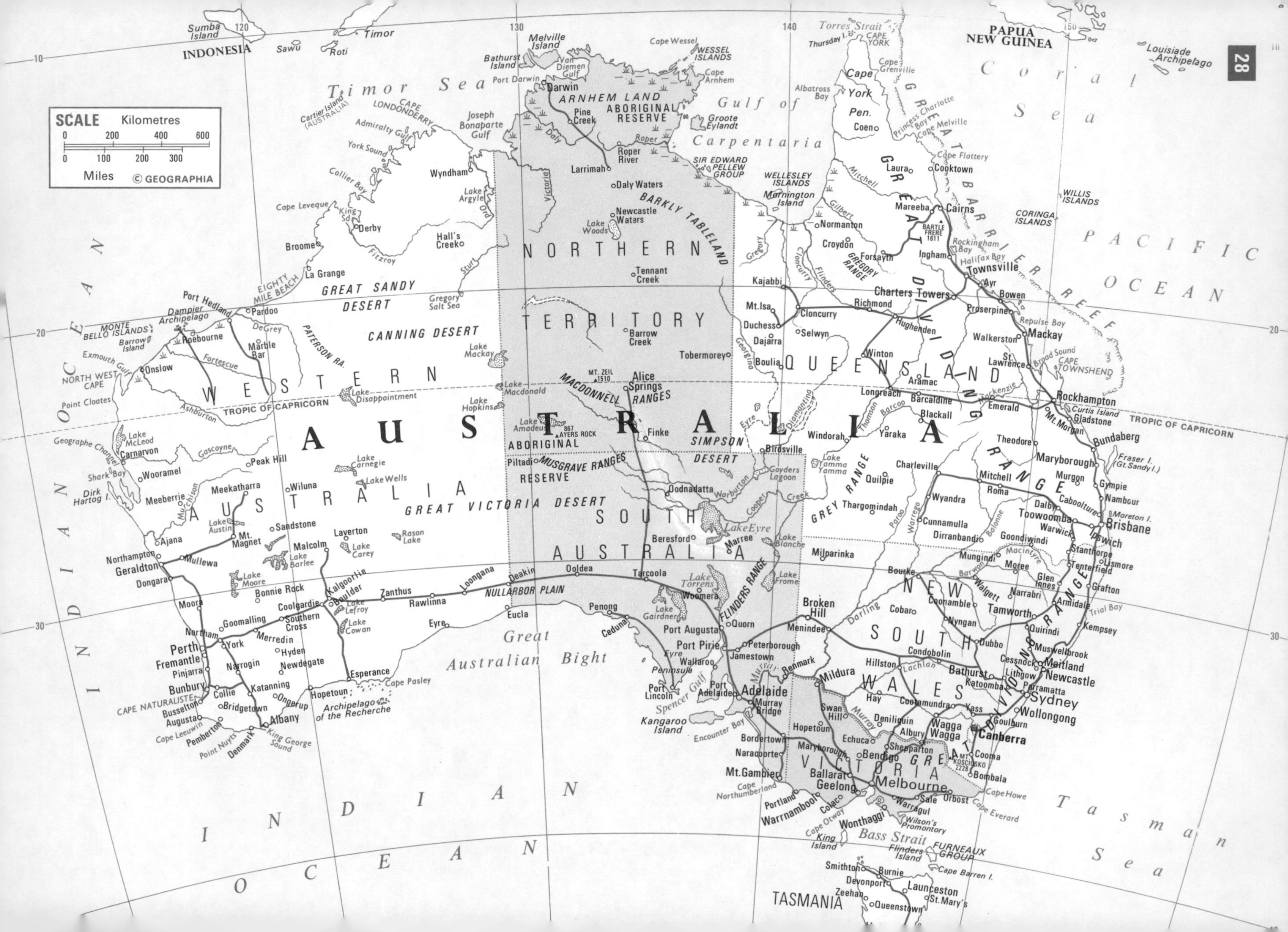
SCALE
Kilometres
0
200
400
600
0
100
200
300
Miles
© GEOGRAPHIA
AUSTRALIA
WESTERN AUSTRALIA
NORTHERN TERRITORY
SOUTH AUSTRALIA
QUEENSLAND
NEW SOUTH WALES
VICTORIA
TASMANIA
INDONESIA
PAPUA NEW GUINEA
INDIAN OCEAN
PACIFIC OCEAN
Timor Sea
Coral Sea
Tasman Sea
Gulf of Carpentaria
Great Australian Bight
Bass Strait
Torres Strait
TROPIC OF CAPRICORN
GREAT BARRIER REEF
GREAT DIVIDING RANGE
GREAT SANDY DESERT
CANNING DESERT
GREAT VICTORIA DESERT
SIMPSON DESERT
NULLARBOR PLAIN
BARKLY TABLELAND
MACDONNELL RANGES
MUSGRAVE RANGES
FLINDERS RANGE
GREY RANGE
GREGORY RANGE
PATERSON RA.
ARNHEM LAND ABORIGINAL RESERVE
ABORIGINAL RESERVE
EIGHTY MILE BEACH
MT. ZEIL 1510
867 AYERS ROCK
BARTLE FRERE 1611
MT. KOSCIUSKO 2228
Sumba Island
Sawu
Roti
Timor
Cartier Island (AUSTRALIA)
CAPE LONDONDERRY
Admiralty Gulf
York Sound
Collier Bay
Cape Leveque
King Sd.
Derby
Broome
La Grange
Port Hedland
Pardoo
Dampier Archipelago
MONTE BELLO ISLANDS
Barrow Island
Roebourne
Marble Bar
DeGrey
Fortescue
Exmouth Gulf
Onslow
NORTH WEST CAPE
Point Cloates
Ashburton
Lake McLeod
Carnarvon
Geographe Channel
Gascoyne
Shark Bay
Wooramel
Dirk Hartog I.
Meeberrie
Murchison
Meekatharra
Peak Hill
Wiluna
Lake Austin
Mt. Magnet
Sandstone
Ajana
Northampton
Geraldton
Mullewa
Dongara
Lake Moore
Lake Barlee
Malcolm
Laverton
Lake Carey
Rason Lake
Lake Carnegie
Lake Wells
Lake Disappointment
Lake Mackay
Lake Macdonald
Lake Hopkins
Lake Amadeus
Piltadi
Moora
Bonnie Rock
Coolgardie
Kalgoorlie
Boulder
Southern Cross
Lake Lefroy
Lake Cowan
Zanthus
Rawlinna
Loongana
Deakin
Eucla
Eyre
Northam
Perth
Fremantle
Pinjarra
York
Goomalling
Merredin
Hyden
Newdegate
Narrogin
Katanning
Ongerup
Esperance
Cape Pasley
Hopetoun
Archipelago of the Recherche
Bunbury
Collie
CAPE NATURALISTE
Busselton
Augusta
Cape Leeuwin
Bridgetown
Pemberton
Point Nuyts
Denmark
Albany
King George Sound
Wyndham
Joseph Bonaparte Gulf
Lake Argyle
Ord
Hall's Creek
Fitzroy
Sturt
Gregory Salt Sea
Bathurst Island
Melville Island
Van Diemen Gulf
Port Darwin
Darwin
Pine Creek
Daly
Victoria
Larrimah
Roper River
Roper
Daly Waters
Newcastle Waters
Lake Woods
Tennant Creek
Barrow Creek
Alice Springs
Finke
Tobermorey
Cape Wessel
WESSEL ISLANDS
Cape Arnhem
Groote Eylandt
SIR EDWARD PELLEW GROUP
WELLESLEY ISLANDS
Mornington Island
Albatross Bay
Thursday I.
CAPE YORK
Cape Grenville
Cape York Pen.
Coen
Princess Charlotte Bay
Cape Melville
Cape Flattery
Laura
Cooktown
Mitchell
Gilbert
Normanton
Croydon
Forsayth
Mareeba
Cairns
Rockingham Bay
Halifax Bay
Ingham
Townsville
Ayr
Bowen
Proserpine
Repulse Bay
Mackay
Broad Sound
CAPE TOWNSHEND
Walkerston
St. Lawrence
Gregory
Kajabbi
Cloncurry
Flinders
Mt. Isa
Duchess
Dajarra
Selwyn
Richmond
Charters Towers
Hughenden
Winton
Boulia
Georgina
Longreach
Barcaldine
Aramac
Mackenzie
Emerald
Blackall
Rockhampton
Curtis Island
Gladstone
Mt. Morgan
Bundaberg
Theodore
Maryborough
Fraser I. (Gt. Sandy I.)
Gympie
Murgon
Nambour
Caboolture
Moreton I.
Brisbane
Ipswich
Toowoomba
Dalby
Warwick
Roma
Mitchell
Charleville
Wyandra
Quilpie
Yaraka
Thomson
Barcoo
Windorah
Diamantina
Eyre
Lake Yamma Yamma
Thargomindah
Warrego
Paroo
Cunnamulla
Dirranbandi
Balonne
Goondiwindi
Macintyre
Mungindi
Moree
Stanthorpe
Tenterfield
Lismore
Grafton
Glen Innes
Armidale
Trial Bay
Kempsey
Narrabri
Tamworth
Walgett
Barwon
Bourke
Coonamble
Quirindi
Muswellbrook
Maitland
Newcastle
Cessnock
Dubbo
Nyngan
Cobar
Darling
Lithgow
Katoomba
Bathurst
Parramatta
Sydney
Wollongong
Condobolin
Hillston
Lachlan
Cootamundra
Yass
Goulburn
Canberra
Wagga Wagga
Hay
Deniliquin
Albury
Cooma
Bombala
Cape Howe
Birdsville
Goyders Lagoon
Cooper
Creek
Warburton
Oodnadatta
Lake Eyre
Marree
Beresford
Lake Blanche
Lake Frome
Milparinka
Broken Hill
Menindee
Ooldea
Tarcoola
Lake Torrens
Woomera
Lake Gairdner
Penong
Ceduna
Quorn
Port Augusta
Port Pirie
Peterborough
Jamestown
Wallaroo
Eyre Peninsula
Port Lincoln
Spencer Gulf
Port Adelaide
Adelaide
Murray Bridge
Murray
Renmark
Mildura
Kangaroo Island
Encounter Bay
Bordertown
Naracoorte
Mt. Gambier
Cape Northumberland
Portland
Warrnambool
Colac
Cape Otway
Hopetoun
Swan Hill
Echuca
Shepparton
Bendigo
Maryborough
Ballarat
Geelong
Melbourne
Warragul
Sale
Orbost
Cape Everard
Wonthaggi
Wilson's Promontory
King Island
Flinders Island
FURNEAUX GROUP
Cape Barren I.
Smithton
Burnie
Devonport
Launceston
St. Mary's
Zeehan
Queenstown
WILLIS ISLANDS
CORINGA ISLANDS
Louisiade Archipelago
10
20
30
120
130
140
150

29
SCALE Kilometres 0 80 160 240
Miles 0 50 100 150 © GEOGRAPHIA
AUSTRALIA
QUEENSLAND
NEW SOUTH WALES
VICTORIA
SOUTH AUSTRALIA
TASMANIA
GREAT DIVIDING RANGE
AUSTRALIAN ALPS
CAPITAL TERRITORY
Canberra
Sydney
Melbourne
Adelaide
Hobart
Newcastle
Wollongong
Bass Strait
KING Island
FURNEAUX GROUP
KENT GROUP
PACIFIC OCEAN
TASMAN SEA
INDIAN OCEAN
NEW ZEALAND
NORTH ISLAND
SOUTH ISLAND
Auckland
Wellington
Christchurch
Dunedin
Cook Strait
Foveaux Strait
Stewart Island
SOUTH PACIFIC OCEAN
(NEW ZEALAND) Bounty Islands
(NEW ZEALAND) Antipodes I.
The Snares
SCALE Kilometres 0 50 150 250
Miles 0 50 100 150 © GEOGRAPHIA
EAST 144 OF GREENWICH
EAST 172 OF GREENWICH

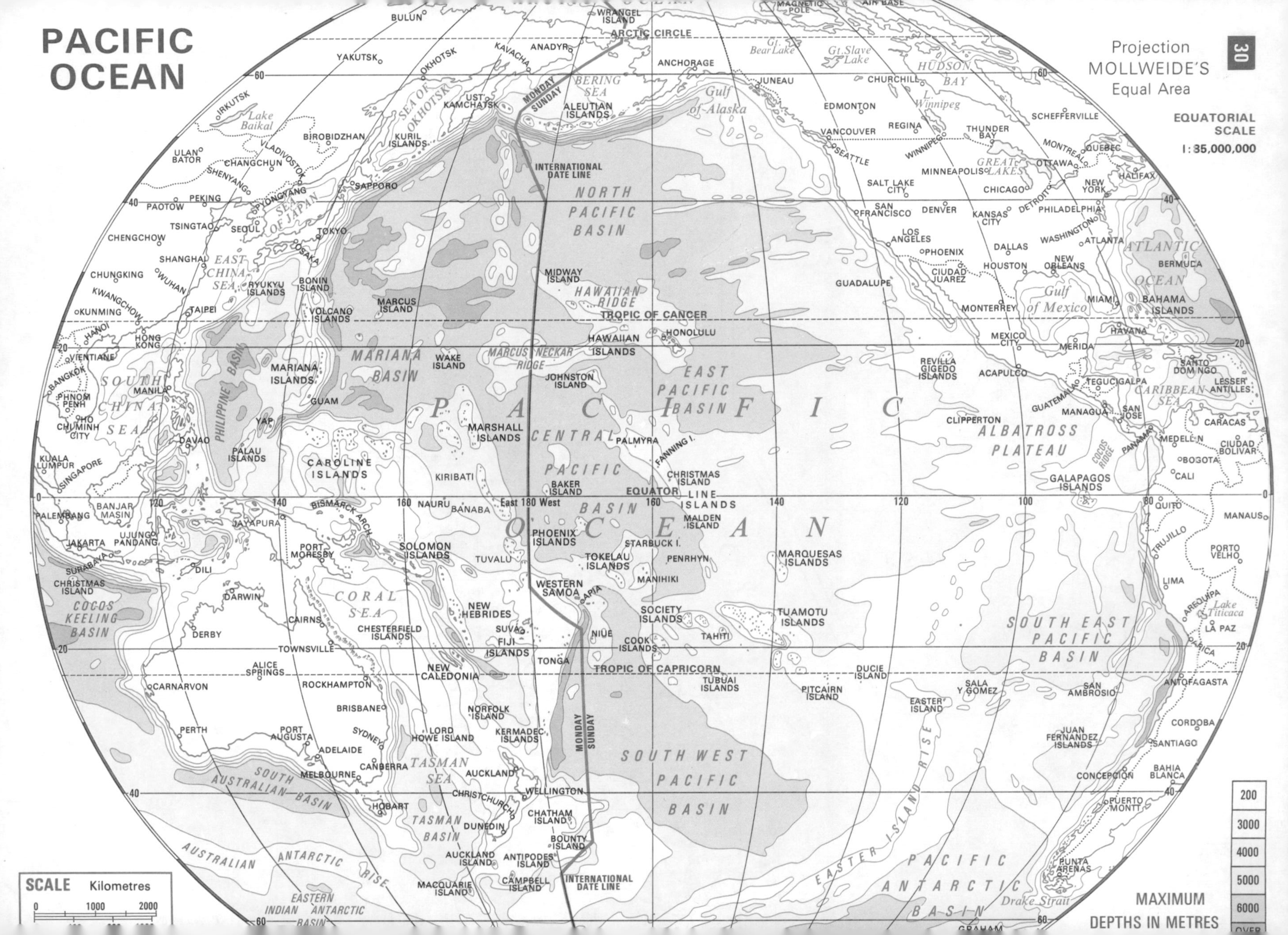

PACIFIC OCEAN
30
Projection
MOLLWEIDE'S
Equal Area
EQUATORIAL SCALE
1: 35,000,000
SCALE Kilometres
0
1000
2000
MAXIMUM DEPTHS IN METRES
200
3000
4000
5000
6000
ARCTIC CIRCLE
TROPIC OF CANCER
EQUATOR
TROPIC OF CAPRICORN
East 180 West
INTERNATIONAL DATE LINE
MONDAY
SUNDAY
P A C I F I C
O C E A N
NORTH PACIFIC BASIN
EAST PACIFIC BASIN
CENTRAL PACIFIC BASIN
SOUTH WEST PACIFIC BASIN
SOUTH EAST PACIFIC BASIN
PACIFIC ANTARCTIC BASIN
MARIANA BASIN
PHILIPPINE BASIN
HAWAIIAN RIDGE
MARCUS NECKAR RIDGE
ALBATROSS PLATEAU
COCOS RIDGE
EASTER ISLAND RISE
AUSTRALIAN ANTARCTIC RISE
SOUTH AUSTRALIAN BASIN
TASMAN BASIN
EASTERN INDIAN ANTARCTIC BASIN
COCOS KEELING BASIN
BERING SEA
SEA OF OKHOTSK
SEA OF JAPAN
EAST CHINA SEA
SOUTH CHINA SEA
CORAL SEA
TASMAN SEA
CARIBBEAN SEA
ATLANTIC OCEAN
Gulf of Alaska
Gulf of Mexico
HUDSON BAY
Drake Strait
Lake Baikal
Gt. Bear Lake
Gt. Slave Lake
L. Winnipeg
GREAT LAKES
Lake Titicaca
MAGNETIC POLE
WRANGEL ISLAND
BULUN
YAKUTSK
OKHOTSK
KAVACHA
ANADYR
UST KAMCHATSK
ALEUTIAN ISLANDS
ANCHORAGE
JUNEAU
CHURCHILL
EDMONTON
REGINA
SCHEFFERVILLE
VANCOUVER
SEATTLE
WINNIPEG
THUNDER BAY
MONTREAL
QUEBEC
OTTAWA
HALIFAX
MINNEAPOLIS
SALT LAKE CITY
CHICAGO
NEW YORK
DETROIT
PHILADELPHIA
WASHINGTON
ATLANTA
SAN FRANCISCO
DENVER
KANSAS CITY
LOS ANGELES
PHOENIX
DALLAS
HOUSTON
NEW ORLEANS
CIUDAD JUAREZ
GUADALUPE
MONTERREY
MIAMI
BERMUDA
BAHAMA ISLANDS
HAVANA
MEXICO CITY
MERIDA
REVILLA GIGEDO ISLANDS
ACAPULCO
SANTO DOMINGO
LESSER ANTILLES
TEGUCIGALPA
GUATEMALA
MANAGUA
SAN JOSE
CLIPPERTON
CARACAS
PANAMA
MEDELLIN
CIUDAD BOLIVAR
BOGOTA
CALI
GALAPAGOS ISLANDS
QUITO
MANAUS
TRUJILLO
PORTO VELHO
LIMA
AREQUIPA
LA PAZ
ARICA
ANTOFAGASTA
SALA Y GOMEZ
EASTER ISLAND
SAN AMBROSIO
CORDOBA
JUAN FERNANDEZ ISLANDS
SANTIAGO
CONCEPCION
BAHIA BLANCA
PUERTO MONTT
PUNTA ARENAS
IRKUTSK
ULAN BATOR
BIROBIDZHAN
KURIL ISLANDS
CHANGCHUN
VLADIVOSTOK
SHENYANG
SAPPORO
PEKING
PAOTOW
PYONGYANG
TSINGTAO
SEOUL
TOKYO
OSAKA
CHENGCHOW
SHANGHAI
WUHAN
CHUNGKING
KWANGCHOW
RYUKYU ISLANDS
BONIN ISLAND
MARCUS ISLAND
MIDWAY ISLAND
KUNMING
TAIPEI
VOLCANO ISLANDS
HONOLULU
HAWAIIAN ISLANDS
HANOI
HONG KONG
VIENTIANE
MARIANA ISLANDS
WAKE ISLAND
JOHNSTON ISLAND
BANGKOK
MANILA
PHNOM PENH
GUAM
HO CHI MINH CITY
YAP
MARSHALL ISLANDS
PALMYRA
FANNING I.
DAVAO
PALAU ISLANDS
KUALA LUMPUR
SINGAPORE
CAROLINE ISLANDS
KIRIBATI
CHRISTMAS ISLAND
BAKER ISLAND
LINE ISLANDS
BANJARMASIN
PALEMBANG
BISMARCK ARCH
NAURU
BANABA
MALDEN ISLAND
JAYAPURA
PHOENIX ISLANDS
STARBUCK I.
JAKARTA
UJUNG PANDANG
PORT MORESBY
SOLOMON ISLANDS
TUVALU
TOKELAU ISLANDS
PENRHYN
MARQUESAS ISLANDS
SURABAYA
DILI
MANIHIKI
WESTERN SAMOA
APIA
DARWIN
NEW HEBRIDES
SOCIETY ISLANDS
TUAMOTU ISLANDS
CAIRNS
DERBY
CHESTERFIELD ISLANDS
SUVA
FIJI ISLANDS
NIUE
COOK ISLANDS
TAHITI
TOWNSVILLE
ALICE SPRINGS
NEW CALEDONIA
TONGA
TUBUAI ISLANDS
DUCIE ISLAND
PITCAIRN ISLAND
CARNARVON
ROCKHAMPTON
BRISBANE
NORFOLK ISLAND
KERMADEC ISLANDS
PERTH
PORT AUGUSTA
SYDNEY
LORD HOWE ISLAND
ADELAIDE
CANBERRA
MELBOURNE
AUCKLAND
WELLINGTON
CHRISTCHURCH
HOBART
CHATHAM ISLAND
DUNEDIN
BOUNTY ISLAND
AUCKLAND ISLAND
ANTIPODES ISLAND
CAMPBELL ISLAND
MACQUARIE ISLAND

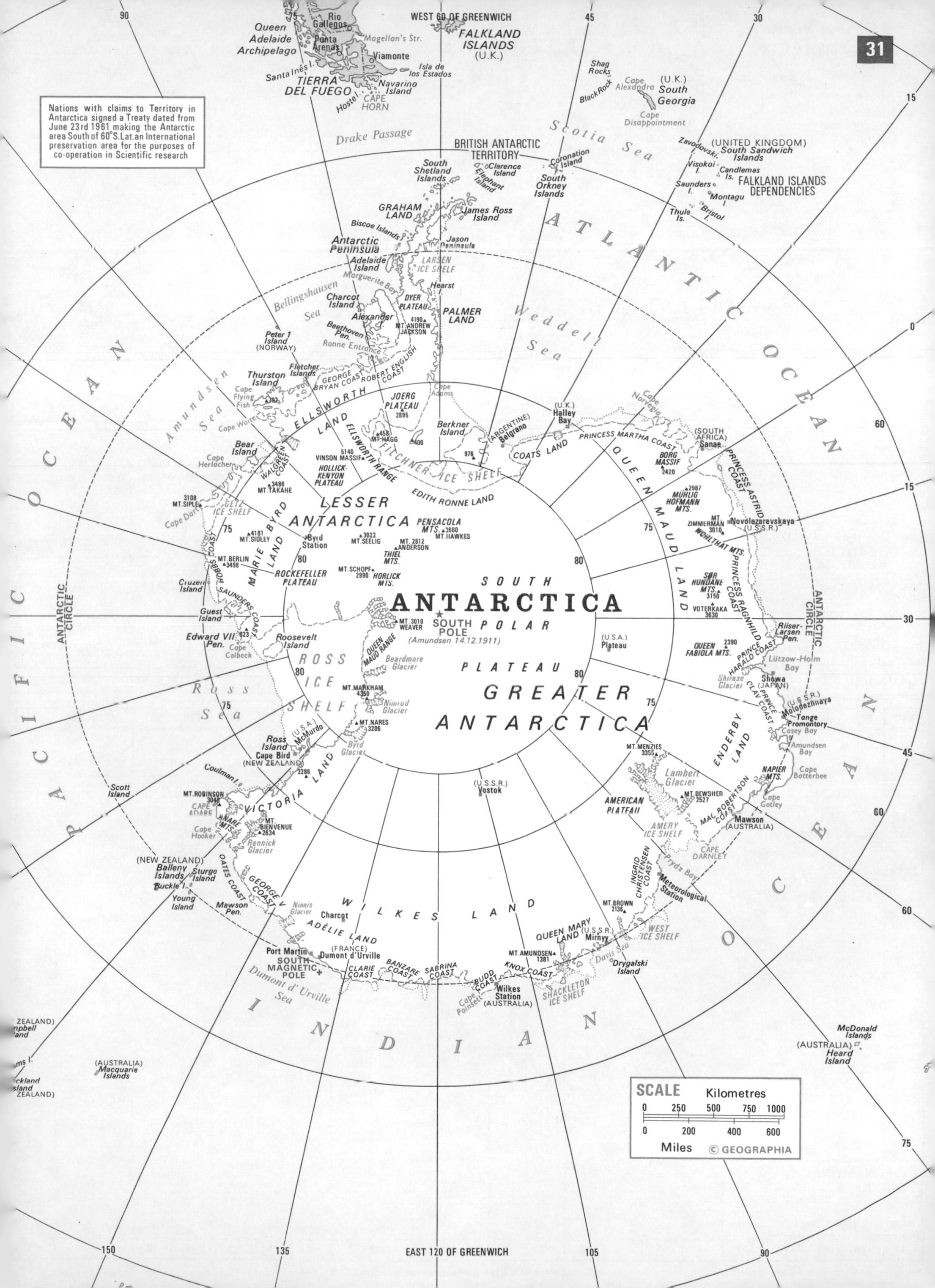

Nations with claims to Territory in Antarctica signed a Treaty dated from June 23rd 1961 making the Antarctic area South of 60°S.Lat.an International preservation area for the purposes of co-operation in Scientific research
WEST 60 OF GREENWICH
EAST 120 OF GREENWICH
ANTARCTICA
SOUTH POLAR PLATEAU
SOUTH POLE
(Amundsen 14.12.1911)
LESSER ANTARCTICA
GREATER ANTARCTICA
ATLANTIC OCEAN
PACIFIC OCEAN
INDIAN OCEAN
ANTARCTIC CIRCLE
FALKLAND ISLANDS (U.K.)
TIERRA DEL FUEGO
CAPE HORN
Drake Passage
Scotia Sea
(U.K.) South Georgia
(UNITED KINGDOM) South Sandwich Islands
FALKLAND ISLANDS DEPENDENCIES
BRITISH ANTARCTIC TERRITORY
South Shetland Islands
South Orkney Islands
GRAHAM LAND
Antarctic Peninsula
PALMER LAND
LARSEN ICE SHELF
Weddell Sea
Bellingshausen Sea
Amundsen Sea
Ross Sea
ROSS ICE SHELF
ELLSWORTH LAND
MARIE BYRD LAND
FILCHNER ICE SHELF
EDITH RONNE LAND
COATS LAND
QUEEN MAUD LAND
PRINCESS MARTHA COAST
PRINCESS ASTRID COAST
PRINCESS RAGNHILD COAST
PRINCE HARALD COAST
ENDERBY LAND
MAC ROBERTSON COAST
AMERICAN PLATEAU
AMERY ICE SHELF
Lambert Glacier
INGRID CHRISTENSEN COAST
QUEEN MARY LAND
WEST ICE SHELF
SHACKLETON ICE SHELF
KNOX COAST
BUDD COAST
SABRINA COAST
BANZARE COAST
CLARIE COAST
ADÉLIE LAND
WILKES LAND
GEORGE V COAST
OATES COAST
VICTORIA LAND
Dumont d'Urville Sea
SOUTH MAGNETIC POLE
Vostok (U.S.S.R.)
Mirnyy (U.S.S.R.)
Mawson (AUSTRALIA)
Wilkes Station (AUSTRALIA)
Showa (JAPAN)
Novolazarevskaya (U.S.S.R.)
Halley Bay (U.K.)
Belgrano (ARGENTINE)
Sanae (SOUTH AFRICA)
McMurdo (U.S.A.)
Byrd Station
Plateau (U.S.A.)
Dumont d'Urville (FRANCE)
Molodezhnaya (U.S.S.R.)
(NEW ZEALAND) Balleny Islands
(AUSTRALIA) Macquarie Islands
(AUSTRALIA) McDonald Islands Heard Island
Peter 1 Island (NORWAY)
SCALE Kilometres 0 250 500 750 1000
Miles 0 200 400 600
© GEOGRAPHIA

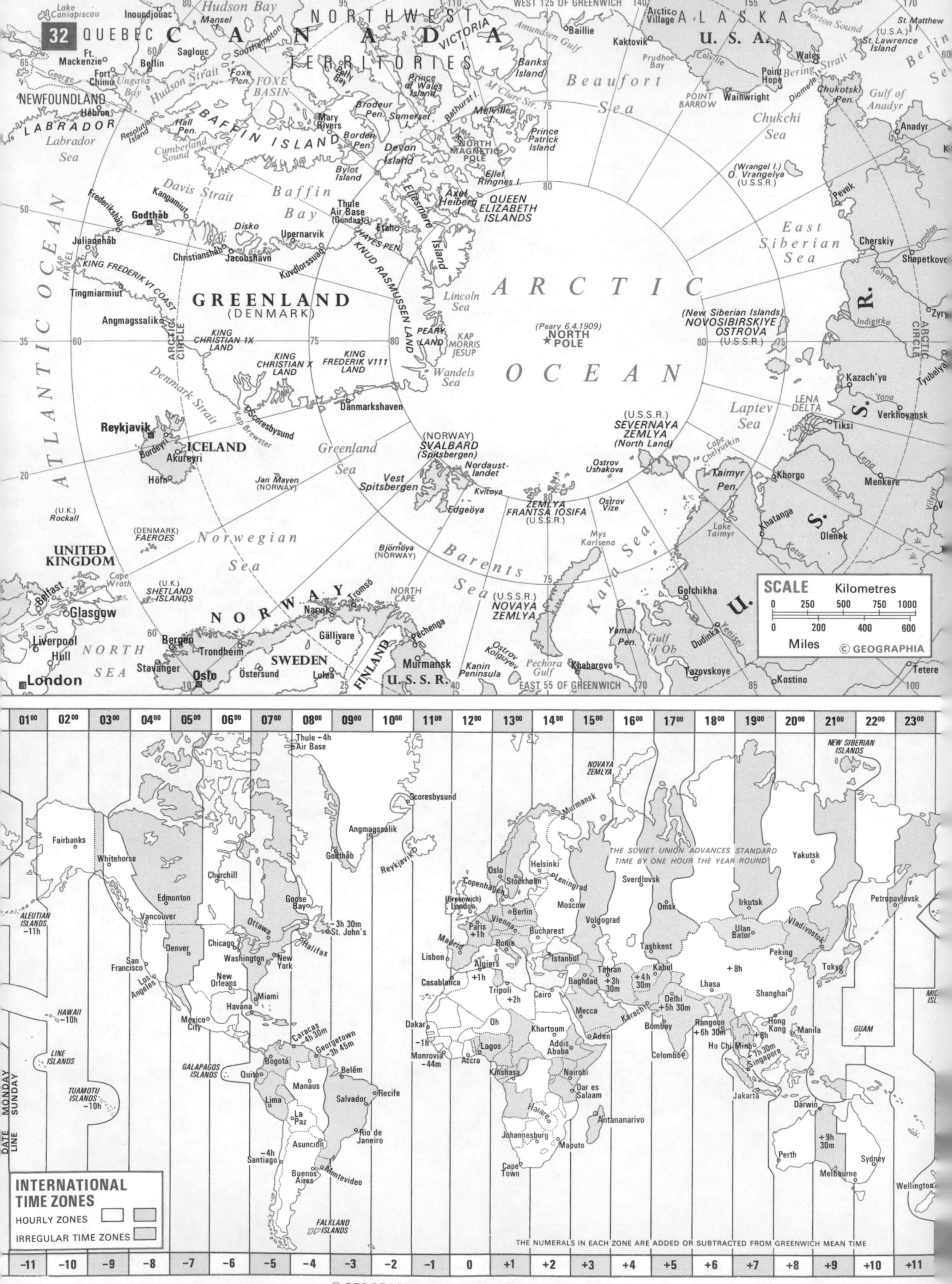

NORTHWEST TERRITORIES
CANADA
ARCTIC OCEAN
GREENLAND (DENMARK)
ATLANTIC OCEAN
NORTH POLE
ICELAND
NORWAY
SWEDEN
FINLAND
U.S.S.R.
ALASKA U.S.A.
SCALE Kilometres 0 250 500 750 1000
Miles 0 200 400 600
© GEOGRAPHIA
INTERNATIONAL TIME ZONES
HOURLY ZONES
IRREGULAR TIME ZONES
THE SOVIET UNION ADVANCES STANDARD TIME BY ONE HOUR THE YEAR ROUND
THE NUMERALS IN EACH ZONE ARE ADDED OR SUBTRACTED FROM GREENWICH MEAN TIME
DATE LINE MONDAY SUNDAY

Counties of Ireland

	Area in sq. km	Pop. (1981 census)	Admin. H.Q.
ULSTER			
Antrim	2,906	717,800	Belfast
Armagh	1,266	133,970	Armagh
Down	2,465	311,880	Downpatrick
Fermanagh	1,701	50,255	Enniskillen
Londonderry	2,082	183,095	Londonderry
Tyrone	3,155	139,075	Omagh
N. Ireland	13,575	1,536,075	
Cavan	1,890	53,855	Cavan
Donegal	4,830	125,112	Lifford
Monaghan	1,290	51,192	Monaghan
MUNSTER			
Clare	3,188	87,567	Ennis
Cork	7,459	266,121	Cork
Kerry	4,701	122,770	Tralee
Limerick	2,686	100,925	Limerick
Tipperary (N)	1,997	58,984	Nenagh
Tipperary (S)	2,258	76,277	Clonmel
Waterford	1,839	50,118	Waterford
LEINSTER			
Carlow	896	39,820	Carlow
Dublin	922	422,786	Dublin
Kildare	1,694	104,122	Kildare
Kilkenny	2,061	70,806	Kilkenny
Laoighis	1,720	51,171	Portlaoghise
Longford	1,044	31,140	Longford
Louth	821	88,514	Dundalk
Meath	2,339	95,419	Trim
Offaly	1,997	58,312	Tullamore
Westmeath	1,764	61,523	Mullingar
Wexford	2,352	99,081	Wexford
Wicklow	2,025	87,449	Wicklow
CONNACHT			
Galway	5,939	149,220	Galway
Leitrim	1,525	27,609	Carrick-on-Shannon
Mayo	5,397	114,766	Castlebar
Roscommon	2,463	54,543	Roscommon
Sligo	1,795	55,474	Sligo
Irish Republic	68,892	2,627,474	

to an understanding with the North and Irish unity. *See* NORTHERN IRELAND. Membership of the Common Market from 1973 initially did much to help commercial expansion, but Ulster complicates I.'s relationships with the 'nine' in other fields, e.g. her abstention from the European Convention on the Suppression of Terrorism in 1976.

The official language is Irish (q.v.), but English is recognized as a second official language. In religion the Irish are overwhelmingly R.C., under 5% belonging to the Protestant Church of Ireland. Area 68,892 sq.km (26,601 sq.m); pop. (1978) 3,220,000. M.U.: Irish punt.

ĪRĒ'NĒ. Greek goddess of peace (Roman 'Pax').

IRENE (*c.* 752-803). Consort of the eastern Roman emperor Leo IV. A poor orphan girl of Athens, her beauty and gifts won the love of the Emperor, who m. her in 769. On his death in 780 she became regent until 802, when her many cruelties led to her banishment. The Greek Orthodox Church canonized her.

IRETON, Henry (1611-51). English general. In 1642 he joined the Parliamentary forces and fought at Edgehill (1642), Gainsborough (1643), and Naseby (1645). He m. Oliver Cromwell's dau. in 1646. After Naseby I., who was opposed to the extreme Republicans and Levellers, strove to reach a compromise with Charles I, but he subsequently played a leading part in the trial and execution of the latter. I. went to Ireland with Cromwell and in 1650 became lord-deputy there. He d. after the capture of Limerick.

ĪRIAN. Indonesian name for NEW GUINEA.

ĪRI'DIUM. Chemical element. Symbol Ir, at. wt. 192.2, at. no. 77. Discovered by Tennant in 1803, I. is a metal of the platinum family; white, very hard and brittle, and usually alloyed with platinum or osmium. It is used for points of fountain-pen nibs, compass bearings, parts of scientific apparatus, and surgical tools. Under neutron bombardment I. becomes a most useful source of gamma rays for industrial radiography, especially for steel up to 5cm (2in) thick, the half-life being 74 days.

Ī'RIS. Plants bearing large flowers of various colours. The plants belong to the monocotyledonous family Iridaceae, Iris genus. The leaves are long and narrow, tapering to a point, the flowers have coloured sepals and petals, and stigmas enlarged into petalloid form which hide the stamens. *See* FLAG.

Ī'RIS. The coloured part of the eye surrounding the pupil. It contains radiating muscle fibres which dilate and circular ones which contract the pupil in response to the stimulus of light or accommodation to longer or shorter distance.

IRISH. Irish Gaelic is the chief representative of the Gaelic branch of the Celtic languages. Its history falls roughly into 3 periods: Old Irish, from about the 7th to the middle of the 9th cent. AD; Middle Irish, from the 9th to the 12th cent.; and Modern Irish from the 13th cent. onwards. In the last period it is usual to distinguish Early Modern Irish, up to the 17th cent. The language of the Ogam inscriptions is earlier than Old Irish.

There are 3 chief dialects, the Southern (Waterford, Cork, Kerry, Clare), the Western (Galway, Mayo) and Northern (Donegal) - the areas to which I. has been driven back in the course of the cents. Although it is the first official language of the rep. and has been taught in schools since 1922, the number of Irish speakers in genuine Irish-speaking districts (the Gaeltacht) is small, and less than 10,000 children speak it at home.

Literature. Early Irish literature consists of the sagas which are mainly in prose and a considerable body of verse. The chief cycles are that of Ulster, which deals with the mythological Conchobar and his followers, and the Ossianic, which has influenced European literature through MacPherson's version.

Early Irish poetry has a unique lyric quality and consists mainly of religious verse and nature poetry, e.g. St Patrick's hymn, Ultán's hymn to St Brigit, etc. A large amount of pseudo-historical verse is also extant, ascribed to such poets as Mael Mura (9th cent.), Mac Liac (10th cent.), Flann Mainistrech (11th cent.), etc. Religious literature in prose incl. sermons, saints' lives, e.g. those in the *Book of Lismore* and in the writings of Mícheál Ó Cléirigh (17th cent.), and visions. History is represented by annals and by isolated texts like the *Cogad Gaedel re Gallaib*, an account of the Viking invasions by an eyewitness.

The Early Modern Irish period is often referred to as the Classical age of Irish literature. The 'official' or 'court' verse of the 13th to 17th cents. was produced by a succession of professional poets, notably Tadhg Dall Ó Huiginn (d. *c.* 1617) and Donnchadh Mór Ó Dálaigh (d. 1244); and Geoffrey Keating (d. *c.* 1646) wrote in both verse and prose.

The bardic schools ceased to exist by the end of the 17th cent. Metre became accentual, and not as before syllabic. The greatest exponents of the new school were Egan O'Rahilly (early 18th cent.), and the religious poet Tadhg Gaelach Ó Súilleabháin. No writers of the modern revivalist movement have achieved internat. fame.

IRISH REPUBLICAN ARMY. Extremist organization, formed Jan. 1919, dedicated to the creation of a united Irish Republic. Its activities in England and Ireland led to stringent measures by the British govt, and it was declared illegal in Eire in 1939. Terrorism sporadically continued, and the IRA was active in the Civil Rights disorders in N Ireland from 1968, when a bitter division developed between the 'official' organization, using slightly more regular means, and the 'provisionals' committed to indiscriminate assassination and bomb outrages.

IRISH SWEEPSTAKE. *See under* LOTTERY.

IRISH TERRIER. A brown or reddish-brown Irish breed of dog. The coat is rough, the head long and narrow, forelegs straight and strong, chest narrow, and back straight.

IRKUTSK (irkootsk'). City of the RSFSR, cap. of I. region, S Siberia, situated on the Angara river, 72km (45m) NW of Lake Baikal. I., founded in 1652, began to grow after the Trans-Siberian railway reached it in 1898. Coal is found nearby; iron and steel, machine tools and gold-dredging machinery for the goldfields lying to the N, and timber are among its products. The city is a cultural centre with a univ. founded in 1918. Pop. (1977) 532,000.

IRON. The most widely spread of all metals except aluminium (Anglo-Saxon iron; Lat. *ferrum*), symbol Fe, at. wt. 55.85, at. no. 26, said to have been worked into implements by the Egyptians *c.* 3000 BC. It is extracted from 4 main ores: magnetite, a black oxide; haematite or kidney ore, another oxide, red in colour; limonite, a brown oxide; and siderite, a carbonaceous ore. Iron is the basis of all steel, and apart from its constructional uses, when mixed with carbon and other elements, I. is most important chemically. In electrical equipment, it forms the basis of all permanent and electromagnets and the cores of transformers and magnetic amplifiers. I. is used for anodes in electronic rectifiers, because it is not corroded by mercury. Traces of I. salts in glass give a sharp cut-off for short UV rays, and the I.-arc contains a large collection of reference wavelengths useful in spectroscopy.

IRON AGE. Iron was being made in Thailand by *c* .1600 BC. but everywhere remained inferior to bronze for strength until *c.* 1000 BC when metallurgical techniques improved. Once steel could be made by the addition of carbon, the period when man's weapons and tools were of iron began.

IRONBARK. Species of trees of the eucalyptus family, so-named in Australia because of their generally hard bark, and producing valuable timber.

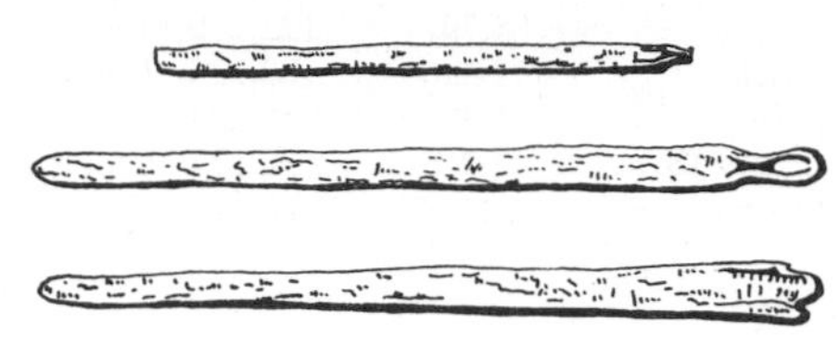

IRON AGE. The volunteers who in 1977 lived the life of ancient Britons in an Iron Age settlement recreated as it would have been *c.* 300 BC at a secret location in the West Country. The project was sponsored by BBC television. *Photo: Press Association*

IRONBRIDGE GORGE. Site, nr Telford New Town in Shropshire, of the Iron Bridge (1779) which marks Britain's emergence as the world's first industrial nation: it is now part of an open-air museum of industrial archaeology.

IRON CROSS. German military decoration, instituted in Prussia in 1813 and consisting of a Maltese cross of iron, edged with silver.

IRON CURTAIN. In Europe after the S.W.W. the division between democratic West and Communist E: first used by Churchill in speech at Fulton, Missouri, 1946.

IRON GATE. Narrow passage, interrupted by rapids, in Romania. A hydro-electric scheme undertaken 1964-70 by Romania and Yugoslavia transformed the gorge to a 145 km (90 m) long lake. An archaeological survey before flooding revealed 1965 Europe's oldest urban settlement, Lepenski Vir (6th millennium BC).

IRON GUARD. *See* ROMANIA.

IRON PYRITES. Common ore of iron, being the sulphide FeS_2, with about 46 per cent iron content. A brass-yellow, metallic mineral resembling gold (hence 'fool's gold'), it occurs in cubic crystals.

IROQUOIS (irohkwoi'). Confederation of N American Indians, the Six Nations (Cayuga, Mohawk, Oneida, Onondaga and Seneca, with the Tuscorora from 1715), traditionally formed by Hiawatha (actually a priestly title) in 1570. Always friendly to the British and Dutch, they played a most important part in the Anglo-French American wars. They now live in reservations on the

Canadian-US border. They are noted for their fringed leather clothing.

IRRĀ'DIATION. The process of exposing to radiation with a definite purpose in view. Ultra-violet I. is used in the food and pharmaceutical industries for making vitamin products. X-radiation and radiation from radium and radioactive isotopes are used in industry and medicine for diagnostic photography and in the treatment of certain malignant conditions. Radiation from particle accelerators and nuclear reactors is used in industry, agriculture and medicine; for making radioactive isotopes; and for preservation and sterilization of foods, drugs and prepacked surgical requirements. Gamma rays are used to control infestation in stored grain and other foodstuffs; I. with electrons, gamma-rays or neutrons is used to produce desired properties in plastics.

IRRAWA'DDY. Chief river of Burma. Its sources are the Mali and N'mai rivers. It crosses the centre of Burma, and flows roughly N to S, for 2,090km (1,300m) into the Bay of Bengal. The chief tributaries are the Chindwin and Shweli.

IRRIGATION. The supplying of water by artificial means to promote agriculture in countries where rainfall is absent or limited, e.g. the classic example of the channelling of the natural flood waters of the Nile practised from time immemorial in Egypt. In modern times the development of engineering has allowed the storage of surplus water by the construction of huge dams, from which it is released as needed, the dams also serving other purposes such as the provision of electric power, carrying highways, creating a lake fishery, etc. One of the most famous is the Aswan High Dam on the Nile, which also illustrates some of the drawbacks of the system. Continuous controlled irrigation tends to cause concentration of salts which adversely affects soil fertility, the rich silt brought by natural flood waters is largely retained at the dam, and marine life, e.g. fisheries, where the river reaches the sea, is impoverished. Impoverishment of the environment can occur along the whole length of a river, which may be too heavily drawn upon even to survive as far as the sea, e.g. the Colorado, USA. Water distribution to the crop through earth channels, etc., is often wasteful, and it is more economical and effective, though more expensive, to use a system of overhead irrigation whereby pipes run among the growing crop and spray it in the fashion of light or heavy rain, according to requirements, as in sugar-growing in Natal. Used with care, however, I. is making an immense contribution to increased food production, especially in the Third World.

IRRIGATION. Contour lines form an attractive abstract design, the irrigated area contrasting strongly with the uncultivated arid area, in the border country of South Australia. *Photo: Axel Poignant*

IRVINE. New town in Strathclyde, Scotland, overlooking the Isle of Arran. Industries incl. trucks and buses, ball and roller bearings, sports goods, diagnostic laboratories, etc. A leisure centre (1975) makes it an attractive holiday resort. Pop. (1974) 46,500, with an eventual target of 120,000.

IRVING, Sir Henry. Stage-name of the British actor John Brodribb (1838-1905). After acting in the provs., he went to London in 1866, and in 1871 began his long connection with the Lyceum Theatre, where he estab. his reputation in *The Bells,* and by his unconventional performance as Hamlet. In 1878 he became manager of the Lyceum, and engaged Ellen Terry as his leading lady, a partnership which lasted until I.'s death. The Lyceum became celebrated for superb and well-mounted productions, incl. *The Merchant of Venice,* with I.'s unusual and sympathetic portrayal of Shylock, *Henry VIII, Lear,* and Tennyson's *Becket.* I.'s acting, coloured by his strong personality, was noted for its versatility, spirit and originality; he was knighted in 1895, the first actor ever to be so honoured.

IRVING, Washington (1783-1859). American author. B. in New York City, of English parents, he pub. in 1809 a mock-heroic *History of New York,* supposedly written by the Dutchman 'Diedrich Knickerbocker'. In 1815 he went to England where his publications incl. the *Sketch Book of Geoffrey Crayon, Gent.* (1820), which contained such stories as 'Rip van Winkle' and 'Legend of Sleepy Hollow', and displayed the delicate humour and clear style which are characteristic of his work. He later visited Spain where he wrote amongst other books a *Life of Columbus* (1828), before returning to America in 1832. He was US ambassador to Spain 1842-6.

ISAAC (ī'zak). Hebrew patriarch, only son of Abraham and Sarah, and father of Jacob and Esau.

ISABE'LLA (1451-1504). Queen of Castile, known as Isabella the Catholic. She m. Ferdinand of Aragon in 1469, and in 1474 became queen of Castile in her own right on the death of her brother Henry IV. Thus the crowns of the 2 Christian states in the Spanish peninsula were united. She was largely responsible for the establishment of the Inquisition in Castile and the persecution of the Jews, and gave financial encouragement to Columbus.

ISABELLA II (1830-1904). Queen of Spain. She succeeded her father Ferdinand VII in 1822. The Salic Law banning a female sovereign had been abrogated by the Cortes, but her succession was disputed by her uncle Don

Carlos. After 7 years of civil war the Carlists were worsted. She abdicated in favour of her son Alfonso XII in 1870.

ISAIAH (īzī'ya). OT prophet of the 8th cent. BC. The son of Amoz, he was probably of high rank, and lived largely in Jerusalem. His call to prophecy is thought to have come *c.* 740, and he saw Assyria as the avenging weapon of Jahweh whom the Israelites had forsaken.

ISCHIA (isk'ia). Volcanic is. *c.* 26km (16m) SW of Naples, Italy, in the Tyrrhenian Sea. It has mineral springs known to the Romans, beautiful scenery, and is a holiday resort. Pop. (1971) 32,000.

ISE (ēs'ā). City SE of Kyoto, on Honshu, site of the most sacred Shinto shrine, dedicated to sun-goddess Amaterasu. It has been rebuilt every 20 yrs in the form of a perfect thatched house of the 7th cent. BC, and contains the octagonal mirror of the goddess.

ISÈRE. River of SE France rising near the Italian frontier and flowing 290km (180m) generally W, to enter the Rhône 11km (7m) above Valence. A dam was completed in 1952 to harness its rapid flow for electricity, and its upper valley (Tarentaise) has major industries. It gives its name to the dept of I.

ISFAHAN (ēsfah-hahn'). City in Iran, chief town of the prov. of I. on the Zaindeh r. The city reached its greatest prosperity and splendour when Shah Abbas I (1586–1628) made it the Persian capital. After the onslaught of the Afghans in 1722 its political significance diminished, and the cap. was moved to Tehran. Notable features are the Great Square, the Grand Mosque, and the Hall of the Forty Pillars. There are steel and textile industries. Pop. (1976) 671,825.

I'SHERWOOD, Christopher William Bradshaw (1904–86). English novelist. Ed. at Cambridge, as described in the autobiographical *Lions and Shadows* (1938), he later spent a fruitful period in Germany which inspired *Mr. Norris Changes Trains* (1935) and *Goodbye to Berlin* (1939). Returning to England, he collaborated with Auden (q.v.) in 3 verse plays. He then went to Hollywood as a scriptwriter, and joined the Huxley-Beard group, who were practising a form of Yoga in the Californian desert, and from 1944 collaborated with Swami Prabhavananda in a translation of the *Bhagavad-Gita,* etc.

ISHMAEL (ish'mā-el). OT character, the son of Abraham and Hagar, his wife's Egyptian handmaid, and regarded as the father of the Arab people. Driven out into the desert with his mother because of Sarah's jealousy, Ishmael grew up to be a famous archer in the wilderness of Paran. Mohammed claimed to be his descendant.

ISHTAR or **Istar.** The 'Lady of Heaven', the chief goddess in the Babylonian and Assyrian pantheon. She was identified with Astarte.

Ī'SINGLASS. Pure form of gelatin obtained from the cleaned and dried swimming-bladder of various fish, particularly the sturgeon. I. is used in the clarification of wines and beer, and in cookery.

Ī'SIS. The principal goddess of ancient Egypt. She was the dau. of Geb and Nut (earth and sky), and as the sister-wife of Osiris searched for his body after his death at the hands of his brother Set. Her son Horus then defeated and captured Set, but cut off his mother's head because she would not allow Set to be killed. She was later identified with Hathor (q.v.). The cult of Isis ultimately spread to Greece and Rome.

ISHERWOOD. Leaders of thought in the Thirties, W. H. Auden (left) with Christopher Isherwood, at the BBC for the programme 'Speaking Personally'. *Photo:Camera Press*

ISIS. Name sometimes given to the upper stretches of the Thames, England, above Oxford.

ISKENDERUN (iskenderoon'). Port, naval base and steel town in Hatay, Turkey. It was founded by Alexander the Great in 333 BC. Pop. (1970) 81,640.

I'SLAM. One of the great world religions (Arabic 'submission', i.e. to the will of Allah). The popular alternative form of Mohammedanism is rejected by believers as suggesting that Mohammed (q.v.) has a similar role to that of Jesus in the Christian Trinity. The fundamental beliefs are contained in the creed: There is no God but Allah, and Mohammed is the Prophet or Messenger of Allah. The Oneness of God is emphasised, as are his omnipotence, beneficence, and inscrutability. He only is divine and idolatry, or worship of saints, is therefore regarded as blasphemous. Moslems also believe in the Creation, Fall of Adam, Angels and the Jinn (q.v.), Heaven and Hell, a Day of Judgment, God's predestination of good and evil, and in a succession of scriptures revealed by Allah to a line of prophets, incl. the Pentateuch given to Moses, and the Gospel of Jesus; the ultimate and perfect revelation is the Koran (q.v.) of Mohammed. The latter embodies the Islamic Law (the Shari'a or 'Highway'), which can be clarified by reference to the *sunna* (practice) of the Prophet as transmitted by his Companions: the Sunni sect also employ ijma' (endorsement by universal consent of practices and beliefs not warranted by the Koran or the sunna).

Each individual Moslem is personally responsible for his religious life; there is no separate 'church' organisation or privileged priesthood, although the descendants of Mohammed, the Hashim family, are a class apart and wield great influence, as do certain holy men (*see* AYATOLLAH). Five practical obligations - 'The Pillars of the Faith' - are demanded of each Moslem: recitation of the Creed, at least once, and with understanding and faith; worship of Allah at the 5 appointed times each day, facing towards Mecca, the Holy City (q.v.); almsgiving; fasting from daybreak till sunset throughout the month of Ramadan (q.v.) for all Moslems except the sick, travellers, soldiers on active sevice, etc.; and at least once in his lifetime the pilgrimage to Mecca.

The Moslem era began with the Hejira (q.v.) in AD 622, and the calendar is solely lunar, the year of 354 days being divided into 12 months (30 and 29 days alternately). This results in the year rotating round the seasons, and when Ramadan falls in midsummer the rule against drinking causes hardship.

The law covers every aspect of life. In diet it forbids alcohol or the eating of pork. In personal life it requires the circumcision of all males; allows up to 4 wives, provided they can be treated equally; enables a man to divorce at will; governs the rules of inheritance; and rules on the status of women (*see* CHADOR). Usury is forbidden, which raises problems in banking, and penalties such as stoning to death for adultery or amputation of a hand for theft, as imposed in the fundamentalist revival in Iran and elsewhere, shock many Moslems as much as they do non-Moslems.

The Koran recognises slavery, but only of non-Moslem captives; the white slaves (*mamlucks*), usually Turks, in the Islamic slave-army were often manumitted and received administrative appointments, occasionally founding their own dynasties, e.g. the slave kings of Delhi and the Mamelukes (q.v.) - in Egypt. (*See also* JANISSARIES). The duty of the Holy War or *jihad* (q.v.) led to the Arab conquests which spread I. to Asia, Russia, N Africa, Spain (Moslems expelled 15th cent. AD), Pakistan and India, the Balkans, Indonesia and China. A Holy War declared in 1914 by the Sultan of Turkey against the Allies in the F.W.W. was of little consequence, and I. subsequently lost ground in the Balkans. However, in the last two cents. I. has been spread by immigrant groups and by missionary work, e.g. by the Ahmadiyya (q.v.) movement, to the rest of Africa, to N and S America, and to W Europe, where it is numerically inferior only to Christianity. The USSR, where the faith is actively discouraged, is numerically (*c.* 45 million) one of the world's most important Islamic countries, and the faith forms a focus for nationalism among the peoples of central Asia - Kazakhs, Tadjiks, Tatars, Turkmens, and Uzbeks. The number of Moslems is est. at *c.* 750 million, of whom *c.* 25 million are in Europe (1.5 million in the UK), *c.* 435 million in Asia, and *c.* 182 million in Africa.

The supreme political and religious ruler of the I. Community was formerly the Caliph (q.v.), aided by the Vizier (*wazir* 'helper'). The three main sects into which I. became divided, the Sunnis (majority party), the Shi'ites or Shiahs (qq.v.), and the Kharijites, originated in the differing theories on the office of the Caliph, but have since developed differences in theology, etc.; later sects incl. the Wahhabis (q.v.) and the Ahmadiyyas. Islam is distinctive in being a comprehensive political, legal and social system based on a religion, as opposed to a religious institution contained within a secular state. In the last 2 cents., nationalism in Turkey, Iran, India and Pakistan, etc., has often come before the idea of a united Islam, and this, together with Western influence on systems of govt. and way of life, led to basic changes in secular matters. However, since the S.W.W. a resurgence of fundamentalist I., often fanatically opposed to the ideas of the West, has become a potent factor in modern politics in those and other countries.

ISLA'MABAD. Cap. of Pakistan from 1967, in the Potwar district of Pakistan, at the foot of the Margala Hills and immediately NW of Rawalpindi. Designed by Constantinos Doxiadis it is well landscaped and the Civic Centre on Capital Avenue is a notable feature. Pop. (1970) 70,000.

ISLANDS, Bay of. West coast harbour of Newfoundland, Canada; and also the bay on the NE side of the N Auckland peninsula, NZ.

ISLAY (i'lā). Most southerly island of the Inner Hebrides, Scotland, in Strathclyde region, separated from Jura by the Sound of Islay. The principal towns are Bowmore and Port Ellen. Area 609 sq.km (235 sq.m); pop. (1971) 3,900.

ISLE OF ELY. *See* ELY, ISLE OF.

ISLE OF MAN. Island in the Irish Sea lying almost equidistant from Scotland to the N, Ireland to the W, Wales to the S, and England to the E. Nearly 50 per cent of the island is cultivated, oats being the principal crop. The cap. is Douglas; other towns incl. Ramsey, Peel, and Castletown. Shipping and air services link the I. of M. with England, Scotland and Ireland. The island is a popular holiday resort, and annual motor-cycle races are held. In recent years it has developed gambling facilities, banking and insurance, and as a tax haven.

Among the island's fauna is the tailless Manx cat. Pile dwellings, etc., show evidence of prehistoric settlement, and Christianity spread throughout the island during the Celtic period. For *c.* 500 years Man and some of the Scottish islands were nominally under the Norwegian kings. Magnus, last king of Man and the Isles, d. in 1265 and *c.* 1266 M. passed to Scotland. From 1290 English and Scottish rule alternated; in 1406 the Stanley family were granted the territory by Henry IV, but were succeeded in 1736 by the dukes of Atholl, when the island became a great smuggling centre. In 1866 the I. of M. obtained home rule. The govt is composed of a Crown-appointed Lieut.-Gov., the Legislative Council, and the representative House of Keys. Together these make up the Tynwald Court, which passes laws subject to the Royal Assent. Acts passed by parliament in London do not affect the I. of M. unless it is specifically named. Area 518 sq.km (221 sq.m); pop. (1979) 63,000.

ISLE OF WIGHT (wīt). Island county off the S coast of England. It is divided from the mainland by the Solent on the NW and Spithead on the NE. The chalk cliffs of the S coast end on the W in the Needles. The island is composed of agricultural and sheep-grazing land, but there are many holiday resorts, e.g. Sandown, Ventnor, Ryde, Shanklin. Inland is Carisbrooke. The cap. is Newport: near Cowes, the chief port, is Osborne House. The Romans called the island Vectis, meaning 'separate division': it was conquered by Vespasian in AD 43. Area 381 sq.km (147 sq.m); pop. (1978) 114,300.

ISMAIL I (ismah-ēl') (1487-1542). Shah of Persia. He founded the Safavi dynasty, ruling 1499-1524, and estab. the first nat. govt since the Arab conquest. Responsible for making Shi'ism the nat. religion, he conquered the Uzbeks 1510, but was defeated by Selim, Sultan of Turkey, in 1514.

ISMAIL (isma-ēl') (1830-95). Khedive of Egypt. A grandson of Mehemet Ali, he became viceroy of Egypt in 1863 and in 1866 received the title of Khedive from the Sultan. In 1875 Britain, at Disraeli's suggestion, bought the Khedive's Suez Canal shares for £3,976,582, and Anglo-French control of Egypt's finances was estab. In 1879 Britain and France persuaded the Sultan to appoint Tewfik, his son, Khedive in his place.

ISMAILIA (isma-ēlē'ah). Town on the shore of Lake Timsah, Lower Egypt, near the entrance into the lake of the Suez Canal. I. came into existence in 1863 as HQ for the construction of the canal, and was named after Khedive Ismail (q.v.). It is the main communications centre of the canal zone. Pop. (1974) 190,000.

I'SOBAR. A line drawn on maps and weather charts linking all places with the same atmospheric pressure. When used in weather forecasting, the distance apart of the Is. is an indication of the barometric gradient. Where they are close together cyclonic weather is indicated, and where far apart anticyclonic. The pressures indicated on the met. charts have generally been corrected to sea-level.

ISO'CRATES (436-338 BC). Athenian orator. One of the pupils of Socrates, he started his celebrated school about 392 BC. Hampered in public life by nervousness, he was unrivalled as a composer of literary speeches. Shortly after Philip's victory at Chaeronea, I. committed suicide.

ISOLA'TION. Segregation of persons exposed to or suffering from an infectious disease, to prevent its spread. Isolation or fever hospitals are kept by many local authorities for patients suffering from the notifiable infectious diseases.

ISOLATIONISM. The section of opinion in the USA which up to 1941 opposed all American intervention in European politics. They were more numerous among the Republicans than among the Democrats, and drew their greatest support from the Republican stronghold of the Middle West. Following the S.W.W. isolationism remained in abeyance and America made her presence felt worldwide, espec. in W Europe and the Pacific area. The Korean War, however, and still more the involvement in Vietnam, led to withdrawal in the Pacific, and a reaction against too great a European commitment.

ISO'MERISM. The existence of more than one compound having the same molecular composition and weight, but with different properties, due to the changed arrangement of the atoms in the molecules. Some organic compounds and complex inorganic salts exhibit this phenomenon.

ISOME'TRICS. System of muscular exercises without apparatus, e.g. by opposing one set of muscles to another. These exercises, some of which can be performed without visible movement, have been advocated as a means whereby sedentary workers can attain fitness, but can be damaging when practised by the unskilled.

ISOMOR'PHISM. Crystalline similarity in chemically related substances. In mathematics it means correspondence between the operations of groups.

ISO'PODA. Order of marine, freshwater, and terrestrial crustaceans, having no exoskeleton.

I'SOPRENE (C_5H_3). A volatile fluid which forms substances similar to rubber by polymerization.

I'SOTHERM. On a map, a line linking all places having the same temperature either at a given time or over a given period. Is. may show either actual temperature relations, or temperatures reduced to sea-level readings, 1.5°C or 2.7°F (moist air) to 3°C or 5.4°F (dry air), is subtracted for every 300m (1,000 ft) of altitude.

I'SOTOPE. Substances having different atomic weights, although chemically identical, with the same atomic number and occupying the same place in the periodic table of the elements, are said to be Is., i.e. the atoms which are Is. of a particular element have a varying number of neutrons in their nuclei, but the same number of protons and orbiting electrons. Is. were shown to exist at the beginning of this century from investigations of natural radioactivity, and their importance has grown enormously, many hundreds now being known. They may be stable or unstable, naturally occurring or man-made. When naturally occurring all the Is. of an element occur in a fixed proportion. *See* ATOM, RADIOISOTOPE.

I'SRAEL. Country of SW Asia, part of Palestine (q.v.). Set up in 1948 immediately on the ending of the British League of Nations mandate, I. was accepted by the UN as a member in 1949, but was promptly attacked by her Arab neighbours (*see* ARAB-ISRAELI WARS). Within the enlarged boundaries secured in armistices in 1949 with Jordan, Lebanon, Syria and Egypt, I. comprised the hills of Galilee in the N, the coastal plain along the Mediterranean, and the desert triangle of the Negev in the south. The major gains, achieved under Gen. Moshe Dayan in the 'Six Day War' of 1967, were: the Golan Heights in the N from Syria; the West Bank (the hill areas known to Israelis by the traditional names of Samaria and Judah) from Jordan, as well as E (Old) Jerusalem; and in the S the Gaza Strip and Sinai Peninsula (qq.v.) from Egypt. In the October War of 1973 a further 1,300 sq.km (500 sq.m) of Egypt and 780 sq.km (300 sq.m) of Syria were occupied.

Under the Peace Treaty between Israel and Egypt of 1979, reached under the Camp David (q.v.) Agreements I. was due to restore the whole of Sinai to Egyptian control in 1982; the Gaza Strip and West Bank were to receive autonomy by negotiation, but this foundered on the interpretation by Begin that such autonomy must be purely local, an Israeli military presence must be maintained, and Jewish settlements remain. The matter of E Jerusalem was not covered, and in 1980 Israel affirmed the united city as the country's capital. No peace agreements have been reached with Jordan or Syria. *See* GUSH EMUNIM.

Fruit, espec. citrus, avocadoes and various vegetables, vines, olives, cotton and sugar beet, are grown in soil rendered fertile by skilled cultivation and irrigation. Large areas are under collective ownership, as in a kibbutz. Minerals incl. the salt deposits (potash, etc.) of the Dead Sea, copper nr Elat, phosphates (Oron), but the oil wells of Sinai have already been returned to Egypt, and nuclear power is being developed to supply the energy shortage. Industries incl. textiles, chemicals, plastics, precision instruments, and avionics (aircraft and missiles). The economy is crippled by defence expenditure and inflation is rampant. Besides the cap. of Jerusalem, large towns incl. Tel Aviv, Haifa, and Beersheba.

The head of state is a pres. elected directly for 5 yrs: the first was Chaim Weizmann (q.v.). A single chamber parliament (Knesset) is elected on a system of proportional representation for 4 years and the cabinet is headed by a Prime Minister, from 1986 Yitzhak Shamir, of the Likud party. The opposition party is the Israel Labour Party, led by Shimon Peres.

Israel is a secular state, but Judaism is the predominant faith. Under the Law of Return (1950) 'every Jew shall be entitled to come to I. as an immigrant'. Those from E and E Europe are known as Ashkenazim, and from Spain and Portugal, Arab N Africa, etc., as Sephardim. An Israeli-born is a Sabra. The official languages are Hebrew and Arabic.

Area (1949) 20,700 sq.km (8,000 sq.m); (1967) 89,350 sq.km (34,500 sq.m); pop (1981) 3,920,000. Economic and other difficulties have resulted in large-scale emigration and by 1980 400,000 Israeli Jews were living in

USA (incl. 250,000 in NYC). Before 1967 the Moslem pop. was *c.* 10%, but the 1967 conquests brought *c.* 1,000,000 additional Arabs within Israel. M.U.: shekel.

Historically, ISRAEL was the name of the northern kingdom of Palestine formed by those Jewish tribes which, after the death of Solomon, seceded from the rule of his son Rehoboam, and elected Jeroboam as their king.

ISSIGŌ'NIS, Sir Alec (1906-). British engineer. B. in Smyrna, he created modern economy motoring by his design of the Morris Minor (1948) and the Mini-Minor (1959), which added the word 'mini' to the language.

ISRAEL. The bulwark of relgious faith - Jerusalem's Wailing Wall - believed to be built of stones from the original Temple of Solomon. *Photo:Leon Herschritt/Camera Press*

ISTANBUL (-bool'). City and chief seaport of Turkey, formerly cap. of the Turkish Empire. Occupying the site of the ancient Byzantium and Constantinople (qq.v.), I. stands on the western shore of the Bosporus at the point where it enters the Sea of Marmara, thus controlling the route between the Mediterranean and the Black Sea. To the N of the promontory on which I. stands is the long harbour of the Golden Horn. There are many varied industries. Notable buildings are the church of Santa Sophia, built by Justinian in the 6th cent. on the same site as the building erected by Constantine: later used as a mosque, it has been a museum since 1934. The Topkapi Palace, residence of the sultans till 1909 (with a Great Harem of 400 rooms) has also been restored as a museum.

In 1453 the city, which for 11 cents. had been the capital of the Roman Empire, was taken by the Turks and remained capital of the Ottoman Empire until 1923, when Ankara became the capital of the Turkish republic. Pop. (1970) 2,312,750.

ITALIAN. One of the main Romance languages derived from Latin, which it closely resembles. It originated in its present form in Tuscany in the Middle Ages, acquiring prestige through its use by Dante, though the renewed use and influence of Latin during the Renaissance period tended to make of written Italian a stilted and artificial language bearing little resemblance to the popular tongue. By the middle of the 19th cent. Florentine usage had come to be universally accepted as a basis for the written language. However, outside Tuscany, dialect is still the general conversational medium. D'Annunzio (q.v.) coined many new words.

ISTANBUL. Overlooking the Bosporus, the graceful dome and minarets of the Dolmabahce Mosque. *Photo: Douglas Dickins*

Literature. It originated in the 13th cent. with the Sicilian school which imitated Provençal poetry. The contemporary works of St Francis of Assisi and Jacopone da Todi reflect the religious faith of the time. Guido Guinicelli (1230-*c.* 1275) and Guido Cavalcanti (*c.* 1250-1300) developed the spiritual conception of love and influenced Dante Alighieri, whose *Divina Commedia* is the greatest work of I.L. Petrarch was a humanist and a poet, while Boccaccio is principally known for his short stories.

The 15th cent. marked the beginning of the Renaissance. Boiardo dealt with the Carolingian epics in his *Orlando Innamorato* which was completed and transformed by Lodovico Ariosto as *Orlando Furioso.* Their contemporaries Niccolo Machiavelli and Francesco Guicciardini (1483-1540) are outstanding historians. Torquato Tasso wrote his epic *Gerusalemme Liberata* in the spirit of the Counter-Reformation.

The 17th cent. was characterized by the exaggeration of the poets Giovanni Battista Marini (1569-1625) and Gabriello Chiabrera (1552-1638). In 1690 the 'Academy of Arcadia' was formed: its members incl. Innocenzo Frugoni (1692-1768) and Metastasio. Other writers incl. Salvator Rosa, the satirist. During the 18th cent. Giuseppe Parini (1729-99) ridiculed the abuses of his day, while Vittorio Alfieri attacked tyranny in his dramas. Carlo Goldoni wrote comedies and Ugo Foscolo (1778-1827) is chiefly remembered for his patriotic verse. Giacomo Leopardi is not only the greatest lyrical poet since Dante, but also a master of Italian prose; the Romantic, Alessandro Manzoni, is best known as a novelist, and influenced amongst others the novelist Antonio Fogazzaro. A later outstanding literary figure and poet, Giosuè Carducci, was followed by the verbose Gabriele d'Annunzio, writing of sensuality and violence, and Benedetto Croce, historian and philosopher, who between them dominated I. literature at the turn of the cent.; other writers were the realist novelist Giovanni Verga, the dramatist Luigi Pirandello, and the novelists Ignazio Silone and Italo Svevo. Poets of the period incl. Dino Campana, Giuseppe Ungaretti and among the modern school are Nobel-prizewinner Eugenio Montale, Salvatore Quasimodo, Attilio Bertolucci (1911-) and Andrea Zanzotto (1921-). Novelists of the post-Fascist period, preoccupied with political and moral problems, incl. Alberto Moravia, Carlo Levi, Cesare Pavese (1908-50), Vasco Pratolini (1913-), Elsa Morante (1916-), Giuseppe Tomasi, Prince of Lampedusa, and the younger writers Italo Calvino (1923-), and Leonardo Sciascia.

ITALIAN LITERATURE. The greatest of all Italian poets - Dante - by Andrea del Castagno, at Florence. *Photo: Mansell Collection*

ITALIAN ART. Italy is rich in examples of the Byzantine style of architecture which is a mixture of oriental and classical elements; such are the monuments of Justinian in Ravenna and the later church of St Mark's in Venice. The Romanesque style was developed in Italy from the 10th to the 13th cents. Examples of this style are the churches of Lombardy; the baptistery, cathedral, and Leaning Tower of Pisa; and the cathedrals of Sicily. The Gothic period in Italy developed from the 13th to the 15th cents. It is based on Romanesque and differs a great deal from the Gothic style of northern Europe. Façades were elaborately decorated; mosaics and coloured marble were used, and sculpture - delicately carved - was placed around windows and doors.

The history of It. painting begins in the latter half of the 13th cent., or in Italian parlance the *Duecento.* Giotto is usually regarded as the first great Italian painter. He broke away from the traditional formal style, and created a world of beauty that is related to the world of everyday life. An earlier painter, Cimabue, may have been Giotto's master. Other great artists of the *Duecento* were the sculptors Niccola Pisano and his son, Giovanni, and the painter Duccio.

The most famous names of the 14th cent. - the *Trecento* - include the Florentines Bernardo Daddi (*c.* 1290-1348); Taddeo Gaddi and his son Agnolo; the Sienese Ambrogio and Pietro Lorenzetti; and the Veronese painter, Vittore Pisano.

The next period in I.A. is called the *Renaissance* (15th and 16th cents.), i.e. 'rebirth' of the classical spirit. The architectural style was developed by Brunelleschi and his contemporaries. The most famous achievement is the basilica of St Peter's, Rome, with which Michelangelo's name is associated.

The great artists of the Renaissance include Ghiberti, the sculptor of the 'Doors of Paradise' of the Florentine baptistery; Donatello, the greatest sculptor of the period; Luca della Robbia; Masaccio, famous for his paintings in the Carmelite church, Florence; Fra Angelico; Uccello who achieved fame as a pioneer in scientific perspective; Pollaiuolo, another famous experimenter; the Bellini family; Mantegna; Andrea del Verrocchio, sculptor of the Colleoni memorial, the greatest equestrian statue of the Renaissance; Sandro Botticelli; Leonardo da Vinci, the great mind of the Renaissance; Michelangelo, the greatest artistic genius of the period; Raphael, painter of the 'Sistine Madonna'; Titian, who was supreme as a colourist; Tintoretto, who was Titian's pupil; Correggio; and Veronese.

The most famous names of the following *Baroque* period are those of the sculptor and architect Bernini, and in painting Caravaggio and the Caracci. The 18th and earlier 19th cents. were dominated by the Neo-Classic movement, seeking inspiration from the works of the past rather than life itself, and it was not until the rise of the Futurist (q.v.) school, e.g. Gino Severini (1883-1966), and succeeding Metaphysical school, e.g. Carlo Carra (1881-1966) that a revival came. Modigliani is an outstanding figure at the beginning of the 20th cent., but the Fascist régime was no breeding ground for great art. In more recent years there have been a no. of interesting sculptors incl. Giacomu Manzu (1908-), Marino Marini, and Emilio Greco: Annigoni is a popular portrait painter.

ITA'LICS. *In printing, the letters sloping towards the right as used in this article. Nowadays they are usually employed, side by side with the erect Roman type, for purposes of emphasis and citation. Aldus Manutius (q.v.) of Venice first introduced italics of the lower case in 1501, and only later also replaced the Roman capitals by capitals of the I. type. Is. were soon in vogue in Italy and imitated in other countries.*

ITALY. Republic of S Europe bordering on France, Switzerland, Austria, and Yugoslavia on the W, N and E,

ITALIAN ART. The lower church of St Francis at Assisi is graced by this 'Madonna and Child with Three Saints' by Lorenzetti. *Photo: Courtesy of the Italian State Tourist Office*

and stretching SE as a long peninsula into the Mediterranean. Area 301,195 sq.km (116,300 sq.m); pop. (1977) 56,600,350.

I. is bounded on the N by the semi-circle of the Alps, from just E of Monaco on the W to the Adriatic on the E; elsewhere by the sea. The coastline is *c.* 7,240 km (4,500 m). The Alps, among which lie the famous lakes Maggiore, Lugano, and Garda, slope down to the northern plain which is drained by the Po and its tributaries, the Adige and the Piave.

The peninsula of central and southern I. consists of the Apennines, which diverge from the maritime Alps round the Gulf of Genoa, and their valleys and foothills. These mountains rise into isolated limestone peaks, e.g. Gran Sasso (2,911 m/9,580 ft). Noted rivers are the Tiber and Arno, on which stand Rome and Florence respectively. The republic of I. incl. the large islands of Sicily and Sardinia and a number of smaller ones, among them Elba, Capri, Ischia, the Lipari Islands. I. contains the only active volcanoes in Europe: Vesuvius, Stromboli, and Etna.

The climate is a good deal hotter in the S than in the N where some of the Alpine heights are covered with perpetual snow. The northern plain has a continental climate - hot in summer, cool in winter. In the peninsula the surrounding sea tempers summer heat; heavy snowfalls are common in winter in the mountainous backbone of the country. The chief rains, *c.* 75cm (30in) in the lowlands to upwards of 125cm (50in) in the mtns, fall Feb.-March.

The cap. is Rome; other large cities incl. Milan, Turin, Florence, Bologna, Verona, Padua, and Ferrara, and the ports of Genoa, La Spezia, Leghorn, Naples, Reggio di Calabria, and Palermo to the W; Taranto on the SE; Brindisi, Bari, Ancona, Venice and Trieste on the E coast.

The main rail lines are state-owned, and electrified and re-equipped since the S.W.W.; there is a motorway system, and Alitalia (chief airline) is state-run.

Economics. A quarter of the working population is engaged in agriculture. The continental plain, the area round Naples and Tuscany, is very fertile. Wheat is the most important cereal and maize is cultivated as an alternative crop. Rice is grown in Lombardy, Piedmont and elsewhere. The vine is cultivated throughout I. Olive oil and chestnuts are universal foods; the orange, lemon, fig, and almond are important in the S. I. produces more silk than any other European country. Hemp, flax, and cotton are grown. Cattle, sheep, goats, and pigs are reared. Emilia and Lombardy produce famous cheeses.

I. has few minerals. Volcanic products include sulphur (Sicily), borax (Tuscany), pumice and lava stone. Tuscany has rich mercury deposits, Sardinia is rich in lead, copper and zinc, and Elba in iron. Carrara and Siena produce marble. Petroleum and natural gas are worked in Sicily; there are small deposits of coal in Sardinia and of lignite in Arezzo, Pisa, and Grosseto; this scarcity of coal has encouraged the development of water power which provides three-quarters of the electricity available. Industry is still concentrated in the N, but the state steelworks at Taranto is part of an attempt to promote large-scale development in the poorer S. The chief manufactures are textiles (cotton, silk, woollen, and man-made fibres), chemicals, motor vehicles, leather goods, food-processing, etc.

Regions of Italy

	Area in sq. km.	*Pop. in 1977*	*Capital*
Abruzzi	10,794	1,227,890	Aquila
Apulia (Puglia)	19,346	3,856,352	Bari
Basilicata	9,992	619,057	Potenza
Calabria	15,080	2,057,913	Catanzaro
Campania	13,594	5,378,777	Naples
Emilia Romagna	22,119	3,956,458	Bologna
*Friuli-Venezia Giulia	7,844	1,245,193	Udine
Latium (Lazio)	17,202	4,997,358	Rome
Liguria	5,413	1,859,227	Genoa
Lombardy	23,797	8,910,389	Milan
Marches (Marche)	9,690	1,403,730	Ancona
Molise	4,438	331,833	Campobasso
Piedmont (Piemonte)	25,399	4,540,685	Turin
*Sardinia (Sardegna)	24,089	1,582,108	Cagliari
*Sicily (Sicilia)	25,709	4,936,249	Palermo
*Trentino-Alto Adige	13,613	872,219	Trento**
Tuscany (Toscana)	22,991	3,587,301	Florence
Umbria	8,456	802,448	Perugia
*Valle d'Aosta	3,262	114,280	Aosta
Veneto	18,367	4,320,886	Venice
	301,195	56,600,354	

*special autonomous regions **also Bolzano-Bozen

Government. I., which had been a monarchy since its unification in 1870, became a rep. in 1946 (*see* History below). It has a parliament of 2 houses - a Chamber of Deputies elected by universal direct suffrage for 5 years and a Senate elected for 6 years. The head of state is a Pres. elected for 7 years by a joint session of the houses of parl.; he must secure a two-thirds majority. He is assisted by a cabinet led by a PM, and may dissolve parl. except during the last 6 months of his term of office.

Under the Italian constitution of 1947 there are 20 regions (incl. Molise), 5 being special regions with a higher degree of autonomy (Friuli-Venezia Giulia, Sardinia, Sicily, Trentino-Alto Adige, Valle d'Aosta) and 15 ordinary regions which elected their first regional councils in 1970. Under a treaty with the Papacy in 1929, Roman Catholicism was the official religion until a new concordat of 1978 gave complete religious freedom: it is still the religion of 90% of the population.

ITALY. A panorama of a typical Italian town – Urbino – still predominantly Renaissance in style. *Photo: Courtesy of the Italian State Tourist Office.*

ITALY. Closest to power of all Europe's Communist leaders was Enrico Berlinguer (general secretary of PCI from 1972 until his death).

History. The varying peoples inhabiting I. - Etruscans in Tuscany, Latins and Sabines in middle I., Greek colonies in the S and Sicily, and Gauls in the N - were united under Roman rule during the 4th-3rd cents. BC. With the decline of the Roman Empire, and its final extinction in AD 476, I. became exposed to the attacks of the barbarians, and passed in turn under the rule of the Ostrogoths and the Lombards. The 8th cent. witnessed the rise of the papacy as a territorial power, the annexation of the Lombard kingdom by Charlemagne, and his coronation as emperor of the west in 800. Henceforward until 1250 Italian history turns in the main on the relations, at first friendly and later hostile, between the papacy and the Holy Roman Empire. During this struggle the Italian cities seized the opportunity to convert themselves into self-governing republics. By 1300 five major powers existed in I.: the city-republics of Milan, Florence and Venice; the papal states; and the kingdom of Naples. Their mutual rivalries and constant wars laid I. open during 1494-1559 to invasions from France and Spain; as a result Naples and Milan passed under Spanish rule. After 1700 Austria secured Milan and replaced Spain as the dominating power, while Naples passed to a Spanish Bourbon dynasty, and Sardinia to the dukes of Savoy. The period of French rule (1796-1814) temporarily unified I., and introduced the principles of the French Revolution, but after Napoleon's fall I. was again divided between Austria, the Pope, the kingdoms of Sardinia and Naples, and 4 smaller duchies. Nationalist and democratic ideals nevertheless remained alive, and inspired attempts at revolution in 1820, 1831 and 1848-9. After this last failure the Sardinian monarchy assumed the leadership of the national movement. With the help of Napoleon III the Austrians were expelled from Lombardy in 1859; the duchies joined the Italian kingdom; Garibaldi overthrew the Neapolitan monarchy; and Victor Emmanuel II of Sardinia was proclaimed king of Italy at Turin in 1861. Venice and part of Venetia were secured by another war with Austria in 1866; in 1870 Italian forces occupied Rome, thus completing the unification of I., and the Pope ceased to be a temporal ruler until 1929 (*see* VATICAN CITY). In 1878 Victor Emmanuel II died, and was succeeded by Humbert (Umberto) I, his son, who was assassinated in 1900. The formation of a colonial empire began in 1869 with the purchase of land on the Bay of Assab, on the Red Sea, from the local sultan. In the next 20 years the Italians occupied all Eritrea which was made a colony in 1889. An attempt to seize Ethiopia was decisively defeated at Adowa in 1896. War with Turkey in 1911-12 gave Tripoli and Cyrenaica. I.'s intervention in the F.W.W. on the Allied side secured her Trieste, the Trentino, and S Tirol. The post-war period was marked by intense political and industrial unrest, culminating in 1922 in the establishment of Mussolini's Fascist dictatorship. The régime embraced a policy of aggression with the conquest of Ethiopia in 1935-6 and of Albania in 1939, and I. entered the S.W.W. in 1940 as the ally of Germany. Defeat in Africa 1941-3 and the Allied conquest of Sicily in 1943 resulted in Mussolini's downfall; the new govt declared war on Germany, and until 1945 I. was a battlefield between German occupying forces and the advancing Allies. In 1946 Victor Emmanuel III, who had been king since 1900, abdicated in favour of his son Humbert (Umberto) II, who abdicated later in 1946 when a referendum rejected monarchy.

A peace treaty between I. and the Allies was signed and ratified in 1947. It deprived I. of its colonial empire and transferred to Yugoslavia Zara (Zadar) and part of

Venezia Giulia; to France 4 small areas in the Alpes Maritimes; to Greece the Dodecanese. Trieste (q.v.), which the Allies proposed to make a free territory, was in 1954 returned to I. Economic expansion was rapid within the Common Market from 1957 until the setbacks of the 1970s. Italy has the largest Communist party in Europe (*see* GRAMSCI), led by Alessandro Natta. There was a 'historic compromise' coalition between Communists and Christian Democrats 1973–9, which resulted in a fall in Communist support from the high reached in the elections of 1976, and in 1979 the Communists withdrew from the official parliamentary majority. By 1980 the Socialists had associated themselves with the Christian Democrats in govt., but the situation remained unstable. In the 1983 elections, Bettino Craxi became Italy's first Socialist Prime Minister, at the head of a left-of-centre coalition government. He was re-elected in 1985, but resigned in 1987 after the longest rule by a single prime minister since 1945. Giulio Andreotti was asked to form a government, but was unsuccessful. The future remains uncertain.

There has also been terrorism on a considerable scale, e.g. the kidnap and murder by the left of premier Aldo Moro in 1978, and the bomb outrage killing 81 at Bologna railway station by the right in 1980.

ITCH. Irritation of nerve endings in skin or mucous membrane not amounting to pain. 'The itch' is scabies, an eruption produced by the burrowing into the skin of the female of the minute parasite *Acarus scabiei.*

IVAN III (ēvahn') (1440-1505), called 'the Great'. Grand duke of Moscow, he succeeded his father in 1462; by some historians he is called the first tsar of Russia. In 1480 Ivan effectually revolted against Tartar overlordship by refusing to pay the customary tribute to the Grand Khan Ahmed, who was slain in battle in the following year. He adopted the double-headed eagle as the symbol of the Russian state.

IVAN IV (1530-84). Tsar of Russia, called 'the Terrible'. Son of the grand duke of Muscovy, he became grand duke on the death of his father in 1533 and was actual ruler from 1544. In 1547 he was crowned the first tsar of Russia, and embarked upon a period of internal consolidation and external conquest of Kazan, Astrakhan and W Siberia. After 1560 he developed into a ferocious tyrant, and from 1564 he lived away from Moscow, his life being passed in alternate debauchery and religious austerities.

IVANOVO. Cap. of I. region, RSFSR, 240km (150m) NE of Moscow; industries incl. textiles, chemicals and engineering. Pop. (1977) 461,000.

IVES, Charles Edward (1874-1954). American experimental composer, in daily life a business man, whose use of smaller intervals than the semi-tone rendered his songs and 5 symphonies hard to perform.

IVES, Frederic Eugene (1856-1937). American inventor. B. in Connecticut, he became manager of the photography laboratory at Cornell university, and there in 1878 invented a half-tone process. By 1886 he had evolved the half-tone process now generally in use. Among his many other inventions was the three-colour process of colour printing.

IVIZA. *See* IBIZA.

Ī'VORY. The hard white substance of which the teeth of certain animals are composed. Most valuable are the tusks of the African and Indian elephants, in which the dentine is of unusual hardness and density. Ivory has been used in carving and other decorative work from prehistoric times, and is today so valuable that poachers continue to destroy the remaining wild elephant herds in Africa to obtain it illegally.

Vegetable I. is used for buttons, toys, and cheap I. goods. It consists of the hard albumen of the seeds of a tropical palm (*Phytelephas macrocarpa*), which is imported from Colombia. Black Ivory was a euphemism for African slaves.

IVORY COAST. Country of W Africa (Côte d'Ivoire), between Liberia and Ghana. Behind a coastal plain, some 65 km (40 m) wide and heavily forested, I.C. rises steeply to a central plateau and mountainous country in the north. Products incl. coffee, cocoa, palm oil, mahogany, diamonds, manganese and offshore oil. The cap. is Yamoussoukro; ports are Abidjan (former cap) and San Pedro, a major deepwater port.

There is a pres. (*see* HOUPHOUËT-BOIGNY) and a single-chamber assembly. France secured trading rights on the coast in 1842, and occupied the interior in 1882. In 1960 the I.C. became independent, but the official language is still French. The majority of the pop are animists, with Moslem and Christian minorities. Pop. (1977) 9,490,000. M.U.: CFA franc.

IVY. Genus of trees and shrubs (*Hedera*) of the Araliaceae family. The European I. (*Hedera helix*) has shiny, evergreen, triangular- or oval-shaped leaves and its clusters of small, yellowish-green flowers are followed by poisonous black berries. It climbs by means of root-like suckers put out from its stem, and is injurious to trees. Ground I. (*Nepeta hederacea*) is a small, creeping plant of the Labiatae family found both in Britain and N America; and the N American poison I. (*Rhus toxicodendron*), also known as poison oak, belongs to the Anacardiaceae.

IXĪON. In Greek mythology, son of a king in Thessaly and husband of Dia, who for his crimes was bound by Zeus to a fiery wheel which rolls endlessly through the underworld.

IXTAPAN DE LA SAL (ist'ahpan). Health resort, 72km (45m) from Toluca, Mexico. The radioactive waters are used in the treatment of rheumatism and skin ailments, and are sometimes identified with the legendary Aztec fountain of youth.

I'ZARD. Another name for the chamois.

IZHEVSK (ēzhefsk'). Russian town, cap. of Urdmurt ASSR, on the Izha, 240km (150m) SW of Perm. A metallurgical centre dating from 1760, it makes steel, agricultural and other machinery, and machine tools. Pop. (1977) 534,000.

IZMIR (ēzmēr'). Ancient port on the W coast of Turkey-in-Asia, cap. of I. il. Originally a Greek colony founded *c.* 1000 BC, it was formerly known as Smyrna. After many vicissitudes (incl. destruction by Tamerlane in 1402), it was taken by the Turks in 1424. A rail terminus with modern harbour facilities, it exports wheat, dried fruit, textiles, etc., and has an oil refinery. Pop. (1970) 520,690.

J

Tenth letter of the modern Roman alphabet. The modern Eng. value of *j* is that of a compound consonant, *d* followed by the sound *zh* (as in pleasure, pron. ple*zh*'ur).

JABIRU (ja'biroo). Species of stork (*Jabiru mycteria*) found in America. It is *c.* 150cm (5ft) high with white plumage. The head is black and red.

JABLONEC (yah'blonets). Town in Czechoslovakia on the Neisse, NE of Prague, famed for glass from 14th cent. Pop. (1970) 30,000.

JABORA'NDI. The dried leaves of several S American plants (genus *Pilocarpus*) which yield pilocarpine, an alkaloid which strongly stimulates sweat and saliva flow.

JA'CAMAR. Small Brazilian birds of the family Galbulidae. They have long sharp-pointed bills and paired toes. The plumage is brilliantly coloured.

JA'ÇANA. Wading birds in the family Parridae, found in S America, Africa, India, and Australasia.

JACARA'NDA. Tree of the family Bignoniaceae found in Brazil, and also several other flowering trees with fragrant wood in the W Indies and S America.

JA'CINTH or **hyacinth.** A red or yellowish-red gem which is a variety of zircon.

JACKAL (jak'awl). Member of the dog family (*Canis aureus*), found in S Asia, Africa and Dalmatia. About 45cm (1.5ft) high and 60cm (2ft) long, it is greyish-yellow, darker on the back. Nocturnal, it preys on smaller mammals and poultry, though packs will attack larger animals. It has a reputation as a scavenger and will follow lions and tigers to finish off the carcases of their kill.

JACKAL. Jackals are scavengers, like the hyenas, but are much more attractive in appearance. They rarely attack live prey, but strip the carcases left by larger predators. *Photo: M. Myers/Camera Press.*

JACKDAW. Species of crow in the genus *Corvus*, found in Europe and W Asia. It is black and grey and often nests in masonry.

JACKSON, Andrew (1767-1845). 7th Pres. of the USA, b. in S Carolina, he defeated the British at New Orleans in 1815, and was elected Pres. in 1828. In 1832 he vetoed the renewal of the US bank charter, and was re-elected, whereupon he continued his struggle against the power of finance.

JACKSON, Glenda (1936-). British actress. B. at Birkenhead, she made her name in *Marat-Sade* (1965). For her film performances in *Women in Love* (1971) and *A Touch of Class* (1973), she was awarded Oscars, and played Queen Elizabeth I in the award-winning television series *Elizabeth R* (1971). In John Mortimer's play *The Collaborators* (1973) she broke into comedy.

JACKSON, John (1769-1845). British pugilist; known as 'Gentleman Jackson', he was champion 1795-1803. He taught Byron boxing.

JACKSON, Lady, *See* WARD, B.

JACKSON, Thomas Jonathan, known as 'Stonewall' J. (1824-63). American Confederate general. After serving in the Mexican War of 1846-8, he became professor of military tactics at the Virginia military institute. In the Civil War he acquired his nickname and his reputation at Bull Run, from the firmness with which his brigade resisted the Northern attack. In 1862 he organized the Shenandoah valley campaign, and assisted Lee's invasion of Maryland. He helped to defeat Hooker's army at Chancellorsville, but was accidentally shot by his own men.

JACKSON. Cap. of Mississippi state, USA, on the Pearl r. It dates from 1821 and was virtually destroyed by Sherman in 1863. The discovery of natural gasfields to the S stimulated industry; products include lumber, furniture, cottonseed oil, iron and steel castings. Pop. (1970) 154,000.

JACKSONVILLE. City, port, and holiday resort of Florida, USA, the business cap. of the state, with some industry. Founded in 1822, J. was named after Andrew Jackson (q.v.), then Gov. of Florida. To the N the Cross-Florida Barge Canal links the Atlantic with the Gulf of Mexico, some 160km (100m) N of Tampa. Pop. (1970) 513,439.

JACK THE RIPPER. Popular name for the unidentified murderer of 5 women prostitutes in the Whitechapel area of London in 1888: the mutilation of the bodies added to the sensation. Speculative identifications incl. the Duke of Clarence (d. 1892), elder brother of George V; the Duke's tutor J. K. Stephen, cousin of Virginia Woolf; and M. J. Druitt, a teacher who committed suicide 1888.

JACOB (jā'kob). Hebrew patriarch. The 2nd son of Isaac and Rebecca, he obtained the rights of seniority from Esau by trickery, and became a pastoral chief. He m. his 2 cousins Leah and Rachel, serving Laban 7 years for each. At the time of the famine in Canaan he joined his son Joseph in Egypt.

JACOBABAD (jāk'-). Town in Pakistan, 400km (250m) NNE of Karachi. It has a very small rainfall (*c.* 5cm/2in annually) and reaches the highest temperature in the Indian sub-continent - as much as 53°C (127°F). Pop. (1972) 130,000.

JACOBEAN. Term applied to a style of architecture and furniture in favour during the reign of James I (1603-25). Following the general lines of Elizabethan design, it used classical features more widely. A fine example is Hatfield House, Herts.

JACOBINS (jak'obinz). A democratic republican club of the French Revolution, which originated at Versailles in 1789, but later moved to Paris where it rented a Jacobin (Dominican) friary. The name 'Jacobin' passed into general use for any supporter of revolutionary or democratic opinions.

JACOBINS. Danton joined in the debates at the Jacobin Club, but rapidly developed even more extreme views. *Photo: Mansell Collection.*

JACOBITES. Those who continued to support the House of Stuart after the dethronement of James II in 1688 (Lat. *Jacobus,* James). Jacobitism was strongest among the Scottish Highlanders, who rose unsuccessfully under Claverhouse in 1689. James, the 'Old Pretender', headed a rebellion in Scotland and N England in 1715, and in 1745-6 his son Charles Edward led a Scottish invasion of England which reached Derby. After the defeat of Culloden, Jacobitism disappeared as a political force.

JACOBS, William Wymark (1863-1943). British author. A professional civil servant, he was b. at Wapping and acquired an intimate knowledge of the docks and their 'characters', such as the rascally 'Bob Pretty', which he exploited in amusing short stories, e.g. *Many Cargoes* (1896). He excelled in the macabre, e.g. *The Monkey's Paw.*

JACQUARD (zhahkahr'), **Joseph Marie** (1752-1834). French inventor of the J. loom, enabling the most complex designs to be woven. He was bitterly attacked by his fellow weavers, but the basic principles of his invention are in universal use.

JACQUERIE (zhahkrē'). Name given to the French peasant rising of 1358. The word is derived from the nickname for the French peasant, *Jacques Bonhomme.*

JADE (jād). Name given to various mineral substances, most commonly jadeite and nephrite, ranging from white to dark green according to the iron content. Long the hardest mineral known, its use by certain races is of ethnological interest and as a measure of their standard of civilization. The Chinese first discovered and used J., bringing it from E Turkestan (so far as is known J. has never been found in China), and carried the art of J. carving to its peak: the Aztecs and Maoris have also used J. for ornaments, weapons and utensils since prehistoric times.

JADE. Princess Tou Wan of the Western Han dynasty, clothed for burial in a suit of jade which is thought to date from *c.* 100 B.C. Every small plaque would take lengthy shaping and polishing before being set in place. *Photo: Society for Anglo-Chinese Understanding.*

JAEN (hahen'). Capital of J. prov., S Spain. It has remains of its Moorish walls and citadel, and makes textiles, leather, soap, alcohol. Pop. (1970) 78,156.

JA'FFA. Ancient port of Palestine dating at least from the 15th cent. BC. It appears as Joppa in Egyptian records and in the Bible, and was captured by the Crusaders in the 12th cent. AD, by Napoleon in 1799, and by Allenby in 1917. It was incl. in the rep. of Israel in 1948 and united with Tel Aviv in 1949 (*see* TEL AVIV-JAFFA).

JĀ'GAN, Cheddi (1918-). Guyanese politician. Descended from Indian immigrants, J. was ed. at Queen's Coll., British Guiana, and in the USA. In 1950 he became leader of the People's Progressive Party, with strong leftish tendencies, and in 1961-4 was the first PM of British Guiana and Min. of Development and Planning. His American-born wife, Janet J., is sec. of the party and in 1963-4 was Min. of Home Affairs.

JA'GUAR. Largest species of cat in America (*Panthera onca*). It is *c.* 1.2m (4ft) long excluding the tail. The ground colour of the fur varies from creamy white to brown or black, and is covered with black spots in rosettes.

JAHANGIR (-gēr') ('Conqueror of the World'). Name adopted on his succession in 1605 by Salim (1569-1627), 3rd Mogul emperor of Delhi. Son of Akbar the Great, during his troubled and tyrannical reign he lost Kandahar to Persia in 1622; and as a result of his addiction to drink and opium he lost power also to his wife Nur Jahan ('Light of the World'). A literary and artistic connoisseur, he designed the beautiful Shalimar Gardens in Kashmir, and gardens and buildings in Lahore.

JAGUAR. Even at two months, the heaviest leather gloves are needed to handle this youngster. *Photo: Popperfoto.*

JAHWEH. Another spelling of Jehovah (q.v.).

JAI ALAI. *See* PELOTA.

JAINISM (jā'nizm). A religion professed by about 2 million and a half Hindus, and sometimes regarded as an offshoot from Hinduism. Its sacred books record the teachings of Mahavira (599-527 BC), the latest of a long series of Tirthankaras, or omniscient saints and seers. B. in Vessali, now Bessarh, he became an ascetic at the age of 30, acquired omniscience at 42, and preached for 30 years.

Jains believe that non-injury to living beings is the highest religion and their code of ethics is based on sympathy and compassion. They also believe in 'karma' (q.v.). In J. there is no deity, and like Buddhism it is a monastic religion. There are 2 main sects: the Digambaras, who originally went about completely nude, and the Swetambaras.

JAIPUR (jīpoor'). Indian city, cap. of Rajasthan state, noted for the colour of its stone buildings - pink for Siva, with touches of yellow for Kali. It is a railway junction with some industry. Pop. (1971) 631,145. J. was formerly the cap. of the princely state of J., merged in Rajasthan 1949.

JAKAR'TA. Capital of Indonesia on the NW coast of Java. Founded by the Dutch in 1610, it was known as Batavia 1619-1949. The president's palace and the govt. offices are here, and from the 1960s there has been remarkable commercial and industrial (textiles, chemicals, plastics, etc) development, as well as hotels and other tourist facilities. There are 2 airports and the city is linked by canal with its port of Tanjung Priok 10 km (6 m) north-east. The main campus of the Univ. of Indonesia is here. Pop. (1975) 6,500,000.

JAMAICA (jamā'ka). Largest is. in the British W Indies, lying *c.* 145km (90m) S of Cuba, in the Caribbean Sea. Of great natural beauty, J. consists of an elevated well-watered plain, bisected by the Blue Mts. running E to W which rise to *c.* 2,255 m (7,400 ft). The cap. is Kingston, founded 1693; the ruins of the nearby 'pirate city' of Port Royal, destroyed and partly submerged by an earthquake in 1692, with a loss of 2,000 lives, were excavated from 1965 by Robert Marx. The chief products are bananas, sugar, coffee, rum, citrus fruits, coconuts, and tobacco. Bauxite is a principal export. Industries are increasingly varied and tourism is important.

Colombus discovered J. in 1494 and it remained Spanish until conquered by Britain in 1655. Representative govt was granted in 1884, and in 1962 J. became independent within the Commonwealth. There is a Gov.-Gen., elected House of Representatives and nominated Senate. The name J. derives from the aboriginal Xaymaca (land of wood and water), but the aboriginal people died out under the hard labour imposed on them by the Spaniards, who then imported Negroes to work for them. Most of the people today are of Negro descent, and the patois in everyday use mingles old and new English, Spanish, French and African. The majority adhere to a variety of Christian sects. Mounting violence between supporters of the ruling People's National Party, led by Michael Manley (q.v.) and the Labour Party (JLP) led to a declaration of emergency in 1976 and the exodus of much of the middle class. A bankrupt economy and resentment at the close ties with Cuba led to a landslide victory for the JLP under Edward Seaga in 1980. Area 11,525 sq.km (4,411 sq.m); pop. (1977) 2,110,000. M.U.: Jamaican dollar.

The Cayman Is. (q.v.) and the Turks and Caicos Is. (q.v.), formerly dependencies of J., were given separate administrations in 1958.

JAMES. Apostle and saint. A son of Zebedee, he was, like his brother John, a fisherman of Galilee. Called as a disciple by Jesus, he became a leader of the Church in Jerusalem after the Crucifixion, and was put to death by Herod Agrippa in AD 44. He is the patron saint of Spain. Another James, the son of Alphaeus, and also a disciple of Christ, is distinguished as 'J. the Little'. A third James was the Lord's brother, and is known as 'J. the Just'. Paul says that Christ appeared to him after the Resurrection, and that he was a leader of the Church in Jerusalem.

JAMES I and **VI** (1566-1625). King of England and Scotland. The son of Mary, queen of Scots, and Lord Darnley, he was proclaimed king of Scotland as J. VI upon his mother's abdication in 1567. After a troubled minority he assumed power in 1583; he estab. a strong central authority, and asserted the supremacy of the State over the Kirk. Succeeding Elizabeth as king of England in 1603, he alienated Puritan sentiment by his High Church views, and Parliament by his assertions of Divine Right. His unpopularity was increased by his fondness for favourites, and by his schemes for an alliance with Spain. He m. Anne of Denmark in 1589.

JAMES II and **VII** (1633-1701). King of England and of Scotland, the 2nd son of Charles I. In 1660 he m. Anne Hyde, by whom he had 2 daus., Mary and Anne. His 2nd wife was the Catholic Mary of Modena. Appointed Lord High Admiral at the Restoration, he was successful both as an administrator and as a commander in the Dutch Wars. His conversion to Roman Catholicism led to

JAMAICA. One of the island's greatest sources of wealth is the attraction to tourists of its palm-fringed beaches and coves. *Photo: Patrick Lichfield/Camera Press.*

attempts to exclude him from the succession. After his accession in 1685 the failure of Monmouth's and Argyll's rebellions strengthened his position, but his attempts at arbitrary rule and his favour to Catholics produced a reaction against him, and in 1688 the Whig and Tory leaders united in an invitation to William of Orange to take the throne. J. fled to France. In 1689 he led a rising in Ireland, but was defeated at the battle of the Boyne (1690), and henceforward remained in exile in France.

JAMES. Name of 7 kings of Scotland. **James I** (1394-1437) was captured by the English on the way to France in 1406, and although he became king the same year was held a prisoner until 1424. Before returning to Scotland he m. Lady Jane Beaufort, and described his wooing in *The Kingis Quair,* a poem in the style of Chaucer. He was murdered by his nobles. **James II** (1430-60) succeeded his father James I, and took over the govt. in 1449. His reign was troubled and he was accidentally killed while besieging Roxburgh Castle. **James III** (1451-88) succeeded his father James II, assumed the royal power in 1469, and was murdered during a rebellion. **James IV** (1473-1513) succeeded his father James III. He m. Margaret, dau. of Henry VII, in 1503, but in 1513 he invaded England, and was defeated and killed at Flodden. **James V** (1512-42) succeeded his father James IV, and took power in 1528. The defeat of his army by the English at Solway Moss in 1542 hastened his end. For James VI and VII *see* JAMES I and II OF ENGLAND.

JAMES I (1208-76). King of Aragon, called 'the Conqueror'. Succeeding his father in 1213, he conquered the Balearic Is. and took Valencia from the Moors.

JAMES, Henry (1843-1916). Anglo-American novelist. B. in New York, the brother of the philosopher William J., he spent much of his youth in Europe. His first novel was *Roderick Hudson* (1876), which like *The American* (1877) and *The Portrait of a Lady* (1881) shows the impact of European culture on the American mind. Other novels of the middle years are the exclusively American *Washington Square* (1881) and *The Bostonians* (1886); and *The Tragic Muse* (1890), *The Spoils of Poynton* (1897), and *The Awkward Age* (1899), all with English backgrounds. Greatest of his later works were *The Wings of a Dove* (1902), *The Ambassadors* (1903), and *The Golden Bowl* (1904). Noteworthy are the short essay in the supernatural 'The Turn of the Screw' (1898), and his valuable literary *Notebooks.* After 1875 he resided permanently in Europe, becoming a naturalized British subject in 1915. His style became increasingly involved - the stages wittily summarized as 'James I, and James II and James the Old Pretender' - and he is popularly best known by the successful posthumous stage adaptation of his books, the medium being one in which he had always wanted to excel. In 1976 he was commemorated in Poet's Corner, Westminster Abbey.

JAMES, Jesse (1847-82). American folk hero. B. on a Missouri farm, J. became, with his brother Frank (1843-1915), leader of the notorious Quantrill gang. Carrying out many daring bank and railroad robberies in the midwestern states, they caused numerous deaths and a large reward was offered for their capture. A hero even during his lifetime, he was killed by an accomplice. Frank was unconvicted and became a respectable farmer.

JAMES, Montague Rhodes (1862-1936). British theologian. Provost of King's Coll., Cambridge, 1905-18, and of Eton 1918-36, he pub. numerous Biblical studies, including the *Apocryphal New Testament* (1924). He was also a master of the uncanny, and the malevolent apparitions of *Ghost Stories of an Antiquary* (1904) and other volumes are unrivalled.

JAMES, William (1842-1910). American psychologist and philosopher, brother of Henry J. He turned from medicine to psychology and taught at Harvard 1872-1907. In 1890 appeared his *Principles of Psychology,* followed by *Will to Believe* (1897), and *Varieties of Religious Experience* (1902), one of the most important works on the psychology of religion. He expounded his pragmatic approach to metaphysics in *Pragmatism* (1907) and *Meaning of Truth* (1909).

JAMES EDWARD (1688-1766). The 'Old Pretender', called by Jacobites James III. The son of James II, he was b. at St James's Palace, and after the revolution of 1688 was taken to France. He landed in Scotland in 1715 to head a Jacobite rebellion, but withdrew owing to lack of support. In his later years he settled in Rome.

JAMESON, Sir Leander Starr (1853-1917). British colonial statesman. B. in Edinburgh, he practised medicine in London and then Kimberley, where he became a friend of Cecil Rhodes. Early in 1896 he led the J. raid from Mafeking into Transvaal, in support of the dissatisfied 'Uitlanders'. Surrendering, he was handed over to the British for punishment, but owing to ill-health he served only part of his sentence of 15 months' imprisonment. Returning to S Africa, he succeeded Rhodes as leader of the Progressive Party of Cape Colony, where he was PM 1904-8. He was created a baronet in 1911.

JAMESTOWN. Site in Virginia, USA, 60km (37m) NW of Norfolk, of the first permanent British settlement in N America, estab. by Captain John Smith in 1607, and cap. of the British colony of Virginia 1624-99. In the nearby J. Festival Park there is a replica of the original Fort James, and models of the ships (*Discovery, Godspeed* and *Constant*), which carried the 105 pioneers.

JAMMU (jumoo'). Winter cap. of the state of J. and Kashmir (q.v.). It stands on the Tavi and is linked by road to Pathankot and India's rail system. An important drug research laboratory is situated at J. Pop. (1971) 155,250.

JAMNAGA'R. Indian city and port, in Gujarat state, on the Gulf of Kutch, WSW of Ahmedabad. It has textile mills, match factories, etc., and an airport. Pop. (1971) 214,853.

JAMSHEDPUR. City of Bihar, Republic of India. Begun in 1909, on land acquired in 1907, J. takes its name from the Parsee industrialist Jamsheedji Tata, founder of the great Bombay firm. The Tata iron and steel works at J. are based on the coal and iron of the neighbouring Chota Nagpur plateau. Pop. (1971) 465,200.

JANÁČEK (yah'nahchek), **Leoš** (1854-1928). Czech composer. He studied the organ at Prague before visiting Leipzig and Vienna in 1878; on his return he organized a series of popular concerts, presenting great masterpieces to his Moravian countrymen, and in 1881 founded and directed an organ school in Brno. He became director of the Conservatoire at Brno in 1919, and prof. at the Prague Conservatoire in 1920. His music, based on the rhythm and melody of the Moravian peasant speech and folk music, incl. arrangements of folk songs, many operas and choral works, e.g. *Jenufa* (1904); *Taras Bulba* for orchestra; and chamber music.

JA'NISSARIES. Bodyguard of the sultan, the Turkish standing army 1330-1826. Until the 16th cent. it was recruited by taking Christian boys who received instruction in the Muslim faith. In 1826, when the sultan decided to raise a regular force, they revolted, whereupon they were suppressed,

JAN MAYEN (yahn mī-en). Norwegian island in the Arctic between Greenland and Norway, named after a Dutchman who visited it *c.* 1610. Area 373 sq.km (144 sq.m).

JANSEN, Cornelius (1585-1638). Dutch theologian who became prof. at Louvain in 1630, and RC bishop of Ypres in 1636. J. gives his name to the RC religious movement known as Jansenism, which originated with his *Augustinus* (1640), in which he argued that the teaching of St Augustine on grace, free will, and predestination was opposed to the doctrines of modern theologians, especially the Jesuits. During the middle years of the 17th cent. the Church in France was distracted by the theological war of Jansenists and Jesuits. Pascal was an ardent Jansenist, together with the Arnaulds of the Port Royal circle. In 1713 a Jansenist work by Quesnel, the leader of the party, was condemned by pope Clement XI as heretical, and after Quesnel's death in 1719 Jansenism as an organized movement in France disappeared. But it survived in Holland where in 1723 a regular Jansenist church was estab. under the bishop of Utrecht.

JANŪĀ'RIUS, St (d. AD 305). Patron saint of Naples; also called San Gennaro. Traditionally, he suffered martyrdom under Diocletian. Two phials of his blood are alleged to liquefy miraculously.

JĀ'NUS. Roman god, the patron of the beginning of the day, month, and year. The first month of the year is named after him, and he is represented in art with 2 faces looking in opposite directions.

JAPA'N. An independent sovereign state of eastern Asia in the N Pacific Ocean. J. consists of a chain of more than 1,000 islands running N to SW and separated from the continent by the Sea of Japan. The chief islands are Hokkaido, Honshu (the mainland), Shikoku, and Kyushu (qq.v.). The chief towns are Tokyo, Osaka, Nagoya, Kyoto, Yokohama, and Kobe. Total area 370,000 sq.km (142,680 sq.m); pop. (1977) 114,150,000. M.U.: yen.

The coastline is deeply indented, particularly on the Pacific shore where the Tuscarora Deep is one of the deepest sea-beds in the world. A mountain range traverses J. from N to SW, the highest peak being Fujiyama in Honshu, 3,778m (12,390ft). J. has a large number of active volcanoes and is subject to earthquakes. Extensive, well-watered plains divide the mountains. The main rivers are the Ishikari, *c.* 645km (400m) and the longest, in Hokkaido; the Shinano, Tone, and Yoshino in Honshu. Lakes are numerous.

By the 1960s the traditional products - rice, silk, and fish - accounted for less than 10 per cent of her national output, and she was among the leading industrial nations, producing ships, motor vehicles, cameras, sewing machines, watches and clocks, electronic equipment, steel, textiles, plastics, paper, chemicals and cement. Minerals incl. some coal, of poor quality; oil and natural gas discovered on Honshu after the S.W.W. but insufficient to meet demand; copper, lead, manganese, iron, gold and silver. Hydro-electric and thermo-electric power is well-developed.

The Japanese are shorter than the Chinese and Koreans, but of similar build. There exists a physical difference between social classes, the majority being descended from the Malay or Indonesian race while the upper minority may have been of Manchu-Korean origin. Earlier than these types are the Ainu. The national religion is Shinto (q.v.), but its profession does not exclude acceptance also of Buddhism (introduced in 6th cent.); there are some half-million Christians (from 16th cent.). Festivals, such as Christmas, are celebrated by many who are not Christian.

Government. Under the constitution which came into effect in 1947, the Emperor divested himself of his former divine attributes and became a constitutional sovereign with no executive powers. Women received the vote, human rights on Western lines were laid down, and war was renounced, but there was agitation for revision of this provision in 1980 rather than passive reliance on US arms. A cabinet led by a PM was given executive power; a house of representatives elected for 4 years and a house of councillors, one-half to be elected every 3 years, were given legislative power.

History. The Japanese nation probably arose from the fusion of 2 peoples, one coming from Malaya or Polynesia, the other from Asia, who conquered the original inhabitants, the Ainu. Japanese history remains legendary until the 5th cent. AD, when the art of writing was introduced from Korea. After the introduction of Buddhism, also from Korea, in the 6th cent., Chinese culture became generally accepted, but although attempts were made in the 7th cent. to diminish the power of the nobles and set up a strong centralized monarchy on the Chinese model, real power remained in the hands of the great feudal families until modern times. In 1192 the ruling noble Yoritomo assumed the title of shogun (commander-in-chief), which until 1867 was usually borne by the real ruler of J. Intercourse with Europe began in 1542, when Portuguese traders arrived; they were followed by the Spaniards, and in 1609 by the Dutch. Christianity was introduced by Francis Xavier in 1549. During the 15th and 16th cents. J. sank into a state of feudal anarchy, until order was restored between 1570 and 1615 by 3 great rulers, Nobunaga, Hideyoshi, and Iyeyasu; the family of the last, the Tokugawa, held power until the abolition of the shogunate. The fear that RC propaganda was intended as a preparation for Spanish conquest led to the expulsion of the Spaniards in 1624, and the Portuguese in 1639, and to the almost total extermination of Christianity by persecution; only the Dutch were allowed to trade with J. under irksome restrictions, while Japanese subjects were forbidden to leave the country. This complete isolation continued until 1853, when the USA insisted on opening trade relations; during the next few years this example was followed by the European powers. Consequently the isolationist party compelled the last shogun to abdicate in 1867, and executive power was restored to the Emperor. During the next 30 years the privileges of the feudal nobility were abolished, a uniform code of law was introduced, and a constitution was estab. in 1889. The army was modernized, and a powerful navy founded. Industry developed steadily and a considerable export trade was built up.

J.'s career of aggression began in 1894 when a war with China secured her Formosa and S Manchuria, as well as control of Korea, which was formally annexed in 1910. A victorious war with Russia in 1904-5 gave J. the S half of Sakhalin, and compelled the Russians to evacuate Manchuria. J. formed an alliance with Britain in 1902, and joined the Allies during the F.W.W.; at the peace settlement she received the German islands in the N Pacific as mandates. The 1920s saw an advance towards democracy and party govt, but after 1932 the govt assumed a semi-Fascist form. As a result of successful aggression against China in 1931-2 a Japanese puppet monarchy under Pu Yi, last Emperor of China, was estab. in Manchuria (*see* MANCHUKUO); war with China was renewed in 1937. J. entered the S.W.W. with the attack on Pearl Harbor on 7 Dec. 1941, and at first won a succession of victories in the Philippines, Malaya, Burma, and the Netherlands Indies. She was finally compelled to surrender in Aug. 1945; an Allied control commission took charge, and J. was under military occupation by Allied (chiefly US) troops until April 1952 when the Japanese Peace Treaty came into force. After J.'s defeat, Korea was made independent; Manchuria and Formosa were returned to China; the islands mandated to J. after the F.W.W. were placed by the UN under US trusteeship. Japan successfully agitated for the return by the USA of the Ryuku Is., and the Bonin and Volcano Is. (qq.v.), and has asked the Soviet Union to return the Northern Territories, i.e., the is. of Shikotan and the Habomai Group, and the southernmost Kurils (q.v.), Kunashiri and Etorofu.

Following the S.W.W. Japan renounced nuclear weapons, but rapidly became Asia's leading economic power, extending aid to her neighbours. The Liberal Democratic Party (LDP) has been in power almost continuously since the S.W.W., although subject to factions: Yasuhiro Nakasone (1911–) became PM in 1982. The LDP leans more to co-operation with USA than China, and the opposing Democratic Party (DSP) reverses this position.

In the arts Japan has made an especial mark in the cinema since the film *Rashomon* (1951), dealing with the Samurai, of Akira Kurosawa, and in architecture has a designer of international reputation, Kenzo Tange (1913–), creator of Olympic buildings in 1964. *See also* JAPANESE ART and LITERATURE.

JAPAN. The Emperor and Empress in the garden of the new imperial palace, which preserves the traditional style. *Photo: Courtesy of the Japanese Information Centre.*

JAPAN, Sea of. The sea between Japan and the mainland of Asia.

JAPAN CURRENT. *See* KUROSHIO.

JAPANESE. The language of Japan. Pure J. is usually considered a member of the Altaic group of languages, showing affinities with Korean. It is of simple, agglutinating structure. As the J. developed no script of their own, they adopted in the 3rd cent. the Chinese ideographs and adapted them, thus evolving an extremely complicated system. Later a simplified system (*Kana*) was introduced, but never ousted the old one. The language of today is a mixture of Japanese and Chinese, with borrowings from modern European languages.

JAPANESE ART. The main periods in the history of J.A. are: *Pre-Buddhist* (before 580): examples of Pre-Buddhist art and simplicity are the *haniwa,* clay grave figures, and *dôtaku,* bronze bells decorated with engravings. *Suiko* period (580-650): together with Buddhism, Korean temple builders, painters, etc., came to Japan. *Hakuohô* period (650-720); during this Japanese art was strongly influenced by Chinese. *Tempyô* period (720-810): in this 'blossom-time of Japanese civilization' there was still a strong Chinese influence, but native genius asserted itself, and a great amount of sculpture was produced. *Jogan* period (810-980): a transitional period in which the chief influences were the religious sects of Shingon and Tendai. *Fujiwara* period (980-1170): in this period of elegance and refinement elaborate temples and mansions were built. *Kamakura* period (1170-1350): a more vigorous style of art was adopted. Sculpture was characterized by great strength and solidity. *Ashikaga* period (1350-1570): Zen Buddhism influenced the art. The rapid ink sketch in line and wash introduced by Zen priests from China became popular. Pottery gained in importance from the introduction of the tea ceremony. *Momoyama* period (1570-1630): the brilliant Kano artists produced beautiful screens to decorate palaces and castles. *Tokugawa* period (1630-1867): colour prints were first produced. Famous artists were Matabei, Kôryusai, Kiyonaga, Utamaro, and Hokusai. *Meiji* period (1868-1912): the influence of Western art, especially Impressionism, is clearly discernible; well-known artists were Gaho (1835-1908) and Kogyo (1866-1919). *Showa* period (1926-): attempts were made by, e.g. Seiho (1864-1942), to adapt the Western methods of objective realism to the traditional J. variety, and by painters such as Taikan (1868-1958) to revive the traditional subjective style; younger painters, e.g. Kokei (1883-1957) tried to combine traditional and foreign styles. *See also* BONSAI, and IKEBANA.

JAPANESE ART. Linear perfection in the art of Ukiyoe — 'Pursuit of Humanity'. *Photo: Courtesy of the Japanese Information Centre.*

JAPANESE LITERATURE. Among its earliest survivals are the 8th cent. *Collection of a Myriad Leaves,* which incl. poems by Hitomaro and Akahito (the principal form being the *tanka,* a 5-line stanza of 5, 7, 5, 7, 7, syllables), the prose *Record of Ancient Matters.* To the late 10th and early 11th cents. belong the women writers Sei Shōnagon and Murasaki Shikibu. During the 14th cent. the Nō drama developed from ceremonial religious dances, combined with monologues and dialogues. The 17th cent. brought such scholars of Chinese studies as Fujiwara Seikwa (1560-1619) and Arai Hakuseki (1657-1725). To this period belongs the origin of *kabuki,* the popular drama of Japan, of which Chikamatsu Monzaemon (1653-1724) is the chief exponent; of *haiku* (the stanza of 3 lines of 5, 7, 5 syllables), popularized by Matsuo Bashō (1644-94); and of the modern novel, as represented by Ibara Saikaku (1642-93). Among those reacting against Chinese influence was the poet-historian Motoori Norinaga (1730-1801). The late 19th and early 20th cents. saw the replacement of the obsolete *Tokugawa* style as a literary medium by the modern colloquial language, and the influence of Western lit., esp. Russian, produced writers such as the 'Realist' Tsubouchi Shōyō (1859-1935), followed by the 'Naturalist' and 'Idealistic' novelists, whose romantic preoccupation with self-expression gave rise to the still popular 'I-novels' of e.g. Dazai Osumu (1909-48).

Reacting against the autobiographical school were Natsume Sōseki (1867-1916), Nagai Kafū (1879-1959), and Junichirō Tanizaki (1886-1965), who instead found inspiration in past traditions or in self-sublimation; later novelists incl. Yasunari Kawabata (1899-1972) and Yukio Mishima (q.v.). Shimazaki Tōson (1872-1943) introd. Western-style poetry e.g. 'Symbolism', but the traditional forms of *haiku* and *tanka* are still widely used. Western-type, modern drama (Shingeki), inspired by Ibsen and Strindberg, has been growing since the turn of the century.

JAQUES-DALCROZE (zhak dalkrōz'), **Émile** (1865-1950). Swiss composer. He is best remembered for his system of physical training by graceful movement to music (eurhythmics), and founded the Institut J.-D. in Geneva.

JÄRNEFELT, Armas (1869-1958). Finnish composer. B. at Vyborg, he became court conductor at Stockholm, and is chiefly known for his 'Praeludium' and the lyrical 'Berceuse'.

JA'RRAH. Wood of the tree *Eucalyptus marginata* found in Australia; dark, close-grained, and durable.

JA'RROW. English industrial town in Tyne and Wear, on the S bank of the Tyne, 10km (6m) E of Newcastle and connected with the N bank by the Tyne Tunnel (1967). It grew with the establishment in the 19th cent. of the Palmer shipbuilding yards, and their closure in 1933 prompted the **Jarrow March** of unemployed protesters. J. was included in a 'special area', and steel rolling, ship repairing, tube manufacture, etc., were introduced. St Paul's Church (686) was the home of Bede until his death. Pop. (1972) 29,070.

JARRY (zhahrē'), **Alfred** (1873-1907). French dramatist. His farce *Ubu Roi* (1896) foreshadows the Theatre of the Absurd, and satirizes the bourgeoisie. Mère Ubu prods Père Ubu into making himself king by a coup, and his antics destroy the kingdom.

JASMINE or **jessamine.** Genus of plants (*Jasminum*) of the Oleaceae family, found in many parts of the world, but mainly in the E. J. oil is used in perfumery. The common J. (*J. officinale*), a native of Iran and N India, but naturalized in Europe, is a climber growing over 4m (12ft) high which bears clusters of white or yellow sweet-smelling flowers. The Chinese winter J. *(J. nudiflorum)* produces brilliant yellow flowers before its leaves appear.

JĀ'SON. In Greek mythology, the leader of the Argonauts who sailed to recover the Golden Fleece of the ram that had been carried away to Colchis. He escaped with the fleece and Medea, with whom he lived at Corinth; when he took a new bride she was slain by Medea's magic.

JA'SPER. Hard, compact variety of quartz, usually coloured red, brown or yellow. J. is opaque, and has been used as a gem.

JASPERS (yas'pers), **Karl** (1883-1969). German philosopher. B. at Oldenburg, he studied medicine and psychology, and in 1921 became prof. of philosophy at Heidelberg. Deprived by the Nazis in 1937, he was rescued in 1945 from the threat of death by the American occupation. His works incl. *General Psychopathology* (1913), and *Philosophy* (1932). As an interpreter of German existentialism, he was ranked next to Heidegger.

JASSY. Another form of IAŞI.

JĀ'TAKA. Name given to a collection of Buddhist legends giving an account of 547 previous incarnations of Buddha.

JAUNDICE. Yellowing of the skin and eyes. The usual cause is the presence of bile in the deeper layers, due to obstruction of the common bile duct, e.g. by gallstones, pressure of a growth on the duct, or swelling of the duct walls through catarrh; or to some disturbance of liver function which prevents the bile from ever reaching the ducts.

JAURÈS (zhohrās'), **Jean Léon** (1859-1914). French Socialist politician. B. in Tarn, he was a lecturer in philosophy at Toulouse until his election in 1885 as a deputy. In 1893 he joined the Socialist Party, and in 1904 founded *L'Humanité* and became its editor. An advocate of international peace, he was assassinated by a half-witted youth.

JAVA (jah'vah). The most important island of Indonesia, situated between Sumatra and Bali. With the is. of Madura, area 132,000 sq.km (51,000 sq.m); pop. (1971) 76,000,000. Along the centre of J. extends a chain of mountains, sometimes rising to 2,750m (9,000ft), which incl. volcanoes. The highest mountain, Semeru, 3,676m (12,060ft), is in the E. About half the island is under cultivation, the rest being thickly forested. Mountains and sea breezes prevent extreme heat, but humidity is high, as is rainfall in Dec. to March. Products incl. rice, coffee, cocoa, tea, sugar, rubber, quinine, teak, and petroleum.

The cap. of J. is Jakarta, also the cap. of Indonesia; important ports are Surabaja and Semarang. The people, of Mongol affinities, comprise Javanese, Sundanese, and Madurese, with differing languages. The majority are Moslems. Fossilized remains of a primitive man (*Homo erectus*) were discovered in 1891-2.

In central J. there are ruins of magnificent Buddhist monuments and of the Sivaite temple in Prambanan. J.'s last Hindu kingdom, Majapahit, was destroyed c. 1520 and followed by a number of short-lived Javanese kingdoms. The Dutch E India company founded a factory in 1610, named Batavia. The British occupied J. in 1811, during the Napoleonic period, returning it to the Dutch in 1816. J. was occupied by the Japanese 1942-5, and after their defeat became part of the rep. of Indonesia (q.v.).

JAW. One of the bony structures, upper and lower, which hold the teeth and form the framework of the mouth. The upper jaw (maxilla) consists of 2 bones united in the middle at an early stage of development. They join the bones of the forehead and cheek and each contains a hollow space, the maxillary sinus. The lower jawbone, the mandible, is hinged at each side to the bone of the temple by ligaments.

JAY. Genus of birds (*Garrulus*) of the crow family, confined to the Old World and common in Europe except in the far N. In the common J. (*G. glandarius*) the body is fawn with patches of white, blue and black on the wings and tail. Its own cry is a harsh screech, but it has considerable powers as a mimic. Allied is the common blue J. (*Cyanocilta cristata*), of N America, found in the pine forests.

JAY, Peter (1937-). British Labour economist. He is the son of Douglas Jay (1907-), who was pres. of the Board of Trade 1964-7, but campaigned zealously against the Common Market. He m. in 1961 Margaret, dau. of James Callaghan, during whose premiership he was ambassador to Washington 1977-9.

JAYAWARDENE (jī-ahwahdē'nē), **Junius Richard** (1906-). Sri Lankan statesman. Leader of the United Nat. Party from 1973, he defeated Mrs Bandaranaike to become PM in 1977. Following a constitutional amendment, he then became the country's first president.

JAZZ. A complete polyphonic, syncopated music originating in New Orleans between 1880-1900. The unusually favourable conditions were: the Spanish and later French domination of the city, with their musical traditions; the American brass band; and the still remembered 'Bamboula' chants from the Congo, whose mournful repetition and variations of short, insistent themes led easily to the blues. With no other entertainment available, music was an essential part of the bars, dance halls and bawdy houses of the red-light district, Storyville; as well as of picnic parties, weddings and funerals, where the marching bands led the procession to the cemetery playing hymns and slow blues, and then returned, swinging with the zest and fire of final salutation that could be heard miles away.

The prodigious techniques of early brass players was due to their natural talent, lack of awareness that their instruments had any limitations, and the competitive spirit that existed among bands. The exodus from New Orleans started in 1917, after the US Navy caused Storyville to be closed. Joe Oliver, Fred Keppard, Louis Armstrong, et al., moved to Chicago and St Louis, later spreading their influence to New York, where the more refined Fletcher Henderson orchestra was in vogue, succeeded by Paul Whiteman. Small dynamic groups survived the swing era of the 1940s, with the big bands of Goodman, Ellington and Herman, to emerge with increased vigour after the S.W.W., when J. had reached across Europe as far as Russia. Under the impetus of Charlie Parker, Dizzy Gillespie, Miles Davis, et al., J. has proliferated in an immense diversity of styles through which it is difficult to see the mainstream. From the revival of Traditional J. in the 1950s - a romantic, unimaginative version of the original - to modern J. there is to be found an increasingly wide range of rhythmic and harmonic content, embracing such diverse elements as the Bach fugue, the Brazilian bossa nova and the atonalities of Bartók. Among the early masters of J., whose compositions achieved recognition only in the 1970s is Scott JOPLIN (q.v.). *See* SWING.

Jazz Dance, developed in the USA in the 1970s. Defined by Matt Mattox, one of its pioneers with his Jazzart Co., as 'free-style dance', it takes in elements of ballet and modern dance, and blends them with Afro-American, Indian classical and Latin American forms.

JAZZ. The jazz festival in New Orleans, when at Mardi Gras the bands march, as in the early days. *Photo: Mireille Vautier.*

JEANS, Sir James Hopwood (1877-1946). British mathematician and astronomer. His original contributions incl. work in physics, on the kinetic theory of gases, forms of energy radiation; and in astronomy, on giant and dwarf stars, the nature of spiral nebulae, and the origin of the cosmos. He did much to popularize astronomy.

JEANS. Working trousers of blue denim which in the 1960-70s became the unofficial unisex uniform of youth throughout the world in its rejection of the uniformity of middle-class values. A heavy canvas cloth, known as jene fustian, from the Fr. form of Genoa (Gênes) where it originated, was first used in Liverpool, England, *c.* 1850 to make working clothes. About the same time Levi Strauss (1830-1902), Bavarian immigrant to USA, used some - which had been intended for tent and waggon covers - for trousers for goldminers in San Francisco. Hence they came to be called J. or 'Levi's'. Later a Fr. fabric, serge de Nîmes (corrupted to 'denim') was used.

JEDBURGH (jed'buro). Small town of Borders region, Scotland, on Jed Water. It has associations with Mary Queen of Scots, the Young Pretender and Burns. Pop. (1971) 3,880.

JEDDA. *See* JIDDA.

JEEP. The popular name for the General Purpose (GP) vehicle of the American Army. It is a small open vehicle which can be driven over rough ground.

JEFFERIES, John Richard (1848-87). British naturalist and writer. After an unsuccessful start, he gained a reputation as a writer in 1872, following a remarkable letter to *The Times* on the Wiltshire labourer. His intimate books on the countryside incl. *Gamekeeper at Home* (1878), *Wood Magic* (1881), *Life of the Fields* (1884); and the autobiographical *Bevis* (1882) and *Story of My Heart* (1883).

JEFFERS, John Robinson (1887-1962). American poet. B. in Pittsburgh, he had a complete mastery of free verse, and demonstrated a lone antagonism to human society which was echoed by the isolation of his home at Carmel in N California. His vols. incl. *Tamar and Other Poems* (1924), *The Double Axe* (1948), and *Hungerfield and Other Poems* (1954).

JEFFERSON, Thomas (1743-1826). Third Pres. of the USA. B. in Virginia, he pub. *A Summary View of the Rights of America* (1774) and as a member of the Continental Congresses of 1775-6 he was largely responsible for the drafting of the Declaration of Independence. He was governor of Virginia 1779-81, ambassador to Paris 1785-9, and Secretary of State 1789-93. J. was the founder of the Democratic Party. He was elected Vice-President 1796-1801 and President 1801-9.

JEFFREY, Francis, Lord (1773-1850). Scottish lawyer and literary critic. B. at Edinburgh, he was a founder and editor of the *Edinburgh Review* 1802-29. In 1830 he was made Lord Advocate, and in 1834 a Scottish law lord. He is chiefly remembered for his hostility to the romantic movement, and wrote of Wordsworth's *Excursion*: 'This will never do.'

JEFFREYS, George, 1st baron (1648-89). British judge. B. in Denbighshire, he became Chief Justice of the King's Bench in 1683, and presided over many political trials, notably those of Sidney, Oates, and Baxter, becoming notorious for his brutality. In 1685 he was raised to the peerage, and conducted the 'bloody assizes' after Monmouth's rebellion, during which 320 rebels were executed and hundreds more flogged, imprisoned or transported. Created Lord Chancellor in 1685, he attempted to flee the country after the revolution of 1688, but was captured and d. in the Tower.

JEHOL. Another name for CHENGDE.

JEHOVAH. The principal name for God in the OT, spelled JHVH or better YHWH in Hebrew; between these consonants were inserted the vowels of the word Adonai (Lord), but modern scholars incline to the pronunciation Jahveh or Yahweh.

JEHOVAH'S WITNESSES. Religious organization originated in the USA in 1872 by Charles Taze Russell (1852-1916). They attach great importance to Christ's second coming, said by Russell to have taken place invisibly in 1874, and by his successor 'Judge' Joseph Rutherford (d. 1942) in 1914. The ensuing Armageddon and Last Judgment, which entail the destruction of all except the faithful, is to give way to the Theocratic Kingdom. Their tenets, involving rejection of obligations such as military service, have often brought them into conflict with authority. The Watch Tower Bible and Tract Soc. and the Watch Tower Students' Assoc. form part of the movement. Membership *c.* 3,000,000.

JELLICOE, John Rushworth, 1st earl (1859-1935). British admiral. B. at Southampton, he entered the navy in 1872. As acting admiral, he commanded the Grand Fleet 1914-16, but the only action he fought was the battle of Jutland (q.v.). He was 1st Sea Lord 1916-17, organizing measures to combat the U-boat menace.

JELLY-FISH. Class of marine animals in the group Coelenterata. The J. has an umbrella-shaped body composed of a semi-transparent gelatinous substance, with a fringe of stinging tentacles. Most of them move freely, but some are attached by a stalk to rocks or seaweed. They feed on small animals which are paralysed by the stinging threads.

JENA (yeh'nah). Old town, first mentioned in the 9th cent., in E Germany, SE of Weimar. Here in 1806 Napoleon defeated the Prussians. Schiller and Hegel taught at

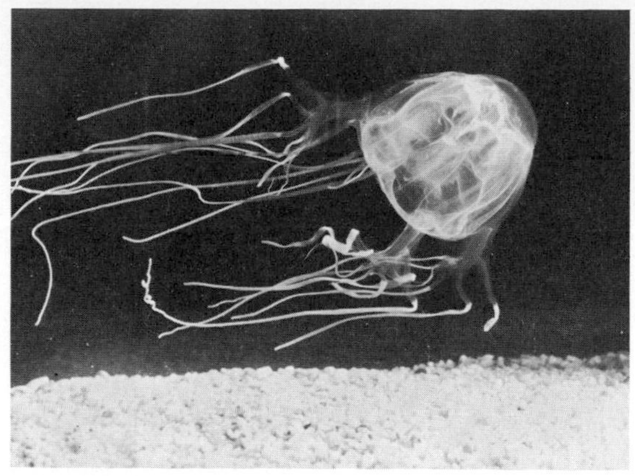

JELLYFISH. The sea wasp grows to the size of a man's head and trails filaments up to 10m (30 ft) long. On the slightest contact these eject thousands of stinging capsules, and until the development of an anti-venene in 1970, many died painfully after meeting these jellyfish while swimming. *Photo: Australian News and Information Service.*

JERBOA. When jumping the jerboa makes use of its tail to give it initial support. *Photo: Popperfoto.*

the univ. which dates from 1558. The Zeiss firm of optical-instrument makers, founded 1846, is among its chief industries. Pop. (1978) 101,000.

JENKINS, Roy Harris (1920-). British Labour politician. Ed. at Balliol Coll., Oxford, he was a close friend of Gaitskell, and has pub. studies of Attlee, Asquith, etc. He was Min. of Aviation 1964-5, Home Secretary 1965-7, and succeeded Callaghan as Chancellor of the Exchequer (1967-70). In 1970 he became deputy leader of the Labour Party, but in 1972 resigned because of disagreement with Wilson on the Common Market issue. Again Home Sec. 1974–6, he was pres. of the Common Market Commission 1977–80, and founder-leader of the 'radical centre' Social Democratic party from 1981 until he resigned after the 1983 election.

JENNER, Edward (1749-1823). British physician. He studied in London under John Hunter and practised all his life in Gloucestershire. From 1775 he made a special study of the cowpox, and in 1796 successfully inoculated a boy with matter taken from cowpox vesicles. He pub. his discovery that vaccination produced immunity from smallpox in 1798.

JENNER, Henry ('Gwas Myhal') (1849-1934). Cornish poet. He revived Cornish as a literary vehicle, and in 1904 pub. a handbook of the Cornish language.

JENSEN, Arthur (1923-). American psychologist. In 1969 he caused a furore by arguing that IQ was 80% inherited, and again in 1980 by *Bias in Mental Testing* by claiming that the IQ of black Americans averaged 15 points below that of whites, and that the underprivileged do best on objective tests.

JERABLUS. *See* CARCHEMISH.

JERBŌ'A. Several genera of rodents, found chiefly in Africa and Asia, and mainly herbivorous and nocturnal. Most typical is the common Egyptian J. (*Jaculus aegyptius*) with a body *c.* 18cm (7in) long and slightly longer tail. At speed it moves in a series of long jumps with its fore-feet held close to the body. *See* DESERT RATS.

JERĒMĪ'AH. Hebrew prophet, b. near Jerusalem, whose ministry continued 626-586 BC. During the siege of Jerusalem by Nebuchadnezzar, J. was imprisoned on suspicion of wishing to desert to the invader, but he was released on the city's fall, and retired to Egypt.

JEREZ DE LA FRONTERA (hereth' dā lah frontā'rah). Town in Cadiz prov., SW Spain, NE of Cadiz, famed for sherry. Pop. (1970) 149,900.

JERICHO (jer'ikō). Ancient city in the Jordan valley, Jordan, north of the Dead Sea. It was the first of the Canaanite strongholds to be captured by the Israelites, the walls of the city allegedly falling down to the blast of trumpets. Excavations by successive archaeologists from 1907 at intervals onwards show that the walls of the city were destroyed many times; little is left of the Late Bronze Age city captured by Joshua. (*See* KENYON, K.). A short distance from the old site is a modern Arab village, in Arabic Eriha.

JEROME (jerōm') (*c.* 340-420). Christian saint and Father of the Church. B. at Strido, he was baptized at Rome in 360, and subsequently travelled in Gaul, Asia Minor, and Syria. Summoned to Rome as adviser to pope Damasus, he revised the Latin translation of the NT and the Latin psalter. On the death of Damasus in 384 he travelled to the east, and settling at Bethlehem translated the OT into Latin from the Hebrew. His Lat. versions form the basis of the Vulgate.

JEROME, Jerome K(lapka) (1859-1927). British author. After being successively clerk, teacher, and actor, he turned to journalism; his *Idle Thoughts of an Idle Fellow* (1889), a collection of essays on such subjects as 'Babies', 'The Weather', etc., and his *Three Men in a Boat* (1889), made his reputation as a humorist. His dramatized story *The Passing of the Third Floor Back* (1907) is more sentimental.

JERSEY. Largest of the Channel Islands. Government is by a lieutenant-governor and an assembly. St Helier is the capital. Farming is the chief occupation. J. was occupied by the Germans 1940-5. Area 117 sq.km (45 sq.m); pop. (1971) 72,532.

JERSEY CITY. City of New Jersey, USA. It faces Manhattan Island, to which it is connected by tunnels. Its many industries incl. foundries, electrical apparatus, chemicals, cigarettes. The decayed dockside area, unsuited to modern port facilities, is being restored (from 1976) as Liberty Park. Pop. (1970) 260,545.

JERICHO. One of the Neolithic skulls with delicately moulded features discovered by Kathleen Kenyon in her excavations 1951-62. These were apparently retained as mementoes of loved relatives. *Photo: Courtesy of Dame Kathleen Kenyon.*

JERUSALEM (jero͞o′salem). Ancient city of Palestine, divided in 1948 between the new rep. of Israel and Jordan. In 1950 the Israelis proclaimed the New City, the western part which they then held, cap. of Israel, and following their capture of the Old City from the Jordanians in 1967, affirmed in 1980 that the united city was the cap. of Israel. The UN does not recognise J. as the cap. of Israel. Area (pre-1967) 37.5 sq.km, (post-1967) 108 sq.km, incl. areas of the West Bank to the N, E and S. Pop. (1967) Jews 195,000 (1980) 290,000; Arabs (1967) 56,000, (1980) 100,000. From the 1920s building extended beyond the old city, and in recent years Jewish 'ring' suburbs have been built.

By 1400 BC J. was ruled by a king subject to Egypt. David made J. the cap. of a united Jewish kingdom *c.* 1000. Nebuchadnezzar captured J. in 586 BC and deported its population. Under Cyrus a new settlement was made, and *c.* 445 the walls were rebuilt. J. passed under Alexander the Great, and later was a pawn in the contest between the Syrian Seleucids and the Egyptian Ptolemies. In 63 BC Pompey captured J., and a Jewish revolt led to the city's utter destruction in AD 70 by Titus. On its site was founded in AD 130 the Roman city of Aelia Capitolina, which was pillaged by the Persian Chosroës II in 615 while under Byzantine rule. J. was conquered by Islam in 637, and Turks and Egyptians held sway until the Crusaders took the city in 1099. Recaptured by Saladin in 1187, J. remained under almost unbroken Islamic rule, through the conquest by the Turks in 1517, until the British occupation in 1917.

There are 7 gates into the old city through the walls built by Selim I. From *c.* the 1920s, J. extended in modern suburbs, especially in the S and W. Notable buildings incl. the Church of the Holy Sepulchre erected by Constantine in 335, and the Mosque of Omar, built in 691 and occupying the site of Solomon's temple. The Hebrew univ. of J. on Mount Scopus was opened in 1925. J. is a Holy City for 3 faiths: Christian, Hebrew and Moslem; it has RC, Anglican, and Greek bishops, and a Coptic Metropolitan. Freedom of access of all faiths to their Holy Places was guaranteed by Israel in 1967. *See* TEMPLE.

JERUSALEM. The Via Dolorosa - the road believed to have been traversed by Christ on his way to Calvary. *Photo: Courtesy of the Israel Government Tourist Office.*

JERUSALEM ARTICHOKE. *See* ARTICHOKE.

JERVIS, John, earl of St Vincent (1735-1823). British admiral. An efficient organizer and rigid disciplinarian with both officers and men, he secured the blockage of Toulon in 1795, and the famed defeat of the Spanish fleet off Cape St Vincent (1797), in which Captain Nelson (q.v.) played a key part.

JERVIS BAY. Deep bay on the coast of New South Wales, Australia, 145km (90m) SW of Sydney. The Federal Govt in 1915 acquired 73 sq.km (28 sq.m) here to create a port for Canberra. J.B. forms part of Australian Capital Territory and is the site of the Royal Australian Naval College.

JESUITS (jez′ū-its) or **Society of Jesus.** An RC religious order. Founded by Loyola (q.v.) in 1534, it received papal approval in 1540. Its main objects were defined as educational work, the suppression of heresy, and missionary work among the heathen. Its members are not confined to monasteries. Loyola infused into the order a spirit of military discipline; training is long and arduous. During the 16th and 17th cents. they achieved success as missionaries to Japan and China, in Paraguay, and among the Red Indians. From the beginning they aimed at political influence, and these activities resulted in their expulsion during 1759-68 from Portugal, France, and Spain, and in 1773 the Pope suppressed the order. It was revived in 1814, but has since been expelled from many of the countries of Europe and America. Younger members working in the 'third world' often support revolution. Under Fr. Pedro Arrupe, general of the order from 1965, unorthodox moral and theological teachings have caused friction with the Pope. The order has *c.* 29,000 members, incl. *c.* 15,000 priests, the remainder being students and lay members.

JESUS CHRIST (jēz'us krīst) (*c.* 4 BC-AD 29 or 30). Jesus - called in Hebrew the Messiah, and in Greek the Christ - was the founder of Christianity (q.v.). The main sources of information on His life and work are the 4 Gospels. B. in Bethlehem, the son of the Virgin Mary of the tribe of Judah and the family of David. He was brought up as a carpenter by Joseph (q.v.) at Nazareth. In AD 26 or 27 His cousin John the Baptist began his preparatory mission, and after baptism at his hands Jesus became fully conscious of His own purpose. The Galilean Ministry incl. 2 missionary journeys through the district and the calling of the 12 Apostles, and culminated in the feeding of the 5,000. His teaching is summarized in the Sermon on the Mount, and was illustrated by homely parables. His apparent disloyalty to the traditional religion roused the opposition of the dominant religious party, the Pharisees, who joined the secular party of the Herodians against Him. Consequently He retired to the non-Jewish territory of Tyre and Sidon, where He probably devoted Himself to training the disciples, and made Himself known to them as the expected Messiah.

He then returned to Jerusalem (probably in AD 29), entering the city a week before the Passover, acclaimed by the populace as the Messiah. Fearing popular anger, the Jewish authorities arrested Jesus privately, aided by the betrayal of Judas, and after a hurried trial He was condemned to death by the Sanhedrin. Ultimate confirmation of this sentence was wrung from the Roman procurator Pontius Pilate by stressing the threat to imperial authority of His teaching. Three days after the Crucifixion, the long series of reported miracles culminated in Christ's Resurrection and His later Ascension.

JET. Mineral substance similar in composition to lignite and anthracite; it occurs in quantity near Whitby and along the Yorkshire coast. Ornaments made of J. have been found in Bronze Age tombs.

JETFOIL. Boat or ship which, as distinguished from the hydrofoil (q.v.) which travels on top of the waves, sinks its foils below the surface. Unaffected by turbulence, they slice through the water, and ensure smooth progress even in waves 4 m (12 ft) high. In both civil and military use, Js. reach speeds of 43 knots (80 kph/50mph).

JETLAG. The effect of a sudden switch of time-zones in jet air travel - not of lack of sleep or fatigue in flight - which means that the traveller is forced to spend his days under the influence of his 'night-metabolism', geared to sleep not activity. *See* CIRCADIAN RHYTHM.

JET PROPULSION. In aircraft propulsion, gas turbines are popularly referred to as J. engines. Air, after passing through a forward-facing intake, is compressed in a compressor or fan, driven by a turbine that absorbs sufficient energy for the purpose from the fast-moving gas stream. It is then heated and expanded rapidly rearwards by burning fuel in it in the combustion chamber, and is finally ejected from a rearward-facing jet pipe or nozzle, at very high speed to produce the opposite-acting force called thrust. Thrust, or engine power output, results from the acceleration of gases through the jet pipe to produce a forward reaction, which acts on the aircraft through its engine-mountings, not from any pushing of the hot gas stream impinging on the static air. Thrust is proportional to the mass of the gas ejected times the acceleration imparted to it, and is stated in units of pounds force (lbf) or kilograms force (kgf), both now being succeeded by the internat. unit, the Newton (N).

Variants of the J. are: 1. *turbojet,* the simplest form of gas turbine, used in aircraft well into the supersonic range. 2. *turboprop,* for moderate speeds and altitudes (up to 725kmph/450mph and 10,000m/30,000ft). Extra stages of turbine absorb most of the energy from the gas stream to drive the propeller shaft via a speed reduction gear. 3. *turbofan,* best suited to high subsonic speeds. It is fitted with an extra compressor, and the resultant excess airflow bypasses the core engine, and mixes with the J. exhaust stream, to give it lower temperature and velocity - hence greater economy, efficiency and quietness than the turbojet, and higher speed than the turboprop. 4. *turboshaft,* used to drive the main and tail rotors of helicopters; and in hovercraft, ships, trains, and in power stations and pumping equipment. It is effectively a turboprop without its propeller, power from an extra turbine being delivered to a reduction gearbox or directly to an output shaft. Most of the gas energy drives the compressors and provides shaft power so residual thrust is low, and turboshaft power is normally quoted as shaft horsepower (shp) or kilowatts (kw). 5. *ramjet,* used for some types of missiles. At twice the speed of sound (Mach 2), pressure in the forward-facing intake of a J. engine is 7 times that of the outside air, a compression ratio which rapidly mounts with increased speed (to Mach 8), with the result that no compressor or turbine is needed. The ramjet comprises merely an open-ended rather barrel-shaped tube, burning fuel in its widest section, and is cheap, light and easily made. However, fuel consumption is high and it needs rocket-boosting to operational speed. 6. *rocket* (q.v.), which unlike other J. engines carries its own oxygen and fuel, and so can operate in space.

Variants and additional capabilities of Js. incl. 1. multi-spool engines, in which compressors may be split into 2 or 3 parts driven by independent turbines, so that each runs at its own optimum speed. 2. vectored thrust (a swivelling of the jet nozzles from vertical to rearward horizontal to achieve vertical take-off followed by level flight) and reverse thrust, used to slow the landing run, and achieved by blocking off the jet pipe with special doors and re-directing the gases forward through temporarily opened cascades. 3. lift and booster Js., which are small, light-weight, high thrust-to-weight ratio gas turbines vertically installed for take off, hovering and landing, or to give increased power for take off, respectively, and are both shut down in normal flight. 4. reheat (afterburning), used espec. in military aircraft to obtain short-duration thrust

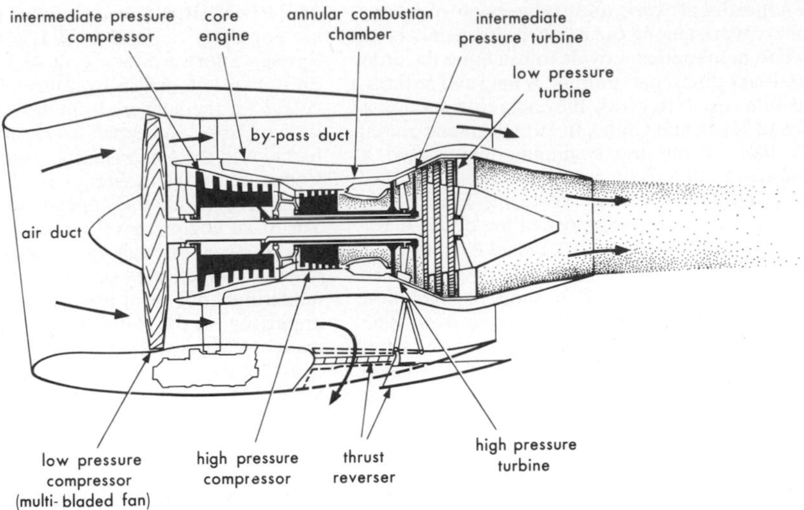

JET PROPULSION. The turbofan combines the advantages of the turboprop and turbojet: above is the Rolls-Royce RB 211 three-shaft turbofan. *Courtesy of Rolls-Royce Ltd.*

increase of up to 70 per cent by the controlled burning of fuel in the gas stream after it has passed through the turbine, but which increases fuel consumption.

The J. engine principle has also been applied to experimental motor-cars, the Rover BRM gas turbine being the first to run (Le Mans, 1963), when it averaged 173kph/108mph over 24 hours.

JEVONS, William Stanley (1835-82). British economist. Prof. of logic and political economy at Manchester from 1866, and at London (1876-81). He introduced the concept of final or marginal utility into economic theory.

JEWISH AUTONOMOUS REGION. Part of Khabarovsk Territory, RSFSR, in the Far East, on the left bank of the r. Amur. The cap. is Birobidjan. Textiles, leather, and clothing are made; there is some non-ferrous metallurgy, light engineering, and agriculture, and timber is worked. Estab. 1934 (nat. dist. 1928), the J.A.R. became only nominally Jewish after Stalinist purges 1936-7 and 1948-9. Area 36,000 sq.km (13,900 sq.m); pop. (1978) 198,000, incl, *c.* 15,000 Jews.

JEWS. Name given to the Semitic people, otherwise Israelites or Hebrews, who claim descent from the patriarch Abraham. Led by him they emigrated from Mesopotamia to Canaan *c.* 2000 BC. During the Hyksos period some settled on the borders of Egypt and were put to forced labour, from which they were rescued by Moses, founder of their religion, who aimed at their establishment in Palestine. The main invasion *c.* 1274 BC was led by Joshua and during the period of Judges ascendancy was estab. over the Canaanites. Complete conquest of Palestine and the union of all Israel was achieved under David *c.* 1000 BC, and Jerusalem became the capital. Solomon, David's son, succeeded and enjoyed a reputation for great wealth and wisdom, but his lack of a constructive policy led after his death to the secession of the north (Israel) under Jeroboam, only Judah remaining under the house of David. A new factor was introduced with the rise of Assyria: Israel purchased safety by tribute, and under Jeroboam II *c.* 785 reached her highest pitch of luxury, but the basis of her society was corrupt, and prophets such as Amos, Isaiah, and Micah predicted destruction. Retribution came at the hands of Tiglathpileser and his successor Shalmaneser IV; the northern kingdom was organized as Assyrian provs. after the fall of Samaria in 721 BC, although Judah was spared as an ally. When the Assyrian power waned, her place was taken by Babylonia, and in 586 BC Nebuchadnezzer took Jerusalem and carried off the major part of the population to Babylon.

Recent archaeological work has raised questions as to the historicity of some stories of the early period, e.g. Abraham and Moses (qq.v.): there is no evidence, for example, from increasingly full Egyptian sources, of Abraham's sojourn in Egypt.

Under Cyrus, the founder of the Persian Empire, they were allowed to return to Palestine; the Temple was restored in 520, and *c.* 444 Ezra promulgated the legal code which was to govern the future of the race. Alexander's conquest of the Persian Empire was followed by a struggle for Palestine between the Syrian Seleucids and Egyptian Ptolemies, and until the end of the 3rd cent. BC Palestine remained under the govt. of Egypt with a large measure of freedom. But with the advance of Syrian power Antiochus IV attempted intervention in Jewish internal quarrels, thus prompting the Maccabean revolt in 165 BC. For a short time Judaea was practically an independent kingdom, but internal dissension led to Pompey's intervention in 63 BC, and Roman suzerainty was estab. After the death of Herod in 4 BC one experiment in govt followed another until the revolt of AD 66-70 led to the destruction of the Temple by Titus.

Further desperate revolts followed, but a new focus of Jewish national sentiment was found in the work of the Rabbi Johanan ben Zakkai (*c.* 20-90), and after his day the President of the Sanhedrin was recognized as the Patriarch of Palestinian Jewry. Greatest of these presidents was Rabbi Judah (*c.* 135-220), who codified the traditional law in the *Mishnah.* A decline followed the Christianization of the Roman Empire, and intellectual supremacy passed to the descendants of the 6th cent. exiles in Babylonia, who compiled the Babylonian Talmud.

European settlements also deteriorated under the Christianization of the Roman Empire, but Jewry enjoyed a golden era during the period of Islamic conquest, producing such men as the philosopher Saadiah, the poet Jehudah Ha-lvei, the codifier Moses Maimonides, etc. In medieval Europe the Jews were increasingly separated from the general life and trade by measures which culminated in the 16th cent. institution of the Ghetto. This persecution has been periodically revived since the period of comparative enlightenment beginning with the extension of the rights of man to the Js. by the French Revolution in 1790. Under the Nazi régime, 1939-45, some 5,000,000 Js were put to death in Europe, leaving 1,500,000 (with a similar number in Russia) out of a former 6,500,000. Zionism (q.v.) was an attempt to solve the Jewish problem. Outside Israel, the main centres of Jewry today are the USA (6,000,000), USSR 2,250,000, and the UK (450,000).

JEW'S HARP. Musical instrument. It is a small iron frame, attached to which is a steel strip, to be twanged by the fingers, while the frame is gripped by the teeth. Only one fundamental note is available, but by changing the shape of the mouth a complete harmonic scale can be produced.

JHANSI (jahn'sē). Indian city in Uttar Pradesh, 286km (178m) SW of Lucknow, a railway and road junction, and a market centre. It was founded in 1613, and was the scene of a massacre of British civilians in 1857. Pop. (1971) 198,100.

JHELUM (jāl'um). One of the five rivers which give its name to Punjab. It is the ancient Hydaspes, on the banks of which Alexander the Great won a great victory in 326 BC. The Mangla dam (1967), one of the world's largest earth-filled dams, stores flood waters for irrigation and hydro-electricity.

JIANGSU (jē-ahngsoo'). Eastern coastal prov. of China (formerly Kiangsu), on either side of the mouth of the Chang Jiang. Much of the area is swampy, but the land is fertile, and rice, wheat, cotton, tea and soya beans are grown. Silk is made, and industries incl. cement, ceramics and textiles. Coal, iron and copper are mined. The cap. is Nanjing, and J. incl. the special municipality of Shanghai. Area 102,200 sq.km (39,450 sq.m); pop. (1979) 57,000,000.

JIANGXI (jē-ahngshē'). Eastern coastal prov. of China (formerly Kiangsi), to the S of the Chang Jiang. Rice, tea, cotton and tobacco are grown, and coal and tungsten mined. The cap. is Nanchang. Area 164,800 sq.km (63,600 sq.m); pop. (1979) 28,000,000.

JIBUTI. *See* DJIBOUTI.

JIDDA (jed'a). Arabian seaport on the Red Sea, in Hejaz, a transit port for pilgrims to Mecca, 72km (45m) to the E; it has an airport. It is linked by road with Mecca, Medina, Riyadh and Taif. The deep-water King Feisal port (1973) serves both commerce and the pilgrim traffic. Pop. (1977) 561,000.

JIHAD (jihahd'). Word (Arabic 'struggle') used in the Koran to cover the duty of Moslems to oppose those who reject Islam (q.v.), and more recently in the Mecca Declaration (1981) when the Islamic powers pledged a J. against Israel, although not necessarily involving a military attack.

JIANGSU. An unusual harvest. Massed silkworm cocoons are gathered from the cut branches by members of a commune, who are striving to diversify the local economy. *Photo: Society for Anglo-Chinese Understanding.*

JILIN (jēlēn'). Prov. (formerly Kirin) of NE Chine, in central Manchuria, with its cap. at Changchun. Area 290,000 sq.km (111,940 sq.m); pop. (1979) 24,000,000.

JIMÉNEZ (khēmān'eth), **Juan Ramón** (1881-1958). Spanish lyric poet. B. in Andalusia, he left Spain during the civil war to live in exile in Puerto Rico. His poetry has great spirituality and artistic purity. Particularly popular are his odes to his donkey 'Platero'. He gained a Nobel prize in 1956.

JINAN (jēnahn'), Cap. (formerly Tsinan) of Shandong prov., China. An ancient walled city, it is a commercial and food processing centre with textile and other industries. Pop. (1973) 870,000.

JINDYWOROBAKS. Name for an Australian literary group (1938-53), derived from Aboriginal 'take-over'. Founded by Reginald Ingamells (1931-55), it was devoted to encouraging an individual Australian character in the country's literature.

JINGDEZHEN (jingdajen'). Town (formerly Fou-liang) in Jiangxi, China, site of a porcelain industry from the 6th cent. *See* KAOLIN. Pop. (1978) 350,000.

JI'NGO. A noisy and bellicose patriot. The term originated in 1878, when Beaconsfield's pro-Turkish policy nearly involved Britain in war with Russia. His supporters adopted as their war-song a music-hall ditty containing the line, 'We don't want to fight, but by jingo if we do . . .' The word is possibly derived from Persian 'war' or Basque 'god'.

JI'NJA. Town in Eastern Province, Uganda, on the Victoria Nile. It has a large copper-smelting works, tobacco and textile factories, and a brewery; also an airport. Nearby is the Owen Falls Dam (1954). Pop. (1970) 38,000.

JINN (Djinn). In Mohammedan mythology, spirits which assume human or animal shapes.

JINNAH, Mohammed Ali (1876-1948). Indian statesman. He was ed. at Karachi and in England being called to the English Bar in 1896, and became pres. of the Moslem League in 1916. From 1934 he was elected annually as pres., and popularized among Indian Moslems the idea of separate Moslem and Hindu states when British rule ended. His views on 'Pakistan' were recognized by the Cripps mission of 1942, and at the 1946 conferences in London he insisted that only partition could solve the Indian problem. J. became Gov.-Gen. of Pakistan on the transfer of power on 15 Aug. 1947.

JINSHA JIANG (jēn'shah jē-ahng'). Alternative name for the upper reaches of the Chang Jiang (formerly Yangtze-Kiang), China, from its sources in Tibet to Yibin, where it is joined by the Min.

JIVARO (jivah'rō). Tribe of S American Indians found in Ecuador and Peru, formerly famous for keeping the shrunken heads of their enemies as battle trophies.

JOACHIM (yō'akhim), **Joseph** (1831-1907). Hungarian violinist. He studied under Mendelssohn, first performed in England in 1844, and was the founder of the J. Quartet (1869-1907). His compositions incl. the 'Hungarian Concerto' and orchestral works.

JOAN. A mythical Englishwoman who was supposed to have become Pope in 855, as John VIII, and to have given birth to a child during a papal procession. The myth was exposed in the 17th cent.

JOANNINA. *See* IOANNINA.

JOAN OF ARC, St (1412-31). French heroine. She was b. at Domrémy, on the Meuse, and was the daughter of a well-to-do farmer. In 1429 she went to Chinon, where she persuaded Charles VII she had received a divine mission to raise the siege of Orléans. At this time all France N of the Loire was held by the English and their allies. Entrusted with a military command, J. raised the siege; defeated the English at Patay; and witnessed Charles's coronation at Reims. The French henceforward took the offensive and by 1453 had expelled the English from France. J. failed to capture Paris, and in May 1430 was captured. She was found guilty of witchcraft and heresy. On 30 May 1431 she was burned by the English in Rouen market-place, her ashes being thrown into the Seine. An official inquiry in 1456 annulled her sentence, and in 1920 she was canonized.

JŌB. An ancient chieftain in the land of Uz, usually identified with Edom, whose name is given to a dramatic poem in the OT (probably 5th cent. BC). The book is one of the first attempts to explain the problem of human suffering in a world created and governed by God, who is all-powerful and all-good.

JOCKEY CLUB. *See* HORSE RACING.

JODHPUR (jōdpoor'). Indian city in Rajasthan, formerly cap. of J. princely state, founded in 1459 by Rao Jodha. It is a market centre with notable buildings and is dominated by its red sandstone fort. The training college of the Indian Air Force is at J. Pop. (1971) 318,900.

JODL (yōdl), **Alfred** (1892-1946). German general. B. at Aachen, he drew up the Nazi government's plan for the attack on Yugoslavia, Greece, and the Soviet Union, and in Jan. 1945 became chief of staff. He headed the delegation which signed Germany's surrender at Reims on 7 May. He was tried at Nuremburg in 1945-6, and hanged.

JOAN OF ARC. A miniature portrait of the warrior saint from a contemporary manuscript. *Photo: Photographie Giraudon.*

JO'DRELL BANK. Site in Cheshire, England, of the pioneer radio-telescope belonging to Manchester univ. Completed in 1957 in time to track the orbit of the first sputnik, its 76m (250ft) diam. paraboloid reflecting bowl has a range 1,000 times greater than the best optical telescopes. *See* LOVELL, SIR BERNARD.

JOFFRE (zhofr), **Joseph Jacques Césaire** (1852-1931). French soldier. B. in the Pyrenees, he was made chief of general staff in 1911. The invasion of Belgium by the Germans in 1914 took him by surprise, but his successful stand on the Marne made him a national hero, and he received the supreme command of all the French armies. His failure to make adequate preparations at Verdun in 1916, and the disasters on the Somme, caused increasing discontent. In Dec. 1916 J. was replaced by Nivelle, although he received the honorary title of marshal of France.

JOGJAKARTA. *See* JOKJAKARTA.

JOHANNESBURG (johan'-). Largest city of S Africa, situated on the Witwatersrand in Transvaal and centre of the world's greatest gold-mining industry. Founded after the discovery of gold in 1886, the town was probably named after Jan (or Johannes) Meyer, first mining commissioner. Notable buildings incl. the law courts, Escom House (Electricity Supply Commission), the S African Railways Administration Building, the City Hall, Chamber of Mines and stock exchange, the Witwatersrand (1921) and Rand Afrikaans (1966) univs., and the Union Observatory. J. is the Republic's biggest centre for local and overseas trade in primary and industrial products and is the most important rail centre. The Jan Smuts international airport, to the NW came into use in 1954. The mines and railways have given rise to engineering works and there are meat-chilling plants, clothing factories, etc. Pop. (1970) 1,432,643, of whom 501,000 were white.

JOHN. Apostle and saint. The son of Zeberdee and Salome, a sister of the Virgin Mary, he was b. in Judaea, and with his brother James became a Galilean fisherman and one of the first disciples called by Jesus. J. was present at the Last Supper and at the Trial, and to him Jesus entrusted His mother at the foot of the cross. According to tradition J. was the author of the 4th Gospel, the Johannine Epistles, and also of the Apocalypse.

JOHN. Name of 23 popes. JOHN XXII, pope 1316-34, who spent his papacy at Avignon, engaged in a long conflict with the emperor, Louis of Bavaria, and with the Spiritual Franciscans, who preached the absolute poverty of the clergy. 'JOHN XXIII', pope 1410-15, was a pirate before entering the Church. In an attempt to end the Great Schism he was elected pope by a council of cardinals at Bologna, but was deposed by the Council of Constance in 1415, together with the popes of Avignon and Rome. He is not recognized by the Church, and the title JOHN XXIII was assumed by Angelo Giuseppe Roncalli (1881-1963). B. near Bergamo, one of a peasant family of 13, he was elected Pope in 1958. Landmarks of his papacy were improved relations with the Soviet Union, establishment of RC hierarchies in newly emergent states, the encyclicals *Mater et Magistra* (*Mother and Teacher:* 1961) and *Pacem in Terris* (*Peace on Earth:* 1963) realistically outlining the role of the Church in modern conditions, and the summoning of the Second Vatican Council.

JOHN (1167-1216). King of England. The youngest son of Henry II, he attempted to seize the kingdom during his brother Richard's absence at the Crusade. On Richard's death in 1199 J. was recognized as king by England and Normandy, while Anjou and Brittany supported the claim of his nephew Arthur. J. captured and murdered Arthur, but lost Normandy to the king of France. J.'s refusal to recognize Langton as archbishop of Canterbury led to the imposition of an interdict on England, and to his excommunication so that in 1213 he surrendered his kingdom to the Pope and became his vassal. His tyranny led to the barons enforcing his signature of Magna Carta (q.v.) in 1215. His repudiation of the charter provoked a civil war which was still in progress when J. d. at Newark.

JOHN II (1319-64), king of France from 1350, was defeated and captured by the Black Prince at Poitiers in 1356. He was released in 1360, but having failed to raise the money for his ransom returned in 1364 to England, where he d.

JOHN III (1642-96), called **Sobieski.** King of Poland. A brilliant soldier, he was elected king in 1674. In 1683 he saved Vienna from the Turks, who were besieging it.

JOHN. Name of 6 kings of Portugal. JOHN I (1357-1433), a natural son of Pedro I, elected king by the Cortes in 1385. His claim was supported by an English army against his rival, the king of Castile, an event which marks the beginning of the Anglo-Portuguese alliance. JOHN IV (1603-56), originally duke of Braganza, was elected king when the Portuguese rebelled against Spanish rule in 1640. JOHN VI (1769-1826) acted as regent for his mother Maria I 1792-1816. He fled to Brazil when the French invaded Portugal in 1807, and did not return until 1822. On his return Brazil declared its independence, with J.'s elder son Pedro as emperor.

JOHN, Augustus Edwin (1878-1961). British painter. B. in Tenby, the son of a solicitor, he studied at the Slade, and in 1903 first exhibited at the New English Art Club. Elected RA in 1928, he was awarded the OM in 1942. Typical of his portraits is 'The Smiling Woman' (his second wife, Dorelia), and 'Galway', also in the Tate Gallery, exemplifies his gifted draughtsmanship as a mural artist. Himself an impressively picturesque figure, he was pres. of the Gypsy Lore Society, and in 1952 pub. a fragmentary autobiography *Chiaroscuro.*

His sister, **Gwen J.** (1876-1939), a Catholic convert, lived mainly in France, and was also a talented artist.

JOHN BULL. An imaginary figure used as a personification of England. The name was popularized by Dr Arbuthnot's *History of J.B.* (1712). He is represented as a prosperous farmer of the 18th cent.

JOHN CHRYSOSTOM (345-407). Christian saint and Father of the Eastern Orthodox Church. B. at Antioch, he was a hermit of the desert before being appointed bishop of Constantinople in 398.

JOHN OF AUSTRIA, Don (1545-78). Spanish soldier, the natural son of Charles V. He won a great naval victory over the Turks at Lepanto in 1571.

JOHN OF DAMASCUS, St (*c.* 676-*c.* 754). Eastern Orthodox theologian. B. at Damascus, he ably defended image-worship against the Iconoclasts.

JOHN OF GAUNT (1340-99). English nobleman, duke of Lancaster from 1362. The 4th son of Edward III, he was b. at Ghent. During the last years of Edward and the minority of Richard II he acted as head of the government and provoked protests from parliament by the corruption of his rule.

JOHN OF THE CROSS, St (1542-91). Spanish mystic. He became a Carmelite friar in 1564, and was several times imprisoned for attempting to impose the reforms laid down by St Teresa. His *Obras espirituales* were pub. in 1618. His verse, full of spiritual ecstacy, is of great beauty.

JOHN O' GROATS HOUSE. Site in the NE of Highland region, Scotland, about 3km (2m) W of Duncansby Head, proverbially regarded as the most northerly point of Britain.

JOHN PAUL II. The first pope to come from Poland, John Paul is an accomplished linguist and author. His works translated into English include *Easter Vigil and other Poems* (1979). *Photo: Rex Features.*

JOHN PAUL I (1912-78), Albino Luciani known from his smile as 'the happy Pope', held the office only 26 Aug.-28 Sept. 1978. He chose his name as the combination of his two immediate predecessors, and was followed in this by his successor **John Paul II** (1920-), Karol Wojtyla, the first non-Italian pope since 1522. B. nr Cracow, of poor family, he lost both parents while still a child. In 1939 he was conscripted for forced labour by the Germans, working in quarries and a chemical factory, but from 1942 studied for the priesthood at a seminary illegally open in Cracow. After the war he taught ethics and theology at the univs. of Lublin and Cracow, and 3 yrs after becoming abp. of Cracow was created a cardinal in 1967. Despite personal charisma, he has been criticised for his traditionalist viewpoint, maintaining papal infallibility, and condemning artificial contraception, women priests, married priests, and modern dress for monks and nuns. He was shot by a Turk in 1981.

JOHNSON, Amy (1904-41). British airwoman. B. at Hull, in 1930 she flew alone from Croydon to Australia in 19½ days, and in 1932 made a record-breaking flight to the Cape. She m. J. A. Mollison in 1932, with whom she flew the Atlantic in 1933. Her greatest achievement was her flight to the Cape and back in 1936. Her aircraft disappeared over the Channel in the S.W.W., while she was serving with the Air Transport Auxiliary, and the mystery of her fate enhanced the legend.

JOHNSON. Amy Johnsons's name was one to conjure with in the Thirties when 'record flights' were one of the excitements of the period. *Photo: Mansell Collection*

JOHNSON, Andrew (1808-75). 17th President of the USA. B. in N Carolina, he was elected to Congress in 1843 as a Democrat, became Vice-President in 1864, and succeeded to the presidency on Lincoln's death, retiring in 1869. His conciliatory policy towards the seceded states involved him in a feud with the Radicals, culminating in his impeachment before the Senate in 1868, which failed by one vote.

JOHNSON, Dame Celia (1908-82). Brit. actress. Making her début in 1928 as *Major Barbara,* she excelled in the delicate subtlety of her performances, e.g. in *The Flowering Cherry* (1957) and the film *Brief Encounter* (1946). She m. in 1935 the author and traveller Peter Fleming (1907-71).

JOHNSON, Lyndon Baines (1908-73). 36th Pres. of the USA. B. in Stonewall, Texas, he worked his way through college, graduating in 1930. After teaching in 1931, he went into politics as sec. to a Texas Congressman, and was himself elected to Congress (1937-49), and to the Senate (1949-60). A gifted and persuasive orator, his appreciation that politics was 'one long accommodation of contesting forces' brought him to Democratic leadership of the Senate. A Democratic nominee for Pres. in 1960, he agreed to stand as Vice-Pres., thus bringing crucial Southern votes for Kennedy and himself in the 1960 election. Following the assassination of Kennedy in 1963, he succeeded as president. After the Tonkin Gulf incident in 1964, he made the first escalatory moves in the Vietnam War, and in the elections in Nov. was given a popular mandate unequalled in US history. At home he introduced civil rights legislation, action against poverty and promotion of education in a 'Great Society' programme which John F. Kennedy had failed to put through. From 1965 he failed in an attempt to promote peace negotiations in Vietnam, and public opinion increasingly saddled him with responsibility for the conflict, so that he declined the presidential nomination in 1968.

JOHNSON, Pamela Hansford (1912-81). British novelist. B. in London, she m. in 1950 as her second husband Lord Snow (q.v.). Like him she had a gift for subtly delineated character, as in *Too Dear for my Possessing* (1940), and *The Honours Board* (1970); and the play *Corinth House* (1948).

JOHNSON, Samuel (1709-84). English lexicographer, author, and critic. B. in Lichfield, he became first an usher and then a literary hack. In 1735 he m. the widow Elizabeth Porter and opened a private school. When this proved unsuccessful he went to London with his pupil David Garrick, becoming a regular contributor to the *Gentleman's Magazine* and publishing the successful poem *London* in 1738. However, he still remained in miserable poverty with companions such as Richard Savage, whose Life he wrote in 1744. In 1755 he pub. his *Dictionary,* still interesting for the vigour of its definitions. While engaged on this he had also pub. the satire *Vanity of Human Wishes* (1749), seen the failure of his tragedy *Irene* (1749), and conducted the periodical *The Rambler* (1750-2), succeeded by *The Idler* (1758-60). In 1759 he wrote the philosophical romance *Rasselas.* He was awarded a pension in 1762, and his first meeting with Boswell in 1763 was followed by the formation of the 'Literary Club' in 1764, to which Reynolds, Burke, Goldsmith, and Garrick belonged. His edition of Shakespeare appeared in 1765. A visit with Boswell to Scotland and the Hebrides in 1773 was recorded in *Journey to the Western*

Isles of Scotland (1775), and in 1779-81 were pub. *Lives of the Poets,* which contain his finest critical comments. J. was buried in Westminster Abbey and his house in Gough Square, London, is preserved as a museum.

JOHNSON (yon′son), **Uwe** (1934-). German novelist. He left East Germany in 1959 to live in West Berlin, and his books deal with the division of Germany, and bridge the gap between pre and post-war life. They incl. *Conjectures about Jakob* and *Anniversaries* (1977).

JOHNSON. Uwe Johnson has opened a new field in the novel by his treatment of historical fact alongside time past and time present in the lives of his characters. *Photo: Friedrich Rauch/Camera Press.*

JOHN THE BAPTIST. Christian saint and prophet. The son of Zacharias and Elizabeth, who was a cousin of Christ's mother, he was a Nazarite from his birth. After preparation in the wilderness, he proclaimed the coming of Christ, baptizing Him in the Jordan. He was executed by Herod Antipas at the instigation of Salome.

JOHORE (johor′). State of the Federation of Malaysia. J. came under British protection in 1885. The southernmost point of the Asiatic mainland, J. is joined to Singapore by a causeway. Its products are rubber, tin, pineapples, copra, etc. The cap. is Johore Bahru. Area 18,960 sq.km (7,320 sq.m); pop. (1970) 1,400,000.

JOINT. An articulation; a structure in which 2 bones meet. Some joints allow no motion (e.g. the sutures of the skull); some allow a very small motion (e.g. the sacro-iliac joints in the lower back); but some other joints allow a relatively free motion. Of this 3rd class (diarthrodial) some allow a gliding motion (e.g. one vertebra of the spine on another); some have a hinge action (e.g. those of the elbow and knee); and others allow motion in all directions (e.g. the hip and shoulder joints), by means of a ball-and-socket arrangement. The ends of the bones at a moving J. are covered with cartilage for greater elasticity and smoothness, and enclosed in an envelope (capsule) of tough white fibrous tissue lined with a membrane which secretes lubricating (synovial) fluid. The J. is further strengthened by ligaments. Js. are easily injured, but heal readily unless infection is introduced.

JOINVILLE (zhwañvēl′), **Jean,** Sire de (1224-1317). French chronicler. B. in Champagne, he accompanied Louis IX on the crusade of 1248-54, which he described in his *History of St Louis.*

JOKJAKARTA (jokyōkahr′tah). Town in Java, Indonesia, 60m S of Semarang. It has an airport and is the seat of a university. Pop. *c.* 300,000.

JOLSON, Al. Stage name of the American singer Asa Yoelson (1886-1950). B. in Russia, he became famous as a star of the early sound-films *The Jazz Singer* and *The Singing Fool.*

JŌ′NAH. Hebrew prophet, whose name is given to a book in the OT. He was sent to prophesy destruction on Nineveh, was cast overboard, and is said to have spent 3 days and nights in the belly of a whale.

JONES, Bobby (1902-71). American golfer. He dominated the game from 1923 until he retired in 1930 after achieving the grand slam, US and British amateur and open championships all in one year. He was the originator of the Masters Tournament.

JONES, Gwyneth (1936-). Welsh soprano. B. in Pontypool, she studied at the Royal College and at Zurich, and incl. among her finest roles Sieglinde in *Die Walküre,* Aïda and Desdemona.

JONES, Henry Arthur (1851-1929). British playwright. His first success was the melodrama *The Silver King* (1882); among his 60 other plays were *The Case of Rebellious Susan* (1894), *The Liars* (1897) and *Mrs. Dane's Defence* (1900), notable as an early realist-problem play.

JONES, Inigo (1573-*c.* 1652). English architect. B. in London, he studied in Italy, and was influenced by the works of Palladio. He was employed by James I in designing the scenery for Ben Jonson's masques, and in 1619 he designed his masterpiece, the banqueting-room at Whitehall; and the church of St Paul, Covent Garden, London.

JONES. Wilton House in Wiltshire, founded by William Herbert, 1st Earl of Pembroke, but later rebuilt according to designs by Inigo Jones drawn up in 1648. *Photo: Courtesy of the British Tourist Authority.*

JONES, John Paul (1747-92). American naval officer. B. in Kirkcudbright, he served at sea as a trader and slaver, but on his return to Scotland from the W Indies, on a ship of which he had become master, he was accused of murdering one of the crew. Searching for evidence of his innocence, he returned to the W Indies, but killed the leader of a mutiny and fled to his brother in Virginia, receiving a privateer's commission from Congress on the outbreak of the War of Independence in 1775. As head of a French naval expedition, he menaced British shipping 1779-81 and returned to America in 1781. He joined the Russian navy as a rear-admiral in 1788, fighting against Turkey, but lost Catherine's favour and d. in France.

JONESTOWN. Commune of the People's Temple Sect, NW of Georgetown, Guyana, estab. 1974 by Jim Jones (1933-78), who originally founded the sect among San Francisco's black community. Complaints of oppression led to a visit by a US congressman who was shot, with his companions, after which Jones enforced mass suicide, mainly by imbibing cyanide, on his followers (914 dead, incl. over 240 children).

JÖNKÖPING (yon'choping). Town at the S end of Lake Vatter, Sweden. It is a great industrial centre. Pop. (1978) 108,600.

JON'QUIL. Name given to a species of the Amaryllidaceae family, *Narcissus jonquilla,* which has yellow flowers with an orange corona, and is found in S Europe and Africa.

JONSON, Benjamin (1572-1637). English dramatist, poet, and critic. B. at Westminster, he entered the theatre as actor and dramatist in 1597. In 1598 he narrowly escaped the gallows for killing a fellow-player in a duel, and in the same year his *Everyman in His Humour* was produced, followed by *Everyman out of His Humour* (1599), *Cynthia's Revels* (1600) and *Poetaster* (1601). His first extant tragedy is *Sejanus* (1603), with Burbage and Shakespeare as members of the original cast. J. collaborated with Marston and Chapman in *Eastward Ho* (1605), and shared their imprisonment when official exception was taken to a derogatory reference to the Scots. There followed the great plays of his middle years *Volpone, or the Fox* (1606), *Epicoene, or The Silent Woman* (1609), *The Alchemist* (1610), *Catiline* (1611), *Bartholomew Fair* (1614). Meanwhile J. had made a great reputation in the presentation of masques, and produced some 30 such pieces before a quarrel with his associate Inigo Jones in 1630 lost him court favour. Failing health overshadowed his later plays, e.g. *The Staple of News* (1626). J. excelled in construction, and was the creator of the English comedy of humours. From 1630 he was virtually poet laureate; he is buried in Westminster Abbey.

JOPLIN, Scott (1868-1917). American Negro ragtime king. He spent ten years as an itinerant musician, and by 1893 was working in the saloons and brothels of Chicago. His 'Maple Leaf Rag' (1899) was the first instrumental sheet music to sell a million, and 'The Entertainer' was the theme tune of the film *The Sting* (1973), which revived his reputation.

JOPPA. Ancient name of JAFFA.

JORDAENS (yor'dahns), **Jakob** (1593-1678). Flemish painter. B. at Antwerp, he is noted for his realistic pictures of Flemish life.

JORDAN, Dorothea (1762-1816). British actress. She made her début in 1777, and retired in 1815. She was a mistress of the duke of Clarence (later William IV) by whom she had 10 children who were given the name FitzClarence.

JORDAN. River in the Levant. It rises on Mount Hermon in Syria at 550m (1,800 ft) a.s.l. and flows S for *c.* 320km (200m) through the Sea of Galilee into the Dead Sea, 390m (1,290 ft) b.s.l. It occupies the northern part of the Great Rift Valley; its upper course forms the boundary of Israel with Syria and the kingdom of Jordan; its lower course runs through Jordan - W Bank occupied by Israel 1967.

JORDAN, The Hashimite Kingdom of. Country of SW Asia, bordered W by Israel (with which J. shares the Dead Sea), N by Syria, E by Iraq and Saudi Arabia, S by Saudi Arabia. It has a 24km (15m) coastline on the Gulf of Aqaba, an inlet of the Red Sea, with one port, Aqaba. The cap. is Amman.

Much of J. is desert, though where there is water the soil is fertile; wheat, millet, sesame, olives and grapes are grown; cattle, sheep, camels, and goats are reared. About a quarter of the inhabitants continue to live nomadically. Minerals incl. the potash of the Dead Sea, phosphate deposits, and large oil shale resources which were potentially profitable by 1980 owing to the oil price rise. The general level of J. is 790m (2,600 ft) a.s.l., rising in the S to over 600m (5,000 ft) and sinking in the W to the Dead Sea. The numerous *wadis* (river beds), most of which drain to the r. Jordan or the Dead Sea, are empty except for the brief period of the winter rains.

The constitution of 1951 estab. a cabinet responsible to a parliament consisting of a senate nominated by the king and a lower house elected by manood suffrage. Although in 1974 King Hussein ceded responsibility for the West Bank area to the PLO, the Jordanian parliament was reconvened in 1976 with West Bank representation, but the lower house was dissolved indefinitely, owing to the impossibility of holding West Bank elections. The UN had in 1974 granted the PLO permanent observer status in the General Assembly.

Total area 98,000 sq.km (38,000 sq.m); total pop. (1976) 2,750,000, incl. *c.* 750,000 Palestinian refugees. Some 92,000 sq.km lies E of the Jordan, pop. (1976) 1,950,000; and 6,000 sq.km W of the Jordan, pop. (1976) 800,000. The majority are Sunni Moslems and the language is Arabic. M.U.: J. dinar.

History. The area forming the kingdom of Jordan was occupied by the independent Nabataeans from the 4th cent. BC, and perhaps earlier, until AD 106 when it became part of the Roman prov. of Arabia. It was included in the Crusaders' kingdom of Jerusalem, 1099-1187, and from the 16th cent. was ruled by the Ottoman Turks until the break-up of the Turkish Empire after the F.W.W. The League of Nations placed it in 1920 under British mandate as part of Palestine; but in 1923 Britain recognized the mandated territory E of the Jordan r. as a separate country, Transjordan, under the Emir Abdullah. Transjordan was given full independence by a treaty of 1946, in which year Abdullah took the title king and changed the name of his country to the Hashimite Kingdom of Jordan (a name that came into general use only in 1949). Abdullah was a prime mover in the formation of the Arab League (q.v.), and in 1948 his forces invaded the newly proclaimed republic of Israel, occupying most of the area of Palestine (q.v.) which the United Nations had proposed to allocate to the Arabs. Abdullah made an armistice with Israel in 1949, but retained the part of Palestine (incl. eastern Jerusalem) which he had occupied, formally annexing it in 1950. Abdullah was assassinated in 1951; his grandson Hussein (q.v.) became king in 1952, his father Talal having been deposed owing to mental illness. J. fought in alliance with Egypt against Israel 5-10 June 1967, when all J. west of the r. Jordan incl. E Jerusalem (q.v.) was occupied by Israel. The 3 districts of J. thus occupied (Jerusalem, Hebron and Nablus - known to

Israelis as Judaea and Samaria) are referred to collectively as the West Bank. Jordan continued to oppose the peace settlement between Israel and Egypt which followed the Camp David Agreements in 1979, and in particular the continued Israeli settlements in the West Bank area, and the affirmation of all Jerusalem (inc. the E sector) as the Israeli capital. Jordan assisted Syria in the Golan Heights during the 1973 Arab-Israeli War, and in 1980 supported Iraq in the Iran-Iraq conflict.

JORDAN. The symmetrical perfection of the Roman forum at Jerash. *Photo: Marc Sharratt/Feature-Pix.*

JOSEPH. Sir Keith Joseph, one of the chief theorists of the Conservative Party and founder of the Centre for Policy Studies in 1974. *Photo: Keystone.*

JOSEPHINE. A portrait of the Empress at La Malmaison, her favourite residence, which Napoleon gave her after their divorce, and where she also spent her later retirement. *Photo: Lauros-Giraudon.*

JOSEPH. The husband of the Virgin Mary. He was a descendant of David, and a carpenter by trade. According to Catholic tradition, he had a family by a previous wife, and was an elderly man when he married Mary, who remained perpetually virgin.

JOSEPH II (1741-90). Holy Roman Emperor. The son of the emperor Francis I and Maria Theresa, he succeeded his father as emperor in 1765, but only attained real power after his mother's death in 1780. He introduced a series of sweeping reforms, but his disregard of traditional privileges, etc., provoked revolts in Belgium, Hungary, and elsewhere.

JOSEPH, Sir Keith Sinjohn (1918-). British Cons. politician. He entered Parliament in 1956, and was Min. of Housing and Local Govt. 1962-4, Sec. of State for Social Services 1970-4, Industry 1979-81, and Education and Science from 1981.

JOSEPH, Père. Religious name of the Capuchin monk François Le Clerc du Tremblay (1577-1638). As secretary-agent to Cardinal Richelieu, he was considered to have such influence with him that he was nicknamed the 'Grey Eminence'.

JOSEPHINE (jō'zefēn) (1763-1814). Empress of France. A native of Martinique, *née* Marie Josèphe Rose Tascher de la Pagerie, she m. in 1779 the vicomte de Beauharnais, who was guillotined during the Revolution. In 1796 she m. Napoleon Bonaparte, with whom she was crowned empress in 1804. As she bore him no child, he divorced her in 1809, and she spent the rest of her life in retirement near Paris.

JOSEPH OF ARIMATHAEA. A wealthy Jew and member of the Sanhedrin, who was a secret supporter of Jesus, and on the evening of the Crucifixion begged his body of Pilate and buried it in his own tomb. According to tradition he brought the Holy Grail to England about AD 63 and erected at Glastonbury the first Christian church to be built in Britain.

JOSEPHSON, Brian (1940-). British physicist. Working at Cambridge, he is an authority on super-conductivity, and in 1973 shared a Nobel prize for his theoretical predictions of the properties of a super-current through a tunnel barrier, espec. the phenomena named after him 'J. effects'.

JOSEPHSON JUNCTION. Device used in 'superchips' to speed the passage of signals by the phenomenon called 'electron tunnelling'. Though these superchips respond a thousand times faster than the silicon chip, they have the disadvantage that the components of the J.Js. operate only at temperatures close to absolute zero.

JOSEPHUS (jōsē'fus), **Flavius** (AD 37-*c.* 100). Jewish historian. B. in Jerusalem, he became a Pharisee. On the outbreak of the Jewish revolt in 66 he was given the command in Galilee, but was defeated and captured. He won the favour of the emperor Vespasian and settled in Rome. He wrote *Antiquities of the Jews* to AD 66; *The Jewish War*; and an autobiography.

JO'SHUA. Hebrew general who led the Israelites after the death of Moses in the conquest and settlement of the land of the Canaanites (Palestine).

JŌS'ĪAH (b. 647 BC). King of Judah. Grandson of Manasseh and son of Amon, he succeeded to the throne when 8. The discovery of a Book of Instruction (probably Deuteronomy) during the repair of the Temple in 621 stimulated thorough reform, which included the removal of all sanctuaries except that of Jerusalem. J. was killed in a clash at Megiddo with Pharaoh-nechoh, king of Egypt.

JOSQUIN DES PRÉS (zhoskań' dā prā) (*c.* 1445-1521). Flemish composer of masses, a pupil of Okeghem; he also wrote secular songs.

JÖTUNHEIM (yö'toonhīm). Mountainous region of S Norway, containing the highest mountains in Scandinavia, Glittertind (2,453m/8,048ft) and Galdhöpiggen (2,468 m/8,097 ft).

JOUBERT (zhoobār'), **Petrus Jacobus** (1831-1900). Boer general. He led the Boer Commandos against the British 1880-1, defeated Jameson in 1896, and was responsible for the early Boer successes in the South African War.

JOULE, James Prescott (1818-89). British physicist. He was a brewery owner, but dedicated to precise scientific research, and his work on the relations between electrical, mechanical and chemical effects, led to the discovery of the first law of thermodynamics. He determined the mechanical equivalent of heat (J.'s equivalent).

JOULE. The unit of work and energy in MKS and SI units. It is the work done - the energy transferred - when the point of application of 1N is displaced a distance of 1m in the direction of the force, also expressed as the work done in one sec. by the current of 1 amp across a potential difference of 1 volt. It is equal to 10^7 erg.

JOURNALISM. The profession of reporting, photographing or editing news for newspapers, magazines, the radio and television. Standards are set by awards such as those founded by J. Pulitzer (q.v.).

JŌ'VIAN (331-64). Roman emperor. Captain of the imperial bodyguard, he was chosen emperor by the soldiers on Julian's death in battle with the Persians (363), and concluded a humiliating peace. He re-estab. Christianity as the state religion.

JOWETT (jō'et), **Benjamin** (1817-93). British scholar. Taking holy orders in 1842, he became in 1855 Regius prof. of Greek at Oxford, and in 1870 Master of Balliol. He was prominent in promoting univ. reform, incl. the abolition of the theological test for degrees, and trans. Plato, Aristotle and Thucydides.

JOYCE, James Augustin Aloysius (1882-1941). Irish writer. B. in Dublin, he studied medicine in Paris, but later became a teacher of languages. In 1907 he pub. a vol. of verse, *Chamber Music*, and in 1914 the realistic stories *Dubliners*. His *Portrait of the Artist as a Young Man* (1916) is semi-autobiographical and anticipates the advanced technique of *Ulysses* (1922), which records the events of a Dublin day, and mingles direct narrative with the unspoken and even unconscious reactions of the characters. The book was banned for obscenity in England and the USA. *Finnegan's Wake* (1939), long known as *Work in Progress*, attempts a synthesis of all existence, using a polyglot language containing impressionistic compounds, e.g. 'polyfizzyboisterous'.

JOYCE, William (1906-46). Fascist. B. in New York, the son of a naturalized American of Irish birth, he carried on Fascist activity in Britain as a 'British subject'. On the outbreak of the S.W.W. he went to Germany and broadcast to Britain, becoming nicknamed 'Lord Haw-Haw'. He was tried in 1945 and hanged for treachery.

JUAN (hoo-ahn') **CARLOS** (1938-). King of Spain. The son of Don Juan, pretender to the Spanish throne, he m. in 1962 Princess Sophia, eldest dau. of King Paul of the Hellenes. In 1969 he was named by Franco to succeed on the restoration of the monarchy intended to follow Franco's own death: his father was excluded because of his known liberal views. He became king in 1975. *See* table under BOURBON.

JUAN FERNANDEZ ISLANDS (hoo-ahn' fern-ahndeth). A group of islands in the S Pacific belonging to Chile. The most important are Santa Clara and Mas-a-Tierra (also sometimes called Juan Fernandez Island) where Alexander Selkirk (q.v.) was marooned 1704-9. The islands were named after the Spanish navigator who discovered them *c.* 1565.

JUAREZ (hoo-ah'reth), **Benito Pablo** (1806-72). Mexican politician, b. of Indian parents. He was governor of Oaxaca 1847-52, but was exiled by Santa Anna. He had a share in the successful revolt of 1855, and in 1858 was elected President of the republic. He declared war on France in 1862 when Napoleon III sent troops to Mexico and as constitutional President opposed the French-supported emperor Maximilian, who was executed in 1867. Juarez was re-elected President, and again in 1871.

JUBA (jo͞ob'a). River in E Africa formed at Dolo, Ethiopia, by the junction of the Ganale Dorya and Dawa rivers. It flows S *c.* 885km (550m) through the Somali Rep. (of which its valley is the most productive area) into the Indian Ocean.

JUBA. Town in Sudan Rep., cap. of Equatoria prov., on the left bank of the White Nile, at the head of navigation above Khartoum 1,200 km (750m) N, J. is an admin. and trade centre. Pop. (1970) 45,500.

JUBBULPO'RE or **Jabalpur.** City of Madhya Pradesh, Rep. of India with textile, oil and flour mills, and a univ. (1957). Pop. (1971) 533,750.

JUDAEA (joodē'-ah). *See* JUDAH.

JUDAH (joo'dah). District of S Palestine, which after the death of Solomon adhered to his son Rehoboam and the Davidic line, whereas the rest of Israel elected Jeroboam as ruler of the northern kingdom. In NT times, J. was the Roman prov. of Judaea, and in modern Israeli usage refers to the southern area of the West Bank.

JUDAISM (joo'da-izm). Term signifying the distinctive religious beliefs and observances of the Jews. It is founded on the Torah, 'direction for living', which combines the Mosaic code and its oral interpretation. During the Babylonian exile of 586 BC the Jews preserved their individual mode of life, and with the return under Cyrus J. was estab. by the code of Ezra. The effect of the destruction of the Temple on J. was countered by the rising importance of the synagogue, of home religious life, and of the lay rabbis.

The creed of J. is based on the fundamental concepts of one God, the revelation of His will in the Torah, and the special relationship of God and the Jewish people: its orthodox formulation is that of Moses Maimonides (1135-1204). Among the distinctive observances of J. are circumcision, the daily services in Hebrew, and the observance of the Sabbath (7th day of the week) and the 3 principal festivals, Passover, Pentecost, and Tabernacles. Dissenting movements in J. include the Pharisees, Sadducees, and Essenes of NT times; the 8th cent. Karaites; the Chasidism of the 18th cent.; the Reform movement begun in Germany in 1810 which reached England in 1842; and the more radical Liberal J. which developed in America and founded its first London synagogue in 1911. As with Christianity and Islam, there has been a reversion to fundamentalism in recent times, e.g. Gush Emunim (q.v.).

JUDAS ISCARIOT (joo'das iskar'i-ot). The one of the 12 Apostles who betrayed Jesus. He was the treasurer of the little band, and at the last Passover arranged with the chief priests to betray Jesus for 30 pieces of silver. The betrayal effected, he was smitten with remorse and committed suicide.

JUDGE. A person invested with power to hear and determine legal disputes. In the UK, Js. are chosen from barristers of long standing (for higher courts), and solicitors. *See* LAW COURTS. Js. of the Supreme Court, of which the Crown Courts function as a branch, and the County Courts, are nominated by the Lord Chancellor (except for the Lord Chief Justice), who is a political appointee. In the USA, apart from the Federal judiciary which are executive appointments, Js. in most states are elected by popular vote.

JUDICIAL SEPARATION. A husband or wife, when the marriage partner has committed certain offences, e.g., adultery, failure to maintain the wife (in certain circumstances the husband) and children, may obtain a declaration from the Magistrates' court that the complainant need no longer cohabit with the defendant, is entitled to maintenance, etc. Neither party is freed to marry again. A similar procedure exists in the USA.

JUDO (jū'dō). Synthesis of the most valuable methods - J. meaning 'gentle way' - from the many forms of jujitsu (jūjit'soo), 'the soft art', the traditional Japanese skill of self-defence and offence without weapons, which was originally practised as a secret art by the feudal Samurai. In modern times J. has been adopted throughout the world as a compulsory subject in the armed forces, the police, and in many schools. When it is practised as a sport the 2 combatants wear special loose-fitting, belted-jackets and trousers to facilitate holds, and the falls are broken by a special square mat: when one estab. a painful hold that the other cannot break, the latter signifies his surrender by slapping the ground with a free hand. Degrees of proficiency are indicated by the colour of the belt: for novices white; after examination, brown (3 degrees); and finally, black (9 degrees). *See* KARATE, KUNG FU.

JUGGERNAUT (jug'ernawt), or **Jagannath.** A name for Vishnu, the Hindu god, meaning 'Lord of the World'. His temple is at Puri, Orissa.

JUGOSLAVIA. *See* YUGOSLAVIA.

JUGULAR (jōō'gular). Belonging to the neck, especially of the external, anterior, and internal J. veins, through which the blood returns from the head and face towards the heart.

JUGU'RTHA (joo-) (d. 104 BC). King of Numidia in N Africa, who, after a long resistance, was betrayed to the Romans in 107 BC, and put to death by strangulation or starvation after being imprisoned in the underground prison beneath the Capitol.

JUJITSU. *See* JUDO.

JUJUBE (jōō'joob). Tree of the *Zizyphus* genus in the family Rhamnaceae, and also its berry-like fruits. The Mediterranean species is *Z. vulgaris*; the Chinese (*Z. jujuba*) has fruit the size of small plums, known when preserved in syrup as 'Chinese dates', but the Indian (*Z. mauritiana*) has a more mediocre fruit. The name is also given to a type of mucilaginous sweet.

JULIAN (jōō'lyan) (*c.* 331-63). Roman emperor, called the 'Apostate'. B. in Constantinople, the nephew of Constantine the Great, he was brought up as a Christian, but in early life became a convert to paganism. Sent by Constantius to govern Gaul in 355, he was proclaimed emperor by his troops in 360, and was marching on Constantinople when in 361 Constantius's death allowed him to succeed peacefully. He revived pagan worship, and infuriated the Christians by refusing to persecute heretics. He was slain in battle against the Persians.

JULIANA (jōōlyah'na) (1909-). Queen of the Netherlands. The dau. of Queen Wilhelmina (1880-1962), she m. in 1937 Prince Bernhard of Lippe-Biesterfeld (q.v.), and ruled 1948-80, when she abdicated and was succeeded by her dau. Beatrix (q.v.).

JULIUS (jōōl'yus) **II.** Pope 1503-13, was a politician who set himself to make the papal states the leading power in Italy, and formed international alliances first against Venice and then against France. He began the building of St Peter's, Rome, in 1506, and was the patron of Michelangelo and Raphael.

JULY REVOLUTION. Name given to the Parisian revolution of 27-9 July 1830 which overthrew the restored Bourbon monarchy of Charles X, and substituted the constitutional monarchy of Louis Philippe, whose rule (1830-48) is sometimes referred to as the July Monarchy.

JU'MNA. River in India, which rises in the Himalayas, in Uttar Pradesh, and joins the Ganges nr Allahabad, where it forms a sacred bathing place: Agra and Delhi are also on its course. Length 1,385 km (860m).

JUMPING HARE. S African rodent (*Pedetes capensis*), similar in appearance and habits to the jerboa, but the head is like that of a hare.

JUMPING MOUSE. N American rodent (*Zapus hudsonius*) in the jerboa family.

JUNCACEAE (jung-kā'sē-ē). Botanical name for the rush family, represented by 2 British genera, *Juncus* (rush) and *Luzula* (woodrush). *See* RUSH.

JUNEAU (joonō). Ice-free port of Alaska, USA on Gastineau Channel in the remote Alaska panhandle. There is salmon fishing, and gold and furs are exported. J. has been the cap. since 1906, but there are plans for a new cap. to the N of Anchorage. Pop. (1970) 6,000.

JUNG (yoong), **Carl G.** (1875-1961). Swiss psychologist. Like Freud he stressed the importance of unconscious memories and early childhood experiences, but he rejected Freud's excessive emphasis upon the sexual instinct. J. developed his own theory of analytical psychology, and wrote *Modern Man in Search of a Soul* (1933), etc. *See* COLLECTIVE UNCONSCIOUS.

JUNGFRAU (yoong'frow). Mtn - 'the maiden' - of exceptional beauty in the Bernese Oberland, Switzerland: 4,166 m (13,669 ft). A railway ascends to the plateau of the Jungfraujoch, 3,456 m/11,340 ft, where there is a winter sports centre.

JUNIPER (jo͞on'iper). Aromatic evergreen shrubs found throughout Britain, Europe, America, and temperate countries of the world. They are members of the Cupressaceae family, genus *Juniperus.*

JUNIUS (jo͞o'nyus), **Letters of.** A series of letters pub. in the *Public Advertiser* 1769-72, under the pseudonym J. Written in a pungent, epigrammatic style, they were intended to discredit the 'king's friends' in the interests of the opposition Whigs. The generally accepted theory attributes them to Sir Philip Francis.

JUNKERS (yoong'kers), **Hugo** (1859-1935). German aeroplane designer. In 1919 he founded in Dessau the aircraft works named after him. J. planes, including dive bombers, night fighters, and troop carriers, were used by the Germans in the S.W.W.

JUNKERS. Name applied to a class of landed gentry in Prussia, given to reactionary views and policy. They constituted a large percentage of the officer corps of the Prussian army.

JUNO (jo͞o'nō). Roman goddess identified with the Greek Hera. The wife of Jupiter, the queen of heaven, she was especially the goddess of women.

JUNTA (jun'ta, or hoon'ta). Spanish word meaning a council, and usually applied to the military rulers of a country after an army takeover, as in Turkey in 1980.

JUPITER (jo͞o'piter), or **Jō've.** Chief god of the ancient Romans, identified with the Greek Zeus. Originally he was god of the sky and associated with the lightning and thunderbolt. Later he came to be known as the protector in battle and the bestower of victory. He was the son of Saturn, m. his sister Juno, and reigned on Olympus as lord of heaven.

JUPITER. The largest planet in the Solar System, 1300 times larger than Earth and 318 times heavier. Its diameter at the equator is *c.* 143,200 km (88,980 m), and it is largely composed of hydrogen (liquefied by pressure) and helium. Nuclear reactions are taking place inside it, producing radiation which would be fatal to unprotected astronauts flying near, and the surface temperature, once thought never to exceed − 129°C (− 200°F), has been shown to rise much higher. The atmosphere is composed of hydrogen, with smaller amounts of methane, ammonia and helium. The surface is hidden by 'cloud belts', which show as reddish-brown and yellow through a telescope. Notable is the Great Red Spot c. 48,000 km (30,000 m) across, which has a small tail attached; first seen 300 yrs ago, it drifts and has circled the planet several times. It may be an intense updraught of gas.

J. takes 11.9 yrs to complete one journey round the Sun (778,000,000 km/483,300,000 m), but its axial rotation period is very short - 9 hr 55 min 29-70 sec. There are 17 satellites or moons, the 4 most recently discovered having been found by the two *Voyager* (US) spacecraft in 1979. The four largest were discovered by Galileo 1609-10, but no detail of their surfaces was known until the *Voyager* photographs. Io (q.v.) apparently has surface deposits of salts which make it the most reflective object known in the Solar System, and both it and Europa (q.v.) are about the size of Earth's Moon. Ganymede and Callisto (qq.v.) are rather larger than Mercury. Radio signals emitted by J. are thought to depend on the relative positions of Io and Europa. Jupiter also has an intense magnetic field.

There has been speculation, from the composition of J.'s atmosphere, that it may be an immense 'chemical laboratory' in which the processes of life may already have commenced.

JUPITER. No signs of life forms having been detected on Mars, attention has been turned to Jupiter. Towards the top left is the Great Red Spot, and above it the shadow of the satellite Ganymede which can be seen top right. *Photo: Courtesy of the Royal Astronomical Society.*

JURA (joo'rah). Series of parallel mountain ranges running SW-NE along the French-Swiss frontier between the Rhône and the Rhine, a distance of 250km (156m). The highest peak is Crête de la Neige 1,723 m (5,650 ft). The J. mountains give their name to a dept of France; and a J. canton was estab. 1979 in Switzerland formed from the French-speaking areas of Berne, where a separatist movement has existed since the 19th cent., but espec. from 1947.

JURA (joo'ra). Island of the Inner Hebrides: separated from the mainland by the Sound of J. The whirlpool Corrievrekin (Gaelic 'Brecan's cauldron) is off the N coast.

JURISPRUDENCE (jo͞orispro͞o'dens). The science of law in the abstract; that is, not the study of any particular laws or legal system, but of the principles upon which all mature legal systems are founded.

JURY. Body of laymen sworn to render a verdict in a court of justice. Of generally Germanic origin, the British J. probably derives most directly from the custom of the Franks, introduced into England by the Normans. Under the Plantagenets it developed from a body of neighbours, familiar with the people and background of the case - almost appearing in the character of witnesses - to an impartial panel rendering a verdict based solely on evidence heard in court. In England common Js. (special Js. are almost obsolete, but *see also* CORONER) are used in the more important criminal and certain civil cases, jurors being selected from men and women of 18-65 on the electoral roll, with exemption for peers, doctors, MPs, ministers of religion, etc. Either prosecution or defence may challenge any juror as unsuitable. Restrictions were introduced in 1980 on the controversial practice of 'J. vetting.' Only in terrorist and national security trials would the checking of potential jurors' records in Special

Branch files be authorised, and checks with local CID files would only be allowed to confirm the identity of a juror against whom other checks had raised doubts. The verdict reached is conclusive, i.e. there can be no retrial on the same charge, and in England had always been unanimous (though Scotland had allowed simple majority verdicts in a J. of 15), but evidence of corruption and intimidation led to the Criminal Justice Act 1967, by which a majority of 10 to 2 convicts, and people with criminal convictions are disqualified from serving. Members of Js. are allowed certain expenses, etc. In 1977 the Criminal Law Act ended J. trial for petty theft to reduce pressure on the overloaded Crown Courts.

The basic principles of the British system have been adopted in the US, most Commonwealth countries, and in some European countries, e.g. France. In the USA the use of a grand J. (abolished in England in 1933) has been retained, both at federal and state level: consisting of 23 persons it hears only evidence for the prosecution to decide whether there is a case to be referred for trial. Witnesses are not represented by counsel, the hearings are in secret, and the judge is not present at the sessions, the J. merely presenting their findings to him. The person whom the J. decide to indict may never appear, and immunity is frequently given to witnesses providing evidence which enables a criminal indictment to be made.

JUS PRIMAE NOCTIS (yoos prē'mī nok'tis) (Lat., right of the first night). The custom of allowing the lord to enjoy the wife of any of his tenants on the wedding night. It existed in Scotland until Malcolm III, in the 11th cent., enacted that the bridegroom might pay a sum of money in lieu; and a similar right has been discovered among many savage races.

JUSTICE OF THE PEACE. In England an unpaid magistrate appointed by the Lord Chancellor. Two or more Js. of the P. sit to dispose of minor charges (formerly their jurisdiction was much wider), to commit for trial by a higher court more serious ones, to grant licences for the sale of intoxicating liquor, etc. In the USA, where they are in receipt of fees and are usually elected, their courts are the lowest in the States, and Js. of the P. deal only with minor offences, such as traffic violations: they may also conduct marriages.

JUSTI'NIAN I (483-562). Byzantine emperor. B. in Illyricum, he was associated with his uncle Justin I in the govt from 518. He m. the actress Theodora, and succeeded Justin in 527. He recovered N Africa from the Vandals, SE Spain from the Visigoths, and Italy from the Ostrogoths, largely owing to his great gen. Belisarius. The greater part of his reign was also taken up by an indecisive struggle with the Persians. J.'s religious zeal led him to build St Sophia at Constantinople, and to close the univ. at Athens in 529. He ordered the codification of Roman law which has exercised a great influence on European jurisprudence.

JU'STIN MARTYR (*c.* 100-*c.* 163). Christian apologist, and a Father of the Church. B. in Palestine, he was converted to Christianity at Ephesus, and spent the rest of his life as an itinerant Christian missionary-philosopher. He was martyred in Rome.

JUTE (joot). Fibre obtained from 2 plants of the genus *Corchorus* - *C. capsularis* and *C. olitorius*. J. is used for sacks and sacking, upholstery, webbing, twine, stage canvas, etc., but in uses such as bulk packaging, and tufted carpet backing, tends to be replaced by synthetic polypropylene. The world's largest producer of J. is Bangladesh.

JUTES. A Germanic people who originated in Jutland but had been settled for some time in Frankish territory before they occupied Kent *c.* 450, according to tradition under Hengist and Horsa, and conquered the Isle of Wight and the coasts of Hants opposite in the early 6th cent.

JUTLAND. A peninsula of N Europe between the N Sea and the Kattegat. The S belongs to Germany, whilst the N part constitutes continental Denmark.

JUTLAND. The greatest naval battle of the F.W.W. fought between the British under Admiral Jellicoe and the Germans under Admiral Scheer, on 31 May 1916, off the W coast of Jutland. After a battle-cruiser action between Beatty and Hipper, the former retired northward and drew the whole enemy fleet on to Jellicoe's battleships. Scheer, however, escaped a perilous situation by retreating S. During the night, with several encounters with British destroyers, he passed astern of Jellicoe's fleet and escaped, aided by the latter's lack of information. Yet J. was a decided British victory since the Germans never again ventured out to battle.

JUVENAL (jōō'venal) (*c.* AD 60-140). Roman satirist and poet. B. probably at Aquinum, he received a good education. Late in life his genius for satire brought him to the unfavourable notice of the emperor Domitian. 16 of his satires are extant, and they give a brutal and sometimes disgusting picture of the Roman society of his day.

JUVENILE DELINQUENCY. Offences against the law committed by young people. The Children and Young Persons Act (1969) introduced in Britain the gradual abolition of the prosecution of children up to the age of 14, and provided 3 options for Juvenile Courts in respect of all care and criminal proceedings involving children up to the age of 17: binding over of parents, supervision orders, and care orders. Community homes were to have replaced the former approved schools, remand homes and probation hostels. It was hoped that the system would reduce the number of children in court, but this was not achieved, to some extent possibly because restrictions on finance did not allow a full back-up system, espec. of the proposed community homes.

Contrary to earlier belief, D. is not solely the product of poverty. It is more probable that the largest factor is family disorganization which creates emotional and psychological difficulties for the growing child. There is a higher D. rate in affluent countries, overcrowded urban populations have a higher rate, and the last year at school is at risk.

JYLLAND (ju'lahn). The mainland of Denmark, the northern section of the Jutland peninsula (q.v.). The chief towns are Aalborg, Aarhus, Esbjerg, Fredericia, Horsens, Kolding, Randers and Vejle. *See also* JUTES.

K

Eleventh letter of the Roman alphabet, in Eng. representing the unvoiced velar stop. It is silent before another consonant at the beginning of a word (e.g. in *knee*), a change accomplished, probably, in the 17th cent.

K2. Second highest mtn in the world, in the Karakorum range, N Kashmir; it is also known as Dapsang, 'Hidden Peak', and formerly as Mt Godwin-Austen (after the eldest son of an English geologist). First climbed in 1954 by an Italian expedition, it is 8,611 m (28,250 ft) high.

KAABA (kah'bah). The oblong building in the quadrangle of the Great Mosque at Mecca (q.v.) into the NE corner of which is built the black stone declared by Mohammed to have been given to Abraham by Gabriel, and devoutly revered by Moslem pilgrims. The name means chamber.

KABBALA (kab'ala) (Heb., 'tradition'). Body of esoteric Jewish doctrine containing strong elements of pantheism, and akin to Neoplatonism. Among its earliest documents are the *Sefir Jezirah* (The Book of Creation), attributed to Rabbi Akiba (d. AD 120). The *Zohar* or Book of Light was first written in Aramaic about the 13th cent., and Kabbalistic writing reached its peak period between the 13th and 16th cents. The most notable writer was Moses ben Nachman (1195-1270).

KABINDA. *See* CABINDA.

KABUL (kah'bool). Cap. of Afghanistan and of K. prov., on the K. r. 2,100 m (6,900 ft) a.s.l. Originally a walled city of importance throughout central Asia, it is a great marketing town, with match, woollen, furniture, and other factories, a military academy, and a univ. (1932). K. is the focal point for the Khyber Pass route to Peshawar, Pakistan. Pop. (1976) 587,600.

KA'BWE. Town in Zambia (formerly **Broken Hill**), on the Copper Belt. Copper, cadmium, lead and zinc are mined. Pop. (1976) 98,000.

KABYLES (kabilz'). Group of Berber tribes in N Africa, chiefly Algeria. Moslems, they formerly served as soldiers in the French forces. *See* ZOUAVES.

KÁDAR (kah'dahr), **János** (1912-). Hungarian politician. A member of the underground in the S.W.W., he afterwards was a leader of the Communist régime (though himself imprisoned for deviation from 'Stalinism' 1951-3), but on the outbreak of the Hungarian revolt of 1956 declared the party dissolved. He then headed a govt under Russian supervision 1956-8 and 1961-5, remaining in 1965 as 1st sec. of the Communist Party.

KADHAFI (kadhah'fi), **Moamer al** (1942-). Libyan statesman. He headed the military coup which overthrew King Idris and estab. a rep. in 1969, and became the equivalent of president. He advocates a purified Islam and the union of all Arab lands and their joint destruction of Israel. In 1974 he relinquished his political and admin. duties to concentrate on ideological functions. Plans for a merger of Libya and Egypt (1973) foundered on a clash between K. and Sadat, and a 'propaganda war' intermittently continued.

KADUNA (kadōō'na). Town in Nigeria, on the K. river, a market centre for grain and cotton: textiles are made and there are car assembly, timber and pottery industries, and an oil refinery. Pop. (1975) 202,000.

KADHAFI. The Libyan president, Moamer al Kadhafi, greeted by Leonid Brezhnev on his visit to Moscow in 1976. *Photo: Popperfoto*

KAFFIR or **KAFIR** (kah'fer). Name given to the Bantu-speaking peoples, incl. the Xhosa and Pondo tribes of Cape Province, living in much of SE Africa. They are primarily agriculturalists, raising cattle and grain. They should not be confused with the Kafirs (Arabic: 'infidels'), a mountain people living on the border between NE Afghanistan and Pakistan, so named because they refused to accept Islam until the 20th cent. They are now known as Nuri: 'people of light'. In modern S. Africa, the word K., as applied miscellaneously to Black people, is regarded as offensive.

KAFKA, Franz (1883-1924). Czech novelist. B. at Prague, he worked for a time in an insurance office, but developed tuberculosis, and d. in a sanatorium nr Vienna. He wrote in German and although short stories appeared during his lifetime he is chiefly remembered for his 3 long, but unfinished, allegorical novels *The Trial* (1925), *The Castle* (1926) and *America* (1927), which were pub. posthumously despite his instructions that they should be destroyed.

KAFUE (kahfōō'e). River in central Zambia, a tributary of the Zambezi: 965 km (600 m) long. Also the town of K., 44 km (27 m) S of Lusaka, centre of Zambia's heavy industry from 1967. Pop. (1980) 35,000.

KAGAN. *See under* BUKHARA.

KAGŌ'SHIMA. Port on K. Bay, Kyushu, Japan. The Satsumayaki porcelain is made there. Pop. (1977) 478,000.

KAHN, Louis (1901-74). American architect. A follower of Mies van der Rohe, he developed a romantically classical style, marked by 'service' towers surrounding the main working spaces. His works incl. the Salk Laboratories, La Jolla, California, and the Palace of Congresses, Venice.

KAIETEUR (kah-etoor') **FALL.** Waterfall on the r. Potaro, a tributary of the Essequibo, Guyana. It is 250m/822ft - i.e. five times as high as Niagara.

KAIFENG (kah-ē-fung') City in Henan prov., of which it was formerly the cap. It lost its importance owing to the silting up of the nearby Huang He river at this point. K. was the cap. of China 907-1127. Pop. (1970) 450,000.

KAIKOURAS (kīkoor'az). Double range of mts in the NE of South Island, NZ, separated by the Clarence r., and reaching 2,885 m (9,465 ft): they have great scenic beauty.

KAINGAROA. State forest to the NE of Lake Taupo in North Island, NZ, one of the world's largest man-made forests.

KAIRWAN (kirwahn'). Moslem holy city in Tunisia, N Africa, S of Tunis. Said to have been founded AD 617, K. ranks after Mecca and Medina as a place of pilgrimage. Pop. (1970) 100,000.

KAISER, Henry J. (1882-1967). American industrialist. He built up steel and motor industries, and his shipbuilding firms became famous for the mass production of vessels, incl. the 'liberty ships' - cheap, quickly produced, transport ships - built for the UK in the S.W.W.

KAISER. A title formerly borne by the Holy Roman Emperors, Austrian Emperors 1806-1918, and German Emperors 1871-1918. The word, like Tsar, is derived from the Lat. *Caesar.*

KAISERSLAUTERN (kī'zerslowtern). W German town in the Rhineland Palatinate, 48km (30m) W of Mannheim. It dates from 882; the castle from which it got its name was built by Frederick Barbarossa in 1152, destroyed by the French in 1703. Industries incl. textiles and cars. Pop. (1978) 100,100.

KAKAPO (kah'kapō). An almost flightless parrot (*Strigops habroptilus*) which lives in burrows in New Zealand. Nocturnal, and a dullish green-brown, it is almost extinct.

KALAHARI (kahlahhah'rē). Semi-desert inland area, comprising most of Botswana, but extending also into SW Africa (Namibia), Zimbabwe and S Africa. In the N the only permanent river, the Okavango flows into the Okavango marshes (formerly Lake Ngami), rich in wild life. Elsewhere game survives only in protected areas. S Africa has a nuclear site here. Area c. 900,000 sq.km (347,400 sq.m).

KALE. A variety of cabbage (*Brassica oleracea,* variety *acephala*) grown as a winter vegetable. The commonest forms are the Scotch K. or borecole and curly K.

KALEVALA (kahlehvah'lah). Finnish national epic first formed from scattered legends and ballads by Elias Lönnrot in 1835. The hero of the poem is Väinamöinen, god of music and poetry.

KA'LGAN. *See* ZHANGJIAKOU.

KALGOO'RLIE. Town in W Australia, 545km (340m) NE of Perth, amalgamated with Boulder in 1966. Gold has been mined since 1893, and it is a Flying Doctor centre. There is a School of Mines. Pop. (1976) 19,000.

KALI (kah'lē). In Hindu mythology, the wife of Siva. She is the goddess of destruction and death.

KÂLIDÂSA (kahlēdah'sah). The most famed of the writers is the 2nd epoch of Sanskrit literature, believed to have flourished about AD 375 at the court of King Vikramaditya at Ujjain. *Sakuntalâ* was his greatest play.

KALIMA'NTAN. Indonesian name of the SE part of Borneo, formerly Netherlands Borneo. It forms a prov. of the rep. of Indonesia and is for the most part low-lying, with mountains in the NW rising in Mt Raya to 2,274 m (7,462 ft). The chief towns, both ports, are Banjermasin at the mouth of the Negara r., and Balikpapan, which is an important petroleumproducing centre. Area 543,900 sq.km (210,000 sq.m); pop. (1971) 5,200,000.

KALININ (kahlē'nin), **Mikhail Ivanovich** (1875-1946). Soviet statesman. Founder of *Pravda,* he was prominent in the October Revolution, and in 1919 became pres. of the Central Executive Committee of the Soviet Govt, then in 1937 pres. of the Presidium of the Supreme Soviet until 1946 - both posts were equivalent to Pres. of the USSR.

KALININ. City of the RSFSR, cap. of K. region. On the Volga, 160km (100m) NW of Moscow, and called Tver until 1933, it was re-named in honour of President K. It is an important transport centre. Pop. (1977) 401,000.

KALI'NINGRAD. City in the RSFSR, cap. of K. region, better known by its German name Königsberg. K. grew up round a castle dating from 1255, a seat of the Teutonic Knights. It was cap. of East Prussia until that area ceased to exist with its division between Russia and Poland in 1945, under the Potsdam agreement. It was re-named in honour of President Kalinin of the USSR. Pop. (1977) 353,000.

KALMAR (kahl'mahr). Port on the SE coast of Sweden. Industries incl. paper, matches and the Orrefors glassworks. Pop. (1978) 53,000.

KA'LMUCK. An ASSR of the RSFSR. Estab. on the Caspian Sea in 1935, it was abolished in 1943, and its inhabitants deported to Siberia for their alleged collaboration with the Germans during the battle of Stalingrad. It was restored in 1957. Area 75,9000 sq.km (29,305 sq.m); pop. (1978) 279,000.

KA'LTENBRUNNER (-brooner), **Ernst** (1901-46). Austrian Nazi leader. After the annexation of Austria he joined Himmler's staff, and as head of the Security Police (SD) from 1943 was responsible for the murder of Allied soldiers, and of millions of Jews. He was tried at Nuremberg, and hanged.

KALUGA (kahloo'ga). Town in the RSFSR, on the Oka, 160km (100m) SSW of Moscow, cap. of K. region. It has hydro-electric installations and engineering works, and makes telephone equipment, measuring devices, etc. Pop. (1977) 262,000.

KAMAKURA (kamakoora). Town in Honshu, Japan to the S of Yokohama. It was the seat of the first Shogunate 1192-1333, which estab. the rule of the Samurai class. Noted are the Hachimangu Shrine, dedicated to the gods of war and the great 13th cent. statue of Buddha (Daibutsu) 13m (43ft) high. From the 19th cent. artists and writers settled here, e.g. Kawabata. Pop. (1975) 175,000.

KAMARA'N. Island in the Red Sea, formerly belonging to S Yemen, but occupied by N Yemen in 1972. The former RAF station is controlled by the USSR. Area 180 sq.km (70 sq.m).

KAMCHA'TKA. Mountainous peninsula of E Asia; name also of a region of the RSFSR covering the peninsula and the Chukchi and Koryak national districts. Agriculture is possible only in the S, and the inhabitants are fishermen and hunters. Petropavlovsk, cap. of region, is the only town.

KAMET. Himalayan mountain 7,756 m (25,447 ft) on the Tibet/India border. F. S. Smythe and Eric Shipton were in the group which made the first ascent in 1931.

KAMAKURA. The great 13th century bronze statue of Buddha the hands are placed in the position which indicates meditation. *Photo: Mireille Vautier.*

KAMIKAZE (kahmikah'zi). Suicide pilots of the Japanese air force in the S.W.W. - the name means 'god wind' - who deliberately crash-dived their planes, loaded with bombs, usually on ships of the U.S. navy.

KAMPALA (kahmpahl'a). African town, commercial centre and, from 1962, cap. of Uganda, cap. of Buganda region; *see* BUGANDA. It is linked by rail with Mombasa, and is a market for cotton, coffee, livestock, etc. Cigarettes are made. The Parliament buildings were opened in 1960. Makerere Univ. (1938) lies to the NW. Pop. (1972) 331,000.

KAMPERDUIN. *See* CAMPERDOWN.

KAMPONG CHAM. Town in Kampuchea, NE of Phnom Penh. Pop. (1971) 35,000.

KAMPUCHEA (kampoochē'-a). Country of SE Asia, between Thailand and S Vietnam on the Gulf of Thailand. The vast central plain comprises the low-lying middle valley of the Mekong towards the E and the area towards the W, formerly a sea gulf, of which the centre is Lake Tonle-Sap. To the N of the lake are the magnificent ruins of Angkor (q.v.) and to the S of it the river Tonle-Sap flows out to link with the Mekong at Phnom Penh. There is higher land adjoining the upper reaches of the Mekong on the E border with Laos and S Vietnam, and the Cardamones Mts. border the Gulf of Thailand. Almost half the country is forested, and only about a fifth of the cultivable area was in use even before the civil war. The central plain owes its immense fertility to the inundation in the monsoon season June-Oct., when the swollen Mekong causes the great lake to overflow, of an area of more than 2,500 sq.km (1,000 sq.m). Rice, maze, soya, etc. are grown, and rubber and timber are produced from the forests. Mineral resources incl. phosphates and iron. There is a large fishing industry, but manufactures are on a limited scale, development in recent years being hindered by the war.

The chief towns are the cap. Phnom Penh; the modern deepwater ocean port of Kompong Som (formerly Sihanoukville) on the Gulf of Thailand; the river ports of Kompong Cham (Mekong) and Kompong Chhnang (Tonle-Sap); and Battambang.

The Kampucheans are fundamentally an Indonesian people, but there has been much infiltration from India. The most ancient monuments date from the 7th cent. AD when the Khmers, the ancestors of the present people, had built up a remarkable civilization. After the 12th cent. the Khmer realm began to fade, and K. continued to decline. The King, formerly a vassal of Siam, in 1863 accepted the protection of France, which lasted until the Japanese overran the country in 1941 during the S.W.W. The independence of the country, then known as Cambodia, was recognised by France in 1955. Prince Norodom Sihanouk (1922-), elected king 1941, then abdicated to become PM as leader of the Popular Socialist Community. In 1960 he was created Head of State, but was deposed 1970, when a rep. was proclaimed under Pres. Lon Nol, supported by the USA. However, Prince Sihanouk and the Communist Khmers Rouges regained control of the govt. by 1975 after a civil war, and Lon Nol fled into exile. Prince Sihanouk remained 'Head of State' until 1976.

Long-known by the European form of its name as Cambodia, K. was styled Khmer Rep. 1970-5, Democratic Kampuchea 1975-9, and People's Rep. of Kampuchea from 1979. Under the regime of Pol Pot (1925-), who was PM 1976-9, untold numbers were executed or d. of starvation in the name of establishing a pure Communist state. In 1977-8 border clashes developed into a full-scale invasion by Vietnam (backed by USSR) and the establishment of an alternative govt. under Heng Samrin. By 1979 the guerrillas, still under the military leadership of Pol Pot, were driven back to the Thai border. Many Kampuchean refugees had already crossed the border, and by 1980 it was feared the conflict might extend into Thailand. World govts were divided as to recognition of the Heng Samrin regime, or that of Khieu Samphan, Chinese-backed and successor as PM to Pol Pot. In 1981 Prince Sihanouk announced his willingness to lead a coalition resistance movement against the Vietnamese occupation army, together with individual Khmer Rouge members. The Khmer Rouge army, headed by Sol Sen from 1985, remains politically isolated.

Area 181,000 sq.km (71,000 sq.m); pop. (1980) *c.* 5,630,000, as against *c.* 7,500,000 in 1975. The people are traditionally Hinayana Buddhists, and the official language is Khmer, although French has been largely used in govt. and trade. M.U.: riel.

KANA'KA. Hawaiian word for man; applied to the natives of the South Sea islands.

KANAZA'WA. City of Honshu island, Japan, 160km (100m) NNW of Nagoya. It has large textile and porcelain industries. Pop. (1977) 393,000.

KANCHENJU'NGA. Himalayan mtn on the Nepal-Sikkim border (8,598 m/28,208 ft), 120km (75m) SE of Everest: the name means '5 treasure houses of the great snows'. K. was first climbed by a Brit. expedition 1955.

KANDAHA'R. City of Afghanistan, 450km (280m) SW of Kabul, cap. of K. prov. and an important trading centre, with wool and cotton factories. It is surrounded by a 8m (27ft) high mud wall. On 1 Sept. 1880 the British under

General Roberts defeated the Afghans there. Pop. (1976) 115,000.

KANDI'NSKY, Vasily (1866-1944). Russian Expressionist artist. B. in Moscow, he travelled widely abroad and by 1910 was producing completely non-representational work. In 1912 he pub. the influential *Concerning the Spiritual in Art* and was joint-originator with Franz Marc of the *Blaue Reiter* movement 1911-12. For some years he taught at the Bauhaus and, after its closure by the Nazis, settled in Paris. His use of colour, and ordered arrangement of spheres and rectangles, affected the work of many other artists.

KANDY (kahn'dē). Town of Sri Lanka, formerly cap. of the ancient kingdom of K. One of its temples contains an alleged tooth of Buddha and is one of the most sacred Buddhist shrines. At Peradenia, 5km (3m) away, is the chief campus of the Univ. of Sri Lanka (1942) and a botanical garden. Pop. (1977) 103,000.

KANGAROO'. Family of marsupials (Macropodidae) found in Australia and Tasmania. All are herbivorous and range from the musk K., similar in size to a large rat, through the medium-sized wallabies - which extend their range to New Guinea - to the familiar great grey K. (*Macropus major*) which stands 2.5m (8ft): some extinct forms must have reached 3m (10ft) or larger. The single young of the great grey K., born usually in Jan. after a very brief gestation period, is *c.* 2.5cm (1in) long at birth and remains in the mother's pouch, with excursions as it matures, until Oct. The developed hind legs and strong tail enable them to travel at speeds in long leaps. Adaptable to rain forest or dry areas, the K. (even 'rare' species) rapidly increases in number when protected, and an annual quota is killed to avoid crop damage, the fur and meat being exported.

KANGAROO PAW. Bulbous plant *(Anigozanthos manglesii)* with a row of small white flowers emerging from velvety green tubes with red bases. It is the floral emblem of Western Australia.

KANIA (kah'nia), **Stanislaw** (1927-). Polish statesman. A specialist in security and foreign affairs, he succeeded Gierek as First Sec. of the United Workers' Party in 1980 following the Gdansk strikes. He promised greater democracy and respect for the agreement reached with the men.

KANŌ'. Cap. of K. state in N Nigeria, centre of an irrigated area. Founded *c.* 1000 BC, K. is walled city where goods still arrive by camel train to a market place holding 20,000 people, and is an important centre for the Sudan. New K. extends beyond the walls and products inc. cycles, glass, furniture, textiles, chemicals. Pop. (1975) 399,000.

KANPUR (kahn'poor). Indian city, on the Ganges, southwest of Lucknow, in Uttar Pradesh, cap. of K. district. It is an important commercial and industrial centre with cotton, woollen, and jute mills, chemical and plastics factories, iron and steel works. During the Indian Mutiny in 1857 it was the scene of a massacre of British civilians who had surrendered to Nana Sahib. Under the *raj* it was spelt Cawnpore. Pop. (1971) 1,273,000.

KANSAS. Central state of the USA. It is the principal winter wheat-producing area in the USA. The chief rivers are the Missouri, Kansas, and Arkansas; the chief towns Kansas City, Wichita, Topeka (the cap.), and Hutchinson; and cattle, coal, petroleum, and natural gas are important; Wichita is a leading producer of aircraft. Area 213,063 sq.km (82,264 sq.m); pop. (1970) 2,249,071.

KANGAROO. A forester or great grey kangaroo *(Macropus major)* with a joey in her pouch. About nine months old he is almost ready to leave the pouch permanently. *Photo: Courtesy of the Australian Information Service.*

KANSAS CITY. Twin city in the USA at the confluence of the Missouri and Kansas rivers, partly in Kansas and partly in Missouri. Founded *c.* 1826 by French fur trappers as a trading post, it is now a market and agricultural distribution centre, and leads the USA for storage and distribution of frozen food and winter wheat marketing. The majority of the offices of K.C. (Ks) are in K.C. (Mo), and the latter is the second city in the USA for car assembly. In the 1920s and 1930s K.C. was run by boss Tom Pendergast, of the Ready-Mix Concrete Co., and in the nightclubs on Twelfth Street under his 'protection' jazzmen such as Lester Young, Count Basie and Charlie 'Yardbird' Parker performed. Pop. (1970) of K.C. (Ks) 168,213; K.C. (Mo) met. area 1,323,800.

KANSU. *See* GANSU.

KANT, Immanuel (1724-1804). German philosopher. B. at Königsberg, he went to the univ. there, and in 1770 was appointed professor in logic and metaphysics. His first book, *Thoughts on the true estimates of living forces,* appeared in 1747, and the *Theory of the Heavens* in 1755. In the latter he combined physics and theology in an argument for the existence of God. Best-known of his works is the *Critique of Pure Reason* (1781), which was followed by the *Prolegomena* (1783), *Metaphysic of Ethics* (1785), *Metaphysic of Nature* (1786), *Of Practical Reason* (1788) and *Of Judgment* (1790). In 1797 ill-health led to his retirement. K. was a transcendental idealist, making a prime distinction between noumenon (object of purely intellectual intuition) and phenomenon (object of perception or experience); phenomena do not exist in themselves but only in relation to the mind. He identified practical reason with morality and the supreme cause is a moral cause. He gave the name of Categorical Imperative to the absolute unconditional command of the moral law, a law binding universally on every rational will.

KANTORŌ'VICH, Leonid (1912-). Russian economist. Leader of the mathematical school of economic research, he demonstrated that decentralization of decisions in a planned economy could only be made with a rational price system, a thesis in conflict with Soviet doctrine. He was awarded a Nobel prize 1975.

KAOHSIUNG (kah-awsyoong'). City and port on the W coast of Taiwan. Industrial products include aluminium ware, fertilizers, cement; there are also oil refineries, iron and steel works, shipyards, and food-processing factories. K. began to develop as a commercial port after 1858; its industrial development came about while it was occupied by Japan, 1895-1945. Pop. (1973) 915,000.

KĀ'OLIANG. Variety of millet grown in NE China and N China as a foodcrop. The plants grow up to 3.5m (12ft) high. The stalks are used for thatch, matting, and fencing.

KĀ'OLIN. Mineral, also called China clay, and named K. from the Chinese for high hill, the place nr. Jingdezhen (q.v.), where it was first mined. It is used in porcelain, paper, paint and cosmetics.

KA'PITZA, Peter (1894–1984). Russian physicist. He held important posts in Britain, e.g. as asst. director of magnetic research at the Cavendish Laboratory, Cambridge, 1924-32, before returning to the USSR to work at the Russian Academy of Science. In 1978 he shared a Nobel prize for his work on magnetism and low temperature physics.

KAPOK (kah'pok). Silky hairs produced round the seeds of certain trees, particularly the K. tree (*Eriodendron anfractuosum*) of India, Java, and Malaya, and the silk-cotton tree (*Ceiba pentandra*), a native of tropical America. K. is used for stuffing cushions, mattresses, and sound insulation. Oil obtained from the seeds is used in food and soap preparation.

KARA BOGAZ GOL (kahra' bogahz' gul). Gulf of the Caspian Sea, Turkmenistan, USSR. Sodium chloride, sulphates and other salts are deposited by evaporation over its area of 20,000 sq.km (8,000 sq.m).

KARACHI (karah'chi). Chief seaport and former cap. of Pakistan, in Sind, N of the Indus delta. It has a fine harbour, and an international airport. Natural gas is brought to K. by pipeline from Sui, 563km (350m) to the N, and there is an oil refinery at nearby Korangi. Pop. (1972) 3,469,000.

KARAFUTO (kahrahfootō). Japanese name for the southern part of the island of Sakhalin (q.v.), annexed by Japan in 1905, restored to Russia in 1945.

KARAGA'NDA. Industrial town in Kazakh SSR, USSR, cap. of K. region, which produces coal, copper, tungsten, manganese, etc. Pop. (1977) 576,000.

KARAJAN (karayahn'), **Herbert von** (1908-). Austrian conductor. Originally a student of the piano, he has for many years been associated with the Berlin Philharmonic Orchestra; directed the Salzburg Festival from 1964, and became director of the Vienna State Opera (artistic manager 1956-64) in 1976.

KARA-KALPAK (kah'ra kahlpahk'). ASSR of Uzbek SSR, USSR, called after the Kara-Kalpak people whose name means black bonnet. They live S of the Sea of Aral and were subdued by Russia in 1867. An autonomous K.-K. region formed in 1926 within Kazakh ASSR, transferred to the RSFSR in 1930, made an ASSR in 1932, was attached to Uzbekistan in 1936. The cap. is Nukus. With the aid of artificial irrigation cotton, rice, wheat and other crops are grown; fish from the Aral Sea is canned at Muynak. Area 158,000 sq. km (61,000 sq. m); pop. *c.* 700,000 (*c.*40 per cent Kara-Kalpaks).

KARAKŌ'RAM. Range of mountains in central Asia. The highest peak is K2 (q.v.). K. was also the name of Genghis Khan's capital, now in ruins.

The *Karakoram Highway* was constructed 1969-78 by Pakistan, branching from the Gilgit-Xinjiang road at Mor Khun in northern Kashmir to form a second link with Xinjiang.

KARA-KUM (kah'rah-koom'; Black Sands). Sandy desert occupying most of Turkmen SSR, USSR. Area *c.*310,800 sq.km (120,000 sq.m).

KARAMANLIS (kahramanlēs'), **Constantinos** (1907-). Greek statesman. A lawyer and an anti-Communist, he was PM Oct. 1955-Mar. 1958; May 1958-Sept. 1961; and Nov. 1961-June 1963, when he went into self-imposed exile. He was recalled as PM on the fall of the regime of the 'colonels' in July 1974-May 1980, when he became president. Elected by a large majority, he held a referendum which rejected a monarchy. He resigned 1985.

KARA (kah'ra) **SEA.** Part of the Arctic Ocean off the N coast of the RSFSR, bounded to the NW by the is. of Novaya Zemlya and to the NE by Severnaya Zemlya. Novy Port on the Gulf of Ob is the chief port, and the Yenisei also flows into it.

KARATE (kahrahtā). Method of unarmed combat, *kara* 'empty' and *te* 'hand', said to have originated in Okinawa in the 17th cent., under the influence of kung-fu (q.v.). The population had been recently conquered by the Japanese and were forbidden to carry weapons: K. was later further developed by the Japanese. It differs from judo in its emphasis on 'striking' with open hand or closed fist, and kicking.

KARBALA. *See* KERBELA.

KARĒ'LIA. ASSR of the RSFSR, formed in 1956 from the Karelo-Finnish SSR set up in 1940 and adjoining the Finnish frontier. K. is rich in sources of water power and forest reserves and fisheries. The cap. is Petrozavodsk. Area 172,400 sq.km (66,500 sq.m); pop. (1978) 742,000.

KARĒ'LIAN ISTHMUS. Strip of land between Lake Ladoga and the Gulf of Finland, RSFSR, USSR, with Leningrad at the S extremity and Viipuri at the northern. Finland ceded it to the USSR 1940-1 and from 1947.

KARENS (kahrenz'). People of the Far East, numbering perhaps 1½ million in all. Most of them live in E Burma near the Thailand border, across which some of them are found, as also are some in the Irrawaddy delta. Their language belongs to the Sino-Thai family, and it is believed that they are descended from the Chinese driven S by the Shan people. The K. strongly resisted integration in Burma after that country became independent in 1948, and Kantarawaddy, Bawlake, and Kyebogyi, three divisions of Burma formerly called the Karenni states, were in 1954 formed into the Kayah state (area *c.* 11,900 sq.km/4,600 sq.m), while parts of the districts of Toungoo, Thaton, and Amherst became the Karen state (area 30,000 sq.km/11,600 sq.m), both states having a measure of autonomy.

KARATE. Defensive moves: against a wrist grip (upper left); warding off a punch with a 'rising block' (upper right); evading a downward blow (lower left); and foiling a grip from the rear (lower right).

KARIBA (karēb'a) **DAM.** Concrete dam on the Zambia-Zimbabwe border, c. 386km (240m) down-stream from the Victoria Falls, constructed 1955-60 to supply power to both countries. The dam crosses K. gorge, and the reservoir, Lake Kariba, has important fisheries.

KARIKA'L. Small port in India, 250km (155m) S of Madras, at the mouth of the right distributory of the Cauvery delta. On a tract of land acquired by the French in 1739, it was transferred to India *de facto* in 1954, by treaty in 1956. *See* PONDICHERRY.

KARL-MARX-STADT. Town in E Germany, cap. of K. district, on the Chemnitz r., 65km (40m) SSE of Leipzig. It is an industrial centre with engineering works, textile and chemical factories. Formerly called Chemnitz, it came within the Russian zone of occupation after the S.W.W. and was renamed in 1953. Pop. (1978) 310,770.

KARLOVY VARY. Spa in the Bohemian Forest, Czechoslovakia, famous from the 14th cent. for its alkaline thermal springs. Pop. (1977) 61,000.

KARLSBAD. German name of KARLOVY VARY.

KARLSBURG. German name of ALBA JULIA.

KA'RLSKRŌNA. Seaport and naval base on the S coast of Sweden, the HQ of the Swedish navy since 1680. Pop. (1978) 60,000.

KARLSRUHE (-rōō-e). Town of Baden-Württemberg, W Germany, 56km (35m) S of Mannheim. K., founded 1715, is an important communication centre, and has large railway shops, breweries, etc. Pop. (1978) 276,000.

KARLSTAD. Town in Sweden, on the is. of Thingvalla, at N end of Lake Vaner. It makes matches, machinery, etc. The conference which ended the union between Norway and Sweden was held there in 1905. Pop. (1978) 73,500.

KARMA (Sanskrit, action or fate). In Indian religion and philosophy, the sum of a man's actions that is carried forward from one existence to the next, and in so doing determines its character for good or for ill. In Hinduism and Jainism there is belief in an individual soul which inherits and passes on the load of K., improved or worsened as the case may be; in Buddhism, however, there is no conception of a permanent personality, but the K. is attached in some way to the *khandas* or elements, both physical and mental, which are carried on from birth to birth until the power that holds them together is dispersed in the attainment of Nirvana.

KA'RNAK. Village of modern Egypt, on the E bank of the Nile, which gives its name to the temple of Ammon (constructed by Seti I and Rameses II) round which the major part of ancient city of Thebes was built. An avenue of rams leads to Luxor (q.v.).

KARNA'TAKA. State in the Rep. of India. Formed in 1956, as the state of Mysore, from the former princely states of Mysore and Coorg, and districts transferred from Bombay, and Madras states, it was renamed K. in 1973. The chief rivers are the Vistna, Tungabadhra, and Cauvery. The state is mainly agricultural, crops incl. rice and other grains, groundnuts, cotton and sugar; and there are valuable forests. Industries incl. iron and steel, aircraft, electronic goods, textiles and paper; and minerals incl. gold, manganese and iron. The cap. is Bangalore. Area 191,757 sq.km (74,210 sq.m); pop. (1971) 29,299,000.

KARRI (ka'ri). Giant eucalyptus tree (*E. diversicolor*) which grows in the extreme SW of W Australia. It may reach over 120m (400ft). Exceptionally strong, the timber is used for girders.

KARROO (karōō'). Two areas of semi-desert in Cape Province, S Africa, divided into the Great K. and Little K. by the Swartberg. The two Ks. together have an area of c. 260,000 sq.km (100,000 sq.m).

KARST. Name originally given to the barren limestone region along the NE shores of the Adriatic, and now applied to similar arid scenery throughout the world, e.g. the French Causses and Jura. Caves are a characteristic of K. lands.

KARTING. Miniature motor racing, originating in the USA *c.* 1955, and introduced to Britain in 1959. These elemental racing cars are *c.* 2m (6ft) long and less than a metre (*c.* 2.5ft) wide. Powered by standard production 2-stroke engines, karts reach speeds of *c.* 130km (80m) ph.

KASAI (kahsī'). River which rises in Angola, and forms the frontier with Zaïre before entering Zaïre and joining the Zaïre r., of which it is the chief tributary. It is rich in alluvial diamonds. Length 2,100 km (1,300 m).

KASHGAR. *See* KASHI.

KASHI (kahshē'). Oasis town (formerly Kashgar) in Xinjiang Uygur autonomous region, China, on the Kaxgar He, cap. of K. district which adjoins the Kirghiz and Tadzik SSRs, Afghanistan and Kashmir. It is a trading centre and focus of Moslem culture. Pop. (1973) 180,000.

KASHMIR (kashmēr'). State in the Himalayas, in the N of the Indian subcontinent, bordering Afghanistan and China. It is drained by the upper waters of the Indus and its tributaries Jhelum and Chenab. There are extensive forests and rice, barley, raw silk, fruit and vegetables are produced.

Most of the people are Moslem, but were formerly ruled by a Hindu Maharajah. In 1947 their ruler acceded to India, but fighting developed between pro-Indian and pro-Pakistan factions, helped by Pakistani troops in the W and by Indian troops in the E. India brought the dispute before the UN in 1948, but failing a settlement, open war broke out in 1965. In 1966 Ayub Khan and Shastri signed the Declaration of Tashkent, pledging the restoration of peaceful relations, but in 1971 during the breakaway of Bangladesh from Pakistan there was further fighting in the area, with some adjustment of the cease-fire line.

The area of K. occupied by India forms the state of *Jammu and K.*, of which the winter cap. is Jammu and the summer one Srinagar. Sheikh Abdullah (q.v.) became PM under Indian sovereignty in 1975, and was succeeded in 1983 by his son Farooq Abdullah. Area 138,236 sq.km (85,896 sq.m); pop. (1971) 4,615,000. The area occupied by Pakistan is known as *Azad (Free) K.*, with its admin. HQ at Muzaffarabad. Area 84,000 sq.km (52,196 sq.m); pop. (est. 1971) 1,500,000.

KA'SSEL. City in Hessen, W Germany, dating from the 10th cent. It has engineering and locomotive works, electronic and chemical industries, etc. Pop. (1978) 199,450.

KASSE'M, Abdul Karim (1914-63). Iraqi politician. He became PM of the rep. in 1958, adopting a pro-Soviet policy. He pardoned the leaders of the pro-Egyptian party who tried to assassinate him in 1959, but was executed after the 1963 coup.

KATANGA. *See* SHABA.

KATHIAWAR (kahtiawahr'). Peninsula on the W coast of India. Formerly occupied by a number of princely states, all K. (60,723 sq.km/23,445 sq.m) had been included in Bombay state by 1956, but was transferred to Gujarat in 1960. Gandhi was b. in K. at Porbandar.

KATHMANDU (kahtmahndōō). Cap. of the Himalayan state of Nepal, founded in the 8th cent. It has an airport, and is linked by road with India and Tibet. Pop. (1971) 353,760.

KATMAI (kat'mī). Active volcano in Alaska, USA, 2,046 m (6,715 ft). Its major eruption in 1912 created the Valley of Ten Thousand Smokes.

KATOWICE (katovit'sa). Industrial city in S Poland. Anthracite and iron are mined and there are iron foundries, smelting works, and machine shops. Pop. (1978) 350,000.

KA'TTEGAT. Sea passage between Jutland and Sweden. It is about 240km (150m) long and 135km (85m) at its broadest.

KATYN (katin') **FOREST.** Forest nr Smolensk, USSR, where 4,500 Polish officer POWs captured in the Ger.-Soviet partition of Poland, were shot in the spring of 1940; 10,000 others were killed elsewhere. The crime was disclosed by the Germans in 1943 and attributed to the NKVD, the Russians attribute it to the Germans. A memorial in London (1976), dated 'Katyn 1940', reflects the larger weight of evidence that the Russians were responsible.

KATHMANDU. The shrine of Kal-Bhairab, the god of terror, stands athwart the main street with its pagoda temples. *Photo: Douglas Dickins.*

KATZ, Sir Bernard (1911-). British biophysicist. In 1970 he shared a Nobel prize with Ulf von Euler of Stockholm and Julius Axelrod of Maryland for work on the elucidation of the biochemistry of the transmission and control of signals in the nervous system, which is of vital importance in the search for remedies for nervous and mental disorders.

KAUFFER, Edward McKnight (1890-1954). American artist. He lived in England 1914-41, and was particularly famous for his posters.

KAUFFMANN (kowf'mahn), **Angelica** (1741-1807). Swiss artist. B. in Grisons, she lived in Italy until 1765 and in England 1765-81, where her neo-classical paintings became popular. She became one of the first RAs in 1796 and returned to Rome in 1781.

KAUNAS (kow'nahs). Town and river port in the Lithuanian SSR, on the Niemen, with a univ. (1922). Textiles, chemicals and agricultural machinery are made. It was the cap. of independent Lithuania 1918-40. Pop. (1977) 359,000.

KAUNDA (kah-oon'dah), **Kenneth David** (1924-). Zambian politician. Son of an African missionary, he was ed. at Lubwa Training School where he became a teacher (headmaster 1944-7), and was in 1950 founder-sec. of the Lubwa branch of the African Nat. Congress. In 1958 he founded the breakaway Zambia African Nat. Congress, but this organization was banned as subversive and K. imprisoned. On his release he founded in 1960 the United National Independence Party, became in 1963 Min. of Local Govt, and in 1964 first PM of N Rhodesia, then first pres. of Zambia. From 1973 he introduced one-party rule.

KAURI PINE (kow'ri). A New Zealand conifer (*Agathis australis*), it often reaches 45m (150ft), and yields valuable softwood timber. *Kauri Gum*, the resinous deposit dug up in areas where K. forest existed previously, is used in varnishes.

KAVA (kah'vah). Non-alcoholic, intoxicating beverage prepared from the roots or leaves of a variety of pepper plant, *Piper methysticum*, in the S Pacific islands.

KAWABATA, Yasunari (1899-1972). Japanese novelist. Influenced by the *Tale of Genji*, which he rendered into modern Japanese, his novels are delicate in technique, e.g.

KAVA. In Fiji, at a ceremony among chiefs, the mixer holds the strainer in his hands and squeezes the fluid from it, holding it so that the guest's herald may see the consistency of the brew. The herald advises whether the additional water should be added or not, calling his instructions to the mixer. *Photo: Rob Wright/Camera Press.*

Snow Country (1947) and *A Thousand Cranes* (1952). He was awarded a Nobel prize 1968.

KAWASAKI (kahwahsahkē). City in Japan, between Tokyo and Yokohama. Iron and steel, chemicals and textiles are made, and there is a famous Buddhist shrine. Pop. (1977) 999,000.

KAY, John (1704-after 1764). British inventor. In 1733 he patented his flying-shuttle, intended to speed up the work of the hand-loom-weaver, but was ruined by the litigation necessary to defend his patent, and in 1753 his house at Bury was wrecked by a mob, who feared the use of machinery would cause unemployment. He is said to have d. in poverty in France.

KAYAH STATE. *See* KARENS.

KAYAK (kī'ak). Long, and light, sealskin-covered boat used by Eskimo fishermen and sealers.

KAYE, Danny. Stage-name of American film and stage comedian Daniel Kominski (1913–87). B. in Brooklyn, NY, of Russian extraction, he made such films as *Wonder Man* (1944), *The Secret Life of Walter Mitty* (1946) and *Hans Christian Andersen* (1952). He excelled in lunatic, apparently multi-lingual monologue, etc.

KAZAKH SSR (kahzahk'). Asiatic rep. of the USSR, bounded on the W by the Caspian Sea. Predominantly low-lying, it rises in the E and SE to the mountains of central Asia. Among its products are cotton, grain, and sugar beet; minerals incl. coal, petroleum, iron, copper, and lead. The cap. is Alma-Ata. Area 2,717,300 sq.km (1,049,150 sq.m); pop. (1979) 14,685,000 (of whom 30 per cent were Kazakhs and 51 per cent Russians and Ukrainians).

KAZA'N, Elia (1909-). American stage and film director. B. in Constantinople of Greek extraction, he became an actor, and made his name by his stage direction of *Skin of Our Teeth* (1942), *A Streetcar Named Desire* (1947), *Death of a Salesman* (1949), and *Cat on a Hot Tin Roof* (1955). His films incl. *A Tree Grows in Brooklyn* (1945), *Gentlemen's Agreement* (1948), *A Streetcar Named Desire* (1951), *On the Waterfront* (1954), *East of Eden* (1954), and *The Visitors* (1972).

KAZAN (kahzahn'). Cap. of the Tatar ASSR, USSR, it was until 1552 cap. of a Tatar Khanate, which was conquered by Ivan IV. A transport and commercial centre, with a univ. (1804), it has engineering, oil refining and petrochemical industries, manufactures textiles, and has a large fur trade. The 'Black Virgin of K.', an icon so-called because blackened with age, was removed to Moscow (1612-1917), where the great K. Cathedral was built to house it in 1631: it is now in the USA. Among miracles attributed to its presence were the defeat of the Poles (1612) and of Napoleon (1812) at Moscow. Pop. (1977) 970,000.

KĒ'A. A hawk-like greenish parrot *(Nestor notabilis)* found in NZ, which sometimes strikes the back of sheep, eating the fat round their kidneys. The Maori name imitates its cry.

KEAN, Edmund (1787-1833). British actor. B. in London, son of a strolling actress, he made a sensationally successful London début as Shylock in 1814, and also excelled as Richard III and Othello. His son, **Charles John K.** (1811-68), made his stage début in 1827, and achieved fame as Hamlet in 1838. In 1842 he m. Ellen Tree (1805-80), who assisted his series of Shakespearian revivals as lessee of the Princess's Theatre, London, 1850-9.

KEATON, Buster. Stage-name of American comedian Joseph Frank K. (1896-1966). A sophisticated, deadpan actor, he began his screen career after the F.W.W. as stooge to 'Fattie' Arbuckle in the Keystone Kops comedies, and became one of the great silent-film comedians; his films incl. *Steamboat Bill Jr.* and *The General,* and later *Round the World in 80 Days* (1957).

KEATS, John (1795-1821). British poet. B. in London on 29 or 31 Oct. 1795, the son of a livery-stable keeper, he attended an Enfield private school before being apprenticed to a surgeon and becoming a student at Guy's Hospital (1815-17). He then abandoned medicine for poetry, publishing his first vol. in 1817, and *Endymion* in 1818: the latter was harshly reviewed by the Tory *Blackwood's Magazine* and the *Quarterly,* largely owing to K.'s friendship with the Radical, Leigh Hunt. In 1818 he wrote *Isabella,* and the first version of *Hyperion;* took a walking tour in Scotland which increased his tubercular tendency; and nursed his brother Tom, who d. of the same disease. To 1819 belong 'The Eve of St. Agnes', 'The Eve of St. Mark', his 'Odes', 'Lamia', and the new version of *Hyperion.* In this year also he fell hopelessly in love with Fanny Brawne. In 1820 he pub. a final vol. of poems, and in Sept. sailed for Italy in an effort to recover his health. He d. in Rome. Valuable insight into K.'s poetic development is provided by his *Letters,* pub. in 1848. His work is noted for its rich imagery: he tried to 'load every rift with ore'.

KEBLE (kēbl), **John** (1792-1866). Anglican divine and religious poet. B. in Glos., he was ordained in 1815, and in 1827 pub. the vol. of poems *The Christian Year.* K. was prof. of poetry at Oxford, 1831-41; and his sermon on national apostasy preached in 1833 is taken as the beginning of the Tractarian movement. K. wrote 4 of the *Tracts for the Times,* and from 1835 was vicar of Hursley, in Hants. K. College, Oxford, was founded in 1870.

KECSKEMET (ketch'kemāt). Town in Hungary, SE of Budapest. Situated on the Hungarian plain, it is a trading centre of an agricultural region. Pop. (1977) 94,000.
KEDAH (ked'a). State ruled by a sultan in the Federation of Malaysia. It was transferred by Thailand to Britain in 1909, and was one of the Unfederated Malay States till 1948. The chief products incl. rice, rubber, tapioca, tin, and tungsten. Alor Star is the cap. Area 9,480 sq.km (3,660 sq.m); pop. (1970) 955,000.
KEELING. Another name for the Cocos Islands.
KEELUNG. Port on the N coast of Taiwan, 24km (15m) NE of Taipei, with shipbuilding, chemical and fertilizer industries. Pop. (1973) 334,000.
KEEPER OF THE GREAT SEAL. An officer who had charge of the Great Seal of England. During the Middle Ages the great seal was entrusted to the Chancellor. Later a special Lord Keeper was appointed to take charge of it, but since 1761 the posts of Chancellor and Keeper have been combined.
KEEWATIN (kēwah'tin). Eastern dist. of North-west Territories, Canada, incl. the islands in Hudson and James Bays. The N is an upland plateau, the S low and level, covering the greater part of the Barren Grounds (Arctic prairies) of Canada. There are a number of lakes; trapping for furs is the main occupation. Trading posts incl. Chesterfield Inlet, Eskimo Point, and Coral Harbour, the last with an air base set up during the S.W.W. K. District was formed in 1876, under the administration of Manitoba; it was transferred to Northwest Territories in 1905, and in 1912 lost land S of 60 deg. N to Manitoba and Ontario. Area 590,935 sq.km (228,160 sq.m).
KEFALLINIA (kefalinē'a). Largest of the Ionian Is. (formerly Cephalonia), off the W coast of Greece. It was devastated by an earthquake in 1953 which destroyed the cap. Argostolion. Area 935 sq.km (360 sq.m); pop. (1973) 46,300.
KEFLAVIK. Fishing port in Iceland, 35km (22m) SW of Reykjavik. It has a large international airport, built during the S.W.W. by US forces (who called it Meeks Field). K. became a NATO base in 1951. Pop. (1978) 6,500.
KEIGHLEY (kēth'li). Town in W Yorks, England. Woollens and worsted are made, and there are engineering industries. Haworth, home of the Brontës, is now part of K. Pop. (1972) 55,690.
KEITEL (kīt'el), **Wilhelm** (1882-1946). German field marshal. He was chief of the supreme command from 1938, and signed the unconditional surrender of the German forces at Berlin on 8 May 1945. He was tried at Nuremberg as a war criminal and hanged.
KEKULE (kek'oole), **Friedrich August** (1829-96). German chemist. B. at Darmstadt, he became prof. at Ghent in 1858, and at Bonn in 1865. His theory of molecular structure revolutionized organic chemistry (1858). In 1865 he conceived the novel idea of the ring structure of benzene from, it is said, a dream he had of a serpent catching its tail.
KELA'NTAN. State, ruled by a sultan, in the Federation of Malaysia. It was transferred by Siam to Britain in 1909, and until 1948 was one of the Unfederated Malay States. The cap. is Kota Bharu. The chief products incl. rice, rubber, copra, tin, manganese and gold. Area, 14,882 sq.km (5,746 sq.m); pop. (1970) 684,740.
KELLER, Helen Adams (1880-1968). American author. B. in Alabama, she lost the senses of sight and hearing through an illness when 19 months old, and of necessity remained dumb. Under the tuition of Anne Sullivan Macy, she became able to speak and graduated with honours at Radcliffe College in 1904. She pub. several books.
KELLS, Book of. Illuminated copy of the Gospels in Latin preserved in the library of Trinity College, Dublin. Of outstanding beauty, it was written at the monastery of K. founded by St. Columba.

KELLS. A page from the Book of Kells which shows St Matthew. *Photo: Mansell Collection.*

KELLY, Edward 'Ned' (1854-80). Australian bushranger. The son of an Irish convict, he wounded a constable in 1878 while resisting the arrest of his brother Daniel for horse-stealing. The two brothers escaped and with two confederates carried out bank-robberies on the Victoria-New South Wales border. In 1880 K. was captured and hanged.
KELLY, Grace Patricia (1929–82). American film actress. B. in Philadelphia, she made her film debut in 1951 in *Fourteen Hours*, and later starred in *High Noon* (1952), *The Country Girl* (1954) for which she received an Academy Award, and *High Society* (1955). In 1956 she m. Prince Rainier of Monaco (q.v.).
KELP. The powdery ash of burned seaweeds, a lesser source of iodine, also collectively the large sea-weeds, particularly the *Fucaceae* and *Laminariaceae*.

The brown K. *Macrocystis pyrifera*, abundant in antarctic and sub-antarctic waters, is one of the fastest growing organisms known, reaching 100m (320ft). It is farmed for the alginate industry, rapid surface growth

KELLY. A contemporary engraving of Ned Kelly at the moment of his capture in 1880. He is wearing the home-made armour, which Sidney Nolan depicted so dramatically in his series dealing with the bushranger. *Photo: Mansell Collection.*

allowing cropping several times a year, but is an alien pest in European waters.

KELVIN, William Thomson, 1st baron K. (1824-1907). British physicist. As prof. at Glasgow 1846-99, he was an inspiring teacher and prodigious researcher in all aspects of physical sciences. Pioneer of the absolute scale of temperature, his work on the conservation of energy (1851) led to the second law of thermodynamics. Popularly known for his contributions to telegraphy, he developed stranded cables and sensitive receivers, greatly improving transatlantic communications. Maritime endeavours led to a tide gauge and predictor, an improved compass, and simpler methods for fixing a ship's position at sea. He was pres. of the Royal Soc. 1890-5. *See* CENTIGRADE.

KEMBLE. British family of actors. **Roger K.** (1721-1802), a strolling player and travelling manager, had 12 children, one of whom was Mrs Siddons (q.v.). **John Philip K.** (1757-1823), the 2nd child, made his début in 1776. In 1788 he became manager of Drury Lane, London, and in 1803 of Covent Garden. He retired in 1817 and lived at Lausanne. Strikingly handsome and intelligent, he was among the greatest English tragedians. **Charles K.** (1775-1854), a younger brother of the above, appeared with success in supporting roles 1792-1840. **Frances Anne (Fanny) K.** (1809-93), the elder dau. of Charles K., first appeared as Juliet at Covent Garden in 1829. After 1848 she made a great reputation by her Shakespeare readings.

KE'MEROVO. Coal-mining town in the RSFSR, in W Siberia and centre of Kuznetz coal basin; it has chemical and metallurgical industries. Pop. (1977) 454,000.

KE'MPE, Rudolf (1910-76). German conductor. Noted for the clarity and fidelity of his interpretations, espec. of Richard Strauss and Wagner's *Ring*, he conducted the Royal Philharmonic from 1961 and was musical director of the Munich Philharmonic from 1967.

KEMPIS. *See* THOMAS À KEMPIS.

KENDAL. Town in Cumbria, England, on the r. Kent. Besides traditional industries, such as the making of woollens introduced in the 14th cent. by the Flemings, and agricultural machinery, K. is a centre of varied light industry. Pop. (1972) 21,830.

KE'NDO. Japanese fencing, using bamboo replicas of samurai swords. Masks and padding are worn.

KENILWORTH. Town in Warwickshire, England, famous for its Norman castle, which became a royal residence and was enlarged by John of Gaunt and later by the earl of Leicester, who lavishly entertained Elizabeth I here. It was dismantled after the Civil War; the ruins were given to the nation by the 1st Lord Kenilworth in 1937. Pop. (1971) 15,000.

KENNEDY, John Fitzgerald (1917-63). 35th Pres. of the USA. The 2nd son of Joseph Patrick K. (1888-1969), millionaire and ambassador to the UK 1938-40; he was b. at Brookline, Mass., and ed. at Harvard and the London School of Economics. A back injury received while playing football was worsened by service with the navy in the Pacific, when he was decorated for gallantry after a Japanese destroyer sank the torpedo-boat he commanded. Elected to the House of Representatives as a Democrat in 1947, he became a Senator in 1952, and in 1960 was elected to the presidency, defeating Nixon in one of the closest contests of US history, the first RC and youngest man ever to be elected. Supported by the academics and intellectuals of the 'New Frontier', he pursued liberal domestic policies in civil rights, medical care for the aged, etc., and in foreign affairs adopted a firm but negotiable attitude, notably in the Cuban crisis of 1962 and in the signature of the nuclear test-ban treaty of 1963. Riding in an open car through Dallas 22 Nov. 1963 he was assassinated (allegedly) by Lee Harvey Oswald, an ex-Marine and Marxist sympathiser, who was in turn shot at Dallas police HQ in full view of a television audience by a night-club proprietor, Jack Ruby. He was the author of *Why England Slept* (1940) and *Profiles in Courage* (1956). His wife, Jacqueline Lee Bouvier (1929-), whom he had m. in 1953, was noted for her restoration of the White House to the decor of 1880: after his assassination, she m. in 1968 the Greek shipping millionaire Aristotle Onassis (1906-75), and subsequently entered the world of publishing. The Kennedy children, Caroline (1957-) and John Fitzgerald, Jun. (1960-), became trend-setters for juvenile America.

The John F. Kennedy Center for the Performing Arts incl. an opera house, concert hall, theatre and cinema, and stands beside the Potomac r., Washington. *See also* K. SPACE CENTER.

His younger brother **Robert Francis K.** (1925-68) was ed. at Harvard and Virginia univs., and was admitted to the Mass. State Bar in 1951 and the US Supreme Court in 1955. He was campaign manager for his brother in 1961, and as Attorney-General 1961-4 pursued a 'racket-busting' policy and promoted the Civil Rights Act of 1964. When Johnson preferred Hubert H. Humphrey for the 1964 Vice-Pres. nomination, K. resigned and became Senator for NY. In 1968 he campaigned for the Presidential nomination, but was assassinated by Sirhan Bissara Sirhan, a Jordanian Arab resident in the USA from 1957.

His youngest brother **Edward Moore K.** (1932-) went into legal practice in Boston, joined with 'Bobby' K. in the management of J.F.K.'s pres. campaign, and in 1963 became the youngest US Senator. His career suffered some setback from 1969, following his delay in reporting a car accident: *see* MARTHA'S VINEYARD. He was asst majority leader in the US Senate 1969-71, and in 1980 failed in a bid for the Democratic presential nomination.

The eldest of the 4 brothers, **Joseph Patrick K.,** Jun. (1915-44), a naval airman, was killed in action in the S.W.W.

KENNEDY. The links between the Kennedy brothers were close. Here (from left to right) Robert, Edward and John are seen in consultation. *Photo: Courtesy of USIS.*

KENNEDY Space Center, John F. Space-flight experimental centre (1962) on Cape Canaveral (known as Cape K. 1963-73, when it reverted to the traditional name), on the Atlantic coast of Florida, 367km (228m) N of Miami. It is separated from the mainland by Banana r., Merritt is., and Indian r. The first US unmanned space flight was made from here 31 Jan. 1958, and the first manned flight to land on the Moon 16 July 1969.

KENNELLY, A. E. (1861-1939). American engineer. An assistant of Edison and later prof. at Harvard, he verified the existence of an ionized layer in the upper atmosphere in 1902, shortly before it had been predicted by Heaviside (q.v.). *See* IONOSPHERE.

KENNELLY-HEAVISIDE LAYER. The lower regions of the ionosphere (q.v.) which refract radio waves (*see line illus. under* EARTH), allowing their reception round the surface of the earth. The K.-H.L. approaches the Earth by day, and recedes from it at night.

KENNETH I (d. *c.* 858). King of Scotland. Traditionally, K. McAlpin is regarded as the founder of the Scottish kingdom by his final defeat of the Picts *c.* 844, after which he reigned until his death.

KENSINGTON and CHELSEA, Royal Bor. of. Bor. of Greater London which contains many of London's major museums - Natural History section of the British Museum, Science Museum, Victoria and Albert Museum, and the Commonwealth Institute. It also incl. K. Palace, although most of K. Gardens in which it stands are in Westminster; this became a royal residence in the time of William III and Queen Victoria was born here. Holland House, last of the great country mansions once surrounding London, was destroyed in an air raid in 1940: a youth hostel stands on the site and the grounds are a public park. Kensal Green Cemetery in N Kensington is famous as the resting-place of Wilkie Collins, Cruikshank, Leigh Hunt, Cardinal Manning, Thackeray and Trollope. Pop. (1972) 183,230. *See* CHELSEA.

KENT, Alexander. *See* REEMAN, Douglas.

KENT, Edward George Alexander Edmund, 2nd duke of (1935-). British prince, son of George (1902-42), 4th son of George V, who was cr. duke of K. just before his m. in 1934 to Princess Marina of Denmark and Greece (1906-68). The second duke, who succeeded when his father was killed in an air crash on active service with the RAF, was ed. at Eton and Sandhurst, and then commissioned in the Royal Scots Greys. In 1961 he m. Katharine Worsley (1933-) and his heir is George (1962-), earl of St Andrews.

His brother, Prince Michael (1942-) became an officer with the Hussars in 1962. His sister, Princess Alexandra (1936-), m. in 1963 Angus Ogilvy, son of the 12th earl of Airlie; they have two children, James (1964-) and Marina (1966-).

KENT, William (1685-1748). British landscape gardener, influential in freeing the art from formalism. B. in Herts, he followed the landscapes of Claude and Poussin, with a fondness for classic temples.

KENT and STRATHEARN, Edward Augustus, duke of (1767-1820). British general. The 4th son of George III, he m. Victoria Mary Louisa (1786-1861), widow of the Prince of Leiningen, in 1818, by whom he had one child, the future Queen Victoria.

KENT. Co. of SE England. Running NW to SE across the county are the N Downs. S of them is the Weald, agricultural land with orchards, hop fields, market gardens, etc. NE Kent produces fruit and wheat. K. is often called the 'Garden of England'. Romney Marsh in the S is celebrated for its sheep. Industrial K. in the NW has large cement and paper-making industries. The principal rivers are the Darent, Medway, and Stour. Inland from Deal is an extensive coalfield.

The admin. HQ is Maidstone; other important towns are Canterbury, Rochester, Chatham, Gravesend, Sheerness, and four of the Cinque Ports (Dover, Sandwich, New Romney, and Hythe). Coastal holiday resorts incl. Folkestone, Margate and Ramsgate. In popular speech, a 'man of K.' hails from E of the Medway, and a 'Kentish man' from the western part of the co. The Univ. of Kent at Canterbury was founded in 1965. Area 3,730 sq.km (1,440 sq.m); pop. (1978) 1,449,000.

KENTIGERN, St (*c.* AD 518-603), also called 'Mungo', a nickname meaning 'dear friend'. First bishop of Glasgow, he was b. at Culross. The pagans forced him to flee to Wales, where he founded the monastery of St Asaph. In 573 he returned to Glasgow, whose cathedral he founded.

KENT. The familiar cones of the old oast houses, used for drying the hops, now part of a private home, Sheerland House. *Photo: J. Allan Cash.*

KENTU'CKY. South-central state of the USA, called the 'Blue Grass State' because of the richness of the 'blue grass' area. There are *c.* 1,300 km (800m) of river boundary, incl. the Ohio in the N. Agriculture (tobacco, maize and soya bean) and mining, incl. coal, petroleum and nat. gas, surpass industrial production, although this incl. tobacco products and food processing, and varied others developing. The cap. is Frankfort; other towns incl. Louisville, Covington and Lexington, famous for its trotting races. Attractive to tourists are the Land Between the Lakes (an isthmus between the man-made K. Lake and Lake Barkley), part of the TVA development; Mammoth Cave (discovered 1799), and the birthplace of Lincoln. Fort Knox (q.v.) is also in the state. Area 104,623 sq.km (40,395 sq.m); pop. (1970) 3,219,311.

KĒ'NYA. Country in E Africa with a coastline on the Indian Ocean; it rises from a coastal plain to a broad high plateau rising from 1,000 to 3,000 m (3,000-10,000 ft), crossed by the Rift Valley. The chief river is the Tana, navigable for about 240km (150m) from its mouth. The climate is tropical on the coastal plain, warm temperate in the highlands. Products incl. coffee, tea, maize, wheat, cotton, sisal, tobacco, rice, and timber from *c.* 8,000 sq.km (3,000 sq.m) of forests. There are also beef and dairy cattle, with hide and skin by-products. Minerals incl. cement, soda ash and fluorite. The development of a varied industry is being encouraged using local produce, e.g. cotton textiles, meat and vegetable products. There is also a luxury trade in fruit, flowers and vegetables air-freighted to Europe. Tourism is very important, with game parks and the Malindini Marine Reserve, and the prehistoric sites (Olduvai Gorge and Lake Rudolf: *see* LEAKEY). The cap. is Nairobi; and the chief port Mombasa. Area 582,600 sq.km (224,960 sq.m); pop. (1977) 14,340,000. The largest tribal group is the Kikuyu. Besides tribal religions there is a large Christian minority, and a number of Moslems. The language is Swahili, with English reintroduced as a practical alternative from 1975. M.U.: Kenya shilling.

K. became a Brit. protectorate in 1895 and a crown colony in 1920. Nationalist agitation ensued from 1946 (*see* MAU-MAU), and following independence in 1963, K. became a rep. within the Commonwealth. The first pres. was Jomo Kenyatta (q.v.), and there is also a single-chambered Nat. Assembly. A one-party state from 1964, K. has numerous candidates competing for parliamentary seats, which ensures a democratic element, within the controlling K. African Nat. Union (KANU). Tribal tension exists, e.g. the assassination of Tom Mboya (q.v.) a Luo, by a member of the dominant Kikuyu. Africanization led to the departure of many Asians 1967-8, large numbers going to Britain. In 1978 vice-pres. Daniel Arap Moi succeeded Kenyatta and was re-elected 1979 and 1983.

KENYA. A view over the Great Rift Valley, the stepped terraces in the distance, showing the kind of country where primitive man once wandered, whose remains have been so dramatically brought to light by the Leakeys. *Photo: J. Allan Cash.*

KENYA, Mt. Extinct volcano from which K. takes its name (5,200 m/17,058 ft); it was first climbed by Sir Halford Mackinder in 1899.

KENYA'TTA, Jomo. Name assumed by Kenya politician Kamau Ngengi (*c.* 1889-1978), *kenyatta* meaning 'beaded belt'. A member of the Kikuyu tribe, he was b. nr Fort Hall, son of a poor farmer and grandson of a magician. Brought up at a Church of Scotland mission, he joined the Kikuyu Central Assocn, devoted to recovery of Kikuyu lands from white settlers, of which he became pres. He spent some years in Britain, and returning to Kenya in 1946 as pres. of the Kenya African Union (successor to the banned KCA), he was in 1953 sentenced to 7 yrs for his management of Mau-Mau (q.v.), though some doubt has been cast on his complicity. Released to exile in N Kenya in 1958, he was allowed to return to Kikuyuland in 1961 and in 1963 became PM (also pres. from 1964) of independent Kenya. His policy is summarized by his slogans 'Uhuru na Moja' (Freedom and Unity) and 'Harambee' (Let's get going), and entailed collaboration with the whites to ensure unbroken economic progress.

KENYON, Dame Kathleen (1906-78). British archaeologist. Her excavations at Jericho showed that the double walls previously associated with Joshua belonged to an earlier period and that a Neolithic settlement had been estab. at J. as early as *c.* 6800 BC.

KEPLER, Johann (1571-1630). German astronomer. B. in Württemberg, he became Tycho Brahe's assistant in 1600 and succeeded him as imperial mathematician in

KENYATTA. A meeting between Kenya's president, and Tanzanian president, Julius Nyerere. *Photo: Popperfoto.*

1601. In his last years he was astrologer to Wallenstein. He d. at Ratisbon.

As the discoverer of the 3 laws of planetary motion that bear his name, K. ranks as one of the founders of modern astronomy. The laws are: (1) The orbit of each planet is an ellipse with the Sun at one of the foci. (2) The radius vector of each planet describes equal areas in equal times. (3) The squares of the periods of the planets are proportional to the cubes of their mean distances from the Sun.

KE'RALA. State of the Rep. of India formed in 1956 from the former princely states of Travancore and Cochin (except for a small area in the E, transferred to Tamil Nadu), plus a small area formerly in S Tamil Nadu. K. is noteworthy as the most literate state in India - more than 50 per cent of men, about a third of women. The name was that of an ancient kingdom in this area which came to an end in 1310 when it was conquered by Mohammedan invaders. Tea, spices, coconuts, oilseeds, and rice are grown; there are extensive mineral deposits (white clay, mica, graphite, lignite, etc.), and industry is developing under govt encouragement. Political instability arises from strong religious and caste divisions. Area 38,855 sq.km (15,000 sq.m); pop. (1971) 21,347,000.

KE'RBELA. Holy city of the Shi'ite Moslems, 96 km (60m) SW of Baghdad, Iraq, on the site of the battlefield where Husein, son of Ali and Fatima, was killed in AD 680 while defending his succession to the Khalifate. His tomb in the city is visited every year by many pilgrims. Pop. (1972) 100,000.

KERCH (kārch). Port in the Crimea, Ukraine SSR, at the E end of K. peninsula, an important iron-producing area. Built on the site of an ancient Greek settlement, K. became Russian in 1783. Pop. (1977) 154,000.

KERE'N. Trading town in Eritrea, Ethiopia, NW of Asmara. Keypoint of the Italian defence line in the S.W.W., it fell to the British Mar. 1941. Pop. 10,000.

KERE'NSKY, Alexander Feodorovich (1881-1970). Russian politician. After holding several ministerial posts, he was premier of the second provisional govt, before its collapse in Nov. 1917, during the Bolshevik revolution. He lived in the USA from 1918.

KERGUELEN (ker'gelen) **ISLANDS.** Volcanic archipelago in the Indian Ocean, part of the French Southern and Antarctic Terrs. Uninhabited except for scientists, they produce abundant birdlife and a unique wild cabbage containing a pungent oil.

KERKYRA. Greek form of CORFU.

KERMA'DEC ISLANDS. Volcanic group, a dependency of NZ, 965km (600m) NE of Auckland. Area 34 sq.km (13 sq.m); uninhabited, except for a met. station on Raoul, the largest is.

KERMAN (kārmahn'). Town in SE Iran, a road centre. Shawls and carpets are made. Pop. (1970) 85,400.

KERMANSHA'H. Town of Iran, cap. of Kermanshahan prov., which is on the borders of Iraq. The prov. is very fertile and inhabited mainly by Kurds. K. is noted for its carpets and weaving, there is also a large petroleum refinery. Pop. (1970) 187,900.

KERN, Jerome (1885-1945). American song-writer. He composed the popular operetta, *Show Boat* (1927), from which comes the song 'Ol' Man River'.

KERNOW (ker'nō). Celtic name for Cornwall.

KE'ROSĒNE. Mineral oil, a mixture of liquid hydrocarbons of sp. gr. about 0.78 to 0.83 and flash point below 67°C, prepared by distillation from petroleum. It is used for illumination and heating, and in the UK is known as 'paraffin oil'.

KE'ROUAC, Jack (1923-69). American novelist. Of French-Canadian extraction, he was b. in Lowell, Mass., and by his football prowess was set for a univ. career. Instead he became a merchant seaman, then wandered the US and Mexico making a living by a miscellany of jobs. His books are the continuing Odyssey of Jack Duluoz, king of the Beatniks, and incl. *On the Road* (1958), *The Dharma Bums* (1959), and *Big Sur* (1963), which shows the crack-up of his hero against a background of modern America, with its neonlit superhighways.

KERRY. Co. in the prov. of Munster, Rep. of Ireland. Its W coastline is deeply indented. The N part is low-lying, but in the S occur the highest mts. in Ireland; Macgillycuddy's Reeks (q.v.). There are many rivers and lakes, incl. the famous lakes of Killarney. There is some engineering, manufacture of woollens, shoes and cutlery, but tourism is the most important industry. Tralee is the co. town. Area 4,701 sq.km (1,815 sq.m); pop. (1971) 112,770.

KESSELRING, Albert (1885-1960). German field marshal. He commanded the Luftwaffe during the invasions of Poland and the Low Countries, 1939-40, and in the early stages of the Battle of Britain. Later he served under Rommel in N Africa, took command in Italy in 1943, and was appointed C-in-C on the western front in March 1945. His death sentence for war crimes (1947) was commuted to imprisonment; he was released 1952.

KE'STĒVEN, Parts of. SW area of Lincs, England, an admin. unit with co. offices at Sleaford 1888-1974, when K. was merged in Lincs.

KESTREL. Bird (*Falco tinnunculus*) in the family Falconidae, which breeds in the British Is. Its head and tail are bluish-grey, and its back is a light chestnut-brown with black spots.

KESWICK (kez'ik). Market town and tourist centre in Cumbria, England, nr Derwentwater. It was the home of Coleridge and Southey, and there is an annual *K. Convention* (from 1875) of Evangelical Christians. Pop. (1971) 4,500.

KETCH, Jack (d. 1686). English executioner. He took over the post *c.* 1663, and carried out the executions of

KESTREL. Kestrels are often trained, as here (note the jesses on each ankle to which the leash is fastened), for falconry. *Photo: Heather Angel.*

Lord Russell in 1683 and Monmouth in 1685. His name became a common nickname for an executioner.

KETONES. Organic compounds containing the carbonyl group CO, differentiated from aldehydes by uniting to 2 atoms of carbon instead of one of carbon and one of hydrogen. They are liquids or low-melting-point solids, slightly soluble in water, and form derivatives in acid solutions.

KETTERING. Town in Northants, England, nr the Ise, 21km (13m) NE of Northampton. Industries incl. printing machinery and footwear. Pop. (1974) 68,980.

KEW. Part of the bor. of Richmond-upon-Thames, in Greater London, containing Kew Palace, once a royal residence, and the Royal Botanic Gardens, which were opened to the public in 1841. In 1964 additional grounds were acquired at Wakehurst Place, Ardingly, Sussex. The gardens not only exhibit unusual plants but serve as a 'plant bank', safeguarding against the extinction of species, or the exhaustion of the potential of cultivated species, when it is necessary to go back to the wild. *See also* PUBLIC RECORD OFFICE.

KEY, Francis Scott (1779-1843). American author of 'The Star-Spangled Banner'. A lawyer by profession, he wrote the song while Fort McHenry was being defended against the British in 1814. It is (since 1931) the national anthem of the USA.

KEYNES (kānz), **John Maynard,** 1st baron (1883-1946). British economist. B. at Cambridge, he was ed. at King's Coll., Cambridge, of which he became a Fellow. He held a Treasury appointment during the F.W.W., and took part in the peace conference as chief Treasury representative, but resigned in protest against the financial terms of the treaty. He justified his action in *The Economic Consequences of the Peace* (1919). His later economic works, e.g. *The General Theory of Employment, Interest, and Money* (1936), aroused much controversy by their proposals to prevent crises by control of credit and currency. **Keynesian Economics** is the reverse of Monetarism (q.v.), and advocates that a fall in national income, lack of demand for goods, and rising unemployment should be countered by increased govt. expenditure to stimulate the economy, popularly 'spending one's way out of recession'. Keynes led the British delegation at the Bretton Woods Conference, and his theories were widely accepted in the aftermath of the S.W.W., but developed flaws in the new economic climate of the 1970s when recession was combined with inflation.

KEY WEST. Town at the tip of the Florida peninsula, USA. In 1967 it became the first in America to take all its fresh water from the sea. As a tourist resort, it was popularized by Hemingway. Pop. (1970) 29,300.

KGB. The Russian secret police, the *Komitet Gosudarstvennoye Bezhopaznosti* (Committee of State Security), in control of frontier and general security, and the forced labour system. Earlier names for the secret police were the Okhrana under the Tsars; Cheka (q.v.) 1918-23; GPU or OGPU *(Obedinyonnoye Gosudarstvennoye Polititcheskoye Upravleniye)* 1923-34; NKVD *(Narodny Komisariat Vnutrennykh Del)* 1934-46; and MVD (q.v.) 1946-53. Smersh (q.v.) was a sub-section. The HQ is 2 Dzerzhinsky Square, Moscow, and the Lubyanka Prison is located behind it: there are admin. offices in every major town.

KHABARO'VSK. Town on the r. Amur, cap. of K. Territory in the far E of the RSFSR. It has refineries for petroleum from Sakhalin, saw mills and flour mills, meat packing, and other industries. Pop. (1977) 524,000.

KHACHATURIAN (kachatyūr'ēan), **Aram Ilyich** (1903-78). Russian composer. B. in Tiflis, he studied under Myaskovsky, and used folk themes strikingly, espec. in the ballets *Gayaneh* (1942: incl. the 'Sabre Dance') and *Spartacus,* which provided theme music for the television series *The Onedin Line.*

KHAKI (kah'ki). Originally the sand- or dust-coloured uniforms worn by British and native troops in India *c.* 1850; recognized particularly in the S African War as useful neutral camouflage, and adopted as standard throughout the world.

KHA'LIFA, The, or **Abdullah el Taaisha** (1846-99). Sudanese dervish leader. Succeeding the Mahdi as ruler of the Sudan in 1885, he was defeated by Kitchener at Omdurman in 1898; the K. escaped, but was killed at Kordofan.

KHAMA (kah'mah), **Sir Seretse** (1921-80). Botswana statesman. Son of the Bamangwato chief Sekoma II (d. 1925), he studied law in Britain and m. an Englishwoman, Ruth Williams. This m. was strongly condemned by his uncle Tshekedi K., regent during his minority, as contrary to tribal custom, and Seretse K. was banished in 1950, returning in 1956 on his renunciation of any claim to the chieftaincy, but in 1965 he became PM of Bechuanaland, and was pres. of the new rep. of Botswana 1966-80.

KHA'MSIN (Arabic 'fifty'). Hot, dry, southerly winds which originate in the Sahara and blow across N Egypt during the spring and summer. The name is derived from the supposed average duration of the winds, i.e. 50 days.

KHAN, Liaquat Ali (1895-1951). Indian statesman. Ed. at Allahabad and Oxford, he studied law, and in 1923 joined the Muslim League. He was deputy leader of the Muslim League Party 1941-7, and in 1947 became first PM of Pakistan. He was assassinated by a Muslim fanatic.

KHA'RGA. Oasis in the Western Desert of Egypt. Known to the Romans, it became in 1960 HQ of the New Valley irrigation scheme. An area twice the size of Italy is being reclaimed for agriculture by use of newly located natural underground reservoirs.

KHA'RKOV. Industrial city of the Ukrainian SSR, cap. of K. Region, 400km (250m) E of Kiev. It is an important railway junction, a great engineering centre, and has a large tractor-making plant. K., founded in 1654, has a univ. and an airport. In recent years coal reserves have been discovered nearby. Pop. (1977) 1,405,000.

KHARTOUM (-toom′). Cap. and trading centre of the Rep. of Sudan, at the junction of the Blue and White Nile. K. was founded in 1830 by Mehemet Ali (q.v.). General Gordon (q.v.) was killed at K. by the Mahdist rebels in 1885. A new city was built after the site was recaptured by the British under Kitchener in 1898. Besides K. Univ., there is also a branch of Cairo Univ. Pop. (1973) 334,000, and of K. North, across the Blue Nile, 150,000.

KHATYN (katin′). Village NE of Minsk, USSR, with a memorial to the many Byelorussian villages destroyed by the Germans in the S.W.W., of which K. was one.

KHAZARS (kazahz′). People of Turkish origin from central Asia who formed a buffer state in the 7-12th cents. AD between the Arabs and the Byzantine Empire, and later between the Byzantine Empire and subsequent Russian pressure from the N. They were converted to Judaism *c.* AD 740, and disappeared from history *c.* 1245, but it has been suggested that they were the ancestors of the E European Jews, themselves the ancestors of the majority of modern Jewry, and hence actually of Aryan and not Semitic origin.

KHEDIVE (kedēv′). Title granted by the sultan of Turkey in 1867 to his viceroy in Egypt, and held by the latter's successors until 1914.

KHERSO′N. Town on the Dnieper r., Ukraine SSR, built by Potemkin as a naval harbour, cap. of K. region. Its industries incl. soap and tobacco manufacture and brewing. Pop. (1977) 324,000.

KHE SANH (kā san). US Marine outpost nr the Laotian border and just S of the demilitarized zone in N Vietnam. Garrisoned by 4,000 Marines, it was under attack by 20,000 N Vietnamese 21 Jan.-7 April 1968.

KHIVA (khē′vah). Town in Uzbek SSR, USSR, cap. of K. khanate (modern Khorezm) till its submission to Russia in 1873. Carpets and textiles are made. Pop. (1970) 25,000.

KHMER REPUBLIC. *See* KAMPUCHEA.

KHŌ′MEINI, Ayatollah Ruhollah (1900-). Iranian Shi'ite Moslem leader. B. in Khomein, central Iran, he opposed the Shah's social and economic programme and was exiled from 1964. He returned when the Shah left the country in 1979, and estab. an Islamic rep. of a fundamentalist type.

KHORA′NA, Har Gobind (1922-). American biochemist. B. in India, and ed. at the Univ. of Punjab and Liverpool Univ., he later worked at Wisconsin Univ., and from 1970 at the Massachusetts Inst. of Technology. In 1968 he shared a Nobel prize for research on the 'interpretation of the genetic code and its function in protein synthesis', and in 1976 led the team which first synthesized a biologically active gene.

KHORRAMSHAHR′. Port and oil-refining centre in Iran, on the Shatt al Arab and linked by bridge with the is. of Abadan. It was captured by Iraqi troops in 1980. Pop. (1975) 135,000.

KHRUSHCHEV (krooshchov′), **Nikita Sergeyevich** (1894-1971). Soviet statesman. B. nr Kursk, the son of a miner, he fought in the Civil War, and in the S.W.W. organized the guerrilla defence of his native Ukraine. As Sec. Gen. of the CCCP (1953-64), he denounced Stalinism in a secret session of the Soviet Communist Party in Feb. 1956. Many victims of the purges of the 1930s were either released or posthumously rehabilitated, but when Hungary revolted in Oct. against Soviet domination, there was immediate Soviet intervention. In 1958 K. succeeded Bulganin as Chairman of the Council of Ministers (PM), and maintained a policy of peaceful co-existence and competition with capitalism, the space achievements of the USSR being outstanding under his leadership. His attitude in foreign policy, however, conflicted with that of China, so that he developed a personal feud with Mao Tse-tung, and when he hastily despatched missiles to Cuba US pressure compelled their withdrawal. He was consequently compelled to resign in 1964, although by 1965 his reputation was to some extent officially restored.

KHOMEINI. The Ayatollah Khomeini giving his final press conference in Paris before returning to Iran to establish the new Islamic republic. *Photo: Keystone.*

KHUFU (koo′foo) (fl. *c.* 3000 BC). Egyptian king of Memphis, who built the largest of the Pyramids. The Gk form of K. is Cheops.

KHUZESTAN (koo′zestahn′). SW prov. of Iran, which incl. the chief Iranian oil resources. Towns incl. Ahwaz (cap.), and the ports of Abadan and Khorramshahr. *See* ARABISTAN.

KHYBER (kīber) **PASS.** A defile 53km (33m) through the mountain range which separates Pakistan from Afghanistan. The K.P. was used by Mahmud of Ghazni, Baber, Nadir Shah, and other invaders of India. The present road was constructed by the British during the Afghan Wars.

KIANGSI. *See* JIANGXI.

KIANGSU. *See* JIANGSU.

KIBBU′TZ. Israeli communal collective settlement, with collective ownership of *all* property and earnings and collective organization of work; a modified version, the *Moshav Shitufi,* is similar to the Collective Farms (q.v.) of Soviet Russia. Other Israeli co-operative rural settlements incl. the *Moshav Ovdim* which has equal opportunity, and the similar but less strict *Moshav* settlement.

KIDD, William (*c.* 1645-1701). British pirate. B. in Greenock, he settled in New York. In 1696 he was commissioned by the Governor of New York to suppress pirates, but he became a pirate himself. Arrested in 1699, he was taken to England and hanged.

KIDDERMINSTER. Market town in Hereford and Worcester, England, on the Stour. It has been famous for carpets since *c.* 1735. Pop. (1972) 48,670.

KIDNAPPING. Originally in the 17th cent. the stealing of people, usually young, to work in the colonial plantations as indentured labour, from which they could be rescued by the payment of a 'ransome'. The offence is usually committed in modern times for money, but in the 1970s and 1980s frequently with an ideological background. *See* LINDBERGH.

KIDNEYS. A pair of reddish-brown organs *c.* 11cm (4.5in) by 4cm (1.5in), situated on the rear wall of the abdomen, which are responsible for water regulation, excretion of waste products and maintaining the homeostasis of the blood. Each K. consists of a number of long tubules; the outer parts filter the aqueous components of blood, and the inner parts selectively reabsorb vital elements, leaving waste products in the remaining fluid (urine) which is collected at the ends of the ducts and passed through the ureter to the bladder. The action of the Ks. is vital to life, although if one is removed, e.g. because of a tumour, the other enlarges to take over its function. A patient with 2 defective Ks. may continue near-normal life with the aid of a K. machine or continuous ambulatory peritoneal dialysis (q.v.), in which the peritoneal membrane takes over K. function with the aid of a plastic bag of dialysis solution, or may receive a K. transplant. Ultrasonics may be used for the painless dispersal of K. stones without surgery.

KIEL (kēl). Port of W Germany on the Baltic 88km (55m) N of Hamburg; cap. of Land Schleswig-Holstein. There are shipbuilding and engineering industries and fisheries. K. Week in June is the Ger. equivalent of Cowes for yachtsmen. The *K. Canal* (97km/60m) opened 1895, links the North Sea with the Baltic. Pop. (1978) 256,500.

KIELCE (kē-elt'se). City in central Poland, NE of Krakow, a rail junction with chemical and metallurgical industries. Pop. (1978) 162,000.

KIERKEGAARD (kye'rkegawr), **Soren Aabye** (1813-55). Danish philosopher. B. in Copenhagen, where he spent most of his life, he was the son of a Jewish merchant, but was converted to Christianity in 1838, although he became hostile to the estab. Church, and his beliefs caused much controversy. His concept of man as an isolated individual before God is largely the basis of Existentialism (q.v.). He regarded sin as self-alienation, the cause of which is 'dread', and discarded the Bible and Reason as proof of God's existence, which he saw only in man's personal relationship with God. Very prolific, he pub. his first important work *Either-Or* in 1843, and notable later are *Concept of Dread* (1844) and *Post-script* (1846), which summed up much of his earlier writings. His many pseudonyms were sometimes used to argue with himself.

KIEV (kē-ef'). Cap. of the Ukrainian SSR, the third largest city of the USSR. Situated at the junction of the Dnieper with the Desna, K. is a great route focus and marketing centre. It has a univ., an airport and a wide range of industries. The Slav domination of Russia began with the rise of K., the 'mother of Russian cities', founded in the 5th cent. and many times conquered and re-conquered. It was also the original seat of Christianity in Russia (988). Pop. (1977) 2,079,000.

KIERKEGAARD. A portrait sketched by his cousin, Christian Kierkegaard. *Photo: Courtesy of the Royal Danish Ministry of Foreign Affairs.*

KIGALI (kigah'li). Cap. of Rwanda, on the hilly central plateau. Pop. (1977) 90,000.

KIGŌ'MA. Town and port on the E shore of Lake Tanganyika, Tanzania, linked by rail with Dar-es-Salaam. Pop. (1970) 10,000.

KILDARE (kildār'). Co. of Leinster prov., Rep. of Ireland, S of Meath. The north is wet and boggy, but in the E and W oats, barley, and potatoes, etc., are grown and cattle are reared. Area 1,694 sq.km (654 sq.m); pop. (1971) 71,980. The co. town is K., which is the centre for the Irish horse-breeding industry. Pop. (1971) 3,750.

KILIMA-NJARO (kilimanjah'rō). *See* TANZANIA.

KILKE'NNY. Co. in Leinster prov., Rep. of Ireland, E of Tipperary. K. is mainly devoted to agriculture, but in the N coal is worked. Area 2,061 sq.km (796 sq.m); Pop. (1971) 61,470. The co. town is K., on the r. Nore. Pop. (1971) 9,838.

KILLA'RNEY. Market town of co. Kerry, Rep. of Ireland, the most famous beauty spot in Ireland. To the SW lie Macgillycuddy's Reeks (q.v.) and the K. lakes. Pop. (1971) 6,500.

KILLER-WHALE. Cetacean (*Orcinus orca*), also called the grampus, one of the Delphinidae, or dolphin family. Black above and white beneath, it breeds in the Arctic and is the sole member of its order to feed on other dolphins and whales, seals, etc.

KILMA'RNOCK. Town in Strathclyde region, Scotland, 32km (20m) SW of Glasgow. It was here that Burns' first book of poems was published in 1786. Pop. (1973) 50,175.

KILMUI'R, David Patrick Maxwell Fyfe, 1st earl K. (1900-67). British lawyer and Cons. politician. Called to the Bar in 1922, he became an MP in 1935 and was Solicitor-Gen. 1942-5 and Attorney-Gen. in 1945 during the Churchill govts. At the Nuremberg trials he was deputy to Sir Hartley Shawcross and for most of the time conducted the British prosecution. He was Home Sec. 1951-4 and Lord Chancellor 1954-62. In 1954 he was created visct and in 1962 earl.

KILO. Prefix denoting in the metric system 1,000 units. *Kilogram* is a unit of weight equal to 1,000 grams or 2.205 lb. *Kilometre* is a unit of length equal to 3,280.89 ft (approx. ⅝ of a mile). *Kiloton* is a unit of explosive force equivalent to 1,000 tons of TNT used in describing atom bombs. *Kilowatt* is a unit of power equal to about 1⅓ horsepower.

KILVERT, Francis (1840-79). British clergyman and diarist. Unpub. until 1938-9, his *Diary: 1870-79* is a useful record of social life.

KI'MBERLEY. Diamond-mining town in Cape Prov., S Africa, 153km (95m) NW of Bloemfontein. It was founded in 1871 and named after the 1st earl of K. who, as Sec. of State for the Colonies, placed the mines at that time under British protection; De Beers Consolidated Mines secured control of the mines in 1887. Pop. (1970) 104,000, of whom 29,400 are white. Also an area in Western Australia, named after the same man, where diamonds were found 1978-9.

KIM IL SUNG (kim'-il-soong') (1912-). N Korean marshal and statesman. He became PM in 1948, and pres. in 1972, but retained the presidency of the Communist Workers' Party; he has campaigned constantly for the reunification of Korea. His son Kim Chong Il (1942-) was in 1980 being groomed as his successor.

KIMŌ'NŌ. Traditional costume of Japanese women, still retained for formal wear - the *homongi* or 'visiting dress'. For the finest Ks. a rectangular piece of pure silk (*c.* 11m/36ft×0.5m/1.5ft.) is cut into 7 pieces for tailoring, the brilliant colouring of the design (which must match perfectly over the seams and for which flowers are the favourite motif) then being painted by hand and enhanced by embroidery or gilding. The accompanying *obi* or sash is also embroidered.

KINCA'RDINESHIRE. Former co. of E Scotland, merged in 1975 in Grampian region. The area is chiefly agricultural, with a large fishing industry at Stonehaven, the former co. town.

KĪNE'TICS. Branch of dynamics dealing with the action of forces producing or changing the motion of a real body, as distinguished from kinematics, which deals with motion without reference to force or mass.

KING, Martin Luther (1929-68). American Negro leader. B. in Atlanta, Georgia, son of a Baptist minister, he also became a pastor. Preaching non-violence - he won the 1964 Nobel peace prize - he campaigned to end segregation. Riots across USA followed his being shot, and a white escaped convict, James Earl Ray, was arrested in England, extradited, and sentenced to 99 years' gaol in 1969.

KING, William Lyon Mackenzie (1874-1950). Canadian Lib. statesman. B. in Ontario, he was PM 1921-30 (excl. June-Sept. 1926) and 1935-48. He took part in the 1926 Imperial Conference which recognized the Dominion's equal status with Britain, and his proposals, that self-governing countries maintain close co-operation but be linked only by allegiance to the Crown, were incl. in the Statute of Westminster. He received the OM in 1947.

KING CRAB. Marine animal (*Limulus*) in the class Arachnida. The upper side of its body is entirely covered by a shell and it has a long spine-like tail. It is unable to swim and burrows in the sand, feeding on worms. K.Cs. measure up to 60cm (2ft).

KINGCUP. Name given to several flowers of the Ranunculaceae family, particularly the buttercup and the marsh marigold.

KINGFISHER. European bird (*Alcedo atthis*) also found in parts of N Africa and Asia. The plumage is brilliant blue-green on the back and chestnut beneath. Ks. feed upon fish and aquatic insects, etc. The nest is made of fish-bones in a hole in a river bank. Australia has a number of species incl. the kookaburra (q.v.), one of the forest Ks. or Dacelonidae.

KING'S/QUEEN'S COUNSEL. In England, barristers appointed to senior rank by the Lord Chancellor and being 'called within the Bar'. They wear silk, as opposed to stuff gowns, and take precedence over the junior Bar.

KING'S COUNTY. Older name of OFFALY.

KING'S EVIL. The popular name in England for scrofula, which disease was supposed to be curable by the touch of the sovereign.

KINGSLEY, Charles (1819-75). British Anglican churchman and author. B. at Holne, Devon, he became curate and then rector of Eversley, Hants (1842-75). His press articles and his campaigning novels *Yeast* (1848), and *Alton Locke* (1850), earned him the title of the 'Chartist clergyman'. His later books incl. *Hypatia* (1851), *Westward Ho!* (1855), a tale of Elizabethan seamen, and *Hereward the Wake* (1866): and for children *The Heroes* (1856) and *The Water-Babies* (1863). He was prof. of modern history at Cambridge 1860-9, and subsequently canon of Chester, and from 1873 of Westminster. In 1864 his controversy with J. H. Newman prompted the latter's *Apologia* (1864). His brother **Henry K.** (1830-76), novelist, b. in Northants, was involved in an escapade which led to his emigrating to the Australian goldfields (1853-8). His novels incl. *Geoffrey Hamlyn* (1859), based on his Australian experiences, and *Ravenshoe* (1862), dealing with the Crimea.

KINGSLEY, Mary Henrietta (1862-1900). British ethnologist. The niece of Charles K., she made extensive expeditions alone in W Africa, and pub. remarkably lively accounts of her findings, e.g. *Travels in W Africa* (1897). She d. of enteric fever while nursing Boer prisoners in Simonstown hospital.

KING'S LYNN. English seaport at the mouth of the Great Ouse, Norfolk, England. The name was changed from Lynn to King's L. by Henry VIII. It is the birthplace of Fanney Burney. Industries incl. agricultural machinery, brewing, fishing and boatbuilding. Pop. (1972) 30,200.

KING'S MEDAL. Two awards initiated in 1945. K.M. for courage in the cause of freedom, and K.M. for service in the cause of freedom, designed for Allied or other foreign civilians who assisted Britain in the S.W.W.

KING'S/QUEEN'S PROCTOR. In England the Official representing the Crown in matrimonial cases. His chief function is to intervene in divorce proceedings to stop a decree *nisi* being made absolute if he discovers that material facts have been concealed from the court or that there has been collusion, or adultery by the petitioner since the decree, or any other cause against the dissolution of the marriage.

KINGSTON. (1) Cap. of Jamaica, W Indies. It has an excellent harbour on the S coast and is the cultural and commercial centre of the is. K. was rebuilt after an earthquake in 1907. It was founded 1693-1703, and made cap.

of Jamaica in 1872. Pop. (1976) 635,000. (2) City of Ontario, Canada, on Lake Ontario, seat of Queen's Univ., with shipbuilding yards, engineering works, and grain elevators. It grew from 1782 round the French Fort Frontenac, captured by the English in 1748, and was named in honour of George III. Pop. (1976) 60,000.

KINGSTON-UPON-HULL. Official name of HULL.

KINGSTON UPON THAMES. Bor. of Greater London, England, on the S bank of the Thames, 16km (10m) SW of London. The coronation stone of the Saxon kings is still preserved here. Industries incl. metalworking, plastic and paint. It is admin. HQ of Surrey. Pop. (1972) 139,420.

KINGSTOWN. *See* DUN LAOGHAIRE.

KING-TE-CHEN. *See* JINGDEZHEN.

KINNOCK, Neil 1942– . Labour politician. Born at Tredegar, and ed at Cardiff Univ, he is strongly left-wing, and a noted orator. In 1983 he became leader of the Labour Party.

KINRO'SS. Former co. of Scotland, merged in 1975 in Tayside region. The area is chiefly agricultural and contains Loch Leven. The former co. town was Kinross. Pop. (1972) 2,830.

KINSHASA (kinshah'sa). Cap. of the Rep. of Zaïre, formerly Léopoldville, on the r. Zaïre, 400km (250m) inland from Matadi. It was founded by Stanley in 1887. A flourishing commercial centre, it also has chemical, textile, engineering, food product and furniture industries. There is a campus of the Nat. Univ. Pop. (1975) 2,000,000.

KINSEY, Alfred (1894-1956). American sexologist. Based on replies to questionnaires, his reports on *Sexual Behaviour in the Human Male* (1948) and *Female* (1953) set a pattern of uninhibited revelation.

KIPLING, Joseph Rudyard (1865-1936). British poet and author. B. in Bombay, the son of John Lockwood K. (1837-1911), curator of the Central Museum at Lahore (1875-93), he was ed. at the United Services College at Westward Ho, which provided the background for *Stalky and Co.* (1899). His *Schoolboy Lyrics* were privately pub. in 1881, and he was engaged as a journalist in India 1882-9; during these years he wrote *Departmental Ditties, Plain Tales from the Hills, Soldiers Three, Under the Deodars, Wee Willie Winkie*, etc. Returning to London he pub. *The Light that Failed* (1890) and *Barrack Room Ballads* (1892), and m. in 1892 Caroline, the sister of the American Wolcott Balestier who collaborated with him in *Naulahka* (1891). He lived largely in the USA 1892-6, where he produced the short stories *Many Inventions* (1893), the two *Jungle Books* (1894-5), and *Captains Courageous* (1897). Prior to the F.W.W. he pub. *Kim* (1901), the *Just So Stories* (1902), *Puck of Pook's Hill* (1906), and *Rewards and Fairies* (1910); and in 1907 was awarded a Nobel prize. Later works incl. the autobiographical *Something of Myself* (1937). His ashes rest in Westminster Abbey. Enjoying in his heyday an enormous popularity, and subsequently almost equal denigration for 'jingoist imperialism', he was yet a superb craftsman, and the variety and range of his achievement can still astonish. His is the ultimate distinction of being quoted daily by people who never realize whom they quote, or even that they do quote at all, e.g. 'The Ballad of East and West', 'Boots', 'If', 'Gunga Din', and 'Mandalay'.

KIRCHNER (kĕrkh'ner), **Ernst Ludwig** (1880-1938). German artist. With a number of other painters he formed the movement Die Brücke (The Bridge) in 1905, which was estab. in Berlin from 1911. Harsh, angular and distorted, his work changed from portraiture and city scenes to mountain landscapes when he settled in Switzerland on being invalided from the army in 1917. His work was attacked as degenerate under Hitler and he committed suicide.

KIRGHIZ SSR. A constituent rep. of the USSR, adjoining the frontier of Sinkiang-Uighur, China. Some two-thirds of the people are Kirghiz, belonging to the Mongolian Tartar family. The introduction of artificial irrigation and hydro-electric power, and of a number of Russian settlers, modified their traditional nomadic way of living, but livestock breeding remains a principal industry. Wheat and other grains, fodder crops, tobacco, etc., are grown; there are sugar refineries, food, timber, and textile factories; and coal and petroleum are worked. The cap. is Frunze. Area 198,500 sq.km (76,100 sq.m); pop. (1979) 3,529,000.

KIRIBATI (kir'ibas). Country in the Pacific Ocean comprising 33 small islands, the Gilbert, Phoenix and Line Islands, and Banaba (Ocean Is.): the new name K. is a modified form of 'Gilberts'. British from 1892, they became an independent rep. within the Commonwealth in 1979. The cap. is the atoll of Tarawa. Area 655 sq.km (253 sq.m); pop. (1975) 53,000.

KIRIN. *See* JILIN.

KIRK, Norman (1924-74). NZ Labour statesman, known as 'Big Norm'. Once an engine-driver, he led the Labour Party from 1965, and was PM 1972–4.

KIRKCALDY (kirkaw'di). Seaport on the Firth of Forth, Fife region, Scotland. Manufactures incl. floor coverings and paper. Pop. (1973) 50,207.

KIRKCUDBRIGHT (kirkoo'bri). Former co. of S Scotland, merged in 1975 in Dumfries and Galloway region. K., on the Dee at the head of K. bay was formerly the co. town, pop. (1973) 2,690. The name means 'chapel of Cuthbert'.

KIRKUK (kirkook'). Town in NE Iraq, centre of a major oilfield with pipelines to Tripoli (Lebanon) and Banias (Syria). Pop. (1970) 176,800.

KIRKWALL. Admin. HQ and port of the Orkneys, Scotland, on the N coast of Mainland. The cathedral of St Magnus dates in part from 1137. Pop. (1973) 4,780.

KIRO'V, Sergei Mironovich (1886-1934). Russian Bolshevik leader. He joined the Bolsheviks in 1904, and took a prominent part in the 1918-20 civil wars. His assassination in 1934 led to the political trials held during the next 4 years.

KIRO'V (kēr'of). Town NE of Gorky, on the Vyatka r., RFSR, USSR. A rail centre, it makes rolling stock, machine tools, etc. Pop. (1977) 381,000.

KIROVABAD (kērovahbat'). Important industrial town in Azerbaijan SSR, producing cottons and woollens and processed foods. Pop. (1977) 216,000.

KIRO'VOGRAD. Town on the r. Ingul in the Ukrainian SSR, USSR. On a lignite field, it processes food and makes agricultural machinery. Pop. (1977) 228,000.

KIRRIEMUIR (kirimū'er). Market town of Tayside, Scotland, noted as 'Thrums' in Sir James Barrie's novels, and his birthplace. Pop. (1973) 4,295.

KISANGANI (kisangah'ni). Town in NE Zaïre (formerly Stanleyville), on the upper Zaïre r., below Stanley Falls. It is an important centre of communications. Pop. (1975) 298,000.

KISHINE'V. Cap. of the Moldavian SSR, USSR. Founded in 1436, it became Russian in 1812. It was taken by **Romania** in 1918; by the Russians in 1940, by the Germans in 1941, when it was totally destroyed: the Russians recaptured the site in 1944, and rebuilding soon began. It has cement and food factories. Pop. (1977) 489,000.

KISSINGER (kis'injer), **Henry** (1923-). American statesman. B. in Bavaria, of Jewish parents, he emigrated to USA with them in 1938. After work in army counter-intelligence, he won a govt. scholarship to Harvard, and subsequently became a govt. consultant. In 1969 he was appointed asst. for National Security Affairs (Sec. of State 1973-77) by Pres. Nixon, and went on secret missions to Peking and Moscow which led to Nixon's visits to both countries and a general detente. In 1973 he shared a Nobel peace prize with Le Duc Tho, the N Vietnamese Politburo member, for his part in the Vietnamese peace negotiations. He was active in the Arab Israeli peace negotiations 1973–5, and in the negotiations in Africa arising from the Angola and Rhodesia crises of 1976. In 1983 Reagan appointed him head of a bipartisan commission on Central America.

KISSINGER. As Secretary of State 1973-77, Henry Kissinger invented the art of 'shuttle diplomacy', going in person to see the heads of state concerned. He is seen here at London airport. *Photo: Courtesy of the USIS.*

KITAKYŪ'SHU. Japanese city and port, on the Hibiki Sea, N Kyushu, formed 1963 by the amalgamation of Moji, Kokura, Tobata, Yawata, and Wakamatsu. It is a great coal port for nearby mines and an industrial centre with steel mills and factories making chemicals, cotton thread, plate glass, alcohol, etc. A tunnel (1942) links it with Honshu. Moji was opened to foreign trade in 1887. Pop. (1977) 1,060,000.

KITCHENER. City in Ontario, Canada, 96km (60m) SW of Toronto. It has foundries, furniture factories, and other works based on power from Niagara Falls. Founded in 1806 as Sand Hills, it was renamed Berlin *c.* 1830, Kitchener in 1916. Mackenzie King was born at K. Pop. (1976) 272,000.

KITCHENER, Horatio Herbert, earl K. of Khartoum (1850-1916). British soldier. B. in Co. Kerry, he was commissioned in 1871, and transferred to the Egyptian Army in 1882. Promoted C-in-C in 1892, he crushed the Sudanese dervishes at Omdurman in 1898, re-occupied Khartoum, and also forced a French expedition to withdraw from Fashoda. During the S African War he acted as Lord Roberts' chief of staff, and as C-in-C 1900-2 brought the war to a successful conclusion. He subsequently commanded the forces in India and acted as British agent in Egypt, and in 1914 received an earldom. Appointed War Minister on the outbreak of the F.W.W., he was drowned while on his way to Russia. He had been created field marshal in 1909.

KITE. Name of several birds of prey in the family Falconidae. The European species (*Milvus milvus*) is a typical example, and may be distinguished by its forked tail. It is *c.* 60cm (2ft) long. Kites are rare in Britain, but are found in Europe, America, and India.

The man-made K. - named after the hovering bird - is at its simplest a roughly diamond-shaped frame of wood, metal or plastic, which is covered with paper, nylon, etc., and balanced by a long tail: it is controlled from the ground by a string. They have been flown as a pastime for many cents., espec. in China and Japan, and have undergone advanced technical development; some important early Ks. were made like windsocks with wings attached, and in recent years striking manoeuvrability and lifting power have been achieved. Ks. have practical use in meteorology and aerial survey, and man-lifting reconnaissance Ks. were devised in the 19th cent.

KITE. An early colour print of Japanese boys flying kites: those in the foreground concentrate on their peg-tops. *Photo: Mansell Collection.*

KI'TIMAT. Port founded 1955 at the head of Douglas Channel, to the SE of Prince Rupert, British Columbia. Alumina from Jamaica is brought to the aluminium smelter - one of the world's largest - powered by the Kemano hydro-electric scheme. Pop. (1971) *c.* 10,000.

KITTIWAKE. Sea-gull (*Rissa tridactyla*), found in the North Atlantic regions. Other species are found in the North Pacific and Bering Sea.

KI'TWE. Town in Zambia, 48km (30m) NW of Ndola, a commercial centre for the copperbelt. Zambia's emerald mines are to the S. Pop. (1975) 315,000.

KITZBÜHEL (kits'bül). Winter sports resort in the Austrian Tirol, 80km (50m) NE of Innsbruck. Pop. (1970) 7,700.

KIVU (kē'voo). Lake in the Great Rift Valley between Zaïre and Rwanda, *c.* 105km (65m) long. The chief port is Bukavu.

KIWI (kē'wi). Native name for a genus of nocturnal flightless birds (*Apteryx*) confined to New Zealand. It has long and hair-like plumage, a very long beak, and the egg is larger, in relation to the size of the body, than that of any other bird.

KIWI. Its nocturnal habits make it not an easy bird for a zoo to display, and there is difficulty in keeping pace with its appetite for earthworms. The cloaks of Maori chieftains are made from its feathers. *Photo: Popperfoto.*

KLAIPEDA (klī'peda). Seaport in the Lithuanian SSR, on the Baltic coast at the mouth of the Dange r., with iron foundries, shipbuilding yards, and other industrial works. It was founded in 1252 as the castle of Memelburg by the Teutonic Knights, joined the Hanseatic League soon after, and has changed hands between Sweden, Russia, and Germany. Lithuania annexed K. in 1923, and after German occupation 1939-45, it was restored to Lithuania. Pop. (1977) 173,000.

KLAPROTH (klahp'rōt), **Martin Heinrich** (1743-1817). German chemist. First prof. of chemistry in Berlin from 1810, he is famous for his discovery of the elements uranium, zirconium, cerium, and titanium.

KLEE, Paul (1879-1940). Swiss artist. B. near Berne, he studied at Munich, Paris, and Rome. In 1920 he went to the Bauhaus in Weimar, and in 1922 he became a prof. at the Düsseldorf academy. When Hitler rose to power in 1933 he returned to Berne. K. dwelt in a dream world, and has been attacked for plagiarizing infant formulas, but many find his work full of profound sensibility.

KLEIST (klīst), **(Bernd) Heinrich Wilhelm von** (1777-1811). German dramatist. B. at Frankfurt-an-der-Oder, he wrote tragedies and a comedy *Der zerbrochene Krug* (1811) as well as stories and poems, but achieved only a posthumous reputation. In a suicide pact, he killed first a girl-friend, and then himself.

KLE'MPERER, Otto (1885-1973). American conductor. B. in Germany, where he became noted for his interpretation of contemporary and classical (especially Beethoven and Bruckner) music, he was director of the Los Angeles Symphony Orchestra 1933-46.

KLEPTOMĀ'NIA. A symptom of insanity revealed by an overpowering desire to steal, and associated with many forms of mental aberration.

KLIEGL (klēgl), **John** (1869-1959) and **Anton** (1872-1927). American brothers, born in Germany, who invented the brilliant carbon-arc (klieg) lights used in television and films.

KLONDIKE. District of Yukon, Canada, E and S of K. river. It was the scene of a gold rush in 1896, which brought some 30,000 people to the area, but by 1910 most of the gold had been removed and the pop. dwindled. Latterly, silver-ore has been found.

KLO'PSTOCK, Friedrich Gottlieb (1724-1803). German poet. His religious epic *Der Messias* (1745-73) and his lyric odes, with their flexible, subtle metres, and impressionistic, subjective vocabulary, prepared the way for the great age of 18th cent. German literature.

KNAPWEED. Wild flower common in Britain, Europe, and W Asia, known also as hardheads. A member of the Compositae family (*Centaurea nigra*), it produces hard, bract-covered buds which break into composite heads of purple flowers.

KNARESBOROUGH. English market town in N Yorks, 6km (4m) NE of Harrogate. Linen and textiles are made. The castle dates from *c.* 1070. Eugene Aram (q.v.) hid the body of his victim in St Robert's cave at K. Pop. (1971) 10,000.

KNEE. The hinge joint between the thigh bone and the shin bone. It consists, roughly, of two smooth, shallow cups (condyles of the tibia) within which fit two smooth rounded protrusions (condyles of the femur); in front, protecting it, is the kneecap.

KNELLER, Sir Godfrey (1646-1723). British portrait painter of German descent. Court painter to Charles II, William III and George I, he showed in his best works a strong grasp of character, e.g. the members of the Whig 'Kit-Cat Club'.

KNIGHT, Dame Laura (1877-1970). Brit. artist. She excelled in detailed, narrative painting of gypsies, of fairground and circus life, and of the ballet. She m. in 1903 Harold K. (d. 1961), a portrait painter, and was created DBE in 1929.

KNIGHTHOOD, Orders of. Fraternities carrying with them the rank of knight, admission to which is granted as a mark of royal favour or as a reward for public services. During the Middle Ages such fraternities fell into 2 classes, religious and secular. The first class, e.g. the Templars (q.v.), and Knights of St John, consisted of knights who had taken religious vows and devoted themselves to military service against the Saracens or other non-Christians. The secular Os. probably arose from bands of knights engaged in the service of a prince or great noble, who wore his badge or the emblem of his patron saint. The Order of the Garter, founded *c.* 1347, is the oldest now in existence: there are 8 other British Os., those of the Thistle (founded 1687), St Patrick (1788), the Bath (1725), the Star of India (1861), St Michael and St George (1818), the Indian Empire (1878: no conferments since

1947), the Royal Victorian O. (1896), and the O. of the British Empire (1917). Most of the ancient European Os., such as the O. of the Golden Fleece, have disappeared as a result of political changes. A knight bachelor belongs to the lowest stage of K., i.e. is not a member of any specially named order. *See also* MERIT, ORDER OF.

KNIGHTHOOD. The resplendent robes of a Knight of the Garter. Sir Harold Wilson (left) and the Duke of Grafton walk in procession to their installation at St George's Chapel, Windsor Castle. *Photo: U.P.I.*

KNIPPER, Lev Constantinovich (1898-). Russian composer His early work shows the influence of Stravinsky, but after 1932 he became a 'popular' composer, as in the symphony *Poem of Komsomol Fighters* (1933-4) with its mass battle songs, etc. Best known in the W is his song 'Cavalry of the Steppes'.

KNITTING. Hand-knitting (using one flexible or several straight needles) and crochet (in which the needle is hooked) are age-old crafts still widely practised as a hobby. K. was mechanized to produce stockings in the late 16th cent., and later developed to produce other types of garment, but the standard was generally uninspired until the introduction of synthetic yarns after the S.W.W. Brilliant dyes, and methods of texturing, elasticizing, and stabilizing, revolutionized the industry, which has estab. a 50 per cent share in the women's clothing industry and a similar share in that of men.

KNOCK (nok). Village in co. Mayo, Rep. of Ireland. In 1879 2 women claimed to have seen a vision of the Virgin with St Joseph and St John at the parish church: its status as a shrine was confirmed by a papal visit in 1979.

KNOSSOS. Site in Crete occupied from *c.* 2500 BC, where Europe's earliest civilization flourished (*see* MINOAN). Excavation of the palace of the legendary king Minos by Sir Arthur Evans 1900-25 revealed that the story of Theseus and the Minotaur kept in a labyrinth had a basis of fact in ancient ritual dances of youths and girls which involved somersaulting over a live bull's horns, and the maze-like palace lay-out. Also spelt Cnossus.

KNOT. Bird (*Calidris canutus*) of the plover family. A wader, about the size of a thrush, it is brick-red in summer, drab in winter, and feeds on insects and molluscs. Breeding in the Arctic, Ks. travel widely in winter, to be found as far afield as Java, S Africa, New Zealand, and Britain.

KNOT. The unit by which a ship's speed is measured, corresponding to 1 nautical mile per hour. The nautical mile is one minute of latitude, and although varying over the Earth's surface, is in practice taken to be 1,853 m/6,080 ft (1kn = *c.* 1$\frac{1}{7}$ of a mile). It is also used in aviation and has not so far been replaced by the SI measurement in m/s (metres per second).

KNOT. An intertwinement of parts of one or more ropes, cords, strings, etc., used to bind them together or to other objects. It is constructed so that the strain borne serves to draw it tighter. 'Bends' or 'hitches' are Ks. used to fasten ropes together or round spars, and splices are used to join 2 ropes together, end to end.

KNOX, John (*c.* 1505-72). Scottish Protestant reformer. B. probably at Haddington, he was ordained priest, but afterwards was converted to Protestantism, probably by the reformer, George Wishart. After Wishart's execution in 1546 he went into hiding, but later joined a group of reformers who had seized the castle of St Andrews, and at their request began to preach the reformed doctrines. When the castle was taken by the French in 1547, K. was sent to the galleys, and only released in 1549 at the intercession of the English govt. In England he exercised his influence to strengthen the Protestant element in the Prayer Book, in the compilation of which he assisted. He was made a royal chaplain in 1551. On Mary's accession he escaped and settled first at Frankfurt, where he was a pastor to English refugees, and later at Geneva, where he was associated with Calvin. In 1559 he returned to Scotland, and was chiefly responsible for the establishment of the Church of Scotland. His *History of the Reformation in Scotland* (1586) is one of the masterpieces of Scottish prose.

KNOX, Ronald Arbuthnott (1888-1957). British RC scholar. Son of an anglican bp of Manchester, he became chaplain to the Univ. of Oxford following his ordination in 1912, but resigned in 1917 on his conversion to Rome and was Catholic chaplain 1926-39. His modern translation of the Bible (1945-9) had a masterly turn of phrase and was officially approved by the RC Church. He combined scholarship with a rare sense of humour, e.g. his dialogues *Let Dons Delight* (1939), and a reputation in detective fiction disapproved by his superiors.

KNOXVILLE. City of Tennessee, USA, the centre of a mining and agricultural region of great beauty, seat of a univ. founded in 1794. It is the admin. HQ of the Tennessee Valley Authority. Pop. (1970) 174,587.

KNUTSFORD. English town in Cheshire 24km (15m) SW of Manchester, of which it is a residential district. Mrs Gaskell, who lived at K. for 22 years and is buried there, wrote of it under the name Cranford. Pop. (1971) 10,000.

KOALA (kō-ahl'a). Marsupial (*Phascolarctos cinereus*) of the family Phalangeridae, found only in E Australia and not easily kept in zoos because it feeds almost entirely on eucaluptus shoots. Resembling a bear 60cm (2ft) long, it has greyish fur which led to its almost complete extermination by hunters. Under protection from 1936 it has rapidly increased.

KOALA. At the Lone Pine Sanctuary near Brisbane, a kindergarten group. Half an inch long at birth, the babies stay in their mother's pouch without emerging until they are about five months old. *Photo: Courtesy of the Australian Information Service.*

KOBE (kō'bi). Port on the S coast of Honshu is., Japan, founded 1868. Industries include shipbuilding, iron and steel manufacture, sugar refining. Pop. (1977) 1,337,000.

KOBLENZ (kōb'lents). City of the Rhineland-Palatinate, W Germany, at the junction of the Rhine and Mosel. It dates back to Roman times. It has shoe and cigar factories, paper mills, and other works, and is noted as a centre of the wine trade. It is a centre of communications. Pop. (1978) 115,725.

KOCH, Robert (1843-1910). German bacteriologist. B. in Hanover, he isolated the tubercle bacillus in 1882, and invented the tuberculin test for cattle. In 1905 he received the Nobel prize for medicine.

KODÁ'LY, Zoltán (1882-1967). Hungarian composer. B. at Kecskemet, he studied at the Budapest Academy, where 1907-42 he was prof. of composition. With Bartok he collected Magyar folk music, and has written much chamber and instrumental music, the comic opera, *Háry János* (1926), 'Dances of Galanta', etc.

KŌ'DIAK. Island off the S coast of Alaska, USA, of which it forms part, site of the first white settlement in Alaska, made by the Russians in 1784, and of a US naval base. Area 9,505 sq.km (3,670 sq.m) K. is the home of the world's largest bear. The town of K. is the largest fishing port of the USA, chiefly salmon. Pop. (1970) 3,800.

KOESTLER (kerst'ler), **Arthur** (1905–83). Anglo-Hungarian author. B. in Budapest and ed. as a scientist in Vienna, he became a foreign correspondent in the Middle East, and elsewhere, and later science editor for a German newspaper chain. He joined the Communist Party in 1931 and travelled in Russia and other Soviet countries, but was disillusioned a few years later and left, as described in *The God That Failed* (1950). His experiences while under sentence of death in Spain during the Civil War are told in *Spanish Testament* (1938: revised as *Dialogue with Death*) and inspired *Darkness at Noon* (1940). In 1940 he was imprisoned by the Nazis in France, the subject of *Scum of the Earth* (1941), but escaped to England and after the S.W.W. became a British subject. His later works incl. *Arrival and Departure* (1943), *The Yogi and the Commissar* (1945), both attacks on Communism; *The Sleepwalkers* (1959), a history of cosmology; *The Lotus and The Robot* (1960), exploring eastern philosophy; *The Act of Creation* (1964) analysing creativity and *The Roots of Coincidence*.

KOH-I-NOOR ('Mountain of Light'). Diamond, the central stone of the British queen consorts crown. It was presented in 1849 to Queen Victoria after the annexation of the Punjab.

KOHL, Helmut (1930–). W German statesman. Leader of the CDU (Christian Democratic Union)/CSU (Christian Social Union) from 1976, he succeeded Schmidt as Chancellor in 1982, and won the 1983 election.

KOHL-RABI (kōlrah'bi). A variety of kale (*Brassica oleracea*). The leaves shoot from a swelling on the main stem. The globular portion is used for food, and resembles a turnip.

KOKAND. Town of the Uzbek SSR, 530km (330m) ENE of Bukhara, the centre of a fertile oasis. Industrial developments incl. a fertilizer factory, cotton and silk mills, and machine shops. K. was the cap. of K. Khanate, annexed by Russia in 1876. Pop. (1977) 155,000.

KOKO NOR. Mongolian form of Qinghai (q.v.).

KOKOSCHKA (kokosh'ka), **Oskar** (1886- 1980). Austro-British artist. As an expressionist artist and dramatist, he was already startling Vienna in his late teens. As a cavalry officer in the First World War, he was badly wounded, and was labelled a degenerate by the Nazis. He fled to England in 1938 and became British in 1947. Kokoschka was specially noted for brilliantly coloured townscapes with the same psychological penetration as his portraits.

KOKURA. *See under* KITAKYUSHU.

KŌ'LA. Peninsula in N Russia, bounded by the White Sea on the S and E, and by the Barents Sea on the N. It is coterminous with Murmansk region of the RSFSR. Apatite and other minerals are exported. To the NW the low-lying granite plateau adjoins Norway's thinly-pop. co. of Finnmark, and Soviet troops are heavily concentrated here. Area 129,500 sq.km (50,000 sq.m).

KOLA NUT. *See* COLA.

KOLCHAK, Alexander Vasilievich (1875-1920). Russian admiral. He commanded the White forces in Siberia, and in 1918 proclaimed himself Supreme Ruler of Russia, setting up a provisional govt at Omsk, and later at Irkutsk. He resigned in Denikin's favour, and was shot by the Bolsheviks.

KOLCHUGINO. *See* LENINSK-KUZNETSKY.

KOLHAPUR (kōlapoor). Indian town in Maharashtra state, a trade, educational, and film-production centre, cap. of K. district. K. was formerly cap. of K. princely state, incorporated in Bombay state in 1949. Pop. (1971) 259,000.

KOLKHOZ. Russian term for collective farm (q.v.).

KÖLN. German form of COLOGNE.

KOLWEZI (kolwā'zi). Copper and cobalt mining town, Shaba prov., Zaïre. In 1978 former police of the prov. invaded Shaba from Angola and massacred *c.* 500 Zaireans and 138 whites: many skilled white engineers then left.

KOMMUNI'ZMA, PIK. The highest mtn in the USSR, in the Akademiya Nauk range of the Pamirs, in Tadzhikistan. Communism Peak (7495 m/24,590 ft) was formerly known as Stalin Peak and Garmo Peak.

KOMPONG SOM. Port and industrial city (fromerly Sihanoukville) in Kampuchea, *c.* 160 km (100 m) from the Thai border and dominating the Gulf of Thailand. Founded in 1956, it has road and rail links with Phnom Penh. In 1980 the USSR was developing it as a submarine base. Pop. (1971) 8,600.

KOMSOMOL. The Russian name for the All-Union Leninist Communist Youth League. Membership is open to all young people between the ages of 14 and 26, and numbers several millions. Founded in 1918, it acts as the youth section of the Communist Party, and its activities include all forms of national service, e.g. the rebuilding of Stalingrad in 1942.

KONGUR SHAN (kongoor' shahn). Mountain in Uygur Zizhiqu auton. region, Xinjiang, China, SW of Kashi. It has 4 peaks (7,719m/25,325 ft) and a Brit. expedition led by Chris Bonington was the first to conquer the summit in 1981.

KO'NIEV, Ivan Stepanovich (1898-1973). Soviet marshal. In the S.W.W. he was celebrated for his brilliant victory in 1943 in the Dnieper bend, liberating the Ukraine, and advanced to link with Anglo-US forces approaching from the W.

KÖNIGSBERG. *See* KALININGRAD.

KONSTANZ. German form of CONSTANCE.

KON-TIKI. Legendary Sun King who ruled the country later occupied by the Incas (q.v.), and was supposed to have migrated, with certain white-skinned and bearded followers, out into the Pacific. *See* HEYERDAHL.

KO'NYA. City in Turkey-in-Asia, *c.* 480km (300m) E of Izmir, on the site of ancient Iconium, said to have been visited by St Paul. Prosperous in the 12th cent., K. decayed with the Seljuk state, but is now a market town for a fertile area: carpets and silks are made. The monastery of the Dancing Dervishes is at K. Pop. (1970) 200,000.

KOO'KABURRA. The largest of the world's kingfishers *(Dacelo novaeguineae),* the K. or laughing jackass, has an extraordinarily human laughing note, which is one of the most familiar sounds of the bush of eastern Australia.

KOOKABURRA. Far less aquatic than the true kingfisher, the kookaburra is often found far from water, and feeding on small reptiles and insects. *Photo: Courtesy of the Australian Information Service.*

KORAN. More properly, Quran, though both are transliterations; the sacred book of Islam (q.v.). Written in the purest Arabic, it contains 114 suras or chapters, and is stated to have been divinely revealed to the prophet Mohammed; the original is supposed to be preserved beside the throne of Allah in heaven.

KORDA, Sir Alexander (1893-1956). British film producer and director. B. in Hungary, he came to England in 1931 (naturalized 1936); his films incl. *The Private Life of Henry VIII* (1933), *The Third Man* (1950), and *Richard III* (1955).

KŌRDŌFA'N. Prov. of the Rep. of Sudan: never an independent state, the 'White Land' nevertheless has a character of its own. It is mainly undulating plain, characterized by acacia scrub producing gum arabic, marketed in the chief town El Obeid, and cattle are raised. Formerly a rich agricultural prov., it has been overtaken by desertification.

KŌRĒ'A. Country in Asia, 'Land of Morning Calm', occupying the peninsula projecting southwards from Manchuria, having the Yellow Sea on the W and the Sea of Japan on the E. The N border is mountainous, and a secondary range runs southward along the E coast. There are large forest reserves in the N, while the streams provide hydro-electric power.

On the division of the country (*see* HISTORY), North K. was left with the richest mineral resources, incl. iron, coal, oil and barytes, and was also the most industrially advanced, iron, and steel, textiles, cement, chemicals, etc., being produced. However, in South K. agriculture (rice, barley, tobacco, ginseng, etc.) has been revolutionized by self-help collective farming, the New Community Movement (*Saemaul Undong*). With foreign aid, South K. has also developed industrially as a workshop of Asia, new mineral resources being exploited, and products incl. steel, ships, chemicals, electronics, silk, cotton and synthetic textiles, sports goods, household appliances and plastics. A fishery industry has also been estab.

The chief religions are Confucianism and Buddhism. North Korea has its cap. at Pyongyang, other towns incl. Kaesong, Wonsan and Heungnam; South Korea has its cap. at Seoul, others towns incl. Inchon, Pusan, and Taegu. Area North K. 121,250 sq.km (46,815 sq.m); pop. (1975) 16,000,000. Area South K. 99,000 sq.km (38,450 sq.m); pop. (1977) 36,400,000. M.U.: won.

History. The foundation of the Korean state traditionally dates back about 2,000 years BC, to the dynasty of Tangun, followed by that of the Chinese Kija, which ruled from *c.* 1122 until the 4th cent. BC. K. was subsequently distracted by internal war and invasion until the 10th cent. AD when it was united within the boundaries it subsequently retained. In the 16th cent. Japan invaded K. for the first time, later withdrawing from a country it had devastated. In 1905 Japan began to treat K. as a protectorate, and in 1910 annexed it. Many Japanese colonists settled in K., introducing both industrial and agricultural development. The Japanese in K. surrendered in 1945, but although Russia withdrew from K. north of the 38th parallel in 1948, and the USA from the south in 1949, the country remained divided. In 1950 the N Koreans invaded South K., but the UN sent troops (mainly American) to drive them back and fighting was almost over when China intervened on the side of North K. The 1953 armistice restored the status quo, but in 1972 a N-S Co-ordinating Committee was estab. to achieve peaceful reunification. Development of closer relations, however, was hindered by various incidents, incl. the discovery in 1974 of a series of tunnels from N to S Korea, passing under the demilitarized zone, and intended to facilitate invasion.

North K. (Democratic People's Rep. of K.) has a Soviet-type constitution; Marshal Kim II Sung (q.v.) became pres. in 1972. South K. (Rep. of K.) has a Pres. and Nat. Assembly. After Synghman Rhee (q.v.) South K. became more democratic under Gen. Park Chung Hee (q.v.), who seized power in an army coup 1961, and was elected pres. 1963. The economic growth of the 1970s concentrated wealth in the hands of a few and in Oct. 1979 Park Chung Hee was assassinated. Eventually Gen. Chun Du Hwan took over as pres. in Sept. 1980 and, while maintaining an autocratic regime, promised a wider distribution of wealth.

KOREAN. The language of Korea, written in Chinese characters from the 5th cent. to 1443, when King Sejong developed a remarkably advanced phonetic alphabet, and a native literature sprung up. It was later discouraged as 'vulgar letters' - Onmun - and banned by the Japanese, but revived after the S.W.W. as 'top letters' - Hangul - so that modern Korea has 95% literacy.

KORINTHOS. Greek form of CORINTH.

KORO'LEV (karawl'yef), **Sergei** (1906-66). Russian designer of space-rockets. B. at Zhitomir, son of a teacher, he designed the first sputnik, the moon-rockets, and the manned space ships

KORTRIJK. Flemish form of COURTRAI.

KOS. *See* COS.

KOSCIUSKO. Highest mt in Australia, 2,229m (7,316 ft), in New South Wales. (Sir) Paul Strzelecki, who was born in Prussian Poland, discovered K. in 1839 and named it after the Polish hero K. (q.v.).

KOSCIUSZKO (kosi-us'kō), **Tadeusz** (1746-1817). Polish leader of the revolutionary forces which fought against Russia in 1794. He was defeated by combined Russian and Prussian forces, and captured at Maciejowice, but was released in 1796.

KŌSHER. Heb. for 'fit', as applied by Jews to meat slaughtered according to Mosaic law.

KOŠICE (kosh'itse). Town on the Hernad, Czechoslovakia. Textiles are made and K. is of strategic importance as a road centre; it has an airport. A large part of the pop. (1977) 181,000 is Magyar-speaking, and K. was in Hungary 1938-45.

KO'SOVO. Auton. region of Serbia, Yugoslavia. It is inhabited by Albanians and borders on Albania, so that there is a demand for unification with that country.

KOSSUTH (kosh'oot), **Lajos** (1802-94). Hungarian patriot. He founded the paper *Pesti Hirlap*, in which he pleaded for social and national reforms, and in 1848 became pres. of the committee of national defence and virtual ruler of the country. In 1849 he proclaimed his country's independence of the Habsburgs. The Hungarians were later defeated by Austrian and Russian troops, and K. fled to Turkey. Later, he went to England.

KOSYGIN (kosēg'in), **Alexei Nikolaievich** (1904-80). Russian statesman. An economic expert, he succeeded Khrushchev as PM (chairman of the Council of Ministers) 1964-80. His moves to give more independence to industry and act with caution in foreign affairs were increasingly over-ruled by Brezhnev and the party machine.

KOSYGIN. Alexei Kosygin addresses a political meeting at the Bolshoi Theatre. Twice a Hero of Socialist Labour, he wears the honour on his left breast. *Photo: Novosti.*

KOTA BHARU (kō'ta bah'roo). Cap. of Kelantan, Malaysia. Pop. (1970) 55,000.

KOTA KINABALU (kō'ta kē'nabaloo). Cap. and port (formerly Jesselton) of Sabah, Malaysia. Rubber and timber are exported. Pop. (1970) 42,000.

KŌTŌ. Rectangular stringed musical instrument, plucked with the fingers, the chief traditional instrument of Japan. It rests horizontally on the floor, the musician being seated behind it: the modern version has 20 strings.

KOTTBUS (kot'boos). Town on the Spree, cap. of K. dist, E Germany. A centre of rail and road communication, with an airport, K. makes cloth, carpets, hats, etc. Pop. (1978) 105,180.

KOUROU (kooroo'). River and second-largest town of French Guiana, NW of Cayenne. Close to the Equator, and so ideally suitable as a launch-site, K. has a space centre engaged in work for ESA. *See* ARIANE. Pop. (1979) 6,000.

KOVNO. Russian form of KAUNAS.

KOWLOO'N. Peninsula on the Chinese coast forming part of the British Crown Colony of Hong Kong (q.v.). The town of K. is a residential area.

KRA, Isthmus of. The narow 'waist' of Thailand proposed as the site for the *K. Canal* to link the Gulf of Thailand and Indian Ocean, and avoid the expensive detour via Singapore.

KRAFFT-EBING, baron Richard von (1840-1902). German pioneer psychiatrist. A neurologist, he pub. his best-known work *Psychopathia Sexualis* in 1886.

KRAGUJEVAC (krahgooyāv'ats). Garrison town of Serbia, Yugoslavia. Pop. (1971) 71,180.

KRAKATŌ'A. Is. volcano in Sunda Strait, Indonesia, between Java and Sumatra, whose eruption in 1883 caused widespread destruction and atmospheric phenomena. A tidal wave hit Java and Sumatra, where some 36,000 people were drowned.

KRAKOW (krak'ō). City of Poland, the cap. from c. 1300 to 1595, on the Vistula. K. is commercially important; railway wagons, paper, chemicals, etc., are made and there are tobacco and food factories. It has the second-oldest univ. in central Europe (1364), at which Copernicus was a student, and a fine 14th cent. Gothic cathedral. Pop. (1978) 713,000.

KRAMATORSK (krahmahtorsk'). Town in the Ukrainian SSR, in the Donbas, N of Donetsk. It produces coal-mining machinery, steel and ceramics, and has railway repair shops. Pop. (1977) 171,000.

KRASNODAR. Cap. of K. territory of the RSFSR, USSR. Situated to the N of the Caucasus, at the head of navigation of the r. Kuban, it is an important industrial town, connected by petroleum pipeline with the Caspian oilfields. Pop. (1977) 552,000.

KRASNOYA'RSK. Cap. of K. territory of the RSFSR, USSR, on the r. Yenisei. The territory is an agricultural area of modern development. Gold was discovered near the town, founded in 1628, and besides locomotive works, paper and saw mills, cement factories, etc., K. has a gold refinery and hydro-electric installations. Pop. (1977) 769,000.

KREBS, Sir Hans (1900-81). British biochemist. B. in Germany, he was prof. at Sheffield 1945-54, and Whitley prof. at Oxford 1954-67. In 1953 he shared a Nobel prize in medicine for discovering the citric acid or 'K' cycle - the route by which food is converted into energy by living tissues.

KREFELD (kreh'felt). Town near the Rhine, 52km (32m) NW of Cologne, W Germany. An important industrial and textile centre, it is on the Westphalian coalfield. Pop. (1978) 224,525.

KREISLER (krīz'-), **Fritz** (1875-1962). Austrian violinist. He was specially noted for his interpretation of the concertos of Brahms and Beethoven, and Elgar's violin concerto is dedicated to him.

KREMENCHUG (krāmenchoog'). Town on the Dnieper, Ukrainian SSR, USSR. Industries incl. production of road-building machines, railway wagons, and processed food; lumber and grain are items in its trade; and it has hydro-electric installations. Pop. (1977) 206,000.

KREMLIN. The citadel or fortress of Russian cities. The Moscow K. dates from the 12th cent., and the name 'the K.' is used as synonymous with the Soviet govt.

KREMLIN. Inside the Teremni Palace within the Kremlin walls, one of the exquisite 17th century bedrooms which were carefully restored in the 19th century. *Photo: Novosti.*

KREUTZER (krötsār'), **Rodolphe** (1766-1831). French violinist and composer of German descent, to whom Beethoven dedicated his violin sonata Op. 47, known as the K. Sonata.

KRILL. Antarctic crustacean, the most common species being *Euphausia superba Dana.* Shrimplike, it is c. 6cm (2.5in) long, with 2 antennae, 5 pairs of legs, 7 pairs of light organs along the body, and is coloured orange above and green beneath. Moving in enormous swarms, K. constitute the chief food of the baleen whale, and have been used to produce a protein concentrate for human consumption and meal for animal feed.

KRISHNA. A Hindu deity, the 8th incarnation of Vishnu, and hero of the Indian epic, *Mahabharata.*

The *K. Consciousness Movement* (1966) was estab. in the USA by His Divine Grace A. C. Bhaktivendanta Swami Prabhupada (1896-1977). Its bible is the Bhagavad Gita, and members shave their heads, wear orange robes, and chant 'Hare Krishna'.

KRIVOI ROG. Town in the Ukrainian SSR, USSR, 130km (80m) SW of Dnepropetrovsk. The surrounding district is rich in iron ore, and there is a metallurgical industry. The name means 'crooked horn'. Pop. (1977) 641,000.

KRŌ'NSTADT. Russian naval base on the is. of Kotlin in the Gulf of Finland, opposite Leningrad, founded by Peter the Great in 1703.

KROPO'TKIN, Peter Alexeivich, Prince (1842-1921). Russian anarchist. B. in Moscow, he served in the army, did important survey work in Asia, joined the revolutionary party in St Petersburg, and in 1874 was imprisoned. He escaped to England in 1876, and later moved to Switzerland. Expelled from Switzerland, he went to France, where he was imprisoned 1883-6. He then lived in England until 1917, when he returned to Moscow. Among his principal works are *Modern Science and Anarchism* and *Mutual Aid.*

KRUGER (kroo'-), **Stephanus Johannes Paulus** (1825-1904). President of the Transvaal Rep. B. at Colesberg, Cape Colony, he accompanied his family on the 'great trek' across the Vaal r., and soon became prominent in Transvaal politics. In 1863 he was appointed Cdr.-Gen. of the forces, in 1883 he was elected Pres., and re-elected in 1888, 1893, and 1898. His refusal to remedy the grievances of the Uitlanders (English and other non-Boer white inhabitants of the rep.) led to war with Britain in 1899. When Pretoria was occupied by British troops K. fled to Europe, where he pleaded vainly for European intervention. He d. in Switzerland.

KRUGER NATIONAL PARK. Game reserve in NE Transvaal, S Africa, between the Limpopo and Crocodile rivers. Estab. by Kruger (1898), it is the largest in the world; *c.* 21,000 sq.km (8,000 sq.m).

KRUGERSDORP. Mining town in the Witwatersrand dist, Transvaal, S Africa. Manganese and uranium are worked as well as gold. Pop. (1970) 91,200.

KRUPP (kroop). Family of German industrialists. The Essen foundries were estab. early in the 19th cent., and the firm developed long distance artillery, e.g. 'Big Bertha' in the F.W.W. (so nicknamed after the Krupp heiress). Between the wars, the firm continued to manufacture armaments in secret and supported Hitler. Attempted deconcentration of its assets after the S.W.W., when the head of the firm was imprisoned, failed, and until 1967 it played a part in German recovery. *See* ESSEN.

KRYPTON (Gk, hidden). A colourless, odourless, inert gas, symbol Kr, at. no. 36, at. wt. 83.8. It was discovered in 1898 by Ramsay and Travers in the residue from liquid air. Occurring in the atmosphere (*c.* 1 to 1,000,000), K. is used to enhance brilliance in miners' electric lamps, and in some gas-filled electronic valves. *See* METRE.

KRYUKOV (kryoo'kof), **Fyodor** (1870-1920). Russian author. Son of a Cossack leader, he began writing a major work on Don Cossack life during the F.W.W., but d. of typhus during the Cossack retreat before the Red Army in the Civil War. The MS was lost. It has been suggested by Solzhenitsyn that this was the original of *Quiet Flows the Don,* the work pub. by Sholokhov (q.v.).

KUALA LUMPUR (kwah'lah loom'poor). Cap. of the Fed. of Malaysia. Formerly within the state of Selangor, of which it was also the cap., it was created a fed. terr. in 1974. There is a large trade in tin and rubber, and the many educational institutions incl. the Univ. of Malaya (1962) and the Nat. Inst. of Technology. Pop. (1970) 451,730.

KUANYIN. The 'goddess of mercy' of the Chinese Buddhists; the Japanese worship her as Kwannon.

KUBAN (koobahn'). A river of the USSR, rising in Georgia and flowing about 800km (500m) N and W to the Black Sea. The name is also applied to the low-lying agricultural dist of Krasnodar Terr. immediately N of the Caucasus.

KUBELIK (koob'elēk), **Jan** (1880-1940). Czech violinist. He performed in Prague at the age of 8, and was one of the world's greatest virtuosos; he also wrote 6 violin concertos, etc.

KUBLAI (kooblī) **KHAN** (1216-94). Mongol emperor of China, grandson of Ghengis Khan. He succeeded his brother Mangu in 1259, estab. himself as emperor of the whole of China, and with little success attempted to extend his rule still further.

KUBRICK (koo'brik), **Stanley** (1928-). British film director. His films, which use such devices as sequences of horrific violence, played against music with the opposite association, incl. *Lolita* (1962), *Dr Strangelove* (1964), *2001: A Space Odyssey* (1968), *A Clockwork Orange* (1971), and *The Shining* (1980).

KUCHING (koo'ching). Cap. and port of Sarawak, on the S. river. Pop. (1970) 63,535.

KUDZU (kood'zoo). Creeper (*Pueraria thunbergiana*) introduced to the southern USA from Japan in the 1930s to stem soil erosion. So rapid in growth as to become a scourge, it nevertheless enriches the soil with nitrogen and is a useful animal feed.

KUFRA (koo'frah). Group of oases in the Libyan Desert, Libya, N Africa, SE of Tripoli. By the 1970s the vast underground reservoirs were being used for irrigation.

KUIBYSHEV (koo͞'bishef, but anglicized kwē'bishef). Cap. of K. Reg., RSFSR, USSR, an excellent river port, at the junction of the Samara with the Volga. K. is the centre of the fertile middle Volga plain; industries incl. making of aircraft, locomotives, cables, synthetic rubber, textiles; petroleum refining, quarrying, and the manufacture of fertilizers in a complex built with US co-operation from 1973. Founded as Samara, K. was renamed K. in 1935, and was the provisional cap. of the USSR 1941-3. Pop. (1977) 1,204,000.

Kuibyshev Sea is an artificial lake *c.* 480km (300m) long, created in the 1950s by damming the Volga river.

KU KLUX KLAN. American secret society. Two have existed; the first, estab. as a social club in Tennessee in 1865, later adopting hooded white robes, etc., developed into an organization for maintaining white supremacy in the S and opposing the US Congress reconstruction programme. It declined after the withdrawal of occupation forces from the S in 1877. The 2nd K.K.K., formed in 1915 on an anti-Jewish-Catholic-Negro basis, also declined from 1928, till racial violence flared in the 1950s and 1960s.

KULAK (koo͞'lak; literally 'fist'). Russian term for a rich peasant who could afford to hire labour, and often acted as village usurer. They resisted the Soviet govt's policy of collectivization, and in 1930 they were 'liquidated as a class', about a million families being banished to eastern Russia.

KUMASI (koomah'sē). Town in Ghana, W Africa, cap. of Ashanti region. There is trade in cocoa, rubber and cattle. In the Fourth Ashanti War, in 1900, Sir Frederic Hodgson, Gov. of the then Gold Coast Colony, with his wife, staff, and a small garrison were besieged in the fort Mar.-June, when they fought their way out. Soon afterwards the Kingdom of Ashanti, of which K. had been the cap. since the 17th cent., was annexed by the British. There is a univ. (1961), and K. is linked by rail with Takoradi and Accra, as well as having a major airport. Pop. (1970) 343,000.

KÜNG, Hans (1928-). Swiss RC theologian. Prof. at Tübingen Univ. from 1963, he was in 1979 debarred by the Vatican from teaching 'in the name of the Church' because he had cast doubt on papal infallibity, and on whether Christ was the son of God.

KUNG-FU (gung-foo). Popular name for the Chinese art of unarmed combat (Manadarin *ch'üan fa*) which originated in the 6th cent., possibly under Indian influence, at the Shaolin temple, Honan province. Of many varied styles, the best-known is *wing chun* 'beautiful springtime', of which the film actor Bruce Lee was an exponent. This is said to have been founded in the 16th cent. by a woman, and is marked by constantly flowing movement to sense in advance moves by an opponent, and the use of offence as a means of defence. *See* KARATE.

KUNLUN SHAN (koonloon' shahn). Chinese mtn range on the edge of the great Tibetan plateau, 4,000 km (2,500 m) E-W; incl. Ulugh Muztag (7,723 m/25,378 ft).

KUNMING (koonmēng'). Cap. of Yunnan prov., China, seat of Yunnan Univ., and an important communications centre. It is the Chinese terminus of the Burma Road, and stands on Lake Dian Chi, *c.* 2,000 m (6,300 ft) a.s.l. Chemicals, textiles, etc., are manufactured, and copper smelted with nearby hydroelectric power. Pop. (1970) 1,700,000.

KUOMINTANG (National People's Party). Chinese nationalist party, founded by Sun Yat-sen (q.v.) in 1894, and responsible for the overthrow of the Manchu Empire 1912. In alliance with the Communists, the power of the warlords was broken and China unified during 1924-7, when Chiang Kai-Shek's right wing launched a reign of terror against the Communists, only interrupted to resist the Japanese invasion of 1937-45, and breaking out again 1945-9, when the K. were driven from the mainland to Formosa, q.v.

KURDAITCHA SHOES. Shoes made of emu feathers which leave no tracks: worn by Australian Aborigines when escaping their enemies and by sorcerers.

KURDISTAN (koordistahn'). Hilly region in SW Asia in the neighbourhood of Mt Ararat, where the borders of Iran, Iraq, Syria, Turkey and the USSR meet. The Kurds, divided among all five countries, have nationalist aspirations, and number *c.* 7,000,000. They are Sunni Moslems.

The Kurds of **Iraq** live in the mountainous NE prov. of Kirkuk, rich in oil, and were in revolt from 1961 to obtain a fully autonomous Kurdish state. In 1980 the first elections were held to the Legislative Council of the Kurdish Autonomous Region estab. in 1974.

The Kurds of **Iran** number *c.* 4,000,000 in the provs. of W Azerbaijan, Kurdistan, Kermanshah and Ilam. In 1946 they briefly achieved a Kurdish rep. with Soviet backing, were repressed under the Shah, and when they revolted against the regime of Ayatollah Khomeini were savagely put down 1979-80. However, it was promised that the 4 provs. would be united in an autonomous unit.

KURDISTAN. A Kurdish mother and child: the dowry, worn in the form of gold ornaments, may be very valuable indeed, passing down from generation to generation. *Photo: Mireille Vautier.*

KURE (koo're). Naval base & port 32km (20m) SE of Hiroshima, on the S coast of Honshu, Japan. K. has shipyards and engineering works. The Japanese fleet surrendered in K. Bay to the Allies 14 Aug. 1945. Pop. (1977) 241,000.

KURIA MURIA (koor'ia moor'ia). Group of 5 is. in the Arabian Sea, off the S coast of Oman. Area 72 sq.km (28 sq.m).

KURILS (koor'ilz). Chain of *c.* 50 small islands stretching from the NE of Hokkaido, Japan to the S of Kamchatka. Some of them are of volcanic origin. They were discovered in 1634 by a Russian navigator and were settled by Russians. Japan seized them 1875-1945, when under the Yalta agreement they were returned to Russia. Japan still claims the southernmost (Etorofu and Kunashiri), and also the nearby small is. of Habomai and Shikotan (not part of the K.). The USSR agreed to the latter in 1972, but the question of Etorofu and Kunashiri prevents signature of a Japan-Soviet Peace Treaty. Area 14,765 sq.km (5,700 sq.m); pop. (1970) 15,000.

KUROPATKIN (koorōpaht'kin), **Alexei Nikolaievich** (1848-1921). Russian general. He won a high reputation during the Russo-Turkish War of 1877-8, was C-in-C in Manchuria in 1903, and resigned after his defeat at Mukden. During the F.W.W. he commanded the armies on the N front until 1916.

KUROSHIO. Warm Pacific current flowing in a great arc from Japan towards the W coast of America.

KURSK (koorsk). Town dating from the 9th cent., cap. of K. reg. of the RSFSR, USSR. Industries incl. chemicals, machinery, alcohol, and tobacco. Pop. (1977) 373,000.

KUT-AL-IMARA (koot'-al-imah'ra). Town on the Tigris, Iraq, a grain market and carpet-manufacturing centre. It was besieged Dec. 1915-April 1916, when Gen. Townshend with his force was compelled to surrender. Pop. (1970) 70,000.

KUTCH (kooch), **Rann of.** Salt, marshy area in Gujarat state, India, which forms 2 shallow lakes, the Great Rann and the Little Rann, in the wet season, and is a salt-covered desert in the dry. It takes its name from the former princely state of K., which it adjoined. An internat. tribunal awarded 90% of the R. of K. to India and 10% (*c.* 800 sq.km (300 sq.m)) to Pakistan, the latter comprising almost all the area above water the year round, in 1968.

KUTUZOV (kootoo'zof), **Mikhail Larionovich,** Prince of Smolensk (1745-1813). Russian field marshal. He commanded an army corps at Austerlitz, and the retreating army in 1812. After the burning of Moscow he harried the French throughout their retreat, and later took command of the united Prussian and Russian armies.

KUWAIT (koo'wāt). Sheikdom on the NW shores of the Persian Gulf. It is mainly low-lying desert country inhabited by nomadic Bedouin. The sheik of K., to prevent possible pressure by the Turks (of whose empire K. was nominally a part), asked Britain for protection in 1897. K.'s independence under British protection was recognized in 1914, and in 1961 K. became a member of the UN and the Arab League. General Kassem of Iraq refused to recognize K.'s independence, claiming it as part of Iraq, and there have been subsequent incursions into Kuwaiti territory. In 1976 the constitution was suspended, but in 1981 parliamentary govt. was restored.

Formerly dependent on dhow building, pearling and maritime trading, this small, barren state assumed international importance following the discovery of a rich petroleum field at Burgan in 1938 (production started in 1946) and subsequently also in the Kuwait-Saudi Arabian Neutral Zone. Since most of the royalties paid to the sheik (amounting to many millions a year) are used for social developments, K. is one of the best-equipped of the world's states in public works, medical and educational services. The giant tankers are accommodated at a man-made floating island terminal. Area 19,000 sq.km (7,400 sq.m); pop. (1978) 1,130,000, only 50% Kuwaitis, the rest Arab immigrants. M.U.: Kuwait dinar.

The cap., also called K., is a flourishing port and is being developed as an outstanding example of town planning. Its seawater distillation plant is the biggest in the world, and there are power stations supplying light industries. An impressive survival of the past is the 'Sif' palace on the seafront. Pop. (1973) 375,000.

KUZBAS. Industrial area in Kemerovo region, RSFSR, USSR, lying on the Tom r. to the N of the Altai mountains. Development began in the 1930s. It takes its name from the old town of Kuznetsk: *see* LENINSK-KUZNETSKY; NOVO KUZNETSKY.

KUZNETS (kooz'nets), **Simon** (1901-). American economist. B. in Russia, he was prof. at Harvard 1960-71, and developed theories of national income and economic growth, used to forecast the future, in *Economic Growth of Nations* (1971). He was awarded a Nobel prize in 1971.

KUZNETSOV (koosnyetsof'), **Anatoli** (1930-79). Russian writer. His novels *Babi Yar* (1966), describing the wartime execution of Jews at Babi Yar, nr Kiev, and *The Fire* (1969), about workers in a large metallurgical factory, were seen as anti-Soviet. Visiting Britain in 1969, he was given permission to settle there.

KWANGCHOW. *See* GUANGZHOU.

KWANGSI-CHUANG. *See* GUANGXI ZHUANG.

KWANGTUNG. *See* GUANGDONG.

KWA'SHIOR'KOR. Ghanaian name for the severe malnutrition common among children in W Africa, resulting in retarded growth, etc. The term was introduced to medical literature by Dr Cicely Williams in the 1930s.

KWEICHOW. *See* GUIZHOU.

KWEIYANG. *See* GUIYANG.

KYD, Thomas (*c.* 1557-95). English dramatist. He followed his father's profession as a scrivener, and *c.* 1588 wrote *The Spanish Tragedy,* which anticipated elements present in *Hamlet.*

KYOGA (kē-ōg'a). Lake in central Uganda: area 2,600 sq.km (1,000 sq.m).

KYŌTO. Japanese city of Honshu situated near Biwa Lake, with which it is linked by canal. Among its industries are silk weaving and manufacture, embroidery, porcelain, and bronze and lacquer ware. K. was founded, as Uda, in the 8th cent. and was the Japanese cap. 794-1868. Pop. (1973) 1,440,000.

KYRENIA (kīrē'nia). Port in Cyprus, *c.* 20km (12m) N of Nicosia. Pop. (1970) 32,700.

KYRENIA. The harbour and, in the background, the Kyrenia Mountains, among which so much Turkish, Greek and British blood was spilt in guerrilla warfare before independence. *Photo: Ken Lambert/Camera Press.*

KYUSHU (kū'shoo). Most southerly of the main islands of Japan, separated from Shikoku and Honshu by Bungo Channel and Suo Bay, but connected to Honshu by bridge and rail tunnel. The coast is very broken. The island is very mountainous, though the peaks are not very high. The active volcano Aso-take (1,592 m/5,223 ft) has the world's largest crater. There are coalfields, and gold, silver, iron and tin are mined. Agricultural products incl. rice, tea, and tobacco. The principal towns are Nagasaki, the cap. (q.v.), Kagoshima, Kumamoto, and Fukuoka. Area, incl. about 370 small islands, 42,079 sq.km (16,170 sq.m); pop. (1970) 13,000,000.

KYUSTENDIL (kē-oost'endil). Town in SW Bulgaria, SW of Sofia, noted for its hot springs. Pop. *c.* 25,000.

KYZYL-KUM (kizilkōōm'). Desert in Kazakhstan and Uzbekistan, USSR. It lies between the Sur-Darya and Amu-Darya rivers, and is being reclaimed for cultivation by irrigation and protective tree-planting. Area *c.* 300,000 sq.km (116,000 sq.m).

L

Twelfth letter of the Roman alphabet. The sound represented is one of the most stable in all languages; in some languages it tends to be lost between a back vowel and a consonant, as in Eng. 'half', 'should', etc.

LABELLED COMPOUND. A compound in which an isotope (usually radioactive) is substituted for a normal atom. Thus labelled, the path taken by the compound can be readily followed, and its quantity measured, by geiger counters, etc. This powerful and sensitive technique is used in medicine, science and industry.

LABIATAE. Family of dicotyledonous plants comprising some 200 genera with 3,000 species. Among their outstanding characteristics are the square stem, the hairy leaves, the arrangement of the flowers in small groups on the stem, and the hooded form of the petals. The family includes lavender, rosemary, thyme, sage and mint.

LABOR PARTY, Australian. Party developing from the trade-union movement in 1891, and deriving its ideas less from European Marxist theory than from English Chartism and (as the spelling indicates) from American labor concepts. In 1957 there was a split when the Democratic Labor Party, mainly RC and anti-Communist, was formed: by 1974 it was no longer represented in either house. The L.P. remained out of office from 1949, except for the brief interlude under Whitlam (1972–5), which ended in a constitutional crisis involving the Gov.-General (*See* CONSTITUTION), until Bob Hawke (q.v.) defeated Malcolm Fraser in the general election of 1983. The party's leaders have included W.M. Hughes, Scullin, Curtin, Chifley, Whitlam and Hayden (qq.v).

LABOUR DAY. The annual festival of the Labour Movement, often linked with 1 May, the immemorial day of popular rejoicing as marking the beginning of summer.

In Britain it was celebrated 1890-1977 on 1 May or the first Sunday in May, but in 1976 the Wilson govt decided that it should be a public holiday on the first Monday in May. In Scotland the Spring 'bank holiday' already being on the first Monday in May, L.D. became the last Monday of the month.

LABOUR PARTY. British working-class and Socialist party. Although Keir Hardie and John Burns entered Parliament independently as Labour MPs in 1892, it was not till 1900 that a conference representing the trade unions, the Independent Labour Party and the Fabian Society (qq.v.) founded the L.P., known until 1906, when 29 seats were gained, as the Labour Representation Committee. All but a pacifist minority of the L.P. supported the F.W.W., and in 1918 a Socialist programme was first adopted, with local branches of the party being set up to which individual members were now admitted. By 1922 the L.P. was recognized as the official Opposition, and in 1924 formed a minority govt (with Liberal support) for a few months under J. R. MacDonald (q.v.). A second minority govt in 1929 followed a conservative policy, completely failing to deal with unemployment, and in 1931 MacDonald and other leaders, faced with a financial crisis, left the party to support the National government. The I.L.P. (q.v.) seceded in 1932. In 1936-9 there was internal dissension on foreign policy, the leadership's support of non-intervention in Spain being strongly criticized, and Sir Stafford Cripps, Aneurin Bevan and others being expelled for advocating an alliance of all left-wing parties against the Chamberlain govt.

The L.P. supported Churchill's wartime coalition, but then withdrew and took office for the first time as a majority govt. under Attlee after the 1945 elections. The Welfare State was developed by nationalisation (q.v.) of essential services and industries, and a system of national insurance (1946) and a National Health Service (1948). Defeated in 1951, the L.P. was split by disagreements on further nationalisation and unilateral/multilateral disarmament, but achieved unity under Gaitskell's leadership 1955-63, and under Wilson returned to power 1964-70 and, very narrowly, 1974-9. Callaghan, who had been elected by Labour MPs to succeed Wilson in 1976 (the first British PM to be elected to the office) attempted to retain power by a consultative pact with the Liberals 1977-8, but was forced to a general election in May 1979 and lost. In Opposition he was confronted by pressure from the constituency organisations and the trade unions (who form a large part of L.P. membership and contribute largely to its funds by a political levy) for increased control. Demands incl. the election of future party leaders by an electoral college (agreed in special Conference Jan. 1981: 40% trade union vote, 30% MPs, 30% constituency parties), instead of by MPs alone; the college (and not as previously the leader) would also prepare the party manifesto; some form of control would also be exercised over the leader's choice of his Cabinet as PM (in Opposition there is already an annual ballot among MPs to elect members of the Parliamentary Committee or 'Shadow Cabinet', who each take responsibility for covering one aspect of govt.); and Labour MPs themselves have to submit to re-selection at each election. Michael Foot, leader 1980–83, stood down after the disastrous general election defeat in 1983, and was replaced by Neil Kinnock.

Within the Labour Party the extreme left-wing Militant Tendency, so-named from its association with the Trotskyite news-sheet *Militant,* had by 1981 become dominant in a number of constituency Labour Parties. In 1982 the party's executive decided that, to safeguard the party constitution, a register of groups should be established.

The L.P., the TUC and the Co-operative movement together form the National Council of Labour, in order to co-ordinate political activities and take joint action on specific issues. The Fabian Society is the most important affiliated political body.

LABRADO'R. Peninsula in NE Canada, lying between Ungava Bay on the NW, the Atlantic on the E, and the Strait of Belle Isle on the SE. Part of it is in the prov. of Quebec, part forms a division of the prov. of Newfoundland, from which it is separated by the Strait of Belle Isle. L. consists for the most part of a plateau sloping gently from the mountains which fringe the irregular coastline. There are important fisheries, espec. for cod. Large forests support a timber and pulp industry, and there are rich

LABOUR PARTY. Neil Kinnock in dominant form at the Labour Party Conference at Brighton in 1983 after his election to the leadership, following the resignation of Michael Foot.

mineral resources, espec. iron. Hydro-electric resources incl. Churchill Falls on Churchill r., where there is one of the world's largest underground power houses. Area (of the L. division of Newfoundland) 285,000 sq.km (110,000 sq.m); pop. (1976) 557,725.

The *L. retriever* probably descends directly from dogs brought to Britain by fishing boat crews *c.* 1835. They are black or tan and stand *c.* 55cm (22in) high.

LA BRUYÈRE (brüyār'), **Jean de** (1645-96). French essayist. B. in Paris, he studied law, took a post in the revenue office, and in 1684 entered the service of the house of Condé. His *Caractères* (1688), satirical portaits of contemporaries, made him many enemies.

LABUAN (lahboo-ahn'). A flat, wooded island off NW Borneo, ceded to Gt Britain in 1846, and from 1963 incl. in Sabah, Fed. of Malaysia. The chief town is Victoria, with a good harbour. Area 90 sq.km (35 sq.m).

LABURNUM. Flowering tree (*L. vulgaris*) a member of the Leguminosae family, native to the mountainous parts of central Europe. The flowers, in long drooping clusters, are bright yellow and appear in early spring; some varieties have purple or reddish flowers. The seeds are poisonous.

LAC. Resinous incrustation exuded by the female lac-insects (*Coccus lacca*), which eventually covers the twigs of trees in India and the Far East. The gathered twigs are known as stick-lac, which yields a useful crimson dye and the commercial shellac formed by melting the separated resin, and spreading it into thin layers or flakes.

LACCADIVE (lak'adīv), **MINICOY and AMINDIVI ISLANDS.** *See* LAKSHADWEEP.

LACE. A plain or decorative textile fabric of an open-work or network type. Needle-point or point laces (which are a development of embroidery) were first evolved in Italy in the late 15th or early 16th cents., whence the craft spread to France and Germany, probably being brought to England by the Flemings. The other chief variety of L. is bobbin or pillow L., which is made by twisting threads together in pairs or groups, according to a pattern marked out by pins set in a cushion, and is said to have been invented by Barbara Uttmann (b. 1514) of Saxony: elaborate patterns may require 1,000 bobbins. From 1589 various attempts were made at producing machine-made L., and in 1809 John Heathcoat achieved success with a bobbin net machine: the principles of this system are kept in modern machines making plain net. The earliest machine for making true L., reproducing the movements of the fingers of the pillow-lace workers in twisting the threads together, was the invention of another Englishman, John Leavers, in 1813. It had a wooden frame and many of the moving parts were of wood, but the principle involved is the same as in the modern machines at Nottingham, the great centre of machine-made L. Early Ls. were principally made from linen thread, enriched with gold, silver, or silk: later materials incl. cotton, wool, rayon, nylon, etc. Among the great centres of L.-making have been Venice, Alençon, and Argentan for point L., and Mechlin, Valenciennes, and Honiton for bobbin L.: both types are made at Brussels.

LACE. The complexities of making pillow lace at Bruges, the pattern being carefully pricked out with pins. These bobbins are severely practical, but many early examples are fancifully carved. *Photo: J. Allan Cash*

LA CEIBA (thā-ēva). The chief port of Honduras on the Atlantic. Pop. (1973) 44,000.

LACERTID (las'ertid). Member of a class of radio-emitting star-like bodies, which show no lines in their optical spectra. They appear to be a variety of galaxy, and are in the process of divesting themselves of excess non-thermal energy.

LACEWING FLY. Insect of the families Hemerobiidae (incl. the brown lacewings) and Chrysopidae (incl. the green lacewings or golden-eye flies), found through-out the world. So named because of the veining of their 2 pairs of semi-transparent wings, they have narrow bodies and long thin antennae. The eggs of the green lacewing are stalked.

LACHISH (lā'kish). Biblical city identified by Albright in 1929 as having occupied the mound of Tell ed-Duweir *c.* 40km (25m) SW of Jerusalem. Most notable find during excavations by J. K. Starkey 1932-8 was a no. of ostraca inscribed in Hebrew which antedate the final destruction of the city in 589 BC and are valuable for comparison with Hebrew MSS.

LACHLAN (lak'lan), River, a tributary of the Murrumbidgee, Australia, which rises in the Blue Mtns: length 1,485 km (920m).

LACLOS (lahkloh'), **Pierre Choderlos de** (1741-1803). French author. An army officer, he wrote a single novel in letter form, *Les Liaisons dangereuses* (1782), an analysis of moral corruption.

LA CONDAMINE. *See* MONACO.

LACQUER (la'ker). A varnish made from the sap of the lacquer-tree (*Rhus vernicifera*), and used for producing a highly polished surface on furniture and other articles. L. is often coloured red, blue, brown, etc., and successive coatings of the varnish are applied to the objects treated. The earliest specimens are Korean, whence the art spread to China and Japan. Many months are needed to produce the finest work.

LACROSSE. Canadian ball game. The name comes from the Fr. *la croix*, a bishop's crozier, which a L. stick somewhat resembles. The game was played by the Red Indians, both men and women, from whom the Canadians adopted it. Introduced into England in 1867, it became particularly popular as a women's game after 1900.

The stick or 'crosse' is a light staff of hickory wood, with the top bent in the form of a hook, from the tip of which a thong is drawn down and fastened to the shaft. Across the frame a loose network of hide is drawn. The pitch is 110.65m (120yd) long and 75.25m (85yd) wide, with a wing area on either side of a central line. The goals, 1.83m (6ft) by 1.83m (6ft), are in circles 5.50m (18ft) in diameter. The ball, made of indiarubber sponge, weighs 127–141 grammes (4.5–5.0oz).

The team consists of 10 men incl. the goalkeeper. To open play, the 2 centres 'face' the ball, and each tries to get it. The ball may be kicked, but not handled, except by the goalkeeper. A player may not be held, tripped, pushed, charged, or shouldered; a 'free position' may be awarded for a foul, or a player may be suspended. The game is controlled by 2 referees on the field, a time-keeper and a scorer.

LACTATION. The secretion of milk. In late pregnancy the cells lining the lobules inside the breasts undergo a change which makes them convert the blood into milk. The supply of milk starts shortly after birth with the production of colostrum, a clear fluid consisting largely of serum, which has a certain purgative effect needed by the infant. The milk becomes established in a few days, and will then continue practically as long as the child continues to suck.

LACTIC ACID. Three acids of the same composition. The ordinary acid is a colourless, almost odourless syrup, soluble in water, alcohol, and ether. It occurs in sour milk, wine, and certain plant extracts. and is always present in the stomach.

LACTOSE, or **milk sugar.** A disaccharide found in the milk of all animals. Cow's milk contains 4.5-5 per cent of the sugar. It is usually prepared from the whey obtained in cheese making.

LADAHK (ladahk'). Subsidiary range of the Karakoram and district of NE Kashmir on the border of Tibet. After the Chinese occupation of Tibet in 1951, China made claims on the area.

LADI'NOS. *See* GUATEMALA.

LADI'NS. Ethnic community in the Dolomites, descended from Etruscans and proto-Italic tribes of the Po valley, and speaking a language directly derived from Latin. Numbering *c.* 16,000, they have links with the Romansch-speakers of Switzerland.

LADOGA (lah'-), **Lake.** Largest lake in Europe, in the RSFSR, just NE of Leningrad. It receives the waters of the Svir, which drains L. Onega, and other rivers, and drains to the Gulf of Finland by the r. Neva. Lake L. forms a link in the White Sea-Baltic Canal. Area 18,400 sq.km (7,100 sq.m).

LADRONES. Spanish name (meaning thieves) of the MARIANAS.

LADY. Feminine title of honour, correlative to that of Lord, and Sir. It is the correct title of the dau. of an earl, marquis or duke, and of any woman whose husband is above the rank of baronet or knight, and is also accorded by courtesy to the wives of these two latter ranks.

LADYBIRD. A migratory beetle of the family Coccinellidae, red or yellow in colour, with black spots. There are several species which, with their larvae, feed upon aphides and scale-insect pests.

LADYBIRD. The 7-spot ladybird *(Coccinella 7-punctata)* in flight, showing the membraneous wings which are concealed beneath the spotty wing-cases. *Photo: Heather Angel*

LADY DAY. 25 March, the festival of the Annunciation of the Virgin Mary. Until 1752 (when 1 Jan. was substituted) it was the beginning of the legal year in England, and it is still a quarter day.

LADYSMITH. Town in Natal, S Africa, 185km (115m) NW of Durban, nr the Klip. It was besieged by the Boers, 2 Nov. 1899-28 Feb. 1900, during the S African War. L. was named in honour of the wife of Sir Harry Smith (q.v.). Pop. (1970) 25,000.

LA FAYETTE (fayet'), **Marie Joseph Gilbert du Motier,** marquis de (1757-1834). French soldier and statesman. He fought against Britain in the American War of Independence. During the French Revolution he sat in the National Assembly as a constitutional royalist, and in 1789 was given command of the National Guard. In 1792 he fled the country after attempting to restore the monarchy, and was imprisoned by the Austrians until 1797. He supported Napoleon during the Hundred Days, sat in the Chamber of Deputies as a Liberal from 1818, and assisted the revolution of 1830. He was a popular hero in the USA, and the towns of L. in Louisiana, pop. (1970) 69,000 and in Indiana, pop. (1970) 45,000, are named after him.

LA FAYETTE, Marie-Madeleine, comtesse de (1634-93). French author. Her *Mémoires* of the French court are keenly observed, and her *La Princesse de Clèves* (1678) is the first French psychological novel and *roman à clef* (novel with a 'key') in that real-life characters were presented under fictitious names, incl. La Rochefoucauld (q.v.) who was for many yrs her lover.

LA FONTAINE (foñtăn'), **Jean de** (1621-95). French poet. B. at Château-Thierry, from 1656 he lived largely in Paris, enjoying the friendship of Molière, Racine, and Boileau. His outstanding works are his *Fables* (1668-94), and his *Contes* (1665-74), a series of witty and improper tales in verse.

LAFORGUE (lahforg'), **Jules** (1860-87). French poet, whose technical innovations greatly influenced T. S. Eliot and also later French writers.

LĀ'GASH. Sumerian city north of Shatra, Iraq. Discovered (1877) and excavated by Ernest de Sarzec, then French consul in Basra, it was of great importance under independent and semi-independent rulers *c.* 3000-2700 BC. Besides objects of high artistic value, it has provided *c.* 30,000 clay tablets giving detailed information on temple administration.

LAGER (lah'ger; Ger. *lager,* store). A light beer. After fermentation L. is stored at a low temperature for periods ranging from a few weeks to several months, and acquires its characteristic flavour. L. is particularly popular in Germany and the USA, and increasingly in Britain.

LAGERKVIST, Pär (1891-1974). Swedish author. Recognition of his lyric poetry, dramas (*The Hangman,* 1935), and novels (*Barabbas,* 1950) has been hindered by their obscurity of expression, but in 1951 he was awarded a Nobel prize.

LAGERLÖF (lah'gerlöf), **Selma** (1858-1940). Swedish novelist. Originally a schoolteacher, she won fame in 1891 with a collection of stories of peasant life, *Gösta Berling's Saga.* She received a Nobel prize in 1909.

LĀ'GOS. Port in Nigeria, W Africa. At the W end of an is. in a lagoon, it is linked by bridges with the mainland, via Iddo Island. There is an excellent harbour and modern airport, and the univ. (1962) has a large medical school. Onikan Museum has one of the world's richest collections of African art. However, the climate is unhealthy, and while it remains the chief commercial centre, it is being replaced from 1976 as the cap. of Nigeria by Abuja (q.v.). Pop. (1975) 1,061,000.

LAGRANGE (lahgroñzh'), **Joseph Louis** (1736-1813). French mathematician. He presided over the commission which introduced the metric system in 1793. His chief writings are *Mécanique analytique* (1788) and *Théorie des fonctions analytiques* (1797).

LA GUARDIA (gwahr'di-a), **Fiorello Henrico** (1882-1947). American politician. Elected mayor of New York in 1933 against the opposition of the powerful Tammany Hall machine, he cleaned up the administration, suppressed racketeering, and organized unemployment relief, slum-clearance schemes, and social services. Although nominally a Republican, he strongly supported the New Deal. L.G. Airport, NY, is named after him.

LA HOGUE (hōg). A naval battle fought off the Normandy coast in 1692 in which the combined English and Dutch fleets defeated the French.

LAHO'RE. Cap. of the prov. of Punjab, Pakistan, and second city of Pakistan. L. has many associations with the Mogul rulers Akbar, Jahangir and Aurangzeb, whose cap. it was in the 16-17th cents., and the Shalimar Gardens are to the NW. There is a univ. (1882), and industries incl. engineering, textiles, carpets, chemicals. Pop. (1972) 2,148,000.

LAHORE. The Shalimar gardens, laid out in the late 17th century by Shah Jehan. *Photo: Courtesy of the office of the High Commissioner for Pakistan.*

LAIBACH. German name of LJUBLJANA.

LAING, Ronald David (1927-). Scottish psychoanalyst. He is noted as the originator of the 'social theory' of mental illness, i.e. schizophrenia is promoted by the family setting of the patient which demands that its members conform to standards alien to the individual. His books incl. *The Divided Self* (1960) and *The Politics of the Family* (1971).

LAISSEZ-FAIRE (lā'sehfair'). The theory that the State should refrain from all intervention in economic affairs. The phrase originated with the 18th cent. French economists, the Physiocrats, whose maxim was *laissez-faire et laissez-passer* (literally 'let go and let pass', i.e. 'leave the individual alone, and let commodities circulate freely'). Before the 17th cent. control by the guild, local authorities, or the State, of wages, prices, employment, the training of workmen, etc., was taken for granted. As capitalist enterprises developed in the 16th and 17th cents., entrepreneurs shook off the control of the guilds and local authorities, and the revolution of 1640-60 weakened the hold of the State on economic life. By the 18th cent. this process was complete.

The reaction against L.-F. began in the mid-19th cent., and found expression in the factory acts, etc. This reaction was inspired partly by humanitarian protests against the social conditions created by the Industrial Revolution, partly by the wish to counter the popular unrest of the 1830s and '40s by removing some of its causes. The last cent. has shown an ever-increasing degree of State intervention to promote social amelioration, which since 1945 has been extended into the field of nationalization of leading industries and services.

LAKE. Sheet of still water lying in depressed ground without direct communication with the sea. Lakes are common in glaciated mountain regions, along the course of gently declining rivers, and in low land near the sea. The main classifications are by origin as follows: glacial Ls., such as in the Alps; barrier Ls., formed by landslides, valley glaciers, etc.; crater Ls.; tectonic Ls., occurring in natural features. Most Ls. are fresh, e.g. the group incl. Superior, Michigan and Huron, but in hot regions where evaporation is excessive they may be salt, e.g. the Dead Sea. The 20th cent. has seen the creation of large artificial

Ls. in connection with hydro-electric and other works. There has also been pollution and sometimes eutrophication (a state of over-nourishment) of Ls., when agricultural fertilizers leach into them, causing an explosion of life, and the Ls. choke and die.

LAKE DISTRICT. The 1,800 sq.km (700m) area in Cumbria, embracing the principal English lakes separated by wild uplands rising to many peaks, incl. Scafell Pike 978 m (3,210 ft).

Windermere, in the SE, is connected with Rydal Water and Grasmere. The westerly Scafell range extends S to the Old Man of Coniston overlooking Coniston Water, and N to Wastwater. Ullswater lies in the NE of the district, with Hawes Water and Thirlmere nearby. The river Derwent flows N through Borrowdale forming Derwentwater Bassenthwaite. W of Borrowdale lie Buttermere, Crummock Water, and, beyond, Ennerdale Water.

The L.D. has associations with Wordsworth, Coleridge, Southey, De Quincey, and Ruskin, and was made a National Park in 1951: once remote, it is now in danger from too many visitors.

LAKE DWELLINGS. Habitations built on piles driven into the bottom of a lake. Such villages are found in W Africa, S America, Borneo and New Guinea. Remains of Stone Age lake villages have been found throughout the Continent, and in Britain, e.g. a lake village of the 1st cents. BC and AD excavated nr Glastonbury.

LAKE HAVASU CITY. Small town in Arizona, USA, being developed as a tourist resort. Old London Bridge was transported and reconstructed there in 1971.

LAKES, Gippsland. Series of shallow lagoons on the coast of Victoria, Australia: the chief are Wellington, Victoria and King (broadly interconnected), and Reeve.

LAKH, Lac, or **Lak.** Indian term for 100,000.

LAKSHADWEEP. Group of 14 coral is., 10 inhabited, in the Indian Ocean, 320km (200m) off the Malabar coast, formerly known as the Laccadive, Minicoy and Amindivi Islands. Discovered by Vasco da Gama in 1499, they were British from 1877 until Indian independence: created a Union Terr. of the Rep. of India in 1956, they were renamed L. in 1973. They produce coir, copra and fish. The admin HQ is Kavaratti Is. Area 28 sq.km (11 sq.m); pop. (1971) 32,000, mainly Moslems.

LAKSHMI (laksh'mē). Hindu goddess of good fortune, love and beauty, and the wife of Vishnu.

LA LÍNEA. Town and port on the isthmus of Algeciras Bay, Spain, adjoining the frontier zone with Gibraltar, and until the closure of the border by Spain 1969 a source of supplies and labour for the latter. Pop. (1970) 55,700.

LA'LLANS. Scottish word meaning 'lowland' and referring espec. to the dialect of that area of the country as used by writers such as Hugh MacDiarmid (q.v.).

LAMAISM (Tibetan, *lama*, a superior priest). The religion of Tibet and Mongolia; a form of Buddhism belonging to the Mahayana school. Buddhism was introduced into Tibet in AD 640, but the real founder of L. was the Indian missionary Padma Sambhava who began his activity about AD 750. In the 15th cent. was founded the sect of Geluk-Pa (virtuous) by Tsongkhapa, which has remained the most powerful organization in the country. The Dalai Lama (q.v.), residing at the palace of the Potala at Lhasa, exercised both spiritual and temporal authority as head of the Tibetan State until 1959, and is considered an incarnation of Bodhisattva Avalokitesvara. *See also* PANCHEN LAMA. On the death of the Dalai Lama great care is taken in finding the infant in whom he has been reincarnated.

L. formerly numbered 1 in 4 of the male population as a monk, but under Chinese Communist rule their numbers were rapidly reduced. Formerly frequent in the Tibetan countryside were prayer-wheels and prayer-flags on which were inscribed prayers; when these were turned by hand or moved by the wind, great spiritual benefit was supposed to accrue.

LAMARCK (lamahrk'), **Jean Baptiste** (1744-1829). French naturalist. B. at Bazentin, he was forced by ill-health to abandon a military career, and studied medicine and meteorology before turning to botany. His greatest works were his *Philosophie Zoologique* (1809) and the *Histoire naturelle des animaux sans vertèbres* (1815-22). His theory that acquired characteristics could be inherited was long discredited, but was revived in the later 20th cent.: *see* EVOLUTION.

LAMARTINE (lahmahrtēn'), **Alphonse de** (1790-1869). French poet. B. at Mâçon he achieved immediate success with his first vol. of musically romantic poems, *Méditations* (1820), which was followed by *Nouvelles Méditations* (1823), *Harmonies* (1830), *Recueillements* (1839), etc. He entered the Chamber of Deputies in 1833, and by his *Histoire des Girondins* (1847) influenced the revolution of 1848.

LAMB, Charles (1775-1834). British essayist and critic. B. in London, he was ed. at Christ's Hospital, where he was a contemporary of Coleridge, and in 1792 became a clerk at India House. In 1796 he pub. some poems together with Coleridge, but in the same year his sister Mary (1764-1847) stabbed their mother to death in a fit of madness, and L. devoted his life to caring for her, since periodic recurrence of the attacks meant that she must at times be placed in an asylum. In 1807 he collaborated with Mary in the *Tales from Shakespeare*, and in 1808 pub. *Specimens of English Dramatic Poets* which assisted the revival of interest in Elizabethan playwrights. In 1820 he began contributing to the *London Magazine* the series of appealingly individual essays under the pseudonym of 'Elia', borrowed from an early office acquaintance, which were collected in 1823 and 1833. In 1825 L. retired from India House, and moved first to Enfield then to Edmonton, where both he and his sister are buried.

LAMBERT, John (1619-83). English gen. B. in Yorks, he joined the parliamentary army in 1642, and distinguished himself as a cavalry commander at Marston Moor, Preston, Dunbar, and Worcester. He co-operated closely with Cromwell until 1657, when his opposition to Cromwell's proposed assumption of the title led to a breach. After the Restoration he was imprisoned for life.

LAMBETH. Borough of Greater London, England, opposite Westminster on the S bank of the Thames. Notable buildings incl. L. Palace, with its 15th cent. Lollard's Tower, on a site which has been occupied by the chief residence of the archbishops of Canterbury from 1197; and County Hall, HQ of the GLC, opened in 1922. Pop. (1972) 301,700.

LAMBETH CONFERENCE. *See* ANGLICAN COMMUNION.

LAMBURN, Richmal Crompton. *See* CROMPTON.

LAMELLIBRANCHIA (lamelibrang'kia). Class of molluscs, also known as bivalves, from the shell which consists of 2 valves joined by a hinge. There are many

LAMB. Charles Lamb, a portrait painted in 1804 by William Hazlitt (q.v.). *Photo: Courtesy of the National Portrait Gallery*

LAMPREY. The river lamprey *(Lampetra fluviatilis)*, showing the suctorial mouth and seven gill slits. Henry I is reputed to have died of a surfeit of this, his favourite fish. *Photo: Heather Angel*

varieties, the best-known being cockles, mussels and oysters, usually found in shallow seawater.

LAMMAS ('loaf-mass'). Medieval festival of harvest, celebrated on 1 Aug. At one time it was an English quarter day, and is still a quarter day in Scotland.

LAMMERGEIER (lamergī-er). Bird of prey (*Gypaëtus barbatus*), half-eagle and half-vulture, with a wing-span of over 3m (10ft). It ranges over S Europe, N Africa and Asia.

LAMMERMUIR HILLS (lammermūr'). A range of hills dividing Lothian and Borders regions, Scotland, from Gala Water to St Abb's Head.

LAMPREY (lam'pri). An eel-like fish belonging to the family Petromyzontidae. They feed on other fish by a type of parasitism, fixing themselves by the round mouth to their host and boring the flesh by their toothed tongue. The sea-L. is a food fish.

LA'NARK. Town in Strathclyde region, Scotland, 35km (22m) SE of Glasgow. William Wallace once lived here, and later returned to burn the town and kill the English sheriff. New L. to the S, founded 1785, was the scene of 'ideal village' socialist experiments by Robert Owen. Pop. (1973) 8,850.

LA'NARKSHIRE. A former southern inland co. of Scotland, merged in 1975 in the region of Strathclyde. The co. town was Lanark.

LANCASHIRE. Co. of England, between N and W Yorks to the E, and the Irish Sea to the W. As reconstituted after the local govt reorganization of 1974, it lost the Furness peninsula to Cumbria in the N, and in the S lost a small area round Warrington to Cheshire; Liverpool and its hinterland to Merseyside; and most of the SW to the new co. of Greater Manchester. To the NE it gained considerably at the expense of the former W Riding of Yorks. The chief river is the Ribble. Towns incl. Preston, the admin HQ; Blackburn and Burnley; the ports of Fleetwood and Heysham; and the seaside resorts of Blackpool, Morecambe and Southport. Formerly L. was the world centre of cotton manufacture, and depended also on other traditional industries, but others of a more varied kind are being expanded or estab., and Central Lancs New Town (1970), which incl. the whole of Preston, Fulwood, Bamber Bridge, Leyland and Chorley (intended pop. 500,000) is to become the focus of the new co. Area 3,005 sq.km (1,160 sq.m); pop. (1978) 1,369,600. L. has a rich vein of humour, e.g. George Formby, Gracie Fields and Les Dawson; *L. hotpot* is meat stew with potatoes cooked in a closed pot.

LA'NCASTER, House and Duchy of. A family descended from Henry III's son, Edmund, earl of L., which ruled England 1399-1461. The family estates passed by marriage to John of Gaunt (q.v.), who was created duke of L. in 1362. His son Henry IV obtained the throne in 1399. The third Lancastrian king, Henry VI, was deposed in 1461 and murdered in 1471, and the Lancastrian claim passed to Henry of Richmond, a descendant of John of Gaunt, who became king as Henry VII in 1485.

The DUCHY OF L. became a county palatine, with its own courts outside the royal jurisdiction, in 1351; these rights have been attached to the Crown since 1399. The office of Chancellor of the Duchy of L. is actually a 'sinecure', usually held by a member of the cabinet with a special role outside the prov. of the regular ministries, e.g. Harold Lever as financial adviser to the Wilson-Callaghan govts from 1974.

LANCASTER, Sir Osbert (1908–86). British artist. Ed. at Charterhouse and Lincoln Coll., Oxford, he went on to study at the Slade, and produced imaginative stage settings for Old Vic and Covent Garden productions. He was popularly best known for his 'pocket' cartoons in the *Daily Express* from 1939, which introduce a series of satirically amusing characters from the Establishment, e.g. Maudie Littlehampton and Canon Fontwater. He was knighted in 1975.

LANCASTER. City in Lancs, England, on the r. Lune. It is the traditional co. town of Lancs, but the modern admin HQ is Preston. The castle incorporates Roman work, and during the Civil War was captured by Cromwell. The Univ. was founded in 1964. Industries incl. textiles, floor coverings, furniture and plastics. Pop. (1971) 49,820.

LANCASTER. City in Pennsylvania, USA, 115km (70m) W. of Philadelphia, producing silk and cotton textiles, electrical goods, etc. Pop. (1970) 57,700.

LANCELET. Animal (*Amphioxus*). Sole representative of the class Cephalochordata or Leptocardia, one of the most primitive groups of the Chordata. Skull, vertebral column, centralized brain, and paired limbs are absent, but there is a notochord which runs from end to end of the body, a tail, and a number of gill-slits. L. is found in all seas; it burrows in the sand, but when disturbed swims freely. In its feeding habits it resembles the sea-squirts (Tunicata).

LANCELOT OF THE LAKE. The most celebrated of Arthur's knights, and the lover of Queen Guinevere. He was originally a folk-hero, and was introduced into the Arthurian cycle in the 12th cent.

LANCHOW. *See* LANZHOU.

LANCRET (loṅkreh'), **Nicolas** (1690-1743). French artist. B. In Paris, he was a follower of Watteau, painting graceful *fêtes galantes* and illustrating the amorous *Contes de la Fontaine.*

LAND (lahnt). A federal unit (plural Länder) of W Germany.

LANDES (loṅd), **The.** Sandy low-lying area in SW France, along the Bay of Biscay, *c.* 12,950 sq.km (5,000 sq.m) in extent. Formerly a furze- and heath-covered waste, it has in many parts been reclaimed by planting with pine and oak forests. It gives its name to a dept, and extends into the depts of Gironde and Lot-et-Garonne. Arcachon is a well-known bathing resort. There is a testing range for rockets and missiles at Biscarosse, 72km (45m) SW of Bordeaux. There is an oilfield at Parentis-en-Born.

LAND LEAGUE. Irish peasant organization, formed by Michael Davitt in 1879 to fight against evictions. It forced Gladstone's govt, by its skilful use of the boycott against any man who took a farm from which another had been evicted, to introduce a law in 1881 restricting rents and granting tenants security of tenure.

LANDLORD AND TENANT. The relationship which exists when an owner of land or buildings (the landlord) gives to another (the tenant) the exclusive right of occupation for a definite limited period, e.g. a year, a term of years, a week or a month. When the terms of the contract are embodied in a deed they are said to be covenants, and the whole agreement is termed a *lease.*

There was formerly freedom of contract between L. and T. in Britain, but wartime shortage of rented accommodation for lower income groups led to abuse by unscrupulous Ls. and from 1914 acts were passed affording protection for Ts. against eviction and rent increases. The shortage was aggravated by the S.W.W. and from 1939 Rent Acts were passed greatly increasing the range of dwellings so protected. Extensive decontrol under the 1957 Rent Act led to hardship, and further legislation followed, notably the Rent Act of 1974, under which tenants of furnished and unfurnished premises were given equal security of tenure. This reflected Labour policy of eliminating the private sector, and the pool of accommodation tended thenceforward to dry up. The Housing Act (1980), introduced by the Conservative govt., attempted to make it more attractive to a landlord to let his property, while still safeguarding the tenant, notably by creating a new category of tenure - the protected shorthold.

LANDOR, Walter Savage (1775-1864). British poet and author. B. in Warwick, he was expelled from Rugby and rusticated from Oxford owing to his uncertain temper. In 1795 he pub. his first *Poems,* followed by the epic *Gebir* (1798), and the verse drama *Count Julian* (1812). In 1808 he raised a force of volunteers to free Spain from Napoleon, and settled at Llanthony, S Wales, in 1809-14: In 1811 he m. unhappily, and lived mainly in Italy 1814-35, when he settled in Bath until 1859. To this period belong the *Imaginary Conversations* (1824-46), *Pericles and Aspasia* (1836), *The Pentameron, The Hellenics* (1846-7), etc. Drawn into a libel action in 1858, he took refuge in Florence, where he d.

LANDRAIL. *See* RAIL.

LAND REGISTRY, H.M. State register of landowners voluntarily submitting titles to their land for examination and approval by the registrar on behalf of the State estab. in 1862. By the L.R. Act of 1897 the principle of compulsory registration was introduced, which makes the future buying or selling of land much easier and cheaper, since absolute titles granted by the L.R. (administered under the Lord Chancellor by the Chief Land Registrar) are guaranteed and lengthy examinations of title are unnecessary.

LANDSEER, Sir Edwin Henry (1802-73). British painter and sculptor. B. in London, he exhibited at the RA in 1815, and achieved great popularity with sentimental studies of animals, e.g. 'Dignity and Impudence'. A masterly draughtsman, he was elected RA in 1831 and knighted in 1850. Best known of his sculptures are the Trafalgar Square lions.

LAND'S END. A promontory of W Cornwall, 15km (9m) WSW of Penzance, the most westerly point of England. Nearby is the Minack open air theatre. An extension of L.E. is a group of dangerous rocks, the Longships, a mile out, marked by a lighthouse.

LAND'S END. Granite cliffs thrust into the Atlantic and dangerous reefs lie close in, as well as the outer group marked by a lighthouse. *Photo: Courtesy of the British Tourist Authority*

LANDS'KRONA. Seaport of Sweden, on the Sound, 32km (20m) N of Malmo. L. makes machinery, chemicals, etc., and has shipbuilding yards and sugar refineries. Charles XI defeated the Danes off L. in 1677. Pop. (1972) 34,700.

LANFRANC (lan'frangk) (*c.* 1005-89). Archbishop of Canterbury. B. at Pavia, he entered the monastery of Bec, Normandy, in 1042, and there opened a school which achieved international fame. His skill in theological controversy did much to secure the Church's adoption of the doctrine of transubstantiation. Appointed archbp of Canterbury in 1070, he rebuilt the cathedral, replaced English clergy by Normans, enforced clerical celibacy, and separated the ecclesiastical from the secular courts.

LANG, Andrew (1844-1912). British author. B. at Selkirk, he went to London as a journalist in 1875. His writings include historical works, e.g. *History of Scotland* (1900-7) and *The Maid of France* (1908), a reply to Anatole France's life of Joan of Arc; anthropological essays, e.g. *Myth, Ritual and Religion (1887)* and *The Making of Religion* (1898), which involved him in controversy with Frazer; translations of Homer; verse and novels; and a series of children's books, beginning with the *Blue Fairy Tale Book* (1889).

LANG, Fritz (1890-1976). American film producer. B. in Vienna, he caused a sensation in 1931 with *M*, in which Peter Lorre starred as a child-killer, fled to Hollywood from Germany in 1936 after his anti-dictator *Dr Mabuse* (1933), and there made *Fury* (1936) with Spencer Tracy and *You Only Live Once* (1937) with Henry Fonda, and others with a strong sense of social realism.

LANGEVIN (lonzhvañ'), **Paul** (1872-1946). French physicist. A pioneer in the field of magnetic theory and the molecular structure of gases, he was prof. of general physics at the Collège de France. Arrested by the Germans as a anti-Fascist in 1940, on his release he escaped to Switzerland, returning after the liberation. *See* GRENOBLE.

LANGLAND, William (*c.* 1332-*c.* 1400) British poet. B. in the W Midlands, possibly near Malvern, he took minor orders, and in later life settled in London. His alliterative *Vision concerning Piers Plowman* appeared in 3 versions *c.* 1362-*c.* 1398, but certain critics believe he was responsible only for the first of these. The poem forms a series of allegorical visions, in which Piers develops from the typical poor peasant to a symbol of Christ, and condemns the social and moral evils of 14th cent. England.

LANGLEY, Samuel Pierpont (1834-1906). American inventor. Prof. of physics and astronomy at Western Univ. of Pennsylvania 1866-87, and sec. of the Smithsonian Inst. 1887-1906, he did valuable research on the infra-red portions of the solar spectrum. His steam-driven aeroplane flew for 90 sec. in 1896, making the first flight by an engine-equipped aircraft, and establishing the 'respectability' of aeronautical research in the USA.

LANGMUIR, Irving (1881-1957). American scientist. Working for the General Electric Co. 1909-50, he invented the mercury vapour pump for producing high vacua and the atomic hydrogen welding process and was a pioneer of the thermionic valve. In 1932 he was awarded a Nobel prize for his work on surface chemistry.

LANGTON, Stephen (d. 1228). English churchman. B. in Lincs, he studied at Paris where he became chancellor of the univ., and in 1206 was created a cardinal. When in 1207 Innocent III secured his election as archbp of Canterbury King John refused to recognize him, and L. was not allowed to enter England until 1213. He supported the barons in their struggle against John, and was mainly responsible for Magna Carta.

LANGTRY, Lillie (1853-1929). British actress. Greatly admired by Edward VII, she was known as 'the Jersey lily', having been born in the island.

LANGUAGES OF THE WORLD. They have been arranged, in a large number of cases, into language families on the basis of their genetic relationship, but many groupings are only tentative. Further information on the chief Ls. and L. families is to be found under their names.

Most practically important and thoroughly investigated is the Indo-European family, which comprises in the *centum* division Greek; the Italo-Celtic group (Latin, whence the Romance languages; Celtic, Gaelic, Manx, etc.); Germanic (Gothic, the North-Germanic or Scandinavian languages,. and the West Germanic, including English, German, Flemish, Dutch, Afrikaans, etc.); and also Tocharian; and in the *satem* division Balto-Slavonic (Lithuanian, Russian, Polish, Slovene, Serbo-Croat, Bulgarian, etc.); Armenian, Albanian; and the Indo-Iranian languages - Zend, Persian, Sanskrit, Pali, and the modern Indian languages. The Caucasian family includes Georgian and perhaps Basque. The Hamito-Semitic contains the Ethiopian tongues, Aramaic, Hebrew, Arabic with Maltese, and also Berber, Egyptian, Somali, etc. The Finno-Ugrian family includes Finnish, Lapp, Estonian, Magyar or Hungarian. The Altaic family contains Turkish, Mongol, Manchu, etc. Eskimo and Aleut form one family, and Korean and Japanese another. In the Sinitic or Indo-Chinese family are placed Tibetan, Burmese, Chinese, Siamese, Annamese, etc. The Malayo-Polynesian family includes the languages of Malaya and the South Seas excluding New Guinea. Tamil is one of the languages in the Dravidian family. The languages of New Guinea and Papua, the Australian aborigines, the Bushmen and Hottentots, are placed in separate families. Yet other families comprise Bantu (Swahili, Zulu, etc.), Sudanian (Nuba, Ewe, Hausa, etc.), and the American (the 'Red Indian' tribes, the Maya, the Inca, etc.).

The most important languages numerically - in tens of millions of speakers - are: Chinese 100 (incl. Mandarin, Cantonese, etc.); English 38; Russian 25 (Great Russian only); Hindi 24; Spanish 24; Arabic 13; Bengali 13; Portuguese 13; German 12; Japanese 12; French 10; Malay 10; Italian 6.

LANGUEDOC (lahñgdok'). Area of southern France in which the dialects of the *langue d'oc* (oc = yes), as opposed to the *langue d'oui* of northern France, were spoken in the Middle Ages, Provencal being the chief. It was the language of the troubadours, and was revived in the 19th cent. In modern times the name **Occitanie** (okitahni') has also been revived to denote this area, still differing in language and temperament from the north, which incl. the major part of the regions of Languedoc-Roussillon and Provence-Côte d'Azur, where - in conjunction with Corsica - separatist aims are popular.

LANIER (lanēr'), **Sidney** (1842-81). American poet. B. in Georgia, he served in the Civil War, and subsequently studied law, which he abandoned for music. His *Poems* (1877) contain some interesting metrical experiments, in accordance with his theories expounded in his *Science of English Verse* (1880), on the relation of verse to music.

LA'NOLIN. Purified wax obtained from the wool of sheep and used in cosmetics, soap, preparation of leather, etc.

LANSBURY, George (1859-1940). British Labour leader. He sat on Poplar borough council from 1903, and went to prison with most of the councillors in 1921 rather than modify the council's policy of more generous unemployment relief. Leader of the Labour Party in the House 1931-5, he resigned (as a pacifist) in opposition to the party's policy in the Ethiopian War.

LANSDOWNE, Henry Charles Keith Petty Fitzmaurice, 5th marquis of (1845-1927). British Cons. statesman. He was Gov-Gen of Canada 1883-8, Viceroy of India 1888-93, War Minister 1895-1900, and For. Sec. 1900-6; while at the Foreign Office he abandoned Britain's isolationist policy, by forming alliances with Japan and France. His publication in 1917 of proposals for a compromise peace led to a violent controversy.

LANSING. Capital of Michigan, USA, at the confluence of the Grand and Red Cedar rivers. L. makes motor-vehicles, diesel engines, pumps, furniture, etc. Pop. (1970) 131,546.

LA'NTHANUM (Gk. *lanthano* to lie hidden). One of the cerium sub-group of the rare earths, it is a white metal: symbol La., at. wt. 138.92 and at. no. 57. Separated from ceria by Mosander in 1839, it occurs in nature in the cerite earths and resembles iron in its physical properties.

LANZHOU (lahnjaw-o͞o'). Cap. (formerly Lanchow) of Gansu prov., China, on the Huang He, *c.* 190 km (120 m) S of the Great Wall. Oil from the Yumen fields 800 km (500 m) to the N is refined, coal is mined nearby, and there are chemical, fertiliser and synthetic rubber industries. Pop. (1975) 1,750,000.

LAOIGHIS (lā-ish). Co. in Leinster prov., Rep. of Ireland. It is flat except for the Slieve Bloom mountains in the NW. Sugar beet is grown and dairy farming practised. Woollens and agricultural machinery are made. Portlaoighise is the co. town. Area 1,7,20 sq.km (664 sq.m); pop. (1971) 45,260.

LAON (loṅ). Capital of Aisne dept, N France, 120km (75m) NE of Paris. There is a fine 12th cent. cathedral. Pop. (1975) 28,600.

LAOS (lah'ōs). Mountainous country of NW Indo-China. It comprises the upper valley of the Mekong r., which for much of its course forms the W boundary with Thailand, and here the majority of the pop. live. The cap. Vientiane, and the former royal cap., Luang Prabang on the 300m/1,000 ft Plain of Jars (so-called because an advanced prehistoric people settled there carved single blocks of stone into 'jars' large enough to hold a man), are on its banks. The mtns are forested, providing ideal country for guerilla infiltration along the Vietnam border, and rise to Phu Bia 2,817m (9240ft) in central Laos. Crops incl. rice, maize, tobacco, citrus, and teak and other timber - worked by elephants, hence the country's early name of Lanxang 'Land of a Million Elephants'. Minerals incl. tin and iron: industry is little developed. For an outlet to the sea, L. formerly relied on Thailand, but there are plans for a highway to the N Vietnamese coast, and a route to Kompong Som in Kampuchea.

L. became an independent kingdom in the 14th cent., and was first reached by Europeans in the 17th cent., becoming first a French protectorate 1893-1946 and then an assoc. state of the French Union 1950-54, when it was accorded full independence at the Geneva Conference. A sporadic civil war followed, the neutralist govt, headed by Prince Souvanna Phouma, negotiating in 1957 the Vientiane Agreement with the Communist Pathet Lao or 'Lao State' forces, headed by Prince Souphanouvong (half-brother of Souvanna Phouma). However, a right-wing force, then headed by Prince Boun Oum, emerged and negotiations among the 'Three Princes' led to another agreement in 1962, also unimplemented. From 1967 N Vietnamese intervention in L. assisted the Pathet Lao, and by the Vientiane Agreement of 1973 a cease-fire line divided the country NW to SE, giving the Communists two-thirds of the country incl. the Plain of Jars and the Bolovens Plateau in the S, but giving the Souvanna Phouma govt two-thirds of the population. All foreign forces (N Vietnamese, Thai, and American), were to be withdrawn, and in Souvanna Phouma's provisional govt of 1974, both sides received equal representation. By 1975 the Pathet Lao (now renamed Lao People's Front) were dominant, and King Savang Vatthana (1908-80), who had succeeded in 1959, abdicated and L. became a People's Democratic Rep. under the presidency of Prince Souphanouvong. Prince Souvanna Phouma, announced that he would not hold office in the govt formed after elections in 1976 to a new Nat. Assembly, although he would advise his successors. In 1977 there were clashes on the Laos-Kampuchean border, and L. leans towards the Vietnam-USSR axis.

Area 235,700 sq.km (91,000 sq.m); pop. (1972) 3,110,000. Many are Buddhist, and the official language is Lao, although French and (increasingly) English are used as second languages. M.U.: kip.

LĀO TZE (lah'ō-tsā'). Chinese philosopher, commonly regarded as the founder of Taoism (q.v.). Many legends gathered round him, but nothing certain is known of his life, and he is variously said to have lived in the 6th and the 4th cent. BC. The *Tao Tê Ching*, the Taoist scripture, is attributed to him, but apparently dates from the 3rd cent. BC.

LA PAMPA. *See under* PAMPAS.

LA PAZ (pahs'). City of Bolivia, the seat of government since *c.* 1900, although Sucre remains the official cap. Founded in 1548, La P. is 3,800 m (12,400 ft) a.s.l., the highest cap. in the world. It has a univ. and an airport. Pop. (1976) 654,700.

LAPIS LAZULI (laz'ūlī) or **lazurite.** Deep blue mineral used in inlaying and ornamental work, and in the manufacture of pigment. Chemically it consists of a sodium aluminium silicate with sodium sulphide. L.L. occurs in metamorphic limestones, and is found in Afghanistan, Siberia, Chile, and Iran.

LAPLACE (lahplahs'), **Pierre Simon,** marquis de (1749-1827). French mathematician and astronomer. B. in Normandy, he was appointed prof. of mathematics at the Paris École Militaire in 1767. He observed the motion of the moon, Jupiter, Saturn, etc., and won universal fame with his *Traité de Mécanique Céleste* (1799-1825).

LAPLAND. Region of N Europe in Norway, Sweden, Finland and Russia without political definition. Within the Arctic Circle, L. has low temperatures, with 3 months' continuous daylight in summer and 3 months' continuous darkness in winter. There is summer agriculture, incl. wheat, but the chief resources of L. are minerals (chromium, copper, iron, etc), timber, hydroelectric

LA PAZ. The strange landscape of the Valley of the Moon on the outskirts of La Paz. *Photo: J. Allan Cash*

power, and tourism. Of Mongolian stock, the true Lapps declined under successive invasions, and although now settled in special villages, form only a small proportion of the population, numbering *c.* 20,000. They live by hunting, fishing, reindeer herding, and handicrafts.

LA PLATA (plah'tah). Capital of Buenos Aires prov., Argentina, founded in 1882, 9km (5.5m) from its port Ensenada. Industries incl. meat packing and petroleum refining. It has a univ. (1897). Pop. (1970) 408,000.

LA PLATA, Rio de. *See* PLATE, R.

LAPTEV (lap'tef) **SEA.** Part of the Arctic Ocean between the Taymur Peninsula and the New Siberian Is off the N Russian coast.

LAPWING. Bird (*Vanellus vanellus*) of the plover family, so named from its slow flight. It is also known as the green plover and - from its call - as the peewit. Bottle-green above and white below, it inhabits moorland in Europe and Asia, making a nest scratched out of the ground.

LARAMIE (lar'ami). Town in Wyoming, USA, on the L. Plains, a plateau 2,300m (7,500 ft) a.s.l., bounded to the N and E by the L. Mtns. The L. river, on which L. stands, is linked with the Missouri via the Platte. On the Overland trail and Pony express route, L. features in Western legend. Pop. (1970) 23,150.

LARCENY (lah'seni). In Britain formerly the name for stealing, the illegal deprivation of the lawful owner of his personal property, which is now incl. in the more comprehensive offence of theft (q.v.). Until 1827 L. was divided into 'Grand L.', punishable by death or transportation for life, and 'Petty L.', when the stolen articles were valued at less than a shilling (5p.). In the USA the distinction survives.

LARCH. Genus of trees (*Larix*) of the Coniferae family. The common L. (*L. decidua*) was introduced to Britain in the 17th cent. and grows 40m (130ft). The small needle-like leaves are replaced every year by new bright green foliage which later darkens. Closely resembling it is the tamarack (*L. americana*), and both are timber trees. The golden L. (*Pseudolarix amabilis*), a native of China, turns golden in autumn.

LARD. An edible fat prepared from the abdomen of pigs, but nowadays the term covers the whole body-fat of the pig. It is used in the manufacture of margarine, soap and ointment. Lard-oil, a clear, colourless liquid, is used for lubrication.

LARDERE'LLO. Site in the Tuscan hills, NE Italy, where the sulphur springs were used by the Romans for baths, and exploited for boric acid in the 18-19th cents. Since 1904 they have been used to generate electricity: the water reaches 220°C.

LARDNER, Ring (1885-1933). American short-story writer. A sporting correspondent, he based his characters on the people he met professionally and his collected vols. of short stories incl. his first *You Know Me, Al* (1916). *Round Up* (1929) and *Ring Lardner's Best Short Stories* (1938), all in a lively argot.

LAREDO (lahrā'dō). City on the Rio Grande, Texas, USA, with oil-refining and meat-processing industries. Pop. (1970) 69,000. On the opposite bank is **Nuevo L.**, Mexico, a textile centre. Pop. (1970) 150,900. The towns are a focus of US/Mexican trade.

LĀ'RĒS. Roman household gods peculiar to each family, and whose shrine was the centre of family worship.

LÁRISA (lahrēs'ah). Town in Thessaly, Greece, a centre of textile manufacture. Pop. (1971) 72,350.

LARK. Song bird (*Alauda arvensis*) found in the northern hemisphere, and migrating south in winter. It is *c.* 18cm (7in) long, with light brown plumage, and nests on the ground. It mounts in the air almost vertically and sings as it rises.

LARKIN, Philip (1922-85). British poet. Ed. at St John's Coll., Oxford, he gained success in 1955 with his vol. of poems, *The Less Deceived,* remarkable for their clarity and sensitivity. His other works incl. his novel *Jill* (1946) and, as ed., *The Oxford Book of Twentieth Century English Verse* (1973).

LARKSPUR. *See* DELPHINIUM.

LARNE. Seaport of co. Antrim, N Ireland, on Lough L., terminus of sea routes to Stranraer, Liverpool, Dublin, etc. Pop. (1971) 17,000.

LA ROCHEFOUCAULD (rōshfookō), **François,** duc de (1613-80). French writer. B. in Paris, he became a soldier, and took part in the *Fronde.* His later years were divided between the court and literary society. His best-known work is his *Réflexions, ou Sentences et Maximes Morales* (1665), a collection of brief, epigrammatic and cynical observations on life and society. *See* LA FAYETTE, MME DE.

LA ROCHELLE. *See* ROCHELLE, LA.

LAROUSSE (lahroos'), **Pierre** (1817-75). French grammarian and lexicographer. His *Grand Dictionnaire universel du XIXe siècle* (1865-76) was an epoch-making achievement and continues in subsequent revisions.

LARVA. The first form of many animals (esp. insects) as it emerges from the egg, as a grub, maggot, or caterpillar. It differs considerably from the adult which appears after metamorphosis.

LARYNGITIS (larinjī'tis). Inflammation of the lining membrane of the larynx (q.v.). The acute form is due to a cold, excessive use of the voice, inhalation of irritating smoke, etc. The voice may be completely lost. With rest the inflammation usually subsides in a few days.

LARYNX. A cavity at the upper end of the windpipe containing the vocal cords, by which sounds are produced. It is stiffened with cartilage and lined with mucous membrane.

LA SALLE (sahl'), **René Robert Cavelier,** Sieur de (1643-87). French explorer. B. at Rouen, he undertook 1670-83 a number of journeys which led to the discovery

LARVA. Clustered larvae of the Mexican bulls-eye moth on a leaf: the effect is of a flower, and serves as useful camouflage from predators. *Photo: NHPA*

of Lakes Ontario and Erie and of the Ohio and the Mississippi. He annexed Louisiana and Illinois to the Crown of France, but during a final expedition was killed by his own men in Texas.

LASCAR. An E Indian seaman. The word derives from the Persian *lashkar*, 'army', 'camp', and Ls. were originally an inferior class of sepoy.

LAS CASAS (lahs-kah'sahs), **Bartolomé de** (1474-1566). Spanish priest, the 'apostle of the Indians'. B. in Seville, he took RC orders in 1510, and sailed for the Spanish colonies in America, where he opposed the ill-treatment and enslavement of the native Indians, and in 1530 persuaded the government to forbid slavery in Peru. He also laboured as a missionary, his *Historia de las Indias* (1875-6) was never completed.

LASCAUX (lahskō'). Cave system nr Montignac in the Dordogne, SW France, discovered in 1940 by one of a party of boys out rabbiting. It has rich paintings of oxen, horses and red deer of the Upper Palaeolithic *c.* 18,000 BC.

LA'SDUN, Sir Denys (1914-). British architect. Ed. at Rugby, he has a versatile distinction in his work which incl. the Royal Coll. of Physicians in Regent's Park, science buildings for Cambridge, the Univ. of E Anglia, and the National Theatre on the South Bank. He was knighted in 1976.

LĀ'SER. Acronym for Light Amplification by Stimulated Emission of Radiation. Device for producing a narrow highly parallel beam of light, capable of travelling over vast distances without dispersion, and of being focused to give enormous power densities (10^8 watts per cm^2 for high-energy Ls.) and operating on a principle similar to that of the maser, q.v.

Many solid, liquid and gaseous substances have been used for L. materials incl. synthetic ruby crystal (used for the first extraction of L. light in 1960 and giving a high-power pulsed output) and a helium-neon gas mixture, capable of continuous operation, but at a lower power. In 1962 a L. was used to throw light at the moon's surface, a reflection being detected 2½ sec. later (Massachusetts Inst. of Tech.).

Some uses of Ls. incl. communications (a L. beam can carry much more information than radio waves), cutting, drilling, welding, more accurate radar, satellite tracking, and in medical and biological research. In espionage, sound wave vibrations from the window glass of a room can be picked up by reflected laser beam, extracted by a receiver within horizon distance, and amplified. *See also* BEAM WEAPONS and BOMB.

LASHIO. Town in the Shan State, Burma, *c.* 200km (125m) NE of Mandalay, with which it is linked by rail. L. is linked by the Burma Road, constructed in 1938, with Kunming in China.

LA'SKI, Harold (1893-1950). British political theorist. Prof. of political science at the London School of Economics from 1926, he taught a modified Marxism, and pub. *A Grammar of Politics* (1925), and *The American Presidency* (1940). He was chairman of the Labour Party 1945-6. His niece, **Marghanita L.** (1915-), has written novels, e.g. *The Victorian Chaise Longue* (1953), and studies of Jane Austen and George Eliot.

LAS PA'LMAS. Tourist resort on the NW coast of Gran Canaria, Canary Islands: it is adjoined by its port of La Luz. Pop. (1970) 287,000.

LA SPEZIA (laspet'sē-ah). Port in Liguria, Italy, on the Gulf of S., where Shelley drowned in 1822. The chief Italian naval base, L.S. has shipbuilding, engineering, electrical and textile industries. Pop. (1978) 120,000.

LA'SSA FEVER. Fever caused by a virus, first detected in 1969 nr the village of L. in N Nigeria. It is spread by a species of rat found only in W Africa, and there is no known cure, the death rate being over 50%. Symptoms, first a sore throat and temperature, develop after 10 days to ulcers, vomiting and acute convulsions of the central nervous system.

LASSALLE (lahsahl'), **Ferdinand** (1825-64). German Socialist. He took part in the 1848 revolution, during which he met Marx, and in 1863 founded the General Association of German Workers (later the Social-Democratic Party). Besides carrying on a tireless propaganda of speeches and pamphlets, he secretly intrigued with Bismarck. He was killed in a duel arising from a love-affair.

LASSETER'S REEF. Legendary gold-bearing area in the Rawlinson Range, Western Australia. Discovered by H.B. Lasseter in 1897, who is said to have produced specimen nuggets of great purity, it could never be relocated, and Lasseter disappeared during an expedition to rediscover it in 1930. More recent prospectors have found evidence of useful mineral deposits in the area indicated in his papers.

LASSUS, Orlande de (*c.* 1530-94). Flemish composer. B. at Mons, he pub. his first book of motets in 1556. Soon after he settled permanently in Munich. His compositions include many songs and madrigals, among them settings of poems by his friend Ronsard.

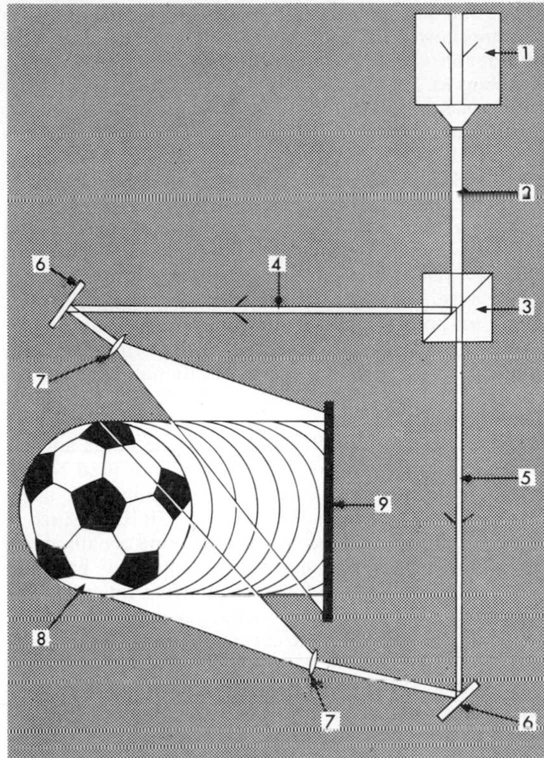

LASER. The use of laser light in making a hologram. (1) Laser; (2) beam of light of regular frequency (i.e. with waves all the same length) generated by laser; (3) light divided into two by crystal 'beam splitter'; (4) the 'reference' half of the beam; (5) the 'object' half of the beam; (6) special optical mirrors reflect the two halves of the beam through convex camera lenses (7) which spread them out. The object beam is directed at the object (8) of which the hologram is being made, whence the light waves are once more reflected, this time toward the light sensitive photographic plate (9), made of glass, perspex, film, etc. and covered with a very special emulsion. The reference beam is directed immediately towards the plate. However, the two beams of light meet before they reach the plate, and an 'interference wavefront' is formed which results in the 'measurements' in breadth and depth of the object being recorded on the plate.

LAS VEGAS (lahs vāg'ahs). City of Nevada, USA, the centre of a vast recreation area, but better known for its nightclubs where performers are paid fabulous sums, and for its gambling casinos in Fremont Street and the 'Strip' outside the city. Pop. (1970) 42,625.

LATAKIA. *See* LATTAKIA.

LA TÈNE. Archaeological site at the E. end of Lake Neuchatel, Switzerland, famous for late Iron Age remains, incl. magnificent swords. It gave its name to a whole culture, existing from the 5th cent. B.C. to the Roman conquest.

LATENT HEAT. Term first used by Joseph Black (*c.* 1760) for the heat which changes the state of a substance (e.g. in melting or vaporization) without changing the temperature.

LA TÈNE. A silver cauldron of the La Tène culture, found at Gundestrup in North Jutland, and moulded in relief with figures of gods and goddesses. *Photo: Courtesy of the National Museum, Copenhagen*

LATERAN CHURCH OF ST JOHN. The Pope's cathedral as bishop of Rome. Little remains of the ancient basilica built by Constantine, *c.* 324.

LATERITE (Lat. *later*, brick). A residual weathering product of basalts, granites and shales, forming a clay-like rock impregnated with ferric hydroxide. It is usually soft and friable, occurring in the tropics.

LĀ'TEX. A lactiferous fluid of angiospermous plants, an emulsion of various substances. It circulates longitudinally in branched tubes conducting plastic substances and acting as reservoir. L. is exuded from the Para rubber tree and worked into rubber. Coagulation is prevented by ammonia or formaldehyde.

LATIMER, Hugh (*c.* 1490-1555). English Protestant reformer. After his conversion to Protestantism in 1524 he was several times imprisoned, but was protected by Wolsey and Henry VIII. He was appointed bp of Worcester in 1535, but resigned in 1539. Under Edward VI his sermons denouncing social injustice won him great influence. He was arrested for heresy in 1553, and burned at Oxford.

LATIN. The language spoken by the Romans, and the parent of the Romance languages, e.g. Italian, French, Spanish, and Portuguese. As Lat. literature had an influence on all subsequent European civilization, L., even beyond the Middle Ages, remained for long as the vehicle for learned works; and until the reforms following the Second Vatican Council was universally used throughout the RC Church in services, etc. The striking merits of L. are its clarity and conciseness. Like Greek it is a highly inflected language, i.e. the grammatical functions of nouns, verbs, pronouns, and adjectives in a sentence is indicated by terminations which vary according to the meaning.

L. was not native to Italy. It was brought there about 1000 BC by wandering tribes from the N who settled in Latium near the mouth of the Tiber. With the growing power of Rome it spread throughout Italy, and other competing languages gradually disappeared (e.g. Oscan, Umbrian, Etruscan). The conquest of Spain and Gaul extended the use and influence of L. outside Italy, but the Roman hold on Britain (AD 43-AD 410) was not firm enough to submerge completely the Celtic speech of the islanders.

From the 3rd cent. AD there has to be distinction between the literary or standard Latin used in speaking and writing by educated people, and the forms, generally known as Low or Vulgar L., spoken by ordinary people in the different parts of the western half of the Empire. A number of *patois* grew from the latter, and slowly became stabilized as the Romance languages. There is a further distinction between the medieval Latin of the Vulgate (the Latin Bible of the RC Church) and also of general educated intercourse of the period, and the classical Latin of the writers of the golden age, which was even in its own day a somewhat rarefied form. At the Renaissance study of the newly available MSS led to stress on the exact revival of the latter, and this pedantry was ultimately effective in stifling the development of L. as a 'universal' second language throughout Europe.

LATIN AMERICA. The countries of S and Central America (incl. Mexico) in which Spanish, Portuguese, and French are spoken. There are three economic organizations: Central American Common Market (1960), the Andean Group (1969), and L.A. Integration Association (1980). The *L.A. Economic System* (1975), known as SELA from the initial letters of its name in Spanish, and with a membership drawn from the Caribbean as well as S and Central American states, aims at integration and industrial co-operation, and co-ordination of existing organizations. The HQ is Caracas.

LATIN LITERATURE. Only a few hymns and inscriptions survive from the primitive period of L.L., before the 3rd cent. BC. Greek influence began with the work of Livius Andronicus (*c.* 284-204 BC) who translated the *Odyssey* and Greek plays into Latin. Naevius and Ennius both attempted epics on patriotic themes; the former used the native 'Saturnian' metre, but the latter introduced the Greek hexameter. Plautus and Terence successfully adapted Greek comedy to the Latin stage. Lucilius (180-103 BC) founded Latin verse satire, while the writings of Cato were the first important works in Latin prose.

In the *De Rerum Natura* of Lucretius, the world's greatest philosophical poem, and the passionate lyrics of Catullus, Latin verse reached maturity. Cicero set a standard for Latin prose, in his orations, his philosophical essays, and his letters. To the same period belong the histories of Caesar.

The Augustan Age (43 BC-AD 17) is usually regarded as the golden age of L.L. There is a strong patriotic feeling in the work of the poets Virgil and Horace, and the historian Livy, who belonged to Augustus's immediate circle. Virgil produced the one great Latin epic in the *Aeneid*, while Horace brought a distinctive charm and polish to both the lyric and satire. Younger poets of the period were Ovid and the elegiac poets Tibullus and Propertius.

The 'Silver Age' of the Empire begins with the writers of Nero's reign: the Stoic philosopher Seneca, Lucan, author of the epic *Pharsalia*, the satirist Persius (AD 34-62), and, by far the greatest, the realistic novelist Petronius. At the end of the 1st and beginning of the 2nd cent. came 2 major writers, the historian Tacitus and the satirist Juvenal; other writers of the period were the epigrammatist Martial, the scientist Pliny the Elder, the letter-writer Pliny the Younger, the critic Quintilian, the historian Suetonius, and the epic poet Statius (*c.* 61-96).

The 2nd and 3rd cents. produced only one pagan writer of importance, the romancer Apuleius, but there were several able Christian writers, such as Tertullian, Cyprian, Arnobius (d. 327), and Lactantius (d. 325). In the 4th cent. there was something of a poetic revival, with Ausonius (*c.* 310-90) and Claudian, and the Christian poets Prudentius (*c.* 348-410) and St Ambrose. The classical period ends, and the Middle Ages begin, with St Jerome's translation of the Bible, and St Augustine's *City of God.*

Throughout the Middle Ages Latin remained the language of the Church, and was normally employed for theology, philosophy, histories, and other learned works. Latin verse, adapted to rhyme and non-classical metres, was used both for hymns and the secular songs of the wandering scholars. Even after the Reformation Latin retained its prestige as the international language of scholars, and was used as such, e.g. by More, Bacon, and Milton.

LATITUDE and LONGITUDE. Latitude is the angular distance of any point from the equator, measured N or S along the Earth's curved surface, equalling the angle between the respective horizontal planes. It is measured in degrees, minutes, and seconds, each minute equalling one sea-mile in length. For map-making latitude is based on the supposition that the Earth is an oblate spheroid. The difference between this (the geographical) and astronomical latitude is the correction necessary for local deviation of plumb-line.

Longitude is the angle between the terrestial meridian drawn from the pole, through a place, and a standard meridian now taken at Greenwich. All determinations of longitude are based on the Earth turning through 360° in 24 hours, or the Sun reaching 15° W each hour.

LATITUDINARIANS. Name applied to those Anglican divines, e.g. Tillotson and Stillingfleet, who after 1660 regarded episcopal govt and forms of worship as things indifferent, and favoured modifications to reconcile Dissenters to the Church.

LATIUM. Ancient division of central Italy, originally the territory of the Latinii. The modern Italian region of L. (or Lazio) incl. the provs. of Viterbo, Rieti, Rome, Frosinone and Latina.

LATOUR (lahtoor'), **Georges de** (1593-1652). French artist. His name was unknown until discovered by an art historian in 1863 and in the 20th cent. nos. of pictures attributed to others were identified as his, although the authenticity of some has been questioned. He served as court painter to the king and to the duke of Lorraine, and is especially noted for his 'night' style using the light of shielded candles, etc.

LA TROBE, Charles Joseph (1801-75). Australian administrator. He was superintendent of Port Phillip district 1839-51, and first Lt.-Gov. of Victoria 1851-4. The **Latrobe River** is named after him, and flows generally SE through Victoria to Lake Wellington, through one of the world's largest deposits of brown coal.

LATTAKIA. Port in NW Syria. A Phoenician city, it was the Roman Laodicea ad Mare, and during the Crusades was captured by Tancred 1102 and re-taken by Saladin in 1188. Modernized in the 1970s as a deepwater port, it has tobacco industries. Pop. (1970) 121,600.

LATTER-DAY SAINTS. *See* MORMONS.

LA'TVIA. An SSR of the USSR. It lies on the Baltic between Lithuania to the S, and Estonia to the N. L. is low-lying and watered by many rivers, e.g. the Daugava, and there are numerous lakes. Formerly dependent on agriculture and forestry, L. has become predominantly industrial since the S.W.W. and produces electric railway rolling stock, telephone equipment and radios, steel and rolled metal, fertilizers, paper, textiles, and cement. Riga is the cap.

Before the F.W.W. L. formed part of the Russian Empire, but in Nov. 1918 it was proclaimed an independent rep., recognized by Russia in 1920. In 1939 Russia demanded military bases, and in 1940 incorporated L. as a constituent rep., which it has remained apart from the German occupation 1941-44. After the S.W.W. there was forcible assimilation, Latvians being deported to other parts of the USSR and Russians being settled in L. By 1970 only about half the people were Latvian and use of the language was discouraged. Area 63,700 sq.km (24,600 sq.m); pop. (1978) 2,500,000.

LATVIAN or **Lettic.** One of the 2 surviving members of the Baltic branch of the Indo-European family, the other being Lithuanian. L. is known from 1585.

LAUD (lawd), **William** (1573-1645). English churchman. As archbp of Canterbury from 1633, his High Church policy, his support for Charles I's unparliamentary rule, his censorship of the press, and his persecution of the Puritans all aroused bitter opposition, while his strict enforcement of the statutes against enclosures and of laws regulating wages and prices alienated the propertied classes. His attempt to impose the use of the Prayer Book on the Scots provoked a revolt which precipitated the English Revolution. Impeached by parliament in 1640 he was imprisoned in the Tower, condemned to death by a bill of attainder, and beheaded.

LAUDANUM (lawd'num). A solution of opium in alcohol (tincture).

LAUDER (law'der), **Sir Henry (Harry)** (1870-1950). Scots comedian. At first a mill worker and miner, he made his reputation with comic songs of his own composition such as 'Stop Yer Ticklin' Jock', and 'I Love a Lassie'.

LAUDERDALE, John Maitland, duke of (1616-82). Scottish statesman. Formerly a zealous Covenanter, he joined the Royalists in 1647, and as High Commissioner for Scotland 1667-79 persecuted the Covenanters. He was created duke of L. in 1672.

LAUE (low-e), **Max Theodor Felix von** (1879-1960). German physicist. He was a pioneer in measuring the wavelength of X-rays by their diffraction through the closely spaced atoms in a crystal, leading to the powerful technique now used to elucidate the structure of complex biological materials, e.g. DNA (q.v.). Awarded Nobel prize 1914. *See* GRENOBLE.

LAUGHARNE (larn). Village at the mouth of the r. Towey, Dyfed, Wales. The home of Dylan Thomas, it features in his work as 'Milk Wood'.

LAUGHING JACKASS. *See* KOOKABURRA.

LAUGHTON (law'ton), **Charles** (1899-1962). Anglo-American character actor. B. in Scarborough, he specialized in larger-than-life roles, such as his film appearances in *The Private Life of Henry VIII* and as Captain Bligh in *Mutiny on the Bounty.*

LAUNCESTON (lahn'ston). (1) English town in Cornwall, 34km (21m) NW of Plymouth. There are ruins of a Norman castle, besieged in the Civil War. Pop. (1972) 4,890. (2) Port in NE Tasmania, Australia, on the Tamar, founded 1805. Its industries incl. woollen blankets, saw milling, engineering, furniture and pottery making; Tasmania's railway workshops are at L. Pop. (1976) 63,400.

LAURACEAE. A family of dicotyledonous plants containing over 1,000 species. They are evergreen and mostly aromatic. Two of the chief genera are *Cinnamomum* and *Laurus.*

LAURASIA. See CONTINENT.

LAUREL. Name given to the bay (q.v.) and to evergreen species of the genus *Prunus* in the family Rosaceae, notably the common cherry L. (*P. laurocerasus*), introduced to Europe from Asiatic Turkey in the 16th cent., and a popular ornamental shrub in N America and Britain. The leaves are either dark green or variegated with yellow, and the small flowers are followed by red berries: the whole plant is poisonous, containing hydrocyanic acid.

LAUREL, Stan (1890-1965) and **HARDY, Oliver** (1892-1957). American film comedians. Laurel (*né* Arthur Stanley Jefferson) was thin and tearful, and always exasperating to the temper of the fat and dominant Hardy. With a minimum of dialogue, and an underlying criticism of society from the position of the underdog, their films were revived as a world-wide cult in the 1970s.

LAUREL and HARDY. A scene from *Leave 'em Laughing* (1928): the infuriated traffic cop is Edgar Kennedy. *Photo: Mansell Collection*

LAURIER (lō'riā), **Sir Wilfrid** (1841-1919). Canadian Liberal statesman. As PM 1896-1911 - the first French-Canadian to hold the office - he supported imperial preference and the building of Canadian warships to co-operate with the British Navy, and sent Canadian troops to serve in the S African War.

LAURUSTINUS (lorestī'nus). Evergreen shrub (*Vibernum tinus*) in the family Caprifoliaceae. It has clusters of white flowers in the winter months, and is of Mediterranean origin.

LAUSANNE (lōzahn'). Cap. of Vaud canton, Switzerland, above the N shore of Lake Geneva. There is a cathedral (consecrated 1275: restored 19th cent.) and univ. (originating 1537), and industries incl. chocolate, scientific instruments, publishing, etc. Pop. (1971) 136,600. The *Treaty of L.* (1923) made peace between Turkey and the Allies after the F.W.W.

LAVA. The molten substance emitted from a volcanic crater. Basic L. containing less silica than acid L., it flows greater distances, taking longer to solidify.

LAVA'L, Pierre (1883-1945). French politician. B. near Vichy, he entered the Chamber of Deputies in 1914 as a Socialist, but after the F.W.W. moved towards the right. He was PM and For. Sec. in 1931-2, and again in 1935-6, his second period of office being marked by the Hoare-L. agreement for concessions to Italy in Abyssinia. He joined Pétain's govt as Vice-Premier in June 1940; dismissed in Dec., he was reinstated by Hitler's orders as head of the govt and For. Min. in 1942. His share in the deportation of French labour to Germany made him universally hated. On the Allied invasion he fled the country, but was arrested in Austria, tried for treason, and shot after trying to poison himself.

LA VALLIÈRE (lah vahlyār'), **Louise de La Baume Le Blanc,** duchesse de (1644-1710). Mistress of Louis XIV from 1661, to whom she bore 4 children. Created a duchess in 1664, she retired to a convent in 1674 when superseded by Mme de Montespan: she was slightly lame and had a sweetly winning personality.

LA VENDÉE. *See* VENDÉE, LA.

LAVENDER. Sweet-smelling herb of the Labiatae family, genus *Lavandula,* a native of the western Mediterranean countries. The bush (*L. vera*) is low-growing with long, narrow, erect leaves of a silver-green colour. The flowers (borne on a terminal spike) vary in colour from lilac to deep purple, and are covered with small fragrant oil glands. The oil is extensively used in pharmacy and perfumes.

LAVOISIER (lahvwahzyā'), **Antoine Laurent** (1743-94). French chemist. B. in Paris, he was appointed a farmer-general of taxes in 1769, and director of the govt gun-powder factory in 1775, and received other important appointments. During the Revolution he was arrested with the other farmers-general, who were hated for their extortions, and guillotined. Although he carried on useful research on meteorology and agriculture, his greatest contribution was the overthrow of the phlogiston theory (a weightless 'fire element' liberated during combustion), which had stifled the development of chemistry for over a century. He showed in 1772 that burned sulphur and phosphorus increased in wt because they absorbed 'air', and later, in burning metals, that only a part of 'common air' was consumed, which he called oxygen (Priestley's dephlogisticated air); the non-vital air, or nitrogen, being left behind. With Laplace he showed that water was a compound of oxygen and hydrogen, and founded on his oxygen theory the basic rules of chemical combination which survive to this day.

LAVRE'NTIEV, Mikhail (1900-). Soviet scientist. Appointed director of the Institute for Precision Mechanics and Computer Engineering in 1950, he was responsible from 1957 for the development of Akademgorodok, the 'science city', near Novosibirsk. He has emphasized the practical application of discoveries, and close links with industry.

LAW, Andrew Bonar (1858-1923). British Cons. statesman. B. in New Brunswick, he made a fortune in Scotland as a banker and iron-merchant, and entered parliament in 1900. Elected leader of the Opposition in 1911, he became Colonial Secretary in Asquith's coalition govt 1915-16, and was Chancellor of the Exchequer 1916-19, and Lord Privy Seal 1919-21, in the Lloyd George coalition. He formed a Conservative cabinet in 1922, but resigned on health grounds in 1923.

LAW, William (1686-1761). English churchman. His Jacobite opinions caused him to lose his fellowship at Emmanuel Coll., Cambridge, in 1714, and later he became tutor in the household of Edward Gibbon, the grandfather of the historian, at Putney. After 1740 he lived in retirement at his birthplace, King's Cliff, Northants. His most famous work is *A Serious Call to a Devout and Holy Life* (1728), which influenced the Wesleys.

LAW. The body of rules and principles by which justice is administered in a state. The 2 main systems of European L. are Roman L. and English L. (qq.v.). English L. is (1) Common L., (2) Statute L. Common L. is unwritten and might be described as the basic code of justice necessary to any community. Statute L. consists of the specific Acts of Parliament enacted from time to time to regulate particular matters. *See* INTERNATIONAL LAW.

LAW COURTS. At the head of the English legal system stands the House of Lords, which hears appeals in both civil and criminal cases. Below it, under the Courts Act (1971) are the Supreme Court of Judicature as the Court of Appeal (civil and criminal) and the High Court of Justice (civil), comprising the Chancery, Queen's Bench and Family Divisions. All more serious criminal work not covered by the Magistrates' Courts is handled by the Crown Courts (as are also certain civil cases), which are organized in six circuits. The towns of each circuit are first-tier (High Court and Circuit Judges dealing with both criminal and civil cases), second-tier (High Court and Circuit Judges dealing with criminal cases only), or third-tier (Circuit Judges dealing with criminal cases only). The former assizes and quarter sessions were abolished, but the Central Criminal Court (the 'Old Bailey') continued to be the Criminal Court for Greater London. Cases are allotted according to gravity among High Court and Circuit Judges and Recorders (part-time judges with the same jurisdiction as Circuit Judges). Solicitors were allowed for the first time to appear in and conduct cases at the level of the Crown Courts, and solicitors as well as barristers of 10 years standing became eligible for appointments as Recorders, who after five years become eligible as Circuit Judges.

County Courts, dealing with minor civil cases, are served by Circuit Judges. Minor criminal cases are heard by 2-7 lay Justices of the Peace, exercising summary jurisdiction, although in London and other large towns trained lawyers sit as Stipendiary ('paid') Magistrates. Juvenile Courts, held in separate buildings, are presided over by specially qualified justices. *See* also COURTS, Small Claims.

At the head of the federal judiciary in the USA is the Supreme Court which also hears appeals from the inferior federal courts and from the decisions of the highest courts of the states. The US Courts of Appeals - organized in circuits - deals with appeals from the US District Courts in which civil and criminal cases are heard. State Courts deal with civil and criminal cases involving state laws, the lowest being those of the justices of the peace, etc.

LAWES (lawz), **Henry** (1596-1662). British composer. He wrote the music for Milton's masque *Comus.*

LAWES, Sir John Bennet (1814-1900). British agriculturist. B. at Rothamsted, he produced 'super-phosphate', the earliest patent manure in 1842, and in 1899 estab. the Lawes Agricultural Trust to supervise the work of the Rothamsted experimental station.

LAWLER, Ray (1911-). Australian playwright. B. in Melbourne, he became a factory hand at 13, then an actor. His play *The Summer of the 17th Doll* (1957) dealt with sugar cane-cutters on leave after the season's work and the passing of one man's physical supremacy: it was successful also abroad.

LAW LORDS. The 10 Lords of Appeal in Ordinary, who, in England, together with the Lord Chancellor and other peers, make up the House of Lords in its judicial capacity.

LAWN TENNIS. A racket-and-ball game invented in 1874 in England, and played on a level court. *See* diagram. The lively inflated rubber ball is about 6cm (2½in) diam. and 56 grammes (2oz) weight, and the racket *c.* 70cm (27in long), its oval head strung with nylon. The object of the game, called L.T. on whatever surface it is played, is to hit the ball into the opponent's area in such a way that he cannot return it to the player's area. The court is divided along its length, and each point is started by one player (standing behind the base line, alternately on the left and right of his own area) serving the ball with a powerful overhead shot into a restricted part of the opponent's court diagonally opposite. The server is allowed 1 failure. The opponent must return the ball, after the first bounce, to any part of the server's area of the court, when play continues on both entire areas until the point is decided, the ball being played after the first bounce or volleyed in the air. The game is won by the first player to win 4 points (called 15, 30, 40, game) unless both players reach 40 (*deuce*) when a player needs 2 consecutive points to win. A set goes to the player who wins 6 games, except that he must win by a margin of 2 games over his opponent, and where necessary a set is extended until this margin is achieved. However, nowadays a 'tie-break' system is often operated when the score reaches 6 games all (sometimes 8 all). A highly specialized sport, fostered by national and international bodies, it is noted for its increasingly high prize money. The chief competition events incl. the Davis Cup (donated 1900) for international competition among men and the Wightman Cup (1923) for US and UK women's teams. Formerly amateur, but professional from 1968, are the All England Championships at Wimbledon where multi-winners have incl., in the men's singles: Fred Perry 1934-6, Rod Laver 1961-2, 1968-9, John Newcombe 1967, 1970-1, Bjorn Borg 1976-80 and John McEnroe 1981, 1983 and in the womens singles Helen Wills Moody 1927-30, 1932-3, 1935, 1938, Louise Brough 1948-50, 1955, Maureen Connolly 1952-4, Maria Bueno 1959-60, 1964, Billie Jean King 1966-8, 1972-3, and 1975, Chris Evert Lloyd 1974, 1976, 1981, Martina Navratilova 1978-9, 1982-3, and Evonne Cawley 1980 (as E. Goolagong 1971). In the USA the National Tennis Centre is at Flushing Meadow, NYC, nr La Guardia airport.

LAWRENCE, St (d. 258). Christian martyr. B. probably in Spain he became a deacon of Rome under Sixtus II, and when summoned to deliver the treasures of the Church displayed the beggars in his charge, for which he was broiled on a grid-iron.

LAWRENCE, David Herbert (1885-1930). British novelist and poet. B. in Notts, the son of a miner, he studied at Nottingham univ., and became a teacher. His earliest novel, *The White Peacock*, appeared in 1911, but he first attracted attention with the semi-autobiographical *Sons and Lovers* (1913). In 1914 he m. Frieda von Richthofen, who is the model for Ursula Brangwen in *The Rainbow* (1915), which was suppressed for obscenity, and in its sequel *Women in Love* (1921). His later years were largely spent in travel in Italy, Australia and Mexico, partly in search of health, partly in the hope of finding peace in a less complex and materialistic society. His travels inspired the novels *Aaron's Rod* (1922), *Kangaroo* (1923), and *The Plumed Serpent* (1926), as well as

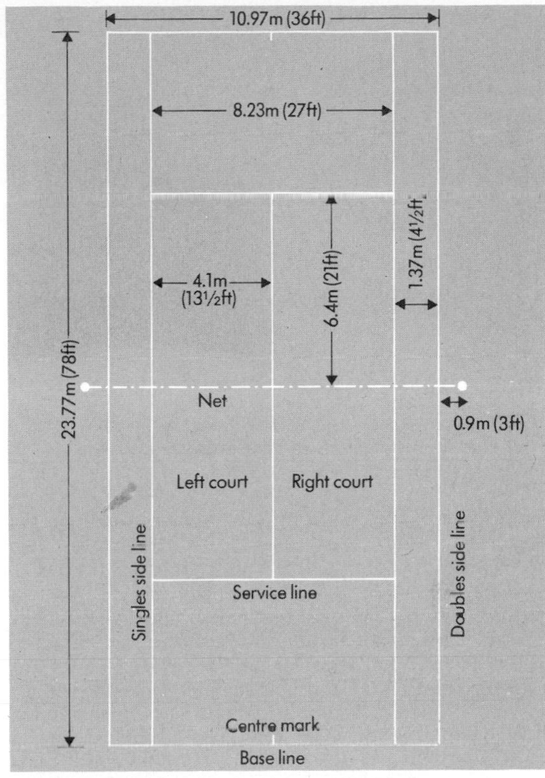

LAWN TENNIS

Etruscan Places (1927-8), and other travel books. *Lady Chatterley's Lover* (1928) gave rise to a long controversy, and the unexpurgated edition was banned as obscene in the UK until 1960. It expresses rather crudely L.'s dominating conviction that emotion and the sexual impulse are creative and true to human nature, and therefore of paramount importance in our increasingly sterile and cerebral society. His philosophy and writing, often irrational and of uneven quality, are shown at their best in his poems and short stories, e.g. 'The Woman Who Rode Away' (1926). L. d. of tuberculosis near Nice.

LAWRENCE, Ernest O(rlando) (1901-58). American physicist. During his long period in California, he was prof. of physics from 1930 and director of the Radiation Laboratory from 1936, which he built up into a large, brilliant school for research in nuclear physics. His invention of the cyclotron pioneered the production of artificial radio-isotopes and led to many new fields of investigation. He was awarded the Nobel prize in 1939.

LAWRENCE, Gertrude (1898-1952). English actress. B. in London, of Danish extraction, she estab. her reputation in the 1920s as a sophisticated stylist in revue and musical comedy. In later years she played mainly in New York. Her greatest success was *Private Lives* (1930-1) written specially for her by Noël Coward.

LAWRENCE, Sir Henry Montgomery (1806-57). British soldier. B. in Ceylon, the brother of John L., he entered the Bengal Artillery in 1823, and served in the Burmese War 1824-6 and the Afghan War, 1842. On the outbreak of the Mutiny he took charge at Lucknow and organized

LAWRENCE. A self-portrait by D.H. Lawrence, and the kitchen of his home in Nottingham, now preserved as a museum. *Photo of Lawrence's home: Robert Holmes*

the defence of the residency, but was killed early in the siege.

LAWRENCE, John Laird Mair, 1st baron (1811-79). Viceroy of India. B. in Yorks, he began his Indian career in 1830, and in 1853 became chief commissioner for the Punjab. During the Mutiny he disarmed the mutinous troops in his area, and was largely responsible for the recapture of Delhi. He was viceroy of India 1864-9.

LAWRENCE, Sir Thomas (1769-1830). British painter. B. at Bristol, the son of an innkeeper, he entered the RA schools in 1787, and was elected RA in 1794, and PRA in 1820. He succeeded Reynolds as principal painter to the king in 1792, and was knighted in 1815. He painted portraits of many of his famous contemporaries, incl. the series of pictures of Allied sovereigns and statesmen in Windsor Castle.

LAWRENCE, Thomas Edward (1888-1935). British soldier, known as 'Lawrence of Arabia'. B. in Wales, he studied at Oxford, and during 1910-14 took part in archaeological expeditions to Syria and Mesopotamia. Appointed to the military intelligence department in Cairo, he took part in negotiations for an Arab revolt against the Turks, and in 1916 attached himself to the Emir Faisal. He showed himself a guerrilla leader of genius, combining raids on Turkish communications with the stirring up of revolt among the Arabs. He joined the RAF in 1922 as an aircraftman under the name Ross, transferring to the tank corps under the name T. E. Shaw in 1923 when his identity became known, then returning to the RAF in 1925. He adopted the name Shaw by deed poll in 1927. In 1935 he was killed in a motor-cycling accident. His account of the Arab revolt, *Seven Pillars of Wisdom*, was pub. privately in 1926, was abridged as *Revolt in the Desert* (1927), and appeared in a public edition after his death in 1935. *The Mint* (1936) was a crude account of life in the ranks.

LAWRENCE. Town in Mass., USA, established in 1845 to utilize power from the Merrimack Rapids on a site first settled in 1655. It makes woollens and other textiles, clothing, paper, radio equipment, etc. Pop. (1970) 66,920.

LAWRENCIUM (loren'sium). Radioactive element, symbol Lr; at. no. 103; mass of isotope of longest known half life 257. It was discovered in 1961 and named after E. O. Lawrence (q.v.).

LAWSON, Nigel (1932–). British Cons. politician. A former financial journalist, he was Financial Sec to the Treasury 1979–81, Sec of State for Energy 1981–3, and Chancellor of the Exchequer from 1983.

LA'XNESS, Halldor. *See* ICELANDIC LITERATURE.

LAYAMON (fl. 1200). English poet. A priest of Arley Regis, Worcs. he wrote the *Brut*, a chronicle of *c.* 30,000 alliterative lines on the history of Britain from the legendary Brutus onwards, which gives the earliest version of the Arthurian story in English.

LĀ'YARD, Sir Austen Henry (1817-94). British diplomatist and archaeologist. B. in Paris, he travelled to the Middle East in 1839, conducted 2 expeditions to Nineveh and Babylon, 1845-51, and sent to England the specimens forming the greater part of the collection of Assyrian antiquities in the British Museum.

LA' YOUN (lah yo͞on'). Cap. of Western Sahara (also El Aaiún). Phosphates from Bu Craa are taken to the port installations 20 km (12 m) SW of the city. Pop. (1975) 24,500.

LAY-READER. In the Church of England a layman permitted to read the lessons, or under licence from the bishop of the diocese to conduct morning or evening prayer.

LAZARUS, Emma (1849-87). American poet, author of the poem inscribed at the base of the Statue of Liberty, incl. the words 'Give me your tired, your poor,/Your huddled masses yearning to breathe free'.

LAZIO. Italian form of LATIUM.

LEA. English river rising in Bedfordshire, flowing past Luton, Hertford and Ware, and bounding Herts and Essex, before it flows through Greater London to join the Thames at Blackwall. It is navigable for 45km (28m). The L. Valley Authority was estab. 1967 to make it a 'playground' for London.

LEACH, Bernard (1887-1979). British potter. His beautifully simple designs, influenced by a period of study in Japan, pioneered the modern revival of the art. He estab. the L. Pottery at St Ives in 1920.

LEACOCK, Stephen Butler (1869-1944). British humorous writer. B. in Hants, he lived in Canada from 1876, and was head of the dept of economics at McGill univ., Montreal, 1908-36. He pub. works on politics and economics, studies of Mark Twain and Dickens, but is best known for his humorous writings, such as *Literary Lapses* (1910), *Nonsense Novels* (1911), and *Frenzied Fiction* (1918).

LEAD. One of the 4 most used and produced metals, the end product of the uranium-radium and thorium series, symbol Pb (Lat. *plumbum*), at. wt. 207.21 and at. no. 82. Known since prehistoric times (mentioned in Exodus), it is a bluish-grey, and the heaviest, softest and weakest of common metals; it lacks elasticity and is a poor conductor of electricity, and is used as a shield for radioactive sources, and in ammunition, batteries, glass, ceramics, and alloys such as pewter and solder. Lead is a cumulative poison within the body, and L. water pipes and L.-based paints are a health hazard, as is the use of L. as an 'anti-knock' petrol additive, esp. for children who have high blood L. levels from breathing L.-polluted air, since they tend to hyperactivity and mental retardation. Galena (PbS) is the chief mineral ore from which L. is obtained by a roasting process.

LEAF. Term applied to any lateral outgrowth on the stems of plants, but chiefly referring to those which constitute the foliage. Foliage leaves are composed of 3 parts: the *sheath* or leaf-base, the *petiole* or stalk, and the *lamina* or blade, the last-named being traversed by a network of veins. The chief leaf structures are: cotyledon (seed leaves); scale-leaf (on underground stems); foliage leaf (having the distinctive functions of assimilating carbon and other nutrient substances, the absorption of light, and constituting the respiring and transpiring organ of the plant); and bract (in the axil of which a flower is produced). A *simple* leaf is undivided, e.g. as in the aspen tree; a *compound* leaf is composed of several leaflets, e.g. the blackberry. Leaves that fall in the autumn are termed *deciduous*, and evergreens are *persistent*.

LEAF INSECTS. Family of insects (Phyllidae) of the order Phasmida, with a depressed and leaf-like body, remarkable for closely resembling the foliage on which they live. They are most common on islands from the Indian Ocean to the Pacific.

LEAF INSECT. Almost invisible among the leaves, even the legs having developed leaf-like forms. *Photo: NHPA*

LEAGUE OF NATIONS. International organization for the prevention of war estab. in 1920 with HQ at Geneva, but superseded by the UN in 1945. Its Covenant, drawn up by a special commission of the Paris Peace Conference, presided over by Pres. Wilson, was inorporated in the Versailles and other peace treaties. Members undertook to preserve the territorial integrity of all, and to submit disputes to the L. of N. or to arbitration.

Although successful in the humanitarian field (aid to refugees; international action against epidemics, drug traffic and slave trading; and improvement of working conditions through ILO, q.v.), it was hampered by internal rivalries and the necessity of unanimity on major political issues. No action was taken against Japan's aggression in Manchuria (1932); attempts to apply sanctions against Italy for her attack on Ethiopia collapsed (1935-6); no move was made against Germany for aggression in Austria, Czechoslovakia and Poland; and expulsion of Russia in 1939 had no effect on the Russo-Finnish War - Japan (1932) and Germany (1933) simply withdrew.

LEAKEY, Louis Seymour Bazett (1903-72). British archaeologist. B. at Kabete, Kenya, he was curator of Coryndon Museum, Nairobi, 1945-61, and in 1958 discovered gigantic animal fossils at Olduvai Gorge (q.v.), as well as sharing with his wife in discovering many early remains of a human type. **Mary L.** discovered in 1948 the first complete skull of an ape-man of the Miocene period on Rusinga Is. in Lake Victoria, known as Proconsul and *c.* 25,000,000 yrs old. After the death of her husband, she returned in 1974 to the Olduvai Gorge and discovered the earliest firmly dated human remains at Laetolil, 40km (25m) to the south. These, which are 3,350,000-3,750,000 yrs old, share many features with true man, and help to confirm that Australopithecus (*see* MAN) is not a direct ancestor of modern man, but an offshoot of the hominid line which died out. Previous evidence in support of this thesis had been provided by the Leakeys' son, **Richard L.**, (1944-) who discovered in 1972, nr Lake Rudolf in N Kenya, a skull *c.* 2,900,000 yrs old, with a capacity of 800cc - much greater than that of hominids of *c.* 1,500,000 yrs ago, such as Australopithecus.

LEAKEY. Richard Leakey holding in his right hand the skull of Australopithecus and in his left the breakthrough '1470' skull of a hominid at least 2.6 million years old, which proved theories that there is more than one branch of Man's family tree and that at least two types of early man co-existed. *Photo: Marion Kaplan/Camera Press*

LEAMINGTON (lem'-): officially **Royal L. Spa.** Health resort in Warwickshire, England, on the Leam, adjoining Warwick. The Royal Pump Room offers modern spa treatment. Pop. (1973) 46,140.

LEAN, David (1908-). British film director. Beginning as a camera assistant in 1928, he was asst director of *Pygmalion* (1938), and director of *Blithe Spirit* (1945), *Brief Encounter* (1946), *The Bridge on the River Kwai* (1957) and *Lawrence of Arabia* (1962).

LEAR, Edward (1812-88). British artist and humorist. B. in Holloway, he first attracted attention by his paintings of birds, and later turned to landscapes. He travelled in Italy, Greece, Egypt and India, pub. books on his travels with his own illustrations, and spent most of his later life in Italy. A vein of fantastic humour appears in his *Book of Nonsense* (1846) which popularized the limerick.

LEASEHOLD. Called in law a 'chattel real', a L. is a tenancy of land from year to year, or for a term of years.

LEASE-LEND. Programme of mutual aid between Britain, the USA, and the other Allies, carried out during the S.W.W. and begun under the Lease-and-Lend Act (1941-5), empowering the President to sell, exchange, transfer, lease, or lend war materials to any country whose defence he considered essential to the defence of the USA. War supplies could thus be sent to Britain on a credit basis instead of the cash-and-carry system introduced by the Neutrality Act of 1939.

In Feb. 1942, after the US's entry into the war, an agreement between Britain and the US provided for mutual L.-L. assistance, and for collaboration to deal with post-war economic problems.

LEATHER. A material prepared from the skins of animals, birds, and fish. L. articles at least 7,000 years old still exist. Methods of preparation vary according to the type of hide or skin and the kind of L. required. 'Hides' are the coverings of larger animals, such as cattle, horse and buffalo; 'skins' those of the smaller, such as calf, pig, goat, and sheep.

Tanning, the 'oldest manufacturing process in the world', prevents a skin from putrefying and turns it into L. Skins from the slaughterhouse are salted for temporary preservation and on arrival at the tannery the surplus flesh, hairs and salt are removed, and the skins dipped in tanning solutions of gradually increasing strength - a process which may take many weeks. Vegetable tanning solutions are generally blends of bark, leaf or nut infusions from various trees, and chrome tanning (basic chromium sulphate) is used for shoe uppers. After drying L. may be dyed or sprayed to any colour; and mechanical treatments provide various physical properties and types of surface texture. L. is used for footwear, harness and saddlery, travel goods, handbags, clothing, upholstery for furniture and cars and industrial goods such as oil seals and drive belting.

LEATHER. Tanners at work curing hides at Fez in Morocco, using the age-old processes. *Photo: Mireille Vautier*

LEATHERHEAD. Town in Surrey, England, SW of London, on the Mole at the foot of the N Downs. There are several industrial research stations and the Thorndike Theatre (1968) named after Sybil Thorndike (q.v.). Pop. (1972) 41,160.

LEAVEN (lev'n). Element inducing fermentation; especially applied to the yeast added to dough in bread making. Hence it is used figuratively of any pervasive influence, ususally in a good sense, although to the Hebrews it symbolized corruption, and unleavened bread was used in sacrifice.

LEAVIS, Frank Raymond (1895-1978), British critic. He ed. the controversial review *Scrutiny* 1932-53, championed the work of D.H. Lawrence and James Joyce, and in 1962 attacked Snow's theory of 'Two Cultures'.

LE'BANON. Country of SW Asia, on the Mediterranean between Israel to the S and Syria to the E and N. It forms a narrow strip *c.* 210km (130m) long and 48km (30m) wide, with the Lebanon Mts running N to S down the centre of the country, and the Anti-Lebanon range and Mt Hermon on the Syrian border to the E. Between the mtn ranges are the fertile valleys of the Orontes and Litani rivers. Irrigation is extending the cultivated area and crops incl citrus and other fruits, vegetables, olives, sugar beet and tobacco. Industries incl. canned and processed foods, textiles, tobacco, electrical goods, petroleum and chemicals. Banking and finance are important, and many tourists visit the sites of Baalbeck, Byblos and Tyre. The famed cedars of L. are now few. The chief towns are Beirut, the cap.; Tripoli, Zahlé and Saida (Sidon). Arabic is the official language, but French and English are widely used. Area 10,400 sq.km (3,400 sq.m); pop. (1978) 3,060,000, who incl. Maronite Christians, and Sunni and Shi'ite Moslems. The official language is Arabic, but French and English are widely used. M.U.: Lebanese pound.

Before the F.W.W. Lebanon was part of the Ottoman Empire; it became a French League of Nations mandate in 1922, and Allied troops under Gen. Catroux having ousted the Vichy French admin. in 1941, the country became independent in 1944. Under the constitution of 1947 there is a pres. (always a Maronite Christian) who appoints the PM (always a Sunni Moslem) and cabinet, and an elected Nat. Assembly always presided over by a Shi'ite Moslem. However, the Moslems are now in the majority, and from the late 1960s Palestine guerrillas were estab. in southern Lebanon. This led to a disastrous civil war between Christians and Moslems 1975–6. In 1976 Syria, originally a supporter of the guerrillas' activity against Israel, intervened militarily (in alliance with the Christians) against an alliance of Palestinians and leftists. The Christians were now mainly in an enclave N of Beirut, and in a strip on the Israeli-Lebanon border, both parts receiving Israeli aid. Israel invaded L. Mar.–June 1978, and again in 1982 (*see* ARAB-ISRAELI WARS), so that in 1983 the PLO under Arafat (q.v.) was compelled to leave. The Christian Pres. Amin Gemayel (q.v.) attempted to avoid partition of Lebanon, but neither Israel nor Syria would withdraw, and in 1984 his own army largely defected to the Druse (under Walid Jumblatt) and Shia Moslem militias. A multinational peacekeeping force proved ineffectual, and was withdrawn by Mar. 1984. Israeli forces finally withdrew by June 1985.

LEBANON. Cedars, as they have grown in Lebanon since biblical times. It was with cedar wood that King Solomon panelled the interior of his temple at Jerusalem 'from floor to rafter', together with that of his palace.

LEBDA. Older name of HOMS.

LEBEDEV (lebād'yef), **Peter Nikolaievich** (1866-1912). Russian physicist. While prof. at Moscow univ. 1892-1911 he succeeded in proving experimentally, and then measuring, the minute pressure which light exerts upon a physical body; confirming Clerk Maxwell's theoretical determination.

LEBENSRAUM (lehbenzrowm') (Ger., living space). A slogan used by the Nazis to justify their annexation of neighbouring states and their demand for the return of the former German colonies, on the ground that Germany was over-populated.

LEBRUN (lebrun'), **Albert** (1871-1950). French statesman. He became Pres. of the Senate in 1931 and in 1932 was chosen as Pres. of the rep. In 1940 he handed his powers over to Marshal Pétain.

LE CARRÉ (le ka'rā), **John.** Pseudonym of British author David John Cornwell (1931-). After teaching at Eton, he was a member of the Foreign Service 1960-4. His books incl. *The Spy Who Came in from the Cold* (1963) and *Tinker, Tailor, Soldier, Spy* (1974), and *Smiley's People* (1979). He coined the word 'mole' for a political traitor within a country.

LECITHIN (le'sithin). Fatty substances, containing nitrogen and phosphorus, occurring in animal and vegetable cell tissues. The name is from Gk *lekithos* 'egg yolk', and ovolecithin is found in eggs; vegelecithin (containing no cholesterol and much used in diets) is found in vegetables such as soya beans.

LECONTE DE LISLE (lekoṅt-de-lēl), **Charles Marie René** (1818-94). French poet. B. on Réunion, he settled in Paris in 1846 and headed Les Parnassiens (q.v.) 1866-76. Distinguished by perfection of versification and form, his work drew inspiration from the ancient world, e.g. *Poèmes antiques* (1852), *Poèmes barbares* (1862) and *Poèmes tragiques* (1884).

LE CORBUSIER (korbüsyā). Pseudonym of the French architect Charles Edouard Jeanneret (1887-1965). B. in Switzerland, he was originally a painter and engraver, but turned his attention to the problems of modern industrial society. For L.C. the house is a habitable machine which should be designed according to functional criteria. He won the contest for the Palace of the Nations at Geneva, devised town-planning schemes for Algiers, Barcelona, Buenos Aires, and Nemours (Algeria), and planned Cité Radieuse, Marseille and Chandigarh, India. *Le Modulor* (1948) explains his mathematical system for proportioning and relating the parts of buildings.

LECOUVREUR (lekoovrör'), **Adrienne** (1692-1730). French actress. She gained fame at the Comédie Française, where she made her début in 1717, and had many admirers, incl. Voltaire. The duchesse de Bouillon, a rival mistress of Maurice de Saxe, is thought to have poisoned her.

LĒ'DA. In Greek mythology the wife of Tyndareus and mother of Clytemnestra. She was loved by Zeus in the form of a swan, and by him became the mother of Helen of Troy, Castor and Pollux.

LE DUC THO (lē-duk-tō) (1911-). N Vietnamese diplomatist. In 1973 he was awarded, but indefinitely postponed receiving, the Nobel peace prize with Kissinger (q.v.).

LEE, Bruce. Stage-name of the American film actor, Lee Yuen Kam (1941-73). He estab. himself as a master of kung-fu (q.v.), the basis of the Chinese Western. *See* FILM.

LEE, Nathaniel (*c.* 1653-92). English dramatist. B. at Hatfield, he was ed. at Westminster and Cambridge. After an unsuccessful attempt to become an actor, he wrote from 1675 a number of bombastic tragedies, the best of which was *The Rival Queens* (1677). His dissipated life led to temporary insanity, and he d. in a fit of intoxication.

LEE, Robert Edward (1807-70). American gen. B. in Virginia, he was commissioned in 1829, served in the Mexican War, and in 1859 suppressed John Brown's raid on Harper's Ferry. On the outbreak of the Civil War he joined the Confederates, and became military adviser to Pres. Davis. In 1862 he received the command of the army of N Virginia and won the Seven Days' Battle against McClellan. During 1862-3 he made several raids into Northern territory, winning victories at Fredericksburg and Chancellorsville, but after his defeat at Gettysburg was compelled to take the defensive. He surrendered in 1865 at Appomattox Court House. He is recognized as one of the world's greatest strategists.

LEECH, John (1817-64). British caricaturist. B. in London, he studied medicine before turning to art. He illustrated many books, incl. Dickens' *Christmas Carol*, and during 1841-64 contributed *c.* 3,000 humorous drawings and political cartoons to *Punch*.

LEECHES. Worms in the class Hirudinea. They inhabit fresh water and in tropical countries infest damp forests. As blood-sucking animals they are injurious to man and beast, to whom they attach themselves by means of a strong suctorial mouth. Formerly the medicinal leech (*Hirudo medicinalis*) was used for bloodletting. Some Ls. live in the sea, e.g. the rock L. which infests sharks, etc.

LEEDS. City in W Yorks. England, on the Aire, a centre of communications where road, rail and canal (to Liverpool and Goole) meet. Since the 14th cent. it has been a centre of woollen manufacture, and clothing, with engineering, printing, chemicals and glass, are leading industries. Noted buildings incl. the Town Hall (Cuthbert Brodrick), Leeds Univ. (1904), the Art Gallery (1844), several fine churches, Temple Newsam (birthplace of

Darnley, now a museum), and the Cistercian Abbey of Kirkstall (1147). Pop. (1974) 748,000.

LEEK. Plant of the Liliaceae family. The cultivated L. (*Allium porrum*) is a variety of the wild *A. ampeloprasum* of Europe and Asia, and the lower leaf-parts are eaten as a vegetable. When fighting the Anglo-Saxons the Welsh, under St David's instructions, wore Ls. in their hats and it remains their national emblem.

LEE KUAN YEW (1923-). Singapore statesman. A third generation Straits Chinese, he studied law at Cambridge, became a founder-member of the left-wing People's Action Party (PAP), and PM of Singapore 1959.

LEEUWARDEN (lā'wahrden). City of the Netherlands, cap. of Friesland Prov. Noteworthy buildings incl. the palace of the stadholders of Friesland, and the church of St Jacob. L. is a marketing centre, and makes gold and silver ware. Pop. (1973) 86,340.

LEEUWENHOEK (lā'wenhook'), **Anthony van** (1632-1723). Dutch anatomist and pioneer microscopist. B. at Delft, he turned from business to microscopic research, investigated the structure of the red blood corpuscules, spermatozoa in animals, yeast, etc.

LEEWARD (loo'ahrd) **ISLANDS.** A general term for the N half of the Lesser Antilles in the West Indies. The British L.I. comprise *Antigua* and *Montserrat* (qq.v.) and the 3 islands of *St Christopher* (St Kitts), area 176 sq.km (68 sq.m), pop. 37,150, cap. Basseterre; *Nevis* area 93 sq.km (36 sq.m), pop. 15,000, cap. Charlestown; and *Anguilla* area 90 sq.km (35 sq.m), pop. 6,500.

The L.I., together with the British *Virgin Islands* (q.v.), were until 1960 a single colony. After attempts at a general West Indian federation (1958-62) failed, the status of Associated State was granted to Antigua (independent 1981), and also to *St Kitts-Nevis-Anguilla.* Anguilla alleged domination by the St Kitts federal admin., and in 1969 declared itself a rep. A small British force restored order, and 1971-5 A. was under direct rule from Britain at her own request. In 1976 Anguilla was granted internal autonomy, while still formally part of the Assoc. State of Kitts-Nevis-Anguilla. In 1981 Anguilla, at her own request, became a separate crown colony, and in 1983 St Kitts-Nevis became independent as St Christopher-Nevis.

LE FANU (lef'anoo), **Joseph Sheridan** (1814-73). Irish writer. B. in Dublin, he wrote novels and short stories, such as *The House by the Churchyard* (1863), *Uncle Silas* (1864), and *In a Glass Darkly* (1872), which rank high among stories of the mysterious.

LEFT WING. Term in politics used for the more radical parties. It originated in the French National Assembly in 1789, where the nobles sat in the place of honour on the president's right, and the third estate on his left; this arrangement has become customary in European parliaments, where the radicals sit on the left and the conservatives on the right. It is also usual to speak of the right, left, and centre, when referring to the different elements composing a single party.

LEGACY. A bequest of personal property made by a testator in his will and passing on his death to the legatee. Specific Ls. are definite named objects, e.g. a piece of jewellery. General L.s are sums of money or items not specially identified, e.g. 'one of my clocks'. A residuary L. is all the remainder of the deceased's personal estate after the other L.s have been distributed.

LEGEND (Lat. *legenda,* things to be read). Term originally applied to the books of readings designed for use in Divine Service, and afterwards extended to the stories of saints read at matins and at mealtimes in monasteries. The best-known collection of such stories was the 13th cent. *Legenda Aurea* by Jacobus de Voragine. The term has since extended its meaning to traditional stories about famous people.

LÉGER (lehzheh'), **Fernand** (1881-1955). French artist. By 1911 he was exhibiting Cubist works, favouring espec. cylindrical and machine forms, and reducing his human beings to puppets. He designed settings for ballets, and was a decorative mural painter.

LEGHORN. Seaport (Italian *Livorno*) of Tuscany, W Italy. 12m to the SW of Pisa. The modern town contrasts with the picturesque old fortress, dating back to before the 12th cent., and the new fortress (16th cent.). L.'s prosperity developed under the Medici who built the first harbour. It has a naval academy, shipyards, iron and steel works, distilleries, and makes motor-cars, macaroni, and copper goods. L. is also a popular resort. Pop. (1978) 177,500.

LEGIONNAIRE'S DISEASE. Pneumonia-like disease, cause by the bacterium *Legionella pneumophila,* so-called because it attacked a convention of an American 'fraternity' in 1976. The incubation period is 10 days, it is sometimes fatal, and only one antibiotic is effective against it.

LEGION OF HONOUR (Légion d'Honneur). French military and civil order, founded by Napoleon in 1802. The pres. of the rep. is grand master, but administration is in the charge of the grand chancellor. Women are eligible and the 5 ascending grades are: chevalier, officer, commander, grand officer and grand cross. In 1963, owing to overcrowding of the lower grades, it was decided to limit award of the L. of H. to 'eminent' services, 'distinguished' and 'honourable' services to be rewarded by the newly created Order of Merit (Ordre de Mérite), which also replaced a number of other decorations awarded by the various ministries. Still retained was the *Palmes Académiques* awarded by the Min. of Education.

LEGITIMACY. Any child born anywhere in lawful wedlock is legitimate, unless the husband successfully repudiates paternity, a proceeding, in the interests of the child, which is not encouraged by the law. In England and Wales an illegitimate child was legitimated on the subsequent marriage of its parents, provided there was no impediment to such marriage at the time of the birth of the child, by an act of 1926 effective 1927; an act of 1959 legitimated an illegitimate child on the marriage of its parents even though at the time of the birth the father or mother was married to a third person. A legitimated person has all the rights and duties of one born in wedlock except that such a person cannot succeed to, or transmit, any dignity or title. The law relating to legitimation is not uniform in the USA, but in general follows the line of the law in England.

LEGITIMISTS. The party in France which continued to support the claims of the house of Bourbon after the revolution of 1830. When the direct line became extinct in 1883 the majority of the party transferred their allegiance to the house of Orléans.

LEGUMINOSAE. Family of dicotyledonous plants, containing 600 genera and 12,000 species. It includes trees, e.g. laburnum and acacia; bushes, e.g. gorse; garden flowers, e.g. lupin, sweet pea; vegetables, e.g. peas and beans; and wild plants, e.g. clover. In some species of L.

leaves may be modified into tendrils which twine round other stems, affording support to the plant. Many species have characteristic flowers in which a large petal is flanked by 2 smaller ones, while in front 2 small petals form a boat-shaped shelter in which the 10 stamens are hidden. The seeds are carried in a pod. The roots of L. plants, e.g. clover, frequently bear small nitrogenous nodules, which restore nitrates to the soil.

LEHÁR (la'hahr), **Franz** (1870-1948). Hungarian composer. B. at Komárom, he studied at Prague conservatoire, intending to become a violinist, but abandoned this for conducting. He wrote many popular operettas, among them *The Merry Widow* (1905), *The Count of Luxembourg* (1909), *Gypsy Love* (1910) and *The Land of Smiles* (1923) and has also composed songs, marches, and a violin concerto.

LE HAVRE. *See* HAVRE, LE.

LEHMANN, Lotte (1888-1976). German-born American soprano. She excelled in Wagner and was the original Marschallin in *Rosenkavalier.*

LEHMANN (lā'man), **Rosamond Nina** (*c.* 1904-). British novelist, author of *Dusty Answer* (1927), *Invitation to the Waltz* (1932), *The Ballad and the Source* (1944), and *A Sea-Grape Tree* (1976).

LEIBNIZ (līb'nits), **Gottfried Wilhelm** (1646-1716). German philosopher and mathematician. B. at Leipzig, he soon showed a versatile genius, and at the age of 20 was offered a professorship at the univ. of Altdorf. He dedicated his *Nova methodus docendi discendique Juris* (1667) to the elector of Mainz, who employed him on political missions. The French king invited L. to Paris, where he met Christian Huygens, who revived his interest in mathematical problems. About this time L. invented a calculating machine, and in 1673, while engaged on a political mission to London, was elected a fellow of the Royal Society. After his return to Paris, he resumed his mathematical investigations, and devised a new form of differential and integral calculus. He also left the service of the elector for that of the dukes of Brunswick-Luneburg. In his *Systema Theologicum* (1686), he sought to promote a reunion of the Protestant and Catholic Churches. *Essais de Théodicée sur la bonté de Dieu, la liberté de l'homme, et l'origine du mal* (1710), *La Monadologie* (1714), and *Principes de la nature et de la grâce* (1714), are his main philosophical works. In his view the universe consists of a number of monads in harmony with each other and with God; therefore this is the best of all possible worlds, and faith and reason are not in conflict.

LEICESTER (les'ter), **Robert Dudley,** earl of (*c.* 1532-88). English courtier. Son of the duke of Northumberland, he was created E. of L. in 1564. His good looks won him the favour of Queen Elizabeth, who might have married him if he had not been previously married to Amy Robsart. When his wife d. in 1560, Dudley was suspected of murdering her. Elizabeth gave him command of the army sent to the Netherlands in 1585-7, and of that prepared to resist the threatened Spanish invasion of 1588.

LEICESTER. City in Leics, England, on the Soar, 156km (97m) NW of London. The Roman Ratae Coritanorum (founded AD 50), it is one of the oldest towns in England. The guildhall dates from the 14th cent. and ruined Bradgate House was the home of Lady Jane Grey. Industries incl. processed food (cheese and pork pies), hosiery, footwear, light and precision engineering, electronics, printing and plastics. There is a univ. (1957), and polytechnic. De Montfort Hall is a superb concert hall, and the Haymarket is a shopping centre with a civic theatre. Since the S.W.W. the city has acquired a large immigrant pop., espec. Indian and Pakistani. It is the admin. HQ of Leics. Pop. (1973) 287,350.

LEICESTER. Able, ambitious and vain, he had a stormy relationship with Elizabeth I. When she discovered in 1579 his secret second marriage in 1576, to the widow of the Earl of Essex, she nearly sent him to the Tower. *Photo: Courtesy of the National Portrait Gallery.*

LEICESTER OF HOLKHAM, earl of. *See* COKE.

LEICESTERSHIRE. A midland co. of England, which retained its boundaries in the local govt reorganisation of 1974, and also incorporated the whole of the co. of Rutland to the E. It is mainly low-lying. The Soar valley runs S to N, dividing Charnwood forest from the E uplands; other rivers are the Avon and Welland. The loamy soil affords rich cattle pasture and in the W wheat and other cereals flourish. Horses are bred and it is a famous hunting co. The Vale of Belvoir (bē'ver) N of Melton Mowbray and Grantham, is of outstanding natural beauty and projected coal extraction there caused fierce controversy in 1979. The Vale is also the home of Stilton cheese. The chief towns are Leicester, the admin. HQ; Melton Mowbray, Market Harborough, Loughborough and Oakham. Area 2,553 sq.km (986 sq.m); pop. (1978) 833,300.

LEICHHARDT (līkh'hahrt), **Friedrich** (1813-48). Australian explorer, b. in Prussia. In 1843 he walked 965 km (600 m) from Sydney to Moreton Bay, Queensland, and in 1844 went from Brisbane to Arnhem Land, but on a further expedition from Queensland in 1848 disappeared, never to be seen again. Patrick White used the character of L. in *Voss.*

LEIDEN (lā-den). City in S. Holland prov., Netherlands. On the Old Rhine, 10km (6m) from its mouth, L. is linked by canal to Haarlem, Amsterdam and Rotterdam. Woollen goods and cigars are made, and it has been a printing centre since the Elzevir works were estab. in 1580. The univ. was founded by William the Silent in 1575, and Rembrandt and Jan Steen were b. here. Pop. (1978) 102,800.

LEIF ERICSSON (lēf er'ikson) (fl. 1000). Viking explorer, the son of Eric the Red, who colonized Greenland. He is said to have discovered 'Vinland', generally identified with Nova Scotia.

LEIGH (lē), **Vivien** (1913-67). British actress, *née* Hartley. Remarkable for her fragile beauty and vivacious fire, she excelled as Sabina in *The Skin of Our Teeth,* and Blanche in *A Streetcar named Desire,* receiving an Oscar for the film of the latter, and in the title-role of the film *Lady Hamilton.* She was m. to Lord Olivier, 1940-60, playing with him in *Antony and Cleopatra.*

LEIGH-MALLORY, Sir Trafford (1892-1944). British air chief marshal. He served in the F.W.W., and subsequently held staff appointments. As AOC No. 12 Fighter Group 1937-40, he aided in the defence during the Battle of Britain. He was C-in-C of Allied air forces during the invasion of France, and was killed in an air crash.

LEIGHTON, Frederick, baron (1830-96). British artist and sculptor. B. at Scarborough, he spent most of his early life on the Continent, and achieved fame in 1855 with his 'Cimabue's Madonna Carried in Procession'. Most of his works represented historical, especially classical, subjects, e.g. 'Captive Andromache' (1888), and 'The Return of Persephone' (1891).

LEINSTER (lin'ster). SE prov. of Rep. of Ireland, incl. the cos. of Longford, Westmeath, Meath, Louth, Offaly, Laoighis, Kildare, Dublin, Carlow, Wicklow, Kilkenny, and Wexford (qq.v.). Area 19,635 sq.km (7,581 sq.m); pop. (1971) 1,497,145.

LEIPZIG (līp'tsig). Cap. of L. dist., E Germany, 145km (90m) SW of Berlin, lying in a fertile plain. The old town has narrow streets with 16th and 17th cent. houses. Near the Gothic Rathaus (1558) is Auerbach's Hof. built about 1530. L. has muscial associations with J. S. Bach and Mendelssohn. The 'Gewandhaus'' concert hall was completed 1884, and the univ. founded in 1409. The famous L. fairs have been responsible for the growth of its varied manufacturers, which incl. furs, leather goods, cloth, glass, motor-cars, and musical instruments, and are the main meeting-place for commercial interests of E and W Europe. L. was the scene of Napoleon's defeat in the Battle of the Nations, 1813. Pop. (1978) 564,300.

LEISHMANIASIS (lēshmanī'asis). Tropical disease identified by Sir William Leishman (1865-1926). Caused by a single-cell parasitic organism spread by sandflies, it takes various forms. It may attack the internal organs (kala-azar), the nose and mouth (espundia - limited to the New World), or cause skin ulcer (oriental sore).

LEITH (lēth). Scottish port, incorporated in Edinburgh in 1920, having been granted to Edinburgh as its port by Robert Bruce in 1329. L. stands on the S of the Firth of Forth.

LEITRIM (lē'trim). Co. in Connacht prov., Rep. of Ireland, Bounded on the NW by Donegal Bay. The N is tableland. The main rivers are the Shannon, Bonet, Drowes and Duff; Lough Allen divides it into two. The main products are potatoes, linen, woollens, and pottery; coal, iron and lead are mined. The co. town is Carrick-on-Shannon. Area 1,525 sq.m (589 sq.m); pop. (1971) 28,360.

LEIX. Spelling used 1922-35 of LAOIGHIS.

LĒ'LAND, John (*c.* 1506-52). English antiquary. B. in London, he became chaplain and librarian to Henry VIII, and during 1534-43 toured England collecting materials for a history of English antiquities. His MSS have formed a valuable source for scholars.

LĒ'LY, Sir Peter (1618-80). Anglo-German portraitist. B. in Westphalia, he came to England in 1641, and was employed both by Charles I and Cromwell. Charles II made him his court painter, and knighted him in 1679. His most famous paintings are those of the beauties of Charles II's court at Hampton Court. His real name was Pieter van der Faes, but L. adopted his father's nickname 'Lely' - from the fleur-de-lis on their house front.

LE MANS. *See* MANS, LE.

LEMBERG. German name of LVOV.

LEMMING. Small rodent found in America, N Europe and Asia. The European lemming (*Lemmus lemmus*), common in Norway, is 12cm (5in) long and yellowish brown. Periodically, when their population exceeds the available food supply, Ls. migrate towards the sea and are drowned in large numbers.

LE'MNOS. Greek island (Gk límnos) of volcanic origin, rising to 430m (1,411 ft), in the N of the Aegean Sea. Mulberries and other fruits and tobacco are grown, and sheep are reared. The main towns are Kastro and Mudros. Area 466 sq.km (180 sq.m).

LEMON. Fruit of the L. tree (*Citrus limone*). It may have originated in NW India, and was introduced into Europe by the Spanish Moors in the 12th or 13th cent. It is now grown largely in Italy, Spain, California, Florida, S Africa, and Australia.

LĒ'MUR. Sub-orders of Primates, Lemuroidea and Tarsioidea. The true Ls. inhabit Madagascar and the Comoro Islands, and certain allied species, e.g. the galagos and loris, are found in E Africa and E Asia. They are arboreal animals, valued for their long soft fur, and many species are nocturnal. They feed upon fruit, insects, birds, etc. The Ring-tailed lemur (*L. catta*) is often kept as a pet.

LĒNA. Longest river in Asiatic Russia, flowing generally NE, then NW from the W slopes of the Baikal mts for nearly 4,800 km (3,000 m), during which it is joined by innumerable tributaries to enter the Arctic Ocean by several mouths. It is ice-covered for 6 months of the year.

LE NAIN (nań), **Antoine** (1588-1648), **Louis** (1593-1648), and **Mathieu** (1607-77). French painters. The 3 brothers were b. at Laon, settled in Paris, and were among the original members of the French Academy. They painted portraits, but mainly devoted themselves to pictures of peasant life.

LENCLOS (lońklō), **Ninon de** (1615-1705). French lady of fashion. As the recognized leader of Parisian society, she was the mistress in turn of many highly placed men, including Condé and La Rochefoucauld.

LENIN (lā'nin), **Vladimir Ilyich.** Pseudonym of Russian statesman V. I. Ulyanov (1870-1924). B. at Simbirsk (renamed Ulyanovsk in his honour), he was the son of a school-inspector. He practised law for a time, but after 1893 devoted himself entirely to revolutionary propaganda, and was banished to Siberia 1895-1900. After his release he ed. the Social-Democratic Party's paper *Iskra*

(*The Spark*) from abroad, visiting London several times after 1902. In *What is to be done?* (1902) he maintained the revolution must be led by a disciplined party of professional revolutionaries; at the 1903 party congress in London this theory was accepted by the majority of delegates, who hence became known as Bolsheviks ('majority'). L. took an active part in the 1905 revolution, but after its defeat again had to leave Russia. In 1914 he settled in Switzerland, whence he attacked those Socialists who supported the F.W.W. on the grounds that it was a purely 'imperialist' struggle; this view he expounded in his most important book, *Imperialism* (1917). On the outbreak of the revolution in March 1917 he returned to Russia, and put forward a programme of immediate peace and transfer of power to the Soviets. As a result, he had to go into hiding until 7 Nov., when the prov. govt was overthrown and a Soviet govt set up under L.'s presidency. Peace was concluded with Germany, but during 1918-21 the new régime was threatened by foreign intervention and 'White' uprisings. Even during the civil war many important reforms were achieved, including the division of large estates among the peasantry and the recognition of the equal rights of all the peoples of Russia, while L. was already planning large-scale electrification schemes. He also took the lead in founding the 3rd (Communist) International in 1919. His health was undermined by overwork and the effects of an attempt to assassinate him in 1918, and after 1922 he became an invalid. He d. on 21 Jan. 1924; his embalmed body was laid in a mausoleum in Red Square, Moscow.

His wife **Nadezhda Konstantinova Krupskaya** (1869-1939) worked with L. at St Petersburg in the illegal Union for the Liberation of the Working Class, m. him in 1898, and shared actively in his work. Her *Memories of Lenin* throws much light on him, both as a political leader and as an individual.

LENIN. A family group: Lenin and his wife, with Lenin's nephew Victor and the daughter of a friend in 1922. *Photo: Novosti*

LENINAKAN (lyenyinakahn'). Industrial town in Armenia SSR, USSR, 40km (25m) NW of Yerevan, a railway junction with textile factories, engineering industries, and an electric power station. Founded in 1837 as a fortress called Alexandropol, it was virtually destroyed by an earthquake in 1926. Pop. (1977) 192,000.

LENINGRAD. Cap. of L. region of the RSFSR, second city of the USSR. Cap. of the Russian Empire 1709-1918. It was founded as an outlet to the Baltic in 1703 by Peter the Great, who took up residence there in 1712. Originally called St Petersburg, it was renamed Petrograd in 1914, and L. in 1924. It stands at the head of the Gulf of Finland, and is split up by the mouths of the Neva, which connects it with Lake Lagoda. The site is low and swampy, and the climate very severe.

L. was the centre of all the main revolutionary movements from the Decembrist revolt of 1825 up to the 1917 revolution. During the German invasion in the S.W.W. the city heroically withstood siege and bombardment from Sept. 1941 to Jan. 1944.

L. is famous for its wide boulevards; most of its fine baroque and classical buildings of the 18th and early 19th cents. survived the S.W.W. siege. L. has a univ. (1819) and is the seat of a Metropolitan of the Orthodox Church. Museums incl. the Winter Palace, occupied by the Tsars until 1917, the Hermitage, the Russian Museum (formerly Michael Palace), and St Isaac's Cathedral. The oldest building in L. is the fortress of St Peter and St Paul, on an island in the Neva, a dreaded political prison. L. became a seaport when it was linked with the Baltic by a ship canal built 1875-93. It is also linked by canal and river with the Caspian and Black Seas, and in 1975 a seaway connection was completed via Lakes Onega and Ladoga with the White Sea nr Belomorsk, so that naval forces can reach the Barents Sea free of NATO surveillance. There is a major airport. Industries incl. shipbuilding and the manufacture of machinery and machine tools, chemicals, textiles, and textile machinery, diesel motors, tyres, and rubber boots. Pop. (1977) 4,425,000.

LENINGRAD. The 'Hermitage' art gallery, which has one of the world's finest collections. *Photo: J. Allan Cash*

LENINSK-KUZNETSKY (lyen'yinskē kōōznyet'skē). Town in Kemerovo region, RSFSR, on the Inya r., 320km (200m) SSE of Tomsk. It is a mining centre in the Kuzbas, with a large iron and steel works; coal, iron, manganese, and other metals, and precious stones occur in the neighbourhood. Formerly Kolchugino, the town was renamed L.-K. in 1925. Pop. (1977) 131,000.

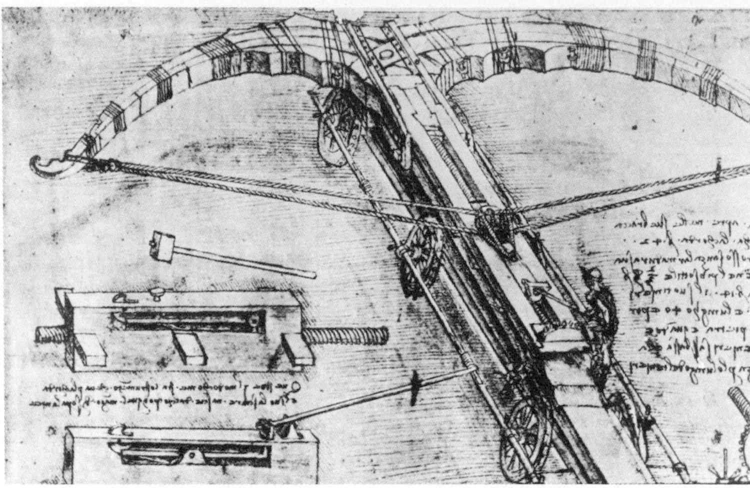

LEONARDO DA VINCI. A self-portrait from his notebooks, and a design for a 'secret weapon', a gigantic crossbow.

LĒ'NŌ, Dan (1861-1904). British comedian. Beginning as an acrobat, he became the idol of the music halls, and the greatest of pantomime 'dames'.

LE NÔTRE (lenotr'), **André** (1613-1700). French landscape gardener, creator of the gardens at Versailles and the Tuileries.

LENS (loṅs). Coal-mining town in Pas-de-Calais dept, France. It was in German occupation and close to the front line from Oct. 1914 to Oct. 1918 in the F.W.W. when the town and its mines were severely damaged. In the S.W.W. it was occupied by the Germans May 1940 to Sept. 1944, but suffered less physical damage. Pop. (1975) 42,000.

LENS. A piece of a transparent medium such as glass with 2 polished surfaces - one of which may be concave or convex, and the other may be either plane, concave or convex - to modify the rays of light, which become more convergent or more divergent according to the type of L. they traverse. Convex Ls. converge the light and concave Ls. diverge it. They are essential parts of spectacles, microscopes, telescopes, cameras and almost all optical instruments. Compound Ls. for special purposes are built up from 2 or more Ls. made of glass (or other suitable medium) of different refractive index.

The image formed by a single L. suffers from several defects or aberrations, notably spherical aberration in which a straight line becomes a curved image, and chromatic aberration in which an image in white light tends to have coloured edges. Aberrations are corrected by the use of compound Ls. For electron L, *see* ELECTRON MICROSCOPE.

In zoology a L. is the part of the eye which focuses the rays of light on to the cornea. *See* EYE.

LENS, gravitational. Object in space which, by its gravitational field, bends light in a similar way to a spectacle lens. For an observer on Earth this may mean that, as in 1979, two quasars are seen which appear physically almost identical. In reality such a twin effect is more probably due to there being double images of a single quasar, which are created by an intervening galaxy, itself to be faintly seen between the 'two' quasars.

Such a lens also produces a magnifying effect, and from a focal point 200,000 million miles out in space objects seen behind the Sun would be magnified 20 million times: it has been suggested that this is the direction of astronomy in the future.

LENT. In the Christian Church, the 40 days' period of fasting which precedes Easter, beginning on Ash Wednesday, but omitting Sundays.

LENTHALL (len'tawl), **William** (1591-1662). British lawyer. Speaker of the House of Commons in the Long Parliament of 1640-60, he took an active part in the Restoration.

LENTIL. Annual plant of the Leguminosae family (*Lens esculenta*) of which the small seeds are widely used for food. The plant, which resembles the vetch, is probably native to the shores of the Mediterranean. It grows 15-45cm (6-18in) in height, and has white, blue, or purplish flowers. The pods are *c.* 4cm (1.5in) long, containing 2 seeds. The commonest varieties are the greyish French L. and the red Egyptian L.

LENYA (lān'ya), **Lotte.** Stage-name of Austrian actress and singer Karoline Blamauer (1905-81). M. to Kurt Weill (q.v.) in 1925, she appeared in several of the Brecht-Weill operas, notably *The Threepenny Opera* (1928).

LĒ'Ō III, the Isaurian (*c.* 680-740). Byzantine emperor. A soldier who seized the throne in 717, he successfully defended Constantinople against the Saracens in 717-18, and attempted to suppress the use of images in church worship.

LEÓN (lā-on'). Cap. of L. prov., Spain, 825m (2,700 ft) a.s.l. It is the see of a bishopric and has a Gothic cathedral (1199) and other fine ecclesiastical buildings. Pop. (1970) 105,235.

The ancient kingdom of LEÓN, dating from the 10th century, incl. not only modern L. prov., but also modern Palencia, Valladolid, Zamora and Salamanca; in 1230 it was united with Castille.

LEÓN. City of Guanajuato state, Mexico, 370km (230m) NW of Mexico City. It dates from 1576 and has a fine cathedral. Pop. (1977) 557,000.

LEŌN. Cultural centre and univ. city of Nicaragua, founded in 1523. Pop. (1977) 212,100.

LEONARDO DA VINCI (vin'chē) (1452-1519). Italian painter, sculptor, architect, musician, engineer, and scientist. B. in Vinci, in the Val d'Arno, the natural son of a lawyer, he studied under Verrochio, and began to work as an independent artist *c.* 1477 under the patronage of Lorenzo the Magnificent. In 1482 he was employed at Milan by Lodovico Sforza as state engineer, court painter, and director of court festivities. He painted the 'Last Supper' on the wall of the refectory of Santa Maria Delle Grazie, and devised an irrigation system for the plains of Lombardy. In 1500 L. returned to Florence, and in 1502 was employed by Cesare Borgia as architect and chief engineer. Commissioned to decorate one of the walls of the council hall in the Signoria, Florence, he chose the 'Battle of Anghiari' as his subject, but abandoned this work after spending 2 years on the cartoon. About 1504 L. completed his portrait of the wife of Zanoki del Giocondo, known as 'Mona Lisa', now in the Louvre. In 1513-15 he was in Rome. At the invitation of Francis I he went to France, and lived at the Château Cloux near Amboise, where he d. There is no other man in history who distinguished himself in so many different fields. *See* RENAISSANCE.

LEONCAVALLO (lāonkahvah'lō), **Ruggiero** (1858-1919). Italian operatic composer. B. at Naples, he played at restaurants, composing in his spare time, until in 1892 *I Pagliacci* was performed and immediately became popular. Of his other operas, only *La Bohème* (contemporary with Puccini's) and *Zaza* enjoyed some success.

LĒO'NIDAS (d. 480 BC). King of Sparta. He was killed while defending the pass of Thermopylae with 300 Spartans, 700 Thespians, and 400 Thebans against a huge Persian army.

LEOPARD. Member of the cat family (*Panthera pardus*), also known as the panther, found over almost all Africa and Asia. The ground colour of the coat is golden and the spots form rosettes which differ according to the variety: black Ls. are simply mutants and retain the patterning as a 'watered-silk' effect, and white specimens have been known. The L. varies in size from 1.5 to 2.5m (5-8ft), incl. the tail, which may measure 1m (3ft).

Closely allied is the snow L. or ounce (*Panthera uncia*) which has irregular rosettes of much larger black spots, and is a native of central Asia. The clouded L. or clouded tiger (*Neofelis nebulosa*) is rather smaller than the ordinary L., with large blotchy markings rather than rosettes, found in SE Asia.

LEOPARDI (lā-ōpahr'dē), **Giacomo,** count (1798-1837). Italian poet. B. at Recanati, of a noble family, he wrote many of his finest poems, incl. his great patriotic odes, before he was 21. His first collection, *Versi*, appeared in 1824, and was followed by his philosophical *Operette Morali* (1827), in prose, and *Canti* (1831). After 1830 his life was divided between Florence, Rome, and Naples, where he d. Throughout life he was tormented by ill-health, by the consciousness of his deformity (he was hunch-backed), by loneliness and a succession of unhappy love-affairs, and by his failure to find consolation in any philosophy. He has nevertheless been called the greatest

LEOPARD. A hunting leopard in Serengeti Park, Tanzania. *Photo: Heather Angel*

lyric poet since Dante.

LĒ'OPOLD. Name of 2 Holy Roman Emperors. **Leopold I** (1640-1705) succeeded his father Ferdinand III in 1657. The greater part of his reign was occupied by wars with Louis XIV of France and with the Turks. **Leopold II** (1747-92), son of Maria Theresa, succeeded his brother Joseph II in 1790. He adopted a hostile attitude towards the French Revolution which led to the outbreak of war a few weeks after his death.

LEOPOLD I (1790-1865). King of the Belgians. The son of the duke of Saxe-Coburg, he served against the French with the Russian Army 1813-14. He m. Charlotte, the dau. of George IV of the UK, in 1816, but she d. in the following year. Elected to the throne when Belgium became independent in 1831, he proved a wise and liberal ruler. He exercised a great influence over his niece Queen Victoria.

LEOPOLD II (1835-1909). King of the Belgians. He succeeded his father Leopold I in 1865. He financed Stanley's explorations in Africa, which resulted in the foundation of the Congo Free State. This was ruled autocratically by L., who derived a huge fortune from it. The scandal caused by his maladministration resulted in its annexation as a Belgian colony in 1908.

LEOPOLD III (1901–83). King of the Belgians. The son of Albert I, he succeeded his father in 1934. When the Germans invaded Belgium in 1940, L. took command of the army, until the enemy compelled him to surrender. He was held a prisoner until 1945. After his liberation a constitutional crisis arose, as the left-wing parties demanded his abdication in view of charges brought against his conduct in 1940; as a result, his brother Prince Charles was appointed regent. In 1950 L. was recalled, but national unrest led him to resign his powers to his son Baudouin.

LÉOPOLDVILLE. *See* KINSHASA.

LEPA'NTO. Italian name of the Greek port of Naupaktos, on the N of the Gulf of Corinth. A famous sea battle was fought in the Gulf of Corinth off L., then in Turkish possession, on 7 Oct. 1571, between the Turks and Christian League forces from Spain, Venice, Genoa, and the Papal States which were commanded by Don John of

Austria (q.v.). Instigated by pope Pius V, the League delivered a crushing blow to Moslem sea power. Cervantes was wounded in the battle, which is the subject of a stirring poem by G. K. Chesterton.

LEPIDOPTERA. Order of insects which includes the moths and butterflies (qqv).

LEPROSY. A disease due to infection by the lepra bacillus. It is most common in hot, damp countries, especially Africa, but is found all over the world. In the nodular type the skin thickens, lumps appear all over it and break down into ulcers: the patient eventually dies of exhaustion, tuberculosis, or kidney disease. In the smooth type the microbe chiefly attacks the nerves of the skin, producing discoloured patches, loss of feeling, paralysis, and the death and shedding of fingers and toes. The bacillus may be transmitted by contact, or enter through stomach and lungs.

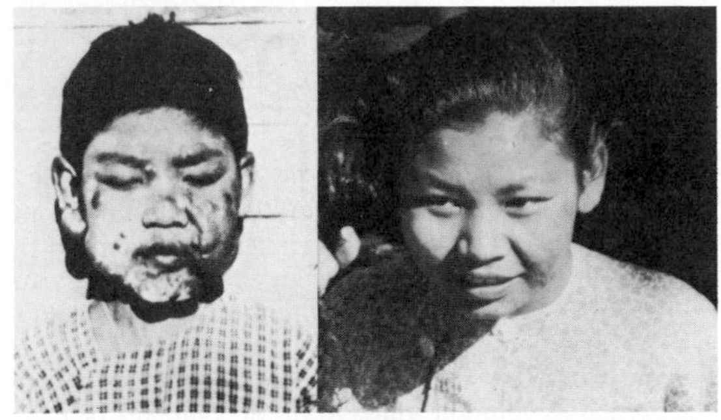

LEPROSY. Eight-year-old Ma Boke Sone on arrival (left) at the Roman Catholic Leprosy Institute in Rangoon, and three years later after sulphone drug treatment. *Photo: Courtesy of W.H.O.*

LE'PTIS MAGNA. Ruined city in Libya, 120km (75m) E of Tripoli. It was founded by the Phoenicians, then came under Carthage, and in 47 BC under Rome. Excavation in the 20th cent. brought to light remains of fine Roman buildings.

LE PUY. *See* PUY, LE.

LÉRIDA (ler'ēthah). Capital of L. prov. in N Spain, on the Segre, 132km (82m) W of Barcelona. The chief manufactures are leather, paper, glass, and cloth. L. was captured by Caesar in 49 BC. It has a palace of the kings of Aragon. Pop. (1970) 347,015.

LE'RMONTOV, Mikhail Yurevich (1814-41). Russian poet and novelist. B. in Moscow, he received a commission in the Guards, but in 1837 was exiled to the Caucasus for a revolutionary poem on the death of Pushkin. The romantic scenery of the Caucasus deeply influenced his poetry. After returning to St Petersburg in 1838 he pub. his psychological novel *A Hero of Our Times* and a vol. of poems. He was killed in a duel.

LERNER, Alan Jay. *See* LOEWE, Frederick.

LER'WICK. Port and admin. HQ of Shetland, Scotland. Situated on the E coast of mainland, it has hand-knit (espec. shawls) and fishing industries, but offshore oil has provided new employment opportunities. Pop. (1973) 6,200.

LE SAGE (sahzh), **Alain René** (1668-1747). French novelist and dramatist. B. in Brittany, he early abandoned law for literature. His novels incl. *Le Diable boiteux* (1707) and his masterpiece *Gil Blas* (1715-35), much indebted to Spanish originals.

LESBIANISM (lez'bianizm). Homosexual relationship between women, so-called from Lesbos, where Sappho (q.v.) was born.

LESBOS. Greek island in the Aegean Sea, near the coast of Turkey, conquered by the Turks from Genoa in 1462, annexed to Greece in 1913. L. was an ancient Aeolian settlement, the home of Alcaeus and Sappho. Mytilene is the cap. L. produces olives, wine, and grain. Area 1,748 sq.km (675 sq.m); pop, (1971) 86,340.

LESOTHO (lesō'tō). Country, formerly known as Basutoland, bounded by the Orange Free State, Natal and Cape Prov., but not part of the Rep. of S Africa. The land is mountainous, rising to 3,350 m (11,000 ft), but crops incl. wheat and maize; and sheep and goats supply wool and mohair for export. Diamonds are mined and there is developing light industry, but *c.* half the male pop. works in the mines of S Africa. The cap. is Maseru.

The founder of the Basuto nation was Chief Moshesh (1790-1870), who united the tribesmen *c.* 1830. From 1835 he waged war on encroaching Boer settlers, but lost some territory and in 1868 Basutoland passed, at his own request, under British protection. It became independent within the Commonwealth under the name L. in 1966, the Paramount Chief becoming head of state as King Moshoeshoe II (1939-). In 1970 the first general elections resulted in the defeat of the govt, but PM Chief Leabua Jonathan suspended the constitution, and a state of emergency continued 1970-3, when an interim Nat. Assembly was called, but a revolt was forcibly quelled in 1974. Area 30,346 sq.km (11,716 sq.m); pop. (1976) 1,246,815. M.U.:S African rand.

LESS DEVELOPED COUNTRIES. Countries (LDCs) late to develop an industrial base, and often heavily dependent on selling such agricultural products or mineral resources as they may have to developed countries where the wealth-creating packaging, processing and distributing may be done. At the 1964 UN conference on Trade and Development, the 'Group of 77' was estab. as a trade union of LDCs to bring pressure by concerted action on developed countries to give aid, etc.

LEPIDOPTERA. In the facing illustration is a selection of species. Nos 1–16 are moths: (1) Austrian emperor, (2) small magpie, (3) oleander hawkmoth, (4) thistle ermine, (5) tiger-moth, (6) great oak beauty, (7) magpie, (8) currant clearwing, (9) six-spot burnet, (10) swallow-tail, (11) *Aclias leto,* Assam, (12) black arches, (13) broad-bordered bee hawkmoth, (14) Kentish glory, (15) green hummingbird hawkmoth, (16) yellow underwing; and nos 17–30 are butterflies: (17) *Papilio ulysses,* New Guinea, (18) zebra swallow-tail (*Papilio Marcellus*), N.America, (19) *Cyclopides silvius,* Europe, (20) *Troides paradiseus,* New Guinea, 13cm (5.25in) across, (21) Lulworth skipper (*Adopaea actaeon*), England, (22) high brown fritillary (*Argynnis adippe*), England, (23) dark clouded yellow (*Colias myrmidone*), Europe, (24) eastern marbled white (*Melanargia larissa*), Europe, (25) *Satyrus achine,* Europe, (26) red admiral (*Pyrameis atalanta*), Europe, Asia, N and S America, (27) large heath or gatekeeper (*Epinephele tithonus*), England, (28) *Heliconius burneyi,* Peru, (29) comma (*Polygonia c-album*), England, (30) *Precis octavia,* Africa. In the centre, the anatomy of a butterfly.

1
2
3
4
5
6
7
8
9
10
11
12
13
14
15
16
apex
antenna
costal margin
eye
cell
thorax
veins
tornus
apex
outer margin
abdomen
inner margin
anal angle
17
18
19
20
21
22
23
24
25
26
27
28
29
30

LE'SSEPS, Ferdinand, vicomte de (1805-94). French diplomat and engineer. In 1854 he obtained a concession for the construction of a canal across the isthmus of Suez. Work began in April 1859, completed Nov. 1869. *See also* PANAMA CANAL.

LE'SSING, Gotthold Ephraim (1729-81). German dramatist and critic. B. at Kamenz in Saxony, he studied at Leipzig, and subsequently lived in Berlin, Leipzig, and Hamburg. His dramatic masterpieces incl. *Miss Sara Sampson* (1755), the first German tragedy of common life; *Philotas* (1759) a one-act prose tragedy; the comedy *Minna von Barnhelm* (1767) with a Seven Years War background; the domestic tragedy *Emilia Galotti* (1772); and the verse play *Nathan der Weise* (1779) which treats the theme of religious tolerance. As a critic he decisively influenced the course of German literature with *Briefe, die neueste Literatur betreffend* (1759), in which Shakespeare is ranked above the French dramatists; with his masterpiece *Laokoon* (1766) in which he analyses the functions of poetry and the plastic arts; and with the *Hamburgische Dramaturgie* (1767-8) in which he re-interpreted Aristotle and again championed Shakespeare. His many theological and philosophical writings include *Ernst und Falk* (1777-80) in which he pleaded for tolerance and understanding in human affairs.

LESVOS. *See* LESBOS.

LETCHWORTH. English town in Herts, 56km (35m) NNW of London, founded in 1903 as the first British garden city. The principal industrial products are clothing, furniture, scientific instruments, and light metal goods, and it is a printing centre. Pop. (1972) 31,540.

LĒ'THĒ. In Greek mythology a river of the underworld whose waters, when drunk, brought forgetfulness of the past.

LE TOUQUET. *See* TOUQUET-PARIS-PAGE, LE.

LETTERS. The art of L.-writing was perfected by the Romans with Cicero, Pliny the Younger, and Seneca. Christianity introduced the pastoral L., of which the exponents include Basil, Chrysostom, and Gregory Nazienzen in the Eastern Church, and Ambrose, Augustine, Jerome, and Gregory in the West. Outside the Church the Middle Ages tended to produce mainly letters of state, apart from exceptions such as the correspondence of Héloise and Abelard (12th cent.), and the Paston Ls, (15th cent.). To the Reformation period belong the notable correspondences of Erasmus, Luther, and Melanchthon. There was a steady development of English Ls. during the 16th and 17th cents. with Donne, Spenser, Sidney, Milton, Cromwell, Wotton, etc., while in France there were Pascal and Mme de Sévigné. The art reached its highest polish in the 18th cent. in the Ls. of Pope, Walpole, Swift, Mary W. Montagu, Chesterfield, Cowper, Gray, and the 'Ls. of Junius': Richardson adapted the form to the use of the novel. French L.-writers of the period incl. Bossuet, Voltaire, and Rousseau. Familiar names of the 19th cent. are those of Lamb, Byron, Keats, Fitzgerald, Stevenson; the American Emerson, and J. R. Lowell; the French George Sand, Saint-Beuve, and the Goncourt brothers; the German Schiller and Goethe; and the Swiss Gottfried Keller. In the 20th cent. we have T. E. Lawrence, G. B. Shaw and E. Terry, K. Mansfield, Rilke, etc., There are several collections of famous letters, e.g. E. V. Lucas's 'The Gentlest Art'. Ownership of a letter, as a document, passes to the recipient; copyright remains with the writer.

LETTRES DE CACHET (let'r-de-kasheh'). French term for orders signed by the king and closed with his seal (*cachet*); especially orders under which persons might be imprisoned or banished without trial. They were used as a means of disposing of politically dangerous persons or criminals of high birth without the embarrassment of a trial. The system was abolished during the French Revolution.

LETTUCE (le'tis). Annual plant (*Lactuca sativa*) belonging to the Compositae family, and believed to have been derived from a wild variety, *L. serriola*. There are 4 common forms, the cabbage L., with round or loose heads, the Cos L., with long, upright heads, the asparagus L., with narrow leaves, and the cut-leaved L., with deeply serrated leaves.

LEUCITE (lū'sī). Mineral occurring frequently in volcanic rocks of recent origin, and others low in silica content and rich in potash. It is dull white to grey, and usually opaque.

LEUCOCYTE (lū'kosīt). A white blood cell. The blood contains about 11,000 leucocytes to the cubic millimetre - about one to every 500 red cells. Generally speaking, the function of the white cells is to eat up invading bacteria and to repair the results of injury. The resistance of the body to injury and disease, therefore, depends on them. Their number may be reduced (leucopenia) by starvation, pernicious anaemia, and certain infections - e.g. typhoid and malaria. An increase in the numbers (leucocytosis) is a reaction to normal events such as digestion, exertion and pregnancy, and to abnormal ones such as loss of blood, cancer and most infections.

LEUKAEMIA (lūkē'mia). A form of cancer of the blood, marked by an increase in the white blood cells. Today it is cured or controlled in many children and young adults by radiotherapy or drugs. There may be an inherited proneness to L. which can be augmented by external factors such as high fever, and nuclear radiation.

LEVA'NT. Name applied to the E. Mediterranean region, or more specifically, to the coastal regions of Turkey-in-Asia, Syria, Lebanon, and Israel.

LEVELLERS. The democratic party in the English Revolution. They found wide support among the New Model Army, and the yeoman farmers, artisans, and small traders, and during 1647-9 proved a powerful political force. Their programme included the establishment of a republic, govt by a parl. of one house elected by manhood suffrage, religious toleration, and sweeping social reforms. Mutinies by the Ls. in the army were suppressed by Cromwell in 1649. They were led by John Lilburne (q.v.).

LĒ'VEN, Alexander Leslie, 1st earl of (*c.* 1580-1661). Scottish general. After a distinguished career in the Swedish service, he led the Covenanters' army which invaded England in 1640. He also commanded the Scottish army sent to aid the English Puritans in 1643-6, and shared in the victory of Marston Moor. In 1641 he was created earl of L.

LEVEN. Town in Fife region, Scotland, at the mouth of the r. Leven. L. is a holiday resort, and has timber, paper and engineering industries. Pop. (1973) 9,500.

LEVEN, Loch. Lake in Tayside region, Scotland, area 16 sq.km (6 sq.m) and 18km (11m) in circuit, with 7 islands, drained by the r. L. Mary Queen of Scots was imprisoned 1567-8 on Castle Island.

LĒVER, Charles James (1806-72). Irish novelist. B. in Dublin, he was ed. at Trinity Coll., and became a doctor. His rollicking novels of Irish and army life, such as *Harry Lorrequer* (1837), *Charles O'Malley* (1840), and *Tom Burke of Ours* (1844), achieved a remarkable popularity. His extravagance made it necessary for him to live on the Continent and support himself by incessant writing. In 1867 he became consul at Trieste.

LEVERKUSEN (la'verkoozen). River port in North Rhine-Westphalia, W Germany, 8km (5m) N of Cologne, with chemical industries. Pop. (1978) 163,400.

LÉVESQUE (levek'), **René** (1922-). French-Canadian politician. A law student, he served as a war correspondent in the S.W.W. and Korea. In 1968 he founded the Parti Québecois, with the aim of an independent Quebec, but a referendum rejected the proposal in 1980.

LÉVI-STRAUSS (le'vi-strows), **Claude** (1908-). French anthropologist. He has soguht to find a universal 'structure' governing man's social life, the way in which he creates his myths, etc. His books incl. *The Savage Mind* (1966).

LEVITATION. To rise and float in air without visible means of support, as alleged to have been done by medieval mystics, or by objects at spiritualistic seances. *Magnetic levitation* has been experimentally used in 'maglev' trains. Magnetic repulsion, achieved by making parts of both track and vehicle like poles of a magnet, supports the vehicle slightly above the surface of the track, and the driving-force is provided by a linear induction motor.

LĒ'VĪTES. One of the 12 tribes of Israel, traditionally descended from Levi, one of the sons of Jacob. They were charged with the lesser services of the Temple, and the priesthood was confined to one Levite family, the descendants of Aaron.

LEWES (lū'es), **George Henry** (1817-78). British philosopher and critic. From acting he turned to literature and philosophy, his works incl. a *Biographical History of Philosophy* (1845-6), and *Life and Works of Goethe* (1855). He m. unhappily in 1840, and after meeting Mary Ann Evans (George Eliot) in 1851, left his wife in 1854 to form a life-long union with her.

LEWES. Town in the co. of E Sussex (of which it is admin. HQ), England, on the Ouse, 72km (45m) S of London. Barbican House nr. the Castle is a museum. Simon de Montfort defeated Henry III here in 1264. L. is famous for its 5th November celebrations. Pop. (1974) 75,440.

LEWIS, Sir Arthur (1915-). British economist. B. on St Lucia, he specialised in the economic problems of developing countries, as in *The Theory of Economic Growth* (1955), and shared a Nobel prize in 1979.

LEWIS, Cecil Day. *See* DAY LEWIS, CECIL.

LEWIS, Clive Staples (1898-1963). British scholar. In 1954-63 he was prof. of Medieval and Renaissance English at Cambridge, and his books incl. the remarkable medieval study *The Allegory of Love* (1936); space fiction *Out of the Silent Planet* (1938); such individual essays in popular theology as *The Screwtape Letters* (1942) and *Mere Christianity* (1952); the autobiographical *Surprised by Joy* (1955) and books for children.

LEWIS, John L(lewellyn) (1880-1969). American labour leader. B. in Iowa, son of a Welsh miner, he worked in the pits, and 1920-60 was pres. of the United Mineworkers of America. He was founder-pres. of the CIO (*see* AFL/CIO) in 1935, and was expelled from the AFL. Later he re-affiliated the UMWA to the AFL until 1947, when it became independent.

LEWIS, Matthew Gregory (1775-1818). British author, known as 'Monk' L. from his terror romance *The Monk* (1795), which enjoyed a vogue.

LEWIS, Meriwether (1774-1809). American explorer. Private sec. to Pres. Jefferson, he was commissioned with William Clark (1770-1838) to find a land route to the Pacific. He followed the Missouri River to its source, crossed the Rocky Mountains, and followed the Columbia River to the Pacific, then returned overland to St Louis, 1804-6. He was rewarded with the governorship of the Louisiana Territory. His death, nr Nashville, Tennessee, has been ascribed to suicide, but was more probably murder.

LEWIS, Percy Wyndham (1884-1957). British author and artist. B. off Maine, in his father's yacht, he was ed. at the Slade and in Paris and pioneered on returning to England the new spirit of art which his friend Ezra Pound called Vorticism: he also ed. *Blast*, a literary and artistic magazine proclaiming its principles. His paintings were as boldly hard and aggressive as his literary style, his portraits being especially memorable, e.g. of Edith Sitwell and T. S. Eliot. Among his novels the best are *Tarr* (1918) and *The Childermass* (1928), but he also wrote a number of theoretical books, e.g. *Time and Western Man* (1927), and the autobiographical *Blasting and Bombardiering* (1937) and *Rude Assignment* (1950). He has a controversial reputation, being assessed by some as a leading spirit of the early 20th cent.: the argument is generally sharpened by his support in the 1930s of Fascist principles.

LEWIS, Sinclair (1885-1951). American novelist. B. in Minnesota, he stayed for a time at Upton Sinclair's socialist colony in New Jersey, then became a freelance journalist. He made a reputation with *Main Street* (1920), depicting American small-town life; *Babbitt* (1922), story of a typical business executive, a real-estate man of the midwest caught in the conventions of his milieu which gave a new word to the American language; and *Arrowsmith* (1925), study of a scientist. His later books incl. *It Can't Happen Here* (1935), *Cass Timberlane* (1945), and *The God-Seeker* (1949). He received a Nobel prize 1930.

LEWIS. N part of Lewis-with-Harris, the largest is. of the Outer Hebrides, off the W coast of Scotland and to the N of Uist. L., incl. in Western Isles, is separated from Harris (q.v.) by a line joining Lochs Resort and Seaforth. Fishing is a main economic activity. Stornoway is the only centre of importance. Area 1,769 sq.km (683 sq.m).

In 1981 it was proposed to upgrade the RAF airfield at Stornoway to a NATO forward-operating base. It was intended to prevent Soviet naval access to the Western shipping lanes to America via the Greenland, Iceland, UK (GIUK) Gap.

LE'XINGTON. (1) Town, centre of the Bluegrass Country, Kentucky, USA. Bloodstock is bred in the area, and races and shows are held. There is a tobacco market and the Univ. of Kentucky and Transylvania (1780). Pop. (1970) 108,137. (2) Town of Mass., USA, with printing and pub. industries. Pop. (1970) 32,000. The Battles of L. and Concord were the earliest engagements of the American War of Independence, 19 April 1775. *See* REVERE, PAUL.

LEYDEN. *See* LEIDEN.

LEYLAND (lā'land). Town in Lancs, England, 8km (5m) S of Preston. British Leyland, largest of British firms producing cars, buses and lorries, has its HQ here. Pop. (1973) 23,700.

LHASA (lah'sa). Cap. of Tibet, on a lofty plateau 3,600 m (11,830 ft) a.s.l. surrounded by mountains: the name means 'Dwelling-place of the Gods'. Weaving, and the manufacture of pottery and gold and silver ware are carried on. It became in the 17th cent. the seat of the Dalai Lama, head of Lamaism; his palace, the 17th cent. Potala, standing high above the town, is the most striking of a number of remarkable buildings; the Jokang temple of Buddha, which attracts many pilgrims, dates from AD 652. When the Chinese invaded Tibet in 1722 they destroyed the walls of L. which were not rebuilt. In 1950-1 the Chinese carried out a more determined conquest of Tibet; following an unsuccessful rebellion in 1959 the Dalai Lama fled to India. The monks who had formed the bulk of the pop. (est. 50,000) were compelled to take up secular occupations.

LHOTE (lōt), **André** (1885-1962). French artist. B. at Bordeaux, he was very influential through his treatises on art in which he explored questions of technique and ultimate artistic aims. His 'Rugby' in the Musée d'Art Moderne, Paris, is an excellent example of his use of colour and geometric style.

LHOTE, Henri. *See* SAHARA.

LIAO (lyow). River of NE China. The main headstream rises in the mts of Inner Mongolia and flows E, then S to the Gulf of Liaodong. It is *c.* 1,450 km (900m) long and is frozen from Dec. to March.

LIAONING (lē-owning'). Chinese prov. in the NE lying about the Gulf of Liaodong; it incl. Liaodong peninsula. The cap. is Shenyang; other large towns are Anshan, Dandong, and Lüda, Agriculture is important, chief crops being millet, wheat, soya beans; heavy industry based on local coal and iron deposits, is found at Anshan. Area 150,996 sq.km (58,300 sq.m); pop. (1973) 28,000,000

LIAO-YANG (lyow-yahng'). City in Liaoning prov., China, on the Taizi. Here in 1904 the Russians were defeated by the Japanese. Pop. *c.* 100,000.

LIBAU. German form of LIEPAJA.

LIBBY, Willard Frank (1908-80). American chemist. His concept of radio-carbon dating in 1947 brought him a Nobel prize in 1960. *See* CARBON.

LIBEL. One of the two types of defamation. In L. the defamatory statement is reproduced in a permanent form, the most common being by writing, in a newspaper, or by broadcasting. Libel is both a crime and a civil wrong, or tort (unlike slander (q.v.), which is a tort only). The more usual remedy is by civil proceedings and until a case heard in 1936 a criminal prosecution was resorted to only where the publication of the libel was likely to bring about a breach of the peace, as where it was so gross that there was a danger that the defamed person would assault the person responsible for publishing it. In civil proceedings, if the person publishing the libel proves its substantial truth, he escapes liability (with some exceptions, e.g. in references to a person's convictions for crime); but in criminal proceedings it is necessary to prove not only that the words used were true, but also that it was in the public interest that they should be known by the public. By the mid-1970s the precedent estab. by the case of 1936 had gained importance because of the greater freedom of comment exercised by journalists.

The civil remedy for libel is extremely comprehensive, for proceedings may be brought not only against the person who was first responsible for the statement, but also against everyone who has subsequently repeated or published it. Moreover, a person may defame another of whose existence he is unaware, for the test is whether the words used could be regarded as applying to the plaintiff by reasonable men, who knew him, but a defendant who can show he pub. the words innocently and without negligence may avoid liability if willing to pub. a reasonable correction and apology, and pay the plaintiff's costs.

Certain transactions and statements are 'privileged', either absolute or qualified. If a proceeding or statement is absolutely privileged, e.g. all proceedings in Courts of Justice, in Parliament, or in reports of parliamentary proceedings, no action can be brought for libel in respect of it, no matter how inaccurate or malicious the words were. Where a statement enjoys 'qualified privilege', a person who has been defamed by it must prove not only that the words used were untrue, but that the person uttering them had a malicious (i.e. an improper) motive. Another common defence to an action is 'fair comment on a matter of public interest'. Considerable latitude is allowed by the law to criticism of matters of general interest (including new books, plays and films, and all public sports and pastimes), but if facts are quoted they must be quoted with substantial accuracy, and the criticism must be reasonably temperate. The stringency of English L. law has been widely attacked as limiting freedom of the press: in the USA the position is much more elastic.

LIBERALISM. The political and social theory associated with the Liberal Party in Britain, and similar parties elsewhere. L. developed during the 17th-19th as the distinctive theory of the industrial and commercial classes in their struggle against the power of the monarchy, the Church, and the feudal landowners. In politics it stood for parliamentary govt, freedom of the press, speech and worship, and the abolition of class privileges; economically it was associated with laissez-faire, a minimum of state interference in economic life, and international free trade. In the late 19th and early 20th cents. these ideas were modified by the acceptance on the one hand of universal suffrage, hitherto opposed by most Liberals, and on the other of a certain amount of state intervention, in order to ensure a minimum standard of living and to remove extremes of poverty and wealth. The classical statement of Liberal principles is found in *On Liberty* and other works of J. S. Mill.

LIBERAL PARTY. One of Britain's 2 historic parties, the successor to the Whig Party (q.v.). The term 'L', used officially from *c.* 1840 and unofficially from *c.* 1815, marked the transfer of control from the aristocrats to the more radical industrialists, backed by the Benthamites, Nonconformists and the middle classes. During the Ls.' first period of power (1830-41), they promoted parl. and municipal govt. reform and the abolition of slavery, but their utilitarian and laissez-faire theories led to the harsh Poor Law of 1834. Lib pressure forced Peel to repeal the Corn Laws in 1846, thereby splitting the Tory Party, and except for 2 short periods the Ls. were in power 1846-66, but the only outstanding figure of the period, Palmerston, was very conservative and the only major change was the general adoption of free trade.

Extended franchise in 1867 and Gladstone's emergence as leader began a new phase, dominated by the 'Manchester school' with a programme of 'peace, retrenchment, and reform'. Gladstone's 1868-74 govt. introduced many important reforms, incl. elementary education and vote by ballot. The party's left, mainly composed of working-class Radicals led by Bradlaugh and Chamberlain, repudiated the laissez-faire ideology and inclined towards republicanism, but the Ls. were split over Home Rule in 1886 and many joined the Conservatives. Except for 1892-5, the Ls. remained out of power until 1906, when reinforced by Labour and Irish support they returned with a huge majority: Old-Age Pensions, National Insurance, limitation of the powers of the Lords, and the Irish Home Rule Bill followed.

From 1914 the L. Party declined, Lloyd George's alliance with the Conservatives 1916-22 dividing them between himself and Asquith, and although reunited in 1923 they continued to lose votes. They briefly joined the Nat. Govt 1931-2, but after the S.W.W. were reduced to a handful of MPs. A revival began under the leadership 1956-67 of Grimond (q.v.), and continued under Jeremy Thorpe (1929-), who resigned after a period of controversy within the party in 1976. After a 'caretaker' return by Grimond, David Steel became the first party leader in British politics to be elected by party members who were not also MPs. in 1977–8 Steel entered into a voting pact with Labour in return for 'consultation', and when the Social Democratic Party was formed, entered into an Alliance, which gained some 25% of the vote in the election of 1983 but only 4% of seats.

LIBERAL PARTY. David Steel started a precedent in English politics by his pact with Labour in 1977. *Photo: Jane Bown/Camera Press.*

LIBERAL PARTY (Australian). Estab. in 1944 by Menzies, following a Labor landslide, it derived from the former United Australia Party. Remaining in power from 1949, with a brief Labor intermission 1972-5, it has been led in succession by Holt (q.v.), Gorton (q.v.), Sir William McMahon (1908-), Sir Billy Snedden (1926-), and Malcolm Fraser (q.v.). The Liberal Party was again returned to power in 1980, but with a reduced majority.

LIBERATION THEOLOGY. Theory developed by Western intellectuals of the primary importance of 'Christ the Liberator', Himself the personification of the poor and devoted to freeing them from the oppression of the rich (Matthew xix 21, xxv 35, 40). Taken up with espec. enthusiasm in S America, it is in some respects indistinguishable from Marxism in its policy of action, and inevitably leads to violence. In 1980 Pope John Paul II combined warnings to priests against involvement in political activity with warnings to the rich against the potential consequences of their position.

LĪBĒ'RIA. Rep. on the W coast of Africa, between Sierra Leone and the Ivory Coast. The interior consists of a densely wooded plateau. The only navigable rivers are the St Paul and the Cavalla. The main settlements are along the coast; here coffee, cacao, palm nuts, indigo, yams, maize, sugar cane, sorghum, and rice are cultivated. Rubber has been worked with American aid from 1926, and in 1970 exploitation of the country's rich timber resources was begun by an American co. Minerals incl. large reserves of iron, and some diamonds and gold. The cap. is Monrovia, and Buchanan is the other chief port. The official language is English. Area 112,820 sq.km (43,700 sq.m); pop. (1977) 1,800,000, of whom *c.* 45,000 are Americo-Liberians, and the remainder indigenous peoples, who did not receive the vote until 1944. M.U.: US dollar.

L. was founded with a settlement in 1822 nr the present Monrovia by the American Colonization Society as a home for Negro freed slaves. The next years were occupied by a bitter struggle against the hostile natives. L. declared its independence in 1847. The economy is still, however, largely American-controlled. The political system is modelled on that of the USA with a Pres. Cabinet, Senate and House of Representatives. Tubman (q.v.) was pres. 1943-71, when he was succeeded by William Tolbert (1913-80), who was assassinated during a coup by the lower ranks of the army led by Master Sergeant Samuel Doe (1952-). The coup represented a revolt by the subjugated indigenous and underprivileged tribes (95% of the pop.) against the freed-slave settlers or Americo-Liberians. Many former govt. members were publicly shot.

LIBERTY, EQUALITY, FRATERNITY. The official motto of the French Republic, adopted in 1793 as a summary of the ideals of the revolution. The Vichy régime of 1940-4 substituted the phrase 'Work, family, fatherland'.

LIBREVILLE (lēbrvēl'). Cap. of Gabon, on the estuary of the r. Gabon. Founded in 1848 as a refuge for freed slaves, L. developed into a port. It has an airport. Pop. (1974) 251,400.

LI'BYA. Country in N Africa, on the Mediterranean, bounded by Tunisia and Algeria to the W, Niger and Chad to the S, and Sudan and Egypt to the E. Until 1963 it comprised the federal provs. of Cyrenaica, Fezzan, and Tripolitania (qq.v.), but in the interests of overall unity was then divided into 10 admin. divisions. From N to S the country consists of a fertile undulating Mediterranean zone where fruits, particularly dates, and cereals thrive; a sub-desert area where alfalfa is cultivated; and the greater part of the Libyan desert, which is broken by fertile oases and the Fezzan Mtns. There are no rivers, and rainfall is infrequent. Traditionally there has been a trade in cattle, hides and skins, with some sponge and tunny fishing, but the discovery of oil in 1959 brought unprecedented income growth. The cap. is Tripoli, other towns incl. Benghazi, Misurata, Homs, Zawia, Gharian and Tobruk. There are magnificent archaeological sites at Shahat (Cyrene), Leptis Magna, Sabratha, etc., and rockpaintings of *c.* 3,000 BC in the Fezzan. The pop. is mainly Arab, with some Berbers in the W. Area 1,780,000 sq.km (680,000 sq.m); pop. (1979) 2,900,000, 95% Sunni Moslems. M.U.: Libyan dinar.

Libya was held in succession by Romans, Vandals and Arabs, before passing in the 16th cent. under Turkish rule. The Turks were ousted in 1911-12 by the Italians who colonised the coastal belt and developed it agriculturally. In the S.W.W. the country was occupied in 1943 by British troops, and was in 1951 the first independent state to be created by the UN, becoming a kingdom under Idris I (1890-). Following a military coup in 1969, L. became a rep. and in 1970 British bases at Tobruk and El Adem were closed. Under Col. Kadhafi (q.v.) a strict Moslem regime was estab., with the Arab Socialist Union as the single permitted party from 1971. In 1976, as an experiment in 'direct democracy', a Gen. People's Congress was estab., comprising leaders of the 'people's congresses' and 'popular committees', and of trade unions and professional organizations, which appointed Kadhafi as president. An invasion of Chad in 1983 was followed by withdrawal and a non-intervention treaty with France in 1984.

LICE. Parasitic insects (Anoplura or Pediculidae). They have flat, segmented bodies without wings, and a sucking tube attached to the head, with which they suck the blood of mammals on whom they live. Several species occur on man including the hair-louse (*Pediculus capitis*), and the body-louse (*P. corporis*) which may be a typhus carrier. Most mammals have their own varieties of L. Bird-lice, or biting-lice, are a different insect (Mallophaga).

LICENCE. Document issued by some govt or other recognized authority conveying permission to the holder to do something otherwise prohibited, and designed to facilitate accurate records, the maintenance of order, and collection of revenue. In Britain examples are those required for marriage, for keeping a dog or gun, and sale of intoxicating liquor.

LICHENS (lī'kenz). Group of plants (*Lichenes*), which consist of a fungus and an alga existing in a mutually beneficial relationship. They are found on trees, rocks, etc., and flourish under very adverse conditions. Some Ls. have food value (e.g. Reindeer moss and Iceland moss), others give dyes such as litmus, or are used in medicine, especially for lung diseases.

LICHFIELD. City in the Trent valley, Staffs, England, 24km (15m) SE of Stafford. It was founded in the 7th cent. by St Chad and the 13th cent. cathedral has a triple spire. Brewing is carried on. Dr Johnson was born here. Pop. (1972) 23,280.

LIDDELL HART, Sir Basil (1895-1970). British military scientist. Gassed during the F.W.W., he had retired from the army by 1927, and was military correspondent to the *Daily Telegraph* 1925-35 and *The Times* 1935-9. He was an exponent of mechanised warfare, and his ideas were adopted in Germany in 1935 in creating the First Panzer Division, combining motorized infantry and tanks: from 1937 he advised the War Office on British Army reorganization. His books incl. biographies of Scipio, Foch and T. E. Lawrence.

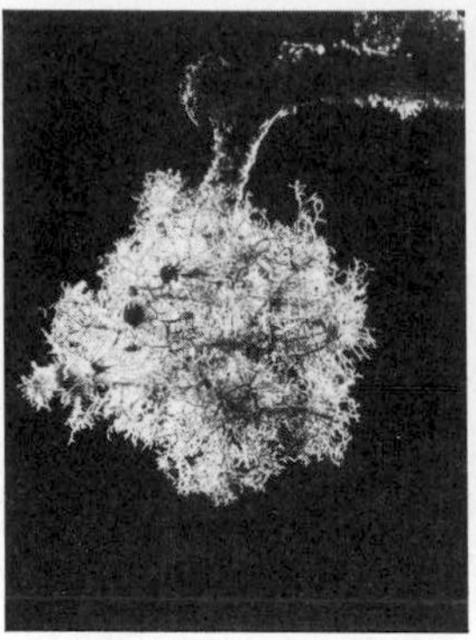

LICHEN On the left, beard lichen *(Usnea)* growing on a twig, and on the right, foliose lichen *(Parmenia)* on tree bark. *Photos: Heather Angel.*

LIDICE (lē'dētseh). Czech mining village, completely destroyed by the Nazis on 10 June 1942 as a reprisal for the assassination of Heydrich. The 192 men of the village were all shot, the 196 women sent to concentration camps where 50 died, and the 105 children to Germany. After the liberation a model mining village was built near the site, which is marked by a monument. Karl Frank, a Sudeten German, was later tried, found responsible for the crime, and hanged at Prague in 1946. The name of L. was taken by many places abroad.

LIE (lē), **Trygve Halvdan** (1896-68). Norwegian statesman. He became sec. of the Lab. Party in 1926, was For. Min. in the exiled govt. 1941-6, when he helped keep the Norwegian fleet for the Allies, and first Sec.-Gen. of UN 1946-53.

LIEBIG (lē'-), **Justus,** Baron von (1803-73). German chemist. After his discovery of the chemical composition of fulminates in 1824 he was appointed prof. at Giessen, and in 1852 at Munich. L. became a baron in 1845.

LIEBKNECHT (lēb'knekht), **Wilhelm** (1826-1900). German Socialist. He took part in the 1848 revolution, and subsequently lived in London until 1861, forming a close friendship with Marx. He was imprisoned for opposing the Franco-Prussian War. From 1874 he led the Social-Democrats in the Reichstag. His son, **Karl L.** (1871-1919), b. in Leipzig, entered the Reichstag as a Social-Democrat in 1912 and during the F.W.W. was imprisoned for organizing an anti-war demonstration. A founder of the German Communist Party, originally known as the Spartacus League, he led an unsuccessful Communist revolt in Berlin in 1919, and was murdered by army officers.

LIECHTENSTEIN (lēkh'tenstīn). Small European principality, situated between Austria and Switzerland. Vaduz is the cap. L. was formed in 1719 from the two counties of Schellenberg and Vaduz. Formerly agricultural, L. developed varied light industries after the S.W.W., with an influx of foreign workers, and is now a highly industrialized country. Generous company law encourages the registration of foreign companies. The language is German. Francis Joseph II (1906-) succeeded to the princedom in 1938. Area 160 sq.km (62 sq.m); pop. (1977) 24,715; M.U.: Swiss franc.

LIE DETECTOR. Registering device for blood pressure, rate of breathing, etc., which tend to alter under stress of telling an untruth.

LIÈGE (lyāzh'). Cap. of L. prov., Belgium, SE of Brussels, on the Meuse. Coal and steel have declined, but L. is still important for its arms industry, incl. specialised weapons. Textiles, paper, and chemicals are other products. There is a univ. (1817) and a number of ancient churches, the oldest, St Martin's, dating from 692. Pop. (1978) 228,000.

LIEPAJA (lyā'pahyah). Port of the Latvian SSR, situated on a narrow peninsula between Lake L. and the Baltic. Shipbuilding, engineering, and the manufacture of steel, textiles, and chemicals are among its industries. The Knights of Livonia founded L. in the 13th cent. Pop. (1977) 100,000.

LIFAR (lē-), **Serge** (1905–86). Russian dancer and choreographer. B. at Kiev, he studied under Nijinska, joined the Diaghilev co. in 1923 and was *premier maître de ballet* at the Paris Opéra 1947-58 and 1962-63. A noted experimenter, he developed the importance of the male dancer in *Prometheus* (1929), produced his first ballet without music, *Icare*, in 1935, and pub. the same year the controversial *Le Manifeste du chorégraphie*.

LIFE. The ability of an organism to go through the processes which enable it to grow, stay in 'working order', and produce energy, as well as reproduce itself and respond to such stimuli as light, heat and sound in a way that shows that it 'means' to stay alive. It is thought that L. began *c.* 4,000,000,000 years ago, and since study of Venus and Mars has been possible, it seems probable that the original atmosphere of Earth consisted of carbon dioxide, nitrogen and water. By passing electric sparks or ultraviolet radiation through flasks of this mixture complex 'biological' molecules have been created, called amino acids. These are the 'building blocks' of life since they combine in complicated ways to form the proteins which are an essential part of all living cells. The earliest kinds of L. were very probably forms of virus, and from these developed the network of plant and animal L. of today. This theory encourages belief that there may be L. of a similar kind elsewhere in the Universe. British scientist James Lovelock has suggested that the Earth's interdependent living matter, air, oceans, and land surface may comprise one giant system which could be regarded as a single organism, which he has named Gaia (at the suggestion of William Golding, q.v.) after the ancient Greek Earth goddess. Earth's existing L. forms are the smallest fraction of those which once flourished, and the reason why dinosaurs, for example, which were once the 'highest' form of L., disappeared is not exactly ascertained.

By 1977 study of the variety of molecules, incl. fairly complex organic molecules, detected by radar astronomy in pre-stellar molecular clouds and interstellar dust, suggested that L. could possibly have been brought to the Earth by means of meteorites or comets.

LIFEBOAT. Small landbased vessel specially built for saving life at sea, or a boat carried aboard a larger ship in case of shipwreck. In Britain the Royal Nat. L. Institution (1824), founded at the instance of Sir William Hillary, provides a voluntarily manned and supported service. The US Coast Guard is part of the govt service. A modern RNLI boat is *c.* 16m (52ft) long and self-righting, so that it is virtually unsinkable. Inflatable mini-Ls. are used for inshore work, and helicopters play an increasing role in search and rescue.

LIFE INSURANCE. *See* INSURANCE and SAVING.

LIFFEY (lif'i). River of the Rep. of Ireland, which rises in the Wicklow Mtns. It flows for 80 km (50 m), first W across Kildare, then E to Dublin Bay.

LIFFEY. Canoeing on the 'white water' of the river makes a crash helmet a useful item of equipment. *Photo: Fionnbar Cannanan/Camera Press.*

LIGAMENTS. Short bands of tough fibrous tissue connecting two bones at a joint, or holding an organ, such as the liver or uterus, in position.

LIGATURE. Suture (nylon, wire, etc.) binding a blood vessel, a limb, the base of a tumour, etc., chiefly so as to stop the movement through it of blood or other fluid.

LIGHT. Electromagnetic radiation in the visible range, i.e. from about 770 nanometres in the extreme red to 400 in the extreme violet. See diagram of frequency spectrum under ELECTROMAGNETIC WAVES. Light is considered to exhibit not only wave but particle properties and the fundamental particle or quantum of light is called the *photon*. The speed of L. in free space is approximately 299,793 km per second/186,000 miles per second (a universal constant denoted by *c*) and allegedly the fastest speed in nature. Newton was the first to discover, in 1666, that sunlight is comprises all the different colours in certain proportions, and that it could be separated into its components by refraction. Earlier it was thought that refraction produced colour, rather than separating those existing.

Heavy light is a form of light discovered at Cern in 1983, and consisting of Z-nought particles. It exists for the tiniest fraction of a second, and travels less than the length of an atomic nucleus before it is converted into energy, i.e. explodes. The **light year** is a measure in astronomy, the distance travelled by L. in one year, a distance of (9,461 × 10^{12} km/nearly 6 million million miles.

LIGHTHILL, Sir James (1924-). British mathematician. Lucasian prof. at Cambridge 1969-79, he has specialized in highspeed aerodynamics and jet propulsion. He was knighted in 1971.

LIGHTHOUSE. Structure carrying a powerful light to aid marine or aerial navigation. Among early Ls. were the Pharos of Alexandria (*c.* 280 BC) and those built by the Romans at Ostia, Ravenna, Boulogne and Dover. In England beacons burning in church towers served as Ls. until the 17th cent., and in the earliest Ls. such as the

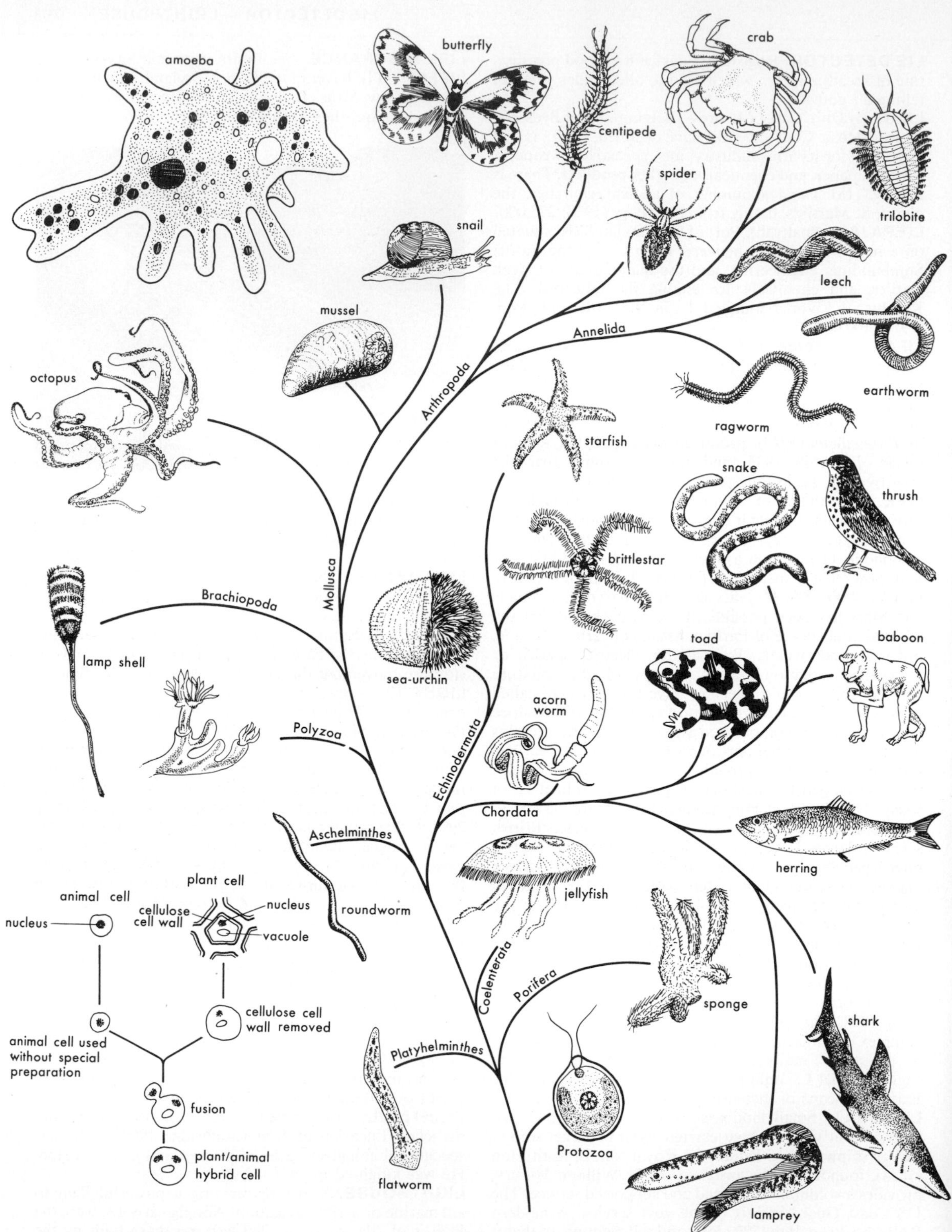

LIFE. A simplified diagram of the related network of the more familiar classes of animals, together with (top left), the amoeba – one of the simplist living animals – in which the nucleus is the large dark spot on the left, and (bottom left) a diagrammatic representation of recent experiments in the fusing of animal and plant cells.

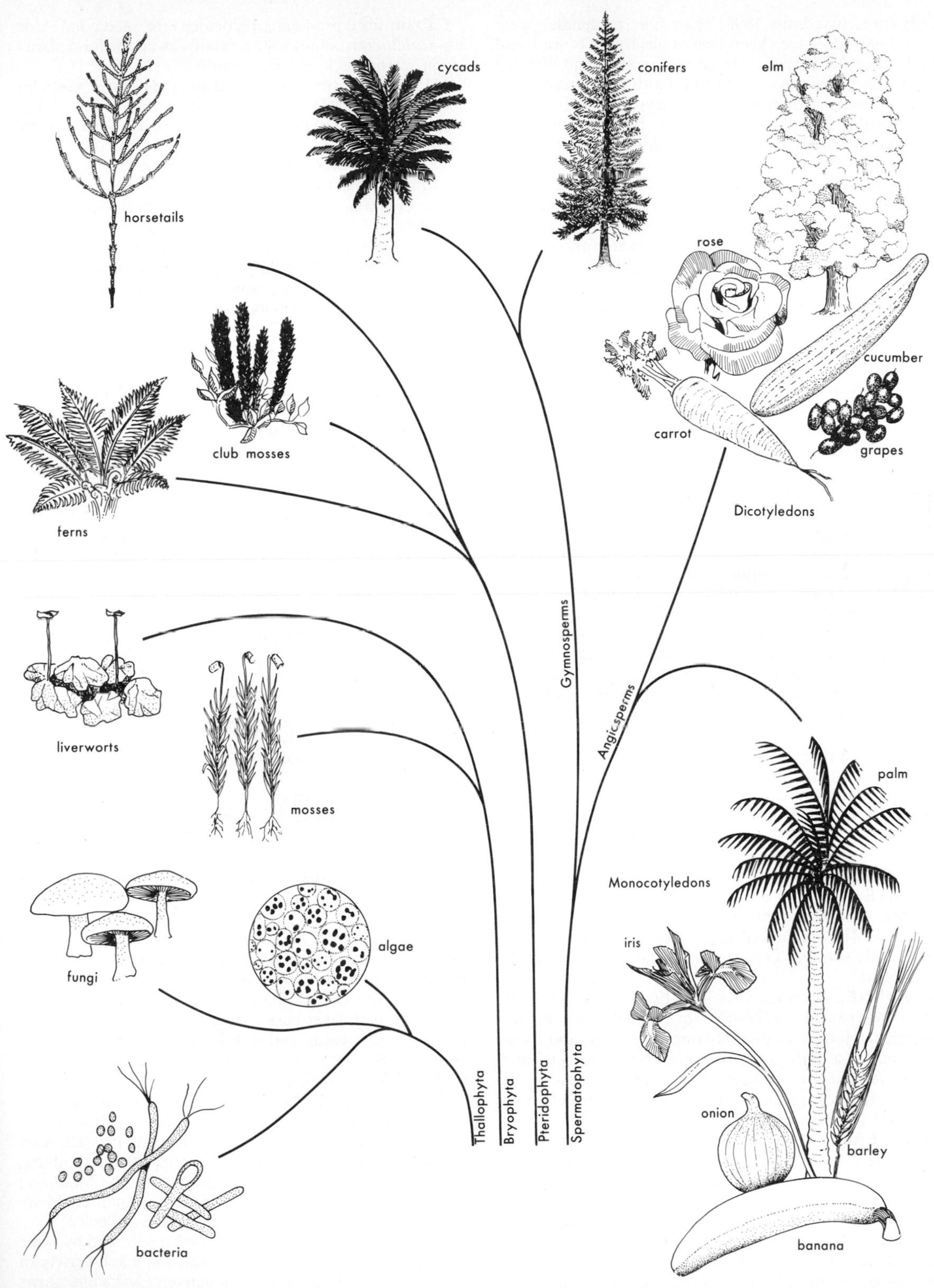
cycads
conifers
elm
horsetails
rose
cucumber
club mosses
carrot
grapes
ferns
Dicotyledons
Gymnosperms
Angiosperms
liverworts
mosses
palm
Monocotyledons
fungi
algae
iris
onion
Thallophyta
Bryophyta
Pteridophyta
Spermatophyta
barley
bacteria
banana

PLANT LIFE

Eddystone, first built 1698, open fires or candles were used. Today dissolved acetylene or electricity is used, and the light of the burner or lamp is magnified and directed out to the horizon (or up to the zenith for aircraft) by a series of mirrors or prisms. For identification lights are individually varied, usually either flashing (the dark period exceeding the light) or occulting (the dark being equal or less): fixed lights are liable to confusion. Manned **lightships** replace Ls. where reefs, sandbanks, etc., make erection of a L. impossible; and, where it is impossible to maintain keepers, unattended lightbuoys equipped for up to a year's service. In fog sound signals are made (horns, sirens, explosives), and in the case of lightbuoys, fog bells and whistles operated by the movement of the waves. In the UK there are 3 general L. authorities - Trinity House, Commissioners of Northern Ls., and Commissioners of Irish Lights: in the USA the supervisory authority is the Coast Guard.

LIGHTNING. A discharge of electricity, accompanied by a visible flash, between 2 clouds or a cloud and the earth, caused by a difference in potential. In dry weather the atmosphere has a positive potential with respect to the earth, increasing with distance. When the usual balance cannot be maintained, water particles coalesce to form drops, concentrating their charge, which under stress results in a flash of L. Forked L. gives the impression of sharp angles but is usually sinuous; sheet L. is usually a distant indefinite illumination. Thunder is the accompanying noise, augmented by echoing. Conduction of the discharge is most likely through isolated buildings or elevated conductors, lesser conducting suffering most damage. However, physicists have recently suggested that the necessary 100 million volts of electricity could not be produced in this way, and that L. is caused by cosmic rays which initiate the process by shattering atoms in the upper atmosphere.

Ball L. is a phenomenon, not yet fully explained, which occurs during thunderstorms. It consists of a luminous sphere, apparently less dangerous the larger it is, which may hover inside a room and emit a rattling sound. If it explodes, it burns anything with which it comes in contact. It has been suggested that it is caused by a vortex ring of plasma.

LIGNITE. *See* COAL.

LILAC. A flowering shrub (*Syringa vulgaris*) of the family Oleaceae. The panicles of small white or purplish flowers are sweetly scented. The smaller Persian L. is also popular in gardens.

LILBURNE, John (*c.* 1614-57). English politician. He was imprisoned 1638-40 for circulating Puritan pamphlets, fought in the parliamentary army, and by his advocacy of a democratic republic won the leadership of the Levellers (q.v.). Under the Commonwealth he was twice tried for sedition and acquitted, and after his acquittal he was imprisoned 1653-5.

LILIACEAE (lili-ā'sē-ē). Family of bulbous plants, including a few shrubs. The genus *Lilium* is typical of the family, and incl. more than 50 varieties. They are monocotyledons, and the leaves may be alternate or in whorls. The stems are erect, the flowers usually appearing at the top. The flowers are regular and frequently bell-shaped. Many varieties are cultivated in gardens, including hyacinth, tulip, Madonna lily, autumn crocus, etc.

Certain fibre-producing plants and the medicinal *Aloe* and *Colchicum* belong to this family, as do the food plants onion, garlic, leek and asparagus.

LILIENTHAL (lēl'yentahl), **Otto** (1848-96). German glider pioneer. He made and successfully flew many gliders and inspired the Wrights. He was killed in a glider crash.

LILITH (Heb. *lilātū,* night). An Assyrian female demon; according to the Talmud she was the wife of Adam before Eve's creation. She was said to entice children to destruction.

LILLE (lēl). Cap. of Nord dept, N France, on the Deûle, 240km (150m) NNE of Paris. Lying in a rich agricultural and industrial plain. L. was long a fortress city, and became the seat of a bishopric in 1913. Its citadel, built by Vauban, and Palais des Beaux Arts, with its collection of pictures, are the most noted historical buildings, while public buildings incl. univs. and a Pasteur institute. There are many important industries and manufactures incl. locomotives, heavy machinery, coal mining, textiles, and sugar. Pop. (1975) 171,000.

LILONGWE (lilong'wā). Cap. of Malawi, 240km (150m) NW of Blantyre, and 80km (50m) W of Lake Malawi. There is a tobacco industry. Pop. (1977) 103,000.

LILY OF THE VALLEY. Plant (*Convallaria majalis*) in the family Liliaceae, growing in woods in Europe, N Asia, and N America, and a common garden plant. The white flowers are scented.

LIMA (lē'mah). Cap. of Peru, on the Rimac r. 10km (6m) E of the Pacific coast, where is its port of Callao. Founded by Francisco Pizarro in 1535, it was rebuilt after destruction by an earthquake in 1746. The univ. dates from 1551, and also dating from the colonial period are the cathedral (1746), govt palace (the rebuilt Palace of the Viceroys) and the ancient Inquisition building now the senate house. Industries incl. chemicals, textiles, glass, cement, etc. Limatambe airport lies to the SE. Pop. (1972) 3,317,650.

LIMASSŌ'L. Seaport in Cyprus, on Akrotiri Bay, to the SW of Nicosia. There is a wine trade and cigarettes are made. Richard I m. Berengaria of Navarre here in 1191. Pop. (1975) 80,600.

LIMBO (Lat. 'border' or 'edge'). In medieval theology, a region for the souls of those who were not admitted to the divine vision; the word was first used in this sense by Thomas Aquinas. *Limbus infantum* was a place where unbaptized infants enjoyed inferior blessedness; and *limbus patrum* was the place where the prophets and fathers of the OT dwelt. Also a West Indian dance in which the performer passes under a pole, the body being bent over backwards, and skilled exponents managing the feat when the pole is only a few inches from the ground.

LIMBURG. An ancient feudal duchy of Lower Lorraine, divided between the Netherlands and Belgium in 1839. The modern provs. are (1) Limbourg, a NE prov. of Belgium in part bounded by the Meuse, cap. Hasselt. Area 2,408sq.km (930 sq.m); pop. (1978) 698,520. (2) Limburg, a SE prov. of the Netherlands, drained by the Maas and Roer, cap. Maastricht; it incl. the only Dutch coalfield. Area 2,219 sq.km (857 sq.m); pop. (1978) 1,060,945.

LIME. Citrus fruit (*Citrus aurantifolia*) regarded by some as a variety of the citron, *C. medica*, and a sub-variety of the sweet lime, *C. limetta.* It is a native of India and grows on small thorny bushes. The white flowers are succeeded by light green or yellow fruits resembling lemons but more globular in shape.

LIME. Calcium oxide (CaO), an alkaline earth, derived from the metal calcium. It is a white, powdery substance, sometimes known as quicklime. Slaked lime or hydrate of lime is calcium oxide combined with water $Ca(OH)_2$. Carbonate of lime $CaCO_3$ in the form of limestone or chalk is generally heated in kilns for the production of calcium oxide.

LIME or **linden.** Genus of deciduous trees (*Tilia*) found in Europe, N Asia, and N America. They are distinguished by the light green leaves and yellowish sweet-smelling flowers, which hang in cymes from the leaf axil, accompanied by an oblong leaf or wing joined to the flower stalk at the base.

LIMEHOUSE. District of the Greater London bor. of Tower Hamlets. It borders on the Thames and the West India dock, and formerly incl. many Chinese.

LIMERICK. Five-line nonsense verse, which first appeared in England *c.* 1820, and was popularized by Edward Lear. An example is:.

There was a young lady of Riga,
Who rode with a smile on a tiger;
They returned from the ride
With the lady inside,
And the smile on the face of the tiger.

LIMERICK. Chief tn and co. bor. in co. L., Rep. of Ireland, on the Shannon, to the SW of Dublin. An ancient town, it was occupied by the Danes from *c.* 820 to *c.* 1100. The cathedral of St Mary was built in the 12th cent., restored 1860. L. is the most important port on the W coast. Pop. (1971) 57,160. The co. of Limerick, in Munster prov., is mainly level but rises in the SE to the Galty mts. The chief river is the Shannon. The Golden Vale is a fertile district. Area 2,686 sq.km (1,037sq.m); pop. (1971) 140,460.

LIMESTONE. Name for sedimentary rocks composed chiefly of carbonate of lime ($CaCO_3$). They may be deposited under sea or fresh water, being the calcareous remains of many aquatic animals, such as crustacea, mollusca, foraminifera, etc. Corals build up into solid masses of limestone rock.

LIMITATION, Statutes of. Under English law Acts of Parliament limiting the time within which certain classes of action may be inaugurated, e.g. in simple contracts and most civil wrongs an action must be started by the aggrieved party within 6 yrs. In principle US law is similar, but varies from state to state.

LIMITS, Territorial and **Fishing.** *See* SEA, Law of the.

LIMOGES (lēmōzh'). Cap. of Haute-Vienne dept, France, 180km (130m) NW of Bordeaux on the Vienne. Its cathedral was begun in 1273. The Black Prince sacked L. in 1370. L. is famous for porcelain. Pop. (1975) 136,000.

LI'MONITE. Hydrated iron oxide. The mineral, also known as brown iron ore, is found in bog deposits.

LIMPET. Species of gasteropod mollusc. It has a conical shell, and adheres firmly to rocks by the disc-like foot. They are marine animals, and the Common L. (*Patella vulgata*) remains in the inter-tidal area. They leave their fixed position only to obtain vegetable food, always returning to the same spot.

LIMPŌ'PŌ. River, also known as Crocodile r., which marks the N boundary of the Transvaal, S Africa, and flows for 1,600 km (1,000 m) to reach the Indian Ocean in Mozambique, NE of Maputo.

LIMPOPO. In Botswana the majority of the people live by stock raising, and especially in this area where the Limpopo marks the border with the Transvaal. *Photo: Central Office of Information*

LINACRE (lin'aker), **Thomas** (*c.* 1460–1524). English humanist scholar and physician. In 1509 he became physician to Henry VIII, and in 1518 obtained from the king a charter constituting the Royal College of Physicians, of which he was the first president. He was one of the leading figures of the New Learning.

LĪ'NAR ('line' + 'star'). In astronomy, point sources discovered 1970 which emit with great energy at wavelengths characteristic of the spectral line of certain chemical compounds. Detectible in any weather, they have potential value in navigation.

LINCOLN (ling'kon), **Abraham** (1809–65). 16th Pres. of the USA. B. in a Kentucky log cabin, he was almost entirely self-educated, but having qualified as a lawyer practised from 1837 at Springfield, Illinois. He sat, as a Whig, in the state legislature 1834–41 and in Congress 1847–9, and joined the new Republican Party in 1856. As a candidate for the Senate in 1858, he held a series of public debates with his opponent, Stephen Douglas, which won him the Republican candidature for the presidency in 1860. He was elected on a minority vote.

Between his election and his inauguration in March 1861, 7 slave states seceded from the Union, and were followed by 4 more. L.'s refusal to evacuate Fort Sumter gave the signal for civil war, which until 1863 went badly, and L. became extremely unpopular. His cabinet and generals were often insubordinate, and even disloyal, yet L. finally imposed his will on them so firmly that he was accused of aiming at dictatorship. The British govt was hostile, and it took all L.'s tact to avert war. The abolitionists considered him luke-warm on the slavery question, for though he hated slavery he considered the fundamental issue to be the preservation of the Union.

Although his proclamation of 1863 freed slaves only in Confederate territory, he nevertheless advocated the constitutional amendment totally abolishing slavery. His view of the war is summarized in his speech at the dedication of the war cemetery at Gettysburg in 1863, in which he said it was being fought to preserve a 'nation, conceived in liberty, and dedicated to the proposition that all men are created equal', and to ensure that 'government of the people, by the people, for the people, shall not perish from the earth'. In 1864 he was re-elected by a 400,000 majority, and as victory approached he advocated a conciliatory reconstruction policy, 'with malice towards none, with charity for all'. Five days after Lee's surrender, L. was assassinated in a theatre at Washington by a Confederate fanatic, John Wilkes Booth. The L. Memorial (1922) contains a large seated statue of the pres. For the L. Center, *see* NEW YORK.

LINCOLN. City in Lincs. (of which it is admin. HQ), England, on the Witham 210km (130m) NW of London. It was the Roman Lindum, and the compact medieval town still runs up Steep Hill. The 11-15th cent. cathedral has the earliest Gothic work in Britain. Industries incl. excavators, cranes, gas turbines, power units for oil platforms and cosmetics. Pop. (1974) 73,260.

LINCOLN. Cap. of Nebraska, USA, it is a grain and livestock centre for an agricultural area, with food processing, engineering, and oil refining industries. The state univ. dates from 1871. Pop, (1970) 149,520.

LINCOLNSHIRE Eastern co. of England which, in the local govt reorganisation of 1974 lost a sector on the Humber in the N to Humberside. The chief rivers are the Witham and Welland, and the fens cover a considerable area of L. Horses, cattle and sheep are reared, and crops incl. barley and garden bulbs. A huge underground reservoir (50°C), discovered in 1978 beneath the L. basin, is of potential commercial use. Formerly it was divided into 3 admin. cos.: Parts of Lindsey, Kesteven, and Holland (qq.v.). The admin. HQ is Lincoln. Area 5,885 sq.km (2,272 sq.m); pop. (1978) 530,100.

LIND, Jenny (1820-87). Swedish soprano singer. B. in Stockholm, she gained the name 'Swedish Nightingale' on account of her remarkable range.

LINDBERGH, Charles Augustus (1902-74). American aviator. In 1927 he made the first solo non-stop flight across the Atlantic, and was created a colonel in the US Army. Before America's entry into the S.W.W. he was prominent as an Isolationist. L.'s first-born son was kidnapped and killed in 1932; a case which led to the passing of the 'Lindbergh Law', making kidnapping a federal instead of a state offence, in the same year. The kidnapper, B. R. Hauptmann, was executed in 1936.

LINDEN TREE. *See* LIME.

LINDISFARNE. Another name of HOLY ISLAND, Northumberland.

LINDSAY, Nicholas Vachel (1879-1931). American poet. B. at Springfield, he adopted a wandering life, supporting himself by lectures and recitations of his own poetry. He gained recognition with *Congo and other Poems* (1914); later books incl. *Chinese Nightingale* (1917), *Johnny Appleseed* (1928), and the autobiographical *Handy Guide for Beggars.*

LINDSEY, Parts of. Former admin. co. within Lincs (q.v.), with its HQ at Lincoln.

LINEAR ACCELERATOR. A machine in which charged particles are accelerated to high speed in passing down a straight evacuated tube or waveguide. Acceleration of the particles is produced by electromagnetic waves in the tube or by electric fields.

LINE ISLANDS. *See* GILBERT ISLANDS.

LINEN. The yarn spun and the textile - one of the oldest known - woven from flax (q.v.). To get the longest possible fibres, F. is pulled (not cut) by hand or machine, just as the seed bolls are beginning to set. After preliminary drying, it is steeped in water so that the fibre can be more easily separated from the wood of the stem, then 'hackled' (combed), classified, drawn into continuous fibres, and spun. Bleaching, weaving, and finishing processes vary according to the final product, which ranges from sailcloth, canvas and sacking to cambric and lawn. Because of its length of fibre, L. yarn has twice the strength of cotton, and is superior in delicacy, so that it is especially suitable for lace making. It mixes well with synthetics.

LINGAM. A phallus, worshipped by the Hindus as the symbol of Siva, the god of destruction yet of generative power. Often it is combined with the Yoni, the female emblem.

LINGUA FRANCA. A simplified language or jargon used in intercourse between peoples of different language who are unable to acquire each other's languages correctly. The term, literally 'Frank language' (Frank being the general Arabic term for Europeans), was originally applied to the hybrid Italian which came to be used in trade in the eastern Mediterranean from Renaissance times onwards.

LINGUISTICS. The science of the phenomena of language in general. Language may be defined as the transmission of ideas by means of articulate sounds, but L. also includes written language, inasmuch as it begins by being dependent on the spoken words.

L. in its widest sense embraces a number of special studies, such as phonetics, etymology, semantics, and comparative grammar.

LINKÖPING (lin'chöping). Town in Sweden, 172km (107m) SW of Stockholm. It is the seat of a Lutheran bishopric, and has a 12th cent. cathedral. Tobacco, hosiery, aircraft and engines are manufactured. Pop. (1978) 110,800.

LINLI'THGOW, John Adrian Louis Hope, 1st marquess of (1860-1908). British administrator. The eldest son of the 6th earl of Hopetoun, he was first Gov.-Gen. of the Australian Commonwealth 1900-2. His son, **Victor A. J. Hope,** 2nd marquess (1887-1952), was viceroy and Gov.-Gen. of India 1936-43.

LINLI'THGOW. Town in Lothian region, Scotland, 27km (17m) W of Edinburgh. L. is a tourist centre, with a distilling industry. The ruined L. palace was at one time a residence of the kings of Scotland; Mary Queen of Scots was born there. Pop. (1973) 6,100.

LINLITHGOWSHIRE. Former name of WEST LOTHIAN, now incl. in Lothian region.

LINNAEUS (linē'us), **Carolus** (1707-78). Swedish botanist, ennobled in 1762 as Carl von Linné, Swedish form of his Lat. name. Son of a Lutheran pastor, he studied at Lund and at Uppsala, where he became in 1741 prof. of medicine (later botany). In his *Species Plantarum* (1753) he achieved the concise method of naming plants and animals by genus, species, etc. which forms the basis of modern classification. His books, MSS and specimens were bought by Sir J. E. Smith, founder of the Linnean Society (1788), and preserved in the Linnean Rooms, Burlington House, London. *See* CENTIGRADE.

LINNET. Bird of the finch family (*Acanthis cannabina*) common in Europe. Its colour changes with the seasons to brown, grey, or pink. It nests in bushes and feeds on fruits and insects.

LĪ'NOTYPE. *See* PRINTING.

LIN PIAO (lin pyow), Marshal (1908-71). Chinese soldier and politician (Pinyin: Lin Biao). Vice-chairman of the Communist Party, and Vice-Premier and Min. of Defence from 1959, he was named as successor to Mao Tse-tung in 1969. He was alleged to have planned a military coup in 1971, which was to have been supported by Moscow in return for territorial concessions, but fled on its failure, his aircraft possibly having been shot down in Russian Mongolia. He d. in the crash.

LINSEED. Seeds of the flax plant (*Linum usitatissimum*), from which linseed oil is expressed, the residue being used as feeding cake for cattle. The oil is used in paint and varnishes, and in the manufacture of linoleum.

LINZ (lints). Cap. of Upper Austria, on the Danube. A river port, it grew up around the Roman fort Lentia. It is a tourist centre. Iron and steel, textiles, chemicals, etc., are manufactured. Pop. (1971) 202,875.

LION. Member of the cat family (*Panthera leo*), found in Africa and NW India and formerly more widely. The coat is tawny, the young having darker strips and spot markings which usually disappear in the adult, and the male has a heavy mane and a tuft at the end of the tail. Head and body measure *c.* 2m (6ft), plus 1m (3ft) of tail, the lionesss being slightly smaller. Ls. produce litters of 2-6 cubs, and often live in parties of several adult males and females with half a dozen young ones. Capable of short bursts of speed, they skilfully collaborate in stalking their prey which consists of the large herbivorous animals. Man-eating is usually the resort of old lions whose teeth and strength are failing. In zoos, a *liger* is the offspring of a male lion and female tiger; a *tigon* of a male tiger and female lion.

LION. A splendid specimen drinks at the waterhole, his eyes still alert, uncertain whether he is hunting or being hunted.
Photo: Courtesy of SATOUR

LIPARI ISLANDS (lē'pahrē). Group of volcanic islands off the NE of Sicily, named Lipari, Vulcano, Stromboli, Salina, Panaria, Filicudi, and Alicudi. They were known to the ancients as the home of Aeolus, god of the winds, and are sometimes called Eolian Is. The largest is L., on which stands the cap. of the same name. Area 114 sq.km (44 sq.m).

LIPCHITZ, Jacques (1891-1973). Lithuanian sculptor. He worked in Paris from 1909, and from 1941 in the USA, becoming a citizen in 1957. His works range from the Cubist 'Femme Assise' (1916) to later more baroque studies of the human figure, his bronzes being especially fine.

LI'PPE. German r., rising in the Teutoburg Forest and flowing generally W to join the Rhine at Wesel. It gave its name to a small state, which was a sovereign principality from the 12th cent. until 1918, and is now part of North Rhine-Westphalia.

LIPPERSHEY (lip'ershī), **Hans.** Dutch spectaclemaker who is said to have invented the telescope by chance, *c.* 1608.

LIPPI, Fra Filippo (1406-69). Italian painter, b. at Florence. His most important works are the frescoes in the choir of the cathedral at Prato, representing the lives of John the Baptist and St Stephen. L.'s 'Vision of St Bernard', formerly attributed to Masaccio, is in the National Gallery, London. His son, **Filippino L.** (1457-1504), was also a painter, studied under Botticelli, and executed frescoes in the Carmine, Florence, and the 'Virgin and Saints' (Uffizi, Florence).

LIP READING. Interpretation of speech by observation of the lips, tongue, and facial expression, enabling a deaf person, when proficent in the art and when the other person fully co-operates to carry on to some extent a normal conversation without the use of electrical or other hearing aids.

LIQUORICE (lik'ōris). Plant (*Glycyrrhiza glabra*) in the family Leguminosae, and the black, hard, sticks of paste prepared from boiled extracts of the crushed root, which are made into confectionery or, in pharmacy, for masking the bad taste of medicine.

LIRA (lēr'ah) (Lat. *libra*, pound). The standard unit of Italian currency, divided into 100 centesimi.

LISBOA. Portuguese form of LISBON.

LISBON (liz'bon). Cap. of Portugal (*Lisboa*) from 1260, and of Estremadura prov. It lies in a beautiful position on the Tagus, which here forms a tidal lake and an estuary. Most of L. is built on low hills. Alfama dist. is the old town, with narrow streets, picturesque but poor. The centre of city life is the Cidade Baixa (lower city): an earthquake in 1755 destroyed this part of the city, with great loss of life; it was rebuilt rapidly at the expense of the marquis of Pombal. Points of interest incl. the Castelo de São Jorge, the cathedral, a Moorish citadel founded 1150, the monastery of São Vicente de Fóra and the church of Nossa Senhora do Monte, the palace of the National Assembly (formerly a Benedictine monastery), the Palacio das Necessidades (formerly the royal palace, from which Manuel II, last king of Portugal, went into exile in 1910), the museums of ancient and of contemporary art, the botanical garden and Edward VII park, and the English cemetery, where Henry Fielding is buried. The city is the seat of an archbishopric, and the univ. was founded 1911, a technical univ. being estab. 1930. It has a fine harbour and is the centre of an important fishing industry. Among other industries are textiles, chemicals, shipbuilding, sugar refining, paper and pottery, and exports incl. wine, olive oil and cork. There is an underground railway, and a rail link with the seaside resort of Estoril, the internat. airport of Portela lies to the NE.

L., an important centre in Roman times, achieved its greatest prosperity in the 16th cent. Pop. met. area (1970) 1,034,140.

LISBURN. Cathedral city and market town in Antrim, N Ireland, on the r. Lagan, noted for linen and furniture. Jeremy Taylor d. here. Pop. (1971) 27,400.

LISIEUX (lēsyö'). Town in Calvados dept., France, to the SE of Caen. Thérèse Martin (1873-97), popularly called the 'little flower', spent all but the first 5 years of her short life in the Carmelite convent of L., and was in 1925 canonized as St Thérèse of L.: her tomb attracts pilgrims. Pop. (1975) 26,675.

LISTER, Joseph, 1st baron (1827-1912). British surgeon. He was prof. of surgery at Glasgow 1860-9, at Edinburgh 1869-77, and at King's Coll., London, 1877-92. The first to use antiseptic treatment for wounds, he introduced antiseptic surgery and the prevention of infection by the utmost cleanliness in the operating-room. He was pres. of the Royal Society 1895-1900, and was created baron L. of Lyme Regis in 1897. In 1902 he received the OM.

LISZT (list), **Franz** (1811-86). Hungarian pianist and composer. B. at Raiding, he was originally taught by his father, but after his first public performance when only 9 he went to Vienna to study under Czerny and Salieri and at 11 claimed even Beethoven among his many admirers. Becoming possibly the greatest virtuoso pianist of all time, he travelled widely in Europe, producing an opera *Don Sancho* in Paris at 14. In 1833 began his 10-year affair with the comtesse d'Agoult, by whom he had 3 children and with whom he lived mainly in Switzerland (*see* WAGNER). As musical director and conductor at Weimar (1849-59), where he lived with the Princess Caroline Sayn-Wittgenstein, he was a propagandist of the music of Berlioz and Wagner. Retiring to Rome, he turned again to his early love of religion and in 1865 became a secular priest (hence his adoption of the title Abbé), but continued to teach, give concert tours and indulge in several love-affairs. He d. at Bayreuth.

L. greatly influenced many younger musicians, incl. Brahms, Bülow, and Grieg, and originated the symphonic poem. His most notable compositions are his lyrical, but often technically very difficult, piano works, incl. the popular *Libesträume* and the *Hungarian Rhapsodies*, based on gipsy music. He also wrote a *Faust* and a *Dante* symphony; masses and oratorios; songs and piano arrangements of works by Beethoven, Schubert, Wagner, etc.

LI T'AI-PO (lē-tī-pō), or **LI PO** (705-62). Chinese poet. B. in Szechwan, he deals mostly with wine and other material joys of life, interspersing beautiful natural descriptions. His poems rarely exceed 12 lines. Li is said to have been drowned by falling from a pleasure-boat while drunk.

LITANY. In the Christian Church, a set form of responsive prayer or supplication.

LITCHI (lēchē'). Tree (*Litchi chinensis*) in the family Sapindaceae. The delicately flavoured ovate fruit is about the size of a walnut, and is encased in a brownish rough outer skin and has a hard seed. The L. is a native of S China, where it has been cultivated for 2,000 years.

LITERARY CRITICISM. The determination of the principles governing literary composition and their application. The earliest systematic L.C. was the work of Aristotle; among subsequent Greek writers is the anonymous author of the treatise *On the Sublime*, usually attributed to Longinus. The most important of the Latin critics were Horace and Quintilian. Medieval L.C. shows few original writers apart from Dante, but the Italian Renaissance produced a new type of Humanist C., beginning with Boccaccio, and the revival of classical scholarship exalted the authority of Aristotle and Horace. The spread of Renaissance ideas stimulated critics such as du Bellay in France and Sidney in England, and the increasing influence of classical writers illustrated in Jonson's work reached its apex in the neo-classicism of Boileau and Rapin, which affected Dryden. The neo-classic tradition was continued in the 18th cent. by Pope, Addison, and Johnson, and in France by la Harpe, Marmontel, and Voltaire. The Romantic reaction at the end of the 18th cent. was represented by Diderot in France, Lessing in Germany, and Wordsworth and Coleridge in England; other Romantic critics include Shelley, Hazlitt, Lamb, and de Quincey. A more scientific spirit was introduced by Sainte-Beuve, who was followed in France by Brunetière and Taine. To the later Victorian Age belong Carlyle, Arnold, and Pater, with Poe and Lowell in the USA, and Tolstoy in Russia. Also influential in European thought were Georg Brandes and Benedetto Croce, English L.C. in the 20th cent. is represented by A C. Bradley, Saintsbury, C. S. Lewis, T. S. Eliot, I. A. Richards, W. Empson, F. R. Leavis; and in the USA Edmund Wilson, Cleanth Brooks, and Lionel Trilling.

LI'THIUM (Gk. *lithos*, stone). The lightest metal known, symbol Li, at. no. 3, and at. wt. 6.940, it was discovered by Arfvedson in 1817. It has a silvery lustre, tarnishing rapidly in air so that it is kept under naphtha, is soft and ductile, and burns in air at 200°C. Never occurring free in nature, it is nevertheless widely distributed, traces being found in nearly all igneous rocks and many mineral springs. It is used as a reducing agent, in batteries, to harden alloys and in producing tritium.

LITHO'GRAPHY. In printing, a process of graphic reproduction discovered by Aloys Senefelder in Munich towards the end of the 18th cent. It is a method of surface printing based on the principle that grease and water repel one another. The drawing is made with greasy ink on an absorbent stone; this is washed with water, and then inked, the watered parts repelling the ink, and the drawing (or greasy parts) attracting it. The drawing is then printed. It has enjoyed a revival in modern times, since it enables the collector to possess an artist's 'original' at a modest price. In the production of modern books, etc., the name is applied to complex processes which now have only a basic principle in common with the original method.

LITHUĀ'NIA. A Soviet Socialist Republic of the USSR. It is situated between Latvia on the N, White Russia on the E, Poland on the S, Kaliningrad region of the RSFSR on the SW, and the Baltic on the W. L. is flat and low-lying, with a few hills and numerous small lakes. It is watered by the Niemen and its tributaries. Forestry and agriculture are both of importance. Crops incl. rye, oats, sugar beet, flax, potatoes, vegetables and fodder crops, and poultry and eggs are exported. Industries incl. textiles (cotton, linen and wool), footwear, paper, sugar refining, and increasingly - shipbuilding, heavy engineering and building materials. The cap. is Vilnius; other towns incl. Kaunas (like Vilnius having a univ.), and Klaipeda. Area 65,200 sq.km (25,300 sq.m); pop. (1978) 3,400,000.

A grand duchy from the 13th cent., Christianized in the 14th, L. was united with Poland 1569-1776, when it passed to Russia. L. proclaimed its independence in 1918, recognized by Russia in 1920. L., like Estonia and Latvia, received demands in 1939 for military bases, and in 1940 was incorporated in the USSR as a SSR. Forcible Russification ensued.

LITHUANIAN. The language of the Lithuanians, an Indo-European tongue, retaining many very ancient features: the free accent, the full complement of cases in the noun, etc. It does not seem to have been reduced to writing before the 16th cent., and it is spoken by about 3 millions.

LITMUS. A colouring matter obtained from various lichens. The aqueous extract of L. is used as an indicator to test the acidic or alkaline nature of aqueous solutions; with acid it turns red, with alkali (hydroxyl) it turns blue.

LITTLE BIGHORN. *See* CUSTER.

LITTLEHAMPTON. Seaside resort in W Sussex, England, at the mouth of the Arun, 16km (10m) SE of Chichester. Pop. (1971) 19,500.

LITTLE ROCK. Cap. of Arkansas, USA, in the state centre, on the Arkansas river. Industries incl. electrical-engineering, rubber, arms, timber and cotton-seed oil. Among the earliest Southern towns in which the Supreme Court ruling on racial integration in schools was carried out, L. was the scene of considerable disorder in 1957, when state and federal authority conflicted. Douglas MacArthur was b. here. Pop. met. area (1970) 333,300.

LITTLEWOOD, Joan. British theatrical director. After early experience with the Manchester Repertory Theatre, she founded Theatre Workshop in 1945. With her professionally 'earthy' and vigorous productions at the Theatre Royal, Stratford (London), she broke through to fame, e.g. *A Taste of Honey* (1959), *The Hostage* (1959-60), *Fings ain't Wot They Used T'Be* (1960-1), and *Oh What a Lovely War* (1963).

LITURGY. In the Christian Church, a term originally limited to the celebration of the Eucharist, but now used of any or all services for public worship.

LIU SHAO-CHI (lē-ōō show-chē) (1898-1974). Chinese statesman (Pinyin: Liu Shaoqi). A schoolfellow of Mao Tse-tung's, he became chairman, i.e. pres., of the republic in 1959, and was named as Mao's successor. Opposing Mao's policy of continuous revolution (as dislocating economic development), he fell into disgrace in 1968 during the Cultural Revolution, and d. in obscurity.

LIVER. The largest gland in man, *c.* 2kg (4lb) occupying the upper right-hand portion of the abdomen, below the diaphragm. A prodigious factory and storehouse, it makes the blood proteins (albumen, etc.) and antibodies; stores vitamins and food as glycogen, which is broken down to sugar and passed into the blood, to supply energy on demand to any part of the body. In addition to filtering and purifying the blood, the L. disposes of some waste products (e.g. urea) directly into the gut, to which it also supplies bile, an emulsifying agent which breaks fat down into minute droplets to aid its digestion.

LIVERMORE VALLEY. Valley in California, USA, site of the Lawrence Livermore Laboratory (named after Ernest Lawrence, q.v.), part of the Univ. of Calif., which shares with Los Alamos Laboratory, New Mexico, all US military research into nuclear warheads and atomic explosives. It has the world's most complex computer.

LIVERPOOL, Robert Banks Jenkinson, 2nd earl of (1770-1828). British Tory statesman. He entered parliament in 1790, and was For. Sec. 1801-3, Home Sec. 1804-6, and 1807-9, War Min. 1809-12, and PM 1812-27. His govt conducted the Napoleonic Wars to a successful conclusion, but its ruthless repression of freedom of speech and of the press aroused such opposition that during 1815-20 revolution frequently seemed imminent.

LIVERPOOL. City and seaport in Merseyside (of which it is admin. HQ), England, on the right bank of the Mersey 5km (3m) from the Irish Sea. Probably founded by the Norsemen, it replaced Chester in medieval times as a port for Ireland, but attained importance only under Charles II with the growth of trade with the American colonies and W Indies. The first dock was opened in 1715 and during the 18th cent. L. became the main centre of the slave trade, and in the 19th and first half of the 20th cent. was notable as the exporting centre for the textiles of Lancs and Yorks. Today, shortened lines of communication by motorway and freightliner train mean that more British exports of all kinds flow out through L. than by any other route and modernization by the Mersey Docks and Harbour Board (1858) makes it Europe's major Atlantic port. There are many miles of quays with specialized berths for 'packaged' softwood timber, petroleum, bananas and other fruit, and the expanding 'container' trade with N America, notably in the Seaforth dock 1967-71 which gives a 48-hr turn-round. There are also modernized facilities for bulk cargoes and commodities which cannot be containerized, and for the conventional carrier to less developed areas as yet unable to handle container traffic, as in Africa, the Far East, and S America, e.g. in the Birkenhead dock across the Mersey. Other imports incl. vegetable oils, grain, iron ore and other metals, sugar and cotton. Industries incl. flour milling, sugar refining, engineering, ship repairing, chemicals, tobacco, and extraction of vegetable oil, with modern factories on the industrial estates at Aintree, Kirkby and Speke. Garston, 6.5 (4m) up-river from L. has also developed as a container port. The Mersey Tunnel (1934) links L. and Birkenhead, and a tunnel to Wallasey was opened in 1971. There is an airport at Speke.

Outstanding buildings incl. Speke Hall, the 18th cent. Town Hall, St George's Hall (1854) in the Greek style, the Walker Art Gallery (1877) with a fine collection, and the Dock Offices, Liver Buildings and Cunard Building on Pier Head. The Anglican Cathedral (1904-79), designed by Sir Giles Gilbert Scott in the Gothic style, is the largest church in England; the RC Metropolitan Cathedral of Christ the King, 1967, is circular and has a lantern-tower carrying glass panels designed by John Piper. The univ. (1881) received its charter 1903. The Beatles (q.v.) were born in L., and made their début here. Pop. (1974) 574,560.

LIVERWORTS. Class of plants (Hepaticae) resembling mosses. They are of world-wide distribution in moist situations, and many are found in Britain.

LIVERY COMPANIES. The guilds of the City of London, whose members formerly wore a distinctive dress on special occasions. The companies have lost almost all their original industrial functions, but they still maintain their social activities. Most of them administer valuable charities, often educational.

LIVINGSTON. Town in W Lothian, Scotland, developed as a 'new town' from 1962, with chemical industries, brass and iron founding, ship repairing, etc. Pop. (1975) 21,000.

LIVINGSTONE, David (1813-73). Scottish missionary and explorer. B. at Blantyre, Lanarkshire, he worked in a cotton mill before studying medicine, Greek, and theology at Anderson's College, Glasgow. In 1838 he was accepted by the London Missionary Society, and in 1840 took his medical degree at Glasgow. L. was first sent to Bechuanaland. In 1844 he m. Mary Moffat, the daughter of the missionary Robert Moffat, and in 1849 discovered Lake Ngami. After a journey with him to the Upper Zambezi his wife and children fell ill and had to return to England. L.'s next journey took him to Loanda, where he arrived in 1854. In 1856 he followed the Zambezi to its mouth, and discovered the Victoria Falls before reaching Tete and Quilimane. During a visit to London he left the service of the London Missionary Society, and was appointed consul at Quilimane, being also chosen to lead an expedition to E and Central Africa, which resulted in the discovery of lakes Shirwa and Nyasa and in the exposure of the slave trade. This journey was saddened by the death of his wife in 1862. In an attempt to find the sources of the Nile he ranged between lakes Nyasa and Tanganyika from 1866, reaching Ujiji in 1871. Here Stanley joined him, and together they explored N Tanganyika. L. d. in May 1873 at Old Chitambo, Zambia. He was buried in Westminster Abbey in 1874.

LIVINGSTONE. Town in Zambia, on the Zambezi r., nr Victoria Falls. Founded in 1905, it is named after the explorer, and there is a Rhodes-Livingstone Museum, a game park, and an internat. airport. Pop. (1976) 58,000.

LIVORNO. Italian form of LEGHORN.

LIVY (Titus Livius) (59 BC–AD 17). Roman historian, famous for his *History of Rome*, from the foundation to 9 BC. It was composed of 142 books, of which 35 survive, viz., 1-10 and 21-45, covering the periods from the arrival of Aeneas in Italy to 293 BC, and 218-167 BC.

LIZARD. Order of reptiles, Lacertilia. The order contains 21 families and over 1,500 species. They are distributed throughout the temperate and tropical regions of the world, being most numerous in warmer climates. Most Ls. have scaly bodies, movable eyelids, and well-developed limbs. Some varieties, e.g. the British blindworm, are legless. The tail is often fragile, but a new tail grows if the old one is shed.

Ls. are generally terrestrial, and usually arboreal, but some are semi-aquatic and one is marine. Their diet varies, some being vegetarian, others feeding on insects, worms, or eggs, etc. They are usually oviparous, but in some varieties the young are completely developed before birth.

LIZARD. The perenty goanna *(Varanus giganteus)*, Australia's largest lizard, which grows up to 2.5 m (8 ft), and is found in the central desert areas. *Photo: Popperfoto*

LIZARD POINT. The most southerly point of Cornwall and England. Lizard Town is the nearest village. The coast is broken into small bays, overlooked by 2 cliff lighthouses.

LJUBLJANA (lublyah'nah). Cap. of Slovenia, Yugoslavia. It still retains its mediaeval fortress, but is a modern industrial city: textiles, leather goods, paper, chemicals, etc. are made and there are iron foundries. There is a univ. (1919). A motorway via the Karawanken Tunnel (1979-83) under the Alps links it wth S. Austria. Pop. (1971) 135,000.

LLAMA (lah'ma). S American animal (*Lama huanacus glama*), used in Peru as a beast of burden. Ls. are white, with brown or black spots, very hardy, and require little food or water. They spit profusely when annoyed. The alpaca (q.v.), is an allied species.

LLAMA. In Peru an Aymara Indian girl looks after a mixed herd of sheep and llamas. *Photo: Mireille Vautier*

LLANBERIS (lanber'is). Village in Gwynedd, Wales, point of departure for ascents of Snowdon. Pop. (1973) 2,000.

LLANDAFF (lan'daf). Town in S Glamorgan, Wales, 5km (3m) NW of Cardiff, of which it forms part. The 12th cent. cathedral was restored 1844-69, and after damage in a German air raid in 1941, again restored 1948-60: it contains Epstein's sculpture 'Christ in Majesty'.

LLANDRINDOD (lanrin'dod) **WELLS.** Spa in Powys, Wales, admin. HQ of the county. Pop. (1973) 3,500.

LLANDUDNO (landid'no). Touring centre for N Wales, in Gwynedd, nr the mouth of the Conway. Great Orme's Head is a spectacular limestone headland. Pop. (1973) 18,000.

LLANELLI (lane'lhi). Welsh seaport in Dyfed, by the Burry estuary, formerly Llanelly. Industries incl. tinplate and copper smelting. Pop. (1971) 26,080.

LLANFAIR P.G. (lan'vīr-). Village in the SE of the Welsh island of Anglesey. The full name is Llanfairpwllgwyngyllgogerychwyrndrobwllllandysilliogogogoch (St Mary's church in the hollow of the white hazel near to the rapid whirlpool of St Tysillio's church, by the red cave).

LLANOS (lah'nōs). Grasslands of tropical and subtropical America, as in the Orinoco basin.

LLEWELLYN, Richard. Pseudonym of the Welsh author and dramatist Richard Vivian Llewellyn Lloyd (1907–83). He sprang to fame in 1939 with *How Green Was My Valley*, a novel about a S Wales mining family.

LLEWELYN (loo-el'in) **I** (d. 1240). Prince who became king of N Wales in 1194, and extended his rule over all Wales not in Norman hands. His grandson, **Llewelyn II** (d. 1282), succeeded in 1246, and was compelled by Edward I in 1277 to acknowledge him as overlord and to surrender S Wales. His death while leading a national uprising marked the end of Welsh independence.

LLEWELYN-DAVIES, Richard, baron (1912-). British architect. He was consultant for the rebuilding of the London Stock Exchange and the new town Milton Keynes. He was created a life peer in 1964.

LLEYN (līn) **PENINSULA.** Peninsula in N Wales between Cardigan Bay and Caernarvon Bay. It incl. the resort Pwllheli, and Bardsey Is. at the tip of P.L. is the traditional burial place of 20,000 saints.

LLOYD, Harold (1893-1971). American film comedian, noted for his 'trademark' of spectacles with thick horn rims, who appeared from 1913 in silent and talking films.

LLOYD, Marie. Stage-name of British music-hall artist Matilda Alice Victoria Wood (1870-1922). First singing at the Grecian music-hall in London's East End in 1885, she embodied the Cockney comedy of the 1890s.

LLOYD, Selwyn. *See* SELWYN LLOYD, Lord.

LLOYD GEORGE, David, 1st earl L.-G. (1863-1945). Welsh Liberal statesman. B. in Manchester, son of a teacher, he became a solicitor, and in 1890 was elected MP for Caernarvon Boroughs, which he represented for 54 years. In parliament he made his reputation as a fiery Radical and Welsh Nationalist, and during the S African War was prominent as a pro-Boer. In the Liberal cabinet of 1905 he became Pres. of the Board of Trade, and in 1908 Chancellor of the Exchequer; the most notable measures associated with his term of office were the introduction of old-age pensions in 1908, and of health and employment insurance in 1911. His budget of 1909 provoked the Lords to reject it, and thereby led to the Parliament Act of 1911.

The F.W.W. brought him to the fore as the dominating figure in the cabinet. As Min. of Munitions 1915-16 he thoroughly reorganized the supply of arms and ammunition, shortage of which had created a national scandal. Succeeding Kitchener as War Min. in June 1916, he advocated a policy of diverting manpower to the eastern front which resulted in the Salonika expedition. By this time he had lost all faith in Asquith as a war leader; in Dec. the breach became an open one, and a new coalition was formed, with L.G. as PM. His aim now became to secure a unified Allied command; this was achieved in May 1918, and enabled the Allies to withstand the last German offensive and conduct the war to a victorious conclusion. As one of the 'Big Three', L.G. was among those primarily responsible for the Versailles peace settlement.

The 1918 elections gave the coalition a huge majority over the Labour Party and Asquith's Liberal followers, but it soon lost its prestige. The growth of unemployment, its interventionist policy in Russia, the use of the 'black and tans' in Ireland, and the failure of L.G.'s pro-Greek policy in the Near East, all lost it support, and in 1922 the Conservatives withdrew. The reunion of Asquith's and L.G.'s supporters failed to stimulate a Liberal revival, and within the party L.G. was widely distrusted. During 1931-5 he withdrew to lead a tiny opposition Liberal group within the Commons. He ceased to be an important figure thereafter, although he occasionally came to the fore, as when in 1940 he helped to overthrow the Chamberlain govt. He was raised to the peerage shortly before his death in 1945. His highly controversial war memoirs appeared in 1933-6. **Dame Margaret L. G.** (1864-1941), *née* Owen, whom he m. 1888, was created DBE in 1919 for her social work. His second wife, **Frances,** countess L. G. (1888-1972), *née* Stevenson, was his private sec. from 1913 until their marriage in 1943. Her *Lloyd George: A Diary* (1971) contains her diaries during his years in office.

L. G.'s younger dau. **Lady Megan L. G.** (1902-66) became a Liberal MP in 1929 and was deputy leader of the party from 1949 until her defeat in 1951. Joining the Labour Party in 1955, she re-entered the House in 1957.

LLOYD'S. Insurance market and centre of the world's shipping intelligence in London, England. A corporation, the members of which, known as underwriters, issue insurance policies for their own account and risk. Business is only transacted through brokers who have been authorized by the committee to carry on business with Lloyd's underwriters. Underwriters must satisfy the committee annually that they are in every way fitted to undertake the financial responsibility which membership involves. Although originally predominantly marine, today there are few risks, life assurance and financial guarantee apart, that cannot be effected.

In 1688 Edward Lloyd kept a coffee house in Tower Street, moving in 1691 to Lombard Street. Frequented by business men willing to insure against sea-risks, this became the acknowledged centre where insurers might be found. *Lloyd's News* incl. marine information in its single sheet which was first pub. in 1696, and *Lloyd's List and Shipping Gazette* started 1734 is still pub. The association was incorporated under an Act of 1871, and stricter regulations, incl. a new 25-strong council, were planned in 1980. A succession of scandals involving Lloyd's members has led to calls for further reform. The HQ is a spectacular new building in Lime Street, designed by Richard Rogers (q.v.), which was completed in 1986. *See* LUTINE.

The American equivalent, the New York Reinsurance Exchange (REX) was estab. in 1978.

LLOYD'S. The Committee Room at Lloyd's is adapted from the original Adam Great Room of Bowood House in Wiltshire. The magnificent ceiling and Adam fireplace were removed in their entirety. *Photo: Courtesy of Lloyd's*

LLOYD'S REGISTER OF SHIPPING. Founded 1760, this international society for the survey and classification of merchant shipping provides rules for the construction and maintenance of ships and their machinery. It is governed by a large committee representing ship-owners, shipbuilders, marine engineers, and underwriters. The register book, published annually, contains particulars of all known sea-going ships of 100 tonnes gross and over.

LOBACHE'VSKI, Nikolai Ivanovich (1793-1856). Russian mathematician. B. at Makariev, he was prof. of mathematics at Kazan univ. 1823-46, and is usually regarded as the founder of non-Euclidean geometry.

LOBĒ'LIA. Genus of plants in the family Lobeliaceae, named after the botanist Matthias de Lobel. About 250 species are known, native of temperate and tropical regions. Some forms, especially those found in Africa, grow to the size of small trees.

LOBENGULA (lō-bengoo'la) (*c.* 1833-94). Matabele king. Succeeding his father in 1870, he accepted British protection in 1888, but in 1893 rebelled. He was defeated near Bulawayo.

LOBI'TO. Seaport in Angola, linked with Beira, Mozambique, by the trans-Africa rlwy, via the copperbelt of Zaïre and Zambia. Pop. (1975) 85,000.

LOBSTER. A family of crustacea, Homaridae, found on the coasts of the N Atlantic and Mediterranean, and used for food. They are distinguished by the pincers on the end of the first 3 pairs of legs, the front pair being very large. When living the outer cuticle is bluish black in colour, but turns red on boiling. They live in shallow water in rocky places, and are caught in wicker lobster-pots. The common European lobster (*Homarus gammarus*) is usually sent to the market fresh.

LOBSTER. Australia is the world's biggest exporter of rock lobster. This specimen, about five years old, is standing beside himself: the moult shell behind him was discarded within the previous twelve hours. *Photo: Courtesy of the Australian Information Service*

LOCAL GOVERNMENT. That part of government dealing mainly with matters concerning the inhabitants of a particular district or place, together with those the administration of which parliament has delegated to local authorities.

HISTORY. The system of L.G. in England developed haphazardly. In the 18th cent. it varied in towns between democratic survivals of the guild system, and the narrow rule of small oligarchies. The Municipal Reform Act (1835) estab. the rule of elected councils, although their actual powers remained small. In the country L.G. remained in the hands of the JPs assembled in Quarter Sessions, until the L.G. Act (1888) set up county councils. These were given a measure of control over the internal local authorities, except the major bodies, which were constituted county boroughs. The L.G. Act (1894) set up urban and rural district councils, and, in the rural districts only, parish councils.

Under the Local Govt Act (1972) the upper range of English L.G., except for Greater London (already reorganized 1965) was estab. on a two-tier basis. There are 40 cos. (46 until 1986, when London and the 6 metropolitan cos. were abolished) in England and 8 in Wales. These in turn are subdivided into districts. *See* COUNTY, COUNTY COUNCIL, DISTRICT COUNCIL. Parish councils (q.v.) in England were largely unaffected, but in Wales parishes were replaced by communities, with similar powers.

On the Continent, L.G. tends to be much more centrally directed and controlled, rather than the 'partnership' prevailing in England, e.g. France, Germany and the Soviet Union, although German cities have a tradition of independent action, as exemplified in Berlin, and France from 1969 moved towards regional decentralization. In the USA a good deal of the English spirit of freedom survives, and the system shows evidence of the early type of settlement, e.g. in New England the town is the unit of L.G., in the South the co., and in the N Central states the combined co. and township. A complication is the tendency to delegate power to special authorities in such fields as education. In Australia, although an integrated system similar to the British was planned, the scattered nature of settlement, apart from the major towns, has prevented implementation of any uniform tiered arrangement.

LOCAL OPTION. The right granted by a government to the electors of each particular area to decide whether the sale of intoxicants shall be permitted. Such a system has been tried in certain states of the USA, in certain Canadian provs., and in Norway and Sweden.

LOCA'RNO. Health resort in the Ticino canton of Switzerland on the N of Lago Maggiore, W of Bellinzona. Formerly in the duchy of Milan, it was captured by the Swiss in 1803. Pop. (1970) 14,100.

LOCARNO, Pact of. A series of diplomatic documents initialled at Locarno on 16 Oct. 1925, and formally signed in London on 1 Dec. 1925. The Pact settled the question of the Rhineland, and the powers - Britain, France, Belgium, Italy, and Germany - guaranteed the existing frontiers between Germany and France, and Germany and Belgium. The prime mover in the Pact was Austen Chamberlain. Following the signing of the Pact Germany was admitted to the League of Nations, but in 1936 the Nazis formally denounced the pact.

LOCHABER (lokhah'ber). Wild mountainous dist of Highland region, Scotland, including Ben Nevis. It is the site of large-scale hydro-electric installations.

LOCHNER (lokh'ner), **Stephan** (fl. 1400-51). German painter. He was b. on the Upper Rhine, and all his principal works are in the cathedral and museums of Cologne, incl. the 'Madonna in the Rose Garden', 'Adoration of the Kings', and 'Presentation in the Temple'. L.'s death marked the end of idealism in Rhenish painting, and the realism coming from the Netherlands took its place.

LOCKE, John (1632-1704). English philosopher. B. in Somerset, he studied at Oxford, practised medicine, and in 1667 became sec. to the earl of Shaftesbury. He consequently fell under suspicion as a Whig and in 1683 fled to Holland, where he lived until the 1688 revolution. In later life he pub. many works on philosophy, politics, theology, and economics; these incl. *Letters on Toleration* (1689-92), *Two Treatises on Government* (1690), *Essay concerning Human Understanding* (1690), and *Some Thoughts concerning Education* (1693).

His *Treatises on Government* supply the classical statement of Whig theory, and enjoyed great influence in America and France. He maintains that governments derive their authority from the people's consent, and that they may overthrow any government threatening their fundamental rights. Among these rights he incl. religious freedom, although he would deny toleration to Catholicism and atheism as dangerous to society. His *Essay concerning Human Understanding*, which deals with the nature, origin, and limits of human knowledge, raised problems which dominated 18th cent. philosophy down to Kant.

LOCKJAW. *See* TETANUS.

LOCUST. Swarming grasshopper, with short antennae and auditory organs on the abdomen, in the family Acrididae. When the larvae ('hoppers') emerge from the eggs, which are laid in the ground, they form into bands. As winged adults, flying in swarms, they may be carried by the wind hundreds of miles from their breeding grounds, and on alighting devour all vegetation. Ls. occur in nearly every continent, the migratory L. (*Locusta migratoria*) ranging from Europe across Russia to China, and even small swarms may cover several sq.m and weigh thousands of tons. Control by spreading poisoned food amongst the bands is very effective, but it is cheapest to spray concentrated insecticide solutions from aircraft over the insects or the vegetation on which they feed. They eat the equivalent of their own weight in a day, and, flying at night with the desert wind, may cover some 500km (300m).

The *L. tree* is the carob (q.v.) which has locust-like seed-pods.

LOCUST. In close-up, a young locust. *Photo: NHPA*

LODGE, Henry Cabot (1850-1924). American statesman. B. in Boston, he was a Republican senator from 1893 until his death. It was largely due to him that the USA refused to join the League of Nations. His grandson **Henry Cabot L.** (1902-) entered journalism, then became Republican senator for Mass. in 1936. Campaign manager for Eisenhower's nomination, he was a member of his cabinet and US representative to the UN 1953-60. He was American ambassador to S Vietnam 1963-4 and 1965-7, and in Bonn from 1968. In 1969 he took over from Harriman as Nixon's negotiator in the Vietnam peace talks, and became special envoy to the Vatican 1970.

LODGE, Sir Oliver Joseph (1851-1940). British physicist. B. in Staffs, he was prof. of physics at Liverpool 1881-1900, and principal of Birmingham univ. 1900-19. His place in physics rests chiefly on his researches on radiation, and the relation between matter and ether. His investigations on the Hertzian waves led him to invent a coherer, which he used to accomplish wireless telegraphy. L. was a prominent psychic research worker.

LODGE, Thomas (*c.* 1558-1625). English author and dramatist. His romance *Rosalynde* (1590) was the basis of Shakespeare's *As You Like it.*

LODI (lō'dē). Town and episcopal see of Italy 30km (18m) SE of Milan, a market for agricultural produce; fertilizers, agricultural machinery and textiles are made. Napoleon's defeat of the Austrians at the battle of L. in 1796 gave him control of Lombardy. Napoleon was first called Le Petit Caporal at L. Pop. (1971) 38,200.

LODZ. Town in Poland, cap. of L. voivodship, 120km (75m) SW of Warsaw. The centre of a group of industrial towns, it produces textiles and textile machinery, dyes, etc., and is the seat of a univ. (1945). Pop. (1978) 818,000.

LOESS (lō'es). A yellow loam, accumulated by wind in periglacial regions during the ice ages. It usually attains considerable depths, and is very fertile. There are large deposits in central Europe, especially Hungary; in China and N America.

LOEWE (lō), **Frederick** (1901-). American composer. B. in Austria, son of an operatic tenor, he studied music incl. the piano under Busoni, and in 1924 went with his father to the USA. In 1942 he joined forces with Alan Jay Lerner (1918–86), and their joint successes incl. *Brigadoon* (1947), *Paint Your Wagon* (1951), *My Fair Lady* (1956), *Gigi* (1958), and *Camelot* (1960).

LOFO'TENS. Group of islands belonging to Norway with which are often included the Vesteralen group, off the NW coast of Norway. Hinnoy, in the Vesteralens, is the largest island of Norway. The seas surrounding the islands are rich in cod and herring. Area 4,530 sq.km (1,750 sq.m).

LOG. An apparatus for measuring the speed of a ship through water. For the original 'common L.', a piece of weighted wood (log-chip) attached to a line, knotted at intervals, was thrown off the rear of the ship, and its progress measured by timing the passage of the knots with a sand-glass. Sophisticated modern Ls. may use electromagnetism, sonar, etc.

LOGANBERRY. Fruit first raised from seed by the American Judge J. H. Logan in 1881, a hybrid between a wild blackberry and a raspberry.

LO'GARITHMS. The exponents of powers to which an invariable number called the base has to be raised to produce the number of which it is the L. To multiply common numbers, their Ls. are added; to divide, they are subtracted; involution is done by multiplication, and evolution by division.

LOGIC (Gk *logos*, reason). The science of accurate thought. The founder of L. as a separate branch of philosophy was Aristotle, whose treatises, known collectively as the Organon, provided the basis for a complete system. The medieval Church, concentrating on Aristotle's method of deduction from certain given premises, produced the modified system known as Scholasticism. This prevailed until the scientific spirit of the Renaissance produced the inductive method of Bacon, which works backward from the accumulated facts to the principle which accounts for them. Hobbes, Locke, and especially J. S. Mill, developed this form. To the school of rationalist philosophers inspired by Descartes belong Spinoza and Leibniz. Exponents of formal L. include Kant, Hamilton, Mansel, Lotze, and Herbart. Among later logicians are Bosanquet, Bradley, Johnson, Russell, and Whitehead.

LO'GOS (Gk 'word' or 'reason'). A term in Greek, Hebrew and Christian philosophy and theology. It was used by Greek philosophers for the divine reason pervading the universe. Under Greek influence the Jews came to conceive of Wisdom as an aspect of God's activity. The Jewish philosopher Philo (1st cent. AD) attempted to reconcile Platonic, Stoic, and Hebrew philosophy by identifying the L. with the Jewish idea of 'Wisdom'. Several of the New Testament writers took over Philo's conception of the L., which they identified with Christ.

LOHENGRIN (lō'engrin). Name of Parsival's son, legendary Knight of the Swan and hero of a German epic of the late 13th cent., on which Wagner based his opera (1848).

LOIR (lwahr). French river, rising N of Illiers in the dept of Eure-et-Loir and flowing SE, then SW to join the Sarthe near Angers. It gives its name to the depts of Loir-et-Cher and Eure-et-Loir.

LOIRE (lwahr). The longest river in France, rising in the Cévennes at 1,350 m (4,430 ft) and flowing for 1,050 km (625 m) first N then W till it reaches the Bay of Biscay at St Nazaire, passing Nevers, Orléans, Tours and Nantes. It gives its name to the depts of Loire, Haute-Loire, Loire-Atlantique, Indre-et-Loire, Maine-et-Loire, and Saône-et-Loire.

LOIRET (lwahreh'). River of France, 11km (7m) long. It rises near Olivet and joins the Loire 8km (5m) below Orléans. It gives its name to L. dept.

LŌ'KI. In Scandinavian mythology, one of the Aesir, but the cause of dissension among the gods, and the slayer of Balder. His children are the Midgard serpent Jörmungander which girdles the earth, the wolf Fenris, and Hela.

LOLLARDS. Name, probably meaning 'mutterers' given to the followers of Wycliffe (q.v.). They condemned transubstantiation, advocated the diversion of ecclesiastical property to charitable uses, and denounced war and capital punishment. Propaganda began *c.* 1377; after the passing of the statute *De Heretico Comburendo* (1401) many Ls. were burned, and in 1414 they raised an unsuccessful revolt in London. Lollardy lingered on in London and E. Anglia, and in the 16th cent. became absorbed into the Protestant movement.

LOMBARDS or **Langobards.** A Germanic people, originating on the Elbe, who invaded Italy in 568, and occupied Lombardy, which is named after them, and central Italy. Their kingdom was conquered by Charlemagne in 774.

LOMBARDY. Region of N Italy, divided into the provs. of Bergamo, Brescia, Como, Cremona, Mantua, Milan, Pavia, Sondrio, and Varese. It incl. Lakes Como and Iseo, part of Maggiore on the W, part of Garda on the E, and is drained by the Po and several of its left-bank tributaries, incl. the Ticino. It has extremes of climate; vines, cereals, and the mulberry tree are cultivated, and silk is produced. Milan, the cap., is the centre of a highly industrialized area. In the N the region is a much favoured holiday resort. The area was taken from the Roman Empire in 568 by the Langobardi or Lombards, from whom it took its name. In the Middle Ages it belonged to the dukes of Milan; later, in succession, to Spain, Austria, and Sardinia. Area 23,797 sq.km (9,191 sq.m); pop. (1977) 8,910,400.

LOMBO'K. Island of Indonesia. Mataram is the chief town and Ampanam the chief port. It rises in Mt. L., a volcano, to 3,773 m (12,379 ft). Area 4,727 sq.km (1,825 sq.m).

Through L. Strait, between L. and Bali, runs Wallace's Line, discovered by the naturalist A. R. Wallace (1823-1913), to the W of which the fauna and flora are predominantly Asian, to the E predominantly Australasian.

LOMBRŌ'SO, Cesare (1836-1909). Italian criminologist. He became a prof. of mental diseases at Pavia in 1862. Subsequently he held chairs in forensic medicine, psychiatry, and criminal anthropology at Turin. His principle work is *L'uomo delinquente* (1889). He held that there was a physically distinguishable criminal 'type'.

LOMÉ (lōmā'). Cap. and port of Togo, on the Bight of Benin. Under the **Lomé Convention** (1975) trading and economic co-operation was estab. between the EEC and the developing African, Caribbean and Pacific countries: renewed 1981. Pop. (1975) 215,000.

LOMÉ. The Lomé Convention in session, a portrait of President Eyadéma on the wall behind the delegates. *Photo: Courtesy of the Commission of the European Community*

LO'MOND. The largest freshwater Scottish loch, 37km (23m) long, partly in Strathclyde and partly in Central region; area 70 sq.km (25 sq.m). It contains 30 islands and is overlooked by Ben Lomond.

LONDON, Jack (1876-1916). American author. B. in San Francisco, he used his own adventurous life as the background of his most popular books, e.g. *The Call of the Wild* (1903), *White Fang* (1906) - the story of a dog - and

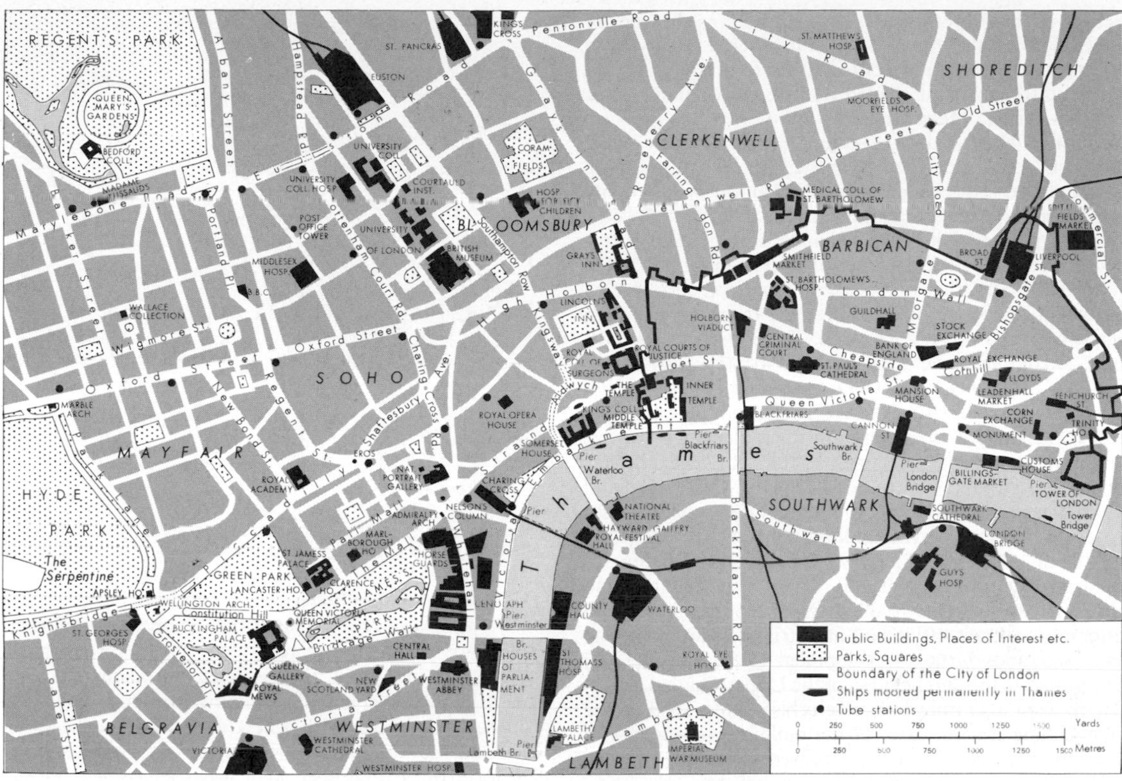

LONDON

Martin Eden (1909). Less familiar are the socialist ideas, influenced by Marx and Nietzsche, of *The People of the Abyss* (1903), etc.

LONDON. The cap. of England, on the r. Thames, c. 80km (50m) W of the sea at the Nore.

The City of London occupies a site probably unsettled before Roman times. Area 274 ha. (677 acres), resident pop. (1971) 4,250 (daytime working pop. est. at 500,000). The City is the commercial and business centre of the UK. Within its 'square mile' lie the Bank of England; the Royal Exchange, the Stock Exchange, the Baltic Exchange, etc.; Lloyd's; the head offices of the principal banks and insurance companies; the Bankers' Clearing House; the Central Criminal Court (popularly called the Old Bailey, from the street in which it stands) and the Inner and Middle Temples; several food markets - Leadenhall (poultry), Billingsgate (fish, being relocated on the Isle of Dogs), Smithfield (meat), Spitalfields (vegetables and fruit); and the HQ of the Port of London Authority. The Mermaid, first theatre within the City for 3 cents., was opened in 1959.

The City is governed by a corporation dating from the 12th cent. and unique in local govt; it consists of 3 courts: (i) the Court of Aldermen, one for each of the 25 wards, elected for life; (ii) the Court of Common Hall, composed of freemen of the City Livery Companies, which chooses annually 2 Sheriffs and other officers, and nominates 2 Aldermen from among former Sheriffs for choice by the Court of Aldermen to fill the office of Lord Mayor; (iii) the Court of Common Council, composed of the twenty-five Aldermen, and 130 Common Councilmen elected annually on St Ignatius's Day (17 Dec.) by citizens who qualify as electors by paying rates on property in the City. This last is the local govt authority for the City and sits at the Guildhall. The Lord Mayor (so called since the 16th cent. without specific grant of the title, which was formerly Mayor) presides over all 3 Courts, and he is also the chief magistrate. He takes office on 8 Nov. and his presentation to the Lord Chief Justice and swearing in at the Royal Courts of Justice (just beyond the City boundary, in Westminster) are the occasion of the annual Lord Mayor's procession, held on the next Saturday. The annual Lord Mayor's banquet at the Guildhall follows. The Lord Mayor's official residence is the Mansion House.

Greater London was redefined in 1965, following the recommendation of a Royal Commission, and enlarged to comprise the former co. of London, the major part of Middlesex, which also disappeared administratively, and parts of Essex, Herts, Kent, and Surrey. The overall authority until 1 April 1986 was the Greater London Council (GLC); its responsibilities have largely reverted to the 32 London Borough Councils. Area 1,580 sq.km (610 sq.m); pop. (1978) 6,918,000.

History. L. first appears in history as 'Londinium' in AD 61, when it was sacked by Boadicea. The origin of the name remains uncertain. Roman L. was a walled city, and an important trading centre from which all roads radiated. It was the seat of a bishopric before 314. After an obscure period in the 5th-6th cents., L. reappears as the cap. of Essex. During the 9th-11th cents. it suffered greatly from Viking raids. The City secured rights of self-government in the 12th cent. and elected its first mayor in 1191, or perhaps earlier. Meanwhile Westminster, which grew up round the 7th cent. abbey, became the seat of govt in the 12th cent., and of parliament in the 13th. The outstanding event of the 16th cent. was the dissolution of L.'s many monasteries. In the struggle against the Stuarts L. played a decisive part, and its trained bands distinguished themselves in the Civil War. The Great Plague of 1665 was followed by the Fire in 1666; rebuilding was entrusted to Wren and Robert Hooke, though the revolutionary plan made by Wren was not followed. The nobility in the 17th cent. abandoned the City as a residential district for Lincoln's Inn and Covent Garden, while in Hanoverian times they moved still farther W. In the 19th cent. the City lost its residential character altogether, and rail transport encouraged spreading suburbs. In the 20th cent. Mayfair and other central areas ceased to be mainly residential and were overtaken by offices, and commuter problems and road congestion correspondingly increased. Remedial measures after the S.W.W. incl. decentralisation of industry and offices, but this led to depopulation and urban decay, so that by the 1980s there was a renewed attempt to attract office and industrial development, e.g. the Docklands Urban Development Corporation (1981) to regenerate the derelict area of the Upper Thames docks. There were also imaginative refurbishments, such as the remodelling for new uses of the buildings on the site of Covent Garden Market (removed to Nine Elms). Improvements to transport facilities incl. new tube lines: Victoria (1969), Jubilee (1978), a link to the docklands (under construction), and Piccadilly line extension to Heathrow Airport (completed, with loop to Terminal 4, 1986). Gatwick and Luton are the two other international airports, with Stansted designated as a fourth. The risk of flooding, from a possible combination of high tides in the Thames, North Sea 'surges' and falling land levels, was met by a barrier spanning the river at Woolwich, officially opened 1984. Its ten gates normally lie level with the riverbed, but can be rotated to an upright position whenever necessary.

L. suffered slightly from air raids during the F.W.W. Raids during the S.W.W., which killed 29,890 people, injured 50,497, and destroyed or damaged many famous buildings, fell into 3 main stages: day raids Aug.-Sept. 1940; night raids Aug. 1940-May 1941, incl. the fire raid on the City on 29-30 Dec.; and flying and rocket bombs June 1944-March 1945.

Architecture. L. contains specimens of all styles of English architecture since the 11th cent. Examples incl. Norman: The White Tower, Tower of London; St Bartholomew's, Smithfield; the Temple Church. Gothic: Westminster Abbey; Westminster Hall; Lambeth Palace; Southwark Cathedral. Tudor: St James's Palace; Staple Inn, Holborn. 17th cent.: Banqueting Hall, Whitehall (Inigo Jones); St Paul's, Kensington Palace, and many City churches (Wren). 18th cent.: Somerset House (Chambers); St Martin-in-the-Fields; Buckingham Palace. 19th cent.: British Museum (classical); Houses of Parliament; Law Courts (Gothic); Westminster Cathedral (Byzantine). 20th cent.: County Hall; Bush House; Waterloo Bridge; Royal Festival Hall; Commonwealth Inst.; and National Theatre.

LONDON

Commerce and Industry. Important from Saxon times, the Port of L. once dominated the Thames from Tower Bridge to Tilbury, but restricted space for modern development in the met. area has led to extension of downstream Tilbury to cope with container traffic, as well as a proposal to continue with a new deep-water port on the reclaimed Maplin Sands off Foulness Is., even when the plan for a third L. airport there was shelved. The prime economic importance of L. is as an internat. banking, commercial, and financial centre, with large-scale industry on the outskirts, e.g. printing, clothing, food processing, paper, chemicals, furniture, electrical and mechanical engineering, plastics, etc. Small-scale specialized products incl. jewellery, gold and silver work, furs, and haute couture and tailoring. There are also recording, broadcasting, television, and film studios; publishing offices, and the works and offices of the national press.

L. has long occupied a unique position in the nation's life as a centre of politics, administration, the law, fashion, pleasure, learning, and the arts. Its great public occasions range from Coronations to Cup finals, the Lord Mayor's show to the Royal Academy exhibition. It contains the headquarters of many learned and artistic societies; among its educational organizations are the British, Victoria and Albert, Natural History, and Science Museums, the National and Tate Galleries, and the Zoological Gardens. L. Univ. is the largest in Britain, while the Inns of Court have been the training-school for lawyers since the 13th cent. L. has been the main centre of English drama ever since its first theatre was built by Burbage in 1576; a replica of his Globe Theatre (1599) was planned in 1980.

LONDON. Canadian city in S Ontario, on the r. Thames, 160km (100m) SW of Toronto. The centre of a good farming district, it has tanneries, breweries, and factories making hosiery, radio and electrical equipment, leather, shoes, etc. It dates from 1826 and is the seat of the Univ. of Western Ontario and of the Stratford Shakespearean Festival. It has an airport. Pop. (1976) 240,400.

LONDON. A view over the Houses of Parliament, with 'Big Ben' to the left and County Hall (headquarters of the Greater London Council) to the right, on the other side of the Thames, beyond Westminster Bridge. The white silhouette of the Royal Festival Hall can be seen set between Hungerford and Waterloo Bridges, and, to the right of the tall 'Shell International' building, the dome of St Paul's in the City is just visible among rising office blocks. *Photo: Courtesy of the British Tourist Authority*

LONDON, Museum of. Formed by the amalgamation of the former Guildhall (Roman and medieval) and London (Tudor and later) Museums, announced in 1962: the exhibits of both, which complement each other, are housed (1976) in a new building at the junction of London Wall and Aldersgate, nr the Barbican.

LONDONDERRY. City in co. L., N Ireland, 101km (63m) NW of Belfast, on the Foyle. Developing from the monastery founded by St Columba in the 6th cent., L. still has the famous walls surrounding the old town. In 1689 it was defended by the Protestants against the besieging army of James II from April to July. Industries incl. textiles, food processing, light engineering and chemicals. In 1968-9 there were 'civil rights' disturbances which led to local govt reform.

The co. of L. borders the Atlantic; its main river is the Roe. Farming is hampered by excessive rainfall. The admin. HQ is L. Area 2,082 sq.km (804 sq.m); pop. (1971) 183,095.

The town of L. was originally called Derry (Irish Dhoire, place of oaks); both town and county took the name L. when land belonging to the O'Neills was given to the City of London Corporation in 1609.

'LONDON GAZETTE.' Twice-weekly publication (which first appeared in 1666) of official announcements, service appointments, decorations, etc.

LONDON UNIVERSITY. L.U. originated with the foundation in 1826 of University Coll., to provide university education free from religious tests. In 1836 a charter set up an examining body with power to grant degrees. L.U. threw open all degrees to women in 1878, being the first British univ. to do so. It ceased to be a pure examining body in 1900, when it took over the existing colleges. It also includes 20 medical schools. Among the chief colleges are University, King's, the Imperial College of Science and Technology, the London School of Economics, the School of Oriental and African Studies, Queen Mary, Birkbeck, and the 3 colleges founded for women: Royal Holloway, Bedford, and Westfield. There are *c.* 46,500 internal and *c.* 29,700 external students. The univ. headquarters are in Bloomsbury.

LONG, Huey Pierce (1893-1935). American 'Share the Wealth' demagogue, gov. of Louisiana 1928-31, when his rule was marked by reforms side by side with corruption and semi-Fascist tendencies. Elected to the senate in 1931 he was celebrated for his filibusters. He was assassinated.

LONG BEACH. Coastal city of California, S of Los Angeles, USA. It is important both as an industrial centre and pleasure resort; Signal Hill oilfield, discovered in 1921, is within the city boundary. L.B. is subject to earthquakes. Pop. met. area Los Angeles-L.B. (1970) 6,970,733.

LONGCHAMP (lońshoń'). Pleasure resort and racecourse of Paris, France, in the Bois de Boulogne. It is on the site of a former nunnery founded in 1260, suppressed 1790.

LONGFELLOW, Henry Wadsworth (1807-82). American poet. B. in Portland, Maine, he was ed. at Bowdoin Coll., where he became prof. of modern languages (1829-35), and subsequently held a similar position at Harvard (1836-54). His first vol. of poems, *Voices in the Night*, appeared in 1839, and was followed by *Ballads and Other Poems* (1842), containing 'Excelsior' and 'The Wreck of the Hesperus'; *Evangeline* (1847); *The Golden Legend* (1851), based on the 12th cent. German work; *Hiawatha* (1855), a Red Indian epic; *The Courtship of Miles Standish* (1858); and *Tales of a Wayside Inn* (1863-74). His popularity in England is witnessed by the erection of a monument to him in Westminster Abbey.

LONGFORD, Frank (Francis) Aungier Pakenham, 7th earl of L. (1905-). Anglo-Irish Labour politician. Ed. at Eton and Oxford, he was brought up in High Tory Protestant circles but is a leading Catholic layman, worked in the Cons. Party Economic Research Dept. 1930-2, yet became a prominent member of the Labour Party (being personal assistant to Sir William Beveridge during the S.W.W.), was Min. of Civil Aviation 1948-51, Lord Privy Seal 1964-5, 1966-8 and Colonial Sec. 1965-6. He is a keen advocate of penal reform. He m. 1931 Elizabeth Harman (1906-) who, as 'Elizabeth Longford' pub. such historical studies as *Victoria R.I.* (1964), and their eldest dau. Lady Antonia Fraser (1932-) pub. *Mary Queen of Scots* (1969).

LONGFORD. Co. of Leinster prov., Rep. of Ireland, whose rivers are the Camlin and Inny; the Shannon marks its W boundary. There are several lakes. Area 1,044 sq.km (403 sq.m); pop. (1971) 28,250. The co. town is L., on the Camlin. Pop. (1971) 4,000.

LONGINUS (lonjī'nus), **Cassius** (*c.* AD 213-73). Greek philosopher and critic. B. probably in Syria, he taught in Athens for many years. While journeying in the East, he became the teacher and adviser of Zenobia of Palmyra. On his instigation she rebelled against Roman rule, and when she was captured L. was put to death. The critical treatise *On the Sublime* is usually attributed to him.

LONG ISLAND. Is. forming part of the State of New York, USA, separated from the mainland by Long Island Sound. There are many pleasure resorts, e.g. Jones Beach and Coney Island. In the W are Brooklyn and Queen's, bors. of Greater New York City. Area 4,463 sq.km (1,723 sq.m). Long Is. City, in Queen's, founded 1640 and a city in its own right 1870-98, is an industrial district.

LONGITUDE. *See* LATITUDE AND LONGITUDE.

LONG MARCH, The. The 10,000 km (6,000 m) trek undertaken by Mao Tse-tung and his troops from SE to NW China, under harassment from Chiang Kai-shek, from 1934 to 1935. It was the prelude to Mao's ascent to power. The **New Long March** is the plan to achieve world leadership for China in science and technology by 2000.

LONG PARLIAMENT. Name commonly applied to the parl. of 1640-60, which carried through the English Revolution. Its Royalist members withdrew in 1642, and the 'Presbyterian' right wing was excluded in 1648. The remaining members, known as the Rump, ruled England until they were expelled by Cromwell in 1653. The L.P. reassembled in 1659-60, and began the negotiations which led to the Restoration.

LONSDALE, Hugh Cecil Lowther, 5th earl of (1857-1944). British sportsman. He was an expert huntsman, steeplechaser, boxer, and yachtsman, and as president of the National Sporting Club laid down the rules of boxing and presented the 'L. belts'.

LONSDALE. Henry Cooper with three Lonsdale belts which he won. *Photo: Courtesy of Henry Cooper.*

LOO'FAH. Fruit of the herbaceous plant *Luffa cylindrica* in the gourd (q.v.) family. Its 'skeleton' is familiar in the bathroom.

LOOS, Anita (1893-1981). American author. B. in California, she scored her greatest success with the fictitious diary of a girl on the make, *Gentlemen Prefer Blondes* (1925).

LOOSESTRIFE. Plants of the Primulaceae family, e.g. the common L. (*Lysimachia vulgaris*) *c.* 1m (3ft) high on river banks in Britain with spikes of yellow flowers; wood L. or yellow pimpernel and creeping jenny: also the striking purple L. (*Lythrum salicaria*) in the family Lythraceae.

LOPE DE VEGA. *See* VEGA.

LÓPEZ (lō'pes), **Carlos Antonio** (1790-1862). Paraguayan statesman. He succeeded his uncle J. G. R. Francia as virtual dictator in 1840, and held supreme power until his death. He was succeeded by his son **Francisco Solano L.** (1827-70), who involved the country in a war with Brazil, Uruguay and Argentina during which five-sixths of the pop. perished. He was himself killed in battle.

LOP-NUR (lawp-nōōr'). Series of shallow lakes (formerly Lop-Nor) with shifting boundaries in the Taklimakan Shamo (desert) in Xinjiang Uygur, China. Marco Polo visited L.-N., then a single lake of considerable extent *c.* 1273. The area is used for atomic tests.

LOQUAT (lō'kwat). Evergreen tree of the Rosaceae family (*Eriobotrya japonica*) native to China and Japan and known also as the Japanese 'plum'. The golden fruit is of delicate sweet-sour taste.

LORCA, Federico Garcia (1899-1936). Spanish poet. B. at Fuentevaqueros, he followed his first *Libro de Poemas* (1921) by *Canciones* (1926) and *Romancero Gitano* (1927). He visited New York in 1930, but returned to Spain in 1931 to found *La Barraca*, a touring theatrical company. Among his plays are *El Maleficio de la Mariposa* (1920), *Bodas de Sangre* (1933), *Yerma*, *Doña Rosita la Soltera*, and *La Casa de Bernada*. His finest poem is his 'Lament' for the bullfighter Sánchez Mejias. He was shot by the Falangists.

LORD. The prefix L. is used informally as an alternative to the full title of a marquess, earl, or viscount, and is normally so used in speaking of a baron, and as a courtesy title before the forename and surname of the younger sons of dukes and marquesses. A bishop is formally addressed as the L. Bishop of A.

LORD-LIEUTENANT. The head of the magistracy of a county. This office, first instituted by Henry VIII, is usually held by a large landowner. Its duties included until 1871 responsibilities for the co. militia. The L.-L. appoints the co. magistrates.

LORD MAYOR. *See* MAYOR.

LORD'S. Headquarters of the Marylebone Cricket Club, regulating body of English cricket since 1788, and also the county ground of Middx. Thomas Lord (1757-1832) first opened the ground in Dorset Square in 1787 and in 1814 it was removed to its present site in St John's Wood.

LORDS, House of. *See* PARLIAMENT.

LORD'S SUPPER. *See* EUCHARIST.

LORELEI (-lī). A rock in the Rhine near St Goar, W Germany, which possesses a remarkable echo. According to a poem written by Brentano (q.v.) in 1802, a maiden who drowned herself because of an inconstant lover became a siren luring fishermen to destruction by her song, a story which developed into a legend used by several subsequent writers.

LORE'NZ, Konrad (1903-). Austrian ethnologist. Director of the Max Planck Institute for the Physiology of Behaviour in Bavaria 1961-73, he is known for his studies of animal behaviour. *King Solomon's Ring* (1952) and *On*

Aggression (1966). In 1973 he shared a Nobel prize with N. Tinbergen and Karl von Frisch (qq.v.).

LORE'TO. Place of pilgrimage in Ancona prov., Italy, containing the *Santa Casa*, or Holy House, of the Virgin, said to have been carried from Nazareth by angels in 1294, first to Dalmatia, and from there to L. Hence, Our Lady of L. is patron saint of aviators. Pop. (1970) 9,500.

LORIENT (lōryoṅ'). Seaport of W France, WNW of Vannes. It is a naval station with state dockyards and a varied trade is conducted via its separate commercial port. Pop. (1975) 68,655.

LORRAIN, Claude. *See* CLAUDE LORRAIN.

LORRAINE. *See* ALSACE-LORRAINE.

LORRAINE, Cross of. A red cross with 2 horizontal crosspieces, on a blue ground. It was the emblem carried by Joan of Arc, and was adopted by the Free French forces in 1940.

LORY. Group of Auralasian, honey-eating parrots (family Loriidae) which are brilliantly coloured.

LOS ALAMOS. Military township in New Mexico, USA, 40km (25m) NW of Santa Fé, where research and designing of the atom bomb were carried out (working on data provided by other research stations) 1943-5. It continued to be a centre of atomic and later of space research. Pop. (1970) 11,310.

LOS ANGELES (loss an-ja-les). City on the coast of S California, third largest in the USA. Founded in 1781, L.A. was then in Mexico; it was taken by a US naval force in 1846 and annexed 1850. Its full name is El Pueblo de Nuestra Señora La Reina de los Angeles de Porciuncula (The Village of Our Lady Queen of the Angels of Porciuncula). It is an important commercial port and naval base, and has the nation's largest fishing industry. Industries incl. aerospace equipment, electronics, electrical goods, film-making, rubber, chemicals, clothing, printing, food products, etc. Largest of many educational institutions is the Univ. of California. The climate is pleasant and there are many visitors to the Mt Wilson and Mt Palomar observatories, Hollywood Bowl concert arena, the Huntingdon Art Gallery and Library, Hollywood (q.v.) and Disneyland. Pop. (1972) 2,895,000; of met. area L.A.-Long Beach 9,700,000.

LOS ANGELES, Victoria de (1923-). Spanish soprano. In opera her roles incl. Manon and Madame Butterfly, and she is celebrated for her concert renderings of Spanish songs.

LŌ'SEY, Joseph (1909-). American stage and film director. After studying medicine, literature and theatre, he produced several short films and plays, incl. *Payment Deferred* (1931) and *Galileo* (1947) - both with C. Laughton, on Broadway. In 1951 he settled in England, where some of his notable films incl. *The Servant* and *Secret Ceremony*.

LOSSIEMOUTH. Fishing port and resort in Grampian region, Scotland, on the Moray Firth. Ramsay MacDonald was b. and buried at L. Pop. with Branderburgh (1971) 5,840.

LOT (loh). French river, rising in the Cévennes in Lozère dept, and flowing for *c.* 480km (300m). W to join the Garonne at Aiguillon. It gives its name to the depts of Lot and Lot-et-Garonne.

LOTHAIR I (795-855). Holy Roman Emperor. He was the son of Louis I, who in 817 associated him with himself in the govt of the Empire. After Louis's death in 840 the Empire was divided between L. and his brothers, L. taking N Italy and the Rhône and Rhine valleys.

LOTHAIR (825-69). King of Lotharingia. He inherited from his father, the emperor Lothair I, in 855 a district W of the Rhine, between the Jura Mts and the N Sea. This became known after him as Lotharingia, later corrupted into Lorraine.

LOTHIAN, The. A name formerly applied to the S Scotland cos. of Haddington, Edinburgh, and Linlithgow (E.L., Mid-L., and W.L.), also incl. Roxburghshire and Berwickshire. This area, part of the kingdom of Northumbria from 547, was annexed by the Scots in 1018. The name was revived in 1975 for the new region created from the cos. of East L.; the major part of Midlothian and West L.; and the city of Edinburgh, the admin HQ. Area 1,813 sq.km (700 sq.m); pop. (1979) 747,737.

LOTTERY. Arrangement in which persons buying tickets are eligible to win prizes in a draw. In England, both govt and private Ls. were held from the 17th cent. onwards, but cheating became so much of a scandal that an act of 1802 made illegal any L. not authorized by parliament; the last state L. was held in 1826. An act of 1934 permitted small Ls. or raffles at e.g. bazaars, and Ls. promoted for a society not connected with gaming, or among people working or living in the same premises; both types were subject to certain conditions, incl. the exclusion of money prizes. Later legislation allowed prizes of up to £1,000, still under stringent conditions. Premium Savings Bonds (*see* SAVING) were in the nature of a L., but large scale Ls. for local govt fund-raising purposes failed to be approved.

Ls. are illegal in the USA and any lottery ticket found in the post is destroyed. But many countries still conduct state Ls., e.g. Italy and Malta. The most successful of Ls. is undoubtedly the Irish Sweepstake, run under govt auspices in aid of the nursing services in the Rep. of Ireland on 3 races in the course of the year; 25 per cent of the receipts, after deduction of expenses, go to the Hospitals Trust Board, the remaining 75 per cent being distributed in prizes. Sale of tickets in the UK is illegal.

LOTUS. Genus of plants in the family Leguminosae, e.g. bird's foot trefoil (*L. corniculatus*); also the shrub *Zizyphus lotus* known to the ancient Greeks who used its fruit to make a type of bread and also a wine supposed to induce happy oblivion - hence L.-eaters; and the water-lilies *Nymphaea lotus*, frequent in Egyptian art, and *Nelumbo nucifera*, the sacred L. of the Hindus which (unlike the Egyptian) does not float but stands erect above the water.

LOUGHBOROUGH (luf'boro). English market town in Leics, 16km (10m) NW of Leicester. Industries incl. engineering, bell founding, and the making of electrical apparatus and hosiery. L. Coll. of Technology (residential) was founded in 1918, expanded in 1959, became in 1966 L. Univ. of Technology. Pop. (1971) 47,110.

LOUIS I (788-840). Holy Roman Emperor, called **the Pious.** He succeeded his father Charlemagne in 814, and counts as Louis I of France.

LOUIS. The name of 18 kings of France. The emperor Louis I (q.v.) counts as Louis I of France. **Louis V** (967-87), who reigned 986-7, was the last of the Carolingian dynasty. **Louis VII** (*c.* 1111-80), who reigned 1137-80, led the 2nd Crusade in 1147-9. **Louis VIII** (1187-1226) was invited to become king in place of John by the English barons, and unsuccessfully invaded England 1215-17. He

LOUIS XIV. The King and his heirs by Nicolas Largillière. The son, grandson and great grandson depicted all died before Louis, and yet another great-grandson succeeded as Louis XV. *Photo: Courtesy of the Trustees of the Wallace Collection*

succeeded to the French throne in 1223. **St Louis IX** (1214-70), who succeeded him, was the ideal medieval king. He led a crusade to Egypt in 1248-50, but was defeated and captured by the Saracens, spending 4 years in captivity. He d. at Tunis while leading another crusade. **Louis XI** (1423-83), who succeeded to the throne in 1461, broke the power of the great nobles headed by Charles the Bold, duke of Burgundy, by a combination of force and unscrupulous intrigue. **Louis XII** (1462-1515) was known as duke of Orléans until he succeeded his cousin Charles VIII in 1499. Throughout his reign he was engaged in Italian wars. **Louis XIII** (1601-43) succeeded his father Henry IV in 1610, and assumed the royal power in 1617. During 1624-42 the control of his policy was entirely in the hands of Richelieu (q.v.).

LOUIS XIV (1638-1715). King of France. He succeeded his father Louis XIII in 1643, but until 1661 France was ruled by Mazarin (q.v.). After his death L. never appointed another prime minister, but planned and supervised the execution of his own policy, which was summed up in his saying *L'État c'est moi* (I am the State). His ministers were drawn from the middle classes, the greatest of them being Colbert, whose work was undone by L.'s policy of military aggrandizement. Louis attempted in 1667-8 to annex the Spanish Netherlands, but was frustrated by an alliance of Holland, England, and Sweden. Having detached England from the alliance, in 1672 he invaded Holland. Led by William of Orange, the Dutch stood firm, and a European alliance was formed against L.; the Peace of Nijmegen (1678) nevertheless brought considerable territorial gains.

War was renewed 1688-97 between L. and the Grand Alliance, including England, formed by William of Orange. On land the French were everywhere victorious, but in 1692 L.'s fleet was almost destroyed at La Hogue. L.'s acceptance in 1700 of the Spanish throne for his grandson led to the War of the Spanish Succession (1701-13). The Peace of Utrecht ended French supremacy in Europe. In 1660 L. m. the Infanta Maria Theresa of Spain, but he was greatly influenced by his mistresses, including Louise de la Vallière, Mme de Montespan, and Mme de Maintenon, whom he m. after his wife's death in 1683.

LOUIS XV (1710-74). King of France. A great-grandson of Louis XIV, he was only 5 when he came to the throne, and until 1723 the duke of Orléans was regent. L. was indolent and frivolous, and left the government in the hands of his ministers, the duke of Bourbon and Cardinal Fleury. On Fleury's death in 1743 he attempted to rule alone, but he fell entirely under the domination of his mistresses, Mme de Pompadour and Mme du Barry. His foreign policy proved humiliating for France, Canada and India being lost.

LOUIS XVI (1754-93). King of France. He succeeded his grandfather Louis XV in 1774. He was dominated by his queen, Marie Antoinette, and the finances fell into such

LOUIS XV. The ineptitude and weakness of his government led surely to the Revolution in the reign of his successor: in Madame de Pompadour's famous words 'After us the Deluge'. A portrait by L. M. van Loo. *Photo: Courtesy of the Trustees of the Wallace Collection*

confusion that in 1789 the States General were summoned, and revolution began. L. remained personally popular until in 1791 he attempted to flee the country; thereafter republicanism grew, and in Aug. 1792 the Parisians stormed the Tuileries and made the royal family prisoners. Deposed in Sept., L. was tried for treason and guillotined.

LOUIS XVII (1785-95). Nominal king of France. The son of Louis XVI, he was imprisoned with his parents in 1792, and probably d. in prison.

LOUIS XVIII (1755-1824). King of France. The younger brother of Louis XVI, he was known before 1795 as the count of Provence. He fled from France in 1791, and assumed the title of king in 1795. He lived in exile until he obtained the throne in 1814. Driven out again during the 100 Days, he returned after Waterloo. He pursued a liberal and conciliatory policy, attempting to restrain the violence of the ultra-royalists, until the assassination of the heir to the throne in 1820 led to a royalist reaction.

LOUIS (loo'is), **Joe.** Professional name of American boxer Joseph Louis Barrow (1914-81). B. nr Lexington, Alabama, he was world heavyweight champion 1937-49: the power of his blows earned him the nickname 'the brown bomber'.

LOUISIANA. South-central state of the USA bordering the Gulf of Mexico. Much of L. is occupied by the delta of the Mississippi. Mineral products incl. petroleum, sulphur, natural gas, salt; industries incl. petroleum refining, food processing, lumbering, paper making; agricultural products incl. rice, cotton, sugar, and maize. The cap. is Baton Rouge, and the largest city, New Orleans. Area 125,675 sq.km (48,523 sq.m); pop. (1970) 3,643,180.

L. takes its name from the old French prov. of LOUISIANA, explored by La Salle and claimed for Louis XIV, in whose honour he named it, in 1682. The prov. extended from the British colonies in the E to the Spanish colonies on the W and from what is now Manitoba to the Gulf of Mexico. France lost to Britain the part of L. east of the Mississippi in 1763, and it became part of the USA in 1783; the part west of the Mississippi, 2,144,500 sq.km (828,000 sq.m) in extent, passed to Spain in 1762, but by a secret treaty of 1800 was restored to France. In 1803 Napoleon sold this area to the USA for £3,000,000; it was divided into the Territory of New Orleans, which became the state of L. in 1812, and the Territory of L., later to become the states of Arkansas, Missouri, Nebraska, Iowa, and S Dakota, and part of N Dakota, Minnesota, Kansas, Oklahoma, Colorado, and Wyoming.

LOUIS PHILIPPE (1773-1850). King of the French. The son of the duke of Orléans, he was known after 1785 as the duke of Chartres. He supported the French Revolution during its earlier stages, but fled the country in 1793, and until 1814 lived in exile. He identified himself with the Liberal opposition, and after the 1830 revolution became king. He relied for support on the rich bourgeoisie, and corruption discredited the régime. Overthrown in 1848, he escaped to England, where he d.

LOUIS PHILIPPE. Charles Philipon's famous caricature of Louis in transition from prince to pear.

LOUISVILLE. City of Kentucky, USA, on the Ohio, SW of Cincinnati. Industries incl. electrical goods, agricultural machinery, motor vehicles, tobacco and baseball bats. The Kentucky Fair and Exposition Center is one of the largest in the USA, and the Kentucky Derby (1875) is run on Churchill Downs. There is a major scheme for its development as a river port, of which the first stage will be completed in 1978. Pop. met. area (1974) 849,000.

LOURDES (loord). Place of pilgrimage in Hautes-Pyrénées dept, SW France. Pop. (1975) 18,100. *See* BERNADETTE.

LOURENÇO MARQUES (lōrañ'so mahr'kes). *See* MAPUTO.

LOUTH (lowth). Market town in Lincs, England, 24km (15m) S of Grimsby. Tennyson attended the 16th cent. school (rebuilt). Pop. (1973) 12,000.

LOUTH. Maritime co. of Leinster prov., Rep. of Ireland. For the most part undulating lowland, the co. is fertile. The chief industries are agriculture, linen manufacture and fishing. The co. town is Dundalk. Area 821 sq.km (317 sq.m); pop. (1971) 74,950.

LOUVAIN (loovañ'). Town in Brabant, Belgium, 24km (15m) NE of Brussels: the Flemish form is Leuven. Founded in 891, it was a great clothmaking centre in the Middle Ages, and has a fine 15th cent. town hall, and a famous univ. (1426). There are brewing, leather and chemical industries. Pop. (1978) 87,125.

LOUVRE (loovr). Art galley in Paris, containing one of the finest collections of paintings, sculptures, and art objects in the world; formerly a palace of French kings. Built on the site of a 13th cent. château, the L. is first mentioned in records of 1204. Napoleon converted the L. into a national art gallery. Two world-famous exhibits are the Venus de Milo and Leonardo da Vinci's 'Mona Lisa'.

LOVAT, Simon Fraser, 12th baron L. (*c.* 1667-1747). Scottish Jacobite. Throughout a political career lasting 50 years he constantly intrigued with both Jacobites and Whigs, and was beheaded for supporting the 1745 rebellion.

LOVECRAFT, Howard Phillips (1890-1937). American author of horror stories. The only son of a travelling salesman who d. when L. was 8, he grew up as a recluse and produced eerie fiction such as *The Shuttered Room,* which became a cult in the 1970s.

LOVELACE (luv'lās), **Richard** (1618-58). English poet. Owing to his responsibility for the Kentish Petition pleading for the re-establishment of the King's rule in 1642, he was committed to the Westminster gatehouse, where he wrote 'To Althea from Prison' etc. During a second imprisonment in 1648 he revised his *Lucasta: Epodes, Odes, Sonnets, Songs, etc.* (1649). He d. in poverty.

LOVELL, Sir Bernard (1913-). British astronomer. During the S.W.W. he worked at the Telecommunications Research establishment (1939-45), and in 1951 became prof. of radio astronomy at the Univ. of Manchester and director of Jodrell Bank Experimental Station (now Nuffield Radio Astronomy Laboratories). His books incl. *Radio Astronomy* (1951) and *The Exploration of Outer Space* (1961). He was knighted in 1961.

LOVER, Samuel (1797-1868). Irish author. B. in Dublin, he became a miniature painter, and in 1835 settled in London where he conquered society by his singing of his own compositions, which he pub. in *Songs and Ballads* (1839), etc. He is also remembered for his humorous novels, *Rory O'More* (1837) and *Handy Andy* (1842).

LOW, Sir David (1891-1963). New Zealand cartoonist. B. in Dunedin, he was noted for his independence and radical views, and the bold, simple lines of his drawings and the gallery of characters he evolved, e.g. Colonel Blimp, Hit and Muss, and the TUC horse, became world-famous.

LOW COUNTRIES. European region comprising the Netherlands and Belgium, sometimes extended to incl. Luxembourg.

LOWELL (lō'-el), **Amy** (1874-1925). American poet. B. in Massachusetts, in 1913 she became attached to the Imagist group, succeeding Ezra Pound in its leadership. A distinguished experimenter in free verse, she pub. *Sword Blades and Poppy Seeds* (1914), and *What's o'Clock?* (1925); and *Tendencies in Modern American Poetry* (1917).

LOWELL, James Russell (1819-91). American author. B. in Massachusetts he was admitted to the Bar 1840, and ed. *The National Anti-Slavery Standard* (1848-52). In 1848 he estab. his reputation with the satirical *Fable for Critics, The Vision of Sir Launfal,* and the first series of *Biglow Papers.* He succeeded Longfellow as prof. of modern languages at Harvard (1855-76), and was ambassador to Spain (1877-80), and to England (1880-5). Among his later works are the essays *My Study Windows* (1871).

LOWELL, Percival (1855-1916). American astronomer. In 1894 he founded the L. observatory at Flagstaff, Arizona.

LOWELL, Robert (1917-77). American poet. A Bostonian, he broke the usual New England links to become a Roman Catholic in 1940 and a conscientious objector in the S.W.W. His vols. incl. *Land of Unlikeness* (1944), *Lord Weary's Castle* (1946), and *Notebook* (1970).

LOWELL. City of Massachusetts, USA, at the junction of the Merrimack and Concord rivers. The textile industry declined from the 1920s, but the old mills have been converted to new uses in the 1970s, and the area became a 'national park' in 1978, as a birthplace of the US industrial revolution. Pop. (1970) 94,250.

LOWER CALIFORNIA. *See* BAJA CALIFORNIA.

LOWER SAXONY. Land of NW Germany, formed in 1946 from Hanover, Oldenburg, Brunswick, and Schaumburg-Lippe. Industries incl. textiles, electrical and mechanical engineering. Hanover is the cap. Area 47,475 sq.km (18,300 sq.m); pop. (1978) 7,224,200.

LOWESTOFT. Seaport and resort in Suffolk, England, 190km (118m) NE of London on Oulton Broad and the North Sea. Benjamin Britten was b. here. Pop. (1972) 52,270.

L. Ness is the point farthest E in England. In a naval battle fought off L. in 1665 the English under James, duke of York (afterwards James II), drove off the Dutch.

LOWRY, Laurence Stephen (1887-1976). British artist. B. in Manchester, he painted the drab industrial Lancashire of the F.W.W. period, peopled with spindly human figures, simple and moving. He was unrecognized until his mid-fifties.

LOYALISTS or **Tories.** The colonists who opposed the break with Britain during the American War of Independence. Altogether they numbered about a third of the pop. After the war many of them removed to Canada, where they became known as 'United Empire Ls.'.

LOY'ŌLA, Ignatius de (Inigo Lopez de Ricalde) (1491-1556). Founder of the Society of Jesus, b. at the castle of Loyola in Guipuzcoa prov., Spain. He became a soldier and was wounded at Pampeluna. While he was recovering he read the Bible. The effect on him was so profound that he abandoned the army and retired to a mountain cave in order to meditate. He went on a pilgrimage to

Jerusalem (1523), and later studied at Salamanca and Paris. He founded the Society of Jesus in 1534, and in 1541 became its first general. His *Spiritual Exercises* was pub. in 1548.

LOZÈRE (lōzār'). Section of the Cévennes Mts., S France. It rises in Finiels to 1,702 m (5,584 ft), and gives its name to a dept.

LP (liquefied petroleum) GAS, a by-product of oil refining, provides gas to 250 times its liquid volume. Butane, for domestic purposes, is increasingly used in remote areas, and propane has many specialized industrial uses, e.g. as an alternative to acetylene in metal cutting.

LSD. Hallucinogen (*ly*sergic acid *d*iethylamide), one of the most powerful mind-changing drugs known, a derivative of ergot (q.v.). Colourless, odourless, and easily synthesized, it is non-addictive, but its effects are unpredictable and may be disastrous.

LUANDA (loo-an'da), (São Paulo de). Port and cap. of Angola. Founded in 1575, it has cotton, sugar, tobacco, timber and paper industries, and exports coffee, sugar, palm oil and diamonds. Pop. (1970) 400,000.

LUA'NG PRABA'NG. Great religious centre in Laos, on the Upper Mekong at the head of river navigation. It was the cap. of the kingdom of L.P., incorporated in Laos in 1946, and the royal cap. of Laos 1946-75. Pop. (1973) 44,250.

LÜBECK. Seaport of Schleswig-Holstein, W Germany, on the Baltic Sea, 60km (37m) NE of Hamburg, founded in 1143. Its 5 main churches are fine Gothic examples, and its cathedral dates from 1173. Once head of the powerful Hanseatic League, it later lost much of its trade to Hamburg and Bremen, but improved canal and port facilities helped it to retain its position as a centre of Baltic trade. The name L. is of Wendish origin, and means lovely one. L. was a free state of both the Empire and the Weimar Rep. Pop. (1978) 227,200.

LUBITSCH (loo'bich), **Ernst** (1892-1947). German-American actor and film director. In the USA from 1922, he directed comedies with stylish touch, e.g. *Ninotchka* with Garbo.

LUBLIN (loob'lin). City in Poland, on the Bystrzyca r., 150km (95m) SE of Warsaw. A trading centre from the 10th cent., it has an ancient citadel, 16th cent. cathedral, and a univ. founded in 1918. There are textile, engineering, aircraft and electrical industries. A council of workers and peasants proclaimed Poland's independence at L. in 1918; and a Russian-sponsored committee of nat. liberation, which proclaimed itself the prov. govt of Poland at L. on 31 Dec. 1944, was recognized by Russia 5 days later. Pop. (1978) 292,000.

LUBRICANTS. Substances insinuated between moving surfaces to reduce friction. A solid L. is graphite (plumbago), either flaked or emulsified (colloidal) in water (aquadag) or oil (oildag). Semi-solid and liquid L. are more important, consisting of animal, vegetable, and mineral oils. The L. most used are recovered from petroleum distillation.

Extensive research has been carried out on chemical additives to reduce corrosive wear, prevent the accumulation of 'cold sludge' (often the result of stop-start driving in city traffic jams), keep pace with the higher working temperatures of aviation gas turbines, and provide radiation-resistant greases for nuclear power plants.

LUBUMBA'SHI. Town in Zaïre, formerly Elisabethville, 40km (25m) from the Zambian border. The cap. of Shaba (formerly Katanga) region, it is the centre of a great copper and uranium-mining area. Pop. (1974) 401,600.

LU'CAN or **Marcus Annaeus Lucanus** (AD 39-65). Latin poet. B. at Cordova, he was a nephew of the philosopher Seneca, and became a favourite of Nero's, until that emperor's jealousy of his poetic powers ended their friendship. He then joined in a republican conspiracy, and on its failure committed suicide. His unfinished epic *Pharsalia* deals with the civil wars between Caesar and Pompey.

LUCAS VAN LEYDEN (līd'en) (*c.* 1494-1533). Dutch artist. B. at Leiden, he executed his first engravings when a boy, and was later influenced by Dürer, whom he met at Antwerp. His principal paintings incl. 'The Chess Players' (Berlin) and 'Virgin and Child' (Munich).

LUCCA (look'kah). City of pre-Roman origin, in Tuscany, Italy. It estab. itself as an independent rep. in 1160, but was finally absorbed in Tuscany in 1847. The city has many fine churches, with richly decorated exteriors, and its cathedral was begun in the 12th cent. Pop. (1971) 90,400.

LUCE, Henry Robinson. *See* BOOTHE, CLARE.

LUCERNE. *See* ALFALFA.

LUCERNE (lūsern'). (1) Cap. and tourist centre of L. canton, Switzerland, standing on the Reuss, where it flows out of Lake L. Growing up round the Benedictine monastery, estab. *c.* 750, it owes its prosperity to its position on the St Gotthard road and railway. There is a 17th cent. cathedral. Pop. (1971) 70,200.

(2) Lake in central Switzerland, of great scenic beauty. Most famous of the surrounding mts are the Pilatus and Rigi. It is 39km (24m) long with an area of 114 sq.km (44 sq.m).

LUCIAN (loo'shian) (*c.* 125-*c.* 190). Greek writer. B. at Samosata in Syria, for a time he was an advocate at Antioch, but later travelled before settling in Athens *c.* 165. He d. in Egypt, where he occupied an official post. L. is chiefly remembered for his satirical dialogues, in which he pours scorn on all religions.

LUCKNOW. Cap. city of Uttar Pradesh, Rep. of India, once cap. of the nawabs of Oudh. It lies on the Gumti, NE of Kanpur. When the Indian Mutiny of 1857 broke out, the residency at L., already fortified and provided with stores by Sir Henry Lawrence, was besieged from 2 July (on which day Lawrence was wounded by a shell, dying 2 days later) until its relief by Sir Colin Campbell on 16 Nov. There is a univ. (1921), engineering, chemical and textile industries, and L. is famed for its handicrafts in leather, embroidery, gold, silks and shawls. Pop. (1971) 826,250.

LUCRETIA (lūkrē'shia). A Roman matron, the wife of Collatinus, said to have committed suicide after being ravished by Sextus, son of Tarquinius Superbus. According to tradition, this incident led to the dethronement of Tarquinius and the establishment of the Roman rep. in 509 BC.

LUCRETIUS or **Titus Lucretius Carus** (99-55 BC). Roman poet and Epicurean philosopher. He is remembered for his splendidly sombre didactic poem *De Rerum Natura*, expounding his materialistic philosophy based on the notion that the whole universe is the result of combinations of atoms.

LŪCU'LLUS, Lucius Licinius (*c.* 110-56 BC). Roman general. As commander against Mithridates of Pontus 74-66 he showed himself one of Rome's ablest generals and administrators, until superseded by Pompey. He then retired from politics. Enormous wealth enabled him to indulge in well-bred luxury, and Lucullan feasts were famous.

LÜDA (loodah'). Port (formerly Lü-ta) in Liaoning prov., China, on Liaodong Peninsula facing the Yellow Sea. It comprises the naval base of Lüshun (formerly Port Arthur) and the commercial port of Dalien (formerly Talien/Dairen). These were both leased to Russia in 1898, but were ceded by the latter to Japan after the Russo-Japanese War, Lushun only surrendering to the Japanese after a lengthy siege June 1904-Jan. 1905. After the S.W.W. Lüshun was occupied by Russian airborne troops, and Dalien was made a free port with half the port installations leased to Russia. Lüshun was returned to China in 1955, and deteriorating relations between the two countries ended the sharing of facilities at Dalien. Lüda is icefree all the year round. Industries incl. engineering, chemicals, textiles, oil refining, shipbuilding, and food processing. Pop. (1977) 4,200,000.

LUDDITES (lud'īts). Name given to those taking part in the machine-wrecking riots of 1811-16. Their main organizer, possibly an imaginary person, was referred to as General Ludd. The movement, which began in Notts and spread to Lancs, Cheshire, and Yorks, was primarily a revolt against the unemployment caused by the introduction of the new machines. Many Ls. were hanged or transported.

LUDENDORFF (lood'en-), **Erich** (1865-1937). German general. B. in Prussian Poland, he entered the army in 1883, and joined the general staff in 1894. As Chief of Staff to Hindenburg on the eastern front during the F.W.W. he was largely responsible for the German victory at Tannenberg in 1914. After Hindenburg's appointment as Chief of General Staff in 1916, and L.'s as Quartermaster-General, the two together largely decided German policy. After the war L. organized the Kapp putsch of 1920, took part in the Nazi rising at Munich in 1923, and sat in the Reichstag as a Nazi.

LÜDERITZ. Town and port on L. Bay, SW Africa, named after Adolf Lüderitz of Bremen, who settled here in 1883 and was drowned off the coast 3 years later. L. developed through the discovery of diamonds nearby; a fish-canning industry was started later. On the coast, 19km (12m) S of L., Diaz placed a cross in 1488 on his return from rounding the Cape of Good Hope. Pop. (1970) 3,450.

LUDLOW (lud'lō). Market town in Salop, on the Teme, 42km (26m) S of Shrewsbury. It was at Ludlow Castle that Milton's masque *Comus* was presented in 1634. Pop. (1971) 7,000.

LUDWIG (lood'vig). Name of 3 kings of Bavaria. **Ludwig I** (1786-1868) succeeded his father Maximilian Joseph I in 1825. His patronage of learning and the arts made Munich an international centre of culture. Although a liberal ruler, his association with the dancer Lola Montez destroyed his popularity and in 1848 he was compelled to abdicate. **Ludwig II** (1845-86) succeeded his father Maximilian II in 1864. He supported Austria during the Austro-Prussian War of 1866, but brought Bavaria into the Franco-Prussian War as Prussia's ally, and in 1871 offered the German crown to the king of Prussia. He became the patron of Wagner and built the Bayreuth theatre for him. Declared insane in 1886, he drowned himself soon after. **Ludwig III** (1845-1921) was proclaimed king in 1913, and abdicated in 1918.

LUDWIGSHAFEN. Town in Rhineland Palatinate, W Germany, on the Rhine opposite Mannheim. Industries incl. chemicals, dyes, fertilizers, plastics, textiles, etc. Pop (1978) 163,670.

LUFTWAFFE. The German air force reorganized in 1933 under Goering. The anti-aircraft defences and forces concerned with launching the V1 and V2 robots were also later included. The strength of the L. was over-estimated in the immediate pre-war and the wartime years. *See* BRITAIN, BATTLE OF. The 3 factors in the decline of the L. were the switch from airfield to city bombing of 1940, the fighter resistance and bomber retaliation of the RAF, and the increased British production figures.

LUGANO (loogah'nō). Lake, partly in Switzerland, partly in Italy, lying between Lakes Maggiore and Como; area 49 sq.km (19 sq.m). The town of L. stands on the lake in the Ticino canton, Switzerland, 101km (39m) NW of Milan. Both the town and lake are renowned for their beauty. Pop. (1970) 21,900.

LUGANSK. *See* VOROSHILOVGRAD.

LUGARD, Frederick John Dealtry, 1st baron (1858-1945). British colonial administrator. He served in the army 1878-89, and then entered the service of the British E Africa Co., for whom he took possession of Uganda in 1890. He later became High Commissioner for N Nigeria (1900-7); Gov. of Hong Kong (1907-12); and Gov.-Gen. of Nigeria (1914-19). He received a barony in 1928. His *Dual Mandate* (1922) was an influential plea for development through the existing African system of chieftainship, rather than western democracy.

LUGWORM. Genus (*Arenicola*) of marine worms (also known as lobworms) common between tide-marks where their whereabouts are known by their castings. They are used by anglers as bait, but are useful - as are earthworms on land - for their cleansing and powdering of the sand, of which they may annually bring to the surface *c.* 1,900 tons per acre.

LU HSÜN. Pseudonym of the Chinese short-story writer Chon Shu-jêu (1881-1936). Grandson of a blameless official at the Manchu court who was executed by the empress dowager, he knew poverty in his youth. In 1926 he fled the long arm of the Peking govt to become dean of the Coll. of Arts at Sun Yat Sen Univ. His 3 vols. of stories, *Call to Arms, Wandering*, and *Old Tales Retold*, reveal the influence of Gogol. His supreme mastery of the form is recognized by the Communist régime and he is widely read.

LUIK. Flemish name of LIÉGE.

LUKE, St. Traditionally the compiler of the third Gospel and of the Acts of the Apostles. He appears to have been a physician and to have accompanied Paul after the ascension of Christ. Of his life little is known, although it is surmised that he was a non-Jewish native of Antioch and that he d. in Bithynia at the age of 74.

LULEÅ (lool'ā-aw). Seaport in Sweden, on the Gulf of Bothnia at the mouth of the r. L. It ships iron ore and timber during the summer when it is free of ice. Pop. (1978) 67,400.

LULLY (lülē), **Jean Baptiste** (1639-87). Italian-born French composer, *né* Giovanni Battista Lulli, who became a French citizen in 1661. B. in Florence, he went to France, and in 1653 became court composer to Louis

LU HSÜN. One of the most popular of modern Chinese writers.

XIV. He supplied music for Molière's plays, and also composed the first notable French opera *Les Fêtes de l'Amour et de Bacchus.*

LUMBĀ'GO. Aching and pain in the lower back. It may be due to spasm of the muscles protecting inflamed spinal joints, or the muscles may be made painful by rheumatism, chill, or the poison of a diseased appendix or other abdominal organ. One of the soft discs which form cushions between the vertebrae may be nipped by the bones.

LUMBINI (loombēn'ē). Birthplace of Buddha in the foothills of the Himalayas near the Nepalese-Indian frontier. A Sacred Garden and shrine was estab. 1970 by the Nepalese govt.

LUMIÈRE (lümyār'), **Auguste** (1862-1954) and **Louis** (1864-1948). French cinema pioneers and brothers. With their father they developed autochrome plates, the stereoscope, colour photography, and in 1894-5 improved the cinematograph sufficiently to herald their invention of the cinema; the production and exhibition of films for public entertainment.

LUMINOUS PAINT. A preparation containing a mixture of pigment, oil, and a phosphorescent sulphide, usually of calcium or barium. After exposure to light it appears luminous in the dark. The L.P. used on watch faces is radioactive and does not require exposure to light.

LUMUMBA (lōōmōōm'bah), **Patrice** (1926-61). Congolese statesman. Imprisoned by the Belgians, but released in time to attend the conference giving the Congo (now Zaïre) independence, he led the Nat. Congolese Movement to victory in the subsequent gen. election and became PM in 1960. He was deposed in a coup d'état, and murdered by Congolese rivals while in custody in Katanga. *See also* INTERNATIONAL.

LUNARDI (loonarhr'dē), **Vincenzo** (1759-1806). Italian balloonist. He came to London as sec. to the Neapolitan ambassador, and made the first balloon flight in England from Moorfields in 1784.

LUND (loond). City in Sweden, 16km (10m) NE of Malmö. It has an 11th cent. Romanesque cathedral, and a univ. founded in 1666. The treaty of L. was signed in 1676 after Charles XI had defeated the Danes. Pop. (1978) 76,970.

LUNDY. Rocky island at the entrance to the Bristol Channel, 19km (12m) NW of Hartland Point, Devon, England. Formerly noted as a stronghold of privateers and pirates, L. also has prehistoric remains and the ruins of Marisco castle (11th-14th cent.). Area 419 ha. (1,047 acres). Pop. (1975) 40.

LÜNEBURG. Town of Lower Saxony, W Germany, 48km (30m) SE of Hamburg. Formerly prominent in the Hanseatic League, it is an industrial centre making ironware, chemicals, etc., and gypsum and lime are mined. On L. Heath, S of the town, all German forces in the Netherlands, NW Germany, Schleswig-Holstein, and Denmark (more than a million men) surrendered to Field Marshal Montgomery on 4 May 1945. Pop. (1972) 60,900.

LUNGFISH. Living 'fossils', 3 genera of the order Dipnoi, related to the coelacanth, found in Africa, S America and Australia. In dry conditions they are able to breathe air with lungs, which they possess in addition to gills.

LUNGFISH. Thought to be extinct in Queensland until a specimen was found in 1870, the species *(Epiceratodus forsteri)* is now strictly protected. They grow to about 2 m (6ft), but this specimen is only about 50 years old. *Photo: Courtesy of the Australian Information Service.*

LUNGS. The organs of respiration. They are 2, and occupy the thorax, the upper part of the trunk. They fit exactly into this conical space, but do not meet in the middle. The heart is placed between them. Their function is to remove the carbon dioxide from the blood and replace it with oxygen. At every beat the heart pumps blood into their veins, which divide into very small branches, where the blood is brought into contact with the air in the air cells at the ends of the smallest divisions of the air tubes (bronchi). The lung tissue, consisting of multitudes of air cells and blood vessels, is very light and spongy. Air is drawn into the Ls. through the wind-pipe and the bronchi by the expansion of the ribs and the contraction of the diaphragm; it is pressed out of the Ls. when the ribs contract and the diaphragm relaxes. The Ls. expand with the thorax because there is normally no air space (*see* PNEUMOTHORAX) between the 2 surfaces. These are formed by the pleura, a smooth membrane lubricated by serous fluid.

The principal diseases of the Ls. are tuberculosis, pneumonia, bronchitis, and cancer (qq.v.).

LUNT, Alfred (1893-1977). American actor. B. in Wisconsin, he went straight from school into the theatre, and in 1922 m. Lynn Fontanne (1887–1983), with whom he subsequently co-starrred in more than 30 brilliant successes incl. *Design for Living* (1933), *There Shall Be No Night* (1940–1) and *The Visit* (1960).

LŪPERCĀ'LIA. A Roman festival celebrated on 15 Feb. Goats and a dog were sacrificed, and the priests ran round the city carrying goatskin thongs, a blow from which was believed to cure sterility in women. The ritual probably combined fertility magic with charms conveying protection against wolves.

LUPIN. Plants of the genus *Lupinus*, comprising about 200 species. They are native to Mediterranean regions and parts of N and S America, and have been naturalized in Britain. The spikes of pea-like flowers may be white, yellow, blue or pink. *L. albus* is cultivated in some places for cattle fodder, and for green manuring. The seeds contain toxic chemicals, which hinder their widespread use as human food, but non-toxic varieties are being bred.

LŪ'PUS Tuberculosis of the skin (L. vulgaris). The organism produces ulcers which spread and eat away the underlying tissues. Treatment is primarily with standard antituberculous drugs, such as streptomycin, but ultraviolet light may also be used. Lupus erythematosus is a chronic inflammation of the skin of the face, with red patches usually on the cheeks and across the nose, with or without scales.

LURÇAT (lürsa'), **Jean** (1892-1966). French artist who revived the traditions of tapestry design, e.g. Le Chant du Monde.

LURGAN. *See* CRAIGAVON.

LURISTAN (looristahn'). Mountainous district in SW Iran, inhabited by Lur tribes (est. at 500,000) who live by their sheep and cattle. Excavation in the area has revealed a remarkable culture of the 8-7th cents. BC with remarkable bronzes decorated with animal forms: its origins are uncertain.

LUSAKA (loosah'ka). Cap. of Zambia from 1964 (of N Rhodesia 1935-64), 370km (230m) NE of Livingstone. A thriving commercial and agricultural centre, it has flour mills, tobacco factories, vehicle assembly, plastics and printing works, and the Univ. of Zambia was estab. here in 1966. Linked by road and rail with Dar-es-Salaam via Zaïre, and also with Benguela in Angola, L. also has an internat. airport. At Kafue 80km (50m) to the S., there is a vast hydroelectric and irrigation project, and textile, fertilizer and steel industries. The L. Commonwealth Conference (1979) reached accords on the Rhodesia-Zimbawe question, which led to the independence of Zimbabwe. Pop. (1974) 400,000.

LÜSHUN-DALIEN. *See* LÜDA.

LUSITĀ'NIA. Cunard liner, built in 1906, and sunk by a German submarine on 7 May 1915. About 1,200 lives were lost. This crime strengthened anti-German feeling in the USA.

LÜ-TA. *See* LÜDA.

LUTE. Name given to a family of stringed musical instruments which was very popular in the 14-18th cents., and includes the mandore, theorbo, and chittarone. Ls. are pear-shaped and the strings are plucked with the fingers: the 20th cent. has seen a revival.

LUTHER (lo͞oth'er), **Martin** (1483-1546). German reformer, usually regarded as the founder of Protestantism. B. at Eisleben, the son of a miner, he studied at the univ. of Erfurt, spent 3 years as a monk in the Augustinian convent there, and in 1507 was ordained priest. Shortly afterwards he attracted attention as a teacher and preacher in the univ. of Wittenberg; and in 1517, after returning from a visit to Rome, he attained nationwide celebrity for his denunciation of the Dominican monk Tetzel, who was one of those sent out by the Pope to sell 'indulgences' as a means of raising funds for the rebuilding of St Peter's at Rome. On 31 Oct. 1517, he nailed on the church door at Wittenberg a statement of 95 theses on indulgences, and in the next year he was summoned to Rome to defend his action. His reply was to attack the papal system even more strongly, and in 1520 he publicly burnt in Wittenberg the papal bull that had been launched against him. Charles V summoned him to the Imperial Diet at Worms in 1521, where he refused to retract anything. On his way home he was taken into 'protective custody' by the elector of Saxony in the castle of the Wartburg. Later he became estranged from Erasmus, and engaged in violent controversies with political and religious opponents. In 1525 he m. Catherina von Bora (1499-1552), an ex-nun. After the drawing up of the Augsburg Confession in 1530, he gradually retired from the Protestant leadership. His literary output was very great. His *Table Talk*, letters, sermons, and commentaries are still read, and his hymns sung, and his translation of the Scriptures into German may be said to mark the emergence of German as a modern tongue.

LUTHERANISM. That form of Protestantism that is derived from the life and teaching of Martin Luther (q.v.); it is sometimes called Evangelical to distinguish it from the other main branch of continental Protestantism, the Reformed. It is the principal form of Protestantism in Germany, and is the national faith of Denmark, Norway, Sweden, Finland, and Iceland. The organization may be episcopal (Germany, Sweden) or synodal (Holland and USA): the Lutheran World Federation has its HQ in Geneva. The most generally accepted statement of Lutheranism is that of the Augsburg Confession (1530) but Luther's Shorter Catechism also carries great weight. L. is also very strong in the Middle West of USA where several churches were originally founded by German and Scandinavian immigrants. It is the largest Protestant body, incl. some 80 million persons, of whom 40 million are in Germany, 19 million in Scandinavia, 8½ million in USA and Canada and most of the remainder in central Europe.

LUTHULI (lo͞oto͞o'li), **Albert** (1899-1967). S African Black leader. A Zulu tribal chief, he became pres. of the African National Congress in 1952, and preached non-violence and multi-racialism. This prompted the formation of the rival militant Pan-Africanist Congress in 1958. Arrested in 1956, L. was never actually tried for treason, although he suffered certain restrictions from 1959. He was under suspended sentence for burning his pass when awarded the Nobel peace prize for 1960.

LUTHER. Luther preaching, as illustrated in a manuscript edition of his prayers. *Photo: Mansell Collection*

LUTINE. British bullion vessel lost off Holland 1799. Its bell, salvaged 1859, is at Lloyd's (q.v.). It is sounded once when a ship is missing and twice for good news.

LUTON (loo'ton). Town in Beds, England, 53km (33m) SW of Cambridge. Besides the traditional manufacture of hats, it has car, chemical, electrical goods, and ballbearing industries. The airport is a secondary one for London. Luton Hoo, a fine Robert Adam mansion, was built in 1762. Pop. (1974) 164,000.

LUTYENS, Sir Edwin Landseer (1869-1944). British architect, whose works incl. country houses, the Whitehall Cenotaph, the govt buildings of New Delhi, and the British Embassy, Washington. Knighted 1918, he was PRA 1938–44. His dau. **Elisabeth L.** (1906–83), who m. Edward Clark (d.1962) in 1942, was a composer.

LÜTZEN. Town in E Germany, to the SW of Leipzig, famous for the victory of 1632 of Gustavus Adolphus (q.v.), king of Sweden, over Wallenstein; Gustavus was killed in the battle. Here also Napoleon overcame the Russians and Prussians in 1813.

LUXEMBOURG. Independent grand-duchy of Europe, situated between France, Germany, and Belgium. Most of the rivers flow into the Moselle which forms part of the eastern border of L. The chief crops are cereals and potatoes, and there are important chemical works, and iron and steel industries based on rich deposits of ore at Esch-Alzette, although the last are declining. Banking is growing by leaps and bounds. The cap. is called L. (q.v.).

L. is a constitutional monarchy. Grand Duke Jean (1921-) succeeded to the throne in 1964 on the abdication of his mother Grand Duchess Charlotte. The Chamber of Deputies is elected for 5 years, and the govt is headed by a Min. of State. There is also a Council of State nominated by the Grand Duke. L. is a member of the Customs Union Benelux (q.v.). Area, 2,586 sq.km (999 sq.m); pop. (1977) 360,200, mainly of Low German stock with a language (Letzburgesch) based on old Teutonic roots, but the official language is French. In addition there are *c.* 90,000 foreign workers. The majority are R. Catholic. M.U.: Luxembourg franc.

LUXEMBOURG. Cap. of the grand-duchy of L. on the r. Alzette. Notable are the 16th cent. Grand Ducal Palace, baroque 16th cent. cathedral, the European Court of Justice, and the European Parliament buildings, where sessions are held alternately with Strasbourg, though by 1981 Strasbourg was favoured. Pop. (1979) 79,300.

LUXEMBOURG, Palais du. Palace in Paris, France, in which the Senate sits. Built 1615 for Marie de' Medici by Salomon de Brosse, it was later enlarged: Watteau used the gardens in his backgrounds.

LUXEMBOURG ACCORD. Political agreement (1966) demanded by the French, that a majority decision of the Council of Ministers of the European Community may be vetoed by a member state if national interests are at stake.

LUXEMBURG (looks'emboorg), **Rosa** (1870-1919). German Communist. B. in Poland, she settled in Germany *c.* 1895, and acquired German nationality by marriage. During the F.W.W. she co-operated with Liebknecht in anti-war propaganda and in founding the Spartacus League. She was imprisoned and wrote a series of prison letters. Released in Nov. 1918, she was murdered together with Liebknecht.

LU'XOR. Town in Upper Egypt, more correctly El-Aksur (The Castles), on the E bank of the Nile, S of Cairo. A tourist centre, with hotels, bazaars, fine parks and an internat. airport, L. and Karnak (q.v.) are on the site of Thebes. The Temple of Luxor was built by Amenhotep III, and part of the decoration was carried out by Tutankhamun, whose tomb is among those in the Valley of the Kings on the other side of the Nile. Pop. (1970) 20,000.

LUZERN. German form of LUCERNE.

LUZON (loozon'). The largest and most northerly island of the Philippine Republic. It is mountainous, with a volcanic peak, Mayon 2,462 m (8,077 ft). There are many rivers and lakes. Spanish settlers arrived in L. in the 16th cent. and the island belonged to Spain until it was ceded to the USA in 1898. Manila, with its suburb Quezon City, cap. of the republic, is on L., which was the scene of fierce fighting in 1942 and 1945 during the S.W.W.: *see* BATAAN and CORREGIDOR. Gold is produced and there is uranium at Larap in southern L. The USA has an air base (Clark Field) used as a logistical base in the Vietnam War, and also a naval base (Subic Bay), for which agreement was renewed in 1979. Area 108,172 sq.km (41,765 sq.m). Pop. (1970) 12,836,000.

LVOV (lvof). City in the Ukrainian SSR, cap. of L. region. Founded in the 13th cent. by a Galician prince (the name means city of Leo or Lev), its German name is Lemberg. It was Polish until taken by Austria 1772; Polish again 1919-39, and then became part of the USSR after the

S.W.W. There are 3 cathedrals (Armenian, Greek and RC), and the univ. dates from 1661. It is a rail junction with an airport, and has textile, engineering and metallurgical industries. Pop. (1977) 642,000.

LWOW. Polish form of Lvov.

LYCANTHROPY (līkan'-). Human transformation to a werewolf; form of insanity involving this belief.

LYCEUM (līsē'um). An ancient Athenian gymnasium and garden, with covered walks, where Aristotle taught. It was SE of the city, and named after the nearby temple of Apollo Lyceus.

LYCEUM. London theatre, situated in Wellington Street, near the Strand. It was opened in 1809 (rebuilt 1834) and under the management of Henry Irving (1878-1902), saw many of Ellen Terry's triumphs. After the S.W.W. it became a dance hall.

LYCURGUS (līker'gus). Spartan lawgiver. He is said to have been a member of the royal house, who, while acting as regent, gave the Spartans their constitution and system of education (9th cent. BC). Many scholars believe him to be purely mythical.

LYDGATE, John (*c.* 1373-*c.* 1450). English poet. B. probably at Lydgate, Suffolk, he entered the Benedictine abbey of Bury St Edmunds, was ordained in 1397, and was prior of Hatfield Broadoak (1423-34). The friend of Chaucer, he produced numerous pedestrian works, often translations or adaptations, e.g. his *Troy Book*, and *Falls of Princes*.

LYDIA (lid'ya). Ancient kingdom of Asia Minor (7th-6th cents. BC), with its cap. at Sardis. The Lydians were the first Western people to use standard coinage. Their last king, Croesus (q.v.), was conquered by the Persians in 546 BC.

LYELL, Sir Charles (1797-1875). Scottish geologist, whose *The Principles of Geology* (1830-3) estab. the conception of the Earth's crust having been gradually brought to its present condition through millennia of change without sudden 'catastrophes'.

LYLY (lil'i), **John** (*c.* 1553-1606). English dramatist and author. B. probably in Canterbury, in his romance *Euphues, or the Anatomy of Wit* (1578), he popularized elaborate stylistic devices, and originated the word 'euphuism'.

LYME REGIS (līm rē'jis). English seaport and holiday resort of Dorset. The duke of Monmouth landed at L.R. in 1685. Pop. (1974) 3,510.

LYMINGTON (lim-). Seaport of Hants, England, 19km (12m) SW of Southampton. It is a yachting centre. Pop. (1972) 36,310.

LYMPH. A clear saline fluid which carries nutriment to the tissues and waste matter away from them. It exudes from the finest blood vessels into the tissue spaces between the cells all over the body, and bathes the cells, which take up from it the nourishment they require and excrete the waste. This is carried through lymph capillaries into larger lymph vessels (lymphatics). These lead to lymph glands, small round bodies chiefly situated in the neck, armpit, groin, thorax and abdomen. Their function is to generate lymphocytes - white blood corpuscles with a protective or repairing capacity - and to filter out harmful substances and bacteria. From the lymph glands, vessels carry the lymph to the thoracic duct and the right lymphatic duct, which lead into the large veins.

LYNCH (linch), **'Jack' (John)** (1917-). Irish statesman. B. in Cork, he became a noted Gaelic footballer and a barrister. In 1948 he entered the parliament of the rep. as a Fianna Fail member, and was P.M. 1966-73 and 1977-9.

LYNCHING. The execution of an alleged offender by a summary court having no legal authority. The origin of the term remains controversial. In the USA the custom originated on the frontiers, where no regular courts existed and outlaws and cattle thieves abounded. Later examples have mostly occurred in the southern states, where it was used after the Civil War as a means of keeping the Negroes in subjection. During 1882-1900 the annual figure for the USA varied between 96 and 231, but it is today an exceptional occurrence for black or white.

LYNN. Industrial city of Massachusetts, USA, situated on Massachusetts Bay. Mary Baker Eddy, founder of Christian Science, lived at L. Founded in 1629, it was called Saugus until 1673 when it was re-named after King's Lynn, England. Pop. (1970) 90,295.

LYNN, Dame Vera (1917-). British popular singer. In the S.W.W. she was the 'Forces' Sweetheart', with such songs as 'Auf Widerseh'n' and 'White Cliffs of Dover'. DBE 1975.

LYNX (lingks). Carnivorous mammal (*Felis lynx*) in the cat family, found in rocky and forested regions of N America and Europe. Larger than a wild cat, it has a short tail, tufted ears, and the long, silky fur is reddish brown or grey with dark spots. The US bobcat or bay L. (*F. rufus*) is a smaller relative. *See also* CARACAL.

LYON. French form of Lyons.

LYONS, Sir Joseph (1848-1917). British business man, the founder of the catering firm of J. Lyons and Co., Ltd., in 1894. He popularized 'tea-shops', with waitresses known as 'nippies', and the 'Corner Houses' incorporating several restaurants of varying types were long a feature of London life. From the 1970s the firm moved into other fields of mass catering.

LYONS, Joseph Aloysius (1879-1939). Australian statesman. A native of Tasmania, he was elected to the Federal Parliament in 1929, and became Postmaster-General and Minister for Works. In 1931 he resigned from the cabinet and formed the United Australia Party. After the general election in the following Dec., L. formed a coalition govt with the Country Party, which was confirmed in office by the 1934 and 1937 general elections. He d. in office in April 1939. His wife **Dame Enid L.** (1897-) was first woman member of the House of Representatives and of the federal cabinet.

LYONS (lyoṅ) (Fr. Lyon). Cap. of Rhône dept., and third city of France, at the confluence of the Rhône and Saône, 275km (170m) NNW of Marseilles. The most notable buildings are the 19th cent. Notre Dame de Fourvière, the Gothic cathedral of St Jean, and the church of St Martin d'Ainay originating in the 6th cent. L. is the seat of an archbishopric, and a law and univ. centre. Formerly a chief fortress of France, L. is a road and rail centre, and is second only to Paris in commercial importance. L. is famous for silk and other fine textiles; it also makes chemicals, dyestuffs, machinery, etc., and has printing works. There is an international fair. It was the ancient Lugdunum, taken by the Romans 43 BC. Pop. met. area (1973) 1,083,000.

LYOPHILISATION (lī-ofilīzā'shun). Freeze-drying process used for foods and pharmaceuticals, and in the preservation of organic archaeological remains.

LYRE. Stringed instrument of great antiquity. It originated in Asia, and was used in Greece and Egypt. It consisted of a soundbox with 2 curved arms joined by a crosspiece. There were 4 to 10 strings which were stretched from the crosspiece to a bridge near the bottom of the soundbox. It was played with a plectrum held with the right hand.

LYRE-BIRD. Genus of Australian birds (*Menura*), similar to a pheasant. The male has a large lyre-shaped tail, brilliantly coloured. They nest on the ground, and feed on insects, worms, and snails.

LYSANDER (līan'der) (d. 395 BC). Spartan general. He brought the Peloponnesian War to a successful conclusion by capturing the Athenian fleet at Aegospotami in 405, and by starving Athens into surrender in the following year. He now aspired to make Sparta supreme in Greece, and himself in Sparta; he set up puppet governments in Athens and her former allies, and intrigued to secure himself the Spartan Kingship, but was killed in battle with the Thebans.

LYTE, Henry Francis (1793-1847). British hymn writer. B. at Kelso, he was ordained in 1815, and in 1823 moved to the parish of Brixham. He d. in Nice. His best-known hymns are 'Abide With Me' and 'Praise, my soul, the King of Heaven'.

LYTHAM ST ANNES (lidh'am). Resort in Lancs, England, on the Ribble, 10km (6m) SE of Blackpool. The Premium Savings Bond head office is at L.StA. Pop. (1972) 40,940.

LYTTON, Edward George Earle Lytton Bulwer-Lytton, 1st baron (1803-73). British author. B. in London, he pub. his first poems in 1820, and in 1827 m. Rosina Wheeler, from whom he separated in 1836. His novels successfully followed every turn of the public taste and incl. *Falkland* (1827), the Byronic *Pelham* (1828), *Paul Clifford* (1830), *Eugene Aram* (1832), *The Last Days of Pompeii* (1834), *Rienzi* (1835), *The Last of the Barons* (1843), *Harold* (1848), and *The Caxtons* (1850). He also achieved success as a playwright with *The Lady of Lyons* (1838), *Richelieu (1838),* etc. He sat in Parl. as a Lib. 1831-41, and as a Cons. 1852-66, and was Colonial Sec. 1858-9. He was created a baron in 1866.

LYRE-BIRD. The more splendid of the two species, the superb lyre-bird. Its song is as beautiful as its appearance, and it is also noted for its courtship display and nest-mounds. *Photo: Popperfoto*

His only son **Edward Robert Bulwer-L.,** 1st earl of Lytton (1831-91), was Viceroy of India (1876-80), where he was noted for his controversial 'Forward' policy. He pub. verse under the pseudonym Owen Meredith.

M

The 13th letter of the Roman alphabet. It corresponds to the Gk *mu* and the Semitic *mem*, and is almost always sounded as a voiced labial nasal. Finally, or before consonants, it disappears in French, Portuguese, and other languages, leaving a trace in nasalization of the preceding vowel. In Roman numerals M equals 1,000.

MAAS (mahs). River of the Netherlands, the lower course of the Meuse (q.v.).

MAASTRICHT (mahs'trikht). Capital of the prov. of Limburg, the Netherlands, on the Maas, near the Dutch-Belgian frontier. It dates from Roman times. Industries incl. metallurgy, textiles and pottery. Pop. (1978) 109,700.

MAAZEL (mah'zel), **Lorin** (1930-). American conductor. B. in France, the son of an American singer, he studied the violin and made his debut as a conductor at the age of nine. He excels in the interpretation of Mozart.

MABUSE (mahbüs'), **Jan.** Name adopted by Flemish artist Jan Gossaert (*c.* 1472-*c.* 1534), derived from his birthplace, Maubeuge. His journey to Italy in 1508 with Philip of Burgundy started a vogue for Italian journeys and the Italian style. His works incl. 'The Adoration of the Magi (National Gallery) and a no. of portraits, in which the hands are used to convey character. His colours are brilliant.

McADAM, John Loudon (1756-1836). Scottish engineer. B. at Ayr, he was appointed general surveyor of roads in 1827. The word 'macadamizing' was coined for his system of constructing roads of broken granite.

MACADAMIA (makadā'mia). Nut from trees of the genus *Macadamia*, native to Queensland, in the family Proteaceae. Carried in long bunches, they are delicious eating, and are increasingly cultivated as a luxury item.

MACAO (mahkah'-ō). Portuguese possession on S coast of China, *c.* 65km (40m) W of Hong Kong, from which it is separated by the estuary of the Canton r. It consists of the town of M., occupying an island peninsula, and 2 small islands. M. was leased by the Portuguese in 1557, annexed by them in 1849, and recognized as Portuguese by treaty in 1887. Under the organic statute of 1975 it was granted practical autonomy. In 1987 it was agreed that Portugal would hand over possession before 2000. Area 15.5 sq.km (6 sq.m); pop. (1975) 260,000.

MacARTHUR, Douglas (1880-1964). American gen. B. in Arkansas, the son of an army officer, he became Chief of Staff 1930-5. As commander of US forces in the Far East he defended the Philippines against the Japanese 1941-2, escaped to Australia, and in March 1942 assumed command of the Allied forces in the SW Pacific. He was responsible for the reconquest of New Guinea in 1942-5 and of the Philippines in 1944-5, being appointed Gen. of the Army in 1944. After the surrender of Japan he commanded the Allied occupation forces there. During 1950 he also commanded the UN forces in Korea, but in April 1951, following his expression of views contrary to US and UN policy, he was relieved of all his commands by Pres. Truman.

MACARTHUR, John (1767-1834). Australian colonist. B. in Devonshire, he went to Sydney in 1790, and began experiments in sheep breeding in 1794, subsequently importing from S. Africa the merino (q.v.) strain. He quarrelled with successive governors of N.S.W., and when arrested by Bligh, stirred up the Rum Rebellion, in which Bligh was himself arrested and deposed. In later years he studied viticulture, and planted vines in Australia from 1817, establishing the first commercial vineyard. His quarrelsomeness developed in 1832 into actual insanity.

MACA'SSAR. *See* UJUNG PANDANG.

MACAULAY, Dame Rose (1881-1958). British novelist. B. in Cambridge, she changed from the serious vein of her early novels to lightly touched satire of a muddled world, as in *Potterism* (1920) and *Keeping up Appearances* (1928). Her later books, very few being novels, incl. *The Writings of E. M. Forster* (1938), and *The Towers of Trebizond* (1956). Brought up in the Church of England, she returned to her lapsed faith through the influence of Father Hamilton Johnson: her letters to him were pub. in 2 vols. (1961-2). She was created DBE in 1958.

MACAULAY, Thomas Babington, baron (1800-59). British historian, essayist, poet, and politician. B. in Leics, he was ed. at Cambridge, and in 1826 was called to the Bar. In 1825 he pub. in the *Edinburgh Review* his essay on Milton, which was followed during the next 20 years by numerous historical and critical essays. He entered parl. as a Whig or Lib. in 1830, and advocated parl. reform and the abolition of slavery. He spent 1834-8 in India as a member of the Supreme Council, and was mainly responsible for the Indian penal code. He again sat in parl. 1839-47 and 1852-6, and in 1857 accepted a peerage. His only vol. of verse, *Lays of Ancient Rome*, appeared in 1842. The 4 vols. of his *History of England* (1848-61) were only completed to 1702. Although charged with showing dogmatism and Whig prejudices, it ranks as a literary masterpiece.

MACBETH (d. 1058). King of Scotland. The son of Findlaech, hereditary ruler of Moray, he was commander of the forces of Duncan, king of Scotia, whom he murdered in 1040. His reign was prosperous until Duncan's son Malcolm led an invasion and killed M. at Lumphanan. Shakespeare's tragedy (*c.* 1606) was based on Holinshed's *Chronicle*.

MACCABEES (mak'abēz). Jewish family, sometimes known as the Hasmonaeans, founded by the priest Mattathias (d. 166 BC). He and his sons led the struggle for Jewish independence against the Syrians in the 2nd cent. BC. Judas (d. 161) reconquered Jerusalem in 165 BC, and Simon (d. 135) estab. Jewish independence in 142 BC.

McCARRAN, Patrick (1876-1954). American Democrat politician. A lawyer, he became senator for Nevada in 1932, and as an isolationist strongly opposed Lend-Lease and sponsored in 1950 the McCarran-Walter Immigration Act, forbidding foreign seamen to land in the US unless willing to submit to interrogation by immigration officers. *See* COMMUNISM.

McCARTHY, Joseph (1909-57). American Republican politician. A lawyer, he became senator for his native Wisconsin in 1946, and in 1950 caused a sensation by claiming to hold a list of *c.* 200 Communists working in the State Dept. He continued a not-uninfluential witch-hunting campaign - 'McCarthyism' - until censured by the senate in 1954.

McCLELLAN (maklel'an), **George Brinton** (1826-85). American general. The incompetent C-in-C of the Union forces in the American Civil War, he was eventually finally removed from his post by Lincoln in 1862. He stood as Democratic presidential candidate against Lincoln in 1864 and was defeated.

MACCLESFIELD. Town in Cheshire, England, on the Bollin, about 29km (18m) NE of Crewe. An industrial centre, it has a reputation for fine silks and other textiles. Pop. (1972) 44,480.

McCLURE (makloor'), **Sir Robert John le Mesurier** (1807-73). British explorer. In 1850 he completed his discovery of the North-West Passage.

McCORMICK, Cyrus Hall (1809-84). American inventor. The son of a Virginian farmer, he invented a mechanical reaper in 1831.

McDIARMID (makdur'mid), **Hugh.** Pseudonym of the Scottish nationalist poet Christopher Murray Grieve (1892-1978). B. in Dumfriesshire, he worked for a time as a labourer: his nationalism emerges in 'A Drunk Man Looks at the Thistle' and his strongly Marxist views in his two 'Hymns to Lenin'. He was a forcefully gifted poet and his prose had the same idiosyncratic power, e.g. the autobiographical *Lucky poet* (1943).

MACDONALD, Flora (1722-90). Scottish heroine who rescued Prince Charles Edward after the Battle of Culloden (1746), and, disguising him as her maid, escorted him from her home in the Hebrides to the mainland. She was arrested, but released in 1747.

MacDONALD, James Ramsay (1866-1937). British Lab. statesman. B. at Lossiemouth, the son of a labourer, he joined the ILP in 1894 and became first sec. of the Lab. Party in 1900. He was elected to parl. in 1906, and led the party until 1914, when his opposition to the F.W.W. lost him his leadership. He recovered it in 1922, and in Jan. 1924 formed a govt. dependent on Lib. support, the withdrawal of which in Oct. forced him to resign. He returned to office in 1929, again as leader of a minority govt; this collapsed as a result of the economic crisis in 1931, and M. left the Lab. Party to form a National govt with Cons. and Lib. backing. He resigned the Premiership in 1935, remaining Lord President of the Council.

MACDONALD, Sir John Alexander (1815-91). Canadian Cons. statesman. B. in Glasgow, he was taken to Ontario as a child. In 1857 he became PM of Upper Canada. He took the leading part in the movement for federation, and in 1867 became first PM of Canada. Defeated in 1873, he returned to office in 1878, and retained it until his death.

MACDONNE'LL RANGES. Mountain range in central Australia, N Territory, in which Alice Springs is situated. Highest peak Mt Zeil 1,510 m (4,955 ft).

MacDOWELL, Edward Alexander (1861-1908). American composer. Encouraged by Liszt while in Germany, he showed much romantic feeling in his works which incl. the *Indian Suite* (1896), and piano concertos and sonatas. Prof. of music at Columbia univ., NY, 1896-1904, he had a mental breakdown in 1905.

MACEDONIA (masedōn'ēa). Name of an ancient country of SE Europe which lay between Illyria, Thrace, and the Aegean Sea. It is used for much the same area in modern geography: one of the fed. reps. of Yugoslavia (cap. Skopje) and a prov. of Greece (cap. Thessaloniki) are both called Macedonia, and the rest forms SW Bulgaria. The area is wild and mountainous, and the chief rivers are the Struma and the Vardar.

MACDONNELL RANGES. Simpson's Gap, in the Macdonnell Ranges, near Alice Springs in the Northern Territory. *Photo: Courtesy of the Australian Information Service*

MACEIÓ (mahsāyō'). Town in NE Brazil, cap. of Alagoas state, with sugar, tobacco, textile and timber industries. Its port is Jaraguá to the E. Pop. (1975) 323,600.

McEVOY (mak'evoi), **Ambrose** (1878-1927). British artist, especially noted as a water-colourist and as a painter of delicately refined portraits of women.

MACGILLYCUDDY'S REEKS (makgilikud'iz-). A group of mts lying W of Killarney, in Co. Kerry, Ireland, which incl. Carrantuohill 1,041 m (3,414 ft), the highest peak in Ireland.

McGINLEY, Phyllis (1905-78). American writer of light verse. Canadian-born, she became a contributor to the *New Yorker* and pub. many equally masterly collections of social satire: *One More Manhattan* (1937) and *The Love Letters of Phyllis McGinley* (1954).

McGO'NAGALL, William (1830-1902). Scottish poet, celebrated for the badness of his verse as the 'Great M.' Among his best-known works, a vogue of the 1960s, was an account of the Tay Bridge disaster of 1879. Quite humourless, he was often hoaxed, e.g. his journey to Balmoral in 1878 to see Qu. Victoria.

MACH (mahkh), **Ernst** (1838-1916). Austrian philosopher. Originally a prof. of mathematics at Graz, he was prof. of philosophy at Prague 1867-95 and Vienna 1895-1901. An empiricist, he laid down that science was a record of facts perceived by the senses, and that acceptance of a scientific law depended solely on its standing the practical test of use: he opposed concepts such as Newton's 'absolute motion'.

MACH (mahk) **NUMBER.** System of speed measurement devised by Ernst Mach (*see* above), Austrian physicist and mathematician. The ratio of the speed of a body to that of sound in the undisturbed medium through which the body travels is its M.N. In an aircraft, when the M.N. passes through 1, i.e. when its velocity is greater than that of sound, it is said to have passed through the sound barrier.

MACHA'DO, Antonio (1875-1939). Spanish poet and dramatist. B. in Seville, he was inspired in his finest lyric verse, contained in *Campos de Castilla* (1912), by the Castilian countryside.

MACHAULT (mahshō'), **Guillaume de** (*c.* 1300-77). French poet and musician. B. in Champagne, he was in the service of John of Bohemia for 30 years, and later of King John the Good of France. He gave the forms of the *ballade* and *rondeau* a new individuality, and ensured their lasting vogue.

MACHEL (mahshel'), **Samora** (1933-). Mozambique statesman. As leader of the Frente de Libertação de Moçambique (Frelimo) from 1966, he organized the guerrilla training programme in Tanzania, and in 1975 became pres. of Mozambique.

MACHEN, Arthur (1863-1947). Welsh author. Characterized by mystic symbolism and the super-natural, his writings incl. *House of Souls* (1906) and *Angels of Mons* (1915; source of the F.W.W. legend).

MACHIAVELLI (makē'ahvel'li), **Niccolo** (1469-1527). Italian statesman and author. B. in Florence, he became second chancellor to the Republic (1498-1512). With the accession to power of the Medici in 1512, he was arrested and imprisoned on a charge of conspiracy, but in 1513 released to exile in the country. He completed his *Il Principe* in 1513; this advocated a unified Italian state under a powerful ruler without reference to moral standards; in *L'Arte della guerra* (1520) he outlined the provision of an army for such a prince; and in *Historie fiorentine* analysed the historical development of Florence till 1492. Among his later works are the comedies *La Mandragola* (1524), and *Clizia.* The theories expressed in *Il Principe* and in his *Discorsi* (1531) influenced political science.

MACHINE GUN. Type of small arm (q.v.) perfected in the US by Gatling in 1860. A number of barrels were arranged about a central axis, and the breech containing the reloading, ejection and firing mechanism was rotated by hand; shots being fired through each barrel in turn. The Maxim of 1883 was recoil operated, but some later types have been gas-operated (Bren) or recoil assisted by gas (some versions of the Browning). The sub-M.G., first exploited by Chicago gunmen in the 1920s, was widely used in the S.W.W., e.g. the recoil-operated Sten. *See* ROCKET.

MACHU PICCHU (mah'chōō pēk'chōō). Inca city, NW of Cuzco, Peru. It was discovered in 1911 by Hiram Bingham at the top of 300m (1,000 ft) high cliffs, and contains well-preserved remains of houses, temples, etc., built *c.* AD 1500.

McINDOE, Sir Archibald (1900-60). New Zealand plastic surgeon. B. at Dunedin, NZ, he worked at the Mayo Foundation before joining St Bartholomew's in 1930, and was subsequently surgeon-in-charge of the Queen Victoria Plastic and Jaw Injury Centre in Sussex. During the S.W.W. he became famous for his remodelling of the faces of badly burned pilots, forming for them the Guinea Pig Club.

MACHINE GUN. The new Light Support Weapon (foreground and detail below) is less than half the weight of the present General Purpose MG (in the background): 5.26 kg (11 lb 9.5 oz) as against 12.39 kg (27 lb 5 oz). It has the advantage also of sharing many components with the new Individual Weapon (rifle), and both use 4.85 mm ammunition. It is hoped that the new British system will also be adopted for use by NATO in the 1980s. *Photo: Crown Copyright*

MA'CINTOSH, Charles (1766-1843). Scottish manufacturing chemist, inventor of a waterproof fabric lined with a rubber solution, who gave his name (but spelt 'mackintosh') to raincoats made of it: other processes have largely superseded this method.

MACKENSEN (mahk'ensen), **August von** (1849-1945). German field marshal. B. in Saxony, in the F.W.W. he accomplished the break-through at Gorlice and the conquest of Serbia (1915), and in 1916 had a big share in the overthrow of Romania. After the war M. retained his popularity to become a symbolical figure of the German Army.

MACHU PICCHU. The breath-taking site of the Inca city that the Spanish conquistadors never found. *Photo: Mireille Vautier*

MACKENZIE, Sir Compton (1883-1972). Scottish author. The son of actor parents, he was ed. at Magdalen College, Oxford, and pub. his first novel *The Passionate Elopement* (1911); later were *Carnival* (1912), *Sinister Street* (1913-14) an outspoken autobiographical novel; and the comic *Whisky Galore* (1947). Invalided from the army in 1915, he returned to serve in intelligence, and his *Greek Memories* led to a farcical trial under the Official Secrets Act. He pub. his autobiography in ten 'octaves' 1963-71, his memory being phenomenal. Fay Compton (1894-78), the actress, was his sister.

MACKENZIE, William Lyon (1795-1861). Canadian politician; grandfather of W. L. Mackenzie King. B. near Dundee, he emigrated to Canada in 1820, and in 1837 led a rising at Toronto. After its failure he lived in the USA until 1849, and 1851-8 sat in the Canadian legislature as a Radical.

MACKENZIE. River of the NW Territories, Canada, discovered by the British explorer, Sir Alexander Mackenzie (*c.* 1755-1820), in 1789; it flows from the Great Slave Lake to the Arctic Ocean, and is about 1,600 km (1,000 m) long. It gives its name to one of the 3 districts of NW Territories; area 1,366,188 sq.km (527,490 sq.m).

MACKEREL. Food fish (*Scomber scombrus*), found in N temperate and tropical seas. It is blue with irregular black bands down its sides, the latter and the undersurface showing a pink metallic sheen. The chief M. fisheries of Britain are off the SW coast.

MACKER'RAS, Sir Charles (1925-). Australian conductor. Noted for his advocacy of the music of Janacek, he became Associate Artist of the English National Opera in 1980, and was knighted in 1979.

McKINLEY, William (1843-1901). Twenty-fifth pres. of the USA. B. in Ohio, he was elected to Congress in 1876 as a Republican, and was Pres. in 1896 and again in 1900. His period of office was marked by America's adoption of an imperialist policy, as exemplified in the Spanish War of 1898, the annexation of the Philippines, etc. M. was assassinated by an anarchist at Buffalo in 1901.

McKINLEY, Mt. Highest peak 6,194 m (20,320 ft) in N America, situated in Alaska, USA, named after Pres. William McKinley.

MACKINTOSH, Charles Rennie (1868-1928). Scottish architect, the influential art nouveau designer of the Glasgow School of Art (1896).

MacLEISH, Archibald (1892-1982). Am. poet. B. in Illinois, he was Asst. Sec. of State in 1944-5 and helped to draft the constitution of UNESCO. He made his name with a poem 'Conquistador' (1932), descriptive of Cortes' march to the Aztec capital, but his later plays in verse, *Panic* (1935) and *Air Raid* (1938), deal with contemporary problems. In 1949-62 he was Boylston Prof. of Rhetoric at Harvard, and his essays *Poetry and Opinion* (1950) reflect his feeling that a poet should be 'committed', expressing his outlook in his verse.

MACLEOD (maklowd'), **Iain Norman** (1913-70). British Cons. politician. He was Min. of Health 1952-5, Labour 1955-9, and as Colonial Sec. 1959-61 forwarded the rapid independence of African terrs. He envisaged a simplified tax structure while Chancellor in 1970 and d. in office.

MACLISE (-les'), **Daniel** (1806-70). Irish artist. B. at Cork, he moved to London in 1827 and painted portraits of famous people, and historical pictures, incl. 'The Meeting of Wellington and Blücher after Waterloo', and 'Death of Nelson' for the Westminster Palace. He was elected RA in 1840.

McLUHAN (makloo'an), **Marshall** (1911-80). Canadian sociologist. Director of the Centre for Culture and Technology, Univ. of Toronto 1963-79, he maintained that by technology and espec. electronics, an extension of the human brain had been achieved which made individualism obsolete and compelled a corporate interdependence. His books incl. *The Mechanical Bride* (1951), *The Medium is the Message* (1967), *War and Peace in the Global Village* (1968), and *Take Today: The Executive as Drop-out* (1972).

MacMAHON (-oṅ), **Marie Edmé Patrice Maurice de** (1808-93). French soldier and statesman. His share in the victory of Magenta in the Franco-Austrian War of 1859 won him the titles of duke of Magenta and marshal of France. In the war of 1870 he was captured at Sedan, and after his release suppressed the Paris Commune. Elected Pres. of the Rep. in 1873, he worked for a royalist restoration, but was forced to resign in 1879.

McMILLAN, Edwin Mattison (1907-). American physicist. Prof. at the Univ. of California 1946-73, he shared a Nobel prize in chemistry with Seaborg (q.v.) in 1951, and in 1963 shared with I. Veksler, director of the Russian Joint Institute for Nuclear Research, an Atoms for Peace award for their independent arrival 20 years before at a method of overcoming the limitations of the cyclotron.

MACMILLAN, (Maurice) Harold (1894-). British Cons. statesman. Member of a family of publishers, he was ed. at Eton and Oxford and served with the Grenadier Guards in the F.W.W. Entering parliament as a Unionist (Stockton-on-Tees 1924-9 and 1931-45, and Bromley 1945-64), he held his first important post as Min. of Housing 1951-4, and was then Min. of Defence until he succeeded Eden as For. Sec. in 1955, and as Chancellor of the Exchequer 1955-7 introduced Premium Bonds. Taking over as PM in 1957, following Eden's resignation after Suez, he led his party to victory in the 1959 elections on the slogan 'You have never had it so good'. (The phrase came from a speech at Bedford in 1957, in which he was actually warning of the coming danger of inflation.) The Cyprus dispute had already been temporarily settled in 1959, but his realization of 'the wind of change' in Africa led to rapid recognition of the independence of new states, and though Britain's entry to the Common Market failed, the securing of the nuclear test-ban treaty just before his resignation through ill-health in 1963 counteracted to some extent the effect at home of the Vassall spy case and the Profumo scandal. Christened 'Supermac' by cartoonist Vicky in 1958, he has in retrospect been recognized as 'the last of the giants'. He received the O.M. in 1976, and an earldom in 1984 as Lord Stockton.

MacMILLAN, Sir Kenneth (1929–). British choreographer. He was Director of the Royal Ballet, Covent Garden 1970–7 and became principal choreographer in 1977: his creations have incl. *Romeo and Juliet, Song of the Earth, Anastasia* and *Gloria* (1980). Kt 1983.

MACMILLAN, Kirkpatrick (d. 1878). Scottish blacksmith who invented the bicycle in 1839. His invention consisted of a hobby-horse fitted with treadles, and propelled by pedalling.

MacNEICE, Louis (1907-63). Anglo-Irish poet. B. in Belfast, he was ed. at Oxford and lectured in classics at Birmingham 1930-6 and London 1936-40. Free of the rigid political alignments of his contemporaries, he made his début with *Blind Fireworks* (1929) and developed a polished ease of expression, reflecting his classical training, in dealing with man in society, as in *Autumn Journal* (1939). Later vols. are the highly original *The Dark Tower* (1946), written for the BBC, for whom he wrote features 1941-9 'like a poet, but with a journalist's instinct for essence'; a verse translation of Goethe's *Faust*, and the radio play *The Administrator* (1961).

MÂCON (mahkoṅ). Cap. of the French dept of Saône-et-Loire, on the Saône, 72km (45m) N of Lyons. A town dating from ancient Gaul, it is famous for wine. Pop. (1975) 40,500.

MACPHERSON, James (1736-96). Scottish author. B. at Ruthven, in 1760, he pub. *Fragments of Ancient Poetry collected in the Highlands of Scotland*, which was followed by the epics *Fingal* (1761) and *Temora* (1763), which he claimed as the work of the 3rd cent. bard Ossian. Challenged by Dr Johnson, M. failed to produce his originals and a committee decided in 1797 that M. had combined fragmentary materials with oral tradition. Nevertheless, the works of 'Ossian' exercised a considerable influence on the development of the Romantic movement in Britain and abroad.

MACQUARIE (makwor'ē), **Lachlan** (1761-1834). Scottish administrator who succeeded Bligh as governor of NSW in 1808, and raised the demoralized settlement to prosperity. In 1821 he returned to Britain in poor health, exhausted by struggles with his opponents. Lachlan r. and M. r. and Is. are named after him. **M. Island** is a Tasmanian dependency, some 1,370 km (850m) SE of Hobart, and uninhabited save for an Australian govt research station.

MACRAMÉ (makrah'mā). The art of making decorative fringes and lacework with knotted threads, from the Arabic word for 'striped cloth', which is often decorated in this way.

MACREADY, William Charles (1793-1873). British actor. In 1816 he made his début at Covent Garden, and rose to become England's leading actor. He was very successful as Macbeth, Lear, John, and Henry IV.

MACRŌBIO'TICS. Zen Buddhist diet plan stressing organically grown wholefoods, and which attempts to balance the principles of yin (female), expressed as 5 parts fruit, vegetables, etc., and yang (masculine), 1 part meat, eggs, etc.

MACQUARIE ISLAND. A wandering albatross is banded by a member of the Wildlife Survey section of the Australian Commonwealth Scientific and Industrial Research Organisation. *Photo: Courtesy of the CSIRO*

McWHIRTER, Norris (1925-). British editor and compiler, with his younger twin brother, **Ross M.** (1925-75), of the *Guinness Book of Records* from 1955. The latter was shot by terrorists following his endeavours to raise £50,000 reward for the arrest of IRA bombers in Britain.

MADAGA'SCAR. Island 400km (250m) off the SE coast of Africa, separated from the mainland by the Mozambique Channel. The interior is mountainous, the Central Plateau rising to 1,200 m (4,000 ft), and the highest of 3 great massifs being Tsaratanana 2,886 m (9,468 ft) in the N. The lower regions are fertile - manioc, rice, coffee, groundnuts, sugar cane, etc. - and cattle are raised. The only r. of any size is the Manoka, which flows out on the W coast; on the E coast a series of lagoons is linked to form the Canal des Pangalanes. Industries being developed incl. textiles, sugar refining, food processing (espec. meat), machinery, and cement, and minerals incl. chromium, graphite, iron, bauxite, mica, and phosphates. The cap. is Tananarive; other towns incl. Majunga, Tamatave (chief port), Fianarantsoa, Diégo-Suarez, and Tuléar.

The first European to reach M. was the Portuguese, Diego Diaz, in 1500, but it was not until 1896 that it became a French colony. From 1946 an overseas terr., it became independent in 1960 within the French Community as the Malagasy Republic, but in 1972, following a referendum in favour of 'direct democracy' a military govt took over. The coastal peoples - animist and Malagasy-speaking - thus ousted the Mérinas - often Christian and French-speaking - of the plateaux: the Mérinas incl. the Hova caste which supplied the dynasty ruling M. from the late 18th cent. until the island's acquisition by the French. The Democratic Rep. of M. was proclaimed in 1975 and Lt-Commander Didier Ratsiraka became M.'s first pres. in 1976. The pres. is elected for 7 years and the Nat. People's Assembly for five. The only official language is now Malagasy (Malayo-Polynesian), but some co-operation with France continues. Claims are maintained on the Indian Ocean Is. of Glorieuses, Juan de Nova, Europa and Bassas da India, currently admin. by France. Area 592,000 sq.km (228,500 sq.m); pop. (1977) 8,520,000. M.U.: Malagasy franc.

MADEIRA (madē'ra). Group of 5 Portuguese is., off the NW coast of Africa *c.* 420km (260m) N of Santa Cruz, Canary Is., which form the district of Funchal. Madeira, the largest, and Porto Santo, are the only inhabited is. Their mild climate makes them a popular winter resort. Pico Ruivo on M. is 1,846 m (6,056 ft) high, and Funchal (also on M.) is the cap.; pop. (1973) 55,250. The products incl. madeira (a fortified wine), sugar cane, fruit, fish and handicrafts such as wickerwork and embroidery. Portuguese from the 15th cent., M. was occupied by Britain in 1801 and 1807-14: the Portuguese name for the group is Funchal. There is an independence movement, possibly in federation with the Azores and Canaries, backed by Kadhafi and USSR. In 1976 M. gained partial autonomy. Total area 790 sq.km (308 sq.m); pop. (1973) 282,000.

MAD'HYA BHA'RAT. State of the Rep. of India 1950-6. It was a union of 19 states of which Gwalior and Indore (qq.v.) were the most important; 5 other small states subsequently joined. In 1956 M.B. was absorbed in Madhya Pradesh.

MADHYA PRADESH'. State of the Rep. of India, so named in 1950 when it consisted of the former British prov. of Central Provs. and Berar and the princely states of Makrai and Chattisgarh. In 1956 it lost some SW districts, including Nagpur (q.v.), and absorbed Bhopal, Madhya Bharat, and Vindhya Pradesh. The cap. is Bhopal; other large towns are Indore, Jabalpur, Ujjain and Gwalior. Area 443,452 sq.km (171,210 sq.m); pop. (1971) 41,650,000.

MADISON, James (1751-1836). Fourth pres. of the USA. In 1787 he became a member of the Philadelphia Convention and took a leading part in drawing up the US constitution and the Bill of Rights. He became Sec. of State in Jefferson's govt 1801-9, the main achievement of his ministry being the Louisiana Purchase; became Pres. in 1809; and was re-elected in 1812. During his period of office the US became involved in the war with Britain of 1812-15.

MADISON. The cap. of Wisconsin, USA, *c.* 193km (120m). NW of Chicago, situated between lakes Mendota and Monona, seat of the state univ. Pop. met. area (1974) 297,700.

MADONNA (Italian, my lady). Italian name for the Virgin Mary.

MADRAS (mahdrahs'). City and port in the Rep. of India, cap. of Tamil Nadu, on the Bay of Bengal. Cotton, cement, chemicals, and iron and steel goods are manufactured, and there is a brisk export trade. Fort St George, nucleus of the city, and Government House, the governor's residence until 1947, then the seat of the legislature, are among the chief buildings. The univ. was constituted in 1857. Fort St George was founded by the E India Co. in 1639. Occupied by the French 1746-8, M. was shelled by the German ship *Emden* in 1914, the only place in India attacked in the F.W.W. Pop. (1971) 2,470,300.

MADRAS. Former name of TAMIL NADU (q.v.).

MADRI'D. Cap. of Spain and of M. prov., on the Manzanares. It is built on an elevated plateau in the centre of the country, and has excesses of heat and cold. It first became important in the times of Charles V and Philip II; the original town was almost square, with rounded corners. The Puerta del Sol is the chief of many plazas, and in the Calle de Alcalá stands the Real Academia de Bellas Artes, founded in 1752. The famous Prado Museum (1785) is near the botanical garden. Some churches are historically interesting, and the royal palace, finished in 1764, contains a celebrated library and tapestry collection. M. has several schools of industry and art, and a univ. transferred from Alcalá de Henares 1836-7. Its suburbs have grown extensively, as have its industries, which incl. leather, chemicals, furniture, tobacco, and paper. During the civil war M. was besieged by the Nationalists 7 Nov. 1936 to 28 March 1939. Pop. (1970) 3,146,071.

MA'DRIGAL. In music, a form of composition for three or more voices without musical accompaniment. It originated in the Netherlands before the middle of the 15th cent., later becoming popular in Italy and in Elizabethan England. The chief English composers incl. Byrd, Weelkes, Kirbye, and Orlando Gibbons. The M. Society was founded in 1741.

MA'DURA. Island of the Rep. of Indonesia, off Surabaya, rising in the central hills to 4,800 m (1,545 ft). It produces rice, tobacco, salt, etc.; cattle breeding and fishing are carried on. Area 4,564 sq.km (1,762 sq.m); with offshore islands, more than 5,000 sq.km (2,000 sq.m); pop. (1970) 2,447,000.

MADURA. Fine cattle are bred in the island, and even take part in these unusual chariot races. *Photo: Mireille Vautier*

MADURAI (mudoorī'). Town on the r. Vaigai in Tamil Nadu state, India, site of the great Hindu temple of Sundareswara, and of M. Univ. (1966). Cotton textiles and brassware are made; rice, tobacco, spices exported. Pop. (1971) 548,300.

MAEANDER (mē-an'der). Anglicized form of the ancient Greek name of a river in Turkey-in-Asia (Turkish, Buyuk Menderes, great Menderes). It rises near Afyonkarahisar (in anc. Phrygia) and flows for *c.* 400km (250m) by a very winding course into the Aegean: hence the word 'meander'.

MAECENAS (mīsē'nas), **Gaius Cilnius** (*c.* 69 BC–8 BC). Roman patron of the arts. The friend and counsellor of Augustus, he encouraged the work of Horace and Virgil.

MAELSTRÖM (māl'strōm). Whirlpool off the Lofoten Is., also known as the Moskenstraumen, which gave its name to the genus.

MAESTRICHT. *See* MAASTRICHT.

MAETERLINCK (maht'erlingk), **Maurice,** count (1862–1949). Belgian poet and dramatist. He achieved internat. fame with his play *Pelléas and Mélisande* (1892), which inspired music by Debussy and Sibelius, *The Blue Bird* (1908), and *The Burgomaster of Stilemonde* (1918), celebrating Belgian resistance in the F.W.W. - a theme which caused his exile to America in 1940. His philosophical essays incl. *The Treasure of the Humble* (1896) and *The Life of the Bee* (1901).

MAFEKING. *See* MAFIKENG.

MAFIA (It. mafē'a; anglicized: maf'ēa). Originally a secret society of 15th cent. Sicily (the name means 'swagger'), hostile to the law and avenging their own wrongs by means of the vendetta. In the 19th cent. the M. was employed by absentee landlords to manage their *latifundia* (landed estates), and through terrorization, etc., soon became the unofficial ruler of Sicily. In spite of loss of power on the *latifundia,* which were expropriated and divided among the peasants after the S.W.W., the M. is still powerful in Sicily, especially in the towns, where they have turned their attention to industry. The govt has waged periodic campaigns of suppression, notably in 1927 and 1963-4. The M. has spread abroad, its biggest offshoot being in the USA, where it is known as *Cosa Nostra* (It. 'our thing'). None but those of Italian descent is eligible for membership, organization is in 'families', each with its own boss or *capo,* and a committee of 12 bosses from NY, Chicago and other leading cities rules nationally. Activities range from 'protection' and illicit gambling to drug peddling and murder. In 1962-3 sensational revelations were made by Joe Valachi, who, while in Atlanta's Federal gaol, killed a fellow-prisoner, whom he thought had been detailed by the M. to kill him. Intimidation of witnesses prevents elimination of the M. and *Cosa Nostra,* although special campaigns are officially undertaken from time to time. The M. features frequently in fiction, e.g. Marlon Brando in the film *The Godfather* (1972).

MAFIKENG (maf'-). Town in NE Cape Province, S. Africa, which in 1980 was incorporated in Bophuthatswana with the original spelling restored. Besieged in the S African War 12 Oct.1899–17 May 1900, it was successfully held by a small garrison under Baden-Powell. Pop. (1970) 7,000.

MAGADA'N. E Siberian port on the Sea of Okhotsk, RSFSR, USSR. Pop. (1975) 103,000.

MA'GADHA. A kingdom of ancient India, roughly corresponding to the middle and southern parts of modern Bihar; it witnessed many incidents in the life of the Buddha, and was the seat of the Maurya dynasty, founded by Chandragupta (q.v.).

MAGALLANES. Another name for PUNTA ARENAS.

MAGDEBURG (mahg'deboorg). Cap. of M. district, E Germany, on the Elbe 130km (81m) SW of Berlin. It has a Gothic cathedral, one of the few buildings to survive the Thirty Years War. Motor-cars, paper, textiles, machinery, etc., are produced, and there are sugar refineries. It dates from the 9th cent. and was captured by the US 9th Army, 18 April 1945. Pop. (1978) 282,000.

MAGELLAN (majel'an), **Ferdinand** (*c.* 1480–1521). Portuguese navigator. He was brought up at court and entered the royal service, but later transferred his services to Spain. His proposal to sail to the E Indies by the W was accepted, and in 1519 he started from Seville. He discovered and sailed through *M. Strait,* crossed the Pacific, to which he gave its name, and in 1521 reached the Philippines. Here he was killed in battle: 18 of his companions reached Seville in 1522, completing the first voyage round the world. In 1964 the wreck of his ship *Concepcion* was thought to have been located off Leyte in the Philippines where she was abandoned.

The *Strait of M.* separates the tip of S America from the island of Tierra del Fuego, and joins the Atlantic and Pacific. Length 595km (370m).

MAGENTA (mahjen'tah). Town in Milan prov., Lombardy, Italy, 24km (15m) W of Milan, the scene of a victory by the French and Sardinians over the Austrians in 1859. Pop. (1971) 21,600.

MAGGIORE (mahjō're), **Lago.** Lake in Piedmont and Lombardy, Italy, and the Swiss canton of Ticino. Locarno is on its N shore. It is 63km (39m) long and up to 9km (5.5m) wide, with fine scenery.

MAGGOT. Name of the footless larvae of insects, especially those of flies, a typical example being the larva of the blow-fly which is deposited on flesh.

MAGHREB (mah'greb). Name for NW Africa (Arabic 'west', 'sunset'): the M. powers - Algeria, Libya, Morocco, and Tunisia - agreed on economic co-ordination 1964-5, Mauritania co-operating from 1970.

MAGI (mā'jī). The name of the priesthood of the Persian (Zoroastrian) religion, used in the Vulgate – where the authorized version gives 'wise men'. The three M. who came to visit the infant Christ with gifts of gold, frankincense, and myrrh were in later tradition described as 'kings'. The 'Adoration of the Magi' has inspired many artists.

MAGIC. The art of controlling the forces of nature by means of charms and ritual. It originated in the idea that like produces like, e.g. the ceremonial sprinkling of water will produce rain, a dance imitating a successful hunt will ensure success in hunting, to destroy the image of an enemy will cause his death. It is now generally accepted that most primitive religious practices are of magical origin. Under Christianity those still practising the ancient rites were persecuted as witches. Traces of M. still survive in folk-custom and in superstitions.

MAGIC NUMBERS. In atomic physics the numbers of neutrons or protons (2, 8, 20, 28, 50, 82, 126) in the nuclei of elements of outstanding stability such as lead and helium. It is accounted for by the neutrons and protons being arranged in layers or 'shells'.

MAGINOT LINE (mahzhēnō'). French system of fortifications along the German frontier from Switzerland to Luxembourg. Built 1929-36 under the direction of the

War Minister, André Maginot, it consisted of semi-underground forts armed with heavy guns, joined by underground passages, and protected by anti-tank defences. Lighter fortifications continued the line to the sea. In 1940 the Germans pierced the Belgian frontier line and outflanked the M.L.

MAGLEV. *See* LEVITATION.

MAGNA CARTA. The charter granted by King John in 1215. As a reply to his demands for excessive feudal dues and attacks on the privileges of the Church, Archbp Langton in 1213 proposed to the barons the drawing up of a charter, and this John was forced to accept at Runnymede on 15 June 1215.

M.C. begins by reaffirming the rights of the Church. Certain clauses guard against infringements of feudal custom, e.g. the king shall not demand any grant beyond those customary, without the consent of his tenants-in-chief. Others are designed to check extortions by officials or maladministration of justice, e.g. no freeman to be arrested, imprisoned or punished except by the judgment of his peers or the law of the land, while others guaranteed the privileges of London and the cities.

As feudalism declined M.C. lost its significance, and under the Tudors was almost forgotten. During the 17th cent. it was re-discovered and re-interpreted by the parliamentary party. Four original copies exist, one each in Salisbury and Lincoln Cathedrals, and 2 in the British Museum.

MAGNĒ'SIA. Magnesium oxide (MgO), obtained from the mineral periclase. It is formed when magnesium is burnt in air or oxygen, appears as a white powder or colourless crystals, and is used medicinally.

MAGNĒ'SIUM. A light, white, fairly tough metal, which tarnishes in air: symbol Mg, at. wt. 24.32 and at. no. 12. First found in Magnesia, a district in Thessaly, and widely distributed as the silicate, carbonate and chloride. It was recognized as an element by Black in 1755, isolated by Davy in 1808, and prepared in coherent form by Bussy in 1831. It is used in alloy, to strengthen aluminium for aircraft construction, and with uranium as a canning material in nuclear reactors. Its incendiary properties are used in flashlight photography, flares and fireworks.

MAGNETIC FLUX. A phenomenon produced in the neighbourhood of electric currents and magnets. The amount of M.F. through an area (measured in Maxwells) equals the product of the area and of the magnetic field strength at a point within that area.

MAGNETISM. Branch of science dealing with the properties of magnets and the magnetic fields. The lodestone acting as a compass, in that one pole seeks N, is thought to have been known to the Chinese, before (but not accepted in Europe until) the 12th cent. P. Peregrinus (fl. 13th cent.), an early experimentalist, inspired the work of William Gilbert (1546–1603) who described in *De Magnete* many fundamental properties of magnets and conceived of the earth itself as a magnet. Significant experiments were made in the 19th cent. by Coulomb, Gauss and Oersted (*see* ELECTRICITY). The general properties of magnets are that they align themselves on a N–S axis, the N seeking pole facing N, but varying from the true geographic meridian (magnetic variation), like poles repel, and unlike poles attract. The force of attraction or repulsion between 2 poles varies inversely as the square of the distance between them. Substances differ in degree and kind in their ability to be magnetized (permeability). Those substances, like iron, which have very high permeabilities, are said to be ferromagnetic. Apart from its universal application to dynamos, electric motors, switch-gear, and so forth, M. has become of considerable importance in modern science, incl. particle accelerators for nuclear research, memory stores for computers, tape recorders, cryogenics (q.v.) and investigations of matter and space.

Experiments have confirmed that homing pigeons and other animals rely on their perception of Earth's magnetic field for their sense of direction (*see* MIGRATION), and by 1979 it was suggested that man shares this sense.

MA'GNETĪTE. An important iron ore, magnetic iron oxide (Fe_3O_4). It is a black metallic mineral, strongly magnetic and sometimes possessing polarity (lodestone). It is widely distributed in igneous rocks.

MAG'NETRON. Thermionic valve (electron tube) for generating very high frequency oscillations, espec. as used in radar.

MAGNI'TOGORSK. Town in Chelyabinsk region, RSFSR, 320km (200m) S of Chelyabinsk town, on the r. Ural and the eastern slopes of the Ural Mountains. It was founded in 1931 to work the iron, manganese, bauxite, etc., in the district, and has blast furnaces and other metallurgical works producing steel, motor-cars, tractors, railway waggons, etc. Pop. (1977) 398,000.

MAGNŌ'LIA. Genus of trees in the family Magnoliaceae, native to China, Japan, N America, and the Himalayas. They vary in height from 50cm (2ft) to 30m (150ft). The large single flowers are white, rose, or purple in colour.

MAGPIE. Genus of birds (*Pica*) in the Crow family. The Common M. (*Pica pica*) has black and white plumage, the long tail having a metallic gloss. It feeds on insects, snails, mice, etc., and is found in Europe, Asia, and N Africa.

MAGRITTE (mahgrēt'), **René** (1898–1967). Belgian artist. A Surrealist, he used a visionary representationalism in such paintings as 'The Eye' (Museum of Modern Art, NY) or the late 'Scheherazade'.

MAGYARS (mod'yars). The largest racial group of Hungary. *See* HUNGARY; HUNGARIAN.

MAHABHA'RATA (Great poem of the Bharatas). Sanskrit epic of 18 books probably composed in its present form *c.* 300 BC. Forming with the *Ramayana* the 2 great epics of the Hindus, it deals with the fortunes of the rival families of the Kauravas and the Pandavas, and contains the Bhagavad-Gita (q.v.).

MAHAR'ASHTRA. State of the Republic of India formed in 1960 from the southern (predominantly Marathi-speaking) part of the former Bombay state. Bombay city is the cap.; other large towns are Poona, Nagpur, and Sholapur. It also includes the famous caves of Ajanta. Agriculture supports the majority of the people, cotton, rice, and ground-nuts being important crops. Area 307,762 sq.km (118,717 sq.m); pop. (1971) 50,412.

MAHARI'SHI (mah-hahrē'shi). Hindu guru or spiritual leader, espec. the Maharishi Mahesh Yogi, who at one time influenced the Beatles (Sanskrit *maha* 'great', *rishi* 'sage').

MAHĀYĀNA. *See* BUDDHISM.

MAHDI (Arab., he who is guided aright). The title of a coming messiah who will establish the reign of justice on earth. It has been assumed by many Moslem leaders, notably by the Sudanese sheik Mohammed Ahmed (1848–85), who headed a revolt in 1881 against Egypt and

MAHARASHTRA. Victoria Station, Bombay, a remarkable example of 19th century Gothic architecture enlivened by typically Indian decoration. *Photo: Peter Fraenkel*

in 1885 captured Khartoum. His great-grandson **Sadiq el M.** (1936-) leader of the Umma party in the Sudan, was PM 1966-7, and imprisoned 1969-74 for attempting to overthrow the military regime. Later reconciled to the ruling Sudanese Socialist Union, he then left the country in opposition to its support for 'Camp David'.

MAH-JONG (mah-dzong'). Originally an ancient Chinese card game, it is now usually played by 4 people with 144 small ivory tiles or 'dominoes', divided into 6 suits. The name means 'sparrows'.

MAHLER, Gustav (1860-1911). Austrian composer. B. in Bohemia, of Jewish extraction, he studied at Vienna conservatoire, conducted in Prague, Leipzig, Budapest, Hamburg (1891-7), and at the Imperial Opera, Vienna (1897-1907), and later went to the USA, becoming chief conductor at the Metropolitan Opera House (1907), and director of the Philharmonic Orchestra, New York. Outstanding among his symphonies is the 4th; *Das Lied von der Erde* is a symphony for solo voices and orchestra; his songs and song-cycles incl. the moving *Kindertotenlieder.*

MAHO'GANY. Timber obtained from several genera of trees found in America espec. in Belize. It is a warm red colour, very durable, and takes a high polish. True M. comes from the *Swietenia* but other types come from the Spanish and Australian cedars, the Indian redwood, and other trees of the family Meliaceae, native to Africa and the E Indies.

MAHÓN (mahōn'). Cap. and port of the Spanish island of Minorca, probably founded by the Carthaginians. It was in British occupation 1708-56 and 1762-82. Pop. (1970) 16,600.

MAHRA'TTAS or **Marathas.** A mixed race living in W and central India, and speaking the Marathi language. In the 17th and 18th cents. they formed a powerful military confederacy, which proved a dangerous rival to the Mogul emperors, until their power was broken by the Afghans in 1761. M. generals founded great states in the Deccan and central India, e.g. Indore, Gwalior, and Nagpur. A series of wars with the British, 1779-1871, ended in the annexation of most of their territory. *See* MAHARASHTRA.

MAIDEN CASTLE. Name of a prehistoric fort and successive later earthworks on Fordington Hill, near Dorchester, Dorset, England. A rampart, about 18m (60ft) high, enclosed an area of 18 ha (45 acres). The site was inhabited from Neolithic times (*c.* 2000 BC), and was stormed by the Romans AD 43.

MAIDENHAIR. A fern (*Adiantum capillusveneris*) with hair-like fronds terminating in small kidney-shaped pinnules containing the spores. It is widely distributed in America, and is sometimes found in the W of the British Isles.

MAIDENHEAD. Town in Berkshire, England, 40km (25m) W of London, on the Thames. A boating and boat-building centre, it manufactures electronic equipment, has a printing industry, etc. Pop. (1972) 47,220.

MAIDS OF HONOUR. In Britain the immediate attendants on the person of a queen. They are chosen generally from the daus. and grand-daus. of peers, but in the absence of another title bear that of Honourable. Queen Elizabeth II was attended by 6 at her coronation.

MAIDSTONE. Town in Kent, England, on the Medway, admin. HQ of the co. There are agricultural machinery, paper and printing, and brewing industries. Notable are the ruins of All Saints' College (1260) and Chillington Manor (Elizabethan), an art gallery and museum. Pop. (1972) 72,000.

MAIKOP (mī'kop). Cap. of Adyge autonomous region of the RSFSR on the Bielaia r., with timber mills, distilleries, tanneries and tobacco and furniture factories. Oilfields, discovered in 1900, are linked by pipeline with Tapse on the Black Sea. Pop. (1973) 122,000.

MAILER, Norman (1923-). American novelist. Born in New Jersey, the son of a South African immigrant, he is best known for his novel of the S.W.W. *The Naked and the Dead* (1949) and *An American Dream* (1964). He ran unsuccessfully for mayor of NY 1969, campaigning for NY as 51st state.

MAILLOL (mahyol'), **Aristide Joseph Bonaventure** (1861-1944). French sculptor. B. at Banyuls, he was a painter and designer before turning his attention to sculpture and held his first exhibition in 1902, becoming the leading sculptor in France. His principal works incl. the figure of 'Fame' for the Cézanne monument at Aix-en-Provence, and 'Flora' and 'Pomona' at Winterthur.

MAIL ORDER. Method of retail selling through specialized M.O. houses, by which the customer orders goods through the mail, usually with the aid of a glossy, illustrated catalogue. Originating as an organized business in the US, where the great distances made it a boon to isolated agricultural communities, it expanded rapidly. Reduced prices to the consumer can follow from bulk buying and elimination of the middleman. Almost all the transactions are on credit, and sales are concentrated in clothing, footwear, household textiles and soft furnishings, though almost every known item is available by this method. In Britain M.O. was comparatively slow to develop and the percentage of retail sales it covers remains far smaller.

MAIMONIDES (mīmon'idēz), **Moses** (Moses Ben Maimon) (1135-1204). Jewish codifier and philosopher. B. at Cordova, he evolved a philosophy of religion of great significance. His Code of Jewish Law is known as the *Mishneh Torah,* and his philosophical classic is *The Guide to the Perplexed.*

MAINE. The north-easternmost state of the USA, and the largest New England state. It has a rugged coast, and there are some 1,300 islands off the shore. The surface is undulating with a number of mountain peaks, culminating in Mt Katahdin 1,606 m (5,273 ft). There are many lakes.

Rivers incl. the Penobscot and Kennebec. In the valleys dairy farming and market gardening are carried on. Eighty per cent of M. is forested, and pulp and paper are the chief products; blueberries, apples and shell-fish are produced, and catering for holiday-makers is an important industry. The cap. is Augusta; the largest city, Portland. Area 86,027 sq.km (33,215 sq.m); pop. (1970) 993,663.

MAINE. Old French prov. bounded on the N by Normandy, on the W by Brittany, and on the S by Anjou. The modern depts of Sarthe and Mayenne approximately correspond with it.

MAINE. French river, 11km (7m) long, formed by the junction of the Mayenne and Sarthe; it enters the Loire below Angers, and gives its name to M.-et-Loire dept.

MAINTENON (mañtnoń'), **Françoise d'Aubigné,** marquise de (1653–1719). Wife of Louis XIV. The dau. of a Protestant, she was m. in 1657 to the poet Scarron (1610–60). Louis XIV employed her as governess, gave her a title in 1678, and soon afterwards made her his mistress. After the death of his queen she was secretly m. to him *c.* 1685.

MAINZ (mīnts). Cap. of Rhineland-Palatinate, W Germany, on the Rhine, 37km (23m) WSW of Frankfurt-am-Main. In Roman times it was a fortified camp and became the cap. of Germania Superior. Printing was invented *c.* 1448 in M. by Gutenberg. The Romanesque cathedral was severely damaged in the S.W.W. Pop. (1978) 186,860.

MAIZE. Plant (*Zea mays*) of the grass family, cultivated by Amerindians - hence its alternative name of Indian corn or in US usage 'corn' - and introduced to Europe by Columbus. It is now grown extensively in all subtropical and warm temperate regions, its range having been extended by hardy varieties in the 1960s to colder zones, and is widely used as animal feed. Sweet corn, a variety in which sugar is not converted to starch, is a familiar vegetable (fresh, tinned or frozen): other varieties are made into hominy, polenta, pop-corn, and corn bread. Industrial uses incl. industrial alcohol, corn oil, and (from the stalks) paper and hardboard.

MAIZE. 'Corn on the cob' piled high as the crop is gathered, not in the native home of the plant in America, but just outside Peking. *Photo: Courtesy of the Society for Anglo Chinese Understanding*

MAJO'LICA. A kind of enamelled pottery (q.v.), so-named from the Italian form of Majorca. The term is especially applied to the richly decorated enamel pottery produced in Italy 15th to 18th cents.

MAJO'RCA. Largest island of the Balearics (q.v.), which rises in Puig Mayor to 1,445 m (4,741 ft). Olives, figs, oranges, etc., are grown, and wine and brandy produced. Minerals incl. coal, iron and slate. The cap. is Palma, pop. 234,100. Area 3,639 sq.km (1,405 sq.m); pop. (1970) 363,200.

MAKA'RIOS III (1913–77). Cypriot Orthodox churchman. Archbishop and ethnarch in Cyprus from 1950, he was exiled by the British to the Seychelles 1956–7 because of his support for the armed struggle for union with Greece. He was President of the republic of Cyprus 1960–77, being briefly deposed for a few months in 1974.

MAKHACH'KALA. City, cap. of Daghestan ASSR, RSFSR, on the Caspian Sea, 145km (90m) ESE of Grozny, from which pipelines bring petroleum to M.'s refineries; shipbuilding, meat packing, and chemicals, matches, cotton textiles are other industries. Pop. (1977) 239,000.

MALABAR COAST. Name of the coastal area of Karnataka and Kerala states, India, lying between the Arabian Sea and the Western Ghats. About 65km (40m) W to E, 725km (450m) N to S, it has fertile soil and heavy rains, and produces food grains, coconuts, rubber, spices. Teak, ebony, and other woods are extracted from the mountain-side forests. Lagoons fringe the shore. A district of Tamil Nadu transferred in 1956 to Kerala was called M.C.

MALACCA. State of W Malaysia, Fed. of Malaysia. Portuguese from 1511, then Dutch from 1641, it was ceded to Britain in 1824, becoming part of the Straits Settlements. It produces rubber. Area 1,650 sq.km (640 sq.m) (about 70 per cent Chinese). The cap., also M., originated in the 13th cent. as a fishing village frequented by pirates, and developed into a trading port before Europeans reached the area. Pop. (1970) 86,360. The *Strait of M.* 965km (600m) long, lies between Sumatra and the Malay Peninsula; for *c.* 320km (200m) it is less than 38km (24m) wide.

MA'LAGA. Spanish seaport, cap. of M. prov., on the Mediterranean, 105km (65m) NE of Gibraltar; its mild and sunny climate makes it a popular holiday resort; other industries incl. sugar refining, distilling, brewing, olive oil pressing, shipbuilding. It has an airport. Founded by the Phoenicians and taken by the Moors in 711, M. was cap. of the Moorish kingdom of M. from the 13th cent. until captured in 1487 by Ferdinand and Isabella who founded the parish church in 1490. Pop. (1970) 374,450.

MALAGA'SY REPUBLIC. *See* MADAGASCAR.

MA'LAMUD, Bernard (1914–86). American novelist. A teacher of English, he first attracted attention with *The Natural* (1952), taking a professional baseball player as his hero, but was more typically represented by *The Assistant*

(1957), with its Yiddish-speaking immigrant characters, *The Fixer* (1966), and *Dubin's Lives* (1979).

MALĀ'RIA. Recurrent fever due to invasion of the blood stream by the minute parasite plasmodium. This develops in the stomach of the anopheles mosquito and passes into the blood when the insect pierces the skin to feed, enters the red corpuscles of the blood, completes its growth, and is then liberated into the blood stream, where its toxins cause the fever. The name derives from the Italian 'bad air', since it used to be believed that this was the cause. From 1955 the WHO organized an urgent eradication campaign, but strains of mosquito have developed which are resistant to DDT, as well as malarial parasites which are resistant to modern drugs, and in the 1970s M. had resurfaced in India, Indonesia, S America and other tropical areas.

MALAWI (malah'wi). Country in central Africa. Mainly plateau country, apart from Lake M. to the E, it averages some 1,000 m (3,000 ft), reaching over 2,500 m (8,000 ft) in Nyika Plateau in the N, and in the SE, across the valley of the Shiré, rises to over 3,000 m (9,850 ft) in the Mlanje Massif. Products incl. tea, tobacco, cotton, groundnuts, maize, and sugar. The cap. is Lilongwe; other towns are the former cap. Zomba, Blantyre-Limbe, and Mzuzu. Area 117,000 sq.km (47,950 sq.m); pop. (1977) 5,571,000. M.U.: kwacha.

First Europeans to visit M. were the Portuguese from the 17th cent., but the British intervened to prevent annexation by them during the late 19th cent., when they wished to link their colonies of Angola and Mozambique. The difficulty of the terrain, and warfare between the rival tribes of the Yao and Ngoni, had prevented any considerable penetration until this period, although Livingstone had reached Lake M. in 1859. The country became a Brit. protectorate in 1891, and from 1907 was known as Nyasaland. Against the wishes of its people, it was linked with N and S Rhodesia in the Fed. of Rhodesia and Nyasaland 1953-63, but then became self-governing, and in 1964 independent as Malawi, becoming a rep. within the Commonwealth in 1966. There is a pres., Hastings Banda being the first to hold the office (pres. for life from 1971), and a Nat. Assembly. The Malawi Congress Party is the only permitted political party.

MALAWI. Lake, for the most part incl. in the Rep. of M., formed in a section of the Great Rift Valley. It is *c.* 500m (1,500 ft) a.s.l., and 560km (350m) long, with an area of 37,000 sq.km (14,200 sq.m). It is intermittently drained to the S by the Shiré into the Zambezi.

MALA'Y PENINSULA. Southern projection of the continent of Asia lying between the Strait of Malacca, which divides it from Sumatra, and the China Sea. The northern portion is partly in Burma, partly in Thailand; the southern forms part of the Fed. of Malaysia (q.v.). The island of Singapore lies off its southern extremity.

The main physical feature is a central limestone range of wooded mountains over 2,000 m (7,000 ft) and flanked by undulating hills and alluvial plains. Mostly jungle-covered, they are watered by innumerable streams incl. the Perak, Bernam, and Muar on the W and the Kelantan, Pahang, and Trengganu to the E. The extremely humid tropical climate has little difference between summer and winter, and there is a profusion of flora and fauna.

In ancient times the M.P. seems to have been dominated by various waves of immigrants from India, and was the centre (9th to 14th cents.) of Sri Vijaya, the great Malay Buddhist empire, which was ultimately overthrown by Majapahit, Java's last Hindu kingdom, which in its turn was destroyed by Islam. Malacca became a centre of Islamic culture and an entrepôt for the spice trade, and a mighty Malay or Johore empire arose. Its growth was checked, however, by the conquest of Malacca by the Portuguese in 1511. In 1641 the Dutch ousted the Portuguese, and in 1773 the surrounding territory broke away from the Malay empire. Penang was founded by British interests in 1786, and Singapore in 1819. From 1874 Britain extended her control over the Malayan states, and before the S.W.W. the political organization of M. comprised the Straits Settlements (Singapore, Penang, incl. Prov. Wellesley, Malacca), the Federated Malay States (Perak, Selangor, Negri Sembilan, Pahang), and the Unfederated States (Johore, Kedah, Perlis, Kelantan, Trengganu). Occupied by the Japanese 1942-5, these various territories became in 1946 a crown colony, reorganized in 1948 as the *Federation of Malaya* which attained full independence 1957, and in 1963 (on the accession of Singapore, Sabah, and Sarawak) became known as Malaysia (q.v.).

MALAY'SIA. Federation in SE Asia, within the Brit. Commonwealth, formed in 1963 by the linking of the Fed. of Malaya, Sarawak, N Borneo (then renamed Sabah), and Singapore (seceded 1965): its establishment was opposed by Indonesia, but militant 'confrontation' ceased 1966. Since 1966 the states of the former Fed. of Malaya have been known as West M., and Sabah and Sarawak as East M. The Supreme Head of the Federation is elected for 5 years by the rulers of the member states from among their number; the fed. parliament consists of a senate (partly elected, partly nominated) and a house of representatives elected by universal adult suffrage. The nat. language is Malay, usually written in Arabic characters, which belongs to the W or Indonesian branch of the Malayo-Polynesian family of languages and originated in Malacca. English is also permitted as an official language in Sarawak, but the question of its use will be reviewed in 1979. Islam is the official religion of M., but religious freedom is guaranteed.

Equatorial rain forest covers three-quarters of both East and West M, and besides the all-important rubber, copra, palm and coconut oil, timber, pine-apples, kapok and rice (universally grown, but also imported) are produced. The chief mineral is tin, but gold, iron ore, bauxite, ilmenite, and coal are also mined, and there is petroleum in Sarawak. Industries are being developed to lessen M.'s dependence on raw material exports to more highly developed countries. Fishing is important. The cap. is Kuala Lumpur, in the fed. terr. of K.L. Area 331,500 sq.km (128,000 sq.m); pop. (1979) 13,000,000, incl. 50% Malays and 35% Chinese (between whom racial tension exists), and the rest Indians, Pakistanis, and indigenous peoples of East M. Five year plans 1966-70 and 1971-5 have given priority to the development of East M. and raising the level of lower income groups, and to increasing the financial stake in the country of the Bumiputras (native-born Malays). There has been Communist guerrilla activity on the Thai-M. border from 1969. M.U.: ringgit.

MALCOLM (mal'kom) **III,** called **Canmore** (d. 1093). King of Scotland. The son of Duncan I, he became king in 1054. He was killed at Alnwick while invading Northumberland.

MALAYSIA. A remarkable feat of Dayak engineering in North Borneo. Erected by rule-of-thumb methods, such bridges outlast many tropical storms. *Photo: Mireille Vautier*

MA'LDIVES. Group of nineteen coral atolls in the Indian Ocean, 725km (450m) SW of Sri Lanka, a republic since 1968. The Moslem inhabitants are famous as navigators and fishermen. The Is., which were a dependency of Ceylon 1645–1948, were under Brit. protection 1887–1965, when they became independent as the Republic of Maldives, and from 1985 a full member of the Commonwealth. Sunni Islam is the state religion. There is a Pres. and House of Representatives. Malé on Kings Island, is the cap. (pop. 15,000). Area 298 sq.km (115 sq.m); pop. (1980) 140,000 mainly Moslem, their language resembling old Sinhalese. M.U.: rupee.

MALDON. English market town in Essex, at the mouth of the Chelmer, the scene of a battle with the Norsemen in 991. Laurence Washington, great-great-grandfather of George Washington, was rector of Purleigh nearby 1632-43; he is buried at M. Pop. (1972) 14,300.

MALEBRANCHE (mahlbroṅsh'), **Nicolas** (1638-1715). French philosopher. B. in Paris, he joined the Congregation of the Oratory in 1660. His *De la Recherche de la Vérité* (1674-8), was inspired by Descartes: he maintained that exact ideas of external objects are obtainable only through God.

MALENKOV (mahl'yenkof), **Georgi Maximilianovich** (1901-). Soviet statesman. B. at Orenburg, he became chairman of the Council of Ministers (PM) in 1953, but resigned in 1955 following agricultural difficulties for which he confessed guilt. He was manager of the Ust-Kameno-Gorsk power station 1957-63. His second marriage was to Elena Khrushcheva, sister of Nikita Khrushchev.

MALHERBE (mahlārb), **François de** (1555-1628). French poet and grammarian. B. in Caen, he became court poet in *c.* 1605 under Henry IV and Louis XIII. He advocated reform of language and versification and estab. the 12-syllable Alexandrine as the standard form of French verse.

MALI, Republic of. Inland country of W Africa, the former French Sudan (*see* SUDAN), which became independent in 1960, outside the French Community. The name derives from the cap. of a medieval Negro kingdom on the Niger which fell before the attacks of other Negro tribes in 1500. M. covers the upper basins of the Senegal and Niger rivers, but is for the most part desert. Bamako, on the Niger, is the cap.; other towns are Mopti and Timbuktu. Cattle, sheep and camels are reared, but since independence rice and sugar-cane cultivation, and also some light industry, have been developed. A rail link Bamako-Conakry is planned to give M. access to the sea. In 1968 there was a military coup, and although there were elections for the presidency and nat. assembly in 1979, Pres. Moussa Traoré and the only official party, UDPM (Union démocratique du peuple malien), were automatically returned to power. Area 1,204,000sq.km (465,000 sq.m); pop. (1976) 6,030,000 mainly Moslem. French is the official language. M.U.: M. franc.

MALI. Bambara women passing a mud-built mosque in the striking local style at Djenné. *Photo: Mireille Vautier*

MALIC ACID. A laevorotatory compound $C_4H_6O_5$, widely distributed in apples, plums, cherries, grapes, and other fruits. It is usually prepared from the unripe berries of the mountain ash, and has the appearance of colourless needle-like crystals.

MA'LIK, Yakob Alexandrovich (1906-80). Soviet diplomat. As permanent representative at the UN 1948-53 and 1968-76, it was his walk-out from the Security Council in Jan. 1950 which allowed the authorisation of UN intervention in Korea to pass.

MALINES (-lēn'). City in the prov. of Antwerp, Belgium on the Dyle, 19km (12m) NE of Brussels. Once famous for its lace, called Mechlin (from Mechelen, the Flemish form of Malines), it makes furniture, carpets, textiles, etc., and is the seat of the archbishop-primate of Belgium. There is a famous carillon school and the cathedral contains Van Dyck's 'Crucifixion'. Pop. (1978) 78,500.

MALINO'VSKY, Rodion Yakolevich (1898-1967). He fought at Stalingrad, commanded in the Ukraine, and led the advance through the Balkans to capture Budapest (1945). He was Min. of Defence 1957-67.

MALLARMÉ (mahlahrmā'), **Stéphane** (1842-98). French poet. B. in Paris, he taught English there until 1892, and with Verlaine founded the Symbolist school. His belief that poetry should be evocative and suggestive was reflected in *L'Après-Midi d'un faune* (1876), which inspired Debussy. Later publications are *Poésies complètes* (1887), *Vers et prose* (1893), and the prose *Divagations* (1897).

MALLEE. Australian Aboriginal term for dwarf eucalyptus trees, characterized by a dense growth of small stems, and thick underground stems which retain water. These and more tree-like forms characterized the M. Region of NW Victoria until the advent of irrigation farming etc.

MALLORCA. Spanish form of MAJORCA.

MALLOW. Family of plants (Malvaceae) found in the N hemisphere. The common M. (*Malva sylvestris*), native to Europe and naturalized in N America, has 5-petalled, purple flowers.

MALMÉDY (mahlmehdē'). Town in Belgium, 40km (25m) S of Aachen. Given to Prussia in 1814, it became Belgian in 1920 after a plebiscite. It was a centre of fierce fighting during the German offensive in the Ardennes Dec. 1944. Pop. (1972) 6,500.

MALMÖ (mal'mo). Port and industrial city (shipbuilding, textiles) in Sweden. Pop. (1978) 238,500.

MA'LORY, Sir Thomas (d. 1471). English author, most usually thought to have been the Warwickshire landowner of that name who was MP for Warwick in 1445, and in 1451 and 1452 was charged with theft, rape and attempted murder. He would have compiled his prose romance *Morte d'Arthur* during his 20 years in Newgate. It is a translation from the French modified by material from other sources, and deals with the exploits of Arthur's knights of the Round Table, the quest for the Grail, etc.

MALPIGHI (mahlpē'gē), **Marcello** (1628-94). Italian physiologist. B. near Bologna, he held professorships at Bologna, Pisa, and Messina, and made many discoveries (still known by his name) in his study of animal and vegetable tissues by means of the microscope.

MALPLAQUET (mahlplahkā'). Village in Nord dept, France, to the NW of Maubeuge, where on 11 Sept. 1709 the Allies, under Marlborough and Prince Eugene of Savoy, defeated the French under Villars.

MALRAUX (mahlroh'), **André** (1901-76). French novelist. B. in Paris, he studied art and oriental languages, then went with an archaeological expedition to Indo-China. Later he became involved in the Kuomintang revolution, and *La Condition humaine* (1933: *Storm over Shanghai*) drew on these experiences. *L'Espoir* (1937: *Days of Hope*) is set in Civil War Spain, where he was himself a bomber-pilot in the International Brigade. In the S.W.W. he was an ardent supporter of the Gaullist Resistance. Min. of Cultural Affairs 1960-9, he pub. vols. of *Antimémoires* from 1967.

MALT. Grain, usually barley, which has been allowed to germinate and then dried. It is used for brewing and fermentation.

MALTA. Largest of a group of is. in the Mediterranean, 93km (58m) S of Sicily and 290km (180m) N of the N African coast. It is fairly low-lying. Agriculture - wheat, vegetables, fruit and flowers - and fishing are important, and lace-making is a traditional craft. Formerly largely dependent on prosperity brought by foreign military bases, M. has developed the dockyards on a commercial basis, and encouraged new industries such as textiles, knitwear, plastics, wine, and increasing exploitation of tourism. Valletta is the cap. and Luqa airport was completed 1958.

M. was colonized in turn by Phoenicians, Greeks, Carthaginians, and Romans - St Paul was shipwrecked here - and fell to the Arabs in 870. It was the HQ of the Knights of St John from 1530, became French in 1798, and British in 1814. A vital link in the S.W.W., being besieged and under air attack, M. was awarded the GC (decoration no longer used). In 1964 M. became independent within the Commonwealth and in 1974 a rep., with a pres. elected for 5 yrs and a House of Reps., elected by proportional representation. The ruling Labour Party policy (under leader Dom Mintoff 1971–84, followed by his former deputy, Carmelo Mifsud Bonnici) has been one of 'positive neutralism' allowing neither US nor Soviet warships to use docking facilities. Close links with Libya ended in 1984 with a dispute over Mediterranean oil-prospecting boundaries. The official languages are Maltese (related to Arabic, but influenced by Italian), and English. The people are RC. Total area 316 sq.km (122 sq.m), incl. Gozo 67 sq.km (26 sq.m) and Comino 2.5 sq.km (1 sq.m); pop. (1977) 308,940. M.U.: Maltese pound.

MALTA, Knights of. *See* ST. JOHN OF JERUSALEM.

MALTHUS (mal'thus), **Thomas Robert** (1766-1834). British economist and churchman. B. near Guildford, Surrey, he is famous for his *Essay on the Principle of Population* (1798; 2nd ed. 1803), in which he maintains that population increases in geometrical ratio, whereas the food supply increases in arithmetical ratio. Hence the necessity for checks, of which moral restraint is one of the chief.

MALVERN (mawl'vern). English spa and inland resort in Hereford and Worcester, on the E side of the Malvern Hills, which extend for *c.* 16km (10m), and have their high point in Worcester Beacon 425m (1,395 ft). The Royal Radar Establishment is here, and an offshoot of the American Boehm porcelain studio. The **M. Festival** (1929-39), assoc. with Shaw and Elgar, was revived in 1977. Pop. (1972) 31,000.

MALVINAS. Argentine name for FALKLAND IS.

MA'MELŪKES. Freed Turkish slaves who long dominated Egypt. They formed the royal bodyguard in the 13th cent., and in 1250 placed one of their own number on the throne. M. sultans ruled Egypt until the Turkish conquest of 1517, and they remained the ruling class until 1811, when they were massacred by Mehemet Ali.

MAMMALS or **Mammalia.** A classification, invented by Linnaeus in 1758, incl. all vertebrates which suckle their young. Most forms are viviparous, but there are still egg-laying species, the Monotremata (platypus, echidna, etc.).

MAMMOTH. Genus *Mammuthus* of extinct elephants (q.v.) whose remains are found world-wide, some being half as tall again as modern species. The woolly mammoth (*Elephas primigenius*), the size of an Indian elephant, had long fur, and huge inward-curving tusks.

MAMMOTH. Although they lived in the Ice Age, we know exactly what mammoths looked like, preserved specimens having been found in the frozen marshes of north-eastern Siberia. *Photo: G. Kinns/AFA*

MAMMOTH CAVE. Huge limestone cavern, in M.C. National Park (estab. 1936), Edmonson co., Kentucky, USA. The main cave is 6.5km (4m) long, and rises to a height of 38m (125ft); it is famous for its stalactites and stalagmites. Indian councils were once held here.

MAN, Isle of. *See* ISLE OF MAN.

MAN, Origins of. Until comparatively recently, it was thought that M. did not appear on Earth until *c.* half a million years ago, e.g. Pithecanthropus from Java (q.v.) and the related Peking Man (q.v.): fragments of the earliest skull found in Europe in 1965 at Vertsszöllös, *c.* 48km (30m) W of Budapest, belong to the same grouping. However, Darwin had predicted that the cradle of M. was Africa, and in 1924 Raymond Dart discovered at Taungs in Cape Province, the southern ape Australopithecus, difficult to date, but at least as old. The revolution in thinking about human origins came with the work of the Leakeys (q.v.) in Olduvai Gorge (q.v.) and later on the shores of Lake Rudolf in N Kenya, and in the Afar Valley in NE Ethiopia, which form part of the Great Rift Valley (q.v.). It now appears that the earliest man-like creature appeared 14 million years ago, but not until 3-5 million years ago did the hominid stock apparently divide into several types, of which all except the direct line of modern man (*Homo sapiens*) died out. The undisturbed stratification of the Rift Valley area makes more accurate dating possible, but bitter controversy rages over interpretation of all the finds connected with early man, and there is no agreement as to whether the differing types represent different genera or species or merely 'varieties'. *See also* PILTDOWN.

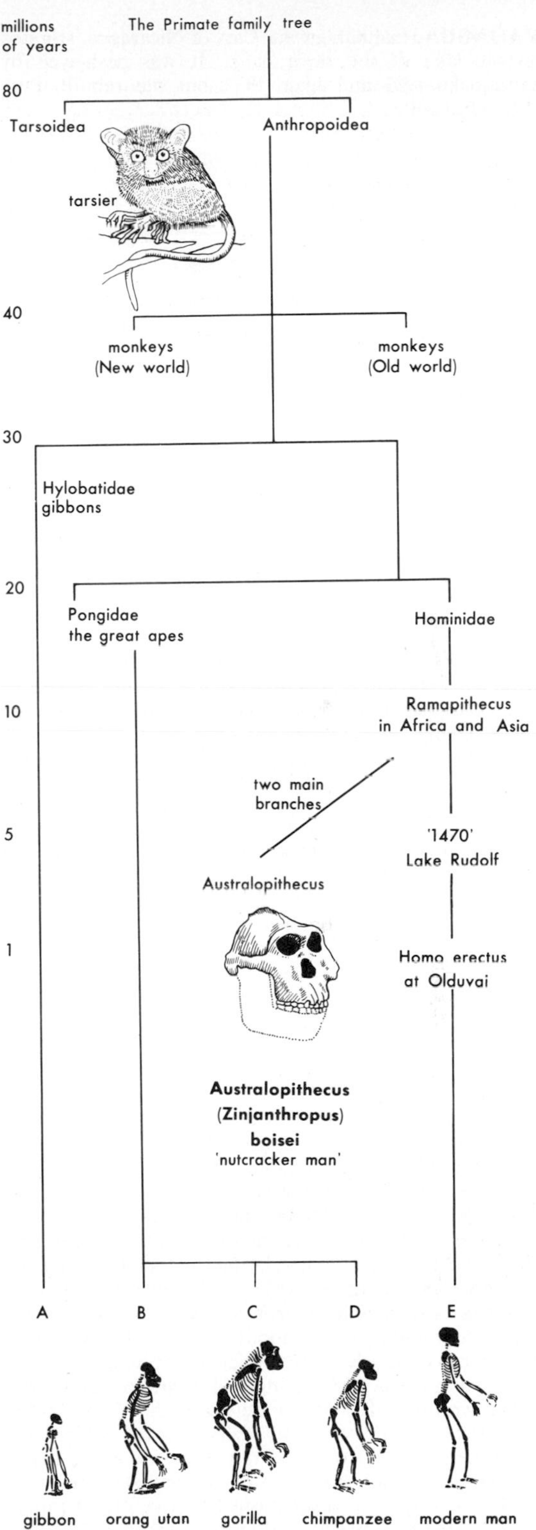

MAN. A tentative outline – much simplified – of the history of man's descent, based on recent discoveries.

MANAGUA (mahnah'gwah). Cap. of Nicaragua, situated on the lake of the same name. It was destroyed by earthquake 1931 and again 1972, but was rebuilt. Pop. (1977) 622,800.

MANAGUA. A city street soon after the earthquake in 1972: the older buildings on the right are comparatively unscathed. *Photo: Mireille Vautier*

MANÁUS (mahnah'os). Capital of Amazonas, Brazil, on the Rio Negro, near its confluence with the Amazon; although 1,600 km (1,000 m) from the Atlantic, it can be reached by sea-going vessels. In the 1970s it developed as a tourist centre. Pop. (1973) 750,000.

MANAWA'TU. River in North Island, NZ, rising in the Ruahine Range. The M. Plain is a rich farming area, specializing in dairying and fat lamb production.

MA'NCHA, La. Old prov. of Spain; the name, still used for the same district which covers the modern prov. of Ciudad Real and parts of Toledo, Cuenca, and Albacete, is derived from Arabic *al mansha*, the dry land.

MANCHE (moṅsh), **La.** French name for the English Channel (q.v.). It gives its name to a Fr. dept.

MANCHESTER. City in the met. co. of Greater Manchester, on the river Irwell, 50km (31m) E of Liverpool. Originally a Roman camp, M. is mentioned in Domesday Book, and by the 13th cent. was a centre for woollens. Its damp climate made it ideal for cotton, introduced in the late 16th cent., and in the 19th cent. (with a period of stagnation during the American Civil War which cut off supplies from the South) the M. area was the world centre of manufacture: in the 20th, espec. after the S.W.W., there was a sharp decline, and the disused mills were used to provide cheap premises for new industries. The varied products of the vast industrial area of which M. is the commercial centre, incl. road vehicles and tractors, aircraft, textile machinery, woollen and cotton goods, chemicals, iron and steel tubing, rubber, paper, flour and processed foods. There is a fine port with an extensive transit trade, which has encouraged M.'s growth as a financial, banking, and insurance centre. It is linked with the Mersey and the sea by the 57km (35.5m) M. Ship Canal (1894), and also served by the Bridgewater and other canals. Road and rail connections are highly developed, and M. Airport is of internat. standard.

M. has long been distinguished as a centre of radical thought (*see* PETERLOO), and in the *Guardian* (1821) has the one 'provincial' English newspaper of national standing. Culturally flourishing, it has the internat. Hallé Orchestra (1857); the City (1829) and Whitworth (1889) art galleries; the Central (1934) and John Rylands (1899) libraries; and Manchester Univ. (Owens Coll. 1851: univ. 1903) and Univ. Inst. of Science and Technology (1824: univ. 1966). Other buildings incl. the 15th cent. cathedral, Royal Exchange (1869), Town Hall (designed by Alfred Waterhouse), and the Free Trade Hall. It is the admin. HQ of Greater M. Pop. (1974) 533,560.

MANCHESTER, Greater. Met. co. created in the local govt reorganization of 1974 from the SE area of Lancashire, incl. M. (the admin. HQ), and NE Cheshire, incl. Altrincham and Stockport. Area 1,284 sq.km (496 sq.m); pop. (1978) 2,663,500.

MANCHUKUO (manchookwō'). Name of a puppet state set up in Manchuria by the Japanese in 1932 with Changchun (Hsinking) as its cap. and the last Chinese emperor, Henry Pu Yi, as ruler. It disappeared with Japan's defeat in 1945.

MANCHURIA (manchoor'ēa). Region of NE China, the modern provs. of Heilongjiang, Jilin, and Liaoning.

The area was originally inhabited by nomadic Tungus, but in the 17th cent. the Manchus obtained control, and a Manchu dynasty occupied the throne of China 1644-1912. Chinese colonisation began in the 18th cent., and by 1900 they formed 80% of the pop. Japan secured a part of S Manchuria in 1895, and Russia secured a lease of the Guangdong (Kwantung) peninsula for 25 yrs, which concession passed to Japan after her victory over Russia in the war of 1904-5. In 1931 the Japanese M. and set up the puppet state of Manchukuo (q.v.), 1932. After the collapse of Japan in 1945, M. was returned to China, and the many Japanese who had settled there were expelled.

MANDAEANS (mandē'anz). The only surviving Gnostic sect; they live near the Euphrates, S Iraq, and their sacred book is the *Ginza*.

MA'NDALAY. Chief town of Upper Burma, on the Irrawaddy, *c.* 495km (370m) N of Rangoon. Founded by King Mindon Min in 1857, it was cap. of Burma 1857-85. It has many pagodas, temples, and monasteries. Pop. (1972) 919,325.

MA'NDARIN. Chinese official. The word was adopted in the 16th cent. from the Portuguese, its ultimate origin being Sanskrit *mantrin*, 'counsellor'. In China the Ms. were chosen from the 7th cent. by examination. The term M. was also applied to the group of dialects, of which the standard form is that of Peking; they have been since the Ming dynasty the standard language of Chinese officialdom.

MANDATE. Under the Treaty of Versailles the system whereby the administration of former German and Turkish possessions was entrusted to Allied States by the League of Nations, the latter being replaced as the responsible authority in 1945 by the UN, when Ms. which had not achieved independence or self-govt became known as Trust Territories (q.v.). SW Africa (q.v.) is an exception in that the Rep. of S Africa does not recognize UN authority in this.

MANDELA (mandā'lah), **Nelson** (1918-). S African Black leader. A citizen of the Transkei, he led the Spear of the Nation (Umkonto We Sizwe), the militant wing of the banned African Nat. Council, and was jailed for life in 1964 for sabotage and plotting to overthrow the SA govt.

MANDELSHTAM, Osip Emilevich (1891-1938). Russian poet. Son of a Jewish merchant, he was sent to a concentration camp by the Communist authorities in the thirties, and the date and manner of his death were long unknown. Once considered a minor master, he was estab. as one of the greatest modern poets by his posthumously pub. work, saved by his widow, which has a classic brevity.

MANDEVILLE (man'devil), **Sir John.** Supposed author of a 14th cent. travel manual for pilgrims to the Holy Land, originally written in French and probably the work of Jean d'Outremeuse of Liège. As well as references to real marvels such as the pyramids, there are tales of headless men with eyes in their shoulders, etc.

MA'NDOLINE. A musical instrument descended from the lute, so called because its body is shaped like an almond (It. *mandorla*). It has 8 or 10 strings.

MANDRILL. W African baboon (*Papio maimon*). The nose is bright red and the cheeks striped with blue. There are red callosities on the buttocks; the fur is brown, with a yellow beard.

MĀ'NĒS. The gods of the underworld in ancient Rome, later identified with the ghosts of the dead.

MANET (mahneh'), **Édouard** (1832-83). French painter. B. in Paris, he came under the influence of Velazquez and Hals, and exhibited with Monet, Renoir and Whistler at the *Salon des Refusés* in 1863. This exhibition marked the beginning of the Impressionist movement, of which M. was the leading spirit. He summed up his aims in the famous dictum, 'The principal person in a picture is the light.' His best-known works incl. 'Déjeuner sur l'herbe', 'Absinthe Drinker', 'Olympia', 'Fife Player', and 'Bar at the Folies-Bergère'.

MANGALO'RE. Port in Karnataka, Rep. of India, on the Malabar coast, with textile and food industries. Pop. (1971) 214,100.

MA'NGANĒSE (Lat. *magnes* magnet). A brilliant white metal, present in small quantities in most rocks: symbol Mn, at. wt. 54.94 and at. no. 25. Discovered by Gahn in 1774 by reducing the dioxide with carbon, M. has a high melting point and is normally very hard and brittle. Chemically it is very reactive, and combines readily with oxygen on heating. Chiefly used in alloys, espc. for M. steel which is very tough, it also serves as a depolarizer in dry batteries, and potassium permanganate (an oxidizing agent) is used as an antiseptic and in quantitative analysis.

MANGEL-WURZEL or **mangold.** A variety of the common beet (*Beta vulgaris*) derived from the sea beet (*B. maritima*). It is used chiefly as feed for cattle and sheep.

MANGO. Tree *(Mangifera indica)* native to India but now widely cultivated for its oval fruits in other tropical and subtropical areas, e.g. West Indies. They do not travel well and in temperate countries are better known preserved unripe in pickles or chutney.

MA'NGROVE. Tree of the family Rhizophoraceae native to tropical coasts and estuaries where, by sending down roots from its branches, it rapidly forms close-growing M. swamps. Its timber is impervious to water and resists marine worms.

MANHATTAN. An island, 20 × 4km (12.5 × 2.5m), lying between the Hudson and East rivers, and forming a borough of New York City, USA. The business centre of the city lies in M., through which runs Broadway, a street famed for its theatre associations. Pop. (1970) 1,539,233.

MANHATTAN PROJECT. The development of the atom bomb in the S.W.W. *See* FERMI, OPPENHEIMER.

MANICHAEISM (man'ikē-izm). Religion founded by Mani (Latinized as Manichaeus), who was b. in Mesopotamia *c.* AD 216, and proclaimed his creed in 241 at the Persian court. Returning from missions to China and India, he was put to death at the instigation of the Zoroastrian priesthood *c.* 276. Despite persecution M. spread and flourished until the 10th cent. Its fundamental tenet was that the material world is an invasion of the realm of light by the powers of darkness: particles of goodness imprisoned in matter were to be rescued by messengers such as Jesus, and finally by Mani himself.

MANILA (mahnē'lah). Chief port of the Philippines, on Luzon: the natural harbour of M. bay is one of the finest in the Far East. Founded in 1571 by Spain, M. was captured by the USA in 1898, and in 1945 during the S.W.W. the old city to the S of the r. Pasig was reduced to rubble in fighting between the American troops and the Japanese. The city is the cap. of the Rep. of the Philippines, but was replaced by Quezon City (q.v.) 1948-76. Industries incl. textiles, tobacco, distilling, shipbuilding, etc. Pop. met. area (1975) 4,500,000.

MANIOC. *See* CASSAVA.

MANIPUR (manipoor'). State (from 1972) of the Rep. of India, to the E of Assam. Most of M. is mountainous and covered with dense forests, but there is a broad fertile valley which incl. Loktak Lake and Imphal, the cap., and produces large quantities of rice. It was the scene of very heavy fighting against the Japanese in March-April 1944. M. is the original home of polo. Area 22,346 sq.km (8,620 sq.m); pop. (1971) 1,070,000.

MANITŌ'BA. Prov. of Canada, situated midway between the Atlantic and Pacific. The territory was within the charter of the Hudson's Bay Company 1670-1869, the prov. being created 1870. It developed rapidly with mechanized grain-farming.

M. is mainly flat, with scattered hills. The prairie area lies to the W and SW, while in the NE the surface is broken by marshes. The prov. has a Hudson Bay coastline, and incl. 3 large lakes, Winnipeg, Winnipegosis, and Manitoba. The main rivers are the Assiniboine, Red, Nelson, and Churchill. The climate is continental. The provincial govt at Winnipeg, the cap., is under a lieutenant-governor and a legislative assembly, while 6 senators and 13 MPs represent M. in the Dom. parliament. Wheat, flaxseed, etc. are grown; poultry reared; and almost half the land area being under timber, lumbering is important. Furs (wild and ranch-bred) and fisheries are also valuable. Minerals incl. nickel, copper, zinc, gold and silver. Industries incl. food processing, iron and steel, clothing, chemicals, electronic equipment, and space probes. After the cap. the chief towns are St James - Assinaboia, St Boniface, St Vital and Brandon. Area 650,088 sq.km (251,000 sq.m); pop. (1976) 1,021,506.

MANITOBA, Lake. In Manitoba prov., Canada, it drains into Lake Winnipeg to the NE through the Dauphin r.: area 4,700 sq.km (1,800 sq.m).

MANIZALES (mahnēthah'les). City in the Central Cordillera in W Colombia at 2,150m (7,000ft) a.s.l., centre of a coffee-growing area. It is linked with Mariquita by the world's longest overhead cable transport system 72km (45m). Pop. (1973) 320,000.

MANLEY, Michael (1924-). Jamaican statesman. The son of Norman M. (1893–1969) – founder of the Peoples Nat. Party and PM 1959–62 – he was PM 1972–80.

MANN, Thomas (1875-1955). German novelist and critic. Son of a Lübeck grain merchant, he worked in an insurance office in Munich and on the staff of the periodical *Simplicissimus*, then returned in imagination to his native Lübeck to portray in his first novel *Buddenbrooks* (1900) the decline of one of the great Hanseatic families. *Der Zauberberg* (1924: *The Magic Mountain*), set in a Swiss sanatorium and concerned with problems of life and death, prepared the way for the award to him in 1929 of a Nobel prize, but his opposition to the Nazi régime forced him to live abroad and in 1940 he became a US citizen. Among his other most impressive works are the biblical tetralogy on the theme of Joseph and his brethren (1933-44), the political novel on the fate of modern Germany *Dr. Faustus* (1947), the comic masterpiece *Confessions of Felix Krull* (1954) and a number of short stories incl. 'Tonio Kröger' (1903) and 'Death in Venice' (1913).

His brother, **Heinrich M.** (1871-1950) was also a novelist, his books incl. *Im Schlaraffenland* (1901), *Professor Unrat* (1904: *The Blue Angel*), depicting the sensual downfall of a schoolmaster; the happier *Die kleine Stadt* (1909); a scathing trilogy dealing with the Kaiser's Germany *Das Kaiserreich* (1918-25); and 2 vols. on the career of Henry IV of France (1935-8). He left Germany with his brother and d. in the USA.

MANNA. A sweetish exudation obtained from many trees such as the ash and larch, and used in medicine. The M. of the Bible is thought to have been from the tamarisk tree.

MANNERHEIM (mahn'erhīm), **Carl Gustav Emil von** (1867-1951). Finnish soldier-statesman. After the establishment of a Finnish Socialist rep. in 1917 he formed a 'white' army, crushed the Socialists with German assistance, and during 1918-19 acted as regent. He commanded the Finnish armies during the Russian wars of 1939-40 and in 1941-4, and as president of Finland 1944-6 negotiated the peace settlement with Russia.

MANNHEIM. Town in Baden-Württemberg, W Germany, at the confluence of the Neckar and Rhine. Heavy machinery, glass, earthenware, chemicals, etc., are manufactured. A fishing village from the 8th cent., M. was made a town in 1606. Pop. (1978) 305,740.

MANNING, Henry Edward (1808-92). British cardinal. Ed. at Harrow and Balliol, he left the Colonial Office for the Anglican Church, becoming in 1840 archdeacon of Chichester. In 1851 he was converted to Rome, founded in 1857 the congregation of the Oblates of St Charles Borromeo, and in 1865 succeeded Wiseman as abp of Westminster. An ardent defender of papal infallibility, he was created a cardinal in 1875, and crossed a polemical sword with Gladstone in *The Vatican Decrees* (1875).

MANNING, Olivia (1911-80). British novelist. Best-known of her books were those telling the story of Harriet and Guy Pringle, inspired by her life with her husband R.D. Smith (whom she m. in 1939) during the S.W.W. These incl. *The Great Fortune* (1960), *The Spoilt City* (1962) and *Friends and Heroes* (1965), forming 'The Balkan Trilogy', and a later 'Levant Trilogy'.

MANOE'L (1469-1521). King of Portugal. He succeeded his uncle John II in 1495, and was known as 'the Fortunate', because his reign was distinguished by the discoveries by Portuguese navigators and the expansion of the Portuguese Empire.

MANOEL II (1889-1932). King of Portugal. He ascended the throne on the assassination of his father, Carlos I, in 1908; was driven out by a revolution in 1910, and lived in England.

MANOM'ETER. Instrument for measuring the pressure of gases, or blood pressure.

MANOR. A type of estate which formed the basic economic unit under the feudal system in England. The M. lands consisted of the lord's demesne, the lands held by the free tenants and villeins, and the meadow and waste lands. Tenure of a M. carried with it the right to hold a manorial court, which dealt with petty offences and disputes.

MANS (moṅ), **Le.** Industrial town in Sarthe dept, France, with a car-racing circuit on which is held an annual 24 hr endurance race (estab. 1923) for GT (grand touring) and sports cars, and their prototypes. Pop. (1975) 150,250.

MANSFIELD, Katherine. Pseudonym of New Zealand writer Kathleen Beauchamp (1888-1923). B. nr Wellington, New Zealand, she was ed. in London, to which she returned after a two-year visit home, where she pub. her earliest stories. Her first marriage to George Bowden in 1909 was immediately disastrous, but a second to John Middleton Murry in 1918 endured. Her delicate artistry emerges not only in her vols. of short stories, e.g. *In a German Pension* (1911), *Bliss* (1920) and *The Garden Party* (1923), but in her *Letters* and *Journal*. She d. of tuberculosis.

MANSFIELD. English town in Notts, on the Maun, nr a coalfield. The chief industries are the manufacture of textiles, boots, machinery, etc. Pop. (1972) 58,300.

MANSLAUGHTER. In both English and US law the killing of a human being either (1) in a sudden affray, or (2) as an outcome of culpable negligence. Charges under the first head are closely allied to murder, and will only be M. if there is no evidence of premeditation.

MA'NSTON. RAF aerodrome in Kent, England, a major diversionary aerodrome for aircraft (civil or military) in distress.

MANSURA (mahnsoo͞'rah). Town in Lower Egypt, the cap. of Dakahlia prov. It lies on the Damietta branch of the Nile, and has a flourishing cotton industry. M. was founded *c.* 1220; St Louis IX, king of France, was imprisoned in the fortress, 1250. Pop. (1974) 232,000.

MANTEGNA (mahntān'yah), **Andrea** (1431-1506). Italian painter of the Paduan school. B. at Vicenza, he came under the influence of Donatello, Uccello, Filippo Lippi, etc., and was the most important painter of the early Renaissance. His masterpiece is the 'Triumph of Caesar' (Hampton Court). The 'Madonna with John the Baptist and the Magdalen' (National Gallery), is one of the best preserved of all his works.

MANTIS. Insect of the family Mantidae. The praying mantis (*M. religiosa*) of S Europe adopts an attitude characteristic of devotion while waiting for its prey - flies, grasshoppers, and caterpillars. The eggs are laid in September and hatch early in the following summer. Ms. have the power of changing their coloration in accordance with their surroundings. There are over 800 species.

MA'NTŪA. Cap. town of M. prov., Lombardy, Italy, standing on an island of a lagoon of the Mincio, 40km (25m) SW of Verona. Among the chief buildings are the cathedral, founded in the 12th cent., the church of St Andrea, and Gothic palaces. Virgil was b. near M., which dates from Roman times. The industries incl. chemicals. Pop. (1971) 65,400.

MANU (ma'noo). In Hindu mythology, the founder of the human race. His preservation by Brahma from a deluge has caused him to be compared with Noah.

MANTIS. The green praying mantis *(Sphodromantis gastrica)* completing her egg case (ootheca), which adheres to the tree trunk behind her. This is a species from the South African Highveld. *Photo: Anthony Bannister/NHPA*

MANUTIUS (manū'shius), **Aldus** (1450-1515). The most famous Italian Renaissance printer. He estab. his printing press in Venice in 1490, and was the first to print Greek books. He made Venice the chief publishing centre of Europe.

MANX. The Gaelic language of the Isle of Man. Known only from the 17th cent., it is nearer akin to Scottish Gaelic than to Irish, and has been considerably influenced by English. Manx-speakers have declined: nearly 5,000 in 1900 and *c.* 100 in 1971. Original literature in M. consists mainly of ballads and carols (known as *carvels*).

MANZŌ'NI, Alessandro, count (1785-1873). Italian writer, author of tragedies but best remembered for his historical love story *I Promessi Sposi* (1825-7).

MAORI (mowri). The aboriginal population of New Zealand. They came from E Polynesia, according to tradition, *c.* 1350, and are tall and muscular, flat-nosed, with brown skin and black hair, At the time of the coming of Europeans they numbered *c.* 150,000. Their civilization was still neolithic, but they had acquired great skill in wood and stone carving and in weaving patterned cloth; women did most of the agricultural work, whilst the chief occupation of the men was warfare. The M. religion incl. some sort of belief in a supreme god, but was concerned mainly with placation of spirits who punished breach of taboo. The chief of a clan was held sacred. Not long ago in decline, their numbers are once more increasing, (1976) 270,000, and although they are full citizens of New Zealand there is some slight 'colour' difficulty.

MAO TSE-TUNG (mow zedong') (1893-1976). Chinese Communist statesman (Pinyin: Mao Zedong). B. in Hunan, he was a founder member of the Chinese Communist Party and became Chief of Publicity and Propaganda under Sun Yat-sen, but, sacked by Chiang Kai-shek, he became leader of the Communists in 1927. He led the 'long march' to Shensi in 1935 and secured an alliance with the Kuomintang from 1936 till the resumption of civil war in 1945. As chairman of the Chinese Communist Party, he held effective power from 1943, inspiring the 'Greap Leap Forward' 1959 and the 'Cultural Revolution' 1966, for which the 'little red book' of thoughts from his writings was the handbook. He m. as his 3rd wife in 1939

MAORI. A festival of song and dance in traditional dress at the model Maori village at Whakarewarewa, Rotorua. *Photo: Courtesy of the High Commissioner for New Zealand*

Jiang Qing (formerly Chiang Ching) (1913-), an actress who had made her debut as Nora in *A Doll's House*, and exercised increasing power after M.'s severe stroke in 1974. After his death, she was tried and received a suspended death sentence for counter-revolutionism in 1981.

MAO TSE-TUNG. Chairman Mao, and Lin Piao, the latter holding the little Red Book of Mao's thoughts. *Photo: Courtesy of the Society for Anglo-Chinese Understanding*

MAPLE. A deciduous tree of the genus *Acer* with opposite, stalked, palmately lobed leaves and green flowers, followed by two-winged samaras. There are about 115 species, chiefly in north temperate regions. The only British species is *A. campestre*; but *A. pseudoplatanus*, the sycamore or great maple, is naturalized. The sugar maple, *A. saccharatum*, is the N American species, and source of M. sugar.

MAPLIN. *See* Essex.

MAPUTO (mahpoo'tō). Cap. and chief port of Mozambique, formerly called Lourenço Marques, on Delagoa Bay. Linked by rail with Rhodesia and Johannesburg, it handles a vast entrepôt trade, and has an international airport. Industries incl. textiles, food processing, and furniture. Pop. (1970) 384,000.

MAQUIS (makē). Name of the scrub in Corsica, among which bandits sought cover. The term Maquis was popularly applied to members of the French Underground Movement (*Forces Françaises de l'Intérieur*) during the German occupation of 1940-5.

MARACAIBO (mahrahkī'bō). Port in Venezuela, on the channel connecting Lake M. with the Gulf of Venezuela. It chiefly exports oil from the fields surrounding the lake, but other products shipped incl. sugar, coffee, cocoa and hardwoods. There is a univ. Pop. (1971) 650,000.

MARAS (mah'rahsh). Town in the Taurus Mtns, Turkey, an agricultural marketing centre. Pop. (1970) 105,200.

MARAT (mahrah'), **Jean Paul** (1743-93). French revolutionary. B. in Switzerland, he practised medicine in Paris. After the outbreak of the Revolution he edited *L'Ami du peuple*, later renamed *Journal de la République Française*. He was the idol of the Paris working-classes, and in 1792 was elected to the National Convention and carried on a long struggle against the Girondins. He helped to bring about their overthrow in May 1793, but in July he was assassinated by the Girondin enthusiast, Charlotte Corday.

MA'RATHON. A plain in Greece on the E coast of Attica, 40km (25m) NE of Athens, where in 490 BC the Greeks defeated the Persian invaders in one of the decisive battles of the world. The news of the victory was conveyed to Athens by a runner, sometimes called Pheidippides, who fell dead as he entered the city. His performance is commemorated by a *Marathon Race* of *c.* 42km (26m 385yds), first included in the Olympic Games at Athens in 1896. The 192 dead infantry were possibly heroised as the Parthenon horsemen. *See* ELGIN MARBLES.

MARBLE. A limestone of pleasant colour and pattern, which takes and retains a good polish. Most marbles were originally limestones of ordinary character which have undergone recrystallization under the action of metamorphism, e.g. the Carrara marbles. An exception is Purbeck M., which is clayey limestone containing abundant remains of the freshwater gastropoda Paludina.

MARBURG. W. German town in Hessen, on the Lahn, 80km (50m) N of Frankfurt-am-Main. Seat of a univ. founded in 1527 as a centre of Protestant teaching; Luther and Zwingli disputed on religion at M. in 1529. Manufactures incl. chemicals, machinery, pottery. Pop. (1972) 48,500.

MARBURG DISEASE. Virus disease of central Africa, first known in Europe in 1967 among research workers in Germany with African green monkeys, hence it is also called 'green monkey' disease. It is characterized by haemorrhage of the mucous membranes, fever, vomiting and diarrhoea: mortality is high.

MARC, Franz (1880-1916). German artist. Closely associated with Kandinsky in preparing the Blue Rider Album in 1911, he repeatedly used the symbolism of animals, e.g. 'The Tower of the Blue Horses'. He was killed at Verdun.

MARCEAU (mahrsoh'), **Marcel** (1923-). French mime. B. at Strasbourg, he is the creator of the clown-harlequin 'Bip', and of mime sequences such as 'Youth, Maturity, Old Age and Death'. *See* PANTOMIME.

MARCH. Market town in the fen country of the Isle of Ely, Cambridgeshire, England, 39km (24m) N of Cambridge. Pop. (1971) 14,000.

MARCHAND (mahrshoṅ'), **Jean Baptiste** (1863-1934). French general and explorer. In 1898 he headed an expedition from the French Congo which occupied Fashoda on the White Nile. The subsequent arrival of British troops under Kitchener resulted in a crisis which nearly led to war between Britain and France.

MARCHES. The boundary areas of England with Wales, and England with Scotland. In the Middle Ages these troubled frontier regions were held by lords of the marches, sometimes called *marchiones* and later earls of March. The first earl of March of the Welsh M. was Roger de Mortimer (*c.* 1286-1330); of the Scottish M., Patrick Dunbar (d. 1285).

M. is also the name in English of a region of NE Italy covering the provinces of Ancona, Ascoli, Piceno, Macerata, and Pesaro e Urbino (in Italian, Marche pron. mahr'kā). The cap. is Ancona.

MARCŌ'NI, Guglielmo (1874-1937). Italian pioneer in the invention and development of wireless telegraphy. B. at Bologna, in 1895 he estab. wireless communication over more than a mile near Bologna. In 1896 he came to England, and conducted successful experiments on the roof of the Post Office building in London, on Salisbury Plain, and across Bristol Channel, and in 1897 the company that is now Marconi's Wireless Telegraph Co. Ltd. was formed. In 1898 M. successfully transmitted signals across the English Channel, and in 1901 estab. communication with St John's, Newfoundland, from Poldhu in Cornwall, and in 1918 with Australia. M. was an Italian delegate to the Peace Conference in 1919, received the Nobel prize for physics in 1909, and was made a senator and in 1929 a marchese.

MARCOS (mahr'kos), **Ferdinand** (1919-). Filipino statesman. B. on Luzon, he was convicted in 1939 while a law student of having murdered a political opponent of his father, but eventually secured his own acquittal. He was elected president in 1965 and ruled through increasing unrest until his oppressive regime was overthrown and he fled the country in 1986.

MARCUS AURĒ'LIUS ANTONĪ'NUS (AD 121-180). Roman emperor and Stoic philosopher. B. in Rome, he was adopted, at the same time as Lucius Aurelius Verus, by his uncle, the emperor Antoninus Pius, whom he succeeded in 161. He conceded an equal share in the rule to Lucius Verus (d. 169). M. A. spent much of his reign warring against the Germanic tribes, and d. in Pannonia, where he had gone to drive back the invading Marcomanni. Although one of the best of the Roman emperors, he persecuted the Christians for political reasons. M. A. is famous for his philosophical 'Meditations'.

MARCUSE (mahrkuz'), **Herbert** (1898–1979). American political philosopher. A Jewish refugee from Hitler's Germany, his books incl. *One Dimensional Man* (1964). A Marxist, he became prof. at the Univ. of California in 1975 and preached the overthrow of the existing social order by non-democratic means, taking advantage of the tolerance of the existing regime. Student revolts on the campus, and elsewhere were inspired by his theories to practical violence which dismayed him.

MARDUK. Chief god of Babylonia. Originally an inferior spirit connected with water magic, he became associated with Babylon, and on the rise of that city to greatness the priesthood gave him the qualities of a sun-god, recognizing him as creator of the earth and man.

MARE (mah'rā). Latin word for 'sea', used in the early maps of the Moon for the dark areas of the surface then thought to be water, but now known to be dry plains.

MARE'NGO. Italian village in Piedmont, where on 14 June 1800 Napoleon inflicted a crushing defeat on the Austrians.

MARGARET, St (*c.* 1045-93). Queen of Scotland. The grand-dau. of Edmund Ironside, she went to Scotland after the Norman Conquest, and soon after m. Malcolm III. Through her influence the Lowlands, hitherto purely Celtic, became largely Anglicized. The marriage of her dau. Matilda to Henry I united the Norman and English royal houses. She was canonized in 1251 in recognition of her benefactions to the Church.

MARGARET (1283-90). Known as the 'Maid of Norway', she was the dau. of Eric II, king of Norway, and Princess Margaret of Scotland. On the death of her grandfather, Alexander III, she became queen of Scotland, but d. in the Orkneys on the voyage to her kingdom.

MARGARET OF ANJOU (oṅzhōō') (1430-82). Queen of England. The dau. of René of Anjou, she was m. to Henry VI in 1445. After the outbreak of the Wars of the Roses in 1455, she acted as the leader of the Lancastrians, her one object being to secure the succession of her son, Edward (b. 1453). She withdrew to France in 1463, but returned during the Lancastrian reaction of 1471, only to be defeated and captured at Tewkesbury, where her son was killed. After 5 years' imprisonment she was allowed in 1476 to return to France, where she d. in poverty.

MARGARET (ROSE) (1930-). Princess of the UK. B. at Glamis Castle on 21 Aug. 1930, she is the younger dau. of George VI (q.v.). Religious and constitutional problems arose when it seemed possible that she might marry Group Captain Peter Townsend, former court equerry, who had been divorced, and in 1955 she announced her decision not to marry him. In 1960 she m. Anthony Armstrong-Jones, later created Lord Snowdon (q.v.), and is officially styled HRH The Princess Margaret, Countess of Snowdon. However, in 1976 they mutually agreed to live apart, and were divorced in 1978. They have a son, David, visct Linley (1961-), and a dau., Lady Sarah Armstrong-Jones (1964-).

MARGATE. Chief seaside resort of a group incl. Cliftonville, Westbrook, Westgate-on-Sea and Birchington, in Kent, England. It has a fine promenade and sands. Pop. (1974) 50,135.

MARGRAVE. German title (equivalent of marquess) for the 'counts of the March', who guarded the frontier regions of the empire from Charlemagne's time. Later it was borne by other territorial princes. The most important were the margraves of Austria and of Brandenburg.

MARGRETHE (mahrgrā'te) II (1940-). Queen of Denmark. The eldest dau. of Frederik IX, she succeeded him in 1972. She m. in 1967 French diplomat Count Henri de Laborde de Monpezat, who took the title HRH Prince Hendrik. Her heir is Crown Prince Frederik (1968-).

MARGUERITE. Popular name for the *Chrysanthemum frutescens*, of the botanical family Compositae. It is a shrubby perennial bearing white ray-florets surrounding a yellow centre.

MARGUERITE D'ANGOULÊME (doṅgoolām') (1492-1549). Queen of Navarre, French poet, and author of the *Heptaméron*, an imitation of Boccaccio. The sister of Francis I, she was b. in Angoulême, and m. as her 2nd husband Henri d'Albret, king of Navarre, in 1527.

MARI (marē'). An ASSR of the RSFSR, in the E of European Russia. The Volga flows through the SW of M., some 60 per cent of which is forested. The chief industries are lumbering, woodworking, paper making, and others associated with timber; grain, flax, potatoes, and fruit are grown. Yoshkar-Ola is the cap. About half the inhabitants are of Mari stock, a people conquered by Russia in 1552. M. was made an autonomous region in 1920, an autonomous rep. in 1936. Area 23,200 sq.km (8,900 sq.m); pop. (1978) 712,000.

MARIANAS (mahrē-ah'nahz). Archipelago in the NW Pacific, comprising Guam (q.v.) and the **Commonwealth of the Northern Marianas** (1978), a scattered group of 14 is. and atolls. The latter were sold to Germany by Spain in 1899, mandated to Japan in 1919, and taken by US Marines 1944-5 in the S.W.W. with espec. fierce fighting on Saipan and Tinian. Under US trusteeship from 1947 as part of the Pacific Is. Trust Territory (q.v.), they voted for commonwealth status in 1975. Fruit, vegetables, fish products, copra and handicrafts are exported. The admin. HQ is Saipan. Area 479 sq.km (185 sq.m); pop. (1974) 14,355, the majority RC Micronesians.

MARIANSKE LAZNE (mahr'ēanskā lahz'nye). Spa in Czechoslovakia, internationally famous before the S.W.W. under its German name Marienbad. The water of its springs, which contains Glauber salts, has been used medicinally since the 16th cent. Pop. (1970) 20,000.

MARIA THERESA (1717-80). Austrian empress. The dau. of the Emperor Charles VI, she m. her cousin Francis of Lorraine in 1736, and succeeded her father as archduchess of Austria and queen of Hungary and Bohemia in 1740. Her claim was challenged by Charles of Bavaria, who was elected emperor in 1742, while Frederick of Prussia occupied Silesia. The War of the Austrian Succession followed, in which Austria was allied with Britain, and Prussia with France; when it ended in 1748, M. T. retained her heritage, except that Frederick kept Silesia, while her husband had succeeded Charles as emperor in 1745. Intent on recovering Silesia, she formed an alliance with France and Russia against Prussia; the Seven Years War of 1756-63, which resulted, exhausted Europe and left the territorial position as before. After 1763 she pursued a consistently peaceful policy, concentrating on internal reforms; although her methods were despotic, she fostered education, codified the laws, and abolished torture. She also expelled the Jesuits. In these measures she was assisted by her son, Joseph II, who became emperor in 1765, and succeeded her in the Habsburg domains.

MARIBOR (mah'rēbor). Yugoslav town and resort in Slovenia, on the Drave, with a 12th cent. cathedral and some industry (boots and shoes, railway rolling stock are among products). M. dates from Roman times. Pop. (1971) 97,200.

MARIE (1875-1938). Queen of Romania. The dau. of the duke of Edinburgh, 2nd son of Queen Victoria of the UK, she m. Prince Ferdinand of Romania in 1893, who was king 1922-7. She wrote a number of literary works, notably *Story of My Life* (1934-5). Her son Carol became king of Romania, and her daus., Elisabeth and Marie, queens of Greece and Yugoslavia respectively.

MARIE ANTOINETTE (1755-93). Queen of France. The dau. of the Emperor Francis I and Maria Theresa, she m. in 1770 the dauphin, who 4 years later became king as Louis XVI. She forfeited her popularity by her frivolity,

MARIA THERESA. A miniature of the Empress with her consort and children, based on a painting by Martyn van Meytens in the Pitti Palace, Florence. The little girl in the crinoline, in the foreground, is the future Queen Marie Antoinette. *Photo: Courtesy of the Trustees of the Wallace Collection*

her extravagance, and her meddling in politics, often in Austrian interests. After the outbreak of the revolution in 1789 she exercised all her influence over her weak-willed husband to prevent concessions: she opposed Mirabeau's plans for a constitutional settlement, and brought about the unsuccessful flight to Varennes, which discredited the monarchy. She now relied on foreign intervention and when war with Austria began in 1792 betrayed the French plans to the enemy. In Oct. 1793 she was tried for treason and guillotined.

MARIE DE FRANCE (mahrē' de froṅs) (fl. *c.* 1150-1215). French poet. B. probably in Normandy, she is thought to have been the natural dau. of Geoffrey Plantagenet and half-sister to Henry II, and to have been abbess of Shaftesbury (1181-1215). She was the author of *Lais*, or verse tales, and *Ysopet* a collection of fables.

MARIE DE' MEDICI (mā'dēchē) (1573-1642). Queen of France. The dau. of the grand duke of Tuscany, she m. Henry IV of France in 1600, and after his murder in 1610 acted as regent for her son, Louis XIII. She left the government to her favourites, the Concinis, until in 1617 Louis seized power and put them to death. Reconciled to him in 1619, she lost all influence after the coming to power in 1624 of Richelieu.

MARIE LOUISE (1791-1847). Second wife of Napoleon I. The dau. of Francis I of Austria, she was m. to Napoleon in 1810 after his divorce from Josephine, and bore him a son, the king of Rome, in 1811. On his fall she returned to Austria. Granted the duchy of Parma in 1815, she proved a comparatively liberal ruler.

MARIENBAD. Ger. name of MARIANSKE LAZNE.

MARIETTE (mahryet'), **Auguste Ferdinand François** (1821-81). French Egyptologist. Beginning excavations in Egypt in 1850, he made many important discoveries, incl. the 'temple' between the feet of the Sphinx. He was the founder of the Egyptian Museum, Cairo, and Director of the Service des Antiquités from 1858.

MARIGOLD. Several plants of the Compositae family, espec. the pot M. (*Calendula officinalis*) in cultivation both in single and double forms for some 300 years, and the African M. (*Tagetes erecta*) and French M. (*T. patula*), both actually natives of Mexico.

MARIJUANA. *See* DRUGS and HEMP.

MARIN, John (1870-1953). American artist. B. in N.J., he was an architect's draughtsman until in 1899 he began to study art, living in Paris 1905-11. His finest works are his water-colour landscapes incl. studies of the Maine coast.

MARINES. Fighting men equally at home on land or sea, and because of their dual role of top calibre and esprit de corps. The Corps of Royal Marines (instituted 1664) is primarily a military force trained also for fighting at sea, providing commando units, landing craft, crews, frogmen, etc. The United States Marine Corps (estab. 1775) is primarily a naval force trained for fighting on land.

MARINE'TTI, Filippo Tommaso (1876-1944). Italian author. B. at Alexandria, in 1909 he pub. the first manifesto of 'Futurism'; he illustrated his theories in *Mafarka le futuriste* (1910), plays, and a vol. on theatrical practice (1916). He recorded his F.W.W. experiences in *Otto anime in una bomba* (1919), and welcomed Mussolini with *Futurismo e fascismo* (1924).

MARI'NI, Marino (1901-80). Italian sculptor. Influenced by primitive sculpture, he worked in an elongated, elegant style, and was particularly well known for his bronze horses, riders, and dancers.

MARIONETTE. Type of puppet (q.v.), a jointed figure controlled from above by wires or strings. They early reached a high artistic level in Burma and Ceylon and at the courts of Italian princes in the 16th-18th cents., and Haydn wrote an operetta such as *Dido* for the Esterhazy M. theatre. In the 20th cent. there has been a revival, especially in television, and Ms. have reverted to being a popular rather than aristocratic entertainment.

MARIONETTE. 'Wayang' marionettes in batik from the museum of batik in Djakarta. *Photo: Mireille Vautier*

MARLBOROUGH. The 1st Duke of Marlborough and Sarah, his tempestuous Duchess, both portraits after Kneller. *Photos: Courtesy of the National Portrait Gallery*

MARITAIN (mahretañ'), **Jacques** (1882-1973). French philosopher. Originally an exponent of Bergson, e.g. *La philosophie bergsonienne* (1914), he later became the best-known of the Neo-Thomists applying to contemporary problems the creative techniques of medieval times, e.g. *Introduction à la Philosophie* (1920).

MARITIME TRUST. Equivalent of the National Trust (q.v.) in the world of ships, estab. 1970 to discover, repair and preserve vessels of historic, scientific or technical interest: pres. the Duke of Edinburgh.

MARITSA (mah'ritsa). River, rising in the Rhodope Mtns, Bulgaria, which forms the Greco-Turkish frontier before entering the Aegean nr Enez: length 440km (275m).

MARIUPOL. *See* ZHDANOV.

MĀ'RIUS, Gaius (155-86 BC). Roman military commander and statesman. B. near Arpinum, he served in Spain in 134, and in the Jugurthine War 109-106. He was elected consul 7 times, the first time in 107. He defeated the Cimbri and the Teutones 102-101. M. tried to deprive Sulla of the command in the East against Mithridates, and as a result civil war broke out in 88. Sulla marched on Rome, and M. fled to Africa, but later Cinna held Rome for M. Cinna and M. created a reign of terror in Rome until the death of the latter.

MARIVAUX (mahrēvō'), **Pierre Carlet de Chamblain de** (1688-1763). French novelist and dramatist. He was b. in Paris, and his polished, sophisticated comedies, such as *Le Jeu de l'amour et du hasard, Les fausses confidences,* and *L'Épreuve,* gave the word *marivaudage* to the French language.

MARJORAM. Aromatic herbs of the Labiatae family. Wild M. (*Origanum vulgare*) is found both in Europe and Asia and has become naturalized in America: the culinary sweet M. is *Majorana hortensis.*

MARK. Christian apostle and evangelist, whose name is given to the 2nd Gospel. His first name was John, and his mother, Mary, was one of the first Christians in Jerusalem. He was a cousin of Barnabas, and accompanied Barnabas and Paul on their first missionary journey. Later, he was a fellow worker with Paul in Rome, and he seems to have attached himself to Peter as his interpreter after Paul's death. According to tradition he was the founder of the Christian Church in Alexandria, and Jerome says that he d. and was buried there.

The Gospel according to St Mark is held to have been written AD 65-70, and used by the authors of the 1st and 3rd Gospels.

MARK ANTONY (Marcus Antonius) (83-30 BC). Roman statesman and soldier. He served under Julius Caesar in the later campaign in Gaul. As tribune he defended Caesar's interests at Rome during the civil war, and when consul (44 BC), tried to secure for Caesar the title of king. After Caesar's assassination, A. with Octavius and Lepidus formed a triumvirate, and in 42 BC A. assisted in the defeat of Brutus and Cassius at Philippi. During 41 BC A. toured the eastern provinces, where he met Cleopatra, with whom he fell in love. When the 3 triumvirs divided the empire between them, A. secured Egypt for his share. In 32 BC the Senate declared war on Cleopatra. Defeated by Octavius at the naval battle of Actium (31), A. committed suicide.

MARKHOR (mahr'kor). Large wild goat (*Capra alconeri*), with spirally twisted horns and long shaggy coat. It is found in the Himalayas.

MARKIEVICZ, Constance Georgina, countess (d. 1927). Irish nationalist, *née* Gore Booth, who m. the Polish count M. in 1900. She fought in the Easter Rebellion of 1916, and was sentenced to death; the sentence was commuted, and she was released in 1917. She was elected to parliament at Westminster as a Sinn Féin candidate in 1918, so becoming the first British woman MP, but did not take her seat.

MA'RKOV, Andrei (1856-1922). Russian mathematician, who formulated the concept of the Markov Chain.

MARKOV CHAIN. In statistics a chain of events in which the transition between each event is a matter only of established probability, uninfluenced by the past history of earlier links in the chain.

MARKOVA (markō'fa), **Dame Alicia.** Name assumed by the first English Ballerina Assoluta, Lilian Alicia Marks (1910-). Trained by Pavlova, she was ballerina with Diaghileff's co. 1924-9, was the first resident ballerina of the Vic-Wells Ballet 1933-5, partnered Dolin in their own Dolin-Markova Co. 1935-7, and danced with the Ballet Russe de Monte Carlo 1938-41 and Ballet Theatre, USA, 1941-6. She was created DBE in 1963, and since 1970 has taught at the Univ. of Cincinnati. Of ethereal grace, she is always assoc. with the great classical ballets, espec. *Giselle.*

MARKS, Simon, 1st baron M. of Broughton (1888-1964). British chain-store magnate. The son of Polish immigrant Michael M., who started with Yorkshireman Tom Spencer a number of 'penny bazaars' in 1887, he entered the business in 1907 and built up a chain of more than 200 stores. Selling specially manufactured goods of high quality, he achieved a democratic revolution in dress for men and women.

MARL. A sedimentary rock sometimes called a clayey limestone, and incl. various types of calcareous clays and argillaceous limestones. Ms. are commonly laid down in freshwater lakes, and are usually soft, earthy, and of a white, grey, or brownish colour. They are used in cement making and as a top dressing for farmland.

MARLBOROUGH, John Churchill, 1st duke of (1650-1722). English soldier. The son of an impoverished Cavalier, he rose rapidly in the army through the favour of James, duke of York, and received a barony in 1685. At the revolution of 1688 he deserted James for William of Orange, who rewarded him with the earldom of M., yet in 1692 he fell into disfavour for intriguing with the Jacobites. He had m. Sarah Jennings (1660-1744), the friend of the Princess Anne, and after Anne's accession was created a duke. In the War of the Spanish Succession, he commanded the English and Dutch forces. His victory at Blenheim in 1704 saved Vienna from the French, and was followed by further victories at Ramillies (1706), Oudenarde (1708), and Malplaquet (1709). The return of the Tories to power in 1710, and a quarrel between Anne and the duchess, resulted in the dismissal of M. in 1711, and his flight to Holland to escape prosecution for corruption. He returned in 1714. The magnificent mansion and estate of Blenheim, in Oxon, were granted in recognition of his services. His London home, *M. House* (1709), was designed by Sir Christopher Wren: it was afterwards leased by Queen Anne, and later provided a home for Queen Adelaide, Edward VII (as prince of Wales), and Queen Mary. In 1959 it was lent to the govt by Elizabeth II to provide a Commonwealth meeting place in London (opened 1962). *See also* CHURCHILL, SIR WINSTON.

MARLBOROUGH. English market town in Wilts, 122km (76m) W of London. M. Coll., opened in 1843, is a public school. Pop. (1972) 6,200.

MARLOWE, Christopher (1564-93). English poet and dramatist. B. in Canterbury, the son of a shoemaker, he left Cambridge for London *c.* 1587, where he joined the earl of Nottingham's theatrical company. His 4 great plays, written 1587-93, are *Tamburlaine,* which gave blank verse the freedom of the English stage; *Dr. Faustus*; *The Jew of Malta*; and *Edward II.* His poems incl. versions of Ovid's *Amores,* and of Musaeus' 'Hero and Leander'. In 1593 he was involved, owing to statements made by Thomas Kyd under torture, in charges of atheism. A warrant had been issued for his arrest, when he was killed by Ingram Frisar in a Deptford tavern, apparently in a brawl over a reckoning, but possibly owing to political intrigue.

MA'RMARA. Small inland sea separating Turkey in Europe from Turkey in Asia, and connected through the Bosporus with the Black Sea, and through the Dardanelles with the Aegean. Length 275km (170m), breadth up to 80km (50m).

MARMES MAN. Human remains found on the ranch of R.J. Marmes in Washington, USA, in 1965. They are the earliest found in the Americas and 11,000 years old. A Mongol type, Marmes Man is thought to have been a cannibal.

MARMONTEL (mahrmoṅte'l), **Jean François** (1723-99). French novelist and dramatist. He wrote tragedies and libretti, and contributed to the *Encyclopédie*; in 1758 he obtained control of the journal *Le Mercure,* in which his *Contes Moraux* (1761) appeared. Other works incl. *Bélisaire* (1767), and *Les Incas* (1777). He was appointed historiographer of France (1771), secretary to the Académie (1783), and Professor of History at the Lycée (1786), but retired in 1792 to write his *Mémoires d'un père* (1804).

MA'RMOSET. Small monkey in the family Hapalidae found in S and Central America. Most species have characteristic tufted ears and handsome tail, and some are full-grown when the body is only 18cm (7in). Best-known is the common M. or ouistiti (*Callithrix jacchus*) of Brazil, often kept there as a pet.

MARMOT. A burrowing rodent of the genus *Marmota,* living in snowy regions, extending from the Alps to the Himalayas, and also in N America. *M. marmota* is the typical M. of the Central European Alps. Ms. live in colonies, make burrows, one to each family, and hibernate.

MARNE (mahrn). French river which rises in the plateau of Langres and joins the Seine at Charenton near Paris. It gives its name to the depts of Marne, Haute Marne, Seine-et-Marne and Val de Marne; and to 2 battles of the F.W.W. (q.v.).

MARONITES. Christian sect probably deriving mainly from refugee Monothelites of the 7th cent. They were subsequently united with the RC Church, and number *c.* 400,000 in the Lebanon and Syria with an equal no. scattered overseas in S Europe, and the Americas.

MAROT (mahrō'), **Clément** (*c.* 1496-1544). French poet. B. at Cahors, in 1524 he accompanied Francis I to Italy, and was taken prisoner at Pavia, but was soon released, and by 1528 was a salaried member of the royal household. Suspected of heresy, he fled to Turin, where he d. His graceful, witty style has been a model for all later writers of light verse.

MARPRELATE CONTROVERSY. Name given to a pamphleteering attack on the clergy of the C of E made in 1588 and 1589 by a Puritan writer or writers, who took the

MARS. 'Mars and Venus' by Botticelli, the richly moulded figures, brilliant colour and precise detail being characteristic of the artist, whose work was ill-appreciated by the art critics until the later 19th century. *Photo: Courtesy of the National Gallery, London*

pseudonym of Martin Marprelate. The pamphlets were printed by John Penry, a Welsh Puritan. His press was seized, and he was charged with inciting rebellion and hanged in 1593.

MARQUAND, John Phillips (1893-1960). American writer. Originally famous for a series of stories featuring the Japanese detective 'Mr. Moto', he made a serious reputation with his gently satirical novels of Bostonian society - *The Late George Apley* (1937) and *H. M. Pulham, Esq.* (1941).

MARQUESAS (mahrkā'sahs). Mountainous archipelago in the central Pacific Ocean, extending *c.* 400km (250m). Mendaña discovered the southern M. in 1595 and named them after his patron, the marquess of Cañete, Spanish viceroy of Peru. The M. were annexed to France in 1842 and used as a penal colony until 1865. The two largest is. are Nuku-hiva and Hiva Oa, and the admin. HQ is Atuona on the latter. Area 1,270 sq.km (490 sq.m); pop. (1970) 5,600, mainly Polynesians.

MARQUESS or **Marquis.** Title and rank of a nobleman who in the British peerage ranks below a duke and above an earl. The first English M. was created in 1385, but the lords of the Scottish and Welsh 'marches' were known as *marchiones* before this date. *See* MARCHES. The premier English marquessate is that of Winchester, and the wife of a M. is a marchioness.

MARQUETTE (mahrket'), **Jacques** (1637-75). French Jesuit missionary and explorer. Going to Canada in 1666, he explored the upper lakes of the St Lawrence, and in 1673 made a remarkable voyage down the Mississippi.

MARQUIS, Donald Robert Perry (1878-1937). American author. B. in Illinois, he is chiefly known for his humorous creations, *Old Soak* (1921), portraying a hard-drinking comic, and *archy and mehitabel* (1927), the type-written verse adventures of the cockroach, archy.

MARQUISES. French form of Marquesas.

MARRAKE'SH. Town in the foothills of the High Atlas *c.* 210km (130m) S of Casablanca, with textile and food processing industries. Founded in 1062, it has a medieval palace and mosques, and was formerly the cap. of Morocco. Pop. (1971) 330,000.

MARRAM-GRASS. A coarse perennial grass (*Ammophila arenaria*) which flourishes on sandy patches and, because of its tough and creeping rootstocks, is largely employed to hold coast dunes in place, particularly in Holland.

MARRA'NOS. The descendants of the Span. Jews converted by force to Christianity in the 14th and 15th cents., who secretly preserved their adherence to Judaism and carried out Jewish rites. Under the Spanish Inquisition thousands were burned at the stake. M. refugees in the 17th cent. founded the Jewish communities in Amsterdam, London, etc.

MARRIAGE. For the community primarily the means of ensuring its own continuation under stable conditions for the care of the young, and because of its importance hedged round by conventions, customs, and religious and civil laws in both 'civilized' and 'primitive' communities. The modern tendency is to freedom of choice in a partner, but modified by age-limits, below which no M. is valid, e.g. in the UK for both sexes 16 and in the USA varying according to state, for example New Hampshire allows girls to marry at 13; by degrees of consanguinity or other special relationships within which M. is either forbidden or enjoined; by economic factors such as ability to pay a father-in-law the required bride price, as in Africa; by rank, caste or religious differences; by medical requirements such as the blood tests of some states of the USA; by the necessity of obtaining parental, family or tribal consent; by the negotiations of a marriage broker in property-conscious and conventional societies, e.g. in Japan or formerly among Jewish communities; or colour, e.g. M. is illegal between European and non-European in S Africa, and until 1967 between white and coloured in some Southern, and white and Mongolian in some Western, states of the USA.

M. may be polyandrous or polygynous (qq.v.), but in modern times the emancipation of women in the W has led to greater emphasis on M as a personal relationship

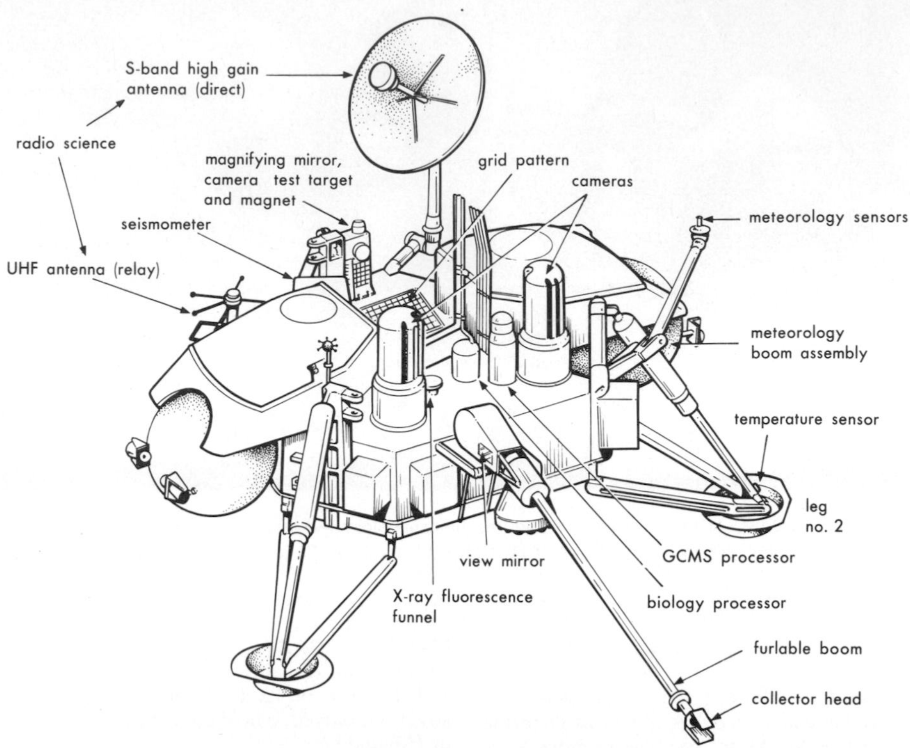

MARS. A diagram of the Viking lander's chief features when prepared to start its survey. The gas chromatograph mass spectrometer (GCMS) was to help search for possible organic compounds which would indicate life. *Courtesy of NASA*

with monogamy increasingly the rule, e.g. even in Moslem countries such as Pakistan where the right of a man to have 4 wives has been much restricted. Women also approach equality in M. in other ways, e.g. married women were enabled to hold property in their own name in England by 1882; in California community property laws entail the equal division of all assets between the partners on divorce; and in England a woman may be required to support a husband unable to support himself, and may be awarded custody of children. Stress on the personal aspect, however, leads to easier divorce (q.v.) notably in the USA and increasingly in the UK so that remarriage is more and more frequent for both sexes within the lifetime of the original partner. In the Soviet Union extreme freedom of divorce was granted at the Revolution in 1917, but these provisions were later progressively modified, until in the 1960s divorce was once again made easy. Illegitimacy, however, is discouraged: paternity suits are restricted and state allowances for unmarried mothers are small.

In England Ms. can be effected according to the rites of the C of E or those of other faiths, or in a superintendent registrar's office, but in most European countries civil registration of M., as well as (or instead of) a religious ceremony is obligatory, but common-law Ms. (i.e. an agreement to marry followed by co-habitation as man and wife) are still recognized in e.g. Scotland, some states of the USA and the USSR. As a step to international agreement on M. law the UN in 1962 adopted a convention on consent to M., minimum age for M., and registration.

MARRIAGE. The wedding of a prince and princess in the traditional ceremonial robes of ancient Japan, revived for the occasion. The full court regalia worn by the prince is the 'sokutai', and the court dress of the lady is the 'junihitoe'. *Photo: Courtesy of the Japanese Information Centre*

MARROW. In zoology, the soft vascular tissue in the central cavities of bones, composed largely of fat and white corpuscles. Another name for it is medulla.

In botany, Ms. are twining plants of the family Cucurbitaceae, producing large pulpy fruits used as a vegetable, and for making jams and preserves. There are bush Ms. and creeping or climbing Ms.

MARRYAT, Frederick (1792-1848). British naval officer and novelist. B. in London, he entered the RN in 1806 and rose to the rank of captain, but resigned in 1830 after the success of his first novel, *Frank Mildmay.* He wrote a number of popular adventure stories, incl. *Peter Simple* (1834), *Mr. Midshipman Easy,* and a series of boys' books, such as *Masterman Ready, Settlers in Canada,* and *Children of the New Forest* (1847).

MARS. The Roman god of war. The month of March is named after him.

MARS. The fourth planet in order of distance from the Sun. Its average distance from the Sun is 227,800,000 km (141,500,000 m), and it may approach Earth to within 54,700,000 km (34,000,000 m), so that it is then closer than any planet apart from Venus; at such times it is very brilliant and recognisable by its red colour. It is, however, much smaller than Venus or Earth: diameter 6,790 km (4,200 m), and mass only 0.11 that of Earth. It resembles E. in having a rotation period of 24 hr 37 min., but its year is 687 days.

The first man-made object to orbit another planet was *Mariner 9* (USA 1971-2), and this and later spacecraft, incl. *Viking 1* and *2* with lander capsules in 1976, provided much information. The planet is pear-shaped, with a low and level northern hemisphere, comparatively uncratered and geologically 'young', and a heavily cratered 'ancient' southern hemisphere: in this it resembles Earth before the break-up of Pangea by continental drift. The landscape is a dusty, red, eroded lava plain, resembling Arizona; red dust in the atmosphere probably accounts for the light pink sky; and winds of 200 kph (125 mph) have been recorded. Volcanic activity possibly still continues, and there are 4 enormous volcanoes near the equator, of which the largest is Olympus Mons 24 km (15 m) high, with a base 600 km (375 m) across, and a crater 560 km (350 m) wide. To the E of these volcanoes lies a high plateau cut by a great rift zone some 5,000 km (3,000 m) long, which incl. a canyon 480 km (300 m) long, 120 km (75 m) wide and 6 km (4 m) deep: these features are apparently caused by water erosion. Radiating from the S pole is a series of grooves, which seems to have been carved by glacial action, and the polar caps themselves, which advance and retreat 'according to season' are predominantly, if not totally water ice, and M. may have a thick ice shell beneath its surface rocks. The atmosphere is mainly carbon dioxide, but incl. 3% nitrogen and 1.5% argon. Temperatures have been recorded from -89°C (-128°F) to -32.2°C (-26°F). All the conditions for life exist: energy, water, nitrogen, carbon and phosphates, but no proof of organic life has been obtained.

M. has 2 satellites: Phobos, a rugged, cratered, elongated piece of rock 16 × 22.5 km (10 × 14 m) which has a greenish tinge, and Deimos 9 × 11 km (5.5 × 7 m). Both were discovered by A. Hall in 1877, and are thought to be captured asteroids.

MARSALA (mahrsah'lah). Italian seaport in the W of Sicily, exporting the sweet, white M. wine. M. was a Carthaginian settlement. Its cathedral is dedicated to St Thomas of Canterbury. Pop. (1971) 82,800.

MARSEILLAISE (mahrseyāz'), **La.** The French national anthem. The words and music were composed in April 1792 by Rouget de Lisle, an army officer stationed at Strasbourg, and were brought to Paris in Aug. by the volunteers from Marseilles, who led the storming of the Tuileries.

MARSEILLE (mahrsāy'). The chief seaport of France, and cap. of the dept of Bouches-du-Rhône, on the Golfe du Lion, Mediterranean Sea, connected with the Rhône by a canal. It is surrounded by hills, and there are several offshore islands incl. If (q.v.). M. was founded by mariners of Phocaea in Asia Minor in 600 BC. Under the Romans it was a free city, and then, after suffering successive waves of invaders, became in the 13th cent. an independent republic, until incl. in France in 1481. Much of the old quarter was destroyed by the Germans in 1943. The French conquest of Algeria and the opening of the Suez Canal stimulated prosperity, and today it is a major importer of oil from N Africa, and the Near East, a passenger port, and industrial centre, incl. chemicals, oil refining, metallurgy, shipbuilding, food processing, etc. To the NW is Fos sur Mer, site of a harbour forming the S focus of a direct Rhône-Rhine route to the North Sea via Rotterdam: *see* DELTA. The univ. was founded 1409. Pop. (1973) 893,770.

MARSH, Dame Ngaio (1899-1982). NZ novelist. Once on the stage, and later with a lively interest in the theatre as a repertory producer, she went to England in 1928 and worked as an interior decorator. Her first detective novel *A Man Lay Dead* (1934) has had many successors. Created DBE 1966.

MARSHAL. A title given in certain countries to a high officer of state, though originally it meant one who tends horses, in particular a farrier. The Earl Marshal (q.v.), is a high officer of state in England. The corresponding officer in Scotland was the Earl Marischal. The rank of a Marshal of the RAF corresponds to that of Admiral of the Fleet in the navy and Field Marshal (q.v.) in the army. In the French Army the highest officers bear the designation of Marshal of France.

MARSHALL, George Catlett (1880-1959). American soldier and statesman. B. in Pennsylvania, he was commissioned in 1901, served in the F.W.W., and in 1939 became chief of staff with the rank of general. On resigning in Nov. 1945 he became ambassador to China, attempting to secure a coalition between the Nationalist and Communist forces against Japan. He succeeded Byrnes as Sec. of State (1947-9), and as Sec. of Defence Sept. 1950-Sept. 1951 (a post never normally held by a soldier), backed Truman's recall of MacArthur from Korea. The Marshall Plan, initiated by him in a speech at Harvard in June 1947 and officially known as the European Recovery Programme, was in fact the work of a State Dept group led by Dean Acheson. It set the pattern for the large-scale foreign aid by the US which was subsequently widened in scope to cover the entire non-Communist world.

MARSHALL, John (1755-1835). American jurist. B. in Virginia, as chief justice of the Supreme Court 1801-35, he laid down interpretations of the US constitution in a series of important decisions, which have since become universally accepted.

MARSHALL, Sir John (1912-). NZ Nat. Party statesman. Noted for his negotiations of a free trade agreement with Australia, he was deputy to Holyoake (q.v.) in both premierships and succeeded him Feb.-Nov. 1972.

MARSHALLS. Two chains of islands in the W Pacific Ocean, comprising Radak and the Ralik groups, with 13 and 11 islands respectively. Occupied by German traders in 1888, they became a German colony 1906; Japanese mandate 1919; part of the Pacific Is. Trust Terr. (q.v.) 1947. In 1986 a compact of 'free association' with USA was signed, allowing the US to maintain missile bases on the islands for 30 years. Pop. (1984) 34,923.

MARSH GAS. *See* METHANE.

MARSH MARIGOLD. Plant (*Caltha palustris*) of the buttercup family Ranunculaceae, known as the kingcup of England and as the cowslip in the USA. The 5-sepalled yellow flowers are brilliant in moist sheltered spots in March.

MARSI'LIUS OF PADUA (1270-1342). Italian scholar. B. at Padua, he studied and taught at Paris, and in 1324 collaborated with John of Jandun in writing the *Defensor pacis*, a plea for the subordination of the ecclesiastical to the secular power. He played a part in the establishment of the Roman republic in 1328, and was made archbishop of Milan.

MARSTON MOOR. Battle fought in the Civil War on 2 July 1644 on M. M., 11km (7m) W of York. The Royalists, under Prince Rupert and the duke of Newcastle, were completely defeated by the Parliamentarians and Scots, under Cromwell and Lord Leven. Lord Fairfax, on the right of the Parliamentarians, was routed; but Cromwell's cavalry charges were decisive.

MARSŪPIĀ'LIA (Gk *marsupion*, little purse or bag). An order of Mammalia, in which the female has a pouch in which she carries her young for some considerable time after birth. The chief members are the kangaroo, wombat, opossum, Tasmanian wolf, bandicoot, and wallaby.

MARTELLO TOWERS. Towers built along the coast, especially in Sussex and Kent, in 1804, as a defence against the threatened French invasion. The name is derived from a tower on Cape Mortella, Corsica, which was captured by the British with great difficulty in 1794, and was taken as a model. They are round towers of solid masonry sometimes moated, with a flat roof for mounted guns.

MARTEN. Small carnivorous mammals belonging to the Mustelidae family, genus *Martes*. They live in wild and rocky regions in the warmer parts of the northern hemisphere, and are hunted for their fur. The pine-marten (*M. martes*), has long, brown fur, and is *c.* 75cm (2.5ft) long. It is found in Britain. The stone or beech M. (*M. foina*) is lighter in colour. The sable (*M. zibellina*) lives in E Siberia, and provides the most valued fur. The largest is the pekan (*M. pennanti*), with black fur and reaching 125cm (4ft), of N. America.

MARTHA'S VINEYARD. Island 32km (20m) long off the coast of Cape Cod, Mass., where once lived the whaling captains whose houses are now owned by the wealthy as summer homes. Edward Kennedy and a girl companion, Mary Jo Kopechne, were involved in a car crash off nearby Chappaquiddick Is. in July 1969; the girl was drowned.

MARTIAL (mahr'shial) **(Marcus Valerius Martialis)** (*c.* AD 41-*c.* 104). Latin epigrammatist. B. in Bilbilis, Spain, he came to Rome in 64, where he lived by his literary and social gifts, retiring to his native place in 98. His poetry reflects contemporary Roman life, and although licentious, is unrivalled in correctness of diction, versification, and form.

MARSUPIAL. The rare Ningaui of the Western Australian desert, first given official zoological classification in 1975. It weighs 5 grams (0.17 oz), has a body 30 mm (1.1 in) long and a tail about 40 mm (1.75 in) long. It can eat its weight in insects in a day. *Photo: Courtesy of the Australian Information Service*

MARTIAL LAW. As distinguished from military law, i.e. the law governing the conduct of the armed forces, whether within the realm or elsewhere, in peace or in war, the legal position as regards M.L. is difficult of definition in England. In effect, when war, rebellion, etc., are in progress in an area the military authorities are recognized as having powers to maintain order by summary means. In the United States M.L. is usually proclaimed by the pres. or the gov. of a state in areas of the country where the civil authorities have been rendered unable to act, or to act with safety. M.L., though neither in the constitution nor laid down in statutes, has frequently been used in the US, e.g. in Hawaii 1941-4 after the bombing of Pearl Harbor.

MARTIN, St (*c.* 316-400). Bishop of Tours. B. in Pannonia, a soldier by profession, he was converted to Christianity, left the army, and lived for 10 years as a recluse. After being elected bishop of Tours *c.* 371, he worked for the extinction of idolatry and the extension of monasticism in France. He is usually represented as dividing his cloak with a beggar.

MARTIN V. Pope, 1417-31. A member of the Roman family of Colonna, he was elected during the Council of Constance, and ended the Great Schism.

MARTIN, Archer John Porter (1910-). British biochemist. He specialized in chromatography, and shared a Nobel prize for his researches with his colleague R. Synge in 1952.

MARTIN, (Basil) Kingsley (1897-1969). British journalist. Son of a Unitarian minister, he was ed. at Magdalene Coll., Cambridge, lectured in political science at LSE 1923-7, and as editor of the *New Statesman* 1931-60 made it the voice of controversy on the Left. His autobiographical *Father Figures* (1966) and *Editor* (1968) throw much light on political issues of his time.

MARTIN, John (1789-1854). British painter of landscapes and religious subjects. B. in Northumberland, he settled in London in 1806, and first exhibited at the RA in 1812. His pictures, such as 'Belshazzar's Feast' and 'The Deluge', show an exaggerated sense of drama. His brother, **Jonathan M.** (1782-1838), became a convert to Methodism, and followed up his warnings to the established clergy of judgment to come by setting fire to York Minster in 1829. He was condemned to an asylum.

MARTIN, Richard (1754-1834). Irish landowner, lawyer and humanitarian, known as 'Humanity Martin'. He founded the Royal Society for Prevention of Cruelty to Animals in 1824.

MARTIN, Violet Florence (1862-1915). Irish novelist known under the pseudonym 'Martin Ross'. B. in Galway, she collaborated with her cousin, Edith Œ. Somerville, in novels of Anglo-Irish provincial life, e.g. *Some Experiences of an Irish RM* (1899), and *In Mr. Knox's Country*.

MARTIN. Several genera of birds, allied to the swallow, in the family Hirundinidae. The European house M. (*Delichon urbica*), a summer migrant from Africa, is blue-black above and white below, distinguished from the swallow by its shorter, less forked tail. The cup-like mud nest is usually constructed under the eaves of buildings. Best-known of other species are the brownish European sand M. (*Riparia riparia*), which tunnels to make a nest in sandy banks, also a migrant from Africa, and the common purple M. of N America (*Progne subis*), a handsome steely-blue bird which often nests in hollow trees.

MARTIN DU GARD (mahrtiṅ' dü gahr), **Roger** (1881-1958). French novelist. B. at Neuilly, of bourgeois stock, he realistically recorded the way of life of his class in the 8 vol. *Les Thibault* (1922-40). He was awarded a Nobel prize in 1937.

MARTINEAU (mahr'tinō), **James** (1805-1900). British Unitarian minister and philosopher. A remarkable preacher, he anticipated Anglican modernists in his theology. His sister **Harriet M.** (1802-76) was a socio-economist, and wrote children's tales.

MARTINET (mahrtineh'), **Jean** (d. 1762). French inspector-gen. of infantry under Louis XIV, whose constant drilling brought the army to a high degree of efficiency - hence the use of his name to mean a strict disciplinarian.

MARTÍNEZ RUIZ, José. *See* AZORÍN.

MARTI'NI, Simone (*c.* 1284-1344). Italian painter, greatest of the Sienese school, whose influence was widespread. B. in Siena, he was a pupil of Duccio, but excelling his master in his development of line and colour. He painted a portrait of Laura for Petrarch and is commemorated by the poet in 2 sonnets. He d. at Avignon.

MARTINIQUE (mahrtēnēk'). French island in the W Indies (Lesser Antilles). Volcanic in origin, it still has several active volcanoes: *see* PELÉE, MONT. Sugar, cocoa, rum, etc., are produced. The cap. and chief commercial centre is Fort-de-France: pop. 99,000.

M. was discovered by Spanish navigators in 1493, became a French colony in 1635, and was an overseas dept 1947-72, when it became an overseas region. There is agitation for total independence. The Empress Josephine was b. in M., and her childhood home is a museum. Area 1,100 sq.km (420 sq.m); pop. (1972) 339,000.

MARTINMAS. In the Christian calendar, the feast of St Martin (11 Nov.). Fairs were frequently held on it, at which farm-workers were hired. In the Middle Ages it was also the day on which cattle were slaughtered and salted for winter consumption.

MARTI'NO, St (1579-1639). Peruvian Spanish/Negro monk, the first RC 'half-caste' saint in 1962.

MARTYR (from the Gk for 'witness'). In the Christian Church, one who voluntarily suffers death for refusing to renounce the Christian faith or a part thereof. The first recorded Christian M. was St Stephen, who was killed in Jerusalem shortly after Christ's ascension.

MARVELL, Andrew (1621-78). English metaphysical poet and satirist. B. in Yorks, while tutor to the dau. of Lord Fairfax 1650-3 he wrote many of his finest nature poems, and was assistant to Milton as Latin Sec. to the Council of State 1657-60. He was MP for Hull from 1659, and devoted his last years mainly to verse satire and controversial prose works.

MARX (mahrks), **Karl Heinrich** (1818-83). German philosopher and Socialist. B. at Trèves, the son of a Jewish lawyer, he studied at Bonn and Berlin, and during 1842-3 edited the *Rheinische Zeitung* until its suppression. In 1844 began his life-long collaboration with Engels (q.v.), with whom he developed the Marxist philosophy, first formulated in their joint works, *The Holy Family* (1844), and *German Ideology* (1846), and M.'s *Poverty of Philosophy* (1847). Both joined the Communist League, a German refugee organization, and in 1847-8 they prepared its programme, 'The Communist Manifesto'. During the 1848 revolution M. ed. the *Neue Rheinische Zeitung*, until in 1849 he was expelled from Prussia.

He then settled in London where he wrote *Class Struggles in France* (1849), *The 18th Brumaire of Louis Bonaparte* (1852), *Critique of Political Economy* (1859), and his monumental work *Das Kapital* (1867: *Capital*). In 1864 the International Working Men's Association was formed, whose policy M., as a member of the general council, largely controlled, and on behalf of which he wrote his defence of the Paris Commune, *The Civil War in France* (1871). Although he showed extraordinary tact in holding together its diverse elements, it was disrupted by the intrigues of the anarchists, and in 1872 collapsed. The 2nd and 3rd vols. of *Capital* were ed. from his notes by Engels, and pub. posthumously. M. was buried at Highgate.

MARX BROTHERS. Team of American film comedians: Leonard 'Chico' (1887-1961), Arthur 'Harpo' (1888-1964), Julius 'Groucho' (1890-1977), Milton 'Gummo' (1897-1977), and Herbert 'Zeppo' (1901-79). Their films incl. *Duck Soup* (1933) and *A Night at the Opera* (1935).

MARXISM. The philosophical system, also known as dialectical materialism or scientific Socialism, founded by Marx and Engels, and developed by Plekhanov, Lenin and Stalin. The main sources of Marx's thought were classical German philosophy, especially that of Hegel; English political economy, notably the works of Adam Smith and Ricardo; and the 'Utopian Socialism' of Saint-Simon, Fourier and Owen. M. is a complete and consistent philosophy, which has profoundly influenced current views on science, history, and literary criticism, even among non-Marxists. Modern British Marxist writers include C. Caudwell in philosophy, R. P. Dutt in politics, M. Dobb in economics, J. B. S. Haldane, J. D. Bernal, and H. Levy in science, V. G. Childe and C. Hill in history, and R. Fox, G. Thomson, B. Farrington and J. Lindsay in literary studies. *See* DIALECTICAL MATERIALISM; also COMMUNISM.

MARY (Blessed Virgin Mary), Mother of Jesus Christ. She was traditionally the miraculous child of Joachim and Anna in their old age; she m. Joseph, the carpenter of Nazareth, and accompanied him to Bethlehem. The question of her perpetual virginity (the 'brethren of Jesus' being presumed as the sons of Joseph by a former marriage) has occasioned much controversy, but is recognized as a dogma of the RC Church, as is her Immaculate Conception and bodily Assumption. Veneration of M. as a mediator has played an increasing part in worship since the Council of Ephesus, AD 431: Pope Paul proclaimed her 'Mother of the Church' 1964.

MARY (1867-1953). Queen consort of George V (q.v.). The dau. of the duke and duchess of Teck, the latter a grand-dau. of George II, she became engaged in 1891 to the duke of Clarence, eldest son of the Prince of Wales (later Edward VII). After his death in 1892, she in 1893 m. his br. George, duke of York, who succeeded to the throne in 1910. She was an art connoisseur and needlewoman.

MARY I (1516-58). Queen of England. The dau. of Henry VIII by Catherine of Aragon, she was b. at Greenwich. When Edward VI d. in 1553, she secured the crown without difficulty in spite of the conspiracy to substitute Lady Jane Grey. In 1554 she m. Philip II of Spain, and as a devout Catholic obtained the restoration of papal supremacy. Although naturally humane, she sanctioned the persecution of Protestants which won her the nickname of 'Bloody M.'.

MARY II (1662-94). Queen of England. The elder dau. of James II, she was m. in 1677 to her cousin, William of Orange. After the 1688 revolution she accepted the crown jointly with William. During his absences abroad she took charge of the government, and showed courage and resource when invasion seemed possible in 1690 and 1692.

MARY, Queen of Scots (1542-87). She succeeded her father, James V, in infancy, and as a child was sent to France, where she m. the dauphin, later Francis II. After his death she returned in 1561 to Scotland, which, during her absence, had accepted Protestantism. She m. her cousin, the earl of Darnley, in 1565, but they soon quarrelled, and Darnley took part in the murder of M.'s secretary, Rizzio. In 1567 he was assassinated as the result of a conspiracy formed by the earl of Bothwell, possibly with M.'s connivance, and shortly after Bothwell carried M. off and m. her. A rebellion followed; defeated at Carberry Hill, M. abdicated and was imprisoned. She escaped in 1568, raised an army, and after its defeat at Langside fled to England. Elizabeth held her a prisoner, while the RCs, who regarded M. as rightful queen of England, formed many conspiracies to place her on the throne. The discovery that she was involved in Babington's plot led to her trial and execution at Fotheringay Castle in 1587.

MARY (1457-82). Duchess of Burgundy. The dau. of Charles the Bold, she m. Maximilian of Austria in 1477, thus bringing the Low Countries into the possession of the Habsburgs, and ultimately of Spain.

MARY (mah'rē). Town in Turkmen SSR, on the Murgab. It dates from the 19th cent. and lies 29km (18m) W of the ancient city of Merv (q.v.). It makes textiles, carpets, and metal goods and has food factories. Pop. (1973) 62,000.

MARY. Mary, Queen of Scots, in mourning for her first husband, Francis II. The portrait is based on a drawing by Francois Clouet. *Photo: Courtesy of the Trustees of the Wallace Collection*

MARYBOROUGH. Australian coastal town in SE Queensland, near coal- and gold-mining fields. It has iron and steel foundries. Pop. (1972) 19,150.

MARYBOROUGH. *See* PORT LAOIGHIS.

MARYLAND. An Atlantic state of USA, between Pennsylvania and Virginia. It has a much-indented coastline, and is penetrated by Chesapeake Bay, a wide arm of the Atlantic. In the W are wooded mountains and coal is mined; the centre is undulating wheatland, and on the coastal plains there are tobacco plantations, fruit orchards, etc. Fish is abundant, and oysters are very plentiful. The cap. is Annapolis; the largest city is Baltimore. The first settlers in M., 1634, were Roman Catholics, following the grant to Lord Baltimore in 1632 of a royal charter to establish a colony N of the Potomac. They called their first township St Mary's; it remained the cap. until displaced by Annapolis, 1694. M. was one of the 13 original states forming the Union. Area 27,394 sq.km (10,577 sq.m); pop. (1970) 3,922,399.

MARY MAGDALENE. Probably from Magdala, she is said in the Gospels to have had 7 demons cast out from her. She was present at the Crucifixion and met the risen Jesus.

MARY OF MODENA (1658-1718). Queen consort of England and Scotland. The dau. of the duke of Modena, she m. James, duke of York, later James II, in 1673. The birth of her son, James, in 1688, which was widely believed to be fraudulent, gave the signal for the Revolution, and M. fled to France.

MASACCIO (mahsah'chō). Name given to the Florentine painter Tomaso di Giovanni di Simone Guidi (1401-28). B. nr Florence, where, with his teacher

Masolino di Panicale (*c.* 1384–1447), he executed his most famous work, the decoration of Santa Maria del Carmine. He was one of the first to apply the laws of perspective, had a good knowledge of anatomy and made effective use of light and shade.

MASA'DA. Rock fortress 396m (1,300 ft) above the W shore of the Dead Sea, Israel. Besieged by the Romans AD 72, its population of 953 committed mass suicide: the site was excavated 1963–5, incl. the palace of Herod.

MASADA. The stepped rock fortress, which provided a supreme example of human courage. In the distance, the Dead Sea. *Photo: Courtesy of the Israel Government Tourist Office*

MASAI (mahsī'). African people remarkable for their fine physique. Originally warriors and nomadic breeders of humped zebu cattle, on which they relied for their diet of milk, meat and blood, they disdained agriculture but are gradually adopting a more settled life. Their territory is divided between Tanzania and Kenya, and at the time of independence in 1963 they unsuccessfully demanded its total inclusion in either one country or the other. Neither Negro nor Bantu, they speak a Hamitic language.

MASARYK (maz'erik), **Thomas Garrigue** (1850–1937). Czech statesman. Always a champion of national minorities, he directed the Czech revolutionary movement, founding with Beneš and Stefanik the Czechoslovak Nat. Council, and in 1918 was elected first pres. of the newly-formed Czechoslovak Republic. Thrice re-elected, he resigned in 1935 in favour of Beneš. His son **Jan Garrigue M.** (1886–1948), a diplomat, became For. Min. to the exiled Czech govt in London in 1940 and continued to hold the post on its return to Prague in 1945. However, when there was reorganization following Communist pressure in Feb. 1948, he allegedly committed suicide. For 20 years no reference was allowed to be made to the Masaryks, but in the liberalization of 1968 tribute was paid and doubt as to Jan's 'suicide' admitted.

MASCAGNI (mahskahn'yē), **Pietro** (1863–1945). Italian composer. B. at Leghorn, he became famous as the composer of the one-act opera *Cavalleria Rusticana*, first produced in Rome in 1890.

MASCARA'. Algerian wine trade centre, after which the cosmetic M. is named, 96km (60m) SE of Oran. It has the HQ of Abd-el-Kader (*c.* 1807–83) who fought the French invasion of Algeria 1830–47, M. being captured 1841. Pop. (1970) 37,000.

MASEFIELD, John (1878–1967). Brit. poet. B. at Ledbury, Herefordshire, he went to sea, and while in the USA worked as a barman in a New York saloon. Returning to England, he joined the *Manchester Guardian* before settling in London. He attracted notice by such vols. of poetry as *Salt Water Ballads* (1902), but fame came with the verse narrative of a drunkard's conversion *The Everlasting Mercy* (1911), with its forcefully colloquial language. Later were the Chaucerian *Reynard the Fox* (1919), and novels such as *Sard Harker* (1924) and *Badon Parchments* (1947); and he essayed drama in *Tragedy of Nan* and *Pompey the Great.* He was appointed Poet Laureate in 1930, and in 1935 was awarded the OM.

MĀ'SER (Acronym for Microwave Amplification by Stimulated Emission of Radiation). A high-frequency amplifier or oscillator dependent on the quantum properties of electrons. By inverting the populations of a pair of electron spin energy levels (i.e. by making the upper level more densely populated than the lower one) the resonance absorption at a frequency corresponding to the energy difference can be changed to emission; an M. results from suitable coupling of this radiation to a microwave cavity or travelling wave structure. The population inversion can be achieved by beam focusing, as in a two-level ammonia gas M., or pumping at a different frequency between another pair of levels, as in a solid-state three-level M. This latter can be tuned magnetically and operates at liquid helium temperatures (−269°C); it is the most sensitive amplifier known.

The two-level M. was first suggested in 1954 by C. H. Townes at Columbia univ. and independently the same year by Basov and Prokhorov in the USSR. The principle of the three-level M. was envisaged by Bloembergen in 1956 at Harvard and Bell Telephone Laboratories embodied it in a cavity M. in the same year and in a travelling wave M. in 1958. The principle has since been extended to other parts of the electromagnetic spectrum. (*See* LASER.) The ammonia M. is used as a frequency standard oscillator (*see* CLOCKS) and the three-level M. as a receiver for satellite communications and radio astronomy.

MASERU (maz'eroo). Cap. of Lesotho, S Africa, on the Caledon r.; it is a trading centre and the Nat. Univ. of Lesotho (1964) is at Roma, 48km (30m) N. Pop. (1974) 30,000.

MASHŌ'NALAND. The E part of Zimbabwe, occupied by the Mashona tribes. It was granted to the British South Africa Company in 1889, and occupied 1890. The company ruled it until 1923 when it came within the self-governing colony of Southern Rhodesia. Here are the ruins of Zimbabwe (q.v.).

MASHRAQ (mash'rak). Name for countries of the E Mediterranean (Arabic 'east', 'sunrise'): the M. power are Egypt, Jordan, Syria, Lebanon.

MASKELYNE (mas'kelin), **Nevil** (1732–1811). British Astronomer Royal from 1765, who devised such instruments as the prismatic micrometer, and was founder-editor of the *Nautical Almanac* from 1766. His scheme to measure the Earth's density was put into practice in 1774.

MASOCH (mah'sokh), **Leopold Sacher von** (1836–95). Austrian novelist. His books dealt with the sexual pleasures to be obtained by having pain inflicted on oneself - hence 'masochism'.

MASON, Alfred Edward Woodley (1865-1948). British novelist and playwright. Originally an actor, he pub. his first novel, *A Romance of Wastdale,* in 1895, and won a great reputation with *The Four Feathers* (1902), a tale of the Sudan. He also created the detective Hanaud, who appears in *At the Villa Rose* (1910), etc.

MASON AND DIXON LINE. In the USA, the boundary line between Maryland and Pennsylvania (lat. 39° 43′ 26.3″ N), named after M. and D., English astronomers who surveyed it 1763-7. It became popularly regarded as dividing the slave states from the free before the Civil War, and generally the N from the South.

MASQUE (mahsk). Form of amateur dramatic entertainment introduced into England from Italy during the reign of Henry VIII. It reached perfection in the Stuart period with the partnership of Inigo Jones and Ben Jonson. Based on a fairy or mythological theme, the plot was overshadowed by the elements of music, dancing, costume, and scenic design. The masked performers were drawn from the court nobility.

MASS. In physics, the quantity of matter in a body. The British unit of M. is the pound, i.e. the quantity of matter in a standard platinum cylinder preserved at the standards office at the Board of Trade; in the SI system, now under adoption in Britain, the base unit of mass is the kilogram. M. determines the acceleration produced in a body by a given force working upon it, the acceleration being inversely proportional to the M. of the body. The M. also determines the force exerted on a body by the gravitational attraction of the earth, although this attraction varies slightly from place to place. At a given place, however, equal M. experiences equal gravitational forces, which are known as the weights of the bodies. M. may, therefore, be compared by comparing their weights at the same place, as in a balance.

MASS. In the Christian Church, the Eucharist, also known as the Lord's Supper, or Holy Communion; since the Reformation, the use of the word has been practically confined to the RC Church, but it is in use amongst Anglo-Catholics. RCs believe that the M. is a real offering in which the bread and wine are transubstantiated, i.e. are converted into the body and blood of Christ. Changes were made to 'popularize' its celebration following the Second Vatican Council, e.g. the priest was to face the congregation, and English and other vernaculars could be used instead of Latin. Anglo-Catholics believe that Christ is really present under the forms of bread and wine. Protestants maintain that Christ's sacrifice was made on Calvary, and that Holy Communion is a commemorative rite.

Low M. is said by the priest without music; at high M. the priest is assisted by deacon and sub-deacon, and there is incense and music.

MASSACHUSETTS (masachoo'sets). One of the New England states of USA, facing the Atlantic Ocean and incl. the 2 large islands of Nantucket and Martha's Vineyard. The N coast is very rocky. Inland the country rises gradually to the Berkshire hills. There are many lakes, and the chief rivers are the Merrimac and the Connecticut. Agriculture is still important, but M. is largely industrial, e.g. electronics and communications equipment, shoes, textiles, and machine tools. Building stone is quarried. The cod fisheries have been famed for centuries. The famous M.I.T. (M. Institute of Technology, 1861) is at Cambridge, Mass., seat also of the Univ. of Harvard (1636).

The Pilgrim Fathers were the first settlers, at Plymouth in 1620, and the narrow Puritan outlook was long predominant. It was one of the original 13 states of the Union. The cap. is Boston. Area 21,385 sq.km (8,257 sq.m); pop. (1970), 5,689,170.

MASSAGE. Manipulation of the tissues and muscles of the body for therapeutic effect. The basic movements are pétrissage (moulding), kneading, friction, effleurage (stroking), tapotement (patting). It is particularly useful in the case of sporting injuries.

MASSA'WA. Chief port of Ethiopia, in Eritrea, on the Red Sea, with a good harbour. Salt is produced and pearl fishing carried on. One of the hottest inhabited spots in the world, the temperature reaching 100°F (37.8°C) in May, it was held by the Italians 1885-1941. Pop. (est.) 30,000.

MASSAWA. Temperatures here reach 46°C (115°F) and water evaporates quickly. About 230,000 tonnes of salt are collected from these pans every year. *Photo: Jennifer Fry/Camera Press*

MASSÉNA (mahsānah'), **André** (1756-1817). Marshal of France. He served in the revolutionary wars, and under Napoleon was created a marshal of France in 1804, duke of Rivoli in 1808, and prince of Essling in 1809. He was in command in Spain 1810-11.

MASS-ENERGY EQUATION. The equation $E = mc^2$, denoting the interconversion of mass and energy, where E is the energy in joules, m is the mass in kg, and c is the speed of light in metres/sec.

MASSENET (mahsnā'), **Jules Émile Frédéric** (1842-1912). French composer. B. near St Étienne, he composed many operas, incl. *Hérodiade* (known in England as *Salomé*), *Manon* (1884), *Le Cid* (1885), and *Thaïs*; and also ballets, oratorios and orchestral suites, incl. *Scènes pittoresques.*

MASSEY, Vincent (1887-1967). Canadian Liberal statesman. He helped to estab. the M. Foundation (1918) which funded the building of M. College, Univ. of Toronto, etc., held diplomatic posts, and was first Canadian-born Gov.-General. His brother **Raymond M.** (1896–1983), a US citizen from 1944, starred in films, eg *Things to Come* and *Mourning Becomes Electra.* Raymond's dau. **Anna** (1937–) is an actress.

MASSIF CENTRAL (mahsef' soṅtrahl'). Mountainous plateau region of S central France: area 93,000 sq.km (36,000 sq.m), highest peak Puy de Sancy 1,886 m (6,188 ft). Still largely remote, it is a source of hydroelectric power, and Clermont-Ferrand is a large industrial centre.

MASSINE (mahsēn'), **Léonide** (1896-1979). Russian dancer-choreographer. In his appearance with the Diaghilev Ballet Russe in Paris 1914-20 and the Ballet de Monte Carlo, 1932-41, he gained fame for his interpretation of character roles. His choreographic works incl. the first Cubist ballet *Parade* (1917); *The Three Cornered Hat* and *La Boutique Fantasque* (1919); *Le Sacre du Printemps* (1920); *Symphonie Fantastique* (1936), based on Berlioz; *Mam'selle Angot* (1943), etc.

MA'SSINGER, Philip (1583-1640). English dramatist. B. at Salisbury, he settled in London *c.* 1606. His masterpiece is *A New Way to Pay Old Debts* (*c.* 1625), in which the usurer, Sir Giles Overreach, appears. He collaborated with Fletcher and Dekker, and some critics credit him with a share in Shakespeare's *Two Noble Kinsmen* and *Henry VIII.*

MASS OBSERVATION. Method of ascertaining general facts bearing on contemporary life, and also the name of a society founded in London in 1937 for this purpose, and employing a panel of observers and a number of trained investigators. *See* GALLUP and HARRISSON.

MASSŌ'RAH. A collection of philological notes on the Hebrew text of the OT. At first merely oral tradition, the M. was committed to writing in the Aramaic language at Tiberias in Palestine between the 6th and the 9th cents AD.

MASS SPECTROMETER. An instrument in which positive ions (q.v.) of a material are separated by an electric-magnetic system which permits accurate measurement of the relative concentrations of the various ionic masses present, and detects non-radioactive isotopes.

MASTER AND SERVANT. Although in Britain common law governs relations between employer and employee in circumstances not covered by special enactments, the latter cover an increasingly large field. Conditions in factories have been covered since the 19th cent., but the Offices, Shops and Railway Premises Act (1963) extended protection to workers in previously neglected areas. The Equal Pay Act (1970), in force from 1975, prevents discrimination between men and women in employment. Redundancy payments were provided for under an act of 1965, and the Contracts of Employment Act (1972) compels an employer to set out details of his contract with an employee incl. wage rates, hours of work, holiday entitlement, injury and sick pay, and length of notice to be given by both parties to end the contract. The Sex Discrimination Act (1975) attempted to secure equality of opportunity for both sexes.

MASTER OF THE ROLLS. Title of an English judge ranking immediately below the Lord Chief Justice; he presides over the Court of Appeal, besides being Keeper of the Records and head of the Public Record Office.

MASTERS, Edgar Lee (1869-1950). American poet. B. in Kansas, he achieved fame with the free verse *Spoon River Anthology* (1915), in which the inhabitants of a small town tell of their frustrated lives.

MASTIFF. British dog, usually fawn, which was originally bred for sporting purposes. It has a large head, wide-set eyes, and broad muzzle.

MA'STODON. The primitive elephant, whose fossil remains have been discovered in all the continents except Australia, particularly in deposits of Pleistocene Age in the USA and Canada. It resembled the modern elephant, but was lower and longer; its teeth suggest that it lived on leaves in the primeval swamps and forests.

MASULIPATNA'M. Indian seaport in Andhra, at the mouth of the N distributary of the r. Kistna. Its name means fish town, and it has a textile industry. Pop. (1971) 112,650.

MASU'RIAN LAKES. Lakes in Poland (former E Prussia) which in 1914-15 were the scene of battles in which the Germans defeated the Russian invaders.

MATABELELAND (mahtahbā'le-). The western portion of Zimbabwe, inhabited by the Matabele. It consists of rich plains watered by tributaries of the Zambezi and Limpopo, with mineral wealth. The chief town is Bulawayo. M. was granted to the British S Africa Company in 1889 and occupied in 1893 following attacks on white settlements in Mashonaland; in 1923 it was included in Southern Rhodesia. Joshua Nkomo is a Matabele.

MATA'DI. Chief port of Zaïre on the r. Zaïre, 115km (70m) from its mouth. It is linked by oil pipelines with Kinshasa and exports coffee, cacao, palm oil, cotton, copal, copper, etc. It has an airport. Pop. (1971) 59,200.

MATA HARI (mah'ta hah'ri) (1876-1917). Dutch spy, *née* Margaretha Geertruida Zella. She m. a Dutch army officer, but left him to win notoriety as a courtesan and 'oriental' dancer under the name M.H., 'Eye of the Day'. In the F.W.W. she was in both French and German pay, but it was the French who finally shot her on espionage charges. She remained the archtype exotic spy.

MATA'NZAS. Port on the N coast of Cuba, with tanning, textile, and sugar industries, and large exports of sugar. Pop. (1970) 160,000.

MATAPA'N. Southernmost cape of the mainland of Greece, off which, on 28 March 1941, during the S.W.W., a British fleet under Admiral Cunningham sank an Italian squadron.

MATCHES. A match is a small strip of wood (usually aspen) or taper tipped with combustible material for producing fire. Friction matches containing phosphorus were first made by John Walker of Stockton-on-Tees *c.* 1826. A 'safety' match is one in which the combustible body and the oxidizing agent are kept apart, the former being incorporated into the striking part and the latter onto the side of the box.

MATÉ (mat'eh) (Paraguay tea). The dried leaves of the Brazilian holly (*Ilex paraguayensis*), an evergreen shrub akin to the common holly, that grows in Paraguay and Brazil. The Jesuits were the pioneers in its cultivation, and it is still sometimes called Jesuits' tea. After roasting, the leaves are powdered and the prepared infusion is drunk through a tube.

MATÉ'RIALISM. The philosophical theory that everything that exists can be explained in terms of matter and motion. Thus it excludes any form of supernaturalism, regarding 'matter' as the one ultimate fact and 'mind' as a product of matter. Like most other philosophical ideas, M. probably arose among the early Greek thinkers. The Stoics and the Epicureans were materialists, and so were the ancient Buddhists. Among modern materialists have been Hobbes, d'Holbach, Büchner, and Haeckel; while Hume, J. S. Mill, Huxley, and Herbert Spencer showed materialist tendencies.

MATHEMATICS. The science of spatial and numerical relations. Pure M. includes, as its main divisions, geometry, arithmetic, and algebra, the calculus, trigonometry, etc.; while mechanics, the mathematical theories of astronomy, electricity, optics, and thermodynamics, etc., are included in the heading of applied M.

Probably prehistoric man had learned to count at least up to the 10 represented by his fingers, and Chinese, Hindus, Babylonians, and Egyptians all evolved methods of counting and measuring which were of practical importance in their everyday life. The first theoretical mathematician is held to be Thales of Miletus (640-546 BC), to whom we owe the first theorems in plane geometry. His disciple, Pythagoras, established geometry as a recognized science among the Greeks, so that the way was prepared for the school of Alexandrian geometers that produced Euclid, Archimedes, and others in the 4th and 3rd cents. BC. Our present numerals are a Hindu-Arabic system which reached Europe about AD 100. The Arab mathematicians of the Near East were the masters from whom European scholars learnt their science, and in the 15th cent. there began an uninterrupted development. Geometry was revivified by the invention of algebraic geometry by Descartes in 1637. Napier invented logarithms, and Newton and Leibniz the calculus. Lobachevski (1793-1856) rejected parallelism and developed non-Euclidean geometry, followed by Einstein in 20th cent.

Modern methods of teaching arithmetic (q.v.) are sometimes referred to as the 'new M.'.

MATILDA (1102-67). Queen of England. The dau. of Henry I, she m. the Emperor Henry V, and after his death Geoffrey Plantagenet, count of Anjou. Although the barons had recognized her as Henry's successor, on his death in 1135 they elected her cousin Stephen king. M. invaded England in 1139, and in 1141 was crowned queen. Civil war followed, until in 1153 Stephen was recognized as king, and M.'s son, Henry II, as his successor.

MATISSE (mahtēs'), **Henri** (1869-1954). French artist. B. at Le Cateau Nord, after becoming an associate of the Salon, he was a member of the group known as *les Fauves*. One of the leading painters of the modern French school, he was essentially a designer or decorator, employing pure colour, distorting natural forms, and subordinating subject matter to pattern. In 1947-51 he designed and decorated a chapel for the Dominicans of Vence.

MATLOCK. English spa and admin. HQ of Derbyshire, 24km (15m) N of Derby on the Derwent. It has warm springs. Pop. (1972) 20,320.

MATO GROSSO. Formerly the largest state of Brazil, between Bolivia on the W and the r. Araguaia on the E., it was split into two in 1979. The northern retains the name M.G., still having its cap. at Cuiaba; M.G. do Sul has Campo Grande as its capital. There are extensive forests (the name means dense forest), from which maté, quebracho, rubber, timber, etc., are extracted; diamonds, silver, gold, lead and other minerals are found, sugar and tobacco are grown, cattle reared.

MATRIARCHY (māt'riahrki). That form of social organization in which the mother and not the father is head of the family, and descent and relationship are reckoned through the female line. M., often associated with polyandry, has been found in certain parts of India, in the South Sea Islands, Central Africa, and among Indian tribes in N America.

MATSYS (mahtsīs') (also Massys or Metsys), **Quentin** (1466-1530). Flemish painter. B. at Louvain, he was influenced by the masters of the Italian Renaissance, and is famous for his sacred pictures, such as the triptych of the 'Pietà', in the Antwerp museum. He also painted portraits, incl. one of Erasmus, which he presented to Sir Thomas More.

MATISSE. The altar and a stained glass window in the chapel at Vence decorated by the artist. *Photo: Courtesy of the French National Tourist Office*

MATTER. In physics, the 'stuff' out of which all objects outside the mind are considered to be composed. The history of science is largely taken up with accounts of theories of matter, ranging from the hard atoms of Democritus to the 'waves' of modern electrophysical theory. *See* ATOM, etc.

MA'TTERHORN. Mtn peak in the Alps on the Swiss-Italian border (Fr. le Cervin, Ital. il Cervino): 4,478m (14,690ft). It was first climbed in 1865 by Edward Whymper: 4 members of his party of 7 were killed when the rope broke during the descent.

MATTHEW. Christian apostle and evangelist, the traditional author of the first Gospel. He is usually identified with Levi, who was a tax-collector in the service of Herod Antipas, and was called by Christ to be a disciple as he sat at the receipt of custom by the Lake of Galilee.

MATTHIAS CORVINUS (1440-90). Greatest of the kings of Hungary. The son of the great warrior, John Hunyadi, he was elected king in 1458. His aim of uniting Hungary, Austria, and Bohemia involved him in long wars with the emperor and the kings of Bohemia and Poland, during which, in 1485, he captured Vienna and made it his capital.

MAUDLING (mawd'-), **Reginald** (1917-79). British Cons. politician. His ministerial posts incl. Chancellor of the Exchequer 1962-4, and he was a contender for the Cons. leadership in 1965, but he resigned as Home Sec. (1970-2) following references to him during the bankruptcy proceedings of architect John Poulsen, since,

MATTERHORN. The ascent by Whymper's party in 1865 was a landmark in mountaineering. From the Swiss side the mountain appears to be an isolated peak, but it is actually the end of a ridge. *Photo: Courtesy of the Swiss National Tourist Office.*

as Home Sec. he would have been in charge of the Met. Police who were to investigate the case.

MAUFE (mawf), **Sir Edward** (1883-1974). British architect. His best-known works are the Anglican cathedral, Guildford, and the Runnymede (q.v.) memorial.

MAUGHAM (mawm), **(William) Somerset** (1874-1965). Brit. author. B. in Paris, he was ed. at King's School, Canterbury, and Heidelberg univ. before studying medicine at St Thomas's Hospital. He practised for a year in the London slums, but after the success of his first novel *Liza of Lambeth* (1897) devoted himself to writing. *Of Human Bondage* (1915) has strong autobiographical elements, although whereas the hero was lame M.'s handicap had been a stammer; *The Moon and Sixpence* (1919), based on the life of Gauguin, was made into an opera by Gardner (q.v.), and *Cakes and Ale* (1930) satirizes Hardy and Walpole. Meanwhile M. had also been establishing a reputation as a fashionable dramatist, often having several plays running at the same time in the West End: *Lady Frederick* (1907), *The Circle* (1921) and *Our Betters* (1923). His cynical disillusion and urbanely ironic style is perhaps seen at its best in his short stories, e.g. *The Trembling of a Leaf* (1921) which incl. 'Rain', the story of an encounter between a missionary and a prostitute which has been dramatized and filmed. In the F.W.W. he was in Switzerland and Russia, where he was attempting to prevent the outbreak of revolution, as a secret agent - a role he again briefly played in the S.W.W. - and his adventures inspired the 'Ashenden' stories. His brother **Frederic Herbert,** 1st visct M. (1866-1958), was a Judge of the High Court from 1928 and was raised to the peerage in 1939: and the latter's son **Robert,** 2nd visct M. (1916-81), was well known as an author under the name 'Robin M.', e.g. his novel *The Servant* (1948, filmed 1963).

MAUGHAM. Somerset Maugham in 1931, a portrait by P. Steegman in which the sitter is placed against the kind of exotic landscape which so often formed the background of his stories. *Photo: Courtesy of the National Portrait Gallery*

MAU-MAU (mow mow). Terrorist secret society with Nationalist aims active in Kenya 1952-60. An offshoot of the Kikuyu Central Assocn, it was banned by the govt at the outbreak of the S.W.W. Its members, chiefly of the Kikuyu tribe, were bound by oaths and ritual as repulsive as their methods of attack on white settlers, their cattle, and black Kenyans who opposed or refused to join them. In 1963 the independent Kenyan govt offered free pardon to all M.-M. terrorists still outlawed.

MAUNDY THURSDAY. The Thursday before Easter. The name has been derived from the Lat. *mandatum*, the first word of the service chanted at the ceremony of washing the feet of pilgrims on that day, which was instituted in commemoration of Christ's washing the apostles' feet. The ceremony was observed in the Church from about the 4th cent., and performed by the English sovereigns until the time of William III. The rite of foot-washing was abandoned in 1754, but the Maundy money (M. pennies) is still presented in Westminster Abbey (elsewhere in alternate years).

MAUPASSANT (mohpahsoṅ'), **Guy de** (1850-93). French author. B. in Normandy, he entered the Civil Service, and was encouraged in his literary ambitions by Flaubert. In 1880 he estab. his reputation with the short story *Boule de Suif.* His later works include many short stories and novels, such as *Une Vie* (1883), *Bel-ami* (1885), and *Fort comme la mort* (1889). Becoming insane in 1892, he d. in a Paris asylum.

MAURIAC (mohrē-ahk'), **François** (1885-1970). French novelist. B. in Bordeaux, he pub. his first important work *Le Baiser au lépreux* in 1922, which shows the conflict of an unhappy marriage. Similarly preoccupied with the irreconcilability of Christian practice and human nature are *Fleuve de feu* (1923), *Désert de l'amour* (1925), and *Thérèse Desqueyroux.* He was awarded a Nobel literary prize in 1952.

MAURICE, (John) Frederick Denison (1805-72). Anglican churchman. Son of a Unitarian minister, he was ordained in the C of E in 1834, but in 1853 was deprived of his professorships in English history and literature and divinity at King's Coll., London, following the publication of his *Theological Essays* attacking the doctrine of eternal punishment. He founded with Kingsley the Christian Socialist movement and promoted popular education. In 1866 he became prof. of moral philosophy at Cambridge.

MAURISTS. A congregation of French RC monks, belonging to the Benedictine order, estab. in 1621 at the Benedictine monastery of St Maur-sur-Loire. Subsequently its chief house was in Paris, and there the M. fathers carried on literary and historical work, while still maintaining the strict monastic discipline. In 1792 the congregation was suppressed.

MAURITĀ'NIA. Country in NW Africa, in full the Islamic Rep. of M., lying N of Senegal. The name M. was that of the Roman prov. of NW Africa, so-called from the Mauri, a Berber people who inhabited it. Under French rule from 1903, it became an independent rep. within the French Community in 1960. Much of M. is part of the Sahara Desert, and crops of millet and maize are subject to drought. Many of the people are still nomadic, living by their flocks and herds. There are great resources of iron and copper. The cap. is Nouakchott. Moktar ould Daddah was pres. 1961 until his Arabisation policy led to a military coup in 1978. Civilian govt. was restored in 1980 and a new constitution with a pres. and nat. assembly was introduced.

Area 1,030,000 sq.km (419,000 sq.m); pop. (1977) 1,481,000. Some 30% are the dominant Arab Berbers; 30% black or mixed-race Haratine (descendants of black slaves who remained in effect slaves until abolition in 1980); and 30% Black Africans. The great majority are Moslem. The national language is Arabic, but French is also to be taught in schools until 1985. M.U.: ougiya.

MAURITIUS (mawrish'us). Island in the Indian Ocean 885km (550m) E of Madagascar. Then uninhabited, it was discovered by the Portuguese *c.* 1510; was occupied by the Dutch 1598-1710 and by the French from 1715 until conquered by the British in 1810, to whom it was ceded in 1814. In 1968 it became a monarchy (with Elizabeth II as queen) within the Commonwealth. Sugar, tea and tobacco are produced. The cap. is Port Louis; pop. 142,500. There is a Gov.-General and Legislative Assembly. The majority of the pop. are Hindus (350,000) originally imported as indentured labour from India after the abolition of slavery in the early 19th cent., and there is some friction with the French Roman Catholic (220,000) and Moslem (110,000) population. Official languages are English and French, Creole French being widely spoken. Most important of several small island dependencies is Rodriguez *c.* 560km (350m) to the E: area 100 sq.km (400 sq.m); pop. (1972) 24,770. The Chagos Archipelago was transferred in 1965 to the Brit. Indian Ocean Terr. (q.v.). Declaration of M. as a rep. within the Commonwealth is under discussion, and the Maoist opposition has demanded the return to M. of the is. of Diego Garcia. Area 1,865 sq.km (720 sq.m); pop. (1979) 900,000. M.U.: M. rupee.

MAUROIS (mohrwah'), **André.** Pseud. of French author Émile Herzog (1885-1967). In the F.W.W. he was attached to the British Army, and the essays *Les Silences du Colonel Bramble* (1918) give humorously sympathetic observations on the British character. His novels incl. the semi-autobiographical *Bernard Quesnay* (1926), but he was best known for his fictionalized biographies, e.g. *Ariel* (1923), a life of Shelley, and for his essays on contemporary problems.

MAVOR, O. H. *See* BRIDIE, JAMES.

MAWSON, Sir Douglas (1882-1958). Australian Antarctic explorer. B. nr Bradford, he was taken to Sydney as a child, and qualified as a mining engineer. As a member of Shackleton's expedition of 1907-9, he discovered the South Magnetic Pole, and in an expedition of his own (1911-14) extended Australia's claim to sovereignty in the Antarctic to *c.* 5,402,480 sq.km (2,472,000 sq.m). Prof. of geology and mineralogy at the Univ. of Adelaide 1920-53, he was knighted in 1914 and in 1954 his name was given to Australia's first permanent Antarctic base.

MAXIM, Sir Hiram Stevens (1840-1916). Anglo-American inventor. A naturalized Briton, he improved lighting methods, experimented with flight and invented the M. machine-gun.

MAXIMILIAN I (1459-1519). Holy Roman Emperor. The son of the Emperor Frederick III, he m. Mary of Burgundy in 1477, thus bringing the Low Countries under Habsburg rule, and became emperor in 1493. His dream of reviving the medieval empire involved him in long wars in Italy and Hungary with little result, but he made the Habsburgs the most powerful house in Europe, especially by marrying his son, Philip, to the heiress to the Spanish throne.

MAXIMILIAN (1832-67). Emperor of Mexico. The brother of the Emperor Francis Joseph of Austria, he was given command of the navy in 1854, and was gov. of Lombardy and Venetia 1857-9. He m. Princess Charlotte of Belgium in 1857. After the occupation of Mexico by French troops he accepted the title of emperor in 1864, but soon found himself a mere puppet in French hands. He met with resistance from the republicans under Juárez, and in 1866 French troops withdrew, at the demand of the USA; M., deserted, was captured by the republicans 1867 and shot.

MAXWELL, James Clerk. *See* CLERK MAXWELL.

MAY, Sir Thomas Erskine (1815-86). English constitutional jurist. Clerk of the House of Commons 1871-86, when he was created baron Farnborough, he wrote the standard *Treatise on the Law, Privileges, Proceedings, and Usage of Parliament* (1844).

MAYA (mah'yah). American Indian civilization which was shown by excavations in 1976 to have originated as early as *c.* 2600 BC in the Yucatan peninsula, and which has left remains also in the nearby highlands, espec. in southern Mexico, Guatemala and Belize. During their 'classic' period AD 325-925, the Maya built remarkable stone buildings and 'stepped' pyramids without the aid of metal tools, developed a form of hieroglyphic writing used in manuscripts and carved stelae, and were skilled in agriculture, pottery, weaving, mathematics and astronomy. Their religion involved human sacrifice, but on a lesser scale than that practised by the Aztecs. Towards the end of the classic period there was an unexplained partial population movement away from the central area, work being abandoned on religious buildings and cities under construction. Mexican influence also became strong at this time, but from AD 1200 was progressively thrown off. However, a general decline of the culture continued accompanied by civil wars, and the Spanish conquest in the 16th cent. completed its downfall, destroying much also of historical value incl. all except 3 of the ancient bark codices. *See* CHICHEN ITZA.

MAYA (mah'ya). Sanskrit word meaning 'illusion', applied frequently in Hindu philosophy, particularly in the Vedanta, to the cosmos which Isvara, the personal expression of Brahma or the Atman, has called into being. This is real, yet it also is illusion, since its reality is not everlasting.

MAYA. The head of a young man, crowned with water-lilies, which was found surrounded by offerings in a secret temple tomb, and is now in the National Museum of Mexico. *Photo: Mireille Vautier*

'MAYAGUEZ' (mī'ahgez). American freighter seized by Cambodian Khmer Rouge Communists in May 1975 and liberated by US Marines at the instance of Pres. Ford: 41 American lives were lost and a congressional report in 1976 was critical of the action taken.

MAYAKOVSKY, Vladimir (1893-1930). Russian poet. He combined revolutionary propaganda with efforts to revolutionize poetic technique, e.g. *150,000* (1920) and the dramatic poem *Mystery-Bouffe* (1918) on the October Revolution. He also wrote the satiric play *Klop* (1928: *The Bedbug*), taken in the West as an attack on philistinism in the USSR. He committed suicide.

MAY DAY. May 1, traditionally the popular festival to celebrate the beginning of summer, which has its origin in pre-Christian magical rites, of which the dance round the maypole (an ancient fertility symbol) is a survivor. In Communist countries it is usually celebrated with political parades, often incl. a show of armed strength. *See* LABOUR DAY.

MAYENCE. French form of MAINZ.

MAYENNE (mahyen'). Town in M. dept, France, 65km (40m) NW of Le Mans, on the river M., with a 12th cent. church and 13th cent. chateau. There are textile, printing and engineering works. Pop. (1975) 13,000.

The r. MAYENNE rises in the W of Orne dept, flows in a generally S direction through the depts of M. (to which it gives its name) and Maine-et-Loire for 125m to join the Sarthe just above Angers and form the Maine.

MAYER, Maria Goeppert- (1906-). American physicist. B. in Kattowitz, Poland, and ed. at Göttingen univ., she became a US citizen in 1933, and was senior physicist at the Argonne Nat. Lab. 1946-60, and prof. in the Univ. of California (La Jolla) from 1960. For her discoveries in the theory of atomic nuclear shell structure, she was awarded a Nobel prize in 1963.

MAYERLING. *See* RUDOLPH.

MAYFAIR. The fashionable quarter in the W of London, England, vaguely defined as lying between Piccadilly and Oxford Street, and including Park Lane, but increasingly devoted to offices.

'MAYFLOWER'. *See* PILGRIM FATHERS.

MAYFLY. Insects in the order Ephemeroptera (Gk *ephemeros* lasting for a day, an allusion to the very brief life of the adult), found in many parts of the world. The larval stage, which can last as long as a year, is passed in water, the adult form developing gradually from the nymph through successive moults. The adult has transparent, net-veined wings, the hind pair being noticeably smaller, and 3 caudal filaments. Both nymphs and adults are important as food for fish, esp. trout.

MAYNOO'TH. Village in Kildare, Rep. of Ireland, 23km (14m) W of Dublin, with a famous training college for RC priests. Pop. (1971) 1,300.

MAYO, William James (1861-1939). American surgeon, founder with his brother, **Charles Horace M.,** of the M. Clinic (1889) in Rochester, Minnesota.

MAYO. A western county of Rep. of Ireland in Connacht prov., facing the Atlantic Ocean and including Achill is. Much of it is wild and barren, and the coast is rocky. Castlebar is the co. town. Area 5,397 sq.km (2,084 sq.m); pop. (1971) 109,525.

MAYOR. Formerly in England, Wales and N Ireland the title of the principal officer of a municipal corporation of a city or borough, it was retained after the local govt reorganization of 1974 by those district councils which petitioned for a royal charter granting the district borough status. The status of city, similarly granted by letters patent, may in certain cases also grant the right to call the chairman of the council the 'Lord M.'. Parish councils which adopt the style of town councils have a chairman

MAYO. Lough Conn in the east of county Mayo is typical of the wildly beautiful scenery of the area. *Photo: Courtesy of the Irish Tourist Authority*

known as the 'town M.'. In Scotland the title of 'provost' and 'Lord P.' are similarly used. There are also 'Lord Ms.' in the chief cities of Australia. The office of M. was revived for Paris for the first time since 1871 when Chirac (q.v.) took office in 1977.

MAYOTTE (mīyot'). Is. of the Comoro group (q.v.), which in 1976 voted in a referendum to become a French overseas dept, rather than join the new Comoro Is. state. Area 374 sq.km (144 sq.m); pop. (1976) 40,000.

MAZARIN (mahzahrań'), **Jules** (1602-61). French statesman. B. at Piscina, he entered the papal diplomatic service, whence in 1639 he passed to that of France. He was created a cardinal in 1641, and succeeded Richelieu as chief minister in 1642. His policy of repressing the power of the nobility provoked the *Fronde* (q.v.), during which he was temporarily exiled. A great diplomatist, he conducted the Thirty Years War to a successful conclusion, and in alliance with Cromwell waged a victorious war against Spain.

MAZZINI (mahtsē'nē), **Giuseppe** (1805-72). Italian nationalist. B. at Genoa, he studied law and later joined the revolutionary society, the Carbonari. He was imprisoned in 1830, then went to France, where he founded 'Young Italy'. This was followed in 1834 by an international revolutionary organization, 'Young Europe'. For many years he lived in exile in France, Switzerland, and England, plotting uprisings in Italy, which all failed. In 1833 he was condemned to death in his absence by the Sardinian govt. On the outbreak of the 1848 revolution he returned to Italy, and for a few months in 1849 was at the head of the repub. govt set up in Rome. After its overthrow he went into exile again. He achieved a widespread moral influence which was among the most potent factors making for Italian unity.

MBOMA. Another spelling of BOMA.

MBOYA (mboi-ya), **Tom** (1930-69). Kenya politician. In 1960 he was among the founders of the Kenya African National Union (KANU) a working alliance of the Kikuyu and Luo tribes. He was Min. of Lab. 1962-4, Justice 1963-4, and Economic Planning from 1964 until killed by a Kikuyu.

MEAD, Margaret (1901-78). American anthropologist. Influential in questioning by comparative anthropology the conventions and customs of the West, she pub. *Coming of Age in Samoa* (1928), *Growing up in New Guinea* (1930), etc.

MEAD (mēd). Beverage made from honey and water fermented with yeast, drunk by the ancient Greeks and Britons, and still occasionally brewed in England.

MEADE, James Edward (1907-). British economist. His *The Theory of International Economic Policy* (1951-5) was a landmark in the study of trade and capital movements. He shared a Nobel prize in 1977.

MEAN. In mathematics, a specific related term intermediate between the first and last terms of a progression. The *arithmetic M.* is the average value of the quantities, i.e., the sum of the quantities divided by their number. The *geometric M.* is the corresponding root of the product of the quantities.

MEAN FREE PATH. The average distance travelled by a particle, atom or molecule between successive collisions.

MEASLES. An acute infective fever caused by a virus, and transmitted usually by coughing, sneezing, etc. Symptoms are severe catarrh, small spots inside the mouth, and a raised, blotchy red rash appearing about the 4th day: patients are isolated for a fortnight. In white children it is comparatively a minor ailment, although serious complications may develop, but among some African peoples it is the most acute infectious disease. *See also* GERMAN M.

MEAT. The flesh of animals taken as food. Modern means of preparation and transport have made its use widespread in all prosperous manufacturing areas, but many eastern peoples rarely or never eat M. Grasslands support mainly cattle and sheep, and grainlands support swine. Heavily peopled countries tend to specialize in high-grade beef or dairy cattle, confining sheep to the non-arable areas. Exporting countries incl. Argentina, Australia, New Zealand, Canada, USA, and Denmark (chiefly bacon).

High M. prices have led to the development of M. substitutes designed to have a similar appearance, taste, texture and nutritive value, and using textured vegetable protein extruded in fibres in the same way as plastics.

MEATH. Co. of Rep. of Ireland, in Leinster prov., facing the Irish Sea. It is mainly agricultural. The co. tn is Trim. Area 2,339 sq.km (903 sq.m); pop. (1971) 71,730.

MEAT PACKING. Name given to the industry in the USA of preparing meat for consumption at a distance, particularly overseas. The industry depends on refrigeration, which was invented in 1861. Frozen beef was first sent to Smithfield from America in 1874. The first frozen meat was dispatched from Argentina in 1878 and from Australia in 1879. Chicago had the world's greatest M.P. plants, until the stockyards closed in 1971.

MECCA. City of Saudi Arabia, the cap. of Hejaz and the holiest city of the Moslem world, where the Prophet was born. It stands in the desert, in a valley about 72km (45m) E of Jidda, its port on the Red Sea, with which it is linked by an asphalted road, and long before the time of Mohammed was a commercial centre, caravan junction, and place of pilgrimage. In the centre of M. is the Great Mosque, in whose courtyard is the Kaaba (q.v.); it also contains the well Zam-Zam, associated by tradition with Hagar and Ishmael, and the Maqām Ibrāhīm, a holy stone supposed to bear the imprint of Abraham's foot. The mosque was occupied by armed Shi'ite minority fundamentalists Nov.-Dec. 1979. Pop. (1970) 301,000. *See* JIHAD.

MEDALS. Left to right: Legion of Honour (France); Iron Cross (Germany); George Cross (U.K.); Waterloo Medal (U.K.); Victoria Cross (U.K.); Medal for Merit (U.S.A.) and Medal of Honor (army and air force) (U.S.A.). *Photo: Courtesy of A.H.Baldwin Ltd., and Spink and Son Ltd.*

MECHANICS. That branch of applied mathematics that deals with the motions of bodies and the forces causing them, and also with the forces acting on bodies in equilibrium. It is usually divided into dynamics and statics. **Quantum M.** is the system based on the quantum theory (q.v.) which has superseded Newtonian M. in the interpretation of physical phenomena on the atomic scale.

MECHELEN. Flemish form of MALINES.

MECKLENBURG. Historic name of an area lying along the Baltic coast of Germany. It was divided into 2 grand duchies, M.-Schwerin (13,126 sq.km/5,068 sq.m) and M.-Strelitz (2,929 sq.km/1,131 sq.m) which became free states of the Weimar Rep., 1918-34, when they were joined to form the state of M. After the S.W.W., M., incl. that part of Pomerania W of the Oder, was in 1946 made a Land of E Germany. In 1952 the historic boundaries were swept away, and parts of M. were incl. in the districts of Rostock, Schwerin, and Neubrandenburg.

MEDAL OF HONOR. Award instituted by the US Congress for the navy (1861) and army (1862) for gallantry in action. Although differing in design, both army and navy medals are bronze stars bearing Minerva encircled in their centres.

MEDALS and DECORATIONS. Pieces of metal, sometimes coinlike, struck or cast in commemoration of victories, coronations, or other historic events; or issued to mark distinguished service in military or civil life - sometimes as a badge of membership of an order of knighthood or similar special group.

Commemorative Ms. originated in Italy in the 15th cent., reaching their highest artistic level in the work of Pisanello, etc. Other schools of medallists flourished in Germany in the 16th cent., and in France, England and Holland in the 17th cent.

Among the best-known British Ms. and Ds. for distinguished service are the Victoria Cross (q.v., military, 1856) and George Cross and M. (q.v., mainly civilian, 1940), and the Order of Merit (q.v.). The UK honours system is also valid in many member states of the Commonwealth, but countries such as Australia and Canada have systems of their own, either co-existent or exclusive. Other high-ranking awards are the American M. of Honor (q.v., military, 1861-2), Medal for Merit (civilian, 1942), Presidential Medal of Freedom (civilian, 1963), and Order of the Purple Heart (q.v., military, originally 1782, revived 1932); the French *Légion d'honneur* (civil and military, with 5 classes, instituted by Napoleon in 1802) and *ordre national du Mérite* (1963, civil and military, replacing earlier merit awards); the German *Pour la Mérite* (military 1740, and since 1842 for science and art, instituted by Frederick the Great), and Iron Cross (q.v., military, 1813); USSR Gold Star M. (civilian and military). Military Ms. may be issued in connection with a particular battle, for individual feats of valour, or to mark service over the period of a campaign. The earliest English one is that issued by Elizabeth I to commemorate the defeat of the Armada, but until the 19th cent. Ms. were awarded only to officers: the first to be issued to all ranks was the Waterloo M. in 1816.

MEDAWAR (med'awahr), **Sir Peter** (1915-). British scientist. As Jodrell prof. of zoology and comparative anatomy 1951-62, he was in 1960 awarded a Nobel prize for medicine (with Sir Macfarlane Burnet, q.v.) for his work in immunology, having discovered that the body's resistance to grafted tissue etc. is undeveloped in the newborn child. Awarded OM 1981.

MĒDĒ'A In Greek legend, a sorceress, dau. of Æetes, king of Colchis. When Jason reached Colchis seeking the golden fleece, M. fell in love with him and by her magic helped him in his aim, and then fled with him on board the *Argo.* But when Jason married Creusa in her place, M. sent the bride a poisoned garment which caused her death, and killed the 2 children she had borne to Jason.

MEDELLIN (mādelyēn'). Town in the Central Cordillera, Colombia, 1,538 m (5,046 ft) a.s.l. The centre of a coffee-growing, and gold and silver mining area, it has a univ. and has textile and steel manufactures, etc. Pop. (1972) 1,270,000.

MEDES (mēdz). An ancient Aryan people of W Persia, on the borders of Mesopotamia. First heard of in the 9th cent. BC as tributaries to Assyria, their cap. was Ecbatana. In alliance with Babylon they destroyed Nineveh, the Assyrian cap., in 612, and extended their dominions as far as central Asia Minor. The Persians, who had been subject to the Ms., revolted in 550 BC, and their king Cyrus became king of the Ms. and Persians, who rapidly merged.

MEDICI (mā'dēchē). Famous Florentine family. Its founder, **Giovanni** (1360-1429), acquired a fortune in commerce and banking, and exercised great political influence as a supporter of the popular party. His eldest son, **Cosimo** (1389-1464), dominated the govt from 1434 onwards, and was succeeded by his son, **Piero** (1416-69), and his grandson, **Lorenzo the Magnificent** (1449-92). Both Cosimo and Lorenzo were munificent patrons of the arts, literature, and scholarship, while the latter was a poet of considerable ability; under their rule Florence was adorned with works of art, and became the centre of European culture. Lorenzo's son, **Giovanni** (1475-1521), became pope in 1513 as Leo X.

MEDICI. The statue of Cosimo I, alongside the Palazzo Vecchio in Florence. He was considered by his contemporaries to be the incarnation of Macchiavelli's *Prince. Photo: Camera Press*

MEDICINE. The science and art of healing bodily and mental diseases; also any substance used in the treatment of disease. Taking the word in its former sense, M. covers every form of curative treatment, and also includes the study of the causes of disease and relative subjects. The basis of M. is anatomy or the structure and form of the body, and physiology, or the study of the body's functions. There are, however, many other sub-divisions, e.g. pathology, pharmacology, obstetrics, surgery, dentistry, etc.

M. as a scientific study had its rise in ancient Greece between 700 and 600 BC, but the first Greek physician was Hippocrates (*c.* 460 BC). He it was who recognized that disease is the result of natural causes; and although his knowledge of the body was slight, he and his followers initiated the careful observation of symptoms out of which clinical M. has developed. In the Alexandrian age the city of Alexandria was the seat of a great medical school, and the knowledge acquired by the Alexandrian doctors was consolidated and extended by Galen, who lived in Rome in the 2nd cent. AD. For more than 1,000 years Galen was chief medical authority, and it was not until the 16th cent. that any considerable additions were made to medical science. The discovery by Harvey in 1628 of the circulation of the blood was of epoch-making importance. John Hunter founded experimental and surgical pathology. Anatomists, botanists and chemists made valuable additions to the growing science, but it was in the 19th cent. that M. was revolutionized by the work of such men as Pasteur, Koch, Lister, and Manson.

In the 20th cent. spectacular advances have been made in the treatment and control of disease. Salvarsan (q.v.), 1909, was the first specific antibacterial agent, and the sulphonamides synthesized by G. Domagk in the 1930s were active against groups of pathogenic bacteria, as were the later antibiotics (q.v.) of natural origin (penicillin, streptomycin, tetracycline, etc.). As a result, pneumonia is no longer fatal, tuberculosis can usually be cured, and diabetes can be controlled indefinitely with insulin (q.v.). All branches of M. and surgery benefited by the growth of effective nationwide blood-transfusion (q.v.) services. A dramatic increase in the understanding of the human mind followed the work of Freud (q.v.) and his successors, in the many branches of psychiatry (q.v.), incl. the effective use of drugs. Transplant surgery, e.g. of the heart and kidneys (qq.v.), developed rapidly from the 1960s. World-wide campaigns to eradicate the viral diseases, smallpox and polio, in the 1970s were remarkably successful, although the development of resistant strains of parasites and viruses gave cause for concern, and there was a resurgence of malaria, the possibility of a revival of a fatal influenza strain, and the emergence of new diseases, e.g. lassa fever. The time and cost of 'westernized' medical training, and its inapplicability to the vast areas and populations of the 'third world' led to the introduction of the 'barefoot doctors', auxiliary medical helpers trained in hygiene and the administration of a limited number of standard drugs for the prevalent diseases of a particular region. In the 1970s to 1980s nuclear M. began to develop, e.g. positron emission tomography.

MEDICINE, Alternative. Despite the recognized advances of orthodox M., there has been widespread public disillusion with such aspects as the formerly too widespread prescription of barbiturates. This has led to a great growth of interest in unorthodox alternative M., e.g. acupuncture (q.v.), herbalism (the sole use of drugs derived from herbs, rather than including also those synthesized in the laboratory), homoeopathy, osteopathy (qq.v.), etc. Some forms, such as acupuncture and osteopathy, have gained increasing countenance from orthodox M. itself, but the absence of enforceable standards in some fields has led to the proliferation of the eccentric and charlatan.

MEDINA (medē'nah). City in Saudi Arabia, *c.* 355km (220m) N of Mecca. To all Moslems it is a holy city second only to Mecca, since it was here that the Prophet lived many years after he fled from Mecca, and here he died. The Mosque of the Prophet contains his reputed tomb, and those of Abu Bekr, Omar, and Fatima, Mohammed's daughter. M. is linked with Jidda by an asphalted road. Pop. (1970) 137,000.

MEDITATION. In modern practice, transcendental M. (TM), the cultivation of a deeply relaxed though wakeful condition, distinct from sleep or a hypnotized state, practised independently of any religious belief or cult. Metabolic changes take place consistent with the release of anxiety, and it is claimed to help withstand stress, and improve learning ability, creativity and efficiency.

MEDICINE. William Harvey, painted by an unknown artist about 1627, when he was working on his theory of the circulation of the blood. *Photo: Courtesy of the National Portrait Gallery*

MEDITERRANEAN. The inland sea that separates Europe from N Africa, with Asia on the E. The Strait of Gibraltar connects it with the Atlantic; the Suez Canal links it with the Red Sea and the Indian Ocean. In the NE, through the Dardanelles and the Sea of Marmara, it is connected with the Black Sea. Its name means surrounded by land, and on its shores western civilization was built up. Its chief divisions are the Tyrrhenian, Ionian, Adriatic, and Aegean seas, and its extreme length is 3,700 km (2,300 m). Shallows stretching from Sicily to Cape Bon in Africa divide it into an eastern and a western basin. It is saltier and warmer than the Atlantic, and nearly tideless. Area 2,966,000 sq.km (1,145,000 sq.m). Pollution from human and industrial waste has reached danger level. Under an internat. treaty (1978) dumping of mercury, cadmium, persistent plastics, DDT, crude oil and hydrocarbons was forbidden.

MEDLAR. A small European fruit tree (*Mespilus germanica*) of the family Rosaceae, with fruits resembling a small brown-green apple. These are eaten when decay has set in and the taste is agreeably acid.

MÉDOC (mehdok'). French dist. bordering the Gironde, N of Bordeaux, famed for its wines; Margaux and St Julien are 2 of the best-known varieties.

MEDUSA. *See* GORGON *and* JELLYFISH.

MEDWAY. River of SE England, rising in Sussex and flowing through Kent to Sheerness, where it enters the Thames. It is about 96km (60m) long. It divides the 'Men of Kent' who live to the E, from the 'Kentish Men', who live to the W.

MEEGEREN (mā'-), **Hans van** (1889-1947). Dutch artist who faked Vermeers, incl. 'Christ at Emmaus', which was sold to Rotterdam's Boymann's Museum. He admitted the forgeries when arrested in 1945 on unfounded suspicion of collaboration with the Nazis. After a year's imprisonment he d. penniless.

MEERSCHAUM (mērshawm; Ger. sea froth). A soft white mineral which, when dry, floats on the water; it is hydrated magnesium silicate, and is obtained chiefly from Asia Minor. It is used for pipe bowls and cigarette holders.

MEERUT (mē'rut). City of Uttar Pradesh, Rep. of India, where the Indian Mutiny began in 1857. It contains many mosques and temples, the Jama Masjid dating from 1019. Pop. (1971) 367,820.

MEGALITHIC MONUMENTS (Gk *megas* great, and *lithos* stone). A term for all prehistoric remains consisting of large stones either standing upright and singly (menhirs), or in rows (alignments), stone circles, generally with a central 'altar stone', or built into the form of a hut. *See* DOLMEN.

MEGATHĒ'RIUM. Extinct genus of Edentata, huge sloth-like beasts which inhabited America in the Pliocene/Pleistocene period.

ME'GHALAYA. State of the Rep. of India, created in 1970 from the Garo, and Khasia and Jaintia tribal hill districts of Assam. The cap. is Shillong. Area 22,445 sq.km (8,666 sq.m); pop. (1971) 1,000,000.

MEGI'DDŌ. Ancient Palestinian fortress, situated in the valley of Esdraelon. Here Thothmes III defeated the Canaanites, *c.* 1450 BC; Josiah was killed in battle, 609 BC; and Allenby broke the Turkish front in 1918.

MEHEMET ALI (mā'hemet ah'lē) (1769-1849). Pasha of Egypt. An Albanian, he commanded a Turkish regiment sent to Egypt in 1799 to fight the French, secured his election as pasha in 1805, built up an army and navy on European models, went to war with his overlord the sultan of Turkey in 1831 and 1839, and conquered the Sudan. He was the founder of the royal house (till 1953) of Egypt.

MEHTA (mā'tah), **Zubin** (1936-). Indian conductor. B. in Bombay, of Parsee parents, he made his US debut in Philadelphia in 1960, and in 1978 became director of the NY Philharmonic.

MEIJI TENNO. *See* MUTSUHITO.

MEIR (mā-ēr), **Golda** (1898-1978). Israeli stateswoman. B. in Kiev, she emigrated as a child to USA, and settled in Palestine in 1921. A founder member of the Labour Party (Mapai), she was Foreign Min. 1956-66, and PM 1968-74. She resigned following criticism of the unpreparedness of Israel in the 1973 war.

MEISSEN (mī'sen). City in Dresden district, E Germany, on the Elbe, 24km (15m) NW of Dresden. It was founded in 929 by Henry the Fowler, has a fine Gothic cathedral and is famed for its china, called Dresden from its original place of manufacture. Pop. (1975) 44,000.

MEISTERSINGERS (Ger. master singers). German lyric poets of the 14th and 16th cents. who formed guilds for the revival of minstrelsy at Nuremberg and elsewhere.

MEITNER (mī'-), **Lise** (1878-1968). Austrian physicist. Driven from Germany because of her Jewish origin, she worked in Sweden, and was the first to realise that Hahn (q.v.) had inadvertently achieved the fission of uranium. She refused to work on the atom bomb.

MEKNÈS (mek'nez). City in Morocco, 57km (36m) WSW of Fez, in a fertile valley, one of the traditional caps. Pop. (1971) 248,000.

MĒKO'NG. River of SE Asia, rising in Tibet and flowing for 4,500 km (2,800 m) generally S into the South China Sea. The 4 riparian powers (Cambodia, Laos, Thailand,

MELBOURNE. 'The Block' in Collins Street, Melbourne by Melton Prior, painted in 1889, and (right) the State reception hall in the art gallery of the Victorian Arts Centre: the ceiling of coloured glass was designed by Australian artist, Leonard French. *Photos: Courtesy of the Australian Information Service*

and Vietnam) are developing the lower M. for irrigation and power projects.

MEKONG. The river at Phnom Penh, with a fleet of fishing boats. *Photo: Mireille Vautier*

MELANCHTHON (melangk'thon), **Philip** (1497-1560). German Protestant reformer and theologian, whose real name was Schwarzerd. He was appointed prof. of Greek at Wittenberg in 1518, and helped Luther in preparing his German translation of the New Testament. From 1519 M. was a chief of the Reformers, and in 1521 he issued the first systematic formulation of Protestant theology. He composed the Augsburg Confession in 1530, and engaged in controversies with both Catholics and Protestants.

MELANĒ'SIA. A division of the islands in the central and western Pacific between Micronesia to the N and Polynesia to the E. It embraces all the islands from the New Britain archipelago to the Fiji Islands, inhabited mainly by Papuans.

MELANOMA (melanōm'a). Skin cancer formed of dark-coloured cells, which is commoner among light-skinned people, especially women who sunbathe. Sunspot activity appears to increase the ultraviolet quality of sunlight, making it brighter and two years later the skin cancer rate shows an increase. Increases also come after sunny summers, such as in Britain in 1976.

MELBA, Dame Nellie. Professional name of Australian soprano Helen Mitchell (1861-1931), prompted by her birthplace having been Melbourne. She made her operatic dèbut in Brussels in 1887, and became the most renowned soprano of her day, notably as Donizetti's *Lucia.* In 1918 she was created DBE (GBE 1927). Her name has been given to fruit M., and M. sauce and toast.

MELBOURNE, William Lamb, 2nd visct M. (1779-1848). British Whig statesman. In 1805 he m. Lady Caroline Ponsonby, who wrote novels under the title Lady Caroline Lamb and became infatuated with Byron from 1812, and from whom in 1825 he won a long fight for separation, following her becoming mad in the previous year. He had entered the Commons in 1806, became Irish Sec. in 1827, and succeeded his father in the title in 1828. He became Home Sec. in 1830 and was briefly PM in 1834, returning to office again as PM 1835-41. Falsely accused in 1836 of seducing C. E. S. Norton (q.v.), he lost William IV's favour, but was the confidential adviser of Victoria on her succession, teaching her statecraft.

MELBOURNE. Cap. of Victoria, Australia, on the Yarra, near its mouth. The settlement began in 1835, and was named M. in 1837, after Lord M.; its growth was accelerated by gold rushes, and M. is the second city of Australia. It was the seat of the Commonwealth government 1901-27, and its buildings incl. the Law Courts, Govt Offices, Houses of Parliament, 2 cathedrals, and 3 univs. (Melbourne 1853, Monash 1958, and La Trobe 1964). Industries incl. engineering, food processing, clothing and textiles, and besides good road, rail, and air links, there are excellent dock facilities at Port M. It has a reputation as a focus of cultural activity, and the Victorian Arts Centre is among the world's finest. Pop. (1976) 2,603,600.

MELILLA (melil'ya). Spanish town in Morocco, on the NE coast. An important military base, it was captured by Spain in 1496. Pop. (1970) 86,000.

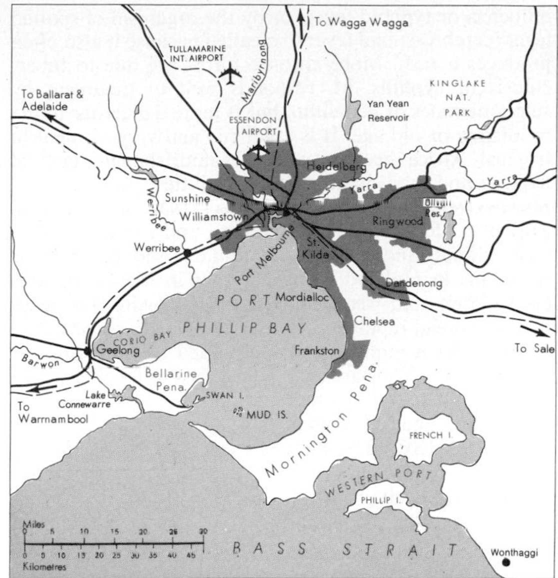

MELBOURNE

MELON. Twining plant of the family Cucurbitaceae. The Musk M. (*Cucumis melo*) and the Water M. (*Citrullus vulgaris*) are common edible varieties.

MĒ'LOS. Greek is. in the Aegean (*Milos*), one of the Cyclades. Among ancient works of art discovered here was the Venus de Milo (1820), now in the Louvre. The cap. is Plaka. Area 155 sq.km (60 sq.m).

ME'LROSE. Town in Borders region, Scotland, *c.* 48km (30m) SE of Edinburgh. The ruins of M. Abbey, founded in 1136, were immortalized in verse by Sir Walter Scott. Pop. (1971) *c.* 2,000.

MELTON MOWBRAY. English market town in Leics, on the Eye, famous as a hunting and horse-breeding centre and for its pork pies and Stilton cheese. Pop. (1971) 16,000.

MELVILLE, Henry Dundas, visct M. (1742-1811). British Tory politician. B. at Edinburgh, he entered parl. in 1774, and as Home Sec. 1791-4 persecuted the parliamentary reformers. He was Sec. of War 1794-1801, and 1st Lord of the Admiralty 1804-5, and received a peerage in 1802. His impeachment for malversation in 1806 was the last in English history.

MELVILLE, Herman (1819-91). American author. B. in New York, in 1837 he sailed to Liverpool as a cabin-boy, as described in *Redburn* (1849), and in 1841 joined the crew of a South Seas whaler, an experience which inspired his masterpiece, *Moby Dick* (1851), story of the contest between Captain Ahab and a great white whale which has symbolic overtones. M. held a post in the New York customs 1866-85. His other books incl. *Typee* (1846), *Omoo, Billy Budd,* and several vols. of verse.

MEMEL. German name of KLAIPEDA.

ME'MLING or MEMLINC, Hans (*c.* 1430-94). Flemish artist, b. probably at M. nr Alkmaar. His masters are said to have incl. Lochner and van der Weyden, and in 1446 he settled in Bruges, where he was town painter 1475-87, and some of his finest works are preserved in the Hospital of St John, e.g. the 'Deposition' triptych (1480), the 'Adoration of the Magi' altar (1479), and the shrine of St Ursula (1489). He has a serene delicacy of touch and invests his madonnas with a rich sensitivity of feeling.

MEMORIAL DAY. Day of remembrance instituted 1863 for those fallen in the American Civil War, but now observed, usually on 30 May, for all Americans killed on active service in subsequent wars.

MEMPHIS (mem'fis). Ruined city beside the Nile, 19km (12m) S of Cairo, Egypt. Centre of the worship of Ptah, it was made the cap. of the united kingdoms of Upper and Lower Egypt by Menes, but was superseded by Thebes under the new empire in 1570 BC. It declined and was subsequently used as a stone quarry, although the necropolis of Sakkara escaped damage under sand.

MEMPHIS. Largest city of Tennessee, USA, on the E bank of the Mississippi, of which it is a major port. Industries incl. timber, cotton, pharmaceuticals, food processing and tobacco. It has an Elvis Presley Plaza, with a statue of the singer by Eric Parks. Pop. met. area (1971) 863,600.

MENAI (men'ī) **STRAIT.** Channel of the Irish Sea, dividing Anglesey from the Welsh mainland. It is *c.* 22km (14m) long, and up to 3km (2m) wide; it is crossed by Telford's suspension bridge (1826), and R. Stephenson's tubular railway bridge (1850).

MENAM. *See* CHAO PHRAYA.

MENA'NDER (*c.* 342-291 BC). Greek dramatist. B. in Athens, he was the most popular exponent of the new comedy of manners, and his highly improbable plots later became fashionable. Only a few fragments of his 105 plays were known until the discovery in 1957 of the *Dyscholos* (Bad-tempered man). Many fragments have been recovered from papyri used as papier mâché for Egyptian mummy cases.

MENCIUS (men'shē-us; Latinized form of Mengtzu) (*c.* 372-289 BC). Chinese moralist. B. in Shan-Tung province, he founded a school in the tradition of Confucius. At the age of 40 he set out with his disciples to find a ruler who would put into practice his enlightened political programme. After 20 years he gave up the search and retired. His teachings (*Book of Mengtzu*) were collected after his death.

MENCKEN, Henry Louis (1880-1956). American critic, known from his birthplace as 'the sage of Baltimore'. His unconventionally phrased, satiric contributions to *Smart Set* and *American Mercury* (both of which periodicals he edited) roused great controversy. His best book was *The American Language* (1918 and often revised).

ME'NDEL, Johann Gregor (1822-84). Austrian monk, abbot of the Augustinian abbey at Brünn from 1868. By experiments with generations of peas in the monastery garden he developed a theory of organic inheritance - Mendelism - governed by dominant and recessive characters. He pub. his results 1865-9, but his work remained unrecognized until the early 20th cent.

MENDELE'YEV, Dmitri Ivanovich (1834-1907). Russian chemist. The framer of the Periodic Law of the atomic weights of chemical elements, he was prof. at St Petersburg univ. (1866-90).

MENDELSSOHN-BARTHOLDY, Jakob Ludwig Felix (1809-47). German composer. B. in Hamburg, the grandson of Moses M., he settled in Berlin. When 11, M. already had numerous compositions to his credit, and a few years later his output included symphonies, operas, etc. M. revered the great classical composers, esp. Bach. At the age of 17, M. wrote the overture to *A Midsummer Night's*

Dream. M. visited England for the first time in 1829, and was enthusiastically received. During later visits to England, he conducted his two oratorios, *St Paul* and *Elijah,* and was fêted. During a tour of Scotland he was inspired to write the overture *Fingal's Cave,* and a tour of Italy resulted in the *Italian Symphony.* He accepted important musical appointments at Düsseldorf, Leipzig, Berlin, and in 1843 founded the Leipzig conservatoire. Among M.'s most popular compositions are the piano pieces *Songs without Words,* numerous songs, an early *Octet,* and the *Serious Variations* and *Rondo Capriccioso,* both for piano.

MENDERES. *See* MAEANDER.

MENDÈS-FRANCE (-frahns), **Pierre** (1907–82). French statesman. A lawyer, he was PM and For. Min. 1954–5, when he concluded the war in Indo-China, and granted Tunisian independence.

MENDICANCY. The solicitation of alms. A perennial problem, even in the Welfare State, M. is particularly widespread in eastern countries and has been fostered in Moslem lands by almsgiving being a religious obligation. Stringent measures are taken against M. in the USSR, and in Britain, where legislation began in the 14th cent., it is an offence to solicit alms on the public highway, to expose any sore or malformation to attract alms, or cause a child to beg, and begging letters containing false statements are also illegal.

MENDICANT ORDERS. In the RC Church, the 4 orders of Mendicant Friars - Franciscans, Dominicans, Carmelites, and Augustinian Hermits (Austin Friars) - all of which arose in the early and middle 13th cents., and were inspired by a resolve to return to the simplicity of primitive Christianity. At first dependent on alms, in course of time they accumulated property. Hinduism also has many MOs.

MENDOZA (mendō'thah), **Antonio de** (1490-1552). First Spanish viceroy of New Spain (Mexico) 1535-51. His rule was enlightened and the system he estab. lasted until the 19th cent. Appointed viceroy of Peru in 1551, he d. there.

MENDOZA (mendō'thah). Cap. of the Argentine prov. of the same name. It was founded in 1561 and has greatly developed owing to its position on the Trans-Andean railway. It is the centre of an irrigated area producing half the country's olives, as well as fruits and cereals, and excellent wine. Pop. (1970) 118,000.

ME'NELIK II (1844-1913). Negus (emperor) of Abyssinia from 1889. He defeated the Italians in 1896, and the independence of his country was fully recognized.

MĒ'NĒS. Traditionally, the first king of the 1st dynasty of ancient Egypt. He is said to have been the founder of Memphis and the organizer of the worship of the gods.

MENIN. Belgian textile-making town in W Flanders, 11km (7m) SW of Kortrijk, on the Lys. The **Menin Gate** at Ypres (q.v.), on the road to Menin, commemorates 54,896 British soldiers missing in the battles of Ypres in 1914-18. Pop. (1978) 22,000.

MENIN'DEE. Village and sheep centre of New S Wales. Australia, on the Darling r. 105km (65m) SE of Broken Hill, centre of a water-conservation scheme conserving the waters of the Darling in M. Lake (155 sq.km/60 sq.m) and lakes nearby.

MENINGĪ'TIS. Inflammation of the meninges, the lining membranes of the base of the brain and spinal cord. An acute attack can be caused by spread of infection from disease of the nose or ear, by other infections, such as influenza or typhoid fever, or by the organism of spotted fever (cerebro-spinal fever), so called because it also often produces a rash. More chronic forms are due to tuberculosis or syphilis. M. responds well to treatment by sulphonamides or penicillin, but is more dangerous to life in infancy or old age. It is epidemic and very virulent in tropical Africa because of under-nourishment, lack of hygiene and inadequate medical facilities.

MENNONITES. A Christian sect that originated in Zürich in 1523. They were baptists, and refused to hold civil offices and undertake military service. Similar sectarians in Holland found a leader in Menno Simons (1496-1559), and were named after him. After his death the Ms. spread rapidly, but their views led to persecution, and in 1683 a number of them settled at Germantown, Pennsylvania. They are fundamentalists in theology, very simple in their ways of life, maintain their pacifism, and speak the languages of their ancestors.

ME'NOPAUSE. The change of life; the cessation of function of the female reproductive organs. The time of onset is usually about 45, but varies very much. Menstruation becomes irregular and ceases. The 'change' is natural and usually uneventful, but some women suffer from troubles such as flushing, excessive bleeding, and nervous disorder. Since the S.W.W. Hormone Replacement Therapy (HRT) has been developed to counteract such effects. Treatment (with oestrogen or an alternation of oestrogen and progestogen) may last 6 months to 5 yrs, must be specially tailored to the individual to avoid side-effects, and is managed so that the patient has regular bleeding, like periods.

MENORCA. Spanish form of MINORCA.

MENO'TTI, Gian Carlo (1911-). American composer. B. in Italy, he has lived in the USA since 1928. His operas are well known for their dramatic sense, excellent libretti (which he writes himself), and for the interdependence of words and music. Best-known are *The Medium* (1946); *The Telephone* (1947); *Amahl and the Night Visitors,* a Christmas story (1951); *The Consul* (1950); and *The Saint of Bleeker Street* (1954).

MENSHEVIKS. The right wing of the Russian Social-Democratic Party. They were so called because they formed the minority (Russ. *menshinstvo*) at the 1903 party congress, the left-wing majority being known as Bolsheviks. During the Russian revolution they succeeded in setting up a govt in Georgia, and after its overthrow disappeared.

MENSTRUATION. The female period; the monthly discharge from the womb of blood and breakdown products of the lining which has been prepared for the development of an egg-cell if fertilized. It starts at puberty, about 14, and ends with the change of life (*see* MENOPAUSE). If conception has taken place, the discharge does not occur. Otherwise M. may fail (amenorrhoea) in association with anaemia, depression, certain glandular disorders, etc. It may be painful (dysmenorrhoea), usually because of spasm of the womb; or the loss may be excessive (menorrhagia) because of inflammation, etc., within the womb. A proportion of women suffer from pre-menstrual tension (PMT), which causes headaches and irritability: treatment is by vitamin B6 (pyridoxine) and a synthetic form of progesterone, a female hormone.

MENTAL DISORDER. Generic term for all forms of mental ill health, of which there are in law 4 main types: **mental illness** in which patients of normal intelligence

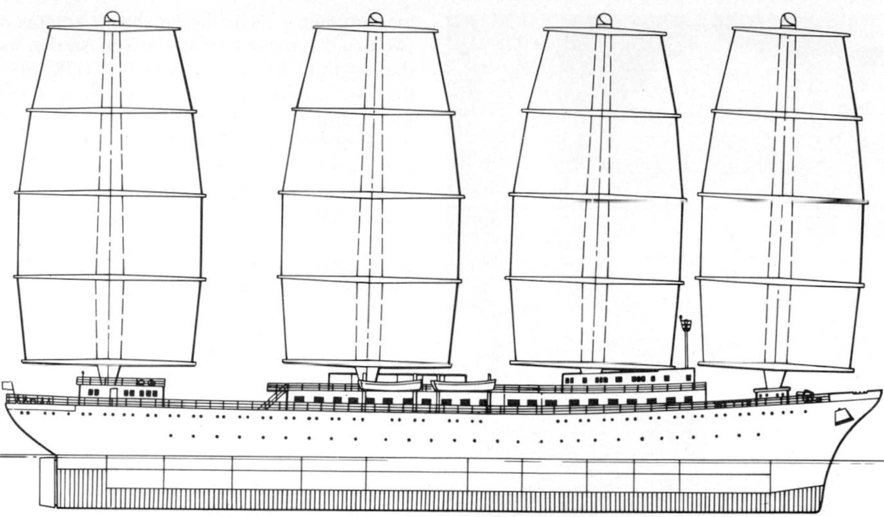

MERCHANT NAVY. The Dyna-Ship, designed by German aerodynamics engineer Wilhelm Prölss to save fossil fuels by once more using sailing ships for cargo. For maximum airfoil effect, there would be no break between the dacron sails which would roll out on tracks from the centre of the masts. The yards would be fixed and the sails set by a single officer exercising remote control from a panel on the bridge.

become disordered **severe subnormality** in which mental development is arrested to such an extent that the patient is incapable of leading an independent life, those formerly called idiots or imbeciles; **subnormality** in which special care and training can to some extent overcome the incomplete development of the mind, many of those formerly called feeble-minded; and **psychopathic disorder** in which the patient may or may not be of normal intelligence, but is characterized by extreme irresponsibility or abnormal aggressiveness which makes it unsafe for others as well as himself if he is not under treatment. Boundaries are difficult to draw, but commonly recognised kinds of mental illness incl: dementia, paranoia, schizophrenia (qq.v.), and manic depressive insanity, an alternation between elation (mania) and depression (melancholia). *See also* DOWN'S SYNDROME SEDATIVES.

MENTAL TEST. Scientifically standardized procedure for measuring a defined characteristic of the mind. Pioneer work was done by Sir Francis Galton and Binet; and later by Burt, Thorndike and others. M.Ts. may measure either intellectual ability or temperamental and moral qualities, and may be subdivided into those testing inborn or acquired characteristics; and cross-classified into those testing general qualities such as 'general intelligence' or more specialized aptitudes and propensities. The first large-scale use of intelligence Ts. for adults was for 2,000,000 drafted men in the USA in 1917. In industry aptitude tests, e.g. for manual dexterity, are practically useful, but conventional intelligence Ts., at one time favoured in deciding suitable education for eleven-year-olds, have drawbacks. Improved results may be contrived by practice; people with unconventional backgrounds are at a disadvantage, and original potentiality or 'creativity' cannot be measured: research is being directed to improved methods.

MENTHOL ($C_{10}H_{19}OH$). Peppermint camphor; an alcohol derivative of menthone. It occurs in peppermint and is responsible for the plant's odour.

MENTON (moṅtoṅ'). Resort (Ital. *Mentone*) on the French Riviera, close to the Italian frontier, in Alpes-Maritimes dept, frequently visited by Queen Victoria for its agreeable climate. It belonged to the princes of Monaco until sold to France in 1861. Pop. (1975) 25,300.

ME'NŪHIN, Yehudi (1916-). American violinist. Of Russian-Jewish parentage, he gave his first concert at 8, dazzling the critics by his maturity and freshness of approach. He retired for a period of intensive study 1935-7, and achieved a depth of interpretation, as in the Elgar and Beethoven concertos, which made him among the world's greatest players. His sister **Hephzibah M.** (1921-81) was a pianist and often accompanied him.

In 1963 he founded the *Y.M. School* at Stoke D'Abernon, Surrey, a boarding school for talented young musicians, the only one of its kind outside Russia. In 1965 he was created hon. KBE.

MENZIES, Sir Robert Gordon (1894-1978). Australian statesman. A successful Melbourne lawyer, he entered politics in 1928, was Attorney-Gen. in the federal parl. 1934-9, and in 1939 succeeded Lyons as PM and leader of the United Australia Party (1939-41). Leading the Opposition from 1943, he in 1944 initiated the formation of a new party - the Australian Lib. Party - to unite all anti-Lab. groups except the Country Party, and in 1949 became PM of a Lib.-Country Party coalition govt, being re-elected 1951, 1954, 1955, 1958, 1961, and 1963. Knighted 1963, he succeeded Churchill as Lord Warden of the Cinque Ports in 1965, and retired as PM 1966.

MEQUINES. *See* MEKNÈS.

MERCĀ'TOR, Gerardus (1512-94). Latinized form of Gerhard Kremer, name of the Flemish map-maker who devised 'M.'s projection' - the first map using it being pub. in 1568. *See* ATLAS.

MERCHANT NAVY. Ships owned by shipping companies and used as trading vessels to provide sea transport for passenger traffic and for export and import cargoes. The chief types of merchant ships are: (1) tramps, which

MENZIES. Sir Robert Menzies, by long service as Prime Minister and strength of personality, was as well-known a figure in Britain as in Australia. *Photo: Camera Press*

may coast between home ports or carry bulk cargoes for voyages of up to 2 years from one port to another throughout the world; (2) tankers (now the largest ships afloat, up to *c.* 500,000 tonnes and 380m/1,245 ft long) and other ships carrying a single specialized cargo; (3) cargo liners, combining cargo and passenger traffic on short or world voyages - liners carrying passengers only are decreasing in modern conditions. Among the most famous passenger ships are the 3 Cunard 'queens', *Queen Mary* (1936) which in 1967 went to Long Beach, California, as a floating hotel; *Queen Elizabeth* (1940), the largest in tonnage (82,998), was taken to Hong Kong for conversion to a floating university but destroyed by fire in 1972; and *Queen Elizabeth II* (1968); the *France* (Fr. 1961) was transferred to Norway in 1980 (at 315m/1,035 ft she is the longest of the giant ships). The world's first atomic-powered merchant ship was the *Savannah* (USA 1959). The first modern merchant ship to be built with sails + diesel engine on the lines estab. by Prölss (see illus) was the *Aitoku Maru* (Japan 1980).

MERCIA (mer'shia). One of the Anglo-Saxon kingdoms, which at its greatest extent included all England between the Humber and the Thames, except E Anglia. It first emerged *c.* 600, and in the 8th cent. dominated all England S of the Humber. From *c.* 825 it came under the overlordship of Wessex. In 886 the E of M. was included in the Danelaw.

MER'CŪRY. Roman god, identified with the Greek Hermes, and like him represented with the winged sandals and caduceus. He was the messenger of the gods.

MERCURY. The nearest planet to the Sun (on average 58,000,000 km/36,000,000 m), its diameter is 4,840 km (3,000 m), and the revolution period 88 days. Radar measurements have shown that it rotates once for every two orbits it makes round the Sun, so that its day is double the length of its year. *Mariner 10* (USA 1973) discovered that M. is two-thirds iron, so that it is half as heavy as Earth, and is also rich in uranium; as it decays radioactive uranium releases helium gas which, plus argon and neon, make up the thin atmosphere. It is like the Moon on the outside, but possibly the interior resembles that of Earth. Large meteors have created craters 160km (100m) or more in diameter, which have been filled by lava rising from beneath the surface. There are also large plains, cliff formations and an intriguing magnetic field.

MERCURY. The only common metal liquid at ordinary temperatures, it was known to the ancient Chinese and Hindus, and is found in Egyptian tombs of *c.* 1500 BC: symbol Hg, at. wt. 200.61, at. no. 80. A dense, mobile, silvery liquid, it is found free in nature, but the chief source is the mineral cinnabar, HgS. Its alloys with other metals are *amalgams.* It is used in drugs and chemicals, for mercury vapour lamps, arc rectifiers, power-control switches, vacuum and other scientific apparatus, barometers, thermometers, etc.

MERCURY FULMINATE. Highly explosive compound used in detonators and percussion caps. It is a grey, sandy powder, and highly poisonous.

MEREDITH (mer'edith), **George** (1828-1909). British novelist and poet. B. in Portsmouth, he was ed. in Germany, articled to a London solicitor, but soon entered journalism, and in 1849 m. Mary Nicolls (d. 1861), the widowed dau. of Thomas Love Peacock, who left him in 1858. In 1851 he pub. *Poems* and in 1855 the prose romance, *The Shaving of Shagpat.* His first realistic psychological novel, *The Ordeal of Richard Feverel* (1859), was followed by *Evan Harrington* (1860), *Rhoda Fleming* (1865), *Harry Richmond* (1871), *The Egoist* (1879), *Diana of the Crossways* (1885), and *The Amazing Marriage* (1895). His later vols. of verse incl. *Modern Love* (1862) and *Poems and Lyrics* (1883). He was reader to Chapman and Hall 1862-94, and in 1867, 2 years after his marriage to Mary Vulliamy (d. 1885), made his home at Flint Cottage, Box Hill. In 1905 he received the OM.

MERGA'NSER. Genus of ducks, mainly marine. The goosander (*Mergus merganser*) is widely distributed in the N hemisphere, though rare in Britain.

MERGENTHALER (merg'entahler), **Ottmar** (1854-99). German-American inventer. B. in Hachtel, Württemberg, where he served his apprenticeship as a watchmaker, he went to USA in 1872 and there developed 1876-86 the first linotype machine.

MERIDA (mer'ĕdhah). Mexican city, cap. of the state of Yucatan and seat of a univ., it has a cathedral founded 1598. M., dating from 1542, is a centre of the sisal industry. Pop. (1970) 253,800.

MERIDIAN. A great circle drawn on the earth's surface so as to pass through both poles, and thus through all places with the same longitude. Terrestrial longitudes are usually measured from Greenwich M. An astronomical M. is a great circle passing through the pole and the zenith. (*See* LATITUDE AND LONGITUDE.)

MÉRIMÉE (mehremeh'), **Prosper** (1803-70). French author. B. in Paris, he entered the public service, and under Napoleon III was employed on unofficial diplomatic missions. Among his best works are the stories *Colomba* (1841), dealing with a Corsican feud, and the

Spanish *Carmen* (1846); and the witty and sceptical *Lettres à une inconnue* (1873).

MERINO (merē'no). Originally a term for sheep-pasture inspectors in Spain, M. now refers to a breed of sheep native to Africa. Its close-set, silky wool is of extremely good quality, and the M., now found all over the world, is the breed on which the Australian industry is built.

MERIO'NETHSHIRE. Former co. of Wales, facing Cardigan Bay on the W, incl. in Gwynedd in 1974. It incl. Cader Idris and Bala Lake, and the r. Dee. Dolgelley was the co. town.

MERIT, Order of. British order of chivalry, founded in 1902 by Edward VII and limited in number to 24. Though not a knighthood, it is very highly regarded. *See* LEGION OF HONOUR.

MERLIN. Small falcon (*Falco columbarius*), which breeds in England and Scotland. Males are steel-blue above and rufous below; females are brown. It nests in the heather. The N American pigeon-hawk (*F. columbanus*) is similar.

MERMAIDS. In folklore, semi-human creatures who live in the sea; their form is that of a beautiful woman with the tail of a fish. The dugong and seal (qq.v.) have been suggested as possible origins for the legends.

MEROE (mer'ō-ē). Ancient city of the Rep. of the Sudan, on the Nile near Khartoum, cap. of Nubia *c.* 600 BC to AD 350. Tombs and inscriptions have been excavated, and because of its iron smelting slag-heaps, it has been called the 'Birmingham of ancient Africa'.

MEROVI'NGIANS. The name of a Frankish dynasty, derived from its founder, Merovech (5th cent.). His descendants ruled France from the time of Clovis (481-511) to 751.

MERSEYSIDE. Met. co. of England created in the local govt re-organisation of 1974, and comprising the SW corner of Lancs, incl. Liverpool and St Helens and the NW half of the Wirral Peninsula, incl. Birkenhead and Wallasey, formerly in Cheshire. The river Mersey is formed by the union of the Goyt and Tame at Stockport, then flows *c.* 115km (70m), expanding to a harbour estuary between Runcorn and Liverpool. The admin. HQ is Liverpool. Area 648 sq.km (250 sq.m); pop. (1978) 1,545,500.

MERSIN (mersēn'). Port in Turkey, also known as Icel, on the Mediterranean, 65km (40m) SW of Adana. Oil is refined, and chrome, copper and agricultural produce are exported. Pop. (1970) 114,300.

MERTHYR TYDFIL (mur'ther tid'vil). Town in Mid Glamorgan, Wales, 38km (24m) NW of Cardiff, in an iron and coal district. Between the 2 world wars it suffered heavily from unemployment. Pop. (1972) 54,530.

MERV. Oasis in Russian Turkmenistan, a centre of civilization at least 1200 BC, and site of a town founded by Alexander the Great. Old M. was destroyed by the Emir of Bokhara 1787, and the modern town of Mary (q.v.), founded by the Russians 1885, lies 29km (18m) W.

MESA (mā'sa). Spanish word for 'table', adopted for flat-topped mts cut away in a steep cliff at the side or sides.

MESA VERDE. The 'green table', a wooded cliff top in Colorado, USA, with the finest of all Pueblo cliff dwellings, the Cliff Palace, built into its side *c.* AD 1000. With 200 rooms, 23 circular ceremonial chambers (kivas), and an original population of *c.* 400 people, it was probably a regional centre.

ME'SCALIN. Drug derived from a turnip-shaped cactus (*Lophophora Williamsii*) of Texas and N Mexico, known locally as peyote (pāyō'tā), etc. The tops, which scarcely appear above ground, are dried and chewed, or added to alcoholic drinks. Allegedly non-habit-forming and without after-effects, M. heightens the perceptions and is used by the Navajos of California and Indians of other states in the ceremonial of the Native American Church. It was used experimentally by Aldous Huxley (q.v.) and others.

ME'SHED. Cap. of the prov. of Khorasan, Iran. It is the holy city of the Moslem Shi'ite sect, and is visited by *c.* 100,000 pilgrims annually. There is a univ. Manufactures incl. carpets, leather goods, woollen and cotton textiles. M. is linked by rail with Tehran and Ashkhabad, cap. of Turkmen SSR, and by road with Herat in Afghanistan. Pop. (1976) 670,180.

MESMERISM. Theory that a subject may be reduced to a state of trance by the consciously exerted 'animal magnetism' of the operator, in which the willpower of the former is entirely subordinated. It is named from the Austrian physician, Friedrich Anton Mesmer (1733-1815). B. at Weil, near Constance, he took a medical degree at Vienna, and conducted experiments there, at first with actual magnets. Driven from Vienna by the police, he settled at Paris in 1778, and created a fashionable sensation. An investigating committee denounced him as a charlatan in 1785, and he d. in Switzerland. M. is now popularly identified with hypnotism.

MĒ'SON. Unstable particle with mass intermediate between those of the electron and the proton, found in cosmic radiation and emitted by nuclei under bombardment by very high-energy particles.

MESOPOTĀ'MIA. Classical name derived from the Greek for 'middle' and 'river' given to the land between the Euphrates and the Tigris. Here the civilizations of Sumer and Babylon flourished, and some consider it the original home of civilized man. It is part of modern Iraq.

MESOZŌ'A. Group of minute parasitic animals of the Metazoa. It is divided into 2 classes, the Rhombozoa and the Orthonectida.

MESRINE (mezrēn'), **Jacques** (1937-1979). French criminal. Of well-to-do family, he became a burglar celebrated for his glib tongue, sadism, and bravado, and most of all for his escapes from the police and prison. Towards the end he had links with left-wing terrorism. Police cornered him in Paris and shot him with 21 bullets.

MESSAGER (mesahzhā'), **André Charles Prosper** (1853-1929). French composer. He studied under Saint-Saëns. M. was successful with his light operas, such as *La Béarnaise* and *Véronique.*

MESSALINA, Valeria (*c.* AD 22-48). Roman empress. She was the third wife of Claudius, and for some years dominated him. Her name has become a byword for immorality. In 48 she forced a noble to marry her, although she was still married to Claudius, and the latter had her executed.

MESSERSCHMITT, Willy (1898-1978). German designer. His ME-109 was a standard Luftwaffe fighter in the SWW, and his ME-262 (1942) was the first mass-produced jet fighter, but Hitler did not see its significance.

MESSIAEN (mesi-aṅ'), **Olivier** (1908-). French composer and organist. He was a pupil of Dukas, and his works, which incl. church music, make use of bird song and Indian themes.

MESSĪ'AH. Word derived from the Hebrew for 'the anointed', the Greek equivalent of which is Christ. The Jews from the time of the exile have looked forward to the coming of the M., who shall be a deliverer. Christians believe that the M. came in the person of Jesus Christ.

MESSINA (mesē'nah). Sicilian city in the NE corner of the is. It was an ancient Greek foundation before it was taken by the Carthaginians and then the Romans. In 1908 it was destroyed by an earthquake in which 77,000 were killed. The Straits of M. separate Sicily and Italy. Pop. (1971) 257,725.

MESTROVIC (mesh'trovitch), **Ivan** (1883-1962). Yugoslav sculptor. In 1947 he went to the US and was naturalized in 1954. His notable works incl. portrait busts of Rodin, Sir Thomas Beecham, Pres. Masaryk, etc.

META'BOLISM. The processes of building up and breaking down constantly taking place in living organisms to sustain life and growth. The 3 principal types relate to: green plants (based on photosynthesis in which complex organic substances are built up from water, carbon dioxide and mineral salts in the presence of chlorophyll and sunlight); plants not containing chlorophyll, e.g. moulds, yeasts, fungi, and bacteria, which secure energy by many different chemical transformations, e.g. oxidation of ammonia to nitrates; and animals dependent for food on complex compounds which they break down partially by digestion, and subsequently resynthesize. Thus animals are dependent on green plants either directly or indirectly.

METALIOUS, Grace (1924-64). American novelist, *née* de Repentigny. B. in Manchester, New Hampshire, she m. at 17 Christopher M. and, after writing many short stories uneventfully, struck the headlines with *Peyton Place* (1956), an exposé of life in a small New England town that roused a storm of protest.

METALLIC GLASS. Substance produced from metallic materials (non-corrosive alloys rather than simple metals) in liquid state which, by very rapid cooling are prevented from reverting to their regular metallic structure. Instead they take on the properties of glass, while retaining the metallic properties of malleability and relatively good electrical conductivity.

METALLURGY. The art of working metals. Process M. is concerned chiefly with their extraction from the ores, and refining and adapting them for man's use, while physical M. is interested in their properties and application. The foundations of metallurgical art were probably laid about 3500 BC in Egypt, Mesopotamia, and India, where the art of smelting metals from ores was discovered, and gold, silver, copper, lead, and tin were worked. The smelting of iron appears to have been discovered about 1500 BC, and the Romans hardened and tempered steel. From the fall of the Roman Empire until the latter part of the Middle Ages, the only advances in M. were due to the Arabian chemists.

Cast iron began to be made in the 14th cent., and in the 18th cent. we find the beginning of the modern blast furnace. The application of steam power resulted in an enormous increase in iron and steel production.

Metals can be extracted from their ores in 3 main ways: (1) dry processes such as smelting, volatilization or amalgamation, (2) wet processes involving chemical reactions, and (3) electrolytic processes.

METALS. Elements which are classified as Ms. have certain characteristics and physical properties which can be increasingly accounted for by modern theories based on studies of their atomic and sub-atomic structures. Ms. are good conductors of heat and electricity; opaque, but reflect light well; malleable, which enables them to be cold-worked and rolled into sheets; and ductile, which permits them to be drawn into thin wires. Generally hard, they are crystalline in their normal pure state, many of them mixing with one another to form alloys with properties depending on the proportions of their constituents. Their hardness, tensile strength, toughness, brittleness, etc., may be varied by physical means such as heat-treatment, work hardening, etc., but their physical properties, such as melting point, coefficient of thermal expansion, density, etc., are constant.

60 to 70 Ms. are known, but only the following are used in commerce: (i) *Precious Ms.:* gold, silver, mercury, platinum, and the platinum Ms., used principally in jewellery. (ii) *Heavy Ms.:* iron, copper, zinc, tin, lead, the common Ms. of engineering. (iii) *Rarer heavy Ms.:* nickel, cadmium, chromium, tungsten, molybdenum, manganese, cobalt, vanadium, antimony, and bismuth; used principally for alloying with the heavy Ms. (iv) *Light Ms.:* aluminium and magnesium. (v) *Alkali Ms.:* sodium, potassium, lithium; and alkaline earth Ms.: calcium, barium, strontium, used principally for chemical purposes.

Other metals have come to the fore because of special nuclear requirements, e.g., technetium, produced in nuclear reactors, is corrosion-inhibiting; zirconium may replace aluminium and magnesium alloy in canning uranium in reactors; titanium is really tough and hard, titanium oxide finds wide application in artistic finishes, because of its inertness and whiteness. Of great importance are the carbides of titanium, zirconium, niobium, and hafnium, alone or in combination, because of their high melting points round 3,000°C. *See* METALLIC GLASS.

METAMORPHISM. Geological term referring to the changes which have occurred in the rocks of the earth's crust, caused by increases of pressure or of temperature, or of both, since the rocks were formed.

METAPHYSICS. A branch of philosophy, concerned with the ultimate nature of reality. It has been maintained that no certain knowledge of metaphysical questions is to be had. Epistemology, or the study of how we know, lies at the threshold of the subject. M. is concerned with the nature and origin of matter and of mind, the interaction between them - i.e. the 'mind-body problem'; the meaning of time and space, causation, determinism and free will, personality and the Self, arguments for belief in God, and human immortality.

The foundations of M. were laid by Plato and Aristotle. St Thomas Aquinas, basing himself on the latter, produced a metaphysical structure that is accepted by the Catholic Church. The subject has been advanced by Descartes, Spinoza, Leibniz, Berkeley, Hume, Locke, Kant, Hegel, Schopenhauer, and Marx; and in modern times by Bergson, Bradley, Croce, M'Taggart, Whitehead, and Wittgenstein.

METASTASIO (metahstah'zē-ō). Pseudonym of the Italian poet, Pietro Trapassi (1698-1782). B. in Rome, from 1730 he was court poet at Vienna, and wrote numerous lyric dramas.

METAXAS, Joannis (1871-1941). Greek soldier and statesman. B. in Ithaca, he opposed co-operation with the Allies during the F.W.W. and was prominent in the restoration of the monarchy in 1935. To combat internal difficulties he estab. a dictatorship when he became PM in 1936, and introduced several important reforms. Refusing to abandon Greece's neutral position, he victoriously led the resistance to the Italian invasion in the S.W.W.

METAZŌ'A. One of the 2 main sections into which the animal kingdom is divided, the other being the protozoa. M. are multi-cellular, and include all the higher forms of animal life.

MĒ'TĒOR. A small particle moving round the Sun. If a M. approaches the Earth to within 240km (150m), it enters the upper atmosphere, and since it is moving very rapidly (up to 70km (45m) per sec.) frictional heat is set up; the M. destroys itself in the streak of radiation known as a *shooting-star.* Most Ms. are smaller than grains of sand. They tend to travel in swarms, and when the Earth passes through a swarm the result is a shower of shooting-stars: the most famous annual shower is that of the Perseids, in early August. Both radar and photographic methods are used in their study.

Very large, bright meteors are known as **fireballs,** and seem more nearly related to minor planets or asteroids. They appear unexpectedly, and when not completely consumed in their descent through the atmosphere reach the Earth as **meteorites.** Meteorites may be chondrites (stony, with metal only in minute grains); achondrites (stony and metal-free - rare); stony irons (equal amounts stone and iron); or irons (almost pure iron-nickel alloys). Many meteorites are large, but these seldom survive intact to reach Earth - the largest (of the iron-nickel type) weighed 30 tonnes - but they supply the vast bulk of cosmic dust reaching Earth's surface. Billions of years ago, however, Earth must have been subject to meteoric impact on a similar scale to that of the Moon, Mars and Venus. Large nos. have been found in Antarctica, where conditions have enabled them to survive without losing volatile compounds, etc. Only 3 M. have accurately known orbits round the Sun: Lost City, Pribram and Innisfree. *See* ASTRON, THERMOLUMINESCENCE.

METEORO'LOGY. The scientific observation and study of the phenomena of weather. At meteorological stations readings are taken of the more important factors determining weather conditions. Atmospheric pressure is measured by a mercury barometer, temperature by a screened thermometer, humidity by a hygrometer, which expresses relative humidity as a percentage of the maximum. Winds are categorized by the Beaufort Scale, and the Beaufort weather code signifies every weather condition by suitable initials, with capitals denoting intensity. Cloud observations gauge how many eighths of sky are covered by each type, and rainfall is measured each 12 hours in a funnel. Specially equipped weather ships maintained by several nations incl. Britain, at a number of ocean stations, report on weather conditions and advise air traffic. They carry radar (q.v.) and twice daily make balloon soundings of wind, temperatures and humidity. Increasing costs have reduced their number, and there is growing reliance on reports from satellites which signal back a wide range of information, and on a broader basis, but offering some practical difficulties of interpretation. All these data are reported to, and collated by central agencies, e.g. Meteorological Office, London; US Weather Bureau, Washington, and then pooled on an international basis, when all nations can be informed on weather conditions as they affect crops, storms, hurricanes, etc., enabling regular weather forecasts to be made. The electronic computer has enabled a promising start to be made in the stupendous task of using physical laws to calculate the future trend and to give long-range weather forecasts. The *World Meteorological Organization* (1950) has weather centres at Suitland, Maryland, USA; Moscow; and Melbourne.

MĒ'TER. A general term for any instrument used for measurement, often compounded with a prefix to denote a specific type of M., e.g. ammeter, voltmeter, flowmeter, pedometer, etc. Ms. may not only indicate but also integrate and/or record measurements.

ME'THĀNE or **marsh gas** (CH_4). The simplest hydrocarbon of the paraffin series; a constituent of the gas which arises in marshy districts from the decomposition of vegetable matter in stagnant water, and also of the explosive 'fire damp' in coal mines. M. is also a product of the distillation of coal, lignite, peat, wood, etc. It is colourless, odourless, and lighter than air, burns with a faintly luminous flame, and explodes when mixed with air or oxygen.

METHANOGEN. *See* ARCHAEBACTERIA.

ME'THANOL. The simplest of the monohydric alcohols, also known as methyl alcohol. It can be made by the dry distillation of wood (hence it also known as wood alcohol), but today is usually made from coal or natural gas. When pure, it is a colourless, inflammable liquid with a pleasant odour, and is highly poisonous. It is used to produce formaldehyde (q.v.); methyl tert-butyl ether (a replacement for lead as an octane-booster in petrol); vinyl acetate (largely used in paint manufacture), petrol, etc. In making petrol it is cheapest to convert the coal or gas first to a mixture of carbon monoxide and hydrogen (synthesis gas), which is then converted in turn to methanol and petrol. Natural gas from New Zealand's Maui field is now being converted to petrol at less than the cost of producing petrol from oil.

METHODISM. The evangelical movement founded by John and Charles Wesley in 1739; the name was originally applied to the Wesleys and their circle at Oxford as a nickname. M. originated within the C of E, and only in 1795 became a distinct body.

The doctrines of M. are contained in John Wesley's *Notes on the New Testament* and sermons. The form of church government is presbyterian in Britain, and episcopal in the USA. The supreme authority is the annual conference, composed of equal numbers of ministers and laymen. Members are grouped under 'class leaders' and churches into 'circuits'.

METHODIUS. *See* CYRIL.

METHŪ'SELAH. One of the antediluvian patriarchs of Hebrew story. From the immense age with which he is credited, 969 years, M. has become the type of longevity.

METHYL ALCOHOL *See* METHANOL.

METHYLATED SPIRITS. Adulterated or 'denatured' alcohol, which has been rendered undrinkable, and is free of duty for industrial purposes. It is nevertheless drunk by advanced alcoholics, and eventually results in death.

METRIC SYSTEM. System of weights and measures developed in France in the 18th cent. and recognized as an internat. system by major industrial countries incl. the UK in the 19th cent. In 1960 an internat. conference on

MEXICO. The great centre of Zapotec culture at Monte Albán (left), where a hill-top was levelled to form a plaza bounded by mounds and terraces, and human sacrifices were carried out. On the right, the Polyforum of Mexico City, which includes a theatre, exhibition hall, etc., and includes this lyric painting by David Siqueiros. *Photos: A.G. Formenti and Mireille Vautier*

weights and measures redefined the basic unit - the metre - as the length measured in vacuo of 1 650 763.73 wavelengths of the orange-red radiation emitted by krypton (isotope 86) corresponding to the unperturbed transition between the $2p_{10}$ and $5d_5$ levels. It also recommended for universal adoption a revised International System (*Système International d'Unités:* abbrev. SI), which has 7 prescribed 'base units', the metre 'm' for length, kilogram 'kg' for mass or weight, second 's' for time, ampere 'A' for electric current, kelvin 'K' for thermodynamic temperature, candela 'cd' for luminous intensity, and mole 'mol' for quantity of matter. Two supplementary units are incl. in the system - the radian (rad) and steradian (sr) - used in the measurement of plane and solid angles. In addition, there are recognized derived units which are those which can be expressed, algebraically, as simple products or divisions of powers of the basic units, with no other integers appearing in the expression, e.g. the watt is a derived unit. Some units, well estab. and internationally recognized, remain in use within SI, or in conjunction with it: minute, hour and day in measuring time; multiples or sub-multiples of base or derived units which have long-estab. names, such as tonne for mass, the litre for volume, and specialist measures such as the metric carat for gemstones. Prefixes used to multiply and divide the M. units are era (T) trillion times (10^{12}); giga (G) billion times (10^9); mega (M) million times (10^6); kilo (k) thousand times (10^3); hecto (h) hundred times (10^2); deka (da) ten times (10); deci (d) tenth part (10^{-1}); centi (c) hundredth part (10^{-2}); milli (m) thousandth part (10^{-3}); micro (μ) millionth part (10^{-6}); nano (n) billionth part (10^{-9}); pico (p) trillionth part (10^{-12}); femto (f) quadrillionth part (10^{-15}); atto (a) quintillionth part (10^{-18}). The metric system was made lawful for most purposes in UK and USA in the 19th cent. The UK govt. agreed to the adoption of SI as the primary system of weights and measures in 1965, but compulsion was abandoned in 1978, although further decisions will be needed in 1989 when Britain will have to conform to certain EEC regulations. A Metric Act was passed in USA in 1975.

METROPOLITAN OPERA COMPANY. Foremost opera co. of USA, founded NY 1883. The M.O. House (opened 1883) was demolished 1966, and the co. transferred to the Lincoln Center.

METSU (met'sü), **Gabriel** (1630-67). Dutch painter. B. at Leyden, he worked in Amsterdam from 1657. His pictures are usually of the anecdotal type and incl. 'The Duet' and 'Music Lesson', both in the National Galley, London.

METTERNICH-WINNEBURG, Clemens Wenzel Lothar, prince (1773-1859). Austrian statesman. He was ambassador to France 1806-9, and Foreign Minister from 1809 until the 1848 revolution forced him to flee to England. At the Congress of Vienna in 1815 he advocated co-operation by the great powers to suppress democratic movements.

METZ. Cap. of Moselle dept, France, on the Moselle. It has a Gothic cathedral, is the centre of a rich agricultural region, and manufactures shoes, metal goods, and tobacco. It was long one of the great frontier fortresses of France. M. was a free city of the Holy Roman Empire until 1552, and was German 1871-1918. Pop. (1973) 113,590.

MEURTHE (mört). Fr. r. 163km/102m long, which rises in the Vosges Mts. and flows in a generally NW direction to join the Moselle at Frouard, 8km (5m) NNW of Nancy. It gives its name to the dept of Meurthe-et-Moselle.

MEUSE (mös). River which rises in the dept of Haute-Marne, France, passes Verdun, and flows in a N direction into Belgium, past Namur and Liège, then enters the Netherlands S of Maastricht, flowing N, then W to join the Waal near Gorkum. The Dutch form of its name is Maas. Its total length is *c.* 900km (560m). The M., which gives its name to a French dept, was a line of battle in the F.W.W. in 1914, and the S.W.W. in 1940.

MEWAR. Another name for UDAIPUR.

MEXICALI (meksikah'li). City in Baja California, Mexico, on the frontier with USA. It is the centre of a fertile area: cotton, citrus and vines are grown under irrigation. Pop. (1974) 391,000.

MEXICO. Federal rep. of North America, lying S of the USA.

Physical. The Gulf of California divides the mainland of the E from the elongated, mountainous peninsula of Lower California to the W. The 2 ranges of the Sierra Madre enclose an extensive central plateau and meet near the isthmus of Tehuantepec, on which both coasts converge. None of the rivers is of any commercial importance. Climatically, the country is divided into: (1) *Tierra Caliente*, a low-lying, tropical region adjacent to the coasts and including the peninsula of Yucatan; (2) *Tierra Templada,* a temperate region including most of the plateau; and (3) Tierra Fría, a cold region rising above 1,800 m (6,000 ft), in which Mexico City is situated. Over much of M. the rainfall is very scanty, almost half having less than 500mm annually.

Economic. M. is still largely agricultural, but requires food imports. The main crops are maize (the staple food), beans, wheat, coffee, sugar, rice, bananas, tobacco, sisal, and cotton. Cattle are bred. Contour-ploughing, re-afforestation, and irrigation are used to conserve and extend cultivable land. Silver, gold, lead, zinc, arsenic, copper, iron ore and uranium are worked. Oil and natural gas resources (nationalized 1938) have proved increasingly rich, and much is supplied to the USA. Iron and steel, textiles, electrical goods, chemicals, etc., are increasingly produced, and traditional handicrafts in silver, pottery, weaving, leather, etc., supply valuable revenue. The chief ports are Tampico and Vera Cruz, and communications by road, rail and air are excellent. M.U.: peso.

Political. M. comprises 31 states, and 1 federal dist. As amended in 1953, the federal constitution provided for a pres. popularly elected for 6 years and ineligible for re-election, and a congress consisting of a number of deputies elected for 3 years and a senate elected for 6 years. Men and women are eligible to vote at 18.

Area and Population. Area 1,979,650 sq.km (763,944 sq.m); pop. (1976) 62,330,000. The official language is Spanish, but some 3,000,000 Amerindians speak Indian languages, of which the most important is Nahuatl, and a third of them speak no Spanish. Most of the people are Roman Catholic, but Church and State have been separated since 1857, and church activities are restricted. Although education is free and theoretically compulsory up to the age of 15, illiteracy remains a problem because of the high birth rate. The most important univ. is the Nat. Univ. of Mexico, founded 1551, which has 100,000 students. Apart from Mexico City, the cap, the largest towns are Guadalajara, Monterrey, León, Ciudad Juárez, Mexicali, Tlalnepantla, Chihuahua and Culiacán. Tourism is increasingly important, the majority of visitors being from USA, and resorts such as Acapulco are world-famous. The great archaeological sites incl. the Pyramid of the Sun at Teotihuacán 66m (216ft) high; the Maya and Toltec ruins of Tula and Chichén Itzá in Yucatan; and the Zapotec city of Monte Albán nr Oaxaca.

History. M. was the scene of the brilliant Indian civilizations of the Mayas, at its height *c.* AD 300-900, the Toltecs (c. 900-1100), and the Aztecs who settled on the central plateau, and whose last emperor, Montezuma II, was killed in 1520 during the Spanish invasion. M. became the viceroyalty of New Spain; Spanish culture and the Catholic religion were firmly established, and the natural wealth of the country was developed, but foreign rule became increasingly oppressive, and Spanish rule was ended in 1821. In 1824 a rep. was set up. Texas separated from M. in 1836, and New Mexico and California were ceded to the USA after the war of 1846-8. After 3 years of civil war, Benito Juarez established himself as ruler over the whole country in 1861. His repudiation of foreign debts led to foreign intervention, and in 1863 Maximilian of Austria was proclaimed emperor; but when the French troops supporting him were withdrawn, 1866, he was captured and executed, 1867. Juarez remained pres. until 1872. His successor, Lardo, was opposed by Porfirio Diaz who, entering Mexico City in force in 1876, was elected pres. 1877-80 and again in 1884 and at each succeeding election until forced to resign in 1911. The stability resulting from Diaz's dictatorship ended with his fall. But in 1920 a period of reconstruction began, based on a new constitution of 1917 which expropriated owners of large estates and let the land to the peasants. Mexico declared war on the Axis powers June 1942, and was an original member of the United Nations. From 1929 the Institutional Revolutionary Party has been predominant, concentrating on the creation of wealth for redistribution. Pres. José López Portillo was elected pres. in 1976.

MEXICO CITY Cap. and largest city of Mexico, situated on the S edge of the central plateau, at 2,255 m (7,400 ft) a.s.l. near Lake Texcoco. It is spacious and regular, and the many fine buildings incl. the 16th cent. cathedral, the national palace, the national library, the Palace of Justice, and national univ. M.C. is an important cultural centre, a vital railway, road, and air service centre, and business and industrial development is growing.

The city dates from c. 1325, when the Aztec cap. Tenochtitlán was begun on an island in Lake Texcoco. This city was levelled in 1521 by the Spaniards, who in 1522 founded a new city on the site. In the 1970s-1980s the remains of the ancient city were excavated on cleared areas for preservation as a museum. The lake has gradually shrunk, and is *c.* 4km (2½m) from the present-day M.C. Pop. (1980) *c.* 13,000,000.

MEYERBEER (mī'-erbār), **Giacomo.** Adopted name of German composer Jakob Liebmann Beer (1791-1864). B. in Berlin, from 1826 he lived mainly in Paris, apart from his work after 1842 as general musical director in Berlin. A talented pianist, he became best known for his spectacular operas, e.g. *Robert le Diable* (1831) and *Les Huguenots* (1836).

MEYNELL (men'el), **Alice** (1847-1922). British poet, *née* Thompson. She pub. *Preludes* (1875) and her collected poems appeared in 1923. Her essays incl. *Rhythm of Life* (1893) and *Second Person Singular* (1921). In 1877 she m. the Catholic author and journalist Wilfrid M. (1852-1948) and with him befriended Francis Thompson. Her youngest son was **Sir Francis M.** (1891-1975), book designer and founder of the Nonesuch Press (1923) for fine editions.

MEZZANINE (mez'anēn). Architectural term derived from the diminutive of the Italian word for middle; it is a low storey in a building between 2 higher ones.

MEZZOGIORNO (metsōdzēor'nō). Italian 'mid-day'; the hot impoverished regions of S Italy.

MEZZOTINT (med'zo-). A method of etching in tone, widely practised during the 18th cent. A copper or steel plate is roughened by means of a rocking tool, which makes indentations and raises a 'burr'. The burr is then scraped away where lighter tones are wanted in the design. The process was used to reproduce the works of Turner, Reynolds, Constable, Romney, Lawrence and others.

MIAMI (mī-am'i). City and port in SE Florida, USA, where the M. river enters Biscayne Bay. In 1895 'Fort Dallas' was a tiny hamlet, but with the coming of the railway and its incorporation as the City of M. (Seminole 'sweet water') in 1896, it grew rapidly as a centre for citrus fruit, tourism, and oceanographic research, and as a commercial and manufacturing 'Gateway to Latin America'.

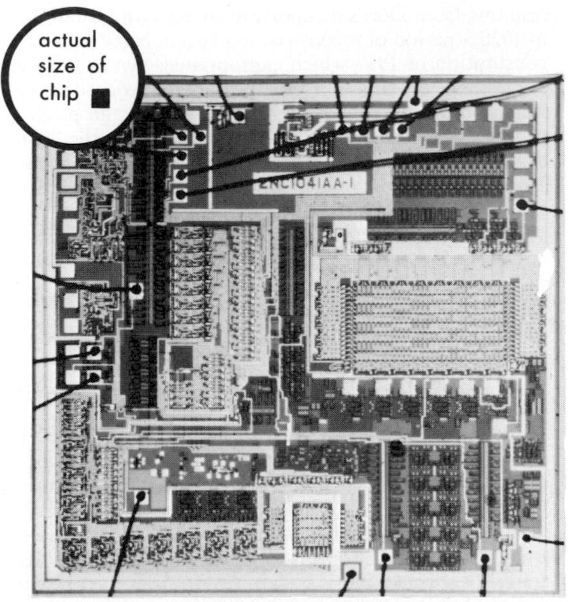

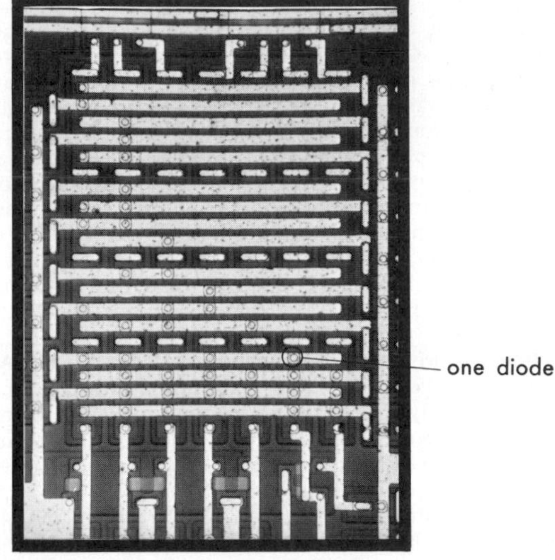

MICROCOMPUTER. The world's first digital electronic fuel injection system to be fitted to a production car (left) is a tiny chip of silicon, wafer thin and less than 5mm (0.2in) square. This enlargement shows the circuitry imprinted into the material, its complexity being emphasised by the area outlined in white being further greatly enlarged (right). The chip acts as a fixed-programme mini-computer, receiving a continuous stream of signals concerning engine condition, such as engine speed, intake airflow, water temperature, etc. It then calculates, by reference to the inbuilt digital memory store, the precise fuel flow required at that moment in time, to provide exactly the right fuel/air mixture. *Photos: Courtesy of the Lucas Group*

Many Cuban refugees (*c.* 125,000) settled here after 1959. Pop. met. area (1970) 1,259,176.

MĪ'CA. A group of minerals distinguished by their perfect basal cleavage causing them to split into thin flakes, and by their vitreous pearly lustre. They are found in schists, gneisses, and granites, and their good thermal and electrical insulation quality makes them valuable in industry. M. can be dated to a few thousand years by its geological context, and muon-neutrino tracks within it confirm evolutionary theories of the solar planetary system.

MĪ'CAH (fl. *c.* 700 BC). Hebrew prophet, whose writings in the OT denounce the oppression of the ruling class of Judah, and plead for justice.

MICHAEL. An archangel, referred to in the Book of Daniel as the guardian angel of Israel. In Revelation he leads the hosts of heaven to battle against Satan. In ecclesiastical art he bears a flaming sword.

MICHAEL (1596-1645). Tsar of Russia. He was elected tsar by a national assembly in 1613, at a time of anarchy and foreign invasion, and founded the house of Romanov, which ruled until 1917.

MICHAEL (1921-). King of Romania. Son of Carol II, he succeeded his grandfather as king in 1927, but was displaced when his father returned from exile in 1930. In 1940 he was proclaimed king again on his father's abdication, and in 1944 he overthrew the dictatorship of Antonescu and enabled Romania to share in the final victory of the Allies at the end of the S.W.W. He abdicated and left Romania in 1947.

MICHAELMAS DAISY. Popular name for *Aster tradescanti* and also for the sea aster or starwort.

MICHAELMAS DAY. Festival of St Michael and all Angels, observed on 29 Sept., and one of the English quarter days.

MICHELANGELO (mīkelan'jelō) (1475-1564). Italian artist and poet, whose full name was Michelagniolo di Lodovico Buonarroti Simoni. B. near Florence, he studied painting under Domenico and David Ghirlandaio, and for a number of years lived in the palace of Lorenzo de' Medici. He worked in Rome 1496-1501, and again was chiefly in Rome 1508-64. His works of sculpture include the *Pietà*, David, and, for the tomb of pope Julius II, Moses, and the Slaves. In Florence he designed the Medici sepulchral chapel. His most important paintings are those on the ceiling and above the altar ('The Last Judgment') of the Sistine Chapel, Rome. In 1547 he was appointed chief architect of St Peter's, and designed the dome. M. was the most gifted artist of the Italian Renaissance. He also wrote sonnets and madrigals, many of which were inspired by his friendship with Vittoria Colonna in his later years.

MICHELANGELO. The 'Tondo Doni', a representation of the Holy Family painted, as his first major work, for Angelo Doni, who also patronized Raphael. It is now in the Uffizi at Florence. *Photo: Courtesy of the Italian State Tourist Office.*

MICHELSON, Albert Abraham (1852–1931). American physicist. Prof. at Chicago from 1892, he was the first American scientist to win the Nobel prize. He invented the M. interferometer, and in conjunction with E. W. Morley performed in 1887 the *Michelson-Morley Experiment* to detect the motion of the earth through the postulated ether. The failure of the experiment led to Einstein's theory of relativity.

MICHIGAN (mish'-). A north-central state of the USA, consisting of 2 peninsulas separated by Lake M. and bordered by lakes Superior, Huron, and Erie, and Canada. The chief highlands are the Porcupine mts., and the rivers incl. the Muskegon, Grand, St Joseph, Kalamazoo. The state, formerly agricultural, is now chiefly industrial, the motor-car industry being prominent. As the producer of iron ore, copper, cement, sand and gravel, gypsum, and salt, M. is one of the leading states in the Union. Detroit is the largest city; other cities are Grand Rapids, Flint, Saginaw, and Lansing (the cap.).

The area was explored by the French from 1618 onwards, their first permanent settlement being made in 1668; it became British in 1763, was organized as a territory 1805 (M. territory, 1787, having incl. parts of other later states), and was admitted to the Union as a state 1837. Area 150,777 sq.km (58,216 sq.m), incl. 4,975 sq.km (1,194 sq.m) of inland water. Pop. (1970) 8,875,083. Lake M. is the third largest of the great lakes of N America, and the only one completely in the USA. It is over 480km (300m) long, and 57,625 sq.km (22,400 sq.m) in area.

MICHIGAN CITY. City and port in the state of Indiana, USA, lying on Lake Michigan, 65km (40m) ESE of Chicago. It was founded *c.* 1830, and is a summer resort with metal and clothing industries. Pop. (1970) 39,370.

MICKIEWICZ (mitskē-ă'vich), **Adam** (1798–1855). Polish poet. B. in Lithuania, he was imprisoned and compelled to live for 5 years in Russia, owing to his revolutionary activities. There he pub. the narrative poem, *Konrad Wallenrod* (1828). He d. at Constantinople, while raising a Polish corps to fight against Russia in the Crimea War. The greatest of his later works is *Pan Tadeusz*, the Polish epic.

MĪ'CRŌBE. In biology, a microscopic organism, a germ, bacillus, micro-organism, or bacterium, instinct with life and power of multiplication. *See* BACTERIA.

MICROBIOLOGICAL WARFARE. *See* BIOLOGICAL/CHEMICAL WARFARE.

MICROCOMPUTER. Microprocessor in which the arithmetic and control units may be made on a single chip (q.v.) or piece of monocrystalline silicon, which measures *c.* 2.5 × 2.5 × 0.01mm. By the mid-1970s they had taken over increasingly complex tasks, which would previously have needed a minicomputer, e.g. control of small switching exchanges, traffic flow, office calculators, etc.

In the 1980s the very high speed integrated circuits (VHSIC) being developed would enable a complete radar system, for example, to be put on one chip. Echoes from enemy radar would be processed before an opponent had time to act to destroy an allied ship, or plane. Making such chips involves drawing lines on it which are only half a micrometre in width, one hundredth that of a human hair.

MICROFORM. Overall term for the output of micropublishing, which usually takes 2 forms: *microfilm* (16 or 35 mm) on which documents, or the pages of a book or journal, are recorded, and which requires complex equipment to screen; and microfiche (Fr. *fiche* 'card' or 'slip'), a sheet of film 105 × 148 mm on which similar items are recorded, usually 98 frames to a fiche and $\frac{1}{24}$th actual size (in ultrafiche and superfiche the degree of reduction is greater), and read by means of a simpler viewing device or 'reader'.

MĪCRO'MĒTER. An instrument for making very small measurements with the greatest accuracy. For astronomical use, it consists of 2 very fine wires, one fixed and the other movable, placed in the focal plane of a telescope; the movable wire is fixed on a sliding plate and can be moved parallel to the other until the object appears between the wires. The movement is then indicated by a scale on the adjusting screw. *M. gauges* are measuring gauges having their adjustment effected by an extremely accurate fine-pitch screw; they are of great value in engineering.

MICROMINIATURIZATION. The reduction in size and weight of electronic components and circuits to meet space, airborne and military needs, and for such devices as electronic computers in which the number of circuits is very large.

MĪCRONĒ'SIA. That part of Oceania lying N of Melanesia, which incl. the Federated States of M., Belau, Kiribati, the Mariana and Marshall Is., Nauru and Tuvalu (qq.v.).

MICRONESIA, Federated States of. The Caroline Is. (Truk, Yap, Ponape, and Kosrae), formerly part of the Pacific Islands Trust Territory (q.v.), which entered into 'free association' with the USA in 1980.

MĪ'CROPHŌNE. The first component in a sound-reproducing system, whereby the mechanical energy of sound waves is converted into electrical energy for the purpose of transmission.

MICROPROCESSOR. *See* MICROCOMPUTER.

MĪ'CROSCOPE. An optical instrument for magnifying small objects for detailed examination. A simple M. or magnifying glass has a single convex lens. A compound M. has 2 sets of lenses, the objective (as being nearer the object) which forms a real, inverted and magnified image of the object, just within the focal length of the eyepiece (the second lens system) which acts as a simple M. to allow the operator to view the image. Light from a source below the object to be examined, which is mounted on a slide, is concentrated by a condenser. Compound lenses are always used to reduce distortion of colour and shape to a minimum. Electron Ms. (q.v.) make visible details 500 times finer than an optical M., but require objects to be viewed in a vacuum and usually damage delicate and live specimens. Acoustic, X-ray, and laser Ms. are now under development to obviate these difficulties.

MĪ'CRŌWAVE HEATING. Form of radio-frequency or dielectric H., using frequencies at least 20 times higher than usually employed. Instead of penetrating from the surface by conduction, heat is generated throughout an object simultaneously. It is used in instantaneous cooking of prepared foods, destruction of insects in grain, destruction of enzymes in processed food, liquid sterilization, pasteurization, and drying of timber and paper.

MĪ'DAS. King of Phrygia, who was granted the gift of converting all he touched to gold, and who, for preferring the music of Pan to that of Apollo, was given ass's ears by the latter. Also instrument (black box) recording flight data in planes.

MID-ATLANTIC RIDGE. Chain of mtns and valleys which runs N-S through the bottom of the Atlantic Ocean for some 65,000 km (40,000 m) almost from the Arctic to the Antarctic. Lava rising *c.* 225 million years ago from within the Earth's mantle along the mid-Atlantic rift valley first began to split N America from Europe, and S America from Africa. The process still continues at the rate of *c.* 25mm (1in) per year. The Azores are out-lying peaks of the M-A.R.

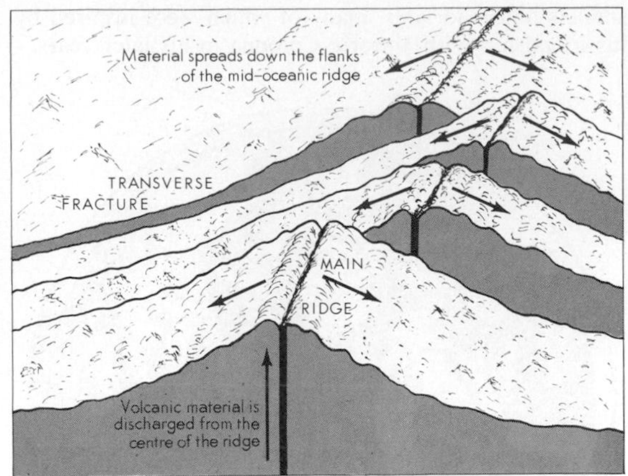

MID-ATLANTIC RIDGE

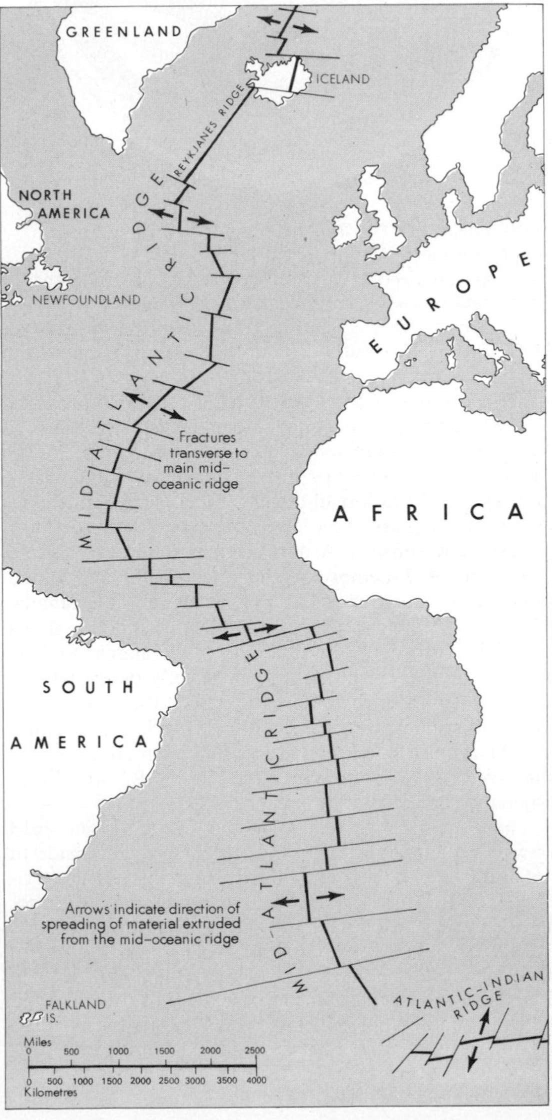

MIDDELBURG. Town in Walcheren Island, Netherlands, cap. of Zeeland prov. It has engineering works and tobacco and furniture factories, and a 15-16th cent. Town Hall. Pop. (1974) 37,500.

MIDDLE AGES. A term which came into use in the 17th cent. for the period of European history between the fall of the Roman Empire and the Renaissance. It is usually regarded as beginning in the 5th cent. and ending in the 15th. Its distinctive features were the unity of W Europe within the RC Church, and the feudal organization of political, social and economic relations.

MIDDLEBACK RANGE. Mtn range in the NE of Eyre Peninsula, South Australia *c.* 65km (40m) long, parallel with the W coast of Spencer Gulf. Iron deposits are mined at Iron Baron, Iron Knob, and Iron Monarch.

MIDDLE EAST. *See* NEAR EAST.

MIDDLESBROUGH. Town in Cleveland, England, on the Tees, the commercial, social and cultural centre of the urban area formed by Stockton-on-Tees, Redcar, Billingham, Thornaby and Eston. Dating from *c.* 1830 it depended on the iron industry, shipbuilding and - from 1920s - chemicals, and entered a depressed phase from the

1930s until diversification in the 1960s. It is the admin. HQ of Cleveland. Pop. (1974) 155,000.

MIDDLESEX. English county, which disappeared as an administrative div. in the re-organization attendant on the creation of the new Greater London 1964-5. Contained within the Thames basin, and where not built over good agricultural land, it was settled in the 6th cent. by Saxon tribes, and its name comes from its position between the kingdoms of the E and W Saxons.

MIDDLETON, Thomas (*c.* 1570-1627). English dramatist. B. in London, he produced numerous romantic plays and realistic comedies, both alone and in collaboration. Best-known are *A Fair Quarrel* and *The Changeling,* with Rowley; *The Roaring Girl* with Dekker; and *Women Beware Women.*

MIDDLE WEST. Name given to a large area in the north-centre of USA, usually taken as comprising the states of Ohio, Indiana, Illinois, Michigan, Iowa, Wisconsin, and Minnesota, and containing about a quarter of the total population. Lord Bryce, who first distinguished the area in 1888, said that the MW is the most distinctively American part of the USA. It tends to be Republican and isolationist.

MIDGE. Name applied in popular speech to many gnat-like insects; in particular to the Chironomidae.

MIDLANDS. A section of England corresponding roughly to the Anglo-Saxon kingdom of Mercia. It is bounded on the N by Yorks and Lancs, on the W by Wales, on the S by the Thames, and the E by Norfolk, Suffolk, Essex, Herts, and Greater London.

The **West Midlands** is a met. co. created round Birmingham in the local govt re-organization of 1974. It took in areas to the NE and S of Birmingham in Warwicks, incl. Coventry; central southern Staffs, incl. Wolverhampton, Walsall and Dudley; and the northernmost projection of Worcs, incl. Smethwick. The admin. HQ is Birmingham. Area 958 sq.km (370 sq.m); pop. (1978) 2,711,600.

MIDLŌ'THIAN. Former Scottish co., lying S of the Firth of Forth, incl. in 1975 in the region of Lothian. It incl. Moorfoot and the Pentland Hills in the S, the rivers Gala and N and S Esk, and the Water of Leith. Edinburgh was the admin. HQ.

MIDNIGHT SUN. Phenomenon seen N of the Arctic Circle and S of the Antarctic Circle when the sun is above the horizon at midnight during summer.

MIDRASH (Heb., inquiry, searching out). Name given to the ancient Jewish homiletical commentaries on the Bible, in which allegory and legendary illustration are freely used. They were compiled principally in Palestine from the 4th cent. onwards.

MIDSHIPMAN. Officer in training in the RN, ranking below the lowest commissioned officer. Ms. are often called 'snotties', traditionally because they wiped their noses with their sleeves rather than handkerchiefs. In the US students training at the naval academy are called Midshipmen.

MIDSUMMER. The summer solstice, about 21 June, but M. Day is 24 June - a quarter day and the festival of St John the Baptist.

MIDWAY. Circular atoll and island group in the N Pacific, *c.* 1,900 km (1,200 m) NW of Hawaii. Discovered by the USA in 1859 and acquired by that country in 1867, M. became a point of call for trans-Pacific aircraft in 1935. Area 5.5 sq.km (2.2 sq.m); pop. (1970) 2,220.

MIDWIFERY. Obstetrics; the assistance of women in childbirth. As one of the principal divisions of the qualifying course for medical practitioners, it incl. all sorts of treatment, medical and surgical, connected with birth, but the functions of a midwife are in most countries limited by law to the making of preparations and examinations, the giving of ordinary assistance and after-care, and the summoning of the doctor in an emergency.

MIES VAN DER ROHE, Ludwig (1886-1969). American architect. Son of a stonemason, he was b. in Aachen, and was director of the Bauhaus 1929-33. He became prof. at the Illinois Institute of Technology (1938-58), for which he designed new logically functional buildings from 1941, and the bronze-and-glass Seagram building, NY.

MIGNONETTE (minyonet'). Sweet-scented garden plant (*Reseda odorata*), bearing usually yellowish-green flowers in racemes, with abundant foliage.

MIGRAINE. Incapacitating disease, characterized by headaches, usually severe, and preceded in 75 per cent of cases by warning symptoms (disturbances of vision, especially flashing lights, and less frequently of sensation affecting the legs, arms or face). In 60 per cent of cases the headache is accompanied by nausea or vomiting. A cure is not available, but paracetamol may be used to reduce pain, together with metoclopramide to reduce vomiting and give the analgesic a better chance to operate. Correct diet may also help prevent attacks.

MĪGRĀ'TION. The movement, either seasonal or as part of a single life cycle, of certain animals, espec. birds and fish, to particular breeding or feeding grounds. Allied to it is the homing ability of pigeons and of bees, etc. The patterns of M. have been estab. by marking specimens which are recovered after death, or pass through scientific stations en route, but the precise methods by which animals navigate and how they know where to go are still obscure. Birds have greater visual acuity and visual memory of ground clues than man, but in long-distance flights appear to navigate by the Sun and stars, possibly in combination with an internal biological 'clock' which acts roughly in the same way as a marine chronometer, and with a 'reading' of the Earth's magnetic field through an inbuilt 'magnetic compass'. The last-named is a tiny mass of tissue between the eye and brain in birds, and similar cells occur in 'homing' honeybees, and in certain bacteria which use it to determine which way is 'down'. *See also* MAGNETISM. Most striking, however, is the M. of young birds which have never flown a route before and are unaccompanied by adults. It is postulated that they may inherit as part of their genetic code an overall 'sky chart' of their journey which is triggered into use when they become aware of how the local sky pattern above the place in which they hatch fits into it. Similar theories have been advanced in the case of fish, such as eels and salmon, with whom vision obviously plays a less important role, but for whom currents and changes in the composition and temperature of the sea in particular locations may play a part, e.g. in enabling salmon to return to the precise river in which they were spawned. *See also* LEMMING.

MIHAILO'VICH, Draga (1893-1946). Yugoslav soldier. He served in the army of his native Serbia in the Balkan and F.W.Ws. After the German occupation of Yugoslavia in the S.W.W., he withdrew to the hills with his guerilla troops ('Chetniks'), but his antipathy to the Croatian Tito's Communist resistance fighters, and the withdrawal in 1943 of the support of the Allies and the exiled Y. govt, forced him to accept aid from the Italians and Germans, and he was eventually captured and shot for treason.

MIKADO (mikah'dō). Title applied by foreigners to the Japanese emperor; the Japanese style is *tenno.*

MILAN (milan'). City of N Italy (Ital. *Milano*), cap. of M. prov., on the r. Olona in the Plain of Lombardy. In the heart of the city is the Piazza del Duomo, at one end of which is the splendid Gothic cathedral - one of the largest churches, area 12,800 sq.m (14,000 sq.yds), and capable of holding 40,000 worshippers. Begun in 1386, it was not finished until 1813, though St Charles Borromeo consecrated it in 1577. The exterior is a mass of pinnacles, statues, etc. Nearby is the famous Scala opera house (1778). Other noteworthy buildings are the Palazzo Reale, the palace of the archbishop, the church of St Ambrose (Ital. Ambrogio) with St Ambrose's tomb, the Casa del Borromei, the Brera picture-gallery, and the castle. Leonardo da Vinci painted his 'Last Supper' in the former refectory of the convent adjoining Santa Maria delle Grazia.

M., which is the seat of 2 univs., is also a great industrial centre, making aircraft, locomotives, motor-cars, bicycles, etc., and is the chief seat of the Italian textile industry. It was the ancient Mediolanum, and for cents. in the Middle Ages was an independent city-state under the Visconti and Sforza families. In 1859 it became part of the kingdom of Italy. Pop. (1978) 1,706,000.

MILAN. The elaborate Gothic construction of the great cathedral, with a myriad turrets and pinnacles, and 4,440 statues. *Photo: Courtesy of the Italian State Tourist Office*

MILANKOVITCH HYPOTHESIS. *See* ICE AGE.

MILDENHALL. Market town in Suffolk, England, on the edge of M. fen 30km (19m) NE of Cambridge. A rich treasure of Roman silverware of the 4th cent. AD discovered in 1942 is now in the British Museum. There is an airport. Pop. (1974) 7,150.

MILDEW. Name given to minute fungi, like a thin whitish coat, which appear as a destructive growth on plants, paper, leather, wood, etc., when exposed to damp. They incl. both parasites and saprophytes. *See* FUNGI.

MILDURA (mildoo'ra). Town in Victoria, Australia, on the Murray r., 480km (300m) NW of Melbourne. It has food processing industries based on the fruit and vegetables of the irrigated land of the surrounding area. Pop. (1971) 13,200.

MILE. Traditional measure of length in English-speaking countries, 1,760 yds or 5,280 ft (1.60934 km), originally derived from the Roman M. of 1,000 paces. The Internat. Nautical (or Air) Mile (INM) is exactly 1.852 km or *c.* 6,076 ft.

MILE END. A part of the Greater London bor. of Tower Hamlets in the district of Stepney in the East End. M.E. Green (later renamed Stepney Green) was the scene of Richard II's meeting with the rebel peasants in 1381, and the exercise ground of the train-bands.

MILES, Bernard, baron (1907-). British actor-producer. After repertory experience, he appeared in such parts as Briggs in *Thunder Rock* (1940) and Iago in *Othello* (1942), and his films incl. *Great Expectations* (1947). He founded a Trust which built the City of London's first theatre for 300 years, The Mermaid (1959). Created life peer 1979.

MĪLĒ'TUS. Ancient Greek city in SW Asia Minor, which carried on an important trade with Egypt and the Black Sea. The scientists Thales, Anaximander, and Anaximenes were born at M.

MI'LFOIL. *See* YARROW.

MILFORD HAVEN, Louis Alexander, 1st marquess of (1854-1921). British sailor. B. Prince Louis of Battenberg, he became a naturalized Briton in 1868, and entered the navy. In 1912 he was 1st Sea Lord, but he had to resign in 1914 owing to 'anti-German' agitation in the press. He gave up his German titles in 1917, assumed the surname of Mountbatten, and was made marquess of M.H. In 1921 he was appointed Admiral of the Fleet. He was the father of Earl Mountbatten, and the grandfather of the duke of Edinburgh. *See also* GUSTAV VI.

MILFORD HAVEN. Welsh seaport in Dyfed, with a fine harbour comprising the estuary of the E and W Cleddau rivers. There are oil refineries, a terminal for giant tankers linked by pipeline with Llandarcy, nr Swansea, where there are also petrochemical works, and an oil-fired power station. Pop. (1971) 13,000. In Welsh M.H. is Aberdaugleddau 'mouth of two harbours'.

MILHAUD (mēloh'), **Darius** (1892-1974). French composer. A member of Les Six, a group of young composers, he had lived for a time in Brazil and his treatment of Latin-American folk song *Le Boeuf sur le Toit* caused a sensation. His other most famous work was the jazz ballet *La Création du Monde.* He was associated with Paul Claudel (q.v.), with whom he collaborated in various ballets. In 1940 he went to the US as prof. of music at Mills College, Calif., and became prof. of composition at the National Conservatoire in Paris in 1947. Much of his later work, which incl. chamber, orchestral, and choral music, is polytonal.

MILITARY LAW. *See* MARTIAL LAW.

MILITIA. A home-defence force, as distinguished from the Regular Army, consisting of ordinary citizens, with usually some military training, who are on call in emergencies.

King Alfred estab. the first M. or *fyrd*, in which every freeman was liable to serve. After the Conquest a feudal levy was estab. in which landowners were responsible for raising the men required. This in turn led to the increasing use of the general levy by English kings to combat the growing power of the barons. In the 16th cent., under such threats as the Spanish Armada, plans for internal defence relied increasingly on the M., or what came to be called 'trained bands', of the general levy. After the Restoration, the M. fell into neglect, but it was re-organized in 1757, and relied upon for home defence during the French wars; and in the 19th cent. it extended its activities abroad, serving in the Peninsular, Crimean and Boer wars. In 1852 it adopted a volunteer status, and in 1908 the M. was merged with the Territorial Army and the Special Reserve forces, to supplement the Regular Army, and ceased to exist as a separate force.

The principle of a M. was introd. into the US with the first settlers, who had to be able to defend as well as build their settlements. After an Act of 1792, it more or less replaced for a time the Regular Army, but was itself supplanted in the late 19th cent. by the volunteer National Guard units of individual states, which are under federal orders in emergencies, and are now an integral part of the US Army. In Switzerland, the M. is the national defence force, and every able-bodied man is liable for service in it.

MILK. The secretion of the mammary glands of female vertebrate animals which suckle their young, for whom it is a complete food. The M. of cows, goats and sheep is that most usually consumed by man: over 80 per cent is water, the remainder comprises protein, fat, milk sugar, calcium, phosphorus, comparatively little iron, and vitamins. Pasteurisation (q.v.) renders M. safe for consumption, and further heat treatment produces 'long life' M. which, while not exposed to the air, will remain 'fresh' in the hottest climate for 6 months without refrigeration. In homogenized M. the fat content has been broken down to distribute the cream evenly for drinking. Besides cream, butter and cheese, the vogue for slimming has led to a great increase in the consumption of other M. products, e.g. *buttermilk*, which consists of the skim M. left after churning butter and which is soured by lactic acid (produced by bacteria from milk sugar), and *yogurt*, made from concentrated whole M., which is fermented and has a low fat content, and is sold either naturally sour or flavoured with fruit. Condensed and other forms of concentrated M. and dried M. in powder form, began to be produced from the mid 19th cent., and are widely sold. Breast-feeding is preferable for babies because the mother's milk contains anti-body proteins vital in warding off disease, epidermal growth factor (EGF), etc. *See* DAIRYING.

MILKY WAY. The luminous band of light stretching around the heavens, and passing through constellations such as Cygnus (the Swan), Gemini (the Twins), Sagittarius (the Archer) and Crux Australis (the Southern Cross). It is composed of stars, together with bright and dark nebulae. These stars are not, however, packed closely together. When we look along the main plane of the Galaxy, we see many stars in more or less the same direction, and it is this which causes the M.W. appearance. In 1962 the magnetic field hitherto only conjectured as the cause of the M.W.'s spiral structure was measured by a research team at Jodrell Bank.

MILL, John Stuart (1806-73). British philosopher and economist. B. in Pentonville, the son of James M. (1773-1836), eminent Utilitarian philosopher, he proved a remarkably precocious student. In 1822 he entered the India House, where he became head of his department before retiring in 1858. In 1826, as described in his *Autobiography* (1873), he passed through a mental crisis; he found his father's bleakly intellectual Utilitarianism emotionally unsatisfying, and abandoned it for a more human philosophy influenced by that of Coleridge. So, too, in his social philosophy he gradually abandoned the Utilitarians' extreme individualism for an outlook akin to liberal socialism, while still laying great emphasis on the liberty of the individual; this change can be traced in the later editions of *Principles of Political Economy* (1848). He sat in Parliament as a Radical 1865-8, and introduced a motion for women's suffrage. His feminist views inspired his *On the Subjection of Women* (1869). His philosophical and political writings incl. *A System of Logic* (1843), *On Liberty* (1859; generally considered his masterpiece), and *Considerations on Representative Government* (1861).

MILLAIS (millā'), **Sir John Everett** (1829-96). British artist. B. at Southampton, he joined Holman Hunt and Rosetti in 1848, founding the Pre-Raphaelite Brotherhood, and all his best works were painted in the Pre-Raphaelite manner, e.g. 'Christ in the House of His Parents' (1850), 'Ophelia' (1852), and 'Autumn Leaves' (1856). In 1855 he m. Effie Gray, Ruskin's divorced wife. Although his early work had provoked fierce criticism, he later achieved great popularity with his story-pictures, such as the 'Boyhood of Raleigh' (1870), and 'The North-west Passage' (1874), sentimental child-studies, e.g. 'Bubbles' (1886), and portraits. He was created a bart. in 1885 and elected PRA in 1896.

MILLAY (millā'), **Edna St Vincent** (1892-1950). American poet. B. in Maine, she pub. her first collection of poems, *Renascence*, in 1917. This was followed by other vols. of direct emotional poetry, such as *The Harp-Weaver* (1922).

MILLENNIUM. A period of 1,000 years, during which (so certain Christian sects believe), Christ will return to govern this Earth in person. This belief, also called Chiliasm (from the Greek for 1,000), was widespread in the early days of Christianity. As hopes were disappointed, belief in the Second Coming tended to fade, but Millennarian views have been expressed at periods of great religious excitement, such as the Reformation. The Fifth Monarchy Men were millennarians, as are Jehovah's Witnesses.

MILLER, Arthur (1915-). American playwright. His concern with family relationships and contemporary American values is reflected in *All my Sons* (1947), and *Death of a Salesman* (1949), and *The Crucible* (1953) is an equation of the Salem witch hunt (q.v.) with political persecution of any age, with particular relevance to 'McCarthyism'. M. himself was convicted of Contempt of Congress in 1957 for refusing to reveal the names of those present at a meeting of Communist writers in 1947. He was m. (1956-61) to Marilyn Monroe (q.v.), for whom he wrote the film *The Misfits* (1960), in which she starred, and with whom Maggie of his play *After the Fall* (1964) has been popularly identified. Other notable plays incl. *A View from the Bridge* (1955).

MILLER, Glenn (1904-44). American bandleader. A trombonist, he launched his band in 1938 and created the 'big band sound' of the era, e.g. 'In the Mood'. He enlisted and disappeared without trace on a flight between England and France.

MILLER, Henry (1891-1980). American writer. B. in New York, he spent some years in the Paris underworld which provided material for the fictionalized *Tropic of Cancer* (1931), and *Tropic of Capricorn* (1938). These were so out-spoken that the first could not appear in England until 1963, and the second was only pub. in the US in 1961.

MILLET (mēleh'), **Jean François** (1814-75). French painter. B. in Normandy of a peasant family, he went to Paris to study in 1837. He settled at Barbizon, in the forest of Fontainebleau, in 1848, and there became the leader of a group of artists who concentrated on naturalistic paintings of peasant life and rustic scenery. He is best known for his studies of peasants, such as 'The Reapers' (1854), 'The Gleaners' (1857) and 'The Angelus' (1859).

MILLET. In botany, members of the family Gramineae (grasses), cultivated in various countries, the grains as a cereal food and the stems as fodder. The most important are *Panicum miliaceum*, extensively cultivated in the warmer parts of Europe, and *Sorghum vulgare*, also known as Durra (q.v.).

MILLIKAN, Robert Andrews (1868-1953). American physicist. B. in Illinois, he held chairs in physics at Chicago and Pasadena, California, and was best known for his atomic research, in which he made the most accurate measurement of the electronic charge of negative electricity (1917). He was awarded a Nobel prize in 1923.

MILLIN, Sarah Gertrude (1889-1968). S African novelist, *née* Liebson. She was noted for her treatment of the problems raised by colour, e.g. *God's Step-Children* (1924).

MI'LLIPĒDE. Animal of worldwide distribution, in the class Diplopoda. It has a segmented body, each segment usually bearing 2 pairs of legs, and the head bears a pair of antennae. The class is divided into a number of orders; some species roll into a ball. Certain orders are provided with silk glands. Ms. feed on decaying vegetable matter, but some species injure crops by feeding on tender roots.

MILLS, Sir John (1908-). British actor-director. Acting in films from 1933, he made a reputation in stiff-upper-lip wartime roles, as in *In Which we Serve*; later were *Great Expectations* (1947), *Scott of the Antarctic* (1949), and *Ryan's Daughter*, for which he received an Oscar as best supporting actor in 1971. He was knighted in 1976.

MILOSZ (mē'wash), **Czeslaw** (1911-). Polish-American poet. B. in Lithuania of Polish parentage, he became a diplomat before defecting and taking US nationality. He was awarded a Nobel prize in 1980, notably for his *Bells in Winter* (1980).

MILNE, A(lan) A(lexander) (1882-1956). British author. Of Scots parentage, he is best-known for his work for children. He brought the toys of his little son (Christopher Robin) to life in *Winnie-the-Pooh* (1926) and *The House at Pooh Corner* (1928), in which Pooh is a whimsical bear; adapted *The Wind in the Willows* for the stage as *Toad of Toad Hall*; and wrote vols. of children's verse, *When We Were Very Young* (1924) and *Now We are Six* (1927).

MILNER, Alfred, visct (1854-1925). British statesman. As Gov. of Cape Colony 1897-1901, he negotiated with Kruger on behalf of the Uitlanders, before the outbreak of the S African War, and undertook, as Governor 1901-5, the remodelling of the civil admin. of the Transvaal and Orange River colonies after their annexation. His concept (later modified) of the Empire as a 'permanent and organic union', not an alliance of self-governing colonies, and his advocacy of colonial trade preferences, etc., influenced his disciples (Geoffrey Dawson, Lionel Curtis, etc.), known as M.'s Young Men. In 1916 he became a member of Lloyd George's War Cabinet, and as Sec. for War 1918-19, was largely responsible for creating a unified Allied command under Foch.

MILTON, John (1608-74). English poet. B. in London, the son of a scrivener, he was ed. at Christ's Coll., Cantab. The best-known of his univ. poems are the ode 'On the Morning of Christ's Nativity' (1629), and his lines on Shakespeare. In 1632 M. retired to his father's house at Horton for 5 years of studious preparation for his poetic vocation, and there wrote the companion pieces *L'Allegro* and *Il Penseroso* (1632); the masque *Comus* (1634); and 'Lycidas' (1637), an elegy on the death of his friend, Edward King. In 1638-9 he visited France and Italy, where he met the imprisoned Galileo. Settling in London in 1640, he limited his creative writing during the next 20 years mainly to pamphlets. Among the chief of these are *Of Reformation Touching Church Discipline* (1641), one of several attacks on episcopacy; *Doctrine and Discipline of Divorce* (1643), and *Tetrachordon* (1644), both occasioned by the desertion of his Royalist wife, Mary Powell, whom he had m. in 1642; *On Education* (1644), a subject of which he had practical experience as tutor to his nephews and others; and *Areopagitica* (1644), a forthright defence of the freedom of the press. His only poetic productions during these years were his sonnets. He was reconciled to his wife in 1645, and 4 years after her death in 1652 m. Catherine Woodcock (d. 1658), and then in 1662 Elizabeth Minshull, who survived him. In 1649 he became Latin Secretary to the Commonwealth, and although blind by 1652, carried on his duties with the aid of assistants such as the poet A. Marvell. Although arrested at the Restoration, he was released on payment of a fine, and while living in obscurity began serious work on his long-projected epic. *Paradise Lost*, the story of the fall of mankind and the hope of ultimate redemption, appeared in 1667, and was followed by *Paradise Regained* and *Samson Agonistes*, a tragedy in the Greek tradition, in 1671. Among his other works are poems in Italian and Latin, the finest of the latter being the *Epitaphium Damonsis*, lamenting the death of his friend, Charles Diodati; and a *History of Britain* (1670). He d. from an attack of gout, and was buried in St Giles, Cripplegate, London.

MILTON KEYNES (kēnz). New town, Bucks, England, planned 1969 on a grid lay-out as 'Los Angeles' in England. It is the HQ of the Open Univ. Pop. (1975) 60,000, with an eventual pop. of 250,000.

MILWAUKEE (milwaw'kē). Largest city in Wisconsin, USA, on Lake Michigan, 135km (85m) N of Chicago.

MILTON. A portrait by an unknown artist, painted *c.* 1629.
Photo: Courtesy of the National Portrait Gallery

With a fine harbour, it is a great grain- and coal-distributing port. Heavy machinery of many kinds is manufactured, and brewing and meat packing are important. Pop. met. area (1970) 1,393,260.

MIMŌ'SA. Genus of the family Leguminosae, found in tropical and subtropical regions and ranging from shrubby plants to large trees. The flowers are small, fluffy, golden balls (tufts of stamens) and the leaves are pinnate, divided into a multiplicity of small leaflets. Certain species, e.g. the sensitive plant of Brazil (*M. sensitiva*), shrink as if withered on being touched, though rapidly recovering.

MI'NARET (Arab. *manāra*). A slender turret attached to a Mohammedan mosque. It has one or more balconies, from which the *muezzin* calls the people to prayer 5 times a day.

MIND. The presumed mental or physical being or faculty that enables one to think, will, and feel; the seat of the intelligence and of memory; sometimes only the cognitive or intellectual powers as distinguished from the will and the emotions. The relation of M. to matter may be variously regarded. Materialists identify the two: mental phenomena equally with physical are to be explained in terms of matter and motion. Dualists hold that M. and matter exist independently side by side. Idealists maintain that M. is the ultimate reality, and that matter is the creation of intelligence, and does not exist apart from it. *See* PSYCHOLOGY.

MINDANAO (mindahnah'ō). The second-largest is. of the Philippine Rep. The mountainous rain forest was found in 1971 to harbour an isolated stone-age tribe, the Tasaday. The active volcano Apo reaches 2,855 m (9,369 ft), and M. is subject to severe earthquakes. The chief town is Davao. There is a Moslem guerrilla resistance movement. Area 94,227 sq.km (36,381 sq.m); pop. (1970) 5,057,300.

MINDEN (min'-). Town of North Rhine-Westphalia, W Germany, 56km (35m) WSW of Hanover, on the Weser. The duke of Brunswick's Anglo-Allied army here defeated the French in 1759.

MINDORO (mindō'rō). Is. of the Philippine Rep., S of Luzon. Mt Halcon rises to 2,590 m (8,500 ft); the chief town is Calapan. Area 10,347 sq.km (3,995 sq.m).

MINDSZENTY, József (1892–1975). RC Primate of Hungary. Imprisoned by the Communists in 1949, he escaped in 1956 to take refuge in the US legation. Persuaded by the Pope to go into exile in Austria in 1971, he was 'retired' when Hungary's relations with the Vatican improved in 1974.

MINE. Explosive charge to detonate as required below ground or water. In deep water moored types may be used; in shallow areas aircraft drop Ms. to lie on the bottom to be detonated by the noise of a ship's propeller, pressure of its hull overhead, or magnetic influence. Detonation can be either by a particular type of ship, or after several ships have passed. Time clocks may be used to 'sterilize' Ms. and avoid damage to the laying power or the need to sweep at sea, or use M. detectors on land. M.-sweepers (with low acoustic signature and anti-magnetic) use wire-cutters or devices simulating a ship's noise or magnetic influence; M.-hunters search the sea bottom with acoustic equipment.

MINEHEAD. Picturesque town and resort in Somerset, England, 34km (21m) N of Taunton, where Exmoor meets the sea. Pop. (1971) 8,100.

MINERALOGY. The study of minerals. A mineral is a natural substance having a characteristic chemical composition. Most of them are crystalline, and in this they differ from rocks. The classification of minerals is based chiefly on their chemical constitution, viz. metallic, ionic, and molecular. In addition, their crystallographic and physical characters, their mode of formation and occurrence, form part of the study. In the case of minerals of economic importance a knowledge of mining and metallurgy is also needed.

MINERAL OIL. Term applied to oils obtained from mineral sources, e.g. coal, petroleum, as distinct from those obtained from vegetable or animal sources.

MINERAL WATERS. Waters with mineral constituents gathered from the rocks over which they flow, and classified by these minerals into earthy, brine, and oil M.Ws. Curative powers are believed to be attached to many M.Ws., the types of these medicinal waters being: alkaline (Vichy), bitter (Seidlitz), salt (Droitwich), earthy (Bath), sulphurous (Aachen), and special varieties, such as barium (Harrogate). The name M.Ws. is also applied to prepared drinks, artificially simulating the natural waters, and charged with carbon dioxide.

MINERVA. The Roman goddess of intelligence, and of the handicrafts and arts, identified with the Greek Athene. From the earliest times she had a temple on the Capitol in Rome.

MINHOW. Name 1934–43 of FOOCHOW.

MINIATURE PAINTING. The term 'miniature' is derived from the Lat. *miniare*, to paint with minium, i.e. a vermilion colour, and is usually applied to portraits of small dimensions; it was formerly used to describe little pictures in the initial letters and borders of medieval manuscripts.

Although practised with exquisite delicacy in Persia and India in the medieval period, M.P. did not reach its height in Europe until the 16th cent. with Hans Holbein the Younger. The first English miniaturist was Nicholas Hilliard (q.v.), later practitioners incl. Samuel Cooper, Richard Cosway and George Engleheart (qq.v.). Notable in France were Jean (1486-1541) and François (*c.* 1522-72) Clouet, Nicolas Lancret and Pierre Prud'hon; in Spain Goya and in America C. W. Peale. Photography led to a decline in demand, but the art is still practised.

MINIATURE. A self portrait by Nicholas Hilliard, at the age of thirty in 1577. The impression of exact detail in the ruff is created by a series of disparate strokes. *Photo: Courtesy of the Victoria and Albert Museum*

MINING. The extraction of minerals from the Earth, carried on from the earliest times, e.g. Neolithic man's galleries through chalk with reindeer-antler picks and flint hammers and wedges, and Egyptian mining of turquoise in the Sinai Peninsula with copper implements during the First Dynasty. Modern M., in view of the growing scarcity of rich, shallow deposits, encounters increasing difficulties of exploitation, e.g. low-grade ores require new methods of mass working, such as the possibility of underground nuclear explosions to break up the rock; deposits at great depth necessitate new drilling methods and involve the overcoming of high temperatures (e.g. at 3,650 m/12,000 ft it is *c.* 55°C/130°F); or deposits under the sea-bed will lead to the evolution of new techniques. Petroleum and natural gas are already extracted from the ocean floor, e.g. North Sea and off Venezuela. *See* COAL, IRON and other minerals, and also BACTERIA.

MINK. Genus (*Mustela*) of the weasel family incl. the European *M. lutreola* and N American *M. vison.* Up to 45cm (1.5ft), excl. their bushy tails which add 25cm (10in), they produce an annual litter of half a dozen in their river-bank burrows. The demand for their rich brown fur led to the estab. from the 1930s of M. ranches, and production of varying shades. 'Escapes' become a destructive pest.

MINING. The world's largest copper mine in Chuquicamata some 3,000 m (10,000 ft) high in the Atacama Desert. *Photo: Armand Latourre/Camera Press*

MINNĒA'POLIS. Largest city in Minnesota, USA, on the Mississippi, seat of Minnesota univ. an institute of arts, the Tyrone Guthrie Theatre, and a symphony orchestra. The old warehouses by the river have been converted to shops and restaurants, and the city-centre is glass-covered against the difficult climate. The main industry is flour milling; cream, electrical machinery, and motor-cars are also manufactured. It forms the large 'twin cities' area with St Paul. Pop. met. area (1970) 1,805,081.

MINNESINGERS. German lyric poets of the 12th and 13th cents., who in their songs dealt mainly with the theme of courtly love without revealing the identity of the object of their affections. Among the best-known M. were Dietmar von Aist, Friedrich von Hausen, Heinrich von Morungen, Reinmar, and, greatest of all, Walther von der Vogelweide (q.v.).

MINNESŌ'TA. A N-central state of the USA with innumerable lakes, and the sources of the Red, St Lawrence, and Mississippi rivers. In the N are pine-forests and the land is high; the remaining two-thirds are prairie. M. produces barley, flax seed, hay, rye, oats, potatoes, and wheat, and even more valuable livestock products - butter, milk, bacon, turkeys - but industry now leads farming. The chief industries are iron mining (60 per cent of US ore), food processing, farm and other machinery, and pulpwood. Minneapolis is the largest city, but St Paul is the cap. Area 217,735 sq.km (84,068 sq.m); pop. (1970) 3,805,069.

MINNOW. Small fish (*Phoxinus phoxinus*) found in streams and ponds in Europe and Asia.

MINOAN. Name applied to the brilliant prehistoric civilization of Crete; it is derived from Minos, reputed son of Zeus, and the most famous of the legendary kings of Crete.

No remains of palaeolithic man have as yet been found in Crete, but in the Neolithic Age some cents. before 3000 BC the island was peopled by men of non-Indo-European stock, coming probably from SW Asia Minor, and akin to the early Bronze Age inhabitants of the Gk mainland. With the opening of the Bronze Age about 3000 BC the M. culture proper begins. This is divided into 3 main periods: Early M., *c.* 3000-2200 BC; Middle M. *c.* 2200-1580 BC; and Late M., *c.* 1580-1100 BC. Each period is marked by cultural advances in copper and bronze weapons, pottery of increasing delicacy and intricacy of design, fresco-painting, and the construction of palaces (notably at Knossos, Phaistos, and Mallia), and of fine houses.

About 1400 BC, in the late M. Period, the civilization was suddenly destroyed by earthquake or war. A partial revival continued till *c.* 1100 BC.

In religion the Ms. seem to have worshipped principally a great mother goddess with whom was associated a young male god. The tales of Greek mythology about Rhea, the mother of Zeus, and the birth of Zeus himself in a Cretan cave seem to be based on M. religion. The Ms. left many documents, in the form of tablets written in a highly developed script, which were long undeciphered. *See* VENTRIS, Michael, KNOSSUS and ATLANTIS.

MINOR. Under the Family Law Reform Act (1969) for England and Wales the age of majority in civil law was reduced to 18, and those under age are described as Ms. instead of infants. The act legalized marriage without parental consent, and the making of a valid will after the age of 18 (both already possible in Scotland), and enabled anyone over 16 to give valid consent to personal medical treatment. In the USA the age of majority is also 18.

MINO'RCA. Second largest of the Balearic Is. (q.v.). The chief town is Mahon. Area 702 sq.km (271 sq.m).

MINOTAUR. In Greek legend, a monster, half-bull and half-man, the offspring of Pasiphaë, wife of King Minos of Crete, and a bull. The M. was housed in a labyrinth, and provided with victims from 7 youths and 7 maidens sent as annual tribute from Athens. It was slain by Theseus, with the aid of Minos' dau., Ariadne. *See* KNOSSUS.

MINSK. Cap. of White Russia SSR. Manufactures machinery, textiles, leather, etc. Dating back to the 11th cent. and in turn held by Lithuania, Poland, Sweden, and Russia, M. was destroyed by Napoleon in 1812 and the Germans in 1944. The White Russian state univ. is at M. Lee Harvey Oswald, killer of J.F. Kennedy, lived here two years. Pop. (1977) 1,231,000.

MINSMERE (minz'mēr). Coastal marshland bird reserve (1948) nr Aldeburgh, Suffolk, attracting a greater number of species than any other in Britain, and noted for the Scrape, a man-made breeding habitat.

MINSTER. Originally, a monastery, and in this sense often preserved in place names, e.g. Westminster; later the word was also applied to the church attached to a monastery, e.g. York Minster.

MINT. Genus of aromatic plants (*Mentha*) in the family Labiatae, widely distributed in temperate regions. The plants have square stems and creeping rootstocks, and the flowers grow in a terminal spike, usually pink or purplish. Garden mint (*M. viridis*) and peppermint (*M. piperita*), are the best-known.

MINT, Royal. Department which manufactures all British coins and also distinctive coinages, official medals and seals for the Commonwealth, foreign countries, etc. For cents. in the Tower of London, the R.M. was housed in a building on Tower Hill from 1810 until the new R.M. was opened at Llantrisant, Mid Glamorgan, 16km (10m) NW of Cardiff 1968. The nominal head is the Master Worker and Warden, who is the Chancellor of the Exchequer, but the actual chief is the Deputy Master and Comptroller, a permanent civil servant. The equivalent in the USA is the Bureau of the M.

MINSMERE. Avocet and shelduck in a confrontation at the reserve. *Photo: Eric Hosking*

MINTON, Thomas (1765-1836). British potter. B. at Shrewsbury, he at first worked under Spode, but in 1789 estab. himself at Stoke-on-Trent as engraver of designs (he was the first to devise the 'willow pattern') and in 1793 founded a pottery there producing exquisite bone china incl. much tableware.

MINUTEMEN. Originally the armed citizens who agreed to act 'in a minute' before the American War of Independence. The name was adopted 1959 by the right-wing organisation estab. by Robert DePugh, a Missouri manufacturer, to combat a Communist invasion or uprising. The New York police seized quantities of arms 1966, and DePugh was sentenced to 3 yrs imprisonment.

MIQUELON ISLANDS (mēklon'). Small group off the S coast of Newfoundland which with St Pierre (q.v.) form a French overseas dept. Cod fishing is the chief occupation; silver fox and mink are bred. Area 216 sq.km (83 sq.m); pop. (1972) 700.

MIRABEAU (mērahbō'), **Honoré Gabriel Riqueti,** comte de (1749-91). French statesman. The son of a Provençal nobleman, he had a stormy career before the Revolution, during which he was 3 times imprisoned, and passed several years in exile. In 1789 he was elected to the States General as a representative of the third estate. His eloquence won him the leadership of the National Assembly; nevertheless, he was out of sympathy with the majority of the deputies, whom he regarded as mere theoreticians, his own aim being to establish a parliamentary monarchy on the English model. From May 1790 he secretly acted as political adviser to the king.

MIRACLE (Lat. *miraculum,* a marvel). An event which seems to transcend the laws of nature, and is regarded as a manifestation of Divine power. Hume attacked the credibility of the miraculous, and there has been a marked decline in its evidential value. In our own day, however, C. S. Lewis and others have argued in favour of the reasonableness of miracles, given belief in a God who is still concerned for His creation.

MIRACLE PLAYS. Medieval religious dramas based on sacred writ or saints' lives, which were performed chiefly on festivals, such as Corpus Christi day or Easter, and reached their highest development in the 15th and 16th cents. Separate episodes were performed by the various guilds of the towns on mobile stages, and in some instances, e.g. the Wakefield, York, and Chester plays, almost complete cycles survive.

MIRANDOLA. *See* PICO DELLA MIRANDOLA.

MIRFIELD. Town in W Yorks, England, on the Calder r., NE of Huddersfield. There is a theological college run by the Anglican Community of the Resurrection, known for its missionary work: its most famous member is Trevor Huddleston, opponent of apartheid in S Africa. There is a second college in Barbados. *See* GORE, CHARLES. Pop. (1974) 18,200.

MIRÓ, Joan (1893–1983). Spanish artist. B. at Barcelona, he was with Dali one of the main originators of the Surrealist movement. His pictures tend to spindly lines and blobs, and primitive colour, e.g. 'Still-life with an Old Shoe' and 'Dog Barking at the Moon'. He designed sets for the Diaghilev co.

MIRZAPUR (mērzahpōōr'). City of Uttar Pradesh, Republic of India, on the Ganges, *c.* 80km (50m) ESE of Allahabad. It is a grain and cotton market, with bathing sites and temples on the river. Pop. (1971) 106,000.

MISCARRIAGE. *See* ABORTION.

MISDEMEANOUR. *See* FELONY.

MISERICORD or **miserere.** In architecture, a bracket on the under-side of a hinged seat of the choir stalls in a church, used as a rest for a priest when standing during long services. Ms. are often decorated with carvings.

MISHIMA, Yukio (1925-70). Japanese author. He often chose homosexual themes, e.g. *Confessions of a Mask* (1949). Obsessed by the tradition of the Samurai, he founded a private army, the Association of Shields. With his followers he broke into a barracks, addressed the soldiers on the corruption of the nation, and committed hara-kiri.

MISHNA. A commentary on written Hebrew law, consisting of discussions between rabbis and handed down orally from their inception in AD 70 until *c.* 200, when with the Gemara, the discussions in schools of Palestine and Babylon on law, it was committed to writing to form the Talmud.

MISKOLC (mish'kolts). Town in Hungary, 145km (90m) NE of Budapest. Seat of a tech. univ. It trades in local wines and tobacco and makes textiles, furniture, paper, etc. Pop. (1978) 206,000.

MISR. Egyptian name for EGYPT and the Egyptian name for CAIRO.

MISSAL. In the RC Church, a service-book containing the complete office of Mass for the entire year. An easier, simplified M. in the vernacular was introduced 1969 (obligatory from 1971). It was the first major reform since 1570.

MISSILE. *See* NUCLEAR WARFARE.

MISSIONS (Lat. *mittere*, to send). Organized attempts to spread religion among the unconverted. During the first 3 cents. Christianity was spread throughout the Roman Empire by missionaries, of whom the greatest was Paul. In the Dark Ages the new faith was spread beyond the Empire by men such as Gregory the Illuminator, Ulfilas, Chrysostom, Patrick, and Martin of Tours. And in addition to the great figures of medieval times, such as

MISHIMA. The author with the Samurai sword with which he ended his life. *Photo: Sven Simon/Camera Press*

Columba, Aidan, Boniface, Cyril, etc., there were combined efforts of the Benedictine, Dominican and Franciscan orders. The explorations of the Renaissance opened new fields, and the foundation of the Jesuit order supplied such missionaries as Francis Xavier (1506-52). Gradually the Protestant churches also showed an interest in missions, the pioneer being the SPCK, founded in 1698, and after 1731 the continental Moravians. In the late 18th and early 19th cents. many Protestant missionary societies were founded, incl. the Baptist (1792), the London (1795), and the Church (1799). Efforts were maintained throughout the cent., notably in the foundation of the China Inland Mission by J. H. Taylor (1865), but renewed impetus came from the career of David Livingstone, and since the World Missionary Conference at Edinburgh in 1910 there has been growing international co-operation. The 19th cent. also saw a growth of activity on the part of the RC and Eastern Orthodox churches.

Christianity's chief rival in the mission-field is Islam, which became in the 20th cent. the second religion in Europe, and made increasing converts in black Africa and in USA.

MISSISSI'PPI. With the Missouri, considered by some the longest river in the world. It is the main arm of the great river system draining the USA between the Appalachians and the Rockies, and was discovered in 1541 by the Spanish explorer Hernando do Soto at a point near present-day Memphis. The M. rises in the lake region of N Minnesota, flowing through marsh and lakeland to St Anthony Falls at Minneapolis. Below the tributaries Minnesota, Wisconsin, Des Moines, and Illinois, the confluence of the Missouri and M. occurs at St Louis. The river turns at the Ohio junction, passing Memphis, and taking in the St Francis, Arkansas, Yazoo, and Red tributaries, en route to its delta on the Gulf of Mexico beyond New Orleans. Length of M. proper, 3,779 km (2,348 m); of the Missouri and the Lower M., 5,863 km (3,643 m).

MISSISSIPPI. A S central state of the USA, bounded on the W by the M. river and on the S by the Gulf of Mexico. It is mainly lowland, rising to 198m (650ft) in the NE. Second only to Texas in cotton, M. also produces sweet potatoes, sugar, rice, pecan nuts, and soya beans. Oil and natural gas are exploited, and other industries incl. food processing, pulpwood and timber, chemicals, and canned seafood, based on Biloxi, also a holiday resort. A 'static test' rocket centre was estab. in Hancock co. 1967.

M. was traversed by De Soto in 1540, settled by the French in 1699, was English 1763-79, Spanish 1779-98, then part of the US territory of M. (which incl. Alabama) until admitted to the Union in 1817. It was the second state to join the Confederacy, 1861; was re-admitted to the Union 1870. Jackson is the cap., Gulfport the chief harbour. Area 123,584 sq.km (47,716 sq.m); pop. (1970) 2,216,912.

MISSISSIPPI. 'A Cotton Plantation on the Mississippi', as represented in a lithograph of 1883 by William Aitken Walker. In the background, on the river, one of the famous steamboats. *Photo: The Harry T. Peters Collection, Museum of the City of New York*

MISSOLO'NGHI. Town in W Greece, on the N shore of the Gulf of Patras. Several times under siege by the Turks in the wars of 1822-26, it was the place of Byron's death. Pop. (1971) 11,650.

MISSOURI (mizōō'ri). The longest tributary of the Mississippi in the USA, rising in SW Montana among the Rockies, and flowing through N and S Dakota, and Missouri; it forms the boundary between Nebraska and Iowa. The main towns in its course are Sioux City, Omaha, Kansas City, Kans., and Kansas City, Mo., its largest tributaries the Yellowstone, Platte and Milk. The M. is navigable to Fort Benton. Length from its formation at the Three Forks confluence to the Mississippi, 3,969 km (2,466 m). Total length from source of Red Rock r. 4,318 km (2,683 m). Dams provide flood control, irrigation, and electric power.

MISSOURI. A central state of the USA, in the agricultural valley of the Mississippi, which forms the E border. The M. river flows across the state from W to E. In the S rises the forested Ozark Plateau, while N are prairies. Maize, soya beans, and wheat are grown, and pigs, cattle and sheep are bred. Minerals incl. lead (largest US producer), barytes, lime, coal and iron ore. Besides a large aerospace industry (space capsules, rocket engines, aircraft etc.), it has motor assembly plants, food processing, chemical, and cement works, and tourism, e.g. the Mark Twain State Park, is very important. The cap. is Jefferson City; other towns are St Louis and Kansas City. Area 180,455 sq.km (69,674 sq.m); pop. (1970) 4,677,399.

MISTINGUETT (mistaṅget'). Stage-name of the French actress and dancer Jeanne Bourgeois (1873-1956). A leading music-hall artist in Paris from 1899, she also appeared in revue at the Folies-Bergère, Casino de Paris, and Moulin Rouge, singing songs such as 'Mon Homme'. Maurice Chevalier often partnered her.

MISTLETOE. Parasitic plant (*Viscum album*) found in Europe. It occurs on deciduous and evergreen trees, most commonly on the apple, where it produces an evergreen bush. *See* DRUIDISM.

MISTRAL (mēstrahl'), **Gabriela.** Pseud. of the Chilean poet Lucila Godoy Alcayaga (1889-1957). Her country's leading educationist, she represented Chile as consul in Lisbon, Los Angeles, Mexico, etc. Her poetry, for which she was in 1945 awarded a Nobel prize, incl. *Sonetos de la Muerte* (1915: *Sonnets of Death*).

MISTRAL. A cold, dry, northerly wind which occasionally blows during the winter on the Mediterranean coast of France. It has reached a velocity of 145kph (90mph) in the Rhône valley.

MITAU. German name of JELGAVA.

MITCHELL, Margaret (*c.* 1900-49). American novelist. B. in Atlanta, Georgia, she joined the *Atlanta Journal* as a reporter (1922-6) and in 1925 m. John R. Marsh. *Gone with the Wind* (1936), is a colourful novel of her home state in the Civil War period.

MITCHELL, Peter (1920-). British chemist. His research on the transmission of biological energy (proticity), and formulation of the chemiosmotic theory, covering conservation of energy by plants during respiration and photosynthesis, led to a Nobel prize 1978.

MITCHELL, Reginald Joseph (1895-1937). British aircraft designer. B. at Stoke-on-Trent, he joined Vickers in 1916, and became its chief designer in 1920. For his designs of the Schneider Trophy seaplanes he gained recognition by the Royal Aeronautical Society in 1927. Later designs incl. RAF flying-boats and the Spitfire I fighter (1936).

MITCHISON, Naomi Margaret (1897-). British novelist. B. at Edinburgh, a dau. of J. S. Haldane (q.v.), she m. G. R. Mitchison (created life peer 1964) in 1916. Her novels, of which *The Corn King and Spring Queen* (1931), and *The Blood of the Martyrs* (1939) are best known, mainly deal with the ancient world.

MITE. In zoology, an order of minute Arachnida. There are many varieties, mostly parasites, which infest birds, animals, and plants, causing diseases and sometimes death.

MITFORD, Mary Russell (1787-1855). British author. B. in Hants, she is chiefly remembered for her sketches, *Our Village* (1824-32), describing Three Mile Cross, near Reading where she lived for years.

MITFORD SISTERS. Of the 6 daus. of the 2nd Baron Redesdale, the best-known are **Nancy** (1904-73), author of the semi-autobiographical *Pursuit of Love* (1945) and *Love in a Cold Climate* (1949), and ed. of, and one of the contributors to, *Noblesse Oblige* (1956), with its serio-comic definitions of 'U' (upper class) and 'Non-U' speech and behaviour; **Jessica** (1917-), author of the autobiographical *Hons and Rebels* (1960) and *The American Way of Death* (1963), and m. first to her cousin Esmond Romilly, nephew of Winston Churchill, with whom in

1937 she ran off in a blaze of publicity to join the Republicans and report on the Spanish Civil War; and **Unity** (1914-48), who joined the British Union of Fascists in the 1930s, becoming associated with Hitler and other leading German Nazis. **Diana** m. Sir Oswald Mosley (q.v.).

MI'THRAS. Persian god of light, whose creed seems to have been an extension of the Zoroastrian dualism. M. represented the power of goodness, and promised his followers compensation for present evil after death. His cult was introduced into the Roman Empire in 68 BC, rapidly developed, particularly among soldiers, and by *c.* AD 250 rivalled Christianity in strength. M. was said to have captured and killed the sacred bull, from whose blood all life sprang, and a bath in the blood of a sacrificed bull formed part of the initiation ceremony. In 1954 remains of a Roman temple dedicated to M. were discovered on a site in the City of London, now occupied by Bucklersbury House, in front of which they were reassembled for permanent exhibition.

MITHRAS. Wearing a Phrygian cap, this marble head was found in the excavation of London's temple of Mithras. *Photo: Courtesy of the Museum of London*

MITHRIDĀ'TĒS VI, called **the Great** (132-63 BC). King of Pontus from 120 BC. His attempt to conquer all Asia Minor led to war with Rome in 88. He overran Asia Minor, massacred 80,000 Romans, and invaded Greece, but was defeated by Sulla and ultimately by Pompey. He was killed by a soldier at his own order.

MITRE (mīt'er). The head-dress worn by bishops, cardinals, and mitred abbots at solemn services. There are Ms. of many different shapes, but in the western Church it usually takes the form of a tall cleft-cap. The M. worn by the Pope is called a tiara.

MITTERAND (mitehraṅ'), **François** (1916-). French politician. During de Gaulle's and Pompidou's presidencies, he organized a joint left-wing front, and in the presidential elections of 1981 defeated Giscard d'Estaing. His implementation of socialist policies, however, was being modified by 1982.

MITYLENE (mitilē'nē). Greek city and port, cap. of the island of Lesbos (to which the name M. is sometimes applied) and a centre of sponge fishing. It has an airport. Pop. (1971) 23,425.

MĪZORA'M. Union terr. of the Rep. of India, formed in 1972 from the Mizo Hill district of Assam. Rebels carried on a guerrilla war 1966-76, but in 1976 acknowledged M. as an integral part of India. Area 21,230 sq.km (8,200 sq.m); pop. (1972) 400,000.

MKS system. System of units in which the base units metre, kilogram, second, replace the centimetre, gram, second of the CGS system (q.v.), which it now supersedes. Its adoption has been advocated since 1901, since it simplifies the incorporation of the electrical units into the metric system, and it was included in SI. For application to electrical and magnetic phenomena the ampere is added, the reference then being to the **MKSA system.**

MŌ'A. Group of extinct birds (Dinorthiformes), once found in NZ. They varied from .5-3.5m (2-12ft), with strong limbs, a long neck, and no wings. They occurred as far back as the Pliocene age. The Maoris used them as food, but the use of European firearms enabled them to be killed in too large numbers.

MŌ'AB. An ancient country situated E of the southern part of the Jordan and of the Dead Sea, in the area of modern Jordan. The region is hilly and in parts is very fertile; cereals and vines were formerly cultivated. The inhabitants were closely akin to the Hebrews in culture, language, and religion, but were often at war with them. M. eventually fell to Arabian tribes. The MOABITE STONE, discovered in 1868 at Dhiban, dates from the 9th cent. BC, and records the rising of Mesha, king of M., against Israel.

MOBILE (-bē'l). City and only seaport in Alabama, USA 217km (135m) ENE of New Orleans. Founded 1702 by the French a little to the N of the present city, M. was cap. of the French colony of Louisiana until 1763, then British until 1780, Spanish to 1813. It has a substantial import and export trade, and possesses dry docks, meat packing and manufacture of paper, cement, clothing, industrial chemicals, etc., are industries. Pop. (1970) 190,000.

MOBUTU (mobōō'tōō), **Sese-Seko-Kuku-Ngbeandu-Wa-Za-Banga** (formerly **Joseph-Désiré**) (1930-). Zaïrean statesman and general. He assumed the presidency by a coup in 1965, converted Zaïre to a unitary state under a centralized govt, and was re-elected in 1970 for 7 yrs. In 1976 he superseded the use of ballot boxes in elections to the Nat. Assembly by a system of 'acclamation' at mass rallies.

MOBUTU SESE SEKO, Lake. On the border of Uganda and Zaïre, it is some 130km (80m) NW of Lake Victoria in the Great Rift Valley. The first European to see it was Sir Samuel Baker, who named it Lake Albert after the Prince Consort. It was renamed in 1973 by Pres. Mobutu after himself. Area 4,275 sq.km (1,650 sq.m).

MOÇAMBIQUE. *See* MOZAMBIQUE.

MOCHA (mō'ka). Seaport of N Yemen (modern **Mokha**), nr the mouth of the Red Sea, formerly famed for its coffee exports. It has declined since the Russians built a new port nr Hodeida. Pop. (1970) 6,000.

MOCKING-BIRD. Genus of American birds (*Mimus*), related to the thrushes. Most familiar in the USA is *M. polyglottus,* brownish grey on the upper part, with white markings on the almost black wings and tail. It often nests in trees close to human homes and courageously defends its young.

MŌ'DENA. City of Emilia, Italy, the cap. of the prov. of M. 37km (23m) NW of Bologna. Fine buildings, incl. the 12th cent. cathedral, the 17th cent. ducal palace, and the univ., founded 1683, which is famed for its medical and legal faculties. Pop. (1978) 179,800.

MODERATOR. The material in a reactor used to reduce the energy, and hence the speed, of fast neutrons, so far as possible without capturing them. Slow neutrons are much more likely to cause fission in a U-235 nucleus than to be captured in a U-238 nucleus, so by using a M. a reactor can be made to work with fuel containing only a small proportion of U-235.

MODERATOR. One who presides over a meeting, especially in the Presbyterian and Congregational churches (e.g. the General Assembly of the Church of Scotland). Also applied to the chairman of town meetings in the USA and to the officials who superintend examinations at Oxford and Cambridge.

MODERNISM. In the C of E a development of the liberal church movement, known as M. since *c.* 1910, which attempts to reconsider Christian beliefs in the light of modern scientific theories and historical methods without abandoning the essential doctrines. Prominent Modernists incl. E. W. Barnes, J. A. Robinson, A. M. Stockwood, J. L. Wilson, and W. R. Inge. Similar movements exist in many non-conformist churches and in the RC Church. M. was condemned by pope Pius X in 1907.

MODIGLIANI (modēlyah'nē), **Amedeo** (1884–1920). Italian artist. B. in Leghorn, of Jewish family, he settled in Paris in 1906, became interested in primitive art, and in 1909 began to produce sculptures showing the influence of Negro masks. His originally conceived, strangely elongated portraits have a mournful attraction. Always penniless, and a prey to drink and drugs, he d. of tuberculosis and his pregnant mistress, Jeanne Hébuterne, threw herself to death from a window the next morning.

MODULATION. In radio, the intermittent change of frequency, amplitude, etc. of a carrier wave, in accordance with the speaking voice, music, or other signal being transmitted.

MO'DULE. Unit of measurement; used in architecture of the size of a structural part which governs the proportion of the remainder, and in space research, e.g. the 3 components in a spacecraft making a moon landing: command M. (working, eating, and sleeping compartment), service M. (containing electricity generators, oxygen supplies and manoeuvring rocket), and lunar M. (for landing astronauts on the surface and returning them to the command ship in lunar orbit).

MOGADISHU (mogudi'shōō). Cap. and chief port of the Somali Republic. It has a cathedral built 1925–8 and mosques dating back to the 13th cent. It also has an airport. Pop. (1972) 200,000.

MŌ'GILEV. Town in White Russian SSR, 193km (120m) E of Minsk, annexed by Russia from the Swedes in 1772. It makes tractors, clothing, furniture, etc. Pop. (1977) 275,000.

MO'GOK. Village of Burma, 114km (71m) NNE of Mandalay, famous for its ruby and sapphire mines.

MOGULS (mōgulz'). A dynasty which ruled in N India from the establishment of their empire by Baber in 1526 till the dethronement and imprisonment of the last M. emperor by the British in 1857. The emperors were called Ms. (Mongols) as being descendants of Tamerlane: among the greatest were Akbar (1542–1605), Shah Jehan (fl. 1614–66), and Aurungzebe (1618–1707).

MOHÁCS (mō'hahch). Town on the Danube, Hungary, 177km (110m) S of Budapest, famous for 2 battles, in 1526 the Turks beating the Hungarians, and in 1687 being beaten by the Austrians.

MŌ'HAIR. The hair of the Angora goat. Fine, white, and lustrous, the fibre is manufactured into fabric. Commercial M. is now obtained from cross-bred animals, pure-bred supplies being insufficient.

MŌHA'MMED, Muhammad or **Mahomet** (Arab., 'praised') (*c.* 570–632). Founder of Mohammedanism or Islam (q.v.). B. in Mecca, he became a shepherd and caravan conductor, before obtaining leisure for meditation by his marriage with a wealthy widow in 595. He received his first revelation in 610, and after some years of secret teaching openly proclaimed himself the prophet of God, *c.* 616. The basis of his teaching was the Koran, a sacred work dictated by him to amanuenses while he remained in a state of trance. His increasing success in gaining converts led to persecution, and M. was forced to flee to Medina in 622. This flight - the Hegira - marks the beginning of the Islamic era. After the battle of Badr, 623, M. was constantly victorious, and in 630 he entered Mecca as the recognized prophet of Arabia. He d. at Medina, and was there buried.

MOHAMMED. Name of 6 sultans of Turkey. MOHAMMED II (1430–81), captured Constantinople in 1453 and conquered Greece. MOHAMMED VI (1861–1926), the last sultan, was deposed in 1922, and d. in exile.

MOHAMMEDANISM. *See* ISLAM.

MOHAWKS. Tribe of the Iroquois (q.v.).

MOHENJO DARO. Site of a city of *c.* 2500–1600 BC, on the lower Indus, Pakistan, where excavations from the 1920s have revealed the Indus Valley civilization (q.v.). Artistically remarkable are the soapstone seals - elephants, snakes, etc. M. has its own airport (1967).

MOHI'CANS and **Mohē'gans.** Two closely related N American Indian tribes, akin to the Algonquins, who formerly occupied Connecticut and the Hudson valley. J. F. Cooper (q.v.) confused the 2 tribes.

MOHOLE. American project for drilling a hole through the Earth's crust, so named from the discovery by the Yugoslav, Andrija Mohorovičić (1857–1936), of the Mohorovicic (abbr. Moho) Discontinuity, which marks the transition from the crust to the Earth's first inner layer or 'mantle'. Initial tests were made in 1961 off Guadelupe

MOLLUSCS. Few species are used industrially, but the rock whelk (left) has been exploited from ancient times as the source of 'Tyrian' purple and occurs widely in warmer waters. The species shown, *Murex ramosus Linne,* occurs in coral lagoons off Australia. The European cuttle (right) with his ten 'arms' and tentacles neatly aligned in front of him, is the source of the artist's pigment, sepia. *Photos: Courtesy of the Australian Information Service and Douglas P. Wilson*

Island in the Pacific, since the thickness of the Earth's crust is least beneath the oceans, lessening to *c.* 5km (3m) in places. Expense and technical difficulties indefinitely postponed achievement of the ultimate aim, but the cores brought up illuminated the geological history of the Earth and aided the development of geophysics.

MOHS (mo͞os), **Friedrich** (1773-1839). German mineralogist. He devised in 1820 a scale classification of minerals in order of hardness, from 1 (talc) to 15 (diamond).

MOI (mō-i), **Daniel Arap** (1924-). Kenyan statesman. A schoolmaster, he became Min. of Home Affairs in 1964, vice-pres. in 1967, and in 1978 succeeded Kenyatta as president.

MOJAVE (mōhah'vi) **DESERT.** Region in S California, part of the Great Basin: area 38,500 sq.km (15,000 sq.m).

MOJI. *See* under KITAKYUSHU.

MOLA'SSES. Strictly the drainings from raw cane sugar, but also used as a synonym for treacle (q.v.). M. from sugar cane produces rum in fermentation; that from beet sugar gives alcohol.

MOLD. Admin. HQ of Clwyd (q.v.), Wales.

MOLDĀ'VIA. The E region of Romania, which was united with Wallachia to form Romania in 1859.

MOLDĀ'VIAN SSR. A constituent republic of the USSR. It is a fertile, well-watered plateau. Vineyards and orchards are its chief wealth; sheep and cattle are reared on the S steppes. M. was created in 1940 from the former Moldavian ASSR, and Bessarabia, ceded by Rumania in the same year, except the area bordering the Black Sea (added to Ukraine SSR). Kishinev is the cap. Area 33,700 sq.km (13,100 sq.m); pop. (1978) 3,900,000.

MOLE. Genus of mammals in the family Talpidae. The common M. of Europe (*Talpa europaea*) has a thick-set body *c.* 18cm (7in) with soft dark fur. Purblind, it lives underground in circular grass-lined nests and excavates extensive tunnels in its search for worms and grubs, throwing up the earth at intervals in 'mole-hills'. The short muscular forelimbs and shovel-like hind feet are adapted for burrowing. Some members of the family are aquatic, e.g. the American shrew M. (*Scalops aquaticus*).

MOLE. Base unit of the SI system, unit symbol mol, indicating amount of substance. The M. is the amount of substance of a system which contains as many elementary entities as there are atoms in 0.012 kg of carbon 12. The entities must be specified (whether atoms, molecules, ions, electrons, etc.).

MOLECULE. The smallest particle of any substance that can exist free yet still exhibit all the chemical properties of the substance. Molecules are composed of a number of atoms (q.v.) ranging from one atom in a helium molecule to many thousands of atoms in the molecules of complex organic substances. The composition of the molecule is determined by the nature of the bonds, probably electric forces, which hold the atoms together.

According to the molecular or kinetic theory of matter, molecules are in a state of constant motion, the extent of which depends on their temperature, and they exert forces on one another.

MOLIÈRE (mōlyār'). Pseudonym of the French dramatist Jean Baptiste Poquelin (1622-73). B. in Paris, he studied law before assisting his father in his trade as an upholsterer. In 1643 he became one of the founders of the *Illustre Théâtre,* of which he was later the leading actor, and in 1655 wrote his first play, *L'Étourdi.* He estab. his reputation with *Les Précieuses ridicules* (1659), which was followed by some 40 comedies, incl. *L'École des femmes* (1662), *Tartuffe* (1664), *Le Festin de Pierre* (1665), *Le Misanthrope* (1666), *Le Médecin malgré lui* (1666), *Georges Dandin, L'Avare* (1668), *Le Bourgeois gentilhomme* (1670), *Les Fourberies de Scapin* (1671), *Les Femmes savantes* (1672), and *Le Malade imaginaire* (1673). His fearless social satire exposed him to many attacks from his enemies, against whom he was consistently protected by Louis XIV.

M. introduced to the stage a new comedy, which relied not on the formal neatness of the Greek plots, but on the exposure of hypocrisy and cant in the eternally recurrent types of human character.

MOLINOS (mōlē'nos), **Miguel de** (1640-97). Spanish mystic. B. near Saragossa, he settled in Rome after being ordained a RC priest, and wrote in Italian several devotional works, incl. the *Guida spirituale,* which aroused the hostility of the Jesuits, who caused him to be arrested in 1685. In 1687 he was sentenced to life imprisonment. His doctrine, known as Quietism, puts particular emphasis on disinterested love and on the attainment of a state of spiritual repose in which we can approach most closely to God.

MOLLUSCS. A large sub-division of the animal kingdom. The majority are marine animals, but some inhabit fresh water, and a few are terrestrial. They incl. shell-fish, snails, slugs, and cuttles. The body is soft, limbless, and cold-blooded. There is no internal skeleton, but most species have a hard shell covering the body. The shell takes a variety of forms, univalve (e.g. snail), bivalve (e.g. mussel), chambered (e.g. nautilus), and many other variations. In some cases, e.g. cuttle and squid, the shell is internal. There is a fold of skin, the mantle, which covers the whole body or the back only, and which secretes the calcareous substance forming the shell. The lower ventral surface forms the locomotory organ, or foot. Ms. vary in diet, the carnivorous species feeding chiefly upon other members of the class. Some are vegetarian. Reproduction is by means of eggs, and is sexual.

Classification of Mollusca

Class Amphineura

Order, Polyplacophora; coat-of-mail shells.
Order, Aplacophora.

Class Gastropoda

SUB-CLASS, Streptoneura.
Order, Aspidobranchia; limpets, top shells, ear-shells.
Order, Pectinibranchia; rock snails, whelks, harp shells, cones, periwinkles.
SUB-CLASS, Euthyneura.
Order, Opisthobranchia; bubble shells, sea hairs, umbrella shells.
Order, Pulmonata; true snails and slugs, false limpets.

Class Scaphopoda

Family: Dentaliidae.

Class Lamellibranchia

Order, Protobranchia; Nucula.
Order, Filibranchia; common mussel, pearl oyster, scallops.
Order, Eulamellibranchia; freshwater mussel, cockle, razor shell, oyster, shipworms.
Order, Septibranchia; Poromya.

Class Cephalopoda

SUB-CLASS, Tetrabranchia; pearly nautilus.
SUB-CLASS, Dibranchia.
Order, Octopoda; octopus; argonaut.
Order, Decapoda; squids, cuttlefish.

Shell-fish (oysters, mussels, clams, etc.) are commercially valuable, espec. when artificially bred and 'farmed'. The Romans, and in the 17th cent. the Japanese, experimented with advanced methods, and raft culture of oysters is now widely practised. The cultivation of pearls, pioneered by Kokichi Mikimoto, began in the 1890s and became an important export industry after the F.W.W.

MŌ'LNÁR, Ferenc (1878-1952). Hungarian novelist and playwright. His best novel is *Paul Street Boys* (1907), but he is most widely known for his play, *Liliom* (1909), a study of a circus barker, adapted as the musical *Carousel.*

MOLOCH (mō'lok), or **Molech.** A Phoenician deity worshipped at Jerusalem in the 7th cent. BC, to which children were sacrificed.

MOLOKAI (mōlōkī'). A mountainous island of Hawaii state, USA, lying SE of Oahu; Kamakou (1,512 m/4,960 ft), is the highest peak. In 1873-89 Father Damien took charge of, and organized, the leper settlement on the N coast, at Kalaupapa. Area 673 sq.km (259 sq.m); pop. (1970) 5,260.

MO'LOTOV, Vyacheslav Mikhailovich. Name assumed by Soviet statesman V. M. Skryabin (1890–1986). He was Chairman of the Council of People's Commissars (PM) 1930-41, and succeeded Litvinov as For. Min. (1939-49 and 1953-6), and was first deputy premier 1953-7. However, in 1957 he was one of the 'anti-party' group expelled from the govt for Stalinist activities. He was famous for the frequency with which he said *niet* 'No' at the UN.

The *M. cocktail,* used by resistance groups in the S.W.W., was a home-made hand grenade, consisting of a bottle filled with inflammable liquid and fired by a wick.

MOLOTOV. Name 1940-57 of PERM.

MOLTKE, Helmuth Carl Bernhard, count von (1800-91). Prussian general. B. in Mecklenburg, he entered the Prussian Army in 1821, became chief of the general staff in 1857, and was responsible for the Prussian strategy in the wars with Denmark (1863-4), Austria (1866), and France (1870-1). He was created a count in 1870 and a field marshal in 1871. His nephew, **Helmuth Johannes Ludwig von M.** (1848-1916), became chief of staff in 1906, and drew up the plans for the invasion of France carried out at the beginning of the F.W.W.

MŌLU'CCAS. Groups of islands, most of them volcanic, forming part of the Republic of Indonesia. The N group comprises Morotai, Halmahera (the largest), Ternate, Tidore, Makian, Bachan, Obi Islands, Sula Islands; the S group, Buru, Ceram, Amboina, Banda Islands, Kai Islands, Aru Islands, Tanimbar Islands, Babar Islands, Kisar, and Wetar. Pepper, cloves, nutmeg (especially from the Bandas) and other spices, for which the M. are still noted, attracted the Portuguese in the 16th cent. The Dutch held the M. 1616-1942, when they were invaded by the Japanese. After the S.W.W. the S Moluccas helped maintain Dutch rule 1945-9 during the Indonesian fight for independence, and in 1950 declared an independent rep. until Indonesia estab. control. The troops, in Dutch service for 300 yrs, were evacuated to the Netherlands and continued to agitate for a separate republic. Area 74,505 sq.km (28,767 sq.m); pop. *c.* 1,000,000.

MOLY'BDENITE. Molybdenum disulphide, MoS_2, the chief ore mineral of molybdenum. It possesses a hexagonal crystal structure, and has a metallic lustre resembling graphite.

MOLYBDENUM (Gk *molybdos* lead). Very brittle and malleable white metal, an electric furnace product of molybdenite (MoS_2) and wulfenite, and one of many fission products from a nuclear reactor: symbol Mo, at. wt. 9595 and at. no. 42. Discovered by Scheele in 1778, it has a melting point of 2,620°C, and is not found in the free state. Producing countries incl. the USA, Canada and Norway. Important in producing specialized steels, it is also used for electrodes (since it is easily welded to soda and Pyrex glass and to other metals), and for filaments (alloyed with tungsten) in thermionic valves. In use as an aid to lubrication, M. disulphide (MoS_2) makes an outstanding reduction in surface friction between ferrous metals.

MOMBASA (mombah'sah). Port of Kenya, E Africa, situated on M. island, and together with the adjacent port of Kilindini handling nearly all the foreign trade of Kenya, Tanzania, and Uganda. Pop. (1980) 342,000.

MOMENT. In physics and engineering the M. is the product of a quantity and a distance. In particular the moment of a force about a point is the product of the force and the perpendicular distance from the point to the line of action of the force, and measures its turning effect or torque. The *M. of inertia* of a body measures its resistance to angular acceleration and depends on the particular axis of rotation being considered.

MOME'NTUM. The M. of a body is the product of its mass and its linear velocity; angular M. is the product of its moment of inertia (*see under* MOMENT) and its angular velocity. The M. of a body does not change unless it is acted on by an external force. The law of conservation of M. is one of the fundamental concepts of classical physics. It states that the total M. of all bodies in a closed system is constant and unaffected by processes occurring within the system.

MONA. *See* ANGLESEY.

MO'NACO. Small principality, under French protection, on the Mediterranean, bounded by the French dept. of Alpes-Maritimes. M. comprises 3 communes, Monaco-Ville, Monte Carlo, and La Condamine. At the old town of M. is the palace, and a remarkable aquarium. M. is governed by a Ministry, Council of State, and elected National Council, under the authority of the reigning prince, Rainier III (1923–), who succeeded his grandfather Prince Louis II in 1949. In 1956 he m. the American film star Grace Kelly (q.v.) and they have 3 children, Prince Albert Alexandre Louis Pierre (1958–), the heir-apparent, and Princess Caroline (1957–) and Princess Stephanie (1965–). If the reigning House of Grimaldi were to die out, with no male or female heir, the principality would pass under French sovereignty. Area 1.5 sq.km (.575 sq.m); pop. (1975) 25,029.

MONA'DNOCK. An isolated hill or mtn, named after Mount M. in New Hampshire, USA: 1,063 m (3,186 ft).

MONAGHAN (mon'ahan). County of Ulster prov., Rep. of Ireland, watered by the Finn and Blackwater. Cereals are grown, and linen made. The co. town is M. Area 1,290 sq.km (498 sq.m); pop. (1971) 46,240.

MONASTICISM (Gk *monachos*, monk). Method of religious life, by which the individual, under vows of poverty, chastity, and obedience, devotes himself to the service of God in retirement. M. was known in pre-Christian times among the Jews, e.g. the Essenes, and forms part of non-Christian religions, e.g. Buddhism. The institution of Christian M. is ascribed to St Anthony in 3rd cent. Egypt, but the inauguration of communal life is attributed to his disciple, St Pachomius. The full adaptation of M. to the conditions of western life was carried out by St Benedict in the 6th cent., and the Benedictine Rule became general. In 910 the foundation of Cluny began the system of orders whereby each monastery was subordinated to the mother institution. During the Middle Ages other forms of M. were estab., incl. the eremitical Carthusians (1084), the Augustinian canons, who were clerics organized under a monastic system (11th cent.); the military Knights Templar and Knights Hospitaller (12th cent.); and in the early 13th the 4 great mendicant orders, Franciscans, Dominicans, Carmelites, and Augustinians, who went out to work in the world.

M. reached the height of its influence during the 13th cent., declining during the 14th, and was severely affected by the Reformation. Renewed life came with the foundation of orders dedicated to particular missions, such as the great weapon of the Counter-Reformation, the Society of Jesus (1540). But the French Revolution exercised a repressive influence. Yet another revival came in the late 19th cent. and continues in the 20th, particularly in the active orders, although by the mid-20th cent. emphasis was moving to a combination of the active and contemplative life. Throughout the history of M. organizations for women have existed on parallel lines with those for men.

MONASTIR. Turkish name of BITOLJ.

MÖNCHEN-GLADBACH (mön'khen-glad'bakh). Town in N Rhine-Westphalia, W Germany, nr Düsseldorf. There are textile and clothing, machine, paper and other industries, and it is the NATO HQ for northern Europe. Pop. (1978) 258,850.

MOND, Ludwig (1839–1909). British chemist. B. at Cassel, Germany, he moved to England in 1862, and, while partner in a chemical works at Widnes, perfected a process for recovering sulphur during the manufacture of alkali. In 1867 he became a British subject, and in 1873 helped to found the firm of Brunner, Mond and Co., which pioneered the British chemical industry.

MONDALE, Walter Frederick (1928–). American Democratic politician. B. in Ceylon, Minnesota, he became a lawyer, was Carter's Vice-President 1977–81, and a candidate for the Democratic nomination 1984.

MONDAY. The first day of the week. It replaced Sunday on the recommendation of the International Standardization Organization, ratified by Britain in 1971. The name derives from its having been considered sacred to the Moon (Old English *Mōnandaeg* and Latin *Lunae dies).*

MONDRIAN (mon'drē-ahn), **Piet** (1872–1944). Dutch abstract painter. B. at Amersfoort, in 1917 he founded with Theo van Doesburg the review and movement known as *De Stijl* (The Style), which sought to apply the principles of geometrical abstract design to painting, sculpture, and architecture. Neo-Plasticism, which he founded in 1920, was a phase of *De Stijl.*

MONET (mōnā'), **Claude** (1840–1926). French Impressionist painter. B. at Paris, he studied under Boudin, and after spending 2 years in Africa with a French regiment, entered Gleyre's studio. He became a prominent member of the French Impressionist group, which incl. Manet, Degas, Renoir, and Sisley. He excelled in painting atmospheric effects, and was fond of depicting the same subject at different times of the day, e.g. his series of haystacks.

MO'NETARISM. The management of a country's economy, espec. in the achievement of a reduced rate of inflation, by control of the money supply. The basic requirement is seen as keeping the growth of the money supply in step with growth in the ability to produce goods. This in turn requires cutting of govt. spending, which is also regarded as in the short-term eliminating waste and in the long-term as a means of returning to the private sector as large a proportion of the economy as possible in order to attain greater efficiency.

Other measures are the restriction of credit in the private sector by high interest rates, and the avoidance of selective assistance to industries which are no longer viable because of inefficient management or production techniques, changes in markets, or such factors as over-manning, excessive wage demands, restrictive union practices, etc. The resultant unemployment, though severe, is believed to be less in amount and less long-lasting than would be the result of the adoption of Keynesian methods. Palliative measures, such as import controls to prevent goods from more efficient overseas industries entering the country are also to be rejected.

The term entered British politics late in 1974 when rising unemployment and strikes ended the attempt of the Heath govt. to apply a monetary policy. From 1979 the Thatcher govt. attempted a more complete application of M., of which the leading academic exponent is Milton Friedman (q.v.).

MONEY. Any commodity which by custom, convention, or law, serves as the common medium of exchange in a community. Coinage is said to have been first used by the Lydians in the 7th cent. BC, and paper M. was in use in China *c.* AD 800 when this 'flying M.' was used to defeat bandits who otherwise easily ran down the imperial messengers whose horses were laden with coin. From the earliest times both coin and notes have been issued as a govt monopoly. Today coins - which are for the most part alloy tokens, rather than of metal such as gold or silver of equivalent intrinsic value - and notes are limited to smaller transactions, and are supplemented by modern developments such as credit cards (q.v.), which link with bank M. transferred by cheque.

Money supply is a vital element in a govt's endeavours to control any economy, strict monetarist theory in fact maintaining that the only reason for the depreciation of M., and consequently inflation, is an excess of M. in circulation with too few goods to meet demand. Govts try to control growth of the M. supply by curbing, or encouraging in deflationary circumstances, the amount of bank lending and deposits at interest. In estimating M. supply coins and notes, and the current bank accounts of individuals and companies, are referred to as M1, and M1 together with term deposits (mainly deposit accounts at banks) is referred to comprehensively as M3 (M2 was a vaguer concept which has dropped out of use). Such an estimate covers only internal monetary conditions, however, so that in any final calculation the increase in M3 is added to the balance of payments deficit, so that the external credit being obtained is also taken into account in what is known as DCE (domestic credit expansion). Govts themselves frequently add to inflationary pressures by largescale borrowing for expenditure in the public sector to stave off unemployment, etc.

INTERNATIONAL MONEY. The problems that faced nations after the S.W.W. of 1939-45 were not dissimilar to those that existed after the F.W.W. Disordered exchanges, depreciated monetary units, with the resulting interference with overseas trade, were the common experience. Various cures for these ills were tried, the suspension of the gold standard among them. Then in July 1944 a United Nations Monetary and Financial conference was held at Bretton Woods, New Hampshire, USA, which led to the establishment of an International Bank for Reconstruction and Development, and the opening of the International Monetary Fund, in Washington, USA, which is designed to assist in the smooth working of trade and in the prevention of crises, in addition to the preservation of exchange stability. The Fund system has many of the advantages of the gold standard, without its rigidity, but distorted balance of payments positions were a marked feature of the late 1960s, e.g. Britain struggling against an adverse balance and Germany in the reverse position. In the 1970s the rise in demand for commodities, and especially for oil, led to more widespread imbalances, and world-wide inflation. These years also saw a switch from fixed exchange rates for the currencies of various countries to a 'floating rate', which limited speculation by those anticipating the devaluation or revaluation of any particular currency, but tended in itself to add to the instability of the internat. monetary situation. The beginnings of an international currency can perhaps be seen in organizations such as the Common Market: *See* EUROPEAN MONETARY SYSTEM. *See also* BANKING, GOLD STANDARD, etc.

MONGŌ'LIA. A vast plateau region of E central Asia, lying between L. Baikal and the Nan Shan mountains. The 3 physical divisions are: (1) the Gobi region, a long central depression within the plateau; (2) the NW mountains; (3) the SE mountains. The plateau climate is dry and subject to extremes of cold and heat, particularly in the Gobi region, where NW winds prevail; the NW and SE mountains receive the rainy winds. The inhabitants are Mongols, mainly nomadic and living in tents, who keep herds of horses, camels, cattle, goats, and sheep and are expert horsemen. The former organization of the Mongols under hereditary princes as a military society has broken down under Communist rule, as has the power of Islam and Lamaism (qq.v.), but in 1967 there was violent opposition to the Maoist Cultural Revolution in both Outer and Inner M. Discoveries made by expeditions in the 1920s confirmed that M. is a main area of world evolution, many remains being found of prehistoric animals and early human culture. The language of M. belongs to the Altaic family, and its literature is mostly colloquial fairy tales.

The name Mongols first appears in Chinese annals in the 6th cent., and their power reached its zenith under Genghis Khan, who became emperor in 1206, and his grandson, Kublai Khan (1216-94), the first Mongol emperor of China. Separation of the N Mongols from the S Mongols dates from the 14th cent., following the overthrow in 1368 of the Mongol dynasty of China by the Mings.

Inner Mongolia (Pinyin: Nei Monggol) is an autonomous region of China, created in 1947. It has varied in size from time to time, the latest change being in 1972 when substantial areas were redistributed among Heilongjiang, Jilin and Liaoning, in conjunction with the creation of new air bases, roads and railways in this strategic frontier area. Millet, soya, sugar beet and oil seeds are grown where possible along the Yellow river, and coal and iron worked. The cap. is Hohhot. Area 450,000 sq.km (173,700 sq. m); pop. (1979) 8,500,000.

Outer Mongolia, the N part of M., is bounded on the N by the RSFSR, elsewhere by China. It was part of China from 1686 until given autonomy at the Chinese revolution of 1911-12. In 1924 it adopted the soviet system of government and proclaimed itself the Mongolian People's

Republic. China recognized its independence in 1946, and M. has a mutual assistance pact with USSR (1966). Agriculture is on the collective system, and new areas are being brought into cultivation. Minerals incl. copper, molybdenum, gold, tungsten, uranium, coal and oil. Ulan Bator is the cap. and chief manufacturing centre, but industry is being developed at Darkhan (nr Soviet border N of the cap.) and Choybalsan (in the E) mainly by Soviet aid. China has accused Russia of making Outer M. a colony. Area 1,560,000 sq.km (600,000 sq.m); pop. (1971) 1,300,000.

MONGOLISM. *See* DOWN'S SYNDROME.

MO'NGOOSE. Mammal in the family Viverridae. The Indian M. (*Herpestes mungo*) is greyish in colour, *c.* 50cm (1.5ft), with a long tail. It may be tamed, and is often kept for its ability to kill snakes. The Egyptian M. or Ichneumon is larger.

MONISM. In philosophy, the belief that the universe may be reduced to a single principle, whether mental, material, or other. It is thus opposed to dualism and pluralism.

MO'NITOR. Armoured vessel of light draught and slow speed, specializing in long-range coastal bombardment, which takes its name from the first of its class, the Federal turret-ship *Monitor*, used in the American Civil War. Ms. were largely used in the F.W.W., especially off the Belgian coast. None was built between the wars, but a few of the larger type were used in the S.W.W. The word M. also denotes a family of lizards (*see* DRAGON), and a professional listener to and reporter of broadcasts. The BBC Monitoring Service was first formally organised 1939 at Evesham, and from 1943 at Caversham Park nr Reading. Since 1945 there has been total exchange with USA, where the Far East and S America are monitored.

MO'NIZ, Antonio Egas (1874-1955). Portuguese diplomat and neurologist. He pioneered the treatment of mental disease by surgery, notably prefrontal leucotomy, which can be useful in treating schizophrenia and paranoia. He was awarded a Nobel prize in 1949.

MONK, or **MONCK, George,** 1st duke of Albemarle (1608-69). English soldier. During the Civil War he fought for the king, but after being captured changed sides and took command of the parliamentary forces in Ireland. He served in Cromwell's Scottish campaign 1650, and at sea against the Dutch 1652-3, and under the Commonwealth became C-in-C in Scotland. Leading his army into England in 1660 he brought about the restoration of Charles II, and was created duke of Albemarle.

MONK, Maria (*c.* 1817-50). Claiming to have escaped from a Montreal nunnery, she pub. palpably false *Awful Disclosures* (1836) of life therein.

MONKEY. Term usually applied to all the Primates except man and the anthropoid apes. Ms. are numerous in tropical parts of Africa, S America, and Asia, and are seldom found elsewhere.

MONKEY-PUZZLE TREE or **Chilean pine.** Evergreen tree (*Araucaria araucana*) native of Chile.

MONMOUTH, James Scott, duke of (1649-85). Leader of 'Monmouth's rebellion'. B. at Rotterdam, the natural son of Charles II by Lucy Walter, he was created duke of M. in 1663. He m. Anne Scott, countess of Buccleuch, and adopted her surname. The Whig opposition attempted unsuccessfully to secure him the succession to the crown by the Exclusion Bill, and in 1684, having become implicated in a Whig conspiracy, he fled to Holland. After James II's accession in 1685, he landed at Lyme Regis, claimed the crown, and raised a rebellion which was crushed at Sedgemoor, in Somerset. M. was captured and beheaded on Tower Hill.

MONMOUTHSHIRE. Former co. of Wales, which in 1974 became, less a small strip on the border with Mid Glamorgan, the new co. of Gwent. The former co. town was Monmouth, birthplace of Henry V.

MONNET (monā'), **Jean** (1888-1979). French economist. The originator of Churchill's offer of union between the UK and France in 1940, he devised the French modernization programme of which he took charge under de Gaulle in 1945, and in 1950 produced the 'Schuman Plan' initiating the co-ordination of European coal and steel production which developed into the 'Common Market'.

MONOCOTYLEDON (monokotilē'don). Plants having one seed-leaf (cotyledon). The stems of such plants are usually hollow or soft, e.g. palms, bamboos, grasses, and cereal plants. The foliage leaves are parallel-veined.

MONOD (monoh'), **Jacques** (1910-1976). French biochemist. Head of the dept of cellular biochemistry at the Pasteur Inst., Paris, he was awarded a Nobel prize in 1965 (with two colleagues) for research in genetics and microbiology. According to his *Chance and Necessity* (1970) 'Pure chance, absolutely free but blind is at the very root of the stupendous edifice of evolution'.

MONOPHYSITES (mono'fisits). Christian heretics of the 5th-7th cents., who taught that Christ had one nature, in opposition to the orthodox doctrine laid down at the Council of Chalcedon in 451, that He had 2 natures, the human and the divine.

MONO'POLY. Originally a grant from the Crown conferring the sole right to manufacture or sell a certain article. The abuse of such grants, which were frequently made to royal favourites, provoked many protests from parliament under Elizabeth, James I, and Charles I. The term is applied today to business organizations or groupings of organizations, formed into trusts or cartels, strong enough to dominate particular industries and so restrict competition and control prices. In the UK the Ms. Commission (1948, reconstituted under the Restrictive Trade Practices Act 1956, which also created a special court to deal with restrictive agreements) inquires into such problems and makes recommendations to the govt. A familiar example is the enforcement by manufacturers of minimum resale prices, which was abolished under the Resale Prices Act (1964), following the example of USA and Canada. The Fair Trading Act (1973) defined a M. supplier as having 'a quarter of the market'.

Monopsony is the opposite position, in which there is only one buyer, as when govt and nationalized industry is the only purchaser in such fields as rail, telephone and military equipment.

MONORAIL. Railway running on a single (usually overhead) rail. Originally invented in 1882 to carry light loads, and when run by electricity called a telpher, in more recent years the M. has been used to solve passenger transport problems in congested city areas, as in Germany and Japan, and in undeveloped areas links mines, etc. to ports and railheads without the heavy construction and maintenance costs of road and ordinary rail facilities.

MONŌSŌ'DIUM GLUTAMATE (gloo'-). Food additive, $NaC_5H_8O_4$, which accentuates the meaty flavour. Its white crystals are a salt of glutamic acid, one of the amino acids.

MONOTHEISM (mon'othē-izm). Belief in one God, as opposed to polytheism, the belief in many.

MONO'THELITES. Christian heretics of the 7th cent., who sought to reconcile the orthodox and Monophysite theologies by maintaining that while Christ possessed 2 natures He had only one will.

MONOTREME (mon'atrēm). Member of the Monotremata, the only living order of primitive egg-laying mammals. Native to the Australian region, they incl. the echidna and platypus.

MONROE, James (1758-1831). Fifth pres. of the USA. B. in Virginia, he served in the War of Independence, was Minister to France 1794-6, and during 1803 negotiated the Louisiana Purchase. He was Sec. of State 1811-17, and was elected Pres. in 1816, and again in 1820. His name is associated with the *Monroe doctrine*, expressed in his message to Congress in 1823, when European intervention against the revolting Spanish colonies in S America was proposed, in which he declared that the American continents 'are henceforth not to be considered as subjects for future colonization by any European powers', and that any attempt to extend European colonies in the Americas would be regarded as dangerous to USA peace and safety.

MONROE, Marilyn. Professional name of Norma Jean Mortensen (1926-62), American film actress and sex symbol. An illegitimate child, suffering wretchedly in early life, she first made her name in *The Asphalt Jungle:* later films incl. *The Seven Year Itch, Bus Stop* and *Some Like it Hot.* Her second husband was Joe Di Maggio, the baseball star, and her third Arthur Miller (q.v.). She d. of an overdose of sleeping tablets.

MONROVIA (munrō'via). Port and cap. of the Liberian rep., Africa. M., founded in 1821, was named in honour of President Monroe (q.v.). Along the coast, 95km (60m) SW, Buchanan handles iron exports from the Nimba mtns. Pop. (1974) 171,680.

MONS (monz). Cap. of the prov. of Hainault, Belgium, situated in the centre of an extensive coalfield, and with textile and sugar industries. The retreat from Mons in Aug. 1914 followed the first important battle (23 Aug.) fought by the BEF in the F.W.W. Pop. (1972) 61,000.

MONSA'RRAT, Nicholas (1910-79). British author. B. in Liverpool, he served in the RN during the S.W.W. 1940-6, and made his name with the war novel *The Cruel Sea* (1951).

MONSOO'N (Arabic *mausim,* season). Term originally applied by the Arabs to a wind which occurs at fixed seasons in the Arabian Sea; now applied to any seasonal wind, particularly those which occur in India and the N Indian Ocean.

MONSTE'RA. Plant of the Arum family (Araceae), a native of tropical America. The small flowers crowd on thick, fleshy spikes, each enclosed by a large leaf. A striking feature is the drying up of areas between the veins of the leaves, which ultimately form holes and deep marginal notches.

MO'NSTRANCE. In the RC Church, a vessel used from the 13th cent. to hold the Sacred Host when exposed at Benediction or in processions.

MONTAGU, Lady Mary Wortley (1689-1762). British letter-writer and society poet. *Née* Pierrepont, she m. Edward Wortley M., ambassador to Constantinople. Returning to England in 1718, she introduced inoculation against smallpox, and quarrelled with Pope, her former friend and correspondent.

MONTAIGNE (moṅtān'), **Michel Eyquem de** (1533-92). French essayist. B. at the Château de Montaigne, near Bordeaux, he studied law, and in 1554 became a counsellor of the Bordeaux parlement. Little is known of his earlier life, except that he frequented the court of Francis II and tasted the pleasures of Paris. In 1571 he retired to his estates, relinquishing his magistracy, and in 1580 pub. the first 2 vols. of his *Essays.* He toured Germany, Switzerland, and Italy 1580-1, returning on his election as mayor of Bordeaux, a post he held till 1585. The third vol. of *Essays* appeared in 1588. He d. of quinsy, and was buried in Bordeaux. The originator of the modern essay form, M. deals with all aspects of life in a mood of urbane scepticism, and as translated by John Florio in 1603, largely influenced English writers and thinkers.

MONTA'LE, Eugenio (1896-1981). Italian poet. His vols. of highly individual poetry - e.g. *Ossi di seppis* (1925: *Cuttlebones*), *Le occasioni* (1939: *The Occasions*), *La bufera* (1956: *The Storm*) - reflect his concern with language and meaning, and explore with stoicism such experiences as isolation, uncertainty and exile, in the context of contemporary life. He was awarded a Nobel prize in 1975.

MONTALE. In its citation when awarding Montale a Nobel prize, the committee singled out the 'indelible feeling of the value of life and the dignity of mankind' in his work. *Photo: Courtesy of the Italian Institute*

MONTANA (montah'nah). State of the USA, on the Canadian border. It is bisected by the Rocky Mts. and their subsidiary ranges: to the E lies the Great Plains region. The chief rivers are the Missouri and Yellowstone. There is extensive irrigation, and wheat is the principal crop, but stock raising is also very important. Forestry supports timber, pulp, and plywood industries. M. is rich in minerals, espec. copper, first worked 1880: others incl. fluorspar, manganese, vermiculite, oil, and natural gas.

The cap. is Helena. The site of 'Custer's last stand', is preserved at Little Big Horn. Area 381,085 sq.km (147,138 sq.m); pop. (1970) 694,409.

MO'NTANISM. A movement within the early Church which strove to return to the purity of primitive Christianity. Originating in Phrygia *c.* 156 with the teaching of a prophet named Montanus, it spread to Asia Minor, Rome, Carthage, and Gaul.

MONTAUBAN (moṅtōboṅ'). Town of S France, dating from 1144, cap. of the dept of Tarn-et-Garonne, 50km (31m) N of Toulouse, long a Protestant stronghold. Pop. (1975) 50,420.

MONT AUX SOURCES (moṅtōsürs'). Highest point of the Drakensberg (q.v.).

MONT BLANC (moṅ bloṅ). The highest mountain in the Alps (4,810 m (15,781 ft)). First ascended by Jacques Balmat and Dr Michel Paccard in 1786. A 12km (7.5m) road tunnel (1965) links France and Italy.

MONTBRETIA (-brēsh'ia). Genus of plants (*Montbretia*) in the family Iridaceae. The yellow or reddish flowers are borne on long stems.

MONTCALM (montkahm'), **Louis-Joseph de Montcalm-Gozon,** marquis de (1712-59). French general. B. near Nîmes, he was appointed commander of the troops in Canada in 1756. He won a succession of victories over the British, but was defeated by Wolfe at Quebec, where he and Wolfe were slain.

MONT CENIS (moṅ senē'). Pass in the Alps between France and Italy at 2,082 m (6,831 ft) a.s.l., on the road between Lyon and Turin.

MONTE BELLO ISLANDS. Uninhabited group in the S Pacific, off the NW coast of Western Australia: the largest is Barrow Is.

MO'NTE CARLO. One of the 3 communes of Monaco (q.v.), famous for its gaming tables.

MO'NTE CRISTO. A small uninhabited island to the W of Italy, 40km (25m) S of Elba. It is chiefly famous because of Dumas' novel, *The Count of M. C.*

MONTĒ'GŌ BAY. Port and tourist resort in NW Jamaica. Pop. (1970) 25,000.

MONTÉLIMAR (montā'limahr). Town in Drome dept, France. It makes the nougat to which its name is given. Pop. (1975) 27,600.

MONTENE'GRO. Fed. rep. of Yugoslavia, between Bosnia-Hercegovina and Albania. Once part of Serbia, it became independent in the 14th cent. It never submitted to the Turks and the treaty of Berlin, 1878, recognized M. as a sovereign principality; Prince Nicholas took the title of king in 1910. M. sided with Serbia in the Balkan wars and in the F.W.W., when it was overrun by the Austrians. After the defeat of Austria in 1918, King Nicholas was deposed and M. voted in favour of joining the new Kingdom of the Serbs, Croats, and Slovenes (renamed Yugoslavia, 1931). The cap. is Titograd. Area 13,807 sq.km (5,330 sq.m); pop. (1971) 531,215.

MONTEREY (monterā'). Town in W California, USA, 145km (90m) SE of San Francisco, cap. of the state until 1849. Pop. (1970) 26,300. **Monterey Park,** also in California, is a residential 'suburb' 10km (6m) E of Los Angeles. Pop. (1970) 49,200.

MONTERREY (monterā'). City in NE Mexico, with iron and steel, and food processing industries, and a univ. (1933). Pop. (1980) 2,000,000.

MONTESPAN (moṅtespoṅ'), **Françoise-Athénais de Pardaillan,** marquise de (1641-1707). Mistress of Louis XIV. The dau. of the duc de Montmartre, she m. the marquis de M. in 1663, became Louis's mistress in 1667, and in 1691 retired to a convent. Her 7 children by Louis were legitimized, but her influence over him waned following her engagement of the future Mme de Maintenon (q.v.) as their governess.

MONTESQUIEU (moṅteskyö'), **Charles Louis de Secondat,** baron de la Brède et de (1689-1755). French philosophical historian. B. near Bordeaux, he became adviser to the Bordeaux parlement in 1714. After the success of his *Lettres persanes* (1721), he adopted a literary career. Later works are *Considérations sur les Causes de la grandeur des Romains et de leur décadence* (1734), and *De l'Esprit des Lois* (1748), a study of the principles of government.

MONTESSORI (montesaw'ri), **Maria** (1870-1952). Italian educationalist. B. near Ancona, she was the first woman to take a medical degree at Rome univ. (1894), and from experience with mentally deficient children evolved a system of spontaneous education adapted to normal infants, as described in her *Montessori Method* (1912).

MONTEUX (montö'), **Pierre** (1875-1964). Franco-American conductor. He estab. a reputation as conductor of Diaghileff's Russian Ballet 1911-14 and 1917, and Ravel's *Daphnis and Chloe* and Stravinsky's *Rite of Spring* were first performed under his direction. He then for many years conducted in America, notably with the San Francisco Symphony Orchestra 1935-52.

MONTEVERDI, Claudio (1567-1643). Italian composer. B. at Cremona, while in the service of the duke of Mantua, he achieved fame with the operas *Orfeo* (1607) and *Arianna* (1608), and became musical director at St. Mark's, Venice, in 1613.

MONTEVIDEO (montividā'-ō). Cap. and chief port of Uruguay, cap. also of M. dept., on the River Plate. Founded in 1726, M. is the seat of an archbishopric; it has a cathedral, a univ. (1849), and an international airport. The chief exports are beef and other animal products. Pop. (1975) 1,230,000.

MONTEVIDEO. The seat of the municipal administration during the period of Spanish colonial rule, this building now houses the Uruguayan Parliament. *Photo: Mireille Vautier*

MONTEZ, Lola. Stage-name of the adventuress Maria Gilbert (1818-61). B. in Ireland, she appeared on the stage as a Spanish dancer, and in 1847 became the mistress of

King Ludwig I of Bavaria, whose policy she dictated for a year. Her liberal sympathies led to her banishment through Jesuit influence in 1848. She later acted in the USA and Australia, and d. in New York.

MONTEZUMA II (montēzoo'mah) (1466-1520). Aztec emperor of Mexico. He became emperor in 1502. When Cortes invaded Mexico in 1519 he made M. a prisoner, and shortly after the emperor was murdered by his subjects while attempting to dissuade them from attacking the Spaniards.

MONTFORT, Simon de, earl of Leicester (*c.* 1200-65). English statesman. The son of Simon de Montfort, leader of the crusade against the Albigenses, he came to England in 1230, and was granted the earldom of Leicester. From 1258 onwards he led the baronial opposition to Henry III's misrule, and in 1264 defeated and captured the king at Lewes. As head of the govt in 1265 he summoned the first parl. in which the towns were represented. He was defeated and killed soon after at Evesham.

MONTGOLFIER (moṅgolfyā'), **Joseph Michel** (1740-1810), and **Étienne Jacques** (1745-99). French balloonists. The 2 brothers were papermakers of Annonay, near Lyons, where on 5 June 1783 they sent up a balloon filled with hot air. The first successful human flight was made in a M. balloon on 21 Nov. 1783. The M. experiments greatly stimulated scientific interest in aviation.

MONTGOMERY OF ALAMEIN, Bernard Law Montgomery, 1st visct (1887-1976). British field marshal. The son of an Ulster clergyman, he served in France during the F.W.W. At the beginning of the S.W.W. he was commanding the 3rd division, which formed part of the BEF in France 1939-40, and he took part in the evacuation from Dunkirk. In Aug. 1942 he took command of the 8th Army, then barring the German advance on Cairo; the victory of El Alamein in Oct. turned the tide in N Africa, and was followed by the expulsion of Rommel from Egypt and rapid advance into Tunisia. In Feb. 1943 M.'s forces came under Eisenhower's command, and during the following months were prominent in the conquest of Tunisia and Sicily and the invasion of Italy. He commanded the Allied armies during the opening phase of the invasion of France in June 1944, and from Aug. the British and Imperial troops which liberated the Netherlands, overran N Germany, and entered Denmark. At his 21st Army Group HQ on Lüneberg Heath, he received the German surrender on 3 May 1945. He was in command of the British occupation force in Germany until Feb. 1946, when he was appointed CIGS. He was promoted to field marshal in 1944, and in 1946 was created a visct. In Oct. 1948 M. became permanent military chairman of the Cs-in-C in Committee for W European defence, and 1951-8 was deputy Supreme Commander, Europe.

MONTGOMERY. US city, cap. of Alabama, on the Alabama r., 240km (150m) NE of Mobile. Settled in 1814, M. became the state cap. in 1847; it was the cap. of the Confederate govt Feb.-May 1861. M. makes fertilizers, cigars, machinery, and cotton textiles. Pop. (1970) 133,390.

MONTGOMERYSHIRE. Former co. of N Wales incl. in Powys in 1974. The co. town was Montgomery. Pop. (1973) 43,600.

MONTH. Originally the time between a new moon and the next, averaging 29½ days, now called a lunar M. The calendar M. is for convenience composed of a complete number of days, 30 or 31 (February 28), the extra 6 hours' time per year being added to February as a day each 4th or leap year.

MONTHERLANT (moṅterloṅ'), **Henri de Millon** (1896-1972). French author. B. in Paris, he was a Nazi sympathizer, and his novels, which are marked by an obsession with physical relationships, include *Aux fontaines du désir* (1927), and *Pitié pour les femmes* (1936). His tempered masterpiece is *Le Chaos et la nuit* (1963), drawn from one man's awareness of death.

MONTMARTRE (moṅmar'tr). Bohemian quarter of Paris, France, dominated by the basilica of Sacré Cœur, 1875. It is situated in the N of the city on a 120m (400ft) high hill.

MONTPARNASSE (moṅpahrnahs'). District in the W of Paris, France, frequented by artists and writers. The Pasteur Institute is also here.

MONTPELLIER (moṅpelyā'). Cap. of the dept. of Hérault, France, 50km (31m) SW of Nîmes. There is a 14th cent. cathedral and a univ. (1289) with a famous medical school. Industries incl. engineering, food processing, textiles. Pop. (1975) 178,150.

MONTREAL (montrē-awl'). Largest city, great inland port, and commercial centre of Canada, in Quebec prov., on the island of Montreal, at the junction of the Ottawa and St Lawrence rivers. A number of bridges, incl. the Victoria Jubilee Bridge, spanning the St Lawrence, link the city with the mainland. M. is linked with the inland canal system, and the Canadian National and Canadian Pacific Rlys. M. was founded as Ville Marie de Montréal in 1642 by Paul de Chomédy, Sieur de Maisonneuve; suffered much from Iroquois hostility; and was the last place surrendered by the French to the British, 1760. Nevertheless, when troops of the rebel Continental Congress occupied M. 1775-6, the citizens refused to rise against the British. French remains the language of the majority of the pop. Mount Royal (or Réal), 230m (753ft), overlooks the city. M. is the seat of both RC and Anglican dioceses, and of the RC M. univ. (formerly a branch of Laval) and the Protestant McGill and Sir George Williams univs. M. has excellent rail, waterway, dock and airline facilities (HQ of ICAO); and industries incl. aircraft, chemicals, oil refining and petrochemicals, flour milling, sugar refining, brewing and meat packing. Carefully preserving its old quarter, M. is also a very modern city, e.g. the Place Ville Marie project, where a skyscraper surmounts a 4-level underground 'city' of shopping arcades, parking space, and station platforms for direct access by rail. The M. Internat. Exhibition (Expo 67) on two man-made is. in the St Lawrence was succeeded by the world's largest permanent exhibition. Pop. met. area (1976) 2,802,500.

MONTREUX (moṅtrö'). Winter resort in Vaud canton, Switzerland, on the E shore of Lake Geneva. Close by is the castle of Chillon. At the annual television festival (1961) the premier award is the *Golden Rose of M.* The *Convention of M.* in 1936 allowed Turkey to re-militarize the Dardanelles. Pop. (1970) 21,000.

MONTROSE (montrōz'), **James Graham,** marquess of (1612-50). Scottish soldier. The son of the 4th earl of M., he supported the Covenanters in their struggle against Charles I, but after 1640 went over to the king's side. In 1644 Charles created him a marquess and lieutenant-general in Scotland, whereupon he rallied the Highlanders and won a succession of brilliant victories. Defeated in 1645 at Philiphaugh, he escaped to the Continent. He returned in 1650, and after attempting to raise a rebellion was hanged at Edinburgh.

MONT ST MICHEL (moṅ-saṅ-mēshel'). Small rocky island (50m/165ft high), situated near the coast of Manche dept, France: man-made polders have converted it to a peninsula, and there are plans to restore the water flow. It is famous for its Benedictine monastery, estab. in 708.

MONTSERRA'T. Mountain of Spain, 39km (24m) NW of Barcelona; so called because its uneven outline resembles the serrated edges of a saw (Sp. *monte serrado*). It rises to a height of 1,240 m (4,070 ft). The Benedictine monastery of M., high on the mountain, contains a famous image of the Virgin.

MONTSERRAT. Volcanic island in the British W Indies, one of the Leeward group. It was discovered by Columbus (1493), who named it after the mountain in Spain. It was first colonized by the Irish, 1632. M.'s principal products are cotton and cotton-seed, citrus and other fruits, and vegetables. The chief town is Plymouth (pop. 1,230). Area 101 sq.km (39.5 sq.m); pop. (1979) 12,500

MONUMENT, The. In London, England, overlooking Billingsgate, a column 62m/202ft, designed by Wren, and completed in 1677 to commemorate the Great Fire of London (1666), near the site of the house in Pudding Lane where the conflagration began.

MO'NZA. City in Italy, 15km (9m) NE of Milan. It was the capital of the Lombard rulers. The cathedral of San Giovanni, founded in 595, contains the iron crown of Lombardy. Pop. (1978) 122,000.

MOODY, Dwight Lyman. *See* HYMN.

MOON. The only natural satellite of the Earth, at an average distance of 384,400 km (238,857 m) and with a revolution period of 27⅓ days. Since it has no light of its own and merely reflects that of the Sun, it shows the familiar phases from 'new' to 'full' as it moves round the Earth, gradually changing its position in relation to the Sun. Because the M.'s axial rotation coincides with its revolution period, part of the surface is permanently turned towards the Earth, while another part (owing to the M.'s oscillatory motion from side to side and backwards and forwards - librations - only 41 per cent of the whole) is permanently averted. The large dark areas on the surface easily seen with the naked eye were formerly thought to be liquid and are still known as 'seas', but are in fact plains overlaid with a volcanic 'dust', which includes a large proportion of glass in the form of microscopic spheres. Craters, some volcanic and others caused by meteoritic impact, occur even in these plains, but much larger ones (over 240km/150m in diameter) occur in the light areas which are rough and frequently mountainous, with peaks of a height comparable with the highest on Earth. Once hot, turbulent and volcanic, the M. still has traces of a hot central core, as well as traces of water vapour trapped in rocks at the time of its formation. Specimen rocks have been dated at 2½ to 4½ billion years old, and analysis suggests that the M. was formed independently of Earth and later 'captured', for although its minerals incl. the same kinds of elements as those of Earth, their composition is different. The M. is almost or quite devoid of atmosphere, and so cannot support life in any form.

Early lunar probes incl. *Lunik I* (USSR), which passed within 6,400km (4,000m) of the M. in Jan. 1959; *Lunik II* (USSR) which crash-landed Sept. 1959; *Luna IX* (USSR), which made the first soft landing Feb. 1966; and *Apollo VIII* (USA 21-27 Dec. 1968) carrying Frank Borman, James Lovell and William Anders, which was the first manned craft to orbit the M. The first manned M. landing was made by *Apollo XI* (USA 16-24 July 1969) near the lunar equator in the Sea of Tranquillity, on 20 July, Michael Collins remaining on board the command module Columbia while Neil Armstrong and Edwin Aldrin descended in lunar module Eagle and successively walked on the surface at 9.17 pm.

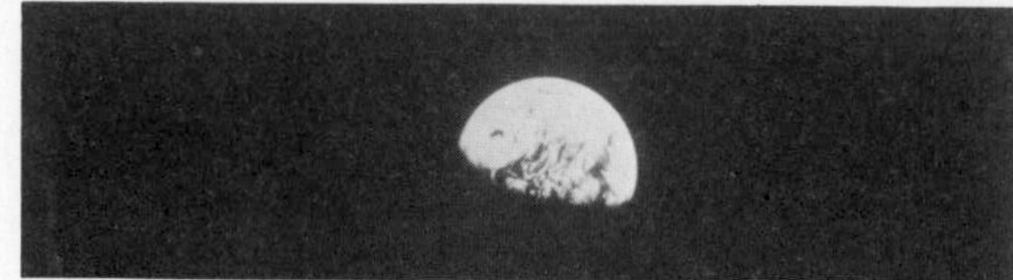

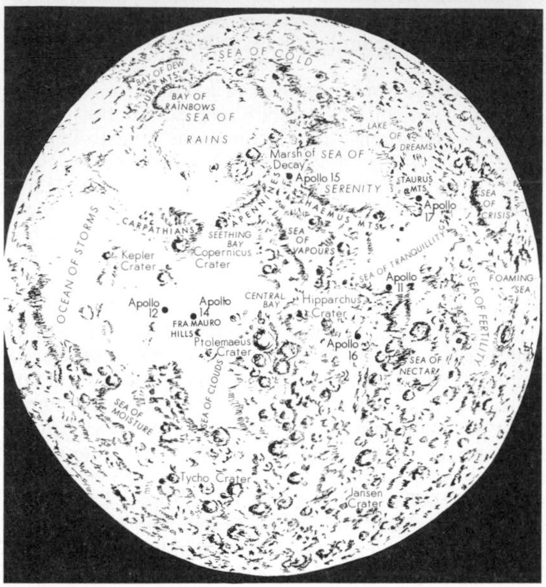

MOON. The face visible from the Earth with the landing sites of the Apollo missions 11-17 (no. 13 was abortive). Above, Earth as seen from the Moon. *Photo: Courtesy of Nasa.*

The M. is the chief force in controlling the tides, its gravitational 'pull' causing the extra high spring tides in combination with the Sun; the low, neap tides occurring when the M. pulls at 'right-angles' to the Sun. Rainfall records indicate that rain is more likely a few days after a new M.

MOON, Sun Myung (1920-). Korean industrialist and founder of the Unification Church (1954), an amalgam of Christianity and Buddhism. From 1973 he launched a major mission in the USA. His mainly youthful followers (Moonies) live a strictly disciplined communal life, give all their possessions to the church, and devote themselves to fund-raising, recruitment and prayer. The church has been attacked for alleged 'brainwashing' techniques.

MOONIE. Town in SE Queensland, site of Australia's first commercial oil strike. Pop. *c.* 100.

MOON TREATY. Popular name for the draft UN treaty proposed by the Soviet Union which restricts free enterprise exploitation of the Moon, asteroids, or any

MOON. The last manned flight in the Apollo series, number 17 in 1972. Jack Schmitt, the first scientist-astronaut, is taking photographs beside an enormous boulder. In the foreground is the front part of the Lunar Rover, with the umbrella-like antenna used to send signals back to Earth, and beneath it is the remotely controlled television camera. *Photo: Courtesy of NASA*

other celestial body. In 1980 the USA strongly opposed ratification.

MOONSTONE. Opalescent variety of potassium sodium feldspar, found in Sri Lanka or Burma, and distinguished by a blue, silvery, or red tint.

MOORE, George (1852-1933). Irish novelist. B. in co. Mayo, he went to study art in Paris (1870), and pub. 2 vols. of poetry there. His first novel, *A Modern Lover* (1883), was startlingly frank regarding sexual relationships and was followed by others, incl. *A Mummer's Wife* (1885); *Esther Waters* (1894); *Evelyn Innes* (1898); the religious *Brook Kerith* (1916); and *Aphrodite in Aulis* (1930). He also pub. the autobiographical *Confessions of a Young Man* (1888); *Memoirs of My Dead Life* (1906); and the trilogy of the Irish revival, *Hail and Farewell* (1911-14).

MOORE, George Edward (1873-1958). British philosopher. Educ. at Trinity Coll., Cambridge, he was prof. of philosophy at the univ. 1925-39, and ed. the journal *Mind*, to which he contributed important articles, 1921-47. His books incl. *Principia Ethica* (1903) and *Some Main Problems of Philosophy* (1953), but his chief influence was as a teacher with immense analytic power.

MOORE, Henry (1898–1986). British sculptor. B. at Castleford, Yorks, he studied at Leeds and the Royal College of Art, but learned more from the works of primitive artists in the British Museum and the simple forms of life in the Natural History Museum. He sought to express his own emotional apprehension in terms of the material in which he worked, and by his originality encountered much hostility. His drawings are also of remarkable quality, especially his London air-raid-shelter scenes of the S.W.W. In 1963 he was awarded the OM.

MOORE, Sir Jeremy (1928–). British soldier. As Major-General Commando Forces, Royal Marines, 1979–82, he commanded the land forces in the Falklands campaign; KCB 1982.

MOORE, Sir John (1761–1809). British commander in the Peninsular War 1808–9. Forced to retreat to Corunna, he was killed in the battle covering the embarkation.

MOORE, Marianne (1887-1972). American poet. B. in Missouri, she edited the literary *Dial* (1925-9), and pub. vols. of intellectual verse of difficult form, e.g. *Observations* (1924), *What are Years* (1941), and *A Marianne Reader* (1961).

MOORE, Thomas (1779-1852). Irish poet. B. in Dublin, he went to England to study law in 1799, and in 1803 was appointed admiralty registrar in Bermuda, but left the post in charge of a deputy, whose subsequent embezzlement (for which he was held liable) sent him into exile on the Continent (1819-22). Among his works are the verse romance, *Lalla Rookh* (1817), and the *Irish Melodies* (1807-35), upon which his reputation now mainly rests. A friend of Byron, of whom he wrote a biography, he allowed the MS of the poet's *Memoirs* to be destroyed by publisher John Murray in 1824 on the grounds of propriety. His own *Memoirs* appeared 1853-6.

MOOREHEAD, Alan McCrae (1910–83). British journalist, brilliantly successful as foreign and war correspondent to the *Daily Express* 1936-45, whose books incl. *Mediterranean Front* (1941), *Montgomery* (1946), *Gallipoli* (1956), and *Darwin and the Beagle* (1969).

MOORHEN. Common water fowl (*Gallinula*), about the size of a bantam, and found throughout the Old World. The M. is black with a red patch on the head and a white patch under the tail.

MOORS. Name (English form of Lat. *Mauri*) originally applied to the inhabitants of the Roman prov. of Mauritania, in NW Africa. Now applied to the people who live N of the Sahara and W of Tripoli, especially the people of Algeria and Morocco, who are principally of Arab and Berber origin. In the 7th cent. the Moors were conquered by the Arabs, and embraced the Mohammedan faith. The Arabs who occupied Spain from 711 to 1492 were called Moors (Sp. *moros*).

MOOSE. *See* ELK.

MOOSE JAW. Town in Saskatchewan, Canada, W of Regina. Settled in 1882, it is a railway centre and has an airport; also extensive stockyards, grain elevators, petroleum refineries, etc. Pop. (1976) 34,245.

MORA'DABAD. Town in Uttar Pradesh, Rep. of India. On the right bank of the Ramganga r., it was founded in the 17th cent. by Rustam Khan, and the Great Mosque dates from 1631. It is a market centre for wheat, cotton, sugar cane and rice, and produces textiles and engraved brassware. Pop. (1971) 272,355.

MORALITY. Didactic medieval verse drama, in part a development of the Miracle Play (q.v.), in which human characters are replaced by personified virtues and vices. The M. flourished in the 15th cent., the most famous example being the *Everyman*.

MORAL REARMAMENT. *See* BUCHMAN, F.N.D.

MORĀ'VIA, Alberto. Pseudonym of Italian novelist Alberto Pincherle (1907-). The son of an architect, he was b. in Rome, publishing his first novel *The Indifferent Ones* (1932) to a burst of acclaim. However, his criticism of Mussolini's régime led to a stifling of his work by the govt. until after the S.W.W. Later books incl. *Woman of Rome* (1949), *Two Women* (1958) and *The Empty Canvas* (1961), a study of an artist's obsession with his model. He is noted for his bare and compelling narrative.

MORĀ'VIA. District of central Europe, part of Czechoslovakia, of which it formed a prov. 1918-49. After division into several regions named after their principal towns, M. was in 1960 re-divided into two: South M. (cap.

Brno), area 15,022 sq.km (5,800 sq.m); pop. (1977) 2,005,000 and North M. (cap. Ostrava), area 11,060 sq.km (4,270 sq.m); pop. 1,899,000. The principal river is the Morava. Forests cover about a quarter of M., which elsewhere is fertile, producing maize and the vine in the S, wheat, barley, rye, flax, sugar beet, etc., farther N. Coal and iron are mined.

By the end of the 6th cent. the Slavs had settled in M., they were converted to Christianity in the 9th cent., when M. became part of the German Empire under Charlemagne. In 874 the kingdom of 'Great Moravia' was founded by Sviatopluk. The country was conquered by the Magyars in 906, but became part of the Holy Roman Empire in 958; in 1029 it was incorporated in Bohemia, in 1526 was brought under the rule of the Habsburgs, and in 1849 became an Austrian crownland. It was incorporated in the new republic of Czechoslovakia in 1918.

MORĀ'VIANS. Protestant episcopal Church founded in Bohemia in 1457, as an offshoot of the Hussite movement. They suffered much persecution after 1620, and were held together mainly by the leadership of their bishop, Comenius. Driven out in 1722 by further persecution, they spread over Germany and into England and N America, while in 1732 missionary work among the heathen was begun. There are *c.* 63,000 Ms. in the USA, and small congregations in England and on the Continent.

MORAYSHIRE (mur'ā-). Former co. of NE Scotland, of which the SW section (incl. Grantown-on-Spey) was incl. in 1975 in Highland region, and the NE area facing the great inlet of the **Moray Firth** (38km/15m wide at its entrance between Burghead and Tarbat Ness), became part of Grampian region. The co. town was Elgin.

MORAZÁN (mōrahthahn'), **Francisco** (1792-1842). Central American statesman. B. in Honduras, he led the successful liberal-federalist revolt of 1827 against the cons. in Honduras and in Salvador and Guatemala in 1828 and 1829. Elected pres. of the Central American Confederation in 1830, he was re-elected in 1834, but Honduras, Nicaragua and Costa Rica seceded in 1838 and Guatemala in 1839. Attempting to hold the union together by force he was driven out by the Guatemalan dictator, Carrera, and a further attempt to revive union in 1842 ended in his capture and execution in Honduras. He is now the symbol of Central American unity.

MORBIHAN (morbē-oṅ'), **Gulf of.** Seawater lake, area 104 sq.km (40 sq.m), in Brittany, W France, linked by a channel with the Bay of Biscay. M. is a Breton word 'little sea'; the gulf gives its name to a dept.

MORDVI'NIAN ASSR. Autonomous rep. of the RSFSR, lying W of the Sura r. Forested in the W, it is fertile elsewhere and produces sugar beet, grains, potatoes, etc. Sheep are reared and dairy farming is important. Timber, furniture, and textiles are produced. Mordvinia was conquered by the Russians during the 13th cent. It was made an autonomous region 1930, an ASSR 1934. A state univ. was set up 1957. The cap. is Saransk. Area 26,200 sq.km (10,100 sq.m); pop. (1978) 976,000.

MORE (mōr), **Hannah** (1745-1833). British author. B. near Bristol, she went to London in 1774, and was one of the most brilliant 'blue-stockings'. After 1782 she again retired to the country to work among the poor and write such edifying books as *Coelebs in search of a Wife* (1809).

MORE, Henry (1614-87). Greatest of the Cambridge Platonists, he became a fellow of Christ's Coll. in 1639. His chief work is the *Divine Dialogues* (1688).

MORE, Sir Thomas (1478-1535). British statesman and author. B. in London, he studied under Linacre and Grocyn at Oxford, and was influenced in his religious beliefs by Colet. In 1497 he first met Erasmus, while studying law at Lincoln's Inn, and in 1504 entered parliament. From 1509 he was favoured by Henry VIII. and employed on foreign embassies, becoming a member of the privy council in 1518 and Speaker of the House of Commons in 1523. He was knighted in 1521, and on the fall of Wolsey became Lord Chancellor in 1529, but resigned in 1532 owing to his failure to agree with the king on his ecclesiastical policy and the marriage with Anne Boleyn. In 1534 he refused as a devout Catholic to take the oath of supremacy to Henry VIII as head of the Church, and after imprisonment in the Tower was executed. Among his writings are the Latin *Utopia* (1516), sketching an ideal commonwealth; the English *Dialogue* (1528), directed against Tyndale; and a *History of Richard III.* M. was canonized in 1935.

MORE. Sir Thomas More in a portrait after Holbein. *Photo: Courtesy of the National Portrait Gallery*

MŌR'ĒA. Name used under Turkish rule for the Greek peninsula of PELOPONNESE.

MOREAU (moroh'), **Jean Victor Marie** (1763-1813). French general. B. at Morlaix, he served in the Revolutionary War, and won a brilliant victory over the Austrians in 1800 at Hohenlinden. His republicanism involved him in intrigues against Napoleon, for which he was banished. In 1813 he offered his services to the Allies, and was killed at the battle of Dresden.

MORECAMBE BAY. Inlet of the Irish Sea, between the Furness Peninsula (Cumbria) and Lancs, England. The rise and fall of the tide over the sands is considerable, and

M.B. is under consideration as a source of tidal electric power. The twin town of **Morecambe and Heysham** is on the mid-Lancs coast, the former being a resort and the latter a port with a ferry service to Ireland. Pop. (1973) 42,000. On the S edge of the bay is the resort of **Fleetwood,** laid out by architect Decimus Burton 1836. There is natural gas 50 km (30 m) offshore. Pop. (1973) 30,000.

MORE'L. Mushroom. The common M., *Morchella esculenta,* grows abundantly in Europe and N America. A yellowish-brown, its edible cap is much wrinkled and *c.* 2.5cm (1in) long. M. is used for seasoning gravies, soups, sauces, etc.

MORESBY, John (1830-1922). British naval explorer and author, remembered for his discovery in 1873 of the finest harbour in New Guinea, on which Port Moresby now stands.

MORGAN, Sir Henry (*c.* 1635-88). Welsh buccaneer. Joining the W Indies Buccaneers, he warred against the Spaniards, capturing and sacking Panama in 1671. In 1674 he was knighted and appointed lieutenant-governor of Jamaica.

MORGAN, John Pierpont (1837-1913). American financier and philanthropist. B. in Conn., he built up one of the greatest international banking-houses, financing gigantic steel, shipping and railway enterprises. He was succeeded in this by his son, **John Pierpont M.** (1867-1943), who raised loans for the Allies during the F.W.W. He assisted the preparation of the Dawes Plan (1922), and was unofficial US delegate to the Reparations Conference (1929). He presented his father's art collection and library to the American Nation.

MORGAN, Thomas Hunt (1866-1945). American biologist. B. at Lexington, he was prof. of biology at Bryn Mawr Coll. 1894-1904, when he transferred to Columbia univ. In 1933 he was awarded the Nobel prize for medicine. He originated the theory of paired elements within the chromosomes which govern heredity, using a fruit fly (*Drosophila melanogaster*) in his experiments.

MORGANATIC MARRIAGE. Marriage between a man of royal birth with a woman of lower rank, who does not share his rank. The marriage is recognized by the Church, and the issue are legitimate, but they cannot succeed to the rank or possessions of their father.

MORI'SCOS. Name given to Spanish Moslems who accepted Christian baptism, and their descendants. They were all expelled from the country in 1609.

MORLAND, George (1763-1804). British painter. B. in London, the son of the artist Henry M., he first exhibited at the RA at the age of 10. After leaving home in 1784 he lived a dissolute life, but was a hard worker, sometimes painting 2 pictures a day. He excelled in country subjects showing gypsies, stable interiors, etc.

MORLEY, John, 1st visct M. of Blackburn (1838-1923). British Liberal statesman and writer. He entered parliament in 1883, and was Sec. for Ireland in 1886 and 1892-5. As Sec. for India 1905-10, he prepared the way for more representative government. He was Lord President of the Council 1910-14, but resigned in protest against the declaration of war in 1914. He pub. lives of Voltaire, Rousseau, Burke, and Gladstone. He received a peerage in 1908.

MORLEY, Thomas (1557-*c.* 1603). English composer. He studied with Byrd, and became organist at St Paul's, obtaining a monopoly of music printing. He wrote madrigals, and songs for Shakespeare's plays. His *Plaine and Easie Introduction to Practicall Music* (1597) is a useful historical source.

MORMONS, or **Latter-Day Saints.** Religious organization founded by Joseph Smith (1805-44). B. in Vermont, he received his first call in 1820, and in 1827 claimed to have been granted the revelation of the *Book of Mormon* (an ancient prophet), inscribed on gold plates and concealed a thousand years before in a hill nr Palmyra, NY state. Christ is said to have appeared to an early American people after His ascension to estab. His church in the New World, and the Mormon Church is a re-establishment of this by divine intervention. The 'Church of Jesus Christ of Latter-Day Saints' (1830) was founded at Fayette, NY, and accepted the book as supplementing the Christian scriptures. Further settlements were rapidly estab. despite persecution, and Brigham Young and the Twelve Apostles undertook the first foreign M. mission in England, the earliest European converts reaching the USA in 1840. Their doctrines met with persecution, and Smith was killed in Illinois. To escape further persecution, Brigham Young led an emigration to the Valley of the Great Salt Lake in 1847 and in 1850 Utah was created a territory with Young as governor (1851-8). Most of the M. who remained in the Middle West (HQ Independence, Missouri) accepted the founder's son Joseph Smith (1832-1914) as leader, adopted the name *Reorganized Church of Jesus Christ of Latter-Day Saints,* and claim to be the true successor of the original church. They do not accept the non-Christian doctrines later proclaimed by Young in 1852, notably that of polygamy, which Young attributed to the original founder in 1843 on no verifiable evidence: Smith is on record as condemning plural wives. The doctrine was formally repudiated by the Utah Mormons in 1890, and Utah was recognized as a State of the Union in 1896. The M. number *c.* 3,250,000; the Reorganized Church *c.* 205,000; both have branches in Britain.

MORNING GLORY. Plant (*Ipomoea purpurea*) of the family Convolvulaceae (*see* CONVOLVULUS), native to tropical America. It has dazzling blue flowers and small quantities of substances similar to LSD (q.v.) are found in the seeds of one variety.

MO'RO, Aldo (1916-78). Italian Christian Democrat statesman. Prime Minister 1963-8 and 1974-6, he was expected to become Italy's pres. when he was kidnapped and shot by Red Brigade urban guerrillas.

MOROCCO (mōrok'ō). Country in NW Africa; its Arabic name Al-Maghreb means farthest west. It has a long coastline to the NW on the Atlantic, continued in the N on the Mediterranean. The High and Middle Atlas, rising to 4,570m (15,000 ft), cross M. from SW to NE; farther S is the Anti-Atlas range, and in the N the Rif Mountains. Chief rivers are the Moulouya, flowing to the Mediterranean, the Sebou and er Abia, flowing to the Atlantic. Much of the land is fertile, the vine, the olive, figs, almonds, dates, citrus fruits, wheat, barley, linseed, and rice being grown; sheep, cattle, goats, mules, horses, and camels are reared. Mineral products incl. phosphates, anthracite coal, iron ore, manganese, antimony, lead, zinc, silver, and petroleum. Fishing (tunny and sardines) is important. The cap. is Rabat; other towns incl. Casablanca, Marrakesh, Fez, and Meknes. Area 458,730 sq.km (166,000 sq.m); pop. (1977) 18,240,000. The official language is Arabic, but Berber is spoken by the mountain peoples, with French and Spanish as recognized auxiliaries in the cities. M.U.: dirham.

History. The sultan of M., last of the Barbary states to maintain independence, accepted French protection in 1912, and the country was divided into three zones: the special zone of Tangier, 240 sq.m (internationalized 1925 under a treaty of 1923); a Spanish protectorate in the N, 11,000 sq.m; the rest a French protectorate. The Spanish and later the French had to contend with serious armed opposition from the tribesmen, but after the surrender of Abd El-Krim (q.v.) in 1926 the country was pacified, and a number of French and Spanish colonists settled in M. The sultan continued to be recognized as ruler. After the S.W.W. there was widespread unrest in M. and in 1956 the country's independence was recognized by France, Spain, and the powers controlling Tangier. In 1957 the sultan Mohammed V (1909-61) changed his title to that of king; he was succeeded by his son Hassan II (1929-). Under the proposed revised constitution of 1972, there was to be a single Chamber of Representatives, two-thirds directly elected, and one-third indirectly elected by an electoral college comprising representatives of local govt, commerce, industry, agriculture and trade unions. Owing to unrest elections did not take place in 1973, and the King has narrowly escaped assassination attempts. In 1975 the King led a march into Spanish Sahara, and following the Spanish withdrawal incorporated two-thirds of the terr. into M. in 1976, and the remaining third (following Mauritania's withdrawal) in 1979; guerrilla resistance by forces claiming independence for Western Sahara continued. In 1980 the OAU called on Morocco to accept a ceasefire under UN supervision there, followed by a referendum.

MŌ'RON. Adult with the mind of a 10-yr-old.

MORŌ'NI. Cap. of the Comoro Is. on Grand Comore. Pop. (1970) 12,000.

MORPHEUS (mor'fūs). In Roman mythology the god of dreams or sleep.

MORPHIA (mor'fē-a). Name generally applied to the alkaloid morphine ($C_{17}H_{19}O_3N$), used to alleviate pain. It can be taken by mouth or injected.

MORRIS, William (1834-96). British poet, Socialist and craftsman. B. at Walthamstow, he was ed. at Oxford, where he formed a lasting friendship with Burne-Jones, and was influenced by Ruskin and Rossetti. He abandoned architecture to study painting, and in 1858 pub. his first book of verse, *The Defence of Guenevere.* He founded his own firm for the manufacture of furniture, wallpapers, church decorations, etc., in 1862, and did much to raise English standards of craftsmanship. He also pub. several more vols. of verse-romances, notably *The Life and Death of Jason* (1867), and *The Earthly Paradise* (1868-70). A visit to Iceland in 1871 inspired his greatest poem, *Sigurd the Volsung* (1876), and his translations of the Sagas. He joined the Social Democratic Federation in 1883, left it as too moderate in 1884, and founded the Socialist League. To this period belong the romances, *A Dream of John Ball* (1888) and *News from Nowhere* (1891); the critical and sociological studies, *Signs of Change* (1888) and *Hopes and Fears for Art* (1892); and the narrative poem, *The Pilgrims of Hope.* Besides active journalistic and propaganda work, he founded the Kelmscott Press.

MORRIS DANCE. An English folk-dance which is still popular. In earlier times it was usually danced by 6 men, one of whom wore girl's clothing. It probably originated in pre-Christian ritual dances.

MORRISON OF LAMBETH, Herbert Stanley Morrison, baron (1888-1965). British Lab. statesman. On leaving elementary school he became a shop assistant, was appointed sec. of the London Lab. Party (1915-45), and was a member of the LCC 1922-45. Entering parl. in 1923, he was Min. of Transport 1929-31, Home Sec. 1940-5, and Lord Pres. of the Council and Leader of the House of Commons 1945-51, briefly succeeding Bevin as For. Sec. (Mar.-Oct. 1951). In 1955 he was defeated by Gaitskell in the contest for leadership of the party.

MORSE (mors), **Samuel Finley Breese** (1791-1872). American inventor of the magnetic telegraph. B. in Mass., in 1836 he produced the first adequate electric telegraph, and in 1843 was granted $30,000 by Congress for an experimental line between Washington and Baltimore. He invented the **Morse Code** for transmitting messages by telegraphy, etc. The table shows the internat. M. alphabet: the dot indicates a signal of short duration and the dash is 3 times this length.

A	•—	M	— —	Y	—•— —
B	—•••	N	—•	Z	— —••
C	—•—•	O	— — —	1	•— — — —
D	—••	P	•— —•	2	••— — —
E	•	Q	— —•—	3	•••— —
F	••—•	R	•—•	4	••••—
G	— —•	S	•••	5	•••••
H	••••	T	—	6	—••••
I	••	U	••—	7	— —•••
J	•— — —	V	•••—	8	— — —••
K	—•—	W	•— —	9	— — — —•
L	•—••	X	—••—	10	— — — — —

THE MORSE CODE

MORTGAGE (mor'gej). A transfer of property - usually land - as a security for repayment of a loan. A M. of land is made by a deed which conveys the full ownership of the land to the mortgagee subject to the mortgagor's right to get his land back on payment of both principal and interest.

MORTIMER, Roger de, 8th baron of Wigmore and 1st earl of March (*c.* 1287-1330). English nobleman. A rebel, he was imprisoned by Edward II for 2 years before making his escape from the Tower to France. There he joined with the English queen, Isabella, who was conducting negotiations at the French Court and returned with her to England. Edward fled when they landed with their followers, and after securing Edward's deposition by parliament, M. ruled England as the Queen's lover. In 1328 he was created Earl of March. He was popularly supposed responsible for Edward II's murder, and when the young Edward III had him seized, while with the Queen at Nottingham Castle, he was hanged, drawn and quartered at Tyburn.

MORTON, John Bingham (1893-1979). British journalist. Ed. at Oxford, he contributed a humorous column to the *Daily Express* 1924-76 under the pseudonym of 'Beachcomber', and pub. many humorous novels.

MOSAIC (mozāk'). A design or picture produced by inlaying variously coloured pieces of marble, stone, glass, or other substances, used chiefly for the decoration of floors and walls, especially in churches. M. was commonly used by the Romans for the decoration of their villas (e.g. Hadrian's villa at Tivoli), and by the Byzantines. The art was revived by the Italians during the 13th cent., when it was used chiefly for the decoration of churches. Examples of modern M. work may be seen in the hall of the Houses of Parliament, and in Westminster Cathedral.

MOSCOW (mos'kō). Russian city (*Moskva*), cap. of the RSFSR from 1918, of the USSR from 1922; cap. also of the M. region, and of Russia from the 14th cent. until 1709, when Peter I transferred the cap. to St Petersburg (renamed Leningrad in 1924). It stands on the Moscow r., 640km/400m SE of Leningrad. The Kremlin (Citadel), which is on the northern bank of the r., is at the centre. First built in the 12th cent., it consists of a walled enclosure containing some of the most important buildings in M., including the cathedral of the Assumption of the Virgin; the cathedral of the Archangel Michael, which was the burial place of the tsars down to Ivan Alexeivich, brother of Peter the Great; the cathedral of the Annunciation; the Ivan Veliki tower (90m/300ft), a famine relief work commissioned by Boris Godunov in 1600; various palaces, incl. the former Imperial Palace, museums, and other buildings. The Tsar Kolokol (king of the bells), 200 tonnes (1735), is also in the Kremlin. The walls of the Kremlin are crowned by 18 towers and have 5 gates. Near the Kremlin stands the Kitai Gorod, containing various govt offices. Lenin's mausoleum is in Red Square (near the Kremlin), a famous open space in M. used for political demonstrations and processions. M. also has 2 univs., one of which was founded in 1755 and is the oldest in Russia, the other opened 1953; the Academy of Sciences, founded at St Petersburg (Leningrad) 1726, moved to M. 1934; the M. Arts Theatre, founded 1898; and the state opera house. M. is the seat of the Patriarch of the Russian Orthodox Church; is linked with Stavropol by oil pipeline (480km/300m), from 1957; is the centre of the railway system, and has an international airport. An underground railway, opened 1935, later extended, is a tourist showpiece. M. is also the largest industrial centre of the USSR, producing machinery, electrical equipment, textiles, chemicals, and many food products. From its foundation in the 12th cent. the city has had a stormy history. It was burnt in 1571 by the Khan of the Crimea, and ravaged by fire in 1739, 1748, and 1753; in 1812 it was burnt by its own citizens to save it from Napoleon's troops, or perhaps by accident. In the S.W.W. Hitler's troops were within 20m of M. on the NW by Nov. 1941, but the stubborn Russian defence and severe winter weather forced their withdrawal in December. The Soviet space centre, Star City (Zvezdnoy Gorodok), is on the outskirts of M. Pop. (1977) 7,819,000.

MOSELEY (mōz'li), **Henry Gwyn-Jeffreys** (1887-1915). British physicist. He did valuable work on atomic

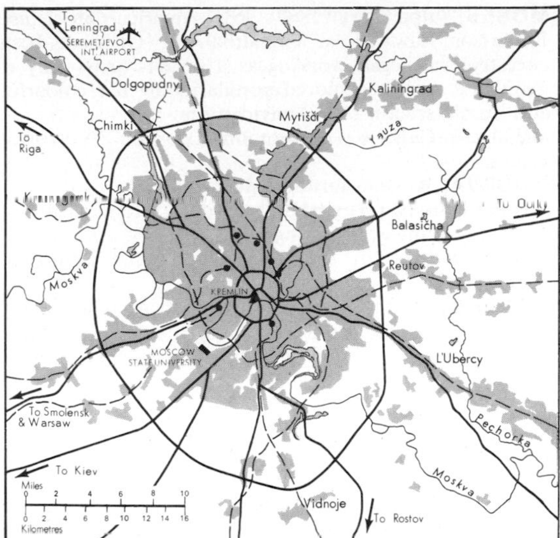

MOSCOW

MOSCOW. A view over the city with the Cosmonauts' Monument soaring skyward to the left: at night the interior is illuminated. *Photo: Novosti*

structure, and in 1913 devised the series of atomic numbers. He was killed in action at Gallipoli.

MOSELLE (mōzel'). River, 515km (320m) long, which rises in the Vosges, France, and is canalized from Thionville to its confluence with the Rhine at Koblenz. It gives its name to the depts of M. and Meurthe-et-moselle.

MOSES (14th cent. BC?). Jewish lawgiver and judge who led the Israelites out of Egypt to the promised land of Canaan. According to the OT, M. was hidden among the bulrushes on the banks of the Nile when the Pharoah commanded that all new-born male Hebrew children should be destroyed. He was found by a dau. of Pharoah, who reared him. Eventually he became the leader of the Israelites in the Exodus, and the 40 years' wandering in the wilderness. On Mt Sinai he received from Jehovah the Ten Commandments engraved on tablets of stone, and died at the age of 120, after having been allowed a glimpse of the Promised Land from Mount Pisgah.

MOSES, Anna Mary (1860-1961). American artist, *née* Robertson, known as 'Grandma' M. Of Scots-Irish ancestry, she began working as a serious artist only *c.* 1927, and rapidly achieved popularity by her colourful and simple scenes from American life.

MOSI-OA-TUNYA (mosiotōōn'ya). *See* VICTORIA FALLS.

MOSKVA. Russian form of Moscow.

MOSLEM BROTHERHOOD. Group of fundamentalist Islamic extremists, operating throughout the Arab world, and specialising in assassination, e.g. the killing of supporters of Pres. Assad of Syria.

MOSLEMS. Adherents of Islam (q.v.). An unorthodox variant of the creed is held by Negro extremists of the USA, the *Black Muslims* or *Nation of Islam,* whose aims are segregation from white America in one or two separate and sovereign Negro states. Christianity is rejected as merely a means of continuing Negro subjection. The movement was founded by Wallace D. Fard, a pedlar who claimed to come from Mecca, and led from 1934 by the Hon. Elijah Muhammad (1897-1975), having its HQ in Chicago. Its growth from 1946 was due to Malcolm X (1926-65), *née* Little, son of a Baptist minister, who was converted while serving 7 yrs imprisonment for larceny and reformed: *Autobiography* ed. Alex Haley 1965. In 1964 he broke away and founded his own Organization of Afro-American Unity, preaching 'Active self-defence', but was shot: 3 Negroes, 2 being B.M., convicted 1966. Elijah Muhammad (*né* Poole) was succeeded by his son, Wallace Muhammad (1933-).

MOSLEMS. The most charismatic of the Black Muslims - Malcolm X - a portrait taken during a visit to Oxford. *Photo: Keystone*

MOSLEY (mōz'li), **Sir Oswald Ernald** (1896-1980). Brit. Fascist. In parl. as a Unionist 1918-22, Independent 1922-4, and Lab. member 1924 and 1926-31, he then founded the British Union of Fascists. Interned during the S.W.W., he was released on health grounds in 1943, and resumed Fascist propaganda with his Union Movement. He m. in 1920 Lady Cynthia, dau. of Lord Curzon (d. 1933), and in 1936 Diana Freeman-Mitford. *See* FASCISM and MITFORD SISTERS.

MOSQUE (mosk; Arabic *mesjid,* temple). Mohammedan place of worship. The earliest Ms. were based on the Christian basilican plan, but many different influences contributed towards their architectural development. Ms. vary a great deal in style in different parts of the world. Chief features are: the dome, the minaret, from which the faithful are called to prayer, the mihrab, or prayer niche, in one of the interior walls, showing the direction of Mecca, and an open court surrounded by porticos.

MOSQUITO. Word of Spanish derivation often used in referring to species of gnat (q.v.).

MOSSA'DEQ, Mohammed (1880-1967). Persian PM 1951-3. He prosecuted the oil dispute with the Anglo-Iranian Oil Co., and when he failed in his attempt to overthrow the Shah was imprisoned: from 1956 he under house arrest. *See* ABADAN.

MOSSES. Class of small non-flowering plants (Musci) forming with the liverworts (q.v.) the lower order Bryophyta. M. are found throughout the world, especially where other vegetation is thin, and each plant comprises a rhizoid and a stem, with leaves on its lower portion and producing sexual organs at its tip. The peat or bog moss (*Sphagnum*) was formerly used for surgical dressings. Moss gardens are popular in Japan, the most famous being at the Moss Temple, nr Kyoto.

MOSTAGANEM (mōstahgahnem'). Port in Algeria, on the Gulf of Arzew, in a vine-growing area. Founded in the 11th cent., it has metal and cement works, and is linked by pipeline with the natural gas fields at Hassi Messaoud. Pop. (1974) 101,700.

MOSTA'R. Town of Bosnia-Hercegovina, Yugoslavia, 80km (50m) SW of Sarajevo, famous for its grapes and wines. On the site of a Roman fortress, M. is on a brown coalfield and produces aluminium and tobacco. Pop. (1971) 89,400.

MOSUL (mōs'ool). City in Iraq, on the right bank of the Tigris, opposite the site of ancient Nineveh, 355km (220m) NW of Baghdad. Once famous for muslin (q.v.), it is the centre of an oilfield. Pop. (1975) 857,000.

MOTEL. Type of hotel first developed (1928) in the USA by A. Heinemann which provides especially for the touring motorist. Accommodation consists of individual self-contained sleeping quarters with bath, toilet facilities and garage. Meals are generally obtainable at a central restaurant.

MOTHER OF PEARL. *See* PEARL.

MOTHERWELL & WISHAW. Town in Strathclyde, Scotland, SE of Glasgow, with iron and steel works and coal mines. The 2 burghs were amalgamated in 1920. Pop. (1973) 72,991.

MOTHS. Insects forming the greater part of the order Lepidoptera. Normally distinguished from butterflies (q.v.) by the absence of a knob on the end of the antennae. When at rest, Ms. commonly hold their wings flat or sloping over the body; butterflies close them vertically. The wings are covered with flat, microscopic scales, but in the bee hawk-Ms. and the clearwings the scales are confined to certain areas. The mouth-parts are formed into a sucking proboscis, and certain Ms. have no functional mouth-parts, and, being unable to feed, rely upon stores of fat and other reserves built up during the caterpillar stage. In many cases the males are smaller and more brightly

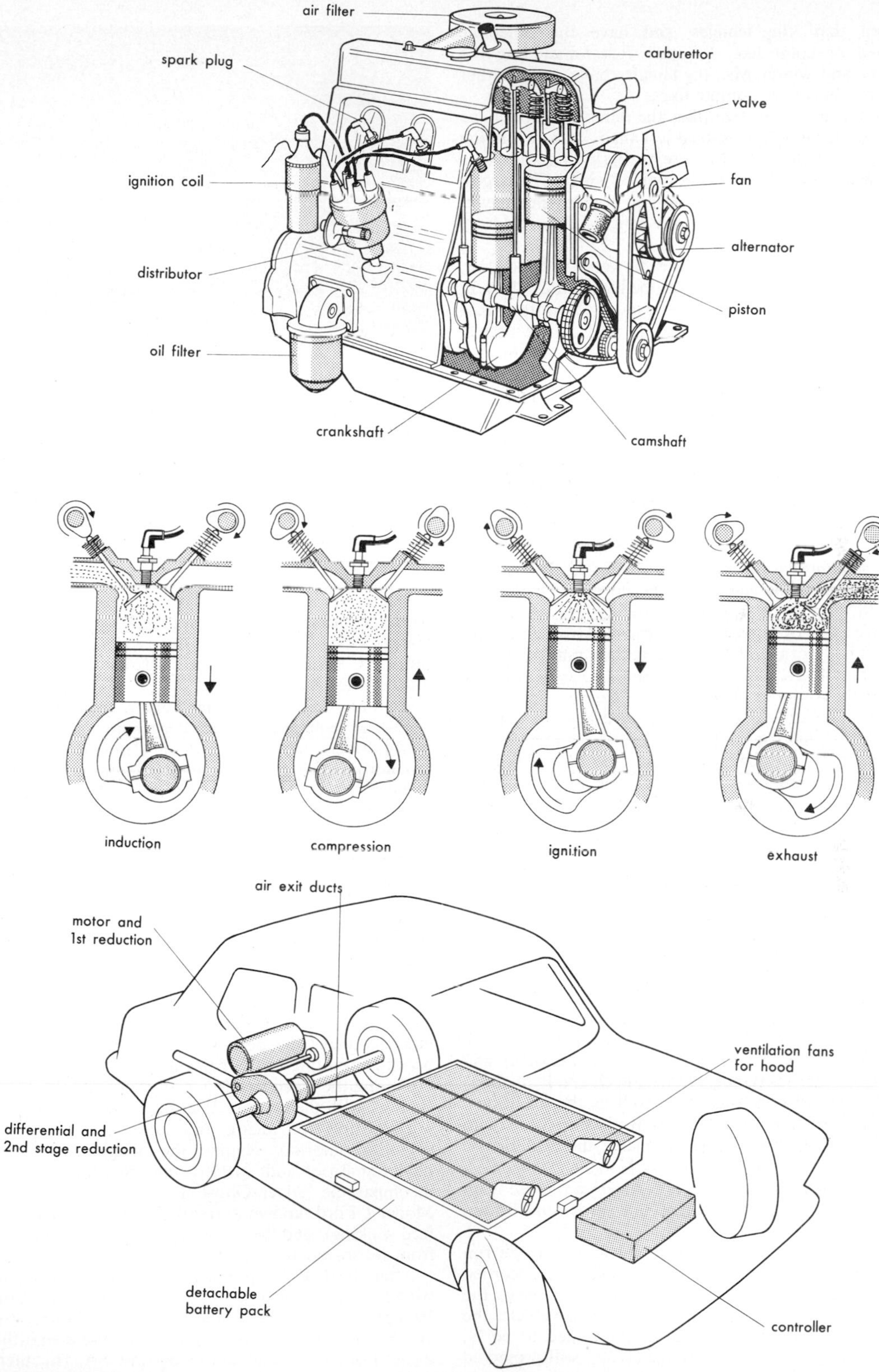

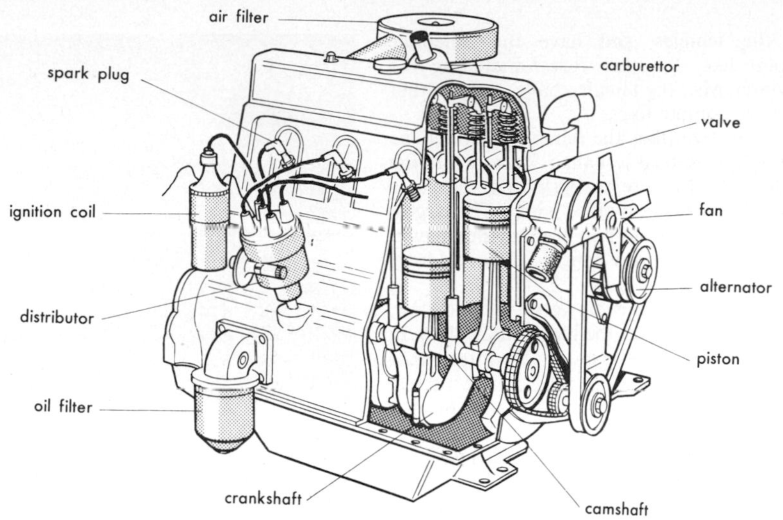

air filter
spark plug
carburettor
valve
ignition coil
fan
alternator
distributor
piston
oil filter
crankshaft
camshaft
induction
compression
ignition
exhaust
air exit ducts
motor and
1st reduction
ventilation fans
for hood
differential and
2nd stage reduction
detachable
battery pack
controller

MOTOR CAR. The main features and working of the internal-combustion engine, and (below) the lay-out of an electric car.

coloured than the females, and have the antennae branched or comb-like. In other cases, including the vapourer and winter Ms., the females have wings either absent or aborted to minute flaps.

Ms. vary greatly in size: thus the minute Nepticulidae sometimes have a wing-spread less than 3mm, while the giant Noctuid or owlet M., *Erebus agrippina*, measures about 280mm (11in) across its extended wings. The largest British Ms. are the death's head and convolvulus hawk-Ms., which have a wing-spread ranging from 114mm (4.5in) to 133mm (5.25in).

Ms. feed chiefly on the nectar of flowers, on honeydew, and other fluid matter: some, like the hawk-Ms., Silver Y, and its relatives, frequent flowers and feed while poised with rapidly vibrating wings.

The larvae or caterpillars have a well-developed head, 3 thoracic and 10 abdominal segments. Each thoracic segment bears a pair of short legs, ending in single claws; a pair of sucker-like abdominal feet is present on segments 3 to 6 and 10 of the hind-body. In the family Geometridae the caterpillars bear the abdominal feet only on segments 6 and 10 of the hind-body. They move by a characteristic looping gait and are known as 'loopers' or geometers. Projecting from the middle of the lower lip of a caterpillar is a minute tube or spinneret, through which silk is emitted to make a cocoon within which the change to the pupa or chrysalis occurs. Silk glands are especially large in the silkworm M. Many caterpillars, including the geometers, which are eaten by birds, etc., are protected by their resemblance in both form and coloration to their immediate surroundings. Others, which are distasteful to such enemies, are brightly coloured or are densely hairy.

Ms. are economically important, owing to the damage caused by the feeding caterpillars, e.g. the winter M. and the codling M., which attack fruit trees; the Mediterranean flour moth, which infects flour mills; and the several species of clothes Ms. At least 100,000 different species of Ms. are known. *See illus. under* LEPIDOPTERA.

MOTOR, Electric. A machine by which electrical energy is converted into mechanical power, which it supplies directly through motor-shaft, gearing, belt-drive, or other form of coupling. The 2 main types are direct-current and alternating-current Ms.

MOTOR BOAT. Small, water-borne craft powered by an internal combustion engine, either of the piston-petrol, compression-ignition oil, or gas-turbine type. Any boat not specially equipped as a M.B. may be converted by a detachable outboard motor. For increased speed, espec. in racing, M.B. hulls are designed to skim the water and reduce frictional resistance. Plastics, steel, and light alloys are now used in construction as well as the traditional wood. In recent designs, drag is further reduced with hydrofins and hydrofoils, which enable the hull to rise clear of the water, at normal speeds. Notable events in M. or 'power-boat' racing incl. the American Gold Cup (1947) over a 145km (90m) course, and the Round-Britain race (1969). *See also* JETFOIL.

MOTOR CAR. A self-propelled vehicle able to be run and be steered on normal roads. Although it is recorded that in 1479 one Gilles de Dom was paid 25 livres by the treasurer of Antwerp, for supplying such a vehicle, the 'father of the automobile' is generally agreed to be N. Cugnot's cumbrous steam carriage (1769), still preserved in Paris.

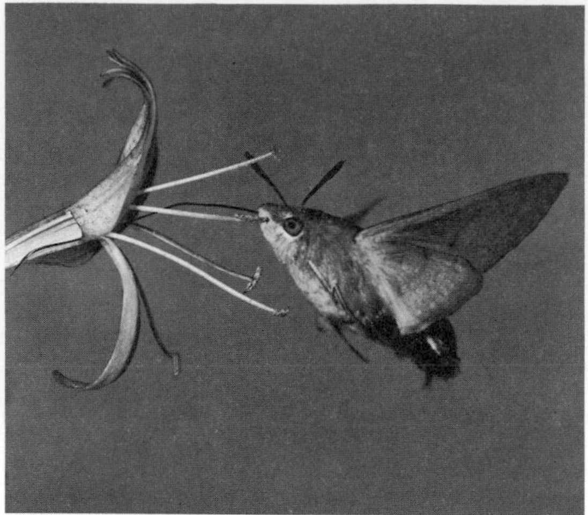

MOTHS. The presence of the humming-bird hawkmoth (*Macroglossa stellatarum*) in the south of England often leads to reports of an influx of humming-birds. The flower has here been cut away, so that the insect's long tongue can be seen. *Photo: NHPA.*

Steam was an attractive form of power to the English pioneers, and in the 19th cent. practical steam coaches by Hancock and Goldsworthy Gurney were used for public transport, until stifled out of existence by punitive road tolls and legislation.

Another Parisian, Étienne Lenoir, made the first gas engine in 1860, and in 1885 Benz built and ran the first petrol-driven motor car; and Panhard 1890 (front radiator, engine under bonnet, sliding-pinion gearbox, wooden ladder-chassis) and Mercédès 1901 (honeycomb radiator, in-line 4-cylinder engine, gate-change gearbox, pressed-steel chassis) set the pattern for the modern car. Emerging with Haynes and Duryea in the early 1890s, US demand was so fervent that 300 makers existed by 1895: many so ephemeral that there were 109 left in 1900.

Meanwhile in England cars were still considered to be light locomotives in the eyes of the law, and theoretically required a man to walk in front with a red flag. Despite this and other iniquities, which put UK development another 10 years behind all others, F. W. Lanchester in 1896 produced an advanced and reliable vehicle, later much copied. The period 1905-6 inaugurated a world boom continuing to the present.

Among the legendary M.Cs. of this cent. are: De Dion Bouton, with the first practical high-speed engines; Mors, notable first for racing and later as a silent tourer (silentium mortis); Napier, the doughty 24 hr-record holder at Brooklands in 1907, unbeaten for 17 years; the incomparable 'Silver Ghost' Rolls-Royce; the enduring Model T Ford (known to rivals as the car which popularized walking); and the many types of Bugatti and Delage, from record-breakers to luxury tourers.

After the F.W.W. popular motoring was inaugurated with the era of cheap light (baby) cars made by Citroën, Peugeot and Renault (France); Austin 7, Morris, Clyno, and Swift (England); Fiat (Italy), and the cheap though bigger Ford, Chevrolet and Dodge in USA. The inter-war years saw a great deal of racing, and experience thus

MOTOR CAR. On the left, the Benz 1888, one of the first production cars, and on the right the original Austin Seven, dating from 1909. *Photos: Crown Copyright*

gained was of benefit to the everyday motorist in improved efficiency, reliability and safety; and also saw the divergence between the lighter, economical European car, with good handling; and the heavier American car, cheap and rugged, well adapted to long distances at speed.

One typical modern European design would have a semi-monocoque construction in which the body panels, suitably reinforced, support the road loads through independent front and rear springing systems, with seats located within the wheelbase for comfort. A vertical 4-cylinder engine is supplied with a suitable petrol-air mixture by the carburettor and cooled by water circulating through the engine block to a front-mounted radiator. From the rear of the engine power is transmitted through a clutch (which disconnects the engine from the rear wheels) to a 4-speed gearbox (which enables optimum engine speed to be maintained for varying road speeds) through a drive shaft to the differential gear, and thence to drive the rear wheels.

After the S.W.W. small European cars tended to be of 3 varieties - front engine and rear drive, front engine and drive, rear engine and drive - in about equal numbers. From the 1950s a creative resurgence produced in practical form automatic transmission for small cars, rubber suspension, and transverse engine mounting, self-levelling ride, disc brakes and safer wet-weather tyres. The drive against pollution from the 1960s and the fuel crisis from the 1970s led to experiments with steam cars (cumbersome), diesel engines (slow and heavy, though economical in city traffic, and producing noise and chemical pollution), and, a more promising development, the hybrid car using both electricity and petrol. Of more immediate application was the stratified charge petrol engine, using a fuel injector to achieve 20% improvement in mileage; weight reduction in the body by the use of aluminium and plastic, and of Perspex rather than glass for windows. Microprocessors were also developed to measure temperature, engine speed, pressure and oxygen content of exhaust gases, and readjust parts of the engine accordingly. *See* INTERNAL COMBUSTION ENGINE and HOVERCRAFT.

MOTOR CYCLE. A bicycle propelled by an internal combustion engine, usually single cylinder and air-cooled, which is noisy but lightweight and capable of high power and speed. M.Cs. are traditionally chain-driven, but there is now a tendency to employ shaft drive with a sprung rear wheel, and to improve comfort by employing two or more cylinders, and screens for the driver and saloon-type passenger sidecars. More recent developments are the powered cycle (less powerful and fast), and the motor scooters.

Most famous of the M.C. races is the Isle of Man Tourist Trophy (TT) race estab. 1907, but other popular types of event are reliability trials and scrambling or roughriding, and scooter rallies.

MOTORING. Between the 2 wars M. developed into a universal pursuit, whether for business or pleasure. The Min. of Transport was estab., roads were improved, and various laws and safety precautions imposed to govern the use of cars. A driver must possess a licence, and his vehicle be registered with the local licensing authority, displaying the number assigned to it. In 1953 a flat-rate duty was imposed, which affected engine and car design, and inadequately powered cars persist in Britain for economic reasons. The law also insists on insurance for third-party risks. Motorists are organized in the Automobile Association (AA), and the Royal Automobile Club (RAC).

MOTOR RACING. Competitive events, beginning with a timed trial from Paris to Rouen in 1894, enjoy great popularity for spectator excitement and for manufacturer's and driver's prestige. Great road races have incl. the mountainous Targa Florio (Sicily), and Mille Miglia (Italy). The 24-hr of Le Mans (1923) is the foremost proving ground for production cars. Famous circuits incl. Brands Hatch, Brooklands (to 1939) and Silverstone, UK; Montlhéry, France; Nurburgring, Germany; and Indianapolis, USA. In Grand Prix M.R. (1906) individual events in numerous different countries, notably the Monaco Grand Prix, count towards the world championship. For the driver of the production car, M. rallies, often time-checked across a continent, are popular, the toughest being the E African Safari (1953) run every Easter.

MOTOR SPEED RECORD. *See* SPEED RECORDS.

MOTT, Sir Nevill (1905-). British physicist. Noted for his research on the electronic properties of glass, and its use in computer materials, he shared a Nobel prize in 1977.

MOULINS (mo͞olaṅ'). Cap. of the dept of Allier, France; 145km (90m) NW of Lyons. It makes cutlery, textiles, glass, etc. M. was cap. of the old prov. of Bourbonnais 1368-1527. Pop. (1975) 26,900.

MOULMEIN (mowlmīn′). Port in Lower Burma, on the Salween estuary, which exports teak and rice. Pop. (1972) 833,655.

MOUNTAIN ASH or **rowan.** Flowering tree (*Sorbus aucuparia*) of the family Rosaceae. Growing to *c.* 9m (30ft), it has pinnate leaves and large cymes of whitish flowers, followed by scarlet berries.

MOUNTBATTEN of Burma, Louis Mountbatten. 1st earl (1900-79). British Admiral of the Fleet. Son of Princess Victoria, a granddau. of Queen Victoria, and Prince Louis of Battenberg, marquess of Milford Haven (q.v.), Lord Louis entered the navy in 1913 and was present at the Battle of Jutland. In the S.W.W. in the battle of Crete, HMS *Kelly* was sunk under him, and he was picked up from the sea. He became Chief of Combined Operations in 1942, being criticised over the Dieppe raid, and in 1943 became C-in-C in SE Asia, receiving the surrender of the Japanese S armies at Singapore in Sept. 1945. As last Viceroy of India 1947, he became first Gov.-Gen. of the Dominion of India, on the granting of independence, until 1948. He was First Sea Lord 1955-9, and Chief of the UK Defence Staff 1959-65. He was created an earl in 1947, and received the OM in 1965. He was killed by an IRA bomb aboard his yacht at Mullaghmore, co. Sligo.

MOUNT EREBUS. *See* EREBUS.

MOUNT ISA (īz′a). Town in W Queensland, Australia. Copper, lead, silver and zinc are mined. Pop. (1976) 25,377.

MOUNT ISA. Australia is one of the world's great copper producers, and seventy per cent of her ore is mined in Queensland, chiefly here at Mount Isa, where silver, lead and zinc are also found. *Photo: Courtesy of the Australian Information Service*

MOUNT LOFTY RANGE. Mtn range in SE South Australia. Mt Bryan 934m (3,064ft) is the highest peak.

MOUNT RUSHMORE. Mtn in the Black Hills, S Dakota, USA. It is 1890m (3,064ft) high, and on its granite face are carved giant portrait heads of Washington, Jefferson, Lincoln and Theodore Roosevelt. The sculptor was Gutzon Borglum (q.v.).

MOUNT ST HELENS. Volcanic mtn NE of Portland, Oregon, USA, which erupted in 1980 after being quiescent for 450 years. Its height was reduced from 2,945m (9,667 ft) to 2,560m (8,400 ft).

MOUNT VERNON. Village in Virginia, USA, on the Potomac, 26km (16m) S of Washington, DC. George Washington lived 1752-99 and was buried on the family estate here, now a nat. monument.

MOUSE. Small rodent of the Muridae family. The house M. (*Mus musculus*) is universally distributed; 75mm (3in) long, with naked tail of equal length, with grey-brown body, it nests in paper and straw. Commonly found in Britain are the long-tailed field M. (*Apodemus sylvaticus*), richer in colour, and the harvest M. (*Micromys minutus*), 65-75mm (2.5-3in) long.

MOUTH. The cavity enclosed by the jaws, cheeks and palate. It is the outer end of the digestive and the respiratory tracts, and in addition to its part in masticating food, and in breathing, has a highly specialized mechanism for producing significant sounds. It is also largely responsible for facial expression, and plays a part in sexual activity. At the back of the M. is a passage (isthmus of the fauces) bounded on each side by 2 folds called the pillars of the fauces; between each pair of folds is one of the tonsils.

MOUTH ORGAN. *See* HARMONICA.

MOZAMBIQUE (mōzambēk′). Country of southern Africa. A wide coastal plain rises to highlands of up to 2,450m (8,000 ft) in the N, and is cut across by the Zambezi and Limpopo rivers: the area is rich in wild life. Sugar, cotton, copra, cashews, and tea are exported, and minerals incl. coal, bauxite and beryl. Power from the Cabora Bassa dam on the Zambezi NW of Tete has stimulated industrial development. The cap. is Maputo (formerly Lourenço Marques), Beira is also an important port.

The indigenous peoples are of the Bantu tribes, but by the 10th cent. Arabs had estab. themselves on the coast. After the discovery of M. by Vasco da Gama in 1498 Portuguese displaced Arab influence, the first colonization being begun in 1505. From 1964 a nationalist organization *Frente de Libertação de Moçambique* (Frelimo) waged a guerrilla campaign, and in 1975 M. became independent of Portugal with the Frelimo leader Samora Machel as the first pres. of the People's Rep. of M. There was an exodus of Portuguese settlers, reduced from 250,000 to *c.* 50,000. The legislative body is the People's Assembly, but as in other Communist regimes the Party rules, and a system of collectivized agriculture, etc., has been introduced. The regime has become increasingly pragmatic owing to its need for western aid. In 1986 Samora Machel was killed in a plane crash.

Area 784,960 sq.km (303,070 sq.m); pop. (1978) 11,000,000. M.U.: metical.

MOZART (mō′tsahrt), **Wolfgang Amadeus** (1756-91). Austrian composer. B. at Salzburg, he showed astonishing precocity, and was trained by his father, Leopold M., who was also a professional musician and composer. With his sister, Maria Anna, he was taken on a number of tours (1762-79) in the course of which they visited Vienna, the Rhineland, Holland, Paris, London, and Italy. Young M. not only gave public recitals, but had already begun to compose a considerable amount of music. In 1770 he was appointed master of the archbishop of Salzburg's court band. He found the post uncongenial, as he was treated as a mere servant, and in 1781 he was suddenly dismissed. From then on he lived mostly in Vienna, and m. Constanze Weber in 1782. He supported himself as a pianist, composer, and teacher, but his lack of business acumen often rendered his existence a hard struggle. He composed prolifically, his works including 25 piano concertos, 25 string quartets, 40 violin sonatas; approx. 50 symphonies, of which the most important are the E flat, G minor, and C major ('Jupiter') symphonies, all composed in 1787; a number of operas, including *Idomeneo* (1781), *Il Seraglio* (1782), *The Marriage of Figaro* (1786), *Don Giovanni* (1787), *Cosí fan tutte* (1790), and *The Magic Flute* (1791), and much other music. His Requiem was left unfinished at his death, and subsequently completed by a pupil. The composer had been in failing health, and regarded its commission (made by an eccentric nobleman in mysterious circumstances) as an evil omen.

MOZART. Tea *à l'anglaise* at the court of the Prince de Conti in the 18th century. The tiny pianist in this painting by Michel Barthélemy in the Louvre is the young Mozart. *Photo: Courtesy of the National Museums of France*

MUBARAK, Hosni (1928-). Egyptian statesman. Commander of the Air Force 1972-5, he was then vice-pres to Sadat, whom he succeeded in 1981.

MUCOUS (mū'kus) **MEMBRANE.** A thin skin containing cells which secrete mucus, a moistening and lubricating fluid. It is found on all internal surfaces of the body, such as the eyelids, breathing and digestive passages, and genital tract.

MUDFISH. N American fish (*Amia calva*) having a highly developed air-sac, enabling it to live out of water for some time. The name is also applied to the lung-fish of the order Dipnoi.

MUDNESTERS. Australian name for a group of birds making their nests from mud, and incl. the apostle bird (*Struthidea cinerea*) so-called from its appearance in little flocks of about 12; the white-winged chough (*Corcorax melanorhamphus*) and the mudlark (*Grallina cyanoleuca*).

MUEZZIN (mōō-ez'in). Moslem official who calls the faithful to prayer from the minaret, etc., of a mosque.

MU'FTI. Moslem official who expounds Islamic law. In Turkey the *Grand M.* had supreme spiritual authority until the estab. of the rep. in 1924. The *M. of Jerusalem,* Haj Amin el-Husseini, elected M. in 1921, assisted the Nazis in subversive activities in the Middle East during the S.W.W., and subsequently directed anti-Zionist activities. Sought as a war criminal, he fled the country.

MUGABE (moogah'bā), **Robert Gabriel** (1925-). Zimbabwian statesman. B. in Zwimba tribal trust land, NE of Salisbury, he is a Shona, and was mission-educated before going to Fort Hare Univ., S Africa. In detention in Rhodesia for nationalist activities 1964-74, he was subsequently based in Mozambique, carrying on guerrilla warfare against Rhodesia. As leader of ZANU (Zimbabwe African Nat. Union), he became PM of independent Zimbabwe in 1980. In 1982 he dismissed his former ally Joshua Nkomo from the govt.

MUGABE. Robert Mugabe, Zimbabwe in his hands, prepares to form the first independent government after his landslide victory in the elections of 1980. *Photo: Keystone.*

MUGGERIDGE, Malcolm (1903-). British journalist. He worked for the *Guardian* and *Daily Telegraph,* ed. *Punch* 1953-7, and in retirement developed a growing interest in religion, becoming RC in 1982. *Chronicles of Wasted Time* (1972–3) is an autobiography.

MU'GWUMP. In US political history Republicans who voted for Cleveland, the Democratic candidate, rather than their own, hence 'non-party or neutral'. From Algonquian Indian 'chief'.

MUJIBUR (moojēb'oor), **Rahman,** Sheikh (1921-75). Bangladeshi statesman. Several times arrested for supporting autonomy for E Pakistan, he won the elections of 1970 as leader of the Awami League (pro-Russian Communist party), but was again arrested when negotiations broke down. After the Civil War of 1971, he became PM of newly independent Bangladesh, but the country declined towards famine and anarchy, and he was presidential dictator Jan.-Aug. 1975, when he was assassinated.

MUKDEN. Former and historical name of SHENYANG.

MULATTO (mūlat'ō). The offspring of parents, one of whom is a European and the other a Negro. *Mestizos* are of mixed European and South American Indian parentage.

MULBERRY. Genus of trees (*Morus*) of the family Moraceae, with a dozen species of which the best-known is black M. (*M. nigra*). Native to Iran, it was introduced into Britain in the 16th cent. It has heart-shaped toothed leaves, and spikes of whitish flowers. The fruit resembles a raspberry in appearance, but is a cluster of small berries. The leaves of the white M. (*M. alba*) are those chiefly used in feeding silkworms.

MULDOON, Sir Robert (1921–). NZ statesman. Minister of Finance 1967–72, he replaced John Marshall as leader of the National Party in 1974, and became PM in 1975, being re-elected with a reduced majority in 1978 and 1981. He was created GCMG in 1984.

MULE. Hybrid animal of the horse family, usually the offspring of a male ass and a mare.

MÜLHAUSEN. German form of MULHOUSE.

MÜLHEIM (mül'hīm). River port on the Ruhr, W Germany, N of Düsseldorf. It has metallurgical and electrical industries. Pop. (1978) 185,900.

MULHOUSE (mül'ooz). Town in Haut-Rhin dept, France, SW of Strasbourg, with textile, electrical and engineering industries. Pop. (1975) 116,500.

MULL. Second-largest is. of the Inner Hebrides, Strathclyde, Scotland. It is separated by the Sound of Mull from the mainland. There is only one town, Tobermory. Area 950 sq.km (367 sq.m).

MU'LLAH. Name given to a judge of the Islamic sacred law; also a title of respect given to various other dignitaries who perform duties connected with the sacred law.

MULLEIN (mul'len). Plant (*Verbascum thapsus*) of the family Scrophulariaceae. It produces lance-shaped leaves a foot or more in length, and in the second year of growth a large spike of yellow flowers. Common in Britain, and found through Europe and Asia, it is naturalized in N America.

MULLER, Hermann (1890-1967). American geneticist. In 1927 he discovered that X-rays produced mutations in the genes and chromosomes of fruitflies. He received a Nobel prize in 1946.

MÜ'LLER, Paul (1899-1965). Swiss chemist. He was awarded a Nobel prize in 1948 for his discovery of the first synthetic contact insecticide DDT (q.v.) in 1939.

MU'LLET. Two genera of food fishes found in river estuaries. The red M. (*Mullus*) contains about 40 species, is red with yellow stripes, and *c.* 40cm (15in) long. The grey M. (*Mugil*) includes about 70 species, which are found in temperate and tropical coastal regions. It is greenish above and grey below.

MULLIKEN, Robert Sanderson (1896-). American chemist and physicist. Professor at Chicago 1931-61, he received a Nobel chemistry prize 1966 for his development of the molecular orbital theory.

MULLINGA'R. Co. tn of Westmeath, Rep. of Ireland. It is an agricultural and trout-fishing centre. Pop. (1971) 6,800.

MULOCK. *See* CRAIK, Dinah.

MULREADY (mul'redi), **William** (1786-1863). Irish artist. B. in co. Clare, he painted genre pictures, e.g. 'Fair Time' and 'Roadside Inn', and illustrated books. In 1840 he designed the first penny-postage envelope, known as the 'Mulready envelope'.

MULRONEY, Brian 1939– . Canadian Progressive Conservative Party leader from 1983. Bilingual and a former labour lawyer, he replaced the more moderate Joe Clark. A former pres. of the Iron Ore Co. of Canada, he was the first PCP leader this century of Quebec origin.

MULTAN (mooltahn'). City in Pakistan, on a site inhabited since the time of Alexander the Great, 205km (190m) SW of Lahore. Textiles, precision instruments, chemicals, pottery and jewellery are made. Pop. (1972) 544,000.

MULTIPLE SCLEROSIS (sklerō'sis). Chronic disease of the central nervous system in which the white fatty substance of the sheath of certain nerve fibres turns to hard scar tissue. It is usually progressive, the consequences incl. weakness of the muscles, tremors, paralysis, and defective sight, speech and sensation. There may be no specific causative virus, but the disease may arise when antibodies to other viruses enter the brain.

MUMFORD, Lewis (1895-). American sociologist. B. on Long Is., he ed. the *Dial* 1919, and studied architecture both in England and the USA, having an especial concern with skylines. His books incl. *Technics and Civilisation* (1934), *The Culture of Cities* (1938), and *Interpretations and Forecasts* (1973).

MUMMY. Human or animal body preserved after death, either naturally or artificially, e.g. mammoths preserved in glacial ice from 25,000 years ago; shrunken heads preserved by the Jivaro tribe in S America; the Ms. of ancient Egypt; and the modern Ms. such as Lenin and Eva Perón.

MUMPS. An acute, highly infectious fever marked by painful inflammation and swelling of one or both of the glands situated in front of the ear (parotid). The cause is probably a virus. It is commonest in young children. Incubation is about 18 days, and isolation should last at least 3 weeks.

MUNCH (moonk), **Edvard** (1863-1944). Norwegian artist. The son of a physician, he studied in Paris, and achieved in his portraits and landscapes the expression of the spirit of the northern peoples.

MÜNCHEN. German form of MUNICH.

MUNCHHAUSEN (munkh'howzen), **Baron** (1720-97). German soldier. B. in Hanover, he had served with the Russian Army against the Turks, and after his retirement in 1760 told exaggerated stories of his campaigning adventures. This idiosyncrasy was utilized by the German writer, Rudolph Erich Raspe (1737-94), in his extravagantly fictitious account of the *Adventures of Baron M.* (1785), compiled while he was taking refuge in London from a charge of theft in his own country. The book was very popular, and was frequently enlarged by other hands.

MUNCHHAUSEN'S SYNDROME. The production of fraudulent medical symptoms by mentally disturbed, but apparently normal, patients, to secure hospital treatment, incl. operations, etc.

MUNICH (mü'nik). Cap. of Bavaria (*München*), W Germany, on the Isar. It is famous for its magnificent buildings and art treasures, many of which it owes to the kings Ludwig I and Maximilian II of Bavaria. The cathedral is late 15th cent. The Old Pinakothek contains paintings by old masters, the New Pinakothek, modern paintings; there is a Bavarian National Museum, the Bavarian State Library, and the *Deutsches Museum* of science and technology. It has a univ. (transferred to M. in 1826), and several other learned institutions. The principal industries incl. brewing and printing and the manufacture of precision instruments, machinery, locomotives, and textiles. M. is also an important railway centre and has an international airport. Developed in 1158, M. became the residence of the dukes of Wittelsbach in the 13th cent. M. was the scene of the Nov. revolution of 1918, the 'Soviet' rep. of 1919, and the Hitler putsch of 1923. It became the centre of the Nazi movement, and the Munich Agreement of 1938 was signed here. Pop. (1978) 1,314,000.

MUNICH AGREEMENT. The agreement between Britain, France, Germany, and Italy, signed by Chamberlain, Daladier, Hitler, and Mussolini, at Munich on 29 Sept. 1938, whereby the Sudeten-German dists. of Czechoslovakia were ceded under duress by that country to Germany without a plebiscite. Although the signatories all guaranteed the new Czechoslovak frontiers, Hitler seized the rest of the country in March 1939.

MU'NNINGS, Sir Alfred (1878–1959). British sporting artist. B. at Mendham, Suffolk, he was outspoken in his dislike of 'modern art', and excelled in racing and hunting scenes.

MUNRŌ', Hugh Hector. *See* SAKI.

MUNSTER. Prov. of Rep. of Ireland, containing the cos. of Clare, Cork, Kerry, Limerick, Tipperary, and Waterford; a kingdom until the 12th cent. Area 24,128 sq.km (9,316 sq.m); pop. (1971) 374,600.

MÜNSTER. Town of N Rhine-Westphalia, Germany, on the Dortmund-Ems Canal; formerly the cap. of Westphalia. The Treaty of Westphalia was signed simultaneously here and at Osnabrück in 1648. Seat of a univ. (1773) M. makes wire, cement, and iron goods and has breweries and distilleries. Damaged in the S.W.W., its ancient buildings, incl. the 15th cent. cathedral and town hall, have been restored. Pop. (1978) 267,200.

MUNTERNIA. Rumanian name of WALLACHIA.

MUNTJAC (-jak). Small deer (*Muntiacus*) found in SE Asia. The buck has short spiked antlers, and two sharp canine teeth forming tusks.

MŪ'RAL PAINTING. (Lat. *murus*, wall). The decoration of walls, and, by extension, of vaults and ceilings, by means of fresco, oil, or encaustic methods. *See* ENCAUSTIC; FRESCO; and TEMPERA.

MURASAKI SHIKIBU (moorahsah'kē shik'iboo) (978–*c.* 1015). Japanese author, whose real name is unknown. Her greatest work is the *Tale of Genji*, the earliest realistic Japanese novel, and a world masterpiece.

MURAT (mürah'), **Joachim** (1767–1815). King of Naples. The son of an innkeeper, he rose rapidly in the French Army through the friendship of Napoleon, and won the reputation of a dashing cavalry commander. He was made king of Naples by Napoleon in 1808, but deserted him in 1813 in the hope that the Allies would recognize him. In 1815 he attempted unsuccessfully to make himself king of all Italy, and when he landed in Calabria in an attempt to recover the throne he was captured and shot.

MURCIA (moor'thē-ah). Cap. of the Spanish prov. of M. on the Segura, 45km (28m) NW of Cartagena. The seat of a univ., M. was founded in 825 on the site of a Roman colony by Abd-ur-Rahman II, caliph of Cordoba; it has a 14th cent. cathedral; silks, metals and glass are manufactured. Pop. (1970) 243,760.

MURDER. The unlawful killing of one person by another, who is of sound mind, has reached years of discretion, and acts with malice aforethought, express or implied.

MURDOCH (mer'dok), **Iris** (1919–). British novelist. B. in Dublin, she specializes in the chessboard intricacies of the adventures of a number of unconventional-type lovers, conveyed in witty prose with a degree of fantasy. Her books incl. *Under the Net* (1954), *The Sandcastle* (1957), *A Severed Head* (1961: dramatized by Priestley in collaboration with M. in 1963), and *The Sea, The Sea* (1978). A student of philosophy, she became in 1948 fellow of St Anne's Coll., Oxford, and pub. in 1953 *Sartre, Romantic Rationalist.* She m. in 1956 J. O. Bayley.

MURDOCK, William (1754–1839). Scottish inventor. B. at Auchinleck, Ayrshire, in 1792 he first used coal-gas to illuminate his house and offices in Redruth, and in 1797 and 1798 he held public demonstrations of his invention.

MURGER (mürzhăr'), **Henri** (1822–61). French writer. B. in Paris, he studied painting, and in 1848 pub. *Scènes de la Vie de Bohème*, which formed the basis of Puccini's opera, *La Bohème*. He d. of overwork and dissipation.

MŪRI'LLŌ, Bartolomé Estéban (1617–82). Spanish painter. B. at Seville, in 1642 he went to Madrid, where he was befriended by Velasquez, then at the height of his fame. After his return to Seville in 1645 he received many important commissions, and founded the academy there (1660). One of the leading painters of the Spanish school, he is famed for his religious and genre pictures.

MURMANSK. Seaport of the Russian SFSR, on the Barents Sea. It is the only port on the Arctic coast of Russia which is ice-free at all times of the year. M. is cap. of M. region, which is coterminous with the Kola peninsula. It is linked with Leningrad by rail, and after the entry of Russia into the S.W.W. in 1941, supplies from Britain and later from the USA were unloaded at M. Pop. (1977) 374,000.

MURNAU (moor'now), **F. W.** Pseudonym of the German film director Friedrich Wilhelm Plumpe (1889–1931). His 'subjective' use of a moving camera to tell the story, through expressive images and without subtitles, in *The Last Laugh* (1924) made him famous.

MURRAIN. *See* FOOT AND MOUTH DISEASE.

MURRAY, Gilbert (1866–1957). British scholar. B. in Sydney, NSW, he was taken to England in 1877, and was prof. of Greek at Glasgow univ. 1889–99 and at Oxford 1908–36. Author of *History of Ancient Greek Literature* (1897), he became best known for his fine verse translations of the Greek dramatists, espec. Euripides. He was awarded the OM in 1941.

MURRAY, Sir James Augustus Henry (1837–1915). Scottish philologist. B. near Hawick, he was pres. of the Philological Society 1878–80 and 1882–4, and compiled and edited the *New English Dictionary*, the first vol. of which was pub. in 1884 at Oxford.

MURRAY, or **Moray, James Stuart,** earl of (*c.* 1531–70). Scottish statesman. An illegitimate son of James V, he was among the leaders of the Scottish Reformation, and after the deposition of his half-sister, Mary, in 1567, became regent. He was assassinated by a supporter of Mary.

MURRAY. Principal river of Australia. It rises in the Australian Alps near Mt Kosciusko, and flows W, forming the boundary between NSW and Victoria. It reaches the sea at Encounter Bay, and is 2,575 km (1,600 m) long. Its chief tributaries are the Darling and the Murrumbidgee (qq.v.). The Dartmouth Dam (1979) in the Great Dividing Range supplies hydroelectric power, and has 'drought-proofed' the Murray river system.

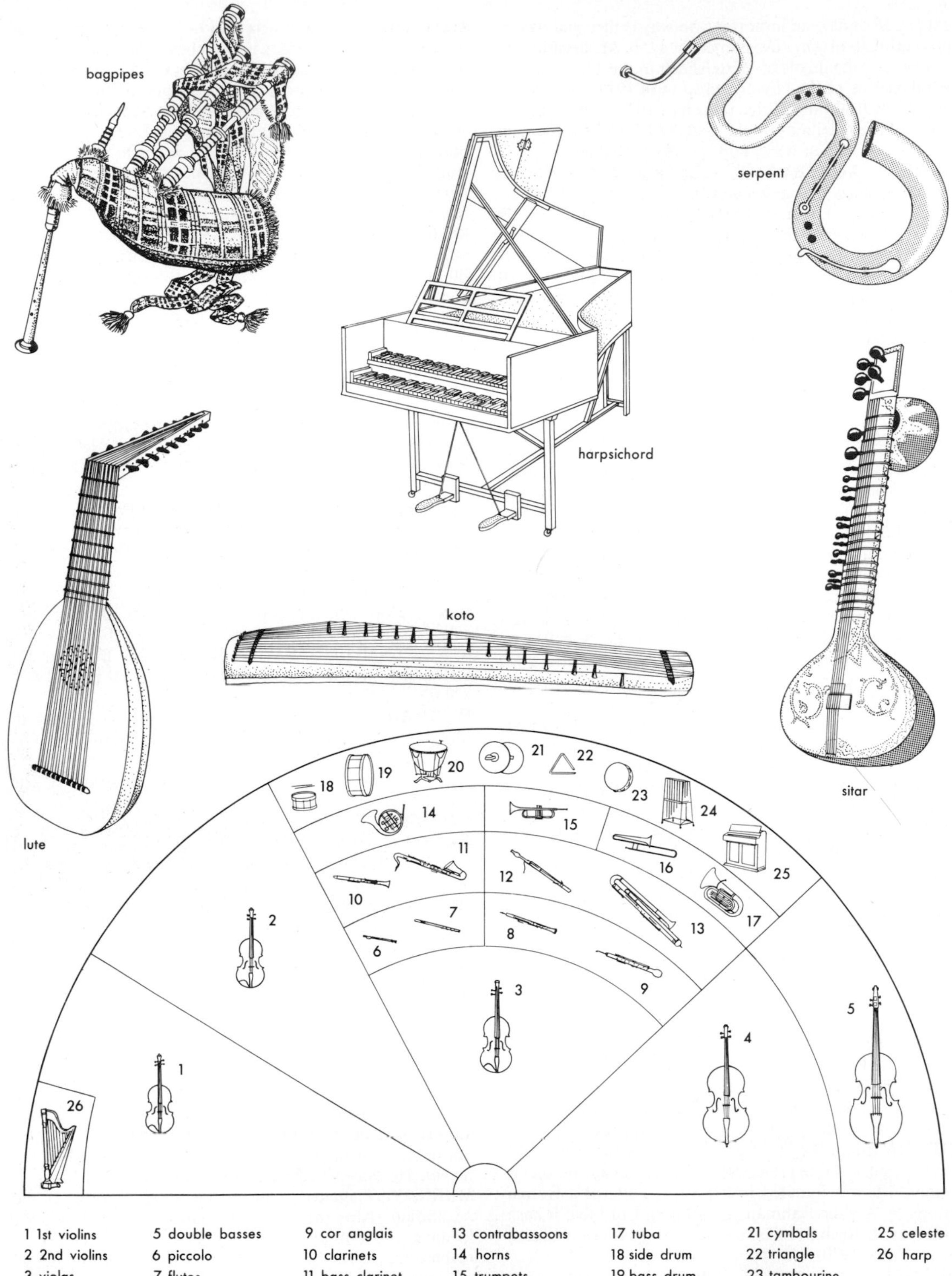

1 1st violins	5 double basses	9 cor anglais	13 contrabassoons	17 tuba	21 cymbals	25 celeste
2 2nd violins	6 piccolo	10 clarinets	14 horns	18 side drum	22 triangle	26 harp
3 violas	7 flutes	11 bass clarinet	15 trumpets	19 bass drum	23 tambourine	
4 cellos	8 oboes	12 bassoons	16 trombones	20 timpani	24 tubular bells	

MUSIC. A selection of musical instruments which illustrates today's interest in those of varied cultures and of earlier periods; and (below) the standard instruments and arrangement of the modern orchestra.

MURRAY. The Sunraysia district in the Murray Valley is Australia's chief area for the production of dried fruit. *Photo: Courtesy of the Australian Information Service*

MURRAY COD. Australian freshwater fish *(Maccullochella macquariensis)* which grows to *c.* 2m (6ft). It is highly valued as food and as a sporting fish, and is named after the river in which it is found.

MURROW, Ed(ward) R. (1908–65). American broadcaster. He is remembered for his radio reports on the London 'blitz' in the S.W.W., and for his television demolition of the power of Senator McCarthy in 1954.

MURRUMBI'DGEE. River of NSW, rising in the Australian Alps, flowing N to the Burrinjuck reservoir, and then W to meet the Murray after covering 1,690 km (1,050 m).

MURRY, John Middleton (1889–1957). British writer. B. in Peckham of humble family, he won a scholarship to Oxford, and in 1913 m. Katherine Mansfield (q.v.), whose biography he wrote. He produced studies of Dostoievsky, Keats, Blake, and Shakespeare, poetry and an autobiographical novel, *Still Life* (1916).

MUSCAT (mus'kat). Cap. of the sultanate of Oman. The adjoining port of Mutrah has a flourishing modern deep-water harbour, Port Qabus, named after the sultan. Pop. (1970) 25,000.

MUSCAT AND OMAN. *See* OMAN.

MUSCLE. Tissue with the special function of contraction. Every M. is made up of collections of large numbers of long spindle-shaped elastic cells, enclosed in coverings of connective tissue (fascia), and contracts and relaxes in response to the impulses reaching the nerves which supply it. All motion in the body is brought about by Ms., which are very numerous and varied in their shape, size and function. The Ms. which move the limbs and trunk in obedience to the will are called voluntary, and also striped, Ms. from the faint cross-shading visible under the microscope. Walls of blood vessels and intestines, hair follicles, the interior of the eye, etc., contain muscle not under the control of the will - involuntary or unstriped M. Muscular dystrophy (dis'trōfē) is a progressive muscular weakness leading to premature death, more frequent in boys than girls.

MŪ'SES. In Greek mythology, the 9 minor divinities who inspired artistic creation. The offspring of Zeus and Mnemosyne, their names and spheres were: Clio (history), Euterpe (lyric poetry), Thalia (comedy), Melpomene (tragedy), Terpsichore (dancing), Erato (love poetry), Polyhymnia (sacred hymns), Urania (astronomy), and Calliope (epic poetry).

MUSGRAVE RANGES. Mountain ranges on the border between South Australia and the Northern Territory. The highest peak is Mt Woodruffe 1,525m (5,000 ft). The area is an Aboriginal reserve.

MUSHROOM. *See* FUNGI.

MUSIC. The art of combining sounds in melodic or harmonic combination, so as to express thought and feeling in an aesthetic form. The Gr. word *mousikē* covered all the arts presided over by the Muses, and not only music in the modern sense. Of ancient Greek music only a few fragments have survived, and scholars are not agreed as to how these are to be deciphered. The various civilizations of the ancient and modern world - such as the Chinese, Hindu and Arabic cultures - developed their own musical systems, which are based on scale-divisions often differing entirely from those of the West. The history of Western M. begins with the liturgical music of the medieval Church, which was derived partly from Greek, partly from Hebrew antecedents. The 4 scales, or modes, to which the words of the liturgy were chanted, were first set in order by St Ambrose in AD 384. St Gregory the Great (*c.* 540–604) added 4 more to the original Ambrosian modes, and this system forms the basis of the Gregorian plainsong still in use in the RC Church. Originally all chants were sung in unison, but *c.* 11th cent. counterpoint was introduced, notably at the monastery of St Martial, Limoges, and in the late 12th cent. at Notre Dame in Paris by Léonin and Perotin the Great. Meanwhile the Provençal and French troubadours had developed a purely secular music, derived from church and folk music.

The 15th and 16th cents. have been called the Golden Age of contrapuntal or polyphonic music. One of the earliest names is that of John Dunstable (d. *c.* 1453), an Englishman, whose works influenced the Frenchman Guillaume Dufay (*c.* 1400–74) and in turn helped to produce the great achievements of the Flemish school whose members incl. Dufay's pupil Joannes Okeghem (*c.* 1420–*c.* 1495) and Josquin des Prés. Other notable composers were the Italian Palestrina and the Fleming Orlande de Lassus, who settled in Italy, the Spaniard Victoria and the Englishmen Tallis and Byrd. The Elizabethan age in England was spec. notable for the flowering of the secular madrigal, and produced such great names as Thomas Morley, Orlando Gibbons, etc.

The beginning of the 17th cent. saw a remarkable development, arising from the ideas of the Florentine Academy, a group of artists and literary men who wished to revive the principles of Greek tragedy. This led to the invention of dramatic recitative, and the beginning of opera. The first great operatic composer was Monteverdi (1567–1643), but before the end of the cent. the form had evolved further in the hands of Alessandro Scarlatti in Italy, and Lully in France. In England a promising start was made by Purcell, but was ended by his premature death which marked a decline in English music. The 17th cent. was also important for the emancipation of instrumental music from purely vocal forms.

The early 18th cent. is dominated by the great figures of J. S. Bach and Handel. The former, perhaps the greatest of all composers, though comparatively neglected in his own day, possessed a complete mastery of harmony and counterpoint, and has exercised a far-reaching influence

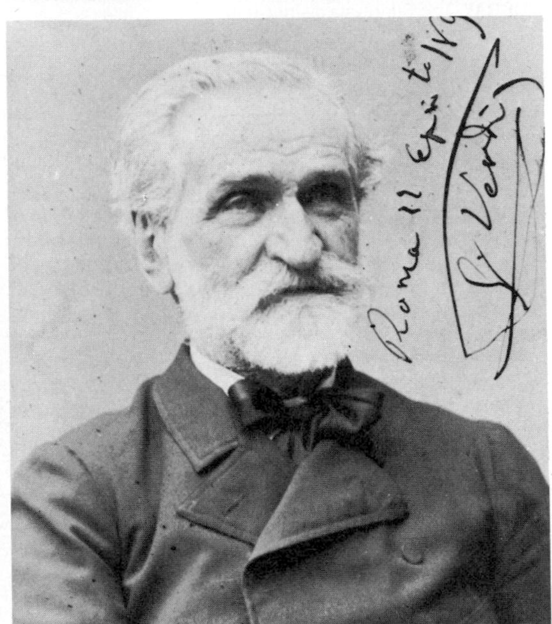

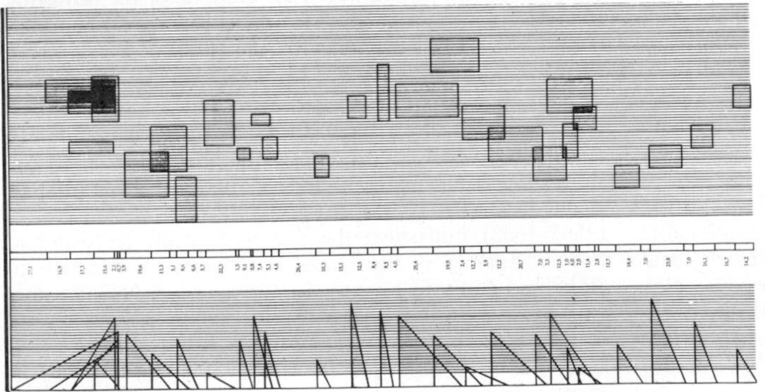

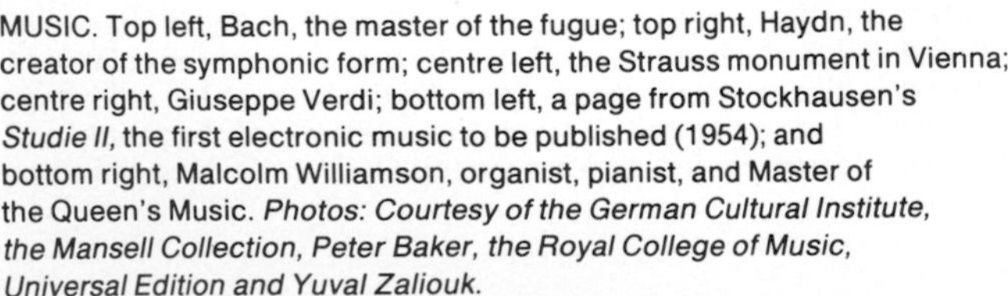

MUSIC. Top left, Bach, the master of the fugue; top right, Haydn, the creator of the symphonic form; centre left, the Strauss monument in Vienna; centre right, Giuseppe Verdi; bottom left, a page from Stockhausen's *Studie II,* the first electronic music to be published (1954); and bottom right, Malcolm Williamson, organist, pianist, and Master of the Queen's Music. *Photos: Courtesy of the German Cultural Institute, the Mansell Collection, Peter Baker, the Royal College of Music, Universal Edition and Yuval Zaliouk.*

on the subsequent development of music. Handel is most noteworthy for his magnificently dramatic oratorios, but had at first written operas based on Italian models, which had then hardened into lifeless conventionality. However, against this, Gluck later exhibited an important reaction.

Bach's great achievements had been in the handling of contrapuntal forms, but the next generation, incl. his own sons, C. P. E. Bach and J. C. Bach, reacted against this way of writing, and began the development of sonata-form, which is the basis of the 'Classical' sonata, quartette, and symphony. In these fields perfection of style was reached by the Viennese school of Haydn and Mozart, who were followed by the commanding figure of Beethoven. With the latter, music assumed dynamic and expressive functions hitherto undreamed of, and the way was opened for the Romanticism of the 19th cent.

'Romantic' music, represented in its earlier stages by Schubert, Schumann, Mendelssohn, Chopin, and Weber, tended to be subjectively emotional. The resources of orchestral colour were increasingly exploited - particularly by Berlioz - and harmony became more and more chromatic in character. National characteristics also became prominent. Thus we have the intense Polish nationalism of Chopin, and the exploitation of Hungarian-gypsy music by Liszt. National schools of composers, such as the Russian, represented by Rimsky-Korsakov, Borodin, Mussorgsky, and, less typically, by Tchaikovsky; the Czech, represented by Dvořák and Smetana, and the Norwegian, represented by Grieg, also emerged. The most revolutionary changes were brought by Wagner into the field of opera, though the traditional Italian lyricism was still perpetuated in the line of Rossini, Verdi and Puccini. Wagner's contemporary, Brahms, stood for Classical discipline of form, though in other respects, he, too, is deeply Romantic in feeling. The Belgian, César Franck, though he went far in the development of chromaticism, also renewed the tradition of polyphonic writing.

At the turn of the cent. there was a certain reaction against Romanticism and a tendency to experiment, which first became apparent in the French 'Impressionist' school, which incl. Debussy and Ravel. In Austria and Germany, Bruckner, Mahler and Richard Strauss, the last great representatives of Romanticism, were succeeded by the highly intellectual 'Atonal' school of Schönberg, Webern and Berg. Other experiments incl. the 'Neo-Classicism' of Stravinsky, Bartók and Hindemith, and the work of the French group known as *Les Six,* which incl. Francis Poulenc and Darius Milhaud. Notable also were the work of Bloch, influenced by Hebrew tradition, and the nordic-tinged romanticism of Sibelius.

The revival in British music begun by Sullivan, Stanford and Parry was continued in the early 20th cent. by Elgar, Delius and Holst. Among the many notable more recent composers in Britain are Vaughan Williams, William Walton, Benjamin Britten, Michael Tippett, Lennox Berkeley, Arthur Bliss, Alan Rawsthorne, Harrison Birtwhistle, Peter Maxwell Davies, John Taverner and Malcolm Williamson; in America Aaron Copland, George Gershwin, Charles Ives, Gian Carlo Menotti, Stravinsky and John Cage; in the USSR Shostakovitch, Prokofiev and Khachaturian; in France Pierre Boulez; in Germany Paul Hindemith, Carl Orff (1895-), Hans-Werner Henze, Karlheinz Stockhausen and Karl Hartmann (1905-63); in Hungary Kodály.

MUSIC, Electronic. Musical sounds produced by audio frequency oscillations of signal generators, electromagnetic instruments, etc. Henck Badings (1907-), a Dutch composer, has produced some of the most attractive romantic use of this, e.g., 'Capriccio for Violin and Sound Tracks'. In more recent years E.M. has been linked to computer composition, as in the later work of John Cage, and the music of Peter Zinovieff.

MUSICAL. A play interspersed with songs and dance sequences, which grew out of the similar, but more farcical, M. comedy, originally developed in the late 19th cent. from the French *opéra bouffe* at the Gaiety Theatre in London by George Edwardes, and spread to the US. It is still largely limited to English-speaking countries; notable writers incl. R. Friml, S. Romberg, J. Kern, I. Berlin, N. Coward, I. Novello, Cole Porter, Sandy Wilson and Lionel Bart. Whereas M. comedy was romantically escapist, Ms. tend since the S.W.W. to deal with contemporary problems, e.g., colour in *South Pacific* (1949) by Rodgers and Hammerstein, gang warfare in *West Side Story* (1957) by Leonard Bernstein.

MUSIC HALL. A theatre offering light entertainment consisting of 'turns', in which singers, dancers, comedians, acrobats, etc., perform in turn. The history of the M.H. begins in the 17th cent., when tavern-keepers acquired the organs which the Puritans had banished from churches. On certain nights organ music was played, and this practice resulted in the weekly entertainment known as the 'free and easy'. Certain theatres in London and the provs. then began to specialize in variety entertainment. The heyday of the M.H. was at the beginning of the present cent., when such artists as Albert Chevalier, Marie Lloyd, and Vesta Tilley performed to full houses. Later stars of M.H. have incl. Sir George Robey, Gracie Fields, the Crazy Gang, Ted Ray, and the American Danny Kaye. The cinema 'killed' M.H., but in the 1960-70s there was a revival in the working men's clubs and in public houses.

MUSIC(K), Master of the King's/Queen's. Appointment to the British Royal Household, the holder being responsible for composing appropriate music for state occasions. The first M. of the K.M. was Nicholas Lanier (appointed by Charles I in 1625): Malcolm Williamson was appointed to the post in 1975.

MU'SIL, Robert (1880-1942). Austrian novelist. B. at Klagenfurt, he devoted long years to *Der Mann ohne Eigenschaften* (3 vols., 1930-43: *The Man Without Qualities*), even then unfinished. Its hero combines the author's background of philosophical study and scientific and military training, and is preoccupied with the problems of the self viewed from a mystic but agnostic viewpoint. M.'s reputation is largely posthumous.

MUSK. Perennial plant (*Mimulus moschatus*) of the family Scrophulariaceae. The small oblong leaves formerly exuded the musky scent which gave it its name, but within the last 20 to 30 yrs the scent has disappeared. It has yellow flowers.

MUSK DEER. Small deer (*Moschus moschiferus*) native to Asia. It has no antlers, does not travel in herds, and is hunted for the musk secreted by an abdominal gland, and used as a medicine or a perfume.

MUSKE'G. Canadian word (of Cree Indian derivation) for swampland. There are some 1,300,000 sq.km (500,000 sq.m) of M. in northern Canada.

MUSK OX. Animal (*Ovibos moschatus*) native to the Arctic regions of N America. It displays characteristics of both the sheep and the ox, is about the size of domestic cattle, and has long brown hair. At certain seasons it exhales a musky odour. Its underwool (qiviut) is almost as fine as vicuna and M.O. farms have been estab. in Alaska, Quebec and Norway.

MUSLIMS. *See* MOSLEMS.

MUSLIN (muz'lin). A light cotton fabric named after Mosul, in Iraq, where it was first made. Its manufacture was introduced into England from India during the 17th cent.

MUSQUASH (mus'kwosh). Rodent (*Ondatra zibethicus*), also named Musk Rat. About 30cm (1ft) long, its body is adapted to aquatic life, having webbed feet and a flattened tail. It builds up a store of food, plastering it over with mud, for winter consumption. The light brown fur is highly valued.

MUSSEL. Popular name for a number of bi-valve molluscs. Most notable of the sea Ms. is the edible *Mytilus edulis*, which is found in clusters attached to rocks around the Atlantic coasts in the N hemisphere and the Mediterranean, and has a blue-black shell. The freshwater pearl Ms. (*Unio*) incl. the *U. margaritiferus* found in some N American and European rivers. The green-lipped M., found only off NZ, produces an extract useful in the treatment of arthritis.

MUSSET (müsā'), **Alfred de** (1810-57). French poet, playwright and novelist. B. in Paris, he abandoned the study of law and medicine to join the circle of writers about Victor Hugo, and achieved success with the vol. of poems, *Contes d'Espagne et d'Italie* (1829). In 1833 he accompanied George Sand to Italy, and his *Confession d'un enfant du siècle* (1835) recounts the story of their broken relations. Most typical of his genius are the verse *Les Nuits* (1835-7) and the short plays *Comédies et proverbes* (1840).

MUSSOLINI, Benito (1883-1945). Italian dictator. B. in the Romagna, the son of a blacksmith, he worked in early life as a teacher and journalist, and became active in the Socialist movement, from which he was expelled in 1914 for advocating Italian intervention in the F.W.W. In 1919 he founded the *Fasci di Combattimento*, whose programme combined violent nationalism with demagogic republican and anti-capitalist slogans, and launched a campaign of terrorism against the Socialists. This movement was backed by many landowners and industrialists, and by the heads of the army and police, and in Oct. 1922 the king and the army leaders installed M. in power as PM. In 1925 he assumed dictatorial powers, and in 1926 all opposition parties were suppressed. During the years that followed the entire political, legal and educ. system was remodelled on Fascist lines. In 1935-6 M. embarked on a career of conquest, with his successful invasion of Ethiopia; this was followed by Italian intervention in the Spanish Civil War of 1936-9, and the conquest of Albania in 1939. This policy drew M. into close co-operation with Nazi Germany, and in June 1940 Italy entered the S.W.W. Italian defeats in N Africa, the Allied invasion of Sicily, and rising discontent at home destroyed M.'s prestige, and in July 1943 he was compelled to resign by the Fascist Grand Council. He was released from his imprisonment by German parachutists in Sept., and set up a 'Republican Fascist' govt in N Italy. In April 1945 he and his mistress were captured at Lake Como by partisans while trying to flee the country, and shot. Their bodies were exposed to the execration of the mob in Milan. *See* FASCISM. His son, BRUNO M. (1915-41), served as a bomber pilot in Ethiopia, Spain, and Greece, and was killed in an air accident. His dau. EDDA, m. Count Ciano (q.v.).

MUSSORGSKY (moosorg'skē), **Modest Petrovich** (1839-81). Russian composer. B. at Karevo, he entered the army in 1856, but resigned his commission in 1858 to concentrate on music while working as a govt clerk. His opera *Boris Godunov* was completed in 1869, although not produced in St Petersburg until 1874. His other works incl. the incomplete operas *Khovanshtchina* and *Sorochintsy Fair*; the orchestral *Night on the Bare Mountain*: the suite *Pictures at an Exhibition*; and many songs. Some of his works were 'revised' by Rimsky-Korsakov, and only recently has their harsh and primitive beauty been recovered. M. d. in poverty, having taken to drugs.

MUSTAFA KEMAL. *See* ATATÜRK.

MUSTAGH. Another name for KARAKORAM.

MUSTARD. Annual plants of the family Cruciferae. The seeds of Black M. (*Brassica nigra*), and White M. (*B. alba*), are used in the production of table mustard, and are cultivated in Europe, N America and England, where wild M. or charlock (*B. arvensis*) is also found. The seedlings of white M. are used as a salad food. M. is frequently grown by farmers and ploughed in to enrich the soil.

MUTATION. In heredity, a new characteristic which suddenly appears in the offspring of a plant or animal and which breeds true is said to be a M. This type of change is one of the bases of evolutionary theory. Mutational changes may be spontaneous, or induced, e.g. by radiation. *See* EVOLUTION.

MUTI (moo'ti), **Riccardo** (1941-). Italian conductor. Assoc. with the London Philharmonia, and the Philadelphia Orchestra (from 1980), he is musically a 'purist', devoted to the carrying out of the composer's wishes to the last detail.

MUTSUHITO (mootsoohē'tō) (1852-1912). Emperor of Japan. He took the title Meiji Tenno (enlightened peace), when he became emperor in 1867. During his reign Japan became a world power.

MUTTON BIRD. Also known as the short-tailed shearwater, the bird (*Puffinus tenuirostris*) migrates from Japan to breed in burrows on islands off SE Australia. The young are very fat, and are harvested as food.

MVD. (Ministerstvo Vnutrennykh Del, Ministry for Internal Affairs). New title from 1968 for the already existing Ministry of Public Order in the USSR, given in an attempt to strengthen the fight of the ordinary police/militia against increasing crime and hooliganism; also the title 1946-53 of the secret police, now the KGB. (q.v.).

MYASTHENIA GRAVIS (mi-asthē'nia grah'vis). Rare disorder marked by muscular weakness. Usually first appearing in muscles round the eye, it sometimes spreads so far through the body as to affect breathing. It is caused by a defect in the body's immune defence system.

MYCENAEAN (mīsinē'an) **CIVILIZATION.** The civilization, also known as the Aegean Civilization, which flourished in Crete, Cyprus, Greece, the Aegean islands, and W Anatolia, *c.* 4000-1000 BC. Its nature was first laid bare by the excavations of Schliemann at Troy, Mycenae (an ancient Greek city in Argolis), and Tiryns after 1870, and of Sir Arthur Evans in Crete after 1899. Originating in Crete, it spread into Greece *c.* 1600 BC, where it continued to flourish, with its centre at Mycenae, after the decline of Crete *c.* 1400. It was finally overthrown by the Dorian invasions, *c.* 1100. The system of govt was by kings, who also monopolized priestly functions; their palaces were large and luxurious, and contained highly efficient sanitary arrangements. Commercial relations were maintained with Egypt throughout. Pottery, fresco-painting, and metal-work reached a high artistic level.

MYCENAEAN CIVILIZATION. The 'Grand Casement' at Tiryns. The rugged style of building with huge stone blocks is known as Cyclopean, since later Greeks felt that only giants could have built such walls. *Photo: Peter Clayton.*

MYERS, Frederic William Henry (1843-1901). British psychic investigator. B. at Keswick, he was one of the founders and the first pres. of the Society for Psychical Research.

MY LAI (mē lī). Village in S Vietnam, destroyed by American troops in 1968 in the incorrect belief that it was occupied by Viet Cong. Lt William Calley, commander of the platoon, was charged with the murder of 102 and convicted of the murder of at least 22. He was sentenced to life imprisonment, but later released on parole.

MYOPIA (mī-ō'pia). Short sight. It is due to a defect in the structure of the eye, so that the incoming light is focused before it reaches the retina. The error can be corrected by concave lenses, and operative treatments are under development.

MYRON (mī'ron) (fl. 500-440 BC). Greek sculptor. B. at Eleutherae in Boeotia, he is remembered for the Discobolus, or discus-thrower.

MYRRH (mer). Gum resin produced by a small tree (*Commiphora myrrha*), of the family Burseraceae, found in Abyssinia and Arabia. In ancient times it was used for incense and perfume, and in embalming.

MYRTLE (mer'tl). Genus (*Myrtus*) of evergreen shrubs in the family Myrtaceae. The common Mediterranean M. (*M. communis*) has oval opposite leaves and white flowers followed by purple berries, all of which are fragrant.

MYSORE (mīsor'). *See* KARNATAKA.

MYSORE. City in Karnataka, Rep. of India, 130km (80m) SW of Bangalore. It produces silks, and engineering goods. Pop. (1971) 355,650.

MYSTERY RELIGIONS. Cults of the ancient world open only to the initiated. The most important of such cults among the Greeks were the Eleusinian mysteries, celebrated annually in honour of Demeter at Eleusis, near Athens, and the Orphic mysteries, in honour of Dionysus. A number of Asiatic mystery cults, such as those of Attis, Cybele, Isis, and Mithras, attained great popularity under the Roman Empire. All these cults derived from primitive fertility rituals; their principal feature was a ritual drama, normally portraying the death and resurrection of the god, while a sacramental meal took place through which the initiate obtained communion with the god by feeding on his flesh and blood, hoping thereby to attain to life beyond the grave. These ideas strongly influenced early Christianity.

MYSTICISM. A mode of religious belief depending on personal spiritual experience of God as the ultimate reality, distinct from all references to thought or reason. The element of M. is common to all the higher religions - Hinduism, Buddhism, Judaism, Islam, and Christianity. M. was first introduced to W Europe through Neoplatonism (q.v.) which was largely affected by Oriental schools of thought, and in its turn influenced the rise of Christian M. through the work of the pseudo-Dionysius the Areopagite. M. flourishes espec. in periods when a civilization is passing through a major crisis, as in Germany in the 14th-16th cents., when feudalism was breaking down, e.g. Thomas à Kempis and Jacob Boehme. Often M. assumed heretical forms, as with the Anabaptists and early Quakers, but the Counter-Reformation also produced mystics such as St Teresa and St John of the Cross. Mystical movements of the 17th cent. incl. those of the Quietists in France, and Henry More and the Cambridge Platonists in England, while the 18th cent. produced two great English mystics in William Law and William Blake. In the 20th cent. there has been a revival of M. in England and the USA, largely due to Hinduism, which is expressed in the works of W. B. Yeats, Gerald Heard, and Aldous Huxley. The scientific study of M. was estab. by the work of Dean Inge, William James, and Evelyn Underhill, and valuable light has been thrown by the use of psychological methods.

MYTHO'LOGY (Gk *muthos*, fable). Science which attempts the interpretation of the stories invented by primitive peoples to express their imaginative conception of the origin of the universe, useful arts, etc., and assess their relationship to similar stories told by other races. The myth is distinguished from the legend (q.v.), which may have an ultimate basis in fact, by being purely fictitious. Great Ms. are those of Egypt, India, Greece, Rome, and Scandinavia.

MYTILENE. *See* MITYLENE.

MYXOEDEMA (miksidē'ma). A disease due to deficiency of the secretion of the thyroid gland chiefly seen in middle-aged women. The mind becomes dull, the temper irritable, and the memory is lost, there is a coarsening of the features, the skin becomes yellow and dry, and the speech thick. The condition can be improved by giving thyroid preparation.

MYXOMATŌSIS (mik'so-). A contagious filterable-virus infection of rabbits, causing much suffering, sometimes deliberately introduced to reduce rabbit population.

N

14th letter of the Roman alphabet, representing a dental nasal sound. In several Romance langages *n* in many circumstances disappears, with nasalization of the preceding vowel.

NAAFI. In full: Navy, Army, and Air Force Institutes. Non-profit-making association, providing canteens for HM Forces at home and overseas; its HQ is at Claygate, Surrey.

NA'BLUS. Town in N Jordan, on the W Bank, 48km (30m) N of Jerusalem. As Shechem, it was in ancient times the cap. of Samaria, and is the largest Palestinian town, after E. Jerusalem, in Israeli occupation. Pop. (1970) 50,000.

NABOKOV (nab'okof), **Vladimir** (1899–1977). Russian author; US citizen from 1945. B. at St Petersburg, he settled in the USA in 1940, and was prof. of Russian literature at Cornell univ. 1948–59, producing a fine translation and commentary on *Eugene Onegin* in 1963. He was also a noted lepidopterist, a pursuit which has something in common with his treatment of his fictional characters. His best-known books incl. *The Real Life of Sebastian Knight* (1945), *Pnin* (1957) and *Lolita* (1955), story of the infatuation of the middle-aged Humbert Humbert for a precociously experienced child of 12 which added the word 'nymphet' to the language.

NACHI'NGWEA. Terrorist training base in Tanzania, *c.* 360km/225m S of Dar-es-Salaam and linked by rail with the port of Mtwara 145km (90m) to the E. It was used by Frelimo 1964–75, and by the African Nat. Council (Zimbabwe) 1975–80.

NĀ'DER, Ralph (1934–). American lawyer, the 'scourge of corporate morality'. His achievements incl. forcing a world revolution in safety standards for cars by his book *Unsafe at any Speed.*

NĀ'DIR. Astronomical term denoting a point in the heavens diametrically opposite to the zenith.

NAEMEN. Flemish form of NAMUR.

NAEVUS (nē'vus). 'Port wine mark'; a bright red tumour of the skin, consisting of a mass of small blood vessels. A N. of moderate size is harmless. Skin grafts, etc., are not very successful, but from 1980 'smooth' Ns. were shown to respond well to argon laser beam treatment.

NAGALAND (nah'gah-). State of the Rep. of India, N of Manipur and bordering Burma on the E. Formerly part of Assam, N. is inhabited by Naga tribes once notorious as headhunters. The British sent 18 expeditions against them 1832–87, and after India attained independence in 1947, they rose against their new ruler. Unable to repress them, the Indian govt entered into negotiations, and the new state was estab. in 1963. Agitation continued for independence, and fighting resumed from 1972: there is also opposition to settlers from Assam. The cap. is Kohima. Area 16,488 sq.km (6,366 sq.m); pop. (1971) 516,000.

NAGASAKI (nahgahsah'kē). Seaport on Kyushu Is., Japan, destroyed by an atom bomb during the S.W.W. on 9 Aug. 1945. Of its pop. of 212,000, 73,884 were killed, 76,796 injured. N. was the only Japanese port open to European trade from the 16th cent. until other ports were opened in 1859. Coal is mined and there are iron works and shipbuilding yards. Pop. (1977) 445,000.

NAGOYA. Seaport of Honshu, Japan, with a Shogun fortress (1610) and a famous Shinto shrine, Atsuta Jingu. Textiles and clocks are made. Pop. (1977) 310,000.

NAGPUR (nagpoor'). City in Maharashtra, Rep. of India, seat of N. univ. (1923) and with an airport. Close to the cotton-growing area of the Deccan, it is a centre for cotton and silk textiles, and there are metallurgical industries. Pop. (1971) 866,145.

NAGY (nahzh), **Imre** (1896–1958). Hungarian leader of the revolt against Soviet domination in 1956. He was executed.

NĀ'HUM (7th cent. BC). Hebrew prophet, possibly b. in Galilee, and author of a prophecy of the destruction of Nineveh incl. in the OT.

NĀ'IADS. Water-nymphs of classic mythology.

NAILS. Hard, smooth, elastic appendages to the skin, made of a horny modification of its outer layer, and protecting and strengthening the tips of the fingers and toes. They are related to the claws and hooves of animals. The N. grows from a bed, or matrix, in the lower germinal layer of the skin.

NAIPAUL (nī'pawl), **Vidiadhar Surajprasad** (1932–). British writer. B. in Trinidad of Hindu parents, he is best known for his novels *A House for Mr. Biswas* (1961), *Mr. Stone and the Knights Companion* (1963), and *A Bend in the River* (1979).

NAIRNSHIRE. Former co. of Scotland, bounded on the N by the Moray Firth, and incl. in 1975 in Highland region. The co. town was Nairn. Pop. (1973) 5,000.

NAIROBI (nirō'bē). Cap. of Kenya, E Africa, 530km (330m) by rail NW of Mombasa. Founded in 1899, it lies in the central Highlands at 1,660 m (5,450 ft). The Univ. of Nairobi was estab. in 1970. There is an internat. airport. Light industries, food processing, etc., are carried on. It is the HQ of the UN Environment Programme (UNEP), and the Internat. Louis Leakey Inst. for African Prehistory was estab. 1977. Pop. (1970) 510,000.

NAKASONE, Yasuhiro (1918–). Japanese Liberal Democratic statesman. Succeeding Suzuki in 1982, he took a Western stance of increasing Japans defence capability. He is a strong advocate of nuclear energy.

NAMA'QUALAND. Great N. is a desert region N of the Orange r., SW Africa. It is inhabited by the sparsely distributed Namaquas, a Hottentot tribe. Area *c.* 388,500 sq.km (150,000 sq.m). Little N. is the desert region S of the Orange r., incl. in Cape Prov. Copper and diamonds are mined. Area *c.* 52,000 sq.km (20,000 sq.m). Pop. *c.* 30,000.

NAMATJIRA (ñamatyē'ra), **Albert** (1902–59). Australian Aboriginal artist. He painted watercolour landscapes of the Australian interior.

NAMIB (nah'mib). The desert coastal strip of SW Africa, averaging *c.* 100km (60m) wide.

NAMIBIA. *See* SOUTH WEST AFRICA.

NAMUR (nahmür'). City and railway junction in Belgium, cap. of the prov. of N., situated at the junction of the Sambre and the Meuse. It has iron and steel foundries and is famous for cutlery. Pop. (1978) 100,296.

NANAIMO (nahn'mō). Coal-mining centre of British Columbia, Canada, on the E coast of Vancouver Is., 95km (60m) NW of Victoria. Pop. (1976) 40,340.

NA'NA SA'HIB (1820-*c.* 1859). Name by which Dandhu Panth, an adopted son of the ex-peshwa of the Mahrattas, was commonly known. He joined the rebels in the Indian Mutiny, and was responsible for the massacre at Cawnpore. After the rebellion he took refuge in Nepal.

NANCHANG (nahnchahng'). Cap. of Jiangxi prov., China, on the Gan r., *c.* 260 km (160 m) SE of Wuhan. A walled 12th cent. city, it is now a road, rail and air junction, and industries incl. textiles, glass, porcelain, soap, etc. It is the seat of a univ. Pop. (1973) 875,000.

NANCY (noṅsi'). Cap. of the dept. of Meurthe-et-Moselle, France, on the Meurthe, 280km (175m) E of Paris. Dating from the 11th cent., N. has a univ. and contains many fine buildings, incl. the Hôtel de Ville and the cathedral (1742). Pop. (1975) 278,000.

NANDA DEVI (nun'da dē'vi). Peak in the Himalayas, Uttar Pradesh, Rep. of India: 7,817 m (25,645 ft).

NANGA PARBAT (nung'a pahr'bat). Peak in the Himalayas, W Kashmir: 8,126 m (26,660 ft).

NANKING. *See* NANJING.

NANJING (nahnjeng'). Cap. (formerly Nanking) of Jiangsu prov., China, on the Chang Jiang, 270 km (165 m) NW of Shanghai. Dating from the 2nd cent. BC, and perhaps earlier, it received the name N. (meaning southern cap.) under the Ming dynasty. It was the cap. of China 1368-1403, 1928-37, 1946-9. An industrial and commercial centre, and hub of communications, it has a univ. (1888), and Sun Yat Sen is buried on Purple Mountain nearby. The bridge (1968) over the Chang is 6,705 m (22,000 ft) long. Pop (1977) 3,000,000.

NANNING (nahneng'). River port, cap. of Guangxi Zhuang autonomous region, China, on the r. You Jiang. A former treaty port (1907), it is also a road centre and trades in fruit and sugar grown in the area. Pop. (1973) 575,000.

NANSEN, Fridtjof (1861-1930). Norwegian explorer, scientist, and statesman. He made his first voyage to Greenland waters in a sealing-ship in 1882, and in 1888-9 attempted to cross the Greenland icefield. He sailed to the Arctic in 1893 in the *Fram,* which was deliberately allowed to drift with an icefloe. Later, N. left the *Fram* and, accompanied by Johansen, continued northwards on foot. They reached 86° 14′ N, the highest latitude then attained, and wintered in Franz Josef Land, returning in 1896. The *Fram* also returned safely. After the F.W.W. N. became League of Nations High Commissioner for refugees, and in 1923 received the Nobel peace prize. The N. inst. for humanist and social research was estab. at Oslo in 1956.

NANTES (noṅt). Seaport of France, cap. of the dept of Loire-Atlantique, on the Loire, 56km (35m) from its mouth. Its buildings incl. the cathedral (1434-1884), built over a 12th cent. crypt, and the castle founded in 938. Here Henry IV signed the EDICT OF N. (1598), granting religious freedom to the Huguenots. Pop. (1975) 252,550.

NANTU'CKET. Is. and pleasure resort area 120 sq.km. (46 sq.m) S of Cape Cod, Mass, USA. In the 18-19th cents. N. was a famous whaling port.

NA'PALM. Fuel used in flame-throwers and incendiary bombs. Produced from jellied petrol, it is named from *na*phthenic and *palm*itic acids.

NAPHTHA (naf'tha). Originally applied to naturally occurring liquid hydrocarbons, the term is now used for the mixtures of hydrocarbons obtained by destructive distillation of petroleum, coal-tar, and shale oil.

NA'PHTHALENE ($C_{10}H_8$). A solid, aromatic hydrocarbon, m.p. 80°C, b.p. 218°C, obtained from the middle oil distillate of coal-tar. A white, shiny, crystalline solid with a penetrating smell, it is used in making indigo and certain azo-dyes; also as a mild disinfectant and insecticide (moth balls have the characteristic smell of N.).

NAPIER, Sir Charles James (1782-1853). British general. After serving in the Peninsular War and capturing a number of vessels in the American War of 1812-14, his great achievement came in his campaigns in Sind 1841-3 which he conquered with a very small force and governed until 1847. He seldom agreed with his superiors, but was liked by his men and was the first to mention in despatches men from the ranks who had distinguished themselves. His brother, **Sir William Francis Patrick N.** (1785-1860), wrote a *History of the Peninsular War* (1828-40) in which he had also served.

NAPIER, John (1550-1617). Scottish mathematician. He was the inventor of logarithms, publishing his Tables in 1614, and of 'N.'s Bones' an early type of calculating device for multiplication and division.

NAPIER. Seaport of N Island, NZ, linked with the town of Hastings to the S, and focus of a farming area. Pop. (1976) 109,000.

NAPIER OF MAGDALA, Robert Cornelis Napier, 1st baron (1810-90). British field marshal. Knighted for his services at the siege of Lucknow, and thanked by parliament for his part in the Chinese War of 1855, he crowned his career in the Abyssinian campaign of 1868 by storming Magdala, and was created a baron.

NAPLES. Seaport and cap. of N. prov., on the Bay of N., 193km (120m) SE of Rome. Formerly the cap. of the kingdom of N., it is the 3rd town of Italy, and as a port second only in importance to Genoa. There are shipbuilding yards, factories making locomotives, textiles, paper, etc.; a famous museum and a marine aquarium. To the S is the Isle of Capri, and behind the city is Mt Vesuvius, with the ruins of Pompeii at its foot. Outstanding buildings of N. incl. the royal palace, the San Carlo Opera House, and the Castel Nuovo (1283). N. has one of the oldest univs. (1224) in the world. Pop. (1978) 1,225,225.

NAPOLEON I (Bonaparte) (1769-1821). Emperor of the French. B. at Ajaccio, Corsica, he received a commission in the artillery in 1785, and first distinguished himself at the siege of Toulon in 1793. N. m. Josephine de Beauharnais in 1796. Having suppressed a royalist rising in Paris in 1795, he received the command against the Austrians in Italy, and by his victories at Lodi, Arcole, and Rivoli (1796-7), compelled them to make peace. The Directory then accepted his plan to conquer Egypt as a halfway-house to India (1798), but although he overran Egypt and invaded Syria his fleet was destroyed by Nelson. In 1799 he returned to France, overthrew the govt of the Directory, and estab. his own dictatorship, nominally as First Consul. He then invaded Italy, defeated the Austrians at Marengo (1800), and broke up the coalition which had been formed against France. Peace was restored in 1802.

Soon afterwards a plebiscite confirmed him in his consulship for life, and another in 1804 granted him the title of emperor. While retaining and extending the legal

NAPOLEON. A portrait of Napoleon I (right) by Vernet, and of his son, Napoleon II, known by the time this portrait was painted by Bazin, as the duke of Reichstadt. Spirited, but without the dominant will of his father, he remained a pawn for Metternich and others in the game of European politics. *Photos: Mansell Collection.*

and educational reforms of the Jacobins, he substituted a centralized despotism for the democratic constitution estab. by the Revolution, and by his Concordat conciliated the Church. The war was renewed by Britain in 1803; Austria and Russia joined the coalition against France in 1805, and Prussia in 1806. Prevented by British sea power from invading England, N. drove Austria out of the war by his victories at Ulm and Austerlitz (1805), and Prussia by the victory of Jena (1806), and after the hard-fought battles of Eylau and Friedland formed an alliance with the tsar at Tilsit (1807).

He now attempted to ruin Britain by his 'Continental System' of excluding British goods from Europe, and to enforce its operation sent an army to occupy Portugal, and in 1808 placed his brother Joseph on the Spanish throne. Spain and Portugal revolted, with British assistance, while in 1809 Austria re-entered the war, only to be defeated at Wagram. To assert his equality with the Habsburgs, N. now divorced Josephine and m. the emperor's daughter, Marie Louise. When the tsar failed to enforce the Continental System, N. invaded Russia in 1812, and occupied Moscow, which was set on fire. The disastrous French retreat encouraged Prussia and Austria to declare war in 1813, and N. was defeated at Leipzig and driven from Germany. After a brilliant campaign on French soil, he abdicated in 1814, and was banished to Elba.

In March 1815 he returned to France and re-assumed power; in June he marched into Belgium to meet the Allies, was defeated at Waterloo, and again abdicated. Having surrendered to the British, he was exiled to St Helena, where he d. and was buried in 1821. His body was reinterred in the Hôtel des Invalides, Paris, in 1840. For his family, *see* BONAPARTE.

NAPOLEON II (1811-32). Title given by the Bonapartists to the son of Napoleon I and Marie Louise; until 1814 he was known as the king of Rome, and after 1818 as the duke of Reichstadt. After his father's abdication in 1814 he was taken to the Austrian court, where he spent the rest of his life. By Hitler's order his body was removed from Vienna in 1940 and reinterred in the Hôtel des Invalides, Paris.

NAPOLEON III (1808-73). Emperor of the French. The son of Louis Bonaparte and Hortense de Beauharnais, brother and step-daughter respectively of Napoleon I, he led two unsuccessful revolts, at Strasbourg in 1836 and at Boulogne in 1840, and after the latter was imprisoned. Escaping in 1846, he lived in London until the 1848 revolution. He was elected president of the republic in Dec., and set himself to secure a following by posing as the champion of order and religion against the revolutionary menace. He secured his re-election by a military coup d'état in 1851, and a year later was proclaimed emperor. Hoping to strengthen his régime by military triumphs, he joined in the Crimean War, waged war with Austria (1859), and attempted unsuccessfully to found a vassal empire in Mexico (1863-7); thereby he aroused the mistrust of Europe and isolated France. At home, his régime was discredited by its notorious corruption; republican and Socialist opposition grew, in spite of severe repression, and forced N., after 1860, to make concessions in the direction of parliamentary govt. Manœuvred by Bismarck in 1870 into war with Prussia, he was forced to surrender at Sedan, whereupon the empire collapsed. After the war he withdrew to England, where he died.

His son by empress Eugénie (q.v.), **Eugène Louis Jean Joseph N., Prince Imperial** (1856-79), was killed fighting with the British Army against the Zulus.

NAPOLI. Italian form of NAPLES.

NARA. Ancient cap. of Japan (AD 710-94), birthplace of Japanese art and literature. Pop. (1973) 191,600.

NARBONNE (nahrbon'). Town in Aude dept, France, chief town of S Gaul in Roman times and a port in medieval times. Pop. (1975) 40,540.

NARCISSUS (nahrsis'us). In Gk legend, a beautiful youth, who rejected the love of the nymph Echo, and as a punishment was made to fall in love with his own reflection in a stream. He eventually pined away for love of himself, and in the place where he d. there sprang up a flower which was named after him. His name is the origin of the psychological term **Narcissism,** meaning an excessive valuation of the self and its attributes, an exaggeration of normal self-respect and pride in oneself into vanity and conceit, which may amount to insanity.

NARCISSUS. Genus of bulbous plants of the family Amaryllidaceae. There are about 35 different species, of which the best-known are the daffodil, jonquil, and poet's N.

NARCOTICS. Drugs that relieve pain and cause deep sleep. The principal are opium and its derivatives and synthetic modifications (morphine, heroin, etc.); the alcohols (paraldehyde, ethyl alcohol, avertin, etc.); and the barbiturates (veronal, luminal, evipan, etc.).

NARRAGA'NSETT BAY. Inlet of the Atlantic, Rhode Is., USA. It encloses a number of is., running inland 45km (28m).

NARSES (nahr'sēz) (*c.* 478-*c.* 573). Byzantine statesman and general, originally a eunuch slave, and later an official in the imperial treasury. He was joint commander with Belisarius in Italy 538-9, and in 552 destroyed the Ostrogoths at Taginae.

NA'RVIK. Seaport in Norway, on Ofot Fjord. It exports iron ore from the Swedish mines. To secure this ore supply the Germans seized N. in April 1940. British, French, Polish, and Norwegian forces recaptured N., but had to abandon it on 10 June owing to the worsening Allied situation elsewhere in Europe; this was the end of fighting in Norway during the S.W.W. Pop. (1973) 14,000.

NARWHAL. A cetacean (*Monodon monoceros*), found only in the Arctic Ocean. The male has a spirally fluted tusk 2-3m (6-10ft) long.

NASEBY (nāz'bi). English village in Northants, 20km (12m) NNW of Northampton, the scene of the decisive battle of the Civil War (14 June 1645), when the Royalists were defeated by Cromwell and Fairfax.

NASH, John (1752-1835). British architect. He laid out Regent's Park, London, and designed many of the terraces nearby. Between 1813 and 1820 he planned Regent Street (subsequently rebuilt), and later repaired and enlarged Buckingham Palace for which he designed Marble Arch, intended as the entrance gateway.

NASH, Ogden (1902-71). American poet. B. in Rye, NY, he pub. numerous vols. of humorous verse of impeccable technique and quietly puncturing satire, e.g. *Hard Lines* (1931), *The Face is Familiar* (1941), and *Collected Verses* (1961).

NASH, Paul (1889-1946). British artist. B. in London, he became famous for his pictures of the F.W.W., such as 'The Menin Road', in the Imperial War Museum, in which he created strange patterns out of the scorched landscape of the Western Front. During the S.W.W. he was appointed official war artist to the Air Ministry. Two of his most celebrated pictures, depicting the struggle in the air, are *Totes Meer*, and 'The Battle of Britain'. His brother, **John Northcote N.** (1893-1977), was also a painter and engraver.

NASH. The Nash terraces round Regent's Park are one of the glories of London. The houses themselves were often not correspondingly well built, and are unsuited to modern living, so that often only the facades are retained, the body of the building being completely reconstructed. *Photo: Courtesy of the British Tourist Authority.*

NASH. 'The Battle of Britain', a vivid impression by Paul Nash of the dogfights of 1940 when Germany attempted to destroy Britain's air bases and communications as a prelude to invasion, and was defeated by the gallantry of the pilots of RAF Fighter Command. *Photo: Courtesy of the Imperial War Museum.*

NASH, Richard (1674-1762). British dandy, known as Beau Nash. As master of ceremonies at Bath from 1705, he made it the most fashionable watering-place in England, and did much to bring a more polished code of manners into general use.

NASH, Sir Walter (1882-1968). New Zealand statesman. B. at Kidderminster, he emigrated to NZ in 1909. In the Labour govt of 1935 he became Min. of Finance, to which he added the post of Deputy PM 1940-9. During the

S.W.W. he was a member of the War Cabinet, and Minister to Washington 1942-4. PM 1957-60, he led the Opposition 1950-7 and 1960-3: knighted 1965.

NASH(E), Thomas (1567-1601). English poet, dramatist and pamphleteer. B. at Lowestoft, he settled in London *c.* 1588, where he was rapidly drawn into the Martin Marprelate controversy, and wrote at least 3 attacks on the Martinists. Among his later works are the satire *Pierce Pennilesse* (1592); the religious *Christes Teares over Jerusalem* (1593); *Jacke Wilton,* the first English picaresque novel; and the comedy, *Summer's Last Will and Testament.*

NASHVILLE. Cap. of Tennessee, USA, on the Cumberland r., NE of Memphis. An important river port, it is in the fertile area of the Tennessee Valley, with a trade in cotton, tobacco, wheat and livestock; is a banking and commercial complex, and has large printing, recording and music publishing industries. It is the HQ of Country and Western music (q.v.). N. dates from 1778, and the Confederate army was badly defeated here in 1864. Pop. (1970) 448,444.

NĀ'SMYTH, Alexander (1758-1840). Scottish portrait and landscape painter. B. in Edinburgh, he is best remembered for his portrait of Burns in the Scottish National Gallery.

NASSAU. Port of New Providence island and cap. of the Bahamas. English settlers founded it in 1629. Pop. (1973) 112,000.

NA'SSER, Gamal Abdel (1918-70). Egyptian statesman. Son of a postal clerk, he entered the army from Cairo Military Academy, and was wounded in the Palestine War of 1948-9. In 1952 he was the driving power behind the Neguib coup, became PM in 1954 and in 1956 pres. of the Rep. of Egypt - of the United Arab Republic from 1958. His appropriation of the Suez Canal (q.v.) and his ambitions for an Egyptian-led Arab union led to disquiet in the area, but his internal policies were generally sound, although a rapidly increasing population lessened their good effect.

NASTURTIUM (naster'shyum). Genus of plants of the family Cruciferae, including *N. officinale,* watercress. The garden species, *Tropaeolum majus,* which has orange- or scarlet-coloured flowers, and *Tropaeolum minus,* which has smaller flowers, belong to the S American Tropaeolaceae. The leaves and buds are sometimes served in salads.

NATA'L. A prov. in the Rep. of S Africa, to the NE of Cape Province, and bounded on the E by the Indian Ocean; so called because it was discovered by Vasco da Gama on Christmas Day, 1497. From the Drakensberg the country slopes to a fertile sub-tropical coastal plain. There are many plantations of sugar cane. Other products incl. the black wattle (*Acacia mollissima*), maize, fruits, vegetables, tobacco, and coal. The cap. is Pietermaritzburg; the chief port and largest town is Durban. N. was a part of Cape Colony 1844-56, when it was made into a separate colony. Zululand was annexed to N. in 1897, and the districts of Vrijheid, Utrecht, and part of Wakkerstroom were transferred from the Transvaal to N. in 1903. In 1910 the colony became a part of the Union of South Africa. Area 86,965 sq.km (33,578 sq.m). Pop. (1970) 4,237,000.

NATAL. Seaport and city of Brazil, cap. of the state of Rio Grando do Norte. It has textile mills and salt refineries. Founded in 1599, N. was made a city in 1822. Pop. (1975) 343,700.

NATCHEZ (natsh'ez). North American Indians of the Mississippi area. They had a highly developed caste system, headed by a ruler priest (the 'Great Sun'), which was once thought alien to N America. This existed until the near destruction of the Natchez by the French in 1731: only a few half-bloods survive in Oklahoma.

NA'TCHEZ. Trading centre in Mississippi, USA, on the bluffs above the Mississippi river. It has many picturesque houses of the period before the American Civil War, and in the heyday of steamboat river traffic was of great importance. Pop. (1970) 19,700.

NATIONAL ACCOUNTS. The organization of a country's finances. In the UK the economy is divided into the public sector (central govt, local authorities and public corporations), the private sector (the personal and company sector), and the overseas sector (transactions between residents and non-residents of the UK). The public sector borrowing requirement (PSBR), as the state took over a larger and larger share of the economy, became a crucial factor in budgets of the UK in the 1970s, and also in that of other countries. It covers both the deficit in sums needed by the central govt to finance its own activities and loans to local authorities and public corporations, and the funds raised by local authorities and public corporations from other sources. The PSBR is financed chiefly by sales of debt to the public outside the banking system (gilt-edged stocks, nat. savings, and local authority stocks and bonds); by external transactions with other countries; and by borrowing from the banking system. Central govt revenue and expenditure is channelled through the Consolidated Fund, which meets expenditure out of revenue that arises largely from taxation, and the National Loans Fund which handles most of the central govt's domestic lending and borrowing.

NATIONAL ANTHEM. A patriotic song employed on official occasions. 'God Save the King/Queen' (q.v.) has been accepted as such in Britain since 1745, although both tune and words are of much earlier origin. The music of the Austrian 'Emperor's Hymn' was written by Haydn in 1797, and was retained after the revolution of 1918, with some new words, until 1948. The German *Deutschland über Alles* is sung to the same tune. In 1951 Pres. Heuss selected a new N.A. for the Federal Republic (Germany having been without one 1945-51): this was unpopular and the old one was revived in 1952. The French N.A., the *Marseillaise* (q.v.), dates from the revolution of 1792, and the Belgian *Brabançonne* from that of 1830. The Internationale (q.v.), adopted as the Russian N.A. in 1917, was replaced by the song 'Unbreakable Union of Freeborn Republics' in 1944. The American N.A., 'The Star-spangled Banner', written during the war of 1812, was officially adopted in 1931. Countries within the Commonwealth have in some cases adopted their own As. as a mark of independent nationhood, the best-known being 'Advance Australia Fair', adopted after a referendum in 1977. The anthem of united Europe is Schiller's 'Ode to Joy', of which Beethoven inserted a setting in his Ninth Symphony.

NATIONAL ARMY MUSEUM. Official museum, estab. in 1960 in Chelsea, London, for the British, Indian and Colonial forces 1485-1914; the Imperial War Museum deals with the period from 1914.

NATIONAL BOOK LEAGUE. British association of authors, publishers, booksellers, librarians, and readers, to encourage the reading and production of better books. Founded as the National Book Council in 1925, it was renamed the NBL in 1944.

NATIONAL COUNTRY PARTY. Australian party representing the interests of the farmers and people of the smaller towns, which developed from c.1860, and holds the power balance between Liberals and Labor. It gained strength following the introduction of preferential voting in 1918, and has been in coalition with the Liberals since 1949, its leader, Douglas Anthony (1929-), being deputy PM in the Fraser government. Re-named *Nat.* C.P. 1975.

NATIONAL DEBT. Debt incurred by the central government of a country. The first issue of government stock in England was made in 1693, to raise a loan of £1,000,000. The main cause of increase in the debt has always been wartime expenditure; thus, after the War of the Spanish Succession, it reached £54,000,000, after the Seven Years War £146,000,000, after the American War £230,000,000 and after the Napoleonic Wars £834,000,000. By 1900 it had been brought down to £610,000,000, but the F.W.W. forced it up, by 1920, to £7,828,000,000, and the S.W.W., by 1945, to £21,870,221,651. In the 1970s it stood at over £35,000 m. The US Public Debt (as it is there called), $2,436,453,269 in 1870, was $1,132,357,095 in 1905, but had risen to $24,299,321,467 by 1920 and, although in 1930 it sank to $16,185,309,831, it has since almost continually risen, reaching $560,000 m. in the 1970s.

NATIONAL FRONT. Extreme right-wing political party founded in Britain in 1967, from a merger of the League of Empire Loyalists and the British National Party. In 1980 dissension arose and splinter groups formed, the N.F. continuing under the leadership of Martin Webster: electoral support in the 1979 general election was minimal. Some of its members had links with the National Socialist Movement of the 1960s: *see* NAZIS.

NATIONAL GALLERY. Art gallery housing the British national collection of pictures, founded in 1824, when parliament voted £57,000 for the purchase of 38 pictures of the Angerstein collection, plus £3,000 for the maintenance of the building in Pall Mall, London, where they were housed. The present building in Trafalgar Square was designed by William Wilkins, and opened in 1838: there have been several extensions. Works of living artists are excluded.

NATIONAL GUARD. *See* MILITIA.

NATIONAL HERITAGE MEMORIAL FUND. Govt. fund estab. in Britain in 1980 to save the countryside, historic houses and works of art, as a memorial to those who gave their lives in the S.W.W.

NATIONALISM. A general term for movements aiming at the strengthening of national feeling and tradition, and particularly at the unification of a nation or its liberation from foreign rule. Under the influence of the French Revolution, strong movements arose in the 19th cent. in favour of national unification in Germany and Italy, and of national independence in Italy, Ireland, Belgium, Hungary, Bohemia, Poland, and the Balkan states, and remained a potent factor in European politics until 1918. Since 1900 N. has become a strong force in Asia and Africa. The term N. is also applied to the exaggerated expression of national pride, and to aggressive movements for national aggrandizement, e.g. imperialism and fascism; this represents a perversion of the outlook of the great 19th cent. nationalists.

A revival of interest in the national language, history, traditions, and culture has accompanied and influenced many political movements, e.g. in Ireland, Czechoslovakia, Poland, and Finland. In recent years a strongly national literary and political movement has developed in Scotland and Wales. N. in music usually takes the form of employing themes and rhythms derived from folk music, as in the works of Dvorák, Sibelius, and Vaughan Williams.

NATIONALIZATION. Policy of bringing essential services and industries under public ownership, pursued by the Labour Govt which held office in the UK 1945-51. Acts were passed nationalizing the Bank of England, coal, and most hospitals (1946); transport and electricity (1947); gas (1948), and iron and steel (1949). In 1953 the succeeding Conservative Govt provided for the return of road haulage to private enterprise and decentralization of the railways; and denationalization of iron and steel - the last-named re-nationalized by Labour 1967. In 1977 the Callaghan govt. nationalised the aircraft and shipbuilding industries. The term is also used for the taking over of assets in the hands of foreign govts or cos. in the newly emergent countries, e.g. Abadan, Suez Canal.

NATIONAL PARKS. Areas set aside and protected from exploitation in order to preserve them for public enjoyment. In England and Wales under the N.P. Act (1949) the Peak District, Lake District, Snowdonia, Dartmoor, Pembrokeshire coast, Yorkshire Dales, Exmoor, and other areas of great natural beauty were designated as N.P. (*See also* NATURE RESERVE.) Port Hacking, NSW, Australia, near Sydney, is the chief N.P. in Australia. N.P. in the USA incl. Crater Lake, Oregon; the Grand Canyon, Arizona; the Mammoth Cave, Kentucky; Mt McKinley, Alaska; Sequoia and Yosemite, California; and Zion Canyon, Utah. Of the 30 N.P. in Canada, the most notable is Jasper, in the Rockies. The Kruger and Natal N.P. were pioneer African examples. The increasing use by the public of N.P. has partly defeated their purpose, and a modern innovation is the reservation of 'wilderness areas' with no motorized traffic; no overflying aircraft; no hotels, hostels, shops or cafés; no industry and the minimum of management.

NATIONAL PHYSICAL LABORATORY. Estab. in 1900 at Teddington, England, the N.P.L. is a research establishment under the control of the Dept. of Industry: the chairman of the visiting committee is the Pres. of the Royal Soc.

NATIONAL PORTRAIT GALLERY. Art gallery in St Martin's Place, Trafalgar Square, London, containing individual portraits of distinguished British men and women of the past. It was founded in 1856: present building opened in 1896.

NATIONAL RESEARCH DEVELOPMENT COUNCIL. Under the Development of Inventions Acts, 1948-65, it exploits inventions deriving from public or private sources, usually acting jointly with industrial firms.

NATIONAL SECURITY AGENCY. Agency handling US communications security, signals intelligence worldwide and codebreaking. Fort Meade, Maryland, is the HQ, and there is a major facility at Menwith Hill, England. The director is Vice Admiral B.R. 'Bobby' Inman.

NATIONAL SECURITY ADVISER. Office created by Pres. Eisenhower in 1953, almost as a 'clerical post', but which became of greater stature when held by McGeorge Bundy 1961-66, and Walt Rostow 1966-69. With the appointment of Kissinger 1969-75, it rivalled that of Sec. of State. In 1986 Admiral J. M. Poindexter resigned after revelations that the US was supplying arms to Iran and using the money to support contra rebels in Nicaragua. He was replaced by Frank Carlucci.

NATIONAL SOCIALISM. *See* GERMANY; HITLER.

NATIONAL TRUST. Founded in 1895, incorporated by Act of Parliament in 1907, it permanently preserves lands and buildings of historic interest or beauty for the people, and is the largest private landowner in Britain. The N.T. for Scotland was estab. 1931. Other similar bodies exist overseas, e.g. in each of the Australian states.

NATIVITY. Name given to 3 Christian festivals: (1) Christmas; (2) the N. of the Virgin Mary, celebrated by the RC and Greek Churches on 8 Sept.; and (3) the N. of John the Baptist, celebrated by the RC, Greek and Anglican Churches on 24 June.

NATURAL HISTORY MUSEUM. The 5 natural history departments of the British Museum: zoology, entomology, geology, mineralogy, and botany. The museum is in a building (designed by Waterhouse and erected 1873-80) in S Kensington.

NATURE RESERVE. Area set aside to preserve its original scenic formation or vegetation, and often to provide a sanctuary and breeding ground for rare birds or animals. The National Parks Act, 1949, gave powers to designate such areas in Britain, to be placed in the charge of the Nature Conservancy estab. 1949.

NAU'CRATIS. Ancient Greek city in Egypt, whose ruins were discovered by Sir Flinders Petrie in 1884, situated in the W extremity of the Nile delta.

NAURU (now'roo). Pacific island 42km (26m) S of the equator in long. 167° E. Discovered in 1798, seized by Germany 1888, it was in 1920 placed under British Empire mandate by the League of Nations, in 1947 under UN trusteeship, Australia being the effective administrator except during Japanese occupation 1942-5. N. achieved independence 1968, becoming 'a special member' of the Commonwealth. N.'s importance is due to its phosphate deposits, which will be exhausted *c.* 1990. Area 21 sq.km (8 sq.m); pop. (1972) 6,800.

NAUSI'CAA. In the *Odyssey*, a daughter of Alcinous, king of Phaeacia, who welcomed Odysseus when he had been cast up by the waves on her island.

NAU'TILUS. Name applied to 2 widely differing cephalopods. The pearly N. (*Nautilus pompilius*), found in the Indo-Pacific Ocean, has a chambered spiral shell and supplies a fine quality mother-of-pearl used in inlay, etc.; the paper N. is also known as the Argonaut (q.v.).

NAVAJO (nav'ahō). N American Indian tribe. Related to the Apache, they were defeated by Kit Carson and American troops in 1864, and were rounded up and exiled. Their reservation, created 1868, is the largest in the USA (65,000 sq.km/25,000 sq.m), mostly in Arizona. They form a vigorous and expanding community (1978) *c.* 140,000, with an income from uranium, natural gas, tourism, rugs and blankets, and silver and turquoise jewellery.

NAVARINO (nahvahrē'nō). Italian and historic name of Pylos Bay, on the W coast of Peloponnese, Greece, famous for a naval victory, the decisive action in the Greek war of liberation, won here in 1827 by the combined fleets of the English, French, and Russians under Codrington, over the Turkish and Egyptian fleets.

NAUTILUS. A flowing symphony of construction - the sectioned shell of a chambered nautilus (*Nautilus pompilius*). *Photo: Heather Angel.*

NAVARRE (navahr'). Mountainous prov. of N Spain, the highest peak being Monte Adi (1,503 m (4,931 ft). The principal rivers are the Ebro and its tributary the Arga. The cap. is Pamplona; Estella, to the SW, where Don Carlos was proclaimed king in 1833, was formerly a centre of agitation by the Carlists (q.v.). N. has the right to join the Basque autonomous region if a referendum should so decide. Area 10,600 sq.km (4,090 sq.m); pop. (1970) 464,900.

This Spanish prov. is part of the old kingdom of N. which incl. also an area in present-day France. N. successfully resisted the Moorish conquerors of Spain and was independent until it became an appanage of the French crown, 1284-1316, by the marriage of Philip IV to the heiress of N. Ferdinand of Aragon annexed Spanish N., 1479, French N. going to Catherine of Foix who kept the royal title. Her grandson became Henry IV of France, and the ancient kingdom of N. was absorbed in the French crownlands in 1620.

NAVIGATION ACTS. A series of Acts passed from 1381 onwards, to protect the Eng. shipping industry against foreign competition. The best-known was that of 1651, forbidding the importation of any goods not carried in English ships or the ships of the country where the goods were produced; this was aimed against the Dutch, who controlled most of the carrying trade. The N.A. were repealed in 1849.

NAVY. A nation's warships and the organization to maintain them. Naval power was an important factor in the struggle for supremacy in the Mediterranean in the 5th cent. BC, e.g. the defeat of Persia by Greece at Salamis, but the first permanent naval organization was estab. by Rome in 311 BC with the appointment of navy commissioners to safeguard trade routes from pirates and eliminate the threat of rival sea power. Next came Byzantine dominance until the Turkish invasions of the 12th cent. AD, and during the Middle Ages the Italian city-states, e.g. Genoa, were influential. From Genoa came the admirals of the first French royal fleet, estab. by Louis IX in the 13th cent., and there was a great deal of cross-Channel raiding during the Hundred Years War (1339-1453) on the part of both sides. The English forces taking part had their origins in the fleet (a few king's ships, plus ships from the shires and a few privileged coastal towns) with which Alfred the Great overcame the Norsemen in 878. Building on the beginnings made by his father, Henry VIII raised a force which incl. a number of proper battleships, created the long-enduring administrative machinery of the Admiralty, and by mounting heavy guns low on a ship's side revolutionized strategy by the use of the 'broadside'. Often compelled to parsimony, Elizabeth yet encouraged Drake, Frobisher, Hawkins, Raleigh and others who were to set the seal on the decline of the great sea power of Spain, which had burgeoned in a great area of exploration and conquest in the early 16th cent., by their defeat of the Armada. In the 17th cent. there was a remarkable development in naval power among the powers of northern Europe, e.g. in the Netherlands, which then founded an empire in the East; in France, where a strong fleet was built up by Richelieu and Louis XIV which maintained the links with possessions in India and Canada; and in England, comparatively briefly under Cromwell. However, effectively reorganized by Pitt in time for the French revolutionary wars, the Royal Navy under Nelson won a victory over the French at Trafalgar in 1805 which ensured British naval supremacy for the rest of the 19th cent.

In the New World the American navy owes its origin to the need for the more exposed provs. to protect their harbours at the outbreak of the War of Independence, and Washington's need to capture British war supplies. Late in 1775 Washington prepared 5 schooners and a sloop, manned with army personnel, and sent them to prey on inbound supply vessels, and by the time of the Declaration of Independence in 1776 these were augmented by armed brigs and sloops from the various colonies: the hero of the period was John Paul Jones. The fleet earned further distinction in actions against Tripoli 1803-5 and Britain 1812-14, and rapidly expanded during the Civil War and again for the Spanish War of 1898.

In the F.W.W. Britain fought off Germany's bid for naval power, but in the inter-war years the American fleet was developed to protect US trade routes, and also with an eye to the renewed German threat and the new danger from Japan. *See* F.W.W. and S.W.W. After the S.W.W. the American fleet emerged as the world's most powerful, but the Cuban crisis, with its demonstration of Russia's impotence at sea led to a striking development under Admiral Sergei Gorshkov (1910-). Today, the Russian fleets (based in the Arctic, Baltic, Mediterranean and Pacific) are more powerful than the combined NATO force, and are completely co-ordinated in their operation with all other Russian sea-going vessels. Russia has one of the world's largest merchant fleets, and the world's largest fishing, hydrographic and oceanographic fleets, in which all ships have intelligence-gathering equipment. The pattern of the new navy reflects that of other modern fleets: over 400 submarines, many with Polaris-type missiles, and over 200 surface combat vessels (mostly of recent date) incl. helicopter carriers, cruisers, destroyers and escort vessels.

NAXALITES (nak'salīts). Indian extremist Communists, so-named from the town of Naxalbari, W Bengal, where a peasant rising was suppressed 1967. The movement was founded by Charu Mazumdar (1915-72).

NAVY. A new concept in naval warfare, the proposed new Harrier Carrier. At just over 7,000 tonnes, it is only marginally larger than a modern destroyer, but could carry either 8 Sea Harrier aircraft - little less than the complement of a cruiser - or 8 large anti-submarine helicopters. Its spacious deck area, hangars, engineering facilities and large electrical generating capacity would also make it suitable for disaster and famine relief. *Photo: Press Association.*

NAXOS (naks'os). An island of Greece, the largest of the Cyclades. Famous since early times for its wine, it was a centre for the worship of Bacchus, who found the deserted Ariadne asleep on its shore. Area 453 sq.km (175 sq.m).

NA'ZARETH. Town in Galilee, Israel, SE of Haifa. Jesus spent his boyhood here. Pop. (1970) 30,000.

NAZARITE or **Nazirite.** A Hebrew under a vow, who in ancient times observed certain rules until it was fulfilled, e.g. not to cut his hair or to drink wine. Samson and Samuel were Ns. for life.

NA'ZCA. Town 435 km (270 m) S of Lima, Peru. On the surface of the nearby plateau are geometric linear markings interspersed with giant outlines of birds, a monkey, etc. Discovered in 1927, they were made By American Indians, possibly in the 6th cent. AD, and the lines seem to lead to sacred places rather than being astronomical. The full effect is visible only from the air, and it is possible the makers used hot air balloons in ceremonial-religious festivals.

NAZE, The. Headland on the coast of Essex, England, 8km (5m) S of Harwich.

NAZIS (nah'tsēz). German Fascist Party. The name is derived from the first two syllables, as pronounced in German, of the full name, *Nationalsozialistiche Deutsche Arbeiterpartei* (National Socialist German Workers' Party). Related were the movements founded in Britain by Sir Oswald Mosley (q.v.) and Colin Jordan (Nat. Socialist Movement 1962), and in USA by George Lincoln Rockwell (American Nazi Party 1958), who was assassinated 1967, allegedly by a party 'officer'. In contrast to the large neo-Fascist movement in Italy, prompted by fear of the large Communist party there, the N. survived in Germany chiefly as a fanatical remnant carrying out terrorist outrages. *See* FASCISM.

N'DJAME'NA. Cap. of Chad, formerly known as Fort Lamy, on the Shari. Pop. (1973) 193,000.

NEAGH (nā), **Lough.** Lake in N Ireland, the largest in the British Isles (396 sq.km/153 sq.m.).

NEAGLE, Dame Anna (1908–86). Brit. actress. B. at Forest Gate, Essex, she was successful as a dancer and in roles as varied as Nell Gwynn (1934), Victoria the Great (1937), and Odette (1950). DBE 1969.

NEALE, John Mason (1818-66). Anglican churchman, famous as a translator of ancient and medieval hymns, incl. 'Jerusalem, the Golden'.

NEANDERTHAL (-tahl) **MAN.** A species of man of the Palaeolithic period. The name derives from the valley to the E of Düsseldorf in the Rhineland where the first skeleton was discovered in 1857. This type of man was much more ape-like than any existing race, though the brain-case was large enough to contain a well-developed brain. It is believed that N.M. became extinct through interbreeding with modern man.

NEAR EAST. Indeterminate area formerly usually taken to incl. the Balkan states, Egypt and S.W. Asia; during the S.W.W. the name Middle East (formerly referring to countries eastward of Iran to Burma) was less accurately applied to the same area and the usage has tended to survive.

NEATH (nēth). Town in W Glamorgan, Wales, nr the mouth of the r. Neath. The site of the Roman fort of Nidum was discovered nearby in 1949, and there are remains of a Norman castle and abbey. Pop. (1972) 27,890.

NEBRA'SKA. A north-central state of the USA, bounded on the N by S Dakota, and on the W by Wyoming and Colorado. In the W are the foothills of the Rocky Mtns (over 1,525 m/5,000 ft); then come sandhills now stable and grass-covered; the prairies, whose fertility is very high, slope to the Missouri, whose tributaries, White, Platte, and Niobrara, with the Big Blue, tributary of the Republican, are the chief rivers. The crops incl. maize, wheat, oats, barley, etc., livestock are important, and the chief industry is food processing, but fertilizers, and oil and natural gas are also produced. B. was purchased by the USA from France in 1803, and it became a state of the Union in 1867. Area 200,036 sq.km (77,227 sq.m); pop. (1970) 1,483,791.

NEBUCHADNEZZAR (nebukadnez'ar) **II,** or **Nebuchadrezzar** (d. 562 BC). King of Babylonia. Shortly before his accession in 604 BC he defeated the Egyptians at Carchemish and brought Palestine and Syria into his empire. Judah revolted, with Egyptian assistance, in 596 and 587-586 BC; on each occasion N. captured Jerusalem and carried off many of the Jews into captivity. N. largely rebuilt Babylon, constructed the famous Hanging Gardens, and carried out ambitious irrigation schemes.

NE'BULA. A luminous patch in the night sky, composed of thinly spread gas and dust. The most famous N. lies below the Belt of Orion, and is clearly visible to the naked eye; large numbers of similar objects may be seen with the aid of telescopes. It is thought that these nebulae are the birthplaces of the stars, and that fresh stars are being created all the time out of the nebular material. A N. shines because of the stars contained in it; if there are no suitable stars, the N. is *dark*, but may be traced because it blocks out the light of stars lying beyond. The 18th cent. astronomer Messier catalogued over 100 nebular objects, incl. true nebulae; *planetary nebulae*, now known to be stars with extensive gaseous surrounds; and *resolvable* or starry nebulae, now known to be galaxies in their own right, and to lie far beyond the boundaries of our own star-system or galaxy.

NEBULA. Planetary nebula in Aquarius, photographed with a 500 cm (200 in) telescope. *Photo: Courtesy of the Hale Observatories.*

NECK. The structures between the head and the trunk. Its bones are the upper 7 (cervical) vertebrae, it comprises many powerful muscles which support and move the head, and in front it contains the pharynx and wind-pipe (trachea), and behind these the gullet (oesophagus). Within it are the large arteries (carotid, temporal, maxillary), and veins (jugular), which supply the brain and head.

NECKER, Jacques (1732-1804). French statesman. B. at Geneva, he made a fortune in Paris as a banker. As Finance Minister, 1776-81, he attempted to introduce certain reforms, and was dismissed through Marie Antoinette's influence. Recalled to office in 1788, he persuaded Louis XVI to summon the States-General; this earned him the hatred of the court, and in July 1789 he was banished. The storming of the Bastille forced Louis to reinstate him, but in Sept. 1790 he resigned and retired to Switzerland. *See* MME DE STAEL.

NE'CTAR. The drink of the Greek gods.

NECTARINE (-ēn or-in). A smooth-skinned peach, usually smaller than other peaches, with firmer flesh.

NEEDLES, The. The name given to a group of rocks lying off the W extremity of the Isle of Wight, England. On the most westerly, 30m (100ft) high, is the N. lighthouse.

NEFERTITI (-tē'tē) or **Nofretiti** (14th cent. BC). Egyptian queen, favourite wife of Ikhnaton (q.v.). She bore 6 daus., and is frequently represented with her husband and children; her name does not appear on monuments later in the reign but it is more probable that she d. than that she was disgraced. The portrait head found at Amarna in 1912 ranks as one of the world's masterpieces, but may be that of one of her daus.

NEGEV. Desert area in S Israel, lying between Beersheba, where it is *c.* 65km (40m) wide, and the Gulf of Aqaba, where it tapers to the port of Eilat; *c.* 195km (120m) long. In ancient times the N. was fertile and Israel has developed the irrigation begun in the 1930s, notably with a water pipeline (1964) from the Sea of Galilee (Lake

Kinnereth). Minerals being exploited incl. oil (1955) at Heletz and copper at Timna, near Elat. N. is a Hebrew word meaning south or arid.

NEGLIGENCE. In law, N. consists in doing some act which a prudent and reasonable man would not do, or omitting to do some act which he would do. N. may arise in respect of a person's duty towards an individual or towards his fellow-men in general. In the first class are such duties as arise from parenthood, guardianship, trusteeship, or a contractual relationship. In the second are the duties owed to the community, such as care upon the public highway, the maintenance of structures in a safe condition, etc. Contributory N. is a defence sometimes raised where the defendant to an action for N. claims that the plaintiff by his own N. contributed to the cause of the action.

NE'GRI SEMBILAN (sembē'lan). State of the Federation of Malaysia, on the W side of the Malay peninsula. It came under British rule in 1873 and entered the Federated Malay States in 1895. Its cap. is Seremban, its harbour Port Dickson. The chief exports are tin, rubber, oil palm, and coconuts. Area 2,550 sq.m; pop. (1970) 481,560.

NEGRO. Term given to a member of the indigenous people of Africa, today distributed around the world. The more commonly used term today is black.

Formerly, the word Negro was used to describe one of three hypothetical human racial groups – the Caucasoid, Mongoloid, and Negroid. Common physical characteristics and pigmentation suggested such a classification, but scientific studies have failed to indicate any genetic confirmation of such a racial division. The attempt to categorize human types (seen in such countries as S Africa for the purposes of segregation) is inevitably doomed by the absence of any straightforward distinction. On the contrary, differences within so-called 'races' are often greater than the distinction between them.

In the USA, blacks comprise some 28.5 million, or 12% of the population. The history of the American Negro is largely one of oppression and survival. Brought to North America in large numbers from Africa to work on plantations in the Atlantic and Southern states, they experienced discrimination before and after the American Civil War. In the 20th century they have moved in large numbers to such cities as New York, Chicago, and Washington. Great efforts have been made by the black population to combat racial discrimination, with some degree of legislative success. The Little Rock incident of 1957 was a major step towards equal rights for blacks, but despite all legislation and 'affirmative action' (the US term for positive discrimination), opportunities for blacks remain demonstrably inferior, particularly in education, employment, and housing. The situation described by US President Johnson's 1968 National Advisory Commission concluded that 'Our nation is moving towards two societies, one Black, one White – separate and unequal', but added that it was not too late to reverse the trend. Social measures to combat racism, such as entrance quotas to enable a larger proportion of blacks to study subjects such as medicine at University, continue to cause controversy.

Black achievement has since the 1960s played a major part in US history. Major black writers include Eldridge Cleaver and James Baldwin; Martin Luther King is acknowledged as one of the greatest civil rights leaders of this century. JAZZ and BLUES music were at one time distinctively black musical genres.

NEGRO, River in S. America. The r. N. flows E from Colombia to Brazil and joins the Amazon near Manaus. Length 2250km (1400m). Also the name of a river in Argentina which rises in the Andes and flows SE across Patagonia and into the Atlantic. Length 1014km (630m).

NĔHEMĪ'AH. Jewish statesman, who was appointed governor of Judaea by the king of Persia, rebuilt the walls of Jerusalem, and carried out religious and social reforms. Some scholars date his appointment in 445-444 BC, others in 384 BC. His memoirs are incorporated in the OT book of N.

NEHRU (nā'rōō), **Jawaharlal** (1889-1964). Indian statesman. B. at Allahabad, and ed. at Harrow and Cambridge, he practised from 1912 at the Allahabad Bar, and soon became prominent in the Congress Party as the leader of its Socialist left wing, acquiring an influence second only to Gandhi's. During 1921-45 he was imprisoned 9 times for his political activities. He became For. Min. in the interim govt set up in Sept. 1946, and PM on the creation of the Dom. (later Rep.) of India in Aug. 1947. In 1951-4 he was also pres. of the Congress Party (a post in which he had succeeded his father in 1929, and had also held in 1936, 1937, and 1946). He pub. an autobiography (1936). His influence over the country remained strong as ever until his death. *See* GANDHI, Indira.

NEHRU. Pandit Jawaharlal Nehru with Mohammed Ali Jinnah, the founder of Pakistan. *Photo: Courtesy of the Indian Information Service.*

NEI MONGGOL (nā mawng-gawl'). *See* MONGOLIA, INNER.

NEISSE (nīs'e). Tributary of the r. Oder in E Europe, 225km (140m) long. It rises in the Iser Mountains, Czechoslovakia, and flows generally N. It marks the S part of the boundary set up in 1945 between E Germany and Polish-occupied Germany. Another trib. of the Oder, the Glatzer Neisse (Polish Nysa Kluz), lies 177km (110m) farther E. On its banks is the town of N. (Polish Nysa), from which the German pop. were expelled in 1945; it was cap. of the prince-bishops of Breslau (Wroclaw) from 1198-1810.

NEJD. Region of central Arabia consisting chiefly of desert. It forms part of the kingdom of Saudi Arabia, and is inhabited by Bedouins. The cap. is Riyadh. Area *c.* 2,720,000 sq.km (800,000 sq.m).

NEKRASOV (nyekrah'sof), **Nikolai Alekseevich** (1821-77). Russian poet. He espoused the cause of the freeing of the serfs and was politically influential.

NELSON, Horatio, viscount (1758-1805). British admiral. He was b. at Burnham Thorpe, Norfolk, where his father was rector, and entered the navy in 1770. While serving in the W Indies he m. Mrs Frances Nisbet. He was almost continuously on active service in the Mediterranean 1793-1800 and as a result of wounds he lost the sight of his right eye in 1794 and his right arm in 1797. His share in the victory off Cape St Vincent in 1797 made him a national hero, and was rewarded by promotion to rear-admiral.

In 1798 he tracked the French fleet to Aboukir Bay, and almost entirely destroyed it in the Battle of the Nile. He then lingered at Naples for a year, during which he helped to crush a democratic uprising, and fell completely under the influence of Lady Hamilton (q.v.). In 1800 he returned to England, and soon after separated from his wife. He was promoted to vice-admiral in 1801, and sent to the Baltic to operate against the Danes, nominally as second-in-command; in fact, it was N. who was responsible for the victory of Copenhagen, and for negotiating peace with Denmark. On his return to England he was created a visct.

In 1803 he received the Mediterranean command, and for nearly 2 years blockaded Toulon. When in 1805 Villeneuve eluded him, N. pursued him to the W Indies and back, and on 21 Oct. totally defeated the combined French and Spanish fleets off Cape Trafalgar, 20 of the enemy ships being captured. N. himself was mortally wounded; his body was brought to England, and buried in St Paul's.

NELSON. Town in South Is., New Zealand, situated on Tasman Bay, with an excellent harbour. It has an airport, saw mills, fruit-canning plants, etc. Pop. (1975) 42,300. Also an industrial town in Lancs, England, N of Manchester. Pop. (1972) 31,360.

NE'MATŌDA. Phylum covering round or thread worms.

NĒME'RTĒA. A group of unsegmented worms, allied to the Platyhelminthes. They are ribbon-shaped and mostly marine.

NEMERY (nemā'ri), **Jaafar Mohammed al-** (1930-). Sudanese statesman. A soldier, he served in campaigns against the rebels in the south, and in 1969 led a successful military coup. He was President of Sudan 1971–85, when he was deposed by the military forces.

NE'MESIS. Greek goddess of retribution. She punished certain moral faults, esp. *hybris*, the arrogant self-confidence which, more than other crimes, excited the hostility of the gods.

NELSON. A portrait of the admiral by L.F. Abbott. *Photo: Courtesy of the National Portrait Gallery.*

NEMI (nā'mē). Lake occupying an extinct volcanic crater in the Alban Hills, some 30km (18m) SE of Rome, near Aricia. Nearby are the sacred woods and ruins of a famous temple of Diana. Two pleasure barges belonging to Caligula were raised from the bed of the lake, 1930-1; they were burned by the Germans in 1944.

NENNIUS (fl. 796). Welsh chronicler, believed to be the author of a Latin *Historia Britonum*, which contains the earliest reference to King Arthur's wars against the Saxons.

NEOLITHIC or **New Stone Age.** *See* STONE AGE.

NĒON (Gk *neos* new). Chemically inert gas, discovered by Ramsay and Travers in 1898: symbol Ne, at. wt. 20.183, at. no. 10. Present in the atmosphere in the proportion 18 parts per million by volume, it is extracted by liquefaction and fractional distillation. It glows bright orange-red in a discharge tube, e.g. its use in advertisement signs. N. is also used in electronics.

NEO-PLASTICISM. A geometric-abstract movement in painting, sculpture, poster design, and interior decoration, founded by Piet Mondrian.

NEO-PLATONISM. Philosophical system, based on the doctrines of Plato and beliefs adopted from Oriental religions, which developed in the 3rd cent. at Alexandria, and was first fully expounded by Plotinus. Its principal doctrine is the attainment of unity with the Deity through purifying ascetic practices. Under Porphyry, N. became the great opponent of Christianity, and its supremacy was almost secured by the advocacy of the emperor Julian. It ceased to exist as an independent system in the 6th cent., but it greatly influenced Augustine, and the whole tradition of Christian mysticism.

NEPAL (nepawl'). An independent kingdom in the Himalayas, bounded on the N. by Tibet, on the E by Sikkim, and on the S and W by India. It is composed of the Tarai, a level strip of land along its S border, and the Himalayan slopes to the N, culminating in Everest and Kanchenjunga (qq.v.), and other immense border peaks, which determine the courses of the 4 groups of rivers that divide the country. Katmandu, the cap., stands in the chief valley; it is linked by air with Calcutta. The people are mixed Mongols, Gurkhas (q.v.) being dominant. Sanatan, an ancient form of Hinduism, and Buddhism are the prevailing religions. The effective ruler of N. from 1846 was the hereditary PM, always a member of the Ráná family; a revolution in 1950 restored power to the king, and a new constitution (1962) provided for a single-chamber national panchayat (council), indirectly elected by local panchayats. All political parties are banned. Major hydroelectric projects power new industries, e.g. chemicals, leather goods, synthetic textiles, iron and steel, and jute and sugar. Roads have been built by foreign aid, e.g. the E-W Highway and Kathmandu-Tibetan border. King Birendra (1946-) succeeded to the throne in 1972, and still exercises almost one-man rule. A constitutional referendum in 1980 left the situation unchanged. Area 141,400 sq.km (54,600 sq.m); pop. (1971) 11,289,000. M.U.: Nepalese rupee.

NEPAL. The eyes of Buddha decorate the small pagoda on the top of a hill outside Kathmandu. *Photo: Barnaby's Picture Library.*

NEPHRITIS. Inflammation of the kidneys, Brights disease, or more accurately glomerulonephritis. It may be caused by infection spreading from elsewhere in the body, eg a streptococcal sore throat, and symptoms incl raised blood pressure and blood in the urine, and swelling caused by retention of fluid (oedema or dropsy). It can become chronic, and may cause uraemia (q.v.).

NE'PTUNE. Roman god of the sea. Most of his myths are borrowed from the Greek stories of Poseidon. According to these, N., Zeus (Jupiter), and Hades (Pluto), the sons of Cronus, dethroned their father and divided his realms, N. taking the sea.

NEPTUNE. The outermost of the giant planets. It is 4,497,000,000 km (2,797,000,000 m) from the Sun, and has a revolution period of 164.8 years. Its diameter is 51,000 km (31,700 m), and in every respect it seems to be similar to Uranus but fainter, and not visible to the naked eye. N. was discovered in 1846 by J. Galle and H. d'Arrest at Berlin, after calculations by U. Le Verrier (Fr.) and J. C. Adams (Brit.) indicated its probable position. The surface temperature has been est. at -184°C, and the atmosphere appears turbulent. There is an outer satellite, Nereid (diameter 300 km/185 m), with a very eccentric orbit, and a much larger inner one – Triton (diameter 4000 km/2485 m), which revolves in a retrograde direction at about the same distance as the Moon from Earth. Voyagers I and II are intended to reach Neptune in 1989.

NEPTŪ'NIUM. Transuranic element, symbol Np, at. wt. 237, at. no. 93. It is produced in atomic reactors as an intermediate in making plutonium. U-238 absorbs a neutron to become U-239 which emits a beta-ray from its nucleus thus turning into Np-239 with a half-life of 2.3 days.

NEREIDS (nē'rē-ids). In Greek mythology, minor goddesses of the sea, one of the classes of nymphs. They sometimes mated with mortals, as in the case of Thetis, who bore Achïlles.

NE'RGAL. A Babylonian and Assyrian sun-god; he was also the god of war and pestilence, and ruler of the underworld. He was symbolized in sculpture by a winged lion.

NERI, St Philip (1515-95). Italian ecclesiastic. B. in Florence, in 1533 he went to Rome, where he devoted himself to good works. Ordained a priest in 1551, he organized the Congregation of the Oratory, and built the oratory over the church of St Jerome, where prayer meetings were held, and scenes from the Bible were performed with music - hence *oratorio.* He was canonized in 1622.

NERO (AD 37-68). Roman emperor, whose full name was N. Claudius Caesar Drusus Germanicus. The son of Domitius Ahenobarbus and Agrippina, he was adopted by his stepfather, Claudius, and succeeded him as emperor in 54. He has become proverbial for cruelty and debauchery, and is said to have murdered Claudius's son, Britannicus, his mother, his wives, Octavia and Poppaea, and many others. He was a poet and an enthusiast for art, and himself appeared on the public stage as an actor and singer. After the great fire of Rome in 64, he persecuted the Christians, who were suspected of causing it, while an aristocratic conspiracy against him in 65 led to the execution or suicide of Seneca, Lucan, and many others. A military revolt followed in 68; the senate condemned N. to death, whereupon he committed suicide.

NERUDA (neroo'da), **Pablo.** Pseudonym of Chilean poet Neftalí Ricardo Reyes (1904-73). A widely travelled diplomat, he ranges in his verse from the intimate lyric to an epic treatment of the history of the American continent *Canto General* (1950). He was awarded a Nobel prize 1971.

NERVA, Marcus Cocceius (C. AD 35-98). Roman emperor. He was a senator who was proclaimed emperor on Domitian's death in 96, and proved a humane ruler. He introduced state schemes for loans for farmers and family allowances, and an agrarian law for the allotment of land to poor citizens.

NERVAL (nervahl'), **Gérard de.** Adopted name of French Romantic poet Gérard Labrunie (1808-55). He pub. short stories, plays, poems, translations, and the semi-autobiographical romance, *Sylvia* (1848-50). He lived a wandering life, darkened by periodic insanity, and committed suicide.

NERVES. The highly specialized cells with their processes through which all the activities of the body are initiated and controlled. The bodies of the cells form most of the grey matter of the brain and spinal cord (central nervous system); long, fine fibres (axons) run out and branch from these to all parts of the body. One set of Ns. transmits the commands of the will to the muscles (motor), another transmits the sensations from the skin, eyes, ears, digestive system, etc. (peripheral nerves), to the brain (sensory). Much of the work of the Ns. is automatic, and never comes into consciousness at all (autonomic nervous system).

NE'RVI, Pier Luigi (1891-1979). Italian engineer and architect. He transformed the use of concrete in buildings by using soft steel mesh internally to give it flowing form. His works incl. Turin exhibition hall (1949), UNESCO building in Paris (1952) and the cathedral at New Norcia, nr. Perth, Australia (1960).

NESBIT, Edith (1858-1924). British writer, best remembered for her children's books, e.g. *The Treasure-Seekers* (1899), *The Would-be Goods* (1901) and *Five Children and It* (1902). Her creation of the Bastable family was a notable departure from the conventional, class-conscious mode of the period. She m. the Fabian Hubert Bland (d. 1914), in 1880, her writing being the mainstay of the marriage, and had 4 children.

NESS, Loch. Very deep lake in Highland region, Scotland, SW of Inverness. Some 37km (23m) long, it averages 1.5km (1m) in width, forms part of the Caledonian Canal, and is surrounded by mountains. There have been reports of a 'monster' since the 15th cent., and similar reports came from Lake Wenbu in Tibet in 1980.

NESTŌ'RIUS (d. *c.* 451). Syrian ecclesiastic. Appointed patriarch of Constantinople in 428, he maintained that Mary was the mother of the man Jesus only, and therefore should not be called the 'Mother of God'. This doctrine was condemned by the council of Ephesus in 431, and N. was deposed and banished. His followers, the NESTORIANS, estab. a powerful Church in Syria and Persia, and successfully carried on missionary work in India, N China, and all over central Asia. They still survive as the Assyrian Church in Syria, Iraq, Iran, etc., and as the Christians of St Thomas in S India.

NETHERLANDS. Kingdom of W Europe, bounded on the N and W by the North Sea, on the S by Belgium, and on the E by Germany. It is often referred to as Holland, the name of its two wealthiest provs., N and S Holland.

PHYSICAL FEATURES. The flatness of the N. is proverbial. Only in S Gelderland, near the German border, and in Limburg are there any hills, the highest part of the country (300m/1,000ft), being in S Limburg. Much land has been wrested from the sea and is below sea-level, esp. in N and S Holland; some of the polders, or drained lands, lie 6m (21ft) b.s.l. A noteworthy feature is the extensive and fertile delta formed by the Rhine and the Maas (Meuse) and their distributaries. Other important rivers are the Ijssel, draining to the Ijsselmeer, and the Scheldt estuary. Off the coast are 2 groups of is.: in the S, Over Flakkee, Schouwen, Tholen, Noord and Zuid Beveland, and Walcheren; in the N the West Frisian Is. incl. Texel, Vlieland, Terschelling, Ameland, Schiermonnikoog, and Rottumeroog. When plans of reclamation are completed, both groups will form part of the mainland. Reclamation of the former Zuider Zee (q.v.), started in 1920, has added 48,450 ha. (120,000 acres) of cultivable land to the country; and the southern part of the ambitious Delta plan to shut off from the sea the river estuaries of S Holland and Zeeland - a scheme launched to prevent a repetition of the disastrous sea floods of 1953 which killed 1,800 people and ruined for several years acres of fertile soil - has been completed, linking Walcheren with N and S Beveland. The E Scheldt Bridge (1965) linking Noord-Beveland and Schouwen-Duiveland is Europe's longest, and an integral part of the plan. The whole Delta scheme, with a sea wall linking Walcheren in the S to a point W of Rotterdam in the N, was planned for completion *c.* 1980.

ECONOMIC LIFE. Both industry and agriculture are thriving. Agriculture concentrates on cattle breeding and the export of cheese, butter, flower bulbs, and vegetables. The chief crops are rye, potatoes, oats, and sugar beet. Industrial activities incl. shipbuilding; the manufacture of textiles, earthenware, cigars, spirits, paper, electrical equipment, margarine, chemicals; iron and steel goods; the cutting and polishing of diamonds, etc.; refining of petroleum. Coal is mined in Limburg; petroleum (discovered in 1943) is worked; salt is extracted at Hengelo in Overijssel; a huge deposit of natural gas, discovered in 1962, exists in Groningen. Shipping and fishing are of great importance, and there is a large trade with Germany, Belgium, and the UK. Amsterdam and Rotterdam are among the most important commercial centres of Europe. M.U.: gulden (guilder).

The N is covered by a network of canals, the larger constructed as a means of transport, many others (some very small) used for drainage. The North Sea Canal (linking Amsterdam with the N Sea), and the New Waterway (running between Rotterdam and the Hook of Holland), can take ocean-going vessels. The state-controlled railways are electrified. Dutch airlines cover the whole world.

AREA AND POPULATION. Area 34,000 sq.km (13,020 sq.m); pop. (1978) 13,897,874 incl. some 300,000 Eurasians of Dutch-Indonesian blood, as well as Amboinese soldiers in the Dutch service, who were absorbed 1949-64. The main towns are Amsterdam (the commercial cap.), Rotterdam, The Hague (the admin. cap. and seat of parliament and the govt), Utrecht, Haarlem, Eindhoven, Groningen, Tilburg, and Nijmegen. The Roman Catholics form the largest single religious group, and preponderate in the S, but over the whole of the country they are outnumbered by Protestants, the majority of whom are members of the Dutch Reformed Church, to which the royal family belongs; Calvinists are also numerous. The standard of educ. is high. There are 5 public univs., at Leiden (1575), Groningen (1614), Utrecht (1636), Amsterdam (1877), and Rotterdam (1966); 2 religious and 6 technical.

GOVERNMENT. The N. is a constitutional monarchy under the house of Orange. Legislative powers are exercised by the 2 chambers of the States-General, and there is also an advisory Council of State under the presidency of the sovereign. Members of the 1st (upper) chamber (Senators) are elected for 6 years (half retiring every 3 years) by the members of the provincial states;

members of the 2nd chamber (Deputies) are directly elected for 4 years by universal suffrage on a system of proportional representation.

For the history and status of the Dutch colonial empire, *see* INDONESIA; NETHERLANDS ANTILLES; NETHERLANDS EAST INDIES; NEW GUINEA; SURINAM.

NETHERLANDS. The Gravensteenbrug in Haarlem, an attractive example of the type of bridge made famous by Van Gogh. *Photo: Courtesy of the Netherlands National Tourist Office.*

History. In Roman times the country S of the Rhine was brought under Roman rule. The Franks followed, and their kings subdued the Frisians and Saxons N of the Rhine in the 7th-8th cents., and imposed Christianity on them. After the break-up of the Frankish Empire the local feudal lords, headed by the count of Holland and the bishop of Utrecht, achieved practical independence, although nominally owing allegiance to the Holy Roman Empire. Many Dutch towns during the Middle Ages became prosperous trading centres, usually ruled by a merchant oligarchy. In the 15th cent. the whole of the Low Countries (present-day N. and Belgium) passed to the dukes of Burgundy, and thence to the Habsburgs and Spain.

In the 16th cent. the religious and secular tyranny of Philip II of Spain led to general revolt in the whole of the Netherlands, in which William the Silent, Prince of Orange (1533-84), and his sons Maurice (1567-1625) and Frederick Henry (1584-1647) were the guiding spirits. The south was re-conquered by Spain, but not north, and at last in 1648 the independence of the north as the Dutch Rep. was recognized under the Treaty of Westphalia (or Munster). The rep., estab. in 1581 as the United Provs., was a confederacy of sovereign provs., and it had become customary to elect the Prince of Orange for the time-being as chief officer (Stadholder) and commander-in-chief for the confederacy. A long struggle took place between the Orangist or popular party, which favoured centralization, and the oligarchical or 'states' rights' party. The oligarchs, headed by De Witt, seized control in 1650, after the death of Frederick Henry, and abolished the stadholderate. Despite the continuing war of independence, during the early 17th cent. the Dutch led the world in trade, in art and in science, and founded an empire in the E and W Indies. Commercial and colonial rivalries led to naval wars with England in 1652-4, 1665-7, and 1672-4.

The French invasion of 1672 enabled William of Orange (William III of England) to recover the stadholderate, and thenceforward until 1713 Dutch history was dominated by the struggle with Louis XIV. These wars exhausted the N., which in the 18th cent. ceased to be a great power. The French revolutionary army was welcomed in 1795. In 1806 Napoleon created his brother Louis king of Holland, and in 1810 annexed the country to France. In 1814 the north and south Netherlands were once more united under King William I (son of Prince William V of Orange); but the S broke away and in 1839 was recognized as independent (*see* under BELGIUM). A liberal constitution was granted in 1814, and the Crown assumed a constitutional position. The sovereigns have been: William I (reigned 1814-40), William II (1840-9), William III (1849-90), Queen Wilhelmina (1890-1948), Queen Juliana (1948-80), and Queen Beatrix, who succeeded on her mother's abdication in 1980. The N. were occupied by the Germans 1940-5. The Christian Democratic Appeal (CDA), centre right, forming the govt. from 1977, became a full political party in 1980.

Art. With the rise of the Dutch nation in the second half of the 16th cent. came the full emergence of Dutch art with Frans Hals, Pieter Lastman (1585-1633) - the teacher of Rembrandt - and Gerard van Honthorst. Among the many masters of the 17th cent. are Rembrandt and his pupil Gerard Douw; Adriaen van Ostade, who transplanted Flemish peasant scenes; Gerard Ter Borch the Younger, first painter of characteristic Dutch interiors; Albert Cuyp; Jan Steen; Jakob van Ruysdael, greatest of the landscapists; Pieter de Hooch; Jan Vermeer van Delft; Willem van de Velde, sea painter to Charles II of England; Jan van der Heyden; and Meindert Hobbema. The houses, market and town halls of this period were fine.

In the 18th and 19th cents. there was a marked decline, except for the genre painters Cornelis Troost (1697-1750) and Jozef Israels (1824-1911), and the outstanding genius of Vincent van Gogh.

Language. A branch of the West Germanic, or, more specially, the German division of the Germanic languages (q.v.), and like Flemish (q.v.) an offshoot of Low Franconian, which is known from *c.* 800. D. is the official language of the Netherlands, whence it spread to the D. colonies; whilst in S Africa 'Cape Dutch' developed into a language of its own, called Afrikaans (q.v.).

Literature. Earliest known poet to use the Dutch dialect was Henric van Veldeke (12th cent.), but the finest example of early Gothic literature is *Van Den Vos Reinaarde* (About Reynard the Fox) by a poet known only as 'Willem-who-made-the-Madoc'. To the Golden Age belong Pieter C. Hooft (1581-1647), lyricist, playwright and historian; Constantijn Huygens (1596-1687), who was knighted by James I in 1622; Gerbrand A. Bredero (1585-1618), gifted in comedy and light verse; the great lyric, satiric and dramatic poet Joost van den Vondel (1587-1679), and the moralizing poet Father Jacob Cats (1577-1660). As in art, the 18th cent. was generally a period of decline, although the epic poet Willem Bilderdijk (1756-1831) ranks high. The Romantic movement found its fullest expression in the nationalist periodical *De Gids* (The Guide) founded in 1837. Among the best-known writers of the period were Nicolas Beets (1814-1903), with his famous sketches *Camera Obscura,* and Eduard Douwes Dekker (1820-87), who wrote novels under the pseudonym 'Multatuli' and was a forerunner of the movement grouped round a second periodical *De Nieuwe Gids* (The New Guide, estab. 1885) which marked the late 19th cent. revival. Among writers of the period were lyricist Herman Gorter (1864-1927), the staider poet Albert Verwey (1865-1937), the poet, playwright and novelist Frederick van Eeden (1860-1932), the novelist Louis Couperus (1863-1923), Marcellus Emants (1848-1923), and Arthur van Schendel (1874-1946). After the F.W.W. Hendrik Marsman (1899-1940), a rhetorical 'vitalist' influenced by German expressionism, led a school counterbalanced by the more sober *Forum* group led by critic Menno Ter Braak (1902-40). No recent writers have attained international standing.

NETHERLANDS ANTILLES. Overseas part of the kingdom of the Netherlands composed of the islands of Curaçao (q.v.), Aruba, and Bonaire, lying off the coast of Venezuela, together with St Eustatius, Saba, and the S part of St Maarten, *c.* 800km (500m) to the NE. Total area 990 sq.km (381 sq.m); pop. (1972) 230,825. Willemstad, on Curaçao, is the cap. Maize, salt, and phosphates are produced, and huge refineries on Curaçao and Aruba treat petroleum from Venezuela. N.A. has full internal autonomy (from 1954), and complete independence is planned by 1980, although Aruba demands separate independence.

NETHERLANDS EAST INDIES. Name used for the East Indian Archipelago until those islands achieved independence as Indonesia (q.v.). The Portuguese were the first European traders to reach the islands, in the early part of the 16th cent. Before the end of that cent. they had been driven out by the English and the Dutch. But the Dutch soon obtained the monopoly of trade there and in 1602 formed their East India Co., which set up a factory at a spot named Batavia in 1619 (renamed Djakarta in 1949). Gradually the company subdued the warring rulers and brought the islands one after another under its rule until in 1798 (during the French occupation of the Netherlands) the company was abolished. The British seized the N.E.I. to prevent them from falling into French hands, restoring them in 1816 when they came under the control of the Dutch govt. In the 20th cent. progress to self-govt was brought to an abrupt end by the Japanese occupation of the N.E.I., 1942-5.

NETSUKE (net'sookā). Toggle used to stop the cords slipping on which Japanese men carried their purse, tobacco pouch, etc., when wearing traditional costume which is without pockets. Made of ivory, wood, etc., they belong mainly to the Edo Period 1601-1867, and are valued as works of art.

NETTLE. Genus (*Urtica*) of plants, many of which have ovate or lanceolate leaves covered with stinging hairs. When lightly touched these penetrate the skin and release an acid juice causing inflammation. The common stinging nettle (*U. dioica*), found in waste places in Europe and naturalized in parts of N America, yields a tough fibre which was made into cloth in ancient Egypt.

NETTLE-RASH. *See* URTICARIA.

NEUCHÂTEL (nöshahtel'). Swiss city, cap. of N canton, nr the NE of N. Lake, 40km (25m) W of Berne. It is the seat of a univ. (1909). Pop. (1971) 38,800.

NEURALGIA (nūral'ja). A severe pain felt along the track of a nerve and not due to inflammation of it (*see* NEURITIS). Some forms are due to exhaustion or illness, others to an unhealthy stimulus, sometimes at a considerable distance - e.g. sciatica - resulting from displacement of one of the discs which lie between the vertebrae. Treatment is by general measures, sometimes by the injection of alcohol into the nerve trunk, and sometimes by cutting or stretching of the nerve.

NEURASTHENIA (nūrasthē'nia). An unscientific term meaning nervous weakness or exhaustion, and used to cover a variety of symptoms of neurosis.

NEURITIS. Inflammation of a nerve or nerves as a result of poison, infection, or injury. Multiple N., the inflammation of a large number of nerves, results from chronic drunkenness (Korsakow's psychosis), or poisoning by lead, arsenic, etc., or the toxins of diseases such as diphtheria or sleepy sickness.

NEURON. Nerve cell of the brain: they number some 100,000 million in human beings - approx. the same number as the stars in the Milky Way. They measure 5-100 microns in diameter, and each have *c.* 1,000 synapses (contacts through which electrical impulses flow to and from other neurons), so that at its most efficient a human brain has *c.* 1,000,000,000,000,000 electrical connections.

NEUROSIS. Mental disorder not amounting to insanity, resulting from unrecognized conflict between the patient's primitive and his ethical impulses. It is often classified into anxiety, marked by irrational apprehension; obsession, in which the will is dominated by compulsive 'rituals' such as the need to wash the hands frequently; and hysteria, in which the trouble is chiefly infantile dependence on others and a lack of emotional control.

NEURO-TOXINS. Substances, such as lead and organolead compounds, organo-chlorines, manganese and mercury, which poison the brain or nervous system. Symptoms of clinical poisoning may be preceded by behavioural abnormalities, such as aggression or rejection of authority, which become evident some years after actual exposure to N.T.

NEUROTRANSMITTER. Chemical in a nerve cell responsible for the transmission of a nervous impulse.

NEUTRA (noi'trah), **Richard Joseph** (1892-1970). Austrian architect. Ed. at the univs. of Vienna and Zürich, he worked in Switzerland 1919-23, when he went to the USA, where he was naturalized in 1929. His works incl. the Lovell Health House, Los Angeles and Mathematics Park, Princeton.

NEUTRALITY. Non-participation in a war between other states. Under international law, neutral states must not supply men, arms, money, or war-supplies to belligerents, or allow the passage of belligerent troops, the establishment of military, naval, or air bases on their territory, or recruiting among their subjects by belligerents. Any favour granted to one belligerent must be extended to the other. Troops entering neutral territory must be interned; belligerent warships may remain in a neutral port for 24 hours, but any prisoners carried must be released. Any violation of N. may be resisted by force. The problem of the rights of neutral goods on belligerent vessels, and vice versa, has been a frequent source of international controversy. An attitude of active sympathy towards a belligerent, known as 'benevolent N.' or 'non-belligerence', is often adopted in practice, although unwarranted by international law; e.g. the attitude of the USA to Britain 1939-41.

NEUTRINO (nūtrē'nō). A very small uncharged fundamental particle (*see* ATOM) of minute mass, very difficult to detect and of great penetrating power, emitted in all radioactive disintegrations which give rise to beta rays. All reactors emit numbers of Ns.

NEUTRON (nū'tron). A nuclear particle having no electric charge and the approximate mass of a hydrogen nucleus. It is found in the nuclei of atoms and plays a vital part in nuclear fission. Outside a nucleus a N. is radioactive, decaying with a half-life of about 12 min. to give a proton and an electron.

Neutron beam machines use either a nuclear reactor or accelerator to produce a stream of Ns., which are then utilised in a similar way to X-rays to 'see' through metals. They have industrial uses, e.g. checking molecular changes in metal as it ages, or lubricant flow in an engine (in which case the Ns. can penetrate the metal, but not the lighter atoms which make up the oil).

A **neutron 'gun',** a cyclotron producing a beam of neutrons, is used in treating certain types of cancer, and has the advantage of minimising damage to the skin and organs next to the tumour.

The **neutron bomb** is a very small H-bomb designed to kill by neutron radiation within a defined target area, but over a very brief period of time and leaving buildings and weaponry uncontaminated. The N. bomb is also referred to as Enhanced Radiation Weapon (ERW).

NEUTRON STAR. The remnant of a star following a supernova outburst, and consisting chiefly of neutrons (protons and electrons having run together). Although massive, it may be under 160 km (100 m) in diameter. *See* NOVA and PULSAR.

NEVADA (nēvah'dah). One of the western states of the USA, lying within the Great Basin between the Rockies and Sierra Nevada, forming a plateau (1,700m/5,500ft) crossed by mountain ranges and intervening valleys. The climate is arid and the soil barren. The Humboldt and its tributaries provide enough irrigation to permit limited agriculture, but the mining of copper, lead, silver, gold, etc., is more important. Its easy divorce law (only 6 weeks' residence necessary) brought it fame. The cap. is Carson City, but the fastest-growing town is Las Vegas. The Nuclear Rocket Development Station is at Jackass Flats in the N. Desert, NW of Las Vēgas. Area 286,300 sq.km (110,540 sq.m); pop. (1970) 488,738.

NEVERS (nevār'). Cap. of Nievre dept, France, on the Loire, about 220km (135m) SSE of Paris. The cathedral was started in the 11th cent., finished *c.* 1500. Pop. (1975) 47,780.

NEW AMSTERDAM. Town in Guyana, on the Berbice, founded by the Dutch. Pop. (1970) 23,000. *See also* NEW YORK.

NEWARK. Largest city of New Jersey, USA, on the Passaic, 13km (8m) W of Manhattan. Its main products are electrical equipment, machinery, fountain pens, chemicals, paints, canned meats. N. dates from 1666, when a settlement called Milford was made on the site. Pop. met. area (1970) 1,845,348.

NEWARK. Town in Notts, England, on the r. Trent, with ruins of the 12th cent. castle in which King John died. There are engineering and brewing industries, and it is a market town. Pop. (1972) 24,580.

NEWBOLT, Sir Henry John (1862–1938). British poet. A barrister 1887–99, he was an authority on naval matters, e.g. *The Year of Trafalgar* (1905) and *A Naval History of the War* (1920) on the F.W.W. His *Songs of the Sea* (1904) and *Songs of the Fleet* (1910) were set to music by Stanford.

NEW BRITAIN. Largest is. in the Bismarck Archipelago, W Pacific, off the NE coast of New Guinea (q.v.), and forming part of Papua New Guinea. There are a number of active volcanoes, incl. Father 2,300 m (7,500 ft), which is the highest peak. The chief town is Rabaul, and the main products are cocoa and copra. Area, incl. the adjacent islands, 36,520 sq.km (14,100 sq.m); pop. (1973) 166,000.

NEW BRUNSWICK. Eastern maritime prov. of Canada, to the NW of Nova Scotia. Its sea coast is *c.* 800km (500m) long, and there are many bays and harbours. It is undulating country, with hills which rise no higher than 275m (900ft) a.s.l. Of the many rivers, the most important are the St John and the St Croix, both of which flow into the Bay of Fundy. There are also many lakes, the largest being the Grand Lake 174 sq.km (67 sq.m). With large forests in the interior, lumbering is of great importance. The soil is fertile, and wheat, potatoes, oats, and turnips are grown. Fredericton is the cap.; St John, the chief port, and Moncton are other towns. The chief industries are paper manufacture, saw milling, fishing and fish curing, and mining (lead, zinc, copper), and oil and natural gas.

Discovered by Cartier in 1534, N.B. was first explored by Champlain in 1604 and remained a French colony until, as part of Nova Scotia, it was ceded to England in 1713. It was separated from Nova Scotia in 1784. It is governed by a Lieut.-Gov. with a Legislative Assembly elected for 5 years by adult suffrage. Area 73,437 sq.km (28,340 sq.m), incl. 1,350 sq.km (520 sq.m) of water; pop. (1976) 677,250.

NEWBURY. Market town in Berks, England, noted for its racecourse and training stables. Aldermaston and Harwell are nearby, and by 1983 the main UK base for US cruise missiles will be RAF Greenham Common. Pop. (1971) 23,634.

NEWBY, P(ercy) H(oward) (1918–). British novelist. Lecturer in English at Cairo 1942–6, he joined the BBC 1949, and became Managing Director BBC radio in 1975. His subtle novels incl. *Something to Answer For* (1968) and *Kith* (1977), set in Egypt in 1941.

NEW CALEDO'NIA. French overseas territory in the S Pacific, situated between Australia and the Fiji Is. Nouméa is the capital. N.C. was discovered by Cook in 1774, and became French in 1853. Surrounded by a barrier reef, it is fertile as well as having nickel, chrome and iron resources. Area 19,200 sq.km (7,400 sq.m); pop. (1979) 133,000, incl. 56,000 Melanesians, 50,000 Europeans, 27,000 Polynesians. The Europeans are mainly supporters of N.C. as an integral part of France; the Melanesians tend to favour independence.

NEWCASTLE, Thomas Pelham-Holles, duke of (1693–1768). British Whig politician. He was Sec. of State 1724–54, and then PM during the Seven Years War, until 1762, although Pitt was mainly responsible for the conduct of the war.

NEWCASTLE. City and port of New South Wales, Australia, NNE of Sydney. Industries incl. the manufacture of iron, steel, and ships, using coal from nearby mines, discovered 1796. There is a univ. (1965). Pop. (1972) 354,630.

NEWCASTLE-UNDER-LYME. Town in Staffs, England, 3km (2m) W of Stoke-on-Trent. The parish church of St Giles rebuilt by Sir Gilbert Scott, retains a 12th cent. tower. Industries incl. coal-mining, clothing, bricks and tiles. Keele Univ. (1962) is nearby. Pop. (1972) 76,900.

NEWCASTLE UPON TYNE. City (admin. HQ) in Tyne and Wear, England, on the r. Tyne, about 13km (8m) from its mouth. It is also admin. HQ of Northumberland. The castle was built by Henry II 1172-7, on the site of an older castle; its keep is still preserved, together with parts of its walls and Black Gate and Watergate. Other noteworthy buildings include St Nicholas's cathedral, which is (apart from the Perpendicular tower) chiefly 14th cent. work; St Andrew's church, which dates back to the 12th cent.; and the Guildhall, built in 1658. N. is connected with the neighbouring town of Gateshead by several bridges. Chiefly famous as a coaling centre, it first began to trade in coal in the 13th cent. In 1826 iron works were estab. by George Stephenson, and the first engine used on the Stockton and Darlington railway was made at N. There are good quay and harbour facilities. Major industries incl. coal mining, shipbuilding, marine and electrical engineering, chemical and metal manufactures. The chief exports are coal, iron and steel goods, chemicals, and copper. The HQ of the Min. of Social Security is here. There is a univ. (1962), art gallery, and a modern Civic Centre (1963). Pop. (1972) 217,220.

NEWCO'MEN, Thomas (1663-1729). British inventor. B. at Dartmouth, he devised an atmospheric steam engine, or 'fire engine', patented in 1705, which was used for pumping water from mines until Watt invented one with a separate condenser.

NEW DEAL. The programme of reforms introduced in USA by F. D. Roosevelt from 1933 onwards, to counteract the effects of the economic crisis that began in 1929. Immediate relief measures included the provision of employment on public works, and of govt loans to farmers at low rates of interest, and the raising of agricultural prices by planned restriction of output. Reforms associated with the programme incl. the introduction of old-age and unemployment insurance, measures to prevent the use of sweated labour and child labour, protection of the right to organize against unfair practices by employers, and the provision of loans to local authorities for slum clearance. A notable feature was the Tennessee Valley scheme (q.v.). The N.D. reduced unemployment from 17 million to 8 million, but met with opposition, and many of its provisions were declared unconstitutional by the Supreme Court in 1935-6.

NEW DELHI. *See* DELHI.

NEW DEMOCRATIC PARTY (NDP). Canadian political party formed in 1961 by a merger of the Labour Congress and the Co-operative Commonwealth Federation (CCF: 1930). It aimed at breaking monopoly control over Canadian resources and industry, with prevention of 'further foreign control'; consumer protection, etc. Led by Edward Broadbent, it gained 32 seats in the elections of 1980.

NEW ENGLAND. The name of a region in the NE of the USA, consisting of the states of Maine, New Hampshire, Vermont, Massachusetts, Rhode Is., and Connecticut (qq.v.), which was originally settled in the main by Puritan groups from England. The name was suggested by Capt. John Smith, who explored it in 1614. The original Puritan immigrant developed into the shrewdly witty Yankee (a name which became current in the 18th cent.).

NEW ENGLAND. District of northern N.S.W., Australia, comprising in particular the tableland area of Glen Innes and Armidale, but regarded by those campaigning for its creation as a new state as extending southward to incl. Newcastle and Tamworth. This proposal originated with Earle Page in 1915, and was the subject of a referendum in 1967, but failed to win a large enough majority of votes.

NEW ENGLISH ART CLUB. Society founded in England in 1886 by a group of painters dissatisfied with the administration of the RA, to secure better representation for younger painters. Its members incl. Sargent, Augustus John, Paul Nash, Rothenstein, and Sickert.

NEW FOREST. Woodland district in Hants, England, W of Southampton. It was a royal hunting-ground in Saxon times, and was enlarged by William I. Oak trees from the forest once supplied the navy. Area 373 sq.km (144 sq.m).

NEWFOUNDLA'ND. Prov. of Canada; it incl. the is. of N., at the entrance of the St Lawrence r., and the coastal region of Labrador, over which N. was given jurisdiction in 1713; the boundary between the part of Labrador attached to N. and the part attached to the prov. of Quebec was settled in 1927. The island is triangular, with Capes Bauld, Race, and Ray forming the angles. It has a rugged coastline indented with many bays. There are many lakes, the largest are Grand 334 sq.km (129 sq.m) and Red Indian 180 sq.km (70 sq.m). The highest mountains, over 760m (2,500 ft), are in the NW. Most of the country consists of barren lands and marshes, but the soil is fertile on the borders of the lakes and rivers, and the valleys of the Gander, Humber, and Exploits, the 3 most important rivers, are densely wooded. The chief exports are timber and paper pulp; others incl. iron ore, zinc, lead, fish products. St John's is the cap.

The is. of N. was discovered by Cabot in 1497, and was the first English colony, Sir Humphrey Gilbert formally taking possession in 1583. The French also estab. settlements, and did not recognize British sovereignty until 1713. The French only surrendered fishing rights under a convention of 1904, and they still retained the offshore is. of St Pierre and Miquelon. Responsible government was granted to the island in 1855, but in 1934, as N. had fallen into financial difficulties, administration was vested in a governor and a special commission. In 1948 a referendum resulted in favour of federation with Canada, and in 1949 N. became the tenth prov. of Canada. Area 404,517 sq.km (156,185 sq.m); pop. (1976) 557,725.

NEWFOUNDLAND. A breed of dog, said to have originated in Newfoundland. There are several varieties, the most important being the black and white, which has a broad muzzle, curly hair and bushy tail.

NEWGATE. A prison in London, England, which stood on the site of the Central Criminal Court. Originally a gatehouse (hence the name), it was estab. in the 12th cent., rebuilt after the Great Fire, and again in 1780, and was demolished in 1903. Public executions were held outside it 1783-1868.

NEW GUINEA. Large is. in the SW Pacific, to the N of Australia - of which it is geologically an extension, and with which it was probably united as recently as the Pleistocene era. It is entirely within the tropics, with a hot climate, very humid in the coastal districts. Very mountainous, it has a central range which reaches over

5,000 m (16,000 ft) in the W: the highest peak is Djaja (formerly Mt Sukarno) 5,029 m (16,500 ft). The tropical rain forest harbours birds of paradise and brilliant butterflies, and various mammals, such as the small kangaroos, show the island's Australian links. The chief rivers are the Fly, which flows across the southern plain into the Gulf of Papua in a maze of mangrove swamps; the Sepik in the NE, and the Mamberano in the NW and Digul in the SW. The native peoples are of Melanesian type, and of many tribes, some in the highlands being pygmies.

The first Europeans to reach N.G. were the Portuguese in 1527, but it was the Dutch East India Co. which laid claim to *western N.G.*, which in 1828 became part of the Netherlands East Indies. The Dutch retained western N.G. after Indonesian independence in 1949, but in 1963 it was ceded to Indonesia by the UN, and remained part of Indonesia by an 'Act of Free Choice' in 1969. The chief town of W Irian (Irian Jaya), as it is now known, is Jayapura (formerly Hollandia). Area 414,000 sq.km (160,000 sq.m); pop. (1971) 8,600,000.

South-eastern N.G. was annexed by Queensland in 1883, and although this was not recognized by the home govt, a British protectorate was set up in 1884, and in 1901 this was transferred to the new govt of the Commonwealth of Australia. In 1906 it was re-named the Territory of Papua. *North-eastern N.G.* was annexed by Germany in 1884, occupied by Australia in 1914, and governed as a mandate 1921-42. It was then in Japanese occupation until 1945, and became an Australian trust terr. in 1946. In 1949 Australia estab. the combined Trust Terr. of Papua-New Guinea (incl. New Britain and Adjacent is.), which became independent in 1975 as Papua New Guinea (q.v.).

NEW HAMPSHIRE. One of the New England states in the NE corner of the USA, bounded on the N by Canada, on the E by Maine, on the S by Massachusetts, and on the W by Vermont. It was one of the original 13 states, and the first colony to declare its independence of Britain, 15 June 1776. Called the 'granite state', it is a mountainous region. The chief rivers are the Connecticut, Androscoggin, Merrimack, Saco, and Piscataqua. Agriculture, formerly the principal occupation, remains important (fruit, poultry, dairy products, etc.); industrial products incl. textiles, paper, leather goods, electrical machinery and apparatus. The state cap. is Concord. Area 24,100 sq.km (9,304 sq.m); pop. (1970) 737,681.

NEWHAVEN. Seaport on the English Channel, in E Sussex, at the mouth of the r. Ouse. There are cross-channel services to Dieppe. Pop. (1973) 10,000.

NEW HAVEN. Town in Conn., USA, 6km (4m) from Long Is. Sound. Founded as Quinnipiac in 1638, it was renamed in honour of N in Sussex, in 1640. It is the seat of Yale University. Pop. (1970) 137,700.

NEW HEBRIDES. *See* VANUATU.

NEW JERSEY. One of the 13 original states of the USA, called the 'garden state', situated on the Atlantic coast between New York and Delaware Bay. The S half of N.J. is a coastal plain, most of it less than 30m (100ft) a.s.l. To the NW is a triassic lowland, with an irregular surface varying in height up to 300m (900ft). The NW corner of the state is hilly, rising to 550m (1,803 ft) at High Point. The rivers include the Hudson, Passaic, Hackensack, Raritan, and Delaware. Along the coast are a number of pleasure resorts, such as Atlantic City and Cape May. The principal towns incl. Trenton (the cap.), Newark, and Jersey City. Agricultural produce (e.g. asparagus, fruits, potatoes, tomatoes, poultry) is important; industrial products incl. chemicals, electrical machinery, clothing, metal goods. N.J. was perhaps visited by Verrazano in 1524. The Dutch were the first to settle, *c.* 1620. N.J. became British in 1664. Area 20,295 sq.km (7,836 sq.m); pop. (1970) 7,168,164.

NEW LONDON. Naval base and yachting centre of SE Connecticut, USA, on the r. Thames, 5km (3m) from Long Island Sound. It was founded 1646, and named N.L. 1658. Pop. (1970) 31,630.

NEWLYN. Seaport near Penzance, Cornwall, England. It gave its name to a group of artists, 'the N. school' (1880-90), who painted its working life. The Ordnance Survey relates heights in the UK to mean sea-level at N.

NEWMAN, John Henry (1801-90). British cardinal. B. in London, he was ordained in the C of E in 1824, and in 1827 became vicar of St Mary's, Oxford. There he came under the influence of R. H. Froude and Keble, and in 1833 pub. the first of the *Tracts for the Times*, which gave their name to the 'Tractarian Movement', and culminated in Newman's celebrated *Tract 90* in 1841. He was received into the RC Church in 1845, and finally settled as an oratorian at Edgbaston. Appointed rector of Dublin univ. in 1854, he pub. lectures on *The Idea of a University*, and in 1864 pub. his autobiography, *Apologia pro vita sua*, defending himself against Kingsley's attack on the RC attitude to truth. His poem, *The Dream of Gerontius*, appeared in 1866, and *The Grammar of Assent*, an analysis of the nature of belief, in 1870. In 1879 he was created a cardinal. His best-known hymn is 'Lead, Kindly Light'. His brother, **Francis William N.** (1805-97), prof. of Latin at Univ. Coll., London, 1846-69, adopted Unitarian views. He wrote the autobiographical *Phases of Faith* (1850).

NEWMARKET. Town in Suffolk, England, 20km (13m) NE of Cambridge. Horse-racing has been held here since James I's reign, and the HQ of the Jockey Club is at N. Important events are the Two Thousand Guineas, the One Thousand Guineas, the Cambridgeshire, the Jockey Club Stakes, and the Cesarewitch. Pop. (1971) 11,350.

NEW MEXICO. State of the USA, lying between Colorado and the Mexican frontier on a rocky tableland, up to 1,800 m/6,000 ft. In the W there are extensive forests, and the NE region is famous for its beautiful 'parks'. The principal rivers are the Rio Grande and its affluent the Rio Pecos, the Canadian, and San Juan; all are dammed for irrigation. The valleys are fertile, the principal crops being wheat, maize, beans, cotton; cattle are raised. Petroleum and natural gas, potash, copper, uranium, gold, silver are among mineral products. Los Alamos is one of several atomic research centres in N.M. The most characteristic forms of vegetation are the yucca and cactus. N.M. is noted for its mild climate. It was colonized by Spaniards in the 17th cent., was acquired from Mexico by the USA in 1848, and became a state in 1912. The cap. is Santa Fé, but the largest town is Albuquerque. D. H. Lawrence's Utopian colony of Kiowa Ranch at Rananim, N of Taos on the slopes of Mt Lobo in the Sangre de Christos has been preserved by the Univ. of New Mexico. Area 315,113 sq.km (121,666 sq.m); pop. (1970) 1,016,000.

NEW ORLEANS (or'le-anz). Chief city of Louisiana, USA, an important commercial centre and port on the Mississippi. At high tide the city is below river-level, and is therefore protected by embankments or levees. It is a market for sugar, rice and cotton; a banking and business

NEW MEXICO. The Pueblo Indian village of Taos built of dried mud, the forerunner of architecture's latest inventions, the sophisticated irregularity of complexes of flats such as Habitat. *Photo: Mireille Vautier.*

centre; has a large oil industry, and produced the Saturn rockets used in *Apollo* spacecraft. There are excellent road, rail and air facilities. Educational institutions incl. Tulane Univ. (1834). N.O. was founded by the French in 1718, and the Vieux Carré or French Quarter with its Mardi Gras celebrations is a tourist attraction. It passed to Spain 1753, was returned to France 1800, and was part of the Louisiana Purchase made by the USA from France in 1803. In the late 19th cent. it was the birthplace of jazz (q.v.). Pop. met. area (1970) 1,034,316.

NEW PLYMOUTH. Town in North Island, NZ, on the W coast of the Taranaki Peninsula, of which it is the chief port. Pop. (1976) 44,000.

NEWPORT. English river-port and market town, cap. of the Isle of Wight, at the head of the estuary of the Medina. SW of the town is Carisbrooke Castle. Pop. (1972) 22,260.

NEWPORT. Seaport in Gwent, Wales, on the r. Usk. It exports iron and coal, has extensive docks, and a steel-works at nearby Llanwern. It is the admin. HQ of Gwent. Pop. (1972) 111,530.

NEWPORT NEWS. City and port of Virginia, USA, on the r. James. It has shipbuilding yards and foundries. Pop. (1970) 138,180.

NEWQUAY (nū'kē). Seaport and holiday resort on the N coast of Cornwall. Pop. (1971) 13,570.

NEW SOUTH WALES. State of the Australian Commonwealth, at first called New Wales by Capt. Cook, who put in at Botany Bay in 1770, and was struck by the resemblance of the coast to that of Wales. It is situated in the SE of Australia. The E and SE coastal district of the country is separated from the inland plains by the Great Dividing Range. In the SE are the Australian Alps, of which the highest point is Mt Kosciusko (q.v.); they extend N as the Snowy Mts. Behind Sydney the Dividing Range is called the Blue Mts., and to the N is the New England Range. The coastal dist. is watered by many rivers, incl. the Hunter, Clarence, and Macleay. The W part of the country is watered by the rivers of the Murray-Darling system, of which the most important are the Murrumbidgee, Lachlan, and Macquarie. The principal towns are Sydney, the most important Australian seaport, in which 60 per cent of the pop. of N.S.W. live, and largest city in the Australian Commonwealth, Newcastle, Wollongong, Albury, Tamworth, Wagga Wagga, Lismore. In 1973 a decentralization programme was instituted to counter the draw of Sydney, and encourage the growth of more medium-sized towns.

N.S.W. is situated in the temperate zone, and has an equable climate. Wheat, rice, maize, oats, sugar cane, tobacco, and fruit are grown. Sheep rearing and forestry are important. There are rich mineral deposits, incl. gold, silver, copper, tin, zinc, and coal. The diversion westward, through the Snowy Mts., of the upper waters of the Snowy r., started in 1949, was planned to provide irrigation and hydro-electric power for large areas of N.S.W. and Victoria.

N.S.W., which was used as a convict settlement 1788-1850, was opened to free immigration 1819, received self-govt in 1856, and became a state of the Commonwealth of Australia in 1901. Legislative power is vested in a parl. of 2 houses, the legislative council of 60 members, and the legislative assembly of 99 members. Voting is compulsory. Area 801,396 sq.km (309,433 sq.m); pop. (1976) 4,777,103.

Lord Howe Is., 700km (435m) NE of Sydney, is a dependency. It is volcanic, highest point Mt Gower 865m (2,840 ft). Area 15 sq.km (6 sq.m); pop. (1973) 260.

NEW SOUTH WALES. The tracking station at Parkes is indicative of the major role played by Australia in the new sciences of the skies. *Photo: Courtesy of the Australian Information Service.*

NEWSPAPER. Publication giving news and comments on it. One of the earliest Ns., the Roman *Acta Diurna*, said to have been started by Julius Caesar, contained announcements of marriages, deaths, military appointments, etc., and was posted up in public places. Not until after the invention of printing, however, were news sheets pub. as commercial undertakings, and, following their introduction into Germany (1609) and the Netherlands (1616), the first English N., *The Weekly News*, ed. by N. Bourne and Thos. Archer, appeared in 1622, followed later by the first daily N., *Daily Courant*, in 1702. Despite the stamp duty imposed on Ns. 1713-1855, with the object of restricting them because of their alleged subversive tendencies, by 1776 there were 53 in London alone. The chief British morning daily papers are: *The Times* (1785),

Guardian (originally *Manchester Guardian,* 1821-1959), *Daily Telegraph* (1855), *Daily Mail* (1896), *Daily Express* (1900), *Daily Mirror* (1903), *The Sun* (*Daily Herald,* 1919–64), and *Financial Times* (1888), *Daily Star* (1978) and *The Independent* (1986); and three evening N.: *The London Standard* (1860), *Evening News,* and *London Daily News* (1987). Important regional dailies are the *Scotsman* (1855) and *Yorkshire Post* (1866). The chief Sunday Ns. are: *Observer* (1791), *Sunday Times* (1822), *News of the World* (1843), *People* (1881), *Sunday Mirror* (1915), *Sunday Express* (1918) and *Sunday Telegraph* (1961).

The PRESS COUNCIL (1953) was estab. to preserve the freedom of the press, to maintain standards and consider complaints, to report on monopoly developments, etc.

Owing to the vastness of the USA, no N. there has a national distribution, and none has a circulation comparable with the largest in Britain. The first successful daily N. was the *Pennsylvania Packet and General Advertiser* (1784). The most notable are the *Baltimore Sun* (1837), *Chicago Tribune* (1847), *Los Angeles Times* (1881), *New York Times* (1851), *Philadelphia Bulletin* (1841), *Philadelphia Inquirer* (1829), *Wall Street Journal* (1889), *Washington Post* (1877). The evening N. pub. in Boston, *The Christian Science Monitor,* has a comparatively small circulation but world-wide reputation.

Ns. of world repute pub. outside the UK and USA incl. *Sydney Bulletin* (1880), Australia; *Times of India* (1838), Bombay; *El Ahram* (1875), Cairo; *La Prensa* (1869), Argentina; *Arbeiter-Zeitung* (1889), Vienna; *Le Figaro* (1826) and *Le Monde* (1944), Paris; *Algemeen Handelsblad* (1828) and *De Telegraaf* (1893), Amsterdam; *Die Welt* (1946), Hamburg; and *Frankfurter Allgemeine Zeitung* (1949), Frankfurt-am-Main; *Corriere della Sera* (1875), Milan, and *Avanti* (1896), Rome; *National-Zeitung* (1842), Basle; *Journal de Genève* (1826), Geneva; and *Neue Zürcher Zeitung,* Zürich; *Izvestiya* (1917) and *Pravda* (1912), Russia; *People's Daily* (1949), Peking.

In a modern press agency communication is screen-to-screen. Journalists write and edit their material on a VDT (visual display terminal), which enables them to correct, delete, insert and transpose sections of text. They then transmit the story by a press of a button to a computer at the agency HQ, using a three-letter originator code, and it is stored there on magnetic disks, ready for final editorial selection, checking and correction. *See also* TELETEXT.

NEWSPAPERS. The archtype Fleet Street journalist, 'not a portrait of a person but a composite of my experiences of the Thirties', says the artist Edmond Kapp. *Photo: Courtesy of Edmond X. Kapp.*

NEWT. Genus of tailed amphibians (*Triturus*) in the family Salamandridae, mainly found in Europe. The common N. (*T. vulgaris*) is *c.* 8cm (3in) long.

NEWTON, Sir Isaac (1642-1727). British natural philosopher. B. at Woolsthorpe, Lincs, he was ed. at Grantham grammar school and Trinity Coll., Cambridge, of which he became a fellow in 1667. During 1665-6 he discovered the binomial theorem and the differential and integral calculus, and began to investigate the phenomena of universal gravitation. He was elected FRS in 1672, and soon afterwards published his *New Theory about Light and Colours. De Motu* was written in 1684, and the next year his universal law of gravitation was completely expounded as follows: 'Every particle of matter in the universe attracts every other particle with a force whose direction is that of the line joining the two, and whose magnitude is directly as the product of the masses, and inversely as the square of their distance from each other.' His greatest work, *Philosophiae Naturalis Principia Mathematica,* was pub. in 3 vols. in 1686-7, with the aid of Halley. N. resisted James II's attacks on the liberties of the univ., and sat in the parls. of 1689 and 1701-2 as a Whig. Appointed warden of the mint in 1696, and master in 1699, he carried through a reform of the coinage. He was elected president of the Royal Society in 1703, pub. his *Optics* in 1704, and was knighted in 1705. N. was buried in Westminster Abbey.

N.'s laws of motion are: (1) Every body continues in its state of rest or of uniform motion in a straight line except in so far as it may be compelled to change that state by the action of some external force; (2) change of motion is proportional to the applied force and takes place in the direction of the line of action of the force, and (3) to every action there is an equal and opposite reaction.

The unit of force in the MKS system (that which would accelerate a mass of 1 kg by 1 metre per sec per sec) is named after him the newton (unit symbol N).

NEWTON ABBOT. Market town in Devon, England, on the r. Teign, with rail repair shops, potteries - clay is mined in the vicinity - and metal works. Pop. (1971) 18,500.

NEWTOWN. Town in Powys, Wales, on the r. Severn. Known in the 13th cent. as Llan, it was enlarged as a market centre under the name of N. in the 15th, and developed as a 'new town' from 1967. Pop. (1975) 6,600.

NEW TOWNS. In the UK towns either newly estab. or greatly enlarged following the S.W.W., when the pop. was rapidly expanding and city centres had either decayed or been destroyed. Fourteen were planned 1946-50, with

NEWTON. The scientist wrote prolifically, and averaged 2,000 words a day throughout his adult lifetime. The portrait is attributed to J. Vanderbank. *Photo: Courtesy of the National Portrait Gallery.*

pop. 25-60,000, and incl. Cwmbran and Peterlee to stimulate employment in depressed areas, and 8 near London to relieve congestion there. Fifteen more, with pop. up to 250,000 were estab. 1951-75, but by then a static pop. and cuts in govt spending halted their creation.

By the later 1970s the policy, which had disrupted family groupings and local communities; destroyed small shops and specialist industries; and led to the decay of city centres, was being reversed, emphasis being on rehabilitation of older towns.

NEWTOWN ST BOSWELLS. Village nr Jedburgh in Borders region, Scotland, SE of Edinburgh. It is a farming centre, with an agricultural college, and the admin. HQ of the region. Dryburgh Abbey, 2km (1.25m) to the E is the burial place of Haig and Sir Walter Scott.

NEW WAVE. Literary movement which arose in the 1950s from a cross-fertilisation of novel and film. Novelists associated with 'la Nouvelle Vague' are Marguerite Duras, Alain Robbe-Grillet and Nathalie Sarraute; film directors Jean-Luc Godard, Alain Resnais and François Truffaut.

NEW WESTMINSTER. Freshwater port in British Columbia, Canada, on the N bank of the Fraser river, S of Vancouver. It was the cap. of BC before it became a prov. Pop. (1976) 42,035.

NEW YEAR'S DAY. 1 January, the first day of the year; celebrations are held in many parts of the world on this day, and in the UK, the USA, and other countries it is a public holiday. In England until 1753 the year began for many purposes on 25 March.

NEW YORK CITY. The largest city in the USA, often abbreviated N.Y.C. It is in New York state, on the Atlantic, at the junction of the Hudson and East rivers. N.Y. Bay was discovered by Giovanni da Verrazano, a Florentine, in 1524, and explored by Henry Hudson in 1609. The Dutch estab. a settlement there in 1613, named New Amsterdam in 1626; this was captured by the English in 1664, and renamed N.Y. During the War of Independence, British troops occupied N.Y. from 1776 until evacuation day, 25 Nov. 1784; it was the cap. of the USA, 1785-9. N.Y.C. was formed in 1898 by the creation and linking of the boroughs of the Bronx, Brooklyn, Manhattan, Queens, and Richmond. N.Y.C. is the commercial and financial cap. of the USA, and probably the busiest port in the world. The docks have a total water frontage of *c.* 1,600 km (1,000 m). The harbour is divided into an outer harbour, called Lower-Bay, and an inner harbour, called Upper-Bay; these are connected by the Narrows, a channel about 1.5km (1m) wide, between Long Is. and Staten Is. The Statue of Liberty stands on Liberty Is. (called Bedloe's Is. until 1956) in the inner harbour. Manhattan Is. forms the business centre. Among the most famous buildings are the HQ of the UN (1951); the World Trade Center (412m/1,350 ft, surpassed in height only by Chicago's Sears Building at 443m/1,454 ft); the Empire State Building (381m/1,250 ft), with television tower 449m/1,472 ft; the Rockefeller Center. The best-known street is the showbusiness centre of Broadway, supplemented by many 'off-Broadway' theatres, but Fifth Avenue, the main shopping district, is the finest thoroughfare. Greenwich Village, Lower Manhattan, is the artist-writer-Bohemian section. On a site between Broadway and the Hudson is the Lincoln Arts Center. The Metropolitan Museum of Art (1870) has the finest collection in the Western hemisphere (*see* CLOISTERS); the Museum of Modern Art (1929) also covers architectural and industrial design, photography and film; and the Pierpont Morgan Library has a research collection based on that of the millionaire (q.v.). Wall Street is the financial centre of the USA. City Hall is the HQ of the Mayor and City Council: *see* TAMMANY HALL. Most famous of the parks is Central Park. The pop. incl. large Negro (*see* HARLEM) and Puerto Rican minorites, as well as large communities of European stock - German, Greek, Hungarian, Irish, Italian, Polish and Russian - and there are *c.* 2,000,000 Jews. The leading newspaper is the *N.Y. Times.* Columbia Univ. (1754) is the most notable of the educational institutions. Largest of the 4 airports is Kennedy International (until 1963 called Idlewild). There are 2 cathedrals: St John the Divine (1892 Protestant Episcopal: Romanesque and Gothic) and St Patrick's (1858-79 RC: Gothic). Industries incl. printing, publishing, clothing, tobacco, electrical etc. Area 780 sq.km (300 sq.m); pop. met. area (1980) 10,716,300.

NEW YORK. The skyscrapers of Manhattan, with the twin towers of the World Trade Center to the far left. *Photo: Mireille Vautier.*

NEW YORK STATE. One of the original 13 states of the USA, the 'Empire State'. Second to California as most populous of the Union, it is situated S of the r. St Lawrence, which forms part of the boundary between N.Y. and Canada, and N of Pennsylvania, and has a coastline on the Atlantic. The central and W regions are low-lying, but in E are the Adirondack and Catskill mts. In the W there are a number of lakes, of which the largest are Lake Seneca and Lake Cayuga; N.Y. also includes part of Lakes Erie and Ontario. In the E are the George and Champlain lakes. The most important river is the Hudson, which is connected with the Greak Lakes by the Erie canal (1825). The largest cities are New York, Buffalo, Rochester, Syracuse, Yonkers, Albany (the cap.), Niagara Falls, and Utica. N.Y. is the 2nd most important manufacturing state in the country, its chief industries being clothing and printing. The administration is in the hands of a Governor, elected for 4 years, and a Senate and Assembly elected for 2.

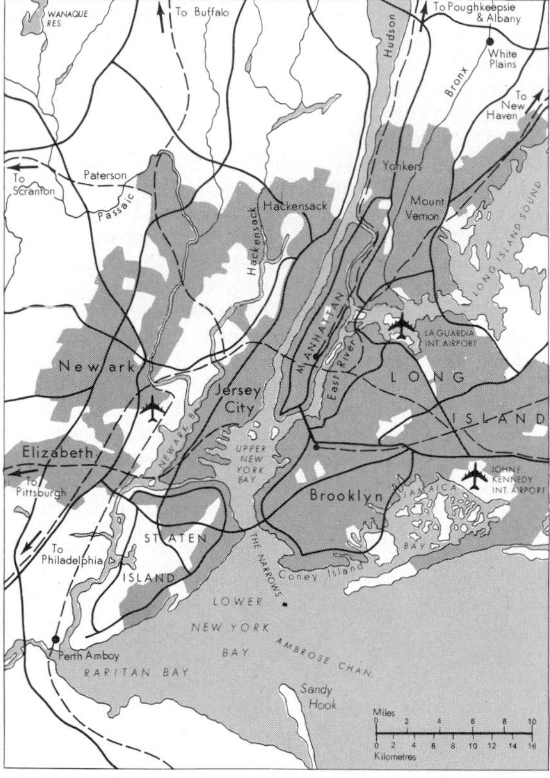

NEW YORK

N.Y. was first explored by Champlain and by Hudson in 1609, was colonized by the Dutch from 1614, and annexed by the English in 1664. The first constitution was adopted in 1777, when N.Y. became a state. Area 128,400 sq.km (49,576 sq.m); pop. (1970) 18,190,740.

NEW ZEALAND. A country of the British Commonwealth, situated in the S Pacific between 33° and 53° S lat. and 167° and 178° E long., and consisting of a group of islands. The most important are North, South, Stewart (separated from S Island by Foveaux Strait) and Chatham Islands (q.v.) 863km (536m) E of N.Z. Outlying is. incl. within N.Z. geographical boundaries are the Kermadec (annexed 1887), Three Kings, Auckland, Campbell, Antipodes, Bounty, Snares and Solander: only the Kermadec and Campbell is. are inhabited. These are grouped with the main is. in 13 statistical areas: *North Island* Auckland (Central and South), East Coast, Hawke's Bay, Northland, Taranaki and Wellington; *South Island* Canterbury, Marlborough, Nelson, Otago, Southland and Westland. The Terrs. Overseas comprise Tokelau Is. (3 atolls transferred 1926 from the former Gilbert and Ellice Is. colony) and Niue Is. (one of the Cook Is., but separately admin. from 1903: chief town Alafi). The Cook Is. (q.v.) are internally self-governing, but share common citizenship with New Zealand. The Ross Dependency (q.v.) is in the Antarctic. *See also* SAMOA.

Physical Features. The coastline of South Is. is almost unbroken, except in the N and SW, but North Is. has more indentations, and has excellent harbours at Auckland and Wellington.

Except for the NW peninsula ending in Cape Maria van Diemen, North Is. is mountainous and incl. 3 active volcanoes - Ruapehu (2,797 m/9,175 ft), erupted 1971, highest point in the is., Ngauruhoe (2,290 m/7,515 ft), erupted 1956, and Tongariro (1,968 m/6,458 ft), erupted 1950 - as well as the remarkable Rotorua district with its geysers and hot springs. In South Is. the Southern Alps (q.v.), incl. Mt Cook and almost 20 other peaks above 3,000 m/10,000 ft. In the higher valleys there are huge glaciers.

Most of the rivers are shallow and rapid, and navigable for only a short distance. The Waikato, in North Is., the largest river in N.Z., rises in the region of Mt Ruapehu, flows northwards and empties into the Tasman Sea; it is navigable for *c.* 115km/70m. In South Is. the important rivers incl. the Wairau, Mataura, and Waitaki: from the hydro-electric station on the Waitaki at Benmore (1965) power is transmitted by under-sea cable across Cook Strait to North Island. There are many lakes, of which the largest is Lake Taupo, in North Is. N.Z. has a temperate climate. Rainfall is moderate, except in the W of the S Alps.

The principal cities are Wellington, the cap., Auckland, Hamilton and Palmerston North in North Is.: Christchurch and Dunedin in South Is.: all have univs. The majority of the inhabitants of N.Z. are of European (chiefly British) descent. The Maoris (q.v.), mainly in North Is., number *c.* 270,000 in 1976. Area 268,675 sq.km (103,736 sq.m); pop. (1978) incl. Maoris 3,145,910.

Economic. The soil is fertile and the most important industry is agriculture, incl. sheep and dairy farming. Exports of wool and leather, of dairy products and other processed foods are high, and lamb and mutton are rivalled in the modern market by N.Z. beef. The effect of Britain's entry into EEC was cushioned for N.Z. by the world rise in demand for commodities, and the high quality of N.Z. products. Crops incl. wheat, oats and barley, fruits and vegetables. In recent years there has been a boom in N.Z.'s 'green gold' (logs, dressed timber, paper, pulp and chemical by-products). There is a light aircraft industry (trainers and crop sprayers), and some machinery and metallurgical industry. 'Expertise' is exported by way of breeding stock, seeds and prepared animal feedstuffs. M.U.: N.Z. dollar.

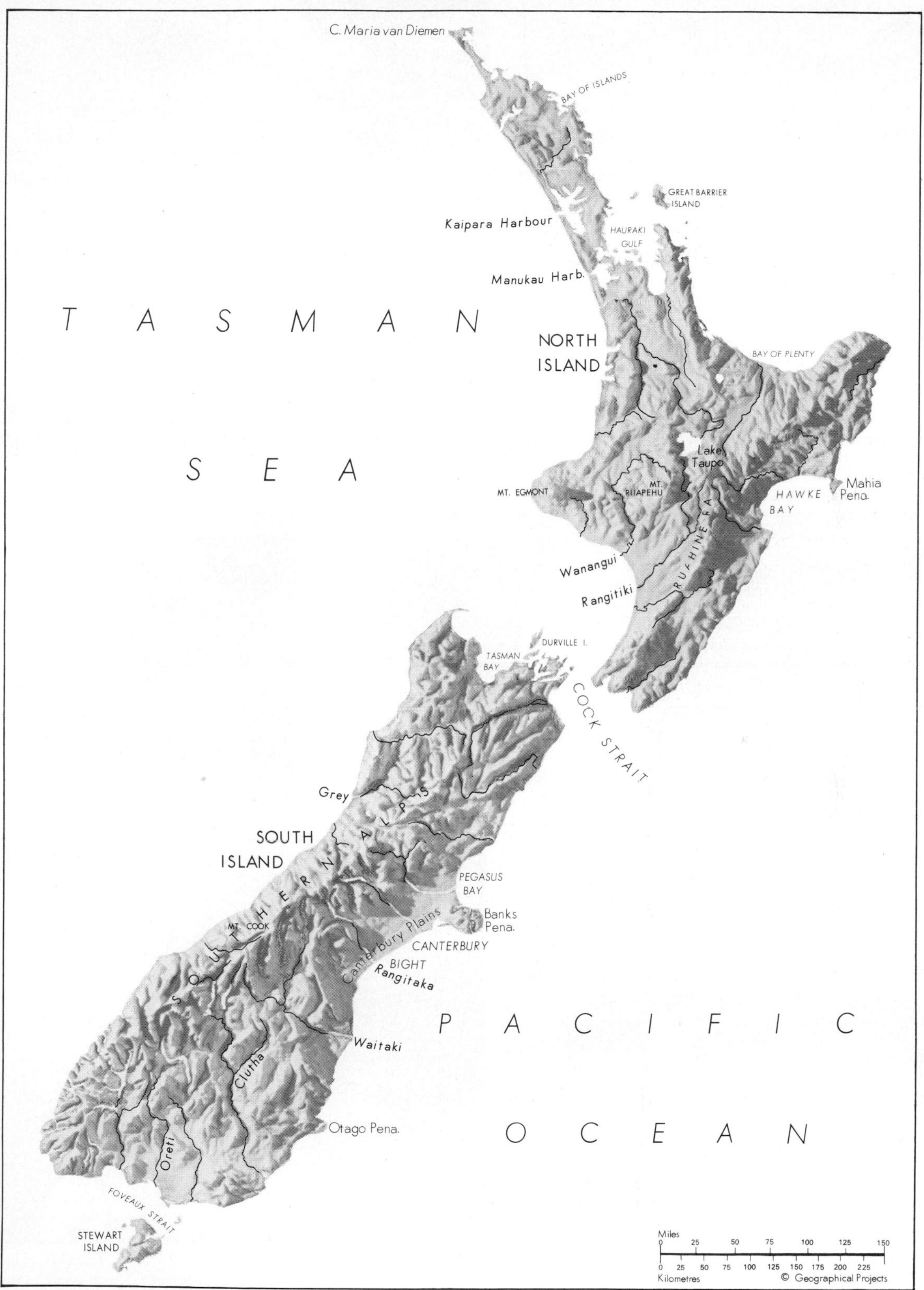

C. Maria van Diemen
BAY OF ISLANDS
GREAT BARRIER ISLAND
Kaipara Harbour
HAURAKI GULF
Manukau Harb.
TASMAN
NORTH ISLAND
BAY OF PLENTY
Lake Taupo
SEA
MT. EGMONT
MT. RUAPEHU
HAWKE BAY
Mahia Pena.
Wanangui
Rangitiki
RUAHINE RA.
DURVILLE I.
TASMAN BAY
COOK STRAIT
Grey
SOUTH ISLAND
SOUTHERN ALPS
PEGASUS BAY
MT. COOK
Banks Pena.
Canterbury Plains
CANTERBURY BIGHT
Rangitaka
PACIFIC
Waitaki
Clutha
Otago Pena.
OCEAN
Oreti
FOVEAUX STRAIT
STEWART ISLAND
Miles
0 25 50 75 100 125 150
0 25 50 75 100 125 150 175 200 225
Kilometres
© Geographical Projects

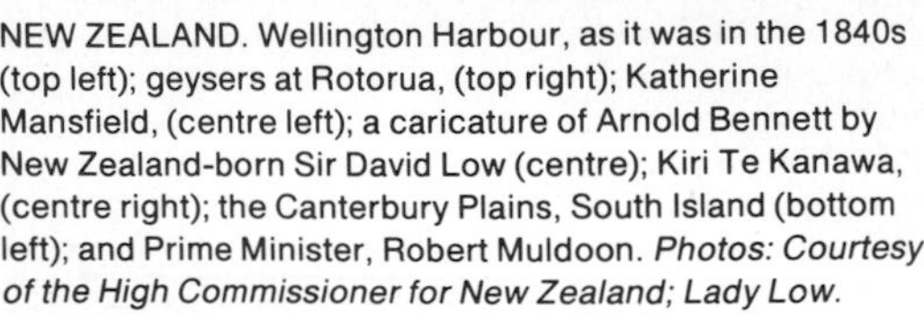

NEW ZEALAND. Wellington Harbour, as it was in the 1840s (top left); geysers at Rotorua, (top right); Katherine Mansfield, (centre left); a caricature of Arnold Bennett by New Zealand-born Sir David Low (centre); Kiri Te Kanawa, (centre right); the Canterbury Plains, South Island (bottom left); and Prime Minister, Robert Muldoon. *Photos: Courtesy of the High Commissioner for New Zealand; Lady Low.*

New Zealand

	Area in sq. km.	Pop. (1978)
North Island	114,688	2,282,800
South Island	150,460	862,000
Stewart Island	1,735	510
Chatham Islands	963	580
Minor Islands	320	20
	268,675	3,145,910
Island Territories:		
Niue Island	260	4,000
Tokelau Islands	10	1,575
Cook Islands	230	18,500
Ross Dependency	453,250	—

*included in N. and S. Island totals

Government. N.Z. is governed by a Gov.-Gen. appointed by the Crown, who is aided by an Executive Council and a General Assembly, or parl., of one house, the House of Representatives, with 87 members including 4 Maoris, popularly elected for 3 years.

Prime Ministers of New Zealand

J. Ballance (Lib.)	1891
R.J. Seddon (Lib.)	1893
W. Hall-Jones (Lib.)	1906
Sir Joseph Ward (Lib.)	1906
T. MacKenzie (Lib.)	1912
W.F. Massey (Reform)	1912
J.G. Coates (Reform)	1925
Sir Joseph Ward (United)	1928
G.W. Forbes (United)	1930
M.J. Savage (Lab.)	1935
P. Fraser (Lab.)	1940
S.G. Holland (Nat.)	1949
K.J. Holyoake (Nat.)	1957
Walter Nash (Lab.)	1957
K.J. Holyoake (Nat.)	1960
J. Marshall (Nat.)	1972
N. Kirk (Lab.)	1972
W. Rowling (Lab.)	1974
R. Muldoon (Nat.)	1975

History. N.Z. was occupied by Polynesian tribes before the 14th cent. Its coasts were explored by Tasman in 1642 and by Cook in 1769, 1773, and 1777. British missionaries began to arrive in 1815. By the Treaty of Waitangi (1840) the Maoris accepted British sovereignty; colonization began, and large-scale sheep farming was developed. Self-govt was granted in 1853. The Maoris resented the loss of their land, and rose in revolt 1845-7 and 1860-72, until concessions were made, incl. representation in parliament. Sir George Grey, Gov. 1845-53 and 1861-70, and Radical PM 1877-84, was largely responsible for the conciliation of the Maoris and the introduction of manhood suffrage. The Cons. held power 1879-90, and were succeeded by a Lib. govt, which with trade union support ruled until 1912; this govt introduced women's suffrage (1893) and old-age pensions (1898), and was a pioneer in labour legislation. N.Z. troops served in the S African War. In 1907 Dominion status was granted. After 1912 the Cons. (Reform) Party regained power, and the trade unions broke with the Libs. to form the Lab. Party. More than 120,000 N.Z. troops fought in the F.W.W., and greatly distinguished themselves at Gallipoli and elsewhere. The Cons. and Libs., who united to form the Nat. Party in 1931, were defeated in 1935 by the Lab. Party, which introduced a comprehensive social security programme. N.Z. declared war against Germany in 1939 a few minutes after the UK; 135,000 New Zealanders served overseas, doing notable work in N Africa and Italy; 10,000 were killed, and there were some 20,000 other casualties. The National Party was almost continuously in power 1949-72, and, after a brief Labour interlude 1972-5, was again returned to power (*see* MULDOON), and re-elected, though with a reduced majority, 1978 and 1981.

Art. N.Z. cannot yet claim to have produced any artist of world-wide fame, except the cartoonist, Sir David Low, but much meritorious work has been done, and there is a lively interest in art, as is evidenced by the many art societies and galleries. The Auckland Society of Arts, founded in 1870, is the oldest art society in N.Z. The N.Z. Academy of Fine Arts and the National Art Gallery are at Wellington. The Maoris are very fine craftsmen, and are noted for their carvings in wood, stone, and bone.

Literature. Among interesting pioneer records are those of Edward Jerningham Wakefield and F. E. Maning; and *A First Year in Canterbury Settlement* by Samuel Butler (q.v.). Earliest of the popular poets was Thomas Bracken, author of the N.Z. national song, followed by native-born Jessie Mackay and W. Pember Reeves, though the latter is better-known as the author of the prose account of N.Z. *The Long White Cloud,* and Ursula Bethell (1874-1945). In the 20th cent. N.Z. literature attained an international appeal with the short stories of Katherine Mansfield (q.v.), produced an excellent exponent of detective fiction in Dame Ngaio Marsh (q.v.), and struck a specifically N.Z. note in *Tutira, the Story of a N.Z. Sheep Station* (1926) by W. H. Guthrie Smith (1861-1940). Poetry of a new quality was written by R. A. K. Mason (1905-71) in the twenties, and in the thirties by a group of which A. R. D. Fairburn (1904-57), with a witty conversational turn, and Allen Curnow (1911-), poet, critic and anthologist, are the most striking. In fiction the thirties were remarkable for the short stories of Frank Sargeson (1903-) and Roderick Finlayson (1904-), and the talent of John Mulgan (1911-45), who is remembered both for his novel *Man Alone* (1939), and for his posthumous factual account of the war in which he died, *Report on Experience* (1947). More recently Kendrick Smithyman (1922-) has struck a metaphysical note in poetry, and James K. Baxter (1926-) has pub. fluent lyrics, and Janet Frame (1924-) has a brooding depth of meaning in such novels as *The Rainbirds* (1968) and *Intensive Care* (1970).

NEY, Michael, duke of Elchingen, prince of the Moskowa (1769-1815). Marshal of France. The son of a cooper, he joined the army in 1788, and rose from the ranks to marshal of France. He served throughout the Revolutionary and Napoleonic Wars, commanding the rearguard during the retreat from Moscow, and for his personal courage was called 'the bravest of the brave'. When Napoleon returned from Elba, N. was sent to arrest him, but instead deserted to him and fought at Waterloo. He was subsequently shot for treason.

NIAGARA FALLS (nī-ag'ara). Two waterfalls on the Niagara r., on the Canadian-USA border, connecting Lake Erie with Lake Ontario; they are separated by Goat Is. The American Fall, to the N, in USA, is 51m (167ft) high, 330m (1,080 ft) wide; the Horseshoe Fall, to the S, in Canada, is 49m (160ft) high, 790m (2,600 ft) across.

On the Niagara r., below the falls, lie (1) on the W bank, N.F., a city of Ontario, Canada, with a large hydro-electric generating plant; pop. (1976) 69,400. (2) on the E bank, N.F., a city of New York state, USA, seat of a univ., with hydro-electric works and a tourist trade; pop. (1970) 85,615.

NIAGARA FALLS. The American Fall in the foreground, and beyond Goat Island, Horseshoe Fall. *Photo: Camera Press.*

NIBELUNGENLIED (nē'beloongenlēd) (Ger., Song of the Nibelungs). Medieval German epic poem composed from older sources, *c.* 1200, by an unknown author. Siegfried, possessor of the Nibelung treasure, marries Kriemhild, sister of Gunther of Worms, wins Brunhild as a bride for the latter, and is murdered by Hagen, Gunther's vassal. Kriemhild obtains vengeance for Siegfried's death by marrying Etzel (Attila) of the Huns, at whose court Hagen and Gunther, with their retinue, are slain. Wagner based his *Ring des Nibelungen* mainly on the Norse versions.

NICAEA (nīsē'a). Ancient city of Bithynia, Asia Minor, founded *c.* 316 BC. Here was held in 325 a famous Council of the Christian Church, convened by the Emperor Constantine I; it promulgated the first version of the Nicene Creed (q.v.). The modern Turkish village of Iznik is on the site.

NICARAGUA. (nikarah'gwah). A republic of Central America, N of Costa Rica, stretching from the Pacific to the Caribbean Sea. Crossing the country from NW to SE is the main cordillera of Central America. The Caribbean coast is swamp land. The most important towns are Managua (the cap.), León, Matagalpa, and Granada. Corinto, on the Pacific, is the chief port. Products incl. bananas, cotton, coffee, cocoa, sugar, timber, gold, silver, and copper.

The first European to reach N. was Gil Gonzalez de Avila (1522), who brought it under Spanish rule. It remained Spanish until 1821, when it gained its independence. The Sandinist Nat. Liberation Front (FSLN: named after Augusto Cesar Sandino, killed by the Nat. Guard 1934) led a revolt 1978-9 against the dictatorship estab. from 1933 by the father of the pres., Gen. Anastasio 'Tacho' Somoza, under the aegis of the USA. Somoza was assassinated in exile in Paraguay in 1980, and non-Marxist liberals were rapidly purged from the govt. estab. in 1979. The head of government from 1985 is Daniel Ortega Saavedra. The US provides aid to the anti-government rebels. Area 148,000 sq.km (57,150 sq.m); pop (1980) 3,000,000.

NICE. French resort on the Riviera, 13km (8m) SW of Monte Carlo, on the Bay of the Angels, the cap. of the dept of Alpes Maritimes. Many festivities are held here, incl. the famous 'Battle of the Flowers', and chocolates and perfume are made. Pop. (1973) 325,400.

NICENE CREED. One of the fundamental creeds of Christianity, promulgated by the Council of Nicaea in 325. It gives the orthodox doctrine of the Trinity as against the Arian heresy. The N.C. was modified by the Council of Constantinople in 381, and the *filioque* clause was added during the 5th and 6th cents. in the western Church.

NICHOLAS, St (4th cent.). Bishop of Myra in Lycia, and patron saint of Russia, children, merchants, and sailors. His festival is 6 Dec. and the custom of giving presents to children on the eve of this day, still retained in some Continental countries, e.g. Germany and the Netherlands, has been transferred in English-speaking countries to Christmas Day; hence the association of his name, Santa Claus (corruption of San Nicolaas), with the latter festival.

NICHOLAS I (1796-1855). Tsar of Russia from 1825. His ambition to dominate the Balkans involved Russia in war with Turkey in 1827-9, and in the Crimean War.

NICHOLAS II (1868-1918). Last Tsar of Russia. Succeeding Alexander III in 1894, he was dominated by his wife, Princess Alix of Hesse, who in turn, was under the influence of Rasputin. His mismanagement of the Japanese War led to the revolution of 1905, which he ruthlessly suppressed. He entered the F.W.W. in 1914, and in 1917 was forced to abdicate. N. and his family were shot by the Bolsheviks at Ekaterinburg in July 1918. The recognised head of the imperial house since 1938 has been Grand Duke Vladimir (1917-), the son of Princess Victoria (dau. of Queen Victoria's 2nd son, Prince Alfred, Duke of Edinburgh and Princess Marie, only dau. of Alexander II of Russia). *See also* ANASTASIA.

NICHOLSON, Ben (1894-). British artist. He is the son of the painter, Sir William N. (1872-1949), remembered for the series of striking posters and other works he produced with his brother-in-law, James Pryde, under the signature 'The Beggerstaff Brothers'. B. at Denham, Bucks, he studied at the Slade, as well as on the Continent and in California. Developing an interest in abstract art, he became known for his geometrical reliefs and as an exponent of Constructivism (q.v.). His work is remarkable for its exquisite control and delicacy. Awarded OM 1968.

NICHOLSON, John (1822-57). British soldier. He was administrative officer at Bannu, in the Punjab, 1851-6, and the justice and firmness of his rule led to his being worshipped as a god. Promoted to brig.-gen. on the outbreak of the Mutiny, he crushed resistance in the Punjab, but was killed during the storming of Delhi.

NICKEL. Lustrous white metal discovered by Cronstedt in 1751, the name being an abbreviation of Swedish *kopparnickel* (false copper): symbol Ni, at. wt. 58.71, at. no. 28. It has a high melting point, low electrical and thermal conductivity, and can be magnetized. N. may be readily forged when hot, and is tough, malleable, and ductile when cold. Canada provides the most extensive deposits, which are usually extracted with copper. Smelting precedes separation, after which the N. is purified. It is used in coinage; in chemical and foodstuff industries for its resistance to corrosion; in electronics and for electroplating. The most important use, however, is in alloys with iron, steel, copper, and chromium, incl. N. steel for armourplating and burglar-proof safes, Monel metal, invar, constantan, nichrome permalloy, perminvar, and other magnetic alloys and stainless steels, cupro-N., N.-silver, and others. Finely divided N. is used as a catalyst in the hydrogenation of vegetable oils.

NICOBARS (nikōbahrz'). Group of 19 islands (7 uninhabited) in the Bay of Bengal, forming with the Andamans (q.v.) a territory of the Rep. of India. The Is. were occupied by the Japanese 1942-5. Area 1,645 sq.km (635 sq.m); pop. (1971) with the Andamans, 115,000.

NICOLSON, Sir Harold (1886-1968). Brit. diplomat and author. Son of Lord Carnock, he entered the Foreign Service, held embassy appointments and served on the British delegation to the Paris Peace Conference of 1919. He was a Nat. Labour MP 1935-45, and in 1947 joined the Labour Party. A distinguished biographer, e.g. *Lord Carnock* (1930), *Curzon: the Last Phase* (1934), and *King George V* (1952), he also pub. studies such as *Monarchy* (1962). He m. in 1913 Victoria Sackville-West (q.v.).

NICOSI'A. Capital of Cyprus to the W of Famagusta. It has leather, textile, pottery and other industries, and an international airport. N. was the residence of the Lusignan kings of Cyprus 1192-1475. The Venetians, who took Cyprus in 1489, surrounded N. with a high wall which still exists; it fell to the Turks 1571. It was again partly taken by the Turks in the invasion of 1974. Pop. (1972) 118,300.

NICOSIA. The double-headed capital of Cyprus. The 'Green Line' separating the Turkish and Greek sectors passes at the foot of the minaret, itself in the Turkish zone while the building in front is in that of the Greeks. *Photo: Holmes-Lebel/Camera Press.*

NICOTINE (nik'otēn). An alkaloid obtained from the dried leaves of the tobacco plant (*Nicotiana tabacum*). A colourless oil, soluble in water, it turns brown on exposure to the air. N. in its pure form is one of the most powerful poisons known: it is named after 16th cent. French diplomat, Jacques Nicot, who introduced tobacco to France.

NIEBUHR (nēbo͞or), **Barthold Georg** (1776-1831). German historian. He was Prussian ambassador at the Holy See 1816-23, and then prof. of Roman history at Bonn until 1831. He wrote a history of Rome (1811-32).

NIEBUHR, Reinhold (1892-1971). American theologian. Prof. of ethics at the Union Theological Seminary, NY, 1928-60, he was influential in his books on Christianity and present-day problems, e.g. *Moral Man and Immoral Society* (1932).

NIEDERSACHSEN. *See* Lower Saxony.

NIELSEN (nel'-), **Carl** (1865-1931). Danish composer. At 14 an army bugler, he became director of the Copenhagen Conservatoire in 1915. His reputation extended outside Scandinavia after the S.W.W., and his works are remarkable for their progressive tonality, as in his opera *Saul og David* and 6 symphonies.

NIEMEYER (nē'mīer), **Oscar** (1907-). Brazilian architect. He was one of the architects employed in designing the HQ of the UN in NY, and from 1957 worked on Brasilia (q.v.).

NIEMÖLLER (ne'möller), **Martin** (1892–1984). German pastor. He led a campaign against the Nazification of the German Church, was dismissed in 1934, and later suffered gaol and the concentration camp, remaining a prisoner throughout the S.W.W. In 1946 he proclaimed Germany's war guilt at the International Missionary Council in Geneva, and was first bp of the newly formed Evangelical Church of Hesse-Nassau 1947-64, and pres. of the World Council of Churches 1961-8.

NIETZSCHE (nē'tshe), **Friedrich Wilhelm** (1844-1900). German philosopher. B. at Röcken, Saxony, he attended Bonn univ. and was prof. of Greek at Basle 1869-80. He had abandoned theology for philology, and was influenced by the writings of Schopenhauer and the music of Wagner, with whom he became on close terms. Both these attractions passed, however, and ill-health caused his resignation from the univ. He spent his later years in N Italy, in the Engadine and in S France. During his mature years till 1889 he pub. *Morgenröte* (1880-1), *Die fröhliche Wissenschaft* (1881-2), *Also sprach Zarathustra* (1883-5), *Jenseits von Gut und Böse* (1885-6), *Genealogie der Moral* (1887), and *Ecce Homo* (1888). He suffered a permanent breakdown in 1889 from overwork and loneliness.

The philosophy of N. is the rejection of the accepted absolute moral values and the 'slave morality' of Christianity. His ideal was the 'Overman' or 'Superman' who would impose his will on those who are too weak and worthless to be anything but slaves. Until this century, his beliefs remained ignored or opposed, by Conservatives and Socialists alike, but support for modern Totalitarianism has often been claimed (possibly wrongly) in N.'s writings.

NIÈVRE (nyāvr'). River in central France rising near Varzy and flowing 40km (25m) S to join the Loire at Nevers. It gives its name to a dept.

NIGER (nī'jer). Third-longest river in Africa, rising 240km (150m) from the W coast, in the highlands bordering Sierra Leone and the rep. of Guinea. It flows NE, then SE, and enters the Gulf of Guinea; 4,185 km (2,600 m). The Benue joins the N. at Lokoja. The N. is a sluggish r., frequently flooding its banks.

NIGER (nēzhār'), **Rep. of.** Country in W Africa. Cattle are raised and groundnuts, millet and coffee grown. In the N, which is part of the Sahara, there are rich uranium and tin deposits. The cap. is Niamey; pop. 102,000. N. was occupied by France in 1912, and became independent outside the French Community in 1960. In a military coup in 1974 Col. Seyni Kountche became Head of State. The country was ravaged by the Sahel droughts of the 1970s, but in the 1980s was recovering prosperity as exploitation of its minerals began. Area 1,187,000 sq.km (459,000 sq.m): pop. (1985) 6,491,000. M.U.: CFA franc.

NIGERIA (nījēr'ia), **Federal Rep. of.** Country in W Africa on the Gulf of Guinea, with Benin to the W, Cameroon to the E, and the rep. of Niger to the N. In 1976 the states of the federation were increased in number and reorganized to obliterate former ethnic and religious (Moslem, Christian, and pagan) divisions. The states with their caps. are now: Anambra (Enugu), Bauchi (Bauchi), Bendel (Benin City), Benue (Makurdi), Cross River (Calabar), Borno (Maiduguri), Gongola (Yola), Imo (Owerri), Kaduna (Kaduna), Kano (Kano), Kwara (Ilorin), Lagos (Lagos), Niger (Minna), Ogun (Abeokuta), Ondo (Akure), Oyo (Ibadan), Plateau (Jos), Rivers (Port Harcourt), and Sokoto (Sokoto). Lagos, though remaining the commercial cap., is being replaced as the admin. HQ by Abuja, more healthily and centrally situated to the SE of Minna.

NIGERIA. A Gelede Society mask (left) from the Yoruba, used in funeral dances; and a 16th century ivory pendant mask, probably representing a King of Benin, with a tiara of miniature heads of Portuguese. Both are from southern Nigeria. *Photos: Courtesy of the British Museum.*

Physical Features. To the S is a coastal strip, a maze of creeks and mangrove swamps, including the delta of the Niger. To the N of this lies a belt of tropical forest. The rest of the country is savannah, becoming arid and treeless towards the N. The E strip is rugged and mountainous. The main rivers are the Niger and its tributary the Benue; both are navigable.

The whole country is hot, in the N the heat is very dry, and in the S damp and enervating. The dry season is characterized by a dust-laden NE wind, the *harmattan.* The annual rainfall, about 180cm (72in) in Lagos, but over 380cm (150in) elsewhere on the coast, is only about 60cm (25in) in the extreme N.

Economic Life. Since 1958 petroleum has steadily overtaken the former staple exports of cocoa, groundnuts, palm oil, cotton, rubber, tin and bauxite in importance, and there are also natural gas deposits, and some coal nr Enugu. Forests supply high-grade timber, and large herds of cattle in the N produce hides for export. M.U.: naira.

Area 924,000 sq.km (357,000 sq.m.); pop. (1980) 100,000,000. The chief groups are the Yoruba in the W, the Ibo in tne E, and the Hausa-Fulani in the N: the N is mainly Moslem and the S mainly Christian. Hausa is a *lingua franca,* English the official language. There is a lively literature, e.g. playwrights Wole Soyinka and Hubert Ogunde, and poet Cris Okigbo. M.U.: naira.

History. Lagos was bought from an African chief by British traders in 1861; in 1886 it became the colony and protectorate of Lagos. Activity in the Niger valley was developed by the National African Co. (later the Royal Niger Co.) which came to an end in 1899; two protectorates, N Nigeria and S Nigeria, were set up in 1900: Lagos was joined to S.N. in 1906. In 1954 N. became a federation which in 1960 achieved independence, becoming in 1963 a federal rep. within the Commonwealth. A military *coup d'état* in 1966 led to the death of Tafawa-Balewa (q.v.). After much unrest Maj.-Gen. Jakabu Gowon became head of the Fed. Military Govt later in 1966, but in 1967 the E region seceded as the Rep. of Biafra (q.v.) and civil war ensued until 1970. Gowon (q.v.) then pursued a policy of reconciliation, but in 1975 was ousted in a bloodless coup by Brigadier Murtala Muhammad. Civilian rule was restored under Pres. Alhaji Shehu Shagari in 1979, but in 1983 Major-Gen. Muhammad Buhari ousted him in a military coup, and headed a Supreme Military Council, with a Federal Executive Council to act as cabinet.

NIGHTINGALE, Florence (1820-1910). British hospital reformer. B. in Florence of wealthy parents, in 1854 she took a staff of nurses to Scutari, where inefficiency and insanitary conditions were causing unnecessary loss of life among the British soldiers from the Crimea, and within 6 months reduced the death-rate in the hospitals from 42 to 2 per cent. For the rest of her life, although living in retirement, she worked constantly to raise the status of the nursing profession. She received the OM in 1907.

NIGHTINGALE. Song-bird (*Luscinia megarhyncos*) which winters in Africa, but breeds in S Europe and S England in the late spring and early summer. The song of the male has a legendary beauty and though to be heard in the daytime is most striking at night when other birds are silent. Allied species are found in E Europe.

NIGHTSHADE. Common name for several plants in the family Solanaceae: best-known are the Black N (*Solanum nigrum*), bittersweet or woody N (*S. dulcamara*), and deadly N. or belladonna (q.v.).

NI'HILISTS. Russian revolutionaries of the reign of Alexander II (1855-81). The name, popularized by Turgenev, means those who approve of nothing (Lat. *nihil*) belonging to the existing order. From 1878 they launched a terrorist campaign which culminated in the murder of the Tsar in 1881.

NIGHTINGALE. A pencil drawing of Florence Nightingale by Sir George Scharf, made just after the end of the Crimean War in 1857. *Photo: Courtesy of the National Portrait Gallery.*

NIIGATA (ni-igahtah). Chief port of W Honshu, Japan, on the Shinano r., with textile, metallurgical, oil-refining and chemical industries. Pop. (1977) 427,000.

NIJINSKY (nēzhin'ski), **Vaslav** (1890-1950). Russian ballet dancer and choreographer. He made his début in 1908, appeared with the Diaghileff company in Paris in 1909, and later in St Petersburg. He turned to choreography in 1912, creating *L'après-midi d'un faune, Jeux,* and *Le Sacre du printemps.* After tours of S and N America, he retired because of insanity.

NIJMEGEN (nī'mākhen). Town in the Netherlands, in the province of Gelderland, on the Waal, 16km (10m) S of Arnhem. The Roman Noviomagus, N. was a free city of the Holy Roman Empire and a member of the Hanseatic League. Brewing is carried on and there are leather and tobacco works. Pop. (1978) 148,000.

NIJNI-NOVGOROD. *See* GORKY.

NIKE (nī'kē). Greek goddess of victory. One of the most beautiful architectural monuments of Athens was the temple of N. Apteros. N. is shown in sculpture with wings, as in the 'Winged Victory' (Louvre).

NIKOLAYEV (nēkōlī'ef). Seaport in the Ukrainian SSR, at the mouth of the S Bug, on the Black Sea, cap. of N region. A naval base, it has important shipyards. Pop. (1977) 447,000.

NILE. The longest river in Africa; its remotest head stream is the Luvironzo branch of the r. Kagera flowing from the SW into Lake Victoria and thence to the Mediterranean. The N. proper begins where the main stream leaves Lake Victoria 4km (2.5m) above Owen Falls (q.v.); it is *c.* 5,600 km (3,500 m) long. From Lake Victoria it flows over rocky country, and there are many cataracts and rapids, including the Murchison Falls, until it enters Lake Mobutu. From here it flows across flat country and in places spreads out to form lakes. At Lake No it is joined by the Bahr el Ghazal, and from this point to Khartoum it is called the White N. At Khartoum it is joined by the Blue N., which rises in the Ethiopian highlands, and 320km (200m) below Khartoum it is joined by the Athara. From Khartoum to Aswan (q.v.) there are 6 cataracts. The N. is navigable to the second cataract, a distance of 1,545 km (960m). The delta of the N. is 190km (120m) wide. In 1980 there was disagreement between Egypt and Ethiopia over the former's plan to pipe N. water under the Suez Canal to Sinai.

NILE, Battle of the. *See* ABOUKIR BAY.

NILGAI (nēl'gī). Large antelope (*Boselaphus tragocamelus*) found in India. The bull has short conical horns and is bluish-grey.

NÎMES (nēm). City of the S of France, cap. of the dept of Gard 29km (18m) NW of Arles, famous for its Roman remains which incl. an amphitheatre dating from *c.* 2nd cent. AD. Pop. (1975) 130,000.

NIMITZ (nim'its), **Chester William** (1885-1966). American admiral. He was responsible for the reconquest of the Solomons (1942-3), the Gilbert Is. (1943), and the Marianas and Marshalls (1944), and as US representative signed the Japanese surrender.

NINEVEH (nin'eve). Cap. of the Assyrian Empire from the 8th cent. BC until its destruction by the Medes under Cyaxares in 612 BC. It was situated on the Tigris opposite the modern town of Mosul, and was adorned with splendid palaces. Excavations from 1842 onwards brought to light the ruins of N. under the mounds, or tells, of Kuyunjik and Nebi Yunus.

NINGBO (nēngbaw'). Fishing port, (formerly Ningpo) in Zhejiang prov., China. Already a centre of foreign trade under the Tang dynasty (618-907), it was one of the original treaty ports in 1842. Pop. (1973) 400,000.

NINGPO. *See* NINGBO.

NINGXIA HUI (neng'shē-ah hoo-ē'). Autonomous region and prov. (formerly Ninghsia-Hui), of NW China. Cap. Yinchuan. Area 170,000 sq.km (65,600 sq.m); pop. (1979) 3,000,000.

NĪ'ŌBĒ. In Greek legend the daughter of Tantalus and wife of Amphion, king of Thebes. Proud of her 12 children, she showed contempt for the goddess Leto who had only two; whereupon Leto induced her own children, Apollo and Artemis, to slay N.'s. N. d. of grief, and was changed into stone by Zeus.

NIOBIUM. Light grey metal closely allied to tantalum, and known in the USA as columbium, which was first prepared by Blomstrand in 1864, though discovered in an ore by Hatchett in 1801: symbol Nb, at. wt. 92.91, at. no. 41. Occurring in a number of rare minerals, it is generally obtained from an African ore, and is a valuable addition to stainless steels, also being used for canning high-temperature nuclear fuel elements, e.g. fast breeder-reactors, espec. when liquid sodium is the coolant.

NIPPON. Transliteration of the native name for Japan.

NIRVANA (nirvah'na) (lit. 'blowing-out'). In Buddhism, the attainment of perfect serenity by the eradication of all desires. To some Buddhists it means complete annihilation, to others it means the absorption of the self in the infinite.

NITHSDALE, William Maxwell, 5th earl of (1676-1744). Jacobite leader who was captured at Preston, brought to trial in Westminster Hall, and condemned to death on 9 Feb. 1716. With his wife's assistance he escaped from the Tower of London in woman's dress, and fled to Rome.

NITRE (nī'tr) or **saltpetre.** Potassium nitrate, KNO_3, a mineral found on the ground and in the soil near the surface of the ground at Bihar, India, Iran, and Cape Province, S Africa. The native salt was formerly used for the manufacture of gunpowder, but the supply of N. for explosives is nowadays largely met by making the salt from nitratine (Chile saltpetre, $NaNO_3$).

NITRE. Mining nitrates in the Atacama Desert near Antofagasta. *Photo: Mireille Vautier.*

NĪ'TRIC ACID. Mineral acid, HNO_3, also called aqua fortis, first prepared by Raimon Lull (q.v.) by heating nitre and clay: its real nature was demonstrated by Cavendish. Obtained directly from the air by the various processes for fixation of atmospheric nitrogen, it is a strong oxidizing agent, dissolves most metals, and is used for nitration and esterification of organic substances; for explosives, plastics, and dyes; in making sulphuric acid and nitrates.

NITRITE (nī'trīt). Any salt or ester of nitrous acid. Nitrites are used as a preservative (e.g. to prevent the growth of botulism spores) and colouring in cured meats, such as bacon and hot dogs. There have been arguments as to their possible role in causing cancer.

NĪ'TROCELLULOSE. Series of esters with 2-6 nitrate groups per molecule, made by the action of concentrated nitric acid on cellulose in the presence of concentrated sulphuric acid: those with 5 or more nitrate groups are explosive (gun cotton), but those with less were used in lacquers, rayon, and plastics, espec. celluloid and photographic film, until replaced by non-inflammable cellulose acetate.

NITROGEN. Colourless, odourless, inert gas isolated by Daniel Rutherford in 1772: symbol N, at. wt. 14.008, at. no. 7. There are an est. 4,000 billion tonnes of N. in the atmosphere of which it forms *c.* 78 per cent by vol. (Gk nitreforming). Many N. compounds, e.g. nitric acid, nitrates, ammonia and the oxides, are of greatest importance in foods, drugs, fertilizers, dyes, and explosives. N. is a constituent of many organic substances, particularly proteins, but is generally obtained from nitrate deposits, e.g. Chile; or from the atmosphere by liquefaction and fractional distillation; or by N. fixation, e.g. the Haber process in which N. and hydrogen are heated under pressure in the presence of a catalyst to form ammonia. The Haber process has become increasingly expensive owing to the increased cost of fuel to produce temperatures as high as 500°C, and there is research to find a less energy-intensive method. In nature atmospheric N. is fixed by certain soil bacteria.

NITROGLYCERINE. Substance,produced by the action of nitric and sulphuric acids on glycerol. Very poisonous, it explodes with great violence if heated in a confined space. It is used in the preparation of dynamite, cordite, and other high explosives.

NIUE (nē-ōō'-ā). One of the Cook Is. (q.v.): in 1974 N. achieved full internal self-govt in free assocn with NZ. Area 260 sq.km (100 sq.m); pop. 4,000.

NIXON, Richard Milhous (1913-). American Repub. politician. B. in California, of Quaker family, he became a lawyer, entered Congress in 1947, and in 1948 attracted attention as a member of the Un-American Activities Committee when he pressed for the investigation of Alger Hiss (q.v.). He was senator from California from 1951 until Vice-Pres. of the US under Eisenhower 1953-61. He failed to defeat J. F. Kennedy in the pres. elections of 1961, but in a 'law and order' campaign defeated Vice-Pres. Humphrey in 1968 in one of the most closely contested elections in US history. In 1969 he formulated at Guam the *N. Doctrine,* abandoning such policies of close involvement with Asian countries as would result in Vietnam-type situations, and the ending of the American commitment in Vietnam was achieved in 1973. Re-elected in 1972 in a landslide victory, he resigned in 1974 - the first US president to do so - following Watergate (q.v.) and the threat of impeachment on 3 counts: 1, obstruction of the admin. of justice in the investigation of Watergate; 2, violation of constitutional rights of citizens, e.g., attempting to use the Inland Revenue Service, FBI, and CIA as a weapon against political opponents; 3, failing to produce 'papers and things' as ordered by the Judiciary committee. He was granted a controversial free pardon by Pres. Ford. *See* WHITTIER.

NKRUMAH (nkrōō'mah), **Kwame** (1909-72). Ghanaian statesman. Originally a schoolmaster, he studied later in both Britain and America, and following his return to Africa, formed in 1949 the Convention People's Party with the aim of immediate self-govt. He was imprisoned in 1950 for incitement of illegal strikes, but was released the same year, becoming PM of the Gold Coast (1952-7), of Ghana (1957-60), and first pres. of the rep. from 1960 until his dictatorial rule led to his deposition while on a visit to Peking in 1966. He remained in exile but from 1973 was posthumously 'rehabilitated'.

NKVD. *See* KGB.

NŌ. The classical, aristocratic Japanese drama, which developed in the 14-16th centuries and is still performed. There is a repertory of some 250 pieces, of which 5 - one from each of the several classes devoted to different subjects - may be put on in a performance lasting a whole day. The players are masked and beautifully costumed.

NŌ'AH. Biblical character. The son of Lamech and father of Shem, Ham, and Japheth, he built an ark so that he and his family and specimens of all existing animals might survive the Deluge (Gen. 6-8). In a Babylonian version the hero is Ut-napishtim.

NŌ'BEL, Alfred Bernhard (1833-96). Swedish chemist. B. at Stockholm, he invented dynamite in 1867, and ballistite, a smokeless gunpower, in 1889. He amassed a large fortune from the manufacture of explosives and the exploitation of the Baku oilfields, the bulk of which by his will he left in trust for the endowment of five **Nobel Prizes.** These are awarded internationally each year for outstanding achievement in chemistry, physics, medicine, literature, and the promotion of peace: a 6th, for economics and financed by the Swedish Nat. Bank, was first awarded 1969.

NODULE (nod'ūl). In geology a rounded or irregular body, such as is often found in igneous or sedimentary rocks, and as has been more recently discovered on the surface of the seabed in certain areas. Theories of the origin of the latter, consisting of manganese etc., incl. precipitation, volcanic activity and creation by organism (as with coral). They grow at a slower rate than the sediment round them, but remain uncovered, possibly pushed up by sea cucumbers. There are schemes to raise them by hydraulic pumping in the Pacific and elsewhere.

NOEL-BAKER, Philip John (1889–1982). British Lab. politician. An ardent supporter of the League of Nations and UN, he pub. *The Arms Race* (1958), and he was in 1959 awarded a Nobel peace prize.

NOGUCHI (nōgoo'chē), **Hideyo** (1876-1928). Japanese bacteriologist, who did much valuable work in connection with syphilitic diseases, and discovered the parasite of yellow fever, a disease from which he died while working in British W Africa.

NOISE. Unwanted sound, an increasing problem in industrialized societies. Permanent, incurable loss of hearing can be caused by prolonged exposure to high N. levels (above 85 decibels in an octave), and even below this, if the N. is in a narrow frequency band: temporary loss occurs when exposure is for shorter periods. Lower levels of N. form an irritant, but seem not to increase fatigue or affect efficiency to any great extent. Roadside meter tests, introduced by the Min. of Transport in Britain in 1968, allowed 87 decibels as the permitted limit for saloon cars and 92 for lorries.

NŌ'LAN, Sir Sidney (1917-). Australian artist. B. in Melbourne, he developed, with little formal training, an individual interpretation of the Australian scene - the explorers and drought landscapes of the outback - but is most famous for his interpretation of the theme of Ned Kelly (q.v.). He was knighted 1981.

NO'LDE, Emil. Name - taken from his native village of N. in Schleswig - adopted by the German Expressionist artist Emil Hansen (1867-1956). Working both in water colour and oil, he excelled in colourful seascapes and such mystic religious works as 'The Last Supper' and 'Joseph tells his Dream'.

NOLLEKENS (nol'ekenz), **Joseph** (1737-1823). British sculptor. B. in Soho, he executed busts of George III, the Prince of Wales (later George IV), Pitt, Fox, Garrick, Sterne, and others.

NOMINALISM. One of the two main trends in the medieval philosophy of Scholasticism. In opposition to the Realists, who maintained that universals, i.e. the distinctive qualities which enable us to group objects into classes, have a real existence, the Nominalists taught that they are mere names invented to describe the qualities of real things. Controversy on this issue continued at intervals from the 11th to the 15th cent.

NON-ALIGNED MOVEMENT. Inaugurated in 1961 at an internat. conference in Belgrade by Tito, its aim was opposition to colonialism, neo-colonialism and imperialism, and to the dominance of dangerously

NOLAN. Sidney Nolan at work in his studio on his famous series of the mid-sixties dealing with bushranger Ned Kelly, who can just be seen wearing his home-made armour. *Photo: Axel Poignant.*

conflicting E and W alliances. However, many members were in receipt of aid from either E or W or both, and some went to war with one another (Vietnam-Kampuchea, Ethiopia-Somalia). By the 1979 conference in Havana, Castro was attempting to make the N.M. the 'natural' ally of the USSR.

NONCONFORMISTS. A term originally applied to the Puritan section of the C of E clergy who in the Elizabethan age refused to conform to certain practices of the Church, e.g. the wearing of the surplice and kneeling to receive Holy Communion. After 1662 the term was confined to those who left the Church rather than conform to the Act of Uniformity. It is now applied mainly to members of the Free Churches.

NONJURORS. Clergymen of the Church of England who after the Revolution of 1688 refused to take the oaths of allegiance to William and Mary. They continued to exist as a rival Church for over a century, and consecrated their own bishops, the last of whom d. in 1805. Notable Ns. were Thomas Ken, Jeremy Collier, and William Law.

NORDENSKJÖLD (nor'denshöld), **Nils Adolf Erik,** baron (1832-1901). Swedish explorer. He made voyages to the Arctic with the geologist Torell, and in 1878-9 discovered the North-East Passage. On his return he was made a baron, and pub. the results of his voyages in a series of books, incl. *Voyage of the Vega round Asia and Europe* (Eng. 1881).

NORDIC. A racial type, characterized by tall stature, long (dolichocephalic) head, and fair skin, hair, and eyes, found chiefly in Scandinavia and adjoining parts of

NORFOLK ISLAND. The British government later transferred some of the descendants of the mutineers of the *Bounty* to Norfolk Island, where this painting of Captain Bligh being set adrift is still treasured. *Photo: Ulli Skoruppa/Camera Press.*

Europe. The N. type is present in its purest form among the Swedes and Finns, somewhat less typically in Norway, Denmark, and the coastal region of Germany, and among the Baltic peoples; it is well represented in Britain, esp. in the north of England and the Western Isles of Scotland.

NORE, The. A sandbank at the mouth of the Thames, England. A lightship - the first of its kind - was placed there in 1732. The 'Mutiny of the Nore' in the British fleet took place in the vicinity in 1797.

NORFOLK, Miles Fitzalan-Howard, 17th duke of (1915-). Earl Marshal of England, and premier duke and earl. As Earl Marshal, he is responsible for the organization of ceremonial on major state occasions. He succeeded his cousin **Bernard Fitzalan-Howard,** 16th duke of N. (1908-75), who organized the coronations of George VI and Elizabeth II.

NORFOLK. Co. on the E coast of England. Its coastline is flat, except at Hunstanton and in the region of Cromer where there are cliffs, and much land has been reclaimed from the Wash near King's Lynn. The chief rivers are the Ouse, Yare, Bure, and Waveney. The series of lakes called the Broads are famous for their wild life, and are favoured for sailing and motor cruises. The soil consists mainly of sand, loam, and chalk. The chief crops incl. oats, wheat, barley, turnips and beet. Turkeys and geese are reared for the London market. Norwich, the co. tn, is the only industrial centre. Other towns incl. Gt Yarmouth, King's Lynn, Cromer, and Hunstanton. From 1965 large natural gas deposits were located off the coast. In 1974 N. acquired a very small area from NE Suffolk. Area 5,515 sq.km (2,129 sq.m); pop. (1978) 679,800.

NORFOLK. A seaport of Norfolk co., Virginia, USA, on the estuary of the r. James. On the opposite bank is the suburb of Portsmouth, where there is a navy yard. Pop. met. area N.-Portsmouth (1970) 633,142.

NORFOLK. The floating gallery established in 1976 on Ranworth Inner Broad being towed to its mooring. The building also houses displays on conservation and the history of the Broads. *Photo: Great Yarmouth Press Agency.*

NORFOLK ISLAND. Is. in the Pacific, midway between New Zealand and New Caledonia, discovered by Capt. Cook in 1774. N.I. was settled in 1856 by descendants of the mutineers of the *Bounty* from Pitcairn Is., and was under the jurisdiction of New South Wales until 1914, when it became a territory of the Australian Commonwealth. It has fertile soil and a mild climate; citrus, bananas, etc, are grown. Area 34 sq.km (13 sq.m); pop. (1978) 2,000.

NORMAN, Montagu, 1st baron (1871-1950). British banker. Governor of the Bank of England 1920-44, he handled German reparations after the F.W.W., and by his return to the Gold Standard in 1925 and other policies was held by many to have contributed to the Great Depression.

NORMAN. Style of architecture used in England from the time of Edward the Confessor until about the end of the 12th cent. N. buildings are massive, the semi-circular arch is used (except in the case of small openings for which trefoil arches are sometimes used), buttresses are of slight projection, and vaults are barrel-roofed. Examples are the Keep of the Tower of London, and parts of the cathedrals of Chichester, Gloucester, Oxford, and Ely.

NORMANDY (Fr. *Normandie*). One of the old provs. of France, on the seaboard of the English Channel, with Rouen as its cap. It now forms the two regions of Basse-Normandie (depts of Calvados, Manche and Orne) and Haute-Normandie (Eure, Seine-Maritime).

Part of Roman Gaul and then of the Frankish kingdom of Neustria, the region was occupied by the pagan Norsemen in the early 10th cent., and in 912 Rouen and some neighbouring land was given to their leader Rollo, who after becoming a Christian took the name of Robert. A descendant of Robert was William the Conqueror. During the Anglo-French wars N. changed hands several times, but it was finally conquered by the French under Charles VII in 1450. N. again became a battleground during the S.W.W. in 1944 after Allied forces had landed on the beaches near Arromanches and Carentan on D-Day (q.v.). There was bitter fighting for weeks, particularly at Caen and Falaise.

NORMANDY. The Abbaye aux Hommes, at Caen, a fine specimen of Romanesque architecture founded by William the Conqueror in 1070. *Photo: Courtesy of the French Government Tourist Office.*

NORMAN-FRENCH. The French dialect used by the Norsemen who settled in Normandy in the 10th cent., and subsequently by the Norman ruling class in England. Although generally replaced by English in the 14th cent., it remained the language of the court until the 15th and the official language of the law courts until the 17th, and is still used in the Channel Is. A considerable literature written in England in N.F. exists, including the 12th cent. chronicles of Gaimar and Wacc, and thc fables of Marie de France.

NORMANS. The Norsemen who were granted Normandy by the king of France in 911, and adopted the French language and culture. During the 11th and 12th cents. they conquered England, parts of Wales and Ireland, S Italy, Sicily, and Malta, settled in Scotland, and took a prominent part in the Crusades. After the 13th cent. they ceased to exist as a distinct people.

NORRIS, Frank (1870-1902). American novelist. B. in Chicago, he completed only 2 parts of his great projected trilogy, the *Epic of Wheat: Octopus* (1901) dealing with the growing of wheat, and *The Pit (1903)* describing the gamble of the Chicago wheat exchange.

NORSEMEN. The early inhabitants of Norway. The term is used in a more general sense for all the Scandinavian Vikings who during the 8th-11th cents. raided and settled in Britain, Ireland, France, Russia, Iceland, and Greenland. The Norse religion (banned in 1000) was recognized by the Icelandic govt in 1973.

NORTH, Frederick, 8th lord (1732-92). British statesman. He entered parl. in 1754, became Chancellor of the Exchequer in 1767, and was PM in a govt of Tories and 'king's Friends' in 1770. Throughout his premiership his policy, supported by the monarch George III, was to maintain a hard line against the American colonies. He was compelled to resign in 1782, returned to office in 1783 in a coalition with Fox (q.v.), and after its dismissal in Dec. of the same year he retired from politics.

NORTH, Sir Thomas (*c.* 1535-1601). English translator. His translation of Plutarch's *Lives* (1579), a masterpiece of Elizabethan prose, formed the source of Shakespeare's Roman plays.

NORTHA'LLERTON. Town in N Yorks, England, admin. HQ of the co., with tanning and flour milling industries. Pop. (1974) 9,100.

NORTH AMERICA. A continent covering 18 per cent of the earth's land area, whose physical bounds reach Panama, Alaska, and Labrador, and divided into N America proper (Canada, the USA and Mexico) and CENTRAL AMERICA (q.v.).

N.A. bears marked physical features. The Laurentian region is disordered rock structure in a low-lying ring round Hudson Bay, from Labrador on the E to the Arctic. Lakes and streams abound amid wild afforestation. The Appalachian area is a mountainous range running from Newfoundland SW to Alabama. Called the Appalachians from Nova Scotia to Pennsylvania, and the Allegheny plateau S to Alabama, the area is occupied by large coal deposits. A coastal plain borders the Gulf of Mexico and the Atlantic. The Western Highlands or Cordilleras are complex ranges forming a vast interior barrier down the W of the continent from Alsaka to Central America. Rising to over 6,000 m (20,000 ft) in Mt McKinley, Alaska, the individual ranges are the Alaska range, Brooks range, Mackenzie mts., Rocky mts., Colorado plateau, and Mexican plateau. Parallel to the Rockies are the Coast range, Cascade range, and Sierra Nevadas, which bound narrow, fertile, Pacific-coast plains. The Central Plains are a wide belt stretching from the Arctic to the

ARCTIC OCEAN
GREENLAND SEA
ASIA
WRANGEL I.
ELLESMERE ISLAND
QUEEN ELIZABETH ISLANDS
GREENLAND
ICELAND
BEAUFORT SEA
DEVON I.
BANKS I.
PARRY IS.
BERING STR
BROOKS RA.
Alaska
Yukon
MT. McKINLEY
AMUNDSEN G.
VICTORIA I.
G. OF BOOTHIA
BAFFIN ISLAND
DAVIS STR.
Mackenzie
Great Bear L.
KODIAK I.
Great Slave L.
HUDSON STR.
Ungava Pena.
ALEXANDER ARCHO.
HUDSON BAY
Labrador
L. Athabasca
Laurentian Shield
Peace
Nelson
QUEEN CHARLOTTE IS.
NEW-FOUNDLAND
MT. ROBSON
JAMES BAY
G. OF ST. LAWRENCE
LAURENTIAN MTS.
VANCOUVER ISLAND
L. Winnipeg
CAPE BRETON I.
ROCKY MOUNTAINS
S. Saskatchewan
Columbia
Lake Superior
Nova Scotia
St. Lawrence
Mississippi
L. Michigan
L. Huron
L. Ontario
C. Cod
Niagara Falls
Great Basin
Missouri
L. Erie
SA. NEVADA
Platte
APPALACHIAN MTS.
ATLANTIC OCEAN
MT. WHITNEY
Arkansas
Ozark Plateau
Ohio
BERMUDA
SANTA BARBARA IS.
Colorado
Mississippi
Lower California
G. OF CALIFORNIA
SIERRA MADRE OCCID.
SA. MADRE OR.
Rio Grande
Florida
BAHAMA ISLANDS
STR. OF FLORIDA
GULF OF MEXICO
CUBA
CAYMAN ISLANDS
HISPANIOLA
JAMAICA
GULF OF CAMPECHE
Yucatan
G. OF HONDURAS
CARIBBEAN SEA
PACIFIC OCEAN
L. Nicaragua
Isthmus of Panama
Panama Canal
SOUTH AMERICA
Miles
0 200 400 600 800 1000
0 200 400 600 800 1000 1200 1400
Kilometres
© Geographical Projects

Gulf of Mexico, averaging 2,400 km (1,500 m) in breadth and including the Canadian and USA wheat and plantation areas; roughly along the US-Canadian border they slope gently downwards to N and to S.

The chief river systems are the E-flowing St Lawrence, Missouri, Arkansas, and Rio del Norte; the W-flowing Yukon, Snake, and Colorado rivers; the S-flowing Mississippi, and the N-flowing Mackenzie. Between Canada and the USA lies the unique lake system, comprising Superior, Michigan, Huron, Erie, and Ontario, from which issues the St Lawrence. The climate varies greatly with latitude.

The American Indians, incl. the Eskimo, share Mongoloid physical characteristics which show that they entered North America in successive waves from Asia via the land bridge which once crossed the Bering Strait. The date of the first arrivals was once thought to be a few thousand years BC, but the period has been steadily pushed back by further research at least to 20,000 years ago, and even more recently to probably 70,000 years ago. Archaeological discoveries in N America incl. the communal stone houses and richly decorated pottery of the Pueblo era, and the skilled copper work of the 'mound-builders' of the Mississippi basin, all at their best in the 12-14th cents. AD, but there is nothing to compare with the advanced cultures of Central and South America. The Amerindians are thought to have numbered *c.* 1,000,000 when Europeans first arrived, and although some tribes declined into extinction, there has been a general increase in the 20th cent. Their social-economic plight in the reserves of the USA - usually carved out of the poorest and most remote land - prompted the admin. to make attempts to assist them after the S.W.W., and among Indians themselves there was a nationalist revival. This incl. the militant American Indian Movement, as well as peaceful commercial development: *see* ALCATRAZ, WOUNDED KNEE. Today they number *c.* 250,000 in Canada; 764,000 in USA; and 3,000,000 in Mexico: the Indian languages have survived in great diversity.

By successive waves of immigration from Europe from the 17th cent. White settlers estab. their predominance throughout North America. Their introduction of slave labour from Africa in the southern states of the USA, however, resulted in about 11 per cent of the present pop. being 'Black'. Only about a quarter of this Black pop., which is now more evenly distributed, is now without an admixture of White or other blood. In Mexico the majority of the pop. is of Spanish descent and Spanish-speaking, and the second largest minority in the USA consists of Hispanic Americans. The only other language and culture to survive as a coherent entity on a considerable scale is that of French Canada. Most later European settlers in N.A. adopted the language and culture of their new country, but after the S.W.W. there was a reversal to some extent of this total assimilation and a new pride in national origins. During the peak period of European immigration 1880-1930, it averaged more than half a million annually, chiefly to the USA, which now imposes an annual limit of 170,000 from the Eastern Hemisphere and 120,000 from the Western.

NORTHAMPTON. Town in Northants, of which it is the admin. HQ, England, on the r. Nene. In 1965 there was a decision to expand the town, and engineering has taken over as the main industry instead of the traditional boots and shoes. Other new industries incl. food processing, and brewing. Pop. (1975) 141,000.

NORTH AMERICA. The highest mountain in North America, Mount McKinley: it is very rarely that its head appears so spectacularly above the clouds. *Photo: Mireille Vautier.*

Countries of North America

	Area 1,000 sq.km.	*Population*	*Capital*
Canada	9,975	22,992,604	Ottawa
St. Pierre and Miquelon (French)	.2	6,260	St. Pierre
United States of America (incl. Hawaii)	9,364	218,059,000	Washington DC
Mexico	1,980	64,594,400	Mexico City
Great Lakes	246	—	
	21,565.2	305,652,264	

NORTHAMPTONSHIRE or **Northants.** Midland county of England, which incl. the sources of the Cherwell, Avon, Leam, Welland, and Nene. Its churches with broached spires are famous. The N. climate is mild, the soil fertile, and cattle are raised, and wheat and barley grown. There is some industry at Northampton, the admin. HQ, and Kettering. Area 2,367 sq.km (914 sq.m); pop. (1978) 516,400.

NORTH ATLANTIC TREATY. Treaty signed in Washington, DC, on 4 April 1949 by Belgium, Canada, Denmark, France, Iceland, Italy, Luxembourg, Netherlands, Norway, Portugal, UK, and USA. The signatories agreed that 'an armed attack against one or more of them in Europe or North America shall be considered an attack against them all'. Greece and Turkey acceded in 1952, and Germany in 1955.

The chief body of the NAT Organization is the Council of Foreign Ministers which holds periodic meetings and also functions in permanent session through the appointment of permanent representatives. The unified international secretariat has its HQ at Brussels from 1967 (formerly Paris) as does a Military Committee consisting of chiefs of staff (until 1967 in Washington). The military HQ is called Supreme Headquarters Allied Powers, Europe (SHAPE) and moved from Rocquencourt,

France, to Chièvres-Casteau, nr Mons, 1967. The Supreme Allied Commanders, Europe and Atlantic, are Americans, but there is also an Allied Commander, Channel - a British admiral. France withdrew from the organization, but not from the alliance, 1966, and Greece withdrew militarily, but not politically, in 1974 over the Cyprus issue. Greece re-entered NATO in 1981, and Spain, unofficially a member from 1980, was seeking a Parliamentary mandate in 1981.

NORTH CAROLĪ'NA State of the USA on the Atlantic seaboard, one of the original 13. It is fertile, and agriculture, incl. the production of tobacco and cotton, is the principal industry. Kaolin, mica, feldspar, tungsten, and granite are worked; timber is important; textiles, cigarettes (about half those produced in the whole Union), furniture, paper, chemicals, and artificial fibres are produced. The fisheries are valuable. The cap. is Raleigh, the largest city Charlotte, and the chief port is Wilmington. Verrazano, 1524, and De Soto, 1540, were the earliest European visitors; the first English settlement in America was made on Roanoke Is. in 1585, but it was wiped out. Area 136,523 sq.km (52,712 sq.m); pop. (1970) 5,082,059.

NORTHCLIFFE, Alfred Charles William Harmsworth, 1st visct N. (1865-1922). British newspaper proprietor. Founding the *Daily Mail* (1896), he revolutionized popular journalism with attractive make-up and writing, and with the *Daily Mirror* (1903) originated the picture paper: in 1908 he also obtained control of *The Times.* He was created a baron in 1905 and visct in 1917. His brother Harold Sidney Harmsworth, 1st visct **Rothermere** (1868-1940), was associated with him in many of his newspaper projects.

NORTH DAKŌ'TA. West North Central state of the USA, bounded in the N by Canada, situated in the Great Plain region, and consisting of 3 huge tablelands, viz. the Red River valley in the E, the Pembina mts. in the NE, and the Missouri plateau which covers the western half of the state. In the SW are the Bad Lands, so called because the pioneers had great difficulty in crossing them. The valley of the Red River is very fertile, and grain production is the chief industry of the state. The cap. is Bismarck, the largest town Fargo. Area 183,020 sq.km (70,665 sq.m); pop. (1970) 617,761.

NORTH-EAST FRONTIER AGENCY. *See* ARUNACHAL PRADESH.

NORTH-EAST INDIA. Tribal area of India, land-locked by Bangladesh and Burma, with China to N, and linked with the rest of India only by a narrow corridor between Bangladesh and Nepal. It comprises the states of Meghalaya, Assam, Mizoram, Tripura, Manipur, and Nagaland, and the Union Terr. of Arunachal Pradesh. There is opposition to immigration from Bangladesh, and from the rest of India, and there is considerable support for secession.

NORTH-EAST PASSAGE. The sea route from the Atlantic round the N of Asia to the Pacific, followed successfully for the first time by A. E. Nordenskjöld (q.v.) in 1878-9. Since 1935 the use of this route has been extensively developed by the Soviet govt, in connection with its colonization of N Siberia.

NORTHERN AREAS. Districts to the N of Azad Kashmir, directly admin. by Pakistan but not merged with it, incl. Baltistan and Gilgit (autonomous districts 1947-72) and Hunza (ruled by a Mir as a principality for 900 years until 1974).

NORTHERN IRELAND. A self-governing country within the UK estab. in 1920 and comprising the counties of Antrim, Down, Armagh, Tyrone, Londonderry, and Fermanagh, and the co. bors. of Belfast, the cap., and Londonderry, all in the prov. of Ulster. Area 14,147 sq.km (5,462 sq.m); pop. (1971) 1,536,075. The largest single group, predominant near the border with the Irish Rep., is RC, but overall the Protestant denominations are in the majority, Presbyterians being the most numerous. There are 2 univs., Queen's (1849) at Belfast and the New Univ. of Ulster at Coleraine (1968).

Physical. Most of N Ireland occupies a peninsula of Ireland projecting NE towards Scotland. Its centre is the fertile basin of Lough Neagh, joined to Belfast Lough by the valley of the Lagan. To the N are the plateau of Antrim extending to the rugged coast, and the valley of the Bann. Farther W the Sperrin mts. (Sawel, 683m/2,240 ft) rise above boggy plateaux, while in the SE of the country the Mourne mts. culminate in Slieve Donard (880m/2,796 ft). A low temperature range and high humidity and precipitation are characteristic of the climate.

Economics. The traditional industries of N.I. are shipbuilding, hit by economic depression and linen, enjoying a revival. The synthetic fibres industry has been affected by Third World competition, but others incl. shoes, chemicals, electronics, cars (notably the DeLorean sports car project), plastics, machine tools, aircraft and tobacco. One quarter of the land surface is mountain and bog - producing peat and used for rough grazing - but on the remainder a thriving agriculture supports a growing food processing industry. Formerly on a basis of smallholdings, agriculture now moves towards amalgamation in large farms, highly specialized and mechanized. Products include milk, butter, cheese, beef, bacon, eggs and chicken; and the chief crops are barley, oats, hay, potatoes, flax, and - in co. Armagh - fruit. Tourism has been affected by the bomb outrages.

History. The recent history of N.I. dates from the early 17th cent. when Protestant Scottish and English 'planters' settled there and gave the region an outlook very different from that of the rest of the island. Separation from the S came in 1920, the border (agreed on in 1925) excluding the 3 Catholic Ulster counties. Apart from spasmodic outbreaks of activity on the part of the IRA (q.v.), agitation remained largely in abeyance, but in 1968-9 serious Civil Rights disturbances in protest against discrimination against RCs in employment and housing, and restricted franchise in local govt elections, led to reform. However, renewed rioting in Belfast and Londonderry necessitated despatch of a British peacekeeping force and in 1972 direct rule by the UK was estab. and the separate N.I. parliament at Stormont, nr Belfast, was prorogued. A constitutional convention elected in 1975 failed to agree on a revised system of govt. amidst increasing violence, and 'direct rule' from Westminster was maintained. However, N.I. continued throughout to send members to the British Parliament. In 1982, under N.I. Secretary, James Prior, an elected Assembly of 78 members was established, but was boycotted by Provisional Sinn Fein (political wing of the IRA), which had gained 5 seats, and by the SDLP (Social Democratic and Labour Party). It was intended eventually to resume legislative and executive functions, but little progress had been made by 1984.

NORTHERN RHODESIA. *See* ZAMBIA.

NORTHERN TERRITORY. A territory of the Commonwealth of Australia, bounded on the N by the Arafura Sea and lying between Queensland and W Australia. Darwin is the cap. Most of the N.T. is within the tropics, and the climate is hot, with considerable variations in temperature in the S. There is an insufficient rainfall, but beef cattle are reared, with the help of water from artesian bores; fishing and pearl fishing are carried on on the coast; and gold, copper, tungsten, manganese, bauxite, and uranium are among minerals worked. Mineral discoveries on land occupied by Aborigines led to a royalty agreement 1979. Area 1,356,165 sq.km (523,620 sq.m); pop. (1976) 97,090.

NORTH POLE. *See* ARCTIC.

NORTH RHINE-WESTPHALIA. Land of W Germany, to the W, in the valley of the Rhine, and including the Ruhr (q.v.) industrial dist. It was formed in 1946 from the N part of the former Rhine prov. and the prov. of Westphalia (q.v.). Sugar-beet and potatoes are the biggest crops, coal and iron the chief mineral products. All kinds of iron and steel goods, fertilizers, artificial fibres, textiles are made. Düsseldorf is the cap.; other large towns are Cologne, Essen, Dortmund, Duisburg and Wuppertal. Area 34,150 sq.km (13,110 sq.m); pop. (1978) 17,030,300.

NORTH SEA. Sea bounded by the E coast of Britain, and the coasts of Belgium, the Netherlands, Germany, Denmark, and Norway. In the NE it joins the Norwegian Sea, and in the S it meets the Strait of Dover; average depth 55m (180ft), greatest depth 660m (2,166 ft), off Norway. There are a series of banks extending from the coast of Yorkshire to the Skagerrak, the most important being the Dogger Bank. There are rich fisheries, and oil and natural gas resources. Area *c.* 523,000 sq.km (202,000 sq.m).

NORTH SHIELDS. Seaport in Tyne and Wear, England, at the mouth of the Tyne, opposite S Shields, NE of Newcastle.

NORTH UIST. *See* UIST.

NORTHUMBERLAND, John Dudley, duke of (*c.* 1502-53). English statesman. Son of Edmund Dudley, he was created duke of N. in 1551, and was chief minister until Edward VI's death in 1553, when he attempted to place his daughter-in-law Lady Jane Grey on the throne. His misrule had made him so hated that the scheme immediately collapsed, and N. was beheaded.

NORTHUMBERLAND. Co. in the N of England, separated from Scotland by the Cheviot Hills and the Tweed. The surface in the E is flat, but it rises to the central moorland region, and in the NW there are mountains which culminate in the Cheviot (898m/2,676 ft). The chief rivers are the upper Tyne and Tweed. In the SW are the Northumbrian lakes, of which the largest is Greenlee Lough, and there are coal mines at Hexham in the SE. In 1974 N. lost Newcastle on Tyne (which remains the admin. HQ) and the coastal towns of Tynemouth and Whitley Bay to Tyne and Wear. Area 5,034 sq.km (1,944 sq.m); pop. (1978) 289,200.

NORTHUMBRIA. An Anglo-Saxon kingdom covering NE England and SE Scotland. It originally comprised two independent kingdoms founded in the 6th cent., Bernicia, extending from the Forth to the Tees, and Deira, from the Tees to the Humber, which were united in the 7th cent. During the 7th-8th cents. N., under the influence of Irish missionaries, became a cultural centre of European fame. It accepted the supremacy of Wessex in 827, and during the later 9th cent. was conquered by the Danes.

NORTH-WEST FRONTIER PROVINCE. Prov. of British India, formed in 1901, which lay between Afghanistan and Punjab. Predominantly Moslem, it became part of Pakistan in 1947. Containing the Khyber and other passes, this mountainous area was strategically vital to successive Mogul and British rulers who waged constant warfare against the Pathan (q.v.) tribesmen. The cap. was Peshawar.

NORTH-WEST PASSAGE. The sea route from the Atlantic round the N of Canada to the Pacific. Many attempts were made to discover it from that of Frobisher (1576-8) onwards. Franklin's failure to return in 1847, as planned, from his search for it led to the organization of 39 expeditions in the next 10 years. R. McClure discovered the passage 1850-3, though he did not cover the whole route by sea: this was done for the first time by Amundsen (1903-6). It was first used commercially by the US tanker *Manhattan* 1969 following Alaskan oil discoveries.

NORTHWEST TERRITORIES. The NW region of Canada, situated between Yukon on the W and Baffin Bay on the E, and bounded on the S by British Columbia, Alberta, Saskatchewan, and Manitoba. In the W is the r. Mackenzie. There are many lakes, of which the largest are the Great Slave Lake and the Great Bear Lake. The area was the northern part of Rupert's Land, bought by the Canadian govt from the Hudson's Bay Co. in 1869, and is divided into Mackenzie, Keewatin, and Franklin dists. An Act of 1952 placed the N.W.T. under a commissioner acting at Ottawa under the Min. of Northern Affairs and National Resources. Mining, fur trapping, and fishing are the chief industries. Mineral products incl. gold, silver, pitchblende, and petroleum. The Mackenzie r. and its tributaries are an important means of transport; regular air services operate internally. Area 3,379,689 sq.km (1,304,903 sq.m); pop. (1976) 42,609, two-thirds Indian or Eskimo.

NORTHWICH. Market town in Cheshire, England, on the Weaver, NE of Chester, famous for salt mines and brine springs, and an important centre of chemical production. There are beautiful old houses. Pop. (1972) 10,500.

NORTON, Caroline Elizabeth Sarah (1808-77). British author. The granddau. of R. B. Sheridan, she m. the Hon. George N. (1800-75) in 1827. In 1836 her husband falsely accused Lord Melbourne of seducing her, and subsequently tried to obtain the profits from her books. In 1877 she m. Sir Maxwell Stirling. Her best works were *Undying One* (1830), dealing with the Wandering Jew; and *Voice from the Factories* (1836), attacking child labour.

NORWAY. Kingdom occupying the N and W portion of the Scandinavian peninsula, bounded on the E by Sweden, Finland, and the USSR, on the N by the Arctic Ocean, on the NW by the Norwegian Sea, and on the W by the North Sea.

Physical. The surface is mountainous, the highest part of the country (over 2,450 m/8,000 ft) being in the region of the Sogne fjord. There is an extensive coastline, deeply indented with fjords; and numerous islands lie offshore. Some of the most beautiful fjords are Hardanger, Sogne (largest and deepest), Nord, Trondheim, Vest, and Ofoten. The Midnight Sun (q.v.) is seen in northern N., and at the North Cape part of the Sun's disc is continuously above the horizon from mid-May to the end of July, and there is no sunrise for 2 months in winter. During the long winter nights the Northern Lights appear (*see* AURORA). The only river of any length is the Glomma (560km (350m)); from the numerous short, rapid rivers with many waterfalls, N. harnesses an ample supply of electric power.

NORWAY. A restored fan-loft stave church at Birkeland, near Bergen. *Photo: Barnaby's Picture Library.*

Economic. Forests cover 20 per cent of the area, and there are paper, wood pulp, and furniture industries. Only a small area is suitable for cultivation, but agriculture is important, hay, potatoes, barley and oats being grown, and cattle and sheep are raised. Minerals incl. copper, pyrites, nickel, iron and zinc, and the oil and natural gas from the North Sea, which supports petrochemical industries. The last-named is now more important than farming, fishing and forestry together. The economy generally relies on high technology, e.g. engineering (gas turbines), electrical goods such as television sets, manufacture of fertilizers, aluminium, etc., sporting goods, pleasure craft, textiles, and foodstuffs. The merchant fleet is among the world's largest, and there are fisheries. The chief towns incl. Oslo, the cap.; Trondheim, Bergen, Stavanger, Kristiansand and Haugesund. The climate is modified by the Gulf Stream.

Area 324,219 sq.km (125,064 sq.m); incl. Svalbard, Jan Mayen, Bouvet Is., and Peter I Island, 386,190 sq.km (149,285 sq.m); pop. (1978) 4,051,208. The Evangelical Lutheran Church is endowed by the state. M.U.: krone.

Government. N. is a constitutional monarchy. Under the constitution of 1814 legislative power is vested in the Storting (Parl.), elected every 4 yrs by men and women over 20. The Storting is then divided by election among its own members into a Lagting (upper committee of one quarter of its members) and Odelsting (lower committee). *See* OLAV V.

History. N. was originally inhabited by a Finnish people, who were gradually conquered by Teutonic invaders from *c.* 1700 BC. The country remained under local chieftains until Harald Fairhair (reigned 872-*c.* 930), the most powerful of them, unified N. and introduced the feudal system. Christianity was introduced by Olaf II in the 11th cent.; he was defeated by rebel chiefs backed by Canute in 1030, but his son Magnus I regained the throne 5 years later. Haakon IV (1217-63) estab. the authority of the Crown over the nobles and the Church and made the monarchy hereditary. Denmark and N. were united by marriage in 1380, and in 1397 N., Denmark and Sweden were united under one sovereign; union with Denmark continued after Sweden, following a long struggle, was recognized as independent in 1523. The Reformed religion was introduced in 1536.

Denmark in 1814 ceded N. to Sweden, but the Norwegians declared their independence and adopted a parliamentary constitution. The Swedes then invaded N., and a compromise was reached whereby N. was to remain an independent kingdom, with its own parl., united with Sweden under a common king. Conflict between the Norwegian parl. and the Swedish monarchy continued until 1905, when the parl. declared N. completely independent. This was confirmed by plebiscite, and Prince Charles of Denmark was elected king under the name Haakon VII.

N. was invaded by Germany in April 1940, and in spite of armed resistance by the Norwegian Army, assisted by British and French forces, completely overrun by June. The king and govt escaped to Britain, while a puppet govt was set up under Quisling (q.v.), and a strong resistance was maintained inside the country. After a referendum (1972) N. refused to enter the Common Market, but sought trade agreements. Labour Party predominance since the mid-1930s has been interrupted by non-socialist coalitions since the 1960s, and new parties have grown up, but a new Labour govt. was formed in 1976.

Language. A member of the Scandinavian branch of the Germanic family of languages. As a consequence of the political union of Norway with Denmark (1380-1814), Danish became the literary medium of Norway, until in the 19th cent. the scholar Ivar Aasen (1813-96) produced the *Landsmål,* which he based on the local dialects of Norway; it has been accepted in many dists. of Norway, in schools, in churches, and for speeches in the Storting; but Dano-Norwegian, or the *Riksmål* continues to be used side by side with it.

Literature. The most remarkable production of N. L. before the eclipse which followed the union with Denmark in 1380 are the Skaldic genealogical poems of the 10th cent., the poetic Edda (q.v.) assembled in the 12th, and the prose sagas such as the *Heimskringla* of Snorri Sturlason in the 13th. A revival came in the 17th cent. with the descriptive poetry of Petter Dass (1647-1708), but the work of Ludwig Holberg and Johan Wessel (1742-85) belonged rather to the joint Dano-N. tradition. In the 19th cent. J. S. Welhaven (1807-73) still looked to the Danish connection, but the great national poet Henrik Wergeland turned to Norway's own spiritual resources for inspiration. The national revival became more vigorous through the work of the great folklorists and under the influence of vernacular writers such as Aasmund Vinje (1818-70) and Arne Garborg (1851-1924) who adopted Ivar Aasen's *Landsmål.* The great figures of the later 19th cent. were Björnstjerne Björnson, Henrik Ibsen, and the novelists

Jonas Lie and Alexander Kielland. To the earlier 20th cent. belong the novelists Knut Hamsun and Sigrid Undset. Later prominent figures are Helge Krog (1889-1962), dramatist and critic; the poets Arnulf Overland (1889-1968) and Olaf Bull (1887-1933); the novelists Johan Falkberget (1879-1967), Cora Sandel (1880-1974), and Sigurd Hoel (1890-1960); and the poet, playwright, and novelist Nordahl Grieg.

Music. Among well-known names are those of the violinist-composer Ole Bull (1810-80), Grieg, Sinding and Svendsen (qq.v.).

NORWEGIAN SEA. Part of the Arctic Ocean between Greenland and Norway.

NORWICH, Alfred Duff Cooper, 1st vist. N. (1890-1954). British diplomat. Entering parl. as a Unionist (later Cons.) in 1924, he was War Min. 1935-7, and then 1st Lord of the Admiralty, resigning in 1938 in protest against the Munich agreement. Under Churchill he was Min. of Information (1940-1); govt rep. with the French Committee of National Liberation 1943-4, and ambassador to France 1944-7. Knighted in 1948, he was created a visct in 1952, and pub. his memoirs, *Old Men Forget,* in 1953. He m. in 1919 Lady Diana Manners (1893-), a celebrated beauty, who created a sensation in Max Reinhardt's production of *The Miracle* (1924).

NORWICH (nor'ij). City in Norfolk, England, admin. HQ of the co., on the Wensun, just above its confluence with the Yare. Notable buildings incl. the cathedral (founded 1096), Norman castle (the keep housing a museum and collection of paintings by the Norwich School), Guildhall (15th cent.), medieval churches, Tudor houses, Georgian Assembly House, City Hall (1938), and Central Library (1963). The Univ. of E Anglia (1963) is at Earlham to the W of the city. Industries incl. footwear, engineering, printing, chemicals, clothing, and foodstuffs; and it is a marketing, banking, insurance, and commercial centre. Pop. (1974) 121,700.

NOSE. The upper orifice of the respiratory tract; the organ of the sense of smell. It is divided down the middle by a septum of cartilage. The nostrils or outer portion contain plates of cartilage which can be moved by muscles and have a growth of stiff hairs at the margin to prevent foreign bodies from entering. The whole nasal cavity is lined with mucous membrane which warms and moistens the air and ejects dirt. Inside the nose 3 wide air sacs, separated by plates of bone, lead back to the nasopharynx at the head of the windpipe. The lining of the lower, or respiratory, part of the cavity is covered with cilia; that of the upper part is furnished with olfactory cells which receive impressions of smell from particles in the entering air and transmit them though special nerves to the brain. The cavity communicates with various sinuses.

NOSTRADĀ'MUS. Latinized name of Michel de Notredame (1503-66). French astrologer. He was consulted by Catherine de' Medici and was physician-in-ordinary to Charles IX. His reputation was greater than his accuracy, but his supposed long-term prophecies were used by Goebbels in propaganda for Hitler.

NOTT, John (1932-). British Conservative politician. After studying law, he entered merchant banking, became Sec. of State for Trade 1979-81, and succeeded Pym as Min. for Defence in 1981.

NOTTINGHAM. City in Notts (of which it is the admin. HQ), England, at the confluence of the Leen and the Trent. Industries incl. engineering, coalmining and ironworking, cycles, textiles, knitwear, pharmaceuticals, tobacco, electronic equipment, and lace. The city is linked by canal with the Atlantic and North Sea. The 17th cent. castle, built on the site of a Norman fortress, is a museum; the RC cathedral (1844) is by Pugin; and there is an attractive modern Playhouse and shopping district. Newstead Abbey to the N was Byron's home, and N. has links with D. H. Lawrence and Alan Sillitoe. Nottingham Univ. was estab. 1881. Pop. (1974) 294,700.

NOTTINGHAMSHIRE or **Notts.** Midland county of England. Most of the county is undulating, rising to 180m (600ft) in the SW. Sherwood Forest, famous for its association with Robin Hood, is in the SW; what remains of the forest is incl. in the region called the 'Dukeries'. The chief rivers are the Trent and its tributaries, the Idle, Erewash, and Soar. In the W are Cresswell Crags where remains of prehistoric man have been found. The chief industrial town is Nottingham, the admin. HQ of the co.; other towns incl. Mansfield, Retford and Worksop. In 1974 N. lost two minor projections in the NW to the new co. of South Yorkshire. Area 2,108 sq.km (814 sq.m); pop. (1978) 973,700.

NOUAKCHOTT (noo-ahkshot'). Cap. of Mauritania, W Africa, nr the Atlantic Coast. It is linked by caravan route with Senegal to the S, and with Morocco to the NE. Pop. (1970) 70,000.

NŌ'VA. A star which suffers an outburst, and flares up for a period which may amount to several weeks - after which it subsides to its former state. In novæ such an expansion causes a light increase of 10-15 magnitude; in supernovæ (q.v.), the result of the explosion of a complete star, up to 20 magnitudes. *See* NEUTRON STAR.

NOVALIS (novah'lēs). Pen-name of Friedrich Leopold, Freiherr von Hardenberg (1772-1801), German poet. The most genuinely inspired poet of the older Romanticists, he approached the great problems of God and Nature, life and death, with profound intuition.

NŌ'VA LISBŌ'A. *See* HUAMBO.

NOVA SCOTIA (nōv'ahskōsh'iah). A prov. of Canada, consisting of a long, narrow peninsula and the island of Cape Breton, S of the Gulf of St Lawrence. Its E and S shores are washed by the Atlantic, and an isthmus, 18.5km (11.5m) wide links the prov. with New Brunswick. The Cobequid mts. stretch across the interior. The coastline is about 3,200 km (2,000 m); there are many rivers, most of them under 80km (50m), lakes, and fine harbours. The cap. and chief port is Halifax. Agriculture is the most important industry, particularly dairying, poultry rearing and fruit growing. The fisheries are valuable. Lumbering is carried on, and wood pulp for paper is manufactured. Coal, gypsum, lead, zinc, and copper are mined, and there are iron and steel works, paper mills, food factories, and shipyards.

History. N.S. was visited by Cabot in 1497, but it was not until 1604 that a permanent settlement was established by Europeans. In that year the French under De Monts established themselves on the peninsula. In 1613 they were expelled by English colonists from Virginia. The name N.S. was given to the colony, which had hitherto been called Acadia, by Sir William Alexander in 1621. England and France subsequently contended for possession of the territory. In 1713, N.S. (which then incl. present-day New Brunswick and Prince Edward Is.) was ceded to the English; Cape Breton Is. remained French until 1763. N.S. was one of the 4 original provs. of the dominion of Canada, 1867. Area 54,558 sq.km (21,065 sq.m); pop. (1976) 828,571.

NŌ'VAYA ZEMLYA'. Group of is., RSFSR, off the N coast of Russia in the Arctic Ocean. A few Samoyed live there, but it is chiefly known for its rich bird life, seals, walrus, etc. Area 90,650 sq.km (35,000 sq.m).

NOVEL. A full-length fictitious prose narrative. Probably inspired by Oriental story-telling, the European N. originated in Greece in the 2nd cent. BC. Best-known of the Greek examples is the *Daphnis and Chloë* of Longus, and almost the only surviving specimen of the Latin N. is the *Golden Ass* of Apuleius, based on a Greek model. But the modern N. took its name and inspiration from the Italian *novella*, the short tale of varied character which became popular in the late 13th cent. Most famous of these It. writers were Boccaccio and Bandello, whose works were translated into English in such collections as Painter's *Palace of Pleasure* (1566-7), and inspired the Elizabethan novelists, e.g. Lyly, Sidney, Greene, Nash, and Lodge. In Spain, Cervantes' *Don Quixote* (1604) made an outstanding contribution to the development of the N., but the 17th cent. was largely dominated by the French romances of La Calprenède and Mlle de Scudéry, although Congreve and Aphra Behn continued the English tradition.

In the 18th cent. the realistic novel came to maturity in the work of Defoe, Richardson, Fielding, Sterne, and Smollett. Walpole, and later Mrs Radcliffe, by their development of Gothic romance, prepared the way for Sir Walter Scott, while Jane Austen perfected the domestic N. of manners. The great representatives of the Victorian Age are Dickens, Thackeray, the Brontës, Kingsley, Charles Reade, George Eliot, Trollope, and Stevenson. The 19th cent. was also a great period for the N. on the Continent, with Hugo, Balzac, the two Dumas, George Sand, and Zola in France; Goethe and Jean Paul in Germany; Gogol, Turgenev, Dostoievsky, and Tolstoy in Russia; and in America with Cooper, Melville, Hawthorne, Twain, and Howells.

To the transition period from Victorian to modern times belong the rebels Meredith, Butler, Hardy, and Gissing; the slightly alien genius or subject-matter of Henry James, Kipling, Conrad, and George Moore; and the sober realism of Wells, Bennett, and Galsworthy. Slightly later are W. S. Maugham, E. M. Forster, Hugh Walpole, James Joyce, D. H. Lawrence, I. Compton-Burnett, and Virginia Woolf - the last three being particularly influential in the development of N. technique. Among those who began writing in the '20s are J. B. Priestley, Richard Hughes, Aldous Huxley, Christopher Isherwood, Graham Greene, William Plomer, V. S. Pritchett, and Evelyn Waugh; and the women writers E. Bowen, Rose Macaulay, and Rosamund Lehmann. The next decade produced Nigel Balchin, Joyce Cary, Lord Snow, Lawrence Durrell, and George Orwell, and more recent names incl. Anthony Powell, John Fowles and Anthony Burgess. Twentieth-cent. novelists abroad incl. (German) Lion Feuchtwanger, Thomas Mann, Franz Kafka, Ernst Wiechert, and Stefan Zweig; (French) André Gide, Marcel Proust, Jules Romains, François Mauriac, and Alain Robbe-Grillett; (Italian) Gabriele d'Annunzio, Ignazio Silone, and Alberto Moravia; (Russian) Maxim Gorky, Mikhail Sholokhov, Aleksei Tolstoi, Boris Pasternak, and Alexander Solzhenitsyn; (Spanish) Arturo Baréa, Pío Baroja and Ramón Pérez de Ayala; and (American) Edith Wharton, Theodore Dreiser, Ernest Hemingway, Upton Sinclair, Sinclair Lewis, William Faulkner, Bernard Malamud, Eudora Welty, Vladimir Nabokov, and Saul Bellow.

NOVELLO, Ivor. Stage-name of British actor, manager, and composer I. N. Davies (1893-1951). B. in Cardiff, son of the singer Clara Novello Davies, he made his name as a song-writer, e.g. 'Keep the Home Fires Burning', in the F.W.W., and author of straight plays, e.g. *The Truth Game* (1928), but is best remembered for the spectacular musical plays in which he often appeared with romantically handsome charm, e.g. *Glamorous Night* (1925), *The Dancing Years* (1939), *Perchance To Dream* (1945-7), *King's Rhapsody* (1949) and *Gay's The Word (1951).*

NO'VGOROD. Town of the RSFSR, cap. of N region, on the Volkhov, 3km (2m) N of Lake Ilmen. N. dates from the 9th cent. and was an important and prosperous city from the 12th cent. until destroyed by Ivan the Terrible in 1570. It is an agricultural centre and has distilleries, meat-packing works, etc. Pop. (1978) 170,000.

NOVGOROD. Inside the Novgorod Kremlin. On the left is the theatre, in the centre the monument to the thousandth anniversary of the foundation of the Russian state in 862, and in the background the cathedral of Saint Sophia, built in the 11th century. *Photo: Novosti.*

NOVI SAD. Cap. of the autonomous prov. of Voivodina, Yugoslavia. Pottery and cotton goods are manufactured. Pop. (1971) 142,000.

NOVOCAINE. A synthetic drug widely used as a local anaesthetic. It has replaced cocaine, being equally strong when injected but only one-third as toxic and not habit-forming. It is, however, not nearly so effective when used as a surface anaesthetic. It is always used with adrenaline.

NOVO KUZNETSK (nov'o kooznyet'sk). Town in Kemerovo region, RSFSR, on the r. Tom, 360km (225m) SSE of Tomsk, an important centre of steel and iron manufacture in the Kuzbas. A town of less than 4,000 in 1939, it had a pop. of 537,000 in 1977. It was called Stalinsk 1932-61.

NOVOROSSII'SK. Seaport of the RSFSR, of the NE coast of the Black Sea. Cement, bicycles, furniture, etc., are made. Pop. (1977) 153,000.

NOVOSIBIRSK. City in W Siberia, RSFSR, on the Ob. It has mechanical engineering, textile and food processing industries, and advanced research is carried on at Akademgorodok. *See* LAVRENTIEV. Pop. (1977) 1,304,000.

NOVOYA BUKHARA. *See* BUKHARA.

NOYES (noiz), **Alfred** (1880–1958). British poet. B. at Wolverhampton, he was ed. at Oxford, and was prof. of modern English literature at Princeton univ. 1914–23. His first vol. of verse, *The Loom of Years* (1902), was followed by many others, equally smooth in versification and traditional in theme, e.g. *Drake, an English Epic* (1906–8). His best-known poems incl. 'The Highwayman' and 'Barrel Organ'. Other works incl. the prose *The Unknown God* (1934), telling of his conversion to R. Catholicism.

NŪ'BIA. A region of NE Africa, probably named from *nub*, the ancient Egyptian word for gold. It was one of the chief battlegrounds of the ancient world, where the struggle for supremacy in N Africa was waged between the black and white peoples, and the great rock-cut temple at Abu Simbel and such forts as Buhen are relics of Egyptian occupation: to the Egyptians northern N. was known as Wawat and southern N. as Kush, and of modern N. the north is part of Egypt and the south part of the Rep. of Sudan. Of particular interest are the mysterious X-group, people who occupied the greater part of N. *c.* AD 250–550, and whose royal tombs were excavated by W. B. Emery. Mistaken by earlier investigators for natural mounds created by wind erosion, the graves contained rich treasures in jewellery and the remains of numerous slaughtered attendants and horses. By the building of the Aswan High Dam the greater part of N. was submerged beneath the extended reservoir (Lake Nasser).

NUCLEAR ENERGY. Energy obtained from the inner core or nucleus of atoms, as opposed to energy released in chemical processes, which is derived from the electrons surrounding the nucleus.

If a high-speed alpha particle (q.v.) strikes another nucleus it can cause it to disintegrate, e.g. by the emission of a proton or a neutron. The released neutron, having no electric charge, can pass freely through matter unless it strikes a nucleus, which it can easily enter since the protons do not repel it as they would a positively-charged particle. It may leave the nucleus again, or may stay in it, in which case it may or may not cause a practically immediate nuclear disintegration. What actually happens depends on the kind of nucleus it strikes and the velocity with which it strikes it. If a neutron enters a nucleus of uranium-235 the latter may undergo fission into 2 roughly equal fragments which fly apart, while at the same time a small number of free neutrons (often 2 or 3) are released and travel out through the material. If the material is pure U^{235}, then they may enter other nuclei, causing further fissions, more released neutrons, and so on; an ever-branching 'chain' of nuclear fission spreads with great rapidity through the material with enormous evolution of energy. A certain minimum amount of U^{235} is required to support the nuclear explosion; this critical amount is a military secret. In practice 2 lumps of the material, each smaller than the critical size, are brought close together, forming a lump above the critical size; as soon as a neutron enters the system, there is a nuclear explosion.

When such a chain reaction is produced under control, however, inside a nuclear power reactor, a commercial electricity supply can be generated. Among the various types of nuclear reactor are: (1) The *gas-cooled*, e.g. Calder Hall, in which the necessary control is achieved through absorption of excess neutrons in control rods of boron (often as an alloy with steel), and through a slowing down ('moderating') of the speed of the escaping neutrons, to make it easier for them to split the nuclei, by surrounding the 'natural' uranium fuel with a graphite moderator. The heat produced as the nuclei in the uranium metal fuel rods split is removed by circulating carbon dioxide gas under pressure, from which the heat is removed by transfer to water which converts to steam for driving electricity generators. Advanced gas-cooled reactors (AGRs) use uranium oxide fuel in which the uranium is slightly 'enriched', thus increasing efficiency. The escape of harmful radiation from all reactors is prevented by an enclosing concrete shield.

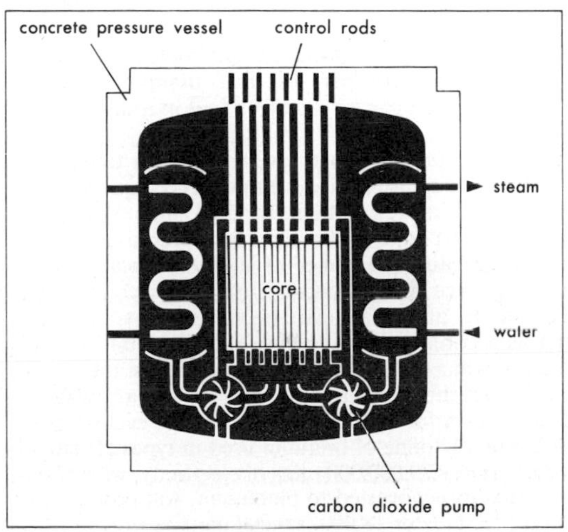

advanced gas-cooled reactor (AGR)

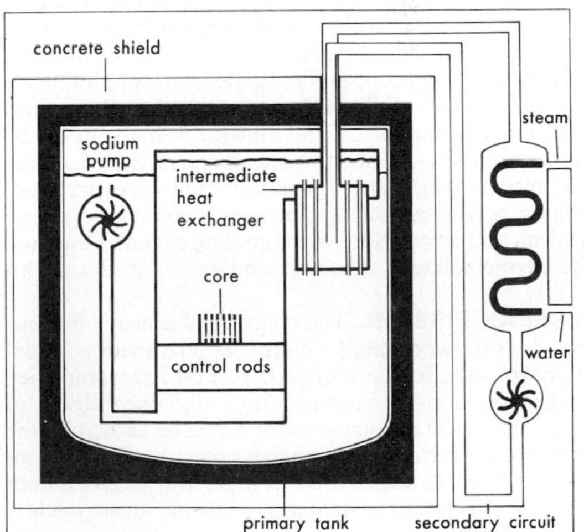

fast breeder reactor

(2) The *water-cooled*, or steam generating heavy water reactor (SGHWR), e.g. Winfrith, Dorset. In this the rods of uranium fuel are contained in pressure tubes, and the

latter are immersed in 'heavy' water as a moderator. 'Light', i.e. ordinary, water is then circulated through the pressure tubes, is converted to steam by the heat of the fuel elements, and at 280°C is passed directly to a normal turbo-alternator to generate electricity. In the UK work on an SGHWR system was abandoned in 1978 and provision made in 1979 for adoption of the *pressurized water reactor* (PWR). In this, uranium in the form of rods is contained in zirconium alloy tubes, and nuclear fission creates intense heat which is carried away by a sealed and highly pressurised primary loop of irradiated water (chiefly 'heavy' water) to steam generators where the heat is transferred to non-radioactive water. The resultant steam, channelled through a conventional turbine and generator, then produces electricity. It was a PWR which broke down at Three Mile Island (*see* HARRISBURG) in 1979, and those ordered by Britain were to incorporate additional safeguards. Both the gas-cooled and water-cooled reactors turn part of their uranium fuel into plutonium, which can be used as a fuel in a third type of reactor.

(3) The *fast breeder reactor,* which is closer to the atom bomb in its operation, since it employs no moderator and the neutrons move at their original high speed, e.g. Dounreay, Scotland. It 'breeds' more plutonium than it consumes because a 'blanket' of uranium is placed round the fuel charge in the reactor core and is converted to plutonium by absorbing spare neutrons. Instead of gas or water as a coolant, this type uses liquid metal - usually sodium - which carries the heat generated in the reactor core through heat exchangers to heat ordinary water to produce steam for turbines. These are the reactors of the future, since 1 tonne of uranium used in types (1) and (2) produces only 480,000,000 units of electricity, whereas the same quantity, converted to plutonium, will produce in a fast breeder reactor 18,000,000,000 units.

As reserves of natural fuels, such as coal and oil, decrease and also become more costly because of increased labour charges, etc., nuclear power becomes increasingly essential and competitive. The initial cost of power station construction is greater, but running costs are less, and although reserves of uranium are limited, breeder reactors produce more fissile atoms of plutonium than they 'burn'. Difficulties arise in that the excess plutonium is highly toxic and difficult to make safe; fast breeders operate at much higher temperatures than the non-breeders which are now in use; their cores are more compact, so that a nuclear explosion is possible in case of accident, and any rupture of the cooling channels involves a dangerous mixture of sodium and water. *See* NUCLEAR WASTE.

NUCLEAR FISSION. The splitting of a heavy nucleus into 2 (or very rarely more) approximately equal fragments - the fission products. Fission is accompanied by the emission of neutrons (q.v.) and the release of energy. It can be spontaneous, or it can be caused by the impact of a neutron, a fast-charged particle or a photon.

The drawbacks which arise from nuclear fission do not apply to the power potentially available from nuclear fusion *See* ATOM.

NUCLEAR WARFARE. For the use of nuclear weapons in the S.W.W. *see* BOMB. Nuclear weapons now exist in many varied forms: aircraft bombs, warheads for missiles, e.g. short range surface-to-surface missiles such as the Lance, artillery shells, anti-aircraft missiles, depth charges and high-powered landmines called 'atomic demolition munitions' to blast craters in the path of advancing armies. Problems of safety arise and weapons are kept in special ammunition storage (SAS) sites, and made ready to fire only by a secret code transmitted through a special device, known as Permissive Action Link. Destruction of the weapons would scatter highly poisonous plutonium. Defence against inter-continental ballistic missiles (ICBMs) is by anti-ballistic missile (ABM) system, i.e. comprising a radar system, and two types of missile, one short range with high acceleration, and one comparatively

NUCLEAR ENERGY. The steam generating heavy water reactor at Winfrith in Dorset. Above, the fuel storage pond, showing Cerenkov radiation from irradiated fuel and, below, a 45- tonne transport flask for irradiated fuel in transit in the reactor hall. *Photos: Courtesy of the UKAEA.*

long range, able to intercept above the atmosphere. Clusters of warheads, which can be directed to individual targets, and known as multiple independently targetable re-entry vehicles (MIRVs) were developed by 1968. An internat. Treaty of Nuclear Non-Proliferation (1968) tried to prevent the spread of weapon manufacture, and there was an attempt to limit the arms of the USA and USSR by Strategic Arms Limitation (q.v.) talks.

The most recent long-range weapon of the USA is the MX missile, of which it plans to have 200, stored on a 'loading dock' system, i.e. with each missile shuffled at random among 23 possible locations on transporters while dummies mislead the enemy (by simulating a real missile's heat output, magnetic field, radiation and weight) as to its actual location. Periodically, all shelters would be uncovered at once to show only one real weapon.

To retain an independent nuclear deterrent the UK decided in 1980 to buy Trident missiles from USA to replace Polaris. To be carried on 4 submarines, each has 8 independently targetable re-entry vehicles over a range of c. 6,400 km (4,000 m) to separate targets within range of c. 240 km (150 m) from the central aiming point.

See also Army, Penetration Technology.

The whole concept of N.W., however, was modified by the development in 1976 of the cruise missile. A pilotless plane c.6 m (19ft) long and c. 50 cm. (21 in) wide, it carries 15 times the equivalent of the original bomb used against Japan over a range of more than 3,000 km (2,000 m). It travels at a speed of c. 800 kph (500 mph.) after launching from land, sea or air, and by a pre-set computer programme can approach its target by a course designed to change, or even reverse, so as to confuse the defence. Delivery is accurate to within 10 m (30 ft). These are being deployed in Europe by USA. *See* Newbury.

NUCLEAR WARFARE. An Air Launched Cruise Missile is ejected from the weapons bay of a B-52G bomber over the White Sands Missile Range in New Mexico. Just over 4 m (14ft) long they travel at subsonic speeds, powered by small turbofan engines. They are intended to be launched in large numbers to assist manned strategic bombers in penetrating to targets. *Photo: Courtesy of Boeing Aerospace.*

However, although cruise missiles are much cheaper than Trident, and have greater accuracy, they have at present less range, are slower in flight, possess only one warhead, and require more expensive back-up. To achieve the same destructive effect with cruise missiles as with Trident would also require hours rather than minutes of firing time, and allow an enemy to be alerted to the source of the missiles.

NUCLEAR WASTE. *See* Radioactive Waste.

NUCLEIC ACIDS. Complex organic acids with long-chain spiralling molecules, some of which like DNA (deoxyribonucleic acid) and RNA (ribonucleic acid) play an important part in protein synthesis and in the transmission of hereditary characteristics.

The kind of molecular structure — the double helix — suggested for DNA by Francis Crick (q.v.) and his fellow workers was challenged by NZ researchers in 1976. They suggested that the 4 basic building blocks or nucleotides formed 2 parallel chains, and were held together like a zip fastener.

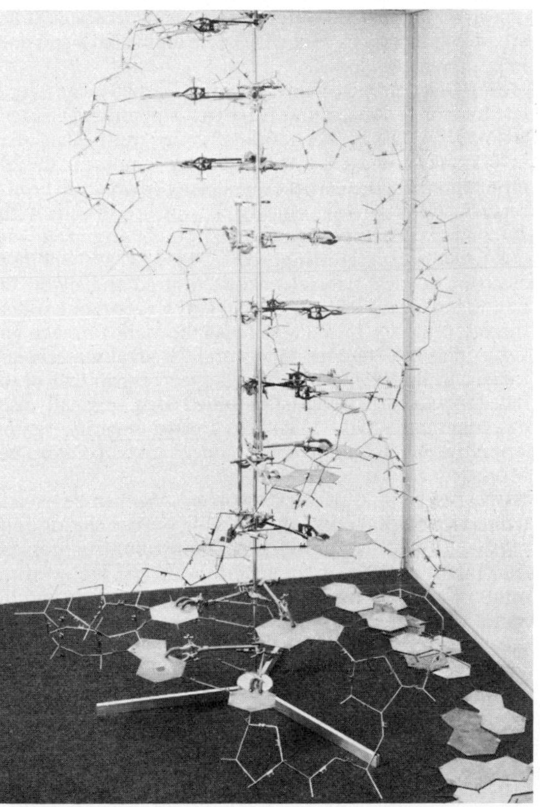

NUCLEIC ACIDS. A reconstruction of the 'double helix' model used by Watson and Crick in 1953 to represent the nucleotide bases in DNA, made up from the original metal plates, and also incorporating several features later recognized as inaccurate. A few 'left-over' plates lie on the floor. *Photo: Crown copyright, Science Museum, London.*

NUFFIELD, William Richard Morris, visct. N. (1877-1963). British manufacturer and philanthropist. Starting with a small cycle-repairing business, he planned in 1910 a car to run at low cost for the ordinary man, and built up Morris Motors Ltd at Cowley, Oxford - now merged in British Motor Holdings. His benefactions incl.

establishment of the Oxford Medical School Trust, Nuffield Coll., Oxford, and the Nuffield Foundation (1943).

NUJŌ'MA, Sam (1929-). Namibian politician. Exiled in 1960, after founding SWAPO (South West African People's Organization) in 1959, he controls the guerrillas which cross the border from Angolan bases.

NUKU'ALOFA (nōō'koo-alō'fa). Cap. and port of Tonga, on Tongatapu. Pop. (1976) 20,000.

NU'LLARBOR PLAIN. Arid coastal area between the Great Victoria Desert and the Great Australian Bight, partly in Western and partly in South Australia. It is *c.* 560km (350m long) and 240km (150m) wide. Underlying it is a network of caves.

NŪ'MA POMPI'LIUS. Legendary king of Rome, whose reign is traditionally dated 716-679 BC. He succeeded Romulus and instituted religious rites.

NUMBAT. Aboriginal name for the 2 marsupial species of Australian banded termite-eater (*Myrmecobius*). They are brown, boldly striped with white on the back and have long tubular tongues.

NŪMI'DIA. Roman name, meaning nomads' land, for a territory of N Africa, the E part of modern Algeria.

NŪMISMA'TICS. The study of coins and medals. The invention of coinage is attributed to the Chinese in the 2nd millennium BC, the earliest types being small-scale bronze reproductions of barter objects - knives, spades, etc. In the W coinage of stamped, guaranteed weight originated with the Lydians of Asia Minor (early 7th cent. BC) who used electrum, a local natural mixture of gold and silver: the first to issue gold and silver coins was Croesus of Lydia in the 6th cent. BC. In modern times the right to make and issue coins is a state monopoly and the great majority are tokens, in that their face value is greater than that of the metal of which they consist. A milled edge, originally used on gold and silver coins for greater security against 'clipping', is retained in some modern token coinage. *See* MONEY.

NUN (Lat. *nonna*, an elderly woman). Woman devoted to the service of God under the vows of poverty, chastity, and obedience, and living under a certain rule. It is possible that the institution of communities for Ns. preceded the establishment of monasteries (*see* MONASTICISM), and the majority of the male orders have their feminine counterparts. The convent is ruled by a superior (often elected), who is subject to the authority of the bishop of the diocese or sometimes directly to the Pope.

NUNEATON (nunē'ton). Town in Warwicks, England, 15km (9m) NE of Coventry. There are coal-mining, brick, and textile industries. Pop. (1973) 69,000.

NUREMBERG (Ger. Nürnberg). A city of Bavaria, W Germany. It lies on the Pegnitz, to the NW of Munich, and was noted for its ancient walls and fine old buildings, incl. the castle; the churches of St Lorenz, St Sebald, and Our Lady; the town hall; and the houses of Hans Sachs and Albrecht Dürer, until it suffered some 75 per cent devastation in the S.W.W. Manufactures incl. toys, electrical and other machinery, precision instruments, calculating machines, pencils and fountain pens, textiles, beer. The hop trade is of importance.

A castle was founded on the site in 1050, and in 1219 N. became a free imperial city. During the Middle Ages it attained great importance both as a commercial and a cultural centre, but it decayed after the 30 Years War and was annexed by Bavaria in 1806. Nazi Party rallies were held here from 1933, and in 1945 the N. Trials (q.v.). Pop. (1978) 488,755.

NUREMBERG TRIALS. The trials held in judgment of the leading Nazi war criminals Nov. 1945-Oct. 1946. The International Military Tribunal consisted of 4 judges and 4 prosecutors; 1 of each from UK, USA, USSR and France. The main charges in the indictment were: (1) conspiracy to wage wars of aggression; (2) crimes against peace; (3) war crimes, e.g. murder and ill-treatment of civilians and prisoners of war, deportation of civilians for slave labour, and killing of hostages; (4) crimes against humanity, e.g. mass-murder of Jews and murder and ill-treatment of political opponents. An appendix accused the German Cabinet, General Staff, and High Command, Nazi leadership corps, SS, SA, and Gestapo of criminal responsibility. Of the 24 men accused, Krupp was too ill to be tried; Ley committed suicide during the trial, and Bormann, who had fled, was sentenced to death in his absence. Fritsche, Schacht and Papen were acquitted. The other 18 were found guilty on one or more counts. Hess, Funk and Raeder were sentenced to life imprisonment, Shirach and Speer to 20 yrs, Neurath to 15 yrs, and Doenitz to 10 yrs. The remaining 11 men, sentenced to death by hanging, were Goering (committed suicide before execution), Ribbentrop, Kaltenbrunner, Rosenberg, Frank, Frick, Sauckel, Seyss-Inquart, Streicher, Keitel, and Jodl. The leadership corps, SS, and Gestapo were declared criminal organizations.

NUREYEV (noorā'yef), **Rudolf** (1939-). Russian dancer. B. at Ufa, son of a farmer, he was trained at the Kirov Ballet School, then danced with the co. until he sought political asylum in the West while they were appearing in Paris in 1961. He subsequently made a series of appearances with Dame Margot Fonteyn in *Giselle, Marguerite and Armand,* etc.

NURSERY RHYMES. Jingles current among children. Usually limited to a couplet or quatrain with strongly marked rhythm and rhymes, they have often been handed down by oral tradition from remote antiquity. Some of the oldest N.Rs. are connected with a traditional tune and accompanied the ancient ring games, e.g. 'Here we go round the mulberry bush', which were part of the May Day festivities. Others preserve in a mutilated form the memory of incantations and other rites; and yet other, e.g. Jack Sprat, Jack Horner, and Mary with her little lamb, have a factual basis and have commemorated popular figures.

NURSING. The care of the sick, very young or old and disabled. Originally practised by members of religious orders, N. became progressively secularized following the Renaissance and Reformation, but organized training was first instituted in Germany in 1836. The work done there influenced Florence Nightingale (q.v.) who, during the Crimean War, estab. standards of scientific, humanitarian care in military hospitals, which had a beneficial effect throughout the world. In Britain the General Nursing Councils, estab. by the Nurses Registration Act of 1919, register nurses qualified by examination, incl. those qualified in special fields of N., e.g. sick children, mental N., etc., and there are a large number of registration programmes for health visiting, midwifery, etc., many organized by the Royal College of Nursing (1916). In the US, although registration is the responsibility of individual states, an almost uniform standard has been estab. by the National League for N. (1952).

NUSA TENGGARA (nū'za tengah'ra). Volcanic archipelago, Indonesia, also known as the Lesser Sunda Is., and incl. Bali, Lombok and Timor.

NUT. A fruit consisting of a kernel with a hard outer shell which decays when ripe, releasing the seed. It may be situated in a whorl of bracts (e.g. filbert), a cupule (e.g. acorn), or fibrous covering (e.g. coconut); embedded in the flesh of a fruit (e.g. almond); or with a bristly outer covering (e.g. chestnut). Most Ns. contain nutritive oils.

NUTHATCH (nut'-). European bird (*Sitta europaea*) about the size of a sparrow, having a blue-grey back and buff breast. It is a climber and feeds chiefly upon nuts. The nest is placed in a hole in a tree, and 5 to 8 white eggs with red spots are laid in early summer.

NUTMEG. Kernel of the seed of the evergreen tree (*Myrista fragrans*), native to the Moluccas. Both the N. and its secondary covering (known as mace) are used as a spice in cookery.

NYASA (nyah'sah). *See* MALAWI, LAKE.

NYA'SALAND. *See* MALAWI.

NYERERE (nyerār'e), **Julius Kambarage** (1922-). Tanzanian statesman. Ed. at Makerere Univ. Coll. and at Edinburgh, he became a schoolmaster until devoting himself in 1954 to the formation of the Tanganyika African National Union and subsequent campaigning for independence. He became Chief Min. in 1960, was PM 1961-2, and was elected first pres. of the Tanganyika Rep. 1962 (re-elected 1965, 1970, 1975, and 1980). He introduced one-party govt in 1963, as more suited to the situation, but is noted for his wisdom and moderation: he is a Christian.

NYLON. Name given to a group of synthetic fibre-forming substances which are similar in chemical structure to proteins and were developed in the USA by W. H. Carothers and his associates. N. is used in the manufacture of toilet articles, textiles, medical sutures, etc. N. fibres are stronger and more elastic than silk, and relatively insensitive to moisture and mildew. N. is particularly suitable for hosiery and woven goods simulating other materials such as silks and furs; it is also used in carpets.

NYLON. Dr Wallace Carothers, the Du Pont Scientist who in 1938 invented the synthetic fibre, nylon.

NYMPHS (nimfz). In Greek mythology, the guardian spirits of various natural objects. Hamadryads or Dryads were tree Ns., the Naiads were Ns. of springs and pools, the Oreads of hills and rocks, and the Nereids of the sea.

O

15th letter of the Roman alphabet, whose form was derived from the Semitic alphabet. In modern Eng. it represents a wide range of sounds, from the diphthong ō (*so*) to the open sounds in *or, on,* etc., and the oo-sound in *wolf,* etc.

OAHU (wah'hoo). Island in the Hawaiian group, formed by two great volcanoes now extinct, on which is Honolulu, cap. of the state of Hawaii, USA. Third largest of the is., it is agriculturally important, sugar and pineapples being grown for export, and has the great concentration of population, and the Pearl Harbor naval base. It is a tourist paradise and has Waikiki and other bathing beaches. Area 1,525 sq.km (589 sq.m); pop. (1970) 630,500.

OAK. Genus of trees and shrubs (*Quercus*) in the beech family (Fagaceae). Widely distributed in temperate zones, over 300 species are known. They are valuable for their timber, the wood being durable and straight grained, but *O. wilt,* the result of a symbiotic partnership between a beetle and a fungus, resembles Dutch elm disease and is equally virulent. The English oak (*Q. robur*), also found in Europe, grows to 36m (120ft) and girth of 15m (50ft). Other European varieties are the evergreen oak (*Q. ilex*), the Turkey oak (*Q. cerris*), and the cork oak (*Q. suber*), of the W Mediterranean region; valuable American timber Os. are the white O. (*Q. alba*) and the evergreen live O. (*O. virginiana*).

OAKLAND. Port in California, USA, on the E coast of San Francisco Bay. It is linked by bridge (1936) with San Francisco, and has vehicle manufactures, textile, chemical and food processing industries and builds ships. Jack London Square is named after the novelist, who lived on O.'s waterfront. Pop. (1970) 361,560.

OAK RIDGE. Town in Tennessee, USA. The O.R. Nat. Laboratory (1943) was estab. to manufacture plutonium for atom bombs, and the American Museum of Atomic Energy is here. Pop. (1970) 28,300.

OAKS. Horse-race, run at Epsom by fillies of 3 years old, usually on the Friday of Derby Week.

OASTLER, Richard (1789-1861). British social reformer. B. at Leeds, he opposed child-labour and the Poor Law of 1834, winning the nickname of 'the Factory King', and was largely responsible for securing the Factory Act of 1833 and the Ten Hours' Act of 1847.

OATES, Laurence Edward Grace (1880-1912). British Antarctic explorer who accompanied Scott on his final dash to the South Pole and died, 'a very gallant gentleman', alone in the blizzard. The museum at the home of Gilbert White (q.v.) contains a Captain O. room with relics.

OATES, Titus (1649-1705). British perjurer. A clergyman, he entered the Jesuit colleges at Valladolid and St Omer as a spy in 1677-8, and on his return to England announced he had discovered a 'popish plot' to murder Charles II and re-estab. Catholicism. Although this story was almost entirely false, many innocent RCs were executed during 1678-80 on O.'s evidence. In 1685 he was flogged, pilloried and imprisoned for perjury. He was pardoned and granted a pension after the revolution of 1688.

OATH. A solemn promise to tell the truth or perform some duty, combined with an appeal to a deity or something held sacred. Primitive peoples often swear on a weapon or the body of a beast of prey, which is appealed to to kill the person swearing if he breaks his word.

In English courts a witness normally swears to tell the truth holding a NT in his right hand; in the USA a witness raises his right hand in taking the O. Sects which object to the taking of Os., e.g. Quakers, and atheists, etc., give a solemn promise to tell the truth. A Jew swears holding the Pentateuch, with his head covered. Moslems, Hindus, etc., swear by their respective sacred books; a Chinese witness breaks a saucer before giving evidence. In Scottish courts witnesses swear to tell the truth 'as I shall answer to God at the great day of judgment'.

OATS. Genus of plants (*Avena*); an important cereal food. The plant has long, narrow leaves, and stiff straw stem; the panicles of flowers, and later of grain, hang downwards. The cultivated O. (*A. sativa*) is produced for human food and for feeding horses and domestic animals and birds.

OB. A river of Asiatic Russia, flowing 3,380 km (2,100 m) from the Altai mts. through the W Siberian Plain to the Gulf of Ob in the Arctic Ocean.

Ō'BAN. Seaport on the Firth of Lorne, Strathclyde, Scotland, sometimes called the holiday cap. of the Western Highlands. Pop. (1971) 8,000.

OBEID (ō'bā-id), **El.** City in central Sudan, a trading centre for cattle, grain, and gum arabic. The Mahdi defeated the Egyptians here in 1883. Pop. (1971) 76,500.

OBERAMMERGAU (oh'berahm'ergow). Village of Bavaria, Germany, 72km (45m) SW of Munich noted for the performance approx. each decade since 1634 of a Passion play.

OBERHAUSEN (ō'berhowzen). Industrial and coal-mining city in the Ruhr valley, North Rhine-Westphalia, W Germany. Pop. (1978) 232,558.

Ō'BERON. King of the fairies. He figures in the 13th cent. French *Huon of Bordeaux,* was adopted by Shakespeare in *A Midsummer Night's Dream,* and was made the hero of an epic by Wieland and an opera by Weber.

OBĒSITY. Being over-weight - which renders one more susceptible to disease and lessens life expectancy. Slimming diets and exercises vary in effect because of variation in the structure of fatty tissue itself in different individuals, and also because the rate of the natural metabolic processes varies.

Ō'BI. A form of witchcraft practised by the Negroes of the W Indies. It combined Christian elements with pagan ceremonies imported from Africa, such as snake-worship.

OBOE (ō'bō). Musical instrument of the woodwind family. Played vertically, it is a wooden tube with a bell, is double-reeded, and has a yearning, poignant tone. The range is almost 3 octaves. There are O. concertos by E. Goossens and G. Jacob.

OBŌ'TE, (Apollo) Milton (1924-). Uganda statesman. A migrant to Kenya in 1950, where he worked as a labourer, salesman and clerk, he was a founder member of the Kenya African Union. Returning home he led the opposition 1961-2, and became PM in 1962, and pres. from 1966 until overthrown by Idi Amin in 1971. In 1980 he returned after Amin's fall and was again elected president.

OBRE'NOVICH. Name of a Serbian dynasty which ruled 1816-42 and 1859-1903. They were engaged in a feud with the rival house of Karageorgevich, which obtained the throne by the murder of the last O. in 1903.

OBSERVATORY. A building designed for observation of natural phenomena, especially astronomical. The earliest O. was at Alexandria, built by Ptolemy Soter, *c.* 300 BC. The erection of Os. was revived in W Asia *c.* AD 1000, and extended to Europe. That built on Hveen island, Denmark, in 1576, for Tycho Brahe, was elaborate, but survived only till 1597. It was followed by those at Paris (1667), Greenwich (1675), and Kew (1769).

Among the most famous modern Os. are the Hale at Palomar Mtn, California; Kitt Peak in Arizona, and Mt Semirodniki in the Caucasus, which have the most powerful optical telescopes covering the sky from the northern hemisphere: famous radioastronomic Os. incl. Jodrell Bank (q.v.), the Mullard at Cambridge, England, and Narrabri to the N of Sydney, Australia. Until recently the skies of the southern hemisphere were comparatively neglected, although study of them could help to solve some of astronomy's greatest problems, but in 1975 important optical Os. were estab. at Cerro Tololo, Chile; La Silla, Chile; and Siding Spring, Australia.

O'CASEY, Sean (1884-1964). Irish dramatist. B. in Dublin, he worked as a labourer in early life, and was largely self-educated. His first plays, *The Shadow of a Gunman* (1922), and *Juno and the Paycock* (1925), created a sensation by their realistic picture of Dublin slum life during the 'troubles'; they were followed by *The Plough and the Stars* (1926), an unromantic depiction of the Easter Rebellion, which led to riots when first produced. His later plays incl. *The Silver Tassie* (1929), *Within the Gates* (1934), *The Star Turns Red* (1940), *Red Roses for Me* (1943), *Oak Leaves and Lavender* (1946) and *The Drums of Father Ned* (1960). O.'s work is unique in its harmonious blending of stark realism with symbolism, tragedy with comedy and Dublin slang with a richly poetic diction.

OCCAM (o'kam), or Ockham, William of (*c.* 1300-49). English philosopher, known as the Invincible Doctor. B. at Ockham, Surrey, he became a Franciscan monk, defended the doctrine of evangelical poverty against pope John XXII, and was imprisoned at Avignon on charges of heresy in 1328, but escaped to Munich, where he d. In philosophy, he revived the fundamentals of Nominalism.

OCCITANIE (ōkitahnē'). *See* LANGUEDOC.

OCEAN. The continuous water surface of the Earth, *c.* 363,000,000 sq.km (140,000,000 sq.m), or 70.8% of the total area; mean depth 3,660 m (12,000 ft). There are strictly 3 oceans - Atlantic, Indian, and Pacific (qq.v.) - to which the Arctic (q.v.) is usually added. Their surface temperature varies with latitude; between −2°C and 29°C; beneath the surface temperature decreases rapidly to 370m (1,200 ft), more slowly to 2,200 m (7,200 ft), and hardly at all deeper still. Changes of temperature are less extreme than those of land, a factor greatly affecting the climate of countries bordering the Os., and prevailing winds and the positioning of land masses affect surface currents which produce further modifications. Salinity averages about 3½%. Beyond the continental shelves, shallow ledges to 180m (600ft), the continental slope reaches down to the abyssal zone, the largest area, at 1,800-5,500 m (6,000-18,000 ft). Only a small area lies deeper, the greatest recorded depth being 11,000 m (36,198 ft) by the *Vityaz* (USSR) in 1957 in the Mariana Trench in the W Pacific. Study of the O. floors has provided confirmation, e.g. the extension of the 'break' in the Earth's crust beneath the Atlantic round the Cape of Good Hope, that *c.* 20,000,000 yrs ago the Earth had a single land mass (Pangea: *see also* WEGENER), with N America bordering (with Greenland between) on Eurasia; and with Africa's west coast adjoining S America, and her east coast adjoining India, Antarctica, and Australia.

James Cook (q.v.), the American Matthew Maury (1806-73), and John and James Ross (qq.v.) were pioneers in the study of the Os., known as oceanography or oceanology. Mid-19th cent. submarine cable-laying gave a useful impetus, but the most rapid advances have come since the S.W.W. with the development of new techniques in undersea photography, drilling of cores from the O. floors (*see* MOHOLE), use of sonic sounding devices, and the perfection of manned submersibles - the ships of inner space - able to move about the sea floor at depths of up to 1,800 m (6,000 ft). Besides pure research (*see also* ARCHAEOLOGY), there have been military and commercial incentives, the latter including sea farming (*see* FISHING) and the lure of mineral wealth - under the sea bed (coal, petroleum, natural gas, etc.); in the sediment of its floor and in the natural continuing deposition of valuable metals there (for example, self-forming manganese nodules which are in effect a 'mine' perpetually renewed); and in the waters themselves (bromine, magnesium, potassium, salt, etc. already commercially extracted, and aluminium, calcium, copper, gold, manganese, silver, etc. potentially recoverable). Research centres incl. the British Inst. of Oceanography at Godalming and in the USA the Naval Oceanographic Office co-operates with the Scripps Inst. (California) and Woods Hole Inst. (New England); international co-operation is assisted by an Oceanographic Commission under UNESCO.

OCEANĀ'RIUM. Large size display tank in which aquatic animals and plants live, not separated according to species as in the conventional aquarium, but living together much as they would in their natural environment. The world's first O. was founded by the explorer and naturalist W. Douglas Burden in 1938 at Marine Studios, Marineland, Florida.

OCEANIA (ōsē-ā'nia). Term embracing the islands of the S Pacific Ocean. The divisions are Micronesia, Melanesia, and Polynesia; Australasia is often included.

OCEAN ISLAND. One of the Gilbert Is., part of Kiribati, it is also known as Banaba, and has rich phosphate deposits. The islanders were driven out by the Japanese in the S.W.W., and were resettled by Britain in 1945 on Rabi in the Fiji group. The islanders claimed improved royalties and return to O.I. after mining damage had been made good, and in 1976 were awarded damages for govt failure to replant with fruit-bearing trees.

OCĒ'ANUS. In Greek mythology, a river supposed to encircle the earth.

O'CONNELL, Daniel (1775-1847). Irish politician, called 'the Liberator'. B. in Kerry, he was educ. for the priesthood, but adopted a legal career. In 1823 he founded

OCEANOGRAPHY. The *Glomar Challenger*, launched in 1968, was named after the first oceanographic research vessel, the converted British warship *HMS Challenger*, fitted out in 1872. Owned by Global Marine Ltd., and directed by the Scripps Institution, she is designed to operate in very deep waters, drilling and coring for ocean sediment, which may be mineral rich. Maximum operating water depth was 6,243 m (20,483 ft) and maximum penetration of the ocean floor 1,290 m (4,265 ft). *Photo: Courtesy of the Scripps Institution of Oceanography.*

OCEANARIUM. Hand-feeding ensures fair shares, otherwise this fine grouper specimen might lose his lunch to the dolphins hovering in the background. *Photo: Courtesy of Marine Studios, Marineland, Florida.*

the Catholic Association to press RC claims. Although ineligible as an RC to take his seat, he was elected MP for co. Clare in 1828, and so forced the govt to grant Catholic emancipation. In parliament he co-operated with the Whigs in the hope of obtaining concessions until 1841, when he launched his campaign for repeal of the union. His timid and vacillating leadership and conservative outlook on social questions alienated his most active supporters, who broke away and formed the 'Young Ireland' movement. He d. at Genoa.

O'CONNELL. A portrait miniature of Ireland's 'Liberator', Daniel O'Connell, painted in 1836 by B.Mulrenin. *Photo: Courtesy of the National Portrait Gallery.*

O'CONNOR, Feargus (1794-1855). Irish politician. B. in Ireland, he sat in parliament 1832-5 as a follower of O'Connell, but then, as editor of the *Northern Star* and a powerful speaker, made himself the most influential figure in the English Chartist movement, and its collapse in 1848 helped unsettle his reason and he d. insane.

OCTAVIAN. *See* AUGUSTUS.

O'CTOPUS. Genus of Cephalopoda having a round or oval body, and 8 arms with 2 rows of suckers on each, though the word is sometimes used to cover other members of the order. Occurring in all temperate and tropical seas, where they feed on crabs, etc., they can vary their coloration according to their background and may either swim with their arms or proceed through a type of jet propulsion by means of their funnel. The common O. (*O. vulgaris*), relished as a delicacy in S Europe, may reach 2m (6ft) and is sometimes found off Britain. Generally speaking the perils of O. attack are exaggerated, but off the Pacific coast the giant *O. apollyon* may span more than 8m (26ft).

ODE. Lyric poem containing the spontaneous expression of emotional fervour. Originating in ancient Greece as a chant sung to a musical accompaniment, it was brought to perfection by Sappho and Pindar, and by Horace and Catullus among the Romans. Among the modern writers of Os. are Spenser, Milton, Dryden, Collins, Coleridge, Wordsworth, Shelley, Keats, Tennyson, and Swinburne.

ODENSE (ō'dhense). Port on the is. of Fünen, Denmark. It is the birthplace of Hans Andersen, and its industries incl. shipbuilding, electrical goods, glass and textiles. Pop. (1973) 137,275.

Ō'DER. European river, 885km (550m) long, rising in Czechoslovakia. It flows generally NW past Wroclaw and Frankfort-on-O. to Szczecin, on the Baltic Sea. It was chosen in 1945 as the German-Polish border N of its confluence with the Neisse.

ŌDE'SSA. Seaport in the Ukrainian SSR on a bay in the NW corner of the Black Sea, cap. of O. region. It is an important commercial air and railway centre, and has excellent harbour facilities. Lying between the Dnieper and Dniester estuaries, O. was founded by Catherine II in 1795 near the site of an ancient Greek settlement. In German occupation 1941-4, O. suffered severe damage under the Russian 'scorched earth' policy and from German destruction. It has a univ. Pop. (1977) 1,039,000, incl. *c.* 100,000 Jews.

ODETS (ōdets'), **Clifford** (1906-63). American playwright. B. in Philadelphia, he was brought up in the Bronx, New York, and went on the stage at 15. He won fame with *Waiting for Lefty* (1935), a one-act play depicting a strike.

Ō'DIN. One of the chief gods of the ancient Germanic tribes, called Woden in Anglo-Saxon. The husband of Frigga and father of Baldur and Thor, he lives in Asgard when he is a sky-god, or in Valhalla when he is conceived as a god of the dead and as receiving the ghosts of brave warriors.

ODY'SSEUS. The chief character of the *Odyssey* (*see* HOMER), mentioned also in the *Iliad* as one of the most prominent leaders of the Greek forces at the siege of Troy. He is said to have been the ruler of the island of Ithaca. Among the Greek heroes O. was distinguished for his sagacity.

OEDIPUS (ēd'ipus). Legendary king of Thebes. As his father, King Laius, had been warned by an oracle that his son would kill him, O. was exposed at birth and left to die, but was rescued and brought up by the king of Corinth. When grown to manhood O. killed Laius, whom he did not know, in a quarrel. Having saved Thebes from the Sphinx, he was granted the kingdom, and in ignorance married his mother, Jocasta. After 4 children had been born, the truth came out, whereupon O. blinded himself and Jocasta hanged herself. In his later wanderings O. was led by his dau. Antigone. The story of O. forms the subject of 2 of Sophocles' tragedies.

OEDIPUS COMPLEX. Term invented by Freud for the emotional conflict set up by a young child's relations with his parents. The child develops a sexual passion for his mother, and a feeling of jealousy and hostility towards his father; the unconscious conflicts created by this problem are a major cause of neuroses, and one of the most important factors in the development of character. *Hamlet* has been interpreted as a study of the O.C.

OERSTED (ör'-), **Hans Christian** (1777-1851). Danish scientist. Prof. of physics at Copenhagen from 1806, in 1820 he discovered magnetic fields, thus founding the science of magnetism. The *oersted*, the CGS electromagnetic unit of magnetizing or magnetic force named after him, is equal to the force in dynes on a unit magnetic pole at any point in a vacuum. In SI units O. = $10^3/4\pi$A/m.

OESOPHAGUS (ēso'fagus). The gullet; the passage by which food travels from mouth to stomach. It is about 23cm (9in) long, and its upper end is at the bottom of the pharynx, immediately behind the windpipe.

OESTROGEN. A hormone which produces oestrus, i.e. menstruation in women and heat in the females of the lower mammals. Three principal oestrogens have been isolated - oestrone, oestriol, and oestradiol. *See* MENOPAUSE.

OFFA (d. 796). Anglo-Saxon king of Mercia in 757. He conquered Essex, Kent, Sussex, and Surrey, defeated the Welsh and the West Saxons, and estab. Mercian supremacy over all England S of the Humber. **Offa's Dyke** is an earthwork along the Welsh border attributed to him, and remains of its defences still stand along the line from the mouth of the Dee to that of the Severn.

O'FFALY. Co. of Rep. of Ireland, in the prov. of Leinster, between Galway on the W and Kildare on the E. The Shannon flows along its W boundary; other rivers incl. the Brosna, Clodagh, and Broughill. In the SE are the Slieve Bloom mts. The co. town is Tullamore. Area 1,997 sq.km (771 sq.m); pop. (1971) 51,830.

OFFENBACH (ofenbahk'), **Jacques** (1819-80). French composer. B. at Cologne, he studied at Paris, became a member of the orchestra of the Opéra Comique, and later conductor at the Théâtre Français. He wrote light opera for presentation at the Bouffes Parisiens, of which he held the lease, and afterwards for various theatres. His most widely known works are *Orphée aux enfers* (1858), *La belle Hélène* (1864), and *Les contes d'Hoffmann* (1881).

O'FLAHERTY (ō-flah'herti), **Liam** (1897-). Irish author. B. on the Aran Is., he has written novels of Irish life, notably *Thy Neighbour's Wife*, *The Informer*, and *Land* (1946), dealing with Fenian activities in co. Mayo.

O'GADEN. Region in Harar prov., SE Ethiopia, which juts into Somalia, and is claimed by the latter state. It is a desert plateau, rising to 1,000 m (3,000 ft); arid farming is practised by nomads.

O'GAM or **Ogham.** System of alphabetic writing once in use in the British Isles. The name O. is sometimes extended to the oldest-known form of the Gaelic languages. Some 300 funerary inscriptions in O. are known, mainly from the SW parts of Ireland, but also from Wales, Scotland, the Isle of Man, and Hampshire. The script developed during the 5th cent. and consists of a system of strokes or notches suited to be carved in rough stones.

OGBOMOSHO (ogbawmō'shō). Town in Nigeria, 80km (50m) NE of Ibadan. It is a commercial centre. Pop. (1973) 320,000.

OGDEN, Charles Kay (1889-1957). British originator, with Ivor Armstrong Richards (1893-1979), of Basic English (q.v.). Together they wrote *Foundations of Aesthetics* (1921) and *The Meaning of Meaning* (1923).

OGDON, John (1937-). British pianist. Son of a schoolmaster, he created sensation in Moscow in 1962 when he won the Tchaikovsky award with Ashkenazy (q.v.). He is noted for his interpretation of Busoni.

Ō'GILVY, Angus James Bruce (1928-). British businessman. Second son of the earl of Airlie, he m. in 1963 Princess Alexandra (1936-), sister of the Duke of Kent (q.v.).

OGLETHORPE, James Edward (1696-1785). English soldier. He joined the Guards, and in 1732 obtained a charter for the colony of Georgia, intended as a refuge for debtors and for European Protestants, and administered it himself until 1743.

OGPU. *See* GPU.
O'HIGGINS, Bernardo (1776-1842). Chilean soldier and statesman. Of Irish descent, he was foremost among the leaders of the Chilean struggle for independence from Spanish rule 1810-17, and headed the first permanent national govt 1817-23.
OHIO (ōhī'ō). North-central state of the USA, S of Lake Erie, between Indiana on the W and Pennsylvania on the E. It takes its name from the r. Ohio. An important farming state - livestock products, maize, oats, tomatoes, grapes, soya beans, etc. - it is also one of the industrial leaders, producing cars, aircraft, boats, machine tools, industrial and office machinery, electrical goods, hardware and glass, tyres and plastic goods, etc. Minerals incl. bituminous coal, lime, clay, and natural gas. The chief towns are Akron, Cleveland, Cincinnati, Dayton, Toledo, and Columbus, the cap. It became a state 1803. Area 106,714 sq.km (41,222 sq.m); pop. (1970) 10,652,017.
OHIO. River of the USA, second-largest affluent of the Mississippi. It is formed by the union of the Allegheny and Monongahela at Pittsburgh, Pa., and is 1,580 km (980m) long. Its name is Indian and means 'beautiful river'.
OHM, Georg Simon (1787-1854). German physicist. He was prof. successively at Cologne, Nuremberg, and Munich, and in 1827 promulgated what is known as OHM'S LAW: the steady current in a metallic circuit is directly proportional to the constant total electromotive force in the circuit. If a current I flows between two points in a conductor across which the potential difference is E, then by O.'s law E/I is a constant which is known as the *resistance* R between the two points. Hence E/I = R. Equations relating E, I and R are often quoted as O.'s law but the term resistance did not enter into the law as originally stated.
OHM. In electricity, the practical unit of resistance, named after G. S. Ohm. A circuit's resistance is 1 ohm when a potential difference of 1 volt is required to produce a current-flow of 1 ampere.
OIL. Three main classes of oils are distinguished: essential oils, mineral oils (*see* PETROLEUM), and fixed or fatty oils. All Os. are composed chiefly of carbon and hydrogen, are inflammable, and usually are insoluble in water. They may be solid at ordinary temperatures, when they are termed fats, or liquid. Most essential oils are liquids and are obtained from vegetable sources. Fixed oils are products of varying consistency, widespread in the animal and vegetable kingdoms. Vegetable oils are generally obtained from the nuts or seeds of plants, and animal oils and fats occur in the fat-containing tissues; fish oils are important in this group. They are widely used as food, in soap manufacture, in paint and varnishes, lubrication and illumination.
OISE (wahz). European river which rises in the Ardennes, Belgium, and flows through France in a generally SW direction for 300km (186m) to fall into the Seine *c.* 65km (40m) below Paris.
OI'STRAKH, David Fyodorovich (1908-74). Russian violinist. B. at Odessa, he became prof. at the Moscow Conservatory in 1939, and was world renowned as an executant, often playing with his son **Igor O.** (1931-). Shostakovich wrote both his violin concertos for him.
OKAPI (okah'pi). Animal (*Okapia johnstoni*) of the giraffe family though with much shorter legs and neck, found in central Africa, but very rare and strictly protected. Purplish brown, with creamy face and black and white stripes on the legs, it is beautifully camouflaged.
OKAYAMA (ōkahyahmah). Port in W Honshu, Japan, on the Asahi r. 11km (7m) from its mouth. It makes textiles and is noted for its fine park and three Buddhist temples. Pop. (1973) 476,000.
ŌKEECHŌ'BEE. Lake in the N Everglades, Florida: 65km (40m) long and 40km (25m) wide.
ŌKEFENŌ'KEE. Swamp in SE Georgia, USA, rich in alligators, bears, deer, birds, etc. Much of its 1,700 sq.km (660 sq.m) forms a Nat. Wildlife Refuge.
ŌKHO'TSK, Sea of. Arm of the N Pacific between the Kamchatka Peninsula and Sakhalin, and bordered southward by the Kurile Is. Free of ice only in summer, it is often fogbound. Area 937,000 sq.km (582,000 sq.m).
ŌKINA'WA. Largest of the Ryukyu Islands (q.v.) in the Pacific Ocean, *c.* 300m SW of Japan, of which it was a prefecture until captured by US forces in a violent battle lasting 1 April-21 June 1945, in which there were 47,000 US casualties (12,000 killed and missing) and the Japanese garrison of 60,000 were all killed except for a few hundred taken prisoner. O. and the rest of the Ryukyu Islands continued to be admin. by the USA, but by an agreement 1969 reverted to Japan in 1972. The chief town is Naha (pop. 258,000), cap. of the Ryukyus. In 1973 Japan announced plans for relocating mainland industry on O.; and development of sugar-growing, a tourist resort, and aviation and communication networks. Area 1,256 sq.km (485 sq.m). Pop. (1970) 934,000.
OKLAHŌ'MA. South-central state of the USA, deriving its name from an Indian word meaning 'red people'. The surface is for the most part an upland prairie. The principal rivers are the Arkansas, Red, and Canadian. The most important mountains are the Wichita range in the S and the Ozark range in the E. The climate is continental with considerable extremes between summer and winter temperatures; the O. 'panhandle' is part of the dustbowl area of the USA. Minerals incl. petroleum, natural gas, coal and lead. The chief crop is wheat, and cattle are raised. The principal cities are Oklahoma City (the cap.), and Tulsa. O., part of the Louisiana Purchase of 1803, was admitted to the Union as a state in 1907; it was 'dry' from then until, as the result of a referendum, prohibition was abolished in 1959. Area 181,088 sq.km (69,919 sq.m); pop. (1970) 2,559,253.
OKLAHOMA CITY. Cap. of Oklahoma, USA, on the Canadian river. Situated in an oilfield, its chief industry is oil refining and manufacture of oil mining machinery, but aircraft, telephone equipment, etc. are also made. There are several univs., and it has the Nat. Cowboy Hall of Fame. Pop. met area (1970) 669,000.
OKOVA'NGO SWAMP. *See* BOTSWANA.
OLAF. Name of 5 kings of Norway. **Olaf I** Tryggvesson (969-1000), elected king in 995, began the conversion of Norway to Christianity, and was killed in a sea battle against the Danes and Swedes. **Olaf II** Haraldsson (995-1030), king from 1015, offended his subjects by his centralizing policy and zeal for Christianity, and was killed in battle by Norwegian rebel chiefs backed by Canute (q.v.) of Denmark. He was declared the patron saint of Norway in 1164. **Olaf V** (1903-) succeeded his father Haakon VII (q.v.) in 1957.

OLD AGE. The progressive degeneration of bodily and mental processes associated with the later years of life. Its cause is still not precisely known (*see* AGEING), but every one of the phenomena can occur at almost any age, and the process does not take place throughout the body at an equal speed. Normally, however, ageing begins after about 30. The arteries start to lose their elasticity, so that a greater strain is thrown upon the heart. The resulting gradual impairment of the blood supply is responsible for many of the changes, but, between 30 and 60 there is a period of maturity in which, if life is lived sensibly and in accordance with natural law, ageing makes little progress. Research into the causative process of O.A. (gerontology) incl. genetic and diet factors, and the mechanisms behind structural changes in arteries and bones. Geriatrics is the branch of medicine dealing with O.A. and its diseases.

OLD BAILEY. Properly the name of a street in the City of London, England, leading off Ludgate Hill, but more usually applied to the Central Criminal Court (q.v.) which is there situated.

OLD CATHOLICS. RCs who refused to accept the dogma of papal infallibility, declared in 1870, and set up their own ecclesiastical organization. The movement originated in Bavaria, and still survives in Germany, the Netherlands, Austria, Czechoslovakia, and in Switzerland. Its organization is episcopal. Certain modifications of R.C. practice were adopted, e.g. the use of the vernacular in services anticipated subsequent RC practice, and priests are allowed to marry.

OLDENBURG. City in Lower Saxony, W Germany, 37km (23m) W of Bremen on the Hunte, once cap. of O. duchy. It dates from the 9th cent. Pop. (1978) 134,800.

OLDHAM (ōl'dam). Town in Greater Manchester, England, 11km (7m) NE of Manchester. It makes cotton and other textiles, and textile machinery, plastics, electrical goods, electronic equipment, etc. Pop. (1972) 104,860.

OLD MOORE'S ALMANAC. Annual publication in Britain containing 'prophecies' of the events of the following year. It was first pub. in 1700, under the title *Vox Stellarum,* by Francis Moore (1657–*c.* 1715), astrologer and quack-doctor, to advertise his pills.

OLD STONE AGE ART. Paintings, engravings, and sculptures of the palaeolithic or O.S.A. - i.e. 20,000 to 8,000 years ago - found in caves and rock shelters in SW France, Spain, and Africa. The usual subjects are animals, such as the mammoth, bison, elephant, and horse, but the human figure is occasionally depicted. The finest examples, distinguished for their great vigour and naturalistic treatment, are the paintings at Altamira, Lascaux, and the Central Sahara (qq.v.). Cave paintings also form part of Indian art (*see* BHOPAL), and that of the Aborigines of Australia. It is supposed that the paintings were in the nature of 'sympathetic magic', designed to increase the food supply.

OLD STYLE. A qualification, often abbreviated as 'O.S.', applied to dates before the year 1752 in England as quoted in later writers. In that year the calendar in use in England was reformed by the omission of 11 days, in order to bring it into line with the more exact Gregorian system, and the beginning of the year was put back from 25 March to 1 Jan. *See* CALENDAR.

OLDUVAI GORGE. Deep cleft in the Serengeti steppe, Tanganyika. In 1958-9 Leakey (q.v.) discovered here Pleistocene remains of gigantic animals - sheep similar in size to a carthorse, pigs as big as a rhinoceros, a gorilla-sized baboon, and a skull (*Zinjanthropus*) with huge teeth that led to the nickname 'Nutcracker Man'. It is thought that conditions in the O.G. enabled creatures of the Pliocene to survive to a comparatively late date.

OLD VIC. Theatre S of the Thames in Waterloo Rd, London, founded in 1818 as the Coburg. Taken over by Emma Cons in 1880, when it was known as the Royal Victoria Hall, it became a popular centre for opera and drama, and was affectionately dubbed the Old Vic. In 1898 Lilian Baylis, niece of Emma Cons, assumed the management, and in 1914 began the celebrated series of Shakespeare productions, which continued until the S.W.W. The theatre was badly damaged by enemy action in 1940, but the O.V. company continued to appear at the New Theatre, and in 1950 the O.V. was re-opened, becoming the temporary home of the National Theatre 1963-76.

OLEA'NDER. Evergreen shrubs of the genus *Nerium,* native to the Mediterranean region. The pink flowers grow in clusters, and the lance-shaped leaves contain a poisonous juice, oleandrin.

OLGA, St (d. *c.* 969). The wife of Igor, the Scandinavian prince of Kiev, her baptism (*c.* 955) was an important step in the Christianization of Russia.

OLIVARES (ōlēvahr'es), **Gaspar de Guzman,** count-duke of (1587–1645). Spanish minister. Favourite of Philip IV, he ruled the country 1621–43.

OLIVE (o'liv). An evergreen tree (*Olea europaea*) of the family Oleaceae. It grows to *c.* 7.5m (25ft) high, has spiny branches and opposite, lance-shaped leaves. The white flowers are followed by bluish-black oval fruits, from which O. oil is expressed: pale yellow, it is chiefly composed of glycerides and, besides being edible, is used in soap, ointments, and as a lubricant. It is native to Mediterranean regions, but is now of wide distribution in warm climates.

OLIVENITE (oliv'enīt). Hydrated copper arsenate, occurring as a mineral in olive-green prisms.

OLIVES, Mount of. A range of hills E of Jerusalem. Gethsemane was at its foot, while a chapel (now a mosque), marks the traditional site of the Ascension.

OLI'VIER, Laurence, baron (1907–). British actor. B. at Dorking, Surrey, son of a clergyman, he made his début as Katherine in 1922 at Stratford-on-Avon in a boys' performance of *The Taming of the Shrew.* Among his most famous parts are Romeo, Sir Toby Belch, Macbeth, Hamlet, and Archie Rice in *The Entertainer.* His films include *Wuthering Heights* and *Rebecca,* and he has produced, directed and played the leading role in film versions of *Henry V, Hamlet,* and *Richard III.* Knighted in 1947, he was for many years associated with the Old Vic and was director of the National Theatre 1962-73. He m. the actresses Jill Esmond (1930-40), Vivien Leigh (1940-61), with whom he played in *Anthony and Cleopatra,* etc., and in 1961 Joan Plowright. He was created a life peer 1970, and awarded OM in 1981.

O'LIVINE. A pale green mineral, magnesium iron silicate $(Mg,Fe)_2SiO_4$. Transparent O. is called chrysolite, and used in jewellery.

OLNEY (ōl'ni). Town in Bucks, England, on the r. Ouse NE of Buckingham. The house in which William Cowper lived is a museum. Every Shrove Tuesday housewives run a pancake race, which since 1946 has also been run in a time contest with Liberal, Kansas. Pop. (1975) 2,400.

OLIVIER. Although the star of many films, it is nonetheless as a Shakespearean actor that Lord Olivier is best remembered. The title role of *Othello* gave full scope to his versatility. *Photo: Camera Press.*

OLOMOUC (ōlōmōts'). Town in Czechoslovakia, at the confluence of the Bystrice and Morava. There are sugar-refining, brewing, and metal goods industries. Pop. (1977) 98,000.

OLSZTYN (ol'shtin). Industrial town in NE Poland: it was formerly in E Prussia, when it was known as Allenstein. Pop. (1978) 100,000.

OLYMPIA (olim'pia). An ancient Greek sanctuary, in the W Peloponnese on the Alpheus, and the scene of the original Olympic Games. It contained temples of Zeus Olympius, Hera, etc. The events of the Games were contested in the Stadium and Hippodrome; the former for foot-races, boxing, wrestling, etc., the latter for chariot- and horse-races. The Games were held every 4 years (*olympiad* - this method of reckoning time ceased to be used with the abolition of the games in AD 394) during a sacred truce and from 776 BC continuous records were kept. Religious offerings were followed by the contest, originally only foot-races, but subsequently greatly enlarged. Women were forbidden to be present and contestants were men of Hellenic descent only, until in later years Romans were admitted.

The revival of the Games was initiated by the French Baron Pierre de Coubertin in 1894; an International Olympic Committee organized the meetings which it was intended should be held each 4 years, but they were interrupted by both world wars. The Olympic emblem of 5 interlaced circles represents the 5 continents. The first modern Olympic Games (1896) were held in Athens, and abstentions (as a result of the Soviet invasion of Afghanistan) when they were held in Moscow in 1980 led to a proposal to make Greece the permanent venue.

The modern O.G. cover a much wider range of events, e.g. swimming, skating, equestrian events, football, rowing. Similar games on a limited basis are the Commonwealth, European and Asian G.

OLYMPUS (ōlim'pus). Name of a large number of mountains in Greece and in neighbouring countries. The most famous of them, identified with the abode of the gods in the *Iliad,* is a group of hills, the highest point of which reaches 2,918 m (9,570 ft) in the N of Thessaly.

There is a Mt Olympus, 2,424 m (7,954 ft), in the Olympic mts., Washington state, USA, which forms Olympic National Park (1938). Another Mt Olympus, on the planet Mars, is c.24,000 m (80,000 ft) high.

OMAGH (ō'ma). Co. tn of Tyrone, N Ireland, on the r. Strule, 48km (30m) S of Londonderry. Growing up round an abbey founded in the 8th cent., O. has dairy industries and is a market centre. Pop. (1971) 12,000.

Ō'MAHA. City in E Nebraska, USA, on the Missouri. It is a major livestock market and has food processing and meat-packing industries. The Joslyn Art Museum has a major collection and Boys Town, founded by Father Flanagan for orphan and other deprived children, is 18km (11m) to the W. Pop. met area (1974) 583,600.

The landing-point in France of the US 5th Corps on 6 June 1944, between Port-en-Bressin and the estuary of the Vire r., Calvados dept, was given the code name O. beach.

OMAN (omahn'). Sultanate occupying the eastern corner of Arabia, until 1970 known as Muscat and Oman. A mtn range rising to more than 2,745 m (9,000 ft) runs NW to SE, but the coastal plain NW of the cap. of Muscat is fertile and famous for its dates. Oil was discovered in 1964, and other minerals incl. copper and manganese. Oil is refined and Omani silverware is famous. The reactionary sultan was deposed in 1970 by his son, who succeeded him as Sultan Qabus bin Said (1941-), and with British and Iranian aid suppressed left-wing guerrilla activity (continuous 1965-75) in the mountainous W prov. of Dhofar, on the border with S Yemen. The chief town of Dhofar is Salalah, with its port of Raysut. Masirah Is. off the SE coast of O. is used in aerial reconnaissance of the Arabian Sea and Indian Ocean. The Kuria Muria Is. were a Brit. cable station 1854-1967. Area 212,000 sq.km (82,000 sq.m); pop. (1970) *c.* 1,000,000; M.U.: Omani rial.

Ō'MAR (*c.* 581-644). Arabian caliph. He was one of Mohammed's ablest advisers, and in 634 succeeded Abu Bekr as the second of the caliphs. During his reign Syria, Palestine, Egypt, and Persia were conquered by the Arabs. He was assassinated. The mosque of O. at Jerusalem is attributed to him.

OMAR KHAYYĀM (khīyahm') (*c.* 1050-1123). Persian astronomer and poet. B. in Nishapur, he founded a school of astronomical research and assisted in reforming the calendar. The result of his observations was the *Jalālī* era, begun in AD 1079. In the West, O.K. is chiefly known as a poet through Edward FitzGerald's translation of his *rubā'īs* as *The Rubáiyát,* also trans. by Robert Graves 1967.

OMAYYADS (ōmī'yadz). An Arab dynasty which held the caliphate 661-750. They were overthrown by Abbasids, but a member of the family escaped to Spain, and in 756 assumed the title of emir of Cordova. His dynasty, which took the title of caliph in 929, ruled at Cordova until the early 11th cent.

OMBUDSMAN (om'bōōdsman). Post of Scandinavian origin instituted to safeguard citizen rights against encroachment by the govt or its employees: introduced in Sweden 1809, Denmark 1954, and Norway 1962. The O. investigates complaints of injustice which would otherwise have no hope of redress. First Commonwealth country to appoint an O. was NZ 1962; the UK followed 1966 with a Parliamentary Commissioner (Sir Edmund Compton); and Hawaii was the first US state to appoint an O. 1967. The U.K. Local Govt Act (1974) set up a Local O., or Commissioner for Local Admin., to investigate maladmin. by local councils, police, health or water authorities.

OMDURMAN (omdoor'mahn). City in the rep. of Sudan, on the White Nile, opposite Khartoum. It was the residence of the Mahdi, 1884-98, and is an important trading centre. Pop. (1973) 299,400. The Battle of O. (1898) was a victory for Kitchener over the forces of the Mahdi.

OMNIBUS (abbr. bus). A road conveyance for all. Originating in Paris in the reign of Charles X, the first English O. travelled between Paddington and the Bank. The London General O. Co. (founded in 1856) became the most prominent, and its horse Os. survived until 1911. Since then, the growth of single- and double-decker motor Os. has been universal. Strict safety precautions now govern their usage, and their originally limited journeys extend to transcontinental vehicles usually called motor-coaches.

OMSK. Town in the RSFSR, cap. of O. region, at the confluence of the Om and the Irtysh. Agricultural and other machinery is made and O. has food-processing factories and saw-mills; also oil refineries linked with Tuimazy in Bashkiria by a 1,600 km (1,000 m) pipeline. It developed round a fortress dating from 1716. Pop. (1977) 1,026,000.

ONASSIS. *See* KENNEDY, JACQUELINE.

ONEGA (on'egah). Second-largest lake in Europe, situated partly in Leningrad region, partly in Karelia ASSR. Area 8,030 sq.km (3,820 sq.m). The O. canal, along its S shore, is part of the Mariinsk system linking Leningrad with the r. Volga.

ONEIDA (ōnī'dah). Town in NY state, USA, on O. Creek, to the E of Syracuse. It makes silverware, fertilizers, paper, etc., but is best known as the site of the O. community, moved here from Vermont in 1848. Members of the community held all things in common, and practised a form of 'complex marriage' much criticized outside the community, which was dissolved in 1879. A co-operative company took over its commercial activities in 1881. Pop. (1970) 11,660.

O'NEILL (ō-nēl'), **Eugene Gladstone** (1888-1953). American playwright. B. in NY City, son of the actor James O., he had varied experience as gold prospector, seaman, actor, etc., and began learning his craft at George Pierce Baker's drama school at Harvard in 1914. His first full-length play *Beyond the Horizon* (1920), an immediate success, was followed by the expressionist study in fear *The Emperor Jones* (1920); the realistic *Anna Christie* (1921); *The Hairy Ape* (1922). *All God's Chillun Got Wings* (1924) dealt with miscegenation, and this, together with the peasant sensuality of *Desire under the Elms* (1924), provoked the censor. Symbolism predominated in *The Great God Brown* (1926) and *Lazarus Laughed* (1927); *Strange Interlude* (1928) used a stream of consciousness method; and the trilogy *Mourning Becomes Electra* (1931) developed the Orestean theme of Greek drama. *Ah, Wilderness!* (1933) approached the norm of New England comedy, *Days Without End* (1934) returned to Catholic inspiration, and *The Iceman Cometh* (1946) struck again a confused note. Events of his own early life, e.g. his mother's mental instability, are portrayed in *Long Day's Journey into Night*. In 1936 he was awarded a Nobel prize and was undoubtedly America's leading dramatist between the wars.

O'NEILL of the Maine, Terence, baron (1914-). Irish statesman. Member for Bannside, co. Antrim, from 1946 he held many posts in the Ulster govt and was Min. of Finance from 1956 until he succeeded Brookeborough as PM (1963-9). Life peer 1970.

ONION (un'yen). Bulbous plant (*Allium cepa*) of the family Liliaceae. Cultivated from ancient times, it probably originated in Asia. The edible part is the bulb, containing an acrid volatile oil, giving a strong flavour. The O. is a biennial, the common species producing a bulb in the first season and seeds in the second.

ONSĀ'GER, Lars (1903-76). Norwegian-born American chemist. Prof. of theoretical chemistry at Yale 1945-72, he was the discoverer in 1931 of the 'reciprocity relations of O.', fundamental to the process of turning heat into energy. He received a Nobel prize in 1968.

ONTĀ'RIO. Province of Canada, between the Great Lakes and Hudson Bay. It has an undulating surface, with a range of hills extending towards Lake Huron. The principal rivers are the St Lawrence and Ottawa. The climate of O. is healthy, the soil in the S is fertile, and large areas are under cultivation. There are dairy and fruit farms, and cattle and poultry are raised. Tobacco is cultivated. The chief minerals include gold, nickel, copper, and uranium. More than a quarter of the region is covered by forests, and lumbering is one of the most important industries. O. is the most important manufacturing centre in Canada because of its great water-power resources. Railway rolling-stock, agricultural implements, motor-cars, textiles, tannery and rubber products, pulp and paper are among the main manufactures. The chief cities are Toronto (the cap.), Ottawa, Hamilton, Windsor, and London. O. became British in 1763, and after the War of American Independence many British loyalists settled in the region, from 1791 called Upper Canada until renamed O. in 1867. Area 1,068,587 sq.km (412,582 sq.m); pop. (1976) 8,264,465.

O'NYONG-NYONG. Virus disease transmitted by mosquitoes in East Africa. Symptoms: pains in the joints and glands, an itching rash and fever. It first appeared in 1961.

ONYX (on'iks). A cryptocrystalline variety of silica having straight parallel bands of different colours; milk-white, black, and red. Sardonyx has layers of sard or red carnelian alternating with lighter layers of O. It can be used for cutting cameos.

OÖLITE (ō'olīt). A calcareous rock formed of small grains of carbonate of lime, resembling the hard roe of a fish: the name derives from the Gk for 'egg' and 'stone', coarse-grained Os. are termed pisolites from Gk for 'pea' and 'stone'. The structure may arise from the accretion of carbonate of lime round grains of sand or particles of shell in moving water. It may also be formed from calcareous algae deposited in hot springs. The term is also used to indicate the middle and upper layers of the Jurassic system.

OOSTENDE. Flemish form, meaning east end, of OSTEND (q.v.).

OPAL. A non-crystalline form of silica, occurring in stalactites in volcanic rocks. The common O. is opaque, milk-white, yellow, red, blue, or green, and lustrous. The precious O. is colourless, having innumerable cracks from which emanate brilliant colours produced from minute crystals of cristobalite. Os. are found in Hungary, New South Wales (black Os. were first discovered here in 1905) and Mexico, noted for fire Os.

OP ART. Form of art, espec. popular in the early sixties, which is based on the creative use of scientifically-based optical illusions, as in the work of Jeffrey Steele and Bridget Riley. Such patterns can be adapted by computer to give fascinating variations on the original theme.

OP ART. Jeffrey Steele's painting 'Baroque Experiment - Fred Maddox', also known as 'Harlequinade', produced in 1962–3. *Photo: Courtesy of Hon. Anthony Samuel.*

OPENCAST MINING. *See* COAL.

OPEN SHOP. A factory or other business employing people not belonging to trade unions, as opposed to the 'closed shop' (q.v.), which employs trade unionists only.

OPERA. A dramatic work in which singing takes the place of speech, and in which the music accompanying the action has paramount importance, although dancing and spectacular staging may also play their part. It originated in late 16th cent. Florence when a number of young poets and musicians attempted to reproduce in modern form the musical declamation, lyrical monologues, and choruses of classical Greek drama. One of the earliest composers was Jacopo Peri (1561-1633), whose *Euridici* influenced Monteverdi (q.v.). At first solely a court entertainment, O. soon became popular and in 1637 the first public O. house opened in Venice. In the later 17th cent. the elaborately conventional aria, designed to display the virtuosity of the singer, became predominant over the dramatic element, composers of this type of O. incl. Cavalli, Cesti, and Scarlatti. In France O. was developed by Lully and Rameau, and in England by Purcell, but the Italian style retained its ascendance, as in the career of Handel (q.v.).

Comic O. (*opera buffa*) was developed in Italy by such composers as Pergolesi, while in England *The Beggar's Opera* (1728) started the vogue of the Ballad O., using popular tunes and spoken dialogue, of which *Singspiel* was the German equivalent.

The revolt against artificiality began with Gluck, who insisted on the pre-eminence of the dramatic over the purely vocal element. Mozart learned much from Gluck in his serious operas, but his greatest triumphs were won in the field of Italian *opera buffa*, and in those works, such as *The Magic Flute*, in which, taking the *Singspiel* as a basis, he laid the foundations of a purely German O. This line was continued by Beethoven in *Fidelio*, and in the work of Weber, in which the Romantic style appears for the first time in O. The Italian tradition, which placed the main stress on vocal display and melodic suavity, continued unbroken into the 19th cent. in the Os. of Rossini, Donizetti, and Bellini.

It is in the Romantic O. of Weber and Meyerbeer that the work of Wagner has its roots. Dominating the contemporary operatic scene, he attempted to create, in his 'music-dramas', a new art-form, and completely transformed the 19th cent. conception of O. In Italy, Verdi succeeded in assimilating, in his mature work, much of the Wagnerian technique, without sacrificing the Italian virtues of vocal clarity and melody, and this tradition was continued by Puccini.

French O. in the mid-19th cent., represented by such composers as Delibes, Gounod, Saint-Saëns, and Massenet, tended to be of rather secondary importance. More serious artistic ideals were put into practice by Berlioz in *The Trojans*, but the merits of his work were largely neglected in his own time. Bizet's *Carmen* began a fashion for 'realism' in O.; his lead in this respect was followed in Italy by Mascagni, Leoncavallo, and Puccini. Debussy's *Pelléas and Melisande* represented a reaction against the over-emphatic emotionalism of Wagnerian Os. National operatic styles were developed in Russia by Glinka, Rimsky-Korsakov, Mussorgsky, Borodin and Tchaikovsky, and in Bohemia by Smetana, and several notable composers of light O. emerged, incl. Sullivan, Lehar, Offenbach, and Johann Strauss.

In the 20th cent. the atonal school produced an outstanding O. in Berg's *Wozzeck* and the Romanticism of Wagner was revived by Richard Strauss, e.g. *Der Rosenkavalier*. Notable modern composers incl. in Britain Delius, Britten, John Gardner and Phyllis Tate, and the Australian, Malcolm Williamson; in the US Gershwin, Menotti, Kurt Weill, and Stravinsky; in Germany Werner Egk; in the USSR Prokofiev: and in Italy Mascagni.

OPERA. Maria Callas in the role of Tosca, one of her greatest triumphs at the Royal Opera House at Covent Garden. Here she is seen with her co-stars, Tito Gobbi (left) and Renato Cioni. *Photo: Popperfoto.*

OPHTHA'LMIA (of-). Inflammation of the eye. O. neonatorum (newborn) is an acute inflammation of a baby's eyes at birth with the organism of gonorrhoea caught from the mother. Sympathetic O. is the diffuse inflammation of the sound eye which is apt to follow septic inflammation of the other. To prevent it, surgeons remove a damaged eye if there is no hope of its sight being restored.

OPIE, John (1761-1807). British artist. B. in St Agnes, Cornwall, he became famous as a portrait painter in London from 1780, later painting historical pictures such as 'The Murder of Rizzio'.

OPINION POLL, Public. The political equivalent of commercial market research. Originating in crude form in the 19th cent. in the USA, they were developed more scientifically in the 20th cent. with the use of statistical sampling techniques, and became popularly known through the work of George Gallup (q.v.). By the 1960s and 1970s they had become a controversial feature of election campaigns on the grounds that they influence the voting, e.g. by establishing one party as likely to win and making the voters wish to 'join the winning side', or by making the lead of one party seem so great that its supporters feel victory is ensured and fail to turn out to play their part in the voting, and so on. Some countries have tried to ban them, with the result that the poll results were published abroad and then reported by their own media notwithstanding.

OPIUM. A narcotic drug obtained from the juice of the opium poppy (*Papaver somniferum*). The unripe seed capsules are cut and the milky juice exuded from them is dried and compressed. Turkey is the main source of medicinal O.: illicit sources incl. the Golden Triangle and Mexico. *See* DRUGS. It is dangerous and habit-forming, containing a high percentage of morphine.

OPIUM WARS. Wars waged against China to enforce the opening of Chinese ports to trade, espec. the opium traffic. Opium from British India paid for Britain's imports from China, such as porcelain and silks, but above all tea, then only obtainable in bulk from China. The *First Opium War* 1840-2, between Britain and China, resulted in the cession of Hong Kong to Britain and the opening of 5 'treaty ports'. A *Second Opium War* 1857-60 followed between Britain and France in alliance against China, when there was further Chinese resistance, notably in Canton, one of the treaty ports. At its close the Summer Palace in Peking was fired on the orders of Lord Elgin, son of the appropriator of the Elgin Marbles.

OPO'LE. Town in Poland, on the Oder, some 80km (50m) SE of Wroclaw. An agricultural market centre, it has textile, chemical and cement industries. It was the cap. of the German prov. of Upper Silesia 1919-45. Pop. (1975) 97,000.

OPOR'TO. Second city (Portuguese *Porto*) in Portugal, on the Douro, 5km (3m) from its mouth. It is famed for the export of port wine, mainly to Britain; and has textile, leather and pottery industries. There is a 12th cent. cathedral, a univ. (1911), and an internat. airport at Pedras Rubas. Pop. met area (1970) 693,200.

OPO'SSUM. Marsupial of the family Didelphidae. Os. are small arboreal animals, with prehensile tails, hands and feet well adapted for grasping, and yellowist-grey fur. These true Os. are confined to N and S America, but the name is popularly applied to the somewhat similar members of Phalangeridae found in Australia, New Zealand, etc.

OPPENHEIMER (op'enhīmer), **Robert** (1904-67). American physicist. The son of a German immigrant, he worked with Rutherford at Cambridge. As director of the Los Alamos Science Laboratory 1943-5, he was in charge of the development of the first atom bomb and director 1947-66 (senior prof. theoretical physics from 1966) Inst. of Advanced Study, Princeton. Objecting to the development of the H-bomb, he was declared a security risk in 1953 by the US Atomic Energy Commission - an incident of the McCarthy era - but was rehabilitated in 1963 when the Commission granted him the Fermi (q.v.) Award.

OPPOSITION, Leader of His/Her Majesty's. In Britain the official title borne since 1937 by the leader of the largest opposition party in the Commons. The post carries a salary of £24,100, plus parl. salary £7,670.

OPTICS. The scientific study of the phenomena of light and vision, e.g. shadows cast by opaque objects, images formed in mirrors, and lenses, microscopes, telescopes, cameras, etc. Light rays are for all practical purposes straight lines, although Einstein has demonstrated that they may be 'bent'. On striking a surface they are reflected or refracted with some attendant absorption, and the study of these facts is the subject-matter of geometrical optics. *See* FIBRE OPTICS, LIGHT.

In **fibreoptics** light is reflected down the inside of bundles of very fine optically insulated glass fibres and transmits an undistorted image from one end to the other. The technique can be used in inspecting parts of machines, or the human body itself, which are hard to examine in any other way.

OPUNTIA. *See* PRICKLY PEAR.

OPUS DEI (ō'pus dā'ē). An RC secular institution aiming at the dissemination of the ideals of Christian perfection, particularly in intellectual and influential circles. Founded in Madrid in 1928, and still especially powerful in Spain, it is now international. Its members may be of either sex, lay or clerical.

O'RACLE. In Greek religion, the answer given by a deity to an inquirer, also used of the place where the answer is given. The earliest O. referred to in classical writings is that at Dodona, where priests expounded the meaning of sounds made by the sacred oaks of Zeus; but the best-known is the O. of Apollo at Delphi. The name O. was adopted by ITV for its teletext (q.v.) system.

ORADEA (orah'dyah). Ancient town in Romania, 130km (80m) NW of Cluj. A railway junction with an airport, it is the centre of a wine-producing area and varied industries incl. agricultural machinery, chemicals, non-ferrous metallurgy, leather goods, printing, glass, textiles, clothing, beer, etc. Made the seat of a bishopric by St Ladislas in 1083, it was destroyed by the Turks in 1241 and rebuilt. Many of its buildings date from the time of Maria Theresa. It was ceded to Romania in 1919, held by Hungary 1940-5. Pop. (1977) 173,620.

ORAN (orahn'). Seaport in Algeria, and on a hill rising above the Mediterranean, *c.* 370km (230m) W of Algiers, with a fine harbour. It was under Spanish rule 1509-1708 and 1732-91, being under Turkish rule in the interval. O. was occupied by France in 1831. After the surrender of France to Germany in 1940, the French warships in the naval base of Mers-el-Kebir nearby were put out of action by the RN to prevent them from falling into German hands. A univ. was estab. 1967. Pop. (1974) 485,200.

ORANGE, House of. The royal family of the Netherlands. The title is derived from the small principality of O., in S France, held by the family from the 8th cent. to 1713. They held considerable possessions in the Netherlands, to which, after 1530, was added the German county of Nassau. From the time of William the Silent the family dominated Dutch history, bearing the title of stadholder for the greater part of the 17th and 18th cents. The son of the Stadholder William V was made King William I by the Allies in 1815.

ORANGE (oronzh'). Town in Vaucluse dept, France, 24km (15m) N of Avignon. It has remains of a Roman theatre and arch. Pop. (1975) 26,470.

ORANGE (or'anj). Co. Metropolitan area of southern California, USA, the fastest-growing in the country. Oranges and strawberries are grown, and there is a vast aerospace and electronics industry. Disneyland is here, and Santa Ana is the chief town. Pop. met area (1976) 1,706,000.

ORANGE. Town in NSW, Australia, 200km (125m) NW of Sydney. There is a woollen textile industry based on local flocks, and fruit is grown. Pop. (1976) 24,500.

ORANGE. Special species of evergreen tree in the genus *Citrus,* remarkable for bearing blossom and fruit at the same time. They are commercially cultivated in Spain, Israel, Brazil, S Africa, USA, etc., but seem to have originated in SE Asia. Among the principal types are the Jaffa, Maltese blood, tangerine, mandarin, and Seville - the bitter O. used in making marmalade. Os. yield several essential oils.

ORANGE (or'ānj). River of S Africa, rising on the Mont aux Sources in Lesotho and flowing in a W direction to the Atlantic. It runs along the S boundary of the Orange Free State, and was given its name in 1779 in honour of the Dutch stadholder. Length 2,100 km (1,300 m). In 1975 water from the O. was diverted via the O.-Fish River Tunnel to irrigate the semi-arid eastern Cape Province (*see* TUNNEL).

ORANGE, Project. Plan (1980) for a white S African 'homeland' (Projek Oranje) to be estab. on the border between Orange Free State and the Northern Cape. No black would be allowed to live or work there.

ORANGE. Research scientist Peter Bacon with a dwarf orange tree at the New South Wales Department of Agriculture research centre at Yanco. Despite their size, they may be over a dozen years old, and yet bear more fruit than normal trees and new mechanical harvesters are under development to gather the crop. *Photo: Courtesy of the Australian Information Service.*

ORANGE FREE STATE. Prov. of the Rep. of S Africa, to the N of the prov. of the Cape of Good Hope, from which it is separated by the r. Orange. Its surface consists chiefly of plateaux, extending SW from the Drakensberg mts. in the E. The principal rivers are the Vaal and Orange. The most important industry is stock farming, and in the E there is a large area under cultivation. Coal is mined at Vereeniging and at Sasolburg oil fuel is produced from coal; diamonds are found near Jagersfontein and Koffiefontein, and gold at Odendaalsrust. The chief towns are Bloemfontein (the cap.), Harrismith, Smithfield, Kroonstad, and Jacobsdal. The first Boers settled N of the r. Orange about 1820. During the Great Trek of 1836 some 10,000 emigrants settled in this region to get away from British rule. The country was annexed by Sir Harry Smith in 1848, but was granted its independence in 1854, when it became the 'Orange Free State'. As the ally of the S African Republic (Transvaal), it joined in the struggle against the British in the S African War of 1899-1902. In 1900 it was annexed as a British Crown Colony, named the Orange River Colony. In 1910 it became a prov. of the Union of S Africa, and reverted to its old name. Area 129,152 sq.km (49,866 sq.m); pop. (1970) 1,716,350, of whom *c.* 300,000 were white.

ORANGEMEN. An Ulster Protestant society founded in 1795 to combat the United Irishmen and the peasant secret societies, a revival of the Orange Institution (1688) formed in support of William (III) of Orange, the anniversary of whose victory over the Irish at the Boyne (1690), is celebrated by O. on 12 July.

ORANG-UTAN (o'rang-ōō'tahn). Anthropoid ape (*Pongo pygmaeus*), found solely in Borneo and Sumatra. Up to 1.65m (5.5ft) in height, it is covered with long red-brown hair, and lives mainly a solitary arboreal life, feeding chiefly on fruit. It is lethargic, and since it is hunted by local tribesmen for food, as well as by animal collectors, is increasingly rare. It is of amiable temperament and is sometimes considered the most intelligent of the apes: the name means 'man of the forest'.

ORANG-UTAN. A fine example of the female of the species. *Photo; Zoological Society of London.*

ORASUL STALIN. Name 1948-56 of BRASOV.

ORATORIANS. An RC order of secular priests, called in full Congregation of the Oratory of St Philip Neri, formally constituted by St Philip Neri in 1575 at Rome, and characterized by the degree of freedom allowed to individual communities. It was first estab. in England by Cardinal Newman in 1848, and in 1884 Brompton Oratory in London was opened. All churches of the O. are famed for their music.

ORATŌ'RIO. A musical setting of religious incidents, scored for orchestra, chorus, and solo voices, on a scale more dramatic and larger than a cantata. The term derives from St Philip Neri's Oratory in Rome, where settings of the *Laudi spirituali* were performed in the 16th cent. The definite form of O. began in the 17th cent. with Cavalieri, Carissimi, Scarlatti, and Schütz, and reached perfection in such works as J. S. Bach's Christmas O. and St Matthew Passion, and Handel's *The Messiah,* etc. Other famous examples of Os. are Haydn's *Creation* and *Seasons,* Mendelssohn's *Elijah,* and Elgar's *Dream of Gerontius.*

ORCHESTRA (ōr'kestra). A composite group of instruments combining to play music. The 4 sections into which it is divided are the strings, wood-wind, brass, and percussion. Development of the O. is wrapped up with that of music, particularly with opera and symphony. The bowed strings proved its lasting foundation, and during the 17th and 18th cents. wind, percussion, and plucked instruments were gradually added. The strings have 5 separate subsections, first violins, second violins, violas, violon-cellos, and double basses, in strength proportionate to maintain a balance of tone. The wood-wind became standardized by the end of the 18th cent., consisting of a pair each of flutes, oboes, clarinets, and bassoons. Later modifications to

ORATORIO. The composer of several oratorios, it is for the 'Dream of Gerontius' that Sir Edward Elgar is best remembered which, after its initial failure in 1900, has since been recognised as a masterpiece. *Photo: Popperfoto.*

these were the piccolo, cor anglais, bass clarinet, and double bassoon.

A pair each of trumpets and horns sufficed till the late 18th cent., when trombones began to be specified, appearing in triplicate. Since then 2 extra horns and 1 tuba have been added. Two kettledrums were used during the 17th cent., and their number was later raised to 3. From Turkey came the bass drum, cymbals, side-drum, and triangle.

The harp is the only permanent plucked instrument. Other instruments sometimes incl. are the xylophone, celesta, piano, organ, etc.

Instruments of the Orchestra

1st violin	16	Bassoon	2	Tuba	1
2nd violin	16	Piccolo	1	Timpani	3
Viola	12	Cor Anglais	1	Side Drum	1
Violoncello	12	Bass Clarinet	1	Bass Drum	1
Double Bass	8	Double Bassoon	1	Triangle	1
Flute	3			Cymbals	1
Oboe	2	Horn	4	Gong	1
Clarinet	2	Trumpet	4	Harp	1
		Trombone	3		

ORCHID (or'kid). Family of monocotyledonous plants (Orchidaceae) containing some 5,000 species, distributed throughout the world except in the coldest areas, and most numerous in damp equatorial regions. The flowers have 3 sepals and 3 petals. The lowest petal, the labellum, is usually large, and may be spurred, fringed, pouched, or crested. The flowers are sometimes solitary, but more usually are borne in spikes, racemes or panicles, either erect or drooping. Tropical Os. are epiphytes (attached to trees, etc., although nonparasitic), but temperate Os. commonly grow on the ground, e.g. the spotted orchis (*Orchis maculata*) and other British species. Os. are cultivated under glass for the luxury flower trade, and among private collectors, some specimens commanding very high prices.

ORCZY (ort'si), **Baroness** (1865-1947). Hungarian-born novelist, dau. of baron Felix O., she m. an Englishman, Montague Barstow. Going to London in 1881 to study art, she began to write in 1900, and is best remembered as the author of *The Scarlet Pimpernel* (1905). Sir Percy Blakeney, apparently a foppish weakling but actually bold rescuer of victims of the French Revolution, appeared in many sequels.

ORDEAL. A primitive mode of trial and of testing the guilt of an accused person. It is based on the belief that heaven will protect the innocent, and methods used included walking barefoot over glowing ploughshares, carrying a red-hot iron, and dipping the hand into boiling water. In England such tests were largely superseded after the Norman Conquest by trial by battle. Os. are still used among the Indians, Arabs, and Africans.

ORDER. In classical architecture, the column (incl. capital, shaft, and base), and the entablature, considered as an architectural whole. The 5 orders are Doric, Ionic, Corinthian, Tuscan, and Composite. *See also* COLUMN.

ORDER IN COUNCIL. In Britain an order issued by the sovereign with the advice of the Privy Council; in practice it is issued only on the advice of the cabinet. Acts of parliament often provide for the issue of Os. in C. to regulate the detailed administration of their provisions or they may be used to introduce wartime emergency legislation.

ORDNANCE SURVEY. The official mapping of Britain. Its establishment in 1791 followed the making of military surveys in Scotland and elsewhere. The first map - of Kent - was pub. in 1801. Maps of large and small scales have since been produced, and their revision is now the main task of the O.S. Dept, the administration of which is controlled by the Dept of the Environment. A modern survey, begun in 1945, is due for completion in 1982.

Ō'REGON. Mountainous NW state of the USA. The extensive forests are one of the state's principal sources of wealth. The chief rivers are the Columbia (which flows along most of the N boundary) and its tributary, the Snake. The chief towns are Portland, Salem (the cap.), and Eugene. The state of O. is the S part of the much larger O. Country, over the N boundary of which there was a long-standing dispute with Britain, settled in 1846 when it was agreed that the frontier should be extended to the W coast along lat. 49° N. O. Country was made a Territory 1848 from which Washington Territory was detached 1853. O. with its present boundaries entered the Union 1859. Spanish explorers visited the coast in the 16th cent. Robert Gray, a US navigator, discovered and named the Columbia r. in 1792. The state is noted for its strong conservation policy, and for its opposition to further permanent settlement. Area 251,180 sq.km (96,981 sq.m); pop. (1970) 2,091,385.

Ō'REL. Town in the RSFSR, cap. of O. region, situated on the Oka, 320km (200m) SSW of Moscow. It is an important grain market and rail centre with engineering industries. Pop. (1977) 289,000.

O'RENBURG. Town in the RSFSR, cap. of O. region, on the right bank of the Ural r. *c.* 370km (230m) ESE of Kuibyshev. It dates from the early 18th cent. and is an important trading and mining centre. It was called Chkalov 1938-57 in honour of a long-distance flyer. Pop. (1977) 446,000.

ORE'NSE. Town in NW Galicia, Spain, on the r. Miño. Pop. (1970) 73,400.

ORESTES (ōres'tēz). In Greek legend, the son of Agamemnon, and of his wife, Clytemnestra (qq.v.).

ÖRESUND (eresund'). Strait between Sweden and Zealand Is., Denmark, linking the Baltic and North Sea.

ORFORD, Earl of. *See* WALPOLE.

ORGAN. A musical wind instrument of ancient origin, developed from the Pan-pipe and hydraulus, mentioned as early as the 3rd cent. BC. Leather bags and bellows were added, and the hydraulic type more favoured than the pneumatic O., which has since prevailed. Os. were imported to France from Byzantium in the 8th and 9th cents., after which their manufacture in Europe began. The supersession of the old drawslides by the key system dates from the 11th-13th cent., the first chromatic keyboard from 1361. The more recent designs date from the 1809 composition pedal.

The modern O. produces sound from varying-sized pipes under applied pressure. One note only is sounded by each pipe, but these are grouped into stops, which are ranks or scales of pipes prepared to 'speak' by a knob. These, in turn, form part of a sectional O., one of the tonal divisions comprising the whole O. These separate manuals are the great, swell, choir, solo, echo, and pedal Os., controlled by the player's hands and feet. By this grouping and sub-division extremes of tone and volume are obtained.

Apart from its continued use in churches, the O. has been adapted for entertainment. The electrically controlled O. substitutes electrical impulses and relays for some of the air-pressure controls. Those, such as the Hammond Os., built during the 1930s for the large cinemas of the period, incl. many special sound effects as well as colour displays. They are now museum pieces.

ORGANIC CHEMISTRY. The chemistry of carbon compounds. The great number and diversity of these compounds render it convenient to group them separately. They are built up chiefly through the combination of carbon with hydrogen, oxygen and nitrogen. Compounds containing only carbon and hydrogen are known as hydrocarbons.

O.C. is largely the chemistry of a great variety of homologous series, in which the molecular formulae, when arranged in ascending order, form an arithmetical progression with the common difference CH_2. The physical properties undergo a gradual change from one member to the next.

The chain of carbon atoms forming the backbone of an organic molecule may be built up from beginning to end without branching; or it may throw off branches at one or more points. This division of organic compounds is known as the *Open-Chain*, or *Aliphatic* compounds. Sometimes, however, the ropes of carbon atoms curl round and form rings. These constitute the second division of organic compounds known as *Closed-Chain, Ring*, or *Cyclic*, compounds. Other structural varieties are known. Upon the capacity of carbon atoms to form molecular rings and chains depends the infinite variety of organic nature.

In inorganic chemistry a specific formula usually represents one substance only, but in O.C. it is exceptional for a molecular formula to represent only one substance. Substances having the same molecular formula are called *isomers*, and the relationship is known as *isomerism*. Where substances have the same molecular formula, but differ in their structural formulae, they are called *structural isomers*. *Spatial isomers*, or stereoisomers, have the same molecular formula, and also the same structural formula, the difference lying in their spatial dispositions. The study of spatial isomers led to the recognition of a new and extensive field of chemistry, known as *stereochemistry*, or 'chemistry in space'.

Hydrocarbons form one of the most prolific of the many organic types. Typical groups containing only carbon, hydrogen, and oxygen are alcohols, aldehydes, ketones, ethers, esters, carbohydrates, etc. Among nitrogenous types are amides, amines, nitro-compounds, amino-acids, proteins, purines, alkaloids, and many others, both natural and artificial. Other organic types contain sulphur, phosphorus, halogens, etc.

The most fundamental of organic chemical reactions are oxidation, reduction, hydrolysis, condensation, polymerization, and molecular rearrangement. In nature, such changes are often brought about through the agency of promoters known as *enzymes*, which act as catalytic agents in promoting specific reactions. The most fundamental of all natural processes is *synthesis*, or building up. In living plant and animal organisms the energy stored in carbohydrate molecules, derived originally from sunlight, is released by slow oxidation and utilized by the organisms. The complex carbohydrates thereby revert to carbon dioxide and water, from whence they were built up with absorption of energy. Thus, a so-called carbon food cycle obtains in nature. In a corresponding nitrogen food cycle, complex proteins are synthesized in anture from carbon dioxide, water, soil nitrates, ammonium salts, etc., and these proteins ultimately revert to the elementary raw materials from whence they sprung, with the discharge of their energy of chemical combination.

Originally it was believed that carbon compounds derived from plant and animal sources could not be artificially prepared in the laboratory, but now many organic compounds can be synthesized, some of which are unknown in nature.

ORGANIC FARMING. Farming without the use of chemical sprays or fertilizers. Crop yields may be a third less, but whereas the conventional system uses up fertility, so that chemical fertilizers must be perpetually used, the organic system builds it up.

ORGANISATION DE L'ARMÉE SECRÈTE (OAS). French terrorist organization formed in 1961 with the aim of overthrowing the constitutional régime in Algeria and establishing *Algérie française*. It was headed by Gen. Raoul Salan (imprisoned 1962–8).

ORGANIZATION FOR ECONOMIC CO-OPERATION AND DEVELOPMENT (OECD). New title of the OEEC from 1961, when the USA and Canada became full members and its original scope was extended to incl. development aid. Its HQ are in Paris.

ORGANIZATION OF AFRICAN UNITY. By its charter, adopted at the Addis Ababa Conference of Heads of African States (30 independent countries were represented) in 1963, it is pledged to eradicate colonialism, emancipate still dependent territories, and improve conditions in the economic, cultural and political spheres throughout Africa and its adjoining islands. The permanent HQ is at Addis Ababa.

There is also a French-speaking Joint African and Mauritian Organization (*Organization Commune africaine et mauritienne:* OCAM), originating in 1962, which works within the framework of the OAU for African solidarity: HQ Yaoundé.

ORGANIZATION OF AMERICAN STATES. In 1890 at Washington, under the auspices of the US Sec. of State James G. Blaine, the *International Union of the American Republics* was estab. to encourage friendly relations. Its central office at Washington, known from 1910 as the *Pan-American Union,* became in 1948 the central and permanent organ of the more comprehensive O. of A.S.

ORGANIZATION OF CENTRAL AMERICAN STATES (*Organizacion de Estados Centro Americanos:* ODECA). The first organization of this name, estab. in 1951, was superseded by a new one in 1962: membership – Costa Rica, El Salvador, Guatemala, Honduras, and Nicaragua, provision being made for Panama to join at a later date. The permanent HQ is in Guatemala City.

ORGANIZATION OF THE PETROLEUM EXPORTING COUNTRIES. Organization (OPEC) estab. in 1960 to co-ordinate the interests of oil-producing states world-wide. It also regards itself as a vehicle for economic justice and improving the position of Third World states by forcing the developed world to provide them with technology and open their markets to the goods which would then be produced.

ORIENTEERING. Sport of pedestrian route-finding, developed in Scandinavia and introduced to Britain *c.* 1960. Competitors start at minute intervals, with a large-scale map marked with the exact location of control points about .8km (0.5m) apart, where their control cards are stamped.

ORIGAMI (origah'mi). The art of folding paper into various shapes and forms, such as dolls and birds, with a minimum of cutting and drawing. Popular in Japan from the 10th cent., it is now practised both as an art and an educational activity for children.

ORIGEN (ō'rijen) (*c.* 185–*c.* 254). A Father of the Christian Church. He was b. probably at Alexandria, and his father was the Christian martyr, Leonidas, beheaded in 202. After teaching at Alexandria 204–32 he was banished and settled in Caesarea, where he founded another school. Under Decius in 250 he was arrested and put to torture at Tyre, where he d.

His writings covered every aspect of Christianity, but he is chiefly remembered for his fanciful method of allegorical exegesis of the Bible.

ORIGINAL SIN. The Christian doctrine that, as a result of Adam's fall, man is by nature corrupt, and can obtain salvation only through divine grace.

ORINŌ'CO. River of northern S America, flowing for *c.* 2,400 km (1,500 m) through Venezuela, and forming for *c.* 320km (200m) the boundary with Colombia in which rise the Guaviare, Meta, Apure, and other left-bank tributaries incl. the Ventuari, Caura and Caroni. The O. is navigable by large steamers for 1,125 km (700m) from its Atlantic delta. Rapids obstruct the upper river.

ORIOLES (ō'ri-ōlz). Passeriform birds of the Oriolidae family, well known in Europe. They are shy and restless, with brilliant plumage. Other species extend to Asia and Africa, while in America the name is applied to the Icteridae family. The golden O. visits Britain.

ORI'SSA. State of the Rep. of India, between W Bengal to the NE and the Bay of Bengal and Andhra to the SW. The Mahanadi flows through the state, and iron is mined. The state of O. includes the former British prov. of O., conquered 1803 and made an autonomous prov. 1937, and 22 former princely states. Cuttack, the largest city, was replaced as cap. by Bhubaneswar in 1956; Puri is famous for its temple of Jagannath or Juggernaut. Area 155,825 sq.km (60,164 sq.m); pop. (1971) 21,935,000.

ORIZABA (ōrēthah'bah). City of Veracruz state, Mexico, 105km (65m) SW of Veracruz. It is a popular resort and industries incl. brewing, paper making, and textiles. O. peak to the N of the city, now known by its Aztec name Citlaltepec 'star mtn', erupted 1687 but is now dormant: at 5,700 m (18,700 ft) the highest mtn in Mexico. Pop. (1970) 90,000.

ORKNEY. Former co. of Scotland, created in 1975 an islands area. It comprises a group of is. off the N coast, separated from the mainland by the Pentland Firth 9.5km (6m) wide. Of *c.* 90 islands and islets, 28 are inhabited. The most important are Pomona (or 'Mainland'), largest of the group, N and S Ronaldsay, Hoy, Rousay, Stronsay, Westray, Shapinsay, Eday and Sanday. The admin. HQ is Kirkwall on Pomona. The climate is comparatively mild because of the Gulf Stream. The highest point is Ward Hill (475m/1,560 ft) on Hoy. Fishing and farming are carried on. Inhabited since prehistoric times (*see* SKARA BRAE), the Os. are the *Orcades* of ancient geographers. They were conquered by Harold I (Fairhair) of Norway in 876, pledged to James III of Scotland for the dowry of Margaret of Denmark 1468, and the dowry not being paid, annexed by Scotland in 1472. Scapa Flow, used as a base by the RN in both world wars, is between Pomona and Hoy. It was here that the surrendered German fleet scuttled itself on 21 June 1919. Area 984 sq.km (380 sq.m); pop. (1979) 18,055.

ORKNEYS. The houses of the Neolithic village of Skara Brae are of drystone construction, which was covered with clay in exposed areas. The alleyways linking them, one of which runs off to the left, were only 1.2 m (4 ft) high. *Photo: Courtesy of the British Tourist Authority.*

ORKNEY CAUSEWAY. Construction put up in the F.W.W., completed in 1943 during the S.W.W., joining 4 of the Orkney Is., built to protect the fleet from intrusion through the eastern entrances to Scapa Flow. It links Kirkwall and the is. by road.

ORKNEYS, South. *See* SOUTH ORKNEYS.

ORLA'NDO, Vittorio Emanuele (1860-1952). Italian politician. As PM 1917-19 he attended the Paris Peace Conference, forming one of the 'big four' with Lloyd George, Wilson, and Clemenceau, but dissatisfaction with his handling of the Adriatic settlement led to his resignation. He at first supported Mussolini, but was in retirement 1925-46, when he returned first to the assembly and then the senate.

ORLANDO. City of Florida, USA, named in 1857 after Orlando Reeves, a soldier killed in a clash with Indians. Centrally situated at the hub of communications, it has grown phenomenally industrially. Pop. (1970) met. area 595,000.

ORLÉANS (orlā-oń'). Capital of Loiret dept, France, formerly the cap. of the old prov. of Orléanais, situated on the Loire, 115km (70m) SW of Paris. O., of pre-Roman origin, is famous for its association with Joan of Arc (q.v.), who liberated it from the English in 1429, and is an important commercial centre, industries incl. textiles, engineering and processed foods. Pop. (1975) 88,500.

ORMANDY, Eugene (1899–1985). American conductor. B. in Budapest, he became a violin virtuoso, then went to USA, and was music director to the Philadelphia Orchestra 1936–80.

ORMOLU (or'mol o͞o; Fr. *or moulu,* ground gold). A gold-tinted alloy of copper, zinc, and sometimes tin, used for mountings of furniture.

ORMONDE (awr'mond), **James Butler,** duke of (1610-88). Irish general. He commanded the royalist troops in Ireland 1641-50 during the Irish rebellion and the English revolution, and was Lord-Lieut. 1644-7, 1661-9, and 1677-84. He was created a marquess in 1642 and a duke in 1661. His grandson, **James,** 2nd duke (1665-1745), succeeded Marlborough as C-in-C in 1711, but was impeached in 1715 for Jacobite intrigues, and exiled.

ORMUZD. *See* AHURA MAZDA.

ORNE (orn). French river rising E of Sées and flowing NW, then NE to the English Channel below Caen. A ship canal runs alongside it from Caen to the sea at Ouistreham. The O. is 152km (94m) long and gives its name to a dept.

ORNITHO'LOGY. The section of zoology concerned with the study of birds (q.v.). It covers not only scientific aspects relating to the structure and classification of birds, but also the activities of the many amateurs in all countries interested primarily in the natural beauty of birds, their habits, song, flight, etc., secondarily in their value to agriculture as destroyers of insect pests. This interest has led to the formation of societies for their protection (developing into their study), of which the Society for the Protection of Birds (1889) in Britain was the first; it received a royal charter in 1904. The Audubon Society (1905) in the USA has similar aims. Other countries now have similar societies, and there is an International Council for Bird Preservation with its HQ at the Natural History Museum. The HQ of the British Trust for O. is at Beech Grove, Tring, Herts. Migration, age, pollution effects on birds, etc., are monitored by ringing (trained govt.-licensed operators fit numbered metal rings to captured specimens with a return address). Legislation in various countries to protect wild birds dates from a British Act of 1880.

ORONTES (oront'ēz). River rising in Lebanon, nr Baalbek, and flowing through Syria to the Mediterranean: 400km (250m). It is chiefly used for irrigation.

ORPEN, Sir William Newenham Montague (1878-1931). Irish artist. He studied at Dublin and London, became famous as a portraitist, was knighted in 1918, and was elected RA in 1919.

ORPHEUS (-fūs). Mythical Greek poet and musician. He was the son of Apollo and a muse, and m. Eurydice, who d. from the bite of a snake. O. went down to Hades to bring her back, relying on his sweet singing to charm the nether gods. Her return to life was granted on condition that he walked ahead of her without looking back. O. broke this condition, and Eurydice was irretrievably lost. In his grief, he despised the Maenad women of Thrace, and was torn in pieces by them.

The Orphic religion was one of the mystical cults of Greece, its most distinctive features in doctrine being the belief in a future life in which the condition of O.'s worshippers could be bettered by asceticism and the performance of mystical rites. Remains of an Orphic temple were identified 1980 nr. Hungerford, England.

ORRIS ROOT. The underground stem of species of iris grown in S Europe. Violet-scented, it is used in perfumery.

ORSK. Town in Orenburg region, RSFSR, at the junction of the Or and Ural rivers. Originally a fortress, it has large petroleum refineries fed by a pipeline from Guriev, locomotive and aluminium plants, etc. Pop. (1977) 244,000.

ORTEGA Y. GASSET (awrtā'gah-ē-gah'set), **José** (1883-1955). Spanish philosopher and critic. He considered Communism and Fascism the cause of the downfall of western civilization. His *Toward a Philosophy of History* (1941) contains philosophical reflections on the State, and an interpretation of the meaning of human history.

ORTHOPAEDICS (-pē'diks). The science of correcting deformities. It progressed tremendously during both world wars. Among its most important techniques are the treatment of fractures, bone and nerve grafting, the restoration of function after any type of paralysis, the reconstruction of joints, and especially rehabilitation, in which the patient is treated as a whole and all the resources of surgery, medicine, psychology, physical training and occupational therapy are concentrated on him. Electronics play an increasing role.

ORTHO'PTERA. Order of terrestrial insects, incl. grasshoppers, crickets, and locusts (qq.v.).

O'RTOLAN. A bird (*Emberiza hortulana*) of the bunting family, common in Europe and W Asia. Migrating southward or returning, it is netted, then fed and killed for the table. It is variously coloured, with a grey head.

ORVIETO (orvē-ā'tō). City in Terni prov., Italy. It stands on an eminence, NE of Lake Bolsena. The magnificent 14th cent. cathedral contains sculptures by Orcagna and frescoes by Luca Signorelli and Fra Angelico, and doors (1963) by Emilio Greco (q.v.). It is on the site of Volsinii, one of the 12 Etruscan cities, which was destroyed by the Romans 280 BC; it has many Etruscan remains. Pop. (1977) 25,500.

ORWELL, George. Name adopted by British author Eric Blair (1903-50). B. in India, he was ed. at Eton as a King's Scholar, and for 5 yrs served in the Burmese police force, an experience reflected in the novel *Burmese Days* (1935). Adventures as dishwasher, schoolmaster, and bookshop assistant were related in *Down and Out in Paris and London* (1933) and service for the Republican cause in the Spanish Civil War in *Homage to Catalonia* (1938). His greatest book is the satire *Animal Farm* (1945) which incl. such sayings as 'All animals are equal, but some are more equal than others', but the greatest sensation was made by *1984* (1949) which carries state control of existence to the ultimate.

ORYX (or'iks). Genus of large African desert antelope, incl. 3 species, which extend to Syria and Arabia, but are almost extinct. Attempts are being made to breed them in captivity. In profile the 2 long horns appear as one and the O. may have given rise to the legend of the unicorn.

OSAKA (ōsah'ka). Second-largest city and a port of Japan. Situated on the island of Honshu, and lying on a plain sheltered by hills and opening on to O. bay, O. is honeycombed with waterways. Oldest city of Japan, it was at times the seat of govt 4-8th cents., was a mercantile centre in the 18th, and in the 20th set the pace for Japan's revolution based on light industries. Manufactures incl. iron and steel, ships, chemicals, and textiles. It is a tourist centre for Kyoto and the Seto Inland Sea, and linked with Tokyo by fast electric train 200kph (124 mph). An underground shopping and leisure city (1951) was so successful it was a model for others throughout Japan. The univ. was founded 1931. Pop. (1973) 2,681,000.

OSAKA. Osaka Castle, completed in 1586, but destroyed several times, took 40,000 workmen 3 years to construct. The donjon, above, was rebuilt in 1931. *Photo: Courtesy of the Japan Information Centre.*

OSBORNE, Dorothy (1627-95). English letter-writer. In 1655 she m. Sir William Temple (1628-99), to whom she wrote her letters (1652-4), first pub. in 1888.

OSBORNE, John James (1929-). English dramatist and actor. He became well known as an 'angry young man' when his first play, *Look Back in Anger* (1956), in which the hero satirises middle-class life, was produced. His later plays incl. *The Entertainer* (1957), and *Luther* (1960). He was m. to the actress Mary Ure (1957-63), film critic Penelope Gilliat (1963-8), and actress Jill Bennett from 1968.

OSBORNE HOUSE. A favourite residence of Queen Victoria, for whom it was built in 1845, 1m SE of Cowes in the Isle of Wight, England. It was presented to the nation by Edward VII.

OSCAR. The name of 2 kings of Sweden and Norway. **Oscar I** (1799-1859) succeeded his father, Charles XIV, in 1844, while his younger son, **Oscar II** (1829-1907), came to the throne in 1872. He abandoned the title of king of Norway on the separation of the two kingdoms in 1905.

OSCAR. Annual cinema award in various fields (10in bronze-gilt statuette) estab. 1927 by the American Academy of Motion Pictures, and nicknamed O. 1931 because a new secretary exclaimed, 'That's like my uncle Oscar!'

OSCILLATOR. An O. is a generator producing a desired oscillation. It is an essential part of a radio transmitter, as it generates the high-frequency carrier signal necessary for radio communication. There are many types of O. for different purposes involving various arrangements of valves or transistors, inductors, capacitors, and resistors, and the frequency is often controlled by the vibrations set up in a crystal, e.g. quartz.

OSCILLOGRAPH (osil'ograf). Instrument for recording oscillations, electrical or mechanical; an **oscilloscope** shows variations in electrical potential on the screen of a cathode ray tube, by means of deflection of a beam of electrons.

OSHO'GBŌ. Town in western Nigeria, 200km (125m) NE of Lagos. It is a market for palm products and cocoa, and cotton textiles are made. Pop. (1975) 282,000.

OSIER (ō'zhier). A tree or shrub of the willow genus (*Salix*), cultivated for basket making.

OSIJEK (osē'yek). Town and r. port in Croatia, Yugoslavia, on the Drava, with textile and other industries. Pop. (1971) 94,000.

OSĪ'RIS (Egypt. *Ausar*). Ancient Egyptian god who personified the power of good; he was the enemy of Set, the god of evil. He was united in the sacred triad with his wife Isis, and his son Horus. Slain by Set, he was avenged by Horus, and went to rule over the dead in the underworld.

OSLO (oz'lō). Cap. of Norway, on the SE coast, at the head of Oslo fjord. The first recorded settlement was made by Harald III (Hardrada) *c.* 1050 in Ekeberg, but the modern city lies mainly to the N and W of the fortress of Akershus, built by Haakon V in the late 13th cent. This change was due to Christian IV who re-planned the city after the fire of 1624; in his honour it was called Christiania from 1624 to 1924. Important buildings incl. the Royal Palace, the Parl. House, the univ. (1811), the national theatre, and the new town hall (1931-50). O. is a prosperous seaport and has considerable shipbuilding, engineering, and textile industries. Pop. (1978) 460,400.

OSMAN or **Othman I** (1259-1326). Turkish sultan. He began his career in the service of the Seljuk Turks, but in 1299 he set up a kingdom of his own in Bithynia and assumed the title of sultan. He conquered a great part of Asia Minor, so founding the Turkish Empire. His successors were known as 'sons of O.', whence the term 'Ottoman' is derived.

O'SMIUM (Gk *osme*, odour). Bluish-white, hard, crystalline metal, very heavy and infusible: symbol Os, at. no. 76, at. wt. 190.2. Discovered in 1803 by Tennant in residue left when crude platinum was dissolved in aqua regis (concentrated nitric and hydrochloric acids), it is found in platinum-bearing river sands and with iridium in osmiridium. Heated in air it gives off a pungently irritating poisonous vapour. It is used for lamp filaments, with iridium to form a very hard alloy suitable for pen-nibs and fine machine bearings, and, when finely divided, as a catalyst.

O'SNABRÜCK. City and episcopal see in the Land of Lower Saxony, W Germany, 115km (70m) W of the city of Hanover. Before the S.W.W., when O. was severely damaged, it had fine examples of both Gothic and Renaissance architecture; O. bishopric was founded by Charlemagne, 783. Industries incl. engineering, iron and steel, textiles and clothing, paper, and processed foods. The Treaty of Westphalia was signed at O. and Münster in 1648. Pop. (1977) 160,000.

OSPREY. Bird of prey (*Pandion haliaetus*), known in America from its diet as the fish hawk, and formerly breeding in Scotland. Dark brown above and a striking white below, it measures 0.6m (2ft), with a 2m (6ft) wingspread. The 'O.' plumes of the milliner are those of the egret (q.v.).

OSSA. Mtn in Thessaly, Greece, 1,978 m (6,490 ft). The vale of Tempe separates it from Olympus. Mt Pelion, to the S, is said to have been piled on O. by the Giants to enable them to scale Olympus. **Mount O.** 1,620 m (5,305 ft) is the highest peak in Tasmania.

OSSETIA (osēsh'ia). Area in the Caucasus inhabited chiefly by a people called Ossets or Alans. It is divided into **North O.**, an ASSR of the RSFSR, cap. Ordzhonikidze; and **South O.**, an autonomous region of Georgian SSR, cap. Tshkinvali. N.O. has some industry served by water-power from the r. Terak and grows maize, fruit, and market-garden crops; S.O. is a mountain health resort with lumbering, fruit growing and livestock rearing. Ossets may be of Persian origin, amd speak Ossetic, a language of the Iranian group. They were first conquered by the Russians in 1802.

OSSIAN (osh'ian). Irish hero and poet, properly called Oisin. He is represented as the son of Finn Mac Cumhaill, *c.* AD 250, and as having lived to tell the tales of Finn and the Ulster heroes to St Patrick, *c.* 400. The publication, from 1760 onwards, of the 'Ossianic' poems of J. Macpherson (q.v.), has made O.'s name familiar throughout Europe.

O'SSORY. Ancient kingdom, lasting until 1110, in Leinster, Ireland; the name is preserved in existent Church of Ireland and RC bishoprics.

OSTADE (ostah'de), **Adriaen van** (1610-85). Dutch painter and engraver, famous for his pictures of tavern scenes, village fairs, etc. B. at Haarlem, he studied under F. Hals. His brother, **Isaac van O.** (1621-49), excelled in winter landscapes, and roadside and farmyard scenes.

OSTEND. Seaport and pleasure resort of Belgium, in the prov. of W Flanders, 108km (67m) NW of Brussels. It has a fine promenade over *c.* 5km (3m) long, and a casino and royal chalet on the sea front. There are large docks, and the Belgian fishing fleet has its headquarters here. Pop. (1978) 71,320.

O'STEO-ARTHRITIS. Degenerative disease of the joints in later life, often resulting in disabling stiffness and wasting of muscles. Formerly thought to be due to wear and tear, it has been shown to be less common in the physically active. It appears to be linked with crystal deposits, in the form of calcium phosphate, in cartilage, a discovery which in the late 1970s suggested hope of eventual prevention.

OSTEOLOGY. Part of the science of anatomy, dealing with bones and their uses. *See* BONE.

OSTEOMYELITIS (o'stē-ōmī-elī'tis). Infection of bone. The organism may be introduced through an injury or through the blood-stream, especially shortly after an illness. The symptoms are high fever, severe illness, and pain over the limb. If the infection is at the surface of the bone it may quickly form an abscess; if it is deep in the bone marrow it may spread into the circulation and set up fatal blood poisoning.

OSTEOPATHY. A system of unorthodox medical teaching and practice which regards the chief cause of disease as a disorder of structure, a 'lesion' in tissue of any kind, but most commonly a minor displacement of one or more vertebrae. The treatment combines manipulation of the lesion, with other more orthodox remedies. In Great Britain osteopaths have no legal standing.

O'STIA. Ancient Italian town and harbour near the mouth of the Tiber. Dating from *c.* 330 BC, it was the port of Rome and at one time had a pop. of *c.* 100,000; in modern times a seaside resort (Ostia Mare) has been estab. nearby.

OST'POLITIK. German 'eastern policy': W German Chancellor Brandt's policy of rapprochement with the Communist bloc from 1971, pursued to a modified extent also by Schmidt.

O'STRACISM (-siz-). Political device to preserve order in ancient Athens. As a result of votes written on oyster-shells (Gk *ostraka*, whence the name), political personages might be exiled for a period of 10 years.

OSTRACŌ'DA. A sub-class of Crustacea. Found in both salt and fresh water, these minute animals have a bivalve shell enclosing the body and limbs.

O'STRAVA. Town in Czechoslovakia, cap. of N Moravian region created 1960, NE of Brno, in a coal-mining district. It has heavy iron works and furnaces. Pop. (1970) 280,000.

OSTRICH. Genus (*Struthio*) of flightless birds found in Africa and Arabia. The male may be *c.* 2.5m (8ft) tall and weigh 135kg (300lb), and is the largest of extant birds. Living in family groups of 1 cock with several hens, the O. has exceptionally strong legs and feet (2-toed) which enable it to run at high speed and are also used in defence. The beautiful tail feathers have commercial value and Os. are bred in farms, especially in S Africa. *See* RATITAE.

OSTROGOTHS. *See* GOTHS.

ŌSTWALD (ōst'valt), **Wilhelm** (1853-1932). German chemist. He specialized in electrochemistry, and estab. the importance of catalysts, such as those forming the basis of the petrochemical industry. He was awarded a Nobel prize in 1909.

OSTRICH. A two-week-old ostrich surveys its shell at the Tropical Bird Garden at Rode. A second chick died in its egg, unable to break through. *Photo: The Times.*

OSWALD, St (*c.* 605-42). King of Northumbria. While exiled in Iona, he was converted to Christianity, and in 634 won the Northumbrian crown. With the assistance of St Aidan he furthered the spread of Christianity until he was defeated and killed by the heathen king Penda of Mercia.

OSWESTRY (oz'estri). English market town in Salop, near the Welsh border. There is a church dedicated to St Oswald, king of Northumbria, who was killed here in 642. Agricultural machinery, plastics, clothing, etc., are made. Pop. (1974) 12,000.

OTARU (ōtahroo). Fishing port on W coast of Hokkaido, Japan, with paper mills; processes fish and makes sake. Pop. (1977) 187,000.

OTHMA'N (*c.* 574 656). Arabian caliph. A son in law of Mohammed, he was elected caliph in 644. Under his rule the Arabs became a naval power and captured Cyprus, but his personal weaknesses led to his assassination.

OTHMAN I. *See* OSMAN.

OTRA'NTO. Seaport and archiepiscopal see in Apulia, Italy, on the Strait of O. The cathedral was begun in 1080. Pop. (1970) 4,300.

O'TTAWA. Cap. of Canada, in the prov. of Ontario, occupying a hilly region overlooking the r. Ottawa, 160km (100m) W of Montreal. It is divided by the Rideau Canal - to the W Upper Town, to the E Lower Town. There are 2 falls providing power for the city, viz. the Chaudière Falls, on the Ottawa, and the Rideau Falls. The principal buildings are the govt buildings on Parl. Hill, the RC cathedral of Notre Dame, Christ Church cathedral, the Nat. Museum, the Nat. Art Gallery, the Observatory, Rideau Hall - the gov.-gen.'s residence - and the Nat. Arts Centre (1969). The chief industry is lumbering, and wood pulp and paper are manufactured. The city was founded when a body of men under John By were building the Rideau Canal, 1826-32, and was named Bytown in By's honour; it was renamed O. (from the Outaouac Indians who traded furs with the French in the 17th cent.) in 1854 and chosen by Queen Victoria as cap. of Canada in 1858. Pop. (1976) met. area 693,500.

OTTAWA AGREEMENTS. The trade agreements concluded at the Imperial Economic Conference, held at Ottawa in 1932, between Britain and the Dominions (except the Irish Free State), India, and S Rhodesia. The

Dominions agreed to lower their preferential tariffs on British manufactures, while Britain admitted almost all Dominion produce free of duty, granted preferences to the rest, and increased duties on foreign imports competing with Dominion produce. The agreements marked the abandonment by Britain of her traditional free-trade policy.

OTTER. Aquatic carnivore of the weasel family. The O. of Europe and Asia (*Lutra lutra*) has a broad head, elongated body covered by grey-brown fur, short legs, and webbed feet: incl. a 45cm (1½ft) tail, it measures over a metre (*c.* 3½ft). It lives on fish and in Britain is hunted. There are a no. of American species, e.g. the larger *L. canadensis* of N America and the commercially valuable fur-bearing sea O. (*Latax lutris*) of the N Pacific.

OTTO. Name of 4 Holy Roman emperors. **Otto I** (912-73) succeeded in 936, restored the power of the empire, asserted his authority over the Pope and the nobles, ended the Magyar menace by his victory at the Lechfeld in 955, and re-founded the East Mark, or Austria, as a barrier against them. **Otto IV** (*c.* 1182-1218), elected emperor in 1198, engaged in controversy with Innocent III, and was defeated by the Pope's ally, Philip of France, at Bouvines in 1214.

OTTOMAN EMPIRE. Moslem Empire founded in Turkey *c.* AD 1300, succeeding the Seljuk Empire. Driven out of central Asia in 1402, the Turks recovered and captured Constantinople in 1453, destroying the remnants of the Byzantine Empire. After various conquests the O.E. by the end of the 16th cent. extended from Hungary to Egypt and parts of Persia. From then a period of disintegration followed until in 1920 the O.E. came to an end, being replaced by the Rep. of Turkey (q.v.). *See* SULEIMAN.

OTWAY, Thomas (1652-85). British dramatist. B. near Midhurst, Sussex, he wrote for the stage from 1675, his chief plays being *The Orphan* (1680) and *Venice Preserved* (1682). He d. destitute in London.

OUDENAARDE (ow'denahrde). Small town of E Flanders, Belgium, on the Scheldt, 28km (18m) SSW of Ghent. O. was the site of Marlborough's victory over the French in 1708. Pop. (1970) 23,000.

OUDH (owd). E part of a former prov. of British India, the United Provs. of Agra and Oudh, 1901-47. O. lay between the Nepal frontier and the Ganges; Lucknow was the cap. Anciently a kingdom, it was under Mogul rule until it regained independence 1732-1856 when the British deposed the king. Area 62,000 sq.km (24,000 sq.m). From 1950 it formed part of the state of Uttar Pradesh.

OUESSANT. French form of USHANT.

OUAGADOUGOU (wagadōō'gōō). Cap. of Upper Volta, a commercial and industrial centre. Pop. (1975) 168,600.

OUIDA (oo-ē'da). Pseudonym of British novelist Marie Louise de la Ramée (1839-1908), author of highly coloured romances, e.g. *Under Two Flags* (1867) and *Moths* (1880).

OUJDA (oojdah'). Town in N Morocco. Close to the frontier with Algeria, it has lead and coalmining industries. It is linked by rail with the Mediterranean at Ghazaouet, E to Algeria, and S with Colomb-Béchar in Algier on the Sahara route. Pop. (1971) 175,530.

OULU. Port in Finland, cap. of O. dept. It stands on the Gulf of Bothnia at the mouth of the r. O., which drains Lake O. It grew up round a castle built by the Swedes in 1375 (the Swedish name for the town being Uleåborg), and has a cathedral (1830) and univ. (1958). There are saw mills, flour mills, tanneries, shipbuilding yards, etc. Pop. (1977) 92,460.

OUNCE. A unit of weight, the 12th part of a pound troy = 480 grains; in avoirdupois, the 16th part of a pound = 437.5 grains; in metric, 28 grams. The fluid O. is a measure of capacity, in the UK equivalent to an avoirdupois O. of distilled water at 62°C.

OUSE (ōōz). Name of several British rivers. The Great O. rises in Northants, and after winding some 250km (160m) it enters the Wash N of King's Lynn. A huge sluice across the Great O., near King's Lynn, part of extensive flood-control works, was opened in 1959. The Yorkshire O. is formed by the junction of the Ure and Swale near Boroughbridge, and joins the Trent to form the Humber. The Sussex O. rises between Horsham and Cuckfield, and flows through the S Downs to enter the English Channel at Newhaven.

OUSEL or **ouzel** (ōōzl). Ancient name of the blackbird, now applied to the dipper (or water-O.) and ring-O. Water-Os. occur in Europe and in the Americas.

OUTBACK. Any unspecified inland region of Australia away from the settled areas, and unsuited to settlement unless irrigation, etc., becomes possible.

OUTBACK. Dogged by drought, dust-storms and despair, a picture that sums up the spirit of the outback, that daunts the settler and haunts the artist. *Photo: Fred Combs/Camera Press.*

OUTLAWRY. Ancient punishment, now virtually obsolete, for felony and misdemeanour, which meant that the outlaw might be apprehended by any person, and lost all his civil rights, his lands and goods were forfeit to the Crown.

OUTRAM (ōōt'ram), **Sir James** (1803-63). British general. B. in Derbyshire, he entered the Indian Army in 1819, served in the Afghan and Sikh Wars, and commanded in the Persian campaign of 1857. On the outbreak of the Mutiny he co-operated with Havelock to raise the siege of Lucknow, and held the city until relieved by Sir Colin Campbell.

OVAL, The. A cricket ground, dating from 1846, the headquarters of the Surrey County Cricket Club, at Kennington, London, England. The first Test Match between England and Australia was played here in 1880.

OVARIES. The pair of organs which in the female generate the ova, or egg-cells, from which, if they are fertilized, grow the offspring. In woman they are 2 whitish rounded bodies *c.* 25mm (1in) by 35mm (1.5in) near the ends of the Fallopian tubes. The ovum develops in the Graafian follicle and bursts out about the 13th day after menstruation starts. In its place grows the 'yellow body' (*corpus luteum*). If the ovum is fertilized this persists until near full term; otherwise it dies off. The Os. also secrete the hormones responsible for the secondary sexual characteristics of the female, such as smooth, hairless skin and large breasts.

OVENS RIVER. River in Victoria, Australia, a tributary of the Murray: the valley attracts tourists.

OVERIJSSEL (ō'verīsel). A prov. of the Netherlands, lying N of Gelderland, S of Drenthe, and watered by the Ijssel and the Vecht. Zwolle is the cap. Sheep and cattle rearing and dairy farming are the chief occupations. Area 3,800 sq.km (1,470 sq.m); pop. (1977) 1,001,270.

OVERLANDERS. Australian drovers who in the 19th cent. opened up new territory by driving their cattle to new stations, or to market, before the establishment of regular stock routes.

OVERLAND TELEGRAPH. The cable erected 1870-2 linking Port Augusta in S. Australia and Darwin in Northern Territory, and the latter by undersea cable to Java: it ended the communications isolation of the continent.

OVERTURE. A piece of instrumental music, usually preceding an opera. There are also Os. to suites, plays, etc., and 'concert' overtures such as Elgar's *Cockaigne* and John Ireland's descriptive *London Overture.* The use of an O. in opera came into being during the 17th cent., the 'Italian' O. consisting of 2 quick movements interspersed with a slow one, and the 'French' of a quick movement between 2 in slower tempo.

O'VID (43 BC-AD 17). Roman poet, whose full name was Publius Ovidius Naso. B. at Sulmo, he studied rhetoric in Rome in preparation for a legal career, but soon turned to literature. In AD 8 he was banished by Augustus to Tomi, on the Black Sea, where he d.: this punishment was supposedly for his immoral *Ars amatoria,* but was probably due to some connection with Julia, the profligate dau. of Augustus. Among his works are the youthful *Amores;* the *Heroides,* fictitious love-letters of legendary heroines; the *Metamorphoses,* mythical stories of miraculous transformations; the *Fasti,* forming an incomplete poetic calendar; and the fruits of his exile, the elegiac *Tristia* and *Epistulae ex Ponto.*

OVIEDO (ōvē-ā'dō). An episcopal city, cap. of O. prov., Spain, 25km (16m) S of the Bay of Biscay. The cathedral dates from the 14th cent., and there is a univ. (1604). O. makes textiles, matches, chocolate, sugar, etc. Pop. (1970) 154,120.

OVUM. An egg-cell which, if it is fertilized by fusion with a spermatozoon (conception), attaches itself to the rich lining of the womb; there it grows by cell division and differentiation into a child.

OWEN, Alun (Davies) (1925-). British writer. A Bevin boy in the mines during the S.W.W., he gained stage experience in repertory at Perth and Birmingham, spent a year with the Old Vic, and then in 1957 started to write. Beginning in radio, he became well known for his TV plays, e.g. *No Trams to Lime Street* (1959) and *You Can't Win 'Em All* (1962).

OWEN, David (1938-). British Labour statesman. A doctor, he became a research fellow at the medical unit of St Thomas's Hospital (1966-8), also entering Parliament in 1966. He was Min. of State, Health and Social Security 1974-6, transferred to the Foreign Office in 1976, and in 1977 on the death of Crosland, succeeded as Foreign and Commonwealth Secretary until 1979. In 1981 he was associated with Shirley Williams, William Rodgers, and Roy Jenkins in founding the Social Democratic Party, and in 1983 succeeded Jenkins as its leader.

OWEN. David Owen (far right) with Shirley Williams and Roy Jenkins, associated with him in the foundation of the Social Democratic Party. *Photo: Press Association.*

OWEN, Robert (1771-1858). British Socialist and Co-operator. B. at Newtown, Montgomery, he became manager in 1800 of a mill at New Lanark, where by improving working and housing conditions and by providing schools he created a model community. From 1817 he proposed that 'villages of co-operation', self-supporting communities run on Socialist lines, should be founded; these, he believed, would ultimately replace private ownership. After an unsuccessful attempt to run such a community in the USA, he organized the Grand National Consolidated Trades Union in 1833, in order that the unions might take over industry and run it co-operatively. Although this scheme collapsed in 1834, O.'s ideas did much to stimulate the co-operative movement.

OWEN, Wilfred (1893-1918). British poet. B. at Plas Wilmot, Oswestry, in 1913 he went to France as a tutor, returning to England to enlist in 1915, and was killed in action a week before the Armistice. His poetry expresses his hatred of war.

OWEN FALLS. Cataract in Uganda on the White Nile, 4km (2.5m) below the point at which the river leaves Lake Victoria. A dam, built 1949-60, provides hydro-electricity for Uganda and Kenya, and helps to control the flood waters.

OWENS, James 'Jesse' (1913-80). American Black athlete. Of superb grace and versatility, he excelled in running on the flat and over hurdles, and in the long jump. At the Olympics in Berlin in 1936 he won 4 gold medals to the disgust of Nazi racists.

OWL. Bird of prey in the sub-order Striges, the majority being nocturnal. The Os. are characterized by large eyes encircled by radiating feathers set in a forward position (though the head has a compensating mobility); short, hooked beak; and soft, thick plumage which gives them a soundless flight. The diet consists mainly of rodents consumed whole, the indigestible remains being disgorged in pellets or 'castings'. All species lay white eggs, and, contrary to the habit of most birds, incubation begins as soon as first is laid. Familiar species are the tawny O. (*Strix aluco*) of Europe and the Near East; the large eagle O. (*Bubo bubo*) of Europe and Asia - both with closely allied species in America - and the long-eared O. (*Asio otus*) and short-eared O. (*A. flammeus*) which have a wide range in both the old and new worlds. Also of interest are the little O. (*Athene noctua*), symbol to the Greeks of the goddess of wisdom and naturalized in Britain, and the handsome snowy O. (*Nyctea scandiaca*), which moves south in winter from the Arctic. Generally Os. are sombrely coloured, and have a reputation as birds of ill-omen from the unearthly quality of their cries.

OWL. The powerful owl *(Ninox strenua)*, found through Queensland, New South Wales and Victoria, is Australia's largest owl, c.75 cm (30 in) long. *Photo: Courtesy of H. Frauca/Australian Information Service.*

OX. The castrated male of domestic species of cattle (q.v.), used particularly in underdeveloped countries for ploughing and other agricultural purposes, also the extinct wild O. or aurochs of Europe, and extant wild species.

OXA'LIC ACID. One of the oldest known organic acids, $(COOH)_2.2H_2O$, it is a white, crystalline, poisonous solid, soluble in water, alcohol, and ether. Salts occur in wood sorrel and other plants. It is used in the leather and textile industries, in dyeing and bleaching, ink manufacture, metal polishes, and for removing rust and ink stains.

OXENSTJERNA (oks'enshārna), **Axel Gustafsson,** count (1583-1654). Swedish statesman. As Chancellor from 1612, he ably seconded Gustavus Adolphus's foreign policy by his organizing and diplomatic ability. He acted as regent for Queen Christina, and conducted the Thirty Years War to a successful conclusion.

OXFORD, Edward de Vere, 17th earl of (1550-1604). English lyric poet, to whom Shakespeare's plays have been attributed by some.

OXFORD. Cathedral city and admin. HQ of Oxfordshire, England, on the Thames, 82km (51m) NW of London. The tower of the Saxon church of St Martin stands close to Carfax, the intersection of the 4 main roads. During the 13th cent. O. was the meeting-place of several parliaments, and during the Civil War was the Royalist headquarters. The city has greatly expanded with the advent of the large Morris motor works at Cowley, developed under Lord Nuffield. Pop. (1974) 114,220. *See* OXFORD UNIVERSITY.

OXFORD AND ASQUITH, Earl of. *See* ASQUITH.

OXFORD GROUP. *See* BUCHMAN, F. N. D.

OXFORD MOVEMENT. Known also as the Tractarian Movement and Catholic Revival, it attempted to revive Catholic religion in the Church of England. Newman dated the movement from Keble's sermon at Oxford in 1833. The O.M. by the turn of the cent. had transformed the face of the Anglican communion, and is represented today by Anglo-Catholicism.

OXFORDSHIRE. Southern midland co. of England, which, following the local govt reorganization of 1974 incl. a large area of NW Berkshire. It now encloses much of the Thames Basin, takes in the Chiltern Hills in the SE and spurs of the Cotswolds in the W, and the Vale of the White Horse in the S. It is good farming country, and cars, paper, bricks and cement are made. The admin. HQ is Oxford; other towns are Banbury, Chipping Norton and Abingdon. Area 2,612 sq.km (1,008 sq.m); pop. (1978) 540,600.

OXFORD UNIVERSITY. Oldest of the British univs., it was estab. during the 12th cent., the earliest existing coll. being founded in 1249. After suffering from land confiscation during the Reformation, it was reorganized by Elizabeth in 1571. Besides the colls., notable academic buildings are the Bodleian Library (with the New Bodleian, opened in 1946, with a capacity of 5 million books), the Divinity School, and the Sheldonian Theatre. The U. is governed by the Congregation of the Univ.; Convocation, composed of Masters and Doctors, has a delaying power. Normal business is conducted by the Hebdomadal Council. There are *c.* 8,000 undergraduates.

OXIDE. A binary compound of oxygen and another element. The 3 main classes are: (1) Acidic Os., which combine with basic Os. to form salts; (2) basic Os., reacting with acids to form salts; and (3) neutral Os., possessing neither acid nor basic properties.

OXLIP. A wild plant (*Primula elatior*), in character between the primrose and cowslip.

OXUS. Ancient name of AMU DARYA.

OXY-ACETYLENE WELDING. The fusion of metals by burning acetylene in pure oxygen, producing high-temperature flames. In the high-pressure system the gases are delivered to a blowpipe from cylinders in correct proportion.

OXFORDSHIRE. Named after the battle, Blenheim Palace was built to the designs of Hawksmoor and Vanbrugh. It retains the landscaped grounds laid out by 'Capability' Brown, as well as the formalised patterns typical of the 18th century in the gardens close to the house. It was the birth-place of Sir Winston Churchill. *Photo: Courtesy of the British Tourist Authority.*

Oxford Colleges

	Founded in		*Founded in*
University	1249	Wadham	1612
Balliol	c. 1263	Pembroke	1624
Merton	1264	Worcester	1714
St. Edmund Hall	c. 1278	Hertford	1740
Exeter	1314	Keble	1870
Oriel	1326	Lady Margaret Hall	1878
The Queen's	1340	Somerville	1879
New	1379	St. Anne's	1879
Lincoln	1427	St. Hugh's	1886
All Souls	1438	St. Hilda's	1893
Magdalen	1458	St. Peter's	1928
Brasenose	1509	Nuffield	1937
Corpus Christi	1517	St. Antony's	1950
Christ Church	1546	St. Catherine's	1962
Trinity	1555	Linacre	1962
St. John's	1555	St. Cross	1965
Jesus	1571	Wolfson	1966

OXYGEN (Gk. *oxys* acid, and *genes* forming). Colourless, odourless, tasteless, non-toxic gas, slightly soluble in water; symbol O, at. no. 8, at. wt. 16.00. Discovered by Priestley in 1774 by heating mercuric oxide using the Sun's rays and a burning glass (and independently in the same year by Scheele), it is the most abundant element, and both free and combined makes up nearly one-half of the total material on the surface of the Earth - 21 per cent by volume of the atmosphere, nearly 50 per cent by weight of the rocks, and 89 per cent by weight of the water. The only gas able to support respiration, it is just as essential for almost all combustion, and is used in high-temperature welding, improving blast-furnace working, low-temperature work, and aiding respiration. Liquefied O. is pale blue and magnetic.

O. is obtained by fractional distillation of liquid air, by electrolysis of water, or by heating manganese dioxide with potassium chlorate. It is very reactive, and combines with all other elements except the inert gases and fluorine.

OYSTER. Bivalve mollusc of the family Ostreidae, the upper valve being flat, the lower concave, hinged by an elastic ligament. The mantle, lying against the shell, protects the inner body, which incl. respirative, digestive and reproductive organs. Os. are distinguished by their change of sex, which may alternate annually or more frequently, and by the no. of their eggs - a female may discharge up to a million eggs during a spawning period. Among the species commercially exploited for food are the European O. (*Ostrea edulis*) - there are famous beds at Whitstable, Kent, and Colchester - and the American (*O. virginica*) of the Atlantic coast: the former is larviparous (eggs and larvae remain in the mantle cavity for a period before release) and the latter oviparous (eggs are discharged straight into the water). O. farming is increasingly practised, the beds being specially cleansed for the easy setting of the free-swimming larva (which then as a miniature O. is known as 'spat'), and the Os. later properly spaced for growth and fattened. Pearls (q.v.) are not obtained from members of the true O. family.

OYSTER CATCHER. Wading bird of the plover family. The common O.C. of European coasts (*Haemotopus ostralegus*) is black and white, with a long red beak to open shellfish; the allied American species has an even longer bill and a less musical cry.

Ō'ZARK MOUNTAINS. Area of ridges and valleys, with intersecting streams, the highest points no more than 645m (2,300 ft), divided among 5 states (Arkansas, Illinois, Kansas, Mississippi, Oklahoma): 130,000 sq.km (50,000 sq.m). Varied scenery makes it popular with tourists.

Ō'ZONE. Blue gas O_3 of characteristic odour, a form of oxygen, found in the atmosphere. Slightly soluble in water, it is produced when oxygen or air is subjected to a silent electrical discharge, ultra-violent ray action (e.g. the O. layer in the upper atmosphere is caused by the ultra-violet rays of the Sun), or radium emanation. It is a powerful oxidizing agent, and is also used in bleaching and air-conditioning. Because of fears that chlorofluorcarbons (CFC), the propellant used in aerosols, wears down the O. layer which protects Earth against ultra-violet rays from the Sun (which cause skin cancer), attempts are being made to phase out the use of such containers.

P

Sixteenth letter of the Roman alphabet. In Semitic languages, in Gk, and in Latin *p* had much of the same sound as it normally has today in English when final, or when following *s* at the beginning of a word, the sound of an unvoiced labial stop. In other positions in English, and especially when initial, *p* is aspirated.

PACARAIMA (pahkahrī'ma), **Sierra.** Range of mtns running some 620km (385m) along the Brazil-Venezuela frontier, and into Guyana: the highest point is Mount Roraima (q.v.).

PACHOMIUS (pakōm'ius), **St** (292-346 AD). Egyptian monk. He founded the first Christian monastic community living under a rule.

PACIFIC ISLANDS, Trust Terr. of. UN Trust Terr. comprising over 2,000 is. and atolls (a Japanese mandate 1919-47), which was admin. by USA 1947-80, when all its members, the Carolines, Marianas (except Guam) and Marshalls (qq.v.), had achieved independence. Area 1,800 sq.km (700 sq.m); pop. (1973) 115,000.

PACIFIC OCEAN. The largest ocean of the world, extending from Antarctica to the Bering Strait. Area 166,242,500 sq.km (64,186,300 sq.m); average depth 4,188 m (13,739 ft); greatest depth 11,000 m (36,198 ft) in the Mariana Trench.

PACIFIC SECURITY TREATY. *See* ANZUS.

PACIFIC WAR (1879-83). War conducted by Bolivia and Peru in alliance against Chile, in which Chile seized Antofagasta and the coast between the mouths of the rivers Loa and Paposo, thus rendering Bolivia completely landlocked. Peru also lost much of her southern coastline - from Arica to the mouth of the r. Loa. Bolivia has since tried to regain Pacific access, either by a corridor across her former Antofagasta prov. or a twin port with Arica at the end of the rail link from La Paz. Brazil supports the Bolivian claims which would facilitate her own transcontinental traffic. *See* PERU.

PACIFISM. The belief that violence should never be resorted to as a means of settling disputes. Among the holders of pacifist views are some Christians, e.g. the Soc. of Friends, Jehovah's Witnesses; some Hindus, e.g. Gandhi and his followers.

PADANG (pahdahng'). Port on the W coast of Sumatra, Indonesia, seat of a univ. (1951), with an airport. It exports coffee, copra, rubber, tea, resin, etc. The Dutch secured trading rights here in 1663, and built a factory *c.* 1680. Pop. (1975) 225,000.

PADERBORN (pah'der-). Town of N Rhine-Westphalia, W Germany, already the seat of a bishopric in Charlemagne's time. The 11th-13th cent. cathedral was destroyed in the S.W.W. A former Hanseatic town, it makes textiles, leather goods, precision instruments. Pop. (1972) 58,200.

PADEREWSKI (pahderef'skē), **Ignacz Jean** (1860-1941). Polish pianist, composer and statesman. The son of a Polish patriot, he gained European and American fame after his début in Vienna in 1887 and became a noted exponent of Chopin. After the F.W.W., during which he organized the Polish army in France, he became in 1919 PM of the newly independent Poland, which he represented at the Peace Conference, but continuing opposition forced him to resign the same year. Having resumed a musical career in 1921, he was Pres. of the Polish National Council in Paris in 1940 and d. in NY.

PADUA (pad'ūa). City (It. *Padova*) of N Italy, 45km (25m) W of Venice. The 13th cent. Palazzo della Ragione, and the basilica of St Antonio, are notable. The univ., founded in 1222, is famous. Pop. (1971) 232,270.

PAESTUM (pes'tum). Ancient Greek city, near Salerno in S Italy, founded *c.* 600 BC. There are a number of temple ruins.

PAGAN. Village in Burma, SW of Mandalay. It lies close to the ruins of a former Burmese cap., founded 847, taken by Kublai Khan 1287.

PAGANINI (pahgahnē'nē), **Nicolo** (1782-1840). Italian violinist. B. at Genoa, he first appeared at 9 years old, and from 1805 took Europe by storm. His appearance, his amours, and his virtuosity, especially his performances on a single string, created the legend of his being in league with the Devil. He composed works for the violin notable rather for their ingenious exploitation of the instrument than intrinsic value.

PAGE, Sir Earle Christmas Grafton (1880-1961). Australian statesman. He led the Country Party 1920-39, was PM of a caretaker govt in April 1939 following Lyons's death, represented Australia in the British War Cabinet 1941-2, and as Min. of Health under Menzies, 1949-55, introduced the Australian health scheme in 1953.

PAGE, Sir Frederick Handley (1885-1962). British aircraft engineer, founder of one of the earliest manufacturing cos. in 1909, and designer of long-range civil aircraft and multi-engined bombers in both wars, e.g. the Halifax in the S.W.W.

PAGO PAGO (pā'gō-pā'gō). Port of American Samoa; a harbour in the island of Tutuila. It was acquired by the USA in 1872. The nearby village of Fagatogo is the seat of govt. of American Samoa. Pop. (1970) 1,5000.

PAHANG (pah-hahng'). State of the Federation of Malaysia, ruled by a sultan. Rubber, tin, gold, etc., are exported. Kuantan, the cap., has a deepwater port at Tanjung Gelang 25km (16m) to the N. Area 35,930 sq.km (13,873 sq.m); pop. (1970) 505,000.

PAHLAVI (pahlah'vi) **dynasty.** Iranian dynasty founded by **Riza Khan** (1977-1944), an army officer who seized control of the govt. in 1921 and was proclaimed Shah in 1925. During the S.W.W. Britain and Russia were nervous of his German sympathies, and, compelling him to abdicate in favour of his son, occupied Iran 1941-6. His son **Mohammed Riza Shah Pahlavi** (1919-80), encountered strong political opposition. In 1953 he attempted the arrest of Mossadeq (q.v.), but was himself forced to flee the country and returned only with CIA assistance. Given massive aid by the USA, he pushed forward modernisation, to make Iran a major military and industrial power. He used Savak (contraction of the Farsi words for 'security'), the secret police he founded in 1957, to suppress opponents. In 1978 relaxation of his autocratic rule, under pressure from Carter, led to explosive unrest,

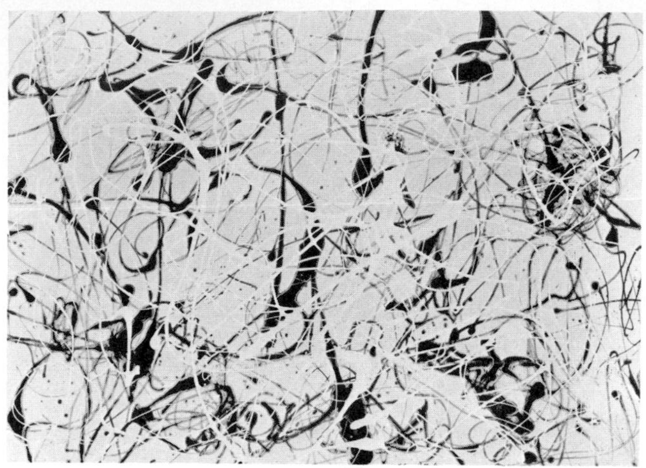

PAINTING. Two examples of modern art: an example of action painting by Jackson Pollock in 'Number 23', in which the subject content is reduced to a minimum, and David Hockney, foremost English figurative painter, with his 'Atlantic Crossing', in which the 'v' shapes are not seagulls but arrows to indicate the wind direction. *Photos: Courtesy of the Tate Gallery and Popperfoto*

and in Jan. 1979 he went into exile, and d. of cancer in Egypt. His heir is Crown Prince Riza (1960-), his son by his 3rd wife, Farah Diba.

PAHSIEN (pahsyen'). *See* CHONGQING.

PAIN. Sensation of hurt or discomfort caused by a message to the brain, as a result of accident, illness, etc., which travels along the nerves as electrical impulses. When these reach the gap between one nerve and another, special chemicals govern whether this gap is bridged, and may also either increase or lessen the attention the message receives, or modify its intensity in either direction. The main type of transmitter is known simply by an initial as 'substance P', and the chief pain inhibitors are the natural painkillers, the enkephalins and endomorphins, which were discovered in 1975.

PAINE, Thomas (1737-1809). British author. B. at Thetford, he went to America in 1774, where he pub. 'Common Sense' (1776), an influential republican pamphlet, and fought for the colonists in the War of Independence. In 1787 P. returned to England, and in 1791 he pub. *The Rights of Man*, an answer to Burke's *Reflections on the Revolution in France.* In 1792 he was indicted for treason but escaped to France, to represent Calais in the Convention. Narrowly escaping the guillotine, he regained his seat after the fall of Robespierre. In 1793 he pub. *The Age of Reason*, opposing Deism to Christianity and Atheism. He returned to America in 1802, and d. in New York.

PAINTING. The chief traditional methods of P. are tempera or distemper, fresco, oil P. (discovered by the Van Eyck brothers in Flanders), and water colour, which evolved from the wash drawings of the 15th-17th cents. and reached its highest development with Turner. Modern technology is adding increasing numbers of new media, such as the brilliant acrylic colours. The chief kinds of P., apart from those dealing with religious and mythological subjects, are *historical*, as seen in the work of David, Ingres, Delacroix; *portrait*, Van Dyck, Rembrandt, Velasquez, Goya, Reynolds, Gainsborough, Sargent, Sutherland; *landscape*, Claude Lorrain, Corot, Turner, Constable, Cotman; *seascape*, Jan van de Cappelle, van de Velde the Younger, Turner; *genre*, Brueghel, Vermeer, de Hooch; *still life*, Jan and Cornelius van Heem, Chardin, Courbet, Manet, Braque; *abstract*, Picasso, Ernst, Klee, Nicholson.

Various movements and schools are dealt with under individual headings, e.g. Action Painting, Blaue Reiter, Die Brücke, Impressionism, Op Art, Pointillism, Pop Art, Post-Impressionism, Pre-Raphaelite Brotherhood, Primitivism, etc.

PAISLEY. Town in Strathclyde, Scotland, on the White Cart 11km (7m) SW of Glasgow, famous for the manufacture of thread, introduced c. 1810. There are also distilleries, engineering works, and shipyards. P. grew up round an abbey founded 1160. Pop. (1973) 94,883.

PAISLEY, Ian (1926-). Ulster politician. Minister of the Martyrs Memorial Free Presbyterian Church from 1946, he entered the N. Ireland Parliament in 1970 and became MP at Westminster in 1974. His extreme Protestant position has made him a controversial figure.

PAKHTOONISTAN. *See* PATHANS.

PAKISTAN (pahkistahn'). Islamic Republic in south Asia. It comprises the provs. of Punjab, Sind, Baluchistan, and NW Frontier, and the centrally admin. tribal areas (*see* NORTHERN AREAS): these were formerly collectively known as West Pakistan 1947-72 to distinguish them from East Pakistan, the prov. lying east of West Bengal, India, which estab. its independence as Bangladesh (q.v.) in 1972. The cap. (formerly Karachi 1947-59 and Rawalpindi 1959-67) is Islamabad: other important towns are Lahore, Hyderabad, Multan, Peshawar and Quetta.

To the N and W are mountain ranges, the remainder of P. is a fertile plain watered by the Indus and its tributaries, aided by complex irrigation systems. The chief crops are wheat, rice, millet and sugar cane, with fruit and dates in the mountainous west. Cattle, sheep, goats, horses and camels are reared. Minerals incl. coal in the NW, chromite, iron, gypsum, and some oil and natural gas. Industrial growth is being encouraged, and there are cotton and woollen mills, and lacquered goods, pottery and embroidered articles are produced.

Schools of Painting

Italian, 13th—18th cents. *Florence:* Cimabue, Giotto, Orcagna, Taddeo Gaddi, Fra Angelico, Uccello, Masaccio, Filippo and Filippino Lippi, Botticelli, Michelangelo, Sarto. *Siena*: Duccio. *Umbria*: Francesca, Perugino. *Milan*: Leonardo da Vinci, Borgognone, Luini. *Parma*: Correggio. *Venice*: Bellini, Carpaccio, Giorgione, Titian, Palma Vecchio, Tintoretto, Veronese, Tiepolo, Canaletto. *Padua*: Mantegna. *Verona*: Pisano. *Bologna*: The Carracci, Reni, Domenichino. *Rome and Naples*: Raphael, Caravaggio, Sassoferrato, Rosa.

Spanish, 16th—19th cents. El Greco, Ribera, Zurbarán, Velasquez, Murillo, Goya, Picasso.

Flemish, 14th—20th cents. Van Eyck, Weyden, Bouts, Memlinc, Bosch, Brueghel, Mabuse, Patinir, Rubens, Van Dyck, Brouwer, Teniers.

Dutch, 16th—19th cents. Rembrandt, Hobbema, Hooch, Vermeer, Hals, Ostade, Ruisdael, Steen, Hondecoeter, Van Gogh.

German, 15th—20th cents. Lochner, Lucas Cranach, Schongauer, Grünewald, Dürer, Holbein, Elsheimer, Chodowiecki, Kandinsky, Klee, Ernst, Kokoschka.

French, 16th—20th cents. Clouet, Poussin, Claude, Watteau, Chardin, Boucher, Fragonard, David, Ingres, Corot, Géricault, Delacroix, Manet, Monet, Degas, Renoir, Camille Pissarro, Cézanne, Gauguin, Matisse, Rouault, Braque, Utrillo, Vuillard, Vlaminck.

British, 17th—20th cents. Hilliard, Lely, Kneller, Hogarth, Wilson, Reynolds, Stubbs, Gainsborough, Romney, Rowlandson, Raeburn, Blake, Morland, Crome, Lawrence, Girtin, Turner, Constable, Cotman, Cox, Etty, Bonington, Watts, Frith, Hunt, Rossetti, Millais, Burne-Jones, Brangwyn, Sickert, Wilson Steer, Duncan Grant, Augustus John, Paul Nash, Stanley Spencer, Graham Sutherland, Sir Alfred Munnings, Ben Nicholson, John Bratby, Francis Bacon, Victor Pasmore, David Hockney.

American, 18th—20th cents. John S. Copley, Benjamin West, Charles W. Peale, Gilbert Stuart, Washington Allston, John James Audubon, Winslow Homer, Thomas Eakins, J.A.M. Whistler, Mary Cassatt, John S. Sargent, John Marin, Rockwell Kent, Diego Rivera, Lyonel Feininger, Laszlo Moholy-Nagy, Jackson Pollock, Ben Shahn, Edward Giobbi.

Australian, 19th—20th cents. Tom Roberts, Sir William Dobell, Russell Drysdale, Sydney Nolan, Albert Namatjira.

Area 803,900 sq.km (310,400 sq.m); pop. (1978) 75,620,000, the majority Sunni, 25% Shi'ite. The official language is Urdu, but English is widely used. M.U. Pakistani rupee.

History. The name P., for a Moslem division of British India, was put forward at the time of the Round Table Conference of 1930-1; it was made up by Choudhary Rahmat Ali (1897-1951) from the names of the predominantly Moslem parts of the subcontinent: *P*unjab, NW Frontier (inhabited chiefly by *A*fghans), *K*ashmir, *S*ind, and Baluchi*stan* (*stan* in Urdu meaning land; the fact that *pak* means pure in Urdu probably added to the attraction of the name). Moslem fear of domination by the vast Hindu majority in British India brought in 1940 a serious demand for a separate Moslem state which delayed for some years the transformation of India into a dominion. This was at last effected in 1947 by the passing

PAKISTAN. The waterfront at Dacca still has quiet stretches where traditional craft ply, and people can wash and bathe. *Photo: Philip Boucas/Camera Press*

of an Act of the Imperial Parliament in London which divided British India into 2 dominions, predominantly Hindu India and predominantly Moslem P. See JINNAH.

In accordance with the distribution of the Moslem population, P. was divided into 2 sections, West Pakistan, which constitutes since 1972 the whole of Pakistan, and East Pakistan, an independent state since 1972 as Bangladesh. The two were separated by a thousand miles of Indian territory. The drawing of the frontiers entailed violent religious disturbances, and the flight of thousands of refugees from India to P. and vice versa, with many deaths and acute distress. These tragic beginnings were overcome, and in 1956 P. became a rep., although choosing to remain within the Commonwealth. However, there was increasing divergence between the eastern and western divisions of the country, under presidents Ayub Khan 1958-69 and Yahya Khan 1969-71. Plans were announced for a new constitution, but in 1971 E Pakistan proclaimed secession as Bangladesh, and the forces of W Pakistan were defeated with Indian aid 3-16 Dec. 1971. West P., now the whole of Pakistan, left the Commonwealth in 1972, under the leadership of the new pres., Bhutto (q.v.), when the independence of Bangladesh was recognized by the Commonwealth. In 1973, under the new constitution of P. (which provided for a fed. parliamentary system and the encouragement of regional languages as well as Urdu), he became PM. By 1975 he had rendered P. self-sufficient in food, and subdued the level of insurgency. However, unrest aimed at the establishment of new independent states was still continued by the Baluchis in Baluchistan; by the Pathans (q.v.) for Pakhtoonistan; and the people of Sind for Sindhudesh. In 1977, following a military coup, Bhutto was condemned to death, and under the presidency of Gen. Mohammed Zia ul-Haq (1924-) from 1978, elections were postponed and martial law reintroduced. An Islamic state was imposed, and a nuclear programme pursued. The invasion of Afghanistan brought the USSR into direct contact with the Pakistan border.

PA'LAMAS, Kostes (1859-1943). Greek poet. He enriched the Gk. vernacular as a literary language by his use of it, particularly in his poetry, e.g. *Songs of my Fatherland* (1886) and *The Flute of the King* (1910), expressing vivid awareness of Gk history.

PALATE. The ceiling of the mouth. The bony front part is the hard, the muscular rear part the soft, P.; this contains in the middle line a short appendage called the uvula. Incomplete fusion of the P. causes interference with speech.

PALA'TINATE. An historic division of W Germany, dating back before Charlemagne. It was ruled by a county palatine (hence the name) and varied in size. When it was attached to Bavaria in 1815 it consisted of Rhenish (or Lower) P. on the Rhine (cap. Heidelberg), and Upper P. (cap. Amberg on the Vils) 210km (130m) to the E. In 1946 Rhenish P. became an administrative division of the Land of Rhineland-Palatinate with cap. at Neustadt; Upper P. remained an administrative div. of Bavaria with cap. at Regensburg.

PALDISKI (pahl'dēskē). Small, ice-free port in Estonia, a Soviet naval base 40km (25m) W of Tallinn at the entrance to the Gulf of Finland.

PALEMBA'NG. Indonesian town, cap. of S Sumatra prov., centre of petroleum production, with large refineries. Coffee and pepper are important articles of trade. P. was the cap. of a sultanate when the Dutch estab. a trading station there in 1616. The large mosque dates from 1740. Pop. (1970) 583,000.

PALE'RMO. Cap. and seaport of Sicily, founded by the Phoenicians. Notable buildings incl. the Capella Palatina built by King Roger II in the 12th cent., univ. (1805) and museum. Pop. (1971) 651,650.

PALESTINE. Historic name of a region in SW Asia lying between the Mediterranean and the Jordan-Dead Sea-Araba depression, *the* Holy Land of Jews and Christians, and a holy land to Moslems.

Geography. Along the W coast lies a fertile plain up to 32km (20m) wide, and to the E the central plateau, which is interrupted only by the plain of Esdraelon. The Jordan runs through a deep rift, which at the Dead Sea is 395m (1,292 ft) below sea-level. In the S. is the semi-desert Negev.

The climate varies from the semi-tropical to the sub-alpine. The summer is hot and dry, and most of the heavy winter rains percolate through the limestone rock, so that artificial irrigation is essential for cultivation. Citrus and other fruits, and olives, are grown. Potash and other chemicals come from the Dead Sea area.

History. P.'s position on the main route connecting Egypt with the Euphrates valley, and with Asia Minor, caused it to come in turn under the domination of Egypt, Assyria, Babylonia, Persia, Macedonia, the Ptolemies, the Seleucids, and Rome. P. formed part of the Roman and later of the Byzantine empire until AD 636, when it was conquered by the Arabs. The Crusaders occupied Jerusalem 1099-1187, after which P. came under the rule of the Mamelukes. The Turks conquered the land in 1516, and held it until the F.W.W. when the British conquered it, 1917-18, and estab. a military administration replaced by civil administration in 1920; in 1922 Britain received a League of Nations mandate (which incorporated the BALFOUR DECLARATION, q.v.) to administer an area described as P., but incl. historic P. and lands across the Jordan that were in 1923 recognized by Britain as a separate country (*see* JORDAN, Hashimite Kingdom of). Some 300,000 Jewish immigrants were allowed to enter P. during 1920-39; under the care of the Jewish Agency they developed agriculture and industry. Discontent, in particular over the admission of Jewish settlers to a land that had become Arab in 636, resulted in serious Arab rebellions in 1929 and 1936-8. Various plans were made, one drawn up in 1939 recommending independence for P. within 10 years, further Jewish immigration after 1944 to be only with Arab consent. The outbreak of the S.W.W. brought the troubles to a temporary end, and both Arab and Jewish Palestinians served as volunteers in the Allied forces. The war over, Jewish terrorist organizations staged a series of outrages. Britain put the problem before the UN which proposed partition, accepted by neither Arabs nor Jews; and in 1947 Britain announced its intentions to give up the mandate on 15 May 1948. On 14 May, eight hours before the mandate ended, the Jewish Agency broadcast a proclamation of a Jewish state of ISRAEL (q.v.).

A series of Arab-Israeli Wars (q.v.) ensued, and the Palestinians developed liberation forces to continue resistance, terrorist outrages also being committed inside and outside Israel. In 1974 the Palestine Liberation Organization led by Yassir Arafat (q.v.) was recognized by the Arab League as having authority over Palestinian territory on the W. Bank, and in 1974 it became the first non-governmental delegation to be admitted to a plenary session of the UN Gen. Assembly. The stance of the P.L.O. varies between insistence on eradication of Israel and acceptance of a Palestinian state in certain territories - the W Bank and Gaza strip - to be recovered from Israel.

Although the name P. derives from the Philistines, the Palestinians are descendants of the Canaanites (q.v.). Recent archaeological research suggests that the early history of the Israelis and Palestinian Arabs is much more intermingled than the Biblical version suggests, but the evidence is hotly contested. *See* ABRAHAM.

There are *c.* 4,000,000 Palestinians: 1,300,000 in the W. Bank, Gaza Strip and E. Jersualem; 1,000,000 in Jordan; 650,000 in Israel; 450,000 in Lebanon; 650,000 in camps (Lebanon, Syria, Jordan, W Bank and Gaza Strip), and 100,000 in USA. Owing to their high birth rate, Palestinian Arabs form an increasingly large minority inside Israel's extended boundaries.

The Palestinian situation has been complicated by the economic pressure applied to the rest of the world by Arab control of major oil supplies, and by the electoral victory in Israel in 1977 of Menachem Begin (q.v.). The Egypt-Israel Peace Treaty (1979) had failed by 1980 to lead to positive moves to estab a Palestinian state, and there had been further Israel-Palestinian hostilities in Lebanon (q.v.).

PALESTRINA (pahlestrē'nah), **Giovanni Pierluigi da** (1525-94). Italian composer. B. at Palestrina, he became choirmaster at the Vatican in 1551. A master of contrapuntal composition, P. composed masses, motets, hymns, magnificats, and litanies.

PALI (pah'lē). The sacred language of the Buddhist canonical texts. Of uncertain origin, it shows the influence of Vedic Sanskrit.

PALISSY (pahlēsē), **Bernard** (*c.* 1510-89). French potter, noted for his richly coloured rustic pottery, e.g. dishes with realistic modelled fish and reptiles or with the network piercing, and a favourite of Catherine de' Medici. Imprisoned in the Bastille as a Huguenot in 1588, he d. there.

PALLADIO (pahlad'dē-ō), **Andrea** (1508–80). Italian architect, whose country houses (e.g. Malcontenta, and the Villa Rotonda nr Vicenza), designed from 1540 for patrician families of the Venetian Rep. influenced the

PAMIRS. Frontier guards join forces with local militia in Xinjiang province to defend the Western Gateway to the Chinese Motherland. *Photo: Courtesy of the Society for Anglo-Chinese Understanding*

architecture of Washington's home at Mount Vernon, the palace of Tsarskoe Selo, and in England, Holkham, Prior Park, Stowe, etc.

PALLĀ'DIUM. White metal of the platinum family, discovered in 1803 by Wollaston, and found in platinum ore in Brazil, California and the Urals, and in nickel ores of Canada: symbol Pd, at. wt. 106.4, at. no. 46. It is also a non-radioactive product of a slow neutron nuclear reactor. P. does not tarnish in air, and when finely divided or spongy absorbs up to 3,000 times its volume of hydrogen and is used as a catalyst. Other uses incl. non-magnetic springs in clocks and watches; parts of delicate balances and surgical instruments; dental fillings; and as alloy with gold to make white gold.

PALLIUM, or **pall.** A pure wool vestment worn by the Pope and by Catholic metropolitans, primates, and archbishops. It is in the shape of a Y, falling across the shoulders back and front.

PALM. Plant of the family Palmaceae characterized by a single tall stem carrying a thick cluster of large palmate or pinnate leaves at the top. The majority of the some 1,500 species are tropical or sub-tropical, have products of great economic importance, e.g. the coconut, date, sago, and oil (*Elaeis guineensis*) Ps.

PALMA (pahl'mah). Cap. and port of the Balearic Is., Spain, on Majorca. A Roman colony founded 276 BC, P. has a cathedral begun in 1229. Products incl. silk and woollen textiles, cement, paper, pottery. There is an airport at Son San Juan. Pop. (1970) 234,100.

PALMA. One of the Canary Islands, Spain, a fertile, wooded island producing wine, fruit, honey, and silk. Area 728 sq.km (281 sq.m); pop. (1970) 80,000.

PALMAS (pahl'mahs), **Las.** Cap. of the Spanish Canary archipelago, on Gran Canaria. The port of La Luz is an important fuelling depot. Pop. (1970) 287,000.

PALM BEACH. Winter resort in Florida, USA, on an island between Lake Worth and the Atlantic. Pop. (1970) 9,086.

PALMER, Samuel (1805-81). British artist, whose landscapes show the influence of Blake.

PALMERSTON, Henry John Temple, 3rd visct. P. (1784-1865). British Whig statesman. He succeeded to an Irish peerage in 1802, and became a Tory MP in 1807. He was Secretary-at-War 1809-28, broke with the Tories in 1830, and sat in the Whig cabinets of 1830-4, 1835-41, and 1846-51 as For. Sec. His foreign policy was marked by distrust of France and Russia, against whose designs he upheld the independence of Belgium and Turkey. He became Home Sec. in 1852, and was PM from 1855 until 1858. His final period as Premier (1859-65) was marked by the 2nd war with China, and by the American Civil War, in which he nearly involved Britain on the side of the South. Popular with the people, for he made good use of the press, he was a constant source of annoyance to the Queen and other ministers because of his high-handed attitude.

PALMERSTON NORTH. City of N Island, N Zealand, centre of a timber-growing and dairy-farming dist. Massey Univ. was estab. in 1963, and has a famous agricultural college. Pop. (1976) 88,724.

PALM SPRINGS. Resort and spa in California, USA, *c.* 160km (100m) E of Los Angeles. Pop. (1970) 21,000.

PALM SUNDAY. The Sunday before Easter, and first day of Holy Week; so called because in the RC Church palm branches are carried to commemorate Christ's entry into Jerusalem on that day.

PALMYRA (palmī'ra). Ancient city and oasis in the desert of Syria, *c.* 240km (150m) NE of Damascus. P., the Biblical Tadmor, was flourishing by *c.* 300 BC, but was destroyed in AD 272 after Queen Zenobia had led a revolt against the Romans. Extensive ruins of the Temple of Bel exist. On the site is a village called Tadmur in Arabic.

PALMYRA. Coral atoll 1,600 km (1,000 m) SW of Hawaii, in the Pacific, purchased by the USA from a Hawaiian family in 1979 for the storage of highly radioactive nuclear waste from 1986.

PALOMAR, Mount. The location of an observatory, 80km (50m) NE of S. Diego, California, having a 508cm (200in) diam. reflector, when dedicated in 1948 the largest telescope in the world.

PAMIRS (pahmērz). A treeless plateau of C Asia, most of which is in the USSR, the rest in China and Afghanistan. The P. are traversed by mountain ranges 7,495 m (24,590 ft); to the S lies the Hindu Kush.

PALMERSTON. A portrait of Lord Palmerston, aged fifty, by J. Partridge. *Photo: Courtesy of the National Portrait Gallery*

PALMYRA. Laid waste by Aurelian when taken in 272, the city was subsequently restored by the emperor, but never regained its earlier importance.

PAMPAS. Flat treeless Argentine plains, lying between the Andes and the Atlantic, and rising gradually from the coast to the lower slopes of the mountains. In the E.P. are the great cattle ranches and the flax- and grain-growing area of Argentina; to the W the P. are arid and unproductive. Characteristic of the P. is P. grass. The prov. of La Pampa is in the E. part of the Pampas plains.

PAMPAS GRASS. Genus of S American grasses (*Cortaderia*). *C. argentea* is grown in gardens and has tall leaves and large panicles of white flowers.

PAMPLŌ'NA. Cap. of the Spanish prov. of Navarre and of the old kingdom of Navarre. A pre-Roman town, P. was rebuilt by Pompey in 68 BC, captured by the Visigoths 476, sacked by Charlemagne 778, and taken by Wellington 1813. It makes wine, leather and shoes, textiles, etc. An annual event is the 'running of the bulls' through the streets in July. Pop. (1970) 147,200.

PAN. Greek deity, the patron of flocks and herds, worshipped mainly in Arcadia. He is represented as a man with the horns, ears, and hoofs of a goat, and usually playing upon a shepherd's pipe.

PANAMA. A rep. of C. America, forming an isthmus divided at its narrowest point by the P. Canal (q.v.) and the Canal Zone. It is traversed by a chain of mountains running parallel to the coasts. The climate is tropical; products incl. bananas, cacao, pearl shell, etc. P. is governed by a president, and an elected national assembly. Spanish is the official language. The cap. is P. City. Formerly part of Colombia, P. declared its independence in 1903 with the encouragement of the USA, which was interested in the Canal Zone. Remains of Fort St Andrews, built by Scottish settlers 1698-1701 in an attempt to colonize P., were discovered in 1976. Area 76,614 sq.km (31,293 sq.m); pop. (1980) 1,830 000. The language is Spanish and the people are RC. M.U.: balboa.

PANAMA CANAL. Canal across the Panama isthmus in Central America, connecting the Pacific and Atlantic; length 80km (50m). The original construction company, headed by the French engineer Ferdinand de Lesseps, began construction in 1879, but collapsed in 1889 owing to financial scandals and yellow fever. The work was taken over by the USA in 1904, and the canal was opened 1914, formally 1920.

The P.C. runs SE through the Canal Zone from Cristobal on the Atlantic to Balboa on the Pacific, and has 12 locks. Nationalist feeling in Panama led to anti-American riots in 1964 and in 1974 agreement was reached that the USA should surrender the 'sovereignty in perpetuity' over the Canal Zone (extending for 5 km/3 m on either side of the canal: area 1,432 sq.km/553 sq.m) granted in 1903. Panama would participate in canal admin. and have a just share of the profits. A larger sea-level canal, to avoid the present costly system of 12 locks between Cristobal and Balboa, is planned, but the disappearance of the locks and the consequent interchange of Atlantic/Pacific marine life forms may have far-reaching effects.

Alternative sites in N Colombia, and on the Nicaragua/Costa Rica border have also been considered by the USA for a new canal.

The **Panama Canal Zone** (land area 964 sq.km/372 sq.m) was acquired 'in perpetuity' by the USA in 1903, and comprised land on either side of the canal itself. It was designed to ensure free passage to international shipping in a turbulent area, but from the 1960s aided US strategy in S America as a training ground for Special Forces, devised by Pres. Kennedy to fight irregular wars. Nationalist feeling in Panama led to anti-American riots in 1964, and under the treaty of 1978 negotiated by Carter, the Zone passed to Panama in 1979. The USA retains control of the management and defence of the canal itself until 1999, and the use of about 25% of the former land area of the Zone for these purposes. Pop. (1970) 50,500.

PANAMA CANAL. A container cargo ship passes through Pedro Miguel lock on the Canal. *Photo: Mireille Vautier*

PANAMA (pahnahmah') **CITY.** Cap. of the rep. of P., situated near the Pacific end of the P. Canal. Founded on the present site in 1673, P. has its port at Balboa, which is in the Canal Zone. An earlier P., to the NE founded 1519, was destroyed 1671 by the Welsh buccaneer Morgan. Pop. (1976) 460,000.

PAN-AMERICAN HIGHWAY. Roadway, a large part of it suitable for all-weather motoring, linking the USA with Central and South America. It was suggested at the 5th International Conference of American States, 1923. Starting from Nuevo Laredo, Texas, it runs through Mexico City to Panama City, then down the W side of S America to Valparaiso, Chile, where it crosses the Andes and goes to Buenos Aires, Argentina. Total length 25,300 km (15,700 m), most of it completed by 1960. *See* DARIEN.

PAN-AMERICAN UNION. *See* ORGANIZATION OF AMERICAN STATES.

PANAY (pahnī'). One of the Philippine Islands, lying between Mindoro and Negros. The cap. is Iloilo. P. is mountainous, 2,215 m (7,265 ft) in Madiaás. The chief occupation is agriculture; rice, sugar, pineapples, bananas, and copra are important products. Copper is mined. The Spaniard Legaspi took P. in 1569; it was occupied by the Japanese 1942-5. Area 11,515 sq.km (4,446 sq.m).

PANCHEN LAMA, 10th Incarnation (1935-). Tibetan spiritual leader, 2nd in importance to the Dalai L. (q.v.). A protégé of the Chinese since childhood, he is not indisputably recognized. On the flight of the Dalai L. in 1959, he was deputed by the Chinese to take over, but stripped of power for subversion 1964, and said to be deported to China 1965.

PANCREAS (pang'krē-as). A gland which secretes ferments necessary for the digestion of starch, protein, and fat. It is about 178mm (7in) long and lies behind and below the stomach. It contains groups of cells called the islets of Langerhans, which secrete insulin. *See* INSULIN and DIABETES.

PA'NDA. Herbivorous mammal (*Ailurus fulgens*) of the family Ailuridae, found in the region of the Himalayas. Similar to a bear, it is *c.* 45cm (1.5ft) with a bushy tail of equal length. The rich chestnut fur darkens on the underside and the legs are black: there are light-coloured rings on the tail and white markings on the face. The rare giant P. (*Ailuropoda melanoleuca*), with striking black and white fur, also a native of NW China and Tibet, seldom survives in zoos since it needs a diet of special bamboo shoots, etc.

PANDA. A lively interpretation of a giant panda cub enjoying its diet of bamboo shoots, produced by the Malvern branch of the Boehm (pron. bem) porcelain studio of Trenton, New Jersey. *Photo: Courtesy of Boehm*

PANDO'RA. The first woman, according to Greek mythology. Zeus sent her on earth with a box filled with evils, to counteract the blessings brought to man by Prometheus's gift of fire. When her box was opened the evils flew out, only Hope remaining.

PANGŌ'LIN or **scaly anteater.** Family of scale-covered, toothless mammals (Manidae), resembling large lizards, and up to 1m (3ft) long. Nocturnal in habit, they are found in Africa and S Asia.

PANIPA'T. Town in Punjab, Rep. of India. Scene of 3 decisive battles: 1526, when Babar was the victor; 1556, won by Akbar; 1761, when the Mahrattas were defeated by Ahmad Shah of Afghanistan. Pop. (1971) 70,000.

PANKHURST, Emmeline (1858-1928). British suffragette, *née* Goulden. Founder of the Women's Social and Political Union in 1903, she launched in 1906 the militant suffragette campaign, and was several times imprisoned and then released after hunger-strikes. She was supported by her daus. DAME CHRISTABEL P. (1880-1958) the political leader of the movement and SYLVIA P. (1882-1960) who suffered 9 times under the 'Cat and Mouse Act', was a pacifist in the F.W.W., and a staunch supporter of the Ethiopian cause against Italy.

PANSY. Perennial garden flower, also known as heart's ease, derived from the European wild P. (*Viola tricolor*), and known as *V. tricolor hortensis.* The flowers are usually yellow, cream or purple, or a mixture, and there are many highly developed varieties bred for size, colour or special markings.

PANTELLERIA (pahntellerē'ah). Volcanic is. in the Mediterranean, 100km (62m) SW of Sicily, with which it is admin. Primitive dry stone dwellings date from prehistoric times, and because of its strategic position P. has been much fought over. It was strongly fortified by Mussolini in the S.W.W., and was the first part of metropolitan Italy to surrender to the Allies 11 June 1943. The chief town is P. Area 115 sq.km (45 sq.m); pop. (1971) 11,000.

PANTHEISM (pan'thē-izm) (Gk. *pan*, all; *theos*, God). A mode of thought which regards God as a pervading presence immanent in the universe. It is expressed in Egyptian religion and Brahmanism, while Stoicism, Neo-Platonism, Judaism, Christianity, and Islam can be interpreted in pantheistic terms. Modern pantheist philosophers incl. Bruno, Spinoza, Fichte, Schelling, and Hegel. A strong pantheistic element is found in the work of many modern poets.

PA'NTHĒON. A temple for the worship of all the gods. The Roman P., begun in 27 BC and rebuilt by Hadrian, is still used as a church. The term P. also denotes a building in which many great men are buried, e.g. the Panthéon at Paris.

PANTHER. Name given in India to the leopard.

PANTOMIME. Among the Romans P. signified a masked actor who performed by means of dumb show, and the tradition continued, notable being the 19th cent. pantomimist Debureau, whose techniques have been revived in the 20th by Marcel Marceau and Jean-Louis Barrault (who played the role of Debureau in the film *Les Enfants du Paradis*). In England P. is a species of dramatic Christmas entertainment, diversified with songs, dances and comedy which, from beginnings connected with the 18th cent. harlequin spectacles, developed in the 19th cent. on fairy-tale and folk-tale themes. After Grimaldi, the clown predominated over the harlequinade. Later in the cent. came the era of music-hall P. with stars such as Dan Leno, Harriet Vernon, and Vesta Tilley, and magnificent 'transformation' scenes. In the 20th cent. Ps. are fewer, because of the decline of live theatre, but Ps. on ice became popular after the S.W.W. Provincial Ps. are truer to tradition than London productions.

PANZER (pahn'tser). German word meaning 'armour', used in connection with armoured vehicles, regiments, etc. The Nazi P. divisions overwhelmed the French, English, and Belgians in 1940.

PAPACY. The office of the Pope or bishop of Rome, as head of the RC Church. According to the RC claim, the leadership or 'Keys' of the Church was entrusted by Christ to Peter, who became the first bishop of Rome. For many cents., however, Rome was recognized as only one of the great patriarchates of the Church, and Constantinople never accepted the primacy of Rome, breaking away in 1054. The missions of Gregory I (590-604) marked the P.'s first attempt to extend its authority outside Italy. Its position was strengthened in the 8th-9th cents. by the support of the Frankish kings, and reached its height in the 11th-13th cents. under Gregory VII and Innocent III. In the 14th cent. the P. fell completely under French control; its headquarters were removed to Avignon (1309-78), and this 'Babylonian Captivity' was followed by the Great Schism (1378-1417) between rival popes at Rome and Avignon. The reformation withdrew much of N and W Europe from the Roman obedience, and throughout the 17th and 18th cents. the P. lost prestige and political influence. Under Pius IX the Papal States (territory ruled by the Pope as sovereign) were annexed to Italy in 1870, and the conflict with the Italian monarchy lasted until the Lateran Treaty (1929) recognized papal sovereignty over the Vatican City. The Vatican Council (1870) proclaimed the doctrine that the Pope is infallible when he speaks *ex cathedra*. The Pope is elected by the Sacred College of Cardinals, and his pontificate is dated from his coronation with the tiara, or triple crown, at St Peter's. Following the Second Vatican Council (1962-6) an Episcopal Synod (200 bishops elected by the local hierarchies) was estab. 1967 to collaborate with the Pope in the govt of the Church. By 1977 it was tentatively agreed that in the event of a reunion of the RC Church and the Anglican Communion, the latter would accept the primacy of the Pope, but that he would exercise it in 'collegial association with his brother bishops'.

PAPAW'. *See* PAWPAW.

PAPEETE (pahpē'ti). Cap. of Fr. Polynesia, the name means 'little water', on Tahiti in the Society Is., of which it is also cap. and port. Pop. (1977) 62,735.

PAPEN (pahpen), **Franz von** (1879-1969), German politician. Chancellor in 1932, he negotiated the Nazi-Conservative alliance which put Hitler in power, and was Vice-Chancellor 1933-4, envoy to Austria 1934-8, and ambassador to Turkey 1939-44. At the Nuremberg Trials 1945-6, he was acquitted, but was imprisoned by a denazification court.

PAPER. Sheet of vegetable fibre, the name deriving from Lat. *papyrus*, a form of writing material made from the water reed and used in ancient Egypt. The invention of true P., made of pulped fishing nets, rags, etc., is credited to Tsai Lun, a Minister of Agriculture under the Han dynasty of China, in AD 105. Its use gradually spread from the 8th cent. and the 1st English paper mill was estab. at Stevenage in the 15th cent. The spread of literacy led to the invention by Louis Robert in 1799 of a machine to produce a continuous reel of paper, since production by hand of single sheets could no longer keep pace with demand. Apart from its obvious uses in writing, printing and packaging, P. is today also employed in towels and toilet tissues, hardboard, roofing felt, insulating panels and drainpipes; and in electrical work as an insulator.

PAPHOS (pā'fos). Ancient city of Cyprus, originally a Phoenician colony. According to legend Aphrodite landed here after her birth from the sea waves. Modern P. is 16km (10m) to the E. Pop. (1972) 12,100.

PAPINEAU (pahpēnō'), **Louis Joseph** (1786-1871). Canadian politician. B. in Montreal, he organized the unsuccessful rebellion in Lower Canada in 1837, then fled the country, but returned in 1847 to sit in the United Canadian legislature until 1854.

PAPUA (papoo'a). Name originally given to the island of New Guinea, later particularly to its SE section. *See* NEW GUINEA.

PAPUA NEW GUINEA. Country in the SW Pacific, comprising the eastern part of the is. of N.G. (q.v.) and the N.G. islands, of which the chief are New Britain and New Ireland; part of the Solomon Is. (incl. Bougainville, q.v.); and the Admiralty Is. (Manus, etc.). Admin. by Australia as the UN Trust Terr. of Papua-New Guinea (q.v.) from 1949, it became an independent member of the Commonwealth in 1975. Products incl. coconuts, cocoa, coffee and rubber; timber and prawns, but the predominant source of wealth in the area is the copper of Bougainville. The cap. is Port Moresby. Area 462,000 sq.km (178,260 sq.m); pop. (1975) 2,700,000. M.U.: kina. *See* PIDGIN ENGLISH.

PARÁ. *See* BELÉM.

PARACELS (paraselz'). Group of *c.* 130 small islands (Chinese: Xisha/Vietnamese Hoang Sa), 266km (165m) SE of Hainan. They are disputed between China and

Vietnam because they lie in an oil-bearing area. They were occupied by the Chinese after a naval skirmish in 1974.

PARACE'LSUS (1493-1541). Swiss physician and theosophic philosopher, whose real name was Theophrastus Bombastus von Hohenheim. In 1526 he became lecturer in medicine at Basle, and revolutionized the theoretic basis of medicine. From 1529 onwards he wandered Europe, and he d. at Salzburg.

PARACHUTE (par'ashoot). Umbrella-shaped device, basically consisting of some 2 dozen panels of nylon with shroud lines to a harness. It is used to slow down the descent of a human being, supplies, etc., from a plane or missile to a safe speed for landing, or sometimes to aid the landing of a plane or missile itself. Modern designs enable the parachutist to exercise considerable control of direction, etc. *See* FREE-FALLING. Leonardo da Vinci sketched a P. design, but the first descent from a balloon was not made until 1797 by Garnerin, and from an aircraft by Berry in 1912. In *parascending* the parachuting procedure is reversed, the canopy (parafoil) to which the sportsman is attached being towed behind a vehicle to achieve an ascent.

PARADISE. Persian word for a park or pleasure garden, and hence applied to the Garden of Eden, the Messianic kingdom, and the heaven of after life.

PARAFFIN. A hydrocarbon (or mixture of hydrocarbons) of the P. series, general formula C_nH_{2n+2}. The lower members are gases, e.g. methane (marsh gas). The middle ones (mainly liquid) form the basis of petrol (gasolene), kerosene (q.v.), lubricating oils, and the higher ones (P. waxes) are used in ointment and cosmetic bases. *See* KEROSENE.

PARAGUAY (pa'ragwī). Inland republic of S America, bounded by Boliva to the N, Brazil to the NE, and Argentina to the SW and S. The chief rivers are the Paraná and its tributary, the P., which divides the country in two. The climate is tropical to sub-tropical, with an abundance of summer rain. For the most part, P. is below 150m (500ft) a.s.l.; hills in the E rise to *c.* 450m (1,500 ft). Much of the land is forested, timber, quebracho (used in tanning), and yerba maté being natural products important commercially. Crops for home consumption incl. maize, mandioca, beans, sugar cane, rice; cotton (for export) and tobacco are also grown, and yerba maté plantations have been estab. Hides and meat are other exports. Minerals found but little worked incl. iron, manganese, and copper.

Under the constitution of 1967 there is a pres. elected for 5 yrs. and a senate and chamber of deputies, also popularly elected. The cap. is Asunción. Both Spanish and Guarani, the language of the Indian inhabitants at the time of the Spanish conquest, are commonly spoken by Paraguayans, the races having mixed. Area 406,752 sq.km (157,042 sq.m); pop. (1977) 2,800,000, mainly RC. M.U.: guarani.

P. was discovered by Sebastian Cabot in 1526, and Asunción was founded by Spanish settlers in 1537. From *c.* 1600 until 1767, when they were expelled, Jesuit missionaries administered much of the country as a semi-theocratic state. At first a prov. subordinate to the Spanish viceroyalty of Peru, then from 1776 part of the viceroyalty of Buenos Aires, P. in 1811 declared its independence from Spain. J. G. R. Francia, an able lawyer, established himself as despotic president, 1816-40; he was followed by his nephew, C. A. López, and he in turn (1862) by his son, F. S. López, who involved P. in a war with Brazil, Argentina, and Uruguay. After 5 years of war P. was invaded and López killed at Aquidaban in 1870. When hostilities ceased the Paraguayan people consisted mainly of women and children. Recovery was slow with many revolutions; and continuing disputes over the frontier with Bolivia in the torrid Chaco zone of the N flared up into war, 1932-5; arbitration by the USA and 5 S American reps. brought a frontier settlement and a peace treaty 1938. Under Pres. Alfredo Stroessner, who achieved power by a military coup in 1954, there was a liberalisation of regime from 1968; re-elected for 6th term 1978.

PA'RAKEET. *See* PARROT.

PARALDEHYDE. A colourless liquid $(CH_3CHO)_3$ formed from acetaldehyde. It is soluble in water and is a safe hypnotic.

PARALYSIS. Failure of action of muscle, due to injury or disease of the nerves supplying it. Paresis is partial P. *See* POLIOMYELITIS; and SLEEPY SICKNESS. In hysterical P. the nerves are sound and the disorder is in the emotions and will.

PARAMA'RIBO. Port and cap. of Surinam, 24km (15m) from the sea on the Surinam r., an important trading and commercial centre with an airport at Zanderij 40km (25m) to the S. Pop. (1971) 110,000.

PARANÁ (pahrahnah'). River of S America, formed by the confluence of the Rio Grande and Paranaiba. It is joined by the Paraguay at Corrientes, and flows into the Rio de la Plata with the Uruguay. It is about 4,000 km (2,500 long. It is being exploited jointly by Argentina, Brazil and Paraguay for hydroelectric power: Itaipu being the world's largest scheme.

PARANÁ. River port in Argentina, on the P. river, 560km (350m) NW of Buenos Aires. It has a handsome cathedral; also flour mills and meat canneries. Pop. (1970) 189,000.

PARANOIA. Monomania; a serious form of mental disorder in which the patient believes himself to be an especially superior person menaced by a conspiracy. Around this belief he builds up an elaborate delusional system embracing the whole of his life. Occasionally he will realize that the ideas are false and remain sane, but usually he is possessed by them and may attack one of his 'persecutors'.

PARAPSYCHOLOGY (parasīkol'oji). Scientific study of the phenomena of extra-sensory perception, which are not within the range explicable by estab. science (Gk. *para* 'beside'). They incl. telepathy (q.v.), telekinesis (controlling the movement of objects), precognition of events, levitation, dowsing, mediumship, etc.

PARAQUAT (par'akwat). Non-selective herbicide (l-dimenthyl-4, 4-bipyridium) used by farmers. Quickly degraded by soil micro-organisms, it is deadly to human beings in the smallest quantity, even if merely dropped on the skin. There is no antidote, and painful death over days follows ingestion, since irreversible, proliferative changes take place in lung tissue, etc.

PARASITE. A creature depending on another for the necessities of life, e.g. lice, fleas, the acarus that causes scabies, tape-worms, and the microscopic organisms that cause syphilis and malaria. Plants, too, may be parasitic.

PARATHYROIDS (-thī'roid-). Two pairs of small endocrine glands situated in the neck above and beside the thyroid. They control the use of lime (calcium) by the body.

PARATYPHOID (-tī'foid) **FEVER.** An infective fever like typhoid but milder and less dangerous.

PARIS, Henri d'Orléans, comte de (1909-). Head of the House of Bourbon: *see* BOURBON TABLE. He served in the Foreign Legion under an assumed name 1939-40, and in 1950 on the abrogation of the *loi d'exil* (1886) banning pretenders to the French throne, returned to live in France.

PARIS, Matthew (d. 1259). English chronicler. He entered St Albans Abbey in 1217, and wrote a valuable history of England down to 1259.

PARIS. Cap. of France in a fertile plain at the confluence of the Marne with the Seine. The City of P. (*Ville de P.*) forms a dept (area 105 sq.km/40.5 sq.m; pop. (1972) 2,461,000), one of the 8 making up the Île de France region.

HISTORY. P., the Roman Lutetia, cap. of the Parisii, a Gaulish tribe, was occupied by Julius Caesar, 53 BC. Clovis made it his cap. *c.* 508, but it attained importance only under the Capetian kings (987-1328). P. was occupied by the English 1420-36, strongly supported the Catholics during the Religious Wars, and was besieged by Henry IV, 1590-4. The Bourbon kings did much to beautify the city. Napoleon adorned it with new boulevards, bridges, and triumphal arches, as did Napoleon III. P. was the centre of the revolutions of 1789-94, 1830, and 1848. It was besieged by the Prussians 1870-1, and by govt troops under the Commune, and during the F.W.W. suffered from air raids and bombardment. In the S.W.W. it was occupied by the Germans June 1940-Aug. 1944.

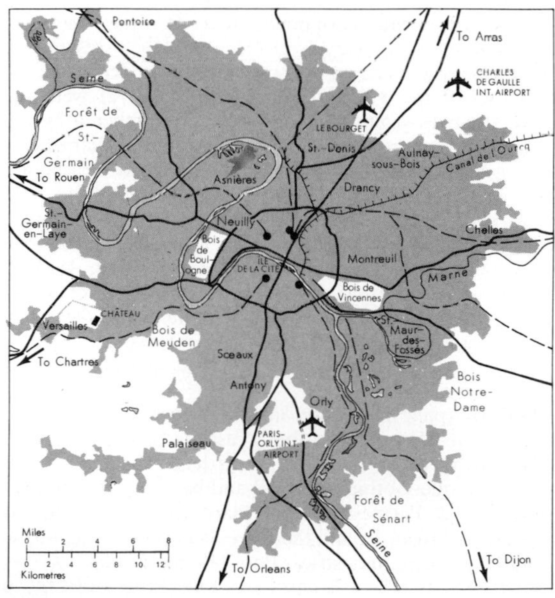

PARIS

MODERN P. The Seine is spanned by 32 bridges, the oldest being the Pont Neuf (1578). On the Ile de la Cité stand Notre-Dame (begun 1163), the seat of the archbishopric, and the Palais de Justice. On the N. bank are the Hôtel de Ville; the former palace of the Louvre, now one of the world's finest art galleries; the Tuileries gardens; and the Place de la Concorde. Thence the Champs Elysées leads to the Place de l'Étoile, in the centre of which is the Arc de Triomphe, with the tomb of the Unknown Warrior under it. Farther W is the Bois de Boulogne. On the S bank are the univ. (founded *c.* 1150); the Panthéon; the Invalides, with the tomb of Napoleon; the Champ de Mars, in which stands the Eiffel Tower; the Luxembourg Palace and Gardens; and the Jardin des Plantes. Montmartre, in the N of the city, on which stands the 19th cent. basilica of Sacré Cœur, rises to 125m (410ft). P. is one of France's main industrial centres, producing metal goods, chemicals, leather goods, glass, tobacco, food products, and luxury goods. It is also an important port, being connected by a modernized canal system with many other parts of France. There are airports at Orly and Roissy-en-France ('Charles de Gaulle'); Le Bourget was closed to commercial air traffic in 1978. Pop. (1975) 8,424,092.

PARIS. The National Centre for Art and Culture, designed by Renzo Piano and Richard Rogers, and opened in 1977 on the Beaubourg plateau. Five storeys high with four more underground, it is a mass of glass and concrete garlanded with coloured pipes and with many escalators linking the various levels, enclosed in plastic tubing. *Photo: Keystone Press Agency*

PARIS, Treaties of. Name given to a number of peace treaties signed in P., the chief being those concluding the Seven Years War (1763), the American War of Independence, the Napoleonic Wars, and the Crimean War. The peace conference after the F.W.W. which drew up the Treaty of Versailles was held in P. in 1919-20. The P. Peace Conference of 1946 drew up the peace treaties between the Allies and Italy, Romania, Hungary, Bulgaria, and Finland.

PARISH COUNCIL. Local govt body in English rural districts estab. by the Local Govt Act (1894) and largely unaffected by the 1974 reorganization. They function in parishes of 200 or more electors, may impose a limited local rate, and are elected every 4 years. In Wales they are called 'community' Cs.

PARIS-PLAGE. *See* TOUQUET-PARIS PLAGE, LE.

PARK, Merle (1937-). Rhodesian-British ballerina. B. in Salisbury, Rhodesia, she joined Sadler's Wells in 1955, and by 1959 was a principal soloist with the Royal Ballet. She combines elegance with sympathetic appeal in such roles as *Cinderella.*

PARK, Mungo (1771-1806). Scottish explorer. B. near Selkirk, he explored the course of the Niger 1795-7, and d. during a second expedition in 1805-6. He pub. *Travels in the Interior of Africa* (1799).

PARK CHUNG HEE (1917-1979). Pres. of S Korea 1963-79. Under his rule S Korea had the world's fastest-growing economy and the wealth was widely distributed, but recession and his increasing authoritarianism resulted in his assassination in 1979 by his chief of intelligence, who was nervous about losing his job.

PARKER, Dorothy (1893-1967). American poet and wit. She presided over a New York 'salon' in the 1920s, incl. Ring Lardner, Ogden Nash and James Thurber; pub. sadly penetrative verse, and wrote mordant reviews of the theatre for *Vanity Fair* and the *New Yorker*.

PARKER, Matthew (1504-75). English churchman. B. at Norwich, he was converted to Protestantism at Cambridge. He received high preferment under Henry VIII and Edward VI, and, as abp. of Canterbury from 1559 was largely responsible for the Elizabethan religious settlement.

PARKINSON, Cecil Edward (1931–). British Cons. politician. As chairman of the Cons. Party organization 1981–Sept 1983 he aided Tory success in the 1983 election, and was a member of the Falklands 'war cabinet' in 1982. He resigned as Min. for Trade and Industry (June–Oct 1983) after revelations concerning his relationship with his former secretary Miss Sara Keays, by whom he was the father of a dau. born in Jan 1984.

PARKINSON, Cyril Northcote (1909-). British historian and satirist. Raffles prof. of history at the Univ. of Malaya, Singapore, 1950-8, he sprang to fame with *Parkinson's Law* (1958), a study of the world of public and business administration, which laid down that 'work expands to fill the time available for its completion' with its corollary 'subordinates multiply at a fixed rate regardless of the amount of work produced'.

PARKINSON, James (1755-1824). British neurologist and palaeontologist. Parkinson's disease (*paralysis agitans*) is named after him.

PARLIAMENT. The supreme legislature of Great Britain. P. originated under the Norman kings as the Great Council of royal tenants-in-chief, to which in the 13th cent. representatives of the shires were sometimes summoned. De Montfort's parliament (1265) set a precedent by incl. representatives of the boroughs as well as the shires, which was followed by Edward I from 1275 onwards. Under Edward III the burgesses and knights of the shires began to meet separately from the barons, thus forming the House of Commons. By the 15th cent. P. had acquired the right to legislate, vote and appropriate supplies, examine public accounts, and impeach royal ministers. The powers of P. were much diminished under the Yorkists and Tudors, but under Elizabeth I a new spirit of independence appeared. The revolutions of 1640 and 1688 estab. parliamentary control over the executive and the judiciary, and finally abolished all royal claim to tax or legislate without parliamentary consent. During these struggles the 2 great parties emerged, and after 1688 it became customary for the king to choose his ministers from the party dominant in the Commons.

The English P. was united with the Scottish in 1707, and with the Irish during 1801-1922. The franchise was extended to the middle classes in 1832, to the urban working classes in 1867, to agricultural labourers in 1884, and to women in 1918 and 1928. Payment of members was introduced in 1911. The duration of Ps. was fixed at 3 years in 1694, at 7 in 1716, and at 5 in 1911, but any P. may extend its own life, as happened during both world wars. Constituencies are kept under continuous review by the Parliamentary Boundary Commissions (1944): no. of MPs 635.

The House of Lords comprises the temporal peers, i.e. all hereditary peers of England (created to 1707), all hereditary peers of Great Britain (created 1707-1800), and all hereditary peers of the UK (1801 onward); all hereditary Scottish peers (under the Peerage Act 1963); all peeresses in their own right (under the same act); all life peers (both the Law Lords and those created under the Life Peerages Act of 1958); and the spiritual peers - the 2 archbps. and 24 of the bps. (London, Durham and Winchester by right, and the rest by date). *See* PEERAGE. Since the P. Act of 1911 the powers of the Lords have been restricted, in that they may delay a bill passed by the Commons for a limited period but not reject it. Its abolition is proposed by the Labour Party, but the Conservative Party would prefer reform of the hereditary element.

The Lords are presided over by the Lord Chancellor, and the Commons by the Speaker. A public bill is given a preliminary first reading and discussed in detail at the second reading; it is then referred to a select or standing committee, after which it is considered by a committee of the whole House. After the third reading it is sent to the Lords, whose procedure is similar. If it passes both houses, it receives the royal assent and so becomes law. *See also* SELECT COMMITTEE. Selective sound broadcasting of parliamentary proceedings on a permanent basis began in 1978.

The European Parliament was at first mainly a consultative body, but direct elections (1979) resulted in an increase in its powers, as provided for under the Rome Treaty. Of the 410 seats the Socialists (112) were the largest single group, but they were outnumbered by the aggregate strength of the centre and right. Parliamentary sessions alternate between Luxembourg and Strasbourg, parliamentary committees meet in Brussels.

PARLIAMENT, Houses of. The present H.P. were designed by Sir C. Barry, and built in 1840-60, the previous building having been burnt down in 1834. It incorporates portions of the medieval Palace of Westminster. The Commons debating chamber was destroyed by incendiary bombs in 1941: the rebuilt chamber (opened 1950) is the work of Sir G. G. Scott, and preserves its former character.

PARMA (pahr'mah). City in Emilia-Romagna, Italy, on the P. river. Founded by the Etruscans, it was the cap. of the Duchy of P. 1545-1860, and has a fine 12th cent. Romanesque-Gothic cathedral and baptistry, and a univ. estab. 1502. Parmesan cheese (hard and flavoursome) is distributed from P., and there are food processing, textile and engineering industries. Pop. (1978) 178,000.

PARNASSIENS (pahrnashi-eṅ), **Les.** School of French poets incl. Leconte de Lisle, Mallarmé, and Verlaine, which flourished 1866-76. Named from the review *Parnasse Contemporain*, it advocated 'Art for art's sake' in opposition to the ideas of the Romantics.

PARNASSUS. Mountain in central Greece, 2,457 m (8,062 ft) revered as the abode of Apollo and the Muses. Delphi lies on its S flank.

PARNELL (pahr'nel), **Charles Stewart** (1846-91). Irish politician. B. in co. Wicklow, he was elected MP for Meath in 1875. P. supported a policy of obstruction and violence, and became the president of the Nationalist Party in 1877. In 1879 he approved the Land League, and his attitude led in 1881 to his imprisonment. He welcomed Gladstone's Home Rule Bill, and continued his agitation after its defeat in 1886. In 1887 *The Times* failed to prove P.'s complicity in the Phoenix Park murders, but in 1889 Captain O'Shea petitioned for divorce on the grounds of his wife's adultery with P.; in 1891 Parnell m. Mrs. O'Shea. For fear of losing the support of Gladstone, his party deposed him in Nov. 1890.

PARR, Catherine (1512-48). 6th wife of Henry VIII. She had already lost 2 husbands when in 1543 she m. Henry VIII. She survived him, and in 1547 m. Lord Seymour of Sudeley.

PARRAMA'TTA. River, W arm of Port Jackson, New South Wales, Australia. It is 24km (15m) long and is lined with industrial suburbs of Sydney: Balmain, Drummoyne, Concord on the left bank, P., Ermington and Rydalmere, Ryde, and Hunter's Hill on the right.

PARROT. Order of birds, Psittaci, abundant in the tropics, espec. in Australia and S America: the smaller species are commonly referred to as parakeets. They are vegetarian, except for the New Zealand kea (*Nestor notabilis*) which has become carnivorous since the settlement of white farmers. Their strong, hooked bills cope easily with fruit and seeds, which they characteristically clasp in their claws while feeding. The plumage is generally very colourful, although the call is commonly a harsh screech: the talent for imitating human speech is most marked in the comparatively sober grey P. (*Psitticus crithacus*) of Africa. The white eggs are usually laid in holes in trees, but the grey-breasted parakeet - though remaining monogamous - combines with the rest of the flock to build enormous nests of twigs in trees, rather like a block of flats. *See* BUDGERIGAR and COCKATOO.

PARRY, Sir Charles Hubert Hastings (1848-1918). British composer. B. at Bournemouth, from 1883 he taught at the RCM, becoming director in 1894, and was prof. of music at Oxford 1900-8. He was created a baronet in 1902. His works incl. songs, motets, and the setting of Milton's 'Blest Pair of Sirens'.

PARRY, Sir William Edward (1790-1855). British explorer. In 1819-20 he led an expedition described in his *Journal of a Voyage to Discover a North-West Passage*, and similar explorations in 1821-3 and 1824-5. In 1827 P. attempted to reach the North Pole, attaining a latitude of 82° 45′.

PARSEES. The followers of Zoroaster (q.v.) who fled from Persia after its conquest by the Arabs, and settled in India in the 8th cent. AD. They now live mainly in Bombay state, maintaining their cult of the sacred fire and the exposure of their dead. They are proverbial for their business ability and philanthropy. They number about 100,000.

PARSLEY. Biennial herb (*Petroselinum crispum*), cultivated for flavouring: 45cm (1.5ft), it has bipinnate, aromatic leaves and yellow umbelliferous flowers.

PARSNIP. Biennial plant (*Pastinaca sativa*), up to 1.2m (4ft) high, cultivated for its edible tap-root. The leaves are ovate, serrated, and downy beneath, and the flower umbels yellow.

PARROT. The Kea has taken to living on offal from sheep stations and may attack live sheep to eat the kidneys. *Photo: Topham/Coleman.*

PARSONS, Sir Charles Algernon (1854-1931). British engineer, inventor of the P. steam turbine, who estab. his own firm nr Newcastle upon Tyne in 1889. He was knighted in 1911 and received the OM in 1927.

PA'RTHENON. The temple of Athena Parthenos (the Virgin) on the Acropolis at Athens. It was built in 447-438 BC, under the supervision of Phidias, and is considered the most perfect example of Doric architecture. Later it was used as a Christian church and by the Turks as a mosque, then as a powder magazine, as a result of which it was reduced to ruins when the Venetians bombarded the Acropolis in 1687. *See* ELGIN MARBLES.

PA'RTHIA. Ancient name for a country of W Asia in what is now NE Iran. Originating *c.* 248 BC, it reached the peak of its power under Mithridates I in the 2nd cent. BC. Ctesiphon was the cap. of P. which was annexed to Persia in AD 226.

PARTICLE, sub-atomic. Any of the sub-divisions of the atom. They are frequently classified in 3 groups of elementary Ps.: baryons, which incl. the massive Ps. (proton, neutron, anti-proton, anti-neutron); mesons, which incl. the intermediate mass Ps. (pion); leptons, which incl. the light Ps. (electron, positron, neutrino); and the ultra-elementary Ps., or quarks (q.v.). *See* BEAM WEAPON.

PARTNERSHIP. A P. in English law is the relation of 2 or more persons carrying on a common business for profit. It differs from a company in that it may not consist of more than 20 members, and that members (and not only the directors) commonly take part in the conduct of the business. In the USA the sharing of profits is regarded as the distinctive feature.

PARTHENON. Devoted to the cult of Athena Parthenos, 'the Virgin', the temple housed an enormous statue of the goddess in gold and ivory. *Photo: J. Allan Cash*

PARTRIDGE, Eric (1894-1979). New Zealand lexicographer. He studied at Oxford after serving in the F.W.W. and settled in England to write with entertaining scholarship *A Dictionary of Slang and Unconventional English* (1934), *Dictionary of the Underworld, British and American* (1950), and many others.

PARTRIDGE. Game bird, 2 species of which are found in Great Britain. The grey P. (*Perdix perdix*) is mottled brown above, with grey speckled breast, and patches of chestnut barred on the sides. The French P. (*Alectoris rufa*) is distinguished from the grey P. by red legs, bill, and eyelids. The back is plain brown, with a white throat edged with black. The sides are barred chestnut and black.

PASADĒ'NA. City in California, USA, 18km (11m) NE of Los Angeles, originally a Spanish settlement. There is an annual Tournament of Roses, and on 1 Jan. the East-West football game (1902), has been held in the Rose Bowl (85,000 seats) from 1923. The Mt Wilson observatory is 8km (5m) NE. Pop. (1970) 113,000.

PASCAL (pahskahl'), **Blaise** (1623-62). French philosopher and mathematician. B. at Clermont-Ferrand, he was a precocious student, and produced a treatise on conic sections in 1640. Coming under Jansenist influence, he took refuge at Port Royal in 1655, and defended the Jansenist doctrines against the Jesuits in the *Lettres Provinciales* (1656). He investigated the laws governing the weight of air, the equilibrium of liquids, the hydraulic press, the infinitesimal calculus, and the mathematical theory of probability. His *Pensées*, a fragmentary apology for the Christian religion, appeared in 1670.

PAS-DE-CALAIS (pah-de-kahlā'). French name for the Strait of Dover; name also of a French dept bordering the Strait of which Arras is the cap., Calais the chief port.

PASHA. A Turkish title of honour borne originally by military commanders, and later by high civil officials. Abolished in Turkey in 1934, it was in use in other Middle East countries until 1952.

PASMORE, Victor (1908-). British artist. B. in Surrey, he was in local govt service with the LCC 1927-37, taught 1949-53 at the Central School of Arts and Crafts, London, where he had once attended evening classes, and was Master of Painting, Durham university, 1954-61. He is noted for abstract compositions and as an exponent of the 'classic' tendency in British art.

PASSAU (pahs'sow). Town of Bavaria, W Germany, at the junction of the Inn and Ilz with the Danube, close to the Austrian frontier. The *Treaty of P.* (1552) between Maurice, Elector of Saxony, and the future Emperor Ferdinand I, allowed the Lutherans full religious liberty, and prepared the way for the Peace of Augsburg: *see* REFORMATION.

PASSCHENDAELE (pa'shendāl). Village in W Flanders, Belgium, near Ypres. The P. ridge before Ypres was the object of a costly, but unsuccessful, British offensive, July-Nov. 1917; British casualties numbered nearly 400,000 (17,000 officers).

PASSFIELD, Sidney Webb, baron P. (1859-1947). British Socialist theorist. B. London, he was till 1891 a civil servant, and in 1895 was the principal founder of the London School of Economics, where he was prof. of public administration 1912-27. Among the founders of the Fabian Soc. in 1884, he was a member of the Labour Party executive 1915-25, entered parliament in 1922, and was pres.of the B of T 1924, Dominions Sec. 1929-30, and Colonial Sec. 1929-31. He received a peerage in 1929. He m. in 1892 Beatrice Potter (1858-1943), who collaborated with him in a series of books, e.g. *History of Trade Unionism* (1894), *English Local Government* (1906), and *Soviet Communism* (1935), and whose own writing incl. *My Apprenticeship* (1926) and *Our Partnership* (1948).

PASSION FLOWER. Genus of climbing plants (*Passiflora*). The name is derived from the likeness of certain parts of the flower to symbols of the crucifixion of Christ.

PASSIONISTS. RC religious order founded in 1720 by St Paul of the Cross (1694-1775), which combines the active and the contemplative life.

PASSION PLAY. A play representing the death and resurrection of a god. In ancient Egypt there were plays in honour of Osiris held at Abydos, and in Greece the mysteries of Dionysus were performed. Christian plays depict the crucifixion and resurrection of Christ, e.g. certain of the medieval miracle plays, and that held at Oberammergau, in Bavaria.

PASSOVER. An ancient Jewish spring festival, which commemorates the Exodus from Egypt. Its 2 main features are a family feast eaten at home on the first evening of the festival, and abstention from leaven throughout the 7 days which it lasts. Formerly a lamb was eaten at the feast, but a shank bone is now substituted.

PASSPORT. Document issued by the foreign office of any country authorizing the bearer to go abroad and guaranteeing him the state's protection. A British P. is generally available for travel to all countries, but some countries require the intending visitor to obtain a special endorsement or *visa*. For the citizen of the UK and Colonies a cheaper, simplified travel document is available for short visits to certain countries. From 1978 uniform European Community Ps. were to be introduced as an alternative to nat. Ps., although their utility in the absence of a common immigration procedure, would be limited. They will be issued from 1985 in the UK.

PASTERNAK, Boris Leonidovich (1890-1960). Russian author. B. in Moscow of Jewish parentage, he remained in Russia when his artist father **Leonid P.** (1862-1945) emigrated to Germany, dying in Oxford. His reputation as his country's chief lyric poet mounted from his first vol. *A Twin Cloud* (1914), through *Life is My Sister* (1922), and

On Early Trains (1941) to the pub. of his selected poems (1945), and he produced excellent translations of Shakespeare's tragedies and Goethe's *Faust*. A Nobel prize in 1958 followed the pub. in the W of his novel *Dr Zhivago*, which had been banned in the USSR as a 'hostile political act'. His work had previously suffered indirect attack and now, although he refused the prize, he was expelled from the Union of Soviet Writers for his portrayal of the degeneration of a scientist who passes from support of the Revolution to increasing disillusion.

PASTEUR (pahstör'), **Louis** (1822-95). French chemist. B. at Dôle, he became director of scientific studies at the École Normale in 1857, where he announced his discovery of the causes of fermentation in alcohol and milk. His proof that the organisms stimulating it were contained in the atmosphere inspired Lister's work in antiseptic surgery. P. was prof. of chemistry at the Sorbonne 1867-89. Among his later researches were those on silkworm disease, anthrax, and hydrophobia; the Institut Pasteur was founded in 1888. *See* PASTEURIZATION.

PASTEURIZATION. Treatment of milk to reduce the number of micro-organisms it contains, and so protect consumers from disease. A temperature of between 62.8°C and 65.5°C is maintained for at least 30 min, then the milk is rapidly cooled to 10°C or lower. The harmful bacteria are killed and the development of the others is delayed.

PASTON LETTERS. A collection of letters and documents, written by or to members of the Norfolk family of P. during 1422-1509.

PASTORAL STAFF. A staff shaped like a shepherd's crook carried by cardinals and bishops on certain formal occasions as a sign of office.

PATAGO'NIA. Geographical area S of lat. 40° S and extending westward through Chile to the Pacific. Argentinian P. is divided into the provs. of Chubut, Rio Negro, Santa Cruz, and Tierra del Fuego; Chilean P. into the provs. of Chiloé and Magallanes (which incl. Chilean Tierra del Fuego). Magellan sighted P. in 1520. Both Chile and Argentina claimed P. (over 1,036,000 sq.km/400,000 sq.m) but agreed to a division in 1881, Chile receiving 186,500 sq.km (72,000 sq.m). Most of Argentinian P. is sterile with a chilly climate and frequent high winds; Chilean P. is cold and damp with dense forest on the lower slopes of the Andes. Sheep rearing is the principal occupation throughout P.; minerals incl. coal and petroleum.

PA'TEN. Flat dish of gold or silver used for holding the consecrated bread at Holy Communion.

PATENT. Letters patent, more usually called a P., are documents conferring the exclusive right to make, use, and sell an invention for a limited period. It is not possible to patent an *idea* nor anything which is not *new*. International coverage was given under a convention of 1883, procedure being simplified following the Washington Conference of 1970. A central office (estab. in Munich, with a branch at The Hague, in 1977) grants Ps. for 20 years in 16 European countries: designs and trade marks are also covered. The London office will close by 1992. In the USA the period of P. is 17 years. *See also* FRANKENSTEIN LAW.

PATER, Walter Horatio (1839-94). British critic. B. in London, he became a fellow of Brasenose Coll., Oxford, in 1864. A noted stylist and supporter of 'art for art's sake', he pub. *Studies in the History of the Renaissance* (1873); *Marius the Epicurean* (1885); *Imaginary Portraits* (1887), etc.

PA'TERNO'STER. Name for the Lord's Prayer, from the opening words of the Latin version.

PATERSON, Andrew Barton (1864-1941). Australian journalist, known as 'Banjo' P., author of vols. of light verse and 'Waltzing Matilda', adapted from a traditional song.

PATHAN (patahn'). Warrior people of Afghanistan and the former NW Frontier Prov. of British India, now part of Pakistan. They were a constant threat to the security of the *raj*, and under the rule of Pakistan continued to agitate for a state of their own, Pakhtoonistan, in which they would be joined by the P. tribesmen of Afghanistan.

PATIALA (patiah'la). City in Punjab, Rep. of India, with textile and metalwork industries. Pop. (1970) 152,000.

PATMORE, Coventry (1823-96). British poet and critic. He was a librarian at the British Museum 1846-66, and as one of the pre-Raphaelites achieved fame with the poem *The Angel in the House* (1854-63), and the collection of odes *The Unknown Eros* (1877).

PA'TMOS. Greek is. of the Dodecanese. St John is said to have written Revelation while in exile here, and the monastery of St John commemorates his stay.

PA'TNA. The cap. of Bihar state, Rep. of India, on the Ganges. It has remains of a hall built by Asoka in the 3rd cent. BC, and is the seat of a univ. (1917). Pop. (1971) 490,265.

PĀ'TON, Alan (1903-). S African writer. B. at Pietermaritzburg, he became first a schoolmaster, and in 1935 principal of a reformatory nr Johannesburg, which he ran on enlightened lines. His novel *Cry, the Beloved Country* (1948) touched the heart of S Africa's problems: later books incl. the study *Land and People of South Africa* (1956), *The Long View* (1968).

PATRA'S. Town (Gk *Patrai*) in Greece on the Gulf of P. In the NW Peloponnese, 72km (45m) W of Corinth. The ancient Patrae, it is the only one of the 12 cities of Achaea to survive. It has hydroelectric installations, and textiles and paper are made. Pop. (1971) 111,600.

PATRIARCH (Gk 'Ruler of a family'). The mythical ancestors of the human race and of the Jews, from Adam to the sons of Jacob. In the Orthodox Church the term is used for the primates of 7 of the 10 national Churches.

PATRICIANS. Privileged class in ancient Rome, descended from the original citizens. After the 4th cent. BC the rights formerly exercised by the Ps. alone were thrown open to the plebeians, and patrician descent became only a matter of prestige.

PATRICK, St (*c.* 389-461 or 493). The patron saint of Ireland. B. in Britain, probably in S Wales, he was carried off by pirates to 6 years' slavery in Antrim before escaping either to Britain or Gaul - his poor Latinity suggests the former - to train as a missionary. He is variously said to have landed again in Ireland in 432 or 456, and is credited with founding the diocese of Armagh, though this was probably the work of a 'lost apostle' (Palladius or Secundinus), of which he was bp. The later, traditional date of death is probably correct. His work was a vital factor in the spread of Irish Christian influence. Of his writings only his *Confessio* and an *Epistola* survive.

PATTI (pat'ē), **Adelina** (1843-1919). British soprano. B. at Madrid, she made her debut in America in 1859, and was celebrated in such roles as Lucia and Amina in *La Sonnambula*. She became a British subject in 1898.

PATTON, George Smith (1885-1945). American gen., known for his fiery daring as 'blood and guts' P. He commanded the 2nd Armoured Division in 1940, and in 1942 led the W Task Force which landed at Casablanca. After commanding the 7th Army, he led the 3rd Army in France, Belgium, and Germany, and in 1945 took over the 15th Army. He d. following a motor accident.

PAU (poh). Town and resort, cap. of Pyrénées-Atlantiques dept in SW France, nr the Spanish border. It is the centre of the Basque (q.v.) area of France, and there have been terrorist outrages. Hydroelectric power services electrochemical and metallurgical industries. Pop. (1973) 76,230.

PAUL (*c.* AD 3-*c.* 64 or 68). Christian saint and apostle, whose real name was Saul. B. in Tarsus, the son of well-to-do Pharisees, he possessed Roman citizenship, and was ed. at Jerusalem at the school of Gamaliel. He took part in the stoning of Stephen, but while on a journey to Damascus was himself converted by a vision. After 3 years' meditation in Arabia, he returned to Damascus to begin his work as an apostle. After some 12 years of preparatory work he set out from Antioch on the first missionary journey among the Gentiles with Barnabas, journeying through Cyprus and Pamphilia. On a 2nd journey he revisited the churches estab. during the first, and founded further churches in Greece. The 3rd journey covers similar ground, but is chiefly concerned with his return to Ephesus, which became one of the great centres of Christian teaching. Returning to Jerusalem, he was arrested, appealed to Caesar, and was sent to Rome for trial *c.* 57 or 59. After 2 years' imprisonment he was possibly released before his final arrest and execution under Nero. Thirteen epistles in the NT are attributed to him.

PAUL. Name of 6 popes. Paul VI (Giovanni Battista Montini, 1897-1978). B. nr Brescia, the son of a banker and journalist, he spent more than 25 years in the Secretariat of State under Pius XI and Pius XII before becoming archbp of Milan in 1954. In 1958 he was created a cardinal by Pope John, and in 1963 he succeeded him as pope and was crowned in St Peter's Square - thought to be the first open-air coronation in the history of the Church - taking the name of Paul as symbolic of ecumenical unity.

His encyclical *Humanae Vitae* (Of Human Life) in 1968, re-affirmed the Church's traditional teaching on birth control, thus following the minority report of the commission originally appointed by Pope John, rather than the majority view.

PAUL I (1754-1801). Tsar of Russia. The son of Peter III and Catherine II, he succeeded his mother in 1796. His mind was already unhinged, and his foreign policy was capricious. He was assassinated.

PAUL (1901-64). King of the Hellenes. The son of King Constantine, he served in the navy for some years and in 1947 he succeeded his brother George II. He m. in 1938 Princess Frederika (1917-), dau. of the duke of Brunswick, whose political role brought her under attack. He was succeeded by his son Constantine II.

PAULI (pow'li), **Wolfgang** (1900-58). Austrian-American physicist. Awarded a Nobel prize in 1945 for his work on atomic structure, he originated P.'s *exclusion principle* in quantum mechanics that in a given system no 2 electrons, protons, or neutrons can be characterized by the same set of quantum numbers.

PAULING (pawl'-), **Linus Carl** (1901-). American chemist. Professor at the California Institute of Technology 1931-63, he was noted for his fundamental work on the nature of the chemical bond and was awarded the Nobel prize for chemistry in 1954. An outspoken opponent of nuclear testing, he received the Nobel peace prize in 1962.

PAULI'NUS (d. 644). Missionary. B. in Rome, he joined Augustine in Kent in 601, and converted the Northumbrians in 625, becoming first archbp of York. He returned to Kent in 633. In 1978 excavation revealed the church he built in Lincoln.

PAULUS (pow'lus), **Friedrich** (1890-1957). German field marshal, commander of the forces besieging Stalingrad 1942-3. He gave evidence at Nuremberg, and later lived in E Germany.

PAUSĀ'NIAS (2nd cent AD). Greek geographer. B. probably in Lydia, he based his *Description of Greece* on his own travels.

PAVIA (pahvē'ah). Town in Lombardy, Italy, on the Ticino. Among its many fine buildings are the 11th cent. church of San Michele and the cathedral of San Martino 1488-1898. The law school, from which the univ. developed, was traditionally founded by Lanfranc (q.v.). An agricultural centre, P. also has modern industries. In the *Battle of Pavia* (1525) Emperor Charles V defeated and captured Francis I of France. Pop. (1971) 84,400.

PA'VLOV, Ivan Petrovich (1849-1936). Russian physiologist. B. near Ryazan, he became a director of the Institute of Experimental Medicine at St Petersburg in 1913. He carried out research on digestion, for which he received a Nobel prize in 1904. His study of conditioned reflexes in animals influenced the behaviourist school of psychology.

PAV'LOVA, Anna (1885-1931). Russian dancer. B. at St Petersburg, she made her début in 1899, appeared in London in 1910, and subsequently toured the world with outstanding success, espec. in *The Swan* (*Le Cygne*), popularizing the Russian ballet everywhere. She d. in Holland.

PAWNBROKER. One who lends money on the security of goods held, the traditional sign of the premises being 3 gold balls which were the symbol used in front of their houses by the medieval Lombard merchants.

PAWPAW or **papaya.** Tropical tree (*Carica papaya*), originating in S America and grown in many tropical countries. The edible fruits resemble a melon, with orange-coloured flesh and numerous blackish seeds in the central cavity, and may weigh *c.* 9kg (20lb). The fruit juice or the tree sap are often used to tenderize meat for the table. In the USA the name 'pawpaw' is given to *Asimina triloba*, which has an unpleasant odour but carries fleshy edible oval berries *c.* 75mm (3in) long.

PAXTON, Sir Joseph (1801-65). British architect, garden superintendent to the duke of Devonshire from 1826 and designer of the Great Exhibition building of 1851 (*see* CRYSTAL PALACE), which was revolutionary in its structural use of glass and iron.

PAYE (Pay As You Earn). System whereby a proportional amount of Income Tax is deducted by the employer and handed over to the Inland Revenue before wages are paid, reliefs due being notified to him by a code no. for each employee. Introduced in Britain in 1944 to spread the tax burden over the year for the increasing no. of wage-earners becoming liable, it was devised by Sir Paul Chambers (q.v.).

PAWPAW. Although native to South America it ripens well in commercial cultivation elsewhere. This plantation is in Queensland, Australia. *Photo: Courtesy of the Australian Information Service.*

PAYMASTER-GENERAL. Head of the P.-G.'s Office, the British govt dept (estab. 1835) which acts as paying agent for most other depts.

PAYSANDU'. Second city of Uruguay, cap. of P. dept, situated on the r. Uruguay *c.* 340km (210m) NW of Montevideo. Tinned meat is the main product. It dates from 1772, and is linked by bridge with Puerto Colón in Argentina (1976). Pop. (1975) 80,000.

PAZ (pahth), **Octavio** (1914-). Mexican poet. B. in Mexico City, his *Piedra de Sol* (1957, *Sun Stone*) is a personal statement comparable with Hart Crane's *The Bridge,* and takes as its basic symbol the Aztec Calendar Stone. He has also pub. a study of Mexican culture *The Labyrinth of Solitude* and ed. anthologies.

PEA. Two allied genera in the family Leguminosae, both climbing plants. The garden P. (*Pisum sativum*) has white, lipped flowers, and has been cultivated since ancient times for its seeds, gathered unripe; it grows at its best in England. Cultivated for their flowers are the fragrant sweet P. (*Lathyrus odoratus*), and the scentless everlasting P. (*L. latifolius*).

PEACE, Charles (1832-79). British criminal. He carried out many burglaries around Manchester, and in 1876 murdered a policeman during a robbery, another man being sentenced to death, though afterwards reprieved for the crime. After killing Arthur Dyson in a quarrel he removed to London, and continued his burglaries until he was arrested, tried, and hanged.

PEACE. Canadian river formed in British Columbia by the union at Finlay Forks of the Finlay and Parsnip rivers and flowing through the Rockies and across Alberta to join the Slave r. just N of Lake Athabasca; length 1,600 km (1,000 m). Discovered *c.* 1780 and explored 1792-3 by Sir Alexander Mackenzie (*c.* 1755-1820), it was used as a means of transport by fur traders. The W.A.C. Bennett dam, completed in 1968 is one of the world's largest: 160m (600ft) high, crest length 2,042 m (6,700 ft).

PEACE CORPS. A body of trained men and women, first estab. in the US by Pres. Kennedy in 1961, providing the necessary skilled manpower required in developing countries, especially in the fields of teaching, agriculture and health. Living among, and at the same level as, the country's inhabitants, volunteers are paid only a small allowance covering their basic needs and maintaining health. The P.C. was inspired by Voluntary Service Overseas (*see* BRITISH VOLUNTEER PROGRAMME), and similar corps have since been formed in other countries.

PEACH. A tree (*Prunus persica*) in the family *Rosaccac.* It has ovate leaves and small white flowers. The yellowish edible fruits have thick velvety skins; the nectarine is a smooth-skinned variety.

PEACOCK, Thomas Love (1785-1866). British satirist. B. at Weymouth, he worked for the East India Company 1819-56. He pub. several books of verse, and the satiric novels *Headlong Hall* (1815), *Melincourt, Nightmare Abbey,* and *Crotchet Castle* (1831).

PEACOCK. Genus of gallinaceous birds, native to India and Sri Lanka. The common P. (*Pavo cristatus*) is rather larger than a pheasant and has a large fan-shaped tail, brightly coloured with blue, green, and purple 'eyes' on a chestnut ground. The female is brown with only a small tail.

PEAK DISTRICT. Tableland of the S Pennines in NW Derbyshire. England. It is a tourist region and a National Park. The highest point is Kinder Scout 636m (2,088 ft).

PEAK DISTRICT. Cattle grazing in the dales of the Peak District. *Photos: A. G. Hutchinson/Camera Press*

PEANUT. *See* GROUNDNUT.

PEAR. Tree (*Pyrus communis*), closely related to the apple (to which it is second in importance as a fruit producer in temperate countries), in the family Rosaceae. Blooming earlier than the apple, it is less hardy.

PEARL. Calcareous substance (nacre) secreted by many molluscs, which when deposited in thin layers on the inside of the shell forms the mother-of-pearl used in ornamental and inlay work, and when deposited round some irritant body forms Ps. Although commercially valuable Ps. are obtained from freshwater mussels, etc., the precious P. comes from the various species of *Margaritifera* in the family Aviculidae, found in tropical waters off N and W Australia, the Californian coast, and in the Indian Ocean.

Artifical Ps. were first cultivated by Kokichi Mikimoto in Japan in 1893, although full development of the industry was not undertaken until after the S.W.W. A tiny bead of shell from the pigtoe clam, plus a small piece of membrane from another P. oyster's mantle (to stimulate the secretion of nacre) is inserted in a 3-yr-old oyster. The Os. are kept in cages in the sea for 3 yrs, and then the Ps. are harvested.

PEARL HARBOR. US Pacific naval base in Oahu, chief of the islands forming Hawaii state, USA, the scene of a Japanese attack on 7 Dec. 1941, which brought America into the S.W.W., and which took place while Japanese envoys were holding 'peace' talks at Washington. The local commanders Admiral Kummel and Lt-Gen. Short were relieved of their posts and held responsible for the fact that the base, despite warnings, was totally unprepared at the time of the attack. *See also* FBI.

PEARS, Sir Peter (1910-). British tenor. A cofounder with Britten of the Aldeburgh Festival, he is closely associated with the composer's work and played the title role in *Peter Grimes*: he has also often been the first performer of works by Tippett and Berkeley. Knighted 1978.

PEARSE, Patrick Henry (1879-1916). Irish poet and republican. B. in Dublin, he was prominent in the Gaelic revival, and led the Easter Rebellion of 1916. He was proclaimed president of the provisional govt, and after its suppression was court-martialled and shot.

PEARSON, 'Mike' Lester Bowles (1897-1972). Canadian Liberal statesman. Appointed For. Min. by St Laurent (1948-57), he effectively represented Canada at the UN and only Soviet opposition prevented his becoming Sec.-Gen.: in 1957 he was awarded a Nobel peace prize principally because of his role in the creation of the UN Emergency Force. Leader of the Liberal Party from 1958, he was PM 1963-8.

PEARY, Robert Edwin (1856-1920). American Polar explorer. B. in Pennsylvania, at his 7th attempt he was the first man to reach the North Pole, on 6 April 1909. He sailed to Cape Sheridan in the *Roosevelt*, and then made a sledge journey to the Pole.

PEASANTS' REVOLT. The rising of the English peasantry in June 1381. Led by Wat Tyler and John Ball, the rebels occupied London and forced Richard II to abolish serfdom, but after Tyler's murder were compelled to withdraw. The movement was then suppressed, and the king's concessions revoked.

PEAT (pēt). Deposit, which varies from compacted fibre to a type of woody brown coal or lignite, formed by the decomposition of aquatic plants, e.g. sphagnum moss and *Thacomitrum lanuginosum.* It may reach a depth of 9m (30ft) and extend great distances, Russia, Canada and Finland having large deposits. In Scotland and Ireland, dried P. has been used as fuel from time immemorial and in Scotland P. fuel is used for malting the barley for Scotch whisky: the peat 'reek' contributes to the flavour.

PECAN (pikan'). Nut-producing tree (*Carya illinoensis*), native to southern USA and possibly N Mexico, and now widely cultivated. The tree grows to over 45m (150ft), and the edible nuts are smooth-shelled, the kernel resembling a smoothly ovate walnut. *See* HICKORY.

PECCARY. American genus of pig-like animals (*Tayassu*), having a gland in the middle of the back which secretes a strong-smelling substance. Blackish in colour, they are covered with bristles, and the skins make a useful leather. Travelling in herds, they are often belligerent.

PECHENGA (pye'chenga). Ice-free fishing port in Murmansk region, RSFSR, on the Barents Sea, more familiar under its Finnish name Petsamo. Russia ceded P. to Finland in 1920, recovered it under the peace treaty with Finland, 1947. Pop. (est.) 5,000.

PECHÓ'RA. River in the USSR, which rises in the N Urals. It carries coal, timber and furs (June-Sept.) to the Barents Sea 1,800 km (1,125 m) to the N, but would be more economically useful if it flowed in the opposite direction. *See* VOLGA.

PÉCS (pāch). Town in SW Hungary, centre of a coal-mining area on the Yugoslavia frontier, and with metallurgical industries and a univ. Dating from Roman times, it was under Turkish rule 1543-1686. Pop. (1978) 169,000.

PEDIATRICS. Branch of medicine dealing with diseases of children and the study of childhood.

PEDIMENT. In architecture, the triangular part crowning the fronts of buildings in classic styles. The P. was a distinctive feature of Greek temples.

PEDO'METER. Instrument for measuring the distance covered by a pedestrian from the number of his steps and their average length. It is so arranged that each step moves a swinging weight, which in turn causes a mechanism to rotate and move a pointer step by step over a dial.

PEDRO. Name of 2 emperors of Brazil. **Pedro I** (1798-1834), the son of John VI of Portugal, escaped to Brazil on Napoleon's invasion, and was appointed regent in 1821. He proclaimed Brazil independent in 1822, and was crowned emperor, but abdicated in 1831 and returned to Portugal. His son **Pedro II** (1825-91), who succeeded him, proved an enlightened ruler, but his anti-slavery measures alienated the landowners, who in 1889 compelled him to abdicate.

PEEBLESSHIRE. Former co. of S Scotland, incl. from 1975 in Borders region. Peebles was the co. town. Pop. (1971) 6,000.

PEEL, Sir Robert (1788-1850). British Cons. statesman. B. in Lancs, he entered parliament as a Tory in 1809. As Home Sec. 1822-7 and 1828-30, he founded the modern police force and in 1829 introduced RC emancipation. After the passing of the Reform Bill (1832), which he had resisted, he reformed the Tory Party under the name of 'Conservatives', on a basis of accepting necessary reforms and seeking middle-class support. He was Premier 1834-5 and 1841-6; he fell owing to his repeal of the Corn Laws (1846) which was opposed by the majority of his party. He and his followers then formed a third party standing between the Liberals and Conservatives; the majority of the Peelites, including Gladstone, joined the Liberals.

PEEL. Seaport in the Isle of Man, 19km (12m) NW of Douglas. The principal occupation is fishing. Pop. (1971) 3,080.

PEELE, George (*c.* 1558-97). English dramatist. B. in London, he wrote a pastoral, *The Arraignment of Paris*; a fantastic comedy, *The Old Wives' Tale*; and a tragedy, *David and Bethsabe.*

PEENEMÜNDE (pē'nemünde). Fishing village in Rostock district, E Germany, in the NW of the is. of Usedom, where guided missiles of the S.W.W. were under development 1936-45.

PEEPUL. *See* BO-TREE.

PEERAGE. In the UK the body of nobility holding the hereditary temporal dignities of duke, marquess, earl, viscount and baron: certain hereditary Ps. may be held by a woman in default of a male heir. To these were added in the later 19th cent. the Lords of Appeal in Ordinary, who are life peers, as well as from 1958 a number of specially created life peers of either sex. Since 1963 it has been

PEEL. Sir Robert Peel founded the modern police-force, hence the early nicknames given to the men of 'Peelers' or 'Bobbles'. This portrait is by H. W. Pickersgill. *Photo: Courtesy of the National Portrait Gallery*

possible for a peer to disclaim his title (*see* Home, Sir Alec Douglas, and Lord Hailsham), usually to enable him to be elected to the Commons, and in 1964 it was ruled that his children need not discontinue use of their courtesy titles. *See* Parliament.

PE′GASUS. In Greek mythology, a winged horse which sprang from the blood of Medusa. Hippocrene, the spring of the Muses on Mt Helicon, is said to have sprung from a blow of his hoof. He was transformed to a constellation.

PEGU (pegōō′). Town of Burma, on the river P., NE of Rangoon, founded AD 573. It is famous for the Shwe-mawdaw pagoda. Pop. (1970) 125,000.

PÉGUY (pehgwē′), **Charles** (1873–1914). French author and poet. B. at Orléans, he estab. a socialist publishing house in Paris, and from 1900 pub. *Les Cahiers de la Quinzaine,* which aimed at regenerating French republicanism. His works incl. *Notre Patrie* (1905) and *Mystère de la Charité de Jeanne d'Arc.*

PEIPING. Name, meaning northern peace, 1928–49 of Peking.

PEIPUS (Pī′pus). Lake on the Estonian-RSFSR frontier, in Estonian Peipsi and in Russia Chudskoye. Alexander Nevski defeated the Teutonic Knights (1242) on its frozen surface.

PĒKI′NG. Cap. of China (Pinyin: Beijing), in Hubei prov. It covers the site of Yenking, cap. of the 10th cent. Liao dynasty, and the 13th cent. cap. of Kublai Khan, called by the Mongols Khanbaligh (Marco Polo's Cambaluc), by the Chinese Taitu. The first emperor of the Ming dynasty made Nanking (southern capital) his cap. but in 1421 Peking (northern capital) once more became cap. of the Chinese Empire, and remained so except for 1928–49 when P. was renamed Peiping (northern peace) and the cap. was once more removed to Nanking. The northern Inner or Tatar City, encloses in turn the old Imperial City or official district, and the purple-walled Forbidden City comprising palaces, pavilions and gardens which were once the home of the emperors and are still the seat of the modern govt. In the southern Outer or Chinese City are the 15th cent. Altar of Heaven and Temple of Agriculture, where the Emperor used to sacrifice on behalf of his people. Banquets on great state occasions, are given in the Great Hall of the People. The restored Summer Palace, a complex of lakes, pavilions and mansions, is 11km (7m) NW, and just outside Peking, scattered round a great valley, are the 14–17th cent. tombs of the Ming emperors. Industries incl. iron and steel, engineering, textiles, printing, and food processing. There is an airport. Pop. (1979) 8,000,000.

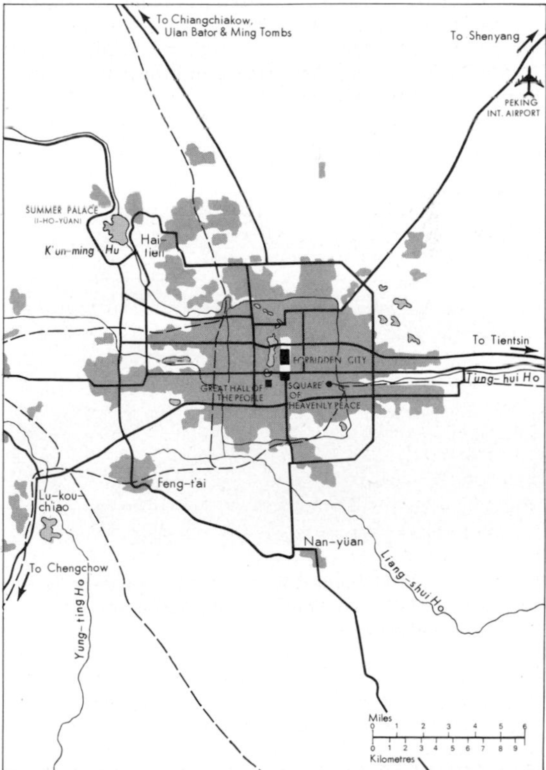

PEKING

PEKINGESE (pekingē'z). Toy dog first bred at the Chinese court as the 'Imperial Lion Dog'. They are long-haired, large-eyed, snub-nosed, and variously coloured, tan being the most common. The first specimens were brought back when the Summer Palace in Peking was looted in 1860.

PEKING MAN. Skull found nr Peking in 1927. Although with a more developed brain, it was thought to be of the same period as Pithecanthropus (*see* JAVA) and *c.* 500,000 yrs old. Doubt was cast on this dating by the discovery of an apparently almost identical skull in N Kenya in 1976, est. at 1,500,000 yrs. The skull of P.M. disappeared in 1941 during the Japanese invasion of China.

PELAGIUS (pēlāji-us) (*c.* 360–*c.* 420). British theologian. He went to Rome *c.* 400, and there taught that every man possesses free will, denying Augustine's doctrines of predestination and original sin. Cleared of heresy by a synod at Jerusalem in 415, he was later condemned by the Pope and the emperor.

PELÉ (pel'ā). Pseudonym of Edson Arantes do Nascimento (1940–), Brazilian footballer. Of a poor Negro family, he achieved worldwide fame as inside left and goal scorer.

PELÉE (pelā'), **Mont.** Volcano (1258 m/4,428 ft) on Martinique, which destroyed the town of St. Pierre during its eruption 1902.

PELHAM, Henry (1696–1754). British Whig statesman. He held a succession of offices in Walpole's cabinet 1721–42, and was PM 1743–54.

PELICAN. Genus of water-fowl, remarkable for the pouch beneath the bill used to store its catches of fish, and incl. the pinkish common P. (*Pelecanus onocrotalus*) of Europe, Asia and Africa; the Australian black-backed P. (*P. constricillatus*); and the American brown P. (*P. occidentalis*), which is marine.

PELICAN. The world's largest species, the black-backed, is found in Australia. *Photo: Courtesy of the Australian Information Service*

PELLĀ'GRA. A disease of sub-tropical countries in which the staple food is maize, due to deficiency of nicotinic acid (vitamin B), which is contained in protein foods and yeast.

PELOPONNESE (pel'ōponēz). Peninsula forming the S part of Greece. It is joined to the mainland by the narrow isthmus of Corinth, and is divided into the nomes of Argolis, Arcadia, Achaea (Akhaia), Elis, Corinth, Lakonia, and Messenia, representing its 7 ancient states. Area 21,549 sq.km (8,320 sq.m); pop. (1971) 986,912.

PELOPONNESIAN WAR. *See* GREEK HISTORY.

PELŌ'TA. Very fast ball-game (the name means 'ball') of Basque derivation, also known as jai alai (pron. hī-lī) meaning 'merry festival', popular in Latin-American countries. It is played in a walled court or cancha, and in some respects resembles squash, but the players use a long, narrow, curved wickerwork basket or cesta, which is strapped to the hand, to hurl the ball (about the size of a baseball) against the walls.

PELSAERT (pel'saht), **François** (*c.*1570–1630). Dutch East India Company official. He sailed to the Indies aboard the *Batavia* (1629), which was wrecked on the W Australian coast. With a few survivors he went on to Batavia in open boats to fetch help for the rest, and on his return had to suppress a mutiny among them. Two offenders were left behind as the first involuntary white 'settlers'. The castaways were lost without trace, but the wreck site was rediscovered in 1963. He d. in Sumatra.

PE'MBA. Coral island in the Indian Ocean, 48km (30m) NE of Zanzibar, and forming with it part of Tanzania. Cloves and copra are the chief products. Area 984 sq.km (380 sq.m); (1978) 168,000.

PE'MBROKE. Seaport and engineering centre in Dyfed, Wales. There is a fine medieval castle, begun 1200, and it was here that Henry VII was born. Pop. (1972) 14,310.

PEMBROKESHIRE. Former extreme SW co. of Wales, which became part of Dyfed in 1974. The co. town was Haverfordwest.

PE'MMICAN. A preparation of dried fatless beef or venison pressed into cubes, used as a food by Arctic explorers and N American Indians.

PEN. Literary association estab. in 1921 by C. A. Dawson Scott, to promote international understanding between writers. The initials stand for Poets, Playwrights, Editors, Essayists, Novelists.

PENANCE. Term in theology used for repentance for sin; an RC sacrament, involving confession of sins and the reception of absolution; and works performed or punishment self-inflicted in atonement for sin. In the RC Church, C. (now also called the Rite for Reconciliation) was formerly always anonymous in a 'confessional box', but is now optionally face-to-face with the priest. Penance is worked out now in terms of good deeds rather than routine recitation of 'Hail Marys' and 'Our Fathers'. *See* CONFESSION.

PENA'NG. State of W Malaysia, Fed. of Malaysia, formed of P. Island (bought by the British from the ruler of Kedah 1785), Province Wellesley (acquired 1800) and the Dindings on the mainland. The cap. is Georgetown, the official name of the major port of P., with which it is conterminous, on Penang Island. Area 1,034 sq.km (400 sq.m); pop. (1970) 776,125.

PENARLAG. Welsh name of HAWARDEN.

PENA'RTH. Seaport in S Glamorgan, Wales, across the mouth of the Ely from Cardiff. Pop. (1972) 23,640.

PENĀ'TES. The household gods of a Roman family.

PENDA (d. 655). King of Mercia from 626. He raised Mercia to a powerful kingdom, and defeated and killed 2 Northumbrian kings, Edwin and Oswald. He was killed in battle with the Northumbrians.

PENDLEBURY, John Devitt Stringfellow (1904-41). British archaeologist. Working with his wife, he became the world's leading expert on Crete. In the S.W.W. he was deputed to prepare guerrilla resistance on the island, was wounded during the German invasion and shot by his captors.

PĒNE'LŌPĒ. Wife of Odysseus. During his absence after the siege of Troy she kept her many suitors at bay by asking them to wait until she had woven a shroud for her father-in-law, but undid her work nightly. When Odysseus returned, he slew her suitors.

PENETRATION TECHNOLOGY. The development of missiles, etc., which have low radar, infra-red and optical signatures, and can penetrate an enemy's defences undetected. In 1980 the USA announced that it had developed such manned aircraft.

PENGUIN. Family of flightless seabirds found only in Antarctic regions. Designed for speed in and under the water, they are awkward on land, where they congregate in 'rookeries' to breed. One or two eggs are laid in a hole in the ground or 'nest' of stones. Well known among smaller species is the black-footed P.: the largest are the king P. (*Aptenodytes longirostris*) and emperor P. (*A. fosteri*).

PENGUIN. Emperor penguins on sea ice near Mawson coast in Antarctica. Scientists from the Australian research centre are seen in the background with their dog team. *Photo: Courtesy of the Australian Information Service.*

PENICI'LLIN. An organic acid formed during the growth of the common mould, *Penicillium notatum.* Even in very weak dilutions it prevents the growth of certain bacteria, many of which are harmful to man, e.g. some of the staphylococci and streptococci, and the organisms of pneumonia, gonorrhoea, meningitis, anthrax and tetanus. Extremely valuable in medicine and surgery, it played an important part in the S.W.W. It was discovered by Sir Alexander Fleming, and its practical use was developed by Sir Howard Florey and E. B. Chain at Oxford.

PENINSULAR WAR. The war of 1808-14 caused by Napoleon's invasion of Portugal and Spain. Portugal was occupied by the French in 1807, and in 1808 Napoleon placed his brother Joseph on the Spanish throne. Armed revolts followed all over Spain and Portugal. A British force under Sir Arthur Wellesley was sent to Portugal and defeated the French at Vimeiro; Wellesley was then superseded, and the French were allowed to withdraw. Sir John Moore took command and advanced into Spain, but was forced to retreat to Corunna, when his army was evacuated. Wellesley took a new army to Portugal in 1809, and advanced on Madrid, but after defeating the French at Talavera had to retreat. During 1810-11 Wellesley (now Visct Wellington) stood on the defensive; in 1812 he won another victory at Salamanca, occupied Madrid, and forced the French to evacuate S Spain. The victory at Vittoria (1813) drove the French from Spain, and in 1814 Wellington invaded S France. The war was ended by Napoleon's abdication.

PENIS. The male organ of generation in reptiles and mammals; it also carries the passage through which urine is discharged from the bladder.

PENN, William (1644-1718). British Quaker and founder of Pennsylvania. B. in London, the son of the Admiral Sir William P. (1621-70), he joined the Quakers in 1667. In 1681 he obtained a grant of land in America, in settlement of a debt owed by the king to his father, on which he estab. the colony of Pennsylvania as a refuge for the persecuted Quakers.

PENNEY, William, baron (1909-). Brit. scientist. He worked at Los Alamos (q.v.) 1944-5, and for his design of the first British atom bomb was knighted in 1952. Director of Atomic Weapons Research Establishment 1953-9, he was chairman of UKAEA 1964-7: created life peer 1967, awarded OM 1969.

PENNINES. System of mountains which has been called 'the backbone of England'. The chain is broken in the centre by a gap through which flow the Aire to the E and Ribble to the W. The P. stretch from the Scottish border to the Peak in Derbyshire. The section N of the gap is broader and higher than the S, with Cross Fell 893m/2,930 ft the highest of several peaks. Britain's first long-distance footpath was the 400km (250m) *Pennine Way* (1965: Edale, Derbyshire to Kirk Yetholm, Borders region).

PENNSYLVANIA. One of the original 13 states of the USA. Crossed by the Alleghenies, P. is drained by the Ohio, Susquehanna and Delaware. Lumbering and agriculture are important, but P. has a vast bituminous and anthracite coal output, and is the largest steel-producing state, Pittsburgh being the great centre for its manufacture. Other mineral products incl. petroleum and natural gas. Among agricultural products are cigar leaf tobacco, buckwheat, maize, wheat, potatoes, fruits. P. was founded and named in 1682 by the Quaker William Penn who had been granted land by Charles II in 1681. The chief towns are Philadelphia, Pittsburgh, Erie, Scranton, Allentown and Harrisburg, the cap. Area 117,412 sq.km (45,333 sq.m); pop. (1970) 11,793,090.

PENNYROYAL. Perennial moorland plant (*Mentha pulegium*). It has ovate leaves, whirls of purplish flowers, and the characteristic scent of mint.

PENSACŌ'LA. Seaport of Florida, USA, on the Gulf of Mexico. There is a large naval air-training station. P. was founded by the Spanish in 1696. Pop. (1970) 59,510.

PE'NTAGON. The HQ of the American Dept of Defense, Washington. One of the world's largest office buildings, it is constructed in 5 'rings' with a pentagonal central court. The *P. Papers* were 'classified' documents pub. by the US press in 1971 on US involvement in Vietnam.

PENTATEUCH (pen'tatūk) (Gk 5 books). The first 5 books of the OT, ascribed to Moses.

PENTAGON. One of the most heavily guarded military headquarters in the world. *Photo: Courtesy of the US Govt.*

PE'NTĒCOST (Gk fiftieth). Jewish festival marking the close of the wheat harvest in Palestine, celebrated on the 50th day after the Passover. It was at P. that the Holy Spirit descended on the Christian Church, an event commemorated on Whit Sunday.

PENTECOSTAL MOVEMENT. Christian revivalist movement inspired, as the name shows, by the baptism in the Holy Spirit with 'speaking in tongues' experienced by the Apostles at the time of the Jewish Feast of Pentecost, or Feast of Harvest (Acts 2). Hence it is sometimes also known as the Tongues movement: *See* TRANCE. Other gifts of the Spirit incl. interpretation of the 'tongues', which are otherwise unintelligible to the rest of the congregation and the speaker; faith healing, performance of miracles and prophecy. Montanism (q.v.) was an earlier expression of this seeking for primitive fervour, and individual saints are said to have spoken with tongues.

The modern P.M. movement dates from 4 April 1906 when members of the Azusa Street Mission in Los Angeles met, under their Negro minister W.J. Seymour, in a private house and experienced 'baptism in the Spirit'. The movement spread, and was brought to the UK by Thomas Barratt, a Cornish-born Methodist minister who had settled in Norway, and had come into contact with P.M. members during a fund-raising mission in the States. It found fertile soil in revivalist areas of Wales and northern England, but was less successful there than in Scandinavia, South America (espec. Brazil and Chile), and S Africa. In the USA, where the largest grouping is the Assemblies of God, members of the movement total more than half a million, and world-wide membership is more than ten million, so that it has been spoken of as the 'third force' in Christendom, and a serious challenge to Roman Catholicism and Protestantism. The P.M. represents a reaction against the rigid theology and formal worship of the traditional churches, the services being noted for informality and gospel hymns with insistent refrains and exclamations of Hallelujah, etc. There is belief in the literal word of the Bible, and a moral code which frowns on alcohol, tobacco, dancing, the theatre, and so on. It is an intensely missionary faith, and recruitment has been spectacularly rapid since the 1960s.

PENTLAND FIRTH. The channel separating the Orkney Islands from N Scotland.

PENZA. Town in the RSFSR, cap of P. region, 560km (350m) SE of Moscow, at the junction of the P. and Sura rivers. Founded as a fort in 1663, it has saw mills, and factories making bicycles, watches, calculating machines, and textiles; also an airport. Pop. (1978) 443,000.

PENZANCE. English seaport and resort in Cornwall, on Mount's Bay, the most westerly town in England. It has a mild climate in which palm trees flourish. Pop. (1972) 19,110.

PĒ'ONY. Genus of perennial plants in the family Ranunculaceae, remarkable for their brilliant and showy flowers. Most popular are the common P. (*Paeonia officinalis*) and the white P. (*P. albiflora*).

PEORIA (pē-ōr'ia). City in Illinois, USA, on the Illinois r. It is a transport, mining, and agricultural centre, seat of Bradley univ. (1897). Fort Crève Cœur was built about here by La Salle in 1680, and became a trading centre; the first American settlers arrived in 1818. Pop. (1970) 127,000.

PEP (Political and Economic Planning). Non-political association publishing reports on aspects of British life, e.g. the press and the health services. Sir Gerald Barry (1899–1968) was one of the founders.

PEPIN (d. 768). King of the Franks. The son of Charles Martel, he acted as mayor of the palace to the last Merovingian king, Childeric III, until in 751 he deposed him and himself assumed the royal title, founding the Carolingian line.

PEPPER. Climbing plant (*Piper nigrum*) native to the E Indies. When gathered green, the berries are crushed to produce the condiment black P.; when ripening and turning red, the berries produce white P. *See* CAPSICUM.

PEPPERMINT. Perennial herb (*Mentha piperita*), with ovate aromatic leaves, and purple flowers. Oil of P. is used medicinally and in confectionery.

PEPTIDE. Small molecule made from the basic sub-units of protein – amino acids. Peptides incl. enkephalin and endorphin, the 'natural painkillers', and others are involved in breathing, digestion and reproduction. Their function was thought to be limited to carrying messages to the organs via the blood, but it is now believed some may also be neurotransmitters, that is, they transmit signals from one nerve cell to another.

PEPUSCH (pā'poosh), **Johann Christopher** (1667–1752). German composer. B. in Berlin, settled in England *c.* 1700 and is best remembered for the anthem 'Rejoice in the Lord', and music for *The Beggar's Opera* and *Polly*.

PEPYS (pēps), **Samuel** (1633–1703). British diarist. B. in London, he entered the navy office in 1660 a few months after beginning his diary. He was appointed secretary to the Admiralty in 1672, imprisoned with loss of office in 1679 on suspicion of being connected with the Popish Plot, reinstated in 1684, and finally deprived at the 1688 Revolution, when he retired to Clapham. His diary, in a personal version of Shelton's shorthand undeciphered until 1825, and discontinued in 1669 owing to failing sight, is unrivalled for its intimacy and the human picture it presents of daily life in the 17th cent.

PERAK (pē'ra). State of the Federation of Malaysia. It is ruled by a sultan. Towns incl. Ipoh the cap. and centre of the Kinta tin-mining fields and Taiping. It exports tin and rubber. Area 20,668 sq.km (7,980 sq.m); pop. (1970) 1,570,000.

PERCEVAL, Spencer (1762-1812). British Tory statesman. The son of the earl of Egmont, he became Chancellor of the Exchequer in 1807, and PM in 1809. He was shot in the lobby of the House of Commons in 1812 by a madman.

PERCH. Genus of spiny-finned fish in the family Percidae. The common freshwater P. (*Perca fluviatilis*), found in Europe, N Asia, and N America, is olive-green or yellowish in colour, with 5 or more dark bands across the back.

PERCY, Sir Henry, called **Hotspur** (1364-1403). English soldier. The son of the 1st earl of Northumberland, he defeated the Scots at Homildon Hill in 1402, and was killed at Shrewsbury while in rebellion against Henry IV.

PERCY, Thomas (1729-1811). British scholar and bishop of Dromore from 1782. B. at Bridgnorth, he discovered a MS collection of songs, ballads, and romances, from which he pub. a selection as *Reliques of Ancient English Poetry* (1765), largely influential in the Romantic revival.

PERFUME. Fragrant essence in which more than 100 natural aromatic materials may be blended from a range of c. 60,000 flowers, leaves, fruits, seeds, woods, barks, resins and roots, linked by natural animal fixatives and various synthetics, the latter increasingly used even in expensive Ps. Favoured ingredients incl. balsam, civet, hyacinth, jasmine, lily of the valley, musk, orange blossom, rose and tuberose.

PERFUME. The part of the Chiris factory at Grasse, where some of the finest perfumes are made. Mosaic windows for ventilation give it the air of a church. On the floor are several tons of violets, ready to go into the rows of batteries on the left, in which the essence is extracted. *Photo: Desmond O'Neill/Camera Press*

PERGA. Ruined city of Pamphylia, 16km (10m) NE of Adalia, Turkey, noted for its local cult of Artemis. It was visited by St Paul.

PE'RGAMUM. Ancient Greek city in W Asia Minor, which became the cap. of an independent kingdom in 283 BC. As the ally of Rome it achieved great political importance in the 2nd cent. BC, and became a famous centre of art and culture. On its site is the Turkish town of Bergama, pop. (est.) 17,000.

PE'RI. In Persian mythology, a species of beautiful harmless beings, between angels and evil spirits, but ruled by Eblis, the greatest of the latter.

PE'RICLĒS (c. 490-429 BC). Athenian statesman. He dominated Athenian politics from 461 as leader of the democratic party. He created a confederation of cities under Athens' leadership, but the disasters of the Peloponnesian War led to his overthrow in 430, and although quickly reinstated he d. soon after. The period of his rule marks the climax of Greek culture. *See* ASPASIA.

PÉRIGUEUX (pehrēgö'). French town, cap. of Dordogne dept, 127km (79m) ENE of Bordeaux. The Byzantine cathedral dates from 984; there is trade in wine and truffles. Pop. (1975) 40,150.

PERIM (pārēm'). Island in the strait of Bab-el-Mandeb, the S entrance to the Red Sea; part of S Yemen. Area 13 sq.km (5 sq.m).

PERIODICAL. Publication brought out at regular intervals, which may be informative, entertaining, religious, etc. One of the earliest Ps. pub. in Britain was the *Compleat Library* (1691/2), which contained articles and reviews of books. Notable later were Steele's *Tatler* (1709), Addison's *Spectator* (1711), the *Gentleman's Magazine* (1731), John Wilkes's *North Briton* (1762), the *Edinburgh Review* (1802-1929), *Quarterly Review* (1806), *Blackwood's Magazine* (1817-1980), *Spectator* (1828), *Punch* (1841), *Economist* (1843), *Contemporary Review* (1866), *New Statesman* (1913), *Now* (1979), etc. The increasing spread of literacy at the end of the 19th cent. was accompanied by a demand for light reading matter, and there are today a large number of popular P. at various levels.

In the US periodicals, unlike newspapers, circulate all over the country and some achieve vast circulations, e.g. *Reader's Digest* (1922) sold some 18 million copies in 1973. Other notable American Ps. are *Saturday Evening Post* (1728-1969), *Nat. Geographic Magazine* (1888), *New Yorker* (1925), *Time* (1923) and *Newsweek* (1933).

PERIODICAL TABLE OF THE ELEMENTS. A classification following the statement by Mendeleyev (q.v.) in 1869, that 'the properties of elements are in periodic dependence upon their at. wt.'. In each of 9 main groups there are striking similarities among the elements, based on electronic structure and nuclear charge. *See* INORGANIC CHEMISTRY for chart of P.T.

PERISCOPE. An optical instrument designed for observation from a concealed position. The essence of a P. consists of a tube with parallel mirrors at each end inclined at 45° to its axis. It attained prominence in naval (especially in submarines) and military operations of the F.W.W.

PERIWINKLE. Genus of gastropods found between tidemarks in brown seaweed. The common edible species of 'winkle' (*Littorina littorea*), abundant in Britain, has spread to the Atlantic coast of America. Also genus of plants (*Vinca*), of which the lesser P. (*V. minor*), with light blue flowers, is found in Europe.

PERJURY. The offence of deliberately making a false statement on oath when appearing as a witness in legal proceedings, on a point material to the question at issue. In Britain it is punishable by a fine, imprisonment up to 7 years, or both.

PERKIN, Sir William Henry (1838-1907). British chemist. B. in London, he discovered in 1856 the mauve dye which originated the aniline dye industry.

PERLIS. Most northerly state of W Malaysia, Fed. of Malaysia. Transferred by Siam to Britain in 1909, it is ruled by a raja. Kangar is the cap. Its products are rubber, rice, coconuts, and tin. Area 803 sq.km (310 sq.m); pop. (1970) 121,100.

PERM. Town of the RSFSR, cap. of P. region, on the Kama near the Urals. It has shipbuilding yards, aircraft and chemical factories, saw mills, etc., and is a centre of petroleum production. It was called Molotov 1940-57. Pop. (1978) 972,000.

PERNAMBUCO. *See* RECIFE.

PERO'N, Juan Domingo (1895-1974). Argentine statesman. He took part in the military pro-fascist coup of 1943, and his popularity with the *descamisados* 'shirtless ones' led to his election as pres. in 1946. He lost popularity after the death of his 2nd wife **Eva** 'Evita' (1919-52), was deposed in 1955, but returned from exile to the presidency in 1973. He was succeeded by his third wife **Maria Estela** 'Isabel(ita)' (1930–), as president until her overthrow in 1976 and subsequent detention until 1981.

PERPENDICULAR. Name given to a period of English Gothic architecture lasting from the end of the 14th to the middle of the 16th cent. The chief characteristics of the style are: window tracery consisting chiefly of vertical members; arches which are either 'four centred' - i.e. consisting of 4 arcs - or of 2 arcs forming a blunt point; vaults which are lavishly decorated; and wall surfaces covered with traceried panels. Good examples of the style are the choir and cloister of Gloucester cathedral, and King's College chapel, Cambridge.

PERPIGNAN (perpēnyoń'). Cap. of the Pyrénées-Orientales dept of France, on the Têt, 65km (40m) S of Narbonne. Overlooking P. is the castle of the counts of Roussillon; the cathedral was founded 1324 by Sancho II, king of Majorca, in whose dominions P. then was. Pop. (1975) 101,200.

PERRAULT (pārō'), **Charles** (1628-1703). French author, chiefly remembered for his prose *Histoires ou Contes du Temps Passé* (1697), which incl. Sleeping Beauty, Red Riding Hood, Blue Beard, Puss in Boots, and Cinderella.

PERRY, Matthew Calbraith (1794-1858). US naval officer, who commanded the expedition which in 1853 reopened communication between Japan and the outside world after 250 years' isolation. In 1854 he negotiated the first US-Japanese treaty.

PERRY. An alcoholic liquor made from pears, mainly in the W Country of England and Normandy.

PERSE, Saint-John. Pseudonym of the French poet Alexis Saint-Léger Léger (1887-1975). His first book of verse *Éloges* (1911) reflects the colour of the West Indies, where he was b. and raised. Entering the Foreign Service in 1914, he was Sec.-Gen. 1933-40. He then emigrated permanently to the USA, and was deprived of French citizenship by the Vichy govt. His later works incl. *Anabase* (1924), a long poem of epic sweep trans. by T. S. Eliot in 1930. He was awarded a Nobel prize in 1960.

PERSE'PHONĒ. Greek goddess, the dau. of Zeus and Demeter. She was carried off to the underworld by Pluto, who later agreed that she should spend 6 months of the year with her mother. The story is a myth for the growth and decay of vegetation.

PERSE'PŌLIS. Ancient cap. of the Persian Empire, 65km (40m) NE of Shiraz. It was burned down, by accident or design, after its capture in 331 BC by Alexander. Impressive ruins of the city have been excavated by the Oriental Institute of Chicago.

PERSEUS (per'sūs). Mythical Greek hero, the son of Zeus and Danae. He slew Medusa, the Gorgon, saved Andromeda from a sea-monster, and became king of Tiryns.

PERSHING, John Joseph (1860-1948). American gen. B. in Missouri, he served in the Spanish War of 1898, the Philippines 1899-1903, and Mexico 1916-17. He commanded the American Expeditionary Force sent to France 1917-18.

PERSIA (persh'ia). Official name of Iran until 1935.

PERSIAN. The earliest language to be used in Persia was the so-called Old Persian (Achaemenian), which used a cuneiform script and appears to date from the period 550-340 BC. It was followed by Avestic or Zend, the language of the sacred books of Zoroaster. Avestic, which appears to have originated in the NW of the country and to have survived until the 3rd cent. AD, gave way in turn to Pahlavi (3rd-7th cent. AD), which shows marked Semitic affinities and incl. much Zoroastrian literature. Parsee or Farsi (AD 700-1100) was the immediate predecessor of modern Persian. The latter belongs to the Indo-european group of languages, uses the Arabic alphabet with a few additional letters, has many Arabic words, and was once widely used in India. This modern language is also called Farsi.

Persian literature before the Arab conquest is represented by the sacred books of the Parsees known as the Avesta and later translated into Pahlavi, in which language there also appeared various secular writings. After the conquest the use of Arabic became widespread. The P. language was revived during the 9th cent. and the following cents. saw a succession of brilliant poets incl. the epic writer Firdousi (q.v.), Nizami (1140-1203), who excelled in romance, the didactic S'adi (1184-1291), the mystic Rumi (1207-73), the lyrical Hafiz (q.v.), and Jami who combined the gifts of his predecessors and is considered the last of the classical poets. Omar Khayyam (q.v.) whose name is so well known outside Persia is less considered there. In the 16th and 17th cents. many of the best writers worked in India, still using classical forms and themes, and it was not until the revolutionary movements and contact with the West of the present cent. that Persian literature moved forward again. None has as yet attained international reputation in translation.

PERSIAN ART. Persian art dates from the foundation of the Persian nation by Cyrus in 550 BC. At first the dominant influence was Assyrian art, but throughout its history Persian geographical boundaries have been constantly shifting, and Persian art has been influenced by many different peoples. In pre-Islamic times the Persians were celebrated for their architecture, e.g. the palaces of Darius and Xerxes. Persian carpets, with their beautiful designs based on animal forms, hunting scenes, etc., are the best expression of Persian craftsmanship, but the

Persians are also famous for their pottery, especially the ware made at Rhages, probably in the 12th cent. AD, and their exquisite miniature paintings.

PERSIAN GULF. *See* GULF.

PERSI'MMON or **Virginian date plum.** Tree (*Diospyros virginiana*) of the family Ebenaceae, native to N America. Some 12m (40ft) high, the P. has alternate oval leaves, and yellow-green unisexual flowers. The small sweet orange fruits are edible.

PERSPIRATION. Sweat, the secretion of the sweat glands. These microscopic structures are found all over the skin; they secrete all the time and the 'insensible' P. may be 3-4 pts/1.7-2.3 l a day. The sweat consists of water-containing cells and also fatty acids from the sebaceous glands. In a warm atmosphere or on exertion the output is raised to keep the body temperature down by evaporation, and the sweat then becomes visible (sensible). Inflammation of the sweat glands is prickly heat.

PERTH. City in Tayside, Scotland, 52km (32m) NW of Edinburgh, on the Tay. There are textile and dye-works. Pop. (1971) 42,438. (2) Cap. of W Australia, 19km (12m) NE of the mouth of the Swan where its port Fremantle lies. P., founded in 1829, is the commercial and cultural hub of the state; it has an airport. Pop. (1973) 723,500.

PERTH. The Perth city centre skyline makes an impressive backdrop for these yachts competing on the beautiful Swan river. *Photo: Courtesy of the Western Australian Government Office.*

PERTHSHIRE. Former inland co. of central Scotland, of which the major part was incl. in 1975 in Tayside, the SW being incl. in Central. Perth was the admin. HQ.

PERU (perōō'). Republic of S America, bordering the Pacific Ocean and lying wholly within the Tropics. There are 3 main divisions: the narrow coastal belt, rendered fertile by irrigation; the Cordillera de los Andes, rising in Mt Huascarán to 6,777 m (22,205 ft), and the forested montaña region of the E slopes of the Andes in which the headstreams of the Amazon rise, and which descends to the jungle or selva of the Amazonian basin. Lake Titicaca is partly in P., partly in Bolivia, and others are the Junin and Parinacochas.

The chief crops are sugar, cotton and coffee, and the forests are rich in cedar, mahogany, etc. Besides the hides and skins of cattle, sheep and goats, there is a luxury trade in alpaca and llama wool, and the rare vicuna hair. The plankton of the Peru current, on which anchovy feed, makes P. the world's leading fishing nation, though most of the catch is turned to fishmeal. Minerals incl. very rich copper resources, iron, lead, silver and zinc, and oil is found both offshore and in various parts of the mainland. Industry is fast growing, incl. iron and steel, non-ferrous metals, chemicals, vehicle assembly, textiles, radios, television receivers, and cement. The chief towns are Lima, the cap. and its port of Callao; Arequipa, the port of Chiclayo on the NW coast, and the great inland port of Iquitos on the Amazon.

The constitution (1979) provides for a pres., and a senate and chamber of deputies, elected for 5 years. Area 1,332,000 sq.km (514,060 sq.m); pop. (1977) 16,580,000. Spanish and (from 1975) Quechua are the official languages. The RC religion is state-protected. M.U.: sol.

History. The remarkable early history of P. incl. both the pre-Inca civilization of the Chimu (q.v.) and that of the Inca civilization itself, with impressive remains at Cuzco and Machu Picchu. Civil war among the Incas helped to enable Francisco Pizarro to seize most of the country before his assassination in 1541, and Spanish rule was firmly established. An Indian revolt by Tupac Amaru (q.v.) in 1780 failed, and during the successful rebellions by the European settlers in other Spanish possessions in S America 1810-22, P. remained the Spanish govt HQ, being the last to achieve independence, 1824. Since then the main events in P.'s history have been the abortive union with Bolivia (1836-9), the naval war against Spain (1864-6), the Pacific War (q.v.) over the nitrate fields of the Atacama Desert, in which P. was defeated and lost 3 provs. (one, Tacna, was returned in 1929). Other boundary disputes were settled by arbitration in 1902 (with Bolivia), 1927 (with Colombia), 1942 (with Ecuador: renewed 1981 over Santiago and Zamora rivers area). A bloodless military coup in 1968 led to the expropriation of American oil and mining interests; and vast estates with sugar plantations, cattle and sheep ranches, were taken over as co-operatives. Military rule ended in 1980 with the re-election of Fernando Belaunde Terry who had been overthrown in 1968 by the army. Terry was in turn defeated in the presidential elections of July 1985 by the social democrat Alan García.

PERU CURRENT. *See* HUMBOLDT CURRENT.

PERUGIA (pehrōō'jah). City in Umbria, Italy, 520m (1,700 ft) above the Tiber, *c.* 137km (85m) N of Rome. One of the 12 cities of Etruria, it surrendered to Rome 309 BC. There is a univ. (1276), a 15th cent. cathedral, a municipal palace begun in 1281, and other fine buildings with many art treasures. Industries incl. silk and wool textiles, liqueurs, chocolate, etc. Pop. (1978) 137,860.

PERUGINO (pehroojē'nō), **Pietro** (1446-1524). Italian painter, whose real name was Vanucci. He worked chiefly in Perugia, and helped to decorate the Sistine Chapel, Rome. Raphael was his pupil.

PESCADORES (peskedaw'rēz). Group (Chinese: P'eng-hu) of *c.* 60 is. off Taiwan, of which they form a dependency. Area 130 sq.km (50 sq.m).

PESCARA (peskah'rah). Town in Abruzzi e Molise, Italy, at the mouth of the P. river, on the Adriatic. It is the birthplace of d'Annunzio. Hydroelectric installations supply Rome with electricity. Pop. (1978) 136,580.

PESHAWAR (peshowr'). Cap. of NW Frontier Prov., Pakistan, 18km (11m) E of the Khyber Pass. Strategically placed, it has been an important city since the 2nd cent.

AD, and was taken by the British in 1849. It is a communications centre. Pop. (1971) 220,000.

PESTALOZZI (pestahlots'ē), **Johann Heinrich** (1746-1827). Swiss educationist. B. at Zürich, he estab. an experimental school at Burgdorf in 1799, and moved it to Yverdon in 1805. Among his writings are *How Gertrude Teaches her Children*, etc.

PÉTAIN (pehtañ'), **Henri Philippe** (1856-1951). French soldier. After studying at St Cyr, he was commissioned in 1878, and was promoted to general in 1915. His defence of Verdun in 1916 during the F.W.W. made him a national hero, and in 1917 he was created French C-in-C, although he became subordinate to Foch in 1918. He suppressed a rebellion in Morocco in 1925-6. As a member of the Higher Council of National Defence he advocated a purely defensive military policy, and was strongly cons. in politics. He became PM in June 1940, following the disastrous Battle of France, and immediately signed an armistice with Germany. Removing the seat of govt to Vichy, he estab. a repressive régime on the Fascist model. On the Allied invasion he was taken to Germany, but returned in 1945 and was sentenced to death for treason, the sentence being commuted to life imprisonment.

PETER, St. One of the 12 Apostles. Originally called Simeon or Simon, he was given the nickname of Cephas (a rock: Gk *petros*) by Jesus. He was a fisherman of Capernaum, and may have been a follower of John the Baptist. It was he who first acknowledged Jesus as the Messiah, and his force of character made him a leader among the Apostles. According to tradition, he settled in Rome in later life, and was crucified there during Nero's persecution in AD 64; he is regarded as the first bishop of Rome. Excavations under the Basilica of St Peter's revealed bones, accepted as those of the Apostle by Pope Paul 1968. Of the Epistles attributed to him, the first is probably spurious, and the second certainly is.

PETER I (1672-1725). Tsar of Russia; called the Great. He succeeded to the throne in 1682 on the death of his brother Tsar Feodor, and assumed control of the govt in 1689. After a successful campaign against the Turks in 1696, he visited Holland and England to study western techniques, and himself worked in Dutch and English shipyards. On his return to Russia he set out to reorganize the country on western lines; the army was modernized, a fleet was built, the admin. and the legal system were remodelled, educ. was encouraged, and the Church was brought under state control. In order to secure an outlet to the Baltic, P. undertook a war with Sweden (1700-21), which resulted in the acquisition of Estonia and part of Latvia and Finland. On the Baltic coast P. built his new capital, St Petersburg. A war with Persia (1722-3) added Baku to Russia.

Peter's eldest son Alexius (1690-1718) had d. in prison for opposition to his father's reforms, and the son of Alexius, later **Peter II** (1715-30), was passed over in the succession to the throne in favour of Peter I's consort Catherine I (q.v.). However, the boy did succeed Catherine in 1727, but d. of smallpox. **Peter III** (1728-62) was the son of Peter I's eldest dau., Anne, wife of the duke of Holstein-Gottorp. In 1741 he was adopted by his aunt, Elizabeth (q.v.), on her succession to the throne and at her behest m. in 1745 the future Catherine II (q.v.). He was deposed in 1762 and d. at the castle of Ropsha, probably murdered by Alexius Orlov.

PETER I. A portrait engraved from a painting by I. Kupetsky in 1737. One of the boats this practical Tsar built is still preserved in the Maritime Museum. *Photo: Novosti*

PETER I (1844-1921). King of Serbia. He was the son of Prince Alexander Karageorgevich, and was elected king when the last Obrenovich king was murdered in 1903. He took part in the retreat of the Serbian Army in 1915, and in 1918 was proclaimed first king of the Serbs, Croats, and Slovenes.

PETER II (1923-70). King of Yugoslavia. He succeeded his father, King Alexander, in 1934, and assumed the royal power after the overthrow of the regency in 1941. He escaped to England following the German invasion, and m. Princess Alexandra of Greece in 1944. He was dethroned in 1945.

PETERBOROUGH. Town in Cambridgeshire, on the W edge of the Fen country. The cathedral is of the 12-16th cents., industries incl. engineering. Pop. (1975) 95,500. The *Soke of P.* was an admin. co. 1888-1965.

PETER DĀ'MIAN, St (1007-72). Italian monk, Pietro Damianai, who was associated in the initiation of clerical reform with Gregory VII.

PETERHEAD. Seaport in Grampian, Scotland, 54km (33m) NE of Aberdeen. Industries incl. fishing, shipbuilding, light engineering, whisky distilling, making of woollen textiles. The Old Pretender landed at P. in 1715. The harbour, built by convict labour (1886-1921; extended 1958), has been increasingly used by service industries for North Sea oil. Pop. (1973) 14,846.

PETER I ISLAND. Uninhabited is. in the Bellingshausen Sea, Antarctica, belonging to Norway. Area 180 sq.km (69 sq.m).

PETERLEE. 'New town' estab. in Durham, England, in 1948. A mining centre, it was named after Peter Lee, first Labour chairman of a co. council. Pop. (1975) 26,300.

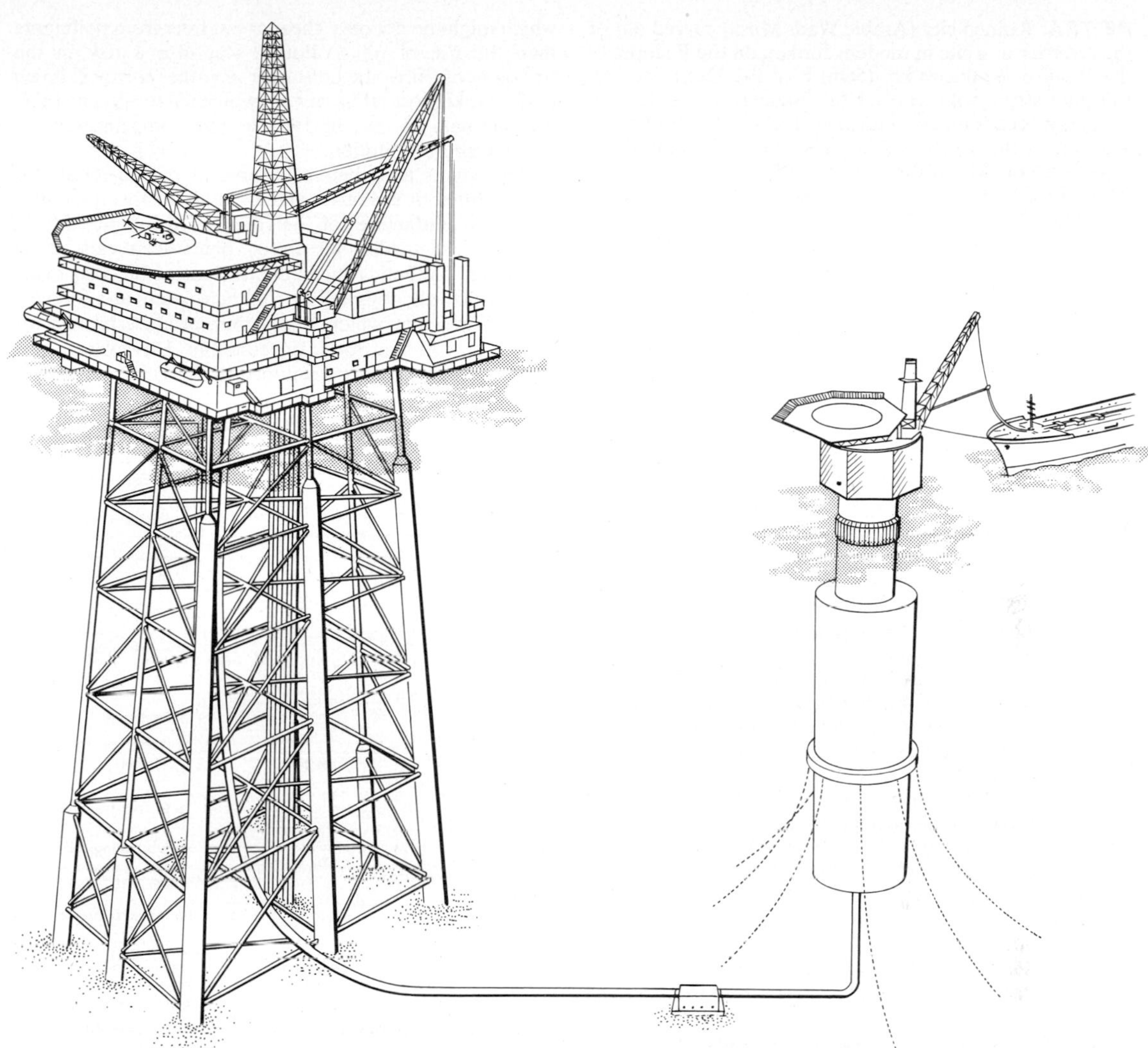

PETROLEUM. A North Sea oil production platform of the type erected by Shell/Esso in the Brent field. The steel base is fixed in place by 32 steel piles 1.8 m (6 ft) in diameter and driven 34 m (111 ft) into the seabed, and the top of the drilling derrick is 226 m (741 ft) above the seabed. Initially, until the establishment of a pipeline link, oil is loaded into tankers from a specially-designed floating storage and loading 'spar', such as that shown right.

PETER LOMBARD (*c.* 1100-60). Italian theologian. B. at Novara, he lectured on theology in Paris, and became bishop of Paris in 1159. His *Sententiarum libri* considerably influenced Catholic doctrine.

PETERLOO. Name given, in reference to Waterloo, to the 'massacre' in St Peter's Fields, Manchester, England, on 16 Aug. 1819, when an open-air meeting in support of parliamentary reform was charged by yeomanry and hussars.

PETER'S PENCE. Voluntary anuual contribution to the cost of papal administration, originally a compulsory levy of one penny per household.

PETER THE HERMIT (fl. 1095-9). French preacher. He was a priest of Amiens, who by his eloquence in preaching the 1st Crusade induced thousands of peasants to march against the Turks. They were cut to pieces in Asia Minor, but P. escaped and accompanied the main body of crusaders to Jerusalem.

PETITION OF RIGHT. The procedure whereby, before the passing of the Crown Proceedings Act (1947), a subject petitioned for legal relief against the Crown, whether for money due under a contract, or for property of which the Crown had taken possession. Also the petition of parliament accepted by Charles I in 1628, declaring illegal taxation without parliamentary consent, imprisonment without trial, billeting of soldiers on private persons, and use of martial law.

PETÖFI (pet'öfi), **Sándor** (1823-49). Hungarian national poet. B. at Kiskörös, he pub. his first vol. of poems in 1844, and settled in Pest. He expressed his revolutionary ideas in the semi-autobiographical poem 'The Apostle', and fell fighting the Austrians in the battle of Segesvár.

PĒ'TRA. Ruined city (Arabic Wadi Musa) carved out of the red rock at a site in modern Jordan, on the E slopes of the Wadi el Araba, 90km (56m) S of the Dead Sea. An Edomite stronghold, cap. of the Nabataeans in the 2nd cent., it was captured by Trajan AD 106 and wrecked in the 7th cent. by the Saracens. It was lost to knowledge until rediscovered in 1812 by the Swiss traveller J. L. Burckhardt.
PETRARCH (It. Petrarca), **Francesco** (1304–74). Italian poet and scholar. B. at Arezzo, he was taken to Avignon in 1313, studied law, was ordained in 1326, and entered the service of the Colonnas. In 1341 he was crowned poet in Rome. Later he lived in Milan with the Viscontis, and died at Arqua, near Padua. An ardent patriot, he was inspired by the greatness of ancient Rome. He wrote *Il canzoniere*, sonnets in praise of 'Laura'; *I trionfi*, a moral allegory in *terze rime*; *Africa*, a Lat. epic on Scipio the Elder; and philosophical treatises, etc.
PE'TREL. Two families of seabirds (Procellariidae and Oceanitidae) so called from their skimming the water surface as St Peter did. Most familiar is the stormy P. of the N Atlantic (*Hydrobates pelagicus*), also known as Mother Carey's chicken. Seldom coming to land except to breed, the Ps. lay a single egg in holes among the rocks. They are sooty-black with a white patch on the tail.
PĒ'TRIE, Sir William Matthew Flinders (1853–1942). British archaeologist. Grandson of Matthew Flinders (q.v.), he is remembered for his work in Egypt (Tanis, the Pyramids, Tell el Amarna, Abydos, etc.) 1880–1926 and as first Edwards prof. of Egyptology, Univ. Coll., London, where his collections are still used for teaching purposes. He was noted for his skilled use of minute observation.
PETROGRAD. Name 1914–24 of LENINGRAD.
PETROLEUM or **mineral oil.** A thick greenish-brown liquid occurring underground in permeable rocks into which it has probably been forced by pressure, and accumulated in anticlines and other 'traps' below impervious rock layers. Flowing wells are due to gas pressure from above, or water pressure from below the oil, which causes it to rise up the borehole; many wells require artificial aids to bring the oil to the surface. The origin of P. is uncertain, but it is thought to be derived from organic material which has been converted by bacterial action, followed by the effects of heat and pressure.

From the crude P. or rock oil various products are made by distillation and other processes, e.g. fuel oil, gasoline (petrol), kerosene, diesel or gas oil, lubricating oil, paraffin wax, petroleum jelly. Aviation spirit is a very volatile form of petrol.

The occurrence of mineral oil was known in ancient times, but the exploitation of oil-fields began with the first commercial well in Pennsylvania in 1859. In the early years the USA held the lead, but in the 1960s the Near East became dominant, huge reserves leading to worldwide dependence on cheap oil for transport and industry. In 1961 the Organization of Petroleum Exporting Countries (OPEC) was estab. to avoid exploitation of member countries, but in the 1970s oil price rises became crippling to the developed nations, and the International Energy Agency (IEA) was estab. in 1974 to protect the interests of oil-consuming countries. By 1975 consumer resistance to high prices, reversion to alternative energy sources, such as coal, and the exploitation of oil reserves widely scattered throughout the world were beginning to readjust the balance, and in the long term intensive research was being carried on into new energy sources which might be not only cheaper but freer from pollutants than the use of oil. Pollution was also a risk in the transport of oil to the consumer, e.g. the *Torrey Canyon* (1967) tanker lost off Cornwall, which led to agreement by the internat. oil cos. in 1968 to pay compensation for massive shore pollution.

P. products and chemicals serve as raw materials for widely different industries and are used in large quantities in the manufacture of detergents, man-made fibres, plastics, insecticides, fertilizers, pharmaceuticals, toilet requisites, synthetic rubber, etc. Increasing oil costs made the planned use of paraffin (from petroleum) as a food for micro-organisms, which would then produce protein for animal and human food, uneconomic. However, a new kind of bacterium was developed in the USA, capable of 'eating' oil, as a means of countering spillage. Its creation gave rise to the so-called Frankenstein Law (q.v.).

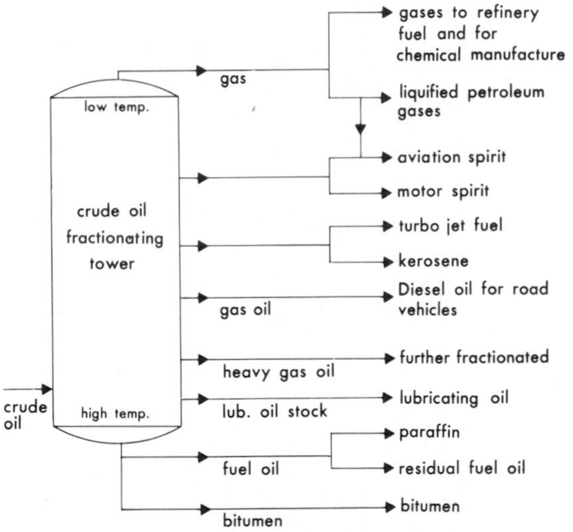

PETROLEUM. A scheme of the basic elements of refining, omitting all the complex mixing and purifying stages. In the fractionating tower a temperature gradient is maintained – highest at the bottom, and lowest at the top. 'Fractions', boiling at various temperatures, are tapped off the column at intervals; from the low-boiling-point gases passing out of the top of the column, to the heavy tar-like substances drained out of the bottom.

PETRONIUS ARBITER, Gaius (d. AD 65). Roman author, the companion of Nero, and supervisor of his licentious pleasures. He committed suicide. His *Satyricon* is a satiric, licentious romance.
PETROPAVLO'VSK. Town in the Kazakh SSR, USSR, on the Ishim, the Trans-Siberian railway, and the Transkazakh line, opened 1953. A former caravan station, it was founded as a Russian fortress, 1782: it produces flour, agricultural machinery, leather. Pop. (1978) 199,000.
PETROPAVLOVSK'-KAMCHA'TSKI. Russian port and naval base on the SE Kamchatka peninsula. Pop. (1978) 207,000.
PETRO'POLIS. Hill resort in Brazil, to the N of Rio de Janeiro, with textile, chemical, ceramic, and tobacco factories, diamond-cutting works, and a trade in flowers,

vegetables, and dairy products. Founded 1845 by immigrants from Bavaria, it was named after Pedro II of Brazil whose favourite summer residence it became. Pop. (1975) 220,000.

PETROVSK. *See* MAKHACHKALA.

PETROZAVO'DSK. Cap. of Karelia ASSR, RSFSR, on the W shore of Lake Onega. It makes metal goods, cement, prefabricated houses, etc., and has saw mills. Peter the Great estab. the township in 1703 as an iron-working centre; it was named P. in 1777. Pop. (1978) 220,000.

PETSAMO. *See* PECHENGA.

PEVENSEY. English village in Sussex, 8km (5m) NE of Eastbourne, the site of William the Conqueror's landing in 1066. The walls remain of the Roman fortress of Anderida, later a Norman castle, and prepared against German invasion in the S.W.W.

PE'VSNER, Sir Nikolaus (1902–83). Anglo-German art historian. B. in Leipzig, he fled from the Nazis, and devoted himself to English art and architecture. In his series *Buildings of England* (1951-74), he achieved a first-hand report on every worthwhile building in the country.

PEWTER. An alloy of lead and tin, much used formerly for ornaments and domestic utensils.

PFALZ. German name of the PALATINATE.

PFORZHEIM (pforts'hīm). Town of Baden-Württemberg, W Germany, 26km (16m) SE of Karlsruhe. Gold and silver ware and jewellery are made. It was a Roman settlement, and the residence of margraves of Baden 1300-1565. Pop. (1978) 107,000.

pH. Scale (*p*otential of *H*ydrogen) ranging 0-14 for measuring acidity or alkalinity, where 7 = a chemically neutral solution. Numbers above 7 denote degrees of alkalinity, those below increasing acidity, and each figure represents a tenfold increase.

PHĀ'ETHON. In Greek mythology, the son of Helios, who was allowed for one day to drive the chariot of the sun. Losing control of the horses, he almost set the earth on fire, and was killed by Zeus with a thunderbolt.

PHAGOCYTES (fag'osīts). White blood cells having the property of devouring bacteria. They are lymphocytes and polynuclear cells, and one of the body's chief defences against infection.

PHALARIS (fl. 570-554 BC). Tyrant of Agrigentum, Sicily. He is said to have built a brazen bull in which victims were roasted alive. He was killed in a popular revolt. The letters attributed to him were proved by Bentley (q.v.) to be a later forgery.

PHA'LAROPE. Genus of seabirds. Of the 3 species the red-necked (*Phalaropus lobatus*) and grey (*P. fulicarius*) visit Britain from the Arctic and *P. tricolor* is exclusively American. The male is courted by the female and hatches the eggs.

PHALLUS. A model of the male sexual organ, used in fertility rituals in ancient Greece and Asia Minor, in India, and in many other parts of the world.

PHARAOH (fā'rō). Hebrew form of the Egyptian royal title Per-'o. This term, meaning 'great house', was originally applied to the royal household, and after *c.* 950 BC to the king.

PHARISEES (far'izēz) ('separated'). Jewish sect which arose in the 2nd cent. BC, in protest against all movements towards compromise with Hellenistic culture. Their main emphasis was on strict observance of the law, rather than on ritual; hence they came into conflict with the priestly caste, or Sadducees. Although they believed in a coming Messiah, they rejected political action, and in the 1st cent. AD the left wing of their followers, the Zealots, broke away to pursue a revolutionary nationalist policy. After the fall of Jerusalem, P. ideas became the basis of orthodox Judaism.

PHARMACOLOGY (farmakol'ojē). Study of the origin, application and effect of chemical substances on animals and man. These products of the pharmaceutical industry range from aspirin to anti-cancer agents, and about 3 per cent of gross sales in the UK are devoted to research, which in some fields, e.g. chemotherapeutics, is both costly and complex - 4,000 new substances may have to be synthesized to find one or two useful products. Well-proven formulations are listed in the official pharmacopoeia.

PHARYNX (far'ingks). The interior of the throat, the cavity at the back of the mouth. Its walls are made of muscle strengthened with a fibrous layer and lined with mucous membrane. It has an opening into the back of each nostril (choanae) and downwards into the gullet and (through the epiglottis) into the windpipe. On each side the Eustachian tube leads from it to the middle ear. The upper part (naso-pharynx) is an airway, but the remainder is a passage for food. Inflammation of the P. is pharyngitis.

PHASMIDA (fas'mida). An order of insects comprising the Stick Insects and Leaf Insects (qq.v.).

PHEASANT (fez'ant). Genus of game birds (*Phasianus*) incl. with the peacock and guinea fowl in the family Phasianidae. The common P. (*P. colchicus*) was introduced from Asia to Europe, according to legend by the Argonauts who brought it from the banks of the r. Phasis. The plumage of the male is richly tinted with brownish green and yellow and red markings, but the female, like other hens of the genus, is a camouflaged brownish colour; the nest is made in the ground, and the P. is polygamous. In England Ps. are semi-domesticated and the shooting season is 1 Oct.-1 Feb.: the P. is naturalized in N America. Among the more exotically beautiful Ps. of other genera, often kept as ornamental birds, are the golden P. (*Chrysolophus pictus*) from China and the argus pheasant of Malaya (*Argusiana argus*) which has metallic spots or 'eyes' on the wings.

PHENACETIN (fena'setin). Painkilling drug banned for general use in the UK from 1980 because long-term use may lead to kidney damage.

PHENOL. *See* CARBOLIC ACID.

PHENYLKETONURIA (fēn'ilketonoor'ia). Condition (PKU) discovered in the 1930s, arising from genetic causes, in which the liver of a child cannot control the level of phenylanine (found in protein foods) in the blood-stream in the normal way by excretion in urine. It is controlled by special diet.

PHEROMONE (fer'ōmōn). Chemical signal (a hormone-like substance) used by numerous animal species to attract their mates. In the fruit-fly (*Drosophila melanogaster*) Ps. are also used to avoid incest and consequent inbreeding.

PHIDIAS (fīd'ias). Greek sculptor. B. at Athens *c.* 500 BC, he was a friend of Pericles who made him superintendent of public works. He constructed the Propylaea and the Parthenon, and executed the colossal statue of Zeus at Olympia which was one of the seven wonders of the world.

PHILADE'LPHIA. City of the USA, in Pennsylvania, 127km (79m) SW of New York. The Delaware connects it with the Atlantic 160km (100m) downstream through

PHEASANT. All the pheasants are handsome birds with beautiful markings, fully displayed in courtship. This handsome fellow is a specimen of Elliot's pheasant. *Photo: Zoological Society of London*

Delaware Bay. Wm. Penn founded the city in 1682 as a Quaker settlement; its name means brotherly love. Notable are the grave of Franklin; Independence Hall (1732-59) in which the Declaration of Independence was adopted, 1776; City Hall (1872) with a tower surmounted by a statue of Penn, total height 167m (548ft); and the US Mint, estab. 1792. P. was temporarily capital of the USA 1790-1800, and attained high eminence in culture. There are the Franklin institute for applied science (1824), and the Univ. of P. (1740); the P. orchestra (1900); the library and the Museum of Art. The port facilities are extensive. The leading industries incl. textiles, oil refining, chemicals, machinery, shipbuilding, food processing, printing and publishing. Pop. met. area (1970) 4,854,200.

PHILAE (fi'lē). Is. in the Nile, Egypt, above the first cataract, famed for the beauty of its Temple of Isis (founded *c.* 350 BC and in use until the 6th cent AD), set among palm trees. Later damming of the river meant that it was submerged for several months of the year, and in 1977 the temple was re-erected on the nearby is. of Agilkia above flooding caused by the Aswan Dam.

PHILATELY. The collection and study of postage stamps. Originating in France *c.* 1860, it became popular throughout the world, London being the world centre. The world's largest collection is in the British Museum, the runner-up being in Smithsonian Institution, Washington: probably the world's finest private collection is that of Queen Elizabeth II. Many countries earn extra revenue and cater for the philatelist by issuing special sets of stamps to commemorate special events, anniversaries, etc., and there are many specialized fields of collection from particular countries to specimens which have some defect, e.g. contemporary issues which are accidentally unperforated.

PHILBY (fil'bi), **Harry St John Bridger** (1885-1960). British explorer. As chief of the British political mission to central Arabia, 1917-18, he carried out extensive exploration and was the first European to visit the southern provs. of Najd; and in 1932 crossed the Rub 'al Khali desert. He wrote *The Empty Quarter* (1933), *Forty Years in the Wilderness* (1957), etc. His son **Harold P.** (1912-), known as Kim P., entered the Foreign Service, but became a Soviet agent and was asked in 1951 to resign: in 1963 he was named as having warned Guy Burgess and Donald Maclean of govt investigations into their activities in 1951, and took Soviet citizenship. He was promoted General in the KGB.

PHILHARMONIC SOCIETY. The Royal P.S. was founded in London in 1813 by the pianist Johann Baptist Cramer (1771-1858) for the purpose of improving musical standards by means of orchestral concerts organized on a subscription basis. Another P.S. was founded in New York in 1842.

PHILIP. One of the 12 Apostles. He was an inhabitant of Bethsaida, and is said to have worked as a missionary in Asia Minor.

PHILIP (382-336 BC). King of Macedonia. After ruling as regent for his nephew, he seized the throne in 359, conquered the Greek cities on the Macedonian coast, Thessaly and Phocis, and defeated the Athenians and Thebans at Chaeronea in 338. He formed the Greek states into a league, and prepared for war with Persia, but was assassinated. He was succeeded by his son, Alexander the Great. His tomb was discovered nr. Vergina in N Greece in 1978.

PHILIP. Name of 6 kings of France. **Philip II** called AUGUSTUS, succeeded in 1180, took part in the 3rd Crusade, conquered Normandy, and defeated a powerful alliance at Bouvines in 1214.

PHILIP IV (1268-1314). King of France. Called the Fair, he engaged in a feud with pope Boniface VIII, whom in 1303 he made a prisoner. Clement V, elected Pope through P.'s influence, transferred his residence to Avignon, and collaborated with P. to suppress the Templars. P. allied with the Scots against England, and attempted to conquer Flanders. **Philip VI** (1293-1350), the first king of the house of Valois, was elected by the barons on the death of his cousin, Charles IV, in 1328. His claim was challenged by Edward III of England, who in 1346 defeated him at Crécy.

PHILIP II (1527-98). King of Spain. The son of the emperor Charles V, he was b. at Valladolid, and in 1554 m. Queen Mary of England. On his father's abdication in 1556 he inherited Spain, the Netherlands, and the Spanish possessions in Italy and America, and in 1580 he annexed Portugal. His intolerance and lack of understanding of the Netherlanders drove them into revolt. Political and religious reasons combined to involve him in war with England, and after 1589 with France. The defeat of the Armada marked the beginning of the decline of Spanish power. P. was buried in the Escorial, which he founded.

PHILIP V (1683-1746). King of Spain. A grandson of Louis XIV of France, he inherited the Spanish crown in 1700, but was not recognized by the Powers until 1713.

PHILIP (1396-1467), known as the Good. Duke of Burgundy from 1419. He engaged in the Hundred Years War as an ally of England and made the Netherlands a centre of art and learning.

PHILIP (1921-). Prince of the UK. A grandson of George I of Greece and a great-great-grandson of Queen Victoria, he was b. in Corfu but raised in England and ed. at Gordonstoun and Dartmouth Naval Coll. During the S.W.W. he served in the Mediterranean, taking part in the battle of Matapan, and in the Pacific. A naturalized British subject, taking the surname Mountbatten, in March 1947, he m. Princess Elizabeth (from 1952 Elizabeth II) in Westminster Abbey on 20 Nov. 1947, having the previous day received the title Duke of Edinburgh. In 1956 he founded the Duke of Edinburgh's Award Scheme to encourage creative achievement among young people, and is also greatly interested in the Commonwealth. He was created a prince of the UK in 1957, and awarded the OM in 1968. Vols. of his speeches appeared in 1957 and 1960.

Descent of the Prince Philip

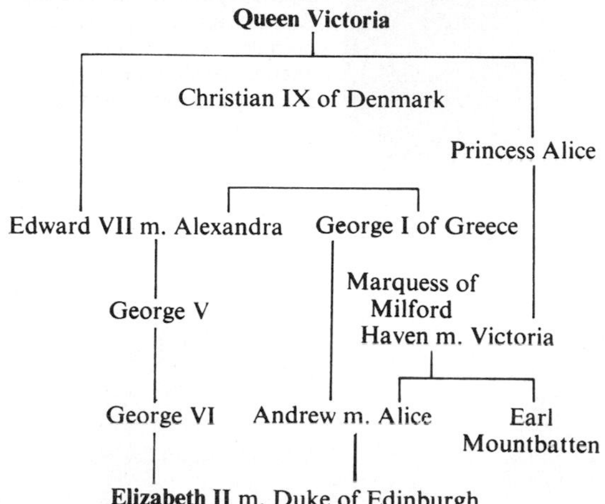

PHILIPPEVILLE (fēlēpvēl'). *See* SKIKDA.

PHILIPPI'. Ancient city of Macedonia, founded by Philip of Macedon, 358 BC. Near P. Antony and Octavius defeated Brutus and Cassius in 42 BC. It was the first European town where St Paul preached (*c.* AD 53), founding the congregation to which he addressed the Epistle to the Philippians.

PHILIPPINES, Republic of the. Independent country consisting of more than 7,000 is. lying N of the equator, between the Pacific Ocean to the E and the S China Sea to the W. The main islands are Luzon in the N and Mindanao in the S; others incl. Mindoro, Masbate, Samar, Panay, Leyte, Cebu, Negros, Bohol, and Palawan. The is. of the main chain are traversed from N to S by volcanic mtn ranges,: the highest point is Mt Apo 2,954 m (9,690 ft) on Mindanao. Forests cover about half the land surface and timber, gums, and resins, bamboo, vegetable oils, dye woods are important products. The main crops are coconuts (copra), cane sugar, rice, maize, tobacco, and hemp. Mineral wealth incl. gold and silver, copper, lead, iron ore, coal, chromite, and quicksilver. There is hydro-electric power, and factories process the local products.

Corazon Aquino (1932–), heads a government set up in 1986 after several years of despotic rule by martial law under Federico Marcos (q.v.). The prominent opposition leader Benigno Aquino was murdered in 1983, allegedly by a military conspiracy, and Marcos declared himself the victor of the 1986 presidential elections. Marcos' own allies resigned in protest against the rigged elections, he fled the country and Aquino's widow was declared President. There was much rejoicing at the change of leadership, but violence and corruption are still widespread.

Area 300,000 sq.km (115,700 sq.m); pop. (1985) 56,808,000, most of Malay stock and RC, but there is a 1,300,000 Moslem minority. Filipino (based on the Malay dialect, Tagalog) is the nat. language, but English and Spanish are also official languages. The cap. is Manila (formerly Quezon City, q.v., 1948-76); other towns are Cebu, Davao and Iloilo. M.U. peso.

History. The P. were visited by Magellan in 1521, and Spanish rule and Catholicism were estab. in the 1560s, during the reign of Philip II, in whose honour the islands were named. During the 19th cent. a series of armed revolts occurred. On the conclusion of the Spanish-American War the P. were ceded to the USA, 1898. In 1935 a semi-independent Commonwealth of the P. was estab., and in 1946 an independent republic was set up; the USA was in 1947 granted the use of a number of military bases in the is. The Japanese occupied the P. 1942-5 after overcoming a fierce resistance by American and Filipino troops under General MacArthur.

After the S.W.W. the P. entered on a troubled period, and the army was actively engaged against the Communist New People's Army (formerly known as the Hukbalahap) active 1945-54 and from 1967 in N Luzon; and also against the Moslem Black Shirt Movement (active from 1970) in Mindanao, the Sulu Archipelago, and Palawan, which they wished to estab. as an independent state, Minsupala. The P. maintain a claim to the Malaysian state of Sabah. It has been proposed that the name P. should eventually be changed to Maharlika (Tagalog 'noble').

PHILIPPOPOLIS. Greek name of PLOVDIV.

PHILISTINE (fil'istīn). Originally a contemptuous term applied by German students to non-members of the univ.; hence a person with no interest in intellectual or artistic matters.

PHILISTINES. A people who inhabited the coastal plain of Palestine from the 12th cent. BC, forming a league of city-states. Coming probably from Asia Minor, they adopted a Semitic language and religion, struggled with the Israelites in the 11th-10th cents. BC, were temporarily subdued by David, and later passed under Assyrian supremacy. They were non-Semitic in origin.

PHILLIP, Arthur (1738-1814). British founder of New South Wales. He entered the navy in 1755 and rose to vice-admiral. He founded the convict settlement at Sydney in 1788, and was governor until 1792.

PHILO JUDAEUS (fī'lō joodē'-us) (fl. 1st cent. AD). Jewish philosopher of Alexandria, who in AD 40 undertook a mission to Caligula to protest against the emperor's claim to divine honours. In his writings P. attempts to reconcile Judaism with Platonic and Stoic ideas.

PHILOLOGY. A Greek term, originally meaning 'love of learning and literature'. It is often used in the sense of linguistics (q.v.), but more often defines the critical study of the literary remains of the past, esp. of Gk and Roman antiquity. In this sense the scholars of Alexandria, who e.g. edited Homer, were philologists. The Renaissance gave great impetus to this kind of study. Dutch scholars took the lead in the 17th cent. whilst Richard Bentley in England held a place of his own. From the study of Sanskrit arose at the beginning of the 19th cent., under Bopp's leadership, what is called comparative P., originally mainly concerned with the Indo-European (q.v.) family of languages, whilst the Romantic movement greatly inspired the establishment of national Ps. - Germanic and German (Grimm), Romance (Diez), Celtic (Zeuss), etc.

PHILOSOPHY. An idealised portrait bust of Plato (top left; St. Thomas Aquinas by Fra Angelico (top right); René Descartes, an engraving from a portrait by Frans Hals (centre left); Thomas Hobbes, after a portrait by J.M. Wright (centre); G.W.F. Hegel, engraved from a portrait by Xeller (centre right); John Stuart Mill (bottom left); and Existentialists Jean Paul Satre and Simone de Beauvoir *Photos: Mansell Collection, National Portrait Gallery (Hobbes and Mill), and Popperfoto (Sartre).*

PHOENICIA. An ivory box-lid and a bronze statuette of Baal, 14th cent. BC, both found at Ugarit (Ras Shamra), and the 'Lady of Elche' found in 1897 in Spain, the work of a Graeco-Phoenician sculptor of the 5th cent. BC. *Photo: Mansell Collection.*

PHILOSOPHY (Gk love of knowledge). The field of theoretical studies which incl. metaphysics, epistemology (theory of knowledge), ethics and aesthetics, but which continually contracts as specific studies acquire their own estab. disciplines, e.g. mathematics, physics, chemistry, biology and (until this cent.) psychology were formerly incl. in P., and logic is in process of separation. Oldest of all philosophical systems is the Vedic *c.* 2,500 BC, but like many other eastern systems it rests on a primarily mystic basis. The first scientific system originated in Greece in the 6th cent. BC with the Milesian school (Thales, Anaximander and Anaximenes). Both they and later pre-Socratics (Pythagoras, Xenophanes, Parmenides, Zeno of Elea, Empedocles, Anaxagoras, Heraclitus and Democritus) were lively theorists, and ideas such as atomism, developed by Democritus, crop up in later schemes of thought. In the 5th cent. among the teachers known as the sophists there emerged in Socrates the apostle of the ideal of reason, and Plato and Aristotle complete the trinity of the golden age of Greek P. Later schools incl. the epicureans (Epicurus), stoics (Zeno) and sceptics (Pyrrho); the eclectics - not a school, but selecting what appealed to them from various systems (Cicero and Seneca) - and the neo-Platonists, infusing a mystic element into the system of Plato (Philo, Plotinus and, as disciple, Julian the Apostate). The close of the Athenian schools of P. by Justinian in AD 529 marks the end of ancient P., though many of its teachers moved eastwards and Greek thought emerges in Moslem philosophers such as Avicenna and Averroes, and the Jewish Maimonides. For the West the work of Aristotle was transmitted through Boethius, and the roll of medieval scholastic philosophers, mainly concerned with the reconciliation of ancient P. with Christian belief, begins in the 9th cent. with John Scotus Erigena, and incl. Anselm, Abelard, Albertus Magnus, Thomas Aquinas (greatest of them all), his opponent Duns Scotus, and William of Ockham.

In the 17th cent. Descartes, with his rationalist determination to doubt, and faith in mathematical proof, marks the beginning of modern P., and was followed by Spinoza, Leibniz and Hobbes, but the empiricists, principally an 18th cent. English school (Locke, Berkeley and Hume), turned rather to physics as indicating what can be known and how, and led up to the transcendental criticism of Kant. In the early 19th cent. classical German idealism (Fichte, Schelling, Hegel) repudiated Kant's limitation of human knowledge; and in France Comte developed the positivist thought which attracted Mill and Spencer. Notable also in the cent. are the pessimistic atheism of Schopenhauer; the dialectical materialism of Marx and Engels; the work of Nietszche and Kierkegaard, which led towards 20th cent. existentialism; the pragmatism of William James and Dewey; and the absolute idealism at the turn of the cent. of the neo-Hegelians (Bradley, Bosanquet, M'Taggart, Royce, Blanshard and Creighton). Among 20th cent. movements are the logical positivism of the Vienna circle (Carnap, Popper, Ayer); the creative evolution of Bergson; neo-Thomism, the revival of the medieval philosophy of Aquinas (Gilson, Maritain); existentialism (Heidegger, Jaspers, Sartre, Marcel); the phenomenology of Husserl, who influenced Ryle; realism (Russell, Moore, Broad and Wittgenstein), and the isolated genius of Whitehead.

PHIZ. Pseudonym of British artist, Hablot Knight Browne (1815-82). B. at Lambeth, he illustrated the greater part of Dickens' *Pickwick Papers*, and others of Dickens' works, as well as novels by Lever and Harrison Ainsworth.

PHLEBITIS (flĕbī'tis). Inflammation of the lining of a vein. It causes the blood in the neighbourhood to clot (thrombosis). Simple or non-infective P. may be caused by an injury or pressure, and is common in the main thigh

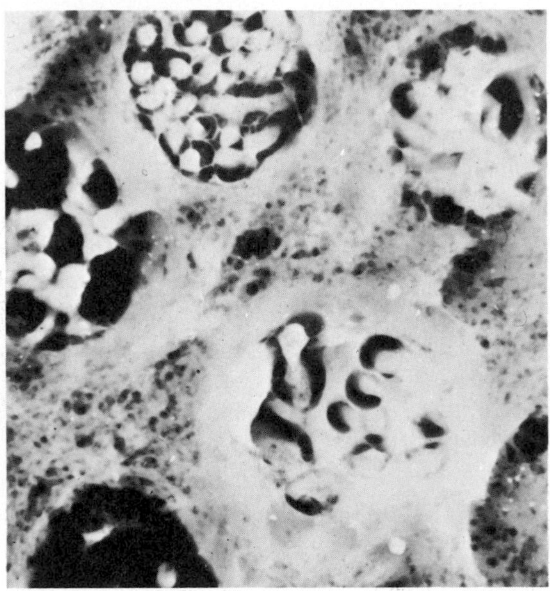

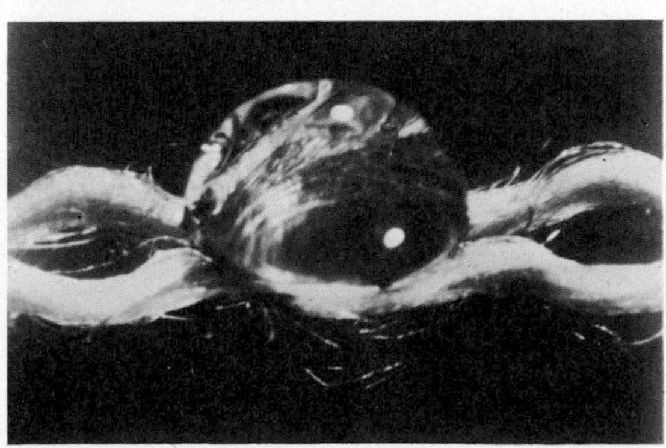

PHOTOGRAPHY. Louis Daguerre (top left); the latest development in instant photography – a cassette of special colour film is exposed in the movie camera, which has a 2:1 zoom lens, then inserted in the solid state Polavision player ready for viewing on the 30cm (12in) screen (top right); Alfred, Lord Tennyson, in the famous camera study by Julia Cameron (middle left); a drop of oil balances, without being absorbed, on two strands of fabric treated with rain and stain repeller (bottom left); and a cavity in a tooth (x7,500), showing bacteria in each of the dental tubules (bottom right). *Photos: Mansell Collection, Polaroid (UK) Ltd., National Portrait Gallery, Minnesota Mining and Manufacturing Co., Miss K. Little of the Nuffield Orthopaedic Centre, Oxford.*

veins of women after childbirth. The blood clots and obstructs the circulation (white leg). Septic P. is caused by infection, e.g. in the lateral sinus and the jugular vein by infection from the middle ear. Fragments of the clot may carry infection to the lungs and cause an abscess.

PHLOX. Genus of plants native to Siberia and N America. The British varieties are half-hardy annuals cultivated from *Phlox drummondi.* They have lanceolate, opposite leaves, and the flowers, borne in panicles, are red, white or mauve.

PHNÔM-PENH (nompen'). Cap. of Cambodia, on the Mekong, 210km (130m) NW of Saigon. It is an important trade centre with buildings in European style, built while Cambodia was under French protection, as well as Buddhist temples, etc. There is a regular river service to Saigon, and an airport at nearby Pochentong. There are textile and food processing industries. At the time of its fall to the Khmer Rouge in 1975, P. P. had a pop. of c. 3 million, reduced (by dispersal etc.) to 20,000 in 1976.

PHOENICIA (fēnish'a). Ancient Greek name for the seaboard of Lebanon and Syria, N of Mt Carmel, inhabited in ancient times by a people who called themselves Canaanites. *See* CANAAN. They were seafaring traders and craftsmen, who visited the Scillies (and possibly Cornwall) and are said to have circumnavigated Africa, and their cities (Tyre and Sidon being the chief) were independent states ruled by hereditary kings, but dominated by merchant oligarchies. Documents found at Ugarit in 1929 give much information on their civilization, and their deities incl. El, Baal, Anat, Astarte or Ashtaroth, and Melkart or Moloch. Their colonies were estab. in Cyprus, N Africa (e.g. Carthage), Malta, Sicily and Spain, and competition from these combined with the attacks of the Sea Peoples, the Assyrians and Greeks, on the cities in P. led to their ultimate decline: the fall of Tyre to Alexander in 332 BC ended the separate history of P. Their exports incl. Tyrian purple cloth, furniture (from the timber of Lebanon), and jewellery: Solomon brought workmen from P. to construct and decorate the Temple at Jerusalem.

PHOENIX (fē'niks). Miraculous Egyptian bird which, according to legend, burnt itself to death on a pyre of aromatic woods after 500 years of life, to arise rejuvenated from the ashes.

PHOENIX. Cap. of Arizona, USA. It handles dairy products and citrus fruit from the surrounding irrigated area, is a tourist centre, and has steel, aluminium, electrical and electronic industries. Pop. (1970) 963,132.

PHOENIX ISLANDS. Group of 8 is. in the S Pacific, incl. in Kiribats (q.v.). Drought has rendered them all uninhabitable. Total land area 18 sq.km (11 sq.m).

PHONETICS. The science which deals with the identification, description, and classification of sounds used in articulate speech. P. owes its origin in large measure to A. M. Bell (1819-1905), and much of the pioneer work was done in England. As the letters of the Rom. alphabet are a quite inadequate means of fixing the definite value of speech sound, special phonetic alphabets have been invented of which the International Phonetic Script is best known.

PHONOGRAPH. *See* RADIOGRAM.

PHOSPHATES. Salts of phosphoric acid. They combine with water in 3 proportions to form metaphosphoric acid, pyrophosphoric acid, and ordinary phosphoric acid. Each of these acids gives origin to other series of salts, of which ordinary phosphoric acid is of the greatest importance.

PHOSPHORUS (Gk *phosphoros,* light-bearing). Element essential to life, discovered by Brand in 1669: symbol P, at. wt. 30.975, at. no. 15. It occurs in several forms, the commonest being white P. (a waxy solid, emitting a greenish glow in air, burning spontaneously to P. pentoxide, and very poisonous) and red P. (neither igniting spontaneously nor poisonous). Production of P. and its compounds has greatly increased since the S.W.W., e.g. the use of soluble phosphates as fertilizers and of other P. compounds in detergents, prevention of scale and corrosion in pipes and boiler tubes, and in certain organic preparations.

PHOTOELECTRIC CELL or **photocell.** A device for measuring or detecting light. There are 3 main types: in the *photoemissive* cell, radiant light energy causes electrons to be emitted, and a current to flow; in the *photovoltaic* cell, a semiconductor device, it causes an electromotive force to be generated; and in the *photoconductive* cell it causes the resistance to vary.

PHOTOFIT. System aiding the identification of 'wanted' criminals. Witnesses select from variant photographs of a single feature (hair, eyes, nose, mouth, etc.), their choices resulting in a composite likeness, then re-photographed and circulated. It is a more sophisticated development by Jacques Penry in 1970 for Scotland Yard of the identikit system evolved by an American, Hugh C. McDonald (1913-), which used drawings not photographs, and which was first used by the police in Los Angeles in 1959.

PHOTOGRAPHY. Modern P. embraces all useful processes for producing images on sensitized materials by radiant energy which may be visible light, ultra-violet, infra-red or X-rays; radiation from radioactive substances, and beams of electrons.

J. N. Niepce produced the first successful photograph in 1822 using silver chloride. Daguerre partnered him in 1829 and discovered that an image could be produced by fuming with mercury vapour an exposed iodized silver plate in a camera (1839), and Fox Talbot independently announced his calotype method also in 1839. From Scott Archer's collodion (wet plate) process (1851) research on emulsions and gelatine reduced the exposure time from 10 sec. to 1/100 sec. by 1900. The invention of the gelatine dry plate, by R. L. Maddox in 1871, was the next great milestone. Panchromatic plates covered the whole spectrum, glass plates were superseded by roll film and box cameras appeared. Colour P. was produced practically in 1891 by Lippman, but Maxwell's tri-colour separation process has prevailed as the basis of modern reproduction.

Enormous advances have been made in all branches of P., in equipment, processes and techniques necessitated by the dependence on photography of television, the cinema industry, news pictures, medical, scientific and research requirements, microfilm recording and new processes in the printing industry and for office copying machines.

The most recent developments in cameras incl. the introduction of automatic loading and the production of a colour print inside the camera 50 sec. after exposure and, in 1980, three-dimensional P. (which uses 4 lenses set in a horizontal line) was under development.

PHOTOSYNTHESIS. Process by which plants first use photons of sunlight to split water into oxygen, protons and electrons - the so-called 'light reaction'. They then use the electrons to convert carbon dioxide into carbohydrates - the 'dark reaction'. Scientists, who achieved artificial P. in the laboratory in 1977, are endeavouring to utilise the electrons instead to convert the protons into hydrogen. Hydrogen can be burned as a fuel in the right type of aircraft or motor engine, and is also non-polluting and easy to store.

The plant mechanism for P. is universally based on the green pigment chlorophyll, except in halobacteria, which use a purple pigment in a similar way. The latter resembles the pigment which, in the retina of the eye, converts light energy to nerve impulses.

PHRENO'LOGY. The theory, now discredited, that by examination of the skull a person's mental development can be measured. It was first propounded by Franz Joseph Gall, a Viennese physician, *c.* 1796.

PHRYGIA (frij'ia). Former kingdom of W Asia covering the Anatolian tableland, inhabited in ancient times by an Indo-European people; it achieved great prosperity in the 8th cent. BC under a line of kings bearing in turn the names Gordius and Midas, but then fell under Lydian rule. From P. the cult of Cybele was introduced into Greece and Rome.

PHRYNE (frī'nē) (4th cent. BC). Athenian courtesan famous for her beauty.

PHYLLOXĒ'RA. Genus of insects in the order Hemiptera similar to aphides. The species *P. vitifolia* a native of N America, attacks grape vines, laying its eggs under the bark. European vines are especially susceptible and many French vineyards suffered terribly on the arrival of the pest in Europe in the 19th cent. The insects may be destroyed by spraying with carbon disulphide or petroleum.

PHYSICS. P. (sometimes called 'natural philosophy') is a branch of science which is concerned with the ultimate laws which govern the structure of the universe and forms of matter and energy and their interactions. For convenience P. is often divided into branches such as nuclear P., solid and liquid state P., electricity, electronics and magnetism, optics, acoustics, heat and thermodynamics.

PHYSIOLOGY. That branch of medicine and biology that deals with the functioning of the healthy human body. *See* HUMAN BODY.

PHYSIOTHERAPY. Use of heat (infra-red lamps, hot water, etc.), electrical stimulation (low-voltage currents), massage and exercise to treat patients suffering from rheumatic conditions, leprosy, poliomyelitis, lung complaints, accidental injuries, war wounds, etc. Qualified practitioners are registered with the Chartered Soc. of P. (England and Wales) and Faculty of Physiotherapists (Scotland); in the USA, where they are more commonly called physical therapists, the central body is the American P. Association.

PIACENZA (pē-ahchen'za). City in Emilia-Romagna, Italy, on the Po, 65km (40m) SE of Milan. The Roman Placentia, P. dates from 218 BC, and has a 12th cent. cathedral. Agricultural machinery, textiles, pottery, etc. are among its industries. Pop. (1978) 109,200.

PIAF (pē-ahf'), **Edith** (1915-63). French diseuse. Embodiment of the defiant, Parisian gamine, she was nicknamed P. (Fr. slang for 'sparrow') because of her small size. Her life was emotionally full but tragic, as suggested by her most famous song *Je ne Regrette Rien* (I Regret Nothing).

PIAGET (pe-ahzha'), **Jean** (1896–1980). Swiss psychologist. By closely recorded observation of his own children, he threw much light on the development of memory, intelligence, and identity in the young.

PIANOFORTE. A stringed musical instrument, whose keyed hammers make it percussive and capable of soft or strong tones - hence its name. The clavichord and the 16th cent. virginal were forerunners of the design evolved in 1709 by Bartolommeo Cristofori, a Paduan harpsichord-maker. Subsequent improvement has been closely linked with the names of famous P. makers, such as Broadwood and Stodart, Pleyel, Érard, Collard, Steinway, Blüthner, and Bechstein. The practice of some designers building the strings vertically has prevailed in the modified form of the upright P. The horizontally strung grand P. is recognized as superior in tone and is used for concert performance. The player P., invented 1842, operated by a mechanism involving a perforated paper roll. Many concert pianists of the day 'recorded' their performances in this form, and such rolls give a very good idea of their style. In modern times there has been a revival of earlier forms of P. to recreate classical music on the instruments for which it was composed, and the latest contemporary instruments tend to incl. some of the advantages of the old in the new.

PICABIA (pikah'bia), **Francis** (1879-1953). Spanish-French artist. Of Spanish origin, he was born and died in Paris. Ever in search of new ideas, he was associated with Impressionism, with Marcel Duchamp and the Dadaist revolt in New York in 1915; with Surrealism; with representational art, and finally with a return to abstract painting. He anticipated many developments of American art in the 1960s.

PICARDY. Former province of France; it covered all the Somme department and parts of Pas de Calais, Aisne, and Oise. The modern P. region incl. Aisne, Oise and Somme.

PICA'SSO (RUIZ), Pablo (1881-1973). Spanish artist. Son of an art teacher José Ruiz Blasco, and an Andalusian mother Maria Picasso López, he discontinued use of the name Ruiz in 1898. B. at Malaga, he was a mature artist at 10, and at 16 was holding his first exhibition. In 1900 he made an initial visit to Paris, where he was to settle, and during his Blue Period 1901-4 painted mystic distorted figures in blue tones; a brief, more supple, Rose Period 1905-6 followed, but in 1907 he completed the revolutionary 'Les Demoiselles d'Avignon' by which Cubism was fully launched. His subsequent development has been kaleidoscopic, rather than moving along any one path, incl. by turns Classicism, Romanticism, Realism, Expressionism, Abstractionism and Naturalism, and ranging through ceramics, sculpture, sets for ballet (e.g. *Parade* in 1917 for Diaghilev), book illustrations (e.g. Ovid's *Metamorphoses*), portraits (Stravinsky, Valéry, etc.), to his generally acknowledged masterpiece 'Guernica' (1937) a nightmare mural interpretation of the agony of the Civil War in Spain. He is unique in the fertile vigour of his invention, and in his appeal to the amateur as well as the expert, his exhibitions attracting a large popular following.

PICCARD, Auguste (1884–1962). Swiss scientist. B. in Basle, he became prof. of physics at the Univ. of Brussels in 1922. In 1931-2 he made ascents to 16,800 m (55,000 ft) in a balloon of his own design, resulting in important discoveries concerning such stratospheric phenomena as cosmic rays. Subsequently he built and used bathyscaphes for undersea research.

PICKFORD, Mary (1893-1979). American actress, *née* Gladys Smith. B. in Toronto, she became the first star of the silent screen to be known by name, and on her marriage - her second - to Douglas Fairbanks senior in 1920, they were called 'the world's sweethearts'.

PICO DELLA MIRANDOLA (pēkō-dellah-mērahn'dōlah), **Giovanni** (1463-94). Italian mystic philosopher. B. at Mirandola, of which his father was prince, he studied Hebrew, Chaldean, and Arabic, showing particular interest in the Kabbala.

PICRIC ACID. Yellow crystalline solid $C_6H_2(NO_2)_3OH$, 2, 4, 6-trinitrophenol. It is a strong acid, dyes wool and silks yellow, is used to treat burns and in the manufacture of explosives.

PICTON. Small port at the NE extremity of South Island, NZ, with a ferry to Wellington in North Island.

PICTS. An early people inhabiting Scotland, probably of pre-Celtic origin, and speaking a non-Celtic language. They were united with the Celtic Scots under the rule of Kenneth MacAlpin in 844.

PIDGIN ENGLISH. Business jargon ('pidgin' being the Chinese corruption of the English word business) used in dealing with Chinese and other Oriental traders, which utilizes simplified English forms arranged according to Chinese idiom. It has developed a character of its own through continued use among local peoples who themselves have different languages, particularly in Papua New Guinea.

PIECK (pēk), **Wilhelm** (1876-1960). German Communist. A leader of the 1919 Spartacist revolt, he was a founder of the Socialist Unity Party in 1946 and from 1949 was pres. of the German Democratic Rep.: the office was abolished on his death.

PIEDMONT. A region of N Italy, bordering Switzerland on the N and France on the W and surrounded, except on the E, by the Alps and the Apennines. The most fertile land is near the Po. The main towns are Turin (the capital), Alessandria, Asti, Vercelli, and Novara. From P., under the House of Savoy, the movement for the unification of Italy started in the 19th cent. Area 25,399 sq.km (9,804 sq.m); pop. (1978) 4,541,000.

PIERNÉ (pē-ārneh), **Gabriel** (1863-1937). French composer and conductor. B. in Metz, he succeeded Franck as organist to Ste Clothilde, Paris, and conducted the Colonne orchestra from 1903. His numerous compositions incl. the 'Entry of the Little Fauns'.

PIETERMARITZBURG (pētermār'itsboorg). Cap. of Natal, S Africa, 66km (41m) WNW of Durban, founded in 1838 by Boer trekkers from the Cape, and was named in 1839 in honour of their leaders, Piet Retief and Gert Maritz. Made cap. of Natal 1842, it is an industrial centre with breweries, and factories making boots and shoes, furniture, etc. Pop. (1970) 158,920.

PĪ'ETISM. Movement within the German Lutheran Church originated by Philip Jacob Spener (1635-1705), and intended to revive practical Christianity as against increasing theological dogmatism.

PĪEZŌELE'CTRIC EFFECT. The property of some crystals of developing an electromotive force or voltage across opposite faces when subjected to a mechanical strain, and, conversely, of altering in size when subjected to an electromotive force. This effect is utilized in devices used for frequency control and measurement, crystal filters and transducers (q.v.).

PIG. Family of mammals (Suidae) in the order Ungulata. Domesticated Ps. are derived from the European wild boar (*Sus scrofa*), crossed with Asiatic breeds. The chief modification is the concave face, the wild swine having a long snout. The modern housewife's preference for lean meat has led to the development of a hybrid heavy P. combining the good qualities of the Landrace, Saddleback and Large White breeds.

PIGALU (pigaloo'). Is. (formerly Annobon) in Equatorial Guinea. Area 17 sq.km (7 sq.m); pop. (1970) 1,500, descended from slaves of the Portuguese and still speaking a form of that language.

PIGEON. General term for members of the family Columbidae, sometimes also called doves, distinguished by their large crops which, becoming glandular in the breeding season, secrete a milky fluid (so-called 'P.'s milk') which aids digestion of food for the young. There are many species, one of the most important being the blue rock-P. (*Columba livia*) from which the domesticated varieties derive (pouter, fantail, homer, etc.). Similar is the stock-dove (*C. oenas*), but the wood-P. (*C. palumbus*) is much larger and has white patches on the neck. The American species incl. the passenger-P. (*Ectopistes migratorius*), once millions strong but extinct from 1914, and the mourning-doves, which (like the European turtle-doves) live much on the ground. The painted Ps. and fruit Ps. of Australasia and the Malay regions are beautifully coloured.

P.-flying is a popular sport in many Continental countries, as well as Britain (where the National Homing Union dates from 1896 and Elizabeth II has a racing P. manager), and the USA. *See also* MAGNETISM, MIGRATION.

PIGGOTT, Lester (1935-). British jockey. A master of management and timing, he was many times champion, and had 8 Derby wins (Never Say Die 1954, Crepello 1957, St Paddy 1960, Sir Ivor 1968, Nijinsky 1970, Roberto 1972, Empery 1976, and The Minstrel 1977).

PIGOTT (pig'ot), **Richard** (1828-89). Irish forger, who sold *The Times* in 1886 a number of documents purporting to prove the complicity of Parnell and other Irish leaders in political murders. These were proved to be forgeries, and P. committed suicide.

PIGS, Bay of. Inlet on the S coast of Cuba *c.* 145km (90m) SW of Havana, site of an unsuccessful invasion attempt by 1,500 anti-Castro Cuban exiles 17-20 April 1961; 1,173 were taken prisoner. The creation of this anti-revolutionary force in the USA by the CIA had been authorized by the Eisenhower admin. and the project executed under that of J. F. Kennedy.

PIKE. Genus of freshwater fish (*Esox*). Found both in Europe and N America the common P. (*E. lucius*) has a long body, and broad flattened head with a large mouth studded with backward-pointing teeth: grey-green mottled yellow above, it is white underneath. Sluggish in habit except when pursuing its prey, it is a voracious feeder and mature specimens may reach over 22.5 kg (50 lb). Some of the smaller species of American P. are known as 'pickerel'.

PIKE-PERCH. Genus of freshwater fish (*Lucioperca*) of the order Percomorphi. The European P.-P. (*Lucioperca lucioperca*) reaches over a metre (3ft), is very voracious, and of some value as a food fish. Related species are found in N America.

PIKES PEAK. Strikingly beautiful mtn in the Rampart range of the Rocky Mtns, Colorado, USA. It was discovered by Lt Zebulon M. Pike while exploring the area in 1806: 4,300 m (14,110 ft).

PILATE, Pontius. Roman procurator of Judaea AD 26-AD 36. Unsympathetic to the Jews, his actions several times provoked riots, and in AD 36 he was recalled to Rome to account for disorder in Samaria. Eusebius says he committed suicide.

PILCHARD. Fish (*Sardina pilchardus*) of the herring family (*Clupeidae*). Bluish-green above and silvery beneath, it grows to *c.* 255mm (10in) long: the chief P. fisheries are off Spain and Portugal.

PILES. Haemorrhoids; varicose veins of the anus. They may be external (covered with skin) or, more commonly, internal (covered with mucous membrane). The cause is increase of pressure in the abdomen, as in childbirth, or constipation. The veins often bleed on defecation; or are extruded from the anus. The remedy is either to remove the piles by cutting or cauterizing, or to harden and close the veins off by injection of a 'sclerosing' fluid.

PILGRIMAGE. Journey to sacred places inspired by religious devotion. For Hindus the holy places incl. Benares and the purifying Ganges; for Buddhists the spots connected with the crises of Buddha's career; for the ancient Greeks the shrines at Delphi, Ephesus, etc.; for the Jews, the sanctuary at Jerusalem; and for Mohammedans, Mecca. Among Christians, Ps. were common by the 2nd cent., and as a direct result of the estab. necessity of making Ps. there arose the numerous hospices catering for pilgrims, the religious orders of knighthood, and the Crusades. The great centres of Christian P. have been, or are, Jerusalem, Rome, the tomb of St James of Compostella in Spain, the shrine of Becket at Canterbury, and the holy places at La Salette and Lourdes in France.

PILGRIMAGE. Hindu pilgrims bathe in the Ganges from the ghats at Varanesi in the ritual of purification. *Photo: J. Allan Cash*

PILGRIMAGE OF GRACE. The rebellion of 1536-7 in Lincs. and Yorks. In character it was both a movement of the feudal nobility and clergy against the dissolution of the monasteries and Henry VIII's centralizing policy, and a peasant revolt against the enclosure of common lands. The rebels were dispersed by promises, and then executed in large numbers.

PILGRIM FATHERS. Name given to the emigrants who sailed from Plymouth in the *Mayflower* on 16 Sept. 1620 to found the first colony in New England at New Plymouth, Mass. Of the 102 passengers less than a quarter were Puritan refugees. They originally set sail in the *Mayflower* and *Speedwell* from Southampton on 5 Aug. 1620, but had to put into Dartmouth when the latter needed repair. Bad weather then drove them into Plymouth Sound where the *Speedwell* was abandoned. The voyage was duplicated in 1957 with *Mayflower II*, a replica presented by Britain to form part of the national shrine at Plymouth, Mass.

PILGRIMS' WAY. Track running from Winchester to Canterbury, England, which was the route of medieval pilgrims visiting the shrine of Thomas à Becket. Some 195 km (120m) long, the P.W. can still be traced for more than half its length.

PILGRIM TRUST. *See* HARKNESS, EDWARD.

PILLORY. Instrument of punishment consisting of a wooden frame set on a post, with holes in which the prisoner's head and hands were secured. Its use was abolished in England in 1837.

PILSEN. German form of PLZEN.

PILSUDSKI (pilsood'ski), **Joseph** (1867-1935). Polish statesman. B. in Russian Poland, he founded the Polish Socialist Party in 1892, and was twice imprisoned for anti-Russian activities. During the F.W.W. he commanded a Polish force to fight for Germany, but fell under suspicion of intriguing with the Allies, and in 1917-18 was imprisoned by the Germans. When Poland became independent he was elected Chief of State, and led the unsuccessful Polish attack on Russia in 1920. He retired in 1923, but in 1926 led a military coup which estab. his dictatorship until his death.

PILTDOWN MAN. Fossilized, fragmentary skull which Charles Dawson (d. 1916) 'discovered' at Piltdown in Sussex in 1912. Long believed to represent the oldest human species found in Europe, it was proved a hoax in 1953. The jaw was that of an orang-utan and the cranial bones (though both human and ancient) could not have come from this site. These assorted items subsequently remained in the Natural History Museum.

PIME'NTO. Genus of trees found in tropical America. The dried fruits of the species *Pimenta officinalis* are used as spice.

PIMPERNEL. Genus of plants (*Anagallis*) in the family Primulaceae. The Scarlet P. (*A. arvensis*) grows in cornfields and is easy to overlook, since the flowers open only in full sunshine. It is naturalized in N. America.

PINCUS (pink'us), **Gregory** (1903-67). American biologist. Specializing in reproductive biology, he played a major role in the development of oral contraceptives.

PINDAR (*c.* 522 BC-442 BC). Greek lyric poet. B. near Thebes, he excelled in the choral lyric.

PINDLING, (Lynden) Oscar (1930-). Bahamas statesman. After studying law in London, he returned to the is. to join the newly-formed Progressive Liberal Party, and then became the first Negro Prime Minister of the Bahamas in 1967.

PI'NDUS MOUNTAINS. Range in N central Greece, between Epirus and Thessaly: highest point Smolikas 2,637 m (8,652 ft).

PINE. Genus (*Pinus*) of some 70 species of evergreen coniferous trees, of which the Scots P. (*P. sylvestris*) is grown commercially for soft timber (deal) and its yield of turpentine, tar, pitch, etc. The oldest living thing is probably the bristlecone P. (*P. aristata*), native to California, of which some specimens are said to be *c.* 4,600 years old.

PINEAL (pin'e-al) **GLAND.** Gland at the centre of the brain. About the size of a pea, it secretes a hormone-like substance (melatonin), which has a probable function in the process of reproduction. The P.G. also controls the physiology of time in human beings, i.e., whether they are at their best in the daytime or are 'night-owls'. In fish and lizards the P.G. enables them to change colour to match their background.

PINEAPPLE. Plant (*Ananas comosus*) native to S and Central America, now cultivated in many other tropical areas, e.g. Queensland. The mauvish flowers are produced midway in the 2nd year, and subsequently consolidate with their bracts into a fleshy fruit. For export to world markets the fruits are cut unripe and lack the sweet juiciness typical of the tinned P. (usually the smoother-skinned Cayenne variety) which is allowed to mature fully.

PINEAPPLE. Needing more care than any other fruit in cultivation, the pineapple takes up to eighteen months to mature. Here paper bags full of fertiliser are being placed alongside the rows in a plantation in Puerto Rico, where pineapples rank third behind sugar and tobacco in importance to the economy. Most are exported to the USA. *Photo: Camera Press*

PINE'RO, Sir Arthur Wing (1855-1934). British dramatist. B. in London, of Jewish extraction, he became an actor, beginning to write for the stage in 1877. He wrote farces such as *Dandy Dick* (1887), the sentimental *Sweet Lavender*; and the problem plays *The Second Mrs Tanqueray* (1893), *The Notorious Mrs Ebbsmith* (1895), and *Mid-Channel* (1909); and *Trelawny of the Wells* (1898).

PINK. *See* CARNATION.

PINKERTON, Allan (1819-84). American detective. B. in Glasgow, he emigrated to the USA in 1842, where in 1852 he founded P.'s National Detective Agency. In 1861 he prevented a plot to assassinate Lincoln, and from his espionage system, built up in the Civil War, created the Federal secret service.

PINKIE. Spot near Musselburgh, Midlothian, Scotland, which was the scene of a defeat of the Scots by the English in 1547.

PINT. Liquid measure of capacity (0.6 litre), ½ of a quart, ⅛ of a gallon: equivalent to 20 fluid oz in imperial measure UK, and 16 fluid oz in USA.

PI'NTER, Harold (1930-). British dramatist. Of Jewish stock, he had a rigorous training as an actor in provincial repertory 1949-57. *The Caretaker* (1960) brought him success as a playwright, but *The Birthday Party*, produced in 1958, while he was actually working as a caretaker, was a dismal failure. Always concerned with the breakdown of communication between individuals, he essayed a sophisticated sexual level in the acid *The Lover* (1962). He writes also for radio and television.

PINTURICCHIO (pintoorik'kē-ō) (1454-1513). Italian painter whose real name was Bernardino di Betti. B. at Perugia, he assisted Perugino in decorating the Sistine Chapel, Rome.

PINYIN. The Chinese phonetic alphabet approved in 1956, and used from 1979 in transcribing all names of persons and places (Pinyin 'transcription') into foreign languages using the Roman alphabet, e.g. Chou En-lai becomes Zhou Enlai, Hua Kuo-feng becomes Hua Guofeng, Teng Hsiao-ping becomes Deng Xiaoping.

PIO'ZZI, Hester Lynch (1741-1821). British author. B. in Caernarvonshire, *née* Salisbury, she m. Henry Thrale in 1763, and in 1765 was introduced to Samuel Johnson, whose friendship she retained until after 3 years' widowhood she m. the musician Gabriele P. in 1784. In 1786 she pub. *Anecdotes of the late S. Johnson*, and in 1788 her correspondence with him.

PIPER, John (1903-). British artist. B. at Epsom, the son of a solicitor, he studied at the RCA and the Slade. From early landscapes of southern England, he went on in the 'thirties to two-dimensional abstracts; to pictures of air-raid destruction in the S.W.W., such as the House of Commons and Bath; then to architectural compositions against romantic backgrounds; theatrical settings, e.g. for the operas of Britten; and a window for Coventry Cathedral and panels for the lantern at Liverpool RC Cathedral.

PIPIT. Several genera of birds in the family Motacillidae allied to the wagtails, but looking like larks. The European meadow P. (*Anthus pratensis*) is about the size of a sparrow and streaky brown.

PIRACY. The taking of a ship, or any of its contents, from lawful ownership while on the high seas, punishable under international law by the court of any country where the pirate may be found or taken. Algiers (*see* CORSAIRS), the West Indies (*see* BUCCANEERS), the coast of Trucial Oman (the Pirate Coast), Chinese and Malay waters, and such hideouts as Lundy Is., were long pirate haunts, but modern communications and the complexities of supplying and servicing modern vessels tend to eliminate P. On land similar techniques, known as hijacking, have been applied to long-distance lorries or trucks. In the case of aircraft the Montreal Convention (1971) provides for internat. co-operation against those sabotaging aircraft and the extradition of offenders.

PIRAEUS (pīrē'us). Port of both ancient and modern Athens and first port of Greece, on the Gulf of Aegina. Constructed as the port of Athens, *c.* 493 BC, it was linked with that city by the Long Walls (built *c.* 460 BC). After the sack by Sulla in 86 BC, P. declined. Modern P. is an industrial suburb of Athens.

PI'RAN, St (fl. 500). Patron saint of tin miners, and so of Cornwall and the Cornish nationalist movement. He was sent as a missionary by St Patrick, and there are remains of his oratory at Perranzabuloe. His feast day is 5 March.

PIRANDELLO (pērahndel'lō), **Luigi** (1867-1936). Italian writer. B. in Sicily, he settled as a teacher in Rome, and won fame with the novel *The Late Mattia Pascal* (1904) and with numerous short stories. His first venture in the field of drama was *La Morsa* (1912), which was followed by *Six Characters in Search of an Author* (1921), *Henry IV* (1922), etc. In 1934 he received the Nobel prize for literature.

PIRANHA (pirah'nya). S American fresh-water fish (*Serrasalmo piraya*) found in the Amazon. About 30cm (1ft) long and with razor-edge teeth, they rapidly devour men or animals, espec. if attracted by blood.

PISA (pē'sah). City in Tuscany, Italy, on the Arno, 11km (7m) from the sea. It has an 11th-12th cent. cathedral, the Leaning Tower or campanile, and a univ. (1338). Cotton and silk are manufactured. Founded by Greek colonists, then an Etruscan and a Roman city, P. was in the 11th-14th cents. an independent naval rep. Gombo, off which Shelley was drowned in 1822, is to the W. Pop. (1978) 103,570.

PISA. The famous leaning tower is some 54 m (179 ft) high, and has foundations only about 3 m (10 ft) deep. Galileo did not make experiments, as legend claims, from the top of the tower. *Photo: Courtesy of the Italian State Tourist Office*

PISANO (pēzah'no), **Andrea.** Assumed name of the Italian sculptor Andrea da Pontaderra (1270-1348), whose works incl. one of the doors of the Florentine baptistery and sculptures in the campanile.

PISANO, Niccola (*c.* 1225-*c.* 1278). Italian sculptor who produced pulpits at Siena and Pisa, which marked a renaissance in Italian sculpture. His son, **Giovanni P.** (1250-1317), was also a sculptor, and designed pulpits.

PISANO, Vittore (1397-1455). Italian artist, called **Pisanello,** chiefly celebrated as a medallist.

PISI'STRATUS (*c.* 605-527 BC). Athenian statesman. Although of noble family, he assumed the leadership of the peasant party, and seized power in 561. He was twice expelled, but recovered power from 541 till his death. Ruling as a dictator under constitutional forms, he first had the Homeric poems written down, and founded Greek drama by introducing the Dionysiac peasant festivals into Athens.

PISSARRO, Camille (1830-1903). French painter. B. in the West Indies, he studied under Corot, and became a leader of the Impressionist movement. His son **Lucien P.** (1863-1944), a landscape painter and engraver, came to England in 1890 and in 1916 became a naturalized Englishman.

PISTOIA (pistō'yah). City in Tuscany, Italy, 16km (10m) NW of Florence. It is surrounded by walls (1302) and has a cathedral dating from the 12th cent. Steel and small arms, paper, macaroni, and olive oil are produced. P. was the site of Catiline's defeat, 62 BC. Pop. (1978) 95,000.

PISTOL. Small firearm (q.v.) designed for one-hand use. Ps. were in use from the early 15th cent. and their evolution closely parallels that of the corresponding shoulder arm. The problem of firing more than once without reloading was tackled by using many combinations of multiple barrels, both stationary and revolving, and although a breech-loading, multi-chambered revolver of 1650 still survives, the first practical solution was Samuel Colt's six-gun (1847). Behind a single barrel, a short 6-chambered cylinder was rotated by cocking the hammer, and a fresh round brought into place. The automatic pistol, operated by gas or recoil, was preferred by the military in many countries, but others still favoured the revolver.

PITCAIRN. Island in the Pacific, *c.* 5,300 km (3,300 m) NE of New Zealand. Discovered in 1767, it was uninhabited until occupied in 1790 by the *Bounty* mutineers, whose presence was discovered in 1808; the present inhabitants are descended from them. Area 5 sq.km (2 sq.m); pop. (1978) 68. The uninhabited islands of Henderson, Ducie, and Oeno, annexed in 1902, were attached to P., which is a British colony.

PITCH Residues from tar distillation, used in roads, waterproofing roofs, etc. *See also* ASPHALT, BITUMEN.

PITCH (acoustics). The position of a note in the musical scale; this depends on the frequency of the predominant sound wave. A standard P. was agreed at an international conference in 1939, A above middle C having a frequency of 440.

PITCHBLENDE, or **uranite.** An ore consisting mainly of uranium oxide U_3O_8, but also containing radioactive salt of radium $RaBr_2$, first separated by the Curies in 1898 from P. from N. Bohemia, in which it occurs in about 1 part in 3 million.

PITMAN, Sir Isaac (1813-97). British phonographer. B. in Wilts, he became a teacher, and after studying Samuel Taylor's scheme for shorthand writing, pub. in 1837 his own system, *Stenographic Soundhand,* speedy and accurate, and adapted for use in many languages. A simplified *PitmanScript,* combining letters and signs, was devised 1971 by Emily D. Smith. His grandson **Sir (Isaac) James P.** (1901-) devised the 44-letter Initial Teaching Alphabet in the 1960s to help children to read.

PITT, William (1759–1806). British Tory statesman. The son of Lord Chatham (q.v.) he entered Parliament in 1781 as a 'Chathamite' Whig, and took office as Chancellor of the Exchequer in Shelburne's govt of 1782-3. He became PM, with the support of the Tories and 'king's friends', in 1783. His main achievements were his reorganization of the national finances and his commercial treaty with France for reciprocal reduction of tariffs. He allowed the country to drift into war with France in 1793 and had little success in his conduct of the war. After 1792 he conducted a policy of repression of all advocates of reform, which in Ireland provoked a rebellion in 1798. To solve the Irish question he carried through the Act of Union in 1800, but resigned in 1801 when George III refused to accept Catholic emancipation. He returned to office in 1804, and set himself to build up a coalition with Austria and Russia against Napoleon. The news of the defeat of Austerlitz destroyed his hopes; he d. broken-hearted, and was buried in Westminster Abbey.

PITT-RIVERS, Augustus Henry (1827-1900). British archaeologist, *né* Lane-Fox, who assumed the surname P.-R. on succeeding to the estates of his great uncle, the 2nd Lord Rivers. Entering the Grenadiers, he later became a lieut-gen., and his earliest interests were in firearms, but on his accession to lands rich in archaeological sites he commenced a series of model excavations recorded in *Excavations in Cranbourne Chase* pub. privately from 1887. He was remarkable for his brilliant pioneer recording methods, use of stratification, and recognition of the importance of humble objects. The best of his collection is now in the Pitt-Rivers Museum, Oxford University.

PITTSBURGH. Second city of Pennsylvania, USA, at the confluence of the Allegheny and Monongahela to form the Ohio. It is a great port, at the centre of a region producing coal, natural gas, and petroleum. Steel is the main product, but P.'s many industries also incl. shipbuilding; making of glass, aluminium, bricks, pottery; and nuclear energy. P., on the site of Fort Duquesne estab. by the French in 1754, was substantially reconstructed under the Renaissance plan of the 1940-50s, so that the 'golden triangle' where the Allegheny and Monongahela meet is one of the world's most concentrated business centres. The Frick and the Carnegie museums have fine art collections, and P. Univ. dates from 1787. Pop. met. area (1970) 2,382,477.

PITU'ITARY GLAND. The most important of the endocrine or ductless glands. About the size of a pea, it is attached to the base of the brain in the 'Turkish saddle', and is divided into 2 distinct lobes. From the anterior lobe hormones are obtained which control the activities of other glands (thyroid, gonads and adrenal cortex); and direct-acting hormones affecting milk secretion, and controlling growth. Secretions of the posterior lobe regulate body water balance, contraction of the uterus, etc. A highly complex gland, and 'Master of the Endocrine Orchestra'.

PIUS. Name of 12 popes. **Pius II** (1405-64) achieved fame in early life as an author under the name of Aeneas Silvius. As pope 1458-64 he attempted unsuccessfully to organize a crusade against the Turks. **Pius IV** (1499-1565), a member of the Medici family, became pope in 1559; he reassembled the Council of Trent, and completed its work in 1563. **Pius V** (1504-72), elected in 1566, excommunicated Queen Elizabeth, and organized the expedition against the Turks which won the victory of Lepanto. **Pius VI** (1717-99), elected in 1775, strongly opposed the French Revolution, and d. a prisoner in French hands. His successor in 1800, **Pius VII** (1740-1823), concluded a concordat with France in 1801, and took part in Napoleon's coronation, but was a prisoner 1809-14. After his return to Rome in 1814 he revived the Jesuit order. **Pius IX** (1792-1878) became pope in 1846. He never accepted the incorporation of the Papal States and of Rome in the kingdom of Italy, and proclaimed in 1854 the dogma of the immaculate conception of the Virgin and in 1870 that of papal infallibility. His pontificate was the longest in history. **Pius X** (1835-1914), pope from 1903, canonized 1954, condemned modernism in a manifesto of 1907. **Pius XI** (Achille Ratti, 1857-1939). Nuncio to Poland in 1919 and archbp of Milan in 1921, he was elected pope in 1922. The Lateran Treaty with Italy was signed in 1929. In his encyclicals he condemned Nazism and anti-Semitism as well as Communism. **Pius XII** (Eugenio Pacelli, 1876-1958). After distinguishing himself as papal nuncio from 1917, he was appointed cardinal in 1929, and Papal Sec. of State in 1930. Elected pope in 1939, he opposed anti-Semitism during the S.W.W. (though his attitude has been the subject of controversy) and made many peace appeals. His proclamation of the new dogma of the bodily assumption of the Virgin Mary (1950) and his restatement of the doctrine that the life of an infant must not be sacrificed to save a mother in labour (1951) roused Protestant criticism. He was subject to visions.

PIZARRO (pēthahr'rō), **Francisco** (*c.* 1475-1541). Spanish conqueror of Peru. He took part in the expeditions of Balboa and others. In 1526-7 he explored the NW coast of S America, and in 1530 with 180 followers conquered Peru. The Inca was treacherously seized and murdered. In 1535 P. founded Lima. A feud now began between the Spanish leaders, and P. was assassinated. His half-brother **Gonzalo P.** (*c.* 1505-48) explored the region E of Quito 1541-2. He made himself governor in Peru 1544, but was defeated and executed.

PLACE, Francis (1771-1854). British Radical. A tailor by trade, he showed great powers as a political organizer and made Westminster a centre of Radicalism. He secured the repeal of the Combination Acts in 1824.

PLAGUE (plāg). Severe infectious disease marked in the classic form by swelling of the buboes or lymphatic glands, hence 'bubonic' P. It is most common in the tropics, India, China, S America, etc. In medieval Europe it was known as the Black Death (q.v.), but died out when the black rat, through whose fleas it was principally transmitted, was exterminated by the brown: in the US it has seldom occurred. Incubation is 2-5 days, followed by fever and a state like drunkenness, and death within a week in 25 per cent of cases. Even more virulent are the septicaemic and pneumonic forms, the latter being

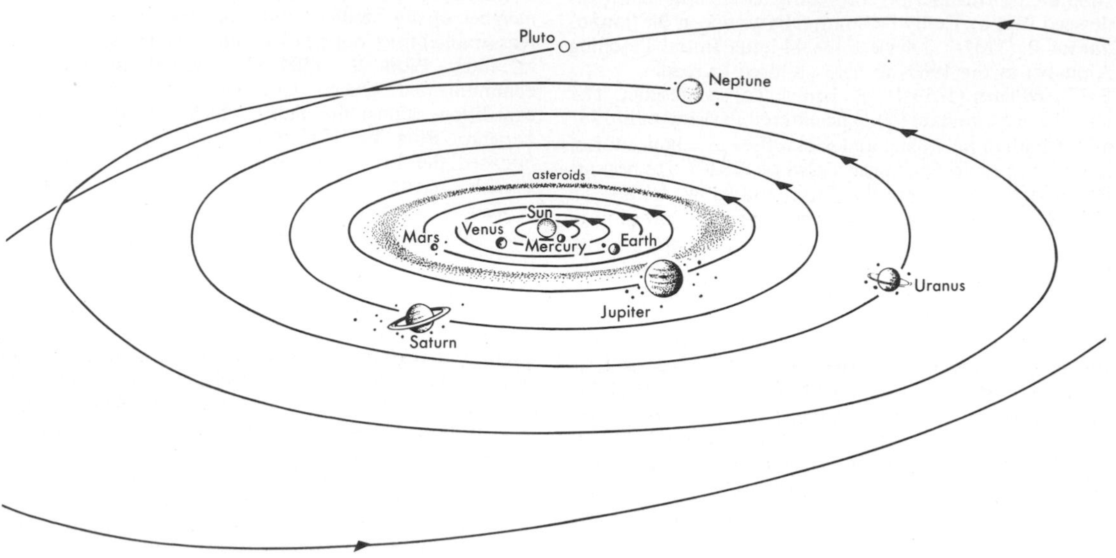

PLANETS. The planets in their orbits round the Sun, which is shown much smaller in relation to them than it really is, just as it is impossible to show the distances of the planets from the Sun to scale within the limits of the page.

invariably fatal until the introduction of sulpha drugs and various antibiotics.

PLAICE. Food-fish (*Pleuronectes platessa*) belonging to the flat-fish group, abundant in N European waters. It is white beneath and brownish with orange spots on the 'eyed' side.

PLAINS. Town in Georgia, U.S.A., 87 km (54 m) from Columbus in a peanut-growing area. Pres. Carter's family settled here in the 18th cent. Pop. (1970) 700.

PLAINS INDIANS. N American Indians of the High Plains which run over 3,000 km (2,000 m) from Alberta to Texas. They shared a horse-riding, buffalo-hunting culture which reached its peak from 1700 to mid 19th cent., and incl. the Blackfoot, Cheyenne, Comanche, Pawnee and Sioux. They are the romantic, ideal American Indian, living in skin tents (*tipi*), and wearing war (and peace) paint, buffalo robes, and eagle-feather warbonnets, so that these characteristics have now been adopted by many tribes who never originally had them. They took scalps and demanded extreme bravery in war and raiding which was beyond some of their males, who adopted women's tasks and clothing (*berdache*). One of their most important rituals was the Sundance (q.v.). The last conflict between whites and Indians was fought out on the Great Plains: *see* LITTLE BIGHORN and WOUNDED KNEE.

PLANCK (plahnk), **Max** (1858-1947). German physicist and framer in 1900 of the Quantum Theory. B. at Kiel, he was appointed to the chair of physics at Kiel in 1885, and at Berlin in 1889, and 1930-7 was Pres. of the Kaiser Wilhelm Institute. His writings incl. *Prinzip der Erhaltung der Energie, Einleitung in die theoretische Physik*, and *Where is Science Going?* An FRS from 1926, he was awarded the Nobel prize for Physics in 1918.

PLANE. Genus of trees (*Platanus*). Species incl. the Oriental P. (*P. orientalis*), a favourite plantation tree of the Greeks and Romans; the hybrid London P. (*P. X hispanica*), with palmate 3-lobed (instead of 5-lobed) leaves, which throws off city smog by the smoothness of its foliage and shedding its bark annually in large flakes; and the American P. or buttonwood (*P. occidentalis*). All have pendulous burr-like fruit and are capable of growth to 30m (100ft) high.

PLANETĀR'IUM. Optical projection device by means of which the motions of the stars and planets are reproduced for educational purposes on a domed ceiling representing the sky as it appears from Earth.

PLANETARY NEBULA. Evanescent phase of adjustment undergone by stars of moderate mass before settling down as white dwarfs. They are in no way planets, the name having been given to them by Sir William Herschel solely because the gas thrown off from them gives a disc-like apperance.

PLANETARY PROBE. A vehicle sent near, or to, another planet. The guidance and launching techniques are much more complex than with lunar probes, owing to the distances involved; communication problems are also increased. The first really successful vehicle of this type was the US Mariner II, which passed within 40,000 km

PIZARRO. Francisco Pizarro, conquerer of Peru and founder of Lima. *Photo: Mansell Collection.*

(25,000 m) of Venus in 1962. Pioneer X (USA 1972) reached Jupiter (1974), continued towards Uranus (1979), and will then continue into space. It carries a plaque showing a naked man and woman, and a diagram of the solar system, in case it reaches another civilization.

PLANETS. Non-luminous globes revolving around the Sun at various distances and in various periods. Nine Ps. are known; in order of distance from the Sun, they are Mercury, Venus, the Earth, Mars, Jupiter, Saturn, Uranus, Neptune and Pluto. Of these, the first 4, and Pluto, are relatively small, solid bodies; the rest are giants, much larger than the Earth, and with gaseous surfaces. Five planets were known from very ancient times: Uranus was discovered in 1781, Neptune in 1846 and Pluto in 1930.

It has been suggested, by the deflection of the course of comets, that 2 further Ps. may exist beyond Pluto. One might be the same size as Earth, but over 50 times more distant from the Sun, and the other double the size of Earth and 100 times farther from the Sun.

PLANIMETER. A simple integrating instrument for measuring the area of a plane surface. It consists of 2 hinged arms; one is kept fixed and the other is traced round the boundary of the area. This actuates a small graduated wheel and the area is found from its change in position.

PLANKTON. A term used first by Victor Hensen to denote those small forms of animal and plant life which float or drift in water.

PLANT. Many of the lower plants consist of a single body or thallus upon which the organs of reproduction are borne. Simplest of all are the threadlike waterplants, e.g. *Spirogyra,* which consist of a chain of cells containing chloroplasts, which are responsible for the green colour of the P. and for the provision of its food. The seaweeds and

Table of the Planets

Name	*Mean dist. (millions of km. from Sun)*	*Period of sidereal revolutions in years*	*Mean diam. in km.*	*Axial rotation (sidereal)*
Mercury	58	0.24	4,840	59 days
Venus	108	0.62	12,300	243½ days
Earth	150	1.00	12,756	23 h 56 m
Mars	228	1.88	6,790	24 h 37 m 23 s
Jupiter	778	11.86	143,200	9 h 55 m
Saturn	1,427	29.46	119,300	10 h 14 m
Uranus	2,870	84.02	47,100	10 h 48 m
Neptune	4,497	164.8	51,000	15 h 48 m
Pluto	5,950	248	c. 2,500	6 days 9 h

mosses possess a further development of the simple chain of cells in their multi-cellular, simple bodies which have specially modified areas in which the reproductive organs are carried. Higher in the morphological scale are the ferns, which produce leaf-like fronds bearing on their under-surface incrustations in which the spores are carried. The spores are freed and germinate to produce small independent bodies carrying the sexual organs; thus the fern has 2 generations in its life cycle.

The flowering Ps. are by far the largest group, and structurally the most complex. The flowering P. is divided into 3 parts, root, stem, and leaves. Roots may be scattered and fibrous, as in the majority of garden annuals, or developed into a swollen food reserve such as the carrot, turnip, or sugar beet. Stems grow above or below ground. Their cellular structure is designed to carry water and salts in solution from the roots, which have obtained the nourishment from the soil, to the leaves, where they are manufactured into P. food. Underground stems sometimes bear tubers, e.g. potatoes, or fruits, e.g. groundnuts, while some are prized as economic products, e.g. ginger. Aerial stems occasionally develop food reserves as in the sugar cane, but are more usually merely a means of support for the leaves. The leaves, which are often highly modified, manufacture the food of the P. by means of the chlorophyll which they contain. Flowers are modified leaves arranged in groups and enclosing the reproductive organs from which the fruits and seeds result.

Man's use of seeds, tubers, etc. as food, or the feeding of plants or grain to animals, which are in turn eaten, is wasteful, and green crop fractionation is under study. After harvesting, food plants such as lucerne are crushed to rupture the cells of the leaves and stem, and the sap, which contains sugars, salts, protein, lipids and vitamins, is released and separated. The fibre residue still contains protein and digestible carbohydrates suitable for cows, and the separated juice is suitable for pigs, or can be further fractionated to precipitate the protein for use either moist or dried. This protein can then be used either as pig food or, with further processing for human consumption, and the remaining liquor is still usable either as pig food or fertilizer.

Growing Ps. from a single cell cultured in a laboratory dish is not only faster and more reliable than from seed (*see* CLONE), but could also lead to the creation of new plants. Carnations, orchids, etc., are already grown by this method.

Classification. The classification of Ps. is based on a number of characters. Ps. are grouped by their similarities of constitution into species, within which minor differences are marked as strains and varieties. Species bearing a resemblance to one another are grouped into genera, and similar genera into families. These are classed in the larger divisions cohorts and classes. The principal groups are shown in the Table. *See also* BOTANY; BREEDING; FLOWER.

Classification of Plants

		Phylum I: **Thallophyta**
		Class
1	**Algae**	Algae, diatoms, etc.
2	**Charophyta**	Stoneworts.
3	**Myxomycetes**	Slime fungi.
4	**Bacteria**	
5	**Fungi**	Moulds, toadstools, puff-balls, lichens, etc.
		Phylum II: **Archegoniatae**
1	**Bryophyta**	Liverworts, mosses.
2	**Pteridophyta**	Ferns, fossils, horsetails, club mosses.
		Phylum III: **Spermophyta**
1	**Pteridospermeae**	Fossils.
2	**Gymnospermeae**	Cycads, fossils, maidenhair tree, cone-bearing trees.
3	**Angiosperms**	Flowering plants: (i) Monocotyledons—orchids, grasses, sedges, lilies. (ii) Dicotyledons—families of daisy, pea, coffee, spurge, carrot and sage.

PLANTA'GENET. Name commonly applied to the royal house of England reigning 1154-1399. It was originally a nickname of Geoffrey, count of Anjou, father of Henry II, who usually wore a sprig of broom (*planta genista*) in his hat, and it was revived *c.* 1450 as a surname by Richard, duke of York, to emphasize the superiority of his claim to the throne to that of Henry VI.

PLANTAIN. Genus of plants (*Plantago*) which are troublesome weeds in lawns, etc., e.g. the great P. (*P. major*) with oval leaves, grooved stalks and a spike of green flowers with purple anthers followed by seeds liked by cage-birds. The name is also given to the genus *Musa* in the tropics: *see* BANANA.

PLA'SMA. The liquid part of the blood; in physics an ionized gas produced at extremely high temperatures, as in the Sun and other stars, and which contains positive and negative charges in approx. equal numbers, is affected by a magnetic field and is a good electrical conductor.

PLA'SMAPHERESIS (-ferē'sis). Process allowing a blood donor to provide 69 litres (120 pts) of plasma annually taken at twice weekly intervals, instead of 0.6 litre (1 pt) of blood 5 times a year. Since it is only the loss of red cells, with haemoglobin and iron that the body finds it difficult to replace, these cells are removed and restored to the body, and the rest (water, salts, albumen, globulins, etc.) are replaced by the body within hours.

PLASSEY (plas'ē). Village in W Bengal, India, on the Bhagirathi r., 50km (31m) NNW of Krishnagar; it has sugar mills and produces rice, jute, and linseed. It gave its name to Clive's victory in 1757 over Suraj-ud-Dowlah,

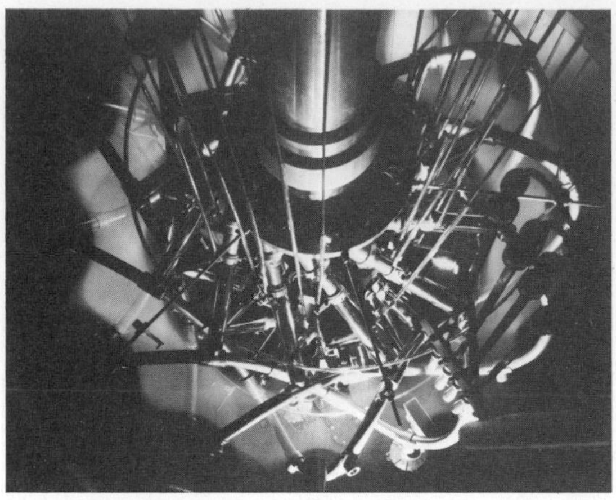

PLASMA. High temperature plasma confined by magnetic fields in the Torso apparatus at Culham Laboratory, which is part of the UK fusion research project. The magnetic field is produced by passing large currents through the specially shaped helical windings, seen here through a window in the top of the large vacuum tank. *Photo: Courtesy of the UKAEA*

but the site of the battle had by 1801 been eaten away by the river.

PLASTER OF PARIS. Calcined gypsum which is mixed with water (1 part gypsum, 2½ parts water) to form a thin paste which later hardens. It is used for taking casts, moulds, etc., and in orthopaedic surgery for setting fractured bones. It is manufactured near Paris: hence the name.

PLASTICS. Synthetic materials which are normally stable, but are plastic at some period during their manufacture. Formerly plastic materials were derived from coal, but from the 1950s the basic materials, espec. for thermoplastics, derive from petroleum (q.v.) derivatives. Fast replacing metal and wood in many fields, Ps. (mostly polymers) are used particularly in household equipment, the construction of houses, ships, aircraft (notably the lightweight carbon-fibre-reinforced Ps. developed in the 1960s), and cars, and the electrical industry. They are processed by extrusion, injection moulding, vacuum forming and compression, and can be formed with different consistencies, ranging from hard and rigid, to soft and rubbery. *See also* ACETIC ACID, ACRYLIC, CELLULOID, NYLON, POLYESTER, POLYETHYLENE, POLYMERIZATION, POLYSTYRENE, POLYURETHANE, PVC, RESIN.

PLASTIC SURGERY. The surgical repair of seriously damaged tissues. During the 2 wars a wide variety of methods have been developed whereby surgeons can restore faces that have been almost entirely destroyed, replace burnt skin, mend damaged nerves, and perform many other surgical marvels. These operations need careful planning and often take months or years to complete.

PLATA, Rio de la. Spanish name for the river PLATE.

PLATE, River. The estuary into which flow the Parana and Uruguay rivers, on the E coast of S America. It is 320km (200m) long and 32-240km (20-145m) wide, and drains much of Paraguay, Argentina, Uruguay, Bolivia, and Brazil; all 5 countries agreed 1968 to co-operate in developing the P. basin. Diaz de Solis discovered the estuary *c.* 1515. In Dec. 1939 the German 'pocket-battleship' *Admiral Graf Spee* (14,000 tons) was scuttled here by her commander rather than engage the British cruisers HMS *Exeter, Achilles,* and *Ajax.*

PLATINUM (Span. *platina,* little silver). Greyish-white, ductile and malleable metal, density 21.45, melting point 1773.5°C, untarnishable in air and very resistant to heat and strong acids: symbol Pt., at. no. 78, at. wt. 195.09. P. occurs as the metal, and alloyed with iridium, osmium and other metals of the same group, and with gold and iron, especially in the Urals, S Africa, Canada and the USA. Both pure and in alloy, it is used extensively in jewellery, dentistry and the chemical industry (in finely divided form, P. acts as a catalyst). It is employed for switch contacts because of its durability; and is valuable in scientific apparatus because P. wires can be sealed gas-tight, through glass.

PLĀ'TO (*c.* 428–*c.* 348 BC). Athenian philosopher. He early entered politics on the aristocratic side, and in philosophy became a follower of Socrates. He travelled widely, and on his return to Athens, *c.* 387, he founded his Academy, in order to train a new ruling class. He twice visited Syracuse in the hope of playing a part in politics, without success. Of P.'s works *c.* 30 dialogues survive, in which ethical and philosophical problems are discussed. Typical examples are the *Symposium,* on love; the *Ion,* on poetry; the *Phaedo,* on the immortality of the soul; and the *Apology* and *Crito,* on Socrates' trial and death. In many dialogues Socrates is the central figure, and it remains uncertain how far the views attributed to him are his, and how far they are P.'s. P.'s philosophy marks a reaction against the scientific rationalism of the Ionian philosophers. He maintained that mind, not matter, is fundamental, and that material objects are merely imperfect copies of abstract and eternal 'ideas'; hence he rejected experiment as a scientific method in favour of argument. His political philosophy is expounded in the *Republic* and the *Laws,* both descriptions of ideal states.

PLATYPUS (plat'ipus). Small mammal (*Ornithorhynchus anatinus*) of the order Monotremata, found in Tasmania and E Australia. Semi-aquatic, it has naked jaws resembling a duck's beak, small eyes and no trace of an external ear. It lives in long burrows in banks of rivers, where it lays eggs in a rough nest. It feeds on water worms, insects, etc., and when full-grown is *c.* 45cm (18in) long.

PLAUTUS, Titus Maccius (d. 184 BC). Roman dramatist. B. in Umbria, he settled in Rome and worked in a bakery before achieving success as a dramatist. He wrote at least 56 comedies, freely adapted from Greek originals, of which 20 survive. Shakespeare based *The Comedy of Errors* on the *Menoechmi.*

PLAYING CARDS. They originated in China, India, or with the Arabs, and appeared in Europe at the end of the 14th cent. In the 15th cent. the pack was gradually simplified and reduced to the present 52. Among the chief card games are Whist, Bridge, Poker (qq.v.), and Rummy. Canasta, a variant of the last-named, was introduced to the US from Argentina in 1949 and later became very popular in Britain.

PLEASENCE, Donald (1919-). British actor. B. in Yorks, he has been especially successful as Leone Gola in Pirandello's *The Rules of the Game,* Davies in Pinter's *The Caretaker,* and in the film *Dr Crippen,* conveying the sinister aspect of the outcast from society.

PLATYPUS. Looking as if put together from the parts of other animals as a hoax, the platypus was at one time threatened with extinction. It is now bred in captivity and has begun to establish itself again. *Photo: Courtesy of the Australian Information Service*

PLEBEIANS. The unprivileged class in ancient Rome, composed of aliens and freedmen, and their descendants. During the 5th–4th cents. BC they waged a long struggle with the patricians, until they secured admission to the offices formerly reserved for the patricians.

PLEBISCITE (pleb'isit). A direct vote by all the electors of a country or district on a specific question. Since the 18th cent. it has been employed on many occasions to decide to what country a particular area should belong, e.g. in Upper Silesia and elsewhere after the F.W.W., and in the Saar in 1935.

PLÉIADE (plāyahd'), **La.** Group of 7 poets in 16th cent. France led by Ronsard, who were inspired by classical models to the improvement of French verse. They were so called from the 7 stars of the P. group.

PLEIADES (plī-adēz). The 7 daus. of Atlas, who on being pursued by Orion were changed by the gods at their own request to a cluster of stars.

PLENTY, Bay of. Broad inlet on the NE coast of North Island, NZ, on which the port of Tauranga stands. One of the first canoes bringing Maori immigrants made landfall here.

PLESE'TSK. Town S. of Archangel in the RSFSR, a launch site for cosmonauts.

PLEURISY (ploo͞'risi). Inflammation of the pleura - a secreting membrane which covers the lungs and also lines the space in which they rest; the 2 surfaces move easily on one another, being lubricated by small quantities of fluid. When it is inflamed the surfaces may dry up or stick together, making breathing difficult and painful. A large volume of fluid may collect in the 'pleural cavity', the space between the 2 surfaces. Pus in the pleural cavity is called empyema. P. occurs in pneumonia and tuberculosis, but may also be a consequence of scarlet fever or rheumatism.

PLE'VEN. Industrial town in N Bulgaria. In the Russo-Turkish War of 1877 Osman Pasha was forced by starvation to surrender P. to the Russians after a siege of 5 months. Pop. (1972) 108,180.

PLIMSOLL, Samuel (1824-98). British social reformer. B. in Bristol, he sat in parliament as a Radical 1868-80, and through his efforts the Merchant Shipping Act was passed in 1876, providing for Board of Trade inspection of ships, and the compulsory painting of a load line, or P.'s mark, to show the limit to which a ship may be loaded.

PLINLI'MMON or **Plynlimon.** Mountain in Powys, Wales, with 3 summits, the highest 752m (2,468 ft).

PLINY. Name of 2 Roman writers. GAIUS PLINIUS SECUNDUS, or **P. the Elder** (*c.* AD 23-79), b. in N Italy, held political and military posts, and was killed during the eruption of Vesuvius. Besides histories now lost, he wrote a *Natural History* dealing with astronomy, geography, zoology, and mineralogy. His nephew, GAIUS PLINIUS CAECILIUS SECUNDUS, or **P. the Younger** (*c.* 61-113), was gov. of Bithynia. *c.* 111-13, and carried on a correspondence of great historical interest.

PLISETSKAYA, Maiya (1925-). Russian ballerina. Educ. at the Moscow Choreographic School, she succeeded Ulanova as prima ballerina to the Bolshoi Ballet.

PLOESTI (plō'yeshti). Town in Romania, 56km (35m) N of Bucharest; it is the centre of the country's oil wells. Pop. (1977) 201,270.

PLOTĪ'NUS (*c.* AD 204-70). Greek philosopher. B. in Egypt, he settled in Rome in 244, and opened a school of philosophy. His lectures were ed. by his follower Porphyry, who also wrote his life. P. was the founder of the Neoplatonic system, which profoundly influenced early Christian thought.

PLOUGH. The agricultural implement most normally used in tilling the soil. The hand P. consists essentially of a continuous beam, the front of which is attached to the horse, and the rear branches made into guiding handles. In the central depression are the blades designed to cut the soil, first vertically, and then to turn over the subsoil. The P. is of iron, and cuts to a depth of about 7in, but there are many variants for special uses. The steam P. was patented in 1855. The 20th cent. has brought tractor and multi-furrow Ps.

PLOVDIV (plov'dif). City in Bulgaria, on the Maritsa, with textile, chemical, leather and tobacco industries. It was founded by Philip of Macedon in the 4th cent. BC and was known as Philippopolis (Philip's city). Pop. (1976) 309,240.

PLOVER. Bird in the family Charadriidae, *c.* 255mm (10in) long, with a short bill. The golden P. (*Pluvialis apricaria*), common on British moorlands, has almost black plumage with yellow spots, the underparts being white in winter and black in summer: there are 2 allied American species. The ringed P. (*Charadrius hiaticula*) with a black and white face, and black band on the throat, is found on British shores, but largest of the ringed Ps. is the killdeer of N America (*Charadrius vociferus*), so called because of its cry.

PLUM. A tree (*Prunus domestica*), bearing an edible drupe. There are many varieties, including the greengage, damson, and sloe. The dried P. is a prune.

PLUMBAGO. *See* GRAPHITE.

PLUTARCH (ploo'tahrk) (*c.* AD 46-120). Greek biographer. B. at Chaeronea, he lectured on philosophy at Rome, and was appointed procurator of Greece by Hadrian. His *Parallel Lives* consist of pairs of biographies of Greek and Roman soldiers and statesmen followed by comparisons between the two. North's translation inspired Shakespeare's Roman plays. P. also wrote essays, known as the *Moralia.*

PLUTO (plōō'tō). In Roman mythology, the lord of Hades. He was the brother of Jupiter and Neptune.

PLUTO. The outermost planet. Its average distance from the Sun is 5,950,000,000 km (3,666,000,000 m), but its orbit is decidedly eccentric, and when at its nearest to the Sun it may be closer in than Neptune. It was discovered in 1930 by C. Tombaugh, at the Flagstaff Observatory, as a result of earlier calculations made by Percival Lowell. Pluto is a small planet, with a diameter of *c.* 2,500 km (1,550 m), the surface temperature is 240°C, and the surface consists of methane ice. It has a moon (Charon) rather smaller than our own, which is synchronous in orbit, i.e. remains above the same place on Pluto. From P. the Sun would appear only as an intensely bright star, and it has been conjectured that it is a lost moon of Neptune.

PLUTŌ'NIUM. Element discovered in 1940 by Seaborg and his co-workers at the Univ. of Calif. by bombarding uranium with deuterons: symbol Pu, at. wt. 242, at. no. 94. Its most stable isotope Pu-239 (discovered 1941) has a half-life of 24,000 years, is fissile, and usually made in reactors by bombarding U-238 with neutrons. It is used in atom bombs, as a fissionable material in reactors, and for enriching the abundant U-238, but has awkward physical properties, and is very poisonous to animals, being absorbed in bone.

In 1977 Pres. Carter banned commercial production of P. in the US, and called for a general ban in the hope of preventing the spread of nuclear weapons, espec. the chance of their coming into terrorists' hands, and in concern as to the safety of the fuel itself.

PLYMOUTH. City and seaport in Devon, England, at the mouth of the Plym. Hawkins, Drake and the Pilgrim Fathers sailed from P. Sound. The 'Three Towns' of P., Devonport, and Stonehouse were amalgamated in 1914. The city rises N from the Hoe headland. Devonport has a dockyard, barracks, and large establishments of the Royal Navy; P. is also an important port for civilian shipping. Following heavy bombing in the S.W.W. the city centre was reconstructed, incl. shopping area, law courts, and municipal offices. The Tamar Bridge now gives P. a direct road link with Cornwall, and there has been major post-war industrial development. Pop. (1974) 246,850. *See* LADY ASTOR.

PLYMOUTH BRETHREN. Christian Protestant sect characterized by extreme simplicity of belief, founded in Dublin *c.* 1827 by the Rev. John Nelson Darby (1800-82). The movement gained strength and an assembly was held in Plymouth in 1831 (hence the name P.B.) to celebrate its arrival in England, but by 1848 the movement had split into 'Open' and 'Close' B. The latter refuse communion with all those not of their persuasion, and from 1959, under the leadership of 'Big Jim' Taylor of New York, achieved notoriety through such edicts as those forbidding members to belong to any organized body or to eat with unbelievers. The P.B. are found throughout the world, but notably in the fishing villages of NE Scotland: membership 80,000.

PLYNLIMON, PLYNLIMMON. *See* PLINLIMMON.

PLZEN (pil'sen). Town in W Czechoslovakia, at the confluence of the Radbuza and Mze, 84km (52m) SW of Prague. Famous for its lager beer, it makes heavy machinery, cars, and is the site of the Skoda armaments works. Pop. (1970) 147,000.

PNEUMONIA. Term is used to describe inflammation of the lung. Based on cause, Ps. are divided into the Specific Ps., which are caused by a specific pathogenic organism; and the Aspiration Ps., in which some abnormality of the lung respiratory system allows the lung to be attacked by non-specific bacteria of low virulence. Treatment of all forms of P. consists of testing the bacteria in sputum, for sensitivity to antibiotics when an appropriate one is applied.
PNEUMOTHORAX. Invasion of the pleural cavity by air. Normally this cavity contains only a very slight quantity of lubricating substance, so that a vacuum is complete, and when the chest expands the lungs also expand.
PNOM-PENH. See PHNÔM-PENH.
PŌ. Longest river in Italy, which rises on the Cottian Alps and flows E to enter the Adriatic through a wide delta. It irrigates the plains of Piedmont and Lombardy. Navigable as far as Cremona, it forms part of an important inland waterway system, linking with the Cremona-Milan and Padua-Venice canals. Length *c.* 668km (415m). There are natural gas fields in the Po Valley.
POCAHO'NTAS (*c.* 1595-1617). Red Indian princess who is said to have saved the life of John Smith when he was captured by her father Powhatan; in fact Smith probably invented the story. P. became a Christian, m. an Englishman, and d. at Gravesend.
PŌ'CHARD. Genus of diving ducks incl. the common P. (*Aythya ferina*) in which the male has a rich red head, black breast and whitish body and wings with black markings; the canvas-back (*Aythya valisineria*), a related species, is especially prized in America as a table bird.
PODGORICA. Older name of TITOGRAD.
PODO'LSK. Town in Moscow region, RSFSR, 40km (25m) SW of Moscow, an industrial centre with petroleum refineries and factories making machinery, sewing machines, cables, cement, ceramics, etc. Pop. (1978) 193,000.
POE (pō), **Edgar Allan** (1809-49). American author. B. at Boston, he was left an orphan in 1811, and brought up by a Mr and Mrs Allan, whose surname he used as a middle name from 1824. After 3 years in the army 1827-31, he attempted to earn his living by writing, but continued poverty, his addiction to alcohol, and the death of his wife in 1847, seem to have unhinged his mind. His poems have a melancholy lyric beauty and influenced the French symbolist school. His popular reputation rests on his short stories, which specialize either in the creation of horrific atmosphere, e.g. 'The Fall of the House of Usher', or in displays of acute reasoning, e.g. 'The Gold Bug' and 'The Murders in the Rue Morgue', which with their investigators Legrand and Dupin laid the foundation of modern detective fiction.
POET LAUREATE. Poet attached to the royal household. Among the Greeks and Romans the pre-eminent poet or warrior was awarded a laurel wreath, hence the modern title of P.L. Among early English poets who had an unofficial status as P.L. were Chaucer, Skelton, Spenser, and Daniel; Jonson had a more definite position, and with Dryden the post was officially estab. There is a stipend of £70 a year, with an extra £27 in lieu of the traditional butt of sack. Although such effusions are no longer obligatory, the P.L. still sometimes produces verses on great national occasions, and is chairman of a committee of 5 poets which awards (usually annually) the King's/Queen's Gold Medal for Poetry, instituted by George V (1933) at the suggestion of Masefield.

Poets Laureate

Sir Wm. Davenant	1638	Robert Southey	1813
John Dryden	1668	Wm. Wordsworth	1843
Thomas Shadwell	1689	Alfred, Lord Tennyson	1850
Nahum Tate	1692		
Nicholas Rowe	1715	Alfred Austin	1896
Laurence Eusden	1718	Robert Bridges	1913
Colley Cibber	1730	John Masefield	1930
Wm. Whitehead	1757	Cecil Day Lewis	1968
Thomas Warton	1785	Sir John Betjeman	1972
Henry Pye	1790	Ted Hughes	1984

POETRY. The imaginative expression of emotion or thought, usually in metrical form. In all literatures P. develops to perfection much earlier than prose, largely because it offers greater aids to accurate memorizing before the appearance of writing materials. Most direct in its interpretation of the emotions is lyric P., which incl. such forms as the song, sonnet, ode, elegy, and pastoral. Halfway between lyric and the narrative of the ballad, lay, and epic, is the use of verse in drama. Appealing largely to the intellect on the other hand are moral and didactic P., which incl. satire, parody, and those expositions of philosophical theory, religious doctrine, and practical subjects, which in England have for the most part been confined to prose since the 18th cent.
POGRO'M. Russian term, lit. meaning 'devastation', applied to unprovoked attacks on the Jews, especially those carried out with official connivance. The Russian Ps. began in 1881, and were common throughout the country down to the Revolution.
POINCARÉ (pwahṅkahreh'), **Jules Henri** (1854-1912). French mathematician. He developed the theory of differential equations.
POINCARÉ, Raymond Nicolas Landry (1860-1934). French statesman, a cousin of Jules Henri P. (q.v.). He became PM in 1912, was pres. 1913-20, and again PM 1922-4, when he carried out the occupation of the Ruhr, and 1926-9.
POINSE'TTIA. Winter flowering shrub (*Euphorbia pulcherrima*, also known as Mexican Flame-leaf and Christmas-flower), with large red leaves encircling small greenish-yellow flowers. Named after its discoverer, J. R. Poinsett, in 1836, it has recently become a Christmas symbol in the USA and Canada, although in Mexico it had been known as the Flower of the Holy Night for many years.
POINTE NOIRE (pwaṅt nwahr'). Chief port of the Congo, with shipbuilding yards, and a rail link to Brazzaville. Pop. (1970) 150,000.
POINTILLISM (pwaṅ'tilizm). Technique in oil painting in which dabs of pure colour are applied to the canvas, and arranged in such a way that when viewed from a distance they would blend into harmonious tones. This technique, also known as Neo-Impressionism, was adopted by Seurat, Signac, and others.
POISONS. Substances which when introduced into or applied to the body are capable of injuring health or destroying life, irrespective of temperature or mechanical action. The majority may be divided into *corrosives*, e.g. sulphuric, nitric, hydrochloric acids, caustic soda, and

corrosive sublimate, which burn and destroy the parts with which they come into contact; *irritants* such as arsenic, copper sulphate, zinc chloride, silver nitrate, and green vitriol, which have an irritating effect on the stomach and bowels; *narcotics*, e.g. opium, prussic acid, potassium cyanide, chloroform, carbon monoxide, sewer gases, etc., which affect the brain and spinal cord, inducing a stupor; *narcotico-irritants* which combine intense irritations and finally act as narcotics, e.g. carbolic acid, foxglove, henbane, deadly nightshade (belladonna), tobacco, and many other substances drawn from the vegetable kingdom. In non-corrosive poisoning every effort is made to remove the P. from the system as soon as possible, e.g. usually by vomiting induced by tickling the back of the throat with a feather or administering an emetic. For some corrosive and irritant Ps. there are chemical antidotes, but for recently developed Ps. in a new category, e.g. paraquat (q.v.), which produce proliferative changes in the system, there is no antidote. When the P. is unknown, tepid water and an emetic may be administered. In most countries the sale of P. is carefully controlled by law, and, in general, only qualified and registered pharmacists and medical practitioners may dispense them.

POITIERS (pwahtyā'). Town in the Loire basin, cap. of Vienne dept., France. In 507, Alaric II was defeated by Clovis nr P. and here Charles Martel stemmed the advance of the Saracens in 732. At P. in 1356 Edward the Black Prince defeated the French King John. The cathedral was commenced in 1162. There is a univ. (1431). Pop. (1975) 78,750.

POKER. Universally played card game, originating in 19th cent. America. It has numerous variations. The object is to win stakes, which are almost invariably played for, by obtaining a hand of 5 cards which rank higher than those of opponents. 2 to 8 players participate, bet on their hands, and exchange cards from the pack in turn, until everyone has exactly called the last bet, which is levied for each turn by each player, or has dropped out. The player with the best scoring hand wins the central pool of money. The combinations are as follows: royal flush, ace to ten of one suit; straight flush, 5 of one suit in sequence; 4 of a kind; full house, 3 of a kind, and 2 of a kind; flush, 5 of one suit; straight, 5 cards in sequence; 3 of a kind; 2 pairs; 1 pair.

POLAND. A rep. of E Europe, bounded on the W by Germany, on the S by Czechoslovakia, on the N by the Baltic and Kaliningrad region of the RSFSR, on the E by the Lithuanian, White Russian, and Ukrainian SSRs. For the most part undulating, P. is part of the great plain of central Europe, though in the S it rises, through hills stretching E from near Wroclaw to the Ukrainian border, into the heights of the Sudeten, Tatra, and Carpathian Mountains on the southern frontier. Of the many rivers, the most important are the Vistula and its chief tributary the W Bug and the Warta, tributary of the Oder, the lower course of which and its tributary the Neisse form the W frontier set up in 1945.

Economic Life. P., as it existed before the S.W.W., was predominantly agrarian, but changes in its physical structure, particularly the acquisition of almost the whole of the 2 German provs. of Upper and Lower Silesia (a small part of former German Silesia had been allotted to P. after the F.W.W.), and the introduction of govt planning, enhanced its industrial potential, and by 1970 less than one third of the pop. was dependent on agriculture. Minerals incl. copper, coal, iron, lead, zinc, silver, oil and natural gas; cement, fertilizers, steel, textiles, shoes, soap are the chief manufactured products. Potatoes, sugar beet, rye, oats, wheat are the heaviest crops; cattle, pigs, sheep, and horses are reared. There are state farms, but collectivization has been abandoned in favour of less rigid co-operation in 'agricultural circles'. Fishing is important.

POLAND. In the heart of the medieval stronghold of Wawel in Cracow, is this vast renaissance courtyard, perhaps unrivalled in Western Europe, where tournaments were watched from three storeys of galleries, supported by the slenderest of columns. *Photo: Courtesy of 'Orbis' Travel.*

Chief towns are Warsaw, the cap., Lodz, Krakow, Wroclaw, Poznan, Katowice, Bydgoszcz, Lublin, and the ports of Gdansk, Szczecin, and Gdynia.

Government. Under the constitution of 1952 the former pres. was replaced by a 15-member Council of State elected by the Sejm (parliament), itself elected by all citizens over 18. A Council of Ministers is also chosen by the Sejm; but real power rested with the Politbureau (Communist Party Committee). However, an amendment of 1976 encouraged participation of non-party members in political and social life, regardless of any religious affiliation.

Area 312,600 sq.km (120,600 sq m); pop. (1978) 34,850,000, of whom some 80% are practising RCs. MU: zloty.

History. In the 10th cent. the Polish tribes were first united under one ruler, and Christianity was introduced. Under the Jagellion dynasty (1386–1572) P. was united with Lithuania, and became a great power, being the largest and most tolerant country in Europe at the death of Sigismond, last Jagellion, in 1572. Elected kings followed and P.'s strength declined. But Stephen Bathory defeated Ivan the Terrible of Russia in 1581 and in 1683 John III Sobieski vanquished the Turks and forced them to raise their siege of Vienna. In the 18th cent. P. was subjected to pressure by Prussia, Russia, and Austria, ending with the first partition, 1772, which left a much-reduced P. still in existence. A second partition followed in 1793, Prussia and Russia seizing further areas, and, after defeating Tadeusz Kosciuszko who led a patriotic rising, they occupied the rest of the country in 1795 and P. ceased to figure on the map of Europe though it lived on in the spirit of the Polish people. Risings in Russian P. in 1830 and

1863 led to intensified repression and an increased attempt to Russianize the pop.

P. was revived as an independent rep. in 1918, under the leadership of Pilsudski, and was recognized by the Treaty of Versailles, 1919. P. took advantage of Russia's weakness at that time, through war and revolution, to advance into Lithuania and the Ukraine, the Red Army stopping the Poles before Kiev and driving them back inside P. where in its turn it was defeated by Pilsudski. Russia and P. agreed on a frontier 240km (150m) E of the 'Curzon Line' (q.v.); and Pilsudski remained semi-dictator of P. from 1926 until his death in 1935. In April 1939 the UK and France concluded a pact with P. to come to its assistance with military aid if it was attacked. Germany invaded P. from the W on 1 Sept. and the UK and France declared war on Germany on 3 Sept. Russia invaded P. from the E on 17 Sept.; and by the end of the month Polish resistance was at an end and the country was occupied by Germany and Russia. A govt in exile was estab. in France, then moved to London in June 1940, and free Polish forces did much to assist the Allied cause.

The Russians drove the Germans from P. 1944-5, and after taking Lublin, 24 July 1944, set up there a national liberation committee which they recognized in Jan. 1945 as the provisional govt. At the Potsdam Conference 1945 the Allies agreed that the part of Germany E of the Oder-Neisse line and the S part of E Prussia should be placed under Polish admin. Nearly half the German pop. of *c.* 4½ million had fled from these regions before the advancing Russians; the rest were expelled 1946-7. A treaty between Russia and P. in 1945 (ratified 1946) gave P. as E frontier the Curzon Line with slight modifications in P.'s favour.

By 1947 the Communists, with Russian backing, had gained control of the country, and moderates fled or were imprisoned. Although Wlasyslaw Gomulka attempted a more liberal independent line 1956-70, he was replaced after food price riots by Edward Gierek. There were renewed food price riots in 1976, and in 1980 widespread strikes, espec. in Gdansk, led to his replacement by Stanislaw Kania (q.v.). Kania was pledged to the more democratic regime demanded by the strikers, incl. independent trade unions, the right to strike, less censorship and access to the media by the RC Church. When the govt. attempted to superimpose Communist Party control on the new unions, the workers enforced their will (under Lech Walesa) by renewed strike threats, and the crisis continued under Kania's successor (from 1981) Gen Wojciech Jaruzelski.

See also Polish Literature, and P. has a sensitive tradition of film-making, e.g. Andrzej Wajda (q.v.). In music Chopin is the greatest name although Witold Lutoslawski (1913-) and Krzystof Penderecki (1933-) have recently made an internat. reputation. In art the most original genius is that of the wood carver Wit Stwosz (*c.* 1440-1533), creator of the altar-piece at Krakow, who is sometimes claimed as German (Veit Stoss).

POLAR BEAR. *See* Bear.

PŌ'LARIZED LIGHT. Ordinary light can be regarded as electromagnetic vibrations at right angles to the line of propagation but in different planes. Light is said to be P. when the vibrations are oriented in a particular direction. Ordinary L. may be plane P. by reflection from a polished surface or by passing it through a Nicol prism or a synthetic polarizing film such as Polaroid, P.L. is used to test the strength of sugar solutions, in the measurement of stresses in transparent materials, to prevent glare, etc.

POLDHU (poldū'). Point overlooking Mount's Bay in Cornwall, England, site of Marconi's wireless station (designed by J. A. Fleming, q.v.), from which the first transatlantic signal - 's' in the Morse code - was transmitted to Signal Hill, Newfoundland, on 12 Dec. 1901. A commercial station from 1905, P. maintained vital links with Atlantic convoys during the F.W.W., and its programme broadcasting in 1920 led to the formation of the BBC in 1922. Public transmission ceased in 1922, complete closure following in 1934: the cleared site is now preserved by the National Trust.

POLE, Reginald (1500-58). English churchman. The grandson of the duke of Clarence, brother of Edward IV, he enjoyed the favour of Henry VIII until he opposed his divorce and the royal supremacy. In 1536 he was created a cardinal and settled in Rome. After Mary's accession he returned to England as papal-legate, re-admitted England to the RC Church, and succeeded Cranmer as archbp of Canterbury in 1556.

POLECAT. Species of weasel (*Mustela putorius*) with light-coloured back and dark belly. The body is *c.* 45cm (18in) long and they have a strong smell.

POLES. The geographic N and S points of penetration of the Earth's surface by the axis about which it revolves. The magnetic Ps. are in directions N and S at angles of declination to the geographic P. They are the directions towards which a freely suspended magnetic needle will point, and vary continually, both in relation to the geographical poles and according to the point at which the magnetic needle is held. Periodically changes in the dynamics of Earth's core cause the magnetic Ps to reverse themselves, the last occasion having been 700,000 yrs ago. It has been calculated that the next reversal will be in 1,200 yrs time, when the N magnetic P. will become the S magnetic P.

POLE STAR. The star which is nearest to the celestial N pole, about 1° distant. It is the brightest of the Ursa Minor constellation, and varies in position slowly. Its position is indicated by the 'pointers' in Ursa Major.

POLICE. Force entrusted with the protection of life and property, the preservation of law and order, and the apprehension of offenders. In addition, the P. are responsible for control of traffic. Forces of this type were known in anc. Egypt, Greece, and Rome. In England the first organized P. force was the Bow Street Runners, introduced by Henry Fielding (q.v.) when he was JP for Westminster; elsewhere constabulary duties were discharged by individual constables and watchmen commissioned by their local area. In 1829 Peel's govt passed an act setting up a P. force in London (hence the popular appellation 'peelers'), and an act of 1856 made the provision of P. forces compulsory. Women police were introduced in 1919, motor-cycle patrols 1921, mobile patrols with two-way radio cars 1927, and the 'man on the beat' began to be equipped with radio from 1965 and might use a 'panda' car - named from its stripe marking - from 1966. Special Patrol Groups of experienced men, travelling in their own squad cars, and patrol wagons, and concentrating on a specific problem were introduced in 1970; New York has a similar Tactical Patrol Force. Admin. is by the Home Office in England and Wales, except for the City of London police controlled by the City Corporation, and by the Scottish Office in Scotland.

There is no central control, Scotland Yard (q.v.) acting only on the invitation of local forces. *See* INTERPOL.

In the USA there are local, county, and state law-enforcement agencies, plus the FBI (q.v.), subordinate to the Dept of Justice, which can act directly only in offences against Federal law, though it co-operates with other P. forces when called upon to do so. Some states have no state force, and state governors as a rule have no control over local P.

British P. carry no weapon except a truncheon in normal circumstances, but are armed on occasion; some though not all US police are armed, as are the Royal Canadian Mounted P., the Carabinieri in Italy, the Civil Guards in Spain, some sections of the rather complicated P. forces in France, etc.

POLICE. Japan's first mounted policewomen parade in 1976 in front of the Imperial Palace in Tokyo. *Photo: Pana Photo and The Press Association.*

POLICY UNIT. Secretariat of the British Prime Minister, devoted not to policy-making but assisting the carrying out of the premier's policies. Its forerunner was the 'Garden Suburb' of Lloyd George in the First World War. Under Wilson and Callaghan it was headed 1974-9 by Bernard Donoughue, and under Thatcher from 1979 by John Hoskyns. The US equivalent is the White House staff.

POLIOMYELITIS (pol'iomī-elī'tis). Inflammation of the anterior horn cells of the spinal cord, those governing muscle action, producing paralysis, and particularly affecting children. The cause is a filtrable virus carried in the spray of sneezing or coughing and entering the nervous system by the nerve endings in the lining of the upper part of the nose. Infection comes from a carrier, never a patient. The practical elimination of P. was ensured by the production of vaccines, an injected one by Jonas Salk in 1953 and an oral one by A. E. Sabin in 1955.

POLISH. A member of the western branch of the Slavonic family of languages. P. literature begins in the 14th cent., but the golden age came in the 16th when Mikolaj Rej of Naglowice (1505-69) developed the language in prose and verse, and Jan Kochanowski (1530-84) emerged as Poland's Renaissance poet. A decline followed until the partial revival under French influence in the 18th cent., and the great Romantic period in the 19th with the poets Adam Mickiewicz (1798-1856), Juljusz Slowacki (1809-49), and Zygmunt Krasinski (1812-59), and the comic dramatist Aleksander Fredro (1795-1876). To the later 19th cent. belongs the historical novelist and Nobel prizewinner Sienkiewicz (q.v.), and the realist novelist Wladyslav Remont (1868-1925), also a Nobel laureate, in 1924. Poland's isolation from the West and her troubled periods of revolt and repression have not allowed more recent names to become internationally known, except the exiled poet Czeslaw Milosz (q.v.). Most familiar of the writers of Polish origin to English readers is Joseph Conrad (q.v.).

POLISH LITERATURE. His great works are all in English, but Joseph Conrad retained in his writing the spirit of his Polish heritage *Photo: Courtesy of the National Portrait Gallery.*

POLISH CORRIDOR. A strip of territory connecting Poland with the Baltic, and dividing E Prussia from the rest of Germany, allotted to Poland by the Treaty of Versailles, 1919. With the inclusion of the S part of E Prussia in Poland in 1945, the P.C. ceased to exist.

POLITBUREAU. A contraction for 'political bureau', a sub-committee of the Central Committee of the Communist Party of the USSR, responsible for laying down the lines of party policy. It was known 1952-66 as the presidium, and the gen. sec. was then known as the first sec. *See* RSFSR.

POLITIAN or **Angelo Poliziano.** Literary name for the Italian poet and scholar Angelo Ambrogini (1454-94). He became tutor to the family of Lorenzo de' Medici and prof. at the Univ. of Florence, and wrote commentaries on classical authors, essays on philology and criticism, and Latin, Greek, and Italian verse.

POLK, James Knox (1795-1849). 11th President of the USA. B. in N Carolina, he was elected President as a Democrat in 1844, admitted Texas to the Union, and forced the war on Mexico which resulted in the annexation of California and New Mexico.

POLKA. A dance in lively 2/4 time, originating *c.* 1830 in Bohemia.

POLLAIUOLO (pollahyoo-ō'lō), **Antonio** (1429-98). Italian artist. B. at Florence, he produced many objects of art such as crosses, chasubles, etc., and executed frescoes and paintings incl. the 'Martyrdom of St Sebastian' in the National Gallery, London.

POLLOCK, Jackson (1912-56). American artist. Of Scots-Irish origin, he was the son of a Wyoming farmer. From 1943, following the drive of the unconscious, he adopted increasingly unconventional techniques, e.g. paint thrown or dribbled on to a surface, and became the recognized exponent of 'action painting'. His death - in a Long Is. car crash - echoed the violence of his art, in which he used jewel colours, metal paints, and great abstract freedom.

POLLUTION. The effect on the environment of by-products of all industrial, agricultural and living processes, e.g. noise, smoke, gases, chemical effluents in seas and rivers, indestructible pesticides, sewage and household waste. Natural regeneration counters P. to a degree, but it rapidly escalates to danger level. Complete control would involve drastic reduction of population, and a halt to industrial development.

PŌ'LŌ. Game played between 2 teams of 4 on horseback, originating in Persia, whence it spread to the East and India: the name derives from Tibetan *pulu* ball. Played by British soldiers in India to improve their horsemanship, it was brought back to England in 1869, and a code of rules was evolved by the Hurlingham club in 1875. The Westchester Cup (1886) was estab. for representative British and US teams. The playing time is roughly an hour, divided into periods (chukkas) of 7½ min. The positions of the players are fairly elastic, and the ball (8.25cm/3.25 in diameter) is struck with the side (not the end) of a mallet 1.32m (52in) long. The famous Hurlingham and Ranelagh grounds no longer exist, but those at Roehampton, Cowdray Park, and elsewhere flourish, aided by royal patronage.

POLO, Marco (*c.* 1254-1324). Venetian traveller. His father and uncle, Nicolo and Maffeo P., travelled overland to China in 1260-9, and returned there in 1271-5, taking with them M.P., who entered the imperial service, and was employed on official missions. They returned to Venice in 1292-5. P. was captured while serving against the Genoese in 1298, and while in prison dictated an account of his travels which gives the earliest European description of the Far East.

POLONAISE (polonā'z). A Polish dance, in stately 3/4 time, which dated from the 16th cent. Chopin developed the P. as a musical form.

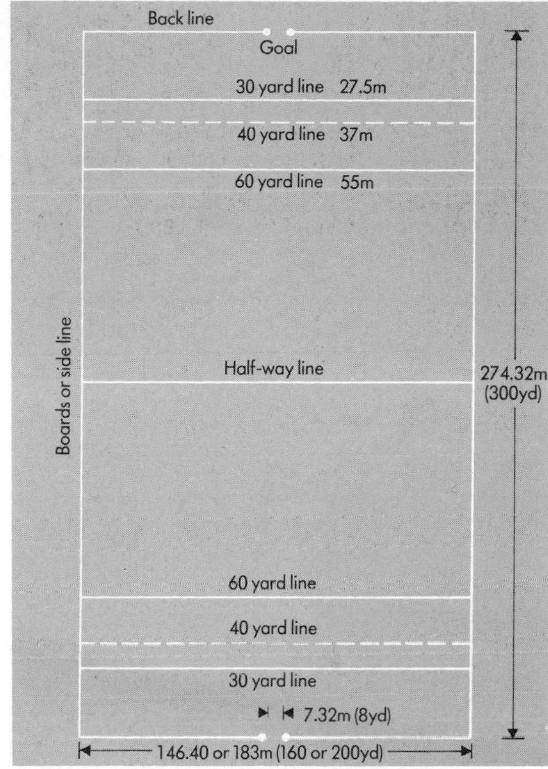

POLO

POLŌ'NIUM. The first radioactive element discovered by the Curies in 1898 (in pitchblende residues) and named after Mme Curie's native Poland: symbol Po, at. no. 84, at. wt. 210. There are some 19 known isotopes, both natural (the most stable being radium F with a half-life of 138.3 days, which emits 5 MeV alpha-particles and is radioactively useful) and man-made.

POLPERRO. Picturesque fishing village and holiday resort in Cornwall, England, 26km (16m) W of Plymouth, much frequented by artists.

POLTAVA (poltah'vah). Town in the Ukrainian SSR, cap. of P. region, on the Vorskla. It is in an agricultural area growing grain, sugar, and fruit. Peter the Great here defeated Charles XII of Sweden in 1709. Pop. (1978) 274,000.

POLTERGEIST (Ger. noisy ghost). In psychic research, name given to the unseen agent, believed by many to be a mischievous spirit or ghost, by means of which objects are moved or hurtled through the air. Famous P. phenomena that occurred at Borley rectory, Suffolk, were described by Harry Price.

PO'LYANDRY. The system whereby a woman is the wife of several men at the same time. It is found in many parts of the world, e.g. in Madagascar, Malaya, and certain Pacific isles, and among certain Eskimo and S American Indian tribes. In Tibet and certain parts of India P. takes the form of the marriage of one woman to several brothers.

POLYANTHUS. Garden flower in the family Primulaceae, thought to be a cross between the primrose

POLO. A sixteenth century Persian impression of the game from a manuscript. *Photo: The Mansell Collection.*

and cowslip. It occurs in many shades from cream to dark red.

POLYBIUS (polib'ius) (*c.* 201-120 BC). Greek historian. B. in Arcadia, he was taken as a prisoner to Rome in 168, but returned to Greece in 151. He was present at the capture of Carthage by his friend Scipio in 146. His history of Rome in 40 books, covering the years 220-146, has largely disappeared.

PO'LYCARP (*c.* AD 69-155). Christian martyr. As bishop of Smyrna for over 40 years he carried on a vigorous struggle against various heresies, and was burned alive at a public festival.

POLYCHLORINATED BIPHENYLS (PCBs). Dangerous industrial chemicals, valuable for non-inflammable qualities, but an environmental hazard because of persistent toxicity. From 1973 their use was limited by internat. agreement.

POLYESTER. Complex compound of hydrocarbons used in making synthetic fibres, such as Dacron and Terylene, resins, and constructional plastics. Glass fibre is used as reinforcement in car bodies, boat hulls, etc.

POLYETHYLENE. A polymer of ethylene, best-known under the trade-name Polythene (*see* Ziegler). Either rigid or highly flexible, it is widely used for containers, protective wrapping, and because it may be made completely transparent and lends itself to colouring, for decorative packaging. When high temperatures are involved, and the ability to stand repeated flexing, polypropylene (related to the rigid type of polyethylene) is used. It has a glass-like finish, and can be used in the sterilization of surgical instruments, etc.

POLY'GAMY or **polygyny.** The system whereby a man may marry several women at the same time. It is found among many primitive hunting, pastoral and agricultural peoples, especially in Africa. Normally it is confined to chiefs and nobles, as in Ancient Egypt and among the primitive Teutons, Irish, and Slavs. Among the Hebrews a man could have any number of wives, but Islam limits a man's legal wives to 4. Certain Christian sects, e.g. the Anabaptists of Münster and the Mormons, have practised polygamy.

PO'LYGON. A plane figure bounded by straight lines. Although incl. a triangle and quadrilateral, it is normally restricted to those figures having more than 4 sides, regular or irregular.

POLYMERIZATION. The chemical union of 2 or more (usually small) molecules to form a new compound of larger molecular wt. There are 3 types: *addition* P., simple multiples of the same compound; *condensation* P. in which molecules are joined together by the elimination of water; and *co*-P. in which the polymer is built up from 2 or more different molecules. There are many important polymers, both natural (e.g. cellulose) and synthetic, e.g. Polythene, nylon, etc. *See* Plastics.

POLYNĒ'SIA. Easternmost of the 3 ethnic divisions of Pacific Ocean isls., of which the other 2 are Micronesia and Melanesia. It comprises all Oceania lying E of approx. 170° E lat., incl. Hawaii, Kiribats, Tuvalu, Fiji, Tonga, Tokelau, Samoa, Cook Is. and French Polynesia. The Maori of New Zealand are also Polynesian. Polynesians are probably of Asiatic origin, and distinct from the Negroid Melanesians with whom there has been a degree of mixture. They are tall and possess fine physique. Their skin is brown, and their hair wavy. They are skilled in house- and shipbuilding, carving and fishing.

French Polynesia. An overseas terr. of France, cap. Papeete. It comprises the Society Is. (q.v.), Tuamotu (q.v.) and Gambier groups; Austral Is.; and the Marquesas (q.v.). Proposals for increased autonomy reached impasse in 1976. Area *c.* 4,000 sq.km (1,500 sq.m); pop. (1970) 120,000.

POLYPROPYLENE. *See* Polyethylene.

POLYPUS. A small benign tumour of the skin due to local overgrowth of cells.

POLYSTYRENE. Synthetic polymer forming a clear plastic used in kitchen utensils, or when expanded by the injection of gas, a stiff foam used in insulation or ceiling tiles.

POLYTECHNICS. Institutions providing comprehensive degree and non-degree courses in art and technology, both full and part-time. Most famous is the Regent Street P., London, founded by Sir George Cayley in 1838, and reconstituted by Quintin Hogg in 1882. From 1966 a series of Ps., initiated by the Labour govt of the day, was estab. at univ. level in the UK.

PO'LYTHĒISM. The worship of many gods, as opposed to monotheism. Examples are the religions of ancient Egypt, Babylon, Greece and Rome, Mexico, and modern Hinduism.

POLYURETHANE. Light synthetic polymer which, prepared in liquid form as a paint or varnish sets extremely hard. In foam form it is used in lining materials, upholstery, etc., when it presents some dangers as it is much more highly inflammable than clothing and furnishing materials of traditional type.

POMEGRANATE. The fruit of a deciduous tree (*Punica granatum*) found in W Asia and N Africa. The edible seeds of the reddish-yellow fruit can be made into wine.

POMERĀ'NIA. District, formerly a prov. of Germany, along the S shore of the Baltic Sea. The area was 30,250 sq.km (11,680 sq.m) and it stretched W to E roughly from just W of Stralsund to Stolp (Pol. Slupsk); it incl. the is. of Rügen, Usedom (Uznam), and Wollin (Wolin). By the Potsdam agreement, 1945, the part of P. E of the Oder-Neisse line was placed under Polish administration. The Ger. form of P. is Pommern, the Pol. Pomorze.

POMERANIAN. Breed of dog resembling a small chow. Claimed to be of German origin, it may be black or white or light brown.

POMFRET. Another form of PONTEFRACT.

POMMERN. German form of POMERANIA.

POMMY or **POM.** Derogatory term for an Englishman, current in Australia from the period of the F.W.W., and of uncertain origin, but possibly from Pompey, an old sailors' name for Portsmouth.

PŌMŌ'NA. Roman goddess of fruit trees.

POMORZE. Polish form of POMERANIA.

POMPADOUR, Jeanne Antoinette Poisson, marquise de (1721-64). Mistress of Louis XV. B. in Paris, she became the king's mistress in 1744, and largely dictated the government's policy procuring the reversal of France's anti-Austrian for an anti-Prussian policy. She acted as the patroness of Voltaire and the *philosophes*.

POMPEII (pompā'yē). Ancient city in Italy, near Vesuvius, 21km (13m) SE of Naples. In AD 63 an earthquake destroyed much of the city which had been a Roman port and pleasure resort; it was completely buried beneath lava when Vesuvius erupted in AD 79. Over 2,000 people were killed. P. was rediscovered in 1748 and the systematic excavation begun in 1763 still continues. The small modern town of P. lies just to the E; it makes macaroni and packing boxes, and caters for tourists. Pop. (1970) 6,500.

POMPEY (Gnaeus Pompeius Magnus) (106-48 BC). Roman soldier and statesman, known as 'the Great'. In early life he supported Sulla and the aristocratic party, but as consul with Crassus in 70 joined the democrats. He conquered Mithridates of Pontus, and annexed Syria and Palestine. In 60 he formed the 1st Triumvirate with Caesar and Crassus. When it broke down after 53, P. returned to the aristocratic party. On the outbreak of civil war in 49 he withdrew to Greece, was defeated by Caesar at Pharsalia in 48, and was murdered in Egypt.

POMPIDOU (pompēdōō'), **Georges** (1911-74). French statesman and scholar. An adviser on De Gaulle's staff 1944-6, he held admin. posts until he became director-general of the French House of Rothschild in 1954, and even then continued in close association with De Gaulle. In 1962 he became PM, but resigned after the Gaullist victory in the elections of 1968, and was elected to the presidency in 1969 as the Gaullist candidate on De Gaulle's resignation.

PONCE (pon'thā). Port on the S coast of Puerto Rico, with textile, and sugar and rum industries. Pop. (1978) 188,500.

PONCE DE LEÓN, Juan (*c.* 1460-1521). Spanish soldier and explorer, discoverer of Florida (1513). He is believed to have sailed with Columbus in 1493, and served 1502-4 in Hispaniola whence in 1508 he conquered Puerto Rico, of which he was made gov. in 1509. He returned to Spain in 1514 to report his discovery of Florida (which he thought was an is.), and was given permission by King Ferdinand to colonize it. In the attempt (1521), he received a severe arrow wound of which he d. in Cuba.

POMPEII. A man and his wife, sometimes called 'The Baker and his Wife', since this attractive dual portrait was discovered on the site of a bakery. *Photo: Courtesy of Imperial Tobacco Ltd.*

PONDICHE'RRY (Fr. pondēshārē'). Port on the E coast of India, 137km (85m) S of Madras, cap. of the union terr. of P. It was founded by the French in 1674 and changed hands several times between French, Dutch, and British before being returned to France in 1814 at the close of the Napoleonic wars. With Karikal, Yanam, and Mahé it formed a French colony until 1954 when all were transferred to the government of India. Since 1962 they have formed a union terr., cap. P. City; pop. 90,650. French remains the chief language. Area 469 sq.km (186 sq.m); pop. (1971) 471,000.

PONDWEED. Genus of aquatic plants (*Potamogeton*) either floating or submerged. The leaves are leathery and elliptical; the flowers grow in green spikes.

PO'NTA DELGADA (delgah'dah). Resort and port on the S coast, also cap., of S Miguel is. in the Azores, Portugal. Pop. (1970) 21,347.

PONTEFRACT. Town in W Yorks, England, 34km (21m) SW of York. There are remains of the Norman castle where Richard II died. Liquorice P. 'cakes', a form of sweet, are noted. Pop. (1972) 31,320.

PO'NTIAC (*c.* 1720-69). American Indian, chief of the Ottawa from 1755. He led in 1763-4 the 'Conspiracy of P.' in an attempt to stop British encroachment on Indian lands. He achieved remarkable success against overwhelming odds, but eventually signed a peace treaty in 1766, and was murdered by an Illinois Indian at the instigation of a British trader. His home was on Apple Is.

in Orchard Lake, Michigan, 8km (5m) SE of the modern car-manufacturing city of P., nr Detroit.

PONTINE (pon'tīn) **Marshes.** Formerly malarial marshes in Latium Italy, nr the coast some 40km (25m) SE of Rome. They defied the attempts of the Romans to drain them, and it was not until 1926 that Mussolini's admin. brought them into cultivation: cereals, fruit and vines, and sugar beet.

PONTUS. Ancient kingdom of NE Asia Minor, bordering the Black Sea, founded *c.* 300 BC. Under Mithridates VI (120-63 BC) it became a great power, but it was conquered by Pompey in 65 BC.

PONTYPOO'L. Town in Gwent, Wales, 15km (9m) N of Newport, where industries, besides coal-mining, incl. the manufacture of iron and steel goods, tinplate and glass, and synthetic textiles. Pop. (1972) 36,910.

PONTYPRIDD (pontaprēdh'). Town in Mid Glamorgan, Wales, on the Taff, 19km (12m) NW of Cardiff. Industries incl. coalmining, chain and cable works, and the light industries of the Treforest trading estate (1937). Pop. (1972) 34,390.

PONY. Small horse under 14.2 hands, i.e. 1.47m (58in). Although of Celtic origin, all the P. breeds have been crossed with thoroughbred and Arab stock, except for the smallest - the hardy Shetland - less than 105cm (42in) Other British breeds incl. the small Exmoor and Dartmoor, the slightly larger New Forest, and the large Welsh cob, and similar native breeds are found elsewhere in Europe and the East. Often ridden by adults, e.g. in polo, or used to pull carts, Ps. are favourites with children, and in 1929 the *P. Club* was estab. to encourage good horsemanship among the young. Now spread throughout the world, it holds instructional rallies and inter-branch championships. Since the S.W.W. pony trekking - following routes of scenic beauty, etc - has been popular for holidays.

POODLE. A highly intelligent breed of dog, incl. the standard (above 38cm/15in at shoulder); miniature (below 38cm/15in) and toy (below 28cm/11in) types.

The P. probably originated in Russia, was naturalized in Germany, where it was used as a sporting dog and gained its name from *Puddler* (one who splashes around in water), and finally became a luxury dog in France, whence it has spread around the world. Their long curly coats, usually cut into elaborate styles, are mostly either black or white (the only colours acceptable in France), although greys and browns are also bred.

POOL. Game derived from billiards, and played with multi-coloured balls, of which the most popular form is snooker (q.v.).

POOLE. Town on P. harbour, Dorset, England, 8km (5m) W of Bournemouth. Characteristic pottery is made of local clay, and there are chemical, engineering, boatbuilding and confectionery industries. The first Boy Scout camp was held in 1907 on Brownsea Is. in the harbour, and P. is a yachting centre. Pop. (1974) 112,000.

POO'NA. Hill city in Maharashtra, Rep. of India, 192km (119m) SE of Bombay. There are rice, sugar, cotton and paper mills, chemicals and jewellery are made and there is an airport. It has long been a military centre and the Nat. Defence Academy is at Khadakvasla nearby. A univ. was estab. in 1948. Pop. (1971) 853,225.

POOR LAW. In England, law for the relief of the destitute poor. The first act for the levy of a compulsory poor rate was passed in 1572, and under the consolidating act of 1601 parish overseers were empowered to provide materials on which to set the unemployed to work, to raise money to relieve the aged, to apprentice pauper children and to build poorhouses. The P.L. of 1834 reorganized the system with boards of guardians elected by the ratepayers, and forbade the relief of the able-bodied except within a workhouse, where conditions were deliberately made repellent: there was violent popular opposition, but the basis of administration remained the same until responsibility was transferred in 1929 to the Min. of Health operating through co. and co. bor. councils. The P.L. system was replaced 1947 by a single relief service admin. by the Nat. Assistance Board, and in 1966 the sharp distinction between contributory and non-contributory benefits was ended by the merger of the board with the Min. of Pensions and Nat. Insurance as the Min. of Social Security.

POP ART. Art movement, so named by art critic Lawrence Alloway, that developed in the late 1950s, and to which Andy Warhol and Liechenstein belong. It represents a direct and representational response to items from advertising (e.g. soup tins), comics, television and films, which form pop culture.

POPE. *See* PAPACY.

POPE, Alexander (1688-1744). British poet. B. in London, son of an RC linen-draper, he was embittered by his personal deformity which made him the butt of his opponents. He attained a rapid reputation with his precocious *Pastorals* (1709), and *Essay on Criticism* (1711), which were followed by the mock-heroic *Rape of the Lock* (1712: enlarged 1714), *Windsor Forest* (1713), and the 'Elegy to the Memory of an Unfortunate Lady' and 'Eloisa to Abelard'. He estab. his financial position for life with the great success of his translation of the *Iliad* (1715-20) and the *Odyssey* (1725-6), and in 1719 settled on his estate at Twickenham which he developed as a miniature compendium of landscape gardening. His edition of Shakespeare (1725) roused the scholarly ridicule of Theobald, and P. revenged himself by making him the hero of his satire on dullness, the *Dunciad* (1728), which was revised in 1743 with Colley Cibber as the chief victim. The *Essay on Man* (1733-4) and *Moral Essays* (1731-5), each consisting of 4 epistles, were shallowly brilliant expositions of philosophy largely influenced by his friend Bolingbroke. The greatest productions of his mature years are the *Imitations of the Satires of Horace* (1733-38). In 1735 also P. manœuvred the publisher Curll into issuing an unauthorized edition of his personal letters, and after denouncing the publication brought out his own version in which the text was judiciously 'improved'. The beloved friend of Swift, Arbuthnot, Gay, and Atterbury, he is outstanding for his workmanship, especially as the creator of the perfectly balanced heroic couplet.

PO'PERINGHE. Ancient town in the prov. of W Flanders, Belgium, 13km (8m) W of Ypres. It was British HQ on the Flanders front during the F.W.W. The Toc H movement originated here in 1915. Pop. (1972) 12,600.

POPLAR. Genus of deciduous trees (*Populus*), with broad leaves. The White P. (*P. alba*) has a smooth grey trunk and the leaves are white below. Other varieties are the aspen (*P. tremula*), grey P. (*P. canescens*), Lombardy P. (*P. nigra* var. *italica*).

POP MUSIC. The emergence of Pop Music, as distinct from traditional 'popular music', coincided with the arrival in their teens of the exceptionally high number of

POPE. A portrait by Jervas of the 'little Queen Anne's man' painted between 1715 and 1727 when Alexander Pope was at the height of his career. *Photo: Courtesy of the National Portrait Gallery.*

children born during the S.W.W. They enjoyed higher teenage earnings or pocket-money than had ever been known before, and the electronic media - the record, the radio and television show - provided an easy means of commercial exploitation. The key instrument - the electronic guitar - also belonged to the new age.

The first manifestation of P.M. was *Rock and Roll,* which had its roots in the Blues (*see* JAZZ), noted exponents being the Negro Chuck Berry and the white Bill Haley and his Comets, the latter reaching an apogee of thumping excitement in 'Rock Around the Clock'. Elvis Presley (q.v.) was the most enduring star to rise from this era. The *Mersey Beat* or Liverpool Sound took part of its inspiration from Rock and Roll and part from both English and Irish folk tradition, and is synonymous with the Beatles (q.v.). Their songs represented a new life style, a 'dropping out' of conventional routine, and a seeking after new religious experiences (from the East rather than the West) linked with ventures into drug-taking. In Bob Dylan (q.v.) the 'message' became all-important, talk taking over from song, and from American 'folk' Country and Western (q.v.) grew. A more earthy rebellion than that of the shampooed Beatles came in the *Rhythm and Blues* period which ensued, and of which the Rolling Stones were the epitome: they derived, oddly enough, from the 'soft' South rather than the 'harsh' North, and their leader, Mick Jagger (1944-), yelled rather than sang. Even more patently derived from the Blues was *Soul,* of which Ray Charles (1930-) and Aretha Franklin (1942-) were famed exponents. Meanwhile, the electronic potential of newly devised equipment was pushed to the utmost in *Psychedelic Pop* by a group such as the Pink Floyd. This rarefied development had its counterpart in *Reggae* (q.v.) from the West Indies, in which the blast of sound assailed the eardrums to damage level. The mutations of P.M. are endless, but the period of original expansion seemed to have lost impetus by the mid-seventies, until the advent of punk (Am. 'rotten') rock in 1976-7 which returned to its unsophisticated origins. In contrast was such a spectacular stage-show as the Pink Floyd's *The Wall* (1980), combining a storyline with modern rock composed by bassist Roger Walters, and selling 10 million copies. In the mid-1980s, the dominant group as live performers were the Police, exponents of rock-reggae, whose songs incl 'Every Breath You Take,' 'Roxanne,' and the elaborate 'Synchronicity.'

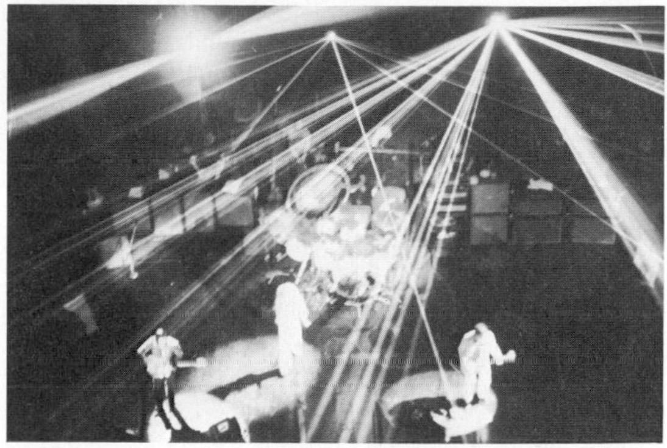

POP MUSIC. To achieve novelty and so maintain interest, the top groups range widely. The Who make discriminating use of laser light—restricted for maximum effect to a few 90-second bursts in each performance— to enhance the impact of their way-out rock music on the audience. *Photo: Courtesy of Graham Hughes.*

POPOCATÉPETL (popokata'petl: Aztec, 'smoking mountain'). Volcano, 65km (40m) SE of Mexico City, Mexico. Its 5,340 m (17,520 ft) summit is snow-clad.

POPOV (popof'), **Alexander** (1859-1905). Russian physicist. He devised the first aerial from a suspended wire, and a detector for radio waves.

POPPER, Sir Karl (1902-). British philosopher. B. in Austria and educ. at Vienna univ., he was prof. of logic and scientific method at London 1949-69. His best-known works are *Logik der Forschung* (1934: *The Logic of Scientific Discovery*), maintaining that the growth of science depends on intellectual daring and rational criticism, *Conjectures and Refutations* (1963), and *Objective Knowledge* (1972).

POPPY. Genus of plants (*Papaver*) having a milky sap, and incl. the crimson field (*P. rhoeas*) and opium Ps. (*see* OPIUM), found in parts of Europe and Asia. Closely related are the California P. (*Eschscholtzia californica*) and the yellow horned or sea P. (*Glaucium flavum*). A large number of cultivated varieties have been developed.

POPULAR FRONT. A political alliance of Liberals, Socialists, Communists, and other centre and left-wing parties against Fascism. This policy was proposed by the Communist International in 1935, and was adopted in France and Spain, where P.F. governments were elected in 1936; that in France was overthrown in 1938, and in Spain in 1939. In Britain a P.F. policy was advocated by Sir Stafford Cripps and others, but rejected by the Labour Party. The resistance movements in the occupied countries during the S.W.W. represented a revival of the P.F. idea, and in post-war politics the term tends to recur whenever a strong right-wing party can only be counterbalanced by an alliance of those on the left.

PORCELAIN (Italian *porcella* small, lustrous seashell). Type of ceramic ware distinguished by its translucence, and traditionally invented in China in the 2nd cent. BC, but the earliest examples of true P. belong to the late 6th-early 7th cent. AD, when it may have been discovered by chance in the attempt to copy imported Indian glassware. It was at its finest under the Sung Dynasty, e.g. the blue-green Celadon ware, and the Ming Dynasty, when colouring was particularly brilliant. During the 17th cent., when the Chinese art had begun to lose its inspiration, though technique continued to improve until the 20th, Portuguese trade contacts with Canton led to the first importation of P. to western Europe. A 'soft paste P.' - actually a mixture of clay and finely ground glass - was first made in Italy as an imitation, but reached great beauty in its own right in France at St Cloud and Sèvres. True P. of the Chinese type was first rediscovered by John Böttger of Meissen, nr Dresden *c.* 1709, and 'Dresden' as the type of delicacy in china became of world-wide fame: German technicians are still in the forefront of the field. In England, Chelsea, Bow and Derby were noted for their soft paste, but in 1768 true P. was first manufactured at Plymouth, and just as in France P. of Limoges had ousted Sèvres soft paste, so in England the 18th cent. saw the triumphs in P. of the Staffordshire potters Thomas Minton and Josiah Spode (famous for his bone china), and beautiful work at Coalport, Lowestoft, Nantgarw, etc. The individual quality was lost during the 19th cent. to a large extent under the impact of mass-production techniques, but the 20th has seen a fresh approach. In recent years the demand for 'limited edition' pieces (bird groups, royal portrait statuettes, etc.) by old-established houses such as Doulton and Worcester, has been stimulated by their investment value.

PORCUPINE. Family of large rodents. True Ps., in the family Hystricidae, are found only in the Old World and are terrestrial in habit. They are characterized by long spines in the coat. The colouring is brown with black and white quills. American Ps. constitute the family Erethizontidae and differ from the European varieties in being arboreal, having a prehensile tail, and much shorter spines.

PORI. Town on the Gulf of Bothnia at the mouth of the r. Kokemäki, Finland, kept ice-free all the year. It has saw mills, nickel and copper refineries, and paper, textiles, matches are made. Pop. (1977) 80,356.

PORNOGRAPHY (porno'grafi). Offensive literature, art or photography, intended to arouse sexual desire, and in the case of 'hard' P., desire of a perverted kind. Precise definition is difficult because standards are subjectively variable as to what is offensive, hence the difficulty in agreement on lines of censorship. Advocates of censorship abolition maintain that P. has no effect on the serious sex crime rate, citing Denmark; others, such as John Court, a clinical psychologist working in Australia, argue that although the well-adjusted may not be affected, the sexually ill-adjusted are, and that there is a strong association between the availability of P. and serious sex crime.

PORPHYRIA (porfir'ia). Rare metabolic disorder, known as the 'royal disease' (Gk *porphyra* purple) found in the houses of Stuart, Hanover and Prussia. Sufferers have incl. Mary Queen of Scots, James I, and George III.

PORPHYRY. A red volcanic rock, of Egyptian origin, much used in Roman ornamentation. It occurs as a thick dyke rediscovered at Jebel Dokhan.

PORPOISE (por'pus). Genus (*Phocaena*) of Cetaceans found in the Atlantic and Pacific. The common P. (*P. phocaena*) is blue-black above, and whitish below, up to 2m (6ft) and feeds on fish. Schools of Ps. leaping together on the surface often foretell stormy weather. In the USA the dolphin (q.v.) is commonly referred to as the P.

PORSCHE (porsh'e), **Ferdinand** (1875-1951). German designer of motor cars. For Hitler he designed the Volkswagen (People's Car), which came on the market actually only after the S.W.W., and famous sports cars under his own name.

PORSON, Richard (1759-1808). British scholar. B. in Norfolk of poor parents, he was sent to Cambridge by a patron, and became prof. of Greek there in 1792. His editions of Aeschylus and Euripides are outstanding achievements of Greek scholarship.

PORT ADELAIDE. Port in S Australia, Australia. It lies on Gulf St Vincent, 11km (7m) NW of Adelaide, and has cement and chemical industries. Pop. (1972) 40,000.

PORT ARTHUR. Deep-water port in Texas, USA, 24km (15m) SE of Beaumont. Founded 1895, it has petroleum refineries, shipyards, brass foundries, chemical factories. It rose to importance with the discovery of petroleum near Beaumont in 1901. Pop. (1970) 57,370. *See* also THUNDER BAY, Canada, and LÜDA, China.

PORT AUGUSTA. Port in S. Australia, at the head of Spencer Gulf. Pop. (1973) 11,000.

PORT-AU-PRINCE (-ō-prins'). Cap. and port of Haiti, W Indies. It has a univ. and industries incl. sugar refining, rum distilleries, textiles and plastics. Pop. (1975) 458,675.

PORT-AU-PRINCE. The statue of the unknown Maroon — the Maroons were Negro slaves who fled their chains to hide in the forests. *Photo: Ministry of Tourism, Haiti.*

PORT DARWIN. *See* DARWIN.

PORT ELIZABETH. Port in Cape prov., S Africa, *c.* 710km (440m) E of Capetown on Algoa Bay. It was founded in 1820 by British settlers and named after the wife of Sir Rufane Donkin, then gov. of the Cape. It exports wool, fruit, ostrich feathers and makes boots, flour, and jam. There is a bilingual univ. (1964). Pop. (1970) 468,600 incl. 150,000 whites.

PORTER, Cole (1893–1964). American composer. B. in Indiana, he wrote the music and lyrics for musical comedies, incl. *Gay Divorce, Around the World in Eighty Days* and *Kiss Me, Kate,* and the film *High Society.* 'Night and Day' is his best-known song.

PORTER, Katherine Anne (1890–1980). American writer. B. at Indian Creek, Texas, she leapt to fame with a vol. of short stories *Flowering Judas* (1930), her reputation for economy and power being maintained in *Pale Horse, Pale Rider* (1939).

PORTER, Rodney Robert (1917–). British biochemist. He was awarded a Nobel prize (with G. M. Edelman of New York) in 1972 for work in discovering the chemical structure of antibodies, which has assisted the diagnosis and treatment of infectious disease.

PORT HARCOURT. Deepwater port and industrial city in Rivers state, Nigeria, on the Bonny r., in the Niger delta. It is linked by rail with the coal and tin mines of the interior. Pop. (1975) 242,000.

PORT KLANG. Rubber port (formerly Port Swettenham), on the Strait of Malacca, 40km (25m) SW of Kuala Lumpur.

PORTLAND, William Bentinck, 1st earl of (*c.* 1649–1709). Dutch statesman. A friend of William of Orange, he took part in the invasion of England in 1688, and received the earldom of P. in 1689. He served in William's campaigns, and negotiated the Treaty of Ryswick and the Partition Treaties.

PORTLAND, William Henry Cavendish Bentinck, 3rd duke of (1738–1809). British statesman. He began his political career as a Whig, and in 1783 became PM in the Fox-North coalition govt. During the French Revolution he joined the Tories, becoming PM (1807–9).

PORTLAND. (1) Largest city in Oregon, USA, on the Columbia, 173km (108m) from the sea, at its confluence with the Willamette. Ocean-going vessels can reach P. which has excellent harbour facilities and road, rail and air links. Industries incl. metal processing, espec. aluminium; paper, timber, and lumber machinery; and electronics. Pop. met. area (1970) 1,064,000. (2) Port and largest city of Maine, USA, on Casco Bay. It has shipbuilding and other industries; the chief export is timber. A first settlement was made on the site in 1633, but wiped out by Indians and French in 1690; re-settlement began in 1718, the place being called Falmouth until 1786. Longfellow was born at P. Pop. (1970) 141,625.

PORTLAND, Isle of. A rocky 'island' off the Dorset coast, England, opposite Weymouth, joined to the mainland by the Chesil Bank (q.v.). It has a 14th cent. castle; a prison, opened 1848, converted into a Borstal 1921; and a naval harbour of refuge. P. stone is quarried. Area 12 sq.km (4.5 sq.m).

PORT MAHON. *See* MAHON.

PORT MORESBY. Cap. and port of Papua New Guinea, on the Coral Sea. It was founded in 1873, and the Univ. of Papua New Guinea was estab. 1965. Pop. (1971) 76,500.

PÔRTO ALEGRE (por'too aleg'rā). Port at the head of a tidewater lake (Lago dos Patos) in SE Brazil. Industries incl. chemicals, meat-packing, tanning and textiles, and there are 2 univs. founded in 1934 and 1948. Pop. (1975) 1,044,000.

PORT-OF-SPAIN. Port and cap. of Trinidad, West Indies. There are 2 cathedrals, and it exports cocoa, sugar, asphalt, copra, rum, petroleum, and angostura bitters. Pop. (1970) 117,000.

PO'RTON DOWN. Site of the Microbiological Research Establishment of the Min. of Defence in Wilts: as a 'germ warfare' centre it came under political attack in the 1960s.

PORTO RICO. Another form of PUERTO RICO.

PORT PHILLIP BAY. Inlet off Bass Strait, Victoria, Australia, on which Melbourne stands.

PORT PIRIE (pi'ri). Port in SE South Australia, Australia, on Germain Bay. Industries incl. the smelting of ores from the Broken Hill mines, and chemicals. Pop. (1973) 16,500.

PORT RASHID (rahshēd'). *See* DUBAI.

PORT ROYAL DES CHAMPS. A former Cistercian convent, SW of Paris, founded in 1204. In 1626 its inmates were moved to Paris, and the buildings were taken over by a male community which became a centre of Jansenist teaching and was in 1638 compelled to vacate the premises; the buildings were destroyed in 1710 by order of Louis XIV.

PORT SAID (sah-ēd'). Port of Egypt, on reclaimed land at the N end of the Suez Canal, founded in 1859. Unused following the blocking of the canal in 1967, P.S. was evacuated by 1969, but by 1975 had been largely reconstructed. Pop. (1974) 342,000.

PORTSMOUTH, Louise de Kéroualle, duchess of (1649–1734). Mistress of Charles II. B. in Brittany, she came to England in 1670. She was acting as Louis XIV's agent, and was generally hated. On Charles's death she returned to France.

PORTSMOUTH. English city and naval port of Hampshire, 119km (74m) SW of London. It covers Portsea Is., which lies between P. and Langstone harbours, and spreads on to the mainland. The Royal Dockyard and naval station occupy the SW area of the is., and the RN barracks bear the name of Nelson's flagship, HMS *Victory,* preserved in dry dock nearby. In 1980 *HMS Warrior,* the world's first armoured battleship was being restored to be berthed near her. P. harbour opens through a bottleneck with Gosport on its W side and P. on the E side. Southsea is a seaside resort with fine views of shipping in the Solent, and the castle is used as a museum of military history. P. was already a port in the days of King Alfred, and in the reign of Henry VIII a French attempt to take it led to the capsize in battle of the warship *Mary Rose* in 1545: there are plans to raise the wrecked vessel for preservation. In the S.W.W. German air raids caused heavy damage and P. was an important mounting base for the Allied invasion of France in 1944. Charles Dickens was born in P. and his birthplace in Commercial Road is a museum. Pop. (1974) 200,380.

PORTSMOUTH. (1) Port of New Hampshire, USA, on the estuary of the Piscataqua. Founded in 1623, P. was the state cap. 1679–1775. The treaty which ended the Russo-Japanese war of 1904–5 was signed here. Pop. (1970) 25,700. (2) City in Ohio, at the junction of the Ohio and Scioto rivers. Founded in 1803, it is a mining centre with boot and shoe, furniture, and other factories. Pop. (1970)

27,650. (3) City and port in Virginia, on Elizabeth r., seat of an important US navy yard and training centre, descended from a navy yard set up by the British in 1752. It also makes textiles and raises oysters. Pop. (1970) 111,000.

PORT SWETTENHAM. *See* PORT KLANG.

PORT TALBOT. Port in W Glamorgan, Wales, at the mouth of the Avon, SE of Swansea. Coal from nearby mines is exported, and there are tinplate and other metallurgical industries. There were cutbacks at the Margam steelworks in 1980. Pop. (1974) 50,000.

PORTUGAL. Republic of Europe, situated between the Atlantic to the W and S, and Spain to the E and N. P. is an elongated area on the W coast of the Iberian peninsula. It has a length of 580km (360m) and breadth of 225km (140m), and is crossed from NE to SW by several parallel ranges of mountains between which pass the valleys of the main rivers, viz. the Minho, Douro, Tagus and Guadiana. The Serra da Estrélla incl. the highest ground in P., 1,936 m (6,532 ft). The climate is temperate.

P. is still mainly agricultural. Wheat, maize, potatoes, rye, rice and olives are grown, and P. produces most of the world's cork. Wine, espec. port wine, and sardines are important exports. Minerals incl. coal, copper, iron, wolfram, etc., and the foundry industry, under the impetus of the S.W.W. and assisted by low wages and a disciplined work force, flourishes. Textiles, pottery, glass, leather goods, furniture, and chemicals are also growing manufactures.

The chief towns are Lisbon, the cap.; Oporto, Vila Nova de Gaia, Coimbra and Setubal; and Funchal (Madeira) and Ponta Delgada (Azores).

Area (incl. the Azores and Madeira) 91,920 sq.km (35,490 sq.m); pop. (1976) 9,730,000, mainly R Catholics. There are univs. at Coimbra (1290), Lisbon, and Oporto (both 1911).

Under the constitution of 1976 P. is a rep., which aims at a 'classless society' and the socialization of the 'means of production and resources'. The pres. (who is also head of the armed forces and of the consultative Supreme Revolutionary Council) is elected by universal suffrage for a 5-year term, and appoints the PM in accord with elections (also by universal suffrage) to the Legislative Assembly.

OVERSEAS POSSESSIONS. Following the revolution of 1974 the remnants of the Portuguese empire rapidly disintegrated. Guinea-Bissau (formerly Portuguese Guinea) became independent in 1974; Angola, the Cape Verde Is., Mozambique, and São Tomé and Príncipe in 1975. Goa (Portuguese India) had in fact long been part of the Rep. of India, but was formally transferred in 1975; Portuguese Timor was effectively absorbed by Indonesia in 1976; and only Macao (q.v.), with greater autonomy, remains Portuguese with the tacit agreement of China.

History. P. originated in the 11th cent. as a county subject to León, while the S was ruled by the Moors. Alfonso I (1128-85) captured Lisbon (1147) and made the Tagus the frontier, assuming the title of king in 1140. Alfonso III (1248-79) finally expelled the Moors. During the 13th cent. the Cortes, representing nobles, clergy and cities, began to meet, and secured control of taxation. A commercial treaty with England was signed in 1294, and an alliance estab. in 1373. During the 15th cent. Portuguese mariners explored the African coast, opened the sea route to India, and discovered Brazil; as a result, in the 16th cent. P. founded colonies in Brazil, Africa, India, and the E Indies. By the 16th cent. the Portuguese kings had become absolute, but when the royal family became extinct in the male line, in 1580, Philip II of Spain seized the crown. The Portuguese rebelled against Spanish rule in 1640, placed the house of Braganza on the throne, and after a long war forced the Spaniards to recognize their independence in 1668. P. fought as the ally of Britain in the War of the Spanish Succession. A period of decadence was ended by the sweeping reforms of Pombal, chief minister 1750-77.

PORTUGAL. Edward VII park in Lisbon, so-called because the King visited the city in 1903. On the left is the Alfama, or old town, crowned by the former Moorish citadel. *Photo: Courtesy of EFTA.*

The French invaded P. in 1807, and were not finally expelled by Wellington until 1811. A strong democratic movement developed, and after a civil war (1828-34) constitutional govt was estab. King Carlos and the Crown Prince were assassinated in 1908; Carlos's younger son Manoel II was driven from the country by a revolution in 1910 and a rep. was proclaimed. It successfully faced armed opposition. In 1932 Dr Salazar became PM and estab. a semi-Fascist dictatorship. During the F.W.W. P. declared war on Germany in 1916 and contributed troops in France and Africa; during the S.W.W. P. remained neutral, but under the treaty of 1373 gave the UK in 1943-6 facilities for air bases in the Azores. On the incapacity of Salazar in 1968, Caetano took office, and a peaceful revolution followed in April 1974. In the 1976 elections the Communists were eliminated, and in 1979 the right-of-centre Democratic Alliance (AD) came to power. In June 1985 the government coalition between the socialists and the social democrat party broke down, and the PM, Mario Soares, resigned, six months before the presidential elections. Portugal entered the EEC on 1.1.86.

PORTUGUESE. A member of the Romance family of languages, ultimately deriving from Latin, but later subjected to a considerable Arabic influence.

Under Provençal influence, medieval P. literature produced popular ballads and troubadour songs, and the Renaissance stimulated the outstanding work of the dramatist Gil Vicente, and the lyric and epic poet Camöens (qq.v.). In the 17th and 18th cents. there was a decline to formality, but the *Letters of a Portuguese Nun* by Marianna Alcoforado (q.v.) were a poignant exception, and found echoes in the modern revolutionary period. No single figure stands out internationally among the varied writers of the 19th and 20th cents, although there is a lively journalistic tradition in Brazil, and Angola developed its own school of Portuguese-African poetry.

PORTUGUESE EAST AFRICA. *See* MOZAMBIQUE.

PORTUGUESE GUINEA. *See* GUINEA-BISSAU.

PORTUGUESE WEST AFRICA. *See* ANGOLA.

PORT WINE. A rich, sweet, dessert wine, red, tawny, or white, grown in the Douro basin of Portugal and exported from Oporto.

POSEIDON. *See* NEPTUNE.

POSEN. German form of POZNAN.

POSITIVISM. The philosophical system of Auguste Comte (q.v.) based on the idea that man has no knowledge of anything but phenomena, and such knowledge is relative not absolute. In every department of human knowledge 3 stages may be discerned: the theological, in which everything is referred to the gods; the metaphysical, in which abstract ideas are of supreme importance; and the positive, when science takes the place of metaphysics and philosophy. On the basis of P. Comte erected his 'Religion of Humanity', in which the object of adoration was the Great Being, i.e. the personification of humanity as a whole. *Logical P.* or empiricism developed in the 1920s: it rejected any metaphysical world beyond everyday science and common sense, and confined statements to those of formal logic or mathematics. *See* CARNAP, MACH.

POST-IMPRESSIONISM. Term applied to various styles of painting which followed Impressionism, and first used by Roger Fry to describe the works of Cézanne, van Gogh, and Gauguin in 1911. Post-Impressionists often distorted natural appearance for the sake of design or to express their own emotions.

POST OFFICE. Organization originally concerned solely with the conveyance of written communications. Since every centrally organized state depends on a speedy flow of information and instructions, early and efficient systems were devised by the rulers of Assyria, China, Rome, etc. In medieval Europe royal couriers and private messengers were frequently used, but major permanent systems waited on the establishment of the nation state. In England in 1516 Henry VIII appointed Sir Brian Tuke as his Master of the Posts with the task of maintaining not only a constant link between the mobile monarch and his capital, but of maintaining a regular service along the main roads from London: postmasters (usually innkeepers) were appointed, with the duty of passing on mail to the next post and of providing horses for royal couriers. Private persons wishing to send letters (both within the kingdom and across to the Continent) or to travel 'post haste' were permitted to use these services: private posts were consistently discouraged as involving loss of revenue for the state service and facilitating treasonable activities.

In 1635 Charles I briefly appointed Thomas Witherings, already a successful 'Postmaster General for Foreign Parts', to improve the domestic services, public correspondence being accepted for the first time for conveyance by messengers at fixed rates. After the Civil War an ordinance of 1654 reaffirmed the repeatedly challenged concept of state monopoly, e.g. the London penny post organized in 1680-2 (when legal action compelled him to desist) by William Dockwra, which was so successful it was continued as part of the official service, Dockwra eventually being appointed comptroller. The uniform penny post advocated by Rowland Hill was instituted in 1840 to replace the former charge varied according to distance - the rate remained unchanged until 1918 - and pre-paid adhesive stamps were introduced.

In the 19th and 20th cents. the P.O. greatly extended its services: savings bank (1861), telegraphs (1870), postal orders (1881), parcels post (1883), telephone service (1912), overseas telegraph service (1950), transatlantic telephone cable (1956), facilities for data processing by computer (1967), and giro (q.v., 1968). The P.O. acts as agent for govt. depts. in the collection of certain revenue, disbursement of pensions and allowances, issue of some licences, etc. In 1969 the former General P.O. had ceased to be a govt. dept., and become the P.O., a public corporation, and in 1980 was split into two - the P.O. and British Telecom, the latter responsible for telecommunications, incl. radio and television broadcasting. The London Telecom Tower (1966) is the highest building in Britain (189 m/620 ft), and its microwave equipment is capable of handling 150,000 simultaneous telephone conversations and 40 television channels. Letters and documents, increasingly uneconomic by ordinary post, can be transmitted at high speed over telephone lines in facsimile by digital electronic signals to an automatic receiver, e.g. Intelpost (1980) which can transmit London-Toronto via satellite in one minute. *See also* VIEWDATA.

In America the first postal service was estab. in Massachusetts in 1639, and in 1692 Thomas Neale opened a P.O. at Philadelphia to convey mail to other colonies, but in 1707 his patent was acquired by the govt and the service gradually expanded. Benjamin Franklin was PMG 1753-74 (deputy 1736-53), becoming in 1775 first PMG of the newly formed P.O. Dept which was replaced 1970 by a US Postal Service, an independent govt agency.

International co-operation is ensured through the Universal Postal Union estab. at Berne in 1875.

POST-TRAUMATIC STRESS. Disordered psychological state (PTSD), the equivalent of shell shock in the F.W.W. and combat fatigue in the S.W.W. It is used in the USA for veterans of Vietnam who suffer from mental flashbacks to wartime experiences, accompanied by feelings of guilt and helplessness.

POTASSIUM (Eng. *potash*, Lat. *kalium*). Soft, silvery-bright, highly reactive metal of the alkali group, symbol K, at. no. 19, at. wt. 39.1. Discovered in 1807 by Sir Humphry Davy by electrolysis of caustic potash (KOH) - the first instance of a metal being isolated by an electric current - it reacts violently with water, forming potassium hydroxide and hydrogen which ignites and burns spontaneously with a violet flame due to the volatilized P. It is, therefore, kept under kerosene or naphtha. Widely distributed in nature in combination with other elements, it is found in salt deposits (carnallite and kainite) and minerals (feldspar, greensand, alunite, leucite), and forms *c.* 2.9 per cent of the Earth's solid crust. The salts are important, especially as essential constituents of fertilizers. Alloyed with sodium, it may be used as a coolant in nuclear reactors.

POTATO. Perennial plant (*Solanum tuberosum*) of the Solanaceae, bred by Andean Indians for some 5,000 yrs to eliminate bitterness and toxicity. It was traditionally introduced to Ireland *c.* 1588 by Sir Walter Raleigh but known rather earlier in Spain. The tuberous roots are used as a vegetable, and are also an important commercial source of alcohol, the residue of the process being useful as cattle food. The sweet P. (*Ipomoea batatas*) of the family Convolvulaceae, is a perennial native to tropical America, difficult of cultivation in adverse conditions. The flesh of the tuberous roots is usually white to orange, and like that of the common P. is used as a source of starch and alcohol, as well as for food.

PO'TCHEFSTROOM. Town in S Africa, on the r. Mooi, the oldest town in the Transvaal, founded in 1838 by Boers trekking from the Cape. Pop. (1970) 43,000.

POTEEN (potēn'). Irish alcoholic liquor traditionally made from potatoes, or barley and yeast, in illicit stills. It is so potent that the drinker may remain drunk after a session for days, though drinking only water.

POTE'MKIN (Russ. potyom'kim) **Grigory Aleksandrovich, Prince** (1739-91). Russian statesman. B. near Smolensk, he entered the army and attracted the notice of Catherine II, whose favourite he was for some years, never losing her friendship throughout his life. His activities as administrator, army commander (introducing reforms), builder of the Black Sea Fleet, conqueror of the Crimea, developer of S Russia, founder of the Kherson arsenal, etc., compel admiration.

POTŌ'MAC. River of the USA, rising in the Allegheny mountains, and flowing SE through Washington, DC, into Chesapeake Bay. It is formed by the junction of the N.P. *c.* 153km (95m) and S.P. *c.* 209km (130m), and is itself 459km (285m) long.

POTOSÍ (pōtōsē'). Town in SW Bolivia. Standing on the Cerro de P. slopes at 4,020 m (13,189 ft), it is among the highest towns in the world. It is famed for its tin and silver mines. Pop. (1976) 77,200.

POTSDAM. Cap. of Potsdam district, East Germany, on the Havel, 26km (16m) SW of Berlin. Its buildings include the New Palace (1763-70), and Sans Souci, both built by Frederick the Great. The Third Reich (Hitler's régime) was proclaimed in P. garrison church on 21 March 1933. Pop. (1978) 124,600. At P. was held in July 1945 a conference of representatives of Britain, the Soviet Union, and the USA, which laid down the political and economic principles governing the treatment of Germany in the initial period of Allied control. From the P. conference also went out the ultimatum to Japan demanding unconditional surrender on pain of utter destruction.

POTTER, Beatrix (1866-1943). British writer and illustrator of children's books, beginning with *Peter Rabbit* (1900): her code diaries were pub. 1966. She m. solicitor William Heelis 1913, and bequeathed her Lake District property to the Nat. Trust.

POTTER, Paul (1625-54). Dutch animal painter, the son and pupil of Pieter P., a landscape painter.

POTTER, Stephen (1900-70). British author. A student of Coleridge, e.g. *Coleridge and S.T.C.* (1935), and a literary critic, he was best known for *Gamesmanship* (1947), *Lifemanship* (1950), and *One Upmanship* (1952), humorous studies in how to outwit and outshine the other fellow which added new words to the language.

POTTERIES, The. The centre of the china and earthenware industry in England, lying in the upper Trent basin of N Staffordshire. Wedgwood and Minton are famous names associated with the P., which covers the area about Stoke-on-Trent, and incl. the formerly separate towns of Burslem, Hanley, Longton, Fenton, and Tunstall.

POTTERY. Objects fashioned from clay and baked hard: *see also* CERAMICS and PORCELAIN. The earliest known pottery was made by the Egyptians *c.* 5,000 BC, and they also developed the potter's wheel, but the making of P. is one of the most widespread ancient crafts and its remains are invaluable to the archaeologist, since each culture usually develops its own types which can be dated and so date objects found in association with them, etc. The Greeks were producing P. by the 8th cent. BC, derived from Egyptian examples, but most typical of their work were the black and red figured vases of *c.* 600-450 BC. Roman P. was largely imitative of Greek, but particularly notable is their Samian ware, made by a special process involving firing in the moulds. After the fall of Rome there was a hiatus until the conquering Arabs, in their movement westward, brought to Spain in the 8th cent. AD the lustrous blue and green glazes used in Persia in the previous cent., but which trace their origin to the brilliant colour oxides developed long before and the skills of Babylon and Nineveh. Especially striking in this period is majolica, ware with an opaque tin-oxide glaze which was exported from Majorca - hence the name. Italy at first merely copied such exports, but in the Renaissance developed her own style of P., notably the coloured relief work executed by the Della Robbia family. Faience, a glazed porous ware, owes its name to an Italian P. town (Faenza), but is peculiarly associated with France, cf. Bernard Palissy, though later spreading to centres such as Delft in Holland and Nuremberg in Germany. In England there is an honestly utilitarian medieval P. with green and yellow glazes, more highly decorated Cistercian ware in the 16th cent., and attractive slip ware in 17th, but the 18th cent. saw a remarkable flowering with the cream and jasper ware of Wedgwood and the stoneware - a type of P. which had reached its height on the Continent in 15th cent. Germany - of John Dwight of Fulham, continued into the 19th by Sir Henry Doulton. The mass manufacture of porcelain as the 19th cent. continued tended to eclipse P., but in the 20th cent. it has regained artistic standing, e.g. the work of Bernard Leach (q.v.), Hans Coper, and Lucie Rie.

POULENC (poolońk'), **Francis** (1899-1963). French composer B. in Paris, he became a member of *Les Six.* His works have a light-hearted vitality and incl. songs, *Rapsodie Nègre* (1916) for piano, wind, strings and voices, and the operas *Les mamelles de Tirésias* and *Les Dialogues des Carmélites* (1937).

POULSEN (pool'sen), **Valdemar** (1869-1942). Danish engineer. He was the first to demonstrate, in 1900, that sound could be recorded magnetically - originally on a moving steel tape: this was the forerunner of the tape recorder.

POULTRY. Term applied to domestic birds in the order Gallinae, incl. ducks, geese, turkeys (q.v.) and fowls. Good egg-laying breeds of chicken are Leghorns, Minorcas, and Anconas; varieties most suitable for the table are Dorkings and Indian Game; those useful for both purposes are Orpingtons, Rhode Island Reds, Wyandottes and Plymouth Rocks. Since the S.W.W. the development of battery-produced eggs and intensive breeding of broiler fowls - and more recently turkeys - for the table introduced into Britain and other countries from the US, have roused a public outcry against these 'animal factories'.

POTTERY. Bernard Leach, at work in his pottery at St. Ives. His unmistakeable style owed much to his early studies in Japan. *Photo: Peter Kinnear.*

POUND, Sir (Alfred) Dudley Pickman Rogers (1877-1943). British admiral of the Fleet. As First Sea Lord and Chief of the British Naval Staff 1939-43, he was responsible for the effective measures taken against the U-boats, and was awarded the OM shortly before his death.

POUND, Ezra (1885-1972). American poet. B. at Hailey, Idaho, he studied the Romance languages and in 1907 was briefly lecturer in French and Spanish at Wabash Coll., Crawfordsville. Going to Europe, he made his home in London for some 13 years, influenced T. S. Eliot, Yeats, and Joyce, and by his first two vols. of verse *Personae* and *Exultations* (1909) estab. the lines of the Imagist movement. During 1921-5 he lived in Paris, his friends incl. Gertrude Stein and Hemingway, and then settled in Rapallo. His sympathy with Mussolini's régime and his anti-Semitism aroused resentment in the USA and UK, and his broadcasts from Italy in the S.W.W. led to his arrest by American troops in 1945. On the eve of his Washington trial he was found unfit to plead and confined in a mental hospital until, in 1958, the treason charges were dismissed on the ground that he was never likely to be so. On his release, he returned to Italy. His first completely 'modern' poem, and for some his best, was *Hugh Selwyn Mauberley* (1920), but his biggest is the series of *Cantos* intended to reach a 100, which comprise a selective view of history: beginning in 1919 they incl. *The Pisan Cantos* (1949), *Section Rock-Drill* (1956) and *Thrones* (1960). Scholars often disapprove his versions from Old English, Provençal, Chinese, ancient Egyptian, etc., but they have definite value as poetry.

POUND. (1) Before metrication the standard unit of weight avoirdupois in the UK, USA and Canada, composed of 7,000 grains or 16 oz and equal to 0.45359237 kg. (2) The British standard of currency, equivalent to 100 pence (before 1971 240 old pence), which is issued in note form (before 1914 as a gold sovereign). After the abandonment of the gold standard in 1931, its internat. exchange

POULTRY. A freak of nature, the Onagadori is a protected bird in Japan and special perches are constructed for the cocks since the tail, which when fully developed can grow to 60ft long, never moults. *Photo: Courtesy of the Japan Information Service.*

value was regulated by the Treasury, but in 1972 sterling was allowed to 'float', i.e., the market rate was not necessarily to be confined within announced limits either in respect of the US dollar or EEC currencies. The green pound of the Common Market is the exchange rate for converting EEC farm prices into sterling. From 1983 the P. will be a coin of yellow metal alloy.

POUSSIN (poosañ'), **Nicolas** (1594-1665). French artist. B. at Les Andelys, he went to Rome in 1624, spending the rest of his life there apart from a brief period as court painter to Louis XIII, 1640-3. His landscapes, historical and religious subjects are some of the finest works of the classical tradition and were immensely influential in his native country. His brother-in-law and pupil **Gaspard Dughet** (1613-75), also a landscape painter, adopted the name Gaspard P.

POVERTY BAY. Inlet on the E coast of North Island, NZ, on which Gisborne stands. It was here that Captain Cook first landed in 1769.

POWELL, Anthony (1905-). Brit. novelist. His Proustian *A Dance to the Music of Time* series, portraying Nicholas Jenkins and his circle of upper class friends began with *A Question of Upbringing* (1951), and was completed in 1975 with *Hearing Secret Harmonies.*

POWELL, Cecil Frank (1903-69). British physicist. In 1950 he received a Nobel prize for his development of a new photographic method for the study of nuclear particles.

POWELL, Enoch (1912-). Brit. Cons. politician. Prof. of Greek at Sydney 1937-9, he became MP for Wolverhampton 1950, was Min. of Health 1960-3, and stood for the party leadership in 1965. His views on defence, nationalisation, and taxation are controversial, and a Birmingham speech on immigration 1968 led to his dismissal from the shadow cabinet. He declined to stand at the Feb. 1974 election, his attacks on the Heath govt promoting its defeat at the polls, and later resigned from the Cons. Party. In Oct. 1974 he returned to Parliament as United Ulster Unionist Council member for S Down.

POWER. The rate of doing work or consuming energy expressed in units of work per unit time.

POWER OF ATTORNEY. A formal instrument, executed under seal, and attested by 2 witnesses, whereby a person gives another authority to act on his behalf, either in a specified number or class of transactions, or generally for a limited period.

POWYS (poo'is), **John Cowper** (1872-1963). British author. B. at Shirley, Derbyshire, he was the brother of the versatile writers Theodore Francis P. (1875-1953) and Llewelyn P. (1884-1939). His verse incl. *Wolfsbane, Mandragora* and *Samphire* - titles which, with those of his critical and philosophical works (e.g. *The Religion of a Sceptic, In Defence of Sensuality,* and *The Meaning of Culture*), and his interest in Rabelais (of whom he pub. a study in 1947), indicate the mystical fantasy and lusty richness of his novels, which incl. *Wolf Solent* (1929) and *A Glastonbury Romance* (1933).

POWYS. Co. of central Wales created in 1974 from Brecknock, Montgomery and Radnor. The admin. HQ is Llandrindod Wells. Area 5,079 sq.km (1,961 sq.m); pop. (1978) 106,000.

POYNTER, Sir Edward John (1836-1919). British painter. B. in Paris, son of the architect Ambrose P. (1796-1886), he became first head of the Slade School (1871-5). On Millais' death in 1896, he was elected PRA. Noted for his decorous nudes, he also designed mosaic panels in Westminster Palace (1870), and painted 'Israel in Egypt', 'The Golden Age' and 'Atlanta's Race'.

PO'ZNAN. City in Poland on the Warta, 275km (170m) W of Warsaw, the seat of a univ. (1919). Manufactures incl. locomotives and farming machinery, precision instruments, bicycles, aircraft, beer. Settled by German immigrants in 1253, it was a residence of the dukes of Poland from 1296; it passed to Prussia in 1793 and was restored to Poland in 1919. Hindenburg was born at P. Pop. (1975) 510,000.

POZZUOLI (potswol'i). Port in Campania, Italy, 11km (7m) SW of Naples, with iron and steel industries. Pop. (1970) 60,000.

PRADO. A famous thoroughfare of Madrid, Spain, which gave its name to the picture gallery *Real Museo de Pintura del Prado,* containing the national collection of pictures, founded by Charles III in 1785.

PRAETOR (prē'tor). A Roman magistrate, elected annually, who assisted the consuls and presided over the civil courts. The number of Ps. was finally increased to 8, who after a year of office acted as provincial governors for a further year.

PRAGMATISM. Name given to the philosophical doctrine advanced by the American philosopher William James (q.v.) that the truth of a conception may be judged from its bearing upon human conduct. James derived the idea from C. S. Peirce (1839-1914) who introduced the term and the principle into philosophy in 1878.

PRAGUE (prahg). French form of Praha, cap. of Czechoslovakia, on the Vltava. Germans were settled here in the 13th cent. when the kings of Bohemia made it their cap. It was a residence of the Holy Roman Emperors during the 14th to 17th cents. Hitler occupied P. in 1939. The city, which is exceptionally pleasing, rises in terraces from the river. On the left bank is the Hradčany with the castle, and the old town has a profusion of palaces, bridges, and churches. The univ. was founded by the Emperor Charles IV in 1348. Since the time of the Austro-Hungarian empire, P. has been the venue quinquennially of the Spartakadia, a physical education spectacle at the Strahov stadium in which 250,000 take part. Industries incl. cars and aircraft, chemicals, paper and printing, clothing, brewing and food processing. Pop. (1977) 1,176,000.

PRAIRIE. The central N American plains, formerly grass-covered, extending over most of the region between the Rockies on the W and the Great Lakes and Ohio river on the E, and extending northward into Canada.

PRÂKRIT (prah'krit). The popular languages of ancient India, as opposed to Sanskrit. The best-known P. is Māhārastri, used for the later Jain sacred books. The Ps. were also used in lyric poetry and for certain characters in Sanskrit drama.

PRATO (prah'tō). Town in Tuscany, Italy, NW of Florence. The 12th cent. cathedral has masterpieces by Donatello, Filippo Lippi, and Andrea Della Robbia. Woollen textiles are made. Pop. (1978) 155,800.

PRAWN. Crustacean in the family Palaemonidae, allied to the shrimp. The common P. (*Leander serratus*), translucently colourless, and 50-75mm (2-3in) long, is found in shoals in shallow off-shore water in the temperate zone, and is good eating. In tropical rivers, e.g. in the W Indies and Central America, there are Ps. approaching the size of lobsters.

PRAXI'TELĒS. Greek sculptor who lived in Athens during the 4th cent. BC. The works credited to him incl. the statue of Hermes carrying Dionysus and the bas-relief of Aphrodite of Cnidus.

PRAYER. Address to a divine power, whether of supplication, adoration, confession, or thankfulness. Among primitive peoples, P. is often merely a magic formula, compelling the deity to perform the wishes of the worshipper, but with the advance of religion it develops towards disinterested communication with a higher power. The RC and Greek churches sanction prayer to the Virgin, angels, and saints, to secure their intercession for the devotee, but Protestant churches limit P. to God alone. Protestant churches also make no provision for prayer for the dead, since this implies belief in Purgatory.

PREDESTINATION. In theology, the doctrine which asserts the foredetermination by God of all events, and of the ultimate election to glory or reprobation to perdition of the individual soul. The theory of P. was elucidated in the controversy between Augustine, who claimed the absolute determination of election by God, and Pelagius, who upheld the doctrine of freewill. Luther and Calvin adopted the Augustinian view at the Reformation, although in differing degrees, but Arminius adopted the Pelagian standpoint.

PREFECT (Fr. *préfet,* prāfeh'). In France the govt's representative in each dept, the office being first estab. in 1800. In each *commune* (the unit of local govt) a mayor is elected by the municipal council (themselves elected by universal suffrage), who is head of the local police, and acts with his assistants under the orders of the P. *See* LOCAL GOVT.

PREGNANCY. The condition in which a child is growing within the womb. It begins at conception and ends at birth, and the normal length is forty weeks, though abortion or premature birth may occur at any time, and the period may be much exceeded. Menstruation stops on conception. After the second month the breasts become tense and tender, the area round the nipple becomes dark brown. Enlargement of the womb can be felt about the end of the third month, and thereafter the abdomen enlarges progressively.

PREMINGER, Otto (Ludwig) (1906–86). American producer-director. B. in Vienna, he was associated with the Josefsteater before going to the USA. His films show a highly developed and intricate technique of story-telling, which clearly presents the issues, without judging them; and a masterly use of the wide screen and the travelling camera: they incl. *Margin for Error* (1942), *Anatomy of a Murder* (1959), *Advise and Consent* (1961), *Skidoo* (1968) and *Rosebud* (1974).

PREMIUM SAVINGS BONDS. *See* LOTTERY and SAVING.

PREMONSTRATENSIANS or **White Canons.** An RC monastic order founded by St Norbert at Prémontré, France, in 1120. Their rule was a stricter version of that of the Augustinian Canons.

PREMPEH I (d. 1931). Ashanti chief. He became king in 1888, and later opposed British rule. He was deported and in 1900 the Ashanti were quelled. Converted to Christianity, he returned to Kumasi in 1924, being made head chief of the people. *See* ASHANTI.

PRE-RAPHAELITE BROTHERHOOD. A group of Victorian artists who abandoned the rules of art developed under Raphael, and painted biblical and literary subjects in a naturalistic style. The Brotherhood, founded in 1848, had only 3 members - Dante Gabriel Rossetti, John Everett Millais, and Holman Hunt - though many other artists came under their influence, notably Ford Madox Brown, Burne-Jones, Frederick Sandys, and Arthur Hughes. The Brotherhood broke up in 1853 when Millais became a ARA and abandoned the Pre-Raphaelite technique.

PRESBYTERIANISM. That system of government of the Christian Church that is based on elders as distinguished from Episcopalianism with its rule by bishops. At the Reformation, P. was expounded by John Calvin, and from his teaching and influence derive the present Presbyterian churches in Scotland (where the estab. Church is Presbyterian), England, the Commonwealth, USA, etc. Each congregation is governed by elders, clerical or lay, who are of equal rank; and congregations are grouped in presbyteries, synods, and general assemblies.

PRESCOTT, William Hickling (1796–1859). American historian. B. in Mass., he was almost completely blinded by an accident, but produced the popular *History of Ferdinand and Isabella, Conquest of Mexico* (1843), and *Conquest of Peru* (1847).

PRESCRIPTION. The legal acquisition of title or right by uninterrupted use or possession from time immemorial.

PRESCRIPTION. An order written in a recognized form by a practitioner of medicine, dentistry, or veterinary surgery to a pharmacist for a preparation of drugs to be used in treatment. By tradition it is written in Latin, except for the directions addressed to the patient. It consists of (1) the superscription *recipe* (take), contracted to R; (2) the inscription or body, containing the names and

PRE-RAPHAELITE. Working on this picture at the time of his divergence from Morris over socialism, Sir Edward Burne-Jones wrote 'To put on the beggar maid a sufficiently beggarly coat that will not look unappetising to King Cophetua... that I hope has been achieved..' When exhibited in Paris at the *Exposition Universelle* (1889) it was hailed, surprisingly, by one French critic as 'the symbolic expression of the scorn of wealth'. *Photo: Courtesy of the Tate Gallery.*

quantities of the drugs to be dispensed; (3) the subscription, or directions to the pharmacist; (4) the signature, consisting of the contraction *Signa,* followed by directions to the patient; and (5) the patient's name, the date and the practitioner's name.

PRESIDENT. The usual title of the head of state in countries without a monarch. The office may range from the equivalent of a constitutional monarch to the actual head of the govt. For presidents of the US *see* UNITED STATES OF AMERICA.

PRESIDENTIAL MEDAL OF FREEDOM. Highest peacetime civilian award in the USA, instituted in 1963, conferred annually on Independence Day by the Pres. on those making significant contributions to the 'quality of American life'. It replaced the Medal of Freedom (1945) awarded for acts and service aiding US security.

PRESLEY (prez'li), **Elvis** (1935-77). B. in Tupelo, Mississippi, he estab. himself from 1956 as the archetype, dominant-voiced, electric-guitar backed 'pop' singer, and was nicknamed Elvis the Pelvis because of his gyrating hips. Best-known of his earlier songs was 'Hound Dog'. As he matured he graduated to a softer ballad style.

PRESS. *See* NEWSPAPERS.

PRESSBURG. German name of BRATISLAVA.

PRESTER JOHN (John the Priest). Fabulous Christian prince who in the 12th-13th cents. was believed to rule a powerful empire in Asia. In the 14th-16th cents. P. J. was identified with the king of Ethiopia.

PRESTON. Seaport in Lancs, England, on the Ribble nr its mouth, 34km (21m) S of Lancaster. Cromwell defeated the Royalists at P. in 1648. Industries incl. textiles, chemicals, electrical goods, aircraft and shipbuilding. It is admin. HQ of Lancs. Pop. (1972) 95,450.

PRESTONPANS. Town on the Firth of Forth, Lothian, Scotland, 15km (9m) E of Edinburgh. Nearby in 1745 the royal troops were routed by the Jacobites. Pop. (1971) 3,210.

PRESTWICK (prest'wik). Town on the Firth of Clyde, Strathclyde, Scotland, 5km (3m) N of Ayr, known for its championship golf course, and as an airport for transatlantic services. Pop. (1971) 13,438.

PRETORIA. Administrative capital of the Rep. of S Africa, and cap. of Transvaal prov. Founded in 1855, and called after the Boer leader A. Pretorius (1799-1853), it became cap. of Transvaal in 1860, and administrative cap. of the Union in 1910. P. univ. was founded in 1930; P. is also the seat of the Univ. of South Africa (1873). The Loftus Versfeld rugby stadium is the citadel of Afrikanerdom. Pop. (1970) 561,700.

PREVIN (prā'vin), **André** (1929-). American conductor and composer. B. in Berlin, he studied there and in Paris, and was principal conductor of the London Symphony Orchestra 1968-79. He has done much to popularize classical music.

PRÉVOST D'EXILES (prāvō' degzēl'), **Antoine François** (1697-1763). French author, known as Abbé P. He was a monk, an army officer, lived in England and Holland (1728-33), and in 1754 became prior of St-Georges-de-Gesnes. Of his sentimental novels, *Manon Lescaut* (1731) is best remembered.

PRIAPUS (prī-ā'pus). Greek god of fertility, usually represented as a grotesquely ugly man with an exaggerated phallus. He was also a god of gardens, where his image was frequently placed as a scarecrow.

PRI'BILOF ISLANDS. Group of 4 islands in the Bering Sea, of volcanic origin, 320km (200m) SW of Bristol Bay, Alaska, USA; named after Gerasim Pribilof who discovered them in 1786, they were sold by Russia to the USA in 1867 with Alaska, of which they form part. They were made a fur-seal reservation in 1868.

PRICKLY HEAT. Inflammation of the sweat glands; a minor disorder of hot, wet climates, due to excessive sweating. Small vesicles are formed, but quickly dry up and heal.

PRICKLY PEAR. Genus of cacti (*Opuntia*) native to America, especially Mexico and Chile, but naturalized in southern Europe, northern Africa, and Australia, where they are a pest (*see* CACTOBLASTIS). The common P.P. (*O. vulgaris*) is low-growing, with red or white flowers, and has pleasant-tasting oval fruit.

PRIDE, Thomas (d. 1658). A London drayman or brewer, he rose to be a colonel in the Parliamentary Army in the Civil War, and on Cromwell's orders executed in 1648 'Pride's Purge' of the House of Commons of its Presbyterian and Royalist members.

PRIESTLEY, John Boynton (1894-). British author. B. in Bradford, son of a schoolmaster, he was educ. at Trinity Hall, Cambridge, and served in the F.W.W. He estab. his reputation as a novelist with *The Good Companions* (1929), which he dramatized with E. Knoblock in 1931, and reinforced it with *Angel Pavement* (1930) and later books. As a playwright he has often been preoccupied with theories of time, as in *Dangerous Corner* (1932), *Time and the Conways* (1937), *Johnson over Jordan* (1939) and *An Inspector Calls* (1945), but has also a gift for family comedy, e.g. *Laburnum Grove* (1933) and *When We Are Married* (1938), and in 1962 made a stage adaptation with the author of the novel by Iris Murdoch *A Severed Head.* He is also noted for his broadcasts, especially those in wartime, and for his excellent literary criticism, as in *Literature and Western Man* (1960). He m. in 1953 Jacquetta Hawkes (q.v.). Awarded OM 1977.

PRIESTLEY, Joseph (1733-1804). British chemist and Nonconformist divine. B. in Leeds, he became a Presbyterian (Unitarian) minister in 1755 and from 1767 was minister of a chapel in Leeds. About 1774 he discovered oxygen, and was elected FRS in 1766. In 1780 he removed to Birmingham, and in 1791 his chapel and house were sacked by the mob because of his support of the French Revolution. In 1794 he emigrated to America.

PRIEST'S HOLE. In Britain, in the time of the penal laws against Roman Catholic priests, a secret room or hiding-place for them. Many still exist in old houses, and a good example is that at Speke Hall.

PRIMARY (prīm'ari). In presidential election campaigns in the USA, the means by which a preliminary sorting out of the candidates who will be chosen by the major parties to undertake the main campaign is achieved. Held in some 35 states, they begin with New Hampshire in February and continue till June, and operate under varying complex rules. Generally speaking the number of votes received by a candidate governs the number of delegates who will vote for him at the National Conventions in July/August, when the final choice of candidate for both the Democratic and Republican parties is decided.

PRIMATE. The official title of metropolitans in the Christian Church. The archbishop of Canterbury is the P. of all England, and the archbishop of York the P. of England.

British Prime Ministers

Sir Robert Walpole (*Whig*)	1721
Earl of Wilmington (*Whig*)	1742
Henry Pelham (*Whig*)	1743
Duke of Newcastle (*Whig*)	1754
Duke of Devonshire (*Whig*)	1756
Duke of Newcastle (*Whig*)	1757
Earl of Bute (*Tory*)	1762
George Grenville (*Whig*)	1763
Marquess of Rockingham (*Whig*)	1765
Duke of Grafton (*Whig*)	1766
Lord North (*Tory*)	1770
Marquess of Rockingham (*Whig*)	1782
Earl of Shelburne (*Whig*)	1782
Duke of Portland (*Coal.*)	1783
William Pitt (*Tory*)	1783
Henry Addington (*Tory*)	1801
William Pitt (*Tory*)	1804
Lord Grenville (*Whig*)	1806
Duke of Portland (*Tory*)	1807
Spencer Perceval (*Tory*)	1809
Earl of Liverpool (*Tory*)	1812
George Canning (*Tory*)	1827
Viscount Goderich (*Tory*)	1827
Duke of Wellington (*Tory*)	1828
Earl Grey (*Whig*)	1830
Viscount Melbourne (*Whig*)	1834
Sir Robert Peel (*Con*)	1834
Viscount Melbourne (*Whig*)	1835
Sir Robert Peel (*Con.*)	1841
Lord J. Russell (*Lib.*)	1846
Earl of Derby (*Con.*)	1852
Lord Aberdeen (*Peelite*)	1852
Viscount Palmerston (*Lib.*)	1855
Earl of Derby (*Con.*)	1858
Viscount Palmerston (*Lib.*)	1859
Lord J. Russell (*Lib.*)	1865
Earl of Derby (*Con.*)	1866
B. Disraeli (*Con.*)	1868
W.E. Gladstone (*Lib.*)	1868
B. Disraeli (*Con.*)	1874
W.E. Gladstone (*Lib.*)	1880
Marquess of Salisbury (*Con.*)	1885
W.E. Gladstone (*Lib.*)	1886
Marquess of Salisbury (*Con.*)	1886
W.E. Gladstone (*Lib.*)	1892
Earl of Rosebery (*Lib.*)	1894
Marquess of Salisbury (*Con.*)	1895
A.J. Balfour (*Con.*)	1902
Sir H. Campbell-Bannerman (*Lib.*)	1905
H.H. Asquith (*Lib.*)	1908
H.H. Asquith (*Coal.*)	1915
D. Lloyd George (*Coal.*)	1916
A. Bonar Law (*Con.*)	1922
Stanley Baldwin (*Con.*)	1923
J.R. MacDonald (*Lab.*)	1924
Stanley Baldwin (*Con.*)	1924
J.R. MacDonald (*Lab.*)	1929
J.R. MacDonald (*Nat.*)	1931
Stanley Baldwin (*Nat.*)	1935
N. Chamberlain (*Nat.*)	1937
Winston Churchill (*Coal.*)	1940
Clement Attlee (*Lab.*)	1945
Sir W. Churchill (*Con.*)	1951
Sir Anthony Eden (*Con.*)	1955
Harold Macmillan (*Con.*)	1957
Sir Alec Douglas-Home (*Con.*)	1963
Harold Wilson (*Lab.*)	1964
Edward Heath (*Con.*)	1970
Harold Wilson (*Lab.*)	1974
James Callaghan (*Lab.*)	1976
Margaret Thatcher (*Con.*)	1979

PRIMATES. The highest order of mammals; it includes man, the apes, monkeys, tarsiers, and lemurs.

PRIME MINISTER or **Premier.** In Commonwealth countries, and other states with parliamentary constitutions, the head of the government. The first English PM is generally considered to have been Walpole (1721-42), but not until 1905 was the office officially recognized, PMs up to then holding some other office in addition, generally that of First Lord of the Treasury. In the UK the PM is usually the leader of the largest party in the House of Commons. Since 1902 PMs have invariably been commoners. The salary is £26,250, plus parl. salary £7,670. In certain Commonwealth countries, e.g. Australia, a distinction is drawn between the Fed. PM and the Premier of the individual states. *See* POLICY UNIT.

PRIMITIVISM. The influence on modern art (Kirchner, Modigliani, Picasso, etc.) of tribal Africa, Australasia, and South and Central America, and also of European or N American European-derived peasant cultures.

PRIMO DE RIVERA, Miguel (1870-1930). Spanish soldier and statesman. He was captain-general of Catalonia when in 1923, following the disaster of the Morocco campaign, he became in effect dictator of Spain with the support of Alfonso XIII. In 1925 he became premier, and effected some useful material reforms. He resigned in 1930.

PRIMROSE. Woodland plant (*Primula vulgaris*) common in Britain and Europe, bearing pale yellow flowers in spring. Related to it is the cowslip, and the oxlip may be a hybrid of the two.

PRINCE (Lat. *princeps*, 'first'). A royal or noble title. In Rome and medieval Italy it was used as the title of certain officials, e.g. *princeps senatus*, 'leader of the Senate'. The title was granted to the king's sons in 15th cent. France, and in England from Henry VII's time. The sovereign's eldest son is normally created P. of Wales, and the eldest dau. has often been created Princess Royal: the title is not held by 2 princesses at the same time.

PRINCE EDWARD ISLAND. Island prov. of Canada, in a bay of the Gulf of St Lawrence, separated from New Brunswick and Nova Scotia on the mainland by Northumberland Strait. It is mainly flat with a deeply indented coast. Dairying and fishing are the chief industries; silver-fox breeding is also important, and there are fish-canning factories and timber mills. Charlottetown is the cap. Discovered by Cabot in 1497, the prov. was claimed in 1603 by the French who called it Île Saint-Jean; taken by the British in 1758 and made a separate colony in 1769, it was re-named P.E.I. in 1798 in honour of Edward, fourth son of George III, at that time serving as lieut-general in Canada, duke of Kent 1799 and later father of Queen Victoria. P.E.I. entered the confederation in 1873. A road

PRIME MINISTER. Four prime ministers who faced major constitutional issues: W.E.Gladstone (top left), who devoted his last great speech in the Commons to the coming confrontation of Lords and Commons; J.R.MacDonald, first Labour PM, who in 1931 remained in office when most of his socialist colleagues resigned; Stanley Baldwin, whose handling of the Abdication crisis in 1937 was so controversial; and J.Malcolm Fraser, the Australian Liberal PM who took office in 1975 in the greatest constitutional crisis of the continent's history. *Photos: Courtesy of the National Portrait Gallery (Gladstone and MacDonald), Popperfoto, and the Australian Information Service*

and rail tunnel bridge and causeway is planned across Northumberland Strait to link P.E.I. with the New Brunswick coast. Area 5,657 sq.km (2,184 sq.m); pop. (1976) 118,229.

PRINCE IMPERIAL. *See* NAPOLEON III.

PRINCE RUPERT. Port at the mouth of the Skeena r., in Brit. Columbia, Canada, on Kaien Island, W side of Tsimpsean peninsula. A fishing centre with dry dock and cold-storage facilities. Pop. (1976) 14,754.

PRINCESS ROYAL. *See* PRINCE.

PRINCETON. Borough in New Jersey, USA, 80km (50m) SW of New York, the seat of Princeton univ. founded in 1746 at Elizabethtown, moved to Newark 1784, to P. 1756. Pop. 12,310.

PRINCETOWN. English village on the W of Dartmoor, Devon, containing Dartmoor prison, opened 1809.

PRINTED CIRCUIT. Electronic circuit produced by electrically depositing (or etching) a metallic network on an insulating board to link electronic components.

PRINTING. The reproduction of text or illustrative material on paper, as in books and newspapers, or on an increasing variety of materials, e.g. on tins and plastic containers.

In China the art of P. from a single wooden block was known in the 6th cent. AD, and moveable type was being used by the 11th century. In Europe P. was unknown for another 3 cents., and it was only in the 15th cent. that moveable type was re-invented, traditionally by Johannes Gutenberg (q.v.). It was William Caxton (q.v.) who introduced P. to England. There was no further substantial advance until in the 19th cent. steam power replaced hand operation of the presses, making possible long 'runs', and hand composition of type (each tiny metal letter being taken from the case and placed individually in the narrow stick which carried one line of text) was replaced by machines operated by a keyboard. The Linotype, used in newspapers (it produced a line of type in a solid slug) was invented by Ottmar Mergenthaler in 1886, and the Monotype, used in bookwork (it produced a series of individual characters, which could be hand corrected) by Tolbert Lanston in 1889.

Revolutionary as these inventions were, they represented no fundamental change, but simply a faster method of carrying out the same basic operations. The next revolution, which began in 1960, was the introduction of electronic photo-typesetting machines, which allowed the entire process of setting and correcting to be done in the same way that a copy-typist operates, thus eliminating the composing room, and leaving only the making of plates and the running of the presses to be done traditionally. By the 1970s the final steps were taken to plateless P., using various processes, such as a computer-controlled laser beam, or continuous jets of ink acoustically broken up into tiny equal-sized drops which are electrostatically charged under computer control.

PRIOR, James (1927-). British Conservative politician. He was Min. of Agriculture 1970-2, Lord Pres. of the Council 1972-4, as Employment Secretary 1979-81 curbed trade union activity with his Employment Act (1980), and became Northern Ireland Secretary 1981.

PRIOR, Matthew (1664-1721). British poet-diplomat. B. in E Dorset, he was associated under the Whigs with the negotiation of the treaty of Ryswick and under the Tories with that of Utrecht ('Matt's Peace'), but on the return of the Whigs to power was imprisoned by Walpole 1715-17. His greatest gift as a poet was for light occasional verses.

PRIPET (prē′pet). River of W Russia, a tributary of the Dnieper which it joins 80km (50m) above Kiev, Ukrainian SSR, after a course *c.* 800km (500m). The P. marshes near Pinsk were of strategic importance in both world wars.

PRISM. In mathematics, a solid figure (polyhedron) with two equal polygonal faces (bases) in parallel planes; the other faces being parallelograms, of the same number as there are sides to one of the bases. In optics triangular Ps. are widely used in a variety of intruments incl. spectroscopes, binoculars, periscopes, and rangefinders, their properties depending on the refractive index of the material of which they are made and the angles at which they are cut.

PRISON. Place of confinement for those contravening the laws of the state. Until the late 18th cent. criminals were commonly sentenced to death, mutilation or transportation rather than imprisonment, so that the growth of criminal Ps. as opposed to places of detention for those awaiting trial, confined for political reasons, etc., was a late development. One of the greatest reformers in Britain was John Howard (q.v.), whose P. Act of 1778 estab. the principle of separate confinement combined with work in an attempt at reform. Though long a dead letter, it was carried out when Pentonville was built in 1842. Penal servitude was introduced in 1857, as an additional deterrent, after the refusal of the colonies to accept transported convicts, but this and hard labour were finally abolished in Britain by the Criminal Justice Act of 1948, so that there is only one form of prison sentence, viz. imprisonment. Under the Criminal Justice Act of 1967 courts may suspend P. sentences of 2 years or less, and, unless the offender has previously been in prison or borstal (q.v.), will normally do so, i.e. sentence only comes into effect if another offence is committed. Persistent offenders may receive an extended sentence for the protection of the public. After serving one-third of their sentence (minimum 12 months), selected prisoners may be released on licence. In certain circumstances the facilities of adult Ps. may be used at the court's discretion for juveniles, but sentences of detention centre and Borstal training are usually imposed.

The Criminal Justice Act (1972) required the Courts to consider information about an offender before sentencing him to prison for the first time, and introduced the concept of community service (q.v.) to replace prison for non-violent offenders, and of day training centres for the social education under intensive supervision of the inadequate.

All enlightened countries aim at rehabilitation and in Russia, for example, great stress is laid on constructive work and the assimilation of the prisoner to a normal life, e.g. wives may be allowed to live with good-conduct men. Notable experiments have also been made in Britain and elsewhere in 'open Ps.' without bars, release of prisoners to work in ordinary jobs outside the P. in the final stages of their sentence, and after-care on release. *See* PROBATION.

PRISONERS OF WAR. By international convention P.o.W. are entitled to food on the same scale as the captor country's rear-line troops; supply of clothing and footwear; medical attendance; and the right to send and receive letters, and to receive food parcels and reading matter. P.o.W. who are seriously wounded or ill may be repatriated if a medical board, on which 2 doctors out of 3 are neutrals, certifies they are permanently incapacitated as fighting men. These rights are safeguarded by the International Red Cross Committee at Geneva, representatives of which inspect prison-camps.

PRITCHETT, Sir Victor Sawdon (1900-). British novelist, short-story writer and critic. His works incl. *You Make Your Own Life*, and *It May Never Happen*, collections of his short stories, and *The Living Novel* (1946) criticism. As a critic he is associated with the *New Statesman*. He was knighted in 1975.

PRIVACY. The right of the individual to be free from secret surveillance (by scientific devices, etc.), and the disclosure to unauthorised persons of personal data, as accumulated in computer data banks. Always an issue complicated by considerations of state security, public welfare (in the case of criminal activity), etc., it has been rendered more complex by modern technology.

In the USA a Privacy Act (1974) resulted from Watergate. The code required that there should be no secret databanks, and that agencies handling data must ensure their reliability and prevent misuse (i.e. information gained for one purpose must not be used for another). The public must also be able to find out what is recorded, how it is used, and be able to correct it.

In 1981 Britain was the only Western country without computerised data protection and legislation was under consideration, supported by civil liberties organisations, the computer industry and big business, since the OECD recommends that computerised information should flow freely only between countries protecting the privacy of the data by law.

PRIVATE ENTERPRISE. System whereby economic activities are in private hands and are carried on for private profit, as opposed to national, municipal, or co-operative ownership.

PRIVET. Genus of shrubs. The common P. (*Ligustrum vulgare*) has lanceolate leaves and small spikes of white flowers followed by black berries. Cultivated species are used for hedging.

PRIVY COUNCIL. A body of royal advisers. It originated in England in Norman times as the council of the chief royal officials, and under the Tudors and early Stuarts became the chief governing body. After 1688 it was replaced by the cabinet, which originated as a committee of the P.C. Its powers are now formal, e.g. royal proclamations and orders-in-council, and membership is an honour granted automatically to Cabinet Ministers - who for the most part comprise the acting council - and to others who have held high political, ecclesiastical or judicial offices in Britain and the Commonwealth. It is presided over by the Lord President of the Council. The function of the *Judicial Committee of the P.C.* as a final court of appeal for members of the Commonwealth is almost completely obsolete.

PRIVY PURSE. The personal expenditure of the British sovereign, and also the office dealing with such expenses. The Civil List (q.v.) now finances only expenses incurred in pursuance of official functions and duties, and personal expenditure derives from the sovereign's own resources.

PRIVY SEAL, Lord. An English officer of state, through whose hands all letters-patent had to pass before the great seal was affixed. The title is now an honorary one, borne by a member of the cabinet entrusted with special non-departmental duties.

PROBABILITY. *See* CHANCE.

PROBATE. Formal proof of a will. If its validity is unquestioned, it is proved in 'common form'; the Executor, in the absence of other interested parties, obtains at a P. Registry a grant upon his own oath. Otherwise, it must be proved in 'solemn form': its validity estab. at a P. Court (in the Family Division of the High Court) those prejudiced under it being made parties to the action. In the US the 'solemn form' is the more usual, although there may be no question as to validity, and P. is granted generally by courts of special jurisdiction.

PROBATION. A procedure adopted in lieu of prison sentence, in certain cases, e.g. first offenders, where the offender is placed under the supervision of a P. Officer appointed by the court, and undergoes certain restrictions. This method is used where it is believed that it will benefit the offender's future behaviour. In respect of juveniles P. is no longer used, 'supervision' orders being substituted.

PROCARYOTE (prō'kari-ōt). One of the 2 classes of living cell, that in which there is no definite nucleus, as in bacteria and blue-green algae. *See* EUCARYOTE.

PROCESSOR. Originally synonymous with 'computer', the term is now often limited to the arithmetic and control units of a computer. *See* MICROCOMPUTER.

PROCONSUL. *See* ANTARCTICA and LEAKEY.

PROCRU'STĒS ('the stretcher'). In Greek legend, a robber who tied his victims to a bed, and if they were longer than the bed, cut off their limbs, and if they were shorter, stretched them.

PROCURATOR-FISCAL. An officer attached to the sheriff's court in Scotland charged with the preliminary questioning of witnesses regarding crimes, and also inquiring into the circumstances of suspicious deaths.

PROFIT-SHARING. A system whereby an employer pays his workers a fixed share of his profits. It originated in France in the early 19th cent., and under the influence of the Christian Socialists was widely practised for a time within the co-operative movement.

PROGRESSION. A series of numbers each formed by a specific relationship to its predecessor. An *arithmetical* P. has numbers which increase or decrease by a common sum or difference, e.g. 2, 4, 6, 8 . . . A *geometric* P. has numbers each bearing a fixed ratio to its predecessor, e.g. 3, 6, 12, 24 . . . A *harmonic* P. is a series with numbers whose reciprocals are in arithmetical P., e.g. 1, $\frac{1}{2}$, $\frac{1}{3}$, $\frac{1}{4}$ . . .

PROHIBITION. Laws making illegal the sale of intoxicating liquor, which originated in the USA. Legislation was passed in Maine in 1846, and throughout many states thereafter, but later became a dead letter. Revival of the campaign at the end of the cent. led to a sustained agitation for legislation, which was nourished by the F.W.W. and need for cereals. In 1920 a P. amendment (known as the Volstead Act, after Congressman V. who introduced it) to the US constitution became operative. Apart from loss of revenue, it led to bootlegging, the illicit distilling of usually bad quality liquor for illegal distribution, and gangsters such as Al Capone made fortunes. Public opinion insisted on repeal of the act in 1933. In literature it prompted novels such as Fitzgerald's *The Great Gatsby* and Hemingway's *To Have and Have Not.* On religious grounds, P. is practised with varying degrees of severity in Moslem countries, and in 1975 measures were taken to facilitate the eventual introduction of total P. throughout India.

PROKO'FIEV, Serge (1891-1953). Russian composer. B. nr Ekaterinoslav, he studied at St Petersburg under Rimsky-Korsakov and achieved fame as a pianist. For some time he lived in London, in the USA, and in Paris, but returned to Moscow in 1934. He composed operas such as *The Love of Three Oranges*; ballets for Diaghileff; symphonies incl. the *Classical Symphony*; the *Scythian Suite*; music for films; piano concertos, of which the 3rd is best known; violin concertos; songs and cantatas, e.g. that for the 29th anniv. of the Oct. Revolution; *Peter and the Wolf*, a fairy tale, etc.

PROLETARIAT. Those classes which possess no property, and therefore depend upon the sale of their labour-power, as opposed to the capitalists or bourgeoisie, who own the means of production, and the petty bourgeoisie, or working small property-owners. They are usually divided into the industrial, the agricultural and the intellectual P. The term is derived from the Lat. *proletarii*, the class possessing no property, who served the state by producing offspring (*proles*).

PROMENADE CONCERTS ('Proms'). Originally, concerts during the performance of which audiences are allowed to walk about. The London P.Cs. (since 1895) are the premier musical activity of England. They were given in the Queen's Hall until it was destroyed by enemy action in 1941, and then in the Royal Albert Hall, and were conducted by Sir Henry Wood until his death. They have fostered the 20th cent. renaissance of music appreciation in England.

PROMETHEUS (promē'thūs). Greek hero, who stole fire from heaven to give to men, and taught them the useful arts. Zeus to punish him chained him to a rock in the Caucasus, where an eagle preyed on his liver, until he was rescued by Hercules.

PROMETHIUM. Element of the rare earth group, of which the existence in nature is unconfirmed: symbol Pm, at. no. 61, at. wt. uncertain (probably 147). Several isotopes, obtained by fission of uranium and by neutron bombardment of neodymium, have been reported by different groups of workers.

PROMISSORY NOTE. A written promise to pay on demand or at a fixed future time a specific sum of money to a named person or bearer. Like a cheque, it may be negotiated by endorsement by the payee.

PRONGBUCK or **pronghorn.** Only surviving member of a family (Antilocapridae) between deer and cattle. The P. (*Antilocapra americana*) is 1m (3ft) high, sheds its horns annually, and is a swift runner. It inhabits the N American plains.

PROPERTIUS (prōper'shius), **Sextus Aurelius** (fl. 30-15 BC). Roman poet. B. at Assisi, he settled in Rome, and became a member of the literary circle of Maecenas. The majority of his poems deal with his love for his mistress 'Cynthia'.

PROPHETS. Name given to the succession of Hebrew saints and seers who preached and prophesied in the Hebrew kingdoms in Palestine from the 8th cent BC until the suppression of Jewish independence in 586 BC and possibly later. The chief were Elijah, Amos, Hosea, and Isaiah. The prophetic books of the OT constitute a division of the Hebrew Bible.

PROPORTIONAL REPRESENTATION. An electoral system designed to ensure that minority votes are not lost, and that the distribution of seats corresponds to that of votes. It should not be confused with a system such as the single transferable vote (STV) as used in Australia (*see* VOTE).

True P.R. requires that constituencies should each return 3 or more members, and has 2 main forms: (a) the party list (common on the Continent), of which a modification similar to that adopted in W Germany was recommended for the UK by the Hansard Soc. in 1976. This is the additional member system (AMS) under which three-quarters of the members would be elected as at present in single-member constituencies, and the remaining seats would be allocated according to the overall number of votes cast for each party. (b) the single transferable vote (STV) system, as used in the Rep. of Ireland, under which candidates are numbered by the elector according to his preference, and surplus votes (over the quota required by a candidate to win) are then transferred to second preferences, as are second preference votes from the successive candidates at the bottom of the poll until the required number of candidates has been achieved.

PROPYL ALCOHOL (C_3H_7OH). Two compounds, normal P.A., and isopropyl A. The former is also known as ethyl carbinol. It is a colourless liquid, hygroscopic, has density 0.8, and is miscible with water. P.A. is used in perfumery preparations.

PROSE. The expression of thought in written language without attempt at metrical form. English P. first appeared in the 8th cent., reached a simple perfection under Alfred in the 9th, suffered eclipse following the Conquest, revived by the 14th cent., and attained flexibility and precision with Dryden.

PROSE. John Dryden, the creator of modern English prose style, painted by Kneller in 1693. *Photo: Courtesy of the National Portrait Gallery*

PROSTAGLANDIN (prostaglan'din). Any of a group of acidic lipids formed in all tissues of the body, but espec. in seminal fluid, and which act as messengers between and within cells, although some, e.g. prostacyclin, may act as circulating hormones. They occur in excess in arthritis, play an important role in the perception of pain and production of inflammation, and a deficiency of Ps. seems to occur in cases of schizophrenia.

PROSTITUTION. The provision of sexual gratification by a person in return for payment. P., both male and female, has probably existed in all human societies, although attitudes towards it have varied widely. In some countries (such as Holland and W Germany) P. is officially recognized by the licensing of brothels and the registration of prostitutes, particularly as a means of combating venereal diseases by enforced regular medical examination. In Britain, since 1959, it is not an offence to be or to become a prostitute, but fines (with possible imprisonment for repeated offences) are imposed for soliciting in a public place; there are also fines for procuring a person not a prostitute for the purpose of P., and for anyone living on the earnings of a prostitute, and for keeping a brothel.

PROTACTINIUM (Gk *protos* first). The first element of the actinium series of radioactive elements, symbol Pa, at. no. 91, at. wt. 231: found in nature in all uranium ores, and discovered by Soddy and Cranston (independently by Hahn and Meitner) in 1917. It forms actinium by the loss of an alpha-particle.

PROTECTION. The discouragement by heavy duties of the import of foreign goods likely to compete with home products. The opposite practice is Free Trade (q.v.).

PROTECTORATE. In international law, the relationship between a large state and a small or backward one, over which the former exercises a direct or indirect control. In English history, the term the P. is applied to the rule of Oliver and Richard Cromwell 1653-9.

PROTEINS (prō'tē-inz). Organic substances containing carbon, hydrogen, oxygen, and nitrogen. They constitute an important part of living cells, and are essential in animal diet. The most common examples are egg-albumin, casein in milk, haemoglobin in blood, and ossein in bone. Single-cell protein is obtained by drying micro-organisms (algae, bacteria, fungi or yeasts) grown on waste substances, e.g. animal waste, waste paper and mill liquor, and sewage sludge; and also on petroleum and liquefied natural gas. It is used to supplement animal feeds and is potentially for direct use as human food.

PROTESTANTISM. One of the main divisions of Christianity, the others being Roman Catholicism and the Eastern Orthodox Church. Its name is usually derived from the protest made by Luther and his supporters at the Diet of Spires in 1529 against the decision to reaffirm the Edict of the Diet of Worms against the Reformation. The Protestant Churches incl. the Church of England and the Nonconformist or Free Churches in Britain, the Lutheran and Reformed (Calvinist) Churches on the Continent and the great majority of Christians other than Roman Catholics in the Commonwealth, USA, etc.

PROTEUS (prō'tūs). In Gk mythology an old man, the warden of the sea beasts of Poseidon, who possessed the gift of prophecy, but could transform himself to any form he chose to evade questioning. Also the eel-like, white, eyeless amphibian (*P. anguinus*) found in the caves of Dalmatia, which has 4 rudimentary legs and external gills; on exposure to light it develops dark pigmentation and becomes fully eyed.

PROTOCOLS OF ZION. An anti-Semitic falsification, purporting to be the notes of a plan for the Jewish world conquest submitted by Herzl in 1897 to the 1st Zionist Congress at Basle, and first pub. in Russia in 1905. In 1921 the London *Times* conclusively proved that the Ps. are a plagiarism of an attack on Napoleon III, pub. in Geneva in 1864.

PROTOPLASM. Greyish, translucent, jelly-like material within and incl. the plasma membrane of a cell, the basis of all living things. Always containing carbon, oxygen, hydrogen, nitrogen and a large proportion of water, it may also comprise sulphur, iron, phosphorus, calcium and iodine, as well as such complex chemical compounds as proteins and fats in colloidal form. Chemical interactions constantly take place in all living matter, and P. is capable of repeatedly reproducing itself.

PRŌTOZŌ'A. Group of unicellular animals. Each cell is capable of individual existence, but many types live in colonies. The body is composed of protoplasm, and in the Foraminifera and Radiolaria a skeleton of calcium carbonate or silica is deposited.

PROUDHON (proodoṅ'), **Pierre Joseph** (1809-65). French anarchist. B. at Besançon, he sat in the Constituent Assembly of 1848, was imprisoned for 3 years, and had to go into exile in Brussels. His ideas, which envisaged a highly decentralized society of small property owners, greatly influenced French Socialist thought. He pub. *What is Property?* (1840) and *Philosophy of Poverty.*

PROUST (proost), **Marcel** (1871-1922). French author. B. at Auteuil, son of a wealthy doctor, he was a martyr to asthma from the age of 9. Mixing in society, he gained a reputation as a dilettante, but following the deaths of his father and mother (in 1904 and 1905 respectively) he retired to devote himself to his mammoth autobiographical study, reflecting also the life of his time, which appeared as *A la recherche du temps perdu* (1913-27: *Remembrance of Things Past*). A cork-lined workroom for absolute isolation from the world and various other eccentricities, besides his homosexuality, have made him as much written about as writer. A fragmentary early novel *Jean Santeuil* (written 1899) was pub. in reconstructed form in 1951.

PROVENÇAL. A Romance langugage, also known as *langue d'oc*, in use in S France from the early Middle Ages until the 16th cent., when it was replaced by French, although individual dialects survived. P. resembles the Catalan dialect of Spanish, and is closer than French to the original Latin forms.

P. literature originated in the 10th cent., and flowered in the 12th cent. with the work of the troubadours (q.v.), e.g. Bernart de Ventadorn, Arnaut Daniel, Giraud de Borneil, Raimbaut d'Orange, and Bertran de Born. The Albigensian War in the 13th cent. destroyed the troubadours, and P. disappears as a literary medium from the 14th until the 19th cent. when Jacques Jasmin (1798-1864) and others paved the way for the Félibrige group of poets, of whom the greatest are Joseph Roumanille (1818-91), Frédéric Mistral (1830-1914), and Félix Gras (1844-1901).

PROVENCE (prōvoṅs'). Ancient prov. of France, on the Mediterranean. Already a Roman *provincia* (hence its name), it varied in size through its history and for a short time *c.* AD 900 was a kingdom. Later it was a county held by Alphonso, king of Aragon, Charles of Anjou, king of Naples, and others. The last count bequeathed it in 1482 to Louis XI of France, and his son Charles VIII secured control of it. Today, as the region Provence-Côte d'Azur, it comprises the depts of Alpes-de-Haute-Provence, Hautes-Alpes, Alpes-Maritimes, Bouches-du-Rhône, Var and Vaucluse. It still has its own tongue.

PROVERB. A short familiar expression of a well-estab. ethical or practical truth. The most notable collection of Ps. is in the OT book of that name, which forms part of the Wisdom Literature of the ancient Hebrews. Solomon is said (on slender grounds) to have been the author of some of them.

PROVIDENCE. Cap., port and trade centre of Rhode Is., USA, on Providence r., 43km (27m) from the Atlantic. Jewellery, silverware, textiles and textile machinery, watches, chemicals, etc., are manufactured, and meat packing is carried on. P. was settled by Roger Williams in 1636. The first Baptist chapel in the American colonies was built in 1638 at P., which is the seat of Brown Univ. (1764). Pop. met. area P.-Pawtucket-Warwick (1970) 900,569.

PROVINCE WELLESLEY. *See* PENANG.

PROXY. A person legally authorized to stand in another's place; also the instrument of conferment thereof. The term usually refers to voting at meetings, but there may be marriages by P.

PRU'DHOE BAY. Site on the coast of N Alaska where oil was struck beneath the frozen tundra in 1968. The Arctic Wildlife Range to the E. has the only large herd of N. American caribou. *See* NORTH-WEST PASSAGE.

PRUNUS. Genus of trees in the family Rosaceae. The white or pink flowers are followed by drupes, often edible. Plums, peaches, apricots, almonds, and cherries all belong to this genus.

PRUSSIA. Former state of Germany, bordering the Baltic, and formed out of a union in 1618 of the Mark of Brandenburg and the Prussian state of the Teutonic Order. The Mark of Brandenburg originated in the 12th cent. under the Ascanians, who were followed by the Wittelsbachs, and in 1415 by the Hohenzollerns. John Sigmund (1608-19) m. Anna, dau. of Albert Frederick, duke of Prussia and last grandmaster of the Teutonic Order, and so united the territories. Frederick William (1640-88), known as the Great Elector, laid the foundations of P.'s military power. Frederick III (1688-1713) assumed the title of King Frederick I of Prussia in 1701. Frederick William I (1713-40) concentrated his energies on the development of P.'s military might and commerce. During the reign of his son Frederick the Great (1740-86) Silesia, E Frisia, and W Prussia were annexed. The reign of Frederick William III (1797-1840) was marked by the disaster of Jena (1806); his possessions were reduced, but after the Congress of Vienna (1815) P. regained its lost territories and also acquired lands in the Rhineland and Saxony. The year 1848 was marked by revolutionary outbreaks. In 1864 war with Denmark resulted in the acquisition of Schleswig and Holstein, while after the defeat of Austria in 1866 Hanover, Nassau, Frankfurt-am-Main, and Hesse-Cassel were annexed to P. which became the head of the N German Confederation. In 1871 William I of P. became emperor of all Germany. In 1918 P. became a rep. and a democratic constitution was adopted in 1920. In 1932 the Prussian govt was removed from office by the Reich govt of von Papen, and after 1933 P. lost its local independence. The Allies abolished the state of P. in 1946.

PRUSSIC ACID. *See* HYDROCYANIC ACID.

PRYNNE, William (1600-69). English puritan. He pub. in 1632 *Histriomastix*, a work attacking stage-plays, and containing aspersions on the queen for which he was pilloried and lost his ears. In 1637 he was again pilloried and branded for an attack on the bishops. He opposed the execution of Charles I, and actively supported the Restoration.

PRZEMYSL (pzhem'isl). Town in SE Poland, 96km (60m) W of Lvov, on the San. Traditionally founded in the 8th cent., it belonged alternately to Poland and Kiev in the 10-14th cents. Austrian 1722-1919, it was a frontier fortress besieged by the Russians, except for a brief respite, from Sept. 1914 to March 1915. It was in German occupation June 1941 to July 1944. Industries incl. timber, ceramics, flour milling, tanning, distilling and food canning. Pop. (1975) 55,000.

PSALMS. Book of the OT consisting of 150 poems, the majority of which are songs of praise and were intended to be sung to a musical accompaniment. The Psalter was probably completed in its present form in the 1st cent. BC, and is divided in 5 books, containing Ps. 1-41, 42-72, 73-89, 90-106, and 107-150. The authorship of many of the Ps. is ascribed to David, but no absolute evidence for this exists.

PSI (psī). Twenty-third letter of the Gk alphabet, but used as a term in parapsychology to denote a hypothetical faculty common to man and other animals responsible for such phenomena as extra-sensory perception and telekinesis; and also in atomic physics (*See* ATOM).

PSILOCYBIN (silosī'bin). Hallucinogen derived from the mushroom *Psilocybe semilanceata* or liberty cap (from a supposed resemblance to the caps worn during the French Revolution); its effects are similar to those obtained from Mexican species, and to those of LSD. Less potent than the latter, it is sometimes used in treating mental disorder.

PSKOV. Town in the RSFSR, USSR, on the Velikaya, 15km (9m) SE of Lake P. and 260km (160m) SSW of Leningrad, famous for leather and a trade centre for hemp, flax and timber. It dates from AD 965 and was independent 1348-1510, when it became Russian. In the S.W.W. it was in German hands 1941-4. Pop. (1978) 160,000.

PSORIASIS (sorī'asis). An inflammation of the skin marked by raised red patches, usually on the arms and legs, covered with whitish scales. The first attack usually takes place in childhood and attacks recur at irregular intervals. Treatment with long wave ultraviolet light is helpful.

PSYCHE (sī'kē). The personification of the soul in later Gk literature and art, generally represented as a winged girl. The love story of Cupid and P. is told in Apuleius's 'Golden Ass'.

PSYCHIATRY. *See* PSYCHOLOGY.

PSYCHIC RESEARCH. The investigation of phenomena inexplicable by recognized scientific laws. Formerly this was limited to phenomena produced at séances - levitation, ectoplasm, telepathy and supernormal cognition in trance and clairvoyant mediums, activities of apparitions and poltergeists - and useful work was done by the British Society for Psychical Research (1882). Between the wars, however, the study of extra-sensory perception in particular emerged from the séance room to the science laboratory and famous centres are the Parapsychology Laboratory of Duke Univ., N Carolina (*see* RHINE, J. B.) and the Psychophysical Research Unit at Oxford.

PSYCHOANALYSIS (sīkō-anal'isis). Technique originated by Freud for the treatment of his patients which involves free association of thoughts in the waking state, and analysis of the contents of dreams, as a means of revealing the unconscious - ideas and emotions existing beneath the realm of consciousness. It is assumed that the patient's mental illness is caused by one or more repressed childhood experiences, and that he can be cured if these are brought to light, and he is helped by the analyst to deal with them rationally.

PSYCHOLOGY (sīkol'oji). The study of all forms of behaviour in animate beings, incl. the role of instinct and heredity, environment and culture; the operation of sensation and perception, learning and memory; the bases of motivation and emotion; and the functioning of thought, intelligence and language. Abnormal types of behaviour, diagnosed and treated by **psychiatry** and **psychotherapy**, incl. addiction to alcohol and drugs, anxiety, autism (a state of withdrawal, espec. in children, for which shock treatment has been used with some success), depression, neuroses, obsessions (from rituals such as hand-washing to the executive who cannot stop working), psychopathy (q.v.), schizophrenia (q.v.), and sexual deviations and inadequacies.

PSYCHOLOGY. The duality of human nature was recognised long before Freud. This crowned hermaphrodite figure in a 16th century manuscript devoted to alchemy symbolises the 'inner duality' of a female element ('anima ') in the male unconscious. *Photo: Courtesy of Leiden University Library*

The foundation of P. as a science is generally attributed to Wilhelm Wundt (1832-1920), who estab. the first experimental institute; other pioneers incl. Gustav Fechner (q.v.), founder of psychophysics, and the group of *gestalt* 'whole' psychologists concerned with the organizational law governing our perception of objects, e.g. Wolfgang Köhler (1887-1967). Most famous of all is Sigmund Freud, and the group linked with him, incl. Jung, Adler and Rorschach (qq.v.). The treatment devised by Freud (*see* PSYCHOANALYSIS) is too time-consumingly expensive for wide use, and Kurt Lewin (1890-1947) developed 'group therapy' in which patients in effect treat each other, e.g. Alcoholics Anonymous works on these lines by mutual understanding and support among sufferers. Other forms of treatment incl. corrective conditioning (deriving from the work of Pavlov, and J. B. Watson and the Behaviourist school, qq.v.), drugs such as tranquillizers and anti-confusional agents, electric shock treatment for depression, psychosurgery (q.v.), modification of home and family background (*see* LAING, R. D), and - for the future - genetic engineering to correct inherited mental defect. *See also* PSYCHOSOMATIC MEDICINE.

Much light on instinct and heredity has been thrown by such specialists in animal behaviour as Konrad Lorenz and Niko Tinbergen (qq.v.), and controversy continually

PSYCHOLOGY. Sigmund Freud, the founder of modern psychological studies, whose theories have passed into the vocabulary of popular speech. *Photo: Courtesy of Ernst Freud*

rages concerning the comparative importance of heredity and environment, espec. in such questions as the possible link between race and intelligence (*see* EYSENCK, H. J.). Useful early studies of memory were made by Hermann Ebbinghaus (1850-1909) with the aid of nonsense material, and later work incl. that of Roger Brown and David McNeil in the late 1960s on the familiar 'tip-of-the-tongue' failure to achieve recall. The growth of human intelligence has been explored by Piaget (q.v.), and it is possible to look forward to the use of artificial 'intelligences' in the future (*see* CYBERNETICS): *see also* INTELLIGENCE, MENTAL TESTS. Even creativity has not escaped analysis, as in the 'lateral thinking' concept of Edward de Bono The basic problems of language have been illuminated by experiments such as that of Beatrice and Allan Gardner at the Univ. of Nevada in 1966 with the chimpanzee Washoe, whose physical inability to produce human sounds was overcome by substitution of the sign language of the deaf, and the more sophisticated level has been tackled by Noam Chomsky (q.v.). Emotion and motivation were among aspects of P. covered by the classic writers Charles Darwin and William James (qq.v.), and modern studies have been infinitely varied, e.g. the psychological causes of obesity, and the under-achievement of women seen as the result of social pressures, previously inescapable physical conditions, and so on. There have also been fascinating explorations of sleep and dreams, of unusual extensions of the senses, e.g. echo-location, which humans practise crudely, and bats and dolphins at a superbly high level, and extrasensory perception in the wider sense, which remains controversial (*see* PARAPSYCHOLOGY).

The greatest expansion of the subject, however, has been in social psychology, from the work of Durkheim (q.v.), who recognized the importance of group affiliations to the adjustment of the individual, to that of Margaret Mead (q.v.) on the differences of human behaviour in differing cultures; of Gordon W. Allport (1896-1967) on the nature of prejudice; and of Kinsey (q.v.) on sex. The techniques of P. are also being applied to internat. issues, e.g. the analysis by Stanley Milgram at Yale in the 1960s of the nature of obedience as it underlies totalitarian regimes such as Nazism (many subjects were willing to inflict torture on fellow subjects in experiments at bidding of an instructor), or the Irving Janis concept of 'group-think' which shows how pressure for consensus suppresses useful dissent and promotes disastrous decision-making, as with Kennedy and his circle of advisers in the invasion of Cuba. *See also* CATASTROPHE THEORY.

PSYCHOPATHY (sīkop'athi). Mental illness. The psychopath has no sense of social responsibility, and no sense of guilt or shame for what he does in a ruthless achievement of his ends.

PSYCHOSOMATIC (sīkōsōmat'ik) **MEDICINE.** The study of the interaction between mind and body. It covers illness caused by psychological factors, e.g. emotional stress which may result in skin disease, etc., and the cure of illness by the administration of a placebo (plasē'bō), from Lat. 'I will please', a dummy pill with no medical ingredient given to pacify a patient or to a 'control' patient in medical experiments.

PSYCHOSURGERY. Surgical operation on the brain intended to change the subject's personality by the relief of anxiety and so on, e.g. leucotomy (separation of the white fibres in the prefrontal lobe of the brain), which is also known, espec. in the US, as lobotomy. There is wide medical difference of opinion as to its justification, since results are not predictable and are irreversible.

PTAH (tah). Ancient Egyptian god, one of the Memphis triad; he was the divine potter or artificer, the personification of creative force.

PTARMIGAN (tar'migan). The smallest grouse (*Lagopus mutus*) found in Britain. It also inhabits the Arctic, and its colour changes with its surroundings.

PTERIA. Classical name for BOGHAZKOI.

PTERODACTYL (terōdak'til). Extinct creature of the order Pterosauria, existing in the Mesozoic age. It was formerly assumed to have been a type of smooth-skinned flying lizard of up to 6m (20ft) wingspan, but more recent discoveries have shown the P. to be a highly intelligent, furry creature, with a gliding flight on wings which might have a span of up to 17m (50ft), and that it may have been warm-blooded.

PTOLEMY (tol'emi). Name of a dynasty of Macedonian kings who ruled Egypt. Ptolemy I, one of Alexander's generals, seized Egypt in 323 BC, and was succeeded by 12 kings of the same name. Ptolemy XIII was put to death in 47 BC by his sister Cleopatra, with whose death in 30 BC the dynasty ended.

PTOLEMY or **Claudius Ptolemaeus** (2nd cent. AD). Astronomer and geographer. A native of Egypt, he carried out observations in Alexandria, and pub. a *Geography*, which was a standard source of information until the 16th cent. The *Ptolemaic system*, which was not superseded by

PTERODACTYL. An artist's reconstruction showing both the bird and bat-like propensities of this extinct creature. *Photo: Courtesy of the Natural History Museum.*

the Copernican until 1543, assumed that the earth was the fixed centre of the universe, with the Sun, Moon, and stars revolving round it.

PTOMAINE (tō'mā-īn). A class of chemical substances produced by putrefaction. Ps. do not really play a part in food poisoning. 'P. poisoning' is, in fact, usually caused by bacteria of the *Salmonella* group.

PUBERTY (pū'-). The stage of human development in which the secondary sexual characteristics begin to appear and the individual becomes capable of reproduction. In boys it occurs at about 14; in girls usually a little earlier. Better nutrition in W Europe, the USA, etc., has tended to make P. occur at an ever-earlier age.

PUBES. The lowest part of the front of the trunk, the region where the external generative organs are situated. The underlying bony structure, the pubic arch, is formed by the union in the mid line of the two pubic bones, which are the front portions of the hip bones. In women it is more prominent than in men, to allow more room for the passage of a child's head at birth, and carries a pad of fat and connective tissue, the *mons veneris* (mountain of Venus), for its protection.

PUBLIC HOUSE. In England a house licensed for the consumption of intoxicating liquor, which may be either a 'free' or 'tied' house, according to whether supplies are bought from a particular co. owning the P.H. or whether the landlord has a free choice of suppliers.

PUBLIC SCHOOLS. Term used in a specialized sense in Britain to denote the independent schools which developed principally during the 18th and early 19th cents., although some, such as Eton and Harrow, are ancient foundations originally intended for poor scholars. P.S. are predominantly boarding schools for boys of 12–18 years, which are divided into houses, each in the care of a housemaster. Much of the discipline is entrusted to senior boys or prefects, though this system and the former stress on classical subjects, sports and games, have been much modified in recent years. The heads are members of the Headmasters' conference. Since 1965 the Labour Party has been committed to their integration into the state system.

PUBLIC SECTOR. *See* NATIONAL ACCOUNTS.

PUBLISHING. The production of books for sale. The publisher arranges for the printing, binding and distribution, to booksellers or through direct mail - the latter being a growing field - but may also share in the creative aspect of book production by commissioning books, by editing otherwise unpublishable work, e.g. Thomas Wolfe, but exercise of this function is controversial, etc. Although all rights in a book may be purchased by the publisher for a single outright fee, it is more usual and generally more fair to publisher and author if a fixed 'royalty' is paid on every copy sold, in return for the exclusive right to pub. in an agreed territory. Rising costs in book production have tended to discourage worthwhile books with a relatively small sale in favour of the best-seller, most markedly in the USA; other features of modern P. are the growth of non-fiction titles, and the great increase of paper-backs. In Britain most leading publishers are members of the Publishers' Association.

PUCCINI, Giacomo (1858–1924). Italian composer. B. at Lucca, he achieved success with the opera *Manon Lescaut* (1893), which was followed by *La Bohème, Madame Butterfly, Tosca,* and the unfinished *Turandot.*

PUDOVKIN, Vsevolod Illationovich (1893–1953). Soviet film director. His films incl. *Mother, Storm Over Asia,* and *Suvorov.* One of the fathers of Soviet cinema, he wrote *Film Technique* and *Film Acting.*

PUEBLA (pūe'vlah). City in Mexico, SE of Mexico City, on the Pan-American Highway. There are pre-Columbian remains nearby. The modern city was founded *c.* 1535 as P. de los Angeles, but was re-named P. de Zaragoza in honour of Gen. Zaragoza who defeated the French here in 1862. There is a univ. (1537) and a 16–17th cent. cathedral. Industries incl. textiles, sugar refining, metallurgy, and beautiful hand-crafted pottery and tiles. It is a market for livestock, fruit and vegetables. Pop. (1977) 516,200.

PUEBLO (pwā'blō). American Indian tribes of Arizona and New Mexico (Hopi, Zuñi, etc.) living in communal villages built of adobe or stone. This type of village is also found in areas of Latin America.

PUEBLO (poo-e'blō), **USS.** American intelligence vessel captured without resistance by the N Koreans Jan. 1968, allegedly within their territorial waters: the crew, but not the ship, were released Dec. 1968. A naval court recommended no disciplinary action.

PUERPERAL FEVER. Infection by pus-producing cocci, which enter raw surfaces of the womb and genital tract left by the passage of the child. The mortality used to be severe, but the sulpha drugs and penicillin have made mortality almost negligible.

PUERTO RICO (pūer'tō rē'kō). Is. commonwealth in assoc. with the USA, the easternmost of the Greater Antilles, West Indies: there are a number of nearby small islands. Mountainous, with a range running E-W across its almost quadrilateral surface, P.R. has a fertile coastal plain and valleys, though much land needs irrigation. Dairy and livestock farming are now more important than sugar, and coffee, pineapples and other fruit, vegetables and tobacco are grown. There are also important industries - textiles, plastics, chemicals, electric and electronic goods, cement, and food processing - and tourism earns much currency. The cap. is San Juan.

Discovered by Columbus in 1493, when it was known by the Arawak Indian name Boriquen, it was annexed by Spain in 1509, and ceded to the USA by a treaty of 1898. In 1952 it achieved commonwealth status, and confirmed this, in preference to independence, by referendum in 1967: the constitution is similar to that of the USA. Recent industrial and agricultural development has led many emigrant Puerto Ricans to return home, but they still form a substantial number of the Hispanic minority in the USA. The people are RC and Spanish-speaking, but English is also almost universal, and both are official languages.

Area 8,891 sq.km (3,435 sq.m); pop. (1977) 3,319,000.

PUFF ADDER. A venomous reptile (*Bitis arietans*) in the family Viperidae. Native to Africa and S Arabia, it is *c.* 1.6m (5ft) long, and yellowish-brown.

PUFFIN. Sea-bird (*Fratercula arctica*), of the auk family, found on the coasts of the northernmost countries of the Atlantic. About 32cm (13in) long, it has orange legs, black plumage above and white underparts. In the breeding season the large beak is increased in size, and coloured red, yellow, and blue. One dirty-white egg is laid in a burrow in the soil.

PUFFIN. Comically attractive in their clown-like breeding 'make-up', puffins were formerly commercially exploited. The young were taken from the nest and salted down for food. *Photo: E.K. Thompson/Aquila*

PUG DOG. Toy dog resembling a small bulldog. Sandy or silvery-fawn in colour, it was introduced into England, from China, by the Dutch East India Co. in the 16th cent.

PUGIN (pū'jin), **Augustus Welby Northmore** (1812-52). British architect. A convert to R Catholicism, he was a pioneer of the Gothic revival, assisting Barry (q.v.) with the Houses of Parliament.

PUGLIA Ital. form of APULIA.

PULA (po͞o'lah). City and port in Croatia, Yugoslavia, with both commercial and naval harbours. Already in Roman days a naval port, Colonia Pietas Julia, it was taken by the Venetians in 1148. It passed to Austria in 1815, to Italy in 1919, to Yugoslavia in 1947. It has a Roman theatre, a temple of Augustus (19 BC), and a castle and cathedral constructed under Venetian rule. Pop. (1971) 47,425.

PULITZER, Joseph (1847-1911). American newspaper proprietor. B. in Hungary, he in 1883 became proprietor of the *New York World.* In 1903 he estab. the school of journalism at Columbia Univ. which awards the annual P. prizes in journalism and letters.

PU'LSAR. Oscillating radio star sending out precisely regular radio pulses, although with wide variation in individual frequency, first discovered by Cambridge astronomers 1967. They are now recognised as neutron stars.

PULSE. The impulse transmitted by the heartbeat throughout the arterial system. When the heart muscle contracts it forces blood into the aorta; because the arteries are elastic, the sudden rise of pressure causes a throb or sudden swelling through them all. It can be felt at points where an artery is near the surface of the body, as in the wrist, and is a good indicator of the strength and rate of the heartbeat. The P. is distinct from the actual flow of the blood, which continues more or less uniformly at about 60 cc. a sec. The P. rate is generally about 70 per minute.

PŪ'MA. Carnivorous mammal (*Felis concolor*) of the cat family, found in America. Tawny in colour, the young have black spots and ringed tails. In S America it is known as the cougar or mountain lion.

PUMICE. A volcanic igneous rock. It is very porous and composed mostly of cavities, and has various commercial applications.

PUMPKIN. Genus of annual plants (*Cucurbita*) in the family Cucurbitaceae, probably native to the warmer regions of America and some of which are known in the USA as squashes, especially the more bushy kinds. The chief species are the common P. (*C. pepo*), of which the vegetable marrow is probably a variety, which has broad, lobed leaves on long trailing stems, and yellow flowers followed by an edible fruit weighing up to 45kg (100lb); the great gourd (*C. maxima*) which may have a fruit double this size; and the musk P. (*C. moschata*) with a musky smell and more elongated fruit: all are commercially important, and are also cultivated in warmer parts of Europe.

PUNCH. Alcoholic liquor compounded of spirits, fruit juice, sugar, spice, and hot water. P. originated in India.

PUNCH. Shortened form of the name Punchinello. The hero of the puppet play 'P. and Judy', in which he overcomes or outwits all opponents, P. has a hooked nose, hunched back, and a squeaky voice. The play is performed by means of glove puppets, manipulated by a single operator concealed in a portable canvas stage frame. P. originated in Italy, and was probably introduced to England at the Restoration.

PUNIC WARS (pū'-). The wars between Rome and Carthage. The first (264-241 BC) resulted in the cession of Sicily to Rome. During the second (218-201 BC) Hannibal invaded Italy, but was finally defeated at Zama. The third (149-146 BC) ended in the destruction of Carthage.

PUNJAB (punjahb′). Division of the Indian subcontinent in the NW. P., meaning 'five rivers', so called from the tributaries of the Indus (Jhelum, Chenab, Ravi, Beas, Sutlej) flowing through it. The chief crops are cotton, sugar, wheat, rice.

Punjab was annexed by Britain in 1849, after the Sikh Wars of 1845–6 and 1848–9, and formed into a prov. with its cap. at Lahore, area 256,000 sq.km (99,000 sq.m). After the partition of British India, West P. became the Pakistan prov. of Punjab, still with its cap. at Lahore. Area 133,400 sq.km (51,500 sq.m); pop. (1972) 37,374,000. East P. became part of the Indian state of Punjab.

PUNJAB. Indian state formed in 1956 from East P. and a number of princely states in the area, the largest of which was Bahawalpur. Violent agitation led in 1966 to the state being split on a linguistic basis into two new states, the Punjab-speaking Punjab: area 50,376 sq.km (19,450 sq.m); and the Hindi-speaking Haryana (q.v.); with certain hill areas being transferred to Himachal Pradesh. The two new states continued to share the cap. of Chandigarh, pending the construction of a new one for Haryana. Punjab is chiefly agricultural; manufactures incl. textiles, sewing machines, bicycles, etc. Pop. (1971) 13,510,000.

PUNTA ARENAS (poon'tah ahra'nahs). Chilean seaport, cap. of Magallanes prov., on Magellan Strait, most southerly town on the American mainland. It is the centre for an area producing coal, copper, gold, timber, wool, meat, and other animal products. The name (Spanish) means sandy point. Pop. (1972) 67,600.

PUPPET. Human, animal, or fantasy figure manipulated on a miniature stage by an unseen operator, although in Japan (*bunraku*) 4 operators, dressed in black to convey invisibility, may combine to manipulate one large puppet, sharing body, head, arms and legs among them. Ps. are of great antiquity (10th cent. BC in China) and of world-wide distribution. The main forms are the glove Ps. (*see* PUNCH), string marionettes (q.v.), and rod-operated Ps. which may be seen only as shadows on a screen - the shadow plays of Java being of this type.

PUPPET. A *bunraku* puppet play in which the black-clad operators disappear from the consciousness of the audience in their 'willing suspension of disbelief'. *Photo: Courtesy of the Sanwa Bank Ltd.*

PURANAS. Religious Sanskrit epics dealing with the mythology of the Hindus, and dating probably from the 8th cent. AD.

PURBECK, Isle of. A peninsula in Dorset, England, between the English Channel, and Poole Harbour to the N. It is *c.* 13km (8m) N to S, 19km (12m) E to W. P. marble and china clay are obtained from the 'isle', which incl. Corfe Castle and Swanage.

PURCELL, Henry (1659–95). English composer. B. at Westminster, he became a chorister at the Chapel Royal, and subsequently was a pupil of Dr John Blow. In 1677 he was appointed composer to the Chapel Royal, and in 1679 organist at Westminster Abbey. As composer to the king, P. set to music odes or anthems. *Dido and Aeneas* (1689) was a landmark in the history of opera. P. wrote music for Dryden's *King Arthur* (1691), and for *The Fairy Queen* (1693). The 'Trumpet Voluntary' often attributed to him is actually the work of Jeremiah Clarke.

PURCHAS, Samuel (*c.* 1575–1626). English compiler of travel books, rector of St Martin's, Ludgate, 1614–26. His collection *P. His Pilgrimage* (1613), was followed by another in 1619, and in 1625 by *Hakluytus Posthumus, or P. his Pilgrimes,* largely based on MSS left by Hakluyt.

PURDAH. *See* CHADOR.

PURGATIVES. Drugs which accelerate or make easier the emptying of the bowels. Laxatives (mild Ps.) incl. bran and agar (bulk laxatives), and liquid paraffin, or agar (lubricants). Saline Ps. incl. Epsom salts and sodium phosphate. Mild irritant Ps. are castor oil, cascara, aloes, rhubarb, and senna.

PURGATORY. Theological term for a state of place of purification of the souls after death. It is held by Roman Catholics, who also believe that its duration may be lessened by the prayers of the faithful.

PURI (poor'ē). Town in Orissa, India, on the Bay of Bengal. The shrine of Juggernaut (q.v.) is there, dating from *c.* AD 318; the annual festival attracts thousands of pilgrims. Pop. (est.) 50,000.

PURITANS. Term applied after 1564 to those members of the C of E who wished to eliminate Catholic survivals in its ritual, or who wished to substitute a presbyterian for the episcopal form of church govt. The term is used to cover also the Separatists, who withdrew from the Church altogether. Under James I and Charles I the Ps. came to be identified with the parliamentary opposition. After the Restoration they were driven out of the Church, and the term P. was replaced in general use by 'Dissenter' or 'Nonconformist'.

PURPLE HEART, Order of the. The earliest American military award for distinguished service beyond the call of duty, estab. by Washington in 1782, when it was the equivalent of the modern Congressional Medal of Honor. Of purple cloth bound at the edges, it was worn on the facings over the left breast. After the American Revolution it lapsed until revived by Pres. Hoover in 1932, when it was issued to those wounded in the F.W.W. and subsequently; the modern P.H. is of bronze and enamel.

Also slang parlance for a stimulant P.H.-shaped pill, formerly used by junior drug-addicts.

PURPURA (per'pūra). Spontaneous bleeding below the skin. The condition is like bruising, but the blood is localized in spots which may be as large as a coin. They occur in smallpox and kidney disease, but are also the main symptoms of certain recognized ailments.

PUS. Thick, yellowish fluid formed by the bodies of white blood cells killed in conflict with invading bacteria, and of superficial cells of granulation or mucous membrane which die and are shed off. P. is formed wherever infection exists, and an enclosed collection of P. is an abscess.

PUSA'N. The chief port of S Korea, nearest point to Japan on the Asiatic mainland, a railway and industrial centre (textiles, rubber, salt and, at nearby Pohang, iron and steel); fishing also is important. P. was invaded by the Japanese in 1592, opened to foreign trade in 1883. It was a UN supply port during the Korean War of 1950-2. Pop. (1975) 2,454,000.

PUSEY, Edward Bouverie (1800-82). British churchman. Ed. at Eton and Christ Church, Oxford, he was ordained in 1828 when he became Regius prof. of Hebrew at the univ., and in 1835 joined J. H. Newman (q.v.) in issuing the *Tracts for the Times.* After Newman's secession to Rome, P. became leader of the High Church Party or Puseyites, striving until his death to keep them from final conversion. His work is continued through P. House at Oxford, founded in his memory, which contains his library.

PUSHKIN (poosh'-), **Alexander Sergeievich** (1799-1837). Russian poet. B. at Moscow, he held administrative posts, was exiled several times for his liberal views, and d. of wounds he received in a duel. At first influenced by Byron, the study of Shakespeare later led him towards realism. The great national poet of Russia, P. was a supreme lyricist, and wrote verse novels such as *Robber Brothers, The Gypsies,* etc., and the great verse romance *Eugene Onegin* (1822-33); the novel *The Captain's Daughter* (1836), and the tragedy *Boris Godunov* (1825).

PUSHKIN. A portrait of the founder of modern Russian literature by Vasily Tropinin dated 1827. Pushkin is best-known in the West by the number of his works made into operas which include *The Queen of Spades* (Tchaikovsky), *The Golden Cockerel* (Rimsky-Korsakov) and *Russlan and Ludmilla* (Glinka). *Photo: Novosti*

PUSHKIN. Town in Leningrad region, RSFSR, south of Leningrad. P. was founded by Peter the Great as Tsarskoe Selo (tsar's village); it became the imperial summer residence under Elizabeth and Catherine the Great, and both Catherine and Alexander I (1792-6) built palaces there. In the 1920s the place was re-named Detskoe Selo (children's village), in 1937 Pushkin in honour of the poet. Paper, clothing, and chemicals are made. P. was held 1941-4 by the Germans who devastated it before retreating; it was subsequently restored. Pop. *c.* 60,000.

PUSHTU. The language of the Afghans, belonging to the E Iranian group.

PUTREFACTION (pū-). Decomposition of organic matter through the action of a large variety of micro-organisms. The P. in a human corpse will often give reliable information on the time and cause of death.

PUTTING THE SHOT. Ancient sport in which a round weight or 'shot' (7.2kg/16lb) is hurled from a circle (5.42m/7ft) boarded 10cm (4in) high.

PUVIS DE CHAVANNES (püvēs' de shahvahn'), **Pierre Cécile** (1824-98). French painter. B. at Lyons, he first exhibited in the Salon in 1850, and subsequently estab. a reputation as a decorative painter.

PUY-DE-DÔME (pü-ē'-de-dōm'). Extinct volcano in the Auvergne Mountains, central France, 1,465 m (4,806 ft) high. It lies 10km (6m) W of Clermont-Ferrand and on its slopes are ruins of a temple of Mercury. Pascal carried out experiments on air pressure in 1648 on the P.-de-D., which gives its name to a dept.

PU YI, Henry (1906-67). Emperor of China and Manchukuo. He succeeded to the Chinese throne in 1908 under the name Hsuan Tung, and was deposed in 1912, but restored for a week in 1917. In 1932 he became pres. of the Japanese puppet state of Manchukuo, assumed the title of emperor in 1934 and was captured by the Russians in 1945 and taken to Siberia. In 1949 he was handed over to Mao Tse-tung, was freed in 1959, and became in 1964 a deputy in the Chinese Parliament.

PVC. Abbreviation for polyvinyl chloride, a plastic made in various degrees of flexibility for use in drainpipes, floor tiling, records, shoes and handbags, etc.

PWLLHELI (po͝olhel'i). Seaside resort in Gwynedd, Wales, on Cardigan Bay. The Welsh Nat. Party, Plaid Cymru, was founded here in 1925. Pop. (1973) 4,000.

PYELITIS (pī-elī'tis). Inflammation of the pelvis of the kidney, a hollow chamber in which the urine is collected before discharge.

PYGMALION (pigmā'lion). In Greek legend, a king of Cyprus who fell in love with an ivory statue he had made. Aphrodite breathed life into the statue, which P. married.

PYGMY (pig'mi). A member of a race of diminutive humans. There are African and Asiatic Ps., Negrillos and Negritos respectively.

PYLOS. Greek name of NAVARINO.

PYM (pim), **Barbara** (1913-80). British novelist. B. in Shropshire, she wrote a sextet of novels 1950-61, incl. *Some Tame Gazelle* (1950), treating Civil Service life, etc., with comic irony. Fame came in 1977 when Philip Larkin and Lord David Cecil both chose her as the most underrated novelist of the century. Her later books were *The Sweet Dove Died* (1978) and *A Few Green Leaves* (1980).

PYM, Francis (1922–). British Cons. politician. Defence Secretary 1979–81, he succeeded Carrington as Foreign Min. 1983–4.

PYM, John (1584-1643). English statesman. B. in Som., he first entered parliament in 1614, and was largely responsible for the Petition of Right. As leader of the Puritan opposition in the Long Parliament, he moved the impeachment of Strafford and Laud, and drew up the Grand Remonstrance. He was the chief of the 5 members whom Charles I attempted to arrest in 1642. Shortly before his death he negotiated the alliance between parliament and the Scots.

PYONGYANG. Cap. and industrial city of N Korea, on the Taedong r., with coal mines nearby, and iron and steel, textile, and chemical industries. It has been entirely rebuilt since the Korean War. Pop. (1978) 1,500,000.

PYORRHOEA (pī-orē'a). Discharge of pus from tissues between the tooth substance and the gum.

PYRAMID. A massive building of pyramidal shape erected as a royal tomb to protect the body and thereby to preserve the spirit. Such Ps. are found only in Egypt and the most famous at Gizeh, nr Cairo, incl. the Great P. of Khufu (Gk Cheops), the P. of Khafra (Gk Chephren) and that of Menkaura (Gk Mycerinus). As ritual centres of worship, Ps. were erected by the Aztecs and Mayas, e.g. Chichen Itza (q.v.) and Cholula, 113km (70m) from Mexico City, where in 1967 the world's largest P. in ground area (300m/990ft base with a height of 60m/195ft) was discovered, in the midst of 4 smaller Ps. and many other buildings.

PYRAMID. The pyramids at Gizeh all belong to the 5th millennium BC. Earliest is the Great Pyramid, to the right, which is 230m (755 ft) square and 147m (481 ft) high; next is the pyramid of Khafra, still with part of the original casing at its apex, and — in the distance — the much smaller pyramid of Menkaura. *Photo: Barnaby's Picture Library.*

PYRAMIDS. A game played on a billiard table, in which 15 coloured balls are arranged pyramidally, the apex-ball resting on the 'pyramid-spot'. The object of the game is to pocket more balls than one's opponent.

PY'RAMUS AND THI'SBE. Babylonian lovers whose story is told by Ovid. T. lost her veil when pursued by a lion, which tore it to pieces. It was found covered with blood by P., who believing her to be dead stabbed himself. On finding his body she killed herself.

PYRENEES (pir'enēz). Mountain range of SW Europe, separating the Iberian peninsula from France. The Ps. extend *c.* 435km (270m) from the Bay of Biscay to the Mediterranean. The central P. incl. Aneto, Fr. Néthon (3,404 m/11,168 ft) and other peaks. The range gives its name to 3 Fr. depts, P.-Atlantiques, Hautes-P., and P.-Orientales. The Basque country is on the Fr./Span. frontier to the W. There are few passes, but a tunnel links Aragnouet, SE of Tarbes, France with Bielsa, Spain. Hydroelectric power has fostered industrial growth in the foothills.

PYRETHRUM (pīrē'thrum). Sub-division of the genus Chrysanthemum in the family Compositae. The ornamental species *C. coccineum* is commonly grown in gardens, and feverfew (*C. parthenium*) is a British wild flower. P. powder is a powerful contact insecticide for aphides, mosquitoes, etc.

PYRIDINE (pir'idīn). A liquid base (C_5H_5N) occurring in coal tar and bone oil. It has a sickly odour, is soluble in water, and is used as a solvent.

PYRITES. *See* IRON PYRITES.

PYROGA'LLIC (pīrō-) **ACID** or **pyrogallol.** An acid ($C_6H_3(OH)_3$) prepared from gallic acid. It is used in photographic developers and for the estimation of oxygen in gas analysis.

PYROMETER. Instrument for measuring high temperatures: 3 typical types are thermoelectric, optical, and radiation. Resistance thermometers are sometimes used as Ps.

PYROXE'NE (pī'roksēn). An important group of minerals, occurring as brown, green, or black rocks. They are silicates of calcium, magnesium, iron, etc.

PYRRHON (pir'o) (*c.* 360–270 BC). Greek philosopher. B. at Elis, he maintained that as it was impossible to attain certainty, man should seek peace of mind by renouncing all claims to knowledge.

PYRRHUS (pir'us) (*c.* 318-272 BC). King of Epirus, who in 280 invaded Italy as the ally of the Tarentines against the Romans. Although he twice defeated them, he suffered heavy losses (hence 'a Pyrrhic victory'). Defeated at Beneventum in 275, he returned to Greece.

PYTHAGORAS (pīthag'ōras) (*c.* 570-500 BC). Greek philosopher. B. in Samos, he settled in Croton in S Italy, and there founded a religious brotherhood which exercised great influence in politics until it was suppressed in the 5th cent. Their doctrines incl. the immortality of the soul and its transmigration. They devoted much attention to mathematics, and anticipated much of Euclid's work in geometry. *P.'s theorem* states that in a right-angled triangle the square on the hypotenuse is equal to the sum of the squares on the other 2 sides.

PYTHAGORAS OF RHEGIUM (rē'ji-um). Greek sculptor of the 5th cent. BC. B. at Samos, he settled in Rhegium, Italy, and estab. a reputation for his statues of athletes.

PYTHEAS (pith'e-as) (4th cent. BC). Greek navigator of Marseilles, who explored the W coasts of Europe at least as far as Denmark, travelled through Britain, and visited 'Thule', probably the Shetlands.

PYTHIAN GAMES (pith'ian). Ancient Greek festival in honour of Apollo, celebrated near Delphi every 4 years.

PYTHIAS. In Greek story, a Pythagorean whose friend Damon offered his own life as security when P. was condemned to death by a tyrant.

PYTHON (pī'thon). Genus of tropical snakes in the Boa family. They are non-poisonous, but kill their prey by constriction. They grow to 9m (30ft) in length.

PYX. Vessel used in RC churches for the reservation of the blessed sacrament. The Trial of the P. is the test of the coinage by a goldsmith, at the hall of the Goldsmiths' Company, London, and is so called from the P. or box, in which specimens of each variety of coin are preserved.

Q

17th letter of the alphabet, representing *koppa* of the earliest Greek alphabet. In Latin, as in English, it is always followed by *u*: *qu*, pron. *kw*.

QADISIYAH (kad'-) **Battle of.** Battle in S Iraq in AD 637 in which a Muslim Arab force defeated a larger Zoroastrian Persian army and ended the Sassanian Empire. The defeat is still resented in modern Iran, where modern Muslim Arab nationalism threatens the break-up of the Iranian state.

QAT (kat). Shrub (*Catha edulis*) related to coffee. The leaves are chewed as a mild narcotic in some Arab countries.

QATAR (katahr'). Emirate occupying Q. peninsula in E Arabia, which stretches c. 210 km (130 m) into the Arabian Gulf. Less than 3% is fertile, and surface water and rain are negligible, but there are experimental farms for fruit and vegetables. Industries incl. fertilisers, steel, and petrochemicals. Oil discoveries since the S.W.W. have made the country rich, and Sheikh Khalifa (1930-), who deposed his cousin in 1972, has introduced reforms. The cap. is Dohar, and the Dohar Regional Training Centre gives vocational training to students from all the Gulf states, and the Gulf (football) Tournament is played in Khalifa Stadium. Area 11,437 sq.km (4,250 sq.m); pop. (1978) 200,000, mainly in Dohar. M.U.: Q riyal.

QATTARA (kahtah'rah) **DEPRESSION.** A tract of the W Desert, Egypt. It lies up to 125m (400ft) b.s.l. and consists of very soft sand and, being virtually impassable to vehicles, it afforded protection to the left flank of the Allied armies before and at the battle of Alamein in 1942. Area 20,000 sq.km (7,500 sq.m).

QINGDAO (chĕngdah-aw'). Port on Jiazhou Bay in Shandong prov., China, with cotton and flour mills, engineering and locomotive works, etc. The chief town is Jiazhou (formerly Kiaochow) terr., ceded to Germany in 1898, it was captured in 1914 by British and Japanese forces and only returned to China by Japan in 1922. Pop. (1973) 1,500,000.

QINGHAI (chĕnghī'). NW prov. of China (formerly Chinghai), bordering Tibet: the people are nomadic graziers. There have been oil discoveries. The cap. is Xining. Area 721,000 sq.km (278,000 sq.m); pop. (1979) 3,500,000. A shallow lake, Qinghai Hu, lies in the NE at 3,200 m (10,500 ft), area 4,200 sq.km (1,600 sq.m).

QIN SHIH HAUNG TI. *See* CH'IN SHIH HUANG TI.

QISARAYA (kīzarē'a). Small port in Israel, on the Mediterranean coast 27km (17m) N of Tel Aviv-Jaffa. It is on the site of ancient Caesarea, founded by Herod 13 BC, where Paul was imprisoned for two years.

QUAESTOR (kwē'-). A Roman magistrate whose duties were mainly concerned with public finances. The Qs. originated as assistants to the consuls. Both urban and military Qs. existed, the latter being attached to the commanding generals in the provinces.

QUAGGA. Extinct species of wild horse (*Equus quagga*), resembling the zebra. Excessive hunting caused its dying out after 1858, when the last one was sent to the London Zoo from Cape Colony. Reddish-brown, with darker stripes on the fore-parts, it was whitish beneath.

QUAI D'ORSAY (kā-dorsā'). Part of the left bank of the Seine in Paris, where the French Foreign Office and other government buildings are situated.

QUAIL. Smallest species of the partridge family. The common Q. (*Coturnix coturnix*) is reddish-brown, and is found in Europe, Asia, and Africa. They are highly valued as food, and are netted while migrating to and from N Africa.

QUAKERS. Popular name for the Religious Society of Friends; the name Q. was applied to the Society's founder George Fox when he was before the magistrates at Derby in 1650, because he bade Judge Bennet to quake at the name of the Lord. In practical Christian living Qs. broke with many conventions and suffered fierce persecution. They dressed simply, refused to take oaths and to take off their hats in the presence of social superiors, and abandoned all titles. They still refuse to take any part in war. They have no professional ministry, and are guided by the 'inner light'. The meetings for worship begin with a period of silence, which continues until a member (of either sex) is guided to utter a word of exhortation or teaching, of prayer or praise. The Qs. are organized in 'meetings' composed of representatives of the congregations; the Yearly Meeting carries greatest weight. HQ is Friends' House, Euston Road, London.

QUANGO (kwang'o). In the UK the acronym of *qua*si-*a*utonomous *n*on-*g*overnmental *o*rganisation, e.g. the Location of Offices Bureau (1963 - abolished 1979). By the late 1970s the proliferation of such bodies, membership of which offered wide areas of political patronage, was a cause for concern, and there were some reductions under the Thatcher govt.

QUANT (kwont), **Mary** (1934-). British designer. From 1955, through her Chelsea boutique Bazaar, she achieved a practical but off-beat revolution in fashion clothing for women, combining it with her own make-up range. She epitomized the Swinging London of the 1960s.

QUANTRILL (kwon'tril), **William Clarke** (1837-65). American guerrilla. B. in Ohio, he had been a teacher, gambler and horse thief before commanding a unit on the Confederate side in the Civil War, said to have incl. Jesse and Frank James. He assisted in the capture of Independence, Mo., in 1862 and in Kansas in 1863 led the sack of Lawrence and put to death 17 captives after defeating a Union cavalry force at Baxter Springs. Wounded in a skirmish with Union troops in Kentucky in 1865, he probably d. there shortly after, but ballad legend (which also converts him to a kindly hero) maintains he returned to teach school in Texas.

QUANTUM THEORY. In physics, a theory advanced by Max Planck (q.v.) in 1900 to account for the phenomena of the distribution of the radiant energy from a 'black body' (one whose surface absorbs all the radiation of any wavelength that falls upon it) between the various wavelengths in the spectrum of the radiation. Planck assumed that the energy emitted consisted of separate multiples of a fundamental unit or *quantum* of energy. The theory was eventually supported by research into X-rays and the theory of spectra, and was applied in photo-electricity. Attention was then directed to its reconciliation with the wave-theory of light. The development of modern physics and its applications particularly in nuclear power and electronics is largely based on the Q.T. and developments from it.

Quantum mechanics is a mathematical system for describing the statistical behaviour of subatomic particles and systems not directly observable by man.

QUARANTINE (kwo'rantēn). A term derived from the Fr. *quarantaine* (40 days), and applied to any period during which persons, animals, and vessels suspected of carrying disease are detained and isolated.

QUARK (kwork). Sub-atomic particle, the theoretical basic building block of matter. It has so far been impossible to produce them in isolation, but they are said to have fractional charges of one-third or two-thirds of the basic charge of an electron or proton, and by 1980 five kinds had been identified. They were named by physicist Murray Gell-Mann in 1963, from a passage in James Joyce's *Finnegans Wake*, which has a kind of play on the word 'quarts', hence the pronunciation.

QUARRYING. The commercial exploitation of rock deposits, e.g. marble, slate, granite. Machine cutting is used to minimize damage when dimension stone, i.e. blocks or slabs of definite size, is required for ornamental or specialized uses (paving, wall finishes, roofing, etc.); for the broken or crushed stone used in concrete, road beds, etc., and which in modern times forms the greater part of the Q. industry, explosives are the most frequent method.

QUART. An imperial capacity measure consisting of 2 pints, or a ¼ of a gallon (1.2 litres).

QUARTER DAYS. The appointed dates on which quarterly rents, etc., become due. These are 25 March, 24 June, 29 Sept., and 25 Dec., or Lady, Midsummer, Michaelmas, and Christmas Days respectively.

QUARTZ. Rock occurring most frequently in the oldest geological strata. As a mineral it is one of the most common of the Earth's crust and consists of silica (SiO_2), sometimes with oxides. There are numerous different forms and colours incl. rock crystal, amethyst, rose Q., yellow Q., smoky Q., etc., tourmaline, agate, bloodstone, cornelian, jasper, onyx, sard, chalcedony, calcite, fluorite, granites, granite porphyries, felsites, gneisses, schists, quartzite and sand. Generally hard and crystalline, it is used for jewellery and ornamental purposes, and extensively in the ceramic arts, in optical and scientific instruments, and electronics in which Q. crystals are used for frequency standards.

QUASAR (kwā'zar). Very brilliant, very distant, core of a radio galaxy (quasi-stellar source, QSS), emitting an enormous quantity of energy in light and radio waves. It is thought that Qs. emit beams of fast electrons which broadcast radio waves when they hit the magnetised gas extensions on either side of the galaxy. The largest object in the Universe is thought to be quasar 3C 345, which has radio-emitting regions extending across 78 million light years of space. Quasars are made brilliant by giant black holes (q.v.) devouring stars in their midst, and it has been suggested that some Qs. are supermassive and that, as they move past another galaxy, drawn in by gravity, they distort it as they gather up matter from it to power their quasar activity. Some Qs. also occur in groups and may have different red shifts. Such differences normally indicate that the objects are at different distances in the sky, but these grouped Qs. appear to be physically associated and astronomers are trying to find an explanation.

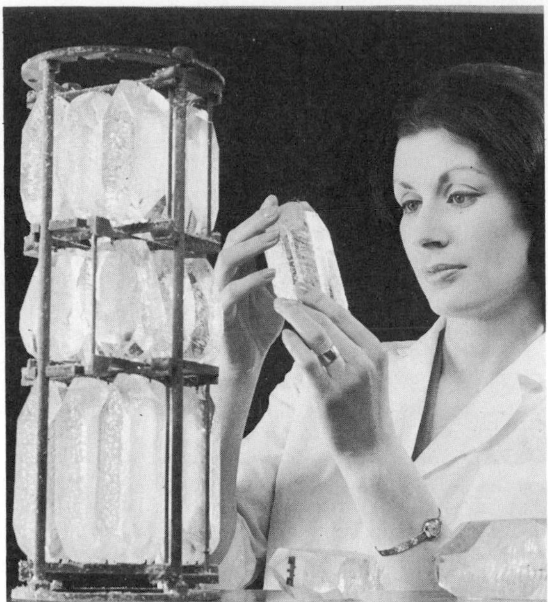

QUARTZ. Natural quartz crystals of this size take 3,000,000 years to form, but using specially designed pressure vessels and control equipment, Standard Telephones 'grow' radio quality quartz suitable for use in the manufacture of frequency control units in less than a month. *Photo: Courtesy of Standard Telephones and Cables Ltd*

Quasars were first discovered 1964–5, when radio measurements made by Cyril Hazard of the Institute of Astronomy, Cambridge, led to the identification of the first known quasar 3C 273. The existence of Qs. supports the 'big bang' theory of the Universe.

QUASIMODO (kwahsimō'dō), **Salvatore** (1901–68). Italian poet. He first became known with *Acque e terre* (1930), and his later books, e.g. *Nuove Poesie* (1942) and *Il falso e vero verde* (1956), reflect a growing preoccupation with contemporary political and social problems. He won a Nobel prize 1959.

QUASSIA (kwas'ia). The bark and wood of the tropical trees *Quassia amara* and *Picrasma excelsa*, formerly used as a tonic infusion, and in modern use as an insecticide.

QUATERNIONS. A form of calculus devised by Sir William Rowan Hamilton (1805–65), of Dublin. As a geometry it is primarily concerned with the operations whereby one quantity or vector is changed into another, direction being taken into account as well as magnitude. The method is of great use in geometrical and dynamical problems.

QUATHLAMBA. The Sesuto name for the DRAKENSBERG.

QUATRE BRAS (kahtr-brah'). A hamlet in Brabant, Belgium, 32km (20m) SE of Brussels, where Wellington defeated Ney on 16 June 1815.

QUEBEC (kwebek'). Cap. and port of Q. prov., Canada, at the confluence of the St Lawrence and St Charles rivers, c. 645km (400m) from the Gulf of St Lawrence. It was founded in 1608 by Champlain, and the picturesque old town lies below the citadel some 110m (360ft) above the river. In 1759 Q. was captured by the British (under Wolfe) from the French (under Montcalm), after a battle on the Plains of Abraham nearby in which both commanders were killed. Q. is a flourishing centre of French-Canadian culture, and has both Anglican and RC cathedrals, and 2 univs., Laval (1663: royal charter 1852), the first in N America, and Quebec (1969). Industries incl. textiles and clothes; timber, pulp and paper; printing and publishing; iron and steel; and leather. Pop. of met. area (1976) 542,160.

At the *Q. Conference* (1943) Roosevelt, Churchill, Mackenzie King and Tse-ven Soong approved Mountbatten as supreme Allied commander SE Asia and plans for the invasion of France, for which Eisenhower was to be supreme commander.

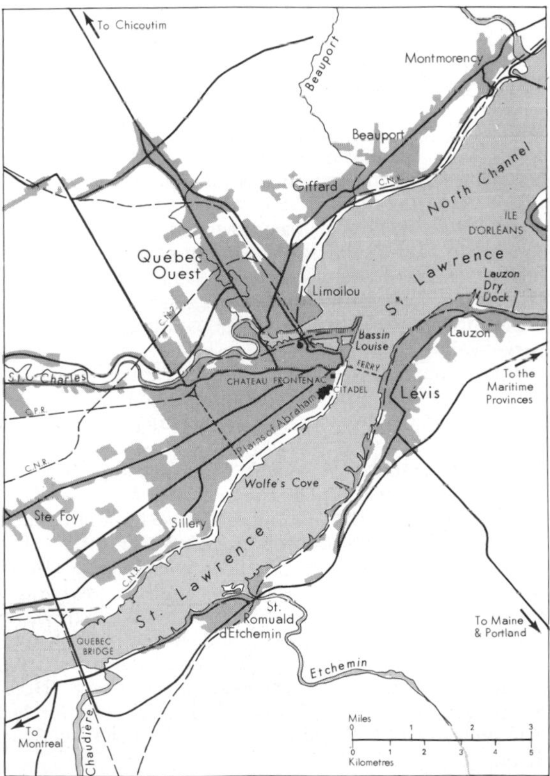

QUEBEC

QUEBEC. Eastern province of Canada, bounded by the USA to the S, Ontario to the SW, Hudson Bay and Strait to the W and N, and Newfoundland (Labrador) to the NE. The lowlands of the St Lawrence, which flows NE to the Gulf of St Lawrence, are bounded to the S by the Notre Dame mountains, an extension of the Appalachians, and to the N by the Laurentian plateau, much of which is densely forested, and which forms the major portion of the province. The chief natural resources are abundant timber and water power, provided by the many rivers and lakes, vast iron deposits in Ungava region, asbestos, mica, copper, lead-graphite, and other mineral deposits. The climate is severe but healthy. Growing industries incl. pulp and paper, chemicals, non-ferrous metals, textiles, electrical goods, aircraft, railway rolling stock, and food processing. Agriculture remains important, with oats and other grain, fodder crops, dairy produce, maple sugar and fruit; and forestry, fishing, fur-trapping and fur-ranching are also carried on. The largest cities are Q., the cap., Montreal, Laval, Sherbrooke, Verdun, Trois-Rivières, and Hull. There are 4 RC univs., Laval (1852), Montreal (1920), Sherbrooke (1954) and Quebec (1969), and 3 Protestant, McGill (1821), Bishop's (1845) and Sir George Williams Univ. (1929). The educational system is organized throughout on a denominational basis. In 1980, despite the resurgence of nationalism since the 1960s, and the adoption of French as the only official language in 1974, a referendum rejected the Quebec govt.'s proposal to negotiate 'sovereignty-association' with the rest of Canada. *See* LÉVESQE.

Area 1,540,676 sq.km (594,860 sq.m); (1976) 6,234,445. the majority Roman Catholics of French stock.

QUEBRACHO (kebrah'cho). the name of several S American trees with very hard wood. The bark of the white Q. (*Aspidosperma quebracho*) is used medicinally; the red Q. (*Schinopsis lorentzii*) is used in tanning.

QUECHUA (ketsh'wa). South American Indians of the Andean regions, whose ancestors incl. the Inca. The Q. language is the second official language of Peru, and is also spoken in Ecuador. Alternative spellings are Quichua, and Kechua.

QUEEN CHARLOTTE ISLANDS. Canadian group of is. lying c. 100m off the coast of British Columbia, to which it belongs politically. Graham and Moresby are the largest is. Lumbering, fishing, and cattle raising are the chief industries. The Q.C.I. were visited by Juan Perez in 1774, by Cook in 1778.

Area 9,790 sq.km (3,780 sq.m).

QUEEN'S AWARD. Estab. in 1965 as the Q.A. to Industry, it was replaced from 1976 by 2 separate awards for Export Achievement and for Technological Achievement. Made to organizations, not individuals, the Q.A. entitles the holder to display a special emblem for 5 yrs. Awards are made annually on the birthday of Qu. Elizabeth II (21 April).

QUEENSBERRY, John Sholto Douglas, 8th marquess of (1844–1900). British administrator and sportsman. He succeeded to the title in 1858, and 1872–80 served as a Scottish representative peer. In 1867 he drew up the Q. rules which govern boxing. *See* DOUGLAS, LORD ALFRED.

QUEEN'S COUNSEL. *See* KING'S COUNSEL.

QUEEN'S COUNTY. *See* LAOIGHIS.

QUEENSLAND. A state of the Commonwealth of Australia, comprising the whole NE portion of the continent. The Great Dividing Range runs parallel to the E coast for 1,600 km (1,000 m) to the frontier with New South Wales in the S, rising to Mt Bartle Frere 1,657 m (5,438 ft). The Great Barrier Reef (q.v.) lies off the NE coast. The main rivers are the Burdekin, Fitzroy, Flinders, and Mitchell. The climate of most of Q. is tropical but not unhealthy. Almost all land is state owned and leased. Cattle and sheep are reared; cereals, fruit, cotton, sugar and tobacco grown; and dairying and forestry are important. Minerals incl. bauxite, coal, gold, copper, lead, zinc, and oil and natural gas W of Brisbane. Tourism is increasingly important. There are factories for processing the primary products. The chief towns are Brisbane (the cap.), Townsville, Rockhampton, TooWoomba and Ipswich. Until 1859 Q. formed part of New South Wales. Area 1,736,524 sq.km (670,500 sq.m); pop. (1976) 2,037,197.

QUEENSLAND. Among the world's greatest cattle-rearing areas is Queensland, Australia, although severe drought may still have disastrous effect. Helping to round up this herd, is Prince Charles. *Photo: Keystone*

QUEEN'S PROCTOR. *See* KING'S PROCTOR.

QUEENSTOWN. Former name of COBH.

QUEMOY (kemoi'). Is. off the SE coast of China, and admin. with Matsu by Taiwan. Area 130 sq.km (50 sq.m); Matsu 40 sq.km (17 sq.m); pop. *c.* 40,000. In 1960 they were shelled from the mainland, and the USA announced they would be defended if attacked.

QUENEAU (kenoh'), **Raymond** (1903-76). French author. His poetry bears the enduring impress of his early Surrealist associations, and he is most accessible to the English reader in his humorous novels, e.g. *Zazie dans le Métro* (1959), portraying a precocious little Parisienne.

QUENNE'LL, Peter (1905-). British author. Son of Marjorie and C. H. B. Quennell, joint authors of the historical series incl. *Everyday Things in England,* he edited *History Today* 1951-79. He is an authority on the 18th cent., e.g. his edition of *The Memoirs of William Hickey* (1960), and Byron, e.g. *Byron, the Years of Fame.*

QUESNAY (kānā), **François** (1694-1774). French economist and physician. B. near Paris, he became physician to Louis XV, and *c.* 1750 founded the group of *Économistes* with Jean de Gournay. His chief work *Tableau Économique* (1758) advocated physiocracy, government according to natural order.

QUETTA (kwet'tah). Town in Baluchistan, Pakistan, near the Afghanistan border. There is a military staff college (1907). Coal is mined nearby. Pop. (1972) 156,000.

QUETZALCOATL (kātzahlkōwahtl'). Mexican god. In human form, he was said in Toltec legend to have been fair-skinned and bearded, to have reigned on earth during a golden age and to have disappeared after promising to return. Cortez was thought by the Mexican Indians to have been Q. when he invaded their land.

QUETZALCOATL. The feathered serpent god of air and water in the pre-Columbian Aztec and Toltec cultures, an interpetation in stone from the Quetzalcoatl Temple at Teotihuacan in Mexico. *Photo: A.G. Formenti*

QUEZON (kāzon') **CITY.** Cap. of the Philippines 1948-76. Laid out from 1940 in a NE suburb of Manila, it was named after the first pres. of the rep. Manuel Quezon (1878-1944). Pop. (1975) 960,350.

QUIBERON (kēbroṅ'). Coast town in the Morbihan dept, France. In 1759 Q. Bay saw the defeat of the French fleet under Conflans by Hawke. Pop. (1975) 5,000.

QUICKSILVER. *See* MERCURY.

QUIETISM (kwī-etism). A religious attitude, displayed periodically in the history of Christianity, consisting of passive contemplation and meditation to achieve union with the Divine. The founder of modern Q. was the Spanish priest Molinos who pub. a *Guida Spirituale* in 1675.

QUILLER-COUCH (-kooch), **Sir Arthur Thomas** (1863-1944). British author. B. at Bodmin, he was prof. of English literature at Cambridge from 1912, and besides editing *The Oxford Book of English Verse* (1900), etc., made a name as a novelist, e.g. *The Splendid Spur* (1889) under the pseudonym 'Q'.

QUILTER, Roger (1877-1953). British composer. B. at Brighton, he was educ. at Eton, and studied under Knorr at Frankfurt Conservatoire. He is best known for song settings from Dowson, Shakespeare, etc., incl. 'Now Sleeps the Crimson Petal' and 'To Daisies', and for his 'Children's Overture' and music for *Where the Rainbow Ends.*

QUIMPER (kaṅpār'). Cap. and port of Finistère dept, France. The cathedral dating from the 15th cent. is a fine example of Gothic architecture. Pop. (1975) 60,500.

QUINCE. A spreading tree (*Cydonia oblonga*), bearing a bitter, yellow, pear-shaped fruit, used as a preserve, either individually or with apples.

QUINCEY, de. *See* DE QUINCEY.

QUININE (kwinēn'). Chief alkaloid in cinchona bark, introduction to Europe from Peru (1639) for treating the ague. Later it was used to kill the blood parasites causing malaria, but has been supplanted by the less toxic and more powerful synthetics.

QUINQUAGESIMA (kwinkwajes′ima). The Sunday before Lent. The name is probably due to Q. being 50 days before Easter.

QUINSY. Old name for acute tonsillitis, particularly the type where a tonsillar abscess forms.

QUINTANA ROO (kintah′nah roo). Isolated area of the Yucatan peninsula, Mexico. There are Maya remains.

QUINTERO (kintăr′o), **Serafin Alvarez** (1871-1938) and **Joaquín Alvarez** (1873-1945). Spanish dramatists. B. near Seville, these brothers always worked together and from 1897 they produced some 200 successful plays, principally dealing with Andalusia. Among them are *Papá Juan: Centenario* (1909) and *Los Mosquitos* (1928).

QUINTI′LIAN (Marcus Fabius Quintilianus) (*c.* AD 35-95). Roman rhetorician. B. at Calagurris, Spain, he taught rhetoric in Rome from 68 and later composed the *Institutio Oratorio,* in which he advocated a simple and sincere style of public speaking.

QUI′PUS. A system of knotted cords of one or several colours used by the Incas of ancient Peru. The knots, arranged as in our decimal system, recorded granary and warehouse stores, etc.

QUI′RINAL. One of the 7 hills on which ancient Rome was built. Its summit is occupied by a palace built in 1574 as a summer residence for the Pope and occupied 1870-1946 by the kings of Italy. The name Q. is derived from that of the god Quirinus.

QUI′SLING, Vidkun (1887-1945). Norwegian politician. Leader from 1933 of the Norwegian Fascist Party, he aided the Nazi invasion in 1940 by delaying mobilization and urging non-resistance. Made premier by Hitler in 1942, he was arrested and shot as a traitor by his countrymen in 1945. His name became used to stigmatize all guilty of his type of treason.

QUITO (kē′tō). Cap. of Ecuador, already a town before the Incas took it *c.* 1470. The Spaniards captured it in 1534. It lies at 4,300 m (9,350 ft) in the Cordillera, and although only 14′ S of the equator, has a climate of perpetual spring owing to its height. Notable are the cathedral, univ. (1787) and Jesuits' church. Q. is the principal textile centre of Ecuador; it also makes beer, flour, leather, ceramics, chemicals, soap; gold, silver and other metal articles. Pop. (1974) 560,000.

QUIXOTE, Don. *See* CERVANTES.

QUM (koom). Holy city of the Shi'ite Moslems in central Iran, 145 km (90 m) S of Tehran. The Islamic academy of Madresseh Faizieh (1920) became the HQ of Ayatollah Khomeini.

QUMRAN (koomrahn′), **Khirbet.** Ruined site, excavated from 1951, in the foothills on the NW shores of the Dead Sea. Originally an iron age fort (6th cent. BC) it was occupied in the late 2nd cent. BC by a monastic community, the Essenes (q.v.), until the buildings were burnt down in AD 68. The Dead Sea Scrolls (q.v.) comprise their library, hidden for safekeeping and never reclaimed.

QUOITS (koits). Game in which a heavy, sharp-edged, iron ring or quoit is thrown, over or near to an iron 'hob' from 16m (18yds) distance, where is placed a second hob. A circular clay area surrounds each hob, and play proceeds as in bowls, from end to end, 2 points being awarded for a 'ringer' and 1 for the quoit nearest the hob.

QUORUM (kwō′rum). A minimum number of members required for the validity of the proceedings of any assembly.

R

Eighteenth letter of the alphabet, corresponding to the Semitic *resh* and Greek *rho.* A liquid, pronounced with the tip of the tongue on the palate, it is sometimes 'trilled' by vibration of the tongue, especially in Scotland, but in S England is often weak when used medially and silent finally.

RA. Ancient Egyptian sun-god and king of the gods, later identified with the Theban sun-god Ammon. He was depicted with a hawk's head.

RABA'T. Cap. and port of Morocco, on the Atlantic coast, 177km (110m) W of Fez. Industries incl. cotton textiles, carpets and leather goods. There is a fine 12th cent. mosque and a secular univ. (1957). Pop. (1974) 703,000.

RABAUL (rahbowl'). Largest port of Papua New Guinea, on New Britain; also an airport. It was destroyed by the RAF after its occupation by the Japanese in 1942, but rebuilt. Copra and cocoa beans are exported. Pop. (1970) 1,500.

RABBI (ra'bī). Jewish doctor of the law, particularly one dealing with ecclesiastical affairs.

RABBIT. Lagomorph (*Oryctolagus cuniculus*) of the family Leporidae. Widely distributed in Europe and America, it has become a pest because of its destructive feeding and prolific breeding (several litters in a season), man having destroyed its natural enemies or introduced it to a country such as Australia where these are largely non-existent. Until the advent of myxomatosis (q.v.) the flesh was commonly eaten in Britain: the disease also modified the mode of life of surviving Rs. which tended to move from the ramified underground burrows or 'warrens', where they formed large colonies, to living and breeding in the open. The natural coat is grey, but this is treated and dyed commercially to imitate more costly furs. Many specialized forms are bred for show purposes, etc., e.g. the English lop-eared, and the long-haired Angora. *See* RODENTS.

RABELAIS (rahbelā'), **François** (*c.* 1495-1553). French author. B. at Chinon, Touraine, he became a monk, and, having studied medicine, lectured on anatomy. His great works are *La Vie inestimable de Gargantua* (1535) and *Faits et dits héroiques du grand Pantagruel* (1533), satiric allegories laced with coarseness, broad humour, and philosophy, which tell the adventures of the 2 giants, Gargantua and Pantagruel, father and son.

RABIES (rā'bēz). A disease of animals transferable to man by biting, the saliva of the sick animal, usually a dog, fox or wolf, carrying the virus. If the wound is cauterized at once or proper serum treatment (Pasteur) is given, the disease may be prevented, and in 1975 a new, more effective type of vaccine was evolved in France. Otherwise, the patient will die after a painful illness, marked by spasms of the throat brought on by drinking or the sight of water, hence the alternative name hydrophobia (meaning 'aversion to water'). A rabies epidemic, originating in Poland in the S.W.W., had spread across Europe to northern France by the 1970s, and in Britain precautions were strengthened to stop its crossing the Channel. Oral vaccination (by bait) of foxes, rather than their destruction, is recommended as a control measure.

RABIN (rahbēn'), **Itzhak** (1922-). Israeli statesman. He succeeded Golda Meir as PM in 1974 but resigned in 1977 following his involvement with his wife in a currency scandal.

RĀ'CHEL. Character of the OT. A dau. of Laban, she was the favoured wife of Jacob, by whom she was the mother of Joseph and Benjamin.

RACHEL (rahshel'). Stage-name of the French tragedienne Elizabeth Félix (1821-58). B. in Switzerland, of Jewish extraction, she achieved success in Racine's *Phèdre* in 1843, and won a European reputation for the fierce passion of her acting.

RACHMAN (rakh'man), **Peter** (1920-62). Polish immigrant to Britain. Buying up cheaply rented houses in London controlled under the 1957 Rent Act, he used blackmail and physical violence to evict the tenants, and sold the then decontrolled property at great profit, let it at exorbitant rates to prostitutes, etc. These tactics became known as Rachmanism.

RACHMANINOV (rahkhmahn'ēnof), **Sergei Vassilievich** (1873-1943). Russian composer. B. at Oneg, Novgorod, he studied at the St Petersburg and Moscow conservatoires, and toured as a concert pianist. At the Revolution he went to the USA. His dramatically emotional music has a strong melodic basis and incl. operas, e.g. *Francesca da Rimini* (1906) based on Pushkin's play; 3 symphonies; piano pieces and songs. Among his most familiar works are the 'Prelude in C sharp minor', the 2nd piano concerto in C minor, and 'Rhapsody on a Theme by Paganini' for piano and orchestra.

RACIAL DISCRIMINATION. National or personal prejudice due to differences of religion, colour or blood, or to historical enmity, and leading to unfavourable distinctions socially, politically, economically, or legally. R.D. on religious or intellectual grounds is found in e.g. anti-Semitism; in the traditional Chinese contempt for European barbarism; in the Moslem wars against the infidel, etc. R.D. is usually automatically practised by stronger against weaker races, e.g. Indian Hindu *caste* ('varna' means 'colour') system probably developed from the conquest of the (darker) aborigines by the advancing Aryan peoples; the Untouchables are the darkest Indians. Discrimination against the Negro is largely the aftermath of the European slave trade, but is also practised by Indians and others; and American light-skinned Negroes tend to look down on the darker. On the other hand, anti-White feelings are manifested by the Black Muslims in the US, and by some newly emergent African nations. Even within Israel there are complaints of discrimination by the European Jews against the darker-skinned less-educated Jews of the Middle Eastern countries. As a result of the 'Yellow Peril' scare of the late 19th and early 20th cents. there is general prejudice by Caucasian peoples against Mongolian as well as Negroid peoples. Traditional race hatred between many countries is the result of wars, occupation, etc., for example in the UK there is still prejudice

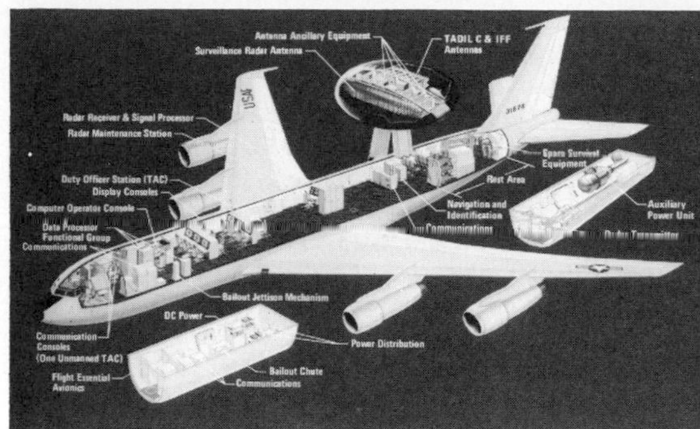

RADAR. The USAF Airborne Warning and Control System (AWACS), showing the basic operational configuration of the advanced surveillance, command and control platform. The airframe is a modified 707-320 Intercontinental topped by a 9.1 metre (30 ft) rotating radome assembly: TADIL & IFF - TActical Data and Information Link & Indication Friend or Foe. *Courtesy of Boeing Aerospace*

against Irish, Welsh, etc., and vice versa. Expression of R.D. may range from complete segregation of races as in S Africa until increasing relaxation in the 1970s and 1980s, through unofficial but effective discrimination, which defies the law, to the hard-to-isolate, mainly social disabilities. As a rule, R.D., where recognized, is generally regarded as harmful on practical as well as on moral grounds and may be combated by legislation, e.g. in the UK a series of Race Relations Acts from 1965 and in the USA the Civil Rights Acts of 1964 and 1968, and the Voting Rights Act of 1965. A United Nations convention on the elimination of R.D. came into force 1969. Reverse R.D. occurs when attempts are made to rectify the effects of previous long-term discrimination by measures favouring the group concerned: *see* BAKKE.

RACINE (rahsēn'), **Jean** (1639–99). French dramatist. B. at La Ferté-Milon, he became the friend of Boileau, La Fontaine, and Molière. His earlier tragedies incl. *Andromaque* (1667), *Britannicus* (1669), *Bajazet* (1672), *Mithridate* (1673), *Iphigénie* (1674), and *Phèdre* (1677). After the failure of the last-named he no longer wrote for the secular stage, but influenced by Mme de Maintenon produced the 2 religious dramas, *Esther* (1689) and *Athalie* (1691).

RACKETS or **racquets.** Game played in an enclosed court usually 18.3m (60ft) long by 9.1m (30ft) wide, by 2 or 4 persons each with a racket about 75cm (2.5ft) long, weighing 255 grammes (9oz). The ball is 25mm (1in) in diameter and weighs 28 grammes (1oz). Play begins from a service box, one of which is marked at each side of mid-court, and the ball must be hit above a 2.75m (9ft) line on the endwall. After service it may be played anywhere above a 68.5cm (27in) high line on the endwall the general rules of tennis applying thereafter. *See also* SQUASH.

RACOO'N or **raccoon.** American carnivorous mammal *(Procyon lotor)* of the Procyonidae, *c.* 60cm (2ft) long, with a greyish-brown body, and black and white ringed tail, the R. is an omnivorous feeder, and is nocturnal in habit.

RACOON-DOG. Small wild dog *(Nyctereutes procyonides)*, found in the Far East. The pelt is fawnish, with black markings. They are nocturnal and hunt in packs.

RAD. Dosage unit of absorbed radiation, 1 rad equalling 0.01 J/kg. Everyone receives a dose of 0.1 rad per year from natural sources of radiation.

RACOON-DOG. Kept on fur-farms in the U.S.S.R., the racoon-dog has 'escaped' and has spread across Europe as a potential pest. *Photo: Michael Lyster/The Zoological Society of London*

RADAR. A process of locating the position of an object in space, of direction finding and navigation by short radio waves. The name 'radar', standing for the phrase *R*adio *D*irection *a*nd *R*ange, was adopted from USA. All solids and liquids reflect radio waves, which are uninfluenced by darkness, clouds or fog. To detect any reflecting object it is necessary to send out a beam of small-wavelength (1cm–100cm) short-pulse radio waves and to use receivers to pick up the reflected beam. It is then possible to determine the direction of arrival of the reflected waves and thus the direction of the object with respect to the receiving station. The distance (range) may be determined by timing the journey of the radio waves to the reflecting object and back.

Some of the first experiments on distance measurement by radio location were carried out by Appleton (q.v.), and the military application of radar was begun by Robert Watson-Watt (q.v.) in 1935. The technique was further improved during the S.W.W., and subsequently R. equipment became standard in ships and aircraft to increase navigational safety in darkness, cloud and fog. It was also used in air traffic control, production of aerial maps, study of meteorological conditions, etc. During the 1970s and 1980s missiles and aircraft began to be produced which were able to evade R. detection, e.g. by modification of shape (to reduce R. cross-section), use of radar-absorbent paints; and electronic jamming devices. *See* PENETRATION TECHNOLOGY.

RADAR ASTRONOMY. The application of radar principles to astronomical research. Contact was first made with the Moon during the S.W.W., and timing the delay in receiving echoes from the Sun and planets improved determination of their distance from Earth.

RADCLIFFE, Anne (1764-1823). British novelist (*née* Ward), the chief exponent of the Gothic novel, or romance of terror. Her best-known work is *The Mysteries of Udolpho* (1794).

RADIATION. *See* ELECTROMAGNETIC WAVES.

RADIATION SICKNESS. Illness caused by exposure of the body to high energy radiation in large doses, e.g. in radiotherapy, fall-out from an atom bomb, or accident in a nuclear reactor. The symptoms incl. preliminary nausea, followed by haemorrhage, weakened resistance to infection, prostration and eventual death in severe cases. Those who survive may produce children who are affected in varying degrees. *See* FALLOUT.

RADIC (rah'dich), **Stjepan** (1871-1928). Yugoslav politician. B. near Fiume, he led the Croat national movement within the Austro-Hungarian Empire, and supported union with Serbia in 1919. His opposition to Serbian supremacy within Yugoslavia led to his murder in the parliament house.

RADICAL. A chemical structure, formed by 2 or more elements, which partakes in reactions without disintegration, yet often cannot exist alone. The behaviour of compound Rs. forms a vital part of organic chemistry.

RADICALS. Before 1832 in Britain the supporters of parliamentary reform, and subsequently the advanced wing of the Liberal Party. During the 1860s the Rs., led by Cobden, Bright, and J. S. Mill, stood for extension of the franchise, free trade, and laissez-faire, but after 1870, under the leadership of J. Chamberlain, Dilke, and Bradlaugh, they adopted a republican and semi-Socialist programme. With the growth of Socialism in the later 19th cent. Radicalism lost its popular basis, and ceased to exist as an organized movement. In the USA the term R. is applied to any holder of left-wing opinion.

RADIO. The transmission and reception of radio waves. James Clerk Maxwell first developed the theory of electromagnetic waves in 1864, confirmed practically in the laboratory in 1888 by Heinrich Hertz. Marconi developed the work, in 1896 succeeding in establishing communication between Penarth amd Weston-super-Mare; 5 years later he received a signal in Newfoundland transmitted from Poldhu in Cornwall. The phenomenon of waves moving round the curvature of the earth was simultaneously explained by Heaviside and Kennelly in their theories of a layer of upper atmosphere which acts as an electrical conductor instead of an insulator. The invention of the radio valve by Fleming (1904) laid open the way for broadcasting, which began in Britain in 1920. Later evolution has produced television in 1934, and radar (qq.v.).

When an electric charge is made to surge up and down a transmitting aerial, electric and magnetic 'strains' or waves are produced, which travel outwards at 300,000,000 metres (186,000 m) per sec. One such wave is emitted for each oscillation of the charge, whose frequency is expressed by the number of these 'cycles' completed per sec. The wavelength is thus equal to the velocity (metres per sec.) divided by frequency (cycles per sec.), in terms of metres. Radio waves range in wavelength from 20 kilometres to less than a centimetre.

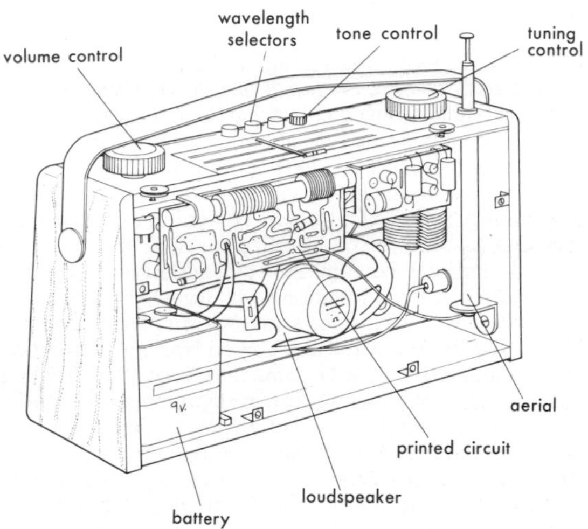

RADIO. The interior of a modern battery portable.

The ground waves radiated are weakened by loss of energy over the land. The sky waves (those which travel upwards) traverse greater distances by rebounding from the ionosphere in 'hops'. Medium and long waves are used for restricted ranges, and short waves, which suffer greatest loss over ground, for long-distance telephony and broadcasting.

In modern transmitters the electrical oscillations are generated by means of a thermionic valve set in a circuit consisting of an inductance (usually a wire coil) and capacitance (usually a capacitor of sheets of metal with air between). To prevent the dying away of the oscillations when the energy is expended, a valve is coupled which maintains them by injections of energy. They are then amplified further until powerful enough to transmit. The oscillations alone, however, are merely carrier waves and must be 'modulated' by the impression of the desired intelligence which is conveyed forth as part of the radiated wave. The aerial transmits the high-frequency oscillations into a relatively great volume of space; short waves are suited to 'beaming' or directive transmission. (*See* BROADCASTING.)

The receiving aerial intercepts some of the transmitted waves, which set up a minute current, conducted to the receiver, whose purpose is to separate from these high frequencies the low frequencies containing the transmitted intelligence, and reconvert them through a loud-speaker into sound. The receiver must be adjusted so that its electrical characteristics are similar to those of the transmitting circuits. It is set at the desired, or resonant, frequency, when it receives these oscillations much more violently than any others. As in transmission, the circuit consists of inductance coils and air or mica capacitors. Tuned circuits are devised to allow a small band only of frequencies to be received. The currents set up by the incoming wave are oscillating at high frequency, and to modulate the oscillations so that only low frequencies are applied to the loud-speaker, a detector - a one-way device - is used, consisting of one or more valves or transistors. The simple 'diode' suppresses the requisite frequencies, conveying the remainder on for conversion. To boost the current to the strength to enter the speaker, audio frequency amplifying valves or transistors are used.

The low-frequency impulses are finally applied to the loud-speaker, consisting of a coil of thin wire mounted on a 'former' rigidly attached to a paper cone. The coil is suspended in a powerful magnetic field and the whole left free to move. The currents fed to the coil produce a magnetic field which interacts with the permanent magnetic field to cause coil movement and vibrations in the cone. These are identical with the vibrations produced by the original sounds, and as they occur also in air are reproduced identically by the receiver.

See SINGLE SIDEBAND TRANSMISSION.

RADIOACTIVE WASTE. Waste is produced in the course of a nuclear power programme in solid form (e.g. irradiated fuel element cans and other equipment); liquid (radioactive liquid solutions arising from the separation of fission products from irradiated fuel in reprocessing plants, as at Windscale in Cumbria); and gaseous (produced during reactor and fuel plants operation). Gas is still produced in a small enough quantity to be released to the air; low activity solid waste is packaged for sea disposal c. 450 km (300m) off Land's End; high activity solid waste may be combustible, the plutonium being recovered from the incinerator, or may be buried; the chief problem is with high activity liquid wastes, and a favoured method of dealing with these is by vitrification into solid glass cylinders for storage in salt mines, on or under the seabed, or eventually in dead planets in space.

RADIOACTIVITY. The phenomena exhibited by a small class of substances, e.g. uranium, thorium, radium, and actinium, which spontaneously emit radiations that penetrate substances opaque to normal light, affect a photographic plate in the dark, produce phosphorescence in certain minerals, and ionize gases. These same properties are exhibited by other radiations such as X-rays, but only when the exciting agent is external. The spontaneous emission is due to the disintegration of the actual atoms of the radioactive element, and may be accompanied by explosive violence which produces new atoms differing in properties from the parent element.

Röntgen discovered X-rays in 1895, and in 1896 Becquerel found that uranium radiations affected a photographic plate in darkness. The next year Mme Curie separated radium, beginning the search for the elements subsequently discovered. Rutherford investigated these radiations, and classified them into alpha, beta, and gamma rays. In atom-bomb research great strides were made in the study of R. Since 1940 numbers of transuranium elements (q.v.) have been produced, in addition to hundreds of artificial radioactive isotopes: *See* ATOM; ISOTOPE.

RADIOACTIVE WASTE. Incorporation of highly active liquid wastes in a very durable glass, which would then be stored indefinitely in leak-proof stainless steel vessels is a partial solution to the problem. This section of a vessel contains experimental vitrified waste with simulated fission products. *Photo: Courtesy of the UKAEA*

RADIOASTRONOMY. Branch of astronomy which deals with the electromagnetic radiations received from celestial objects. These are focused and studied by means of radio telescopes, one of the most famous of these being the 75m (250ft) metal paraboloid or 'bowl' at Jodrell Bank in Cheshire (q.v.). Various other designs have since been adopted, some measuring several kilometres across, and new types have been evolved for special purposes, e.g. the radio-heliograph (1966) for Sun research invented by Englishman Paul Wild and erected at Narrabri, 500km (310m) N of Sydney, Australia. This was used to forecast for American astronauts on Moon flights when dangerous solar and cosmic radiation could be expected. Radio sources incl. not only 'objects' within our own Galaxy, but other galaxies, and outer space beyond the reach of vision. All sources so far identified are natural, but many astronomers believe it possible that other intelligences may be attempting to communicate across space, and a 'watch' is maintained with this in mind.

The pioneer in R. was Karl Guthe Jansky (1905-49), an American of Czech ancestry, who in 1932 detected radio signals from the constellation of Sagittarius at Holmdel in New Jersey. Valuable work was done in Britain by James Stanley Hey (1909-), who discovered during S.W.W. research on jamming enemy radar that sun spots emitted radio waves, etc. The British climate being unfavourable to optical astronomy, effort was concentrated on R. (unaffected by cloudy weather) and rapid advances were made after the S.W.W.

RADIO BEACON. A radio transmitter whose radiations enable a craft to determine its direction or position relative to the beacon by means of a communications receiver or direction finder.

RADIOCARBON DATING. *See* CARBON and LIBBY.

RADIOCHEMISTRY. The chemical study of radioactive elements and their compounds, whether produced from naturally radioactive or irradiated materials, and their use in the study of other chemical processes.

Radiochemicals enable the biochemical functioning of different parts of the living body to be observed, incl. the brain, heart and lungs; help in the testing of new drugs, showing where the drug goes in the body and how long it stays there; and help in reading the genetic code. Their main use, however, is in diagnosis, e.g. cancer, foetal abnormalities, and heart disease.

RADIO FREQUENCIES AND WAVELENGTHS. Classification of. In order to name them it is convenient to group frequencies and wavelengths together in bands, each band referring to waves having similar propagation characteristics, and for which similar techniques are used in the radio terminal equipment. The radio frequency spectrum internationally agreed in 1959 was (in kHz):

Very low frequency (VLF) 10-30.
Low frequency (LF) 30-300.
Medium frequency (MF) 300-3,000.
High frequency (HF) 3,000-30,000.
Very high frequency (VHF) 30,000-300,000.
Ultra high frequency (UHF) 300,000-3,000,000.
Super high frequency (SHF) 3,000,000-30,000,000.
Extremely high frequency (EHF) 30,000,000-300,000,000.

RADIOGRAM. Combined unit of radio and gramophone in a single cabinet; an X-ray photograph or radiograph.

RADIO'GRAPHY. The production of shadows on sensitized film by X-rays. They are produced when a high unidirectional voltage is applied to the electrodes in a vacuum tube - giving rise to a stream of electrons from the cathode - which when stopped at the anode produce X-rays. These penetrate matter according to its atomic weight, density and thickness. In doing so they cast shadows on the film and are used to examine the internal parts of the body, or in industry to examine solid materials, e.g. weld seams, pipelines, etc.

RADIOISOTOPE. A radioactive isotope: the majority of natural isotopes (q.v.) of mass below 208 are not radioactive. Most Rs. are made by bombarding an ordinary inactive material with neutrons in the core of a nuclear reactor. The radiations given off are easy to detect, can in some instances penetrate substantial thicknesses of materials, and may have profound effects on living matter, hence Rs. are very useful in many fields of medicine, industry, agriculture and research. *See* COBALT, LABELLED COMPOUND.

RĀDIŌTHE'RAPY. The treatment of disease by radiation obtained from X-ray machines or radioactive sources. The effect of the radiation is to reduce the activity of dividing cells and is of especial value for its effect on certain malignant tissues, certain non-malignant tumours and some diseases of the skin. Generally speaking the rays of the ordinary diagnostic X-ray machine are not penetrating enough to be very efficient in treatment, and for this purpose more powerful machines are required operating from 10,000 to over 30 million volts. The lower-voltage machines are similar to conventional X-ray machines, the higher-voltage ones may be of special design, e.g. linear accelerators and betatrons.

Much R. is now given using artificially produced radio isotopes (q.v.). Radioactive cobalt (symbol Co) is the most useful, as this produces gamma rays (very penetrating), and machines with sources of this material are used instead of very high-energy X-ray machines. Similarly certain radioactive substances may be used by actual administration to patients, e.g. radioactive iodine for thyroid disease.

RADIOISOTOPE. The United Kingdom Atomic Energy Authority's Radiochemical Centre at Amersham is the world's largest international supplier of radioisotopes. Here radio pharmaceutical compounds labelled with mercury-197 are prepared in a standard shielded cell. *Photo; Courtesy of U.K.A.E.A.*

In the past much use was made of radium, but this has now been largely supplanted by artificially produced radioactive substances, which are more easily obtainable. Small sources may actually be implanted into the tissue being treated, in an attempt to localize the irradiation.

RADISH. Cultivated biennial herbs (*Raphanus sativus*) of the Cruciferae family, with fleshy, edible roots. The latter may vary in colour through white, red, and black, and have a pungent taste.

RĀ'DIUM (Lat. *radius* ray). A brilliant white radioactive metal, symbol Ra, at. wt. 226, at. no. 88. The salt R. bromide was first separated by M. and Mme Curie in 1898 from Bohemian pitchblende, but R. itself was not isolated until 1911 (by Mme Curie and Debierne). More volatile than barium, which it resembles chemically, its m.p. is 700°C. It is obtained commercially as bromide or chloride from pitchblende (q.v.), which occurs in Czechoslovakia, E Africa and Colorado. R. disintegrates spontaneously with the emission of alpha particles and forms the radioactive chemically inert gas radon (q.v.). Both were used for cancer therapy, but have been replaced by radioactive Co. 60. Both R. and Co. 60 are used extensively in industrial radiography.

RADIUM HILL. Mining site SW of Broken Hill, NSW, Australia, formerly a source of radium and uranium.

RADNORSHIRE. Former border co. of Wales, incl. in Powys 1974. Part of the high central plateau, the area rises to its greatest height in the Forest of Radnor, and is famed for sheep. The chief rivers are the Wye and Teme, and Presteign was the co. town.

RADOM (rah'dōm). Town in Poland, 96km (60m) S of Warsaw. There are iron works and tanneries, and bicycles, machinery, boots and shoes, beer, flour, and tobacco are manufactured. R. became Austrian in 1795, Russian in 1825, and was returned to Poland in 1919. Pop. (1978) 184,000.

RĀ'DON. Radioactive gas formed by the disintegration of radium (q.v.), formerly called radium emanation, then niton (Lat. *nitens* shining) and from 1923 radon: symbol Rn, at. no. 86, at. wt. 222. Discovered in 1900 by Dorn, it was isolated by Ramsay and Gray 8 years later.

RAEBURN (rā'-), **Sir Henry** (1756-1823). Scottish artist. B. in Edinburgh, he travelled in Italy, returning to his native city in 1787 as a portrait painter. In 1815 he was elected RA, and in 1822 was knighted.

RAEDER (rā'der), **Erich** (1876-1960). German Admiral. Chief of Staff to Hipper in the F.W.W., he became head of the navy in 1928, but was dismissed by Hitler in 1943 because of his failure to prevent Allied Arctic convoys reaching Russia. Sentenced to life imprisonment at Nuremberg, he was released on grounds of ill-health in 1955.

RAFFLES, Sir Thomas Stamford (1781-1826). British administrator. He entered the E India Co.'s service in early life, took part in the capture of Java from the Dutch in 1811, and while gov. of Sumatra 1818-23 was responsible for the acquisition and foundation of Singapore in 1819. He was a founder and first pres. of the Zoological Society.

RAGLAN, FitzRoy James Henry Somerset, 1st baron R. (1788-1855). British general. In the Peninsular War under Wellington, he was foremost in the storming of Badajoz, and at Waterloo lost his right arm. He commanded the British forces in the Crimea, being created field marshal after Inkerman, but the later losses and privations of his troops were said to have accelerated his death from dysentery. The R. sleeve, with no shoulder seam but cut right up to the neckline, is named after him.

RAGTIME. Syncopated music (ragged time = syncopated), created by American Blacks in the later 19th cent., and influenced by folk music traditions, the minstrel shows, and the marching bands. It later merged into jazz. *See* JOPLIN.

RAGUSA (rahgōō'zah). Italian town in Sicily, 54km (34m) SW of Syracuse. It stands over 450m (1,500 ft) above the r. R. It makes cotton and woollen textiles, but chief interest is in the ancient tombs in caves nearby. Pop. (1971) 59,300. Also the Italian name of DUBROVNIK. The word argosy comes from this R. famed under Turkish rule in the 16th cent. for its trading fleets: at that time, R. was called in England Arrogosa.

RAGWORT. Perennial plant (*Senecio jacobaea*), of the Compositae. Over a metre (3ft) high it produces brilliant yellow flowers, and is an abundant weed.

RAHERE (d. 1144). Ministrel and favourite of Henry I, who in 1123 founded St Batholomew's priory, Smithfield, and St Bartholomew's hospital, London.

RAH'MAN PUTRA, Tunku (meaning 'prince') **Abdul** (1903-). Malaysian statesman. As leader of the Alliance Party he took part in the independence negotiations in 1955, became PM of Malaya in 1957, and was the prime mover in the creation of Malaysia 1963. In 1964 he was again returned to power by an overwhelming majority as PM of Malaysia, in face of the threat to the existence of the new federation from Sukarno; resigned 1970.

RAIKES, Robert (1735-1811). British educationist. B. at Gloucester, where he ran a printing business, he started a Sunday school in 1780, the beginning of the Sunday-school movement.

RAIL. A general name for birds of the Rallidae family. The corncrake or Land-R. (*Crex crex*) has a grating cry, and is brown above and whitish below. Others are the coot, moorhen, and water R.

RAILWAYS. Track laid for the passage of trains conveying passengers and goods. The use of rails to reduce friction was recognized early, iron rails being utilized at collieries in the 18th cent. The imaginative abilities of the English steam pioneers, Newcomen, Watt, *et al.*, led to the realization of self-propelled steam rail vehicles, by Trevithick (1804), Hedley (1813) and Stephenson (1825), whose 'Rocket' drew a coach along part of the Manchester-Liverpool line at 30 mph in 1829. The widespread and haphazard building which followed - at enormous cost in money and engineering skill - resulted in 250 separate companies; which resolved into 4 systems in 1921, and became the nationalized 'British Railways' in 1948, known as 'British Rail' from 1965. European R. developed quickly during the 19th cent., and in the USA and Canada the growth of R. made full exploitation of the central and western territories possible, as well as enabling the North to win the American Civil War, sometimes referred to for this reason as the 'Railway War'. Some of the world's most remarkable R., in South America, were built by British engineers.

The supremacy of R. in freight and passenger transport was rapidly destroyed after the S.W.W. by the phenomenal growth of motor car ownership and internal air services, which took away passenger traffic, and by road haulage door-to-door, which took over in freight. The picturesque era of steam ended over the same period, except for revivals by enthusiasts and where electricity was cheap, systems were electrified (since it is more efficient to centralize power than carry it around). Elsewhere, diesel engines were adopted, as being cleaner, easier to control, and capable of running round the clock as required. Nevertheless, increasing labour and maintenance costs meant ever higher fares and fewer passengers, and declining freight traffic. By 1980 many rural and urban train services in the UK were under threat of extinction, and the 'railbus' was developed as a countermeasure. It consists of a single-decker bus, longer than a normal bus, but shorter than a railway carriage, and fitted with railway wheels. A pair will run as a 'two-coach train' carrying *c.* 100 passengers in each coach, and have a driver and conductor-guard. Two 200 hp diesel engines give a top speed of *c.* 120 kmph (75 mph). Only in less developed areas, where enormous distances were involved over difficult terrain, and there were problems of bulk transport of minerals, etc., to specific industrial centres and port

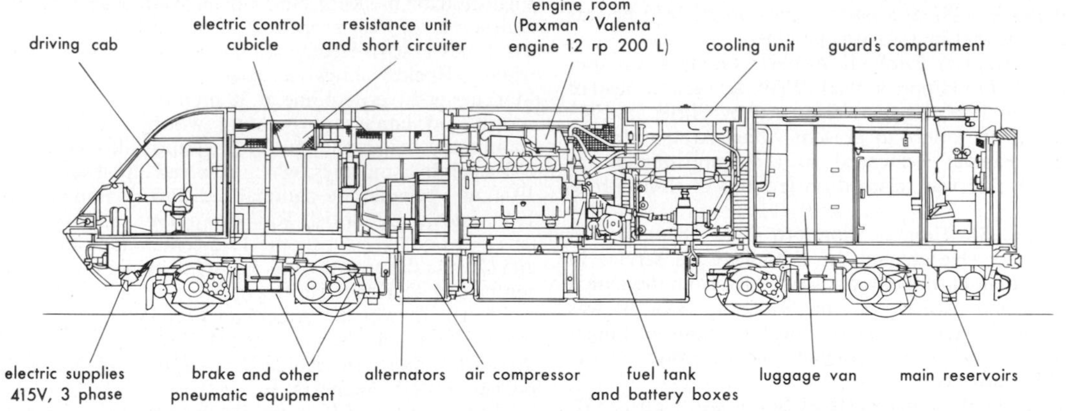

RAILWAYS. One of the first production high speed trains (HSTs) for Inter-City services at 200 kph (125 mph) which began on 4 Oct 1976 between London-Bristol and South Wales. The prototype established a world speed record for diesel trains at 229 kph (143 mph) in 1973. *Photo and diagram: Courtesy of British Railways Board*

outlets, were new R. constructed, e.g. the Tanzam Railway in Africa, and the second Trans-Siberian in the USSR. *See also* LEVITATION, MAGLEV.

RAIN, acid. Weak solution of sulphuric and nitric acids which falls as rain or snow when sulphur dioxide (from coal-burning power plants, smelters and factories) and nitrogen oxides (from car exhausts and factories), rise to mingle with water vapour. It affects the food chain in fresh-water lakes, plant growth, and buildings (by corrosion).

RAINBOW. An arch formed in the sky showing the prismatic colours in their order. It is caused by the refraction of rays of light by rain globules. The colours of the R. are the same, and in the same order, as in the spectrum.

RAINE, Kathleen (1908-). British poet. Dau. of a schoolmaster, she was educ. at Girton Coll., Cambridge. Her vols. of poetry incl. *Stone and Flower* (1943) and *The Lost Country* (1971) and reflect both the Northumberland landscape of her upbringing and the religious feeling which led her to the Roman Catholic Church in 1944. She was formerly m. to the poet and sociologist Charles Madge, and has written vols. of autobiography.

RAINIER III, Prince. *See* MONACO.

RAINIER. Mountain in the Cascade Range, Washington state, USA, 4,392 m (14,408 ft) crowned by 14 glaciers and carrying dense forests on its slopes. It is a quiescent volcano. Mount R. national park was dedicated in 1899.

RAISIN. Dried grape; the chief kinds are the common R., the sultana or seedless R., and the currant. They are produced in the Mediterranean area, California, Australia, etc.

RAJASTHAN (rah'jastahn). State of the Rep. of India, formed in 1948 and later enlarged: it incl. the former princely states of Bikaner, Jaipur, Jodhpur and Udaipur. The cap. is Jaipur. Grains and sugar are grown with irrigation. India's first underground nuclear test was carried out in the R. desert. Area 342,274 sq.km (132,152 sq.m); pop. (1971) 25,766,000.

RAJPUT. High-caste Hindus of India, predominantly soldiers and landowners. They are widespread over N India. The Rajput states of W India are now merged in Rajasthan. The Rana family (ruling aristocracy of Nepal until 1951) is also Rajput.

RALEIGH or **Ralegh** (raw'li), **Sir Walter** (*c.* 1552-1618). English adventurer. B. in Devon, he served in early life in France and Ireland, and at sea against the Spaniards. He won Elizabeth I's favour, and in 1584 was knighted. He made several unsuccessful attempts 1584-7 to establish a colony in 'Virginia' (now N Carolina). He led an exploring expedition to S America in 1595, which he described in his *Discovery of Guiana,* and distinguished himself in the expeditions to Cadiz in 1596 and the Azores in 1597. After James I's accession in 1603 he was condemned to death on a charge of conspiracy, but reprieved and imprisoned in the Tower, where he wrote his unfinished *History of the World.* Released in 1616, he led a gold-seeking expedition to the Orinoco, which failed disastrously, and on his return was beheaded under his former sentence.

RALEIGH. Cap. of N Carolina, USA, with electrical machinery, food processing and textile industries. Pop. met. area (1974) 500,000.

RALEIGH, Fort. Site at the N end of Roanoke Is., NC, USA, to which in 1585 Sir Walter Raleigh sent out 108 colonists from Plymouth, under his cousin Sir Richard Grenville. The first English settlement was estab. here, but in 1586 Drake took the dissatisfied survivors back to England. The outline fortifications are preserved.

RAMADA'N or **Ramazan.** The 9th month of the Moslem year, throughout which a strict fast is observed during the hours of daylight.

RAMAN (rah'man), **Sir Venkata** (1888-1970). Indian physicist. Awarded a Nobel prize in 1930 for his discovery in 1928 of the *R. Effect*: the scattering of monochromatic light when passed through a transparent substance. He became in 1948 director of the R. Research Institute and national research prof. of physics.

RAMAT GAN (ramat gan'). Town in W Israel, NE of Jaffa-Tel Aviv. There are textile and food processing industries. Pop. (1972) 117,500.

RAMAYANA (rahmay'yana). A Sanskrit epic poem of the 6th-4th cents. BC. Consisting of 48,000 lines, it describes the adventures of the hero Rama, later identified with the god Vishnu, and incorporates both mythical and historical elements.

RAMBERT (ronbār'), **Dame Marie** (1888-1982). Brit. ballet dancer and teacher. B. in Warsaw, she danced with the Diaghilev ballet 1912-13, opened the R. School in 1920, and in 1926 founded the *Ballet R.* which she directed. She m. in 1918 Ashley Dukes (1885-1959), playwright and producer, and was created DBE in 1962.

RAMBOUILLET (roṅbōōyā'), **Catherine de Vivonne,** marquise de (1588-1665). French society woman, whose *salon* at the Hôtel de R. in Paris incl. Descartes, La Rochefoucauld, and Mme de Sévigné.

RAMBOUILLET. Town in Yvelines dept, France, in the S of the forest of R. The royal château is now the presidential summer residence. Pop. (1975) 16,500.

RAMÉE, Louise de la. *See* OUIDA.

RAMESES (ram'esēz). Name of 11 ancient Egyptian kings. **Rameses II** (reigned *c.* 1300-1225 BC), the son of Seti I, successfully waged war on the Hittites, and carried out colossal works of art such as the rock temple at Abu Simbel.

RAMESES II. The entrance to the temple of Rameses II at Abu Simbel, in its original magnificent setting, before its removal to safety (in sections) above the flood waters of the Aswan Dam. The four colossi represent the king wearing the double crown of Egypt. Beneath the king's knees are figures of Queen Nefertari and some of the royal children.

Rameses III (reigned *c.* 1200-1168 BC) won a naval victory over the Philistines and other barbarian peoples, and asserted his suzerainty over Palestine.

RAMILLIES (ram'ilēz, Fr. rahmēyē'). Village in Brabant, Belgium, 21km (13 m N of Namur, scene of Marlborough's victory over the French on 23 May 1706, during the War of the Spanish Succession.

RAM MOHUN ROY. *See* BRAHMA SAMAJ.

RAMPHAL (ram'fahl), **Sir Shridath Surendranath** (1928-). Guyanese statesman. He studied law at the Univ. of London and Harvard Law School, and was Min. of Foreign Affairs and Justice in Guyana 1972-5. He became Sec.-General of the Commonwealth in 1975.

RAMSAY, Allan (1686-1758). Scottish poet. B. in Lanarkshire, he became a wig-maker and then a bookseller in Edinburgh. He pub. *The Tea-Table Miscellany,* and *The Evergreen,* collections of ancient and modern Scottish song.

RAMSAY, Sir William (1852-1916). British chemist. B. at Glasgow, he became prof. of chemistry at Bristol in 1880, and London (1887-1913). He became an FRS in 1888, was knighted in 1902, and received a Nobel prize in 1904. Together with Lord Rayleigh he discovered argon in 1894. In 1895 R. manufactured helium, and in 1898, in cooperation with M. Travers, identified neon, krypton, and xenon. With F. Soddy he noted the transmutation of radium into helium in 1903. This discovery led in 1910 to that of the density and atomic weight of radium.

RAMSGATE. English port and seaside resort in the Isle of Thanet, Kent. 'The royal harbour' (1795) was named by George IV. Pop. (1972) 40,000.

RANCE (raṅs). River in Brittany, France, flowing into the Channel between Dinard and St Malo, where a dam built 1960-7 (with a lock for ships) uses the 13m (44 ft) tides to feed the world's first successful tidal power station.

RAND. Dutch word for edge or brink. It is used as an abrreviation for the Witwatersrand, a gold-bearing ridge in Transvaal, S Africa, extending for *c.* 65km (40m) W and E of Johannesburg. Gold was first found here in 1854. The R. became the basic unit of S Africa's new decimal currency in 1961.

RANGOON. Cap. of Burma on the R. river, 32km (20m) from the sea. It is a great commercial centre, exporting rice, teak, and petroleum. There is a univ. (1920). The golden Shwe Dagôn pagoda, founded according to tradition in 585 BC, is a centre of pilgrimage for Burmese Buddhists. A city called Dagôn was founded on the site in 746; the name R. (meaning end of conflict) was given to it by Alaungpaya in 1755 when he made it his cap. The E India Co. set up a factory in 1790 at R., which was captured by the British in 1852. Pop. (1973) 3,662,000.

RANJIT SINGH (1780-1839). Indian maharajah. He succeeded his father as a minor Sikh leader in 1792, and created a Sikh army which conquered Kashmir and the Punjab. In alliance with the British, he estab. himself as 'Lion of the Punjab', ruler of the strongest of native Indian states.

RANSOM, John Crowe (1888-1974). American poet. B. in Tennessee, he was a Rhodes scholar, and was prof. of English at Vanderbilt Univ. 1927-37 and then Carnegie prof. of poetry at Kenyon Coll. His vols. of romantic but anti-rhetorical verse incl. *Poems about God* (1919), and *Two Gentlemen in Bonds* (1926).

RANSOME, Arthur (1884-1967). British author. Once a journalist - he was correspondent in Russia for the *Daily News* during the F.W.W. and the Revolution - he was best known for his books for children, beginning with *Swallows and Amazons* (1930), and incl. in the series *Peter Duck* (1932) and *Great Northern?* (1947). These are marked by depth of characterization and technical accuracy, and for many of them the author was his own illustrator.

RANUNCŪLĀ'CEAE. A family of dicotyledonous plants, with distinctive flowers and divided leaves, which incl. the clematis, anemone, buttercup (Ranunculus), delphinium, and peony.

RAPALLO (rahpah'lo). A port and winter resort of Liguria, Italy, 24km (15m) SE of Genoa on the Gulf of R. A treaty signed here by Italy and Yugoslavia in 1920 settled their common frontier; and a treaty signed by Germany and Russia at R. in 1922 cancelled their claims on one another for war indemnities.

RAPA NUI. Another name for EASTER ISLAND.

RAPE. Two plant species, *Brassica campestris* and *Brassica napus*, grown for their seeds, which yield the pungent mustard R. oil. The common turnip is a variety of the former, and the swede turnip of the latter.

RAPE. Sexual intercourse with a woman without her consent. The increasing frequency of the crime in modern society, combined with the reluctance of women to face the publicity of the courts, led in 1976 in Britain to legislation that the victim should remain anonymous, her sex history should not be in question, and there should be a shift of stress to emphasize that her 'absence of consent' rather than proof of her 'resistance to violence' is the criterion of the crime. The anonymity of the accused was also to be preserved unless he were convicted.

RAPHAEL SANZIO (ra'fā-el sahn'zē-ō) (1483-1520). Italian painter. B. at Urbino, the son of Giovanni Santi, a court painter, he at first studied under his father, and in 1499 went to Perugia, where he entered the studio of Perugino. The influence of the latter is shown in R.'s paintings of St Michael, St George, the Three Hesperides, and the Coronation of the Virgin. In 1504-8 he was in Florence, where he studied the works of Leonardo da Vinci, Michelangelo, Massaccio, and Fra Bartolommeo. Paintings of this period incl. the 'St Catherine' and the 'Ansidei Madonna' in the National Gallery. In 1508 he went to Rome where he was employed by pope Julius II to redecorate a number of rooms in the Vatican. Thenceforward he painted a great many works - frescoes, easel pictures, etc. - of which some of the most famous incl. 'St Cecilia', the 'Disputa', 'School of Athens', and the 'Sistine Madonna' at Dresden. His works are distinguished for their beauty of form and colour, and he ranks as one of the greatest figures in the history of art.

RARE EARTHS. The oxides of metals found in certain rare minerals. The elements incl. under the heading of R.E. are those nos. 21, 39, and 57-71: *see* table under Inorganic Chemistry.

RARE GASES. The name applied to the elements helium, neon, argon, krypton, xenon, and radon, characterized by their lack of chemical affinity.

RASPBERRY. A prickly cane-plant (*Rubus idaeus*) of the Rosaceae family with white flowers followed by white or red fruits. These are used for jam and wine.

RASPŪ'TIN, Gregory Efimovich (1871-1916). Russian monk. The illiterate son of a poor peasant, he claimed divine powers, and in 1907 was presented at court, where he acquired great influence over the Tsarina because of her belief that he could cure her son, the Tsarevitch, of haemophilia. The control he exercised through her over political and ecclesiastical appointments, and his notorious debauchery, created a scandal which did much to discredit the monarchy. He was murdered by a group of nobles.

RAT. Name given to the larger members of the family Muridae. The brown R. (*Rattus norvegicus*) is *c.* 200mm (8in) with a tail of almost equal length. It frequents sewers, docks, and warehouses, and in the country hedges, ricks, granaries, and other food stores. Brown Rs. also infest ships, by which they have been spread over the world. The black or long-tailed R. (*Rattus rattus*) is smaller than the brown R., by which it has largely been replaced. Some black Rs. are still found in docks and on ships. They do not interbreed with the brown Rs. *See* PLAGUE.

RATES and **RATING.** Rates are a form of local taxation imposed by local authorities to finance their various activities. In England and Wales a 'General Rate' is levied to cover expenditure on all purposes by district councils and by the City Corporation and the boroughs of London (incl. of the amount required by the Greater London Council and the county councils). It is levied at an appropriate figure in the pound on the assessment of all rateable property, and is supplemented under the Local Govt. Act (1974) by govt grant aid. Rebates for lower income groups were introduced in 1966, and in 1976 the Layfield Committee recommended rating assessment on market value rather than an assumed rental value, and the introduction of a supplementary local income tax. Property taxes are the US equivelent of rates.

RATHENAU (rah'tenow), **Walter** (1867-1922). German Jewish statesman. A leading industrialist, he was appointed economic director during the F.W.W. and developed a system of economic planning in combination

RAVENNA. Brilliant in colour as when it was first created, this mosaic gains a living quality from the variation in depth of the surface, and an added richness from the gold leaf layered in glass used in depicting crowns. The emperor Justinian is here shown with the members of his court. *Photo: Courtesy of the Italian State Tourist Office.*

with capitalism. After the war he founded the Democratic Party, and became For. Min., 1922. He signed the Rapallo Treaty of friendship with Russia in 1922, and soon after was murdered by right-wing fanatics.

RATHLIN. An is. 6.5km (4m) off the N coast of N Ireland and incl. in the co. of Antrim. St Columba founded a church on R. in the 6th cent.; and Robert Bruce went into hiding there after his defeat by the English at Methven in 1306.

RATIBOR (rah'tēbōr). German form of RACIBORZ.

RATIONALISM. In the history of human thought, the belief that reason is the most important, if not the only, means of ascertaining truth. The name is usually applied to the system of thought which interprets religious doctrines by the light of reason, questioning traditional and rejecting supernatural authority. The Rationalist movement arose in Germany in the 18th cent., and in the 19th it extended to Britain and USA.

RA'TISBON. French name of REGENSBURG.

RATITAE (rāti'tē). One of the 2 main divisions of birds. It is represented by the ostrich, rhea, emu, cassowary, and kiwi. *See* BIRDS.

RATTIGAN, Sir Terence (1911-77). Brit. playwright. B. in London, he wrote naturalistic plays of the English middle class, believing that a play stands or falls artistically as well as commercially by the judgement of the wider audience. They incl. the comedy *French Without Tears* (1936); *The Winslow Boy* (1945) based on a real-life incident of a naval cadet wrongly accused of theft; *The Browning Version* (1948), study of a schoolmaster; *Separate Tables* (1954), set in a Bournemouth hotel; and *Ross* (1960) dealing with T. E. Lawrence. He was knighted in 1971.

RATTLESNAKE. A snake of the N American genus *Crotalus*, distinguished by the horny flat rings of the tail, which 'rattle' when vibrated. The venom injected by the R. is fatal.

RAVEL (rahvel'), **Maurice** (1875-1937). French composer. B. at Ciboure, he achieved a reputation with the piano pieces *Pavane pour une Infante défunte* (1899), and *Jeux d'eau* (1901). Among his later works are the sensational *Boléro*; the ballet *Daphnis et Chloé; the operas L'Heure espagnole* and *L'Enfant et les sortilèges*; and the piano compositions *Gaspard de la nuit, Miroirs,* etc.

RAVEN. Bird (*Corvus corax*) in the crow family. About 60cm (2ft) long, the R. has black and lustrous plumage. Found only in the northern hemisphere, it is rare in Britain, breeding chiefly in N Scotland.

RAVE'NNA. City of Emilia, Italy. It lies in a marshy plain and is famous for its Byzantine churches with superb mosaics, e.g. San Vitale. R. was a Roman port and naval station, and 404-93 was the cap. of the W Roman emperors, 493-526 of Theodoric, and later of the Byzantine exarchs 539-750. Byron lived for some months at R., home of the Countess Guiccioli, during the years 1819-21. Pop. (1978) 138,560.

RAVI (rah′vē). River in the Indian sub-continent, a tributary of the Chenab which it joins above Multan. It rises in India, forms the boundary between India and Pakistan for some 95km (70m), and enters Pakistan above Lahore, the chief town on its course of 725km (450m). It is an important source of water for the Punjab irrigation canal system.

RAWALPINDI. City in Pakistan, in the foothills of the Himalayas. It is a great military, road, and rail centre and 1959-67 was cap. of Pakistan pending the construction of Islamabad immediately to the NW. Pop. (1972) 615,400.

RAWLINSON, Sir Henry Creswicke (1810-95). British orientalist. B. in Oxfordshire, he became political agent in Baghdad in 1844, and translated Darius' cuneiform inscription at Behistun. He continued the work of excavation begun by Layard, and pub. a *History of Assyria*, etc.

RAWSTHORNE, Alan (1905-71). British composer. B. in Lancs., he first became known by his 'Theme and Variations for Two Violins' (1938), which was followed by other tersely virile works incl. 'Symphonic Studies', the cantata *Kubla Khan*, the 'Concerto for String Orchestra', and a vigorously inventive 'Sonata for Violin and Piano' (1959).

RAY or **Wray, John** (1627-1705). British botanist, whose *Methodus plantarum* (1682) was the first to divide flowering plants into monocotyledons and dicotyledons, etc. The R. Society, founded in 1844, perpetuates his memory.

RAY, Satyajit (1921-). Indian film director. B. in Bengal, and a commercial artist before he turned to films, he is well known for his interpretation of Bengali life, e.g. *Asparajito* (1956: *The Unvanquished*), and *Distant Thunder* (1973).

RAY. Fish with a flattened body, wing-like pectoral fins, and a tail like a whip, e.g. the stingrays, which have a serrate, poisonous spine on the tail, and the torpedo fish (q.v.).

Also the path along which a wave may be considered to travel, i.e. perpendicular to the wave front.

RAYLEIGH (rā′li), **John W. Strutt,** 3rd baron R. (1842-1919). British physicist. He was prof. of experimental physics at Cambridge 1879-84, and of natural philosophy at the Royal Institution 1887-1905. He wrote the standard *Treatise on Sound* and experimented in optics and microscopy. With Sir William Ramsay, R. discovered argon. He was awarded the OM, and was president of the Royal Society 1905-8, when he became chancellor of Cambridge Univ. In 1904 he received a Nobel prize.

RAYON. The name which has superseded artificial silk for the filaments made from the solidification of solutions of modified cellulose. The 3 types of commercial importance are viscose, acetate, and copper R.

RAZORBILL. A resident British seabird (*Alca torda*), of the auk family, which breeds on cliffs. It has a curved beak, and is black above and white below.

RAZOR-SHELL or **razor-fish.** Genera (*Ensis* and *Solen*) of bivalve molluscs, with narrow elongated shells, resembling a razor handle and delicately coloured. They are found in sand among rocks.

READE, Charles (1814-84). British author. B. in Oxfordshire, he was called to the Bar in 1843, but devoted himself to writing in London. As a dramatist his great successes were *Mask and Faces* (1852: pub. in novel form as *Peg Woffington* in 1853), and *The Lyons Mail* (1854). Among his novels are *It's Never too Late to Mend* (1856); his historical masterpiece *The Cloister and the Hearth* (1861); and *Hard Cash* (1863). His nephew **William Winwood R.** (1838-75) wrote the extremely popular *Martyrdom of Man* (1872), a rationalistic survey of history.

READING, Rufus Daniel Isaacs, 1st marquess of (1860-1935). Liberal statesman. Son of a Jewish merchant, he was called to the Bar and entered parliament in 1904. He became Attorney-Gen. in 1910 and Lord Chief Justice in 1913. Raised to the peerage in 1914, he was Viceroy of India 1921-6. On his return to England he was made a marquess, and in the National govt he was For. Sec. in 1931. His widow, **Stella** (1894-1971), dowager marchioness of R., was created a baroness (life peerage) in her own right in 1958, and was the founder (1938) of the Women's Voluntary Services for Civil Defence.

READING. English town, admin. HQ of Berks, on the Thames at its junction with the Kennet. An important railway junction and agricultural centre, noted for biscuits and electronics. The univ. (1926), founded as a univ. coll. in 1892, specializes in agriculture and horticulture, but has also faculties in arts, science, music, etc. Oscar Wilde passed his 2 years' imprisonment at R. Pop. (1972) 135,000.

READING. City of Pa., USA, important as a manufacturing centre. It was founded in 1748 by two sons of Wm. Penn. Pop. (1970) 87,650.

REAGAN (rā′gan), **Ronald** (1911-). American Republican statesman. B. in Tampico, Illinois, he was a star from the thirties of some fifty films and later also in television. Politically, he made the transition from Rooseveltian liberalism to down-the-line Republicanism, becoming Rep. gov. of California 1967-74, when his term was marked by battles against insurgent students of the Univ. of California. In 1968 and 1974 he made bids for the Rep. presidential nomination, losing first to Nixon, then to Ford, but in 1980 succeeded and won a landslide victory over Carter. He pledged to free American enterprise at home and to enable the country to negotiate from a 'position of strength' abroad.

He survived an assassination attempt in 1981, and in 1984 won a landslide victory against Mondale to become re-elected for a further four-year term as president. He has adopted a policy of intervention in central America, particularly in Nicaragua (q.v.).

REALISM. In the medieval philosophy known as Scholasticism, the theory that the only truly real things are 'universals'; it is thus opposed both to Nominalism and to Conceptualism. In modern philosophy the term stands for the doctrine that there is an intuitively appreciated reality apart from what is presented to consciousness, that what is experienced through the senses has an independent existence. As such it is opposed to Idealism. Modern realists incl. C. D. Broad and (although their views were later modified) Russell and G. E. Moore: Wittgenstein has been an important later influence.

REAL PRESENCE. The belief that there are present in the properly consecrated Eucharist the body and blood of Jesus Christ. It is held by Roman Catholics, and in some sense by Anglo-Catholics.

RÉAUMUR (rā-ōmür′), **René Antoine Ferchault de** (1683-1757). French scientist. B. at La Rochelle, his researches assisted the development of French industry, and included a method of tinning iron. He invented the R.

REAGAN. Practising a foreign policy of military and financial intervention, Ronald Reagan was re-elected President in 1984.

thermometer scale, in which freezing point is 0° and boiling point 80°.

RECALL. A political device providing for the immediate recall of an elected delegate if he acts contrary to the wishes of his constituents. It originated in Switzerland, and since 1903 has been adopted in a number of states of USA. A certain percentage of the electorate must sign an application for a fresh election.

RÉCAMIER (rehkahmyā'), **Jeanne Françoise** (1777-1849). French leader of society. B. at Lyons, *née* Bernard, she m. at 15 Jacques R., an elderly banker. She was the 'queen' of a salon of literary and political celebrities.

RECIFE (resē'fe). Seaport in Brazil, cap. of Pernambuco state, at the mouth of the r. Capibaribe. Its proximity to Europe and good harbour give it great commercial importance. It has an airport. Founded in 1504, R. is intersected by waterways. It is the seat of a univ. (1946) and is a naval base. Industries incl. sugar refining, fruit canning, and the making of cotton textiles and flour. Pop. (1970) 1,060,700.

RECKLINGHAUSEN (-howsen). Town in North Rhine-Westphalia, W Germany, 24km (15m) NW of Dortmund. Coal mines and iron foundries are nearby and it has chemical and textile factories, engineering works, etc. R. is said to have been founded by Charlemagne. Pop. (1972) 125,000.

RECORDER. In England, a part-time judge who may sit alone, or in specified circumstances, with justices of the peace, to exercise jurisdiction in the Crown Courts in less serious cases. They are chosen from barristers of standing and also, since the Courts Act of 1971, from solicitors: Rs. may eventually become Circuit judges.

Also, name applied generally to the flute family and in particular to the true Rs. of English origin.

RECORD OFFICE, Public. Estab. in 1838 in Chancery Lane, London, the P.R.O. contains the English national records since the Norman Conquest, brought together from Courts of Law and Govt Depts, incl. Domesday Book, the Gunpowder Plot papers, and the log of HMS *Victory* at Trafalgar. Modern records from the 18th cent. have been housed at Kew from 1976. *See* ARCHIVES.

RECORD PLAYER. Device for reproducing sound recorded as a spiral groove on a disc or 'record'. A motor-driven turntable rotates the record at a constant speed, and a stylus or 'needle' on the tone arm is made to vibrate by the undulations as it touches the record. These vibrations are then converted to electrical signals by a transducer, and, after amplification, pass to a loudspeaker which converts them into sound.

The pioneers of the R.P. were Edison, with his phonograph and Emile Berliner, who invented the disc record (1896). The most recent developments are in stereophonic sound (*see* HI-FI), and digital recording.

Digital recording does not record the vibrations of sound waves directly, but picks up the sound by microphones and then feeds it through amplifiers to a computer. The computer converts the sound waves to a series of numbers equivalent to the character of the wave form, stores them as binary words, and plays them back into re-created sound waves which cause the membrane of the speaker to vibrate. Distortion is completely avoided because there are no imperfections, as in magnetic tape or record surfaces. *See also* TAPE RECORDING.

RECTIFIER. Device for obtaining unidirectional current from an alternating source of supply, either by inversion of or suppression of alternate half-waves. Rs. are necessary in the conversion of a.c. supply to d.c. The many different types all depend on being able to pass current in one direction and unable to pass it in the reverse direction.

RECTOR. Term applied to an Anglican clergyman who receives the whole of the tithes levied in his parish, as against a vicar who draws only part; also to the head of certain universities and colleges.

RECYCLING. The reclamation of potentially useful material from household and industrial waste, preventing pollution and saving expenditure on scarce raw materials and depletion of often non-renewable resources. Also, the investment by oil-producing nations of surplus funds in the industries, etc., of oil-importing nations, so rectifying the shortfall in their profit and loss accounts.

RED. Slang term for a revolutionary, Anarchist or Communist, which originated in the 19th cent. in the form 'red republican', meaning a republican who favoured a social as well as a political revolution, generally by armed violence.

RED ARMY. Title formerly borne by the army of the USSR. It developed from the Red Guards, or volunteers who carried out the Bolshevik revolution, and received its name because it fought under the red flag. The name R.A. was abolished in 1946, 'Soviet Army' being substituted.

RED CROSS, The. International agency founded to assist wounded and prisoners in war. Prompted by war horrors described by the Swiss, Henri Dunant, the Geneva Convention of 1864 laid down the principles ensuring the safety of ambulances, hospitals, stores, and personnel distinguished by the emblem of the red Geneva Cross on a white ground. The British R.C. Society was founded in 1870, and incorporated in 1908. In addition to dealing with associated problems of war, e.g. refugees, and the care of the disabled, the R.C. is increasingly concerned with the disasters of peace - epidemics, floods, earthquakes, accidents, etc. The R.C. also works in close association with the St John Ambulance Association. The American National R.C. was founded 1881. The Moslem equivalent is the Red Crescent.

RED DEER. Woodland deer (*Cervus elaphus*) of Europe and W Asia which in Britain is kept ornamentally in parks, but is also hunted on Exmoor and 'stalked' in Scotland as 'sport'. The male is antlered, and 140cm (4½ft) at the shoulder: in the rutting season in autumn its 'bell' or roar is formidable. The young are spotted, but adults lose these markings *See also* DEER.

REDDITCH. Town in Worcs, England, famous for needles, fishing tackle, car and aircraft components, cycles and motor cycles, and electrical equipment. It was developed from 1965 as a 'new town' to take Birmingham's overspill. Pop. (1975) 45,760.

RED DUSTER. Popular name for the Red Ensign, flag of the British mercantile marine. First used in 1674, it was shared with the RN until 1864, when it became the exclusive symbol of merchant ships.

RED FLAG. The international symbol of Socialism. In France it was used as a revolutionary emblem from 1792 onward, and was adopted officially as its flag by the Paris Commune of 1871. Since the revolution of Nov. 1917, it has been the national flag of the USSR; as such it bears a golden hammer and sickle crossed, symbolizing the unity of the industrial workers and peasants, under a gold-rimmed 5-pointed star, signifying peace between the 5 continents. 'The Red Flag', the Labour Party anthem, was written by Jim Connell during the 1889 London strike.

REDGRAVE, Sir Michael (Scudamore) (1908–85). British actor. B. in Bristol, the son of an actor, he made a reputation for sensitive playing in *Thunder Rock* (1941: filmed 1942), is noted for his stylish, well-balanced Shakespearian performances, and has appeared with special distinction in his own stage adaptation of James's *The Aspern Papers* (1959) and in Chekhov's *Uncle Vanya* (1962-3). He was knighted in 1959. His dau. **Vanessa R.** (1937-), with whom he has sometimes appeared, became famous for her interpretation of Ophelia, and appeared in such films as *Morgan - A Suitable Case for Treatment* (1966) and *Mary, Queen of Scots* (1972).

RED GUARDS. In the USSR the armed workers who took part in the Bolshevik revolution 1917: in China from 1966 the school and college students with red armbands who furthered the Cultural Revolution by attacking old ideas, culture, habits and customs.

RED INDIANS. *See* INDIANS, AMERICAN.

REDL, Alfred. *See* SECRET SERVICE.

REDMOND, John Edward (1856-1918). Irish statesman, leader of the Nationalist Party from the death of Parnell until after the Easter Rebellion in 1916. He was elected an MP in 1881, and from 1900 was the acknowledged head of the Irish parliamentary party. After the general elections of 1910 he held the balance of power in the House of Commons, and was able to secure the introduction of a Home Rule bill. Strong opposition was encountered in Ulster, and in 1914 the Ulster Covenanters and R.'s Nationalist Volunteers seemed likely to come to open war. When the F.W.W. broke out, however, R. flung all his influence into the country's war effort, and in recognition of his patriotism the Home Rule bill was passed, although its operation was to be suspended until the end of the war. The rise of Sinn Féin and the Easter Rebellion were bitter blows, and R. d. a disappointed man.

REDOUTÉ (redootā'), **Pierre Joseph** (1759-1840). French artist, the 'Raphael of Flowers'. Patronized by the Empress Josephine and the Bourbon court, he produced superb volumes of flower paintings, the finest being *Les Roses* (1817-24). To delicacy of touch, he added a profound knowledge of plant structure.

RED RIVER. Western tributary of the Mississippi, USA, so-called because of the reddish soil sediment it carries. The stretch which forms the Texas-Oklahoma border is known as Tornado Alley because in the spring warm air from the Gulf of Mexico colliding with cold fronts from the north leads to tornado formation.

REDRUTH. *See* CAMBORNE-R.

RED SEA. A strip of water about 2,000 km (1,200 m) long and 160-320km (100-200m) wide, running SE from Suez to the straits of Bab-el-Mandeb. Occupying part of the Great Rift Valley, it separates Egypt, the Sudan Republic, and Ethiopia in Africa from Arabia in Asia. The R.S. is referred to in the OT, notably in Exodus, chap. 14, which relates the story of the escape of the Israelites across the R.S. from Pharaoh and his chariots. The sludge of its floor is mineral-rich.

REDSHANK. Bird (*Tringa totanus*) of N Europe and Asia, where it nests in swampy areas, although wintering farther south. Named from its long red legs, it is greyish and speckled black.

REDSTART. Bird (*Phoenicurus phoenicurus*) which winters in Africa and spends the summer in Europe. Named from its red tail, it has a dark grey head (with white mark on the forehead) and back, and brown wings with lighter underparts. The American R. (*Setophaga ruticilla*) belongs to a different family.

RED TAPE. Phrase descriptive of bureaucratic methods, derived from the 'pink' fastening for departmental bundles of documents in Britain.

REDWING. Member of the thrush species (*Turdus iliacus*), rather smaller than the song thrush, and with reddish wing and body markings. It breeds in the north of Europe and Asia, moving south in winter.

REDWOOD. *See* SEQUOIA.

REED, Sir Carol (1906-76). British film producer and director. His films incl. *Odd Man Out* (1947); *The Fallen Idol* (1950) and *The Third Man* (1950), both written for him by Graham Greene; and *The Running Man* (1962).

REED. Perennial aquatic grasses. The common R. (*Phragmites communis*) attains 3.5m (12ft) or more, having stiff erect leaves, and straight stems bearing a plume of purplish flowers.

REED. In music, the sound-producing medium of various families of instruments, so called because it is made from the outer layer of the R. (*Arundo donax*). The 'beating' R., which vibrates against the side of the instrument tube, is used in the organ (the R. in this case being metal), clarinet, etc., and the 'free' R. which vibrates from side to side within the tube, in the mouth organ, harmonium, accordion, etc.

REEMAN, Douglas (1924-). British novelist. He served in the Navy in the S.W.W., and his books, beginning with *A Prayer for the Ship* (1958) reflect this experience. He is also the author, under the pseudonym Alexander Kent, of a series set in the Napoleonic period and dealing with the career of Admiral Richard Bolitho.

REEVES, William Pember (1857-1932). New Zealand statesman and writer. He was Minister of Education in N.Z. (1891-6), and director of the London School of Economics (1908-19). He wrote poetry and the classic description of N.Z., *Long White Cloud* (1898).

REEMAN. Douglas Reeman, whose books not only have authenticity, whether in period or modern setting, but an unusual depth of conception in their characterisation.

REFEREE. An arbitrator. The term is most commonly used of the official in charge of a game, such as football, but may also be applied in law to members of the court of Rs. appointed by the House of Commons to give judgment on petitions against private bills, etc., and to the 3 official Rs. to whom cases before the High Court may be submitted.

REFERENDUM. The procedure whereby a decision on proposed legislation is referred to the electorate for settlement by direct popular vote. It is most frequently employed in Switzerland, but has also been used in Canada, Australia, New Zealand, and certain states of the USA. It was used for the first time in the UK in 1975 on the Common Market issue.

REFORMATION, The. The movement which in the 16th cent. ended the religious unity of W Europe, and resulted in the establishment of the Protestant Churches. Reforming movements akin to Protestantism had existed since the 12th cent., e.g. the Waldenses in France and Germany, the Lollards in England, and the Hussites in Bohemia, but these had all been driven underground. The success of the R. in the 16th cent. was due partly to the rise of centralized absolute monarchies, which resented the political power of the papacy, and partly to the price revolution, which impelled kings and nobles to confiscate the Church's enormous wealth.

The R. began in Germany in 1517 with Luther's (q.v.) protest against the sale of indulgences; the title of 'Protestants' came into general use in 1529. The Peace of Augsburg (1555) left N and W Germany Protestant, and E and S Germany RC. An offshoot of German Protestantism was the Anabaptist movement. Lutheranism was officially adopted by Sweden in 1527 and by Denmark in 1536. In Switzerland the R. was begun by Zwingli (q.v.) in 1518; it later came under the leadership of Calvin (q.v.). Calvinism found many followers in France, where the Huguenots (q.v.), although a minority, were strong enough to carry on a religious war, 1562-98. Both Calvinism and Anabaptism were strong in Holland, where resentment of religious persecution was a main cause of the war of independence (1568-1609). The English R. was begun under Henry VIII, who repudiated papal authority in 1534, and dissolved the monasteries. Under Edward VI Protestantism was established, and after a reaction under Mary, the process was completed by Elizabeth. The Scottish R., led by Knox (q.v.), triumphed in 1560. In Italy, Spain, and Portugal Protestantism was crushed by the Inquisition; in Bohemia, Poland, and Hungary it won considerable support, but was almost stamped out in the 17th cent.

REFORMATION. On the left, Cromwell and Cranmer, the latter presenting his bible to the king who crushes pope Clement VII beneath his feet. In vain, Pole and Fisher endeavour to rescue him, while monks in the foreground bewail their fate. *Photo: Mary Evans Picture Library*

REFRIGERATION. The process of absorbing heat at a low temperature and rejecting it at a higher temperature. R. is used in the food industries for the preservation of foodstuffs by chilling or freezing, the storage time which can be tolerated varying with the character of the foodstuff and, in general, increasing as the storage temperature is lowered. R. is also used in industrial processes and in air-conditioning (comfort cooling). *See also* DEEP FREEZING.

The R. process may be effected by gas expansion, by absorption cycles or most commonly by the vapour compression cycle. This is based on the fact that a fluid will absorb heat in changing from the liquid to the gaseous state, and reject heat when changed from gaseous to liquid state: absorption can take place at a low temperature and heat rejection can take place at a higher temperature. Fluids used as refrigerants in the vapour compression cycle incl. carbon dioxide (used most in R. plants on ships), ammonia (generally in industrial and marine equipment), and Refrigerant-12 (dichlorodifluoromethane), the most useful fluid in domestic and small commercial plants such as are used in shops and markets. *See also* CRYONICS.

REFUGEES. *See* DISPLACED PERSONS.

RĒGĀ'LIA or **Crown Jewels.** The symbols of royal authority. The British R. were broken up during the Commonwealth, with the exception of the ampulla and anointing spoon, and the present set mainly dates from after the Restoration. A daring attempt to steal them was made in 1671 by Colonel Blood, who was subsequently pardoned and pensioned by Charles II. Formerly kept in the Wakefield Tower, they were moved 1967 to the newly-built Crown Jewel House, in the Tower of London, and are elaborately guarded. Among the chief items are St Edward's Crown; the Imperial State Crown; the jewelled Sword of State used only at the Coronation; the Sword of State used at the opening of Parliament and on other State occasions; the Curtana (Sword of Mercy); the Swords of Temporal and Spiritual Justice; the Orb; the Royal Sceptre or Sceptre with the Cross (containing the great Star of Africa, cut from the Cullinan diamond); the Rod with the Dove; St Edward's Staff; the Spurs; the Coronation Ring (the 'Wedding Ring of England'); the Armills (gold bracelets, given by the Commonwealth countries in 1953); the Ampulla (which contains the holy oil for the anointing); and the Anointing Spoon.

REGENCY STYLE. Style of architecture which prevailed in England during the latter part of the 18th cent. and the early part of the 19th cent. The style is characterized by its restrained simplicity, and its imitation of ancient classic architecture, especially Greek. The most famous architects of the period were Henry Holland, who designed many domestic buildings, John Nash (q.v.), and Decimus Burton, who designed the screen at Hyde Park Corner.

REGENSBURG (reh'gensboorg). City in Bavaria, W Germany, on the Danube at its confluence with the Regen, 100km (63m) NE of Munich. Many fine medieval buildings remain. It is on the site of a Celtic settlement going back to 500 BC, became the Roman Castra Regina in AD 179, a free city in 1245, and seat of the German Diet from the 16th cent. to 1806. It was incl. in Bavaria in 1810. Pop. (1978) 133,500.

REGENT. One who discharges the royal functions during the king's minority or incapacity. Since Henry VIII's reign a R. or council of regency has always been appointed by act of Parliament. The Prince of Wales, later George IV, acted as R. during George III's insanity, 1811-20; hence this period is usually referred to as 'the Regency'.

REGER (reh'ger), **Max** (1873-1916). German composer and pianist. He was b. in Bavaria, and became organist at Weiden. He taught at Munich, 1905-7, was professor at the Leipzig Conservatoire from 1907, and conductor of the Meiningen ducal orchestra 1911-13. He composed prolifically, but alcoholic excess led to his early death. His works incl. fine organ and piano music, chamber music and songs.

REGGAE (re'gā). Jamaican music, with its roots in Black Africa, which is particularly assoc. with the anti-White religious sect, the Rastafarians. Believing in Haile Selassie, the Emperor of Ethiopia as their deity, they demanded repatriation to Africa: the emperor was crowned as Ras Tafari - hence the sect name. The instruments are made from bamboo, hoops from salt-fish barrels, etc., and the musical themes are crude and the rhythm thumpingly insistent. Taken to Britain in the 1960s by immigrants, it became a White cult in the 1970s.

REGGIO (rej'ō). Port of Calabria, Italy, on the Straits of Messina, producing wine, oil, silk and perfumery. Pop. (1978) 179,000. Also, a town of Emilia, at the foot of the Apennines. Pop. (1978) 130,000.

REGINA (rejī'na). Cap. of Saskatchewan prov., Canada, 575km (357m) W of Winnipeg. It is in a grain and oil producing region, and growth has been stimulated by the development of potash resources of the prov.; industries incl. oil refining, cement, steel, farm machinery, fertilizers, and flour. It was founded 1882 on a site where Indians had piled the bones of slain buffalo, hence nicknames such as Bone Creek, but was called Regina in honour of Victoria, and is known as Queen City of the Plains. The Mounties' museum is a tourist attraction. Pop. (1978) 159,260.

REGIONAL CRIME SQUAD. *See* CRIMINAL INVESTIGATION DEPT.

REICH (rīkh), **Wilhelm** (1897-1957). Austrian doctor, advocate of sexual freedom. He combined Marxism and psychoanalysis, and in *The Sexual Revolution* gave a detailed account of the change in this sphere which accompanied the Russian economic revolution. His ideas on *The Function of the Orgasm* were controversial. He emigrated to USA in 1939, and d. in prison, following committal for contempt of court.

REICH (rīkh). The German state. The Nazi régime was known as the 3rd R., the 1st generally being identified with the Holy Roman Empire, and the 2nd with the German Empire of 1871-1918.

REICHSTADT, Duke of. *See* NAPOLEON II.

REICHSTAG (rīkhs'tahg) **FIRE.** The burning of the Reichstag building at Berlin on 27 Feb., 1933, which was probably organized by Nazis, led by Goering, and by them attributed to the Communists. Van der Lubbe, a half-witted Dutchman who was probably a Nazi tool, Torgler, a Communist deputy, and Dimitrov (q.v.), Popov, and Tanev, Bulgarian Communists, were tried at Leipzig. Dimitrov's defence forced the court to acquit all the prisoners except Van der Lubbe, who was executed.

REID, Thomas (1710-96). Scottish philosopher. B. in Kincardineshire, he became a Presbyterian minister, and in 1764 succeeded Adam Smith as prof. of moral philosophy at Glasgow. He wrote an *Enquiry into the Human Mind on the Principles of Common Sense* (1764), and other works in which he elaborated his 'commonsense philosophy'. There are certain self-evident things, he maintained, such as the material external world and the human soul, which are believed to exist by 'the consent of ages and nations, of the learned and unlearned'.

REIGATE (rī'gāt). Town in Surrey 32km (20m) S of London, at the foot of the North Downs, forming with Redhill a residential suburb. Pop. (1973) 55,600.

REIMS (rēmz; Fr. raṅs). City in Marne dept, NE France, 130km (80m) NE of Paris on the Vesle, the Roman Durocorturum; from 987 all but six French kings were crowned at R. Ceded to England by the 1420 treaty of Troyes, the city was retaken by Joan of Arc, who in 1429 had Charles VII consecrated in the cathedral built during the 13th cent. The Mars Gate dates from the 4th cent. R. is the centre of the great champagne industry. Woollen and other textiles are manufactured. Pop. (1975) 177,320.

REINCARNATION. The doctrine that the soul after death may enter another human body or that of an animal. It has appeared in the teachings of many religions and philosophies, e.g. Buddhism, Hinduism, Jainism, the philosophies of Pythagoras and Plato, certain Christian heresies, and Theosophy.

REINDEER. Deer of the Arctic and sub-Arctic, common to both E and W hemispheres. About 120cm (4 ft) at the shoulder, it has a thick, brownish coat and broad hoofs well adapted to travel over snow. It is the only deer in which antlers are also present in the female: up to 150cm (5ft) long, they are shed in winter. The Scandinavian form (*Rangifer tarandus*) has been domesticated by the Lapps for cents., and has been introduced to Alaska and the Canadian Arctic. The American form (*R. caribou*), known as caribou, occurs in 2 forms - the large woodland caribou of the more southerly region and the barren-ground caribou of the north. R. migrate southward in winter, moving in large herds, and it is in Dec.-March that the Lapps round them up for sorting by their owners: a frilly greyish lichen (*Cladonia rangiferina*), popularly known as R. moss, is their main food.

REINHARDT (rīn'hahrt), **Max** (1873-1943). Austrian-American theatrical producer. Besides the classics - Shakespeare, Molière, Ibsen - he was celebrated for his romantically lavish London production of *The Miracle* (1911) with Lady Diana Cooper, and from 1933 worked in America, becoming a naturalized citizen and making such films as *A Midsummer Night's Dream.*

REITH, John Charles Walsham, 1st baron (1889-1971). Brit. public servant. As 1st general manager (1922-7) and 1st director-general (1927-38) of the BBC, he supervised the creation and development of British radio services and of the world's first regular TV service (1936): the annual series of broadcast *R. Lectures* (1947), given by outstanding leaders of contemporary thought, were named in his honour. He was a pioneer advocate of the publicly owned but independently operated utility corporation.

RELATIVITY. Theory of physics, associated with the name of Albert Einstein (q.v.), based on the requirement that the laws of physics should be unaffected by the uniform motion of the observer. The need for such a theory became apparent in 1887, when Michelson and Morley performed an experiment to determine the velocity with which the Earth moved through the hypothetical ether. No such velocity was, however, detected; and Lorenz and Fitzgerald suggested that this was because a measuring rod or body in motion suffers a contraction in length in the direction of its motion - a correction just sufficient to account for the negative result of the Michelson-Morley experiment. This suggestion was given rational justification by Einstein in the Special Theory of R. in 1905. It may be impossible to determine absolute motion by any experiment whatever, he said; the phenomena of nature will be the same to 2 unaccelerated observers moving with any uniform velocity relative to one another. Ten years later Einstein advanced his General Theory of R., which was even more revolutionary in its impact on the world of physics. Newton's theory of gravitation had to be abandoned because it was incompatible with the Special Theory of R. Einstein now explained gravitation in terms of the properties of space and time, and not by the idea of a gravitational force of attraction. The idea of 'force of gravitation' is abandoned. The planets, stars, etc., move as they do, not because they are influenced by forces coming from other bodies in the universe, but because of the special nature of the world of space and time in the neighbourhood of matter. Einstein's theory, furthermore, led to the remarkable conclusion that light-rays are 'bent'. In the vast interstellar spaces unaffected by gravitating masses, light-rays travel in straight lines; but when they come within the field of influence of a star or other massive body they are deflected by the latter's gravitational field by an amount directly proportional to the body's mass.

The Einstein theory was carefully tested by expeditions despatched by the observatories of Greenwich and Cambridge to observe the eclipse of the Sun of 1919, and the results were conclusively in its favour. The theory also predicts the 'shift' of certain lines in the solar spectrum, the precession in the orbit of Mercury, and the bending of light-rays in the neighbourhood of the Sun, and these results admit of experimental verification. In recent years it has been suggested that the general theory might be revised to take account of Mach's principle that the properties of space and time in our vicinity are governed by the distribution of matter in the remote nebulae.

RELAY, Electrical. Switching device operated by an electric current, causing abrupt changes, e.g. making or breaking the circuit, changing of the circuit connections, or variation in the circuit characteristics.

RELICS. Objects associated with Christ or a saint, or parts of a saint's body, preserved as objects of religious veneration. The cult of R. gave rise to many abuses in the Middle Ages, and it was condemned by the Protestant reformers but upheld by the Council of Trent. Relic-worship is widely practised in Lamaism, Mahayana Buddhism, etc.

RELIEF. In architecture, a term applied to carved figures and other forms which project from the background. The Italian terms *basso-rilievo* (low relief), *mezzo-rilievo* (middle relief), and *alto-rilievo* (high relief) are used according to the thickness of the sculpture from the background. The French term *bas-relief* is commonly used for low relief.

RELIGION. Term usually derived from the Latin *religāre*, to bind, that is used to describe man's attitude towards the gods or God. In original Buddhism, there is no Deity; yet Buddhism, like atheistic Jainism, and Confucianism, which is primarily a code of good behaviour, is always included in the list of the world's religions. E. B. Taylor gave as 'the minimum definition of religion, the belief in spiritual beings'. Matthew Arnold defined it as 'morality touched with emotion', but, as Prof. W. K. Clifford pointed out, some religious facts are immoral, e.g. human sacrifices to the gods, sacred prostitution, suttee, and thuggery. Prof. J. E. M'Taggart thought of R. as a feeling of harmony between oneself and the universe. Some modern theologians find the essence of R. to lie in a feeling of awe or reverence for the Unseen Power who or which is believed to be making for righteousness.

The chief religions are: (a) the Oriental faiths: Hinduism, Buddhism, Jainism, Sikhism, Parseeism, Confucianism and Taoism in China, Japanese Shinto; and (b) Judaism, Christianity, and Islam (Mohammedanism) - 'religions of a book'. Of Christianity the principal divisions are the Roman Catholic, the Eastern Orthodox, and the Protestant.

Marxist Communism, or dialectal materialism, is sometimes incl. among religions, since it requires belief in the revelation of Marx and Engels and in its interpretation by the 'priesthood' of the party, and offers the believer the reward of absorption into the heaven of a classless, egalitarian society. The god or other 'illusions' in competing faiths are seen as created by the need for some escape from the evils of capitalism, and when man becomes his own 'god' in a perfect society the need for such myths disappears. The concept lacks logic and has no more produced even its own kind of perfection in any existing experiment than other faiths.

RELIGION, Comparative. The impartial study of the various religions of the world. The first-known surviving attempt of a kind of philosophy of religious beliefs is contained in fragments of the Greek thinker Xenophanes (6th cent. BC). Herodotus and Aristotle contributed to the study. The Middle Ages provided nothing but naive tales and observations, and the Reformation had a narrowing influence. Really serious comparative work did not begin until the 17th cent., when the Jesuits in China produced some interesting studies. Towards the end of the 18th cent. a little body of English missionary scholars in Calcutta began to study the sacred books of India. An immense stimulus was given to the investigation of religious beliefs by the Darwinian theory of Evolution. Notable workers in the field incl. Max Müller, Sir James Frazer, Sir E. B. Tylor, Andrew Lang and R. C. Zaehner. Much of the raw material of the science has been provided by Christian missionaries. The more recent observers have been field anthropologists.

REMARQUE (rehmahrk'), **Erich Maria** (1898-1970). German novelist. B. at Osnabrück, he was a soldier in the F.W.W., and his anti-war sentiments, expressed in his most famous book *All Quiet on the Western Front* (1929), led to his being deprived of his German nationality in 1938; he eventually settled in the USA in 1939, and later became an American citizen.

REMBRANDT, Harmensz van Rijn (1606-69). Dutch painter and etcher. B. in Leyden, the son of a wealthy miller, he studied under Swanenburch, an architectural painter of Leyden, and for a short time under Peter Lastman in Amsterdam. The greatest painter of the Dutch school, he is famous for his masterly treatment of light and shade, his portraits of old people, and his great gift for depicting objects which are commonly regarded as ugly - e.g. 'Sirloin of Beef', and 'Slaughtered Ox' - as things of beauty. He is also the greatest of etchers. His earliest pictures - e.g. 'St Paul in Prison' and 'St Jerome' - were painted in Leyden, but most of his work was executed in Amsterdam, where he settled in 1631. He is said to have visited England about 1661-2. In 1656 he was declared bankrupt, and a collection of his etchings and drawings were sold for a fraction of their value. But he continued to work diligently, and in the closing years of his life he produced some of his best works. Besides those mentioned, his most famous works incl. 'Presentation in the Temple', the 'Anatomy Lesson', 'The Night Watch', 'Woman Taken in Adultery', 'The Good Samaritan', and a number of self-portraits.

REMEMBRANCE SUNDAY. National Day of Remembrance for both world wars. A 'two-minute silence' is observed at the actual time of the signature of the Armistice with Germany on 11 Nov. 1918 in the F.W.W., and services of commemoration are held, with wreaths of

REMBRANDT. A detail from 'An old man as St Paul', a penetrating study of the experience of the sorrows of life. *Photo: Courtesy of the National Gallery, London*

'Flanders poppies' being laid at the Whitehall Cenotaph and elsewhere. The poppies are also worn by individuals and are made and sold by disabled members of the British Legion in aid of war invalids and their dependants. Observed 1919-45 as Armistice Day (always on 11 Nov.), it was then renamed R.S. and since 1956 it has been fixed as the 2nd Sunday of the month.

RENAISSANCE (Fr. rebirth). The intellectual movement which originated in 14th-16th cent. Italy, and spread over W Europe in the 16th cent. Among its outstanding characteristics were an emphasis on the potentialities of the individual and this life; the belief in the power of education to produce the 'complete man', the man of action who is also master of all the culture of his age; the desire to enlarge the bounds of learning; the growth of scepticism and free thought; and the acceptance of Greek and Latin literature and art as models.

The beginning of the Italian R. is usually dated in the 14th cent. with the work of Dante, Petrarch, and Boccaccio; in the 16th it was almost extinguished by the Counter-Reformation. From Italy the humanists, such as Erasmus, spread the enthusiasm for classical learning through W Europe, and during the 16th cent. the ideals of the R. came gradually to dominate French, Spanish, and English culture. The invention of printing and the geographical discoveries gave a further impetus to the new spirit. Biblical criticism of Erasmus and others contributed to the Reformation, and although the 2 movements often came into conflict, such writers as Spenser and Milton successfully reconciled their ideas. Apart from those named, typical figures of the R. were Machiavelli, Ariosto, da Vinci, Michelangelo, Tasso, Bruno, Galileo and Campanella in Italy; Rabelais and Montaigne in

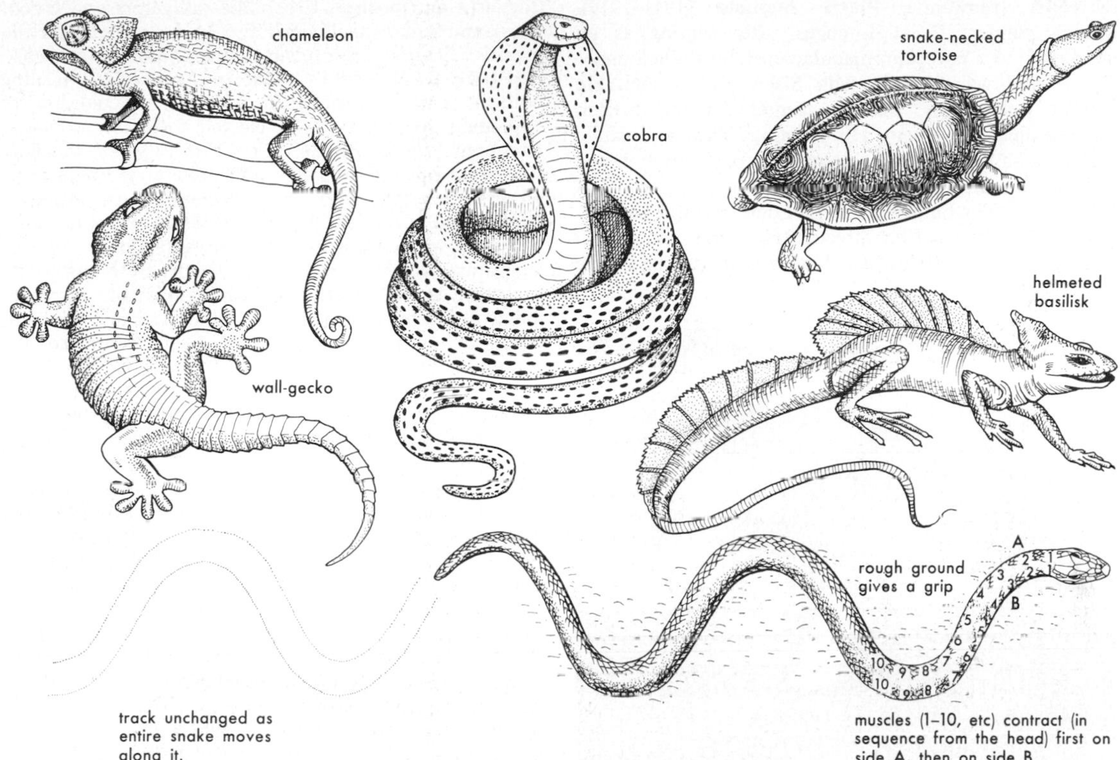

REPTILES. Representative species, and the undulatory movement used by the majority of snakes.

France; Cervantes in Spain; Camoens in Portugal; Copernicus in Poland; and More, Sidney, Marlowe, Shakespeare and Bacon in England.

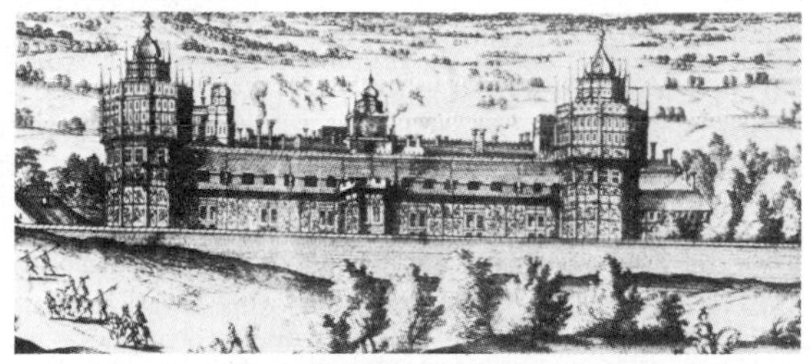

RENAISSANCE. Built by Henry VIII, Nonsuch Palace in Surrey was the embodiment of the splendour of Renaissance architecture. It was eventually given by Charles II to Lady Castlemaine who sold it to be demolished for the price of the building materials. This engraving was made in 1582 by Joris Hoefnagel.

RENAULT, Mary. Pseudonym of novelist Mary Challans (1905–83). Originally a nurse, she became famous for her re-creations of the myths and history of ancient Greece, e.g. the triology dealing with Theseus: *The Last of the Wine* (1956), *The King Must Die* (1958), and *The Bull From the Sea* (1962), and *The Persian Boy* (1972) and *The Nature of Alexander* (1975), both dealing with Alexander.

RENFREW (ren'froo). Town in Strathclyde, on the Clyde, 8km (5m) NW of Glasgow, with shipbuilding and engineering industries. It was formerly the co. town of Renfrewshire. Pop. (1973) 19,000.

RENFREWSHIRE. Former W county of central Scotland, bordering the Firth of Clyde. It was incl. in the region of Strathclyde in 1975. The co. town was Renfrew.

RENI (rā'nē), **Guido** (1575-1642). Italian painter of the Bolognese school. B. at Calvenzano, he was influenced by Caravaggio, and in *c.* 1602 settled in Rome where he painted his masterpiece, 'Phoebus and the Hours preceded by Aurora'. He eventually returned to Bologna where he founded a school.

RENNES (ren). Cap. of Ille-et-Vilaine dept, W France, at the confluence of the Ille and Vilaine, 56km (35m) SE of St Malo. It was the old cap. of Britanny, and the univ. specializes in Breton culture. The second Dreyfus trial was held at R. in 1899. Pop. (1975) 194,100.

RENNIE, John (1761-1821). Scottish engineer. His best-known works incl. old Waterloo Bridge and old London Bridge (reconstructed in USA).

RĒ'NŌ. City of Nevada, USA, on the Truckee. It dates from 1868 and is best known as a place of temporary residence in order to take advantage of the state divorce laws, which require only 6 weeks' residence and provide extensive grounds on which to sue. R. is also the seat of the state univ. (1874), and has some industry, e.g. meat packing. Pop. (1970) 72,870.

RENOIR (renwahr'), **Pierre Auguste** (1841-1919). French painter. B. at Limoges, after serving as an apprentice to a porcelain manufacturer, he studied under Gleyre and was friendly with Sisley and Monet. He became one of the leading painters of the French Impressionist movement. His paintings show a sensitive touch, and a fine sense of colour; he is particularly noted for his nudes. Among his best-known works are 'Les Parapluies', 'The Bathers', and 'La Loge'. His son, **Jean R.** (1894-1979), was a film director. His films include *La Grande Illusion* (1936), *La Marseillaise*, and *La Bête Humaine.*

RENOIR. An appealing example of this artist's work, always sensitive to the aura of femininity: 'Girl in Black'.

REPARATIONS. Indemnities paid by countries defeated in war, as by Germany in both world wars.

REPRIEVE. The legal temporary suspension of the execution of a sentence pronounced after conviction of a capital offence. It is usually associated with the death penalty. In Britain it used to be made by the Crown on the advice of the Home Sec., and in the USA it is the prerogative of state govs.: the Pres. having this power in the case of federal offences, e.g. treason.

REPTILES. Class of vertebrates (Reptilia) including the snakes, lizards, crocodiles, turtles and tortoises. They are distinguished from the Amphibia by the absence of gills, breathing by means of lungs. They are cold-blooded, produced from eggs, and the skin is usually covered with scales. Many extinct forms are known, including the orders Pterosauria, Rhynchocephalia (containing one living form, the tuatara), Plesiosauria, Ichthyosauria, and Dinosauria. The chief living orders are the Chelonia (tortoises and turtles), Crocodilia (alligators and crocodiles), and Squamata, divided into 3 sub-orders, Lacertilia (lizards); Rhiptoglossa (chameleons); Ophidia (snakes).

REPUBLICAN PARTY. One of America's 2 leading political parties, formed in 1854 by a coalition of opponents to slavery, who elected their 1st president, Abraham Lincoln in 1860. In the early years, the R.P. supported protective tariffs; and preference for genuine settlers (homesteaders) over speculators for unsettled public land. Coupled with these liberal measures were conservative tendencies and an antagonism of the legislature to the executive, which were markedly expressed after Lincoln's assassination in the impeachment of Andrew Johnson, his Democratic and southern successor, and the election of Gen. Grant to the presidency in 1868 and 1872, which were both residues of civil-war bitterness - the party being divided into those who considered the South a beaten nation, and those who did not recognize the secession, and wished to reintegrate the South into the country as a whole. Towards the end of the century the R.P. was identified with US imperialism, and industrial expansion. The era of President Theodore Roosevelt saw attempts at regulation and control of big business, and in forming the Progressive Party in 1912 he effectively removed the liberal influence from the R.P. until the 1940s. With few intermissions, the R.P. controlled the legislature from the 1860s until defeated by the 'New Deal' Democrats in 1932. The R.P. remained in eclipse until the election of Eisenhower in 1952, rather a personal triumph than that of the party which only narrowly managed to secure an initial control of Congress, soon lost and not regained by the next R. pres., Richard Nixon, in 1968. After an isolationist period before the S.W.W., the R.P. adopted an active foreign policy under Nixon and Ford, but the latter struggled under the aftermath of Watergate (q.v.), and was defeated by Carter when he stood as R. presidential candidate in 1976. However, the party achieved a landslide victory under Reagan in the 1980 presidential election, and also carried the Senate.

REREDOS (rēr'dos). An ornamental screen or wall-facing at the back of the altar of a church.

RESERPINE (res'erpēn). Tranquilliser and depressant, an alkaloid derived from the root of the plant *Rauwolfia serpentina* of SE Asia.

RESIN. A substance exuded from pines, firs, and other trees, in gummy drops which harden in air. Varnishes are the commonest products of the hard resins, and ointments those of the soft resins. Rosin is the solid residue of distilled turpentine, a soft R. The name R. is also given to many synthetic products used in adhesives, plastics and varnishes, which have similar characteristics. However, they differ chemically, being manufactured by polymerization.

RESISTANCE, electrical. The property of a substance which restricts the flow of electricity through it, associated with conversion of electrical energy to heat; also the magnitude of this property. A *resistor* is an element whose principal characteristic is R., which depends on many factors which may include any or all of the following: the nature of the material, its temperature, dimensions, and thermal properties; degree of impurity, the nature and state of illumination of the surface and the frequency and magnitude of the current. The practical unit of R. is the ohm.

RESIN. The two halves of Lotus Elite, Esprit and Eclat glass-fibre car bodies are assembled with Araldite adhesive. Unfortunately, production line models, though they have the same strength, are not equipped, as was James Bond's Lotus Esprit in *The Spy who Loved Me*, for travel under water. *Photo: Courtesy of Ciba-Geigy*

RESISTANCE MOVEMENTS. The opposition movements in Axis-occupied countries during the S.W.W. In E Europe these took the form of guerrilla warfare, among the most successful being the partisan movement led by Tito in Yugoslavia, the guerrillas in Greece and Poland, and the partisan bands behind the German lines in Russia. In more industrialized countries, such as France, Belgium, and Czechoslovakia, sabotage in war factories and on the railways, combined with underground propaganda and the assassination of particularly obnoxious Germans and collaborators, was more important. In these countries also, however, guerrilla activity was maintained, the groups affording a refuge for men resisting conscription for forced labour. Most of the R.Ms. were based on an alliance of all anti-Fascist parties, but in some countries, such as Yugoslavia and Greece, serious conflict arose between left-and right-wing movements. After the S.W.W. the tactics of the R. were used by countries under colonial rule to gain independence.

RESPIGHI (respē'gē), **Ottorino** (1879-1936). Italian composer. B. at Bologna, he studied under Rimsky-Korsakov, and in 1913 became prof. of composition at the Accademia di Santa Cecilia in Rome. He composed operas, and orchestral works of a descriptive nature, e.g. *Fontane di Roma*, etc.

RESPIRATION. The process by which the blood gives up carbon dioxide and is charged with oxygen. Used blood is forced into the lungs by the contraction of the right ventricle of the heart; there it passes through fine capillary vessels with very thin walls in contact with the air cells. From these the blood takes up oxygen (about 4 per cent of the total volume of the air), giving up the same quantity of carbon dioxide, together with water and small quantities of ammonia and waste matter. The rate of R. at rest in the adult is about 18 to the minute; during sleep it becomes slower, and during exertion, emotion, or fever it may be much increased.

RETRIEVER. Breed of sporting dog. The flat or wavy-coated R. was derived from the Labrador R. and the setter or collie. The head and neck are long, the body rather short, and the coat black or liver-coloured. The curly-coated R. is partly derived from the poodle and is usually black.

RETZ (rās), **Jean François Paul de Gondi,** Cardinal de (1614-79). French politician. A churchman with political ambitions, he stirred up and largely led the insurrection of the Fronde (q.v.). After a period of imprisonment and exile he was restored to favour in 1662 and created abbot of St Denis. His *Memoirs* are of great historical interest.

RÉUNION (rā-ünyoṅ'). Is. in the Indian Ocean, 915km (570m) E of Madagascar. In Piton de Neiges, it rises to 3,069 m (10,068 ft). Sugar, maize, vanilla and tobacco are grown, and rum is made. St Denis, pop. 86,000, is the cap. Discovered by the Portuguese in 1513, R. was annexed by Louis XIII in 1642. It became an overseas dept in 1946, and an overseas region in 1972. Area 2,500 sq.km (970 sq.m); pop. (1977) 492,400.

REUTER (roi'ter), **Paul Julius,** baron de (1816-99). Founder of Reuters international news agency. B. at Cassel, Germany, he began a continental pigeon post in 1849, and in 1851 he set up a news agency in London. Not until 1858, however, did he persuade the Press to use his news telegrams from the Continent, in which year the service also became world-wide. Under Sir Roderick Jones (1877-1962), Reuters became a private trust in 1916, and was taken over by the Newspaper Proprietors' Association 1926-41.

REVAL, REVEL. *See* TALLIN.

REVERE (revēr'), **Paul** (1735-1818). American patriot. A Boston silversmith and member of the Sons of Liberty, he was one of the official couriers who carried the news of the approach of British troops to Lexington and Concord on the night of 18 April 1775. Longfellow commemorated the event in 'Paul Revere's Ride'. The first shots of the American War of Independence were fired at L. next day.

REVOLVER. *See* FIREARMS.

REVUE. A stage presentation originating as a loosely constructed satire on current events. Although in some measure retaining this form the R. often implies merely a variety of scenes.

REYKJAVÍK (rā'kyahvik). Cap. and chief port of Iceland, on its SW coast. It has a univ. founded in 1911, and a cathedral. Many of the houses are wood. It is a modern city, heated by underground mains fed by the volcanic springs to the E. Pop. (1977) 83,900.

REYNAUD (rānō'), **Paul** (1878-1966). French politician. He succeeded Daladier as PM in March 1940, but resigned in June, after the German break-through. He was held a prisoner until 1945, first in France, and later in Germany.

REYNOLDS, Sir Joshua (1723-92). British artist. B. near Plymouth, he went to London at the age of 17, and was apprenticed to Thomas Hudson, a mediocre portrait painter. From 1743 he was active as a portrait painter in London and Plymouth, but in 1749 went abroad to complete his studies. He spent over 2 years in Rome, visited other Italian cities, and settling in London in 1752 he became the most famous portrait painter of his day and the first president of the RA (1768). He was a life-long friend of Dr Johnson, and at R.'s suggestion the 'Literary Club' was founded in 1764. He painted portraits of Johnson, Goldsmith, Garrick, and other famous people of his day, in a style synthesized from that of the old masters, but overlaid with his own inventiveness. He was knighted in 1768. His artistic theories are propounded in his *Discourses*.

RHĒ'A. Family of birds (Rheidae), found only in S America. They are incapable of flight, and differ from the ostrich in having a feathered neck and head and three-toed feet, and in their smaller size. There are 2 species *Rhea americana* and the smaller *Pterocnemia pennata*.

RHEE, Syngman (1875-1965). Korean politician. A rebel under Chinese and Japanese rule, he became pres. of the Korean Rep. from 1948 until riots forced him to resign and leave the country in 1960. He estab. a repressive dictatorship and was an embarrassing ally for the USA.

RHEIMS. *See* REIMS.

RHENIUM (Lat. *Rhenus*, Rhine). Hard grey metal; symbol Re, at. no. 75, at. wt. 186.22. Discovered in 1925 by Noddack, Tacke and Berg in the minerals columbite, tantalite and wolframite, it is used in thermocouples and as a catalyst for dehydrogenation.

RHESUS (re'sus) **MONKEY.** A macaque (*Macaca mulatta*) also known as the bandar, found in N. India. It has long, straight brown-grey hair, pinkish face and red buttocks. The Rhesus or Rh factor is an agglutinogen first found in the blood of R. monkeys, and which is also present in 85% of human beings, who are said to be Rh-positive - the remaining 15% are Rh-negative.

See BLOOD GROUPS.

RHEUMATISM. A term loosely applied to a large variety of ailments associated with inflammation of the joints and muscles. **Rheumatic fever** is caused by a streptococcal throat infection which appears to trigger the formation of antibodies which attack the patient's own tissues. It is commonest between 15 and 30, and is marked by a high temperature and inflammation of the joints, which passes rapidly from one to another. It lasts about 2 weeks, and the chief danger is of possible damage to the heart muscle.

RHINE (rīn), **Joseph Banks** (1895-1980). American parapsychologist. His work at Duke Univ., Ohio, involving controlled laboratory experiments in telepathy, clairvoyance, precognition and psychokinesis, described in *Extra-Sensory Perception* (1934) made ESP a household word, but later research cast doubt on his results.

RHINE. River of Europe (Ger. *Rhein*, Dutch *Rijn*). It rises in Switzerland, and forms the frontier between Switzerland and (i) Liechtenstein, (ii) Austria from Liechtenstein to Lake Constance, (iii) Germany from Lake Constance to Basle, and the Franco-German frontier from Basle to near Karlsruhe, where it enters Germany. It receives the Neckar, Main, Moselle, Ruhr. Crossing the Dutch border, it becomes a wide delta covering the SW of the Netherlands, and with many branches which link and divide and link again. One branch, the Ijssel, runs N from just E of Arnhem to the Ijsselmeer; the others, of which the chief are the Lek and the Waal, link eventually with the Maas (Meuse) and Scheldt (Escaut) to fall into the North Sea by a number of mouths, the most important being the canalized New Waterway and the Scheldt estuary. It is navigable as far as Basle. Length *c.* 1,300 km (800m). The *Rhine-Rhône Waterway*, destined for completion in the mid-1980s, is a direct canal link between Rotterdam and Marseilles; and the *Rhine-Main-Danube Waterway*, also intended for completion in the mid-1980s, links Rotterdam with Constanza on the Black Sea.

RHINELAND-PALATINATE. Land of Germany formed in 1946 of the Rhenish Palatinate (*see* PALATINATE) and parts of Hessen, Rhine prov. and Hessen-Nassau. Much of it is wooded mountain country, and forestry is carried on; cattle, pigs and poultry are reared; wheat, rye, barley, oats and potatoes are grown; and wine and tobacco are produced. The chief industries are chemicals, leather goods and machinery. The cap. is Mainz. Area 19,400 sq.km (7,500 sq.m); pop. (1978) 3,639,300.

RHINOCEROS (rīno'seros). Ungulate mammal of the family Rhinocerotidae. Best-known are the one-horned Indian R. (*Rhinoceros unicornis*), 150cm (5ft) at the shoulder and with a tubercled skin, folded into shield-like pieces; the African black R. (*Diceros bicornis*), bad-tempered and with a prehensile upper lip for feeding on shrubs; and the docile broad-lipped or 'white' R. (*Diceros simus*), actually slaty-grey and with a squarish mouth for browsing grass. Both the latter are smooth-skinned and two-horned, but the white is rare and at 2m (6ft) the largest R.: an extinct species reached 4.5m (15ft).

RHINOCEROS. A pair of black rhinoceros in Kenya. The two cattle egrets are welcome visitors since they cleanse their hosts of pests. *Photo: Topham/Coleman*

RHODE ISLAND. Smallest state of the USA, on the Atlantic coast. One of the original 13 states, R.I. was founded in 1636 by Roger Williams, who had been exiled from Massachusetts Bay Colony for religious dissent. The coastline is indented by Narragansett Bay, running 45km (28m) inland. Industries incl. textiles, formerly most important but declining after the S.W.W. and overtaken by varied manufactures, jewellery, silverware, machinery, rubber and plastics. Poultry (espec. R.I. reds) and dairying flourish; apples and potatoes are grown; and there are valuable fish and shellfish resources. The cap. is Providence, and Newport is a noted seaside resort. Area 3,144 sq.km (1,214 sq.m); pop. (1970) 949,723.

RHODES, Cecil John (1853-1902). S African statesman. B. at Bishop's Stortford, Herts, he went to Natal in 1870. As head of De Beers Consolidated Mines and Goldfields of S Africa Ltd, he amassed a large fortune. He entered the Cape legislature in 1881, and became Prime Minister in 1890. Aiming at the formation of a S African federation and of a block of British territory from the Cape to Cairo, he was largely responsible for the annexation of Bechuanaland in 1885, and formed the British S Africa Co. in 1889, which occupied Mashonaland and Matabeleland, thus forming Rhodesia. The discovery of his complicity in the Jameson Raid forced him to resign the premiership in 1896. The R. Scholarships were founded at Oxford under his will, for students from the Commonwealth, USA, and Germany. They are his most lasting achievement. Ahead of his time in advocating Anglo-Afrikaner co-operation, he was less alive to the rights of black Africans, despite the final 1898 wording of his dictum: 'Equal rights for every civilized man south of the Zambezi'.

RHODES. Prime Minister of the Cape from 1890 to 1896, Rhodes is here caricatured following his achievement of a telegraphic link between the Cape and Cairo in 1892. *Photo: Ikon*

RHODES, Zandra (1940-). British designer. B. in Chatham, Kent, she is best known for the extravagant fantasy and luxury of her dress creations.

RHODES. Largest of the Dodecanese, in the E Aegean Sea. It was first settled by Greeks *c.* 1000 BC, held by the Knights Hospitallers of St John 1306-1522, taken from Turkish rule by the Italian occupation in 1912, and ceded to Greece in 1947. Grapes and olives are grown. R. is the cap., pop. (1971) 32,000. Area 1,412 sq.km (545 sq.m).

RHODESIA. *See* ZIMBABWE.

RHŌ'DIUM (Gk *rhodon*, rose). Silvery-white metal of the platinum family, symbol Rh, at. no. 45, at. wt. 102.91, discovered in 1803 by Wollaston. Its salts form red solutions, and it is found native with platinum in river sands in the Urals and the Americas. Used in thermocouples and in electro-plating, it gives a corrosion-free highly polished surface, superior to that of chromium.

RHODODE'NDRON. A genus of evergreen and deciduous shrubs in the family Ericaceae. The ovate leaves are often dark and leathery, and the large racemes of flowers occur in all colours except blue.

RHONDDA (ron'dha). Welsh coal-mining town in Mid Glamorgan, comprising 2 main valleys in the E of the S Wales coal area; it also has many light industries. Pop. (1972) 88,450.

RHÔNE (rōn). Large river of S Europe. It rises in Switzerland, flows through the Lake of Geneva to Lyons in France, where at its confluence with the Saône the upper limit of navigation is reached. The river turns due S, passes Vienne and Avignon, and takes in the Isère and other tributaries. Near Arles it divides into the Grand and Petit R., flowing respectively SE and SW into the Mediterranean W of Marseilles, and forming a two-armed delta; the area between the distributaries is the Camargue, a desolate, mosquito-plagued marsh *c.* 780 sq.km (300 sq.m), the haunt of flamingo and other birds. Drainage has brought parts of it under cultivation, especially for rice, and there is a threat to the rich wildlife. The Rhône is harnessed for hydroelectricity, the chief dam being at Genissiat in the dept. of Ain, constructed 1938-48.

RHUBARB (roo'-). Perennial plant (*Rheum rhaponticum*) grown for its edible leaf stalks. The leaves are poisonous. The roots of *R. palmatum* are used medicinally.

RHYME or **rime.** A feature of verse which arises from identity in sound of the endings of certain words. Although avoided in Japanese verse as a blemish, it exists in most Asiatic and modern European languages. It was, however, unknown in classical Greek and Latin verse, and in Anglo-Saxon and other old Teutonic poetry its place was taken by alliteration. R. first appeared in W Europe in late Latin poetry.

RHYS (rēs), **Jean** (*c.*1894-1979). British novelist. Dau. of a Creole (Dominica) mother and a Welshman, she pub. *Voyage in the Dark* (1934) and other books before the S.W.W., but made a wide reputation with *Wide Sargasso Sea* (1966), recreating the early life of the mad Creole wife of Rochester in *Jane Eyre*.

RIBBENTROP, Joachim von (1893-1946). German Nazi leader. B. in the Rhineland, he served in the F.W.W., and subsequently became a champagne-salesman. He joined the Nazi Party in 1932, acted as Hitler's adviser on foreign affairs, and was German ambassador to Britain 1936-8. As For. Min. 1938-45, he was largely responsible for Germany's aggressive foreign policy. He was tried at Nuremberg as a war criminal in 1946, and hanged.

RIBERA (rēbā'rah), **Jusepe** (1591-1656). Spanish painter and etcher. B. near Valencia, he went to Italy where he was known as *Spagnoletto* ('Little Spaniard'). He was a realistic painter, and was fond of depicting gruesome subjects, e.g. the 'Martyrdom of St Bartholomew'. His etchings show great originality.

RIBS. Twelve curved bones with cartilage on each side of the chest. At the rear each pair is joined to one of the vertebrae of the spine. The upper 7 are 'true' ribs, because they are joined by cartilage directly to the breast bone (sternum); the 8th, 9th and 10th are each joined by cartilage to the rib above; the 11th and 12th ('floating ribs') are not attached in front at all. The Rs. protect the lungs and

RICHARD II. A very early oil painting showing Richard II in 1377. He is being presented to the Virgin by his patron saints, John the Baptist, Edward the Confessor and Edmund. *Photo: Courtesy of the National Gallery, London*

heart and at the same time allow the chest to expand and contract easily.

RICARDO, David (1772-1823). British economist. After making a fortune on the London Stock Exchange, he pub. in 1817 *Principles of Political Economy,* in which 'laws' of rent, value, and wages, long generally accepted, were clearly enunciated.

RICE, Elmer (1892-1967). American playwright. B. in New York City, he was best known for the Expressionist *The Adding Machine* (1923) and *Street Scene* (1929), which was made into an opera by Kurt Weill.

RICE, Tim. *See* WEBBER, Andrew Lloyd.

RICE. The principal cereal of the wet regions of the tropics; the yield is very large, and R. is said to be the staple food of one-third of mankind. It is derived from grass of the genus *Oryza,* which is probably native to India and SE Asia. It has been cultivated since prehistoric days in the East, and has now been introduced into suitable lands in other parts of the world. It is a crop that matures quickly, taking 150-200 days in warm, very wet conditions. During its growing period it needs to be flooded either by the heavy monsoon rains or by adequate irrigation. This restricts the cultivation of swamp rice, the usual kind, to level land and terraces. A poorer variety, known as hill rice, is grown on hillsides. Paddy, or unhusked R., has valuable vitamins which are lost in husking or polishing, but it is only in the polished state that R. enters into European trade. Outside Asia there is some R. production in the Po valley of Italy, and in the United States in Louisiana, Carolina, and in California. New varieties with greatly increased protein content have been developed by gamma radiation for commercial cultivation and yields are much higher. Rice husks when burnt provide a silica ash which, mixed with lime, produces an excellent cement, more acid resistant than Portland cement.

RICHARD I, called **Coeur-de-Lion** (1157-99). King of England. The third son of Henry II, against whom he twice rebelled, he succeeded to the crown in 1189. In the third Crusade 1191-2 he showed courage and generalship, although he failed to recover Jerusalem. While returning overland he was captured by the duke of Austria, who handed him over to the Emperor Henry VI, and he was held prisoner until a large ransom was raised. His later years were spent in warfare in France, and he was killed while besieging Châlus. Himself a poet, he became a hero of romances after his death.

RICHARD II (1367-1400). King of England. B. at Bordeaux, the son of Edward the Black Prince, he succeeded his grandfather Edward III in 1377, the govt being in the

RICE. Rice-growing on terraces on the island of Bali, Indonesia. *Photo: Mireille Vautier*

hands of a council of regency. During the Peasants' Revolt in 1381 he showed much courage. His fondness for favourites resulted in conflicts with parliament, and in 1388 the baronial party headed by the duke of Gloucester had many of his friends executed. R. recovered control in 1389, and ruled moderately until 1397, when he had Gloucester murdered, and his leading opponents executed or banished, and made himself absolute. In 1399 his cousin the duke of Hereford (later Henry IV) returned from exile to lead a revolt; R. was deposed by parliament and imprisoned in Pontefract Castle, where he d. mysteriously.

RICHARD III (1452-85). King of England. The son of Richard, duke of York, he was created duke of Gloucester by his brother Edward IV, and distinguished himself in the Wars of the Roses. On Edward's death in 1483 he was created protector to his nephew Edward V, and soon secured the crown on the plea that Edward IV's sons were illegitimate. He proved a capable ruler, but the suspicion that he had murdered Edward V and his brother undermined his popularity. In 1485 Henry, earl of Richmond, raised a rebellion, and R. was defeated and killed at Bosworth. Modern scholars tend to minimize the evidence for his crimes as Tudor propaganda.

RICHARDS, Frank. Pseudonym of British author Charles Hamilton (1875-1961). Writing for the boys' papers *Magnet* and *Gem,* he invented the Greyfriars public school at which the most famous pupil was the immortal fat boy, always in trouble, Billy Bunter.

RICHARDS, Ivor Armstrong. *See* OGDEN, C.K.

RICHARDS, Sir Gordon (1905-). British jockey. First riding in 1920, he had 21,834 mounts and 4,870 winners before his retirement in 1954. He was 26 times champion jockey, and was knighted in 1953, the year he won the Derby with Pinza.

RICHARDSON, Henry Handel. Pseudonym of Australian author Ethel Henrietta R. (1880-1946). B. in Melbourne, she left Australia at the age of 18, and never returned, although her books have a predominantly Australian outlook. Her best-known books are *Maurice Guest* (1908), *The Fortunes of Richard Mahony* (1917-29), and the *Young Cosima* (1939).

RICHARDSON, Sir Owen Williams (1879-1959). British physicist. At Cambridge he worked under J.J. Thomson in the Cavendish Laboratory, and studied the emission of electricity from hot bodies, giving the name thermionics (q.v.) to the subject. He received a Nobel prize in 1928.

RICHARDSON, Sir Ralph David 1902–83. British actor. He achieved success as actor- director of the Old Vic 1944–7, with roles incl. Peer Gynt, Cyrano de Bergerac and Falstaff. His films incl *Anna Karenina* (Karenin: 1948) and *The Heiress* (Dr Sloper: 1949). Knighted 1947.

RICHARDSON, Samuel (1689-1761). British novelist. B. in Derbyshire, he was apprenticed to a printer, setting up his own business in London in 1719, and becoming printer to the House of Commons. His *Pamela* (1740-1), written in letter form, achieved a sensational vogue both in England and on the Continent, and was followed by *Clarissa* (1747-8), and *Sir Charles Grandison* (1753-4). Remarkable for his analysis of the feminine mind, R. exercised great influence on the development of the novel.

RICHARDSON, Tony (1928-). British director and producer. With George Devine he estab. the 'English Stage Co.' in 1955 at the Royal Court Theatre, London, where his productions incl. *Look Back in Anger* (1956). In 1958, he founded with John Osborne (q.v.) Woodfall films, and has produced or directed *A Taste of Honey* (1961), *Saturday Night and Sunday Morning* (1960), and *Dead Cert* (1974).

RICHBOROUGH. Former seaport (Roman Rutupiae) in Kent, England, now marooned in salt marshes, but reactivated militarily in both world wars.

RICHELIEU (rēshlyö'), **Armand Jean du Plessis de** (1585-1642). French cardinal and statesman. B. at Paris of a noble family, he entered the Church, and was created bishop of Luçon in 1606, and a cardinal in 1622. Through the influence of Marie de' Medici he became Louis XIII's chief minister in 1624, a position he retained until his death. At home he aimed to make the monarchy absolute; he ruthlessly crushed opposition by the nobility, and destroyed the political power of the Huguenots, while leaving them religious freedom. Abroad he sought to establish French supremacy by breaking the power of the Habsburgs; he therefore supported Gustavus Adolphus and the German Protestant princes against Austria, and in 1635 brought France into the 30 Years War.

RICHLER, Mordecai (1931-). Canadian novelist. Of Polish Jewish extraction, he was born in the poorer quarter of Montreal, which served as a setting for *The Apprenticeship of Duddy Kravitz* (1959). Later books incl. *Joshua Then and Now* (1980).

RICHMOND. (1) Town in N Yorks, England, on the Swale. Henry VII took his earlier title, earl of R. from the town. Pop. (1972) 7,260. (2) Cap. of Virginia, USA, on the r. James, *c.* 70m from the Atlantic. R. is the centre of the vast Virginian tobacco trade and manufactures immense quantities of cigarettes. It was the Confederate cap. 1861-5; a museum commemorates Edgar Allan Poe's association with R. Pop. (1970) 249,430.

RICHMOND-UPON-THAMES. Bor. in the SW of Greater London. Little remains in Richmond of the 14th cent. palace where Elizabeth I died, but the riverside gardens and Richmond hill and park make it a favourite resort of Londoners. The bor. incl. Barnes and Twickenham (q.v.). Pop. (1973) 170,940.

RICHTER (rik'ter), **Charles Francis** (1900–1985). American seismologist. He developed the *R. Scale,* graded 0 - 10, for measuring the strength of the wave motion of an earthquake; 8.6 is the severest so far known.

RICHELIEU. A triple portrait of Cardinal Richelieu by Philippe de Champaigne. An inscription on the back says that it was painted for the use of the sculptor Franchesco Mochi at Rome and the right hand profile is marked as 'the better of the two'. *Photo: The Mansell Collection*

RICHTER (rikh'ter), **Johann Paul Friedrich** (1763-1825). German author, commonly known as Jean Paul. B. in Bavaria, he created a series of comic eccentrics only rivalled by Dickens. His books incl. *Hesperus* (1794), a fictitious biography which estab. his fame; *Quintus Fixlein* (1796); *Siebenkäs* (1796-7); *Titan* (1800-3); *Die Flegeljahre* (1804-5: *The Awkward Age*); and *Dr Katzenbergers Badereise* (1809: *Dr Katzenberger's Journey to the Watering-place*).

RICHTER, Sviatoslav (1915-). Russian pianist. He is noted for his remote detached approach, and is an outstanding interpreter of Schumann.

RICHTHOFEN (rikht'hōfen), **Manfred,** freiherr von (1892-1918). German airman. B. at Schweidnitz, Silesia, he commanded in the F.W.W. a crack fighter squadron known as the R. circus, and shot down 80 aircraft before being killed in action.

RICIN. *See* CASTOR OIL.

RICKETS. A vitamin D deficiency disease of young children, marked by softening of the bones. Formerly frequent in British slum children, it is sometimes seen in the children of Negro immigrants, since pigmentation of the skin lessens ability to make best use of the limited sunlight, which acts on fats to produce the vitamin D necessary to enable lime to be deposited in the bones, so hardening them.

RIDGEWAY, The. Grassy track dating from prehistoric times which runs along the Berkshire Downs in England from White Horse Hill to near Streatley.

RIDING, Laura (1901-). American poet. A member of the Fugitive Group of poets, which flourished in the Southern US 1915-28, she went to England in 1926, remaining abroad until 1939, during which time she collaborated with Robert Graves (q.v.) on *A Survey of Modernist Poetry* (1927). She pub. her *Collected Poems* in 1938.

RIDLEY, Nicholas (*c.* 1500-55). English Protestant bishop. He became chaplain to Henry VIII in 1541, and bishop of London in 1550. He took an active part in the Reformation and supported Lady Jane Grey's claim to the throne. After Mary's accession he was arrested and burned as a heretic.

RIEL (rē-el'), **Louis** (1844-85). French-Canadian rebel. B. at St Boniface, he championed the cause of the Métis (half-breeds), and in 1869-70 led an unsuccessful revolt and set up a provisional govt at Winnipeg. After leading a second rising in Saskatchewan in 1885 he was hanged for treason.

RIEMANN (rē'mahn), **Georg Friedrich Bernhard** (1826-66). German mathematician. B. in Hanover prov., he studied theology at Göttingen, but soon turned to mathematics. He was prof. at Göttingen from 1857, and originated what is called Riemannian geometry - a non-Euclidean system.

RIENZI (rē-en'zē), **Cola di** (*c.* 1313-54). Roman political reformer. At a time when the Papacy was estab. at Avignon, he proclaimed in 1347 the restoration of the ancient Roman republic. In a few months he was expelled from the city, and a second attempt was ended by his assassination.

RIESMAN (rēz'man), **David** (1909-). American sociologist. He was prof. of social sciences at Chicago 1946-58 and at Harvard from 1958. His best-known book is *The Lonely Crowd: A Study of the Changing American Character* (1950).

RIF, Er. Mountain range about 290km (180m) long on the Mediterranean seaboard of Morocco. The Riffs, under Abd el-krim (q.v.), put up a prolonged resistance to Spaniards and French.

RIFT VALLEY, Great. Volcanic 'valley formed 10-20 million years ago by a crack in the Earth's crust, and running from the Jordan valley to Mozambique. The Red Sea forms part of it, and also the series of lakes, incl. Lake Rudolf, which provided early man with a helpful environment and preserved his stratified remains. At some points it is merely a depression, but elsewhere has 2 vertical fault lines with an 'in-fill' of volcanic material.

RIFT VALLEY FEVER. Virus disease originating south of the Sahara. Hosted by sheep and cattle, it is spread by mosquitoes, and a virulent strain had reached Egypt by 1977.

RIGA (rē'gah). Cap. and seaport of the Latvian SSR, USSR, on the Daugava (W Dvina), 13km (8m) from the Gulf of R. It has Hanseatic League remains. There is a univ. (1919). A member of the Hanseatic League from 1282, R. has belonged in turn to Poland 1582, Sweden 1621, and Russia 1710. The name means 'tortuous'. Pop. (1977) 876,000.

RIGG, Diana (1938-). British actress. B. in Doncaster, she spent her childhood in India. She reached stardom as Emma Peel in the television series, *The Avengers* 1965-7, and stage successes incl. *Abelard and Héloïse* (1970).

RIGHT OF WAY. A public R. of W. is a right exercisable by any member of the public to pass over land. Such rights arise from the dedication of the land (e.g. a road) to public use. Also relevant to motorists approaching an intersection. There is rarely any clear-cut ruling as to who has priority, but in France, with certain exceptions, a motorist must give way to traffic entering the road from his right.

RIGHTS OF MAN AND THE CITIZEN, Declaration of the. Statement issued by the French National Assembly in 1789. It lists as fundamental rights: representation in the legislature; equality before the law, and of opportunity; freedom from arbitrary imprisonment; religious freedom, and freedom of speech and the Press; taxation in proportion to ability to pay; and security of property. The preamble to the French constitution of 1946 reaffirms these rights, and adds others, e.g. equal rights for women; the right to work, to join a trade union, to strike, and to social security, leisure, support in old age, and free education.

RIGI (rē'gi). Mtn in central Switzerland, nr Lake Lucerne: highest point, Kulm, 1,800 m (5,908 ft).

RIJEKA (rīyak'ā). Port in Yugoslavia, on the E coast of the peninsula of Istra, at the mouth of the Rečina r. It has oil refineries, distilleries, paper mills, chemical and tobacco factories, etc. Acquired by the Habsburg rulers of Austria in 1465, it was given to Croatia in 1776, incorporated in Hungary 1807, re-united with Croatia in 1848, seized by Gabriele d'Annunzio (q.v.) in 1919, annexed by Italy in 1924, ceded to Yugoslavia in 1947. Its Italian and historic name Fiume is derived from its original name, St Vitus in Flumine. Pop. (1971), with the suburb of Susak on the other side of the river, 133,000.

RILEY (rī'li), **Bridget** (1931-). British artist. A leading exponent of Op Art (q.v.) in black-and-white and colour, she has produced particularly original 2-colour silk screen prints on plexiglass.

RILKE (rēl'ke), **Rainer Maria** (1875-1926). Austrian poet. B. at Prague of Carinthian stock, he was intended for a military career, but soon turned to literature. He travelled widely, especially in Russia, and was for a time Rodin's secretary. His prose works incl. the semi-autobiographical *Notebook of Malte Laurids Brigge*, and his poetical works the *Sonnets to Orpheus* and the *Duino Elegies*. His verse is characterized by a form of mystic pantheism which seeks to achieve a state of ecstasy in which existence can be apprehended as a whole. He d. in Switzerland.

RIMBAUD (rańbō'), **Jean Nicolas Arthur** (1854-91). French Symbolist poet. B. at Charleville, he went to Paris where he became the friend of Verlaine, who tried to murder him when they quarrelled. He then wandered Europe, travelled to the E Indies and Abyssinia, and d. at Marseilles. His verse is often obscure, but it has exerted an enormous influence on 20th cent. poets. His best-known vol. is *Illuminations* (1886).

RIMET (rēmeh'), **Jules** (1873-1956). French football administrator. Pres. of the French Football Assocn 1919-49, he founded FIFA (Fédération Internationale de Football Association), and promoted the World Cup competition, the trophy being named after him.

RIMINI (rē'mēnē). Seaport and holiday resort of Emilia, Italy, on the Adriatic 112km (69m) SE of Bologna. Macaroni, shoes, furniture, textiles, ships are made. As the Roman Ariminum, it was the terminus of the Flaminian and Aemilian Ways. Francesca da Rimini was assassinated there in 1285. R. was very badly damaged in Sept. 1944: it formed the eastern strongpoint of the German 'Gothic' defence line, and was taken by the Allies only after severe fighting. Pop. (1971) 120,000.

RIMSKY-KORSAKOV (rimz'ki korsahkof'), **Nikolai Andreievich** (1844-1908). Russian composer. B. at Tikhvin, Novgorod, he served in the navy some years. In 1872 he finished his first opera, but previously he had written the symphonic poem *Sadko* (1867) and the programme symphony *Antar* (1868). He often utilized Russian folk idioms and rhythms, and may be regarded as a nationalist composer. His operas incl. *The Maid of Pskov, The Snow Maiden,* and *The Golden Cockerel.*

RINEANNA. *See* SHANNON AIRPORT.

RING. A circlet, usually of precious metal, sometimes set with gems, worn on a finger as a decoration or token. The origin of the wedding R. is uncertain, but in Roman times betrothal Rs. were bestowed. Rs. were used for money in ancient Egypt and elsewhere, and their connection with the Church still survives in instances such as the English Coronation.

RING OF FIRE. The several island arcs surrounding the Pacific Ocean where regular and violent volcanic eruptions take place.

RINGWORM or **tinea.** The results of infestation by one of a group of parasitic microscopic fungi. In R. of the scalp the fungus (trichophyton) produces round patches of slight inflammation from which the hair falls out or breaks off. The treatment is by drugs which destroy the fungus. R. of the skin, commonly called athlete's foot, starts in the cracks between the little and the 4th toes, and may spread over the foot and other parts of the body, to produce a weeping eczema and an intolerable itch.

RINTELEN, Fritz von (d. 1949). German spy. He led a spy ring in USA during the F.W.W., sabotaging the shipment of Allied munitions until captured in 1915. He later settled in England and pub. the reminiscent *Dark Invader.*

RIO DE JANEIRO (rē'ō de zhahnā'rō). City and seaport of Brazil, cap. of R. de J. state, situated on the W of a fine natural harbour. The name commemorates its discovery on 1 Jan. 1502, though there is in fact no river. Portuguese and French settlers strove for supremacy in the 16th cent., the former prevailing. R. de J. became cap. of independent Brazil in 1822, and remained cap. until replaced by Brasilia (q.v.) in 1960. The harbour, with the impressive Sugar Loaf mt. at its entrance, is ringed by a 20m boulevard. The older parts of the city contain the commercial section, modern development producing such spacious thoroughfares as the Avenida Rio Branco. Some buildings of the colonial period and some 17th cent. Jesuit churches survive. The docks deal with the produce of large parts of Brazil including coffee, sugar, hides, etc. The city's own products are of the domestic-consumer type. It has 3 univs. and an airport, and is a naval base. Copacabana is a luxurious beachside suburb. Pop. (1975) 4,857,700.

RIO DE LA PLATA. Spanish name for the r. PLATE.

RIO DE ORO. Former southern district of the prov. of Spanish Sahara (q.v.). *See* SAHARA, WESTERN.

RIO GRANDE (rē'ō gran'di *or* grand). River 2,800 km (1,800 m) flowing from the Rockies in S Colorado to the Gulf of Mexico, and forming along the last 2,400 km (1,500 m) of its length the Texas-Mexico border. Changes in the course of the river led to disputes between USA and Mexico, settled 1970.

RIO GRANDE DO SUL (rē'ō grahn'dā doo sool). *See* PORTO ALEGRE.

RIOM (ryoń'). Town in the Puy-de-Dôme dept of central France on the Ambène. A pleasant town with many handsome 15th and 16th cent. houses, it was the scene in Feb.-April 1942 of a 'war guilt' trial of several prominent Frenchmen, incl. Blum, Daladier, and Gamelin (qq.v.), organized by the Vichy govt. Instead of a trial of the accused men, the proceedings developed into an argument as to the reasons for France's unpreparedness, and, soon at Hitler's instigation, the court was adjourned, then dissolved. The defendants were kept in prison until released by the Allies in 1945. Pop. (1973) 16,650.

RIO MUNI. *See* GUINEA, EQUATORIAL.
RIO NEGRO (nāg'ro). River 2,250 km (1,400 m) long which rises in E Colombia, and joins the Amazon at Manaus.
RIOT ACT. Act passed in 1714 to suppress Jacobite disorders. Under it, if 12 or more persons assemble unlawfully to the disturbance of the public peace, a magistrate may read a proclamation ordering them to disperse; if the rioters nevertheless continue together for an hour after the reading of the proclamation they are guilty of felony, and may be dispersed by force: repealed 1967.

Modern methods of **R. control** incl. plastic or rubber bullets; stun bags (soft canvas pouches filled with buckshot which spread out in flight); water cannon; and CS gas.
RIO TINTO. Town in Huelva, Spain, famous for its copper mines, first exploited by the Phoenicians but now almost worked out. Pop. (1970) 8,400.
RIPON. English cathedral city and market town in N Yorks, 40km (25m) N of Leeds, on the Ure. The cathedral was built 1154 to 1520. Pop. (1972) 11,870.
RISORGIMENTO (rēsōrjēmen'tō) (Ital. resurrection). The movement for Italian national unity and independence which began after 1815. The risings of 1848-9 failed, but the Austrian War of 1859 was followed by the foundation of the Italian kingdom in 1861. The addition of Venetia to Italy in 1866, and of Rome in 1870, completed the R.
RIVA DEL GARDA (rēvah del gah'da). Town on Lake Garda, Italy, where the Prix Italia broadcasting festival has been held since 1948.
RIVERA (rēvār'ah), **Diego** (1886-1957). Mexican artist. A convinced Communist, he expressed his ideas in the vast and vivid fresco murals he executed in Mexico and the USA, making this form widely popular.
RIVERA, Primo de. *See* PRIMO DE RIVERA.
RIVERINA. District of New South Wales, Australia, between the Lachlan and Murray rivers, through which runs the Murrumbidgee. On fertile land, artificially irrigated from the 3 rivers, wool, wheat, and fruit are produced.
RIVER PLATE. *See* PLATE.
RIVERSIDE. City in California, USA, on the Santa Ana r. 93km (58m) E by S of Los Angeles. Founded in 1870, it is the centre of a citrus-growing district and has a citrus research station. The seedless orange was developed at R. in 1873. Pop. met. area (1970) San-Bernadino-R.-Ontario 1,121,074.
RIVIERA (rēvē-ā'rah). The Mediterranean coast of France and Italy from Marseille to Spezia, the rest of the French Mediterranean coast being merely 'South of France'. The most exclusive section, with the finest climate is the Côte d'Azur, Menton-St Tropez, which incl. Monaco. It has the highest property prices in the world.
RIYADH. Cap. of Saudi Arabia, and of Nejd, in an oasis, connected by rail with Damman on the Arabian Gulf and by road with Kuwait and Hail. It is surrounded by a high wall with six fortified gates, outside which are date gardens irrigated from deep wells. There is a large royal palace, and university. Pop. (1976) 666,840.
RIZZIO (rēt'sē-ō), **David** (1533-66). Italian adventurer at the court of Mary Queen of Scots. After the queen's marriage to Darnley in 1565, his influence increased so as to arouse jealousies that ended in his murder by certain nobles.
RNA. *See* NUCLEIC ACID.
ROACH. Freshwater fish (*Rutilus rutilus*) of N Europe, dark green above, whitish below, and with reddish lower fins.
ROANOKE (rōnōke). City in Virginia, USA, on the R. r. 88km (55m) W of Lynchburg. Founded in 1834 as Big Lick, it was a small village until 1881 when the repair shops of the Virginia Railway were set up there, after which it developed rapidly. Besides doing railway repairs, it produces chemicals, steel goods, furniture, and textiles. The name is Indian and means shell money. Pop. (1970) 92,115.
ROBBE-GRILLET (rōb grēyeh'), **Alain** (1922-). French author. B. at Brest, he qualified as an agronomist and worked in Africa and the West Indies as a research biologist before turning to writing. He is the leading theorist of *le nouveau roman,* e.g. his own *Les Gommes* (1953: *The Erasers*) and *Dans le Labyrinthe* (1959), which concentrates on detailed description of physical objects, etc. Other members of the school (for whom, as literary director of *Les Editions de Minuit,* he is publisher) incl. Butor and Sarraute. He also wrote the script for the film *L'Année Dernière à Marienbad* (1961).
ROBBERY. In English law, a variety of theft: stealing from the person, with force used to intimidate the victim: maximum penalty, life imprisonment.
ROBBIA (rob'bē-ah), **Della.** Family of Florentine architects and sculptors. **Luca della R.** (1400-82) executed a number of important works of sculpture in Florence, and produced some beautiful sculptured work in terracotta, now known as D.R. ware. **Andrea della R** (1435-1525), the nephew and pupil of Luca, also produced enamelled reliefs. Five of Andrea's sons carried on the family tradition; the most famous were **Giovanni della R.** (1469-1529), who equalled his father, and **Girolamo della R.** (1488-1566), also an architect and sculptor.
ROBBINS, Jerome (1918-). American dancer and choreographer. A chorus-boy on Broadway, and then soloist with the newly formed American Ballet Theatre 1941-6, he became in 1949 associate artistic director of the NY City Ballet. Among his ballets are *Fancy Free* (1944; with Leonard Bernstein), *Facsimile* (1946), *The Age of Anxiety* (1950; again with Bernstein and based on Auden's poem). He also choreographed the musicals *The King and I, West Side Story,* and *Fiddler on the Roof.*
ROBERT. Name of 3 kings of Scotland. For **Robert I** *see* BRUCE, ROBERT. **Robert II** (1316-90), the son of Walter, steward of Scotland, and Marjory, daughter of Robert I, became king in 1371. He was the founder of the house of Stuart. **Robert III** (*c.* 1340-1406) succeeded his father Robert II in 1390.
ROBERT. Name of 2 dukes of Normandy. **Robert I,** called the Devil (d. 1035), became duke in 1028, and was the father of William the Conqueror. He is the hero of several romances. **Robert II** (*c.* 1054-1134), eldest son of William the Conqueror, succeeded him as duke of Normandy, but not as king of England, in 1087, and took part in the 1st Crusade. He was deposed by his brother Henry I in 1106.
ROBERTS, Frederick Sleigh, 1st earl (1832-1914). British field marshal, known as 'Bobs'. B. at Cawnpore, he joined the Bengal Artillery in 1851, and served through the Indian Mutiny, receiving the VC, and the Abyssinian campaign of 1867-8. During the Afghan War of 1878-80 he occupied Kabul, and subsequently made a famous march

to Kandahar, where he won a complete victory. After serving as C-in-C in India 1885-93, and Ireland 1895-9, he received the command in S Africa, where during 1900 he forced Cronje to surrender at Paardeberg, and by his occupation of Blomfontein and Pretoria made possible the annexation of the Transvaal and Orange Free State. On returning to England he received an earldom, and was C-in-C 1900-5. In later life he strongly advocated conscription. Early in the F.W.W. he d. at St Omer while visiting the trenches.

ROBERTS, Tom (Thomas William) (1856-1931). Australian artist, introducer to Australia of plein-air impressionism. B. in England, he arrived in Australia in 1869, returning to Europe to study in 1881 (*see* RUSSELL, J. P.). He painted the official picture of the opening of the first Federal parliament.

ROBERTSON, Thomas William (1829-71). British dramatist. At first an actor, in his family tradition, he had his first success as a dramatist with *David Garrick* (1864), which set a new, realistic trend in English drama of the time: later plays, in many of which the Bancrofts acted, incl. *Society* (1865) and *Caste* (1867).

ROBESON, Paul (1898-1976). American bass singer. He graduated at Columbia Univ. as a lawyer, but limited opportunities for Negroes led him instead to the stage, e.g. *The Emperor Jones* (1924), and *Showboat* (1928) in which he sang 'Ol' Man River'. He was a superb *Othello* (1930), and his films incl. *Sanders of the River* and *King Solomon's Mines*. An ardent advocate of his people's rights, he had his passport withdrawn 1950-8 because of his association with left-wing movements.

ROBESPIERRE (rōbe-spyãr'), **Maximilien François Marie Isidore de** (1758-94). French statesman. B. at Arras, he had a distinguished legal career, and was elected to the National Assembly of 1789-91. His defence of democratic principles made him widely popular in Paris, while his disinterestedness won him the nickname of 'the Incorruptible'. As leader of the Jacobins in the National Convention he supported the execution of Louis XVI and the overthrow of the Girondins, and in July 1793 was elected to the Committee of Public Safety. His zeal for social reform, his attacks on the anti-religious and other excesses of the terrorists, made him enemies on both right and left; a conspiracy was formed against him, and in July 1794 he was overthrown and guillotined.

RŌ'BEY, Sir George. Stage-name of British comedian George Edward Wade (1869-1954), the 'Prime Minister of Mirth'. Dressed in close-buttoned frock coat and semi-clerical bowler, he sang such songs as 'Tempt Me Not!' and - in the F.W.W. Bing Boys show - 'In Other Words' and was a master of significant gesture and voice inflection. He was also renowned as an amateur violin maker, and was knighted in 1954.

ROBIN. Song-bird (*Erithacus rubecula*) in the thrush family. It is found in Europe, W Asia, Africa, and the Azores. Both sexes are olive-brown, with a red breast. The nest is constructed in a sheltered place, and from 5 to 7 white freckled eggs are laid. The much larger N American R. belongs to the same family, but in Australia members of several unrelated genera have been given the familiar name, and may have white, yellowish or red breasts.

ROBIN HOOD. Legendary outlaw, who from the 13th cent. on became the hero of many popular ballads. It is doubtful whether his story has any historical basis; in their anticlericalism and defiance of authority the ballads reflect the revolutionary spirit of the peasantry in the years preceding the rebellion of 1381. R.H. was also the hero of folk-plays, customarily performed on May Day, and was sometimes identified with the May King.

ROBINSON, Edwin Arlington (1869-1935). American poet. B. in Maine, he dealt mainly with psychological themes in the manner of Browning. Among his publications are *The Children of the Night* (1897), which estab. his reputation, *The Man Against the Sky*, *Tristram*, *The Man Who Died Twice*, and *King Jasper* (1935).

ROBINSON, Henry Crabb (1775-1867). British writer, whose diaries, journals, and letters are a valuable source of information on his friends Lamb, Coleridge, Wordsworth, and Southey.

ROBINSON, John Arthur Thomas (1919-83). British Anglican churchman. Son of a clergyman, he was bp of Woolwich 1959–69 and lecturer in theology, Trinity Coll., Cambridge, from 1969. A left-wing Modernist, he wrote several books incl. the controversial *Honest to God* (1963), which was interpreted as denying a personal God.

ROBINSON, Sir Robert (1886-1975). British scientist. Waynflete prof. of chemistry at Oxford in 1939-55, he was pres. of the Royal Society 1945-50, and won a Nobel prize for researches in plant biology, especially in the structure of alkaloids (1947), receiving the OM in 1949. He was knighted in 1939.

ROBINSON, W(illiam) Heath (1872-1944). British black-and-white artist, famous for his humorous drawings of fantastically complex machinery for performing simple operations, e.g. raising one's hat.

ROBOT. Term coined by dramatist Karel Capek (from Czech 'work'), and meaning a worker automaton in human form. Modern industrial robots do not resemble human beings. They are essentially mechanical 'arms' with a range of human-like movements which are controlled by a computer (programmed to differing degrees of complexity), and powered electrically, hydraulically, or pneumatically. The 'first generation' began to be used in the 1960s to carry out unpleasant or heavy jobs, such as paint spraying or arc welding, and were expensive and clumsy. The 'second generation' of the 1980s are smaller, cheaper and capable of positioning items to within 0.1 mm, so that they can be used in precision work such as the assembly of typewriters. The 'third generation' will be able to 'see', for example to enable them to pick up components lying jumbled in any position in a container.

ROB ROY MACGREGOR (1671-1734). Scottish Highland outlaw, nominally a grazier who lived for years by cattle-lifting and blackmail.

ROBSART, Amy (*c.* 1532-60). The first wife of Robert Dudley, earl of Leicester (q.v.), whom she m. in 1550. She d. mysteriously at Cumnor Hall, Oxon. It was widely believed Leicester had had her murdered because he hoped to marry Elizabeth I.

ROBSON, Dame Flora (1902-). British actress. B. at S Shields, she made her début in 1921, and her many deeply sensitive interpretations incl. Miss Tina in *The Aspern Papers* (1959). She was created DBE in 1960.

ROCHDALE. Town in Greater Manchester, England, on the Roch 16km (10m) NE of Manchester. The 'R. Pioneers' founded the first Co-operative Society in England, in Toad Lane, Rochdale in 1844. Textiles, machinery, asbestos, etc., are manufactured. Gracie Fields was born here and a theatre is named after her. Pop. (1972) 93,000.

ROCHEFORT (rōshfor′). Port in Charente-Maritime dept., W France, SE of La Rochelle and 15km (9m) from the mouth of the Charente. Metal goods and machinery are made; grain, wine, dairy produce are exported. The port, at which Napoleon embarked for England in 1815, dates from 1666. Pop. (1975) 29,200.

ROCHELLE (rōshel′), **La.** Seaport and cap. of Charente-Maritime dept, W France. The cathedral, completed 1762, and episcopal palaces are of note, and industries incl. ship-building and saw-milling. It was a stronghold of the Huguenots, who defended it unsuccessfully against Richelieu in 1627–8. Pop. (1975) 72,950.

ROCHESTER, John Wilmot, 2nd earl of (1647–80). British poet. Although he showed gallantry at sea in the 2nd Dutch War, he spent most of his time at court, where he became notorious for debauchery. His poems incl. many graceful lyrics and some powerful satires, the best of which *A Satire against Mankind,* shows a spirit akin to Swift's.

ROCHESTER. City of Kent, England, on the Medway, just W of Chatham. The castle keep (12th cent.) is one of the finest specimens of Norman architecture in England. The cathedral was built in the 12th–15th cents. The nearby Borstal prison gave its name to a system of treatment of juvenile delinquents introduced in 1908. The site was already a port in pre-Roman days. R. has many associations with Dickens. Pop. (1972) 56,000.

ROCHESTER. City of New York state, USA, on the Genesee S of Lake Ontario. There are flour mills, and Kodak films and cameras are manufactured. R. has a univ. (1850). Pop. met. area (1970) 875,636. Also a city in SE Minnesota, USA. A commercial centre, with dairy and other food processing industries. It is the site of the Mayo Clinic: *see* MAYO, W. J. Pop. (1970) 53,800.

RO′CHET. A vestment worn mainly by RC and Anglican bishops and abbots. The RC type reaches to the knee, while the Anglican is nearly to the feet.

ROCK′ALL. Islet in the Atlantic about 24m (80ft) across and 370km (230m) W of N Uist in the Hebrides, annexed by Britain in 1955. Part of a fragment of Greenland which broke away 60 million years ago, it is in a potentially rich area for oil and gas. It is also claimed by Denmark.

ROCKEFELLER, John D(avison) (1839–1937). American millionaire, pres. of Standard Oil, which by 1878 controlled 90 per cent of US refineries. His son John D(avison) R., Jnr. (1874–1960), devoted himself to the management of the philanthropic R. Foundation (1913). The latter's son Nelson (Aldrich) R. (1908–79) entered politics as a Republican and was governor of New York State 1958–73, but he failed to win the Republican presidential nomination in 1964 and 1968. In 1974 he became Ford's vice-president, but his liberal views alienated some Republican support, and in 1975 he withdrew as vice-presidential candidate for 1976.

The **R. Center** in Manhattan, NY, is the largest privately owned business and entertainment centre in the world, and incl. Radio City Music Hall.

ROCKET and **ROCKET WARFARE.** Projectile driven through space by the reaction on the rocket of the fast-burning fuel within. Rs. have been valued for their pleasing effect as fireworks, over the last 7 cents., but their intensive development as a means of propulsion to high altitudes – carrying payloads – started only in the inter-war years, e.g. the state-supported work in Germany (*see* VON BRAUN, WERNHER), and of Prof. R. H. Goddard (1882–1945) in the USA.

In warfare the head of the R. carries an explosive device. Such weapons were first used by the Chinese *c.* AD 1100, and were encountered in India in the 18th cent. by the British forces. The R. missile was then re-invented by Sir William Congreve (1772–1828) in England *c.* 1805, and remained in use by various armies in the 19th cent. In the S.W.W. they were effectively used by aircraft, and by the Germans in their V2 attacks on the London area in 1944–5: the V2 (15m/50ft long and carrying 1 tonne of high explosive in its warhead) as the first guided missile.

Since the S.W.W., the devastating combination of refined, precise guidance systems with atomic war-heads has produced missiles which are the key to international power politics. They are designed for short, medium and long range; and may be for surface to surface, air to surface, or surface to air use. The latest development is the cruise missile. *See* NUCLEAR WARFARE.

Rockets are also used to supplement conventional artillery, e.g. the US multiple-launch rocket system (MLRS). Armed with 2 pods of 6 Rs, which can be fired individually or otherwise, it has the advantage over guns in firepower, mobility and cost, but is restricted to long-range.

The only form of propulsion available which can function in a vacuum, Rs. are essential to research in outer space, e.g. the giant 3-stage Saturn 5 rocket used to launch the *Apollo* space craft. The 'space shuttle' being developed by the USA in the 1970s was the first rocket plane designed for routine service.

ROCKHAMPTON. Port of Queensland, Australia, on the Fitzroy estuary. It is in a region producing dairy products and coal, gold and copper; it has meat-canning factories. Pop. (1972) 49,800.

ROCKINGHAM, Charles Watson Wentworth, 2nd marquess of (1730–82). British Whig statesman. He succeeded his father as marquess in 1750. As PM 1765–6 he repealed the Stamp Act, and subsequently supported the Americans' claim to independence. He again became PM in 1782, but d. in office.

ROCKY MOUNTAINS. The dominating section of the N American mountain system. They extend from the junction with the Mexican plateau, northward through the W central states of the USA, through Canada to the Alaskan border. Many large rivers rise in the R.M. incl. the Missouri. The R.M. Nat. Park (1915) in Colorado has more than 100 peaks over 3,350 m (11,000 ft); Mt Logan on the Canadian-Alaskan border is 6,050 m (19,850 ft). In the 1980s computer techniques enabled natural gas to be located in the 'western overthrust belt' in large quantities.

ROCOCO (rokō′ko). Style of architecture and decoration which prevailed in France at the time of the Regency and the reign of Louis XV. It is characterized by bizarre ornamentation, and complete lack of restraint. It is a degenerate form of Baroque (q.v.).

RODENTS. Order of gnawing mammals (Rodentia), incl. the squirrels, dormice, mice, voles and guinea-pigs. Rabbits and hares are distinguished from these true rodents by having two pairs of double incisors in the upper jaw instead of one, and are now technically classified in a separate order, Lagomorpha (Gk *lagos* hare *morphos*

ROCKY MOUNTAINS. The dramatically broken splendour of the 'Rockies' in their Canadian section. Castle Craigs and Mount Lefroy, near Lake Louise in Alberta. *Photo: Courtesy of Mcgill University*

form). Most species are burrowers and are vegetarian in habit. Hibernation is common.

RODEO (rōdā'-ō). Originally a round-up of cattle on the western ranges of America, it has developed into a cowboy tournament, in which challenges are thrown out by the men of various herds at round-ups.

RODGERS, Richard (1902-80). American composer. In collaboration with Lorenz Hart (1895-1943), he wrote songs such as 'Blue Moon' and the pioneer realistic musical with a squalid hero *Pal Joey* (1940); and with Hammerstein the musicals *Oklahoma* (1943), *South Pacific* (1949), *The King and I* (1951) and *The Sound of Music* (1959).

RODIN (rōdań'), **Auguste** (1840-1917). French sculptor. B. in Paris, he studied under Barye and Carrier-Belleuse, and visited Italy in 1875, where he studied the works of Donatello and Michelangelo. In 1877 he made a tour of the French cathedrals, and was much influenced by Gothic sculpture. He settled near Paris. His best-known works incl. 'The Thinker', 'The Kiss' and 'The Burghers of Calais' (copy in Embankment Gardens at Westminster). Many of his works are in the R. Museum, Paris.

RODNEY, George Brydges Rodney, baron (1718-92). British admiral. His first action was under Hawke against the French off Ushant in 1747. In 1762 he captured Martinique, St Lucia, and Grenada, and received a baronetcy in 1764. In 1780 he relieved Gibraltar by defeating a Spanish squadron off Cape St Vincent. In 1782 he crushed the French fleet under count de Grasse off Dominica, for which brilliant victory he was raised to the peerage.

ROEBUCK. Species of deer (*Capreolus capreolus*), found in Europe and Asia. Still occurring wild in Scotland, it is *c.* 0.6m (2ft) high, has short three-pronged antlers which are shed in December, and in summer is reddish, in winter greyish-brown.

ROESELAERE. Flem. form of ROULERS.

ROGATION DAYS. The 3 days before Ascension Day in the Christian calendar. The processions marking the occasion in England have mostly lapsed.

ROGERS, Richard (1933-). British architect. His works incl. the Georges Pompidou Centre for the Visual Arts in Paris (jointly), and the new Lloyds building in London (1986).

ROGERS, Samuel (1763-1855). British poet. He succeeded his father as head of a banking firm in 1793, and having estab. his poetical reputation with *The Pleasures of Memory* (1792), retired from business in 1803, and devoted himself to literary and social life, giving celebrated 'breakfasts' at his home near Green Park. His poetry is correct but cold, and he now lives mainly in his *Table Talk* and *Recollections*.

ROGET (rozhā'), **Peter Mark** (1779-1869). British physician, one of the founders of the Univ. of London, and author of a *Thesaurus of English Words and Phrases* (1852).

RÖHM, Ernst (1887-1934). German leader of the Nazi 'Brown Shirts', the S.A. (*Sturm Abteilung*) whose brawling and blatant homosexuality had embarrassed Hitler. On the pretext of an intended S.A. *putsch* some hundred of them were killed 29-30 June, 1934, sometimes referred to as 'the night of the long knives'.

ROHMER, Sax. Pseudonym of British crime writer Arthur Sarsfield Ward (1886-1959), creator of the sinister Chinese Dr Fu Manchu (1913).

ROKOSSO'VSKY, Konstantin (1896-1968). Polish-born soldier, prominent in the battles of Moscow, Stalingrad and Orel, and the liberation of Poland in the S.W.W. Though created a marshal of the Soviet Union, he assumed Polish citizenship in 1949 and was Polish C-in-C and War Min. until 1956. He subsequently served again in the Russian defence ministry.

ROLAND (d. 778). French soldier, killed by the Basques during Charlemagne's invasion of Spain. He subsequently became the hero of the 11th cent. *Chanson de Roland*, Ariosto's *Orlando Furioso*, and many other romances.

ROLAND DE LA PLATIÈRE (rōloń' de la plahtyār'), **Manon Jeanne** (1754-93). French politician. *Née* Phlipon, she m. JEAN MARIE R. (1734-93), a leader of the Girondins during the French Revolution, and set up a salon which became the party's centre. She was guillotined in 1793, and on hearing of her death her husband, who had escaped from Paris, committed suicide. Her memoirs, written in prison, are of interest.

ROLFE, Frederick (1860-1913). British writer, known under his assumed style of Baron Corvo. In early life he studied for the RC priesthood, but was diverted into a literary career. Not until the publication in 1934 of A. J. A. Symons's *The Quest for Corvo*, was there any general appreciation of Rolfe's *Hadrian VII, Desire and Pursuit of the Whole, Weird of the Wanderer*, strange creations of a tortured mind.

ROLLAND (roloń'), **Romain** (1866-1944). French novelist and dramatist. B. at Clamecy, he was prof. of the history of music at the Sorbonne 1904-10. He wrote works on Beethoven and Handel, novels such as the voluminous *Jean-Christophe* (1904-12), for which he received a Nobel prize in 1915, and the plays *Danton* and *Le 14 juillet*.

ROLLE (rōl) **de Hampole, Richard** (*c.* 1300-1349). English hermit, author of English and Latin works, incl. the mystic *Meditation of the Passion*.

ROLLER. Group of birds in the family Coraciidae, resembling crows. They are found in the Old World, and the species *Coracias garrulus* is an occasional British visitor. The name is derived from their habit of rolling over in flight.

ROLLER-SKATING. *See* SKATING.

RO'LLO (*c.* 860-932). First duke of Normandy from 912 until his retirement to a monastery in 927; he was a Viking leader who received the province from Charles III of France.

ROLLS-ROYCE. *See* ROYCE.

RŌ'MA. Town in SE Queensland, in a wheat-growing and natural gas producing area, linked by rail and pipeline to Brisbane. Pop. (1971) 5,860.

ROMAGNA (romah'nya). Area of Italy on the Adriatic coast, under papal rule 1278-1860, and now part of the region of Emilia-Romagna.

ROMAINS (rōman'), **Jules**. Pseudonym of French novelist, playwright and poet Louis Farigoule (1885–1972). B. in the Cévennes, he lectured in philosophy in Paris and the provs. (1909-19), and developed the theory of Unanimisme, i.e. that every group has a communal existence greater than that of the individual, which intensifies their perceptions and emotions. He expressed this in the verse *La Vie unanime* (1908), the novel *Mort de quelqu'un* (1911: *Death of a Nobody*), etc. Of his plays, the farce *Knock, ou le Triomphe de la médecine* (1923: *Dr Knock*) is best known. His later work is contained in the cycle of *c.* 30 novels *Les Hommes de bonne volonté* (1932-47: *Men of Good Will*).

ROMAN ART. The development of R.A. dates from about the 4th cent. BC. Before that time the art of Rome was chiefly Etruscan or Graeco-Etruscan. The Romans learnt a great deal from their Etruscan neighbours, e.g. realistic portraiture, and in architecture the characteristic form of Roman temples, which was based on Etruscan models. Later, Greek influence dominated R.A.; after the conquests of the later Republic, Roman generals returned with examples of Greek art, and Greek craftsmen were employed in the decoration of Roman palaces. At the time of Augustus Greek influence was still dominant, but art was enlisted in the service of the State, and sculpture and other forms of art of this period show great technical skill. Roman painting was confined to interior decoration, e.g. the wall paintings of Pompeii and of the houses and tombs of Rome. The Romans were skilful mosaic artists, and mosaics were produced in most places in the Empire, especially in Africa, Gaul, and Antioch.

ARCHITECTURE. Architecture was the dominant Roman art. It had its rise in the last decades of the Republic; it developed during the Empire and attained ostentatious magnificence at the time of Augustus and Hadrian. The Romans derived the principle of arched construction from the Etruscans. From Greek art they acquired the classic orders, the generic type of circular buildings, the portico, the theatre, the monumental gateways, the circus, and the public place. In Rome the chief feature of planning was the variety of the Fora. These were the market places and were surrounded by shops, temples, and public buildings. Every provincial city had its forum, that at Pompeii being famous. Roman temples were of two types, rectangular and circular, the latter deriving from Etruscan and Greek precedent. The chief circular temple is the Pantheon of Agrippa in Rome. The basilica, which was adapted from Greek examples, became the most important of the Roman public buildings. It served as a general place of assembly for purposes of law and of exchange. The Roman theatre also followed Greek models, though there were certain modifications such as the more monumental treatment of the stage, and the use of a pit with seats reserved for senators in place of the ancient orchestra. The amphitheatre is essentially a Roman creation - the most famous example is the Colosseum in Rome. The triumphal arch was built to commemorate great victories - those erected in honour of Trajan and Marcus Aurelius are exceptionally fine. Among the Roman works of utility, which are great feats of engineering skill, are the aqueducts. Palaces, residences, and villas were highly developed, and attained to a spendour hitherto unknown.

ROMAN BRITAIN. Roman relations with Britain began with Caesar's invasions of 55 and 54 BC, but the actual conquest was not begun until AD 43.

England was rapidly Romanized, but N of York fewer remains of Roman civilization have been found. After several unsuccessful attempts to conquer Scotland the N frontier was fixed at Hadrian's Wall (q.v.). During the 4th cent. Britain suffered from raids by the Saxons, Picts and Scots. The Roman armies were withdrawn in 407 but there were partial re-occupations 417-*c.* 427 and *c.* 450. Roman towns incl. London, York, Chester, Caerleon, St Albans, Colchester, Lincoln, Gloucester, and Bath. The most permanent remains of the occupation were the system of military roads radiating from London.

ROMAN CATHOLICISM. The largest Christian denomination; it is estimated that there are about 585 million Roman Catholics in the world today. They describe themselves not as Roman Catholics, but as Catholics, i.e. members of the Universal, One, Holy Catholic and Apostolic Church, founded by Jesus Christ. The doctrinal basis of the Church is the 3 creeds, the Bible (q.v.), and Christian tradition. The Church claims to preach a set of doctrines that were revealed in the lifetime of the Apostles and have been preserved by continuous tradition ever since; but doctrine has developed in the sense that beliefs that were once implicit have been made explicit, e.g. the doctrine of the Immaculate Conception of the Virgin Mary, (1854) and of her Assumption (1950). The characteristic function of the Church is the offering of public prayer; the clergy are bound to recite certain prayers at fixed times daily. The central act of worship is the Mass - the representation to God of the Sacrifice made on the Cross. It is believed that when the priest repeats Christ's words spoken at the Last Supper, the bread and wine on the altar become Christ's body and blood, although no change takes place in their outward appearance. The Host, or Sacred Bread, is referred to as the Blessed Sacrament. There are 6 other sacraments, viz., baptism, confirmation, the rite for reconciliation (confession and penance), matrimony, holy orders, and the anointing of the sick, formerly extreme unction. The Church is intimately concerned with the preservation of the moral law; it is opposed to the remarriage of divorced persons, and certain forms of birth control. Great emphasis is laid on the ascetic tradition and on the religious life of retirement from the world; there are more than 300 different Orders of men, e.g. the Benedictine monks, the Franciscan and Dominican friars, the Jesuits, and many more Orders of women. From the earliest times high honours have been paid to those Christians who had proved themselves worthy of the name of saint; the process of official canonization was simplified in 1969. It is believed that miracles constitute one of the hallmarks of sanctity; and public prayers may be addressed to the saints asking them to intercede with God on the behalf of men. It is held that at death the soul passes into the intermediate

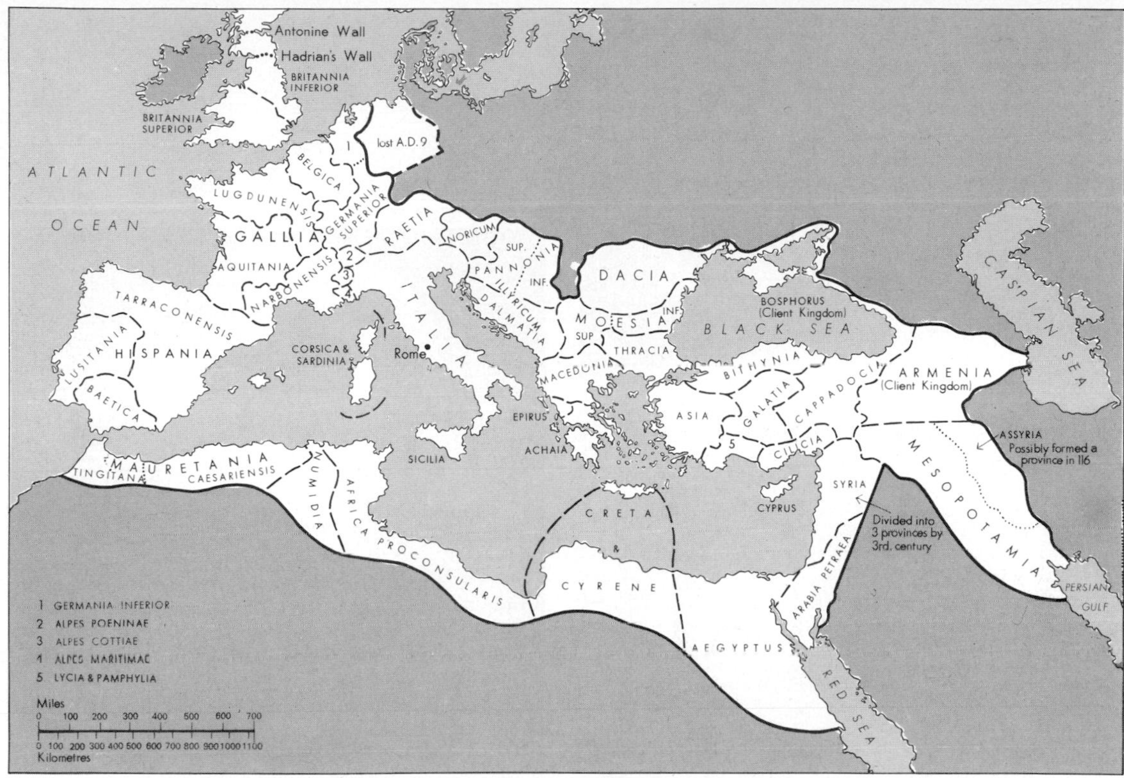

ROMAN HISTORY. The Roman Empire in A.D. 117, the time of its greatest expansion.

state of Purgatory, where it is cleansed from the stain of sin. The eternal home of the blessed is Heaven, while the incorrigibly wicked are doomed to Hell. The head of the Church is the Pope, who is primarily the bishop of Rome. Since 1870 it has been a Catholic dogma that the Pope as Christ's Vicar is infallible when he makes solemn pronouncements on matters of faith and morals. However, after the S.W.W. there was a tendency to widen the source of authority (*see* PAPACY), and to co-operation in the oecumenical movement which assisted a review of the tenets of the faith. Issues incl. the form of church govt and services, incl. the adoption of the vernacular in the Mass (q.v.), the rules and dress of monastic orders (some of which have been controversially modernized), the role of 'worker' priests and the possibility of married priests (women priests have not been seriously considered), birth control and divorce. With the accession of John Paul II in 1978 there was a strong reversion to a traditionalist position. *See* VATICAN CITY.

ROMANCE. Term applied in modern usage to any highly coloured prose fiction remote from the conditions of everyday life, and in medieval times to the lengthy stories in verse and prose which became popular in France *c.* 1200, and spread throughout Europe. The Rs. usually dealt with the adventures of Charlemagne and his heroes, King Arthur and his knights, or the classical themes of Troy, Thebes, etc.

ROMANCE LANGUAGES. A group of languages all of which descend directly from Popular (Vulgar) Latin, the spoken language of the Roman Empire. They incl. Italian, Spanish, Portuguese, Provençal (and Catalan), French, Rumanian, and Romansh (Rhaeto-Romanic).

ROMANESQUE. Style of architecture which prevailed in western Europe from the 9th to the 13th cent. The style varied in different countries, but everywhere the round arch was employed. In planning, different methods of subdivision were favoured to accord with experiments in vaulting. Arches were introduced to spring directly from the capitals of columns, and a system of arching was devised. The basilican plan was in general use for the early buildings, but in the 12th cent. the cruciform found acceptance. For towers square, octagonal, and circular plans were followed.

ROMAN HISTORY. According to tradition Rome was founded in 753 BC, and was ruled in succession by 7 kings. The Etruscan dynasty of the Tarquins was expelled in 510, and a republic was estab., governed by 2 chief magistrates, or consuls, who were elected annually by the popular assembly, and a council of elders, or Senate. The concentration of power in the hands of the patrician aristocracy, who monopolized the magistracies and membership of the Senate, aroused the opposition of the plebeian masses. By a long struggle they secured the right to elect tribunes to defend their interests, the codification of the laws, and the right to marry patricians; in 367 it was enacted that one consul must be a plebeian, and by 300 all the magistracies were thrown open to them.

Meanwhile Rome was extending her power over her neighbours. The cities of Latium were formed into a

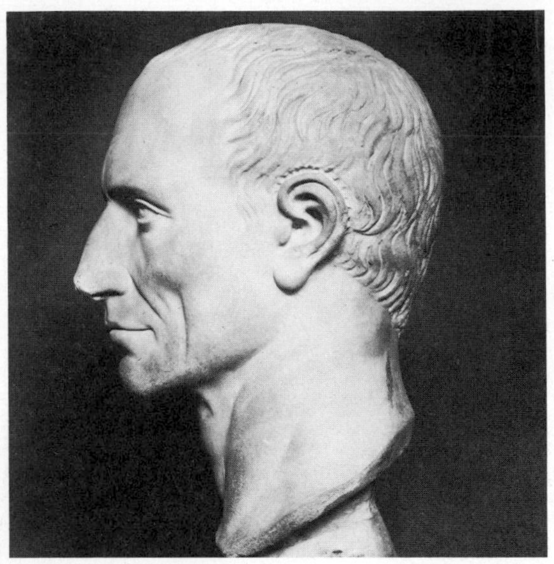

ROMAN HISTORY. The ruins of the Colosseum at Rome (top left); the Roman kitchen reconstructed at the Museum of London at the Barbican (lower left); and a portrait bust, perhaps more attractive than authentic, of Julius Caesar. *Photos: J. Allan Cash, Kenneth Mason, Mansell Collection*

league, under Roman suzerainty. The temporary occupation of Rome by the Gauls in 390 failed to check her advance. The Etruscans to the N were subdued during the 5th-4th cents., and the Samnites to the SE during 343-290. The Greek cities of the S, in spite of the assistance granted them by King Pyrrhus of Epirus, were conquered in 280-272. With the conquest of Cisalpine Gaul (Lombardy) in 226-222, Rome became mistress of Italy.

Inevitably she came into conflict with Carthage, which was attempting to conquer Sicily. The 1st Punic War (264-241), during which the Roman navy was founded, ended in a Roman victory and the annexation of Sicily, to which in 238 Sardinia was added. These new possessions were treated, not as self-governing 'allies', but as provinces ruled by Roman governors. The Carthaginian attempt to found a new empire in SE Spain aroused Roman suspicions, and in 218 war was renewed. Hannibal invaded Italy and won a brilliant series of victories, until a Roman invasion of Africa forced him to withdraw. The victory of Zama in 202 was followed by Carthage's surrender and the cession of her Spanish colonies. By 133 most of Spain had been subdued. Rome now became drawn into Greek and Asiatic politics. Three wars with Macedon were followed by its conversion into a province in 148, while after a revolt in 146 Greece also became in effect a Roman province. In the same year Carthage was destroyed and its territory annexed. On the death of the king of Pergamum in 133, Rome succeeded to his kingdom, which incl. half Asia Minor.

The continual wars had ruined the Italian farmer class while enriching the aristocracy, who built up huge estates cultivated by slave labour. In 133 Tiberius Gracchus, to meet this evil, put forward proposals for agrarian reforms, and was murdered by the senatorial party. His policy was taken up in 123 by his brother Gaius Gracchus, who added proposals for limiting the powers of the senatorial oligarchy, and was likewise murdered. The leadership of the democrats passed to Marius, who had conquered Numidia in 109-106 and saved Italy from a German invasion in 102, while the senate found a champion in Sulla. A revolt of the Italian cities in 91-88 compelled Rome to grant them the franchise. While Sulla was repelling an invasion of Greece by Mithradates of Pontus (87-84) Marius seized power; on his return in 82 Sulla launched a reign of terror and revised the constitution in the Senate's interests.

His changes were reversed in 70 by Pompey and Crassus, but the social struggle continued; Spartacus led a dangerous slave revolt in 73-71, and the democratic extremists, led by Catiline, rebelled in 63. Having crushed Mithradates and annexed Syria and the rest of Asia Minor during 66-62, Pompey returned to form an alliance in 60 with the democratic leaders Crassus and Caesar. The latter received the command in SE Gaul, annexed in 121, and by 51 had conquered Gaul as far as the Rhine. During his absence, Pompey drifted into the senatorial party, and

Caesar's return to Italy in 49 was the signal for civil war, from which Caesar emerged as master of Rome. His programme of social and political reform was interrupted by his assassination in 44. The empire was now divided between his nephew Octavian, who ruled the W, and Antony, who as Cleopatra's lover ruled the E from Egypt; war between them began in 32, and with the deaths of Antony and Cleopatra in 30 Egypt was annexed.

Octavian, henceforward known as Augustus, was now absolute, although in theory he was only *princeps* (first citizen), and republican forms were retained. The establishment of an efficient centralized govt, in place of that of the corrupt senatorial oligarchy, proved an immense gain to the empire. Augustus made the Rhine and the Danube its frontiers; Claudius in AD 43 added Britain. The dynasty founded by Augustus held power until AD 68, and was succeeded by the Flavian house (69-96). Under Nerva, Trajan, Hadrian, Antoninus Pius, and Marcus Aurelius (96-180) the empire enjoyed a golden age of peace and prosperity. Trajan added Dacia and Mesopotamia to the empire, the latter was abandoned by Hadrian, and thereafter expansion ceased.

A cent. of war and disorder followed Marcus Aurelius's death, during which a succession of generals were placed on the throne by their armies. A deep-rooted economic crisis sapped the empire's vitality, while the frontiers were threatened by Franks, Goths, and Parthians. Diocletian (284-305) reorganized the empire as a centralized autocracy ruling through an ubiquitous bureaucracy. Constantine I (324-37) recognized the political value of Christianity, which Diocletian had persecuted as subversive, and himself became a convert. He removed the capital to Constantinople, and from 364 the empire, as too large to administer, was divided between emperors at Constantinople and Rome. Reforms failed to check inner decay or aggression from without. The Goths overran Greece and Italy, sacked Rome in 410, and finally settled in Spain. The Vandals conquered Italy. Britain was abandoned in 407. The Huns raided Gaul and Italy in 451-2. When the last emperor was deposed, in 476, the western empire ceased to exist even in name.

ROMANIA (rōmā'nia). A republic of SE Europe, bounded by Bulgaria, the Black Sea, the USSR, Hungary, and Yugoslavia.

PHYSICAL FEATURES. R. is traversed from N to S by the Carpathians and from E to W by the Transylvanian Alps, the 2 ranges forming a great arc separating Transylvania to the NW from the plains of Wallachia and Moldavia. The main rivers are the Danube, which reaches the Black Sea through an extensive delta; its tributaries the Prut (which forms the boundary with the USSR), Siret, Ialomita, Arges, Olt, and Jiu; and the Mures and Somesul in Transylvania. There are numerous lakes in the vicinity of the lower Danube. The plains of the E and S are exposed to great extremes of climate.

ECONOMIC LIFE. Since the S.W.W. industry has overtaken agriculture in importance, workers being directed to factories from agriculture. By the 1980s this had led to a shortfall in Romanian coal and oil, and the growth of the chemical industry (synthetic yarns, plastics, fertilisers), and light and heavy industry (incl. iron and steel), encountered depressed world trade which has reduced the market for those products abroad. Minerals also incl. copper, lead, manganese, and zinc. Agriculture has been reorganised, with special emphasis on the raising of cattle, sheep and pigs. Wheat, maize, sunflower, sugar beet, and grapes are important crops; and forests (covering ¼ of the country) supply a large timber industry. There is a road and rail network, and an international airport at Bucharest, and river and maritime transport developed via the Danube and Black Sea, which also support a fishing industry. Tourism is encouraged by the scenery, and rich remains of earlier cultures: resorts incl. Mamaia snd the spa Eforie, both on the Black Sea, and winter sports centres such as Sinaia.

The cap, is Bucharest; other towns incl. Cluj, Iasi, Timisoara, Ploesti, Braila, Galati Oradea, Brasov, Arad and Constanta. Area 237,500 sq.km. (91,699 sq.m); pop. (1977) 21,650,000, the majority of whom belong to the Romanian Orthodox Church. M.U.: leu.

GOVERNMENT. Under the Constitution of 1965 (more liberal than the Soviet model of 1952) the Grand Nat. Assembly is elected for 4 yrs by workers over 18, and the PM and other members of the Council of State are responsible to the assembly. The Council was headed by a pres., but not until 1974 was a pres. of the republic appointed: *see* CEAUSESCU.

History. The Romans conquered Dacia, now R., in AD 101-7, and introduced colonists (who incl. Ovid); many of these inter-married with the native population. After the withdrawal of the Romans in 275, R. was occupied by the Goths, and during the 6th-12th cents. was overrun by Huns, Bulgars, Slavs, and other invaders. In the 14th cent. the principalities of Wallachia, in the S, and Moldavia, in the E, were founded. Wallachia fell under Turkish suzerainty in the course of the 15th cent., Moldavia early in the 16th. From 1829-56 Turkish suzerainty was exchanged for Russian protection. In 1859 both principalities elected as prince Alexander Cuza who proclaimed their union; he was deposed in 1866, and Prince Charles of Hohenzollern-Sigmaringen elected. After the Russo-Turkish War (1877-8), in which R. sided with Russia, the great powers recognised R's independence, and in 1881 Prince Charles assumed the royal title as Carol I.

R. fought against Bulgaria in the Second Balkan War (1913) and annexed S Dobruja. It entered the F.W.W. on the Allied side in 1916, was occupied by the Germans 1917-18, and received Bessarabia and Transylvania under the peace settlement. During the 1930s the pro-Fascist Iron Guard became prominent; to counter them Carol II in 1938 estab. his own dictatorship, but when in 1940 he had to surrender Bessarabia, N Transylvania, and S Dobruja to Russia, Hungary, and Bulgaria respectively, the Iron Guard seized power, and forced him to abdicate in fabour of his son Michael. R. was occupied by the Germans in 1940, and declared war on Russia in 1941. When the Germans were expelled by the Red Army in 1944 a coalition of left and centre parties took power, and R. declared war on Germany. By the peace treaty of 1947 between R. and the Allies, R. recovered Transylvania; Bessarabia and N Bukhovina went to Russia, S Dobruja to Bulgaria. Michael abdicated later that year, and a rep. was estab. of which the Communists rapidly gained control. Russian occupation forces remained in R. until 1958, but thereafter R. took a more independent attitude, e.g. condemnation of the Soviet invasion of Czechoslovakia, and forged closer trading links with the West. There was increasing stress on both political and economic independence in the 1970s and 1980s and even the question of the territories lost to Russia in 1947 was raised: *see* BESSARABIA, BUKHOVINA.

ROMANIA. Castle Bran, alias Castle Dracula, in the Carpathians, a worthy setting for Bram Stoker's legendary creation. *Photo: Courtesy of the Romanian National Tourist Office.*

ROMANIAN. One of the Romance languages, it developed from the Popular Latin spoken by the Roman settlers of Dacia, but later was strongly influenced by Slav languages. Only in the 19th cent. was the Cyrillic alphabet abandoned in favour of the Roman. The most important dialect is Daco-R., spoken in Wallachia, Moldavia, Bessarabia, Transylvania, Bukhovina, and the Dobruja; Macedo-R. is spoken in Macedonia, Albania, Thessaly, and Epirus.

Romanian Literature. It was not until the 16th cent. that Church Slavonic was replaced by R. in the translation of the Gospels (1560) issued by Diakonus Koresi: a complete Bible appeared in 1688. Of the chronicle writers and translators the best is Dmitrie Cantemir (1673-1723). The greater part of the 18th and early 19th cents. was dominated by Greek influences, and was a period of decline. Ion Radulescu (1802-72) brought the new 'romantic' inspiration to R.L., and a new interest in R. folk songs arose. Other writers of the time were Vasile Cârlova (1809-31), the lyric poet; the historical novelist Dimitrie Bolintineanu (1826-73); and the versatile Vasile Alecsandri (1819-90). Typical of the new period following the achievement of national union was critic Tito Maiorescu (1840-1917), who influenced the greatest R. poet Milhail Eminescu (1850-89). Other popular writers are the dramatist Ion Caragiale (1852-1912); the novelists Carmen Sylva (1843-1916), Duiliu Zamfirescu (1858-1922), and Mihail Sadoveanu (1880-1961); and the great poet Tudor Arghezi (1880-1967). Recent writers such as novelist-dramatist Camil Petruscu, deal with the alliance of intellectuals and workers, etc.

ROMAN LAW. One of the 2 great European legal systems, English law being the other. It originated under the republic, was developed under the empire, and continued in use in the Byzantine Empire until 1453. The first codification was that of the 12 Tables (450 BC), of which only fragments survive. R.L. assumed its final form in the codification of Justinian (AD 528-34). An outstanding feature of R.L. was its system of international law (*jus gentium*), applied in disputes between Romans and foreigners or provincials, or between provincials of different states. During the Middle Ages R.L. was adopted, with local modifications, all over Europe, mainly through the Church's influence; its later diffusion was largely due to the influence of the French *Code Napoléon*, based on R.L., which was adopted in the 19th cent. by several states of E Europe and Asia, and in Egypt. Inside the Commonwealth, R.L. forms the basis of the legal systems of Scotland and Quebec, and is also the basis of that of S Africa, the 2 latter being of French and Dutch origin respectively.

ROMANOV (rōmahn'of). Name of the dynasty which ruled Russia from 1613 to the revolution of March 1917.

ROMAN RELIGION. In the religion of the ancient Romans, traces are found of fetishism, e.g. reverence paid to stones and trees, and totemism, e.g. the wolf-cult. Its strongest element was the domestic cults, e.g. of Janus, Vesta, and the Penates, deities of the threshold, hearth, and store-cupboard respectively. Agricultural elements were the spring fertility rites, the harvest and sowing festivals, and the worship of Jupiter, Mars, and Ceres, who were originally agricultural deities. Other cults were introduced from Etruria (Minerva, Juno), Latium (Diana), and Greece (Apollo), and native gods became identified with those of Greece. Under the empire the state religion was a purely political instrument, typified by the deification of dead emperors. While the educated classes turned to Stoicism or scepticism, the masses found solace in such Oriental mystery cults as that of Isis, in Mithraism, and in Christianity, which made their appeal to the senses, the mind, and conscience.

ROMA'NSH. A Romance language (q.v.), which in 1937 was added to French, German, and Italian, to become the 4th national language of Switzerland. It is spoken by some 50,000 people in the eastern cantons.

ROMANTICISM. Term applied in all arts to the tendency which puts imagination before reason, and abandons the classical ideals of absolute clarity and perfection of form. In literature R. emerged with increasing strength during the later 18th cent., reaching an open declaration with the publication of the *Lyrical Ballads* by Wordsworth and Coleridge in 1798, and inspired the work of Byron, Shelley, and Keats. In prose R. is represented by the 'terror' romances of the Radcliffe school, and the historical novels of Scott. Among the great representatives of R. abroad are Arnim, Brentano, Novalis, Eichendorff, and Tieck in Germany; Chateaubriand, Lamartine, Musset, de Vigny, and Hugo in France; and Manzoni and Foscolo in Italy. In music R. may be found in Schubert, but is generally considered to begin with Weber, to incl.

Schumann, Wagner, and Brahms, and to close with Mahler. In art R. especially denotes the movement which began in France in 1830 as a reaction against the classicism of David and his followers. Its chief exponents were Delacroix and Géricault.

ROMANTICISM. A blending of French and English romantic feeling in Gustav Doré's interpretation of the Arthurian legend in his illustrations of Tennyson's *Idylls* - 'The Ride to Camelot'. Doré's work has enjoyed a revival in the 1970s. *Photo: Mary Evans Picture Library*

ROMANY. *See* GYPSIES.

ROME (*Roma*). Cap. of the Italian Republic and R. prov. and Latium region, on the Tiber, 27km (17m) from the Tyrrhenian Sea. To the E of the river lies the main part of the city, incl. the 7 hills (Quirinal, Aventine, Caelian, Esquiline, Viminal, Palatine, and Capitol) on which the ancient city stood; to the W the popular quarter of Trastevere, the more modern residential quarters of the Prati, and the Vatican (q.v.). The Forum, Colosseum, Pantheon (at present a church), Castel Sant' Angelo (the mausoleum of the Emperor Hadrian), and baths of Caracalla are among the remains of ancient R., while the Lateran, Quirinal, Colonna, Borghese, Barberini, Doria Pamfili, and Farnese palaces date from the Renaissance period. Notable buildings of more recent times incl. the monument to Victor Emmanuel II on the Capitol hill, University City, Policlinico, Palace of Justice, Parliament, and Italian Forum. Apart from St Peter's the main ecclesiastical edifices incl. St John Lateran, St Paul's, S Lorenzo, S Maria Maggiore, and S Maria degli Angeli. Via dei Fori Imperiali (which traverses the Forum), Via Nazionale, Corso Vittorio Emmanuele, and Corso Umberto are fine thoroughfares. Piazza Venezia (where is situated the Palazzo Venezia, *c.* 1455), Piazza del Popolo, Piazza Navona, Campo dei Fiori, Piazza Barberine, Piazza di Spagna, and Piazza Colonna are among the fine squares, many of which are adorned with beautiful fountains. The main open spaces are the Villa Borghese, which adjoins the Pincio terrace from which there is a good view of the Vatican and the heights of Monte Mario, and the Janiculum, which is the site of an immense statue of Garibaldi. Academic institutions incl. the univ. and British and French schools of art. R. has few industries but is an important road, rail and air centre. An underground rlwy 11km (7m), built in 1938-55, runs from the central railway station, which was constructed 1938-50, to Laurentina, SW of the city. A new international airport was opened at Fiumicino in 1961. A large section of the pop. finds employment in govt offices. Pop. (1971) 2,800,500.

ROME. The basilica of St Peter's, looking across St. Peter's Square to the Via della Conciliazione. *Photo: J. Allan Cash*

History. For the early history of R. *see* ROMAN HISTORY. After the deposition of the last emperor, Romulus Augustulus, in 476 the papacy (q.v.) became the real ruler of R., and from the 8th cent. was recognized as such, although attempts were made, e.g. by Arnold of Brescia (1143-55) and Rienzi (1347-54), to revive the rep. As a result of the French Revolution R. temporarily became a republic in 1798-9, and was annexed to the French Empire 1808-14, until the Pope returned on Napoleon's fall. During the 1848-9 revolution, a republic was estab. under Mazzini's leadership, but in spite of Garibaldi's defence was overthrown by French troops. In 1870 R. became the cap. of Italy, the Pope retiring into the Vatican until 1929 when the Vatican City was recognized as a sovereign state. The occupation of R. by the Fascists in 1922 marked the beginning of Mussolini's rule. After his fall in 1943 R. was occupied by the Germans, but was captured by the Allies in 1944.

ROME, Treaties of. After discussions at Messina, Sicily, in 1955, two treaties were signed at Rome in March, 1957 which estab. the European Economic and Atomic Energy Communities. *See* EUROPEAN UNION.

ROMMEL, Erwin (1891-1944). German field marshal. B. in Swabia, he served in the F.W.W., later joining the Nazi Party. He was prominent in the annexations of central

Europe and the fall of France, commanded the N African offensive from 1941 (when he earned the nickname 'desert fox') until defeated by Montgomery at Alamein, and was C-in-C for a short time against the Allies in Europe in 1944. He was a sympathizer in the Stauffenberg plot, and was forced to commit suicide, although officially announced as dying of wounds received in an RAF raid.

ROMNEY, George (1734–1802). British artist. B. near Dalton-in-Furness, Lancs, the son of a carpenter and cabinet-maker, he was practically self-taught. He set up as a portrait painter in 1757, and deserting his wife and children in 1762 he went to London where he became one of the most successful portrait painters of his day. His most famous sitter was Lady Hamilton.

ROMNEY. Lady Hamilton in a more demure interpretation than usual by George Romney.

ROMNEY MARSH. A stretch of drained marshland on the Kent coast, England, between Hythe and Rye, used for sheep pasture. The seaward point is Dungeness. R.M. was reclaimed in Roman times, and is famed for its churches. **New Romney,** formed by the amalgamation of R., one of the Cinque Ports (q.v.), with Littlestone and Greatstone, is now more than a mile from the sea. Pop. (1974) 4,000.

ROMSEY (rum'zi). English market town in Hampshire, on the Test, 13km (8m) NW of Southampton. R. Abbey was founded by Edward the elder; the main surviving feature is the fine Norman church. The mansion of Broadlands nearby, seat of Earl Mountbatten, was formerly the seat of Lord Palmerston. Pop. (1972) 11,160.

RO'MŪLUS. The legendary founder and first king of Rome, the son of Mars by Rhea Silvia. R. and his twin brother Remus were exposed by their great-uncle Amulius, but were suckled by a she-wolf and rescued by a shepherd. On reaching manhood they killed Amulius and founded Rome. Having murdered Remus, R. reigned alone until he disappeared in a storm, and thereafter was worshipped as a god under the name of Quirinus.

ROMULUS AUGUSTULUS (*c.* AD 461–?). Last Roman emperor in the West. When about 14 he was made emperor by his soldier father Orestes in 475, but compelled to abdicate in 476 by Odoacer, leader of the barbarian mercenaries, who nicknamed him Augustulus. Orestes was executed and R. confined to a Neapolitan villa where he d. at an unknown date.

RONCESVALLES (ronthesvahl'yes). Village of N Spain, in the Pyrenees 8km (5m) S of the French frontier, celebrated as the scene of the defeat of the rearguard of Charlemagne's army under Roland, who with the 12 peers was slain.

RONSARD (roṅsahr'), **Pierre de** (1524–85). French poet. B. near Couture, he was a page at the French court and spent some years in Britain. His intended diplomatic career was cut short by deafness, and he retired to study the classical writers, emerging in 1550 as the leader of the Pléiade (q.v.). An original and lightly sensitive stylist, he pub. *Odes* (1550), *Amours,* and *Abrégé de l'art poétique français.* He was patronized by Charles IX, but was bitterly opposed by the followers of Marot.

RÖNTGEN, Wilhelm Konrad (1845–1923). German physicist. B. at Lennep, he became in 1879 director of the Physical Institute at Giessen, and in 1885 at Würzburg, where he conducted his experiments which resulted in the discovery of the rays named after him, in 1895. While investigating the passage of electricity through gases, he noticed the fluorescence of a barium-platinocyanide screen. This radiation R. found would pass through some substances opaque to light, and affect a photographic plate. As the X-ray, the development of this invention has revolutionized surgery. He received a Nobel prize in 1901.

The unit of electromagnetic radiation (x-ray) is named after him, and $1R = 2.58 \times 10^{-4}C/kg$.

ROOD. Alternative name for the Cross of Christ specially applied to the large crucifix which was placed above the R.-screen in medieval churches. Also a surface measure, denoting a quarter of an acre.

ROODEPOORT-MARAISBURG (rūrdepūrt-marit'z-börkh). Town in Transvaal, S Africa, 15km (9m) W of Johannesburg. At a height of 1,745 m (5,725 ft), it is a gold-mining and residential town. Leander Starr Jameson (q.v.) and his followers surrendered here in 1896. Pop. (1970) 114,190, incl. 56,750 White.

ROOK. Bird (*Corvus frugilegus*) of the crow family. The plumage is black and lustrous, and the face bare. Rs. live in colonies at the tops of trees, usually near human habitation.

ROOKE, Sir George (1650–1709). British admiral. He took part in the actions off Beachy Head, 1690, and La Hogue, 1692, and in 1702 destroyed the French and Spanish fleet at Vigo. Together with Sir Clowdisley Shovell, he captured Gibraltar and defeated the French at Malaga in 1704.

ROON (rōn), **Albrecht Theodor Emil,** count von (1803–79). Prussian field marshal. B. near Kolberg, he was War Minister from 1859 and reorganized the army so thoroughly that the 1866 and 1870-1 victories were made possible.

ROOSEVELT, Franklin Delano (1882-1945). 32nd president of the USA. B. at Hyde Park, New York, of a landowning family, he was educ. in Europe and at Harvard and Columbia univs. In 1905 he m. Anna Eleanor R. In 1907 R. was admitted to the Bar and began practising in New York. He entered politics in 1910, when he was elected to the state senate as a Democrat. He held the Assistant Secretaryship of the navy in Wilson's govts 1913-21, and did much to increase the efficiency of the navy during the F.W.W. He was nominated for the vice-presidency in 1920, but with the Democratic defeat returned to his legal practice. The infantile paralysis from which he suffered till his death afflicted him in 1921, but extensive treatment lessened its effect. He served as Governor of New York 1929-33.

He was nominated as Democratic candidate for the presidency in 1932, and won a decisive victory. Amid a grave economic depression he took office in 1933, and at once displayed determined leadership. Surrounding himself by a 'brains trust' of the experts, he launched a carefully spaced legislative programme, which Congress had to accept. Banks, which he closed during the crisis, were reopened; Federal credit was restored, and when the New Deal got under way, the gold standard was abandoned, and the dollar devalued. In 1935 R. introduced the Utilities Act, directed against abuses in the large holding companies, and the Social Security Act, providing for unemployment and old-age insurance.

The presidential election of 1936 was fought entirely on the record of the New Deal, and resulted in a sweeping victory for R. During 1935-6 he was involved in a long conflict with the Supreme Court, who declared several of his measures unconstitutional, until the retirement or death of certain of its members enabled him to secure the support of a liberal majority. In 1938 R. introduced measures for farm relief and the improvement of working conditions. In his foreign policy he endeavoured to use his influence to restrain Axis aggression, and to establish 'Good Neighbour' relations with the American countries.

Soon after the outbreak of war he launched a vast rearmament programme, introduced conscription, and provided for the supply of armaments to the Allies on a 'cash-and-carry' basis. In spite of strong isolationist opposition, and the fact that he was breaking a long-standing precedent in standing for a 3rd term, he was re-elected in 1940. He then introduced his 'lease-lend' plan for the supply of war materials to the Allies, announced that the US would become the 'arsenal of democracy', and in 1941 drew up with Mr Churchill the Atlantic Charter as a statement of Allied war aims. In that year he defined the 'Four Freedoms' (q.v.). From the Japanese attack on Pearl Harbor in Dec. 1941, he devoted himself solely to the conduct of the war. He participated in the Washington (1942) and Casablanca conferences (1943), to plan the Mediterranean assault, and in those at Quebec, Cairo, Tehran (1943), and Yalta (1945), at which the final preparations were made for the Allied victory. He was re-elected for a 4th term in 1944. His sudden death on 12 April 1945 was the cause of worldwide mourning. *See also* New Deal.

His wife **Eleanor R.** (1884-1962) whom he m. in 1905, actively furthered his political career. A prominent social worker and lecturer, her newspaper column 'My Day' was widely syndicated, and she was a US delegate to the UN general assembly, and later chairman of the UN commission on human rights 1946-51. Within the Democratic Party she formed the left-wing Americans for Democratic Action group in 1947. Her books incl. *This I Remember* (1950), and *You Learn By Living* (1960).

ROOSEVELT, Theodore (1858-1919). 26th President of the USA. B. in New York, he was elected to the state legislature as a Republican in 1881. He was Assistant Secretary of the Navy 1897-8, and during the Spanish War of 1898 commanded a volunteer force of 'rough riders'. After serving as Governor of NY 1898-1900 he was elected Vice-President in 1900 to McKinley, whom he succeeded as President on his assassination in 1901, and was re-elected in 1904. In office he campaigned against the great trusts, and initiated measures for the conservation of national resources, while carrying on a jingoist foreign policy designed to enforce US supremacy over Latin America. Alienated after his retirement in 1909 by the conservatism of his successor Taft, he formed the Progressive or 'Bull Moose' Party, as whose candidate he unsuccessfully ran for the presidency in 1912 against Taft and Wilson. During the F.W.W. he strongly advocated American intervention. He wrote historical and other works, incl. *The Naval War of 1812* (1882) and *The Winning of the West* (1889-96). On an expedition to Mississippi in 1902 he refused to shoot a bear cub, and Teddy bears were named after him.

ROOT. The underground extremities of plants. Rs. often form the storehouse of nutritious food substances, as well as absorbing moisture, etc., from the soil. The main R. is known as the tap-root, and has various qualifying names according to the form it assumes, e.g. conical, napiform (turnip-shaped), fusiform (spindle-shaped). The subsidiary Rs. are known as fibrous Rs. and may be divided as follows: (a) non-tuberous and (b) tuberous, including moniliform (necklace- shaped), nodolose (bearing knobs towards the extremities), and annulated (divided into rings).

ROPE. Stout cordage over 2.5cm (1in) circumference. It is made similarly to thread or twine, by twisting yarns together to form strands, which are then in turn twisted round each other in the direction opposite to that of the yarns. Although hemp is still the commonest material used to make R., nylon is increasingly used.

ROQUEFORT-SUR-SOULZON (rokfohr′-sur-sool-zoń′). Village in Aveyron dept, France, famous for its strong cheese, made of sheep and goats' milk and matured in caves. Pop. (1973) 1,500.

RORAIMA (rorī′ma), **Mount.** Plateau (Indian 'Mother of Rivers') *c.* 50 sq.km (20 sq.m) and 2,629 m (8, 625 ft) a.s.l. at the conjunction of Guyana, Brazil and Venezuela. It is thought to have taken its present form 300 million years ago, and the isolation due to its 300m (1,000 ft) cliffs has ensured a largely unique fauna and flora. However, the inhospitable, eroded rock supports only some grasses, bushes, flowers, insects and small amphibians. Conan Doyle's *The Lost World*, inspired by reports of its strange character, was entirely fanciful in envisaging it still as it was in the palaeozoic period, with prehistoric monsters roaming primeval forest.

RORQUAL (rōr′kwawl). A species of *Balaenoptera* - large, long, fin-whales. The blue whale (*B. sibbaldi*) is the largest of all animals, measuring 30m (100ft) and more.

The common R. (*B. physalas*) is slate-coloured and not quite so long.

RORSCHACH (ror'shakh), **Hermann** (1884-1922). Swiss psychiatrist, influenced by Freud and Jung, whose methods of diagnosis incl. the *Formdeutversuch* or R. test consisting of 10 bilaterally symmetrical, amorphous, ink-blot patterns (5 black and white, 5 coloured) which the subject is asked to interpret, his answers revealing personality type, degree of intelligence and emotional stability.

ROSA, Salvator (1615-73). Italian painter. B. near Naples, he spent much of his time when a youth travelling in southern Italy, where he copied from nature. He went to Rome in 1635, and estab. a great reputation as a landscape painter. He also wrote verse satires.

ROSACEAE (rōzā'sē-ē). A large family of seed-bearing plants which produce many temperate fruits e.g. the apple, pear, plum, cherry, peach, and almond, as well as the rose and other flowers.

ROSARIO (rōsah'rē-ō). River port of Argentina, 280km (175m) NW of Buenos Aires, on the Parana. Founded in 1725, it has sugar refineries, meat-packing and maté-processing factories, etc. Wheat, flour, meats, etc., are exported. Pop. (1970) 798,000.

ROSARY. Form of prayer used by RCs consisting of 150 Aves and 15 Paternosters and Glorias; also a string of 165 beads for keeping count of the prayers.

ROSCELLINUS (roselī'nus), **Johannes** (*c.* 1050-*c.* 1122). Medieval thinker; regarded as the founder of the Scholastic philosophy because of his defence of Nominalism against Anselm.

ROSCIUS (rosh'ius) **GALLUS, Quintus** (*c.* 126-62 BC). Roman actor, originally a slave, who achieved fame and fortune by his acting ability. His name has become proverbial for a great actor.

ROSCOMMON. County of Rep. of Ireland in the prov. of Connacht, bounded on the E by the Shannon. A number of lakes (e.g. Gara, Key, Allen) lie partly or wholly in R., which is noted for its pastures. The co. town, also R., has remains of a castle put up in the 13th cent. by English settlers. The name, originally Ros-Comain, means wood round a monastery. Area 2,463 sq.km (951 sq.m); pop. (1971) 53,520.

ROSE. Genus of flowering plants (family Rosaceae). Many cultivated forms have been derived from the sweet briar (*Rosa rubiginosa*) and the dog-rose (*R. canina*). There are many climbing varieties, but the more cultivated forms are bush roses and standards. These are cultivated roses grafted on to a briar stem. By a Royal Nat. Rose Socety ruling in 1979 (as received by the World Fed. of Rose Societies), the hybrid tea (so-called from its scent since the early 19th cent.) was renamed the large flowered rose, and the floribunda became the cluster flower rose. Individual names, such as Peace, were unchanged.

ROSEBERY, Archibald Philip Primrose, 5th earl of (1847-1929). Liberal statesman. Educ. at Eton and Oxford, he succeeded to the title in 1868, and was appointed Commissioner of Works 1885, and For. Sec. 1886 and 1892-4. He succeeded Gladstone as PM in 1894, but his govt survived less than a year. After 1896 his imperialist views gradually estranged him from the Liberal Party. He was also a noted racehorse-owner, winning the Derby 3 times.

ROSEMARY, Evergreen shrub (*Rosmarinus officinalis*) bearing small scented leaves. An aromatic oil is extracted from the clusters of pale purple flowers.

ROSENBERG (rōzenberg), **Alfred** (1893-1946). German politician. B. at Tallinn, he became the chief Nazi ideologist. He supervised the training of the party, and 1941-4 was Reich Minister for eastern occupied territories. He was tried at Nuremberg in 1946 as a war criminal and hanged.

ROSENBERG, Julius and **Ethel.** *See* SECRET SERVICE.

ROSES, Wars of the. The civil wars fought between the adherents of the House of Lancaster, which ruled England 1399-1461, and the House of York, which claimed the throne. The two parties used the red and the white rose respectively as their badges. The first battle was fought at St Albans in 1455. War was renewed in 1459-61, ending in the Yorkist claimant's accession as Edward IV, and the destruction of the Lancastrians at Towton. A Lancastrian rising in 1464 was crushed at Hexham. A temporary Lancastrian restoration took place in 1470-1, ended by the Yorkist victories at Barnet and Tewkesbury. Peace reigned until Henry of Richmond's victory at Bosworth in 1485 restored a branch of the House of Lancaster; as Henry VII he m. Elizabeth of York, and so united the two Houses. Yorkist rebellions continued, however, until 1497.

ROSETTA (Arab. Rashid). Town in Egypt, on the main W arm(to which it gives its name) of the Nile delta, NW of Cairo. Pop. (1970) 33,000. The Rosetta Stone with a trilingual inscription was found here in 1799 by one of Napoleon's officers, captured by the British in 1801, and in 1802 placed in the British Museum. *See* HIEROGLYPHIC.

ROSEWOOD. The name of several kinds of ornamental timber, produced and exported in large quantities from Brazil, Jamaica, and Honduras. It is a rich brown, and polishes well.

ROSH HASHA'NA. The two-day holiday at the start of the Jewish New Year (first new moon after the autumn equinox).

ROSICRUCIANS (rōzikroo'shianz). Name adopted by certain early 17th cent. philosophers, who claimed occult powers, and employed the terminology of alchemy to expound their mystical doctrines. The name comes from certain books pub. in 1614 and 1615, which were attributed to Christian Rosenkreutz ('rosy cross'), most probably a pen-name, but allegedly a writer living *c.* 1460. Several societies have been founded in Britain and the USA which claim to be their successors, e.g. the Rosicrucian Fraternity (1614 in Germany, 1861 in USA).

ROS'KILDE. Historic town on R. Fjord, Denmark. It was the Danish cap. from the 10th cent. until 1443, and the much restored cathedral contains the remains of the Danish kings. Pop. (1975) 51,000.

ROSS, Sir John (1777-1856). Scottish rear-admiral and explorer. He served in the wars with France and made voyages of Arctic exploration in 1818, 1829-33 and 1850. His nephew **Sir James R.** (1800-62) made several Arctic voyages with his uncle and with Parry (1819-27), determined the position of the magnetic north pole in 1831, and in 1839-43 commanded an Antarctic expedition. *See* ROSS ISLAND AND DEPENDENCY, named after him.

ROSS, Sir Ronald (1857-1932). British physician and bacteriologist. B. in India, he served 1881-99 in the Indian

ROSETTA STONE. A decree of the priests of Memphis conferring divine honours upon Ptolemy V, King of Egypt 196 BC. The top inscription is in classical hieroglyphic; the centre panel repeats the decree in the contemporary cursive script – demotic; and the bottom section repeats it yet again in classical Greek. *Photo: Courtesy of the trustees of the British Museum*

Medical Service, and 1895-8 discovered the malaria parasite and studied its life-history. He received a Nobel prize in 1902.

ROSS. English market town in Hereford and Worcester, 19km (12m) SE of Hereford. Agricultural implements are manufactured. The philanthropist John Kyrle (1637-1724), who made his home at R. and was chosen sheriff in 1683, is called the Man of R. He was celebrated by Alexander Pope. Pop. (1971) 6,000.

ROSS AND CRO'MARTY. Former co. of Scotland. In 1975 Lewis, in the Outer Hebrides, became part of the Western Isles, and the mainland area was incl. in Highland region. The coastline of the latter is indented by many sea lochs and has many islands off the western shore. Peaks incl. Ben Wyvis in the NE, striking in its isolation; Glomach Falls (113m/370ft) are the highest in Britain; and Loch Maree is renowned for its beauty. Dingwall was the admin. HQ.

ROSS DEPENDENCY. All the islands and territories between 160° E and 150° W long. S of 60° S lat.; it incl. Edward VII Land, Ross Sea and its islands, and parts of Victoria Land. It was placed under New Zealand jurisdiction by an Order in Council of 1923. There are a few scientific bases with *c.* 250 staff. Area 453,000 sq.km (175,000 sq.m).

The **Ross Ice Shelf** or Barrier is a permanent layer of ice across the Ross Sea *c.* 425 m (1400 ft) thick. It is probable that marine organisms beneath it have been undisturbed from the Pleistocene period until drillings were made in 1976.

ROSSETTI, Christina Georgina (1830-94). British poet. The sister of Dante R., and a devout Anglican, she produced much popular lyric and religious verse, e.g. *Goblin Market* and other poems (1862).

ROSSETTI, Dante Gabriel (1828-82). British poet and artist whose full name was Gabriel Charles Dante R. B. in London, the son of the Italian patriot Gabriele R. (1783-1854), who settled in England in 1824, he studied at the RA schools and under Madox-Brown, and in 1848 formed the Pre-Raphaelite brotherhood together with Millais and Hunt. He early began writing verse, and pub. *The Blessed Damozel* in 1850, but on the death in 1862 of the beautiful Elizabeth Siddal (whom he had m. in 1860) he buried his verse MSS. with her. These were recovered in 1869, and when pub. as *Poems* (1870) were attacked on the grounds of morality as belonging to the 'fleshly school of poetry'. *Ballads and Sonnets* appeared in 1881, and he also pub. translations from Dante, Villon, and others. His best-known paintings incl. 'Beata Beatrix', 'Monna Vanna', 'The Beloved', and 'Dante's Dream'. His brother, **William Michael R.** (1829-1919), was one of the later members of the Pre-Raphaelite Brotherhood, and pub. art and literary criticism.

ROSSINI (rossē'nē), **Gioachino Antonio** (1792-1868). Italian composer. B. at Pesaro, his first success was the opera *Tancredi* (1813). In 1816 his *Il Barbiere di Siviglia* was produced at Rome, and was at first a failure. During his fertile composition period, 1815-23, he produced 20 operas, but after *Guillaume Tell* (1829) gave up writing opera. His later years were spent in Bologna and Paris. Among the works of this period are the *Stabat Mater* (1831-41), and the piano music first pub. in 1919 and arranged for ballet by Respighi as *La Boutique fantasque.*

ROSS ISLAND. Name of 2 islands in Antarctica, one in Weddell Sea, discovered 1903 by Nordenskjöld, area *c.* 3,885 sq.km (1,500 sq.m); the other in Ross Sea discovered 1841 by Ross, area c. 6,475 sq.km (2,500 sq.m), and incl. the active volcano Mt Erebus (4,204 m/13,202ft).

ROSSLARE. Port of co. Wexford, Republic of Ireland, 15km (9m) SE of Wexford. Founded by the English in 1210, it was made the Irish terminus of the steamer route from Fishguard in 1906.

ROSTAND (rostahṅ'), **Edmond** (1869-1918). French dramatist. B. at Marseilles, he achieved immediate success with *Les romanesques* (1894), which was followed by *La Princesse lointaine* (1895); *La Samaritaine* (1897); *Cyrano de Bergerac* (1897), his greatest triumph; *L'Aiglon* (1900), which provided Bernhardt with one of her greatest roles; and *Chantecler* (1910), in which Lucien Guitry appeared.

ROSTOCK (ro'stok). Port in E Germany, on the Warnow, 13km (8m) S of the Baltic. Founded in 1189 on a long-inhabited site, it became in the 14th cent. a powerful member of the Hanseatic League. It has a univ. (1419). Pop. (1978) 220,875.

ROSTOV-ON-DON (rostov'-). Seaport in the Russian SFSR, cap. of R. region, on the Don, 23km (14m) E of the Sea of Azov. R. has shipyards; tobacco, motor-car and locomotive and textile factories. It dates from 1761, and is linked by river and canal with Volgograd on the Volga.

ROSS ISLAND. An historic photograph taken by members of Scott's Antarctic expedition in 1911. Mount Erebus, seen here from the ship *Terra Nova,* was first climbed by Sir Douglas Mawson with two companions on Shackleton's Antarctic expedition of 1908. *Photo: Popperfoto*

Part of R. region is within the Donbas (q.v.). Pop. (1977) 921,000.

ROSTROPŌ'VICH, Mstislav Leopoldovich (1927–). Russian cellist and conductor. B. at Baku, he was first taught by his father. His mastery of his instrument has prompted a number of composers to write for him, incl. Prokofiev (his unfinished 'Concerto for Cello' was completed by R.), Shostakovich, Khachaturian and Benjamin Britten. He was deprived of Russian citizenship in 1978.

ROSYTH (rōsīth'). A naval base and dockyard in Fife, Scotland, built 1909, on the N shore of the Firth of Forth, 3km (2m) S of Dunfermline.

RŌ'TA. Fishing port and naval base on the Atlantic coast of Spain, NW of Cadiz.

ROTARY CLUB. Society founded to foster the ideal of service to others and composed of business and professional men. The first R.C. (so called because the meetings were held at the offices of each member in rotation) was estab. by Paul Harris in 1905 in Chicago; the first British R.C. was founded in 1911. The R. International had in 1975 some 750,000 members throughout the world.

ROTHAMSTED. English agricultural experimental station 6.5km (4m) NW of St Albans, founded by Sir James Bennet Lawes (1816–1900) to carry out soil research. Its records go back to 1843. Lawes endowed the station in 1889, and in 1899 formed the Lawes Agricultural Trust to continue the work.

ROTHENBURG (rō'tenboorg) **OB DER TAUBER** (tow'ber). Town in Bavaria, W Germany, 65km (40m) W of Nuremberg, famous for its medieval buildings, churches, and walls. Pop. (1978) 13,000.

RŌ'THENSTEIN, Sir William (1872–1945). British artist, son of a German immigrant who settled in Bradford. His work, now out of favour, incl. decorations for St Stephen's Hall, Westminster, and portrait drawings. He was Principal of the Royal College of Art 1920–35, and helped Epstein, Paul Nash, and Henry Moore. His elder son **Sir John R.** (1901–) was Director of the Tate Gallery 1938–64, his younger son **Michael R.** (1908–) is an artist, noted as a print-maker.

ROTHERHAM. Town in S Yorks, England, 8km (5m) NE of Sheffield, on the Don and Rother. Industries incl. iron and steel, pottery, glassworks, brewing. Pop. (1972) 84,570.

ROTHERMERE. *See* under NORTHCLIFFE.

ROTHESAY (roth'si). Cap. of the Isle of Bute, which was incl. in 1975 in Strathclyde region. It is a touring centre for Scotland's W coast. Pop. (1971) 6,373.

ROTH'KŌ, Mark (1903–70). American artist. B. in Russia, he was the founder of abstract expressionism, and produced large, simple canvases in a limited number of strong-toned colours, designed for spiritual contemplation.

ROTHSCHILD (roths'-chīld). The name of a Jewish family, famed for its activity in the financial world for 2 cents. Mayer Anselm (1744–1812) set up as a moneylender in Frankfurt-am-Main, and important houses were estab. throughout Europe by his 10 children. Nathan Mayer (1777–1836) settled in England, and his grandson Nathaniel (1840–1915) was created a baron in 1885. Lionel Walter (1868–1937) succeeded his father as 2nd baron R. and was a noted naturalist. The 2nd baron's nephew, Nathaniel (1910–), 3rd baron R., is a scientist. During the S.W.W. he was with military intelligence and was awarded the GM for work in bomb disposal. He was head of the central policy review staff in the Cabinet Office – the 'think tank' set up by Edward Heath – 1970–4. James de R. (1878–1957), originally a member of the French branch, but who became a naturalized Briton, bequeathed to the nation Waddesdon Manor, near Aylesbury.

ROTORUA (rotoroo'a). Town in North Island, NZ, in the Hot Spring District, near Lake R. There are medicinal springs, and active volcanoes, which, with hills and lakes, form a vast scenic attraction for many visitors. Pop. (1976) 46,650.

ROTTERDAM. Second city and chief port of the Netherlands, on the Rotte and the Maas mouth of the Rhine-Maas delta; the Nieuwe Waterweg (new waterway), constructed 1866–90, links R. with the North Sea for shipping. R. dates from the 12th cent. or earlier, and developed as a port threaded with waterways. There is a statue of Erasmus, who was born at R., in the market place; the Groote Kerk (great church) or Church of St Lawrence, begun early in the 15th cent., was gutted in the German air attack of 14 May 1940, and subsequently restored. R.'s museums and art collections are notable. Industries incl. brewing, distilling, shipbuilding, sugar and petroleum refining, and the manufacture of margarine and tobacco. The city centre was destroyed by German air attack in 1940, but has been completely rebuilt, and an underground railway system constructed (opened 1968). The dockyards have been greatly extended, with modern container and bulk cargo handling facilities, and the R.-Europort complex is one of the premier ocean cargo ports of the world. Pop. (1978) 590,312.

ROUAULT (roo-ō), **Georges** (1871–1958). French artist. B. in Paris, the son of a cabinet-maker, he was apprenticed to a stained-glass maker – the influence of this craft being obvious in his later paintings – and studied under Gustave Moreau. His works incl. 'Aunt Sallies' and 'The Three Judges', both in the Tate, and moving religious subjects, e.g. 'The Holy Face' as imprinted on the veil of St Veronica.

ROUSSEAU 'Tropical storm with a tiger', dated 1891, was the first of the *Douanier*'s jungle scenes, the genre which established his present fame. *Photo: Courtesy of the National Gallery, London*

ROUBAIX (roobā'). Town in Nord dept, N France NE of Lille, important centre of French woollen textile production. Pop. (1975) 110,000.

ROUBILLAC (roobēyahk'), **Louis François** (1695-1762). French sculptor. B. at Lyons, he went to England where he was patronized by Walpole, becoming the most popular sculptor of his day. His principal works incl. statues of Handel, Newton, and George I, and busts of Shakespeare and Pope. His name is sometimes less correctly spelled Roubiliac.

ROUEN (roo-oṅ'). French port, cap. of Seine-Maritime dept, on the Seine, to the NW of Paris. It was also cap. of Normandy from 912. Lost by King John 1204, it was in English possession 1419-49; Joan of Arc was burned in the market place 1431. The cathedral (13th-16th cent.) is famous (its right-hand tower, Tour de Beurre, was paid for by the sale of indulgences to eat butter during Lent), and there are other notable buildings. R. is a centre of the wine trade. Industries incl. cotton spinning and weaving, distilling, and petroleum refining. Pop. (1975) 113,535.

ROUGET DE LISLE (roozhā' de lēl), **Claude Joseph** (1760-1836). French author and army officer. B. at Lons-le-Saunier, he composed, at Strasbourg, *La Marseillaise*, the French national anthem and song of the revolution.

ROULERS (roolā'). Town in W Flanders prov., Belgium, 21km (13m) NW of Courtrai. Linen, jute, and other textiles are made. R. was an important German base during the F.W.W. Pop. (1972) 40,400.

ROULETTE (roolet'). A gambling game, associated with Monte Carlo, consisting of betting on the numbered divisions of a turning wheel into which an ivory ball will fall. They are coloured alternately black and red, with numbers from 0-36. The table, on which bets are laid, is designed in 3 columns of numbers corresponding to those of the wheel, and many methods of betting exist, with the odds appropriate to the chances against the number appearing. The play is under the control of a croupier.

ROUNDHEADS. Nickname applied to the parliamentary party during the revolution of 1640-60. It has a sneering implication, since at the time only the lower classes wore their hair short.

ROUP. A contagious disease of poulty and game. Caused by unhealthy conditions, it is characterized by swelling of the face and purulent catarrh.

ROUSSEAU (roosō'), **Henri** (1844-1910). French artist known as *Le Douanier* (customs official) because this was for a time his profession. B. in Laval, he exhibited at the

Salon des Indépendants from 1886 to 1910, and was associated with the group which was led by Apollinaire and Picasso. He painted landscapes, animals and jungle scenes.

ROUSSEAU, Jean Jacques (1712-78). French philosopher. B. in Geneva, he was apprenticed in turn to a lawyer and engraver, but ran away and from 1728 led the wandering life described in his *Confessions.* The first of many ill-repaid patrons was Mme Warens, whose lover he became. On the breakdown of this relationship he went to Paris, where he took as his mistress the servant girl, Thérèse le Vasseur: their 5 children were deposited in the foundling hospital. In 1754 he pub. a *Discourse on the Origin of Inequality,* denouncing civilized society, which made him famous, but retired to country seclusion to produce the sentimental romance *La Nouvelle Héloïse* (1760); the revolutionary *Du Contrat social* (1762); and the educational treatise *Émile* (1762). The democratic political implications and the deistic viewpoint of the latter caused it to be condemned by Church and State, and R. fled abroad, living for a time in England under the patronage of Hume. He later returned to France, but suffered from an increasing persecution mania until his death. R. was buried in the Panthéon.

ROUSSEAU, Pierre Étienne Théodore (1812-67). French landscape painter of the Barbizon School. B. in Paris, he studied under Rémond and Guyon Lethière. He came under the influence of Constable and Bonington, sketched from nature in many parts of France, and settling in Barbizon in 1848 he became one of the pioneers of Romanticism.

ROWAN. *See* MOUNTAIN ASH.

ROWE (rō), **Nicholas** (1674-1718). English dramatist and poet. He entered the Middle Temple in 1691, and inherited a fortune from his father. His most famous dramas are *The Fair Penitent* (1702), and *Jane Shore* (1714), in which Mrs Siddons played. He ed. Shakespeare, and was Poet Laureate from 1715.

ROWING. Propulsion of a boat by successive strokes of oars. A rower may handle either 2 oars (sculling) or more commonly 1 oar, especially in racing boats, which consist of 2-, 4-or 8-man crews, with or without coxswain (steersman). The first recorded English race, still surviving, was Doggett's Coat and Badge, initiated in 1715 between Thames watermen: there were similar races between ferrymen of the Hudson river, New York, in 1811 and 1823. Amateur rowing as a sport, developing early in England (Leander club 1817) and later in the USA (Detroit boat club 1839), has become internationally popular. In the UK the chief annual events incl., the Oxford and Cambridge boat race, the Thames head of the river race, and the Henley Royal regatta, also a major international event. In the USA the Harvard-Yale boat race, held on the Thames at New London, and the Poughkeepsie regatta, are the premier events, while international contests in all classes are held during the Olympic Games.

ROWLANDSON, Thomas (1756-1827). British caricaturist. B. in London, he studied at the RA Schools and in Paris. Impoverished by gambling, he turned from portrait painting to caricature. His *Tour of Dr Syntax in Search of the Picturesque,* and its 2 sequels, proved very popular. Other works incl. 'The Dance of Death', and illustrations for Smollett, Goldsmith, and Sterne.

ROWLEY, William (*c.* 1585-*c.* 1642). English dramatist. He became an actor, wrote *All's Lost by Lust,* and collaborated with Thomas Middleton in *The Changeling* and *The Spanish Gypsie.*

ROWLING, Wallace 'Bill' (1927-). NZ Labour statesman. He became pres. of the Labour party in 1969, and succeeded to the premiership when Kirk d. in 1974. He was defeated in the elections of Nov. 1975.

ROWSE, Alfred Leslie (1903-). British historian. A fellow of All Souls Coll., Oxford 1925-74, he has made a popular as well as a scholarly reputation with books on the Tudor period. He pub. a biography of Shakespeare in 1963, and in 1973 made a controversial claim to have identified the 'Dark Lady' of the sonnets as Emilia Lanier, half-Italian dau. of a court musician, with whom the poet is alleged to have had an affair 1593-5.

ROXBURGH (-buro). Former border co. of Scotland, incl. in 1975 in Borders region. A mainly upland area, where sheep are raised, it incl. the fringes of the Cheviots. Jedburgh was the co. town.

ROYAL ACADEMY OF ARTS. An institution founded in London in 1768 by George III to encourage painting, sculpture, and architecture, the first pres. being Sir Joshua Reynolds. In 1771 the academy was granted quarters in Somerset House, but in 1836 it moved to the National Gallery, and in 1867 was granted a lease of Old Burlington House. An annual summer exhibition is held at the academy for the works of contemporary artists. The R.A. Schools give instruction in painting, sculpture, and architecture free of charge.

ROYAL ACADEMY OF DRAMATIC ART. Founded by Herbert Beerbohm Tree in 1904, it is the foremost academy of its kind in Britain. Its headquarters have been in Gower Street, London, since 1905, and a Royal Charter was granted in 1920.

ROYAL ACADEMY OF MUSIC. The senior music school in the British Commonwealth (1822). It provides a full-time complete musical education.

ROYAL AERONAUTICAL SOCIETY. The oldest British aviation body, formed in 1866. Its members discussed and explored the possibilities of flight long before its successful achievement.

ROYAL AIR FORCE. *See* AIR FORCE.

ROYAL BALLET. Title under which the Sadler's Wells Ballet (the senior co. estab. at Covent Garden), Sadler's Wells Theatre Ballet (the junior co. at Sadler's Wells), and the Sadler's Wells School (Richmond, Surrey) were incorporated in 1957.

ROYAL COLLEGE OF MUSIC. A London college, opened in 1883, which combines with the Royal Academy of Music for local examinations.

ROYAL HORTICULTURAL SOCIETY. Instituted in 1804 for the improvement of horticulture, it holds a series of flower shows at Vincent Square, London, the great annual show at Chelsea being a social event, and has 120 ha. (300 acres) of gardens, orchards and trial grounds at Wisley in Surrey. The Lindley Library is probably the world's finest horticultural collection, and the soc. itself pub. many books.

ROYAL HOUSEHOLD. Name given to those persons who are in the personal service of the sovereign. The chief officers of the R.H. are the Lord Chamberlain, the Lord Steward, and the Master of the Horse. Separate Hs. are maintained by other principal members of the Royal Family.

ROYAL INSTITUTION OF GREAT BRITAIN. An organization for the 'promotion, diffusion, and extension of science and useful knowledge', founded in London in 1799. Faraday and Davy are among distinguished scientists who have used the laboratories.

ROYAL MARINES. *See* MARINES.

ROYAL MILITARY ACADEMY. *See* SANDHURST.

ROYAL OPERA HOUSE. The leading English opera house, in Covent Garden, London. The original theatre was opened in 1732, a second in 1809, and the present one in 1858.

ROYAL SOCIETY. The oldest and premier scientific society of Britain. It originated in 1645 and its charter dates from 1660. The Copley and other medals are awarded periodically, and scientific papers are read at Burlington House, London. The Scottish counterpart is the R.S. of Edinburgh.

ROYAL SOCIETY FOR THE PREVENTION OF CRUELTY TO ANIMALS (R.S.P.C.A.). A society formed in 1824 to improve the conditions under which animals were kept and to abolish the gross cruelties which flourished on all sides. Since then further legislation has been initiated by the R.S.P.C.A. to strengthen the efforts of its inspectors and clinic workers.

ROYAL WARRANT HOLDERS. An association of business firms authorized to display the royal crest, signifying royal patronage by appointment.

ROYCE, Sir Frederick Henry (1863-1933). British self-styled 'mechanic'. Originally a manufacturer of electric dynamos and cranes, he so impressed Charles Stewart Rolls (1877-1910) by the car he built for his own personal use in 1904 that the Rolls-Royce partnership was formed. Suffering in later life from ill-health he designed his most famous car the Phantom II Continental - remarkable for silence, speed and refinement - without ever visiting the factory, but his greatest achievement was the R.-type engine which powered the Schneider Trophy-winning seaplane in 1929 and 1931, and was later developed into the Merlin engine which enabled the RAF Hurricanes and Spitfires to defeat the Luftwaffe in the S.W.W.

ROYCE, Josiah (1855-1916). American philosopher. B. at Grass Valley, California, he became professor of philosophy at Harvard in 1892, and Alford professor in 1914. His writings reveal a deep consideration of human nature and its varied ideals.

RUANDA. *See* RWANDA.

RUAHINE (roo-ahē'ne). Mountain range in North Island, NZ. The Manawatu r., on which Palmerston North stands, rises here.

RUAPEHU (rōō-a-pē'hōō). Volcano in Tongariro Nat. Park, N Island, New Zealand. Lying to the SW of Lake Taupo, it is the highest peak in North Island, 2,797 m (9,175 ft).

RUB' AL KHALI (roob-al-kha'lē). Vast sandy desert (Arabic 'empty quarter') in south Saudi Arabia. Bertram Thomas was the first European to cross it in 1930-1. Area 650,000 sq.km (250,000 sq.m).

RUBBER. The coagulated latex of a great range of plants, mainly from the New World. Most important is Para R. (so called from its original place of export) which derives from the tree *Hevea brasiliensis.* It was introduced from Brazil to SE Asia, where most of the world supply is now produced, the chief exporters being Malaysia, Indonesia, Sri Lanka, Cambodia, Thailand, Sarawak, and Brunei. At about 7 years the tree, which may grow to 20m (60ft), is ready for 'tapping', small incisions being made in the trunk and the latex dropped into collecting cups. Other sources of R. are: *Manihot glaziovii,* another Brazilian tree, which supplies Ceara R., and *Koksagyz,* or Russian dandelion, which grows in temperate climates and can yield about 45kg (100lb) of R. per tonne of roots, and guayule *(Parthenium argentatum)* which grows in south-west USA and Mexico. In the 20th cent. world production of R. has increased a hundredfold, and the S.W.W. stimulated the production of synthetic R. to replace the supplies from Malayan sources overrun by the Japanese.

There are an infinite variety of synthetic Rs. adapted to special purposes, but overwhelmingly the most important economically is SBR (styrene-butadiene rubber). Cheaper than natural R., it is preferable for some purposes (e.g. car tyre treads, where its higher abrasion-resistance is useful), and is either blended with natural R. or used alone for industrial moulding and extrusions, shoe soles, hosepipes, latex foam, etc.

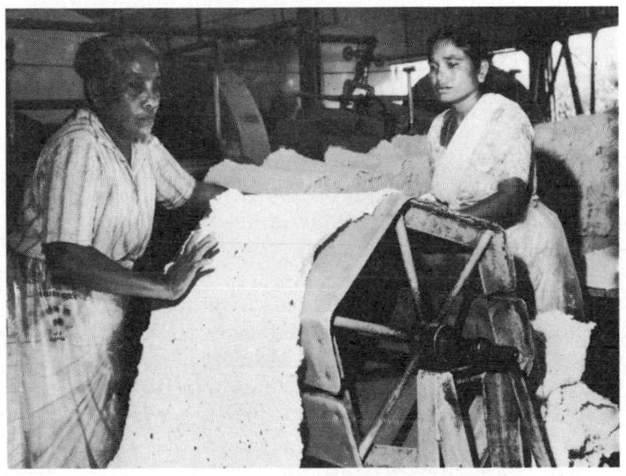

RUBBER. Indian women working in a rubber factory in Malaysia. In the preparation of this crêpe rubber (straw-coloured rather than the dark brown of sheet rubber), the coagulum passes through rollers rotating at different speeds, so producing the crêping effect. *Photo: Mireille Vautier*

RUBBRA, Edmund Duncan (1901-). British composer. B. at Northampton, he studied under Holst and is a master of contrapuntal writing, cf. his study *Counterpoint* (1960). His compositions incl. 8 symphonies, the opera *Bee-bee-bei,* chamber music, songs, etc.

RUBENS (roobenz), **Peter Paul** (1577-1640). Flemish painter. B. at Siegen, Westphalia, he was taken to Antwerp in 1587, and after studying under Verhaecht, Adam van Noort, and O. van Veen went to Italy in 1600. In 1605 he visited Spain, and at Madrid painted many portraits of the Spanish nobility. He settled in Antwerp in 1609, and became court painter to the Archduke Albert and his wife Isabella. His masterpiece, the 'Descent from the Cross', in the Antwerp cathedral, was painted in 1611-14. In 1620 he went to France at the invitation of Marie de' Medici, and painted a number of pictures commemorating her marriage to Henry IV. In 1628 he again went to Madrid where he met Velasquez. In 1629-30 he was in London as envoy to Charles I, and painted a portrait of the king and his queen, and the 'War and Peace', now in the National

Gallery. He is noted as a fine colourist, and excelled in the use of the pencil.

RUBIACEAE (roobi-ā'sē-ē). Large family of plants mainly found in the tropics; its typical genus is *Rubia*, or madder.

RUBICON (roo'bikon). Ancient name of the small river flowing into the Adriatic which, under the Roman republic, marked the boundary between Italy proper and Cisalpine Gaul. When Caesar led his army across it in 49 BC he therefore declared war on the republic; hence to 'cross the R.' means to take an irrevocable step. Its identity is not certain, but the Fiumicino is officially recognized as the R.; it rises in the Etruscan Apennines 16km (10m) WNW of San Marino and enters the Adriatic 16km (10m) NW of Rimini.

RUBIDIUM (Lat. *rubidius*, dark red). Soft white metal of the alkali group which tarnishes instantly in air and ignites spontaneously: symbol Rb, at. no. 37, at. wt. 85.48. Discovered spectroscopically by Bunsen and Kirchoff in the mineral lepidolite, it is slightly radioactive, and is used as a photo-sensitor, having the closest colour response to that of the eye.

RUBINSTEIN, Arthur (1888–1982). Polish-American pianist. He studied in Warsaw and Berlin, and appeared with the worlds major symphony orchestras, specializing in Chopin, Debussy and the Spanish composers. Hon KBE 1977.

RUBUS (ro͞o'bus). Genus of shrubs or herbs, whose white or pink flowers are followed by edible fruits. It includes *R. idaeus*, the raspberry, and *R. fruticosus*, brambles and blackberries.

RUBY. With the emerald (q.v.) probably the most precious of gem stones, of red transparent corundum, crystallizing in the hexagonal system; it is without true cleavage. The true R. is found mainly in Burma, but Rs. have been produced artificially and are widely used in lasers (q.v.).

RUDA SLASKA. Town in Silesia, Poland, with metallurgical industries, created 1959 by a merger of Ruda and Nowy Butom. Pop. (1973) 147,000.

RUDD or **red-eye.** Freshwater fish, *Scardinius erythrophthalmus*, common in lakes and slow rivers of England and N Europe. Coppery-coloured with red fins and eyes, it reaches a length of 45cm (18in).

RUDOLF, Lake. Lake in the Great Rift Valley, 375m (1,230 ft) a.s.l., with its northernmost end in Ethiopia and the rest in Kenya. Area *c.* 9,000 sq.km (3,500 sq.m), it is saline and shrinking by evaporation. Its shores were a hunting ground of primitive man, and valuable remains have been found which are accurately datable because of the undisturbed stratification.

RUDOLPH. Name of 2 Holy Roman Emperors. **Rudolph I** (1218-91), originally count of Habsburg, was elected emperor in 1273. He was the first Habsburg emperor, and founded the greatness of his House by investing his sons with the duchies of Austria and Styria. **Rudolph II** (1552-1612) succeeded his father Maximilian II in 1576. His intolerant policy led to unrest in Hungary and Bohemia, which compelled R. to surrender Hungary to his brother Matthias in 1608, and to grant the Bohemians religious freedom.

RUDOLPH (1858-89). Crown Prince of Austria. The only son of the emperor Francis Joseph, he early showed progressive views which brought him into conflict with his father. In 1889 he and his mistress, Marie Vetsera, were found shot in his hunting lodge at Mayerling. The official verdict was suicide.

RUDOLF. Turkana fishermen on Lake Rudolf, their methods varying little from those practised by early man whose remains have been found along the lake boundaries. *Photo: J. Allan Cash*

RUE. A shrubby herb (*Ruta*), of the family Rutaceae, native to S Europe and temperate Asia. Common R., *R. graveolens*, formerly called herb of grace, was much used in medieval medicine.

RUEIL-MALMAISON (rü-ā' mahlmāzoṅ). NW suburb of Paris, France. The chateau of M., now a museum, was a favourite residence of Napoleon, and Empress Josephine retired here on her divorce.

RUFF. Bird (*Philomachus pugnax*) of the snipe family (Scolopacidae). The name is taken from the frill of erectile feathers developed in breeding-time round the neck of the male. The R. no longer breeds in Britain, but is found across N Europe and Asia, and migrates S in winter.

RUGBY. English market town in Warwickshire, near the Avon, 16km (10m) SE of Coventry. It is an important rail junction and has engineering works. R. School, founded in 1567 under the will of Lawrence Sheriff, attained fame during the headmastership, 1828-52, of Thomas Arnold (q.v.); R. football originated at the school. Pop. (1972) 59,680.

RÜ'GEN. Is. in the Baltic, off Stralsund, in Rostock bezirk, E Germany, linked by causeway to the mainland. The chief town is Bergen: it is a holiday centre.

RUHR (ro͞or). River of Germany, a right-bank tributary of the Rhine. It rises N of Winterberg and flows NW then W to Arnsberg and Neheim. Entering the R. coalfield about Hagen, it passes near Essen and through Mülheim to join the Rhine at Duisburg-Hamborn. The R. valley (228km/142m) was formerly a great iron and steel centre. The area was occupied by French and Belgian troops 1923-5 in an unsuccessful attempt to force Germany to pay reparations laid down in the Treaty of Versailles. During the S.W.W. the R. district was severely bombed from the air and was conquered by the Allies 1-18 April 1945, 325,000 German troops being taken prisoner. Allied control of the area came to an end with the setting up of the European Coal and Steel Community in 1952. Mining in the R. has declined, and iron and steel is now concentrated at Duisburg and Dortmund. New industries incl. petrochemicals, cars, etc.

RULE OF THE ROAD. In Britain, this states that vehicles should be kept to the left of the road or be liable for any ensuing damage. The reverse procedure applies nearly everywhere else in the world, all traffic keeping to the right. This latter is the rule at sea, and for 2 ships crossing, the one having the other on her starboard must give way.

RUM. Island of the Inner Hebrides, Highland region, Scotland, a nature reserve from 1957. Haskeval is 741m (2,659 ft) high. Area 109 sq.km (42 sq.m). Ardnamurchan Point is 24km (15m) to the S.

RUM. Spirit fermented and distilled from sugar cane. Scummings from the sugar-pans produce the best R., molasses the lowest grade.

RUMANIA. *see* ROMANIA.

RUMFORD, Benjamin Thompson, count R. (1753-1814). Scientist and administrator. B. in Mass, he served on the English side in the War of American Independence, and later was an official of the duke of Bavaria, for whom he effected civil and military reforms. He became a count of the Holy Roman Empire in 1791. Returning to England in 1798 he announced his theory that heat is a mode of motion and not a substance, and in 1799 helped found the Royal Institution. From 1804 he lived in France.

RUM JUNGLE. Uranium mining centre in the NW of Northern Territory, Australia.

RUNCIE (run'si), **Robert Alexander Kennedy** (1921-). In 1979 he became the first archbishop to be appointed on the suggestion of the church group, the Crown Appointments Commission (formed 1977), rather than by political consultation. A High Churchman, he is opposed to the ordination of women at the present time, but favours ecclesiastical remarriage for the divorced.

RUNCIMAN, Walter, 1st viscount (1870-1949). Liberal politician. The son of the 1st baron R., a prominent ship-owner, he entered parliament in 1899, and was President of the Board of Education 1908-11; of Agriculture 1911-14; and of Trade 1914-16. He returned to the Board of Trade in 1931-7, and was Lord President of the Council 1938-9. In 1938 he undertook a mission to Czechoslovakia to persuade the Czechs to make concessions to Germany.

RUNCORN. Town in Cheshire, England, 24km (15m) upstream from Liverpool and on the Manchester Ship Canal. As a 'new town' it coped with Merseyside overspill from 1964, the chief product is chemicals. Pop. (1975) 45,860.

RUNDSTEDT (roond'stet), **Karl Rudolf Gerd von** (1875-1953). German field marshal. He took part in the Polish campaign in 1939, and was largely responsible for the German break-through in France in 1940. Defeated on the Ukrainian front in 1941, he was appointed C-in-C in France in 1942. He stubbornly resisted the Allied invasion in 1944 and in Dec. launched a temporarily successful offensive in the Ardennes. He was captured, but in 1949 war-crime charges were dropped owing to his ill-health.

RUNES. The oldest Germanic script, chiefly adapted from the Lat. alphabet. Rs. were scratched in wood, metal, stone, or bones. The earliest runic inscriptions date from the 3rd cent. and were found in Denmark. Rs. were used in England in Anglo-Saxon times, and the Bewcastle and Ruthwell crosses are among the most notably runic monuments. Several 11th cent. Norse runestones are claimed to have been found in the USA.

RUNNYMEDE. A meadow on the S bank of the Thames near Egham, Surrey, England, where on 15 June 1215 King John put his seal to Magna Carta. Part of it was dedicated as memorial to J. F. Kennedy in 1964, in combination with a scholarship scheme for sending students to American univs. Overlooking R., on Cooper's Hill, is a memorial to 20,455 men and women of Commonwealth air forces who died during the S.W.W. and have no known grave.

RUNYON, Damon (1884-1946). American writer. B. in Manhattan, Kansas, he was a war correspondent in Mexico and Europe, and a sports and crime reporter in New York. His collection of short stories, *Guys and Dolls* (1932), was an immediate success, and was followed by others. Dealing with the seamier side of New York life, the stories are told with wry humour in the racy, specialized argot developed by R. for the purpose.

RUPERT, Prince (1619-82). English general and admiral. Son of the Elector Palatine and James I's dau. Elizabeth, he came to England in 1642, to fight for his uncle Charles I, and proved a dashing cavalry leader. Defeated by Cromwell at Marston Moor and Naseby, he commanded a royalist privateering fleet 1649-52 until driven from the seas by Blake. He returned to England in 1660, and distinguished himself as an admiral in the Dutch Wars.

RUPERT. Prince Rupert was not only a skilled cavalry leader, but an ingenious scientific experimenter, and one of the earliest mezzotinters. This portrait is from the studio of Lely. *Photo: Courtesy of the National Portrait Gallery*

RUPERT'S LAND. Name given in honour of Prince Rupert (q.v.), to a large area of N Canada granted to the Hudson's Bay Company in 1670, sold by the company to the Dominion of Canada in 1869, and subsequently divided between Quebec, Ontario, Manitoba, and the Northwest Territories, when the name disappeared.

RUPTURE. *See* HERNIA.

RUSE (roo'se). Bulgarian river port on the right bank of the Danube. It is familiar historically by its Anglicized Turkish name, Rustchuk. The Turks built a great fortress here. R. has an airport and is linked with Giurgiu, Romania, on the opposite bank of the Danube by a railway and road bridge opened in 1954. Pop. (1976) 163,000.

RUSH. Genus of plants (*Juncus*) in the family Juncaceae (q.v.), found in wet places in cold and temperate regions. The common R. has hollow stems which have been used for mat-making and basket work since ancient times.

RUSK, Dean (1909-). American Democratic statesman. During the S.W.W. he fought in the army in the Burma-China theatre and became Deputy Chief of Staff of US Forces. After the war he served in the Dept of State, and as Asst Sec. of State for Far Eastern Affairs was prominent in Korean War negotiations. He was Sec. of State 1961-9, and in 1971 became prof. of internat. law in the Univ. of Georgia, his native state.

RUSKIN, John (1819-1900). British writer. B. in London, only child of a prosperous wine-merchant, he was able to travel widely and was ed. at Oxford. The first vol. of his *Modern Painters* appeared in 1843. Many works followed, incl. *The Seven Lamps of Architecture* (1849) in which he stated his philosophy of art, and *The Stones of Venice* (1851-3). His writings hastened the appreciation of unorthodox painters such as Turner and the Pre-Raphaelites. In 1848 he m. Euphemia Chalmers Gray, but the marriage proved a failure; 6 years later Mrs R. secured a decree of nullity and later m. Millais. The 5th and final vol. of *Modern Painters* appeared in 1860, and the remaining years of R.'s life were devoted to social and economic problems, in which he adopted a radical outlook. To this period belong a huge series of lectures, pamphlets, *Unto this Last* (1862), *Sesame and Lilies* (1865), *The Crown of Wild Olive* (1866), etc. From 1869 to 1879 R. was Slade prof. of Art at Oxford, and he made a number of social experiments, such as 'St George's Guild', for the establishment of an industry on socialist lines. His last years were spent at Brantwood, Coniston.

Ruskin College was founded in Oxford in 1899 by an American, Walter Vrooman, to provide education in the social sciences for working men. It is supported by contributions from trade unions, etc.

RUSSELL, Bertrand Arthur William, 3rd earl (1872-1970). Brit. philosopher and mathematician. B. at Trelleck, the grandson of the 1st earl, he was ed. at Trinity College, Cambridge, where he specialized in mathematics and became a lecturer. R.'s pacifist attitude in the F.W.W. lost him the lectureship, and he served 6 months' imprisonment for an article he wrote in a pacifist journal. His *Introduction to Mathematical Philosophy* (1919), was written in prison. After visits to USSR and China, he went to USA in 1938 and taught at many univs. He later returned to England, and was a fellow of Trinity College, Cambridge. Among his most important works are *Principles of Mathematics* (1903); *Principia Mathematica* (1910: with A. Whitehead); *Problems of Philosophy* (1911); *Principles of Social Reconstruction* (1917); *Marriage and Morals* (1929); *An Enquiry into Meaning and Truth* (1940); *History of Western Philosophy* (1946), and *New Hopes for a Changing World* (1951). He succeeded his brother in the earldom in 1931, and was awarded the OM in 1949 and the Nobel literary prize for 1950. From 1949 he advocated nuclear disarmament, and until 1963 was on the Committee of 100, a militant branch of the Campaign for Nuclear Disarmament.

RUSSELL, Charles Taze. *See* JEHOVAH'S WITNESSES.

RUSSELL, George William (1867-1935). Irish poet and essayist. Editor of *The Irish Homestead* 1904-23, and *The Irish Statesman* 1923-30, he was an ardent nationalist and agricultural organizer. He helped found the Irish national theatre, and his poetry, pub. under the pseudonym 'AE', incl. *Gods of War* (1915) and reflects his interest in mysticism and theosophy.

RUSSELL, John, 1st earl (1792-1878). British Liberal statesman, known as Lord John Russell. The son of the 6th duke of Bedford, he entered the Commons in 1813, and supported Catholic Emancipation and the Reform Bill. He was Paymaster-General 1830-4, Home Sec. 1835-9, Colonial Sec. 1839-41, and PM 1846-52. He entered Aberdeen's cabinet as For. Sec. in 1852, and was Colonial Sec. in 1855. In Palmerston's 2nd govt of 1859-65 he was For. Sec. and gave valuable assistance to Italy's struggle for unity, although his policies on Poland, Denmark and the American Civil War provoked much criticism. He succeeded Palmerston as PM in 1865, but on the defeat of his Reform Bill in 1866 retired. He received an earldom in 1861.

RUSSELL, John (1795-1883). British 'sporting parson', who developed the short-legged, smooth-coated Parson Jack Russell terrier. They do not breed true and so are not recognized by the Kennel Club.

RUSSELL, John Peter (1858-1931). Australian artist. B. in Sydney, he met Tom Roberts (q.v.) in 1881 on the voyage to England, and became a member of the French post-impressionist group. His portrait of Van Gogh is in the Stedelijk Museum, Amsterdam.

RUSSELL, Lord William (1639-83). British Whig statesman. The son of the 1st duke of Bedford he was among the founders of the Whig Party, and actively supported the Exclusion Bill in parliament. He was accused of complicity in the Rye House Plot, on dubious evidence, in 1683, and executed.

RUSSELL, Sir William Howard (1821-1907). British journalist. B. in Ireland, he acted as *The Times* correspondent during the Crimean War, and created a sensation by his exposure of the mismanagement of the campaign. He was knighted in 1895.

RUSSELL OF KILLOWEN, Charles, 1st baron (1832-1900). British lawyer. In 1887 he appeared for Parnell before the commission investigating *The Times* allegations against the Irish leader, and in 1893 he represented Britain before the Behring Sea Commission. He became Lord Chief Justice in 1894.

RUSSELL OF LIVERPOOL, Edward Frederick Langley Russell, 2nd baron (1895-1981). Brit. barrister. As Deputy Judge Advocate-General BAOR 1946-7 and 1948-51, he was responsible for all war-crime trials in the British Zone of Germany 1946-50, and has pub. *The Scourge of the Swastika* (1954), *The Trial of Adolf Eichmann* (1962), etc.

RUSSIA. The popular name for the pre-revolutionary Russian Empire (before 1917), and the Soviet Union (q.v.) although it is more accurately restricted to the Russian

RUSSIA. A view over the roofs of the Kremlin in Moscow (top left); the statue of Peter the Great by Falconet in Dekabrist Square, Leningrad, which inspired Pushkin's poem 'The Bronze Horseman' (top right); 'Whitsuntide' by the greatest of Russia's painters of icons, Andrei Rublyov (left centre); Catherine the Great, her hair flowing down her back in contrast to the masculinity of her attire, by Erikson (centre); a portrait of the composer Modest Mussorgsky by Ilya Repin (1844-1930), the finest of the realist painters (right centre); a portrait of Leo Tolstoy by I. Kramskoy (bottom left); and Alexander Solzhenitsyn studying at Stanford University, USA, following his deportation from the Soviet Union. *Photos: Novosti (Moscow, Catherine the Great, Mussorgsky) and Popperfoto (Solzhenitsyn).*

Soviet Federal Socialist Republic, the largest and predominant republic within the USSR.

RUSSIAN. A member of the Slavonic branch of the Indo-European family of languages. It represents the eastern group of Slavonic, and incl. Great Russian, the general literary idiom; Little R. or Ukrainian; and White R., centring round Vilna, Minsk, Vitebsk, and Smolensk.

RUSSIAN ART. From the 10th cent., when Russia was organized as an independent state, until the time of Peter the Great, Russian architecture and painting followed the Byzantine style, and was dominated by the Greek Orthodox Church. Sculpture did not flourish because it was not allowed in churches. The Russians, however, displayed good taste in the art of icon-painting, for which they are famous, and the greatest master of this art was Andrea Rublyov (1370-1430). In the 17th cent. Peter the Great introduced western ideals into Russia, and foreign architects were employed to build his new cap. of St Petersburg. For 2 cents. the art of Russia reflected tendencies in Italy, France, Germany, and England. In the Soviet Union art has been enlisted in the service of the State. Extreme forms of modern art are not encouraged, though they were in the early days of the Soviet régime, when the Russians sought to free art from all traditional slavery, and replaced the Imperial Academy by a Free College of Art.

Early Russian modernism 1910-30 is increasingly recognised in the West as having anticipated later trends there by half a century. Artists incl. Kasimir Malevich, (1878-1935), founder of Suprematism, Ivan Klium (1873-1943) and Kandinsky (q.v.). There were also remarkable women painters: Alexandra Exter, Natalya Goncharova, Lyubov Popova, and Olga Rozanova. The work of those who remained in Russia was suppressed by Stalin, and remains unseen in the USSR, though exhibited abroad by the Soviet govt., as in Paris in 1979.

Unofficial recent artists incl. Oscar Rabin and Edward Zelenin, and Ivan Glazunov created a sensation with 'The Return of the Prodigal Son' (1978) in which a blue-jeaned youth sought forgiveness of a Christ figure for the blood and carnage of modern times.

RUSSIAN HISTORY. The southern steppes of R. were originally inhabited by nomadic peoples, and the northern forests by Slavonic tribes, who slowly spread southward. Viking chieftains in the 9th-10th cents. estab. their own rule in Novgorod, Kiev, and other cities, and in the 10th-12th Kiev temporarily united the Russian tribes into an empire. Christianity was introduced from Constantinople in 988. In the 13th cent. the Mongols (the Golden Horde) overran the southern steppes, compelling the Russian princes to pay tribute, while in the 14th Byelorussia and the Ukraine came under Polish rule. Ivan III, prince of Moscow (1462-1505), threw off the Mongol yoke, and united the NW, while Ivan IV (1547-84) assumed the title of tsar and conquered Kazan and Astrakhan. During his reign the colonization of Siberia began, and by 1700 it had reached the Pacific. A period of anarchy succeeded Ivan's death, until the first Romanov tsar was elected in 1613. Following a Cossack revolt, the E Ukraine was reunited with R. in 1667.

Peter I (1682-1725) modernized the administration and army, founded a navy, introduced western education, and wrested the Baltic seaboard from Sweden. Catherine II (1762-96) annexed the Crimea and part of Poland, and recovered the W Ukraine and White Russia. Russia intervened in the Revolutionary and Napoleonic Wars (1798-1801, 1805-7), and after repelling Napoleon's invasion took part in his overthrow (1812-14). During the 19th cent. revolutionary ideas steadily spread, in spite of harsh repression. A rapid development of industry followed the abolition of serfdom (1861); a working-class movement developed, and in 1898 the Social Democratic Party was founded. A revolution in 1905, although suppressed, compelled the tsar to accept a parliament with limited powers. Abroad, Russian attempts to dominate the Balkans led to wars with Turkey in 1827-9, 1853-6, and 1877-8, and provoked the hostility of Britain, France, and Austria. Russian expansion in central Asia also aroused British suspicions, while in the Far East the treaties of Aigun (1858) and Peking (1860) were imposed on China, annexing territories N of the Amur and E of the Ussuri rivers, and the occupation of Manchuria resulted in war with Japan in 1904-5. Russo-German rivalries in the Balkans nevertheless brought Russia into an alliance with France (1895) and Britain (1907), and were a main cause of the F.W.W. in 1914.

A revolution in March 1917 estab. a republic, but the provisional govt's failure to make peace rallied popular support to the Bolsheviks, led by Lenin, who in Nov. seized power. Peace was concluded with Germany at Brest-Litovsk in March, 1918. During 1918-21 British, French, US, and Japanese forces invaded Russia, while 'White' armies carried on civil war; Poland, Lithuania, Latvia, Estonia, and Finland became independent, Romania occupied Bessarabia, and Poland seized the W Ukraine and White Russia. A federal constitution was adopted in 1923. The 'war communism' policy was replaced in 1921 by the 'New Economic Policy' (NEP) of tolerating some private business. Inner party controversies followed Lenin's death, ending with the adoption of Stalin's policy of 'Socialism in one country' and the inauguration of the 1st 5-year plan. During 1928-39 heavy and light industries were developed, and agriculture collectivized.

From 1933 Russia put forward a policy of collective resistance to aggression. In 1939 she concluded a non-aggression pact with Germany, and after the German conquest of Poland reoccupied the W Ukraine and White Russia. There was a short Russo-Finnish War in 1939-40. During 1940 Bessarabia, Lithuania, Latvia and Estonia were taken into the Soviet Union. For events 1941-5, *see* SECOND WORLD WAR.

Russia, was startled by the Hungarian Revolution of 1956 into savage repression that antagonized the West and embittered relations with Yugoslavia, but on becoming PM, in 1958, Krushchev extended his de-Stalinization campaign, begun in 1956. His policy of 'peaceful co-existence in competition with capitalism' led to the Sino-Soviet ideological rift, which from 1960 worsened, with Russian opposition to China's Cultural Revolution and bloodshed on the frontier (notably on the Ussuri, q.v.) accompanied by demands for revision of the Aigun/Peking treaties. Relations with the West remained uneasy, e.g. the Cuban crisis of 1962, but the nuclear test-ban agreement of 1963 marked some amelioration. At home there were splendid achievements in space research (q.v.), and improvement in supplies of consumer goods. Krushchev's fall in 1964 marked a return to Cold War attitudes under Brezhnev and Kosygin (qq.v.). The naked military expediency of the invasion of Czechoslovakia in

1968 shocked both Communist and non-Communist opinion, and the rapid increase in Soviet naval power with acquisition of naval bases abroad on Western shipping routes, contradicted agreements on co-operation with the West achieved at the Helsinki Conference (1975). At the same time bad harvests and technically defective development led to increasing indebtedness to the West, and as the fount of Communist dogma, Russia was challenged by 'socially scientific' Communism (q.v.). Afghanistan was invaded in 1979, and the instability of Poland from 1980 led to greater centralised control, both at home and abroad. Brezhnev replaced Kosygin as PM by the elderly Tikhonov, and his own successor, Andropov (q.v.), did not live long enough to do more than ease the situation with China. He was in turn succeeded by Chernenko (q.v.), who died only 13 months after becoming leader. The new leader from Mar. 1985, Mikhail Gorbachev (q.v.), represents a younger generation of Soviet politicians.

RUSSIAN LITERATURE. The earliest productions of R.L. are the sermons and chronicles and the unique prose poem 'Tale of the Armament of Igor', belonging to the period in 11th and 12th cents. when the centre of literary culture was Kiev. By the close of the 14th cent. leadership had passed to Moscow, which was completely divorced from developments in the West until the 18th century: most noteworthy in this period are the political letters of Ivan the Terrible, the religious writings of the priest Avvakum (1620-81), who was the first to use vernacular Slavonic in literature, and the traditional oral folk-poems dealing with legendary and historical heroes which were collected in the 18th and 19th cents. Modern Russian literature begins with Mikhail Lomonosov (*c.* 1711-65), who fused elements of the elaborate Church Slavonic with colloquial Russian to create an effective written medium. Greatest of these earlier writers, working directly under French influence, were the fabulist Ivan Krylov (1768-1844) and the historian Nikolai Karamzin (1765-1826). Poetry reached its greatest height with Alexander Pushkin, and the tempestuously Byronic Mikhail Lermontov, while prose was dominated by Nikolai Gogol. Typical of the intellectual unrest of the mid-19th cent. is the prose writer Alexander Herzen, but to this generation also belong the great realist novelists Ivan Turgenev, Ivan Goncharov, Fyodor Dostoievsky, and Leo Tolstoy. Among their followers are the humorous Nikolai Leskov (1831-95), the morbid Vsevolod Garshin (1855-88), and Vladimir Korolenko (1853-1921), and in drama the isolated genius of Anton Chekhov. Rising from the pervading pessimism of the '80s came Maxim Gorky, and his followers Alexander Kuprin and Ivan Bunin; in contrast are the depressingly negative Leonid Andreyev and Mikhail Artsybashev. To the more mystic school of thought belong the novelist Dmitri Merezhkovsky and the poet philosopher Vladimir Soloviev, who moulded the thought of the greatest of the Symbolist poets, Alexander Blok.

Many writers left the country at the Revolution, but in the 1920s two groups emerged - the militantly Socialist LEF led by the Futurist Mayakovsky (q.v.) and the fellow-travellers of NEP incl. Pilnyak, Pasternak, Alexei Tolstoy, and Ehrenburg (qq.v.). Literary standards sank to a very low ebb during the first 5-year plan 1928-32, when facts were compulsorily falsified to present a rosy view of contemporary life in the effort to fortify Socialism, but the novelist Sholokhov and poets O. E. Mandelshtam, Anna Akhmatova (1888-1966) and Nikolai Tikhonov (1896-) were notable. More freedom was allowed by the subsequent Realism, e.g. Simonov (q.v.) and the work of the poet Tvardovsky (1910-71) during the S.W.W. Censorship closed down again from 1946 until the thaw after Stalin's death, during which Vladimir Dudintsev (q.v.) pub. his *Not by Bread Alone,* but was then soon renewed. Landmarks were the controversy over the award of a Nobel prize to Pasternak (q.v.), the public statements by the poet Yevtushenko, and the imprisonment in 1966 of the novelists Andrei Sinyavsky (1926-) and Yuli Daniel (1926-) for smuggling their works abroad for publication. Others fled the country, e.g. Anatoly Kuznetsov (1929-), whose novel *The Fire* (1969) obliquely criticized the regime, and Solzhenitsyn (q.v.), who found a different kind of disillusion in the West. To evade censorship there has also been a resort to allegory, e.g. Vasili Aksyonov's *The Steel Bird* (1979) grotesquely satirising dictatorship. Among those apart from all politics was the nonsense verse writer Kornei Chukovsky (q.v.) beloved of all Russians.

RUSSIAN SOVIET FEDERAL SOCIALIST REPUBLIC (RSFSR). A constituent republic of the USSR. It is by far the largest of the Soviet states, and reaches from the Gulf of Finland to the Pacific and from the Arctic to the Black and Caspian Seas. Its area accounts for about three-quarters of that of the USSR. Most of its surface is occupied by the great plain of E Europe and Siberia. In Europe the Black Earth district to the S and SE of Moscow is famed for its rich soil and is of great agricultural importance. Farther N extensive forests provide the main economic resource of the area, though there are extensive mineral deposts, espec. in the Urals. The Volga rises in the Valdai Hills between Leningrad and Moscow, and later flows through a steppe-like area which incl. many manufacturing centres. Farther S, in the Kuban and the foothills of the Caucasus, is a warm temperate region of great fertility. The Caucasus rises to over 4,875 m (16,000 ft); the Urals form the geographical boundary between Europe and Asia, seldom exceed 1,525 m (5,000 ft), and are the nucleus of a region of immense mineral wealth and industrial activity. The Siberian portion (q.v.) of the RSFSR has been much developed since the Revolution, especially during the S.W.W. and after, and, with its increasingly exploited mineral wealth, has become of exceptional industrial importance. Agriculture and stock raising thrive in the S half of the region; to the N of this are forests, although the area under cultivation is extending every year; the far N lies within the Arctic Circle. In the far east forestry, fishing and trapping are carried on; in the peninsula of Kamchatka fishing, and in the S some agriculture. The Altai, Abakan, Tannu, Baikal, Yablonoi, Kolyma, and Anadyr ranges are the loftiest in Asiatic RSFSR. The main rivers are, in Europe: the Don, Volga, Moskva (or Moscow), N Dvina, and Pechora; in Asia: the Ural, Kama, Ob, Tobol, Irtish, Yenisei, Angara, Lena (famous for its goldfields), and Amur. A number of the rivers, in both Europe and Asia, have been harnessed for irrigation and power. The Gulf of Finland is linked by seaway with the White Sea and by canal and the Volga and Don rivers with the Caspian and Black Seas.

The largest towns incl. Moscow, the cap. (cap. also of the USSR), Kaliningrad, Leningrad, Gorki, Rostov-on-Don, Volgograd, Sverdlovsk, Novosibirsk, Kazan,

Kuibyshev, Saratov, Voronezh, Yaroslavl, Ivanovo, Archangel, Omsk, Chelyabinsk, Tula, Perm, Astrakhan, Ufa, and Irkutsk.

POLITICAL STRUCTURE. The RSFSR proper is made up of 6 territories and 49 regions; within it also are the ASSRS and autonomous regions listed in the table, and 10 national areas.

Russian Soviet Federal Socialist Republic

	Area in sq. km.	*Pop. in 1,000s*	*Capital*
Autonomous Soviet Socialist Republics			
Bashkir	143,600	3,847	Ufa
*Buriat	351,300	896	Ulan Ude
Chechen-Ingush	19,300	1,169	Grozny
Chuvash	18,300	1,288	Cheboksary
Daghestan	50,300	1,600	Makhachkala
Kabardino-Balkar	12,500	674	Nalchik
Kalmuck	75,900	279	Elista
Karelian	172,400	742	Petrozavodsk
Komi	415,900	1,083	Syktyvkar
Mari	23,200	712	Yoshkar-Ola
Mordvinian	26,200	976	Saransk
N. Ossetian	8,000	604	Ordzhonikidze
Tatar	68,000	3,383	Kazan
*Tuva	170,500	259	Kyzyl
Udmurt	42,100	1,496	Izhevsk
*Yakut	3,103,000	842	Yakutsk
Autonomous Regions:			
Adyge	7,600	410	Maikop
Karachai-Cherkess	14,100	361	Cherkesk
Gorno-Altai	92,600	171	Gorno-Altaisk
*Jewish	36,000	198	Birobidjan
*Khakass	61,900	492	Abakan

**In Asia*

Govt is by the presidium of the elected Supreme Soviet; the pres. of the presidium is pres. also of the RSFSR; there is also a council of ministers and a political bureau of the central committee of the Communist Party.

AREA AND POPULATION. The RSFSR covers 17,076,000 sq.km (6,590,000 sq.m); pop. (1979) 137,552,000, the great majority Russians but incl. Tartars, Mordovians, Chuvashis, Bashkirs, Poles, Chechens, and others. In spite of strong official discouragement of religion a number of Russians still profess the Russian Orthodox faith, and there are many Moslems in N Caucasia and parts of Asia. The Jewish pop., considerable before the S.W.W., was much reduced during the German occupation of W European Russia.

EDUCATION. This is free and compulsory from 7 to 15 or 16, and in large towns up to 17. Of the many univs. those of Moscow, Leningrad, Odessa, Gorki, and Sverdlovsk are notable; there are also numerous institutes of higher technical and scientific instruction.

HISTORY. The All-Russian Congress of Soviets was set up by a coup d'état of the Bolsheviks on 7 Nov. 1917 (25 Oct. O.S. - hence the 'October Revolution'), and a govt consisting of a council of people's commissars was formed, led by Lenin. In elections held later in Nov. the Bolsheviks were defeated - only 215 Bolsheviks and supporters were returned out of 707 deputies; but the Bolsheviks knew their own minds and early in 1918 they dispersed the constituent assembly, made peace with Germany, and proceeded, in the face of famine, civil war, and foreign attack, to estab. a strong Communist govt. With the agreement for the formation of the USSR, reached in 1922, ratified 1924, the history of the RSFSR becomes part of that of the USSR. *See* SOVIET UNION.

RUSSO-JAPANESE WAR. This struggle was brought about by Russian penetration in Manchuria, culminating in the lease of Port Arthur in 1896, and the occupation of the Amur prov. in 1900. In 1904 diplomatic relations were broken off by the Japanese, who then without warning attacked the Russian fleet at Port Arthur. The outstanding events of the subsequent fighting were the siege and surrender of the Russian garrison in Port Arthur (May 1904-Jan. 1905) and the destruction of the Russian Baltic fleet in the Tsushima Straits (May 1905). Peace was concluded at Portsmouth, USA, in 1905. Russian rights in Port Arthur passed to Japan, together with the Manchurian railway; Korea became a Japanese sphere of influence, and Sakhalin was divided between Russia and Japan.

RUST. Common name for the minute parasitic plants of the order Uredineae, which appear on the leaves of their hosts as orange-red spots, later becoming darker, when they are known as mildew. The best-known is the wheat R. (*Puccinia graminis*).

RUST. Reddish deposit formed on iron by the action of water, oxygen, and 'impurities', i.e. carbon dioxide in the air, or carbon, sulphur, etc., in the metal. The impurity forms a conducting solution with the water; causing an electrolytic effect by which salts of iron are formed and then decomposed by the oxygen. Oil painting provides protection as do various chemical preparations.

RUTH. Character of the OT whose story is told in the Book of R. The daughter-in-law of Naomi, she m. Boaz, and became the ancestress of David.

RUTH, George Herman (1895-1948). American baseball player, known as 'Babe' R. B. at Baltimore, he joined the Boston Braves in 1914, becoming one of the best batters of all time, and in 1920 was sold to the NY Yankees. He returned to Boston in 1934 but left the team the same year. A baseball 'idol', he played in 10 world series and made 714 home runs (60 in one season in 1927).

RUTHĒ'NIA. Region in central Europe, home of the Ruthenes or Russniaks. Before the F.W.W. it was within Austria-Hungary. After the dual monarchy split up in 1918, part of R. was incl. in Czechoslovakia, part in Poland, part in Romania. All 3 were ceded to Russia after the S.W.W., Czech and Polish R. in 1945, Romanian R. in 1947, and were incorporated in the Ukrainian SSR.

RUTHĒ'NIUM. Metallic element discovered in 1843 in platinum ore. Its symbol is Ru, atomic no. 44, atomic weight 101.1.

RUTHERFORD, Ernest, 1st baron (1871-1937). N Zealand physicist. He was prof. at Montreal 1898-1907, at Manchester 1907-19, and at Cambridge 1919-37, where he was also director of the Cavendish Laboratory. He was awarded the Nobel prize in 1908 and knighted in 1914, and became a fellow of Trinity College, Cambridge, in 1919. In 1925 he received the OM, and became pres. of the Royal Society, of which he had been a fellow since 1903, and in 1931 was created Baron R. of Nelson, NZ. A pioneer of modern atomic science, his main researches were in the field of radioactivity, and he was the first to recognize the nuclear nature of the atom.

RUTHERFORD, Dame Margaret (1892-1972). Brit. actress. Specializing in formidable yet jovially eccentric females, she incl. among her best roles Mme Arcati (1941) in *Blithe Spirit,* Miss Prism (1939) and Lady Bracknell (1947) in *The Importance of Being Earnest.*

RUTHERFORDIUM. Chemical element, at. no. 104, named after Ernest Rutherford, but known in the USSR as kurchatovum (after scientist Igor Kurchatov).

RUTILE (ro͞ot'īl). Mineral, a native form of titanium dioxide, TiO_2. Formerly of little economic value, it is now greatly sought after for producing white pigments used to give brilliant whiteness to paint, paper, and plastics, and for making titanium (q.v.). The sands of Australia's E and W coasts are a major world source.

RUTLAND. Formerly the smallest co. of England, between Leics and Northants, R. was merged with Leics in the local govt reorganization of 1974. This met with strong local opposition and R. remained a separate admin. district. The admin. HQ was Oakham.

RUWENZŌ'RI (roo-). Mountain mass, the name meaning 'cloud king', nr the Equator between Zaïre and Uganda. It is 105km (65m) long and upwards of 48km (30m) wide: Margherita (5,110 m/16,763 ft) in the Stanley group is the highest peak. Stanley reached R. in his expedition of 1887-9. R. is believed to be the legendary 'Mtns of the Moon.'

RUYSDAEL (rois'dahl), **Jacob** (*c.* 1628-82). Dutch landscape painter. B. at Haarlem, he painted rural scenes near his native town and in Germany, and excelled with trees. The figures in his pictures were painted by other artists. His works are noted for their poetic feeling, and he is regarded as the greatest landscape painter of the Dutch school.

RUYTER (roi'ter), **Michael Adrianszoon de** (1607-76). Dutch admiral. B. at Flushing, he went to sea at the age of 11, and saw service against Spain in 1640-2, and the English in 1652-4. In the next war with England, he forced Rupert and Albemarle to retire into the Thames (1-4 June 1666), but on 25 July was heavily defeated off the N Foreland. He had his revenge in 1667, when he suddenly sailed up the Medway, burnt 3 men-of-war at Chatham, and captured others. He was again given the command when France and England declared war in 1672. He was mortally wounded in an action against the French fleet off Messina, and d. at Syracuse.

RWA'NDA. Country in central Africa, between Tanzania and Zaïre. It incl. part of beautiful Lake Kivu in the W, to the NE of which are volcanic mtns, the highest point Mt Karisimbi 4,507m (14,786ft). ft). Eastern R. forms part of the E African plateau, and is bounded by the Kagera r., whose headwaters SW of Kigali, the cap., are the source of the Nile. The Kagera Nat. Park in the NE has a wealth of untouched flora and fauna. Coffee, cotton, tea, and pyrethrum are grown, and cattle raised, and there are mineral reserves of tin, gold, and wolframite, with methane gas under Lake Kivu.

Part of German East Africa until 1918, and then of the Belgian mandate and trusteeship of Ruanda-Urundi (*see* URUNDI) from 1920, R. became independent in 1962. Area 26,338 sq.km (10,169 sq.m); pop. (1978) 4,460,000. Some 80% are the short-statured agrarian Bahutu, and most of the remainder are the very tall, pastoral Watutsi, the warlike aristocracy whose dominance was broken by a Bahutu revolt in 1960. There are a very few pygmies. Official languages are the Bantu tongue, Kinyarwanda and French. M.U.: R. franc.

Under the constitution of 1978 the republic has an executive president, with a National Development Council of 12 ministers, and a National Assembly. There is only one political party, and there have been a number of attempted coups.

RYAZAN (rē-ahzahn'). Town dating from the 13th cent., cap. of R. region, in the RSFSR, on the Oka. Agricultural machinery, leather, shoes, etc., are made. Pop. (1977) 442,000.

RYBINSK (rübensk'). City (formerly Schcherbakov) on the Volga, RSFSR. Pop. (1977) 237,000. The *R. Reservoir* was completed 1941 as part of the Mariinsk canal system. Fishing and shipbuilding are carried on. Area *c.* 5,200 sq.km (2,000 sq.m).

RYDE (rīd). English resort on the NE coast of the Isle of Wight. It lies on the Solent opposite Portsmouth, with which there is steamer and hovercraft connection. Pop. (1972) 23,000.

RYE. English town in Sussex, on the Rother, a member of the Cinque Port of Hastings. It was once a flourishing port, but silt brought down by the river has caused the sea to retreat 3km (2m) from the harbour. Henry James lived at R. for many years. Pop. (1972) 4,450.

RYE. A grain cereal (*Secale cereale*), grown extensively in N Europe. The flour is used to make black bread, but in Britain R. is grown only as a forage crop.

RYE HOUSE PLOT. An alleged plot formed by the Whigs in 1683 to murder Charles II, and his brother James, duke of York, while passing the Rye House, Herts. Although the plot possibly never existed, Lord Russell, Algernon Sidney, and many others were executed on charges of complicity.

RYLE, Gilbert (1900-76). British philosopher. Waynflete prof. of metaphysical philosophy at Oxford 1945-68, he is known for his influential *The Concept of Mind* (1949), which sets out to show that the distinction between the inner and the outer world that has haunted philosophy and psychology since Descartes cannot be sustained.

RYLE, Sir Martin (1918–84). British radioastronomer Prof. at Cambridge from 1959, he estab. British pre-eminence in this field, and was in 1974 awarded a Nobel prize jointly with Antony Hewish (q.v.). In 1972 he was appointed Astronomer Royal.

RYUKYU (rēyuk'yoo) **ISLANDS.** Chain of islands stretching between Taiwan and Japan, and numbering 73, of which 47 are inhabited; the main is. are Okinawa, Miyako and Ishigaki. They were under Chinese suzerainty until 1874 when Japan seized them: R. is the Chinese name still used by the USA, but the Japanese refer to them as the Okinawa Islands. After the S.W.W. they were occupied by the USA from 1945, the northernmost Oshima group (area *c.* 260 sq.km/100 sq.m) being returned to Japan in 1953. Okinawa (q.v.) is the largest. Following an agreement of 1969, the R. reverted to Japan 1972. Sugar, pineapples, and marine products, are exported. Area 2,200 sq.km (848 sq.m).; pop. (1980) 1,300,000.

S

19th letter in the English alphabet, and its principal sibilant. It represents an unvoiced fricative which has become voiced in English when intervocalic. Its normal sound is the s in *this.*

S.A. (Ger. *Sturm Abteilung*). The 'storm troops' of the Nazi Party. Formed in 1922, the S.A. became the basis of the Nazi armed strength, but many of its leaders were killed in the 'purge' of 1934, and it was largely superseded by the S.S. At the Nuremberg trials it was acquitted of the charge of being a criminal organization. *See* RÖHM, ERNST.

SAAR. River of France and Germany; length 240 km/ 149 mi.

SAARBRÜCKEN (sahrbrü'ken). Cap. of Saarland (since 1919), W Germany, on the Saar on a large coalfield, it is a centre of heavy industry, iron and steel, etc., and also electrical goods, etc. Pop. (1980) 193 700.

SAARINEN, Eero (1910-61). American architect. B. in Finland, he was the son of the architect and town planner Eliel S. (1873-1950), who founded the Finnish Romantic school of architecture, especially with his design of Helsinki Railway Station (1905-14), and contributed greatly to American skyscraper design, turning later to Functionalism. S. was taken to the US by his father in 1923 (becoming naturalized in 1940) and collaborated with him on a number of projects. His works incl. the US embassy, London and Dulles Airport, Washington.

SAARLAND. Land of W Germany, bordering Moselle dept of France on the SW, and crossed from NW to S by the r. Saar. The traditional steel industy has been modernised and its coal has new importance in the energy shortage, but there are many new manufacturing industries. About half its area is cultivated for wheat, rye, oats, potatoes, etc.; cattle, pigs, poultry are reared, and one-third is forested. The cap is Saarbrucken. Area 2,695 sq.km (1,040 sq.m); pop. (1978) 1,081,100.

After the F.W.W. the Saargebiet (Saar district) was placed under French administration for 15 years by the Treaty of Versailles; following a plebiscite it was returned to Germany in 1935. Hitler gave it the name S. At the end of the S.W.W. it was in the French zone of occupation and following elections in 1947 was in 1948 given autonomous status but linked economically with France. A referendum in 1955 went against the proposed 'Europeanization' of the area, and in 1957 it became a Land of W Germany.

SABAH (sab'a). State of the Fed. of Malaysia, occupying the NE corner of Borneo and forming (with Sarawak) E Malaysia. Admin by the Brit. N Borneo Co. from 1881 (which took over rights ceded to a British syndicate by the Sultan of Sulu in 1878), it became a Brit. protectorate in 1888, and with the is. of Labuan was the crown colony of N Borneo from 1946 until accession to Malaysia in 1963 under the name Sabah. The Philippines have advanced territorial claims on S. (1962 and 1968) on the ground that the original cession by the Sultan was illegal, Spain having then been sovereign in the area. Most of S. is mountainous and forested (highest peak Mt Kinabalu 4,098m/13,445ft, where copper was discovered 1968), supplying ¼of the world's hardwood. Other products incl. rubber, hemp, copra and cocoa, and there are unexploited mineral resources. The chief towns are the cap. Kota Kinabalu and Sandakan. Area 80,500 sq.km (29,400 sq.m); pop. (1970) 655,300.

SABATINI (-tē'nē), **Rafael** (1875-1950). British novelist. B. in Italy of Italian and British parents, he pub. many popular historical novels, such as *Scaramouche* (1921) and *Captain Blood* (1922).

SABBATH. The 7th day of the week, celebrated by the Jews as a sacred day of rest. It is reckoned from sunset Friday to sunset Saturday.

SABINES (sa'bīnz). People of ancient Italy, who dwelt in the mountains beyond the Tiber. They were subjugated by the Romans, and amalgamated with them in the 3rd cent. BC. The legendary 'Rape of the S. Women' is famous in Roman history.

SABLE. *See* MARTEN.

SACCHARIN (sa'karin); (ortho-sulpho benzimide, $C_6H_4SO_2NHCO$). An intensely sweet, white crystalline solid, obtained from toluene: it is 300 times as sweet as sugar. Widely used in soft drink manufacture, etc., and as a 'slimming aid' because it contains far fewer calories than sugar, it has produced cancer when used in massive quantities to feed laboratory rats. Following proposals to ban its use in the USA, no conclusive findings were reached as to its effect on humans.

SACCO-VANZETTI CASE (sahk'kō-vahnzet'tē). Murder trial in Massachusetts, USA, 1920-7, ending with the execution for murder of Nicola Sacco and Bartolomeo Vanzetti, Italian immigrants. The Mass. court declared in 1977 that the trial had been unjust, the accused being the victims of prejudice because of their anarchist views.

SACHS (sahks), **Hans** (1494-1576). German poet and dramatist. B. at Nuremberg, he became a master shoemaker, and a prominent Meistersinger, composing no fewer than 4,275 *Meisterlieder.*

SACHSEN. German form of SAXONY.

SACKBUT. Musical instrument, in essentials the modern trombone, common from the 14th cent.

SACKVILLE, Thomas, 1st earl of Dorset (1536-1608). English poet. He collaborated with Thomas Norton in *Gorboduc* (1561), the first English tragedy, and the first English play in blank verse; became Lord Treasurer in 1599, and earl of Dorset in 1604.

SACKVILLE-WEST, Victoria (1892-1962). British author. Dau. of the 3rd baron Sackville, she is remembered for her novels *The Edwardians* (1930) and *All Passion Spent,* and the pastoral poem *The Land* (1927). She m. in 1913 Sir Harold Nicolson (q.v.).

SACRAMENT. In Christian usage, a holy ordinance instituted by Christ as an outward and visible sign of an inward and spiritual grace. In the RC Church 7 sacraments are recognized, viz. baptism, Holy Communion (Eucharist or mass), confirmation, rite of reconciliation (confession and penance), holy orders, matrimony, and the anointing of the sick. Of these the first 2 only are held by the C of E to be generally necessary to salvation.

SACRAME'NTO. Cap. and port of California, USA, 130km (80m) NE of San Francisco, on the Sacramento r., which flows 615km (382m) through S. Valley to San Francisco Bay. The newly constructed Port of S. affords a deepwater channel to the Pacific, and S. has a metropolitan airport. Founded as Fort Sutter in 1839, S. became state cap. in 1854, and Old S. is now being carefully restored. Manufactures incl. processed foods from the surrounding area (almonds, peaches, pears, etc.), detergents, and jet aircraft. Pop. met. area (1975) 889,000.

SACRAMENTO. The State capitol, where the legislature meets, in California's capital city. Built 1860–9 in fine classical style, it stands in parkland. *Photo: Mireille Vautier*

SADA'T, Anwar (1918–81). Egyptian statesman. He succeeded Nasser as pres. in 1970, expelled Soviet military advisers, and by his handling of the Egyptian campaign in the October War of 1973 restored morale. Re-elected in 1976, he visited Israel in 1977, and could have been re-elected for life under the revised constitution of 1980, but was assassinated by Islamic fundamentalists. In 1978 he shared a Nobel peace prize with Begin (q.v.).

SADDUCEES (sad'usēz). A Jewish sect of NT times opposed to the Pharisees. They denied the immortality of the soul and maintained the religious Law in all its strictness.

SADE (sahd), **Marquis de** (1740-1814). French writer. B. in Paris, he became a soldier. Condemned to death for an unnatural offence, he twice escaped from prison, and was committed to an asylum, where he wrote obscene plays and novels. 'Sadism', a form of sexual perversion that delights in the infliction of cruelty, is named after him.

S'ADI or **Saadi.** Assumed name of the Persian poet Sheikh Moslih Addin (*c.* 1184-1291). B. at Shiraz, he travelled widely before settling there finally *c.* 1256. *Bustan* (Tree-garden) and *Gulistan* (Flower-garden) are the most celebrated of his works.

SADLER'S WELLS. Mineral springs in Finsbury, N London, England, known in medieval times, but re-discovered by a man called Sadler in 1683 and exploited in connection with a music-hall. Lilian Baylis developed a later theatre on the site as a northern annexe to the 'Old Vic'. The S.W. Opera Co. (re-named English Nat. Opera Co. 1974) moved to the Coliseum in 1969, but S.W. continued to stage visiting opera and ballet cos. *See* ROYAL BALLET.

SADOVA (sah'dōvah). Village in Czechoslovakia, 13km (8m) NW of Hradec Kralove (Ger. Königgrätz), better known in its German form Sadowa (sah'dōvah) for the battle fought nearby on 3 July 1866, in which the Prussians defeated the Austrians.

SAFETY LAMP. A portable L. designed for use in places where inflammable gases may be encountered, e.g. coal mines. The electric cap L. used as a miner's working light has the bulb and contacts in specially protected enclosures while the flame S.L., now used primarily for gas detection, has the wick enclosed within a strong glass cylinder surmounted by wire gauzes. Sir Humphry Davy in 1815 and George Stephenson each invented flame S.L.s.

SAFFRON. Plant (*Crocus sativus*) native to Asia Minor. Similar to a purple crocus, S. flowers in late autumn. It yields an extract used for orange colouring and flavouring.

SAFI (sahfē'). Port on the Atlantic coast of Morocco, with a sardine industry, boatbuilding yards, and fertilizer plants: phosphates are exported. Pop. (1974) 130,000.

SAGA. Prose narrative written down in the 11th-13th cents. in Norway and Iceland. They vary from family chronicles, e.g. the *Landnamabok* of Ari (1067-1148), the *Heimskringla* of Snorri Sturlason (1178-1241), and the *Sturlunga* of Sturla Thordsson (1214-84), to the legendary and anonymous *Njala*, *Laxdaela*, and *Grettla*.

SAGAMIHARA. Town on Honshu, Japan. There is a large silkworm industry. Pop. (1977) 391,000.

SA'GAN, Carl (1934-). American physicist and astronomer. He became known as a populariser, with such books as *The Cosmic Connection* and *Broca's Brain;* and the television series *Cosmos* (1980). He was responsible for the plaque depicting a man and a woman affixed to space probes *Pioneer* 10 and 11 in case they encountered intelligent life.

SAGAN (sahgań'), **Françoise** (1935-). French novelist, author of femininely psychological studies of love relationships incl. *Bonjour Tristesse* (1954), *Aimez-vous Brahms?* (1959) and *Scars on the Soul* (1974). She has also ventured into ballet (*Le Rendezvous manqué*) and the drama (*Château en Suède*).

SAGE. Perennial herb (*Salvia officinalis*). The grey-green aromatic leaves are used as a seasoning: up to 120cm (4ft) high, it has blue flowers.

SA'GO. The starchy material obtained from the pith of the S. palm, which forms a nutritious food, and is used for manufacturing glucose.

SAGUENAY (sag'enā). River in Quebec, Canada, which flows SE from Lake St John to the St Lawrence. It is an important source of hydroelectric power: length 765km (475m).

SAHARA (sahah'rah). The largest desert in the world, 5.5 million sq.km (3.5 million sq.m) of N Africa from the Atlantic to the Nile, covering southern Morocco, Algeria, Tunisia and Libya; western Egypt, much of Mauritania, Mali, Niger, and Chad; and part of W Sudan. Small tracts in NE Algeria and Tunisia are below sea level, but the major part is plateau with a central mtn system which incl. the Ahaggar Mtns in SW Algeria, the Aïr Massif in Niger, and the Tibesti Massif in N Chad, of which the highest peak is Emi Koussi 3,415 m (11,204 ft). Oases round natural springs punctuate the ancient caravan routes N and S, which are being adapted to modern roads. Discovery from the 1950s of mineral wealth, espec. oil and natural gas in the northern S. has transformed the economic aspect of the desert and the prospects of its nomadic peoples. In prehistoric times the S. was fertile, supporting rich animal and human life, and remarkable rock paintings were discovered from 1956 by Henri Lhote, espec. in the area of the NE Ahaggar known as the Tassili: they date from *c.* 5450–2500 BC. In Tunisia espec. reafforestation is being attempted.

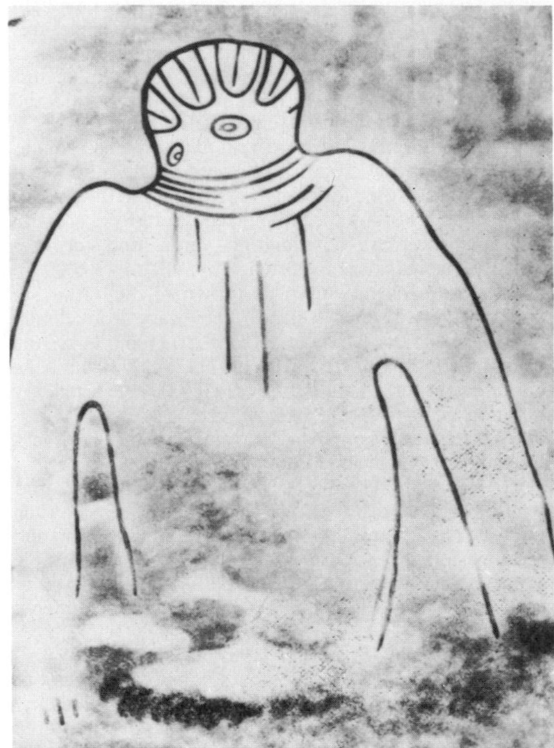

SAHARA. One of the brilliantly coloured rock paintings discovered in the Tassili by Henri Lhote. Some 6 m (18 ft) high, he named it 'The Great Martian God', since it looks as if it represents a creature from another world. *Photo: Courtesy of Henri Lhote*

SAHARA, Western. Country on the Atlantic coast of N Africa, a Spanish possession 1884–1976. Following Spanish evacuation, two-thirds (all the district of Saguia el Hamra and the district of Rio de Oro to the N of Dakhla, incl. the rich Bu Craa phosphate mines) was occupied by Morocco, and one-third by Mauritainia (the southern part of the district of Rio de Oro), which also received a share in exploitation of the mineral deposits. However, the Popular Front for the Liberation of Saguia el Hamra and Rio de Oro (Polisario) proclaimed a Saharan Arab Democratic Republic, and guerrilla activity continued, based at Tindouf in Algeria with Algerian support. In 1979 Mauritania withdrew, southern Rio de Oro being taken over by Morocco, but guerrilla activity persisted. The cap. is La'Youn (also El Aaiún), and the chief port is Dakhla (formerly Villa Cisneros). Area 266,000 sq.km (102,680 sq.m); pop. (1980) 100,000, the majority evacuated to Algeria.

SA'HEL. Marginal area to the S of the Sahara desert, stretching from Senegal to Somalia. A population explosion, with poor agricultural practice, destruction of the scrub, and also climatic change, has led to southward extension of the desert.

SAIDA. *See* SIDON.

SAIGON (sīgon'). Former name of Ho Chi-minh City (q.v.). The *Battle of S.* 29 Jan.- 23 Feb. 1968 involved the expulsion of 5,000 infiltrating Viet Cong by S Vietnamese and US forces. In 1975, following the evacuation by S Vietnamese forces of the central highlands, S. finally fell to N Vietnamese forces 30 April 1975.

SAINT. A man or woman eminent for piety, usually one who has been canonized by the Catholic Church. The lives of many thousands of Ss. have been collected by the Bollandists, and the number is added to by the process of canonization (q.v.). A new Calendar of Ss.' days was approved by Paul VI from 1970: among those excluded as probably never existing were Ss. Barbara, Catherine, Christopher and Ursula; Ss. George, Januarius, Nicholas (Santa Claus) and Vitus were among those listed only for optional veneration; and among new Ss. for obligatory veneration were St Thomas More and the Uganda martyrs.

ST ALBANS. City of Herts, England, 32km (20m) NW of London, which grew up round an abbey founded by King Offa II in 793 in honour of St Alban (q.v.). Nearby are remains of Roman Verulamium on Watling St. The battle of St A. in 1455 opened the Wars of the Roses. Pop. (1974) 52,600.

ST ANDREWS. Town in Fife, Scotland, on the coast 19km (12m) SE of Dundee. It is the HQ of golf, and of the Royal and Ancient Club (1754), and the univ. (1411) is the oldest in Scotland. Pop. (1973) 10,000.

ST AUGUSTINE. City in Florida, USA, 60km (37m) SSE of Jacksonville. A port and a holiday resort, it is the oldest town in the USA, having been founded in 1565 by Pedro Menendez de Aviles near the site of Juan Ponce de Leon's landing place (1513). Drake burned it in 1586, Capt. John Davis burned it in 1665. It was ceded to the USA, in 1821. St A. incl. the oldest house (probably late 16th cent.) and the oldest masonry fort (1672) in the USA. Pop. (1970) 12,350.

ST AU'STELL. English market town in Cornwall, 22km (14m) NE of Truro, the centre of the China clay area which supplies the Staffordshire potteries. *See* FOWEY. Pop. (1972) 30,000.

ST BARTHOLOMEW, Massacre of. *See* BARTHOLOMEW.

ST BERNARD. Name of 2 passes in the Alps. (1) Great St B. Pass (2,472 m/8,110 ft) is in the Pennine Alps between Piedmont, Italy, and Valais, Switzerland. Near the crest is the famous hospice founded in the 10th cent. for pilgrims. A road usable by pack-horses crossed it by AD 69; Napoleon I marched across the pass into Italy in 1800. A road tunnel under the Great St B. was opened 1964. (2) Little St B. Pass (2,188 m/7,179 ft) crosses the Graian Alps, between Piedmont and Savoie, France. Hannibal is said to have invaded Italy by this route.

ST BERNARD DOG. Large mastiff named after the monks of St Bernard, who kept them for finding lost travellers and to act as guides. They are squarely built, with pendulous ears and lips and large feet.

ST CHRISTOPHER. Another name for St Kitts. *See under* LEEWARD ISLANDS.

ST CLOUD (san kloo'). Western suburb of Paris on the Seine. The 17th cent. palace was the favourite residence of Napoleon, and he here m. Marie Louise: it was destroyed during the Siege of Paris in 1870. Within the beautiful park is the nat. Sèvres porcelain factory.

ST CYR (san sēr). The military coll., founded by Napoleon in 1808 at the village of St Cyr, nr Versailles, was destroyed by bombing from the air during the S.W.W.; it was transferred to Coëtquidan in Morbihan dept in 1946.

ST DAVID'S. Cathedral city in Dyfed, S Wales. The cathedral, founded by St David, the patron saint of Wales, was rebuilt between 1180 and 1522. It is the largest church in Wales. Pop. (1972) 1,700.

ST DENIS. Town in Seine-St Denis dept, France, 6.5km (4m) N of Paris. The abbey church, founded in 626, is Gothic and contains the tombs of many of the kings of France. Abelard was a monk in the abbey of St D. Pop. (1975) 97,000.

ST DUNSTAN'S. Welfare organization, founded in 1915 by newspaper proprietor Sir Arthur Pearson (1866-1921), for British servicemen blinded through the F.W.W. or subsequent military operations. Blindness had caused his own retirement in 1910.

SAINTE-BEUVE (san-böv'), **Charles Augustin** (1804-69). French critic. B. at Boulogne-sur-Mer, he contributed to the *Revue des deux mondes* from 1831. In 1840 he was appointed a keeper of the Mazarin library, and was elected to the French Academy in 1844. His chief work was *L'Histoire de Port Royal* (1840-8) his *Causeries du lundi* are masterpieces of criticism.

ST ELIAS MOUNTAINS. Range on the Yukon/British Columbia/Alaska border, which incl. the peak of St Elias 5,489 m (18,008 ft), Mt Logan (q.v.), and Mt Fairweather 4,663 m (15,300 ft). There is also the largest icefield outside the polar regions, incl. the Malaspina Glacier 3,885 sq.km (1,500 sq.m).

ST ÉTIENNE (sant ātyen'). Cap. of Loire dept, France. It has an important silk and rayon industry; coal and iron-ore are mined, and there are heavy industries. Pop. (1975) 218,300.

SAINT-EXUPÉRY (sant-āksüperē'), **Antoine de** (1900-44). French airman and author. He served in the S.W.W. with the French Air Force, and disappeared on a mission over France from Corsica. His works incl. the autobiographical *Vol de Nuit* and *Lettre à un Otage*; and *Le Petit Prince*.

ST GALL. Cap. of St G. canton, Switzerland. It grew up about a Benedictine abbey built round a cell inhabited by an Irish hermit, Gall, 614-640, and was famous as a centre of learning in the 8th-10th cents. The library of its ancient abbey is renowned for early MSS. Pop. (1971) 81,200.

ST GEORGE'S. Cap. and port of Grenada, on the SW coast. Pop. (1975) 8,600.

ST GEORGE'S CHANNEL. Between SW Wales and SE Ireland, it links the Irish Sea with the Atlantic. It is 160km (100m) long, and 80-150km (50-90m) wide.

ST GERMAIN-EN-LAYE (san-zherman'-on-lā). Town 21km (13m) W of Paris, France. Pop. (1975) 38,500. The Treaty of St G. (1919) condemned the war between Austria and the Allies. Representatives of the USA (an associated power) signed it, but after the Senate failed to ratify the Treaty of Versailles, the Treaty of St G. was not submitted to it. The USA made a separate peace with Austria in 1921.

ST GOTTHARD PASS. A famous road and rail route from N Europe to Italy, connecting the lakes Lucerne and Maggiore. The hospice on the pass (2,112 m/6,929 ft) dates from 1331. The rail tunnel (1872-82) rises to 1,154 m (3,786 ft); a road tunnel 16.3 km (10.1 m) at an average height of 1,146 m (3,760 ft) was completed 1970-80.

ST HELĒ'NA. Island in the S Atlantic, 1,900 km (1,200 m) W of Africa. It became a British possession in 1673. Napoleon d. in exile here in 1821; his body was taken to France in 1840. The cap. is Jamestown. Area 122 sq.km (47 sq.m); (1977) 5,216. Ascension and Tristan da Cunha are dependencies.

ST HELENS. Town in Merseyside, England, 19km (12m) NE of Liverpool, and connected to the Mersey by canal. It is the chief English centre for the manufacture of sheet glass. Pop. (1972) 104,450.

ST HELIER (hel'yer). Seaside resort and cap. of Jersey, Channel Islands. The Jersey legislature sits in the *salle des états* here. Pop. (est.) 28,000.

ST IVES. (1) English fishing port and holiday resort with an artists' colony (*see* BARBARA HEPWORTH), in Cornwall, on St I. Bay. It took its name from an Irish princess called Ia (5th cent.). Pop. (1973) 9,710. (2) English market town in Cambridgeshire on the Ouse, 8km (5m) E of Huntingdon. Cromwell lived at St I. 1631-6; it took its name from a 6th cent. missionary. Pop. (1971) 16,000.

ST JAMES'S PALACE. Situated in Pall Mall, London, this was a royal residence from 1698 to 1837, and royal levées are still held there. Foreign ambassadors are accredited to the Court of St James's.

SAINT JOHN. Largest city of New Brunswick, Canada, on the St J. r. It is an important fishing centre and port for an agricultural and lumbering area. Founded by the French as Saint-Jean in 1635, it was taken by the British in 1758. Pop. (1976) 85,960.

ST JOHN OF JERUSALEM, Knights Hospitallers of. The oldest order of Christian chivalry, named after the hospital founded at Jerusalem *c.* 1048 by some merchants of Amalfi for the benefit of pilgrims. A military side developed with the need to protect pilgrim routes from the Saracens. In 1291 the knights were forced to leave Palestine, and went first to Cyprus, in 1309 to Rhodes, and then were granted Malta by the Emperor Charles V in 1530. Napoleon expelled them from the island on his way to Egypt in 1798, but the order survives in Rome, HQ Palazzo di Malta. It has *c.* 8,000 knights and women are admitted. The Grand Master is the highest ranking RC layman in the world. A Protestant English offshoot, chartered 1888, works mainly through the St John Ambulance Assocn and Brigade, carrying out hospital work and first aid.

ST JOHN'S. Cap. city and chief port of Newfoundland, on the E coast, in the peninsula of Avalon. Its main industries depend on the cod fisheries. Sir Humphrey Gilbert founded St J. in 1582. Pop. (1976) 143,400.

ST JOHN'S WOOD. Residential suburb of NW London. Lord's cricket ground, HQ of the MCC is here.

SAINT-JUST (san-zhüst), **Louis Antoine Léon Florelle de** (1767-94). French revolutionary. A close associate of Robespierre, he became a member of the Committee of Public Safety in 1793, and was guillotined with Robespierre.

ST KILDA. A group of small islands 80km (50m) W of Harris, westernmost of the Outer Hebrides, incl. in 1975 in Western Isles, Scotland. The last 35 inhabitants were moved to the mainland in 1930, but in 1957 a missile tracking station was established here in connection with the S Uist rocket range; the same year, under the will of the 5th Marquess of Bute (1907-56), St K. was acquired by the National Trust for Scotland, under whose auspices summer-working parties visit the is. The islands are noted for seabirds.

ST KITTS. *See under* LEEWARD ISLANDS.

ST LAURENT (lōroṅ'), **Louis Stephen** (1882-1973). Canadian Liberal politician. Called to the Quebec Bar in 1905, he became Min. of Justice in 1941, took over the additional post of For. Min. in 1946, and was PM from 1948 to his defeat in 1957, when he was succeeded in the party leadership in 1958 by Lester Pearson.

ST LAWRENCE. River of N America which, with the Great Lakes at its head, forms one of the world's great river highways. Leaving Lake Ontario, it marks the USA-Canadian frontier for nearly 160km (100m); the rest of its course to the Gulf of St L. lies in Canada. Montreal is built on a large island near the confluence of the Ottawa r. The St L. is ice-bound for 5 months of the year. Length *c.* 1,046 km (650m). The St L. Seaway, 217km (135m) long, constructed 1954-9, made it possible for seagoing ships to reach the ports on the Great Lakes; it also added immensely to the hydro-electric capacity of the r.

ST LEGER (le'jer). One of the 5 classic British horse races. It was instituted by Colonel St Leger in 1776, and is run at Doncaster in Sept. The distance is 2.9km/1¾m 127yds.

ST LEONARDS. *See* HASTINGS.

ST LÔ (saṅ loh). Cap. of Manche dept, France, on the Vire. An important agricultural and road centre, it was destroyed 10-18 July 1944, when US forces captured it from the Germans in the S.W.W. The name comes from a bishop of Coutances who built a church on the site. Pop. (1975) 25,000.

ST LOUIS (loo'-is). Chief city and river port of Missouri, USA, on the Mississippi *c.* 16km (10m) below its confluence with the Missouri. Founded as a trading post by the French in 1764, it passed to the USA in 1803 by the Louisiana Purchase, and has many important industries. The Gateway Arch (1965) is a memorial by Saarinen to the pioneers of the W. Industries incl. cars, steel, aerospace equipment, electrical goods, shoes, brewing and food processing. Pop. met. area (1970) 2,331,371.

ST LUCIA (loo'sha). One of the Windward Islands, West Indies. Discovered by Columbus 1502, settled by the French 1635, it became British 1803 and independent within the Commonwealth in 1979. With Grenada and Dominica, it is one of the 'progressive' independent govts. of the E Caribbean. It produces bananas and other fruits, and coconuts. Castries is the cap. Area 603 sq.km (233 sq.m), pop. (1979) 113,000.

ST MALO (saṅ mahlō'). Seaport in the Ille-et-Vilaine dept, W France, on the Rance estuary. The town is noted as a tourist resort. It took its name from a Welshman, who was bishop there in the 6th cent. Pop. (1973) 43,725.

ST MICHAEL AND ST GEORGE. A British order of knighthood founded in 1818, and usually awarded for services rendered in the British Commonwealth countries overseas. The 3 grades are: Knight Grand Cross (GCMG), Knight Commander (KCMG), and Companion (CMG).

ST MICHAEL'S MOUNT. Is. in Mount's Bay, Cornwall, connected at low tide by a causeway to the mainland. A castle stands on the summit. It was presented by Lord St Levan to the National Trust in 1954. Also, **Mont St-Michel** (q.v.), off the NW coast of France.

ST MICHAEL'S MOUNT. It was from the dangerous quicksands off Mont St-Michel that Earl Harold rescued two Norman soldiers while the future William the Conqueror watched. *Photo: Barnaby's Picture Library*

ST MORITZ. Village and winter-sports centre in Grisons canton, Switzerland, on the St M. lake. The Cresta Run dates from 1885. Pop. (est.) 3,750.

ST NAZAIRE (saṅ nahzār'). Seaport in Loire-Atlantique dept, France, at the mouth of the Loire on the Bay of Biscay. Used as a submarine base by the Germans during the S.W.W., it was the scene of a British Commando raid, 28 March 1942, in which 212 out of 353 taking part were lost (killed or missing). Pop. (1975) 65,300.

ST OMER (saṅt-ōmār'). A town in Pas-de-Calais dept, France, on the Aa, 42km (26m) SE of Calais. From 1914-16 the British GHQ was located at St O. Pop. (1973) 19,600.

ST PAUL. Cap. city of Minnesota, USA, on the Mississippi adjoining Minneapolis. A road, rail and air centre, its industries incl. electronics, publishing and printing, petrochemicals, cosmetics, and meat-packing. Pop. (1970) 309,830.

ST PAUL'S CATHEDRAL. The cathedral church of the City of London, and the largest Protestant church in England. A Saxon church on the site was replaced by a Norman by 1240, which was destroyed by the Great Fire in 1666. The present building was designed by Wren and built 1675-1710. Interior features are the whispering gallery, and the tombs of Wellington and Nelson in the crypt.

ST PETER PORT. The chief town and port of Guernsey, Channel Is. Victor Hugo lived here 1855-70. Pop. (1970) 16,000.

ST PETERSBURG. *See* LENINGRAD.

ST PETERSBURG. Coast town of Florida, USA. Nicknamed Sunshine City, it is a flourishing resort, and mushroomed industrially with the development of space industry in the 1950s. Pop. (1970) 216,250.

SAINT-PIERRE (sań-pyār'), **Jacques Henri Bernardin de** (1737-1814). French writer. He is best known for his romantic *Paul et Virginie* (1789).

ST PIERRE. Group of small barren is. off SW Newfoundland. Cod-fishing and cod-salting, drying, and canning are the main occupations. Area 26 sq.km (10 sq.m); pop. (1978) 6,260. With Miquelon (q.v.) it forms an overseas dept of France.

ST QUENTIN (sań końtań'). Town in Aisne dept, N France, on the Somme 34km (21m) S of Cambrai. The Prussians defeated the French in 1871 at St Q. which suffered badly during the F.W.W. Pop. (1975) 69,000.

SAINT-SAËNS (sań-sahńs'), **Camille** (1835-1921). French composer. B. in Paris, he studied at the Conservatoire and under Gounod, and in 1857 became organist at the Madeleine. He achieved success as a pianist, and estab. his reputation as a composer with the 4 symphonic poems *Le Rouet d'Omphale, La Danse Macabre, Phaéton,* and *La Jeunesse d'Hercule.* Among his other works are 3 symphonies, 5 piano concertos, and the opera *Samson et Dalila.*

SAINT-SIMON (sań-sēmoń'), **Claude Henri,** comte de (1760-1825). French Socialist. B. in Paris, he fought in the American War of Independence, and was imprisoned during the French Revolution. He wrote prolifically, e.g. *Du système industriel* (1821) and *Nouveau christianisme* (1825), advocating a state of society ruled by technicians and industrialists.

ST SIMON, Louis de Rouvroy, duc de (1675-1755). French writer. B. in Paris, he served with the Household Corps, and in his *Mémoires* (1691-1723) gives an acute portrayal of the French court.

ST TROPEZ (trōpez'). Fishing port in Var dept., on the Côte d'Azur, France. It was made a fashionable resort by Brigitte Bardot in the 1960s, and topless sunbathing began on Pamplona Beach in 1972.

ST VINCENT. *See* JERVIS, JOHN.

ST VINCENT. One of the Windward Is., West Indies. It became a British possession in 1783 and independent as St Vincent and the Grenadines in 1980. Best-known of the Grenadines (q.v.) associated with St Vincent is Mustique, an exclusive holiday resort where Princess Margaret has a villa. The cap. is Kingstown. Bananas, arrowroot, copra, and spices are produced. Area 388 sq.km (150 sq,m); pop. (1978) 114,000.

ST VINCENT, Gulf. Inlet of the Southern Ocean, S Australia. Adelaide stands half-way along its E shore.

ST VITUS' DANCE. Chorea; a disease of the nervous system associated with rheumatic fever. The chief symptoms are involuntary movements of the face and limbs, sometimes so violent as to interfere with sleep and feeding. The saint was allegedly a martyr in Rome under Diocletian, and the patron saint of dancers.

SAINT-SIMON. Ahead of his time, the Comte de Saint-Simon advocated a 'meritocracy', the equality of women, and a plan to link the Atlantic and Pacific by canal. *Photo: The Mansell Collection*

SAKAI (sakī). Industrial city in S Honshu, Japan, with aluminium, engineering, chemical and fertilizer industries. Pop. (1977) 764,000.

SAKE (sak'ā). Japanese rice-wine; yellowish-tinted, with 15 per cent alcohol content, it is drunk hot.

SAKI. Pseudonym of British author Hugh Hector Munro (1870-1916). B. in Burma, where he served an unhappy year with the Military Police, he became a journalist, was foreign correspondent to the *Morning Post* 1902-8, and was killed in action on the Western Front. He produced a number of ingeniously witty short stories set in the Edwardian fashionable world and the brilliant novel *The Unbearable Bassington* (1912), with its playboy hero Comus Bassington.

SAKHALI'N. Island in the N Pacific, 965km (600m) long from N-S. Two parallel mountain ranges, rising to over 1,525 m (5,000 ft), extend throughout its length. The N is much colder than the S, where dairy farming is carried on and leguminous crops, oats, barley, sugar beet, etc. are grown, with rice and wheat in the central valley. Fishing is very important. S. also produces timber, petroleum in the NE, coal in the W centre. Area 76,400 sq.km (29,500 sq.m); pop. (1973) 650,000, incl. aboriginal Ainus and Gilyaks.

A Russian explorer Poyarkov visited S. in 1644 and subsequently it was colonized by Russians and Japanese. South S. was in 1875 ceded by Japan to Russia, which used the is. as a political convict settlement. Japan regained S.S. in 1905, but again ceded it to Russia in 1945. In 1947 the isl. together with the Kuriles (q.v.) was formed into the S.

region of the RSFSR, cap. Yuzhno-Sakhalinsk (Jap. Toyohara).

SAKHAROV (sahkh'arof), **Andrei** (1921-). Soviet physicist. Known as 'the father of the Russian H-bomb', he nevertheless protested against Soviet nuclear tests and was a founder of the Soviet Human Rights Committee. He was awarded a Nobel peace prize in 1975. In 1980 he was exiled to Gorky for his criticism of Soviet action in Afghanistan. He returned to Moscow in 1986.

SAKKA'RA. A village of Egypt, 16km (10m) S of Cairo, with 20 pyramids of which the oldest (3rd dynasty) is the 'Step Pyramid' designed by Imhotep (q.v.), whose own tomb here was the nucleus of the Aesklepieion, a centre of healing in the ancient world.

SA'LADIN or **Sala-ud-din** (1138-93). Sultan of Egypt. He entered the service of the atabeg of Mosul, on whose behalf he conquered Egypt in 1164-74, and after his death was proclaimed sultan in 1175. He conquered Syria in 1174-87, and in 1187 recovered Jerusalem from the Christians. The 3rd Crusade followed, led by Richard I of England, but it failed to capture Jerusalem, and in 1192 S. and Richard made peace.

SALA'DO. Two rivers of Argentina. The *S. del Norte* and *S. del Sud* both rise in the Andes and have a length of some 2,000 km (1,200 m) during the rainy season. The former joins the Parana at Sante Fé, and the latter the Rio Colorado.

SALA'M, Abdus (1926-). Pakistani physicist. He became prof. at Imperial College, London, in 1957, and director of the International Centre for Theoretical Physics at Trieste in 1964. In 1979 he was the first of his countrymen to receive a Nobel prize. *See* FORCES.

SALAMA'NCA. Cap. of S. prov., W Spain, on the Tormes, 260km (160m) NW of Madrid. It has a univ. (founded *c.* 1230) and a 12th cent. cruciform cathedral. Pop. (1970) 125,220. Wellington's most important victory against the French in the Peninsular campaign was won here on 22 July 1812.

SALAMANDER. Genus of old-world amphibians. Best-known is the spotted or fire S. (*Salamandra maculosa*), black with bright yellow markings: the old legend that Ss. are unharmed by fire, or even extinquish it, is unfounded. Among the related species of America is the axolotl (q.v.).

SA'LAMIS. Greek is. in the Gulf of Aegina. It was the scene in 480 BC of a naval battle in which the Persians were defeated by the Greeks. The town of S., on the W coast, is a modern naval station. Area of is. 101 sq.km (39 sq.m); pop. (1971) 17,800. Also, an ancient city on the E coast of Cyprus, rebuilt by Constantius II in the 4th cent AD and known as Constantia.

SAL AMMŌ'NIAC. Another name for ammonium chloride (NH_4Cl). It occurs in mineral form as a white sublimation round the crater of a volcano and may be prepared synthetically. Its chief use is in 'dry-cell' batteries.

SALAZAR (-thahr'), **Antonio de Oliveira** (1889-1970). Portuguese dictator. He was PM 1932-68, exercising a virtual dictatorship. A corporative constitution on the Italian model was introduced in 1933, and until 1945 S.'s National Union, which he founded in 1930, remained the only legal party. S. was also For. Min. 1936-47, and during the S.W.W. maintained Portuguese neutrality. He was incapacitated 1968 by a cerebral stroke.

SALE (sāl). A residential suburb of Manchester, and also a town in Victoria, Australia, linked by canal via the Gippsland Lake to Bass Strait. It is a market and processing centre for dairy produce, livestock and grain from the surrounding area. Pop. (1971) 10,500.

SALAMIS. Once the chief city of ancient Cyprus, with a good harbour, it had a Christian community founded by Paul and Barnabas. Above is the early Byzantine gymnasium. *Photo: J. Allan Cash*

SĀ'LEM. City in Tamil Nadu, Rep. of India. Iron and manganese are mined, and there is a textile industry. Pop. (1971) 308,000.

SĀ'LEM. City of Mass., USA, 24km (15m) NE of Boston. It is an important manufacturing centre. Dating from 1626, In 1692 it was the scene of famous witchcraft trials. Roger Williams (q.v.) was pastor here 1631 until expelled 1636. Hawthorne was b. at S. Pop. (1970) 40,555.

Another SALEM, in Oregon, USA, was settled *c.* 1840, made state cap. 1860. It is a lumbering and fruitpacking centre, and has flourmills. Pop. (1970) 68,855.

SALE'RNO. Seaport of Campania, Italy, 48km (30m) SE of Naples. Founded by the Romans *c.* 194 BC, S. was destroyed by Charlemagne, and sacked by the Emperor Henry VI in 1194. Both its school of medicine and its univ. (1150-1817, revived 1944) were famous in medieval times. On 9 Sept. 1943, the Allies made an important landing in the Gulf of S. To the SE are the ruins of Paestum (q.v.). Pop. (1978) 162,000.

SALFORD. City in Greater Manchester, England, on the r. Irwell. It forms part of the port of Manchester and the ship canal's largest docks are in S. Textiles and chemicals are manufactured and coal is mined. Salford Univ. (1966) was founded 1896 as the Royal Tech. Inst. Pop. (1972) 128,740.

SĀ'LIAN. One of the northern divisions of the Franks (q.v.): the later, wrongly-called, *Salic Law* excluded succession by or through females. This provision was abrogated in Sweden in 1980 to enable Princess Victoria to become Crown Princess.

SALICY'LIC ACID (Orthohydroxybenzoic acid, HO.C_6H_4.COOH). White solid, crystallizing into prismatic needles at 159°C. It is used as an antiseptic, in food preparation, dyestuffs and in the preparation of aspirin.

SALIERI, Antonio (1750–1825). Italian composer. He was the teacher of Beethoven, Schubert and Liszt, and, as a composer, the rival of Mozart. It has been suggested, without foundation that Mozart's mysterious death was due to Salieri's having poisoned him.

SALINGER (sāl'injer), **J(erome) D(avid)** (1919-). American writer. B. in New York he contributed to the *New Yorker* and estab. his reputation with the novel *The Catcher in the Rye* (1951), which was followed by a vol. of short stories, and *Franny & Zooey* which deals in 2 stories with members of the Jewish Glass family already introduced in earlier work. His key characters are often children and his adults psychologically complex.

SALISBURY, Robert Arthur Talbot Gascoyne-Cecil, 3rd marquess of (1830-1903). British Cons. statesman. B. at Hatfield, he entered the Commons in 1853, and succeeded to the title in 1868. He was Indian Sec. 1866-7 and 1874-8; and as For. Sec. 1878-80 took part in the Congress of Berlin. As PM 1885-6, 1886-92, and 1895-1902 he gave his main attention to foreign policy and for most of the time was For. Sec. His grandson, **Robert Arthur James Gascoyne-Cecil,** 5th marquess (1893-1972) sat in the Commons 1929-41, when he was created Baron Cecil. He was Dominions Sec. 1940-2 and 1943-5, Colonial Sec. 1942, and Lord Privy Seal 1942-3 and 1951-2, and Lord Pres. of the Council 1952-7.

SALISBURY, Robert Cecil, 1st earl of. *See* CECIL, ROBERT.

SALISBURY. Cathedral town in Wilts, England, 135km (84m) SW of London. The cathedral of St Mary, built 1220-66, is one of the finest specimens of Early English architecture; its decorated spire 123m (404ft) is the highest in England. S. grew up round the cathedral and has many old and interesting buildings. It makes beer, hardware, carpets, etc., and is an agricultural centre. Another name for it is New Sarum, Sarum being a medieval Latin corruption of the ancient Romano-British name Sorbiodonum. Old Sarum, on a 90m (300ft) hill to the N, was deserted when New Sarum was founded in 1220, but was later again inhabited; it was brought within the town boundary in 1953. Pop. (1972) 35,890.

SALISBURY. *See* HARARE.

SALISBURY PLAIN. A 775 sq.km (300 sq.m) area of open downs in Wiltshire, England, between Salisbury and Devizes. For many years it has been a military training area. It rises to 235m (770ft) in Westbury Down, and incl. Stonehenge (q.v.)

SALIVA. Slightly acid moistening secretion of the 3 pairs of salivary glands in the mouth, aiding the swallowing and digestion of food.

SALK, Jonas Edward (1914-). American physician. B. and ed. in New York, he in 1963 became director of the S. Institute for Biological Studies, California. A specialist in poliomyelitis (q.v.), he developed the S. vaccine in 1954.

SA'LLUST, or **Gaius Sallustius Crispus** (86-34 BC). Roman historian. He had an active political career as a supporter of Caesar, and his histories of Catiline's conspiracy and the Jugurthine War are written in a condensed and epigrammatic style.

SALISBURY. A sketch in oils by John Constable of the cathedral as seen from the river meadows. It is interesting to compare this treatment with the less lively effect in the more familiar finished picture. *Photo: Courtesy of the National Gallery, London*

SALMON. Fish family Salmonidae, espec. the Atlantic S. (*Salmo salar*) The normal colour is silvery, blue-grey above with a few dark spots, but the colour changes at the spawning season. S. spawn up rivers in fresh water where the eggs hatch, but most of their life is spent in the sea. The spawning season is between Sept. and Jan., although they occasionally spawn at other times. The orange eggs are *c.* 6mm (.25in) in diameter, are laid on the river bed, fertilized by the male, and then covered with gravel by the female. The incubation period is from 5 weeks to 5 months. On hatching from the egg the young fish are known as *alevins,* and when they begin feeding they are called *parr.* At about 2 years old the coat becomes silvery, and the young parr are then *smolts.* When the young fish return to the river to spawn between 3 and 3½ years of age they are *grilse.*

SALO'NIKA. Form often used in English for THESSALONIKA.

SA'LOP. *See* SHROPSHIRE.

SALSIFY. Hardy biennial *Tragopogon porrifolius* often called 'vegetable oyster' and eaten as a vegetable.

SALT. Sodium chloride (NaCl), found in sea water, as rock salt, in brine deposits, etc. In chemistry, salts are compounds comprised of an acid and a base united in definite proportions, e.g. hydrochloric acid and caustic soda unite to form the salt sodium chloride, and water.

SALT LAKE CITY. Cap. of Utah, USA, and HQ of the Mormons (q.v.), on the Jordan, 18km (11m) SE of the Great Salt Lake. In 1847 Brigham Young laid out the city as a Mormon settlement, and the great granite temple was built 1853-93. To the W is a vast open pit copper mine and the city has smelters and refineries, meat-packing and printing plants, and salt and oil refineries. Pop. (1970) 175,885.

SALT'ON SEA. Brine lake SE of Los Angeles, California, USA: area 650 sq.km (250 sq.m). It was accidentally created in the early 20th cent. when the Colorado r. overwhelmed an irrigation scheme. It is being used, by the creation of solar ponds, to supply electrical energy.

SALT LAKE CITY. The Mormon temple was dedicated in 1893 and took forty years to build. *Photo: Mireille Vautier*

SALUKI (saloo'ki). Breed of dog, also called the gazelle hound, descended from the hound of the Bedouins of the African deserts. As bred today it resembles the greyhound, is *c.* 65cm (26in) high, and coloured fawn, cream, or white.

SALVADO'R. Port and naval base in Brazil on the inner side of a peninsula separating Todos Santos Bay from the Atlantic. There are flour, sugar and tobacco industries. Founded in 1510, it was the cap. of Brazil 1549-1763, and has a univ. (1946). Pop. (1970) 1,007,200.

SALVADO'R, EL. The smallest and most thickly populated Central American republic, bounded by Guatemala on the W, Honduras on the N, and the Pacific on the S. Inland from a narrow coast plain is a high, fertile plateau, with active volcanoes. El S. lies within the Tropics, but alt. moderates temps. over a large part of the country. Coffee, cotton, sugar and sisal are grown, and there are sugar refineries and textile factories. About one-third of El S. is forested. Chief towns are the cap. San Salvador and Santa Ana; on the coast are the ports of La Union, La Libertad and Acajutla. The constitution of 1962 provided for the election by universal suffrage of a pres. for 5 years with a single chamber legislative assembly elected for 2 years. El S., part of the Central American Federation from 1821, became independent in 1839. General Carlos Romero, of the conservative Party of National Conciliation, was elected President in 1972. He held power, amid allegations of human rights violations, until 1979, when a coup replaced him with a military-civilian junta. Democracy and free elections were proposed, but were postponed as the violence continued. In 1980 Abp. Romero, a champion of human rights, was murdered, and the country was on the verge of civil war. Jose Duarte became president with a left-of-centre coalition. As an anti-communist, he received backing from the US. Elections in 1982 were boycotted by left-wing parties and won by the extreme right-wing National Republican Alliance. Duarte won an election in 1984, won a convincing majority in the National Assembly in 1985, and in 1986 continued to seek a settlement with the rebels. Area 21,393 sq.km (8,260 sq.m); pop. (1976) 4,000,000. M.U.: colón.

SALVAGE. Saving for re-use, either as a whole or in part, of any property threatened with destruction, especially important at sea and against fire. Also the compensation payable to those who by voluntary effort have saved a ship and/or its cargo and passengers from complete loss through shipwreck, fire, or enemy action.

SALVARSAN. An organic compound; the first specific anti-bacterial agent, discovered by Paul Ehrlich in 1909; chemical formula $C_{12}H_{12}N_2O_2As_2.2Hco.2H_2O$ 3, 3'-diamino 4, 4'-dihydroxy-arseno-benzene dihydrochloride. Because of its destructive effect on *Spirochaeta pallida*, it was widely used in the treatment of syphilis, prior to the development of antibiotics (q.v.). Another name for it is 606, referring to the number of experiments performed by Ehrlich in its discovery.

SALVATION ARMY. Christian evangelical, social service, and social reform organization, originally British but later worldwide. It began with revivalist services in a tent in Whitechapel, London, in 1865 conducted by William Booth who, with his wife and other helpers, formed the Christian Revival Association, renamed the East London Christian Mission, extended to cover all London in 1870. Booth used the expression 'salvation army' in a leaflet pub. in 1878, and it was soon accepted as the name of the body, which adopted military titles for its officials, and called its weekly journal the *War Cry*. The organization is now world-wide.

SAL VOLATILE (volat'ilē). A mixture of ammonium carbonate, bicarbonate and carbamate; smelling salts. It is a strong reflex stimulant and is of value in restoring consciousness after a fainting attack or narcotic poisoning.

SA'LWEEN. River rising in E Tibet, China, and flowing through Burma to the Andaman Sea, nr Moulmein. Length 2,800 km (1,750 m), but subject to great rise and fall in level and rapids.

SALZBURG (sahlts'boorg). City in Austria, cap. of S. prov. on the Salzach, seat of an archbishopric founded *c.* 700. There is a 17th cent. Cathedral. Mozart's birthplace is a museum, and since 1920 an annual music festival has been held. Pop. (1971) 128,845.

SAMA'RA. Name until 1935 of KUIBYSHEV.

SAMĀ'RIA. Hilly region of ancient Israel. The town of S., 10km (6m) N of Nablus, was cap. of the kingdom of Israel 10th-8th cents. BC, and was re-named Sebaste by Herod the Great: extensive remains have been excavated. In modern Israeli usage, the term refers to the northern West Bank.

SAMA'RITANS. The descendants of the colonists settled by the Assyrians in Samaria, after the destruction of the Israelite kingdom in 722 BC. They adopted Judaism, but rejected all sacred books except the Pentateuch, and regarded their temple on Mt Gerizim, not that at Jerusalem, as God's true sanctuary; hence much ill-feeling existed between Ss. and Jews. A very small community still exists at Nablus.

SAMARITANS, The. Voluntary organization to help those tempted to suicide or despair, founded in 1953 at St Stephen's Church, Walbrook, London, by the Rector, Chad Varah (1911-), and subsequently extended throughout Britain and overseas. The S. consist of groups of trained lay people, each directed by a professional (usually a clergyman) in consultation with psychiatrists, psychotherapists and doctors. They offer friendship and counselling to 'clients' who may use their emergency telephone numbers by day or night.

SAMĀ'RIUM. A rare earth element, symbol Sm, at. no. 62, at. wt. 150.35. It is hard, grey, brittle metal, found in cerite, samarskite, and gadolinite, and is slightly radioactive.

SAMARKA'ND. City of the Uzbek SSR, USSR, cap of S. region, nr the r. Zerafshan, 217km (135m) E of Bukhara. From 1369 it was the cap. of the empire of Tamerlaine (Timur) whose mausoleum and summer palace still exist, and it was then ruled by the Chinese and emirs of Bukhara before the Russians occupied it in 1868. It remained a centre of Moslem culture until the Revolution. Cotton-ginning and silk manufacture, and engineering are carried on. Pop. (1977) 312,000.

SAMA'RRA. Ancient town in Iraq, on the Tigris, 105km (65m) NNW of Baghdad. Founded in 836 by the Abbasid Caliph Motassim, it was the Abbasid cap. until 876, and is a place of pilgrimage for Shiah Moslems. Pop. (1971) 15,000.

SA'MIZDAT. Russian 'self-published', meaning the typed material circulated underground in the Soviet Union to circumvent the censorship, e.g. reviews of Solzhenitsyn's banned novel *August, 1914* (1972).

SAMŌ'A. Group of volcanic islands in the SW Pacific, to the NNE of Fiji. They are in 2 groups. (1) the rep. of Western Samoa which incl. Savaii and Upolu. The cap. is Apia, on Upolu. Copra, bananas, and cocoa are exported. The people are Christians. The islands were German before the F.W.W., after it under New Zealand League of Nations mandate, then UN trusteeship. Independent from 1962, S. became a full member of the Commonwealth in 1970. Area 2,842 sq.km (1,097 sq.m); pop. (1976) 151,275. M.U.: tala.

(2) US Samoa to the E, incl. Tutuila, Tau, and (320km (200m) NNW of Samoa) Swain's Island. It was acquired by the USA in 1899 by agreement with Britain and Germany. Fagatogo on Tutuila is the cap. Area 197 sq.km (76 sq.m); (1977) 28,700.

SA'MOS. Greek island in the Aegean Sea, *c.* 1.5km (1m) off the W coast of Asiatic Turkey. Mountainous but fertile, S. produces wine, olive oil, etc. Limén Vathéos is the cap., and Teganion is on the site of the ancient city of S. destroyed by Darius. Area 466 sq.km (180 sq.m); pop. (1971) 41,710.

SA'MOYED. Arctic breed of dog, similar to a chow, but with more pointed face and a white coat.

SAMPHIRE (sam'fīr). Perennial plant (*Crithmum maritimum*) found on sea cliffs of Europe. The aromatic leaves are fleshy and sharply pointed; the flowers grow in yellow-green umbels. It is used in salads, etc.

SAMSON. A hero of the ancient Hebrews, one of the 'judges' who ruled Israel in Palestine before the establishment of the monarchy. His story is told in the OT book of Judges.

SA'MŪEL. The last of the 'judges' who ruled the Israelites before the establishment of the Hewbrew kingdom in Palestine, and the first of the line of prophets. His story is told in the first book of the OT that bears his name; this, and 2 Sam., cover the reigns of Saul and David.

SAMUEL, Herbert Louis, 1st visct (1870–1963). British Liberal statesman. Son of a Liverpool banker, he became High Commissioner of Palestine 1920–5 and was the first Jew to govern the Holy Land for *c.* 2,000 years. He suggested the formation of the National Govt set up in 1931, but resigned as a Free Trader in 1932, leading the Liberal Opposition until 1935.

SAMUELSON, Paul (1915–). American economist. He became prof. at the Massachusetts Inst. of Technology in 1940, and was awarded a Nobel prize 1970 for his application of scientific analysis to theory. His books incl. *Economics* (1948) and *Linear Programming and Economic Analysis* (1958).

SA'MURAI. Feudal military caste in power in Japan from the 12th cent. until the fall of the Tokugawa shogunate, in which they had assisted. They obeyed the bushido code of bravery, honour, and service. *See* MISHIMA, YUKIO.

SAMURAI. A figure of a Samurai warrior at the Toshugu Shrine dedicated to Tokugawa Ieyasu, the founder of the Tokugawa Shogunate. *Photo: Douglas Dickins*

SAN'A (sahnah'). Cap. of N Yemen, SW Arabia, 320km 200m N of Aden. A walled city, with fine mosques, it is a jewel of old-style Arab architecture, threatened with destruction by modernization. Pop. (1973) 125,000.

SAN ANDREAS FAULT. Vertical break in the Earth's surface 32km (20m) deep and 965km (600m) long: Los Angeles rests on the W half (moving NW) and San Francisco on the E half (moving SE): in 50 million yrs the two will meet. Meanwhile built-up pressure causes earthquakes.

SAN ANTŌNIŌ. Town of S Texas, USA, a commercial and financial centre. Industries incl. aircraft maintenance, oil refining, and meat packing, and the US Air Force has a base and School of Aerospace Medicine here. The city grew up around the Alamo (q.v.). Pop. met. area (1970) 863,669.

SAN BERNARDINO. City in California, USA, 80km (50m) E of Los Angeles. There are citrus and other food industries, and engineering. Pop. met. area (1975) 1,225,000.

SAN CRISTO'BAL. Town in Venezuela, nr the Colombian border, on the Pan-American Highway. Pop. (1971) 152,240.

SANCTIONS. In international law, measures used to enforce the fulfilment of treaty obligations. The Covenant of the League of Nations provided for the use of the economic boycott against aggressors, but attempts to apply it against Italy during the Abyssinian War of 1935–6 proved

SAN'A. At least half the population live within the old city walls. The houses, built of massive stone blocks for the first two floors may have another six built in brick, as above. Ornate fretted windows, tracery and balustrades are delicately picked out in whitewash. *Photo: Ian Yeomans/Daily Telegraph*

ineffective. The UN Charter similarly provides for the application of economic and military S. *See* ZIMBABWE.

SAND (sońd), **George.** Pseudonym of French authoress Armandine Lucile Aurore Dupin (1804-76), adopted from the name of Jules Sandeau, one of her early companions in Paris. She m. in 1822 Casimir Dudevant, but separated from him after 9 years and henceforth lived in Paris as a writer. Among her early liaisons were those with Alfred de Musset and Chopin. From 1848 she lived at the château of Nohant. Her novels reflect her own marital and intellectual experiences, and incl. *Valentine* (1832), *Consuelo* (1842), *Le Péché de M. Antoine* (1847), and *La Mare au diable* (1846). She also pub. *Histoire de ma vie, Elle et lui* (which describes her love affair with de Musset) and 'Letters'.

SAND. The accumulation of fine-grained fragmentary mineral matter chiefly composed of quartz grains (impure silica SiO_2). It is derived from the rocks of the land surfaces, and is especially characteristic of shallow water and land deposits, to which it is carried by running water, wind or ice. The origin of the grains may be detected by their shape, e.g. sand deposit by running water has a subangular nature, while wind-blown Ss. are well-rounded. Ss. are classified into marine, freshwater glacial, and terrestrial.

SANDBURG, Carl August (1878-1967). American poet. B. in Illinois, he served an apprenticeship to realism as farm labourer, bricklayer, etc., and the open, factual construction of his poetry bears its lasting impress from *Chicago Poems* (1916) onward to *Complete Poems* (1950). He wrote an interesting autobiography *Always the Young Stranger* (1953).

SANDHURST. Small English town in Berks, 7km (4.5m) SSE of Wokingham. In the vicinity are the Royal Military Academy (for which S. is often used as a synonym) and Wellington Coll., a public school.

SAN DIEGO (dē-ā'gō). City in California, USA, an important military and naval base, nr the Mexican border, with a fine natural harbour where long distance tuna trawlers are based. There are fish canneries, aircraft missile plants, and a notable zoo. Pop. (1970) 675,788.

SAND PAINTING. A picture made by preparing an adhesive ground on which coloured sands are laid. In Japan, from at least the 18th cent., natural and artificially coloured sands have been used to depict all types of scene, and the technique has also been used by European artists. Very striking are the S.Ps. used as temporary altars during certain phases of Navajo Indian ceremonial.

SANDPIPER. Group of birds in the snipe family Scolopacidae. The common S. (*Tringa hypoleucus*) is a small graceful bird with long slender bill and short tail, drab above and white below. In summer it breeds in Britain and most of the rest of Europe nr water, and winters far south.

SANDRINGHAM. English village in Norfolk, NE of King's Lynn. S. House, a private residence of the British sovereign, was built by the Prince of Wales (afterwards Edward VII) 1869-71 on the estate which he had bought in 1863. George V and George VI both died at S, and Elizabeth II completely modernised the house and estate.

SANDSTONE. Rocks formed of the consolidation of former sands. The principal component is quartz, and Ss. are classified according to the materials that cement together the grains of quartz, etc., e.g. ferruginous, siliceous, calcareous, barytic, gypseous, and pyritic.

SANDU'SKY. City and resort in Ohio, USA, on S. Bay, Lake Erie. It is an important grain-shipping port and makes chemicals, paper, agricultural machinery, etc. Pop. (1970) 32,675.

SANDWICH, John Montagu, 4th earl of (1718-92). British politician. He was 1st Lord of the Admiralty 1771-82, and the Sandwich Is. were named after him, as are sandwiches, which he invented in order to eat without leaving the gaming-table.

SANDWICH. English market town in Kent, one of the Cinque ports, on the r. Stour. An important port for cents. before the Norman Conquest, it lost its usefulness through the silting up of the harbour in the 16th cent. It has a number of medieval buildings. Pop. (1972) 4,500.

SANDWICH ISLANDS. Another name for HAWAII.

SANDYS, Duncan. *See* DUNCAN-SANDYS, LORD.

SAN FRANCISCO. Principal port on the Pacific coast of the USA, in California, on S.F. Bay. The city stands on a peninsula S of the Golden Gate, a strait 1.5km (1m) wide, 8km (5m) long, giving access to the Bay and crossed by the second longest single-span bridge (1,280 m/4,200 ft) in the world, completed 1937. In the bay is Alcatraz (q.v.) island. Industries incl. meat-packing, fruit canning, printing and publishing, and the manufacture of metal goods. There is a large international airport. S.F. dates from 1776; it was a trading post when captured by the

USA in 1846 during the war with Mexico. An earthquake in 1906 almost completely destroyed the city and killed 452 people. The UN Charter was drawn up at S.F. internat. conference in 1945, and the peace treaty between the Western Allies and Japan, in force from 1952, was signed there in 1951. The city is also noted for its large homosexual community, and strange religious sects (*see* JONESTOWN). *See also* SAN ANDREAS. Pop. met. area S.F.-Oakland (1970) 3,068,403.

SAN FRANCISCO. A replica of Sir Francis Drake's flagship, sailing under the Golden Gate Bridge in San Francisco after a 5-month voyage from Plymouth via the Panama Canal, to become a floating museum. In 1578 Drake took the *Pelican*, now renamed the *Golden Hind*, through the Straits of Magellan, landing north of San Francisco in his voyage round the world. *Photo: The Associated Press*

SANGER, Frederick (1918-). British biochemist. The first to win a Nobel chemistry prize twice, he received the award in 1958 for his elucidation of the structure of insulin, and in 1980 shared it with 2 American scientists for his work on the chemical structure of genes and the decoding of DNA.

SANHEDRIN (san'ēdrin). The supreme Jewish court at Jerusalem during the 2nd cent. BC-1st cent. AD. It consisted of members of the priestly aristocracy, and was presided over by the high priest.

SAN JOSÉ (san hōzā). A city of California, USA, 80km (50m) SE of San Francisco; it has a major flower industry and important fruit canneries, and after the S.W.W. grew industrially, notably as a centre for aerospace research and development. Pop. met. area (1970) 1,057,023.

SAN JOSÉ. Cap. of Costa Rica; the main trade is in coffee, cacao, and sugar cane. The univ. of Costa Rica (1843) is near by. Pop. (1978) 240,000.

SAN JUAN (san hwan'). Cap. of S.J. prov., Argentina, on the S.J. r., 156km (97m) N of Mendoza. It is a centre of the wine industry, gold and copper are mined in the vicinity. S.J. was virtually destroyed by an earthquake in 1944. Pop. (1970) 106,700.

SAN JUAN. Cap. of the Commonwealth of Puerto Rico, on an is. off the N coast. The fortresses of El Morro and San Cristóbal, the governor's palace Fortaleza, and the cathedral are of interest. Pop. met. area (1970) 851,250.

SANKEY, Ira David. *See* HYMN.

SANKT GALLEN. German form of ST. GALL.

SAN LUIS POTOSI (san lwēs potosē'). City in Mexico, centre of a silver-mining area. Founded 1586, it was the colonial admin. HQ and has fine buildings of the period. Pop. (1977) 303,570.

SAN MARINO (mahrē'nō). Independent republic bounded by Italian territory, lying some 19km (12m) SW of Rimini. It claims to be the oldest state in Europe, having been founded in the 4th cent. AD, and is one of the world's smallest states. S.M., the cap., stands on Mt Titano 808m (2,650 ft), a spur of the Apennines. Govt is by a Great and General Council of 60 elected members, two of whom are appointed biannually to act as regents (*Capitani reggenti*). Women may vote (from 1960).

San Marino, which entered into a customs union with Italy in 1862, is under Italian protection. Area 58 sq.km (22.5 sq.m); pop. (1981) 21,600. M.U.: Italian lira.

SAN MARTIN (mahrtēn'), **José de** (1778-1850). S American soldier. B. in Argentina, he served in the Spanish army during the Peninsular War, but after 1812 devoted himself to the S American struggle for independence, playing a large part in the liberation of Argentina, Chile, and Peru.

SAN REMO (rā'mō). Seaport and popular winter resort on the Gulf of Genoa, Liguria, N Italy. There is a casino; perfumes and mosaics are made. Pop. (1971) 61,400.

SAN SALVADOR. Cap. of the republic of El Salvador in Central America, 48km (30m) inland from the Pacific at the foot of S.S. volcano (2,548 m/8,360 ft). S.S. was founded in 1525; it has several times suffered badly from earthquakes. There are food processing and textile industries. Pop. (1976) 500,000.

SANSCŪLO'TTES (French, without knee-breeches). Term applied during the French Revolution to the working classes, who wore trousers, as opposed to the aristocracy and bourgeoisie, who wore knee-breeches.

SAN SEBASTIÁN. Seaport and resort, cap. of the prov. of Guipúzcoa, on the Bay of Biscay, Spain. It became fashionable after Queen Maria Christina, mother of the posthumous Alfonso XIII, made it the summer residence of the court in 1886. S.S., formerly a walled town, was besieged by Wellington in 1813; its walls were removed in 1863. Pop. (1970) 165,830.

SANSKRIT. The literary language of ancient India, belonging to the Indo-Iranian or Aryan branch of the Indo-European family of languages. The oldest form of S. is Vedic (*c.* 1500 BC), the medium in which the 4 Vedas (q.v.) and the associated Brahmanas, Aranyakas, and Upanishads were written. Classical S., with its fixed vocabulary and grammar, was the creation of the grammarians, notably Panini in the 4th cent. BC, but Vedic also continued to be used for several cents. Works written in Classical S. incl. the national epics, the *Mahabharata* and *Ramayana* (qq.v.), and the later artificial epics, of which Kalidasa's *Family of Rama* and *Birth of the War God* are the most famous. In lyric poetry the names of Jayadeva and Bhartrihari, and in drama that of Bhavabhuti, are noteworthy, but in both fields Kalidasa is again considered to excel all others. Other interesting literary forms are the prose romance, represented by Dandin's *Adventures of the Ten Princes*; the beast fables of the *Panchatantra*; and Somadeva's collection of verse fairy tales in the *Kathasaritsagara*. There is practically no historical writing in S., but there are many works dealing with philosophy, law, grammar, astronomy, algebra, and medicine.

SANTA ANA. Industrial city in El Salvador, NW of San Salvador. Pop. (1970) 163,000. Also a fruit-processing centre in California, USA, SE of Los Angeles. Pop. (1970) 156,600.

SANTA ANNA, Antonio Lopez de (1795-1876). Mexican revolutionary. A leader in achieving independence from Spain in 1821, he pursued a checkered career of victory and defeat in and out of office as president or dictator for the rest of his life, and was responsible for the massacre of the Alamo (q.v.).

SANTA BARBARA. Town in S California, USA, with a campus of the Univ. of California. In the Santa Ynez Mtns to the N, is Pres. Reagan's Rancho del Cielo. Pop. (1970) 70,215.

SANTA CLAUS. *See* NICHOLAS, ST.

SANTA CRUZ DE LA SIERRA (sahnta krooth de lah sie'rah). Cap. of S.C. dept in E Bolivia. Sugar cane and cattle were the chief base of local industry until newly discovered oil and natural gas led to phenomenal growth. Pop. (1976) 255,600.

SANTA CRUZ DE TENERIFE (sahnta krooth de ten'erif). Cap. of Tenerife and of the Canary Isls, it is a fuelling port and cable centre. S.C. was bombarded by Blake in 1657; by Nelson in 1797 - the action in which he lost his arm. Pop. (1970) 151,360.

SANTA FÉ (fā). Cap. of New Mexico, USA on the r. Santa Fé, 65km (40m) W of Las Vegas. It has a number of buildings from the Spanish period, incl. a palace (1609-10); the cathedral (1869) is on the site of a monastery built 1622. S.F. is noted for its Indian jewellery and textiles; tourism is its chief industry. Pop. (1970) 41,200, many Spanish-speaking.

SANTA FÉ (fā). Cap. of S.F. prov., Argentina, on the Salado 153km (95m) N of Rosario. Founded in 1573, it has shipyards and exports timber, cattle, and wool. Pop. (1970) 312,000.

SANTANDER (-dār'). Port in Spain on the Bay of Biscay, cap. of S. prov., which is traversed by the Cantabrian Mountains. It was sacked by Soult in 1808, and a fire in 1941 led to the re-planning of the town. There is an automobile industry, shipyards, etc. Pop. (1970) 150,000.

SANTAYANA (-yah'na), **George** (1863-1952). Spanish philosopher. B. at Madrid, he graduated at Harvard, where he taught the history of philosophy, 1889-1911. His books incl. *The Life of Reason* (1905-6), *The Realm of Truth* (1937), *Background of my Life* (1945), vols. of poems, and the novel *The Last Puritan*.

SANTIAGO (santē-ah'gō). Cap. of Chile and major industrial centre (textiles, chemicals, food processing, etc.), about 96km (60m) SE of Valparaiso. Founded in 1541, it is a handsome city, well laid out with broad avenues, e.g., the Alameda, or Avenida de las Delicias, and fine public buildings and a cathedral. There are 2 univs. Pop. of Great S. (1972) 3,700,000.

SANTIAGO de Compostela (kompostāl'ah). Spanish city in Galicia, to the SW of Corunna. It has a univ. and is an archiepiscopal see. The cathedral (begun in 1078) was built above the reputed grave of Sant Iago el Mayor (St James the elder), patron saint of Spain. Pop. (1970) 70,895.

SANTIAGO de Cuba. Port on the S coast of Cuba, with sugar, rum, and cigar industries. Pop. (1970) 292,250.

SANTIAGO de los Caballeros (kabayār'os). City in the Dominican Rep., NW of Santo Domingo, with tobacco, coffee industries, etc. Pop. (1970) 352,000.

SANTINIKETAN. *See* TAGORE, R.

SANTO DOMI'NGO. Cap. city and chief seaport of the Dominican Republic, also formerly called S.D. It stands on the S coast of the is., and was founded in 1496 by Bartholomew Columbus. Its cathedral was built 1515-40. It was called Ciudad Trujillo 1936-61. Pop. (1970) 823,000.

SA'NTOS. Seaport of Brazil, 72km (45m) SE of São Paulo. It is the world's greatest coffee port, and is free to Bolivia and Paraguay. Pop. (1975) 395,700.

SAÔNE (sōn). French r. 430km (268m) long, which rises in the Vosges and joins the Rhône at Lyons.

SÃO PAULO (sowṅ pow'lō). City in Brazil 900m (3,000 ft) a.s.l., 2′ S of the Tropic of Capricorn and 72km (45m) NW of its port Santos (q.v.). Originating as a Jesuit mission in 1554, it is the centre of the coffee trade of Brazil and has meat-packing plants. Pop. (1975) 7,200,000.

SÃO TOMÉ and Príncipe (sowṅ tomā', prē'nsipā). Two is. in the E Gulf of Guinea, an overseas terr. of Portugal until independence 1975. The cap is São Tomé, pop. 3,200. Angolan and Guinea-Bissau troops were stationed in S.T. from 1978 at the request of Pres. Pinto da Costa against an alleged danger of invasion from Gabon. Area 964 sq.km (372 sq.m); pop. (1970) 74,550.

SAPPER. Pseudonym of British author Cyril McNeile (1888-1937). Entering the Royal Engineers in 1907, he retired with the rank of lieut-col in 1919. In 1920 he pub. *Bulldog Drummond*, and continued the adventures of the hero in numerous sequels.

SAPPHIRE (saf'īr). Transparent blue precious stone, a variety of corundum, the less valuable forms being yellow, green, and colourless. Sri Lanka and Burma provide the best stones, usually found in alluvial soil. Ss. are made artificially on a large scale for industry and used almost universally as points in gramophone record reproducing heads (pick-ups).

SAPPHO (b. *c.* 600 BC). Greek lyric poet. B. at Mytilene or Lesbos, she was the centre of a feminine literary coterie at Mytilene, and was the friend of Alcaeus. She is said to have thrown herself from the Leucadian rock, owing to her love for Phaon being unrequited. Her poems survive only fragmentarily.

SAPPŌRŌ. Cap. city of Hokkaido, Japan, nr the E coast. Industries incl. rubber manufacture and food processing, its beer being famous. It is also a winter sports centre, with a snow festival remarkable for giant figures sculptured in ice. There is a univ. (1918). Pop. (1977) 1,256,000.

SAPROPHYTE (sap'rōfīt). Plant feeding on organic compounds in solution, and wholly or partly lacking in chlorophyll. Ss. are generally fungi and live upon dead plants and animals. The moulds on foodstuffs and the dry-rot of timber are caused by saprophytic fungi. Ss. are useful scavengers, and in sewage farms and refuse dumps break down organic matter into nutrients easily assimilable by green plants. Many orchids, also, are incl. among Ss.

SAPPORO. Demons and castles carved in solid ice and some 12 m (40 ft) high form the most striking feature of the snow festival. Army assistance in building them is called in, and also to help clear them away before they become a morass of slush. *Photo: Courtesy of the Japanese Information Centre*

SA'RACENS (-s-). Greek and Roman term for the Arabs, hence used in medieval Europe for all Moslems.

SARAGO'SSA. City in N Spain, on the Ebro, cap. of S prov. It has 2 cathedrals, one dating from the 12th cent., and a univ. It makes leather and leather goods, textiles, machinery, glass, porcelain, beer, etc. Founded as Salduba in pre-Roman days, it was named S. after the Roman conqueror Caesar Augustus; later it was captured by Suebi, Visigoths, and Moors, and was taken in 1118 by Alfonso the Warrior, King of Navarre and Aragon, after a nine months' siege; it remained cap. of Aragon until the end of the 15th cent. S. held out against the French 1808-9 when Agustina (d. 1859) became a national heroine: her story is told in Byron's *Childe Harold.* Pop. (1970) 480,000.

SARAJEVO (-jă'vō). City of Yugoslavia, cap. of Bosnia-Herçegovina federal republic, on the Miljačka. The assassination at S. of Archduke Francis Ferdinand, heir apparent to the throne of Austria-Hungary, by Gavrilo Princip, a Bosnian, on 28 June 1914, precipitated the F.W.W. Pop. (1971) 244,000.

SARA'NSK. Cap. of the Mordovian ASSR, USSR, an industrial centre, it produces electrical goods, machinery, etc. Pop. (1977) 248,000.

SARATO'GA SPRINGS. City and spa in New York State, USA, 61km (38m) N of Albany. Pop. (1970) 18,845.

Near by in 1777 Gen. John Burgoyne (q.v.) was defeated in 2 engagements by Horatio Gates to whom he surrendered. He and some 6,000 men remained prisoners until the end of the War of American Independence.

SARATOV (sahrah'tof). City of the RSFSR, on the Volga, cap. of S. region, 370km (230m) NE of Volgograd. The centre of a petroleum field with a pipe-line supplying Moscow 800km (500m) W, it has also shipbuilding, engineering and printing industries; and a univ. (1909). Pop. (1977) 856,000.

SARAWAK (sarah'wak). State of the Fed. of Malaysia, occupying the NW sector of Borneo and forming (with Sabah) E Malaysia. The coast is backed by a broad plain, but inland is broken, mountainous country. The climate is hot and wet. S. was ceded to Sir James ('Rajah') Brooke by the Sultan of Brunei in 1841 in return for his aid in a campaign against the Dayaks (q.v.), and was placed by his nephew Sir Charles under British protection in 1888. The Japanese occupied S. 1941-5 and following a period of military rule the Rajah, H.H. Sir Charles Vyner Brooke, was reinstated in 1946; five weeks later he ceded S. to the Crown. It was a Crown colony 1946-63, when it acceded to Malaysia. The cap. is Kuching, on the S. r.; Sibu is a port on the Rejang. The principal products incl. petroleum from the Miri oilfield, and natural gas which is liquefied and shipped from the port of Bintulu, as well as rubber, timber, bauxite, and one-third of the world's pepper. Area *c.* 122,000 sq.km (47,000 sq.m); pop. (1970) 976,000, incl. 386,000 Dyaks, 294,000 Chinese and 183,000 Malays.

SARD, and **SA'RDONYX.** *See* ONYX.

SARDINE. Name for several small fish in the herring family, though legally restricted in the UK, following a court ruling of 1915 in favour of an application by a French firm, to the young of the pilchard, caught off Sardinia (hence the name) and Brittany. In 1980 there were attempts to change this ruling which adversely affects packers of other small fish in the group which are indistinguishable in taste, and which are now marketed as sild, brisling, etc.

SARDI'NIA. Is. in the Mediterranean (Ital. *Sardegna*) to the S of Corsica. It is mountainous and largely barren, but many sheep are reared, and in the SW cereals, olives and vines are grown. Cork is exported, and minerals incl. lead, zinc and coal; bauxite is imported for aluminium smelting, and there is a petrochemical industry. Already settled in the Bronze Age, from which many *nuraghi* (fortified dwellings) survive, S. was ruled from the 15th cent. successively by Spain, Austria and Savoy, until absorbed in Italy when Victor Emmanuel II became King of Italy in 1861 (autonomous region from 1948). The Costa Smeralda (Emerald Coast) in the NE is being developed for tourism. The cap. is Cagliari. Area 14,964 sq.km (9,298 sq.m); pop. (1977) 1,582,000.

SARDOU (sahrdōō'), **Victorien** (1831-1908). French dramatist. His plays, many of which were written for such stars as Bernhardt and Irving, incl. *Fédora* (1882), *La Tosca* (1887) and *Robespierre* (1902).

SARGASSO SEA. That part of the N Atlantic lying between 40° and 80°W and 25° and 30°N which is notorious for its floating seaweed (*Sargassum natans*). Ocean currents sweep round the area clockwise leaving the centre virtually still.

SARGENT, Sir (Harold) Malcolm (Watts) (1895-1967). British conductor. From 1923 he was prof. at the RCM, was chief conductor of the BBC Symphony Orchestra 1950-7, and then continued as chief guest conductor and conductor-in-chief of the 'Proms'. He had an easy, polished style.

SARGENT, John Singer (1856-1925). American artist. B. in Florence of American parents, he studied there and in Paris. He settled in London, and was elected RA in 1897. His principal works incl. intimately perceptive portraits of the Wertheimer family, Lord Ribblesdale, T. Roosevelt, Rockefeller, and others and the F.W.W. picture 'Gassed'.

SARGESON, Frank (1903-). NZ short-story writer, novelist and dramatist. B. in Hamilton, he was ed. at Auckland Univ., and pub. his first story in 1933. His work, technically skilled and sensitive, has had a great liberating influence in NZ, and notable later works incl. *The Hangover* (1967) and *Man of England Now* (1972).

SA'RGON. Name of 2 Mesopotamian kings. **Sargon I** (*c.* 2700 BC), king of Akkad, founded the first Babylonian empire. **Sargon II** (reigned 722–705 BC), king of Assyria, carried the Israelites into captivity.

SARK. One of the Channel Islands, 10km (6m) E of Guernsey. It is divided into Great S. and Little S. connected by an isthmus called the Coupée, and is of great natural beauty. The Seignurie of S. was estab. by Elizabeth I, the ruler being known as Seigneur or Dame, and there is a parliament, the Chief Pleas. There is no income tax and cars are forbidden. Area 5 sq.km (2 sq.m); pop. (1971) 590.

SARO'YAN, William (1908–81). American author. B. in California, he told of his childhood there in *The Bicycle Rider in Beverly Hills* (1950), and made his name as a short-story writer, e.g. *The Daring Young Man on the Flying Trapeze* (1934), idealizing the hopes and sentiments of the 'little man', and later collections. His work as a playwright incl. *The Time of Your Life* (1939) and *Talking to You* (1962).

SARRAUTE (sahrōt), **Nathalie** (1902–). French novelist. B. in Ivanovo, N of Moscow, she was taken to France when 2 yrs old, and m. a French barrister, Raymond S. Her books try to give the live, half-conscious interactions of minds in contact with one another, and she is comparatively uninterested in plot, character and style: they incl. *Portrait of a Man Unknown* (1948), *The Golden Fruits* (1964), and *Do You Hear Them?* (1973).

SARRELOUIS. French form of SAARLAUTERN.

SARSAPARI'LLA. A drink prepared from the long twisted roots of plants in the genus *Smilax*, native to Central America.

SARTHE (sahrt). French r. which rises in the E of Orne dept and flows generally SSW to join the Mayenne nr Angers and form the Maine.

SARTRE (sahrtr), **Jean-Paul** (1905–80). French author and philosopher. B. in Paris, he became a teacher, publishing his first novel *La Nausée* in 1937. In the S.W.W. he was taken prisoner for 9 months, but returned from Germany to work for the resistance. Founder of the philosophical school of Existentialism (q.v.), he edited its journal *Les Temps Modernes*, and its tenets are expressed in the novels - a trilogy - of *Les Chemins de la Liberté* (1944–5) and in his strongly dramatic plays, e.g. *Les Mouches* (1947: *The Flies*); *Huis Clos* 1944: *In Camera*), 2 women and 1 man confined in the hell they make for each other; *Le Putain respectueuse* (1947: *The Respectful Prostitute*), attacking racial discimination in the South of the USA; *Crime Passionnel* (1948), an attack on certain aspects of Communism with which S. yet retained his general sympathy, and *Politics and Literature* (1973). Awarded the Nobel prize for literature in 1964, he refused it in advance for 'personal reasons'.

SA'RY-SHAGA'N. Weapons-testing area in Kazakhstan, USSR, nr the Chinese border. In 1980 beam weapons were detected as on trial there.

SĀ'RUM. *See under* SALISBURY, Wilts, England.

SASĒBŌ. Seaport and naval base on the W coast of Kyushu, Japan. Pop. (1977) 254,000.

SASKATCHEWAN (saskach'e-wan). Prairie prov. of Canada, between Alberta and Manitoba. The N is an area of forest, lakes, and sub-arctic tundra. Minerals incl. oil, potash, cadmium, copper, gold, silver, zinc, uranium, coal and salt, and there is natural gas incl. helium. Southern S. is Canada's greatest wheat-growing area: other crops are oats, barley, rye and flax. The Gardiner Dam (1967) on the South S. river, S of Saskatoon, provides irrigation and hydroelectricity. The towns incl. Regina (the cap.), Saskatoon, and Moose Jaw. The name comes from the Indian name Kis-is-ska-tche-wan (fast flowing) of the S. r. formed by the junction nr Prince Albert of the North S. and South S., which rise in the Rockies, to flow into Lake Winnipeg. Area 651,901 sq.km (251,700 sq.m); pop. (1979) 955,500.

SASKATOO'N. City in Saskatchewan, Canada, on the S Saskatchewan r., 240km (150m) NW of Regina. It is the seat of the univ. of Saskatchewan (1907) and makes cement, chemicals, and metal goods. Pop. (1979) 144,300.

SĀ'SOLBURG. Town in S Africa, 50 km (30 m) S of Johannesburg, site of the original oil-from-coal plant which requires a 'tied' coalfield. There are now 2 other plants at Secunda, 115 km (70 m) E of Johannesburg.

SASSANIAN EMPIRE. Ardashir, a local chieftain in the neighbourhood of modern Fars in Iran, estab. the Sassanid dynasty in 224 (naming it after his grandfather Sasan), when he took over the domains of the Parthian Empire. The S.E., after a rapid rise in which it contested supremacy with Rome, was destroyed in 637 by the Moslem Arabs at the Battle of Qadisiyah (q.v.).

SASSOON, Siegfried (1886–1967). British poet. Ed. at Cambridge, he enlisted in 1915, serving in France and Palestine, and expressed in his *War Poems* (1919) the disillusion of his generation. He pub. his *Collected Poems 1908–56* (1961), and as a prose writer is known for his *Memoirs of a Foxhunting Man* (1928).

SATELLITES. Natural Ss. accompany all the planets of the Solar system except Mercury and Venus. Solar tides will eventually cause the orbit of Earth's Moon, which is disproportionately large, to decay, and it is calculated that, in the case of Mercury and Venus, tidal forces have been sufficient to halt their original spin as primary planets, so that their satellites or moons have been lost by impact. Such an impact of a S. would account for the 'backward' rotation of Venus. **Artificial Ss.,** of which the first was the Soviet Union's Sputnik, vary greatly in size from a few pounds to the giant space station launched by the USA in 1973. From 1976 'hunter-killer' satellites were developed to intercept and destroy enemy Ss. which might be used to guide missiles to their target; other possibilities for the destruction of Ss. were laser and X-rays. *See* TELECOMMUNICATIONS.

SATIE (sahtē'), **Erik** (1866–1925). French composer. B. at Honfleur, he became a member of *Les Six.* His compositions incl. 'Limp preludes for a dog' and 'Pieces in the shape of a pear'.

SATO, Eisaku (1901–75). Japanese statesman. Son of a brewer of saké, he opposed the policies of Ikeda in the Liberal-Democratic Party, and succeeded him as PM (1964–72), pledged to a more independent foreign policy. He shared a Nobel peace prize in 1974, for his rejection of nuclear weapons. His brother **Nobosuke Kishi** (1896–), who changed his name from S. on adoption into the Kishi family when young, was PM 1957–60, being forced to resign when the revised security treaty he negotiated with the USA was unpopular.

SATURN. Roman god of agriculture, later identified with the Greek god Cronus. He was believed to be the father of Jupiter, Neptune, and Pluto, who dethroned him, and his reign was identified with the Golden Age of equality and plenty. At his festival, the Saturnalia, in Dec., gifts were

SATURN. A photograph of the rings taken as Voyager 1 neared the planet in 1980. It shows the A and B-rings, with the 4 thin rings which exist within the broad, dark band of the Cassini Division beginning to be seen, and the C-ring. To the left is the bright spot of S14, with S13 in the foreground, two of the newly-discovered satellites. The black spots are an effect produced in transmission by the spacecraft's cameras. *Photo: Consolidated News Pictures.*

exchanged, and slaves were treated as their masters' equals.

SATURN. The second of the giant planets. It has a mean distance from the Sun of 1,427,000,000 km (886,100,000 m); its revolution period is 29.46 yrs, its equatorial diameter is 119,300 km (74,100 m), and its mass is 95 times that of Earth. Like Jupiter, S. is appreciably flattened at the poles, as a result of its rapid axial rotation period (10¼ hrs). It also resembles Jupiter in the belts seen crossing the disc, winds at the surface reaching 1,450 kmph (900 mph), and also has similar 'red spots', one being 16,000 km (10,000 m) across. The planet has an inner core of iron and rock, an outer core of ammonia, methane and water, and above the core a region of metallic liquid hydrogen and helium. The temperature is low, about -180°C (-300°F). The magnetic field is a thousand times as strong as Earth's.

White when seen through a telescope, S. became lemon-yellow as spacecraft Voyager 1 (USA 1980) approached it. The unique, brightly-coloured ring system, hitherto thought to be divided into individual features, was shown to be linked together by hitherto invisible rings, giving it the close-up appearance of a grooved gramophone record, some even being twisted or 'braided' in apparent defiance of the usual laws of physics. The rings themselves, once thought to be dust, consist of countless boulders of ice and rock, the spacecraft itself being hit, though undamaged, several times. These are thought to be the debris of the fragmentation by tidal forces of a former satellite or satellites.

Of the three bright main rings round S., A-ring is the outermost, and is divided from B-ring (brightest of the 3) by the Cassini Division (named after its discoverer). Contiguous with B-ring is C-ring, also known as the Crêpe Ring because of its semi-transparency. Within C-ring is D-ring, which extends down towards the planet and comprises much smaller particles which consequently reflect much less light. Outside A-ring is the thin, 'braided', near-invisible F-ring, discovered in 1979 by Pioneer 11 (USA), and beyond F-ring a diffuse, optically invisible ring which may extend 480,000 km/300,000 m into space.

There are 15 known satellites or moons, the largest being Titan (q.v.); Rhea (diameter 1,500 km/930 m), the most heavily cratered; Dione (1,100 km/685 m), with large craters and cracks in an icy surface; Tethys (1,020 km/635 m), crossed by a valley 750 km/465 m long and with an enormous mtn, at first thought to be a crater, 200 km/125 m across; Iapetus (1,000 km/620 m), apparently crusted on one side with shining ice; Enceladus (520 km/325 m) unusual in being uncratered; and Mimas (350 km/220 m), which has a massive impact crater with shock lines. The others are Hyperion, Phoebe, and a number of small ones which are known only as numbers: S10 and S11, which were formerly thought to be one satellite (known as Janus) and may, since they follow almost identical orbits, once have been so; S12; S13 and S14, which are located on either side of the F-ring and very close to it, and may gravitationally control it; and S15, the closest satellite to Saturn, 800 km/500 m outside the A-ring. The last 3 were all discovered by Voyager 1 in 1980, and many more such small satellites may exist. Further information is expected from Voyager 2 which reaches the gaseous (mainly hydrogen and helium) planet in 1981.

SATYAGRAHA. Term applied in India to non-violent resistance. It was first employed by Gandhi in 1918, and the idea owes much to Tolstoy.

SATYR. In Greek mythology, woodland beings characterized by pointed ears, 2 horns on the forehead, and a tail, who were supposed to attend Dionysus. In Roman writers they are confused with the goat-footed fauns.

SAUDI ARABIA (sow'di). Kingdom of SW Asia occupying the greater part of the Arabian peninsula. Most of the area is desert. Nejd in the interior and Hejaz on the Red Sea coast were in 1927 united under Ibn Saud, former Sultan of Nejd, who proclaimed himself king of both. He was succeeded by his son Saud Ibn Abdul-Aziz (1902-69) in 1953, but the latter proved reactionary and was replaced by his brother Faisal, who became a progressive and stabilizing force in the Arab world. On Faisal's assassination in 1975, he was succeeded by his brother Prince Khaled (1913-82), in turn succeeded by his brother, Prince Fahd (1925-), who is also PM.

Although the country's main wealth derives from the oil discovered in the Arabian Gulf in 1936, surveys indicate that there are considerable reserves of other minerals, incl. iron, gold and phosphates. Agriculture is being extended by irrigation, and camels and sheep are reared. Industries are chiefly oil and mineral-related. The cap. is Riyadh; other towns incl. Hufuf, Medina, Mecca and the ports of Jidda, Damman and Ras Tannura.

Area 2,400,000 sq.km (927,000 sq.m); pop. (1977) 9,520,000, of whom only *c.* 3,000,000 are now nomadic. The great majority are Sunni Moslems, but in the Eastern Province, there are a number of Shi'ites, among whom agents of Ayatollah Khomeini are active. The language is Arabic, considered the purest type because closest to the Koran. M.U.: rial.

SAUL. First king of Israel (d. about 1010 BC). The son of Kish, he was anointed by Samuel, and after his victory against the Ammonites was made king by the people at Gilgal. He lost the favour of God and committed suicide.

SAULT STE MARIE (soo sānt mahrē'). Twin cities on the US-Canadian frontier, at the falls in St Mary's river joining lakes Superior and Huron. S. Ste M., Ontario, manufactures steel and paper. Pop. (1971) 80,330. S. Ste M., Michigan, had a pop. of 15,150 in 1970. Two international canals bypass the falls, which were discovered by Étienne Brulé in 1612, *sault* (modern Fr. *saut*) meaning falls.

SAUMUR (sōmür'). Town in Maine-et-Loire dept, France, on the Loire, famous for its sparkling wines. The cavalry school (1768), has since 1942 also been a training school for the French armoured forces. Pop. (1973) 23,175.

SAUNA (saw'na). Finnish bath. Known for a thousand years and once a sacred cult, the S. bath is traditionally still taken on Saturday. Above a wood fire specially selected black cobblestones, about the size of a man's fist, are heated on an iron grate and water is thrown on them to produce a steam bath at *c.* 90°C (200°F). Perspiration begins in *c.* 10 mins. and, after a beating with whisks made of birch twigs, the bather cools off with a plunge into cold water.

SAUNDERS, Clarence (1881-1953). American retailer. Working as a boy in a grocery store, he conceived the idea of the self-service supermarket. The first opened in Memphis, Tennessee, in 1919.

SAUTERNES (sōtărn'). A village of Gironde dept, SW France, which has given its name to the sweet white table wines of the district. Pop. (1973) 585.

SAVAGE, Michael Joseph (1872-1940). New Zealand Labour statesman. As Prime Minister 1935-40, he introduced much social security legislation.

SAVANNAH. City and port of Georgia, USA, on the S. river 29km (18m) from its mouth. Founded in 1733, it exports cotton, and makes cottonseed oil, fertilizers, machinery, etc. The *Savannah,* first ship fitted with steam power to cross the Atlantic, was built at S.; she made most of the journey (1819), which took 25 days, under sail. The first nuclear-powered merchant ship, launched by the USA in 1959, was given the same name. S. was the first planned 'grid-iron' city in the USA. Pop. (1970) 118,350.

SAVA'NNAH or **savanna.** Term, perhaps of Carib origin, applied by the Spaniards to treeless plains of tropical American prairies, now denoting any extensive tropical grassland.

SAVING. The reservation of a portion of income for future needs, seldom in modern times the massing of a money hoard, because of dangers of fire and theft, but tending to be synonymous with investment. The purchase of precious stones, antiques, works of art, property, etc., for appreciation of value has also been practised as a counter to inflation. Small-scale savers have an increasingly large field opening to them. Very frequent is the acquisition of a home by regular payments on a mortgage obtained through a building society or bank, the house passing to the mortgagor when the purchase price plus interest is paid off. Popular also are life insurance policies producing at the end of a specified time a lump sum or annuity; the majority now issued are 'with profits', i.e. the people insured benefit through profits from the investments of the company. For unit and investment trusts, *see* TRUST.

For small savers who wish to have their money at ready call, but also to secure a modest interest, the most usual recourse is the Trustee Savings Banks (regulated by acts of Parliament) which date from the early 19th cent.; the Post Office (now National) Savings Bank (1861); or the Building Societies (q.v.). The govt, which makes certain tax concessions to people investing in these and in home ownership and insurance policies, also offers the small saver Premium Savings Bonds (1956) repayable at par, earning no interest, but eligible for prizes awarded monthly to holders in a draw made by ERNIE (q.v.); British Savings Bonds, carrying in addition to regular interest a tax-free bonus after a given number of years; and Nat. Savings Certificates (1916) with graduated tax-free interest payable on encashment and a Save As You Earn (1969) scheme with a tax-free terminal bonus - both revised in 1975 to incl. a scheme relating repayments to the monthly retail price index (the former for people of retirement, or near retirement, age only).

Similar methods of savings are available in other countries incl. the USA, where the govt has issued a number of series of savings bonds.

SAVONARŌ'LA, Girolamo (1452-98). Italian reformer. B. at Ferrara, he became a Dominican friar in 1474, and was elected prior of St Mark's Convent at Florence in 1491. His eloquent preaching, and his reputation as a visionary and prophet won him immense popular influence, and in 1494 he led a revolt which expelled the Medicis and estab. a democratic republic. But his denunciations of Pope Alexander VI led to his excommunication in 1497, and in 1498 he was arrested, tortured, hanged, and burned for heresy.

SAVOY. Area, formerly a prov. of the kingdom of Sardinia which, with Nice, was ceded to France in 1860 by Victor Emmanuel II (king of Italy from 1861) in return for French assistance in driving the Austrians from Italy. It lies between the Alps, the Lake of Geneva, and the r. Rhône, and was formed into the depts of Savoie and Haute-Savoie, in Rhône-Alpes region, but there is an S. separatist movement.

SAWFLY. Family of insects in the order Hymenoptera. The name is derived from the saw-like edge of the female's ovipositor. There are about 2,000 species which damage plants either by feeding on them or by the larvae burrowing in the tissues.

SAXE, Maurice, comte de (1696-1750). Soldier. The natural son of the elector of Saxony, he served under Marlborough and Eugène, and for his brilliant exploits in the War of the Austrian Succession was created a marshal of France in 1743.

SAXE. French form of SAXONY.

SAXE COBURG-GOTHA (gōta). A ducal title held by members of the Wettin family. Albert the Prince Consort was the son of Ernest, the 1st duke; and Alfred the duke of Edinburgh, succeeded his uncle in 1893. On his death in 1900, the title passed to his nephew, the duke of Albany, who abdicated in 1918.

SA'XIFRAGE. Genus of plants (*Saxifraga*) in the family Saxifragaceae. They occur in rocky, mountainous, and alpine situations. London Pride (*S. umbrosa*) is a familiar example.

SAXONY. English form of Sachsen, a former kingdom, later state, of Germany. It lay between Prussia, Bavaria, and Bohemia; Dresden was the cap. It got its name from its Saxon inhabitants and originally reached as far W as the Rhine, covering most of the Land of W Germany formed in 1946 and named Lower Saxony. S. was conquered by Charlemagne, but when his empire broke up after his death became a dukedom. This itself was broken up in the 12th cent., and the area called S. subsequently underwent many fluctuations. The Reformation originated in S., Luther being a native. In the 16th cent. the ruler of S. became an Elector and later a king. S. supported Napoleon I and half the kingdom was given to Prussia by the Congress of Vienna, 1815, becoming the Prussian prov. of S. The remaining kingdom joined the German Empire, founded 1871. At the end of the F.W.W. the king abdicated and S. became one of the federal states of the German Republic. After the S.W.W., S. lay in E Germany and in 1946 was, with part of Silesia, made a new Land of S., abolished in 1952.

SAXONY, Lower. *See* LOWER SAXONY.

SAXONY-ANHALT. Land of E Germany, 1946-52. It consisted of Anhalt, a former duchy and state, and most of the former Prussian prov. of Saxony.

SAXOPHONE. A wind instrument made of brass and possessing woodwind characteristics. It was invented by Adolphe Sax (1814-94) as one of a series of such instruments which also included the saxhorn. Several varieties of S. exist, all having a conical brass tube, curved at each end and with 20 keys controlling notes.

SAYAN (sahyan') **MTNS.** Range in the far south of the RSFSR, USSR, on the Mongolian border: highest peak Munku Sardik 3,489 m (11,447 ft). Coal, gold and lead are worked.

SAYERS, Dorothy Leigh (1893-1957). British author. Ed. at Somerville Coll., Oxford, where she read history, she made her name with her creation of Lord Peter Wimsey, the dilettante detective with a taste in wines and 1st editions, who appeared initially in *Whose Body?* (1923); other crime stories incl. *The Nine Tailors* (1934) and *Busman's Honeymoon* (1937). She also wrote the radio series on the life of Christ *The Man Born to be King* (1942), controversially realistic in its time.

SCĀ'BIOUS. Two genera of plants in the family Dipsacaceae, incl. the garden plant *Scabiosa atropurpurea*, and the field S. (*Knautia arvensis*).

SCAFELL (scawfell') **PIKE.** Highest mountain in England (978 m/3,210 ft). It is in Cumbria in the Lake District and is separated from Scafell (964 m/3,162 ft) by a ridge called Mickledore. The summit of S.P. was presented to the Nat. Trust by the 3rd Lord Leconfield, as a war memorial, in 1919.

SCALAR QUANTITY. *See* VECTOR.

SCALLOP. Family of bi-valve molluscs the Pectinidae found in all seas. The shell is fan-shaped with 2 ear-like projections near the hinge. The edible S. (*Chlamys opercularis*) is sedentary but not fixed; *Pecten jacobaeus* was used as a badge by pilgrims from Compostela.

SCAMPI. Large prawns (*Nephrops Norwegicus*) ideal for processing and freezing: the word is the plural of Italian *scampo* 'shrimp'.

SCANDINĀ'VIA. Peninsula of NW Europe, comprising the kingdoms of Norway and Sweden. Politically and culturally it also includes Denmark and is sometimes considered to include Finland.

SCA'NDIUM. A scarce metal element of the rare metallic earth group; symbol Sc, at. no. 21, at. wt. 44.96. was discovered in 1879 in the Scandinavian mineral euxenite.

SCANNER. *See* TOMOGRAPHY and X-RAYS.

SCAPA FLOW. Expanse of sea in the Orkney Islands, Scotland, formerly a base of the RN. The main base of the Grand Fleet during the F.W.W., in 1919 it was the scene of the scuttling of 71 surrendered German warships. It remained the principal base of the home fleet until 1957.

SCAPOLITE (skap'ōlīt). Group of white or greyish minerals, consisting essentially of silicates of aluminium, calcium, and sodium, which probably come from the deep Earth and which possibly act as a subterranean storehouse for gases such as carbon dioxide and sulphur dioxide.

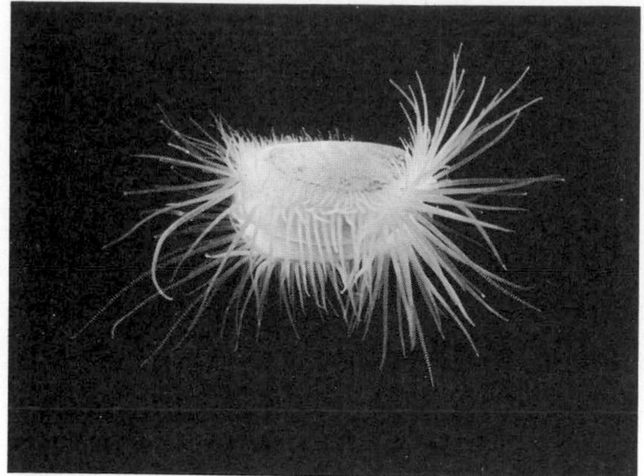

SCALLOP. The gaping file shell *(Lima hians)*. The long marginal tentacles cannot be drawn within the shell, and the animal protects itself by building a 'nest' around itself among rocks or seaweed holdfasts. *Photo: Douglas P. Wilson*

SCARAB (skar'ab). Name for the dung-beetles of the family Scarabeidae, of which *Scarabeus sacer* was reverenced by the ancient Egyptians as the symbol of resurrection. They feed on balls of dung.

SCARAB. The beetle lays its eggs in a ball of dung, afterwards pushing the ball backward up a slope with its hind legs to compact it before lodging it in a safe place for the eggs to hatch. *Photo: Stephen Dalton/NHPA*

SCARBOROUGH. Spa and holiday resort in N Yorks, England. A ruined Norman castle overlooks the town, a touring centre for the Yorkshire Moors. Edith and Sacheverell Sitwell were born at S. Pop. (1974) 44,370.

SCARLATTI (skahrlaht'tē), **Alessandro** (1659-1752). Italian musician. B. at Trapani, he became master of the chapel at the court of Naples and founded the Neapolitan school of opera, writing more than 100 operas himself and some notable church music. His eldest son, **Domenico S.** (1685-1757), was also a composer and is best remembered for his harpsichord sonatas.

SCARLET FEVER. Scarlatina; an infective fever caused by a haemolytic streptococcus. It is transmitted usually by direct infection in spray from speaking or coughing. The incubation period is under a week. The rash is a uniform redness, with small bright red points. Ear-ache due to inflammation is a common complication. Peeling of the skin occurs in convalescence. The disease is currently much less severe, and treatment is often assisted by antibiotics, e.g. penicillin.

SCHAFFHAUSEN (shahf'howzen). Cap. of the most northerly Swiss canton, nr the celebrated falls in the Rhine. Watches, chemicals and textiles are made. Pop. (1970) 38,000.

SCHEER (shehr), **Reinhard** (1863-1928). German admiral. B. in Hesse-Nassau, he was appointed commander of the High Sea Fleet in 1916, and was in command at the battle of Jutland.

SCHELDT (skelt). English name for the European r. called in Dutch Schelde, in French Escaut. It rises in Aisne dept, N France, and flows 400km (250m) N, NE, then W, through Belgium and the Netherlands to enter the North Sea by the W Scheldt S of Walcheren, a wide estuary of great importance to shipping. Antwerp is the chief town on the S.

SCHENECTADY (skenek'tadi). City in New York State, USA, on the r. Mohawk. It dates from 1662 and is an industrial centre with well-known scientific research laboratories. Pop. (1970) 77,960.

SCHEVENINGEN. *See* HAGUE, THE.

SCHICK TEST. A means of ascertaining by the injection of a small dose of diphtheria toxin whether a person is immune to diphtheria or not. In a susceptible person a local flush appears.

SCHIEDAM (skhēdahm'). Town of S Holland, Netherlands, 5km (3m) W of Rotterdam, and famous for its gin. It received its charter in 1273 and about the turn of the 18th-19th cents. sent much gin to the USA. Pop. (1978) 76,000.

SCHILLER (shil'ler), **Johann Christoph Friedrich von** (1759-1805). German author. B. at Marbach (Württemberg), he qualified as a doctor but, after the success of his drama *The Robbers*, devoted himself to literature and became theatrical director at Mannheim, where he produced his tragedies *Fiesco* and *Love and Intrigue*, and began the more mature drama *Don Carlos*. In 1789 he settled at Jena, where he was prof. of history and completed *The History of the Thirty Years War*, and in 1799 at Weimar, where he developed his close friendship with Goethe. His later works incl. the classical dramas *Wallenstein* (a trilogy), *Maria Stuart*, *The Maid of Orleans*, and *William Tell*, and *Naive and Sentimental Poetry*, an outstanding work of literary criticism. S., a high-minded idealist and lover of freedom, also attained great popularity with his shorter poems.

SCHIPPERKE (shi'perke). A tailless watchdog, bred in Belgium. It has black fur and erect ears.

SCHIRACH (shē'rakh), **Baldur von** (1907-74). German Nazi leader. He acted as youth leader of Germany 1936-40, and as gauleiter of Vienna 1940-5, where he carried out the policy of deporting all Jews. He was tried at Nuremberg in 1945-6, and sentenced to 20 years' imprisonment; released 1966.

SCHIST (shist). Foliated rock, crystalline in nature, which presents layers of various minerals easily divisible into thin lenticular plates. The dominant mineral normally names each variety.

SCHISTOSOMIASIS (shi'stosōmī'asis). Alternative name for bilharzia, a disease contracted by washing or swimming in water containing snails, etc., which are hosts to the embryonic stage of flukes of the family

Schistomatidae. These parasites pass through the human skin and attack organs within the body. The disease is common in tropical and subtropical areas, and has spread more widely in Egypt in areas irrigated by the Aswan High Dam. It was first named after Theodor Bilharz of the Cairo School of Medicine who discovered its nature *c.* 1860.

SCHIZOPHRENIA (skitsofrē'nia). 'Split personality', a psychological disorder which involves a fundamental inability to face life: symptoms incl. depression, social withdrawal, delusions and hallucinations. The cause may be defects in the brain's neurotransmitter system, i.e. an insufficiency of prostaglandins (q.v.), since S. improves during fever when levels of prostaglandin in the brain rise. This improves the hope of more effective treatment than tranquillising drugs, etc. at present in use.

SCHLEGEL (shleh'gel), **August Wilhelm von** (1767-1845). German author. B. at Hanover, he was an important figure in the Romantic movement. His Vienna lectures on *Dramatic Art and Literature* were epoch-making, and he is also remembered for his translations of Shakespeare. His brother, **Friedrich von S.** (1772-1892), studied Greek and Sanskrit literature, and wrote extensively on literary history.

SCHLESWIG-HOLSTEIN (shlesvig hol'stīn). Land of W Germany, bounded by Denmark to the N and traversed by the Kiel Canal. Cereals, potatoes and sugar-beet are grown, but S.-H. is predominantly industrial with most of her pop. engaged in shipbuilding, mechanical and electrical engineering and textiles. The largest towns are Kiel (the cap.), Lübeck, Flensburg, and Schleswig. Area 15,785 sq.km (6,095 sq.m); pop. (1978) 2,587,200.

History. Schleswig (Danish Slesvig) and Holstein were 2 duchies held by the kings of Denmark from 1460, but were not part of the kingdom; a number of the inhabitants were German, and Holstein was a member of the German Confederation formed in 1815. Possession of the duchies had long been disputed by Prussia, and when Frederick VII of Denmark died without an heir in 1863, Prussia, supported by Austria, fought and defeated the Danes in 1864, and in 1866 annexed the two duchies. A plebiscite held in 1920 gave the N part of Schleswig to Denmark which made it into the provs. of Haderslev and Aabenraa; the rest, with Holstein, remained part of Germany.

SCHLIEMANN (shlē'mahn), **Heinrich** (1822-90). German archaeologist. Fascinated from an early age by the Homeric epics, he retired from business in 1863 to study archaeology, and in 1871 began excavating at Hissarlik, which he estab. as the site of Troy, although the 'palace and treasure of Priam' which he discovered belong to an earlier settlement on the site than the one which Homer describes. His most important later excavations were at Mycenae, where he thought he had discovered the grave of Agamemnon, though again the find was of an earlier period.

SCHMIDT (shmit), **Helmut** (1918-). German statesman. B. in Hamburg, he became economic adviser to the city, and in 1968 leader of the Social Democratic Party. He was Min. of Defence 1969-72, of Finance 1972-4, and in 1974 succeeded Brandt as Chancellor, being re-elected in 1976 and 1980, but standing down for Kohl (q.v.) in 1982. He was an 'Atlanticist', supporting Nato, but also attempted to pursue a modified form of Ostpolitik (q.v.).

SCHMIDT. Helmut Schmidt, Federal Chancellor of West Germany 1974–82. As leader of the most economically successful nation in Europe, he exercised great influence in the affairs of the Common Market. *Photo: Courtesy of the West German Government.*

SCHNABEL (shnah'bel), **Artur** (1882-1951). American pianist. B. in Austria, he taught music at the Berlin State Academy 1926-31, but settled in the USA in 1939, and composed symphonies and other works. He excelled in Beethoven.

SCHNEIDER TROPHY (shnī'der). An aviation trophy presented by Jacques Schneider in 1913 for competition between seaplanes of any nation. From the first holder, M. Prévost in 1913, who averaged 45.75 mph, the trophy changed hands several times before being won outright by Britain, after victories in 1927, 1929, and 1931, the last creating a world's record of 340.08 mph.

SCHOENBERG (shön'bārg), **Arnold** (1874-1951). Austro-American composer of Jewish descent. B. in Vienna, he developed the twelve-note system (*see* ATONALITY), and taught at the Berlin State Academy 1924-33. Driven from Germany by the Nazis, he settled in the USA in 1933. Among his works are the *Gurrelieder*, the opera *Moses and Aaron* and *Pierrot Lunaire* for voice and chamber orchestra.

SCHOLASTICISM (sk-). Name given to the theological and philosophical system of Christian Europe in the Middle Ages. John Scotus (Erigena) is sometimes regarded as the founder, but the succession of 'Schoolmen' definitely opened with Roscellinus at the end of the 11th cent., when in his advocacy of Nominalism he was countered by Anselm, the champion of Realism. The controversy over 'Universals' thus begun continued for several cents. William of Champeaux, Abélard, Alexander of Hales, Albertus Magnus, and Peter Lombard played prominent parts, but the greatest names are those of Thomas Aquinas, whose writings became the classical textbooks of Catholic doctrine, and the Franciscan Duns Scotus. The last of the Schoolmen is usually reckoned to have been William of Occam, who, in the first half of the 14th cent., restated Nominalism. In the present cent. there has been a revival of interest in Scholasticism, as seen in the writings of Jacques Maritain and other Catholic scholars.

SCHOOL. A place in which instruction is given to the young in preparation for life. Schooling is compulsory in the UK from 5 to 16, the majority of children being educated in Ss. run by local education authorities with govt. aid, the usual division being nursery (under 5) primary (5-11) and secondary (11-18): but by 1980 about 10% of those 16-18 were attending a tertiary college (the courses being mainly job-related), which covers a wider catchment area than a single school. Some 80% of children in the last group attend 'comprehensive' all-ability schools, but in 1979 the compulsion imposed on local authorities by Labour to reorganize all secondary education on comprehensive lines was removed by the Conservatives. An act of 1980 also imposed a statutory duty on local education authorities to comply with parental choice of school, and introduced an 'assisted places' scheme for the govt. to meet the fees of selected pupils at certain independent fee-paying schools on a means-test basis. These independent Ss., which Labour are committed eventually to abolish as 'socially divisive'. incl. the famous 'public' schools, such as Eton, Harrow, Winchester, Rugby, and Repton, many of which are ancient foundations set up originally for poor scholars. All Ss. are subject to govt. inspection and inefficient independent Ss. may be closed. In Scotland the pattern is similar, but 'public' school there equals 'state'.

In France attendance is compulsory 6-16; elementary from 6 to 11, and *enseignement du second degré* 11-18, the *lycées* providing a seven-year course for the gifted leading to the *baccalauréat.* In Germany full-time S. attendance is compulsory 6-15, as is part-time vocational study to 18 for those not continuing at secondary S., which incl. Gymnasien for the more academic. In the USSR schooling is compulsory from 7, usually to 17, with great stress on technical education, and is co-educational. In China, where courses were cut, standards lowered, and study combined with half-time work on factory or farm during the Cultural Revolution, there was a reversal of policy from 1977. A special system of schools for the specially talented was introduced in 1978, and many students are being sent to the West for advanced study.

In the USA attendance at S. is generally compulsory 6-16, the majority of children attending the free public school system, often in a 3-tier system of 6 elementary 'grades' or years, followed successively by 3 yrs at junior high school and 3 yrs at senior high, the courses leading to 'graduation' at 17 or 18. About a third go on to college or university.

SCHOPENHAUER (shō'penhow-er), **Arthur** (1788-1860). German philosopher. B. at Danzig, he graduated at Jena and pub. in 1813 his *Fourfold Root of the Principle of Sufficient Reason*; and in 1818 his chief work, *The World as Will and Idea,* in which his pessimistic philosophy is expounded.

SCHREINER (shrī'ner), **Olive** (1862-1920). S. African writer. B. in Basutoland, the dau. of a missionary, she was the sister of **William Philip S.** (1857-1910), who was PM of Cape Colony 1898-1900, and m. in 1894 S. C. Cronwright. In 1883 she pub. *The Story of an African Farm,* a powerful novel describing life on the S African veldt.

SCHRÖDINGER (shrö'dinger), **Erwin** (1887-1961). Austrian physicist. B. at Vienna, he became in 1940 senior prof. at the Dublin Institute for Advanced Studies. He greatly advanced the study of wave mechanics, and was awarded a Nobel prize in 1933.

SCHUBERT (shōō'bārt), **Franz Peter** (1797-1828). Austrian musician. B. at Vienna, the son of a school-teacher, he himself was a school-teacher for 3 years, but composed busily in his spare time. In 1816 he gave up teaching to compose, and in 1818 was appointed music teacher to the Esterházy family on their estate in W Hungary. Very shortly he was back in Vienna, where he lived henceforth a Bohemian existence. He was only 31 when he died, but his musical output was prodigious. Greatest of the 9 known symphonies are the incomplete B minor and the C major. He contributed much to chamber and pianoforte music, including sonatas and fantasias, but his most treasured works are his songs, of which he wrote over 600, including 3 great cycles.

SCHUBERT. A water colour, dated 1825, by W.A. Rieder in the Historical Museum, Vienna, the city where Franz Schubert composed the majority of his works. *Photo: Courtesy of the Historical Museum, Vienna*

SCHUMAN (shoomaṅ'), **Robert** (1886-1963). French statesman. He was PM 1947-8, and as Foreign Min. 1948-53 created the Coal and Steel Pool (the 'S. Plan' treaty of 1951) and prepared the basis of the Common Market.

SCHUMANN (shōōmahn), **Robert Alexander** (1810-56). German musician. B. at Zwickau, Saxony, he taught at Leipzig conservatoire and was musical director at Düsseldorf 1850-3. As a composer he excelled in pianoforte compositions and in *Lieder*; his piano concerto Op. 54 and sonatas Opp. 11 and 22 are particularly famous. He wrote also much chamber music. His musical criticisms were pub. in his *Neue Zeitschrift für Musik.* From 1854 he was confined in an asylum near Bonn, following a suicide attempt, and there he died. His wife, the pianist **Clara Josephine Wieck** (1819-96), whom he

m. in 1841, devoted herself to the popularization of his work, and appeared frequently in London 1865-88.

SCHUSCHNIGG (shoosh'nig), **Kurt von** (1897-1977). Austrian statesman. A lawyer, he was elected a Christian Social deputy in 1927, and succeeded Dollfuss as Chancellor in 1934, when he was confronted with the Nazi menace from within and without. In Feb. 1938 he was forced to accept a Nazi Min. of the Interior, and a month later Austria was invaded and annexed. S. was imprisoned in Germany until 1945, when he went to USA.

SCHWARZKOPF (shvah'rtskopf), **Elisabeth** (1915-). German soprano. Educated at the Berlin High School of music, she is noted for her dramatic interpretation of operatic roles, such as Elvira in *Don Giovanni* and Marschallin in *Der Rosenkavalier*, and is also a concert singer.

SCHWARZWALD (shvah'rtsvahlt) (Ger., black forest). See BLACK FOREST.

SCHWEITZER (shvīt'ser), **Albert** (1875-1965). French theologian, organist and missionary surgeon. He founded a hospital in 1913 at Lambaréné, Rep. of Gabon, where he afterwards remained, except for brief intervals spent giving recitals of organ music, mainly Bach, to raise funds for his medical work. His many books incl. a standard life of Bach (1905), *The Quest of the Historical Jesus* (1906), *On the Edge of the Primeval Forest* (1921), *My Life and Thought* (1931). He was awarded the Nobel peace prize in 1952 and the OM 1955. His nephew **Pierre-Paul S.** (1912-) was 1963-73 managing director of the International Monetary fund.

SCHWERIN (shvārēn'). Cap. of S. dist., E Germany, situated on Lake S., 52km (32m) SE of Lübeck. S. received its charter from Henry the Lion in 1161; once the cap. of Mecklenburg-S., it has the former grand-ducal palace and a 15th cent. cathedral. Pop. (1978) 113,000.

SCHWITTERS (shwit'erz), **Kurt** (1887-1948). German artist and poet. Originally a portraitist, he developed the art of collage from 1918 using discarded trash such as buttons, bus tickets, stamps, etc., and of poems consisting of sounds without words.

SCHWYZ (shvits). Cap. of S. canton, one of the 3 original cantons, of the Swiss Confederation, which gave its name from *c.* 1450 to the whole country. Pop. (1970) 12,100.

SCIASCIA (shiah'shiah), **Leonardo** (1921-). Sicilian novelist. He often uses the detective novel, not merely as an exploration of a crime, but of the hidden workings of Sicilian life, e.g. *Mafia Vendetta* (1961) and *Equal Danger* (1974).

SCIATICA. Persistent pain felt along the course of the sciatic nerve. It is sometimes due to inflammation of the nerve itself (neuritis), but often to the effects of pressure or inflammation (rheumatism, gout, fibrositis, etc.) on one of the nerves leading out of the lower spine.

SCIENCE MUSEUM. The British Nat. Museum of Science and Industry, estab. 1853, in South Kensington, London. The collections of the Patent Museum were added in 1883; the art collections transferred to the Victoria and Albert Museum in 1909; and the Wellcome Museum of Medical Science moved into a newly-built wing 1980-81.

SCIENCE RESEARCH. In the UK there are 4 research councils: *Medical* (1913), *Agricultural* (1931), and (replacing the Dept of Scientific and Industrial R. under the S. and Technology Act 1965) *Science Research* and *Natural Environment.* The S.R.C. deals with fundamental R. not allocated to the others and, like them, supports R. at the univs. and its own establishments, incl. the Rutherford and Appleton Laboratories (Chilton, Oxfordshire), the Daresbury Laboratory (Daresbury, Cheshire), and the Royal Observatories (Hurstmonceux and Edinburgh): N.E.R.C. deals with ecology and the earth sciences. The *Nat. R. Development Corporation* (1948) secures exploitation of inventions derived from publicly supported research. In the USA a *Nat. R. Council* (1916) estab. by the privately organized Nat. Academy of Ss. is drawn from the univs., industry and govt.

SCIENTOLOGY (sī-ent-). An 'applied religious philosophy', its name derived from Lat. *scire* 'to know' and Gk *logos* 'branch of learning', founded in California in 1954 by Lafayette Ronald Hubbard (1911-) as the *Church of S.*, its HQ from 1959 being at Saint Hill Manor, East Grinstead, Sussex. It claims to 'increase man's spiritual awareness', but the movement has met with criticism.

SCI-FI. The genre of Science Fiction, of which the classic practitioners were Jules Verne and H.G. Wells, but which following the S.W.W. developed as a major section of modern literature with writers such as Brian Aldiss, Ray Bradbury, and Arthur C. Clarke (qq.v).

SCILLA (sil'a). Genus of bulbous plants of the Liliaceae family bearing blue, pink, or white flowers; it incl. the wild hyacinth or bluebell.

SCILLY ISLANDS (sil'i). Group of islands, forming a dist. of Cornwall, England; they lie 40km (25m) SW of Land's End. Only 5 of the 140 islands and islets are inhabited, viz. St Mary's, Tresco, St Martin, Bryher, and St Agnes. Hugh Town on St Mary's is the cap. The mild climate and rich soil enable early vegetables and spring flowers to be produced. Area 16km (6.3 sq.m); pop. (1971) 2,428.

SCIPIO (sip'io), **Publius Cornelius** (d. 211 BC). Roman general. Elected consul in 218, during the 2nd Punic War, he was defeated by Hannibal at Ticinus and killed by the Carthaginians in Spain.

SCIPIO, Publius Cornelius, known as Scipio Africanus Major (237-*c.* 183 BC). Roman general, who destroyed the Carthaginian armies in Spain during 210-206. He invaded Carthage in 204, and defeated Hannibal at Zama (202).

SCIPIO, Publius Cornelius (*c.* 185-129 BC), known as Scipio Africanus Minor. Roman general. Appointed supreme commander during the 3rd Punic War, he took Carthage in 146, and razed it to the ground. As Governor of Spain he subdued that country in 134.

SCLEROSIS (sklerō'sis), **multiple.** Organic disease of the central nervous system producing recurrent paralysis, incontinence and eventually severe paralysis. There is at present no cure.

SCOLIOSIS (skoli-ō'sis). Curvature of the spine. Formerly corrected in young children by a series of operations to insert grafted bone to produce a rigid spine, from 1980 a new electronic technique, the insertion of a stimulative device in the lower back to contract the muscles, has been used to straighten the curve.

SCONE (skoon). Village in Tayside, Scotland, on the Tay, 3km (2m) N of Perth. In its ancient abbey and royal palace most of the Scottish kings were crowned on the stone of destiny, now in the Coronation Chair at Westminster. A modern palace now occupies the site. Pop. (1971) 3,000.

SCOTLAND. Ben Nevis, its tremendous mass given scale by the picturesque old granary, now demolished (top left); Stirling Castle (top right); Sir Walter Scott (a portrait by J. G. Gilbert) and his favourite view towards the Eildon Hills in the Border Country near Abbotsford (centre left and centre); the Guizer Jarl, or leader, polishes his armour for the ancient Shetland ceremony of Up Helly A', when a Viking longboat is annually burnt (centre right); and an aerial view of Edinburgh. In the foreground is the former High School (1829) on Calton Hill, designed by Thomas Hamilton, considered as the home of a revived Scottish parliament, was from 1981 the seat of the Crown Office; in the background are the twelve pillars of what was intended to be a full reconstruction of the Parthenon to commemorate the Napoleonic Wars, and the domes of the observatory. *Photos: Courtesy of the British Tourist Authority (Ben Nevis, Stirling, Scott's view), the National Portrait Gallery (Scott), Paul Harrison (Guizer Jarl), and* The Scotsman *(Edinburgh).*

SCOPOLAMINE (skopo'lamēn). Alkaloid ($C_{17}H_{21}O_4N$), extracted from plants of the Solanaceae family and used in surgery and obstetrics (with morphine) as a sedative, and to prevent travel-sickness.

SCORPION (skŏr'-). Order (Scorpiones) in the class Arachnida. Common in tropical and sub-tropical regions, they may be up to 15cm (6in) in length, and are viviparous and nocturnal. The sting is poisonous, but not usually fatal to healthy persons.

SCOTLAND. That part of Great Britain lying N of the border with England. In addition to the mainland, it comprises numerous islands, incl. Arran, Bute, in the Firth of Clyde, the Inner and Outer Hebrides off the W coast; and the Orkneys and Shetlands to the N. The W coast is very broken, with numerous sea lochs, but the E coast is comparatively regular. Among the main rivers are the Spey, Don, Dee, Esk, Tay, Forth, and Tweed, flowing into the North Sea; the Annan, Nith, Cree, and Esk into Solway Firth; and the Ayr, Clyde, Carron, etc., flowing into the Atlantic. The largest inland lochs are the Lomond, Maree, Ericht, Awe, Katrine, Tay, Rannoch, and Ness.

PHYSICAL. Most of the surface is highland except in the centre and extreme NE. The Cheviot Hills lie on the border with England, and farther N are the Lammermuir and other ranges of the Southern Uplands. These are bounded on the N by the central Lowlands watered by the Clyde and Forth, and containing most of the country's population and industries. Farther N still, rise the Ochill and Sidlaw Hills, and the Campsie Fells, while to the NW of a line running from the mouth of the Clyde to the mouth of the S Esk lie the Highlands, a mountainous area which in turn is divided into SE and NW portions by Glen More traversed by the Caledonian Canal and Lochs Ness and Lochy. The Grampians, in the SE portion, incl. Ben Nevis (q.v.), highest mountain in the British Isles, and Ben Lomond, Ben Lawers, Ben Macdhui, Cairngorm, and other heights.

In 1975 the cos. of S. were re-organized in 9 regions and 3 islands areas (*see Table*), but a number of the cos. reappeared as districts having the same or similar area. The new districts were as follows: *Borders* Berwickshire, Ettrick and Lauderdale, Roxburgh, Tweeddale; *Central* Clackmannan, Falkirk, Stirling; *Dumfries and Galloway* Annandale and Eskdale, Merrick, Nithsdale, Stewartry; *Fife* Dunfermline, North-East Fife, Kirkcaldy; *Grampian* City of Aberdeen, Banff and Buchan, Gordon, Kincardine and Deeside; *Highland* Badenoch and Strathspey, Caithness, Inverness, Lochaber, Nairn, Ross and Cromarty, Skye and Lochalsh, Sutherland; *Lothian* City of Edinburgh, East Lothian, Midlothian, West Lothian; *Strathclyde* Argyll, Bearsden and Milngavie, Bishopbriggs and Kirkintilloch, Clydebank, Cumbernauld, Cumnock and Doon Valley, Cunninghame, Dumbarton, Eastwood, City of Glasgow, Hamilton, Inverclyde, East Kilbride, Kilmarnock and Loudon, Kyle and Carrick, Lanark, Monklands, Motherwell, Renfrew; *Tayside* Angus, City of Dundee, Perth and Kinross.

ECONOMIC. The narrow, diagonal central belt between the Firths of Clyde and Forth contains some 4 out of the 5 million population, and it was here that prosperity arose in the Industrial Revolution with shipbuilding, and the iron and coal fields that supported Scotland's heavy industry. Since the S.W.W. and particularly from the 1960s there has been rationalization and modernization of

Regions of Scotland

	Area in sq. km.	*Pop. (1979)*	*Admin. H.Q.*
Regions:			
Borders	4,662	99,902	Newtown St. Boswells
Central	2,590	271,023	Stirling
Dumfries and Galloway	6,475	142,427	Dumfries
Fife	1,295	332,933	Glenrothes
Grampian	8,702	463,130	Aberdeen
Highland	25,149	189,858	Inverness
Lothian	1,813	747,737	Edinburgh
Strathclyde	13,727	2,424,189	Glasgow
Tayside	7,511	400,451	Dundee
Islands Areas:			
Orkney	984	18,055	Kirkwall
Shetland	1,424	21,835	Berwick
Western Islands	2,901	29,255	Stornoway
	77,233	5,140,795	

the traditional industries, and an attempt to stem the continuing pop. decline through emigration by bringing in new industries such as aluminium smelting, petrochemicals and plastics, and - largely through American investment - electronics and business machines. Development of Tayside has been undertaken, and also promotion of a linear city from Tain to Inverness in the Moray Firth area, and a remarkable series of new towns has sprung up along the central belt - Cumbernauld (q.v.), East Kilbride, Glenrothes, Irvine and Livingston. Most significant for S.'s economic future are her offshore oil and natural gas resources.

The Highlands, besides their commercial value as a source of hydroelectric power, are one of Europe's greatest tourist attractions for their scenery; their grouse, deer and salmon; and their winter sport facilities. Here, and in Grampian and W Strathclyde, fine cattle are raised; miniature ponies come from the Shetlands; and sheep are widely grazed. The chief crops are oats, barley, wheat and roots, and there is dairy farming in the SW. Forestry and fishing are important. Among specialized products which are valued exports are the tweeds of Harris and Scotch whisky. The road and rail systems are good - the bridges over the Forth and Tay being remarkable feats of engineering - and there is a major airport at Prestwick. The chief towns are Edinburgh, the cap., and Glasgow (each with 2 univs.), and St Andrews, Aberdeen, Dundee and Stirling are also univ. cities: the general standard of education is traditionally high.

POPULATION. Descendants of the original Celtic inhabitants form the majority of the population, though in the extreme N and the Orkneys and Shetlands the Norse strain is marked; *see* SCOTTISH GAELIC. During the 19th and 20th cents. there has been a strong current of emigration to England and other parts of the Commonwealth and to the USA. At the same time many Irish settled in the industrial areas of the Lowlands. The majority of the people belong to the (Presbyterian) Church of S. (q.v.). Area (incl. 1,577 sq.km/609 sq.m of inland water), 78,810 sq.km (30,427 sq.m); pop. (1979) 5,140,795.

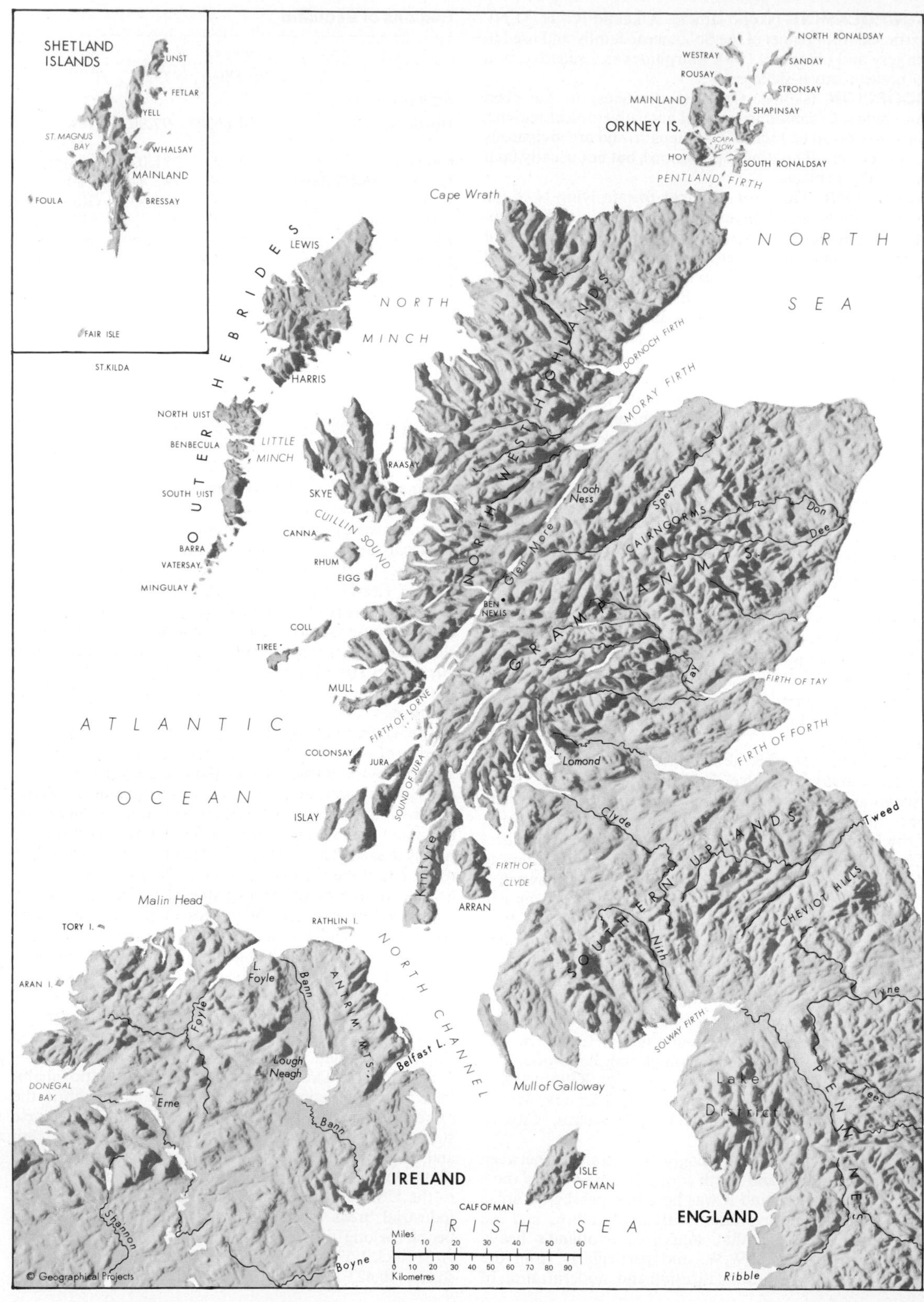
SHETLAND ISLANDS
UNST
FETLAR
YELL
ST. MAGNUS BAY
WHALSAY
MAINLAND
FOULA
BRESSAY
FAIR ISLE
NORTH RONALDSAY
WESTRAY
SANDAY
ROUSAY
STRONSAY
MAINLAND
SHAPINSAY
ORKNEY IS.
SCAPA FLOW
HOY
SOUTH RONALDSAY
PENTLAND FIRTH
Cape Wrath
NORTH SEA
OUTER HEBRIDES
LEWIS
NORTH MINCH
ST. KILDA
HARRIS
NORTH UIST
BENBECULA
LITTLE MINCH
RAASAY
SOUTH UIST
SKYE
CUILLIN SOUND
CANNA
BARRA
RHUM
VATERSAY
EIGG
MINGULAY
NORTH WEST HIGHLANDS
DORNOCH FIRTH
MORAY FIRTH
Loch Ness
Spey
Don
CAIRNGORMS
Dee
Glen More
GRAMPIAN MTS.
BEN NEVIS
COLL
TIREE
Tay
FIRTH OF TAY
MULL
ATLANTIC OCEAN
FIRTH OF LORNE
FIRTH OF FORTH
COLONSAY
JURA
SOUND OF JURA
Lomond
ISLAY
Clyde
SOUTHERN UPLANDS
Tweed
Kintyre
FIRTH OF CLYDE
CHEVIOT HILLS
Malin Head
ARRAN
TORY I.
RATHLIN I.
NORTH CHANNEL
L. Foyle
Bann
ANTRIM MTS.
Nith
ARAN I.
Foyle
Tyne
SOLWAY FIRTH
Belfast L.
Lough Neagh
PENNINES
DONEGAL BAY
L. Erne
Mull of Galloway
Lake District
Tees
Bann
IRELAND
ISLE OF MAN
CALF OF MAN
IRISH SEA
ENGLAND
Shannon
Miles
0 10 20 30 40 50 60
0 10 20 30 40 50 60 70 80 90
Kilometres
Boyne
Ribble
© Geographical Projects

History. Before the Roman conquest of South Britain in the 1st cent. AD, what is now S. was inhabited by Goidelic Celts, later called Picts. The Romans made some attempts at conquest, and during the 2nd cent. temporarily occupied the Lowlands. In the 6th cent. the Angles overran the SE up to the Firth of Forth; the Britons, driven northward, occupied the SW, while Scots from Ireland settled in Argyllshire. Christianity was introduced from Ireland during the 5th-6th cents. The Picts and Scots were united by Kenneth MacAlpin in c. 844; the SE was conquered by Malcolm II in 1015, and in 1034 the Britons were brought into the Scottish kingdom. S. suffered during the 9th cent. from raids by the Norsemen, who held the Hebrides until the 13th cent., and the Orkneys and Shetlands until the 15th. From the 11th cent. many Englishmen and Normans settled in S.; the English language spread over the Lowlands, and the feudal system was estab. in the 12th cent.

Edward I's attempt to annex S. led to a series of revolts led by Wallace and Bruce (1296-1314), ending in the Scottish victory at Bannockburn, although England did not recognize Scottish independence until 1328. Anglo-Scottish relations continued unfriendly until the Reformation; Scottish foreign policy was based on a French alliance, which sometimes, as at Flodden (1513), resulted in disaster. The Scottish parliament, of one house, originating as a council of barons and clergy, assumed its final form with the admission of burgess representatives in the 14th cent. The Stuart dynasty, founded by Robert II who came to the throne in 1371 (N.S.), attempted with little success to control the turbulent nobles; several met violent deaths, and a succession of regencies weakened the monarchy. James IV (reigned 1488-1513) m. Margaret, dau. of Henry VII of England, in 1503.

Under Knox's leadership Calvinism was estab. as the national religion in 1560, and its victory was consolidated by Queen Mary's deposition in 1567. James VI, who, as a great-great-grandson of Henry VII inherited the English crown in 1603 from the childless Elizabeth I, and Charles I sought to bring the democratic Presbyterian Church under royal control by remodelling it on Anglican lines. The Scots rebelled in 1638, and during the Civil War were allied with the English parliamentarians; after Charles's execution, however, they supported his son Charles II, and were conquered by Cromwell, who brought them under English rule 1651-60. Throughout the Restoration period the Presbyterians were persecuted, until the revolution of 1688 brought relief. The Scottish parliament was united with the English in 1707.

Dislike of the union was largely responsible for the Jacobite risings of 1715 and 1745. The latter was followed by the destruction of the clan system, and the eviction of many Highland farmers to make way for sheep-runs. The Union stimulated trade with America, while the coal, iron, shipbuilding and textile industries all expanded greatly during and after the Industrial Revolution. During the 18th cent. S.'s political representation was notoriously corrupt, and S. was prominent in the Radical movement from 1792 to the Reform Bill.

The later 19th cent. saw a new wave of 'clearances' in the Highlands, as sheep-farms gave way to deer forests. There has been a strong working-class movement in the industrial districts of S. since Chartist days; Glasgow in particular long remained an ILP stronghold. During the 20th cent. a nationalist movement demanding the re-establishment of the Scottish parliament has developed. The first Scottish Nationalist MP was elected 1945, but in a referendum in 1979 as to whether Scotland should have its own directly elected assembly in Edinburgh only 33% voted 'yes', not the required 40%. In the recession of the late 1970s and early 1980s unemployment was particularly high in Scotland.

Sovereigns of Scotland

(From the unification of Scotland to the union of the crowns of Scotland and England.)

Celtic Kings			
Malcolm II	1005	Edgar	1097
Duncan I	1034	Alexander I	1107
Macbeth	1040	David I	1124
Malcolm III Canmore	1057	Malcolm IV	1153
Donald Ban	1093	William the Lion	1165
Duncan II	1094	Alexander II	1214
Donald Ban		Alexander III	1249
(restored)	1095		
Margaret of Norway	1286-90		
English Domination			
John Balliol	1292-6	Annexed to England	1296-1306
House of Bruce			
Robert I Bruce	1306	David II	1329
House of Stuart			
Robert II	1371	James IV	1488
Robert III	1390	James V	1513
James I	1406	Mary	1542
James II	1437	James VI	1567
James III	1460	Union of Crowns	1603

SCOTLAND, Church of. The body of Christians recognized by the State as the established and national C. of S. Protestant in theology and presbyterian in organization, it was estab. in 1560 at the Reformation and after attempts to impose episcopacy, re-estab. in 1690. In 1929 the United Free C. of S., which was the result of a large secession in 1843, was re-united with the original body. The country is divided into some 2,400 parishes, in each of which there is a kirk session consisting of the minister and of several laymen called elders. Parishes are grouped into presbyteries; and these again into synods. The supreme court is the General Assembly of clergymen and laymen chosen by the presbyteries; it meets in May under a Moderator, and a Lord High Commissioner attends as the Queen's representative. The Bible is the supreme rule of faith and life, and a subordinate standard is based on the Directory issued in 1645 and the Book of Common Order 1940. There are 1 million members, and in 1968 the Gen. Assembly voted that women be admitted to the Ministry.

SCOTLAND YARD. Headquarters of the Metropolitan Police, at Broadway, Westminster, London. Originally in S.Y. off Whitehall, it was removed to New S.Y. on the Embankment, close to the Houses of Parliament, in 1890, and in 1967 to a new building at Victoria which retained the same name. As the seat of the Criminal Investigation Dept, S.Y. is a synonym for the force of detectives.

SCOTS LAW. As compared with English law, Scottish law differs in particular in the extent to which actions involving large sums are initiated in the lower courts, and the absence of the separate system of Equity. In criminal law the principal distinguishing feature is the all-pervading system of public prosecution. The supreme civil court of Scotland is the House of Lords. Below this comes the Court of Session, possessing an original and an appellate jurisdiction; its judges have the honorary title of Lord, and a division of the Inner House, as the appeal court is called, is presided over by the Lord President, or by the Lord Justice-Clerk. Below the Court of Session is the Sheriff Court, one of which is found in every county. The supreme criminal court is the High Court of Justiciary. Other courts are the Burgh courts (criminal) where the bailies preside, and there are also justices' courts (civil and criminal). There are considerable differences in court procedure. The jury consists of 15 and may arrive at its verdict by a majority. A verdict of 'not proven' is competent. There is no coroner: the Procurator-Fiscal inquires into all suspicious deaths.

SCOTS PINE. *See* PINE.

SCOTT, Elizabeth Whitworth (1898-1972). British architect. She designed (after winning an international competition) the Royal Shakespeare Theatre at Stratford.

SCOTT, Sir (George) Gilbert (1811-78). British architect. Largely responsible for the mid-19th-cent. Gothic revival in England, he renovated many churches incl. Ely cathedral and Westminster Abbey with debateable results; and designed the Albert Memorial, the Foreign Office and St Pancras Station. His grandson **Sir Giles Gilbert S.** (1880-1960), also an architect, received as his first commission Liverpool Anglican cathedral, and besides many other churches, designed Cambridge Univ. Library, Waterloo Bridge, and with his brother **Adrian Gilbert S.** (1882-1963) rebuilt the House of Commons after the S.W.W. He was awarded the OM in 1944.

SCOTT, Robert Falcon (1868-1912). British Antarctic explorer. B. at Devonport, he entered the navy in 1882. He commanded 2 Antarctic expeditions, in the *Discovery*, 1901-4, and in the *Terra Nova*, 1910-12. On 18 Jan. 1912 he reached the S Pole, shortly after Amundsen, but on the return journey he and his companions, Wilson, Oates, Bowers, and Evans, perished. His journal was recovered and pub. in 1913. His wife, **Kathleen,** later Lady Kennet (d. 1947), was a sculptor, e.g. her statue of her husband in Waterloo Place, London.

Their son **Sir Peter Scott** (1909-), is a naturalist, artist and explorer. His paintings are usually either portraits or bird studies, and he is founder-director of the Wildfowl Trust at Slimbridge, Glos., also having published many books on birds. He was nat. gliding champion in 1963 and is a keen yachtsman. *The Eye of the Wind* (1961) is autobiographical. He was knighted in 1973.

SCOTT, Sir Walter (1771-1832). Scottish poet and novelist. B. in Edinburgh, the son of a lawyer, he was educ. at the high school and univ., and in 1792 qualified as an advocate. An early attack of infantile paralysis lamed him slightly for life. His first literary works were translations of German ballads, and in 1797 he m. Charlotte Charpentier or Carpenter, of French origin. His *Minstrelsy of the Scottish Border* appeared in 1802, and henceforth he combined the practice of literature with legal appointments. *The Lay of the Last Minstrel* (1805) was an immediate success, and so too were *Marmion* (1808), *The Lady of the Lake* (1810), *Rokeby* (1813), and *Lord of the Isles* (1815). Out of the proceeds he purchased and rebuilt the house of Abbotsford on the Tweed, but Byron had to some extent now captured the lead with a newer style of verse romance, and S. turned to prose fiction. *Waverley* was issued in 1814, and gave its name to a long series of historical novels, incl. *Guy Mannering, The Antiquary, Old Mortality, Rob Roy, The Heart of Midlothian* and *The Bride of Lammermoor. Ivanhoe* (1819) transferred the scene to England; *Kenilworth, Peveril of the Peak, The Talisman* (1825), and *The Fair Maid of Perth* (1828) followed. In 1820 S. was created a baronet, but in 1826 he was involved in financial ruin through the bankruptcy of Constable his chief publisher, with whom fell Ballantyne & Co., the firm of printers and publishers in which S. had been for many years a sleeping partner. Refusing to accept bankruptcy, he set himself to pay off the combined debts of over £120,000. *Woodstock* (1826), a life of Napoleon, and *Tales of a Grandfather*, are among the chief products of these last painful years. The last outstanding liabilities were cleared after his death on the security of copyrights. Continuous over-work ended in a nervous breakdown. He d. at Abbotsford on 21 Sept. 1832. His *Journal* was issued in 1890, and his life by J. G. Lockhart, his son-in-law, in 1837. His finest works were the books dealing with the troubled times of the Covenanters, still in living memory in his boyhood, and he excels in depicting the speech and character of ordinary, fundamentally good, people.

SCOTTISH GAELIC. This forms with Irish Gaelic and Manx the Gaelic branch of the Celtic languages, and often agrees with Manx where it differs from Irish. S.G. was introduced to Scotland by warriors from Ireland at the end of the 5th cent. It attained its widest extent in the 11th cent. After a long decline the speaking of G. is reviving, also taking root outside the traditional G. districts of the Western Isles and the fringes of the N and W: Gaelic speakers (1961) 76,587, (1971) 88,415.

LITERATURE. The earliest examples of S.G. prose belong to 1000-1150, but the most important early original composition is the history of the MacDonalds in the Red and Black Books at Clanranald. The first printed book in S.G. was a translation of Knox's Prayer Book in 1567. Prose Gaelic is at its best in the folk-tales, proverbs, and essays by writers such as Norman MacLeod in the 19th cent. and Donald Lamont in the 20th.

S.G. poetry falls into 2 main categories. The older syllabic verse was composed by professional bards. The chief sources of our knowledge of this are the Book of the Dean of Lismore (16th cent.), which is also the main early source for the Ossianic ballads; the panegyrics in the Books of Clanranald; and the Fernaig MS. Modern S.G. stressed poetry began in the 17th cent. but reached its zenith during the Jacobite period with Alexander MacDonald, Duncan Macintyre, Rob Donn, and Dugald Buchanan. Only William Livingstone (1808-70) kept alive the old nationalistic spirit in the 19th cent. Emergent during and after the S.W.W. was a new school impatient of tradition, incl. Somhairle MacGilleathain, George Campbell-Hay and Ruaraidh MacThómais.

SCOTTISH TERRIER. Breed of dog, formerly known as the Aberdeen T. because many early show dogs were bred there. Small and sturdy, it has a harsh, wiry outercoat, and may be black, wheaten or brindle.

SCOUTS. Non-military and non-political youth organization originating (as the Boy Scouts) with an experimental camp held in 1907 for 24 boys from every class of society by Baden-Powell (q.v.) on Brownsea Is., Poole Harbour, Dorset. The island was in 1962 acquired by the National Trust. Baden-Powell's book *Scouting for Boys* (1908) led to the incorporation of the B.S. Assocn by royal charter in 1912, and the movement has spread throughout the Commonwealth as well as to foreign countries. In 1966 the rules of the B.S. Association (now the Scout Association) were revised to embody a more adult and 20th cent, image, and the dress was up-dated, e.g. the traditional shorts were exchanged for long trousers. The corresponding organization for girls is the Girl Guides (q.v.), inc. by royal charter in 1922, The scheme was introduced to the US by William D. Boyce, a Chicago publisher who had visited England and met Baden-Powell, and the Boy Scouts of America were inc. in 1910: a similar organization for girls, the Girl Scouts of the USA, was founded in 1912. World membership: Scouts 3,000,000.

SCRABBLE. Board game for 2-4 players, in which counters of varying point values are used to form words. Played by the British royal family, it gained such popularity that internat. competitions are now held.

SCRAMBLING CIRCUIT. A transmitting circuit which renders signals unintelligible unless received by the corresponding unscrambling circuit.

SCRANTON. City in Pennsylvania, USA, on the Lackawanna r., with anthracite mines nearby and heavy industry. Pop. (1970) 103,570.

SCRIABIN (skrē-ahbin'), **Alexander Nicolas** (1871-1915). Russian composer. B. at Moscow, he wrote *Prometheus* and other tone-poems, employing a revolutionary system of harmony. He profoundly affected Russian music, and was also a pianist.

SCRIBE (skrēb), **Augustin Eugène** (1791-1861). French dramatist. B. in Paris, he achieved fame with the *Nuit de la Garde nationale*, and with numerous assistants produced many plays of technical merit but little profundity, incl. *Verre d'eau, Adrienne Lecouvreur*, and *Bertrand et Raton*.

SCRIBES. A Jewish group, incl. both priests and laymen, who devoted themselves to the study of the law of Moses, and who sat in the Sanhedrin. In the NT they are associated with the Pharisees.

SCULLIN, James Henry (1876-1953). Australian Labour statesman. B. at Ballarat, he sat in the House of Representatives 1910-13, and was re-elected in 1922. He was leader of the Federal Parliamentary Labour Party 1928-35, and PM and Min. of Industry 1929-31.

SCULPTURE. Traditionally the artistic shaping in relief or in the round of static materials such as wood, stone, metal and plastic. All the ancient civilizations - Assyrian, Egyptian, Indian, Chinese, Maya, etc. - have left examples of great sculpture, for the most part by unknown artists, and even in the case of the more recent masterpieces of European Gothic the craftsmen are un-named. Traditional European S. descends through that of Greece, Rome and Renaissance Italy, but particularly influential in the development of modern S. in the W has been the work of Negroes of E Africa, the natives of the South Sea Islands, and other 'primitive' peoples. An unusual departure in the 20th cent. has been the invention by Alexander Calder (q.v.) of the *mobile* in which the suspended components move spontaneously with the currents of air. An extension is the *structure vivante,* of which the leading exponents are Bury, Soto and Takis. In this motion is achieved by some mechanism which follows a set pattern devised by the artist, the materials used incl. such unusual items as magnets, lenses and bubbles, and the artistic impression created incl. also a certain element of sound.

Among the world's most famous sculptors are: *Classical Greek:* Phidias, Praxiteles, and Scopas; *Renaissance:* Donatello, Verrocchio, Della Robbia, and Michelangelo; *Baroque:* Bernini, Girardon, and Houdon; *Neo-Classic:* Canova, Thorwaldsen, and Flaxman; and *20th cent.:* Rodin, Maillol, Gill, Epstein, Meštrović, Henry Moore, Hepworth, Ayrton, Brancusi, Lipchitz, Butler, Borglum, Anthony Caro and Marino Marini.

SCUNTHORPE. Industrial town in Humberside, England, 39km (24m) W of Grimsby. It has one of Europe's largest iron and steel works, which has been greatly expanded with EEC help. Pop. (1974) 69,330.

SCURVY. A disease due to lack of vitamin C that is contained in fresh vegetables, fruit and milk. The symptoms are bleeding into the skin, swelling of the gums, and drying up of the skin and hair. Treatment is by giving the vitamin.

SCUTARI (skōō'tahrē). (1) Italian form of Üsküdar, Turkey; (2) Shkodër, Albania.

SCYLLA (sil'a) and **CHARYBDIS** (karib'dis). In classical mythology a sea-monster and a whirlpool, between which Odysseus had to sail. Later writers located them in the Straits of Messina.

SCYPHOZOA. Large group of jelly-fish in the phylum Coelenterata, some over 2m (6ft) across.

SCYTHIA (sith'i-a). Regions N of the Black Sea varying in extent from time to time, and between the Carpathians and the Don, inhabited by the Scythians from the 7th-1st cents. BC. Darius I made an unsuccessful attempt to conquer the Scythians in the 6th cent. BC; from the middle of the 4th they were slowly superseded by the Sarmatians. They produced ornaments and vases in gold and electrum with animal decoration.

SEA, Law of the. Traditonally, fishing and territorial limits, over which a country has absolute juridiction, were set by the Geneva Convention (1882) at 5 km/3 m from the shore - the distance a gun could then reach. In 1980 a draft UN treaty laid down a 19 km/12 m territorial limit, a 320 km/200 m exclusive economic zone (EEZ), and jurisdiction also over marine resources, e.g. oil and fisheries, beyond the latter limit on the continental shelves. Freedom of passage is guaranteed internationally, espec. in narrow straits.

An International Seabed Authority is to be set up to control exploration and exploitation of deep seabed resources (e.g. the est. 22 billion tonnes of copper and nickel at *c.* 3,000 m/10,000 ft), in particular by a UN-chartered mining co. (Enterprise) from which revenues will be allocated to developing countries. A Law of the Sea Tribunal, to arbitrate disputes, is also to be established.

SEA-ANEMONE. A section of the class Anthozoa in the phylum Coelenterata. Tube-like, they are attached at one end to some substratum, the other end being open and fringed with tentacles. They feed on crustaceans and other minute organisms. S.-As. occur in many beautiful colours, especially in tropical waters.

SEABORG, Glenn T(heodore) (1912-). American nuclear chemist. While director of nuclear chemistry research at Berkeley (1946-58), he was awarded with E. M. McMillan (also of the Univ. of California) a Nobel prize in 1951 for discoveries of 3 transuranium elements; and the production of radio-isotope U.233. In 1971 he became prof. of chemistry at the Univ. of California, Berkeley.

SEA CUCUMBER. Slug-like echinoderm of the class Holothuroidea. The cylindrical body may be several feet in length, and dried S.Cs. from N Australia and the Pacific seaboard of the USA are esteemed for the table by the Chinese.

SEAGA (se-ah'gah), **Edward** (1930-). Jamaican Labour party statesman. He won a landslide victory in the 1980 elections to become PM, and spoke of himself as 'very much in the centre'.

SEAGULL. *See* GULL.

SEAHAM. Seaport in Durham, England, 8km (5m) S of Sunderland. Coal mines were developed from the 19th cent. Byron m. Anne Isabella Milbanke at S. Hall nearby. Pop. (1972) 23,370.

SEA-HORSE. Several genera of fishes of which *Hippocampus* is typical. They range from the Atlantic through the Mediterranean to Australia. The body is compressed and covered with bony plates raised into tubercles or spines. There is a crest on the head, and the tail is prehensile.

SEA-HORSE. Ranging in size from a few inches to a foot in length, the sea-horses usually remain in the vertical position as they move. They are excellent fathers, carrying the female's eggs in a pouch on the underside of their tail until hatching. *Photo: Heather Angel*

SEA ISLANDS. Islands in the Atlantic Ocean off the S Carolina-Florida coast. Best quality S.I. cotton with a long 'staple' (fibre), was originally grown here.

SEA KALE. Perennial plant (*Crambe maritima*) of the family Cruciferae cultivated in Europe as a vegetable. The young shoots are forced and blanched.

SEAL. Group of carnivorous marine mammals which are subdivided into the eared fur Ss. or Otariidae, and the earless hair or true Ss., the Phocidae. The fur Ss. or sea lions are found chiefly in the N Pacific and the Bering Sea, and have been ruthlessly persecuted for the sake of their skins. They have sharper muzzles than the true Ss., and use their hind limbs in moving on land. The hair or true Ss. belong to the N Atlantic and the Arctic Oceans, and incl. the 2 species known in Britain, the intelligent common S. (*Phoca vitulina*), and the grey S. (*Halichoerus grypus*); and the valuable Greenland S. (*Pagophilus groenlandicus*). The streamlined body has the limbs converted to flippers, and in the hair Ss. the posterior limbs are joined with the tail. The elephants. or sea-elephant (*Mirunga*), so-named because of its enlarged proboscis, is the largest of all Ss., and is found in the S. Atlantic and Pacific. The male grows much larger than the female: 6m (20ft) and over. It was hunted almost to extinction, but under conservation numbers have recovered.

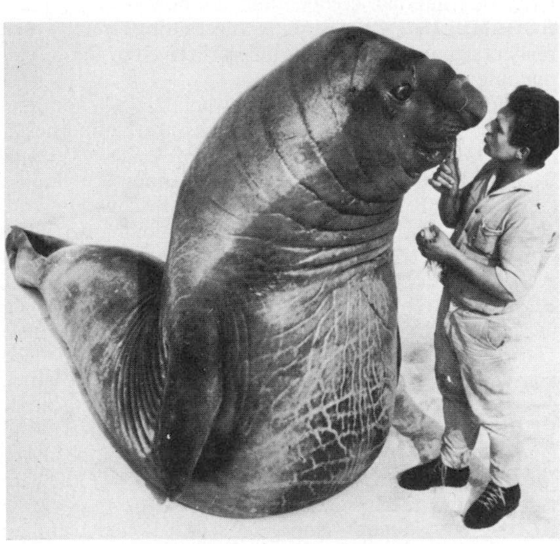

SEAL. Tristan the elephant seal, so named because he was captured off Tristan da Cunha. Becoming a popular inmate of Stuttgart Zoo, he reached more than 4 m (12ft) in length and a weight of 1.5 tonnes, with an appetite for fish in proportion. *Photo: Courtesy of Wilhelma, Stuttgart*

SEA LILY. Class (Crinoidea) of deep water echinoderms. Their rayed bodies are often borne on a stalk.

SEA LION. *See* SEAL. *Seelöwe* was the Ger. cover name for Hitler's projected invasion of Britain in 1940.

SEALYHAM. Breed of terrier dog, named after the place in Pembrokeshire where it originated as a cross of the Welsh and Jack Russell terriers.

SEAPLANE. An aeroplane capable of taking off from, and alighting on, water. There are 2 classes, viz. float-planes and flying-boats. The float-plane is similar to a land-plane but has floats in place of wheels; the flying-boat has a hull shaped like a boat, and may also have floats attached to the wing tips. Although Ss. have the advantage of needing no airfield, they depend on smooth water for a good landing and since the S.W.W. have not often been built.

SECOND WORLD WAR. Australians advancing (left), under cover of a smoke-screen, at the crucial Battle of Alamein in July 1942; and (right) Leslie Cole's painting of the 14th army in Burma. In contrast to the dusty heat of the desert, the armed patrol of the Queen's Own (RWK) wade waist-deep in the flooded Sittang bend. *Photos: Courtesy of the Imperial War Museum*

SEARLE (serl), **Ronald** (1920-). British artist. A skilled draughtsman and cartoonist, he is well known for his sketches of places and people, e.g. *Paris Sketch Book* (1950), *Rake's Progress* (1955); and for the creation of the schoolgirls of St Trinian's in 1941, whom he abandoned in 1953.

SEASON, London. Period May-July when the fashionable world was formerly in residence, and when young women originally made their social début (hence, débutantes) by being presented at Court in a special white dress and head-dress of 3 white ostrich feathers (the Prince of Wales' feathers). The latter custom ceased in 1959, and the S. has faded, but débutantes still start their season by appearing as models at the Berkeley Hotel Dress Show in April and by attending a series of parties and social events, such as Ascot and Henley.

SEATTLE (sē-atl'). Port of the state of Washington, USA, situated between Puget Sound and Lake Washington. First settled 1851, as the nearest port for Alaska, S. grew in the late 19th cent. under the impetus of the Gold Rush. In the 20th it has become a major centre for the manufacture of jet aircraft (Boeing), and also has shipbuilding, timber and paper industries. There are 2 univs., Washington (1861) and Seattle (1891). Pop. (1970) 524,263.

SEA URCHINS. Popular name for a class of Echinoderms, marine animals in which the rays are not free as in star fishes, and brittle stars, but united to form a globular, heart-shaped, or shield-shaped and flattened body, enclosed with plates of lime and covered with spines. Sometimes the spines are holding organs, and they also assist in locomotion. S.Us. feed on seaweed and the animals frequenting them, and are edible.

SEAWEED. General name for a vast collection of lower plant-forms that belong to the Algae (q.v.) division of the Thallophyta. They grow from about high-water mark to depths of 1-200m (3-600ft), and are green, blue-green, red or brown. Many have traditionally been gathered for food, e.g. purple laver (*Porphyra vulgaris*), green laver (*Ulva latissima*), and carragheen moss (*Chondrus crispus*). From the 1960-70s, however, Ss. have been farmed, and the alginates extracted are used in convenience foods, ice-cream, animal feed, etc., as well as in toothpaste, soap, and the manufacture of iodine and glass. *See also* KELP.

SEBASTIAN, St. Christian martyr, first shot with arrows and then beaten to death *c.* 288.

SEBA'STOPOL. *See* SEVASTOPOL.

SECOND WORLD WAR. The war of 1939-45 between the United Nations, headed by Britain, the USA, the USSR, France, and China, on the one side, and the Axis powers, Nazi Germany under Hitler, Fascist Italy under Mussolini, and Japan under Hirohito, with their satellites, on the other. The war was preceded by a long series of acts of aggression by the Axis powers: the Japanese conquest of Manchuria (1931), the Italian conquest of Ethiopia (1935-6), German and Italian intervention in the Spanish Civil War (1936-9), the Japanese invasion of China (1937), the German annexation of Austria (March 1938), Sudetenland (Sept. 1938), and Czechoslovakia (March 1939), and the Italian conquest of Albania (April 1939). Britain and France attempted to meet this menace with an 'appeasement' policy, culminating in the Munich agreement (Sept. 1938). The reaction of public opinion to the annexation of Czechoslovakia forced the British and French govts to open negotiations with the USSR for a peace bloc; these broke down in Aug. 1939, when the USSR concluded a non-aggression pact with Germany. On 1 Sept. Germany invaded Poland and, 2 days later Britain and France declared war. By 10 Sept. all the Dominions, except Eire, had also declared war.

The Conquest of Poland and the West 1939–40. Polish resistance speedily collapsed before the German blitzkrieg, although Warsaw held out gallantly until 27 Sept. After the Polish débâcle Russian forces reoccupied the W Ukraine and Byelorussia, which had been annexed by Poland from Russia in 1920. On the W front both sides remained almost completely inactive behind the Maginot and Siegfried lines until May 1940.

A new stage opened on 9 April 1940, with the German invasion of Denmark, which capitulated without resistance, and of Norway. British and French forces were landed to support Norway's resistance, but in June the invasion of France compelled their withdrawal. British dissatisfaction at the conduct of the campaign caused the fall of the Chamberlain govt, which was succeeded on 10 May by a coalition headed by Winston Churchill.

On the same day the Germans invaded the Netherlands, which surrendered on 15 May, and Belgium. German panzer divisions broke through the French line at Sedan and raced to the Channel, thus cutting off the Allied forces which had entered Belgium from the main French forces. The surrender of King Leopold of Belgium on 28 May compelled them to fall back on Dunkirk (q.v.), whence they were evacuated by a hurriedly collected rescue fleet. The French position was rendered hopeless by Italy's declaration of war on 10 June, and an armistice was signed on 22 June, whereby the Germans occupied N France and the W coast. Meanwhile in London the Free French movement was founded by Gen. de Gaulle.

Britain fights alone 1940–1. From Aug.-Oct. the Battle of Britain (q.v.) raged, as the Luftwaffe launched their mass daylight raids; when it ended they had lost nearly 2,000 aircraft destroyed in daylight. Night raids followed, directed first against London, and then against such provincial cities as Coventry, Birmingham, Bristol, Manchester, Liverpool, Plymouth, Glasgow and Hull. In May 1941 the attack subsided, having completely failed to break the resistance of the British people.

The Italians invaded Greece in Oct. 1940, only to be driven back far into Albania. Germany, in order to complete her control of the Balkans, attacked both Greece and Yugoslavia on 6 April 1941, and by 1 May had overrun both and compelled the British forces sent to the assistance of Greece to withdraw. A month later Crete had been invaded and occupied by German parachutists in spite of stubborn resistance by British and Commonwealth troops.

Russia and the USA enter the War 1941–2. A new stage opened on 22 June 1941 when Germany, in alliance with Finland, Hungary, and Rumania, attacked Russia. By Dec. the invaders, standing on a line from Lake Ladoga to the mouth of the Don, were within 40km (25m) of Moscow, and Leningrad was besieged. A Russian counter-offensive in Dec. 1941-March 1942 forced the Germans to retreat along their whole line, but in June they launched a new offensive designed to secure control of the Caucasian oilfields. Sevastopol was stormed, and by Aug. they had reached the Caucasus and were attacking Stalingrad.

Since the Battle of Britain American opinion had inclined ever more strongly, in spite of isolationist opposition, towards Roosevelt's policy of making the USA 'the arsenal of democracy', which was put into operation with the passage of the Lease-Lend Act in March 1941. On 7 Dec. Japan attacked the US naval base at Pearl Harbor, and declared war on Britain and the USA, and 4 days later Germany and Italy declared war on the USA. The war in Europe, and the Sino-Japanese War which had been in progress since 1937, now became 2 aspects of a single world-wide struggle.

Africa and the Near East, 1940–3. The long campaign in N Africa opened in Sept. 1940, with an Italian drive from Libya into Egypt, which reached Sidi Barrāni. Gen. Wavell counter-attacked during Dec. 1940-Feb. 1941, and advanced into Cyrenaica. The withdrawal of troops for the Balkan campaign then weakened his army, while German forces under Rommel were poured into Africa, and during March-April pushed the British back into Egypt. A new offensive by the 8th Army in Nov. 1941-Jan. 1942 drove into Libya, but was halted at Gazala, whence during May-July Rommel launched a counter-offensive which ended 115km (70m) from Alexandria. In Oct.-Nov. Gen. Montgomery, commanding the 8th Army, won a resounding victory at El Alamein, and began a rapid advance westward, while on 8 Nov. large British and US forces under Gen. Eisenhower landed in Morocco and Algeria. Caught between converging armies, the last Axis forces in Africa surrendered in May 1943.

In E Africa the Italians had occupied British Somaliland in Aug. 1940. Forces from Kenya entered Italian Somaliland in Feb. 1941, while Eritrea was invaded from the Sudan. By May the Italian empire in E Africa, incl. Ethiopia, was in British hands, and British Somaliland had been recovered.

The control of the Middle East was of vital importance to the British position in the Mediterranean, and vigorous measures proved necessary to counteract German intrigues in that area. Following the seizure of power by a pro-Axis premier in April 1941 British forces occupied Iraq, and in June Syria, where a pro-Vichy administration held power, was also occupied. In Aug. British and Russian troops entered Persia, where the shah was under German influence, and converted it into an important supply-line to Russia.

Italy 1943–5. Allied forces from N Africa overran Sicily in July-Aug. 1943, and invaded the Italian mainland on 3 Sept. On 25 July Mussolini was overthrown; the new govt signed an armistice on 8 Sept., and declared war on Germany on 13 Oct. Large German forces entered Italy, and put up a stubborn resistance, first on the Gustav Line, S of Rome, and after it was broken in May 1944 on the Gothic Line, from Pisa to Rimini. This in turn was breached in Sept., and after a final Allied offensive in April 1945 the Germans surrendered on 29 April.

Victory in the East 1943–5. The failure of the Germans to capture Stalingrad, together with the victory of El Alamein and the landings in N Africa, marked the turning-point of the war. A Russian offensive in Nov. 1942-March 1943 cleared the Caucasus and drove the Germans back to the Donetz, while at Stalingrad 330,000 of the invaders were killed or captured. A new German drive in July was halted within a week; the Russians then opened an offensive which continued until Nov., and recaptured Kiev and Zhitomir. During Jan.-April 1944 they liberated the Ukraine and entered Rumania. A general offensive in June-Oct. expelled the invaders from Russian soil, forced Finland, Rumania, and Bulgaria out of the war, and entered E Prussia, Poland and Yugoslavia. British forces entered Greece in Oct., and by the end of 1944 the Germans had been expelled from the greater part of the Balkans. Valuable assistance was rendered to the Allies by Tito's partisans, and by the Greek and Albanian resistance movements. A last Russian offensive in Jan.-May 1945 liberated Poland and Austria, entered Czechoslovakia, and reached Berlin.

Victory in the West 1944–5. The way had been prepared for the opening of the 'second front' in the W by Allied mass bombing raids on Germany, which since 1940 had steadily increased in number and size. On 6 June 1944 the invasion was launched, under the supreme command of Gen. Eisenhower. A bridgehead was estab. in NW France between Cherbourg and Le Havre, and after much hard fighting the Americans broke through the German lines at St Lô, and the British at Caen. On 15 Aug. US and Free French troops landed on the Mediterranean coast and advanced rapidly northwards. The people of Paris rose, and compelled the Germans to surrender on 25 Aug. By the end of Sept. the Allies had liberated most of France, and entered Belgium and the Netherlands, but the airborne operation at Arnhem (q.v.) was a failure, and on the German frontier they were halted by the Siegfried

Line. After a temporary set-back caused by Rundstedt's counter-offensive in the Ardennes in Dec., they launched a new offensive in Feb. 1945 which broke the Siegfried Line. In March the Rhine was crossed; the Canadians advanced through the Netherlands, the British into N Germany, the Americans and French into Central and S Germany. On 24 April the Russians entered Berlin, which surrendered on 2 May. On 7 May Germany surrendered unconditionally.

SECOND WORLD WAR. The headquarters of the 'Secret War'. Bletchley Park in Buckinghamshire, England, known as 'Station X', where mathematicians and engineers worked on the German secret codes. The huts to the right housed the special purpose electronic computer Colossus and other code-breaking devices. *Photo: Courtesy of Dominic Flessati*

The War at Sea. In the Atlantic British merchant ships had to contend with German submarines and surface raiders, who from 1940 controlled the coastline from Norway to France. Shipping losses reached their height in 1942; thereafter they declined, as more escort vessels and aircraft became available for convoys. Outstanding engagements in the Atlantic were the battle of the river Plate (13 Dec. 1939), when 3 cruisers badly damaged the *Admiral Graf Spee*; the engagements in Narvik harbour (10 and 13 April 1940); and the sinking of the *Hood* by the *Bismarck* (24 May 1941) and of the *Bismarck* by the *Dorsetshire* (27 May). Italy's entry into the war created a dangerous situation in the Mediterranean until 1943, and Malta, the chief British naval base, suffered continual bombing. A spectacular victory over the Italian fleet was won off Cape Matapan on 28 March 1941. The delivery of vital supplies to Russia via the Arctic Ocean and the Barents Sea was maintained in face of heavy opposition and natural difficulty.

The Japanese War 1941–5. The attack on Pearl Harbor, which put the US Pacific fleet out of action, air raids on the Philippines, and the sinking of the *Prince of Wales* and the *Repulse* on 10 Dec. 1941 temporarily gave the Japanese naval and air supremacy in the Pacific. They immediately overran Malaya from Thailand, where they had estab. bases, and captured Singapore with 60,000 British troops in Feb. 1942. Hong Kong had surrendered on 25 Dec. The conquest of the Philippines was completed by 6 May, when Corregidor fell, although guerilla resistance continued, and that of the Dutch E Indies by 10 March. Burma was also invaded from Thailand, and after the fall of Mandalay in May the British forces there were withdrawn to India. During Jan.-March Japanese troops were landed in New Britian, the Solomons, and New Guinea.

The first Allied successes against the Japanese were the naval victories in the Coral Sea (4-7 May) and off Midway (4-7 June), when US aircraft inflicted heavy losses on Japanese fleets. Another victory followed on 2-5 March 1943, when a Japanese convoy was destroyed in the Bismarck Sea. A successful offensive was launched in New Guinea in Sept. 1942-Jan. 1943, while during Aug. 1942-Feb. 1943 US marines expelled the Japanese from Guadalcanal, in the Solomons. After occupying certain of the Aleutian Is. in June 1942, the Japanese were forced to withdraw in May-Aug. 1943.

From 1943 the command against Japan was divided between Lord Mountbatten in Burma, Admiral Nimitz in the Central Pacific, and Gen. MacArthur in the SW Pacific. A threatened invasion of India was averted in March-June 1944 by Gen. Slim; the reconquest of Burma was begun in Jan. 1945, and was practically completed with the fall of Rangoon in May. In the Central Pacific, the Gilbert, Marshall, and Mariana Islands were seized by the Allies in 1943-4, and in the SW New Guinea was slowly reconquered. In Oct. 1944 the reconquest of the Philippines began, and was completed by July 1945. The seizure of Iwo-Jima in Feb.-March 1945, and of Okinawa in April-June, supplied the necessary bases for the final attack on Japan.

The end came suddenly. An atom bomb was dropped on Hiroshima on 6 Aug., and another on Nagasaki on 9 Aug. Russia declared war on Japan, and invaded Manchuria on 8 Aug. Hirohito announced his acceptance of the Allied terms on 14 Aug., and the formal surrender was signed on 2 Sept.

In the 1970s much information was released on the 'secret war' waged by the Allies in breaking German codes (*see* COMPUTER and ULTRA), and the significance of their successes in this field has yet to be fully assessed.

SECRET AGENT. *See* SECRET SERVICE.

SECRETARIES. Officials of public companies and societies, etc., whose chief professional organizations in Britain are the Chartered Institute of Ss. and the Corporation of Ss.

SECRETARY BIRD. Bird of prey *(Sagittarius secretarius)* native to S Africa, whose erectile crest of feathers bears some fancied resemblance to a pen behind a clerk's ear - hence the name. Mainly grey, with black and white tail feathers, it stands *c.* 120cm (4ft) high, and is officially protected on account of the deadly way in which it hunts poisonous snakes.

SECRETARY OF STATE. Originally the title given under Elizabeth I to 2 officials conducting the royal correspondence. It is now borne by a number of the more important ministries, e.g. the S. of S. for Foreign and Cw. Affairs, etc. In the US the Foreign Minister is called the Secretary of State.

SECRET SERVICE. Govt organization maintained by most countries to keep a check on the activities of foreign agents (counter-espionage) and to secure information from foreign countries relating to activities considered likely to endanger the safety of the state (espionage).

Spies may be (i) citizens sent abroad to work in the interests of their own country; (ii) citizens spying on their own country for the benefit of another; (iii) double spies working simultaneously for their own and another country. The first kind are usually persons of integrity (T. E. Lawrence was a famous British example who worked against the Turks in the Near East during the F.W.W.; another was the German naval capt. Franz von Rintelen (q.v.) who carried out sabotage in the USA on behalf of Germany and against the Allies in the same war); the second kind are traitors to their own country and often work for money but, especially in the 20th cent., may be actuated by a misplaced idealism (e.g. Klaus Fuchs (1911-), a German refugee and brilliant scientist who became a British subject and in 1950 pleaded guilty to having given the Russians the secret of the atom bomb, receiving only £100 for information which only he could supply); the third kind usually work for money, though not always for substantial amounts: the most notorious double spy was probably Colonel Alfred Redl, who while head of espionage in the Austro-Hungarian secret service before the F.W.W. (and very successful in his job) also spied on his own country for Russia, among other things passing to the Russians the Austro-Hungarian mobilization plans in the event of war.

In war-time spies are normally executed, generally after civil or military trial, though in the actual battle area they are likely to be shot out of hand. Among the most notorious war-time spies was Mata Hari (q.v.). In peace-time the punishment of a convicted spy may vary from imprisonment (Fuchs was released in 1959 and went to E Germany) to expulsion. Among the few spies executed in peace-time were Julius Rosenberg (1918-53) and his wife Ethel (1915-53), who were executed at Sing Sing, NY, in 1953 for passing atom bomb secrets to Russia.

The operations of the S.S. depend on codes (in which groups of letters or numbers represent words, sentences, or a definite combination of word sequences) and ciphers, in which a letter (or number) represents another letter. The easier a cipher or code is to use, the easier it is to break, and vice versa. At the time of the Japanese attack on Pearl Harbor, the Americans had broken the code used by the Japanese who, because of the extreme difficulty of basing a code on the Japanese language, were in fact using one based on English. Invisible ink, microfilm records, secretly installed listening and recording apparatus are other adjuncts of the S.S. One method of counter-espionage is to plant false information on known agents of another country - and this false information, having gone the rounds, has been known to deceive the originator on its return home, at least momentarily.

Espionage is age-old, but it was in the later 19th cent. and early 20th that modern departmentalized organization began, in itself a target for infiltration. In Britain the Secret Intelligence Service (SIS), as it was known from 1911, of the Foreign Office, incl. MI6 (MI = Military Intelligence) for the active collection of information and D Dept for sabotage and subversion. The latter was combined 1940-6 with MI/R (R = Research) as the SOE (Special Operations Executive). Counter-espionage was handled by MI5, known from 1945 as the Directorate of Security Service, which has as its executive arm Scotland Yard's Special Branch (1887), under the control of the Home Office. The best-known spies in this field were the Establishment figures Guy Burgess (1911-63) and Donald Maclean (1913-), who operated within the British FO and several depts of the Secret Service until they fled to the Soviet Union in 1951, and tipped off by Kim Philby (q.v.). A 'fourth man' was identified in 1979 as Anthony Blunt (q.v.), and Sir Roger Hollis (1905-73), head of MI5 1956-65, was alleged without confirmation to be a fifth.

The French counter-intelligence organization is the Direction de la surveillance du Territoire (DST) and the W German equivalent is the Bundesamt für Verfassungsschutz (BfV), or Federal Office for the Protection of the Constitution. In the USA the FBI (q.v.) deals with domestic security, and the CIA with overseas intelligence. Russia had an elaborate system of international espionage before the 1917 Revolution, which has since been elaborated internally and externally: *see* KGB.

SECRET SOCIETIES. Societies, often originally founded for religious or mutual benefit motives, which tend to become politically or otherwise corrupt. Most famous are the Chinese, referred to in the USA as tongs (Cantonese pron of *t'ang* 'office'), which led among the Chinese settled in California to open conflicts in the 1850s known as 'tong wars': *see also* TRIAD. Other S.S. are the MAFIA and OPUS DEI (qq.v.).

SECUNDERABA'D. N suburb of Hyderabad city, Andhra Pradesh, India, formerly a separate town. It was founded as a British army cantonment, with a parade ground where 7,000 troops could be exercised. It was by experiments at S. that Sir Ronald Ross estab. that malaria is carried by the anopheles mosquito.

SEDAN (sedoń'). Frontier town on the Meuse, in Ardennes dept, France. In 1870 S. was the scene of Napoleon III's surrender to the Germans. It has textile mills, dyestuffs, and other industrial plants. Its prosperity dates from the days when it was a Huguenot centre. Turenne was b. at S. It was the focal point of the German advance in 1940. Pop. (1975) 25,450.

SEDAN CHAIR (sedan'). Portable vehicle accommodating one person, and carried on 2 poles by 2 bearers. It is said to have been invented at Sedan, was introduced into England during the reign of James I, and was in general use in the 18th cent.

SEDATIVES. Drugs and other measures which calm the nerves and produce a soothing effect. Some have bad side effects, e.g. reserpine (q.v.) produces depression and barbiturates (q.v.) are addictive. Among the most frequently used today are the benzodiazepine derivatives.

SEDDON, Richard John (1845-1906). New Zealand Liberal statesman. B. in Lancs, he emigrated to Australia, and in 1866 to New Zealand. He entered the legislature in 1879 and was PM 1893-1906.

SEDGE. Genus (*Carex*) of perennial grasslike plants, of the Cyperaceae family, that grow for the most part in wet and swampy ground, fens and marshes. Some are used in paper-making.

SEDGEMOOR. Tract of land, formerly marshy, 5km (3m) SE of Bridgwater, in Somerset, England, where in 1685 Monmouth's rebellion was crushed.

SEDITION. In the UK, S. is an offence against the Crown and govt, differing from treason (q.v.) in that it is not capital. Attempts to bring into contempt or hatred the person of the reigning monarch, the govt as lawfully estab., or either house of parl.; or to incite the sovereign's subjects to bring about a change of govt other than by lawful means are Ss. The raising of discontent between different sections of those subjects is also S. In the 18th and 19th cents. it was held by the courts that any criticism of the govt was seditious, and in 1758 John Shebbeare was imprisoned for libelling William III (d. 1702) and George I (d. 1727); this attitude has entirely changed, and it is accepted that any criticism of the govt aimed at reform is allowable. In the USA, under a wartime act of 1917, reinstated 1950, S. is (i) making a false report intended to interfere with the operations of US armed forces or to assist the enemy; (ii) attempting to seduce the armed forces from their allegiance or to obstruct recruiting.

SEE'GER, Pete (1917-). American singer and 'protest' song-writer of the sixties: notably: 'We shall overcome' (1960), 'Where have all the flowers gone?' (1961), and 'Little Boxes' (1962).

SEELAND. The main island of Denmark on which Copenhagen is situated. It is low-lying with an irregular coastline. Dairy farming is the main occupation. Area 7,000 sq.km (2,700 sq.m).

SEFERIS (sefā'ris), **George.** Pseudonym of the Greek poet and diplomat Georgios Seferiades (1900-71). Ambassador to the Lebanon (1953-7) and then to the UK (1957-62), he did much to help resolve the Cyprus crisis. He pub. his first vol. of lyrics in 1931 and his *Collected Poems* in 1950, his work having a deep feeling for the Hellenic world and showing the influence of the French symbolists and of T. S. Eliot, whose *The Waste Land* he trans. into modern Greek. He received a Nobel prize 1963.

SEGŌ'VIA, Andrès (1894-). Spanish guitarist. He estab. the guitar as a serious instrument by his arrangements for it of classical works by Bach, Handel, Scarlatti, etc., and many works have been composed for him by De Falla, Villa-Lobos and others.

SEGŌ'VIA. Town of central Spain, cap. of S. prov., *c.* 65km (40m) NW of Madrid, and famous for its Moorish alcázar, 16th cent. cathedral and Roman aqueduct. Textiles are made. Isabella of Castile was crowned at S. in 1474. Pop. (1970) 34,700.

SEINE (sān). River of France which rises NW of Dijon on the plateau of Langres and flows 674km (481m) in a NW direction, to the English Channel near Le Havre, passing through Paris and Rouen and receiving the Yonne, Marne, Oise, etc.

SEISMOGRAPH. Instrument for recording earth tremors.

SEISMO'LOGY (sīz-). Study of earthquake phenomena. *See* EARTHQUAKE.

SEKHMET. Egyptian goddess of heat and fire. She was represented with the head of a lioness, and worshipped at Memphis as the wife of Ptah.

SEKONDI-TAKORADI (sekundē' takorah'di). Seaport of Ghana: the old port of S. was founded by the Dutch. Takoradi has an artificial harbour opened 1928. Pop. (1970) 161,000.

SELA'NGOR. State of the Fed. of Malaysia, it was under British protection from 1874, and a Federated State 1895-1946. The cap. was transferred to Shah Alam from Kuala Lumpur in 1973. Klang is the seat of the Sultan and a centre for rubber-growing and tin-mining, and Port Klang (formerly Port Swettenham) exports tin. Area 8,202 sq.km (3,167 sq.m); pop. (1970) 1,630,370.

SELBORNE. English village in Hampshire, 8km (5m) SSE of Alton, made famous by *The Natural History of S.* (1789) of Gilbert White (1720-93) who was b. here. The S. Society (founded 1885) promotes the study of wild life.

SE'LBY. Town in N Yorks, England, on the Ouse. The nearby S. coalfield, discovered in 1967, consists of 2,000 million tonnes of pure coal. Pop. (1975) 12,000.

SELDEN, John (1584-1654). English jurist and statesman. B. in Sussex, he was an ardent Parliamentarian and opponent of Divine Right, and wrote legal works. His *Table Talk* (1689) consists of short essays on political and religious questions.

SELĒ'NĒ. Greek moon-goddess, in later times identified with Artemis.

SELĒ'NIUM (Gk *Selene* Moon). Element discovered in 1817 by Berzelius, associated with telurium and the sulphur family, and existing in several allotropic forms, the grey being a conductor of electricity when illuminated and its conductivity increasing markedly with the brightness of the incident light: symbol Se, at. no. 34, at. wt. 78.96. It occurs as selenides and in many sulphide ores, and is used in making red glasses and enamels, and as a semiconductor used extensively in photocells and rectifiers.

SELECT COMMITTEE, House of Commons. Committee incl. members of any party which deal with a particular subject. In 1979 the Thatcher govt. augmented them by 14 new committees covering agriculture; defence; education; science and arts; energy; environment; foreign affairs; home affairs; industry and employment; social services; trade and consumer affairs; transport; Treasury affairs; Scottish affairs; and Welsh affairs. These new committees were intended to restore Parliamentary control of the executive, improve the quality of legislation, and scrutinise public spending and the work of govt. depts. Departmental ministers attend to answer questions and if information is withheld on a matter of wide concern a debate of the whole House may be called. They represent the major parliamentary reform of this cent., and a possible means - through their all-party membership - of avoiding the automatic repeal of one govt.'s measures by its successor.

SELFRIDGE, Harry Gordon (1857-1947). American business man. B. in Wisconsin, USA, he founded in 1909 the Selfridge Store, the first mammoth department store in Britain.

SELKIRK, Alexander (1676-1721). Scottish sailor. While serving in 1704 as a privateer under Dampier he was marooned on Juan Fernandez island, where he remained until rescued in 1709. This episode suggested Defoe's *Robinson Crusoe.*

SELKIRKSHIRE. Former inland co. of Scotland, incl. in 1975 in Borders region. The area is mainly hilly, sheep being grazed, and industries incl. wool and tanning. The chief rivers are the Tweed, Yarrow, and Ettrick. The admin. HQ was Selkirk. Pop. (1971) 5,700.

SELLERS, Peter (1925-80). British comedian and film actor. Specialising in impersonations and disguises, he first made his name in the zany radio *Goon Show* (1949-60). His films incl. *I'm Alright Jack* (1960), *The Millionairess* (1961), *Dr Strangelove* (1964), *The Pink Panther* (1963, as the bumbling Inspector Clouseau), and *Being There* (1980).

SELOUS, (seloo͞'), **Frederick Courtney** (1851-1917). British hunter-explorer. His pioneer journey in modern Zambia/Zimbabwe opened up the country to Europeans, and he fought in the first Matabele War (1893) and was killed in the East African campaign in the FWW.

The **Selous Scouts** were a multi-racial counter-insurgency force in Rhodesia in 1973-80. When it was disbanded many white scouts went to S Africa.

SELWYN LLOYD, (John) Selwyn Lloyd, baron (1904-78). British Cons. politician. For. Sec. 1955-60 during the Suez Crisis, he became Chancellor of the Exchequer in 1960, when he was responsible for the creation of the Nat. Economic Development Council, but the unpopularity of his policy of wage restraint in an attempt to defeat inflation led to his being asked by Macmillan to resign in 1962. He was Speaker 1971-6.

SELZNICK, David Oliver (1902-1965). American film producer. B. at Pittsburgh, he produced for various companies before himself organizing Vanguard Films Inc., Selznick Studio, etc. His productions incl. *King Kong* and *Gone with the Wind.*

SEMA'NTICS. Branch of philology dealing with the changing meaning of words, also known as semasiology.

SEMAPHORE (sem'afor). A signalling apparatus consisting of a post with movable arms, the position of which conveys the message. By night lights are employed. In the army and navy signallers convey messages by their arms with or without the aid of flags.

SEMARA'NG. Indonesian town in Java, cap. of Central Java prov., 435km (270m) SE of Djakarta. Its exposed harbour is not safe in the time of the monsoon. There are shipbuilding yards; exports incl. coffee, teak, sugar, tobacco, kapok, and petroleum from nearby oilfields. Pop. (1971) 646,500.

SE'MELĒ. In Greek mythology, the daughter of Cadmus and mother of Dionysus by Zeus. At Hera's suggestion she demanded that Zeus should appear to her in all his glory, but when he did so she was consumed by lightning.

SEMICONDUCTOR. Crystalline material whose electrical conductivity lies between that of metals and insulators and increases with temperature over a certain range, and in some cases upon illumination. Some common Ss. are germanium, silicon, selenium, cuprous oxide, cadmium sulphide, boron, lead telluride; their most important applications are in transistors and light-sensitive cells.

SEMIPALATI'NSK (semē-). Town in Kazakh SSR, cap. of S. region, on the Irtysh r. Founded 1718 as a Russian frontier post, it has meat-packing factories, tanneries, and flourmills. The region produces nickel and chromium and includes the Kvzyl Kum atomic testing ground. Pop. (1977) 282,000.

SEMI'RAMIS (*c.* 800 BC). Assyrian queen, who was later identified with the goddess Ishtar.

SĒ'MITES. Traditionally, the descendants of Shem, one of the sons of Noah, but in ethnology the name of a number of Caucasian peoples of the Near and Middle East. Most widely distributed are the Jews; closely related to them were the Ammonites, Moabites, and Edomites; also in the ancient world were the Babylonians, Assyrians, Chaldaeans, Carthaginians, Phoenicians, and Canaanites, and in the modern world are the Arabs, Ethiopians, Syrians, etc. Typical features are a whitish skin, black hair, prominent nose, full lips, and dolichocephalic skull. From the Ss. have sprung the great world religions of Judaism, Christianity and Islam.

SEMITIC LANGUAGES. A family of languages consisting of 4 chief divisions: (1) the eastern, including Babylonian and Assyrian; (2) the northern, including Aramaic and its offsprings Palmyrene, Nabataean, Samaritan, etc.; (3) the western, mainly represented by Hebrew and Phoenician (whence Punic); and (4) the southern, with Arabic and its offsprings, also Ethiopic whence Amharic, Tigré, etc., and Sabaean and Minaean.

SEMOLINA (-lē'na). Hard grains of wheat, too coarse to be sieved in the bolting of flour. The food is used in the form of puddings, and also is an integral part of macaroni, etc.

SENANA'YAKE, Don Stephen (1884-1952). Ceylonese statesman. He was first PM of the Dominion 1947-52, and was succeeded in the office by his son **Dudley Shelton S.** (1911-73) 1952-3, 1960, and 1965-70.

SENATE (sen'at). The Roman 'council of elders'. Originally consisting of the heads of patrician families, it was recruited from ex-magistrates and persons who had rendered notable public service, but was periodically purged by the censors. Although nominally advisory, it controlled finance and foreign policy. Under the empire it lost all real power.

The US Senate consists of 100 members, 2 from each state, elected for a 6-year term. The Italian upper chamber is also known as the S., as is that of France under the 5th Republic. The name is also given to the governing bodies in some univs., e.g. Cambridge and London.

SENDAI (sendī'). City in NE Honshu, Japan. Industries incl. metal goods (a Metal Museum was estab. 1975), textiles, pottery and food processing. The city is espec. assoc. with the Tanabata (q.v.) festival, Pop. (1977) 609,000.

SE'NECA, Lucius Annaeus (*c.* 4 BC-AD 65). Roman philosopher. B. at Cordova, he was the son of Seneca the Elder (d. AD 39), author of books on rhetoric. S. was Nero's tutor but after his accession fell into disfavour and committed suicide at Nero's order. He wrote essays on ethical subjects from the Stoic standpoint, and 9 tragedies which in 16th cent. England were accepted as classical models.

SENEFELDER (sā'ne-), **Alois** (1771-1834). German engraver. B. at Prague, he is famous for his discovery in 1796 of the art of lithography.

SENEGAL (senegawl'). River of W Africa, formed by the confluence of the Bafing and the Bakhoy and flowing for 1,125 km (700m) NW and W to reach the Atlantic near St Louis. In 1968 the Organization of Riparian States of the River S. (Guinea, Mali, Mauretania and S.) was formed to develop the river valley, incl. a dam for hydroelectric power and irrigation at Joina Falls in Mali: its HQ is in Dakar. The river gives its name to the **Republic of Senegal** which lies S of the r. with a coastline on the Atlantic. Except on the coast, it surrounds Gambia. Cattle, sheep, goats, pigs, camels and horses are reared; groundnuts, millet, maize are grown. Minerals incl. phosphates, titanium, bauxite and iron ore. The cap. is Dakar. Area 197,000 sq.km (76,000 sq.m); pop. (1976) 5,090,000. M.U.: CFA franc.

The French estab. themselves on the coast of S. early in the 17th cent. and gradually extended their authority inland. Made a colony 1895 and a territory 1946, S. became independent within the Fr. Community 1960. The first pres. was Léopold Senghor (1906-), also a poet and essayist; he was succeeded in 1981 by Abdou Diouf (1936-). A Confederation of Senegambia (*see* GAMBIA) was proclaimed 1982.

SENILE DEMENTIA. *See* DEMENTIA.
SENNA. *See* CASSIA.
SENNACHERIB (sena'kerib) (reigned 705-681 BC). King of Assyria. He crushed revolts in Tyre, Sidon and Babylon, but failed to capture Jerusalem, and was murdered by his sons.
SENNA'R. Town of Sudan Republic on the Blue Nile, *c.* 260km (160m) SE of Khartoum. It is a railway junction, and nearby is the Sennar dam (1926), part of the Gezira irrigation scheme. Pop. *c.* 10,000.
SENS (soṅs). Cathedral town in Yonne dept, France, on the Yonne, famous for its cathedral and old walls. Manufactures incl. chemicals and cutlery. Pop. (1973) 24,600.
SENUSSI (senoo'se), **Sidi Mohammed ben Ali es** (*c.* 1796-1860). Moslem religious reformer. B. in Algeria, he preached a return to the puritanism of early Islam and met with much success in Libya, where he made Jaghbub his centre and founded the sect called after him. The S., who attacked the British during the F.W.W., were subdued by the Italians in 1931, and in the S.W.W. they joined a Libyan Arab Force formed by Britain.
SEOUL (se-ool'). Cap. of S Korea, nr the Han r., and with its port at Inchon. There is a 14th cent. palace, univ., and exhibition centre (1979), and industries incl. engineering, textile, and food processing. Pop. (1980) 8,000,000.
SEPHARDIM (sefah'dim). Jews descended from those expelled from Spain and Portugal in the 15th cent., or from those forcibly converted to Christianity (Marranos) at that time. Many settled in N Africa, and some in other mediterranean countries or in England.
SEPTICAEMIA (-sē'-). Blood poisoning; the invasion of the circulating blood by bacteria, as may occur in bacterial endocarditis. The condition is serious, but made less so by the advent of antibiotics.
SEPTUAGESIMA. The 3rd Sunday before Lent; the 70th day before Easter.
SEPTUAGINT (Lat. *septuaginta*, seventy). Oldest Greek version of the OT, traditionally made by 70 scholars.
SEQUOIA (sekwoi'a). Two genera of conifers in the family Taxodiaceae, native to California, and named after Sequoya (*c.* 1760-1843), the Cherokee Indian who gave his people an 'alphabet' for their language. The redwood (*Sequoia sempervirens*) is a valuable long-lived timber tree, and the Howard Libbey redwood is the world's tallest tree 110 m (362 ft), with a circumference of 13.4 m (44 ft). The big tree (*Sequoiadendron giganteum*) is the largest of living trees, having enormous bulk, up to some 30 m (100 ft) at the base, as well as being almost as tall as the redwood. It is also, except for the bristle cone pine, the oldest, some specimens being known to have lived more than 3,000 years.
SERANG. Alternative form of CERAM.
SERAPHIM (ser'afim). Celestial beings, of a high order of angelic hierarchy, mentioned in Isaiah.
SERĀ'PIS. Graeco-Egyptian god, a combination of Hades and Osiris, invented by the Ptolemies; his finest temple was the Serapeum at Alexandria.
SERBIA. Federal republic of Yugoslavia, including the autonomous areas of Vojvodina and Kossovo (Metohija). It includes the federal cap., Belgrade. In the N are fertile plains watered by the Danube but the S is mountainous. Wheat, maize, fruit, flax, tobacco, and vines are cultivated. Copper, chrome and antimony are mined. Area 88,267 sq.km (34,080 sq.m); pop. (1971) 8,437,000.

History. The Serbs settled in the Balkans in the 7th cent., and accepted Christianity in the 9th. They were united into one kingdom *c.* 1169, and under Stephen Dushan (1331-55) founded an empire covering most of the Balkans. After their defeat at Kossovo (1389) they became tributary to the Turks, who in 1459 annexed S. Uprisings in 1804-16, led by Kara George and Milosh Obrenovich, forced the Turks to recognize S. as an autonomous principality under Milosh. The assassination of Kara George by his orders gave rise to a long feud between the 2 houses. After a war with Turkey in 1876-8 S. became an independent kingdom. On the assassination of the last Obrenovich in 1903 the Karageorgevich dynasty came to the throne. The Balkan Wars of 1912-13 greatly enlarged S.'s territory at the expense of Turkey and Bulgaria. S.'s designs on Bosnia and Herzegovina, backed by Russia, led to friction with Austria, culminating in the outbreak of war in 1914. S. was completely overrun in 1915-16, and was occupied until 1918, when it became the nucleus of the new kingdom of the Serbs, Croats and Slovenes, later Yugoslavia (q.v.). In modern Yugoslavia there is still bitter rivalry between Croats and Serbs, the latter being predominant.
SERFDOM. The legal and economic status of peasants under feudalism (q.v.). The serf was normally bound to the soil; while he could not be sold like a slave, he was not free to leave his lord's estate. He had to give a certain number of days' unpaid labour every week on his lord's land, in addition to extra labour at harvest time and other busy seasons, and to pay tribute in kind; in return he was allowed to cultivate a portion of the estate for his own benefit. In England S. died out during the 14th-17th cents., but it lingered on in France until 1789, in Russia until 1861, and in most European countries until the early 19th cent.
SERGIUS OF RADONEZH, St (1314/19-1392). Russian saint, founder of the monastery of the Blessed Trinity in the forest near Radonezh. Prior from 1334, he personified the Russian monastic ideal, and besides acting as mediator among Russian feudal princes, inspired Dmitri's victory over the Tartars at Kulikovo.
SERIALISM. *See* DUNNE, JOHN WILLIAM.
SERINGAPATA'M. Town in Karnataka, Rep. of India, on an is. in the Cauvery r. It was the cap. of Mysore State 1610-1799, when it was taken from Tippoo Sahib (who d. of wounds) by Cornwallis.
SERPENT. *See* SNAKE.
SERPENTINE. A mineral, hydrated magnesium silicate, occurring usually in soft rocks. The green mottled appearance resembles that of a serpent. The rare precious S. is used for ornamentation. Fibrous varieties are known as asbestos (q.v.) and chrysotile.
SERPENT MOUND, Great. Embankment up to 4 ft in height, 1,330 ft from jaw to tail and 15-20 ft across, created by Hopewell Indians in Ohio, USA, about 1st-2nd cents. AD.
SĒ'RUM. (1) The clear part of the blood left after clotting and removal of blood corpuscles and fibrin; and the exudate in blisters. It contains the substances which protect against disease (antibodies), and also other proteins; as well as the fats and sugars of the blood. (2) The fluid which lubricates the peritoneum, pleura and other body cavities not open to the air.

SERVAN-SCHREIBER (sārvaṅ-shrībėr'), **Jean Jacques** (1924-). French Radical politician. He created a furore with his *Le Défi americain* (1967), maintaining that US economic and technological dominance would be challenged only by a united left-wing Europe. Pres. of the Radical Party 1971-75, and from 1977.

SERVĒ'TUS, Michael (1511-53). Spanish theologian. B. in Navarre, he practised medicine at Vienne. In his theological writings he put forward unitarian and Anabaptist views, for which he was persecuted by the Inquisition at Lyons, and burned alive by Calvin at Geneva.

SERVICE, Robert William (1874-1938). Anglo-Canadian author. B. in Preston, he emigrated to Canada at 20, and achieved great popularity with ballads of the Yukon in gold-rush days, e.g. 'The Shooting of Dan McGrew'.

SERVICE TREE. Tree *Sorbus domestica* of the Rosaceae, found in Europe and Asia. It has pinnate leaves and small oval fruit. The wild S.T. (*Sorbus torminalis*) is a native of Britain.

SERVO SYSTEM. An automatic control system in which the output follows the input in a desired way, and incorporating a feedback to the input derived from the difference between the actual and the desired output.

SESAME (ses'amē). Annual plant (*Sesamum indicum*) of the family Pedaliaceae, which originated in the East. The Indian variety (*S. orientale*) produces oily seeds used for food and soap making.

SESSION, Court of. *See* COURT OF SESSION.

SESSIONS, Roger (1896–1985). American composer. He studied under Bloch, became prof. of music at California 1945-53 and at Princeton 1953-65. His works incl. chamber music, symphonies, and the spectacular opera *Montezuma* (1941-62).

SET. Egyptian god of night, the desert, and of all evils; he was the murderer of Osiris, and is portrayed as a grotesque animal.

SÈTE (set). Seaport on the Mediterranean coast of France, in Hérault dept, SW of Montpellier. A fishing centre, it has sardine canneries and trades in wine, brandy, chemicals, etc. It was founded in 1666 as an outlet to the Canal du Midi. Pop. (1975) 53,500.

SETŌ INLAND SEA. Japanese sea surrounded by Honshu, Shikoku and Kyushu. It is a transport artery, but also of great beauty, with some 3,000 islands, and a Nat. Park. Fish farming is carried on.

SĒ'TON, Elizabeth (1774-1821). First RC saint of the USA. A convert from Protestantism and wife of a wealthy Wall Street merchant, she founded in Maryland the Sisters of Charity of St Joseph (modern dress and working in social welfare programmes, schools and prisons). She was canonized in 1975.

SETON, Ernest Thompson (1860-1946). British author, whose name was originally Ernest S. Thompson. B. in England, he was brought up in Canada, became noted for his animal drawings and books.

SETTER. Breed of dogs, so called because they are trained in crouching or 'setting' on the sight of game to be pursued. The English S. may be black, tan, or liver and white; the Scottish S. is of a much heavier type; and the Irish S. is usually a rich red.

SETTLEMENT, Act of. Act passed in 1701 confining the succession to the throne of Great Britain to Protestants, and settling the succession, after William III and Anne, on the house of Hanover.

SEURAT (sörah'), **Georges** (1859-91). French artist. B. in Paris, he introduced with Signac the technique of Pointillism (q.v.), an outstanding example of his work being 'La Baignarde' (Tate Gallery).

SEVASTOPOL (sēvast'opol). Port and fortress in the Crimea, Ukraine SSR, base of the Russian Black Sea fleet and a seaside resort, with shipbuilding yards and a wine-making industry. S. was founded by Catherine II in 1784. The fortress was besieged by the English and French Oct. 1854-Sept. 1855 before S. fell; the Germans took it after a siege from Nov. 1941-4 July 1942; the Russians re-took it in 1944. Pop. (1977) 283,000.

SEVENOAKS. Town in Kent, England, 32km (20m) SE of London. Nearby are the 17th cent. houses of Knole, given to the Nat. Trust by the 4th baron Sackville in 1946, and Chevening (q.v.). Pop. (1972) 18,000.

SEVENTH DAY ADVENTISTS. Religious sect having its main following in America, whose distinctive tenet is that Saturday is the Sabbath.

SEVEN WEEKS WAR. War in 1866 between Austria and Prussia, engineered by Bismarck over the Schleswig-Holstein question. The Battle of Sadowa was the culmination of von Moltke's victories. By the Treaty of Prague, Prussia took both Holstein, previously seized by Austria, and Schleswig.

SEVEN WONDERS OF THE WORLD. In antiquity, the pyramids of Egypt; the hanging gardens at Babylon; the temple of Artemis at Ephesus; the statue of Zeus at Olympia; the mausoleum at Halicarnassus; the Colossus of Rhodes; and the Pharos (lighthouse) at Alexandria.

SEVEN YEARS' WAR. The war of 1756-63 between Britain and Prussia on the one hand, and France, Austria, and Russia on the other. Its military interest centres on the successful struggle of Frederick II of Prussia against great odds. Britain's part in the war, under the direction of Chatham, was mainly confined to operations at sea, notably the victory of Quiberon Bay (1759), and in the colonies. The victories of Wolfe and Clive resulted in the conquest of Canada and the foundation of the Indian empire.

SEVERE COMBINED IMMUNE DEFICIENCY. Rare condition (SCID) in which a baby is born without the body's normal defences against infection, and must be kept within a transparent plastic tent until a matched donor can provide a bone marrow transplant. In the USA cells from an aborted foetus are used.

SEVERN. River of Wales and England, 338km (210m). It rises in N Wales on the NE side of Plynlimmon, and flows through Shrewsbury, Worcester and Gloucester to the Bristol Channel. It is famous for its bore (2m/6ft tidal wave): S England and S Wales are linked nr Chepstow by a rail tunnel (1873-85) and road bridge (1966). A barrage has been proposed (seaward of Cardiff and Weston-super-Mare) which would provide electric power, improve dock developments in Cardiff, Bristol, etc.

SEVE'RUS, Lucius Septimius (146-211). Roman emperor. B. in N Africa, he held a command on the Danube when in 193 the emperor Pertinax was murdered. Proclaimed emperor by his troops, S. proved an able administrator. He d. at York while campaigning against the Caledonians.

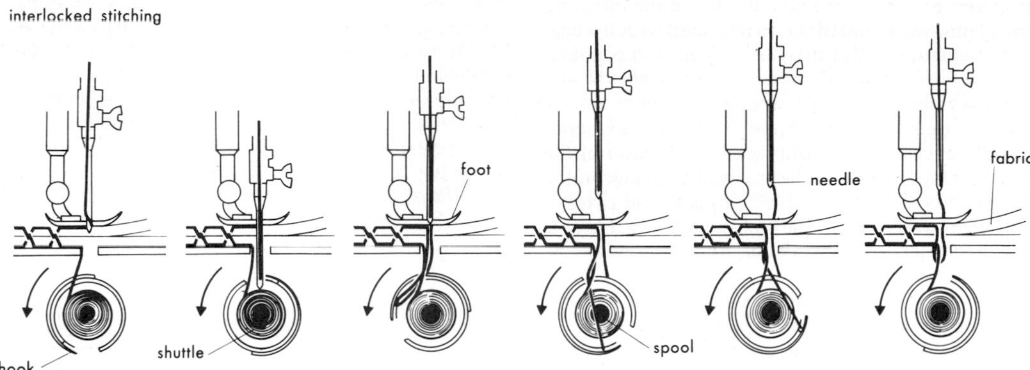

SEWING MACHINE. The making of a 'lockstitch' which prevents the threads pulling apart, and produces a uniform appearance on both sides of the material.

SEVESO (sevā'sō). Town in Lombardy, Italy, site of a factory manufacturing the herbicide hexachlorophine. In 1976 one of the byproducts escaped in a cloud with disastrous contamination of the area, resulting in severe chloracne and deformed births.

SÉVIGNÉ (savenyā), **Marie de Rabutin-Chantal,** marquise de (1626-96), French letter-writer. B. in Paris, in her letters to her dau., the comtesse de Grignan, she gives a vivid picture of contemporary customs and events.

SEVILLE (sev'il). City of Spain (*Sevilla*), on the Guadalquivir 96km (60m) N of Cadiz. Once the centre of a Moorish kingdom, it is famous for the Alcázar, 15th-16th cent. cathedral, church of La Caridad, univ. (1502), and museum. Machinery, spirits, porcelain, silk, and tobacco are made. Pop. (1970) 548,000.

SEVILLE. The art treasures of its museums and the intricate beauty of its architecture, which owes much to Moorish influence, render Seville one of the most interesting cities in Europe. *Photo: Mireille Vautier*

SÈVRE. Name of 2 French rivers from which the dept of Deux Sèvres takes its name. The S Nantaise joins the Loire at Nantes; the S Niortaise flows into the Bay of Biscay.

SÈVRES (sāvr). *See* ST. CLOUD.

SEWAGE DISPOSAL. Sewage - the waste products and refuse from houses, factories, establishments of every kind, streets, etc. - is conveyed through sewers and subjected to purification before being discharged into rivers or the sea. S. works are the responsibility of local authorities. The sludge may be spread over fields attached to the works, or it may be processed and sold as a fertilizer. In places near the coast, raw S. may be flowed or dumped into the sea. The use of S. (as long practised in China), or of sludge, as a fertilizer, has the drawback that the virus of polio and other diseases may survive in the soil and be taken into the body by consumption of subsequent crops.

SEWELL, Anna (1820-78). British author, known for her story of a horse, *Black Beauty* (1877).

SEWING MACHINE. Apparatus for the mechanical sewing of cloth, leather, etc., by a needle, powered by hand, treadle, or belted electric motor. Among early inventors was the Englishman Thomas Saint in 1790. The popular modern lockstitch machine, using a double thread, was invented independently in America by both Walter Hunt (1834) and Elias Howe (1846). Howe's machine was the basis of the machine patented in 1851 by the American Isaac Singer (1811-75). In the Singer microprocessor-controlled S.M., any of 25 different stitching patterns can be selected by pushbutton, and buttonholes, etc., are produced automatically. *See also* ULTRASONICS.

SEX and REPRODUCTION. S. may be defined as the distinction between male and female that forms the basis of sexual reproduction. Amongst the more lowly organisms, and even in some insects, reproduction is a process in which S. may have no part. S. only appears as an essential to reproduction much higher up in the evolutionary scale, and sexual union may be looked upon as being a method of pooling the germ plasm of 2 different lines of descent, thus providing a far greater number of useful mutations. In the higher animals the sexual union of male and female is necesary for the appearance of new life.

Amongst mammals the ova, or egg-cells, are all alike, but the sperms are of 2 kinds, and the sex of the offspring will depend on which kind of sperm has fused with the egg-cell. Sexual characteristics may be divided into primary, i.e. the genital organs and the primary sexual glands, and secondary, which incl. in the woman the more roomy pelvis and the more even distribution of the subcutaneous fat, and differences in the quality and distribution of the hair. The development of the larynx is also greater in the male. At puberty there are marked physical and psychological changes in the body. The emotion of sexual love is aroused or accompanied by visual, auditory, olfactory, and tactile impressions.

Reproduction. The end to which the sexual act is directed is the production of a new individual through the union of an ovum and a spermatozoon. A spermatozoon is about 0.05mm ($\frac{1}{500}$ in) long and consists of a rounded head, a tail by means of which it propels itself, and a middle or connecting piece. In a cubic centimetre of fertile human semen more than a hundred million spermatozoa may be present. The female gamete, or ovum, very much larger than the spermatozoon, is a spherical nucleated cell surrounded by a transparent capsule. The ova are developed in round collections of cells, known as Graffian follicles, which are scattered throughout the substance of the ovary. As these follicles become mature they slowly approach the surface of the ovary and each month one ruptures, discharging its contained ovum into the trumpet-shaped end of the Fallopian tube. This act of ovulation usually occurs about midway between 2 successive menstruations. If intercourse has taken place about the time of ovulation, one of the spermatozoa may succeed in reaching the ovum during its passage along the Fallopian tube. It burrows into the capsule of the ovum and its nucleus unites with that of the ovum. A single nucleus is thus formed, half of the chromosomes being derived from the mother and half from the father. The oosperm (the product of this fusion) then begins rapidly to divide, and by the end of the 5th week the rudiments of all the more important organs of the embryo have been laid down. When pregnancy has lasted approximately 280 days the act of parturition begins. *See* CHILDBIRTH.

The beginning of the reproductive life of a woman is marked by the first appearance of the menstrual flow, and its end by the menopause and the cessation of this flow between the ages of 35 and 55. A man may be able to beget children to a very advanced age.

SE'XTANT. An instrument, invented by John Hadley in 1730, used in navigating and surveying, to measure the Sun's altitude at noon and the angular distances between objects. It has 2 mirrors, one half-silvered, the other rotatable, to coincide the direct vision of an object with a reflected image, the angle being read on to a graduated vernier scale.

SEYCHELLES (sāshel'). Group of *c.* 100 islands in the Indian Ocean to the NE of Madagascar. The chief products are copra, vanilla, cinnamon, patchouli and guano. The cap. is Victoria, pop. 14,500, on the largest is. Mahé, which is used by the USA for tracking and telemetry facilities; the second largest is. is Praslin, famous for its double coconuts. Tourism is being developed.

Colonized by the French in the mid-17th cent., the S. were seized by the British in 1794, made a dependency of Mauritius in 1810, and a separate crown colony in 1903. Independence, as a republic within the Commonwealth, was achieved in 1976, and the is. of Aldabra, Farquhar and Desroches, detached in 1965 to form part of the British Indian Ocean Terr., were returned to the Seychelles. Following a left-wing coup in 1977, a new constitution was adopted under which the S. became a socialist one-party state. There is a pres., France Albert René, elected for 5 years, and a Nat. Assembly. Area 277 sq.km (107 sq.m); pop. (1980) 65,000. English and (from 1976) French are official languages, and Creole is spoken. M.U.: S. rupee. *See* BRITISH INDIAN OCEAN TERRITORY.

SEYCHELLES. Coconut palms along the shoreline of the islands. *Photo: Heather Angel*

SEYMOUR, Jane (*c.* 1509-37). Third wife of Henry VIII, whom she m. in 1536. She d. soon after the birth of her son (Edward VI).

SFAX (sfahks). A port of Tunisia, N Africa, cap. of S. dist., on the Gulf of Gabès, *c.* 240km (150m) SSE of Tunis. S. exports phosphates, olive oil, dates, almonds, esparto grass, and sponges. It has an airport and makes leather, soap, carpets, etc.; there are also salt works, and phosphate workings nearby. A Phoenician and later a Roman colony, S. was occupied by the French in 1881. Pop. (1980) 500,000.

SFORZA. Name of a famous Italian family who held the duchy of Milan 1450-99 and 1522-35. Their court was a centre of Renaissance culture, **Ludovico S.** (1451-1508) being famous as the patron of Leonardo da Vinci and other artists.

's GRAVENHAGE. *See* HAGUE, THE.

SHAANXI (shänshē'). Prov. (formerly Shensi) of NW China, S of the Great Wall. It is mountainous, and the Huang He valley forming the NE boundary of the prov. is an important commercial route: its tributary the Wei He crosses the province. Grain, cotton and tobacco are grown, livestock reared, and minerals incl. coal, iron, salt, gold, nickel and oil. The cap. is Zian: *see also* YAN'AN. Area 195,800 sq.km (75,579 sq.m); pop. (1979) 27,000,000.

SHABA (sha'ba). Region (known before 1972 as Katanga) in Zaïre, the name being Swahili 'copper'. It incl. some of the world's richest copper reserves, as well as uranium and other minerals. Kolwezi is the chief mining town. There was an unsuccessful attempt at secession by K. 1960-3 under Moise Tshombe (1919-69), PM of the Congo (now Zaïre) 1964-5.

SHACKLETON, Sir Ernest (1874-1922). British Antarctic explorer. B. in co. Kildare, Ireland, he was a member of Scott's Antarctic expedition of 1901-4. In 1907-9 he commanded an expedition which reached 88° 23′ S lat., and next commanded the expedition of 1914-16 when he had to abandon his ship, the *Endurance*, in the Weddell Sea. He d. on board the *Quest* on another expedition to the Antarctic.

SHAD. A food-fish (*Alosa*) of the herring family. *A. alosa*, the allice, and *A. finta*, the twaite, are the Brit. species.

SHADWELL, Thomas (1642-92). English dramatist and poet. His plays incl. *Epsom Wells* and *Bury Fair.* He was involved in a violent feud with Dryden whom he attacked in 'The Medal of John Bayes' (1682) and succeeded as poet laureate.

S.H.A.E.F. Abbreviated form of the Supreme Headquarters Allied Expeditionary Force which came into being on 15 Feb. 1944, at Norfolk House, St James's Square, London. In March 1944 it was moved to Bushy Park, near Kingston upon Thames, where the final plans for the Allied invasion of Europe were worked out. The Supreme Commander was General Dwight D. Eisenhower.

SHAFFER, Peter (1926-). British playwright. Ed. at St Paul's School, London and Trinity Coll., Cambridge, he combined journalism as a literary and music critic with his work as a dramatist, which incl. *Five Finger Exercise* (1958), *The Royal Hunt of the Sun* (1964) and *Equus* (1973), which deals with the psychiatric treatment of a boy who has blinded 6 horses.

SHAFTESBURY, Anthony Ashley Cooper, 1st earl of (1621-83). English Whig statesman. B. in Dorset, he served in the Civil War first on the royalist and later on the parliamentary side, supported the Restoration, and received a barony in 1661 and an earldom in 1672, when he became Lord Chancellor. In 1673, he went into opposition, and began to organize the Whig Party. He led the agitation for the exclusion of the duke of York from the succession, and in 1679 secured the passage of the Habeas Corpus Act. Accused of treason in 1681, he fled to Amsterdam, where he d.

SHAFTESBURY, Anthony Ashley Cooper, 3rd earl of (1671-1713). English philosopher, author of *Characteristics* (1711) and other ethical speculations.

SHAFTESBURY, Anthony Ashley Cooper, 7th earl of (1801-85). British philanthropical statesman. He entered parliament as a Tory in 1826, and succeeded to the title in 1851. He strongly supported the Ten-Hours' Act of 1847 and other factory legislation, and was largely responsible for the Act of 1842 forbidding the employment of women and children underground in mines. He was associated with the movement for the establishment of 'ragged' schools for the poor.

SHAFTESBURY. English market town in Dorset, 30km (19m) SW of Salisbury. Alfred is said to have founded an abbey on the site in 880; Canute d. at S. in 1035. It is an important agricultural centre. Pop. (1972) 4,000.

SHAG. *See* CORMORANT.

SHAH Traditional title of the rulers of ancient Persia, meaning 'king', and also used by recent rulers of Iran (*See* PAHLAVI DYNASTY). More formally, the title is Shahanshah 'King of Kings'.

SHAH. The Shah of Iran and Queen Farah leaving the Parliament building in Tehran in 1963. The Queen's presence marked the granting of votes to women, and was the first occasion in Iranian history when a queen had attended the Majlis. *Photo: Camera Press*

SHAH-JEHA'N (1592-1666). Mogul emperor of India from 1627, when he succeeded his father Jehangir. He warred successfully in the Deccan, but was not so fortunate in his campaigns against the Persians. From 1658 he was a prisoner of his son Aurungzebe.

SHAHN, Ben (1898-1969). American artist. B. in Lithuania, he was taken to the US as a child. His work has a sharp photographic realism, and shows an interest in social issues, e.g. his series on Dreyfus, Sacco and Vanzetti and Prohibition; and as a mural artist he worked at Radio City (with Diego Rivera) and the Federal Security Building 1940-2.

SHAKERS. Popular name for the Christian sect of the United Society of Believers in Christ's Second Appearing, founded by James and Jane Wardley in England about 1747, and carried into N America in 1774 by Ann Lee (1736-84), the wife of a Manchester blacksmith. The name was applied because of the ecstatic shakings of the sectaries in their worship. They anticipated modern spiritualist beliefs, and, mainly owing to their doctrine of celibacy, their membership eventually shrank.

SHAKESPEARE, William (1564-1616). English dramatist and poet. B. at Stratford-on-Avon, he was the son of John S., a prosperous wool-dealer, and after an education at Stratford grammar school may have become a schoolmaster. In 1582 he m. Anne Hathaway, who bore him 3 children. Having joined a company of players, probably Leicester's, by 1589 he was estab. in London as a playwright. His earliest plays, written *c.* 1589-93, were the tragedy *Titus Andronicus,* the comedies *The Comedy of Errors, The Taming of the Shrew,* and *Two Gentlemen of Verona*, the 3 parts of *Henry VI,* and *Richard III.* The earl of Southampton became his patron *c.* 1593; S. dedicated to him his poems *Venus and Adonis* (1593) and *Lucrece* (1594), and wrote *Love's Labour's Lost,* satirizing Raleigh's circle, for his amusement. Southampton seems to be the man addressed in S.'s sonnets (written *c.* 1593-6).

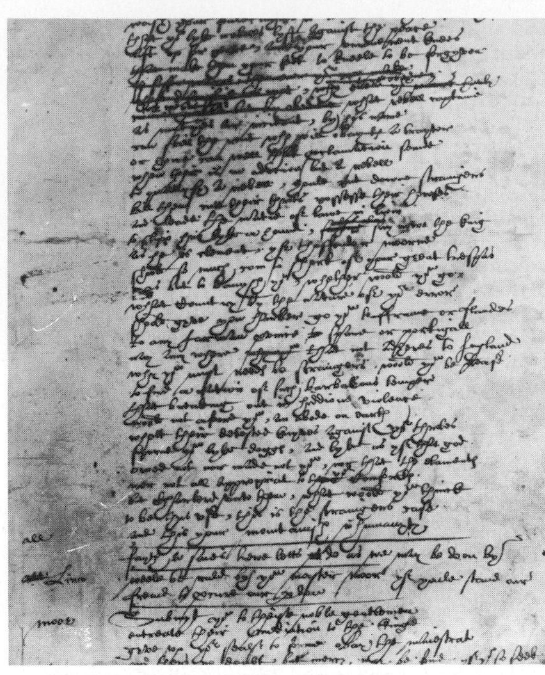

SHAKESPEARE. A miniature by George Vertue (1684–1756) derived from the Chandos portrait, and rediscovered in 1963; and part of a page of Anthony Munday's play *The Booke of Sir Thomas More*, which was revised and enlarged by several other hands. This particular passage is said to be in the autograph of Shakespeare. *Photos: Courtesy of Lois Avery Gaeta of Wyckhoff, New Jersey, and the British Museum*

There has also been speculation as to the identity of the 'Dark Lady' of the Sonnets: *see* ROWSE, A.L.

From 1594 onwards S. was a member of the Chamberlain's (later the King's) company of players. During 1593-8 he had no serious rival as a dramatist, and prospered sufficiently to buy a coat of arms in 1596, and New Place, Stratford, in 1597. Three plays containing a strong lyrical element - *Romeo and Juliet, Midsummer Night's Dream,* and *Richard II* - appeared 1594-5, and were followed by *King John* and *The Merchant of Venice* in 1596. The Falstaff plays of 1597-9 - *Henry IV* (parts I and II), *Henry V,* and *The Merry Wives of Windsor* - brought his popularity to its height. About the same time he collaborated in *Sir Thomas More,* and wrote *Julius Caesar* (1599). Three romantic comedies, unparalleled in their combination of wit and lyricism - *Much Ado about Nothing, As You Like It,* and *Twelfth Night* (*c.* 1598-1601) - brought this predominantly comic period to an end.

The plays which followed, beginning in 1601 with *Hamlet,* show an obsession with the darker side of human nature. The 'dark' comedies *Troilus and Cressida, All's Well that Ends Well,* and *Measure for Measure* (*c.* 1601-4) are bitter and cynical. *Othello, Macbeth,* and *King Lear* followed 1604-6, together with *Timon of Athens,* in which S.'s pessimism reaches its depths. The last 2 tragedies, *Antony and Cleopatra* and *Coriolanus* (*c.* 1607-8), show a striking reaction towards a calmer acceptance of life.

The final group of plays, *Pericles* (which is only partly S.'s), *Cymbeline, The Winter's Tale,* and *The Tempest* (*c.* 1608-11), have many features in common; all but the first are in Fletcher's manner, and were written for an aristocratic audience. During 1613 S. collaborated with Fletcher in *Henry VIII,* and probably in *Two Noble Kinsmen* and the lost *Cardenio.* His last years were spent in Stratford, where he d. on 23 April 1616, and was buried in the parish church. A collected edition of his plays (the 1st Folio) was pub. by 2 of his fellow-actors, Heminge and Condell, in 1623. The only authentic portraits are that in the 1st Folio and the bust on his tomb.

SHALLO'T. A plant (*Allium ascalonicum*) allied to the onion. Its bulbous roots are used in pickles.

SHALMANĒ'SER. Name of 5 Assyrian kings. **Shalmaneser III** (reigned 859-824 BC) pursued an aggressive policy, and made Babylon and Israel tributary to Assyria.

SHAMANISM (shah'manizm). Name (possibly derived from the Hindustani *shaman,* an idolater) applied to the religious beliefs and practices of the aboriginal tribes of N Asia, and by extension other similar systems, espec. among the N American Indians. The outstanding figure is the *shaman,* or medicine-man, a seer and sorcerer, who is believed to make contact with spirits of good and evil.

SHAMIR, Yitzhak (1915–). Israeli statesman. Polish-born, and a leader of the Stern Gang terrorists under the Mandate, he was For. Min. under Begin from 1980, and in 1983 succeeded him as PM.

SHAMROCK. Name given to several trifoliate plants of family Leguminosae. One is said to have been used by St Patrick to illustrate the doctrine of the Holy Trinity, and it was made the national badge of Ireland.

SHAMYL (shahmil') (*c.* 1797-1871). Caucasian soldier. He led the tribesmen of Daghestan in a fight for independence from Russia from 1834 until, when the

Russians were able to deploy greater forces after the Crimean War, he was taken in 1859. His not-too-rigorous captivity in Russia ended with his death at Medina on pilgrimage to Mecca. The official Russian attitude to his campaigns varies according to whether local nationalism is at the moment being encouraged or repressed.

SHANDONG (shahndawng'). Heavily populated maritime prov. of E China, incl. S. peninsula. It is crossed by the Huang He and Grand Canal. Crops incl. cotton, tobacco, wheat, barley and vines, and wild silk is spun. Minerals incl. coal, iron, oil, gold and kaolin. The cap. is Jinan. Ports incl. Yantai, Weihai, Qingdao, and Shigiusuo - being constructed with Japanese aid in 1980. Area 153,300 sq.km (59,170 sq.m); pop. (1979) 70,000,000.

SHANGHAI (shahnghī'). Great port within Jiangsu prov., China, on the Huang-pu 24km (15m) from its entry into the Chang Jiang estuary. A city from 1360, it became important only after 1842 when the treaty of Nanking opened it to foreign trade and an important international settlement developed which remained the commercial centre of the city after extra-territorial rights were given up by the powers, 1943-6. Industries incl. manufacture of textiles, paper, chemicals, steel, agricultural machinery, precision instrument; shipbuilding, flour and vegetable-oil milling, petroleum refining. The port handles *c.* 50 per cent of China's imports and exports. S., a special municipality, is second only to Peking in size. Area 5,800 sq.km (2,240 sq.m); pop. (1980) 12,000,000.

SHA'NKAR, Ravi (1920-). Indian composer-musician. A virtuoso of the sitar, he has composed film music, etc., and founded music schools in Bombay and Los Angeles.

SHANNON. Longest river in Ireland. Rising in co. Cavan, it flows through Loughs Allen and Ree and past Athlone, and reaches the Atlantic through an extensive estuary below Limerick. Famous for salmon, it is also the major source of electric power in the rep., works for which were constructed 1924-30 at and above Ardnacrusha, 5km (3m) N of Limerick.

SHANNON AIRPORT. Transatlantic airport on the r. Shannon in co. Clare, Irish Republic. Its Irish name is Rineanna.

SHANS. Name given to tribesfolk who live in the mountainous borderlands between China, Thailand, and Burma. They are akin to the Laos and the Thais. 41 semi-dependent states in the N of Burma are called the Shan States; they were annexed by Britain in 1885, and now form part of the Burmese Union. Area 149,740 sq.km (57,815 sq.m).

SHANSI. *See* SHANXI.

SHANTUNG. *See* SHANDONG.

SHANXI (shahnshē'). Prov. (formerly Shansi) of N China, partly surrounded by the older section of the Great Wall (246-209 BC). It forms a loess-covered plateau, rising in the N to 1,500 m (5,000 ft). Cotton, tobacco, wheat, barley and grapes are grown, and minerals incl. bituminous coal, iron and salt. The cap. is Taiyuan. Area 157,100 sq.km (60,640 sq.m); pop. (1979) 23,000,000.

SHAPI'RO, Karl (1913-). American poet. B. at Baltimore, he first attracted attention in 1934 with 5 poems under the title 'Noun', and after services in the S.W.W. wrote the striking *V Letter* (1945). He ed. *Poetry* (1950-5) and *Prairie Schooner* 1956-63.

SHARE. In finance, that part of the capital of a company held by a member (shareholder). Shares may be numbered and are issued as units of definite face value; shareholders are not always called on to pay the full face value of their shares, though they bind themselves to do so if called upon. Preference shares carry a fixed rate of dividend and have first claim on the profits of the company; ordinary shares have second claim, and if profits have been good may attract a higher dividend than the preference shares; deferred shares rank for dividend only after the rights of preference and ordinary shareholders have been satisfied. Fully paid-up shares can be converted by the company into stock (q.v.).

SHARIA. *See* ISLAM.

SHAR'JAH. One of the United Arab Emirates, on the Arabian Gulf NE of Dubai: from 1952 incl. Kalba. In 1974 oil was discovered offshore. The cap., also S., has a newly constructed port. Pop. (1980) 125,000.

SHARKS. Name given to the bigger members of the order Pleurotremata, a large group of marine fish with cartilaginous skeletons. Worldwide in distribution, they incl. the 'maneater' white S. (*Carcharodon carcharias*) of tropical waters, which reaches about 12m (40ft), the basking S. (*Cetorhinus maximus*) of temperate seas, found off Britain, which reaches a similar size, but eats only marine organisms, and the equally harmless whale S. (*Rhincodon typus*) which at 18m (60ft) is the largest living fish. Superbly designed as hunters, Ss. have high-speed manoeuvrability. Their eyes, though lacking acuity of vision or sense of colour, are highly sensitive to light; sounds or movements made by their prey are picked up at long distances; their sense of smell is so acute that one-third of the brain is given up to interpreting its signals and the slightest trace of blood in water will attract them; it has recently been discovered that they have special organs, particularly round the mouth, to alert them to the magnetic field created by another fish. Relatively few attacks on man are pursued to a fatal conclusion, and research suggests that they are not in search of food, but attempting to repel 'rivals' from their territory. The liver forms the organ of balance, and their habit of swallowing miscellaneous heavy objects may represent a taking on of ballast to correct some defect in its action. Game fishing for 'sport', the eradication of Ss. in swimming and recreation areas, and their industrial exploitation as a source of leather, oil and protein have reduced their numbers. *See* DOGFISH.

SHĀ'RON. Coastal plain in Israel between Haifa and Tel Aviv, noted since ancient times for its fertility.

SHARP, Cecil (1859-1924). British collector of folk song. B. in London, he travelled the country to record and so save from extinction the folk-song tradition, e.g. *English Folk Song* (1921: 2 vols.), and when in the USA tracked down survivals of English song in the Appalachians, etc. Cecil Sharp House, the HQ in London of the English Folk Song and Folk Dance Society, commemorates his work. More recently he has been criticized for conventionalizing more earthy originals.

SHARP, Granville (1735-1813). British philanthropist. B. at Durham, he was prominent in the anti-slavery movement, and in 1772 secured a legal decision 'that as soon as any slave sets foot on English territory he becomes free'.

SHARP, William (1855-1905). Scottish author. B. in Paisley, he wrote literary criticism, poetry, and novels under his own name, but is best remembered for his mystic romances, e.g. *The Mountain Lovers* (1895); and plays,

SHARKS. A great white shark rises to bait, well illustrating the terror it inspires. However, modern theory suggests that most shark attacks on man are made less in search of food than in an attempt to repel an imagined invasion of territory. *Photo: Ron Taylor/Ardea*

e.g. *The Immortal Hour* (1900), written under the pseudonym Fiona Macleod.

SHARPEVILLE. Town of the Rep. of S Africa, north of Vereeniging. On 21 March 1960 a crowd of black S Africans, variously est. at 5-20,000, was fired upon by police during a campaign against the pass laws.

SHASTON. *See* SHAFTESBURY.

SHA'STRI, Lal Bahadur (1904-66). Indian politician. Several times imprisoned for civil disobedience before independence, he later held various ministerial posts, and in 1964 succeeded Nehru as PM. He d. of a heart attack in Tashkent, following signature of a peace agreement with Pakistan. Small of stature, he was known as the 'Sparrow'.

SHATT AL'ARAB. The joint river ('river of Arabia'), formed by the confluence of the Euphrates and the Tigris, which flows *c.* 190 km (120 m) to enter the Arabian Gulf. Basra, Khorramshahr and Abadan stand on it, and its lower reaches form the border between Iran and Iraq, the demarcation being disputed. In 1975 the two countries reached agreement on the deepest water line as the frontier, but in 1980 this was repudiated by Iraq (q.v.).

SHAW, George Bernard (1856-1950). Irish dramatist. B. in Dublin, the son of a civil servant, he came to London in 1876, where he became a brilliant debater among the Fabians. Of the 5 novels he wrote 1879-83, the least unsuccessful was *Cashel Byron's Profession* (1866). His alliance with the new thought in the theatre was illustrated by his *Quintessence of Ibsenism* (1891), and in 1892 his first play *Widowers' Houses* was produced. It was the first of the *Plays: Pleasant and Unpleasant* (1898), which incl. *The Philanderer*; *Mrs Warren's Profession*, dealing with prostitution; and the pleasant comedies *Arms and the Man*, *Candida*, *You Never Can Tell*, and *Man of Destiny*, a Napoleonic incident. The *Three Plays for Puritans* of 1901 contained the witty *Devil's Disciple*; *Caesar and Cleopatra*; and *Captain Brassbound's Conversion*, written for Ellen Terry. The epic *Man and Superman* (1903), expanding his theme of Creative Evolution, was followed by *John Bull's Other Island* (1904), and *Major Barbara* (1905). *The Doctor's Dilemma*, *Getting Married*, and *The Shewing-up of Blanco Posnet* were pub. in 1911. His next vol. (1914) contained *The Dark Lady of the Sonnets*, touching the Shakespeare problem; *Misalliance*, and *Fanny's First Play*.

Androcles and the Lion was pub. in 1916 with the comedy *Pygmalion*, written for Mrs Patrick Campbell. *Heartbreak House* (1917) symbolizes the breakdown of European civilization, and in *Back to Methuselah* (1921) S. once more faced the problems of social evolution. Latest of his great dramas is *St Joan* (1924). Among the plays of the last years are *The Apple Cart* (1929), *Village Wooing*, *Geneva*, *In Good King Charles's Golden Days*, *Buoyant Billions*, and *Far-Fetched Fables*.

Important for the understanding of S.'s thought are the voluminous prefaces to the plays; *The Intelligent Woman's Guide to Socialism and Capitalism* (1928); *Adventures of a Black Girl in Search of God* (1932); *Sixty Years of Fabianism* (1947); and the vol. of music criticism *The Perfect Wagnerite* (1898). His letters to the actress Ellen Terry (pub. 1931) are also of great interest. In 1925 he received a Nobel prize.

SHCHERBAKO'V. *See* RYBINSK.

SHEARWATER. Genus of birds related to the petrels. The Manx S. (*Puffinus puffinus*) is the only species which breeds in Britain.

SHĒ'BA. Biblical name for Sabaea, in modern Yemen, SW Arabia, formerly famous as a source of gold and spices. According to 1 Kings 10, its queen visited Solomon; Ethiopian tradition traces the former royal house of Ethiopia to their union.

SHECHEM (shē'kem). Ancient town of Palestine, near Samaria, the traditional burial place of Joseph; nearby is Jacob's well. S. was destroyed *c.* AD 67 by Vespasian; on its site stands Nablus (a corruption of Neapolis, built by Hadrian), q.v. Allenby's defeat of the Turks in 1918 in the battle of S. completed the conquest of Palestine.

SHEEP. Bovid mammals of the genus *Ovis*. Domesticated S. are derived from wild species native to the drier uplands of central Asia. They can be reared on many lands unfit for arable agriculture, and their use in rotation on arable land also helps to maintain its fertility. They do well in most temperate regions, especially on hilly land. Several well-known cheeses, such as Roquefort and Parmesan, are made from sheep's milk. Breeds are specialized either for wool or flesh production: most of these are of British origin, except the Merino of the Mediterranean, now raised in Australia, New Zealand, S Africa, and the USA, and the Astrakhan. In Great Britain the best S. lands are in the southern uplands, the Cheviots, the Welsh uplands, the Pennines, and the Cotswolds. Other S.-raising lands are the USSR, Argentine, and Spain.

SHAW. A caricature of George Bernard Shaw by Sir Bernard Partridge, dated 1925. *Photo: Courtesy of the National Portrait Gallery*

SHEEP. The same animal once herded by Laban's shepherd, according to the Bible, the Jacob sheep has a brown and off-white fleece which needs neither bleaching nor dyeing before weaving. Lady Aldington founded a society to encourage this rare, but beautiful breed in 1969. *Photo: National Sheep Association*

SHEEPDOG. A rough-coated, tailless breed of dog, formerly much used by shepherds, farmers, and drovers in the S of England and in Wales, but now mainly a show dog. In colour it is grey or blue-grey.

SHEERNESS. Seaport and resort on the Isle of Sheppey, Kent, England, at the confluence of the Thames and Medway, it has developed its trade with Europe from the 1970s. Originally a fortress (1660), it was briefly captured and held by the Dutch admiral de Ruyter in 1667 and was a royal dockyard till 1960. Pop. (1972) 14,500.

SHEFFIELD. Industrial city in S Yorks, England 29km (18m) SW of Doncaster. Iron smelting has been carried on since the 12th cent., and by the 14th cent. S. cutlery was famous. During the Industrial Revolution its iron and steel manufactures developed rapidly. Cutlery of all kinds, permanent magnets, drills, precision tools are among S.'s products. Other industries incl. electro-plating, type-founding, and the manufacture of optical glass. The parish church of SS. Peter and Paul (14th-15th cents.) is the cathedral of S. bishopric (1914). The fine City Hall was opened in 1932. Mary Queen of Scots was imprisoned at S. 1570-84, part of the time in the Norman castle, which was captured by the Parliamentarians 1644 and subsequently destroyed. There are two art galleries, a museum, and a fine theatre The Crucible (1971); there is also a univ. (1905) and polytechnic (1969). The city is a touring centre for the Peak District. Pop. (1973) 565,500.

SHEFFIELD PLATE. Articles produced by fusing copper with silver, giving a beautiful surface like that of standard silver. The process, invented by Thomas Boulsover (1704-88), a Sheffield cutler, in 1742-3, was displaced by electro plating in the 1840s.

SHELBURNE, William Petty FitzMaurice, 2nd earl of (1737-1805). British Whig statesman. B. at Dublin, he entered the House of Lords in 1761 and became a follower of Chatham. He opposed George III's American policy, and as PM 1783 concluded peace with the USA. He was created marquess of Lansdowne in 1784.

SHELDUCK. Duck (*Tadorna tadorna*) with dark green head and red bill and the rest of the plumage strikingly marked in black, white and chestnut. Of widespread distribution in the Old World, it lays its eggs in rabbit burrows in sandy coasts and may be protected for the sake of these and its down by the local people.

SHELLAC. *See* LAC.

SHELLEY, Mary Wollstonecraft (1797-1851). British author; dau. of William Godwin and his wife Mary Wollstonecraft, and 2nd wife of P. B. Shelley. She eloped with him in 1814 and was m. in 1816. Her *Frankenstein,* the story of a man who created a monster and gave it life, was pub. in 1818. She wrote other novels and ed. the poet's works.

SHELLEY, Percy Bysshe (1792-1822). British lyric poet. B. at Warnham, he was ed. at Eton and University Coll., Oxford, where his collaboration in a pamphlet on *The Necessity of Atheism* (1811) caused his expulsion. While living in London he fell in love with 16-year-old Harriet Westbrook whom he m. in 1811. He visited Ireland and Wales writing pamphlets defending vegetarianism and political freedom, and in 1813 pub. privately the revolutionary poem *Queen Mab.* Meanwhile he had become estranged from his wife and in 1814 left England with Mary Wollstonecraft Godwin, whom he m. in 1816 after Harriet had drowned herself. *Alastor,* written in 1815, was followed by the epic *The Revolt of Islam,* and by 1818 S. was living in Italy. Here he produced the tragedy *The Cenci*; the satire on Wordsworth, *Peter Bell the Third* (1819); and the lyric drama *Prometheus Unbound* (1820). Other works of the period are 'Ode to the West Wind', 'The Cloud', and 'The Skylark'; 'The Sensitive Plant' and 'The Witch of Atlas'; 'Epipsychidion'; 'Adonais' (1821) and the lyric drama *Hellas* (1822); and the prose *Defence of Poetry* (1821). In July 1822 S. was drowned while sailing near Spezia, and his ashes were buried in Rome.

SHELLEY. A portrait of the poet by Amelia Curran, painted three years before his death. *Photo: Courtesy of the National Portrait Gallery*

SHELLFISH. Popular name for edible molluscs and crustaceans, incl. the whelk and periwinkle, mussel, oyster, lobster, crab, shrimp, etc.

SHELL-SHOCK. An obsolete name for various forms of nervous disorder, chiefly hysterical (*see* HYSTERIA), seen in soldiers exposed to heavy explosions or buried, but not confined to them. Such 'war neuroses' are often an aggravation of a previous neurotic conflict. Skilled psychotherapy has been effective in their cure.

SHENANDO'AH. River in Virginia, USA, a trib. of the Potomac which it joins at Harper's Ferry. The S. valley was the site, 1862-4, of important operations in the American Civil War. *See* SHERIDAN, P. H.

SHENSI. *See* SHAANXI.

SHENSTONE, William (1714-63). British poet. B. in Worcestershire, his most popular poem was the Spenserian *Schoolmistress* (1742). His country estate at the Leasowes was a famous example of landscape gardening.

SHENYANG (shenyahng'). Cap. of Liaoning prov., China. It was the Manchu cap. 1644-1912, and their tombs are nearby. Historically known as Mukden, it was taken from Russian occupation by the Japanese in the Battle of Mukden 20 Feb.-10 March 1905, and was again taken by the Japanese in 1931. Pop. (1973) 4,000,000.

SHEPARD, Ernest Howard (1879-1976). British artist. He was chiefly celebrated for his book illustrations, espec. for *Winnie-the-Pooh* and *The Wind in the Willows.*

SHEPHERD'S PURSE. Annual plant (*Capsella bursa-pastoris*) of the Cruciferae family, interesting for its world-wide distribution in the temperate zones. It is a persistent weed with white flowers followed by 2-valved seed pouches from which the name derives.

SHEPPARD, Jack (1702-24). British criminal. B. in Stepney, he was an apprentice carpenter, but turned early to theft and by 4 escapes from prison became a popular hero. He was finally caught and hanged.

SHEPPEY. English island off the N coast of Kent, at the mouth of the Medway. It is linked with the mainland by Kingsferry road and rail bridge over the Swale, completed 1960. *See* SHEERNESS.

SHERATON, Thomas (*c.* 1751-1806). English furniture designer. B. at Stockton-on-Tees, he went to London and pub. his *Cabinet-maker's and Upholsterer's Drawing Book* in 1791, and *The Cabinet Dictionary* in 1802. He was influenced by Hepplewhite and Chippendale and his work has grace and simplicity.

SHERIDAN, Philip Henry (1831-88). American general. Grant gave him command of his cavalry in 1864, and soon after of the army of the Shenandoah Valley, which he cleared of Confederates and entirely laid waste. In the final stage of the war, it was S. who forced Lee's retreat to Appomattox, where he surrendered to Grant.

SHERIDAN, Richard Brinsley (1751-1816). British dramatist. B. in Dublin, he was ed. at Harrow, and m. Elizabeth Linley, dau. of the composer, in 1773. Turning to the stage he wrote the brilliant social comedy *The Rivals* in 1775, and in 1776 became lessee of Drury Lane theatre, where he produced *The School for Scandal* (1777) and *The Critic* (1779). In 1780 he entered Parliament as an adherent of Fox, directed the impeachment of Warren Hastings, and was treasurer to the navy 1806-7. His last years were clouded by the burning down of his theatre in 1809, the loss of his parliamentary seat in 1812, and by complete financial ruin and mental breakdown.

SHERIFF ('shire-reeve'). The chief administrative officer of an English co.; in Scotland the judicial duties of the office have survived with greater importance. The office (elective until Edward II) and name are of pre-Conquest origin. The S., who is appointed annually by royal patent, and is chosen from the leading landowners, acts as returning officer for parliamentary elections, and attends the judges on circuit. His duties of keeping prisoners in safe custody, preparing panels of jurors for assizes, executing writs and death sentences, are supervised by the Under-S. The City of London has 2 Ss. elected by the Liverymen. In the USA the S. of the co. is generally elected and combines some judicial authority with administrative duties.

SHERMAN, William Tecumseh (1820-91). American general. B. in Ohio, he received a command in the Federal army on the Mississippi front early in the Civil War, and collaborated with Grant in the Vicksburg campaign. In 1864 he captured Atlanta, whence he marched to the sea, laying Georgia waste, and then drove the Confederates northwards. He was Commander-in-Chief from 1869 to 1883.

SHER'PA. Member of a tribe of Mongolian origin in NE Nepal, famous for their mountaineering skill. *See* EVEREST.

SHERRIFF, R(obert) C(edric) (1896-1975). British playwright. B. at Kingston-on-Thames, he achieved fame with the anti-heroic war play *Journey's End* (1929). A later success was *Home at Seven* (1950).

SHERRINGTON, Sir Charles Scott (1857-1952). British physiologist. B. in London, he was prof. at Liverpool 1895-1913 and Waynflete prof. of physiology at Oxford 1913-35. He wrote *The Integrative Action of the Nervous System* (1906), which formulated the principles of reflex action. He was also a poet. He received the OM in 1924, and was made GBE in 1922.

SHERRY. A dry, white wine from the vineyards of S Spain between the Guadalquivir and Guadelete. The name derives from the town of Xeres, or Jerez de la Frontera, the centre of the region.

'sHERTOGENBOSCH. *See* 'S HERTOGENBOSH.

SHERWOOD, Robert (1896-1955). American dramatist. After fighting with the Canadian forces in France in the F.W.W., he became a journalist in New York, and achieved his first great success with *The Petrified Forest* (1934). Later plays incl. *Idiot's Delight* (1936), *Abe Lincoln in Illinois* (1938) and *There Shall Be No Night* (1940) - for each of which he received a Pulitzer prize.

SHERWOOD FOREST. A hilly stretch of parkland in W Nottinghamshire, England, formerly a royal forest, area *c.* 520 sq.km (200 sq.m). It is associated with Robin Hood.

SHETLAND ISLES. A group of more than 100 islands, lying NE of the Orkneys and forming from 1975 the islands area of Shetland; admin. HQ Lerwick on Mainland, the largest of the 19 inhabited islands (979 sq.km/378 sq.m): Yell (215 sq.km/83 sq.m) is the second largest. Coloured hand-knit woollens from Fair Isle and Unst, fishing and fish-processing make a prosperous economy. Industrial development, made inevitable by oil discoveries, is concentrated at Sullom Voe, a deep water fiord on Mainland, Europe's largest oil port. Muckle Flugga (60° 51′ 30″ N lat.) is the northernmost of the Brit. Isles. They were under Scandinavian rule 875-1468, and the dialect is derived from Norse. There was opposition in S. to devolution for Scotland, owing to fears of domination by Strathclyde. Area 1,424 sq.km (550 sq.m); pop. (1979) 21,835.

SHIAH (shē'ah) or **SHI'ITE** (shē'īt). One of the 2 branches into which the Moslem world is divided, the other being the Sunni: Sunnis outnumber Shiahs by nine to one. The distinctive Shiah tenet is belief that Ali was the first true successor or caliph of Mohammed, whereas the Sunni branch hold that Ali's three predecessors were legitimate caliphs. The Shiahs also reject the Sunna, or verbal utterances of the prophet. The Shiah stronghold is Iran, where Ayatollah Khomeini has called on Shiahs in other Arab countries to overthrow their Sunni rulers, e.g. in Bahrein. The Alawite sect is a breakaway subdivision of the Shiah branch, to which Pres. Assad of Syria and members of his ruling party belong.

SHIELD. Any material used to reduce the amount of radiation (electrostatic, electromagnetic, heat, nuclear, etc.) reaching from one region of space to another, or any material used as a protection against falling debris, as in tunnelling, etc. Electrical conductors are used for electrostatic Ss., soft iron for electromagnetic Ss., and poor conductors of heat for heat Ss. Heavy materials such as lead and concrete are used for protection against X-ray and nuclear radiation. *See* BIOLOGICAL S.

SHIHCHIACHUANG. *See* SHIJIAZHUANG.

SHIJIAZHUANG (shējē-ahjōo-ahng'). Cap. (formerly Shihchiachuang) of Hebei prov., China. A communications and industrial centre (textiles, chemicals, light engineering) it uses local coal. Pop. (1973) 1,000,000.

SHIKOKU. One of the 4 main islands of Japan, S of Honshu, E of Kyushu. With a mild climate and rainfall up to 266cm (105in) a year in the S, it rises in Mt Ishizuchi to 1,980 m (6,497 ft). There are forests; crops incl. rice, wheat, soya, sugar cane and orchard fruits; and salt and copper are mined. The chief town is Matsuyama. A suspension bridge was completed in 1985 linking Shikoku with Awajishima Is., over the famous Naruto whirlpool in the Inland Sea. Area 17,790 sq.km (6,869 sq.m); pop. (1973) 4,750,000.

SHILLELAGH (shilā'li). Village in Wicklow, Rep. of Ireland, which gave its name to a rough cudgel of oak or blackthorn.

SHILLO'NG. Cap. of Meghalaya, Rep. of India. Pop. (1970) 110,000.

SHIMONOSEKI (shimōnōsek'ē). Japanese seaport in the extreme SW of Honshu, opened to foreign trade 1890. The first of the Sino-Japanese Wars (q.v.) ended with a treaty signed at S. in 1895. Pop. (1977) 263,000.

SHINGLES. *See* HERPES.

SHINTO. The Chinese transliteration of the Japanese for Kami-no-Michi, the Way or Doctrine of the Gods, the indigenous religion of Japan. This is a mixture of nature-worship and loyalty to the reigning dynasty as descendants of the Sun-goddess, Amaterasu-Omikami. State S. was the national faith of Japan; its holiest shrine is at Ise, where in the temple of the Sun-goddess is preserved the mirror that she is supposed to have given to Jimmu, the first emperor, in the 7th cent. BC. Sect. S. consists of 130 sects, each founded by an historical character; the sects are officially recognized, but are not State-supported, as was State S. until its disestablishment by Gen. MacArthur's decree after the S.W.W. Unquestioning obedience and devotion to the emperor is inculcated, but there is also an exemplary ethic.

SHINTY. A winter game popular in the Scottish Highlands, played between teams of 12 players with sticks and a ball. It resembles hockey and lacrosse.

SHIP. Sea-going vessel of considerable size. Greeks and Phoenicians built wooden Ss., propelled by oar or sail. The Romans and Carthaginians fought in galleys equipped with rams and rowed by tiers of oarsmen. The oaken Ss. of the Norsemen were for rough seas, and the fleet of Richard Cœur de Lion was largely of sail. The compass was invented in the 14th cent. and the 15th cent. saw the beginnings of Britain's Royal Navy; Henry VIII built the *Great Harry*, the first double-decked English warship. In the 16th cent. Ss. were short and high-sterned, and despite Pett's 3-decker in the 17th cent. English Ss. did not bear comparison with Spanish and Dutch until the era of Sir Robert Seppings, a shipbuilding pioneer in the early

19th cent. By 1840 iron had largely replaced wood, but fast-sailing clippers survived, built with wooden planks on iron frames. America and Britain made steam experiments as the 19th cent. opened. The *Comet* appeared in 1812, the Canadian *Royal William* crossed the Atlantic in 1833, and the English *Great Western* steamed from Bristol to New York in 1838. Pettit Smith applied the screw to the *Archimedes* in 1839, and after 1850 the paddle-wheel became obsolete. The introduction of the compound engine and turbine, the latter in 1902, completed the revolution in propulsion until the advent of nuclear-powered vessels after the S.W.W., chiefly submarines. More recently hovercraft (q.v.) have been developed for specialized purposes, more espec. for short-distance ferries, e.g. on the English Channel: *see also* HYDROFOIL. Sailing Ss. in automated form for cargo purposes are also being developed (*see* MERCHANT NAVY).

SHIP MONEY. Tax for support of the navy, levied on the coastal districts of England in the Middle Ages. Charles I's attempts to levy it on the whole country in 1634–6, without parliamentary consent and in time of peace, aroused strong opposition, J. Hampden and others refusing to pay. S.M. was declared illegal by parliament in 1641.

SHIRAZ (shē'rahz). Ancient walled city of S Iran, the cap. of Fars prov. It is noted for its wines, carpets, and silver-work, and for its many beautiful mosques. There is a univ. It has suffered from earthquakes. Pop. (1976) 414,500.

SHIRÉ (shirā') **HIGHLANDS.** Area E of the S. river in southern Malawi, up to 1,750 m (5,800 ft) a.s.l., with tea and tobacco plantations. Zomba is the chief town.

SHIZUŌKA. Centre of the tea industry in central E Honshu, Japan: also metal and food processing industries. Pop. (1977) 451,000.

SHKODËR (shkö'drah). Albanian town, on the Bojana, SE of Lake S., 19km (12m) from the Adriatic. It makes woollens and cement, and trades in hides, salt, tobacco, etc. During the F.W.W. it was occupied by the Austrians 1916–18; during the Second by the Italians. Its Italian name is Scutari. Pop. (1976) 62,500.

SHOCK. A dangerous condition due to over-stimulation of the sensory nerves by severe injury or operation, or to loss of blood or plasma (as in burning), or to overpowering emotion. The blood-vessels dilate and the pressure falls below that necessary to supply the tissues of the body, especially the vital nerve-centres of the brain. Treatment is by rest, and, in the case of blood loss, by restoration of the normal circulating volume.

SHOCKLEY, William (1910–). American physicist. He worked with Bardeen and Brattain (qq.v.) on the invention of the transistor.

SHOEBURYNESS. Promontory on the Essex coast, England, N of the Thames estuary, occupied by a school of gunnery.

SHŌ'GI. Japanese game, probably deriving from the same Indian sources as chess, but more complex.

SHOGUN. Formerly, the hereditary C-in-C of the Japanese Army. Though nominally subject to the emperor, he was the real ruler of Japan. In 1867 the emperor re-assumed power.

SHŌLAPU'R. Town in Maharashtra state, India, on the Deccan. It makes textiles, leather goods, chemicals, etc. A nearby reservoir counters recurrent water shortage. Pop. (1971) 398,250.

SHOL'OKHOV, Mikhail Aleksandrovich (1905–84). Russian novelist. He pub. the work that made his name *And Quiet Flows the Don (Tikhi Don)* in 4 vols. 1926–40, telling realistically of the Don Cossacks, and how their lives were affected by the Revolution and Civil War. His other works, short stories and the novel *Virgin Soil Upturned* (1932–9), are inferior, and it has been suggested that the real author of the major work was Kryukov (q.v.). He received a Nobel prize 1965.

SHOP. Building for the retail sale of goods. Until the later 19th cent. S. development had been almost static since ancient times, but with the growth of manufactured goods and the concentration of population in big towns came the development of the department store, in effect a number of small specialist shops under one roof, and of the chain store, with many Ss. scattered in different towns or counties and able to buy wholesale in such quantities that prices could be lowered below those of smaller competitors. As a development of wholesale purchase came direct links with factories producing goods, often under the same ownership, which further cut costs and even the elimination of the S. itself by direct mail or mail order (q.v.). Self-service, originating many years earlier in USA (*see* SAUNDERS, CLARENCE), developed rapidly after the S.W.W. as a result of staff shortages, and in particular in supermarkets for groceries and hypermarkets outside towns with a very wide range of goods. In the 1970s there developed in the USA the 'controlled shopping environment' of an air-conditioned enclosed mall of up to 250 shops in carpeted arcades, often on several levels, with music, free parking, cinemas, restaurants and child-care facilities, e.g. Woodfield Mall, Chicago. The idea was adopted in the UK and elsewhere. Trading stamps, originating in Britain *c.* 1851, were developed in the USA and re-exported to the UK (Green Shield) in 1958, but became a casualty of the recession and changed shopping habits in the late 1970s. Gradually being introduced are direct debit from a customer's bank account by use of a plastic card inserted in a computer terminal at the point of sale, and laser check-outs, which automatically 'read' a line-pattern on the packaging of the goods and deliver an itemised bill to the customer, as well as recording for the store the deduction of the item from shelf stock.

SHOP STEWARD. A trade union representative in a 'shop' or department of a factory, who recruits for the union, inspects contribution cards and reports grievances to the district committee. Originating in the engineering industry, this form of organization has spread to all large industrial undertakings.

SHOREHAM BY SEA. Seaport in E Sussex, England, 10km (6m) W of Brighton, nr the mouth of the Adur. Wine is imported in quantity. Pop. (1971) 18,000.

SHORTHAND. System of rapid writing specially adapted to recording the spoken word. The Greeks and Romans practised systems of abbreviated writing, but the earliest S. system to be based on the alphabet and to follow the spelling of words was that of John Willis pub. in 1602. Later orthographic systems were those of Thomas Shelton (pub. 1630), which was used by Pepys, and that of Thomas Gurney (pub. 1750), which was used by Dickens. Phonetic systems, based entirely on the sound of words, began to appear in the 18th cent., and were perfected by Isaac Pitman. Speeds of approx. 300 words are attainable, and equal speed and accuracy is reached by operators of stenotype machines, which have selective keyboards enabling several word contractions to be printed at a time. The principle of stenotyping has been adapted to enable the deaf to follow speeches, e.g. in the House of Commons. An easily learnt system of abbreviations is used by the machine operator to transfer them at spoken speed to a television screen.

SHOSTAKŌ'VICH, Dmitry Dmitrievich (1906-1975). Russian composer. B. in Leningrad, where he studied the piano and composition at the Conservatoire, he wrote 15 symphonies, the 1st in 1926 and the most famous of the others being the 5th (with its sub-title 'A Soviet Artist's Reply to Just Criticism') in 1937, the patriotic 7th or *Leningrad* (1941) which marked a temporary return to favour; and the moving 10th (1955). He also wrote ballets and operas, most famous of the latter being *The Nose* and *A Lady Macbeth of Mtensk* (1936) which was found by authority too divorced from the proletariat, but after years of suppression was revived in 1963 as *Katerina Ismailova.*

SHOVELL (shuv'-), **Sir Cloudesley** (*c.* 1650-1707). English admiral. He took part with Rooke (q.v.) in the capture of Gibraltar in 1704, and as admiral and C-in-C of the fleet shared in the destruction of the French Mediterranean naval forces. His flagship *Association,* with 4 other ships of the homeward bound fleet (some 2,000 men), was lost off the Scillies in 1707, the admiral himself coming safely ashore, where he was strangled by a woman of the is. for his rings. Cannon and treasure from *Association* were recovered 1967-8.

SHOVELLER. Fresh-water duck (*Spatula clypeata*), so named from its broad flattened beak, with green head and white and brown body plumage. Spending the summer in N Europe or America, it winters farther S. and visits Britain.

SHOW JUMPING. Competitive horse jumping over a course of fences. In the post-S.W.W. years S.J. has become an important part of most horse shows, the winner usually being the competitor with fewest 'faults', i.e. penalty marks given for knocking down or refusing fences, etc., but in time competitions is the competitor completing the course most quickly, additional seconds being added for such mistakes. Famous riders have incl. Col. Harry Llewellyn, Pat Smythe, David Broome, Harvey Smith, Ann Moore, and Princess Anne and her husband Mark Phillips; the German Alwin Schockemohle; the Italian Graziano Mancinelli; and the American Bill Steinkraus.

SHRAPNEL, Henry (1761-1842). Inventor of the S. shell. He served in the RA and became a lieut.-gen. in 1837. His shell was first used in 1804.

SHREVEPORT. City in NW Louisiana, USA on the Red river. It was founded in 1836, named after Henry Shreeve, a riverboat captain who cleared a giant logjam. Industries incl. oil and natural gas, steel, telephones, glass and timber. Pop. (1974) 193,800.

SHREW. Insectivorous mammal of the family Soricidae, resembling a mouse and renowned for its insatiable appetite. The common S. (*Sorex araneus*) is *c.* 7.5cm (3in) long. The pigmy shrewmouse (*S. minutus*) is the smallest British mammal. There are many other species in the N hemisphere and some are aquatic.

SHREWSBURY (shrōz'buri), **earl of.** Title in the peerage of England, held by the family of Talbot since 1442. It is the premier earldom of England.

SHREWSBURY. Town in Salop, England, on the Severn, admin. HQ of the co. The Roman city of Uriconium to the E (larger than Pompeii) has been safeguarded for excavation, and it was at S. that Caractacus fought Nero's legions in AD 51. As Pengwern, S. was cap. of the kingdom of Powis in the 5th cent., which was later part of Mercia. At the battle of S. in 1403 Henry IV defeated the rebels led by Hotspur (Harry Percy, son of the earl of Nortumberland) who was killed. Pop. (1972) 56,670.

SHRIKE. Family of birds (Laniidae), distinguished by a long-toothed bill, and incl. many species, e.g. the Great Grey S. (*Lanius excubitor*) and Lesser Grey S. (*L. minor*), the Woodchat S. (*L. senator*), the Red-backed S. (*L. collurio*), etc. They feed on insects, small birds, and other small animals which they impale on thorns - whence their popular name of butcher-birds.

SHRIMP. A salt-water crustacean of the family Crangonidae, closely allied to the prawn (q.v.), and hunting for food at night. The edible Common S. of N Europe (*Crangon vulgaris*) is grey, changes its colour to brown when boiled, and is *c.* 50mm (2in) long. In Japan and on the Atlantic coast of southern USA they form the basis of a large industry.

SHROPSHIRE. Co. of England bordering Wales, and bisected NW to SE by the Severn. In 1974 it was officially redesignated Salop, a previously less used alternative, but popular protest led to the restoration of the form Shropshire. It is flat to the N; Ellesmere is the largest of several lakes in the SW; and the Clee Hills rise to *c.* 610 m (1800 ft) in the SW. Coal and iron ore are mined, but the co. is chiefly agricultural, sheep and cattle being reared. Shrewsbury is the admin HQ. Area 3,490 sq.km (1,348 sq.m); pop. (1978) 365,900.

SHROVE TUESDAY. The day before Ash Wednesday. The name comes from the Anglo-Saxon *scrifan,* to shrive, and in olden days it was the time for confession before Lent. Another name for it is Pancake Tuesday; the pancakes are a survival of merrymaking in anticipation of Lenten abstinence.

SHRUB. Woody plant smaller than a tree and usually divided into separate stems near the ground.

SHUTE, Nevil. Pseudonym of British novelist N. S. Norway (1899-1960). B. in Ealing, son of a civil servant, it was not until during the S.W.W., in which he served in the RNVR, that he became a best-seller. His always technically accurate books incl. *Pied Piper* (1942), *No Highway* (1948) and *A Town Like Alice* (1949). In 1950 he settled in Australia.

SIALKOT (sē-ahlkōt'). Town and trade centre of Pakistan, nr the Chenab. Surgical and sports goods, metal ware, carpets, textiles and leather goods are produced. Pop. (1972) 203,800.

SIAN (sē-an'). Chinese city, cap. of Shensi prov., a great trade centre with cotton mills. S. was cap. of China under the Chou dynasty (*c.* 1100 BC); under the Han dynasty (206 BC to AD 220), when it was called Changan (long peace); under the Tang dynasty (618-906), as Siking (western cap.). The Manchus named it Sian (western peace); it reverted to the name Changan 1913-32; Siking 1932-43; Sian in 1943. The imperial court retired to S. following the Boxer rising, 1900. In 1974 the tomb of China's first emperor Shih Hwang Ti (reigned 221-210 BC) was discovered nearby with life-size models of his soldiers and war chariots. Pop. (1973) 1,700,000.

SIBELIUS (sēbā'le-us), **Jean Christian** (1865-1957). Finnish composer. Intended by his father for the law, he studied the violin and composition at Helsingfors and went on to Berlin and Vienna. Recognized as a major composer only in Britain and the USA, he has a simple austerity in his work which incl. the orchestral *En Saga* and *Karelia*; the tone-poems *Finlandia* and *Night Ride and Sunrise*; the appealing *Valse Triste*; *Voces Intimae*, a string quartet; and 7 symphonies.

SIBELIUS. At his home in Finland, Sibelius receives a visit from Sir Thomas Beecham, a pioneer of his work in Britain. *Photo: Camera Press*

SIBERIA. Geographical name for Asiatic RSFSR from the Urals to the Pacific. Much of it is within the Arctic Circle and it incl. Lake Baikal (q.v.). Overrun by Russia in the 17th cent., it was used from the 18th as a place of exile for political and criminal prisoners, but the Trans-Siberian rlwy (1892-1905) led to more voluntary settlement. Under Soviet rule many prisoners continued to be sent there, but colonization was undertaken, and after the S.W.W. this was stepped up in an effort to exploit one of the richest of the world's under-developed areas. A second Transiberian Rlwy, the Baikal-Amur Magistral (BAM) has been intermittently under construction from 1934 and is due to operate from 1983. It runs N of Lake Baikal 4,500 km (2,800 m) from Taishet on the existing line via Bratsk, Ust-Kut, Udokan, Tynda, Urgal, Komsomolsk-na-Amur to Sovietskaya Gavan on the Pacific. It will tap resources of coal, copper, iron, nickel, cobalt, molybdenum, gold, diamonds, oil and natural gas. Agriculture is limited by the severity of the climate, but projects such as the possibility of reversing the flow of rivers which drain to the Arctic Ocean could modify climate and fertility. Novosibirsk (q.v.) is the largest city: others incl. Omsk, Krasnoyarsk, and Irkutsk. The Pacific coastline and the Amur basin is frequently referred to as the Soviet Far East. Area 12,050,000 sq.km (4,650,000 sq.m); pop. (1973) 32,850,000.

SIBLEY, Antoinette (1939-). British dancer. Joining the Royal Ballet in 1956, she became senior soloist in 1960. Her roles incl. Odette/Odile, Giselle, the betrayed girl in *The Rake's Progress*, and in 1964 she appeared in the première of Ashton's *The Dream*. She was m. to Michael Somes 1964-73.

SIBYL. In classical mythology, a priestess of Apollo, who was supposed to prophesy under his inspiration. One Sibyl in particular, the Cumaean Sibyl, appears in Roman story as offering to sell to King Tarquin the Proud nine books of prophecies; the price was too high, but at length the king bought the three books that she had not destroyed for the price originally demanded for the set. These **Sibylline Books,** kept at Rome, were consulted in state emergencies. The alleged cave of the Cumaean S. was discovered in 1932 on Monte Cuma, nr Naples.

SICHUAN (sechōō-ahn'). Prov. (formerly Szechwan) of SW China. It lies high, surrounded by mountains, and is well-forested and drained by the Chang Jiang and its tributaries. The Red Basin forms the heart of the province. Products incl. timber, rice, cereals, groundnuts, cotton, sugar, tea, coal, iron, copper, salt, and some oil and natural gas. In 1972 China's nuclear research centres were moved from Xinjiang Uygur on the Russian frontier to sites nr. Chengdu, cap. of S., and Chongqing. Area 569,000 sq.km (219,634 sq.m); pop. (1979) 90,000,000.

SICHUAN. A convoy of lorries on the hair-raisingly steep bends of the busy Sichuan-Tibet highway. *Photo: Courtesy of the Society for Anglo-Chinese Understanding.*

SICILY. The largest island in the Mediterranean, forming with Lipari, Egadi, Ustica, and Pantelleria islands an autonomous region (1946) of Italy. Separated from the mainland by the Strait of Messina, S. is roughly triangular, tapering towards the W. The N and centre are mountainous incl. Etna (3,323 m/10,902 ft after the eruption of 1971); elsewhere undulating hills and river valleys are found. The Simeto, Platani, and Salso are the main rivers. Water shortage owing to low rainfall, a hot climate and extensive deforestation have been partially countered by harnessing mtn streams, and by greenhouse culture. Cereals, citrus, olives, vines (for Marsala wine), and almonds are grown and stock raising is being developed. Industries are based on the sulphur, oil and natural gas resources of the is., and also incl. cars and heavy vehicles, cement, hosiery, knitwear, shipbuilding and food processing. There are tunny fisheries, and fish farms in coastal lagoons and freshwater reserves. The cap. is Palermo; the chief ports are Catania, Messina, Syracuse and Marsala. During the S.W.W. the is. was conquered by the Allies 10 July-8 Aug. 1943. In the post-war period social worker Danilo Dolci (1924-) assisted in combating the Mafia stranglehold on the economy. Area 25,709 sq.km (9,976 sq.m); pop. (1977) 4,936,249.

SICILY. A timeless scene of shepherd and sheep near a temple at Segesta, in Sicily. *Photo: Douglas Dickins.*

SICKLE CELL DISEASE. Form of anaemia common in African peoples, and their descendants elsewhere. In those with 2 genes producing such distorted-shape red blood cells, serious illness results; in those with one healthy gene and one that is abnormal, there may be no sign of illness, rather the reverse, since this form gives resistance to malarial infection. Variant forms occur in Asia.

SICKERT, Walter Richard (1860-1942). British artist. B. in Munich, the son of a Danish painter, he was taken to London and studied at the Slade School and under Whistler. He estab. a reputation as a painter of Impressionistic pictures, his works incl. 'Mamma Mia Poareta', 'The Area Steps', 'The Evening Primrose', and 'Bath'. He became president of the Royal Society of British Artists, and was elected RA in 1934.

SIDDONS, Sarah (1755-1831). English actress. B. at Brecon, Wales, the dau. of Roger Kemble, she m. in 1773 William Siddons. Her first success in Otway's *Venice Preserved* in 1774 led to her engagement in 1775 to appear with Garrick at Drury Lane. The majesty of her presence made her a superb Lady Macbeth, and her other parts incl. Desdemona, Ophelia and Volumnia. She appeared with acclaim until her retirement in 1812, her admirers incl. Johnson and Walpole: Reynolds painted her as 'The Tragic Muse'.

SIDEWINDER. Snake (*Crotalus cerastes*) of N America, so-named because of its sideways forward movement; also a heat-seeking air-to-air missile with a similar motion.

SIDI BARRÂNI (sid'i barah'nē). Coastal settlement of Egypt, about 370km (230m) W of Alexandria, the scene of much fighting 1940-2, during the S.W.W.

SIDI-BEL ABBÈS. Town and trade centre in Algeria, 56km (35m) S of Oran. When Algeria was French, it was the HQ of the Foreign Legion. Pop. (1974) 151,150.

SIDING SPRING MTN. Site 400km (250m) NW of Sydney, NSW, of an Anglo-Australian telescope (1974), which enables the central sector of our Galaxy to be adequately observed for the first time. Since these central regions exert a considerable controlling influence, the 3.81m (150in) telescope is expected to throw light on cosmic origins.

SIDNEY, Sir Philip (1554-86). English poet and soldier. B. at Penshurst, Kent, he entered Parliament in 1581, and in 1583 was knighted. In 1585 he was made governor of Flushing, and was mortally wounded at Zutphen, fighting the Spaniards. Among his works are the sonnet sequence *Astrophel and Stella* (1591); the romance *Arcadia* (1590); and the *Apologie for Poetrie* (1595), the earliest work of English literary criticism.

SIDNEY. This portrait of Sir Philip Sidney by an unknown artist captures the qualities of both soldier and poet. *Photo: Courtesy of the National Portrait Gallery*

SĪ'DON. Chief city of ancient Phoenicia, bitter rival of Tyre from *c.* 1400 BC until conquered by Sennacherib, 701 BC. Later a Roman city, taken by the Arabs AD 637, fought over during the Crusades. On the W part of it stands Saida, Lebanon.

SIEGFRIED (sēg'frēd). Germanic hero. It is uncertain whether his story has a historical basis, but it was current about 700. In the poems of the Norse Elder Edda and in the prose Völsunga Saga S. appears under the name of Sigurd. The best-known version is in the German *Nibelungenlied.*

SIEMENS (sē'mens). Family of 4 brothers, creators of a vast industrial empire: most famous were the eldest, **Ernst Werner von S.** (1812-92), who founded in 1847 the original electrical firm of Siemens und Halske and made many inventions in telegraphy; and **Wilhelm** (1823-83), who became in 1859 a British subject and was knighted in 1883 as Sir William S. He was manager of the firm S.

Brothers, and was concerned with the development of the dynamo, etc.

SIENA (sē'ā'nah). City of Tuscany, Italy, 50km (31m) S of Florence. The city, which dates back to Roman times, is famous for its architecture, and for a school of painting which flourished from the 13th to the 16th cent. There is a univ. (1300) and a Gothic cathedral, completed 1243. An annual race on horseback, the Palio, has been held in the main square since the Middle Ages. Pop. (1978) 70,000.

SIENA. The historic procession begins to form before the race, held in honour of the Virgin, the city's patron saint, and to commemorate ancient victories. The prize is a *palio,* or banner. *Photo: Pepi Meriso/Camera Press*

SIENKIEWICZ (syenkye'vich), **Henryk** (1846-1916). Polish author. His books incl. the 17th cent. historical trilogy *With Fire and Sword, The Deluge* and *Pan Michael* (1890-3); *Quo Vadis?* (1895), set in Rome in the time of Nero, and *Without Dogma* (1891).

SIERRA LEONE (sē-er'ra lēōn' or lā-'ōnā). Country of W Africa, between Rep. of Guinea in the N and Liberia in the SE. It has a very hot and moist climate. Agriculture supports more than half the pop., main products being palm-kernels, ground-nuts, kolanuts, rice, cocoa, coffee, ginger, and cassava. There are vegetable-oil mills, furniture workshops, and various village industries incl. fishing and weaving. Diamonds (about half of gem quality), the most valuable export, iron-ore, and chromite are mined. S.L. is the former British colony, a small area acquired 1788 for repatriating homeless Africans from London and, later, rescued from slave ships, and protectorate (1896) over the hinterland, which achieved self-govt 1958, and independence within the British Commonwealth 1961. In 1971 S.L. became a rep., following a period of military govt, and by 1973 was a one-party state with all opposition suppressed. The position was formalised under a new constitution in 1978, following a referendum, with Dr Siaka Stevens as President (from 1971, re-elected 1976). The current president (elected 1985) is Joseph Saidu Momoh. Capital: Freetown. Area 73,325 sq.km (27,925 sq.m); pop. (1980) 4,000,000. The majority follow tribal religions, but 25% are Moslem. The official language is English. M.U.: leone.

SIERRA MADRE (sē-er'ra mad'rā). Chief mtn range of Mexico, comprising 3 ranges. Two of them, the S.M. Occidental, which follows the line of the Gulf of California, and the S.M. Oriental (incl. the highest point, Pico de Orizaba 5,700 m/18,700 ft), which follows that of the Gulf of Mexico, enclose the country's central plateau. The S.M. del Sur (meaning 'of the south') runs along the SW Pacific coast.

SIERRA NEVADA (nevah'da). Mtn range in southern Spain, the highest peak being Mulhacén 3,481 m (11,421 ft); and also a range in E California, highest peak Mt Whitney 4,418 m (14,495 ft), which incl. the King's Canyon, Sequoia, and Yosemite nat. parks.

SIGNAC (sēnyahk'), **Paul** (1863-1935). French artist. Parisian-born, he was influenced by Monet, and in 1884 joined with Seurat in founding the Société des Artistes Indépendants. Fond of sailing, he expanded his brilliant water-colours made on the spot into large canvases instinct with colour and light, often composed of squarish 'mosaic' blobs.

SIGNALS. Method of communication using flags, light, radio telephony, radio telegraphy, etc. The International Code of S. used by shipping was drawn up by an international committee and pub. in 1931. The codes and abbreviations used by aircraft are dealt with by the International Civil Aviation Organization (1944). *See* MORSE CODE and SEMAPHORE.

SIGNORELLI (sēnyore'li), **Luca** (*c.* 1450-1523). Italian artist. He is famous for his large-scale frescoes, e.g. those in Orvieto cathedral, and his powerful treatment of the nude.

SIKHISM (sē'kizm). The religion professed by some 10 million Indians living for the most part in the Punjab. It was founded by Nanak (1469-*c.* 1539). Its basis is the Unity of God and the Brotherhood of Man, and in it caste plays a comparatively small part. On Nanak's death he was followed as Guru - chief priest - by a succession of rulers who converted the Sikhs - the word means disciple - into a military confraternity which established itself as a political power. Guru Gobind Singh instituted the Khanda-di-Pahul, the Baptism of the Sword, and established the Khalsa ('the pure'), the Brotherhood of the faithful, the Singhs. The Singhs wear the 5 Ks: *kes,* long hair; *kangha,* a comb; *kirpan,* a sword; *kachh,* long drawers; and *kara,* a steel bracelet. The last of the Gurus, Gobind Singh, was assassinated by a Moslem in 1708, and since then the Granth Sahib, the holy book of the Sikhs, has taken the place of a leader. On the partition of India many Sikhs migrated from W to E Punjab, and in 1966 the efforts of Sant Fateh Singh (*c.* 1911-72) led to the creation of a separate Sikh state by partition of Punjab (q.v.).

SI-KIANG. *See* XI JIANG.

SIKKIM (sik'im). Small state in the Himalayas, bordering Nepal, Bhutan, and Tibet (China). Maize and rice are grown. Following a popular uprising in 1973 the King or 'Chogyal' requested India, the protecting power, to take over the admin. In 1975 the legislature voted to abolish the monarchy and S. became a state of India, but in 1979 there was a proposal to reverse the union with India, The cap. is Gangtok. Area 7,298 sq.km (2,818 sq.m); pop. (1971) 208,000. The majority are Nepalese Mahayana Buddhists.

The language of govt. is English, but Nepali, Lepcha and Bhutia are also official languages. M.U.: Indian rupee.

SIKO'RSKI, Wladyslaw (1881-1943). Polish gen. and statesman. B. in Galicia, he organized in 1909 the nationalist military organization, which during the F.W.W. fought for the central powers. He served in the Russian war of 1920, and was PM 1922-3 and War Min. 1923-5. He became PM in Sept. 1939 of the exiled Polish govt, which transferred to London in 1940. He was killed in an air crash. The intransigence of his govt was a cause of Anglo-Russian friction, but allegations that his death was not accidental are unsubstantiated. *See* HOCHHUTH, ROLF.

SĪ'LAGE. Fodder preserved in a silo, an airtight structure for pressing green crops. It is now extended to refer to stacked crops which may be preserved indefinitely.

SILBURY HILL. Steep, rounded, artificial mound in the Kennet Valley, Wilts, not far from Avebury. Dated *c.* 2660 BC and 40 m (130 ft) high, it was long thought to be a barrow, but excavation has shown it not to be sepulchral. One theory is that it is part of a representation of a pregnant mother goddess, the hill itself being her womb, her body being outlined in the surrounding quarry, and connected with Moon worship.

SILBURY HILL. Intriguing in its lack of ascertainable purpose, impressive in its size and the human labour that went to create it, Silbury is a satisfyingly unsolved mystery bequeathed to us by the Bronze Age. *Photo: Anthony Marshall/Daily Telegraph*

SILCHESTER. Archaeological site in Hants, England, 10km (6m) N of Basingstoke. One of the most important towns in Britain in the Roman period. S. is the only town in the prov. known in such detail.

SILD. Norwegian word for small fish of the herring family which are virtually indistinguishable from the sardine (q.v.) when canned.

SĪLĒ'NUS. In Greek mythology, the son of Hermes, or Pan, and companion of Dionysus. He is portrayed as a jovial old man, usually drunk.

SĪLĒ'SIA. Region of central Europe. Before the F.W.W. all except a small part of S. had belonged to Germany since it was wrested from Austria (which had held it since 1675) by Frederick II of Prussia in 1745. In 1919 *c.* 2,750 sq.km (1,700 sq.m) went to newly-formed Czechoslovakia; *c.* 2,575 sq.km (1,600 sq.m) to revived Poland; *c.* 21,000 sq.km (13,000 sq.m) remained part of Germany. Following the S.W.W. all German S. lying E of the Order-W Neisse line was transferred to Polish administration, 1945, and most of its German inhabitants were expelled, as were those of German origin in Czechoslovak S. The largest towns are Wroclaw (Breslau), Katowice, Zabrze (Hindenburg), Chorzow (Königshütte), Gliwice (Gleiwitz), and Bytom (Beuthen) in Poland and Opava (Troppau) in Czechoslovakia.

SILHOUETTE (siloo-et'). A profile or shadow portrait filled in in black or a dark colour, named after Étienne de Silhouette (1709-67), a French finance minister whose economy led to his name being applied to cheap things.

SI'LICON. A non-metallic chemical element, symbol Si (Lat. *silex*, flint), at. no. 14. and at. wt., 28.09. It is used in glass-making, as a hardener in steel alloys, and in S. chips for microcomputers, etc., so that *Silicon Valley* is the nickname of Santa Clara co., California, where there has been a concentration of high technology electronic firms since the late 1950s.

Silicones are synthetic chemical products, characterized by their chemical inertness, good electrical properties, and ability to repel water. They are based on a chain of oxygen and silicon atoms, the latter having organic groups attached to them. These groups and the basic silicone structure can be varied to produce silicone rubber, longer-lasting electrical material, paints, industrial grease, domestic polishes, water-repellent fluids for treating masonry, stain-resistant fabric finishes, etc.

SILICŌ'SIS. A condition affecting workers who inhale flint dust, e.g. anthracite miners and stone cutters. The lung tissue becomes fibrous through constant small injury and repair, less capable of aerating the blood and less resistant to tuberculosis.

SILK. Fine, soft thread produced by the larva of the silkworm moth, the most commonly cultivated species being *Bombyx mori,* and used in the manufacture of textiles. The 'worm' or larva attains maturity within a month of hatching from the egg, feeding on the leaves of white mulberry trees, and then 'spins' a protective cocoon of fine silk thread. Before it can emerge as the perfect insect, when it would in the natural state live for a few days (mating and egg-laying then taking place), the silk maker ensures its death by plunging the cocoon in hot water or in a hot oven. To allow it to emerge would damage the thread: from such damaged cocoons the inferior spun S. is made. The thread from a number of cocoons is then reeled together to form a strong filament of raw S.: one cocoon has *c.* 275 m/300 yds of thread. The introduction of synthetics originally harmed the S. industry, but S. has properties synthetics do not possess and rising standards of living have produced an increased demand for real S. Japan produces just over half the world's S. (mostly for domestic use in kimonos, etc.) followed by China (23 per cent) and the Soviet Union (9 per cent): Italy and France, as having climates best suited to the trees on which the larvae must feed and to the requirements of the insect's own development, are European producers. More recently India has scientifically developed the production of wild silk (tasar or tussah), valued for the irregularities which pattern the surface of the finished textile. Special strains of silkworm (*Antheraea mylitta* or *provlei*) are reared on plantations of oaks beneath nylon nets, the worms being later transferred to open forest to mature. Lights are used to kill the larvae before emergence. In 1978 Japan produced a solution for silkworm diet problems by developing a cell culture of mulberry tissues for feeding, so eliminating the cultivation and harvesting of plantations.

SILK. Silkworm larvae bred on a farm at Ranaghat in West Bengal, India. *Photo: The Times.*

SILLITOE, Alan (1928-). English novelist. Raised in Nottingham, he set there his first book, *Saturday Night and Sunday Morning* (1958), which reflected in its hero, Arthur Seaton, the complete transformation of working-class status in England since the S.W.W. Later books incl. *The Loneliness of the Long Distance Runner* (1959).

SILLS, Beverly (1929-). American operatic soprano. She was one of the world's most dramatically gifted singers, as in *Lucia di Lammermoor* and *Traviata.* In 1980 she became manager of NY City Opera.

SILONE (sēlōn'ā), **Ignazio.** Pseudonym of Italian author Secondo Tranquilli (1900-78). Once a Communist, he later became a non-party socialist. His best-known novel, *Fontamara* (1933), described the hopes and disillusionment of a peasant village.

SILVĀ'NUS. A Roman woodland deity, identified in later times with Pan.

SILVER. A lustrous silvery metal extremely malleable and ductile: symbol Ag (Lat. *argentum*), at. no. 47, at. wt. 107.873, Known since prehistoric times, S. occurs native in Peru, but the chief ores are sulphides, from which the metal is extracted by smelting with lead. It is the best metallic conductor of both heat and electricity, and its most important compounds are the chloride and bromide which darken on exposure to light, the basis of photographic emulsions. S. is used for tableware, jewellery, coinage, electrical contacts and electro-plating, and as a solder it makes good metallic joints at 720°C. The world's greatest producer of silver is Mexico (*c.* 40,000,000 troy oz. p.a.), followed by the USA, Canada, Peru, the USSR, Australia and Japan.

SIMENON (sēmenoṅ'), **Georges** (1903-). Belgian author. B. in Liège, of Dutch and Breton blood, he is the son of an insurance salesman. On his father's death he had to cut short his education, but rebelled against being apprenticed to a baker, and became a bookstore assistant for a time before joining the staff of a local newspaper. At 20 he went to Paris and started writing pulp fiction, then at 30 began the realistic and psychologically sound series of detective novels built round the character of Inspector Maigret of the Paris Sûreté, and his loyal assistants. These have been translated, filmed, and televised the world over. He has also written numerous 'plain novels', as he terms them, without the prop of police detection, such as *A Wife at Sea, The Stain on the Snow,* and *The Woman in the Grey House.*

SIMENON. Georges Simenon, the novelist of the world of crime for whom the human element is overwhelmingly the most important in the mystery equation.

SIMEON STYLITES, St (*c.* 390-459). Syrian Christian ascetic, who lived for 37 years on a pillar.

SIMFEROPOL (simferō'poly). Town in the Crimea, Ukrainian SSR, 65km (40m) NE of Sevastopol, cap. of Crimea region. Soap, tobacco, etc., are manufactured. The military academy provides sabotage and terrorist training for foreigners, e.g. members of the PLO. S. was occupied by the Germans Nov. 1941-April 1944. It is on the site of the Tartar town of Ak-Mechet, conquered by the Russians 1783 and renamed. Pop. (1977) 291,000.

SI'MLA. Cap. of Himachal Pradesh (from 1948), Rep. of India, 2,300 m (7,500 ft) a.s.l. in the Himalayan foothills, 275km (170m) N of Delhi. It was the summer seat of the govt of British India 1864-1947. Pop. (1971) 45,000.

SIMON, Herbert (1916-). American psychologist and computer expert. Researching into the decision-making process in business corporations, he discovered that maximum profit was seldom the chief motive: Nobel prize in economics 1978.

SIMON, John Allsebrook, visct (1873-1954). British Liberal politician and lawyer. As Home Sec. in 1915 he resigned in protest against conscription in 1916 and served in the RFC. Entering the Nat. Govt in 1931 as For. Sec., he was Home Sec. 1935-7, and Chancellor of the Exchequer 1937-40. His chief mark was made by his judgments as Lord Chancellor 1940-5.

SIMON, Neil (1927-). American playwright. B. in NY, he was until 1946 an air force engineer, and began his literary career by working in the mail room of Warner Brothers Pictures in New York. His plays incl. *Barefoot in the Park* (1963), *The Odd Couple* (1965) - a study of a male homosexual ménage - and *The Sunshine Boys* (1972), all of which have been filmed.

SIMONSTOWN. Naval base (1814) in S Africa on False Bay, 37km (23m) S of Capetown. Under the S. Agreement (1955) Britain used its facilities until 1975, when the arrangement was terminated by the Labour govt as a mark of disapproval of S African racial policy.

SĪ'MONY. Name given to the buying and selling of presentation to an ecclesiastical benefice, preferment, etc. It is derived from Simon Magnus, who (as told in Acts viii) offered the Apostles money in return for the power of the Holy Ghost.

SIMPLON (sańploń'). Pass on the borders of Switzerland and Italy. It runs in a SE direction from Brig to Domodossola, rises to 2,006 m (6,582 ft) and is followed by a road built by Napoleon I 1800-5. Under it runs the S. tunnel 19.8 km (12.3m).

SIMPSON, Sir James Young (1811-70). British physician. He took his MD at Edinburgh in 1832, became pres. of the Royal Medical Soc. 1835, and prof. of midwifery 1839. He was largely instrumental in the introduction of chloroform as an anaesthetic in 1847. He was created a baronet in 1866.

SIMPSON, Norman Frederick (1919-). British dramatist. A lecturer in history and English for adult education, his plays *A Resounding Tinkle* (1957), *The Hole* (1958), and *One Way Pendulum* (1959) show the logical development of an abnormal situation, and belong to the 'Theatre of the Absurd'.

SIMPSON DESERT. Area of sand-hills in wave-like formation, with stiff-leaved grasses growing in the troughs, chiefly in Australia's Northern Territory, but partly in Queensland and S Australia. It was named after a pres. of the S Australian Geographical Society who financed its exploration. Area 145,000 sq km (56,000 sq. m).

SINAI (sī'nī). Egyptian peninsula between the gulfs of Suez and Aqaba, at the head of the Red Sea. The Mount Sinai, on which Moses received from Jehovah, the tables of the Law, has been identified with Gebel Mûsa (2,285 m/7,497 ft), near the tip of the peninsula. Sinai was occupied by Israel in 1967, and in 1973 was the scene of the **Battle of S.** 14-19 Oct. between Egyptian and Israeli forces, in which more tanks were used than at Alamein. Israel withdrew, under the disengagement agreement of 1975, and the Camp David peace treaty of 1979, from the area W of a line El 'Arīsh Rās Muhammad, and restored the whole of Sinai to Egyptian control in April 1982. Egypt established a religious complex (Jewish-Moslem-Christian) at Mt Sinai in 1979. There are oil and natural gas resources, and an aqueduct carrying Nile water to S. was begun in 1979.

SINA'TRA, Frank (1917-). American singer. B. in Hoboken, NJ, the son of a former prizefighter, he achieved fame as a heart-throb singer - 'Night and Day', 'You'd Be So Nice to Come Home To', etc., and then estab. himself as an actor, as in *From Here to Eternity* (1953) which won him Oscar. Greatest of his later song successes is 'My Way'.

SINCLAIR, Upton (1878-1968). American novelist. B. in Baltimore, he attracted attention with *The Jungle* (1906), dealing with the Chicago stockyards. Among his later works are *Boston* (1928), and the Lanny Budd series, incl. *Presidential Agent* (1944).

SIND. Prov. of Pakistan, mainly in the Indus delta. Annexed in 1843, it became a prov. of British India, and part of Pakistan on independence. There is agitation among its people for the establishment of a separate S. state, Sindhudesh. Area 122,000 sq.km (47,000 sq.m); pop. (1972) 13,965,000.

SI'NDING, Christian (1856-1941). Norwegian composer. His works incl. 3 symphonies, piano pieces and songs. **Otto** (1842-1909) and **Stephan** (1846-1922), his brothers, were painter and sculptor respectively.

SINGAPORE. Island state of Asia, lying off the southern tip of Malaya and joined to the mainland by a causeway across the Strait of Johore. Leased 1819 from the sultan of Johore by the British East India Co., on the advice of Stamford Raffles, when it was merely a swampy jungle, it passed to the Crown in 1858. During the S.W.W. Singapore was in Japanese occupation 15 Feb. 1942-12 Sept. 1945; its defences had been designed to defeat attack by sea from the south, and the eventual invasion was by land from the north. By 1946 it was created a separate crown colony, became independent in 1959, and was incl. in Malaysia, but seceded to become a rep. within the Commonwealth in 1965. The People's Action Party, led by Lee Kuan Yew (q.v.), achieved power on self-govt. and retained it on independence, but an opposition to their policies soon developed. In March 1985, the president, Devan Nair, resigned on grounds of alcoholism and was succeeded in Aug. by Mr Wee Kim Wee.

The cap. Singapore City, is on the S coast and was founded by Raffles in 1819, developing into a major port, serving the whole of Malaya and exporting rubber, tin, copra, etc. in quantity. There are dockyards, and a major shipbuilding yard at Sembawang in the N of the island, and Jurong, to the W of the city has factories, a new deep-water port, oil refineries and residential development. The internat. airport is at Paya Lebar NE of the city. The city has a Raffles Museum, a univ. (1949), and is a major financial centre of the Far East.

Area 581.5 sq.km (225.6 sq.m); pop. (1973) 2,200,000, the great majority Chinese. M.U.: S. dollar.

SINGLE SIDEBAND TRANSMISSION. Method of transmitting radio waves under consideration by the Internat. Telecommunications Union, using either the frequency band above the carrier frequency, or that below, instead of both (double sideband transmission) as is done now. The technique would reduce airwave congestion, but requires the replacement or conversion of all existing receivers.

SING SING. Name until 1901 of the US village of Ossining, New York, famous as the site of a state prison (1825, rebuilt 1930).

SINING. *See* XINING.

SINKIANG-UIGHUR. *See* XINJIANG UYGUR.

SINN FEIN (shin fān) (Gaelic, 'We ourselves'). Irish nationalist party, founded by Arthur Griffith in 1905, with a policy of resistance to British rule. After 1917 it became under De Valera the centre of the republican movement, and ousted the old Home Rule Party in the 1918 elections.

SINGAPORE. A young boy paints the shaman, who will then take on the divinity of the monkey-god. Drawing blood by self flagellation and cutting his tongue, he will immerse pieces of paper in the sacred fluid and sell them to his faithful followers. *Photo: Mireille Vautier*

It survived only as a small extremist group after the creation of Fianna Fáil.

SINO-JAPANESE WARS. The first war between China and Japan, in 1894-5, ended in a Japanese victory and the annexation of Formosa and the Pescadores. In 1931-2 the Japanese occupied Manchuria, which they formed into the puppet state of Manchukuo, and attacked Shanghai. War was renewed in 1937, when the Japanese overran NE China and seized Shanghai and Nanking. In 1938 they captured Hankow and Canton, and the Chinese cap. was transferred to Chungking. A period of stalemate followed. The Japanese attack on Britain and the USA in 1941 was followed by the extension of lease-lend aid to China, but the loss of Burma cut off a valuable source of supplies. A Japanese offensive in 1944 seriously threatened Chungking. The Chinese shared in the final offensive in 1945, and received the Japanese surrender at Nanking in Sept.

SIOUX (soo) **CITY.** City of Iowa, USA, on the Missouri near its junction with the Big Sioux r. Founded 1849, it is an important livestock and dairy-products centre. Pop. (1970) 85,925.

SIOUX FALLS. Largest city in S Dakota, USA on the Big Sioux r., near the 30m (100ft) high Sioux Falls, which supply power for its industry. Pop. (1970) 72,500

SIOUX INDIANS. Principal tribe of the Dakota family of N American Indians, now confined to S Dakota and Nebraska. Gen. George Custer (1839-76) was killed with 250 men when he moved against a S. camp at Little Bighorn, Montana (under chiefs Crazy Horse and Sitting Bull): the site of Custer's 'Last Stand' is a nat. monument. Following this S. revolt, Congress abrogated the Fort Laramie treaty of 1868 which had made over to the Indians a large area in the Black Hills of Dakota where gold was to be found. Today uranium, coal, oil and natural gas are also found there, and the S. were awarded $160 million compensation in 1980.

SIRENS. In Greek mythology, sea nymphs who lured sailors on to the rocks by their singing. When Odysseus passed them he tied himself to the mast and stuffed his companions' ears with wax, while the Argonauts escaped them because Orpheus' singing surpassed theirs.

SIRO'CCO. A hot, normally dry and dust-laden wind which blows from the highland of Africa to N Africa, Malta, Sicily, and Italy. It occurs mainly in the spring. The name S. has been applied to southerly winds in the E of the USA.

SISAL HEMP. *See* HEMP.

SI'SKIN. Bird (*Carduelus spinus*) in the finch family Fringillidae, found in the Old World from Britain to Japan: it is greenish yellow with an attractive song. The American S. is more accurately the pine-finch (*Spinus pinus*).

SISLEY (sis'li), **Alfred** (1840-99). French artist. B. in Paris, of English parents, he studied under Gleyre, and became associated with Monet and Renoir. He met with little success in his lifetime, but he is now regarded as among the best of the Impressionists. A landscape painter, he painted the effects of light at different times of the day.

SISYPHUS (sis'ifus). A mythical king of Corinth, who was condemned in the underworld to roll uphill a huge stone which always rolled down again when it reached the top.

SI'TAR. Indian instrument of the guitar family: *see illus. under* MUSIC.

SITWELL, Sir Osbert (1892-1969). Brit. poet and author. B. in London, the son of Sir George S. (1860-1943), he went to Eton, and served in the Grenadier Guards 1912-19. He pub. his *Selected Poems* in 1943, and wrote art criticism, novels, e.g. *A Place of One's Own* (1941); and a series of autobiographical vols.: *Left Hand! Right Hand!, The Scarlet Tree, Great Morning, Laughter in the Next Room, Noble Essences* and *Tales My Father Taught Me* (1945-62). His brother, **Sir Sacheverell S.** (1897-), was b. at Scarborough, and has pub. art criticism, e.g. *Southern Baroque Art* (1924), and *British Architects and Craftsmen* (1945); poetry; and prose miscellanies such as *Sacred and Profane Love,* and *Splendours and Miseries.* His sister **Dame Edith S.** (1887-1964), also b. in Scarborough, pub. *Collected Poems* (1930), and *Shadow of Cain* (1948); the prose *Life of Alexander Pope* (1930), and *Aspects of Modern Poetry* (1934); and the autobiography *Taken Care Of* (1965).

SIVA (sē'vah) or **SHIVA** (Skr. for 'propitious'). The 3rd person in the Hindu triad. As Mahadeva (great lord), he is the creator, symbolized by the phallic *linga,* who restores what as Mahakala he destroys. He is often sculptured as Nataraja, performing his fruitful cosmic dance. His consort or female principle (*sakti*), is Parvati, otherwise known as Durga or Kali.

SIXTUS. Name of 5 popes. **Sixtus IV** (1414-84), who became pope in 1471, built the Sistine Chapel, which is named after him. **Sixtus V** (1521-90), who became pope in 1585, supported the Spanish Armada and the Catholic League against Henry IV.

SJAELLAND. *See* SEELAND.

SKA'GERRAK. Arm of the North Sea between the S coast of Norway and the N coast of Denmark. In May 1916 it was the scene of a naval action called in Britain the battle of Jutland.

SKANE (skaw'ne). Densely peopled prov. of S Sweden. A fertile agricultural region, Danish until ceded to Sweden in 1658, it comprises the counties of Malmöhus and Kristianstad; Malmö and Hälsingborg are important centres.

SKARA BRAE (skah'ra brā). Remarkably preserved Neolithic village to the N of Stromness, on Pomona, Orkney Is. Both houses and furniture are of stone construction; the houses are linked by roofed alleys; and the whole is concealed under a refuse mound, so as to be 'underground'.

SKATE. The name of several species of flat fish of the ray family. The common S. (*Raia batis*) is from 60-125cm (2-4ft), greyish, with black specks. Found off the British coasts, it is eaten. The egg-cases ('mermaids' purses') are often thrown up by the tide.

SKATEBOARD. Single flexible board of glass-fibre, aluminium, laminated wood, etc., rather longer and broader than the human foot, with 4 cast-moulded urethane wheels mounted on axle units to allow for accurate steering by weight positioning. First developed in the early 1960s in California, as a land alternative to surfing, they became a world-wide craze in the 1970s.

SKATING. Self-propulsion on ice by means of bladed skates, or on some artificial composition surface by means of skates with 4 small rollers. Ice S. probably originated in Scandinavia, the first skates being animal bones, was popular on the canals of medieval Holland, and in the 17th and 18th cents. in England and on the Continent. The first English S. club was founded in London in 1842, followed in 1849 by one in Philadelphia, where the first all-iron skate was invented in 1850 by E. W. Bushnell: the first artificial ice rink was opened in London in 1876. National bodies incl. the National S. Assocn of Gt Britain (1879), US Figure S. Assocn (1886) and the Canadian Figure S. Assocn (1888), all subject to the International S. Union. Competitive S. events incl. figure (comprising compulsory figures and free S.) for men, women and pairs; dance - for pairs; speed - for men and women. Roller S. first developed in the 18th cent., but the modern 4-wheel skate was the invention of the American James L. Plympton who also opened the first rink at Newport, Rhode Island, in 1866. Events are as for ice S., and in Britain the NSA is the governing body: international control is exercised by the Fédération Internationale de Patinage à Roulettes. *See also* ICE HOCKEY.

SKEGNESS. Holiday resort on the coast of Lincs, England, site of the first Butlin (q.v.) holiday camp. Pop. (1974) 13,560.

SKELMERSDALE. Town in Lancs, W of Wigan, developed as a 'new town' from 1962, with many light industries. Pop. (1975) 40,000.

SKELTON, John (*c.* 1460-1529). English poet. He became tutor to Prince Henry, later Henry VIII, and took orders in 1498. Among his poems are *Colyn Cloute, Phylyp Sparowe,* and *The Tunning of Elynour Rumming.*

SKI'DDAW. Mtn. (930 m/3,053 ft) of Cumbria, England, in the Lake district, N of Keswick.

SKIING. Self-propulsion on snow by means of elongated wooden, metal or plastic skis, *c.* 100mm (4in) wide, *c.* 2m (7ft) long and bent upward at the tip, usually with the assistance of ski poles held in the hands. Prehistoric types of ski date in Sweden to *c.* 3,000 BC, but they were primarily a means of civil or military transport until the sport developed in Norway *c.* 1860. Competition events incl. slalom, in which flags (placed to make the turns as difficult as possible) mark out a course of varying gradient; cross-country racing; and ski jumping - over 150 m (400 ft) being achieved. The Fédération Internationale des Skieurs (1924) is linked with the Ski Club of Great Britain (1924), the Canadian Amateur Ski Assocn (1920), the Nat. Ski Assocn of America (1904), etc. Allied to the ski is the N American Indian snow shoe, a broad frame work covered with a thong web, and useful for travel in thick forest. In water S. the skis are wider and shorter than snow skis, and the skier is towed by a motorboat.

SKATING. John Curry, the world champion amateur, who became professional to devote himself to skating as theatrical expression. *Photo: Colorsport*

SKIING. Ideal for the learner or the expert limbering up for winter sports is the plastic slope now often installed, either in the open air or in large stores. *Photo: Courtesy of Bakelite Ltd.*

SKI'KDA. Port (formerly Philippeville) in Algeria, founded by the French in 1838, and re-named after independence. It is a trade centre for wine, citrus, and vegetables. Pop. (1974) 128,000.

SKIN. The covering of the body. Its outer layer, the epidermis, is insensitive and protective, and the cells of this are constantly being rubbed away and replaced from below; the lower layer, the true skin or corium, is full of blood-vessels and nerves of sensation, touch and temperature control. It contains the hair roots, and the sweat and sebaceous glands, and is supported by a network of fibrous and elastic cells. Skin diseases may be the result of infection, e.g. impetigo, herpes or rarely tuberculosis; tumours, e.g. cancer; fungus invasion, e.g. ringworm; rashes from a multiplicity of common drugs, or contact or allergic dermatitis from furs, hair dyes and some detergents. Skin-grafting is the repair of injured skin by placing pieces of skin taken from elsewhere on the body so that the cells may multiply and cover it.

SKIPTON. Town in N Yorks, England, about 35km (22m) NW of Leeds. Textiles are made. Pop. (1972) 13,000.

SKITTLES. A game with the object of knocking down 9 wooden S. forming a square at one end of an alley by means of a ball hurled from the other. An angle of the square faces the alley. The game resembles tenpin bowling (q.v.).

SKOPJE (skop'yā). Cap. of Macedonia, Yugoslavia, on the Vardar. On the site of an ancient town destroyed by earthquake in the 5th cent., it was taken by the Serbian king Milutin in the 13th cent.; he made it his cap. Again destroyed by earthquake 1963, S. was rebuilt on a safer nearby site. There are chromium mines, iron and steel-works, and an airport. S. is a Moslem centre. Pop. (1972) 400,000.

SKUA (skioo'a). Genus of seabirds, of which the largest is the great S. (*Catharacta skua*) of the N Atlantic, 60cm (2ft) long and dark brown on the upper parts. Very aggressive, the Ss. seldom fish for themselves but force gulls to disgorge their catch.

SKULL. The collection of flat and irregularly shaped bones (22 in all) which enclose and protect the brain and form the face. The brain case (cranium) consists of plates of bone joined by sutures. The bones of the face carry the upper teeth and enclose some air spaces (sinuses) and form the framework for the eyes, nose and mouth. The lower jaw is hinged to the middle of the cranium at its lower edge. Inside, the cranium is hollowed into various shallow cavities into which fit different parts of the brain; the plate corresponding to the back of the head (occipital) is jointed at its lower edge with the upper section of the spine (atlas and axis). The floor of the skull is pierced by a great hole for the spinal cord and a number of apertures through which pass other nerves and blood-vessels.

SKUNK. N American mammal of the family *Mustelidae*. The common S. (*Mephitis mephitis*) has a long, arched body, short legs, a bushy tail, and a black fur with white streaks on the back. In self-defence it discharges a foul-smelling fluid.

SKYDIVING. *See* FREEFALLING.

SKYE (skī). Largest is. of the Inner Hebrides, in Highland region, Scotland, separated from the mainland by the Sound of Sleat. The chief port is Portree. Area 1,665 sq.km (643 sq.m).

SKYE TERRIER. Variety of Scotch terrier. It is rather small with a long coat, varying from dark blue to light grey in colour.

SKYLAB MISSION. Space programme undertaken by the USA on the directive of Nixon (1970) to estab. an experimental space station in orbit 435km (270m) above the Earth. It remained in orbit 14 May 1973-11 July 1979, being visited by manned spacecraft, but then re-entered Earth's atmosphere, and disintegrated, fragments falling on Western Australia. Solar energy was used to power scientific instruments for the first time on board Skylab.

SKYLARK. *See* LARK.

SKYROS (skī'ros). Greek island, one of the N Sporades, in the Aegean. Rupert Brooke (q.v.) is buried here. Area 207 sq.km (79 sq.m).

SKYSCRAPER. *See* UNITED STATES: ARCHITECTURE.

SLADE, Felix (1790-1868). British art collector. B. in London, he bequeathed most of his art collection to the British Museum and endowed Slade art professorships at Oxford, Cambridge, and University College, London. The Slade School is a branch of University College.

SLANDER. One variety of defamation, the other being libel (q.v.). Defamatory spoken words or gestures constitute S., but if broadcast, constitute a libel. Such Ss. as imputing incapacity to a person in his profession, or unchastity to a woman, are actionable without proof of pecuniary loss. As in the case of libel, the S. must be pub. to some person other than the person defamed for it to be actionable.

SLATE. Kind of fine-grained, bluish-purple rock which splits readily into thin slabs suitable for roofing. It is highly resistant to atmospheric conditions, and is also used for writing purposes with chalk. The N Welsh kind is finest.

SLAVERY. The legal and economic status of being another's property. S. probably originated in early agricultural societies, the slaves being recruited from prisoners of war. In Greece and Rome S. formed the economic basis of society. From the 2nd cent. BC conquest flooded Rome with slaves, who in the 1st cent. AD outnumbered free men in Italy, and several slave revolts occurred. The economic crisis of the 2nd cent. AD onwards led to alleviation of the slaves' lot, and serfdom replaced S. It nevertheless died out slowly, surviving in England until the 11th cent. The colonization of America led to a revival of S. in the 16th cent., and to the establishment of a traffic in Negro slaves. Humanitarian agitation led to the prohibition of the slave trade in the British dominions in 1807 and of slave-holding itself in 1833. Leaders of the movement were Granville Sharp, Thomas Clarkson and Wilberforce. In the USA the Civil War turned largely on slavery, which was declared illegal by Lincoln in 1865. Slavery was not officially abolished in Saudi Arabia until 1963, and in Mauritania not until 1980, and still lingers in parts of the world.

SLAVKOV. Czech name of AUSTERLITZ.

SLAVS (slahvz). Indo-European race. They appear to have originated in the Carpathian regions, and by the 7th cent. had occupied an area lying between the Baltic, Elbe, Adriatic, and Black Sea. During the 9th cent. they embraced Christianity, and in the course of the Middle Ages they were expelled from what is now E Germany. After the 16th cent. S. settled in Siberia on an increasingly large scale. The S. have for long been divided into well-defined national groups, among which the Russians (E Slavs) are by far the largest. Others incl. the Poles, Czechs, Slovaks, and Wends (W Slavs), and Serbo-Croats, Slovenes, and Bulgars (S Slavs).

SLEEP. Unconscious state which follows naturally after mental and physical activity, and acts as a restorative of both. It may be prevented by worry and stress, and may be

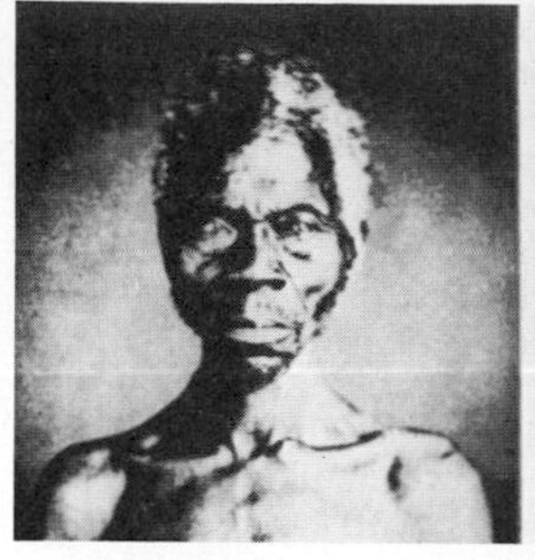
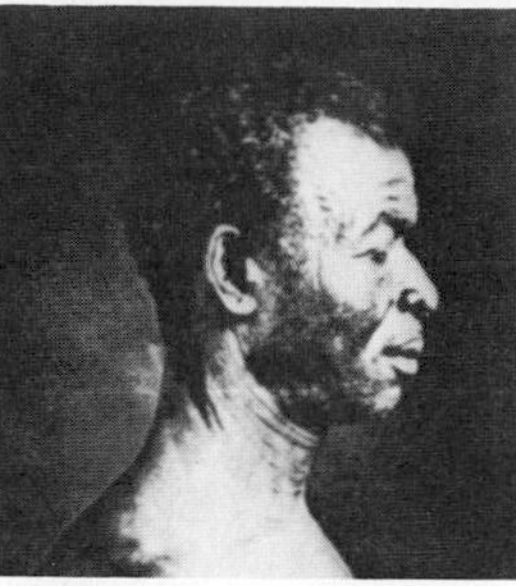

SLAVERY. Two daguerrotypes, possibly the earliest known photographs of American slaves, discovered at Harvard University in 1977. On the left, a Congo slave called Renty, and on the right Jack, from the Guinea Coast, who bears ritual scars decorating his cheek. *Photos: Popperfoto*

induced by drugs. Its mechanisms are still imperfectly known, but it is divided into alternating periods of non-rapid eye movement (NREM), when the heartbeat is regular and no dreams (q.v.) apparently occur, and of rapid eye movement (REM) when the heartbeat is irregular and dreams occur. Both types are essential to health, and the body seems to try to make up any loss in the 7 hours S. which is the average adult requirement: in infancy and sickness longer is required, and the old sleep less. Sleeping drugs tend to reduce the amount of dreaming-type sleep, which is one reason for their long-term use being regarded as harmful.

SLEEPING SICKNESS. Trypanosomiasis; acute disease caused by blood parasites carried by the tsetse fly, etc. When the parasites enter the cerebrospinal fluid, the patient becomes apathetic, and sleeps continually until he dies. The chief symptoms are fever, rash, illness, and sensitivity of the bones to blows. Treatment is with such drugs as Suramin and Mel B.

SLEEPY SICKNESS. Encephalitis lethargica; disease chiefly affecting the central nervous system. Inflammation of the brain, caused by a number of different viruses is followed by death in 40 per cent of cases and invalidism in a large proportion of others. No treatment has yet been developed.

SLIDE RULE. A mathematical instrument used for rapid calculations; incl. multiplication, division, and the extraction of square-roots.

SLĪ'GŌ. Maritime co. of Connacht, Rep. of Ireland. The Darty mtns in the NE rise to 644m (2,113 ft) in Ben Bulben, and Loughs Arrow, Gill and Gara are of striking beauty. There is dairying and stock rearing, and coal, lead, copper and iron ore are mined. The cap. is S., on the Garrogue. Area 1,795 sq.km (694 sq.m); pop. (1971) 50,275.

SLIM, William Joseph, 1st visct (1891-1970). British field marshal. In the F.W.W. he fought at Gallipoli. As commander of the 14th 'forgotten' army 1943-5, he stemmed the Japanese invasion of India at Imphal and Kohima, and then recovered Burma, his forces killing more Japanese than the rest of the Allies in the Pacific theatre. He was CIGS 1948-52, and Gov.-Gen. of Australia 1953-60.

SLOANE (slōn), **Sir Hans** (1660-1753). British physician. B. in Co. Down, he settled in London, and in 1721 founded the Chelsea Physic Garden. He was president of the Royal College of Physicians 1719-35, and in 1727 succeeded Newton as president of the Royal Society. His library, etc., which he bequeathed to the nation, formed the nucleus of the British Museum.

SLOE. *See* BLACKTHORN.

SLŌTH. Family (Bradypodidae) of mammals of the order Edentata, confined to S America. They have small rounded heads, rudimentary tails, and prolonged fore-limbs: each foot has long curved claws adapted to clinging upside down from trees. The fur is greyish-brown, and the diet vegetarian. The chief species are the 3-toed S. or aï (*Bradypus tridactylus*), and the 2-toed S. (*Choloepus didactylus*) of Brazil.

SLOUGH (slow). Town in Berks, England, nr Windsor. There is a large trading estate with engineering and other factories. Pop. (1974) 101,580.

SLOVAKIA. Region in the E of Czechoslovakia settled in the 5th-6th cents. by Slavonic tribes; occupied by the Magyars in the 10th cent.; part of the kingdom of Hungary until 1918 when it became a prov. of Czechoslovakia (q.v.). S. was a puppet state under German domination 1939-45, and was abolished as an administrative division in 1949. Its cap. and chief town was Bratislava.

SLOVĒNES (slōvēnz'). Slav people, inhabiting Slovenia and parts of Styria, and Carinthia. They speak a language akin to Serbo-Croat, and number *c.* 1,750,000. There was dispute between Austria and Yugoslavia over the rights of S. in S Carinthia.

SLOVĒ'NIA. Federal rep. of Yugoslavia, lying between Austria to the N, and Croatia to the S. The surface is mountainous, and agriculture and forestry are important. Ljubljana is the cap. Before 1918 S. was the Austrian prov. of Carniola. Area 20,245 sq.km (7,817 sq.m); pop. (1971) 1,697,500.

SLOW-WORM. *See* BLINDWORM.

SLUG. An air-breathing gastropod of the families Limacidae and Arionidae, and related families. The grey field S. (*Limax agrestis*) is the commonest British species, and a pest to crops and garden plants.

SMALL ARMS. One of the 2 main divisions of firearms (q.v.), S.A. came into use in the late 14th cent. as portable hand-guns, supported on the ground and ignited by hand. The matchlock, evolved during the 15th cent., used a match of tow and saltpetre gripped by an S-shaped lever which was rocked towards the touch hole with one finger, enabling the gun to be held, aimed and fired in much the same way as today. Front and back sights, followed by a curved stock which could be held against the shoulder (in the hackbut or Hookgun), gave increased precision. The inherent difficulty involved in keeping a match alight in wet weather was overcome by the introduction of the wheel lock, *c.* 1515, in which a shower of sparks was produced by a spring-drawn steel wheel struck by iron pyrites. This cumbrous and expensive mechanism evolved into the simpler flintlock *c.* 1625, operated by flint striking steel and in general use for 200 years until a dramatic advance, the 'percussion cap', invented in 1810 by a sport-loving Scottish clergyman, Alexander Forsyth, removed the need for external igniters. Henceforth, weapons were fired by a small explosive detonator placed behind or within the base of the bullet, struck by a built-in hammer. The principles of rifling, breech loading and the repeater, although known since the 16th cent. were not sucessfully exploited until the 19th cent. It was known that imparting a spin made the bullet's flight truer, but the difficulty of making the bullet bite the grooves had until then prevented the use of rifling. The Baker rifle, issued to the Rifle Brigade in 1800, was loaded from the front of the barrel (muzzle), and had a mallet for hammering the bullets into the grooves. The first breech loader was Von Dreyse's 'needle gun', issued to the Prussian army in 1842, in which the detonator was incorporated with the cartridge. By 1870 breech loading was in general use, being quicker, and sweeping the barrel out after each firing. An early rifle with bolt action was the Lee-Metford (1888) followed by the Lee-Enfield, both having a 'magazine' beneath the breech, containing a number of cartridges. With modifications this model is still used by the British army. US developments favoured the repeater (Winchester *et al.*) in which the fired case was extracted and ejected, the hammer cocked, and a new charge inserted into the chamber, all by one reciprocation of a finger lever. In the semi-automatic, part of the explosion energy performs the same operations: the Garand, used by the US army, is of this type. Completely automatic weapons were increasingly adopted during the S.W.W. From 1954 the British army standardized upon the Belgian FN 30 which is gas operated and can fire shots singly or automatically at 650-700 rounds per min. *See* MACHINE GUN.

SMALLPOX. Virus disease, highly contagious and giving rise to fever and a thick eruption, mostly on the arms, legs and face, resulting in permanent pitting and scarring. It was endemic in Europe until the development of vaccination, and remained so in Asia, where the virulent form of the disease (variola major) entailed a fatality rate of 30%, until the worldwide WHO campaign from 1967 which resulted in its eradication by 1980.

SMART, Christopher (1722-71). British poet. He became a fellow of Pembroke Coll., Cambridge, but settled in London as a hack writer. He was confined in 1756 to an asylum, where he wrote his greatest poems, 'A Song to David' and 'Rejoice in the Lamb'.

SMELT. Small fish of the family Osmeridae and the genus *Osmerus.* The most common European S. is the sparling (*Osmerus eperlanus*), which is noted for its delicate flavour: related species occur on the coasts of the USA.

SMERSH. In the Soviet Union, the Main Admin of Counter-Intelligence, estab. 1942 on the basis of the existing Main Admin of the Special Branches of the State Security Service. The name is an acronym, said to have been devised by Stalin from the Russian words (SMERt' SHpionam) meaning 'death to spies'. Its functions were later taken over by other groups. *See* KGB.

SMETANA (smet'ahnah), **Friedrich** (1824-84). Czech composer. B. at Litomyšl, he was largely ed. in Germany, and became conductor of the Gothenburg Philharmonic Society in 1856. He settled in Prague in 1863, where in 1866 he became conductor at the national theatre, and his music developed a national character. He became deaf in 1874, lost his reason in 1883, and d. in an asylum. His finest works are the operas *The Bartered Bride* (1866) and *Dalibor,* and the symphonic suite *My Country.*

SMILES, Samuel (1812-1904). Scottish author. B. at Haddington, he became in turn a doctor, journalist, and sec. to railway companies. He achieved fame with a life of Stephenson (1857), and the popular didactic work, *Self Help* (1859).

SMITH, Adam (1723-90). Scottish economist. B. at Kirkcaldy, he was prof. of moral philosophy at Glasgow 1752-63, publishing his *Theory of Moral Sentiments* in 1759. In *The Wealth of Nations* (1776), the basic idea is of manual labour being the source of a nation's necessaries, and the case is put for free trade in opposition to mercantilist theories; this originated the classical British school of political economy, and largely estab. economics as a separate science.

SMITH, Bessie (1894-1937). American Negro singer. B. in Mississippi, she became known in the 1920s as the 'Empress of the Blues', recording with Louis Armstrong and others.

SMITH, Sir Henry George Wakelyn (1787-1860). British gen. He served in the Peninsular War, and m. a Spanish lady. Subsequently he fought in S Africa and India, and was governor of Cape Colony 1847-52. Ladysmith is named after his wife and Harrismith after himself.

SMITH, Ian Douglas (1919-). Rhodesian statesman. A farmer, b. at Selukwe, Rhodesia, he served in the RAF during the S.W.W. In 1948 he became a member of the S Rhodesia legislative assembly, was a foundation member of the Rhodesian Front 1962, and Min. of the Treasury under Winston Field (1962-4), whom he succeeded as PM. In 1965 he made a unilateral declaration of Rhodesia's independence, and despite UN sanctions and various other pressures, internal and external, maintained his regime with remarkable tenacity. In May 1979 he was succeeded as PM by Bishop Abel Muzorewa, when the country was re-named Zimbabwe-Rhodesia.

SMITH, John (1580-1631). English colonizer. After an adventurous early life, he took part in the colonization of Virginia, acting as president of the colony 1608-9. During an expedition among the Indians his life is said to have been saved by Pocahontas (q.v.). He explored New England in 1614, and pub. pamphlets on America and an autobiography.

SMITH, Joseph. *See* Mormons.

SMITH, Sir Matthew (1879-1960). British artist, known for his exuberant treatment of nudes, luscious fruits and flowers, and landscapes.

SMITH, Sir Ross Macpherson (1892-1922), and **Sir Keith Macpherson S.** (1890-1955). Australian airmen. Brothers, they were the first to fly from England to Australia in 1919, and for this exploit were knighted.

SMITH, Stevie (Florence Margaret) (1903-71). British poet. For 30 years, she worked as personal secretary in a publishing house, making her first literary success with *Novel on Yellow Paper* (1936), but being best known for her poems, beginning with *A Good Time Was Had By All* (1937). She often sang her verse in an idiosyncratic way, which gave her a renewed reputation among young people in the 1960s.

SMITHFIELD. Site of a meat market (1868) and poultry and provision market (1889), in the City of London, England. Formerly an open space, it was the scene of the execution of many Protestant martyrs in the 16th cent., and of the murder of Wat Tyler in 1381, while the annual Bartholomew Fair was held here from 1614 to 1855.

SMITHSON, James (1765-1829). British chemist and mineralogist. The **Smithsonian Institution** in Washington, DC, was estab. in 1846, following his bequest of £100,000 for this purpose, and incl. a museum, art gallery, zoo park, and astrophysical observatory. There is also a Tropical Research Institute in Panama.

SMITH. Stevie Smith, the attractively eccentric poet whose world was the conventional London suburb of Palmers Green. *Photo: Jane Brown/Camera Press*

SMOG. Natural fog plus impurities (unburned carbon and sulphur dioxide) from domestic fires, industrial furnaces and internal combustion engines (petrol or diesel). The use of smokeless fuels, the treatment of effluent and penalties for excessive smoke from poorly maintained and operated vehicles can be extremely effective, as in London, but many cities still suffer, with substantial loss of life, e.g. among chronic bronchitics.

SMOLENSK. City of the RSFSR, cap. of S region, on the Dnieper, 370km (230m) SW of Moscow. Dating from 882, Russian from 1667, it is an educational centre with a 17th-18th cent. cathedral. Its many industries incl. textile and clothing factories, distilleries, and flour mills. Napoleon defeated the Russians at S. in 1812; and fierce fighting centred on the city in 1941 and 1943. Pop. (1977) 264,000.

SMO'LLETT, Tobias George (1721-71). British novelist. B. in Dunbartonshire, he was apprenticed to a Glasgow surgeon, and sailed to the W Indies in 1740 as a naval surgeon. Returning in 1744, he made his name by the picaresque novels *Roderick Random* (1748), *Peregrine Pickle* (1751), *Ferdinand Count Fathom* (1753), *Sir Lancelot Greaves* (1760–2), and *Humphry Clinker* (1771). His methods and vivid characterization greatly influenced Dickens. Among his other works are a *History of England*; a translation of *Don Quixote*; *Travels through France and Italy* (1766), utilizing his experiences in search of health in 1763; and the satire, *Adventures of an Atom* (1769). He d. near Leghorn.

SMUGGLING. The illegal import or export of prohibited goods, or the evasion of customs duties on dutiable goods. Restrictions on imports, originally a means of preventing debasement of coinage (e.g. in 14th cent. England), were later used for raising revenue, mainly on luxury goods, and led to a flourishing period of S. during the 18th cent., in spirits, tobacco, lace, etc. Certain regions were famed for their activities - until the mid-19th cent. the islanders of Scilly, England, poor in natural resources, thought little of the round trip to France in their long boats to bring back contraband - and even today the state of Andorra exists on its 2 principal industries of tourism and S. Modern S., on both the national and international scale, is concerned with such items as watches, diamonds, gold, and narcotics; and is punishable by fines, and in some cases by imprisonment. *See* COASTGUARD.

SMUT and **BUNT.** Parasitic fungi, of the order Ustilaginales, which infect flowering plants, especially cereals.

SMUTS, Jan Christian (1870-1950). S African statesman and soldier. B. in Cape Colony, he studied at Cambridge, and was admitted to the Bar. Having settled in the Transvaal, he was appointed state attorney in 1898, and during the S African War commanded the Boer forces in Cape Colony. He subsequently worked for reconciliation between Boers and British and became Min. of the Interior 1910-12 and Defence Min. 1910-20, on the establishment of the Union. He commanded the S African forces in E Africa 1916-17, and entered the imperial war cabinet in 1917. He was PM 1919-24, and Min. of Justice 1933-9, and on the outbreak of war succeeded Gen. Hertzog as Premier. He held office until defeated at the general election in 1948. He was created a field marshal in 1941 and received the OM in 1947.

SMYRNA (smer'nah). *See* IZMIR.

SMYTH (smīdh), **Dame Ethel** (1858-1944). British composer. B. in London, she studied in Leipzig, and in 1893 her Mass in D was performed in London. Her works incl. the operas *Fantasio*, *The Wreckers*, *The Boatswain's Mate*, *Fête Galante*, and *Entente Cordiale*. She suffered imprisonment as an ardent suffragette. In 1922 she was made DBE. She wrote the autobiographical *Female Pipings in Eden* and *What Happened Next* (1940).

SNAEFELL (snā-). Highest mountain in the Isle of Man, 620m (2,034 ft) high.

SNAIL. Species of air-breathing gastropods, with spiral shells. The more typical Ss. of the genus *Helix*, and family Helicidae, embrace over 1,600 species. The common garden S. (*Helix aspersa*), is very destructive to plants; the Roman S. (*Helix pomatia*) cannot be bred, but is 'corralled' for the gourmet market. Over-collection has depleted the population.

SNAIL. The *Helix pomatia*, or Roman snail, thought to have been introduced into Britain by the Romans for culinary purposes. *Photo: Steven Dalton/NHPA*

SNAKE. A member of the reptilian order Ophidia, characterized by an elongated limbless body possibly evolved because it is advantageous in progression through dense vegetation: one of the most striking internal modifications is the absence or greatly reduced size of the left lung. There are some 3,000 species found in the tropic and

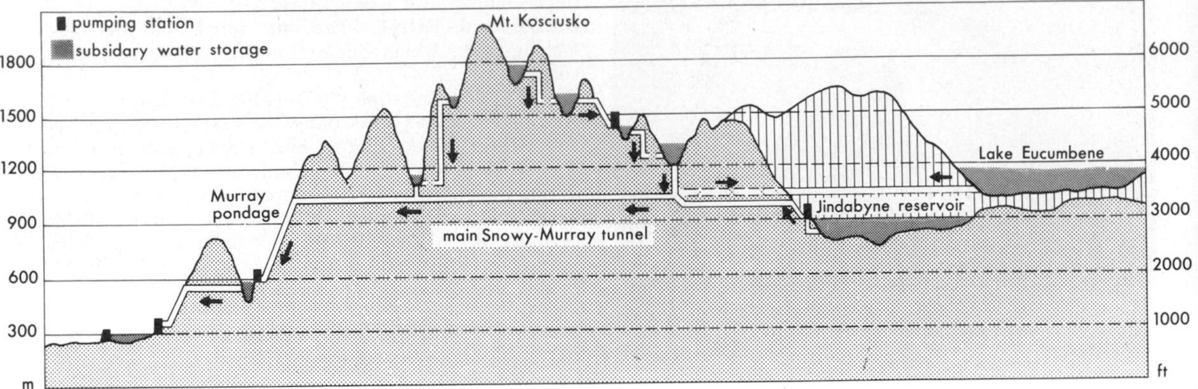

SNOWY MOUNTAINS. Detail of the vast Snowy Mountains hydroelectric and irrigation project. The waters of the Snowy River catchment area are diverted via Lake Eucumbene (which, with Jindabyne reservoir, forms the major storage area) to the Murray River.

temperate zones, but none in New Zealand, Ireland, Iceland, and near the poles. The skin is covered in scales which are markedly wider underneath where they form, in all except a few species, an essential aid to locomotion, e.g. a S. is helpless on glass where these scales can effect no 'grip' on the surface: progression may be undulant, 'concertina' or creeping, or a combination. Detailed vision is limited at a distance, though movement is immediately seen; hearing is restricted to ground vibrations (sound waves are not perceived); the sense of touch is acute; besides the sense of smell through the nasal passages, the flickering tongue picks up airborne particles which are then passed to special organs in the mouth for investigation; and some, e.g. rattlesnakes, have a cavity between eye and nostril which is sensitive to infra-red rays (useful in locating warm-blooded prey in the dark). All Ss. are carnivorous, and often camouflaged for better concealment in hunting as well as their own protection. Some are oviparous and others ovoviviparous, i.e. the eggs are retained in the oviducts until development is complete; in both cases the young are immediately self-sufficient.

The majority of Ss. belong to the Colubridae, chiefly harmless, e.g. the common grass snake of Europe, but incl. the deadly African boomslang *Dispholidus typus.* The venomous families incl. the Elapidae comprising the true cobras (q.v.), the New World coral Ss., and the Australian taipan, copper-head and death adder; the Viperidae (*see* VIPER), and the Hydrophidae, aquatic sea Ss. Anti-sera against snake-bite (made from the venom) are expensive to prepare and store, and specific to one S. species, so that experiments have been made with more widely valid treatment, e.g. trypsin, a powerful protein-degrading enzyme, effective against the cobra/mamba group. Among the more primitive Ss. are the Boidae, which still show links with the lizards and incl. the boa constrictor, anaconda and python: these kill by constriction but only comparatively small animals.

SNAKE. A king brown snake being 'milked' at the Commonwealth Serum Laboratories, Victoria. The venom – the clear fluid at the bottom of the glass – is used in making antivenins. *Photo: Courtesy of Gary C. Lewis*

SNAKE. Affluent of the Columbia r., USA (1,670 km/1,038 m); it flows 65km/40m through Hell's Canyon.

SNAPDRAGON. *See* ANTIRRHINUM.

SNIPE. Marsh bird (*Capella gallinago*) distinguished by its long straight bill, found throughout Europe and valued for the table. Wilson's S. (*C. delicata*) of N America is almost identical. Other species are the rare great S. (*C. media*) and the small jack S. (*Lymneryptes minimus*).

SNOOKER. Derivative of billiards, devised in 1875 at Jubbulpore, India, by Sir Neville Chamberlain (1856-1944), an army officer. The name derives from the derisory nickname for a first-year cadet, 'a snooker', which Sir Neville applied to an opponent who landed him with an unplayable shot. There are 22 balls: 15 'reds' (value 1); the single 'pool' balls, black (value 7), pink (6), blue (5), brown (4), green (3), yellow (2), and the 'cue ball', which is white. The accepted maximum 'break' is 147, reds and pool balls being pocketed alternately. The greatest player was Joe Davis (1901-78), world prof. champion 1927-40 and 1946. The game is now more popular than billiards, and colour television has made it a 'spectator' sport.

SNORING. A loud rattling noise during sleep made by vibration of the soft palate caused by streams of air entering the nose and mouth at the same time.

SNORRI STURLASON (snor'rē stoor lāson) (1179-1241). Icelandic author of the *Heimskringla*, a saga chronicle of Norwegian kings until 1177, and the Prose Edda.

SNOW, Charles Percy, baron (1905-80). British novelist. B. at Leicester, he was tutor at Christ's Coll., Cambridge 1935-45, chief of scientific personnel at the Min. of Labour in the S.W.W. and parliamentary sec. to the Min. of Technology 1964-6. His sequence of novels 'Strangers and Brothers' ranges the British social scale from the 1920s, as seen through the eyes of the narrator 'Lewis Eliot'. It incl. *Time of Hope* (1949), *The Masters* (1951: dramatized 1963) dealing with the election of the master of a Cambridge college; *The New Men* (1954) in which scientists face the problems of nuclear fission, and *Corridors of Power* (1964). His Rede lecture at Cambridge in 1959 'The Two Cultures and the Scientific Revolution' discussed the absence of communication between literary and scientific intellectuals in the West and added a phrase to the language. He received a knighthood 1957 and a life peerage 1964. In 1970 *Last Things* completed the Strangers and Brothers sequence, and *The Malcontents* (1972) turned to the anti-Establishment. In 1950 he m. Pamela Hansford Johnson (q.v.).

SNOW. Flaked particles formed by the condensation in air of excess vapour below freezing point. Light reflecting in the crystals of the flake gives S. a white appearance.

SNOWDEN, Philip, 1st visct (1864-1937). British Labour statesman. B. in Yorks, he worked as a civil servant, and entered parliament in 1906. He stood on the extreme right of the Labour Party, and as Chancellor of the Exchequer, 1924 and 1929-31, pursued a strongly orthodox financial policy. He entered the National Govt in 1931 as Lord Privy Seal, but resigned in 1932.

SNOWDON, Anthony Armstrong-Jones, earl of (1930-). British photographer. The son of Ronald Armstrong-Jones, QC, and his first wife, later countess of Rosse, he was ed. at Eton and Cambridge. He m. HRH Princess Margaret in 1960 and was created earl of S. in 1961. They were divorced in July 1978, and in Dec. 1978 he m. Mrs Lucy Lindsay-Hogg.

SNOWDON. Highest mountain in Wales, 1,085 m (3,560 ft) a.s.l. It consists of a cluster of five peaks. At the foot of S. are the Llanberis, Aberglaslyn, and Rhyd-ddu passes. A rack railway ascends to the summit from Llanberis. Snowdonia the surrounding mountain system, is a Nat. Park (1951).

SNOWDROP. Plant (*Galanthus nivalis*) of the Amaryllidaceae. A spring-blooming bulb, it bears single, white, bell-shaped flowers.

SNOWY MTNS. Range of the Australian Alps. Chiefly in NSW, but with a section across the border in Victoria, it incl. Mt Kosciusko (q.v.), nr which the S. River rises. The river (425km/625m long) flows across Victoria to Bass Strait, but its upper waters were diverted 1949-72, N to the Murrumbidgee and W to the Murray, to provide irrigation and electricity: the scheme incl. 16 large dams.

SNUFF. Powdered tobacco inhaled as a stimulant or sedative. It was common in 17th cent. England, and became universal in the 18th.

SOAMES (sōmz), **Sir Christopher** (1920-). British Cons. politician. He was Sec. of State for War 1958-60, Min. of Agriculture 1960-4, ambassador to Paris 1968-72, vicepres. of the Commission of the European Communities. 1973-7, and Gov. of (Southern) Rhodesia in the period of its transition to independence as Zimbabwe Dec. 1979-April 1980. He m. in 1947 Mary, dau. of Sir Winston Churchill, and in 1978 was created a life peer.

SOANE (sōn), **Sir John** (1753-1837). British architect. B. near Reading, he rebuilt the Bank of England, and was elected RA in 1802. He presented his house in Lincoln's Inn Fields - now the Soane Museum - and his art treasures to the nation.

SOAP. A chemical compound, yielding a lather used in washing; a mixture of the sodium salts of palmitic, stearic, and oleic acids. Made by the action of caustic soda or caustic potash on fats, of animal and vegetable origin. Household Ss. are variously shaped, coloured and usually perfumed.

SOAPSTONE. *See* STEATITE.

SOARES (sō-ahr'esh), **Mario** (1925-). Portuguese statesman. Exiled in 1970, he returned to Portugal in 1974, and in 1976, as leader of the Portuguese Socialist Party (PSP), was PM 1976-8. pledged to achieve a 'socialist democracy'. He resigned as Socialist leader in 1980.

SOBIESKI, John. *See* JOHN III, king of Poland.

SOCIAL CONTRACT. Term in political philosophy for the theory that civil society originated when men agreed to surrender the complete freedom they enjoyed in a state of nature. Hobbes used this theory to justify absolute monarchy, whereas Locke and Rousseau derived from it the inference that all govt rests on the support of the governed.

The term was revived in the UK to denote the unofficial agreement between the Wilson govt. of 1974 and the trade unions that wage demands would be moderated to avoid disruption of the economy. It broke down in 1977.

SOCIAL CREDIT. Economic theory put forward by C. H. Douglas (1879-1952) which finds the cause of crises in the control of money by the banks, leading to a shortage of purchasing power, which could be remedied by payment of a social dividend. It has little success in Britain, but there have been S.C. govts in Canadian provs., although the carrying out of the theory has been vetoed by the central govt.

SOCIAL DEMOCRATIC PARTY. British breakaway party formed in March 1981 following the special Labour Conference in Jan. 1981 which introduced an electoral college to decide the party leadership, and other left-wing measures. The chief founders were Roy Jenkins, David Owen, Shirley Williams (qq.v.), and Bill Rodgers, who objected to the leftward swing in the Labour Party.

SO'CHI. Most popular seaside resort in the RSFSR, USSR, on the Black Sea. In 1976 it became the world's first 'no smoking' city. (1977) 255,000.

SOCIALISM. A movement aiming at the establishment of a classless society through the substitution of common for private ownership of the means of production, distribution, and exchange. The term is used both to cover all movements with this aim, e.g. Communism, Anarchism,

Syndicalism, etc., and more narrowly for Evolutionary S., or Social Democracy.

Anticipations of S. can be found in the ideas of many religious sects, e.g. the Anabaptists and Diggers, and in such Utopias as those of Plato and More. Modern S. originated 1789–1848, in the revolutionary Communism of Babeuf, and the 'Utopian S.' of Owen, Saint-Simon, and Fourier, to which the term was first applied *c.* 1830. Marx and Engels placed S. on a scientific basis, and formed the first Socialist International (1864–72). The Paris Commune (1871) estab. a Socialist govt for a few weeks.

In the later 19th cent. Socialist parties arose in most European countries, the strongest being the German Social Democratic Party; in Britain the Social Democratic Federation was founded in 1881, and the ILP in 1893. This period witnessed a reaction against Marxism, typified by the Fabians and the German Revisionists, at the time when in Russia the Bolsheviks were reviving the original revolutionary significance of Marx's teachings. Weakened by these divisions, the second International (founded in 1889) collapsed in 1914, right-wing Socialists in all countries supporting participation in the F.W.W. while the left opposed it. The Russian revolution removed S. from the sphere of theory to that of practice, and was followed in 1919 by the foundation of the third International, which completed the division between right and left. This lack of unity, in spite of the temporary successes of the Popular Fronts in France and Spain in 1936–8, facilitated the rise of Fascism.

After the S.W.W. Socialist and Communist parties tended to formal union in E Europe, although the rigid Communist control that ensued was later modified in some respects, e.g. Poland, Romania and Yugoslavia. Subsequent tendencies to broader Communism were suppressed in Hungary (1956) and Czechoslovakia (1968). An attempt at a Communist take-over of the Portuguese revolution was defeated 1975–6, and elsewhere in the West there was an uneasy see-saw between alliance and opposition, e.g. the development of a strong near-Communist 'left-wing' element in Britain's Labour Party, the challenge to Socialist domination in Italy in 1976, and the consolidation of their position by the French Communists.

SOCIAL SECURITY. Term for freedom from want through state provision, first used officially in the S.S. Act of the US Congress (1935), passed to enable the Federal govt to cope with the effects of the Great Depression of 1929. The principle involved is, however, a good deal older than that: in Germany compulsory social insurance was estab. in 1883; in Britain compulsory health and unemployment insurance in 1911, non-contributory old-age pensions in 1909.

The term S.S. was first used officially in Britain in 1944, and following the Beveridge (q.v.) Report in 1942, a series of acts was passed from 1945 to widen the scope of S.S., in covering family allowances, supplementary benefits where the family income is below a prescribed level, unemployment, sickness and industrial injury, retirement, provision for dependants on death. It is financed by the state and compulsory contributions from both employer and employee. The S.S. Act (1973) in force from 1975, and the S.S. Pensions Act (1975) replaced the existing largely 'flat-rate' nat. scheme by a basic scheme of earning-related benefits and contributions.

SOCIALISM. Sidney and Beatrice Webb, the pioneers of Fabian Socialism in England, portrayed by Sir William Nicholson. They are seen working on the galley proofs of one of their many books. *Photo: Courtesy of Elizabeth Banks*

In the USA Federal provision for S.S. (medicare, old-age, survivors and disability insurance) is less comprehensive and retains a large voluntary element; unemployment insurance is covered by a joint Federal-State system for industrial workers, but few in agriculture are covered.

SOCIETY ISLANDS. French archipelago in the S Pacific, incl. the Leeward (Huahiné, Raiatéa, Tahaa, Borabora, and Maupiti) and Windward (Tahiti and Moorea) groups. Papeete on Tahiti is the cap. Discovered by the British 1767, the S.I. became a Fr. protectorate 1843 and were annexed by France 1880; they form part of Fr. Polynesia. Area 1,685 sq.km (650 sq.m); pop. (1977) 117,700.

SOCINUS (sōsī'nus). Latinized name of **Lelio Francesco Maria Sozini** (1525–62), Italian Protestant theologian. He adopted Unitarian views on the nature of Christ, which were developed by his nephew, **Fausto Paolo Sozzini** (1539–1604). The latter taught pacifist and anarchist doctrines akin to Tolstoy's; his beliefs are known as Socinianism.

SOCIOBIOLOGY (sō'siō-). Systematic study of all forms of social behaviour, in both animals and humans. It tends to assume that aspects of human behaviour, such as aggression, altruism, male dominance, sexual division of labour and xenophobia, are equally the product of evolution with the size of the human brain, or the development of the hand. It has been criticized on this ground for 'justifying the status quo', but it does also involve a belief that what has developed under certain conditions in the past is not necessarily desirable in meeting changed conditions of the present and future. One of its foremost exponents is Edward Wilson, prof. of zoology at Harvard Univ., author of *Sociobiology: the new synthesis.*

SOCIOLOGY. The study of society, which is the network of human interactions and interrelations. *See* SOCIOBIOLOGY.

SOCOTRA (sōkō'trah). Island in the Indian Ocean 965km (600m) E of Aden. Formerly part of the Mahri sultanate of Qishn and S., which was under Brit. protection from 1886, S. was merged in the rep. of Southern Yemen in 1967. The cap. is Tamridah. The former RAF facilities for anti-submarine patrols are now used by the USSR. Area 3,625 sq.km (1,400 sq.m); pop. (1970) 15,000.

SOCRATES (sok'ratēz) (*c.* 469-399 BC). Athenian philosopher. He is said to have been a sculptor, and served as a soldier, but the greater part of his life he devoted to philosophical discussion. Our main sources of biographical information are Plato's dialogues, Xenophon's *Memorabilia*, and Aristophanes' satirical picture in *The Clouds*; it is uncertain how far Plato attributed his own opinions to S. In philosophy he rejected the search for scientific knowledge, and set himself to guide men to clear thought on ethics and politics; his method was by pretending ignorance to encourage others to talk, and then by cross-examination to expose their inconsistencies. He was accused in 399 of impiety and corrupting the young, and in spite of an eloquent defence condemned to die by drinking hemlock. His trial and death are movingly described by Plato.

SŌ'DA. Common name for sodium carbonate. S.-water is made effervescent by an infusion of carbonic acid under pressure.

SODDY, Frederick (1877-1956). British physical chemist. After working for Rutherford and Ramsay, he was prof. of chemistry at Aberdeen 1914-19 and at Oxford 1919-36. A pioneer of research into atomic disintegration - he coined the term 'isotopes' - he did classic work on radioactivity (*Chemistry of the Radio-Elements*, 1912-14), and was awarded a Nobel prize in 1921. Other scientific books incl. *The Interpretation of the Atom* (1932), and *The Story of Atomic Energy* (1949). Having strong views on education, economics and finance, he also pub. *Cartesian Economics* (1922) and *The Arch Enemy of Economic Freedom* (1943).

SŌ'DIUM. A soft bright silvery reactive metal tarnishing quickly on exposure to air and reacting violently with water to form S. hydroxide: symbol Na (Lat. *natrium*), at. wt. 22.991, at. no. 11. First isolated by Sir Humphry Davy in 1807, it is found abundantly in combination, the commonest form being S. chloride (NaCl - common salt). S. metal is used to a limited extent as a spectroscopic reference, in discharge lamps, and alloyed with potassium as a heat-transfer medium in nuclear reactors.

S. compounds are of the widest industrial importance and thousands of tons are manufactured annually. Among the more important are common salt, S. carbonate (Na_2CO_3 - washing soda), and bicarbonate ($NaHCO_3$ - baking powder), S. hydroxide or caustic soda (NaOH), S. nitrate or Chile saltpetre ($NaNo_2$ - fertilizer), S. thiosulphate or hypo ($Na_2S_2O_3.5H_2O$ - photographic fixer).

An artificial isotope of S., with a half-life of 15 hr is a valuable tracer in the human body.

SO'DOM and **GOMO'RRAH.** 2 of the 5 'cities of the plain' in the Dead Sea area, which according to Genesis were destroyed by fire and brimstone for their wickedness.

SOFIA (sōfē'ah). Cap. of Bulgaria since 1878. It lies at the foot of Vitosha Mts., 130km (80m) NW of Plovdiv, and has many fine modern buildings, incl. the univ. (1880) and the 19th cent. cathedral. Industries incl. textile, rubber, leather, machinery, and electric-equipment making and food processing. There are 2 airports. Pop. (1972) 927,835.

SOFTWARE. The set of instructions produced by a programmer to enable a computer to carry out a given task, as opposed to the 'hardware' of the metal and transistors of the computer itself. It has to be tailored to the needs of the customer, is labour-intensive and demands high skill.

SOGNE (song'ne). Longest and deepest Norwegian fjord: 185km (115m) long and 1,245m (4,080ft) deep.

SOHO (sō'hō). Quarter of W London, between Charing Cross Rd and Regent St. There are many foreign restaurants, night clubs, film co. offices (Wardour Street) and teenage fashion (Carnaby Street).

SOISSONS (swah'soṅ). French town, in Aisne dept, 105km (65m) NE of Paris. It has a 12-13th cent. cathedral and markets agricultural produce. Clovis defeated the Romans at S., 486, ending Roman rule in France. Pop. (1975) 32,000.

SO'KOL ('falcon'). Czech educational and athletic organization founded in 1862, which plays an important part in public life. The movement also flourishes in Poland, Bulgaria, Yugoslavia, and other Slav countries. Until 1948 it was non-political.

SŌ'KŌTO. Town in NW Nigeria, on the S. river. A modern trading centre, it was the cap. of a Fula sultanate from the 16th cent. until occupied by the British in 1903. Pop. (1973) 90,000.

SOLANACEAE. Family of dicotyledonous plants of the tropical and temperate zones, many being native of the Americas, e.g. the potato, tobacco and tomato; *see* NIGHTSHADE.

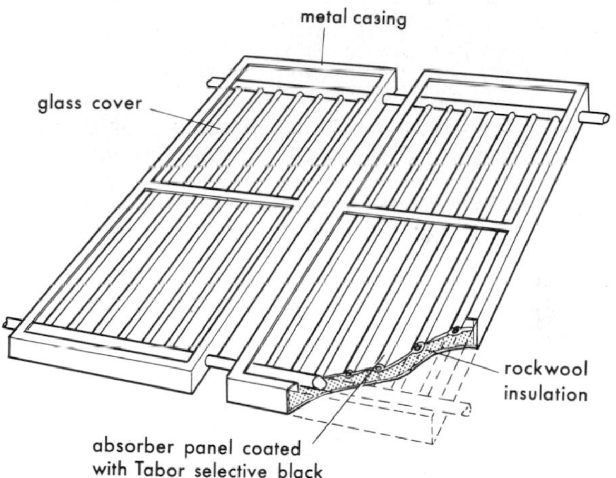

SOLAR ENERGY. For heating water in the home, solar panels of the type illustrated above, may be installed in roof or walls. Installations for space heating in the home would need to cover the entire roof area, and tend to be less satisfactory unless the house has been purpose built for solar heating. *Diagram: Courtesy of the Solar Trade Association.*

SOLAN-GOOSE. *See* GANNET.

SOLAR ENERGY. Attempts to harness the Sun's energy have been made ever since Archimedes is said to have used mirrors to set fire to a Roman fleet attempting to conquer Syracuse. A modern specialist in this field is Felix Trombe, whose solar furnace at Odeillo in the French Pyrenees (1970) uses 20,000 mirrors to generate temperatures of many thousand degrees. As a source of intensive heat for both industrial and scientific experimental purposes, solar furnaces are ideal because the heat is uncontaminated, i.e. it is free from carbon adulteration which occurs in normal high-intensity furnaces. Solar cells producing electric current directly from the Sun's rays have been developed particularly for satellites and space research. *See* SKYLAB. The energy crisis gave added impetus to the use of S.E., which is non-polluting, for heating water in homes, etc., using panels fixed to roofs or walls. Such solar cells on Earth, however, operate best in clear daylight, and a giant antenna in space has been suggested to ensure round-the-clock operation. Comprising hundreds of thousands of solar cells, it would convert sunpower directly to electricity, so powering microwave generators to beam radiation through any intervening cloud to Earth receiving stations. The focusing of the beam would be controlled from Earth by radio pulses, but exposure of the population to microwaves might have biological disadvantages.

SOLAR ENERGY. The solar furnace at Font Romeu, near Odeillo, in the French Pyrenees. Located at 1,800 m (5,900 ft), the parabolic mirror is 45 m (148 ft) high, and made up of a total of 8,570 panels, each about 6 m (18 ft) high. The heat generated is about 3,500°C (6,300°F), sufficient to melt a hole 30 cm (1 ft) across in steel plate 1 cm (3/8th in) thick in 60 sec. *Photo: Courtesy of the Foxboro Co*

SOLAR POND. Natural or artificial 'pond', such as the Dead or Salton Seas (qq.v.), in which salt becomes more soluble in the Sun's heat. Water at the bottom becomes more salty and hotter, and is insulated by the less salty water layer at the top. Temperatures at the bottom reach *c.* 100°C (200°F) and can be used to generate electricity.

SOLAR SYSTEM. *See* PLANETS.

SOLAR WIND. Continuous outward projection from the inner corona of the sun of high-speed streams of low-density hot ionized gas or plasma. The velocity, temperature and density of the S.W. appear to be much higher when solar flares occur, and it is thought to be the cause of radio blackouts, geomagnetic storms, and auroral displays. First detailed information on the structure of the S.W. was obtained during the flight of the US spacecraft *Mariner 2* in 1962.

SOLE. Genus (*Solea*) of flat fish in the family Pleuronectidae. The Common S. (*S. solea*) is up to 150cm (2ft) long, feeds at night on worms, etc., and is a valued European food-dish, as is the rarer lemon S. (*S. lascaris*); the little American Ss., in the genus *Achirus*, have no food value.

SOLENT, The. Strait between the Isle of Wight and the mainland of Hampshire, England. It is a famous yachting centre.

SOL-FA (-fah), **Tonic.** System of musical notation, invented by John Spencer Curwen, *c.* 1840, and utilized by many choral singers as a simpler alternative to staff-notation. Both in its restriction to single parts and in its limited interpretation of the composer's intentions, the system possesses drawbacks. The notes are named *doh, ray, me, fah, soh, lah, te,* and the key is indicated so that the singers know how their keynote *doh* is to be interpreted. Time divisions are indicated by bar-lines.

SOLFERINO (-rē'nō). Village in Verona, N Italy, 8km (5m) S of Lake Garda, site of the battle in which Napoleon III defeated the Austrians in 1859.

SOLICITOR. A member of one of the 2 branches of the English legal profession, the other being barristers (q.v.). A S. conducts legal work on behalf of clients, but until the Courts Act (1971) had a right to represent him only in the inferior courts. He may now appear in and conduct cases in the Crown Courts, and is eligible, in the same way as a barrister of 10 yrs standing, to be appointed a Recorder, and eventually a Circuit judge. *See* LAW COURTS. The **Solicitor-Gen.** is a law officer of the Crown, acting as deputy to the Attorney-Gen.: he is a political appointee with ministerial rank. In the USA the term S. may be used for practitioners in the courts of equity, and, as in England, some public offices have special Ss., and there has been since 1870 a S.-Gen.

SOLID CIRCUIT. Formerly an electronic circuit was always made by joining together by wire separately made electronic components. In a S.C. all the components (resistors, capacitors, transistors and diodes) and interconnections are made at the same time and by the same processes in or on one piece of single crystal silicon. The small size of this construction accounts for its use in electronics for space vehicles and aircraft.

SOLINGEN (zō'lingen). Town of North Rhine-Westphalia, Germany, 21km (13m) E of Düsseldorf, noted in the Middle Ages for its sword blades and still famous for its high-quality steel used for razor blades, cutlery, etc. Pop. (1978) 138,350.

SO'LITON. A non-linear wave, so-named from a 'solitary' wave seen on a canal by British engineer John Scott Russell in the 19th cent., who raced after it on his horse. Before he lost it, it had moved on for over a mile as a smooth, raised and rounded form, rather than widening and dispersing in the normal way. Such behaviour is characteristic of the waves of energy which constitute the particles of atomic physics, so that the mathematical equations which sum up the behaviour of Ss. are being used to further research in nuclear fusion, superconductivity, etc.

SO'LOMON (reigned *c.* 974-*c.* 937 BC). King of Israel. The son of David by Bathsheba, he acquired great wealth by trade, which he employed in building the temple at Jerusalem. His heavy taxation and use of forced labour aroused discontent, and his kingdom disintegrated. He became proverbial for wisdom, as is shown by the attribution of the much later *Proverbs, Ecclesiastes,* and *Song of Songs* to him. King S.'s Mines were formerly thought to have been at Aqaba (anc. Ezion-geber), but these are of later date: copper and iron ore was smelted.

SOLOMON ISLANDS. Archipelago in the W Pacific, lying E of New Guinea. The northern members of the group, incl. Bougainville, Buka, and adjacent islands, which belonged to Germany 1899-1918, form part of Papua New Guinea (q.v.). They are very mountainous, with several volcanoes, and produce bananas, coconuts, taros and sweet potatoes. Kieta, Rawa, and Tinputs (on Bougainville), are the main harbours. Area 11,200 sq.km (4,100 sq.m); pop. (1970) 77,880.

The southern members - Guadalcanal (q.v.), Malaita, San Cristobal, New Georgia, etc. - came under British protection 1893-9: formerly the British S.I. Protectorate, they were re-named the S.I. in 1975, and became independent in 1978. Products incl. fish, timber, palm oil and copra. The cap. is Honiara on Guadalcanal: pop. (1978) 15,000. Area 29,785 sq.km (11,500 sq.m); pop. (1978) 214,000, of whom 93% are Melanesian. MU.: S.I. dollar.

In 1942-5 the S.I. witnessed fierce fighting between Japanese and Allied forces (US and later Australian).

SO'LON (*c.* 638-558 BC). Athenian statesman. Elected archon *c.* 594, he carried out a revision of the constitution which laid the foundations of Athenian democracy.

SOLSTICE (sol'stis). Either of the 2 points reached by the Sun, when its declination is greatest N or S. It has also come to imply the time at which each of these occur, namely 21 June and 21 Dec.

SOLTI (shol'ti), **Sir Georg** (1912-). British conductor. B. in Budapest, he was musical director at Covent Garden (1961-71), where he was noted for glittering productions, and of the Chicago Symphony Orchestra from 1970. He also became principal conductor of the London Philharmonic Orchestra from 1979.

SOLWAY FIRTH. Arm of the sea more than a mile long formed by the estuary of the Esk, and dividing England from Scotland at the W end of the border. It also receives the Dee, Eden, Annan, and Nith, and merges into the Irish Sea.

SOLYMAN II (sōōlāmahn'), called the **Magnificent** (1494-1566). Sultan of Turkey. Succeeding his father in 1520, he greatly extended the Turkish Empire. Belgrade was captured in 1521, and Rhodes in 1522: the victory of Mohacs (1526) brought much of Hungary under Turkish rule, and in 1529 Vienna was unsuccessfully besieged. Baghdad and Armenia were captured from the Persians in 1534.

SOLZHENITSYN (solzhenit'sin), **Alexander** (1919-). Russian novelist. He was in a forced labour camp 1945-53 and sent to Siberia 1953-7, but Khrushchev ensured publication of *One Day in the Life of Ivan Denisovich* (1962) dealing with Stalin's prison camps. *Cancer Ward* (1968) again attacked restrictions on freedom; *August 1914* (1972) dealt with the Russian defeat by Prussia at Tannenberg; and *The Gulag Archipelago* (1973) exposed the Russian concentration camp system, leading to his deportation in 1974. He was awarded a Nobel prize in 1970. *See* WAR.

SŌ'MA. Indian intoxicating drink obtained from the fermented sap of *Asclepias acida* plant. In ancient times it was worshipped as a deity and used in sacrifices to Indra.

SOMALILAND, French. *See* AFARS AND ISSAS.

SOMALI (sōmah'lē) **REPUBLIC.** Country of E Africa, extending along the coast of the Gulf of Aden and the Indian Ocean, occupying the 'horn' of Africa. The climate is hot and dry, but where water is available the soil is productive. The interior is barren and rises to 1,800 m (6,000 ft). The Juba and its trib. the Shebelli are the chief rivers. Rearing of cattle, camels, sheep, and donkeys is the principal occupation; rice, dates, and sugar are grown; gums and resins, hides and skins are exported. Mogadishu is the cap. and chief port; other towns are Berbera and Kismayu (both naval bases) and Obbia, also on the coast; and Hargeisa in the N inland.

The S.R. was formed in 1960 by the union of British and Italian Somaliland. The former (176,000 sq km/68,000 sq m) was made a protectorate 1885-7. Ital. Somaliland was estab. as a colony 1927, incorporated 1936 in Ital. E Africa, conquered 1941 by the British who administered it until 1950 when it was again administered by Italy under UN trusteeship until it became independent as the S.R. in 1960. Brit. Somaliland, accorded independence in the same year, elected to join the S.R. The S.R. has claims to various terrs. with Somali pops.: the NE prov. of Kenya (100,000); Djibouti (58,000); and Ethiopia's Ogaden district (50,000), which the S.R. invaded in 1977. Russian and Cuban military advisers were expelled in 1977 because of Soviet links with Ethiopia, and in 1980 fighting in the Ogaden still continued.

Under the constitution of 1979, S. is a socialist nation, the S. Democratic Rep., in which the Somali Revolutionary Socialist Party is the sole political party. There is a pres., elected by popular vote, and a parliament with legislative powers.

Area 700,000 sq.km (270,000 sq.m); pop. (1977) 3,350,000, mainly nomadic Sunni Moslems. The national language is Somali. M.U.: Somali shilling.

SOMERSET (sum'-), **Edward Seymour,** duke of (*c.* 1506-52). English statesman. The son of a Wilts gentleman, he was created earl of Hertford after Henry VIII's marriage to his sister Jane, and in 1547 became regent for Edward VI, with the title of Protector, and duke of S. A liberal and tolerant ruler, he offended the landowners by his attempts to check enclosure, and the Protestants by his moderate religious policy. He was overthrown in 1549, and beheaded in 1552 on a trumped-up charge of treason. The duchy was restored in 1660 to his descendants.

SOMERSET. County in SW England, on the Bristol Channel. Its coastline consists of low cliffs and marshy tracts of land, whence the sea is kept out by a system of dykes and sluices. The principal rivers are the Avon, Parret, and Exe. In the N are the Mendip Hills (in which are the Cheddar caves) and in the W the Quantock Hills and Exmoor, with Dunkery Beacon (520m/1,708 ft) the highest point. The co. is famed for dairy products, cider, and Exmoor ponies. The chief towns are Taunton, the admin. HQ, Wells and Bridgwater. In 1974, S. lost a considerable area in the N to Avon (q.v.). Area 3,458 sq.km (1,335 sq.m); pop. (1978) 411,100.

SOMERSET HOUSE. Government offices in the Strand, London, built in 1775. It is used by the Inland Revenue, Principal Probate Registry, where wills are kept, and - the E wing - by King's College. The river facade was designed by Sir William Chambers (q.v.). The General Register Office (births, marriages and deaths), formerly at S.H. was merged with the Govt Social Survey Dept as the Office of Pop. Census and Surveys in 1970, and transferred to St Catherine's House.

SOMERVILLE, Edith Oenone (1861-1949). Irish novelist, best known for her stories of Irish life written jointly with her cousin, Violet Martin (q.v.).

SOMME (som). River of N France 240 km (150 m) long, which rises in Aisne dept near St Quentin, flows in a N and W direction past Amiens and Abbeville, and reaches the English Channel through a broad estuary. It gives its name to a dept.

SOMME, Battle of the. Allied offensive in the F.W.W., on the western front, between Beaumont-Hamel and Chaulnes, in July-Nov. 1916, during which tanks were used for the first time. Comparatively slight gains were made, at very heavy cost. The German offensive around St Quentin in March-April 1918 is sometimes called the second battle of the S.

SONAR. In the F.W.W. an Allied Submarine Detection Investigation Committee was estab. and the apparatus perfected *c.* 1920 for detecting the presence of enemy U-boats beneath the sea-surface by the use of ultrasonic echoes was named from its initials ASDIC. In 1963 the name was changed, to accord with NATO practice, to S. (SOund NAvigation and Ranging). The process is similar to that used in radar. The time taken for an acoustic beam in the audible or supersonic range to travel to the underwater object, whose distance is required, and back to the source, enables the distance to be found since the velocity of sound under water is known.

SONATA (sonah'ta). Term originally used to describe a composition for instruments, as opposed to the cantata, which is a composition for voices. The S. is usually played on one or two instruments, and consists of a series of related movements.

SONG. Musical setting of a poem for accompanied or unaccompanied single voice. Among the composers of Ss. are, English: Dowland, Lawes, Purcell, Arne, Sterndale-Bennett, Parry, Stanford, Quilter, Vaughan Williams, Delius, Moeran, Warlock, Ireland, Britten, Tippett, and Phyllis Tate; German: Mozart, Beethoven, Schubert, Schumann, Brahms, Wolf, Richard Strauss, Mahler, Hindemith and Webern; French: Gounod, Debussy, Duparc, Fauré, Poulenc and Ravel; Hungarian: Liszt; Russian: Moussorgsky, Tchaikovsky, Rachmaninoff, Glinka and A. S. Dargomïzhsky (1813-69); and American: Edward MacDowell, Sidney Homer (1864-1953), Charles Ives, and George Gershwin.

SONNET. Poetic form introduced from Italy to England by Sir Thomas Wyatt, who followed in principle the Petrarchan mode, which, strictly interpreted, has the rhyme scheme abba abba, cdcdcd, with a turn of thought at the close of the octave; Milton and Wordsworth are exponents of this type. The Elizabethan form, as used by Shakespeare, has the rhyme scheme abab, cdcd efef gg.

SOOCHOW. *See* SUZHOU.

SOPER, Donald, baron (1903-). British Methodist Minister, supt of the West London Mission, Kingsway Hall, 1936-78 he is well known for his readiness of wit in debate and through television appearances. His books incl. *All His Grace* (1957) and *Aflame with Faith*, and as a speaker at Hyde Park Corner he has influenced many. In 1965 he became a life peer.

SOPHĪ'A (1630-1714). Electress of Hanover. The dau. of the Elector Palatine and Elizabeth, dau. of James I of England, she m. the elector of Hanover. She was recognized as in the succession to the English throne in 1701. Her son, George I, founded the Hanoverian dynasty.

SOPHISTS (sof'ists). Greek teachers of the 5th cent. BC who lectured on culture, rhetoric, and politics. Owing to the picture of them drawn by Plato, 'sophistry' now means dishonest reasoning.

SOPHOCLES (sof'ŏklēz) (495-406 BC). Athenian tragic poet. He produced his first plays in 468, when he won the prize in competition with Aeschylus, and wrote over 120 plays, of which only 7 survive; these are *Ajax, Electra, The Trachinian Maidens, Philoctetes,* and the Theban tragedies *Antigone, King Oedipus,* and *Oedipus at Colonus.* He modified the form of tragedy by the introduction of a third actor and speeded the action by lessening the role of the chorus. Whereas he said of Euripides 'He paints men as they are', he said of himself 'I paint men as they ought to be' and is noted for his noble grandeur and preservation of traditional values.

SOPWITH, Sir Thomas Octave Murdoch (1888-). British aviator. In 1910 he won a £4,000 prize for a flight from England to the Continent, and in 1912 founded the Sopwith Aviation Co. of which he was chairman 1925-7. He was chairman of the Hawker Siddeley Group 1935-63.

SORBIC ACID. Tasteless acid found in the fruit of the mountain ash (q.v.), widely used in the preservation of food, e.g. cider, wine, soft drinks, animal feedstuffs, bread and cheese.

SORBONNE (sorbon'). Alternative name for the Univ. of Paris. The S. was founded in 1253 by Robert de Sorbon, chaplain to Louis IX, as an institution for theological studies. Richelieu reconstructed the buildings in 1626, which were again rebuilt in 1885. In 1808 the S. became the seat of the Académie of Paris and of the Univ. of Paris.

SOREL, Georges (1847-1922). French philosopher. B. at Cherbourg, he glorified violence in his writings, notably *Reflections on Violence* (1908), and taught that an élite must lead the people by means of myths. He championed the Syndicalist movement before 1914, and in later life showed Fascist sympathies.

SORGHUM (sor'gum). A genus of grasses - also called Indian millet, guinea-corn, or durra - grown in Africa, India, China, USA, and S Europe.

SORO'RITIES. *See* FRATERNITIES.

SORREL. Several species of plants in the genus *Rumex*, especially the garden S. (*R. acetosa*) native to N Europe and Asia, and cultivated for its leaves, used in salads, etc.

SORRE'NTO. Coast resort on the Gulf of Naples, Italy, noted for its climate, scenery, and wine. Pop. (1975) 30,000.

S.O.S. International Morse distress signal, transmitted by any available means, e.g. flags, semaphore, radio: chosen because '3 short, 3 long, 3 short' is the most distinctive and easiest signal to transmit, it is popularly regarded in English as representing 'Save our Souls'. 'Mayday', corresponding to Fr. m'aider, is the distress code by radio telephone.

SŌ'TŌ, Ferdinando de (*c.* 1496-1542). Spanish explorer, who in 1539 led an expedition which explored Florida, Georgia, and the Mississippi.

SOULT (soolt), **Nicolas Jean de Dieu** (1769-1851). Marshal of France. He entered the army in 1785, served in the Revolutionary Wars, and was created a marshal in 1804 and duke of Dalmatia in 1808. He held high commands in Spain throughout the Peninsular War, and was chief of staff at Waterloo. He was War Minister 1830-4 and 1840-4.

SOUTH AFRICA. Johannesburg (left) seen from the white mounds of the refuse dumps of the gold mines which established the country's chief prosperity; and the attractive outline of a Cape Dutch farmstead against a mountain background. The style has its roots in the Netherlands but developed characteristically in Africa.

SOUND. A physiological sensation received by the ear, which originates in a vibration which communicates itself to the air, and travels in every direction, spreading out as an expanding sphere. All S. waves travel with a speed which depends on the temperature of the atmosphere, and is *c.* 340m (1,120 ft) per second under ordinary conditions. The pitch of the S. depends on the number of vibrations imposed on the air per second, but the speed is unaffected. The loudness of a S. is dependent primarily on the extent of the to and fro vibration of the air - what is known as the amplitude of the waves. In man, the lowest audible note has a frequency of about 26 vibrations per second, and the highest one of about 18,000: the lower limit of this range varies little with age, but the upper range falls steadily from adolescence onward. *See* ACOUSTICS, DECIBEL, and NOISE.

SOUND, The. Arm of the sea which runs from the Kattegat in the N to the Baltic in the S, and separates Denmark from Sweden: 48km (30m) long, 5-60km (3-37m) wide.

SOUPHANOUVONG (soofanoovong'), **Prince** (1902–). Laotian statesman. He fled abroad after an abortive revolt against the French in 1945, and led the Pathet Lao sometimes fighting against the right-wing forces in alliance with the neutralist forces led by his half-brother Prince Souvanna, and sometimes with the latter against him. He became first pres. of the rep. of Laos in 1975.

SOUSA (soo'zah), **John Philip** (1854-1932). American composer. B. in Washington, he became bandmaster of the US Marines in 1880, and of his own band in 1892. He is best known for his many marches, e.g. 'Washington Post' and 'Stars and Stripes'.

SOUTH AFRICA, Rep. of (Afrikaans *Republiek van Suid Afrika*). Country occupying the S extremity of the African continent.

PHYSICAL FEATURES. Most of S Africa is occupied by the High Veld, *c.* 1,300 m (4,000 ft). In the S the lesser plateaux of the Little and Great Karroo step down from the Veld. On the S and E these plateaux are rimmed by mountain ranges variously named (from S to N) the Swarteberg, Sneeuwberg, Stormberg, Drakensberg (incl. Mont aux Sources, 3,299 m (10,822 ft), highest point in the Rep.), and Zoutpansberg. In Transvaal the Veld is crossed by the long ridge of Witwatersrand, on which stands Johannesburg. Close to Capetown stands Table Mtn, 1,082 m (3,550 ft). The main rivers are, from N to S, the Limpopo, Vaal, and Orange. Over much of the country the climate is temperate, though N Natal is semitropical. Big game is common in many districts, and is preserved in national parks. The Veld is a natural grassland.

ECONOMIC. A world leader in trade and industrial growth, S.A. produces cereals (maize and wheat), fruit (citrus, pears, peaches, apples, grapes, etc.), sugar and tea (in Natal), and excellent wines, the vine having been introduced to the Cape by 17th cent. Huguenot settlers. Cattle and sheep are bred on a large scale, wool being important. Enormous mineral resources incl. gold (q.v.), mainly from the Witwatersrand mines of Transvaal, diamonds, from the Kimberley district, and platinum; and antimony, asbestos, chromite, coal, copper, corundum, graphite, iron ore, lead, magnesite, manganese, nickel, phosphates, tin, titanium, tungsten, and uranium. S.A. has the world's largest oil-from-coal project, since very little natural gas and oil has been discovered. Industries incl. iron and steel, tobacco, textiles and clothing, jams and fruit canning, fertilizers, pharmaceuticals, synthetic rubber, plastics, leather, furniture, and explosives (the world's largest plant is at Modderfontein). Railways, airways, and harbours are govt-operated. The chief towns are Johannesburg, Capetown (the seat of the legislature), Durban, Pretoria (the administrative cap.), Port Elizabeth, Bloemfontein, East London, and Pietermaritzburg. M.U.: rand.

GOVERNMENT. S.A. is a republic with a state pres. elected for 7 yrs by an electoral college consisting of the President's Council, nominated by the state pres. for a 5-yr term and the House of Assembly, elected by white citizens from among their number also for 5 years. The President's Council was introduced to replace the Senate in 1981, and its members (representative of the White, Coloured, Indian and Chinese communities) are nominated by the state pres.: a proposal for a separate council for the majority Black community was rejected by the leader of the Black Homelands. The Black Homelands (q.v.) have their own elected Legislative Assemblies.

History. S.A. was discovered by Diaz who rounded the Cape in 1488. The Dutch E India Co. occupied the site of Capetown in 1652 as a port of call on the way to the

Divisions of the Republic of South Africa

	Area in sq. km	*Population (1970 census)*	*Capital*
Provinces			
Cape of Good Hope	721,000	6,731,820	Cape Town
Natal	86,965	4,237,000	Pietermaritz-burg
Transvaal	286,064	8,717,530	Pretoria
Orange Free State	129,152	1,716,350	Bloemfontein
	1,223,181	21,402,700	
Administered territory			
SW Africa (Namibia)	823,167	746,330	Windhoek
Walvis Bay	1,124		
	2,047,472	22,149,030	

Indies. Occupied by the British 1795 when the Netherlands was occupied by French, restored 1802-6, Capetown and the hinterland were acquired by Britain in 1814 for a sum of £6,000,000. The first European settlers in Natal, on the coast near Durban, were British, 1824. In 1836 some 10,000 Dutch, wishing to escape from British rule, set out on the 'Great Trek' and founded the rep. of Transvaal and the Orange Free State; they also settled in N Natal, which became part of Cape Colony in 1844, and a separate colony in 1856. The discovery of diamonds at Kimberley, in Cape Colony, and of gold in Transvaal, attracted numerous prospectors, between whom and the Dutch farmers (Boers), who had no interest in this mineral wealth, conflict developed. Britain attempted to occupy Transvaal, 1877-81, but withdrew after a severe defeat at Majuba (1881). Denial of citizenship rights to the temporary mining settlers (Uitlanders) in Transvaal, and the imperialist ambitions of Cecil Rhodes and others, led to the Jameson Raid (*see* L. S. JAMESON) and the S African War (1899-1902). This opened with a series of British defeats, but in 1900 Lord Roberts forced Cronje to surrender at Paardeberg; Bloemfontein, Johannesburg, and Pretoria were captured; and Kimberley, Ladysmith, and Mafeking were relieved after long sieges. The Boers, led by Smuts and Botha, continued guerrilla resistance until 1902 when peace was made at Vereeniging, and Transvaal and the Orange Free State acknowledged British sovereignty. In 1910 the Union of S.A. was formed to incl. the provinces of Cape of Good Hope, Natal, Orange Free State, and Transvaal. The outbreak of the F.W.W. was marked by a Boer rebellion, speedily crushed by Smuts. German SW Africa was occupied, and Union forces served with distinction in E Africa and in France. Between the wars the political life of the Union was marked by the alternating terms of office of the republican nationalists under Hertzog and the S African Party under Smuts, who wished to maintain the Commonwealth connection.

On the outbreak of the S.W.W. in 1939, Smuts, having secured the defeat in the S.A. parl. of a motion for neutrality put forward by the PM, Hertzog, took over the premiership. S.A. troops played a major part in the conquest of Ital. E Africa and served with distinction in N Africa and in Italy. The Nationalist Party returned to office in 1948 with a small majority, later much increased, and in 1960 a referendum resulted in a vote for a republic. Unable to accept Commonwealth opposition to apartheid, S.A. left the organization in 1961 (*see* VERWOERD), and on Verwoerd's assassination 1966 the same policy was initially maintained by Vörster (q.v.). However, pressure of world opinion, the economic need for a wider pool of skilled labour and the extension of Black majority rule in other areas of Africa, culminating in the creation of Zimbabwe in 1980, led to an increasing demand for similar equal rights in South Africa. This meant popular rejection of the idea of the Black Homelands (*see also* PROJECT ORANGE), expressions of unrest, as in Soweto (q.v.), and the refusal of Blacks to accept a separate council instead of participation in the President's Council created in 1981. The govt. response has been to re-name apartheid (q.v.), the policy of 'separate development' for the races, as 'plural democracy', and under P.W. Botha (q.v.) there were measures to mitigate 'petty apartheid' or 'unnecessary and hurtful racial discrimination'. These incl. in 1980 bills to modify the 'pass laws' to control the number of Blacks in the cities. Under these every Black was compelled to carry a 'pass' or identity document (*see* SHARPEVILLE), which had to be stamped officially giving permission to the holder to enter particular urban areas. In this way a Black's taking a city job, or moving from one job to another was regulated, and the time for which a husband or wife, or children, might visit a Black working in an urban area, was restricted. There have also been various relaxations in Black participation in sport.

Area 1,223,181 sq.km (472,294 sq.m); pop. (1980) 27,000,000, incl. 20,000,000 Black; 4,410,000 White, mainly of British or Afrikaner descent; 2,500,000 Coloured, of mixed European and African descent; 800,000 Asians, mainly descendants of immigrants from India. The Blacks speak various Bantu languages, but they dislike the word 'Bantu', formerly officially used to refer to them as a people, as derogatory, and it was discontinued in 1978. The official languages are Afrikaans and English, spoken by about 60% and 40% respectively of Whites, but English is also spoken by many Blacks and is preferred by them to Afrikaans as a language of education. The largest church is the Dutch Reformed Church (Nederduits Gereformeerde Kerk), which has modified its separation of congregations into White and non-White, and there are large congregrations both Black and White among the other Christian sects, incl. Anglican, Methodist and R.C. Of 16 univs., 11 are White, 3 Black and 1 each Coloured and Asian.

Art. S.A. can boast of a number of accomplished artists, incl. Gwelo Goodman, Rowarth, Naude, Volschenk, Neville Lewis, and Pieter Wenning, though no distinctive S African school of painting has developed. There are fine collections of European paintings, e.g. at Capetown and Johannesburg.

The architecture of S.A. has remained under Dutch influence, early domestic buildings were similar in style to buildings in Amsterdam. After 1815 a sort of classic Renaissance took place, but architecture deteriorated in style after the discovery of diamonds in 1867, when many buildings were erected hastily and haphazardly. The most noteworthy individual contribution to the architecture of

CARIBBEAN SEA
CURAÇAO
GRENADA
TOBAGO
TRINIDAD
Mouths of the Orinoco
Isthmus of Panama
Panama Canal
Lake Maracaibo
NORTH ATLANTIC
OCEAN
Llanos
Orinoco
GUIANA HIGHLANDS
Casiquiare Canal
Selvas
Mouths of the Amazon
MARAJÓ I.
COTOPAXI
Putumayo
Negro
GULF OF GUAYAQUIL
Amazon
Marañón
Amazon Basin
Tapajoz
Xingu
Caatinga
Ucayali
Madeira
Planalto do Borborema
Tocantins
Campos
SÃO FRANCISCO
BRAZILIAN HIGHLANDS
Yungas
Grande
L. Titicaca
Poopó
Planalto do Mato Grosso
Gran Chaco
Paraguay
Parana
PACIFIC
OCEAN
Atacama Desert
Uruguay
Mar Chiquita
Lagos dos Patos
Mirim Lake
ACONCAGUA
Pampas
Salado
River Plate
ANDES
Colorado
Negro
BAHÍA BLANCA
SOUTH ATLANTIC
OCEAN
SAN MATÍAS G.
Valdés Pena.
CHILOÉ I.
CHONOS ARCHO.
GULF OF SAN JORGE
Taitao Pena.
Patagonia
WELLINGTON I.
FALKLAND ISLANDS
STR. OF MAGELLAN
STR. OF MAGELLAN
TIERRA DEL FUEGO
DESOLATION I.
SANTA INES I.
STATEN I.
Cape Horn
SCOTIA SEA
SOUTH GEORGIA
Miles
0 100 200 300 400 500 600 700
0 100 200 300 400 500 600 700 800 900 1000
Kilometres
© Geographical Projects

S.A. was made by Sir Herbert Baker, who was commissioned by Rhodes to reconstruct *Groote Schuur* (originally built in the 17th cent.), Dutch in style, and later designed Government House and Capital Buildings at Pretoria, the Rhodes Memorial on Table Mountain, and the cathedrals at Capetown and Johannesburg.

Literature. Founder of S African literature in English was Thomas Pringle (1789-1834), who pub. lyric poetry and the prose *Narrative of a Residence in S Africa.* The missionary, Arthur S. Cripps, and the Scot, Charles Murray, also produced excellent verse, but the finest of the more recent poets, Roy Campbell and Francis C. Slater, are S African-born. The first work of S African fiction to achieve fame outside the country was Olive Schreiner's *Story of an African Farm* (1883); later writers in English of international repute incl. Sara G. Millin, Pauline Smith (author of *The Little Karroo*), William Plomer, Laurens van der Post, Alan Paton, and Nadine Gordimer.

Original writing in Afrikaans (q.v.) developed rapidly after the South African War, and incl. the lyricists C. L. Leipoldt, J. F. E. Celliers and E. N. Marais; the satirical sketch and story writer C. J. Langenhoven, and the student of wild life 'Sangiro' (A. A. Pienaar), author of *The Adventures of a Lion Family,* which became popular in English translation. In more recent years the intellectual barriers imposed by the isolation of South Africa internationally have prevented her writers being more widely known, but there has been much spirited work, e.g. that of the *Sestigers* 'People of the Sixties' - novelists André P. Brink and Étienne Leroux, and poetess Ingrid Jonker. In 1976 the first full television service was introduced, and brought a new stimulus in the cultural field.

SOUTH AMERICA. Continent covering 14 per cent of the Earth's land area, joined to Central and N America by the Panama isthmus; it is almost entirely to the E of the northern continent. The relief is divided into 3 longitudinal areas. The Andes in the W run parallel to the Pacific coastline, and rise to more than 6,000 m (20,000 ft); the great central plains, the Llanos, Selvas, Chaco, and Pampas, stretch from the Orinoco basin to Patagonia; and the Brazilian and Guiana highlands.

S of the Orinoco basin the Amazon river system, flowing through dense forest land to the Atlantic, dominates the N of the continent. In Brazil deep valleys are cut in the highland by many rivers flowing E and N; thence, too, the Parana, Paraguay, and Uruguay flow S to form the La Plata estuary, draining the fertile central plains. S of the Colorado and Negro is the Patagonian desert, covering the tapering strip of S.A. to Tierra del Fuego.

The Amazon belt has an equatorial type of climate with a heavy rainfall. The rainfall generally is heavy, except in the narrow coastal strips of Peru and N Chile which, with most of Patagonia, are virtually desert.

Although many pure Indians exist, mainly in Bolivia, Peru, and Ecuador, the introduction of Negroes and Europeans has brought about a thorough racial mixture. Except in Brazil, where Portuguese is spoken, Spanish is the common tongue. The Indian language origins remain obscure; Chibcha, Quechua, and Araucan are the main groups of the W, in Colombia, Peru, and Chile, and other distinct groups exist in the E. Ethnologically and linguistically there are slight affinities with Melanesia and aboriginal Australia.

History. Archaic cultures are still coming to light (*see* CHIMU), but the most remarkable of the later peoples were the Incas (q.v.), who had an imperial concept suggestive of the Old World (*see* HEYERDAHL). In the 16th cent. Spanish (*see* PIZARRO) and Portuguese conquest was rapid, the Amerindians being killed, assimilated or, where not numerous enough to utilize as slave labour, replaced by Negroes from Africa. The Amerindian tradition persisted, however, as in the 18th cent. revolt of Tupac Amaru (q.v.), and in the 20th has revived to a striking degree. Napoleon's toppling of the throne of Spain prepared the way for Bolivar and San Martín (qq.v.) to estab. the independence of S.A., obtained peacefully in the case the Portuguese possession of Brazil. Large-scale immigration from Europe ensued, and the modern Latin-American states, with their uncertain politics, sensational economic developments, and rich variety of culture came into being. The effects of inter-state wars in the 19th cent. are still felt and represent live issues: *see* PARAGUAY and PACIFIC WAR.

Countries of South America

	Area in 1,000 sq. km.	*Pop. in 1,000s*	*Capital*
Argentina	2,780	30,708	Buenos Aires
Bolivia	1,098	6,195	La Paz
Brazil	8,512	135,000	Brasilia
Chile	742	12,042	Santiago
Colombia	1,139	29,347	Bogotá
Ecuador	301	9,378	Quito
Guiana, incl. Inini	91	82	Cayenne
Guyana	210	768	Georgetown
Paraguay	407	3,989	Asunción
Peru	1,332	19,698	Lima
Surinam	143	395	Paramaribo
Uruguay	187	2,936	Montevideo
Venezuela	912	17,317	Caracas
	17,854	267,852	

SOUTHA'MPTON, Henry Wriothesley, 3rd earl of (1573-1624). English courtier and patron of Shakespeare, who dedicated 'Venus and Adonis' and 'Lucrece' to him, and possibly addressed him in the sonnets.

SOUTHAMPTON. City and seaport in Hants, England, 127km (79m) SW of London, on S. Water, between the estuaries of the Itchen and Test. The major passenger port - The Gateway to Britain - S. is also being developed as a great cargo port: there is also an airport. Industries incl. engineering, chemicals, plastics, flour milling and tobacco. There is a univ. (1952). Pop. (1974) 212,000.

SOUTH AUSTRALIA. State of the Commonwealth of Australia. Dairying and wheat and fruit growing are carried on, especially in the irrigated area in the Murray Valley, but 80 per cent of the state is given to cattle and sheep grazing. S.A. produces 75 per cent of Australia's wine, and 90 per cent of its brandy. Fruit canning is important, and there are also factories making textiles and clothing, metal goods and machines, paper, chemicals, etc. The Middleback Range (q.v.) has iron resources, there is coal at Leigh Creek, and natural gas in the NE; other minerals incl. copper, pyrites and gypsum. The cap. is

SOUTHAMPTON. The hydrofoil ferry *Sheerwater* on Southampton Water. Once a certain speed is reached, the ski-like structures at the front of boat support the hull above the water surface, cutting down drag, and so increasing speed. *Photo: Courtesy of the British Tourist Authority*

Adelaide; Whyalla and Port Pirie are also industrial centres, and in the arid N is the experimental rocket range at Woomera. Area 984,341 sq.km (380,054 sq.m); pop. (1976) 1,244,756.

SOUTH BEND. City in Indiana, USA, on the St Joseph r., SE of Chicago. Agricultural machinery, cars, and aircraft equipment are manufactured. Pop. (1970) 125,600.

SOUTH CAROLĪ'NA. A southern, Atlantic state of the USA, one of the original 13. Tobacco, cotton, and soya beans are the principal crops. Industries incl. manufacture of textiles and clothing, paper and wood pulp, furniture, bricks, meat products. The first settlers (1526) were Spaniards; as Carolina, the area was given by Charles I to Robert Heath in 1629. Columbia, the cap., Greenville, and Charleston are the largest towns. Area 80,432 sq.km (31,055 sq.m); pop. (1970) 2,590,576.

SOUTH DAKŌ'TA. A northern-central state of the USA. It is for the most part broad prairie, and W of the 'Bad Lands' rise the Black Hills. The state is drained by the Missouri. Wheat, maize, oats, etc. are grown, and there are agriculture-linked industries. Minerals incl, gold, mica, uranium, natural gas and oil (*see* SIOUX). Sioux Falls is the largest town, and Pierre is the cap. Area 199,550 sq.km (77,047 sq.m); pop. (1970) 666,257

SOUTH-EAST ASIA TREATY ORGANIZATION (SEATO). Collective defence system, analagous to NATO (q.v.), estab. 1954 (Australia, France, NZ, Pakistan, the Philippines, Thailand, UK and USA, with Vietnam, Cambodia and Laos as protocol states). It was phased out after the Vietnam débacle in 1975, and its non-military aspects were assumed by the Assocn of SE Asian Nations (q.v.).

SOUTH-EAST CAPE. The most southerly extremity of Australia, in Tasmania.

SOUTHEND-ON-SEA. Seaside resort in Essex, England, 56km (35m) E of London, at the mouth of the Thames. The pier is more than 2km (1.25m) long. There are light engineering, radio, and boatbuilding industries. Pop. (1974) 162,200.

SOUTHERN CROSS. A constellation in the southern hemisphere of the heavens, consisting of four principal stars arranged in the shape of a cross.

SOUTHEY (sow'dhi), **Robert** (1774-1843). British poet and author. B. at Bristol, he settled at Keswick, to be near Coleridge. He abandoned his early revolutionary views, and from 1808 contributed regularly to the Tory *Quarterly Review.* In 1813 he became poet laureate, but his verse is forgotten, and he is better known for his life of Nelson, and his Letters.

SOUTH GEORGIA. Island 1,300 km (800m) SE of the Falkland Is. (q.v.), from which it is admin., although a dependency of the UK. It was briefly invaded and occupied by Argentina on 3-25 April 1982. Area 3,775 sq.km (1,450 sq.m); pop. *c.* 20 scientists of the Brit. Antarctic Survey based at Grytviken

SOUTHLAND PLAIN. Plain in the extreme S. of South Island, NZ, the chief town being Invercargill.

SOUTH ORKNEYS. Island group (uninhabited) in the Southern Ocean, part of the Brit. Antarctic Terr. (q.v.), discovered in 1821 by George Powell.

SOUTHSEA. A district of Portsmouth (q.v.).

SOUTH SEA BUBBLE. The financial crisis of 1720. The South Sea Co., founded in 1711, which enjoyed a monopoly of trade with S America, offered in 1719 to take over the national debt in return for further concessions. Its £100 shares rapidly rose to £1,000, and an orgy of speculation followed. When the 'bubble' burst, thousands were ruined. The discovery that cabinet ministers had been guilty of corruption led to a political crisis; Walpole became PM and restored financial confidence.

SOUTH SHETLANDS. Archipelago of 12 uninhabited islands in the Southern Ocean, part of the Brit. Antarctic Terr. (q.v.). Area 337 sq.km (130 sq.m).

SOUTH SHIELDS. Seaport in Tyne and Wear, England, on the Tyne. Manufactures incl. cables and chemicals. Pop. (1972) 98,600.

SOUTH UIST. *See under* UIST.

SOUTHWARK (suth'ark). Inner bor. of Greater London - commonly called The Borough - and incorporating from 1965 Bermondsey and Camberwell. It is on the S of the Thames opposite the City: St Saviour's cathedral dates from the 12th cent. and the George Inn (1677) is London's last galleried inn. *See* GLOBE THEATRE. Pop. (1972) 253,260.

SOUTH WEST AFRICA. Territory of S Africa on the Atlantic S of Angola, from which it is separated in the W by the r. Kunene, N of the Cape of Good Hope prov., from which it is separated by the Orange r. Most of the area is barren upland, and in the E is the Kalahari Desert, but there is some good grazing. Cattle, sheep, and goats are raised, and there is an important trade in skins. Mineral wealth incl. diamonds, vanadium, tin, and copper. Windhoek is the cap., and the chief ports are Lüderitz and Walvis Bay (admin with SWA though part of Cape Prov.). Area 823,167 sq.km (317,825 sq.m), excl. Walvis Bay; pop. (1977) 908,800, incl. 418,300 Ovambo, 105,600 White, 80,500 Damaro, 61,400 Kavango, 58,900 Herero.

S.W.A. was annexed by Germany in 1884, and in 1904-7 it was the scene of the Herero rebellion, which was put down with great harshness. In the FWW South African forces under Botha occupied all S.W.A. 1914-15. The terr. was mandated by the League of Nations to South Africa in 1920, and a declaration by the UN in 1966 that the mandate was terminated was rejected by South Africa: the UN declared 1968 that S.W.A. would in future be known as Namibia. Although S Africa accepted plans for UN-Supervised elections in 1979, negotiations were protracted because S Africa supported the multi-racial Democratic Turnhalle Alliance, and the South West African People's Organisation (SWAPO), led by Sam Nujoma (Q.v.), refuses to talk to the S African supported group. In the meantime SWAPO continues guerrilla warfare.

SOVEREIGN. British gold coin, introduced by Henry VII, which became the standard monetary unit in 1817. Minting ceased for currency purposes in the UK in 1914, but it is still struck for use as 'unofficial' currency in the Middle East. The value is notionally £1, but the actual value is that of the weight of the gold at current rates. Like the Mexican 50-peso piece, S African kruger rand, and Soviet chervonetz of 10 roubles, sovereigns are bought by investors suspicious of falling values of paper currencies.

SOVIET (Russian, council). The original Ss. were strike committees elected by the Russian workers during the 1905 revolution. After the deposition of the tsar in 1917 local Ss. were set up by peasants, soldiers, and industrial workers, and they selected delegates to an All-Russian Congress of Ss., which in Nov., under Bolshevik leadership, took over the govt. (*See* SOVIET UNION.) Ss. have been set up in many other countries during periods of crisis, e.g. in Germany in 1918 and Hungary in 1919, and the Councils of Action during the British general strike in 1926. And at the present day similar systems exist in other Communist states.

SOVIET CENTRAL ASIA. *See* ASIA, Soviet Central.

SOVIET FAR EAST. Geographical (not admin.) division of Asiatic RSFSR, on the Pacific coast. It covers the Amur, Lower Amur, Kamchatka, and Sakhalin regions, and Khabarovsk and Maritime terrs.

SOVIETSK (sovyetsk'). Town in Kaliningrad region, RSFSR, 96km (60m) NE of Kaliningrad city. Saw milling, paper and wood-pulp making, distilling, cheese making are among its industries. The former Tilsit (renamed S. in 1946), it was the site of a meeting in 1807 at which Napoleon made peace with Russia and Prussia. Pop. (1973) 50,000.

SOVIET UNION. Abbreviation for the Union of Soviet Socialist Republics (USSR). The Russian Soviet Federated Socialist Republic (RSFSR; q.v.), was formed after the 1917 revolution, and in 1924 the union with the Ukrainian and White Russian Republics and the Transcaucasian Soviet Federal Socialist Republic to form the USSR was ratified. There are now 15 constituent republics (*see* table), and the pop. (1980) was 265,000,000, of whom some 64,000,000 are baptised members of the Orthodox Church, 4,000,000 Roman Catholic, 3,000,000 Protestant, 2,000,000 Jewish; and 43,000,000 Moslem, making the S.U. the fifth largest Moslem country in the world. Under the 1936 constitution the central govt at Moscow is responsible for defence, foreign policy, foreign trade, communications, and heavy industries, while the govts of the constituent republics deal with all other subjects. National groups within several of the constituent republics have a measure of self-govt, the RSFSR incl. the largest number of such autonomous units. A revision of the constitution in 1977 openly recognized for the first time the dominance of the Communist Party by combining in Brezhnev (q.v.) the offices of president and party secretary.

The highest organ of govt is the Supreme Soviet of 2 chambers elected for 5 years – the Soviet of the Union (elected on a basis of 1 deputy for every 300,000 of the pop.) and the Soviet of Nationalities consisting of 32 deputies from each constituent rep., 11 from each autonomous rep., 5 from each autonomous region, and 1 from each national area. The Supreme Soviet elects its Presidium, which acts as an executive committee between its sessions, and the Council of Ministers, or Cabinet. Each constituent republic and autonomous republic has its own Supreme Soviet, of one chamber, and Council of Ministers. All citizens over 18 may vote by ballot. Deputies may be recalled by a majority of their constituents. Local govt is in the hands of district, town, and village soviets.

All industries and means of communication are State-owned, and are normally organized under either an all-Union ministry or a ministry of a constituent republic. Local authorities often run industrial and trading enterprises. Agriculture is carried on chiefly by means of the collective farm (kolkhoz), of which there are 29,000, and the state farm (sovkhoz), of which there are 18,000, but there is increasing dependence in the 1980s on the surplus produced by the private plots which the workers are allowed to retain. Both agricultural workers and craftsmen may work on their own account, provided they do not employ the labour of others. Trade in the countryside is largely in the hands of co-operative societies. Industry and agriculture are run in accordance with a plan, usually covering 5 years, drawn up by the State Planning Commission. Kosygin (q.v.) attempted economic reform with greater managerial freedom in 1965, but this was not followed up because of the example of Czechoslovakia in 1968. Nevertheless, there was a general improvement in living standards under Brezhnev until a series of poor harvests and an industrial slowdown resulted in the 1976–80 plan not being met. Inflation, from which isolation had hitherto shielded the Communist bloc, was gradually having an effect. As an oil producer, the S.U. is the world's largest, but production is expected to peak in the 1980s, and oil is being sought offshore in the Arctic, Caspian and Pacific areas. Siberia may have undiscovered reserves but, as with other minerals, extraction is difficult and costly here. *See also* the constituent republics.

Of the major powers, the Soviet Union is the most completely organized on a war footing with close to two million men in the army, another half million in both the strategic rocket forces, and the border guards and internal security troops, and probably another million in the navy and air force. The manpower is 75% conscript, call-up being at 18 for 2–3 years. After many indirect interventions in the Third World, via Cuba and military advisers, the S.U. intervened directly in Afghanistan in 1979. Troops were also massed on the Polish border in 1980, on the pattern of intervention to maintain orthodox Communist regimes in Hungary and Czechoslovakia (qq.v.), but Brezhnev then disclaimed the use of military force.

SOWETO (sōwā'tō). Black city to the SW of Johannesburg, S Africa. Originating in shanty towns of the 1930s, it developed by govt housing schemes into a city, but until 1976 its pop. could have status only as

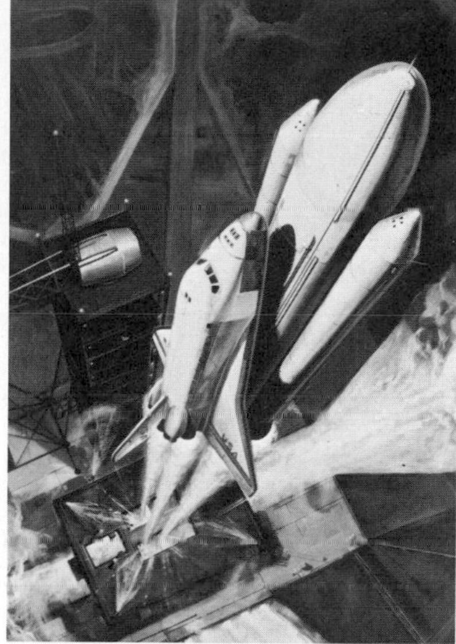

SPACE. The reusable spacecraft of the future, the Space Shuttle developed for NASA. The first orbiter (top left), which has an overall length of 37.19 m (122 ft) and a wingspan of 23.7 m (78 ft), nearing completion at Palmdale, California. The launch (top right) achieved by the orbiter's own three liquid oxygen-liquid hydrogen engines and the two solid rocket boosters on either side of the giant external fuel tank containing the ascent propellant, used by both the main engines and the boosters - the tanks and boosters are later jettisoned. The Spacelab (bottom left), built by the European Space Agency, is carried into space in the cargo bay of the orbiter for use in conducting experiments in the physical sciences, the health sciences and manufacturing processes. At low altitude the Shuttle orbiter goes into horizontal flight (bottom right) for an aircraft type of approach and landing on its return to Earth. *Photos: Courtesy of Rockwell International*

temporary residents, serving as a workforce for Johannesburg. There were serious riots in June 1976, sparked by a ruling that Afrikaans be used in African schools there. Reforms followed. The name derives from SOuth WEst TOwnship Pop. (1976) 1,000,000.

SOYA (soi'ah) **BEAN.** Leguminous plant (*Glycine hispida*), native to E Asia, particularly to Japan and China. Originally grown as a forage crop, it is increasingly used for human consumption in cooking oils and margarine, as a flour, or processed and extruded as textured vegetable protein (TVP).

Union of Soviet Socialist Republics

	Area in sq. km.	*Pop. (1979) in 1,000s*	*Capital*
R.S.F.S.R.	17,075,000	137,552	Moscow
Armenia	29,800	3,031	Yerevan
Azerbaijan	86,600	6,028	Baku
Byelorussia	207,600	9,559	Minsk
Estonia	45,100	1,466	Tallinn
Georgia	69,700	5,016	Tbilisi
Kazakhstan	2,717,300	14,685	Alma-Ata
Kirghizia	198,500	3,529	Frunze
Latvia	63,700	2,521	Riga
Lithuania	65,200	3,339	Vilnius
Moldavia	33,700	3,948	Kishinev
Tadzhikistan	143,100	3,861	Dushanbe
Turkmenistan	488,100	2,759	Ashkhabad
Ukraine	603,700	49,757	Kiev
Uzbekistan	447,600	15,391	Tashkent
U.S.S.R.	22,274,700	262,442	

SOYA BEAN. The Chinese have for centuries grown and eaten the soya bean. It is the richest of all known sources of protein, containing more than fillet steak, turkey or caviar. *Photo: Courtesy of Cadbury Typhoo Ltd.*

SPA. Town in Liège prov., Belgium, famous since the 14th cent. for its mineral springs. It has given its name to similar centres elsewhere. Pop. (1972) 9,600.

SPAAK (spahk), **Paul-Henri** (1899-1972). Belgian Socialist. From before the S.W.W. he consistently held high office, being For. Min. 1936-8, PM 1938-9, For. Min. 1939-46, PM and For. Min. 1947-9, For. Min. 1954-7, and assistant PM and For. Min. 1961-6. An ardent advocate of international peace he was awarded the Charlemagne prize in 1957.

SPACE. The continuum which incl. the galaxies. It used to be thought that S. must be empty, but this is now known not to be the case. In the Solar System, there is a great deal of thinly spread matter; there is also a vast amount of gas and dust between the stars of our Galaxy, and probably there is also appreciable matter in intergalactic space. The absorption of light by this tenuous material has to be taken into account in any astronomical investigation involving large distances.

Air S. is the volume of space between the surface of the earth and an altitude of 80,000 metres. Beyond is *Outer S.*, and in 1967 Britain, Russia and the USA signed a treaty banning nuclear weapons there, and the use of the Moon and other celestial bodies for military purposes. A further UN treaty (*see* MOON TREATY), opened for ratification 1979, would incl. prohibition of mining without permission of Third World countries, whose entitlement to a share of the profits could render the enterprise uneconomic. The European Space Agency (ESA) was estab. in 1975 by the 10 members of the European Community, superseding earlier bodies.

Space Research. The first practicable paper in the history of astronautics was pub. by Tsiolkovsky (q.v.) in 1903 and actual experiments with rockets were first carried out by Robert Hutchings Goddard (1882-1945) in 1914, culminating in his launching the first liquid fuel rocket (independently of Tsiolkovsky's ideas) in 1926. Another theoretical pioneer was Romanian, Hermann Oberth (1894-), whose work inspired that of the German team led by Wernher von Braun (q.v.), in the S.W.W., which was later continued in the USA.

Earth satellites, space probes, etc. incl. *Sputnik I* (USSR) 4 Oct. 1957 which orbited at a height of 229-898km (142-558m) in 96.2 min; *Explorer I* (USA) 31 Jan. 1958, discovered the Van Allen radiation belts; *Vostok I* (USSR: Gagarin, q.v.) 12 April 1961, first manned space ship, recovered after a single orbit at 175-142km (109-88m) in 89.1 min; *Telstar* (USA) 10 July 1962, communications satellite which sent first live television transmission between USA and Europe; *Soyuz I* (USSR) 24 April 1967, Vladimir Komarov, first man to be killed in space when his ship crashlanded; *Apollo XI* (USA) 16-24 July 1969, Neil Armstrong the first man to walk on the Moon (q.v.); *Luna 17* (USSR) 10 Nov. 1970 - 4 Oct. 1971, unmanned lunar vehicle *Lunokhod* took photos and made soil analyses on Moon; *Skylab Mission* (q.v., USA); joint link-up Soyuz (USSR) and Apollo (USA) space ships, achieved July 1975; *Pioneer 10* (USA, launched 28 Feb. 1972–), acted as pathfinder for *Voyagers 1* and *2*, and left the Solar System 13 June 1983, carrying a plaque depicting a man and a woman, in case it encounters intelligent life; *Voyager 1* (USA 5 Sept. 1977–) passing Jupiter and Saturn (qq.v.), with potential for Uranus 1986 and Neptune 1989; *Voyager 2* (USA 20 Aug.1977–), on a slower trajectory, reached Saturn 1981; *Pioneer Venus*

1 (20 May 1978) and *2* (8 Aug. 1978) both reached Venus (q.v.) in Dec. 1978; Space Shuttle project (USA), first launch 12 April 1981; 1984 Reagan announced the building of a permanent US Space Station. *See* PLANETS.

SPAIN (Estado Español, Spanish State). State of SW Europe, occupying most of the Iberian peninsula, from the Pyrenees to the Strait of Gibraltar. Most of its area is occupied by the Meseta, a plateau sloping to the SW and crossed by several mountain ranges, incl. the Sierra de Guadarrama, the Sierra de Toledo, and the Sierra Morena. This plateau is bounded on the S by the Sierra Nevada (Mulhacen 3,477 m/11,411 ft is the highest mtn in continental Spain); and to the N by the Pyrenees and Cantabrian mtns. The Guadalquivir, Guadiana, Tagus, Douro, and Mino flow to the Atlantic; and the Ebro and its tributaries to the Mediterranean. The Balearic and Canary Islands are incl. in S. The interior has extremes of temperature in summer and winter. The main plateau is very dry, but the NW enjoys an equable climate with very much rain, while Andalusia is sub-tropical.

SPAIN. King Juan Carlos and Queen Sophia. Despite prophecies of doom, the King handled an incredibly difficult position, following the restoration of the monarchy, with tact and wisdom. *Photo: Press Association*

ECONOMIC. Two-thirds of the pop. depend on agriculture. Many fruits are cultivated, incl. grapes, oranges, dates, olives, and pomegranates; as well as wheat, barley, potatoes, and sugar beet. Sheep and cattle are raised. Lead and silver are found in Murcia in the SE, copper at Rio Tinto (q.v.), mercury nr Almaden, iron in the Basque country and coal in the Asturias; manganese, tin, wolfram, zinc, and oil (nr Burgos) are also found. Not fully developed industrially, S. is an important manufacturer of cars and other vehicles, textiles, paper, cork, chemicals, leather goods, and ceramics. There are valuable fisheries. Madrid is the cap., and other towns incl. Barcelona, Valencia, Seville, Bilbao, Cordoba, Malaga, Murcia and Saragossa. M.U.: peseta.

GOVERNMENT. Dictator of S. from 1939, Franco embodied in an Organic Law of 1966 his announcement of 1947 that S. was once more a monarchy, with himself acting as regent and Head of State (*Caudillo*) till death or incapacity. The single permitted political party (*Falange Española*) was headed by Franco until his death in 1975, when Juan Carlos (nominated by Franco as the future king of Spain in 1969) acceded. Under the constitution of 1978 S. is a parliamentary monarchy with a senate elected by majority vote, and a congress of deputies elected by proportional representation. Both are elected for 4 yrs and together form the Cortes Generales.

History. Pre-Roman S. was inhabited by Iberians, Celts, and Celtiberians. The Phoenicians and Greeks early estab. colonies on the coast, and the Carthaginians attempted to found an empire in the SE. This fell into Roman hands in *c.* 200 and after a long struggle all S. was absorbed into the Roman Empire. At the invitation of Rome the Visigoths entered S. in AD 414 and set up a kingdom there, *c.* 530-700. In 711 the country was overrun by the Moors. The Christians maintained their resistance from the northern mountains, and by 1250 had reconquered all S. except the kingdom of Granada. During this struggle a number of small Christian kingdoms were founded, all of which by the 13th cent. had been absorbed by Castile and Aragon. The marriage of Ferdinand of Aragon to Isabella of Castile, 1469, brought their domains together on their accession, 1479; and the conquest of Granada in 1492 completed the unification of S.

Under Ferdinand and Isabella, Charles I (*see* CHARLES V, Holy Roman Emperor), and Philip II, S. became the greatest power in Europe, and the mistress of a world-wide empire. Columbus's discoveries made on behalf of S. were followed by the conquest of most of Central and S America; Naples and Sicily were annexed in 1503, Milan in 1535, and Portugal in 1580, while Charles I inherited the Netherlands. But with the revolt in the Netherlands and the defeat of the Armada (1588), S.'s power began to decline; the loss of civil and religious freedom, constant wars, inflation, a corrupt bureaucracy, and the expulsion of the Jews and Moors undermined her economic life, and in the 17th cent. she ceased to be a great power. By the peace of Utrecht (1713) S. lost the S Netherlands (the N had been recognized as independent in 1648), Naples, Sicily, Milan, and Gibraltar. During the 18th cent. reforms were undertaken, and considerable economic progress was made. S. became involved in the Revolutionary and Napoleonic Wars, first as the ally, later as the opponent, of France; the French occupied S. in 1808, and it was not until 1814 that they were expelled, with British assistance.

Throughout the 19th cent. conflict raged between monarchists and Liberals; revolutions and civil wars occurred in 1820-3, 1833-9, and 1868, besides many minor revolts, and a republic was temporarily estab. in 1873-4. S. lost her American colonies during 1810-30, and after the war with the USA of 1898 ceded Cuba and the Philippines to the USA. Republicanism, socialism, and anarchism grew after 1900; Primo de Rivera's dictatorship (1923-30) failed to save the monarchy under Alfonso XIII, and in 1931 a republic was estab.

In 1936 the Popular Front, an alliance of centre and left parties, took office, and introduced agrarian and other reforms which aroused the opposition of the landlords and the Church. A military revolt followed, headed by Gen. Franco (q.v.); the insurgents or Nationalists seized power in the S and NW, but revolts in Madrid, Barcelona, and elsewhere were suppressed by the workers' militia. Madrid held out for 2½ years. Italian troops and German air forces fought on the Nationalist side, while the Republicans or loyalists received minimal assistance from Russia, and volunteers from many countries formed the International Brigade to fight for the govt. Bilbao and the

Basque country were bombed into submission by the Nationalists in 1937, and in 1938 they cut off Catalonia from the main Republican territory. Barcelona fell in Jan. 1939, and the war ended with the surrender of Madrid in April. Although a Fascist dictatorship, S. was nominally neutral in the S.W.W. Gibraltar remains an issue between Britain and Spain. In Franco's declining years there was some liberalization of the regime, and following his death, the National Movement (or Falange) was abolished. In 1977 Adolfo Suarez (q.v.) was victorious in S.'s first general election for 41 years, but in 1982 the Union of the Democratic Centre (UCD) lost heavily, and Felipe González Márquez (Spanish Socialist Workers' Party, PSOE) headed the first left-wing admin since 1936. Attempted military coups failed in 1981 and 1982, and Spain entered the Common Market in 1986.

Area (incl. the Balearic and Canary Is.) is 503,556 sq.km (194,424 sq.m); pop. (1977) 36,350,000. The people are mainly of Iberian stock, but there are strong regional differences, and autonomy has been granted to the Basque and Catalan regions (qq.v.). Pre-autonomy statutes also exist for other regions, but fear of the disintegration of the country has led to a slowdown in the granting of autonomy. The national language is Spanish (Castilian), but a number of regional languages are also recognised. The legal status of the R.C. Church is recognised by a revised concordat with the Vatican (1979).

Of the former vast overseas possessions only Ceuta and Melilla in Morocco, which form part of metropolitan Spain, remain. *See* GUINEA (Equatorial), IFNI, and SAHARA (Western), as well as the many countries of the New World, where Spanish (q.v.) is still spoken.

SPALATO. Ital. form of SPLIT.

SPALDING (spawld'-). Market town in Lincs, England, 23km (14m) SW of Boston. The bulb farms are famous and S. has a flower festival in May. Pop. (1971) 15,000.

SPANDAU (shpahn'dow). Suburb of W Berlin. The chief war criminals condemned at Nuremberg in 1946 were imprisoned in the fortress here. The last of them was Rudolf Hess.

SPANIEL. A group of dogs, characterized by large, drooping ears and a long, silky coat. The Clumber S. takes its name from the estate of the duke of Newcastle, who imported them from France; it is lemon and white, and very silent when hunting. The Sussex S., believed to be the oldest variety, is a golden liver colour. The cocker is a small S., which varies in colour from liver or liver and white to black. Toy Ss., kept as pets, are divided by colour, e.g. the black-and-tan King Charles, and the red and white Blenheim.

SPANISH. The S. language is of Latin origin, and also borrowed much from the Moors during their occupation of the peninsula. The dialect of Castile was adopted as the official language towards the end of the 13th cent., but it has never supplanted the other regional idioms, among which Catalan has achieved the status of an independent language, while Galician is very close to Portuguese. Basque, which is spoken in the extreme NE of Spain, is unrelated to any other European language. S. is the official language of all the Latin American republics except Brazil, and is also spoken in the Philippines and among Sephardic Jews in N Africa, the Middle East, and the Balkans. An official language of the United Nations, S. is spoken by about 200 million persons.

Regions and provinces of Spain

	Area in sq. km.	*Population*
Andalusia		
Almería, Cádiz, Córdoba, Granada, Huelva, Jaén, Málaga, Sevilla	87,268	5,971,277
Aragón		
Huesca, Teruel, Zaragoza	47,669	1,152,708
Asturias		
Oviedo	10,565	1,045,635
Basque		
Álava, Guipúzcoa, Vizcaya	17,682	2,343,503
*Navarra		
Castilla la Nueva		
Ciudad Real, Cuenca, Guadalajara, Madrid, Toledo	72,363	5,164,026
Castilla la Vieja		
Avila, Burgos, Logroño, Santander, Segovia, Soria	49,976	1,542,450
Catalonia		
Barcelona, Gerona, Lérida, Tarragona	31,930	5,122,567
Extremadura		
Badajoz, Cáceres	41,602	1,145,376
Galicia		
La Coruña, Lugo, Orense, Pontevedra	29,434	2,583,674
Murcia		
Albacete, Murcia	26,175	1,167,339
Léon		
Léon, Palencia, Salamanca, Valladolid, Zamora	54,594	1,783,597
Valencia		
Alicante, Castellón, Valencia	23,305	3,073,255
Balearic Islands		
Baleares	5,014	558,287
Canary Islands		
Santa Cruz de la Tenerife, Las Palmas	7,273	1,170,224
	504,750	33,823,918

*Option to join Basque region

Literature. Of the classical epics, the 12th cent. *El Cantar de Mio Cid* is the only complete example. The founder of Castilian prose was King Alfonso X, the Wise, who also wrote lyric poetry in the Galician dialect. The first true poet was the 14th cent. satirist, Juan Ruiz (c. 1283-1350), archpriest of Hita. To the 15th cent. belong the marquis of Santillana (Iñigo López de Mendoza), poet, critic, and collector of proverbs; the chivalric romances, e.g. the *Amadis de Gaula*; the ballads dealing with the struggle against the Moors; and the *Celestina*, a novel in dramatic form. The flowering of the verse drama began with Lope de Rueda (d. 1565), and reached its height with Lope de Vega and Calderon de la Barca. In poetry the Golden Age of the 15th-16th cents. produced the lyrical Garcilaso de la Vega; the patriotic Fernando de Herrera (1534-97); the mystics Santa Teresa and Luis de Léon; Luis de Gongora (1561-1627), whose elaborate style popularized the decadent 'gongorism'; and the biting satire of Francisco de Quevedo. In fiction there developed the pastoral romance, e.g. Jorge de Montemayor's *Diana*;

SPANISH ARMADA. An engraving by Pine from one of a series of tapestries in the House of Lords, which were destroyed in the fire of 1834. The first engagement between the two fleets is shown in the top left-hand corner, after which the English gave chase to the Spaniards, who drew themselves up into a roundel. *Photo: The Mansell Collection*

the picaresque novel, estab. by the anonymous *Lazarillo de Tormes*; and the work of Cervantes. In the 18th cent. the Benedictine Benito J. Feijóo introduced scientific thought to Spain, and French influence emerged in the comedies of Leandro F. de Moratin (1760-1828), etc. Typical of the romantic era were the poet-dramatists Angel de Saavedra (duque de Rivas) (1791-1865), and José Zorilla (1817-93); and the lyricist José de Espronceda (1810-42). Among 19th cent. novelists are Pedro de Alarcón (1833-91), Emilia, condesa de Pardo Bazán (1852-1921), and Vicente Blasco Ibáñez (1867-1928); a 19th cent. dramatist is José Echegaray (1832-1916).

The 'Generation of 1898' incl. the philosophers Miguel de Unamuno (1864-1936) and José Ortega y Gasset (1883-1955); the novelist Pío Baroja (1872-1956); the prose-writer Azorín (José Martínez Ruiz: 1874-1967); the Nobel prizewinning poet Juan Ramón Jiménez (1881-1958). The Nicaraguan Rubén Dario (1867-1916) did much to revolutionise 20th cent. S. poetry, introducing new rhythms, vers libre, etc. The next generation incl. novelist Camilo José Cela (1916–); the poets Antonio Machado (1875-1939), Rafael Alberti (1902-), Luis Cernuda (1902-63), and the Nobel prizewinner Vincente Aleixandre (1898-); and the dramatists Jacinto Benavente (1866-1954), the brothers Quintero (q.v.), and - the most striking - F. García Lorca. The Civil War and the strict censorship of the Franco govt. disrupted mid-20th cent literary life, but later names incl. the novelists Rafael Sánchez Ferlosio (1927-), and Juan Goytisolo (1931-); and the poets Blas de Otero (1916-), and José Hierro (1922-).

In Central and S America there is vigorous life and the growth of a new tradition, especially in poetry. Mexico has been particularly fertile in poetic talent, e.g. Salvador Diáz Mirón (1858-1928) who influenced Darío, Ramón López Verlarde (1888-1921), Alfonso Reyes (1889-1959), Xavier Villaurrutia (1904-42), Alberto Quintero Alvarez (1914-44) and Octavio Paz. Other notable names incl. the Nobel prizewinners Gabriela Mistral and Pablo Neruda - both of Chile; the Argentinian Jorge Luis Borges (q.v.); Julio Herrera y Reissig (1875-1910) of Uruguay; César Vallejo (1895-1937) of Peru; Jorge Carrera Andrade (1903-) of Ecuador; and Nicolás Guillén, a Cuban of Spanish and African descent.

SPANISH ARMADA. The fleet sent by Philip II of Spain against England in 1588. Consisting of 130 ships, it sailed from Lisbon, and carried on a running fight up-Channel with the English fleet of 197 small ships under Howard of Effingham and Drake. The A. anchored off Calais, but was forced to put to sea by fireships, and a general action followed off Gravelines. What remained of the A. escaped round the N of Scotland and W of Ireland, suffering many losses by storm and shipwreck on the way. Only about half the original fleet returned to Spain.

SPANISH ART. Painting. Little pre-10th cent. painting still exists, but many examples of Romanesque art (10th-13th cent.), mainly brilliantly coloured church murals, survive. Gothic murals and altar panels (13th-15th cent.) are more freely natural.

Italian and Flemish influences contributed to Spanish Renaissance painting, and the great masters of this period (end of 15th-16th cent.) incl. Bartolomé Bermejo (*c.* 1440-95), Alonzo Sánchez Coello (1515-90), Luis de Vargas (1502-68), Francisco de Herrera the Elder, Juan de Juanes (1523-79), Juan Navarrette (1526-79), Luis de Morales (1509-86), and the greatest of all, El Greco.

Whereas previously there had been regional distinctions in style, in the 17th cent. a national school developed, of which the greatest names were Ribera, Zurbaran, Velasquez and Murillo.

SPANISH ART. El Greco's 'The Agony in the Garden of Gethsemane', with its moonlit yellow and mauve tints, creates an unforgettable impression. Some art critics have suggested that the artist's elongated figures are the result of a specific eye defect. *Photo: Courtesy of the National Gallery London*

The greatest Spanish artist of the 18th cent. was Goya, who exerted a great influence on European art of the following cent. Painters of the 20th cent. incl. the cubist Juan Gris (1887-1927), the surrealists Joan Miró and Salvador Dali (qq.v.), the impressionist Joaquín Sorolla y Bastida (1863-1923) and, most notably, Pablo Picasso (q.v.). In Spanish America an important school of mural painting emerged in Mexico with the work of the 'Big Four' - José Orozco (1883-1949), Diego Rivera (q.v.), David Siqueiros (1898-1974), and Rufino Tamayo (1899-).

Architecture. The various styles of Spanish architecture are: *Roman* (3rd-5th cent., the period of Roman rule); *Asturian* (9th cent.), which takes its name from the district in NW Spain which was unconquered by the Moors; *Mozarabic* (9th-11th cent.), a style of Spanish Christian architecture, which shows the influence of Mohammedan architecture; *Romanesque* (11th and 12th cents.); *Gothic* (13th-16th cent.); *Renaissance* (15th-17th cent.), which is uninspired though based on Italian models; *Baroque* (17th-18th cent.), a style which the Spaniards delighted in, but carried to excess in the fantastic designs of Churriguera and his followers; *Neo-Classic (18th and 19th cents.); Modern* Oscar Niemeyer and Antonio Gaudi (qq.v.).

Sculpture. The most outstanding sculptors incl. Borgoña (d. *c.* 1543), Berruguete (*c.* 1486-1561), Gregorio Fernandez (1566-1636), Montañes (1564-1649), and Alonso de los Rios.

SPANISH GUINEA. *See* GUINEA, Equatorial.

SPANISH SAHARA. *See* SAHARA, WESTERN.

SPANISH SUCCESSION. Name given to the war of 1701-14 between Britain, Austria, the Netherlands, Portugal, and Denmark on the one side, and France, Spain, and Bavaria on the other, that was caused by Louis XIV's acceptance of the Spanish throne on behalf of his grandson, Philip, in defiance of the Partition Treaty of 1700, whereby it was to pass to the archduke Charles of Austria. The French attempted in 1704 to end the war by a march on Vienna, but were defeated at Blenheim by Marlborough and Eugène of Savoy. The main campaigns were fought in Belgium, where Marlborough won victories at Ramillies (1706), Oudenarde (1708), and Malplaquet (1709). The Allies invaded Spain in 1705, and twice occupied Madrid, but failed to hold it. By the Treaties of Utrecht (1713), and Rastatt (1714), the Allies recognized Philip as king of Spain; Gibraltar, Minorca, and Nova Scotia were ceded to Britain, and Belgium, Milan, and Naples to Austria.

SPANISH TOWN. Town in Jamaica, 24km (15m) WNW of Kingston. Founded by Diego Columbus *c.* 1525, it was the cap. of Jamaica 1535-1871. Pop. (1971) 41,600.

SPARK, Muriel (1918-). Scottish novelist. B. in Edinburgh, she is a convert to Catholicism, and exercises a stylish gift of enigmatic satire in *Memento Mori* (1959), and *The Prime of Miss Jean Brodie* (1961), the story of an Edinburgh school mistress.

SPARK CHAMBER. Electronic device used by physicists in recording tracks of atomic particles. In combination with a stack of photographic emulsion, S.Cs. enable the precise point, within a cubic cm, where an interaction has taken place to be located. The most elementary type of S.C. consists of 2 smooth thread-like electrodes which are positioned 1-2 cm apart, the space between being filled by gas. *See* CHARM.

SPARROW. Bird of the genus *Passer* in the family Fringillidae. The house S. (*P. domesticus*) is numerous in N Europe and Asia, and is naturalized in N America, Australia and New Zealand. The tree S. (*P. montanus*), less common in Britain, is the prevalent species in parts of Europe and in China. Rearing several families a year, the S. rapidly becomes a pest when natural enemies are few. The American Ss. are buntings.

SPARROW-HAWK. Genus (*Accipiter*) of birds in the family Falconidae. The common S. (*A. nisus*) is a woodland bird, preying on smaller birds and mammals, and so much persecuted by gamekeepers.

SPARTA. Ancient Greek city state in Peloponnese, on the r. Eurotas *c.* 32km (20m) from the sea. The Dorians formed the ruling race, the original inhabitants being divided into perioeci, tributaries without political rights, and helots or serfs. The state was ruled by 2 hereditary kings, and under the constitution attributed to Lycurgus all citizens were trained for war from boyhood; hence the Spartans became proverbial for their indifference to pain or death, their contempt for luxury and the arts, and their harsh treatment of the helots. They distinguished themselves in the Persian and Peloponnesian wars, but in the 2nd cent. BC sank into insignificance. The modern town of S. was founded in 1834. Pop. (1971) 10,550.

SPARTACUS (d. 71 BC). A Thracian gladiator, who in 73 BC led a revolt of gladiators and slaves at Capua. After defeating several Roman armies, he was himself defeated and killed by Crassus, and thousands of his followers were crucified. The *Spartacus League*, a German Socialist organization founded by Liebknecht in 1916 to carry on anti-war activity, in 1919 became the German Communist Party. The student arm of the W German Communist Party (DKP) has been known from the 1960s as 'Spartakus', and is Stalinist in ideology.

SPARTA'KIAD. The quadrennial games held by the USSR, so-named because of the stress on physical fitness for state service in ancient Sparta. Some 10,000 Soviet athletes qualify to compete, and in 1979 foreign entrants were admitted for the first time.

SPARTE. Another form of mod. SPARTA.

SPASTICS. Those suffering from cerebral palsy and who consequently have difficulty in moving their arms and legs, and sometimes in speech and swallowing, too. The condition is caused by interference with the development of the brain while it is actively growing before birth, at birth, or in the first year or so of life. It is not progressive, and good training helps to combat the extent of damage. It is more common in cases of premature birth.

SPEAKER. The title applied to the presiding officer charged with the preservation of order in the legislatures of various countries. In the UK the Lord Chancellor fills the office in the House of Lords; in the House of Commons Mr Speaker is elected each parliament, usually occupying the position for considerable periods. The original appointment dates from 1377.

SPECIAL AIR SERVICE. Specialist British regiment (SAS) recruited mainly from parachute regiment volunteers, it was founded by Col. David Stirling in North Africa 1942-5, and revived from 1952. Its HQ is at Bradbury Lines nr Hereford on the Welsh border. It has served in Malaya, Northern Ireland, and against internat. terrorists, as in the siege of the Iranian embassy in London 1980. Members are anonymous, but Col. Charlie Beckwith of the US Special Forces, who led the abortive attempt to rescue the American hostages from Iran in 1980, is an honorary member. Their motto is 'Who dares wins' under a winged dagger.

SPECIFIC GRAVITY. The ratio of the weight of a given volume of a substance at a given temperature to an equal volume of some standard substance, usually at the same temperature. The standard substance for liquids and solids is water, normally at 4°C or 20°C, and is therefore an abstract number independent of units. For scientific work *density,* the mass of unit volume, is preferred.

SPECIFIC HEAT. The quantity of heat required to raise unit mass of a substance by one degree.

SPECTACLES. A pair of lenses fitted in a frame and worn in front of the eyes to correct or assist defective vision. They are said to have been invented in the 13th cent. by a Florentine monk. Few people found the need for S. until printing was invented, when the demand for them increased rapidly. It is not known when S. were introduced into England, but in 1629 Charles I granted a charter to the Spectacle Makers' Guild. Common defects of the eye corrected by spectacle lenses are short sight or myopia by concave (spherical) lenses, long sight or hypermetropia by convex (spherical) lenses, and astigmatism by cylindrical lenses, the direction of the axes of the cylinders being specified. Spherical and cylindrical lenses may be combined in one lens. For convenience bifocal S. provide for correction both at a distance and for reading by combining 2 lenses of different curvatures in one piece of glass. Using photosensitive glass, lenses are produced which darken in glare and return to normal in average conditions: some dangers arise with these, e.g. in driving, since the change is not instantaneous. *See* CONTACT LENS.

SPECTRO'SCOPY. A branch of physics dealing with methods of excitation, detection and study of spectra (*see* SPECTRUM), covering the complete range of electromagnetic wavelengths from radio through infra-red, visible light, ultra-violet and X-rays to gamma rays (*see* FREQUENCY SPECTRUM OF ELECTRO-MAGNETIC WAVES), and of arrangements in order of the energies of collections of atomic particles (electrons, neutrons, etc.). S. is of fundamental importance and wide application in academic research, industry, medicine and forensic science. It provides a rapid and accurate method of detecting, analysing and identifying minute quantities of materials non-destructively, yielding valuable information on the structure of atoms and molecules and the composition and motions of heavenly bodies.

SPECTRUM. An arrangement in order of magnitude of radiated frequencies of electromagnetic waves, or of the energies of atomic particles. The visible S. was first studied by Newton who showed in 1672 that a band of white light (sunlight) passing through a glass prism could be broken into a band of coloured light, ranging from violet through indigo, blue, green, yellow, and orange to red. Light can be regarded as electromagnetic waves and most sources emit waves of complex shape which can be broken up or 'dispersed' by suitable means, such as by a spectroscope, an instrument containing a collimator, a prism or diffraction grating, and a telescope, into a succession of individual waves arranged in order of wavelength.

There are many types of S., both emission and absorption, for radiation and particles. A few common examples may be cited: an incandescent body gives rise to a *continuous S.* where the dispersed radiation is distributed uninterruptedly over a range of wavelengths. An element gives a *line S.* - one or more bright discrete lines at characteristic intervals. Molecular gases give *band S.* in which there are groups of close-packed lines shaded in one direction of wavelength. In an *absorption* S. dark lines or spaces replace the characteristic bright lines of the absorbing medium. The *mass* S. of an element is obtained from a mass spectrograph and shows the relative proportions of its isotopes. (*See also* SPECTROSCOPY).

SPEE (shpā), **Maximilian,** count von (1861-1914). German admiral. B. in Copenhagen, he held North Sea and Far Eastern commands before the F.W.W. He went down with his flagship in the 1914 battle of the Falkland Islands, and the *Graf Spee* battleship was named after him.

SPEEDO'METER. Indicating instrument attached to the gear-box of a vehicle by a flexible drive to give the speed of the vehicle in miles or kilometres per hour on a dial easily visible to the driver.

SPEED RECORDS. Among animals, the swift can fly at up to 160kmph (100mph); the cheetah can reach 105km (65m) over short distances; and the Sei whale can cruise at 65km (40m) on the surface - other species of whales hold the long distance speed record, maintaining *c.* 30km (20m) for 1,600 km (1,000 m). Man - over a 10 sec. sprint - reaches 36.2kmph (22.5mph).

The rail S.R. is held by a French locomotive, the TGV Electrique 23001, which in 1981 reached 310 kph (236 mph) at Pasily. In a conventional car Donald Campbell reached 648.7km (403.1m) at Lake Eyre salt flats, Australia, in 1964; and in a jet-car (1970) Gary Gabelich (USA) reached 1,014.5 km (630.388m). In 1979 Stan Barrett (USA) first broke the sound barrier on land in the Mojave Desert, California, when he reached 1,191 kmph (739.66 mph) in a cigar-shaped vehicle powered by rocket motor, plus a Sidewinder (q.v.) military missile. The water S.R. claimed the lives of 3 eminent car drivers (Segrave, Cobb, and Donald Campbell), and in 1967 on Lake Guntersville,

SPENCER. Sir Stanley Spencer (left) in a self-portrait, and his macabre interpretation of the dead rising from the village churchyard at Cookham in 'Resurrection'. *Photo: Courtesy of the Tate Gallery (Resurrection)*

Alabama, Lee Taylor, jr (USA) reached 458.9km (285.2m). In the air William Knight (USA) in the North American Aviation rocket plane X-15 reached the S.R. for winged aircraft with 7,296 km (4,534 m) in 1967 nr Edwards Air Force Base, California, but an Apollo spacecraft, at the stage of acceleration to 'escape velocity' from Earth orbit to deep space, reached 38,950 km (24,200 m).

SPEENHAMLAND SYSTEM. Method of poor relief in England started by Berkshire magistrates in 1795, whereby wages were supplemented from the poor-rates. It encouraged farmers to pay low wages, however, and was superseded by the 1834 Poor Law. A more sophisticated modern equivalent is the concept of negative income tax (q.v.).

SPEKE (spēk), **John Hanning** (1827-64). British explorer. B. in Somerset, he served with the Indian army and in the Crimea, and in 1856 joined Burton (whom he had previously accompanied to Somaliland) in an expedition to the African lakes. When Burton became ill, S. went on to discover the Victoria Nyanza, but his claim that it was the source of the Nile was disputed by Burton even after Speke and Grant made a second expedition 1860-3 to confirm the point. He accidentally shot himself while shooting near Bath, where he was to have disputed publicly with Burton the next day.

SPELEOLOGY (Gr. spēlaion cave). The scientific study of caves, incl. their origin, development, physical structure, flora, fauna, folk-lore, exploration, surveying, photography, cave-diving, rescue work, etc. It first developed in France in the late 19th cent., where the Société de Spéléologie was founded in 1895, and in the form of 'potholing' - which involves following the course of underground rivers or streams - has in the 20th cent. become a popular sport. In 1963 a world underground depth record of 1,135 m (3,723 ft) was achieved by a British team exploring the Berger cave nr Grenoble.

SPENBOROUGH. Town in W Yorks, 8km (5m) SE of Bradford. Industries incl. textile, leather goods, chemicals, and machinery. Pop. (1972) 41,430.

SPENCE, Sir Basil (1907-76). British architect. He was prof. of architecture at the Royal Academy 1961-8, and his controversial works incl. Coventry Cathedral, Sussex Univ., the British embassy in Rome, the Home Office and Knightsbridge Barracks. He was knighted in 1960: OM in 1962.

SPENCER, Herbert (1820-1903). British philosopher. B. at Derby, he was an engineer before entering journalism. While sub-editor on *The Economist*, he wrote *Social Statics* (1851), expounding his *laissez-faire* views on social and political problems, and in 1855 *Principles of Psychology* appeared. His *Education* (1861) is still of practical value. In the same year he began his *System of Synthetic Philosophy*, in which he applied the evolutionary principle of 'the change from homogeneity to heterogeneity' to the whole field of human knowledge. The chief of the 10 vols. are: *First Principles* (1862), and *Principles* of biology, psychology, sociology, and ethics. Other works are *The Study of Sociology*, *Man v. the State*, *Essays*, and an autobiography.

SPENCER, Sir Stanley (1891-1959). British artist. B. at Cookham-on-Thames, where he spent most of his life apart from his service in the F.W.W., he made village life there his means of interpreting the Christian faith to which he held, e.g. 'Christ Carrying the Cross' and 'Resurrection' (both in the Tate Gallery). His major work is the series of mural paintings for the oratory of All Souls' at Burghclere in Berks, completed 1933. His work combines regard for detail with disregard for reality, achieving a sense of innocence. He was knighted in 1959. In 1962 the *S.P. Gallery*, devoted to his work was opened at Cookham. His brother **Gilbert** (1892-1979) was a landscape artist.

SPENDER, Sir Stephen (1909–85). British poet. Ed. at Univ. Coll., Oxford, he founded with Cyril Connolly the magazine *Horizon* (of which he was co-editor 1939-41) and 1953-67 was co-editor of *Encounter*. His vols. of verse, characterized by introspective sensitivity, incl. *Twenty Poems* (1930), *Vienna* (1934), *The Still Centre* (1939) and *Poems of Dedication* (1946). Other works incl. the verse drama *Trial of a Judge* (1938), and the autobiography *World within World* (1951). He was prof. of English at Univ. Coll., London 1970–77 and knighted 1983.

SPENGLER (shpeng'ler), **Oswald** (1880-1936). German philosopher. In his *Decline of the West* (1918), and his political writings, he maintained civilization was doomed, and glorified primitive man. He was much admired by the Nazis.

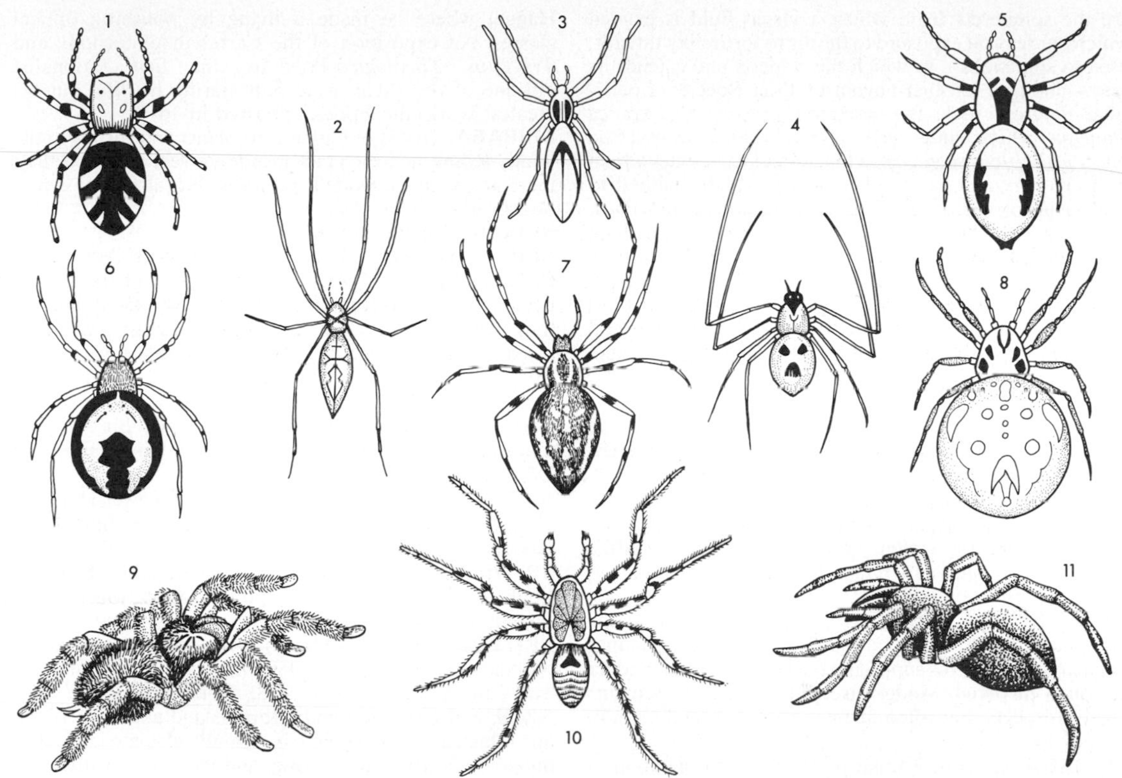

SPIDERS. 1, Salticus scenicus (zebra spider); 2, Tetragnatha solandrii; 3, Tibellus oblongus; 4, Ero theoracica; 5, Evarcha falcata; 6, Araneus pyramidatus; 7, Araneus diadematus (garden spider); 8, Araneus quadratus; 9, Avicularia vestiaria (bird-eating spider, S America); 10, Lycosa tarantula (tarantula, q.v.), 11, Atrax robustus (funnel web – lethally poisonous – Australia)

SPENSER, Edmund (1552–99). English poet. B. in London, he was ed. at Cambridge, entered the service of the earl of Leicester, and in 1579 pub. *The Shepheard's Calendar.* In 1580 he became secretary to the Lord Deputy in Ireland, and at Kilcolman Castle completed the first 3 books of the great moral allegory *The Faerie Queene* (1590). He twice visited England in the vain hope of preferment at court. In 1598 Kilcolman Castle was burnt down by rebels, and S. with his family narrowly escaped. Three further books of *The Faerie Queene* were pub. in 1596, but the remaining 6 were probably lost in the fire. He d. in London, and was buried in Westminster Abbey. S.'s other works incl. the elegy on Sidney, *Astrophel* (1586); the love sonnets or *Amoretti* and the *Epithalamion* (1595); and a prose *View of the Present State of Ireland.* The modern reader is often deterred by the element of allegory, but S. remains the 'poet's poet' in his versification, richness of language, and fertile imagery.

SPERMACETI. Glistening wax-like substance, not a true oil, contained in the cells of the huge, almost rectangular S. case in the head of the sperm whale, and amounting to *c.* 2.5 tonnes. It rapidly changes in density according to temperature, and is used by the whale to enable it to dive a thousand metres to feed on squid, and stay there easily for half an hour. Before the introduction of whaling restrictions it was much used in lubricants and cosmetics. In 1980 a blend of fatty acids and esters from tallow, coconut oil, etc. was developed as a substitute in cosmetics. For sperm whale, *see* CACHALOT.

SPEY (spā). River in Highland region, Scotland. Rising SE of Fort Augustus, it flows 172km (107m) to the Moray Firth between Lossiemouth and Buckie, and is famed for salmon fisheries at its mouth.

SPEYER (shpīr). Ancient city in Rhineland-Palatinate, W Germany, on the Rhine, 26km (16m) S of Mannheim. The name Protestant originated here, from the protests of the Lutherans to the diet of Spires, 1529. Pop. (1972) 50,000.

SPEZIA. *See* LA SPEZIA.

SPHINX (sfinks). A fabulous monster, represented in Egyptian art as a lion with a man's head. It also figures in the art of Greece, Assyria, Persia, etc. The best-known example is the Great S. at Gizeh, Egypt, 58m (189ft) long, built *c.* 2900–2750 BC.

SPHYGMOMANO'METER (sfig'-). Instrument for measuring blood pressure, particularly of the arteries.

SPICE ISLANDS. Old name for the MOLUCCAS.

SPICES. Aromatic vegetable substances used as condiments and for flavouring food. They are obtained from tropical plants, and include pepper, cayenne pepper, nutmeg, ginger, and cinnamon.

SPIDER. Animal of the order Arachnida - not an insect - in which the head and breast are merged to form the cephalothorax, connected to the abdomen by a characteristic narrow waist. On the under-surface of the abdomen are the spinnerets from which a viscid fluid is exuded which hardens on exposure to the air to form silky threads, used to spin webs - in which the S. nests and catches its prey - and as a safeguard against falling. Species of particular interest incl. the common garden S. (*Aranea diadema*) which spins webs of remarkable beauty; the zebra S. (*Salticus scenicus*), a longer-sighted species which stalks its prey and has pads on its feet which enable it to walk even on glass; the poisonous tarantula and black widow (qq.v.); the water S. (*Argyroneta aquatica*) which fills a 'diving bell' home with air trapped on the hairs of the body; and the largest members of the group, the bird-eating Ss. of S. America (*Mygale*), with bodies *c.* 5cm (2in) long and a leg-span of 30cm (1ft). Ss. are generally useful to man in their destruction of harmful insects and an acre of English grassland may contain *c.* 2¼ million.

SPĪ'KENARD. Perennial herb (*Nardostachys jatamansi*), of the family Valerianaceae, also called nard, the source of a famous perfume used in ointments by eastern people and the Romans.

SPILLANE, Mickey (1918-). American writer. B. in Brooklyn, NJ, he began by writing for pulp magazines and became known for violent crime novels featuring Mike Hammer, the 'one-man police force', e.g. *Vengeance is Mine* and *The Long Wait*.

SPĪ'NA BĪ'FIDA. Birth defect, a failure of the developing spinal canal to close completely: bifida = divided into two parts. The nerves supplying the legs, arms and bladder are often involved. Modern treatment has increased survival prospects, but often at the cost of a heavily handicapped life.

SPINACH (spin'ej). Annual plant (*Spinacia oleracea*) in the family Chenopodiaceae. A native of Asia, it is cultivated for its leaves which are used as a vegetable, especially in the USA.

SPINE. The backbone. It contains 26 bones called vertebrae, including the sacrum and coccyx. The vertebra has a semicircular, thick rounded body at the front to take weight, a bony ring behind through which passes the spinal cord, and 3 projections of bone (processes), one on each side and one to the rear. The lowest part of the S. is the sacrum, a broad triangular structure consisting of 5 rudimentary vertebrae fused together, jointed to the hip bones and ending in the tail bone (coccyx), which consists of 4 fused vertebrae. The S. in man has four curves (front to rear), which allow for increased size of chest and pelvic cavities; also permit springing, to minimize jolting of internal organs.

SPI'NEL. A group of minerals possessing cubic symmetry and consisting chiefly of magnesia and alumina. The alumina S. contain the gem varieties, such as the ruby, and occur in Sri Lanka and Burma.

SPINET. A keyboard instrument, smaller than a harpsichord, and distinguished from the larger instrument by having only one string for each note.

SPINNING. The art of drawing out and twisting fibres into threads, by hand or machinery. Synthetic fibres are extruded as a liquid through the holes of a spinneret.

SPINOZA (spinō'zah), **Benedict** (or **Baruch**) (1632-77). Dutch philosopher. B. at Amsterdam of Portuguese-Jewish stock, he abandoned Judaism for a rationalistic pantheism that owed much to Descartes. He taught that all that we know, mind and matter, is a manifestation of the all-embracing substance that is God. Persecuted by the Jews, he had to leave Amsterdam and finally settled at The Hague, where he made a living by polishing optical glasses. An exposition of the Cartesian philosophy and *Tractatus Theologico-Politicus*, the first rationalist critique of the Bible, were pub. during his life, but his greatest work, the *Ethics*, appeared in 1677.

SPIRAEA. Genus of herbaceous plants and shrubs in the family Rosaceae which incl. meadow sweet (*S. salicifolia*): there are many cultivated species with ornamental cymes of flowers.

SPIRES. French form of SPEYER.

SPIRITS OF SALTS. *See* HYDROCHLORIC ACID.

SPIRITUALISM. A belief in the survival of the human personality and in communication between the living and those who have 'passed on'. The spiritualist movement originated in America in 1848. In England the Society for Psychical Research was founded in 1882 by W. H. Myers and Henry Sidgwick to investigate the claims of S. Famous spiritualists incl. D. D. Home, Sir William Crookes, Sir Oliver Lodge, Sir A. Conan Doyle, and Lord Dowding.

SPITALFIELDS. District of the bor. of Tower Hamlets, Greater London, England. It was once famed for Huguenot silk weavers.

SPITHEAD. An anchorage in the Solent, off Portsmouth, England. The name is often applied to the whole of the eastern arm of the Solent (q.v.).

SPITSBERGEN (Svalbard). Group of Norwegian islands in the Arctic Ocean 480km (300m) E of Greenland. The 4 main islands are West S., North East Land, Edge Island, and Barents Island; Hope Island and Bear Island are attached to S., which is heavily glaciated. Coal is mined by Norway and Russia, and there are weather and research stations, incl. a telemetry station for artificial satellites (1967). The chief settlement is Long Year City. There is rich wildlife, incl. walrus and polar bear. Area 62,000 sq.km (24,000 sq.m); pop. (1977) 3,430 incl. 1,200 Norwegians and 2,230 Russians.

SPITZ DOG. *See* POMERANIAN.

SPLEEN. An organ *c.* 12.5 × 7.5cm (5 × 3in) under the diaphragm on the left of the body. Its function is not well known, but is in part concerned with the production and destruction of blood cells.

SPLIT. Yugoslav port and tourist centre, on the Adriatic, founded by Diocletian AD 300. It manufactures cement. Pop. (1971) 152,000.

SPOCK, Benjamin McLane (1903-). American child-care expert. His *Common Sense Book of Baby and Child Care* (1946) influenced a generation to less restrictive up-bringing of children, but in later work he lays more stress on a need for discipline.

SPODE (spōd), **Josiah** (1754-1827). British potter. Son of Josiah S., who had been an apprentice of Thomas Whieldon, and started his own works at Stoke-on-Trent in 1770, he succeeded him in 1797. He was responsible for developing bone porcelain (bone ash, china stone and china clay) *c.* 1800, which was produced at all English factories in the 19th cent., and became potter to George III in 1806.

SPOKANE (spōkan'). City of Washington, USA at the falls of the S. river, which are harnessed for its many industries. It is the centre of a lumbering and mining region and the seat of Gonzaga univ. Pop. (1970) 170,500.

SPOLETO (spōlā'tō). Ancient town in Perugia, Umbria, Italy, of great architectural interest, a papal possession 1220-1860. Pop. (1971) 40,000.

SPONGES. Many-celled animals forming the sub-kingdom Porifera. A simple sponge is vase-shaped, supported by three-rayed spicules. There is a constant flow of water through the pores of the sponge, leaving again by the oscule, or opening at the top. The more complex Ss. are colonized, the body cavity being lined with cells which absorb nutritious material in the water, or have reproductive functions. Ss. are classified according to the chemical nature and arrangement of the spicules into Calcareous Ss., Glass Ss., Common Ss., Four-rayed Ss., Fleshy Ss., Single-rayed Ss., and Horny Ss. Most Ss., are marine, but some are found in fresh water. The toilet S. is the prepared skeleton of a colony.

SPOONBILL. A family of birds, Threskiornithidae characterized by their long, flat bills, dilated at the tip in the shape of a spoon.

SPOONER, William Archibald (1844-1930). British scholar. Warden of New Coll., Oxon, 1903-24, he was famed for lapses of the tongue, e.g. 'Kinquering congs their titles take'. These were exaggerated by repute, and similar errors became known as Spoonerisms.

SPORADES (spor'adēz). Alternative name for the Dodecanese (q.v.).

SPORE. The one-celled reproductive body of Cryptogams or flowerless plants. They are generally light enough to be carried by the wind. Under certain conditions they are produced by bacteria.

SPORE. Looking rather like a Martian invader preparing for take-off, this is an earthstar *(Geastrum triplex)*, so-called because the outer covering splits into a star-shape. A water droplet has just landed on top of the fungus inducing it to expel a spore cloud. *Photo: Heather Angel*

SPOROZOA. A large division of unicellular parasitic protozoa. They readily produce reproductive spores which are transmitted from one host to another. Many of them cause serious diseases, such as malaria and sleeping sickness.

SPRAIN. An injury to ligaments or tendons round a joint without dislocation. Its usual cause is a wrench or twist.

SPRAT. European fish (*Clupea sprattus*) of the herring family. The full-grown S. is *c.* 10cm (4in) long, and occurs in large numbers in British seas.

SPRATLY ISLANDS. Group of is. in the S China Sea, 480km (300m) E of Vietnam and W of the Philippines. Both countries, and the Chinese (to whom they are known as the Nanshan Is.), have claimed sovereignty. In 1975 the Vietnamese, who call them Truong Sa, occupied six of them.

SPRINGBOK. Species of S African antelope (*Antidorcas marsupialis*), *c.* 75cm (30in) high and with lyrate horns. The coat is tawny, but a stripe of white, erectile hair runs down the middle of the back and the underparts are also white. The name derives from the animal's sudden leaps in the air. It is the national emblem of S Africa, and her national football team and her soldiers are known as Ss.

SPRINGFIELD. Name of a number of places in the USA, the chief of which are: (1) Cap. of Ill., on the Sangamon river SW of Chicago. It was the home of Abraham lincoln 1837-61, and is a manufacturing and agricultural centre, with bituminous coal mines in the vicinity. Pop. (1970) 91,750. (2) City of Mass., on the Connecticut; settled in 1636, it has many industries. Pop. (1970) 163,900. (3) City of Mo., an agricultural centre founded 1830. Pop. (1970) 120,100. (4) City of Ohio, to the NE of Dayton. Founded 1799, it has heavy industry, and makes leather goods, paper products, measuring instruments, etc. Pop. (1970) 81,950.

SPRINGS. Town in the Transvaal, S Africa, SE of Johannesburg. Gold, coal, and uranium are mined. Pop. (1970) 104,100.

SPRING-TAILS or **Collembola.** Order of wingless insects, belonging to the section Apterygota, commonly known as Ss., from their having the cerci on the abdomen modified into a forked organ which enables the insect to jump. Widely distributed, they may feed on decaying vegetable matter or (in some species) on the living plant.

SPRUCE. Coniferous trees in the genera *Picea* and *Tsuga*. The Norway S. (*P. abies*) and the hemlock S. (*T. canadensis*) are important timber-trees.

SPURGE. Genus of trees and shrubs in the family Euphorbiaceae. Many have fleshy leaves and a milky juice.

SPURN HEAD. Promontory in Humberside, England, forming the N shore of the Humber estuary.

SPURS, Battle of the. Victory won by Henry VIII at Guinegate, NW France, in 1513; the name recalls the speed of the French retreat.

SPY. *See* SECRET SERVICE.

SPY SHIP. High-speed warship specialising in surveillance of enemy warships, monitoring their radar and sonar, and guiding anti-ship missiles of her own fleet fired from beyond the radar horizon at *c.* 55-55 km (30-35 m).

SQUASH. *See* PUMPKIN.

SQUASH RACKETS. A game played in an enclosed court 9.75m (32ft) long and 6.40m (21ft) wide, normally by 2 persons (doubles played in a larger court where available) each with a racket 685mm (27in) long with a wooden head and strings. The soft 'squashy' ball is 40mm (1.6in) in diameter and weighs 24 grammes (just over an oz.). Play begins from a service box, one of which is marked at each side of mid-court, and the ball must be hit above a line 1.83m (6ft) high on the front wall. After service it may be played anywhere, above the board (a line set out on the upper edge of a band of resonant material .48m/19in high), within the boundary of the court. The general rules of lawn tennis, with points scored by the server up to 9, apply thereafter.

The S.R. Assocn was founded in 1928, but the game remained of limited appeal as a spectator sport, owing to the necessarily small size of the gallery at the rear of the court, until televised games led to a phenomenal increase in its popularity in the 1970s and 1980s.

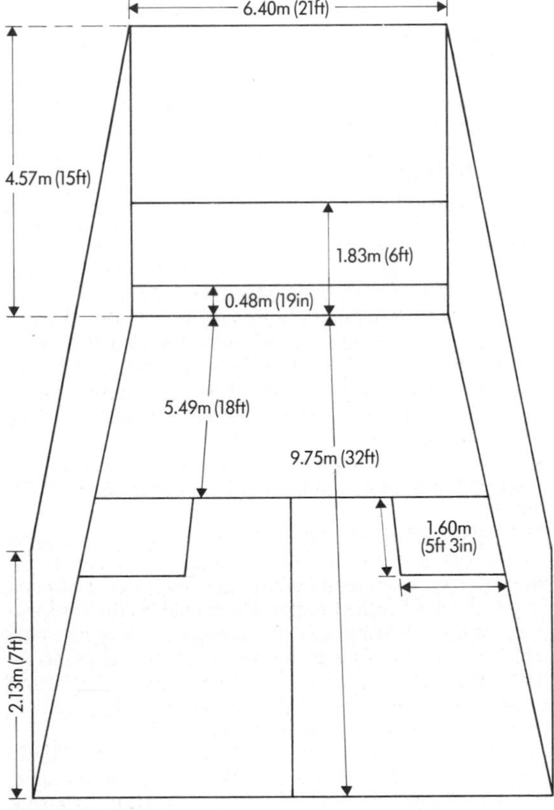

SQUASH RACKETS

SQUATTER. Basically someone illegally settling on land. By the mid-19th cent., however, it was used in Australia and NZ as synonymous with pastoralist or grazier, without an illegal imputation. Those who survived droughts and held on to their wealth estab. a politically powerful 'squattocracy', built elegant mansions, etc. (*see* ARMIDALE). As closer agricultural settlement spread at the close of the century, their influence waned. In the UK during the 1970s the word was applied to those taking over publicly or privately owned houses and other premises, either on grounds of homelessness or as a political manoeuvre, and special legislation was enacted to deal with the problem.

SQUID. Group of marine cephalopod molluscs. The common S. (*Loligo vulgaris*) of the Mediterranean extends in the Atlantic to British waters: the 2 long tentacles are used to seize its prey and the 8 smaller to hold it while feeding. Origin of many tales of sea monsters in the N Atlantic is the giant S. (*Architeuthis princeps*) up to 15m (50ft), but reliably reported to 55m (175ft), of which 7.5m (25ft) would be body length. The flying S. (*Ommastrephes bartrami*) leaps on the surface rather than flies. A number of species carry light organs at certain points on the body and produce striking phosphorescent effects.

SQUIRE or **Esquire.** Originally a young man training for knighthood, who acted as attendant on a knight. From the later Middle Ages the term was loosely applied to a rank between those of knight and gentleman; hence, 'esquire' is used in England after the surname on letters, etc., purely as a courtesy title.

SQUIRREL. Family of rodents (Sciuridae). The common or red S. (*Sciurus vulgaris*) occurs throughout Europe and northern Asia: the fur is a rich red, and the tail handsomely bushy. Omnivorous, it rears its young in nests or 'dreys', and although less active in winter, when it relies for food mainly on stores of nuts, etc., made in the summer, does not hibernate. In Britain the red S. has been almost entirely superseded by the larger grey S. (*S. carolinensis*) introduced from N America.

SRI LANKA. Island 32km (20m) off the SE tip of India, formerly known as Ceylon. In the N low-lying, with a swampy coastline, it rises to a south central mountain mass, where the highest peak is Mt Pidurutalagala 2,528 m (8,294 ft), and Adam's Peak (q.v.) is a centre of pilgrimage. The chief river is the Mahaveli-ganga 335km (208m), rising in the central mtns, and flowing into the sea nr Trincomalee, but navigable only in the lower reaches. The climate is warm 15°C (60°F) in the hills to 27°C (80°F) in the lowlands, and humidity is high. Rainfall is heavy, except in the N, reaching well over 5,000 mm (200in) in the SW. About 20 per cent of the land is forested, valuable timber incl. ebony, satinwood and rosewood, and the ruins of the ancient caps. of Anuradhapura and Polonnaruwa are concealed in the jungle. Crops incl. rice, mainly for home consumption, and the export commodities tea (the most important), rubber, coconut products (oil, copra, dessicated coconut, etc.), cocoa, and cinnamon. Minerals incl. graphite, and such varied gems as sapphire and ruby; and pearls are obtained on the Gulf of Manaar. There are traditional crafts in gold, silver, brass, ivory and tortoiseshell work, but also growing modern industries such as vehicle assembly, textiles, pharmaceuticals, and refining of imported oil. The chief towns are the cap. and chief port of Colombo, Jaffna, Kandy, Galle, Negombo and Trincomalee.

Under the constitution of 1978 there is a presidential system on the French model. The Pres. (popularly elected for 6 yrs) is assisted by a PM, and the unicameral Parliament is elected by proportional representation. The state is secular, but in religion Buddhism has the foremost place: the Tamil minority is Hindu. The official language is Sinhala, but Tamil is recognised as a national language.

History. Only a handful of the Veddas, the original people of S.L., remain in jungle areas, the majority of the population are Sinhalese - an Aryan people from the N of India - who invaded and conquered the island in the 6th cent. BC under their king Vijaya. The Portuguese estab. settlements in the early 16th cent., but were replaced by

SRI LANKA. Although mechanisation will eventually replace the labour of the elephant, they are still greatly used. Here one of the hardworking team settles to a modest lunch. *Photo. Douglas Dickins*

the Dutch from 1602, until the areas the latter governed were annexed by the British in 1796. Briefly admin. as an adjunct of Madras presidency, S.L. became a separate British crown colony in 1802 when it was formally ceded to Britain under the Treaty of Amiens, although it was not until 1815 that the ruler of the central kingdom of Kandy acknowledged British sovereignty. S.L. became independent within the Commonwealth in 1948, and in 1972 adopted a rep. constitution, reverting at the same time from Ceylon to the traditional name of Sri Lanka 'Resplendent Island'. There is a minority problem in that the 2.5 million Tamils, who either arrived in later invasions from the Indian mainland over the cents., or came more recently to work on the tea plantations in the Northern and Eastern provs., claim a separate Tamil state: their HQ is Jaffna. A proportion are being repatriated to India. Mrs Banaranaike's Freedom Party was defeated at the 1977 elections by the United Nat. Party of Junius Jayawardene. Area 65,600 sq.km (25,332 sq.m); pop. (1971) 12,747,755. M.U.: Sri Lanka rupee.

SRINAGAR (srinug'ger). Cap. of Jammu and Kashmir, on the Jhelum, a beautiful city and resort intersected by waterways. It makes carpets, papier mâché, leather goods, etc. Pop. (1971) 403,600.

S.S. (Ger. *Schutz-Staffel*, 'protective squadron'). Nazi élite corps, organized in 1928. Under Himmler's command it reached 500,000, incl. both full-time members (*Waffen-S.S.*, 'armed S.S.'), who fought in the S.W.W., and spare-time members. It carried out police duties, and became infamous for its share in the persecution of the Jews, the brutalities of the concentration camps, and the administration of occupied territories. The Nuremberg court condemned it in 1946.

STABILIZERS. Fins fitted to the sides of a ship and governed automatically by gyro mechanism, which can reduce a 30° side-to-side roll to 3°.

STAËL (stahl), **Anne Louise Germaine de** (1766–1817). French author. B. in Paris, the dau. of the financier Jacques Necker, she m. the baron de S. in 1786. An ardent advocate of political freedom, she was banished from Paris by Napoleon, but gathered round her at Coppet on Lake Geneva men such as A. W. von Schlegel, Byron, and Benjamin Constant. Her relationship with the last-named inspired her novels *Delphine* and *Corinne*. Her most influential work was *De l'Allemagne* (1810), which revealed to France the richness of German literature.

STAFFA. Uninhabited island of the Inner Hebrides, Strathclyde, Scotland, 87km (54m) W of Oban, with remarkable caves.

STAFFORDSHIRE. Midland co. of England. Apart from hills in the extreme N, and to the S in Cannock Chase, it is flat, being the Vale of Trent and its tributaries. The North and South S. coalfields formerly supported two important industrial areas. In the N the Potteries round Stoke-on-Trent, and in the S the Black Country between Birmingham and Wolverhampton, but in 1974 the latter was transferred to W Midlands. The admin. HQ is Stafford. Keele Univ. (1962), nr Newcastle-under-Lyme in N Staffs, has been noted for its enterprise. Area 2,660 sq.km (1,027 sq.m); pop. (1978) 997,000.

STAGHOUND. Breed of dog used for hunting stags. The old English S. was a type of bloodhound, but now a large foxhound is given the name.

STAINED GLASS. Term applied to the coloured transparent glass which is cut into various shapes and joined by lead strips to form a pictorial window design. The art is said to have originated in the Near East. At first it was usual for only one monumental figure to be represented on each window, but by the middle of the 12th cent. incidents in the life of Christ or of one of the saints were commonly depicted. Some of the most beautiful examples of medieval S.G. are to be found in the cathedrals of Canterbury, Lincoln, Chartres, Cologne, and Rouen. Modern designers incl. Morris, Burne-Jones, and James Hogan. Since the S.W.W. the 6th cent. use of thick, faceted glass joined by cement has been revived.

STAINED GLASS. The development of modern transparent resins has made possible fresh imaginative uses for coloured glass in unexpected settings. These screens separate hotel reception rooms. *Photo: Courtesy of Ray Bradley*

STAINER, Sir John (1840–1901). British organist and composer. B. in London, he became organist of St Paul's in 1872, receiving a knighthood on his resignation in 1888. Most notable among his religious choral works are *The Crucifixion*, an oratorio and *The Daughter of Jairus*, a cantata.

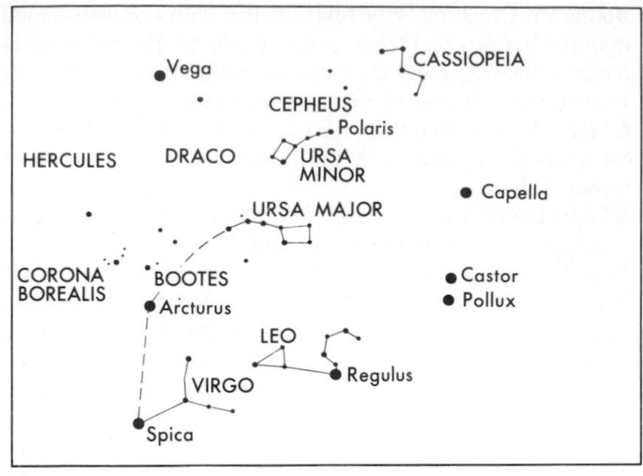

1 Ursa Major region

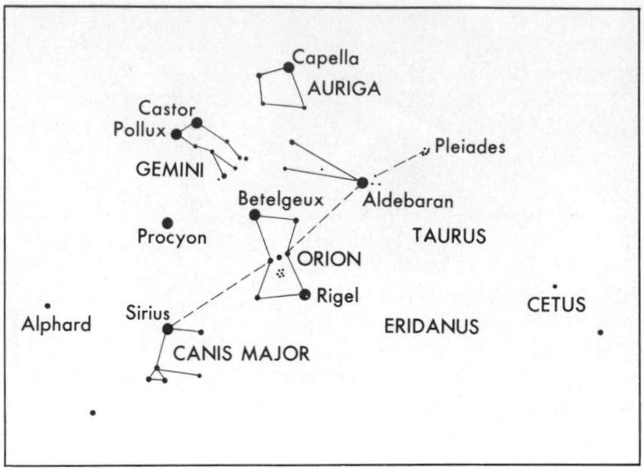

2 Orion region

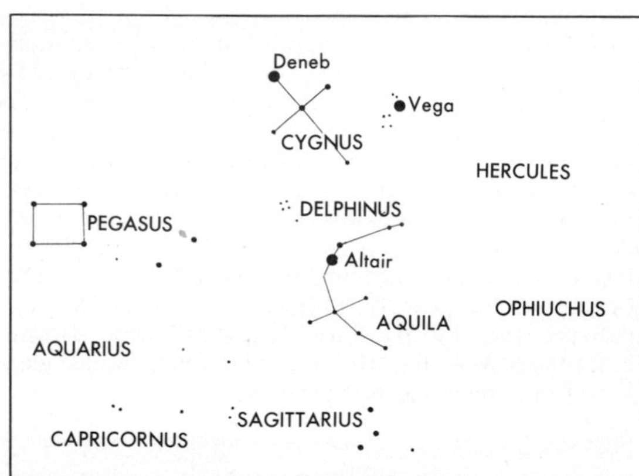

3 Vega Deneb and Altair region

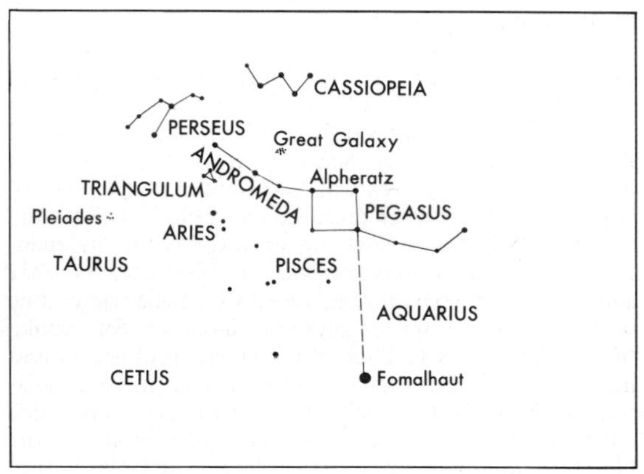

4 Pegasus region

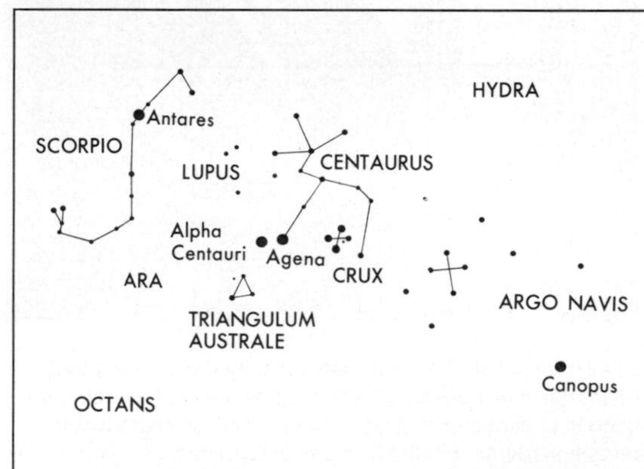

5 Centaurus – Crux region

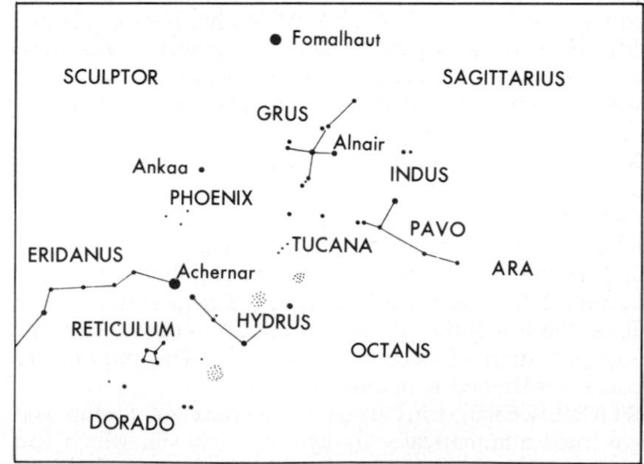

6 Achernar and Grus region

STAKHANOV (stakahn'of), **Aleksei** (1906–77). Russian miner. A worker in the Donbas, he gives his name to *Stakhanovism*, a movement in the 1930s through which workers improved production on their own initiative.

STALACTITE and **STALAGMITE.** A deposit of lime formed in caves by the downward trickling of water containing carbonate of lime. Stalactites are those hanging from the roof, and stalagmites those accumulated on the floor.

STALIN ('steel'). Adopted name of Soviet statesman **Joseph Vissarionovich Djugashvili** (1879–1953). B. at Gori, near Tiflis, the son of a Georgian shoemaker, he was ed. for the priesthood, but was expelled from his seminary for carrying on Marxist propaganda. He joined the Social Democratic Party in 1898, and was exiled to Siberia 5 times 1903–12, but on each occasion escaped and resumed his revolutionary activities. By 1913 he was editing *Pravda* and directing the Bolshevik group in the Duma, while his book, *The National and Colonial Question*, attracted Lenin's attention. From 1913 until the revolution of March 1917 he was an exile in Siberia. He then became a member of the Communist Party's political bureau, and sat on the committee which directed the Nov. revolution. Appointed Commissar for Nationalities in the Soviet govt he was responsible for the decree granting equal rights to all peoples of the Russian Empire. During the civil wars he held various commands, and distinguished himself by his defence of Tsaritsin (now Volgograd) against the 'Whites'. He was appointed gen. sec. of the Communist Party in 1922. Lenin's death in 1924 was followed by prolonged controversies within the party between S., who advocated the industrialization of Russia and the construction of a fully Socialist society, and Trotsky, who denied the possibility of Socialism inside Russia until revolution had occurred in western Europe. S.'s policy was finally accepted in 1927, and was put into operation from 1928 onwards in the five-year plans. The constitution of 1936 was largely his work. S. held no govt post until 1941, when he became chairman of the Council of People's Commissars, a position equivalent to PM. He was largely responsible for Soviet strategy during the S.W.W., and received the rank of marshal of the Soviet Union in 1943, and that of generalissimo in 1945. He met Churchill and Roosevelt at Tehran in 1943 and at Yalta in 1945, and took part in the Potsdam conference. His writings incl. *Foundations of Leninism* and *Dialectical and Historical Materialism*. After his death his 'cult of personality' and the harshness of his one-man rule were condemned.

STALINGRAD. *See* VOLGOGRAD.

STAMBOUL. *See* ISTANBUL.

STAMP. *See* PHILATELY and POST OFFICE.

STANDARD. *See* FLAG.

STANISLAVSKY, Constantine (1863–1938). Stage-name of the Russian actor-producer Constantine Alexeev. B. in Moscow, he was a founder of the Moscow Art Theatre and excelled as the interpreter of Chekhov and Gorky. His 'method', expressed in *My Life in Art* (1934) and other books, has had an immense influence on modern acting, e.g. Marlon Brando.

STANLEY. *See* DERBY, EARL OF.

STANLEY, Sir Henry Morton (1841–1904). British explorer. B. at Denbigh, reared in a workhouse, and adopted by a cotton broker named S.; he went to New Orleans in 1859, was appointed correspondent for the *New York Herald* in 1867, and was commissioned by Gordon Bennett to go to Africa to find Livingstone. He arrived at Zanzibar in 1871, met Livingstone at Ujiji, and together they explored the N end of Lake Tanganyika. His book, *How I Found Livingstone* (1872), was a best-seller. He later traced the course of the Zaïre (Congo) to the sea, and in 1879 founded the Congo Free State.

STANLEY. Cap. of the Falkland Islands, S Atlantic, at the extreme E of the group. Pop. (1974) 1,080.

STANLEY FALLS. Series of 7 cataracts in under 100 km (60 m) in the Lualaba (upper Zaïre river), above Kisangani. They total a drop of over 60 m (200 ft), with great hydro-electric potential.

STANLEY POOL. *See* ZAÏRE RIVER.

STANLEYVILLE. *See* KISANGANI.

STAR. A globe of extremely hot gas, radiating because of nuclear processes taking place inside it. The Sun, which is an average star, has a surface temperature of 6,000°C, and a central temperature of between 12,000,000° and 15,000,000°C; it is at least 6,000 million years old, and will continue radiating in its present form for several thousands of millions of years to come. However, many Ss. are known to be much more luminous than the Sun: S. Doradûs, in the southern hemisphere, is equal to at least one million Suns, and yet is so remote that it cannot be seen without a telescope. Even the nearest S., Proxima Centauri, is more than 4 light-years (roughly 25 million million miles) away. The Ss. are of different types, and are divided broadly into Giant and Dwarf branches; the Sun is classed as a dwarf. No telescope yet constructed will show a S. as anything but a point of light, and our knowledge of them is gained from studies carried out with instruments based upon the principle of the spectroscope. It is thought that many Ss. may well have planetary systems essentially similar to our own Solar System. However, since a planet has no light of its own, the only way it can be detected at present is by its gravitational pull on its star. Such a perturbation is seen in the case of a faint red dwarf S. only 6 light-years away from Earth. It is known as Barnard's star, because particularly studied by E.E. Barnard, and the evidence suggests that it may have 2 planets, but no direct proof is available.

Observation with infra-red telescopes suggests that Ss. are born when a dense cloud of interstellar gas passes among the clustered stars of the spiral arm of a galaxy. The cloud is then compressed to an even greater density, and collapses successively, in a kind of chain reaction, into a series of new stars.

STARCH. A widely distributed carbohydrate, that occurs in granular form in cereals and pulses, fruits of leguminous plants, and potato tubers. Separation is achieved by macerating potatoes, and fermenting grains. The white powder is then subjected to chemical processes which suit it for use as a stiffener in the textile, paper, and laundering industries.

STAR CHAMBER. Tribunal consisting of members of the king's council which met in an apartment of Westminster Palace, which had a starred ceiling. Under the Tudors it dealt with offenders strong enough to defy the ordinary courts, and was generally respected for its speedy administration of justice. Its harsh persecution of Puritans under Charles I made it unpopular, and in 1641 it was abolished.

STAR CLUSTER. A group of stars, much more closely crowded than is usual in the Galaxy. Cs. may be 'loose' or 'open', such as the Pleiades (Seven Sisters) or 'globular', such as Omega Centauri. Among famous naked-eye open clusters are the Pleiades (q.v.), the Hyades, and Praesepe. Large numbers of telescopic clusters are known.

STARFISH. Class of echinoderms, Asteroidea. The body is extended into 5 arms, and is covered with spines and small pincer-like organs. There are also a number of small tubular processes on the skin surface which assist in respiration, and small tube-feet sometimes with suckers at the end. The poisonous and predatory 'crown of thorns' S. of the Pacific, once rare, is very destructive to coral, and did great damage to Australia's Great Barrier Reef when it multiplied disastrously in the 1960-70s.

STARFISH The Crown of Thorns starfish, famous predator of the Great Barrier Reef. *Photo: Valerie Taylor/Ardea*

STARLING. Bird (*Sturnus vulgaris*) common in N Europe and Asia and naturalized in N America from the late 19th cent. The black, speckled plumage is glossed with green and purple. Its own call is a bright whistle, but it is a mimic of the songs of other birds. Strikingly gregarious in feeding, flight and roosting, it often becomes a pest in large cities, e.g. London, where it becomes attached to certain buildings as 'dormitories', returning each night from omnivorous foraging in the countryside.

STATE DEPARTMENT. *See* FOREIGN RELATIONS.

STATEN (stat'n) **ISLAND.** Island in New York harbour, USA, constituting the bor. of Richmond. Pop. (1970) 295,500.

STATIC ELECTRICITY. Electric charge acquired by a body by means of electrostatic induction or friction. Its effects are due to the electrostatic forces produced by the charge. Separation of electric charge is often brought about in everyday life by rubbing different materials together, and this is rendered visible by the sparks produced on combing one's hair in the dark or removing a nylon shirt. S.E. produces serious effects in many industries, e.g. in printing works where measures have to be taken to discharge the S.E. to prevent papers sticking together. In other processes S.E. is useful as in paint spraying where the parts to be sprayed are charged with electricity of opposite sign to that on the paint droplets, and in xerography (q.v.).

STATICS. The branch of mechanics concerned with the behaviour of bodies at rest and forces in equilibrium, and distinguished from dynamics.

STATIONERY OFFICE, HM. An office estab. in 1786 to supply books, stationery, etc., to British govt depts, and to superintend the printing of govt reports, etc., and books and pamphlets in an increasingly wide field from national works of art to industrial and agricultural processes. The corresponding estab. in the USA is the Govt Printing Office.

STATIONS OF THE CROSS. A series of pictures or images, usually 14, depicting the closing scenes of the Passion of Christ.

STAUDINGER (stow'dinge), **Hermann** (1881-1965). German scientist. Prof. of organic chemistry at Freiburg 1926-51, he founded macro-molecular chemistry by researches into the structure of albumen, cellulose, and rubber. Nobel prize 1953.

STAUFFENBERG (stow'fenberg), **Claus von** (1907-44). German resistance leader. A Swabian army officer, he planted a bomb on 20 July 1944 in a briefcase in Hitler's conference room in the Wolf's Lair at Rastenburg. A table leg deflected the force of the blast, and S. was shot the following day.

STAVA'NGER. Fishing port of SW Norway, now one of Europe's foremost oil-prospecting cities. There are also fish-canning, shipbuilding, and other industries. Pop. (1978) 88,000.

STAV'ROPOL. Town in the N Caucasus, RSFSR, USSR, SE of Rostov: known as Voroshilovsk 1935-43. A market centre for an agricultural area, it makes agricultural machinery, textiles, and food products. Pop. (1977) 245,000.

STEAM. A dry, invisible gas formed by vaporizing water. The visible cloud which normally forms in the air when water is vaporized is due to minute suspended water particles. In this state it is called wet S. The 'saturation temperature' is the temperature at which droplets begin to form from water vapour. S. is widely used in chemical and other industrial processes and for the generation of power.

STEAM ENGINE. A machine which uses steam as the working agent in order to convert heat energy into mechanical work. An account of a S.E. was pub. by the marquis of Worcester in 1663, and a Frenchman, Papin, described what was unquestionably the first cylinder and piston engine in 1690. Captain Savery patented an engine in 1698. The S.E. was later improved by Newcomen, Beighton, and others, but it remained imperfect until James Watt introduced the separate condenser and air-pump, patented in 1769, and made various other improvements. Richard Trevithick invented the first steam-propelled vehicle in 1801. George Stephenson successfully applied the S.E. to locomotives in 1829 and in 1802 William Symington built the first steamboat, a pioneer attempt which was followed up by Robert Fulton and Henry Bell.

STĒA'RIC ACID ($C_{17}H_{35}COOH$). A saturated fatty acid, soluble in alcohol and ether, but not water. When pure, it is colourless and waxy.

STĒ'ARIN ($(C_{17}H_{35}COO)_3.C_3H_5$). The name given to the solid first separated on the cooling of many liquid fats or oils; to a mixture of stearic and palmitic acid; and to glycerides of stearic acid.

STĒ'ATĪTE. A hydrous magnesium silicate, usually occurring in beds of metamorphosed serpentine. A massive form of talc, it has a greasy feeling, accounting for its other name, soapstone.

STEBARK. Polish name of TANNENBERG.

STEED (sted), **Henry Wickham** (1871-1956). British journalist. Foreign correspondent for *The Times* in Vienna 1902-13, he was then foreign editor 1914-19 and editor 1919-22. The dismemberment of the Austro-Hungarian

Empire after the S.W.W. has been attributed partly to his influence.

STEEL. Iron containing from 0.05 to 1.5 per cent carbon, ranging through mild Ss. used in tinplate or structural work, e.g. reinforcing rods; carbon steels used for rails, axles, etc.; high carbon Ss., used in cutting tools, etc.; and high-alloy Ss. for special purposes.

In the 1970s the making of low and medium carbon Ss. was revolutionised by the introduction of pneumatic processes (notably the Austrian LD - initials of Linz and Donawitz, where it was first developed, which is also known as the basic oxygen furnace or BOF process). In addition continuous casting of S. now allows iron to go from blast furnace to converter to slabs ready for rolling, without the need for setting into ingots on leaving the converter, which formerly had to be reheated before being made into finished steel plates, etc. Steel strip, in demand for cars and household appliances, is now made by blowing the molten metal (direct from the converter) into a fine powder, which is then stirred with water to form a slurry, which is deposited as a film on a moving belt. High-carbon Ss. are made by electric arc processes which allow precise control during the refining period. High alloy Ss., such as high-speed steels (Ss. which retain their hardness at high temperatures, and so can be used in machines working at high speed), are made by electric induction furnaces. Corrosion resistance (stainless Ss., etc), high tensile properties, etc, are obtained by the addition of nickel, chromium, molybdenum, manganese, tungsten, vanadium, etc, and to prevent the separation and clotting of the alloy a gas atomisation process is used. This reduces the molten metal to fine powder form before compacting it into ingots of more uniform quality and greater strength than could otherwise be obtained.

STEEL, David (1938-). Liberal politician. A journalist and broadcaster, he was the youngest member of Parliament 1965-66, and in 1976 succeeded Jeremy Thorpe as leader of the party. In 1977-8 he entered into a compact to support the Labour govt. In the 1979 general election the Liberal vote was reduced and the no. of Liberal MPs. was reduced from 14 to 11. *See* LIBERAL PARTY.

STEEL BAND. Type of band popular in the West Indies, espec. Trinidad, in which the percussion instruments are made from oildrums.

STEELE, Sir Richard (1672-1729). Irish essayist. B. in Dublin, he entered the guards, and then settled in London, and originated *The Tatler* (1709-11), in which Addison collaborated. They continued their joint work in *The Spectator* (1711-12), and *The Guardian* (1713). He also wrote plays, e.g. *The Conscious Lovers* (1722). He was knighted in 1715.

STEEN (stān), **Jan** (1626-79). Dutch painter. B. at Leiden, he painted genre pictures from all walks of life e.g. 'The Music Master', and 'Tavern Company'.

STEEPLECHASE. *See* HORSE-RACING.

STEEP POINT. The most westerly extremity of Australia, in Western Australia, NW of the Murchison River.

STEER, Philip Wilson (1860-1942). British artist. B. at Birkenhead, he studied in Paris, and was influenced by the Impressionists, becoming a leader (with Sickert) of the English movement. A founder member of the New English Art Club, he had a delicately sharp individualized style in his landscapes and portraits, e.g. 'The Beach at Walberswick' (Tate Gallery). In 1931 he was awarded the OM.

STEIN (stīn), **Gertrude** (1874-1946). American author. B. in Pennsylvania, she studied medicine, and in 1904 went to Paris, where she became acquainted with Picasso. In her work she adopted a cinematic technique, using repetition, absence of punctuation, etc., to convey instantaneous continuity. Her works incl. the self-portrait, *The Autobiography of Alice B. Toklas* (1933).

STEINBECK, John Ernst (1902-68). American novelist. B. in California, he first achieved success with *Tortilla Flat* (1935), a humorous study of the lives of Monterey *paisanos*, following this with *In Dubious Battle* (1936), dealing with the brutal development of a strike by migrant fruit pickers; *Of Mice and Men* (1937), a compassionate vignette of 2 migrant farm labourers, one a feeble-minded giant, which was dramatized by the author and also filmed; and *The Grapes of Wrath* (1939), the saga of a farming family, refugees from the Oklahoma 'dust bowl', who struggle vainly against the inequitable conditions of the California they once regarded as their 'Promised Land'. Later books incl. *Cannery Row* (1944), *East of Eden* (1952), and *Winter of our Discontent* (1961). In 1962 S. was awarded a Nobel prize.

STEINER (shtīner), **Rudolf** (1861-1925). Austrian philosopher. B. in Austria, he became leader of the German theosophists, but broke with them and developed his own teaching, known as 'Anthroposophy'. His school, the Goetheanum, near Basle, was destroyed by fire in 1922, but has since been rebuilt.

STELLENBOSCH (-bos). Town of Cape Prov., S. Africa, 50km (31m) E of Capetown, centre of a wine-producing dist., seat of a univ. (1918), and, next to Capetown, oldest European settlement in S.A. (1679). Pop. (1970) 30,000.

STENDHAL (stoṅdahl'). Pseudonym of French novelist Marie Henri Beyle (1783-1842). B. in Grenoble, he served in Napoleon's armies, taking part in the ill-fated Russian campaign, and, failing in his hopes of becoming a prefect, lived in Italy from 1814 until suspicion of espionage drove him back to Paris in 1821, where he lived by literary hack-work. The reputation of his novels *Le Rouge et le Noir* (1830) and *La Chartreuse de Parme* (1839), pioneer in their psychological subtlety, began with a review of the latter by Balzac in 1840. From 1830 he was a member of the consular service, spending his leaves in Paris.

STEPHEN (c. 1097-1154). King of England. A grandson of William I, he was elected king in 1135, although he had previously recognized Henry I's dau. Matilda as heiress to the throne. When in 1139 Matilda landed in England, a war began which reduced England to anarchy. It ended in 1153, when S. acknowledged Matilda's son, Henry, as his heir.

STEPHEN I (975?-1038). Hungarian king. He succeeded his father in 997, completed the conversion of Hungary to Christianity, and was canonized in 1803. In 1978 the crown of St. S., symbol of Hungarian nationhood, was returned to Hungary by the USA, by whom it had been held since 1945.

STEPHEN, Sir Leslie. *See* WOOLF, VIRGINIA.

STEPHENSON, George (1781-1848). British engineer. B. near Newcastle, he became engine-wright at Killingworth Colliery, and here built his first locomotive in 1814. He also invented a safety lamp in 1815. He was appointed engineer of the Stockton and Darlington Railway, the world's first public railway, in 1821, and of the Liverpool and Manchester Railway in 1826. In 1829 he won a £500 prize with his famous 'Rocket'. His son, **Robert S.** (1803-59), achieved distinction as a civil engineer, constructing railway bridges, notably the high-level bridge at Newcastle, and the Menai and Conway tubular bridges.

STEPNEY. District of the Greater London bor. of Tower Hamlets, on the N of the Thames, E of the City. It incl. the Tower, and large docks.

STEREOPHONIC SOUND. *See* HI-FI.

STERILIZATION. Destruction of the power of reproduction. A man may be sterilized by tying off the tubes carrying seed from the testicles to the seminal vesicles, a woman by tying the Fallopian tubes. Fertility can be restored by removal of the ligatures, if the tubes are still open. Either sex may be permanently sterilized by cutting out a portion of each tube (vasectomy) or by removing the testicles or ovaries (castration), or by giving them a sufficiently powerful dose of X-rays. Male sterilization is much used as a birth control measure in India. The word S. is also applied to the killing of bacteria by heat (asepsis) or disinfectants.

STERNE. Laurence (1713-68). Irish writer. B. at Clonmel, Ireland, he took orders in 1737 and became vicar of Sutton-in-the-Forest, Yorks, in the next year. In 1741 he m. Elizabeth Lumley, an unhappy union largely because of his wandering amorous propensities, e.g. his sentimental love affair with Eliza Draper, of which the *Letters of Yorick to Eliza* (1775) is a record. His chief work is *The Life and Opinions of Tristram Shandy, Gent.* (1760-7), an eccentrically whimsical and bawdy novel which made him a London 'lion'. Also very popular was his *A Sentimental Journey through France and Italy* (1768), born of his journeys abroad in 1762 and 1765 in search of a cure for his tuberculosis.

STE'ROL. An organic solid alcohol, such as ergosterol or cholesterol, which is physiologically very active. A *steroid* is any of the large group of fat soluble organic compounds, incl. the sterols, various hormones and vitamin D., which occur naturally or may be synthesized. *See* ANABOLIC STEROID.

STE'THOSCOPE. Instrument used to ascertain the condition of the heart and lungs by listening to their action. It was invented by R. T. Laënnec (1781-1826), in 1819, and as now used consists of a small plate to be placed against the body and connected by flexible tubes with 2 ear-pieces.

STETTIN (shtetēn'). Ger. form of SZCZECIN.

STEVENAGE. Town in Herts, England, 45km (28m) N of London. Dating from medieval times, S. was in 1946 the first place chosen for development as a 'new town'. Pop. (1974) 74,000.

STEVENS, Wallace (1879-1955). American poet. B. in Reading, Penn., and ed. at Harvard and the NY Law School, he became a lawyer, eventually specializing in insurance. His vols. of poems incl. *Harmonium* (1923) - his first and very badly received - *The Man with the Blue Guitar* (1937) and *The Necessary Angel* (1951). A sensuous technician, he had an obscurity that yielded to intimate study.

STEVENSON, Adlai (1900-65). American statesman. B. in Los Angeles, he was ed. at Princeton, and from Northwestern Univ. Law School went on to be admitted to the Bar in 1926. As gov. of Illinois 1949-53 he campaigned vigorously against corruption in public life, and as Democratic candidate for the presidency in 1952 and 1956 was twice beaten by Eisenhower. In 1945 he had been chief US delegate at the founding conference of the UN.

STEVENSON, Robert (1772-1850). Scottish engineer. B. in Glasgow, he built many lighthouses, incl. that on Bell Rock, 1807-11.

STEVENSON, Robert Louis (1850-94). Scottish author and poet. B. in Edinburgh, he studied at the univ., and became an advocate, but never practised. He travelled on the Continent to improve his health, as recounted in *An Inland Voyage* (1878), and *Travels with a Donkey* (1879). In 1879 he went to the USA, m. Mrs Osbourne, and returning to Britain in 1880, pub. the vol. of stories, *The New Arabian Nights* (1882), and essays, e.g. *Virginibus Puerisque* (1881), and *Familiar Studies of Men and Books* (1882). Fame came to him with *Treasure Island* (1883), which was followed by *Kidnapped* (1886; with its sequel *Catriona* in 1893), *The Black Arrow* (1888), *The Master of Ballantrae* (1889), *Dr. Jekyll and Mr. Hyde* (1886); and the incomplete *Weir of Hermiston* (1896) and *St. Ives* (1897). The humorous *Wrong Box* and the novels *The Wrecker* and *Ebb-tide* were written in collaboration with his stepson, Lloyd Osbourne (1868-1920). In 1890 he settled at Vailima, in Samoa, where he d. His *A Child's Garden of Verses* appeared in 1885, and his Letters in 1899.

STEWART, James (1908-). American actor. B. in Indiana, Pa., he served in the American air force during the S.W.W., and then resumed a career in which his usual film role was the gangly, stubbornly honest, ordinary American, e.g. *Mr. Smith Goes to Washington.*

STEWART ISLAND. Volcanic is. divided from South Island, NZ, by the Foveaux Strait. There is farming, fishing and granite quarrying. The main settlement is Oban. Area 1,735 sq.km (670 sq.m); pop. (1974) 410.

STICK INSECTS. Family of insects (Phasmidae) of the order Phasmida, closely resembling sticks, twigs, etc. Many species are wingless.

STICKLEBACKS. Fishes in the family Gasterosteidae; the popular name is derived from the spines which take the place of the dorsal fin.

STI'GMATA. Impressions of marks corresponding to the 5 wounds of Christ received at His crucifixion, which are said to have been received by St Francis and other saints.

STILICHO (sti'likō), **Flavius** (*c.* AD 359-408). Roman gen. A Vandal by birth, he distinguished himself in campaigns against the Goths and other barbarian invaders, and under Honorius virtually ruled the western empire. He was executed on a charge of treason.

STILTON. Village in Cambridgeshire, on the Great North Road, 10km (6m) SW of Peterborough. It gives its name to a cheese brought to S. in coaching days for transport to London, and still made at and around Melton Mowbray.

STILWELL, Joseph Warren (1883-1946). American gen., nicknamed 'Vinegar Joe'. B. in Florida, he became in 1942 US military representative in China, led the Chinese armies operating with the British in Burma, and later commanded all US forces in the Chinese, Burmese and Indian theatres. Recalled to USA in 1944 because of differences with Chiang Kai-shek, he commanded the US 10th Army on Okinawa, so sharing in Japan's final defeat.

STICK INSECTS. This 28cm-long Giant African stick insect is perfectly camouflaged during the day and moves to feed only at night. *Photo: Anthony Bannister/NHPA*

STIMSON, Henry Lewis (1867-1950). American statesman. B. in New York, he was War Sec. in Taft's cabinet 1911-13, and 1929-33 Hoover's Sec. of State. In 1940-5 he was War Sec.

STINKHORN. Species of fungus (*Ithyphallus impudicus*). It first appears as a white ball, which breaks, and a cylindrical column of white spongy substance shoots from it. The upper cells are filled with an olive jelly which gives off a penetrating odour attracting blowflies, which assist in its propagation.

STINKWOOD. South African tree (*Ocotea bullata*). The timber smells unpleasant when first felled, but is fine-grained and durable, so that much early S African furniture was made from it.

STIRLING. Town in Central region, Scotland, of which it is admin. HQ, 47km (29m) NE of Glasgow. There is some industry, a univ. (1964), and S. castle is of immemorial antiquity and was long the residence of the kings of Scotland. Bannockburn is nearby and Wallace won a victory at S. Bridge in 1297. Pop. (1971) 29,800.

STIRLING, James (1926-). British architect. He designed the engineering building at Leicester Univ., and the Tate Gallery extension.

STIRLINGSHIRE. Former co. of Scotland, merged for the most part in Central region in 1975, but with a SW section, incl. Kilsyth, going to Strathclyde. The area lay between the Firth of Forth and Loch Lomond, and besides the outlying Lennox hills incl. the fringe of the Highlands. The co. town was Stirling.

STOAT. *See* ERMINE.

STOCK. Popular garden flower, whose species have been derived from the wild genus *Matthiola*. The chief varieties are simple-stemmed, queen's, and ten-week, derived from *M. incana*; night-scented S. is *M. bicornis*.

STOCK. In finance, the fully paid-up capital of a company. It is bought and sold by subscribers not in units or shares (*see* SHARE), but in terms of its current cash value.

STOCK EXCHANGE. Institution for the buying and selling of stocks and shares. There are S.Es. in London, Glasgow, Cardiff, and other cities of the UK; in Montreal, Sydney, and other British Commonwealth cities; in NY (usually referred to as Wall Street, from its location) and other US cities; in Paris (Bourse), Amsterdam (Beurs), and other Continental caps. and big towns. The London S.E., opened 1801, is the oldest; before 1801 securities were bought and sold in the coffeehouses in Change Alley. The London S.E. is owned by a private company and controlled by a council, elected annually, which is responsible for the rules governing business transactions. Members, totalling some 4,000, pay heavy fees and must provide sureties; they are re-elected annually and are divided rigidly into brokers (who buy and sell stocks and shares for the public on commission) and jobbers (who as a rule deal only with brokers). Strangers are not allowed on the floor of the house. The *S.E. Official List*, pub. daily, is made up from the day's transactions. There are 2 settlement days in each month, when settlement of accounts must be made.

In S.E. terms a *bear* is a speculator who has sold securities he does not as yet possess in the expectation of buying them back at a lower price before Settling Day; a *bull* buys securities he does not intend to 'take up', i.e. pay for, but hopes to sell at a higher price and pocket the difference; and a *stag* applies for shares in new issues to sell them at a profit as soon as possible to members of the investing public.

STOCKHAUSEN (stok'howsen), **Karlheinz** (1928-). German composer. He studied under Messiaen, and from twelve-note music progressed to electronic composition, e.g. *Kontakte* (1968). Besides pure electronic sound, he advocates supplementation of standard instruments with sound-transforming equipment (timbre filters, modulators, etc.).

STOCKHOLM (stok'hōlm). Cap., important port, and cultural centre of Sweden, on the mainland and island fringe where Lake Mälar discharges into the Baltic. Staden island, the original settlement, contains the market place, the royal palace (1697-1754), a church dedicated to St Nicholas (1264), and the imposing town hall (1923). On Norrmalm are the houses of parl. and the bank of Sweden. A network of bridges links the islands and the mainland; an underground railway was completed in 1957; there is an airport at Bromma. S. is the usual residence of the king, the seat of most of Sweden's educational institutions and of the Nobel Institute. The Swedish warship *Wasa* built for Gustavus II Adolphus, which sank in the harbour on her maiden voyage in 1628, was raised in 1961 in a remarkable state of preservation and is exhibited in a special museum. Industries incl. iron and steel manufacture, engineering, shipbuilding, textile and paper making, sugar refining, printing. Pop. (1972) 1,486,000.

STOCKPORT. Town in Greater Manchester, England, on the Mersey. Textiles, chemicals, plastics, machinery and metal goods are made. Pop. (1972) 138,750.

STOCKS. Wooden device used until the 19th cent. to confine the legs or arms of minor offenders, who were exposed to public ridicule.

STOCKTON. Inland deepwater port in California, USA, on the San Joaquin r., centre of a fertile area of fruit and vegetables, with agricultural machinery and food processing industries. Pop. (1970) 107,650.

STOCKTON-ON-TEES. Town in Cleveland, England, 8km (5m) above the mouth of the Tees. There are shipbuilding, steel, chemical and other industries. Pop. (1974) 162,580.

STOCKWOOD, Arthur Mervyn (1913-). British Anglican churchman. He was bp of Southwark 1959-80, expressing controversial views on homosexuality, and in favour of the ordination of women.

STOICS (stō'iks). Greek school of philosophy, founded *c.* 300 BC by Zeno; it derived its name from the Stoa, or porch, at Athens in which he taught. The Ss. were pantheistic materialists who believed that happiness lies in accepting the law of the universe. In ethics they emphasized human brotherhood; their outlook was internationalist, and they denounced slavery. In the 3rd and 2nd cents. BC Ss. took a prominent part in Greek and Roman revolutionary movements. After the 1st cent. BC Stoicism became the philosophy of the Roman ruling class, and lost its revolutionary significance; outstanding Ss. of this period were Seneca, Epictetus, and Marcus Aurelius.

STOKE-ON-TRENT. City in Staffs, England, formed in 1910 by the amalgamation of Burslem, Hanley, Longton, Stoke-upon-Trent, Fenton and Tunstall - the largest ceramic centre in the world, the Potteries or 'Five Towns' of Arnold Bennett. The Gladstone Pottery Museum (1975) is the world's only working pottery museum. There are also iron and steelworks; chemical, paper and rubber industries, and one of Europe's richest coalfields. Pop. (1972) 262,120.

STOKE POGES. English village in Berks, 3km (2m) N of Slough. The poet Gray is buried in the churchyard, probably the scene of his 'Elegy'.

STOKER, Bram (i.e. Abraham) (1847-1912). British novelist. He studied pure mathematics at Trinity College, Dublin, qualified as a barrister, and worked in the Irish Civil Service - the Registrar of Petty Sessions Clerk's Department - from 1866 until 1878. In the latter year he became business manager to Henry Irving, remaining with him for 27 years. His most famous book is *Dracula* (1897), a tale of were-wolves and vampires, but he pub. a number of other novels as well as personal *Reminiscences of Henry Irving*. *See* DRACULA.

STOKOWSKI (stokof'ski), **Leopold** (1882-1977). American conductor. B. in London of British and Polish parentage, he became an American citizen in 1915. An outstanding experimentalist, he introduced much contemporary music into the US (notably Mahler's 8th Symphony) and appeared in several films (e.g. Walt Disney's *Fantasia*, 1940).

STOMACH. The first receptacle of food after swallowing. It is a bag of muscle situated just below the diaphragm and pear-shaped. Food enters it by the gullet (oesophagus), is digested by the acid juice secreted by the S. lining, and then passes through the pylorus into the duodenum.

STONE AGE. Name given to the period in prehistory before the discovery of the use of metals, i.e. when men's tools and weapons were made chiefly of flint. It is divided into the Old S.A. or Palaeolithic and the New S.A. or Neolithic; in the latter the flint implements were more finely chipped. Sometimes an Eolithic or Dawn Stone Age is distinguished. The men of the Old S.A. were hunters, and their few remains have been found in the deposits of caves, river gravel, and so on. The period is divided into Upper, Middle, and Lower, each of which is subdivided into stages whose names are usually derived from the sites where the characteristic implements were first discovered, viz. *Upper*: Magdalenian, Solutrean, and Aurignacian; *Middle*: Mousterian; *Lower*: Acheulean and Chellean. Palaeolithic men lived in caves, and the most striking survivals of their culture are their wall paintings, e.g. at Altamira and Lascaux. They were contemporary with the mammoth, woolly rhinoceros, reindeer, and cave bear, and lived before and during the ice ages. Neolithic man lived in a milder climate, and made the first steps in agriculture, domestication of animals, weaving, and pottery making. In Europe the S.A. merged into the Bronze Age about 2000 BC.

STONECHAT. Small bird (*Saxicola torquata*) of the thrush family (Turdidae) frequently found in Europe and Asia. The male has a black head and throat, tawny breast, and dark back; the female has a brown head and a speckled throat.

STONEFISH. Fish (*Synanceja verrucosa*) of the Indian and Pacific oceans, *c.* 35cm (14in) long and camouflaged to resemble encrusted rock. The envenomed spines inflict such a painful sting that bathers may drown, even in shallow water.

STONEHENGE. Prehistoric megalithic monument on Salisbury Plain, near Amesbury, Wilts. Several different monuments of differing date have been erected on the site from *c.* 1900 BC, and the structure illustrated belongs to the third period *c.* 1500-1400 BC. Its main feature consisted originally of a circle of 30 upright stones, their tops linked by lintel stones to form a continuous circle about 30m (100ft) across. Within the circle was a horseshoe arrangement of 5 trilithons (each of 2 uprights plus a lintel, but set as separate entities), so-called 'altar-stone' - an upright pillar - on the axis of the horseshoe which was open to the north-east, etc. Though probably having a religious purpose, S. was not a Druid temple; the stones are so arranged that they could have been used to make astronomical calculations.

STOOLBALL. An ancient game, considered the ancestor of cricket, the main differences being that in S. bowling is underhand, and the ball is soft.

STOPES, Marie Carmichael (1880-1958). British advocate of birth control. B. in Edinburgh, she m. in 1918 H. V. Roe and in 1921 founded in London the mothers' clinic for birth control. Her publications incl. plays and verse as well as such best-sellers as *Married Love* (1918).

STOPPARD, Tom (1937-). British playwright. Originally a journalist, he made his reputation with the fantasy extension of *Hamlet* - *Rosencrantz and Guildenstern are Dead* (1967); later works incl. *Jumpers* (1972) and *Travesties* (1975).

STOREY, David (1933-). British novelist and playwright. Son of a Yorkshire miner, he pub. his first book *This Sporting Life* in 1960; later vols. incl. *Saville*

STONEFISH. A masterpiece of camouflage, the stonefish, its back covered in poisonous spines, is barely distinguishable from the rocks and coral of its natural habitat. *Photo: Australian Official Photograph*

STONEHENGE. The local sandstone, or 'sarsen', was used for the uprights, which measure 5.5 by 2m (18 by 7ft), and each weigh some 26 tonnes. To give true perspective, they were skilfully made slightly convex. A secondary circle and horseshoe within the sarsens was built of bluestones, originally brought from Pembrokeshire. *Photo: Courtesy of the British Tourist Authority*

(1976) about the career of a Yorkshire pitman's son. His plays incl. *In Celebration* (1969), and *Early Days* (1980).

STORK. Bird, of which the best-known species is the white S. (*Ciconia ciconia*), which is encouraged to nest on roofs as a symbol of good luck and fertility, hence the popular association with childbirth. About 1m (3ft) high, it has black and white plumage and red bill and legs. It winters in Africa, returning to Europe (not to Britain) in spring. The black S. (*C. nigra*) nests in trees and though white beneath, is bronze-black above and is also found throughout most of Europe. The New World has a single S American species.

STORK. In many parts of Europe storks are encouraged to nest on roofs because of their reputation as luck bringers. A wheel is often fixed to the roof ridge to make nest construction easier. *Photo: Courtesy of the National Travel Association of Denmark*

STORNOWAY. Fishing port of the Outer Hebrides on the E coast of Lewis, admin. HQ of Western Isles. S. was founded by James VI (I of England). Pop. (1971) 5,266.

STOSS, Veit (*c.* 1440-1533). German sculptor. B. in Nuremberg, he worked for many years in Poland, where he is known as Wit Stwosz. His wood carvings, e.g. the Krakow altarpiece, are movingly realistic.

STOURBRIDGE. Town in W Midlands, England, 23km (14m) W of Birmingham. There are iron works and glass is made. Pop. (1972) 55,660.

STOWE, Harriet Beecher (1811-96). American author of the anti-slavery novel, *Uncle Tom's Cabin*, first pub. as a serial 1851-2. She was a dau. of Lyman Beecher (q.v.), and m. in 1836 C. E. Stowe, a theological prof.

STRĀ'BO (*c.* 63 BC-AD 24). Greek geographer. B. in Pontus, he travelled widely to collect material for his *Geography*, which has survived almost entire.

STRACHEY, Giles Lytton (1880-1932). British author. Ed. at Trinity Coll., Oxford, he wrote the attractive *Landmarks in French Literature* (1912), but won fame and set a vogue by his graceful denigration in *Eminent Victorians* (1918) of Cardinal Manning, Florence Nightingale, Thomas Arnold, and Gen. Gordon. In *Queen Victoria* (1921), however, he was almost conquered by his subject.

STRADIVARI (strahdēvah'rē), **Antonio** (1644-1737). Italian violin-maker, who set up his workshop at Cremona during the 1660s. His sons carried on his work, but the secret of his soft varnish was never revealed.

STRAFFORD, Thomas Wentworth, earl of (1593-1641). English statesman. He sat in James I's and Charles I's parliaments, and was among the leaders of the opposition. In 1628 he went over to the king's side and was created visct Wentworth. As Lord Deputy of Ireland from 1632 he pursued a despotic policy. On returning to England in 1639 he became Charles's chief adviser, pressed him to take repressive measures, and in 1640 received an earldom. When the Long Parliament met he was impeached and beheaded.

STRAITS SETTLEMENTS. Former British crown colony, 1867-1946, a prov. of the East India Co., 1826-58, consisting of Singapore, Malacca, Penang, Cocos Is., Christmas Is., and Labuan (qq.v.).

STRALSUND (strahl'soond). Baltic port of Rostock dist., E Germany, opposite the island of Rügen. Founded 1209, it was a Hanse town. Pop. (1972) 69,000.

STRANRAER (stranrahr'). Seaport in Dumfries and Galloway, Scotland, at the head of Loch Ryan. There are regular sailings to and from Larne, N Ireland. Pop. (1972) 9,900.

STRASBOURG (straz'boorg; Ger. Strassburg). Cap. of Bas-Rhin dept, France, on the Rhine, historic cap. of Alsace. There is a Gothic cathedral, and the House of Europe (1950) is the meeting-place of the Council of Europe. Sessions of the European Parliament alternate between S. and Luxembourg. Seized by France in 1681, it was surrendered to Germany 1870-1919 and 1940-4. It is noted for preserves and has motor-car and tobacco factories, printing and publishing works, etc. Pop. (1973) 254,000.

STRATEGIC ARMS LIMITATION (SALT). Talks suggested by Pres. Johnson 1967 for the mutual limitation and eventual reduction of strategic nuclear weapons. They were delayed by the Soviet invasion of Czechoslovakia, but began in 1969, and Salt I was operative 1972-7; Salt II was mainly negotiated by Ford, and signed by Brezhnev and Carter at Vienna in 1979, but not ratified following the Soviet invasion of Afghanistan. Reagan proposed to scrap Salt II and re-negotiate.

STRATEGIC ISLANDS. Islands (Azores, Canary Is., Cyprus, Iceland, Madeira and Malta), which have great political and military significance likely to affect their stability. The first internat. conference among them was held at Funchal in 1979.

STRATFORD-UPON-AVON. English market town in Warwicks, the birthplace of Shakespeare whose grave is in the parish church. The Royal Shakespeare Theatre (1932) replaced an earlier building (1877-9) burnt down in 1926. Shakespeare's birthplace, purchased 1847, contains relics of his life and times. Pop. (1971) 19,450. **Stratford,** city and port of Ontario, Canada, also has a Shakespeare festival.

STRATHCLYDE. Region of Scotland created in 1975 from the cos. of Ayrshire, Bute, Dumbartonshire, Lanarkshire and Renfrewshire, and parts of Argyll and Stirlingshire. It contains half the pop. of Scotland, and is varied in character incl. the excellent agricultural land of Ayrshire in the S, the mining districts of Lanark to the E, and the wild beauty of Glencoe and the is. of Arran, Bute, Mull, etc. to the N and W. There is light and heavy engineering, shipbuilding, oil-related services, and Glasgow (the admin. HQ) is a banking and insurance centre. Area 13,727 sq.km (5,300 sq.m); pop. (1979) 2,424,189.

STRATOSPHERE. That part of the atmosphere beyond 10km (6m) from Earth, wherein the temperature is constant. After the minimum $-55°$C ($-67°$F) is reached, there is even a slight rise up to 40km (25m) in the extremely rarefied air.

STRAUS (strows), **Oscar** (1870-1954). Austrian composer. B. at Vienna, he composed operettas, e.g. *The Chocolate Soldier.*

STRAUSS, Johann (1825-99). Austrian composer. B. in Vienna, he was the son of Johann Strauss (1804-49), a composer of waltz music. In 1862 he relinquished conducting for composition, and wrote operettas, such as *Die Fledermaus,* and numerous waltzes, e.g. 'The Blue Danube', 'Tales from the Vienna Woods', etc., which gained him the title 'The Waltz King'.

STRAUSS, Richard (1864-1949). German composer. B. at Munich, he wrote the symphonic tone poems *Don Juan, Death and Transfiguration,* and *Till Eulenspiegel* (1895), and many songs. His operas incl. *Salome, Elektra, Der Rosenkavalier, Ariadne auf Naxos,* and *Arabella.* He became president of the Reichsmusikkammer, but resigned in 1935 when his opera *Die schweigsame Frau* was boycotted because the libretto was written by the Jewish writer Stefan Zweig.

STRAVINSKY, Igor (1882-1971). Russo-American composer. B. near St Petersburg, he studied under Rimsky-Korsakov and, for the Diaghilev ballet, wrote *The Firebird* (1910), *Petrushka* (1911) and *The Rite of Spring* (1913), which aroused controversy on account of their unorthodox rhythm and harmony. Having lived in Paris from 1920, he went to the US in 1939 and in 1945 took American citizenship. His works incl. symphonies, concertos (for violin and piano), chamber music, a mass (1948) and operas, e.g. *The Rake's Progress* (1951) and *The Flood* (1962).

STRAWBERRY. Genus (*Fragaria*) of fruiting plants of the Rosaceae family which incl. the wild S. of Europe *(F. vesca),* and the N. American meadow S. (*F. virginiana*) and the Chilean (*F. chiloensis*) from which the modern cultivated hybrids derive. Although naturally a dwarf perennial, in commercial cultivation the S. is allowed to produce only 2 or 3 crops before being replaced by new stock or 'runners' allowed to develop from selected plants.

STREETON, Sir Arthur (1867-1943). Australian artist. As one of the Heidelberg School, he pioneered powerful impressions of Australian landscape. His later work, after a period abroad 1898-1923, was less happy.

STREPTOMYCIN. Antibiotic (q.v.). Discovered in 1944 by Dr Selman Waksman at New Jersey, it is prepared from micro-organisms in earth-mould, and is used in the treatment of tuberculosis, influenzal meningitis, and other infections, some of which are unaffected by penicillin.

Houses of Stuart, Hanover, and Windsor

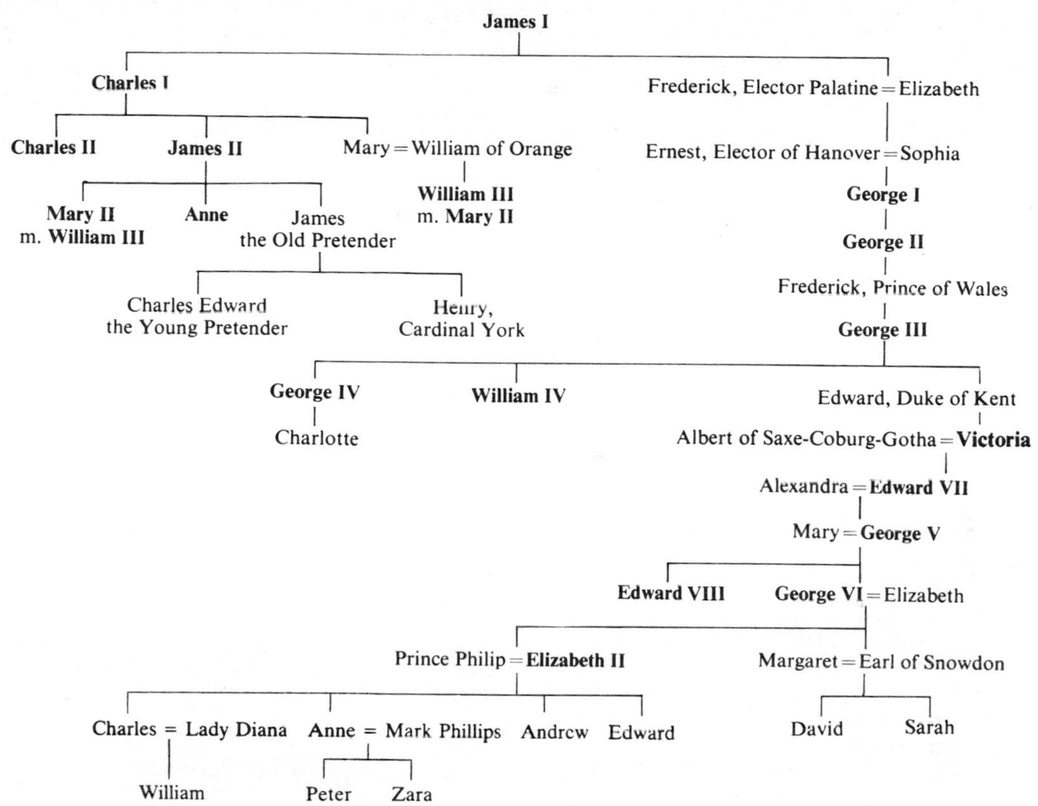

STRETFORD. Town in Greater Manchester, England, 6.5km (4m) SW of Manchester. Old Trafford, the famous cricket ground is here. Pop. (1972) 53,470.

STRIKES and **Lock-outs.** A S. is a stoppage of work by workpeople in order to obtain or to resist a change in their wages, hours, or conditions; a L. occurs when employers shut out their employees to force them to accept such a change, e.g. the L. of the miners in Britain in 1926. A stay-in, sit-down, or stay-down S. occurs when the strikers occupy a factory or mine, and refuse to leave it until their demands are accepted; this method was widely used in France in 1936, and in the USA. A sympathetic S. is one in support of 'strikers' in another industry. A variant of the S. is 'working to rule', and there may be 'work-ins', e.g. when the govt. or an employer wish to close a plant against the will of the workers.

In the UK increasing trade union power in the 1970s and 1980s made the regulation of the strike weapon controversial, e.g. whether there should be a secret ballot of members before a strike be called. Also hotly debated was the use and number of pickets (originally sharpened stakes used in tethering horses or in outer defence works, then used for small parties of troops sent to watch out for the enemy, and today men stationed by trade unions to prevent strike breaking). 'Flying pickets' are those coming from a distance to workplaces not their own, and 'secondary pickets' are stationed at works unconnected with the original dispute. *See* TRADE UNIONS.

STRINDBERG (strind'-), **August** (1849-1912). Swedish dramatist and novelist. B. in Stockholm, he held a post in the Royal Library there 1874-82, but after 1883 he lived as a writer, mainly abroad. He was a strong critic of contemporary Swedish society, and, having been three times married and divorced, a woman hater and deep pessimist. He made a reputation with his novel *The Red Room* (1879, but suffered great shock when unsuccessfully prosecuted for blasphemy following publication of his stories *Married* (1884). He owes his greatest fame to his plays *The Father* (1887), in which a dominating wife drives her husband to insanity; *Miss Julie* (1887); *The Dance of Death* (1901); and *The Ghost Sonata* (1907), which were widely influential in the later development of dramatic technique.

STROBOSCOPE (strō'boskōp). Instrument for studying periodic motion by illuminating an object with flashes at the same frequency as that of its motion. Strobe lighting, flashing in time to the music's beat, is used in many discotheques, but continued for any length of time espec. at a critical frequency, it may cause hallucinatory fits (photic epilepsy).

STROMBOLI (strom'bōlē). Italian island, one of the Lipari Islands, on which is an active volcano, 926m (3,038 ft) high. The island produces Malmsey wine and capers. Area 12.2 sq.km (4.7 sq.m); pop. 1,200.

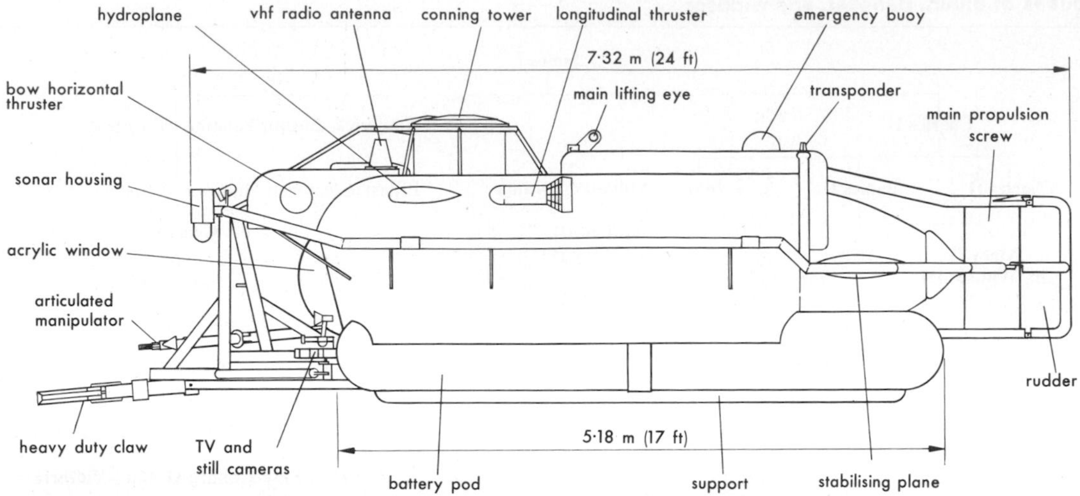

SUBMARINE. The LR2, the world's first plastic submarine, built entirely of glass-reinforced plastic, and designed for North Sea oil exploration and maintenance.

STRONTIUM (Strontian, town in Scotland). A silver-white ductile metal, symbol Sr, at. no. 38, at. wt. 87.63. Discovered by a Scot named Crawford in 1790, and isolated electrolytically by Davy in 1808, it is widely distributed in small quantities as the sulphate and carbonate. The metal resembles calcium and its salts give a brilliant red colour to a flame, are used for fireworks, and the oxide is used in sugar refining.

A long-lived radioactive isotope Sr-90 is produced in the fission of uranium and is a dangerous component of fallout since it is taken up by plants and ingested by cattle which pass it to their milk. When ingested by humans it accumulates in bones causing tumours.

STRYCHNINE (strik'nin). A bitter-tasting alkaloid ($C_{21}H_{22}O_2N_2$), usually obtained by powdering the seeds of plants of the genus *Strychnos*, e.g. *S. nux vomica*. It is a violent tetanizing poison. *See* also the related drug CURARE.

STUART or **Stewart, House of.** Royal family who inherited the Scottish throne in 1371, and the English in 1603. *See* Table.

STUART, John McDougall (1815-66). Australian explorer. He went with Sturt on his 1844 expedition, and in 1860, after 2 unsuccessful attempts, succeeded in crossing the centre from Adelaide to the coast of Arnhem Land. He almost lost his life on his return journey. The *Stuart Highway* in the Northern Territory, Darwin-Alice Springs (1943) and Mt Stuart on the route commemorate him.

STUBBS, George (1724-1806). British artist. B. in Liverpool, son of a currier, he was originally a portrait painter, but in 1758 rented a farm and carried out a long series of dissections which resulted in his book of engravings *The Anatomy of the Horse* (1766). Henceforward he had no lack of commissions, and his paintings are a record of the turf, the hunting field and the golden age of English country life, e.g. 'Phaeton and Pair', 'Gimcrack on Newmarket Heath', 'Haymakers' and 'Reapers'.

STUART HIGHWAY. Straight as an arrow through Australia's Northern Territory, the Stuart Highway was completed during the Second World War as part of the country's aids to military defence. *Photo: Axel Poignant*

STUD, National. Establishment at Newmarket, Suffolk, England (until 1964 at Gillingham, Dorset), maintained by the Horserace Betting Levy Board (until 1963 by the Min. of Agriculture). Founded in Dec. 1915 when Lord Wavertree presented to the nation his stud at Kildare, it removed to England in 1943, and produced thoroughbreds, incl. many notable racehorses, but since 1964 only stallions have been kept for visiting mares.

STURGEON. Genus (*Acipenser*) of fish incl. the common European S. (*A. sturio*) which reaches *c.* 4m (14ft), and in England is a royal fish, traditionally belonging to the Crown, but actually poor eating. The most valuable species, source of the finest caviare (q.v.) are those of the rivers of the Black and Caspian seas, now often artificially raised, being recaught in the breeding season, and the laying of the eggs promoted by the injection of hormone. The S. of The Great Lakes of N America are also used for caviare.

STURM ABTEILUNG (shtoorm' ap'tīloong). The terrorist militia (SA), 'storm section', of the Nazi Party: also known from their uniform as Brownshirts. They were responsible for physical training and political indoctrination.

STURT, Charles (1795-1869). Australian explorer. B. in India, he served in the army, and in 1827 discovered with Hume the r. Darling. In 1828 he sailed down the Murrumbidgee to the estuary of the Murray in circumstances of great hardship, elucidating the entire river system of the region. Drawn by his concept of a great inland sea, he set out for the interior in 1844, crossing the Sturt Desert, but failing to penetrate the Simpson Desert.

STUTTGART (shtoot'gahrt). Capital of Baden-Württemberg, W Germany, on the river Neckar. There is a publishing trade, and important factories and rail yards. Pop. (1978) 584,555.

STYLE, Old and **New.** *See* CALENDAR; OLD STYLE.

STYRIA (stir'ia). Prov. of Austria, in the eastern Alps. An independent state from 1056 until it passed to the Habsburgs in the 13th cent., it was annexed by Hitler in 1938.

STYX (stiks). In Greek mythology the river surrounding the underworld. *See* CHARON.

SUAREZ GONZALEZ (swah'reth gonzah'leth), **Adolfo** (1933-). Spanish statesman. A personal friend of the king, he worked in the Nat. Movement for 18 years, but in 1975 became pres. of the newly-estab. Unión del Pueblo Español (UPE). He took office as PM in 1976, at the request of the king, to speed the reform programme. He retained office in the general election of 1977 and was re-elected in 1979. On his resignation in 1981, he was created Duke of Suarez.

SUBLIMINAL MESSAGE. Message delivered below the level of human consciousness, which may be visual (words or images flashed between the frames of a film in a cinema or on television); or aural (a radio message broadcast 9,000 times an hour at very low volume). The aim may be commercial, to sell a product, or psychological, e.g. to reinforce the horror of a story, or to persuade a patient to give up alcohol or smoking.

SUBMARINE. An underwater ship, espec. a warship designed to operate long-range and at high speed. An early venture was an underwater boat constructed for James I by Dutchman Cornelius van Drebel in 1620, but serious development of S. warfare began in the 18th century. The first naval S. or submersible torpedo boat, the *Gymnote*, was launched by France in 1888 and John P. Holland, an Irish emigrant to the USA, designed a submarine *c.* 1875 which was adopted by both the US and British navies for their warships of this kind at the turn of the century. In both World Wars the S., from the ocean-going to the midget type, played a vital role and in 1954 the USA launched the first nuclear submarine, the *Nautilus* (*see* ARCTIC). The modern nuclear submarine *Ohio* (USA), in service from 1981, is 170 m (560 ft) long, displacement *c.* 18, 700 tonnes, and carries 24 Trident missiles, each with a dozen warheads with a range that is being extended to 11,000 km (6,750 m). Operating depth is usually up to 300 m (1,000 ft), and with nuclear power speeds of 30 knots (55 kmph) are reached. In oceanography (q.v.), salvage, pipe-laying, etc, less wide-ranging and speedy submersibles are used. The Royal Navy's surface diving ship *Challenger* (1980) not only supports divers operating at 300 m (1,000 ft), but acts as mother ship for deep-diving submersibles which are hauled up a stern ramp, and has a moon pool or cylindrical vertical internal shaft, down which a 3-man diving bell can be lowered. Depths of 6,000 m (20,000 ft) are reached.

SUBMARINE. The LR3, the LR2's first successor, ready for launching. The normal operating depth for these craft is 450m (1,500ft), and a crew of 3 is carried. *Photo: Courtesy of Vickers Ltd.*

SUBOTICA. Largest town of Vojvodina, Yugoslavia. It is an agricultural centre with many manufactures. Pop. (1971) 88,800.

SUBPOENA (-pē'na) (Lat. 'under penalty'). A writ issued early in litigation requiring a person to be present at a specified time and place to give evidence before a court or a judicial officer.

SUBWAY. *See* UNDERGROUND.

SUCEAVA. *See* under BHUKOVINA.

SUCKING FISH. Several genera of fishes having an adhesive disc on the head by means of which they attach themselves to ships, sharks, or turtles.

SUCKLING, Sir John (1609-42). English poet. B. at Whitton, he was an ardent Royalist. His chief lyrics appeared in *Fragmenta Aurea* (1646).

SUCRE (sōō'krā). Nominal cap. of Bolivia (*see* LA PAZ), on the central plateau at 2,840 m (9,330 ft). Founded in 1538, S. has a cathedral dating from 1553, and the Univ. of San Francisco Xavier (1624) is probably the oldest in S America. Revolt against Spanish rule in S America first began here 25 May 1809. Pop. (1970) 84,900.

SUDAN (soodahn'). Geographical term used to describe N Africa, S of Algeria, Libya, and Egypt from the Atlantic to the Red Sea.

Sudan Republic lies S of Egypt, N of Uganda, with a coastline on the Red Sea. The climate is tropical, hot, and dry. Desert in the N, it is fertile in the S, producing dura, maize, ground-nuts, cotton, etc. Gum arabic is gathered from a species of acacia. The Nile traverses the rep. from S to N and is important both for irrigation and transport; there is a rail link from the chief port, Port Sudan, via Khartoum (the cap.) with Egypt, and also air services.

Subdued by an Anglo-Egyptian army under Kitchener 1896-8, S was admin. as an Anglo-Egyptian condominium 1899-1956, when it became a rep. The South (Negroid and Pagan) aimed at secession from the North (Arab and Moslem) as Anzania, but after continuous revolt 1956-72, it was agreed that the 3 southernmost of the country's provs. (Bahr el Ghazal, Equatorial and Upper Nile) should form an autonomous Southern Region, with its cap. at Juba. Under the constitution of 1973 there is a pres., and a People's Assembly elected on a limited franchise: the Sudanese Socialist Union (SSU) is the only political party. In 1979 there was agitation for greater political freedom. Arabic is the official language, but English is the agreed 'common language', and is taught in the schools of the South. Area 2,500,000 sq.km (967,500 sq.m); pop. (1977) 17,000,000. M.U.: Sudanese pound. *See* also MALI, Republic of, and NEMERY.

SUDAN. Camel-racing is an eagerly watched event in Arab countries, the competitors being, not the more heavily-built beasts of burden, but lightweight white dromedaries with a fine turn of speed. *Photo: John Bulmer/ Camera Press*

SUDBURY. Town in Ontario, Canada, N of Lake Huron, where most of the world's nickel is mined. Pop. (1976) 167,700. Another S. in Suffolk, England, on the r. Stour, is a market town and birthplace of Thomas Gainsborough. Pop. (1974) 9,000.

SUDETENLAND. (soodeh'ten-). Term applied to an area of Czechoslovakia close to the Sudeten mts., many of whose inhabitants before the S.W.W. were of German origin, settled in the district for generations. Nazi agitation among them led to the Munich crisis in Sept. 1938, following which the S. was ceded to Germany which annexed all Czechoslovakia in 1939. After the S.W.W., S. was returned to Czechoslovakia and more than 2 million of its German-speaking inhabitants were expelled.

SUETONIUS TRANQUILLUS (swētō'nius), **Gaius** (fl. 2nd cent. AD). Latin historian, whose *Lives of the Caesars* gives much personal information.

SUEZ (soo'ez). Port in Egypt at the Red Sea terminus of the S. Canal. Evacuated in the Arab-Israeli Wars, it was reconstructed in the mid 1970s. There are oil refineries and fertilizer plants. Pop. (1974) 368,000.

SUEZ CANAL. Artificial waterway from Port Said to Suez, linking the Mediterranean and Red seas, separating Africa from Asia, and providing the shortest sea route from Europe to the East, to Australasia, and to the E coast of Africa. The French S.C. Company was formed in 1858 to execute the scheme of Ferdinand de Lesseps. The canal was opened in 1869, and in 1875 Disraeli acquired for Britain from the khedive of Egypt 177,642 (out of 400,000) shares for £4 million. The 1888 Convention of Constantinople opened it to all nations. The S.C. was admin. by a co. with offices in Paris controlled by a council of 33 (10 of them British) until 1956 when it was forcibly nationalized by Pres. Nasser. It was blocked by Egypt during the Arab-Israeli war (1967) and not re-opened until 1975. There are plans to widen and deepen the channel more especially to allow the passage of giant tankers.

SUEZ CANAL. The canal was in the front line of hostilities during the Arab-Israeli Wars. During a ceasefire an Israeli guard scrutinises the Egyptian-held bank. *Photo: Camera Press*

SUFFOLK. An eastern county of England. It has a low undulating surface, and a flat coastline. Most is under plough, producing barley, wheat, and sugar beet. It is noted for its horses (S. Punches), formerly much used in agriculture. Industries incl. sugar refining, fertilizers, and agricultural machinery. The principal rivers are the

Waveney, Alde, Deben, Orwell, and Stour; part of the Broads (q.v.) is in S. A very small area SW of Great Yarmouth was transferred to Norfolk 1974. The admin. HQ is Ipswich; other towns are Bury St Edmunds, Lowestoft, Sudbury and Aldeburgh. Area 3,807 sq.km (1,470 sq.m); pop. (1978) 592,700.

SUFISM (sōō'fizm). Islamic mystical movement which rejected ritual and sought a return to primitive simplicity. It originated in Persia, was influenced by Neoplatonism, and coloured the thought of Hafiz, Sadi, Omar, and other writers. Sufi doctrines are a kind of pantheism.

SUGAR. A substance that, in one or another form, occurs in many plants as they approach maturity. It most commonly occurs in fruits, but the sugar of commerce is derived chiefly from the stems of the sugar cane or the roots of the S. beet. S. cane (*Saccharum*) is native to SE Asia, but is now cultivated in many tropical and subtropical lands. It grows to 4m (12ft), and is 4cm (1.5in) thick. Paper products are made from bagasse, the fibre residue of the cane after extraction, and molasses, the uncrystallized syrup drained from the sugar is used in making rum and also in animal feed. Sugar beet (*Beta*) is a root crop of temperate regions.

Over-production of S. has led to a search for alternative uses and a detergent is being developed - effective, gentle, and biodegradable, so that it disperses with less harm to the environment than the ordinary synthetic detergent.

SUGAR. Harvesting sugar cane by hand, using a machete, ready for transport to the refinery. *Photo: Courtesy of the Sugar Bureau*

SUHARTO (soohahr'tō) (1921-). Indonesian general. Anti-Communist, he became army commander 1965, and in 1966 ousted Sukarno, himself becoming president in 1968. He ended confrontation with Malaysia, in Dec. 1975 undertook the invasion of E timor and in 1979 reached a co-operation agreement with Papua New Guinea.

SUICIDE. Self-murder. In English law it was until 1960 a criminal offence if committed while of sound mind: technically a felony (*felonia de se*) it was at one time punished by confiscation of the S.'s goods and until 1823 burial was at night, without burial service, and with a stake through the heart. Hence the frequency with which the coroners' juries often found a verdict that the S. committed the act while insane.

SUKARNO (sookahr'nō), **Achmed** (1901-70). Indonesian statesman. He took part in the nationalist movement before the S.W.W., co-operated in the native administration set up by the Japanese during their occupation, and became pres. of the Indonesian Rep. set up in 1945. He became PM 1959 and was created head of state for life 1963, but was deprived of the premiership 1966 and of the life presidency 1967 by Suharto (q.v.).

SUKKUR (sookoor'). River port in Pakistan, on the Indus: the Sukkur-Lloyd Barrage 1923-32 lies 3km (2m) W. There are railway workshops. Pop. (1972) 159,000.

SULAWESI (soolawā'si). Island in E Indonesia, (formerly Celebes), one of the Great Sunda Is. (q.v.). Mountainous and forested, it produces copra and nickel. Area with dependent is. 190,000 sq.km (73,000 sq.m). Pop. (1971) 8,500,000.

SULEIMAN (soolāmahn') **I** (1494-1566). Ottoman sultan, known as 'the Magnificent'. It was under his rule from 1520 that the Ottoman Empire reached its zenith. He captured Belgrade in 1521, Rhodes in 1523, defeated the Hungarians at Mohacs in 1526, and was only halted in his advance into Europe by his failure to take Vienna after a siege Sept.-Oct. 1529. In 1534 he turned more successfully against Persia, and then in campaigns against the Arab world took almost all North Africa and even Aden. Only the Knights of Malta inflicted severe defeat on both his army and fleet when he tried to take Valetta in 1565. A patron of the arts, himself a poet, he was renowned as a law-giver and administrator.

SULGRAVE. English village in Northants, 4km (2.5m) NW of Helmdon. S. Manor, ancestral home 1539-1610 of George Washington's family, was presented in 1914 to the S. Institute and opened as a Washington Museum.

SU'LLA, Lucius Cornelius (138-78 BC). Roman soldier and statesman. He distinguished himself in the Jugurthine, Teuton, and Social wars, and became the leading figure in the senatorial party. After forcibly suppressing the democrats in 88, he successfully waged war on Mithradates of Pontus. During his absence the democrats seized power, but on his return in 82 he captured Rome and massacred his opponents. Declared dictator, he carried out constitutional reforms, strengthening the senate.

SULLIVAN, Sir Arthur Seymour (1842-1900). British composer. B. in London, he became a choirboy at the Chapel Royal, and studied at Leipzig. He composed oratorios, but became famous for the light operas written in collaboration with Sir W. S. Gilbert (q.v.). These incl. *H.M.S. Pinafore* (1878), *The Pirates of Penzance* (1879), *Patience* (1881), *The Mikado* (1885), *The Yeoman of the Guard* (1888), and *The Gondoliers* (1889), and have achieved a deservedly lasting popularity. The partnership broke down owing to temperamental incompatibility. S. also wrote the serious opera *Ivanhoe*, the ballad 'The Lost Chord', etc.

SULLIVAN, John L(awrence) (1858-1918). American heavyweight boxer. He was world champion from 1882 until his defeat by Corbett in 1892: his defeat of Jake Kilrain in 1889 (commemorated by Vachel Lindsay in verse) was the last bareknuckle championship contest.

SULLIVAN. A bareknuckle fight between John L. Sullivan and Charlie Mitchell of England at Chantilly in 1888 in which the thirty-nine rounds ended in a draw. *Photo: Courtesy of the American History Picture Library*

SULLY (sülē'), **Maximilien de Béthune,** duc de (1560-1641). French statesman. He served on the Huguenot side during the Wars of Religion, and as Henry IV's superindendent of finances 1598-1611 contributed greatly to France's recovery.

SULLY-PRUDHOMME (-prüdom'), **Armand** (1839-1907). French poet. B. in Paris, he wrote philosophical verse showing psychological insight. *Les Solitudes, Les Vaines Tendresses, La Justice,* and *Le Bonheur* are outstanding.

SULPHA DRUGS. Sulphonamides; synthetic Ds. allied to the aniline dyes, which prevent certain bacteria from multiplying, used in the prevention and treatment of childbirth fever, pneumonia, and wound infection.

SULPHUR. Known from ancient times, it is a pale yellow, odourless, brittle solid; insoluble in water, soluble in carbon disulphide and a good electrical insulator; symbol S, at. no. 16, at. wt. 32.066. Widely distributed as the element in volcanic regions, and as sulphides of many metals. There are two crystalline forms and an allotropic plastic form. It is essential to life, resembles oxygen chemically and can replace this element to form innumerable organic and inorganic compounds. It is widely used in the manufacture of sulphuric acid and in chemicals and explosives, matches, fireworks, dyes, fungicides, drugs, etc., and in vulcanizing rubber, particularly for tyres.

SULPHŪ'RIC ACID (H_2SO_4) or **oil of vitriol.** A colourless, oily liquid, used in the manufacture of hydrochloric acid, nitric acid, explosives, coal-tar derivatives, and in many industrial processes.

SULU (so͞o'lo͞o) **ARCHIPELAGO.** Island group (*c.* 870) off SW Mindanao in the Philippines: the largest is Jolo, on which is the chief town of the same name. Until 1940, the S.A. was an autonomous sultanate. Area 2,815 sq.km (1,087 sq.m). The pop. is overwhelmingly Moslem.

SUMATRA (soomah'tra). Largest island of Indonesia. E of a longitudinal mountain range is a wide plain; both are heavily forested. Northern S. is rapidly being industrialized, and the Asakan r. (rising in Lake Toba) has been dammed for power (1974). Rubber, rice, tobacco, tea, timber, tin and petroleum are produced. The chief towns are Palembang, Padang and Benkuelen. Area 427,350 sq.km (165,000 sq.m); pop. (1971) 20,800,000.

SUMĒ'RIANS. A people possibly akin to the Dravidians of India, who inhabited S Babylonia from *c.* 4000 BC, and founded Babylonian culture.

SUMMER TIME. The practice introduced in the UK in 1916, whereby legal time from spring to autumn is an hour in advance of Greenwich mean time. It was permanently in force Feb. 1940-Oct. 1945 and Feb. 1968-Oct. 1971. Double S.T. (2 hours in advance), was in force 1941-5 and 1947. *See* TIME.

SUMMONS. Legal term denoting the citation to appear in court on a certain date, which is served on a person by an official, and which states the claim made by the plaintiff.

SUN. The star around which Earth revolves. It oscillates, changing in diameter slightly every 2 hrs 40 min, but in round figures its diameter is 1,392,000 km (865,000 m), and it is 149,500,000 km (93,000,000 m) from Earth. Like all stars it is composed of intensely hot gas; hydrogen is a major constituent. The surface temperature is 6,000°C and the central temperature between 12,000,000 and 15,000,000°C. It produces its energy by nuclear reactions, resulting in the conversion of hydrogen into helium with a steady loss of mass amounting to 4,000,000 tonnes per sec. Only a small proportion of the released energy reaches Earth: *see* SOLAR ENERGY.

Telescopically, the S. is seen to show various dark patches, known as sunspots. These are cooler areas (around 4,000°C), and are relatively short-lived, though they may become very large. Associated with spot-groups are the bright patches termed *faculae.* The S. shows semi-regular cycles of activity, with maxima occurring about every 11 years. At solar maxima, spot-groups are very frequent, whereas at solar minima the disc may be entirely clear for several days consecutively. Examination of earlier records shows an absence of sunspots coinciding with Earth's cold spell 1650-1715. Their disappearance has been ascribed either to some unexplained change far below the surface, or to a cloud of material entering the solar system and absorbing some of the Sun's radiation: on this latter theory the major ice ages would have been the result of the solar system having entered galactic dust lanes.

With spectroscopic equipment it is possible to examine the *prominences,* masses of glowing hydrogen rising from the S.'s bright surface or *photosphere,* as well as the short-lived but violent outbreaks known as *flares,* usually associated with spot-groups. Only during the total eclipse may prominences be seen with the naked eye. This also applies to the outer surround or *corona,* composed of highly tenuous gas at a remarkably high temperature.

Modern astronomers regard the S. as a dwarf star and certainly it is in no way exceptional in the Galaxy. Since it possesses a system of planets, there is no reason to doubt that other stars have planetary systems of their own.

SUNBELT. In the USA the region between the Californian and Atlantic coasts, S of Washington, DC.

SUNBURY-ON-THAMES. English market town and boating centre in Surrey, 27km (17m) SW of London, with petroleum research laboratories opened in 1962, and film studios. Pop. (1972) 40,200.

SUNDA ISLANDS. Name given to the islands of Indonesia W of the Moluccas. The Greater S.I. incl. Sumatra, Java, Borneo, Celebes, and Billiton; the Lesser S.I., Bali, Lombok, Sumbawa, Flores, Sumba, Timor.

SUNDANCE. Religious rite of the Plains Indians, on the day of the summer solstice, in which a warrior was tied to a sacred pole by ropes ending in wooden skewers thrust through the flesh of the chest. He then danced, straining from the pole, until the flesh gave way. In return he received supernatural aid.

SUNDAY. Seventh day of the week (*see* MONDAY); for Christians the first, and set apart for divine worship (in memory of Christ's resurrection), thus replacing the Jewish sabbath. In the UK labour, the sale of certain goods, and other activities were regulated by law from medieval times, most notably the Sunday Observance Acts of 1625 and 1780 - infringements continuing to be opposed in the 20th cent. by the Lord's Day Observance Society - but under the Sunday Entertainments Bill (1969) curbs on sports, theatres and dancing were lifted, introducing the 'Continental Sunday'. In the USA similar laws to those of England were general in colonial times, but subsequent enforcement has been lax.

Sunday Schools, of which the first was estab. at Gloucester, England, by Robert Raikes in 1780, were valuable originally, not merely as sources of religious instruction, but as enabling the poorest children to learn to read and write before the introduction of free day schools. The movement passed to the USA early in the 19th cent. and still continues, although the tendency is to replace them by special services for the young or combined family worship.

SUNDERLAND, Robert Spencer, 2nd earl of (1640-1702). British politician. He became James II's Sec. of State, and embraced Catholicism. He fled to Holland in 1688, but returned in 1691 and re-entered politics as a Whig. On his advice William III adopted the system of choosing the govt from the dominant party in the Commons.

SUNDERLAND. Seaport in Tyne and Wear, England, at the mouth of the Wear, 22.5km (14m) NE of Durham. With diversification, coalmining and shipbuilding have become less important. There is a polytechnic (1969) and a civic theatre - the S. Empire. Pop. (1974) 295,160.

SUNDEW. *See* INSECTIVOROUS PLANTS.

SUNDIAL. An instrument for measuring time by means of a shadow cast by the sun. It consists of a dial-plane marked with the hours, and a style or gnomon from which the shadow is cast. The style is parallel to the Earth's axis, and points to the N.

SUNDSVALL (soonds'vahl). Seaport with timber and wood-pulp industries in the Västernorrland district of Sweden on the Gulf of Bothnia, 418km (260m) N of Stockholm. Pop. (1979) 94,500.

SUN-FISH. Fish in the marine Molidae or mainly N American freshwater Centrarchidae families which have compressed, almost circular bodies. The latter are nestbuilders and avid predators.

SUNFLOWER. Genus of plants (*Helianthus*) in the family Compositae. The common S. (*H. annus*) is a native of N America, grows to 4.5m (15ft) in favourable conditions, and is commercially cultivated in central Europe and the USSR for the oil-bearing seeds which follow the yellow-petalled flowers.

SUNGARI (soongahri). River of NE China (Manchuria), which joins the Amur on the Siberian frontier: length *c.* 1,300 km (800m).

SUNNIS. Followers of the Sunni rite, the more orthodox of the 2 main divisions of Islam (q.v.) and predominant in most Islamic countries except Iran. The name derives from the *Sunna*, a book of rules inspired by Mohammed.

SUNSPOT. *See* SUN.

SUNSTROKE. Heat stroke (q.v.) caused by exposure to brilliant, hot sunlight.

SUN YAT-SEN (1867-1925). Chinese statesman. The son of a Christian farmer, he founded the Kuomintang party in 1894. After many years in exile he returned to China during the 1911 revolution, and was provisional pres. of the rep. in 1912. When the reactionaries obtained control he estab. a republican govt at Canton in 1921, in which he was proclaimed pres. His '3 people's principles' of nationalism, democracy, and social reform are accepted by both the Kuomintang and the Chinese Communists. His widow Soong Ching-ling (1890-81), ed. in USA, remained influential in Chinese politics, being Vice-Chairman of the Rep. from 1959, but was under attack in 1967 in the Cultural Revolution. After the death of Chu Teh, she served as acting 'Head of State'.

SUPERCONDUCTIVITY. The phenomenon of S., discovered by Kamerlingh Onnes in 1911, is exhibited by some metals and metallic compounds whose resistance decreases uniformly with decreasing temperature until at a critical temperature (the superconducting point), within a few degrees of the absolute zero, the resistance suddenly falls to zero. In this superconducting state an electric current induced by a magnetic field in a closed circuit or ring of the material will continue after the magnetic field has been removed, so long as the material remains below the superconducting point. Important industrial applications of this phenomenon are being actively explored, and in 1979, S. was produced in a synthetic organic conductor which would operate at much higher temperatures, thus cutting costs. *See* CRYOGENICS.

SUPERIOR, Lake. The largest freshwater lake in the world, one of the Great Lakes of N America. Two-thirds lie in the USA, the rest in Canada. It discharges via the St Mary into Lake Huron. Area 82,415 sq.km (31,820 sq.m); 406m (1,333 ft) deep.

SUPERNOVA. Stellar explosion on a vast scale which throws out gases that emit radio waves and X-rays for thousands of years. Afterwards the collapsed core remains as a pulsar (small, very dense neutron star) or a black hole, or possibly a 'star' of an as yet undefined type with peculiar properties. Only 3 supernovae have been observed in our Galaxy since AD, 1000, though they have frequently been detected in external galaxies.

SUPERSONIC SPEED. Speed greater than that of sound, which at sea-level is about 1,220 kph (760mph) and decreases with altitude until at 12,000 m (40,000 ft) it is only *c.* 1,060 kph; above that it remains constant. The first airman to achieve S.S. was Englishman Squadron Leader John Derry in a De Havilland 108 research aircraft on 6 Sept. 1948, in a 35 min. flight; at about 12,000 m (40,000 ft) he dived steeply and reached a speed of *c.* 1,085 kph (675mph). *See* MACH NUMBER.

When an aircraft exceeds the speed of sound (passes the sound barrier) shock waves are built up round the aircraft giving rise to a sonic boom, often heard at ground-level. Supersonic flight with its attendant complexities developed from the 1960s. *See* SPEED RECORDS.

SUPRARĒ'NAL GLANDS. *See* ADRENAL GLANDS.

SUPRE'MATISM. Abstract-art movement founded in 1913 by the Russian painter Malevich, who expressed its aims as 'the supremacy of pure feeling or perception in the pictorial arts - the experience of non-objectivity'.

SUPREME COURT. The highest judicial tribunal in the USA, composed of a chief justice (Warren Burger from 1969), and 8 associate justices. Vacancies are filled by the pres. and members can be removed only by impeachment. *See* LAW COURTS.

SUR. Arabic name of TYRE.

SURABAYA (soorabah'ya). Chief port of Indonesia, cap. of E Java prov., on the N coast of Java. It is an important naval and military base, with shipbuilding yards; also a centre of the petroleum industry. Pop. (1971) 1,320,000.

SURAJ-UD-DOWLAH (soorahj ood dow'lah). *See* CALCUTTA and PLASSEY.

SURAT (sooraht'). City in Gujarat state, India, 269km (167m) N of Bombay, at the mouth of the Tapti, site of the first E India Co. factory in India (1612). Textiles are made. Pop. (1971) 471,815.

SURFING. The sport of riding on the crest of large waves. The narrow, keeled, plastic surfboard is *c.* 1.k m (5 ft) long, and may have a sail (windsurfing). *See illus.* HAWAII, and SKATEBOARD.

SURGERY. The art of treating bodily injuries or disorders by manual means - traditionally the knife. During the S.W.W. plastic surgery was greatly advanced, and more recent developments incl. operations on heart, lung and kidney, using artificial equipment as substitute organs and, increasingly during the 1960s, using organs from live or dead donors - transplant S.: *see* HEART. Instruments are more varied - in addition to the scalpel and electric cautery, beamed high-energy ultrasonic waves may be used, as well as the intense light energy of the laser.

In **microsurgery** a binocular microscope, magnifying 25 times, is used, e.g. in rejoining a severed limb. Sewing of the nerves and blood vessels is done with a nylon thread so fine that it is only just visible to the naked eye. Restoration of movement and sensation may be comparatively limited.

SURINAM. Country in the N of S America, between Guyana and French Guiana, also chief r. of the country at the mouth of which stands the cap. Paramaribo. Sugar, coffee, rice, bananas, and other tropical crops are grown; bauxite is the chief mineral product. Founded as a colony by the English (1650), S. became Dutch in 1667, and under the constitution of 1954 was an autonomous part of the kingdom of the Netherlands until its independence in 1975. In 1980 there was a military coup, and although a mainly civilian govt. was estab. the military in effect retained control. The official language is Dutch, but there is a lingua franca Surinamese (Sranan Tongo). Area 142,819 sq.km (55,143 sq.m); pop. (1977) 450,000. M.U.: S. florin.

SURRĒ'ALISM. Art movement which developed from Dadaism, and was founded *c.* 1924, when André Breton issued its first manifesto. It repudiated all aesthetic values, and derived a great deal from Freudian theories. The movement spread to poetry and had an influence on photography, the film, commercial art, and stage scenery. Its leading exponents incl. Salvador Dali, Hans Arp, Georgio de Chirico, and others - e.g. Picasso, Henry Moore, and Edward Burra - were influenced by it.

SURREY, Henry Howard, earl of (*c.* 1517-47). English poet. The son of the 3rd duke of Norfolk, he served in France 1544-6, and was executed on a poorly based charge of high treason. He shared with Wyatt the honour of introducing the sonnet to England, and through his translation of the *Aeneid* pioneered the use of blank verse.

SURREY. A southern co. of England. The chalk North Downs span the county from Farnham in the W to Caterham in the E, the Wey and Mole flowing N through 2 gaps into the Thames. Market-gardening and agriculture are carried on. The admin. HQ is Kingston upon Thames. Under the reorganization by the London Govt Act (1963) S. lost its metropolitan areas to the new Greater London, but in 1974 lost only a very small area about Horley to W Sussex. Area 1,665 sq.km (639 sq.m); pop. (1978) 995,000.

SURTEES, Robert Smith (1803-64). British sporting novelist. He created Jorrocks, a sporting grocer, and in 1838 pub. *Jorrocks's Jaunts and Jollities.*

SURVEYING. The art of determining the value of all descriptions of landed and house property and of the various interests therein; the practice of managing and developing estates and the science of admeasuring and delineating the physical features of the Earth; the valuation, management, development and survey of mineral property and the measuring and estimating of artificer's work.

SURYA (soor'ya). In Hindu mythology the personification of the Sun.

SUSA (soo'sah). Port in NE Tunisia (Fr. Sousse). A commercial centre, it was founded by the Phoenicians, and has Roman remains. Pop. (1970) 90,000.

SUSQUEHANNA (suskwihan'a). River in USA, rising in central NY state and flowing into Chesapeake Bay: length 715km (444m). It is used for hydroelectric power. The musical name appealed to poet S. T. Coleridge who planned to settle there with Southey and practise Pantisocracy, a form of communism.

SUSSEX. A south-coast co. of England. The chalk South Downs extend E to Beachy Head, rising at Duncton Beacon to 255m (837 ft). The rivers incl. the Arun, Adur, Ouse, and Rother. According to tradition, a Saxon chief Ella landed in what is now S. in 477, defeated the inhabitants, and founded the kingdom of the South Saxons which was absorbed by Wessex in 825. Among the historic remains are the earthwork at Cissbury; castles at Arundel, Pevensey, Hurstmonceux, Lewes, etc. S. is well wooded; root and cereal crops are grown; and cattle and sheep reared. Coast resorts, Brighton being the largest, range from Bognor Regis to Hastings. S. is divided into the 2 admin. cos. of East and West S., which have their admin. HQs at Lewes and Chichester respectively. The Univ. of Sussex is at Brighton. Area of East S. 1,795 sq.km (693 sq.m); pop. (1978) 652,500; West S. 2,017 sq.km (779 sq.m); pop. 633,600.

SUTHERLAND, Earl Wilbur (1915-74). American physiologist, discoverer of a chemical 'messenger' made by a special enzyme in the wall of cells. Many hormones operate by means of this messenger, also instrumental in the adaptation of cells to fresh circumstances, such as

SUSSEX. The only hill figure of human form is the 'Long Man' of Wilmington in East Sussex. Its original date is unknown, and one suggestion is that it represents Pol, god of the underworld, who stands at its gate. This is derived from a neighbouring place-name, Polegate. *Photo: Courtesy of the British Tourist Authority*

environmental changes. It may thus have assisted evolution. Nobel prize 1971.

SUTHERLAND, Graham Vivian (1903-80). British artist. B. in London, he studied at the Goldsmiths' School of Art, and in his early work was influenced by Blake and the Surrealists. After 1936 his style suddenly matured and broadened, and the detailed presentation of some unusually coloured insect, vegetable or mineral form assumed symbolic force. In his portraits, e.g. Maugham, Beaverbrook, Helena Rubinstein, he has usually achieved popular as well as artistic success, but his study of Churchill (1954) was burnt on the instructions of Lady Churchill. In 1960 he was awarded the OM and his tapestry design for Coventry Cathedral was acclaimed in 1962.

SUTHERLAND, Dame Joan (1926-). Australian soprano. Going to England in 1951, she made her début the next year as First Lady in *The Magic Flute*: other successes incl. *Lucia di Lammermoor,* Donna Anna in *Don Giovanni,* and Desdemona in *Otello.* DBE 1979.

SUTHERLANDSHIRE. Former extreme N maritime co. of Scotland, with deep sea lochs and mountainous in the W, Ben More Assynt rising to 999m (3,278 ft). In 1975 it was merged in Highland Region. Dornoch was the admin. HQ.

SU'TLEJ. One of the 'Five Rivers' of the Punjab, flowing through India and Pakistan. It rises in Tibet, China, at 4,633 m (15,200 ft), traverses the Punjab plains, and joins the Chenab nr Madwala. Length 1,450 km (900m).

SUTTEE (sutē'). Custom whereby a Hindu widow throws herself alive on her husband's funeral pyre. Forbidden under British rule in 1829, it enjoys sporadic illegal revivals in modern India.

SUTTON COLDFIELD. Town in W Midlands, with TV transmitter (1949). Pop. (1972) 84,160.

SUTTON HOO. Village nr Woodbridge, Suffolk, England, where in 1939 an E Anglian ship-burial was excavated. It is the funeral monument of Raedwald, King of the East Angles (d. AD 624/5). The objects discovered - jewellery, armour, weapons - were placed in the BM.

SUTTON IN ASHFIELD. English industrial town in Notts, 21km (13m) N by W of Nottingham; hosiery is the chief product; plastics are made and coal is worked. Pop. (1972) 40,240.

SUVA. City, seaport, and cap. of Fiji on S coast of Viti Levu. Pop. (1978) 66,000.

SUZHOU (so͞ojaw-o͞o'). City (formerly Soochow) in Jiangsu prov., China, on the Grand Canal 80 km (50 m) W of Shanghai. The seat of a univ., it makes cotton and silk textiles, paper, chemicals, and has old-estab. crafts in embroidery and jade carving. The city dates from *c.* 1000 BC, and the name S. from the 7th cent. AD, though it was known as Wuhsien 1912-49. Marco Polo visited S. Pop. (1973) 650,000.

SUZUKI (soozooki), **Zenko** (1911-). Japanese statesman. Originally a socialist member of the Diet in 1947, he became a conservative (Liberal Democrat) in 1949, and in 1980–2 succeeded Ohira as PM.

SVALBARD. Norwegian name of SPITSBERGEN.

SVERDLO'VSK. Town of the Russian SFSR, E of the Urals. Copper, iron, platinum, etc., are mined, and there are heavy industries, and a number of micro-biological plants. S has a univ. Formerly called Ekaterinburg, it was the site of the murder of Nicholas II and his family (1918). Pop. (1977) 1,187,000.

SWABIA. Historic region, a duchy 1079-1268, in SW Germany, covering parts of SW Bavaria, Württemberg-Hohenzollern, and S Baden. The part in Bavaria is an admin. div. of that Land, cap. Augsburg.

SWAHILI (swahē'li). Moslem people of mixed Bantu and Arab descent, predominant in Kenya and Tanzania. Their language, of Bantu origin, is a lingua franca in E Africa, and the official language of both Kenya (1973) and Tanzania (1967).

SWALLOW. Family of birds (Hirundinidae) incl. the common S. (*Hirundo rustica*) which winters in Africa and visits Europe April-Sept. Steel-blue above and creamy white beneath, it has a red-brown throat and deeply forked tail. Two broods a year are reared in nests of mud and straw shaped like a half-saucer and built on ledges.

SWAN, Sir Joseph Wilson (1828-1914). British inventor (in the UK) of the incandescent filament electric lamp. B. at Sunderland, he also made discoveries in photographic development and printing.

SWAN. Genus of birds (*Cygnus*) in the duck family, of which they are the largest members. The mute S. (*C. olor*) is up to 150cm (5ft) long, has white plumage, an orange bill with a black knob surmounting it, and black legs; the voice is a harsh hiss. Mating is generally for life and the young (cygnets) are at first grey, later brownish. Wild in eastern Europe, it is half tame in the west and in England is a royal bird, since it was once highly valued for the table. On the Thames, at the annual swan-upping, the cygnets are still marked on the beak as either the property of the Crown or of the 2 privileged City cos., the Dyers and Vintners. Other species incl. the whooper (*C. cygnus*) of N Europe and Asia, and Bewick's S. (*C. bewicki*) both rare in Britain; the black S. of Australia (*C. atratus*); and N American trumpeter S. (*C. buccinator*).

SWANAGE. Holiday resort in Dorset, England, on the Isle of Purbeck, with stone quarries nearby. Pop. (1974) 8,550.

SWANSEA. City and port in W Glamorgan, of which it is admin. HQ, Wales, 72km (45m) NW of Cardiff, which serves the S Wales coalfield. S. is the tinplate centre for the

SWAN. A flotilla of black swans at Williamstown on Port Phillip Bay, Victoria. Unlike many of the world's large birds, they flourish in close company with man. *Photo: Courtesy of the Australian Information Service*

country, and copper, zinc, etc., are smelted. Pop. (1974) 190,370.

SWASTIKA. A symbolic ornament of ancient origin. It consists of a cross, at the end of whose lines perpendiculars extend all in the same clockwise or anti-clockwise direction. The S. was used by the Aryans and by Buddhists as a mystic symbol. Hitler decreed that it should become the German flag in 1935, it having previously only represented the Nazi Party. For this purpose the cross was also represented upright.

SWAZILAND (swah'zē-). Kingdom in SE Africa, bounded N, W, and S by Transvaal prov. of S Africa, E by Mozambique. Mountainous in the W, veld country in the E, it has a good climate, except for great heat in the lower-lying areas, and is free of malaria. Cattle and goats are raised; sugar, rice, citrus and cotton are grown, and wood pulp and timber exported. Minerals incl. iron (deposits at Ngwenya being linked by rail with Lourenço Marques), anthracite, asbestos, tin, calcite and barytes. The cap. is Mbabane, pop. (1976) 22,250.

Formerly a High Commission Terr., it became independent as a sovereign kingdom within the Commonwealth in 1968. The reign of Sobhuza II (1904–82), was followed by a regency (by one of his 100 wives) for his son Prince Makhosimvelo (1968–). Under the 1978 constitution, the king nominates part of both the Senate and House of Assembly, the rest being elected by an electoral college from their own number. English is the official language, but Swazi is spoken by the majority. Area 17,400 sq.km (6,704 sq.m); pop (1981) 580,000, most of them Swazi. M.U.: emalangeni.

SWEDEN. A kingdom occupying the E part of the peninsula of Scandinavia in N Europe with a coastline *c.* 7,560 km (4,700 m) long on the Baltic Sea.

PHYSICAL FEATURES. A mountain range runs along most of the Norwegian border, and the main regions are the mountainous two-thirds in the N, incl. Sarjektjäkko 2,125 m (6,971 ft); the central lowlands; the Småland highlands; and the fertile Skane in the extreme south. Lakes are numerous, the largest being Väner, Vätter, Mälar, and Hjälmar, all in the central region. The main river is the Göta. Öland and Götland are S.'s largest islands. The climate varies greatly. An almost treeless region in the extreme N gives place to a zone of birch forests, while much of the centre of the country is covered by dense coniferous forests.

ECONOMIC. Agriculture is mainly limited to the south, where crops incl. cereals, potatoes and sugar beet, and cattle and pigs are reared. The northern forests support a pulp and timber industry. There are large iron resources, espec. within the Arctic Circle, but steel and shipbuilding generally have suffered from recession and Third World competition, though special steels still have a market. Manufactures incl. Saab-Scania aircraft, carts and trucks, Volvo cars, Electrolux domestic equipment, missiles, electronics, textiles, petro-chemicals, etc., but there is increasing stress on small industries. These, which incl. high quality ornamental glass, form a third of the country's industrial output. There is also massive investment abroad. Hydro-electric power is supplemented by nuclear, the country's reserves of uranium being as large as Australia's. Other minerals incl. copper, lead, and zinc.

The chief towns are Stockholm (the cap.), Göteborg, Malmö, Uppsala, Norrköping, and Västerås.

SWEDEN. A view of the capital from the Kaknäs television and observation tower in East Stockholm. In the foreground on the left is Stockholm's Maritime Museum. *Photo: Courtesy of EFTA*

History. S. was divided in early times between 2 peoples, the Swedes in the N and the Goths in the S, who were united under one king by Sverker (1134-55). Christianity became generally accepted about the same time, and a series of crusades in the 12th-14th cents. brought Finland under Swedish rule. The Riksdag, incl. representatives of the nobles, clergy, and burgesses, was founded in 1359; peasant representatives were added in 1435. The Union of Kalmar (1397) united Denmark, Norway, and S. under a Danish dynasty, but Swedish national feeling led to several revolts, the last of which, in 1520-3, ended the union, and placed Gustavus Vasa on the throne. Lutheranism became the national religion in 1527.

S.'s ambitions to dominate the Baltic coastline involved her in the 16th-18th cents. in many wars with Denmark, Poland, Russia, and Brandenburg, which in spite of the victories of Gustavus Adolphus (1611-32), Charles X (1654-60), and Charles XII (1697-1718), left her exhausted and impoverished. Ruled by a corrupt oligarchy, S. sank into insignificance until Gustavus III

(1771-91) estab. an enlightened despotism. When in 1818 the Vasa line became extinct the crown passed to the French marshal Bernadotte, who reigned as Charles XIV (1818-44) and estab. the present dynasty: see CARL XVI Gustaf. In 1980 the Salic Law (*see* SALIAN) was abrogated and Crown Princess Victoria (1977-) became first in line to the succession.

S. lost Finland to Russia in 1809, but seized Norway in 1814, a union dissolved in 1905. Since 1814 S. has pursued a policy of neutrality. The constitution of 1809 ended the period of absolute monarchy, and under the Constitution of 1975 the powers of the monarchy were made merely nominal. There is a unicameral Riksdag. After 44 yrs of almost uninterrupted power the Social Democrats were defeated in the 1976 elections, and in 1979, after a brief interlude, the Centre Party under Thorbjörn Fälldin was again returned to power. This reflected a demand for less govt. interference, taxation to support a comprehensive welfare system having led to the growth of an underground 'black economy'.

Area 449,700 sq.km (173,629 sq.m); pop. (1980) 8,300,000, mainly of Nordic stock, but with 1,100,000 post-war immigrants (world-wide) and their children. Most belong to the estab. Evangelical Lutheran Church. The Educational system is good, with univs. at Uppsala, Lund, Göteborg, Stockholm, Umeå and Linköping. M.U.: krona.

SWĒ'DENBORG, Emanuel (1688-1772). Swedish philosopher. B. at Stockholm, son of an unorthodox bp, he distinguished himself as a scientist - in geology, magnetic theory, functions of the brain, etc. - being much ahead of his time, and then from 1747 devoted himself to scriptural study, living much in London. His writing (in Latin) incl. *Divine Love and Wisdom,* in which he taught that the Last Judgment having taken place in 1757 there had succeeded The New Church signified by the New Jerusalem in the Revelation of which he was the prophet. An actual sect, for which his writings are the scriptures (Swedenborgians), was not estab. until 1788 by a Clerkenwell printer Robert Hindmarsh.

SWEDISH. A member of the northern or Scandinavian division of the Germanic languages. By the 14th cent. there were a number of rhymed chronicles, ballads and folk songs, but modern literature begins in the 17th cent. with the epic poet Georg Stjernhjelm (1598-1672). In the 18th cent. the names of Linnaeus, Celsius and Swedenborg typify the country's intellectual ferment, and the poet-historian Olof von Dalin was an outstanding literary figure. The period 1771-1809, covering the reigns of Gustavus III (himself a playwright) and Gustavus IV, saw much literary activity, e.g. the song lyrics of Karl Michael Bellman (1740-95), and the dramas of Gudmund Jöran Adlerbeth (1751-1818) and Henrik Kellgren (1751-95), who assisted the king in the royal theatre. Outstanding names of the Romantic era are those of poet-playwright Per Daniel Amadeus Atterbom (1790-1855), the poets Esaias Tegnér and Eric G. Geier (1783-1847) who sought inspiration in the legendary heroic past, and Afzelius, editor of national folk songs. To the period of romantic transition belong the novelist and poet Viktor Rydberg, the classic poet Carl Snoilsky (1841-1903), and the Finnish epic poet Johan Ludwig Runeberg (1804-77), but realism emerged in the novels of Carl Almqvist and Frederika Bremer (1801-65), and broke through in tortured agony in the work of Strindberg. A new romantic idealism followed, e.g. the poets Gustaf Fröding (1860-1911), Erik Axel Karlefeldt and Verner von Heidenstam (1859-1940), and the novelist Selma Lagerlöf - the last 3 all Nobel prizewinners. Among more recent writers, also Nobel prizewinners, are Harry Martinson (1904-78), author of a novel of tramp life, *The Road,* and *Aniara,* a space-fiction epic that was adapted as an opera; and Pär Lagerkvist (1891-1974), lyricist, novelist (*Barabbas*), and playwright.

SWEDISH ART. The rise of Sweden in the 17th cent. ushered in a great cultural era. In the environs of Stockholm are the royal residences of Ulriksdal (1660), Karlsborg (1696-1718), and Drottningsholm. Renaissance churches of Stockholm incl. Maria Magdalen (1650), St Catherina (1725), and the church of Adolphus Frederick (1751-71). Towards the end of the 18th cent. French influence is apparent. From 1830 to 1880 Swedish architecture reflected various tendencies in fashion in Germany and Denmark, but from 1890 the teachings of William Morris were influential on Swedish arts and crafts, and in the 20th cent. Sweden became a world leader in industrial art and produced a notable sculptor in Carl Milles (1875-1955). Contemporary Swedish architecture has also attracted much attention, the tendency is towards austerity.

SWEET, Henry (1845-1912). British philologist, author of works on Old and Middle English, who transplanted to England German scientific techniques of study. He was said to be the original of Prof. Higgins in *Pygmalion.*

SWEET WILLIAM. Garden plant (*Dianthus barbatus*), also called bearded pink because of its bearded petals. The clusters of small flowers are pink, red or white, the leaves elliptical and dark green. The S.W. is named after William, duke of Cumberland, also known as 'Butcher' Cumberland.

SWEYN (swān) (d. 1014). King of Denmark. Succeeding to the throne *c.* 986, he repeatedly raided England, and conquered it in 1013, being accepted as king. His early death led to the recall of Ethelred to the throne.

SWIFT, Jonathan (1667-1745). Irish writer and churchman. B. in Dublin, he became sec. to Sir William Temple at Moor Park, Surrey, where began his friendship with 'Stella' - Hester Johnson (1681-1728). Returning to Ireland, he was ordained in the English Church (1694), and in 1699 was made a prebendary of St Patrick's, Dublin. His satirical *Battle of the Books* and *Tale of a Tub* were pub. in 1804. In 1710 he became a Tory pamphleteer, and obtained the deanery of St Patrick in 1713. His *Journal to Stella* is a series of letters, 1710-13, in which he described his life in London. In 1714 he returned to Ireland, where he wrote *The Drapier's Letters,* opposing the introduction of inferior copper coins into Ireland. In 1726 appeared his best-known work, *Gulliver's Travels.* For some years before his death he was insane. He may have m. Stella, but was deeply involved 1708-23 with Esther Vanhomrigh (1690-1723), whom he called 'Vanessa'.

SWIFT. Family of birds (Micropodidae), the fastest creatures alive, with a flying speed of up to 160kmph (100mph). The common S. (*Apus apus*) migrates from Africa to Europe in summer: drab-coloured, it has a short forked tail, poorly developed feet and legs, and curved wings longer than the body. The nests of the related genus *Collocalia* are used in China for soup.

SWIMMING. The self-propulsion of the body through water. The dog paddle is probably the original 'instinctive' stroke, but the first to be developed in Europe as a skilled technique was the breast stroke in the 16th cent., still used in competitive S., as is the faster but exhausting variant originating in the USA in the 1930s, the butterfly breast stroke, although the other developments from it - the side and overarm strokes - are out of fashion. The crawl was developed by the Australians at the beginning of this cent. from a method in use by the South Sea Islanders, from which in turn came the back crawl in the 1920s, the latter being espec. popular in competition S. because it allows the swimmer to breathe freely throughout. The water is entered by the 'racing plunge' or by diving, the latter being divided for competition purposes into springboard and firmboard events. Earliest of competitive S. bodies was the English Amateur S. Assocn (1869), and the Fédération Internationale de Natation Amateur (1908) was founded in London. With the invention of frogman equipment - flippers for the feet, breathing apparatus, and even mechanical propulsion, underwater S. has developed special techniques of its own. *See also* CHANNEL SWIMMING.

SWINBURNE, Algernon Charles (1837-1909). British poet. B. in London, he was ed. at Eton and Balliol Coll., Oxford, and attained fame with the tragedy *Atlanta in Calydon* (1865), *Poems and Ballads* (1866) was also acclaimed for its lyric fire, but in both Britain and the USA its pagan spirit brought unfavourable comment. In a wrangling controversy that lasted some years he and Rossetti were attacked in 1871 by Robert W. Buchanan, as leaders of 'the fleshly school of poetry'. Among the best of later verse are *Songs Before Sunrise* (1871), revolutionary in its political attitude, and 2 further vols. of *Poems and Ballads* (1878 and 1889). In 1879 he moved to the home of Watts-Dunton (q.v.) at Putney, where he lived in retirement after a career of excess.

SWINDON. Town in Wilts, 124km (77m) W of London. It has Britain's first American-type leisure centre (1976), the Wyvern theatre, and although the British Rail Engineering Works (1841) are now less important S. has diversified since 1950 into heavy engineering, electronics, and electrical manufacture. The birthplace of Richard Jefferies at Coate Farm has been restored. Pop. (1972) 90,330.

SWINE FEVER. Virus disease of pigs, also known as hog cholera: it was almost eradicated in Britain by a policy of slaughter from 1963. **Swine flu** is a virulent form of influenza (q.v.) virtually indistinguishable from a type found in man. **Swine vesicular disease** is a virus disease (porcine enterovirus) closely resembling foot and mouth disease. Known in Italy and Hong Kong, it first occurred in Britain in 1972, and a slaughter policy was pursued. It is communicable to humans, and may have originated in the infection of pigs by a virus causing flu-like symptoms in man.

SWING MUSIC. An offshoot of jazz (q.v.) which flourished from *c.* 1930 to the late 1940s; characterized by a simple harmonic base (of varying tempo) supplied by the rhythm section (percussion, guitar, piano), with a superimposed melodic line carried usually by a solo instrument, e.g. trumpet, clarinet or saxophone.

SWINTON, Sir Ernest (1868-1951). British soldier and historian. Entering the army in 1888, he served in S Africa and the F.W.W., rising to the rank of major-gen., and was the inventor of the tank in 1916. Knighted in 1923, he was Chichele prof. of military history at Oxford, 1925-39.

SWITHIN or **Swithun, St** (d. 862). A chancellor of King Ethelwolf, he was bp of Winchester 852-62. In 971 his body was to be reburied, but the day chosen, 15 July, now St S.'s Day, was so wet that the translation was delayed. This gave rise to the superstition that if it rains on that day it will be rainy for 40 days.

SWITZERLAND. Confederate republic of W Europe, bounded by Germany on the N, Austria on the E, Italy on the S, and France on the NW.

PHYSICAL FEATURES. S. is extremely mountainous; a central plain traversed by the Aar is shut in by the Alps to the S and by the Jura to the N. The Upper Rhine and Rhône lie between the Bernese Oberland and the main chain of the Alps. The Swiss Alps culminate in Monte Rosa (*see* ALPS). The Rhine, its tributary the Aar, the Rhône, and the Ticino, are the main rivers. There is a large number of lakes: Lake Geneva, through which flows the Rhône, lies partly in France; Lake Constance, which is traversed by the Rhine, is shared with Germany and Austria, and Lakes Maggiore and Lugano with Italy.

SWITZERLAND. The redoubtable north face of the Eiger, the ambition of so many climbers in the Bernese Oberland. Seen here from the air, it has the Finsteraarhorn rising above its crest. *Photo: Courtesy of the Swiss National Tourist Office*

The climate shows considerable variations. The *föhn* is a warm, dry southerly wind, while the *bise* is cold and northerly.

ECONOMIC LIFE. Lakes, rivers and mountains, forests and areas suitable only for pasturage take up three-quarters of the country, but the remainder serves to render S. agriculturally almost self-sufficient. Wheat, barley, potatoes, tobacco and vines are grown, and dairy farming is highly developed.

There are almost no industrial raw materials or fuel resources, but hydro-electric power is cheap and industry relies on processing raw materials and semi-manufactured goods, and specialized sophisticated products. The chief industries are machinery, metal-working, chemicals, precision instruments, watches (affected by US encroachment in the field of digitals) and textiles, with smaller specialities incl. chocolates and perfumery. Some 90 per cent of goods are for export and one-third of the labour force is foreign, mainly Italian. Also very important are tourism, foreign investment, banking and insurance. Communications are excellent. The principal towns incl. Berne (the cap.), Zürich, Basle, Geneva, Lausanne, Fribourg, and Neuchâtel, each of which is the seat of a univ.

CONSTITUTION. Two chambers, a national council, elected directly, and a Council of States, with members chosen by the cantons, together form the Federal Assembly, which elects the executive Federal Council for 4 years and the President of the Confederation for 1 year. Extensive powers are reserved for the cantons and the communes. Women were enfranchized 1971.

History. S. originally politically in 1291, when the 'forest cantons' of Schwyz, Uri, and Lower Unterwalden formed the Everlasting League for the defence of their liberties against their Habsburg overlords; practical freedom from Habsburg control was secured in 1389, and from the suzerainty of the emperor in 1499. The entry of new towns and districts, incl. Lucerne, Zürich, and Berne, brought the number of cantons to 8 by 1353 and to 13 by 1513. The Reformation was accepted during 1523-9 by Zürich, Berne, and Basle, but the rural cantons remained RC. S.'s complete independence was recognized by the Treaty of Westphalia, 1648.

After the suppression of the Peasant War (1653), the cantonal govts fell increasingly into the hands of small oligarchies. A French invasion in 1798 estab. a centralized govt; this was modified by Napoleon's Act of Mediation (1803), which made S. a democratic federation. Under the 1815 peace settlement S. received Geneva and other territories, increasing the number of cantons to 22, a new constitution was adopted whereby S. again became a confederation, and the powers guaranteed Swiss neutrality. Following a struggle between the Liberals and Catholics a revised federal constitution, giving the central govt wide powers, was introduced in 1848; a further revision in 1874 increased its powers, and introduced the principle of the referendum. S. maintained its neutrality during both world wars. In 1979 Jura (q.v.) became the 23rd canton.

Area 41,288 sq.km (15,941 sq.m); pop. (1979) 6,300,000, of whom, excl. non-Swiss nationals (*c.* 1,000,000) - 75% speak German, 20% French, 4% Italian, and 1% Romansch.

SWORD-FISH. Family of fishes (Xiphiidae). They are characterized by the long sword-like weapon protruding from the upper jaw. The common S. (*Xiphias gladius*) sometimes reaches Britain. The sail-fishes and spear-fishes are of the closely related family Istiophoridae.

SYCAMORE (sik'amor). Species of tree (*Acer pseudoplatanus*). The leaves are five-lobed, and the hanging racemes of flowers are followed by winged fruits. The timber is used for furniture making.

SWORD-FISH. The sword-fish has a high reputation as a 'game' fish, and is greatly sought after by fishermen who wear out its strength in contests from motor-boats.

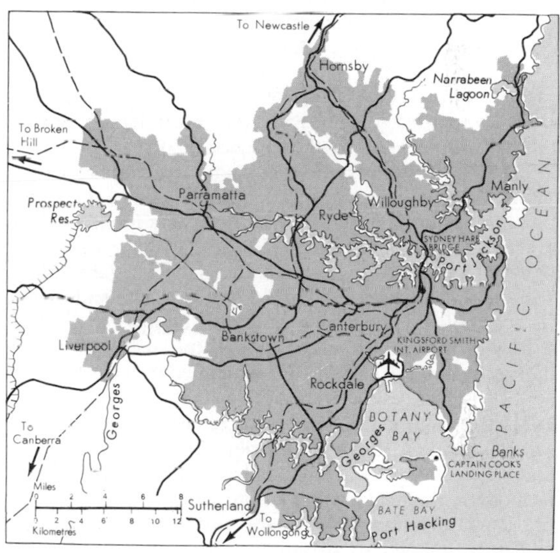

SYDNEY

SYDNEY (sid'ni). Major seaport and cap. of NSW, largest city of Australia. It lies on Port Jackson, 6.5km (4m) W of the Pacific Ocean, and through it passes a large proportion of Australia's exports. Although the streets still follow the lines of the wagon tracks of 150 yrs ago, there are few survivals of the Regency town, e.g. Bligh House, in the modern skyscraper city. Major landmarks are the single span (503.5m/1,652ft) S. Harbour Bridge (1923-32), the Opera House (1959-73), and Centre Point Tower (1980). The city is Australia's prime internat. airport, and is linked by rail with Perth (3,960 km/2,461 m). There are engineering and metal processing industries; scientific equipment, chemicals, furniture and clothing are manufactured; and S. is a wool and wheat mart, as well as a major financial and educational centre with 3 univs. - Sydney (1850), NSW (1958) and Macquarie (1967). Pop. (1976) 3,021,300.

SYDNEY. The Sydney suburb of Paddington is a study in the social regeneration of an urban area. These terrace houses, with fine decorative ironwork (often brought out as ballast in sailing ships) became slums in the 1950s, but have now been restored to fashionable Victorian stylishness. *Photo: Courtesy of the Australian Information Service*

SYENITE (sī'enīt). A group of grey, crystalline, plutonic rocks, composed of feldspar and hornblende, distinguished from granite by the absence of quartz.

SYKTYVKAR (siktifkahr'). Russian city, cap. of Komi ASSR, on the Vychegda r., a lumbering centre with saw mills, paper factories, tanneries, etc. It was founded 1740 as a Russian colony. Pop. (1979) 171,000.

SYLHET (silhet'). Town in NE Bangladesh, in the valley of the Surma r., in a fertile area of tea, rice, jute and sugar. The cap. of a Hindu kingdom until conquered by the Moslems in the 14th cent., it was the scene of bitter fighting in the civil war in 1971 which led to the establishment of Bangladesh. Pop. (1975) 46,000.

SYMBOL. Sign used to save time in conveying information, eliminating language barriers or overcoming illiteracy. In art Ss. have always held an important place, and for modern practical use there is an internat. organization for standardization. Many are used in science and medicine; all motorists are familiar with road signs; housewives make use of those indicating methods of handling fabrics for cleaning; and the code used in the transport of goods is worldwide, e.g. a wineglass to denote fragility, an open umbrella to show which way up the package should be placed, and a skull and crossbones to indicate dangerous contents.

SYMBOLISTS. School of French poets, represented by Verlaine, Mallarmé, and Rimbaud, who used words for their symbolic rather than their concrete meaning: the intimate, personal interpretations employed tended to produce obscurity.

SYMINGTON, William (1763-1831). British inventor. B. in Lanarks, he invented the road locomotive, and in 1788 a steamboat engine, building in 1802 at Grangemouth the first successful steamboat.

SYMONDS (si'mondz), **John Addington** (1840-93). British writer. B. at Bristol, he spent much of his life in Italy and Switzerland, and pub. *The History of the Renaissance in Italy* (1875-86), literary criticism, and a translation of Cellini's autobiography.

SYMONS (si'monz), **Arthur** (1865-1945). British writer. Son of a Methodist minister, he developed a precocious literary gift, and wide friendships with Toulouse-lautrec, Mallarmé, Beardsley, Yeats and Conrad. He introduced Eliot to the work of Laforgue and, of his numerous books, *The Symbolist Movement in Literature* (1900) is best known. In 1908 he suffered a severe mental breakdown, but partially recovered.

SYMPHONY (sim'foni). A musical composition for orchestra, traditionally in 4 contrasted but closely related movements. It developed from the smaller sonata form, the Italian overture, and the dance suite of the 18th cent. Haydn estab. a mature form of S. in his later works, written in allegro, slow, scherzo, and allegro movements. Mozart in lyrical mood, and Beethoven with dramatic tones, expanded the classical form, which has been developed further by successive composers, such as Brahms, Tchaikovsky, Brückner, Dvořák, Mahler, Sibelius, Vaughan Williams, Rubbra, Piston, Prokoviev, Shostakovich, Stravinsky, Copland.

SYNAGOGUE (sin'agog). The building used by Jews for their religious worship. As an institution it dates from the destruction of the temple in Jerusalem in AD 70, though it had been in course of development from the time of the Exile.

SYNCLINE (sing'klīn). *See* ANTICLINE.

SYNCOPE (sin'kopi). Name for FAINTING (q.v.).

SYNDICALISM (sin'dikalizm). Revolutionary labour movement advocating the ownership and control of each industry by the workers in it, organized in their trade union. It rejects parliamentary activity in favour of 'direct action' by means of strikes, culminating in a revolutionary general strike. S. originated in England under Robert Owen's influence in the 1830s, but first became widespread in France after 1900. It exercised considerable influence in England *c.* 1910-24, Tom Mann being its principal spokesman, and was preached in the US by the Industrial Workers of the World. After 1918 S. was absorbed by Communism or Anarchism.

SYNERGY (sin'erji). In medicine the 'co-operative' action of two or more drugs, muscles or organs; in architecture, etc., the augmented strength of systems, where the strength of a wall is greater than the added total of its individual units, e.g. the stone walls of early S American civilisations, not held together by cement or mortar.

SYNGE (sing), **John Millington** (1871-1909). Irish playwright. B. nr Dublin, he was ed. at Trinity Coll., Dublin, and when living in Paris in 1898 was persuaded by Yeats to go to the W of Ireland and the Aran Is. Absorbing the characteristic poetic turns of speech of the local people, he wrote plays incl. *The Shadow of the Glen* (1903), *Riders to the Sea* (1904), *The Well of the Saints* (1907), *The Playboy of the Western World*, and the unfinished *Deidre of the Sorrows*. His presentation of the Irish tended to upset his compatriots, and when *Playboy* (1907) was first presented at the Abbey Theatre there were riots.

SYNOVITIS (sinovī'tis). Inflammation of the lining of a joint, caused by injury or infection.

SYNTHESIZER. Device which uses electrical components to produce sounds, either such as conventional musical instruments produce physically, or in free creativity. In *pre-set Ss.*, the sound of the various instruments is produced by a built-in computer-type memory which triggers all the control settings required to produce the sound of a trumpet or violin. For example, the 'sawtooth' type sound wave produced by a violin is artificially produced by an electrical tone generator, or oscillator, and then fed into an electrical filter which is set to have the resonances characteristic of a violin body. In *programmable Ss.* any number of new instrumental or other sounds may be produced at the will of the performer. *See* ELECTRONICS.

SYPHILIS (si'filis). The principal venereal disease, due to infection of the blood by the parasite *treponema pallidum.* It is communicated almost entirely by sexual intercourse. The first sign is a nodule, sometimes ulcerated (chancre); some weeks afterwards a rash appears all over the body, with ulcers in the mouth and throat. Later, swellings occur under the skin and in the internal organs, and destroy the surrounding tissues, incl. bone. The brain cells may be affected (general paralysis of the insane, *locomotor ataxia*).Treatment, difficult before the discovery of antibiotics, is now simple, quick and effective, except that the large-scale spread of venereal diseases encouraged by the 'permissive' society has led to the emergence of resistant strains.

SYRACUSE (sī'rakūz). Port of E Sicily, Italy, 130km (81m) SW of Messina. Chemicals, salt and wine are produced. It has a cathedral and remains of temples, aqueducts, catacombs, and an amphitheatre. S. was founded in 734 BC and became a centre of Greek culture and power, especially under the elder and younger Dionysius (406-343 BC). S. was taken by the Romans in 212 BC, and was destroyed by Saracens in 878. The rebuilt town was taken by the Normans in the 11th cent. Pop. (1979) 124,000.

SYRACUSE (sir'akūz). City in New York state, USA, to the W of Albany at the S end of Lake Onondaga, and connected with the Great Lakes, the Hudson, and the St Lawrence by canals. Manufactures incl. typewriters, agricultural implements, clothing, furniture. S. was founded 1805 on the site of an Iroquois cap. Pop. met. area (1970) 629,190.

SYRIA (sir'ia). Country of Asia in the Near East. It consists mainly of a desert plateau, rising in the SW to the Anti-Lebanon Mts., and to Mt Hermon and the Golan Heights (qq.v.) on the Israeli border. S. is drained by the Euphrates and its tributaries. Crops incl. cotton, cereals, sugar beet, olives and tobacco. Sheep, goats, camels and cattle are reared. Surveys are discovering new minerals and there are phosphates and some oil. Industrialisation is rapid, and products incl. textiles, footwear, sugar, tobacco, plastics, leather goods and brassware. The cap. is Damascus; Lattakia (on the Mediterranean coastline of 190km/120m) is the chief port and other towns incl. Aleppo, Homs and Hama.

There have been frequent military coups, but under the constitution of 1973 there is a single-chamber elected People's Council, and the Ba'ath Party, predominant from 1963, is recognised as the leading political organization of the 'socialist state'. The pres. (who must be a Moslem) is Lt. Gen. Hafez el Assad (1930-), elected for 7 yrs in 1971, and re-elected 1978 and 1985. Arabic is the language, and most Syrians are Sunni Moslems, but Pres. Assad and the majority of the govt. are Alawite (*see* SHIAH).

History. S. was originally divided between various small kingdoms which fought against Israel, and were subdued by the Assyrians. It was subsequently occupied by the Babylonians, Persians, and Macedonians, but gained importance under Seleucus Nicator (301 BC) founder of Antioch, and Antiochus the Great. After forming part of the Roman and Byzantine empires, it was conquered by the Saracens in 636. During the Middle Ages it was the scene of many of the Crusaders' exploits. The area forming S. belonged to Turkey 1516-1918. It was occupied by Brit. and Fr. troops 1918-19, and in 1920, with Lebanon, was placed under Fr. mandate. The 2 terrs. were separated in 1925, S. becoming fully independent in 1946. The Ba'athists are divided between those favouring continued hostilities with Israel, and those wishing to concentrate on economic development. In 1976 S. intervened directly in the civil war in Lebanon, where support had previously been given to the Palestinians there, and encountered hostility both from the Palestinians themselves and from the Arab League: *see* LEBANON. In 1970 Syria attempted to intervene against Jordan's suppression of Palestinian terrorist groups, and during the Iran-Iraq war of 1980 (in which S. supported Iran), troops were briefly massed on the border of Jordan (a supporter of Iraq).

Area 186,000 sq.km (72,000 sq.m); pop. (1978) 8,100,000. M.U.: Syrian pound.

SYRIAC (sir'iak). One of the Semitic languages, originally the Aramaic dialect of Edessa. From *c.* 700 BC-*c.* AD 700, it was spoken over a large area of C. Asia.

SYRINGA (siring'ga). Genus of shrubs. Lilac (*S. vulgaris*) is the best-known, but the name is given to a number of other plants, notably mock orange, which is in the family Saxifragaceae.

SZCZECIN (sche'chin). Baltic port of Poland, on the Oder, 27km (17m) above its entrance into the Zalew Szczecinska (Stettiner Haff). Under the Ger. form of its name, Stettin, it was Germany's chief port on the Baltic until after the S.W.W. when it came under Polish admin. A member of the Hanseatic League from 1278, it was Swedish 1648-1720 when it was occupied by Prussia. The Russians captured it, 1945. Catherine the Great was b. at S. Pop. (1978) 381,000.

SZECHWAN. *See* SICHUAN.

SZEGED (seg'ed). City in Hungary nr the confluence of the Maros and Tisa, 160km (100m) SE of Budapest. It is an industrial and commercial centre with a univ. Pop. (1979) 178,000.

SZYMANOWSKI (shimanov'ski), **Karol** (1883-1937). Polish composer. B. in the Ukraine, he became director of the Conservatoire at Warsaw in 1922. S. composed orchestral works, operas, and piano music.

T

The 20th letter of the alphabet, whose sound is the unvoiced dental stop. The earliest form was X, which the Phoenicians called *tau*, a cross or sign, but in the Gk alphabet its form was T.

TABLE BAY. Inlet in the SW coast of the Cape of Good Hope, SA, on which stands Capetown. It is overlooked by Table Mountain, of which the highest point is Maclear's Beacon 1,087 m (3,567 ft), and which is covered by cloud - the 'tablecloth'.

TABLE TENNIS. Indoor game developed in Britain *c.* 1880, possibly from real T., which was known until the adoption of the present name by the International T.T. Assocn in 1926 as ping pong. It is played by 2 or 4 players using solid-headed wooden bats and celluloid balls on a rectangular table 2.74m (9ft) long by 1.52m (5ft) wide, and 76cm (2.5ft) from the floor, with a net 15.25cm (6in) high dividing the table into 2 equal courts. Points are scored if the opponent makes a fault (fails to return a ball, strikes into the net, etc.), and 21 points make a game, a match being 2 out of 3 games. In competition additional speed is gained with rubber-covered (first used 1903) or sponge-covered bats.

TABO'RA. Town in W Tanzania. It was founded by Arab traders *c.* 1820 for traffic in slaves and ivory, and is a modern commercial centre. Pop. (1970) 21,000.

TABRIZ (tahbrēz'). City and commercial centre in NW Iran. There is a univ. and industries incl. carpets, cotton and silk textiles, metal casting, etc. Pop. (1976) 598,575.

TABU or **taboo.** Polynesian word meaning 'forbidden', applied to magical and religious objects and practices which are generally prohibited.

TACHOGRAPH (tak'ōgrahf) Combined speedometer and clock which records on a small card disc the speed at which a vehicle travels; how long it is moving or stationary. It is used to monitor the number of hours a lorry-driver is working, when he exceeds the speed limit, etc.

TACITUS (tas'itus), **Cornelius** (*c.* 55-120?). Roman historian. An eminent lawyer, he m. a dau. of Julius Agricola, and in 97 was consul under Nerva. He wrote a life of Agricola; the *Germania*, describing the German tribes; the *Historiae*, a history of the empire from Galba to Domitian (69-97), and the *Annales*, reaching from Tiberius to Nero. He is famed for the succinct compression of his style.

TA'CNA. City of S Peru, on the T. river. Near T., Chile in 1880 defeated a combined Peruvian-Bolivian army and occupied T. until 1929. It is designated for industrial development. Pop. (1972) 42,000.

TACŌ'MA. Port of Washington state, USA on Puget Sound. Founded 1868, it became important through its choice as the terminus of the NPR (1873). Pop. (1970) 154,580. T. is also another name for Mt Rainier.

TADEMA. *See* ALMA TADEMA.

TADZHIK (tahjik') **SSR.** Asiatic rep. of the USSR, separated on the S from Afghanistan and China by the Amu-Darya r. Pik Communizmu (Communism Peak) is the highest mtn in the USSR (7,495 m/24,590 ft). Cotton, fruit, cereals, etc. are grown with irrigation, and industries incl. mining (lead, zinc, radium, mica, sulphur, etc.), engineering, clothing and textiles, and food processing. The cap. is Dushanbe. T. was admitted to the Union in 1929. Area 143,100 sq.km (55,250 sq.m); pop. (1978) 3,700,000.

TAFA'WA BALĒ'WA, Alhaji Sir Abubakar (1912-66). Nigerian statesman. Entering the House of Representatives in 1952, he was Min. of Works (1952-4) and of Transport (1954-7). In 1957 he became PM of the Fed. of Nigeria, but was abducted and assassinated in the *coup d'état* of Jan. 1966.

TA'FFETA (Persian *tafta*, twisted). Light plainly woven silk fabric with a high lustre; the term may be applied to silk and wool mixtures, etc.

TAFT, William Howard (1857-1930). 27th President of the USA. B. at Cincinnati, he was Secretary of War 1904-8, and was elected president in 1908 as a Republican. He was defeated in the election of 1912, and served as chief justice of the Supreme Court, 1921-30. His son, **Robert T.** (1889-1953), a Republican senator from 1939, was a candidate for the Presidential nomination in 1940, 1944, 1948, and 1952, and was sponsor of the T.-Hartley Labor Act of 1947 (bitterly opposed by organized labour).

TAGANRO'G. Port of the RSFSR, on T. Gulf, an arm of the Sea of Azov. T. is icebound in the winter. It makes metal goods, aircraft, machinery, shoes. Russia annexed it 1769. There is a museum devoted to Chekhov who was b. at T. Pop. (1979) 277,000.

TAGLIONI (tahlyō'nē), **Maria** (1804-84). Italian dancer. She was particularly successful in *La Sylphide*, composed by her father, and was noted for her ethereal grace.

TAGORE (tagōr'), **Sir Rabindranath** (1861-1941). Indian writer. B. in Calcutta, in 1901 he estab. the 'Abode of Peace', Visva Bharati Univ. (1922) at Santiniketan 145km (90m) from Calcutta. His translations of his collection of lyrics *Gitanjali* and his verse play *Chitra* brought him world fame, and in 1913 he received a Nobel prize. An ardent social reformer and nationalist, in 1919 he resigned the knighthood he had received in 1915 in protest against British repression. His nephew **Abanindranath T.** (1871-1951) was the father of modern Indian painting. He drew his subjects from Indian history and mythology.

TĀ'GUS. River which rises in Spain, in the mountains of Albarracin, and flows 910km (566m) through Portugal to the Atlantic at Lisbon; longest river in the Iberian peninsula. It is crossed by the April 25 Bridge (1966: formerly the Salazar, but renamed in honour of the revolution in 1974). The Tagus-Segura project (1968) channels water *c.* 240km (150m) to the rainless Murcia/Alicante region for the production of early fruit and vegetables.

TAHITI (tahē'ti). Largest of the Society Islands, part of Fr. Polynesia. T. was visited by Captain Cook (1769) and by Bligh of the *Bounty* (1788). T. came under French protection in 1843, becoming a colony in 1880. Papeete is the cap. Area 1,040 sq.km (402 sq.m); pop. (1977) 95,600.

TAIGA (tīgah'). Russian term for virgin, heavily forested territory, much of it in the permafrost zone, in Siberia (q.v.). There is rich and varied fauna and flora, in delicate balance because the conditions of life are so precarious, and there are fears that the destruction involved in rlwy construction may lead to erosion, etc. The name is also applied to similar regions elsewhere.

TAINE (tān), **Hippolyte Adolphe** (1828-93). French critic and historian. He was appointed prof. at the École des Beaux Arts, in 1864. In his critical writings, e.g. *History of English Literature* (1863) and *Philosophy of Art* (1865-9), he analyses literary works as the products of period, race, and environment. He also pub. *Origins of Contemporary France.*

TAIPAN (tī'pan). Australia's deadliest snake (*Oxyuranus scutellatus*), also found in New Guinea. Some 3m (10 ft) long, it is brown with yellow spots beneath.

TAIPEI (tīpā). Cap. of Taiwan, nr the N coast. It is a commercial centre, and the Nat. Palace Museum (1965) houses the world's greatest collection of Chinese art, evacuated from the mainland in 1948. Pop. (1976) 2,090,000.

TAIWAN (tīwahn'). Pacific is. 145 km (90 m) off the SE coast of China, and long known as Formosa, the name given to it by early Spanish explorers. It was settled by the Chinese from the 15th cent. and annexed by China in 1683, but ceded to Japan in 1895 and only regained by China after the Japanese defeat in 1945. When the Communist forces completed their conquest of mainland China in 1947-9, the Nationalist govt and its followers fled to T., where it continued to be recognized as the legal Chinese govt. by the USA till 1978. In 1971, however, the Communist Chinese govt. was admitted to the UN and the Nationalist Chinese govt. expelled, and T. was acknowledged as a prov. of Communist China by Britain in 1972. Nevertheless, T. continued in fact under Nationalist rule, and there was a mutual defence treaty between the US and T. Govts. (1954-79).

With American aid, T. has achieved economic prosperity. Rice, tea, sugar, fruits, jute, camphor, etc. are produced and, with coal and hydro-electric power, there are growing industries incl. textiles, petrochemicals, steel, glass, brick-making, flour and sugar milling. Minerals incl. gold, copper, aluminium, and some oil and natural gas. The cap. is Taipeh; the chief ports are Keelung in the N and Kaohsiung in the S.

The first pres. was Chiang Kai-shek (q.v.), and the Kuomintang or Nationalist Party exercises near dictatorial rule. Real power was held, after Chiang's death, by his eldest son, Gen. Chiang Ching-kuo (1910–), PM from 1972 and then pres. from 1978. Native Formosans, nearly 85% of the pop., tend to resent their domination by the mainland minority, and to conciliate them a small admixture of elected members was admitted in 1972 to the Nat. Assembly, elected 1947 with indefinite life. Area 35,975 sq.km (13,890 sq.m); pop. (1978) 17,140,000, incl. *c.* 2,000,000 mainlanders. Also controlled by the T. govt are the Pescadores Is. (Penghus) 56 km (35 m) to the W (area 130 sq.km/50 sq.m; pop. *c.* 110,000); and Quemoy (155 sq.km/60 sq.m) and Matsu (28 sq.km/11 sq.m). The 2 latter are within loudspeaker distance of the mainland. M.U.: Taiwan dollar.

TAIYUAN (tah-ēyōō-ahn'). Cap. of Shanxi prov., China. A walled city, founded in the 5th cent. AD, on the Fen He, it is the seat of Shanxi univ. There is bituminous coal nearby, and industries incl. iron and steel, agricultural machinery, cotton textiles, etc. Pop. (1973) 1,450,000.

TAIZÉ (tāzā'). Village of Saône-et-Loire, Burgundy, France. A Protestant monastic community, first founded 1940 by Swiss theologian Roger Schutz (1915-), developed in the 1960s into an ecumenical centre for young people interested in communal Christianity combining 'struggle and contemplation'.

TAJ MAHAL (tahzh mahahl'). *See* AGRA.

TAKAO (tahkow'). Japanese name of KAOHSIUNG.

TAKORA'DI. *See* SEKONDI-TAKORADI.

TALAVERA DE LA REINA (tahlahvā'rah dā lah rā'ēnah). Town of central Spain, on the Tagus, 120km (75m) SW of Madrid. In 1809 Wellesley defeated the French here. Pop. (1970) 31,900.

TALBOT, William Henry Fox (1800-77). British photographic pioneer. His discovery of the negative/positive Calotype process (1839) - contemporary with Daguerre's experiments - laid the foundation of modern photography; he also made instantaneous photographs in 1851 and photo engravings in 1852. He lived at Lacock Abbey, Wilts, 1833-77, and a museum of his work was opened there in 1975.

TALC. A magnesium silicate, $3MgO.4SiO_2.H_2O$, occurring in crystals, but the massive form known as steatite or soapstone is more common. French chalk and potstone are varieties of T. It is used in cosmetics, for lubricants, and as a filler in paper manufacture.

TALIEN. *See* LÜDA.

TALLAHA'SSEE. Cap. of Florida, USA, from 1823, 257km (160m) W of Jacksonville. De Soto discovered an Indian settlement on the site in 1539, and the name is Creek Indian for 'old town'. Centre of an agricultural and lumbering area, it still has many pre-Civil War mansions. Pop. met area (1970) 103,000.

TALLEYRAND-PÉRIGORD (tahlāroṅ'-pārēgōr'), **Charles Maurice de** (1754-1838). French statesman. B. in Paris, he was bp of Autun, 1789-91. He was a supporter of moderate reform, but fled to the USA during the Terror. Returning to France in 1796, he served as For. Min. under the Directory 1797-9, and under Napoleon 1799-1807. He represented France at the Congress of Vienna 1814-15, and was ambassador to London 1830-4.

TA'LLIN. Seaport and cap. of the Estonian SSR on the Gulf of Finland, with a fine harbour closed by ice for 3 months every year. Founded 1219 as Reval, it was a Hansa town, passed to Sweden 1561, to Russia 1750. There is a 13th cent. castle and many other medieval buildings, and metal-working industries. It is a great yachting centre. Pop. (1979) 430,000.

TALLIS, Thomas (*c.* 1505-85). English organist and composer. He was organist at Waltham Abbey until 1540, and with his pupil Byrd was joint organist at the Chapel Royal from 1572. T. wrote masses, anthems, and much other church music.

TA'LMUD (late Heb. for 'teaching'). Chief work of Jewish post-Biblical literature, based on the *Mishnah.* To this was added the *Gemara*, discussions centring on its texts, during the 3rd and 4th cents.

TAMALE (tamah'li). Industrial town and commercial centre in NE Ghana, with a trade in rice, cotton and peanuts. There is an airport. Pop. (1975) 125,000.

TĀ'MAR. River rising in N Cornwall, England, and flowing into the English Channel via Plymouth Sound, where its estuary is known as the Hamoaze. For most of its 97km (60m) length it forms the Cornwall/Devon border. Also, a river in Tasmania, Australia, formed by the union of the N and S Esk, which flows into Bass Strait: length 65km (40m)

TA'MARIND. Species of tropical tree (*Tamarindus indica*) in the family Leguminosae. An evergreen, it has pinnate leaves, reddish-yellow flowers, followed by pods, the pulp of which is used medicinally.

TAMARISK. Genus of shrubs (*Tamarix*), which flourish in warm, salty, desert regions where no other vegetation is found. The common T. or salt cedar (*T. gallica*) has evergreen, scale-like leaves and spikes of very small, pink or white flowers. *See* MANNA.

TAMATAVE (tahmahtahv'). Chief port of Madagascar, on its E coast. Pop. (1972) 60,000.

TAMBOURINE (tam'boorēn). Musical instrument of an ancient origin, almost unchanged since Roman times. A shallow drum with a single skin and loosely set jingles which increase its effect.

TAMBO'V. Cap. of T. region, RSFSR, on the Tsna in the black-earth area, with flour mills, distilleries, railway workshops, artificial-rubber factories, etc. Pop. (1979) 270,000.

TAMERLĀ'NE or **Timur i Leng** (1336-1405). Mongol conqueror. B. in Turkestan, he made himself ruler of Samarkand in 1369, conquered Persia, Azerbaijan, Armenia, and Georgia, and broke the power of the Golden Horde. In 1398-9 he invaded the Punjab and sacked Delhi; he then invaded Syria and Asia Minor, and captured the sultan at Angora.

TA'MIL. Chief of the Dravidian languages; spoken by *c.* 50 million in S India and Sri Lanka.

TAMIL NADU (ta'mil nah'doo). State of the Rep. of India, until 1968 called Madras. It consists of part of the British Madras presidency (later prov.) formed from areas conquered in the 18th cent. from the French and from Tippoo Sahib (q.v.), which became a state of the Rep. of India in 1950. The NE was detached to form Andhra Pradesh in 1953; further areas went to Kerala and Mysore (now Karnataka) in 1956, and the Laccadives (now Lakshadweep) became a separate Union Terr. Products incl. timber from *c.* 22,000 sq.km (14,000 sq.m) of forests; rice and other grains; sugar, groundnuts and cotton. Industries incl. cotton textiles, silk, electrical machinery, tractors, rubber, and sugar refining. The cap. is Madras; other towns incl. Madurai, Tiruchirappalli, Coimbatore and Salem. Area 130,357 sq.km (50,331 sq.m); pop. (1971) 41,103,000. Tamil is the state language.

TA'MMANY HALL. Democratic Party organization in New York. It originated in 1789 as the Society of St Tammany, named after a Red Indian chief. Dominant from 1800 till the 1930s, it gained a reputation for gangsterism. *See* LA GUARDIA.

TA'MMUZ. Sumerian vegetation deity, who died at midsummer and was brought back from the underworld in spring by his lover Ishtar. His cult spread over Babylonia, Syria, Phoenicia, and Palestine. In Greek mythology T. appears as Adonis.

TAMPA. City, port, and resort on the W coast of Florida, USA, famous for its cigars; it also has fruit and vegetable canneries, shipyards, and factories making boxes, fertilizers, clothing, etc. Pop. met. area T.-St Petersburg (1970) 999,613.

TAMPERE (tahm'pārā). City of Finland between Lakes Näsi and Pyhä, important industrially (textiles, paper, shoes, turbines, etc.). Pop. (1979) 165,500.

TAMPICO (tahmpē'kō). Port and airport of Mexico, on the Pánuco, 10km (6m) from the Gulf of Mexico. It is surrounded by oilfields. Pop. (1977) 240,540.

TAMWORTH. Market town in Staffs, on the Tame, 25km (15m) NE of Birmingham. Cars, paper, clothing, etc. are made. Pop. (1974) 48,900. Another T. is in NE New South Wales, Australia, on the Peel river. It is a dairying centre, furniture is made, etc. Pop. (1973) 24,800.

TANA (tah'na). Lake of Ethiopia, the source of the Blue Nile, at 1,800 m (6,000 ft), area 3,625 sq.km (1,400 sq.m).

TANABA'TA. The Japanese 'star festival' celebrated annually on the night of 7 July. It is dedicated to Altair and Vega, 2 stars in the constellation Aquila, who are united once yearly in the Milky Way, according to legend, and represent 2 star-crossed lovers allowed by the gods to meet on that night. Of Chinese origin, T. was introduced to Japan in the 8th cent.

TANAGER (tan'ajer). Family of birds (Thraupidae) similar to finches. Found in Central and S America, they all have brilliant plumage.

TA'NAGRA. City of ancient Greece, in E Boeotia, where Sparta defeated Athens, 457 BC. Many terracotta statues and statuettes were excavated towards the end of the 19th cent.

TANANARIVE (tahnanarēv') or **Antanarivo.** Cap. of Madagascar on the interior plateau, linked by rail with the port of Tamatave. Pop. (1978) 400,000.

TANGA. Port in NE Tanzania, on T. Bay, on the Indian Ocean. In the F.W.W. a British force failed to take it in 1914, but it was seized by Smuts with British troops in 1916.

TANGANYIKA. The mainland of Tanzania (q.v.).

TANGANYIKA (tanganyē'ka). Lake in E Africa, in the Great Rift Valley, between Zaïre to the W and Tanzania and Burundi to the E. It is 772m (2,534 ft) a.s.l., the deepest lake in Africa (1,435 m/4,708 ft), and the mtns round its shores rise to some 2,700 m (9,000 ft). The chief ports are Bujumbura (Burundi), Kigoma (Tanzania), and Kalémié (Zaïre). It is *c.* 645km (400m) long; area 31,000 sq.km (12,700 sqm).

TANGERINE (-nj-). A type of orange (*Citrus reticulata*) similar to a mandarin.

TANGIER (tanjēr'). Free port (1962) and commercial city in Morocco, on the Straits of Gibraltar. Taken by the Portuguese in 1471, it passed to England in 1662 as part of the dowry of Catherine of Braganza, but was abandoned in 1684, becoming later a centre of Barbary pirates. A convention signed 1923, effective 1925, made T. and a small area behind it an international zone. Spain administered it 1940-5; in 1956 it was restored to independent Moroco. Pop. (1971) 215,500.

TANGO. A slow dance of African origin, in 2-4 time, resembling the Spanish Habanera.

TANGSHAN (tahngshan'). Industrial city in Hebei prov., China. Industries incl. steel, pottery, cement, etc., and power is supplied by local coal. In an earthquake in 1976, some 200,000 were killed, and T. is being rebuilt on a new site, coal seams being opened up under the old city. Pop. (1973) 1,000,000.

TANIZA'KI, Junichirô (1886-1965). Japanese novelist. B. in Tokyo, son of a family of printers, he was ed. at Tokyo Imperial Univ. His earlier work has a melodramatic and lurid quality, but after the earthquake of 1923 he moved to the Kyoto-Osaka region where ancient tradition is stronger, and his genius flowered. His books incl. a modernized version of *The Tale of Genji* (1939-41), *The Makioka Sisters* (3 vols., 1943-8), and *The Key* (1956).

TANK. Originally a code name given to the first successful tracked armoured fighting vehicle used in the battle of the Somme in 1916. A T. consists of a body or hull of thick steel, on which are mounted machine guns and a larger gun. The hull contains the crew (usually consisting of a commander, driver, and 2 or 3 men), engine, radio, fuel tanks, ammunition, etc. The T. travels on endless bands, or 'tracks', to traverse rough terrain. *See* SWINTON, SIR ERNEST.

TANKER. Ship with a tank for carrying mineral oil, liquefied gas, molasses, etc., in bulk.

TANNENBERG (tahn'nenberg). Village in Polish-occupied E Germany where in 1410 the Poles and Lithuanians defeated the Teutonic Knights, and in 1914 Hindenberg defeated the Russians.

TANNIC ACID or **tannin** ($C_{14}H_{10}O_9$). Astringent substance occurring in gall nuts, tree barks, and roots, fruits, etc. Its most important property is that of precipitating gelatin to give an insoluble compound, used in the manufacture of leather from hides.

TANNU-TUVA. *See* TUVA.

TANSY. Perennial plant (*Tanacetum vulgare*) in the family Compositae, found in Europe and naturalized in N America. The heads of yellow flowers grow in clusters, and the deeply indented leaves are used in cooking for their bitter flavour.

TA'NTALUM. Bluish-white metal, ductile and malleable, and resembling platinum when polished: symbol Ta, at. no. 73, at. wt. 180.95. Discovered in 1802 by Ekeberg, it occurs chiefly in the mineral tantalite. T. can be drawn into wire with a very high melting point and great tenacity (useful for filament lamps subject to vibration), and is used in alloys; for corrosion-resistant laboratory apparatus and chemical equipment; as a catalyst in the manufacture of synthetic rubber; in tools and instruments; as a getter in vacuum technique; and in rectifiers and capacitors. T. carbide is an important abrasive.

TA'NTALUS. In Greek mythology, a king who was punished in the underworld for his crimes by being tormented with hunger and thirst.

TANZANIA (tanzanē'a), **United Rep. of.** Country in E Africa, formed in 1964 by the union of Tanganyika and Zanzibar (q.v.).

The narrow coastal plain rises to a plateau with the mountain mass of Kilima-njaro ('shining mountain' because of the glaciers and perpetual snow which crown it) to the N and the Livingstone Mts to the SW. Kilima-njaro incl. two extinct volcanic craters, of which Kibo, the higher, rises to 5,895 m (19,340 ft), the highest mtn in Africa. Tanzania also incl. parts of Lakes Victoria and Tanganyika, and the Serengeti National Park has the greatest remaining concentration of plains game in Africa. Mainland crops incl. cotton, cashews, citrus, coffee, cocoa, maize, wheat, sugar, coconuts, and timber (hard and softwood). Mineral resources incl. gold and diamonds, coal and iron, cobalt, copper, mica, nickel and tin, and some offshore natural gas. The cap. is Dodoma, and the chief port Dar es Salaam; other towns incl. Tanga, Zanzibar Town, and the lake ports of Kigoma and Mwanza. Dar es Salaam is linked with the Zambian copperbelt by highway, and the Tanzara (formerly Tanzam) Rlwy.

During the F.W.W. Tanganyika (then part of German E Africa) was conquered from the Germans by Britain, and held as a League of Nations mandate (1921) and UN trusteeship (1946) until becoming an independent republic in 1962. The President (Julius Nyerere, succeeded by Ali Hassan Mwinyi 1985) is both head of state and of Govt., and the Tanganyika African Nat. Union (TANU) is the one party allowed. A policy of Ujamaa (familyhood) is being followed, the rural pop. being concentrated in groups of 250-600 families, working on common land, with common marketing organization, etc.

Area of T. 942,580 sq.km (373,700 sq.m); area of Tanganyika 939,340 sq.km (362,680 sq.m); pop. (1978) 17,552,000 (mainland 17,076,000). Swahili is the official language, with English as the second language. M.U.: Tanzanian shilling.

TANZANIA. At the port of Kilwa, the ruins of the capital of the Zenj Empire, which flourished in the 10-15th centuries, survive on an island in the bay. *Photo: Courtesy of the Royal Commonwealth Society*

TAOISM (tow'-izm or tah'-ō-izm). Chinese philosophical system and religion, said to have been founded by Lâo Tze probably in the 4th cent. BC. Tao, meaning 'road' or 'way', denotes the hidden Principle of the Universe. Less stress is laid on doing good deeds than on harmonious interaction with the environment.

TAORMINA (tah-awmē'na). Resort on the E coast of Sicily, Italy, at the foot of Mt Etna: there is an ancient Greek theatre. Pop. (1975) 8,500.

TAPE RECORDING, magnetic. Method of recording electric signals on a layer of iron oxide, or other magnetic material, coated on to thin plastic tape. The electrical impulses are fed to the electromagnetic recording head, which magnetizes the tape in proportion to the frequency and amplitude of the original signal, and may be audio (for sound recording), video (for television), or data (for computer).

For playback, the tape is passed over (the same or) another head to convert magnetic into electrical impulses, which are then amplified for reproduction. The higher the frequency to be recorded the faster the tape must be passed over the heads. Tapes are easily demagnetized (erased) for re-use, and come in cassette/cartridge form.

TAPESTRY. Ornamental textile used for wall-hangings, furniture, and curtains. The T. design is threaded into the warp, and various shades of wool are used. Many ancient peoples made Ts., and during the Dark Ages the art was practised in the monasteries. European Ts. of the 13th cent. were frequently ornamented with oriental designs brought back by the Crusaders. The great European centres of T. weaving were at Arras, Brussels, Aubusson, Beauvais, and Mortlake. The Gobelin T. factory of Paris was made a royal establishment in the 17th cent. In England, William Morris estab. the Merton Abbey looms in 1877. Many fine Ts. are still made in France, e.g. the tapestry designed by Graham Sutherland for Coventry cathedral which was made at Felletin, where Ts. have been woven since the 15th cent.

TAPESTRY. A fifteenth century French tapestry in the Cluny Museum in Paris, 'The Lady with the Unicorn'. In medieval belief the unicorn was a symbol of purity, what passed as material from its horn being used as a test of poison at the royal table. *Photo: Courtesy of the French National Tourist Office*

TAPE-WORM or **cestode.** Flat parasitic worm with no digestive organs. They have a complicated life-history, and usually reach man within imperfectly cooked meat or fish, causing anaemia and intestinal disorders.

TAPIŌ'CA. *See* CASSAVA.

TĀ'PIR. Genus of ungulate mammals (*Tapirus*), having a short trunk, thick hairy skin, and 4 toes on the front and 3 on the hind feet. The 4 S American species are black; the Malayan T. has white hindquarters.

TAR. A dark brown or black viscous liquid, obtained by the destructive distillation of coal, shale, wood, etc. From wood T., creosote and paraffin are produced. Ts. consist of hydrocarbons, acids, and bases. *See* COAL TAR.

TARA (tah'rah) **HILL.** Site in co. Meath, Rep. of Ireland, 155m (507ft), of a palace and coronation place of many kings of Ireland, abandoned in the 6th cent. St Patrick preached at T.

TARANA'KI (taranah'ki). Peninsula in North Island, NZ, dominated by Mt Egmont. The volcanic soil makes it probably the richest dairying region in the world, and it is noted for cheese. *See* NEW PLYMOUTH.

TARA'NTO. Seaport and naval base of Apulia, S Italy, on the Gulf of T., site of the ancient Greek Tarentum, founded by Sparta in the 8th cent. BC. In 1940 the Brit. Fleet Air Arm sank or severely damaged 6 Italian naval vessels during a night air-torpedo attack. Its steelworks is part of the new industrial complex of S Italy. Pop. (1979) 247,000.

TARANTULA. Poisonous spider (*Lycosa tarantula*) with a 2.5cm (1in) body, so named from its occurrence nr Taranto in Apulia, Italy. It spins no web, relying on its speed in hunting. In the Middle Ages its bite was thought to cause hysterical ailments for which dancing was the cure, hence the dance named tarantella.

TARBES (tahrb). Cap. of Hautes-Pyrénées dept, SW France, a tourist centre for the Pyrénées. It belonged to England 1360-1406. Théophile Gautier and Marshal Foch were b. at T. Pop. (1975) 57,800.

TARE. Another name for VETCH (q.v.).

TAREE. Town on the Manning r., NSW, Australia: a centre for dairy products. Pop. (1978) 14,000.

TARIM (tahrēm') **BASIN.** Internal drainage area in Xinjiang Uygur prov., NW China, between the Tyan Shan and Kunlun Mts. It is crossed by the Tarim He, and incl. Lop Nur. Area *c.* 900,000 sq.km (350,000 sq m).

TARKINGTON, Booth (1869-1946). American novelist. B. in Indiana, he won popularity with his romantic *Monsieur Beaucaire* (1900), and novels of the Middle West, e.g. *The Magnificent Ambersons* (1918).

TARN (tahrn). Fr. river, rising in the Cévennes and flowing 350km (220m) to the Garonne.

TARO (tah'rō), **cocco** or **eddoes.** Names given to a plant (*Colocasia antiquorum*) of the family Araceae, native to the South Seas: the tubers are eaten.

TAROT (tar'ō). Card game originating in Italy in the 14th cent. using 22 emblematic cards, e.g. the hanged man, and 56 numerals. The former have been used in fortune-telling only since the 18th cent.

TA'RPON. Large fish (*Megalops atlanticus*) found in the S Atlantic. It is *c.* 2m (6 ft) long.

TARQUINIUS (tahrkwin'ius) **SŪPE'RBUS.** The last king of Rome, who according to legend reigned 534-510 BC, and was expelled following the violation of Lucretia by his son Sextus.

TARRAGŌ'NA. Port in Catalonia, Spain, 88km (55m) SW of Barcelona. There is a cathedral, and Roman remains incl. an aqueduct. It is noted for wine, as a petrochemical centre and for electrical goods and pharmaceuticals. Pop. (1970) 78,250.

TARRASA (tahrah'sah). Town in NE Spain, NW of Barcelona. An agricultural centre: textiles and textile machinery, and fertilizers are made. Pop. (1970) 139,000.

TA'RSHISH. A city mentioned in the OT, probably the Phoenician settlement of Tartessus in Spain.

TA'RSIER. Small primate (*Tarsius spectrum*) intermediate on the evolutionary scale between lemurs and anthropoids. About the size of a rat, it has thick, light brown fur, very large eyes, and long feet and hands. Nocturnal and arboreal, it moves by leaping. It is found in the Malayan islands.

TARSUS. Town of Turkey. On the T. r., *c.* 16km (10m) from the sea. Cap. of the ancient Roman prov. of Cilicia, and famous as St Paul's birthplace, it was a meeting place for Greek and Asiatic culture. Pop. (1970) 78,000.

TARTAN. A worsted cloth woven in a chequered pattern, consisting of stripes of different colours and widths crossing one another. T. kilts and plaids were worn by the Scottish highlanders from the 15th cent., clans having distinctive patterns. After the 1745 rebellion the use of the T. was illegal until 1782.

TARTA'RIC ACID ($C_4H_6O_6$). Commonly occurring vegetable acid, present in fruit juices in the form of salts of potassium, calcium, and magnesium, and used in effervescent drinks and baking powders.

TARTARS. *See* TATARS.

TA'RTARUS. In Greek mythology, a part of the underworld where the wicked are punished.

TARTU (tahr'tōō). Town in Estonian SSR, on the Emback, said to date from 1030. It belonged to the Teutonic Knights until taken by Russia 1558; Poland and Sweden held it for periods, Russia recovering it in 1704. It has a univ. (1632) founded by Gustavus Adolphus of Sweden. Pop. (1973) 85,000.

TARZA'NA. Town in S California, USA, where Edgar Rice Burroughs, creator of Tarzan, once owned a ranch. It is today the HQ of the Tarzan enterprise.

TASHKE'NT. Cap. of Uzbek SSR, and of T. region, 255km (160m) N of Samarkand. Dating from the 7th cent., it became Russian in 1865. It has a univ., manufactures textiles, metal and leather goods, etc. Pop. (1979) 1,779,000 *Declaration of T.: see* KASHMIR.

TASMAN (tahs'mahn), **Abel Janszoon** (*c.* 1603-59). Dutch navigator. In 1642-3 he discovered Tasmania (which he called Van Diemen's Land in honour of the Gov.-Gen. of the Netherlands Indies, but was re-named Tasmania in 1853 in T.'s honour), New Zealand, and the Tonga and Fiji Islands.

TASMĀ'NIA. Smallest state of the Commonwealth of Australia, which comprises the is. of T. itself, a number of small is. in Bass Strait (incl. Bruny Is., the Furneaux group, Hunter Is. and King Is.), which separates it from the mainland of SE Australia, and also Macquarie Is. (*see* MACQUARIE, LACHLAN). The is. of T. is triangular in shape, and the interior is mountainous, rising to its highest point in Mt Ossa (q.v.). There are numerous lakes, e.g. Great Lake and Lake Sorell, and many rivers, incl. the Derwent, Huon, Gordon and Tamar, which are utilized for hydroelectric power. The climate is mild, with moderate rainfall, except in the mtns of the W where rainfall is heavy.

Wool from its fine flocks and dairy products are exported, and cereals, vegetables and fruit - Tasmanian apples from the orchards of the S are famous - are grown, and the forests provide timber and pulp for papermaking. Mineral wealth is varied, incl. coal and iron, silver and gold, and copper, lead and zinc, and metal refining is carried on. The cap. is Hobart, seat of T. univ. (1890), and Launceston is the chief port. Area of state 68,331 sq.km (26,383 sq.m); pop. (1976) 407,360. There are no Aboriginals, the last having d. in 1876.

Discovered by Tasman in 1642, T. was settled in 1803, and formed part of NSW until 1825. Responsible govt was introduced in 1856 and in 1901 T. joined the Commonwealth of Australia.

TASMANIAN DEVIL. Marsupial (*Sarcophilus ursinus*) found in Tasmania. Similar to a bear, it has dark brown fur with white patches on the chest and hind parts, and is nocturnal and carnivorous.

TASMANIAN DEVIL. Renowned for its ferocity, this marsupial is peculiar to Tasmania although fossil remains have been found on the mainland of Australia. *Photo: Courtesy of the Australian News and Information Bureau.*

TASMAN SEA. Area of the Pacific Ocean, lying between SE Australia and Tasmania to the W, and New Zealand to the E.

TASS. Soviet news agency: *T*elegrafnoye *A*gentstvo *S*ovyetskovo *S*oyuza.

TASSO (tahs'so), **Torquato** (1544-95). Italian poet. At first a law student at Padua, he was enabled to overcome his father's opposition to a literary career by the success of his romantic poem *Rinaldo* (1562), dedicated to Cardinal Luigi d'Este, who took him to Paris, where he met the members of the Pléiade (q.v.). Later he was under the patronage of the cardinal's brother, Duke Alfonso d'Este of Ferrara, for whose court theatre he wrote his pastoral play *Aminta* in 1573. His great work is his romantic epic of the First Crusade *La Gerusalemme Liberata* (1574: *Jerusalem Delivered*), much superior to the *Gerusalemme Conquistata*, written in the stress of mental instability and delusion which set in from 1576.

TATARS (tah'tahrz). Although sometimes loosely used to incl. other Turkic and Mongol peoples, the name applies more accurately to those speaking a language of the NW branch of Turkic. Mainly Moslem, they represent in the USSR, where they live mainly in the Tatar ASSR (cap. Kazan), but also in the Uzbek SSR (whence they were deported from the Crimea, q.v., in 1944) and SW Siberia, the remnant of the 'Mongol' invasion of the 13th cent. The Crimean Ts. (*c.* 400,000) agitated for the restoration of the Crimean ASSR 1957-72; those attempting to go back were returned to Central Asia.

TATE, Nahum (1652-1715). Irish poet. B. in Dublin, he wrote an adaptation of *King Lear,* to which he gave a happy ending, a version of the psalms, and hymns; his best-known poem is 'While shepherds watched'. He became poet laureate in 1692.

TATE, Phyllis (1911-). British composer. B. nr London, she studied at the Royal Academy of Music. Her principal works incl. *Concerto for Saxophone and Strings* (1944), the opera *The Lodger* (1957-8), based on the story of Jack the Ripper, and *Serenade to Christmas* for soprano, chorus and orchestra (1972).

TATE GALLERY. Art gallery at Millbank, London. It contains national collections of pictures and sculpture, those of the British school from the late 16th cent., and of modern foreign art from 1800. Built by the generosity of sugar-merchant Sir Henry Tate (1819–99), it was opened in 1897; later enlargements incl the Clore Gallery for Turner paintings 1983, and sculpture and 'new art' galleries to be built on an adjoining site. A 'Tate in the North' in Liverpool's Albert Docks is planned.

TATI (tahti'), **Jacques** (1908–82). French film director and actor, né Tatischeff. B. in Paris, he was the grandson of diplomat Count Dimitri Tatischeff. He created Hulot, embodiment of courteous opposition to modern mechanization, e.g. *Les Vacances de Monsieur Hulot*.

TATRA (tah'tra) **MTNS.** Section of the central Carpathians (q.v.) on the Czech/Polish frontier: the highest point is Gerlachovka 2,663 m (8,737 ft).

TATTERSALL'S. Bloodstock auctioneers estab. at Knightsbridge Green, SW London, since 1864. It is named after Richard T. (1724-95), who founded T. at Hyde Park Corner in 1766.

TATTING. Lace-work in cotton, etc., made by knotting with a small shuttle of ivory, metal, or - in the modern revival of this craft of medieval to Victorian times - plastic.

TATUM, E(dward) L(awrie) (1909-75). American microbiologist. *See* BEADLE, GEORGE WELLS.

TAUNTON. Market town in Somerset, England, admin. HQ of the co., 48km (30m) NE of Exeter. The Elizabethan hall survives in which Judge Jeffreys held his 'Bloody Assize' in 1685 after the Duke of Monmouth's rebellion. Pop. (1972) 38,300.

TAUNUS (taw'nus) **MTNS.** Range in Hesse, W Germany, rich in mineral springs, e.g. Homburg and Wiesbaden, and bounded by the Rhine, Main and Lahn.

TAUPO (taw'po). Largest lake in New Zealand, in a volcanic area of hot springs; area 616 sq.km (238 sq.m). It is the source of the Waikato.

TAURANGA (tow'ronga). Port in North Is., NZ, on the Bay of Plenty. Citrus, dairy produce and timber are exports from the surrounding area. Pop. (1975) 48,400.

TAURUS. Mt. range in S Asia Minor, forming the S edge of the Anatolian plateau, and rising to over 3,650 m (12,000 ft).

TAVERNER, John (*c.* 1495-1545). English composer. Organist at what was later Christ Church Coll., Oxford, he was imprisoned for heresy in 1530. Later, as an agent of Thomas Cromwell, he assisted in the dissolution of the monasteries. He wrote masses and motets, but as a Protestant renounced his art. *See* DAVIES, P.M.

TAVISTOCK. Market town in Devon, England, 24km (15m) N of Plymouth. Pop. (1971) 6,500.

TAXATION. The part of the national revenues raised by compulsory dues and charges, as distinct from that derived from public property. From the 19th cent. when govts came into existence based on a wide electorate and broadened the scope of legislation needing to be supported by T. (education, transport, defence, health, and social security) the scheme of T. became increasingly comprehensive, and by the mid-20th cent. T. was used by govts as a means of stimulating or restraining the national economy, or to modify the national life in any desired direction, e.g. the encouragement by reduction of T. of any type of manufacture or discouragement by heavy T. of consumption of any commodity. In newly emergent countries T., therefore, tends to be very light, because incomes are low and services, etc., undeveloped.

Direct taxes, which are for the most part graduated according to income, etc., are very widely used in the West; more expensive to collect because individually assessed, they compensate by being the most productive. Most important is *income tax,* collected by the Inland Revenue in Britain, as are the other direct taxes, i.e. *corporation tax* on company profits; *capital gains tax,* introduced to prevent the use of capital as untaxed income in 1961; and *capital transfer tax,* introduced in 1974 to replace estate duty on death (which had become known as a 'voluntary tax' because of the ease of avoidance by gifts during life, etc.) and covering all gratuitous transfers of capital both by lifetime gift and on death. A controversial proposal of the Labour govt in 1974-5 was the introduction of a *wealth tax* which, unlike those operating elsewhere in Europe and intended as supplementary to income tax, would be confiscatory in intention. Another form of direct T. is the rates (q.v.) collected by local authorities which are based on the value of buildings on a site: it has been suggested that these be replaced by a local (state) income tax as in the USA.

Indirect taxes, the most favoured method of T. in the USSR, incl. in Britain the taxes on tobacco, spirits, wine, beer, petrol (*see* CUSTOMS AND EXCISE); and *value-added tax* (VAT). The European Common Market adopted 1967 a VAT system based on the French TVA (Taxe sur la Valeur Ajoutée), and this was adopted in the UK in 1973 as a means of conforming with European practice. It is a tax paid on the value added to any goods or services at each particular stage of the process of production or distribution, and although collected from traders at each stage, it is in final effect a tax on consumers' expenditure. In the USA a sales tax is deducted by the retailer at the moment of sale to the customer.

Tax avoidance is legal, tax evasion is illegal, and tax avoision is sometimes used for the blurred area between.

TAXŌ'DIUM. Genus of trees in the family Taxodiaceae. The American deciduous cypress, *Taxodium distichum,* grows in or near water, and is a timber tree.

TAYLOR, Alan John Percivale (1906-). British historian. Lecturer in international history at Oxford 1953-63, he has made a popular as well as a scholarly reputation by such books as *From Napoleon to Stalin* (1956) and *The Origins of the Second World War* (1961), and by his lectures on TV.

TAYLOR, Elizabeth (1932-). British actress. Going to Hollywood, she estab. her position as the world's most highly paid actress with *A Place in the Sun* (1950), *Giant* (1956), *Butterfield 8* (1960), for which she gained an Academy Award, and *Cleopatra* (1963). She m. (1) Conrad Hilton, Jnr, (2) actor Michael Wilding - both being divorced - (3) impresario Mike Todd, killed in an air crash, (4) singer Eddie Fisher, (5) and (6) actor Richard Burton - a divorce intervening - and (7) John Warner, Rep. senator for Virginia. She became US citizen 1978.

TAYLOR, Jeremy (1613-67). Anglican divine. B. at Cambridge, he was deprived of his living by the Puritans in 1644, and thrice imprisoned as a royalist under the Commonwealth. His books incl. *Liberty of Prophesying* (1646), a defence of toleration, and *Holy Living* (1650) and *Holy Dying* (1651). He became bp of Down in 1661.

TAYLOR, Zachary (1784-1850). 12th President of the USA. B. in Virginia, he commanded the invasion of Mexico in 1846-7, and was elected president as a Whig in 1848.

TAYSIDE. Region of Scotland, created in 1975 from the former cos. of Angus, Kinross and the major part of Perthshire, except for the SW section incl. Ben More, the Trossachs and Callander, which became part of the Central region. It is traversed NW-SE by the **Tay** (Scotland's longest river, 188km/117m, and famous for its salmon) and its tributaries; and Dundee (admin. HQ) lies on the r. estuary. It incl. part of the Grampians, and lochs Tay and Rannoch to the NW, the Ochil and Sidlaw Hills to the SE, and the vales of the N and S Esk, and Barrie's birthplace at Kirriemuir, to the NE. Area 7,511 sq.km. (2,899 sq.m); pop. (1979) 400,451.

TBILISI (tbilyē'sē). Cap. of Georgian SSR, on the Kura, close to the foothills of the Caucasus. It dates back to the 5th cent. The seat of a univ., it manufactures textiles, machinery, ceramics, tobacco, etc. Pop. (1979) 1,066,000.

TCHAIKOVSKY (chīkov'ski), **Peter Ilyich** (1840-93). Russian composer. B. at Kamsko-Votinsk, he became a prof. of harmony at Moscow in 1865, and later met Balakirev and the nationalist circle. The 2nd symphony was performed in 1873, and the piano concerto in B flat minor in 1875. T. wrote several operas, incl. *Eugene Onegin*; ballet music, *The Swan Lake, The Sleeping Beauty,* and *The Nutcracker*; orchestral fantasies, *Romeo and Juliet, Francesca da Rimini,* and *Hamlet*; 3 piano concertos and a violin concerto; and chamber and vocal music. All these enjoy wide popularity, as do the 4th, 5th and 6th symphonies.

TEA. Plant (*Camellia sinensis*) from the leaves of which the beverage of the same name is made. Left to itself it reaches 12m (40ft), but is restricted in cultivation to bushes *c.* 1.5m (4ft) high from which at *c.* 5 yrs the young shoots and leaves are picked. After 24 hrs spread on shelves in the 'withering' lofts, the leaves are broken up by rolling machines, which release the essential oils, and allowed to ferment. This process is then halted by passing the leaves through ovens where moisture is removed and the blackish-brown T. emerges ready for sifting into the various grades.

Known in China as early as 2737 BC, T. was first brought to Europe in AD 1610, but was not in use in England until 1657. It rapidly became a fashionable drink but remained expensive because cargoes had to be brought from China in the specially fast T. clippers. In 1823, however, T. was found growing wild in northern India, and some 10 years later plantations were estab. in Assam and then in Sri Lanka: other modern producers incl. Africa, S America, Russia, Indonesia and Iran. Methods of consumption vary: in Japan special T. houses and an elaborate T. ceremony have evolved; in England 'afternoon' T. had its own ritual; and in Tibet hard slabs of compressed T. are used as money before being finally brewed. Tea bags, perforated sachets (made of paper with 'wet strength') enclosing specially fine tea, have become increasingly popular, but 'instant' tea never estab. itself.

TEA. Picking tea in China, the original home of the beverage, as the mist rises over the junks at sea in the early morning, and the dew is fresh on the plants. *Photo: Courtesy of the Society for Anglo-Chinese Understanding*

TEAK. Timber tree (*Tectona grandis*) grown in India, Burma, and Java. The wood is very hard and is used for shipbuilding.

TEAL. Small duck (*Anas crecca*). The drake has a reddish-brown head with green and buff markings on either side, and a black and white line on the wing. The female is buff and brown.

TEASEL. Species of plant (*Dipsacus fullonum*). It grows in waste places to a height of 2m (6ft). The purple flowers grow in an egg-shaped head, divided by hooked bracts. T. brushes are made from the heads.

TEBA'LDI, Renata (1922-). Italian soprano, remarkable for the controlled purity of her voice and excelling in roles from Puccini.

TEBBIT, Norman 1931- . British Cons. politician. A former RAF and civil airline pilot, when he held various trade union posts, he was Min. for Employment 1981–83, when his proposals for trade union reform met opposition, and for Trade and Industry from 1983.

TECHNETIUM. The first artificially made element (Gk *technetos,* artificial), symbol Tc, at. no. 43, at. wt. of most stable isotope 99. Originally produced by Perrier and Segré (California) in 1937 by bombarding molybdenum with deuterons or neutrons, it was later isolated in large amounts from the fission products of uranium and may have importance in alloys.

TECHNO'CRACY. Govt by technical experts. Certain contemporary writers, e.g. J. Burnham in *The Managerial Revolution,* have maintained that modern society is tending towards T.

TECHNOLOGY. The practical application of the arts and sciences in industry and commerce. Britain's industrial revolution preceded that of Europe by half a century, and her prosperity stimulated Continental countries to encourage technological education in order to emulate her. France estab. the École Polytechnique, the first technological univ., in 1794 and Germany founded the remarkable series of Technische Hochschulen with one in Berlin in 1799. In Britain education in T. was

TELECOMMUNICATIONS. British Telecom Internationals new Satellite Earth Station in London distributes broadcasts via satellite to cable television networks within the UK and across Europe. When completed, it will also be used to provide businesses with advanced digital communications services. Here, work is being carried out on Aerial 1 (*above left*), the Station is shown complete in the artist's impression (*lower left*), and (*right*) the latest generation of satellite in the Intelsat system. Intelsat V has a capacity of approximately 12,000 telephone channels plus two colour television channels. *Photo: British Telecom International.*

catered for by the mechanics institutes, notably the Univ. of Manchester Inst. of Science and T. (founded 1824, created univ. 1966) which, together with the Imperial College of Science and T. (estab. 1907), still form the focus of technological work. America was quick to grasp the importance of T., most of her univs. having schools of engineering and T., and also estab. a number of institutes on European lines of which the most famous are the Massachusetts (1861) and California Institutes of T. and the Rensselaer Polytechnic Institute (founded at Troy, NY, in 1824). The mass production of technologists, exceeding the pace of both western Europe and the USA, has been concentrated upon by the Soviet Union and increasingly by China.

TECUMSEH (tekum'se) (1768-1813). Shawnee Indian chief. He attempted to unite all the Red Indian tribes into a confederation, and was killed while fighting the Americans as an ally of the British.

TEDDER, Arthur William, 1st baron (1890-1967). Marshal of the Royal Air Force. He was Air Officer Commanding RAF Far East 1936-8, and Middle East 1941-3, where his method of pattern bombing known as 'Tedder's carpet' became famous. As Deputy Supreme Commander under Eisenhower 1943-5, he was largely responsible for the initial success of the 1944 Normandy landings.

TEDDINGTON. Part of Twickenham, in the Greater London bor. of Richmond upon Thames. T. Lock, 119km (74m) upstream, is the highest point reached by the tide. The National Physical Laboratory (1900) is at T.

TEES. River, rising in Cumbria, England, which flows 130km (80m) to reach the North Sea via Tees Bay in Cleveland, a new co. created in 1974 to take in the highly industrialized area of its lower reaches, incl. Stockton on Tees, Thornaby, Middlesbrough and Billingham.

TEESSIDE. The industrial area at the mouth of the r. Tees, Cleveland, England. Traditional shipbuilding and heavy engineering have made way for high technology, capital intensive steelmaking (Redcar has Europe's largest steel complex, 1979); Europe's biggest chemical site (ICI); a massive oil fuel terminal at Seal Sands; and the main North Sea natural gas terminal. Middlesbrough is a major port.

TEETH. Hard structures within the mouth, growing from each jaw in 2 semicircular rows and meeting (occlusion) in the act of biting. The first set, the milk teeth, appear from age 6 months to 2½ yrs, and number 20. The permanent dentition replaces these from the 6th year onwards, the wisdom teeth (3rd molars) sometimes not appearing until the age 25 or 30. It consists of 32 teeth: 2 incisors, 1 canine (eye tooth), 2 premolars, and 3 molars on each side of each jaw. A tooth is made of bony substance called dentine. It has a root or roots set in a socket of fine bone (alveolus), a neck covered by gum, and a crown covered with hard white enamel. It is hollow and filled with a highly sensitive pulp made of nerves and blood vessels. The chief diseases of teeth are misplacements resulting from defect or disturbance of the tooth-germs before birth; eruption out of the proper places; caries (decay), and pyorrhoea.

TEGUCIGALPA (tāgoos'igahl'pa). Cap. of Honduras 975m (3,200 ft) a.s.l. on the S central plateau. Formerly famous for its gold and silver mines, it is now a commercial and industrial centre, with textile industries and food processing plant. Pop. (1974) 267,755.

TEHRAN (tārahn'). Cap. of Iran, 96km (60m) S of the Caspian Sea, a univ. city, centre of communications, and with textile, chemical, engineering, tobacco and other industries. In 1943 T. was the scene of the first meeting between Stalin, Roosevelt and Churchill. Pop. (1976) 4,500,000.

TEIGNMOUTH (tin'muth). Coastal centre and port in S Devon, England, on the Teign estuary with fine Georgian architecture. Pop. (1974) 12,700.

TEILHARD DE CHARDIN (tāyahr de zhahrdiṅ'), **Pierre** (1881-1955). French mystic and palaeontologist. B. in the Puy-de-Dôme, of well-to-do parents, he entered the Society of Jesus in 1899, was ordained in 1911, and during the F.W.W. was a stretcher bearer, taking his final vows in 1918. His books on philosophical themes were not allowed to be pub. by his superiors as they seemed to tend to pan-psychism. He attempted to relate psychic and physical energy, and evolved his concept of the *noosphere* - the union of thought of human beings.

TE KA'NAWA, Kiri (*c.* 1947-). New Zealand soprano. B. in Gisborne, of a European mother and Maori father, she was adopted as an infant, and m. an Australian, Desmond Park. Her reputation was estab. by her performance as the Countess in *The Marriage of Figaro* at Covent Garden in 1971.

TEKTITE (tek'tīt). Small, rounded glassy stone (from Gk *tektos* 'molten'), found in certain regions of Earth, espec. Australasia. They are thought to be the scattered drops of molten rock thrown out by the impact of a large meteorite or comet, or more probably, launched by a volcanic explosion on the Moon.

TEL AVIV-JAFFA (avēv'). City in Israel, on the Mediterranean, NW of Jerusalem. Textiles, sugar, chemicals are made; printing and publishing are important. T.A. (founded 1909) was combined with Jaffa (q.v.) 1949: their sister ports were superseded by Ashdod 1965. Pop. (1978) 348,100.

TELECOMMUNICATIONS (Gk *tele*, afar). The first apparatus used for communication over a distance, apart from such devices as semaphore, heliograph, etc., was the *telegraph.* The earliest practicable instrument was invented by Cooke and Wheatstone in 1837, and used by railway cos., the first public line being laid between Paddington and Slough in 1843. Morse invented a signalling code (still used), and a recording telegraph, first used commercially between England and France in 1851. As a result of Hertz's discoveries using electromagnetic waves, Marconi estab. wireless communication between England and France (1899) and across the Atlantic (1901). Today the keyboard-operated teleprinter is supplemented by the facsimile machine linked to the telephone: *see* POST OFFICE.

The *telephone* was invented in 1876 by Alexander Graham Bell, as a result of Faraday's discovery of electromagnetism. Transmission is by cable and microwave radio, and overseas, where the curvature of the Earth otherwise presents problems, by satellite.

This solution was outlined in 1945 by Arthur C. Clarke in *Wireless World,* when he proposed the modern system of international communications satellites (comsats), also sometimes called synchronous satellites (syncoms) or geostationary satellites, because when in orbit they have the same speed as the Earth and so remain over the same place. The first to be successfully launched, by Delta rocket from Cape Canaveral, was Syncom 2 on 26 July 1963. Numbers of such satellites are now in use, concentrated over heavy traffic areas such as the Atlantic, Indian and Pacific Oceans. Telephony and television transmissions are carried simultaneously, and as the satellite spins clockwise to maintain stability, the antenna (which enables the satellite to receive and transmit signals) spins anti-clockwise at the same speed, so keeping it always pointed towards Earth in the correct communications position. Procedure, technical standards, frequencies, etc., are controlled by the International Telecommunications Union (ITU). The number of Earth stations continually increases, Etam, USA, and Goonhilly, q.v., being noted for research.

In 1980 the PO opened its first System X (all electronic, digital) telephone exchange in London, a method already adopted in the USA, and copper core cables for transmitting calls were due to be replaced by a beam of laser light passing through a fine glass fibre.

TELEGAMES. *See* VIDEOGAMES.

TEL EL AMARNA. *See* AMARNA TABLETS.

TELE'PATHY (Gk for 'feeling from afar'). The term was coined by F. W. H. Myers who defined it as 'the communication of impressions of any kind from one mind to another, independently of the recognized channels of sense'. The card-guessing experiments of Prof. J. B. Rhine (q.v.) of Duke univ., N Carolina, in the 1930s, considered to have proved the phenomenon, were under suspicion in the 1980s. In the USSR, experiments have been made with T. as a means of communication between astronauts.

TE'LESCOPE. An instrument for magnifying distant objects optically, and - in astronomy - for collecting various other kinds of data from space. Types of T. are: 1) *optical,* first developed by Lippershey in 1608, and consisting basically of an object-glass (a lens or concave mirror to collect and focus light) and an eyepiece for magnifying this image. The world's largest is the 610 cm (240 in) reflector at the Special Astrophysical Observatory on Mt. Pastukhov, N Caucasus, USSR. The distorting effects of the atmosphere will be avoided by the Large Space T. (LST) (254 cm/100 in) to be launched by NASA into orbit round the Earth in 1983. 2) *infra-red,* which detects any fractional heating of matter above absolute zero, and can detect black holes, or record the birth of new stars. The largest is the British instrument (1979) on Hawaii. 3) *radio,* which can pick up and analyse radio waves from space, and first detected pulsars and quasars. These may take specialised forms, such as the radioheliograph (1966) for Sun research invented by Englishman, Paul Wild, and erected at Narrabri, N of Sydney. It was used to forecast dangerous solar and cosmic radiation for American astronauts on Apollo flights. The world's largest radio T. was built in New Mexico USA, 1977. 4) *ultra violet,* which pick up radiation in the range between ordinary light and X-rays, and enable the distribution of chemical elements in the Universe to be charted. 5) *X-ray,* which have to be placed aboard a balloon, rocket or satellite to be beyond the range of atmospheric absorption, and which pick up the X-ray activity of black holes, quasars, etc. In 1979 satellite

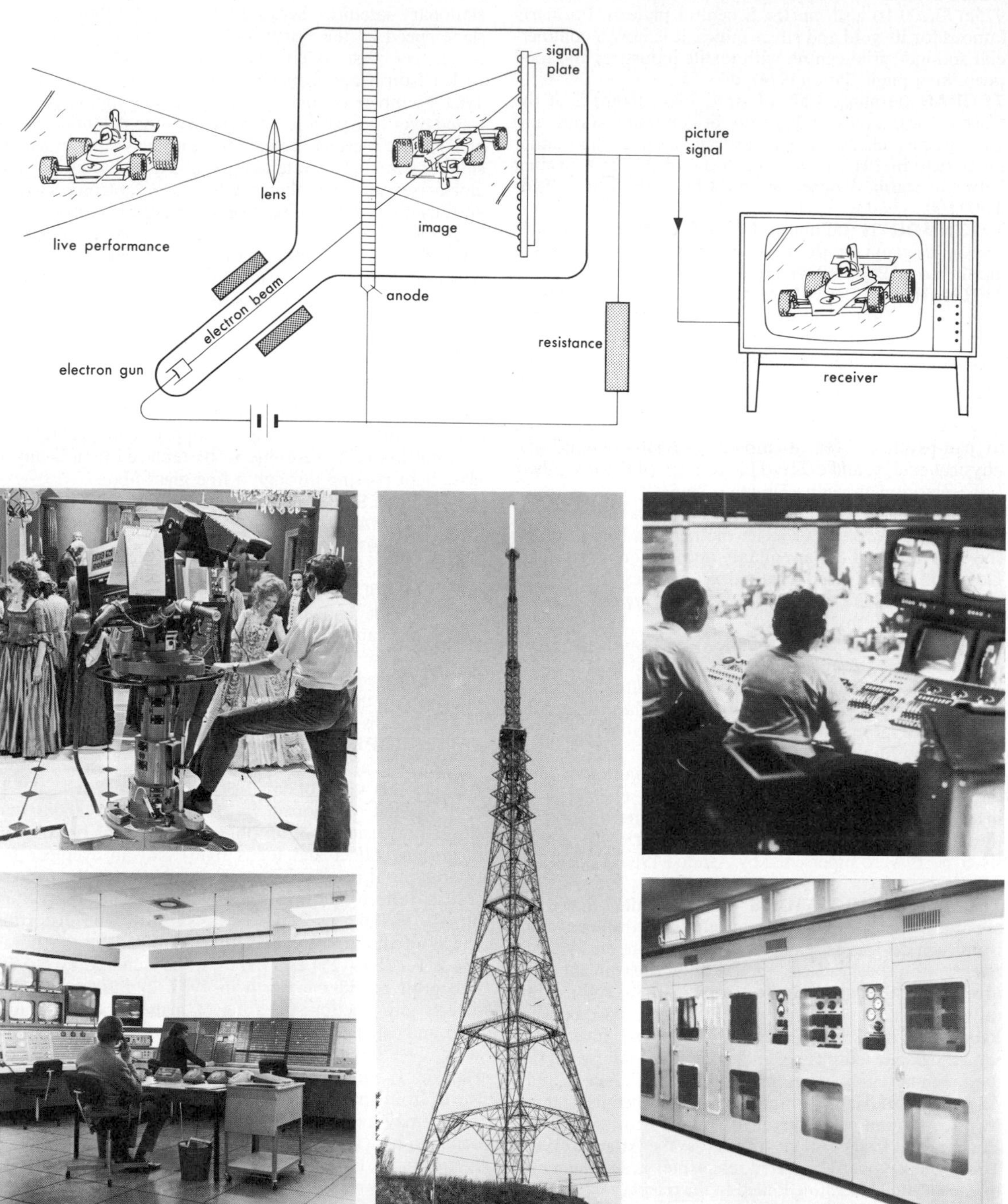

TELEVISION. Above, a simplified diagram of the way in which the television picture passes through the eye of the camera to the home television screen. Below, other links in the complex chain which brings the programme to the viewer: (top left) Norma Streader and Angharad Rees rehearse the ball scene in *Poldark*; (top right) the production gallery; (bottom left) switching control for radio and television networks at Pebble Mill, Birmingham; (bottom right) the vision transmitter - the final radio frequency stage is grid-modulated and is capable of a peak power output of approx. 40 kw; (centre) the tower and transmitting aerial system (with VHF extension) at the Crystal Palace station. *Photos: Courtesy of the BBC*

Einstein (USA) carried the first high resolution imaging X-ray T. to be placed into orbit round Earth.

TELETEXT. Broadcast system of displayed information on the nation's television screens (entertainment, sport, finance, etc.) which is constantly updated, e.g. CEEFAX (q.v.) and ORACLE (ITV). *See also* VIEWDATA.

TELETEXT. A sub-editor of Ceefax operates one of the visual display unit keyboards. The screen shows the 'page' as it is received in the viewer's home. *Photo: BBC.*

TELEVISION. The reproduction at a distance by radio waves of visual images. In 1873 it was realized that since the electrical properties of selenium vary according to the amount of light to which it is exposed, light could be converted into electrical impulses, making it possible to transmit such impulses over a distance and then re-convert them into light. The chief difficulty was seen to be the 'splitting of the picture' so that the infinite variety of light and shade values might be transmitted and reproduced. In 1908 Campbell-Swinton pointed out that the transmission and reception would be better done by the use of cathode-ray tubes. Mechanical devices were used at the first practical demonstration of actual television, given by J. L. Baird in London on 27 Jan. 1926, and cathode-ray tubes used experimentally by the BBC from 1934. The world's first public T. service was started from the BBC station at the Alexandra Palace, in N London, on 2 Nov. 1936. Both sound and vision programmes are received on the same aerial. The vision programme is taken to the vision receiver, at whose output end is a cathode-ray tube whose flattened end constitutes the viewing screen. The minute currents set up by the incoming vision signals are magnified in order to bring them up to a workable strength. The end of the tube, upon which the scene is to appear, has its inside surface coated with a fluorescent material which is bombarded by a stream of electrons emitted by a gun in the neck; light is thereby produced; a separate signal being used to control brightness. The resulting light and shade patterns give an effective reproduction of the original scene. This is built up by an electronic beam tracing out half the lines in the picture (625 in the UK and the Continent, 525 in the USA and Japan) 50 or 60 times per sec, then going back to the top of the screen to trace out the rest. The 2 halves are then interleaved (interlaced scanning).

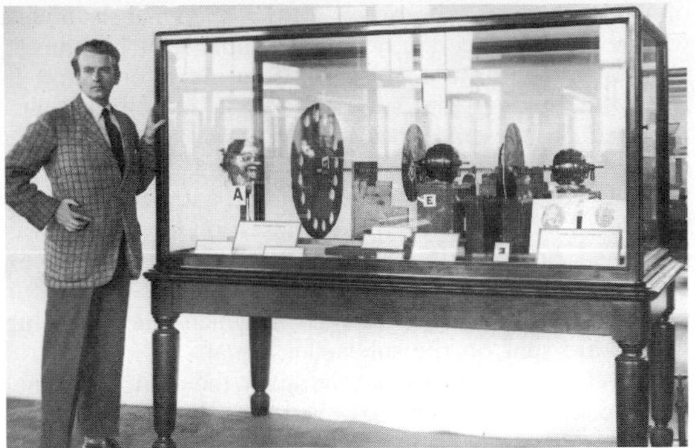

TELEVISION. J.L.Baird, the British pioneer of television, photographed in 1926 with the apparatus with which he successfully demonstrated the world's first instantaneous living moving scenes by wire and wireless. *Photo: Popperfoto*

For colour T. the scene to be transmitted is similarly analysed by the T. camera into a large number, 625, of horizontal lines and the information along each line is transmitted in sequence. In black and white T. it is only the brightness of each part of the line which is important. In colour T. it is necessary to measure the characteristics of the colour at every point along each scanning line, to transmit signals which are a measure of these characteristics, and at the receiver to build up a colour picture based on these signals.

Baird gave a demonstration of colour T. in London in 1928, but it was not until Dec. 1953 that the first successful system was adopted for broadcasting, in the USA. This is called the NTSC system, since it was developed by the National Television System Committee, and variations of it have been developed in Europe, e.g. SECAM (sequential and memory) system in France and the PAL (phase alternation by line) in W Germany. All 3 differ only in the way colour signals are prepared for transmission. Agreement on a universal European system failing in 1964, the UK in 1967 adopted PAL (as did W Germany, Netherlands and Switzerland) and France and the USSR adopted SECAM.

The method of colour reproduction is related to that used in painting, colour photography and printing. Just as the artist uses a palette with only a few basic colours which he combines to form a full range of hues in his picture, so in colour T. the receiver reproduces only three basic colours: red, green and blue. The effect of yellow, for example, is reproduced by combining equal amounts of red and green lights, while white is imitated by a mixture of all 3 basic colours. It is then possible to specify the colour which it is required to transmit by sending signals which indicate the amounts of red, green and blue lights which are to be generated at the receiver.

To transmit each of these 3 signals in the same way as the single brightness signal in black and white T. would need 3 times the normal bandwidth, and reduce the number of possible stations and programmes to one-third of that possible with monochrome T. The 3 signals are therefore coded into one complex signal which is transmitted as a more or less normal black and white signal, and which produces a satisfactory - or compatible - picture on ordinary black and white receivers. A fraction of each primary red, green and blue signal is added together to produce the normal brightness, or luminance signal. The minimum of extra colouring information is then sent by a special subcarrier signal which is superimposed on the brightness signal. This extra colouring information corresponds to the hue and saturation (*see* COLOUR) of the transmitted colour, but without any of the fine detail of the picture. The impression of sharpness is conveyed only by the brightness signal, the colouring being added as a broad colour wash. The various colour systems differ only in the way in which the colouring signals are sent on the subcarrier signal.

The colour receiver has to amplify the complex signal and decode it back to the basic red, green and blue signals; these primary signals are then applied to a colour cathode-ray tube. The colour display tube is the heart of any colour receiver. Many designs of colour picture tube have been invented and the most successful of these is known as the shadow mask tube. It operates on similar electronic principles to the black and white T. picture tube, but the screen is composed of a fine mosaic of over one million dots arranged in an orderly fashion. One-third of the dots glow red when bombarded by electrons, one-third glow green and one-third blue. There are 3 sources of electrons, respectively modulated by the red, green and blue signals. The tube is so arranged that the shadow mask itself shadows the green and blue glowing dots from the red electrons, and so on. The glowing dots are so small that from a normal viewing distance the colours merge into one another and a picture with a full range of apparent colours is seen.

By the 1980s the original broadcasting stations had diversified into video systems (q.v.); subscription services, incl. a viewer 'response' button to cut off unpopular performers, as in the Qube system in the USA; cable television; and direct broadcasting by satellite (DBS), for which the viewer requires a 'dish' antenna, receiver, amplifier, and a de-scrambler. *See* TELECOMMUNICATIONS.

TELFORD, Thomas (1757-1834). Scottish civil engineer. A shepherd's son, and erstwhile poet, mason and surveyor, he opened up N Scotland by building new roads; constructed many aqueducts and canals incl. the famed Caledonian (1803-23); and erected the Menai bridge on the suspension principle, scarcely tried previously in England. In 1963 the New Town of T., 32km (20m) NW of Birmingham in E Salop, was named after him; it has iron and engineering works, and the Ironbridge Gorge Museum of Industrial Archaelogy is nearby. Pop. (1975) 94,000.

TELL, William. Swiss hero, who is said to have been sentenced, for refusing to salute the Habsburg badge, to shoot an apple off his son's head. Having accomplished this, he shot the tyrannical Austrian ruler. This story has no historical basis, but the legendary setting is Altdorf, at the head of Lake Lucerne.

TELLŪ'RIUM. Silver-white, brittle, semi-metallic element of the sulphur group, discovered by Müller von Richtenstein in 1782 and named by Klaproth in 1798 from Lat. *tellus,* earth; symbol Te, at. no. 52, at. wt. 127.61. It is used in colouring glass (blue to brown) and in the electrolytic refining of zinc. Its strength and hardness are greatly increased by addition of 0.1 per cent lead, when it is used for pipes and cable sheaths.

TEMA (tā'ma). Port in Ghana, E of Accra, in the Accra/Tema city area. Opened 1962, it superseded the 'surf' ports at Accra, Cape Coast, etc., and has oil refineries and a fishing industry.

TEMPERA. A method of painting in which a gelatinous substance is employed. A form of T. was used in ancient Egypt, and by many Italian masters.

TEMPERATURE. The state of hotness or coldness of a body (in degrees Centigrade officially from 1948 called Celsius - or Fahrenheit) and the condition which determines whether or not it will transfer heat to, or receive heat from, another body according to the laws of thermodynamics (q.v.). The normal temperature of the human body taken in the mouth is 36.8°C (98.4°F). Variation by more than a degree or so indicates ill-health, a rise signifying excessive activity (usually due to infection), and a decrease signifying deficient heat production (usually due to lessened vitality). To convert °C to °F multiply by 9/5 and add 32 (below 32°F subtract 32); °F to °C subtract 32 then multiply by 5/9. A useful quick approx. for converting °C to °F is to double the Centigrade and add 30, e.g. 12°C = 24 + 30 = 54°F.

TEMPLARS. A religious order, founded in 1119, of knights who took vows of poverty, chastity, and obedience and devoted themselves to the recovery of Palestine from the Saracens. They played a distinguished part in the Crusades of the 12th and 13th cents. The enormous wealth of the order aroused the envy of Philip IV of France, who arranged for charges of heresy to be brought against its members in 1307, and the order was suppressed.

TEMPLE, Shirley (1928-). American film star. B. in Santa Monica, Calif., she became the singing and dancing star of many films incl. *Bright Eyes* (1934), in which she sang 'On the Good Ship Lollipop', and received a special Academy Award the same year. As Shirley T. Black, she was active in the Rep. party, and was US Chief of Protocol 1976-7.

TEMPLE, Sir William (1628-99). English statesman. He had a distinguished diplomatic career, and negotiated the Triple Alliance with Holland and Sweden in 1668, and the marriage of Princess Mary to William of Orange in 1677. After 1681, disapproving of Charles II's policy, he retired to Moor Park, Surrey, where he wrote his attractive essays.

TEMPLE, William (1881-1944). British churchman. Son of Frederick T. (1821-1902), liberal theologian and abp of Canterbury 1896-1902, he won a high reputation for his application of Christian beliefs to social matters. He was abp of York 1929-42 and of Canterbury 1942-4, and wrote *Christianity and the State* (1928) and *Nature, Man and God* (1934), more influential than intellectually sound.

TEMPLE. A group of buildings S of Fleet St, London, which formed the English headquarters of the Templars 1185-1313, and since the 14th cent. has been occupied by 2 of the Inns of Court, the Inner T. and the Middle T. The round church, built 1185, bombed 1941, was restored 1958.

TEMPLE. The centre of Jewish national worship at Jerusalem. Three Ts. occupied the site: Solomon's T., which was destroyed by Nebuchadrezzar; Zerubbabel's T., built after the return from Babylon; and Herod's T., which was destroyed by the Romans in AD 70. The Mosque of Omar occupies the site. The Wailing Wall is the surviving part of the western wall of the platform of the enclosure of the T. of Herod, so-called by tourists because of the oriental chanting style of the Jews in their prayers there. Under Jordanian rule Jews had no access to the spot, but took this part of the city in the 1967 campaign.

TEMPLE BAR. Western gateway of the City of London, England, standing between Fleet St and the Strand. Rebuilt by Wren in 1672, it was removed in 1878 to Theobold's Park, Herts. The heads of traitors were formerly displayed on spikes on T.B. A figure of a griffin marks the site.

TEMPLER, Sir Gerald (1898-1979). British field marshal. He served in both world wars, but is especially remembered for his work as High Commissioner in Malaya 1952-4, following the assassination of his predecessor, Sir Henry Gurney, when he won the war against the Communist guerrillas.

TENCH. Freshwater fish (*Tinca tinca*). A member of the carp family, it is *c.* 45cm (18in) long, olive-green above and grey beneath. The scales are small, and there is a barbel at each side of the mouth.

TENERIFE (tenerif'). The largest of the Canary Islands (q.v.), Spain. Santa Cruz is the main town, and Pico de Teyde is an active volcano. Area 2,060 sq.km (795 sq.m).

TENG HSIAO-PING. *See* DENG XIAOPING.

TENIERS (tenērs'), **David** (1582-1649), the Elder. Flemish painter. B. at Antwerp, he studied under Rubens and Elsheimer, and painted scenes of everyday life in Flanders. His son, **David T.** (1610-90) the Younger, was influenced by Rubens and Brouwer, became court painter to Archduke Leopold William, and is considered the finest of Flemish genre painters.

TENNESSEE (tenesē'). S central state of the USA, having the Unaka and Great Smoky mountains (part of the Appalachians) as its E boundary, and the Mississippi as the W. The T. river waters the valley between the Appalachians and the Cumberland plateau, and re-enters the W of the state, joining the Ohio in Kentucky: length 1,050 km (652m). The **Tennessee Valley Authority** (TVA), estab. by Act of Congress 1933, is charged with development of the river system for navigation, flood control, and generation of hydroelectric power. In the N, the Cumberland is the main river. Lumbering is important, and maize, wheat, cotton, tobacco are grown. Coal, zinc, pyrites and phosphate are among minerals worked, and there are iron and steel and chemical industries. Research centres incl. Oak Ridge (q.v.) and the Arnold Engineering Development Centre for aircraft. The cap. is Nashville, the largest town Memphis. Area 109,412 sq.km (42,244 sq.m); pop. (1970) 3,924,164.

TENNIEL (ten'i-el), **Sir John** (1820-1914). British humorous artist. B. in London, he joined *Punch* in 1850, and for over 50 years he was a leading cartoonist on that magazine. He illustrated *Alice in Wonderland* and other books.

TENNIS. An ancient game played by the English and French aristocracy from the 14th cent. It is now called Royal, Court, Lord's, or Real T. It is played indoors on a court bisected by a net. Inlet into each end and one side of the court is a sloping roof, against which the ball may be hit. *See* LAWN TENNIS.

TENNYSON, Alfred, 1st baron (1809-92). British poet. B. at Somersby, Lincs, he was ed. at Trinity Coll., Cambridge, where he became the friend of A. H. Hallam. In 1827 he pub. *Poems, by Two Brothers,* written with Charles T. (1808-79), and in 1830 *Poems, chiefly Lyrical.* His full power emerged in the *Poems* of 1832. The death of Hallam in 1833 inspired the *In Memoriam,* not published until 1850. A further vol. of *Poems* appeared in 1842, and the less successful *Princess* in 1847. In 1850 T. m. Emily Sellwood, and succeeded Wordsworth as poet laureate. *Maud* followed in 1855, and the series of Arthurian legends *The Idylls of the King* appeared 1857-85. Among the later vols. are *Enoch Arden* (1864), *Lucretius* (1868), *The Revenge* (1878), *Ballads and other Poems* (1880), *Tiresias* (1885), *Demeter* (1889), and *The Death of Oenone* (1892). He also wrote verse dramas, the most successful being *Becket* (1884). In 1884 T. was raised to the peerage. He was buried in Westminster Abbey. His poetry is characterized by craftsmanship and musical utterance. His brother Charles T. (1808-79) adopted the additional surname of Turner in 1830, and is remembered for his fine sonnets.

TENPIN BOWLING. A game of very early origin, said to have been taken to the USA by Dutch settlers in the 17th cent. Modern bowling lanes measure 18.30m (60ft) to the nearest pin and have an extra 4.57m (15ft) approach area; they are 1m (3ft 6in) wide. Balls weighing up to 7.25kg (16lb) are made of rubber composition and drilled with holes for thumb and two fingers. Pins made of maple are 38.1cm (1ft 3in) high. The game is usually between two players or teams of 3, 4, or 5 players a side. A game of tenpins is made up of 10 'frames'. The frame is the bowler's turn to play and in each frame he may bowl twice. He scores one point for each pin knocked down, with bonus points for knocking all ten pins down in either one ball or two. The player or team making the greater score wins.

The US National Bowling Association was formed in 1875. The game, in its modern form, has found considerable popularity in Britain.

TEPLICE. Industrial city and spa in Czechoslovakia 16km (10m) W of Usti. Peat and lignite are mined, glass, porcelain, cement, paper, etc., made. Its springs give warm radioactive water. Goethe and Beethoven met at T. in 1812. Pop. (1970) 53,000.

TEQUILA (tekēl'a). Alcoholic drink made in Mexico from the agave (q.v.). It is a more sophisticated version, prepared by the conquistadors, of the native Aztec pulque, and was named from the place, *c.* 55km (35m) from Guadalajara, where it was first made.

TE'RATORN. Group of extinct birds (Gk 'wonder bird'), which incl. the largest known flying bird, of which the fossilised bones (5-8 million years old) were found in Argentina in 1980. It measured 3.3 m (11 ft) from beak to tail, had a 7.6 m (25 ft) wingspan, and weighed 75 kg (12 stone.)

TERBIUM. A metallic element, symbol Tb, at. no. 65, at. wt. 158.93. It is one of the group of rare earths.

TER BORCH (ter borkh), **Gerard** (1617-81). Dutch painter. B. at Zwolle, the son of a painter, he came under the influence of Frans Hals, visited England, and painted studies of refined Dutch life, e.g. 'A Lady at Her Toilet' in the Wallace Collection.

TERE'DO. The shipworm *(Teredo),* a bivalve mollusc which uses the valves of its shell to rasp tunnels through timber. A scourge in the days of wooden sailing ships, its activities are now mainly limited to harbour works of timber construction.

TERENCE (Publius Terentius Afer) (*c.* 190-159 BC). Roman dramatist. B. at Carthage, he was brought to Rome as a slave. After receiving his freedom he devoted himself to literature, and enjoyed the patronage of Scipio. His surviving 6 comedies, mostly imitated from Greek models, are distinguished for their subtle characterization and purity of style.

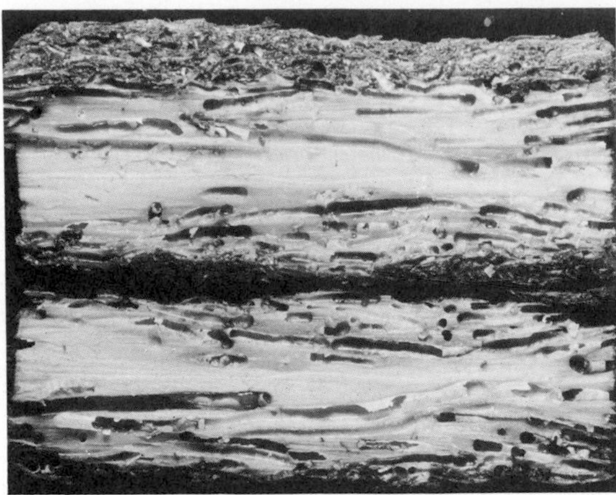

TEREDO. Timber affected by *Teredo navalis*. A jetty pile has here been split open, and a live 'worm' can be seen (upper left), its shells open, ready for the next bite. *Photo: Douglas P. Wilson*

TERMITE. The mounds of magnetic termites in northern Australia reach some 5 m(15ft), and are aligned north/south. In this way they are spared the burning heat of the mid-day sun, but the broad sides of the nest catch the warmth in early morning and evening. *Photo: Richard Harrington/Camera Press*

TERESA, St (1515-82). Spanish mystic. B. at Avila, she entered a Carmelite nunnery, and in 1562 founded a new and stricter order. She was subject to fainting fits, during which she claimed to see visions. She wrote *The Way to Perfection*, and an autobiography. In 1622 she was canonized and became the first woman 'Doctor of the Church' in 1970.

TERMITES. Soft-bodied insects forming the order Isoptera, also known as white ants. They are different in structure and metamorphosis from ants, but are social in habit, often building huge nests or *termitaria*. There are 5 chief castes or types, comprising 2 sterile forms and 3 reproductive forms. In the chief reproductive caste both males and females are winged; other reproductive members are short-winged or wingless. The sterile castes are wingless and are divided into *soldiers* which defend the colony, and *workers* which construct the termitarium and provide food. Ts. feed largely on wood and do much damage in tropical and sub-tropical countries.

TERN. Genus of sea-birds (*Sterna*). Of the 8 species, 5 breed in Britain. They are characterized by long wings and a forked tail. The underparts are white or grey and the crown of the head black.

TE'RRA CO'TTA. A form of baked clay used in building, sculpture, and pottery. It was first employed in ancient countries where there was no stone available. The term is specifically applied to small figures or figurines, e.g. those found at Tanagra (q.v.).

TE'RRAPIN. Name commonly given to fresh-water members of the tortoise order. The diamond back T., a N American coastal species, is considered a delicacy.

TERRE HAUTE (tera hōt'). City in Indiana, USA, on the Wabash r., SW of Indianapolis. Plastics, chemicals, glass, etc. are made. Pop. (1970) 70,300.

TERRIER. Group of dogs formerly used in hunting rabbits and game. Small and fleet-footed, they are highly intelligent. They incl. the bull, Cairn, fox, Irish, Scottish, sealyham, Skye and Yorkshire terriers.

TERRITORIAL ARMY. Created in Britain as the T. Force (1908) from volunteer regiments formally incorporated in 1872, it was raised and admin. by County Associations and intended primarily for home defence: it was renamed T.A. in 1922. Merged with the Regular Army in the S.W.W., it was revived 1947, but replaced 1967 by a smaller, more highly trained Territorial and Army Volunteer Reserve, again re-named T.A. in 1979.

TERRORISM. The use of systematic violence espec. by small groups to further political aims. The most notorious incl. **Baader-Meinhof group** originating in W Germany (so-called after its leading members Andreas Baader and Ulrike Meinhof, but calling itself Red Army Faction) and active from 1968 - Ulrike Meinhof committed suicide in 1976 during her trial in Stuttgart; **Black September** (named from the month in 1970 when guerrillas active in Jordan were suppressed by the Jordanian army), who massacred 11 Israelis at the Munich Olympic Games in 1972 (*see* PALESTINE); **Irish Republican Army** (q.v.); **Quebec Liberation Front,** who kidnapped and killed minister Pierre Laporte in Canada in 1970; **Symbionese Liberation Army** (named from 'symbiosis', the living together of two different organisms for mutual benefit) who kidnapped Patricia Hearst, grand-dau. of W. R. Hearst (q.v.) in 1974; **Tupamaros** who kidnapped British ambassador Sir Geoffrey Jackson in Uruguay 1971.

By 1980 such predominantly left-wing organisations had their right-wing counterparts, responsible for the assassination of Archbishop Romero in El Salvador; the bomb outrage in Bologna rlwy. station (81 dead), and the right-left civil war in Turkey which led to a military takeover, all in 1980.

TERRY, Dame Ellen (1847-1928). British actress. She made her début in 1856, and from 1878 was Irving's leading lady, portraying Shakespearian roles. In 1864 she

m. G. F. Watts (q.v.), but separation and divorce followed. While she lived with E. W. Godwin 1868-74, 2 children were born to her (*see* CRAIG, E. G.); and she subsequently made 2 further unsuccessful marriages. Later she appeared in plays by her friend, G. B. Shaw, with whom she had a delightful correspondence.

TERTIARIES. Associations of RC laymen who, without abandoning their family life or their usual callings, attempt to live in accordance with the teachings of the friars. The first such order was founded by St Francis in 1221.

TERTU'LLIAN (*c.* 155-222). Christian father. B. at Carthage, he was converted *c.* 192. His theological works are the earliest important Christian writings in Latin. In later life T. became a Montanist.

TERZA RIMA. Italian metre used in Dante's *Divine Comedy*, consisting of 3-line stanzas in which the 2nd line rhymes with the 1st and 3rd of the following stanza. The best-known English example is Shelley's 'Ode to the West Wind'.

TEST ACT. Act passed in England in 1673 requiring all holders of public office to renounce transubstantiation and take the sacrament in an Anglican church, thus excluding RCs and Nonconformists from office. Its clauses were repealed in 1828-9.

TESTOSTERONE (testost'erōn). Steroid hormone secreted chiefly by the testes. Synthetic or animal T. is used to treat inadequate development of male characteristics or to give athletes (illegitimately) additional energy. In the latter use it is not so far detectable in drug tests.

TE'TANUS. Lockjaw; an acute infectious disease caused by a bacterium chiefly found in richly manured soil. Its toxins affect the central nervous system, producing violent and painful spasm of the muscles.

TETUAN (tetoo-ahn'). Town in NE Morocco, near the Mediterranean coast, 64km (40m) SE of Tangier. Pop. (1971) 285,000.

TEUTONIC KNIGHTS. German military order, founded in 1190, which from 1228 devoted itself to crusading against the pagan Prussians and Lithuanians. They ruled Prussia until the 15th cent.

TEXAS (tek'sas). Southern state of the USA, on the Mexican border and the Gulf of Mexico, until Alaska became a state (1959) largest in the Union. The Rio Grande del Norte and Red river form the SW and NE boundaries respectively; most important of the other rivers are the Trinity, Brazos and Colorado. In the extreme W is the arid Llano Estacado plateau or Staked Plains, where much land has been reclaimed by irrigation, which falls rapidly to the Great Plains and prairies. Texas leads all states in cattle (*see* AMARILLO) and sheep, in rice, cotton and sorghum, and quantities of peanuts, pecans, vegetables and fruits are grown. It produces a third of America's oil needs, and also has great resources of natural gas, asphalt, graphite, sulphur, salt, helium, etc., so that the leading industry is chemicals: others are oil refining, food processing, machinery, and transport equipment. The cap. is Austin; the largest city Houston (q.v.), nr which is the self-contained city of the Texas Medical Center with a pop. of 36,000. Other towns are Dallas, San Antonio, Fort Worth and El Paso.

The first settlement was made by the Spaniards in 1682 nr El Paso. Mexico, of which T. was then part, won independence from Spain in 1821, and there was considerable American immigration. Friction arose, Santa Anna (q.v.) massacred the Alamo garrison in 1836, but was himself defeated by Sam Houston at San Jacinto in the same year. Houston then became pres. of the T. republic, which was admitted to the Union in 1845 - the only state to have been recognised as an independent rep. before annexation.

TEXAS. Dallas, one of the world's wealthiest cities, is the banking centre of Texas and has department stores so lavishly equipped that it leads America in 'giftware' which only oil millionaires can afford. *Photo: Camera Press*

Area 692,407 sq.km (267,339 sq.m); pop. (1970) 11,196,730.

TEXEL (tek'sel). Dutch is., largest and most westerly of the Frisians (q.v.).

TEXTILES. Materials woven from spun thread. The art of weaving textiles is one of the earliest developed by man. Sheep's wool, linen, and silk were used in the Old World, cotton and animal fibres (from e.g. the llama) in the New. Spinning and weaving (qq.v.) remain essentially what they have always been, but the adaptation of machinery to both processes from the 18th cent. onwards not only made possible much quicker production, but also added greatly to fineness and variety of texture. The basic materials - wool from various animals, silk, linen, cotton - continue to be used, but from the invention in 1883 of artificial silk (rayon) thread by Hilaire de Chardonnet, man has developed a number of synthetic threads, most of them derived chemically from coal or mineral oil, and marketed under trade names, e.g. nylon, terylene, and orlon; these are sometimes used alone, often together with natural fibres. Fabrics made by hand or machine knitting, though not strictly textiles (from Lat. *texere*, to weave) are much used in a similar way, especially for clothing and furnishings. Among the most welcome advances in 20th cent. T. manufacture have been the development of flame resistant and easy-care fabrics - crease resisting, permanently pleated, easily washable, and 'drip-dry', and treated with water and stain repeller. Spun-bonded fabrics eliminate the need for weaving or knitting: a web of fibre is created, and fuse-bonding is induced by passing it through a controlled heating process.

TEYTE (tāt), **Dame Maggie** (1888-1976). British lyric soprano. Having studied under Jean de Reszke in Paris, she made an inimitable reputation in Mozartian roles, e.g. Cherubino in *The Marriage of Figaro,* and was coached as Mélisande by Debussy himself. In 1958 she was created DBE.

THACKERAY, William Makepeace (1811-63). British novelist. Son of an E India Co. official, he was b. in Calcutta, and ed. at Charterhouse and Trinity Coll., Cambridge. After a brief essay at the law in the Middle Temple, he went to study art in Paris, and ultimately settled to journalism in London. For *Fraser's Magazine* he wrote 'The Yellowplush Correspondence' (1837-8), and 'The Great Hoggarty Diamond' (1841), and for *Punch* 'Mr. Punch's Prize Novelists' (1847) and 'The Snobs of England' (1847), using such pseudonyms as Michael Angelo Titmarsh. In 1836 he had m., but in 1840 his wife became insane in childbed, leaving him with 2 daus. for whom he wrote the fairy tale *The Rose and the Ring* (1855). The first and greatest work to appear under his own name was *Vanity Fair* (1847-8), with its splendidly vixenish heroine Becky Sharp; later novels are *Pendennis* (1848), *Esmond* (1852: with a sequel *The Virginians* 1857-9), and *The Newcomes* (1853-5), in which T.'s tendency to sentimentality is most marked.

THACKERAY. A pencil drawing of William Makepeace Thackeray by D. Maclise, dating from c. 1840. *Photo: Courtesy of the National Portrait Gallery*

THAILAND (tī'-). Independent kingdom in SE Asia, long familiar in the W as Siam. The name Muang T'ai, meaning Land of the Free People and translated Thailand, was adopted in 1939. T. is mountainous in the N, barren in the E, has a central fertile alluvial plain, and a narrow hilly strip in S which is part of the Malay peninsula. The main rivers are the Menam (r.) Chao Phraya (important for transport) and its tribs.; the Mekong marks *c.* 965km (600m) of the E frontier, the Salween *c.* 320km (200m) of the W. The climate is tropical.

Crops incl. rice, tobacco, sugar, oil seeds, fruit for canning, and tobacco, and cattle are reared. Forests incl. teak and support a timber industry, and minerals incl. tin, tungsten, rubies, sapphires, and offshore natural gas.

Rice is by far the most important crop; others incl. sugar, tobacco, cotton, peanuts; oxen, buffaloes, and pigs are reared. The forests of the N produce teak; mineral deposits incl. tin. wolfram, rubies, sapphires. There is an inland waterway system, a rail system linked with that of Malaysia, and good modern roads. Bangkok is the capital and chief port, with a modern air port at Don Muang: other important towns are Thonburi and Chiengmai. Area 514,000 sq.km (198,247 sq.m); pop. (1978) 44,035,000. The people are predominantly Buddhist. M.U.: baht.

History. Finds of bronze artifacts in N Thailand 1974-6 showed that a stage of metallurgy had been reached there in 4,000 BC, which was not reached in Mesopotamia and the rest of the Middle East (formerly thought to be the cradle of the Bronze Age) until 3,000 BC.

THAILAND. A hill tribe family at Chiengmai in northern Thailand. While the mother prepares thread, the father amuses their child by playing the flute. *Photo: Courtesy of the Thai National Tourist Office*

The Thai monarchy, which until 1932 was absolute, originated *c.* 1350; the present dynasty dates from 1782. The Portuguese reached Siam in 1511, the Dutch followed in the 17th cent., in which cent. the (Eng.) East India Co.

had a factory at Ayuthia for some years. A treaty of friendship and trade between Britain and Siam was signed in 1826; treaties with other European powers followed. After the F.W.W. increasing national consciousness led in 1932 to the promulgation of a constitution restricting the absolute power of the king. The country was occupied in 1941-44 by the Japanese. King Ananda Mahidol was assassinated in 1946 and was succeeded by his brother Bhumibol Adulyadej (q.v.). A series of coups d'état, generally bloodless, led to rule by a military junta, but this was overthrown by the king in 1973. Communist guerrillas have been active from 1965, mainly in the N and E on the Laotian border, and in the far S on the Malaysian border; in the latter area Moslem separatists also operate. By 1979 the Communists claimed control of many 'liberated zones'. Following the further military coup of Oct. 1976 T. remained a monarchy, the new constitution providing for a Senate appointed by the King on the PM's recommendation, and a House of Representatives elected by universal suffrage. All US forces were withdrawn, though some co-operation continued, but relations with Kampuchea, Laos and Vietnam are uneasy.

THAÏS (thā-is) (4th cent. BC). Greek courtesan, mistress of Alexander the Great and later wife of Ptolemy, king of Egypt. She was supposed to have instigated the burning of Persepolis.

THALASSAEMIA (-ē'mia). Form of anaemia in which an abnormal haemoglobin molecule results in distortion of the red blood cells, and untreated children die in infancy. It is one of the world's most common genetic diseases.

THALES (thā'lēz) (640-546 BC). Greek philosophic scientist who fl. at Miletus in Asia Minor, made important advances in geometry, and as a materialist in philosophy put forward a theory that all matter and life originated from water.

THALĪ'A. The muse of comedy in ancient Greece.

THALI'DOMĪDE. Tranquillizer developed by a W German pharmaceutical firm in 1957: more than 5,000 expectant mothers gave birth to malformed children as a result of taking it, and the drug was withdrawn in 1961.

THALLIUM (Gk *thallos* budding twig). Bluish-grey metal which tarnishes in air, is soft like lead, malleable but of low tenacity: symbol Tl, at. no. 81, at. wt. 204.39. Discovered spectroscopically and isolated by Crookes in 1861 (by Lamy 1862), it is a poor conductor of electricity and its compounds are poisonous, being used as rat poison and insecticide. Tl-104, a strong beta emitter, is used to gauge thickness of materials which absorb beta rays.

THAMES (temz). English river on which London stands. Its headstreams rise in the Cotswold hills above Cirencester and unite above Lechlade. The total length to the Nore is 338km (210m). It is tidal as far as Teddington. Tributaries from the N are the Windrush, Evenlode, Cherwell, Thame, Colne, Lea and Roding; and from the S, Kennet, Loddon, Wey, Mole, Darent, and Medway. High storm surge tides threaten central London with flooding, and a flood barrier is under construction at Woolwich for completion 1982.

THAMES, Firth of. Inlet between Auckland and the Coromandel Peninsula, NZ.

THANET, Isle of. The NE corner of Kent, England, bounded by the North Sea and the r. Stour. It was an is. until the 16th cent., and incl. the coastal resorts of Broadstairs, Margate and Ramsgate.

THAMES. In more recent years there has been a new appreciation of the river as a source of amenities, even in the built-up areas. The 'new town' of Thamesmead uses the river to supply a large lake which small boats can use in safety. *Photo: Courtesy of the Greater London Council*

THANKSGIVING DAY. In USA, a national holiday observed on the 4th Thursday in Nov. It was first celebrated in 1621 by the Pilgrim Fathers.

THANT, U (1909-74). Burmese diplomat. Together with his close friend U Nu (q.v.), he worked for his country's independence, and as Sec.-Gen. of the UN 1962-71 made the controversial decision to remove the UN peacekeeping force from the Egypt-Israel border 1967.

THAR (tah) **DESERT.** Sandy region on the western Indian (Rajasthan) border. Area 260,000 sq.km (100,000 sq.m).

THATCHER, Margaret (1925-). British Cons. politician. Née Roberts, the dau. of a grocer, who was later mayor of Grantham, she was ed. at Somerville Coll., Oxford, qualified as a research chemist and barrister, and m. in 1951 Denis Thatcher, a director of Burmah Oil. She entered Parliament in 1959, was Sec. of State for Education 1970-4, and defeated Heath in the contest for leadership of the Cons. Party in 1975.

She succeeded Callaghan as Britain's first woman PM after the Cons. victory in the 1979 election. Application of strict monetarist theory (*see* MONETARISM) cut inflation, but unemployment rose to a high level. Abroad the Rhodesia question was settled by the creation of Zimbabwe, Britain's problems within the Common Market were tackled, and the Falklands (q.v) were retaken from Argentina. In 1983 she achieved a landslide victory in the general election.

THEATRE. The place or building in which dramatic performances are given. The first European Ts. were in Greece and were originally open spaces round the altar of Dionysus. The great stone theatre at Athens was begun *c.* 500 BC, and its semicircular plan provided for an audience of 20,000 or 30,000 people sitting in tiers on the surrounding slopes; it served as a model for the Ts. that were erected in all the important cities of the Graeco-Roman world. After the collapse of the Roman Empire the Ts. were deserted, but extant Roman Ts. are at, e.g. Orange, France, and near St Albans, England. In medieval times, several stages of wood and canvas, one for each scene, were set up side by side in fairgrounds and market squares

THEATRE. A No theatre of about 1600 (left). Even today the performers (all male) spend a lifetime in the perfection of their highly specialised roles, in which music and dance play an important part. And, on the right, London's National Theatre on the South Bank of the Thames, with Sir Peter Hall, Director of the Theatre Company in the foreground. *Photos: Yasuda Trust and Banking, and Keystone*

THATCHER. Margaret Thatcher presenting the party programme in 1983 with William Whitelaw (left) and Cecil Parkinson (right), and (left to right behind her) Norman Tebbit, Geoffrey Howe, Francis Pym, and Michael Heseltine. *Photo: Srjda Djukanovic/ Camera Press.*

for the performance of mimes and miracle plays. Small enclosed Ts. were built in the 16th cent., and that at Vicenza, built by Palladio (1518-80), still exists. The first London T. was the 'Theatre' in Shoreditch built in 1576 by James Burbage (d. 1597), who also opened the first covered T. in London, the Blackfriars (1596). Famous London Ts. incl. the Haymarket (1720, rebuilt 1821), Drury Lane (1663), and Her Majesty's (1705), both several times rebuilt. In the USA the centre of the theatrical world is NY City, with numerous Ts. on Broadway, e.g. the Biltmore, Booth, Lunt-Fontanne, Helen Hayes, and Lyceum, although Williamsburg, Va. (1716), and Philadelphia (1766) had Ts. earlier.

In the 20th cent. the large commercial theatres have been affected by the cinema and TV, but there have also been developments resulting in a new infusion of life. These incl. the 'little Ts.' off Broadway, which often give a dramatist his first production, and of which the first was the Theater Guild (1919), others being the Gate, Phoenix, Greenwich, Mews, and Bouwerie Lane; in Britain the work of the repertory theatres, e.g. Birmingham, and of the Old Vic (q.v.); and in Ireland the Abbey (q.v.). Since the S.W.W. in Britain Ts. have often been built as a symbol of civic pride, e.g. at Chichester, Coventry and Guildford; and since *c.* 1925 the USA has acquired a number of community, regional and univ. Ts., e.g. the Alley Playhouse, Houston; Margot Jones's T., Dallas; the Actors Workshop, San Francisco; Penthouse T., Univ. of Washington, Seattle. Ts. are also often incl. as part of larger cultural centres, e.g. the Lincoln Center, NY; Place des Arts, Montreal; and the National T. (1975) on London's South Bank the home of the National T. co. launched in 1963. National Ts., of which the Comédie Française (founded by Louis XIV in 1690 and with a permanent home from 1792) was the first, also exist in Stockholm, Moscow, Athens, Copenhagen, Vienna and elsewhere.

THEBAINE (thē'bā-in) ($C_{19}H_{21}NO_3$). A highly poisonous alkaloid contained in opium.

THEBES (thēbz). Ancient city of Upper Egypt on both banks of the Nile, probably founded under the 1st dynasty. About 1600 BC it became the capital of all Egypt. The present villages of Luxor and Karnak mark its site, and contain magnificent ruins.

THEBES. Capital of Boeotia in ancient Greece. In the Peloponnesian War it was allied with Sparta against Athens, and for a short time after 371 BC it was the most powerful state in Greece. Alexander the Great destroyed it in 336 BC and although it was restored it was never again important. Pindar (q.v.) lived at T.

THEFT. In Britain, under the Theft Act (1968), the dishonest appropriation of another's property with the intention of depriving him of it permanently: maximum penalty 10 years. The act placed under a single head forms of T. which had formerly been dealt with individually, e.g. burglary and larceny.

THEISM (thē'izm). Belief in the existence of a God, usually conceived of as a personal being, who has revealed Himself to the world in a special revelation. In its widest use the term means belief in the existence of gods. *See* DEISM.

THĒ'MIS. In Greek mythology, personification of law and order. She was the dau. of Uranus and Ge.

THEMI'STOCLĒS (*c.* 514–449 BC). Athenian soldier and statesman. In 483 he was largely responsible for the ostracizing of Aristides, and for 10 years he exercised almost supreme power in the state. In the Persian War he played a distinguished part in the battle of Salamis (480) and then rebuilt and strengthened the walls of Athens. About 470 Spartan influence secured his banishment, and he fled into Asia, where Artaxerxes, the Persian king, received him with favour. Henceforth he lived at Magnesia.

THEŌ'CRITUS (fl. *c.* 270 BC). Greek poet. B. probably at Syracuse, he spent much of his life at Alexandria. His *Idylls*, truthful pictures of rustic life distinguished by deep feeling for nature, have served as a model for all subsequent pastoral poetry.

THEODOLITE (thē-o'dolīt). Instrument used in surveying for the measurement of horizontal and vertical angles. It consists of a small telescope mounted so as to move on 2 graduated circles, one horizontal and the other vertical, while its axes pass through the centres of the circles.

THEODORA (thē-ōdō'ra) (*c.* AD 508–548). Byzantine empress, consort of Justinian, whom she m. *c.* 523; earlier she had been his mistress and a common courtesan. As queen she earned a high reputation for courage and charity.

THEODORA'KIS, Mikis (1925–). Greek composer. He gained an internat. reputation by 'Zorba's dance', etc. Active in left-wing politics, he was imprisoned 1967–70 for attempting to overthrow the military régime.

THEŌ'DORIC I. King of the Visigoths, 418–51. He was a grandson of Alaric, warred successfully against the Romans, but united with them against the Huns under Attila and fell at Châlons.

THEODORIC (455–526). Founder of the Ostrogothic monarchy in Italy; called Theodoric the Great. Succeeding his father as king about 474, he warred intermittently against the Romans and was given permission by the Emperor Zeno to secure Italy from Odoacer. With 250,000 Ostrogoths he overran the peninsula, and on Odoacer's murder was accepted as king. For 33 years he ruled with ability.

THEODOSIUS (thē-ōdō'shius) **I** (*c.* 346–395). Roman emperor of the East, called the Great. B. in Spain, he served under his father, a Roman general, in Britain and the Balkans, and in 379 was called to become emperor of the East as the colleague of Gratian, the emperor of the West. In 4 years T. completely dispersed the Goths, concluding peace with them in 382. In 394 T. became sole emperor. The chief blot on his fame is his massacre of 7,000 citizens of Thessalonica in 390 after there had been rioting in the circus.

THEODOSIUS II (401–50). Byzantine emperor 408–50. He defeated the Persians, but from 441 had to pay heavier tribute to Attila the Hun.

THEOLOGY. The science of religion, concerned chiefly with God and with man's relationship to Him. Natural T. deals with what may be discovered by reason and a study of the natural world; Revealed T. has for its subject the specific doctrines of Christianity, Islam, and the other world faiths.

THEORBO (thē-ōr'bo) or **archlute.** Musical instrument, a large member of the lute (q.v.) family.

THEŌ'SOPHY. Name applied to various systems of 'divine wisdom', but in particular to the doctrines of the Theosophical Society founded in 1875 by Mme Blavatsky (q.v.) and Col. H. S. Olcott. These are based on the Hindu principles of karma and reincarnation, with Nirvana as the goal of the aspiring soul.

THEOTOCOPULI. *See* GRECO, EL.

THERESA, Mother. Indian RC nun, *née* Agnes Bojaxhiu (1910–). Of Albanian parentage, she was b. in Skopje, and at 18 entered a convent in Calcutta and became a teacher. In 1948 she became an Indian citizen and obtained leave to work instead in the city slums, founding a new order the Missionaries of Charity for both men and women. They live in great poverty, succour the sick and abandoned children, and are noted for their care of the dying. The order is based in Calcutta. She was awarded a Nobel Peace prize in 1979; honorary OM 1983.

THÉRÈSE OF LISIEUX (1873–97). French saint. B. at Alençon, dau. of a watchmaker, she entered a Carmelite convent at L. at 15, where her holy life induced her superior to ask her to write her spiritual autobiography. She advocated the Little Way of Goodness in small things in everyday life, and is known as Little Flower of Jesus. She d. of tuberculosis and was canonized in 1925.

THERMIC LANCE. Tube of mild steel, enclosing tightly-packed small steel rods and fed with oxygen. On ignition temperatures above 3000°C are produced and the T.L. becomes its own sustaining fuel. It rapidly penetrates walls and a 23cm (9in) steel door can be cut through in less than 30 sec. Criminals have used T.Ls. but alarm systems can detect the radiation emitted by a T.L. in operation.

THERMIO'NICS. That branch of science that deals with the emission of electrons from matter under the influence of heat. A thermionic valve, used in telegraphy and telephony and in radio and radar, is a device using space conduction by thermionically emitted electrons. Classification is into diode, triode, and multi-electrode valves, but in many applications valves have been replaced by transistors (q.v.). *See* O. W. RICHARDSON.

THERMODYNAMICS. The science of the transfer of heat into other forms of energy, on which is based the study of the efficient working of engines, e.g. the steam and internal combustion. The 3 laws of T. are: (1) energy can be neither created nor destroyed: heat and mechanical work being mutually convertible; (2) it is impossible for an unaided self-acting machine to convey heat from one body to another at a higher temperature; (3) it is impossible by any procedure, no matter how idealized, to reduce any system to the absolute zero of temperature in a finite number of operations. Put into mathematical form these have widespread applications in physics and chemistry.

THERMOGRAPHY (thermo'grafi). The recording of heat patterns, as developed in the 1970s and 1980s, using a photographic method (the Aga system) developed by the army to assist night vision, by detecting the body heat of any enemy, or the hot engine of his tank. British doctor, Ray Clark, has used it to record the complex, rhythmic, but apparently independent, patterns in the way the parts of the human body heat up and cool down during sleep.

THERMOLUMINESCENCE. Light released by irradiated material when later heated. It occurs with most crystalline substances to some extent. In the case of ceramics, it is used in archaeology to date pottery, and is used by geologists in dealing with terrestrial rocks and meteorites.

THERMOMETER. An instrument for measuring temperature (q.v.) depending on the nearly uniform change in physical properties, of expansion in a solid liquid or gas; or the change in electrical properties such as resistance with temperature. The commonest form used at ordinary temperatures is the mercury or alcohol-in-glass T. reading directly against a scale marked in degrees Centigrade or Fahrenheit. (*See* TEMPERATURE for conversion factor.) Other instruments incl. *thermocouples* depending on the voltage generated between the junctions of 2 dissimilar metals; *resistance thermometers* depending on the change of electrical resistance of a conductor with temperature; *pyrometers* (q.v.); *thermistors* depending on the change of electrical resistance of a semiconductor with temperature; *bimetallic strips* depending on dissimilar rates of expansion of 2 metals, and *gas thermometers* depending on the gas laws.

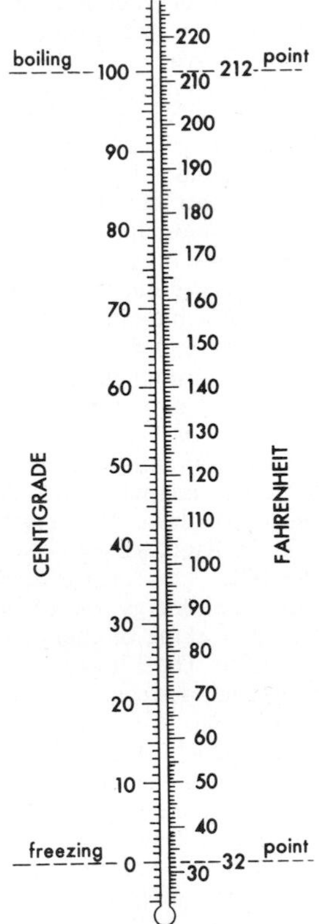

THERMOMETER

THERMOPYLAE (thermo'pilē). A narrow pass in Greece from Thessaly to Locris, famous for its heroic defence against the Persians in 480 BC by Leonidas, King of Sparta, and *c.* 1,000 men, who fought to the death.

THESSALONĪ'KI. Port in Greek Macedonia at the head of the Gulf of T. with some industry - textile making, shipbuilding, brewing, tanning, etc. It is on the site of Thessalonica, the Roman city to whose inhabitants St Paul addressed 2 famous epistles. Founded from Corinth 315 BC, captured by Saracens AD 904, by the Turks 1430, it was restored to Greece 1912. It was an Allied base in the F.W.W., and was occupied by the Germans 1941-44. Pop. (1971) 345,800.

THE'SSALY. Region of Greece, bordering the Aegean, a fertile plain enclosed by mts. and comprising the towns of Kardhitsa, Larisa, Magnesia, and Trikkala.

THE'TFORD. Town in Norfolk, England, where the Little Ouse and Thet rivers meet: there is some engineering. Pop. (1974) 17,000. **Thetford Mines** in Quebec, Canada, is the site of the world's largest asbestos deposits.

THIBAULT, J. A. *See* FRANCE, ANATOLE.

THIERS (tyār'), **Louis Adolphe** (1797-1877). French statesman and historian. B. at Marseilles, he achieved fame with his *History of the French Revolution* (1823-7) and *History of the Consulate and Empire* (1845-60). He held cabinet posts under Louis Philippe, and from 1863 led the parliamentary opposition to Napoleon III. As head of the provisional govt in 1871 he negotiated peace with Prussia and suppressed the Paris Commune. He was first President of the 3rd Republic 1871-3.

THIMPHU (tim'poo). Cap. of Bhutan (q.v.), nr the NW borders with China. Pop. (1971) 10,000.

THIRD WORLD. Countries, numbering *c.* 114, which are comparatively undeveloped industrially, mainly those outside Europe and North America. In 1977 the 24 wealthiest nations (with 19% of the world population) created 65% of the world's production. *See* THREE WORLDS THEORY.

THIRD WORLD WAR. *See* WAR.

THIRTY-NINE ARTICLES. *See* ANGLICAN COMMUNION.

THIRTY YEARS' WAR. The war fought in Germany 1618-48. Nominally a religious war, it originated in the ambition of the Habsburgs to obtain political control of all Germany. The war began with a revolt of the Bohemians against Austrian rule in 1618-20, and after their defeat was continued by certain Protestant princes, who were aided during 1625-7 by Denmark. Gustavus Adolphus of Sweden intervened on the Protestant side in 1630, and overran N Germany before he was killed in 1632. After the Swedish defeat at Nördlingen (1634) France entered the war in 1635, and inflicted several defeats on the emperor's Spanish allies. By the Treaty of Westphalia (1648) France received S Alsace, and Sweden certain provinces on the Baltic, while the emperor's authority over Germany became purely nominal. The war was largely fought by armies of mercenaries, such as those of Wallenstein, Tilly, and Mansfeld, which devastated Germany.

THISTLE. Several genera of plants in the family Compositae, the best-known being *Carduus* and *Cirsium*, found in the N hemisphere. The flower heads are purple and cottony, the leaves are deeply indented and spiny: a T. is the Scottish national emblem.

THISTLE, Most Ancient and Most Noble Order of the. Scottish order of knighthood (KT) founded in 1687. There are sixteen knights, and the Queen is sovereign of the order. Its motto is *Nemo me impune lacessit* (No one provokes me with impunity).

THISTLEWOOD, Arthur (1770-1820). English Radical. A follower of Thomas Spence, he was active in the Radical movement and was executed as the chief leader of the Cato St conspiracy.

THOMAS, St. One of the 12 apostles. He is said to have preached Christianity in Parthia or India; hence the ancient S Indian churches are called 'the Christians of St T.'. He is not the author of the so-called Gospel of St T. *See* BIBLE.

THOMAS, Dylan Marlais (1914-53). Welsh poet. B. in Swansea, son of the English master at the local grammar school where he was ed., he worked as a reporter on the *South Wales Evening Post,* then settled as a journalist in London and pub. his first vol. *Eighteen Poems* in 1934. He reached a lilting mastery of his medium in *Deaths and Entrances* (1946) and the radio 'play' *Under Milk Wood* (1954): the short stories of *Portrait of the Artist as a Young Dog* (1940) are autobiographical. A dipsomaniac, he d. in NY where he had made a number of reading and lecture tours. Repeatedly anthologized, e.g. his celebration of his 30th birthday 'Poem in October' and 'Fern Hill', an evocation of his youth, he has become a legend. His detective story *The Death of the King's Canary* (1976), written with his friend John Davenport, is a satire of the contemporary literary and artistic world.

THOMAS, (Philip) Edward (1878-1917). British poet and author of books on the English countryside. In 1916 he pub. *Six Poems* under the pseudonym of Edward Eastaway; vols. under his own name were *Poems* (1917) and *Last Poems* (1918), dealing with nature idealistically. T. was killed in action in the F.W.W. at Arras. His wife **Helen T.** (1877-1967) pub. the biographical vols. *As it was,* and *World without End.*

THOMAS, Ronald Stuart (*c.* 1914-). Welsh poet. Vicar of St Hywyn, Aberdaron, from 1967, he has made a reputation with such vols. as *Song at the Year's Turning* (1955), which illustrated the conflict between traditional Welsh values and 'English' sterilely encroaching civilization.

THOMAS À KEMPIS. Alternative name of THOMAS HAMMERKEN (*c.* 1380-1471), German monk. B. at Kempen, near Düsseldorf, he entered the Augustinian monastery of Zwolle. His *Imitation of Christ* is perhaps the best-known devotional work ever written.

THOMPSON, Francis (1859-1907). British poet. B. at Preston, he settled in London, where he fell into poverty and ill health. Wilfrid and Alice Meynell procured the publication of his poems in 1893, incl. 'The Hound of Heaven'. In this and later vols. (*Sister Songs* and *New Poems*) T., who was a Roman Catholic, expressed a mystic view of life.

THOMPSON, John Taliaferro (1860-1940). American colonel, and inventor of the T. sub-machine-gun, predecessor of the tommy-gun. B. in Kentucky, he retired from the army in 1914.

THOMSON, Elihu (1853-1937). American inventor. B. in England, he lived in USA from 1858, and was prof. of chemistry and mechanics at Philadelphia (1876-80). He founded, with E. J. Houston, the Thomson-Houston Electric Co. in 1882, later merging with the Edison Co. to form the General Electric Co. As director of the research laboratory, he made important advances into the nature of the electric arc, invented the first high-frequency dynamos and transformers. He also contributed to improvements on many aspects of incandescent lighting and radiology.

THOMSON, James (1700-48). British poet. B. in Roxburghshire, he wrote the influential descriptive poem *The Seasons* (1726-30) in blank verse, and the song, 'Rule, Britannia'.

THOMSON, James (1834-82). Scottish poet, who wrote as 'B.V.' (Bysshe Vanolis). B. in Renfrewshire, he became an army schoolmaster and a journalist. His poem 'The City of Dreadful Night' (1880) reflects deep despair.

THOMSON, Sir Joseph John (1856-1940). British physicist. Ed. at Manchester and Cambridge, where he became Cavendish prof. of experimental physics (1884-1918), he organized the Cavendish research laboratory which became a world-famous centre of atomic research. His work resulted in the discovery of the electron which inaugurated the electrical theory of the atom, and his elucidation of positive rays and their application to an analysis of neon led to Aston's discovery of isotopes. He is regarded as the founder of modern physics, and was awarded a Nobel prize in 1906 and the OM in 1913. His son **Sir George Paget T.** (1892-1975), ed. at Cambridge, was prof. of physics at the Imperial Coll. of Science 1930-52, where he carried out aeronautical and atomic research, and in 1937 received (with C. J. Davisson) a Nobel prize for work on interference phenomena in the irradiation of crystals by electrons.

THOR. The Norse god of thunder. He was represented as a man of enormous strength, who defended mankind against demons.

THOREAU (thō'rō), **Henry David** (1817-62). American author and naturalist. B. at Concord, Mass., he is best known for his *Walden, or Life in the Woods* (1854). Some 30 vols. of later works are based on his daily journals of walks and nature observations.

THŌ'RIUM. Dark grey, naturally radioactive metal, widely distributed throughout the world in minerals, particularly monazite beach sands: symbol Th, at. no. 90, at. wt. 232.05. Discovered by Berzelius (1828), it has a half-life 1.39×10^{10} years, and its greatest potential use is breeeding from it uranium-233, an excellent fuel for power reactors.

THORN APPLE. Plant *(Datura stronomium),* also called jimsonweed, which grows to 5 m (15 ft), and has white or violet trumpet-shaped flowers. Native to the USA and Canada, it has spread to Africa and Europe. The leaves are poisonous.

THORNDIKE, Dame Sybil (1882-1976). British actress. She is best remembered for her splendid St Joan, in the play Shaw wrote for her, and often appeared with her husband Sir Lewis Casson (1875-1969). She was created DBE in 1931. The T. Theatre, Leatherhead (1969), is named after her, and the theatre workshop after her husband. Her brother **Russell T.** (1885-1972) was also an actor, and wrote the series of novels featuring the 18th cent. smuggling parson 'Dr Syn'.

THORWALDSEN (tōr'-), **Bertel** (1770-1844). Danish sculptor. B. at sea, he studied in Rome where he became friendly with Canova. His output was enormous, and he excelled in classical and mythological subjects, e.g. 'The Triumph of Alexander'.

THOTH (tōt). The Egyptian god of wisdom and learning. He was represented as a scribe with the head of an ibis, the bird sacred to him.

THOTHMES (tōtmes). Name of 4 Egyptian kings of the 18th dynasty. THOTHMES I (reigned 1540-1501 BC) founded the Egyptian empire in Syria. His grandson, THOTHMES III, reigned *c.* 1500-1446 BC, extended the empire to the Euphrates, and conquered Nubia.

THOUSAND ISLANDS. Some 1,500 is. scattered on the US-Canadian border in Lake Ontario, where the St Lawrence flows out of the lake.

THRACE. The heart of the Thracian Empire, which endured from 6,000 BC to AD 300, and originally covered a much greater area, was modern Bulgaria, where there have been magnificent tomb finds of gold and silver treasure since 1945. The Thracians were fine horsemen, and these and other animals, appear on dishes, drinking vessels and jewelry. The legend of Orpheus, the unwarlike musician hero, as well as the cult of Dionysus, were derived by the Greeks from Thrace. They had made trading settlements - apparently peaceably - along the coast in the 8th-1st cents. BC. The rest of T. was to some extent conquered by Persia in the 6th-5th cents., and by Macedon in the 4th-2nd cents., but the break-up of the Empire was finally ensured by the Celts who swarmed in upon the Thracians in 279 BC. From AD 46 T. was a Roman prov., later forming part of the Byzantine Empire. The Turks held it from the 15th cent. until 1878 when Bulgaria secured the N, Greece the S. After the F.W.W. Thrace was divided between Greece, of which it forms a nome or prov., and Turkey.

THREE RIVERS. *See* TROIS RIVIÈRES.

THREE WORLDS THEORY. Allegedly first formulated in 1974 by Mao Tse-tung, it sees the First World as the USA and USSR; the Second World as the smaller developed countries, Canada, Japan and Europe; and the Third World as Africa, Latin America and Asia (except Japan). An equitable and peaceful world is eventually to be secured by the extension of socialism through to the First World (USSR being seen as having reverted to capitalist imperialism), and by collaborative measures between second and third world powers, since changing times and circumstances have made many second rank powers more amenable. By 1979 co-operative effort was to be directed mainly against USSR, as the greatest danger to peace.

THRIFT. Genus of plants (*Armeria*) in the family Plumbaginaceae. Sea T. (*A. maritima*) occurs on seashores and cliffs in Europe. The leaves are small and linear. The pink flowers rise on straight stems.

THROAT. The structures in front of the neck, incl. the wind pipe (trachea), the gullet (oesophagus), the blood vessels passing to the head from the heart, the thyroid gland, and the tissues at the back of the mouth.

THROMBŌ'SIS. Development during life of a blood-clot within a vessel or the heart, causing restriction of blood flow.

THRUSH. Family of birds (Turdidae). The song T. (*Turdus musicus*) is 20cm (8in) long, brown above and with a paler throat and breast speckled with dark brown: it is one of Britain's finest songbirds. Slightly larger is the missel T. (*T. viscivorus*), nicknamed the storm cock because it often sings before and during wild, wet weather. N American species incl. the hermit T. (*Hylocichla guttata*), a beautiful songster, and the wood T. (*T. mustelina*).

THUCYDIDES (thūsid'idēz) (*c.* 460-400 BC). Athenian historian. He held a command in the Peloponnesian War in 424, but met so little success that he was banished until 404. In his *History of the Peloponnesian War* he attempted a scientific and impartial history of his own time.

THUGS. Hindu sect who sacrificed travellers to Kali, the goddess of destruction, by strangling them. They were suppressed *c.* 1830.

THU'LĒ. Greek and Roman name for the most northerly land known. It was applied to the Shetlands, the Orkneys and Iceland, and by later writers to Scandinavia.

THULIUM. A metallic element, symbol Tm, at. no. 69, at. wt. 168.94. It is one of the rare-earth metals.

THUNDER BAY. City and lake port on Lake Superior, Ontario, Canada, formed by the union of Port Arthur and its twin city of Fort William to the S. It is an industrial centre. Pop. (1971) 50,000.

THUNDERBIRD. Among Plains Indians, USA, the mythical creator of the storms of the great plains.

THURBER, James Grover (1894-1961). American humorist. B. in Columbus, Ohio, he made his name with short stories in the *New Yorker*, perhaps the most famous of these being 'The Secret Life of Walter Mitty'. His doodle drawings also first appeared in this magazine, and incl. preposterous impressions of dogs whom T. placed above the human species. Blind in one eye from boyhood he was totally blind in the last decade but continued his work.

THURINGIA (tooring'ia). A German Free State, 1919-34, a gau under the Nazis, it was enlarged and made a Land, 1946-52, of E Germany; then its historic boundaries were obliterated in the new dists. of Erfurt, Gera, and Suhl. It contained the fertile Saale plain and, in the S, the beautiful Thüringer Wald: the cap. was Weimar.

THURSDAY ISLAND. Pearl fishing is. in Torres Strait, Queensland, Australia: chief centre, Port Kennedy. Area 3 sq.km (1.2 sq.m).

THURSO. Seaport in Highland region, Scotland, on T. bay. It is the mainland terminus of the steamer service to the Orkneys, and the experimental atomic station of Dounreay lies to the W. Pop. (1971) 9,025.

THYME (tīm). Genus of plants (*Thymus*) in the Labiatae family. Garden T. (*T. vulgaris*), a native of the Mediterranean, has aromatic leaves used for seasoning, white or reddish flowers, and a slightly woody growth under a foot high.

THYMUS (thī'mus). A ductless gland near the root of the neck. It develops early in embryonic life, continues to grow after birth, but atrophies before adult life. In 1978 it was shown that it is the T. which teaches the body's immune system the difference between 'self' and 'foreign' tissues: it is vital to the body's resistance to infection. The food known as 'sweetbread' is an animal thymus.

THYROID (thī'roid). One of the principal endocrine glands, situated in front of the throat. It secretes thyroxin, a hormone containing iodine. This stimulates growth, metabolism, and other functions of the body. Abnormal action produces Graves' disease, deficient action produces myxoedema and cretinism.

TIANJIN (tē-ahnjēn'). Port and industrial city (formerly Tientsin), a special municipality within Hubei prov., of which it was formerly the cap. It stands where the Grand Canal joins the Hai He (32 m) from the Yellow Sea, to the SE of Peking. It was opened to foreign trade in 1860, and was occupied by the Japanese in 1937. There is a univ. Area 4,000 sq.m (1,545 sq.m); pop. (1979) 7,000,000.

TIARA (ti-ah'ra). The triple crown worn by the Pope. The term was originally applied to a head-dress worn by the ancient Persians.

TĪ'BER. River of Italy on which Rome stands. It rises in the Apennines and flows for 400km (250m) in a S direction before reaching the Tyrrhenian Sea by 2 mouths, the chief 27km (17m) SE of Rome.
TĪBĒ'RIUS, Claudius Nero (42 BC–AD 37). Roman emperor. The stepson and adopted son of Augustus, he had a distinguished military career, and on Augustus's death in AD 14 succeeded to the empire. He was a conscientious ruler under whom the empire prospered. In later life he retired to Capri.

TIBERIUS. The emperor and his mother, Livia, are enthroned in the guise of Jupiter and Ceres, receiving a young warrior. Above them, Germanicus, who died in A.D. 19, is carried on a winged horse to join the deified Augustus who reclines in heaven. This complex cameo is carved in sardonyx.

TIBE'STI MTNS. Range in the central Saharan system, N Chad: highest peak Emi Koussi 3,415 m (11,204 ft).
TIBE'T. Country of central Asia (Chinese Pinyin form: Xizang), occupying a lofty barren plateau bounded by the Himalayas to the S and SW and the Kunlun Mts. to the N, traversed from W to E by the Bukamagna, Karakoram, and other ranges, and having an average elevation of 4-4,500 m (13-15,000 ft). The Sutlej, Brahmaputra, and Indus rise in T., which has numerous lakes, many salty. The yak is the main domestic animal. Wool is exported, and other products incl. borax, salt, horn, musk, herbs, and furs. Gold, iron pyrites, lapis lazuli and mercury are mined. Lhasa is the cap.

T. was an independent kingdom from the 5th cent. AD. From *c.* 1700 to 1912 it was under nominal Chinese suzerainty, a claim made effective in 1951 when the historic ruler, the Dalai Lama, was driven from the country and the monks (perhaps a quarter of the pop.) were forced out of the monasteries: *see* LAMAISM. In 1965 T. became an autonomous region of C., industrialization (textiles, chemicals, agricultural machinery, etc.) has been encouraged, and many Chinese have settled there. Chinese rule continued to be resented and the economy languished, so that in 1980 under the slogan 'relax, relax and relax again' traditional patterns of agriculture, livestock raising and trade were restored. Repeated attempts were also made to persuade the Dalai Lama to return. Area 1,221,600 sq.km (471,540 sq.m); pop. (1979) 1,700,000. Polyandry (q.v.) was common.

TIBET. Unlike the women of other eastern races, those of Tibet have always held high status. Physically active and strong, they play a major part in all aspects of life. *Photo: Courtesy of the Society for Anglo-Chinese Understanding*

TICKS. Two families of Acari in the Arachnida. Allied to the mites T. are blood-sucking disease-carrying parasites on men, animals, and birds.
TIDES. Rise and fall of waters due to the gravitational forces of the Moon and Sun. High water occurs at an average interval of 12 hours 24½ min. The highest or spring tides are at or near new and full moon, and the lowest or neap tides when the moon is in the 1st or 3rd quarter. Some seas, e.g. the Mediterranean, have very small tides. Gravitational T. - the pull of nearby groups of stars - have also been observed to affect the galaxies.

Phenomena dangerous to population centres, but not true Ts., are (1) a combination of naturally high Ts. with storm surge, e.g. the Thames area and adjacent low-lying coasts of Germany and the Netherlands; (2) the water 'walls' created by typhoons and hurricanes, such as often hit Bangladesh; (3) underwater upheavals in the Earth's crust which may cause 'Ts'. travelling at 1,000 kph (400mph), known as *tsunami* (a Japanese name, pron. tsoonah'mi) because frequent in that country; and (4) the long-term general rise of sea-level caused by a global temperature change melting the polar ice caps.

TIECK (tēk), **Johann Ludwig** (1773-1853). German writer. One of the leaders of the Romantic movement, he wrote much poetry, and collected folk-tales, some of which he dramatized, e.g. *Puss in Boots.*

TIEN-SHAN. *See* TYAN SHAN.

TIENTSIN. *See* TIANJIN.

TIEPOLO (tē-ā'pōlō), **Giovanni Battista** (1692-1769). Italian artist. B. at Venice, he was a master of colour and executed delightful decorations in churches and palaces, with transparent atmospheric effects, e.g. the episcopal palace Würzburg.

TIERRA DEL FUEGO (tē-er'rah del fwā'gō). Group of is. separated from the S tip of S America by Magellan Strait. The W is part of the Chilean prov. of Magallanes; the E is a prov. of Argentina. The name (Span.) means land of fire. The southernmost point of the group is Cape Horn. *See also* BEAGLE CHANNEL.

TI'FFANY, Louis Comfort (1848-1933). American artist and glassmaker. He produced stained glass windows, iridescent Favrile (OE fabrile 'craftsman') glass, and lampshades. He used glass which contained oxides of iron and other impurities to get richness of colour.

TIFLIS. Russian form of TBILISI.

TIGER. Largest of the great cats (*Leo tigris*), formerly found in much of Central Asia but increasingly rare. The striped markings - black on reddish fawn - are present from birth, though rare cream or black specimens have been known. The T. reaches a length of 3-3.6m (10-12 ft), may be either solitary or one of a family party, is a good swimmer, and feeds for preference on deer or cattle, man-eating being the result of weakened powers.

TĪ'GRIS. River of Turkey and Iraq, one of the two great rivers of Mesopotamia (q.v.). The T. rises in the Anti-Taurus and flows for more than 1,600 km (1,000 m) to join the Euphrates 72km (45m) above Basra. Mosul and Baghdad stand on it.

TIJUANA (tikhwah'na). Town in Baja California, Mexico, close to the US border, with horse racing and gambling casinos. Pop. (1974) 335,100.

TIKHONOV (tē'khonof), Nikolai (1905-). Russian statesman. Once a locomotive engineer, he became a close associate of Brezhnev, joining the Politburo in 1979. In 1980 he succeeded Kosygin as PM (chairman of the Council of Ministers). He resigned in September 1985.

TILBURY. Port in Essex, England, on the N bank of the Thames. In 1976 major extension was undertaken.

TILLY, Jan Tserklaes, count (1559-1632). Imperialist general in the Thirty Years War. Notorious for his storming of Magdeburg in 1631, he was defeated by Gustavus Adolphus at Breitenfeld, and at the Lech, in which latter battle he was mortally wounded.

TILSIT. *See* SOVIETSK.

TIMBER. Name given to woods used for building, furniture making, pulp making, etc. It is divided into 3 groups: 1. Tropical hard woods, e.g. mahogany, teak, ebony, and rosewood, obtained from Central America, W Indies, W Africa, and Asia. 2. Hardwoods of temperate regions in Europe and N America, include oak, elm, beech, and the hard eucalyptus woods of Australia, known as jarrah and karri. 3. Timber of coniferous trees - pine, fir, spruce, larch, etc., which are the easiest of all trees to work. Sawdust and shavings compacted into sheets with synthetic resins, and often veneered on both sides, are used for their strength and stability. *See also* FORESTRY.

TIKHONOV. Nikolai Tikhonov, chosen in 1980 as a conservative successor to Kosygin as Soviet Prime Minister. *Photo: Keystone.*

TIMBU'KTU. Town in Mali Rep., 14.5km (9m) N of the Niger on the S edge of the Sahara. Founded in the 11th cent., it is an important caravan centre. Pop. (1970) 10,000.

TIME. For the purposes of everyday life, the alternation of day and night consequent upon the rotation of Earth on its axis. The natural unit of time is the true or apparent solar day, the period in which the Earth makes a complete rotation relative to the Sun. Apparent solar time suffers from the disadvantage that the days are not of equal length; a fundamental unit of time was adopted, therefore, the mean solar day, equal to the average length of the apparent solar day. Since the Sun crosses different meridians at different moments there is a local apparent time and a local mean time, the local noon being defined as the passage of the Sun across the meridian passing through that place. From 1884 Greenwhich meridian was adopted as the prime meridian, from which all longitudes were measured. The local mean time of places W of Greenwich was earlier than that of Greenwich, and vice versa. A system of standard or zone times was adopted by most countries, the standard of time differing from Greenwich mean time by an integral number of hours. Each hour corresponds to 15° longitude. The meridian of 180° longitude more or less - the date line - separates the half-zone in which the time is 12 hours fast on Greenwich mean time from that in which it is 12 hours slow. The interval of time taken by the Earth to make one complete rotation relative to the stars is called the sidereal day. Today standard time is co-ordinated Universal Time (UT), introduced in 1972, which is atomic time (q.v.), adjusted to keep in step with the regular seasonal variation of the period of Earth's rotation by the insertion of leap seconds.

TIMISOARA (tēmēshwah'rah). Town in W Romania. It has a univ. (1962). Pop. (1972) 200,000.

TĪ'MOR. Largest and most easterly is. of the lesser Sunda group in the Malay archipelago. West T. forms the Indonesian prov. of Nusu Tenggara, cap. Kupang. East T. (the NE of the is., together with the western enclave of

Ambeno) was an overseas prov. of Portugal until the civil war of 1975, when it was annexed by Indonesia as the prov. of Loro Sae in 1976. The cap. is Dili. Guerrilla warfare continues. Total area 33,610 sq.km (12,977 sq.m); pop. (1971) 2,905,000.

TIMOSHENKO, Semyon Konstantinovich (1895-1970). Marshal of the Soviet Union from 1940. Known as the 'baldheaded eagle', as Defence Minister he reorganized the Soviet army in 1940, and from 1941 first delayed then destroyed the German attack.

TI'MOTHY. The companion of St Paul on his missionary journeys, and in his imprisonment, to whom 2 of the Pauline epistles are addressed.

TIN. The most usual of the several varieties of T., is a silver-white, crystalline metal, malleable and somewhat ductile, which crumbles to a greyish powder at low temperatures: symbol Sn (Lat. *stannum*), at. no. 50, at. wt. 118.70. It is found chiefly in the mineral cassiterite SnO_2 in Malaysia, Indonesia and Bolivia, and is chiefly used as a protective coating to resist corrosion on iron and steel, i.e. the 'tin can' food container. Its use was known in the ancient world and the mines in Cornwall, where working was renewed in the 1960s, were being worked in the Bronze Age. Other important alloys, besides bronze, incl. solder, type metal, pewter, and metals for bearings.

TI'NBERGEN, Jan (1903-). Dutch economist. He shared a Nobel prize in 1969 with Ragnar Frisch for his work on econometrics (the mathematical-statistical expression of economic theory). His brother **Nikolaas T.** (1907-) is a zoologist, specializing in the organization of instinctive behaviour, and shared a Nobel prize with Konrad Lorenz and Karl von Frisch in 1973.

TINDOUF (tēndōōf'). Oasis in W Algeria, nr the Moroccan border. There are large iron deposits nearby.

TINNĪ'TUS. Internal sounds, inaudible to others, which are heard by sufferers from malfunctions of hearing, e.g. spasm of an inner-ear muscle. In some cases there is a hum at a frequency of *c.* 40 Hz which resembles that heard by people troubled by environmental hum (q.v.). There is little relief possible, except in being in a place where external noise drowns out the internal one.

TINTAGEL (tinta'jel). English village on the Atlantic coast near Camelford, Cornwall. Its castle is associated with the Arthurian legends.

TINTORE'TTO. Name given to the Venetian painter Jacopo Robusti (1518-94) because his father was a dyer (*Tintore*). Chief of the later Venetian school, he painted portraits and biblical scenes.

TIPPERĀ'RY. Inland co. of Munster, Rep. of Ireland, watered by the Shannon and Suir. It is partly mountainous, but the Golden Vale in the SW is a fertile dairy region. It is administratively divided into North T. (area 1,997 sq.km/771 sq.m; pop. in 1971 being 54,340), with its admin. HQ at Nenagh; and South T. (area 2,258 sq.km/872 sq.m; pop. 62,230), admin. HQ Clonmel. The town of T. is in South T.

TIPPETT, Sir Michael (1905-). Brit. composer. Ed. at the RCM, he was director of music at Morley College 1940-51, and the same sensitive concern for humanity which led to his brief imprisonment as a conscientious objector in 1943 appears in his oratorio *A Child of Our Time* (1941). Later works incl. operas, notably *King Priam* (1961) and *The Ice Break* (1977), two piano sonatas, a Magnificat and Nunc Dimittis written for St John's

TIPPERARY. Ireland's ancient status as an early home of Christianity in Europe is illustrated by the beautiful Celtic crosses, with their characteristic intertwined ornamentation found in the countryside. This is the east face of South Cross at Ahenny in Tipperary. *Photo: Courtesy of the Commissioners of Public Works in Ireland*

Coll., Cambridge (1961), and incidental music for *The Tempest* (1962). He was knighted 1966.

TIPPOO' SAHIB (1753-99). Sultan of Mysore, India, from 1782, when he succeeded his father Hyder Ali. He was killed in a war with the British. His formidable 1,000 strong rocket brigade led to the re-invention of the rocket missile by Congreve: *see* ROCKET.

TIRANA (tērah'na). Cap. of Albania, 32km (20m) E of Durrës. Founded in the 17th cent., T. makes cotton textiles, soap, cigarettes, etc., and is the seat of a univ. Pop. (1970) 171,000.

TIROL. Former prov. of the Austrian Empire, divided 1919 between Austria (Austrian prov. of T.: cap. Innsbruck) and Italy (*see* TRENTINO-ALTO ADIGE).

TIRPITZ (tir'pits), **Alfred von** (1849-1930). German admiral. As Sec. for the Navy 1897-1916 he was largely responsible for the F.W.W. U-boat campaign.

TIRSO DE MOLINA (tērsō de mōlē'nah). Name taken by Gabriel Tellez (1571-1648), Spanish dramatist, who wrote some 400 comedies.

TIRUCHIRAPALLI (tiroochirapa'li). Town in Tamil Nadu, Rep. of India, on the r. Cauvery. It makes cotton textiles, cigars, gold and silver filigree. A place of pilgrimage, it was cap. of Tamil kingdoms from the 10th-17th cent. The name means three-headed demon. Pop. (1971) 306,250.

TIRYNS. Site of Greek city in Argolis, with massive remains of the Mycenaean culture.

TISSOT (tēsō'), **James Joseph Jacques** (1836-1902). French artist. Serving in the Franco-Prussian War, he subsequently went to London and produced a number of highly detailed and attractive renderings of the Victorian social scene.

TISZA (tē'sah). River rising in the USSR, and flowing through Hungary to Yugoslavia, where it links with the Danube above Belgrade. Length 1,300 km (800m).

TIT or **titmouse.** Name given to members of the Passerine family Paridae, of birds. Six species, all insect eaters, are found in Britain, viz. the crested, blue, cole, great, marsh and long-tailed.

TĪ'TAN. The largest moon of Saturn and the largest in the Solar System (diameter 4,820 km/3,600 m), it was discovered by C. Huygens in 1655. It is also the only moon in the Solar System to have an atmosphere, which was thought to consist of methane, until spacecraft Voyager 1 (USA 1980) showed that it consists mainly of nitrogen. There is a covering of thick cloud and the position of any solid surface is not known. The temperature at the lowest point measured is *c.* $-200°$C ($-330°$F).

'TĪTA'NIC'. The supposedly unsinkable British White Star liner that struck an iceberg off the Grand Banks of Newfoundland on her maiden voyage 14/15 April 1912: 1,513 lives were lost.

TĪTĀ'NIUM. Lustrous, steel-like white metal resembling iron, burning in air, and the only metal to burn in nitrogen: symbol Ti, at. no. 22, at. wt. 47.90. Discovered by Gregor (1791), it was named by Klaproth in 1795 and obtained pure by Hunter in 1910. Its compounds occur in practically all igneous rocks and their sedimentary deposits. The oxide is used in high-grade white pigments, and some barium compounds are used in high value capacitors. Of great strength and corrosion-resistance, although lightweight it is used in Concorde and spacecraft, and was found on the Moon in the Sea of Tranquillity.

TĪ'TANS. In Greek mythology, the sons and daus. of Uranus and Ge, who warred against Zeus, but were thrust into the underworld.

TITHES (literally, tenths). In England payment exacted from the inhabitants of a parish for the maintenance of the church and its incumbent. Originally it was payable in kind, and was levied on all yearly profits, but in the 19th cent. a rent charge was substituted. By the Tithe Act, 1936, rent charge was replaced by 'redemption annuities' payable to the Crown, govt stock being issued to T.-owners.

TITIAN (tish'an). Anglicized form of the name of Italian artist Tiziano (Vecellio) (*c.* 1477-1576). He studied under the Bellinis, and was strongly influenced by Giorgione. In 1548 he painted the equestrian portrait of Charles V, and later executed many pictures for Philip II of Spain. His most important works incl. 'Bacchus and Ariadne', 'Venus and Adonis', and the 'Entombment of Christ'.

TITICACA (tētēkah'kah). Mountain lake in the Andes, part in Bolivia and part in Peru, over 3,815 m (12,500 ft) a.s.l.; 210km (130m) long and area 8,300 sq.km (3,200 sq.m). It is used for irrigation and hydro-electric power. Peru has ports at Puno and Huancane, and Bolivia at Guaqui. Giant, edible frogs abound in its waters.

TITIAN. A portrait of Charles V, the Holy Roman Emperor, which has a delightful informality, and is preserved in Munich. *Photo: The Mansell Collection*

TITO (tē'tō). Assumed name of the Yugoslav soldier and statesman Josip Broz (1892-1980). B. in Croatia, he served in the Austrian army during the F.W.W., was captured by the Russians, and fought in the Red Army during the Civil Wars. Returning to Yugoslavia in 1923, he became prominent as a Communist. After the German invasion of 1941, he organized the National Liberation Army which carried on guerrilla warfare against the occupying forces. He received the title of marshal in 1943. In 1946 he became PM of the Federal Rep. and C-in-C of the armed forces, and was largely responsible for the settlement of the Yugoslav minority question on a federal basis. Under a new constitution in 1953 he became Pres. (for life from 1974). Denounced by the Cominform, particularly the USSR, in 1948 for his (successful) system of decentralized, profit-sharing workers' councils, very popular with the peasantry, his belief that there are different national roads to socialism, and his subsequent foreign policy of 'positive neutralism', Tito became one of the principal leaders of the uncommitted nations in world politics.

TITICACA. The characteristic reed boats used by the Aymara Indians of the lake. The women are also as attached to their 'bowler' type headgear as City financiers once were. *Photo: Mireille Vautier*

TITOGRAD (tē'tograd). Yugoslav town, cap. of Montenegro, on the Moracha. A commercial centre with tobacco factories and sawmills, it is on the site of Diocletian's birthplace. Until the S.W.W., when it was badly damaged, it was called Podgorica; it was rebuilt, and renamed in 1948 in honour of Tito. pop. (1971) 54,500.

TITUS, Flavius Sabinus Vespasianus (AD 40–81). Roman emperor. Eldest son of Vespasian, he was a distinguished soldier and stormed Jerusalem in AD 70. He became emperor in 79.

TIVOLI (tē'vōlē). Ancient town of Italy, 32km (20m) ENE of Rome, with ruins of Hadrian's villa and other Roman remains; also the Villa d'Este (1549) with its gardens.

TLEMCEN (tlemsen'). Town in NW Algeria, an important religious centre with medieval mosques. Carpets and leather goods are made. Pop. (1970) 90,000.

TLI'NGIT. Largest group of American Indians on the NW coast, others being the Tsimshian and Chinook. They are noted for their carving, as in the totem poles which bear the crests and titles of the owner, painting and weaving. Frequent motifs are the raven and mythical 'thunderbird', whale, octopus, beaver, bear and wolf. Their canoes were traditionally hewn from a single log. They anticipated modern pop stars by using glittering mica flakes, added to bear's grease, as a protective cosmetic. Their most famous custom was the **potlatch,** a formal distribution of food and goods to guests, which had in turn to be surpassed by the chief guest. Today many run prosperous salmon canneries.

TNT ($C_6H_2(NO_2)_3CH_3$). Short for trinitrotoluene, a powerful high explosive; a yellow crystalline solid, prepared from toluene acted upon by sulphuric and nitric acids.

TOAD. Genus of amphibians, of world-wide distribution, except in Australia and Madagascar. The common T. (*Bufo vulgaris*) of Europe and Asia has a rough, usually dark brown skin in which there are glands secreting a poisonous fluid which makes it unattractive as food for other animals: it needs this protection as its usual progress is a slow, ungainly crawl. The eggs are laid, not in a mass as with frogs, but in long strings. The common T. of N America, *B. lentiginosa*, is very similar.

TOADSTOOLS. *See* FUNGI.

TOBACCO. A narcotic plant of the genus *Nicotiana*, family Solanaceae, whose dried leaves are prepared for smoking, chewing, and as snuff. The generally cultivated species is *N. tabacum*, a native of America: it was introduced to Europe as a medicinal plant in the 16th cent. and the habit of smoking T. was probably brought to England *c.* 1556 by Hawkins. *See* CIGAR; CIGARETTE. The best-known Ts. are grown in USA (Virginia, N and S Carolina, Georgia, Kentucky, Tennessee); the Commonwealth (Ontario, Zimbabwe, Malawi); and Turkey, Greece, and Bulgaria. By 'topping' the plants about a dozen large leaves are produced which are cured by exposure to the sun, air currents, or artificial heat, and subsequently mature for 2 or 3 years in the warehouse. T.-smoking, espec. in the form of cigarettes, is now recognized as leading to disease, particularly affecting the heart and lungs.

TOBACCO. In eastern China large quantities of tobacco are grown and production is increasing, since it does not yet seem to have attracted the same health campaign veto as in the West. *Photo: Courtesy of the Society for Anglo-Chinese Understanding*

TOBĀ'GO. *See under* TRINIDAD.

TOBATA. *See under* KITAKYUSHU.

TOBOGGAN. Flat-bottomed sledge, curving upward at the front, and carrying runners, used in coasting down snow slopes, or on artificial curved courses of high-banked snow or ice, e.g. the Cresta run. As incl. in the Olympics, tobogganing incl. runs with two types. Luge (lōōj) Ts. seat 1 or 2, are not enclosed, have no brakes and are steered only by altering the body position and by footwork. Bobsleighs, seating 2 or 4, are of steel or aluminium, with streamlined 'cowls' enclosing the lower fore-part; steering is by a pivoting front section and the action of the 'brakeman' from behind, and there are emergency brakes. Courses for the former events are usually more labyrinthine than for the second. Skibobs resemble a bicycle in which a ski replaces each wheel, and the rider wears foot skis up to 50cm long. The word T. derives from Canadian Algonquin Indian.

TOBO'LSK. Town in the RSFSR, USSR, nr the confluence of the Irtysh with the Tobol. A Cossack settlement, founded in 1587, it is still noted for peasant crafts, and produce synthetic rubber. Pop. (1970) 50,000.

TOBRUK (tobrook'). Port in Libya, 96km (60m) W of Bardia, with an excellent harbour. Occupied by the Italians in 1911, it was taken by the British in the S.W.W. in 1941, and unsuccessfully besieged by Axis forces April-Dec. 1941. It was captured by the Germans in June 1942 after the retreat of the main British force to Egypt, and this precipitated the replacement of Auchinleck by Montgomery. Pop. (1970) 16,000.

TOC H. Organization for Christian fellowship, founded at Poperinghe in 1915 by the Rev. Neville Talbot and the Rev. P.T.B. Clayton (1885-1972); it was named Talbot House in memory of Gilbert Talbot who was killed in action in July 1915. Toc H is the army signaller's designation of the initials.

TOCQUEVILLE (tokvēl'), **Aléxis Charles Henri Clérel de** (1805-59). French historian, author of *Démocratie en Amérique* (1835) and *L' Ancien Régime et la Révolution* (1856).

TODD, Alexander Robertus, baron (1907-). British organic chemist. B. in Glasgow he was prof. at Manchester 1938-44, and Cambridge 1944-71. Elected FRS in 1942, he was awarded a Nobel prize in 1957 for his work on the nucleic acids: important in inherited characteristics - for transmitting and putting them into effect. OM 1977.

TODT (tōt), **Fritz** (1891-1942). German engineer. He was responsible for the Siegfried Line and the great autobahn roads, and as Min. for Armaments 1940-2 built the Atlantic Wall.

TOG. Measure of thermal insulation used in the textile trade, e.g. a light summer suit provides 1.0 tog.

TOGLIATTI (tolyah'ti), **Palmiro** (1893-1964). Italian politician, a founder of the Italian Communist party. The river port and industrial town of T. in the RSFSR, USSR, on the Kuibyshev Reservoir, is named after him. Pop. (1979) 502,000.

TŌ'GŌ. Country in W Africa between Ghana and Benin, with a 56km (35m) coastline on the Gulf of Guinea, on which the cap. Lomé (pop. 135,000) stands. Cocoa, coffee, coconuts and copra are exported, but phosphate and bauxite are now much more important.

T. was formerly part of the German colony of Togoland, which in 1922 was divided between France and Britain under League of Nations mandate. It was then under UN trusteeship from 1946 until in 1956 Brit. Togoland voted for integration with Ghana (q.v.), where it became Volta region, and in the 1970s developed a secessionist movement; and Fr. Togoland chose independence as the Rep. of Togo outside the Fr. Community. Under the constitution of 1980 T. has a Pres. (Gnassingbe Eyadéma, elected for 7 years in 1979), a unicameral Nat. Assembly, and the Rassemblement du peuple Togolais (RPT) is the only legal political party.

Area 56,000 sq.km (21,850 sq.m); pop. (1977) 2,350,000, about 75 per cent Christian and 25 per cent Moslem. The official language is French, but the people speak a variety of African languages. M.U.: CFA franc.

TŌ'JŌ, Hideki (1884-1948). Japanese politician. As PM 1941-4 he was mainly responsible for the attack on Pearl Harbor. He was tried and hanged as a war criminal.

TOKAJ (tō'koi). Hungarian town at the confluence of the Bodrog and the Tisa, famous for its wine. Pop. (est.) 6,500.

TOKELAU ISLANDS (tōkelow'). Group of 3 atolls in the central Pacific, admin. by New Zealand since 1926, and declared part of NZ in 1949: Atafu, Fakaofo, and Nukunono. Their resources are scant, and most of the pop. is being voluntarily resettled in NZ. Area 10 sq.km (4 sq.m); pop. (1976) 1,575.

TŌ'KYŌ. Cap. of Japan, on T. Bay on the island of Honshu. The delta of the Sumida r. separates the city proper from the suburb of Honjo. Formerly called Yedo and founded in the 16th cent., it was named T. (eastern city) in 1868 when the emperor removed his court there from Kyoto. T., badly damaged by an earthquake in 1923 when some 58,000 people were killed, was 80 per cent destroyed from the air in the S.W.W. Rebuilding was rapid, and from the 1960s there was a movement of pop. to the perimeter, and the growth of Shinjuku to rival the central Ginza shopping area. Within T. are the Imperial Palace, National Diet, Nat. Theatre, T. Univ. (1877) and many others (incl. from 1974 the HQ of the United Nations univ.), museums, the Nat. Athletic Stadium, and it is the HQ of broadcasting, publishing and economic life. There are internat. airports at Narita to the NE, and at Haneda. Pop. (1978) 8,266,000.

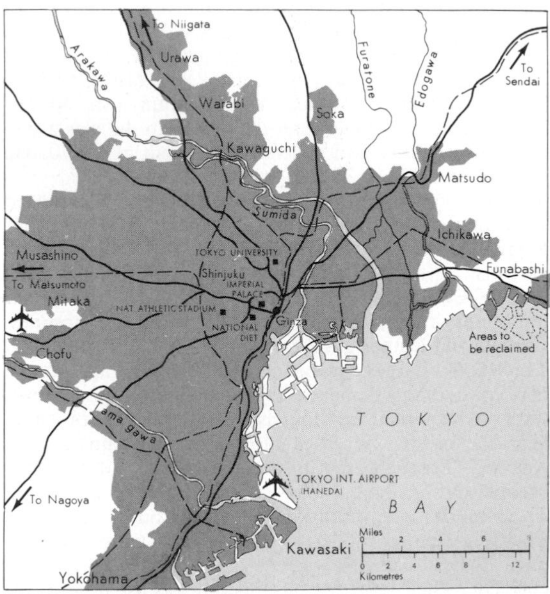

TOKYO

TOLEDO (tōlā'dō). (1) City in Spain on the Tagus, 68km (42m) SW of Madrid. There is a Gothic cathedral 1227-1493, and there are fine buildings of the Moorish period. For centuries T. sword blades were famous. Pop. (1970) 41,000.

(2) City and port in Ohio, USA, on Maumee Bay at the W end of lake Erie. Very important industrially (motor vehicles, electrical appliances, glass, food processing, etc.). Pop. met. area (1970) 685,387.

TOLKIEN (tol'kēn), **John Ronald Reuel** (1892-1973). British scholar. Merton prof. of English at Oxford 1945-59, he is celebrated for his creation of a world -

Middle-Earth - peopled with Hobbits, Dwarfs, Men, etc., with their own language, history and myth, as described in *The Hobbit* (1937), *The Lord of the Rings* (1954-5), and *The Silmarillion* (1977; ed. Christopher Tolkien).

TOLPUDDLE MARTYRS. Six farm labourers of Tolpuddle, nr Dorchester, who in 1834 were transported to Australia for forming a Trade Union. After a nation-wide agitation they were pardoned 2 years later.

TOLSTOY (tol'stoi), **Alexei Nikolaievich** (1882-1945). Russian author. B. at Kuibyshev, he trained as an engineer, and in 1907 pub. a vol. of symbolist lyrics. After being a soldier in the White army, he went to Paris, and before returning to Russia in 1922 wrote the 1st part of his trilogy *Khozhdeniye po mukam* (*Road to Calvary*), awarded a Stalin prize in 1942. Other works are the historical novel *Peter the Great* (1929-34) and the play *Ivan the Terrible.*

TOLSTOY, Leo Nikolaievich (1828-1910). Russian novelist. B. of noble family at Yasnaya Polyana in Tula, he fought in the Crimean War. A series of *Tales from Sebastopol* made him famous. His masterpieces are *War and Peace,* dealing with the Napoleonic struggle (1866), and *Anna Karenina* (1877). Later he devoted himself to preaching a gospel of brotherhood and love. Such books as *What is Religion?* and *The Kreutzer Sonata* have a didactic and religious purpose. *Resurrection,* his last novel, appeared in 1900. Excommunicated for his heretical views, he gave up the use of his property, lived as a peasant, and d. a fugitive from his home at Astapovo.

TO'LTECS. Ancient people of Central America whose culture preceded that of the Aztecs and Mayas.

TOLUENE (tōl'ū-ēn). A colourless, inflammable liquid, $C_6H_5CH_3$, b.p. 110°C, and insoluble in water. Obtained as a by-product in the distillation of coal-tar, it is used as a solvent, and as a starting point in the manufacture of many substances incl. explosives (*see* TNT), dyes, perfumes and sulphonic acids.

TOMASI (tōmah'si), **Giuseppe, Prince of Lampedusa** (1896-1957). Italian writer. He became famous for his novel *Il Gattopardo* (1958: *The Leopard*), pub. posthumously, which describes the Bourbon regime, Garibaldi's victory, and the dawn of modern Italy, in his native Sicily, as experienced by the vividly portrayed character of Prince Fabrizio and his family.

TOMATO. Annual plant (*Lycopersicon esculentum*) of the Solanaceae family, native to S America, sometimes also known as the 'love-apple' although any aphrodisiac quality of the globose red or yellow fruits is imaginary. As a salad crop Ts. are grown in N America and Europe under glass.

TOMBSTONE. Desert town in SE Arizona, USA. It flourished 1879-83 until its silver mines were exhausted, and its decline was then arrested by the 'Western' legend of T. as the place where sheriff Wyatt Earp, his brothers and 'Doc' Holliday shot to death the Clanton gang at the OK corral in 1881. Pop. (1972) 1,283.

TOMLINSON, H(enry) M(ajor) (1873-1958). British author. B. in London, he was a and *Athenaeum F.W.W. and literary editor of the Nation and Athenaeum* 1917-23. His books, which have the tang of the sea he loved in their writing, incl. *The Sea and the Jungle* (1912), *Gallions Reach* (1927), and *Morning Light* (1946).

TOMMY-GUN. Name for any light automatic carbine or rifle from hip or shoulder, derived from the US Thompson sub-machine gun.

TŌMO'GRAPHY. Use of X-rays to obtain a 'slice' or plane section (Gk. *tome* 'a cutting') photograph of the brain or other organs of the body. The crystal detectors and amplifiers have a sensitivity a hundred times greater than ordinary X-ray films, and the method - computerised axial tomography (CAT) scanning - defines the size and shape of deep-lying tumours. It was developed independently by Allan Cormack (USA/S African-born) and Godfrey Hounsfield (UK), who shared a Nobel prize in 1979. In advanced positron-emission tomography (PET), biochemical activity is mapped by introducing radioactive tracers into tissue, and the method is useful as a means of selecting patients for brain surgery, e.g. operations to bypass blocked arteries.

TOMSK. Industrial city on the r. Tom, Siberia, USSR. It has a univ. (1888), and although specialising from 1980 in synthetic fibres, also has sawmilling, distilling, plastics, and electric motor manufactures. Pop. (1979) 421,000.

TOM THUMB. Name from an English folk tale frequently given to dwarfs, in particular Charles Sherwood Stratton (1838-83), known as General T.T.

TON. The imperial English or long T. is 2,240 lb, the American or short T. is 2,000 lb and the metric tonne is 1,000 kg or 2,204.6 lb.

TONE, Theobald Wolfe (1763-98). Irish nationalist. Called to the Bar in 1789, he was prominent in the revolutionary society of the United Irishmen. In 1798 he accompanied the French invasion of Ireland, was captured and condemned to death, but cut his throat in prison.

TO'NGA. Polynesian kingdom in the S Pacific consisting of 3 groups of islands; cap. Nukualofa on Tongatapu. They were visited by Captain Cook in 1773, who called them the Friendly Islands, and came under British Protection in 1900 and became a sovereign member of the Commonwealth in 1970. King Tungi (1918-) succeeded his mother, Queen Salote, in 1965. He is assisted by a cabinet, privy council, and legislative assembly of 21. The state religion is Wesleyanism. Copra and bananas are produced. Area 700 sq.km (270 sq.m); pop. (1976) 90,128.

TONGUE. Muscular organ in the floor of the mouth. It has a thick root attached to a U-shaped bone (hyoid) behind; a thin fold of mucous membrane connects its lower middle line with the floor of the mouth. It is covered with mucous membrane containing many nerves and also the 'taste buds', which distinguish the qualities called salt, sweet, sour and bitter. It directs food to the teeth, presses food and drink back into the throat in the act of swallowing and by modifying the voice forms articulate speech.

TONKA. Tree (*Coumarouna odorata*) of the family Leguminosae, native to Guiana. Its fruit, a dry, fibrous pod, contains a single aromatic seed used in perfumery.

TONKIN. Name of a former Fr. protectorate, from 1950 part of Vietnam (q.v.). It was in the **T. Gulf,** after a minor engagement on 2 Aug. 1964, that the US destroyers *Maddox* and *Turner Joy* reported a night attack on 4 Aug. by N Vietnamese torpedo boats. It has been suggested that radar and sonar effects were misinterpreted, but a retaliatory air attack was made on N Vietnam which led to the eventual despatch of over 1,000,000 US troops to battle in S Vietnam. There is disagreement between China and Vietnam over territorial limits in the Gulf, which has oil resources.

TONLE SAP (ton'la sap). Lake in W Kampuchea with rich fisheries, fed by the Mekong during the monsoon season, and drained by it for the rest of the year. Area from 2,600 sq.km (1,000 sq.m) to 6,500 sq.km (2,500 sq.m) at its height.

TONSILS. A pair of gland-like bodies between the 2 arches (fauces) of the soft palate at the back of the mouth. They may become infected, and it was formerly common for them to be removed, even when not strictly necessary, but it is now considered that they serve some protective function.

TONSURE. Ritual shaving or cutting of the hair as a symbol of dedication to the clerical state in the RC and Eastern Orthodox churches. In the former, the crown was shaved, leaving a fringe all round to resemble Christ's crown of thorns, but the practice ceased from 1973; in the latter the hair is merely shorn close.

TONYS. Annual awards (the Antoinette Perry Awards) by the League of New York Theatres to actors, authors, etc. in both musical and 'straight' plays on Broadway.

TOOLS, Machine. Strictly the term incl. wood-working M. Ts., but is generally used for all tools operated by power. They are the basis of industrial production, and their most important use is in the manufacture of engines and machines. The chief M.T. is the lathe, from which the others have developed. The industrial potential of a country is often calculated by the number of M.Ts. available. Automatic control of M.Ts. is an important modern development. *See* AUTOMATION.

TOOWOO'MBA. Town in SE Queensland, Australia. Set among the Darling Downs, it is a commercial and industrial centre (coal-mining, iron-working, engineering, and clothing factories), as well as an agricultural market for a fertile area. Pop. (1978) 71,900.

TŌ'PAZ. Mineral valued as a gemstone. It crystallizes in the rhombic system and has a perfect basal cleavage. It varies from yellow to white, blue or pink, and is found in Brazil, Peru, Sri Lanka, and Siberia.

TOPE. Small shark (*Galeorhinus galeus*) ranging through temperate and tropical seas. Dark grey above and white beneath, it reaches 2m (7ft): the young are born alive, sometimes 50 at a time.

TOPE. Kind of tumulus found in India and SE Asia; a Buddhist monument usually built over a relic of Buddha or his disciples. They date from 300 BC-AD 400, and the most famous are at Sanchi, near Bhilsa, C India.

TOPĒ'KA. Cap. of Kansas, USA, on the r. Kansas, 90km (55m) W of Kansas City. Laid out in 1854, T. became state cap. in 1861. It has textile and engineering industries. Pop. (1970) 125,000.

TOPLADY, Augustus Montague (1740-78). British Anglican clergyman. B. at Farnham, he pub. his famous hymn 'Rock of Ages' in 1775.

TORBAY. District in S Devon, England, created in 1968 by the union of the seaside resorts of Paignton, Torquay and Brixham. Pop. (1974) 108,700.

TORGAU (tor'gow). Town in Leipzig dist., E Germany. Here Frederick the Great defeated the Austrians in 1760, and US and Russian forces first made contact in the S.W.W. Pop. (1970) 20,000.

TORINO. Ital. form of TURIN.

TORNĀ'DO. Extremely violent revolving storm, caused by a rising column of warm air propelled by strong wind. The diameter may be a few hundred metres or less, but the T. rises to a great height, and is marked by swirling funnel-shaped clouds. Moving at speeds up to 400 kph (250 mph), Ts. are common in the Mississippi basin and cause great destruction. The most severe are always accompanied by thunderstorms.

TORONTO. Canadian city, cap. of Ontario (1797), on the N shore of lake Ontario. It is an important port, and industries incl. making of farm machinery, motor cars, meat packing and other food processing. Cheap power is drawn from Niagara Falls. It is also a great commercial, banking, and publishing centre. Central T. has been re-developed, with underground shopping streets linking the giant complex, of which T.-Dominion Center and New City Hall form part. It has theatres (O'Keefe Center, Massey Hall and Royal Alexander Theater), is the nat. television centre, and mounts an annual Canadian Nat. Exhibition. There is a univ. (1827). T. dates from 1794, built on the site of a French fort (1749); it was constituted a city 1834. Pop. (1976) 633,320; met. area 2,803,100.

TORONTO. The world's tallest free-standing structure, the CN tower (1975) which rises to 553 m (1,815 ft). The transmission mast at its top has antennae for radio, television and speeding vital business communication. The 'bulge' houses observation galleries, a restaurant, etc. *Photo: Courtesy of Canadian National Railways.*

TORPEDO. Self-propelled submarine projectile used in naval warfare. Invented in 1805 by R. Fulton, the first T. consisted of an explosive charge only, and propulsion mechanism was added in 1862 by R. Whitehead. In the S.W.W. 'human Ts.' were piloted by suicide crews. The modern T. is a homing missile, e.g. the British Sting Ray, coming into service in the 1980s, which is launched from a ship, helicopter, etc., and uses a computer brain to assist in finding an enemy submarine.

TORPEDO FISH or **electric ray.** Family of fishes, the Torpedinidae, whose electric organs between the pectoral fin and the head can give a powerful shock. *T. hebetans* is found off England.

TORQUAY (torkē'). English seaside resort and residential town in S Devon on Tor Bay. Once a fishing village, T. dates from the 12th cent., and in 1968 became part of Torbay (q.v.).

TORQUEMADA (tōrkāmah'dah), **Tomás de** (1420-98). Spanish inquisitor. B. at Valladolid, he became a Dominican, revived the Inquisition, and is said to have been responsible for the burning of 10,000 persons. T. also expelled the Jews from Spain.

TORRENS (tor'enz). Salt lake in eastern South Australia, which is reduced to a marsh in dry weather. It is *c.* 8m (25ft) b.s.l.; area 5,775 sq.km (2,230 sq.m).

TORRES STRAIT. A 130km (80m) wide channel separating New Guinea from Australia, scattered with reefs, discovered by Torres in 1606.

TORRES VEDRAS. Town of Portugal, 40km (25m) N of Lisbon. The 'lines of T. V.' were built by Wellington in the Peninsular War. Pop. (1970) 13,100.

TORRICELLI (tor-rēchel'lē), **Evangelista** (1608-47). Italian physicist. B. at Faenza, he discovered the principle of the barometer, inventing the T. tube and the T. vacuum in 1643.

TORSION. The state of strain set up in a material by virtue of being twisted, e.g. when a thread wire or rod is twisted, the T. which is set up in the material returns or tends to return it to its original state. An instrument which makes use of this is the T. balance, a sensitive device for measuring small gravitational or magnetic forces, or electric charges, by balancing these against the restoring force set up by them in a suspended fibre.

TORTOISE. Reptile of the order Chelonia. Marine and freshwater forms are known as turtles or terrapins. It has a characteristic 'shell' consisting of a curved upper carapace and flattened lower plastron which are joined at the sides, and the head and limbs may be retracted within it, to a greater or lesser extent, in time of danger. Herbivorous it has no teeth but the mouth forms a sharp edged 'beak': eggs are laid in mud and hatched by the sun. Best-known species are the small N African T. (*Testudo graeca*), also found in Asia Minor, often imported to languish in British gardens, and the giant species of the Galapagos and Seychelles which reach a great age, may be 120cm (4ft) long, and yield *c.* 90kg (200lb) of meat - hence their almost complete extermination by passing ships.

Tortoiseshell is the semi-transparent shell of the hawksbill turtle.

TORTUGA (tortōō'gah). Island (Fr. La Tortue) off the N coast of Haiti (q.v.), formerly a pirate lair.

TORTURE. The infliction of bodily pain, esp. to extort evidence or confession. At one time a feature of most judicial systems, it was abolished in England *c.* 1640, in Scotland in 1708, and in France in 1789, but was revived by the Nazis and Japanese during the S.W.W. The usual instruments of T. in Europe were the rack, wheel, thumb-screw, and boot.

After the S.W.W. forms of mental T. were scientifically developed. The KGB and other Communist interrogators used 'brain-washing' procedures from the 1950s which involve arrest of the suspect during the night, his isolation in featureless, soundless cells, without sleep and with little food. In the West, by the early 1960s, a similar technique had been perfected in which isolation was replaced by severe sensory deprivation. The suspect is prevented from seeing by a hood, from feeling by being swathed in a loose-fitting garment, and from hearing by a continuous loud 'white' noise at *c.* 85 decibels, while being forced to maintain himself in a 'search' position against a wall by his finger-tips. Long-lasting psychiatric effects are alleged. The European Convention for the Protection of Human Rights and Fundamental Freedoms forbids T., and in 1971 the Rep. of Ireland brought charges against Britain for using these techniques in N Ireland. The European Commission of Human Rights in 1976 found Britain guilty of T. in its interrogation techniques, but the European Court of Human Rights ruled that it was 'inhuman and degrading treatment'.

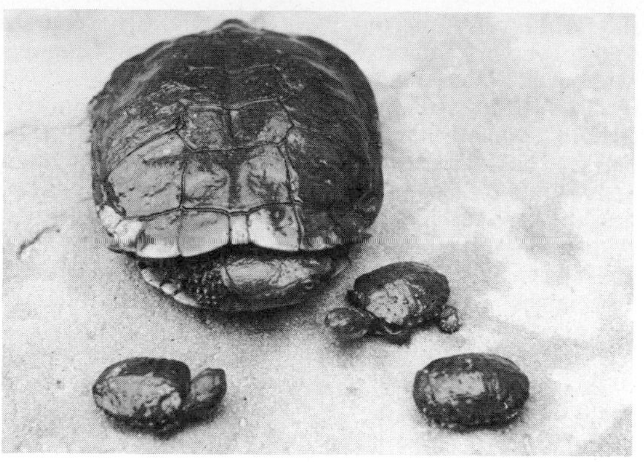

TORTOISE. All members of the order found in Australia are aquatic. The western swamp tortoise was thought to be extinct until a small boy brought in his newly captured pet for identification. The little ones will take ten years to reach maturity. *Photo: Courtesy of the Australian Information Service*

TORUN (to'rōōny). Town in Poland on the Vistula, 48km (30m) ESE of Bydgoszcz, founded by the Teutonic Knights (13th cent.). It has a univ. Copernicus was b. at T. Pop. (1978) 164,000.

TORY PARTY. Name applied *c.* 1680-1830 to the fore-runner of the present Conservative Party. The original Tories were Irish guerrillas who warred on the English; hence the name was transferred, at first in a derogatory sense, to the Royalists who opposed the Exclusion Bill. The T.P. largely supported the revolution of 1688, but fell under suspicion of Jacobite sympathies and were excluded from office 1714-60. Under George III they regained power, which they held almost continuously until 1830. They were traditionally the party of squire and parson, as opposed to the Whigs, who drew their support largely from the trading classes and Nonconformists. Of late years the name has been revived as an alternative to Conservative. In the history of the USA a T. was an opponent of the break with Britain in the War of American Independence 1775-1883.

TOSCANINI (toskahnē'ni), **Arturo** (1867-1957). Italian conductor. B. in Parma, he made La Scala, Milan - where he conducted 1898-1903, 1906-8, and 1920-9 - the world's leading opera house. However, he was opposed to the Fascist régime, and in 1936 returned to America, where he had conducted at the Metropolitan 1908-15, the NBC Symphony Orchestra being formed for him in 1937. He retired in 1954.

TOTALIZATOR or **Tote.** Device on horse-racing courses and greyhound tracks to record bets and pay winnings without the intervention of a bookmaker.

TOTEMISM. System of belief common among primitive peoples, whereby the members of a clan believe themselves to be descended from an animal or plant: this totem (Algonquin Indian, 'my guardian spirit') is sacred to them, and they are forbidden to eat it. T. is usually associated with exogamy, i.e. members of the same clan are forbidden to inter-marry. It still exists among the Australian Aborigines and the American Indians, and formerly prevailed over most of Europe and Asia.

TO'TILA (d. 552). King of the Ostrogoths, who warred with Justinian for Italy, and was killed by Narses at the battle of Taginae.

TOTTENHAM. District of the Greater London bor. of Haringey. Settled in Danish times, it has a church (All Hallows) dating in part from the 12th cent. Bruce Castle (16th cent.) was built on a site belonging to Robert Bruce's father. T. Hotspur is a famous football team.

TOUCAN (tookahn'). Bird of the family Ramphastidae with very large, often brilliantly coloured beak, espec. in the genus *Rhamphastos.* Living in small flocks in S America forests, Ts. often have handsome plumage, are omnivorous, and lay their eggs in holes in trees.

TOULON (tooloń'). Seaport and cap. of Var dept, France, on the Mediterranean, 48km (30m) SE of Marseilles. It is the chief Mediterranean naval station of France, with defences commanding the sea and large dockyards. Petroleum refining, and the making of chemicals, furniture, and clothing are among its industries. The Roman Telo Martius, T. was made a port by Henry IV. It was occupied by the British in 1793, and Napoleon first distinguished himself in driving them out. Pop. (1975) 180,510.

TOULOUSE (toolo͞os'). Cap. of Haute-Garonne dept, S France, on the Garonne SE of Bordeaux, T. was an important place before the Roman conquest. Cap. of the Visigoths and later (781–843) of Aquitaine, it has a 12–13th cent. cathedral and a univ. (*c.* 1230). Wellington repulsed Soult at T. in 1814. Textiles are made and the French aerospace industry is here, e.g. Concorde. Pop. (1975) 371,145.

TOULOUSE-LAUTREC (-lawtrek'), **Henri Raymonde de** (1864–1901). B. at Albi, where a L. Museum commemorates him, he was dwarfed and crippled by both his thighs having been broken in boyhood. Of noble descent - the counts of T. - he now preferred to plunge himself into the unquestioning and convivial life of Montmartre and produced posters and colour lithographs of striking linear dexterity showing can-can dancers, circus acrobats, brothel scenes, etc. His life was shortened by his heavy drinking.

TOUQUET-PARIS-PLAGE (tookā'), **Le.** Fashionable resort of France, Pas-de-Calais dept, on the Channel coast with fine sands and pinewoods. Pop. (1973) 4,500.

TOURAINE (toorān'). Ancient prov. of France whose cap. was Tours. It is covered by Indre-et-Loire dept and part of Indre.

TOURCOING (toorkwań'). Town in Nord dept, France, near the Belgian border, an important textile centre since the 12th cent. Pop. (1975) 102,500

TOUR DE FRANCE (toor de frońs). French road race for professional cyclists estab. in 1903. The route (*c.* 4,000 km/2,400 m) is variable, taking about 3 weeks to cover in stages of *c.* 200km (120m) each day, but always ending in Paris after passing over terrain of varying difficulty, with time trials at intervals. The rider with the shortest overall time at the conclusion of each stage wears a yellow jersey. The competitors form about a dozen teams with a dozen riders in each, each commercially sponsored. Famous riders incl. Fausto Coppi (Italian), Jacques Anquetil (French), and Eddy Merckx (Belgium). In Britain a shorter simpler version is known as the *Milk Race.*

TOUR DE FRANCE. Few events arouse as much excitement in France as this annual cycle race, and the town chosen as the departure point is in ferment for days before the 'off'. *Photo: Courtesy of the French National Tourist Office*

TOURMALINE. Hard, brittle mineral, a complex of various metal silicates, and containing aluminium and boron. Small Ts. are generally found in granites and gneisses. The common varieties are opaque, ranging from black (schorl) to pink, and the transparent gemstones may be colourless (achroit), rose pink (rubellite), green (Brazilian emerald), blue (indicolite, Brazilian sapphire), or brown (dravite).

TOURNAI (to͞ornā') (Flem. Doornik). Town in Hainaut prov., Belgium, on the Scheldt. On the site of a Roman relay post, it has a Romanesque cathedral dating from the 11th cent. Carpets, cement, leather are made. Pop. (1979) 70,000.

TOURNAMENT or **tourney.** Martial sports popular in the Middle Ages. Events incl. mounted combats and mock fights with sword, spear or dagger. The T. was introduced into England from France in the 11th cent., and flourished until the 16th cent.

TOURNEUR (tur'ner), **Cyril** (*c.* 1575–1626). English dramatist. His *Revenger's Tragedy* (pub. 1607) and *Atheist's Tragedy* (pub. 1611) are among the most powerful of Stuart dramas.

TOURS (toor). Cap. of Indre-et-Loire dept., France, in the Loire valley, historic cap. of Touraine. There is a 13–15th cent. cathedral, and engineering and chemical industries. Balzac was born in the town. Pop. (1975) 139,560.

TOUSSAINT L'OUVERTURE (toosań' loovertür'), **Pierre Dominique** (*c.* 1746–1803). Negro soldier. B. at Haiti, he was a slave and joined the insurrection of 1791. He helped the French when they abolished slavery, became C-in-C of St Domingo in 1796, and turned against the French when they re-imposed slavery. He was captured and d. in prison in France.

TOWER OF LONDON. Fortress on the Thames bank to the E of the City. The keep, or White Tower, was built *c.* 1078 by Bishop Gundulf on the site of British and Roman fortifications. It is surrounded by 2 strong walls and a moat (now dry), and was for cents. a royal residence and the principal state prison. The T.o.L. is today a barracks, an armoury, and a museum. Among prisoners executed there were More, Anne Boleyn, Katherine Howard, Lady Jane Grey, Essex, Strafford, Laud, and Monmouth. *See* REGALIA.

TOWN PLANNING. System of land use in the best interests of the community, with especial stress on aesthetic as well as practical considerations, such as the separation of traffic and pedestrians, provision of easily accessible shops, schools, cinemas, theatres, etc.

TOWNSVILLE. Port in N Queensland, Australia, on Cleveland Bay. Founded in 1868, it was under attack by Japanese aircraft in the S.W.W. in 1942. Exports incl. meat (canned, chilled, etc.), wool, sugar, and minerals, incl. gold and silver. Pop. (1978) 85,300.

TOXAEMIA (toksē'mia). Invasion of the blood by poison, especially that generated within the body.

TOXOCARĪ'ASIS. Infection of humans by a canine intestinal worm which results in a swollen liver and sometimes eye damage.

TOYNBEE, Arnold (1852-83). British economist. He lectured widely in industrial districts on social problems. Toynbee Hall, the first of many social and educational settlements in E London, was named after him in 1885. His nephew **Arnold Joseph T.** (1889-1975), was director of studies at the Royal Institute of Internat. Affairs 1925-55. In his *A Study of History* (12 vols. 1934-61) he attempted as a metaphysician, to discover the laws governing the rise and fall of civilizations. The latter's son **Philip T.** (1916-), a novelist and critic, became for. correspondent of the Observer in 1950.

TRABZON (trahbzon'). Port in NE Turkey, on the Black Sea, 355km (220m) SW of Batum. The Black Sea Univ. was estab. 1963, and exports incl. fruit, tobacco, hides, etc. Pop. (1970) 81,500.

TRACHOMA (trakōm'a). The greatest single world cause of blindness, a severe form of conjunctivitis (q.v.) caused by a micro-organism.

TRACTARIANISM. *See* OXFORD MOVEMENT.

TRACTOR, In agriculture, a motor vehicle, commonly having two very large rear wheels, used in ploughing, and so on. A military **combat tractor** usually has two drivers (one forwards, one backwards), and can excavate 2 tonnes in a single action, so as to hide a Chieftain tank in 11 minutes. It can also cross rivers, operate in nuclear radiation, and clear minefields by discharge of an 'explosive hosepipe'.

TRADE MARK. Distinctive indication (either a name or 'mark') attached to the product of a particular proprietor who must register a legal claim.

TRADES UNION CONGRESS. Voluntary organization of trade unions, founded in Britain in 1868, in which delegates of affiliated unions meet annually to consider matters affecting their members. Today there are some 100 affiliated unions, with an aggregate membership of 10,000,000.

TRADE UNIONS. Organizations of employed workers, formed primarily for the purpose of collective bargaining, and also to provide trade and friendly benefits for members. Trade unions of a kind existed in the Middle Ages as journeymen guilds, and combinations of wage earners were formed in the 18th cent., but modern trade unionism is a product of the Industrial Revolution. Five cents. of repressive legislation in Britain culminated in the passing of the Combination Acts (q.v.), but on the repeal of these in 1824-5, organizations of workpeople were permitted to engage in collective bargaining although still subject to legal restrictions and with no legal protection for their funds until the enactment of a series of Trade Union Acts, 1871-6. Successive Acts of Parliament broadened the unions' field of action, e.g. the 1913 Act which allowed the Unions to engage in political activities. The TUC was for many years mainly representative of unions of craftsmen but in the last decade of the 19th cent. the organization of unskilled labour spread rapidly. Industrial Unionism, meaning the organization of all workers in one industry or trade began about this time; but the characteristic feature of the so-called New Unionism at the time of the 1889 dock strike was the rise of the general labour unions (e.g. the Dock Workers and General Labourers in the gas industry, etc.). In more recent years trade unionism has spread to professional workers, technicians, farm workers, administrative and clerical workers, as well as women. The restrictive Trade Disputes and TU Act (1927) passed after the general strike of 1926, was repealed in 1946. The Wilson govt abandoned plans for legislative reform of TU in 1969, and the Industrial Relations Act (1971) of the Heath govt (incl. registration of TU, legal enforcement of collective agreements, compulsory 'cooling off' periods, and strike ballots) led to confrontation and the govt's fall. It was repealed in 1974 by the succeeding Wilson govt, and the Industrial Relations Court abolished, a new Conciliation and Arbitration Service being set up. *See* SOCIAL CONTRACT. The industrial disputes of the 'winter of discontent' 1978-9, however, undermined the succeeding Callaghan govt., and the Thatcher govt. passed the Employment Act (1980) which restricted the closed shop, picketing and 'secondary action' against anyone other than the employer. *See* STRIKES.

The great growth of American TU, apart from the abortive Knights of Labor 1869-86 (*see also* AFL/CIO) came in the post-Depression years. The movement has a record of greater bitterness and violence than in Britain, but at the present-day has the reputation of being more open to the acceptance of new techniques, taking a broader view of these as conducive to eventual greater prosperity. Probably the most advanced TU system is that of Sweden where conflicts of Us. within an industry - frequent in Britain - are largely eliminated, and where employers and Us. co-operate more freely.

In 1973 a European Trade Union Confederation (ETUC) was estab. with membership 29,000,000: the first pres. was Vic(tor) Feather, baron (1908-76), gen. sec. of the TUC 1969-73. *See* INTERNAT. T.U.

TRAFALGAR, Cape. Low headland in SW Spain off which Nelson defeated a Franco-Spanish fleet on 21 Oct. 1805, near the W entrance to the Straits of Gibraltar. Nelson was mortally wounded.

TRAHER'NE, Thomas (*c.* 1637-74). English metaphysical writer. B. at Hereford, he was vicar of Teddington 1667-74. His moving lyric poetry and his prose *Centuries of Meditations* (1908), were undiscovered until the late 19th cent.

TRAIL. Town in Brit. Columbia, Canada, on the Columbia r. Nearby are giant non-ferrous smelters. Pop. (1971) 11,150.

TRĀ'JAN or **Marcus Ulpius Trajanus** (*c.* AD 52-117). Roman emperor. B. near Seville, he distinguished himself as a soldier, and was adopted as heir by the emperor Nerva, whom he succeeded in AD 98. A just and conscientious ruler, he carried on a correspondence with Pliny on the Christians. He conquered Dacia 101-106, and much of Parthia 114-117. T.'s column at Rome commemorates his victories.

TRAMWAYS. The conveyance system, characterized by the running of wheeled vehicles along parallel rails laid on or alongside public highways. It originated in the colliery vehicles which ran on iron rails from 1776. The earliest passenger T. system was in 1832, in New York, and in the 1860s horse-drawn trams plied in London and Liverpool. The first electric trams, between Portrush and Giant's Causeway, were opened in 1883. Ts. are now powered either by conductor rails below ground or conductor arms connected to overhead wires. Their lack of manœuvrability in traffic has led to their supercession by buses.

TRANCE. Mental state in which the subject loses the ordinary perceptions of time and space, and even of his own body. In this highly aroused state, often induced by rhythmic music, 'tongue-speaking' (often equated with the speaking 'in other tongues' of the disciples at Pentecost) may take place: it usually consists of the rhythmic repetition of meaningless syllables, and return to consciousness is accompanied by euphoria. It is practised by some Christian sects (hence the Pentecostal Movement), and also by Bushman healers, Afro-Brazilian spirit mediums and Siberian shamans.

TRANQUILLIZERS. *See* SEDATIVES.

TRANSCAUCASIA. Area of the USSR to the S of the Caucasus. Here lie Armenia, Azerbaijan (qq.v.), and Georgia which in 1922 formed the Transcaucasian SFSR, broken up in 1936 when each of its members became a separate rep. of the USSR.

TRANSCENDENTALISM. A mode of thought, originating with Kant, 'concerned not with objects, but with our mode of knowing objects'. From Germany T. was introduced into England, and influenced Coleridge and Carlyle. In New England T. developed *c.* 1840-60 into a mystical doctrine which saw God as immanent in nature and the human soul, e.g. Thoreau and Emerson (qq.v.).

TRANSDUCER. A power-transforming device which enables energy in any form (electrical, acoustical, mechanical) to flow from one transmission system to another. The energy flowing to and from a T. may be of the same or of different forms, e.g. an electrical motor receives electrical energy and delivers it to a mechanical system; a gramophone pick-up crystal receives mechanical energy from the needle and delivers it as electrical energy; and a loudspeaker receives an electrical input and delivers an acoustical output.

TRANSFER ORBIT. The orbit followed by a planetary probe. To send such a vehicle by the shortest route would mean continuous expenditure of fuel, which is clearly impossible; it is therefore necessary for the vehicle to move, for most of the journey, in free fall. A probe aimed at Venus has to be 'slowed down' relative to the Earth, so that it enters an elliptical transfer orbit with its perigee (point of closest approach to the Sun) at the same distance as the orbit of Venus; with Mars, the vehicle has to be 'speeded up' relative to the Earth, so that it reaches its apogee (furthest point from the Sun) at the same distance as the orbit of Mars. The need for moving in a transfer orbit, in free fall, means that journeys to the planets are somewhat protracted, but the only way to overcome this difficulty will be to develop nuclear fuels - which will not be an easy matter.

TRANSFORMER. Piece of apparatus without moving parts in which by electromagnetic induction an alternating or intermittent current of one voltage is transformed to another voltage, without change of frequency. A T. has 2 coils, a primary for the input, and a secondary for the output. The ratio of the primary to the secondary voltages (and currents) is directly (and inversely) proportional to the number of turns in the primary and secondary coils. Ts. are widely used in electrical apparatus of all kinds and in particular in power transmission where high voltages and low currents are utilized.

TRANSISTOR. A semiconductor device with 3 or more electrodes. It can act as an amplifier, oscillator photoelectric cell or switch, and usually operates on a very small amount of power. The T. was invented at Bell Telephone Laboratories in America by John Bardeen and Walter Brittain, developing the work of William Shockley. Present-day Ts. commonly consist of a tiny sandwich of semiconductor material, usually germanium or silicon, specially prepared so that the alternate layers have different electrical properties.

A crystal of pure germanium or silicon would act as an insulator. By introducing impurities in the form of atoms of other materials (e.g. boron, arsenic or indium in minute amounts of the order of 1 part in 100 million) the layers may be made either n-type, having an excess of electrons, or p-type, having a deficiency of electrons. This enables electrons to flow from one layer to another in one direction only.

Ts. have had a tremendous impact on the electronics industry and although only invented in 1948 are now made in thousands of millions each year. They perform many of the same functions as the thermionic valve, but have the advantages of greater reliability, long life, compactness and instantaneous action, no warming-up period being necessary. They are widely used in most electronic equipment, but especially for portable radios and television computers, satellites, space research and in microminiaturization.

TRANSJORDAN. Name 1923-46 of the Hashimite kingdom of JORDAN.

TRANSKEI (trans'kī). Independent rep. within S Africa, extending NE from the Great Kei r., on the coast of Cape Province to the border of Natal. The cap. is Umtata, on the Umtata r., pop. 24,800, and there are ports at Port St. Johns and (under construction) Umngazana.

One of the Black Homelands, it became the self-governing territory of T. in 1963, and in 1975 opted for full independence in 1976. Chief Kaisêr Matanzima, the chief minister, (Pres. from 1979) adopted a policy of full citizenship regardless of colour (contrary to the S African concept of 'separate development'), and envisaged

Table of Transuranium Elements

At. No.	*Name*	*Symbol*	*Year discovered*	*Source of first preparation*	*Isotope identified*	*Half Life of first isotope identified*
93	NEPTUNIUM	Np	1940	Irradiation of uranium 238 with neutrons	Np^{239}	2.35 days
94	PLUTONIUM	Pu	1941	Bombardment of uranium 238 with deuterons	Pu^{238}	86.4 years
95	AMERICIUM	Am	1944	Irradiation of plutonium 239 with neutrons	Am^{241}	458 years
96	CURIUM	Cm	1944	Bombardment of plutonium 239 with helium ions	Cm^{242}	162.5 days
97	BERKELIUM	Bk	1949	Bombardment of americium 241 with helium ions	Bk^{243}	4.5 hours
98	CALIFORNIUM	Cf	1950	Bombardment of curium 242 with helium ions	Cf^{245}	44 minutes
99	EINSTEINIUM	Es	1952	Irradiation of uranium 238 with neutrons in first thermonuclear explosion	Es^{253}	20 days
100	FERMIUM	Fm	1953	Irradiation of uranium 238 with neutrons in first thermonuclear explosion	Fm^{255}	16 hours
101	MENDELEVIUM	Md	1955	Bombardment of einsteinium 253 with helium ions	Md^{256}	1.5 hours
102	NOBELIUM	No	1958	Bombardment of curium 246 with carbon ions	No^{255}	3 seconds
103	LAWRENCIUM	Lr	1961	Bombardment of californium 252 with boron ions	Lr^{257}	8 seconds
104	RUTHERFORDIUM	Rf	1969	Bombardment of californium 249 with ions of of carbon-12	Ru^{257}	4 seconds
105	HAHNIUM	Ha	1970	Bombardment of californium 249 with nuclei of nitrogen-15 atoms	Ha^{260}	1.6 seconds

eventual federation of the homelands. Area *c.* 44,000 sq.km (17,000 sq.m); pop. (1976) 1,900,000 Xhosa, but with those working in other areas *c.* 3,000,000.

TRANSMIGRATION OF SOULS or **metempsychosis.** The belief that after death the soul may pass into another human being, an animal or a plant, and that it has so passed on innumerable earlier occasions. The belief was held by the ancient Egyptians, by Pythagoras, Plato, and their followers, and by the Cathars and other heretical Christian sects, and is an integral part of the teachings of Hinduism and Buddhism, and of the Theosophists.

TRANSPLANT. In modern surgery the tranfer of an embryo, genetic material, an organ, tissue, etc., from one part of a body to another, or to another body. A transplant code was issued in the UK in 1979 covering the T. of human organs. Two doctors must certify the brain death of the donor, those doctors being both independent of the transplant team and clinically independent of each other. *See also* EMBRYOLOGY and GENETIC ENGINEERING.

TRANSPORT AND GENERAL WORKERS UNION. Trade union founded in 1921 by the amalgamation of a number of dockers' and road transport workers' unions, previously associated in the Transport Workers' Federation. The largest T. Union in Britain, its gen. secs. have incl. Bevin, Cousins, and from 1969 Jack Jones (1913-).

TRANSPORTATION. Punishment which involved the sending of convicted persons to overseas possessions either for life or for shorter periods. It was introduced in England towards the end of the 17th cent. and was abolished in 1864 after many thousands had been transported, especially to Australia.

TRANS-SIBERIAN RAILWAY. Line connecting the cities of European Russia with Omsk, Novosibirsk, Irkutsk, and Khabarovsk, and terminating at Vladivostok on the Pacific. It took 1891-1905 to build; from St Petersburg (Leningrad) to Vladivostok is *c.* 8,700 km (5,400m). A second line is under construction: *see* SIBERIA.

TRANSUBSTANTIATION. The RC doctrine that the bread and wine at the Eucharist are transformed into the body and blood of Christ. This doctrine, which evolved during the 9th-13th cents., is rejected by Protestant Churches.

TRANSURANIUM ELEMENTS. Family of synthetic elements following the natural series ending with uranium (at. no. 92), which are produced by bombarding uranium or other T.Es. with various atomic particles.

TRANSVAAL. N prov. of the rep. of South Africa bordering Zimbabwe on the N. The S and SW are occupied by the high veld, rising to Witwatersrand, then sinking northward to the low veld. The main rivers are the Vaal and Limpopo with their tributaries. The economic life is dominated by the gold fields of the 'Rand'. Near Pretoria are diamond mines, discovered 1886; coal, iron ore, copper, lead, tin, manganese are among other minerals worked. Cattle and sheep are reared; maize, tobacco, and fruit are grown espec. with irrigation. There are iron and steel works at Pretoria, brick, tile, and pottery factories, etc. The largest towns are Pretoria (the cap.), Johannesburg, Germiston, Brakpan, Springs, Benoni, Krugersdorp, and Roodepoort.

The T. was settled from 1836 by Boers from Cape Colony. After subduing the Zulus they set up a rep. recognized by Britain as independent in 1852. Owing to troubles with the Zulu inhabitants, T. was in 1877 annexed by Britain at the request of some of the settlers; but in 1880 the T. rebelled, inflicting a severe defeat on the Brit. at Majuba Hill (1881), and republican rule was restored, though subject to British suzerainty. After the S.A. War of 1899-1902, T. became a British colony, and in 1910 a prov. of the Union of S.A. Area 286,064 sq.km (110,450 sq.m); pop. (1970) 8,717,530, incl. *c.* 2,000,000 White.

TRANSYLVĀ'NIA. Area of Romania, once a prov., bounded S by the Transylvanian Alps and E and NE by the Carpathians. The Bihar Mountains rise in the centre of T., the surface of which is hilly except in the extreme W. Agriculture, stock-breeding, and forestry thrive, and wine and brandy are produced. Exploitation of mineral wealth, natural gas, lignite, gold, silver, copper, iron, etc. has been rapid since the S.W.W.

Cluj is the chief town. Area 62,000 sq.km (24,000 sq.m). T., which had been part of Hungary from *c.* 1000-1526, 1691-1848, 1868-1918, was united with Romania in 1918 by the vote of its inhabitants. The Vienna Award of 1940, made by Ribbentrop and Ciano, gave most of T. back to

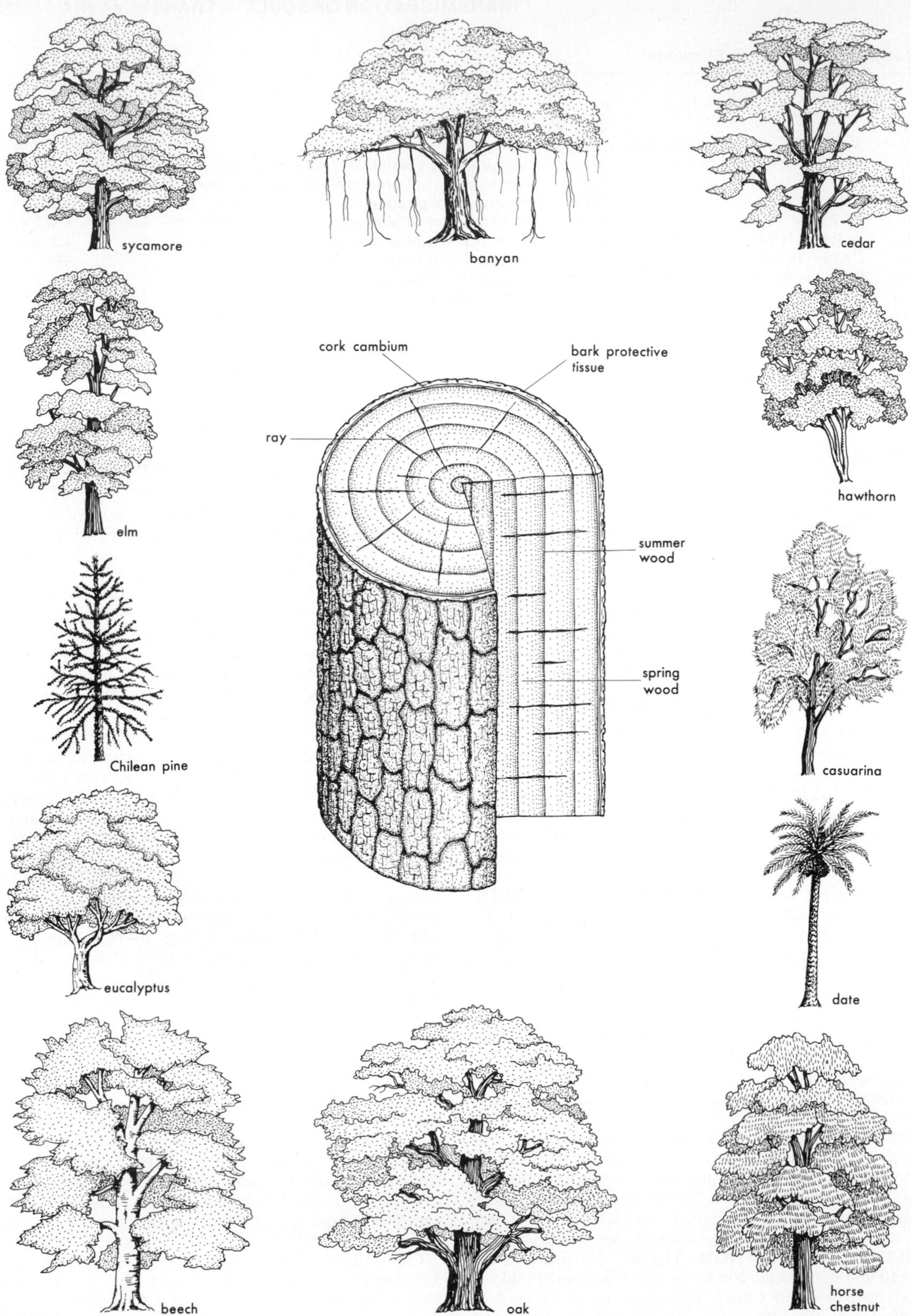

TREES. Typical species, and a trunk section showing growth rings.

Hungary, a gift cancelled in the peace treaty with Hungary, 1947.

TRAPANI (trah'pahnē). Port and naval base in NW Sicily, Italy, *c.* 48km (30m) N of Marsala. Pop. (1971) 79,400.

TRAPPISTS. RC order of monks and nuns, renowned for the strictness of their rule, which incl. the maintenance of silence. It originated in 1664 at La Trappe, in Normandy, as a reformed version of the Cistercian rule, and is now absorbed again in the latter.

TRASIMENO (trasēmē'nō). Lake in central Italy, W of Perugia. Hannibal defeated the Romans here 217 BC. Area 130 sq.km (50 sq.m).

TRAVEL SICKNESS. Nausea and vomiting caused by travelling in trains, buses, aeroplanes, cars, and ships. The constant vibrations and movements are thought to stimulate changes in the semicircular canals forming the labyrinth of the middle ear, and failure of the individual to adapt to this stimulation, which may be reinforced by visual stimulation as well as psychological factors, is thought to be the cause of T.S., although the exact mechanisms involved remain obscure. There are many proprietary cures on the market, some of which contain anti-histamine drugs.

TRAVEN (trah'ven), **B(en).** Pseudonym of the proletarian novelist Herman Feige (1882-1969), whose true identity was unrevealed until 1979. B. in the part of Germany now in Poland, he was in turn known as anarchist Maret Rut, Traven Torsvan, and Hollywood scriptwriter Hal Croves. His books incl. *The Death Ship* (1926), and *The Treasure of Sierra Madre* - basis of the film for which he wrote the script.

TRAVERS, Benjamin (1886-1980). Brit. dramatist. B. in London, he wrote farces for Tom Walls, Ralph Lynn and Robertson Hare, incl. *A Cuckoo in the Nest* (1925), *Rookery Nook* (1926), and *Thark* (1927), known from the theatre at which they were played as the 'Aldwych' farces. A later success was *The Bed Before Yesterday* (1975).

TREACLE. Brown viscid syrup obtained during sugar refining: the paler 'golden syrup' is obtained at a later stage. *See* MOLASSES.

TREADMILL. Penal appliance devised in 1818 by Sir William Cubitt (1785-1861), and long disused. It consisted of a large hollow cylinder around which were steps; by treading on these the prisoner caused the cylinder to revolve and thus pump water, grind corn, etc.

TREASON. An act of betrayal, generally used only of acts against the sovereign or the state to which the perpetrator owes allegiance. In this sense T. was defined in England by the Statute of Treasons, 1352, the principal Ts. being (1) compassing the wounding, imprisonment, or death of the sovereign; (2) seducing the king's wife or eldest dau. or the wife of the heir; (3) levying war against the sovereign in his (her) realm; (4) being adherent to the sovereign's enemies within the realm, giving them aid or comfort in the realm or elsewhere. The punishment on conviction of T. is death. The Treachery Act, 1940, supplemented the law of T. by making it an offence punishable by death for any persons, whether owing allegiance to the British crown or not, to assist the naval, military, or air operations of the enemy, or to impede the forces of the Crown: 16 spies (not normally capable of T., though liable to be shot in the field) were convicted under this act, which expired in 1946. During the 20th cent., persons hanged for T. or treachery in the UK have incl. Casement (1916), John Amery (1945), and William Joyce (1946) who, though he claimed to be a US citizen by birth, carried a British passport valid until 1940 at the time he went to Germany in August 1939.

In the USA, T. is defined in Article III, Section 3, of the Constitution: 'T. against the United States shall consist only in levying war against them, or in adhering to their enemies, giving them aid and comfort. No person shall be convicted of treason unless on the testimony of 2 witnesses to the same overt act, or on confession in open court. The Congress shall have power to declare the punishment of treason.'

TREASURE TROVE. In England, any gold or silver, plate or bullion found concealed in a house or the ground, the owner being unknown. Normally, treasure originally hidden, and not abandoned, belongs to the Crown, but if the treasure was casually lost or intentionally abandoned, the first finder is entitled to it against all but the true owner. Objects buried with no intention of recovering them, e.g. in a burial mound, do not rank as T.T., and belong to the owner of the ground.

TREASURY. Govt dept constituted in 1612 to collect and manage public revenue. The PM is generally the First Lord of the T., the Chancellor of the Exchequer is the financial head; with 5 junior lords these form the Lords Commissioners of the T.

TREBIZO'ND. Another form of **Trabzon.**

TREE, Sir Herbert Beerbohm (1853-1917). British actor-manager. B. in London, the half-brother of Max Beerbohm (q.v.), he managed the Haymarket theatre 1887-96, and Her Majesty's 1897-1917, building the latter entirely from the profits of *Trilby.* He appeared both in Shakespeare and modern roles, often with his wife, **Lady T.,** *née* Maud Holt.

TREE. Name given to perennial plants characterized by a woody stem and branches, and larger than shrubs. Gymnosperm Ts. are classified in 4 divisions: cycads or sago-palms; the maidenhair tree; gnetums; and conifers. Angiosperm Ts. are divided into monocotyledons, incl. palms, bamboos, etc., and dicotyledons, comprising the largest group.

Trees as symbols of fertility play a large part in primitive religion; thus the carrying of green boughs round the village as a fertility rite, and the maypole dance, originally performed round the sacred T., figured in the English May Day festival. Trees or groves were the scene of festivals or the home of oracles, e.g. at the oak of Dodona, in Epirus. The oak was the sacred T. of Jupiter, and was also venerated by the Druids. Many peoples believe that Ts. are inhabited by spirits, who die with them, e.g. the Dryads of the Greeks.

TREE CREEPER. *See* CREEPER.

TREITSCHKE (trītsh'ke), **Heinrich von** (1834-96). German historian. At first a Liberal, he later adopted a Pan-German standpoint. His best-known work is the *History of Germany in the 19th Cent.*

TREMATODES. *See* FLUKE.

TRENCHARD, Hugh Montague, 1st visct (1873-1956). British airman and administrator, nicknamed 'Boom', because of his loud voice. As GOC of the RFC 1915-17 he was responsible for air operations in the F.W.W., and as Chief of Air Staff 1918-29 organized the RAF in preparation for its role in the S.W.W. In 1927 he was created first Marshal of the RAF and in 1930 received a viscounty. As Commissioner of the Metropolitan Police, he carried out

TREE. This juniper is a fine example of the Japanese art of bonsai in which forest trees are reduced to miniatures. *Photo: Courtesy of Tokonoma Bonsai Nursery.*

TREE. A grove of sequoia in California; the 'Grizzly Giant' in the centre is the world's largest tree and, except for the bristle-cone pines of the SW USA, the oldest. *Photo: Camera Press.*

the 'T. Reforms' incl. the estab. of the Police Coll. at Hendon and the application of more scientific methods in detection. In 1951 he was awarded the OM.

TRENGGANU (-gah'noo). State of W Malaysia, on the E coast. The cap. is Kuala Trengganu. Copra, black pepper, tin and wolfram are exported. Area 13,080 sq.km (5,050 sq.m); pop. (1970) 53,355.

TRENT, Council of. A council of the RC Church held at Trento, N Italy, Dec. 1545 to Dec. 1563, incl. adjournments. It defined many Catholic doctrines, and reformed abuses within the Church.

TRENT. Third longest river of England. It rises in the S Pennines and flows first S and then generally NE through the Midlands to enter the Humber. Length 275km (170m). It is navigable by barges for nearly 160km (100m).

TRENTI'NO-ALTO ADIGE (adē'zhā). Autonomous region in N Italy, once part of the old rep. of Venice, then part of Austria until ceded to Italy under the Treaty of Saint-Germain-en-Laye, 1919. It consists of the provs. of Bolzano and Trento. Bolzano (S Tirol) remained German-speaking in spite of attempts at forcible Italianization by the fascist govt and the migration to Germany in 1939 of some 70 per cent of the pop.; Trento has always been Italian-speaking. The peace treaty between Italy and the Allies, 1947, provided that the German-speaking inhabitants of the region should have equal rights, and in 1948 the region was made autonomous. Continued agitation by the German-speaking pop. in the N led to its division into 2 largely autonomous provs. Bolzano/Bozen (the German-speaking Südtirol), with its cap. at Bolzano, area 7,400 sq.km (2,857 sq.m); pop. (1978) 431,122 and Trento (Italian), with its cap. of the same name, area 6,213 sq.km (2,399 sq.m); pop. (1978) 442,873.

TRE'NTŌ. Cap. of Trentino-Alto Adige autonomous region, Italy, and of T. prov., on the Adige, a city famous in history for the Council of Trent (Ger. form of its name), 1545-1563, which issued decrees, confirmed by Pope Pius IV in 1564, settling many points of RC dogma as part of the so-called Counter-Reformation. Pop. (1978) 92,000.

TRENTON. Cap. of New Jersey, USA, on the Delaware, 48km (30m) NE of Philadelphia. Pottery and steel cable are manufactured. Washington defeated the British at T., 1776. Pop. (1970) 104,650.

TREPA'NG. Dried and smoked sea cucumber (*see* ECHINODERMA) used in soup by the Chinese.

TRESPASSER. Technically, a trespass is an unlawful interference with the person or property of another, but in general speech a T. is a person who goes on the land of another without lawful authority. A land-owner has the right to eject a T. by the use of reasonable force. Alternatively, he may sue him for trespass. If a T. is injured whilst on the land of another, he cannot recover damages from the landowner, unless the landowner has done some positive act of injury to him. In English law, a trespass to land is not a crime.

TREVELYAN (trevil'yan), **Sir George Otto** (1838-1928). British liberal statesman. A nephew of Lord Macaulay, whose biography he wrote (1876), he was Chief Sec. for Ireland 1882-4, Chancellor of the Duchy of Lancaster 1884-5, and Sec. for Scotland 1892-5. His other books incl. *The Early History of C. J. Fox* (1880) and *The American Revolution* (1909). His son **George Macaulay** (1876-1962), Regius prof. of history at Cambridge 1927-40, wrote an illuminating *English Social History* (1944): he was awarded the OM in 1930.

TRÈVES. Fr. form of TRIER.

TREVISO (trāvēsō). Town in Veneto region, Italy, 29km (18m) N of Venice. It dates from Roman times. The cathedral, founded 1141, was enlarged in the 15th cent. Pop. (1978) 90,000.

TREVITHICK, Richard (1771-1833). British engineer, constructor of a steam road locomotive (1801), and the first steam engine running on rails (1804).

TREVOR-ROPER, Hugh Redwald. *See* DACRE, Lord.

TRIAD (trī'ad). Chinese secret society, the largest in the world. Originally founded as the Hung Society in AD 386 to promote the cult of Amithabha Buddha (a superhuman holy personage presiding over a 'Blessed Land' in the W of the Universe), it became known as the T. because of the vital part played by the triangle in the initiation ceremony. Gradually it developed as a revolutionary society aiming at the overthrow of the Manchus, was behind the Taiping Rebellion (1851), and organized backing for Sun Yat-sen in London and the USA in the final estab. of the Republic. Now in a dominant position among overseas Chinese (HQ Hong Kong), its various branches, of which the most notorious is the 14K, moved into drugs, gambling and prostitution.

TRIANON (trē'anoṅ). Two palaces in the park at Versailles: Le Grand T. (where peace was signed between Hungary and the Allies 1929) built for Louis XIV, and Le Petit Trianon for Louis XV.

TRIBUNAL. A court of justice, but more espec. in England a body estab. by the govt. to arbitrate in disputes, such as over the siting of new roads or airports, the amount of compensation for industrial injury or unfair dismissal, or appeal against deportation by immigrants. Members are usually local and unpaid, and the chairman is usually the only lawyer. By 1980 over 300,000 cases were being heard annually, and tribunals are usually claimed to be less formal than a court, more speedy, less expensive, and more easily understood because using lay terms.

TRIBUNE (tri'būn). Roman magistrate of plebeian family, elected annually to defend the interests of the plebeians. When the office was instituted in 494 BC there were 2 Ts.; the number was later increased to 10. They could veto the decisions of any other magistrate.

TRICHINA (tri'kina). Parasitic nematode which breeds in rats, pigs, and man. If the larvae enter the intestine they will spread through the bloodstream into the muscles, remaining for long periods, and causing the disease called trichinosis.

TRICHINO'POLY. *See* TIRUCHIRAPALLI.

TRIER (trēr). City in Rhineland-Palatinate, W Germany, on the Moselle near the Luxembourg frontier. It has notable Roman remains. Its cathedral, founded in the 11th cent., was destroyed in the S.W.W. Karl Marx was b. here. Pop. (1978) 101,000.

TRIESTE (trē-est'; Ital. trē-e'stā). Italian city and free port on the Adriatic, in Friuli-Venezia Giulia region. The Roman Tergeste, T. became Austrian in 1382 and, except for occupation by Napoleon 1809-14, remained so until 1918 when the Allies occupied it and it was transferred to Italy under the treaty of Saint-Germain-en-Laye. Yugoslavia claimed T. and after the S.W.W. the city and its surrounding terr. (772 sq.km/298 sq.m) were divided in 1954 between Italy (210 sq.km/80 sq.m, incl. the port) and Yugoslavia, and this division was accepted as final in 1975. Pop. (1979) 263,000. incl. a large Slovene minority.

TRIGONO'METRY. Branch of mathematics which solves problems relating to plane and spherical triangles. Its principles are based on the fixed proportions of angles and sides in a right-angled triangle. It is of importance in surveying. Invented by Hipparchus (q.v.), it was developed by Ptolemy of Alexandria (q.v.) and was known to Hindu and Arab mathematicians.

TRILOBITE (trī'lobīt). Extinct marine arthropod (class Trilobita) of the Palaeozoic period. The Ts. had segmented bodies and might be over 30cm (1ft) long.

TRIMURTI (trimoor'ti). The Hindu triad, representing the Absolute Spirit in its 3 aspects: Brahma, personifying creation; Vishnu, preservation; Siva, destruction.

TRINCŌMALEE'. Seaport on the NE coast of Sri Lanka, with a fine natural harbour, an early Tamil settlement. It was a Brit. naval base until 1957. Pop. (1971) 38,800.

TRINIDAD. Town in Bolivia, nr the r. Mamoré, 400km (250m) NE of La Paz. It is built on a vast man-made earth mound, above flood-level, the work of a little-known early Amerindian people. Pop. (1971) 41,800.

TRINIDAD AND TOBĀ'GŌ. Independent state within the Brit. Commonwealth comprising Trinidad, second largest and most southerly of the W Indian Islands, Tobago, 30km (19m) NE of Trinidad, and some smaller islands. Trinidad lies 11km (7m) N of the nearest point of Venezuela and rises to 940m (3,085 ft) in Mt Aripo. The climate is tropical with cool nights. Sugar, cocoa, coconuts, citrus and timber are produced. A major export is Angostura bitters, first blended from herbs in Angostura in 1824 as a stomach remedy for soldiers by Johann Siegert, a Prussian army doctor. Made in Trinidad since 1875, it is now used to season food and fruit, and flavour 'pink' gin, etc. The Pitch Lake is a major source of asphalt, perpetually renewing itself: Sir Walter Raleigh used it to repair his ships. Oil is also found, and refined together with crude from abroad.

Discovered by Columbus in 1498, and colonized by Spain in 1532, Trinidad was taken by the British in 1797 and ceded to them in 1802. Tobago was ceded to Britain by France in 1814 and amalgamated with Trinidad in 1888. T. and T. became independent in 1962 and a rep. in 1976. There is a Senate and House of Representatives. The country was led to independence by Eric Williams (1911-81), PM 1961-81. The cap. is Port of Spain; other towns incl. San Fernando and (on Tobago) Scarborough.

Area of Trinidad 4,828 sq.km (1,864 sq.m); pop. (1978) 1,130,000; of Tobago 300 sq.km (116 sq.m); pop. 40,000. The majority are of African descent, although Indians are almost as numerous: the language is English. M.U.: T. and T. dollar.

TRINITY. In Christian theology, the doctrine that while God is one in nature, He is three distinct persons, the Father, the Son, and the Holy Ghost. It became Catholic doctrine in the Nicene Creed (q.v.).

TRI'POLI. Port of the Lebanon, 65km (40m) NNE of Beirut, the terminus of an oil pipe-line from Kirkuk. It stands on the site of a Phoenician city. Pop. (1971) 210,000.

TRIPOLI. Cap. of Libya on the Mediterranean. It was developed by the Italians from 1911 as their chief port. There are light manufactures. The magnificent ruins of Leptis Magna are 112km (70m) to the E nr Homs. Pop. (1973) 551,500.

TRIPOLITA'NIA. Former prov. of Libya, N Africa, stretching from Cyrenaica in the E to Tunisia in the W. Tripoli was the cap. Italy captured T. from Turkey in 1912. The Brit. 8th Army made a rapid advance through T. Dec. 1942-Jan. 1943 during the N Africa campaign. In 1963 T. was subdivided into admin. divisions.

TRINITY. The Hindu trinity of Brahma the creator, Vishnu the preserver, and Siva the destroyer, is symbolised by god with one body but three heads, as here in the Elephanta Caves, Maharashtra. *Photo: Courtesy of the Govt of India Tourist Office*

TRIPURA (tri'poorah). State of the Rep. of India (union terr. 1956-71), formerly a princely state, between Bangladesh and Assam. It grows rice, cotton, tea, sugar cane, etc. The cap. is Agartala. Area 10,453 sq.km (4,036 sq.m); pop. (1971) 1,557,000. Bengalis entering from Bangladesh from 1950 now far outnumbered the local tribespeople, and in 1980 the latter revolted, demanding the expulsion of the Bengalis.

TRISTAN or **Tristram.** Legendary Celtic hero. His story is laid mainly at the court of King Mark of Cornwall. His love for Iseult of Ireland has inspired many medieval and modern versions, especially Wagner's opera *Tristan und Isolde.*

TRI'STAN DA CUNHA (koon'ya). Group of 4 small islands in the Atlantic, midway between S Africa and S America, a dependency (1938) of St Helena (q.v.). T. da C. proper is a volcano (2,184 m/7,164 ft), thought to be extinct, which erupted in 1961. Evacuated to Britain, the people returned in 1963. Area 105 sq.km (40 sq.m); pop. (1976) 304. T. da C., then uninhabited, was occupied by the Brit. in 1814. Gough Is. is a weather station, but Inaccessible and Nightingale Is. have only rich wild life.

TRISTEARIN. *See* STEARIN.

TRĪ'TON. In Greek mythology, a merman, son of Poseidon and Amphitrite.

TRĪU'MVIRS. Two groups of 3 magistrates governing the Roman republic. The first T. (60 BC) were Julius Caesar, Pompey, and Crassus, the 2nd (43 BC), Augustus, Antony, and Lepidus.

TRIVA'NDRUM. Indian city, cap. of Kerala state 80km (50m) NW of Cape Comorin. Once cap. of the former princely state of Travancore, it has a univ. (1937), an old fort, and a famous shrine. It is noted for ivory and wood carving. Pop. (1971) 410,000.

TROGLODYTES (trog'lōdīts). Greek term for cave-dwellers, designating certain tribes in the ancient world. The best-known were those of S Egypt and Ethiopia, a primitive pastoral people.

TROGONS. Beautiful tropical birds of the New and Old World in the family Trogonidae. The Central American quetzal (*Pharomacrus mocinno*) has golden-green tail plumes 1m (3ft) in length, and is Guatemala's national emblem: for the Aztecs and Mayas it was a sacred bird.

TROIS RIVIÈRES (trwah rēvyār). City in Quebec, Canada, a lumber port 138km (86m) NE of Montreal with paper, and cotton mills and iron foundries. Champlain founded it 1634. Pop. (1976) 51,200.

TROLLEYBUS. Type of bus conventionally driven solely by electric power collected from overhead wires. They have greater manoeuvrability than a tram, but their obstructiveness in modern traffic conditions led to their use being abandoned, espec. since they are less efficient in their use of energy than diesel buses. However, their quietness in operation and freedom from pollution made them attractive, and Germany has developed new types which operate, by means of 3 tonnes of batteries, for 10km (6m) without drawing current from an overhead wire.

TROLLOPE, Anthony (1815-82). British novelist. B. in London, he entered the Post Office as a clerk in 1834, invented the pillar box, and rose to a responsible position as surveyor before retiring in 1867. His first successful novel was *The Warden* (1855), which began the series set in the imaginary co. of Barsetshire: *Barchester Towers* (1857), *Doctor Thorne, Framley Parsonage, The Small House at Allington,* and *The Last Chronicle of Barset* (1867) - his masterpiece. Other books incl. *The Three Clerks, Orley Farm, The Belton Estate, The Claverings, The Eustace Diamonds,* and *Dr. Wortle's School*; and a political group including *Phineas Finn* and *The Prime Minister.* He delineated the English middle classes with mellowed insight in an easy pleasant style. His *Autobiography,* pub. in 1883, shocked the public by its workman-like attitude to his art. His mother **Frances Milton T.** (1780-1863) was also a novelist and wrote a caustic account of the *Domestic Manners of the Americans* (1832).

TROMBŌ'NE. A brass wind musical instrument, developed from the sackbut. It consists of a tube bent double, varied notes being obtained by an inner sliding tube. The 4 sizes are alto, tenor, bass, and contra-bass.

TROMP, Maarten Harpertszoon (1597-1653). Dutch admiral. B. at Brielle, he twice defeated the Spaniards in 1639. He was defeated by Blake in May 1652, but in Nov. triumphed over Blake in the Strait of Dover. In Feb.-June 1653 he was defeated by Blake, Monck, and Deane, and was killed off the Dutch coast. His son, **Cornelius T.** (1629-91), also an admiral, won fame in 1673 for his battle against the English and French fleets.

TRO'MSÖ. Fishing port in NW Norway, situated on T. island off the mainland. The battleship *Tirpitz* was sunk by British bombers in 1944 when at anchor in T. fjord. There is a univ. (1968). Pop. (1979) 45,360.

TRONDHEIM (tron'dhīm). Fishing port with fish canneries; textile, margarine, soap factories, etc., at the mouth of the Nid, on T. fjord. It was cap. of Norway in the 10-11th cent. and has a univ. (1968). Pop. (1979) 134,683.

TROPICS. The Ts. of Cancer and Capricorn (parallels of latitude 23° 28′ N and S of the equator) prescribe the northernmost and southernmost limits of the area of the Earth's surface in which the Sun can be directly overhead.

TROPINE (trōpīn). ($C_8H_{15}ON$). A white crystalline solid formed by the hydrolysis of alkaloid atropine.

TROPISMS. Automatic movements of plants in reaction to certain influences. Two common T. are the growth toward water (hydrotropism) and toward light (heliotropism).

TROPOSPHERE (trōp'ōsfēr). The lower part of the Earth's atmosphere extending *c.* 10.5km (6.5m) from the Earth's surface, in which temperature decreases with height except in local layers of temperature inversion. The *tropopause* is the upper boundary of the T. above which the temperature is constant or even increases slightly with respect to height.

TROSSACHS. Woodland glen between Lochs Katrine and Achray in Central region, Scotland 3km (2m) long, a favourite tourist spot.

TROTSKY, Leon Davidovitch. Assumed name of Russian revolutionary Lev D. Bronstein (1879-1940). B. nr Elizavetgrad, of Jewish parentage, he was twice exiled to Siberia for Marxist activities, and with Lenin organized the revolution of Nov. 1917, and conducted the peace negotiations with Germany. As Commissar for War he was responsible for the raising of the Red Army. T. differed with the Communist Party on policy, and was expelled from the Council of People's Commissars in 1925, and from the party in 1927. Exiled in 1929, he settled in Mexico, where he was assassinated possibly at Stalin's instigation. He wrote many works criticising the Soviet régime, notably his *History of the Russian Revolution.*

TROUBADOURS (troo'badoorz). Class of poets of Provence and S France, who fl. in the 11th-13th cents., and included both nobles and inferior minstrels. The Ts. originated a type of lyric poetry, devoted mainly to themes of exalted love and the idealization of women, and to the glorifying of the deeds of their patrons. Contemporary with the Ts. were the *Trouvères,* the epic poets of N. France.

TROUT. Fish closely related to the salmon. The common T. (*Salmo trutta*) is widely distributed in Europe, occurring in British fresh and coastal waters. Sea T. are generally silvery and river T. olive-brown, both having spotted fins and sides. In the USA the name T. is given to various species, notably to the rainbow T. (*Salmo gairdneri irideus*) which has been naturalized in many other countries.

TROUVILLE (troovēl')**-SUR-MER.** Summer resort and fishing port in Calvados dept, France, on the estuary of the Seine, linked by bridge to Deauville. Pop. (1975) 6,700.

TROWBRIDGE (trō'-). Town in Wilts, England, admin. HQ. of the co., 13 km (8 m) SE of Bath. Industries incl. processing of dairy products, bacon and ham, brewing and printing. Pop. (1973) 20,150.

TROY or **Ilium.** Ancient city of Asia Minor, in the district called the Troad. Homer's *Iliad* tells of the siege which led to the destruction of T. by the Greeks. After a 10 years' investment it fell to the Greeks through the strategem of the wooden horse, *c.* 1184 BC. Excavations by H. Schliemann revealed 9 different cities buried one beneath the other, of which the 7th, a post-Mycenaean fortress, was probably the Homeric T.

TROYES (trwah). French city, cap. of Aube dept, on the Seine, wealthiest city of the anc. prov. of Champagne. The treaty of T. (1420) granted the French crown to Henry V of England. Pop. (1975) 71,600.

TRUCIAL STATES. Seven small sheikhdoms (*see* ARAB EMIRATES, United) on the former 'pirate coast' of the Arabian Gulf. The name derives from the agreements made in 1820 with Britain to ensure truce in the area, and suppression of piracy and slaving.

TRUDEAU (troodoh'), **Pierre Elliott** (1919-). Canadian Liberal statesman. Called to the Quebec Bar in 1943, he became Min. of Justice and Attorney-General in 1967, and in 1968 succeeded Pearson as PM. Returned with an overall majority in 1968, he lost this in 1973, but regained it in 1974 after a campaign fought on the inflation issue. Defeated at the election of May 1979 by Joe Clark, he achieved a landslide victory in that of Feb. 1980, and following the rejection of separatism by Quebec in the referendum of that year, pledged himself to revision of the constitution asking Britain for its 'patriation'. Noted for his technique of 'vitesse et panache', he favours détente abroad.

TRUDEAU. The Canadian Prime Minister Pierre Trudeau, with his young wife Margaret, before their separation in 1977. *Photo: Colin Davey/Camera Press*

TRUFFLE. Subterranean fungus, highly valued in cookery and confectionery. The finest (*Tuber melanosporum*) comes from Périgord, generally growing under oak trees: it is rounded, blackish brown and covered with warts externally, and with blackish flesh. Pigs like Ts. and are used to locate them, as are dogs. Success in inoculating tree roots with T. spores suggests that Ts. may become less of a luxury.

TRUJILLO (trōōhē'yō). City and port, founded 1535, in Peru, 515km (320m) NW of Lima. Exports incl. sugar and copper. Pop. (1972) 242,000.

TRUJILLO MOLINA (trōōhē'yō mōlē'nah), **Rafael Leonidas** (1891-1961). Dominican dictator. Pres. of the rep. 1930-8 and 1942-52, he was also generalissimo of the armed forces from 1933, and retained control behind the scenes even after handing over the presidency to his brother in 1952. Although under his regime the island was transformed to a modern state by the erection of schools and hospitals and by public works programmes, his suppression of political opponents led to his assassination.

TRUMAN, Harry S. (1884-1972). 33rd President of USA. His middle initial was a compromise tribute to the names of both his grandfathers, but stood for neither in particular. B. at Lamar, Missouri, he became partner in a Kansas City clothing store, but was bankrupted during the Great Depression: it took him 15 yrs to pay off his debts. A Democrat, he was elected senator in 1934, became Vice-Pres. in Jan. 1945, succeeded to the Presidency on the death of F. D. Roosevelt in April, and in 1948 was elected for a second term in a surprise victory over Thomas Dewey. He made the decision in 1945 to use the atom bomb against Japan in order to shorten the war. On signing a bill giving financial aid to Greece and Turkey to avoid a Communist takeover, he enunciated the *T. Doctrine* (1947) that the US would 'support free peoples who are resisting attempted subjugation by armed minorities or by outside pressures', and launched the Marshall Plan for Western Europe. When S Korea was invaded, he intervened with US troops on behalf of the UN, but in 1951 when Gen. Macarthur's policies threatened a Third World War, he removed him from command. He pub. his memoirs *Years of Decision* and *Years of Trial and Hope* 1955-6, and was consulted by Kennedy in the Cuban crisis. He is buried at Independence, Missouri, long his home. His most famous saying was 'If you can't stand the heat get out of the kitchen'.

TRUMPET. Brass wind musical instrument; a doubled tube with valves.

TRUMPETER. A genus of crane-like birds. *Psophia crepitans* is found in Guyana.

TRURO. City of Cornwall, England, at the head of the Fal estuary, admin. HQ of the co. The cathedral was built 1880-1910. T. was the traditional meeting place of the Stannary (*see* CORNWALL), and in the 1980s the nearby tin mines were being redeveloped. Pop. (1972) 15,100.

TRUST. (1) Legal term for an arrangement by which A is empowered to administer property belonging to B for the benefit of C. A and B may be the same person; B and C may not be. (2) In business, the linking of several companies either by transferring shares of the separate cos. to trustees or by the creation of a holding co. whose shares are exchanged for those of the separate cos. Either method prevents the competition that would exist if the cos. involved had remained independent, and in the USA both were made illegal by the Sherman Anti-T. Act, 1890, enforced with vigour for the first time by 'T. buster' Pres. Theodore Roosevelt. A notable application of the act was the dissolution into its component cos. of the Standard Oil Co. of NJ by the Supreme Court, 1911. (3) A unit T. holds and manages a number of marketable securities; by buying a 'unit' in such a trust, the purchaser has a proportionate interest in each of the securities so that his risk is spread. (4) An investment T. is not in modern times a T., but a public co. which invests in marketable securities money subscribed by its shareholders who receive dividends from the income earned by the T. (5) A body formed with some special, usually charitable, object: e.g. the National T. (q.v.); the Carnegie UK T. (1913), whose chief object is the provision of free libraries. Similar bodies in the USA are the Rockefeller (1913) and Ford (1936) Foundations.

The PUBLIC TRUSTEE (1908, under an act of 1906) is an English official empowered to act as executor and trustee, either alone or with others, of the estate of anyone who appoints him.

TRUST TERRITORY. Non-self-governing territory, either held under mandate (q.v.); or detached from an enemy state after the S.W.W.; or voluntarily placed under the UN trusteeship system by the state responsible for its administration, on terms agreed between the latter and the UN. The T.Ts. are progressively prepared for independence.

TSAR. Title of the Russian emperors. It derives from the Lat. *Caesar.*

TSARI'TSYN. Old name of VOLGOGRAD.

TSCHAIKOVSKY. *See* TCHAIKOVSKY.

TSETSE. Fly of the genus *Glossina,* related to the house fly, species of which transmit the disease nagana to cattle and sleeping sickness to man.

TSINA'N. *See* JINAN.

TSINGTAO. *See* QINGDAO.

TSIOLKOV'SKY, Konstantin Eduardovich (1857-1935). Russian scientist, father of astronautics. B. in Izhevsk, he became permanently deaf at ten, following scarlet fever, but studied mathematics, and in 1903 pub. an article on rocket space travel, using liquid propellants (petrol and liquid oxygen) rather than gunpowder. This method, and his concept of space stations, are among ideas which have since been proved sound.

TSUSHIMA (tsoo'shimah). Island of Japan, SE of Korea. It is mountainous and consists of 2 halves, united at low tide. In the T. Strait the Russian fleet was destroyed by the Japanese in 1905.

TSUNAMI. *See* TIDES.

TUAMOTU (too͞'ahmō'too͞) **ISLANDS.** Group of *c.* 80 atolls stretching 2,100 km (1,300 m) in the central Pacific, part of French Polynesia. Discovered 1606 by Span. explorers, they were annexed by France in 1881. They produce pearls and copra. Area 1,064 sq.km (411 sq.m); pop. (1977) 8,500.

TUATARA (too͞-atah'ra). A small lizard-like reptile, *(Sphenodon punctatus)* now found only in certain offshore islands of New Zealand. The most ancient of living vertebrates, it has many unusual internal features, e.g. the pineal body reaches the skin of the top of the head, and has definite eye-like structure.

TUBERCULOSIS (TB). Disease caused by different species of tubercle bacillus affecting birds, cattle and man. Bovine T., carried in milk, affects bones, joints and glands, chiefly of young people, and has largely been eradicated in highly developed countries by efficient control of dairying and pasteurization. Human T., an airborne infection, attacks mainly the lungs; also intestines, skin, brain, etc., of persons of any age. Highly successful treatment is available by a combination of the drugs *Isoniazid* (INH), *Streptomycin* and *para amino sulphonic acid* (PAS), and lengthy bed rest is seldom necessary.

Diagnostic methods incl. regular chest X-ray; and the tuberculin test, in which an extract of a tubercle bacillus is implanted under the skin, causing a reaction in men or animals suffering from T.

TÜBINGEN. Town in Baden-Württemberg, W Germany, on the Neckar south of Stuttgart. It has factories making paper, textiles, surgical instruments, etc. T. dates from the 11th cent. and has a univ. (1477). It was cap. of

TUATARA. Olive-green with yellow spots, the tuatara reaches a length of about 60cm (2ft), is nocturnal and feeds on small animals. *Photo: Popperfoto*

the French zone of occupation after the S.W.W. Pop. (1972) 53,000.

TUBMAN, William V. S. (1895-1971). Liberian statesman. The descendant of American slaves, he was an Assoc. Justice of the Supreme Court 1934-7, and from his election to the presidency in 1944 concentrated on uniting the various races. Frequently re-elected, he d. naturally in office despite frequent assassination attempts.

TUCSON (tōōson'). Town and resort in the Sonoran Desert in southern Arizona, 760m (2,500 ft) a.s.l., and with the Santa Catalina Mts. to the NE rising to *c.* 2,750 m (9,000 ft). Industries incl. aircraft, electronics, copper smelting. Pop. (1974) 263,000.

TUCUMÁN (tookooman'). Cap. of T. prov., Argentina, on the Sali, in the foothills of the Andes. It has sugar mills, distilleries, etc. Founded 1565, T. was the site in 1816 of the signing of the Argentine declaration of independence from Spain. There is a univ. (1914). Pop. (1970) 326,000.

TUDOR. English dynasty descended from the Welshman Owen T., the 2nd husband of Catherine of France, the widow of Henry V. Their son Edmund m. Margaret Beaufort, the great-granddau. of John of Gaunt, and was the father of Henry VII, who ascended the throne in 1485.

TUGELA (tōōgā'la). River in Natal, Rep. of S Africa, flowing, with fine waterfalls, from the Drakensberg 480km (300m) to the Indian Ocean.

TULA (tōō'lah). Cap. of T. region, RSFSR, S of Moscow. It has a govt ordnance factory founded 1712 by Peter the Great. Pop. (1979) 541,000.

TULIP. Genus of plants (*Tulipa*) in the family Liliaceae. The garden T. (*T. Gesneriana*) probably originated in the Near East, and, quickly adopted in Europe during the 16th cent., became a craze in 17th cent. Holland (*cf.* Dumas *The Black Tulip*) when extravagant prices were paid for rarely coloured bulbs. It is today commercially cultivated on a large scale in the Netherlands and E Anglia. The T. tree (*Liriodendron tulipifera*) is a member of the magnolia family, with large tulip shaped blooms.

TULL, Jethro (1674-1741). British agriculturalist. Farming in his native Berkshire, he developed *c.* 1701 a drill enabling seeds to be sown mechanically, and so spaced that cultivation between was possible in the growth period. He pub. *Horse-hoeing Husbandry* (1731).

TU'LSA. City in Oklahoma, USA, on the r. Arkansas. Its port of Catoosa is America's most inland 'seaport', being linked to the Gulf of Mexico via the Mississippi, under the recently completed Arkansas River Navigation System. Founded in 1880, T. developed rapidly following oil discoveries, and has aviation and aerospace industries, as well as being a major oilrefining centre. Pop. met. area (1975) 492,000.

TUMBS, The. Two is., the Greater and Lesser T., in the Strait of Hormuz, formerly held by Ras al Khaimah. Together with a third is., Abu Musa, formerly held by Sharjah, they were annexed by Iran in 1971 when Britain withdrew from the Arabian Gulf. Their recovery for their former owners was a war aim of Iraq in the Iran-Iraq war of 1980.

TŪ'NA. *See* TUNNY.

TUNBRIDGE WELLS, Royal. Spa in Kent, England with chalybeate springs discovered in 1606. The shopping Parade, or Pantiles (paved with tiles in the reign of Queen Anne) was long the resort of fashion. Pop. (1972) 44,950.

TUNDRA (toon'dra). A region of high latitude almost devoid of trees. The term, formerly applied to part of N Russia, is now used for all such regions.

TUNG OIL. Oil used in paints and varnishes, obtained from trees of the genus Aleurites, family Euphorbiaceae, native to China.

TUNGSTEN. *See* WOLFRAM.

TUNICATA. Subphylum of invertebrate marine animals in the phylum Chordata. The sea squirts (Ascidiacea) are the most familiar.

TŪ'NIS. Cap. of Tunisia, on T. bay, linked by a 11km (7m) canal (1893) with La Goulette on the Mediterranean. An old Arab city, T. was occupied by the Fr. in 1881. It was in Axis occupation 1942-3. *See* CARTHAGE. Pop. (1975) 505,500.

TUNI'SIA. Independent rep. in N Africa, situated between Algeria to the W, Libya to the SE, and the Mediterranean to the E and N. The N is traversed by mountain ranges and incl. fertile areas near the coast, while to the S of the Shott el Jerid salt lakes most of the land is desert. T. was once heavily forested, and a re-afforestation programme is sponsored by the UN. Crops incl. cereals, olives, citrus, grapes (used in wine), dates and almonds; horses, cattle, sheep and goats are reared; and traditional manufactures incl. carpets, pottery and copper ware. Minerals incl. phosphates, iron, lead, zinc and oil; modern industries incl. iron and steel and oil refining. The cap. is Tunis; other towns incl. Sfax, Bizerta, Sousse, Kairouan and Gabès. Under the constitution of 1959, there is a unicameral Nat. Assembly: in 1975 Bourguiba (q.v.) became pres. for life. Islam (Sunni) is the state religion;

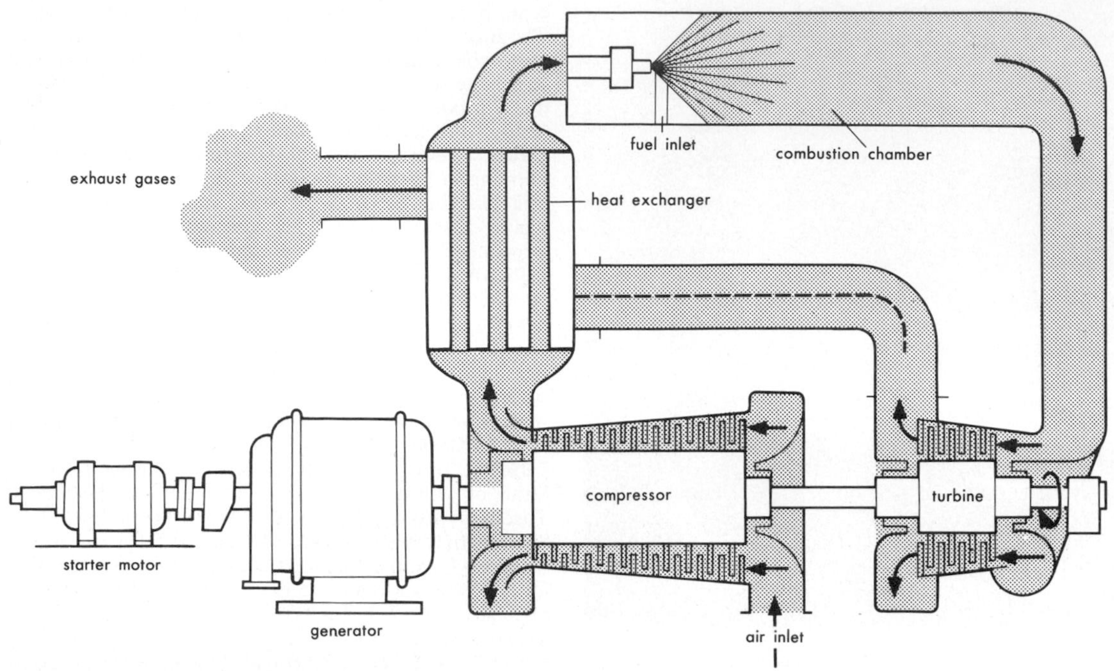

TURBINE. The working of a gas-turbine.

the official language is Arabic, but French is widely used. Area 164,000 sq.km (63,300 sq.m); pop. (1978) 6,030,000. M.U.: dinar.

TUNNEL. Tunnelling is an increasingly important branch of civil engineering in mining, transport, etc. In the 19th cent. there were 2 major advances: the use of compressed air within the T. to balance the external pressure of water and of the T. shield to support the face and assist excavation. In recent years there have been notable developments in linings, e.g. concrete segments and steel liner plates, and in the use of rotary diggers and cutters, and of explosives. Famous Ts. incl.: the world's longest road tunnel, the St Gotthard (1980) 16.3 km (10.1 m); the world's longest rail tunnel, the Seikan (1975) under Tsugaru Strait linking Honshu and Hokkaido 53.85km/33.5m, of which 23.3km/14.5m is under the sea; the Orange-Fish River T. (1975) 82km (50m) constructed for irrigation; and the Chesapeake Bay Bridge-T. (1963) 28km/17.5m.

TUNNY. Fish of the mackerel family (*Thunnus thynnus*), also known as tuna, up to 5m (14ft) long and *c.* 800kg (1,800 lb). It has been fished since ancient times in the Mediterranean as food, and in the 20th cent. fishing for T. with rod and line from a motor-boat has become fashionable on the Pacific coast of N America and elsewhere.

TUPAC AMARU (tōō'pahk ahmahrōō') (1743–81). Name assumed by the Peruvian Indian leader José Gabriel Condorcanqui, who revolted against Spanish rule in 1780 and was executed in Cuzco: he claimed to be a descendant of the last of the Incas. The name *Tupamaros* was adopted by the urban left-wing guerrilla organization founded *c.* 1960 by Raul Sendic, operating in Montevideo.

TURBINE. A rotary steam engine in which the kinetic energy of steam (or water) is converted into work. Essentially it consists of a shaft, wheel, or rotor, carrying a number of vanes or blades; against the latter are directed jets of steam which cause the shaft to rotate at a high speed. Ts. are classified as impulse or reaction. The former, e.g. the de Laval T. patented in 1882, works purely by impulse; steam is expanded in a nozzle or nozzles from the initial steam pressure to a certain back-pressure, thereby converting its heat and pressure energy into kinetic energy of flow. Some part of this kinetic energy is then absorbed by the moving blades attached to the wheel or rotor, which is mounted on a shaft supported within a casing. In reaction Ts. there is a combination of impulse and reaction effects. Fixed and moving blades are attached alternately to the casing and the rotors, and the steam suffers a gradual fall in pressure as it flows through the blade channels, when the corresponding heat drop results in an increase in its velocity. The steam engine of Hero of Alexandria (130 BC) was the prototype of the reaction T. Modern development is largely due to Sir C. Parsons (q.v.). Ts. are used in steamships, electricity generation, etc.

Later is the *gas-turbine* in which a compressed mixture of air and gas, or vaporized fuel, is ignited and, in expanding through the T., generates mechanical power; the compression is effected by a turbo-blower on the same shaft.

First developed for aircraft, they were subsequently used also for land and water locomotion, and in power stations.

TURBOT. Flat-fish (*Scophthalmus maximus*) found in the Mediterranean and especially in the North Sea. Some 60cm (2ft) long and weighing more than 14kg (30lb), it is an epicure's dish.

TURE'NNE, Henry de la Tour d'Auvergne, vicomte de (1611-75). French marshal, one of the ablest of Louis XIV's generals.

TURGENEV (toorgān'yef), **Ivan Sergeievich** (1818-83). Russian author. B. in Orel prov., son of an army officer, he studied at Moscow, St Petersburg, and Berlin, and worked for 2 yrs in the Ministry of the Interior before finally devoting himself to literature. Among his works are the play *A Month in the Country* (1849); the series *A Sportsman's Sketches* collected 1852 which helped to bring about the abolition of serfdom; and the novels *A Nest of Gentlefolk* (1858), *Fathers and Sons* (1862), and *Virgin Soil* (1877). His poetic realism has a pessimism which did not accord with the optimism of the coming revolutionary era and he left the country in 1856, returning only for visits. His characterization, especially of women, is excellent.

TURGOT (tūrgō'), **Anne Robert Jacques** (1727-81). French statesman. B. in Paris, he was appointed Comptroller-General of Finance in 1774, but his drastic economies led to his dismissal in 1776.

TŪRI'N. Chief city of Piedmont (It. Torino), Italy, on the Po, in a fertile plain at the foot of the Alps. It has a univ. (1404) and a cathedral (15th cent.). It was cap. of the kingdom of Sardinia from 1720, of Italy 1861-4. Motor-cars, silk and other textiles, iron and steel goods, are manufactured. Pop. (1979) 1,172,500.

The *Holy Shroud of T.* is an ancient piece of linen, long revered as the 'clean linen' in which Christ's body was wrapped. Brown and reddish stains suggest the imprint of a crucified body, and photographs (1898-1931) show the perfect form of a man with the traditional face of Christ. Tests suggest chemical action might produce such an image in the circumstances of the crucifixion.

TŪ'RING, Alan Mathison (1912-54). British mathematician. A fellow of King's College, Cambridge, he worked at Bletchley Park during the S.W.W.: *see* ULTRA. It was on his theoretical base, developed from the work of Babbage, that the modern computer was based. He also developed the concept of machine learning, and the use of mathematical models in biology.

TURKANA. *See* LAKE RUDOLF.

TURKESTAN. Geographical name for a large area in central Asia divided between the USSR (Kazakh, Kirghiz, Tadzhik, Turkmen, and Uzbek SSRs), Afghanistan (anc. Bactria), and China (part of **Xinjiang Uygur**).

TURKEY. Genus of birds (*Meleagris*) in the pheasant family. The domesticated T. (*M. gallopavo*) derives from the American wild species, introduced to Europe in the 16th cent., and the name may have been adopted from its cry. It is the traditional bird eaten at American Thanksgiving and in Britain at Christmas, but since the S.W.W. has been intensively bred in the same way as chicken.

TURKEY. Republic of Europe and Asia, occupying Asia Minor and Turkish Thrace in Europe. European T. is separated from Asia Minor by the Bosporus, the Sea of Marmara, and the Dardanelles. The interior of Asia Minor is an extensive plateau. The Taurus and Anti-taurus mts. lie in the S, rising to over 3,600 m (12,000 ft), the Egri Dagh range to the E, and the mts. of Pontus to the N along the Black Sea. The main rivers are in Europe the Maritsa and in Asia the Euphrates and Tigris, Kizil, Irmak Buyuk and Menderes (Maeandes). There are numerous lakes. Ankara, in the central plateau, is the cap.; Istanbul (Constantinople) in Europe, the largest city.

Wheat is grown on the central plateau, and sugar, cotton, tobacco, olives, tea, and vines in the fertile coastal belt. Sheep, goats and cattle are reared. The chief minerals are coal, chromite, iron, manganese and sulphur. Industries incl. iron and steel, vehicle assembly, textiles (cotton, wool and silk), glass, cement, and leather goods.

Under the constitution of 1961 there is a senate and Nat. Assembly which jointly elect the pres. for 7 years. Area 780,350 sq.km (301,300 sq.m), of which 23,300 sq.km (9,000 sq.m) are in Europe; pop. (1980) 45,442,000, the majority Sunni Moslems, though with a Shiah minority, but T. is a secular state. M.U.: Turkish lira.

TURKEY. Cave houses at Göreme cut out of the solid rock, and having the look of another planet about them. *Photo: Courtesy of the Turkish National Tourist Office*

History. The Turks originated in Mongolia, whence in the 6th cent. they spread into Turkestan. During the 7th cent. they adopted Islam. The Seljuk Turks in 1055 secured political control of the caliphate, and estab. an empire in Asia Minor. The Ottoman Turks, driven from Central Asia by the Mongols, entered the service of the Seljuks, and Osman I in 1299 founded a kingdom of his own. Having overrun Asia Minor, the Ottomans began their European conquests by seizing Gallipoli in 1354, captured Constantinople in 1453, and by 1480 were masters of the Balkans. By 1550 they had conquered Egypt, Syria, Arabia, Mesopotamia, Tripoli, and most of Hungary; thereafter the empire ceased to expand, although Cyprus was taken in 1571 and Crete in 1669.

The Christian counter-offensive opened in 1683 with the defeat of the Turks before Vienna; in 1699 the Turks lost Hungary, and in 1774 Russia ousted T. from Moldavia, Wallachia, and the Crimea. In the Balkans there was an unsuccessful revolt in Serbia in 1804, but in 1821-9 Greece threw off Turkish rule. Russia's attempts to exploit this situation were resisted by Britain and France, which in the Crimean War (1854-6) fought on T.'s side. The Bulgarian rising of 1876 led to a new war between T. and Russia, and by the Treaty of Berlin (1878) T. lost Bulgaria, Bosnia, and Herzegovina. A militant nationalist group, the Young Turks, secured the grant of a constitution in 1908; Italy took advantage of the ensuing crisis to seize Tripoli in 1911-12, while the Balkan states in 1912-13 expelled the Turks from Albania and Macedonia. T. entered the F.W.W. on the German side in 1914, only to lose Syria, Arabia, Mesopotamia, and its nominal suzerainty in Egypt.

The Greek occupation of Smyrna (Izmir) in 1919 provoked a patriotic reaction; Mustapha Kemal (Atatürk) estab. a provisional govt at Angora (Ankara) in 1920, expelled the Greeks, and in 1923 a national assembly proclaimed T. a rep., with Kemal as first pres. The new republic carried out a sweeping policy of westernization: Islam ceased to be the state religion, polygamy was abolished, and a new legal code was introduced. Kemal's People's Party ruled until 1950, but govt. was subsequently less stable, frequently under coalitions, and the military intervened in 1960, 1971, and 1980, when terrorism by extremists of right and left had led to 5,000 political deaths 1979-80. A junta under Gen. Kenan Evren took unlimited powers under an interim constitution. Turkey became assoc. with the Common Market in 1980, and is a member of NATO, although relations became strained by an invasion of Cyprus Jan.-Sept. 1974.

Archaeological sites incl. Troy (Hissarlik) and Catal Hüyük, fortified city of *c.* 6,000 BC discovered with painted temples and objets d'art in 1961.

TURKISH. A member of the Altaic family of languages, agglutinative in character. Originally it was written in Arabic script, but in 1928 the Latin alphabet became compulsory. For cents. T. literature was based on Persian models, but under Suleiman the Great began the Golden Age of which the poet Fuzuli (d. 1563) is the great exemplar, and which continued in the following cent. with the great poet satirist Nef'i of Erzerum (d. 1635) and others. During the 19th cent. westernization overtook T.L., e.g. the following of French models by Ibrahim Shinasi Effendi (1826-71), poet and prose writer. Joined with him as a founder of the New School was Mehmed Namik Kemal (1840-80), poet and author of the revolutionary play *Vatan* (*The Fatherland*), which caused his exile by the sultan. Unlike these in turning rather to Persian and Arabic than native sources for his vocabulary was the poet Tevfik Fikret (1867-1915). Among more recent names are those of the poet Mehmed Akif (1873-1936), author of the words of the Turkish national anthem; and the poet and novelist Yasher Kemal (1923-).

TURKMEN SSR. Republic of the USSR formed (1924) from part of Russian Turkestan; admitted to the Union in 1925. It lies E of the Caspian Sea. Its Turkmen inhabitants, the majority nomadic before the F.W.W., have been settled under Soviet rule; many are Moslems. The Kara Kum desert covers a great part of the rep., but artificial irrigation is increasing the area under cultivation. Cotton, wool, Astrakhan fur, etc., are produced, and carpets made. The cap. is Ashkhabad. Area 488,100 sq.km (187,000 sq.m); pop. (1978) 2,700,000.

Other Turkmens live in N Afghanistan, NE Iran, N Iraq, Syria and Turkey. In Iran they revolted against the Khomeini regime 1979-80, demanding the return of land alienated by Shah, recognition of their language, etc.

TURKS AND CAICOS ISLANDS. Group of small W Indian islands forming a Brit. Crown Colony; they lie 725km (450m) NE of Jamaica, of which they were a dependency 1873-1962. The Gov. is assisted by a State Council (the majority elected). Internal self-govt. as an assoc. state of the UK was planned for 1981, and full independence in 1982. Salt, crawfish and conch are exported, and tourism is being developed. The seat of govt is Grand Turk. Area 430 sq.km (166 sq.m); pop. (1977), 7,200. M.U.: Jamaican dollar.

TURKU (toor'koo). Finnish port on the r. Aurajoki, near its mouth. It has a castle, cathedral, and 2 univs. (Swedish, 1919, and Finnish, 1922). Pop. met. area (1979) 240,000.

TU'RMERIC. The tuberous rhizomes of *Curcuma longa*, a perennial plant cultivated in India. It is used in curries and as a dyestuff.

TURNER, Dame Eva (1899-). British soprano. B. in Lancs, she was prima donna of the Carl Rosa Opera Co. 1916-24, and has appeared throughout the world in *Turandot*, *Aīda*, etc. She was created DBE in 1962.

TURNER, Joseph Mallord William (1775-1851). British landscape artist. B. in London, son of a barber, he studied at the Academy School, was elected RA in 1802, and in 1809 became prof. of perspective at the Academy. He travelled widely on the Continent, the effect of his time in Italy can be seen in 'Crossing the Brook' (Nat. Gallery), and beautiful Venetian scenes, but in later life he developed an increasing freedom in capturing effects of weather and light in sea and sky with breath-taking grandeur e.g. 'Rain, Steam and Speed', 'Snow Storm'. Always solitary - he never m. - he was not greatly appreciated in his lifetime, though championed by Ruskin, but greatly influenced the development of English art and the work of the Impressionists. He worked with equal effect in oil and water colour. He left a collection of his works to the nation and in 1980 there were plans to house it complete in the former Queen Alexandra Military Hospital beside the Tate Gallery.

TURNER, Nat (1800-31). American Negro rebel. He led 60 slaves in the most important slave revolt, in Southampton, Virginia - the 'Southampton Insurrection'. Before he and 16 of the others were hanged, 54 Whites had been killed. He thought himself divinely inspired.

TURNIP. Biennial plant (*Brassica rapa*) cultivated in temperate climates for its edible white or yellow-fleshed 'root' and the young leaves, which are used as a green vegetable: closely allied is the swede-T. or rutabaga (*Brassica napobrassica*), of greater food value, firmer-fleshed and longer-keeping. Both types are valuable both for human food and livestock fodder.

TURNPIKE. *See* HIGHWAY.

TURPENTINE. A solution of resins obtained by distillation from the sap of conifers. Its chief uses are as a diluent of paint and in varnish.

TURPIN, Dick (1706-39). English highwayman. B. at Hempstead, Essex, the son of an innkeeper, he turned to highway robbery, cattle-thieving, and smuggling, and was hanged at York. His legendary ride from London to York on his mare Black Bess, described by W. H. Ainsworth in *Rookwood*, is probably based on one of c. 305km (190m) from Gad's Hill to York completed in 15 hr in 1676 by the highwayman John Nevison (1639-84).

TURQUOISE (tur'kwoiz). A precious stone: hydrous phosphate of aluminium and copper, bluish-green in colour, found in Iran, Turkestan, Mexico, etc.

TURPIN. Dick Turpin on Black Bess clearing the Hornsey Toll-bar gate, from a contemporary print. *Photo: Radio Times Hulton Picture Library*

TURTLE. A green turtle lays her eggs on the shore in northern Australia, scooping out a hole under cover of darkness before returning to the sea. Aborigines share the Lord Mayor's liking for turtle soup, and the number of turtles grows less. *Photo: Courtesy of the Australian Information Service*

TURTLE. Name for marine and freshwater species of tortoise (q.v.). The legs are modified to oar-like flippers for swimming, and the 'shell' is a more streamlined heart shape than that of the tortoise. Many are carnivorous: the eggs are laid in the sand of the sea shore. Well-known species are the green T. (*Chelonia mydas*), source of T. soup; the hawkbill (*Eretmochelys imbricata*), source of 'tortoise-shell'; the loggerhead (*Caretta caretta*); the snapper (*Chelydra serpentina*) which lives up to its name; and the giant leathery T. (*Sphargis coriacea*) which reaches 2.50m (8ft) and weighs half a tonne.

TU'SCANY. An Italian region, a former grand duchy, in the NW of the peninsula. It corresponds in large part to anc. Etruria. The Apennines reach into it; the Arno is the chief river. Tuscan was adopted as standard, literary Italian. Towns incl. Florence, Pisa, Leghorn, and Siena. Area 22,991 sq.km (8,877 sq.m); pop. (1977) 3,587,301.

TUSSAUD, Madame (1760-1850). French wax-modeller. B. Anne Marie Grosholtz in Berne, she went in 1766 to Paris to live with her famous wax-modeller uncle, Philippe Curtius, whom she soon outshone, and during the French Revolution they were forced to take death masks of many victims and leaders (some still exist in the modern Chamber of Horrors). In 1794 she m. François Tussaud, but they separated, and in 1802 she estab. her exhibition in the Strand, London. It was transferred to Baker St in 1883 and to Marylebone Rd in 1884 (destroyed by fire 1925, but reopened 1928).

TUTANKHAMEN (tootankah'men) (reigned 1360-1350 BC). King of Egypt. A member of the royal house of the 18th dynasty, and a son of Ikhnaton or of Amenhotep III, he may have succeeded to the throne when 11 yrs old and was aged approx. 20 at his death. Little is known of his reign, but in 1922 his tomb was discovered by Lord Carnarvon and Howard Carter in the Valley of the Kings at Luxor. Although robbers had entered it shortly after the funeral, it had been then resealed by his officials and escaped further rifling - the only ancient royal tomb to have done so. The richness of the find, incl. the solid gold coffin, captured the imagination of the world.

TUVA (to͞o'va). ASSR of the RSFSR. It lies NW of Mongolia (Mongolian People's Rep.) of which it was part until 1911. It was declared a Russian protectorate 1914. After the 1917 revolution it was the independent Tannu-Tuva rep. 1920 until incorporated in the RSFSR as an autonomous region in 1944. It was made the T. ASSR in 1961. There is good pasture; gold and asbestos are worked, and there are hydroelectric installations. The cap. is Kyzyl. Area 170,500 sq.km (65,800 sq.m); pop. (1978) 259,000.

TUVALU (toovaloo') Group of is. in the W Pacific, the name meaning 'cluster of eight', for although there are actually nine, one is very small. Under the name Ellice Is., they were part of the Gilbert and Ellice Is. colony 1915-75, when they became a separate Brit. colony, gaining independence 1978. The cap. is on Funafuti. Area 24.6 sq.km (9.5 sq.m); pop. (1979) 7,900.

TVER. Old name of KALININ.

TWAIN, Mark. Pseudonym (a call used for depth sounding by Mississippi pilots) of the American writer Samuel Langhorne Clemens (1835-1910). B. at Florida, Missouri, he was a printer, Mississippi pilot, and goldminer before turning to writing. After a tour of Europe he wrote *The Innocents Abroad* (1869), establishing his reputation as a humorist. He subsequently wrote *The Adventures of Tom Sawyer* (1876), *The Adventures of Huckleberry Finn* (1885), and *A Connecticut Yankee at King Arthur's Court* (1889).

TWEED. River rising in W Borders region, Scotland, and entering the North Sea at Berwick in Northumberland. Length 156km (97m).

TWEED. Cloth made of woollen yarn, usually of several shades, but in its original form without regular pattern and woven on a hand-loom in the remoter parts of Ireland, Wales and Scotland, the most famous being Harris T.; it is highly durable and largely weather-proof. In modern times it is often machine woven, patterned, and processed.

TWEEDDALE. Another name of PEEBLESSHIRE.

TWEEDSMUIR, Lord. *See* BUCHAN, John.

TWELFTH DAY. In the Christian calendar the feast of the Epiphany kept on the 12th day after Christmas, 6 Jan. In olden times many convivial ceremonies were connected with Twelfth Night.

TWICKENHAM. District in the Greater London bor. of Richmond-upon-Thames. Famous residents have incl. Alexander Pope, J. M. W. Turner, Horace Walpole at Strawberry Hill, and Clarendon at York House. T. incl. Hampton Court and a famous ground of the Rugby Union.

TWILIGHT SLEEP. A method of partial anaesthesia used in childbirth, involving the hypodermic injection of analgesics and narcotics.

TWINS. Two individuals produced at one birth. Strictly speaking, two animals developed and born at the same time are T. only if they are the products of the division of a single fertilized ovum or egg cell. Human T. resulting from the simultaneous development of two fertilized eggs are not true T. The latter are always of the same sex.

TYAN SHAN (tē-ahn shan'). One of the great mtn systems (Chinese Tien-Shan) of Central Asia, on the borders of USSR and China, and extending E across Xinjiang Uygur. Pik Pobedy (Victory Peak) is 7,439 m (24,406 ft).

TYBURN (tī'-). An English stream running underground from Hampstead to the Thames at Westminster; T. gallows stood near the present junction of Oxford St and Edgware Rd, from the 12th cent. until 1783.

TYLER, John (1790–1862). 10th Pres. of the USA. B. in Virginia, he was elected Vice-Pres. in 1840 and became Pres. in 1841. In 1845 Texas was annexed. In the Civil War he adhered to the Confederates.

TYLER, Wat (d. 1381). English leader of the peasants in the revolt of 1381. B. in Kent or Essex, he served in the French wars. After taking Canterbury he led the peasants to Blackheath and occupied London. At Mile End Richard II met the rebels and promised to redress their grievances. At a further conference at Smithfield, Tyler was murdered by the 'Lord Mayor', Sir William Walworth.

TYNAN (tīn'an), **Kenneth** (1927–80). British author and critic. The incarnation of the 'swinging sixties' in his advocacy of permissive theatre, he devised the nude revue *O Calcutta!* (1969) first staged in New York.

TYNDALE (tin'dal), **William** (*c.* 1492–1536). English translator of the Bible. B. probably in Glos., he studied at Oxford and Cambridge and was ordained. In 1525 he began to print his English NT at Cologne and had to flee to Worms, where the work was completed. In 1530 was pub. his Pentateuch at Antwerp. The first vol. of Holy Scripture printed in England was his revised NT in 1536. He was seized at Antwerp, and imprisoned at Vilvorde, where he was tried as a heretic, and strangled and burnt.

TYNE (tīn). River formed by the union of the N Tyne (rising in the Cheviots) and S Tyne (rising in Cumbria) nr Hexham, Northumberland, and reaching the North Sea at Tynemouth: length 72 km (45 m). Kielder Water (1980) in the N Tyne Valley is Europe's largest man-made lake, 12 km (7.5 m) long and 0.8 km (0.5 m) wide, and supplies the industries of Tyneside, Wearside and Teesside.

TYNE AND WEAR (tīn and wēr). Met. co. created in 1974 from the SE corner of Northumberland, incl. Newcastle upon Tyne (the admin. HQ) and NE Durham, incl. South Shields, Gateshead and Sunderland, and bisected by the rivers T. and W. The **T. and W. Metro** (1975–81) has continental-type 'supertrams' running on rail lines for 54 km (34 m), beneath Newcastle and Gateshead. The two cities are linked with eath other and with the coast on both sides of the estuary. Area 567 sq.km (912 sq.m); pop. (1978)1,165,100.

TYNEMOUTH (tin'muth). Port and pleasure resort in Tyne and Wear, on the N bank of the Tyne. Pop. (1972) 67,880.

TYNWALD (tin'wold). *See* ISLE OF MAN.

TYPEWRITER. A hand-operated machine for producing characters similar to those of printing. The first practicable T. was built at Milwaukee, Wisconsin, by C. L. Sholes, C. Glidden and S. W. Soulé in 1867, and by 1874 E. Remington and Sons, the gun makers whose name was soon given to the Ts., produced under contract the first machines for sale. Later developments incl. tabulators from *c.* 1898, portable machines *c.* 1907, gradual introduction of electrical operation (allowing increased speed, since the keys are touched not depressed), proportional spacing in 1940, and rotating typehead with stationary platen in 1962.

TYPEWRITER. The typewriter links up with the computer. The operator selects a standard letter or combination of paragraphs from a set 'library', and the machine takes over. An ink-jet printer directs ink droplets onto paper at a rate of 117,000 per second, and letters can be sent by telephone line to a compatible machine at the rate of 1,200 characters per second. *Photo: Courtesy of IBM*

TYPHOID FEVER (tī'foid). An infectious disease contracted by swallowing the specific bacillus. This may be present in the urine or faeces of a patient or a carrier, or may be conveyed by flies. Ulcers form in the small intestine and may bleed internally or perforate with great danger to life. Treatment is by antibiotics: only one is really effective, chloramphenicol, and bacilli resistant to it are being encountered.

TYPHOON (tīfo͞on′). A violent revolving storm that occurs, chiefly in autumn, along the eastern seaboard of Asia between the Philippines and Japan.
TYPHUS (tī′fus). Types of infectious disease caused by organisms of which fleas, lice or mites are transmitters, and which enter the body through abrasions, etc. Treatment is by antibiotics.
TYR (tir). The Scandinavian god of battles. The Anglo-Saxons called him Týw, hence 'Tuesday'.
TYRE (tīr). Town in Lebanon (modern Sûr), *c.* 80km (50m) S of Beirut, formerly a port until its harbour silted up. Pop. (1971) 14,000. T. stands on the site of anc. T., a seaport of Phoenicia. Built partly on the mainland and partly on 2 small islands, the city was a great commercial centre and famous for its purple dye. Besieged by Alexander the Great 333-332 BC and captured, it came under Roman rule 64 BC and was taken by the Arabs AD 638. The Crusaders captured it 1124, and it never recovered from the destruction it suffered when the Arabs recaptured it, 1291. In the 1970s it became a Palestinian guerrilla stronghold, and was shelled by Israel in 1979.
TYRE. The rubber hoop fitted round the rims of bicycle, motor-car and road vehicle wheels. The first pneumatic rubber T. was patented by R. W. Thompson in 1845, but it was John Boyd Dunlop of Belfast who independently re-invented pneumatic Ts. for use with bicycles 1888-9.
TYROL. *See* TIROL.
TYRONE (tirōn′). Co. of Northern Ireland. Chief rivers are the Derg, Blackwater, and Foyle. Agriculture is the principal industry; linens, woollens, soap, etc., are manufactured. Omagh is the co. town. Area 3,155 sq.km (1,218 sq.m); pop. (1971) 139,075.
TYUMEN (tyo͞omen′). Town in W Siberia, RSFSR, USSR, on the r. Tura. Founded 1586, it is the oldest in Siberia, with timber, chemical, and tanning industries. Pop. (1979) 359,000.
TZU-HSI (tsoo-shē) (1836-1908). Dowager empress of China. Of humble birth, she was sold as a slave to a general who presented her to the emperor Hsien-Feng as a concubine. On his death in 1861 she became regent for her son; he d. in 1875 and she became regent for her nephew Kwang-hsu. She was held responsible for the Boxer rebellion in 1900.

U

The 21st letter of the English alphabet, and the 20th in the ancient Roman, in which it was identical with *V*. Not until the 19th cent. were *U* and *V* definitely separated in English dictionaries. It has various sounds, e.g. as in *truth* (ōō), *bull* (*oo*), *but* (*u*), *duke* (*yū*), short *i* (*busy*), short *e* (*bury*).

UBANGI-SHARI. *See* CENTRAL AFRICAN REPUBLIC.

U-BOAT. Name given to the German submarine (*Unterseeboot*) in both world wars, because they were named U followed by a number.

UCCELLO (oochel'lō), **Paolo.** Name used by Italian artist Paolo di Dono (1397-1475). Apprenticed to Ghiberti, he is celebrated for his decorative use of perspective, and his works incl. the 'Nativity' fresco (Florence) and 3 battle pictures for the Palazzo Medici, one of which is in the National Gallery.

UDAIPUR (oodipoor'). Indian city in Rajasthan, once cap. of the former princely state of U., incorporated in Rajasthan 1948. A fine city with several palaces (2 on islands in a lake), and the Jagannath temple (*c.* 1640), it was founded 1568. Pop. (1971) 162,934.

Ū'DALL, Nicholas (1504-56). English schoolmaster and playwright, author of *Ralph Roister Doister* (*c.* 1553), the first known English comedy.

UDINE (oodē'nā). Italian city, 130km (80m) NE of Venice. U. was the cap. of Friuli in the 13th cent., passed to Venice 1420. It makes textiles, leather goods, chemicals, paper, sugar. Pop. (1971) 95,200.

UDMURT (oodmoort'). ASSR of the RSFSR, in the W Ural foothills. Its products incl. timber, flax, potatoes, peat, quartz; there is some industry, e.g. metallurgy at Izhevsk (the cap.). Area 42,100 sq.km (16,200 sq.m); pop. (1978) 1,496,000.

UCCELLO. One of very few paintings on canvas which have survived from the mid-15th century, this rendering of 'St. George and the Dragon' by Uccello combines two episodes of the story in one: the attack on the dragon and its later harnessing to the girdle of the princess, as taken from the *The Golden Legend*, which gives the standard version of the story, written in the 13th century. *Photo: Courtesy of the National Gallery, London*

UFA (oo'fah). Cap. of Bashkir ASSR, RSFSR, in the W Urals on the r. Bielaia, founded by the Russians 1574. It has engineering, oil refining, petrochemical, distilling and timber industries. Pop. (1979) 969,000.

ŪGA'NDA. Rep. of Central Africa. With an average altitude of 1,200 m (4,000 ft) a.s.l., it forms a savannah plateau drained by the White Nile, and incl. Lakes Kyoga and Salisbury, as well as a great part of Lakes Albert (Mobutu Sese Soko), Edward (Idi Amin Dada 1973-9), and Victoria. The country is still predominantly agricultural, 90 per cent of the pop. living in rural areas. Chief crops are cotton, coffee, sugar, tea and tobacco: sugar and cotton mills have been estab. Minerals incl. copper, iron, tin, cobalt, manganese, tungsten and gold. Tourism is encouraged by nat. parks (Qu. Elizabeth, Murchison Falls and Kidepo Valley). The former kingdom of Buganda (q.v.), now divided into N and S Buganda, forms 2 of the 10 admin. provs. The cap. is Kampala in Buganda; other towns are Mbale, Jinja and Entebbe. *See* OWEN FALLS.

A Brit. Protectorate from 1894, U. became independent in 1962, and formally a rep. within the Commonwealth in 1967. Pres. Milton Obote (q.v.) was deposed following a military coup by Idi Amin (q.v.) in 1971. Under Amin's rule the Asian community was expelled, many of the refugees settling in Britain, the economy moved towards breakdown, and relations with other African states, espec. Kenya, deteriorated. He also terrorised his own people, and in 1979 was defeated by combined Ugandan exile and Tanzanian invading forces. After a period of political instability, Obote (Uganda People's Cougress: UPC) was returned to power in the elections of 1980. He was deposed in a military coup in July 1985, and replaced by Lt. Gen. Tito Okello, the head of the armed forces.

Area 236,000 sq.km (93,980 sq.m); pop. (1978) 12,400,000, of Bantu, Hamitic, Nilotic and Sudanese stock. About 50% are Christian, 45% traditionalists, and 5% Moslem. The eventual official language will be Swahili, but English is in general use. M.U.: Uganda shilling.

UGANDA MARTYRS. Twenty-two African Negroes, of whom 12 were boy pages, who were put to death 1885-7 by King Mwanga of U. for refusal to renounce Christianity. They were canonized as the first African saints of the RC Church in 1964. *See* SAINT.

Ū'GARIT. Small kingdom (modern Ras Shamra) on the coast of Syria to the N of Latakia, excavated by Claude Schaeffer from 1929. It was a commercial centre, and in the palace numerous documents in cuneiform have been discovered, as well as an early Ugaritic alphabet of 22 letters - the earliest alphabet known - closely related to the Phoenician from which our own ultimately derives. Most of the discoveries are 15-13th cent. BC, but some *c.* 7000 BC.

UHLAND (ōō'lahnt), **Johann Ludwig** (1787-1862). German poet, author of ballads and lyrics in the Romantic tradition.

UIST (ū'-ist). Two small is. in the Outer Hebrides, Western Isles, Scotland. There is a guided missile range on S.U.

UJIJI (ōōjē'ji). Port on Lake Tanganyika, Tanzania, linked by rail with Dar es Salaam. It was originally an Arab trading post for slaves and ivory, and Stanley found Livingstone here in 1871. Pop. (1970) 17,000.

UGANDA. Rising coffee prices throughout the world make the crop increasingly important in Uganda. Here the beans are washed before drying. *Photo: Douglas Dickins*

UJUNG PANDANG (ōō'joong pan'dang). Chief port (formerly Macassar) of Sulawesi, Indonesia. It has fishing and food processing industries, and a univ. (1956). Pop. (1978) 564,500.

UKELELE. *See* HAWAII.

UKRAINE (ūkrān'). A constituent republic of the USSR, lying in the SW, reaching from the Black Sea to Poland. The U. is the great cereal-growing area of Russia, and sugar-beet and other crops flourish. The Donetz coalfield is the richest in the Soviet Union; iron ore is also mined, and steel and pig-iron are important products. Chief rivers are the Dnieper, which is harnessed at the Dnieper dam (1932) to supply hydro-electric power, the Donetz and the Bug. Natural gas is exported to Austria. The cap. Kiev is the historic centre of Ukrainian culture. Other cities are Kharkhov, Odessa, Dnepropetrovsk, Donetsk, and Nikolayev. Area 603,700 sq.km (233,000 sq.m); pop. (1978) 49,500,000.

The majority of the people are Ukrainians, or Little Russians; the official language is Ukrainian, a Slavonic dialect. Ukrainian literature goes back to the Middle Ages. The first modern Ukrainian writer was Ivan Kotlyarevsky (1769-1838); the great national writer is Taras Shevchenko (1841-61).

U. was a state already in the 9th cent. Russia absorbed E U. in 1667, the rest in 1793. U. proclaimed itself a people's rep. in 1917, a soviet rep. in 1919; from 1923 it formed one of the reps. of the USSR. The Germans overran it in the S.W.W. For additions to U. after the S.W.W., *see* BESSARABIA, BUKHOVINA, RUTHENIA; *see also* CRIMEA.

ULAANBAATAR (oolahn' bah'taw). Cap. (formerly Ulan Bator, and until 1924 Urga) of the Mongolian Rep., linked with Ulan Ude by rail. It has a univ. (1942), and is also a trading centre producing carpets, textiles, vodka, etc., and has an airport. Pop. (1978) 400,000.

ULAN BATOR. *See* ULAANBAATAR.

ULA'NOVA, Galina (1910-). Russian dancer. Prima ballerina of the Bolshoi theatre ballet 1944-61, she continued as ballet master to the company.

ULAN UDE. Cap. of Buriat ASSR, RSFSR, on the r. Uda, and the Trans-Siberian rly. It has industrial plants incl. sawmills and factories making motor-cars and glass. Pop. (1979) 300,000.

ULBRICHT (ool'brikht), **Walter** (1893-1973). E German statesman. A cabinet-maker, he helped to found the German Communist Party, and lived in the USSR during the Nazi era. From 1950 he was first sec. of the Socialist Unity Party, and, as Chairman of the Council of State 1960-73, built the Berlin Wall in 1961 and estab. E Germany's prosperity and recognition outside the Soviet bloc.

ULCER. Sloughing of skin or mucous membrane. It is caused either by infection (e.g. syphilitic ulcer), inadequate blood supply (e.g. varicose ulcer), or irritation (e.g. gastric ulcer).

ULEÅBORG. Swedish name of OULU.

ULM (oolm). German city and fortress in Baden-Württemberg, on the Danube. A free imperial city from the 14th cent. to 1802, it has a fine Gothic cathedral (1377) which escaped damage in the S.W.W. when two-thirds of U. was destroyed. It makes vehicles, agricultural machinery, precision instruments, textiles, etc. Pop. (1978) 94,500.

ULSTER. Northernmost of the Irish provinces, divided into 9 counties, of which 6 (Antrim, Armagh, Down, Fermanagh, Londonderry, and Tyrone) constitute Northern Ireland, while 3 (Cavan, Donegal, and Monaghan) are in the Republic. From Jacobean times it was a centre of English, later Scottish, settlement. Total area 21,585 sq.km (8,335 sq.m); pop. (1971) 1,743,280. The courtesy title *Earl of U.* is borne by Alexander (1974-), eldest son of the Duke of Gloucester.

ULTRA. Name (abbreviation of Ultra Secret) used by the British from spring 1940 in the S.W.W. for intelligence gained by deciphering German signals at the interception centre at Bletchley Park. *See* S.W.W.

ULTRAMONTANISM ('beyond the mountains', i.e. the Alps). Term applied to the Italian party in the RC Church who lay great stress on papal claims.

ULTRASONICS. Ultrasonic rays are physical vibrations in matter occurring at frequencies above 20,000 hertz (cycles per sec.) which is the approximate limit of human hearing. Propagation of U. in air or other gas is very poor and nearly all practical applications are in liquids or solids. The earliest practical application was to detect submarines during the F.W.W. but recently the field has greatly expanded.

The lower frequencies of 20,000-80,000 hertz are mainly used for cleaning in industry and in hospitals. Higher frequencies have been used in the form of pulses to produce echoes as a means of measuring the depth of the sea, to detect flaws in metal and to show displacement of the brain in surgery.

High power U. has been used with focussing arrangements to destroy tissue at a depth in the body, and extremely high frequencies of 1,000 megahertz or more are used in ultrasonic microscopes.

ULTRA-VIOLET RADIATION. Light rays invisible to the naked eye, of a wavelength less than 3,900 Angström units, the lower limit being about 10 Å when the X-ray range begins. Physiologically they are extremely powerful, producing sunburn and causing the formation of vitamin D; they are strongly germicidal and may be produced artificially by mercury vapour and arc lamps for therapeutic use. U.V.R. may be detected with ordinary photographic plates or films down to 2,000 Å. Below this Schumann plates and special vacuum apparatus must be used. It can also be studied by its fluorescent effect on suitable materials.

ULYSSES. *See* ODYSSEUS.

UMBELLI'FERAE. Plant family of dicotyledons containing about 200 genera and 2,700 species, characterized by an inflorescence in which all the foot stalks of a flower cluster radiate from a common point at the top of the stem. They include hemlock, celery, fool's parsley, and carrot.

UMBERTO II (Humbert) (1904–83). Last king of Italy. He succeeded on the abdication of his father, Victor Emmanuel III, on 9 May 1946, and abdicated on 13 June and left the country. From 1944 he had been Lieut.-Gen. of the realm. He subsequently settled in Portugal as the Count di Sarre.

UMBRELLA. Portable protection against the rain - when used against the sun usually called a parasol or sunshade. They were used by the Chinese more than 1,000 yrs BC and also by the rulers of ancient Egypt and Assyria, when they were also a symbol of power, as they are still regarded in parts of Africa, etc. Revived in clerical use in 16th cent. Italy, Us. were first carried as an everyday protection in England by Jonas Hanway (1712-86), and are still part of 'regulation City uniform'.

UMBRELLA. Making umbrellas at Chiengmai in Thailand. A coat of varnish over the paper covering renders them waterproof, and the structure is bamboo. *Photo: Mireille Vautier*

UMBRIA. A region of Italy in the central Apennines, drained by the Tiber. Perugia is the cap. Area 8,456 sq.km (3,265 sq.m); pop. (1977) 802,448.

UMTALI (oomtah'li). Town in E Zimbabwe, nr the Mozambique border. There is some goldmining, and textiles are made. Pop. (1977) 62,000.

UMTATA (oomtah'ta). Cap. of the Transkei (q.v.).

UNAMUNO (oonahmoo'nō), **Miguel de** (1864–1936). Spanish writer. B. at Bilbao and proud of his Basque origin, he was prof. of Greek at Salamanca from 1892 and rector of the univ. from 1900, but was exiled 1924–30 for criticism of the military directorate of Primo de Rivera. His works incl. a mystic poem on survival of death *El Cristo de Velazquez* (1920: *The Velazquez Christ*); the key philosophical study *Del Sentimiento Trágico de la Vida* (1913: *The Tragic Sense of Life*); an interpretation of Cervantes, travel books, plays, stories and novels (e.g. *Niebla*). He is widely influential in the Spanish-speaking world, but an individualistic style has made translation difficult.

UNCERTAINTY PRINCIPLE. The principle (also known as the Indeterminacy Principle) laid down by Heisenberg (q.v.), which plays an important role in quantum physics. Essentially it states that, owing to a particle's ability to behave also like a spread-out wave, its exact rate of motion and precise position are incapable of being measured simultaneously, and consequently the outcome of any experiment in which particles are involved can never be predicted exactly. Similarly, happenings on a larger scale can only be predicted as the result of averaging, e.g. an insurance company can say that a certain percentage of their customers will die before retirement age, but cannot say that any particular customer will, or will not, do so. This undermines the concept of determinism (q.v.) and makes it possible to believe in the Universe as not constructed as an inevitably acting machine, but as possessed of a creative potential of its own.

UNCLE SAM. Nickname for the USA. It originated during the war of 1812, probably from the initials U.S. placed on government property.

UNDERGROUND. Name for London's city and suburban rail services, operated by the London Transport Executive, but with the Greater London Council controlling finance and overall policy. The world's first U. (1863), it was the conception of a London solicitor to relieve traffic congestion. For latest extensions, *See* LONDON.

UNDERWOOD, Leon (1890–1975). British artist and sculptor. B. in London, he travelled widely to Iceland, the US, Mexico and W Africa, devoting several books to the masks, wood carvings and bronzes of the last-named. His rhythmic figures are powerful symbols of human myth.

UNDSET (oond'set), **Sigrid** (1882–1949). Norwegian novelist. B. in Denmark, she was a clerk in Oslo 1899–1909, and first won fame with *Jenny* (1912). Her masterpiece is *Kristin Lavransdatter* (1920–2), set in the 14th cent., which is strongly Catholic - she was in 1925 received into the RC Church. In 1928 she was awarded a Nobel prize.

UNEMPLOYMENT. Lack of employment on a large scale. A certain proportion of U. is 'frictional', i.e. due to the flow of labour from a depressed to a prosperous industry, but the term as used today relates to U. of a different character, i.e. long-term mass U., such as became a permanent feature of economic life in all industrial countries between the two world wars, e.g. in the USA there were 3–4 million unemployed even during the 1929 boom. In Britain, for at least 150 years before 1939, the supply of labour always exceeded the demand except in war-time, and economic crises accompanied by mass U. were recurrent from 1785. The percentage of unemployed (in trade unions) averaged 6 during 1883–1913 and 14.2 (of those covered by the old U. Insurance Acts) 1921–38. The S.W.W. and the rebuilding and expansion that followed meant shortage of labour rather than U. in Britain and on the Continent, as well as in USA, although in the last-named certain areas, espec. those with a large Negro population have chronic U. problems, and this pattern has been repeated more recently in Britain where coloured immigrants predominate. Fluctuation in employment returned in the 1960s, and in the recession of the mid-1970s to 1980s was a world-wide problem. In the UK in 1980 over 2 million were unemployed. An initial strengthening of left-wing reaction lessened when Communist countries, such as Poland, handled the situation even less effectively than capitalist states, whose recourse to increased govt. spending or increased money supply had further weakened already weak economies.

In under-developed countries with high population growth 'under-employment' is always chronic, e.g. S Italy and Latin America; and in newly emergent Africa, India, etc., there is lack of high-grade employment to absorb the new student pop., with resultant govt instability in both circumstances. *See* SOCIAL SECURITY.

UNGARE'TTI, Giuseppe (1888–1970). Italian poet. B. in Alexandria, and later living in Paris and São Paulo, he shows in his lyrics a cosmopolitan independence of Italian poetic tradition, and they are noted for their spare simplicity, esp. the poems (pervaded by a horror of war), in his best-known collection *Allegria di naufragi* (1919: *L'Allegria*).

UNGĀ'VA. Region of N Quebec and Labrador, E of Hudson Bay, noted for iron deposits.

UNGŪLĀ'TA. Large order of mammals including all the hoofed forms, ranging from pigs to elephants.

UNIATE (i.e. united Greek or Eastern Orthodox and RC Church). Name given to those Christian Churches which accept the full Catholic faith and the supremacy of the Pope, and are in full communion with the RC Church, but retain their own liturgy and separate organization.

Ū'NICORN. Fabulous animal referred to by classical writers, said to live in India and to be like a horse but with one straight horn. *See* ORYX.

UNIDENTIFIED FLYING OBJECTS (UFOs). Aerial phenomena which are usually assumed to be 'manned' spacecraft despatched to Earth by civilizations estab. on other planets: they are also referred to because of the shape of the majority of craft in such alleged sightings as 'flying saucers'. Seeing UFOs became a craze in the 1950s, but the vast majority are explicable in mundane terms, e.g. the effect of sunlight on escaped weather balloons. A small residue remains, but although there is nothing inherently improbable in beings from other planets doing what we are ourselves attempting to do with our own space probes, there is no convincing evidence acceptable to the majority of scientists.

UNIFIED FIELD THEORY. In physics the attempt to find a theory which reduces the 4 natural forces (q.v.) to a single unified force. *See* CLERK MAXWELL, James, EINSTEIN, Albert and WEINBERG, Steven.

UNIFORMITY. Name given to 2 acts of parliament. The first (1559) imposed the Prayer Book on the whole English kingdom; the second (1662) required the Prayer Book to be used in all churches, and some 2,000 ministers who refused to comply were ejected.

UNION. The Act of Union of 1707 effected the union of England and Scotland, and that of 1801 of England and Ireland. The latter was abrogated when the Irish Free State was constituted in 1922.

UNION FLAG. The British national flag, popularly called the *U. Jack*, although this is accurate only when it is flown on the jackstaff of a warship. *See* FLAG.

UNION MOVEMENT. Political group in Britain. Originating with the New Party founded by Sir Oswald Mosley (q.v.) and a number of Labour MPs in 1931, it later developed into the British Union of Fascists (1932). An attempt by the 'blackshirts' to march through the East End of London in 1936 led to the Public Order Act, forbidding the wearing of such political uniforms. In 1940 the organization was declared illegal and its leaders interned, but at the end of the S.W.W. it was revived as the U.M., its anti-Jewish and anti-colour doctrines leading to disorder at its meetings.

UNION OF SOVIET SOCIALIST REPUBLICS (USSR). *See* SOVIET UNION; RUSSIA.

UNITARIANS. A Christian denomination which rejects the orthodox doctrine of the Trinity, asserts the Fatherhood of God and the Brotherhood of Man, and gives a pre-eminent position to Jesus Christ as a religious teacher, while denying his Deity. Us. also reject the doctrines of original sin, the atonement, and eternal punishment, and they have no creeds. The various congregations are linked in the General Assembly of Unitarian and Free Christian Churches.

UNITED ARAB REPUBLIC. Union formed 1958, broken 1961, between Egypt and Syria. Egypt continued to use the name after the breach until 1971.

UNITED AUSTRALIA PARTY. Party formed by J.A. Lyons (q.v.) in 1931 from the right-wing Nationalist Party (founded by Hughes and in power 1917-29). Led after the death of Lyons by Menzies, it was considered to have become too dominated by financial interests, lost heavily to Labor in 1943, and was reorganized in 1944 as the Liberal Party (q.v.).

UNITED KINGDOM. Name for England and Scotland together from the accession of James VI of Scotland as James I of England, 1603, confirmed by the Act of Union, 1707, and extended to incl. Ireland, 1801, the full title being U.K. of England, Scotland, and Ireland; from 1927 the form U.K. of England, Scotland and N Ireland was used.

UNITED NATIONS. An association of states pledged to maintain international peace and security, and to promote international co-operation. Its charter, which was drawn up by the San Francisco Conference in 1945, is based on proposals drafted at the Dumbarton Oaks Conference. It succeeded the League of Nations (q.v.).

The 6 principal organs of the U.N. are (1) the *General Assembly* of representatives of all member states, which meets regularly once a year, and may discuss any matter within the scope of the charter, but may not make recommendations on anything already being dealt with by the Security Council. Decisions on important questions are made by a two-thirds majority of members voting, and on other questions by a simple majority, each member having one vote. (2) the *Security Council* consisting of 5 permanent members (UK, USA, USSR, France and Communist China), and 6 others elected for 2 years by the General Assembly. Its decisions must be supported by at least 7 of its members, incl. all permanent members, who thus exercise the right of veto. Taking cognizance of disputes, it may undertake investigations into the circumstances and make recommendations to the parties concerned, and may call on all members to take economic or military measures to enforce its decisions. (3) the *Economic and Social Council,* consisting of representatives of 18 member states, elected for 3 years by the General Assembly, which initiates studies of international economic, social, cultural, educational, health and related matters, and may make recommendations to the General Assembly. It operates largely through specialized commissions of international experts on economics, transport and communications, human rights, status of women, etc. It also co-ordinates the activities of such specialized intergovernmental agencies as the U.N. Educational, Scientific and Cultural Organization (UNESCO 1946) to combat illiteracy, raise living standards through education, etc.; International Labour Organization (q.v.); Food and Agriculture Organization (FAO 1945), to help the nations improve food production and distribution, raise nutritional standards, etc.; International Atomic Energy Agency (IAEA 1957) to develop the peaceful uses of atomic energy; World Health Organization (WHO 1946), to prevent the spread of, and eliminate, such diseases as malaria and tuberculosis; International Monetary Fund and International Bank for Reconstruction and Development, which promote international economic co-operation, etc. (4) the *Trusteeship Council,* consisting of members administering Trust Territories (q.v.), other permanent members of the Security Council, plus sufficient other elected members to balance the administering powers. (5) the *International Court of Justice* (q.v.) at The Hague which is U.N.'s principal judicial organ: the 15 judges are elected by the General Assembly and the Security Council, and U.N. members are pledged by the charter to comply with the decisions of the court in cases to which they are a party. (6) the *Secretariat,* the administrative body, consisting of the Secretary General, appointed by the General Assembly on the recommendation of the Security Council for 5 years, and an international staff.

Members contribute according to their resources, an apportionment being made by the General Assembly, with the addition of voluntary contributions from some govts - to the funds of the U.N. which finance the programme of assistance carried out by the U.N., intergovernmental agencies, the U.N. Children's Fund (UNICEF), the U.N. refugee organizations, and the U.N. Special Fund for undeveloped countries. There are 6 official working languages: English, French, Russian, Spanish, Chinese and Arabic.

The preponderance of influence in the U.N., originally with the Allied States of the S.W.W., is now more widely spread. Although part of the value of the U.N. lies in recognition of member states as sovereign and equal, the rapid increase in membership of minor - in some cases minute - states was causing concern by 1980 (154 members) as lessening the weight of voting decisions. Taiwan (Nationalist China), formerly a permanent member of the Security Council, was expelled 1971 on the admission of Communist China. The U.N. also suffers from the lack of adequate and independent funds and forces, the latter having been employed with varying success, e.g. in Korea, Cyprus, and Sinai, and the intrusion

NITED STATES OF AMERICA. Rainbow ridge, a natural feature in Utah (top left); illiamsburg, the restored 18th century apital of Virginia (top right); Lee arrenders to Grant at the end of the Civil ar (centre left); Jesse James, Robin Hood the Wild West (centre); 'Summertime' . 1895) by Mary Cassatt (centre left); the g cabin comes into its own again, towed house Alaskan settlers in the latest oil oom (centre right); and the Watergate ilding. *Photos: USIS, Mireille Vautier Villiamsburg, log cabin, Watergate), ansell Collection (Lee, James), The untingdon Hartford Collection, Gallery of odern Art.*

of the Cold War which divides members into adherents of the E or W and the uncommitted.

UNITED PROVINCES OF AGRA AND OUDH. Prov. of British India which formed the major part of the state of UTTAR PRADESH.

UNITED STATES OF AMERICA (USA). Federal republic in North America, extending from the Atlantic to the Pacific and from Canada to Mexico, plus the outlying states of Alaska and Hawaii.

Physical. The USA proper, occupying the central part of the N American land mass, is c. 4,345 km (2,700 m) long, and has a greatest width of 2,575 km (1,600 m). The surface consists of vast central plains, bounded by great mountain ranges, the Rockies in the W and the Appalachians in the E. To the E of the Appalachians are the Atlantic coast lowlands. W of the Appalachians is the 'Central Valley', extending from the Great Lakes to the Gulf of Mexico and taking up about half the entire area of the country; here are the Prairies and the Great Plains, constituting one of the most important agricultural areas on the globe. The only considerable exception to its level uniformity is the Ozark mts. in Arkansas and Oklahoma. W of the plains rises the great system of mountains, to the E the Rockies, to the W the Sierra Nevada and the Cascade mts. and Coast ranges, with a great plateau, much of it desert, in between. The highest point in the USA (and in N America) is Mt McKinley (6,194 m/20,320 ft) in Alaska; the lowest Death Valley (86 m/282 ft) b.s.l. The highest peak in continental USA excl. Alaska is Mt Whitney, Calif. (4,418 m/14,494 ft); and the highest in the US Rockies is Mt Elbert (4,490 m/14,433 ft). A narrow, fertile strip borders the Pacific. The main river system is the Missouri-Mississippi basin, flowing through the central plains; the chief rivers flowing into the Pacific are the Columbia (which rises in Canada) in the N and the Colorado in the S. The many rivers of the Atlantic slope are comparatively short, though of great importance. In the N are the Great Lakes, of which Michigan is wholly in the USA, the others being partly in Canada.

CLIMATE. In the centre and the mountains of the Cordillera (Rockies, Sierra Nevada, etc.) the climate is one of extreme cold and heat. The Pacific coastal area has a more uniform climate than the Atlantic seaboard, where the winters are severe. California and Florida are renowned for their geniality. Tropical conditions prevail in the S states. In the E rainfall is abundant, and conditions for urban and agricultural life are excellent. The Plains are liable to drought, and areas in the mtns and plateaux are almost rainless.

REGIONS. There are traditionally some ten great regions, although the development of new industries independent of local resources, e.g. synthetic textiles and electronics; mineral discoveries in agricultural areas; new crops and farming methods; pop. shifts and injection of capital for industrialization, tend to blur the older dividing lines. (1) New England, the historic core of the Union. Maine, Vermont, New Hampshire, Massachusetts, Rhode Island, and Connecticut cover most of the area of original British settlement, and are still one of the chief centres of population and industry. (2) New York, the 'Empire State', formerly the undisputed leader in population, is now second to California, with whom it also shares supremacy in industrial production. (3) The Middle Atlantic States comprise Pennsylvania, New Jersey, and Delaware, and incl. the vast coal, iron and steel area of Pittsburgh, as well as much farm land. (4) The Middle West is industrially great, and often thought of as the most typically American region, it incl. Ohio, Indiana, Illinois, Michigan and Wisconsin; agriculture is important, but more so are the industries based on the iron ore of Michigan. (5) The Prairie States (Minnesota, Iowa, N Dakota, S Dakota, Nebraska and Kansas) are one huge granary, but N Dakota now also has oil and new processes make the taconite (low grade iron) ores of Minnesota workable. (6) The Mountain States (Montana, Wyoming, Colorado, New Mexico, Utah, Arizona, Nevada and Idaho) are the traditional country of sheep and cattle ranches and mineral mines, with desert land on the plateaux, but Montana and Wyoming are now oil producers, and dry farming and irrigation have made formerly arid lands productive, so that Arizona is a leading cotton state. (7) The Pacific States are California (once famous only for fruit and films, but now one of the first three oil states and a leading cotton producer), Oregon, Washington, Alaska (moving into the front rank in oil), and Hawaii, the only extra-continental state, with tropical produce of cane sugar and pineapples. (8) The South comprises Virginia, N Carolina, S Carolina, Georgia, Alabama, Mississippi, Louisiana, and Florida. Its rapid industrialization is illustrated by Louisiana, now one of the three leading oil states, and Florida and Georgia with their growing varied industries; and the domination of tobacco, rice and cotton, is now diversified with citrus, soya, peanuts, etc. (9) The SW contains Texas and Oklahoma, home of the cowboy, but now more remarkable for its vast oil industry, and with extending agriculture under new methods. (10) The Border States (i.e. states separating the traditional differing economic areas): Maryland, West Virginia, Arkansas, Kentucky, Tennessee, Missouri. Here, although West Virginia has coal and Arkansas oil, there is a balance of agriculture and industry, although in Tennessee the latter had moved into predominance by 1975. One of the most remarkable factors in population movement has been the attraction of sunshine, which made California a magnet in the 1950s and Florida in the 1960s, with a large retirement element.

Government. The USA comprises 50 states, and the District of Columbia. Each state is self-governing in local matters, but confides to the central government at Washington the control of foreign affairs and the army and navy. Police, education, public health, etc. remain within the scope of the individual states, but since the Roosevelt 'New Deal' in the 1930s the federal govt has concerned itself with social provisions of one kind and another. The cap. is Washington, DC, which belongs to no state, being administered directly by the Federal govt. Executive power is vested in the President, elected by popular vote every 4 years, and by the 22nd amendment (1951) eligible to stand for 2 terms only; he chooses the members of the Cabinet, who may not be (as in Britain) members of the legislature. Legislative power is vested in Congress, composed of 2 houses: the Senate, with 2 members from each state, elected to serve 6 years, one-third re-elected every 2 years; and the House of Representatives of 435 members, distributed according to pop. among the states, and elected for 2 years.

POPULATION. The original settlers in New England and Virginia were mainly of British stock, but subsequent immigration from all countries to 1980 totalled more than 43 million. Between 1820 and 1975 immigrants came

United States of America

State with date of admission to Union	Area in sq. km.	Pop. est. (1977)	Capital
Alabama (1819)	133,665	3,690,000	Montgomery
Alaska (1959)	1,518,539	407,000	Juneau
Arizona (1912)	295,023	2,296,000	Phoenix
Arkansas (1836)	137,533	2,140,000	Little Rock
California (1850)	411,013	21,896,000	Sacramento
Colorado (1876)	270,240	2,619,000	Denver
Connecticut (1788)	12,973	3,108,000	Hartford
Delaware (1787)	5,328	582,000	Dover
Florida (1845)	151,700	8,452,000	Tallahassee
Georgia (1788)	152,500	5,048,000	Atlanta
Hawaii (1959)	16,705	895,000	Honolulu
Idaho (1890)	216,412	857,000	Boise
Illinois (1818)	146,075	11,245,000	Springfield
Indiana (1816)	93,994	5,330,000	Indianapolis
Iowa (1846)	145,790	2,879,000	Des Moines
Kansas (1861)	213,063	2,326,000	Topeka
Kentucky (1792)	104,623	3,458,000	Frankfort
Louisiana (1812)	125,675	3,921,000	Baton Rouge
Maine (1820)	86,027	1,085,000	Augusta
Maryland (1788)	27,394	4,139,000	Annapolis
Massachusetts (1788)	21,385	5,782,000	Boston
Michigan (1837)	150,777	9,129,000	Lansing
Minnesota (1858)	217,735	3,975,000	St. Paul
Mississippi (1817)	123,584	2,389,000	Jackson
Missouri (1821)	180,455	4,801,000	Jefferson City
Montana (1889)	381,085	761,000	Helena
Nebraska (1867)	200,036	1,561,000	Lincoln
Nevada (1864)	286,300	633,000	Carson City
New Hampshire (1788)	24,100	849,000	Concord
New Jersey (1787)	20,295	7,329,000	Trenton
New Mexico (1912)	315,113	1,190,000	Santa Fé
New York (1788)	128,400	17,924,000	Albany
North Carolina (1789)	136,523	5,525,000	Raleigh
North Dakota (1889)	183,020	653,000	Bismarck
Ohio (1803)	106,714	10,701,000	Columbus
Oklahoma (1907)	181,088	2,811,000	Oklahoma City
Oregon (1859)	251,180	2,376,000	Salem
Pennsylvania (1787)	117,412	11,785,000	Harrisburg
Rhode Island (1790)	3,144	935,000	Providence
South Carolina (1788)	80,432	2,876,000	Columbia
South Dakota (1889)	199,550	689,000	Pierre
Tennessee (1796)	109,412	4,299,000	Nashville
Texas (1845)	692,407	12,830,000	Austin
Utah (1896)	219,931	1,268,000	Salt Lake City
Vermont (1791)	24,887	483,000	Montpelier
Virginia (1788)	105,711	5,135,000	Richmond
Washington (1889)	176,615	3,658,000	Olympia
West Virginia (1863)	62,629	1,859,000	Charleston
Wisconsin (1848)	145,438	4,651,000	Madison
Wyoming (1890)	253,595	406,000	Cheyenne
District of Columbia	179	690,000	
	9,363,404*	216,326,000	
Outlying Territories:			
Puerto Rico, CW. of	8,891	3,319,000	San Juan
Guam	535	104,400	Agaña
Virgin Islands	342	118,960	Charlotte Amalie
American Samoa	197	30,600	Fagatogo
Wake Island	8	1,650	—
Midway Islands	5.5	2,200	—
Marianas, Cw. of the Northern	479	16,260	Saipan
Micronesia, Fed. States of	702	47,200	Moen Is.
Marshall Islands	181	23,000	
Belau	497	11,200	
Johnston and Sand Island	2.5	1,000	—
	11,840	3,675,470	

**Excl. the part of the Great Lakes in USA (157,370 sq. km./60,760 sq. m.), but incl. other inland water.*

mainly from Europe, espec. Germany, UK, Italy and Ireland. More recently the chief immigrant sources have been the Philippines, Mexico and Cuba. Blacks, chiefly descendants of imported African slaves, numbered 22,700,000 in 1970, and American Indians 791,800. The largest religious denomination is the Roman Catholic (over 51,000,000 in 1980), followed by the Baptist and Methodist. Jews numbered some 6,000,000. The total preliminary census pop. figure for 1980 was 226,000,000.

History. Spaniards made (in Florida), in 1565, the first white settlements in what became the USA. The first permanent English settlement was at Jamestown, Virginia, in 1607. In 1620 the 'Pilgrim Fathers' landed at Plymouth, and eventually founded Massachusetts. English RCs founded Maryland in 1634, English Quakers founded Pennsylvania in 1682. A Dutch settlement (1611) on Manhattan Is., named New Amsterdam 1626, was renamed New York after it was taken by the English in 1664. Throughout most of the 18th cent. the English colonies were threatened by French expansion from the Great Lakes in Canada to Louisiana, but the threat from the French ended with the Seven Years War (1756–63). In 1775 the 13 colonies (N.H., Mass., R.I., Conn., N.Y., N.J., Pa., Del., Va., N.C., S.C., Md., and Ga.) rose against the

Presidents of USA

1. George Washington(*Federalist*)	1789
2. John Adams (*Federalist*)	1797
3. Thomas Jefferson (*Democrat Rep.*)	1801
4. James Madison (*Democrat Rep.*)	1809
5. James Monroe (*Democrat Rep.*)	1817
6. John Quincy Adams (*Democrat Rep.*)	1825
7. Andrew Jackson (*Democrat*)	1829
8. Martin Van Buren (*Democrat*)	1837
9. William Henry Harrison (*Whig*)	1841
10. John Tyler (*Whig*)	1841
11. James Knox Polk (*Democrat*)	1845
12. Zachary Taylor (*Whig.*)	1849
13. Millard Fillmore (*Whig*)	1850
14. Franklin Pierce (*Democrat*)	1853
15. James Buchanan (*Democrat*)	1857
16. Abraham Lincoln (*Republican*)	1861
17. Andrew Johnson (*Democrat*)	1865
18. Ulysses Simpson Grant (*Republican*)	1869
19. Rutherford Birchard Hayes (*Republican*)	1877
20. James Abram Garfield (*Republican*)	1881
21. Chester Alan Arthur (*Republican*)	1881
22. Grover Cleveland (*Démocrat*)	1885
23. Benjamin Harrison (*Republican*)	1889
24. Grover Cleveland (*Democrat*)	1893
25. William McKinley (*Republican*)	1897
26. Theodore Roosevelt (*Republican*)	1901
27. William Howard Taft (*Republican*)	1909
28. Woodrow Wilson (*Democrat*)	1913
29. Warren Gamaliel Harding (*Republican*)	1921
30. Calvin Coolidge (*Republican*)	1923
31. Herbert C. Hoover (*Republican*)	1929
32. Franklin Delano Roosevelt (*Democrat*)	1933
33. Harry S. Truman (*Democrat*)	1945
34. Dwight D. Eisenhower (*Republican*)	1953
35. John F. Kennedy (*Democrat*)	1961
36. Lyndon B. Johnson (*Democrat*)	1963
37. Richard M. Nixon (*Republican*)	1969
38. Gerald R. Ford (*Republican*)	1974
39. 'Jimmy' Carter (*Democrat*)	1977
40. Ronald Reagan (*Republican*)	1981

home govt, declaring themselves in 1776 to be 'free and independent states'. Led by George Washington, they defeated George III's armies in the War of American Independence (called by US citizens the War of the Revolution). By the Treaty of Paris, 1783, Britain recognized the independence of the 13 colonies. A constitution drawn up in 1787 came into force in 1789 and, with amendments, remains in force. Washington was chosen first pres. In 1803 Louisiana (q.v.) was bought from Napoleon and in 1819 Florida from Spain. In 1812-14 a war was fought with England because of commercial disputes arising out of the conflict with Napoleon in Europe, and the British captured and burnt Washington. Later expansion westward carried the terrs. of the USA to the Pacific and the war with Mexico, 1846-8, secured from that country the vast lands eventually organized as (US) California, Utah, New Mexico, and Texas. Alaska was purchased from Russia in 1867. *See* also HAWAII.

In 1861-5 was fought the Civil War, or the War between the States between 11 of the Southern States (S.C., Miss., Fla., Ala., Ga., La., Tex., joined later by Va., Ark., Tenn., and N.C.), the Confederate States, which wished to maintain their 'states' rights', in particular the peculiar institution of Negro slavery, and claimed the right to secede from the Union; and the Northern or Federal States which fought to maintain the Union. The Confederate States chose Jefferson Davis as President; the leader of the North was President Lincoln. For 4 years the conflict went on. At first the Confederates were successful under Lee at the battles of Bull Run (1861 and 1862), but Lee suffered a repulse at Gettysburg in 1863; Grant overran the Mississippi states and Sherman marched through Georgia to the sea. On 9 April 1865, Lee surrendered to Grant at Appomattox Court House, and a month later the war was over. Casualties on both sides incl. *c.* 600,000 dead. Slavery was ended, but the war, and in particular its aftermath when the S was occupied by the N as if it had been a foreign conquered country, left behind bitterness that lingered a hundred years later.

The war had immensely stimulated the industrial development of the N and had led to the construction of roads and railways. With the end, a great outburst of economic activity began. The country's vast natural resources were exploited. Thousands more miles of railway were laid. The prairies were peopled. Americans referred with pride to 'God's own country', and extolled the virtues of private enterprise. Occasional depressions broke the tide of prosperity, but progress was vast and rapid until 1929 when the greatest of slumps engulfed America. When F. D. Roosevelt became President in 1933 he embarked on a 'New Deal' which broke with American tradition.

The USA had come into the F.W.W. in 1917, and a majority of the Senate voted for the Treaty of Versailles (which incl. Pres. Wilson's League of Nations), but not the two-thirds majority required by the Constitution for the making of a treaty, and a period of isolationism followed. Peace was made with the Central Powers by separate treaties in 1921. Brought into the S.W.W. by the Japanese attack on Pearl Harbor in 1941, the USA played a major part in the winning of that war, and in the peace-making (*see* MARSHALL, G. C.). Direct military action on behalf of the UN was taken in Korea (q.v.), but resources were strained by Vietnam (q.v.) and continued overseas aid. Kennedy and Johnson had moved to alleviate poverty at home and the Negro problem, and with Nixon came greater stress on military withdrawal and elimination of internal disruption. The trauma of Watergate (q.v.) accelerated disentanglement from overseas commitments. Under Ford there was a shift in power from pres. to Congress, and concentration on fighting the threat of recession, and a real break with the past, as represented by Watergate (q.v.), was attempted with the election of Carter, a 'born-again Christian'. However, a poor economic record and vacillation in foreign affairs, led to a landslide Republican victory in 1980, both in the Senate and in the election of Reagan to the presidency. He was pledged to a stronger USA in military terms and to 'getting the Govt. off the back of the American people' at home. Reagan was re-elected in 1984.

Art. The first American-born artist was the portraitist Robert Feke (*c.* (1705-50), but best-known of early masters is Benjamin West - working mainly in England - who encouraged the portraitist John Singleton Copley, and whose pupils incl. Gilbert Stuart, Thomas Sully, and Charles Willson Peale. To the 19th cent. belong the dramatic landscapes of Washington Allston, the nature pictures of Audubon, the seascapes of Winslow Homer, the realism of Thomas Eakins, and the romantic landscapes of the Hudson River school, e.g. English-born Thomas Cole (1801-48) and later George Inness (1825-94). Appreciated abroad were the markedly individual gifts of Whistler, Mary Cassat and John Singer Sargent towards the end of the cent., and the mysticism of the recluse Albert Pinkham Ryder (1847-1917). Notable in the early 20th cent. was the Ashcan school, so nicknamed because of its concern with slum squalor, e.g. George B. Luks (1867-1933) which influenced the work of George W. Bellows (1882-1925) and Rockwell Kent. A pioneer of European movements such as Expressionism was Max Weber (1881-1961) and more recent artists who blend such influences in their work incl. John Marin; Grant Wood; the Mexican Diego Rivera, who worked in the States; Lyonel Feininger; the apostle of Action painting, Jackson Pollock; the politically concerned Ben Shahn, and the spiritual Mark Rothko. In sculpture the best-known names incl. Hiram Powers (1805-73), Horatio Greenough (1805-52), Thomas Crawford (1814-57), Augustus St Gaudens, Lorado Taft (1860-1936), George Grey Barnard (1863-1938), Gutzon Borglum, Carl Milles, Lipchitz, Mestrovic, Archipenko, and Calder, inventor of mobiles.

Architecture. Early influences derived from England, e.g. early buildings at Harvard and William and Mary resemble Oxford and Cambridge; the Georgian-type houses of Virginia and Pennsylvania; and the churches in the style of Wren. The purely classic phase was introduced by Thomas Jefferson towards the end of the 18th cent., e.g. the Federal Capitol at Washington by William Thornton (1761-1828), and the White House by James Hoban (1762-1831). After the Civil War came a generation of French-trained architects, e.g. H. H. Richardson, chief exponent of a modified Romanesque. A revival of 'Queen Anne' style followed, and then towards the end of the 19th cent. a second classical revival, e.g. Columbia Univ., NY and Pennsylvania Terminal Station. Most characteristic of the US is the skyscraper (the word was first used in 1891) which owed its origin to the development of a method of building in which walls are carried on a framework of steel combined with the high cost of land in city centres: *see* GILBERT, CASS. The most individual of earlier 20th cent. US architects was Frank Lloyd Wright, but impressive work was also produced by Richard Buckminster Fuller, Gropius and Mies Van der Rohe, successive directors of the Bauhaus, the Saarinens (father and son), Richard Neutra, and Philip C. Johnson; and more recently by John Portman (1924-), Peach Tree Center, Atlanta, Chinese-born Ieoh Ming Pei (1917-), Nat. Center for Atmospheric Research, at Boulder, Colorado, and Minoru Yamasaki (1912-), New York's World Trade Center.

Literature. American literature of the colonial period (1607-1765) includes travel books and religious verse, but was mainly theological: Roger Williams, Cotton Mather, and Jonathan Edwards were typical Puritan writers. Franklin's *Autobiography* is the first work of more than historical interest. The revolutionary period (1765-1800) produced much political writing, e.g. by Paine, Jefferson, and Hamilton, and one noteworthy poet, Philip Freneau. In the early 19th cent. the influence of the English Romantics became evident, notably in Washington Irving's tales and Fenimore Cooper's novels of Redskin life.

During 1830-60 intellectual life centred on New England, which produced the essayists Emerson, Thoreau, and Holmes; the poets Bryant, Longfellow, Lowell, and Whittier; the historians Parkman, Prescott, and Motley; and the novelist Hawthorne. Outside the New England circle stood Poe, Melville, and Whitman.

The disillusionment of the post-Civil War period (1865-1900) found expression in the realistic or psychological novel. Ambrose Bierce and Stephen Crane wrote realistic war stories; Mark Twain and Bret Harte dealt with western life; and the growth of industrialism led to the rise of the sociological novel, notably in the work of W. D. Howells, while Henry James, and his disciple Edith Wharton, developed the novel of psychological analysis. A major poet of this period was Emily Dickinson.

Since 1900 the main trend in the novel has been realistic, and American writers have exerted a growing influence in Europe, e.g. Jack London, Upton Sinclair, and Theodore Dreiser, and after the F.W.W. by Sherwood Anderson, Sinclair Lewis, and Ernest Hemingway; the southern writers Erskine Caldwell and William Faulkner; and the proletarian James T. Farrell, John Dos Passos, and John Steinbeck. Aside from the main tradition is the romantic or subjective fiction of Thornton Wilder, J. B. Cabell, and Henry Miller. Among the more important writers emerging after the S.W.W. were Truman Capote, J. D. Salinger, John Updike, Norman Mailer, Nelson Algren, Saul Bellow, Vladimir Nabokov, Bernard Malamud, Jack Kerouac, apostle of the Beat generation, and Gore Vidal. Black protest writers have incl. James Baldwin, Richard Wright and LeRoi Jones. The short story has attracted many of the major novelists from James onward, and was popularized as a form by O. Henry: writers specializing in it incl. Ring Lardner, Katharine Anne Porter, William Saroyan, James Thurber, and Eudora Welty (1909-).

In drama the USA produced a powerful group of dramatists between the wars, incl. Eugene O'Neill, Maxwell Anderson, Lillian Hellman, Elmer Rice and Clifford Odets; and the work of Wilder led towards the post-war work of Tennessee Williams and Arthur Miller, and the later generation of which Paddy Chayefsky, Edward Albee, Neil Simon, and William Inge (1913-73), author of *Bus Stop*, are representative. Traditional poets incl. E. A. Robinson, R. Frost, Elinor Wylie, E. St Vincent Millay, with more experimental work being done by E. L. Masters, Carl Sandburg, Ezra Pound, T. S. Eliot and Amy Lowell, and attempts at the great American epic in Hart Crane's *The Bridge* and S. V. Benet's *John Brown's Body*. Among the most striking of later writers are Conrad Aiken, Archibald MacLeish, Karl Shapiro, Robinson Jeffers, Wallace Stevens, Marianne Moore, Robert Lowell, and Theodore Roethke (1908-63). In the field of literary criticism Irving Babbitt, George Santayana, H. L. Mencken and Edmund Wilson were outstanding; more recent names incl. Lionel Trilling, Cleanth Brooks, Yvor Winters (1900-68), and J. C. Ransom (1888-1974), author of *The New Criticism* (1941), with its stress on structural and linguistic factors.

UNIVERSE. The overall celestial system, containing thousands of millions of star-systems or *galaxies*. Each galaxy is composed of thousands of millions of stars, together with interstellar material. It may be assumed that our own Galaxy is typical, and that our Sun is an average star. It has been found that galaxies tend to congregate in groups, and that each group is receding from each other group, so that the whole universe is expanding. The distances involved are, of course, very great, and modern techniques can probe out to approximately 5,000 million light-years.

The 'steady state' theory of the U. (*see* HOYLE, Sir Fred) is now generally less accepted than the 'big bang' theory, which envisages the U. originating in an outward burst over 13 thousand million years ago. Controversy now concentrates on whether the U. is 'open', and will expand indefinitely, or whether it is 'closed', containing sufficient matter for gravity to halt its expansion and cause it to collapse back again, possibly eventually to expand once more, repeating the process indefinitely. Evidence in 1980 suggested that the 'open' theory was the more likely.

UNIVERSITY. A community or corporation of men and women devoted to higher learning. The first European university was Salerno (9th cent.), followed by Bologna, Paris, Oxford, and Cambridge in the 12th cent. St Andrew's, the first Scottish U., was founded in 1411, and Trinity Coll., Dublin, in 1591. A number of univs. were founded in the 19th and earlier 20th cents. (London 1836, Manchester 1851, Wales 1893, Liverpool 1903, Bristol 1909, Reading 1926, etc), and became known as the 'red brick' Us., as opposed to the ancient stone of Oxford and Cambridge, often popularly referred to as 'Oxbridge'. After the S.W.W. many more univs. were founded in the provs. (Nottingham 1948, Exeter 1955, Sussex 1961, etc), and were nicknamed from their ultra-modern buildings, the 'plate-glass' universities. The oldest Us. in USA are: Harvard (1636), William and Mary (1693), Yale (1701), and Princeton (1746). Recent innovations incl. Us. serving international areas, e.g. the Middle East Technical U. (1961) at Ankara, supported by the UN; the UN university in Tokyo (1974); and the British Open U. (1969) combining correspondence packages, radio, television and brief residence periods for young and old. The last-named has been widely copied, incl. in 1980 the National U. Consortium (NUC) in the USA.

UNKNOWN WARRIOR. Name given to a fallen soldier who was taken as representative of all those killed in the F.W.W., and was given a national funeral. The British U.W. or Soldier was buried in Westminster Abbey in 1920. France, Belgium, USA, and other countries each have their U.Ws.

UNTOUCHABLES. *See* CASTE.

UPANISHADS. The most spiritual division of the Vedic texts which form the scriptures of Hinduism. They number nearly 200.

ŪPAS TREE. A tree (*Antiaris toxicaria*) of the fig family, whose gum is very poisonous and was used by the E. Indian natives to tip their arrows.

UPDIKE, John (1932-). American author. Ed. at Harvard and the Ruskin School of Drawing and Fine Art at Oxford, he was on the *New Yorker* staff 1955-7, and besides the novels (*Rabbit, Run*, 1961, *Couples*, 1968, etc.) and short stories (*The Same Door*, 1962 and *Pigeon Feathers*, 1963) which have estab. his reputation for polished overtones, has written poetry, e.g. *Telephone Poles* (1964).

UPPER VOLTA. *See* VOLTA, Upper.

UPPSALA (up'sah'la). Swedish city, to the NW of Stockholm, with a univ. (1477) and a 13th cent. cathedral long used in the crowning of kings of Sweden; Linnaeus lived at Uppsala. Pop. (1979) 143,386.

UR. Ancient city of Mesopotamia, the Ur of the Chaldees of the Bible; c. 225km (140m) SE of Babylon and 10km (6m) from the Euphrates. Excavations by Sir Leonard Woolley show that it was inhabited 3,500 BC. Chief ruin is a ziggurat or temple tower.

UR. The impressive remains, 18 m (60ft) high, of the lowest of the seven stages which once were comprised in the Great Ziggurat at Ur. The temple on the summit was used only on the rare occasions when the god, in whose honour it was built, descended from heaven to pass the night with its high priestess. *Photo: R. Dalmaine/Barnaby's Picture Library*

URAE'MIA. Condition due to the retention in the blood of substances usually eliminated by the kidneys.

Ū'RALS. Mountain system running from the Arctic to the Caspian Sea and separating Europe from Asia. The highest peak is Naradnaya 2,799 m (6,182 ft)). The middle Urals is one of the most important industrial regions of the USSR, owing to its vast mineral wealth. Perm, Chelyabinsk, Sverdlovsk, Magnitogorsk and Zlatoust are important industrial centres.

ŪRĀ'NIUM. Lustrous white metal, malleable and ductile, tarnishing in air: symbol U, at. no. 92, at. wt. 238.07. It was discovered by Klaproth in 1789 in pitchblende and first prepared by Peligot in 1842. The chief ore is uranite (pitchblende U_3O_8), and recent technological advances have made possible its extraction from low-grade ores. Small amounts of its compounds are used in the ceramics industry to give yellow glazes, and as a mordant in dyeing.

U. isotopes have been of vital importance in the production of atomic energy. Although U-238 is most abundant (99 per cent), U-235 is the only naturally occurring readily fissible isotope (1 part in 140) and U-233 is a fissile material that can be produced by the neutron irradiation of thorium-232. Most of the non-Communist producers (excl. USA) are members of the *U. Institute* (1975) in London. The USA is the largest supplier, and Australia potentially the second largest.

Ū'RANUS. In Gk mythology, the sky-god, responsible for rain and warming sun. He was the husband of Ge and father of Cronus and the Titans.

URANUS. The seventh planet of the Solar System. It is 2,870,000,000 km (1,783,000,000 m) from the Sun, and has a revolution period of 84 years. Though it is a giant, with a diameter of 47,100 km (29,300 m), it is barely visible to the naked eye, and was not known in ancient times; it was discovered by W. Herschel in 1781. In constitution it seems to be similar to the larger giants, Jupiter and Saturn. It has at least 12 satellites. Five are named (Miranda, Ariel, Umbriel, Titania and Oberon), and seven more were discovered by the spacecraft Voyager 2 in Jan. 1986. In 1977 it was found to have a ring system, but one differing from that of Saturn in that the 5 rings (Alpha, Beta, Gamma, Delta and Epsilon) are thin, narrow, and dark, and consist of particles.

URBAN II. Pope 1088-99; he launched the 1st Crusade at Clermont in 1095.

URDU (oor'doo). Indian language, a variety of Hindustani that has borrowed largely from Persian and Arabic and is spoken mostly by Moslems.

Ū'REA. A crystalline substance found in urine and the other body fluids. It is the chief material by means of which the body excretes waste nitrogen. Produced synthetically, it forms a valuable nitrogenous fertilizer, and is used in the production of drugs, explosives, etc.

UREY (ū'rē), **Harold Clayton** (1893-1981). American chemist. In 1932 he isolated heavy water and discovered deuterium (q.v.), receiving a Nobel prize in 1934; and was director of the War Research Atomic Bomb Project, Columbia, 1940-5. His books incl. studies of nuclear and atomic structure, and the origin of the planets and of life.

URGA. Former name for ULAANBAATAR.

Ū'RIC ACID. A substance formed from the breakdown of food and body protein. It is a normal constituent of urine, but if formed in excess and not excreted it is deposited in sharp crystals in the joints and other tissues, causing symptoms of gout; or it may form stones in the kidneys or bladder (calculi).

Ū'RIM and **THU'MMIM.** Two mysterious objects in the breastplate of the High Priest of the ancient Hebrews, whereby they exercised divination.

Ū'RINE. An amber-coloured fluid made by the kidneys from the blood. It contains excess water, salts, protein, waste products, a pigment and some acid. The kidneys pass it through 2 fine tubes (ureters) to the bladder, which may act as a reservoir for up to 0.7 litre (20 oz) at a time. It then passes into the urethra, which opens to the outside by a sphincter (constricting) muscle under voluntary control.

URSA MAJOR and **MINOR.** The Great and the Little Bear; 2 constellations of the N hemisphere. The former consists of 7 bright stars, and a line joining the 2 outermost (the pointers), if produced, passes close to the Pole Star (q.v.) which is in U. Minor.

URSULA, St. A British virgin saint and martyr supposed to have been martyred with her maidens by the Huns in the Rhineland, in 238 or about 451.

U'RSULINES. A RC religious order founded at Brescia, by St Angela Merici in 1537, and renowned for its educational work among girls.

URTICĀR'IA. Nettle rash: an irritant skin condition characterized by the spontaneous appearance of weals. It may or may not be allergic in origin. Treatment is by soothing lotions and by injections of adrenalin. *See* ALLERGY.

URUGUAY (oorugwī). Smallest of the South American republics, lying between Brazil and the estuary of the River Plate, and separated from Argentine by the r. Uruguay. The chief river is the Negro. Hilly in the N, U. is mainly an extension of the Pampas, and cattle-breeding and sheep-farming are the chief occupations, wool, leather, and meat (incl. canned meat) being exported. The cap. is Montevideo; other towns are Salto, Paysandu, and Rivera.

The area of modern U. was settled by both Spain (1624) and Portugal (1680), but Spain secured the whole in the 18th cent., until in 1814 Spanish rule was overthrown under the leadership of José Artigas, dictator until driven out by Brazil in 1820. Disputed between Argentina and Brazil 1825-8, U. was declared independent 1828, though not recognized by its neighbours until 1853. A tradition of democracy was maintained until the growth of corruption after the S.W.W. led to the formation of the left-wing urban guerrilla movement of the Tupamaros (*see* TERRORISM). In 1976 the army intervened to depose Pres. Juan Bordaberry, after his refusal to accept the existence of political parties, and in 1980 a constitution proposing 'restricted democracy' under the army was rejected in a referendum. The Liberal Julio Sanguinetti was elected President in 1985. Area 186,945 sq.km (22,180 sq.m); pop. (1972) 2,960,000. The language is Spanish. M.U.: peso.

URUGUAY. River rising in S Brazil, and forming the border of Brazil and Uruguay with Argentina before joining the Parana in the Rio de la Plata estuary: length 1,600 km (995 m). It is being used for hydroelectricity by Argentina and Brazil.

URUMCHI. *See* URÜMQI.

URÜMQI (oorumchē'). Cap. (formerly Urumchi) of Xinjiang Uygur autonomous region, China. At the N foot of the Tyan Shan, it has coalmines nearby, and produces cotton textiles, cement, chemicals, iron and steel. Pop. (1975) 500,000.

USHANT. French island 18km (11m) W of Brittany off which Howe defeated the French, 1794 ('the glorious First of June').

USHUAIA (ooshoo-ī'-a). Southernmost town in the world, at the tip of Tierra del Fuego, Argentina, less than 1,000 m from Antarctica. It is a free port and naval base.

USKÜB. Turkish name of SKOPJE.

USKÜDAR. Suburb of Istanbul, Turkey, formerly a separate town which became well known under the form Scutari as the site of the hospital set up by Florence Nightingale in the Crimean War.

USSR. Abbreviation for the Union of Soviet Socialist Republics. *See* SOVIET UNION.

USSU'RI RIVER. Tributary of the Amur, rising N of Vladivostok, which joins it S of Khabarovsk, and forms part of the border between the Chinese prov. of Heilongjiang and the USSR. There were military clashes 1968-9 over the sovereignty of Damansky Is. (Chenpao) in mid-river.

USTINOV (oost'inof), **Peter** (1921-). British actor-dramatist. B. in London, he has ventured into almost every aspect of film and theatre life. His plays incl. *House of Regrets* (1942) and *The Love of Four Colonels* (1951), in which latter he appeared, and he was author, director, producer and principal actor in the film *Private Angelo* (1949).

UST-KAMENOGORSK. Chief centre of the atomic industry in the USSR in the Altai Mtns. Pop. (1979) 274,000.

UTAGAWA, Kuniyoshi (1798-1861). Japanese artist of the Ukiyoye or Popular school of painting and print designing. He produced some 8-10,000 prints concerning figures of history and legend, and was in trouble for lampooning the govt. His studies of cats are excellent.

UTAH (ū'taw). A Rocky Mountain state of USA. In the W is the great Basin which incl. the Great Salt Lake and the Great American Desert. E of the Wasatch range lies the plateau at *c.* 3,000 m (10,000 ft), deeply dissected by the Colorado river system. Less than 5 per cent of the land is under crops (wheat, oats, alfalfa, sugar beet, etc.), and half of that is made productive by artificial irrigation; cattle and sheep are raised, wool being important. Minerals incl. gold, silver, uranium, coal, and salt; steel is among manufactures. Salt Lake City is the cap. Area 219,931 sq.km (84,915 sq.m); pop. (1970) 1,059,273.

U. is part of the area ceded by Mexico in 1848; it was colonized and developed by the Mormons (Latterday Saints) who first entered Salt Lake valley in 1847, and remain the largest religious body in the state. Organized as a terr. 1850, it was not admitted to the Union as a state until 1896 because of the long refusal of the Mormons to give up plural marriage.

UTAMARO, Kitagawa (1753-1806). Japanese artist, famed for his designs of colour-prints.

Ū'TICA. City in N. York state, USA, cap. of Oneida co. on Mohawk r. Incorporated as a village 1798, a city 1836, U. makes textiles, firearms, etc. The pop. (1970) 91,610 incl. a large Welsh group who hold an annual eisteddfod.

UTILITARIANISM. *See* BENTHAM, J.

ŪTŌ'PIA (Gk, nowhere). Name given by Sir Thomas More to the imaginary commonwealth described in his *Utopia* (1516), and hence applied to similar dream-countries of other writers, e.g. Plato's *Republic,* Bacon's *Atlantis,* and Campanella's *City of the Sun. See also* WELLS, H. G.

UTRECHT (ū'trekt). Capital of U. province, Netherlands, on the Kromme Rijn (crooked Rhine) 35km (22m) SE of Amsterdam. There is a Gothic cathedral, univ. (1636), metallurgical and textile industries. Pop. (1979) 236,000. The Peace of U. in 1713 concluded the War of the Spanish Succession.

UTRILLO (ootrēl'yō), **Maurice** (1883-1955). French artist. Son of a trapeze-performer who became an artist's model after she suffered a fall, and later an artist herself, he was born following an assault on her by a drunken man, and was himself a drug addict and dipsomaniac from an early age. He is most celebrated for his townscapes of his native Paris, especially Montmartre, often painted from postcard photographs, but intensely and individually realized, e.g. 'Au Lapin Agile', 'Moulin de la Galette', and 'Nôtre-Dame de Paris'.

UTTAR PRADESH. State of the Republic of India formed in 1950 from the United Prov. of Agra and Oudh and neighbouring small princely states. It lies in central N India and comprises the upper plain of the Ganges. Agriculture, helped in the W by artificial irrigation, is the main occupation. Lucknow is the capital, Kanpur the largest city, followed by Agra, Varanesi, Allahabad, Bareilly, and Meerut. Area 294,336 sq.km (113,654 sq.m); pop. (1971) 88,299,000.

UZBEK SSR. Constituent republic of the USSR in central Asia, lying between Kazakh SSR to the N and Turkmen SSR to the S. Much of it is desert, but artificial irrigation is highly developed and more than 60 per cent of the Soviet Union's cotton is grown in U., as well as much rice and lucerne. A pipeline carries natural gas from U. to Chelyabinsk in the Urals. Tashkent is the cap.; it also incl. Bukhara, Samarkand, Khiva, and Kokand. About 60 per cent of the inhabitants are Uzbeks, a Turkic people; many are Sunni Moslems. Area 447,600 sq.km (157,400 sq.m); pop. (1978) 14,800,000.

UZBEK SSR. Riding out by camel to hunt with golden eagles in the desert is still practised in Soviet Central Asia. Accompanied by their dog, the hunters may be away from home for several days, but a portable solar kitchen supplies them with cooking facilities. In operation, the underside of the 'umbrella' is turned towards the sun, and the vessel containing water to be boiled for tea is placed where the reflected rays concentrate. *Photo: A. Varfolomeyev/Novosti Press Agency*

V

Twenty-second letter of the alphabet. It was not differentiated from U until about the 16th cent. In sound it is the voiced dentilabial spirant. In the Roman notation V equals 5.

VAAL (vahl). S African river, the chief tributary of the Orange. It rises in the Drakensberg and for much of its course of *c.* 1,200 km (750m) it separates Transvaal from Orange Free State. Harnessed to produce electric power, it joins with the coalfields alongside to make the valley the equivalent of the Ruhr.

VACCINATION. The insertion into the skin of a small quantity of lymph from a calf immune to cowpox, with a view to producing a general reaction by which the subject develops immunity to smallpox. The practice dates from an experiment by Edward Jenner (q.v.) in 1796. V. of children was compulsory in Britain 1853–1948, unless parents made a declaration of objection.

VACCINATION. A modern vaccine jet injector in use among African villagers. This swift, hygienic method of vaccination has played a major role in ending the toll of smallpox. *Photo: Courtesy of WHO*

VACUUM (vak'u-um). Strictly speaking, a region completely empty of matter; in physics the term means any enclosure in which the gas pressure is considerably less than the atmosphere. The V. CLEANER was invented by the Scotsman Hubert Cecil Booth (1871–1955) who was prompted by seeing an American dust-blowing machine in 1901 to reverse the process and invent a device for the extraction of dust from carpets and upholstery by suction: his first machine was on wheels and operated from the street, tubes being taken into the house. V. FLASKS, originally known as Dewar vessels after Sir James Dewar, their inventor, are glass vessels with double walls, the space between which is a V.

VADODARA (wahdō'dara). Industrial city and rail junction in Gujerat, Rep. of India, until 1976 known as Baroda. Pop. (1971) 467,500.

VADUZ (fah-doots'). Capital of the European principality of Liechtenstein; pop. (1977) 4,700.

VALDIVIA (vahldē'vē-ah). Chilean port, industrial town, and resort. It has shipyards, tanneries, breweries, soap factories, etc. It was founded 1552 by Spanish conquistador Pedro de V. (*c.* 1500–54), conqueror of Chile. Pop. (1975) 89,500.

VALENCE (vahlońs'). French town and river port on the Rhône, cap. of Drôme dept. It is of pre-Roman origin, and has a Romanesque cathedral consecrated 1095. Pop. (1975) 67,100.

VALENCIA (valen'sya). (1) Third city of Spain, cap. of V. prov., near the mouth of the Guadalaviar. It is the seat of an archbishopric and a univ. (1411). Pop. (1970) 653,690. (2) Cap. of Carabobo state, Venezuela, standing 478m (1,568 ft) a.s.l. Founded 1555, V. is a tourist and trading centre and makes textiles, leather, sugar, etc. Pop. (1971) 367,155.

VALENCIA. The city is noted for its gaiety, and the lavishness of giant displays, such as this in the Plaza Mercado, attracts huge crowds as the people make a processional tour of the streets. *Photo: Courtesy of the Spanish National Tourist Authority*

VALENCIENNES (vahlońsyen'). French town in Nord dept on the Escaut (Schelde) in the centre of a rich coal-field. It has many industries, and was formerly famous for its lace. It became French in 1678. Pop. (1975) 42,000.

VALENCY. In chemistry, a measure of the atom-binding capacity of the atoms in an element; or the number of atoms of hydrogen or of any other standard univalent element capable of uniting with one atom of the element.

The elements are described as uni-, di, tri-, and tetravalent when they unite with 1, 2, 3, and 4 univalent atoms respectively.

VALENTINE (d. 270). Christian saint and martyr, supposed to have perished at Rome. The custom of sending 'valentines' on 14 Feb., his festival, seems unconnected with the saint, deriving from the Roman Lupercalia, a festival celebrated in mid-Feb. His name has been dropped from the calendar of saints' days because of doubt that he ever existed.

VALENTINO (valentē'nō), **Rudolf** (1895-1926). Italian film actor in USA, who was famed for his 'handsome lover' parts in *The Four Horsemen of the Apocalypse* (1921), *The Sheik* (1922), and *Blood and Sand* (1922).

VALERA. *See* DE VALERA.

VALĒ'RIAN. Genus of perennial plants found in the temperate northern hemisphere. The root of common V. (*Valeriana officinalis*) is used medicinally as a carminative and sedative.

VALÉRY (vahlārē'), **Paul** (1871-1945). French poet. B. at Sète, he became a member of the circle of symbolists of which Mallarmé was the centre, but for many years abandoned poetry and turned to mathematics and philosophy. In 1917 he pub. the poem *La Jeune Parque*, followed by *Charmes, Le Cimetière Marin*, etc., and by critical studies and philosophical dialogues. V.'s poetry became of the greatest importance for its intellectual content.

VALHA'LLA. In Scandinavian mythology, the 'Hall of the Slain' in Odin's palace, to which were conducted the souls of those who fell in battle. At doomsday (Ragnarök) they will fight with Odin against the giants.

VALKYRIES (val'kirēz). In northern mythology, divine maidens who transport to Odin the souls of heroes who have died in battle.

VALLADOLID (vahl'ahdōlid'). Spanish city, cap. of V. prov. It has a cathedral (1595) and univ. (1346). It was cap. of Castile and Leon in the 14th-15th cents., then of Spain until 1560. Ferdinand and Isabella were married at V. (1469); Columbus died there. V. is a centre of agricultural trade. Pop. (1970) 236,340.

VALLE D'AOSTA (vahl'e dah-os'tah). Autonomous region in NW Italy; most of its inhabitants are French-speaking. Area 3,262 sq.km (1,260 sq.m); pop. (1978) 114,537.

VALLE-INCLÁN (vahl'yā ēnklahn'), **Ramon del** (1866-1936). Spanish writer. A brilliant stylist, he is remembered for his poetic prose *Sonatas* (1902-5), telling the story of the amorous marquis of Bradomín and *Tirano Banderas* (1926), a novel set in S America.

VALLE'TTA. Port and cap. of Malta, on the N coast. The Grand Harbour is one of the world's finest: it was formerly an important British naval base and is now a port of call for ships passing through the Mediterranean via Suez, with large repair yards. V. was founded in 1566 by the Knights Hospitallers, and was named after their Grand Master Jean de la Valette (1494-1568), who successfully defended Malta against the Turks May-Sept. 1565: the 16th cent. palace of the Grand Masters survives. In the S.W.W. the port installations were frequently bombed. There is a univ. (1769). Pop. (1978) 14,000.

VALLEY FORGE. Site some 32km (20m) NW of Philadelphia, USA, where Washington's army spent the winter of 1777-8 in terrible hardship during the American War of Independence.

VALLEY OF TEN THOUSAND SMOKES. Valley in Alaska, USA, where in 1912 the eruption of Mt Katmai, one of the largest volcanic explosions ever known, took place, though without loss of life since the area was uninhabited. It was dedicated in 1918 as the Katmai Nat. Monument; the many fissures on the valley floor still emit steam jets.

VALLEY OF THE KINGS. Valley opposite Thebes, Egypt, on the left bank of the Nile. The tombs of 18-20th dynasty kings are here, incl. Tutankhamen.

VALMY (vahlmē'). French village in the Marne dept where the army of the French Revolution under Dumouriez defeated the Prussians in 1792. Pop. (1975) 300.

VALOIS (vahlwah'). French family, originally counts of V. in the Oise dept, members of which occupied the French throne, 1328-1589.

VALONA. Italian form of VLONË.

VALPARAISO (vahlpahrī'zo). Second city of Chile, capital of V. prov., on the Pacific. It has many factories, and is the busiest commercial port on the W coast of S America. Founded in 1536, it was occupied by Drake 1578, by Hawkins 1595, pillaged by the Dutch 1600, bombarded by Spain 1866; it has also suffered much from earthquakes. Pop. (1975) 248,970.

VA'MPIRE. In the demonology of the Slavonic peoples, a ghost or spirit who emerges from the grave at night and sucks the blood of sleeping men. The name was transferred to the V. bats of S and Central America which suck the blood of sleeping cattle or human beings: the most common species is the Central American *Desmodus rotundus*, about 7.5 cm (3 in) long. The effect of their attacks has been much exaggerated.

VAN (vahn). Turkish city on Lake V. On a site that has been inhabited for more than 3,000 years, it was the scene of Armenian massacres 1895-6. It makes cotton textiles. Pop. (1970) 46,750.

VANĀ'DIUM (Scandinavian goddess Vanadis). Silver-white hard metal, discovered by Del Rio in 1801, and isolated by Roscoe in 1869: symbol V, at. no. 23, at. wt. 50.95. It occurs in the rare minerals vanadinite and patronite, and its chief use is in alloying steel to which it imparts toughness, elasticity and tensile strength. V. compounds (vanadates) are used in the preparation of aniline black for colouring glass.

VAN ALLEN, James Alfred (1914-). American physicist, a pioneer in high-altitude research with rockets, and prof. of physics at the State Univ. of Iowa since 1951. In 1958, following examination of data obtained by 2 *Explorer* earth satellites, he discovered the V.A. belts (of particles from the Sun trapped by the Earth's field). These were 2 zones of intense radiation between altitudes 2,400 km (1,500 m) and 20,000 km (12,000 m). In 1962 an American high altitude nuclear test resulted in the creation of a temporary artificial 'little' V.A. belt of trapped electrons, prejudicial to astrophysical and geophysical research and space flight.

VANBRUGH, Sir John (1664-1726). English dramatist and architect. B. in London, he designed Blenheim Palace and the first Haymarket Theatre, London. Of his many comedies the most notable are *The Relapse* (1696) and *The Provok'd Wife* (1697).

VAN BU'REN, Martin (1782-1862). 8th President of the USA. Secretary of State (1829-31) and then Minister to

England, he was elected President on the Democratic ticket in 1835 and held office until 1840.

VANCE, Cyrus (1917-). American statesman. A lawyer and Democrat, he became Sec. of State in 1977, resigning in 1980 because unable to support Carter's abortive mission to rescue the US hostages in Iran.

VANCOUVER (vankōō'ver), **George** (*c.* 1758-98). British navigator. Entering the navy at 13, he accompanied Cook on his 2nd and 3rd voyages of discovery, and 1791-4 voyaged about the Pacific. He circumnavigated V. Island, which is named after him.

VANCOUVER. Canadian is. off the Pacific coast, part of Brit. Columbia, the cap. of which, Victoria, is sit. on V. Coal is mined and timber is produced; fishing is important. V. was first visited by Capt. Cook, 1778, and was surveyed, 1792, by Capt. George Vancouver (q.v.). Area 32,136 sq.km (12,408 sq.m).

VANCOUVER. Third city of Canada and its chief Pacific seaport, on the mainland of Brit. Columbia, Pacific terminus of the Canadian Pacific rly; it has an internat. airport, and is a major tourist centre. There are 2 univs. (Brit. Columbia and Simon Fraser). Industries incl. the refining of oil pipelined from Alberta (1953), engineering, shipbuilding, aircraft, timber, pulp, and paper, textiles, and fisheries. The site was taken possession of by George Vancouver for Britain in 1792, and V. was founded by the Hudson's Bay Co. in 1825. Pop. met. area (1976) 1,166,348.

VA'NDALS. A Teutonic people akin to the Goths, who early in the 5th cent. AD moved from N Germany to invade the Roman provinces in Gaul and Spain. Many settled in Andalusia (*Vandalitia*), and others moved on to N Africa in 429. In the next cent. they acknowledged Roman overlordship.

VANDERBILT, Cornelius (1794-1877). American millionaire. B. at Staten Island, NY, he made his fortune in steamships and railways.

VAN DER POST, Sir Laurens Jan (1906-). S African writer. His books are concerned with the duality of man's existence, which is symbolized in Africa by the tension between black and white, Boer and Briton, city and veld, as in *Flamingo Feather* (1955), in which the hero is a Boer whose best friend is a Briton. Knighted 1981.

VAN DER WAALS (van dur wah'ls), **Johannes Diderik** (1837-1923). Dutch physicist. He made considerable discoveries in the physical properties of matter, especially intermolecular attractions, and the relation between the pressure and volume of a gas in the transition between liquid and gas phases. He received a Nobel prize in 1910. His *equation of state*: $(P+a/V^2)(V-b) = nRT$ (where P = pressure, V = volume, T = temperature on the Kelvin scale, R = the gas constant, n = the number of moles, and a and b are corrections for the particular gas), gives a close approx to the behaviour of ordinary gases.

VAN DE VELDE. Family of artists. Both **William V.** the elder (1611-93) and his son **William V.** the younger (1633-1707) painted sea battles for Charles II and James II. Another son **Adriaen V.** (1636-72) executed landscapes, and figures in works by Ruysdael, and others.

VAN DIEMEN. *See* DIEMEN.

VAN DYCK (dīk), **Sir Anthony** (1599-1641). Flemish painter. B. at Antwerp, he was for 4 years an assistant to Rubens. He visited England 1620-1, and was painter to James I. He then worked for a time in Italy, but in 1628 returned to Antwerp where he painted many religious works and portaits. In 1632 he was invited to England by Charles I, became court painter, and was knighted.

VANE, Sir Henry (1613-62). English statesman. In 1640 elected a member of the Long Parliament, he was prominent in the impeachment of Laud, and 1643-53 was in effect the civilian head of the Parliamentary government. At the Restoration he was executed as a chief of the Republican Party.

VAN EYCK. *See* EYCK.

VAN GOGH. *See* GOGH.

VANILLA. Genus of orchids, several of which bear pods which when dried are the source of V. flavouring, used in confectionery, etc. The finest V. comes from *V. planifolia*, a native of Mexico, now cultivated elsewhere.

VA'NNIN, Ellan. Gaelic name for Isle of Man.

VANSI'TTART, Robert Gilbert, 1st baron (1881-1957). British diplomat. Entering the diplomatic service in 1902, he was Permanent Under Sec. of State for Foreign Affairs 1930-8 and Chief Diplomatic Adviser to the For. Sec. 1938-41. He was noted for his anti-German polemic. He was created baron 1941.

VAN T'HOFF, Jacobus Henricus (1852-1911). Dutch physical chemist. He explained the 'asymmetric' carbon atom occurring in optically active compounds, and his greatest work - the concept of chemical affinity as the maximum work obtainable which results from a reaction - was shown with measurements of osmotic and gas pressures, and reversible electric batteries. He was the first recipient of the Nobel prize in 1901.

VANUATU (vanoo-ah'too), Rep. of. Group of is. to the NE of Australia. The chief are Espiritu Santo, Malekula, Epi, Ambrym, Efate or Sandwich, Erromanga, Tanna, and Aneityúm. The cap. is Vila (pop. 12,700), on Efate, and the chief port is Santo on Espiritu Santo.

Formerly known as the New Hebrides, the is. were under the joint admin. of Britain and France 1906-80, when they became the Rep. of V. (the name meaning 'Our Land'). Just before the planned independence date there was a brief declaration of separate independence by Espiritu Santo. Area 14,750 sq.km (5,700 sq.m); pop. (1979) 112,600, plus *c.* 5,000 French, and *c.* 2,000 British, Australians, etc.

VAR (vahr). River in S France, rising in the Maritime Alps and flowing generally SSE for 134km (84m) into the Mediterranean near Nice. It gives its name to a dept.

VARANASI. Indian city on the Ganges r. in Uttar Pradesh, more familiar in the W under the form Benarés. It is holy to Hindus with a 5km (3m) frontage of stairways (ghats), leading up from the river to innumerable streets, temples, and the 1,500 golden shrines. The ritual of purification is daily practised by thousands of devout Hindus, who bathe from the ghats in the sacred river. At the burning ghats, the ashes, following cremation, are scattered on the river, a ritual supposed to ensure a favourable reincarnation. Pop. (1971) 582,915.

VARGAS (vahr'gahs), **Getulio** (1883-1954). Brazilian lawyer and statesman. He led the revolution of 1930, and was president 1930-45 and from 1951 till his suicide following a political crisis.

VARIABLE STAR. A star whose brightness changes, either regularly or irregularly, over a short period. Apart from the eclipsing Ss., where the light-change is due to the periodical eclipse of the S. by a binary companion, variables do actually change in luminosity and in radius. Particularly interesting are the *Cepheids,* whose periods are perfectly regular, and range from a few hours up to a few weeks. There are also the less precise long-period variables, such as Mira Ceti (period about 331 days) and the irregular variables such as Betelgeuse in Orion.

VARICOSE VEINS. Dilated or stretched veins, espec. on the inner side of the leg, knee and thigh. The cause is not known, although the condition may be aggravated by prolonged standing. There is no cure, but the symptoms can be alleviated by injection-compression sclerotherapy. An injected fluid helps the vein to collapse of its own accord and compression bandaging aids the process. Surgery may also be undertaken.

VARNA. Bulgarian fortress, and seaport, on an inlet of the Black Sea. A training centre nearby for sabotage and terrorism takes foreign students. Pop. (1976) 251,600.

VARNISH. Name given to resins or resinous gums dissolved in linseed oil, turpentine, etc., that are used in house decoration, furniture making, etc. and to modern synthetic forms.

VASARI (vahsah'rē), **Giorgio** (1511-74). Italian painter and architect, remembered for his *Lives of the Painters, Sculptors, and Architects* (1550).

VASCO DA GAMA. *See* GAMA.

VATICAN CITY STATE, The. Independent sovereign state, created by the Lateran Treaty, 1929, of which the Pope is the head. The Holy See covers the V. palace (the Pope's official residence) and the basilica and square of St Peter's in the heart of Rome, several other basilicas in and near Rome, and the Pope's summer residence at Castel Gandolfo. The Sovereign Pontiff appoints a layman as governor. Area 0.4 sq.km (109 acres); pop. 1,000.

VAUBAN (vōboṅ'), **Sébastien le Prestre de** (1633-1707). French marshal and military engineer. In Louis XIV's wars he conducted many sieges, and rebuilt many of the fortresses on France's E frontier.

VAUCLUSE (vōklüz'). Mt. range in SE France, part of the Provence Alps, to the E of Avignon, rising to 1,242 m (4,075 ft). It gives its name to a dept. Petrarch lived in the Vale of Vaucluse 1337-53, and the name V. has been given to a similarly beautiful location on Sydney Harbour, Australia, now a fashionable suburb.

VAUGHAN (vawn), **Henry** (1622-95). Welsh poet, called the Silurist, because he was a native of the land of the ancient Silures. B. in Brecknockshire, he was a physician, and pub. several vols. of religious verse and prose devotions. A disciple of Donne, V. is ranked as a metaphysical poet, and his mystical outlook on nature influenced Wordsworth and others.

VAUGHAN WILLIAMS, Ralph (1872-1958). British composer. B. at Down Ampney, Glos, he studied at Cambridge and the RCM, and also learnt from Max Bruch in Berlin and Ravel in Paris. Early works incl. the choral and orchestral settings of Whitman 'Towards the Unknown Region' (1907) and 'A Sea Symphony' (1910); and 'A London Symphony' (1914). After the F.W.W. came the 'Pastoral' symphony; the Mass in G minor for unaccompanied choir; the ballad opera *Hugh the Drover* (1924) and several symphonies. In 1951 his operatic morality *The Pilgrim's Progress* which incl. the earlier cantata 'The Shepherds of the Delectable Mountains' was performed for the Festival of Britain. Later works incl. 'Sinfonia Antarctica', developed from his film score - one of several - for *Scott of the Antarctic* and a Ninth Symphony. His genius was very English, owing much to folk song, and music of the Tudor period and Purcell; he received the OM in 1935.

VECTOR. Any physical quantity that has both magnitude and direction, such as the velocity or acceleration of a body, as distinct from a scalar quantity which has magnitude and no direction, such as speed, density, or mass. The direction of a V. is often indicated by an arrow on a line of length equal to its magnitude and in technical writing it is denoted by heavy (Clarendon) type.

VEDA (vā'da) (Sanskrit, divine knowledge). The most sacred of the Hindu scriptures, hymns written in an old form of Sanskrit; the oldest may date from 1500 or 2000 BC. The 4 main collections are: the Rigveda (hymns and praises); Yajurveda (prayers and sacrificial formulae); Sâmaveda (tunes and chants); and Atharvaveda, or V. of the Atharvans, the officiating priests at the sacrifices.

VEGA (vā'gah), **Garcilaso de la** (*c.* 1540-*c.* 1616). Spanish writer. Son on a Spanish conquistador and an Inca princess, he wrote an account of the conquest of Florida and *Commentarios* on the history of Peru.

VEGA CARPIO (kahr'pē-ō), **Lope Felix de** (1562-1635). Spanish poet and dramatist. B. at Madrid, he served with the Armada in 1588, and in 1613 took orders. He wrote epics, pastorals, odes, sonnets, and novels, and over 1,500 plays.

VEGETARIANISM. The practice of restricting diet to foods of vegetable origin, for humanitarian or health reasons. The stricter vegetarians abstain from all food which comes from animals, incl. eggs, milk, butter, and cheese.

VEIL (vāy), **Simone** (1927-). French politician. A victim of Hitler's concentration camps, she was Min. of Health 1974-9, and framed the French abortion bill. In 1979 she became pres. of the European Parliament.

VEINS. Thin-walled muscular tubes which carry blood from all parts of the body to the heart. They contain valves which prevent the blood from running back when moving against gravity. With the exception of the Vs. leading from the lungs to the heart, they always carry blood which has lost oxygen and is therefore dark.

VELAZQUEZ (velath'keth or velas'kwiz), **Don Diego de Silva y** (1599-1660). Spanish painter. B. in Seville, he became in 1623 court painter to Philip IV, whom he painted repeatedly, and in 1652 was appointed court-marshal. He owed much to Titian, Rubens, and Tintoretto.

VELVET. A plain silk fabric with a short thick pile, largely used for rich draperies, hangings, etc. Utrecht and Genoa are famed centres of manufacture.

VE'NDA. Black Homeland nr. the Zimbabwe border in South Africa. Maize and timber are produced and there are reserves of coal, copper, graphite and magnesite. Home of the Vhavenda people, its cap. is Thohoyandu. It became independent in 1979, but received no internat. recognition. Area 7,410 sq.km (2,860 sq.m); pop. (1977) 461,000.

VENDÉE (voṅdā'). R. of W France which rises near the village of La Châtaigneraie and flows 72km (45m) to join the Sèvre Niortaise 11km (7m) E of the Bay of Biscay. It gives its name to a dept where a peasant rising against the revolutionary govt (the War of the Vendée) began in 1793 and spread to other parts of France, lasting until 1795.

VENDE'TTA. Name given to a survival of the blood feud that existed until recently in Corsica and parts of Sardinia and Sicily.

VELASQUEZ. As court painter to Philip IV of Spain, most of Velasquez's life was occupied with portraits of the royal family and courtiers. 'The Lady with a Fan' is one of very few portraits of a lady outside the circle of the Spanish Court and critics have suggested that she was a member of the artist's family, perhaps his daughter Francisca. *Photo: Courtesy of the Trustees of the Wallace Collection*

VENDÔME (voṅdōm'), **Louis Joseph,** duc de (1654-1712). Marshal of France. In the war of the Spanish Succession he was defeated by Marlborough at Oudenarde in 1708, but was successful later in Spain.

VENEREAL DISEASE. *See* SYPHILIS; GONORRHOEA.

VENETIA (venē'shia). Roman name of that part of NE Italy which later became the rep. of Venice and covers approx. the 'three Venices' - in Ital. Venezia-Tridentina (Trentino-Alto-Adige, q.v.); Veneto (called Venezia Euganea 1919-47) which incl. the delta of the Po, a fertile territory at the foot of the mountains, and portions of the Dolomites, Carnic and Julian alps. Its cities incl. Venice, Padua, Verona, and Vicenza. Area 18,367 sq.km (7,095 sq.m); pop. (1978) 4,338,300; and Venezia Giulia (*see* FRIULI-VENEZIA GIULIA).

VENEZIA. Ital. form of VENICE.

VENEZUELA (venizwā'la). Federal rep. of S America on the Caribbean coast, between Brazil and Colombia, occupying the whole of the lower basin of the Orinoco, and the coastal plain bordering Lake Maracaibo - the latter being responsible for V.'s name, which means 'little Venice'. In the SE is the vast Auyan-tepui tableland, still largely unmapped and over 1,000 m (3,000 ft) high: it incl. the world's highest waterfall, Angel Falls 979 m (3,212 ft) high, and 250m SE of Ciudad Bolivar. There are many uniquely differentiated animal and plant species, and the annual rainfall is over 7,600 mm (300in). Coffee, cocoa, maize, rice, sugar, and bananas are grown; beef cattle and horses are raised; and the forests are rich in timber and wild products, such as rubber, balata, tonka beans and vanilla. However, V.'s emergence as a major power in Latin America has been made possible by her oil reserves, in and around Lake Maracaibo, and also the less easily exploited 'heavy' oil belt which runs for 600km (375m) along the N bank of the Orinoco. Other minerals incl. high grade iron ore, e.g. in the E at Cerro Bolivar, which is being used to build up a steel industry; bauxite, which is being processed by the hydroelectric power of the Caroni r., a southern tributary of the Orinoco, into aluminium; and quantities of manganese, phosphate, nickel, gold and diamonds. The cap. is Caracas, other important towns are Maracaibo, Barquisimeto, Valencia, Maracay, Ciudad Guayana, and San Cristobal.

VENEZUELA. A lost lagoon in the Venezuelan jungle, not far from the River Amazon, ringed by table-top mountains. *Photo: Ken Schiff*

Under the constitution of 1958 there is a pres., and a Congress comprising a senate and chamber of deputies. The country is divided into 20 states, 2 terrs. and a fed. district. The majority of the people are mestizos, Spanish-speaking, and RC in religion. Area 912,068 sq.km (352,150 sq.m); pop. (1979) 13,200,000. M.U.: bolívar.

Columbus visited V. in 1498, and it was the Spanish captaincy-general of Caracas 1550-1822, when (led by Simon Bolivar, q.v.), it rebelled, and, as part of Colombia, was freed from Spain. It became an independent rep. in 1830. Under Juan Vicente Gomez whose dictatorship endured 1910-35, the country was exploited for the benefit of the oil cos. and the dictator. Popular opposition developed and a democratic regime was established. The Democratic Action party, almost continuously in power from 1959, was defeated in 1978 when Luis Herrera Campins (Social Christian) became pres. There are border disputes with Colombia over the potentially oil-rich Gulf of V., and with adjoining Guyana, half of whose terr. V. claims. V. was the founder of the Latin American Economic System (SELA). *See* LATIN AMERICA.

VENICE (ven'is). Italian city (*Venezia*), seaport, and naval base. It stands on a group of low-lying islands at the head of the Adriatic, built for the most part on piles, and is connected with the mainland, and its industrial suburb of Mestre, by a rail and road viaduct. The Grand Canal divides V. into 2; the 'streets' are canals, and motor boats and gondolas are the means of conveyance. It is possible to walk all over the city whose quietness is one of its great charms. In the Piazza of St Mark are situated the campanile, the Doge's palace, and the cathedral of St Mark, dating from the 4th cent. There are Byzantine palaces, Gothic churches, and gems of Renaissance architecture. The Lido, *c.* 3km (2m) SE of V., is a popular holiday resort. Among V.'s oldest industries are the making of glass and fine textiles. The gradual flooding of the city is being caused by the slow sinking of the plain and the consequent rising sea-level, and also by the development of Mestre and Porto Marghera as an industrial area and port on marshland to the W of the lagoon. Pop. (1971) 364,000.

V. was founded by refugees from mainland cities sacked by the Huns in the 5th cent. For many cents. V. was an independent rep., stretching at one time to the Alps (*see* VENETIA) and governed by an aristocratic oligarchy and dependent upon Mediterranean commerce for its prosperity. At the head of the rep. was the Council of Ten and the Senate, which appointed the Doge. The rep. was overthrown by Napoleon in 1797. In 1815 V. became Austrian, and in 1866 part of the kingdom of Italy.

VENIZELOS (venizā'los), **Eleutherios** (1864-1936). Greek statesman. B. in Crete, he entered politics, becoming Premier of Greece in 1911. He resigned in 1915 when King Constantine refused to join the Allies in the F.W.W., but became Premier under Alexander in 1917, and brought Greece into the war. Defeated in 1920, he was again Prime Minister in 1924, 1928-32, and 1933. He was exiled in 1935.

VENT, Îles du. Fr. name for the SOCIETY IS.

VENTRIS, Michael George Francis (1922-56). British architect and archaeologist, remembered for his decipherment of Minoan Linear B, the language of the tablets found at Knossos and Pylos. He showed that it was a very early form of Greek and so led the way to a revision of existing views on early Greek history. He was killed in a road accident.

VENUS. The 2nd planet in order of distance from the Sun. It has a mean distance from the Sun of 108,000,000 km (67,000,000 m), and a revolution period of 243½ days; it may approach the Earth to within 38,000,000 km (24,000,000 m), and is then nearer than any other important celestial body, apart from the Moon. Its diameter is 12,300 km (7,600 m), and its mass 0.83 of that of the Earth. Venus differs from the other planets in being quite round and in rotating more slowly than any other planet. It also rotates in the opposite direction to all except Uranus, possibly because a moon travelling counter to its original rotation may have been drawn into a narrowing orbit round V., first retarding, then reversing the spin. Tidal movements involved would have caused heat by friction, with volcanic eruptions giving rise to the brilliantly coloured clouds of sulphuric acid droplets surrounding V., and eventually the moon would have crashed into the planet. The atmosphere is carbon dioxide, but incl. water vapour and surprisingly large amounts of argon. The surface temperature is 480°C (900°F), high enough to melt lead, and Venus apparently radiates 15% more energy than it receives from the Sun. Probe Venus III (USSR) in 1966 was the first man-made object to land on another planet. In 1978-80 Pioneer (USA) probes penetrated the thick clouds with radar to map over 80% of the surface, which consists mainly of rolling upland plains which rise up to 2,000 m (6,560 ft) above the average surface. The granitic crust is heavily cratered, either by volcanic activity or impact, but the craters are eroded or lava-filled. The continent of Aphrodite Terra near the Equator is the largest highland area, being half the size of Africa, and has mountain ranges to the E and W. The highest mtns on V., however, are on the northern 'continent' of Ishtar Terra, where the massif of Maxwell Montes rises to 10,600 m (35,000 ft) above the average surface level.

VENICE. One of Venice's more than 400 bridges, the Bridge of Sighs, built by Contino in the 16th century, joins the ducal palace to the state prison, hence the name. *Photo: A. W. Kerr*

VENUS. Roman goddess of beauty, growth, and love, identified with the Greek Aphrodite.

VENUS' FLY TRAP. *See* INSECTIVOROUS PLANTS.

VERONESE. His work gives an overwhelming sense of spacious opulence, and he was a skilled portraitist. The chief figures in the classical tragedy portrayed here are based on members of the Pisani family. *Photo: Courtesy of the National Gallery, London*

VENUS. This view of Venus from 420,000 km was made by Mariner 10 (USA) television cameras, as the spacecraft flew past on its way to Mercury. Individual frames, taken in invisible ultraviolet light, were computer enhanced, then combined in a mosaic to highlight the swirling patterns of cloud cover. The south pole is at lower left. *Photo: Courtesy of NASA*

VERACRUZ (ve'rakrooz). City and seaport of Mexico, on the Gulf of Mexico. Cortez founded Villa Nueva de la Vera Cruz (Span., New Town of the True Cross) nearby in 1519; it was transferred to its present site 1599. Pop. (1977) 288,815.

VERBĒ'NA. Genus of plants of the Verbenaceae family, having tubular flowers arranged in close spikes. Colours range from white to rose, violet, and purple. There are about 100 species, mostly in the American tropics. The garden V. is a hybrid annual.

VERCINGETORIX (versinjet'eriks) (*d.* 45? BC). Gallic chieftain. Leader of a revolt against the Romans in 52 BC, he was displayed in Caesar's triumph in 46 BC, and later executed.

VERCORS (vārkōr'). Pseudonym adopted by French writer and artist Jean Bruller (1902-) while a member of the French resistance during the S.W.W. Under the occupation he estab. in 1941 a clandestine publishing house, Les Editions de Minuit, from which appeared his novel *Le Silence de la mer* (1942), of the resistance, smuggled abroad.

VERDI (vār'dē), **Giuseppe (Fortunino Francesco)** (1813-1901). Italian composer. B. near Busseto, the son of a village innkeeper, he wrote his first symphony at 15 and then studied in Milan. His first opera *Oberto* was given at La Scala in 1839, and was followed by *Ernani* (Venice, 1844). After visiting London and Paris he returned to Italy and wrote *Rigoletto* (1851), *Il Trovatore* (1853), *La Traviata* (1853), *Don Carlos* (1867), *Aïda* (1871), *Otello* (1877), *Falstaff* (1893), and other operas, as well as religious music, e.g. the *Requiem.* He is remarkable, not merely for the advanced age to which he continued to compose, but for the continued richness of his development as a musician.

VE'RDIGRIS. A basic copper acetate, used as a wood preservative, in anti-fouling compositions, and formerly in green paint. It is an irritant poison.

VERDUN (verduṅ'). Fortress town of NE France on the Meuse. During the F.W.W. it became the symbol of French resistance, withstanding a terrific German onslaught in 1916. Pop. (1973) 24,715.

VERHAEREN (verhah'ren), **Émile** (1855-1916). Belgian poet. B. near Antwerp, he was a leader in the Belgian literary revival of the 1880s.

VERLAINE (verlăn'), **Paul** (1844-96). French poet. B. at Metz, he became an insurance clerk in Paris. His first vol. of poems, *Poèmes saturniens*, appeared in 1866, followed by *La bonne chanson* (1870) and *Sagesse* (1881). Other

VERSAILLES. The great palace of Louis XIV as it appeared in 1650 during the course of its construction, which was not completed by the addition of a chapel (1696–1710) until long after Louis moved in 1682. *Photo: Mary Evans Picture Library*

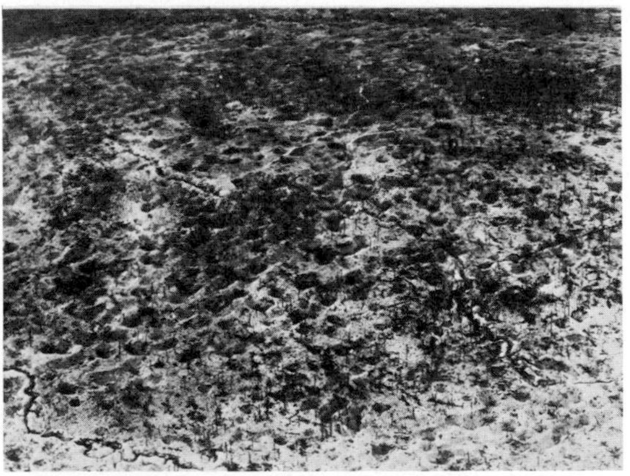

VERDUN. An aerial view of the Verdun area, showing the thousands of cannon craters which turned the countryside into a lunar landscape. *Photo: Popperfoto*

works are *Romances sans paroles* (1874), *Amour* (1888), and *Bonheur* (1891). From 1871 he wandered about France, Belgium, and England with Rimbaud until an attempt to shoot his fellow-traveller brought V. 2 years' imprisonment.

VERMEER (vermār'), **Jan** (1632-75). Dutch artist. B. at Delft, he spent most of his life and d. there. His paintings are distinguished by their harmonious colouring and technical excellence. 'Lady at the Virginals' is in the National Gallery. *See* MEEGEREN, HANS VAN.

VERMO'NT. A N Atlantic state of USA, traversed by the Green Mts. (from which it derives its name). Lake Champlain lies on the W. Dairy products are important; china clay, asbestos, and granite, marble and slate are worked; and business machines, furniture and paper made. V. entered the Union in 1791. Montpelier is the cap. Area 24,887 sq.km (9,608 sq.m); pop. (1970) 444,732.

VERMOUTH (ver'muth). A white wine flavoured by the maceration of bitter herbs and fortified by alcohol. It is prepared in France and Italy.

VERNE (vārn), **Jules** (1828-1905). French author. B. in Nantes, he went to Paris and estab. a reputation as a writer of travellers' tales which show scientific prevision: *Five Weeks in a Balloon* (1862), *Journey to the Centre of the Earth, Twenty Thousand Leagues under the Sea, Around the World in Eighty Days* (1872), etc.

VERNEY, Sir Edmund (1590-1642). English courtier, knight-marshal to Charles I from 1626. He sat as an MP in both the Short and Long parliaments, and though sympathizing with the Parliamentary position remained true to his allegiance: he d. at his post as royal standard bearer at Edgehill. His son Ralph (1613-96) adhered to the opposing party, and his industry was responsible for the preservation at Claydon, the family home in Bucks, of the Verney Papers, a valuable record of this and later periods.

VE'RNIER. A device for taking readings on a graduated scale to a fraction of division; a short divided scale which slides along the main scale and carries the index or pointer. It was invented by Pierre V. (*c.* 1580-1637), who lived at Ornans in Burgundy.

VERNON, Edward (1684-1757). English admiral who captured Portobello in 1739, with a loss of only 7 men.

VERŌ'NA. Cap. of V. prov., Veneto, Italy, on the Adige. It has a 12th cent. cathedral and fine Roman remains. It is an agricultural market town with printing and paper works and makes plastics, furniture, macaroni, etc. A school of painting flourished at V. in the 15th and 16th cents, and there has been an open-air opera festival since 1922. Pop. (1979) 270,860.

VERONESE (vārōnā'ze), **Paolo** (1528-88). Italian painter. B. in Verona, he delighted in painting gorgeous banquets, pageantry, and material splendour. His 'Family of Darius at the feet of Alexander' is in the National Gallery, London. He d. at Venice.

VERO'NICA. Christian saint, a woman of Jerusalem who lent her veil or kerchief to Jesus to wipe the sweat from his brow on the road to Calvary; whereupon the image of the Lord's face was printed upon it. What is alleged to be the actual veil is preserved in St Peter's, Rome.

VERROCCHIO (vārok'kē-ō), **Andrea del** (1435-88). Italian artist, whose real name was Cioni. His only surviving painting is the 'Baptism of Christ' at Florence; his sculptures incl. the equestrian statue of Colleoni at Venice.

VERRUCA. *See* WART.

VERSAILLES (vārsī'). French town, cap. of the Les Yvelines dept, 19km (12m) SW of Paris. Its palace was built mainly by Louis XIV; here the German Empire was proclaimed in 1871 and the Peace Conference was held after the F.W.W. *See* TRIANON. Pop. (1975) 97,130.

The TREATY OF V. was signed on 28 June 1919, between the Allies and Associated Powers (the USA being an Associated Power) on the one hand and Germany on the other. In the forefront of the treaty were the clauses to establish the League of Nations. Germany surrendered Alsace-Lorraine (q.v.) to France, large areas to Poland, and smaller areas to Czechoslovakia, Lithuania, Belgium, and Denmark. The Rhineland was demilitarized, and restrictions were put on German armaments. Germany accepted responsibility for war damage, and provision was made for the payment of reparations. The USA never ratified the treaty, but made a separate peace with Germany and Austria, 1921.

VERSE. The arrangement of words in a rhythmical pattern. Besides metre (q.v.) an important element in verse is provided by *rhyme* which arises from identity in sound of the endings of certain words. Rhyme first made its appearance in western Europe in late Latin poetry, and from thence passed into use in the modern European languages. The binding together of lines into groups by means of a unified rhyme-scheme leads to the creation of the *stanza*.

Classical Greek verse depended upon quantity, a long syllable (indicated thus -) being regarded as occupying twice the time taken up by a short syllable (◡). Long and short syllables were combined in *feet*, such as:

(1) Dactyl: -◡◡ ; (2) Spondee: --;
(3) Anapaest: ◡◡-; (4) Iamb: ◡-;
(5) Trochee: -◡.

Blank verse consists of unrhymed five-stress lines. It was introduced by Surrey, and later became, as perfected by Marlowe, Shakespeare, and Milton, the standard metre for English dramatic and epic poetry.

The *Spenserian Stanza*, rhyming ababbcbcc - the last line being of 12 syllables, was used by Spenser in *The Faerie Queen*. The *Shakespearean Sonnet* consisted of 4 quatrains and a couplet, thus: abab, cdcd, efef, gg. It was first devised by Surrey. The *Pindaric Ode* was modelled on the ancient Greek form with its structure of *strophe*, *antistrophe*, and *epode*. Gray's 'The Bard' and 'The Progress of Poesy' are the best-known examples. *Free Verse* is applied to any verse the rhythmical basis of which is not obvious. *See also* BALLAD; ODE; POETRY, SONNET, etc.

VERTEBRATA. A main sub-division of the animal kingdom, incl. all the backboned animals - mammals (incl. man), birds, reptiles, amphibians, fish.

VERULĀ'MIUM. Roman-British town whose remains have been excavated close to St Albans. Boadicea burnt it in AD 61, but it was rebuilt.

VERWOERD (fervoort'), **Hendrik Frensch** (1901-66). S African statesman. B. in Amsterdam, the son of missionary parents, he held chairs of applied psychology and sociology at Stellenbosch (1927-37), before devoting himself to building up the Nationalist paper *Die Transvaler* (1938-48). He was Min. of Native Affairs 1950-8, and although he did much to improve African housing in the cities, he was chief promoter of apartheid legislation. As PM in 1958 he pledged himself to estab. a rep., achieving this in 1961. He was assassinated in the House of Assembly by a parliamentary messenger Dimitri Tsafendas, a Portuguese b. in Mozambique.

VESPĀ'SIAN (Titus Flavius Vespasianus) (AD 9-79). Roman emperor. Son of a moneylender, he had a distinguished military career and was proclaimed emperor by his soldiers in AD 69 when he was campaigning in Palestine. He reorganized the eastern provinces, and was a capable administrator.

VESPERS. The 7th of the 8 canonical hours in the Catholic Church. The *Sicilian V.* is the name given to a massacre of the French rulers in Sicily in 1282.

VESPUCCI (vespoo'chē), **Amerigo** (1454-1512). Florentine navigator, who in 1497 sailed for the New World, and claimed to have reached the mainland of N America a few days before John Cabot. America is named after A.V.

VESTA. Roman hearth goddess, identified with the Greek Hestia. In Rome her shrine stood in the Forum where was the sacred hearth, whose fire was never allowed to go out. The tenders of the flame were the 6 Vestal Virgins.

VESŪ'VIUS. Active volcano in Italy, *c.* 16km (10m) ESE of Naples, and 1,186 m (3,890 ft) high. It caused the destruction of Pompeii (AD 79) and from 1967 the remains of the larger city, Oplonti, buried in the same catastrophe, were being excavated, part lying beneath modern Torre Annunziata. *See* HERCULANEUM.

VETCH or **tare.** A leguminous annual plant (*Vicia sativa*) with trailing or climbing stems and reddish purple flowers. Winter V. produces spring fodder, and spring V. is cut for hay.

VETERINARY SCIENCE. The science that treats the diseases of domestic animals; more generally it covers their anatomy, breeding, and relations to man. Professional bodies: Royal Coll. of V. Surgeons (1844) and American V. Medical Assocn. (1883).

VETO. Name given to the right of a sovereign, branch of the legislature, or other political power, to prevent the enactment or the operation of a law. In Britain the House of Lords has a suspensory V. over all legislation with the exception of finance measures; in theory the sovereign may V. any Act, but the right has not been exercised since the 18th cent. The V. is used in the Security Council of the UN.

VĪ'AN, Sir Philip (1894-1968). Brit. Admiral of the Fleet. In 1940 he was the hero of the *Altmark* (q.v.) incident, and in 1941 commanded the destroyers which chased the *Bismarck*.

VIBORG (vē'-). Town in Jutland, Denmark, on V. lake. Industries incl. brewing, textiles, tobacco. Pop. (1970) 36,100. *See also* VYBORG.

VĪBU'RNUM. Genus of shrubs of the honeysuckle family. *V. lantana* is the wayfaring tree and *V. opulus* the cranberry tree, or guelder rose.

VICAR. In the C of E a parish priest. *See* RECTOR.

VICENZA (vēchen'tzah). Italian city and episcopal see in Veneto, cap. of V. prov. It has a 13th cent. cathedral and makes textiles and musical instruments. It was the Roman Vicetia. Pop. (1979) 118,200.

VICHY (vē′shē). Health resort with thermal springs already known to the Romans, in Allier dept, France. In 1940-4 it was the seat of Marshal Pétain's govt - whence the phrase Vichy France, i.e. that part of France not occupied by German troops until Nov. 1942. Pop. (1975) 32,250.

VICTOR EMMANUEL II (1820-78). First king of united Italy. B. in Turin, he became king of Sardinia on the abdication of his father Charles Albert, following defeat in war with the Austrians in 1849. In 1855 he allied Sardinia with France and Britain in the Crimean War. In 1859 in alliance with the French he defeated the Austrians and annexed Lombardy. By 1860 most of Italy had come under his rule, and in 1861 he was proclaimed king of Italy. In 1870 he made Rome his capital.

VICTOR EMMANUEL III (1869-1947). King of Italy. B. at Naples, he became king in 1900 on the assassination of his father, King Humbert I. He acquiesced in the Fascist régime, but co-operated with the Allies from 1943, and in 1946 abdicated. The claim to the Italian throne is maintained by his son Umberto II (1904-).

VICTORIA (1819-1901). Queen of the UK and Empress of India. Only child of Edward, duke of Kent, 4th son of George III, she was b. 24 May 1819 at Kensington Palace, and became queen in 1837 on the death of her uncle William IV. In 1840 she m. Prince Albert of Saxe-Coburg and Gotha, and had 4 sons and 5 daus., viz. Victoria, Princess Royal (1840-1901), wife of Frederick III, German emperor; Edward VII; Alice, Grand-duchess of Hesse; Alfred, Duke of Edinburgh and Saxe-Coburg-Gotha; Helena, Princess Christian; Louise, Duchess of Argyll; Arthur, Duke of Connaught; Leopold, Duke of Albany; and Beatrice, Princess Henry of Battenberg. The Prince Consort d. in 1861, and for many years the queen was in retirement - a fact which led to the growth of republican sentiment. Of all her Prime Ministers, Disraeli (Lord Beaconsfield) proved himself the most agreeable, and in 1876 he proclaimed her Empress of India. From 1848 she regularly visited the Scottish highlands, where she had her seat at Balmoral, built to Prince Albert's designs; another favourite home was Osborne House in the Isle of Wight. By 1887, the year of her jubilee, she had regained the public's affection, and something more than affection was shown at the diamond jubilee in 1897. A detailed picture of her life is given in her *Letters* and in her *Journal of Our Life in the Highlands*, etc. She d. at Osborne, 22 Jan. 1901, and was buried at Windsor.

VICTORIA. A state of the Australian commonwealth, in the SE of the continent. It is traversed from E to W by a chain of mountains, part of the Great Dividing Range; for the rest the surface is fertile lowland. Dairy farming and sheep rearing are important, but there is also good wheat country and beef cattle are produced. Large areas are also devoted to orchard fruits, vineyards and vegetables. The gold workings are moving towards exhaustion, but there is coal in the Latrobe Valley, and a steel plant has been estab. Immensely more valuable, however, are the oil and gas resources discovered from 1965 in Bass Strait, with their potential for a petrochemical industry. Other industries incl. food processing and clothing. The pop. is mainly concentrated in Melbourne, the cap., which with Geelong handles almost all exports and imports, and in Ballarat and Bendigo.

VICTORIA. A study in unexpected youthful sophistication and elegance. Queen Victoria visits the opera in 1839, the year before her marriage to Albert. The portrait was painted on marble by the court painter E.T. Parris. *Photo: Lowndes Lodge Gallery*

V. was discovered by Capt. Cook in 1770 and was settled in the 1830s. In 1851 it was created a separate colony, after being part of NSW, and was named after Queen Victoria. In 1901 it became one of the states of the Commonwealth of Australia. The state legislature consists of a Governor, a Legislative Council, and a Legislative Assembly. Area 227,620 sq.km (87,884 sq.m); pop. (1978) 3,818,400.

VICTORIA. Cap. of British Columbia, Canada, on Vancouver Is. It is a great port, an industrial centre, and a railway junction with factories making furniture, clothing, chemicals, etc., and shipyards. V. was founded as Fort V. in 1843 by the Hudson's Bay Co. and has a univ. (1963). Pop. (1976) 218,250.

VICTORIA. Cap. of Hong Kong (q.v.), commonly itself called Hong Kong.

VICTORIA, Lake. Africa's largest lake, on the equator at an altitude of 1,136 m (3,726 ft); area over 69,400 sq.km (26,800 sq.m); 410km (255m) long. Most important of its affluents is the Kagera, the Nile's remotest headstream; the Nile issues from it. The first European to see the lake was Speke in 1858, who named it after Queen Victoria; originally V. Nyanza (Bantu 'great water'). It is partly in Uganda, in Kenya, and in Tanzania. *See* OWEN FALLS.

VICTORIA CROSS. British decoration for conspicuous bravery instituted by Queen Victoria in 1856. Bronze, 4cm (1.5in) diameter, it has a crimson ribbon. Until the supply

VICTORIA. Australia's past lives again. At Emu Bottom, not far from Melbourne, the state's oldest homestead, built in 1836, has been restored to its original condition. The farm itself is also being run as it used to be, and cultivated with farm equipment of a bygone age. *Photo: Courtesy of the Australian Information Service.*

was exhausted in 1942 all V.Cs. were struck from the metal of cannon captured from the Russians at Sevastopol: they are now made from gunmetal supplied by the Royal Mint. Those eligible incl. members of the army, navy, and air force; members of the nursing services; and civilians under the direction of the 3 fighting services.

VICTORIA FALLS. Falls on the r. Zambezi, on the Zambia/Rhodesia border. The river is *c.* 1,700 m (5,580 ft) wide, and drops 120m (400ft) to flow through a 30m (100ft) wide gorge. The Falls were discovered by Livingstone in 1855, and named after Queen Victoria, but are also known in Zambia as Mosi-oa-tunya.

VICTORIAN ORDER, Royal. A British order of chivalry instituted in 1896 by Queen Victoria as a reward for personal services to the sovereign. It comprises Knight or Dame Grand Cross (GCVO), Knight Commander (KCVO), Dame Commander (DCVO), Commander (CVO), Member (MVO).

'VICTORY.' British battleship, 2,198 tonnes (2,164 tons), launched in 1765, and now in dry dock in Portsmouth harbour. She was the flagship of Nelson at Trafalgar.

VICUÑA (vikoon'ya). A small ruminant (*Lama vicugna*) which lives in herds on the Andean plateau. Its soft brown wool is used in textile manufacture.

VIDAL (vē'dahl), **Gore** (1925-). American author. He served in the American army in the S.W.W., and was a member of Kennedy's Advisory Council of the Arts. His works incl. the novel *Myra Breckinridge* (1968), the play, *An Evening with Richard Nixon* (1972), and the screenplays *Suddenly Last Summer* (1958) and *The Lefthanded Gun* (1959) dealing with Billy the Kid.

VI'DEŌGAMES, or **telegames.** Games played, by means of special additional or built-in components, on the screen of the home television set. The first commercially sold was a simple bat and ball game developed in the USA in 1972, but complex variants are now available in colour and with special sound effects. In television 'tennis' a quartz crystal oscillator supplies a clock pulse input to the microprocessor in the component, so that the speed of the 'ball' across the screen can be controlled, and the player uses a simple potentiometer to control the movement of the 'racket'.

VIDEOGRAPHY. Filming with a lightweight camera, producing a videotape that can immediately be played back in colour and sound on a television set. The tape can be wiped and re used.

VIDEO (disc/tape) **SYSTEMS.** Video tape cassette systems (*see* TAPE RECORDING) are used to record broadcast programmes for future viewing, and in addition, like video discs (originated by Baird 1928, commercially used from 1978) give a library of original viewing material. The Philips system has a 30 cm (12 in) rotating vinyl disc coated with a reflective material: information is recorded on the surface as a spiral of miniature pits from which it is recovered by scanning with a miniature laser.

VIDOCQ (vēdok'), **François Eugène** (1775-1857). French detective. B. at Arras, he was a criminal, but in 1809 enlisted as a spy in the Paris police. He rose to be chief of the detective dept.

VIENNA. Capital (Ger. *Wien*) of the Austrian republic, on the Danube at the foot of the Wiener Wald. It consists of an old city, nearly circular, whose former fortifications were replaced (1860) by the Ringstrasse. The cathedral of St Stephen dates from the 13th cent. The Hofburg, the former imperial palace, contains the national library. Among the most notable buildings are the houses of parliament (1883), the royal palace of Schönbrunn (started 1696); the Rathaus (1873-83); the univ., founded 1365; the Burgtheater, many museums, etc. V. was until 1918 the cap. of the Austro-Hungarian Empire and the commercial centre of eastern Europe. It became the Habsburg capital in 1278. In 1934 it was the scene of a Socialist and of a Fascist rising. V. suffered much destruction during fighting in the S.W.W., after which it was divided into US, Brit., Fr., and Russian zones of occupation 1945-55. The UN city (1979) houses the UN Industrial Development Organization (UNIDO) and the Internat. Atomic Energy Agency (IAEA). Psychoanalysis, atonal music and modern Zionism originated in Vienna. (1971) 1,614,340.

The CONGRESS OF V. 1814-15 effected the settlement of Europe after the Napoleonic Wars.

VIENTIANE (vē'enti-ahn'). Port and admin. cap. of Laos on the Mekong r. Pop. (1973) 176,650.

VIETNAM (vē-etnahm'). Country of SE Asia, the name meaning 'distant south'. The people are concentrated mainly in the Red r. delta in the N and the Mekong r. delta in the S, and in the coastal plain. Rice is the chief crop, but sugar, sweet potatoes, coffee, tea, cotton, tobacco, etc., are also grown. Minerals incl. coal (espec. in the N), iron, manganese, chromite, bauxite and phosphates, with some oil and natural gas. Tropical rain forest provides timber (incl. teak), and there are important fisheries. The chief towns are the cap. Hanoi, and the ports of Ho Chi Minh City (formerly Saigon), Da Nang and Haiphong.

The original state of V. was founded in 208 BC in the Red River delta, under Chinese overlordship. It was under direct Chinese rule 111 BC-AD 939 and was thereafter at times nominally subject to China, although extending its rule to the S., and in 1288 defeating the forces of Kublai Khan. Conquered by France 1858-84, it formed the colonies of Tonkin, Annam and Cochin-China, which were occupied by the Japanese 1940-45. Ho Chi Minh (q.v.), who had built up the Vietminh (Independence) League, then overthrew the Japanese (and later French) supported régime of Bao Dai, who had formerly been emperor of Annam only. French attempts to exercise continued control led to bitter fighting 1946-54, and final defeat at Dien Bien Phu (q.v.). The Geneva Conference divided V. along the 17th parallel of latitude into North V. (Communist), cap. Hanoi, and South V. (democratic), cap. Saigon. Within South V. the Communist guerrilla Nat. Liberation Front, or Vietcong, gained strength, and increasing military aid to it by China via North V. and to the South V. govt. by the USA led, after the Tonkin (q.v.) Gulf incident, to direct American intervention. Pres. Johnson offered to negotiate in 1968 and Nixon followed up the offer, peace being concluded in Jan. 1973 following negotiation by Kissinger and Le Duc Tho (qq.v.). US forces were withdrawn from South V., but the International Control Commission proved ineffective, and fighting between North and South resumed until in March 1975 the South was overrun by the North, and American withdrawal of all aid was complete. In 1976 the country was reunited as the Socialist Rep. of Vietnam.

The country remained economically a shambles, but (backed now by the USSR) V. embarked on full-scale war with Kampuchea 1977-78 to topple the régime of Pol Pot which was backed by China, so that China mounted a brief punitive invasion of Vietnam 17 Feb.-16 Mar. 1979. The large Chinese community within V. had been under pressure from 1977, and with other middle-class Vietnamese fled the country 1978-9, often by sea (the 'boat people'), in large numbers (*c.* 1,000,000). Laos also came virtually under Vietnamese control, and Thailand was under threat. Vietnam ranks as the world's third Communist power.

Area 336,000 sq.km (129,000 sq.m); pop. (1979) 52,000,000; of whom 85% are Vietnamese, whose traditional religions are Taoism and Buddhism. M.U.: dong.

VIETNAM. The aftermath of the war in Vietnam. A camp of Vietnamese refugees at Camp Pendleton in California. *Photo: Mireille Vautier*

VIEW DATA SYSTEM. Electronic system using an ordinary telephone line to link the user of a specially adapted television set to a large store of information held on computers, and provided (in the case of Britain's Prestel) by hundreds of independent organisations. Such systems may allow the viewer to 'respond', e.g. ordering and paying for advertised goods and services, or for certain pages to be restricted to listed subscribers in the case of confidential business information.

VIGNY (vēnyē), **Alfred de** (1797-1863). French poet. B. at Loches, he joined the army at 16 and had 12 years' service. His first vol. of poems appeared in 1822, his prose romance *Cinq-Mars* in 1826, and his drama *Chatterton* in 1835. The title of the latter illustrates his interest in England, where he lived some years, and in 1828 he m. an Englishwoman. Some of his best poems are in *Les Destinées* (1864).

VIGO (vē'gō). Spanish seaport and naval station on V. bay in Galicia with petroleum refineries, tanneries, paper mills, distilleries, etc. Pop. (1970) 197,145.

VIIPURI. Finnish name of VYBORG.

VĪ'KINGS. Name given to the Scandinavian 'sea-warriors' who in the 8th-10th cents. raided and settled the coasts of G. Britain and W Europe, later extending their attacks to include Spain and Italy, going as far south as Constantinople and N Africa and as far east as Russia. *See* NORSEMEN.

VILLA CISNEROS. *See* DAKHLA.

VILLA-LOBOS (vē'lah lō'bōs), **Heitor** (1881-1959). Brazilian composer. He developed a nationalistic style, based on folk tunes gathered on his travels through the country, and used orchestras of hundreds and choirs of thousands.

VILLEHARDOUIN (vēlahrdoo-aṅ'), **Geoffroy de** (*c.* 1160-*c.* 1213). The first historian to write in the French language. He was b. near Troyes and wrote a chronicle of the 4th crusade.

VILLEINAGE. The system of serfdom that prevailed in Europe in the Middle Ages. At the time of the Domesday Book, the villeins were the most numerous element in the English population, providing the labour force for the manors. By the 15th cent. V. had been supplanted by a system of free tenure and labour, but it continued in France until 1789.

VILLIERS DE L'ISLE ADAM (vēyā' de lēl ahdoṅ'), **Philippe Auguste Mathias,** comte de (1838-89). French poet, the inaugurator of the Symbolist movement. He wrote the drama *Axel*; *Isis*, a romance of the supernatural; verse, and short stories.

VILLON (vēyoṅ'), **François** (1431-85). French poet. B. at Paris of apparently humble parentage, he dropped his own surname (Montcorbier or de Logos) to assume that of a canon - a relative who sent him to study at the Sorbonne, where he graduated in 1449 and took his MA in 1452. In 1455 he stabbed a priest in a street fight and had to flee the city. About this time he was a member of the Brotherhood of the Coquille, using their argot in some half dozen of his ballades. Pardoned the next year he returned to Paris - the *Petit Testament* belonging to this time - but was soon in flight again after robbing the Collège of Navarre, and was briefly at rest at the court of the duke of Orléans until sentenced to death for an unknown offence from which he was saved by the amnesty of a public holiday. Theft and public brawling continued to occupy his time, in addition to the production of the *Grand Testament* (1461), but in 1463 a sentence of death in Paris, which he managed to have commuted to 10 yr banishment, is the last that is really known of him. His satiric humour, matchless pathos, and fertile lyric power make him a world poet.

VILNIUS. Cap. of Lithuanian SSR. An important fortress already in the 12th cent., cap. of Lithuania from 1323, Polish 1447–1795 (when Russia annexed it) and a centre of Polish and Jewish culture, it was claimed by both Poland and Lithuana after the F.W.W., was given to Poland 1921, occupied by Russia 1939, and immediately transferred to Lithuania. Pop. (1979) 481,000. The Russian form Vilna is often used.

VIMY. French town in Pas-de-Calais dept. Pop. (1973) 3,270. V. Ridge nearby, a spur of the ridge of Notre Dame de Lorette, 8km (5m) NE of Arras, was taken by Canadian troops during the battle of Arras, April 1917: 11,285 Canadians were lost.

VINCENNES (vañsen'). Suburb of E Paris, noted for the Univ. of Paris VIII, usually known as V., founded in 1970 (following the 1968 student rebellion) for blue-collar workers. By 1980 it had 32,000 students, and had attracted a number of drop-outs and drug addicts. In June 1980 it was removed to the industrial suburb of St-Denis.

VINCENT DE PAUL (1576–1660). French RC saint. B. in Gascony, he was ordained in 1600, was captured by Barbary pirates and was a slave in Tunis until 1607. He founded the 2 charitable orders of Lazarists (1625) and Sisters of Charity (1634). He was canonized in 1737.

VINE. A climbing plant (*Vitis vinifera*) of the family Viticeae, a native of Asia Minor, cultivated from antiquity for its fruit, which is eaten or made into wine (q.v.) or other fermented drinks; dried fruits of certain varieties are raisins and currants.

VINEGAR. A weak solution of acetic acid containing salts and colouring matter. White V. is obtained from inferior wines, malt V. from beer.

VINLAND. Norse name for the Hudson Straits/Gulf of St Lawrence area of N America, which Leif Ericsson (q.v.) believed an 'island-continent'.

VINSON MASSIF. Highest point in Antarctica (q.v.).

VIOL. Family of bowed musical instruments, resembling the violin, but with a flatter back.

VIOLET (*Viola*). Large genus of plants which includes the sweet V. (*V. odorata*), dog V. (*V. canina*), wild pansy (*V. tricolor*), and the viola (*V. cornuta*).

VIOLIN. A stringed musical instrument played with a bow. It superseded the viol from the 17th cent.; famous early makers were the Amati family in Cremona, Stradivari, and G. A. Guarnieri. It consists of a resonant body comprising belly and back, a neck with fingerboard attached and 4 catgut strings carried from a tailpiece over a bridge to tuning-pegs on the neck. The **Viola** is slightly larger and thicker than the violin; like the violin it is tuned in 5ths, but is a 5th below. The **Violoncello** is much larger than either of the above and is held between the player's knees. The **Double Bass** is the largest of the family.

VIOLLET-LE-DUC (vyawlā-le-dük'), **Eugène Emmanuel** (1814–79). French architect. Noted as the leader of the Gothic revival in France, and for restoration of medieval buildings.

VIPER. Family of poisonous snakes. The true Vs. (*Viperinae*), abundant in Africa and SW Asia, incl. the adder (*Vipera berus*), Britain's only poisonous snake; the African puff adder (*Bitis arietans*) and the horned V. of N Africa (*Cerastes cornutus*). The second sub-family (*Crotalinae*) incl. the pit vipers and rattlesnakes of the Americas, which have a pit between the eye and nostril.

VIRCHOW (vēr'khō), **Rudolf** (1821–1902). German pathologist. B. in Pomerania, he was a prof. at Berlin and from 1880 leader of the opposition to Bismarck in the Reichstag. His *Cellular Pathology* (1858) opened a new chapter in pathology.

VIRGIL (Publius Vergilius Maro) (70–19 BC). Roman poet. B. near Mantua, he belonged to the yeoman class whose life he eulogized in his poems. His *Eclogues*, 10 pastoral poems, appeared in 37 BC. The *Georgics* or 'Art of Husbandry' followed in 30 BC. and confirmed his position as the chief poet of the age. The last years of his life were spent in composing the Aeneid, an epic poem in 12 books intended to glorify the Julian dynasty, whose head was Augustus, V.'s imperial patron. Horace was his friend. His superbly musical and moving gift of language ensured his acceptance as the voice of imperial Rome for succeeding cents., and by the 3rd cent. his works were used for divination - the Sortes Virgilianae. The apparent forecast of the birth of Christ in the 4th eclogue led to his acceptance as an 'honorary' Christian by the medieval Church and hence as approved reading, and in popular legend he became a powerful magician.

VIRGINIA. One of the 13 original states of the USA, in the S Atlantic group. It comprises a coastal plain, the Piedmont plateau, and the Allegheny Mts. Chief rivers are the Potomac, Rappahannock, York, and James. The chief crops are sweet potatoes, corn, tobacco, apples, peaches and peanuts. Coal is mined, and growing industries incl. furniture, paper, chemicals, processed food, textiles and cigarettes. There are also shipyards and a fishing industry. The cap. is Richmond; other towns are Norfolk, Roanoke, Portsmouth, and Newport News. Area 105,711 sq.km (40,814 sq.m); pop. (1970) 4,648,494.

V. was named in honour of Elizabeth I; it was settled in 1607, the first permanent English settlement in N America. It took a leading part in the revolutionary struggle against England, and was a Confederate state in the American Civil War.

VIRGIN ISLANDS. Group of *c.* 50 islands in the West Indies, of which St Thomas, St Croix, and St John were bought by USA from Denmark in 1917. The cap. is Charlotte Amalie on St Thomas. There is a gov., elected by the islanders, and an elected unicameral legislature, but in 1980 a new constitution was under consideration. Area 342 sq.km (132 sq.m); pop. (1980) 119,000. The other V. Is. are a Brit. colony, cap. Road Town on Tortola. Under the 1967 constitution govt is exercised through the Chief Minister, advised by an Executive Council, and there is a Legislative Council with elected majority. Area 130 sq.km (59 sq.m); pop. (1975) 10,000.

VIRUS (vī'rus). Organism, a thousandth the size of a bacterium. Their existence was deduced in 1898, but they could only be seen after the invention of the electron microscope in the 1940s. Viral diseases incl canine distemper, common cold, foot and mouth, hepatitis, herpes, influenza, measles, mumps, rabies, smallpox, typhus, and yellow fever (qq.v.); and viruses probably play a contributory role in cancer.

Viruses consist of a 'core' of nucleic acids enclosed in a protein 'shell', and outside a living animal cell remain completely inert. To function and reproduce they must force their way into a cell. The healthy human body reacts to such an 'invasion' by producing an anti-viral protein, interferon, which prevents the infection spreading to adjacent cells and gives rise to substances which destroy the virus.

Viroids, discovered in 1971, are even smaller (a single strand of genes, which reproduces solely through the action of enzymes in the cell it infects). They cause stunting, etc, in plants and some rare diseases in animals and man.

VISCONTI, Luchino (1906–76). Italian film and theatrical director. He pioneered the 'neo-realist' film with *Ossessione* (1942); later were *The Leopard* (1963) and *Death in Venice* (1971), and his powerful social comment in documentaries led to clashes with the Italian govt and RC Church.

VISCOSITY. The internal friction or resistance to relative motion of the parts of a fluid. Fluids like pitch, treacle and heavy oils are highly viscous, but a perfect fluid would be non-viscous.

VISCOUNT. In the peerage of the United Kingdom, the 4th degree of nobility, between earl and baron.

VISHNU (vish'noo). Second of the 3 gods constituting the Hindu triad. He is the Preserver, and is believed to have assumed human form on a number of occasions; 10 of such avataras or incarnations are described, the most famous being as Rama and as Krishna. His worshippers are the Vaishnavas (q.v.).

VISIGŌTHS. *See* GOTHS.

VI'STŪLA. Polish river which rises in the Carpathians and runs SE, across Poland to the Baltic at Gdansk. Length 1,090 km (678m).

VITAMINS. Organic substances normally present in small and variable amounts in different foods and of which the absence or partial deficiency in the diet leads to various characteristic diseases and disturbances. Although in 1662 Admiral Hawkins was aware of the value of 'sower oranges and lemmons' against scurvy, it was not fully estab. until about 1915 that several deficiency diseases were preventable and curable by extracts from certain foods. By then it was known that two groups of factors were involved, one being water-soluble and present, for example, in yeast, rice-polishings and wheat-germ, and the other fat-soluble and present in egg-yolk, butter, fish-liver oils and so on. The water-soluble substance, known to be effective against beriberi, was named vitamin B. (The name 'vitamine' later changed to 'vitamin' was chosen to indicate it was an amine and essential to life.) The fat-soluble vitamin complex was at first called vitamin A. With improving analytical techniques these have been subsequently separated into their various components, and others have been discovered. Not all are amines, but the term V. remains.

Of over 20 known Vs., the majority are found in different related forms, and are prepared industrially either by extraction from natural sources, or artificially by chemical synthesis. As their structures have been identified, most of them are now known by their chemical names; thus vitamin C (anti-scurvy) is ascorbic acid, vitamin B_1 (anti beri-beri) is thiamine, vitamin D_2 (anti-rickets) is calciferol, and so on.

There are also a number of organic compounds, similar in biological function to Vs., but capable of being synthesized by man and so not needed in the human diet. Among these, which are not incl. among the true Vs., is choline, essential to rats and some birds which cannot produce sufficient for themselves.

VITEBSK (vētebsk'). Town, dating from the 10th cent., in White Russian SSR, on the Dvina. It manufactures glass, boots and shoes, etc. It has been Lithuanian, Russian, and Polish. Pop. (1979) 297,000.

VITŌ'RIA. City in N Spain, cap. of Alava prov. Here in 1813 Wellington defeated the French. Pop. (1970) 136,873.

VITRIOL. Oil of V. is sulphuric acid; blue, green, and white Vs. are copper, ferrous, and zinc sulphate respectively.

VITTŌ'RIO VENETO (ven'etō). Italian town in Veneto which gives its name to the final victory of the Italians and British over the Austrians in Oct. 1918. It makes motorcycles, agricultural machinery, furniture, paper, textiles, etc. Pop. (1979) 25,000.

VĪ'TUS. Christian saint, supposed to have been a Sicilian who was martyred at Rome early in the 4th cent. His aid is invoked in Catholic lands against the nervous complaint called St Vitus' Dance (q.v.). *See* SAINT.

VIVA'LDI, Antonio (1675–1741). Italian composer and violinist. Interest in his instrumental concertos (over 250) which influenced Bach has revived in the 20th cent. Although ordained in 1703, he never entered the Church, but this and the colour of his hair account for his nickname 'the red priest'.

VIVISECTION. *See* ANTI-VIVISECTION.

VIZCAYA. Basque form of BISCAY.

VLA'DIMIR (*c.* 956–1015). Russian saint. As grand-duke of Kiev, he was converted to Christianity in 988, m. a Christian princess, and Christianized his subjects.

VLADIVO'STOK. City and port of the RSFSR in the Far East, on Amur Bay; it is the most important naval and commercial centre on the Russian Pacific coast, and is kept open by icebreakers throughout the year. It is the admin. centre of the Far East Science Centre, with subsidiary research centres at Khaborovsk, Petropavlovsk, and Magadan. Pop. (1979) 550,000.

VLAMINCK (vlamink'), **Maurice de** (1878–1958). French artist. B. in Paris, he was persuaded to take up painting as a career by Derain, and became famous for his landscapes, often scenes in snow. He also wrote poetry, novels and essays.

VLISSINGEN. Dutch form of FLUSHING.

VLONË (vlon'a). Albanian town and port, site of the declaration of independence by Albania in 1912. It had been Turkish since 1464. Pop. (1976) 58,400.

VODKA. The Russian national drink; a strong colourless liquor distilled from rye, potatoes, maize, and barley.

VOICE. Sound produced by the passage of air between the vocal cords, 2 folds of mucous membrane stretched across the larynx. The sound is much amplified by the hollow sinuses of the face, and is articulated by the muscles of the tongue and cheek. The use of the V. is controlled by the brain, and it will be lost or impaired if the speech centres are damaged.

VOICEPRINT. A visual pattern of lines recorded by the human voice. First used as evidence in criminal trials in USA in 1966, Vs. were banned in 1974 by the US Court of Appeal as 'not yet sufficiently accepted by scientists'.

VOLCĀ'NO. A vent in the Earth's crust from which are ejected molten rock, lava, ashes, gases, etc. Usually it is cone-shaped with a pit-like opening at the top called the crater. Some Vs., e.g. Stromboli and Vesuvius, eject the material with explosive violence; others are a quiet type in which the lava rises up into the crater and flows over the brim; and some may be quiescent for very long periods, e.g. Mount St Helens (q.v.). Many Vs. are submarine. The chief volcanic regions are the Pacific (Cape Horn to Alaska); central Andes (world's highest Guallatiri 6,060 m (19,882 ft), Chile; North Island, NZ; Hawaii; Japan and Antarctica. There are some 600 volcanoes on Earth, and volcanism has helped shape other members of the Solar System, e.g. the Moon, Mars, Venus, the Jovian moon Io, etc.

VOLE. Family of rodents (Cricetidae), widely distributed over Europe, Asia and N America, and which incl. the hamsters and lemmings. British species incl. the water V. or water 'rat' (*Arvicola terrestris*), brownish above and grey-white below; and the field V. (*Microtus agrestis*).

VOLGA (vol'gah). Longest river of Europe: 3,685 km (2,290 m), 3,540 km (2,200 m) navigable. It drains most of middle and E European Russia, rises in the Valdai plateau and flows into the Caspian 88km (55m) below Astrakhan. It is planned to link the V. with the Pechora r. which naturally flows N from the Ural Mtns to the Barents Sea: nuclear blasting would provide a new channel, and the water would restore the V.'s diminished volume, as well as the level of the Caspian Sea.

VOLGA. Its use for irrigation and industry has accentuated its age-long habit of drying up in summer, to form shallows and islands which interrupt navigation. *Photo: Novosti*

VO'LGOGRAD. Town in the RSFSR, on the r. Volga. Metal goods and machinery are manufactured, and there are saw mills, petroleum refineries, etc. Pop. (1979) 929,000. V. was called Stalingrad 1925-61; its successful defence, 1942-3, against the Germans was a turning point of the S.W.W.

VOLLEYBALL. Team game invented in the USA in 1895, played on a court 18m (59ft) long by 9m (29ft 6in), divided into two by a net 1m (3ft 3in) deep suspended 1.43m (4ft 8in) above the court. The 6 players of each team rotate in position through the 6 sub-sections into which each half of the court is divided behind the attack line. The ball, slightly smaller than a basketball, is hit with palm or fist, the aim being to ground it in the opponents' court.

VOLT. The practical unit of electromotive force (e.m.f.) and potential difference (p.d.). It is defined as the e.m.f. or p.d. which, when steadily applied to a conductor of resistance one ohm, produces a current of one ampere.

VOLTA, Alessandro (1745-1827). Italian physicist and pioneer of electrical science. B. at Como, he was a professor there and at Pavia. He invented the voltaic pile, the electrophorus and an electroscope. The volt (q.v.) is named after him.

VO'LTA. The chief river of Ghana, *c.* 1,600 km (1,000 m) long, with 2 main upper branches, the Black and White V. Under the V. River Project, first envisaged 1924, it has been dammed to provide power for general purposes and for the manufacture of aluminium from the country's bauxite deposits.

VO'LTA, Upper. Inland state of W Africa, N of Ghana. Crops incl. groundnuts, millet, maize, rice and cotton; cattle and sheep are reared. In 1975 a dispute with Mali over a strip on the N border was settled by a neutral commission. Annexed by France in 1896, V. became an independent rep. outside the Fr. Community in 1960. A military coup overthrew Pres. Lamizana Nov. 1980. A committee of 'national recovery' headed by Col. Saye Zerbo suspended the constitution, and dissolved the multiparty nat. assembly. Renamed Burkina Faso, 1985. The cap. is Ouagadougou. Area 274,000 sq.km (106,000 sq.m); pop. (1977) 6,320,000. M.U.: CFA franc.

VOLTAIRE (voltār'). Pseudonym of Fr. writer François-Marie Arouet (1694-1778). B. at Paris, son of a notary, he adopted his pseudonym, probably an anagram of Arouet l(e) j(eune), in 1718. He had already started writing poetry at his Jesuit seminary in Paris, and having left school in 1711 was twice imprisoned in the Bastille and thrice exiled from the capital between 1716 and 1726 for libellous political verse: *Oedipe* his first essay in tragedy was staged in 1718. While in England 1726-9 he dedicated an epic poem on Henry IV, *La Henriade*, to Queen Caroline, and on returning to France pub. the successful *Histoire de Charles XII* (1731), and produced the play *Zaïre* (1732). His *Lettres philosophiques sur les Anglais* (1733), a panegyric of English ways, thought and political practice, led to his taking refuge with his mistress, the marquise de Chatelet (d. 1749) at Cirey in Champagne - where he wrote his best play *Mérope*, 1743, and much of *Le Siècle de Louis XIV*. In 1751-3 he was at the court of Frederick the Great, who had long admired him, but the association ended in deep enmity, and from 1754 he estab. himself near Geneva - after 1758 at Ferney, just across the French border, hence the nickname 'patriarch of Ferney'. Among his other works are *La Pucelle*, a verse libel of Joan of Arc; the satirical tale *Zadig*; *Candide* (1759), a parody on Leibniz's 'best of all possible worlds'; and the tragedy *Irène* (1778), for which his visit to Paris to attend its production was a popular but exhausting triumph which accelerated his death there. In religion a Deist, V. devoted himself to crushing the spirit of intolerance: *see* CALAS. His remains were transferred in 1791 to the Panthéon in Paris.

VON BRAUN (brown), **Wernher** (1912-77). German scientist. Technical director of the liquid-fuel-rocket and guided-missile centre at Peenemünde 1937-45, he developed the V-2 rocket used against England. After the S.W.W. he went to America to work on guided missiles and in 1960 became director of the George C. Marshall Space Flight Center in Alabama for the National Aeronautics and Space Administration, working on the Apollo project. *See* MOON.

VOO'DOO. Among the Negroes of the West Indies, Haiti in particular, a cult of serpent worship, phallicism, magical practices, etc.

VŌRŌ'NEZH. Cap. of V. region of the RSFSR, and administrative centre of the Black Earth area. It stands on the V., near where it joins the Don and has many industries, and a univ. founded at Dorpat (Tartu) in 1803, moved to V. during the F.W.W. There has been a town on the site since the 11th cent. Pop. (1979) 783,000.

VOROSHILOV, Klementiy Efremovich (1881-1969). Marshal of the Soviet Union. He joined the Bolsheviks in 1903, and was many times arrested, exiled, but escaped. Commander NW front in 1941, he failed to deal with the German blitzkrieg. In 1953-60 he was pres. of the Presidium of the USSR.

VOROSHILOVGRAD (vöroshelofgrat'). City in the Ukrainian SSR, known as Lugansk until 1935 and 1958-70. It is a centre of heavy industry making diesel locomotives, mining machinery, etc. Its industrial importance began with the establishment of an ironworks here by an Englishman on behalf of the Tsarist govt. Pop. (1979) 463,000.

VORSTER (forst'-), **Balthazar Johannes** (1915–83). South African statesman. B. in Jamestown, Cape Prov., he was interned during the S.W.W. as a member of the militant Afrikaner nationalist organization Ossewabrandwag. A Nationalist MP from 1953, he was Min. of Justice 1961-66, succeeded as PM on the assassination of Verwoerd, and was pres. 1978-9, when he resigned owing to the Dept. of Information having made unauthorised use of public funds during his premiership. The episode was known as Muldergate, after the Min. of Information Cornelius 'Connie' Mulder.

VORTICISM. A movement (1913-22) in English painting, with aims similar to those of Futurism (q.v.). Its exponents, of whom Wyndham Lewis was the leader, believed that painting should reflect the complexity of the modern industrial world.

VOSGES (vōzh). Mt. range in E France, rising in the Ballon de Guebwiller to 1,422 m (4,667 ft) and forming the W edge of the Rhine rift valley.

VOTE. Expression of opinion by ballot, show of hands, etc. In the UK all British subjects over 18, except peers, lunatics and felons, are entitled to vote in local govt and parliamentary elections. A register is prepared annually, and since 1872 voting has been by secret ballot. Under the Corrupt and Illegal Practices Act (1883) any candidate attempting to influence voters by gifts, loans or promises, or by intimidation is liable to a fine or imprisonment.

The voting system is by a simple majority in single-member constituencies. Critics point out that under this system many electors are 'disenfranchized', since Vs. for a defeated candidate are 'lost'; govts may take office with a minority of the total vote; and confrontation between 2 parties, which are divided along class lines, results in either when in power undoing the legislation of its predecessor. Opponents of change argue the danger of increasing party fragmentation, and the ineffectiveness of continual coalition govts. In 1976 the Hansard Soc. Commission for Electoral Reform recommended either a form of proportional representation (q.v.), i.e. the single transferable vote, or the Australian alternative vote system. Under the latter the candidates are marked by the elector in order of preference. If none has an overall majority, the candidate with fewest 'first preferences' is eliminated, and his 'second preferences' are redistributed until an overall majority is achieved.

In the USA the voting age is also 18, but conditions as to previous residence vary according to state. Until declared illegal in 1965, literacy tests or payment of a poll tax were often used to decrease the Negro vote in the South.

In newly emergent states, as in Africa, there may be problems of literacy or differing local languages, and instead of the names of candidates being printed on the ballot paper, pictorial party emblems may be used. The absence of accurate registers can encourage plural voting, so that the elector, once he has voted, may be marked on the hand with temporarily 'indelible' ink. More recently vote by 'acclamation' has tended to be adopted in African states as more immediately 'democratic', but the method encourages intimidation.

VRIES (vrēs), **Hugo de** (1848-1935). Dutch botanist, a pioneer in the study of plant evolution.

VUILLARD (vüeyahr'), **Edouard** (1868–1940). French artist. B. at Cuisseaux, he lived most of his life in Montmartre, and excels in portraits and homely interior scenes in which his mother - manager of a dressmaker's shop - often features.

VULCAN. *See* HEPHAESTUS.

VULGATE. The Latin translation of the Bible made mainly by St Jerome in the 4th cent., and so called because of its vulgar (general) use in the RC Church.

VULTURE. Group of birds of prey. The head and neck are bare, the plumage shaggy, and the beak and claws are hooked. True Vs. occur only in the Old World; the American forms include the condor (q.v.), turkey buzzard, and black buzzard or carrion crow.

VYBORG (vē'borg). Port and naval base in the RSFSR, on the Gulf of Finland, 112km (70m) NW of Leningrad. Founded by the Swedes 1293, it was at one time Finnish (Viipuri). Pop. (1973) 51,000.

VYSHINSKY, Andrei (1883-1954). Soviet statesman. As Commissar for Justice he acted as prosecutor at the treason trials of 1936-8. He was For. Min. 1949-53 and often represented the USSR at the UN.

W

The 23rd letter of the English alphabet, representing a semi-vowel, viz. a *u* in consonantic function. It is called double *u* because it was written *uu* or *vv* which in ligature resulted in *w*. It is not pronounced before *r* (*write, wren*) and in cases such as *two* and *sword*.

WADDENZEE (vad'enzā). European estuarine area (tidal flats, saltmarshes, islands and inlets) N of the Netherlands and W Germany, and W of Denmark. Rich in birdlife, it is also the nursery for the North Sea fisheries, and is threatened by tourism and other development. Area 10,000 sq.km (4,000 sq.m).

WADI HALFA (wah'dē hal'fa). Frontier town in Sudan Rep., on Lake Nuba (the Sudanese section of Lake Nasser, formed by the Nile dam at Aswan), the N terminus of the Sudan railway. Pop. *c.* 15,000.

WAGGA WAGGA (wo'ga wo'ga). Town in NS Wales, Australia, on the Murrumbidgee, 112km (70m) NNE of Albury, centre of an agricultural area. Pop. (1978) 37,650.

WAGNER (vahg'ner), **Richard** (1813-83). German composer. B. at Leipzig, he became director of the Magdeburg theatre, where he produced, unsuccessfully, his first opera, *Das Liebesverbot*. He lived in Paris, 1839-42. His opera *Rienzi* was produced at Dresden in 1842, followed by *The Flying Dutchman* in 1843. As conductor at the Dresden opera house he composed *Tannhäuser* and *Lohengrin*. In 1849 he fled to Paris to escape arrest for taking part in the 1848 revolutionary riots. Liszt befriended him, and produced *Lohengrin* at Weimar in 1850. W. was later allowed to return to Germany, and in 1864 won the favour of Ludwig II of Bavaria. In 1866-72 W. lived in Switzerland near Lucerne. His *Tristan und Isolde* was produced at Munich in 1865, and W. founded the festival theatre at Bayreuth, where in 1876 *The Ring of the Nibelung* was given its first performance. His last work, *Parsifal*, was produced in 1882. W. d. at Venice.

W. revolutionized the 19th cent. conception of opera, envisaging it as a wholly new art-form, in which musical, poetic, and scenic elements should be unified; and by such devices as the use of *leitmotif* he gave to opera thematic unity and coherence.

The Bayreuth tradition was carried on by W.'s wife **Cosima** (1837-1930), Liszt's daughter, whom he had m. in 1870 after her first husband, Hans von Bülow, had divorced her; by her son **Siegfried W.** (1869-1930), himself a composer of operas such as *Der Bärenhäuter, Der Kobold*, etc.; and by later descendants.

WAGNER-JAUREGG (-yow'rek), **Julius** (1857-1940). Austrian neurologist. He received a Nobel prize in 1927 for his work on the use of induced fevers in treating mental illness, e.g. malaria in cases of general paralysis of the insane.

WAGRAM (vahg'rahm). Austrian village, to the NE of Vienna, the scene in July 1809 of Napoleon's victory over the Austrians under Archduke Charles. Pop. *c.* 4,000.

WAGTAIL. Genus of birds (*Motacilla*). Found mostly in N Europe and Asia, they are small, with a slender bill and long tail. Three species breed in the British Isles: the pied W. (*M. alba*), the grey W. (*M. cinerea*), and the yellow W. (*M. flava*).

WAHHABIS (wah-hah'-bēz). Mohammedan sect founded by Mohammed ibn Abdul Wahab (1691-1787), whose doctrines call for a strict observance of the precepts of the Koran. They predominate in Saudi Arabia today.

WAIKATO (wīkah'tō). River of North Island, NZ, 355 km (220 m) long, and also the dairying area it traverses, where butter is particularly important. The chief town is Hamilton.

WAIN, John Barrington (1925-). British author. Ed. at St John's Coll., Oxford, he lectured in English literature at the Univ. of Reading 1947-55. His books incl. the novels *Hurry on Down* (1953), and *The Smaller Sky* (1967); vols. of poetry and criticism and the autobiography *Sprightly Running* (1962).

WAIRARAPA (wīrahrah'pa). Area of North Island, NZ, round Lake W., specializing in prime lamb and dairying. The chief market centre is Masterton, pop. (1979) 21,100.

WAIRAU (wī'row). River in northern South Island, NZ, flowing 170 km (105 m) NE to Cook Strait.

WAITAKI (wītak'i). River in SE South Island, NZ, which flows c. 215 km (135 m) to the Pacific. The Benmore hydro-electric installation, where the earth dam has created a lake, is a tourist attraction.

WAITANGI (wītang'i), **Treaty of.** The treaty made between Britain and NZ's Maori chiefs in 1840, which ceded sovereignty, although retaining territorial rights, to the British crown, in exchange for British protection.

WAITANGI DAY. The national day of New Zealand: 6 Feb.

WAJDA (vī'dah), **Andrzej** (1926-). Polish film director. His work incl. the cult film *Ashes and Diamonds* (1958), and a television film version of Conrad's *The Shadow Line* (1976).

WAKAMATSU. *See* KITAKYUSHU.

WAKEFIELD, Edward Gibbon (1796-1862). British colonial statesman. B. in London, he was imprisoned for abducting an heiress 1826-9, and became manager of the S Australian Association which founded a colony in 1836. He was an agent for the New Zealand Land Co. 1839-46, and emigrated there in 1853. His son, **Edward Jerningham W.** (1820-79), wrote *Adventure in New Zealand* (1845).

WAKEFIELD. City in W Yorks, England, 10km (6m) S of Leeds. The Lancastrians defeated the Yorkists here in 1460. Worsteds, chemicals, machine tools, etc. are made, and there are collieries. It is admin. HQ of W Yorks. Pop. (1972) 60,000.

WAKE ISLAND. A small Pacific island between the Philippines and Hawaii. Annexed by the USA in 1898, it was uninhabited until in 1935 it was made an air staging point, with a garrison; it was occupied by the Japanese 1941-5. Area 8 sq.km (3 sq.m); pop. (1970) 1,650.

WAKHAN SALIENT. Narrow strip of Afghan territory bordered by USSR, China and Pakistan. It was effectively 'annexed' by the Soviet Union in 1980 to prevent alleged arms supplies to Afghan guerrillas from China and Pakistan.

WALES. Dylan Thomas (upper left) and David Lloyd George (upper right), both portraits by Augustus John; the hall of the Coal Exchange in Mount Stuart Square, Cardiff, projected home of a 'devolutionary' Welsh assembly (upper centre); Llyn Padern and Mount Snowden, near Llanberis (centre left); the investiture of the Prince of Wales in 1969 at Caernarvon (centre); and the installation of the bard at the Royal National Eisteddfod (below). *Photos: British Tourist Authority (Thomas), Aberdeen Art Gallery and Museum (Lloyd George), Percy Thomas Partnership and the Property Services Agency (Cardiff), Peter Baker (Snowden), Popperfoto (Caernarvon and Eisteddfod).*

WAKSMAN (wahk'sman), **Selman** (1888-1973). American biochemist. B. in the Ukraine, he emigrated to the US in 1910. He coined the name 'anti-biotic' for bacteria-killing chemicals derived from micro-organisms, and was awarded a Nobel prize for his isolation of streptomycin.

WALACHIA. *See* WALLACHIA.

WALCHEREN (wahl'kheren). Island of Zeeland, Netherlands, in the estuary of the Scheldt. The surface is flat and for the most part below sea-level. Dairy farming forms the main activity. The chief towns are Flushing and Middelburg, the cap. Its motto is *Luctor et emergo* (I struggle and emerge). A Brit. force seized W. in 1809; after 7,000 of the garrison of 15,000 had died of malaria, the remainder were withdrawn. It was flooded by deliberate breaching of the dykes to drive out the Germans 1944-5, and in 1953 by abnormally high tides. Area 200 sq.km (80 sq.m).

WALDE'NSĒS. Christian Church, founded *c.* 1170 by Peter Waldo, a merchant of Lyons. They lived in voluntary poverty, refused to take oaths or take part in war, and later rejected the doctrines of transubstantiation, purgatory, and the invocation of saints. Although subjected to persecution until the 17th cent., they spread in France, Germany, and Italy, and still survive in Piedmont.

WALDHEIM (valt'hīm), **Kurt** (1918-). Austrian diplomat. He was For. Min. 1968-70, and in 1971 succeeded U Thant as Sec.-Gen. of the UN.

WALES. Principality of Great Britain, lying between England to the E, the Bristol Channel to the S, and the Irish Channel to the W and N. Off the NW of the mainland lies Anglesey.

PHYSICAL FEATURES. With the exception of the island of Anglesey, and of areas near the coast and in the valleys of the larger rivers, the surface is mountainous. The main massif of the Cambrian mountains runs from N to S and includes Snowdon 1,085 m (3,560 ft), the highest point in England and Wales, Cader Idris, Plinlimmon, the Black Mountains, and the Brecon Beacons. Among the rivers are the Dee, Conway, Dovey, Ystwyth, Teifi, Towy, Loughor, Neath, and Taff. The Usk, Wye, and Severn rise in Wales. The Alwen, Vyrnwy and Trawsfynydd Reservoirs are in N Wales, and the Birmingham Corporation Reservoirs are in Powys.

ECONOMIC. Agriculture is important in N Wales, and throughout the principality sheep are reared, and in more level areas cattle are pastured, and oats, barley, wheat and root crops grown. Some coal is mined in the NE nr Wrexham, and slate is quarried and lead mined in the N, with the prospect also of copper in Snowdonia. The slate industry has revived with new uses, e.g. crushed slate in enamel to protect North Sea oil pipelines, as a paint filler, etc. In Snowdonia plans for further reservoirs, and increased development of electrical and mechanical engineering plants, threaten the area's natural beauty. There has been depopulation in mid-Wales, with attempts to restore it by the introduction of light industry, but forestry, agriculture and tourism are still the backbone. In the S abundant coal encouraged the growth of iron and steel, tin-plate, and copper-smelting industries. In the 1980s, however, steel-making was espec. under threat in the recession. The export of coal, reviving in the 1960s, built up and maintained the ports of Cardiff, Penarth, Barry and Port Talbot, and in 1978 an anthracite mine at Bettws was the first to be opened in more than a decade. There is oil refining, notably at Milford Haven, and nickel and aluminium manufacture, as well as shipbuilding and engineering industries. The largest towns are Cardiff, the cap., Swansea, Newport, Rhondda, Merthyr Tydfil, and Port Talbot. Aberystwyth, Colwyn Bay, Llandudno and Tenby are seaside resorts. Aberystwyth, Ffestiniog, Brecon, Welshpool and Radnor are designated growth areas. There has been controversy on the choice of areas in Wales for disposal of nuclear waste. Ferry services to Ireland operate from Holyhead and Fishguard.

POLITICAL STRUCTURE. Administratively W is linked with England, but there is a separate Welsh Office, and the system of local govt (since 1974 W has been re-organized in 8 new cos.) is slightly different, in that W has no metropolitan co. and district councils, and parish councils are known in W as community councils.

Counties of Wales

	Area in sq. km.	*Pop. in (1978)*	*Admin. H.Q.*
Clwyd	2,424	382,100	Mold
Dyfed	5,767	325,000	Carmarthen
Mid-Glamorgan	1,019	537,900	Cardiff
South Glamorgan	416	385,600	Cardiff
West Glamorgan	815	366,900	Swansea
Gwent	1,377	438,000	Cwmbran
Gwynedd	3,865	226,400	Caernarvon
Powys	5,079	106,000	Llandrindod Wells
	20,762	2,767,900	

POPULATION. The Welsh are a Celtic people. The majority belong to various Nonconformist denominations, e.g. the Calvinistic Methodists or Presbyterian Church of Wales, Methodists, Baptists, Independents, and Congregationalists. There are cathedrals at St David's, Bangor, St Asaph, Llandaff, and Brecon. The Anglican Church in Wales has been disestablished since 1914. The University of W., founded in 1893, comprises the colleges of Aberystwyth, Bangor, Cardiff, Lampeter, and Swansea. At Aberystwyth there is also a national library, and at Cardiff a national museum. The general system of education is similar to that of England, but Welsh is used as an additional medium. Welsh is spoken most widely in the N. Area 20,762 sq.km (8,030 sq.m); pop. (1978) 2,767,900. *See* WELSH.

History. Welsh history, as distinct from English, begins with the Anglo-Saxon conquest of the 5th-7th cents. The Anglo-Saxon victories at Deorham (577) and Chester (613) cut off W. from the other areas still held by the Britons, while in the 8th cent. the Mercian frontier was pushed forward to Offa's Dyke. During the 9th-11th cents. the Vikings raided the coasts. At this time W. was divided into small states organized on a tribal basis, although princes such as Rhodri (844-78), Howel the Good (*c.* 904-49) and Griffith ap Llewelyn (1039-63) temporarily united the country. The Norman marcher barons gradually conquered much of the S, but in the N Llewelyn I (1194-1240) and Llewelyn II (1246-82) maintained a stout resistance, until the conquest of W. was completed by Edward I in 1283. A last rising was led by Owen Glendower in 1400-13.

Henry VIII in 1536 incorporated W. politically into England, and gave it parliamentary representation. Although the Reformation and Puritanism aroused little response, and in the 17th cent. W. was mainly Royalist and Jacobite, since the Evangelical Revival of the 18th cent. nonconformity has become a powerful factor in Welsh life. During the 18th cent. a strong coal and iron industry developed in the S; in the 19th cent. the miners and ironworkers were militant supporters of Chartism, and W. has long been a stronghold of trade unionism and Socialism. Between the world wars W. suffered greatly from industrial depression; unemployment reached 21 per cent in 1937, and a considerable exodus of population took place. It recovered during and after the S.W.W., but nationalist agitation grew, the Welsh Nat. Party (Plaid Cymru), founded in 1925 by D. J. Williams (1886-1970) returning its first member to Westminster in 1966. Nevertheless, in a referendum in 1979 on a proposal to give Wales an elected single-chamber nat. assembly, though with more limited powers than one proposed for Scotland, only 11% voted 'yes'.

Wales has a strong culture in literature and music (*see* EISTEDDFOD), and the Welsh Nat. Opera Co. has a European reputation.

WALES, Prince of. Title granted to Prince Edward, afterwards Edward II, in 1301, since when it has normally been conferred on the sovereign's eldest son. Prince Charles (q.v.) was invested as 21st P. of W. at Caernarvon in 1969 by Elizabeth II.

WALESA (vahlā'sa), **Lech** (1943–). Polish leader of the trade union Solidarity; Nobel peace prize 1983.

WALEY, Arthur (1889–1966). British orientalist. He translated from both the Japanese (e.g. Murasaki Shikibu, q.v.) and Chinese.

WALKABOUT. Australian Aboriginal English for the nomadic random urge to be on the move - 'go walkabout' - which still exercises its pull, even when they have accepted a European-style job. The term was adopted for the informal, conversational walks among her people begun by Elizabeth II during her tours of Australia and NZ in 1970.

WALLABY. Member of the kangaroo family (q.v.). The group includes the true Ws. or 'brush' kangaroos of the scrub jungle, and the rock Ws.

WALLABY. The quokka, a rare species of wallaby found only on the southwest coast of Western Australia. *Photo: Courtesy of the Australia Information Service*

WALLACE, Alfred Russel (1823-1913). British naturalist. B. in Usk, he travelled on the Amazon, and in 1858 a joint paper on the theory of evolution by W. and Darwin was read to the Linnean Society. Awarded the OM 1910.

WALLACE, Edgar (1875-1932). British author. B. at Greenwich, he was the illegitimate son of an actress who placed him with a Billingsgate fish porter. After a varied series of jobs, incl. newsboy, and a spell in the army, he was a war correspondent 1899-1902, and in 1905 pub. his first full-length novel *The Four Just Men.* Later books, written on copious supples of weak tea, incl. the African stories *Sanders of the River* (1911); crime thrillers, e.g. *A King by Night* (1926) and a series built round the elderly detective Mr J. G. Reeder; and books with a race-course setting, e.g. *The Flying Fifty-Five.* He was also a brilliantly successful writer of melodramas, e.g. *The Ringer* (1926), *The Squeaker* (1928), and *On the Spot* (1931), inspired by the career of Al Capone.

WALLACE. Edgar Wallace had the gift of totally assimilating an atmosphere, so that even the Chicago gangsters approved the authenticity of *On the Spot. Photo: Courtesy of Penelope Wallace*

WALLACE, George (1919-). American politician. Elected gov. of Alabama in 1963, he contested the presidency in 1968 as an independent, and in 1972 campaigned for the Democratic nomination, but was shot at a rally and became partly paralysed.

WALLACE, Lewis (1827-1905). US general and novelist. He served in the Mexican and Civil Wars, and subsequently became governor of New Mexico and minister to Turkey. He wrote the historical novels *The Fair God* (1873) and *Ben-Hur* (1880).

WALLACE, Sir Richard (1818-90). British art connoisseur. He inherited a valuable art collection from his father, the marquis of Hertford. His widow bequeathed it to the nation and it is on view at Hertford House, London, which was acquired by the govt. The **Wallace Collection,** as it is called, contains many works by the 18th cent. French masters.

WALLACE, Sir William (*c.* 1272-1305). Scottish patriot. B. near Paisley, he led a revolt against English rule in 1297, won a victory at Stirling, and assumed the title of governor of Scotland. He was defeated by Edward I at Falkirk in 1298, and in 1305 was captured and executed.

WALLACHIA (wolāk'iah). Former prov. of S Romania. In the Middle Ages an independent principality, it was then under Turkish rule from 1387 until united with Moldavia in 1861 to form Romania.

WALLENSTEIN (vahl'lenstīn), **Albrecht von** (1583-1634). German general. B. in Bohemia, he commanded the Imperial armies with great success in the 30 Years War, but was dismissed in 1630 by the emperor, who feared his ambition. He was recalled in 1631 to face Gustavus Adolphus, and plotted for a principality of his own. In 1634 he was assassinated by his officers.

WALLER, Edmund (1606-87). English poet. He sat in the Long Parliament, and later eulogized both Cromwell and Charles II. He is remembered mainly for such lyrics as 'Go, lovely rose'.

WALLFLOWER. Perennial plant (*Cheiranthus cheiri*) in the family Cruciferae, cultivated for its fragrant red, yellow, or brown flowers.

WALLIS, Sir Barnes Neville (1887-1979). British aeronautical engineer. He designed the airship R 100, perfected the 'bounce-bombs' used against the Möhne and Eder dams in 1943 by the Dambusters' Squadron, was responsible for the geodetic construction of the Wellington bomber, assisted the development of Concorde supersonic airliner, and developed the swing-wing aircraft. He was knighted 1968.

WALLIS AND FUTUNA. Two island groups in the Pacific which form an overseas terr. of France (1961). Area 255 sq.km (98 sq.m); pop. (1976) 9,200.

WALLOONS. A Romanized Celtic people of SE Belgium, numbering *c.* 3 million and speaking a French dialect. Against W. predominance the Flemish movement arose in the 19th cent.

WALLSEND. Town in Tyne and Wear, England, on the Tyne at the E end of Hadrian's Wall. Industries incl. shipbuilding, engineering, and coal mining. Pop. (1972) 46,000.

WALL STREET. Thoroughfare in New York, so called from a stockade erected 1653. The stock exchange is on it, and it has come to be used as a synonym for stock dealing in the USA.

WALNUT. Tree (*Juglans regia*) probably originating in SE Europe, which may have been introduced to England by Roman times and to N America by the early colonists. It may reach 30m (100ft), and produces a full crop of nuts about a dozen years from planting: the timber is a favourite in furniture making.

WALPOLE, Horace, 4th earl of Orford (1717-97). English author. The son of Sir Robert Walpole, he sat in parliament as a Whig 1741-67, and succeeded to the peerage in 1791. He converted his house at Strawberry Hill into a Gothic castle, and by his novel, *The Castle of Otranto* (1765), set a fashion for 'tales of terror'. His letters are of interest.

WALPOLE, Sir Hugh (1884-1941). British novelist. B. in New Zealand, he was brought to England when 5, and in the F.W.W. served with the Red Cross in Russia, an experience reflected in *The Dark Forest* (1916). Best-known of his books are *The Cathedral* (1922) and *The Old Ladies* (1924), both set in the imaginary cathedral city of Polchester, and marked by a creation of atmosphere and hint of sadism peculiar to him. Less happy is the historical epic series the *Herries Chronicle* (1930-3) set in the Lake District.

WALPOLE, Sir Robert, 1st earl of Orford (1676-1745). British Whig Prime Minister. B. at Houghton, Norfolk, he entered parliament in 1701, and became Secretary at War 1708-10, Treasurer of the Navy 1710, and First Lord of the Treasury and Chancellor of the Exchequer 1715-17 and 1721-42. He is reckoned as the first PM. His rule has become proverbial for corruption. He encouraged trade by pursuing a pacific foreign policy, but in 1739 he was forced into war with Spain. On his resignation in 1742 he received an earldom.

WALPURGIS (val-), **St** (d. 779). English nun who preached Christianity in Germany. **W. Night,** the night before 1 May, her feast day, was associated with witches' sabbaths, and particularly with that held on the Brocken in the Harz mts.

WALRUS. Carnivorous marine mammal (*Odobenus rosmarus*) of the Arctic. It reaches a dozen feet in length, has webbed flippers, a bristly moustache, and large tusks from which ivory carvings are made.

WALSALL (wawl'sel). Town in West Midlands, England, 13km (8m) NW of Birmingham. Castings and tubes, electrical equipment, leather goods, etc., are produced. Pop. (1972) 183,000.

WALSINGHAM, Sir Francis (*c.* 1530-90). English politician. As Sec. of State from 1573, he advocated a strong anti-Spanish policy, and ran the govt's spy system.

WALTER, Hubert (d. 1205). Archbishop of Canterbury 1193-1205. As justiciar 1193-8 he ruled England during Richard I's absence and introduced the offices of coroner and justice of the peace.

WALTER, John (1739-1812). British newspaper editor, founder of *The Times.* Outstanding contributors to the development of the paper were his son JOHN W. II (1776-1847) and grandson John W. III (1818-94).

WALTER, Lucy (*c.* 1630-58). Englishwoman, mistress of Charles II, whom she met while a Royalist refugee at The Hague in 1648. Her son was the duke of Monmouth.

WALTHER VON DER VOGELWEIDE (vah'lter fon der fōg'elvīde) (*c.* 1170-*c.* 1230). German poet, greatest of the Minnesinger. Of noble birth, he lived in his youth at the Austrian ducal court in Vienna, adopting a wandering life after the death of his patron in 1198. His lyrics deal esp. with love, but also with religion and politics.

WALTON, Izaak (1593-1683). English author. B. at Stafford, he settled in London as an ironmonger, and wrote short biographies of Donne, Hooker, George Herbert, etc., and the classic *Compleat Angler* (1653).

WALTON, Sir William Turner (1902–83). British composer. B. in Oldham, he was ed. at the Cathedral Choir School and Christ Church, Oxford. Among his works are *Façade* (1923) to words by Edith Sitwell, later produced as a ballet; a viola concerto; the oratorio *Belshazzar's Feast*; 2 symphonies (1935 and 1960); a violin concerto (1939); a sonata for violin and pianoforte (1949) and variations on a theme by Hindemith (1963). He also composed film

WAR. The Spanish Civil War marked the beginning of modern warfare, in which bombing from the air, including both civilian and military targets, put the entire population of the contending countries in the front line. Picasso's 'Guernica', painted in Paris in 1937, is the symbol of this transformation. Formerly on extended loan to MOMA, NY, it was returned to Spain in 1980.

music, for *Henry V, Hamlet* and *Richard III,* which he estab. as an important form for composition. OM 1967.

WALVIS BAY. Chief port of SW Africa, a detached part of Cape Prov. from 1878, but admin. with SW Africa from 1922 until reincorporated in South Africa in 1977. It handles uranium from Rössing *c.* 65 km (40 m) inland. Area 1,124 sq.km (434 sq.m); pop. (1971) 17,000.

WA'MPUM. Cylindrical beads hand-ground from sea shells and formerly used as currency and in decoration by North American Indians of the NE Woodlands.

WANDERING JEW. A Jew who, according to legend, insulted Christ on His way to Calvary, and was condemned to wander about the world until His second coming. Sometimes he is called Ahasuerus.

WANGANUI (wong-ganoo′-i). City, port and airport in North Island, New Zealand, on the W. river. It makes textiles and clothing. Pop. (1979) 39,800.

WANKIE. Town in Zimbabwe, SE of Livingstone, with rich coal deposits. Pop. (1977) 32,000.

WANTAGE. Market town in Berks, England, birthplace of King Alfred. Pop. (1971) *c.* 6,000.

WAPITI. Species of deer (*Cervus canadensis*), native of N America. It is reddish-brown in colour and *c.* 1.5m (5ft) in height.

WAR. Conflict of arms between nations; between parties within a state, as in civil war; or, very frequently in modern times, between a small element within the state (which may be in receipt of foreign aid) against the state, as in guerrilla war. The aim is usually to inflict maximum damage on the enemy with minimum damage to the attacker, hence there is a constant tendency to increase the striking power, and range of weapons. The foot soldier gives way to the mounted warrior, the cavalry to the tank; primitive hand weapons are succeeded in turn by bows and arrows, guns, cannon, and rocket missiles; and in the intellectual field, shouted abuse becomes the sophisticated weapon of psychological warfare, using radio and television. The basic destructive aim, however, may be modified by the wish to keep the enemy alive as slave labour and to take over his assets of goods and territory in usable condition. These latter considerations were often ignored in the ancient world, e.g. the poverty of southern Italy is said still in some degree to arise from the terrible destruction of the civil wars of the Roman period. Today the problem is much greater, since nuclear or biological/chemical warfare (qq.v.) could eliminate both the combatants and the rest of the world pop., together with the very conditions under which any life can exist. Scarcely less terrifying is the prospect of 'true' environmental warfare in which rain, fog, hurricane, lightning, earthquakes, etc., would be manipulated against an enemy, e.g. the attempts by the USA to make the Ho Chi Minh trails unusable by heavy induced rainfall in the Vietnam War. So far the erratic behaviour of the 'normal' world climate has rendered it difficult to judge success or failure in this field.

The intermittent Cold War of the 1950s and 1960s in the West was an immediate reaction to the prospect of total destruction, i.e. the concentrated use of all means (espec. propaganda and economic competition) short of direct force to achieve the usual aims of war. However, by the 1970s the use of major 'conventional' (as against nuclear) force in the East, where it had never altogether ceased, moved back towards the West, e.g. the Battle of Sinai (1973) and the Angola campaign (1975-6), and a writer such as Solzhenitsyn could maintain that the 'Third World War' has already been lost, in a series of defeats in diplomacy and on the battlefield, by the free world. In the 1970s and 1980s the flexibility and precision of the new electronically-controlled conventional weaponry was being combined with the power of the nuclear arm. The USA led the field with the development of the cruise missile and the neutron bomb (*see* NEUTRON). There was also an increasing use of women in the modern army, not only in medical and communications duties where they had traditionally been used, but in a combat role.

Since man is the only species unthreatened by a natural predator, it has been argued that W. is a necessity for the 'survival of the fittest', and that it spurs the human race to technical advance, e.g. the space programme which arose from the German development of the V2.

WA'RATAH. Australian genus of trees and shrubs of the Proteaceae family, *Telopea speciosissima* bears large heads of crimson flowers in crimson bracts.

WARBECK, Perkin (*c.* 1474-99). Flemish pretender to the English throne. Claiming to be Richard, brother of Edward V, he led a rising against Henry VII in 1497, and was hanged after attempting escape from the Tower.

WARBLER. Two families of song birds, the Old World Muscicapidae and the New World Parulidae. Small, insectivorous birds, generally with plain plumage; species found in Britain incl. the whitethroat, blackcap, garden W. (*Sylvia*); the chiff-chaff, wood and willow Ws. (*Phylloscopus*); the reed and sedge Ws. (*Acrocephalus*); and the goldcrest (*Regulus*). The American Ws. are brighter and more closely allied to the Tanagers.

WAR CRIMES. The United Nations War Crimes Commission was set up in 1943 to investigate German atrocities against Allied nationals, and at the Foreign Ministers' conference in Moscow it was agreed that criminals should be tried at the place of their crimes. For the trial of major criminals *see* NUREMBERG TRIALS. Major Japanese criminals were tried before the International Military Tribunal in Tokyo, and others by the legal section of the Allied supreme command.

WARD, Artemus. Pseudonym of American humorist Charles Farrar Browne (1834-67). B. at Waterford (Maine), he achieved great popularity with comic writings such as *Artemus Ward: His Book, Artemus Ward: His book of Goaks, etc.*

WARD, Barbara (1914-81). British economist. She became pres. of the Inst. for Environment and Development in 1973. She m. Sir Robert Jackson in 1950 and in 1976 received a life peerage as Baroness Jackson of Wadsworth. Her books incl. *Policy for the West* (1951) and *The Widening Gap* (1971).

WARD, Mrs Humphry (1851-1920). British novelist, *née* Arnold, who became well known under her married name for serious didactic books, e.g. *Robert Elsmere* (1888), a study of religious doubt. She was a niece of M. Arnold (q.v.) and an opponent of women's emancipation.

WARD, Sir Leslie (1851-1922). British caricaturist, famous under the pseudonym 'Spy' for his caricatures in *Vanity Fair.*

WARE. Market town, Herts, England, on the Lea, 32km (20m) N of London, best known for the 'Great Bed of Ware' (mentioned by Shakespeare and now in the V. and A. Museum). Surgical goods, plastics, etc. are made. Pop. *c.* 10,000.

WARHOL, Andy (1931–87). American artist. B. in Pittsburgh, of Czech immigrant parents, he studied at the Carnegie Inst. of Technology, and worked as a commercial artist 1950-60. He then led the Pop Art movement with stylized reproductions of Campbell's soup tins, stills of Marilyn Monroe, etc. and from 1963 made films such as *Flesh,* which came under the censor.

WARLOCK, Peter. Pseudonym of British composer Philip Heseltine (1894-1930). B. in London, he composed about 100 exquisite songs, a few orchestral pieces, and 'The Curlew' for tenor and chamber orchestra, and under his own name wrote books on musical subjects and ed. old English music.

WARM SPRINGS. US health resort in Georgia, *c.* 65km (40m) NE of Columbus. F. D. Roosevelt, a victim of poliomyelitis, went to W.S. to recover in 1921, revisited it a number of times and d. there at the Little White House, now preserved as a museum. Pop. (1970) 523.

WARNER, Rex (1905-). British author. Making his début with *Poems* (1937), he has produced translations - Euripides, Aeschylus, Xenophon, Plutarch and St Augustine - and a varied original output incl. novels *The Young Caesar* and *Imperial Caesar* (1958-60) and *Pericles the Athenian* (1963). He was Univ. Prof. at the Univ. of Connecticut 1964-74.

WAR OFFICE. Govt dept. formerly controlling British military affairs. The board of Ordnance, which existed in the 14th cent., was absorbed into the War Dept after the Crimean War and the whole named the W.O. In 1964 its essential core became a subordinate branch of the newly estab. Min. of Defence.

WARRANT OFFICER. Rank between commissioned and non-commissioned officers in the British Army, and the highest non-commissioned rank in ground trades of the RAF and the RAF regiment.

WARREN, Earl (1891-1974). American lawyer. Attorney-Gen. of California 1939-43 and gov. of the state 1949-53, he was Chief Justice of the Supreme Court 1953-69. Under him a body of liberal legal rulings, notably in civil rights, was handed down.

WARRINGTON. Town in Cheshire, England, on the Mersey, 22km (14m) E of Liverpool. Designed for development as a 'new town' in 1969, its industries incl. the making of wire and other metal goods, chemicals, and brewing. Pop. (1972) 130,000.

WA'RRNAMBOUL. Port nr the mouth of Hopkins r., SW Victoria, Australia, with dairy and other farming exports. Pop. (1976) 20,200.

WARRUMBU'NGLE RANGE. Range of volcanic origin in NSW, Australia. The name (Aboriginal 'broken-up small mtns') indicate the scenic beauty which has made it a nat. park since 1953. It incl. Siding Spring Mtn (q.v.) at 859m (2,817 ft) the site of an observatory and the Breadknife, a 90m (300ft) high rock only 150cm (5ft) wide; the highest point is Mt Exmouth 1,228 m (4,028 ft).

WARSAW. Cap. of Poland on the Vistula, 520km (325m) E of Berlin. It is terraced above the river. The anc. city was virtually destroyed during the S.W.W., but with the help of old paintings, etc., was reconstructed on the same lines. W. dates from the 13th cent.; it replaced Cracow as cap. in 1595. It has suffered a number of sieges; in the S.W.W. it fell to the Germans 27 Sept. 1939; there was an heroic but abortive rising of its citizens against the German occupiers on 1 Aug. 1944. W. was not liberated until 17 Jan. 1945. Pop. (1978) 1,532,000. The *Warsaw Treaty* (1955) signed by USSR, Albania (excl. 1962), Bulgaria, Czechoslovakia, E Germany, Hungary, Poland and Romania, estab. a 20-yr alliance on NATO lines.

WARSHIP. A fighting ship armed and manned for war. The battleship, supreme at the beginning of the 20th cent., lost ground during the F.W.W. with the development of submarine attack and was rendered obsolete in the S.W.W. with the growth of long-range air attack. The large-scale aircraft carrier was also temporarily out of favour, as too vulnerable, until the resumption of building, espec. by the USSR in the late 1970s and 1980s.

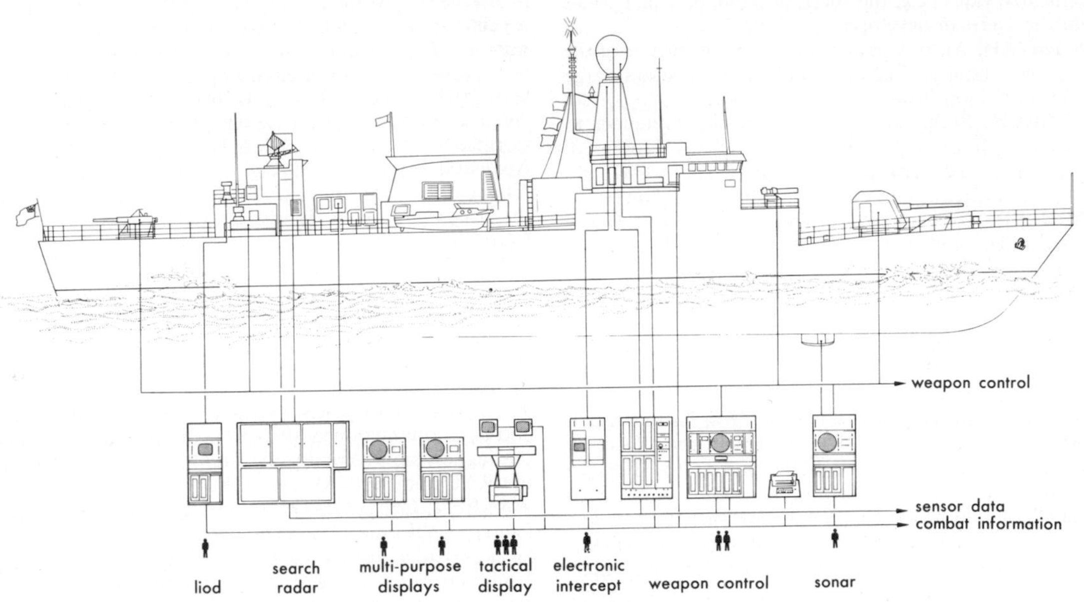

WARSHIP. The modern warship carries three types of sensor system: (1) radar for surface-search and tracking, navigation, air surveillance, and indication of targets to weapon control systems; (2) sonar for detection of surface and sub-surface targets; and (3) optronic (liod - *l*ightweight *o*ptronic *d*etector) for processing the optical contrast of a target against its background, as viewed by a television or infra-red camera. The tactical information thus collected is then processed by computer and presented in logical form to the command through the combat information system, which at the same time collects information from other fleet units, as well as distributing its own data to them. Finally, weapon control systems guide the selected weapons most efficiently to the targets. *Courtesy of Signaal*

WARSAW. The capital is rich in fine buildings, which have been carefully restored even when almost totally destroyed during the Second World War. This is the Lazienki Palace. *Photo: Courtesy of 'Orbis' Travel*

Meanwhile, land-based naval attack aircraft proved inadequate, and in the earlier 1970s the concept of the mini-carrier evolved, using both vertical take-off aircraft, such as the Harrier jump-jet and helicopters with a wide range, such as the Sea King. The Soviet Union has ships of this kind carrying as many as 30 helicopters, and the British navy has 'through deck cruisers' designed for the same purpose, just as the US Navy has 'sea control ships'. The helicopters are equipped with 'dunking' sonar, torpedoes and depth charges. These carriers and other surface ships are increasingly driven by gas turbines, steam turbines being phased out, and include guided missile destroyers and multi-purpose frigates. The latter carry such varied equipment as guns, depth charge mortars, mine-laying rails, variable depth sonar, torpedoes, air defence missiles, and surface to surface missiles. Smaller auxiliaries include mine-hunters for countering blockade of home ports, espec. the base ports of submarines, and in their most modern form are made of glass-reinforced plastic. However, the prime role in future naval warfare will be that of the carriers and the submarine. The latter, increasingly nuclear-powered, fall into two classes, the specially-designed, almost silent attack submarine, intended to release its fast torpedoes and missiles at comparatively close range, and the patrolling submarines with guided missiles of such long range that the submarine itself is virtually undetectable to the enemy. Nuclear power for surface warships still presents safety problems.

WART. Unsightly protuberance composed of a local overgrowth of skin. The common W. (Verruca vulgaris) is due to a virus infection, and usually disappears spontaneously within 2 years, but can be treated with peeling applications or topical liquid nitrogen.

WART HOG. Two species of African wild swine (*Phacochoerus aethiopicus* and *P. africanus*) which have enormous heads with a bristly mane, fleshy pads beneath the eyes, and 4 large tusks.

WARTON, Joseph (1722-1800). English poet, headmaster of Winchester 1766-93, whose verse and *Essay on the Writings and Genius of Pope* (1756-82) marked an 'anti-classical' reaction. His brother, Thomas W. (1728-90), was prof. of poetry at Oxford 1757-67 and pub. the first *History of English Poetry* (1774-81).

WARWICK, Richard Neville, earl of, called the Kingmaker (1428-71). English statesman. During the Wars of the Roses he fought at first on the Yorkist side, and was largely responsible for placing Edward IV on the throne. Having quarrelled with him, he restored Henry VI in 1470, but was defeated and killed by Edward at Barnet.

WARWICKSHIRE. Midland co. of England, whose main rivers are the Avon, to the N of which lies the wooded region or 'Forest of Arden' known to Shakespeare. In the local govt re-organization of 1974, W. lost the industrial area of Birmingham and Coventry to the new co. of W Midlands. There is coal in the NE. The admin. HQ is Warwick, which has a 14th cent. castle and univ. (1965), on the Avon, pop. (1973) 18,000. Other towns incl. Leamington Spa, Rugby and Stratford upon Avon. Area 1,980 sq.km (765 sq.m); pop. (1978) 469,500.

WASH, The. Rectangular bay of the North Sea in England between Norfolk and Lincoln. The coast is marshy. King John lost his baggage and treasure in the W., 1216.

WASHINGTON, Booker Taliaferro (*c.* 1859-1915). American Negro educationalist, who founded in 1881 Tuskegee Institute, a Negro co-educational college in Alabama. He wrote *Up from Slavery* (1901).

WASHINGTON, George (1732-99). 1st President of the USA. B. in Virginia, he distinguished himself as a soldier in campaigns against the French and Indians 1753-7, and was elected to the Virginia House of Burgesses. As a strong opponent of the British govt's policy, he sat in the Continental Congresses of 1774 and 1775, and on the outbreak of war was chosen C-in-C. For the course of the war *see* AMERICAN INDEPENDENCE, WAR OF. After the war he retired to his estate, Mount Vernon, but in 1787 he re-entered politics as president of the Constitutional Convention. He was elected President of the USA in 1789, and re-elected in 1793, but refused to serve a 3rd term, setting a precedent that was followed until 1940. Although he attempted to draw his ministers from all factions, his aristocratic outlook alienated Jefferson, with whose resignation in 1793 the 2-party system originated. In his farewell address (1796) W. maintained that the USA should avoid European quarrels and entangling alliances. He d. and was buried at Mount Vernon, Virginia. Washington's great grandfather, Colonel Augustine Warner of Virginia, is also the great-great-great-great-great-great-great-great-grandfather of Elizabeth II of the UK.

WASHINGTON. Pacific state of the USA, watered by the Columbia and its tributaries. Except for the SW and for the Great Plain of the Columbia r. to the E, nearly all W is mountainous. The Cascade Range runs parallel to the coast, and between Puget Sound and the Pacific are the Olympic Mts. The chief agricultural products are apples and other fruit, wheat, oats, etc. Cattle and sheep are bred. Industries incl. aircraft, ships, road transport vehicles; lumber and paper from extensive forests; processed food, chemicals, cement, and exploitation of zinc, uranium, lead, gold and silver. The cap. is Olympia; the largest towns are Seattle, Spokane, and Tacoma. W., which incl. Mt Rainier and Olympia National Parks, was admitted to the Union in 1889. Area 176,615 sq.km (68,191 sq.m); pop. (1970) 3,409,169.

WASHINGTON. Cap. of the USA, on the Potomac, coterminous with the Dist. of Columbia. The city is laid out according to a uniform plan made by Pierre L'Enfant, a French engineer officer - the first modern cap. city to be designed as such. An underground transport system began operation in 1976. Its many fine buildings incl. the Capitol, Lincoln Memorial, Washington Monument, White House with Blair House (the Presidential guest house) facing it, Supreme Court, Library of Congress, Pentagon (housing the War Department), National Gallery (1941) and Hirschhorn Museum (1974) for modern art, Folger Shakespeare Library, John F. Kennedy Center for the Performing Arts, Nat. Air and Space Museum (1976), Nat. Gallery of Art (1978), and the gothic Nat. Cathedral (1906-). W. was founded in 1790, and has been the federal cap. since 1800. In 1814 it was burnt by the British. Most of the permanent population consists of govt employees. Dulles Internat. Airport (1963) was designed by Eero Saarinen. Pop. (1970) 800,000; met. area 2,856,809.

WASHINGTON. The Capitol, built by William Thornton 1793–1827. The dome is surmounted by a statue of Freedom, and a statue of General Grant stands in the foreground. *Photo: Mireille Vautier*

WASHINGTON. Town on the r. Wear, Tyne and Wear, England, developed as a 'new town' from 1964 from the old village of W., home of George Washington's family. It

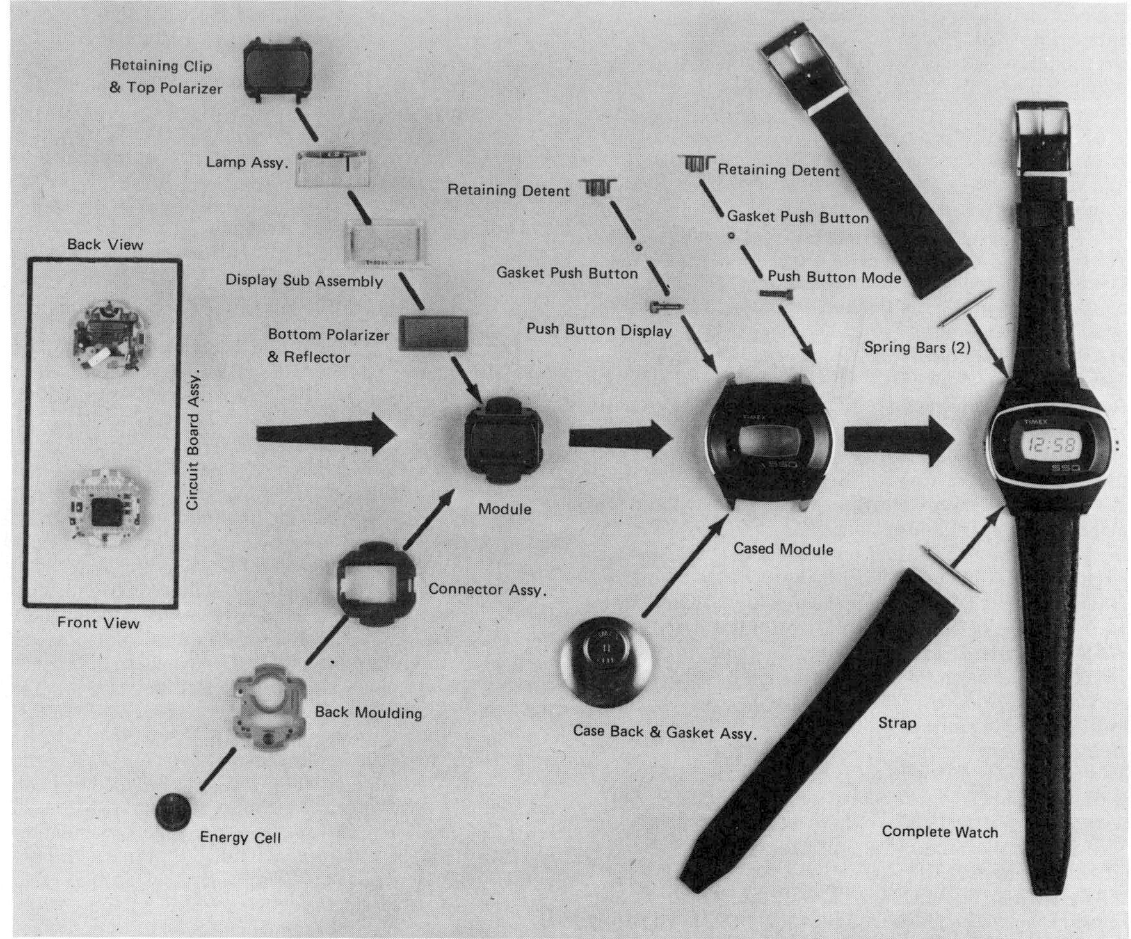

WATCH. A modern digital solid state watch, showing the component parts and the method of assembly. *Photo: Courtesy of Timex*

provides a new focus for industry in an area of declining coal-mining, and for Tyneside overspill. Pop. (1973) 35,000.

WASP. Name of certain stinging insects in the order Hymenoptera. Of the 290 British species, only a few are true Ws. (*Vespidae*); the rest are digger Ws. There are 7 British species of social Ws. in the genus *Vespa*, some nesting below ground, others in trees or bushes, and the largest being the hornet: all the others are solitary. Among social Ws. the queens devote themselves to egg-laying, the fertilized eggs producing female workers; the males arise from unfertilized eggs and have no sting. The larvae are fed on insects, but the mature insects feed mainly on fruit and sugar. In winter the fecundated queens hibernate, but the other Ws. die.

WASSERMANN (vahs'sermahn), **August von** (1866-1925). German prof. of medicine. B. at Bamberg, he became head of the department of experimental therapy and serum research at the Robert Koch Institute in Berlin in 1906 and, in 1913, director of the Kaiser Wilhelm Inst. there. In 1907 he discovered a sero-diagnosis of syphilis (W. reaction).

WATCH. A personally portable timepiece. Miniature sundials were the earliest form, the first true watches being developed in the 15th cent. when they were miniature clocks attached to the girdle. By the 18th cent. the mechanism had been perfected by inventors such as Thomas Tompion (1639-1713) and Thomas Earnshaw (1749-1829), but throughout the 19th cent. Ws. remained articles of value. In the 20th cent. increasing miniaturisation, mass production, and the need for accurate time-keeping in the F.W.W., led to the migration of the W. from the pocket to the wrist of everyman. Between the wars Ws. were given further refinements, e.g. made anti-magnetic, given shock resistance, or made self-winding, and after the S.W.W. came the electric W. in 1957. This had no mainspring, the mechanism being kept in motion by the mutual attraction of a permanent magnet and an electromagnet, which pushed the balance wheel. In the 1970s came the digital watch, in which all moving parts are dispensed with, a crystal oscillator being linked to digital counting and display circuits, and which may be so reduced in size that other elements, such as a calculator, may be incorporated with it in a single wrist-unit.

WATER (H_2O). A liquid, without colour, taste, or odour; an oxide of hydrogen. W. begins to freeze solid at 0°C and 32°F, and to boil at 100°C and 212°F. Liquid, it is virtually incompressible; frozen, it expands by 1/11th of its volume. 1m^3 weighs 1000 kg at 4°C, forming the unit of relative density. It has the highest known specific heat, and acts as an efficient solvent, particularly when hot. It takes the form of sea, rain, and vapour, and tempers and distributes the Sun's heat, and supports all forms of land and marine life. W. covers 70 per cent of the Earth's surface. Water supply in sparsely populated regions comes usually from natural springs, supplemented by pumps and wells. Urban sources are deep artesian wells, rivers and reservoirs, usually formed from enlarged lakes or dammed and flooded valleys, from which W. is conveyed by pipes, conduits and aqueducts (q.v.) to filter beds. By seeping through layers of shingle, gravel and sand, harmful organisms are removed, and the W. is then distributed (sometimes with such additions as chlorine or fluorine, qq.v.) by pumping or gravitation through mains and pipes. In towns, besides industrial demands, domestic and municipal (road-washing, sewage, etc.) needs account for *c.* 135 litres (30 galls) per head each day, and supplies are a pressing problem in dry, fast-developing areas such as California, and in coastal desert area, e.g. Arabia, desalination plants for sea water may be used. In distinction from heavy W. (q.v.), ordinary W. is sometimes referred to as 'light water'.

WATER-BUGS. Several families of aquatic hemipterous insects. They incl. the Hydrometridae (pond-skaters) and Notonectidae, of which the water-boatman is the chief member.

WATERBURY. City of Connecticut, USA, on the Naugatuck, dating from 1674. Clocks, watches, and brass and copper ware are manufactured. Pop. (1970) 108,000.

WATER-COLOUR PAINTING. Method of painting with pigments mixed with water. Known in China as early as the 3rd cent., the art as practised today developed in England, where it was the ideal medium for the expression of shifting vagaries of weather, in the 18th cent. Artists excelling in W.C.P. incl. Sandby, Cozens, Cotman, de Wint, Turner, Constable, Cox, Sargent, Marin, Steer, Cézanne, Signac, Dufy, Nolde, Klee, Paul and John Nash. The Royal Soc. of Painters in Water Colours was founded 1804.

The technique of W.C.P. requires great skill, since its transparency rules out over-painting, and many modern artists who would once have worked in this medium prefer the harsher effects of acrylic (q.v.), which, apart from its rapid drying, is easier to handle.

WATERCRESS. Perennial aquatic plant (*Nasturtium officinale*), found in Europe and Asia, and cultivated as a salad crop. It requires *c.* 4.5 million litres (1 million gallons) of running water daily per hectare (2.5 acres) in cultivation.

WATERFLEA. Aquatic crustaceans in the order Cladocera. The commonest species is *Daphnia pulex.*

WATERFORD. (1) Co. town and port of W county, Rep. of Ireland, on the Suir. Hand-made W. crystal glass (34 per cent lead content instead of the normal 24 per cent) made here until 1851 was revived from 1951. Pop. (1971) 32,000. (2) County of Munster, Rep. of Ireland watered by the Suir and Blackwater. The Comeragh and Monavallagh ranges rise in the N and centre. Cattle raising, brewing and distilling are carried on. Area 1,839 sq.km (710 sq.m); pop. (1971) 77, 315.

WATERGATE. A complex of flats, offices and a hotel beside the Potomac r., Washington, known as The Watergate, was the HQ of the Democratic Party during the 1972 US election. On 17 June five men were caught in these HQ with electronic eavesdropping equipment, and with two accomplices later arrested, were all found to have been paid by the Republican 'Committee for the Re-election of the President' (CREEP). Their trial and the subsequent sequence of disclosures led to the resignation of Nixon, the diminution of the presidential office, and the final abandonment of intervention in SE Asia.

WATERHOLE. In radio the frequency band 1,400-1,700 megahertz which incl. the spectral lines of the constituents of water, and hence the most likely to be used for radio signals from any creatures, with a water-based structure such as our own, who may exist in space. It is threatened with interference from navigational satellites, etc.

WATER LILY. Aquatic plants in the family Nymphaeaceae. The fleshy roots are embedded in the mud and the large round leaves float on the water. The beautiful flowers may be white, pink, yellow or blue: the white *Nymphaea alba* and yellow *Nuphar luteum* are common in Great Britain, and the *Victoria regia*, with leaves about 2m (6ft) in diameter, occurs in the Amazon. *See* LOTUS.

WATERLOO. Village 13km (8m) S of Brussels. Nearby, on 18 June 1815, Wellington defeated Napoleon. Wellington had 68,000 men, of whom 24,000 were British, the remainder being German, Dutch, and Belgian, and Napoleon 72,000. During the last stage of the battle Wellington was supported by the Prussians under Blücher.

WATERLOO CUP. The most important greyhound race in England, known as 'the courser's Derby', and named after the Waterloo Hotel, Liverpool, whose proprietor originated the race in 1836. It is held annually, usually in Feb.

WATFORD. Market town in Herts, England, on the Colne and Grand Union Canal. Industries incl. printing, brewing, flourmilling, and iron founding. Pop. (1974) 77,700.

WATSON, John Broadus. *See* BEHAVIOURISM.

WATSON-WATT, Sir Robert (Alexander) (1892-1973). British physicist. During a long career in govt service (1915-52), he proposed in 1935 a method of radiolocation of aircraft - later developed into radar - a key contribution to victory in the S.W.W.

WATT, James (1736-1819). Scottish engineer. B. at Greenock, he became mathematical instrument maker to Glasgow univ. in 1757. While repairing a model of Newcomen's steam engine in 1764, he devised an exterior condenser to eliminate the loss of power involved in the engine. Patented in 1769, the invention was applied to engines which W. and Boulton manufactured near Birmingham.

WATT. Electrical unit of power, named in honour of James Watt. In the m.k.s. system, it is work done at the rate of 1 joule or 10^7 erg per second, or the amount of energy expended per second by a current of 1 ampere under a p.d. of 1 volt. The power in Ws. is found by multiplying the current in amperes by the p.d. in volts.

WATTEAU (vahtō'), **Antoine** (1684-1721). French painter. B. in Valenciennes, he went to Paris in 1702, and under the influence of the Flemish genre painters painted scenes of tavern and of military life. He later became famous as a painter of the *fête galante*. He was admitted to the French Academy in 1717 and visited London in 1719.

WATTEAU. The first 'peintre des fêtes galantes', Watteau invokes half-real, half-dreamlike combinations of motifs derived from the theatre, the *bal costumé* and aristocratic country pastimes generally in pastoral settings. This is a detail from 'Fête in the Park'. *Photo: Courtesy of the Trustees of the Wallace Collection*

WATTLE. Name given in Australia, where the fluffy golden flowers are the national emblem, to certain species of Acacia (q.v.). Wonderfully adapted to drought conditions, the specially tough leaves further avoid loss of water through transpiration by turning their edges only to the direct rays of the sun. The Ws. are used for tannin and fencing.

WATTS, George Frederick (1817-1904). British artist. B. in London, he studied in the RA Schools. In 1864 he m. Ellen Terry: later the marriage was dissolved. In 1867 he was elected RA. He painted allegorical, biblical, and classical subjects, and portraits, many of which are in the National Portrait Gallery, and others in the Watts art gallery at Compton, nr Guildford. As a sculptor he executed 'Physical Energy' for Rhodes' grave in S Africa, and a replica in Kensington Gardens.

WATTS, Isaac (1674-1748). British Nonconformist churchman and hymn-writer. He wrote 'O God, our help in ages past', and other hymns.

WATTS-DUNTON, Walter Theodore (1832-1914). British writer, author of *Aylwin* (1898) a novel of gypsy life, poems and critical work. He was a close friend of Swinburne, who shared his house at Putney for many years, Rossetti and Borrow, cf. *Old Familiar Faces* (1915).

WAUGH, Evelyn Arthur St John (1903-66). British novelist. Ed. at Oxford, he later became an RC and pub. studies of Edmund Campion and Ronald Knox. During the S.W.W. he served with distinction. His novels incl. satirical studies such as *Decline and Fall* (1928), *Vile Bodies, Put Out More Flags,* and *The Loved One* (1948); also *Brideshead Revisited* (1945), a serious work. His brother, **Alec W.** (1898-1981), was ed. at Sherborne and Sandhurst. He served in the army 1917-18 and also 1939-45. Among his works are *The Loom of Youth* (1917), *No Truce with Time,* and *Island in the Sun* (1956). **Auberon W.** (1940-), son of Evelyn, is a Tory and RC, and has written witty novels incl. *Consider the Lilies* (1968).

WAVE. In the oceans the formation of a ridge or swell by wind, etc. Freak or 'episodic' Ws. form under certain weather conditions at certain times of the year, travelling long distances in the Atlantic, Indian and Pacific oceans. They become extremely dangerous when they reach the shallow waters of the continental shelves at 100 fathoms (200 m), espec. when they meet currents, e.g. the Agulhas Current to the E of South Africa, and the Gulf Stream. A wave height of 34 m (112 ft) has been recorded. They are considered responsible for the sudden disappearance, without distress calls, of many sound ships. *See also* TSUNAMI.

WAVELL, Archibald, 1st earl (1883-1950). British field marshal. He served in the F.W.W. and was appointed C-in-C Middle East in July 1939. He conducted the N African war against Italy 1940-1, and achieved notable successes there as well as in Ethiopia. W. was transferred as C-in-C India in July 1941, and succeeded Lord Linlithgow as viceroy (1943-7), being created visct in 1943.

WAVERLEY, John Anderson, 1st visct W. (1882-1958). British administrator. He organized Civil Defence for the S.W.W., becoming Home Sec. and Min. for Home Security in 1939 (the nationally distributed home outdoor - Anderson - air-raid shelters were named after him). He was Chancellor of the Exchequer 1943-5.

WAXWING. Family of birds (*Ampelidae*) found in the northern hemisphere. The Bohemian W. (*Ampelis garrulus*) is greyish-brown above with a reddish-chestnut crest, black streak at the eye, and variegated wings with 'wax tips'.

WAYNE, Anthony. *See* FORT WAYNE.

WAYNE, John (1907-79). American film actor, né Marion Morrison, and nicknamed 'duke', from the name of a dog he once owned. B. in Iowa, he became doyen of the cowboy world, and in 1969 won an Oscar as Rooster Cogburn in *True Grit.*

WAZIRISTAN. Tribal territory of Pakistan, on the border with Afghanistan. The inhabitants, Waziris and Mahsuds, are warlike, and are a source of trouble to Pakistan, as formerly to British India.

WAZYK (va'zik), **Adam** (1905-). Polish writer. B. in Warsaw, he made his name with *Poem for Adults* (1955), a protest against the régime which preceded the fall of the Stalinists in 1956. In 1957 he resigned with others from the party, disappointed in Gomulka's illiberalism. He is also a novelist and playwright.

WEALD (wēld). District of SE England between the N and S Downs, comprising parts of Kent, Sussex, and Surrey. Its name is from an Anglo-Saxon word meaning wooded tract, but most of the trees which once covered the W. were cut down as fuel for the olden Sussex ironworks. It is occupied by grazing land, hop gardens, and orchards.

WEASEL. Carnivorous mammal in the family Mustelidae, feeding mainly on mice, voles and rats. The common W. (*Mustela nivalis*) of Europe and Asia has an elongated body, short legs and tail. The fur is red-brown above and white beneath, but in winter in cold climates is wholly white, acting as camouflage against snow. There are several American species.

WEATHER. *See* METEOROLOGY.

WEAVING. The production of fabric by means of a loom. It is a craft of world-wide distribution since ancient times, and the products of Egypt and Assyria can compare with modern output. The basic process is the interlacing at right angles of longitudinal threads (the warp) and cross wise threads (the weft), the latter being carried across from one side of the loom to the other by the shuttle. Handlooms may be horizontal or vertical - the latter being the type which has developed industrially in the West - and are still used, e.g. in the manufacture of tweeds in the British Isles. Of great importance in the hand-loom era was the Jacquard machine, the last in a series of inventions for producing complicated designs, which was perfected in the early 19th cent. The power-loom (1786) was essentially the invention of the English clergyman, Edmund Cartwright. There have been many subsequent improvements, but one of the hindrances to yet further increased speed has been the time taken by the passage of the shuttle, which has been partly overcome by the use of water and air jet insertion methods, and by the development in the 1970s of 'multi-phase' looms in which weft insertion occurs in continuous waves across the machine, rather than a single weft being inserted at a time. *See* TEXTILES.

WEAVING. The first looms ever made by primitive man must have looked very much like the one being used here by a Dogon weaver in a Mali village. *Photo: Werner Forman Archive*

WEBB, Sir Aston (1849-1930). British architect, designer of the new front of Buckingham Palace; Admiralty Arch; the chief section of the Victoria and Albert Mus.; and Britannia Royal Naval College.

WEBB, Mary (1882-1927). British novelist. B. in Shropshire, she wrote of country life and characters, e.g. *Precious Bane,* which became known through a recommendation by Earl (Stanley) Baldwin.

WEBB, Sidney. *See* PASSFIELD, LORD.

WEBBER, Andrew Lloyd (1948-). British composer. His musicals, with lyrics by Tim Rice, incl. *Joseph and the Amazing Technicolour Dreamcoat* (1968), *Jesus Christ Superstar* (1970), and *Evita* (1978), based on the life of Eva Perón.

WEBER (veh'ber), **Carl Maria von** (1786-1826). German composer. B. in Eutin, he became kapellmeister at Breslau (1804-6), Prague (1813-16), and Dresden (1816). The originator of the romantic opera, he composed *Abu Hassan* (1811), *Der Freischütz* (1820), *Euryanthe* (1823), as well as instrumental and pianoforte works. He d. during a visit to London where he produced his opera *Oberon,* written for the Covent Garden theatre.

WEBER, Max (1864-1920). German economist. His *The Protestant Ethic and the Spirit of Capitalism* argued that the enemy was not socialism or capitalism, but the bureaucratization inevitable in both.

WEBERN (veh'bern), **Anton von** (1883-1945). Austrian composer. A pupil of Schoenberg, he adopted his 12-note technique, and produced works of extreme brevity, e.g. his oratorio *Das Augenlicht* and songs to words by Stefan George and Rilke. He was killed by a stray shot during the Allied occupation of Austria.

WEBSTER, Daniel (1782-1852). American statesman and orator. B. in New Hampshire, he sat in the House of Representatives from 1813, and in the Senate from 1827, at first as a Federalist and later as a Whig. He became Sec. of State 1841-3 and 1850-2, and negotiated the Ashburton Treaty (1842) which fixed the Maine-Canada boundary.

WEBSTER, John (*c.* 1580-*c.* 1625). English dramatist. He wrote *The White Devil* and *The Duchess of Malfi,* usually considered the greatest English tragedies outside Shakespeare, and the tragi-comedy *The Devil's Law Case.*

WEBSTER, Noah (1758-1843). American lexicographer, b. in Connecticut. His *American Dictionary of the English Language* (1828) standardized American deviations from English spelling.

WEDDELL, James (1787-1834). British Antarctic explorer. In 1823 he reached 75° S lat. and 35° W long. The W. Sea is named after him. This cuts into the Antarctic continent SE of Cape Horn, and much of it is covered with thick pack ice for most of the year; area 8,000,000 sq.km (3,000,000 sq.m).

WEDEKIND (veh'dekint), **Frank** (1864-1918). German dramatist. B. at Hanover, he became in succession journalist, advertising agent, book-keeper to a circus, and actor and producer. He achieved fame with *Frühlings Erwachen, Der Marquis von Keith, Die Büchse der Pandora,* etc. Many of his writings gave offence on account of alleged pornographic tendencies.

WEDGWOOD, Dame Cicely Veronica (1910-). British historian. Dau. of Sir Ralph W. (1874-1956), the railway administrator, she is an authority on the 17th cent. and has pub. fine studies of *Cromwell* (1939), *The Trial of Charles I* (1964), etc. Created DBE 1968, she was awarded the OM 1969.

WEDGWOOD, Josiah (1730-95). British potter. B. at Burslem, Staffs, where he estab. his factory (Etruria) in 1759, he is most celebrated for his jasper ware, a type of unglazed porcelain with the general properties of basalt, capable of being coloured throughout (blue, green or black), with the design in bas-relief in white. From 1775 he employed Flaxman as a designer, but many fine portrait medallions were the work of his chief modeller William

Hackwood. Very famous is his copy of the Portland Vase. Modern W. ware is an important British export.

WEDGWOOD. The annalist of the 'Five Towns', Arnold Bennett, fittingly portrayed on a Wedgwood plaque. *Photo: Courtesy of Wedgwood*

WEEVER. Genus of fish (*Trachinus*) found off European coasts, the greater W. (*T. draco*) and lesser W. (*T. vipera*) off Britain. They bury themselves in sand, and bathers may be wounded by treading on their poison-charged dorsal spines.

WEEVIL. Division of beetles (Rhynchophora) in the order Coleoptera. The head has a prolonged rostrum, which in the female is used to bore a hole in which to place the eggs. The larvae are white; the adult beetles of *Phyllobius* and *Polydrusus*, the common British genera, are bright green. They feed on vegetable matter. In America the granary W. (*Calandra granaria*) attacks grain, the cotton-boll W. (*Anthonomus grandis*) damages cotton crops.

WEGENER (vāg'-), **Alfred** (1880-1930). German polar explorer and geophysicist. He made 3 expeditions to Greenland and d. on a fourth, but is chiefly remembered for 'W.'s Hypothesis', expounded in *Origin of Continents and Oceans* (1915). *See* CONTINENT.

WEIGHTLESSNESS. The condition whereby there is no gravitational force acting on a body, either because gravitational force is cancelled out by equal and opposite acceleration, or the body is so far outside a planet's gravitational field that it exerts no force upon it.

WEIGHTS AND MEASURES. *See* APPENDIX.

WEIHAI (wā'hī). Port in Shantung, China; also a commercial centre. It produces textiles, rubber articles, matches, soap, vegetable oils. It was leased to Britain 1898-1930, during which time it was a naval and coaling station. It was occupied by the Japanese 1938-45. Weihaiwei, its name until 1949, means awe-inspiring seafort. Pop. (1973) 250,000.

WEIL (vīl), **Simone** (1909-43). French author. Of well-to-do Jewish Parisian family, she was for a time a schoolmistress, then plunged into working-class life, tried to help the Republicans in Spain and during the S.W.W. worked briefly for de Gaulle in London. She d. in an English sanatorium. Apart from essays, her works (advocating political quietism) were posthumously pub. incl. *The Need for Roots* (1952), *Waiting on God* (1951) and her notebooks in 1956.

WEILL (vīl), **Kurt** (1900-50). American composer. B. in Germany, he wrote chamber and orchestral music, but is best known for the operas in which he collaborated with Brecht (q.v.), e.g. *The Threepenny Opera* (1928) (an adaptation of John Gay's *The Beggar's Opera*), with its song 'Mack the Knife', and *The Rise and Fall of the City of Mahagonny* (1930), which attacks social corruption and caused a riot at its première in Leipzig. He tried to evolve a new form of musical theatre, using subjects with a contemporary relevance and the simplest possible musical means. With the rise of the Nazis he left Germany for the US, where he wrote a number of successful scores for Broadway. Other important works incl. the opera *Die Burgschaft* (1931). He was m. to the singer Lotte Lenya (q.v.).

WEIMAR (vī'mahr). Town of Erfurt district, E Germany, on the Ilm 21km (13m) E of Erfurt. Before 1918 it was cap. of the grand-duchy of Saxe-Weimar, and was subsequently cap. of Thuringia. In the late 18th and early 19th cents. it was a great cultural centre and the residence of Goethe, Schiller, and Herder. Pop. (1970) 64,500.

WEIMAR REPUBLIC. Name for the republican régime in Germany 1918-33, which was destroyed by Hitler and his followers. It took its name from the city where in Feb. 1919 a constituent assembly met to draw up a democratic constitution.

WEINBERG, Steven (1933-). American physicist. B. in the Bronx, NY, he is best-known for his 1967 paper on the unification of the weak and electromagnetic forces, 2 of the 4 fundamental forces of nature. The same theory was arrived at independently by Abdus Salam, and involved the prediction of a new interaction (the neutral current), which was discovered in 1973, and required the presence of 'charm'. In 1979 they shared a Nobel prize with Sheldon Glashow for their work.

WEINBERGER (vīn'berger), **Jaromir** (1896-1967). Czech composer. B. at Prague he taught composition in New York and Europe. His *Schwanda the Bagpiper* is the most successful of several operas.

WEIZMANN (vīts'-), **Chaim** (1874-1952). Zionist leader - he was Pres. of Israel 1948-52 - and chemist. B. in Russia, he became a naturalized British subject, and as director of the Admiralty laboratories 1916-19 discovered a process for the manufacture of acetone. He conducted the negotiations leading up to the Balfour Declaration.

WELDING. The making of a union between pieces of metal or non-metal, at faces rendered plastic or liquid by heat or by pressure or both. Forge W., employed by blacksmiths since early times, was the only method available until near the end of the 19th cent. The principal modern processes are gas and electric-arc W., in which the heat from a gas flame or an arc melts the faces to be joined and additional 'filler metal' is usually added; and resistance W. in which the weld is formed by a combination of resistance heating from an electric current, and pressure. Recent developments incl. electric-slag, electron-beam, high energy laser, and the still experimental radio wave energy beam W. processes.

WELE'NSKY, Sir Roy (1907-). Rhodesian statesman. B. in Salisbury, S Rhodesia, he became a noted trade union worker among the railwaymen, and was heavyweight boxing champion of the Rhodesias. He succeeded Malvern as PM (1956-63).

WELHAVEN (vel'hahven), **Johan Sebastian Cammermeyer** (1807-73). Norwegian poet. B. at Bergen, he was prof. of philosophy at Christiania 1839-68. A supporter of the Dano-Norwegian culture, he is one of the greatest Norwegian masters of poetic form. His works incl. the satiric *Norges Daemring* (1934), songs based on folklore, etc.

WELLAND SHIP CANAL. Waterway (40km/25m) in Canadian terr., cutting through the Niagara peninsula to link Lakes Erie and Ontario (1932, replacing an earlier canal, 1832).

WELLES, Orson (1915-). American actor, producer and director. In 1937, he collaborated in founding the Mercury Theater, NY, where his productions incl. a modern dress version of *Julius Caesar.* In 1938 his realistic broadcast presentation of H. G. Wells' *The War of the Worlds* caused panic among listeners. In 1940 he wrote, produced, directed and starred in *Citizen Kane,* his first film, and other film roles incl. the character of Harry Lime in *The Third Man* (1950); his film of Kafka's book *The Trial* appeared in 1963.

WELLESLEY, Richard Colley, marquess (1760-1842). British statesman. The brother of the duke of Wellington, he was Gov.-Gen. of India 1798-1805, and by his victories over the Mahrattas greatly extended the territory under British rule. He was For. Sec. 1809-12, and Lord Lieutenant of Ireland 1821-8 and 1833-4.

WELLESZ (vel'ess), **Egon** (1885-1974). Austrian composer and musicologist. He specialized in the history of Byzantine, Renaissance and modern music, and on leaving Austria settled in Oxford, where he was reader in Byzantine music 1948-56. His compositions incl. operas such as *Alkestis*; symphonies, notably the 5th (1956), ballet music, and a series of string quartets; and his writings incl. a biography of Schoenberg, and several studies of Byzantine music.

WELLINGTON, Arthur Wellesley, 1st duke of (1769-1852). British soldier and Tory statesman. B. either in Meath or Dublin, Ireland, he was ed. at Eton, and in 1787 entered the army. Going to India in 1796, he was a major-general by 1802, and achieved victories over the Mahrattas at Assaye and Argaum in 1803. These victories and his negotiation of the peace of 1803 earned him a knighthood, and he returned to England in 1805, but it was as lt.-general and commander of the forces in the Iberian Peninsula (*see* PENINSULAR WAR) that he estab. his reputation. He defeated the French at Vimeiro, but was superseded and recalled, although he again received the command in 1809. He was made visct W. in 1809, earl and marquess of W. in 1812, and having expelled the French from Spain in 1814 was made duke of W. He was appointed ambassador to Paris (1814-15), took part in the Congress of Vienna, and, following Napoleon's escape from Elba, defeated him at Quatre-Bras and at Waterloo (1815). This last victory made him the most influential man in Europe; he again took part in the Vienna Congress, where he opposed the dismemberment of France, and supported the restoration of the Bourbons. He commanded the army of occupation until 1818. As Tory PM 1828-30 he was not a success: he was forced against his will to concede Catholic emancipation, while his opposition to parliamentary reform made him extremely unpopular for a time. He was For. Sec. 1834-5, and was a member of the cabinet 1841-6. He held the office of C-in-C of the forces at various times from 1827, and held it for life from 1842. *See* APSLEY HOUSE.

WELLINGTON. Capital of New Zealand, in N Island, on Cook Strait. It was founded in 1840 by Col. Gibbon Wakefield, as the first settlement of the New Zealand Co., and rises on hills in a fertile volcanic region. The residence of the Governor-General and the seat of govt since 1865, it possesses the Houses of Parliament, Victoria univ., the national museum, and - as the seat of an Anglican bp and an RC archbp - 2 cathedrals. There is an excellent harbour, an airport, and good railway communications. Among its manufactures are woollen goods, soap, shoes, meat, and bricks. Pop. Greater W. (1975) 356,660.

WELLINGTON. Alongside the original Parliament building, the new assembly hall, opened by the Queen in 1977. The preliminary design was prepared by Sir Basil Spence, and the work completed by a New Zealand government architect.
Photo: Courtesy of The Evening Post, Wellington

WELLS, Herbert George (1866-1946). British author. B. at Bromley, Kent, son of a professional cricketer, he took his degree at the Royal College of Science, S Kensington, taught for some years, and then made his name in science fiction with *The Time Machine* (1895), *The Invisible Man* (1897), *The War of the Worlds* (1898), etc. Next he turned to psychological and sociological novels, lively and human - *Kipps* (1905), *Tono-Bungay* (1909), *Ann Veronica* (1909) - in which sexual relationships were frankly treated and which aroused much protest - *The History of Mr. Polly* (1910), and *Mr. Britling sees it Through* (1916). Of his many other books, *The Outline of History* (1920) and *The Shape of Things to Come* (1933), from which a number of his prophecies were fulfilled, are notable. He exerted a vitalizing, releasing effect on his contemporaries, providing them with a new ideology.

WELLS. English city in Somerset, 30km (19m) S of Bristol. The 12th-13th cent. cathedral was built near the site of a Saxon church. W. was made the seat of a bishopric *c.* 900, changed to Bath and Wells in 1244. Pop. (1972) 8,604.

WELSH. A member of the Brythronic group of the Celtic (q.v.) family of languages, known from *c.* 800. In 1971 about 23,000 people in Wales and Monmouthshire spoke W. only; another 542,400 W. and Eng.

The chief remains of early W. literature are contained in the Four Ancient Books of Wales - the Black Book of Carmarthen, the Book of Taliessin, the Book of Aneirin, and the Red Book of Hergest - anthologies of prose and verse of the 6th-14th cents. Characteristic of W. poetry is the bardic system of ensuring the continuance of traditional conventions: most celebrated of the 12th cent. bards was Cynddelw. The English conquest of 1282 involved the fall of the princes who supported them, but after a period of decline a new school arose in S Wales with a new freedom in form and sentiment, the most famous poet being the 14th cent. Davydd ap Gwilym, and in the next cent. the classical metrist Davydd ab Edmwnd. With the Reformation biblical translations were undertaken, and Morgan Llwyd and Ellis Wynn o Lasynys wrote religious prose. Popular metres resembling those of England developed, e.g. the poems of Huw Morys. In the 18th cent. the classical poetic forms revived with Goronwy Owen, and the Eisteddfod movement began: popular measures were used by the hymn-writer William Williams. The 19th cent. saw few notable figures save the novelist Daniel Owen, but the foundation of a Welsh univ. and the work there of Sir John Morris Jones (1864-1929) produced a 20th cent. revival, incl. Thomas Gwynn Jones (1871-1949), W.J. Gruffydd (1881-1954) and Robert Williams Parry (1884-1956). Later poets incl. J. Kitchener Davies (1902-52), Saunders Lewis (1893-), and in the period after the S.W.W. Waldo Williams (1904-71), Euros Bowen (1904-), and Bobi Jones (1929-).

Still best-known outside Wales are those who have expressed the Welsh spirit in English, such as George Herbert, Henry Vaughan, Edward Thomas, Wilfred Owen, Vernon Watkins (1906-67), Dylan Thomas, and Ronald Thomas (qv).

WELSH CORGI. Breed of dog, with a fox-like head, and pricked ears. The coat is dense and any colour except pure white. There are 2 types, the Pembrokeshire and the heavier Cardiganshire.

WELWYN GARDEN CITY. Town in Herts, England, 32km (20m) N of London, founded 1919-20 by Ebenezer Howard. It was developed from 1946 as a 'new town' with chemical, electrical engineering, clothing and food industries. Pop. (1975) 40,700.

WEMBLEY. District of the Greater London bor. of Brent. W. Stadium, opened in 1924, has been the scene of the British Empire Exhibition, the annual FA cup final, and in 1948 of the Olympic Games. A Conference Centre was opened 1977.

WENCESLAS (wen'seslas), **St** (d. *c.* 929). Duke of Bohemia, who attempted to spread Christianity among his people, and was murdered by his brother. He is the patron saint of Czechoslovakia, and the 'good king W.' of the carol.

WENCHOW. *See* WENZHOU.

WENTWORTH, William Charles (1790-1872). Australian statesman. He was the son of D'Arcy W. (c. 1762-1827), surgeon of the penal settlement at Norfolk Is., NSW, who attained great wealth. Ed. in England, he took part in the expedition of 1813 which crossed the Blue Mountains, before completing his studies at Cambridge. In 1855 he was in England to steer the NSW constitution through Parliament, and campaigned for Australian federalism and self-government. He finally settled in England in 1862, but his body was returned to Sydney.

WENTWORTH. Vaucluse House, home of William Charles Wentworth, the campaigner for Australian self-government, is one of Sydney's architectural treasures. The house is a beautiful example of old colonial style. *Photo: Barbara Wace*

WENZHOU (wenjaw-oo'). Port and industrial town in Zhejiang, China. It was opened to foreign trade in 1877, and became prosperous, but has declined in importance. In isolation on the coast, without even a rail link to the prov. cap. at Hangzhou, it staged a revolt against Communism 1976-7. Pop. (1977) 400,000.

WERFEL (ver'-), **Franz** (1890-1945). Austrian poet, dramatist, and novelist. B. in Prague, he lived in Germany, Austria, and France, and in 1940 escaped from a French concentration camp to the USA, where he d. His works incl. the poems *Der Weltfreund, Wir sind, Der Gerichtstag,* etc.; the plays *Juarez und Maximilian, Paulus unter den Juden,* and *Das Reich Gottes in Böhmen*; and the novels *Verdi* and *The Song of Bernadette.*

WERGELAND (văr'gelahnd), **Henrik** (1808-45). Norwegian lyric poet. B. at Christiansand, he was the greatest leader of the Norwegian revival.

WERTH, Alexander (1901-69). British journalist. B. in St Petersburg, he was ed. at Glasgow univ., and became foreign correspondent in Paris and Moscow for the *Guardian, Sunday Times,* etc., excelling in pungent comment also in his books, e.g. *America in Doubt* (1959) and *The Khrushchev Phase* (1961).

WE'SKER, Arnold (1932-). British playwright. Brought up in Hackney, London, he made his name with the trilogy *Chicken Soup with Barley, Roots* and *I'm Talking about Jerusalem* (1959-60), which has an earthy socialist realism derived from his own breadth of human experience as carpenter's mate, farm hand, pastry cook, etc. A later success, *Chips with Everything* (1962), is directed against a prevalent soggy lack of standards. In 1961 he became director of Centre 42.

WESLEY, John (1703-91). British founder of Methodism (q.v.). B. at Epworth, Lincs, where his father was the rector, he went to Christ Church, Oxford, and was ordained in the C of E in 1728. Returning to the college in 1729 as a tutor, he was one of the original band of Methodists. In 1735 he went to Georgia as a missionary. On his return he experienced 'conversion' at a service at the Moravian church in Aldersgate Street, London, on 24 May 1738, and from being a rigid High Churchman developed into an ardent Evangelical. When the pulpits of the Established Church were closed to him and his followers, he took the Gospel to the masses. For 50 years he rode about the country on horseback, preaching daily, largely in the open air, and often several times a day. He is said to have travelled 250,000 m and preached 40,000 sermons. His literary output was great, and his sermons became the doctrinal standard of the Wesleyan Methodist Church. His *Journal* gives an intimate picture of the man and his work. His brother **Charles W.** (1707-88) was one of the original Methodists at Oxford and became a principal preacher and theologian of the Wesleyan Methodists. He wrote some 6,500 hymns, incl. 'Jesu, lover of my soul'. Charles's son, **Samuel W.** (1766-1837), was a celebrated organist, and composer of oratorios, church and chamber music.

WESSEX. The kingdom of the West Saxons, said to have been founded by Cerdic *c.* 500, which comprised Hants, Dorset, Wilts, Berks, Som., and Devon. Egbert in 829 estab. West Saxon supremacy over all England. Thomas Hardy popularized the modern use of the term W. for the SW counties.

WEST, Benjamin (1738-1820). American artist. B. in Pennsylvania, he settled in London in 1763, and became pres. of the RA in 1792. He painted historical pictures, incl. 'The Death of Wolfe', and many early American artists studied with him: *see* UNITED STATES: ART.

WEST, Mae (1892-1980). American actress. Popular in vaudeville, she made a Broadway success in the play *Diamond Lil* (1929), filmed as *She Done Him Wrong* (1933), and was famous for such sayings as 'Come up and see me sometime.'

WEST, Dame Rebecca. Pseudonym of British author Cicily Isabel Fairfield (1892–1983). A perceptive writer on political themes, she pub the study of Yugoslavia *Black Lamb and Grey Falcon* (1942), *The Meaning of Treason* (1949), *The Vassall Affair* (1963), etc. She was created DBE in 1959.

WEST, The. The Great Plains region of the USA to the E of the Rocky Mtns from Canada to Texas. The Indian tribal civilization there had been largely broken by the outbreak of an unidentified disease *c.* AD 1250. Then came the Spanish *conquistadores* who introduced cattle ranching and rodeos, and from whom the Indians adopted the use of the horse *c.* 1650. They were followed by the fur trappers, such as Davy Crockett (q.v.), and the opening up of emigration routes such as the Oregon Trail across the area. The takeover of the prairies themselves was not undertaken on a large scale until after the Mexican War (1846) and the Civil War (1861-5) provided mounted troops who could match the Indian warriors, the Texas Rangers and US Cavalry. The golden era of the cowboy and the Wild West ensued in the 1870-80s, its heroes - often in fact either criminals or operating profitably on both sides of the law - incl. William H. Bonney (1859-81), known as 'Billy the Kid', said to have notched 21 killings in a career as a cattle thief; 'Wild Bill' Hickok (q.v.); Jesse James (q.v.); the Mastersons, tamers of Dodge City, Kansas, and Wyatt Earp (*see* TOMBSTONE). In the late 19th cent. the West became the province of sheepmen and farmers, although much of the land was unsuitable to such use, and large areas have been returning to open desert since the pop. began to fall from about 1930.

WEST AFRICAN STATES, Economic Community of. Organization (ECOWAS), in French *Communauté économique des États de l'Afrique de l'Ouest* (CEDEAO), estab. in 1975, as the enlarged successor to movements from 1972 to end barriers to trade and co-operation in development. Those taking part were Benin, The Gambia, Ghana, Guinea, Guinea-Bissau, Ivory Coast, Liberia, Mali, Mauritania, Niger, Nigeria, Senegal, Sierra Leone, Togo and Upper Volta.

WEST BROMWICH. Town in W Midlands, England, 10km (6m) NW of Birmingham. Industries incl. springs, tubes, foundries, and rolling mills. Pop. (1972) 165,450.

WESTERN AUSTRALIA. The largest state of the Australian Commonwealth (nearly one-third of the total area), covering all of the continent W. of long. 129° E. Towns incl. Perth, the cap., and Fremantle, the chief port, on the W coast, Bunbury, Kalgoorlie, Geraldton, and Albany. The chief rivers are the Fitzroy, Fortescue, Gascoyne, Murchison, and Swan. The shore tends to be rocky and inhospitable, with few good harbours, and the NW coast is subject to hurricanes - 'willy-willies'. In the days of sail many East Indiamen en route from the Netherlands to Batavia were wrecked here, notably the *Batavia* in 1629, and the Museum of W.A. in Perth has a collection of archaeological finds. Most of the interior is desert. In 1826 a convicts' settlement was estab. at King George Sound, but was short-lived. In 1829 Capt., later Sir James, Stirling became Lt.-Gov. of the new colony, and the Swan River Settlement, with Perth and Fremantle, was founded. Conditions were harsh and development slow, however, until the gold strikes at Kimberley 1885 and Kalgoorlie 1893. An enormous fresh impetus to development came in the mid-1960s with the discovery of a wealth of other minerals, espec. large reserves of iron, bauxite nr Perth, and from 1967 oil at Barrow Island, and quantities of ilmenite, manganese, monazite, rutile and zircon. The Aborigines still have a strong tribal organisation and culture, e.g. in the Kimberley area, and there has been strong opposition to mining without compensation, and a determination to preserve sacred areas. Wheat and other cereals are grown, fruit (apples, oranges and pears), and currants and raisins. Large areas are irrigated for dairying and stockraising in the N and along the SW coast. Responsible govt was achieved in 1890, and in 1901 W.A. was one of the states federated in the Commonwealth of Australia. The govt is vested in the Gov., the Legislative Council, and the Legislative Assembly. Area 2,527,632 sq.km (975,920 sq.m); pop. (1976) 832,420.

WESTERN AUSTRALIA. Wave Rock at Hyden resulted from sea action when the land was submerged. The streaks are caused by minerals in the rain that seeps down. *Photo: Richard Harrington/Camera Press*

WESTERN ISLES. Name commonly used for the Hebrides. The Outer Hebrides (Lewis, Harris, N and S Uist and Barra) became an islands area, under the official name W.I., in the local govt reorganization of Scotland in 1975. The admin. HQ is Stornoway. Area 2,901 sq.km (1,120 sq.m); pop. (1979) 29,255.

WESTERN PROVINCES. In Canada the 'producer' provs. Alberta, British Columbia, Manitoba and Saskatchewan. In recent years they have felt alienated by the federal govt. low-cost use or taxation of their primary resources of oil, natural gas, coal and timber.

WEST INDIES. An archipelago lying between the coasts of Florida and Venezuela, and dividing the Atlantic Ocean from the Gulf of Mexico and the Caribbean Sea. They consist of the British W.I.; Curaçao, belonging to the Netherlands; Guadeloupe and Martinique, belonging to France; Puerto Rico, a Commonwealth of the USA; the Virgin Islands, belonging to the USA and Britain; and the independent Cuba, Dominican Republic, and Haiti (qq.v.).

The Federation of the WEST INDIES, comprising Antigua, Barbados, Dominica, Grenada, Jamaica, Montserrat, St Kitts with Nevis and Anguilla, St Lucia, St Vincent, and Trinidad and Tobago (qq.v.), came into existence in 1958. This federation, of which the federal parliament was at Port-of-Spain, Trinidad, came to an end in 1962 when first Jamaica and then Trinidad and Tobago withdrew. Attempts at a new federation were abandoned in 1965, and the new non-colonial status of Associated State (q.v.) was assumed in 1967 by Antigua (independent 1981), Dominica (independent 1978), Grenada (independent 1974), St Kitts-Nevis-Anguilla (St Kitts-Nevis independent 1981, and Anguilla, at its own request, a separate crown colony 1981), and St Lucia (independent 1979).

WEST LOTHIAN. Former central co. of Scotland, bordering the S shore of the Firth of Forth, which was included (except for the Bo'ness area, which went to Central region) in Lothian region. The Almond and tributary Avon were in W Lothian. Agriculture and dairy farming are carried on, and coal and iron worked. Linlithgow was the admin. HQ.

WE'STMACOTT, Sir Richard (1775-1856). British sculptor. He studied under Canova in Rome, was elected RA in 1811, and became a prof. at the Academy. He executed monuments in Westminster Abbey and in St Paul's, and the 'Achilles' in Hyde Park, etc.

WESTMEATH. Inland co. of Leinster, Republic of Ireland. It is drained by the Shannon, Inny, and Brosna, and noted for the Loughs Ree, Sheelin, Ennell, etc. Agriculture and dairy farming are the main occupations; there are limestone quarries; some textiles are manufactured. Mullingar is the co. town. Area 1,764 sq.km (681 sq.m); pop. (1971) 53,570.

WEST MIDLANDS. *See* MIDLANDS.

WESTMINSTER, City of. Most famous of the Greater London boroughs, on the N bank of the Thames between Kensington and the City of London. It contains the London palaces of the sovereign (Buckingham and St James's), Houses of Parliament, Westminster Abbey (*see* below), Whitehall with its many govt offices, and the Cenotaph; Westminster (RC) Cathedral, the Methodist Central Hall, Victoria and Charing Cross stations, the National Gallery, and Trafalgar Square; Westminster, Charing Cross, and St George's hospitals; theatres and clubs, and many other important buildings. It also incl. Hyde, Green, and St James's Parks and part of Kensington Gardens. From 1965 W. has had a Lord Mayor. Pop. (1972) 233,360.

WESTMINSTER BRIDGE, crossing the Thames from the Houses of Parliament to St Thomas's hospital, was rebuilt 1856-62. WESTMINSTER HALL is a relic of the old palace of the English kings; it was originally built by William II in 1097; its magnificent oak roof was erected by Richard II, 1394-9. The hall was the seat of the English law courts until 1882. WESTMINSTER CATHEDRAL, the seat of the RC archbishopric of W., was begun in 1895 and consecrated in 1910; it is in the Byzantine style. WESTMINSTER SCHOOL, one of the great English public schools, was originally a school attached to the abbey, whence its name of St Peter's College. Elizabeth I refounded it in 1560. WESTMINSTER HOSPITAL (1719) was opened on its present site in 1939.

WESTMINSTER ABBEY. Built on a marshy site that was once Thorney Island, W.A. was traditionally founded by Sebert, king of the East Saxons, early in the 7th cent.; its official title is the Collegiate Church of St Peter. The Norman church and monastery were consecrated under Edward the Confessor in 1065, but rebuilding was begun by Henry III in 1245 and was finished in 1528 shortly before the monastery was dissolved. Later additions to what is a fine example of pointed Gothic incl. Henry VII's chapel and the west towers, completed in 1740 to a design by Nicholas Hawksmoor. All the English sovereigns (save Edward V) have been crowned in the abbey since William I, and many of them, incl. Edward the Confessor, Henry III, Edward I, Henry VII, Elizabeth I, Charles II, William III, Anne, and George II, are buried there. The Coronation Chair contains the 'stone of destiny' (traditionally Jacob's pillow at Bethel) on which the Scottish kings were crowned; it was brought to London by Edward I. The

WESTMINSTER. The Queen replies to loyal addresses from both Houses of Parliament, on the occasion of her Silver Jubilee in 1977, in Westminster Hall. Seated beside her is the Duke of Edinburgh. *Photo: Press Association*

abbey is crowded with memorials (incl. the Battle of Britain Memorial Chapel dedicated 1947) and tombs of statesmen, writers, and others, incl. the 'Unknown Warrior', who have left their mark on English history.

WESTMORLAND. Former co. of NW England, created *c.* 1100 but merged in 1974 in the new co. of Cumbria (q.v.). Part of the Fell country and Lake District, it incl. the high peaks of Helvellyn (950m/3,118 ft) and Bow Fell (902 m/2,960 ft); Windermere, part of Ullswater, Grasmere, Rydal Water, and Hawes Water. Appleby was the admin. HQ.

WESTON-SUPER-MARE. Seaside resort in Avon, England, on the Bristol Channel, 34km (21m) SW of Bristol, a fishing village until the early 19th cent. Pop. (1972) 50,730.

WESTPHALIA (-fāl'ia). Former prov. of Prussia, from 1946 part of the Land of North Rhine-Westphalia (q.v.). An independent duchy from the Middle Ages, W. was incorporated in Prussia by the Congress of Vienna, 1815, and made a prov. 1816 with Münster as its cap. W. incl. the Ruhr (q.v.), chief industrial area of Germany, and was the scene of violent fighting during the last stages of the S.W.W.

The kingdom of W., 1807-13, created by Napoleon, did not incl. the duchy, but consisted of Prussian lands W of the Elbe, Hessen, Brunswick, and Hanover.

WEST POINT. Location in NY state, on the Hudson, 80km (50m) N of NYC, site of the US Military Academy (commonly referred to as W.P.), estab. in 1802: women were admitted 1976. W.P. has been a military post since 1778.

WEST VIRGINIA. Mountainous E state of the USA. The Ohio, Monongahela, and the 2 Kanawhas are the chief rivers, while the Alleghenies run SW through the state. This hilly country provides fruit, poultry and dairy products, and is rich in hardwood forests. Resources incl. coal, natural gas and petroleum, which support a chemical industry incl. man-made fibres and plastics, and steel, glass and pottery are manufactured; petroleum refined; and meat packed. Charleston is the cap. W.V. was part of Virginia until 1861 when the western cos. of Va. voted against secession and formed themselves into a separate state, admitted to the Union 1863. Among its tourist attractions is the port of Harpers Ferry (q.v.) restored as it was in 1859 when John Brown seized the US Armory, incl. the fire-engine house in which he was besieged and captured by Robert E. Lee. Area 62,629 sq.km (24,180 sq.m); pop. (1970) 1,744,237.

WEXFORD. Seaport and co. town of Wexford, Rep. of Ireland, on the Slaney. Shipbuilding and fishing are carried on. Founded by the Danes in the 9th cent., W. was devastated by Cromwell in 1649. Pop. (1971) 11,745.

WEXFORD. Co. of the Rep. of Ireland, in the prov. of Leinster, on the SE coast. There are hills in the NW, and the co. is watered by the Barrow and Slaney. The co. town is Wexford. Fishing and the production of oats, barley, potatoes, etc., sheep, pigs and poultry are the chief industries. Area 2,352 sq.km (908 sq.m); pop. (1971) 85,350.

WEYDEN (vīden), **Rogier van der** (*c.* 1399-1464). Flemish painter. B. at Tournai, he settled at Brussels after 1429. His 'Descent from the Cross' is in Madrid.

WEYGAND (vāgoṅ'), **Maxime** (1867-1965). French general. Chief of staff to Foch and chief of the Allied general staff in 1918, he successfully defended Warsaw against the Red Army in 1920, and was appointed C-in-C in May 1940. He advised surrender to Germany, and was subsequently Defence Min. in Pétain's govt, and High Commissioner of N Africa 1940-1. He was a prisoner in Germany 1942-5, and after his return to France was arrested, released in 1946, and in 1949 the sentence of national infamy was quashed.

WEYMOUTH (wā'muth). Seaport and resort in Dorset, England, at the mouth of the Wey, on W. Bay - a fleet anchorage. Dating from the 10th cent., W. was the first place in England to suffer from the Black Death in 1348, was popularized as a bathing resort by George III, and in 1972 was chosen as the Nat. Yacht Racing Centre. Pop. (1972) 41,410.

WHALES. Member of a large group of mammals in the order Cetacea (q.v.), adapted for marine life. They swim chiefly by using the fin-tail, the fore-limbs or flippers maintaining balance, and when rising to the surface to breathe eject a column of exhausted air and water from the blowhole, i.e. nostril. The Mystacoceti feed on plankton, strained through their whalebone plates, but the Odontoceti use their teeth to capture their prey, though not to eat it, since they swallow it whole. Especially ferocious is the killer W., of which one captured specimen had 32 adult seals in its stomach. The milk on which the young are suckled resembles condensed milk, having a water content of only 40-50 per cent. The most important whaling product is oil (used principally in making soap and margarine), and catches are restricted by international agreement to conserve supplies: the high intelligence of Ws. means that their slaughter, usually by shell harpoon guns, involves great cruelty. The herd instinct is strongly developed, and some species are migrant from the polar regions to warmer waters in winter. Whale 'songs' by which the herds seem to keep in touch, are apparently only sung by males, last 20-30 min and have 8-10 themes which form a pattern. The blue W. is the biggest living animal *c.* 26 m (85 ft) long and weighing over 100 tonnes: it is threatened with extinction, as are many other species, and in 1979 a whale sanctuary was estab. in the Indian Ocean. *See* KILLER WHALE.

WHALE. A school of pilot whales stranded in Florida. It is thought that in such cases the leading whale develops an ear disease affecting its sense of direction, and the remainder follow, either blindly, or to help him. Despite the efforts of volunteers to save them, even those successfully refloated will strand themselves again. *Photo: Popperfoto*

WHARTON, Edith (1862-1937). American author, *née* Jones. Her work was greatly influenced by her friend Henry James, and her psychological novels incl. *The House of Mirth,* the tragic *Ethan Frome, The Custom of the Country,* and *The Age of Innocence.*

WHEAT. Cereal plant derived from the wild *Triticum,* a grass native to the Middle East. It has been cultivated since Neolithic times, and is the chief cereal used in bread making in temperate climates which suit its growth. W. is killed by frost, and damp renders the grain soft: warm dry regions produce the most valuable grain. The chief wheat-producing areas of the world are the Ukraine, central and NW United States, the Punjab, the prairie provinces of Canada, parts of France and S Germany, Italy, Argentina, and SE Australia. Flour is milled from the endosperm, the coatings of the grain producing bran and pollard. Semolina is also prepared from W.

WHEATEAR. Small migratory bird (*Oenanthe oenanthe*) found throughout the Old World and also in parts of N America. The plumage is light grey above and white below, with a white patch on the back, a black face-patch, and black and white wings and tail.

WHEATLEY, Dennis Yates (1897-1977). British novelist. B. in London, he served in the F.W.W., and in 1932 sold the family wine business to take up writing. With a gift of narrative that recalls Dumas, he wrote a 'saga' of the adventures of Roger Brook, secret agent in the French Revolutionary period; a series dealing with black magic and occultism and another on wartime espionage - *They Used Dark Forces* (1964) combines both these last themes.

WHEATSTONE, Sir Charles (1802-75). British physicist. B. in Gloucester, he was originally a musical-instrument maker, but became in 1834 prof. of experimental philosophy at King's Coll., London. His inventions incl. the concertina, harmonica, and stereoscope, and he took out the first patent for the electric telegraph with W. F. Cooke in 1837. He measured the speed of electric discharge in conductors, and also devised the *W. bridge* (a special electrical network for measuring resistance) from an idea of S. Hunter Christie's.

WHEELER, Sir Mortimer (1890-1976). British archaeologist. He was keeper of the London Museum 1926-44, when his most notable digs incl. Caerleon 1926-7 and Maiden Castle in Dorset 1934-7, and as director-gen. of archaeology in India 1944-8 revealed the Indus Valley civilization (q.v.). He popularized archaeology, espec. by his television appearances.

WHELK. Family of marine gastropods. The common W. (*Buccinum undatum*) is widely distributed round the N Sea and Atlantic. It is fished for bait and food, and has a thick spiral shell.

WHELK. The common whelk *(Buccinum undatum)* taking a stroll with tentacles outstretched and siphon erect. *Photo: Heather Angel*

WHIG PARTY. The predecessor of the present Liberal Party. The name, first applied to the rebel Covenanters in Scotland, came into use in 1679 for supporters of the Exclusion Bill. The W.P. strongly supported the 1688 revolution, and was in power continuously 1714-60. Led by a group of great land-owning families, it drew its support mainly from the business classes and the Nonconformists; it advocated the development of industry and commerce, a vigorous foreign policy, and religious toleration. During the French Revolution the W.P. adopted a policy of parliamentary reform. After the triumph of this policy in 1832 the name 'Liberal' replaced that of Whig. In

US history the name W.P. was used during 1836-54 by one of the 2 major parties, which opposed the radical policy of Andrew Jackson and defended commercial interests.

WHIP. In Britain an MP employed by his party to secure attendance of members of the party at important debates. The govt chief W., and the 3 junior Ws., are salaried officials; the Ws. of opposition parties are unpaid. The term, which is derived from the whipper-in of a hunt, is also applied to the summons to attend sent to members.

WHIPPET. Breed of dog resembling a small greyhound. The W. was developed, as a cross between the greyhound and fox terrier, by the colliers of northern England, who race them along a straight track, at the end of which their owners stand calling them.

WHIPSNADE. English locality in Beds, 5km (3m) S of Dunstable, site of a zoological park covering 2 sq.km (500 acres) belonging to the London Zoological Society, where wild animals, and birds, are bred and exhibited in their natural state. It was opened to the public in 1931.

WHISK(E)Y. A distilled spirit made from cereals: the name derives from Gaelic *uisgebeatha* 'water of life'. Scotch whisky is distilled from malt; Irish whiskey usually from barley, and American whiskey or bourbon (pron. ber'bon) from Indian corn or rye.

WHIST. A card game played by 2 sides of 2 partners each. Each player is dealt 13 cards. The object of the game is to score tricks, a trick being gained by the partners who play the highest card of a suit, or the highest trump card, the trump suit being determined before the start of the game. Each trick over 6 counts one point to the partners, who score 5 points for a game, and 2 games for a rubber.

WHISTLER, James Abbott McNeill (1834-1903). American artist. B. in Mass., he abandoned a military career for painting, and in 1855 went to Paris where he was associated with the Impressionists. He settled in Chelsea, executed etchings of the Thames, and painted 'Old Battersea Bridge', 'The Symphony in White', and portraits. His 'Nocturnes', 1877, were adversely criticized by Ruskin, and led to the libel trial of 1878 in which W. was awarded a farthing damages. W. retaliated in 1890 with *The Gentle Art of Making Enemies.*

WHISTLER, Rex John (1905-44). British artist, celebrated for fanciful murals, e.g. Tate Gallery Restaurant and Haddon Hall. He was killed in Normandy in the S.W.W. There is a permanent collection of his work at Plas Newydd, Anglesey. His brother **Laurence W.** (1912-), a poet and diamond-point engraver on glass, uses the stippling process invented by the Dutch in the 17th cent., in which the design is composed of small dots hammered into the glass.

WHITBY. Fishing port in N Yorks, England, at the mouth of the Esk. There are remains of the Benedictine abbey built in 1078 on the site of the original foundation by St Hilda in 657, which was destroyed by the Danes in 867. Capt. Cook's ship *Resolution* was built here in W., where he had served his apprenticeship. There are large potash reserves running out under the sea. Pop. (1971) 12,000.

The **Synod of W.** (664) was summoned by King Oswy of Northumbria to decide between the use of the Celtic or Roman forms of Christianity, and resulted in the adoption of the latter, so consolidating a link with continental Christendom.

WHITE, Gilbert (1720-93). English naturalist. B. at Selborne, Hants, he took orders in 1747, and in 1751 retired to his birthplace. His *Natural History and Antiquities of Selborne* (1789) is a classic, and his home 'The Wakes' was opened as a museum and library in 1955.

WHITE, Patrick (1912-). Novelist. B. in London, he was taken to Australia at 6 months, but returned to England and studied at Cambridge before settling in Australia in the 1940s. His first book *Happy Valley* (1939) showed suffering as a condition of existence, and similar allegorical overtones occur in the later *The Aunt's Story* (1946), *Voss* (1957), *The Vivisector* (1970) - an imaginary biography of an artist - *The Eye of the Storm* (1973), and *The Twyborn Affair* (1979). His most important play is *The Ham Funeral* (1947). He was awarded a Nobel prize in 1973.

WHITE. Patrick White has not only established a worldwide literary reputation, but by his interpretation of episodes in Australian history, as in *A Fringe of Leaves* (1976), has made it imaginatively part of the universal heritage. *Photo: Courtesy of the Australian Information Service*

WHITE, T(erence) H(anbury) (1906-64). British writer, best known for his retelling in four volumes of the Arthurian legend, beginning with *The Sword in the Stone* (1938), and published collectively as *The Once and Future King* (1958).

WHITEFIELD, George (1714-70). British evangelist. B. at Gloucester, he came under Methodist influence while at Oxford. He took orders in 1738, but was suspended for his unorthodox doctrines and methods. For many years he travelled through Britain and America, and by his preaching contributed greatly to the evangelical revival. W.'s Tabernacle was built for him in Tottenham Court Rd, London (1756: bombed 1945 but rebuilt). He d. while visiting New England.

WHITEFISH. Name applied to freshwater fishes of the salmon family, belonging to the genus *Coregonus.* Abundant in N American lakes, they also occur in Europe and Asia; 3 species are found in Britain.

WHITEHALL. London street in which is the Cenotaph (q.v.) and many govt offices, the latter making W. symbolic of 'officialdom'.

WHITEHAVEN. Seaport in Cumbria, England, with large docks. There have been several major pit disasters in the coal mines which extend beneath the sea, e.g. 136 men killed in 1910, and 104 in 1947. Some 18km (11m) along the coast to the SE is the Calder Hall atomic power station, and the Windscale plant where spent nuclear fuel from Britain and overseas is reprocessed.

WHITEHEAD, Alfred North (1861-1947). British philosopher and mathematician. He was prof. of applied mathematics at London 1914-24, and 1924-37 prof. of philosophy at Harvard, USA. In his 'theory of organism' he attempted a synthesis of metaphysics and science. Among his works are *Principia Mathematica* (1910-13; with Bertrand Russell), *Concept of Nature*, and *Adventures of Ideas* (1933). W. received the OM in 1945.

WHITE HOLE. The precise opposite of a Black H. (q.v.), formed when a tremendously dense object bursts into view.

WHITEHORSE. Cap. of Yukon Territory, Canada, on Lewes r., centre of a mining and fur-trapping region. W. is the terminus of a railway to Skagway, Alaska, USA, and on the NW Highway; it also has an airport. It replaced Dawson as cap. in 1953. Pop. (1976) 16,200.

WHITE HORSE, Vale of the. Valley of the Ock, which flows into the Thames at Abingdon, England. It takes its name from the figure of a horse, 114m (374ft) long, cut in the chalk at Uffington, Berks. Similar figures are found at Bratton, Wilts, and elsewhere in England; some are probably prehistoric, and of totemic origin.

WHITE HOUSE. Official residence of the president of USA, in Washington, DC. It is a plain edifice of sandstone painted white, built in the Italian renaissance style, 1792-9, to the designs of Hoban, who also restored it after it was fired by the British in 1814. The interior was completely rebuilt 1948-52 and the décor remodelled by Jacqueline Kennedy (q.v.). The name is first recorded in 1811.

WHITE HOUSE. It has been painted white since 1814 to hide the fire marks when it was reduced to a shell during the British capture of the city. The heart of the nation is the President's study, known from its shape as the 'oval office'. *Photo: Mireille Vautier*

The name is often adapted to refer to other residences of the pres., e.g. Little W.H., at Warm Springs, Georgia, where F. D. Roosevelt died; Western W.H., at San Clemente, California, where Nixon had a home; and Florida W.H. denoting Ford's home there.

WHITEHOUSE, Mary (1910-). British Journalist. As honorary sec. of the Nat. Viewers' and Listeners' Assocn., she has campaigned to 'clean-up' these and other media by restoring a more balanced view of sex in programmes for family viewing, etc.

WHITELAW, William, visct (1918–). British Cons. politician. Chief Cons. Whip 1946–70, he was Leader of the House of Commons 1970–2, and as Sec. of State for N Ireland introduced the concept of 'power–sharing', then became Sec. of State for Employment Dec. 1973–4, but failed to conciliate the unions. He was chairman of the Cons. Party 1975–9, and Home Sec. 1979–83.

WHITEMAN, Paul (1891-1967). American danceband leader specializing in 'symphonic' jazz. He wrote an autobiography, *Jazz*.

WHITEOUT. A 'fog' of grains of dry snow caused by strong winds in temperature of 0°-30°F in Canada, USA, etc.

WHITE RUSSIA. *See* BYELORUSSIA.

WHITES. Term applied to the counter-revolutionary party during the French Revolution, when the royalists used the white lily of the French monarchy as their badge, and also during the Russian Civil Wars of 1917-21.

WHITE SEA. Gulf of the Arctic Ocean, on which stands the N Russian port of Archangel. The N Dvina and Onega flow into the W.S. which is frozen in the winter. The W.S. is linked by canal with the Baltic, the Black, and the Caspian Seas. The USSR has a warship construction base (incl. nuclear submarines) at Severodvinsk.

WHITING. Food-fish (*Gadus merlangus*) common in N European waters. It differs from the haddock by the absence of a barbel on the chin.

WHITLAM, (Edward) Gough (1916-). Australian Labor statesman. A barrister, he became leader of the Labor Party 1967, and was PM 1972-5. He promoted closer relations with Asian powers, and attempted redistribution of wealth and the raising of loans to increase nat. ownership of industry and resources. When the opposition blocked finance bills in the Senate, following a crisis of confidence, he refused to call a general election, and was dismissed by the Gov.-General. He was defeated in the general election which followed. *See* CONSTITUTION.

WHITMAN, Walt(er) (1819-92). American poet. B. on Long Island, he worked in printing offices, as a schoolteacher, and as a journalist. In 1855 he pub. his most influential vol., later much enlarged, *Leaves of Grass*. He preached an American vision of freedom in union, expressed in verse stripped of the conventional ornaments of rhyme and regular metre. In 1865 he pub. *Drum-Taps*, a vol. inspired by his work as an army nurse during the Civil War.

WHITSTABLE. Resort in Kent, England, at the mouth of the Swale, 10km (6m) NW of Canterbury, celebrated for its oysters. Pop. (1972) 25,550.

WHITSUNDAY. Church festival held 7 weeks after Easter, corresponding to the Jewish Pentecost and commemorating the descent of the Holy Spirit on the apostles. The name is probably derived from the white garments worn by candidates for baptism at the festival.

WHITTEN-BROWN, Sir Arthur (1886-1948). British airman. After serving in the F.W.W., he took part in the first non-stop flight across the Atlantic as navigator to Capt. John Alcock (q.v.) in 1919.

WHITELAW. Lord Whitelaw, in his robes as a viscount in 1983, the first such hereditary peerage to be created since 1964. *Photo: Press Association.*

WHITTIER, John Greenleaf (1807-92). American poet. B. in Mass, of a Quaker family, he entered politics and journalism, and became a powerful opponent of slavery, as in the verse *Voices of Freedom* (1846). Among his other works are *Legends of New England in Prose and Verse, Songs of Labor and the New England narrative Snow-Bound* (1866).

WHITTIER. City in California, USA, 21km (13m) SE of central Los Angeles. Founded by Quakers in 1887, it was named after the poet. Nixon spent his boyhood here, but the area reserved for a Nixon library-museum became a park. Pop. (1970) 72,870.

WHITTINGTON, Richard (d. 1423). English merchant. B. in Glos, he made a large fortune as a mercer, and was mayor of London 1397-8, 1406-7, and 1419-20. His cat first appears in a play of 1605.

WHITTLE, Sir Frank (1907-). British engineer. He entered the RAF, invented the jet engine in 1930, and was on the special duty list working on jet propulsion 1937-46. In May 1941 the Gloster E 28/39 aircraft first flew with the Whittle jet engine, and in 1948 his pioneer work was recognised by a govt. award of £100,000.

WHO, Dr. Hero of a science-fiction television series conceived in 1962 by Sidney Newman (head of BBC drama) and Donald Wilson, still in progress. He is of variable age and the controls of his space vehicle (TARDIS - Time And Relative Dimensions In Space) are faulty, thus enabling his adventures to range through time on his eternal journey through space. His enemies incl. the Daleks (created by Terry Nation), said to have been named from an encyclopedia section labelled DAL-LEK, mechanical beings with staccato speech, e.g. 'ex-ter-min-ate'.

WHOOPING COUGH. Pertussis; a specific infectious fever due to a bacillus and conveyed by droplets from the nose and throat. It is marked by a peculiar and obstinate cough ending in a long crowing inspiration. The patient should be isolated for 5 weeks, and the cough may persist for months. Antibiotics are ineffective, but a vaccine is used to give active immunity to children under six. In the 1970s there was controversy because of side effects, such as brain damage, attributed to the vaccine. The small number of instances was said to be outweighed by the overall advantages of protection.

WHORTLEBERRY. *See* BILBERRY.

WHYALLA. Port and industrial city in South Australia, with iron and steel works, on the NW shore of Spencer Gulf. Pop. (1976) 33,425.

WHYMPER, Edward (1840-1911). British mountaineer. He made the first ascents of many alpine peaks incl. the Matterhorn (1865), and in the Andes scaled Chimborazo and other mountains. He was a capable wood-engraver, and wrote *Scrambles amongst the Alps* (1871), and *Zermatt and the Matterhorn* (1897).

WICHITA (wē'chēta). Largest city of Kansas, USA, on the Arkansas, a milling centre with petroleum refineries, stockyards, foundries, and factories making aircraft, motor-vehicles, etc. W. has a municipal airport. Pop. met. area (1970) 372,800.

WICK. Fishing port in the far N of Highland region, Scotland, on the E coast, with services to the Orkneys and Shetlands, and an airport. Industries incl. shipyards and distilleries, and there is increased prosperity from the development of N Sea oil. Pop. (1973) 7,805.

WICKHAM, Sir Henry (1846-1928). British planter, who collected rubber seeds in Brazil, which then had a monopoly in rubber production, and so founded the plantations of Sri Lanka, Malaysia, etc.

WICKLOW. Marine co. of Leinster, Rep. of Ireland, S of Dublin. The centre is occupied by W. mtns, Lugnaquilla reaching 926m (3,039 ft). The Slane and Liffey are the chief rivers, cattle are bred, and lead and copper mined. The admin. HQ is the seaport of W. Area 2,025 sq.km (782 sq.m); pop. (1971) 66,295.

WIDGEON. Wild duck (*Anas penelope*). Smaller than the common wild duck, it has a red-brown head with cream crown, greyish-pink breast and white beneath. The bill is blue-grey. In winter it frequents British coasts, but breeds farther south.

WIELAND (vē'lahnt), **Christoph Martin** (1733-1813). German poet and novelist. After attempts at religious poetry, he came under the influence of Voltaire and Rousseau, and wrote graceful novels such as *Agathon,* the satirical *Abderiten,* etc., and tales in verse such as *Oberon, Musarion,* and others, W. was prof. at Erfurt 1769-72, and subsequently became tutor at the court of Weimar. He first trans. Shakespeare into German (1762-6).

WIEN. Ger. form of VIENNA.

WIESBADEN (vēs'bahden). Cap. of the Land of Hessen, W Germany. W. was the cap. of the former duchy of Nassau from the 12th cent. to 1866. Pop. (1979) 271,435.

WIG. Artificial head of hair worn as an adornment, disguise, or to conceal baldness. Ws. were known in the ancient world, and have been found on Egyptian mummies. The 16th cent. periwig imitated real hair, and developed into the elaborate peruke which became part of dress, and under Queen Anne Ws. covering the back and shoulders became fashionable. Ws. are worn in England and some Commonwealth countries as part of the costume of judges, barristers, and some parliamentary officials, and from the 1960s were fashionable (either in real hair or synthetics) for women.

WIGAN (wi'gan). English industrial town, on the Douglas, 19km (12m) N of Warrington. An old town, W. was captured by the Parliamentarians during the Civil War in 1643 and 1651. The W. 'alps', an area of industrial dereliction incl. colliery spoil heaps, has been re-shaped and developed with ski-slopes, boating facilities, etc., and is an outstanding example of reclamation after industrial blight. Coal and textiles have been replaced by food processing, engineering and paper industries. Pop. (1972) 81,420.

WIGGIN, Kate Douglas (1856-1923). American author. B. in Philadelphia, she was a pioneer in the running of kindergartens in America, and wrote *Rebecca of Sunnybrook Farm* (1903), etc.

WIGHT, Isle of. *See* ISLE OF WIGHT.

WIGTOWN. Former co. of SW Scotland extending to the Rhinns of Galloway double peninsula, in the Irish Sea, merged in 1975 in Dumfries and Galloway. The area is moorland to the NE, elsewhere dairying is carried on. The admin HQ was Wigtown, pop. (1973) 1,200; Stranraer the chief port.

WILBERFORCE, William (1759-1833). British reformer. B. at Hull, he began his attacks on slavery while at school, and from 1788 devoted himself to its abolition. He entered parliament in 1780, in 1807 his bill for the abolition of the slave-trade was passed, and in 1833, largely due to his efforts, slavery was abolished throughout the British Empire. His son **Samuel W.** (1805-73) was bp of Oxford 1845-69, and then of Winchester, and was a noted defender of Anglican orthodoxy against the Tractarians.

WILD, Jonathan (*c.* 1682-1725). English criminal, who organized the thieves of London and ran an office which for a payment returned stolen goods to their owners. He was hanged at Tyburn.

WILDE, Oscar Fingal O'Flahertie Wills (1854-1900). Irish writer. B. in Dublin, he was ed. there and at Magdalen Coll., Oxford, where he was a leader of the aesthetic circle burlesqued in Gilbert's *Patience.* His first *Poems* appeared in 1881, the novel *The Picture of Dorian Gray* in 1891, and the series of brilliantly witty comedies *Lady Windermere's Fan* (1892), *A Woman of No Importance* (1893), *An Ideal Husband* (1895), and *The Importance of Being Earnest* (1895). After his conviction in 1895 for homosexuality he was imprisoned for 2 years: *see* DOUGLAS, LORD ALFRED. This experience prompted his *Ballad of Reading Gaol* (1898) and *De Profundis,* written in prison, and pub. in full for the first time in 1949. He latterly lived on the Continent.

WILDEBEEST. *See* GNU.

WILDER, Billy (1906-). Austrian-American film director. B. in Vienna, he was in Hollywood from 1934, where he collaborated with Charles Brackett on film scripts, e.g. *Ninotchka* (1939); he directed, as well as collaborating on the script of *Lost Weekend* (1945) and *Sunset Boulevard* (1950), and such sophisticated comedies as *Some Like it Hot* (1959) and *The Apartment* (1960).

WILDER, Thornton Niven (1897-1975). American playwright and novelist. B. at Madison, Wisconsin, he made his name with the novel *The Bridge of San Luis Rey* (1927), tracing the lives of those involved in a disaster, which had many imitators: best of later books was *The Ides of March* (1942), set in ancient Rome. His plays *Our Town* (1938) and *The Skin of Our Teeth* (1942) were attempts to deepen the content of contemporary drama on lines later taken up by Miller and Williams.

WILFRID, St (634-709). B. in Northumbria, he became bp of York in 665, after defending the Roman cause at the Synod of Whitby.

WILHELMSHAVEN (vil'hehmshahfen). Seaport of Lower Saxony, on Jade Bay. W Germany's chief naval station, it has many small industries and is a holiday resort. Pop. (1979) 100,150.

WILKES, John (1727-97). British Radical politician. B. in Clerkenwell, he entered parliament as a Whig in 1757. His attacks on Bute in his paper, *The North Briton,* led to his outlawry in 1764; he fled to France, and on his return in 1768 was imprisoned. He was 4 times elected MP for Middlesex, but the Commons refused to admit him, and finally declared his opponent elected. This secured him strong working- and middle-class support, and in 1774 he was allowed to take his seat in parliament, where he championed parliamentary reform, religious toleration, and American independence.

WILKIE, Sir David (1785-1841). Scottish genre painter. B. in Fifeshire, he studied at the RA schools, and estab. his popularity with 'Village Politicians' in 1806. Other works incl. 'The Blind Fiddler', 'Village Festival', and 'The Parish Beadle'. He was elected RA in 1811, and became painter-in-ordinary to the king in 1830.

WILKINS, Sir Hubert (1888-1958). Australian explorer. B. in S Australia, he studied engineering, learnt to fly in 1910 and visited both polar regions. In 1928 he flew from Barrow (Alaska) to Green Harbour (Spitsbergen), for which he was knighted, and in 1928-9 made an Antarctic flight which proved that Graham Land is an island: Ben Eielson was his pilot on both flights. He also planned to reach the N pole by submarine.

WILL. An instrument executed by a person (being neither a minor nor lunatic) as a disposition of his property on death. The rules governing the execution of Ws. are mainly contained in the Ws. Act, 1837. A soldier or sailor on active service may make a W. in any clear form, but otherwise the W. must be in writing or print. It must be signed by the testator in the presence of 2 witnesses who also sign, and may not be beneficiaries under the W. Practice in the USA is based on similar lines.

WILLIAM I, called **the Conqueror** (*c.* 1027-87). King of England and duke of Normandy. B. at Falaise, the illegitimate son of duke Robert the Devil, he succeeded his father in the duchy in 1035. Claiming that he had been bequeathed the English throne by his kinsman Edward the Confessor, he invaded England in 1066, defeated and killed Harold at Hastings, and was crowned king. His reign marks the complete establishment of feudalism in England, although W. kept the barons firmly under Crown control. He d. at Rouen after a fall from his horse, and was buried at Caen.

WILLIAM II, called **Rufus** (the Red), (*c.* 1056-1100). King of England. The 3rd son of William I, he inherited England in 1087, and spent much of his reign attempting to conquer Normandy from his brother Robert. His exactions led to baronial revolts, while his methods of extorting money from the Church brought him into conflict with archbishop Anselm. He was killed while hunting in the New Forest, and was buried in Winchester cathedral.

WILLIAM III, called **W. of Orange** (1650-1702). King of Gt Britain and Ireland. B. at The Hague, the son of William II of Orange, and Mary, dau. of Charles I, the French invasion of the Netherlands in 1672 led to his installation as stadtholder. His stubborn resistance forced Louis XIV to make peace in 1678, and from that time he devoted himself to building up a European alliance to resist French aggression. In 1677 he m. his cousin Mary, dau. of James, duke of York. Invited by the opposition, he invaded England in 1688, and accepted the crown, as joint sovereign with Mary, in 1689. He accepted a constitutional settlement whereby parliament secured the main control of policy, although he attempted to safeguard his power by playing off the 2 parties against each other. Much of his reign he spent campaigning, first in Ireland, where in 1690 he defeated James II at the Boyne, and later against the French in Flanders.

WILLIAM IV (1765-1837). King of the United Kingdom. B. at Buckingham Palace, the 3rd son of George III, he was cr. duke of Clarence in 1789, and m. Adelaide of Saxe-Meiningen in 1818. He succeeded George IV in 1830, and during the Reform Bill crisis secured its passage by agreeing to create new peers.

WILLIAM I (1797-1888). King of Prussia and German emperor. B. at Berlin, the son of Frederick William III, he served in the Napoleonic campaigns of 1814-15, and helped to crush the 1848 revolution. He succeeded his brother Frederick William IV in 1861. His policy was largely dictated by Bismarck (q.v.), who secured his proclamation as German emperor in 1871.

WILLIAM II (1859-1941). German emperor. The son of Frederick III and of Victoria, dau. of Queen Victoria, he succeeded his father in 1888. He began his reign by forcing Bismarck to resign in 1890, and his blundering interventions in the field of foreign policy were usually disastrous. During the 1914 crisis, he at first approved Austria's ultimatum to Serbia; then, realizing war was imminent, strove to prevent it when it was too late. On the outbreak of revolution in 1918 he fled to Holland, and spent the rest of his life at the castle of Doorn.

WILLIAM. Name of 3 kings of the Netherlands. **William I** (1772-1844), the son of Prince William V of Orange, lived in exile during the French occupation of 1795-1813, and fought against Napoleon at Jena and Wagram. In 1814 he assumed the title of king; the Austrian Netherlands was added to his kingdom by the Allies in 1815, but secured independence (recognized by the Powers 1839) by the revolution of 1830. W.'s unpopularity led to his abdication in 1840. His son **William II** (1792-1849) served with the British Army in the Peninsular War and at Waterloo. He succeeded his father in 1840, and by conceding a liberal constitution in 1848 averted revolution. William II's son, **William III** (1817-90), reigned 1849-90.

WILLIAM, called **the Lion** (1143-1214). King of Scotland. He became king in 1165. While invading England in 1174 he was captured and forced to do homage for his kingdom to Henry II, but the English claim to suzerainty was abandoned by Richard I in 1189 for a money payment.

WILLIAM. Ger. Crown Prince. *See* FREDERICK WILLIAM.

WILLIAM, called **the Silent** (1533-84). Prince of Orange. The son of the count of Nassau, he inherited the principality of Orange in 1544. He was brought up as a Catholic, and was appointed governor of Holland by Philip II of Spain in 1559. He opposed Philip's tyranny and intolerance, and in 1572 joined the revolt of Holland and Zeeland against Spanish rule; he accepted Protestantism in 1573, and from that time was accepted as the Dutch national leader. His policy of uniting the Protestant and Catholic provinces by religious toleration failed; the S provinces submitted to Spain, while the N formed a federation in 1579, and repudiated Spanish suzerainty in 1581. W. was assassinated at Delft by a Spanish agent. Though talkative, he knew how to hold his tongue on matters of importance - hence his nickname.

WILLIAM OF MALMESBURY (*c.* 1080-*c.* 1143). English historian. A monk of Malmesbury Abbey, Wilts, he compiled the *Gesta regum* and *Historia novella*, together forming a history of England to 1142.

WILLIAM OF WYKEHAM (*c.* 1323-1404). English churchman. B. at Wickham, Hants, he entered the royal service *c.* 1347. He was bp of Winchester from 1367, Lord Chancellor 1367-72 and 1389-91. He founded New Coll., Oxford, in 1379, and Winchester Coll. in 1378.

WILLIAMS, Emlyn (1905-). Welsh actor, playwright, and producer. B. in Mostyn, Flintshire, he made his stage début in 1927, and has since appeared in many plays, including his own *Night Must Fall*, and *The Corn is Green*, and gave a remarkable solo performance as Dickens in readings from the novelist (1951-2) and similarly as Dylan Thomas (1955 and 1957-8). He pub. his autobiography *George* - his own unused first Christian name - in 1961.

WILLIAMS, Sir George. *See* YOUNG MEN'S CHRISTIAN ASSOCIATION.

WILLIAMS, Roger (*c.* 1604-84). English colonizer. B. in London, he emigrated to Massachusetts, but was banished in 1635 for advocating religious toleration. He founded the colony of Rhode Island, on a basis of democracy and complete religious freedom, in 1636.

WILLIAMS, Shirley (1930-). British politician. Dau. of Vera Brittain (q.v.), she was m. to the philosopher, Prof. Bernard Williams 1955–74. Labour Min. for Prices 1974–6 and Education and Science 1976–9, she was a founder of the Social Democratic Party (q.v.), but lost her parliamentary seat in 1983. Her books incl. *Politics is for People* (1981).

WILLIAMS, Tennessee. Pseudonym of American playwright Thomas Lanier W. (1911–83), b. in Missouri. His work was heavy with the frustrations of life in the Deep South, espec. among his women characters, e.g. *The Glass Menagerie* (1945), *A Streetcar named Desire* (1947), and *The Night of the Iguana* (1961).

WILLIAMS, William Carlos (1883-1963). Am. poet. B. in Rutherford, New Jersey, he used spare images and language, and advanced forms of verse in intellectual patterns.

WILLIAMSBURG. City of Va., USA, on a peninsula between York and James rivers, 72km (45m) SE of Richmond. It is the seat of William and Mary College (1693). Dating from 1632, W. was the cap. of the colony of Va. 1699-1779. It has been restored from 1927 chiefly at the expense of John D. Rockefeller Jr, to its 18th cent. appearance, Pop. (1970) 9,070.

WILLIAMS-ELLIS, Sir Clough (1883-1978). British architect, best-known as the designer of the fantasy resort of Portmeirion, N Wales. He was knighted in 1972.

WILLIAMSON, Henry (1895-1977). British author, known for such stories of animal life as *Tarka The Otter* (1927).

WILLIAMSON, Malcolm (1931-). British composer. B. in Australia, he settled in Britain in 1953, and is also a pianist and organist. His works incl. operas (*Our Man in Havana,* 1963), symphonies and chamber music. He became Master of the Queen's Musick 1975.

WILLIS, Ted, baron (1914-). British playwright. B. in London, he became known for his television scripts for the police series *Dixon of Dock Green* (1953-63) and plays of working-class life such as *Woman in a Dressing Gown,* which won the Berlin award as a film (1958). Active in socialist fields, he was in 1963 created a life peer.

WILL-O'-THE-WISP or **ignis fatuus.** Hovering light seen above marshy ground, possibly due to the spontaneous ignition of methane (q.v.).

WILLOW. Genus (*Salix*) of trees and shrubs in the family Salicaceae, which flourish in damp places. The leaves are lance-shaped, and the flowers appear as catkins. Among species found in Britain are the crack W. (*S. fragilis*), the white W. (*S. alba*), the goat W. (*S. caprea*), the weeping W. (*S. babylonica*; a native of China), and the common osier (*s. viminalis*). Cricket bats are made from the white W. (*var. caerulea*).

WILLOW-HERB. Genus of plants (*Epilobium*), well known as weeds. The rose-bay W. or fireweed W. (*Chamaenerion angustifolium*), now placed in a separate genus, is common in woods and waste places. It grows to a considerable height, with long terminal racemes of red or purplish flowers.

WILLOW SOUTH. Projected cap. of Alaska, USA, which lies c. 110 km (70 m) NW of Anchorage.

WILLOW WARBLER. *See* WARBLER.

WILLY-WILLY. Australian Aboriginal term for a cyclonic storm whirlwind.

WILMINGTON. City and port of Delaware, USA, on r. Delaware. Principal industries incl. shipbuilding, and the manufacture of chemicals, leather, iron and steel goods, textiles. The Swedes built Fort Cristina on the site (1638); it passed to the Dutch (1655), the English (1664). Services are still held in the church of Holy Trinity (1698). W. is the HQ of Du Pont enterprises, which started with the foundation of a powder mill (1802) by E. J. du Pont de Nemours. Pop. (1970) 80,400.

WILSON, Sir Angus (1913-). British author. Attached to the Foreign Office during the S.W.W., he was deputy to the superintendent of the B.M. Reading Room 1949-55, and became professor at East Anglia Univ. in 1966. His acidly humorous books incl. *Anglo-Saxon Attitudes* (1956), *The Old Men at the Zoo* (1961), and *Setting the World on Fire* (1980). He was knighted in 1980.

WILSON, Charles Thomson Rees (1869-1959). British physicist. Jacksonian prof. of natural philosophy at Cambridge 1925-34, he was in 1911 the inventor of the W. cloud chamber which enabled the path of an atom to be visibly tracked. In 1927 he shared with A. H. Compton a Nobel prize. *See* CLOUD CHAMBER.

WILSON, Colin (1931-). British author. Leaving school in his native Leicester at 16, he worked as a labourer, in a plastics factory, etc., and then caused a sensation with *The Outsider* (1956), which made the social misfit a hero. Later he made a reputation with thrillers, e.g. *Necessary Doubt* (1964).

WILSON, Edmund (1895-1972). American author. B. in New Jersey, he is best-known as a critic, *Axel's Castle* (1931) being a survey of Symbolism and *The Wound and the Bow* (1941) a study of art and neurosis, and was an early advocate of the work of Dos Passos, Faulkner, Hemingway and Scott Fitzgerald. He also produced original work, e.g. the satiric sketches in *Memoirs of Hecate County* (1946).

WILSON, Sir Henry Hughes (1864-1922). British soldier. He served in Burma, S Africa, and the F.W.W., became CIGS in 1918 and was created field marshal. He was murdered in London by Irish terrorists.

WILSON, Henry Maitland, 1st baron (1881-1964). British field marshal. He served in the S African and F.W.W., and in 1939 became GOC in C Egypt. In 1941 he took command of the 9th Army in the Near East, became C-in-C, Middle East in 1943, and in 1944 was Supreme Allied Commander in the Mediterranean theatre. In 1945-7 he was head of the British Joint Staff Mission in Washington. He was created a baron in 1946.

WILSON, (James) Harold, baron (1916–). Brit. Lab. statesman. B. in Huddersfield, son of a works chemist, he lectured in economics at Oxford in 1937, became a Fellow of Univ. College in 1938, and was elected MP in 1945. He succeeded Sir Stafford Cripps as Pres. of the Board of Trade, but in protest against cuts in social-service spending he resigned in 1951. In 1960 he had a crushing defeat when he challenged Gaitskell's party leadership, but on the latter's death succeeded him. Victorious in the general election of 1964 (increased majority 1966), he encountered opposition to his 'productivity, prices and incomes policy' within his party, and was defeated at the election of June 1970. After the election of Feb. 1974 he formed a minority govt and in Oct. 1974 achieved a majority of 3: his premiership was dominated by the Common Market issue, the Social Contract, and economic difficulties. His memoirs incl. *Final Term: The Labour Government 1974-6* (1979) were controversial. He resigned in 1976, handing over to James Callaghan, and accepted a knighthood (KG). He became a peer in 1983.

WILSON, Richard (1714-82). English landscape artist. He produced Italian and English scenes with an idealist touch and feeling for atmosphere which led towards romanticism.

WILSON, Thomas Woodrow (1856-1924). 28th President of the USA. B. at Staunton, Virginia, he became president of Princeton univ. in 1902. In 1910 he was elected Democratic governor of New Jersey, and in 1912 and again in 1916 he was elected President of the USA. He initiated measures against the Trusts and secured valuable social legislation. He strove to keep the USA neutral during the F.W.W. but the German U-boat campaign forced him to declare war in 1917. In Jan. 1918 he issued his 'Fourteen Points' as a basis for a just peace settlement. At the peace conference in Paris he was successful in securing the inclusion of the League of Nations in the Treaty of Versailles. But on his return to America the treaty, though accepted by a majority of the Senate, failed

WILSON. Sir Harold Wilson entertaining the Prime Minister of Singapore, Lee Kuan Yew, during a visit to Chequers. Both men are keen golfers. *Photo: Popperfoto*

to secure the two-thirds majority necessary, under the Constitution, for ratification.

WILTON. English market town in Wilts, 4km (2.5m) W of Salisbury. W. House, the seat of the earl of Pembroke, was built from designs by Holbein and Inigo Jones, and is associated with Sir Philip Sidney and Shakespeare. W. has been famous for its carpets from the 16th cent. Pop. (1972) 3,960.

WILTSHIRE. SW co. of England, N of Hants and Dorset. In the S is Salisbury Plain; to the NE are Marlborough Downs and Savernake Forest. The principal rivers are the Kennet, Bristol Avon, and Salisbury Avon. The chief crop is wheat, and much of the county is under pasture. Salisbury is the co. town; other centres are Trowbridge (admin. centre), Swindon, Devizes, and Westbury. Stonehenge and Avebury are famous prehistoric monuments. Area 3,481 sq.km (1,344 sq.m); pop. (1978) 516,200.

WIMBLEDON. District of the Greater London bor. of Merton, HQ of the All-England Lawn Tennis Club where world-famous international matches have been held since 1877.

WINCHELL, Walter (1897-1972). American journalist. B. in NY City, he was a columnist on the *New York Mirror* 1929-69, his bitingly satiric writings being syndicated throughout the USA.

WINCHESTER. English cathedral city in Hants on the Itchen, 19km (12m) N of Southampton: it is admin. HQ of the co. It was fortified by the Romans, and became the capital of Wessex. Its cathedral (Gothic and Norman) contains the remains of Saxon kings: built on marshland it was in danger of collapse in 1905 but was saved largely by the efforts of the diver William Walker (d. 1918) who is commemorated by a bronze statue, erected 1964. Jane Austen d. at W., and a window in the cathedral commemorates her. Little of the Norman castle remains, but in the hall King Arthur's Round Table (so-called) is shown. W. College (1394) developed from a 7th cent. grammar school. Pop. (1972) 31,620.

WINDERMERE. Largest lake in England, in Cumbria 17km (10.5m) long and 1.6km (1m) wide. The small town of W. (formerly Birtwaite) is on the E shore.

WINDHOEK (-hook). Capital of SW Africa, 200km (180m) E of Walvis Bay, centre of a dairying region with cold-storage plants and an airport; there are hot springs nearby. Pop. (1970) 60,000.

WINDMILL. A mill with sails or vanes which by the action of wind upon them drive machinery for grinding corn, pumping water, etc. Ws. were used in the E in ancient times, and in Europe they were first used in Germany and the Netherlands in the 12th cent. The main types of W. are the 'post' mill, which is turned round a post when the direction of the wind changes, and the 'tower' mill which has a revolving construction at the top. In the USA a light type of W. with steel sails supported on a long steel girder shaft was introduced for use on farms. The energy crisis has led to modern experiments designed to use wind power on a major scale.

WINDS. Name given to lateral movements of the Earth's atmosphere. Along the equator there is a belt of low pressure, the Doldrums, and towards this belt the Trade Winds blow from the Horse Latitudes - high-pressure areas about 30° N and 30° S of the equator. In the northern hemisphere the Trade Winds blow from the NE, and in the southern from the SE. Also from the Horse Latitudes blow the westerlies towards the poles - N of the equator these are SW winds, and S of the equator they blow from the NW. This theoretical arrangement is affected by the distribution of land and water. There are many local Ws., while on the margin of equatorial calms there may be developed the violent storms known as tornadoes, typhoons, etc. The force of wind is expressed by the Beaufort Scale (q.v.).

WINDSOR, Duchess of (1896-). *Née* (Bessie) Wallis Warfield, in Pennsylvania, she m. in 1916 Earl Winfield Spencer (div. 1927), in 1928 Ernest Simpson (div. 1936), and in 1937 the Duke of Windsor (formerly Edward VIII, q.v.). She pub. her memoirs *The Heart has its Reasons* (1956).

WINDSOR, House of. Official name of the British royal family, adopted in place of 'the house of Saxe-Coburg-Gotha', in 1917. In 1960 Elizabeth II decided that certain of her descendants i.e. those not entitled to the prefix HRH, would in future use the surname Mountbatten-Windsor.

WINDSOR. City and lake port in Ontario, Canada, on the Detroit river, opposite Detroit, USA. It is a great rail and agricultural centre and motor-car engines, iron and steel goods, bricks, etc. are manufactured. Pop. met. area (1976) 247,580.

WINDSOR. Town in Berks, England, on the Thames. It is dominated by W. Castle (q.v.), and has a 17th cent. guildhall of Wren's design. The Treaty of W., 1373, estab. a permanent alliance between England and Portugal. Pop. (1972) 30,900.

WINDSOR CASTLE. The British royal residence in Windsor, Berks. It was founded by William the Conqueror on the site of an even earlier stronghold. In the Lower Ward are St George's Chapel, a fine example of Perpendicular architecture, and the chapel of the Order of the Garter; and the Albert Memorial Chapel, below which are buried George III, George IV, William IV,

George V and George VI. Beyond the Round Tower or Keep is the Upper Ward containing the state apartments and the Queen's private apartments. In the Home Park adjoining the castle is Frogmore House and the Royal Mausoleum where Queen Victoria, the Prince Consort, and Edward VIII rest. Windsor Great Park, with its artificial lake, Virginia Water, lies to the south.

WIND TUNNEL. Laboratory 'tunnel' in which air is blown over a stationary model aircraft to simulate the effects of flight. Lift, drag, and air-flow patterns are observed by the use of special cameras and sensitive instruments, to prepare the way for construction of a full-scale model, which in turn precedes the prototypes which make actual test flights.

WINDWARD ISLANDS. Group of British islands in the W Indies comprising Grenada, St Vincent, St Lucia and Dominica (qq.v.), with the Grenadines, divided between Grenada and St Vincent. Total area 2,100 sq.km (811 sq.m); pop. (1970) 375,000.

Other islands called W.I. are the N group of the Cape Verde Is.; St Martin (St Maarten), St Eustatius and Saba in the Lesser Antilles; Tahiti, Moorea, and Makatea in French Polynesia. The name indicates that they are in the path of the prevailing wind.

WINE. The fermented juice of ripe grapes. The yeast *Saccharomyces ellipsoideus*, which normally lives on the skin of the grape, turns the sugar into ethyl alcohol. For a dry W., fermentation is allowed to go on until the sugar is all or nearly all converted; for a sweet or medium W. the change is arrested at the appropriate time by drawing off the liquor from the grape pulp (*marc*). The quality of W. depends on the type of grape used, the soil, and the climate. The traditional treading of the grapes has been almost entirely replaced by pressing machines.

Red W. is produced from the whole grape, white W. from the juice only. Natural sparkling (actually bubbling) Ws. have been bottled while still fermenting; sparkling champagne is artificially carbonated (natural champagne, rarely met with outside France, is still). Many palatable Ws. do not travel well, and can be found only in the place of origin. France is outstanding as a producer of W.: the finest and the widest variety come from there. Other countries producing excellent Ws. incl. Germany, Hungary, Yugoslavia, Italy, Switzerland, South Africa (where the vine was introduced by Huguenot settlers in 1688), and the USA, where 85 per cent of production is in California. Australian wines have a growing reputation, and also those of S America where the dry, sunny slopes of the central Andes are ideal for vines. The best come from Chile, but Argentina and Uruguay are also good.

W. of a kind can be made from a great many fruits, vegetables, and flowers, and in country districts elderflower, elderberry, parsnip, dandelion, rhubarb, gooseberry, etc., Ws. are regularly made.

WINGATE, Orde Charles (1903-44). British soldier. In 1936 he estab. a reputation for his unorthodox tactics against the ex-Mufti of Jerusalem in Palestine and in the S.W.W. served under Wavell in the Middle East, and later led the 'Chindits' (q.v.) in guerrilla operations against the Japanese in Burma. He was killed in an aeroplane accident in Burma.

A village on Mt Carmel in Israel, inaugurated 1953, was called W. after him.

WINNIPEG. Cap. of Manitoba prov., Canada, at the confluence of the Assiniboine and Red rivers, 72km (45m) S of Lake W., 96km (60m) N of the US border. It is an important railway and financial centre. W. is a great grain market with flour mills, saw mills, foundries, meatpacking works; factories making boxes, bricks, confectionery etc.; printing and bookbinding works. It began as a fur-trading post (1763), and fur auctions are still held. Pop. met. area (1976) 578,220.

Lake W. has an area of 24,500 sq.km (9,465 sq.m).

WINTERGREEN. Genus of plants (*Pyrola*) in the heath family. *P. minor*, with rounded white flowers, is a woodland plant. From the leaves of the N American *Gaultheria procumbens* is extracted oil of W. used in treating rheumatism.

WINTERHALTER (vin'terhahlter), **Franz Xavier** (1806-73). German artist. B. in the Black Forest, he studied at Munich Academy, and was court painter to the Grand Duke Leopold at Karlsruhe. He painted portraits of Queen Victoria, Napoleon III, etc.

WINTERTHUR (vin'tertoor). Swiss town and spa in the canton of Zürich, NE of Zürich, manufacturing rly engines and textiles. Pop. (1971) 92,700.

WIREWORM. *See* CLICK-BEETLE.

WISBECH (wis'bēch). Market town and port on the Nene, in the Isle of Ely, England. Centre of a bulb-growing area, it has fruit and vegetable-canning factories, printing works, etc. Pop. (1972) 17,000.

WISCO'NSIN. N Central state of the USA, a high plain sloping from the Great Lakes in the E to the Mississippi. There are dense forests, esp. in the N; and in the S there is prairie land. W is the premier dairying state of the USA, and much of the grain produced is fed to livestock; wheat growing and milling are also important. Manufactures, based on local supplies of coal, iron, zinc and lead, incl. agricultural machinery, pumps, metal furniture, precision instruments, plumbing equipment. The chief cities are Madison, the capital, and Milwaukee. Area 145,438 sq.km (56,153 sq.m); pop. (1970) 4,417,933.

WISE, Thomas James (1859-1937). British bibliographer. He collected the Ashley Library of first editions, chiefly English poets and dramatists 1890-1930, acquired by the BM at his death, but is chiefly remembered for his forgeries of supposed privately printed first editions of Browning, Tennyson, Swinburne, etc. His activities were revealed by J. Carter and G. Pollard in 1934 and in 1956 it was found that he had perfected his own copies of 17th cent. plays by abstracting leaves from BM copies.

WISEMAN, Nicholas Patrick Stephen (1802-65). British cardinal. B. in Seville, he was rector of the English college at Rome, and became the first abp of Westminster in 1850. Newman was his protégé.

WI'SHART, George (*c.* 1513-46). Scottish Protestant reformer, burned for heresy at St Andrews. He was closely associated with Knox.

WISTER, Owen (1860-1938). American novelist. B. in Philadelphia, a grandson of Fanny Kemble, he was famous for stories of cowboys in the American west, e.g. *The Virginian* (1902).

WISTĒ'RIA. A climbing shrub (*Wisteria chinensis*) in the family Leguminoseae, native to China. It has racemes of pale mauve flowers, and pinnate leaves.

WITAN or **Witenagemot.** The council of the Anglo-Saxon kings, which was composed of officers of the household, the greater land-owners, the bishops, and the abbots of important monasteries.

WITCHCRAFT. The supposed power of working magic with the aid of the devil. Witches were persecuted all over W Europe during the 15th-17th cents., among the best-known cases being those of Joan of Arc and Gilles de Rais. 'White' witches who use 'supernatural' powers for good purposes, e.g. in charming warts, may still be found in England, and after the S.W.W. there was a revival of interest in W. or 'black magic'. Witch 'doctors', as practitioners of traditional medicine, may have considerable skill, and in 1976 the World Health Organization recommended that African govts integrate them into health teams and study their methods.

WITCHCRAFT. Kofi Smart, a much respected witch doctor from Ghana, encourages the use of drums and chanting during his consultations. His herbal remedies are well-known also in neighbouring countries. *Photo: John Moss/Camera Press*

WITCH HAZEL. Flowering shrub (*Hamamelis virginiana*). An astringent extract prepared from the bark or leaves is used in medicine.

WITNESS. One who supplies the testimony in courts of law, on which cases are decided. The rules as to what evidence is admissible are complex, but direct oral testimony of relevant facts, given by Ws. who were present, is required whenever possible.

WITT, John de (1625-72). Dutch statesman. B. at Dort, he became Grand Pensionary of Holland, and virtual Prime Minister, in 1653. By his skilful diplomacy he conducted the English Wars of 1652-4 and 1665-7 to an honourable conclusion, and in 1668 formed the Triple Alliance with England and Sweden against Louis XIV. His brother **Cornelius de W.** (1623-72) distinguished himself as a naval commander in the English Wars. After the Orangist reaction of 1672 Cornelius was imprisoned; John resigned, and while he was visiting his brother both were murdered by the mob.

WITTELSBACH (vit'telsbakh). Bavarian dynasty, who ruled Bavaria as dukes from 1180, electors from 1623, and kings 1806-1918. Prince Rupprecht (1869-1955), son of King Ludwig III and descended from Elizabeth, dau. of James I of England, was technically a claimant to the British throne and the claim descends to his son Prince Albrecht (1905-).

WITTENBERG. Town of Halle district, E Germany, 65km (40m) NE of Halle, on the Elbe. Luther preached in the Stadtkirche (in which he is buried), nailed his 95 theses to the door of the Schlosskirche in 1517, and was prof. of philosophy in the univ. of W. (1502) transferred to Halle in 1815. The painters Lucas Cranach (father and son) lived at W. Pop. (1972) 45,700.

WITTGENSTEIN (vit'genshtīn), **Ludwig** (1889-1951). Austrian philosopher, who worked chiefly at Cambridge. A follower of Frege and pupil of Bertrand Russell (qq.v.), and critic of both, he pub. *Tractatus Logico-Philosophicus,* a classic of analytic philosophy, in 1922. His teaching and posthumous writings, notably *Philosophical Investigations* (1953), completed the work of making language the central subject of philosophic inquiry.

WOAD. Species of plant (*Isatis tinctoria*) in the family Cruciferae. It has arrow-shaped leaves and clusters of yellow flowers. A blue dye, made from the fermented leaves, was used by the ancient Britons to stain their bodies when going into battle.

WODEHOUSE (wood'-), **Sir Pelham Grenville** (1881-1975). British humorist, who became a US citizen in 1955. He wrote a long series of novels, featuring Bertie Wooster and his impeccable man-servant Jeeves, who live in a world of scatty aristocrats and fossilized, upper-class slang. He was knighted in 1975.

WODEN. *See* ODIN.

WOFFINGTON, Margaret (*c.* 1714-60). Irish actress, better known as Peg W. She played in Dublin as a child and made her début at Covent Garden in 1740. She often played male roles.

WOLF, Hugo (1860-1903). Austrian composer. B. at Windischgraz, in Styria, he studied at Vienna conservatoire, became a critic on a Viennese paper, and d. in a Vienna lunatic asylum. His songs belong to the greatest achievements of the Ger. *Lieder* tradition. He also composed the opera *Der Corregidor* and orchestral works, such as 'Italian Serenade'.

WOLF. Wild member of the dog family. The common W. of Europe and Asia (*Canis lupus*) has thick greyish fur: the N American timber W. is a larger variety. Wolves hunt in packs and are now restricted by urban expansion to deep forest country. The prairie W. is the Coyote (q.v.).

WOLFE, Charles (1791-1823). Irish curate, author of one great poem, 'The Burial of Sir John Moore'.

WOLFE, James (1727-59). British soldier. B. at Westerham, Kent, he entered the army in 1741 and served at the battles of Dettingen, Falkirk, Culloden, and Laffeldt. In 1758 he served under Amherst in Canada, and played a conspicuous part in the siege of Louisburg. In 1759 he was promoted major-general, and commanded the victorious expedition against Quebec, in which he lost his life.

WOLFE, Thomas (1900-38). American novelist. B. in N Carolina, he was ed. at the univ. and at Harvard, and travelled to Europe. He believed that good writing was the work of the unconscious, and poured out an enormous quantity of wordage which was cut and shaped by his publisher/editor Maxwell Perkins. His 4 books are *Look Homeward, Angel* (1929), *Of Time and the River* (1935) and the posthumous *The Web and the Rock* (1939) and *You Can't go Home Again* (1940).

WOLF. Relying on each other so much to cooperate in the running down of their prey, the wolf packs form close-knit units, accepting a fixed hierarchy, and indulgent to the young. *Photo: Douglas Corrance*

WOLF-FERRARI (vōlf-ferah'rē), **Ermanno** (1876-1948). Italian-German composer, b. at Venice, whose operas incl. *Il segreto do Susanna*, *I gioielli della Madonna*, and many others.

WOLFIT, Sir Donald (1902-68). British actor-manager. B. at Newark-on-Trent, he formed his own Shakespearian company in 1937, and excelled in the larger-than-life roles of Shylock, Lear, Volpone, etc.

WOLFRAM. Grey, hard metal, ductile and malleable, formerly (until 1949) officially known as tungsten: symbol W, at. no. 74, at. wt. 183.86. Recognized and named by Scheele in 1781, and discovered by the d'Elhujar brothers in 1783, it occurs as wolframite ($FeWO_4$), scheelite ($CaWO_4$) and huberite ($MnWO_4$). Non-magnetic, it is insoluble except in a mixture of nitric and hydrofluoric acids, and has the highest melting point (3370°C) of any metal. W. is used in alloy steels for armour plate, projectiles, high-speed cutting tools, etc., for lamp filaments and thermionic valves. Its salts are used in the paint and tanning industries.

WOLFSBURG. Town NE of Brunswick in W Germany, chosen 1938 as the Volkswagen (Hitler's 'People's Car') factory site. Pop. (1979) 127,330.

WOLFSON, Sir Isaac (1897-). British merchant. Chairman of Great Universal Stores Ltd. from 1946, he estab. the W. Foundation 1955 to advance health, education and youth activities, and endowed 1966 (jointly with Ford Foundation) W. College, Oxford, concentrating on science and technology.

WOLLONGONG (wool'lengong). City (incl. Port Kembla) of NSW, Australia, 65km (40m) S of Sydney. Coal is mined nearby, and there are iron and steel works. Pop. met. area (1976) 211,100.

WOLLSTONECRAFT, Mary. *See* under GODWIN, WILLIAM.

WOLSELEY (wool'zli), **Garnet Joseph,** 1st visct (1833-1913). British field marshal. He entered the army in 1852, and for his victory at the battle of Tel-el-Kebir, 1882, was raised to the peerage. After leading the Gordon relief expedition of 1884-5 he was created a visct. He was C-in-C 1895-1900.

WOLSEY, Thomas (*c.* 1475-1530). English cardinal and statesman. B. at Ipswich, the son of a butcher, he was ed. at Magdalen College, Oxford, and took holy orders. Under Henry VIII he had rapid advancement, being made bp of Lincoln and archbp of York in 1514. Several other sees were conferred on him, and in 1515 he was created a cardinal and became Lord Chancellor of England. During the next 10 years he was one of the most powerful men in Europe. Under him the smaller English monasteries were dissolved, and zeal for the New Learning found expression in Cardinal College (later Christ Church) at Oxford. But his reluctance to further Henry's divorce from Catherine of Aragon led to his downfall in 1529, and in 1530 he was charged with high treason and arrested. He d. at Leicester Abbey.

WOLSEY. A letter from Henry VIII to the Cardinal in July 1518, in which the King plays the role of anxious husband. He is hopeful that the Queen (Catherine of Aragon) is pregnant, and is 'loath to repair to London', since he wishes to move her 'as little as I may now'. *Photo: Mansell Collection*

WOLVERHAMPTON. Town in W Midlands, England, 21km (13m) NW of Birmingham. Industries incl. metal-working, chemicals, tyres, aircraft, commercial vehicles, etc. Pop. (1974) 270,000.

WOLVERINE. Animal (*Gulo gulo*) in the weasel family, Mustelidae, of which it is the largest species, found in Europe, Asia and N America. It covers food it is unable to consume with an unpleasant secretion, hence its alternative popular name of 'glutton'.

WOMBAT. Marsupial of the family Vombatidae, e.g. *Vombatus ursinus* of Tasmania and *V. platyrhinus* of S Australia. They have coarse brownish fur, live in burrows, and are nocturnal and vegetarian.

WOMEN'S INSTITUTES. Local organizations of women in country districts for the purpose of mutual fellowship and practice of useful crafts. The first was founded in 1897 at Stoney Creek, Ontario, under the presidency of Mrs Adelaide Hoodless. The movement is non-class, non-sectarian, and non-party political, and was taken to Britain by Mrs Alfred Watt, the first W.I. being opened in Anglesey.

WOMEN'S LIB(ERATION). The organized campaign for women's equality in all spheres which developed after the S.W.W., and which had its roots in earlier campaigns for Women's Rights (*see* WOLLSTONECRAFT, Mary), and Women's Emancipation (*see* PANKHURST, Emmeline). Leading propagandists incl. Simone de Beauvoir (q.v.), Betty Friedan *The Feminine Mystique* (1963), Eva Figes *Patriarchal Attitudes* (1970) and Germaine Greer *The Female Eunuch* (1970). A constitutional amendment prohibiting sex discrimination was adopted by Congress in the USA in 1972, and was sent to the states for ratification. In the UK there was an Equal Pay Act (1970: effective 1975) and a Sex Discrimination Act (1975) outlawed discrimination against either sex in employment, education, housing and provision of goods, facilities and services to the public.

WOMEN'S SERVICES. The organized use on a large scale of the services of women to assist the prosecution of warfare is of comparatively recent development. They may be used to replace men called to serve in the armed forces in their peacetime occupations, e.g. in factories or agriculture, as with the *Women's Land Army* in Britain 1917-20; to act as volunteer part-time auxiliaries for new tasks created by war, e.g. the *Women's Voluntary Services* (W.V.S.), an amalgamation in Britain in 1938 of already existing bodies which cared for evacuees, gave service in hospitals, assisted air-raid victims, etc., and was continued after the S.W.W. (created W. Royal V.S. 1966); or to enlist as auxiliaries to the armed services. Use of women in actual combat is regarded with repugnance by many civilized states, except in such dire emergency as in the desperate Russian stand against the German invaders in the S.W.W., but may be accepted as routine in such newly emergent states as Cuba and Israel. In Britain there are separate corps for all 3 services: *Women's Army Corps* (WRAC) created in 1949 to take over the functions of the Auxiliary Territorial Service, estab. in 1938 but with a F.W.W. equivalent in the Women's Army Auxiliary Corps (WAAC); *Women's Royal Naval Service* (WRNS) 1917-19 and 1939 onwards; and the *Women's Royal Air Force* (WRAF) estab in 1918 but known 1939-48 as the Women's Auxiliary Air Force (WAAF); and also nursing services, i.e. Queen Alexandra's Army Nursing Corps and Naval Nursing Service, and for the RAF Princess Mary's Nursing Service. In the USA there is a separate Women's Army Corps (WAC), estab. in 1948, which developed from the Women's Army Auxiliary Corps (WAAC), in turn originating in F.W.W. organization on the British model; but although there are nurse corps for the 3 services, there are no separate auxiliary corps for the navy and air force, women being integrated into the general structure.

WOOD, Grant (1892-1942). American artist. A regionalist painter, he struck a note of hard realism in his 'American gothic' studies of farming folk, which were the sensation of the 1930s.

WOOD, Haydn (1882-1950). British composer. A violinist, he wrote a violin concerto among other works, but is best known for his songs which incl. 'Roses of Picardy'.

WOOD, Mrs Henry (1814-87). British novelist, *née* Ellen Price. Dau. of a glove manufacturer, she m. a merchant, but was widowed and settled in London to write. She won early fame with *East Lynne* (1861), later books incl. *The Channings* (1862) and the Johnny Ludlow series of detective stories.

WOOD, Sir Henry (1869-1944). British conductor. B. in London, he studied at the RAM, had experience as an organist and operatic conductor, and from 1895 until his death conducted the London Promenade Concerts, now named after him. He greatly promoted a new national interest in music, and encouraged many young British composers. As a composer he is remembered by the 'Fantasia of Sea Songs' which ends each Promenade season.

WOOD, John (*c.* 1705-54). British architect, known as 'Wood of Bath' because he did his best work for that city. He designed the Royal Crescent, which, like many of his other designs, was carried out by his son, John Wood (d. 1782).

WOOD. The substance beneath the bark of the stem and branches of a tree or shrub: it is hard and fibrous, and in the case of trees is known as timber (q.v.). A super hard wood is produced in wood plastic combinations (WPC), in which W. is impregnated with liquid plastic (monomer) and the whole is then bombarded with gamma-rays to polymerize the plastic.

WOOD-CARVING. The art of carving wood figures in relief or in the round, decorative forms, etc. It was practised in the earliest times, and is practised today by civilized and primitive peoples in most parts of the world. Works of the Negroes of West Africa and of the natives of the South Sea islands are noteworthy. In India, China, and other eastern countries images of deities, etc., have been executed in wood throughout many cents. In Mohammedan countries interior decoration in mosques and other buildings is executed in wood. In Europe, Gothic craftsmen produced much beautiful work such as carved doors, effigies, mouldings, misericords, and reredoses, and many of the great craftsmen of the Renaissance worked in wood, as do many leading modern sculptors.

WOODCUTS and WOOD ENGRAVINGS. In making a woodcut a block of smooth-grained wood is used, the most suitable kinds being lime, cherry, American whitewood, and maple. The block is cut along the grain, and the areas and lines of the design are left in relief. This is probably the oldest printing process, dating from the 15th cent., and it was commonly used by early printers for book illustration.

Wood engravings have not the coarseness of woodcuts; they are usually made in boxwood, though apple and pear are sometimes used. The block is cut across the grain, and it is possible to obtain subtle tonal effects. In the 18th cent. Thomas Bewick developed the medium to perfection. Later wood engravers incl. Eric Gill, Clare Leighton, Rockwell Kent, and Eric Daglish.

WOODFORDE James (1740-1803). British clergyman. He was a fellow and subwarden of New College, Oxon., and held livings in Somerset and Norfolk. His diary covering 1758-1802 is remarkable for its presentation of rural England.

WOOD-CARVING. A detail from the superb 15th century altarpiece in Mariacki cathedral, Krakow, considered to be one of the finest wood carvings north of the Alps. *Photo: Courtesy of 'Orbis' Travel*

WOODLOUSE. Name given to certain Isopoda (Crustaceae) of the family Oniscidae. Unlike all other Isopoda they live on land and breathe air, but damp is necessary to their existence. The eggs are carried by the female in a pouch beneath the thorax.

WOODPECKER. Birds allied to the wrynecks, with whom they form the family Picidae. They live on insects obtained from crevices in the bark of trees. The British green W. or yaffle (*Picus viridis*) is green with red crown and yellow rump, and about the size of a jay. The greater and lesser spotted Ws. (*Dryobates major* and *D. minor*), also British species, have black, red, and white plumage. There are numerous species in N America.

WOODSTOCK. Town in Oxfordshire, England, 13km (8m) NW of Oxford, dating from the 11th cent. It has many associations with the sovereigns of England: Henry I built a palace at W.; Fair Rosamund, mistress of Henry II, is supposed to have lived there; the Black Prince was b. there; and Elizabeth I was imprisoned at W. by Mary I in 1554. Pop. (1971) 2,000.

WOODWORM. The common name for the larval stage of certain wood-boring beetles. Dead or injured trees are their natural target, but they become a serious menace when they attack structural timber and furniture. Most common in Britain are the furniture beetle (*Anobium punctatum*), generally attacking older timber and est. to be present in half the country's buildings; the powder-post beetle (*Lyctus* sp.), attacking newer timber; the death-watch beetle (q.v.), whose presence always coincides with fungal decay; and the wood-boring weevils. Special wood preservatives have been developed to combat W., which has markedly increased since the S.W.W. In warmer countries the greatest danger to timber is from termites (q.v.).

WOOKEY HOLE. Natural cave near Wells, Som., England, in which flint implements of Old Stone Age man with bones of extinct animals have been found.

WOOL. The natural fibrous covering of the sheep, and also of the llama, angora goat, etc. The domestic sheep, *Ovis aries*, provides the great bulk of the fibres used in commerce. In Britain there are some 26 breeds, and the wool is classified as lustre (incl. Lincoln, Leicester, S Devon, Cotswold, Dartmoor), demi-lustre (Cheviot, Exmoor Horn, and Romney Marsh), down (Dorset, Oxford, Suffolk, Hampshire, Southdown, etc.), and mountain (Blackface, Swaledale, Welsh White, Welsh Black, etc.). Lustre Ws. are used for making worsted dress fabrics, linings, braids, and so on. Demi-lustre Ws. are rather finer in quality, and are used for suitings, overcoats, and costumes, and worsted serge fabrics. First of English-grown Ws. are the down; they are used for hosiery yarns, and some for woollen cloths. Mountain Ws. are coarse and poor in quality, often comprising wool and hair mixed; they are useful for making carpets, homespun tweeds, and low-quality woollen suitings and hosiery.

Most of the world's finest W. comes from the merino sheep, which is not successfully aclimatized in Britain. In 1797 it was introduced into Australia, which has become the world's largest producer of Merino Ws.: S Africa and S America are also large producers. Ws. from cross-bred sheep (usually a cross of one of the lustre class with a merino) are produced in New Zealand. Since the S.W.W. blendings of W. with synthetic fibres have been developed.

WOOLF, Virginia (1882-1941). British author. B. in London, she was the dau. of Sir Leslie Stephen (1832-1904), man-of-letters and editor of the *Dictionary of National Biography* 1885-91. She pub. her first novel *The Voyage Out* in 1915. In *Mrs. Dalloway* (1925) she perfected her 'stream of consciousness' technique. Among her later books are *To the Lighthouse, The Waves, The Years,* and the unrevised *Between the Acts* (1941). She also pub. biographies *Flush* and *Roger Fry*; and criticism and essays as *The Common Reader, A Room of One's Own,* and *The Moment* (1948). She m. in 1912 **Leonard Sidney W.** (1880-1969), literary editor of the *Nation* 1923-30, and joint-editor of the *Political Quarterly* 1931-59; she committed suicide on the recurrence of mental illness, drowning herself near her Sussex home. They jointly founded the Hogarth Press in 1917. He pub. a remarkable 5-vol. autobiography 1960-9.

WOOLLETT, William (1735-85). British engraver. One of the greatest masters of the art, in 1775 he was appointed engraver to George III.

WOOLLEY, Sir Leonard (1880-1960). British archaeologist. Although he carried out valuable excavation at Carchemish, Tell El-Amarna, and Atchana (Hatay), he is best remembered for his work at Ur where he discovered evidence of what may have been the biblical flood, and remains of the ziggurats which inspired the story of the Tower of Babel, as well as relics of rich social and cultural life.

WOOLMAN, John (1720-72). American Quaker. B. in Northampton, NJ, he was one of the first anti-slavery agitators, and left an important *Journal.*

WOOLSACK. Name given to the seat of the Lord High Chancellor in the House of Lords; it is a large square bag of wool and is a reminder of the principal source of English wealth in the Middle Ages.

WOOLWICH. District, on both sides of the Thames, divided from 1964 between the Greater London bors. of Newham (the part N of the Thames), and Greenwich. The Royal Military Academy was moved from W. to Sandhurst in 1946. An ordnance depot was set up at W. in 1518, a foundry in 1716, and George III gave it the name Royal Arsenal in 1805: it was closed down 1967.

WOOLWORTH, Frank Winfield (1852-1919). American businessman. He opened his first successful 'five and ten cent' store at Lancaster, Pa., in 1879, and, together with his brother **C. S. Woolworth** (1856-1947), built up a chain of similar shops throughout the USA, Canada, Great Britain, Ireland, and the Continent. His grand-dau., Barbara Hutton (1912-79) was the original 'poor little rich girl': her 7 husbands incl. the actor Cary Grant.

WOOMERA. Small town in S Australia, 177km (110m) NW of Port Augusta, from which W. draws its water supply; centre of a rocket and atomic-weapon proving range estab. 1946 and covering *c.* 8,000 sq.km (3,000 sq.m) to which public access is forbidden. The name (aboriginal) means weapon thrower. Pop. (1971) 4,000.

WOOTTON OF ABINGER, Barbara Frances Wootton, baroness (1897-). British educationist and economist. Prof. of social studies at London 1948-52, she has pub. *Freedom under Planning* (1945), *Social Science and Social Pathology* (1959), etc., and was created a life peer in 1958.

WORCESTER. (1) Cathedral city in Hereford and Worcester, England, admin. HQ of the co., on the Severn. The cathedral is mainly of the 13-14th cents., and the Royal W. Porcelain works was estab. in 1751. Gloves and footwear are made, and W. sauce. At the Battle of W. (1651) Cromwell defeated Charles I. The birthplace of Elgar at nearby Broadheath is a museum. Pop. (1972) 74,260. (2) Port and second-largest city of Mass., USA, on the Blackstone R., founded in 1713. Industries incl. textiles, mechanical engineering, printing, etc. Pop. (1970) 176,570.

WORCESTERSHIRE. Former Midland co. of England, merged with Herefordshire in the new co. of Hereford and W. in 1974, except for a small projection in the N., incl. Smethwick, which went to W. Midlands. Worcester was the co. town.

WORD PROCESSOR. Machine which, by the use of the micro-chip, combines the capabilities of the computer and electric typewriter. It is particularly useful for long reports which may need much amendment in their preparation; documents such as contracts and wills, which must be word-perfect; and long runs of letters which need to be slightly individually varied. The letter, etc., may then be transmitted via a telephone link by the press of a button.

WORDSWORTH, William (1770-1850). British poet. B. at Cockermouth, in Cumberland, he was ed. at Hawkeshead School and St John's Coll., Cantab. Going to France in 1791, he sympathized deeply with the revolutionaries, and fell in love with Marie-Anne Vallon, by whom he had an illegitimate dau. Returning to England just before the Terror he pub. *The Evening Walk* and *Descriptive Sketches* in 1793. In 1797 he settled with his sister Dorothy W. (1771-1855) in Som., in order to be near Coleridge. The 2 friends collaborated in the *Lyrical Ballads* (1798). After visiting Germany 1798-9 he settled at Grasmere in 1799. In 1802 he m. Mary Hutchinson, and in 1805 finished the autobiographical *Prelude*, unpub. till 1850. The *Poems* of 1807 mark the close of his early inspiration. His later vols. incl. *The Excursion* (1814), which together with the *Prelude* was intended to form part of a great poem *The Recluse*; *The White Doe of Rylstone* (1815), *The River Duddon* (1820), *Ecclesiastical Sketches* (1822), and *Yarrow Revisited* (1835). In 1842 W. received a govt pension, and in 1843 succeeded Southey as poet laureate.

WORLD INTELLECTUAL PROPERTY ORGANIZATION. Specialist agency (WIPO) of the UN estab. 1974 to co-ordinate the internat. protection (initiated by the Paris convention of 1883) of inventions, trademarks, and industrial designs, and also literary and artistic works (as initiated by the Berne convention of 1886).

WORKSOP. English market and industrial town in Notts, on the Notts coalfield. Mary Queen of Scots was imprisoned at W. Manor (burned 1761). Pop. (1974) 36,320.

WORLD WARS. *See* First and Second W.W.

WORM. Term popularly used for various elongated limbless creatures. Zoologically Ws. incl. the flat worms such as flukes and tapeworms (qq.v.); the roundworms or Nematoda, e.g. the potato eelworm and the hookworm, an animal parasite; the marine worms or Nemertea (q.v.); and the segmented Ws. or Annelida (q.v.). In 1979 giant sea worms *c.* 3 m (10 ft) long, living within tubes created by their own excretions, were discovered 2,450 m (8,000 ft) beneath the Pacific NE of the Galapagos Is. *See also* Earthworm.

WORMS (vōrms). Town in the Rhineland Palatinate, W Germany, on the Rhine, 21km (13m) N of Ludwigshafen. Luther appeared before a Diet held at W. in 1521 and, with his followers, was outlawed by the emperor. Leather, chemicals, sugar, furniture, etc., are made; and the wines of the dist. are famous. Pop. (1970) 77,100.

WORMWOOD. Name given to aromatic herbs of the genus *Artemisia*, Compositae family. *A. absinthium*, an ingredient of absinth, grows wild in Britain.

WORTHING. English seaside resort in E Sussex at the foot of the S Downs. There are traces of prehistoric and Roman occupation in the vicinity. It is famous for tomatoes. Pop. (1974) 89,630.

WOTTON, Sir Henry (1568-1639). English writer. B. in Kent, he was employed on diplomatic missions under James I, and was provost of Eton from 1624. The *Reliquiae Wottonianae* (1651) contains the lyric 'You meaner beauties of the night'.

WOUNDED KNEE. Site on the Oglala Sioux Reservation, S Dakota, of the last major confrontation between the US Army and the American Indians. Chief Sitting Bull was killed, supposedly resisting arrest, on 15 Dec. 1890, and on 29 Dec. 1890 a group of Indians involved with him in the Ghost Dance Movement (aimed at resumption of Indian control of N America with the aid of the spirits of dead braves) were surrounded and 153 killed. In 1973 the militant American Indian Movement, in the siege of W.K. 27 Feb.-8 May, held hostages and demanded an investigation of the Indian treaties.

WOUVERMAN (wow'vermahn), **Philip** (1619-68). Dutch painter. B. at Haarlem, he painted landscapes and battle pieces. His brothers **Pieter** (1623-82) and **Jan** (1629-66) painted similar scenes.

WRANGEL, Ferdinand Petrovich, baron von (1794-1870). Russian vice-admiral and Arctic explorer, after whom W. Island is named.

WRANGEL, Peter Nicholaievich, baron (1878-1928). Russian general. B. at St Petersburg, he commanded a division of Cossacks in the F.W.W., and in 1920 became C-in-C of the 'White' army in the Crimea operating against the Bolsheviks. Later he became a mining engineer in Brussels.

WRASSE. Fish of the family Labridae, found in temperate and tropical seas. The most common British species is the ballan W. (*Labrus maculatus*).

WREN (ren), **Sir Christopher** (1632-1723). English architect. B. at East Knoyle, Wilts, he studied mathematics, and in 1660 became a prof. of astronomy at Oxford. His opportunity as an architect came after the Great Fire of London (1666). He prepared a plan for rebuilding the city, but it was not adopted. W.'s greatest achievement was St Paul's Cathedral, built 1675-1710. The most noteworthy of his City churches are St Michael's, Cornhill; St Bride's, Fleet St; and St Mary-le-Bow, Cheapside. His other buildings incl. the Royal Exchange, Marlborough House - the W. towers of Westminster Abbey, often attributed to him, were the design of his pupil Hawksmoor - and buildings at Oxford, incl. the Sheldonian Theatre and the Ashmolean Museum.

WREN, Percival Christopher (1885-1941). British novelist. Out of his experiences in the French and Indian armies he wrote such martial novels as *Beau Geste* (1924), dealing with the Foreign Legion.

WREN. Name given to birds of the Passerine family, in particular *Troglodytes troglodytes*, a brown bird, c. 10cm (4in) long, with a cocked-up tail.

WRESTLING. Sport in which 2 contestants strive to throw one another to the ground. It was very popular among the ancient Egyptians and Greeks, and was first made an Olympic sport about 704 BC. The Romans adopted it from the Greeks, and in the Middle Ages it was a favourite English sport. It is widely practised in the Orient, particularly in Japan.

In Britain there are several styles. In N England and S Scotland wrestlers adopt the Cumberland style in which there is no ground play - the wrestler who first touches the ground loses the match. In the West Country (Cornwall and Devon) style, the wrestlers wear a short strong jacket and before one is vanquished 2 shoulders and one hip or 2 hips and one shoulder must touch the ground. 'Catch as catch can', or the Lancashire style, allows ground struggling, and the aim is to force both the opponent's shoulders to the ground. Of recent years 'all-in' W. which recognizes no fouls has enjoyed a considerable vogue in Britain and USA. In Japanese *sumo*, a bout is won by downing an opponent within the circle in the arena, or throwing him outside.

WREXHAM. Market town in Clwyd, Wales, 19km (12m) SW of Chester, the seat of the RC bishopric of Menevia (Wales). Elihu Yale, benefactor of Yale univ., d. at W. and is buried in the 15th cent. church of St Giles. Pop. (1972) 39,140.

WRIGHT, Frank Lloyd (1869-1959). American architect. B. at Richland Center, Wisconsin, the son of a minister and a schoolmistress of Welsh descent, he studied as a civil engineer, but turned to architecture on seeing the newly erected wing of the Wisconsin State Capitol collapse. One of the outstanding architects of the 20th cent., he influenced design all over the world by his freedom from convention and rule. Among his works are his Wisconsin home Taliesin; Falling Water, Pittsburgh, Penn.; and the Guggenheim Museum, NYC (1959).

WRIGHT, Joseph (1855-1930). British philologist. Prof. of comparative philology at Oxford 1901-25, he saved English local speech from oblivion by his 6-vol. *English Dialect Dictionary* (1896-1905).

WRIGHT, Judith (1915-). Australian poet. B. at Armidale, NSW, and m. to the philosopher J. P. McKinney, she has produced vols. of direct verse rooted in the Australian background, e.g. *The Moving Image* (1946) and *Alive* (1972), and ed. *The Oxford Book of Australian Verse* (1954).

WRIGHT, Orville (1871-1948) and **Wilbur** (1867-1912). American flying pioneers. Orville was b. at Dayton, Ohio, and Wilbur in Indiana. Inspired by Lilienthal's gliding, they perfected their glider in 1902, while running a bicycle business at Dayton. Then in 1903 they built and flew successfully their first powered machine (the first to make powered, controlled and sustained flight), nr Kitty Hawk, NC on 17 Dec. 1903. The original machine (now in Washington) was exhibited at the Science Museum, S Ken. 1928-48, and was replaced by an exact replica.

WRIGHT, Richard (1908-60). American Negro author. B. at Natchez, Mississippi, he went to New York in 1937 and in 1940 attracted attention with his portrayal of a Negro murderer as a creature of circumstance in *Native Son*. Later books incl. the autobiographical *Black Boy* (1945) and *The Outsider* (1953). Disillusioned with Communism (cf. his contribution to *The God That Failed*), he d. in Paris where he had settled in 1946 in protest against treatment of his race in the USA.

WRIT. In English law, a precept under seal issued in the name of some executive officer of the Crown, e.g. the Lord Chancellor or a judge, and directed to some public officer such as a county sheriff, or to some private person, commanding him to take certain action in relation to a suit. Thus a W. constitutes the first step in legal proceedings, whether civil or criminal.

WRITERS TO THE SIGNET. A Scottish equivalent of English solicitors: a society of law agents whose predecessors were originally clerks in the Sec. of State's office entrusted with the preparation of documents requiring the signet or seal. The preparation of Crown writs, charters, etc., is the exclusive privilege of the society.

WRITING. The first stage in the development of W., leading to the true alphabet (q.v.), is the picture-W. on wood, rock, etc., examples of which date from *c*. 20,000 BC. Primitive peoples of America, Africa, Polynesia, and Australia combine conventionalized picture-characters to represent simple ideas; Egyptian hieroglyphics, Babylonian and Assyrian cuneiform and Chinese writing use both these ideographs and phonetic word symbols side by side. Syllabic writing, found in the 2 Japanese developments of Chinese writing, grows up by the continued use of a symbol to represent the sound of a short word. Following the phonetic decay of their language the Egyptians evolved single consonant signs, but continued to combine them with ideographs, etc. A more advanced phonetic form of W. than the alphabet, in which each sign theoretically represents one sound, is shorthand.

WROCLAW (vros'lav). Town in Poland, at the junction of the Oder and the Ohle, formerly cap. of German Silesia. Better known under its Ger. name Breslau, it grew up round the cathedral (1148), was in succession Polish, cap. of an independent duchy, Bohemian, Hungarian until Frederick the Great captured it (1742), then part of Prussia until Prussia was abolished in 1945. It suffered badly during the S.W.W. but was subsequently restored. It has a univ. (1811), originally a Jesuit college (1702). Pop. (1978) 593,000.

WRYNECK. Small bird (*Jynx torquilla*), a British summer visitant, which has a peculiar habit of twisting its head and neck - whence its name - and a distinctive call. It is generally grey, spotted and barred with brown.

WUCHANG. *See* under WUHAN.

WUHAN (woohahn'). Chinese city, cap. of Hubei prov., formed by the amalgamation of the anc. cities of Hankou, Hanyang, and Wuchang. It is at the junction of the Chang Jiang and the Han Shui and is a great centre and one of the chief industrial areas of China, with iron and steel and armaments works, cotton and silk textile factories, paper mills, etc. The three cities were in Japanese occupation 1938-45. There was a serious anti-Mao revolt in 1967 during the Cultural Revolution. Pop. (1973) 2,230,000.

WUPPERTAL (voop'pertahl). Industrial town of N Rhine-Westphalia, W Germany, *c.* 32km (20m) E of Düsseldorf, formed 1929 (named 1931) by uniting Elberfield (13th cent.) and Barmen (11th cent.). Pop. (1979) 396,125.

WÜRTTEMBERG (vür'temberg). Former kingdom in SW Germany, 1805-1918, which joined the Ger. Reich in 1870. Its cap. was Stuttgart. Divided in 1946 between the *Länder* of W.-Baden and W.-Hohenzollern, from 1952 it was part of the *Land* of Baden-Württemberg (q.v).

WÜRZBURG (vürts'boorg). Town in Bavaria, W Germany, on the Main, 88km (55m) NW of Nuremberg. W. became the seat of a bishopric in 741 and has an 11th cent. cathedral, an episcopal palace, a univ. (1402-34, refounded 1582). Furniture, leather goods, etc., are made and there are printing and engineering works, breweries and trade in wine. Pop. (1979) 127,260.

WYATT, Sir Thomas (*c.* 1503-42). English poet. He was employed on diplomatic missions by Henry VIII, and in 1536 was imprisoned for a time in the Tower, since he was thought to have been the lover of Anne Boleyn. In 1541 W. was again imprisoned on charges of treason. With the earl of Surrey, he pioneered the use of the sonnet in England. His son **Sir Thomas W. the Younger** (d. 1554) was one of the leaders in the revolt of 1554 intended to prevent the marriage of Queen Mary with Philip of Spain. After attacking the City of London, he was captured and executed.

WYCHERLEY, William (1640-1710). English dramatist. B. near Shrewsbury, he was ed. in France, and his first comedy *Love in a Wood* won him court favour in 1671. His modern reputation rests on the licentious *The Country Wife* and *The Plain Dealer* (1674).

WYCLIFFE, John (*c.* 1320-84). English reformer. B. probably nr Richmond, Yorks, he went to Oxford and about 1360 was Master of Balliol Coll. From 1374 he was rector of Lutterworth. Allying himself with the party of John of Gaunt, who were opposed to ecclesiastical influence at court, he attacked abuses in the Church and about 1378 moved on to criticize such fundamental doctrines as priestly absolution, confession, and indulgences. He sent out bands of travelling preachers, and set disciples to work on translating the Bible into English. Although denounced as a heretic, he d. peacefully at Lutterworth.

WYNNE, David (1926-). British sculptor B. in Hants, he was ed. at Stowe School and Trinity Coll., Cambridge. His works incl. portrait heads of Beecham, Gielgud, Menuhin and The Beatles; the marble 'Breath of Life' and bronze 'Christ and Mary Magdalen'.

WYOMING (wī-ō'ming). One of the Rocky Mountain states of the USA. It is semi-arid, and agriculture is possible only by irrigation and by 'dry-farming'. Mineral wealth is immense; petroleum, tin, natural gas, sodium salts, coal, phosphates, sulphur and uranium. Sheep and beef cattle are raised in large numbers. The state contains the Yellowstone national park, opened in 1872, and the Teton national park; and the tourist industry is next in importance to petroleum. The cap. is Cheyenne. W., admitted to the Union in 1890, gave women the franchise 1869, first representative body to do so. Area 253,595 sq.km (97,913 sq.m); pop. (1970) 332,416.

WYSS (vēs), **Johann Rudolf** (1781-1830). Swiss author. B. at Berne, where he became prof., he is remembered for his *Swiss Family Robinson* (1813).

The 24th letter in the English alphabet, having the sound which can be well represented medially by ks, and initially by z. It is derived through the Latin from the alphabet of western Greece, and was the last letter in the earlier Latin alphabet.

XAVIER (zav'i-er), **St Francis** (1506-52). Jesuit missionary, known as the 'Apostle of the Indies'. B. at his mother's castle of Xavier in the Basque country of Spain, he became a lecturer at the univ. of Paris, and there was one of the first 7 members of the Order of Jesus (1534). Ordained priest in 1537, he went as a Catholic missionary to the Portuguese colonies in the Indies, arriving at Goa in 1542. In 1549-51 he was in Japan, establishing a Christian mission which lasted for 100 years. Returning to Goa in 1552, he sailed for China, and died of fever there. He was canonized in 1621.

XENON (zen'on) (Gk *xenon*, stranger). A heavy inert gas of the argon family, discovered in 1898 by Ramsay and Travers in the residue from liquid air: symbol Xe, at. no. 54, at. wt. 131.30 It occurs in the atmosphere to the extent of about one part in 20 million, and is used in incandescent lamps, in electronic flash lamps, and to give a beautiful blue glow in a discharge tube. It is a fission product of uranium nuclear reactors. Radioactive X. has also been used in a recent technique to measure the flow of blood to the brain during acceleration on a centrifuge in connection with the effects of supersonic speeds on humans.

XENOPHON (zen'ōfōn) (*c.* 430-*c.* 354 BC). Greek historian, philosopher, and soldier. B. in Athens, in his youth he was a friend and ardent disciple of Socrates. In 401 BC he accompanied a body of Greek mercenaries employed by the Persian prince Cyrus in an expedition against Cyrus's brother, the king of Persia. Cyrus was killed in the battle of Cunaxa, and the Greeks were left stranded in the heart of the Persian Empire. X. succeeded to the command, and led them across more than 1,000 m of enemy-infested country to the Bosporus. This 'march of the 10,000 Greeks' is the subject of his famous historical work, the *Anabasis*. Subsequently he served in the Spartan Army, and lived on his estate at Scillus in Elis. Among his other works are the *Memorabilia*, *Apology*, and *Symposium*, consisting of recollections of Socrates.

XEROGRAPHY (zēro'grafi). A dry, non-chemical method of producing images without the use of negatives or sensitized paper. An electrostatically charged photoconductive plate is exposed in a camera to the item to be copied, allowing the charge to remain only in the area corresponding to its image. The latent image on the plate is then developed by contact with powder, which adheres only to the image, and is then usually transferred to

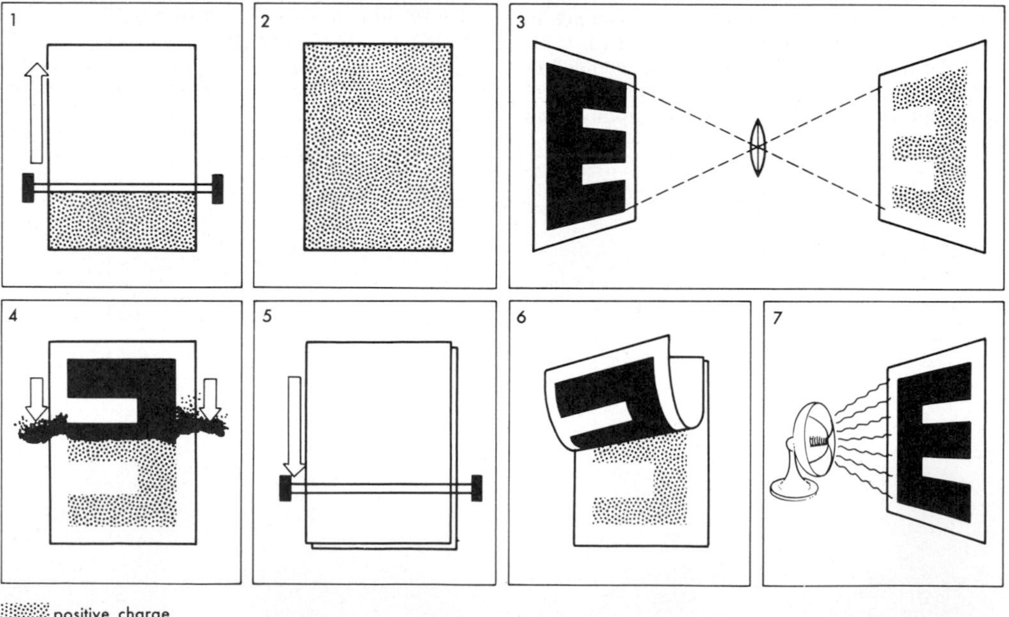

XEROGRAPHY. The surface of the coated plate or drum is sensitised by an electrically charged grid moving across it (1); the plate fully charged (2); the original document 'E' is projected onto the coated plate, the positive charges disappearing in areas exposed to light (3); negatively charged powder is dusted over the plate and adheres to the positively charged image (4); a sheet of paper over the plate receives a positive charge (5); the positively charged paper attracts powder from the plate, forming a direct positive image (6); the print is fixed by heat for a few seconds to form the permanent image (7). *Courtesy of Rank Xerox Ltd.*

ordinary paper or some other flat surface, and quickly heated to form a permanent print. Applications incl. document copying, enlarging from microfilm, preparing printing masters for offset litho and dyeline machines, making X-ray pictures and printing high-speed computer output.

XERXES I (zerk'sēz). King of Persia, 485-465 BC. The son of Darius, he became king on his father's death, and continued with the project of invading Greece. At the head of an army of perhaps 400,000 men, supported by a fleet of 800 ships, X. in 480 BC crossed the Hellespont over a bridge of boats. The Greek fleet was beaten at Artemisium, the pass of Thermopylae was stormed, Athens was taken and burnt. But at Salamis the Persian fleet was annihilated by the Greeks under Themistocles and X. returned to Persia, where he was murdered.

XHOSA (kō'sah). *See* KAFFIR and TRANSKEI.

XIAMEN (shē-ahmun'). Port (formerly Amoy) on Ku Lang island, one of the original 5 treaty ports 1842–1943. In 1980 it was being developed for tourism and for manufacturing projects involving foreign firms. Pop. (1975) 250,000.

XI JIANG (shē jē-ahng'). River (formerly Si-Kiang) of China, the name meaning 'West River', which rises in Yunnan and flows into the South China Sea. Guangzhou lies on the N arm of its delta, and Hong Kong is. at its mouth.

XINGU (shing'oo). River rising in the Mato Grosso, Brazil, and flowing 1,932 km (1,200 m) to the Amazon delta. Also a tribe of South American Indians threatened with extinction by the development of Amazonia.

XINHUA (shēnhoo-ah'). Official Chinese news agency.

XINING (shēnēng'). Cap. (formerly Sining) of Qinghai prov., China. Pop. (1970) 500,000.

XINJIANG UYGUR (shēnjē-ahng' oo-ē'goor). Auton. region (formerly Sinkiang-Uighur) of NW China, Xinjiang meaning 'new frontier'. The semi desert depressions of the Junggar Pendi (Dzungarian Basin) and Tarim Pendi (Tarim Basin) are separated by the Tyan Shan mtn system. Elsewhere cereals, cotton, and fruit are grown; stock are raised, and uranium, coal, iron, copper, tin, and large oil reserves are worked.

The Manchu emperors estab. their rule here in the 18th cent., but Russian expansion forced the cession of large areas by China in 1864 and 1881. The Chinese regard the 480 km (300 m) frontier between X.U. and Russian Tadzikistan as undemarcated. Lop Nur (q.v.) is China's nuclear testing ground, but in 1972 her nuclear research centres were moved to the central prov. of Sichuan. The cap. is Urumqi. Area 1,646,800 sq.km (613,665 sq.m); pop. (1979) 11,000,000, half of them Moslem.

XIZANG (shēzahng'). Chinese name for Tibet (q.v.).

XOCHIMILCO (khōchēmel'kō). Lake about 11km (7m) SSE of Mexico City, Mexico, famous for its floating gardens.

X-RAYS, or Röntgen rays after their discoverer in 1895, are those radiations in the electromagnetic spectrum which are next to ultra-violet rays in the direction of the shorter wavelengths. They are identical in character with radio and light waves, but very much shorter. They can penetrate bodies opaque to ordinary light, even a thin sheet of lead or several feet of wood; this property is made use of in radiography, when the bones of the human body are clearly revealed in an X-ray photograph. Even more valuable is their use in radiotherapy; living cells are more resistant to X-rays than malignant ones, so that deep-seated growths may be successfully attacked and often dispersed or destroyed. Generally speaking they are emitted when high-speed electrons suffer an abrupt loss of energy. Whilst invisible they may be detected by photographic plates, fluorescent screens and by the ionization they produce in gases.

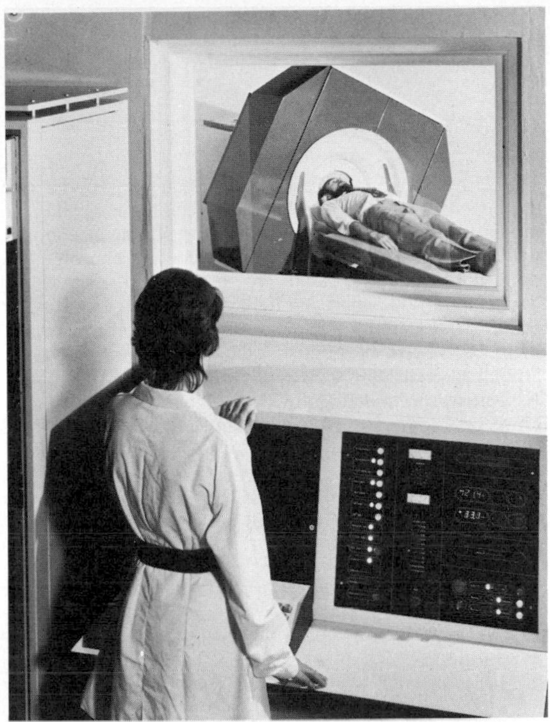

X-RAYS. The most advanced diagnostic system for neuroradiological examination, the EMI-scanner CT1010. The scanning unit, which contains the X-ray source and highly sensitive crystal detectors which measure the X-ray intensity readings for each slice of the brain being studied, can be seen through the window. On this side is the operator's control and viewing console - the television screen being here obscured by the operator's body. *Photo: Courtesy of EMI Medical*

X-ray astronomy has developed since the S.W.W. The Sun and other sources in the universe emit X-rays which are prevented by the atmosphere, which acts as if it were a yard-thick lead shield, from reaching us. The first rocket used to take X-ray photographs was a German V-2, which was captured and used at White Sands, New Mexico, in 1948.

XYLOPHONE (zī'lōfōn). Musical instrument consisting of a number of wooden bars, arranged in rows over resonators, and struck with hammers.

Y

The 25th letter in the English alphabet, derived through the later Latin alphabet from the Greek letter *upsilon.* In modern English it represents the sound of long and short *i,* when used as a vowel, and when used as a consonant in such words as yoke, yacht, etc., is a palatal spirant.

YACHT (yot). A small and light vessel, whether sailing or power-driven, used for pleasure-cruising or for racing. Most prominent of English yacht clubs is the Royal Y. Squadron, estab. at Cowes in 1812, and the Y. Racing Assocn was founded in 1875 to regulate the sport. The *Observer* Singlehanded Transatlantic Race (1960) is held every 4 yrs: the record is held by Philip Weld (USA) 17 days 23 hr 6 min. *See* ADMIRAL'S and AMERICA'S CUP. The royal yacht *Britannia* (1953) has a displacement of 4,000 tonnes (tons) and overall length of 126m (413ft).

YACHT. Ice yachts on Lake Balaton in Hungary. *Photo: Courtesy of the Hungarian Embassy*

YAK. The wild ox (*Bos grunniens*) of Tibet, related to the bisons. When wild it is black, but in domestication it is often black and white. It stands *c.* 2m (6ft) at the shoulder, and has long shaggy hair on the underparts.

YAKUT (yakōōt') **A.S.S.R.** An Asian autonomous rep. of the RSFSR, in the valley of the Lena r. Much of its surface is barren tundra, and the climate is severe, but there is some agriculture in the S. Gold, silver, diamonds, tin, mica, coal, etc., are mined; fur-bearing animals (sable, silver fox, etc.) are both trapped and bred; reindeer are reared. Large natural gas deposits were exploited from 1973: pipeline Yakutsk-Vladivostok. Y. became an autonomous rep. in 1922. The Yakuts, a people of Turkic stock and formerly nomadic, were subdued by Russia in the 17th cent. The cap. is Yakutsk. Area 3,103,000 sq.km (1,197,800 sq.m); pop. (1978) 842,000.

YAKUTSK (yakootsk'). Cap. of Yakut ASSR, RSFSR, on the Lena. It is the coldest point of the Arctic in NE Siberia, and has an institute for studying the permanently frozen soil area (permafrost). There are timber industries. Pop. (1978) 149,000.

YALE. Third-oldest (1701) and one of the most important univs. of USA. It is at New Haven, Conn., and was named after Elihu Yale (1648-1721), b. at Boston, Mass., one-time governor of Fort St George, Madras, who in 1718 sent a cargo of books, pictures, etc., which realized £562. 12s. for the benefit of the then college (univ. 1887).

YA'LTA. Russian holiday resort with a pleasant climate in the Crimea, Ukrainian SSR, 51km (32m) SE of Sevastopol. Livadia, summer palace built by Nicholas II 1910-11, was the site of the Y. conference, 1945, at which Churchill, Roosevelt, and Stalin completed plans for the defeat of Germany and the foundation of the UN. Pop. (1975) 62,500.

YAM. The thick tuberous roots of plants of the genus *Dioscorea,* which in tropical countries, e.g. the S Sea islands, are eaten in the place of potatoes.

YAMOUSSOUKRO (yam'oosoo'krō). Cap. of Ivory Coast from 1983, N of Abidjan. Pres. Houphouët-Boigny was born here. Pop. (1984) 70,000.

YAMUNA (jah'moonah). River in India: rising in the Himalayas, it joins the Ganges nr Allahabad, where it forms a sacred bathing place. Agra and Delhi are on its course, and Nehru and his grandson Sanjay Gandhi were cremated on its banks at Delhi. Length 1,385 km (860 m).

YAN'AN. Town (formerly Yenan) in N Shaanxi prov., China. It was the HQ of the Communists (1936-47) following the Long March (q.v.). Pop. (1973) 50,000.

YANGTZE-KIANG. *See* CHANG JIANG and JINSHA JIANG.

YANKEE. Name often applied by Europeans to the people of the USA in general, although more properly confined to those of the New England states.

YANTAI (yahntī'). Ice-free port (formerly Chefoo) in Shandong prov., China. Pop. (1970) 250,000.

YARD. An imperial measure of length, equal to 3ft or 0.914 metre. It is supposed to have been the length of the arm of King Henry I.

YA'RDANG. Ridge formed by wind erosion from a dried-up river bed, etc., as in Chad, China, Peru, USA. On a more massive scale, they also occur on Mars.

YARKAND (yahrkand') (Chinese Shache). A walled city of Xinjiang Uygur in an oasis of the Tarim basin. Irrigation ensures agriculture and pastoral activity. It is a centre of Islamic culture. Pop. (1970) 90,000.

YARMOUTH, or **Great Yarmouth.** Holiday resort and port in Norfolk, England, at the mouth of the Yare. The staple herring fisheries have been replaced by its position as a leading base for North Sea oil and gas, and it has an increasing container traffic with the Continent. Pop. (1972) 49,830. Another YARMOUTH, a small port in the Isle of Wight, is a yachting centre. The French burned it in 1377 and 1544.

YAROSLAVL (yahrōslahvl'). Town in the RSFSR, cap. of Y. region, on the Volga 250km (155m) NE of Moscow. Industries inc. textiles, rubber, paints, commercial vehicles. Pop. (1979) 597,000.

YARROW, or **milfoil.** A common wayside plant (*Achillea millefolium*) of the Compositae family, found throughout the northern hemisphere usually with flat-topped clusters of white or pink flowers.

YARROW. River in Borders region, Scotland, flowing into the Tweed and famous in poetry.

YAWATA (yahwah'ta). *See* KITAKYUSHU.

YAWS. A contagious disease common in the West Indies, characterized by red, raspberry-like eruptions upon the face, toes, and other parts of the body. A very similar disease is found in W Africa. Treatment is by antibiotics.

YAZD (yahzd). Town of central Iran, *c.* 275 km (170 m) SE of Isfahan, in an oasis on a trade route. There is silk weaving and some other industry. Pop. (1976) 136,000.

YEAR. A unit of time measurement. The calendar Y. consists of 365 days, but a leap Y. - a Y. the date of which is divisible by 4 without remainder - consists of 366 days, an extra day being added to Feb. The last Y. of a cent. is not leap Y., however, unless it is divisible by 400. The tropical, solar, or equinoctial Y. is the time taken by the Earth to revolve round the Sun from equinox to equinox, i.e. 365.2422 mean solar days (365 days, 5 hrs 48 mins 46 secs). The sidereal Y. in which the observation is made on a star is 365 days, 6 hrs 9 mins 9 secs. An historical Y. begins on 1 Jan. but up to 1752 the civil or legal Y. began on 25 March. The fiscal/financial year still ends on 5 April, which is 25 March plus 11 days added under the reform of the calendar in 1752. The regnal Y. begins on the anniversary of the sovereign's accession; it is used in the dating of Acts of Parliament.

YEAST. A mass of minute circular or oval vegetable cells about .000085 m ($\frac{1}{3000}$in) in diameter, each of which is a complete plant capable under suitable conditions of reproducing new cells by budding. When placed in a sugar solution they multiply and convert the sugar into alcohol and carbon dioxide. Ys. are used in leavening bread, fermenting beer, etc.

YEATS (yāts), **William Butler** (1865-1939). Irish poet. Of Anglo-Irish stock, he was b. in Dublin, son of a lawyer turned painter. He became the leading figure of the Celtic revival, helping to found the Abbey Theatre, and as a believer in Irish nationalism sitting in the Irish senate 1922-8. His early poetry, e.g. *The Wind Among the Reeds* (1899) is romantically and exotically lyrical, and he drew on Irish legend for his poetic plays, e.g. *The Countess Kathleen* (1892) and *Deidre* (1907), but broke through to a new sharply resilient style with *Responsibilities* (1914). In his personal life there was also a break: the beautiful Maude Gonne to whom many of his poems had been addressed finally refused to marry him, and in 1917 he m. Georgie Hyde-Lees, whose gifts as a medium reinforced his leanings towards mystic symbolism, cf. the prose *A Vision* (1925 and 1937). His later vols. of verse, of astonishing maturity and lyric inspiration, incl. *The Wild Swans at Coole* (1919), *The Tower* (1927), *The Winding Stair* (1933) and *Last Poems* (1939). His prose works incl. *Autobiographies* (1926), *Dramatis Personae* (1936), *Letters* (1954) and *My Theologies* (1959).

His younger brother, **Jack Butler Y.** (1871-1957), was a well-known artist, using black-and-white to illustrate his own stories, and oil to depict scenes of Irish life, e.g. 'Back from the Races' in the Tate, and later legendary themes.

YEDO. Name until 1868 of TOKYO.

'YELLOW BOOK.' An illustrated quarterly magazine pub. in London 1894-7, in which appeared literary and artistic contributions from Aubrey Beardsley, Max Beerbohm, Henry James, etc.

YELLOW FEVER. Sometimes called yellow jack. An endemic infective F. of the tropics, particularly prevalent in the Caribbean area, Brazil, and the W Coast of Africa. One of the symptoms is a yellowish skin. It has been brought under control following the discovery that it is carried by a mosquito. The first effective vaccines were produced by Max Theiler of NY (Nobel prize 1951).

YELLOWKNIFE. Cap. of NW Territories, Canada from 1967, centre of a gold-mining area discovered in 1934. It is on the N shore of Great Slave Lake and was founded 1935. It has an airport. Pop. (1978) 9,970.

YELLOW RIVER. *See* HUANG HE.

YELLOW SEA. Gulf of the Pacific Ocean between China and Korea. It receives the Huang He (Yellow River) and Chang Jiang. Area 466,200 sq.km (180,000 sq.m).

YELLOWSTONE NATIONAL PARK. A national American reserve, estab. 1872 and maintained by the US govt in NW Wyoming, on a broad plateau in the Rocky Mts. It incl. more than 3,000 geysers and hot springs, and very fine scenery.

YELLOWSTONE NATIONAL PARK. A small herd of bison, which once wandered here in their thousands, graze alongside the Firehole River. *Photo: Courtesy of the United States Travel Service*

YEMEN (yem'en). Two countries occupying the SW corner of the Arabian peninsula: there were hostilities between them until mediation by the Arab League in 1972 led to agreed eventual union. The agreement was renewed 1980, but few practical measures have been taken.

(1) The *Yemen Arab Republic* or North Y. There is a hot moist coastal plain which rises to a plateau, known in classical times because of its fertility as Arabia felix. Cotton, coffee, and grapes are grown for export. The cap. is San'a, and the chief port Hodeida. The king was killed in the revolution of 1962, and a rep. estab., but royalists (with Saudi aid) resisted the new govt (aided by Egypt) until a compromise peace in 1970. By 1980 North Y. was receiving Soviet aid and US aid was withdrawn. Area 195,000 sq.km (75,000 sq.m); (1977) 8,080,000. M.U.: riyal.

(2) The *People's Democratic Republic of Y.* or South Y. Poorer in resources than the N, it is extending its formerly minute fertile area by irrigation: cotton is exported. The cap. is Aden. It comprises the former Brit. colony of Aden and the protectorates of Eastern and Western Aden, from which, after terrorist activity by the

Nat. Liberation Front (with Soviet support) from 1964, Britain withdrew in 1967. Area 160,000 sq.km (62,000 sq.m); pop. (1977) 1,800,000. Also incl. in Y. are the is. of Perim and Socotra (q.v.) and Kamaran (area 180 sq.km/70 sq.m). M.U.: S.Y. dinar.

YENAN. *See* YAN'AN.

YENISEI (yenēsā'-ē). Great river of Asiatic Russia, rising in Tuva region and flowing across the Siberian plain into the Arctic Ocean. Its length is about 3,800 km (2,360 m); its chief tributary is the Angara.

YEOMAN (yō'-). In England, between the break-up of the feudal system and the agricultural revolution of the 18th-19th cents., a small landowner who farmed his own fields.

YEOMANRY. Volunteer cavalry organized 1794, and incl. in the Territorial Army (q.v.) 1907.

YEOMEN OF THE GUARD. A military corps which was founded by Henry VII in 1485 and since then has constituted the bodyguard of the English sovereign. Its duties are purely ceremonial, and the uniform and weapons are much as they were in Tudor times. The nickname of 'Beefeaters' is supposed to have originated in 1669 when the grand-duke of Tuscany ascribed their fine appearance to beef.

YEREVAN (yerevahn'). Cap. of Armenian SSR, in the valley of the Zanga, a few m. N of the Turkish border. It makes tractor parts, machine tools, chemicals, bricks, bicycles, wine, and cans fruit and vegetables. The Armenian state univ. (1921) is at Y. Founded in the 7th cent., Y. was alternately Turkish and Persian from the 15th cent. until ceded to Russia, 1828. Pop. (1979) 1,019,000.

YERSIN (yārsan'), **Alexandre Émile John** (1863-1943). Swiss bacteriologist, who discovered the plague bacillus in Hong Kong in 1894 and prepared a serum.

YEVTUSHE'NKO, Yevgeny (1933-). Russian poet. B. in Siberia, he aroused controversy by his anti-Stalinist 'Stalin's Heirs' (1956), pub. with Khrushchev's support. He pub. his *Autobiography* (1963).

YEW. An evergreen tree (*Taxus baccata*) belonging to the Taxaceae family. It has densely spreading branches with very dark, linear, leathery leaves. The seeds are set in a fleshy, rose-red cup. Both leaves and seeds are poisonous.

YEZD. *See* YAZD.

YEZIDIS (yezē'dēz). A religious sect of Iraq, whose chief centre is near Mosul. Their religion is a mixture of Christianity and Islam; they practise baptism and circumcision, but regard the devil as God's agent and endeavour to keep in his favour.

YEZO (yez'ō). Another name for HOKKAIDO.

Y-FACTOR. All men inherit from their fathers one Y chromosome (q.v.) which gives them their male characteristics, and some (probably 1 in 300) inherit 2, which gives added height, greater emotional instability, inability to bear frustration, and great aggressiveness. Crimes of violence are frequently committed by such men and possession of the Y-factor, immediately detectable under the microscope, has in France and Australia (1968) been successfully pleaded in mitigation in murder cases.

YICHANG (yēchahng'). Port at the head of navigation of the Chang Jiang, Hubei prov., China. Coal and iron are found nearby, and it handles rice, tea, cotton and other local products. There is an airport. Pop. (1973) 120,000.

YIDDISH (Ger. *Jüdisch*, Jewish). The language spoken by Polish and Russian Jews that is based on the German spoken by their ancestors in the Rhineland and has absorbed many Hebrew, Russian, Polish, etc., words. Its literature arose out of the folk songs of eastern Europe and assumed importance in the latter half of the 19th cent. Notable Y. writers incl. novelist and short story writer Isaac Bashevis Singer (1904-), a Pole (US citizen from 1943), awarded a Nobel prize 1978, and Sholem Asch (q.v.).

YIN and YANG. The passive and active principles in nature, regarded as interdependent rather than opposed, as illustrated by the circular symbol, used in both Taoism and Confucianism, of 2 interlocked curved shapes, with a spot of the contrasting colour within the 'head' of each. The white (in Chinese *yang* means 'bright') is thought of as masculine, positive, intellectual and the black (*yin* 'dark') as feminine, negative, intuitive. They do not represent 'good and evil' but an essential balance of equal powers. *See* MACROBIOTICS.

YINCHUAN (yēnchōō-ahn'). Cap. of Ninghsia-Hui autonomous region, NW China. Pop. (1970) 100,000.

YŌ'GA (Sanskrit, union). A system of Hindu philosophy, characterized by belief in a personal deity with whom it is possible to attain mystical and ecstatic union by the practice of hypnosis and a complicated and prolonged system of mortification of the senses, e.g. by abstract meditation, induced apathy, rigidity of posture, ascetic practices, concentration of mind on one particular point, etc. Siva is the Great Yogi. The system is attributed to Patanjali, a Hindu seer who is supposed to have flourished about 150 BC at Gonda, Uttar Pradesh.

YOKOHAMA (yōkohah'ma). Japanese seaport on Tokyo Bay, 29km (18m) SW of Tokyo. Commodore Perry (q.v.) landed at Y. in 1854, and in 1859 it was the 1st Japanese port opened to foreign trade, growing rapidly from a small fishing village to the chief centre of trade with Europe and America. Almost destroyed in an earthquake (1923) it was also rebuilt after S.W.W. air raids. Pop. (1978) 2,686,000.

YOKOSUKA. Japanese seaport and naval base (1884) on Tokyo Bay, S of Yokohama. Pop. (1978) 407,000.

YONI. *See* Lingam.

YONKERS (yung'-). City adjoining New York, USA, on the Hudson. Originally a Dutch settlement dating from c. 1650, it is a busy manufacturing centre, and a residential district. Pop. (1970) 204,300.

YONNE (yon). French river, 290km (180m) long, rising in the Morvan Mts. and flowing N into the Seine near Montereau. It gives its name to a dept.

YORK. A royal dynasty of England, founded by Richard duke of Y. (1411-60), who during the reign of Henry VI (of the House of Lancaster) claimed the throne as the descendant of Lionel duke of Clarence, 3rd son of Edward III, Henry being descended from the 4th son. The Yorkists and the Lancastrians fought out the issue in the Wars of the Roses. Y. was slain at the battle of Wakefield in 1460, but in the next year his son became king as Edward IV, and was followed by his son Edward V and his brother Richard III. The last-named fell at Bosworth in 1485, and the Lancastrian victor became king as Henry VII. To consolidate his claim, Henry m. the eldest dau. of Edward IV.

YORK, Frederick Augustus, duke of (1763-1827). Second son of George III, he was an unsuccessful commander against the French in the Netherlands 1793-9. From 1798 to 1809 he was British C-in-C. The Duke of Y.'s column in Waterloo Place, London, commemorates him.

YORK, Archbishop of. Metropolitan of the northern prov., and Primate of England, the abp. of Y. ranks next to the Lord High Chancellor.

YORK, Duke of. A title often borne by the second or later son of an English king, e.g. George, later George V, 2nd son of Edward VII; and Albert Frederick, 2nd son of George V, later King George VI.

YORK. City in N Yorks, England, on the Ouse, 303km (188m) from London. Traditionally the cap. of the N of England, it was a British city before, under the Romans from AD 71, it became the fortress of Eboracum. Paulinus, 1st bp of Y., was consecrated there in 627, and the see was created an archbishopric in 732. York Minster (*c.* 1230-1474) is built on the site of the wooden church in which Paulinus baptized King Edwin in 627: its stained glass is famous. Much of the 14th cent. city wall survives, with 4 principal gates or bars, and the 15th cent. guildhall (bombed 1942) was reconstructed 1962. The Theatre Royal, site of a theatre since 1765, was restored 1965, and the Univ. of York was chartered 1963. Its commercial prosperity in the Middle Ages rested on control of the wool trade: modern industries incl. rlwy rolling stock, scientific instruments, sugar, chocolate, and glass. Pop. (1974) 104,750.

YORKSHIRE. NE co. of England on the North Sea, formerly divided into N, E and W Ridings (i.e. thirds), but in 1974 reorganized to form a number of new cos.: the major part of **Cleveland** and **Humberside** (qq.v.); **North Y.,** still England's largest co., and incl. the York Moors and Cleveland Hills in the NE, peaks such as Whernside (737 m/2,419 ft) and Ingleborough (723 m/2,373 ft) on the W border, and the towns Scarborough, Whitley, Richmond, Harrogate, York, and Northallerton (admin. HQ), area 8,316 sq.km (3,211 sq.m); pop. (1978) 661,300; **South Y.,** incl. famous metal-working centres such as Sheffield, Doncaster, Rotherham, and Barnsley (admin. HQ), and a very small section of N Derbyshire, area 1,562 sq.km (603 sq.m); pop. (1978) 1,304,100; and **West Y.,** incl. valuable coalfields and the textile centres of Leeds, Bradford, Halifax, Huddersfield, and Wakefield (admin. HQ), area 2,039 sq.km (787 sq.m); pop. (1978) 2,067,900. Small outlying areas also went to Durham, Cumbria, Lancs and Greater Manchester. S and W Yorks are both metropolitan counties.

The Industrial Revolution achieved here some of its greatest transformations, yet in the moors and the dales of the Pennine Range to the W, agricultural and pastoral life goes on as it has done for cents. Area of former geographical co. 16,198 sq.km (6,254 sq.m); pop. (1971) 5,050,000.

YOSEMITE (yōse'mitē) **NATIONAL PARK.** Mountainous area in the Sierra Nevada, California, USA. Dedicated 1890, it incl. Y. and other gorges; Y. Falls (762 m/2,500 ft) in 3 leaps, and many others, and groves of giant sequoias.

YOUNG, Brigham (1801-77). American religious leader. B. in Vermont, he joined the Mormon Church in 1832, and 3 years later was appointed an apostle. After a successful recruiting mission in Liverpool, he returned to USA, and as successor of Joseph Smith, recently murdered, led the Mormon migration to the Great Salt Lake in Utah (1846), founded Salt Lake City, and ruled the colony well until his death.

YOSEMITE. The entrance to the Yosemite Valley, where the first of its beautiful falls descends in a triple cascade. *Photo: Feature-Pix*

YOUNG, Edward (1683-1765). British poet, author of *Night Thoughts on Life, Death, and Immortality,* once universally popular.

YOUNGHUSBAND, Sir Francis (1863-1942). British soldier and explorer. B. in India, he entered the army in 1882 and 20 years later accompanied the mission that opened up Tibet. He wrote travel books and works on comparative religion.

YOUNG MEN'S CHRISTIAN ASSOCIATION (YMCA). Founded in London in 1844 by (Sir) George Williams (1821-1905) in the drapery firm in St Paul's churchyard in which he was a clerk, the YMCA is an association of young men, without distinction of race or colour, who seek to improve themselves spiritually, intellectually, and physically. Women were accepted as members from 1971.

YOUNGSTOWN. City of Ohio, USA, in a rich mining area, with iron and steel plants. Pop. (1970) 141,000.

YOUNG WOMEN'S CHRISTIAN ASSOCIATION (YWCA). Organization for women and girls, formed in 1887 when 2 organizations, both founded in 1855 - the one by Miss Emma Robarts and the other by Lady Kinnaird - combined their work.

YPRES (ēpr), **John Denton Pinkstone French,** 1st earl of (1852-1925). British field marshal. He entered the army in 1874, and in the South African War of 1899 defeated the Boers at Elandslaagte, relieved Kimberley, and captured Bloemfontein. In 1912 he became Chief of the General Staff, but resigned in 1914. Later in the year he was appointed C-in-C of the BEF to France, and held the command until the end of 1915. Lord-Lieut. of Ireland 1918-21, he was created an earl on his resignation.

YPRES. French ēpr; or 'wipers' in British Army pron.; Flem. **Ieper.** Belgian town in W Flanders, 40km (25m) S of Ostend. Its old cloth hall and the cathedral were among the casualties of the F.W.W. The Menin Gate (1927) is a memorial to British soldiers lost in the great battles fought round the town 1914-18. Pop. (1973) 18,300.

YSSELMEER. Alt. spelling of IJSSELMEER.

YTTERBIUM (iter'-). Chemical element. Symbol Yb; at. no. 70; at. wt. 173.04. It is a rare metal occurring in rare earths that contain yttrium.

YTTRIUM (it'-). Chemical element. Symbol Y.; at. no. 39; at. wt. 88.91. is the most basic of the rare earth metals.

YUCATAN (yookahtahn'). A peninsula in Central America, most of it in Mexico but extending into Belize and Guatemala. Tropical crops are grown. It is inhabited by Indians of Maya stock, and there are remains of the civilization which the Spanish conquerors found in decline. Area *c.* 180,000 sq.km (70,000 sq.m).

YUCCA (yuk'a). In botany, a genus of the Liliaceae, with some 30 species occurring in Mexico and the SW of USA. The leaves are stiff and swordshaped and the flowers white and campanulate.

YUGOSLAVIA. A federal rep. (see table for units) of SE Europe in the Balkan peninsula. It has a much indented Adriatic coastline, and mountainous surface save in the N and NE, where are the fertile lowlands of the middle Danube and its tributaries, Drava, Tagiss (Tisa), Sava, and Morava. The climate is continental. The cap. is Belgrade. Many of the people are members of the Eastern Orthodox Church, though there are many Roman Catholics in the NW; 12 per cent of the pop. are Moslems. The Slovene, Macedonian, and Serbo-Croat languages are officially recognized, the last being in general use. About one-third of the pop. work on the land, wheat and maize being the main crops. Minerals incl. coal, copper, lead, iron, aluminium, mercury, petroleum. Iron and steel, cement, fertilizers, and textiles are among industrial products. Horses, cattle, sheep, pigs, and poultry are raised. M.U.: dinar.

CONSTITUTION. The constitution of 1974 estab. a Fed. Assembly with a Fed. Chamber and Chamber of Reps. and Provs.: and replaced direct election by a complex delegational system. After the death of Tito (q.v.) in 1980, the Collective Presidency (formed by representatives from each of the country's divisions) was headed by one of its members as President on a system of annual rotation.

Area 255,874 sq.km (98,740 sq.m); pop. (1976) 21,560,000, of whom *c.* 3 million are Moslem.

Federal Republic of Yugoslavia

	Area in sq. km	*Pop. in 1971*	*Capital*
Bosnia-Hercegovina	51,129	3,717,000	Sarajevo
Croatia	56,470	4,423,000	Zagreb
Macedonia	25,706	1,611,070	Skopje
Montenegro	13,807	531,215	Titograd
Serbia	88,267	8,437,000	Belgrade
Slovenia	20,245	1,697,500	Ljubljana
	255,624	20,416,785	

HISTORY. Y. came into existence in 1918 as the kingdom of the Serbs, Croats, and Slovenes with the Serbian Peter (I) Karageorgevich as king. Peter I died in 1921 and was succeeded by his son Alexander who, faced with difficulties at home and abroad (espec. with Italy), estab. a military dictatorship in 1929. He was assassinated in Marseilles, during an official visit to France, 1934. His young son Peter II (1923-70) succeeded and a regency under his uncle Paul was set up until Peter assumed power early in 1941. German invasion followed, and the whole country was overrun; the king took refuge in England, and Y. became an area of grim guerrilla warfare until the Germans were expelled with the help in the last months of Russian forces. The guerrilla leader Josip Broz (Marshal Tito) estab. a Communist govt, but Y. developed independently of the Soviet Union. In the 1970s violent nationalist separatism grew up, espec. in Croatia, which resulted in purges, and the proclamation of the constitution of 1974 along more orthodox Communist lines.

Literature. The Yugoslav or Serbo-Croat language belongs to the southern branch of the Slavonic languages. Y. literature begins in the 9th cent. with the translation into Slavonic of the church service books. Its great glory is the folk poetry, particularly the song cycles dealing with the battle of Kosovo and the hero Marko Kraljevič. After the cents. of national repression a revival came, notably under Dositej Obradovič (1739-1811). Poets of the earlier 19th cent. incl. the prince-bishop Petar Njegos (1813-51), France Prešern (1800-49), and Ivan Mazuranič (1814-90). Later, Russian influence predominated. More modern writers incl. the novelist Ivan Cankar (1876-1918), dramatist Ivo Vojnovič (1857-1929), and poet Oton Zupančič (1878-1949).

YUKON (yōō'kon). Terr. of NW Canada, named after its chief r. the Y. It incl. the highest point in Canada, Mt Logan (6,050 m/19,850 ft), in the Mt Elias range of the Rockies on the border of Alaska, USA, to the W. Settlement dates from the discovery of gold in the Klondike valley in 1896, and Y. was organized as a political unit in 1898 with Dawson as cap., replaced 1953 by Whitehorse (q.v.). The NW Highway and branches and airlines serve the terr. Petroleum and natural gas, gold and silver are worked; also coal. Fur trapping is important. Area 536,327 sq.km (207,076 sq.m); pop. (1979) 24,000.

YUNGNING. Name 1913-45 of NANNING.

YUNNAN (yoonahn'). Prov. of SW China adjoining Burma and N Vietnam. It is mountainous and well forested. Tin, copper, lead, zinc, coal, salt and other minerals are worked; tea, tobacco, rice, wheat are grown. The Salween and Mekong flow through it, and the Chang Jiang in the N. It is traversed by the Burma Road. The cap. is Kunming. Area 436,200 sq.km (168,370 sq.m); pop. (1979) 30,000,000.

YUZOVKA (yōōz'ofka). *See* DONETSK.

Z

The 26th and last letter in the English and other modern alphabets. It was the 6th in the classical Greek alphabet, but it was found only in the later Roman alphabet. It is used initially and medially in many words of Greek or Oriental origin, and the modern tendency is to employ it in preference to *s* in such words as *baptize, organize,* derived ultimately from the Greek.

ZAANDAM (zahn'dahm). Port in N Holland prov., Netherlands, on the Zaan, NW of Amsterdam. Peter the Great studied shipbuilding here in 1697, and there are timber and paper industries. Since 1974 it has been incl. in the municipality of Zaanstadt. Pop. (1979) 127,700.

ZABALETA (thubulā'tah), **Nicanor** (1907-). Spanish harpist, noted for his efforts to enlarge the repertoire of original harp music by commissioning new works from e.g. Milhaud (q.v.) and Joaquin Rodrigo, and by reviving interest in classical harp music, particularly that of the 15th and 16th cents. in Spain and Portugal.

ZABRZE (zah'bzhe). Town in Silesia, Poland, formerly the German town of Hindenburg. There are coal mines, foundries and chemical works. Pop. (1972) 198,000.

ZADAR (zah'dah). Yugoslav port and holiday resort on the Adriatic Sea. The Roman Jadera, it was alternately held and lost by the Venetian Rep. from the 12th cent. until seized by Austria in 1813 and made cap. of Dalmatia, 1815-1918. It belonged to Italy 1920-47. Pop. (1971) 25,100.

ZADKINE (zad'kēn), **Ossip** (1890-1967). French cubist sculptor. Russian-born, he became French by service in the Foreign Legion, and spent most of his life in Paris, though often exhibiting in London, where he had also studied. Working in varied materials, he represented the human form in abstract terms, e.g. Laocoon and his variations on an Orpheus theme.

ZAGO'RSK. Town 70 km (45 m) NE of Moscow, USSR. The Trinity Monastery of St Sergius (1337), surrounded by a fortified wall, has some of the finest architecture and art of medieval Russia. It has been restored as a tourist attraction and the patriarch of Moscow still lives here. Pop. (1979) 100,000.

ZAGREB (zahg'reb). Yugoslav city, cap. of Croatia, on the Sava. It has a Gothic cathedral and a univ., and was a Roman city. Manufactures incl. leather, linen, carpets, rly wagons. Pop. (1971) 566,084.

ZAIRE (zah-ēr'), **Republic of.** Country of Central Africa, occupying a large part of the Z. river basin. Its central area is a vast flat plain covered by dense forest and jungle swamp, but in the S plateau country rises to 150-300 m (500-1,000 ft) in the Ruwenzori Mts., among which lies a chain of lakes, incl. Mobutu Sese Seko (formerly Albert), Edward (Idi Amin Dada 1973-9) and Tanganyika. The climate on the plain is hot with heavy rainfall: on the plateau it is milder.

The people are for the most part Bantu, and the chief local languages are Swahili in the E, Tshiluba in the S, and Lingala and Kikongo along the Z. river. The official language is French. Rubber, cotton, coffee, tea, cacao, sugar and oil palms are grown, and there is valuable forest timber. The region of Shaba (formerly Katanga) is richest in minerals, espec. copper, but the country also has industrial diamonds, cobalt, gold, uranium, zinc, tin, manganese, and off shore oil. Varied industries incl. cotton textiles, metal goods, vehicle assembly, etc., and the Z. river supplies hydro-electric power. The cap. is Kinshasa (formerly Léopoldville): other towns incl. Lubumbashi (Elizabethville), Kisangani (Stanleyville), the Z. river port of Matadi, and Boma on the Z. estuary. In the stretches free from rapids the river Z. and its tributaries are an important means of transport, but rail, road and air communications are expanding. Area 2,345,000 sq.km (895,000 sq.m); pop. (1977) 26,380,000, of whom the majority speak Bantu languages, and nearly half are Christian (mainly RC), the remainder practising traditional animism. M.U.: zaïre.

ZAÏRE. A Kifwebe mask, carved in wood and painted, and typical in its dramatic power of art from this region. *Photo: Charles Uht/ The Museum of Primitive Art, New York*

History. In the 15th cent. Portuguese explorers reached the coast and Zaïre is the rendering they made of the native Zadi 'big water'. However, the river basin as a whole remained unknown territory to Europeans until the explorations during the 1870s of Livingstone and Stanley (qq.v.). By the time of the arrival of the Portuguese, the great medieval kingdom of Kongo, or Congo, which occupied both banks of the river, and to which Angola and Cabinda were subject, was already in decline. Its further dissolution was aided by civil wars and the drain of the slave trade, and at the Berlin Conference (1885) Portugal (*see* ANGOLA and CABINDA), France (*see* People's Rep. of CONGO), and Belgium formally divided the entire area among themselves. Leopold II, king of the Belgians, had financed Stanley's journeys, and had already estab. personal rule over the so-called Congo Free State, which was now internationally recognized. Local attempts at resistance were suppressed, and there was heavily oppressive exploitation of the native peoples under Leopold's rule. In 1908 the Belgian govt annexed the territory as a colony, and it was generally believed that from that time the Belgian Congo was one of the best-admin. colonies in Africa. Peace was maintained and the territory's resources were developed, but when independence was granted in 1960 the people had received no preparation for self-govt. Old tribal antagonisms revived (*see* LUMUMBA, PATRICE), Belgian settlers were driven out, and rich Shaba (Katanga, q.v.) sought to break away as an independent state. A small UN force remained in the country until 1964, but civil unrest continued, and in 1965 Gen. Mobutu (q.v.) assumed the presidency by a coup. In 1966 he reduced the 21 provs. to 8 regions: Bandundu, Equateur, Kasai E and W, Kivu, Shaba and Bas-Zaïre and Haut-Zaïre, plus Kinshasa city. The constitution of 1967, proclaimed after a referendum, instituted a unitary state under a pres. (Mobutu), with a unicameral legislature and political parties limited to two. Order was restored, and the admin. progressively centralized, Mobutu being re-elected for a further term in 1984. In 1971 the country, which had taken the name Rep. of Congo on independence in 1960, was re-named Zaïre, as was the Congo river. This revival of the old Portuguese name was made to avoid confusion with the People's Rep. of Congo (q.v.). Shaba remained disaffected after its bid for independence, and in 1977 former Katangese insurgents, with Angolan and Cuban aid, attempted a takeover, but later withdrew: a second invasion in 1978 was repulsed by French and Belgian paratroops. There is a territorial dispute with Zambia in the area of Kaputa and Lake Mweru.

ZAÏRE (zah-ēr'). Second-longest river in Africa, formerly the Congo, until re-named in 1971. It has its head in the source of the Lualaba r. (as the upper course of the Z. is known), which rises nr the Zambian border with the Rep. of Zaïre. It then flows 3,475 km (2,718 m) to the Atlantic, running in a great curve which crosses the Equator twice, and discharging a volume of water second only to the Amazon. Navigation is interrupted by dangerous rapids up to 160km (100m) long, notably from the Zambian border to Bukama; below Kongolo, where the gorge known as the Gates of Hell is located; above Kisangani, where the Stanley Falls are situated; and between Kinshasa and Matadi. Boma is a large port on the estuary itself; Matadi is a port for ocean-going ships 80km (50m) from the Atlantic; and at Pool Malebo (formerly Stanley Pool), a widening of the r. 560km (350m) from its mouth which encloses the marshy is. of Bamu, are Brazzaville on the west shore and Kinshasa on the south-western. The Z. is potentially a vast source of hydro-electric power, e.g. the Inga dam supplying Matadi and Kinshasa. The chief tributaries are the Ubangi, Sangha and Kasai.

The mouth of the Z. was discovered by Diego Cão in 1482, but not until the explorations of Livingstone and Stanley did the vast extent of its system become known to Europeans. Swamp, dense jungle, cataract and rapid, prevented its being navigated from source to mouth until the Blashford-Snell expedition in 1974 supported by Pres. Mobutu.

ZÁKINTHOS. Most southerly of the Ionian Is., Greece. Olives, currants, and the vine are grown; carpets are made. Area 400 sq.km (157 sq.m); pop. (1971) 30,190.

ZA'MA. Site of battle fought in 202 BC in Numidia (now Algeria) in which the Carthaginians under Hannibal were defeated by the Romans under Scipio, so ending the Second Punic War.

ZAMBĒ'ZI. River of Africa, *c.* 2,575 km (1,600 m) long, with headstreams in Zambia, Angola, and Zaïre. It flows generally E to the Indian Ocean which it enters through a wide delta near Chinde, Mozambique. Though broken by the Victoria Falls (harnessed for power, 1938) and many rapids, the Z. is important as a highway. *See* KARIBA.

ZA'MBIA. Rep. of S central Africa, formerly Northern Rhodesia. At an altitude of 900-1,500 m (3-5000 ft), except for river valleys, Z. incl. Lake Bangweulu and part of Lake Mweru, and the Kariba Dam (q.v.) and Kafue hydroelectric schemes. Crops incl. maize, groundnuts, cotton, sugar and tobacco, and cattle are reared. Most valuable mineral is the copper from the Copperbelt adjoining Shaba, Zaïre; others incl. emeralds (one third of the world's supply), manganese, lead and zinc. Lusaka replaced Livingstone as cap. in 1935: other towns are Kitwe, Ndola, Kabwe, Chipata, Mufulira, Chingola, Chililabombwe.

The country was visited by the Portuguese in the late 18th cent. and by Livingstone in 1851. It became a Brit. protectorate in 1924, was a member of the Fed. of Rhodesia and Nyasaland 1953-63, and became the independent rep. of Z., within the Commonwealth in 1964. Under Pres. Kenneth Kaunda (q.v.) there has been increased state control of the economy, and the constitution of 1973 provided for a Nat. Assembly and consultative House of Chiefs, and made the United Independence Party the only legal political party. The border with Rhodesia was temporarily closed by Rhodesia in 1973, and Z. continued to use alternative trade routes such as the Tanzam Rlwy.

Area 752,260 sq.km (290,585 sq.m); pop. (1978) 5,500,000. They are chiefly Bantu-speaking, but the official language is English. The majority are Christian (half Protestant, half RC). M.U.: kwacha.

ZAMENHOF (tsah'men-), **Lazarus Ludovik** (1859-1917). Polish-Jewish oculist of Warsaw, who invented the international language, Esperanto.

ZANTE (zahn'te). Ital. form of ZÁKINTHOS.

ZANZIBAR (zanzibahr'). Island (80 km/50 m long; area 1,658 sq.km/640 sq.m) which, together with the is. of Pemba, some adjacent islets, and a strip of coast on the African mainland, formed a sultanate which was placed under Brit. protection 1890-1963, when it became independent. The sultan thereupon handed over to Kenya the mainland strip, but in 1964 was driven into exile, the rep. then estab. being shortly afterwards linked with Tanganyika (q.v.). Cloves are the chief product, followed by copra. The cap. is also Z. on the W coast of the island. Pop. (1978) 475,655.

ZANZO'TTŌ, Andrea (1921-). Italian poet. A teacher from the Veneto, he has pub. much difficult verse incl. the collection *La beltà* (1968), with a strong metaphysical element.

ZAPATA (zapah'ta), **Emiliano** (*c.* 1877-1919). Mexican guerrilla leader finally defeated at Pueblo in 1915.

ZAPOROZHE (zahporozh'ye). City in Ukrainian SSR on the Dnieper, cap. of Z. region, and site of the Dnieper Dam (q.v.). Z. manufactures steel, chemicals, aluminium goods, etc., and is an important centre for pig-iron and magnesium. The Russians did not defend it in 1941, but re-took it from the Germans in 1943. Pop. (1979) 781,000.

ZARAGOZA. Span. spelling of SARAGOSSA.

ZEALAND. *See* SEELAND, Denmark; ZEELAND, Netherlands.

ZĒ'BRA. Name given to striped equine species; the stripes serve as camouflage against the desert and mountainous background. The true or mountain Z. (*Equus zebra*) was once common in Cape Colony and Natal and still survives in parts of S Africa and Angola. It has short legs and long ears and is silvery-white with black or dark brown markings. Grevy's Z. (*E. grevyi*) is much larger, and has finer and clearer markings; it inhabits Ethiopia and the Somali region; Burchell's Z. (*E. burchelli*), which is intermediate in size, has white ears, a long mane, and full tail; it roams the plains N of the Orange river.

ZEBRA The camouflage markings which serve them in good stead among tall grasses, stand out in violent contrast when they come down to the water to drink. *Photo: Heather Angel*

ZĒ'BU. Indian ox (*Bos indicus*), light-coloured with a large fatty hump near the shoulders. It is used for draught, and is held to be sacred.

ZEDEKIAH (zedekī'-ah). Last of the kings of the Hebrew kingdom of Judah. Nebuchadrezzar gave him the throne in 597 BC, but in 586 he was taken away to Babylon as a blinded captive.

ZEEBRUGGE (zābroog'ge). Small Belgian port on the North Sea. The harbour and 14km (9m) canal to Bruges were built 1896-1907. In the F.W.W., when it was a German submarine base, it was attacked on 23 April 1918 by a British force under Admiral Keyes and the canal entrance was blocked.

ZEELAND (zē'-). Prov. of the Netherlands, incl. the estuary of the Scheldt and the is. of Walcheren and N and S Beveland, adjoining Belgium on the S. Most of Z. is below sea-level. Cap. Middelburg. Area 1,709 sq.km (660 sq.m); pop. (1978) 344,400.

ZEFFIRE'LLI, G. Franco (1923-). Italian theatrical director and designer, famous for his beautiful and lavish designs and production of plays, e.g. *Romeo and Juliet* at the Old Vic (1960), of operas, e.g. *Tosca* (1964), and of films, e.g. *The Taming of the Shrew* (1967) and *Jesus of Nazareth* (1977).

ZEISS (tsīs), **Carl** (1816-88). German optician. He opened his 1st workshop at Jena in 1846 and in 1866 joined forces with Ernst Abbe (1840-1905), producing microscopes, field glasses, etc.

ZELE'NKA, Jan Dismas (1679-1745). Bohemian composer. Little of his personal life is known, but he worked at the court of Dresden and became director of church music in 1729. His compositions were rediscovered in the 1970s.

ZELE'NOGRAD. City 145 km (90 m) NE of Moscow, the Soviet equivalent of Silicon Valley.

ZEN. Abbreviation of Japanese *zenna* 'quiet mind concentration', a variant of Buddhism (q.v.) introduced from India to Japan via China in the 12th cent. Zazen or 'sitting meditation' involves periods in the cross-legged lotus position, during which all worldly concerns are banished and a state of selflessness reached which ultimately leads to 'enlightenment'.

ZENDAVE'STA. The sacred scriptures of the Zoroastrians, represented by the modern Parsees. The Avesta consists of liturgical books for the use of the Parsee priests, and the *Gathas* contain the discourses and revelations of Zoroaster. The Zend portion is the commentary thereon.

ZE'NITH. Opposite of nadir; the upper pole of the celestial horizon or the point in the sky immediately above the observer.

ZĒ'NO (fl. *c.* 460 BC). Greek philosopher, one of the Eleatic school. He was a disciple of Parmenides and controverted current views on space and time by such paradoxes as that of Achilles and the tortoise.

ZENO (*c.* 340-265 BC). Greek philosopher, b. at Citium in Cyprus and probably a Phoenician, who founded the Stoic school of philosophy at Athens.

ZENŌ'BIA. Queen of Palmyra in the Syrian desert from AD 266, when on her husband's death she assumed the crown as regent for her sons, until 272 when she was defeated by the Roman emperor Aurelian and taken as a captive to Rome.

ZEPPELIN (tse'pelēn), **Ferdinand,** count von (1838-1917). German airship pioneer. On retiring from the army in 1891, he devoted himself to the study of aeronautics, and his first airship was built and tested in 1900. During the F.W.W. a number of Zeppelins were employed in bombing England, and Z. also helped to pioneer the large multi-engine bomber planes.

ZERMATT (tsermaht'). Swiss tourist and winter centre in the Valais canton at the foot of the Matterhorn. Pop. (1970) 3,100.

ZETLAND. Official form (till 1974) of SHETLAND.

ZEUS (zūs). The supreme god in the Greek pantheon, corresponding to the Roman Jupiter. He was the son of Kronos, and his chief spouse was Hera. As the supreme god he dispensed good and evil and was the father and ruler of all mankind. He is frequently represented holding the thunderbolt and the aegis or shield of fringed goatskin.

ZHANGJIAKOU (jahngjiakaw-oo'). Historic town and trade centre (formerly Changchiakow) in Hebei prov., China, 160 km (100 m) SE of Peking, with which it is linked by rail. Zhangjiakou is on the border of Inner Mongolia, its Mongolian name being Kalgan or 'gate', and it is the S terminus of a road to Ulaanbaatar. It developed

ZEUS. A magnificent head of the god, and that of an eagle - the Jovian bird - carved on a giant scale. They form part of the vanished splendour of Nemrut Dag in Adiyaman il, Turkey, where the Greeks built a hill-top temple, later destroyed by earthquake. *Photo: Fulvio Roiter*

ZHAO ZIYANG. An economic expert with a pragmatic outlook, Zhao Ziyang became Prime Minister in 1980 and General Secretary of the Communist Party in 1987.

under the Manchu dynasty, and was the centre of the long-estab. overland tea trade from China to Russia. Pop. (1973) 300,000.

ZHAO ZIYANG (jah-aw zeyahng') (1919-). Chinese statesman. The nominee of Deng Xiaoping, he succeeded Hua Guofeng in 1980 as Prime Minister. Son of a wealthy landlord, he was purged in the cultural revolution, but in 1975 was appointed to run China's largest prov., Sichuan. He achieved an economic miracle in both agriculture and industry, became the protege of Deng Xiaoping, and after only 6 months as Vice-Premier in 1980, succeeded Hua Guofeng in Sept. 1980 as PM. His policies involve more self-management for farms and factories, greater scope for free market forces, and cash incentives for workers and factories. Following the resignation in 1987 of Hu Yaobang, Zhao Ziyang became General Secretary of the Communist Party, while continuing in the post of PM.

ZHDANOV (zhdah'nof). Port of the Ukraine, USSR, on the Sea of Azov. Formerly Mariupol, it was renamed 1944 in honour of Andrei Zhdanov (1896-1948), statesman and defender of Leningrad, who was born at Mariupol. It has iron and steel industries. Pop. (1979) 503,000.

ZHEJIANG (jejē-ahng'). Smallest prov. (formerly Chekiang) of China, on the SE coast. Rice, cotton, jute, maize and sugar are produced, as well as timber on the uplands. It is densely populated. The cap. is Hangzhou. Area 101,800 sq.km (39,295 sq.m); pop. (1979) 36,000,000.

ZHENGZHOU (jengjaw-oo'). City (formerly Chengchow), cap. of Henan prov. (from 1954), China, on the Huang He. A rail junction, it has cotton textile and food manufactures. In the 1970s the earliest city yet found in China, dating to 1500 BC, was excavated nr. the walls of Zhengzhou. Pop. (1973) 1,100,000.

ZHITO'MIR. Town in Ukrainian SSR, cap. of Z. region, on the Teterev, a trib. of the Dnieper. Dating from the 13th cent., it is a timber and grain centre with furniture factories, etc. Pop. (1979) 244,000.

ZHONGHUA RENMIN GONGHEGUO (jawnghoo-ah' zenmēn gawnghögoo-aw'). People's Republic of China.

ZHOU ENLAI. Pinyin form of Chou En-lai (q.v.).

ZHU DE. Pinyin form of Chu Teh (q.v.).

ZHUKOV (zhōōk'of), **Grigory Konstantinovich** (1896-1974). Marshal of the Soviet Union. Early in 1941 he became Chief of Staff, commanded the armies defending Moscow in 1941, directed the counter-offensive at Stalingrad in 1942-3, and organized the relief of Leningrad in 1943. Appointed commander on the Ukrainian front in March 1944, he led the offensive which ended with the fall of Berlin, headed the Allied delegation which received the German surrender, and subsequently commanded the Russian occupation forces inside Germany, 1945-6. He succeeded Bulganin as Min. of Defence (1955-7).

ZIAN (ze-ahn'). Cap. (formerly Sian) of Shaanxi prov., China. It was the cap. of China under the Chou dynasty (*c.* 1100 BC); under the Han dynasty (206 BC to AD 220), when it was called Changan (long peace); under the Tang dynasty 618-906, as Siking (western cap.). The Manchus named it Sian (Pinyin: Zian - western peace); it reverted to the name Changan 1913-32; Siking 1932-43; and once more Sian (Zian) in 1943. It was here that the imperial court retired following the Boxer rising in 1900. In 1974 the tomb of China's first emperor Ch'in Shih Huang Ti (q.v.) was discovered nearby. Pop. (1973) 1,700,000.

ZIA-UL-HAQ (zē'a-ool-hahk), Mohammad (1924-). Pakistani general and statesman. Following the military overthrow of Prime Minister Bhutto, he became chief martial law administrator in July 1977, and in Sept. 1978 became president. Under his regime Bhutto was executed, civil and political liberties were curtailed, an Islamic code of laws introduced, and elections postponed.

ZIEGLER (zēg'ler), **Karl** (1898-1973). German organic chemist. In 1963 he was awarded a Nobel prize for his work on the chemistry and technology of high polymers, e.g. the combination of many molecules of the simple gas ethylene, into the plastic, Polythene.

ZIGGURAT. In ancient Babylonia and Assyria, a stepped pyramid of sun-baked brick faced with glazed bricks or tiles on which stood a shrine to a deity. The Tower of Babel may have been a Z.

ZIMBABWE (zēmbabh'wē). Bantu word meaning stone house, used originally esp. for extensive ruins near Victoria, in Mashonaland, Zimbabwe. They incl. a massive elliptical enclosure with 10m (30ft) stone walls, known as 'the Temple', and a series of stone-walled enclosures on a granite outcrop known as 'the Acropolis'. There are evidences of a civilized Bantu-speaking people from Zaïre or Ethiopia, and who were smelters of iron, in the area before AD 300. By AD 1200 it was an important settlement of the African Shona people, who had moved in from the N and erected the first stone buildings. In the 15th cent. Mutota, their greatest ruler, extended his empire over modern Zimbabwe, but it fell before the Rozwi tribesmen who then ruled until the 19th cent. They were then in turn defeated by refugee tribes moving N before the Zulu warrior, Chaka. The Z. ruins were then abandoned. The Z. bird, derived from soap-stone sculptures of fish eagles found in the ruins, was the nat. emblem of Rhodesia, and also became that of the new state of Zimbabwe (q.v.).

ZIMBABWE. Country of central Africa bordered by Zambia to the N, S Africa to the S, Mozambique to the E and Botswana to the W. The broad central plateau rises in the NE from c. 1,250 m (4,000 ft) to 1,500 m (5,000 ft), and on the E border, some 70 km (45 m) from Umtali is Mt Inyangani 2,515 m (8,250 ft). To the SE of Bulawayo are the Matoppo Hills, where Rhodes is buried. The healthy climate encouraged European settlement, and the chief crops are cotton, tobacco, sugar, citrus and deciduous fruits, and tea. There is livestock and dairy farming, and fish farming on Lake Kariba. Minerals incl. asbestos, gold, platinum, silver, cobalt, copper, chrome, nickel and coal, and industries, fostered by power from the Kariba dam, incl. textiles, cigarettes, oil refining, vehicle assembly, etc. The cap. is Salisbury; other towns are Bulawayo, Gwelo and Umtali.

Zimbabwe has been occupied from early times by Bantu peoples, notably the Mashona, who built Zimbabwe (q.v.). and estab. an industrial culture, mining gold and working metal with skill. In 1837 the warlike Bantu people, the Matabele, in retreat after unsuccessful battles with the Boers, estab. themselves in the best of the Mashona land. However, in 1889 the combined area later occupied by Zambia and Zimbabwe was incl. in the cession to the British South Africa Company, and the whole was named Rhodesia in 1895 in honour of Cecil Rhodes (q.v.). The Matabele War of 1893 ensued, their leader, Lobengula dying in hiding, but in 1896, following the Jameson Raid, the Matabele once more unsuccessfully attempted the reassertion of their independence. The portion of the area S of the Zambezi, then known as Southern Rhodesia, was granted responsible govt. in 1923, was a member of the Fed. of Rhodesia and Nyasaland 1953-63, and became popularly known simply as Rhodesia in 1964, after the creation of Zambia, when pressure mounted for independence under white rule. The British govt. stipulated that terms for this must be acceptable to all the country's citizens. This was rejected and on 11 Nov. 1965 a unilateral declaration of independence (UDI) was made. Negotiations with Ian Smith (q.v.) leader of the Rhodesian Front regime repeatedly failed, despite the imposition of UN sanctions, and Rhodesia became a rep. in 1970. An 'internal settlement' negotiated by Ian Smith with black moderates in 1978 was rejected by the UN, and guerrilla warfare by the militant black leaders, Robert Mugabe and Joshua Nkomo intensified. Following the London Conference of 1979 Southern Rhodesia became legally independent as the Rep. of Zimbabwe.

Under the constitution of 1980 there is a pres. elected for 6 yrs by members of parliament, which comprises a senate and house of assembly (20 of the 100 members of the latter are elected by white voters). Robert Mugabe (leader of the Z. Nat. African Union ZANU) became the first PM, and Joshua Nkomo (leader of the Z. African People's Union ZAPU) was Min. for Home Affairs 1980-Jan. 1981.

Area 390,622 sq.km (150,820 sq.m); pop. (1977) 6,820,000, of whom c. 230,000 are white. M.U.: Z. dollar.

ZIMBABWE-RHODESIA. Name given to the country, now known as Zimbabwe, Jan.-Nov. 1979, under a constitution approved by a referendum among white voters. Bishop Abel Muzorewa (1925-) was PM May-Nov. 1979.

ZINC. Bluish-white metal, symbol Zn, at. no. 30, at. wt. 65.38. From very early times it has been used as a component of brass but it was not recognized as a separate metal until 1746 by Marggraf, by heating calamine with charcoal. Ores occur in many parts of the world, but the principal source of supply is USA. Its chief modern uses are in the production of galvanized iron and in alloys, especially brass. Its compounds are used in medicine, and in paints, Z. oxide being an important white pigment.

ZI'NNIA. Half-hardy annual of the genus *Zinnia* in the family Compositae, named after the Ger. botanist J. G. Zinn (1727-59). Originally a native of Mexico, it has bright, rounded flower heads.

ZINO'VIEV, Grigory (1883-1936). Russian politician. A prominent Bolshevik, he returned to Russia in 1917 with Lenin and played a leading part in the Revolution. As head of the Communist International (1919) his name was linked with the forged letter inciting Britain's Communists to rise, which helped to topple the Labour govt in 1924. As one of the 'Old Bolsheviks', he was accused of high treason and shot.

ZI'ON. Name of the Jebusite stronghold in Jerusalem that was captured by King David. On the same hill was built the temple and in due course Z. became a synonym for Jerusalem, and the City of God.

ZIONISM. A Jewish movement aiming at the establishment in Palestine of a Jewish state with its cap. at Jerusalem, the 'city of Zion'. As a modern movement it dates from 1896, when Theodor Herzl pub. his *Jewish State,* outlining a scheme for erecting an autonomous Jewish commonwealth under Turkish suzerainty. The Zionist Organization was estab. at Basle in 1897. During the F.W.W. Weizmann was instrumental in securing the Balfour Declaration (q.v.), and in 1948 the Jews in Palestine proclaimed the state of Israel. The General Assembly of the UN condemned Z. as 'a form of racism and racial discrimination' in 1975: those voting against the resolution incl. USA, and the European Community.

ZIRCŌ'NIUM (Arabic *zargun,* gold colour). A rare metal of the titanium family, symbol Zr, at. no. 40, at. wt. 91.22. Discovered in zircon by Klaproth in 1789, and isolated by Berzelius in 1824, it is used in alloys.

ZLATOUST (zlahto-o͞ost′). Town in Chelyabinsk region, RSFSR, in the S Urals, founded in 1754 as an iron- and copper-working settlement, destroyed 1774 by a peasant rising, but developed as an armaments centre from the time of Napoleon's invasion of Russia. Since the Revolution, Z. has become one of the chief metallurgical centres of the RSFSR. Pop. (1979) 198,000.

ZŌ′DIAC. Name given by the ancient Greeks to that zone of the heavens containing the paths of the Sun, Moon and the 5 planets then known. It was about 16° in width, and the stars contained in it were grouped into 12 constellations, viz. Aries, Taurus, Gemini, Cancer, Leo, Virgo, Libra, Scorpio, Sagittarius, Capricorn, Aquarius, Pisces.

ZODIAC. A fifteenth century rendering of the signs of the zodiac, which played such an important role in astrology. *Photo: Mansell Collection*

ZODIACAL LIGHT. A cone-shaped light sometimes seen extending from the Sun along the ecliptic, visible after sunset or before sunrise. It is due to thinly spread material in the central plane of the Solar System. From Britain it is never bright, but it may be conspicuous when observed from countries with clearer atmosphere.

ZO′FFANY, Johann (1733-1810). German portrait painter. Settling in England in 1758, he became RA in 1769, executing many conversation pieces.

ZOG (1895-1961). King of Albania. A member of an important Albanian family, he became PM of Albania in 1922, pres. of the rep. in 1925, and king in 1928. He was driven out by the Italians in 1939 but his son Leka I (1939-) maintains a claim.

ZŌLA, Émile Édouard Charles Antoine (1840-1902). French novelist. B. in Paris, he was a journalist and clerk in Paris until his *Contes à Ninon* (1864) enabled him to devote himself to literature. In 1867 he pub. the masterly study in remorse *Thérèse Raquin*, and in 1871 *La Fortune des Rougon* began the series of some 20 novels portraying the fortunes of a French family under the Second Empire, incl. *Le Ventre de Paris* (1874), *La Faute de l'Abbé Mouret* (1875), *L'Assommoir* (1878), *Nana* (1880), *Germinal* (1885), *La Terre* (1888), and *La Débâcle* (1892). Among later novels are the trilogy *Trois Villes* (1894-8), and *Fécondité* (1899). In 1898 he pub. *J'accuse*, indicting the persecutors of Dreyfus.

ZO′MBA. Former cap. of Malawi, 32km (20m) W of Lake Shirwa, until replaced by Lilongwe in 1975: Z. remains the univ. town. Pop. (1977) 15,700.

ZOO. Short for zoological gardens, i.e. places where wild animals are kept in captivity, whether as an interesting spectacle or in pursuit of scientific knowledge. Henry I started a royal menagerie at Woodstock, Oxon, later transferred to the Tower of London, and in 1831 the king presented the collection in the Tower menagerie to the Zoological Society in Regent's Park, London. *See* HAGENBECK; WHIPSNADE.

ZOOLOGY (zō-o′loji) (Gk. *zōon*, animal). That branch of biology that is concerned with the study of animals. The popular name for it is Natural History, but it comprises not only a description of present-day animals, but the evolution of animal forms, anatomy and physiology, embryology and morphology, geographical distribution, and ecology, etc.

ZOROASTER (zōrō-as′ter), or more correctly **Zarathustra** (600 or 1000 BC?). Persian seer, founder of the religion known after him as Zoroastrianism. He was a Mede or a Persian, and was popularly supposed to be the first of the Magi or Wise Men. In the Zendavesta he features as a religious prophet, the author of hymns (the Gathas) in honour of Ormuzd the Good God. He is said to have found a powerful patron in a prince of eastern Iran, and to have married into the court circle. His date is uncertain.

ZOROASTRIANISM. The religion founded by Zoroaster (q.v.), represented today by the Parsees. Its theology is dualistic, the Good God Ahura Mazda or Ormuzd being opposed by the Evil God, Angra Mainyu or Ahriman. These are represented in the Avesta (*see* ZENDAVESTA) as being perpetually in conflict, but ultimately the victory will be Ormuzd's. A ceremonial was devised for purifying and keeping clean both soul and body. Worship was at altars on which burnt the sacred fire. A priestly caste was instituted. The dead were exposed to vultures. *See* PARSEES.

ZORRILLA (thōr-rēl′yah), **José** (1817-93). Spanish poet and playwright. B. at Valladolid, he based his plays chiefly on national legends.

ZOUAVES (zoo-ahvz′). Corps of French infantry soldiers, first raised in Algeria in 1831 from the Berber Kabyle tribe of Z. Before long, however, the native element was eliminated, and only a half-Arab dress was retained as a characteristic.

ZUCKERMAN (zook′-), **Solly,** baron (1904-). British scientist. B. in Cape Town, he originally specialized in anatomy, but after the S.W.W. was concerned with the wider range of policy, espec. defence, as Chief Scientific Adviser to the govt 1960-71. He was awarded the OM 1968.

ZUIDER ZEE (zoi′der zā; Dutch, south sea). *See* IJSSELMEER.

ZULOAGA (thoo-lo-ah'ga), **Ignacio** (1870-1945). Spanish painter, b. in Vizcaya; he favoured bull-fighters and other Spanish types.

ZULULAND (zoo'loo-). Region in the NE of Natal prov., S Africa, annexed by Britain in 1887 and incorporated in Natal in 1897. The Zulus probably reached the area early in the 17th cent., and under Chaka (1810-28) became a formidable military power. His half-brother Dingaan (q.v.) estab. an even more bloodthirsty regime. Subsequent rulers were Dingaan's half-brother Panda (1840-73), and Panda's son Cetewayo (q.v.) and grandson Dinizulu, who d. in 1913 exiled to the Transvaal. The Zulu Black Homeland (KwaZulu) was estab. in 1970, and a legislative assembly created in 1971. The seat of govt. is Ulundi, site of the final defeat of the Zulus by the British in the Zulu War of 1879. The chief executive officer or PM is Chief Gatsha Buthelezi (1929-), a great-grandson of Cetewayo, who has visualized a confederation of the Black Homelands (q.v.) plus Botswana, Lesotho and Swaziland, and eventually Black majority rule over the whole of S. Africa, with the estab. of a one-party socialist system. Area 31,000 sq.km (12,000 sq.m); pop. (1970) 2,100,000.

ZURBARÁN (thoorbahrahn'), **Francisco de** (1598-?1669). Spanish painter, sometimes called the Spanish Caravaggio. He painted subjects from Church history, e.g. a series (with Herrera) on the life of St Bonaventura.

ZÜRICH (tsü'rikh). Swiss city, cap. of Z. canton, most populous and economically important in the country. It stands beside the lake of Z. It has a univ. (refounded 1833) and is the intellectual cap. of German-speaking Switzerland. Industries incl. machinery, electrical goods, textiles, etc. Pop. met. area (1978) 711,600.

ZUTPHEN (züt'fen). Town in Gelderland prov., Netherlands, near which Sir Philip Sidney was fatally wounded. Pop. (1979) 31,250.

ZWEIG (zvīg), **Arnold** (1887-1968). German novelist, playwright and poet. B. in Silesia, he was Jewish and left Germany on the Nazis coming to power. He is best-remembered for his realistic novel of a Russian peasant in the German army *The Case of Sergeant Grischa* (1927).

ZWICKAU (tsvik'ow). Town in Karlmarxstadt district, E Germany, on an important coalfield. Pop. (1979) 123,500.

ZWINGLI (tsving'lē), **Ulrich** (1484-1531). Swiss Protestant. B. at St Gall, he was ordained an RC priest in 1506, but by 1519 was a Reformer, and led the movement in Switzerland. In a war against the cantons which had not accepted the Reformation he was killed in a skirmish at Kappel.

ZWO'LLE. Cap. of Overijssel prov., Netherlands, a market town with brewing, distilling, butter making and other industries. Pop. (1979) 81,300.

Abbreviations

(For states of the USA both the traditional, and the approved PO two-letter abbreviations introduced 1963 are given.)

A

A ampere, answer; general exhibition, in cinemas, but parents advised might prefer children under 14 not to see it. **AA** exhibition 14 years and over. **Å**, ångström. **A1**, first class (of ships). **AA**, anti-aircraft, Automobile Association. **A. and M.**, Ancient and Modern (hymnal). **AB**, able-bodied seaman. **ABA**, Amateur Boxing Association. **ab init.**, *ab initio* (L. from the beginning). **abl.**, ablative. **ABM**, antiballistic missile. **abp.**, archbishop. **AC**, aircraftman, alternating current. **ACAS**, Advisory, Conciliation and Arbitration Service. **ante Christum** (L. before Christ). **A/C** current account. **acc.**, accusative. **ACF**, Army Cadet Force. **ACGB**, Arts Council of Gt. Britain. **ACP**, African, Caribbean and Pacific countries. **ACT**, Australian Capital Territory. **ACTH**, adrenocorticotrophic hormone. **ACTT**, Association of Cinematograph, Television and Allied Technicians. **ACV**, air cushion vehicle. **AD**, *anno Domini* (L. in the year of the Lord - placed before date). **ad.**, advertisement. **ADB**, Asian Development Bank. **ADC**, aide-de-camp, ADC(P), Personal Aide-de-camp to HM The Queen. **add.**, addendum/addenda. **adj.**, adjective. **ad lib.**, *ad libitum* (L. as much as desired). **Adm.**, Admiral(ty). **admin.**, administer(ed), administration. **adv.**, adverb. **aet.**, *aetatis* (L. of the age). **AEU**, Amalgamated Engineering Union. **AfDB**,African Development Board. **AFLCIO**, American Federation of Labor-Congress of Industrial Organizations. **AG**, Attorney-General, air gunner. **AH**, *anno hegirae* (L. year of the flight - Mohammed, from Mecca to Medina - Moslem calendar). **AI(D)**, artificial insemination (donor). **AK**, Alaska. **AL/Ala.**, Alabama. **Alas.**, Alaska. **alt.**, altitude. **Alta.**, Alberta. **a.m.**, *ante meridiem* (L. before noon). **amp**, ampere. **AMS**, additional member system. **AMESLAN**, *Am*erican *S*ign *Lan*guage (for the deaf). **anon.**, anonymous. **ANZAC**, Australia and New Zealand Army Corps. **ANZUS**, Australian, New Zealand and US Defence Pact (Pacific Security Treaty). **AOC-(in-C)**, Air Officer Commanding (-in-Chief). **AP**, Associated Press. **approx.**, approximate(ly). **aq.**, L. *aqua* (water). **AR**, Arkansas. **arch.**, archaic, architect(ure). **archbp.**, archbishop. **archo.**, archipelago. **Ariz.**, Arizona. **Ark.**, Arkansas. **ARP**, Air Raid Precautions. **arr.**, arranged, arrive(s). **AS**, Anglo-Saxon. **ASDIC**, Allied Submarine Detection Investigation Committee. **ASEAN**, Assocn. of SE Asian Nations. **ASH**, Action on Smoking and Health. **a.s.l.**, above sea-level. **ASLIB**, Assocn. of Special Libraries and Information Bureaux. **assoc.**, associate(d). **assn./assocn.**, association. **ASSR**, Autonomous Soviet Socialist Republic. **asst.**, assistant. **ASTMS**, Association of Scientific, Technical and Managerial Staffs. **ATC**, Air Training Corps. **at. no.**, atomic number. **ATS**, Auxiliary Territorial Service. **at. wt.**, atomic weight. **ATV**, Associated TeleVision. **AUC**, *anno urbis conditae* (L. 'in the year of the founding of the city' (Rome), 753 BC). **Aug.**, August. **aux.**, auxiliary. **AV**, Authorised Version (of the Bible). **avdp.**, avoirdupois. **AVR**, Army Volunteer Reserve. **AWRE**, Atomic Weapons Research Establishment. **AZ**, Arizona.

B

B born, brother. **BA**, Bachelor of Arts, British Academy. **BAAS**, British Assocn. for the Advancement of Science. **BAB**, British Airways Board. **bac.**, *baccalaureus* (L. bachelor). **BAe**, British Aerospace. **BAFTA**, British Academy of Film and Television Arts. **b. and b.**, bed and breakfast. **BAOR**, British Army of the Rhine (formerly *on* the Rhine). **Bart.**, baronet. **Bart's** St. Bartholomew's Hospital, London. **BBB of C**, British Boxing Board of Control. **BBC**, British Broadcasting Corporation (originally Company). **BC**, before Christ (placed after date), borough council, British Columbia, British Council. **BCh**, Bachelor of Surgery (L. *chirurgiae*). **BCL**, Bachelor of Civil Law. **B.Com**, Bachelor of Commerce. **BD**, Bachelor of Divinity. **Bde.**, brigade. **b.e.**, bill of exchange. **Beds**, Bedfordshire. **BEF**, British Expeditionary Force. **BEM**, British Empire Medal. **BEE**, Bachelor of Electrical Engineering. **Berks**, Berkshire. **b.f.**, brought forward. **BFI**, British Film Institute. **BFPO**, British Forces Post Office. **BIS**, Bank for International Settlements. **bk.**, bank, book. **B/L**, bill of lading. **B.Litt.** Bachelor of Letters (L. *literarum*). **BL**, Bachelor of Law. **BM**, Bachelor of Medicine, British Museum. **BMA**, British Medical Assocn. **Bn.**, battalion. **BNEC**, British National Export Council. **BNOC**, British National Oil Corpn., British National Opera Co. **B. of E.** Bank of England. **bor.**, borough. **bos'n.**, boatswain. **BoT**, Board of Trade. **bot.**, botany, botanical. **BP**, British Pharmacopoeia. **bp.**, boiling-point. **Bp.**, bishop. **BR**, British Rail. **Br./Brit.**, British. **Bros.**, brothers. **BRS**, British Road Services. **BS**, Bachelor of Surgery. **BSA**, Birmingham Small Arms (Company). **BSc**, Bachelor of Science. **BSI**, British Standards Institution. **BSL**, British Sign Language (for the deaf). **b.s.l.**, below sea level. **BST**, British Summer Time. **Bt.**, baronet. **Btu**, British thermal unit. **Bucks**, Buckinghamshire. **bus.**, omnibus (L. for all). **BVM**, Blessed Virgin Mary. **Byz.**, Byzantine.

C

C *centum* (L. hundred), Centigrade, Central, Conservative, coulomb. **c.**, cape, centimetre, chapter, *circa* (L. about), cubic. **CA**, California, Central America. **CAB**, Citizen's Advice Bureau, Civil Aeronautics Board (US). **cal.**, calorie, California. **CACM**, Central American Common Market. **Cambs**, Cambridgeshire. **Can.**, canon. **Cantab.**, *Cantabrigiensis* (L. member of Cambridge Univ.). **CAP**, Common Agricultural Policy (EEC). **cap.**, capital, chapter (L.*caput* head). **car.**, carat. **CARE**, Cottage and Rural Enterprises. **CARICOM**, Caribbean Community and Common Market. **CAT**, clear-air-turbulence, computer-assisted typesetting. **cat.**, catalogue. **CB**, confined to barracks, citizens' band (radio). **CBI**, Confederation of British Industry. **CBSI**, Chartered Building Societies Inst. **CC**, Coastal Command, county council(lor), cricket club. **cc**, cubic centimetre, cubic contents. **CCA**, current cost accounting. **CCC**, Central Criminal Court. **CD**, Civil Defence, 400 (Roman), Corps Diplomatique (Fr. Diplomatic Corps). **cd**, candela. **CDC**, Commonwealth Development Corporation. **Cdre**, commodore. **CDS**, Chief of the Defence Staff. **CEAO**, West African Economic Community (Communauté Économique de l'Afrique de l'Ouest). **CECLA**, Latin American Economic Co-ordination Commiccion (Comité Economico para la Coordinación Latinoamericana). **CEGB**, Central Electricity Generating Board. **cent.**, century. **CENTO**, Central Treaty Organization. **CERN**, European Organization (formerly Council) for Nuclear Research (Conseil Européen de la Recherche Nucléaire). **CET**, Central European Time. **cet.par.**, *ceteris paribus* (L. other things being equal). **CF**, Chaplain to the Forces. **c.f.**, carried forward. **cf**, *confer* (L. compare). **CFA**, Communauté Financière Africaine. **CFC**, chlorofluorcarbon. **CFTC**, Commonwealth Fund for Technical Co-Operation. **c.g.**, centre of gravity. **cg**, centigram. **CGS**, Chief of the General Staff, centimetre-gram-second system. **CGT**, Confédération Générale du Travail (Fr. General Federation of Labour). **CH**, Companion of Honour. **c.h.**, central heating. **Ch.**, church. **chap.**, chaplain. **Ches.**, Cheshire. **CI**, Channel Islands. **CIA**, Central Intelligence Agency. **CID**, Criminal Investigation Department. **CIGS**, Chief of the Imperial General Staff (now CGS). **C-in-C**, Commander-in-Chief. **CIO**, see AFL-CIO. **CIPEC**, Intergovernmental Council of Copper Exporting Countries. **cl**, centilitre. **class.**, classical, classification. **cm**, centimetre. **CMG**, Companion of the Order of St. Michael and St. George. Congressional Medal for Gallantry (US). **CMS**, Church Missionary Society. **CND**, Campaign for NuclearDisarmament. **CNRS**, Centre National du Recherche Scientifique. **CO**, Colonial (or Commonwealth) Office, now FCO; commanding officer, conscientious objector, Crown Office, Colorado. **Co.**, company, county. **c/o**, care of. **COD**, cash on delivery. **C of E**, Church of England. **COI**, Central Office of Information. **Col.**, colonel, colonial, Colorado. **Coll.**, college. **Com.**, Communist, commissioner. **Comdt.**, commandant. **COMECON**, Council for Mutual Economic Assistance (Communist). **con.**, *contra* (L. against). **conf.**, conference. **conj.**, conjugation, conjunction. **Conn.**, Connacht, Connecticut. **Cons.**, Conservative. **contd.**, continued. **Co-op.**, Co-operative. **Cor.**, Corinthian(s), coroner. **CORE**, Congress of Racial Equality (US). **Corpn.**, corporation. **COS**, Chief of Staff. **cos.**, cosine. **cox**, coxswain. **CP**, Common Prayer, Communist Party. **c.p.** carriage paid. **CPB**, charged particle beam. **Cpl.**, corporal. **CPP**, current purchasing power. **CPR**, Canadian Pacific Railway, cardiopulmonary resuscitation. **cr.**, created, credit. **CRC,** Cancer Research Campaign, Civil Rights Commission (US). **CRE,** Commission for Racial Equality. **cresc.,** *crescendo* (Ital. becoming louder), crescent. **CSC,** Conspicuous Service Cross (US). **CSE,** Certificate of Secondary Education. **CT,** Connecticut. **CTR,** Controlled Thermonuclear Research, Harwell. **cts.,** cents, centimes. **cttee.,** committee. **cu., cub.,** cubic. **CUP,** Cambridge University Press. **CV,** Cross of Valour (Canada), *curriculum vitae* (L. summary of career). **CVO,** Commander of the Royal Victorian Order. **CWS,** Co-Operative Wholesale Society. **cwt.,** hundredweight. **CZ,** Canal Zone (Panama).

D

D five hundred (Roman). **d.,** daughter, day, dam, decametre, *denarius* (L. penny), died. **DA,** District Attorney (US). **dat.,** dative. **dau.,** daughter. **dB,** decibel. **DBE,** Dame Commander of the Order of the British Empire. **DC,** *da capo* (Ital. from the beginning), Design Council, direct current, District of Columbia (US), District Council. **DCE,** domestic credit expansion. **DCL,** Doctor of Civil Law. **DD,** Doctor of Divinity. **DE,** Delaware. **deb.,** debenture. **dec.,** deceased. **Del.,** Delaware. **del.,** *delineavit* (L. he drew). **dele,** delete. **dept.,** department. **Deut.,** Deuteronomy. **DF,** Defender of the Faith. **DFC,** Distinguished Flying Cross. **DFM,** Distinguished Flying Medal. **DG,** *Dei gratia* (L. by the grace of God), Director General, Dragoon Guards. **DI,** Defence Intelligence. **diam.,** diameter. **dim.,** *diminuendo* (Ital., becoming quieter). **dip.,** diploma. **dir.,** director. **dist.,** district. **div.,** division, divorced. **divi.,** dividend. **DIY,** do-it-yourself. **dl,** decilitre. **D.Litt.,** Doctor of Letters (L. *literarum*). **DM,** Doctor of Medicine, Deutsche Mark. **dm,** decimetre. **DMS,** Diploma in Management Studies. **DMus,** Doctor of Music. **DNA,** deoxy-ribonucleic acid. **DNB,** Dictionary of National Biography. **do.,** ditto. **DOM,** *Deo optimo maximo* (L. to God the best and greatest). **Dom.,** Dominican, Dominion, *Dominus* (L. lord, master). **DORA,** Defence of the Realm Act. **doz.,** dozen. **DP,** displaced person. **DPD,** Diploma in Public Dentistry. **DPP,** Director of Public Prosecutions. **DR,** dead reckoning. **Dr.,** debtor, doctor. **dr.,** dram, drawer (of a cheque). **DS,** *dal segno* (Ital. (repeat) from the mark). **DSc,** Doctor of Science. **DSO,** Distinguished Service Order. **d.s.p.,** *decessit sine prole* (L. died without issue). **DT,** delirium tremens. **DV,** *Deo volente* (L. God willing). **dyn,** dyne.

E

E Earl, east, easter, English, second class (of ships). **e.,** eldest. **e.o.o.e.,** *erreur ou omission exceptée* (Fr. error or omission excepted). **Ebor,** *Eboracensis* (L. of York). **Eccl.,** Ecclesiastes. **ECM,** electronic counter measures. **econ.,** economics. **ECOWAS,** Economic Community of West African States. **ECSC,** European Coal and Steel Community. **ECT,** electroconvulsant therapy. **ECTU,** European Confederation of Trade Unions. **ECU,** acronym for European Currency Unit: coincidentally Fr. medieval coin. **ed.,** editor, edited, educated. **EDC,** European Defence Community. **Edin.,** Edinburgh. **educ.,** educated, education. **EEC,** European Economic Community. **EETPU,** Electrical, Electronic, Telecommunication & Plumbing Union. **EFTA,** European Free Trade Association. **e.g.,** *exempli gratia* (L. for the sake of example). **EHF,** extremely high frequency. **EMA,** European Monetary Agreement. **EMBO,** European Centre for Molecular Biology. **EMS,** European Monetary System. **Eng.,** English. **ENSA,** Entertainments National Service Association. **ER,** *Elisabetha Regina* (L. Queen Elizabeth). *Eduardus Rex* (L. King Edward), Eastern region (British Rail). **ERA,** Equal Rights (for women) Amendment (USA). **ERNIE,** electronic random number indicating equipment. **ERW,** Enhanced Radiation Weapon. **ESA,** European Space Agency. **ESP,** extra-sensory perception. **esp., espec.,** especially. **Esq.,** esquire. **est.,** estimated. **estab.,** established. **et al.,** *et alii* (L. and others). **etc.,** *et cetera* (L. and the rest). **et seq.,** *et sequens* (L. and the following one), and **et sqq.,** *et sequentes* - more than one. **ETU,** Electrical Trades Union. **EURATOM,** European Atomic Energy Agency. **EUTELSAT,** European Telecommunications Satellite Organization. **Exch.,** Exchange, Exchequer. **excl.,** excluding. **exec.,** executive, executed. **ex lib.,** *ex libris* (L.from the library of). **exor.,** executor.

F

F Fahrenheit, farad. **f.,** father, fathom, feminine, *forte* (Ital. loud), frequency. **FA,** Football Assocn. **FAA,** formerly Fleet Air Arm. **fam.,** familiar(ly), family. **FAO,** Food and Agriculture Organization. **FBI,** Federal Bureau of Investigation (US). **FBS,** forward-based systems (military: US in Europe). **FCO,** Foreign and Commonwealth Office. **fcp,** foolscap. **FDR,** Franklin Delano Roosevelt. **fed.,** federal, federated. **fedn.,** federation. **fem.,** feminine. **ff.,** folios, *fortissimo* (Ital. loudest). **fg,** frigorie. **FH,** fire hydrant. **Fid. Def.,** *fidei defensor* (L. defender of the faith). **FIFA,** Fédération Internationale de Football Association. **fig.,** figurative(ly). **FIS,** family income supplement. **FL,** Florida. **fl.,** *floruit* (L. he flourished), fluid. **Fla.,** Florida. **Flt. Lt.,** flight lieutenant. **FM,** field marshal, frequency modulation. **FO,** formerly, Foreign Office. **f.o.b.,** free on board. **foll.,** following. **f.o.r.,** free on rail. **for.,** foreign. **f.p.,** freezing point. **Fr.,** Father, franc(s), French. **fra.,** *frater* (L. brother). **freq.,** frequency. **Fri.,** Friday. **FRS,** Federal Reserve System (US). Fellow of the Royal Society. **ft.,** foot, fort. **fur.,** furlong. **fwd.,** forward. **F.W.W.,** First World War.

G

G gauss, gram, gulf. **GA/Ga.,** Georgia. **Gael.,** Gaelic. **gal.,** gallon. **Gall.,** gallery. **GATT,** General Agreement on Tariffs and Trade. **GB,** Great Britain. **GC,** George Cross. **GCB,** Knight Grand Cross of the Order of the Bath. **GCF,** greatest common factor. **GCM,** greatest common measure. **GDP,** gross domestic product. **Gen.,** general, Genesis. **gen.,** gender, genitive, genus. **geog.,** geography. **geol.** geology. **geom.,** geometry. **Ger.,** German. **Ges.,** Gesellschaft (Ger. company or society). **Gestapo,** *Geheime Staatspolizei* (Ger. state secret police). **GHQ,** general headquarters. **GI,** Government (or General) Issue (US), colloquially a US soldier. **Gib.,** Gibraltar. **Gk.,** Greek. **GLC,** Greater London Council. **Glos.,** Gloucestershire. **GM,** George Medal. **GMC,** General Medical Council. **GMT,** Greenwich Mean Time. **GNP,** gross national product. **GOC(-in-C),** General Officer Commanding (-in-Chief). **GOM,** Grand Old Man (W.E. Gladstone, nickname given ironically by Labouchere). **GOP,** Grand Old Party (the Republican Party, US). **Gov.,** Governor. **Gov.-Gen.,** Governor-General. **govt.,** government. **GP,** general practitioner (medical). **Gr.** Greek. **gr,** grain, gravity. **granddau.** granddaughter. **GRI,** *Georgius Rex Imperator* (L. George, King and Emperor). **g.s.,** grandson. **gt.,** great. **GU,** Guam.

H

H henry (unit of inductance), hour. **ha,** hectare. **hab.,** *habitat* (L. he lives). **h. & c.,** hot and cold (water). **Hants,** Hampshire. **HC,** habitual criminal, House of Commons. **h.c.,** *honoris causa* (L. as a way of honouring). **HCF,** highest common factor. **H.Com.,** High Commissioner. **hd.,** head. **HE,** high explosive, His Excellency. **HEL,** high-energy laser. **Herts,** Hertfordshire. **HF,** high frequency. **HG,** Home Guard. **HH,** His (Her) Highness, His Holiness. **HI,** Hawaii. **hi-fi,** high fidelity. **hist.,** history. **HJS,** *hic jacet sepultus* (L. here lies buried). **HM,** His (Her) Majesty. **hm,** hectometre. **HMS,** His (Her) Majesty's Service or Ship. **HMSO,** His (Her) Majesty's Stationery Office. **HO,** Home Office. **Hon.,** Honorary, Honourable. **HP,** half-pay, high pressure, hire purchase. **hp,** horsepower. **HQ,** headquartes. **hr.,** hour. **HRH,** His (Her) Royal Highness. **HRT,** hormone replacement therapy. **ht.,** height. **h.t.,** high tension. **HWM,** high water mark. **Hz,** hertz.

I

I one (Roman). **I.,** island. **IA/Ia.,** Iowa. **IAEA,** International Atomic Energy Agency. **IATA,** International Air Transport Association. **ibid.,** *ibidem* (L. in the same place). **IBA,** Independent Broadcasting Authority (from 1972), International Bauxite Assocn. **IBRD,** International Bank for Reconstruction and Development (World Bank). **ICAO,** International Civil Aviation Organization. **ICBM,** intercontinental ballistic missile. **ICEM,** Intergovernmental Committee for European Migration. **ICFTU,** International Confederation of Free Trade Unions. **ID/Ida,** Idaho. **IDA,** International Development Assocn. **i.e.,** *id est* (L. that is). **IEA,** International Energy Agency. **IFS,** Irish Free State. **IHS,** popularly *Jesus hominum Salvator* (L. Jesus, Saviour of Mankind), but properly the first 3 letters of the name Jesus in Greek. **IISS,** Internl. Inst. of Strategic Studies. **ILEA,** Inner London Education Authority. **IL/Ill.,** Illinois. **illus.,** illustrated, illustration. **ILO,** International Labour Organization. **ILP,** Independent Labour Party. **IMCO,** Intergovernmental Maritime Consulative Organization. **IMF,** International Monetary Fund. **Imp.,** *imperator* (Lat. emperor). **imp.,** *imprimatur* (L. let it be printed). **IN,** Indiana. **in.,** inch. **Inc.,** incorporated. **incl.,** includes, including, inclusive. **incog.,** incognito (Ital. unknown). **Ind.,** Indiana. **inf.,** infantry, *infra* (L. below). **init.**, *initio* (L. at the beginning). **in loc.**, *in loco* (L. in place). **inns.**, innings. **INRI**, *Jesus Nazarenus Rex Judaeorum* (L. Jesus the Nazarene, King of the Jews). **inst.**, instant (the present month), institute. **int.**, interest. **INTELSAT**, Internat. Telecommunications Satellite Consortium. **inter.**, intermediate. **intercom.**, intercommunications. **intr.**, intransitive. **intro.**, Introduction. **Introd.**, introduced. **IoM**, Isle of Man. **IOU**, I owe you. **IoW**, Isle of Wight. **IQ**, Intelligence Quotient. **IRA**, Irish Republican Army. **IRBM**, intermediate-range ballistic missile. **IRC**, International Red Cross. **IRO**, International Refugee Organization. **IRS**, Internal Revenue Service (US). **is.**, isl(s).., island(s). **ISBN**, International Standard Book Number. **ISO**, International Standards Organization. **It.**, Italian. **ITA**, formerly, Independent Television Authority, Initial Teaching Alphabet. **Ital.**, Italian. **ital.**, italic. **ITN**, Independent Television News. **ITU** Internatioanl Telecommunications Union. **ITV**, Independent Television. **IVF**, *in vitro* fertilisation (for 'test-tube' baby).

J

J joule, judge, justice. **JA**, Judge Advocate. **jeep**, general purposes (g.p.) (car). **JFK**, John Fitzgerald Kennedy. **jnr.**, junior. **JP**, justice of the peace. **jr.**, jun., junior. **JSLS**, Joint Services Liaison Staff. **JWS**, Joint Warfare Staff.

K

K kelvin. **k**, king, knight. **Kan.**, Kansas. **KB**, King's Bench. **KBE**, Knight Commander Order of the British Empire. **KC**, King's Counsel. **KCB**, Knight Commander of the Bath. **KCMG**, Knight Commander of St. Michael and St. George. **KCVO**, Knight Commander of the Royal Victorian Order. **KG**, Knight of the Garter. **kg**, kilogram. **KGB**, *see text.* **kgf**, kilogram force. **KKK**, Ku-Klux-Klan. **km**, kilometre. **km/h**, kilometres per hour. **kn**, knot. **KO**, knockout. **kph**, kilometres per hour. **KR**, King's Regulations. **KS**, Kansas. **KT**, Knight of the Order of the Thistle. **Kt.**, knight bachelor. **kW**, kilowatt. **kWh**, kilowatt hour. **KY/Ky.**, Kentucky.

L

L fifty (Roman), lira. **L.**, lake, Lancers (in regimental names), Latin, left, Liberal, licentiate (in, e.g., **LRAM**, Licentiate of the Royal Academy of Music). **l**, litre, £, *libra* (L. pound - money). **LA**, Local authority, Los Angeles, Louisiana. **Lab.**, Labour, Labrador. **LAFTA**, Latin American Free Trade Assocn. **Lancs**, Lancashire. **Lat.**, Latin. **lat.**, latitude. **lb**, *libra* (L. pound - weight). **lbf**, pound-force. **LBJ**, Lyndon Baines Johnson. **lbw.**, leg before wicket (cricket). **l.c.**, lower case (i.e. small letter). **LCJ**, Lord Chief Justice. **LCM**, lowest common multiple. **L/Cpl.**, lance-corporal. **Ld.**, lord. **ldc**, less-developed country. **Ldg.**, leading (naval). **Leics.**, Leicestershire. **LEP**, electron-positron collider. **LF**, low frequency. **l.h.**, left hand. **LI**, Long Island. **Lib.**, Liberal. **lib.**, library. **Lieut.**, lieutenant. **lin.**, linear. **Lincs.**, Lincolnshire. **lit.**, literally, literary. **Lit. Hum.**, *Literae Humaniores* (L. humane letters: Faculty - classics and philosophy - at Oxford). **Litt.D.**, *Literarum Doctor* (L. Doctor of Literature). **LJ**, lord justice. **LL.D.**, *Legum Doctor* (L. Doctor of Laws). **LMR**, London Midland Region (British Rail). **LOB**, Location of Offices Bureau. **loc.cit.**, *loco citato* (L., in the place cited). **L. of N.**, League of Nations. **log**, logarithm. **long.**, longitude. **loq.**, *loquitur* (L. he speaks). **LP**, long-playing record. **LPO**, London Philharmonic Orchestra. **LS**, *locus sigilli* (L. place of the seal). **LSD**, d-lysergic acid diethylamide tartrate (hallucinatory drug). **L.S.D.**, *librae, solidi, denarii* (L. pounds, shillings and pence). **LSE**, London School of Economics (and Political Science). **LSO**, London Symphony Orchestra. **Lt.**, lieutenant. **LTA**, Lawn Tennis Assocn. **Ltd.**, limited (liability). **LTE**, London Transport Executive. **LW**, long wave. **LWM**, low water mark. **LWT**, London Weekend Television. **lx**, lux.

M

M thousand (Roman), Mach number, marquess, Monsieur (Fr. mister). **m**, married, masculine, metre, mile, million, minute, money, month, mother. **MA**, Massachusetts, Master of Arts. **mag.**, magazine, magneto, magnitude. **Maj.-Gen.**, major-general. **Man.**, Manitoba. **Mar.**, March. **march.**, marchioness. **marge**, margarine. **marq.**, marquess. **maser**, microwave amplification by stimulated emission of radiation. **Mass.**, Massachusetts. **math.**, mathematics. **max.**, maximum. **MB**, *Medicinae Baccalaureus* (L. Bachelor of Medicine), motor-boat. **MBE**, Member of the Order of the British Empire. **MBFR**, Mutual Balanced Force Reduction. **MC**, Military Cross, Master of Ceremonies. **MCC**, Marylebone Cricket Club, Metropolitan County Council. **MD**, Maryland, Doctor of Medicine, mentally deficient. **MDC**, Metropolitan District council. **ME**, Maine, Middle English, marine/mechanical/military/mining engineer. **mech.**, mechanics. **med.**, medical, medieval, medium. **memo**, memorandum. **MEP**, Member of the European Parliament. **mer.**, meridian. **met.**, metropolitan. **Met. Office**, Meteorological Office. **MF**, medium frequency, *mezzo forte* (Ital. moderately loud). **mfd.**, manufactured. **mfg.**, manufacturing. **MFH**, Master of Foxhounds. **MGM**, Metro-Goldwyn-Mayer. **mg**. milligram. **Mgr.**, Monsignor. **MI**, military intelligence. **Middx.**, Middlesex. **mil.**, military. **min.**, minimum, minister, ministry, minute. **Minn.**, Minnesota. **Min. Plen.**, Minister Plenipotentiary. **MIRV**, multiple independently targetable re-entry vehicle. **Miss.**, Mississippi. **MIT**, Massachusetts Institute of Technology. **MKS**, metre-kilogram-second (system of units). **mkt.**, market. **ml**, millilitre. **Mlle**, mademoiselle (Fr. miss). **MLR**, Minimum lending rate. **MLRS**, multiple-launch rocket system. **MM**, Military Medal. **mm**, millimetre. **μm**, micrometre (Gk. 'm'). **Mme**, madame. **MN**, Merchant Navy, Minnesota. **MO**, Missouri. **MoD**, Ministry of Defence. **MOD**, Ministry of Overseas Development. **mod.**, moderate; *moderato* (Ital. at a moderate pace), modern. **MOH**, Medical Officer of Health. **MOI**, Ministry of Information. **mol**, mole (matter). **MOMA**, Museum of Modern Art (NY). **Mon.**, Monday. **Mont.**, Montana. **MP**, Member of Parliament, Metropolitan Police, military police. **m.p.**, melting point, *mezzo piano* (Ital. moderately soft). **mpg**, miles per gallon. **mph**, miles per hour. **MR**, Master of the Rolls. **Mr.**, mister. **MRA**, Moral Rearmament. **MRC**, Medical Research Council. **MRCA**, multi-role combat aircraft. **Mrs.**, mistress. **M/S** or **Ms**, Women's Lib. equivalent of Mr., avoiding reference to marital status. **MS**, manuscript (pl. MSS), Master of Surgery, Mississippi, motor ship. **MSc**, Master of Science. **m.s.l.**, mean sea level. **MT**, Montana. **mt**, mount, mountain. **MTB**, motor torpedo-boat. **MU**, monetary unit. **mun.**, municipal. **mus.**, museum, music(al). **MV**, merchant/motor vessel. **MVO**, Member of the Victorian Order.

N

N newton, north, northern. **n**, name, nephew, neuter, noun. **NAACP**, National Assocn. for the Advancement of Colored People (US). **NAAFI**, Navy, Army and Air Force Institutes. **NALGO**, Nat. and Local Govt. Officers' Assocn., **NAMH**, Nat. Assocn. for Mental Health. **nat.**, national. **NASA**, National Aeronautics and Space Administration (US). **NATO**, North Atlantic Treaty Organization. **NB**, New Brunswick, *nota bene* (L. note well). **NBC**, National Broadcasting Co. (US). **NC**, North Carolina. **NCB**, National Coal Board. **NCO**, non-commissioned officer. **NCP**, National Country Party (Australia). **ND/NDak.**, North Dakota. **n.d.**, no date. **NEA**, Nuclear Energy Agency. **NEB**, New English Bible. **Neb.**, Nebraska. **NEDC**, National Economic Development Council ('Neddy'). **neg.**, negative. **nem. con.**, *nemine contradicente* (L. with no one opposing). **NEP**, New Economic Policy (USSR). **Nev.**, Nevada. **NF**, Newfoundland, Norman French. **NG**, National Giro. **NH**, New Hampshire. **NHS**, National Health Service. **NI**, Northern Ireland. **NJ**, New Jersey. **NKVD**, *see text.* **NM**, New Mexico. **n.o.**, not out (crickt). **no.**, *numero* (L. in number). **nom.**, nominative. **non seq.**, *non sequitur* (L. it does not follow). **Northants**, Northamptonshire. **Notts**, Nottinghamshire. **Nov.**, November. **NP**, Notary Public, National Party (NZ). **n.p.**, new paragraph. **NPA**, Newspaper Publishers' Association. **NPG**, National Portrait Gallery. **NPL**, National Physical Laboratory, Teddington. **nr.**, near. **NRA**, National Rifle Assocn. **NRC**, Nuclear Regulatory Commission. **NRDC**, National Research Development Corporation. **NS**, new style (calendar), Nova Scotia. **NSA**, National Security Agency (USA). **NSB**, National Savings Bank. **NSPCC**, National Society for the Prevention of Cruelty to Children. **NSW**, New South Wales. **NT**, National Theatre (South Bank), New Testament, Northern Territory (Australia). **n.u.**, name unknown. **NUJ**, National Union of Journalists. **NUM**, National Union of Mineworkers. **NUPE**, National Union of Public Employees. **NUR**, National Union of Railwaymen. **NUS**, National Union of Students. **NUT**, National Union of Teachers. **NV**, Nevada. **NY**, New York. **NYC**, New York City. **NYO**, Nat. Youth Orchestra. **NZ**, New Zealand.

O

o/a, on account of. **OAP**, Old Age Pensioner (still often used, although 'senior citizens' now officially have a 'retirement pension'). **OAPEC**, Organization of Arab Petroleum Exporting Countries. **OAS**, on active service, Organisation de l'Armée Secrète, Organization of American States. **OAU**, Organization of African Unity. **ob.**, *obiit* (L. he died). **OBE**, (Officer of the) Order of the British Empire. **obj.**, objective. **obs.**, observation, obsolete. **OC**, officer commanding. **OCAM**, Common African and Mauritian Organization (Organisation commune africaine et mauricienne). **OCAS**, Organization of Central American States (also **ODECA**, qv). **occid.**, **occidental** (Span. western, in place names). **oct.**, octavo. **ODA**, Official Development Aid. **ODECA**, Organizacion de Estados Centroamericanos (Span. Organization of Central American States). **OE**, Old English. **Oe**, oersted. **OECD**, Organization for Economic Cooperation and Development. **OED**, Oxford English Dictionary. **OF**, Old French. **off.**, official. **OGPU**, *see text.* **OH**, Ohio. **OHMS**, on His (Her) Majesty's Service. **OK**, correct or approved (no agreed actual meaning). **OK/Okla.**, Oklahoma. **OM**, (Member of the) Order of Merit. **o.n.o.**, or near(est) offer. **Ont.**, Ontario. **OP**, observation post, out of print, Order of Preachers (Dominicans). **op.**, *opus* (L. work), used for a musical composition. **op. cit.**, *opere citato* (L. in the work quoted). **OPCS**, Office of Population Census and Surveys. **OPEC**, Organization of Petroleum Exporting Countries. **opp.**, opposite. **Ops.**, operations (military). **opt.**, optical, optional. **OR**, other ranks, Oregon. **or.**, oriental (Span. eastern). **Ore.**, Oregon. **orig.**, original. **Ork.**, Orkney Islands. **o.r.**, owner's risk. **OS**, Old Saxon, Old Style (calendar), outsize. **o.s.**, only son. **OSA**, Official Secrets Act. **o.s.p.**, *obiit sine prole* (L. died without issue). **OT**, Old Testament. **OUDS**, Oxford University Dramatic Society. **OUP**, Oxford University Press. **OXFAM**, Oxford Committee for Famine Relief. **Oxon.**, Oxfordshire, *Oxoniensis* (L. of Oxford). **oz.**, ounce.

P

P (car) park, pedestrian crossing, pawn. **p.**, page, past, new pence (UK decimal currency), *piano* (Ital. soft). **PA/Pa.**, Pennsylvania, Press Association, Publishers Association. **p.a.**, per annum (L. yearly). **PAA**, Pan-American Airways. **P & O**, Peninsular and Oriental (Steamship Company). **par.**, paragraph, parallel, parish. **para.**, paragraph. **parl.**, parliament(ary). **part.**, participle. **PAYE**, pay as you earn. **PB**, prayer book. **PBI**, 'poor bloody infantry'. **PC**, parish council, police constable, privy council(lor). **p.c.**, *per centum* (L. by the hundred), postcard. **PDSA**, People's Dispensary for sick Animals. **PEI**, Prince Edward Island. **pen./pena.**, peninsula. **PEN** Club, Poets, Playwrights, Essayists, Editors, Novelists. **per cent.**, *per centum* (L. by the hundred). **per pro**, *per procurationem* (L. by proxy). **PF**, procurator-fiscal. **PG**, paying guest. **PH**, Purple Heart (decoration US). **PhD**, Doctor of Philosophy. **Phil.**, Philadelphia, philosophy. **phys.**, physics. **pinx.**, *pinxit* (L. he painted). **pizz.**, *pizzicato* (Ital. plucked). **PKU**, phenylketonuria. **pl.**, place, platoon, plural. **PLA**, Port of London Authority. **PLR**, Public Lending Right. **P.M.**, *post mortem* (L. after death), prime minister. **p.m.**, *post meridiem* (L. after noon). **PMG**, Paymaster/and formerly Postmaster General. **PMT**, pre-menstrual tension. **PO**, petty officer (RN), Post Office, postal order, pilot officer (RAF). **Pol.**, Polish. **Poly**, polytechnic. **pop.**, population, popular(ly). **Port.**, Portuguese. **pot.**, potential. **POW**, prisoner-of-war. **PP**, parish priest. **p.p.**, *per procurationem* (L. by proxy). **pp.**, pages, *pianissimo* (Ital. very soft). **PPS**, parliamentary, or principal, private secretary, post-post-script. **PQ**, Province of Quebec. **PR**, proportional representation, Puerto Rico. **PRC**, People's Rep. of China. **prec.**, preceding. **prelim.**, preliminary. **prep.**, preparation, preposition. **pres.**, president. **PRO**, Public Record Office, public relations officer. **prof.**, professor. **prom.**, promenade (concert), promontory. **pron.**, pronoun, pronounced. **pro. tem.**, *pro tempore* (L. for the time being). **Prov.** Proverbs, Book of. **prov.**, province, provisional, provost. **prox.**, *proximo* (*mense*) (L. in the next month). **PS**, postscript, private secretary. **Ps.**, Psalm. **pseud.**, pseudonym. **PT**, physical training. **pt.**, pint, past, point, port. **Pte.**, private (military). **PTO**, please turn over, Public Trustee Office. **PTSD**, post-traumatic stress. **Pty**, proprietary (of Australian, South African, etc., companies). **pub.**, public house, published. **PUFA**, poly-unsaturated fatty acids. **PVC**, polyvinyl chloride (plastic).

Q

Q queen, question, the Quarto Shakespeare. **QB**, Queen's Bench. **QC**, Queen's Counsel. **QED**, *quod erat demonstrandum* (L. which was to be proved). **QEF**, *quod erat faciendum* (L. which was to be done). **QGM**, Queen's Gallantry Medal. **Qld**, Queensland. **QM**, quartermaster, Queen's Messenger. **QMG**, quartermaster-general. **QMS**, quartermaster sergeant. **QPM**, Queen's Police Medal. **QR**, Queen's Regulations. **qr.**, quarter, quire. **QS**, quarter sessions. **QSO**, *see* QUASAR. **qt.**, quart. **qto.**, quarto. **qtr.**, quarter. **QUANGO**, *see text.* **QUASAR**, *see text.* **Que.**, Quebec. **quot.**, quotation, quotient. **qv**, *quod vide* (L. which see: plural, qqv).

R

R radius, regiment, **re**, L. with regard to, *rex* (king), *regina* (queen), right, resistance, Röntgen. **r.**, radius, river. **RA**, rear admiral, Royal Academician/Academy, Royal Artillery. **RAC**, Royal Armoured Corps, Royal Automobile Club. **rad**, radian. **rad.**, *radix* (L. root). **RADA**, Royal Academy of Dramatic Art. **radar**, *ra*dio *d*irection *a*nd *r*ange. **RAE**, Royal Aircraft Establishment. **RAF**, Royal Air Force. **RAFVR**, Royal Air Force Volunteer Reserve. **rall.**, *rallentando* (Ital. slowing down). **RAM**, Royal Academy of Music. **ram**, random access memory (chip). **RAMC**, Royal Army Medical Corps. **RASC**, Royal Army Service Corps, now **RCT**. **RBA**, Royal Society of British Artists. **RBS**, Royal Society of British Sculptors. **RC**, Red Cross, Roman Catholic. **RCA**, Royal College of Art. **RCM**, Royal College of Music. **RCS**, Royal College of Surgeons, Royal Corps of Signals. **RCT**, Royal Corps of Transport. **RCVS**, Royal College of Veterinary Surgeons. **R/D**, refer to drawer (of an overdrawn cheque). **Rd.**, road. **RE**, Royal Engineers, Royal Exchange. **recce.**, reconnaissance. **recd.**, received. **ref.**, referred, reference. **reg.**, region(al), registered, regular(ly). **Reg. Prof.**, regius professor. **regt.**, regiment. **REME**, Royal Electrical and Mechanical Engineers. **rep.**, republic(an), representative, repertory (theatre). **Rev.**, Revelation (Book of), reverend, revenue, revolution (political). **rev.** reverse(d), revise(d), revolution (mechanical). **RF**, République française (French Republic). **RFC**, Royal Flying Corps, rugby football club. **RGS**, Royal Geographical Society. **Rh**-positive/negative, either reacting, or not reacting, to blood tests as Rhesus monkeys do. **RHS**, Royal Horticultural Society, Royal Humane Society. **RI**, *rex imperator* (L. king emperor), Rhode Island, Royal Institution. **RIBA**, Royal Institute of British Architects. **RIIA**, Royal Institute of International Affairs. **RIP**, *requiescat in pace* (L. may he rest in peace). **rit.**, *ritardando* (Ital. becoming slower). **riv.**, river. **RLS**, Robert Louis Stevenson. **rly.**, railway. **RM**, Royal Mail, Royal Marines. **RMA**, Royal Military Academy. **RMetS**, Royal Meteorological Society. **RN**, Royal Navy. **RNLI**, Royal National Lifeboat Institution. **RNVR**, Royal Naval Volunteer Reserve. **ro.**, *recto* (L. on the right-(hand page)). **ROC**, Royal Observer Corps. **ROSPA**, Royal Society for the Prevention of Accidents. **RPC**, Royal Pioneer Corps. **RPI**, Retail Price Index. **r.p.m.**, revolutions per min. **RPO**, Royal Philharmonic Orchestra. **RRE**, Royal Radar Establishment. **RPS**, Royal Photographic Society. **RRS**, Royal Research ship. **RS**, Royal Society. **RSA**, Royal Scottish Academy, Royal Society of Arts. **RSC**, Royal Shakespeare Company. **RSFSR**, Russian Soviet Federal (Federative) Socialist Republic. **RSM**, Royal School of Mines, Royal Society of Medicine. **RSPCA**, Royal Society for the Prevention of Cruelty to Animals. **RSV**, Revised Standard Version (Bible). **RSVP**, répondez s'il vous plaît (Fr. reply, if you please). **RTC**, Royal Tank Corps. **Rt. Hon.**, right honourable. **Rt. Rev.**, right reverend. **RU**, rugby union. **Russ.**, Russian. **RYS**, Royal Yacht Squadron. **RZS**, Royal Zoological Society.

S

S saint, socialist, *socius* (L. fellow), south(ern). **s.**, son, second, shilling, singular, succeeded. **SA**, Salvation Army, sex appeal, Society of Antiquaries, South Africa, South Australia, Sturm-Abteilung (Ger. (Nazi) storm troops). **sa.**, sierra. **SALT**, strategic arms limitation. **SAS**, special ammunition storage (nuclear weapons), Special Air Service. **Sask.**, Saskatchewan. **Sax.**, Saxon, saxophone. **SAYE**, Save As You Earn. **SC**, South Carolina. **s.c.**, small capitals. **sc.**, scene, science, *scilicet* (L. let it be understood), *sculpsit* (L. he carved, or engraved, it). **SD/SDak.**, South Dakota. **s.d.**, semi-detached, *sine die* (L. without a day, indefinitely). **SDR**, special drawing rights. **sd.**, signed sewed. **SE**, south-east(ern). **S/E**, stock exchange. **SEATO**, South East Asia Treaty Organization. **sec.**, secant, second(ary), secretary. **SELA**, Latin American Economic System (Sistema Economico Latinamericano). **SEV**, Russian abbreviation for COMECON (Soviet Ekonomicheskoi Vzaimopomoshchi). **sf.**, *sforzando* (Ital. with sudden emphasis). **SF**, science fiction. **SFSR**,

Soviet Federal (or Federated) Socialist Republic. **Sgt.**, sergeant. **SHAEF**, Supreme Headquarters Allied Expeditionary Force. **SHAPE**, Supreme, Headquarters Allied Powers Europe. **SHF**, super high frequency. **SI**, International System (Système International d'Unités) metric. **SIDS**, sudden infant death syndrome (cot death). **sic**, so written (L. thus). **sing** singular. **SIS**, Secret Intelligence Service. **sit.**, situated. **SJ**, Society of Jesus (Jesuits). **Skt.**, Sanskrit. **Slav.**, Slavonic. **SNCF**, Societé Nationale des Chemins de Fer (national railway system of France). **SO**, Scottish Office. **Soc.**, society, socialist. **Som.**, Somerset. **SP**, starting price (betting), *sine prole* (L. without issue). **Span.**, Spanish. **SPCK**, Society for Promoting Christian Knowledge. **spec.**, special(ly), species, speculation. **SPG**, Special Patrol Group. **sp. gr.**, specific gravity. **SPQR**, *Senatus Populusque Romanus* (L. the Roman senate and people). **SPR**, Society for Psychical Research. **sq.**, square. **Sqn/Ldr**, squadron leader. **SR**, Southern Region (British Rail). **sr**, steradian. **SRC**, Science Research Council. **SRN**, state registered nurse. **SS**, steamship, Schutz-Staffel (Ger. Hitler's bodyguard). **SSAFA**, Soldiers', Sailors', and Airmen's Families Assocn. **SSR**, Soviet Socialist Republic. **St.**, saint, street, strait. **st.**, stone. **Sta.**, *santa* (Ital., female saint). **Staffs**, Staffordshire. **STD**, subscriber trunk dialling. **Ste.**, *sainte* (Fr. female saint). **stet** (L. let it stand). **stg.**, sterling. **stn.**, station. **str.**, strait. **STV**, single transferable vote. **sub.**, submarine, subscription, substitute. **subj.**, subject(ive), subjunctive. **Sub-Lt.**, sub-lieutenant. **Suff.**, Suffolk. **sup.**, *supra* (L. above). **SWALK**, signed with a loving kiss. **S.W.W.**, Second World War. **Sx**, Sussex. **Sy**, Surrey. **Syd.**, Sydney. **syn.**, synonym.

T

T, temperature, telephone. **t**, ton/tonne (metric). **TA**, Territorial Army. **TAB**, Technical Assistance Board. **TAF**, Tactical Air Force. **T & AVR**, Territorial and Army Volunteer Reserve. **TAM**, Television Audience Measurement. **tan.**, tangent. **Tas.**, Tasmania. **TB**, tuberculosis. **tech.**, technical. **temp.**, temporary, temperature, *tempore* (L. in the time of). **ten.**, tenor, *tenuto* (Ital. sustained). **Tenn.**, Tennessee. **terr.**, territory. **Tex.**, Texas. **TGWU**, Transport and General Workers Union. **TLS**, *Times Literary Supplement*. **TM**, transcendental meditation. **TN**, Tennessee. **tn.**, town. **TNT**, trinitrotoluene. **Toc H**, Talbot House. **tote**, totalisator. **TPI**, Tax and Price Index. **trans.**, transitive, transitional, translated, translation. **treas.**, treasurer. **TRH**, their royal highnesses. **trib.**, tributary. **trig.**, trigonometry. **trs.**, transfer, transpose. **TSB**, Trustee Savings Bank. **TT**, Tourist Trophy, teetotal, tuberculin tested. **TUC**, trades Union Congress. **TV**, television. **TVA**, Taxe sur la Valeur Ajoutée (Fr. value-added tax), Tennessee Valley Authority (US). **TWA**, Trans-World Airlines. **TX**, Texas.

U

U, Unionist, universal (exhibition, in cinemas). **u.**, uncle. **u.a.**, unit of account (Common Market). **U-boat**, Unterseeboot (Ger. submarine). **u.c.**, upper case (capital letters). **UCL**, University College, London. **UDC**, urban district council. **UDI**, unilateral declaration of independence. **UFO**, unidentified flying object. **UHF**, ultra high frequency. **UK**, United Kingdom. **ult.**, ultimate, *ultimo* (*mense*) (L. in the last month). **UN**, United Nations. **UNA**, United Nations Assocn. **UNCTAD**, UN Commission on Trade and Development. **UNDP**, UN Development Programme. **UNESCO**, UN Educational, Scientific and Cultural Organization. **UNICEF**, UN International Children's Emergency Fund. **UNIDO**, UN Industrial Development Organization. **univ.**, university. **unm.**, unmarried. **unpub.**, unpublished. **UNRRA**, UN Relief and Rehabilitation Administration. **UNWRA**, UN Relief and Works Agency (for Palestine Refugees). **UP**, United Press. **UPU**, Universal Postal Union. **US**, under-secretary, United Services, United States. **USA**, United States of (North) America. **USAF**, United States Air Force. **USIA**, United States Information Agency. **USMC**, United States Marine Corps. **USN**, United States Navy. **USS**, United States ship. **USSR**, Union of Soviet Socialist Republics. **UT**, Universal Time, Utah. **UTH**, ultra-heat tested (long-life milk). **ux.**, *uxor* (L. wife).

V

V five (Roman), volt, **V1** and **V2**, the German flying bomb and rocket in S.W.W. (*Vergeltungswaffe* - reprisal weapon). **v.**, *versus* (L. against), *vice* (L. in place of), *vide* (L. see), verb, verse, very. **V and A**, Victoria and Albert Museum. **VA**, Virginia. **vac.**, vacation. **VAD**, Voluntary Aid Detachment. **van.**, advantage (tennis). **var.**, various. **VAT**, value-added tax. **Vat.**, Vatican. **VC**, Victoria Cross. **VD**, venereal disease. **VDT**, visual display terminal. **VDU**, visual display unit. **VE Day**, Victory in Europe day. **Ven.**, venerable. **verb. sap.**, *verbum sapienti* (*satis*) (L. a word is enough to the wise). **vet.**, veterinary (surgeon). **VHF**, very high frequency. **VHSIC**, very high speed integrated circuits. **Vic.**, Victoria. **VI**, Virgin Is. **VIP**, very important person. **visct.**, viscount. **viz.**, *videlicet* (L. that is to say, namely). **VJ Day**, Victory over Japan day. **VLF**, very low frequency. **VM**, Victory Medal. **vol.**, volume, volunteer. **VR**, *Victoria Regina* (L. Queen Victoria). **v.s.**, *vide supra* (L. see above). **VSO**, Voluntary Service Overseas. **V/STOL**, vertical/short take-off and landing. **VT**, Vermont. **VTR**, videotape recording. **Vulg.**, Vulgate. **v.v.**, *vice versa* (L. the other way round). **vv.**, verses.

W

W Welsh, west(ern), warden, watt. **w.**, week, wife, with. **WA**, Washington (state), Western Australia. **WAAC**, Women's Army Auxiliary Corps (F.W.W.). **WAAF**, Women's Auxiliary Air Force. **WAC**, Women's Army Corps (US). **Warwicks**, Warwickshire. **Wash.**, Washington (state). **WASP**, White, Anglo-Saxon, Protestant (US). **WAVES**, Women Accepted for Volunteer Emergency Service (US Navy). **WC**, water closet. **WCC**, World Council of Churches. **W/Cdr**, wing-commander. **WD**, War Department. **WEA**, Workers' Educational Assocn. **WEU**, Western European Union. **wf.**, wrong fount (of type). **WFTU**, World Federation of Trade Unions. **WHO**, World Health Organization. **WI**, West Indies, Wisconsin, Women's Institute. **Wilts**, Wiltshire. **WIPO**, World Intellectual Property Organization. **Wisc.**, Wisconsin. **WLA**, Women's Land Army. **WMO**, World Meteorological Organization. **WNO**, Welsh National Opera. **WO**, War Office, warrant officer. **WR**, Western Region (British Rail). **WRAC**, Women's Royal Army Corps. **WRAF**, Women's Royal Air Force. **WRNS**, Women's Royal Naval Service. **WRVS**, Women's Royal Voluntary Services. **WS**, writer to the signet. **wt.**, weight. **WV/WVa.**, West Virginia. **WWF**, World Wildlife Fund. **WY/Wyo.**, Wyoming.

X

X ten (Roman), Christ, adults 18 and over (exhibition, in cinemas). **Xmas**, Christmas. **XX**, double strength (of beer). **XXX**, triple strength.

Y

Y yen. **YC**, Young Conservative. **yd.**, yard. **YHA**, Youth Hostels Assocn. **YMCA**, Young Men's Christian Assocn. **Yorks**, Yorkshire. **yr.**, year, your, younger. **YWCA**, Young Women's Christian Assocn.

Z

Z impedance (electricity and magnetism), zero. **zoo**, zoological garden. **zool.**, zoological.

Customary Forms of Address

Ambassador. 'To His Excellency' followed by customary title of the individual. *Begin,* 'Sir' or 'My Lord' (according to rank); *end,* 'I have the honour to be, sir (or My Lord), Your Excellency's most humble and obedient servant.

Archbishop. 'The Most Rev. His Grace the Lord Archbishop of ——.' *Begin,* 'My Lord Archbishop', or 'Your Grace'; *end,* 'I remain, My Lord Archbishop, Your Grace's obedient servant.' The wife of an Archbishop is simply 'Mrs. ——.'

An **R.C. Archbishop** is addressed: 'The Most Rev. the Archbishop of ——.'

Baron. 'To the Rt. Hon. Lord ——.' *Begin,* 'My Lord'; *end,* 'I have the honour to be, My Lord, Your Lordship's obedient servant.' **Baroness.** 'The Rt. Hon. Lady ——.' *Begin,* 'Madam'; *end,* 'I have the honour to be, Madam, Your Ladyship's obedient servant.' Refer to 'Your Ladyship'. **Baroness in her own right:** as for the wife of a Baron.

Baronet. 'Sir John ——, Bt.' *Begin,* 'Sir,; *end,* 'I have the honour to remain, Sir, Your obedient servant.' **Baronet's wife.** 'Lady ——' (omit Christian name). *Begin,* 'Madam'; *end,* 'I have the honour to remain, Madam, Your obedient servant.' Refer to 'Your Ladyship'.

Bishop. 'To the Right Rev. the Lord Bishop of ——.' *Begin,* 'My Lord'; *end,* 'I remain, My Lord, Your Lordship's obedient servant.' Refer to 'My Lord', or 'Your Lordship'. The wife of a Bishop is simply 'Mrs. ——.'

An **R.C. Bishop** is addressed: 'The Rt. Rev. the Bishop of ——.'

Bishop Suffragan. 'To the Rt. Rev. the Lord Bishop Suffragan of ——'; otherwise as for a Bishop.

Cabinet, Members of U.S.: 'To Mr. (or the Hon.) —— ——, Secretary of State.' *Begin,* 'Dear Sir' or 'Dear Mr. Secretary'; *end,* 'Yours faithfully'.

Cardinal. 'To His Eminence Cardinal ——.' *Begin,* 'My Lord Cardinal' or 'My Lord'; *end,* 'I have the honour to remain, My Lord, Your Eminence's obedient child.'

Clergy. 'The Rev. (Christian name and surname).' *Begin,* 'Rev. Sir'; less formally, 'Sir'.

R.C. Clergy. 'To the Rev. Father ——.' *Begin,* 'Dear Rev. Father'; *end,* 'I beg to remain, dear Rev. Father, Your devoted and obedient child.'

Countess. 'The Right Hon. the Countess of ——.' *Begin,* 'Madam'; refer to as 'Your Ladyship'; *end,* 'I have the honour to be, Madam, Your Ladyship's obedient servant.' **Countess in her own right:** as for an Earl's wife.

Dame. 'To Dame Jane ——,' followed by G.C.V.O., D.C.V.O., G.B.E., D.B.E., as appropriate. *Begin,* 'Madam'; *end,* 'I beg to remain, dear Madam, Your obedient servant.'

N.B. Correctly the wife of a Bt. or a Knight is referred to as 'Dame ——' (husband's surname), but this form has fallen into disuse except in legal documents. *See* under Baronet; Knight.

Daughters of Peers. Daus. of Dukes, Marquesses, and Earls are styled 'Lady Jane ——' (family name); daus. of Viscounts and Barons: 'The Hon. Jane ——' (family name). On marriage to a man without title, a Knight, or a Bt., Lady Jane retains her style, substituting her husband's for her father's family name; The Hon. Jane becomes The Hon. Mrs. —— or The Hon. Lady ——, according to whether her husband has no title or is a Knight or Bt. (The title Hon. is never used in speaking.) On marriage to a peer, the dau. of a peer uses the customary form appropriate to her rank.

Dean (of a cathedral). 'The Very Rev. the Dean of ——.' *Begin,* 'Very Rev. Sir'; *end,* 'I have the honour to remain, Reverend Sir, Your obedient servant.'

Doctor. The letters M.D., LL.D., etc., are appended to the ordinary form of address, e.g., 'J. —— (initial and surname), Esq., M.D.' Alternatively, 'Dr. J. ——,' never 'Dr. J. ——, Esq.'

Duke. 'To His Grace the Duke of ——.' *Begin,* 'My Lord Duke' or 'Your Grace'; *end,* 'I have the honour to be, My Lord Duke, Your Grace's obedient servant.' Refer to 'Your Grace'. **Royal Duke.** 'To His Royal Highness the Duke of ——.' *Begin,* 'Sir'; *end,* 'I remain, Sir, Your Royal Highness's obedient servant.' *See* Daughters, Sons of Peers.

Earl. 'The Rt. Hon. the Earl of ——.' *Begin,* 'My Lord'; refer to 'Your Lordship'; *end,* 'I have the honour to be, my Lord, Your Lordship's obedient servant.' An Earl's wife is a Countess (q.v.). *See also* Daughters, Sons of Peers.

Governor of a U.S. State. 'To the Hon. —— ——' or 'To Governor —— ——.' *Begin,* 'Sir'; *end,* 'Yours faithfully'.

Judge. 'The Hon. Mr. Justice ——'; or 'The Hon. Sir (Christian name and surname).' *Begin,* 'Sir'. Only when on the bench is he referred to as 'My Lord' and 'His Lordship'. **In the U.S.A.:** 'The Hon.' followed by the title of office (e.g. Chief Justice of the U.S.A., Associate Justice of the Supreme Court of the U.S.A.). *Begin,* 'Dear Sir', 'Dear Mr. Chief Justice', 'Dear Judge Smith', as appropriate.

Judge of County Court. 'His Honour Judge ——.' When on the bench refer to 'Your Honour'.

Justice of Peace. 'To the Rt. Worshipful —— ——, J.P.' Refer to, when on the bench, as 'Your Worship'.

King. 'To the King's Most Excellent Majesty.' *Begin,* 'Sire', or 'May it please Your Majesty'; *end,* 'I have the honour to remain, Your Majesty's most humble and obedient subject'; refer to as 'Your Majesty'.

Knight Bachelor. As for Baronet, but omitting the abbreviation 'Bt.'

Knight of the Bath, of the Garter, etc. As for Knight Bachelor, but adding the letters K.C.B., K.G., etc.

Knight's wife. As for Baronet's wife.

Lord Chancellor. 'To the Rt. Hon. the Lord Chancellor.' Otherwise according to rank in the peerage.

Lord Chief Justice. 'The Rt. Hon. the Lord Chief Justice of England.' Otherwise according to rank in the peerage.

Lord Provost. 'The Rt. Hon. the Lord Provost of (Edinburgh, Glasgow)'; or 'The Lord Provost of (Aberdeen, Dundee, Elgin and Perth).' *Begin,* 'My Lord Provost', or 'My Lord'; refer to 'Your Lordship'. His wife is sometimes addressed 'The Lady Provost.'

Marchioness. 'The Most Hon. the Marchioness of ——.' *Begin,* 'Madam'; refer to 'Your Ladyship'; *end,* 'I have the honour to be, Madam, Your Ladyship's obedient servant.'

Marquess. 'The Most Hon. the Marquess of ——.' *Begin,* 'My Lord Marquess'; refer to 'Your Lordship'; *end,* 'I have the honour to be, My Lord Marquess, Your Lordship's obedient servant.'

Mayor. 'The Worshipful the Mayor of ——'; or (if the Mayor of a City) 'The Right Worshipful the Mayor of ——.' *Begin,* 'Sir'; refer to 'Your Worship'; in speaking one refers usually to 'Mr. Mayor'; *end,* 'I remain, Sir, Your most obedient servant.'

Member of Parliament. The letters M.P. are added to the ordinary form of address.

Moderator of the Assembly of the Church of Scotland. 'To the Right Rev. the Moderator ——.' *Begin,* 'Right Rev. Sir'; *end,* 'I remain, Right Rev. Sir, Your most obedient servant.'

Officers in the Navy, Army, and Air Force. If a title is held this is added after the military rank, e.g., 'Admiral the Rt. Hon. the Viscount ——,' or 'Air Marshal Sir ——, K.C.B.'

The Pope. 'To His Holiness the Pope.' *Begin,* 'Your Holiness'; *end,* 'I have the honour to remain Your Holiness's most humble child.'

President of the U.S.A. 'To the President, The White House, Washington, D.C., U.S.A.' *Begin,* 'Dear Sir', 'Mr. President', or 'Dear Mr. President'; *end,* 'Yours faithfully'.

Prime Minister. 'The Rt. Hon. —— ——, M.P.' or his personal title if any.

Prince of the British Royal House. 'His Royal Highness Prince (Christian name)'; or if a Duke, 'H.R.H. the Duke of ——.' In either case *begin* 'Sir'; refer to 'Your Royal Highness'; *end,* 'I remain, Sir, Your Royal Highness's most humble and obedient servant.'

Princess of the British Royal House. 'To H.R.H. Princess (Christian name)'; or if a Duchess, 'H.R.H. the Duchess of ——.' *Begin,* 'Madam'; refer to 'Your Royal Highness'; *end,* 'I have the honour to be, Madam, Your Royal Highness's most humble and obedient servant.'

Queen. 'To the Queen's Most Excellent Majesty.' *Begin,* 'Madam', or 'May it please Your Majesty'; refer to 'Your Majesty'; *end,* 'I remain, Madam, Your Majesty's most humble and obedient subject.'

Representatives of the U.S. Congress. 'To the Hon. —— ——.' *Begin,* 'Dear Mr. Representative.'

Secretary of State. 'His Majesty's Principal Secretary of State for the (Defence) Department' or 'The Secretary of State for (Defence).'

Senators of the U.S. Congress. 'To the Hon. —— ——.' *Begin,* 'Dear Mr. Senator'.

Sons of Peers. The eldest son of a Duke, Marquess, or Earl uses, by courtesy, his father's second title and is addressed as though he actually held the peerage; where there is no second title in the family, he is called Lord —— (family name); younger sons of Dukes and Marquesses are styled Lord John —— (family name), their wives become Lady John ——. Younger sons of Earls and all sons of Viscounts and Barons are styled The Hon. John —— (family name), their wives The Hon. Mrs. ——. (The title Hon. is never used in speaking).

Viscount. 'The Rt. Hon. the Viscount ——.' *Begin*, 'My Lord'; refer to 'Your Lordship'; *end*, 'I have the honour to be, my Lord, Your Lordship's obedient servant.'

Viscountess. 'The Rt. Hon. the Viscountess ——.' *Begin*, 'Madam'; refer to 'Your Ladyship'; *end*, as Countess.

Widow of a Peer. If the mother, step-mother or grandmother of the actual peer, she is formally 'The Dowager Duchess of ——,' etc., when the actual peer is married. But it has become much more usual to use the style 'Jane, Duchess of ——,' etc. Similar usage applies to the **widow of a Baronet.**

Weights and Measures

British and metric (SI) systems compared

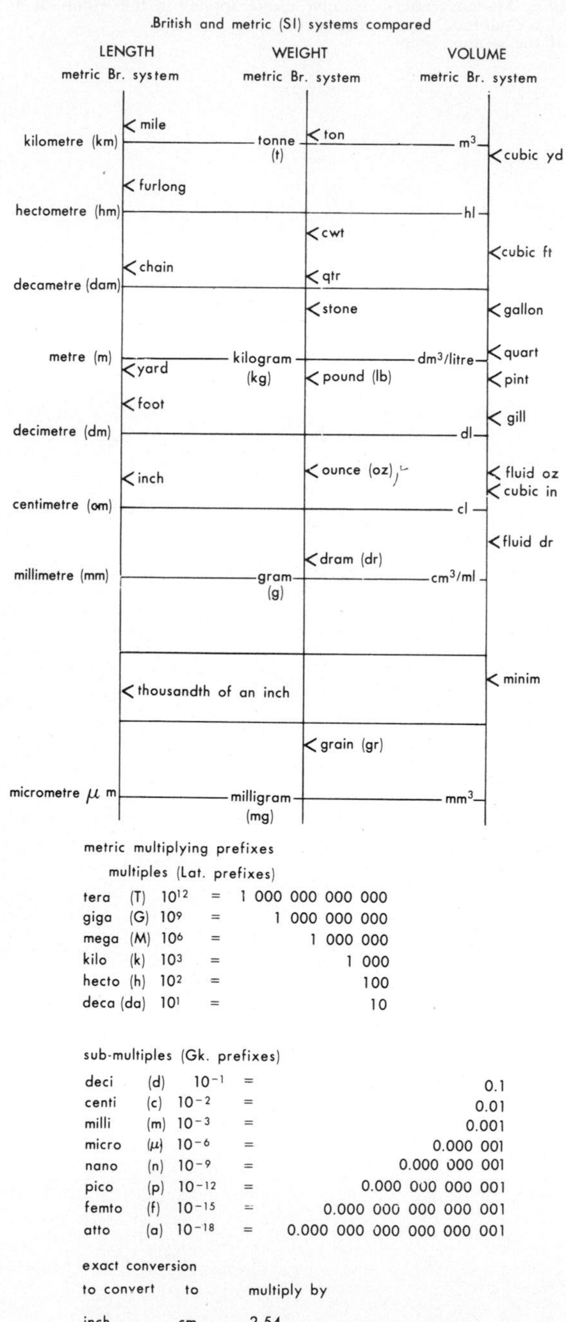

approximate conversion

CENTIMETRES

0 5 10 15 20 25 30

0 2 4 6 8 10 12

INCHES

MILES to KILOMETRES				KILOMETRES to MILES			
Miles	Kms	Miles	Kms	Kms	Miles	Kms	Miles
½	.8	6	9.6	½	.31	6	3.73
1	1.6	7	11.2	1	.62	7	4.35
1½	2.4	8	12.8	1½	.93	8	4.97
2	3.2	9	14.4	2	1.24	9	5.59
2½	4.0	10	16.0	2½	1.55	10	6.21
3	4.8	25	40.2	3	1.86	25	15.53
4	6.4	50	80.4	4	2.49	50	31.07
5	8.0	100	160.9	5	3.11	100	62.14

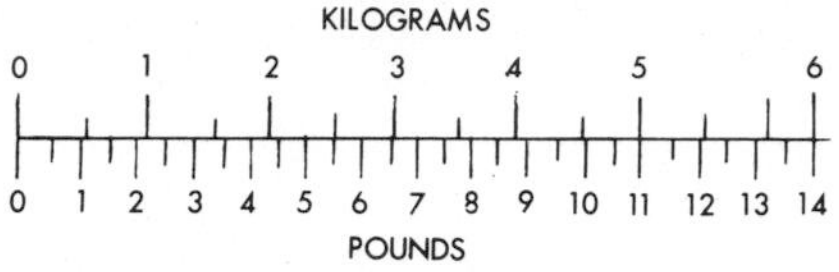

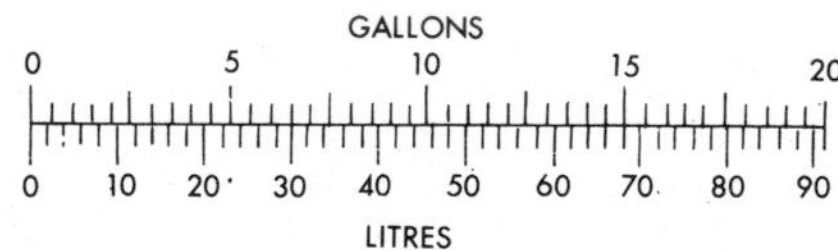

metric multiplying prefixes

multiples (Lat. prefixes)

tera	(T)	10^{12}	=	1 000 000 000 000
giga	(G)	10^{9}	=	1 000 000 000
mega	(M)	10^{6}	=	1 000 000
kilo	(k)	10^{3}	=	1 000
hecto	(h)	10^{2}	=	100
deca	(da)	10^{1}	=	10

sub-multiples (Gk. prefixes)

deci	(d)	10^{-1}	=	0.1
centi	(c)	10^{-2}	=	0.01
milli	(m)	10^{-3}	=	0.001
micro	(μ)	10^{-6}	=	0.000 001
nano	(n)	10^{-9}	=	0.000 000 001
pico	(p)	10^{-12}	=	0.000 000 000 001
femto	(f)	10^{-15}	=	0.000 000 000 000 001
atto	(a)	10^{-18}	=	0.000 000 000 000 000 001

exact conversion

to convert	to	multiply by
inch	cm	2.54
mile	km	1.609
kilometre	m	0.6214
acre	ha	0.40469
ounce	gr	28.35
gram	oz	0.03527
gallon	l	4.546
litre	gal	0.22

NB For temperature conversion, see also text entries TEMPERATURE and THERMOMETER

British and metric units

	metric	British
length		
	100 cm = 1 **metre***	12 in = 1 ft
	10 cm = 1 dam	3 ft = 1 yd
	10 dam = 1 hm	220 yd = 1 furlong
	10 hm = 1 km	8 furlong = 1 mile
area		
	100 sq dm = 1 **sq metre****	144 sq in = 1 sq ft
	100 sq m (m²) = 1 are (m²)	9 sq ft = 1 sq yd
	100 ares = 1 ha	4,840 sq yd = 1 acre
	100 ha = 1 km²	640 acre = 1 sq mile
weight		
	1,000 mg = 1 g	16 dram = 1 oz
	1,000 g = 1 **kilogram** (kg)	16 oz = 1 lb
	1,000 kg = 1 tonne (t)	14 lb = 1 st
		2 st = 1 qtr
		4 qtr = 1 cwt
		20 cwt / 2,240 lb = 1 ton (long)
		2,000 lb = 1 Am. ton (short)
volume		
	1,000 cm³/cc = 1 litre (l)	20 fl oz / 4 gill = 1 pt
	1,000 l = 1 **cubic metre** (m³)***	2 pt = 1 qt
		4 qt = 1 gal

*base units indicated by bold type

**SI base unit = sq metre, but are often used for land measurement

***SI base unit = cu metre, but for general purposes the litre is acceptable